·ALABAMA·COLORADO·ARIZONA·MAINE·TEXAS·UTAH·ALASKA·
·IOWA·LOUISIANA·WISCONSIN·TENNESSEE·IDAHO·

CALIFORNIA·MICHIGAN·MINNESOTA·MISSISSIPPI·MISSOURI·WEST VIRGINIA·NEW YORK·NEVADA
NORTH DAKOTA·PENNSYLVANIA·SOUTH CAROLINA·SOUTH DAKOTA·MARYLAND·ARKANSAS

GEORGIA·DELAWARE·ILLINOIS·KANSAS·NORTH CAROLINA·OREGON·NEBRASKA·KENTUCKY
NEW HAMPSHIRE·NEW JERSEY·NEW MEXICO·CONNECTICUT·FLORIDA·MASSACHUSETTS

1817 1997

The Official Catholic Directory

Anno Domini
1997

Published Annually by
P. J. Kenedy & Sons

·INDIANA·OKLAHOMA·RHODE ISLAND·MONTANA·
·HAWAII·WASHINGTON·VIRGINIA·VERMONT·WYOMING·OHIO·

The Official Catholic Directory

John R. Agel
Publisher

FOREWORD

*We are proud to present the **1997 edition of the Official Catholic Directory** and again wish to thank all the ecclesiastical authorities and diocesan officials involved for their cooperation and participation. We consistently strive to maintain the integrity and credibility of information and offer it in an easy to understand environment.*

*Packaged this year with the Official Catholic Directory, the **Pilgrimage Destination Guide** is being introduced with the coming of the Millennium year. As pointed out by the Bishops Subcommittee on the Millennium, this celebration offers the Church the opportunity to reflect on the meaning of Christianity locally, nationwide and internationally. Many are expected to journey to pilgrimage areas significant both in historical and traditional value to the Christian faith. For your convenience, this booklet has been developed in order to provide information relative to the pilgrim areas and the surrounding regions, as well as maps and contact information.*

***Part II of the Official Catholic Directory**, published in early fall, is included with your subscription. **Part II** contains revisions and updates not found in the main volume; more expanded data for the Pilgrimage section, and a complete list of the dioceses and archdioceses of the world reprinted with permission from the Vatican.*

We are proud to have the honor to visit the Vatican and carry on the rich tradition of providing a detailed and thorough portrait of the Catholic Church. It is our hope to continue to develop this portrayal on a universal level as we endeavor to improve and excel.

John R. Agel

John R. Agel
Publisher

Published by P.J. Kenedy & Sons
121 Chanlon Road ✦ New Providence, NJ 07974

Photo of His Holiness The Pope courtesy of Arturo Mari, L'Osservatore Romano.

His Holiness the Pope John Paul II

P. Sullivan
4-III-91

The Seal of P.J. Kenedy & Sons
The Official Catholic Directory

SIGNIFICANCE:

The shield is the central part of a heraldic device, which is more commonly known as a coat of arms. If that shield is enclosed within a body of text, or other type of surrounding configuration, the device becomes know as a seal, yet it is the shield portion of the design that is the most important, and that which is described technically as the blazon. As the design is examined, it must be remembered that by heraldic tradition the design is described (blazoned) as if being done by the bearer with the shield being worn on the arm. Therefore, the terms dexter and sinister will be reversed as the design is viewed from the front.

The shield of the seal for The Official Catholic Directory has been designed to reflect the character and heritage of this publication of P.J. Kenedy & Sons.

The shield is in two major portions. The right half (sinister impalement) is composed of the blue field on which are seen a silver tree, two candles (in silver or white) in their candleholders (of gold or yellow) and an open book, edged in gold and with a red bookmark. These symbols have been used over the years as the sign of the P.J. Kenedy and Sons publishing organization. These are the traditional symbols of knowledge and learning, so appropriate to a publisher.

The other side of the shield (the dexter impalement) is composed of a silver (white) field on which is seen a red cross, throughout, and a gold eagle. These symbols, combined with the field of the sinister impalement, are represented in the color of the flag of the United States of America and the eagle, the symbol of the United States. The cross represents Christianity and all of this combines to signify that The Official Catholic Directory annually reports on the Catholic Church in the United States.

The shield is surrounded by a laurel wreath of excellence and is enclosed within the legend that states the name of the company, the name of the publication and date (1817) of its founding.

by: Paul J. Sullivan

MASTER COLLECTION

THE I.T. VERDIN CO., CINCINNATI, OHIO

The Savior
Processional Cross
Designed and made by Almy for the 1995 Papal Mass at St. Joseph's Seminary in New York. The Savior Cross is just one selection of Almy's exclusive offering of processional appointments, sacred vessels, eucharistic vestments and clerical clothing. Classic designs for today's church.
For a complimentary copy of the Almy Catalog, please call or write today.
A
C.M. ALMY & SON
OUTFITTERS TO THE CHURCH AND CLERGY SINCE 1892
10 GLENVILLE STREET DEPT YY GREENWICH CT 06836
1.800.225.ALMY

SCULPTWAX®
CHURCH CANDLES
Classical symbolism and expressive liturgical design in the luxurious hand decorated artistry of SCULPTWAX®. . . created and mastercrafted here, in the United States, exclusively at Cathedral Candle Company.
Wedding Candle Ensemble
Holy Trinity™ Christ Candle
Christ Victorious™ Paschal Candle
Holy Trinity™ Paschal Candle
The Christian Rites™ RCIA Candle
Now, In Stock At Your Nearest Church Goods Dealer.
SCULPTWAX®
Only from . . .
SINCE 1897
Cathedral
CANDLE COMPANY

Terra Sancta Guild

serves the Christian people in three different ways:

- custom designs, made-to-order, in answer to individual needs
- limited editions to serve a special public
- substantial inventory of popular, off-the-shelf pieces, always ready for immediate shipment

858 Sussex Boulevard
P.O. Box 300
Broomall, PA 19008
1-800-523-5155

ERRA SANCTA GUILD® is committed to fine design and workmanship in Christian insignia, recognition awards and gifts expressive of religious thought -all graphic signs of faith.

I. A. Serot

I.A. Serot
President

Over 30 years ago*, *Terra Sancta Guild® came onto the market with its own original copyrighted designs. Through our renowned Art Department, we dedicated ourselves to bring forth significant items designed for home, church, and school – pieces that would not add to the glut of kitsch. "What I like about Terra Sancta Guild," said a prominent clergyman in 1965, "is that I can hand these items down to my grandchildren." That comment encouraged us at the time, and now we see succeeding generations who still cherish our products. Today, for example, our responsive clients are requesting us to produce more Celtic designs .

Right: Adé Bethune, Terra Sancta Guild Art Director, is a renowned liturgical artist. Her fame as writer and illustrator, and her expertise in church architecture, are based on a profound grasp of Christian symbolism spoken in the Biblical tradition, in the multi-layered dimensions of Christian worship. Abigail McCarthy says that Adé has done "more than any other artist to rescue twentieth century religious art from the saccharine and the vapid." *The Living Church* writes that Adé should be declared "a national treasure."

ANTHONY JOHN BELLOMO is a sculptor. He works in a wide variety of materials from wood and bronze to fibers, stone and living plant materials. Over the past twenty - five years he has developed the Black Forest Company. Black Forest is a group of artists and artisans, who along with Bellomo, design and build contemporary sculpture and furniture for liturgical spaces. He has developed a series of redwood sand carved exterior pieces for outdoor chapels and meditation gardens. Anthony, along with his team of dedicated crafts persons, pride themselves in listening to the individual community, designing and building pieces to help make their worship a deeper experience.

ST. BARNABAS

ST. JOHN VIANNEY

ST. JOHN VIANNEY
CREDO CROSS

SACRED HEART

310 EUCLID • MOUNT CLEMENS, MICHIGAN 48043 • (810) 954-4800 • FAX (810) 954-4806

Tree of Life
Outstanding, popular fund-raising tool with minimum outlay
Enhances the beauty of your building while helping to pay for it
to Thank & Recognize
to Honor & Memorialize
The Tree of Life is a beautiful piece of art consisting of brass leaves engraved and mounted on tree background
The Tree of Life generates excitement for a new campaign, and acts as a powerful stimulus for ongoing efforts
For a FREE CATALOG, call Carroll Art, Inc. toll-free: 1-800-876-4569

T AG
Granda
Quality Church Supplier from Europe, since 1891.
Liturgical Arts, Inc.
Manufacturers of:
• Chalices and ciboria.
• Tabernacles, monstrances.
• Candlesticks, lamps.
• Stations of the Cross, etc…
Statuary:
Wood carvings.
Vestments:
Chasubles, albs.
Interior design: Church decoration and renovation
Wood carvings
Silver work
Altars, church furniture, etc.
Vestments
Custom made orders: our specialty.
Some of our customers in USA:
• Mother M. Angelica, P.C.P.A., Abbess Our Lady of the Angels Monastery, Birmingham, Alabama.
• St. Aloysius Church, New Canaan, CT
• St. John Fisher Seminary, Stamford, CT
• Christ the King Catholic Church, Houston TX etc…
GRANDA Liturgical Arts, Inc.
2525 Eastwood Avenue, Apt. 8-A
Evanston, Illinois 60201
Phone: 1-800-425.0828
Fax: (847) 492.1374
email: Ruf4granda@aol.com
http://www.hispacom.es/granda
New Tabernacl
for Holy Cross Cathedral Boston, MA
Special design: gold plated finish, enamel decoration
The total height of the tabernacle is 42" and its squar
base measures 20" by 20'
We also designed a matching sanctuary lam
FREE CATALOG (60 PAGES) OR CD-ROM AVAILABLE ON REQUES

Mass Cards

Gold ink, gold foil accents and high quality white vellum envelopes make our Mass Cards a beautiful choice. Mass Cards can be customized and imprinted to suit your needs.

MORE THAN 35 CARD DESIGNS AVAILABLE!

Living

MA 206CD $51.00
Virgin Adoring
(with Gold Foil Embossing)
5" x 7",
packaged 100 to a box

MD 026CD $32.00
Cup of Salvation
3 ¾" x 6 ¼", packaged 100 to a box

MC 464CD $38.00
Our Lady of Iviron
4 ½" x 6 ¼",
packaged 100 to a box

MC 022CD $38.00
Peace of God
4 ½" x 6 ¼",
packaged 100
to a box

Deceased

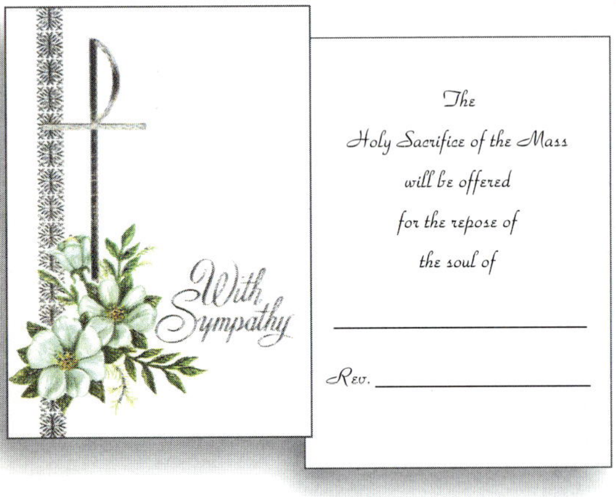

MA 205CD $51.00
With Sympathy
(with Silver Foil Embossing)
5" x 7",
packaged 100 to a box

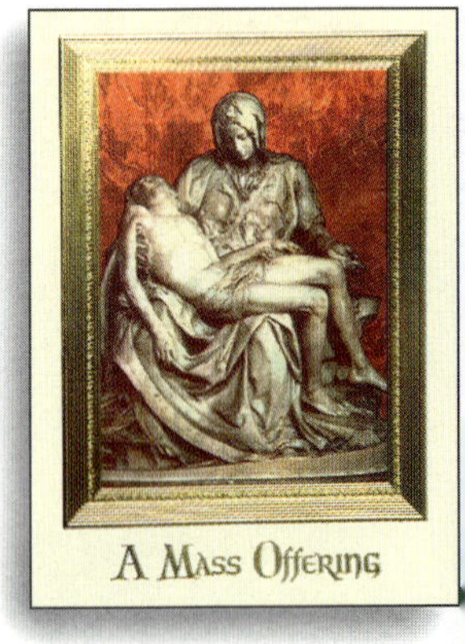

MA 314CD $51.00
Pieta
(with Gold Foil Embossing
5" x 7",
packaged 100 to a box

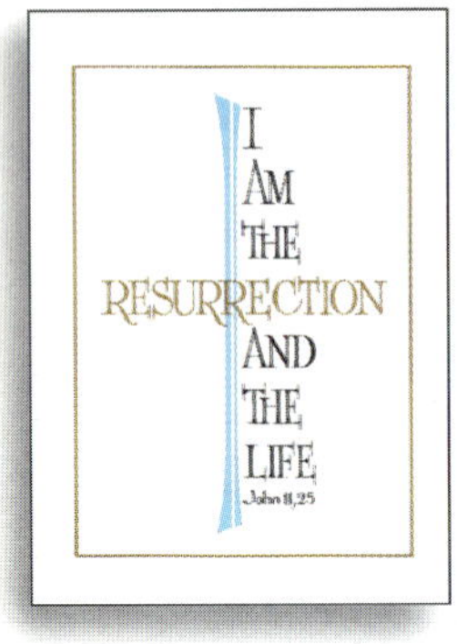

MC 016CD $38.00
I am the Resurrection
4 ½" x 6 ¼",
packaged 100
to a box

MB 001CD $44.00
No Eye Has Seen
5" x 7",
packaged 100 to a box

Christmas Cards

Tastefully designed for personal greetings, our elegant cards will express your faith and joy to family, friends, donors and parishioners. Christmas stationery can be custom imprinted to suit your needs. All cards come boxed with envelopes.

HG 468CD

CS 469-OCD

CP 770CD

Stationery Set

CR 735CD Stationery Set **$31.00**
Includes 100 each: Letterhead, Holy Cards, Offering Envelopes

CP 770CD Christmas Letterhead **$16.00**
8 1/2" x 11", packaged 100 to a box

HG 468CD Holy Cards **$10.50**
2 3/4" x 4 1/4", packaged 100 to a box

CS 469-OCD Offering Envelopes **$8.00**
6 1/2" x 3 3/4", packaged 100 to a box

Verse: May the blessings of the Christ Child be yours this Christmas and throughout the New Year.

You and your loved ones will be remembered in the Holy Sacrifice of the Mass on Christmas Day.

CW 720CD $13.00
Adoration of the Shepherds
(with Gold Ink Accents)
5" x 6 3/4",
packaged 25 to a box

Verse: May the blessings of Christmas be with you today and throughout the New Year

CC 717CD $22.00
Silent Night
(with Gold Ink Accents)
4 1/2" x 6 1/4",
packaged 50 to a box

CA 702CD
$13.00
The Mother and Child
5" x 6 3/4",
packaged 25 to a box

Verse: Wishing you the Love, Peace, and Happiness that the true meaning of Christmas brings.

CX 721CD
$15.00
The Nativity
(with Gold Foil Embossing)
5" x 6 3/4",
packaged 25 to a box

Verse: May all the blessings of the Christ Child be yours this Christmas and may His Divine Presence enrich your life throughout the New Year.

You and your loved ones will be remembered in the Holy Sacrifice of the Mass.

Back Front

CK 727CD $16.00
Pocket Calendar
5" x 4" open, 2 1/2" x 4" folded
packaged 100 to a box

CK 727CD comes with blank inside panels. Imprint with your personal message for a small fee.

Certificates

Four beautiful collections in 3 easy-to-use formats.

For Baptism, Reconciliation, First Communion, Confirmation, and Marriage

Preprinted Certificates

Artwork and preprinted certificate form.

XB 102CD $27.00 Baptism
8" x 10", packaged 50 to a box

NEW! Create Your Own! Certificates

Artwork & Sacramental Title only.

XB 112CD $27.00
Create Your Own!
8" x 10", packaged 50 to a box

All-Purpose Certificates

Artwork Only.

XB 106CD $27.00
All-Purpose (shown blank) 8" x 10"
packaged 50 to a box

inside

XB 107CD $54.00 Godparents Folder
5" x 7", packaged 100 to a box

Matching booklets, folders, holy cards and bookmarks available for some certificates. Printed on lightweight card stock with envelopes. Easy to personalize with typewriter, hand calligraphy and laser printer!

All Certificates are also available in these designs.

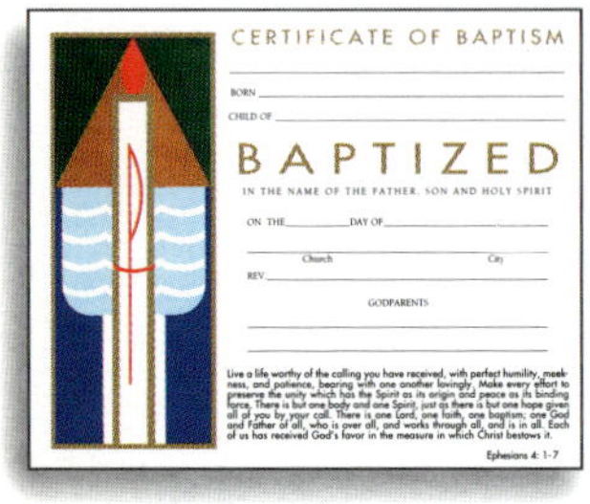

XA 002CD $26.50
Baptism Certificate
8" x 10", packaged 50 to a box

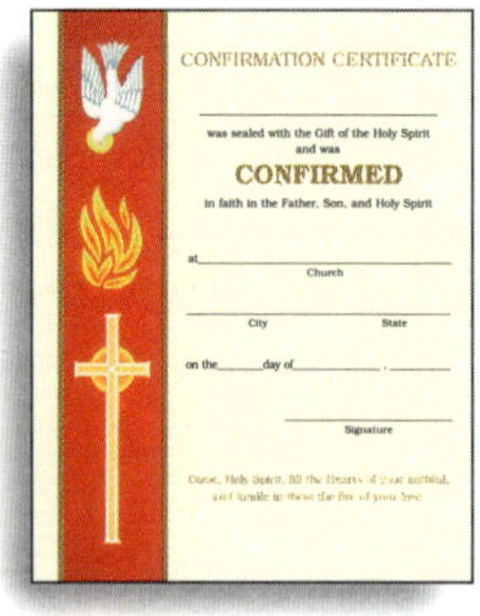

XC 104CD
$27.00
Confirmation
8" x 10",
packaged 50
to a box

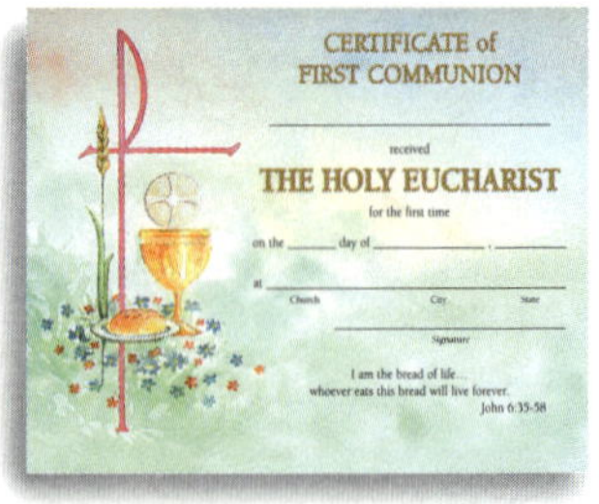

XD 103CD $26.50
First Communion
8" x 10",
packaged 50 to a box

BA 001CD
$25.00
"The Rite of Baptism" Booklet
6" x 9",
packaged 50
to a box

HG 391CD
$10.50
Holy Card
2 3/4" x 4 1/4",
packaged 100
to a box

BK 375CD
$4.00
Bookmark
2 1/4" x 6 1/4",
packaged 5
to a box

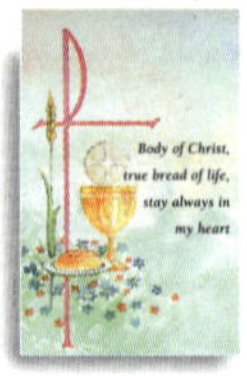

HG 411CD
$10.50
Holy Card
2 3/4" x 4 1/4",
packaged 100
to a box

Cards for Every Occasion

Elegant cards for personal greetings, the ministry of encouragement and fundraising. All cards come boxed with envelopes. Most cards can be customized and imprinted to suit your needs.

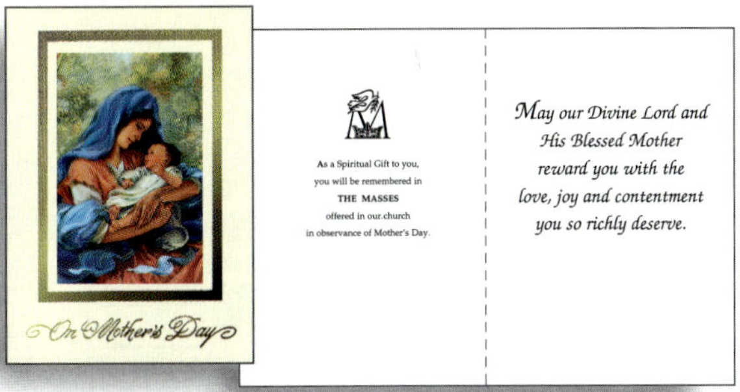

inside

DB 402CD $59.00
Madonna and Child (with Gold Foil)
5" x 6 3/4", packaged 100 to a box

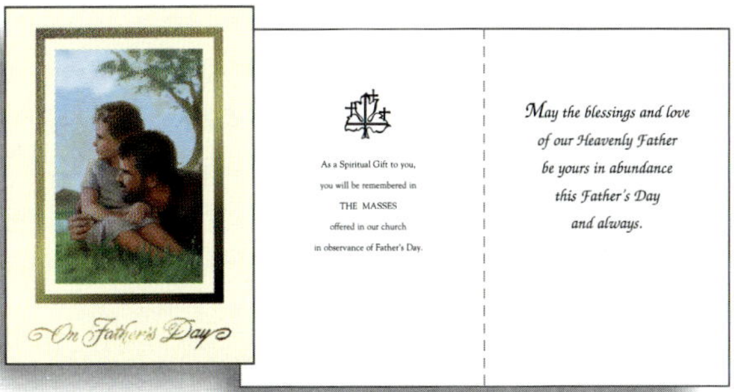

inside

DD 406CD $59.00
St. Joseph and the Christ Child (with Gold Foil)
5" x 6 3/4", packaged 100 to a box

EA 413CD $13.00
Alleluia (with Gold Foil)
4 1/2" x 6 1/4"
packaged 25 to a box

Verse: May the Risen Christ grant you peace and joy at Eastertime and always.

EL 702CD $11.00
Paschal Candle
4 1/2" x 6 1/4",
packaged 25 to a box

Verse: May the Spirit of the Risen Christ live within you now and always. You will be remembered in the Holy Sacrifice of the Mass on Easter Sunday.

MC 359CD $10.50
Birthday
4 1/2" x 6 1/4",
packaged 25 to a box

Verse: God's blessing on your birthday and every day ahead.

MA 208CD
$51.00 Daffodil
(with Gold Foil Embossing)
5" x 7",
packaged 100 to a box

Verse: The Holy Sacrifice of the Mass will be offered for your speedy recovery at the request of
____

MC 362CD $10.50
With Sincere Sympathy
4 1/2" x 6 1/4",
packaged 25 to a box

Verse: Thinking of you at this time of sorrow with warm thoughts and deep sympathy.

MJ 403CD $17.00
May You Be Blessed
4" x 5 1/2",
packaged 50 to a box

Verse: May God bless you for your kindness

Devotional Booklets and Folders

Way of the Cross • Rosary • Wake Service

BP 048CD $26.50
The Way of the Cross
with text from Scriptures
4" x 6",
packaged 50 to a box

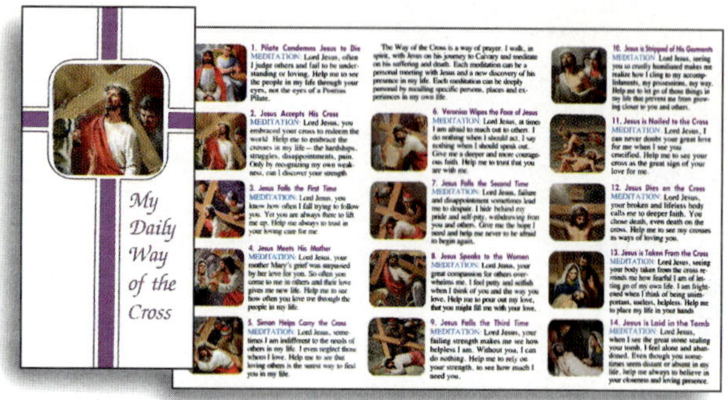

inside

BU 079CD $30.00
My Daily Way Folder—Large Print
4" x 7 1/4" folded,
packaged 100 to a box

inside

BV 060CD $29.00
Rosary Folder
3 1/2" x 6 1/4" folded, packaged 100 to a box

BN 046CD $25.00
Consolation of God
6" x 9",
packaged 50 to a box

Holy Cards and Bookmarks

- Over 70 designs available
- Use for gifts • Mailing enclosures
- Custom imprinting options on Holy Cards

HG 680CD

HG 113CD

ONLY 10.5¢ ea.

Holy Cards
$10.50
2 3/4" x 4 1/4",
packaged 100
to a box

HG 009CD

HG 346CD

BK 442CD
St. Francis

BK 456CD
One
Solitary Life

LAMINATED! ONLY 80¢ ea.

BK 443CD
Hail Mary

BK 373CD
Sacred
Heart Mary

Bookmarks
$4.00
2 1/4" x 6 1/4",
packaged 5
to a box

TOLL FREE ORDERING, CALL 1-800-638-4652
MONDAY through FRIDAY • 8 a.m. to 6 p.m. E.S.T.
or FAX 1-800-807-2954
24 hours a day

BARTON~COTTON • 1405 Parker Road • Baltimore • MD 21227

Adrian Hamers®

One Hundred Years Serving the Clergy
Frapez Toujours
1887

Church Interiors

ɔr those hard to find items, contact Adrian Hamers, Inc.

ɴce 1887, the Hamers name has been synonymous with expert silversmithing throughout the orld in the field of Liturgical Art. We are also experts in: Chruch Interiors from design to execu- ɔn, Renovations, Altars, Sacred Vessels, Appraisals, Gold and Silver Plating & Repairing, ʌbernacles, Marble, Statuary, Woodwork & Woodcarving, Stained Glass, Pews and Chairs, ɔld Leafing, Wall Murals, Heraldic Design and Bishop Regalia.

2 Madison Avenue • Larchmont, N.Y. 10538 • Fax: 914-834-0712 • Tel: (914) 834-7780

St. Teresa's Parish of Palm Springs, CA (Lourdes)

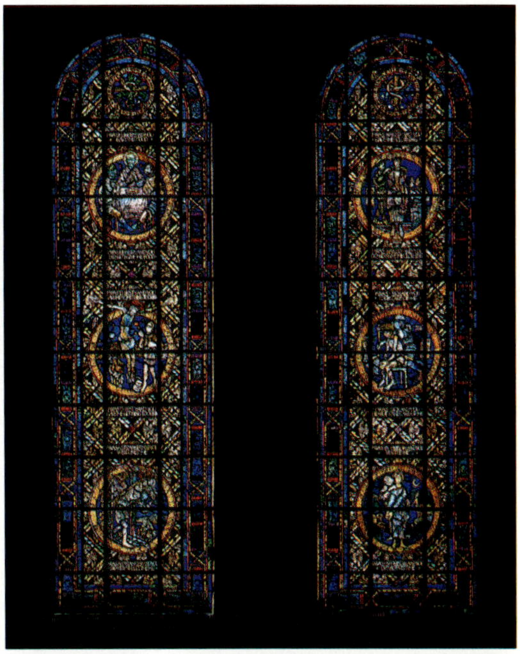

He's outnumbered
2,500 to 1.
THE ARMY NEEDS PRIESTS.
The Catholic soldiers and families in the Army community share the same problems as civilians. Only more so. Most are young, have high pressure jobs, and many are away from home for the first time. But the ratio of parishioners to priests is more than twice as high in the Army as it is in the civilian world. So, if we're going to provide proper spiritual guidance and support, the Army Chaplain Corps needs reinforcements. For more information, call: 1-800-452-7617.
ARMY CHAPLAIN CORPS.
BE ALL YOU CAN BE.

Martin Rambusch, V
MS Historic Preservatio
School of Architectur
Columbia Universi

The Official Catholic Directory

for the Year of Our Lord

1997

GIVING STATUS OF THE CATHOLIC CHURCH AS OF JANUARY 1, 1997

Containing Ecclesiastical Statistics of

THE UNITED STATES, PUERTO RICO,
THE VIRGIN ISLANDS, AGANA, CAROLINE AND MARSHALL ISLANDS,
FOREIGN MISSIONARY ACTIVITIES, CANADA, AND MEXICO.

The information contained in this Directory is derived from reports submitted to the publishers by the ecclesiastical authorities of the countries concerned, and neither the publishers nor the ecclesiastical authorities assume responsibility for any errors or omissions.

P. J. KENEDY & SONS

Publishers to the Holy Apostolic See

For inquiries call: 908-665-3500
or write: 121 Chanlon Rd., New Providence, NJ 07974
To place an order call: 1-800-521-8110

The 1997 edition of *The Official Catholic Directory* was prepared by the Data Base Publishing Group.

John R. Agel, Vice President and Publisher
Publisher's Staff includes:
Jeanne Hanline, Managing Editor
Betty Hromoko, Executive Secretary

Data Base Publishing Staff includes:
Leigh C. Yuster-Freeman, Vice President, Production-Directories
Elizabeth A. Kizar, Editorial Director
Christina Fry Moxley, Managing Editor
Stacy A. Stanford, Senior Editor
Joseph C. Stewart, Associate Editor
Marie-Ange Bovee-Greenberger, Linda Hummer, Kathleen F. Jurcsek,
Jennifer Nagle, Julia Pereira, Cathy Rubino, Faith Shepherd, Editorial Assistants

Photo of His Holiness The Pope courtesy of Arturo Mari, L'Osservatore Romano.

Published by P.J. Kenedy & Sons in association with R.R. Bowker, a division of Reed Elsvier Inc.

International Standard Book Number: 0-8352-4002-9
International Standard Serial Number: 0078-3854
Library of Congress Catalog Card Number: 81-30961
Printed and bound in the United States of America

CONTENTS

Part I

Part II
UNITED STATES

ARCHDIOCESES AND DIOCESES
(Archdioceses are in Bold Face)

MISCELLANEOUS

EASTERN CHURCHES

TERRITORIAL SEES

Part III

CANADA AND MEXICO

Part IV

THE ARCHDIOCESES AND DIOCESES OF THE UNITED STATES—BY STATES

A—Indicates Archdiocese. The Archdiocese of Washington includes the District of Columbia and five Counties of Maryland. Dioceses traverse state lines in the following instances only: Cheyenne includes all of Yellowstone National Park;S Norwich includes Fisher's Island, NY; Wilmington includes the eastern shores of Maryland and Gallup includes parts of Arizona and New Mexico.

Diocesan Abbreviations

ARCHDIOCESES AND DIOCESES

(ALB) ....Albany (New York)
(ALN) ....Allentown (Pennsylvania)
(ALT) ....Altoona-Johnstown (Pennsylvania)
(ALX) ....Alexandria (Louisiana)
(AGN) ....Agana (Guam)
(AMA) ....Amarillo (Texas)
(ANC) ....Anchorage (Alaska)
(ARE) ....Arecibo (Puerto Rico)
(ARL) ....Arlington (Virginia)
(ARM) ....Armenian Catholic Exarchate (Pennsylvania)
(ATH) ....Apostolate To Hungarians (Washington, DC)
(ATL) ....Atlanta (Georgia)
(AUS) ....Austin (Texas)
(B) ....Boise (Idaho)
(BAK) ....Baker (Oregon)
(BAL) ....Baltimore (Maryland)
(BEA) ....Beaumont (Texas)
(BEL) ....Belleville (Illinois)
(BGP) ....Bridgeport (Connecticut)
(BIR) ....Birmingham (Alabama)
(BIS) ....Bismarck (North Dakota)
(BLX) ....Biloxi (Mississippi)
(BO) ....Boston (Massachusetts)
(BR) ....Baton Rouge (Louisiana)
(BRK) ....Brooklyn (New York)
(BUF) ....Buffalo (New York)
(BUR) ....Burlington (Vermont)
(BWN) ....Brownsville (Texas)
(CAM) ....Camden (New Jersey)
(CC) ....Corpus Christi (Texas)
(CGS) ....Caguas (Puerto Rico)
(CHI) ....Chicago (Illinois)
(CHK) ....Chalan Kanoa
(CHL) ....Charlotte (North Carolina)
(CHR) ....Charleston (South Carolina)
(CHY) ....Cheyenne (Wyoming)
(CI) ....Caroline Islands
(CIN) ....Cincinnati (Ohio)
(CLV) ....Cleveland (Ohio)
(COL) ....Columbus (Ohio)
(COS) ....Colorado Springs (Colorado)
(COV) ....Covington (Kentucky)
(CR) ....Crookston (Minnesota)
(DAL) ....Dallas (Texas)
(DAV) ....Davenport (Iowa)
(DEN) ....Denver (Colorado)
(DET) ....Detroit (Michigan)
(DM) ....Des Moines (Iowa)
(DOD) ....Dodge City (Kansas)
(DUB) ....Dubuque (Iowa)
(DUL) ....Duluth (Minnesota)
(E) ....Erie (Pennsylvania)
(ELP) ....El Paso (Texas)
(EST) ....Eparchy of Saint Thomas the Apostle
(EVN) ....Evansville (Indiana)
(FAR) ....Fargo (North Dakota)
(FBK) ....Fairbanks (Alaska)
(FgM) ....Foreign Mission Section
(FR) ....Fall River (Massachusetts)
(FRS) ....Fresno (California)
(FTW) ....Fort Wayne-South Bend (Indiana)
(FWT) ....Fort Worth (Texas)
(GAL) ....Galveston-Houston (Texas)
(GAY) ....Gaylord (Michigan)
(GB) ....Green Bay (Wisconsin)
(GBG) ....Greensburg (Pennsylvania)
(GF) ....Great Falls-Billings (Montana)
(GI) ....Grand Island (Nebraska)
(GLP) ....Gallup (New Mexico)
(GR) ....Grand Rapids (Michigan)
(GRY) ....Gary (Indiana)
(HBG) ....Harrisburg (Pennsylvania)
(HEL) ....Helena (Montana)
(HON) ....Honolulu (Hawaii)
(HRT) ....Hartford (Connecticut)
(HT) ....Houma-Thibodaux (Louisiana)
(IND) ....Indianapolis (Indiana)
(JC) ....Jefferson City (Missouri)
(JKS) ....Jackson (Mississippi)
(JOL) ....Joliet in Illinois
(JUN) ....Juneau (Alaska)
(KAL) ....Kalamazoo (Michigan)
(KC) ....Kansas City-St. Joseph (Missouri)
(KCK) ....Kansas City in Kansas
(KNX) ....Knoxville (Tennessee)
(L) ....Louisville (Kentucky)
(LA) ....Los Angeles (California)
(LAF) ....Lafayette (Louisiana)
(LAN) ....Lansing (Michigan)
(LC) ....La Crosse (Wisconsin)
(LEX) ....Lexington (Kentucky)
(LFT) ....Lafayette in Indiana
(LIN) ....Lincoln (Nebraska)
(LIT) ....Lithuanian Apostolate for Lithuanian Catholics
(LKC) ....Lake Charles (Louisiana)
(LR) ....Little Rock (Arkansas)
(LSC) ....Las Cruces (New Mexico)
(LUB) ....Lubbock (Texas)
(LAV) ....Las Vegas (Nevada)
(MAD) ....Madison (Wisconsin)
(MAN) ....Manchester (New Hampshire)
(MAR) ....Marquette (Michigan)
(MEM) ....Memphis (Tennessee)
(MET) ....Metuchen (New Jersey)
(MGZ) ....Mayaguez (Puerto Rico)
(MI) ....Marshall Islands
(MIA) ....Miami (Florida)
(MIL) ....Milwaukee (Wisconsin)
(MO) ....Military Services (Maryland)
(MOB) ....Mobile (Alabama)
(MRY) ....Monterey in California
(NEW) ....Newark (New Jersey)
(NO) ....New Orleans (Louisiana)
(NOR) ....Norwich (Connecticut)
(NSH) ....Nashville (Tennessee)
(NTN) ....Newton (Melkite, United States)
(NU) ....New Ulm (Minnesota)
(NY) ....New York (New York)
(OAK) ....Oakland (California)
(OG) ....Ogdensburg (New York)
(OKL) ....Oklahoma City (Oklahoma)
(OLD) ....Our Lady of Deliverance *Syriac* (Union City, New Jersey)
(OLL) ....Our Lady of Lebanon of Los Angeles (California)
(OM) ....Omaha (Nebraska)
(ORG) ....Orange in California
(ORL) ....Orlando (Florida)
(OWN) ....Owensboro (Kentucky)
(P) ....Portland in Oregon
(PAT) ....Paterson (New Jersey)
(PBL) ....Pueblo (Colorado)
(PBR) ....Pittsburgh *Byzantine* (Pennsylvania)
(PCE) ....Ponce (Puerto Rico)
(PEO) ....Peoria (Illinois)
(PH) ....Philadelphia (Pennsylvania)
(PHU) ....Philadelphia *Ukrainian* (Pennsylvania)
(PHX) ....Phoenix (Arizona)
(PIT) ....Pittsburgh (Pennsylvania)
(PMB) ....Palm Beach (Florida)
(PP) ....Personal Prelatures
(PRM) ....Parma *Byzantine* (Ohio)
(PRO) ....Providence (Rhode Island)
(PRT) ....Portland (Maine)
(PSC) ....Passaic *Byzantine* (New Jersey)
(PT) ....Pensacola-Tallahassee (Florida)
(R) ....Raleigh (North Carolina)
(RC) ....Rapid City (South Dakota)
(RCK) ....Rockford (Illinois)
(RIC) ....Richmond (Virginia)
(RNO) ....Reno (Nevada)
(ROC) ....Rochester (New York)
(ROM) ....Romanian (Byzantine) (Ohio)
(RVC) ....Rockville Centre (New York)
(SAC) ....Sacramento (California)
(SAG) ....Saginaw (Michigan)
(SAL) ....Salina (Kansas)
(SAM) ....St. Maron of Brooklyn (U.S.A.), Eparchy of
(SAN) ....San Angelo (Texas)
(SAT) ....San Antonio (Texas)
(SAV) ....Savannah (Georgia)
(SB) ....San Bernadino (California)
(SC) ....Sioux City (Iowa)
(SCL) ....St. Cloud (Minnesota)
(SCR) ....Scranton (Pennsylvania)
(SD) ....San Diego (California)
(SEA) ....Seattle (Washington)
(SFD) ....Springfield in Illinois
(SFE) ....Santa Fe (New Mexico)
(SFR) ....San Francisco (California)
(SFS) ....Sioux Falls (South Dakota)
(SHP) ....Shreveport (Louisiana)
(SJ) ....San Jose in California
(SJN) ....San Juan (Puerto Rico)
(SJP) ....St. Josaphat in Parma (Ohio)
(SLC) ....Salt Lake City (Utah)
(SP) ....St. Petersburg (Florida)
(SPC) ....Sprgfld-Cape Girardeau (Missouri)
(SPK) ....Spokane (Washington)
(SPP) ....Samoa-Pago Pago
(SPR) ....Springfield in Massachusetts
(SR) ....Santa Rosa in California
(STA) ....St. Augustine (Florida)
(STF) ....Stamford *Ukrainian* (Connecticut)
(STL) ....St. Louis (Missouri)
(STN) ....St. Nicholas in Chicago *Ukrainian*
(STO) ....Stockton (California)
(STP) ....St. Paul and Minneapolis (Minnesota)
(STU) ....Steubenville (Ohio)
(STV) ....St. Thomas, Virgin Islands
(SUP) ....Superior (Wisconsin)
(SY) ....Syracuse (New York)
(TLS) ....Tulsa (Oklahoma)
(TOL) ....Toledo (Ohio)
(TR) ....Trenton (New Jersey)
(TUC) ....Tucson (Arizona)
(TYL) ....Tyler (Texas)
(VEN) ....Venice (Florida)
(VIC) ....Victoria in Texas
(VNN) ....Van Nuys *Byzantine* (California)
(WCH) ....Wichita (Kansas)
(WDC) ....Washington (District of Columbia)
(WH) ....Wheeling-Charleston (West Virginia)
(WIL) ....Wilmington (Delaware)
(WIN) ....Winona (Minnesota)
(WOR) ....Worcester (Massachusetts)
(Y) ....Youngstown (Ohio)
(YAK) ....Yakima (Washington)

Religious Order Initials for Men

Initials	Order	Code
A.A.	Assumptionists	[0130]
B.C.S.	Brothers of Christian Service	[]
B.G.S.	Little Brothers of the Good Shepherd	[0580]
B.S.O.	Basilian Salvatorian Fathers	[0190]
C.F.A.	Alexian Brothers	[0120]
C.F.C.	Congregation of Christian Brothers	[0310]
C.F.M.M.	Brothers of Our Lady, Mother of Mercy	[0980]
C.F.P.	Brothers of the Poor of St. Francis	[0460]
C.F.R.	Franciscan Friars of the Renewal	[0535]
C.F.X.	Brothers of St. Francis Xavier	[1350]
C.I.C.M.	Missionhurst Congregation of the Immaculate Heart of Mary	[0860]
C.J.	Josephite Fathers	[0710]
C.J.M.	Congregation of Jesus and Mary	[0450]
C.M.	Congregation of the Mission	[1330]
C.M.C.	Congregation of Mother Coredemptrix	[]
C.M.F.	Claretian Missionaries	[0360]
C.M.I.	Carmelites of Mary Immaculate	[0275]
C.M.L.M.	The Congregation of Maronite Lebanese Missionaries	[0785]
C.M.M.	Congregation of Marianhill Missionaries, Marianhill Fathers & Brothers	[0750]
C.M.Vd.	Mekhitarist Fathers	[]
C.O.	Oratorians	[0950]
C.P.	Congregation of the Passion	[1000]
C.P.M.	Congregation of the Fathers of Mercy	[0820]
C.PP.S.	Society of the Precious Blood	[1060]
C.R.	Congregation of the Resurrection	[1080]
C.R.	Theatine Fathers	[1300]
C.R.I.C.	Canons Regular of the Immaculate Conception	[]
C.R.L.	Canons Regular of the Lateran	[0250]
C.R.M.	Adorno Fathers	[0100]
C.R.S.	Somascan Fathers	[1250]
C.R.S.P.	Clerics Regular of St. Paul	[0160]
C.S.	Missionaries of St. Charles-Scalabrinians	[1210]
C.S.B.	Basilian Fathers	[0170]
C.S.C.	Brothers of the Congregation of Holy Cross	[0600]
C.S.C.	Priests of the Congregation of Holy Cross	[0610]
C.S.J.	Congregation of St. Joseph	[1150]
C.S.J.B.	Congregation of St. John the Baptist	[]
C.S.P.	Paulist Fathers	[1030]
C.S.P.X.	Brothers of Saint Pius X	[1180]
C.S.S.	Stigmatine Fathers and Brothers	[1280]
C.S.Sp.	Holy Ghost Fathers	[0650]
C.SS.R.	Redemptorist Fathers	[1070]
C.S.V.	Clerics of St. Viator	[1320]
D.L.P.	Diocesan Labor Priests	[]
Er.Cam.	Camaldolese Hermits of the Congregation of Monte Corona	[0230]
F.C.	Brothers of Charity	[0290]
F.D.P.	Sons of Divine Providence	[0410]
F.F.I.	Franciscan Friars of the Immaculate	[0533]
F.F.S.C.	Franciscan Brothers of the Holy Cross	[0510]
F.I.C.	Brothers of Christian Instruction	[0320]
F.J.	Congregation of St. John	[]
F.M.M.	Brothers of Mercy	[0810]
F.M.M.	Missionary Fraternity of Mary	[]
F.M.S.	The Marist Brothers	[0770]
F.M.S.I.	Sons of Mary Missionary Society	[1270]
F.P.M.	Presentation Brothers	[]
F.S.C.	Brothers of the Christian Schools	[0330]
F.S.E.	Brothers of the Holy Eucharist	[0620]
F.S.P.	Brothers of St. Patrick	[1160]
F.S.R.	Brothers of the Congregation of Our Lady of the Holy Rosary	[0960]
F.S.S.P.	Priestly Fraternity of St. Peter	[1065]
Glmy.	The Glenmary Home Missioners	[0570]
H.J.D.	Los Hermanos de Juan Diego	[]
H.M.C.	Hermits of Mount Carmel	[]
I.C.	Institute of Charity	[0300]
I.C.	Incarnational Consecration	[]
I.H.M.	Brothers of the Immaculate Heart of Mary	[0680]
I.M.C.	Consolata Missionaries	[0390]
I.S.S.S.	Schoenstatt Institute of Secular Priests	[]
L.B.S.F.	Little Brothers of Saint Francis	[1144]
L.C.	Legionaries of Christ	[0730]
M.Afr.	Missionaries of Africa	[0850]
M.C.B.S.	Missionary Congregation of the Blessed Sacrament	[]
M.C.C.J.	Comboni Missionaries of the Heart of Jesus (Verona)	[0380]
M.Des.	Mercedarios Descalzos	[]
M.E.P.	Paris Foreign Mission Society	[0897]
M.G.	Guadalupe Missioners	[]
M.H.M.	Mill Hill Missionaries	[0830]
M.I.C.	Congregation of Marians of the Immaculate Conception	[0740]
M.J.	Missionaries of St. Joseph (Mexico)	[]
M.M.	Maryknoll	[0800]
M.S.	The Missionaries of Our Lady of La Salette	[0720]
M.S.C.	Missionaries of the Sacred Heart	[1110]
M.S.F.	Congregation of the Missionaries of the Holy Family	[0630]
M.S.P.	Missionaries of St. Paul	[]
M.Sp.S.	Missionaries of the Holy Spirit	[0660]
M.Ss.A.	Missionaries of the Holy Apostles	[0590]
M.SS.CC.	Missionaries of the Sacred Hearts of Jesus and Mary	[1120]
O.A.R.	Order of the Augustinian Recollects	[0150]
O.Carm.	Carmelite Fathers and Brothers	[0270]
O.Cart.	Order of Carthusians	[0280]
O.C.D.	Discalced Carmelite Fathers	[0260]
O.Cist.	Cistercian Fathers	[0340]
O.C.S.O.	The Cistercian Order of the Strict Observance (Trappists)	[0350]
O.de.M.	Order of Our Lady of Mercy	[0970]
O.F.M.	Franciscan Friars	[0520]
O.F.M.Cap.	The Capuchin Friars	[0470]
O.F.M.Conv.	Conventual Franciscans	[0480]
O.H.	Hospitaller Brothers of St. John of God	[0670]
O.I.C.	Order of the Imitation of Christ	[]
O.L.P.	Brothers of Our Lady of Providence	[]
O.M.	Minim Fathers	[0835]
O.Mar.	Congregation of Maronite Monks	[0790]
O.M.I.	Oblates of Mary Immaculate	[0910]
O.M.V.	Oblates of the Virgin Mary	[0940]
O.P.	Order of Preachers (Dominicans)	[0430]
O.Praem.	Canons Regular of Premontre	[0900]
O.R.C.	Operarios del Reina de Cristo	[]
O.S.A.	The Augustinians	[0140]
O.S.B.	Benedictine Monks	[0200]
O.S.B.Cam.	Camaldolese Hermits	[]
O.S.B.M.	Order of St. Basil the Great	[0180]
O.S.C.	Canons Regular of the Order of the Holy Cross	[0400]
O.S.Cam.	Camillian Fathers and Brothers	[0240]
O.S.F.	Congregation of the Religious Brothers of the Third Order Regular of St. Francis	[0490]
O.S.F.	Franciscan Brothers of Christ the King	[0500]
O.S.F.	Franciscan Brothers of the Third Order Regular	[0515]
O.S.F.	Franciscan Missionary Brothers of the Sacred Heart of Jesus	[0540]
O.S.F.S.	Oblates of St. Francis de Sales	[0920]
O.S.J.	Oblates of St. Joseph	[0930]
O.S.M.	Servites	[1240]
O.S.P.P.E.	Pauline Fathers	[1010]
O.Ss.S.	Brigittine Monks	[0895]
O.SS.T.	Order of the Holy Trinity	[1310]
P.I.M.E.	Pontifical Institute for Foreign Missions	[1050]
R.C.J.	Rogationist Fathers	[1090]
S.A.	Franciscan Friars of the Atonement	[0530]
S.A.C.	Society of the Catholic Apostolate	[0990]
S.C.	Brothers of the Sacred Heart	[1100]
S.C.	Servants of Charity	[1220]
S.Ch.	Society of Christ	[1260]
Sch.P.	Piarist Fathers	[1040]
S.C.J.	Congregation of the Priests of the Sacred Heart	[1130]
S.D.B.	Salesians of Don Bosco	[1190]
S.D.S.	Society of the Divine Savior	[1200]
S.D.V.	Vocationist Fathers	[1340]
S.F.	Sons of the Holy Family	[0640]
S.F.M.	Scarboro Foreign Missions	[]
S.J.	Jesuit Fathers and Brothers	[0690]
S.M.	Society of Mary (Marianists)	[0760]
S.M.	Marist Fathers	[0780]
S.M.A.	Society of African Missions	[0110]
S.M.M.	Montfort Missionaries	[0870]
S.M.P.	Society of Our Mother of Peace	[]
S.O.Cist.	Cistercian Monks of the Strict Observance	[]
S.O.L.T.	Society of Our Lady of the Most Holy Trinity	[0975]
s.P.	Servants of the Paraclete	[1230]
S.P.S.	St. Patrick Missionary Society	[1170]
S.S.	Society of the Priests of Saint Sulpice	[1290]
S.S.C.	Society of St. Columban	[0370]
SS.CC.	Congregation of the Sacred Hearts of Jesus and Mary	[1140]
S.S.E.	Society of Saint Edmund	[0440]
S.S.J.	St. Joseph's Society of the Sacred Heart	[0700]
S.S.P.	Pauline Fathers and Brothers	[1020]
S.S.S.	Congregation of the Blessed Sacrament	[0220]
S.S.T.	Missionary Society of St. Thomas the Apostle	[]
S.T.	Missionary Servants of the Most Holy Trinity	[0840]
S.X.	Xaverian Missionary Fathers	[1360]
S.V.D.	Society of the Divine Word	[0420]
T.O.R.	Third Order Regular of Saint Francis	[0560]
V.C.	Vincentian Congregation (India)	[]
V.D.C.	Verbum Dei Community	[]

Religious Order Initials for Women

A.B.S.	Auxiliaries of the Blessed Sacrament	[]
A.C.J.	Handmaids of the Sacred Heart of Jesus	[1870]
A.D.	Sisters of the Lamb of God	[2260]
A.I.M.	Association of Mary Immaculate	[]
A.N.G.	A New Genesis	[]
A.P.	Nuns of Perpetual Adoration of Blessed Sacrament	[3190]
A.P.B.	Adorers of the Precious Blood	[0110]
A.P.G.	Sisters of Perpetual Adoration	[3195]
A.R.	Handmaids of the Sacred Heart of Jesus for Reparation	[1880]
A.R.	Augustinian Recollects	[]
A.S.C.	Adorers of the Blood of Christ	[0100]
A.S.C.J.	Apostles of the Sacred Heart of Jesus	[0130]
B.C.	Notre Dame du Bon Conseil (Quebec)	[]
Bethl.	Bethlemita, Daughters of the Sacred Heart of Jesus	[0910]
B.V.M.	Sisters of Charity of Blessed Virgin Mary	[0430]
B.V.M.C.	Blessed Virgin Missionaries of Carmel	[]
C.ach.	Carmelite Sisters of Charity	[0340]
Carmel.D.C.J.	Carmelite Sisters of the Divine Heart of Jesus	[0360]
C.B.S.	Congregation of Bon Secours	[0270]
C.C.	Carmel Community	[0310]
C.C.V.I.	Sisters of Charity of Incarnate Word	[0460]
C.C.V.I.	Sisters of Charity of Incarnate Word, Houston, TX	[0470]
C.C.W.	Carmelite Community of the Word	[0315]
C.D.P.	Sisters of Divine Providence	[0990]
C.D.P.	Sisters of Divine Providence of Kentucky	[1000]
C.D.P.	Sisters of Divine Providence of San Antonio, TX.	[1010]
C.D.P.	Capuchin Sisters (Spain)	[]
C.D.S.	Congregation of Divine Spirit	[1040]
C.F.M.M.	Minim Daughters of Mary Immaculate	[2675]
C.F.P.	Feminine Congregation of the Passion	[]
C.F.P.	Mexican Passionist Sisters	[]
C.G.S.	Contemplatives of Good Shepherd	[1830]
C.H.F.	Sisters of Holy Faith	[1940]
C.H.M.	Congregation of Humility of Mary	[2100]
C.H.S.	Community of the Holy Spirit	[2020]
C.I.C.	Sisters of Immaculate Conception	[2120]
C.I.J.	Congregation of Infant Jesus	[2230]
C.J.C.	Poor Sisters of Jesus Crucified and Sorrowful Mother	[3240]
C.K.	School Sisters of Christ the King	[]
C.L.H.C.	Congregation of Our Lady Help of the Clergy	[3090]
C.M.C.	Congregation of Mother of Carmel	[]
C.M.R.	Congregation of Mary Queen	[]
C.M.S.	Comboni Missionary Sisters	[0690]
C.M.S.	Cashel Mercy Sisters	[2515]
C.M.S.T.	Missionary Carmelites of St. Teresa	[0390]
C.N.D.	Congregation of Notre Dame	[2980]
C.O.C.	Companions of Christ	[]
C.P.	Religious of the Passion of Jesus Christ	[3170]
C.P.	Sisters of the Cross and Passion	[3180]
C.P.C.	Capuchin Poor Clares	[]
C.P.C.	St. Clare Capuchin Sisters	[]
C.PP.S.	Sisters of the Precious Blood (Dayton, Ohio)	[3260]
C.PP.S.	Sisters of the Most Precious Blood (O'Fallon, MO)	[3270]
C.P.S.	Missionary Sisters of the Precious Blood	[2850]
C.R.	Sisters of the Resurrection	[3480]
C.S.	Company of the Savior	[0710]
C.S.	The Christian Sisters (Pious Union)	[]
C.S.A.	Sisters of Charity of St. Augustine	[0580]
C.S.A.	Sisters of St. Agnes	[3710]
C.S.A.	Albertine Sisters (Krakow, Poland)	[]
C.S.A.C.	Sisters of the Catholic Apostolate (Pallottine)	[3140]
C.S.B.	Congregation of St. Brigid	[3735]
C.S.C.	Congregation of Sisters of Holy Cross	[1920]
C.S.C.	Sisters of Holy Cross	[1930]
C.S.C.	Sisters of Holy Cross and Seven Dolors	[]
C.S.E.	Carmelite Sisters of the Eucharist	[]
C.S.F.N.	Sisters of Holy Family of Nazareth	[1970]
C.S.J.	Sisters of St. Joseph (Boston, Brighton)	[3830-01]
C.S.J.	Sisters of St. Joseph (Chicago, Lagrange Park)	[3830-02]
C.S.J.	Sisters of St. Joseph (Orange)	[3830-03]
C.S.J.	Sisters of St. Joseph (Rockville Centre, Brentwood)	[3830-05]
C.S.J.	Sisters of St. Joseph (Cleveland)	[3830-08]
C.S.J.	Sisters of St. Joseph (Lafayette, IN)	[3830-10]
C.S.J.	Sisters of St. Joseph (Pittsburgh, Baden)	[3830-13]
C.S.J.	Sisters of St. Joseph (Salina, Concordia)	[3830-15]
C.S.J.	Sisters of St. Joseph (Wichita)	[3830-18]
C.S.J.	Sisters of St. Joseph of Carondelet	[3840]
C.S.J.	Sisters of St. Joseph of Chambery	[3850]
C.S.J.	Sisters of St. Joseph (Lyons, France)	[3870]
C.S.J.	Sisters of St. Joseph of Medaille	[3880]
C.S.J.B.	Sisters of St. John the Baptist	[3820]
C.S.J.P.	Sisters of St. Joseph of Peace	[3890]
C.S.M.	Sisters of St. Martha of Antigonish N.S.	[3937]
C.S.N.	Congregation of Sisters of Nazareth	[]
C.S.R.	Sisters of Holy Redeemer	[2000]
C.S.S.F.	Felician Sisters	[1170]
C.S.Sp.	Sisters of Holy Spirit	[2030]
C.S.S.T.	Carmelite Sisters of St. Teresa	[]
C.S.T.	Carmelite Sisters of St. Therese of Infant Jesus	[0380]
C.V.D.	Sisters of Bethany	[0250]
C.V.I.	Congregation of Incarnate Word and Blessed Sacrament	[2190]
C.V.I.	Religious of the Incarnate Word	[3449]
D.C.	Daughters of Charity of St. Vincent de Paul	[0760]
D.C.	Daughters of the Cross	[0770]
D.C.M.	Diocesan Carmelites of Maine	[]
D.C.P.B.	Daughters of Charity of Most Precious Blood	[0740]
D.H.M.	Daughters of Heart of Mary	[0810]
D.H.S.	Daughters of the Holy Spirit	[0820]
D.L.F.	Daughters of Our Lady of Fatima	[]
D.L.J.C.	Disciples of the Lord Jesus Christ	[0965]
D.M.	Daughters of Mary of the Immaculate Conception	[0860]
D.M.	Daughters of Our Lady of Mercy	[0890]
D.M.I.	Daughters of Mary Immaculate (Chaldean)	[]
D.M.J.	Daughters of Mary and Joseph	[0880]
D.O.M.	Daughters of Mercy (Croatian)	[]
D.S.F.	Daughters of St. Francis of Assisi	[0920]
D.S.M.P.	Daughters of St. Mary of Providence	[0940]
D.W.	Daughters of Wisdom	[0960]
E.F.M.S.	Eucharistic Franciscan Missionary Sisters	[1150]
E.M.S.	Eucharistic Missionary Society	[]
F.A.S.	Franciscan Apostolic Sisters	[]
F.C.	Daughters of the Cross of Liege	[0780]
F.C.J.	Society of Sisters Faithful Companions of Jesus	[4048]
F.C.S.C.J.	Daughters of Charity of the Sacred Heart of Jesus	[0750]
F.D.C.	Daughters of Divine Charity	[0790]
Fd.CC.	Canossian Daughters of Charity	[0730]
F.D.L.P.	Daughters of Providence	[]
F.D.N.S.C.	Daughters of Our Lady of the Sacred Heart	[0900]
F.D.P.	Daughters of Divine Providence	[0800]
F.D.Z.	Daughters of Divine Zeal	[0795]
F.H.I.C.	Franciscan Hospitaller Sisters of the Immaculate Conception	[1270]
F.H.M.	Franciscan Handmaids of the Most Pure Heart of Mary	[1260]
F.H.M.	Franciscan Sisters Daughters of Mercy	[1235]
F.I.	Daughters of Jesus	[0840]
F.J.	Congregation of the Daughters of Jesus	[0830]
F.L.G.	Franciscan Sisters of Our Lady of Grace	[]
F.M.A.	Daughters of Mary Help of Christians	[0850]
F.M.D.C.	Franciscan Missionaries of the Divine Child	[1340]
F.M.I.	Congregation of the Daughters of Mary Immaculate (Marianist Sisters)	[0870]
F.M.I.	Franciscan Sisters of Mary Immaculate of the Third Order of St. Francis of Assisi	[1500]
F.M.I.J.	Franciscan Missionaries of the Infant Jesus	[1365]
F.M.M.	The Franciscan Missionaries of Mary	[1370]
F.M.S.C.	Franciscan Missionary Sisters of the Sacred Heart	[1400]
F.M.S.J.	Mill Hill Sisters	[1410]
F.M.S.R.	Daughters of Our Lady of Holy Rosary	[]
F.N.S.S.C.	Franciscan Sisters of Our Lady of the Sacred Heart	[]
F.S.E.	The Institute of the Franciscan Sisters of the Eucharist	[1250]
F.S.J.	Religious Daughters of St. Joseph	[0930]
F.S.M.	Franciscan Sisters of Mary	[1415]
F.S.O.L.	Franciscan Sisters of Our Lady	[]
F.S.P.	Pious Society Daughters of St. Paul	[0950]
F.S.P.	Franciscan Sisters of Peace	[1425]
F.S.P.A.	Congregation of the Sisters of the Third Order of St. Francis of Perpetual Adoration	[1780]
F.S.R.	Franciscan Sisters of Ringwood	[1420]
F.S.S.C.	Franciscan Sisters of St. Clare (Pious Union)	[]
F.S.S.E.	Franciscan Sisters of St. Elizabeth	[1460]
F.S.S.J.	Franciscan Sisters of St. Joseph	[1470]
F.S.S.J.	Franciscan Sisters of St. Joseph	[1480]
F.S.S.M.	Franciscan Sisters of the Sorrowful Mother	[]
F.S.Sp.J.	Franciscan Sisters of the Spirit of Jesus	[]
G.H.M.S.	Home Mission Sisters of America (Glenmary)	[2080]
G.N.S.H.	Grey Nuns of the Sacred Heart	[1840]
H.B.S.	Hermanas Contemplativas del Buen Pastor	[]
H.C.G.	Hermanas Catequistas Guadalupanas	[1900]
H.F.deS.J.	Franciscan Sisters of St. Joseph (Mexico City)	[]
H.G.S.	Congregation de Hermanas Guadalupanas de la Salle	[]
H.H.S.	Society of Helpers	[1890]
H.J.	Hermanas Josefinas	[1910]
H.J.D.	Las Hermanas de Juan Diego	[]
H.M.	Sisters of the Humility of Mary	[2110]
H.M.C.	Hermits of Mount Carmel	[]
H.M.S.S.	Sisters of Mercy of the Blessed Sacrament	[2590]
H.M.S.S.	Religious Sisters of the Apostolate of the Blessed Sacrament	[3370]
H.O.Carm.	Hermits of Our Lady of Mt. Carmel	[]
H.P.B.	Congregation of the Handmaids of the Precious Blood	[1860]
H.R.F.	Sisters of the Holy Rosary of Fatima (Mexico)	[]
H.S.H.	Handmaids of the Sacred Heart of Pohang	[]
H.S.M.	Hermit Sisters of Mary	[]
H.Sp.S.	Daughters of the Holy Spirit Nazareth of the Good Shepherd	[]
H.S.S.	Hermanas del Servico Social	[]
H.S.S.R.	Hermit Sisters of Romuald	[]
H.T.	Handmaids of the Most Holy Trinity	[]
H.V.M.	Sisters, Home Visitors of Mary	[2090]
I.B.V.M.	Institute of the Blessed Virgin Mary (Loretto Sisters)	[2370]
I.B.V.M.	Institute of the Blessed Virgin Mary (Loretto Sisters)	[2380]
I.C.	Vietnamese Sisters Incarnational Consecration	[]
I.C.M.	Missionary Sisters of the Immaculate Heart of Mary	[2750]
I.H.M.	Sisters, Servants of the Immaculate Heart of Mary	[2150]
I.H.M.	Sisters, Servants of the Immaculate Heart of Mary	[2160]
I.H.M.	Sisters, Servants of the Immaculate Heart of Mary	[2170]
I.H.M.	Sisters, Servants of the Immaculate Heart of Mary	[2180]

I.H.M.	The California Institute of the Sisters of the Most Holy and Immaculate Heart of the Blessed Virgin Mary	[2930]
I.H.M.	Sisters of the Most Holy and Immaculate Heart of Blessed Virgin Mary (Wichita Foundation)	[]
I.J.	Sisters of the Infant Jesus	[2240]
I.M.	Sisters of Charity of the Infant Mary	[]
I.S.S.M.	Secular Institute of Schoenstatt Sisters of Mary	[]
I.W.B.S.	Congregation of the Incarnate Word and Blessed Sacrament	[2200]
I.W.B.S.	Congregation of the Incarnate Word and Blessed Sacrament	[2205]
J.S.O.P.	Dominican Oblates of Jesus (Spain)	[]
L.B.	Ladies of Bethany	[]
L.C.M.	Sisters of the Little Company of Mary	[2270]
L.H.C.	Lovers of the Holy Cross Sisters	[2390]
L.M.S.C.	Little Missionary Sisters of Charity	[2290]
L.S.	Lasallian Sisters (Vietnam)	[]
L.S.A.	Little Sisters of the Assumption	[2310]
L.S.G.	Little Sisters of the Gospel (France)	[]
L.S.I.C.	Little Servant Sisters of the Immaculate Conception	[2300]
L.S.J.	Little Sisters of Jesus	[2330]
L.S.J.M.	Little Sisters of Jesus and Mary	[2331]
L.S.P.	Little Sisters of the Poor	[2340]
M.C.	Consolata Missionary Sisters	[0720]
M.C.	Missionaries of Charity	[2710]
M.C.	Poor Clare Missionary Sisters	[2840]
M.C.D.P.	Missionary Catechists of Divine Providence, San Antonio, TX	[2690]
M.C.M.	Cordi Marian Sisters	[]
M.C.P.	Missioneras Catequestas de los Pobres	[]
M.C.S.	Missionary Sisters of the Sacred Side	[]
M.C.S.J.M.	Congregation of Missionary Catechists of the Sacred Heart of Jesus and Mary	[]
M.D.	Mothers of the Helpless	[]
M.D.P.V.M.	Missionary Daughters of the Most Pure Virgin Mary	[]
M.E.	Missionary Ecumenical (Rome)	[]
M.C.SS.CC.J.M.	Missionary Catechists of the Sacred Hearts of Jesus and Mary	[2700]
M.E.S.S.T.	Eucharistic Missionaries of the Most Holy Trinity	[]
M.E.S.T.	Eucharistic Missionaries of St. Theresa (Mexico)	[]
M.F.P.	Franciscan Missionaries Our Lady of Peace	[]
M.G.Sp.S.	Guadalupan Missionaries of the Holy Spirit	[1845]
M.H.S.	Sisters of the Most Holy Sacrament	[2940]
M.H.S.H.	Mission Helpers of the Sacred Heart	[2720]
M.I.C.	Missionary Sisters of the Immaculate Conception (Canada)	[]
M.J.	Missionary Sisters of Jesus	[]
M.J.M.J.	Missionaries of Jesus, Mary and Joseph	[2770]
M.M.	Maryknoll Sisters of St. Dominic	[2470]
M.M.D.	Servite Missionary Sisters of the Sorrowful Mother	[]
M.M.M.	Medical Missionaries of Mary	[2480]
M.M.S.	Medical Mission Sisters	[2490]
M.O.M.	Missionary Sisters of Our Lady of Mercy	[2830]
M.P.F.	Religious Teachers Filippini	[3430]
M.P.H.	Missionary Sisters of Our Lady of Perpetual Help	[]
M.P.S.	Misioneras del Perpetual Socorro	[]
M.P.S.	Missionary Sisters of Our Lady of Perpetual Help	[]
M.P.V.	Religious Venerini Sisters	[4180]
M.R.	Marianist Sisters	[]
M.S.	Marian Sisters of the Diocese of Lincoln	[2400]
M.S.B.T.	Missionary Servants of the Most Blessed Trinity	[2790]
M.S.C.	Congregation of the Marianites of the Holy Cross	[2410]
M.S.C.	Missionary Sisters of the Most Sacred Heart of Jesus of Hiltrup	[2800]
M.S.C.	Missionary Sisters of the Sacred Heart	[2860]
M.S.C.Gpe.	Missionaries of the Sacred Heart of Jesus and of Our Lady of Guadalupe	[2865]
M.S.C.K.	Missionary Sisters of Christ the King	[2715]
M.S.F.	Missionary Sisters of the Holy Family	[]
M.S.H.F.	Missionary Sisters of the Holy Family (Poland)	[]
M.S.H.R.	Missionary Sisters of the Holy Rosary	[2730]
M.S.J.	Medical Sisters of St. Joseph	[2500]
M.S.K.C.P.	Missionary Sisters of Christ the King of Polonia	[]
M.S.M.G.	Missionary Sisters of Mother of God	[2810]
M.S.O.L.A.	Missionary Sisters of Our Lady of Africa	[2820]
M.S.S.A.	Missionary Servants of St. Anthony	[2890]
M.S.S.C.B.	Missionary Sisters of St. Charles Borromeo	[2900]
M.S.S.J.	Missionary Servants of St. Joseph (Spain)	[]
M.S.Sp.	Mission Sisters of the Holy Spirit	[2740]
M.SS.S.	Missionary Sisters of the Most Blessed Sacrament	[2780]
M.X.Y.	The Yarumal Foreign Mission Institute (Colombia)	[]
N.A.U.-O.L.C.	North American Unions of Sisters of Our Lady of Charity	[3070]
N.D.	Notre Dame Sisters	[2960]
N.D.S.	Congregation of Notre Dame de Sion	[2950]
O.A.R.	Augustinian Recollect Sisters	[]
O.B.T.	Sisters Oblates to the Blessed Trinity	[3020]
O.C.A.	Carmelite Vietnamese of Our Lady of Mt. Carmel	[]
O.Carm.	Calced Carmelites	[0300]
O.Carm.	Carmelite Nuns of the Ancient Observance	[0320]
O.Carm.	Carmelite Sisters for Aged and Infirm	[0330]
O.Carm.	Carmelite Sisters (Corpus Christi)	[0350]
O.Carm.	Congregation of Our Lady of Mount Carmel	[0400]
O.Carm.	Institute of the Sisters of Our Lady of Mt. Carmel	[0410]
O.C.D.	Carmelite Sisters of the Most Sacred Heart of Los Angeles	[0370]
O.C.D.	Discalced Carmelite Nuns	[0420]
O.C.D.	Carmelitas del Sagrado Corazon	[]
O.Cist.	Cistercian Nuns	[0080]
O.C.S.O.	Cistercian Nuns of the Strict Observance	[0670]
O.D.N.	Company of Mary	[0700]
O.L.C.	Sisters of Our Lady of Charity	[3071]
O.L.C.	Sisters of Our Lady of Charity	[3073]
O.L.G.	Sisters of Our Lady of the Garden	[]
O.L.L.	Sisters of Our Lady of Lourdes	[]
O.L.M.	Sisters of Charity of Our Lady of Mercy	[0510]
O.L.S.	Sisters of Our Lady of Sorrows	[3120]
O.L.V.M.	Our Lady of Victory Missionary Sisters	[3130]
O.M.M.I.	Oblate Missionaries of Mary Immaculate	[]
O.M.O.	Oblates of the Mother of Orphans	[3035]
O.P.	Dominican Contemplative Nuns (Cloistered)	[1050]
O.P.	Dominican Contemplative Sisters (Cloistered)	[1060]
O.P.	Dominican Sisters (St. Catharine, KY)	[1070-01]
O.P.	Dominican Sisters (Columbus, OH)	[1070-02]
O.P.	Dominican Sisters (Sinsinawa, WI)	[1070-03]
O.P.	Dominican Sisters (San Rafael, CA)	[1070-04]
O.P.	Dominican Sisters (Amityville, NY)	[1070-05]
O.P.	Dominican Sisters (Newburgh, NY)	[1070-06]
O.P.	Dominican Sisters (Nashville, TN)	[1070-07]
O.P.	Dominican Sisters (New Orleans, LA)	[1070-08]
O.P.	Dominican Sisters (Racine, WI)	[1070-09]
O.P.	Dominican Sisters (Springfield, IL)	[1070-10]
O.P.	Dominican Sisters (Sparkill, NY)	[1070-11]
O.P.	Dominican Sisters (San Jose, CA)	[1070-12]
O.P.	Dominican Sisters (Adrian, MI)	[1070-13]
O.P.	Dominican Sisters (Grand Rapids, MI)	[1070-14]
O.P.	Dominican Sisters (Blauvelt, NY)	[1070-15]
O.P.	Dominican Sisters (Ossining, NY)	[1070-16]
O.P.	Dominican Sisters (Media, PA)	[1070-17]
O.P.	Dominican Sisters (Caldwell, PA)	[1070-18]
O.P.	Dominican Sisters (Houston, TX)	[1070-19]
O.P.	Dominican Sisters (Tacoma, WA)	[1070-20]
O.P.	Dominican Sisters (Edmonds, WA)	[1070-21]
O.P.	Dominican Sisters (Fall River, MA)	[1070-22]
O.P.	Dominican Sisters (Hawthorne, NY)	[1070-23]
O.P.	Dominican Sisters (Great Bend, KS)	[1070-24]
O.P.	Dominican Sisters (Kenosha, WI)	[1070-25]
O.P.	Dominican Sisters (Oxford, MI)	[1070-26]
O.P.	Dominican Sisters (Justice, IL)	[1070-27]
O.P.	Dominican Sisters (Akron, OH)	[1070-28]
O.P.	Dominican Sisters (Spokane, WA)	[1070-29]
O.P.	Dominican Sisters (Oxford, South Africa)	[1070-30]
O.P.	Marian Society of Dominican Catechists	[1090]
O.P.	Dominican Sisters of Charity of the Presentation of the Blessed Virgin	[1100]
O.P.	Dominican Sisters of Our Lady of the Rosary and of Saint Catherine of Siena, Cabra	[1110]
O.P.	Dominican Sisters of the Roman Congregation	[1120]
O.P.	Dominican Rural Missionaries	[1130]
O.P.	Eucharistic Missionaries of St. Dominic	[1140]
O.P.	Dominican Sisters of Carondelet	[]
O.P.	Religious Missionaries of St. Dominic (Spanish Prov.)	[]
O.P.	Dominican Sisters of Mt. Thabor	[]
O.P.	Dominican Sisters of Our Lady of the Most Holy Rosary	[]
O.P.	Dominican Sisters (Vietnam)	[]
O.P.	Dominican Contemplative Sisters	[]
O.P.	Dominican Sisters (Colombia)	[]
O.P.	Dominican Sisters (Ecuador)	[]
O.P.	Hermanas Dominicanas de la Doctrine Cristiana	[]
O.S.A.	Augustinian Nuns of Contemplative Life	[0160]
O.S.A.	Congregation of Augustinian Sisters Servants of Jesus and Mary	[2145]
O.S.A.	Sisters of St. Rita	[4010]
O.S.A.	Sisters of St. Augustine	[]
O.S.A.	Augustinian Sisters of Our Lady of Consolation	[]
O.S.B.	Benedictine Nuns of the Congregation of Solesmes	[0170]
O.S.B.	Benedictine Nuns of the Primitive Observance	[0180]
O.S.B.	Benedictine Sisters	[0190]
O.S.B.	Benedictine Sisters	[0200]
O.S.B.	Missionary Benedictine Sisters	[0210]
O.S.B.	Congregation of the Benedictine Sisters of Perpetual Adoration of Pontifical Jurisdiction	[0220]
O.S.B.	Benedictine Sisters of Pontifical Jurisdiction	[0230]
O.S.B.	Benedictine Nuns	[0233]
O.S.B.	Olivetan Benedictine Sisters	[0240]
O.S.B.	Congregation of Jesus Crucified	[2250]
O.S.B.	Benedictine Congregation of Our Lady of Monte	[]
O.S.B.	Benedictine Sisters of Sacred Heart	[]
O.S.B.	Contemplative Sisters of St. Benedict	[]
O.S.B.	Benedictine Sisters of Liberty	[]
O.S.B.	Congregation of the Benedictine Sisters of the Sacred Heart	[]
O.S.B.Cam.	Camaldolese Benedictine Sisters	[]
O.S.B.M.	Sisters of the Order of St. Basil the Great	[3730]
O.S.B.S.	Oblate Sisters of the Blessed Sacrament	[3010]
O.S.C.	Order of St. Clare	[3760]
O.S.C.	Sisters of St. Clare	[3770]
O.S.C.Cap.	Capuchin Poor Clares	[3765]
O.S.F.	Franciscan Sisters of Allegany, New York	[1180]
O.S.F.	The Franciscan Sisters of Baltimore	[1200]
O.S.F.	Franciscan Sisters of Chicago	[1210]
O.S.F.	Franciscan Sisters of Christian Charity	[1230]
O.S.F.	Franciscan Sister, Daughters of the Sacred Hearts of Jesus and Mary	[1240]
O.S.F.	Franciscan Sisters of the Immaculate Conception	[1280]
O.S.F.	Franciscan Sisters of the Immaculate Conception and St. Joseph for the Dying	[1300]
O.S.F.	Franciscan Sisters of Little Falls, Minnesota	[1310]
O.S.F.	Franciscan Missionary Sisters for Africa	[1320]
O.S.F.	Franciscan Missionary Sisters of the Immaculate Conception	[1350]
O.S.F.	Missionary Franciscan Sisters of the Immaculate Conception	[1360]
O.S.F.	Franciscan Missionaries of Our Lady	[1380]
O.S.F.	Franciscan Missionary Sisters of Our Lady of Sorrows	[1390]
O.S.F.	Franciscan Sisters of Our Lady of Perpetual Help	[1430]

O.S.F.	Franciscan Sisters of the Sacred Heart	[1450]
O.S.F.	Franciscan Sisters of St. Paul	[1485]
O.S.F.	Sisters of the Third Franciscan Order	[1490]
O.S.F.	St. Francis Mission Community	[1505]
O.S.F.	Sisters of St. Francis	[1510]
O.S.F.	Sisters of St. Francis of Christ the King	[1520]
O.S.F.	Sisters of St. Francis of the Congregation of Our Lady of Lourdes, Sylvania, Ohio	[1530]
O.S.F.	Sisters of Saint Francis, Clinton, Iowa	[1540]
O.S.F.	Sisters of St. Francis of the Holy Cross	[1550]
O.S.F.	Sisters of St. Francis of the Holy Eucharist	[1560]
O.S.F.	Sisters of St. Francis of the Holy Family	[1570]
O.S.F.	Sisters of St. Francis of the Immaculate Conception	[1580]
O.S.F.	Sisters of St. Francis of the Immaculate Heart of Mary (Hankinson, North Dakota)	[1590]
O.S.F.	Sisters of St. Francis of the Martyr St. George	[1600]
O.S.F.	Sisters of Saint Francis of Millvale, Pennsylvania	[1620]
O.S.F.	Sisters of St. Francis of Penance and Christian Charity	[1630]
O.S.F.	Sisters of St. Francis of Perpetual Adoration	[1640]
O.S.F.	The Sisters of St. Francis of Philadelphia	[1650]
O.S.F.	Sisters of Saint Francis of the Providence of God	[1660]
O.S.F.	Sisters of St. Francis of Savannah, MO	[1670]
O.S.F.	School Sisters of St. Francis	[1680]
O.S.F.	School Sisters of the Third Order of St. Francis (Pittsburgh, PA)	[1690]
O.S.F.	School Sisters of the Third Order of St. Francis (Panhandle, TX)	[1695]
O.S.F.	School Sisters of the Third Order of St. Francis (Bethlehem, PA)	[1700]
O.S.F.	The Sisters of St. Francis of Assisi	[1705]
O.S.F.	Congregation of the Third Order of St. Francis of Mary Immaculate, Joliet, IL	[1710]
O.S.F.	Sisters of the Third Order Regular of St. Francis of the Congregation of Our Lady of Lourdes	[1720]
O.S.F.	Congregation of the Sisters of the Third Order of St. Francis Oldenburg, IN	[1730]
O.S.F.	Sisters of the Third Order of St. Francis of Penance and Charity	[1760]
O.S.F.	Sisters of the Third Order of St. Francis (Peoria, IL)	[1770]
O.S.F.	Sisters of St. Francis of the Third Order Regular (Williamsville, New York)	[1800]
O.S.F.	Bernardine Sisters of the Third Order of St. Francis	[1810]
O.S.F.	Hospital Sisters of the Third Order of St. Francis	[1820]
O.S.F.	Servants of the Holy Infancy of Jesus	[1980]
O.S.F.	Consolation Sisters (Highland, CA)	[]
O.S.F.	Franciscan Sisters of Christ the Divine Teacher	[]
O.S.F.	St. Francis Mission Community	[]
O.S.F.S.	Oblate Sisters of St. Francis de Sales	[3060]
O.S.H.J.	Oblate Sisters of the Sacred Heart of Jesus	[3050]
O.S.M.	Mantellate Sisters, Servants of Mary of Blue Island	[3570]
O.S.M.	Servants of Mary	[3580]
O.S.M.	Servants of Mary (Servite Sisters)	[3590]
O.S.M.	Oblates of St. Martha	[]
O.S.P.	Oblate Sisters of Providence	[3040]
O.S.S.	Sacramentine Nuns	[3490]
O.SS.R.	Order of the Most Holy Redeemer	[2010]
O.SS.R.	Oblates of the Most Holy Redeemer	[3030]
O.SS.S.	The Brigittine Sisters	[0280]
O.SS.T.	Sisters of the Most Holy Trinity	[0260]
O.S.U.	Ursuline Nuns (Roman Union)	[4110]
O.S.U.	Ursuline Nuns of the Congregation of Paris (St. Martin, OH)	[4120]
O.S.U.	Ursuline Nuns of the Congregation of Paris (Cincinnati, OH)	[4120-01]
O.S.U.	Ursuline Nuns of the Congregation of Paris (Kansas City, KS)	[4120-02]
O.S.U.	Ursuline Nuns of the Congregation of Paris (Louisville, KY)	[4120-03]
O.S.U.	Ursuline Nuns of the Congregation of Paris (Cleveland, OH)	[4120-04]
O.S.U.	Ursuline Nuns of the Congregation of Paris (Owensboro, KY)	[4120-05]
O.S.U.	Ursuline Nuns of the Congregation of Paris (Toledo, OH)	[4120-06]
O.S.U.	Ursuline Nuns of the Congregation of Paris (Youngstown, OH)	[4120-07]
O.S.U.	Ursuline Sisters of the Congregation of Tildonk, Belgium	[4130]
O.S.U.	Ursuline Sisters of Belleville	[4140]
O.S.U.	Irish Ursuline Union	[4150]
P.B.V.M.	Presentation of the Blessed Virgin Mary Sisters	[3280]
P.B.V.M.	Sisters of the Presentation of the B.V.M.	[3320]
P.B.V.M.	Union of the Sisters of the Presentation of the Blessed Virgin Mary	[3330]
P.C.C.	Order of St. Clare	[3760]
P.C.I.	Pax Christi Institute	[]
P.C.J.	Sisters of the Poor Child Jesus	[3220]
P.C.P.A.	Poor Clares of Perpetual Adoration	[3210]
P.D.D.M.	Pious Disciples of the Divine Master	[0980]
P.F.M.	Little Franciscans of Mary	[2280]
P.H.J.C.	Poor Handmaids of Jesus Christ	[3230]
P.M.	Sisters of the Presentation of Mary	[3310]
P.O.S.C.	Little Workers of the Sacred Heart	[2345]
P.S.N.	Poor Sisters of Nazareth	[3242]
P.S.S.F.	The Little Sisters of the Holy Family	[2320]
P.S.S.J.	Poor Sisters of St. Joseph	[3250]
P.V.M.I.	The Parish Visitors of Mary Immaculate	[3160]
Q.M.H.C.	Quinhon Missionary Sisters of the Holy Cross	[]
R.A.	Religious of the Apostolate of the Sacred Heart	[3380]
R.A.	Religious of the Assumption	[3390]
R.A.	Antonine Sisters	[]
R.A.D.	Sisters of the Love of God	[]
R.C.	Congregation of Our Lady of Retreat in the Cenacle	[3110]
R.C.D.	Sisters of Our Lady of Christian Doctrine	[3080]
R.C.E.	Religious of Christian Education	[3410]
R.C.M.	Sisters of the Immaculate Conception	[2130]
R.C.S.C.J.	Sisters of the Cross of the Sacred Heart of Jesus (Mexico)	[]
R.D.C.	Sisters of the Divine Compassion	[0970]
R.E.	Religious of the Eucharist	[3420]
R.F.	Sisters of St. Philip Neri Missionary Teachers	[]
R.F.R.	Sisters of Our Lady of Refuge	[]
R.G.S.	The Sisters of the Good Shepherd	[1830]
R.H.S.J.	Religious Hospitallers of Saint Joseph	[3440]
R.J.M.	Religious of Jesus and Mary	[3450]
R.M.	Marianitas	[]
R.M.I.	Claretian Missionary Sisters	[0685]
R.M.I.	Religious of Mary Immaculate	[3460]
R.M.M.	Mercedarian Sisters	[]
R.O.D.A.	Sisters Oblates to Divine Love	[]
R.O.L.C.	Our Lady of Charity of Refuge	[3072]
R.S.C.	Religious Sisters of Charity	[3400]
R.S.C.J.	Society of the Sacred Heart	[4070]
R.S.H.M.	Religious of the Sacred Heart of Mary	[3465]
R.S.J.	Religious of St. Joseph of Australia	[]
R.S.M.	Religious Sisters of Mercy of Alma, Michigan	[2519]
R.S.M.	Sisters of Mercy	[2520]
R.S.M.	Sisters of Mercy of Ardagh & Clonmacnois	[2523]
R.S.M.	Sisters of Mercy (Galway)	[2535]
R.S.M.	Sisters of Mercy	[2540]
R.S.M.	Sisters of Mercy (Sligo)	[2549]
R.S.M.	Sisters of Mercy	[2550]
R.S.M.	Sisters of Mercy of the Americas	[2575]
R.S.M.	Sisters of Mercy (Ballyshannon, Ireland)	[]
R.S.M.	Sisters of Mercy (Mayo, Ireland)	[]
R.S.M.	Sisters of Mercy of Mississippi, Inc.	[]
R.S.M.	Sisters of Mercy of Portland	[2655]
R.S.M.	Diocesan Sisters of Mercy	[]
R.S.R.	Congregation of Our Lady of the Holy Rosary	[3100]
R.T.	Theatine Sisters of the Immaculate Conception	[]
R.V.M.	Religious of the Blessed Virgin Mary	[]
S.A.	Franciscan Sisters of the Atonement	[1190]
S.A.A.	Sisters Auxiliaries of the Apostolate	[0140]
S.A.B.	Sisters of St. Anne Bangalone	[]
S.A.C.	Sisters of the Guardian Angel	[1850]
S.A.C.	Pallottine Missionary Sisters Queen of Apostles Prov.	[3150]
S.A.S.V.	Sisters of the Assumption	[0150]
S.B.S.	The Sisters of the Blessed Sacrament for Indians and Colored People	[0260]
S.C.	Sisters of Charity of Cincinnati, Ohio	[0440]
S.C.	Sisters of Charity of Seton Hill, Greensburg, PA	[0570]
S.C.	Sisters of St. Elizabeth, Convent Station	[0590]
S.C.	Sisters of Charity of St. Vincent de Paul, Halifax	[0640]
S.C.	Sisters of Charity of St. Vincent de Paul, New York	[0650]
S.C.C.	Sisters of Christian Charity	[0660]
Sch.P.	Sisters of the Pious Schools	[3200]
S.C.I.C.	Sisters of Charity of the Immaculate Conception of Ivrea	[0450]
S.C.I.M.	Servants of the Immaculate Heart of Mary	[3550]
S.C.K.	Sisters of Christ the King	[]
S.C.L.	Sisters of Charity of Leavenworth, Kansas	[0480]
S.C.M.C.	Sisters of Charity of Our Lady, Mother of the Church	[0530]
S.C.M.M.	Sisters of Charity of Our Lady Mother of Mercy	[0520]
S.C.M.M.	Medical Mission Sisters	[2490]
S.C.N.	Sisters of Charity of Nazareth	[0500]
S.C.O.	Sisters of Charity of Ottawa (Grey Nuns of the Cross)	[0540]
S.C.O.	Sisters of Charity of Quebec (Grey Nuns)	[0560]
S.C.R.H.	Sisters of Charity of Rolling Meadows	[]
S.C.S.J.A.	Sisters of Charity of St. Joan Antida	[0600]
S.C.S.L.	Sisters of Charity of St. Louis	[0620]
S.C.S.H.	Sisters of Charity of St. Hyacinthe (Grey Nuns)	[0610]
S.deP.	Sister Servants of the Poor	[]
S.D.R.	Sisters of the Divine Redeemer	[1020]
S.D.S.	Sisters of the Divine Saviour	[1030]
S.D.S.H.	Sisters of the Society Devoted to the Sacred Heart	[4050]
S.D.V.	Vocationist Sisters	[4210]
S.E.	Sisters of Emanuel	[]
S.E.C.	Sisters of the Eucharistic Covenant	[]
S.F.C.C.	Sisters for Christian Community	[]
S.F.M.A.	Franciscan Missionary Sisters of Assisi	[1330]
S.F.P.	Franciscan Sisters of the Poor	[1440]
S.G.M.	Sisters of Charity of Montreal (Grey Nuns)	[0490]
S.G.S.	Hermanas del Buen Pastor	[]
S.H.C.J.	Society of the Holy Child Jesus	[4060]
S.H.F.	Sisters of the Holy Family	[1960]
S.H.J.M.	Sisters of the Sacred Hearts of Jesus and Mary	[3680]
S.H.S.	Sisters of the Holy Spirit	[2040]
S.H.Sp.	Sisters of the Holy Spirit and Mary Immaculate	[2050]
S.I.M.	Missionaries of the Kingship of Christ	[]
S.I.W.	Sisters of the Incarnate Word and the Blessed Sacrament	[2210]
S.J.	Servants of Jesus	[3560]
S.J.A.	Sisters of Ste. Jeanne D'Arc	[3815]
S.J.B.	Sisters of St. John Bosco (Taylor, TX)	[]
S.J.C.	Sisters of St. Joseph of Cluny	[3860]
S.J.S.	Servants of the Blessed Sacrament	[3499]
S.J.S.M.	Sisters of St. Joseph of St. Mark	[3910]
S.J.W.	Sisters of St. Joseph the Worker	[3920]
S.L.	Sisters of Loretto at the Foot of the Cross	[2360]
S.L.T.	Pious Society of Our Lady of the Most Holy Trinity	[]
S.L.W.	Sisters of the Living Word	[2350]
S.M.	Marist Sisters Congregation of Mary	[2430]
S.M.	Sisters of Mercy	[2516]
S.M.	Sisters of Mercy	[2518]
S.M.	Sisters of Mercy	[2570]
S.M.	Sisters of Mercy (Cork and Ross)	[2600]
S.M.	Misericordia Sisters	[2680]
S.M.	Sisters Servants of Mary	[3600]
S.M.	Sisters of Mercy (Loughrea, Ireland)	[]
S.M.	Sisters of Mercy of Tralee	[]
S.M.D.C.	Sisters of Mercy of Christian Charity of St. Vincent de Paul of Hungary	[2610]
S.M.G.	Poor Servants of the Mother of God	[3640]
S.M.I.	Sisters of Mary Immaculate	[2440]
S.M.I.C.	Missionary Sisters of the Immaculate Conception of the Mother of God	[2760]
S.M.M.G.	Sisters of Mary, Mother of God	[]
S.M.M.I.	Sisters Minor of the Mary Immaculate	[]
S.M.M.S.	Society of Mary Missionary Sisters	[]
S.M.P.	Sisters of Mary of the Presentation	[2450]
S.M.P.	Daughters of Our Mother of Peace	[]
S.M.P.	Society of Our Mother of Peace	[]

S.M.R.	Society of Mary Reparatrix	[2560]
S.M.S.H.	Sisters of Saint Marthe (of St. Hyacinthe)	[3940]
S.M.S.M.	Marist Missionary Sisters	[2420]
S.N.D.	Sisters of Notre Dame	[2990]
S.N.D.deN.	Sisters of Notre Dame de Namur	[3000]
S.N.J.M.	Sisters of the Holy Names of Jesus and Mary	[1990]
S.O.L.M.	Sisters of Our Lady of Mercy	[2670]
S.O.L.P.H.	Sisters of Our Lady of Perpetual Help	[]
S.O.L.T.	Our Lady of the Most Holy Trinity Convent	[3105]
S.P.	Sisters of Providence	[3340]
S.P.	Sisters of Providence	[3350]
S.P.	Sisters of Providence of Saint Mary-of-the-Woods, IN	[3360]
S.P.C.	Sisters of St. Paul of Chartres	[3980]
S.R.	Sisters of Reparation of the Sacred Wounds of Jesus	[]
S.R.C.	Servants of Our Lady, Queen of Clergy	[3650]
S.R.C.M.	Sisters of Reparation of the Congregation of Mary	[3470]
S.S.A.	Sisters of St. Ann	[3718]
S.S.A.	Sisters of St. Anne	[3720]
S.S.C.	Missionary Sisters of St. Columban	[2880]
S.S.C.	Sisters of St. Casimir	[3740]
S.S.C.	Society of the Sisters of the Church	[]
SS.CC.	Congregation of the Sacred Hearts and of Perpetual Adoration	[3690]
S.S.Ch.	Sisters of St. Chretienne	[3750]
S.S.C.J.	Servants of the Most Sacred Heart of Jesus	[3630]
S.S.C.J.	Sisters of the Sacred Heart of Jesus of Saint Jacut	[3670]
S.S.C.K.	Sisters Servants of Christ the King	[3510]
S.S.C.M.	Servants of the Holy Heart of Mary	[3520]
SS.C.M.	Sisters of Saints Cyril and Methodius	[3780]
S.S.D.	Institute of the Sisters of St. Dorothy	[3790]
S.S.E.	Sisters of St. Elizabeth	[3800]
S.S.F.	Congregation of the Sisters of the Holy Family	[1950]
S.S.H.	Sisters Servants of the Most Sacred Heart	[]
S.S.H.J.P.	Servants of the Sacred Heart of Jesus and of the Poor	[3660]
S.S.J.	Servants of St. Joseph	[3595]
S.S.J.	Sisters of St. Joseph (Buffalo)	[3830-06]
S.S.J.	Sisters of St. Joseph (Burlington)	[3830-07]
S.S.J.	Sisters of St. Joseph (Erie)	[3830-09]
S.S.J.	Sisters of St. Joseph (Kalamazoo, Nazareth)	[3830-11]
S.S.J.	Sisters of St. Joseph (Ogdensburg)	[3830-12]
S.S.J.	Sisters of St. Joseph (Rochester)	[3830-14]
S.S.J.	Sisters of St. Joseph (Springfield, MA)	[3830-16]
S.S.J.	Sisters of St. Joseph (Wheeling)	[3830-17]
S.S.J.	Sisters of Saint Joseph of Chestnut Hill, Philadelphia	[3893]
S.S.J.	Sisters of St. Joseph of St. Augustine, Florida	[3900]
S.S.J.C.	Sisters of St. Joseph Benedict Cottolengo	[]
S.S.J.-T.O.S.F.	Sisters of St. Joseph of the Third Order of St. Francis	[3930]
S.S.L.	Congregation of the Sisters of St. Louis, Juilly-Monaghan	[3935]
S.S.LOG.	Seton Sisters of Our Lady of Guadalupe, Tucson	[]
S.S.M.	Sisters of the Sorrowful Mother (Third Order of St. Francis)	[4100]
S.S.M.I.	Sisters Servants of Mary Immaculate	[3610]
S.S.M.I.	Sisters Servants of Mary Immaculate	[3620]
S.S.M.N.	Sisters of Saint Mary of Namur	[3950]
S.S.M.O.	Sisters of St. Mary of Oregon	[3960]
S.S.N.D.	School Sisters of Notre Dame	[2970]
S.S.P.C.	Missionary Sisters of St. Peter Claver	[3990]
S.Sp.S.	Missionary Sisters Servants of the Holy Spirit	[3530]
S.Sp.S.deA.P.	Sister Servants of the Holy Spirit of Perpetual Adoration	[3540]
S.S.S.	Servants of the Blessed Sacrament	[3500]
S.S.S.	Sisters of Social Service of Los Angeles, Inc.	[4080]
S.S.S.	Sisters of Social Service	[4090]
S.S.S.F.	School Sisters of St. Francis	[1680]
S.S.T.V.	Congregation of Sisters of St. Thomas of Villanova	[4030]
S.T.J.	Society of St. Teresa of Jesus	[4020]
S.U.	Society of St. Ursula	[4040]
S.U.S.C.	Sisters of the Holy Union	[2070]
S.V.M.	Sisters of the Visitation of the Congregation of the Immaculate Heart of Mary	[4200]
V.D.C.	Verbum Dei Community	[]
V.H.M.	Visitation Nuns	[4190]
V.S.	Vestiarski Sisters	[]
V.S.C.	Vincentian Sisters of Charity	[4160]
V.S.C.	Vincentian Sisters of Charity	[4170]
V.Z.	Sisters of Charity of St. Vincent de Paul	[0630]
X.M.M.	Xaverian Missionary Society of Mary, Inc.	[4230]
X.S.	Catholic Mission Sisters of St. Francis Xavier	[3810]

A USER'S GUIDE TO THE OFFICIAL CATHOLIC DIRECTORY

Each year the editors of *The Official Catholic Directory* seek added ways of serving their subscribers. Although the book may never answer every question, this is the conscientious goal; its format, arrangement and editorial features are directed toward the convenience and needs of the public. Comments and suggestions are welcome.

* * * *

GENERAL PLAN

For the benefit of the subscriber and a more efficient use of *The Official Catholic Directory* and its cross references, a summary of the contents and their meaning follows:

1. **Ecclesiastical forms of address** recognized in the United States.
   Formal forms of address for correspondence with the clergy in the United States.

2. ***The Official Catholic Directory* Glossary**
   A listing of some of the ecclesiastical terms and organizations found in the *Directory*.

3. **Religious Order Initials for Men** and **Religious Order Initials for Women**
   Indexes of abbreviations relevant to the religious institute name and the applicable identification number.

4. Part I: The Governing Bodies in Vatican City:
   A chronological table of the **Supreme Roman Pontiffs;** the **Pope,** and an alphabetical list of the **College of Cardinals;** the duties of each of the agencies of the **Roman Curia,** and other commissions and institutions associated with the Holy See, along with their officers; a list of the **Seminaries** and **National Colleges** in Rome; the **Apostolic Nunciature** and the **Permanent Observer Mission to the United Nations,** with their staff. As foreign organizations, these entities are not included in the USCC group tax exemption ruling ("Group Ruling").

5. **Part II: Alphabetical Place List**
   The cities, towns, and villages where there is a church with a resident priest, or a Catholic institution, or both, together with the abbreviations of the archdiocese or diocese to which it belongs. A key to the (arch)diocesan abbreviations precedes the *Religious Order Initials for Men* section and the *Alphabetical List of Diocesan and Religious Priests of the U.S.*

6. **The Catholic Church in the United States** (Provinces)
   The archdioceses and dioceses of the United States arranged under the provinces to which they belong, listed with their active archbishops and bishops.

7. **U.S. Cardinals, Archbishops, Bishops, Archabbots and Abbots**
   An alphabetical list of Cardinals, Archbishops, Bishops, Archabbots and Abbots, arranged within their specific title. Also listed is their address and status, followed by a hierarchical/chronological list by year.

8. **National Conference of Catholic Bishops [NCCB]**
   The national body of bishops, with headquarters in Washington, D.C. A listing of the NCCB offices and committees, with their officers.

9. **United States Catholic Conference [USCC]**
   The coordinating body of the American Catholic bishops, with their committees and officers. Also included are the **National Organizations** approved by the USCC and a brief description of their function, and the **National Association of State Catholic Conference Directors.**

10. **Dioceses and Archdioceses** in alphabetical sequence
The most detailed information on the Catholic Church in the United States, including the Military Services, Eastern Churches, Personal Prelatures, and Apostolates to the Hungarians and Lithuanians. Listings are in alphabetical order according to the name of the diocese/archdiocese and include the diocesan curia and administrative offices; a parish-by-parish listing of clergy, churches, missions, and parochial schools; information on institutions, and the religious institutes of men and women located in the diocese/archdiocese; and a statistical profile for each diocese/archdiocese.

11. **United States Territorial Sees**
This section contains information on U.S. territories similar to that found in the preceding section.

12. **Part III: The Catholic Church in Canada and Mexico**
A brief listing of the provinces, archdioceses, dioceses, and administrative organizations in Canada and Mexico. As foreign organizations, these entities are not included in the USCC Group Ruling.

13. **American Foreign Missions**
This section highlights the Religious working specifically in foreign countries. Each Province lists their U.S. members and the countries they serve in. For specific address requests, contact the mission office listed.

14. **Missionary Activities**
Organizations involved in missionary work in the U.S. and foreign countries.

15. **United States Conference of Secular Institutes**
An alphabetical list of secular organizations and their purposes.

16. **U.S. Catholic Mission Association**
An alphabetical list of countries served by the U.S. Catholic Mission Association, detailing the number and religious order or laity personnel working there.

17. **Mission Churches**
A list, by city, of mission churches in the U.S. and the parishes to which they are attached.

18. **Religious Institutes of Men and Women**
An alphabetical list of religious institutes of men and of women, using a P.J. Kenedy identification number. Each listing contains the general headquarters, provinces, provincialates, a summary of legal titles and holdings taken from the individual archdioceses and dioceses within the *Directory,* various forms of ministry and works, statistical data of personnel, and representation in the U.S. dioceses and archdioceses.

19. **Colleges and Universities**
An alphabetical list of colleges and universities by state and diocese, including detailed information on administrative officers, religious and lay faculty, and student body.

20. **Hospitals**
An alphabetical list of hospitals by state and diocese, including information on executive and administrative officers, religious and lay professional staff, bed capacity, and number of patients assisted annually.

21. **Special Care Facilities**
An alphabetical list of special care facilities by state and diocese, including administrators, type of care, religious and lay staff, beds, patients assisted annually, outpatients and residents.

22. **Diocesan and Religious Priests**
An alphabetical list of diocesan and religious priests denoting their year of ordination, the archdiocese or diocese they are assigned to or work in, and the church or institution with which they are affiliated.

23. **Necrology** of U.S. Cardinals, Archbishops, Bishops, Archabbots, Abbots, and Priests
An alphabetical list of the U.S. hierarchy and priests who have died since the last issue of the *Directory,* along with their date of death and last assignment.

24. **Alphabetical List of Institutions**
A list of institutions including the categorical letter indicating where an institution can be found in the *Dioceses and Archdioceses* section along with the diocese/archdiocese abbreviated code and the city and state of the institution.

25. **The General Summary**
A 40+ page general summary of statistics arranged alphabetically by state, listing the archdiocese first within each state, followed by the dioceses. This information, extracted from the Statistical Overview of each diocese/archdiocese, pertains to personnel, parishes, health and welfare, education, and specific sacramental figures, as well as Catholic and total population figures for each diocese/archdiocese. U.S. territories and Eastern Church statistics are also included.

26. **Map of Catholic Diocesan and Province Boundaries in the United States**
Map defining the diocesan, archdiocesan, provincial, and state boundaries.

27. **Products & Services Guide**
Includes a diverse array of products and services offered to the Catholic community.

The Official Catholic Directory Part II
Provides a comprehensive listing of archdioceses and dioceses of the world. Also contains mid-year updates to the U.S. (arch)dioceses. More information on *Official Catholic Directory Part II* can be obtained from the publisher.

* * * *

SPECIAL NOTATIONS USED IN THE DIRECTORY

An asterisk (*) denotes a tax-exempt organization that has its own IRS exemption status and is not covered by the USCC Group Ruling. The Group Ruling allows for the exemption from federal income tax of all Catholic institutions listed in *The Official Catholic Directory* for that year. The exemption was established in 1946 and has been extended every year since then.

[CEM] in a parish listing indicates that a cemetery is connected to the parish. [JC] indicates a joint cemetery, which is a cemetery being utilized by more than one parish. A number following [CEM] or [JC] indicates the number of cemeteries owned by the parish or joint cemeteries shared with other parishes.

A dagger (†) next to a name in the *Necrology* denotes a deceased priest. A Maltese cross (✠) denotes a deceased member of the hierarchy.

* * * *

THE GENERAL SUMMARY

Certain terms used in the General Summary may need additional explanation.

Extern Priests are priests who have not been incardinated into the diocese in which they are currently working and residing.

Health Care Centers include ancillary care systems, medical centers, sanitoriums, and hospices.

Specialized Homes refers to institutions which provide aid to abused children or adults, halfway homes, AIDS patients, ARC patients, ex-offenders, pregnant women, adjudicated delinquents, or runaway youths.

Special Centers for Social Services are institutions or services that provide assistance, such as hotline centers, food banks, homeless centers, legal aid services, or counseling services.

Residential Care of Children refers to orphanages, as opposed to day care centers.

Non-residential Schools for Handicapped are day schools which provide regular and religious education for physically and/or mentally handicapped students.

Received into Full Communion is used to describe people who have been baptized earlier in life and have now been received into full communion in the Catholic Church.

ECCLESIASTICAL FORMS OF ADDRESS RECOGNIZED IN THE UNITED STATES

(These are the formal forms of address used in correspondence.)

CARDINALS:
Address on envelope: His Eminence *(Christian name)* Cardinal *(Surname)*
Salutation: Your Eminence:
Concluding a letter: I have the honor to be, Your Eminence, *etc.*

ARCHBISHOPS:
Address on envelope: Most Reverend *N*_______ *N*_______
Salutation: Your Excellency:
Concluding a letter: I have the honor to be, Your Excellency, *etc.*

BISHOPS:
Address on envelope: Most Reverend *N*_______ *N*_______
Salutation: Your Excellency:
Concluding a letter: I have the honor to be, Your Excellency, *etc.*

ABBOTS:
Address on envelope: Right Reverend *N*_______ *N*_______ *(add religious order initials)*
Salutation: Right Reverend Abbot:
Concluding a letter: I have the honor to be, Right Reverend Abbot, *etc.*

PROTONOTARIES APOSTOLIC:
Address on envelope: Rev. Msgr. *N*_______ *N*_______
Salutation: Rev. Msgr.:
Concluding a letter: I am, Rev. Msgr., *etc.*

PRELATE OF HONOR OF HIS HOLINESS:
Address on envelope: Rev. Msgr. *N*_______ *N*_______
Salutation: Rev. Msgr.:
Concluding a letter: I am, Rev. Msgr., *etc.*

CHAPLAIN TO HIS HOLINESS:
Address on envelope: Rev. Msgr. *N*_______ *N*_______
Salutation: Rev. Msgr.:
Concluding a letter: I am, Rev. Msgr., *etc.*

SECULAR PRIESTS:
Address on envelope: Rev. *N*_______ *N*_______
Salutation: Dear Reverend Father:
Concluding a letter: I am, Reverend Father, *etc.*

RELIGIOUS ORDER PRIESTS:
Address on envelope: Rev. *N*_______ *N*_______ *(add religious order initials)*
Salutation: Dear Reverend Father:
Concluding a letter: I am, Reverend Father, *etc.*

BROTHERS:
Address on envelope: Brother *N*_______
Salutation: Dear Brother *N*_______
Concluding a letter: I am, Respectfully yours, *etc.*

SISTERS:
Address on envelope: Sister *N*_______
Salutation: Dear Sister *N*_______
Concluding a letter: I am, Respectfully yours, *etc.*

TRANSITIONAL DEACONS:
Address on envelope: Rev. Mr. *N*_______
Salutation: Dear Mr. *N*_______
Concluding a letter: I am, Respectfully yours, *etc.*

PERMANENT DEACONS:
Address on envelope: Mr. *N*_______
Salutation: Dear Mr. *N*_______
Concluding a letter: I am, Respectfully yours, *etc.*

THE OFFICIAL CATHOLIC DIRECTORY GLOSSARY

Abbot
The superior of an autonomous community of men religious. He has general and sacramental jurisdiction over his community. The head of a prominent monastery or a congregation consisting of several monasteries is an *archabbot.*

Advocate
An ecclesiastical advocate is someone approved by Church authority to safeguard the rights of a party in a canonical process by arguments regarding the law and the facts of the case. [Cf. c. 1481 and CLSA Comm., p. 967]

Apostolate
Apostolate is the mission of Christ and participation in it. Its object is to bring Christ to others, its goal is the greater glory of God, its scope is universal. The work is carried out by every human agency by which the life of grace may be given or increased in the soul. A mandate from the Church is essential to the Catholic apostolate.

Archbishop
A bishop of a main or metropolitan diocese in an ecclesiastical province. The term is equivalent to *metropolitan* in the Western Church. It may also be granted to other ordinaries and non-residential bishops, and to the ordinary of a diocese outside a province.

Auditor
An official of a diocesan court, who gathers evidence and testimony and draws up a record of an ecclesiastical case.

Bishop
A bishop, by divine institution, carries on the work of the apostles. By reason of episcopal consecration, he shares in the triple apostolic function of teacher of doctrine, priest of sacred worship, and minister of church government. Bishops are responsible for the pastoral care of their dioceses. In addition, bishops have a responsibility to act in council to guide the Church. The term *exarch* is used in Eastern-rite churches.

The bishop to whom a particular or local church is entrusted is called a *diocesan bishop* or a *residential bishop.* All other bishops receive *Titular Sees* over which they exercise no pastoral authority.

When the pastoral needs of a diocese or archdiocese warrant, an *auxiliary bishop* may be assigned to aid the residential bishop in governing his diocese. An auxiliary bishop is assigned when the residential bishop needs assistance in carrying out his duties because of ill health, advanced age, or amount of work. An auxiliary bishop does not have the right of succession within his diocese.

In special circumstances, such as the advanced age or ill health of a diocesan bishop, a *coadjutator bishop* may be appointed to assist the principal bishop of a diocese. Coadjutator bishops have the *right of succession* in the diocese of their appointment from the time the See becomes vacant upon the death or retirement of its bishop.

Brother
A man who is a member of a religious order, but is not ordained or studying for the priesthood.

Cana Conference
A Catholic family movement, originally designed to aid married couples and families in their spiritual and interpersonal relationships. The program is now divided into *Pre-Cana,* for couples engaged to be married, and *Cana Conferences,* programs for married people.

Censor Librorum
A theologian empowered by a bishop to judge a book's soundness in regard to Church teaching before publication.

Chancellor
The office of the chancellor (or the *chancery)* evolved from the practice in the early Church of appointing an official to sign and preserve the letters of the bishop. The first function of the chancellor in the present day is gathering, arranging, and safeguarding the acts of the diocesan curia. Dispensations and other official documents also originate from the chancery. In many dioceses, the chancellor continues to exercise ordinary jurisdiction as delegated by the diocesan bishop. He or she may be assisted by a separate official, the *vice-chancellor.*

Chapter
The *general chapter* of a religious order is an assembly of elected or appointed members and provincials. General chapters are convened for the election of officers, amendments to the constitution, and discussion and legislation of matters of concern to members and the order as a whole.

A *provincial chapter* conducts elections and handles legislation on a provincial level. The assembly is comprised of superiors and representatives of the religious.

A *chapter of canons* is a group of diocesan priests, appointed by the bishop of a diocese, with assigned authority or responsibilities.

College of Cardinals
The College of Cardinals is made up of the cardinals of the Church, who advise the Pope, assist in the central administration of the Church, head the various curial offices and congregations, administer the Holy See during a vacancy, and elect a new Pope. There are three ranks in the College of Cardinals, corresponding to the historical origins of cardinals in the Roman Catholic Church. All cardinals are bishops, but their rank within the College of Cardinals is characterized by one of the hierarchical ranks of bishop, priest, or deacon. Cardinals are given honorary title to churches in the city of Rome. [CF. c. 350; CLSA Comm., pp. 288-289]

1. Cardinal Bishops
There are two types of Cardinal Bishops: 1) those appointed by the Pope as titular bishops to one of the six suburban dioceses of Rome, and 2) Eastern-rite Patriarchs who are heads of Sees with apostolic origins that have been assigned to the College of Cardinals.

2. Cardinal Priests
Heads of Sees outside the city of Rome are assigned a "titular church," one of the churches in Rome. They have no pastoral authority over their titular church.

3. Cardinal Deacons
Cardinals of diaconal rank are bishops without Sees who head the various departments, offices, congregations, committees, and the Secretariat of State of the Roman Curia.

Confraternity of Christian Doctrine [CCD]
A lay organization established for religious education throughout a person's entire life. The term is currently used to describe Catholic parish-based religious education of children from kindergarten through high school. At the diocesan level, the offices are now more commonly known as offices of *religious education* or *Christian formation.* Nationally, the confraternity's religious education component has been taken over by the USCC's Department of Education. It still exists as a separate entity under the USCC Administrative Board, with responsibility for licensing religious and spiritual literature.

Consolidated School
The term, as used in the *Directory,* may refer to a school that takes students from more than one parish, or a school that was formed by the consolidation of two or three other schools. In both cases, it is a means of keeping a Catholic school in a given area open by taking students from the surrounding areas, regardless of parish boundaries.

Convent
In common usage, the term refers to a house of women religious. Originally, it referred to a building where members of religious institutes lived, and was not restricted to communities of women.

Cursillo
The *cursillo de cristianidad,* or "little course in Christianity," is a three-day program for achieving spiritual renewal or spiritual awakening. It seeks to convey a new sense of individual and organized apostolic action. The program, conducted by priests and laypeople, consists of a three-day weekend focused on prayer, study, and Christian action, and a follow-up program known as the *post-cursillo.*

Deacons
The diaconate is the first order or grade in ordained ministry. Its origins are in early apostolic times, when deacons preached and baptized under the direction of the presbyters or bishops. Any man who is to be ordained to the priesthood must first be ordained as a *transitional deacon.* Deacons serve in the ministry of liturgy, of the word, and of charity.

In 1967, Pope Paul VI reinstituted the *Permanent Diaconate* for men who do not plan to become ordained priests. Although men ordained as permanent deacons are sometimes referred to as "married deacons," the permanent diaconate is open to both married and unmarried men, with the understanding that after ordination, they may not marry even after the death of a spouse. Under the authority of the diocesan bishop, they perform the same functions as the transitional deacons while, at the same time, retaining their roles in society as family and business men.

Dean/Vicar Forane
The title of a priest appointed by the bishop to aid him in administering the parishes in a certain vicinity, called a "deanery," or "vicariates forane." The function of a dean, or vicar forane, involves promotion, coordination, and supervision of the common pastoral activity within the deanery or vicariate.

Defender of the Bond
A member of a diocesan tribunal, either a cleric or a lay person, holding a graduate degree in canon law, who is appointed by the diocesan bishop for cases concerning the nullity of sacred ordination or the nullity or dissolution of the marriage bond. The defender of the bond is responsible for a review of

the evidence, scrutiny of the briefs, examination of witnesses, and maintenance of proper procedures during the trial. The defender also deals with some situations concerning the content of the litigation rather than the legal procedures.

Diocesan Consultors
An advisory council of diocesan priests, as appointed by a diocesan bishop, that assists in the administrative affairs of the diocese.

Diocesan Curia
The personnel and offices assisting the diocesan bishop in directing the pastoral activity, administration, and the exercise of judicial power of his diocese. The curia includes among its officers laity and religious as well as clergy. Principal officers of a diocesan curia are the vicar general of the diocese, the chancellor, officials of the diocesan tribunal, examiners, consultors, auditors, the promoter of justice and the defender of the bond.

Diocese
The standard term for a territorial division of the Church, entrusted to a bishop who rules in his own name as local ordinary, and not as a delegate of another. The chief diocese of a province is an *archdiocese.* It is headed by an archbishop. A diocese is usually limited to a definite territory so that it comprises all the faithful who inhabit that territory. [Cf. cc. 369 and 372, #1] In Eastern-rite churches, the term eparchy is used.

Eastern-rite [Oriental] Church
The term used to describe the Catholic churches which developed in Eastern Europe, Asia, and Africa. The Eastern-rite churches have their own distinctive liturgical and organizational systems. Each is considered equal to the Latin rite within the Church.

Ecumenism/Ecumenical Movement
A movement for spiritual understanding and unity among Christians and their churches. The term is also extended to apply to efforts toward greater understanding and cooperation between Christians and members of other faiths.

Exarch/Exarchy
A church jurisdiction, similar to a diocese, established for Eastern-rite Catholics living outside their native land. The head of an exarchy, usually a bishop, is an *exarch.*

Hierarchy
In general, the term refers to the ordered body of clergy, divided into bishops, priests, and deacons. In Catholic practice, the term refers to the bishops of the world or of a particular region.

Holy Name Society
A lay organization which seeks to aid its members in living a genuinely Christian life. The society organizes retreats and other spiritual and devotional exercises.

Holy See
The term refers to the diocese of Rome. Used in reference to the governance of the Church, it refers to the Pontiff, the Roman Curia, and the Sacred College.

Knights of Columbus
A fraternal organization for Catholic men. Knights of Columbus engage in religious and charitable projects in the U.S., Canada, Puerto Rico, Mexico, and the Philippines.

Legion of Mary
A lay organization established to assist the clergy in the sanctification of its members' souls, and the spread of the Christian faith and spiritual service to others. Members participate in almost every form of social service and Catholic action, including evangelization. The organization was founded in 1921.

Metropolitan
The archbishop of an archdiocese in a province. He has limited supervisory powers and influence over the other dioceses and bishops in the province.

Military Ordinariate [Archdiocese for the Military Services, U.S.A.]
A nonterritorial diocese for American Catholics and their dependents who are in the military or affiliated with the armed forces. Personnel employed by or engaged in diplomatic missions for the U.S. government in countries where U.S. military forces are stationed also belong to the Military Ordinariate.

Mission
A mission, or *quasi-parish,* is a parish which has not been established because it lacks one or more of the following qualifications: a resident pastor; necessary financial resources; territorial boundaries; or a natural grouping by way of rite, nationality, or language. Missions are attached to some parishes under the care of their pastors.

Moderator of the Curia
A bishop or priest, appointed by the diocesan bishop, who is concerned primarily with administrative matters and with supervising those working in the curia.

Monastery
An autonomous community house of a religious order, which may or may not be a monastic order. The term is used more specifically to refer to a community house of men religious or women religious in which they lead a contemplative life separate from the world.

Monsignor
An honorary ecclesiastical title granted by the Pope to some diocesan priests. In the United States, the title is given to the vicar general of a diocese. In Europe, the title is also given to bishops.

National Conference of Catholic Bishops [NCCB]
The episcopal conference of U.S. bishops. The membership is comprised of diocesan bishops and their associate bishops. The conference decides matters of ecclesiastical law and issues policy statements on political and social issues.

Newman Apostolate
An apostolate to the Catholic college and university community, now commonly known as "campus ministry."

Notary
An elected or appointed ecclesiastical official who acts as a secretary in formal church proceedings. The notary records the minutes, testimony, etc., of the proceedings.

Opus Dei
A personal prelature dedicated to spreading through society an awareness of the call to Christian virtue, awareness, and witness in one's life and work. The organization was founded in 1928 and in 1950, it received Vatican approval as a secular institution. In 1982, it was designated a personal prelature, the *Prelature of the Holy Cross and Opus Dei.* Members are not members of a religious order, do not take vows, and do not live in community.

Ordinary
Diocesan bishops, religious superiors, and certain other diocesan authorities with jurisdiction over the clergy in a specific geographical area, or the members of a religious order.

Ordination/Ordain
The sacramental rite by which a "sacred order" is conferred (diaconate, priesthood, episcopacy).

Papal Audience
Request for attendance at papal audiences and similar functions may be addressed to: "Bishops' Office for United States Visitors to the Vatican." Postal address: Via dell 'Umilta 30, 00187 Rome, Italy. Tel.: 011-39-6-6678-9184; Fax: 011-39-6-679-1448. Rev. Msgr. Charles W. Elmer, Dir.

Papal Representatives
There are three types of representatives of the Roman Pontiff: 1) those who represent him to particular churches; 2) those who represent him to particular churches and civil government; 3) those who represent him in international organizations or at various conferences and meetings. [Cf. c. 363; CLSA Comm., p. 302]

1. Legate
An individual appointed by the Pope to be his personal representative to a nation, international conference, or local church. The legate may be chosen from the local clergy of a country.

2. Apostolic Pro-Nuncio
In the United States, the papal representative is sent by the Pope to both the local church and to the government. His title is Apostolic Pro-Nuncio. Although he holds the title of ambassador, in U.S. law he is not accorded the special privilege of being the dean of the diplomatic corps.

3. Permanent Observer to the United Nations
The Apostolic See maintains permanent legates below the ambassadorial level to several world organizations. Since the Papal Legate does not enjoy the right to vote within the organization, his title at the United Nations is that of *Observer.*

Parish
A specific community of the Christian faithful within a diocese, which has its own church building, under the authority of a *pastor* who is responsible for providing them with ministerial service. Most parishes are formed on a geographic basis, but they may be formed along national or ethnic lines.

Parish Coordinator
A deacon, religious, or lay person who is responsible for the pastoral care of parish. The parish coordinator is in charge of the day-to-day life of the parish in the areas of worship, education, pastoral service and administration.

Pastor
A priest in charge of a parish or congregation. He is responsible for administering the sacraments, instructing the congregation in the doctrine of the Church, and other services to the people of the parish.

Pastoral Associate
A member of the laity who is part of a parish ministry team.

Pastoral Council
A consultative body which the pastor or bishop consults concerning the pastoral activity within the diocese. Its members include laity, religious, and clergy. The pastoral council's purpose is to study practical situations, difficulties and problems, and make concrete recommendations and proposals to the diocesan bishop. The pastoral council is always subject to the final authority of the pastor or bishop.

Patriarch
The Pope is the traditional "Patriarch of the West." All other bishops in the Latin Rite, even those with the honorary title of "Patriarch," are subject to him. Similarly, patriarchs within nations have only an honorary title unless special provisions are made otherwise. Eastern-rite Patriarchs are subject to the Pope while serving as heads of the faithful belonging to their rites throughout the world.

Personal Prelature
In addition to the territorial arrangement of the Church into particular or local churches or dioceses, canon law also provides for non-territorial areas of religious jurisdiction, incorporating secular clergy and deacons. Membership is also open to lay persons. These *prelatures* are established to meet specific pastoral or missionary needs at the regional, national, or international level without infringing on the rights of the local bishops. A prelature is presided over by a *personal prelate,* who is an ordinary with the right to establish seminaries and ordain priests as members of the prelature.

Canon law also allows for laity to be associated in the works of prelatures without being withdrawn from the jurisdiction of their own diocesan bishop.

Presbyteral Council
Also known as the *priests' council,* the presbyteral council is the principal consultative body mandated by the Code of Canon Law to advise the diocesan bishop in matters of pastoral governance. It consists of bishops and priests serving the diocese.

Propagation of the Faith
An organization, headquartered in Rome, which distributes aid to Catholic missions and organizes the work of missionaries all over the world. The organization has responsibility for fostering missionary vocations, assigning missionaries to field work, defining ecclesiastical boundaries and assigning clergy to them, and encouraging training and installation of native-born clergy.

Promoter of Justice
A cleric or lay person, holding a graduate degree in canon law, who is appointed by the diocesan bishop to serve in the role of a "prosecuting attorney" in trials of crimes against church law and of other judicial litigations in the diocese. A promoter of justice may be appointed for a specific case by the bishop.

Province
A defined geographic area containing an archdiocese, or *Metropolitan See,* and at least one diocese, or *Suffragen See.* The archbishop of the archdiocese has no direct powers over the Suffragen Sees, but does have limited advisory and appellate authority and obligations. The term also refers to a territorial grouping of particular churches or communities, or a territory of a religious order.

Provincial
The superior of the communities of a religious order that constitute a province.

Provincial Council
An assembly of the bishops of an ecclesiastical province, called by the metropolitan archbishop. The term is also used in reference to the provincial superior of a province, along with his or her chief advisors.

Receptions into the Church
Can take two forms: baptism of those not previously validly baptized, or "reception into full communion" with the Church for those who have already been baptized, in which case a profession of faith affects the reception.

Religious Priest/Diocesan Priest
Religious, or regular, priests are those who are professed members of a religious order or institute. Religious clergy live according to the rule of their respective orders. In pastoral ministry, they are under the jurisdiction of their local bishop, as well as the superiors of their order. Diocesan, or secular, priests are under the direction of their local bishop. They commit to serving their congregations and other institutions.

Retreat
A period of time spent in meditation and religious exercise. Retreats may take various forms, from traditional closed forms, to open retreats, which do not disengage the participants from day-to-day life. Both clergy and lay people of all ages participate in retreats. Houses and centers providing facilities for retreats are *retreat houses.*

Rite of Christian Initiation of Adults [RCIA]
The liturgical book containing the norms and rituals of the Catholic Church for people who wish to join the Church. Part of the book is intended for baptized Christians who wish to become Catholics. The term is used in a general sense to refer to the process of entering the Catholic Church.

Roman Curia
The official collective name for the administrative agencies and courts, and their officials, who assist the Pope in governing the Church. Members are appointed and granted authority by the Pope.

St. Vincent DePaul Society
Originally known as the *Conference of Charity,* this is an organization of lay people who serve the poor through spiritual and material works of mercy. The society operates stores, rehabilitation workshops, food centers, shelters, criminal justice and other programs.

Scholastic
A member of a religious order who has completed his novitiate, but has not yet been ordained.

Scholastic Teaching
Usually refers to Scholastic Philosophy, which is the basis for much Catholic Theology. It comes from the canonical "schools" of the 12th-13th centuries, St. Thomas Aquinas, St. Bonaventure, St. Albert the Great, etc., who developed "scholasticism" based mainly on Aristotle. It is the semi-official philosophy of the Church.

Secular Institute
Canonically erected institute of consecrated life for single laity and clerics who strive for the perfection of charity and work for the sanctification of the world while remaining in a lifestyle within the world.

See
The word is taken from the Latin word "sedes" ("seat"), and is used to denote a diocese or ecclesiastical district. The term *Holy See* is reserved to the diocese of Rome whose bishop is the Pope.

Seminary
An educational institution for men preparing for *Holy Orders.* The term originates from the time of St. Augustine, when those preparing for the priesthood were educated in the "cathedral school." During the Middle Ages, the clergy were educated in a university setting where faculties of philosophy, theology, and canon law existed. Eventually individual dioceses or provinces came to establish their own schools for educating their clerical students. Traditional seminaries date from the Council of Trent in the 16th century.

A school for the spiritual, academic, and pastoral education and formation of priesthood candidates is known as a *major seminary* in which the focus is on philosophical and theological education. To prepare for entrance into a major seminary, a period of study is set aside for the required courses in the humanities and the sciences in institutions called *minor seminaries.*

Serra Club
Local units of *Serra International,* an organization which promotes vocations to the priesthood and religious life, and offers instruction to lay leaders.

Sister
The term, in the strictest sense, refers to women religious who belong to institutes which have professed simple vows. However, in everyday usage, the term is used for any woman religious.

Sodality
A group of laity established for the promotion of Christian life and worship, or some other religious purpose.

Special Centers for Social Services
This would seem to overlap with Specialized Homes. Some of the categorization is fairly arbitrary. Catholic Charities might have its own proper distinctions for government or private funding purposes.

Specialized Homes
Includes such institutions as homes for handicapped (e.g., Misericordia Homes), youth homes (e.g., Maryville, Mercy Boys and Girls, Homes), homes for battered women, drug rehab centers, homes for unwed mothers, etc.

Superior
The head of a religious order or congregation. He or she may be the head of a province, or an individual house.

Synod
A gathering of designated officials and representatives of a church, that has legislative and policy-making powers.

1. Synod of Bishops
The Synod of Bishops is a consultative body, unless explicitly stated otherwise by His Holiness, expressing the communion of the hierarchy. A synod of bishops meets in general assembly, either in "Ordinary" or "Extraordinary" session, when the matter for treatment concerns the whole Church

and in "Special Assembly" when the matter deals directly with a definite region or regions.

2. Synod of Oriental Churches
The synods of the Oriental Churches enjoy various prerogatives including the right to elect bishops, regulate discipline and exercise pastoral authority in their respective churches.

3. Diocesan Synod
A diocesan synod is an expression of the communion of the particular church. A diocesan synod enjoys the participation of priests, women and men religious and laypersons; the bishop is the sole legislator.

Theologate
An institution which provides the last four years of study for candidates for the priesthood.

Titular See
A former diocese which no longer physically or geographically exists. Titular Sees are given as an honorary title to any bishop not serving as a chief pastor of a diocese, i.e., auxiliary bishops, papal representatives, and bishops of the Roman Curia.

Tribunal
A tribunal (court) is the name given to the person or persons who exercise the Church's judicial powers. By its very nature, this procedure involves the determination of a legal controversy. A major concern of tribunals is conducting the process leading to the dissolution or annulment of marriages. In ecclesiastical matters, definite procedural norms for conducting a trial are found in the Code of Canon Law to settle disputes. There are various grades of tribunals, including diocesan tribunals, the first court of trial for most cases; regional and metropolitan tribunals, located in an archdiocese, the appellate court for all cases tried within the province; and the tribunals of the Holy See, which act as the Church's central appellate court, try cases reserved to the Holy See, deal with questions of procedure and jurisdiction of the other courts, and act as the Church's supreme court.

United States Catholic Conference [USCC]
The civil corporation and executive agency of the National Conference of Catholic Bishops. The USCC acts as the national public policy organization of the NCCB. Its purpose is to organize and promote Catholic activity in the U.S. and abroad, and to carry out the religious and social action of the Catholic Church in the U.S. The major departments are education, communication, and social development and world peace.

Vicar
The appointment of a priest or a bishop as an *episcopal vicar* is an option given to a diocesan bishop when he needs a deputy for governing a specific territory within the diocese, a group of persons or a specific rite, or a type of apostolic work within the diocese.

By Church law, the diocesan bishop is the judge of all cases in the diocesan tribunal of first trial. He must appoint a priest with ordinary power to judge cases not reserved to the bishop himself. This priest must have a graduate degree in canon law. He is called the *judicial vicar,* and is sometimes referred to as the chief judge or "officialis." He may be given another priest as an assistant with the title of *adjutant judicial vicar.*

A bishop or priest appointed to participate in the executive (administrative) governance of the diocese with executive jurisdiction as a deputy of the diocesan bishop is a *vicar general.* The appointment of a vicar general is mandatory for every diocese. This office is designed to facilitate and unify diocesan administration.

Vicar for Religious
A priest appointed by a bishop to act as his representative in dealing with the religious communities in his diocese.

Information for this glossary was taken from the *Catholic News Service's Stylebook on Religion,* the *Modern Catholic Dictionary,* published by Doubleday and Company, Inc., the *Concise Oxford Dictionary of the Christian Church,* published by Oxford University Press, and the *Encyclopedic Dictionary of Religion,* published by the Sisters of St. Joseph of Philadelphia. The publishers of the *Official Catholic Directory* also wish to thank the Vice Chancellors of the Archdiocese of Chicago for their work in the preparation of this glossary.

The Supreme Roman Pontiffs

St. Peter of Bethsaida in Galilee, Prince of the Apostles, who received from Jesus Christ the Supreme Pontifical Power to be transmitted to his Successors, resided first at Antioch, then at Rome for twenty-five years where he was martyred in the year 64, or 67 of the common reckoning.

END OF PONTIFICATE,	A.D.
St. Linus, M.	76
St. Anacletus or Cletus, M.	88
St. Clement, I, M.	97
St. Evaristus, M.	105
St. Alexander I, M.	115
St. Sixtus I, M.	125
St. Telesphorus, M.	136
St. Hyginus, M.	140
St. Pius I, M.	155
St. Anicetus, M.	166
St. Soterus, M.	175
St. Eleuterius, M.	189
St. Victor I, M.	199
St. Zephyrinus, M.	217
St. Callistus I, M.	222
St. Urban I, M.	230
St. Pontian, M.	235
St. Anterus, M.	236
St. Fabian, M.	250
St. Cornelius, M.	253
St. Lucius I, M.	254
St. Stephen I, M.	257
St. Sixtus II, M.	258
St. Dionysius	268
St. Felix I, M.	274
St. Eutychian, M.	283
St. Caius, M.	296
St. Marcellinus, M.	304
St. Marcellus I, M.	309
St. Eusebius, M.	309
St. Melchiades, M.	314
St. Sylvester I	335
St. Mark	336
St. Julius I	352
Liberius	366
St. Damasus I	384
St. Siricius	399
St. Anastasius I	401
St. Innocent I	417
St. Zozimus	418
St. Boniface I	422
St. Celestine I	432
St. Sixtus III	440
St. Leo I (the Great)	461
St. Hilary	468
St. Simplicius	483
St. Felix III or II	492
St. Gelasius I	496
Anastasius II	498
St. Symmacus	514
St. Hormisdas	523
St. John I	526
St. Felix IV or III	530
Boniface II	532
John II	535
St. Agapitus	536
St. Silverius, M.	537
Vigilius	555
Pelagius I	561
John III	574
Benedict I	579
Pelagius II	590
St. Gregory I (the Great)	604
Sabinianus	606
Boniface III	607
St. Boniface IV	615
St. Deusdeditus or Adeodatus I	618
Boniface V	625
Honorius I	638
Severinus	640
John IV	642
Theodore I	649
St. Martin I, M.	655
St. Eugene I	657
St. Vitalian	672
Adeodatus II	676
Donus I	678
St. Agathonus	681
St. Leo II	683
St. Benedict II	685
John V	686
Conon	687
St. Sergius I	701
John VI	705
John VII	707
Sisinnius	708
Constantine	715
St. Gregory II	731
St. Gregory III	741
St. Zachary	752
Stephen III	757
St. Paul I	767
Stephen IV	772
Adrian I	795
St. Leo III	816
Stephen V	817
St. Paschal I	824
Eugene II	827
Valentine	827
Gregory IV	844
Sergius II	847
St. Leo IV	855
Benedict III	858
St. Nicholas I (the Great)	867
Adrian II	872
John VIII	882
Marinus I	884
St. Adrian III	885
Stephen VI	891
Formosus	896
Boniface VI	896
Stephen VII	897
Romanus	897
Theodore II	897
John IX	900
Benedict IV	903
Leo V	903
Sergius III	911
Anastasius III	913
Landus	914
John X	928
Leo VI	928
Stephen VIII	931
John XI	935
Leo VII	939
Stephen IX	942
Marinus II	946
Agapitus II	955
John XII	964
Leo VIII	965
Benedict V	966
John XIII	972
Benedict VI	974
Benedict VII	983
John XIV	984
John XV	996
Gregory V	999
Sylvester II	1003
John XVII	1003
John XVIII	1009
Sergius IV	1012
Benedict VIII	1024
John XIX	1032
Benedict IX	1044
Benedict IX	1045
Sylvester III	1045
Gregory VI	1046
Clement II	1047
Benedict IX	1048
Damasus II	1048
St. Leo IX	1054
Victor II	1057
Stephen X	1058
Nicholas II	1061
Alexander II	1073
St. Gregory VII	1085
B. Victor III	1087
B. Urban II	1099
Paschal II	1118
Gelasius II	1119
Callistus II	1124
Honorius II	1130
Innocent II	1143
Celestine II	1144
Lucius II	1145
B. Eugene III	1153
Anastasius IV	1154
Adrian IV	1159
Alexander III	1181
Lucius III	1185
Urban III	1187
Gregory VIII	1187
Clement III	1191
Celestine III	1198
Innocent III	1216
Honorius III	1227
Gregory IX	1241
Celestine IV	1241
Innocent IV	1254
Alexander IV	1261
Urban IV	1264
Clement IV	1268
B. Gregory X	1276
B. Innocent V	1276
Adrian V	1276
John XXI	1277
Nicholas III	1280
Martin IV	1285
Honorius IV	1287
Nicholas IV	1292
St. Celestine V	1296
Boniface VIII	1303
B. Benedict XI	1304
Clement V	1314
John XXII	1334
Benedict XII	1342
Clement VI	1352
Innocent VI	1362
B. Urban V	1370
Gregory XI	1378
Urban VI	1389
Boniface IX	1404
Innocent VII	1406
Gregory XII	1415
Martin V	1431
Eugene IV	1447
Nicholas V	1455
Callistus III	1458
Pius II	1464
Paul II	1471
Sixtus IV	1484
Innocent VIII	1492
Alexander VI	1503
Pius III	1503
Julius II	1513
Leo X	1521
Adrian VI	1523
Clement VII	1534
Paul III	1549
Julius III	1555
Marcellus II	1555
Paul IV	1559
Pius IV	1565
St. Pius V	1572
Gregory XIII	1585
Sixtus V	1590
Urban VII	1590
Gregory XIV	1591
Innocent IX	1591
Clement VIII	1605
Leo XI	1605
Paul V	1621
Gregory XV	1623
Urban VIII	1644
Innocent X	1655
Alexander VII	1667
Clement IX	1669
Clement X	1676
B. Innocent XI	1689
Alexander VIII	1691
Innocent XII	1700
Clement XI	1721
Innocent XIII	1724
Benedict XIII	1730
Clement XII	1740
Benedict XIV	1758
Clement XIII	1769
Clement XIV	1774
Pius VI	1799
Pius VII	1823
Leo XII	1829
Pius VIII	1830
Gregory XVI	1846
Pius IX	1878
Leo XIII	1903
St. Pius X	1914
Benedict XV	1922
Pius XI	1939
Pius XII	1958
John XXIII	1963
Paul VI	1978
John Paul I	1978
John Paul II, now reigning.	

PART I
Hierarchy of the Catholic Church

The Hierarchy, as the supreme governing body of the Catholic Church, consists of the Roman Pontiff, the successor of Peter, and the Bishops joined together with him and never without him (canons 330,331,336) in one apostolic college to provide for the common good of the Church. The Roman Pontiff in the exercise of his office is assisted by the College of Cardinals, and further by the departments also called "dicasteries" of the Roman Curia. The bishops, of whom some bear the titles of Patriarch and Archbishop, are united with the Roman Pontiff in the governance of the whole Church; the bishops, when assigned to particular Sees, are individually responsible for the teaching, sanctification and governance of their particular Church. Apostolic Vicars and Prefects together with certain Abbots and other Prelates are also joined in this work.

HIS HOLINESS THE POPE

BISHOP OF ROME AND VICAR OF JESUS CHRIST,
SUCCESSOR OF ST. PETER, PRINCE OF THE APOSTLES,
SUPREME PONTIFF OF THE UNIVERSAL CHURCH.
PATRIARCH OF THE WEST
PRIMATE OF ITALY.
ARCHBISHOP AND METROPOLITAN OF THE ROMAN PROVINCE,
SOVEREIGN OF VATICAN CITY STATE.

JOHN PAUL II

KAROL WOJTYLA

The present successor of St. Peter was born in Wadowice, Diocese of Krakow, May 18, 1920; ordained Priest, November 1, 1946; appointed Titular Bishop of Ombi July 4, 1958; Promoted to Archbishop of Krakow, January 13, 1964; Proclaimed and created Cardinal June 26, 1967. Elected Pope, October 16, 1978; installed October 22, 1978.

VATICAN CITY

Vatican City is the smallest state in the world, occupying 108.7 acres, of which about one third is covered with buildings and is situated on the right side of the Tiber river. Vatican City has territory, population, and sovereignity. This territory, limited as it is, suffices to guarantee the spiritual and temporal independence needed for the exercise of the Holy See's spiritual mission. In 1870 the Kingdom of Italy seized all Vatican possessions which for several centuries had constituted the papal temporal domain. But even after 1870 the Holy See continued to regard itself as a separate entity in international law, and was recognized as such by numerous states with which it retained normal diplomatic relations. After long discussions the Holy See and the then Kingdom of Italy signed the Lateran Pacts on February 11, 1929, so that the complete and independent authority of the Vatican State was and is recognized by the Italian state.

The Sovereign of this small state is His Holiness, the Pope.

The government presently is administered by a Pontifical Commission of which His Eminence Jose Cardinal Castillo Lara is President.

THE COLLEGE OF CARDINALS

The Cardinals constitute a special college and they assist the Roman Pontiff collegially when they are called together to deal with questions of major importance; they do so individually when they assist the Pope especially in the daily care of the universal Church by means of the different offices which they perform (canons 349-350). The Cardinals who are under eighty years of age elect his successor.

The College of Cardinals is divided into three ranks: Cardinal-Bishops, Cardinal-Priests, and Cardinal-Deacons. The College of Cardinals, when complete formerly consisted of 70 members: 6 Cardinal Bishops, 50 Cardinal Priests and 14 Cardinal Deacons, but the late Pontiffs, Pope John XXIII and Pope Paul VI enlarged the College of Cardinals. At the moment the maximum number of Cardinal electors (those under 80 years of age) must not exceed 120.

The Cardinal Bishops (except the Patriarch-Cardinals of the Oriental Rites), have as Titular Sees the Suburban Sees of Rome, which are: *Porto Santa Rufina, Albano, Palestrina, Sabina, Frascati, Velletri, Segni*. The Cardinal Dean has united to his See the See of *Ostia*. The Cardinal Priests take their title from the "Titular Churches" to which they are appointed: the Cardinal Deacons are appointed to other Churches called "Deaconries." The first Cardinal Bishop is *Dean*; the first Cardinal Priest is *First Priest*; and the first Cardinal Deacon is *First Deacon* of the Sacred College. The Dean has the right of ordaining the new Pope if he is not already a bishop; the First Deacon the right of proclaiming him and investing him with the sacred Pallium. On the death of the Pontiff, the Cardinal *Camerlengo* has the Administration of the affairs of the Holy See.

Sometimes the Roman Pontiff promotes a person to the dignity of Cardinal but does not make public his name and keeps it "in pectore." Upon the publication of his name, this Cardinal enjoys his right of precedence from the day on which his name was reserved "in pectore" by the Pope (cfr. Can. 351 3).

The Cardinals of the Holy Roman Church

Listed in Alphabetical Order

Agustoni, Gilberto (Cardinal Deacon), Prefect of the Supreme Tribunal of the Apostolic Signatura; born in Schaffhausen, Switzerland, Diocese of Basel, July 26, 1922. Created and proclaimed November 26, 1994. Address: Via Tiberina, 191, 00188 Rome, Italy.

Angelini, Fiorenzo (Cardinal Deacon), Titular of S. Spirito in Sassia; Former President of the Pontifical Council for Pastoral Assistance to Health Care Workers; in Rome, Italy, August 1, 1916. Created and proclaimed June 28, 1991. Address: 00120 Vatican City State, Europe.

Aponte Martinez, Luis (Cardinal Priest), Titular of S. Maria Madre della Provvidenza a Monte Verde, Archbishop of San Juan; born in Lajas, diocese of Mayaguez, August 4, 1922. Created and proclaimed March 5, 1973. Address: Arzobispado, Apartado S-1967, Calle del Cristo 50, San Juan, PR 00902.

Aramburu, Juan Carlos (Cardinal Priest), Titular of San Giovanni Battista dei Fiorentini, Archbishop Emeritus of Buenos Aires; born in Reduccion, Diocese of Rio Cuarto, February 11, 1912. Created and proclaimed May 24, 1976. Address: La Pampa 4022, 1430 Buenos Aires, Argentina.

Arinze, Francis (Cardinal Priest), Titular of San Giovanni della Pigna; President of the Pontifical Council for Inter-Religious Dialogue; born in Eziowelle, Archdiocese of Onitsha, November 1, 1932.

Created and proclaimed May 25, 1985. Address: Largo del Colonnato 3, 00193 Rome, Italy.

Arns, Paul Evaristo, *o.f.m.* (Cardinal Priest), Titular of S. Antonio da Padova in Via Tuscolana, Archbishop of Sao Paulo; born in Forquilhinha, Diocese of Tubarao, September 14, 1921. Created and proclaimed March 5, 1973. Address: Caixa Postal 916, Rua Alfredo Maia, 195, 01106 Sao Paulo, SP, Brazil.

Bafile, Corrado (Cardinal Priest), Titular of Santa Maria in Portico; born in L'Aquila, July 4, 1903. Created and proclaimed May 24, 1976. Address: Via P. Pancrazio Pfeiffer 10, 00193 Rome, Italy.

Ballestrero, Anastasio Alberto, *o.c.d.* (Cardinal Priest), Titular of S. Maria Sopra Minerva, Archbishop Emeritus of Turin; born in Genoa, October 3, 1913. Created and proclaimed June 30, 1979. Address: Fortino Santa Maria, 19030 Bocca di Magra (La Spezia), Italy.

Baum, William Wakefield (Cardinal Priest), Titular of Santa Croce in Via Flaminia; "Penitenziere Maggiore" born in Dallas, Texas, November 21, 1926. Created and proclaimed, May 24, 1976. Address: Via Rusticucci 13, 00193 Rome, Italy.

Bertoli, Paolo (Cardinal Bishop), Titular Bishop of Frascati; born in Poggio Garfagnana, Diocese of Massa Carrara-Pontremoli, February 1, 1908. Created and proclaimed April 28, 1969. Address: Piazza della Citta Leonina 1, 00193 Rome, Italy.

Bevilacqua, Anthony J. (Cardinal Priest), Titular of Ss. Redentore e S. Alfonso in Via Merulana, Archbishop of Philadelphia; born in Brooklyn, New York, June 17, 1923. Created and proclaimed June 28, 1991. Address: 222 N. 17th St., Philadelphia, PA 19103-1299, U.S.A.

Biffi, Giacomo (Cardinal Priest), Titular of Ss. Giovanni Evangelista e Petronio, Archbishop of Bologna; born in Milan, June 13, 1928. Created and proclaimed May 25, 1985. Address: Arcivescovado, Via Altabella 6, 40126 Bologna, Italy.

Canestri, Giovanni (Cardinal Priest), Titular of St. Andrea della Valle, Archbishop Emeritus of Genoa; born in Castelspina, Diocese of Alessandria, September 30, 1918. Created and proclaimed June 28, 1988. Address: Via Cernaia 9, 00185 Rome, Italy.

Caprio, Giuseppe (Cardinal Priest), Titular of S. Maria Ausiliatrice in Via Tuscolana; born in Lapio, Archdiocese of Benevento, November 15, 1914. Created and proclaimed June 30, 1979. Address: 00120 Vatican City State, Europe.

Carberry, John J. (Cardinal Priest), Titular of S. Giovanni Battista de Rossi a Via Latina, Archbishop Emeritus of St. Louis; born in Brooklyn, New York, July 31, 1904. Created and proclaimed April 28, 1969. Address: 4445 Lindell Blvd., St. Louis, MO 63108, U.S.A.

Carles Gordo, Ricardo Maria (Cardinal Priest), Archbishop of Barcelona, Spain; born in Valencia, September 24, 1926. Created and proclaimed November 26, 1994, Address: Arzobispado, Carrer del Bisbe 5, 08002 Barcelona, Spain.

Carter, Gerald Emmett (Cardinal Priest), Titular of S. Maria in Traspontina, Archbishop Emeritus of Toronto; born in Montreal, March 1, 1912. Created and proclaimed June 30, 1979. Address: 355 Church St., Toronto, Ont., M5B 1Z8, Canada.

Casaroli, Agostino (Cardinal Bishop), Titular Bishop of Porto-Santa Rufina and "in commendam" Titular of SS. XII Apostoli; born in Castel S. Giovanni, Diocese of Piacenza-Bobbio, November 24, 1914. Created and proclaimed June 30, 1979. Address: 00120 Vatican City State, Europe.

Casoria, Giuseppe (Cardinal Deacon), Deacon of S. Giuseppe in via Trionfale; born in Acerra, October 1, 1908. Created and proclaimed February 2, 1983. Address: Via P. Pancrazio Pfeiffer 10, 00193 Rome, Italy.

Cassidy, Edward I. (Cardinal Deacon), Deacon of S. Maria in Via Lata, President of the Pontifical Council for Promoting Christian Unity; born in Sydney, Australia, July 5, 1924. Created and proclaimed June 28, 1991. Address: 00120 Vatican City State, Europe.

Castillo Lara, Rosalio Jose, *s.d.b.* (Cardinal Priest), Titular of Nostra Signora di Coromoto in S. Giovanni di Dio, President of the Pontifical Commission for Vatican City; born in San Casimiro, Diocese of Maracay, September 4, 1922. Created and proclaimed May 25, 1985. Address: 00120 Vatican City State, Europe.

Ce', Marco (Cardinal Priest), Titular of S. Marco, Patriarch of Venice; born in Izano, Diocese of Crema, July 8, 1925. Created and proclaimed June 30, 1979. Address: S. Marco 318, 30124 Venezia, Italy.

Clancy, Edward Bede (Cardinal Priest), Titular of S. Maria in Vallicella, Archbishop of Sydney; born in Lithgow, Diocese of Bathurst, December 13, 1923. Created and proclaimed June 28, 1988. Address: St. Mary Cathedral, St. Mary and College Sts., Sydney, NSW 2000, Australia.

Corripio Ahumada, Ernesto (Cardinal Priest), Titular dell'Immacolata al Tiburtino, Archbishop Emeritus of Mexico City; born in Tampico, June 29, 1919. Address: Apolinar Nieto, 40, Tetlameya, 04730 Mexico, D.F. Mexico.

Daly, Cahal Brendan (Cardinal Priest), Titular of S. Patrizio, Archbishop Emeritus of Armagh; born in Loughguile, Diocese of Down and Connor, October 1, 1917. Created and proclaimed June 28, 1991. Address: Archbishop's House, Ara Coeli, Armagh BT61 7QY, Ireland.

Danneels, Godfried (Cardinal Priest), Titular of S. Anastasia, Archbishop of Malines-Bruxelles; born in Kanegem, Diocese of Brugge, June 4, 1933. Created and proclaimed February 2, 1983. Address: Aartsbisdom, Wollemarkt 15, B-2800 Mechelen, Belgium.

Darmaatmadja, Julius Riyadi, *s.j.* (Cardinal Priest), Archbishop of Jakarta, Indonesia; born in Muntilan, Archdiocese of Semarang, December 20, 1934. Created and proclaimed November 26, 1994. Address: Keus Kupan Agung, Jl. Katedral 7, Jakarta 10710, Indonesia.

Deskur, Andrzej Maria (Cardinal Deacon), Deacon of S. Cesareo in Palatio; born in Sancygniow, Diocese of Kielce, February 29, 1924. Created and proclaimed May 25, 1985. Address: 00120 Vatican City State, Europe.

Dezza, Paolo, *s.j.* (Cardinal Deacon), Deacon of S. Ignazio di Loyola a Campo Marzio, Rector emeritus of Gregorian University; born in Parma, December 13, 1901. Created and proclaimed June 28, 1991. Address: Borgo S. Spirito, 5, 00193 Rome, Italy.

do Nascimento, Alexandre (Cardinal Priest), Titular of S. Marco in Agro Laurentino, Archbishop of Luanda; born in Malanje, March 1, 1925. Created and proclaimed February 2, 1983. Address: Arcebispado, C.P. 87, 1230-C Luanda, Angola.

Echeverria Ruiz, Bernardino, *o.f.m.* (Cardinal Priest), Archbishop Emeritus of Guayaquil; born in Cotacachi, Diocese of Ibarra, November 12, 1912. Created and proclaimed November 26, 1994. Address: Garcia Moreno 548 y Bolivar, Casilla 10-01-04, Ibarra, Ecuador.

Etchegaray, Roger (Cardinal Priest), Titular of S. Leone I, President of Pontifical Council for Justice and Peace, also President of the Central Committee of the Holy Year 2,000; born in Espelette, Diocese of Bayonne, September 25, 1922. Created and proclaimed June 30, 1979. Address: Piazza San Calisto 16, 00153 Rome, Italy.

Etsou-Nzabi-Bamungwabi, Frederic, *C.I.C.M.* (Cardinal Priest), Titular of S. Lucia a Piazza d'Armi, Archbishop of Kinshasa; born in Mazalonga, Diocese of Lisala, December 3, 1930. Created and proclaimed June 28, 1991. Address: Archeveche, B.P. 8431, Kinshasa 1, Rep. du Zaire.

Eyt, Pierre (Cardinal Priest), Archbishop of Bordeaux, France; born in Laruns, Diocese of Bayonne, June 4, 1934. Created and proclaimed November 26, 1994. Address: Archeveche, B.P. 79, 183 cours de la Somme, 33034 Bordeaux Cedex, France.

Fagiolo, Vincenzo (Cardinal Deacon), President of the Disciplinary Commission of the Roman Curia; born in Segni, Italy, February 5, 1918. Created and proclaimed November 26, 1994. Address: Via Rusticucci 13, 00193 Rome, Italy.

Falcao, Jose Freire (Cardinal Priest), Titular of S. Luca a Via Prenestina, Archbishop of Brasilia; born in Erere, Diocese of Limoeira do Norte, October 23, 1925. Created and proclaimed June 28, 1988. Address: QL 12-Cj12, Lote 1, Lago Sul, 71600-325 Brasilia, D.F., Brazil.

Felici, Angelo (Cardinal Deacon), Deacon of Ss. Biagio e Carlo ai Catinari, President of the Pontifical Commission "Ecclesia Dei"; born in Segni, July 27, 1919. Created and proclaimed June 28, 1988. Address: Piazza della Citta Leonina 9, 00193 Rome, Italy.

Fresno Larrain, Juan Francisco (Cardinal Priest), Titular of S. Maria Immacolata di Lourdes a Boccea, Archbishop Emeritus of Santiago, Chile; born in Santiago, Chile on July 26, 1914. Created and proclaimed May 25, 1985. Address: Laura Tromben 5675, Vitacura, Santiago, Chile.

Furno, Carlo (Cardinal Deacon), Grand Master of the Equestrian Order of the Holy Sepulchre of Jerusalem; born in Bairo Canavese, Diocese of Ivrea, December 2, 1921. Created and proclaimed November 26, 1994. Address: Piazza della Citta Leonina 1, 00193 Rome, Italy.

Gagnon, Edouard, *p.s.s.* (Cardinal Priest), Titular of S. Marcello; President of the Pontifical Committee for International Eucharistic Congresses; born in Port-Daniel, Diocese of Gaspe, January 15, 1918. Created and proclaimed May 25, 1985. Address: Via di Porta Angelica 31, 00193 Rome, Italy.

Gantin, Bernardin (Cardinal Bishop), Titular Bishop of Palestrina; Prefect Congregation for the Bishops and President of the Pontifical Commission for Latin America & Dean of the College of Cardinals; born in Toffo, Archdiocese of Cotonou, May 8, 1922. Created and proclaimed June 27, 1977. Address: 00120 Vatican City State, Europe.

Giordano, Michele (Cardinal Priest), Titular of S. Gioacchino ai Prati di Castello, Archbishop of Naples; born in S. Arcangelo, Diocese of Tursi-Lagonegro, September 26, 1930. Created and proclaimed June 28, 1988. Address: Largo Donnaregina 23, 80138 Napoli, Italy.

Glemp, Jozef (Cardinal Priest), Titular of S. Maria in Trastevere, Archbishop of Warsaw; born in Inowroclaw, Archdiocese of Gniezno, December 18, 1929. Created and proclaimed February 2, 1983. Address: ul. Miodowa 17-19, 00-246 Warsaw, Poland.

Gong, Pin-mei Ignatius (Cardinal Priest), Titular of S. Sisto, Bishop of Shanghai and Apostolic Administrator of Soochow; born in P'ou-tong, Diocese of Shanghai, August 2, 1901. Created and reserved "in pectore" in the Consistory of June 30, 1979; proclaimed in the Consistory of June 28, 1991. Address: Our Lady Queen of the Clergy Home, 128 Strawberry Hill Ave., Stamford, CT 06904-1222, U.S.A.

Gonzalez Martin, Marcelo (Cardinal Priest), Titular of S. Agostino, Archbishop Emeritus of Toledo; born in Villanubla, Archdiocese of Valladolid, January 16, 1918. Created and proclaimed March 5, 1973. Address: Arco de Palacio 3, 45002 Toledo, Spain.

Gouyon, Paul (Cardinal Priest), Titular of Nativita di N.S.G.C. a via Gallia, Archbishop Emeritus of Rennes; born in Bordeaux, October 24, 1910. Created and proclaimed April 28, 1969. Address: 181, rue Judaique, 33081 Bordeaux Cedex, France.

Grillmeier, Alois, *s.j.* (Cardinal Deacon), Deacon of S. Nicola in Carcere, Germany. Created and proclaimed November 26, 1994. Address: Kaulbachstr. 31a, D-80538 Munchen, Germany.

Groer, Hans Herrmann, *o.s.b.* (Cardinal Priest), Titular of Ss. Gioacchino ed Anna al Tuscolano, Archbishop Emeritus of Vienna; born in Vienna, October 13, 1919. Created and proclaimed June 28, 1988. Address: Wollzeile 2, A-1010 Vienna, Austria.

Gulbinowicz, Henryk Roman (Cardinal Priest), Titular dell'Immacolata Concezione di Maria a Grottarossa, Archbishop of Wroclaw; born in Szukiszki, Archdiocese of Wilno, October 17, 1928. Created and proclaimed May 25, 1985. Address: ul. Katedralna 11, 50-328 Wroclaw, Poland.

Hickey, James Aloysius (Cardinal Priest), Titular Maria Madre del Redentore a Tor Bellamonica, Archbishop of Washington; born in Midland, Michigan, Diocese of Saginaw, October 11, 1920. Created and proclaimed June 28, 1988. Address: Archdiocesan Pastoral Center, 5001 Eastern Ave., P.O. Box 29260, Washington, DC 20017, U.S.A.

Hume, George Basil, *o.s.b.* (Cardinal Priest), Titular of San Silvestro in Capite, Archbishop of Westminster; born in Newcastle-on-Tyne, Diocese of Hexham and Newcastle March 2, 1923. Created and proclaimed May 24, 1976. Address: Archbishop's House, Ambrosden Ave., Westminster, London, SW1P-1QJ England, Great Britain.

Innocenti, Antonio (Cardinal Priest), Titular of S. Maria in Aquiro, born in Poppi, Diocese of Fiesole, August 23, 1915. Created and proclaimed May 25, 1985. Address: Piazza della Citta Leonina 9, 00193 Rome, Italy.

Javierre Ortas, Antonio Maria, *s.d.b.* (Cardinal Deacon), Deacon of S. Maria Liberatrice a Monte Testaccio, Former Prefect of Congregation for Divine Worship and the Discipline of the Sacraments; born at Sietamo, Diocese of Huesca, February 21, 1921. Created and proclaimed June 28, 1988. Address: Via Rusticucci 13, 00193 Rome, Italy.

Keeler, William Henry (Cardinal Priest), Archbishop of Baltimore; born in San Antonio, Texas, March 4, 1931. Created and proclaimed November 26, 1994. Address: 320 Cathedral Street, Baltimore, Maryland 21201. U.S.A.

Kim, Stephen Sou Hwan (Cardinal Priest), Titular of S. Felice da Cantalice a Centocelle, Archbishop of Seoul; born in Tae Gu, May 8, 1922. Created and proclaimed April 28, 1969. Address: Archbishop's House, 2Ka-1 Myong Dong, Jung Ku, Seoul 100-022, Korea.

Kitbunchu, Michael Michai (Cardinal Priest), Titular of S. Lorenzo in Panisperna, Archbishop of Bangkok; born in Samphan, Archdiocese of Bangkok, January 29, 1929. Created and proclaimed February 2, 1983. Address: Assumption Cathedral, 51 Oriental Ave., Bangkok 10500, Thailand.

Konig, Franz (Cardinal Priest), Titular of S. Eusebio, Archbishop Emeritus of Vienna; born in Rabenstein, Diocese of St. Poelten, August 3, 1905. Created and proclaimed December 15, 1958. Address: Wollzeile 2, A-1010 Wien, Austria.

Korec, Jan Chryzostom (Cardinal Priest), Titular of Ss. Fabiano e Venanzio a Villa Fiorelli, Bishop of Nitra, born in Bosany, Diocese of Nitra, January 22, 1924. Created and proclaimed June 28, 1991. Address: Biskupsky urad, post. schranka 46A, 950 50 Nitra-Hrad, Slovakia.

Kuharic, Franjo (Cardinal Priest), Titular S. Girolamo dei Croati, Archbishop of Zagreb; born in Pribic, Archdiocese of Zagreb April 15, 1919. Created and proclaimed February 2, 1983. Address: Kaptol 31, p.p. 553, 10000, Zagreb, Croatia.

Laghi, Pio (Cardinal Deacon), Deacon of S. Maria Ausiliatrice in Via Tuscolana, Prefect of the Congregation for Catholic Education; born in Castiglione, Diocese of Forli-Bertinoro, May 21, 1922. Created and proclaimed June 28, 1991. Address: 00120 Vatican City State, Europe.

Law, Bernard Francis (Cardinal Priest), Titular of S. Susanna, Archbishop of Boston; born in Torreon, November 4, 1931. Created and proclaimed May 25, 1985. Address: 2101 Commonwealth Ave., Brighton, MA 02135, U.S.A.

Lebrun Moratinos, Jose Ali (Cardinal Priest), Titular of S. Pancrazio, Archbishop Emeritus of Caracas; born in Puerto Cabello, Archdiocese of Valencia, March 19, 1919. Created and proclaimed February 2, 1983. Address: Palacio Arzobispal, Qta. Silvestre, Calle Otama, Valle Arriba, Caracas 1060, Venezuela.

Lopez Rodriguez, Nicolas de Jesus (Cardinal Priest), Titular of S. Pio X alla Balduina, Archbishop of Santo Domingo; born in Barranca, Diocese of La Vega, October 31, 1936. Created and proclaimed June 28, 1991. Address: Arzobispado, Apartado 186, Calle Isabel la Catolica 55, Santo Domingo, Dominican Republic.

Lopez Trujillo, Alfonso (Cardinal Priest), Titular of S. Prisca, President of the Pontifical Council for the Family; born in Villahermosa, Archdiocese of Ibague, November 8, 1935. Created and proclaimed February 2, 1983. Address: Piazza S. Calisto 16, 00153 Rome, Italy.

Lorscheider, Aloisio, *o.f.m.* (Cardinal Priest), Titular of San Pietro in Montorio, Archbishop of Aparecida; born in Picada Geraldo, Archdiocese of Porto Alegre, October 8, 1924. Created and proclaimed May 24, 1976. Address: Curia Metropolitana, C.P. 05, Torre da Basilica 48 andar, 12570-000 Aparecida, S.P., Brazil.

Lourdusamy, D. Simon (Cardinal Priest), Titular of S. Maria delle Grazie alle Fornaci fuori Porta Cavalleggeri; born in Kalleri, Archdiocese of Pondicherry and Cuddalore, February 5, 1924. Created and proclaimed May 25, 1985. Address: Via dei Corridori 64, 00193 Rome, Italy.

Lubachivsky, Myroslav Ivan (Cardinal Priest), Titular of S. Sofia a via Boccea, Major Archbishop of Lviv of the Ukrainians; born in Dolyna, Archdiocese of Lviv of the Ukrainians, June 24, 1914. Created and proclaimed May 25, 1985. Address: Sobor Sviatoho Jura, Ploshcha Sviatoho Jura 5, 290000 Lviv, Ukraina.

Lustiger, Jean-Marie (Cardinal Priest), Titular of S. Luigi dei Francesi, Archbishop of Paris; born in Paris, September 17, 1926. Created and proclaimed February 2, 1983. Address: 8 rue de la Ville l'Eveque, 75384, Paris, Cedex 08, France.

Macharski, Franciszek (Cardinal Priest), Titular of S. Giovanni a Porta Latina, Archbishop of Krakow; born in Krakow, May 20, 1927. Created and proclaimed June 30, 1979. Address: ul. Franciszkanska 3, 31-004 Krakow, Poland.

Mahony, Roger M. (Cardinal Priest), Titular of Ss. Quattro Coronati, Archbishop of Los Angeles; born in Hollywood, California, Archdiocese of Los Angeles, February 27, 1936. Created and proclaimed June 28, 1991. Address: 1531 W. 9th St., Los Angeles, CA 90015-1194, U.S.A.

Maida, Adam Joseph (Cardinal Priest), Archbishop of Detroit; born in East Vandergrift, Pennsylvania, Diocese of Greensburg, March 18, 1930. Created and proclaimed November 26, 1994. Address: 1234 Washington Blvd., Detroit, Michigan 48226, U.S.A.

Margeot, Jean (Cardinal Priest), Titular of S. Gabriele Arcangelo all Acqua Traversa, Bishop Emeritus of Port-Louis; born at Quatre-Bornes, Diocese of Port Louis, February 3, 1916. Created and proclaimed June 28, 1988. Address: Eveche, rue 13 Mgr Gonin, Port-Louis, Ile Maurice.

Martinez Somalo, Eduardo (Cardinal Deacon), Protodeacon of SS. Nome di Gesu', Prefect of the Congregation for Institutes of Consecrated Life and for Societies of Apostolic Life; born at Banos de Rio Tobia, Diocese of Calahorra and Calzada-Logrono, March 3, 1927. Created and proclaimed June 28, 1988. Address: 00120 Vatican City State, Europe.

Martini, Carlo Maria, *s.j.* (Cardinal Priest), Titular of S. Cecilia, Archbishop of Milan; born in Turin, February 15, 1927. Created and proclaimed February 2, 1983. Address: Palazzo Arcivescovile, Piazza Fontana 2, 20122 Milan, Italy.

Mayer, Paul Augustin, *o.s.b.* (Cardinal Priest), Titular of S. Anselmo all' Aventino; born in Altotting, Diocese of Passau, May 23, 1911. Created and proclaimed May 25, 1985. Address: Via Rusticucci 13, 00193 Rome, Italy.

Meisner, Joachim (Cardinal Priest), Titular of S. Pudenziana, Archbishop of Cologne; born in Breslau, December 25, 1933. Created and proclaimed February 2, 1983. Address: Kardinal-Frings-Strasse 10, D-50668 Koln 1, Bundesrepublik, Germany.

Neves, Lucas Moreira, *o.p.* (Cardinal Priest), Titular of Ss. Bonifacio e Alessio, Archbishop of Sao Salvador da Bahia; born in Sao Joao Del Rei, September 16, 1925. Created and proclaimed June 28, 1988. Address: Av. 7 de Setembro 1682, Campo Grande, 40080-001 Salvador, B.A., Brazil.

Noe', Virgilio (Cardinal Deacon), Deacon of S. Giovanni Bosco, Vicar General of Vatican City State, Archpriest of St. Peter Basilica; born in Zelata di Bereguardo, Diocese of Pavia, March 30, 1922. Created and proclaimed June 28, 1991. Address: 00120 Vatican City State, Europe.

Obando Bravo, Miguel, *s.d.b.* (Cardinal Priest), Titular of S. Giovanni Evangelista a Spinaceto, Archbishop of Managua; born in La Libertad of the Prelature of Juigalpa, February 2, 1926. Created and proclaimed May 25, 1985. Address: Arzobispado, Apartado 3058, Managua, Nicaragua.

O'Connor, John Joseph (Cardinal Priest), Titular of Ss. Giovanni e Paolo, Archbishop of New York; born in Philadelphia, January 15, 1920. Created and proclaimed May 25, 1985. Address: 452 Madison Ave., New York, NY 10022, U.S.A.

Oddi, Silvio (Cardinal Priest), Titular of S. Agata de'Goti; born in Morfasso, Diocese of Piacenza-Bobbio, November 14, 1910. Created and proclaimed April 28, 1969. Address: Via delle Grazie 3, 00193 Rome, Italy.

Ortega y Alamino, Jaime Lucas (Cardinal Priest), Archbishop of San Cristobal de La Habana, Cuba; born in Jaguey Grande, Diocese of Matanzas, October 18, 1936. Created and proclaimed November 26, 1994. Address: Calle Habana 152, Apartado 594, La Habana, 10100 Cuba.

Otunga, Maurice Michael (Cardinal Priest), Titular of San Gregorio Barbarigo, Archbishop of Nairobi; born in Chebukwa, Diocese of Kakamega, January 1923. Created and proclaimed March 5, 1973. Address: Arcibishop's House, P.O. Box 14231, Nairobi, Kenya.

Oviedo Cavada, Carlos, *O.de.M.* (Cardinal Priest), Titular of S. Maria della Scala, Archbishop of Santiago de Chile, Chile; born in Santiago de Chile, January 19, 1927. Created and proclaimed November 26, 1994. Address: Simon Bolivar 2843, Santiago, Chile.

Padiyara, Anthony (Cardinal Priest), Titular of S. Maria "Regina Pacis" a Monte Verde, Major Archbishop of Ernakulam of the Syro-Malabar Rite; born at Manimala, Archdiocese of Changanacherry, February 11, 1921. Created and proclaimed June 28, 1988. Address: Cardinal's House, P.O. Box 2580, Ernakulam, Kochi-682031, Kerala, India.

Palazzini, Pietro (Cardinal Priest), Titular of S. Girolamo della Carita'; born in Piobbico, Diocese of Fano-Fossombrone-Cagli-Pergola, May 19, 1912. Created and proclaimed March 5, 1973. Address: Via Proba Petronia 83, 00136 Rome, Italy.

Pappalardo, Salvatore (Cardinal Priest), Titular of S. Maria Odigitria dei Siciliani, Archbishop Emeritus of Palermo; born in Villafranca Sicula, diocese of Agrigento, September 23, 1918. Created and proclaimed March 5, 1973. Address: Arcivescovado, Via Matteo Bonello 2, 90134 Palermo, Italy.

Paskai, Laszlo, *o.f.m.* (Cardinal Priest), Titular of S. Teresa al Corso d'Italia, Archbishop of Esztergom-Budapest; born at Szeged, May 8, 1927. Created and proclaimed June 28, 1988. Address: Uri utca 62, H-1014 Budapest, Hungary.

Pham Dinh Tung, Paul Joseph (Cardinal Priest), Archbishop of Ha Noi, Viet Nam; born in Binh Hoa, Diocese of Phat Diem, June 15, 1919. Created and proclaimed November 26, 1994. Address: Toa Tong Giam Muc, 40 Pho Nha Chung, Ha Noi, Viet Nam.

Pimenta, Simon Ignatius (Cardinal Priest), Titular of S. Maria "Regina Mundi" a Torre Spaccata, Archbishop of Bombay; born in Marol, Archdiocese of Bombay, March 1, 1920. Created and proclaimed June 28, 1988. Address: Archbishop's House, 21 Nathalal Parekh Marg, Bombay-400001, India.

Piovanelli, Silvano (Cardinal Priest), Titular of S. Maria delle Grazie a Via Trionfale, Archbishop of Florence; born in Ronta di Mugello, Archdiocese of Florence, February 21, 1924. Created and proclaimed May 25, 1985. Address: Arcivescovado, Piazza S. Giovanni 3, 50129 Firenze, Italy.

Pironio, Eduardo Francisco (Cardinal Bishop), Titular of Sabina-Foggio Mirteto; born in Nueve de Julio, December 3, 1920. Created and proclaimed May 24, 1976. Former President Pontifical Council for the Laity. Address: Piazza del S. Uffizio 11, 00193 Rome, Italy.

Poggi, Luigi (Cardinal Deacon), Librarian and Archivist of the Holy Roman Church; born in Piacenza, Italy, November 25, 1917. Created and proclaimed November 26, 1994. Address: 00120 Vatican City State, Europe.

Poupard, Paul (Cardinal Priest), Titular of S. Prassede, President of the Pontifical Council of Culture; born in Bouzille, Diocese of Angers, August 30, 1930. Created and proclaimed May 25, 1985. Address: Piazza San Calisto 16, 00153 Rome, Italy.

Primatesta, Raul Francisco (Cardinal Priest), Titular of S. Maria Vergine Addolorata a Piazza Buenos Aires, Archbishop of Cordoba; born in Capilla del Senor, Diocese of Zarate-Campana, April 14, 1919. Created and proclaimed March 5, 1973. Address: Arzobispado, Avda H. Irigoyen 98, 5000 Cordoba, Argentina.

Puljic, Vinko (Cardinal Priest), Archbishop of Vrhbosna- Sarajevo, Bosnia-Hercegovina; born in Prijecani, Diocese of Banja Luke, September 8, 1945. Created and proclaimed November 26, 1994. Address: Nadbiskupski Ordinarijat, Kaptol 7, 71000 Sarajevo, Bosnia Hercegovina.

Quarracino, Antonio (Cardinal Priest), Titular of S. Maria della Salute a Primavalle, Archbishop of Buenos Aires; born in Pollica, Diocese of Vallo della Lucania, August 8, 1923. Created and proclaimed June 28, 1991. Address: Arzobispado, Rivadavia 415, 1002 Buenos Aires, Argentina.

Ratzinger, Joseph (Cardinal Bishop), Titular of Velletri-Segni, Prefect Congregation for the Doctrine of the Faith and President of the Pontifical Bible Commission; born in Marktl am Inn, Diocese of Passau, April 16, 1927. Created and proclaimed June 27, 1977. Address: 00120 Vatican City State, Europe.

Razafindratandra, Armand Gaetan (Cardinal Priest), Archbishop of Antananarivo, Madagascar; born in Ambohimalaza, Archdiocese of Antananarivo, August 7, 1925. Created and proclaimed November 26, 1994. Address: Archeveche, Andohalo, Antanarivo 101, Madagascar.

Ribeiro, Antonio (Cardinal Priest), Titular of S. Antonio da Padova in Via Merulana, Patriarch of Lisbon; born in Gandarela de Basto, Archdiocese of Braga, May 21, 1928. Created and proclaimed March 5, 1973. Address: Campo dos Martires da Patria 45, 1150 Lisboa Codex, Portugal.

Righi-Lambertini, Egano (Cardinal Priest), Titular of S. Maria in Via; born in Casalecchio di Reno, Archdiocese of Bologna, February 22, 1906. Created and proclaimed June 30, 1979. Address: Piazza della Citta Leonina 9, 00193 Rome, Italy.

Rossi, Opilio (Cardinal Priest), Titular of S. Lorenzo in Lucina; born in New York, May 14, 1910. Created and proclaimed May 24, 1976. Address: Via della Scrofa, 70, 00186 Rome, Italy.

Rugambwa, Laurean (Cardinal Priest), Titular of S. Francesco a Ripa Grande, Archbishop Emeritus of Dar-Es-Salaam; born in Bukongo, Diocese of Bukoba, July 12, 1912. Created and proclaimed March 28, 1960. Address: Archbishop's House, P.O. Box 167, Dar-Es-Salaam, Tanzania.

Ruini, Camillo (Cardinal Priest), Titular of S. Agnese, Vicar General of His Holiness of the Diocese of Rome; born in Sassuolo, Diocese of Reggio Emilia-Guastalla, February 19, 1931. Created and proclaimed June 28, 1991. Address: Piazza San Giovanni in Laterano 4, 00184 Rome, Italy.

Sabattani, Aurelio (Cardinal Deacon), Deacon of S. Apollinare alle Terme Neroniane-Allessandrine; born in Casal Fiumanese, Diocese of di Imola, October 18, 1912. Created and proclaimed February 2, 1983. Address: Palazzo del Tribunale, Piazza S. Marta, 00120 Vatican City State, Europe.

Saldarini, Giovanni (Cardinal Priest), Titular S. Cuore di Gesu' a Castro Pretorio, Archbishop of Torino; born in Cantu, Archdiocese of Milan, December 11, 1924. Created and proclaimed June 28, 1991. Address: via Arcivescovado 12, 10121 Torino, Italy.

Sales, Eugenio De Araujo (Cardinal Priest), Titular of S. Gregorio VII, Archbishop of Sao Sebastiao do Rio de Janeiro; born in Acari, Diocese of Caico, November 8, 1920. Created and proclaimed April 28, 1969. Address: Rua da Gloria, 446, C.P. 1362, 20001-970 Rio de Janeiro, R.J., Brazil.

Sanchez, Jose T. (Cardinal Deacon), Titular of St. Pio V, Former Prefect of the Congregation for the Clergy; born in Pandan, Diocese of Virac, March 17, 1920. Created and proclaimed June 28, 1991. Address: 00120 Vatican City State, Europe.

Sandoval Iniguez, Juan (Cardinal Priest), Archbishop of Guadalajara, Mexico; born in Yahualica, Diocese of San Juan de los Lagos, March 28, 1933. Created and proclaimed November 26, 1994. Address: Arzobispado, Apartado Postal 1-331, Liceo 17, 44100 Guadalajara, Jal., Mexico.

Santos, Alexandre Jose Maria dos, *o.f.m.* (Cardinal Priest), Titular of S. Frumenzio ai Prati Fiscali, Archbishop of Maputo; born in Zavala, Diocese of Inhambane, March 18, 1924. Created and proclaimed June 28, 1988. Address: Paco Arquiepiscopal, Avenida Eduardo Mondlane 1448, C.P. 258, Maputo, Mozambique.

Schotte, Jan P., *c.i.c.m.* (Cardinal Deacon), General Secretary of the Synod of Bishops; born in Beveren-Leie, Diocese of Brugge, April 20, 1928. Created and proclaimed November 26, 1994. Address: Palazzo del Bramante, Via della Conciliazione, 34, 00193 Rome, Italy.

Schwery, Henri (Cardinal Priest), Titular of Ss. Protomartiri a Via Aurelia Antica, Bishop Emeritus of Sion; born in Saint Leonard, Diocese of Sion, June 14, 1932. Created and proclaimed June 28, 1991. Address: C.P. 2334, rue Mathieu-Schiner 5, CH-1950 Sion 2, Switzerland.

Sensi, Giuseppe Maria (Cardinal Priest), Titular of "Regina Apostolorum;" born in Cosenza, May 27, 1907. Created and proclaimed May 24, 1976. Address: Piazza S. Calisto, 16, 00153 Rome, Italy.

Sfeir, Nasrallah Pierre (Cardinal Bishop), Patriarch of Antioch of the Maronites, Lebanon; born in Reyfoun, Lebanon, Diocese of Sarba dei Maronitit, May 15, 1929. Created and proclaimed November 26, 1994. Address: Patriarcat Maronite, Bkerke, Lebanon.

Shirayanagi, Peter Seiichi (Cardinal Priest), Archbishop of Tokyo, Japan; born in Hachioji, Archdiocese of Tokyo, June 17, 1928. Created and proclaimed November 26, 1994. Address: Archbishop's House, 16-15 Sekiguchi, 3-chome, Bunkyoku, Tokyo, 112 Japan.

Silva Henriquez, Raul, *s.d.b.* (Cardinal Priest), Titular of S. Bernardo alle Terme, Archbishop Emeritus of Santiago; born in Talca, September 27, 1907. Created and proclaimed March 19, 1962. Address: Calle Los Pescadores 2260, Santiago, Chile.

Silvestrini, Achille (Cardinal Deacon), Deacon of S. Benedetto fuori Porta S. Paolo, Prefect of the Congregation for Oriental Churches; born in Brisighella, Diocese of Faenza-Modigliana, October 25, 1923. Created and proclaimed June 28, 1988. Address: Palazzina della Zecca, 00120 Vatican City State, Europe.

Simonis, Adrianus Johannes (Cardinal Priest), Titular of S. Clemente, Archbishop of Utrecht; born in Lisse, Diocese of Rotterdam, November 26, 1931. Created and proclaimed May 25, 1985. Address: Aartsbisdom, P.B. 14019, 3508 SB Utrecht, Netherlands.

Sin, Jaime L. (Cardinal Priest), Titular of Santa Maria ai Monti, Archbishop of Manila; born in New Washington, Diocese of Kalibo, August 31, 1928. Created and proclaimed May 24, 1976. Address: P.O. Box 132, 1099 Manila, Philippines.

Sladkevicius, Vincentas (Cardinal Priest), Titular of Spirito Santo alla Ferratella, Archbishop Emeritus of Kaunas; born in Zasliai, Diocese of Kaisiadorys, August 20, 1920. Created and proclaimed June 28, 1988. Address: Valanciaus 6, 3000 Kaunas, Lithuania.

Sodano, Angelo, (Cardinal Bishop), Titular of S. Maria Nuova, Secretary of State; born in Isola d'Asti, Diocese of Asti, November 23, 1927. Created and proclaimed June 28, 1991. Address: 00120 Vatican City State, Europe.

Sterzinsky, Georg M. (Cardinal Priest), Titular of S. Giuseppe all' Aurelio, Archbishop of Berlin; born in Warlack, Diocese of Warmia, February 9, 1936. Created and proclaimed June 28, 1991. Address: Wundstrasse 48-50, 14057 Berlin, Germany.

Stickler, Alfons Maria, *s.d.b.* (Cardinal Priest), Titular of S. Giorgio in Velabro; born in Neunkirchen, Archdiocese of Vienna, August 23, 1910. Created and proclaimed May 25, 1985. Address: Piazza del S. Uffizio 11, 00193 Rome, Italy.

Suarez Rivera, Adolfo Antonio (Cardinal Priest), Archbishop of Monterrey in Mexico; born in San Cristobal de las Casas, January 9, 1927. Created and proclaimed November 26, 1994. Address: Apartado Postal 7, Loma Larga 2429 con Sierra Madre, 64000 Monterrey, N.L., Mexico.

Suquia Goicoechea, Angel (Cardinal Priest), Titular of Gran Madre di Dio, Archbishop Emeritus of Madrid; born in Zaldivia, Diocese of San Sebastian October 2, 1916. Created and proclaimed May 25, 1985. Address: Javier Barcaiztegui 7-3, 20010 San Sebastian, Spain.

Swiatek, Kazimierz (Cardinal Priest), Archbishop of Minsk-Mohilev, Apostolic Administrator of Pinsk, Belarus; born in Walga, Amm. Ap. of Estonia, October 21, 1914. Created and proclaimed November 26, 1994. Address: ul. Szewczenki 12/1, 225710 Pinsk, Belarus.

Szoka, Edmund Casimir (Cardinal Priest), Titular of Ss. Andrea e Gregorio al Monte Celio, President of the Prefecture of the Economic Affairs of the Holy See; born in Grand Rapids, Michigan, September 14, 1927. Created and proclaimed June 28, 1988. Address: 00120 Vatican City State, Europe.

Taofinu'u, Pio, *s.m.* (Cardinal Priest), Titular of S. Onofrio, Archbishop of Samoa-Apia; born in Falealupo, Archdiocese of Samoa-Apia, December 9 1923. Created and proclaimed March 5, 1973. Address: Archbishop's House, P.O. Box 532, Apia, Western Samoa, Oceania.

Thiandoum, Hyacinthe (Cardinal Priest), Titular of Santa Maria del Popolo, Archbishop of Dakar; born in Poponguine, Archdiocese of Dakar, February 2, 1921. Created and proclaimed May 24, 1976. Address: B.P. 1908, Villa Les Badamiers, Dakar-Fann, Senegal.

Todea, Alexandru (Cardinal Priest), Titular of S. Atanasio, Archbishop Emeritus of Fagaras and Alba Julia; born in 1913. Created and proclaimed June 28, 1991. Address: Str. P.P. Aron 2, RO-3175 Blaj, A.B., Romania.

Tomko, Jozef (Cardinal Priest), Titular of S. Sabina, Prefect of the Congregation for the Evangelization of People; born in Udavske, Diocese of Kosice, March 11, 1924. Created and proclaimed May 25, 1985. Address: Villa Betania, Via Urbano VIII 16, 00165 Rome, Italy.

Tonini, Ersilio (Cardinal Priest), Titular of Ss. Redentore a Val Melaina, Archbishop Emeritus of Ravenna-Cervia, Italy; born in Centovera di San Giorgio Piacentino, Diocese of Piacenza-Bobbio, July 20, 1914. Created and proclaimed November 26, 1994. Address: Via Santa Teresa 8, 48100 Ravenna, Italy.

Tumi, Christian Wiyghan (Cardinal Priest), Titular of Ss. Martiri dell' Uganda a Poggio Ameno, Archbishop of Douala; born in Kikaikelaki, Diocese of Kumbo, October 15, 1930. Created and proclaimed June 28, 1988. Address: Archeveche, B.P. 179, Douala, Cameroon.

Turcotte, Jean-Claude (Cardinal Priest), Archbishop of Montreal, Canada; born in Montreal, June 26, 1936. Created and proclaimed November 26, 1994. Address: 1071 rue de la Cathedrale, Montreal, P.Q., H2B 2V4 Canada.

Tzadua, Paulos (Cardinal Priests), Titular of Ss. Nome di Maria a Via Latina, Archbishop of Addis Abeba; born in Addifini, Eparchy of Asmara, August 25, 1921. Created and proclaimed May 25, 1985. Address: P.O. Box 21903, Addis Abeba, Ethiopia.

Ursi, Corrado (Cardinal Priest), Titular of S. Callisto, Archbishop Emeritus of Naples; born in Andria, July 26, 1908. Created and proclaimed June 26, 1967. Address: Via Capodimonte 13, 80136 Napoli, Italy.

Vachon, Louis-Albert (Cardinal Priest), Titular of S. Paolo della Croce a Corviale, Archbishop Emeritus of Quebec; born in Saint Frederic-de -Beauce, Archdiocese of Quebec, February 4, 1912. Created and proclaimed May 25, 1985. Address: 1 rue des Remparts, Quebec, Qué., G1R 5L7, Canada.

Vargas Alzamora, Augusto, *s.j.* (Cardinal Priest), Archbishop of Lima, Peru; born in Lima, November 9, 1922. Created and proclaimed November 26, 1994. Address: Calle Los Nogales 249, San Isidro, Lima, Peru.

Vidal, Ricardo J. (Cardinal Priest), Titular of Ss. Pietro e Paolo a Via Ostiense, Archbishop of Cebu; born in Mogpoc, Diocese of Boac, February 6, 1931. Created and proclaimed May 25, 1985. Address: D. Jakosalem Str., P.O. Box 52, 6000 Cebu City, Philippines.

Vlk, Miloslav (Cardinal Priest), Archbishop of Prague, Czech Republic; born in Lisnice-Sepekov, Diocese of Ceske Budejovice, May 17, 1932. Created and proclaimed November 26, 1994. Address: Arcibiskupska Kurie, Hradcanske nam. 16, 119 02, Praha 1, Czech Republic.

Wamala, Emmanuel (Cardinal Priest), Archbishop of Kampala, Uganda; born in Kamaggwa, Diocese of Masaka, December 15, 1926. Created and proclaimed November 26, 1994. Address: Archbishop's House, P.O. Box 14125, Mengo, Kampala, Uganda.

Wetter, Friedrich (Cardinal Priest), Titular of S. Stefano al Monte Celio, Archbishop of Munich & Freising; born in Landau, Diocese of Speyer, February 20, 1928. Created and proclaimed May 25, 1985. Address: Kardinal-Faulhaber Str., 7, D-8000 Munchen 2, Bundesrepublik, Germany.

Willebrands, Johannes (Cardinal Priest), Titular S. Sebastiano alle Catacombe; born in Bovenkarspel, Diocese of Haarlem, September 4, 1909. Created and proclaimed April 28, 1969. Address: Piazza della Citta Leonina 1, 00193 Rome, Italy.

Williams, Thomas Stafford (Cardinal Priest), Titular of Gesu' Divin Maestro alla Pineta Sacchetti, Archbishop of Wellington; born in Wellington, March 20, 1930. Created and proclaimed February 2, 1983. Address: Archbishop's House, P.O. Box 1937, Wellington 6015, New Zealand.

Winning, Thomas Joseph (Cardinal Priest), Archbishop of Glasgow, Scotland; born in Wishaw, Diocese of Motherwell, June 3, 1925. Created and proclaimed November 26, 1994. Address: 40 Newlands Road, Glasgow G43 2JD, Scotland, Great Britain.

Wu Cheng-Chung, John Baptist (Cardinal Priest), Titular of Beata Vergine Maria del Monte Carmelo a Mostacciano, Bishop of Hong Kong; born in Shui-Tsai, Diocese of Kaying, March 26, 1925. Created and proclaimed June 28, 1988. Address: Caritas House, 2 Caine Rd., Hong Kong.

Yago, Bernard (Cardinal Priest), Titular of S. Crisogono, Archbishop Emeritus of Abidjan; born in Pass, Archdiocese of Abidjan July 1916. Created and proclaimed February 2, 1983. Address: Archeveche, 01 B.P. 1287, Abidjan 01, Ivory Coast.

Zoungrana, Paul, *m.afr.* (Cardinal Priest), Titular of S. Camillo, Archbishop Emeritus of Ougadougou; born in Ougadougou, September 3, 1917. Created and proclaimed February 22, 1965. Address: Archeveche, 01 B.P. 1472, Ouagadougou 01, Burkina-Faso.

Patriarchs

Alexandria (Egypt), *Coptic Rite*—His Beatitude Stephanos II Ghattas, born January 16, 1920 in Cheikh Zein-el-Dine; ordained March 25, 1944; elected to Luqsor of the Copts June 9, 1967; consecrated June 16, 1967; elected Patriarch June 9, 1986.

Antioch (Syria), *Syriac Rite*—His Beatitude Ignatius Anthony II Hayek, born in Halab, Archdiocese of Aleppo, September 14, 1910; elected Patriarch, March 10, 1968. Address: Rue Damas, Beyrouth, Lebanon. *Maronite Rite*—His Beatitude Nasrallah Peter Cardinal Sfeir; born in Reyfoun, May 15, 1920; elected Patriarch April 19, 1986.

Melkite Greek Catholic—His Beatitude Maximos V Hakim, born in Tantah, Egypt, May 18, 1908; elected Patriarch, November 22, 1967. Address: Bab Touma, Damascus, Syria.

Jerusalem (Israel)—His Beatitude Michael Sabbah, born in Nazareth, Israel, March 19, 1933; elected Patriarch of Jerusalem of the Latins December 11, 1987; consecrated January 6, 1988.

Babylon of the Chaldeans—His Beatitude Raphael I Bidawid; born in Mossul, April 17, 1922; elected Patriarch, May 21, 1989.

Cilicia of the Armenians—His Beatitude John Peter XVIII Kasparian, born in Cairo, January 20, 1927; elected Patriarch August 5, 1982.

East Indies—Most Rev. Raoul Nicholas Gonsalves; born in Bambolim, Archdiocese of Goa, June 15, 1927; promoted Patriarch January 30, 1978.

Lisbon (Portugal)—His Eminence Antonio Cardinal Ribeiro, born in Gandarela, Archdiocese of Braga, May 21, 1928; appointed Patriarch May 10, 1971. Created and proclaimed Cardinal in the Consistory of March 5, 1973.

Venice (Italy)—His Eminence Cardinal Marco Ce', born in Izano Diocese of Crema, July 8, 1925; ordained March 27, 1948; elected Titular Bishop of Vulturia April 22, 1970; Patriarch December 7, 1978. Created and proclaimed Cardinal in the Consistory of June 30, 1979.

Synod of Bishops

Synodus Episcoporum President: The Holy Father. *Secretary General:* His Eminence Jan Cardinal Schotte, C.I.C.M. *General Secretariat:* Palazzo del Bramante, Via della Conciliazione, 34 00193 Rome, Italy. Tel: 69.88.48.21 or 69.88.43.24. Fax: 69.88.33.92.

Office of Labor of the Apostolic See

Officium Laboris Apostolicae Sedia President: His Eminence Jan Cardinal Schotte, C.I.C.M. *Vice President:* Most Rev. Archbishop Giovanni De Andrea. *Assessor of the Presidency:* Prof. Matteo Dell'Olio. *Assessor of the Presidency:* Prof. Gian Carlo Perone. *Office:* Via dell Conciliazione, 1 00193 Rome, Italy. Tel: 69.88.44.49. Fax: 69.88.38.00.

The Roman Curia

The present norms regarding the Roman Curia were publicly announced June 28, 1988, in the "Pastor Bonus - Constitutio Apostolica de Romana Curia," and published in A.A.S. LXXX/1988, Commentarium Officiale; pp. 841-934. The Supreme Pontiff usually conducts business of the universal Church by means of the Roman Curia, which fulfills its duty in his name and by his authority for the good and the service of the Churches; it consists of the Secretariat of State or the Papal Secretariat, congregations, tribunals and other institutions, whose structure and competency are defined in special law (can. 360). The Roman curia is the complex of departments and institutes which assist the Roman Pontiff in the exercise of his supreme pastoral function for the good and service of the universal Church and of the particular churches, by which the unity of faith and communion of the people of God is strengthened and the mission is promoted which is proper to the Church in the world.

I. THE SECRETARIAT OF STATE TO HIS HOLINESS

The Secretariat of State

The Secretariat of State closely assists the Supreme Pontiff in the exercise of his supreme function. The cardinal secretary of state presides over it. It includes two sections, namely the section for general affairs under the immediate direction of the substitute, assisted by an assessor, and the section for relations with states under the direction of its own secretary, with the assistance of a subsecretary. Attached to this latter section is a body of cardinals and some bishops.

Secretary of State: His Eminence Angelo Cardinal Sodano.

Office: Apostolic Palace, 00120 Vatican City State, Europe. Tel: 69.88.34.38; Fax: 69.88.50.88.

First Section: for General Affairs

The first section handles anything entrusted to it by the Holy Father, as well as matters of daily business which do not fall within the competence of other dicasteries. It fosters relations with these departments, with the bishops, and with the diplomatic missions of the Holy See.

Substitute: Archbishop Giovanni Battista Re.

Assessor: Rev. Msgr. Leonardo Sandri.

Second Section: for Relations with States

The second section of the Secretariat of State handles all matters pertaining to civil governments, fostering diplomatic relations with nations, and maintaining contact with all the diplomatic missions of the Holy See. It takes care also of what concerns the presence and activity of the Holy See in international institutes.

Secretary: Archbishop Jean-Louis Tauran.

Under-Secretary: Rev. Msgr. Celestino Migliore.

II. THE CONGREGATIONS

By the name of "department" (dicasteria) is understood: the congregations, tribunals, councils and offices, namely the Apostolic Camera, the Administration of the Patrimony of the Apostolic See, and the Prefecture of Economic Affairs of the Holy See. The departments are juridically equal among themselves. Attached to the institutes of the Roman Curia are the Prefecture of the Papal Household and the Office of Liturgical Celebrations of the Supreme Pontiff.

The Congregation for the Doctrine of the Faith

The proper function of the Congregation on the Doctrine of the Faith is to promote and safeguard the doctrine of faith and morals in the whole Catholic world; therefore, those things belong to it which touch this matter in any way. Fulfilling the function of promoting doctrine, it fosters studies in order that the understanding of the faith might grow and that a response can be prepared under the light of faith for new questions arising from developments in science and human culture. It is a help to bishops, whether individually or gathered in assemblies, in the exercise of the function by which they are constituted authentic teachers and doctors of the faith as well as the office by which they are held to safeguard and promote the integrity of that faith. This Sacred Congregation reproves doctrines opposed to the principles of the faith after the interested Bishops of a region have been heard. It studies the books referred to it and, if necessary, reproves them after the author has been heard and has had an opportunity to defend himself and after the Ordinary has been forewarned. It also examines whatever concerns"the privilege of the faith" whether in law and in fact. It is competent to pass judgement on errors about the faith according to the norms of an ordinary process. It safeguards the dignity of the sacrament of Penance. The Congregation proceeds administratively or judicially according to the nature of the question to be treated.

Cardinal Prefect: His Eminence Joseph Cardinal Ratzinger.

Secretary: Most Rev. Archbishop Tarcisio Bertone, S.D.B.

Office: Piazza del S. Uffizio 11, 00193 Rome, Italy. Tel: 69.88.33.57; 69.88.34.13; Fax: 69.88.34.09.

The Congregation for the Causes of Saints

The Congregation for the Causes of Saints is competent in all matters which in any way pertain to the Beatification of Servants of God or to the Canonization of the Blessed or to the Preservation of Relics.

This Congregation is divided into three offices.

Pro Prefect: Most Rev. Archbishop Alberto Bovone.

Secretary: Most Rev. Archbishop Edward Nowak.

Office: Piazza Pio XII 10, 00193 Rome, Italy. Tel: 011 39 6 69.88.42.47. Fax: 011 39 6 69.88.19.35.

The Congregation for the Oriental Churches

This Congregation considers those matters, whether regarding persons or things, which touch on the Eastern Catholic Churches. It treats all questions which pertain either to persons, or to discipline, or to the rites of the Oriental Churches, even if they are mixed in that by the nature of the thing or of persons they involve Latins. Territories in which a major part of the Christians belong to Oriental rites are subject only to this Congregation. Even in Latin territories it carefully supervises the faithful of Oriental rites and provides as much as possible for their spiritual needs even by the establishment of their own hierarchy if the number of faithful and circumstances require this.

Cardinal Prefect: His Eminence Achille Cardinal Silvestrini.

Secretary: Most Rev. Archbishop Miroslav Stefan Marusyn, Titular Archbishop of Cadi.

Office: Via della Conciliazione 34, 00193 Rome, Italy. Tel: 69.88.42.82; Fax: 69.88.43.00.

The Congregation for Bishops

This congregation examines what pertains to the constitution and provision of particular churches as well as the exercise of the episcopal function in the Latin Church, except for the competence of the Congregation for the Evangelization of Peoples. It belongs to the Congregation for Bishops to propose to the Roman Pontiff, for approval, the constitution of new dioceses, provinces and regions; to divide, unite and realign them after consulting the interested Episcopal Conferences; it deals also with the erection of the military ordinariates and, after consulting the Episcopal Conference, prelacies for special pastoral ministries for various regions or social groups. This Congregation provides also for the naming of bishops, apostolic administrators, coadjutors and auxiliaries of bishops, military and other vicars and prelates enjoying personal jurisdiction.

It is competent for all things that have to do with bishops and publishes norms which, through the Episcopal Conference, provide for the more urgent needs of the faithful.

Cardinal Prefect: His Eminence Bernardin Cardinal Gantin.

Secretary: Most Rev Archbishop Jorge Maria Mejia.

Office: Piazza Pio XII 10, 00193 Rome, Italy. Tel: 69.88.42.17; Fax: 69.88.53.03.

Pontifical Commission for Latin America

(Directly responsible to Congregation for Bishops).

President: His Eminence Bernardin Cardinal Gantin.

Vice President: Most Rev. Bishop Calderon Polo Cipriano.

The Congregation for Divine Worship and the Discipline of the Sacraments

This congregation does those things which pertain to the Apostolic See as to the moderation and promotion of the sacred liturgy, especially the sacraments, with due regard for the competence of the Congregation on Doctrine of the Faith. It fosters and safeguards the discipline of the sacraments, especially what pertains to their valid and licit celebration; moreover, it concedes favors and dispensations for matters which are not contained in the facilities of diocesan bishops in this line. It alone examines the non-consummation of a marriage and the presence of causes for the granting of a dispensation and everything connected with them. It has competence with regard to the obligations connected with major orders and it examines questions about the validity of sacred ordination.

Pro-Prefect: Most Rev. Archbishop Jorge Arturo Medina Estevez.

Secretary: Most Rev. Archbishop Geraldo Majella Agnelo.

Office: 10 Piazza Pio XII 10, 00193 Rome, Italy. Tel: 69.88.43.16; Fax: 69.88.34.99.

The Congregation for the Evangelization of Peoples or for the Propagation of the Faith

It belongs to this congregation to direct and coordinate throughout the world the work of the evangelization of peoples itself and missionary cooperation, while respecting the competence of the Congregation for Eastern Churches. It is competent for those things which pertain to all the missions established for the spread of the Kingdom of Christ throughout the world and therefore for whatever is connected with the assignment and transferral of the necessary ministers, for describing ecclesiastical boundaries and proposing those who will govern them. It encourages also the development of an indigenous clergy. The congregation sponsors missionary initiatives and promotes missionary vocations and spirituality. In the territories subject to it, the Congregation has charge of all that pertains to the holding of synods and councils, to the establishing of episcopal conferences and to the review of their statutes and decrees. The Congregation has a Supreme Council for the direction of Pontifical Missionary Works, on which depend the general Councils of the Missionary Union of the Clergy, the Society for the Propagation of the Faith, the Society of St. Peter the Apostole, and the Society of the Holy Childhood.

Cardinal Prefect: His Eminence Jozef Cardinal Tomko.

Secretary: Most Rev. Archbishop Giuseppe Uhac.

Adjunt Secretary: Most Rev. Archbishop Charles A. Schleck, C.S.C.

Office: Palazzo di Propaganda Fide, Piazza di Spagna 48, 00187 Rome, Italy. Tel: 011 39 6 69.88.01.01; Fax: 011 39 6 69.88.01.18

The Congregation for Institutes of Consecrated Life and for Societies of Apostolic Life

The principal function of this congregation is to promote and supervise, in the whole Latin Church, the practices of the evangelical counsels as they are exercised in approved forms of consecrated life and at the same time the activities of societies of apostolic life. The Congregation takes care of Religious Institutes of Consecrated Life and Secular Institutes.

Religious Institutes: the Congregation is entrusted with the affairs of all religious institutes of the Latin Rite and their members. It is also competent in matters which pertain to societies of common life, whose members live like religious, or to Third Orders as such.

Secular Institutes: the Congregation is competent in the same way, all else being equal, for Apostolic Societies which, although not religious, make a true and complete profession of the evangelical counsels in the world.

Cardinal Prefect: His Eminence Eduardo Cardinal Martinez Somalo.

Secretary: Most Rev. Archbishop Piergiorgio Silvano Nesti, C.P.

Office: Piazza Pio XII 3, 00193 Rome, Italy. Tel: 69.88.41.28; Fax: 69.88.45.26.

The Congregation for the Clergy

With due regard for the rights of bishops and their conferences, this congregation examines those things which concern priests and deacons of the secular clergy with regard to their persons, pastoral ministry, matters which are in support of the exercise of these things, and in all this provides opportune assistance to the bishops. The Congregation has many functions: studies, proposes and urges the means and aids by which priests strive for sanctity. This office also has charge of everything which concerns the work and discipline of the diocesan clergy. Particularly it promotes the preaching of the Word of God and the works of the apostolate and organization of catechesis, evaluates and approves pastoral and catechetical directories, fosters national and international Catechetical Congresses and indicates the opportune norms for religious instruction of children, young people and adults. The Congregation looks also to the preservation and administration of the temporal goods of the Church without prejudice to the other Congregations which have temporal goods committed to their vigilance.

Pro-Prefect: Most Rev. Archbishop Dario Castrillon Hoyos.

Secretary: Most Rev. Archbishop Crescenzio Sepe.

Office: Piazza Pio XII 3, 00193 Rome, Italy. Tel: 69.88.41.51; Fax: 69.88.48.45.

Pontifical Commission for The Conservation of the Artistic and Sacred Patrimony (Directly responsible to the Congregation for the Clergy).

Secretary: Most Rev. Archbishop Francesco Marchisano.

The Congregation for Catholic Education

This Congregation expresses and exercises the Apostolic See's solicitude for the formation of those who are called to holy orders as well as for the promotion and organization of Catholic education. It is competent for all that pertains to the formation of clerics and the Catholic education both of clerics and of the laity.

The Congregation has many functions and is charged with the direction, discipline and temporal administration of seminaries and whatever touches the education of the diocesan clergy and the scientific formation of religious and secular institutes.

The Congregation oversees universities, faculties, athenaea and any institute of higher learning which has the name "Catholic" in so far as they depend on the authority of the Church, not excluding those directed by religious or the laity.

The Congregation cares for the establishment of parochial and diocesan schools; watches over all Catholic schools below the level of a university and faculty, as well as all institutes of instruction or education dependent on the authority of the Church.

Also within the Congregation is located the Pontifical Work for Vocations, which is charged with coordinating and promoting the work of fostering all ecclesiastical vocations.

Prefect: His Eminence Pio Cardinal Laghi.

Secretary: Most Rev. Archbishop Jose Saraiva Martins.

Office: Piazza Pio XII 3, 00193 Rome, Italy. Tel: 69.88.41.67; Fax: 69.88.41.72.

III. TRIBUNALS

Apostolic Penitentiary

The competence of this Tribunal is concerned with those matters which pertain to the internal forum, for both the sacramental and non-sacramental internal forum. It is competent in matters pertaining to the granting and use of indulgences.

Major Penitentiary: His Eminence William Cardinal Baum.

Regent: Most Rev. Bishop Luigi De Magistris.

Office: Piazza della Cancelleria 1, 00186 Rome, Italy. Tel: 69.88.75.26.

Supreme Tribunal of the Apostolic Signatura

This department, in addition to the function which it exercises as Supreme Tribunal, consults that justice may be correctly administered in the Church.

With the many functions, the Apostolic Signatura judges the matters assigned to it in the Code of Canon Law; it prorogues the competence of tribunals; it extends the forum for strangers in Rome to cases of matrimonial nullity in extraordinary circumstances and for grave reasons; it supervises the proper administration of justice; it provides for the establishment of regional and interregional tribunals; it enjoys the rights assigned to it in concordats between the Holy See and the various nations.

The Tribunal settles questions about the exercise of administrative ecclesiastical power which are referred to it. It also passes on conflicts of competence among the departments of the Holy See; it examines administrative matters referred to it by the Congregations of the Roman Curia as well as questions committed to it by the Holy Father.

Prefect: His Eminence Gilberto Cardinal Agustoni.

Secretary: Most Rev. Archbishop Zenon Grocholewski.

Office: Piazza della Cancelleria 1, 00186 Rome, Italy. Tel: 69.88.75.20; Fax: 69.88.75.53.

Tribunal of the Roman Rota

This tribunal acts as a higher instance at the Apostolic See, usually in the grade of appeal, for safeguarding rights in the Church; it fosters the unity of jurisprudence and, through its own sentences, is a help to lower tribunals. It is also a court of first instance for cases specified in the law and for others committed to the Rota by the Roman Pontiff. The greater part of its decisions concern the nullity of marriage. In such cases its competence includes marriages between two Catholics, between a Catholic and non-Catholic, and between two non-Catholic parties whether one or both of the baptized parties belongs to a Latin or Oriental Rite.

Dean: Rev. Msgr. Francesco Pompedda.

Office: Piazza della Cancelleria 1, 00186 Rome, Italy. Tel: 69.88.75.02; Fax: 69.88.75.54.

IV. PONTIFICAL COUNCILS

Pontifical Council for the Laity

This council is competent in those matters which pertain to the Apostolic See in promoting and coordinating the apostolate of the lay persons and, generally, in those things which look to the Christian life of lay persons as such. The norms were published in the apostolic letter, "Catholicam Christi Ecclesiam" of January 6, 1967 (A.A.S., LIX, pp. 25-28).

President: Most Rev. Archbishop J. Francis Stafford.

Secretary: Most Rev. Bishop Stanislaus Rylko.

Office: Piazza S. Calisto 16, 00153 Rome, Italy. Tel: 69.88.73.22; Fax: 69.88.72.14.

Pontifical Council for Promoting Christian Unity

The function of this Council is to concentrate in an appropriate way on initiatives and ecumenical activities for the restoration of unity among Christians. It has charge of relations with those of other communities; considers the correct interpretation and observance of the principles of ecumenism; promotes Catholic groups and coordinates the efforts at unity, both on the national and international levels; institutes colloquies on ecumenical questions and activities with Churches and ecclesial communities separated from the Holy See; deputes Catholic observers for Christian congresses; invites to Catholic gatherings observers of the separated brethren; orders into practice conciliar decrees on ecumenical matters. Furthermore, it is competent for all questions concerning religious relations with Judaism.

President: His Eminence Edward Cardinal Cassidy.

Secretary: Most Rev. Bishop Pierre Duprey.

President-Emeritus: His Eminence Johannes Cardinal Willebrands.

Office: Via dell' Erba 1, 00193 Rome, Italy. Tel: 69.88.30.71; Fax: 69.88.53.65.

Pontifical Council for the Family

This Council promotes the pastoral care of families and fosters their rights and dignity in the Church and in civil society, in order that they might ever more suitably fulfill their own functions.

President: His Eminence Alfonso Cardinal Lopez Trujillo.

Secretary: Most Rev. Bishop Francisco Gil Hellin.

Office: Piazza S. Calisto 16, 00153 Rome, Italy. Tel: 69.88.72.43; Fax: 69.88.72.72.

Pontifical Council for Justice and Peace

This Council looks to those things which will promote justice and peace in the world according to the gospel and the social teaching of the Church.

President: His Eminence Roger Cardinal Etchegaray.

Secretary: Rev. Msgr. Diarmuid Martin.

Office: Piazza S. Calisto 16, 00153 Rome, Italy. Tel: 69.88.71.91; Fax: 69.88.72.05.

Pontifical Council "Cor Unum"

This Council shows the solicitude of the Catholic Church toward the needy, in order that human fraternity might be fostered and the charity of Christ be made manifest.

President: Most. Rev. Archbishop Paul Josef Cordes.

Secretary: Rev. Msgr. Ivan Marin-Lopez.

Office: Piazza S. Calisto 16, 00153 Rome, Italy. Tel: 69.88.73.31; Fax: 69.88.73.01.

Pastoral Council for the Pastoral Care of Migrants and Itinerant People

This Council directs the pastoral concern of the Church toward the special needs of those who are forced to leave their own native land or who perhaps lack one; it also sees that there is appropriate study of the questions which touch on this matter.

President: Most Rev. Archbishop Giovanni Cheli.

Secretary: Most Rev. Archbishop Francesco Gioia

Office: Piazza S. Calisto 16, 00153 Rome, Italy. Tel: 69.88.71.93; Fax: 69.88.71.11.

Pontifical Council for the Pastoral Assistance to Health Care Workers

This Council shows the solicitude of the Church for the sick by aiding those who carry out a ministry toward the sick and suffering, in order that the apostolate of mercy, which they carry out, may ever more suitably respond to new needs.

President: Most Rev. Bishop Javier Lozano Barragan.

Secretary: Rev. Jose Luis Redrado Marchite, O.H.

Office: Via della Conciliazione, 00193 Rome, Italy. Tel: 69.88.31.38; Fax: 69.88.31.39.

Pontifical Council for the Intepretation of Legal Texts

The function of this Council consists especially in interpreting the Church's laws.

President: Most Rev. Archbishop Julian Herranz Casado.

Secretary: Most Rev. Bishop Bruno Bertagna.

Office: Palazzo delle Congregazioni Piazza Pio XII 10, 00193 Rome, Italy. Tel: 69.88.4008; Fax: 69.88.47.10.

Pontifical Council for Inter-Religious Dialogue

This Council fosters and moderates relations with members and bodies of religions which do not carry the name of Christian, as well as with those who in any way possess a religious spirit. It fosters studies and promotes relations with non-Christians to bring about an increase in mutual respect and seeks ways to establish a dialogue with them; it receives and carefully weighs the wishes of the Ordinaries; it provides for the formation of those who participate in dialogue.

President: His Eminence Francis Cardinal Arinze.

Secretary: Most Rev. Bishop Michael Louis Fitzgerald.

Office: Via dell' Erba 1, 00193 Rome, Italy. Tel: 69.88.43.21; Fax: 69.88.44.94.

Pontifical Council for Culture

The Council embodies the Church's pastoral concern over the relationship between faith and cultures. Its tasks include: studying unbelief and religious indifference, as present in different cultures; supporting the Church's inculturation of the Gospel; promotion initiatives of dialogue between faith and culture, as well as dialogue with those who do not believe in God. Its activities include seminars, intercultural exchanges, and coordinating the activities of Pontifical Academies and the Pontifical Commission for the Cultural Patrimony of the Church. An important hope of the Council is to show faith as the inspiration of science, literature and the arts.

President: His Eminence Paul Cardinal Poupard.

Secretary: Rev. Msgr. Franc Rode, C.M.

Office: Piazza S. Calisto 16, 00120 Vatican City State, Europe. Tel: 69.88.73.21; Fax: 69.88.73.68.

Pontifical Council for Social Communications

This Council is involved in questions touching on the instruments of social communication so that the proclamation of salvation and human progress might be promoted even through them in order to foster civil culture.

President: Most Rev. Archbishop John Foley.

Secretary: Most Rev. Bishop Pierfranco Pastore.

President-Emeritus: His Eminence Andrej Cardinal Deskur.

Office: Palazzo S. Carlo, 00120 Vatican City State, Europe. Tel: 69.88.31.97; Fax: 69.88.53.73.

V. OFFICES

Apostolic Camera

The Apostolic Camera is presided over by the cardinal chamberlain of the Holy Roman Church, assisted by the vice-chamberlain together with certain prelates chamberlain. It chiefly exercises the function which is given to it in the special law on the vacancy of the Apostolic See.

Camerlengo: His Eminence Eduardo Cardinal Martinez Somalo.

Prefecture of the Papal Household

The Prefecture looks after the internal order of the pontifical household and supervises everything which pertains to discipline and service either by clergy or laity who constitute the pontifical chapel and family. It is in charge of the Apostolic Palace and is at the service of the Holy Father, both there and wherever he goes. It arranges audiences with His Holiness and supervises papal ceremonies other than the strictly liturgical.

Prefect: Most Rev. Bishop Dino Monduzzi.

Administration of the Patrimony of the Apostolic See

This Office is competent to administer the goods proper to the Holy See, the income from which is destined to support the expenditures necessary for the functions of the Roman Curia.

Extraordinary Section: Handles the duties committed to it by the Sovereign Pontiff.

Pro-President: Most Rev. Archbishop Lorenzo Antonetti

Secretary: Most Rev. Archbishop Claudio Maria Celli.

Central Office of Statistics of the Church

This Office gathers and organizes the data which seems necessary or useful for a better understanding of the state of the Church and for assistance to its Bishops.

Director: Rev. Msgr. Pietro Silvi.

Prefecture of the Economic Affairs of the Holy See

The Prefecture has the function of supervising and governing the administration of goods which belong to the Holy See or which it is in charge of, no matter what kind of autonomy they may perhaps enjoy. This is directed by a Commission of three Cardinals and coordinates and watches over the administration of the possessions of the Holy See. It receives the reports on the receipts and disbursements of the Church's goods and the various budgets.

President: His Eminence Edmund Cardinal Szoka

Secretary: Most Rev. Bishop Luigi Sposito

Office: Largo del Colonnato 3, 00193 Rome, Italy. Tel: 69.88.42.63; Fax: 69.88.50.11.

Office of the Liturgical Celebrations of the Supreme Pontiff

This Office prepares whatever is necessary for liturgical and other sacred celebrations which are carried out by the Supreme Pontiff or in his name and, in keeping with existing prescription of liturgical law, to supervise them.

Master of Ceremonies: Rev. Msgr. Piero Marini.

Archives of the Second Vatican Council

Director: Rev. Msgr. Vincenzo Carbone.

Archivist: Rev. Msgr. Nazzareno Cinti.

VI. COMMISSIONS AND COMMITTEES

Commission "Ecclesia Dei"

President: His Eminence Angelo Cardinal Felici.

Council of Cardinals for the Study of Organizational and Economic Problems of the Apostolic See

American Members: His Eminence John Cardinal O'Connor; His Eminence Roger M. Cardinal Mahony.

International Theological Commission

President: His Eminence Joseph Cardinal Ratzinger.

General Secretary: Rev. Georges Cottier, O.P.

Commission of Cardinals for the Pontifical Shrines of Pompei, Loreto, and Bari

President: His Eminence Virgilio Cardinal Noe.

Pontifical Biblical Commission

President: His Eminence Joseph Cardinal Ratzinger.

Pontifical Committee for the International Eucharistic Congresses

President: His Eminence Edouard Cardinal Gagnon.

Pontifical Commission for the Revision and Emendation of the Vulgate

Director: Rev. Jean Mallet, O.S.B.

Pontifical Commission for the Vatican City State

President: His Eminence Rosalio Jose Cardinal Castillo Lara.

Pontifical Commission for Sacred Archeology

President: Most Rev. Archbishop Francesco Marchisano.

Secretary: Dr. Fabrizio Bisconti.

Pontifical Committee for Historical Sciences

President: Rev. Msgr. Victor Saxer.

Secretary: Rev. Vittorino Grossi, O.S.A.

Central Committee of the Holy Year 2000

President: His Eminence Cardinal Roger Etchegaray.

Secretary: Most Rev. Archbishop Sergio Sebastiani.

VII. INSTITUTIONS CONNECTED WITH THE HOLY SEE

Vatican Secret Archives

Archivist: His Eminence Luigi Cardinal Poggi.

Prefect: Rev. Joseph Metzler, O.M.I.

Vice Prefect: Rev. Sergio B. Pagaro.

Vatican Apostolic Library

Librarian: His Eminence Luigi Cardinal Poggi.

Prefect: Rev. Leonard Boyle, O.P.

Pontifical Academy of Sciences

President: Prof. Nicola Cabibbo.

Pontifical Academy of Social Sciences

President: Prof. Edmond Malinvaud.

Pontifical Academy for Life

President: Prof. Juan de Dios Vial Correa.

Vice President: Most Rev. Bishop Elio Sgreccia.

Vatican Radio

President of the Coordinating Committee: Rev. Roberto Tucci, S.J.

Director General: Rev. Pasquale Borgomeo, S.J.

Vatican Television Centre

President of the Administrative Council: Dr. Emilio Rossi.

Vice President: Dr. Sandro Baldoni.

Fabric of St. Peter's

President: His Eminence Virgilio Cardinal Noe.

Office of Papal Charities

Almoner: Most Rev. Archbishop Oscar Rizzato.

Vatican Polyglot Press

Director General: Rev. Elio Torrigiani, S.D.B.

Administrative Director: Mr. Giacomo Bonassoli, S.D.B.

Vatican Publishing House

President: Most Rev. Archbishop Giovanni De Andrea.

Director: Rev. Nicolo' Suffi, S.D.B.

Institute for Works of Religion

Director General: Dr. Lelio Scaletti.

Prelate: Vacant.

L'Osservatore Romano

Director: Prof. Mario Agnes.

Secretary: Dr. Carlo DeLucia.

English Language Weekly - Contact Person: Rev. Robert Dempsey.

Translations of English, French, Spanish, German, Portuguese, and Polish editions available.

Press Office of the Holy See

Director: Dr. Joaquin Navarro-Valls.

VIII. AMERICANS WORKING IN THE ROMAN CURIA

Secretariats of State—1. Section for General Affairs: Rev. Msgr. James Harvey; Rev. Msgr. William Millea; Rev. Reginald Foster, O.C.D.; Rev. Steven Zak; Sr. M. Louise Marecka, C.S.S.F.; Sr. Yvonne Mary Loucks, R.S.M.; Sr. Ruth Aubrey, A.S.C.J. *II. Section for Relations with States:* Rev. Msgr. Timothy Broglio; Rev. Msgr. Joseph Marino.

Congregation for the Doctrine of the Faith: Rev. Charles Brown.

Congregation for the Oriental Churches: Rev. Eric Powell.

Congregation for Divine Worship and the Discipline of the Sacraments: Rev. Thomas Fucinaro.

Congregation for Causes of Saints: Rev. Msgr. Robert Sarno.

Congregation for Bishops: Rev. Msgr. Daniel Thomas, Rev. James D. Conley.

Congregation for the Evangelization of Peoples: Most Rev. Archbishop Charles Schleck, C.S.C.; Rev. Joseph McCabe, M.M.

Congregation for the Clergy: Rev. David Ricken; Rev. Anthony McDaid.

Congregation for The Institutes of Consecrated Life and for Societies of Apostolic Life: Sr. Sharon Holland, I.H.M.; Sr. Dionette Werner, C.S.S.F.; Rev. John Ferrin, O.P.

Congregation for Catholic Education: Rev. Msgr. Walter J. Edyvean; Rev. Robert Rapfel.

Apostolic Penitentiary: William Cardinal Baum; Rev. Msgr. James Gillen.

Supreme Tribunal of the Apostolic Signatura: Rev. Msgr. Joseph Punderson; Rev. Salvatore Cordiglione.

Tribunal of the Roman Rota: Rev. Msgr. Kenneth Boccafola; Rev. Msgr. Robert Sable.

Pontifical Council For Promoting Christian Unity: Rev. Msgr. John Radano.

Pontifical Council for the Family: Ms. Joan E. Collemacine-Parenti, Ph.D.

Pontifical Council for Justice and Peace: Sr. Marjorie Keenan, R.S.C.M.

Pontifical Council for the Pastoral Care of Migrants and Itinerant People: Rev. Msgr. Joseph DeAndrea.

Pontifical Council - "Cor Unum": Rev. Msgr. Frank Dewane.

Pontifical Council for the Interpretation of Legislative Texts: Rev. Bernard Hebda.

Pontifical Council for Social Communications: Archbishop John Foley; Dr. Marjorie Weeke.

Administration for the Patrimony of the Apostolic See: Sr. Catherine Danovich, O.S.B.M.; Sr. Judith Zoebelein, F.S.E.

Prefecture for the Economic Affairs of the Holy See: Edmund Cardinal Szoka; Rev. Msgr. Leonard Blair.

L'Osservatore Romano: Rev. Msgr. Robert Dempsey.

Synod of Bishops: Rev. Msgr. John Abruzzese.

Pontifical Commission "Ecclesia Dei": Rev. Arthur Calkins.

Residence for Americans Working in the Roman Curia: Villa Stritch, Via della Nocetta 63, 00164 Rome, Italy. Tel: (011.39.6) 66.16.26.62; 66.16.26.76; Fax: 66.16.27.00.

INSTITUTES OF GRADUATE STUDIES IN ROME

***Pontifical Gregorian University,* with which are associated the *Pontifical Biblical Institute* and the *Pontifical Oriental Institute*—**Constituted in 1552. Address: Piazza della Pilotta 4, 00187 Rome, Italy. Grand Chancellor: Pio Cardinal Laghi; Vice Chancellor: Rev. Peter-Hans Kolvenbach, S.J.; Rector: Rev. Giuseppe Pittau, S.J.; Rector of the Biblical Institute: Rev. Robert O'Toole, S.J.; Rector of the Oriental Institute: Rev. Gilles Pelland, S.J.

***Pontifical Lateran University*—**Founded in 1824. Address: Piazza S. Giovanni 4, 00184 Rome, Italy. Grand Chancellor: Camillo Cardinal Ruini; Rector: Most Rev. Bishop Angelo Scola.

***Augustinianum Instituto Patristico at the Pontifical Lateran University*—**Founded in 1969. Address: Via Paolo VI 25, 00193 Rome, Italy. Rev. Angelo D. Berardino, O.S.A., Pres.

***Pontifical Urban University*—**Founded in 1627. Address: Via Urbano VIII 16, 00165 Rome, Italy. Grand Chancellor: Jozef Cardinal Tomko; Rector: Rev. Msgr. Eric Schmid.

***Pontifical University of St. Thomas Aquinas*—**Founded in 1580. Address: Largo Angelicum 1, 00184 Rome, Italy. Grand Chancellor: Very Rev. Timothy Radcliffe, Master General of the Order of Preachers; Rector: Very Rev. Edward Kaczynski, O.P.

***Pontifical International Institute of St. Anselm*—**Founded in 1687. Address: Piazza Cavalieri di Malta 5, 00152 Rome, Italy. Tel: (06) 57.9.11. Grand Chancellor: Very Rev. Marcel Rooney, Pro-Abbot Primate; Rector: Rev. Pius Tragan, O.S.B.

***Pontifical Salesian University*—**Founded in 1940. Address: Piazza Ateneo Salesiano 1, 00139 Rome, Italy. Grand Chancellor: Vacant.
Rector: Rev. Raffaele Farina.

***Pontifical Antonianum Atheneum*—**Founded in 1933. Address: Via Merulana 124, 00185 Rome, Italy. Grand Chancellor: Very Rev. Schaluck Hermann, O.F.M., Minister General of the Order of Friars Minor; Rector: Rev. Jose Antonio Merino.

***Pontifical Institute of Sacred Music*—**Founded in 1911. Address: Via di Torre Rossa 21, 00165, Rome, Italy. Grand Chancellor: Pio Cardinal Laghi; President: Rev. Msgr. Valentin Miserachs Grau.

***Pontifical Institute of Christian Archeology*—**Founded in 1925. Address: Via Napoleone III 1, 00185 Rome, Italy. Grand Chancellor: Pio Cardinal Laghi; Rector: Rev. Msgr. Patrick Saint-Roch.

***Pontifical Theological Faculty of St. Bonaventure, of the Friars Minor Conventual*—**Erected in 1935. Address: Via del Serafico 1, 00142 Rome, Italy. Grand Chancellor: Very Rev. Gianfranco Gardin; President: Rev. Giovanni Iammarrone, O.F.M.Conv.

***Pontifical Theological Faculty "Teresianum"*—**Founded in 1935. Address: Piazza S. Pancrazio 5-A, 00152 Rome, Italy. Grand Chancellor: Very Rev. Camilo Maccise, O.C.D., Prepositor General of the Discalced Carmelites; President: Rev. Jesus Castellano Cervera, O.C.D.

***Pontifical Theological Faculty "Marianum"*—**Founded in 1955. Address: Viale 30 Aprile 6, 00153 Rome, Italy. Grand Chancellor: Rev. Hubert Moons, Prior General of the Servites; President: Very Rev. Ignacio M. Calabuig Adan.

***Roman Atheneum of the Holy Cross*—**Erected on January 9, 1990. Address: Piazza S. Apollinare 49, 00186, Rome, Italy. Grand Chancellor: Rev. Msgr. Javier Echevarria Rodriguez; Rector: Rev. Lluis Clavell Ortiz-Repisco.

SEMINARIES AND NATIONAL COLLEGES IN ROME

***Pontifical Roman Major Seminary*—**Founded in 1565 by Pius IV. Address: Piazza S. Giovanni in Laterano 4, 00184 Rome, Italy. Rev. Msgr. Luigi Conti, Rector.

***Pontifical Roman Minor Seminary*—**Address: Viale Vaticano 42, 00165 Rome, Italy. Rev. Msgr. Paolo Selvadagi, Rector.

***French Seminary (Pontifical)*—**Founded on October 2, 1853. Address: Via di S. Chiara 42, 00186, Rome, Italy. Rev. Bernard Tenailleau, Rector.

***Lombard Seminary of SS. Ambrose and Charles (Pontifical)*—**Founded in 1863. Address: Piazza S. Maria Maggiore 5, 00185 Rome, Italy. Rev. Msgr. Diego Coletti, Rector.

***North American College (Pontifical)*—**Corporate Title: *The American College of the Roman Catholic Church of the United States.* A Maryland Corporation. Founded in 1859 by Pope Pius IX.
Postal Address: Via del Gianicolo 14, 00120 Vatican City State, Europe. Rev. Msgr. Timothy M. Dolan, Rector. (See AMERICAN COLLEGES ABROAD on the next page for further details.)

***Armenian College (Pontifical)*—**Founded on March 1, 1883. Address: Salita S. Nicola da Tolentino 17, 00187 Rome, Italy. Rev. Andon Saroyan, Rector.

***Beda College (Pontifical)*—**Founded in 1852; separated from the English College in 1917. Address: Viale San Paolo 18, 00146 Rome, Italy. Rev. Msgr. Brian Dazeley, Rector.

***Belgian College (Pontifical)*—**Founded in 1844. Rev. Address: Via G.B. Pagano 35, 00167 Rome, Italy. Rev Msgr. Werner Quintens, Rector.

***Canadian College (Pontifical)*—**Founded in 1888. Address: Via Crescenzio 75, 00193 Rome, Italy. Rev. Martin Belanger, P.S.S., Rector.

***Capranica College (Almo)*—**Founded in 1457 by Cardinal Capranica. Address: Piazza Capranica 98, 00186 Rome, Italy. Rev. Msgr. Luciano Pacomio, Rector.

***Ethiopian College (Pontifical)*—**Founded on October 1, 1919. Address: 00120 Citta del Vaticano, Europe. Rev. P. Teodoro Ghebretensae, Rector.

***German-Hungarian College (Pontifical)*—**Founded on October 28, 1552. Address: Via S. Nicolo da Tolentino 13, 00187 Rome, Italy. Very Rev. Johannes Gunter Gerhartz, S.J., Rector.

***Greek College (Pontifical)*—**Founded on January 13, 1577. Address: Via del Babuino 149, 00187 Rome, Italy. Very Rev. Ambrogio Dolfini, O.S.B., Rector.

***English College (Venerabile)*—**Founded on April 23, 1578. Address: Via Monserrato 45, 00186 Rome, Italy. Rev. Adrian Toffolo, Rector.

***Irish College (Pontifical)*—**Founded in 1628. Address: Via dei Ss. Quattro 1, 00184 Rome, Italy. Rev. Msgr. John Fleming, Rector.

***Lithuanian College (Pontifical)*—**Founded in 1946. Address: Via Casalmonferrato 20, 00182 Rome, Italy. Rev. Msgr. Antanas Algimantas Bartkus, Rector.

***Maronite College*—**Founded on June 17, 1584. Address: Via Porta Pinciana 14, 00187 Rome, Italy.

***Nepomucene College (Pontifical)*—**Address: Via Concordia 1, 00183 Rome, Italy. Rev. Msgr. Karel Janousek, Rector.

***Philippine College (Pontifical)*—**Founded on June 29, 1961. Address: Via Aurelia 490, 00165 Rome, Italy. Rev. Msgr. Jesse Mercado, Rector.

***Pius XI Dutch College (Pontifical)*—**Founded on October 26, 1930. Address: Via Ercole Rosa 1, 00153 Rome, Italy. Rev. Rudolphus Smit, Rector.

***Brazilian College (Pontifical)*—**Founded in 1934 by Pius XI. Address: Via Aurelia 527, 00165 Rome, Italy. Very Rev. Matias Martinho Lenz, S.J., Rector.

***Latin American College (Pio Latino Americano) (Pontifical)*—**Founded in 1858. Address: Via Aurelia Antica 408, 00165 Rome, Italy. Rev. Luis Palomera, S.J., Rector.

***Polish College (Pontifical)*—**Founded on March 9, 1866. Address: Piazza Remuria 2-A, 00153 Rome, Italy. Rev. Msgr. Marian Rola, Rector.

***Portuguese College (Pontifical)*—**Founded on October 28, 1900. Address: Via Nicolo V 3, 00165 Rome, Italy. Rev. Msgr. Jose Tomas Amandio, Rector.

***Russian College of S. Theresa of the Child Jesus (Pontifical)*—**Founded on August 15, 1929. Address: Via Carlo Cattaneo 2, 00185 Rome, Italy. Rev. Richard Cemus, S.J., Rector.

***Ukrainian College of Saint Josephat (Pontifical)*—**Founded in 1897. Address: Passeggiata del Gianicolo 7, 00165 Rome, Italy. Rev. Genesio Viomar, O.S.B.M., Rector.

***College of St. Jerome of the Croatians (Pontifical)*—**Founded on August 1, 1901. Address: Via Tomacelli 132, 00186 Rome, Italy. Rev. Msgr. Anton Benvin.

***St. Thomas Aquinas*—**Founded in 1948. Address: Via Degli Ibernesi 20, 00184 Rome, Italy. Very Rev. Glenn Morris, O.P., Rector.

***Scots College (Pontifical)*—**Founded on December 5, 1600. Address: Via Cassia 481, 00189 Rome, Italy. Rev. Christopher Joseph McElroy, Rector.

***Spanish College (Pontifical)*—**Founded on April 1, 1892. Address: Via Di Torrerrossa 2, 00165 Rome, Italy. Rev. Lope Rubio Parrado, Rector.

***Teutonic College (S. Maria dell'Anima)*—**Founded in 1859. Address: Via della Pace 20, 00186 Rome, Italy. Rev. Msgr. Johannes Nedbal, Rector.

Teutonic College (S. Maria in Camposanto), for the study of Sacred Archaeology and Ecclesiastical History—Founded on November 21, 1876. Address: Via della Sagrestia 17, 00120 Citta del Vaticano, Europe. Rev. Msgr. Erwin Gatz, Rector.

***Polish Ecclesiastical Institute (Pontifical)*—**Founded in 1910. Address: Piazza B. Cairoli 117, 00186 Rome, Italy. Rev. Hieronim Fokcinski, S.J., Rector.

American Church. Santa Susanna—Address: Via Venti Settembre 14. Postal Address: Via Antonio Salandra 6, 00187 Rome, Italy. Tel: 488-2748; Fax: 474-0236. Rev. John J. Foley, C.S.P., Rector.

AMERICAN COLLEGES ABROAD

AMERICAN COLLEGE. LOUVAIN, BELGIUM. Corporate title: *The American College of the Immaculate Conception, Catholic University of Louvain,*— a corporation of the District of Columbia. Founded in 1857. Postal Address: Naamsestraat 100, B-3000 Leuven, Belgium. Tel: 32.16.32.00.11; Fax: 32.16.32.00.12. Very Rev. David E. Windsor, C.M., Psy. D., Rector/Pres.; Rev. Donald M. Hanson, M.A., M.Div., Vice Rector Formation/Dir.- Liturgy and Homiletics; Rev. Francis Kayatta, S.T.B., J.C.L., Vice Rector - Recruitment.

Rev. Msgr. John Scanlan, S.T.B., M.Div., Vice Pres. - Development; Rev. Daniel Tormey, S.T.B., M.A., Dir. - Spiritual Formation; Sr. Rina Cappellazzo, O.P., M.A., Ph.D., Dir. - Pastoral Formation; Rev. Jan Lambrecht, S.J., S.T.D., Theological Advisor; Rev. William A. Traylor, M.A., S.T.B., Pastor, Our Lady of Mercy Parish, Brussels; Prof. John A. Dick, S.T.D., Dir. - Academic Formation; Mr. Daniel J. Frett, S.T.L., Ph.L., Business Mgr. The American College is operated under the auspices of a special committee of the National Conference of Catholic Bishops. Most Rev. Frank Rodimer, Bishop of Paterson, Chairman.

The American College operates in four areas, all in the English language, in conjunction with the Institute of Philosophy, the Faculty of Theology and the Faculty of Canon Law of the Katholieke Universiteit te Leuven (K.U. Leuven) and of the Universite Catholique de Louvain (U.C.L.). *The Seminary Program of Priestly Formation*—both on the level of Philosophy and Theology; graduate studies; monthly and semester sabbatical programs; and a summer session for ministerial renewal.

Office for Development and Recruitment for the American College of Louvain—Postal Address: The Americal College, 3211 Fourth St., N.E., Washington, DC 20017-1194. Tel: 202-541-3108; Fax: 202-541-3322.

The American College is associated with the English-speaking Parish of Our Lady of Mercy in the Brussels area. Parish Postal Address: 64 Avenue Reine Astrid 1410, Waterloo, Belgium. Tel: 32.2.354.5343; Fax: 32.2.351.2314.

NORTH AMERICAN COLLEGE, ROME, ITALY. (PONTIFICAL)—Corporate Title: *The American College of the Roman Catholic Church of the United States.* A Maryland Corporation. Operates under the auspices of a special committee of the National Conference of Catholic Bishops. Chairman: His Eminence James Cardinal Hickey. Founded in 1859 by Pope Pius IX, the express purpose being to bring American seminarians and student priests into close association with the Holy See. Seminarians live and take their priestly formation at the College, while studying at the theological universities in Rome. Three major departments: Seminary, Graduate and Institute for Continuing Theological Education.

Postal Address: North American College, 00120 Vatican City State, Europe. Rev. Msgr. Timothy M. Dolan, Rector; Rev. Msgr. Bernard E. Yarrish, Vice Rector for Administration and Admissions.

Seminary Department: Postal Address: North American College, 00120 Vatican City State, Europe. Tel: 011.39.6.684.931; Fax: 011.39.6.686.75.61. Student Fax: 011.39.6.686.96.65. Rev. Msgr. Timothy M. Dolan, Rector; Rev. William M. Ogrowdowski, Vice Rector for Community Life; Rev. Darr Schoenhofen, Academic Dean; Rev. Jon J. O'Brien, S.J., Staff Psychiatrist; Rev. Thomas Raddloff, S.J., Spiritual Dir.; Rev. Cornelius McRae, Spiritual Dir.; Rev. Joseph Henchey, C.S.S., Spiritual Dir.; Rev. Miles D. Walsh, Apostolic Formation; Dr. Edward Smith, Dir.- Worship; Rev. Ferrando Minoggio, Philosophy Tutor; Bro. Randal Riede, C.F.X., Librarian; Rev. Msgr. Daniel E. Thomas, in residence. Students 144, representing 62 Dioceses and Archdioceses.

Institute for Continuing Theological Education: Postal Address: North American College, 00120 Vatican City State, Europe. Tel: 011.39.6.684.931; Fax: 011.39.6.686.7561. Rev. D. Terrence Morgan, Dir. Fall & Spring 12-week sabbatical sessions for priests. Participants 41.

Graduate Department: Casa Santa Maria, Postal Address: Via dell'Umilta 30, 00187 Rome, Italy. Tel: 011.39.6.69.00.11; Fax: 011.39.6.69.00.18.23. Residence hall of North American College for post-graduate priests from the United States. Rev. Msgr. Charles W. Elmer, Dir. Graduate priests 73, representing 43 Dioceses and Archdioceses.

Bishops' Office for United States Visitors to the Vatican: Postal Address: Via dell'Umilta 30, 00187 Rome, Italy. Tel: (011.39.6)69-00-11; Fax: (011.39.6)6900-1823. Request for attendance at Papal audiences and similar functions may be addressed to this office. Rev. Msgr. Roger C. Roensch, Dir.

Office for Development of the North American College: Postal Address: 3450 Princeton Pike, Lawrenceville, New Jersey 08648. Tel: 609-219-1350; Fax: 609-219-1187. Mr. Patrick Kennedy, Dir. - Development.

The Apostolic Nunciature

Established As Apostolic Delegation January 24, 1893; Nunciature January 10, 1984.
Address: 3339 Massachusetts Ave., N.W., Washington, DC 20008-3687. Tel: 202-333-7121. Fax: 202-337-4036.

APOSTOLIC PRO-NUNCIO
TO THE UNITED STATES

His Excellency
The Most Reverend

AGOSTINO CACCIAVILLAN, J.C.D., J.Civ.D., S.Soc.Lic.
Titular Archbishop of Amiterno
Apostolic Pro-Nuncio

Born in the province of Vicenza, Italy, August 14, 1926; ordained a priest for the Diocese of Vicenza, June 26, 1949. Entered the diplomatic service of the Holy See in 1959; served at the Vatican Secretariat of State, the Philippines, Spain, and Portugal; from 1969 through 1976 he was head of the Documentation and Information Office of the Secretariat of State. On January 19, 1976, he was appointed Apostolic Pro-Nuncio to Kenya, and Apostolic Delegate to the Seychelles. Received episcopal ordination on February 28, 1976. He was named Apostolic Pro-Nuncio to India on May 9, 1981, and, in addition, first Apostolic Pro-Nuncio to the Kingdom of Nepal on April 30, 1985. On June 13, 1990, Pope John Paul II appointed him Apostolic Pro-Nuncio to the United States and Permanent Observer of the Holy See to the Organization of American States.

Rev. Msgr. Renato Volante, S.T.D., J.C.L. *Counsellor;* Rev. Msgr. Dominique Rezeau, J.C.D., *Counsellor;* Rev. Msgr. Giorgio Lingua, J.C.D., *First Secretary.*

Rev. Msgr. John H. Maksymowicz, S.T.L., *Secretary;* Rev. Joseph C. Mulqueen, J.C.L., *Secretary;* Rev. Matthew E. Rzeczkowski, O.P., S.T.L., *Archivist.*

Former Apostolic Delegates:

His Eminence Francesco Cardinal Satolli,	1893-1896.
His Eminence Sebastiano Cardinal Martinelli,	1896-1902.
His Eminence Diomede Cardinal Falconio,	1902-1911.
His Eminence Giovanni Cardinal Bonzano,	1911-1922.
His Eminence Pietro Cardinal Fumasoni-Biondi,	1922-1933.
His Eminence Amleto G. Cardinal Cicognani,	1933-1958.
His Eminence Egidio Cardinal Vagnozzi,	1958-1967.
His Eminence Luigi Cardinal Raimondi,	1967-1973.
His Excellency Most Reverend Jean Jadot,	1973-1980.
His Eminence Pio Cardinal Laghi,	1980-1984.

Apostolic Pro-Nuncios:

His Eminence Pio Cardinal Laghi,	1984-1990.
His Excellency Most Reverend Agostino Cacciavillan,	1990-

The Permanent Observer Mission of the Holy See to the United Nations

Established January 26, 1964

Address: 25 E. 39th St., New York, NY 10016-0903. 212-370-9614. Fax: 212-370-9622.

PERMANENT OBSERVER
OF THE HOLY SEE TO THE UNITED NATIONS

His Excellency
The Most Reverend

RENATO R. MARTINO, J.C.D., D.D.,
Titular Archbishop of Segerme;
Apostolic Nuncio

Born in Salerno, Italy on November 23, 1932; ordained for the Archdiocese of Salerno, June 20, 1957; Entered the diplomatic service of the Holy See July 1, 1962; Served in Nicaragua 1962-64-- Philippines 1964-66-- Lebanon 1966-70-- Canada 1975-78-- Brazil 1978-80; From 1970 to 1975, he was head of the Department for International Organizations in the Vatican Secretariat of State. Appointed Apostolic Pro-Nuncio to Thailand and named Titular Archbishop of Segerme September 14, 1980. Ordained a Bishop on December 14, 1980. Served as Apostolic Pro-Nuncio to Thailand from 1980-86 and also as Apostolic Delegate to Singapore, Malaysia, Laos and Brunei. Apostolic Pro-Nuncio to Singapore June 24, 1981. Appointed Permanent Observer of the Holy See to the United Nations December 3, 1986. Office Address: 25 East 39th St., New York, NY 10016-0903. Tel: 212-370-7885; Fax: 212-370-9622. Residential Address: 20 East 72nd St., New York, NY 10021-4196. Tel: 212-734-2900; Fax: 212-988-3633.

Rev. Msgr. Dominique F. Mamberti, J.C.D., LL.M., *Counsellor;* Rev. Msgr. David J. Malloy, S.T.D., *1st. Secretary;* Rev. Msgr. Carl J. Marucci, M.A.,*Attache;* Rev. James M. Reinert, Ph.D, *Attache;* Mr. Karol Krcmery, *Attache;* Ms. Sommai Tantinarasak, *Secretary;* Ms. Ana Lucia De Campos Charnaux Serta, *Secretary.*

Former Permanent Observers:

Rev. Msgr. Alberto Giovannetti, J.C.D.	1964-1973
Most Rev. Giovanni Cheli, J.C.D., D.D.	1973-1986

Path to Peace Foundation, Inc.--25 East 39th St., New York, NY 10016-0903. 212-370-7885; Fax: 212-370-9622. Board of Directors: Archbishop Renato R. Martino, Pres.; Rev. Msgr. Robert L. Charlebois, Vice Pres.; Rev. Msgr. Eugene V. Clark, Treas.; Mr. John P. Reiner, Sec.

PART II
Alphabetical List of Places in the United States

This comprehensive list includes all cities and towns in the United States in which a Catholic Institution is located.

The abbreviations identify each city or town to the corresponding Diocese or Archdiocese.

Abbeville, LA	LAF
SC	CHR
Abbotsford, WI	LC
Abbott, TX	FWT
Abbottstown, PA	HBG
Aberdeen, ID	B
MD	BAL
MS	JKS
SD	SFS
WA	SEA
Abilene, KS	SAL
TX	SAN
Abingdon, IL	PEO
MD	BAL
VA	RIC
Abington, MA	BO
PA	PH
Abiquiu, NM	SFE
Abita Springs, LA	NO
Abrams, WI	GB
Absecon, NJ	CAM
Ackley, IA	DUB
Acme, MI	GAY
Acoma, NM	GLP
Acosta, PA	ALT
Acton, MA	BO
Acushnet, MA	FR
Ada, MI	GR
MN	CR
OH	COL
OK	OKL
Adair, IA	DM
Adams, MA	SPR
MN	WIN
NY	OG
WI	LC
Adamstown, MD	BAL
Addison, IL	JOL
NY	ROC
Adel, IA	DM
Adelanto, CA	SB
Adell, WI	MIL
Adelphi, MD	WDC
Adena, OH	STU
Adjuntas, PR	PCE
Adona, AR	LR
Adrian, MI	LAN
MN	WIN
Advance, MO	SPC
Affton, MO	STL
Afton, IA	DM
MI	GAY
Agana, GU	AGN
Agana Heights, GU	AGN
Agat, GU	AGN
Agawam, MA	SPR
Agua Dulce, TX	CC
Aguada, PR	MGZ
Aguadilla, PR	MGZ
Aguas Buenas, PR	CGS
Aguilar, CO	PBL
Aguirre, PR	PCE
Ahoskie, NC	R
Aibonito, PR	CGS
Aiea, HI	HON
Aiken, SC	CHR
Ainsworth, NE	GI
Aitkin, MN	DUL
Ajo, AZ	TUC
Akeley, MN	CR
Akron, CO	DEN
IA	SC
NY	BUF
OH	CLV
OH	NTN
OH	PRM
OH	SJP
Alakanuk, AK	FBK
Alameda, CA	OAK
NM	SFE
Alamo, TX	BWN
Alamogordo, NM	LSC
Alamosa, CO	PBL

Albany, GA	SAV
KY	L
LA	BR
MN	SCL
NY	ALB
OR	P
TX	FWT
Albee, MI	SAG
Albemarle, NC	CHL
Albers, IL	BEL
Albert Lea, MN	WIN
Alberta, AL	MOB
Albertville, MN	STP
Albia, IA	DAV
Albion, IN	FTW
MI	KAL
NE	OM
NY	BUF
PA	E
RI	PRO
Albuquerque, NM	SFE
NM	VNN
Alburg, VT	BUR
Alcoa, TN	KNX
Alden, NY	BUF
Alden Station, PA	PHU
Aledo, IL	PEO
Aleppo, KS	WCH
Aleppo Township, PA	PIT
Alexander, IL	SFD
Alexander City, AL	BIR
Alexandria, IN	LFT
KY	COV
LA	ALX
MN	SCL
SD	SFS
VA	ARL
VA	NTN
Alexandria Bay, NY	OG
Alexis, IL	PEO
Alfred, ME	PRT
Algoma, WI	GB
Algona, IA	SC
Algonac, MI	DET
Algonquin, IL	RCK
Alhambra, CA	LA
Alhambra, Ponce, PR	PCE
Alice, ND	FAR
TX	CC
Aliquippa, PA	PBR
PA	PIT
PA	SJP
Allegan, MI	KAL
Allegany, NY	BUF
Allegany State Park, NY	BUF
Allen, TX	DAL
Allen Park, MI	DET
MI	PRM
Allendale, NJ	NEW
Allenspark, CO	DEN
Allenstown, NH	MAN
Allenton, MI	DET
WI	MIL
Allentown, NJ	TR
PA	ALN
PA	PHU
PA	PSC
Alliance, NE	GI
OH	Y
Allison, IA	DUB
Allison Park, PA	PIT
Alma, KS	KCK
MI	SAG
MN	CR
NE	LIN
WI	LC
Alma Center, WI	LC
Almena, WI	SUP
Almond, NY	BUF
WI	LC
Aloha, OR	P
Aloys, NE	OM
Alpena, MI	GAY

Alpha, MI	MAR
NJ	MET
Alpharetta, GA	ATL
Alpine, AZ	GLP
CA	SD
MI	GR
TX	ELP
Alsip, IL	CHI
Alta Loma, CA	SB
Alta Vista, IA	DUB
Altadena, CA	LA
Altamont, IL	SFD
NY	ALB
Altamonte Springs, FL	ORL
Altdorf, WI	LC
Alton, IA	SC
IL	PEO
IL	SFD
NH	MAN
TX	BWN
Altona, NY	OG
Altoona, IA	DM
PA	ALT
PA	SJP
WI	LC
Altura, MN	WIN
Alturas, CA	SAC
Altus, AR	LR
OK	OKL
Alva, FL	VEN
OK	OKL
Alvada, OH	TOL
Alverno, MI	GAY
WI	GB
Alvin, TX	GAL
Alviso, CA	SJ
Ama, LA	NO
Amargosa Valley, NV	LAV
Amarillo, TX	AMA
Amberg, WI	GB
Ambler, PA	PH
Amboy, IL	RCK
Ambridge, PA	PBR
PA	PIT
PA	SJP
Amelia, LA	HT
OH	CIN
Amenia, NY	NY
American Canyon, CA	SR
American Falls, ID	B
American Fork, UT	SLC
Americus, GA	SAV
Amery, WI	SUP
Ames, IA	DUB
TX	BEA
Amesbury, MA	BO
Amherst, MA	SPR
NY	BUF
NY	PSC
OH	CLV
WI	LC
Amite, LA	BR
Amity, OR	P
Amityville, NY	BRK
NY	RVC
Ammannsville, TX	VIC
Amory, MS	JKS
Amsterdam, NY	ALB
NY	STF
OH	STU
Anaconda, MT	HEL
Anacortes, WA	SEA
Anadarko, OK	OKL
Anaheim, CA	ORG
CA	VNN
Anahuac, TX	BEA
Anamoose, ND	FAR
Anamosa, IA	DUB
Anasco, PR	MGZ
Anchorage, AK	ANC
AK	VNN
Anchorville, MI	DET
Andale, KS	WCH

Andalusia, AL	MOB
IL	PEO
Anderson, CA	SAC
IN	LFT
SC	CHR
TX	GAL
Andice, TX	AUS
Andover, MA	BO
NJ	PAT
NY	BUF
OH	Y
SD	SFS
Andrew, IA	DUB
Andrews, NC	CHL
TX	SAN
Aneta, ND	FAR
Angaur, FM	CI
Angelica, NY	BUF
Angels Camp, CA	STO
Angelus, KS	SAL
Angleton, TX	GAL
Angola, IN	FTW
NY	BUF
Aniak, AK	FBK
Anita, IA	DM
PA	E
Aniwa, WI	GB
Ankeny, IA	DM
Ann Arbor, MI	LAN
Anna, IL	BEL
Annandale, MN	STP
VA	ARL
VA	PSC
Annapolis, MD	BAL
Annawan, IL	PEO
Anniston, AL	BIR
Annville, PA	HBG
Anoka, MN	STP
Anselmo, NE	GI
Anson, TX	LUB
Ansonia, CT	HRT
CT	STF
Antelope, CA	SAC
Anthon, IA	SC
Anthony, KS	WCH
NM	LSC
Antigo, WI	GB
Antioch, CA	OAK
IL	CHI
TN	NSH
Antlers, OK	TLS
Anton Chico, NM	SFE
Antonino, KS	SAL
Antwerp, NY	OG
OH	TOL
Anza, CA	SB
Apache Junction, AZ	TUC
Apalachicola, FL	PT
Apalachin, NY	ROC
Apex, NC	R
Apollo, PA	GBG
Apopka, FL	ORL
FL	SJP
Apple Creek, MO	STL
Apple River, IL	RCK
Apple Valley, CA	SB
Applegate, CA	SAC
Appleton, MN	NU
WI	GB
Appomattox, VA	RIC
Aptos, CA	MRY
Arabi, LA	NO
Aragon, NM	GLP
Aransas Pass, TX	CC
Arbor Vitae, WI	SUP
Arcade, NY	BUF
Arcadia, CA	LA
FL	VEN
IA	SC
PA	PBR
WI	LC
Arcata, CA	SR
Archbald, PA	SCR

Archbold, OH	TOL
Arco, ID	B
Arcola, IL	SFD
IN	FTW
Arden, NC	CHL
Ardmore, OK	OKL
PA	PH
Ardoch, ND	FAR
Ardon, IA, IA	DAV
Ardsley, NY	NY
PA	PH
Arecibo, PR	ARE
Arenzville, IL	SFD
Argo, IL	CHI
Argonne, WI	GB
Argusville, ND	FAR
Argyle, MI	SAG
MN	CR
MO	JC
WI	MAD
Arkadelphia, AR	LR
Arkansas City, KS	WCH
Arkansaw, WI	LC
Arlington, IL	PEO
MA	BO
MN	NU
OR	BAK
SD	SFS
TX	FWT
VA	ARL
VT	BUR
WA	SEA
Arlington Heights, IL	CHI
Arma, KS	WCH
Armada, MI	DET
Armonk, NY	NY
Armour, SD	SFS
Armstrong, IA	SC
WI	MIL
Armstrong Creek, WI	GB
Arnaudville, LA	LAF
Arnheim, OH	CIN
Arnold, MO	STL
PA	GBG
Arpin, WI	LC
Arrow Bear Lake, CA	SB
Arroyo, PR	PCE
Arroyo Grande, CA	MRY
Arroyo Seco, NM	SFE
Artesia, CA	LA
NM	LSC
Artesian, SD	SFS
Arvada, CO	DEN
Arvin, CA	FRS
Asan, GU	AGN
Asbury, NJ	MET
Asbury Park, NJ	TR
Ashaway, RI	PRO
Ashburn, VA	ARL
Ashburnham, MA	WOR
Asheboro, NC	CHL
Asherton, TX	SAT
Asheville, NC	CHL
Ashford, CT	NOR
WI	MIL
Ashkum, IL	JOL
Ashland, AL	BIR
IL	SFD
KS	DOD
KY	LEX
MA	BO
ME	PRT
MT	GF
NE	LIN
NH	MAN
OH	CLV
OR	P
PA	ALN
VA	RIC
WI	SUP
Ashland City, TN	NSH
Ashley, ND	FAR
PA	SCR
Ashtabula, OH	PBR
OH	Y
Ashton, IA	SC
NE	GI
RI	PRO
WI	MAD
Ashville, PA	ALT
Askeaton, WI	GB
Aslip, IL	CHI
Aspen, CO	DEN
Aspinwall, PA	PIT
Assinins, MI	MAR
Assonet, MA	FR
Assumption, IL	SFD
OH	TOL
Aston, PA	PH
Astoria, NY	BRK
NY	ROM

OR	P
Astoria-Long Island City, NY	BRK
Atascadero, CA	MRY
Atchison, KS	KCK
Atco, NJ	CAM
Athens, AL	BIR
GA	ATL
IL	SFD
NY	ALB
OH	STU
PA	SCR
TN	KNX
TX	TYL
WI	LC
WV	WH
Atherton, CA	SFR
Athol, MA	WOR
SD	SFS
Athol Springs, NY	BUF
Atkins, AR	LR
Atkinson, IL	PEO
NE	OM
Atlanta, GA	ATL
GA	NTN
GA	SAM
MI	GAY
TX	TYL
Atlantic, IA	DM
Atlantic Beach, FL	STA
Atlantic City, NJ	CAM
Atlantic Highlands, NJ	TR
Atmore, AL	MOB
Attica, IN	LFT
NY	BUF
OH	TOL
Attleboro, MA	FR
Attleboro Falls, MA	FR
Atwater, CA	FRS
Atwood, KS	SAL
Au Sable Forks, NY	OG
Auburn, AL	MOB
CA	SAC
IA	SC
IL	SFD
IN	FTW
MA	WOR
ME	PRT
MI	SAG
NE	LIN
NH	MAN
NY	ROC
NY	STF
NY	SY
WA	SEA
WI	MIL
Auburn Hills, MI	DET
Auburndale, WI	LC
Audubon, IA	DM
NJ	CAM
PA	PH
AuGres, MI	SAG
Augusta, GA	NTN
GA	SAV
IA	DAV
KS	WCH
KY	COV
ME	PRT
MO	STL
WI	LC
Ault, CO	DEN
Auriesville, NY	ALB
Aurora, CO	DEN
IL	JOL
IL	RCK
IL	ROM
IN	IND
KS	SAL
KY	OWN
MN	DUL
MO	SPC
NE	LIN
NY	ROC
OH	Y
SD	SFS
WI	GB
Austin, MN	WIN
TX	AUS
TX	OLL
Austintown, OH	SJP
Ava, IL	BEL
MO	SPC
Avalon, CA	LA
NJ	CAM
PA	PIT
Avella, PA	PBR
PA	PIT
Avenal, CA	FRS
Avenel, NJ	MET
Avenue, MD	WDC
Averill Park, NY	ALB
Avilla, IN	FTW

Aviston, IL	BEL
Avoca, IA	DM
PA	SCR
Avon, CT	HRT
MA	BO
MN	SCL
NJ	TR
NY	ROC
OH	CLV
Avon Lake, OH	CLV
Avon Park, FL	VEN
Avondale, AZ	PHX
CO	PBL
LA	NO
Avonmore, PA	GBG
Awak, Pohnpei, FM	CI
Axtel, KY	OWN
Axtell, KS	KCK
Ayer, MA	BO
Aztec, NM	GLP
Azusa, CA	LA
Babbitt, MN	DUL
Babcock, WI	LC
Babeldaob, FM	CI
Babylon, NY	RVC
Bad Axe, MI	SAG
Baden, MD	WDC
PA	PIT
Badger, MN	CR
Bagdad, AZ	PHX
Bagley, MN	CR
Bailey, CO	COS
Baileys Harbor, WI	GB
Baileyville, KS	KCK
Bainbridge, GA	SAV
NY	SY
Bainbridge Island, WA	SEA
Bainbridge Township, OH	CLV
Bairdford, PA	PIT
Baker, LA	BR
MT	GF
OR	BAK
Baker City, OR	BAK
Bakersfield, CA	FRS
Bakerton, PA	ALT
Bakerville, WI	LC
Bal Harbour, FL	MIA
Bala Cynwyd, PA	PH
Baldwin, KS	KCK
LA	LAF
MI	GR
NY	RVC
Baldwin Boro, PA	PIT
Baldwin Park, CA	LA
Baldwinsville, NY	SY
Baldwinville, MA	WOR
Balfour, ND	FAR
Ball Club, MN	DUL
Ballinger, TX	SAN
Ballouville, CT	NOR
Ballston Lake, NY	ALB
Ballston Spa, NY	ALB
Balltown, IA	DUB
Ballwin, MO	STL
Bally, PA	ALN
Balmorhea, TX	ELP
Balsam Lake, WI	SUP
Balta, ND	FAR
Baltic, CT	NOR
Baltimore, MD	BAL
MD	PHU
MD	PSC
MD	WDC
Bancroft, IA	SC
NE	OM
Bandera, TX	SAT
Bandon, OR	P
Bangall, NY	NY
Bangkok, Thailand	CHI
Bangor, ME	PRT
MI	KAL
PA	ALN
WI	LC
Bankston, IA	DUB
Banning, CA	SB
Bannister, MI	SAG
Bantam, CT	HRT
Bapchule, AZ	PHX
Baptistown, NJ	MET
Bar Harbor, ME	PRT
Baraboo, WI	MAD
Baraga, MI	MAR
Barberton, OH	CLV
OH	PRM
Barbourville, KY	LEX
Barceloneta, PR	ARE
Barclay, IA	DUB
Bardonia, NY	NY
Bardstown, KY	L
Bardwell, KY	OWN
Barefoot Bay, FL	ORL

Baring, MO	JC
Bark River, MI	MAR
Barker, NY	BUF
Barling, AR	LR
Barnegat, NJ	TR
Barnesboro, PA	ALT
PA	PBR
PA	SJP
Barnesville, MD	WDC
MN	CR
OH	STU
PA	ALN
Barnum, IA	SC
Barranquitas, PR	CGS
Barre, MA	WOR
VT	BUR
Barrenspot, VI	STV
Barrett Station, TX	GAL
Barrigada, GU	AGN
Barrington, IL	CHI
NJ	CAM
RI	PRO
Barrio Rio Canas, PR	CGS
Barron, WI	SUP
Barrow, AK	FBK
Barry, IL	SFD
MN	NU
Barrytown, NY	NY
Barryville, NY	NY
Barstow, CA	SB
Bartelso, IL	BEL
Bartlesville, OK	TLS
Bartlett, IL	CHI
Barton, OH	STU
VT	BUR
Bartonville, IL	PEO
Bartow, FL	ORL
Basalt, CO	DEN
Bascom, OH	TOL
Basehor, KS	KCK
Basile, LA	LAF
Basking Ridge, NJ	MET
Bass Lake, CA	FRS
Bassfield, MS	BLX
Bastress, PA	SCR
Bastrop, LA	SHP
TX	AUS
Batavia, IL	RCK
NY	BUF
OH	CIN
Batchtown, IL	SFD
Batesburg, SC	CHR
Batesville, AR	LR
IN	IND
MS	JKS
Bath, ME	PRT
NY	ROC
NY	STF
PA	ALN
Bathgate, ND	FAR
Baton Rouge, LA	BR
Battle Creek, MI	KAL
NE	OM
Battle Ground, WA	SEA
Battle Lake, MN	SCL
Battle Mountain, NV	RNO
Baudette, MN	CR
Bauer, IA	DAV
Baxter Springs, KS	WCH
Bay City, MI	PRM
MI	SAG
TX	VIC
Bay Head, NJ	TR
Bay Mills, MI	MAR
Bay Minette, AL	MOB
Bay St. Louis, MS	BLX
Bay Settlement, WI	GB
Bay Shore, MI	GAY
NY	RVC
Bay Village, OH	CLV
Bayamon, PR	SJN
Bayard, IA	DM
NM	LSC
Bayfield, WI	SUP
Bayonne, NJ	NEW
NJ	PHU
NJ	PSC
Bayou Black, LA	HT
Bayou George, FL	PT
Bayou LaBatre, AL	MOB
Bayou Pigeon, LA	BR
Bayou Vista, LA	LAF
Bayport, MN	STP
Bayside, NY	BRK
Baytown, TX	GAL
Bayville, NJ	TR
NY	RVC
Beach, ND	BIS
Beachwood, OH	CLV
Beacon, NY	NY
Beacon Falls, CT	HRT

Beal City, MI	SAG
Beans Cove, PA	ALT
Bear, DE	WIL
Bear Creek, WI	GB
Bear Creek Township, PA	SCR
Bear Valley, WI	LC
Beardsley, KS	SAL
MN	NU
Beardstown, IL	SFD
Beasley, TX	GAL
Beatrice, NE	LIN
Beattie, KS	KCK
Beattyville, KY	LEX
Beaufort, SC	CHR
Beaulieu, MN	CR
Beaumont, CA	SB
TX	BEA
Beaver, KS	DOD
MI	SAG
PA	PBR
PA	PIT
Beaver Crossing, NE	LIN
Beaver Dam, KY	OWN
WI	MIL
Beaver Falls, PA	PIT
Beaver Island, MI	GAY
Beaver Meadows, PA	ALN
PA	PSC
Beaver Prairie, IL	BEL
Beavercreek, OH	CIN
Beaverdale, PA	ALT
PA	PBR
Beaverton, OR	P
Beaverville, IL	JOL
Bechyn, MN	NU
Bechyne, ND	FAR
Beckemeyer, IL	BEL
Becker, MN	SCL
Beckley, WV	WH
Bedford, IA	DM
IN	IND
MA	BO
NH	MAN
NY	NY
OH	CLV
OH	PRM
PA	ALT
TX	FWT
VA	RIC
Bedford Heights, OH	CLV
Bedford Village, NY	NY
Beech Bottom, WV	WH
Beech Grove, IN	IND
Beemer, NE	OM
Beeville, TX	CC
Bejou, MN	CR
Bel Air, MD	BAL
Belchertown, MA	SPR
Belcourt, ND	FAR
Belding, MI	GR
Belen, NM	SFE
Belfast, ME	PRT
NY	BUF
Belfield, ND	BIS
ND	STN
Belgique, MO	STL
Belgium, WI	MIL
Belgrade, MN	NU
MN	SCL
Belington, WV	WH
Bell City, LA	LKC
Bell Gardens, CA	LA
Bella Vista, AR	LR
Bellaire, MI	GAY
OH	STU
Belle, MO	JC
WV	WH
Belle Chasse, LA	NO
Belle Creek, MN	STP
Belle Fontaine, AL	MOB
Belle Fourche, SD	RC
Belle Glade, FL	PMB
Belle Plaine, IA	DUB
MN	STP
Belle Prairie, MN	SCL
Belle River, MN	SCL
Belle Rose, LA	BR
Belle Valley, OH	STU
Belle Vernon, PA	GBG
Belleair Bluffs, FL	SP
Bellechester, MN	STP
Belledeau, LA	ALX
Bellefontaine, OH	CIN
Bellefontaine Neighbors, MO	STL
Bellefonte, DE	WIL
PA	ALT
Belleview, FL	ORL
IL	SFD
Belleville, IL	BEL
KS	SAL
MI	DET
NJ	NEW
WI	MAD
Bellevue, IA	DUB
KY	COV
MI	LAN
NE	OM
OH	TOL
PA	PIT
WA	SEA
Bellflower, CA	LA
Bellingham, MA	BO
WA	SEA
Bellmawr, NJ	CAM
Bellmore, NY	RVC
Bellows Falls, VT	BUR
Bellport, NY	RVC
Bellville, TX	GAL
Bellwood, IL	CHI
NE	LIN
PA	ALT
Belmar, NJ	TR
Belmond, IA	DUB
Belmont, CA	SFR
MA	BO
MI	GR
NC	CHL
NH	MAN
NY	BUF
WI	MAD
Beloit, KS	SAL
WI	MAD
WI	MIL
Belpre, KS	DOD
OH	STU
Bel-Ridge, MO	STL
Belt, MT	GF
Belton, MO	KC
TX	AUS
Beltrees, IL	SFD
Beltsville, MD	PSC
MD	WDC
Belvidere, IL	RCK
NJ	MET
Belzoni, MS	JKS
Bement, IL	PEO
Bemidji, MN	CR
Bemus Point, NY	BUF
Ben Avon, PA	PIT
Benavides, TX	CC
The Bend, OH	TOL
Bend, OR	BAK
Bendena, KS	KCK
Benedict, MD	WDC
Benedicta, ME	PRT
Benet Lake, WI	MIL
Benicia, CA	SAC
Benkelman, NE	LIN
Benld, IL	SFD
Bennington, NH	MAN
VT	BUR
Bennington Center, NY	BUF
Bensalem, PA	PH
Bensenville, IL	JOL
Benson, AZ	TUC
IL	PEO
MN	NU
VT	BUR
Bentley Creek, PA	SCR
Bentleyville, PA	PIT
Benton, AR	LR
IL	BEL
MO	SPC
WI	MAD
Benton City, WA	YAK
Benton Harbor, MI	KAL
Bentonville, AR	LR
Benwood, MN	CR
WV	WH
Berea, KY	LEX
OH	CLV
Beresford, SD	SFS
Bergen, NY	BUF
Bergenfield, NJ	NEW
Berger, MO	STL
Berkeley, CA	OAK
MO	STL
Berkeley Heights, NJ	NEW
Berkeley Springs, WV	WH
Berkley, CA	OAK
MI	DET
Berlin, MA	WOR
NH	MAN
NJ	CAM
NY	ALB
WI	MAD
Berlinsville, PA	ALN
Bernalillo, NM	SFE
Bernardsville, NJ	MET
Beroun, MN	DUL
Berryville, AR	LR
VA	ARL
Bertha, MN	SCL
Berwick, LA	LAF
ME	PRT
PA	HBG
PA	PHU
Berwyn, IL	CHI
PA	PH
Besancon, IN	FTW
Bessemer, AL	BIR
MI	MAR
PA	PIT
Bethalto, IL	SFD
Bethany, IL	SFD
MO	KC
WV	WH
Bethany Beach, DE	WIL
Bethel, AK	FBK
CT	BGP
OH	CIN
VT	BUR
Bethel Park, PA	PIT
Bethesda, MD	WDC
Bethlehem, CT	HRT
OH	TOL
PA	ALN
PA	PHU
PA	PSC
SD	RC
SD	SAM
Bethpage, NY	RVC
Betram, TX	AUS
Bettendorf, IA	DAV
Beulah, ND	BIS
Bevent, WI	LC
Beverly, MA	BO
NJ	TR
OH	STU
Beverly Hills, CA	LA
FL	SP
MI	DET
Beverly Shores, IN	GRY
Bicknell, IN	EVN
Biddeford, ME	PRT
Biehle, MO	STL
Big Bear, CA	SB
Big Bear Lake, CA	SB
Big Bend, SD	SFS
WI	MIL
Big Clifty, KY	OWN
Big Elbow Lake, MN	CR
Big Lake, LA	LKC
MN	SCL
TX	SAN
Big Long Lake, IN	FTW
Big Pine Key, FL	MIA
Big Rapids, MI	GR
Big River, WI	LC
Big Sandy, MT	GF
Big Spring, TX	SAN
Big Stone City, SD	SFS
Big Stone Gap, VA	RIC
Big Sur, CA	MRY
Big Timber, MT	GF
Big Wells, TX	SAT
Bigelow, AR	LR
Bigfork, MN	DUL
MT	HEL
Billerica, MA	BO
Billings, MO	SPC
MT	GF
Biloxi, MS	BLX
Bingham, ME	PRT
Binghamton, NY	PSC
NY	SY
Birch Coolie, MN	NU
Birch Run, MI	SAG
Birchwood, WI	SUP
Bird City, KS	SAL
Bird Island, MN	NU
Birdsboro, PA	ALN
Birmingham, AL	BIR
AL	NTN
AL	OLL
MI	DET
Birnamwood, WI	GB
Bisbee, AZ	TUC
ND	FAR
Bishop, CA	FRS
TX	CC
Bishop Creek, IL	SFD
Bismarck, ND	BIS
Bismark, OH	TOL
Bison, OK	OKL
SD	RC
Bissell Hills, MO	STL
Biwabik, MN	DUL
Bixby, OK	TLS
Black Brook, NY	OG
Black Canyon City, AZ	PHX
Black Creek, WI	GB
Black Diamond, WA	SEA
Black Eagle, MT	GF
Black Jack, IL	SFD
Black River, MI	GAY
NY	OG
Black River Falls, WI	LC
Blackduck, MN	CR
Blackfoot, ID	B
Blacksburg, VA	RIC
Blackstone, IL	PEO
MA	WOR
VA	RIC
Blackwell, OK	OKL
Blackwood, NJ	CAM
Bladensburg, MD	WDC
Blaine, KS	KCK
MN	STP
OH	STU
Blair, NE	OM
WI	LC
Blairstown, IA	DUB
NJ	MET
Blairsville, GA	ATL
PA	GBG
Blakely, GA	SAV
Blakeslee, OH	TOL
PA	SCR
Blanchester, OH	CIN
Blanco, NM	GLP
TX	AUS
Blasdell, NY	BUF
Blauvelt, NY	NY
Blawnox, PA	PIT
Blenker, WI	LC
Blessing, IA	DUB
TX	VIC
Bliss, NY	BUF
Blissfield, MI	LAN
Block Island, RI	PRO
Bloomer, WI	LC
Bloomfield, CT	HRT
IA	DAV
IN	EVN
NE	OM
NJ	NEW
NM	GLP
Bloomfield Hills, MI	DET
Blooming Prairie, MN	WIN
Bloomingdale, IL	JOL
NY	OG
OH	STU
Bloomington, CA	SB
IL	PEO
IN	IND
MN	STP
TX	VIC
WI	MAD
Bloomsburg, PA	HBG
Bloomsbury, NJ	MET
Bloomsdale, MO	STL
Bloomville, WI	SUP
Blossburg, PA	SCR
Blossom, NY	BUF
Blountstown, FL	PT
Blue Anchor, NJ	CAM
Blue Creek, OH	CIN
Blue Earth, MN	WIN
Blue Grass, IA	DAV
Blue Island, IL	CHI
Blue Point, NY	RVC
Blue Rapids, KS	KCK
Blue Ridge, GA	ATL
Blue Ridge Summit, PA	HBG
Blue Springs, MO	KC
Bluefield, WV	WH
BlueGrass, MN	SCL
Bluffs, IL	SFD
Bluffton, IA	DUB
IN	FTW
MN	SCL
OH	TOL
SC	CHR
Blunt, SD	SFS
Blythe, CA	SB
Blytheville, AR	LR
Boardman, OH	PBR
OH	Y
Bobtown, PA	PIT
Boca Grande, FL	VEN
Boca Raton, FL	PMB
Boerne, TX	SAT
Bogalusa, LA	NO
Bogota, NJ	NEW
Bohemia, NY	RVC
Boise, ID	B
Bokeelia, FL	VEN
Bolingbrook, IL	JOL
Bolivar, MO	SPC
NY	BUF
OH	COL
TN	MEM
Bolton, CT	NOR

MA	WOR
Bolton Landing, NY	ALB
Bombay, NY	OG
Bondsville, MA	SPR
Bonesteel, SD	RC
Bonham, TX	DAL
Bonifay, FL	PT
Bonita, CA	SD
Bonita Springs, FL	VEN
Bonne Terre, MO	STL
Bonneauville, PA	HBG
Bonner, MT	HEL
Bonner Springs, KS	KCK
Bonners Ferry, ID	B
Bonnots Mill, MO	JC
Bono, OH	TOL
Boone, IA	SC
NC	CHL
Booneville, AR	LR
MS	JKS
Boonton, NJ	PAT
Boonville, IN	EVN
MO	JC
NY	SY
Boothbay Harbor, ME	PRT
Boothwyn, PA	PH
Bordelonville, LA	ALX
Bordentown, NJ	TR
Borger, TX	AMA
Boron, CA	FRS
Borrego Springs, CA	SD
Boscobel, WI	MAD
Bossier City, LA	SHP
Boston, MA	ARM
MA	BO
MA	NTN
MA	STF
NY	BUF
Boswell, PA	ALT
Bothell, WA	SEA
Botkins, OH	CIN
Bottineau, ND	FAR
Boulder, CO	DEN
MT	HEL
Boulder City, NV	LAV
Boulder Creek, CA	MRY
Boulder Junction, WI	SUP
Boulevard, CA	SD
Bound Brook, NJ	MET
Bountiful, UT	SLC
Bourbon, MO	JC
Bourbonnais, IL	JOL
Bourg, LA	HT
Bovard, PA	GBG
Bovina, TX	AMA
Bow Valley, NE	OM
Bowbells, ND	BIS
Bowdle, SD	SFS
Bowie, MD	WDC
TX	FWT
Bowling Green, KY	OWN
OH	TOL
Bowlus, MN	SCL
Bowman, ND	BIS
Bowmansville, NY	BUF
Boyce, LA	ALX
Boyceville, WI	LC
Boyd, WI	LC
Boyers, PA	PIT
Boyertown, PA	ALN
Boyes Hot Springs, CA	SR
Boylston, MA	WOR
Boyne City, MI	GAY
Boyne Falls, MI	GAY
Boynton Beach, FL	PMB
Boys Town, NE	OM
Bozeman, MT	HEL
Brackett, WI	LC
Brackettville, TX	SAT
Braddock, PA	PBR
PA	PIT
Braddock Hills, PA	PIT
Bradenton, FL	VEN
Bradenville, PA	PBR
Bradford, IL	PEO
IN	IND
MA	BO
NY	ROC
OH	CIN
PA	E
RI	PRO
VT	BUR
Bradley, IL	JOL
ME	PRT
Bradley Beach, NJ	TR
Bradshaw, MD	BAL
Brady, TX	SAN
Brady's Bend, PA	GBG
Braham, MN	SCL
Braidwood, IL	JOL
Brainard, NE	LIN
Brainerd, MN	DUL
Braintree, MA	BO
Branchdale, PA	ALN
Branchville, NJ	PAT
Brandamore, PA	PH
Brandenburg, KY	L
Brandon, FL	SP
MN	SCL
MS	JKS
SD	SFS
VT	BUR
WI	MIL
Brandy Camp, PA	E
Brandywood, DE	WIL
Branford, CT	HRT
FL	STA
Branson, MO	SPC
Brant, NY	BUF
Brant Beach, NJ	TR
Brasher Falls, NY	OG
Brattleboro, VT	BUR
Brawley, CA	SD
Brazil, IN	IND
Brazoria, TX	GAL
Brea, CA	ORG
Breaux Bridge, LA	LAF
Breckenridge, CO	DEN
MN	SCL
TX	FWT
Brecksville, OH	CLV
OH	PRM
Breda, IA	SC
Breese, IL	BEL
Bremen, IN	FTW
ND	FAR
OH	COL
Bremerton, WA	SEA
Bremond, TX	AUS
Brenham, TX	AUS
Brennyville, MN	SCL
Brentwood, CA	OAK
MO	STL
NY	BRK
NY	RVC
PA	PIT
TN	NSH
Brevard, NC	CHL
Brewer, ME	PRT
MO	STL
Brewerton, NY	SY
Brewster, MA	FR
MN	WIN
NY	NY
OH	Y
WA	SPK
Brewton, AL	MOB
Briarcliff Manor, NY	NY
Briarwood, NY	BRK
Brick, NJ	TR
Brick Town, NJ	TR
Bridal Veil, OR	P
Bridge City, LA	NO
TX	BEA
Bridgehampton, NY	RVC
Bridgeport, CT	BGP
CT	PSC
CT	STF
IL	BEL
MI	SAG
NE	GI
NY	SY
OH	STU
PA	PH
PA	PHU
TX	FWT
WA	YAK
WV	WH
Bridger, MT	GF
Bridgeton, MO	STL
NJ	CAM
Bridgeview, IL	CHI
Bridgeville, PA	PIT
Bridgewater, MA	BO
NJ	MET
SD	SFS
Bridgman, MI	KAL
Bridgton, ME	PRT
Brigantine, NJ	CAM
Briggsville, WI	MAD
Brigham City, UT	SLC
Brighton, CO	DEN
IL	SFD
MA	BO
MI	LAN
WI	MIL
Brilliant, OH	STU
Brillion, WI	GB
Brimfield, IL	PEO
MA	SPR
Brimley, MI	MAR
Brinkley, AR	LR
Brinktown, MO	JC
Bristol, CT	HRT
IN	FTW
NH	MAN
PA	PH
PA	PHU
RI	PRO
SD	SFS
VA	RIC
VT	BUR
WI	MIL
WI	PRM
Bristow, VA	ARL
Britt, IA	DUB
Britton, SD	SFS
Broad Brook, CT	HRT
Broad Run, VA	ARL
Broadalbin, NY	ALB
Broadus, MT	GF
Broadview Heights, OH	CLV
Brocket, ND	FAR
Brockport, NY	ROC
Brockton, MA	BO
MA	LIT
MA	SAM
PA	ALN
PA	PSC
Brockway, PA	E
Brocton, IL	SFD
NY	BUF
Brodhead, WI	MAD
Brodheadsville, PA	SCR
Broken Arrow, OK	TLS
Broken Bow, NE	GI
Bronson, MI	KAL
Bronx, NY	NY
NY	STF
Bronxville, NY	NY
Brook Park, OH	CLV
Brookeville, MD	WDC
Brookfield, CT	BGP
IL	CHI
MA	WOR
MO	JC
WI	MIL
Brookhaven, MS	JKS
PA	PH
Brookings, OR	P
SD	SFS
Brooklandville, MD	BAL
Brooklawn, NJ	CAM
Brookline, MA	BO
PA	PH
Brooklyn, CT	NOR
IA	DAV
MI	LAN
NY	ARM
NY	BRK
NY	LIT
NY	NTN
NY	PSC
NY	SAM
NY	STF
OH	CLV
OH	NTN
Brooklyn Center, MN	STP
Brooklyn Park, MN	STP
Brookneal, VA	RIC
Brooks, MN	CR
WI	LC
Brooksville, FL	SP
KY	COV
MS	JKS
Brookville, IN	IND
KS	SAL
MD	WDC
NY	RVC
PA	E
Broomall, PA	PH
Broomfield, CO	DEN
Brooten, MN	SCL
Brouillette, LA	ALX
Broussard, LA	LAF
Browerville, MN	SCL
Brown Deer, WI	MIL
Brown's Valley, KY	OWN
MN	SCL
Brownfield, TX	LUB
Browning, MT	HEL
Browns Mills, NJ	TR
Browns Valley, MN	SCL
Brownsburg, IN	IND
Brownsdale, MN	WIN
Brownstown, IN	IND
Brownsville, MN	WIN
PA	GBG
PA	PBR
TN	MEM
TX	BWN
Brownville, NY	OG
Brownville Junction, ME	PRT
Brownwood, TX	SAN
Bruce, MS	JKS
WI	SUP
Bruno, NE	LIN
Brunswick, GA	SAV
MD	BAL
ME	PRT
MI	GR
MO	JC
OH	CLV
OH	PRM
Brush, CO	DEN
Brushton, NY	OG
Brusly, LA	BR
Brussels, IL	SFD
WI	GB
Bryan, OH	TOL
TX	AUS
Bryant, IA	DAV
IN	LFT
SD	SFS
Bryantown, MD	WDC
Bryn Mawr, PA	PH
Bryson City, NC	CHL
Buchanan, MI	KAL
ND	FAR
NY	NY
Buchanan Valley, PA	HBG
Buchtel, OH	STU
Buckeye, AZ	PHX
Buckeye Lake, OH	COL
Buckeystown, MD	BAL
Buckhannon, WV	WH
Buckingham, VA	RIC
Buckley, WA	SEA
Bucklin, KS	DOD
Buckman, MN	SCL
Buckner, MO	KC
VA	RIC
Bucksport, ME	PRT
Bucyrus, OH	TOL
Buda, TX	AUS
Budd, IL	PEO
Budd Lake, NJ	PAT
Buena Park, CA	ORG
Buena Vista, CO	COS
WI	LC
Buffalo, IA	DAV
IL	SFD
MN	STP
MO	SPC
ND	FAR
NY	BUF
NY	STF
SD	RC
WY	CHY
Buffalo Center, IA	DUB
Buffalo Grove, IL	CHI
Buford, GA	ATL
Buhl, ID	B
Bulger, PA	PIT
Bullhead City, AZ	PHX
Bunker Hill, IL	SFD
Bunkie, LA	ALX
Bunnell, FL	STA
Buras, LA	NO
Burbank, CA	LA
IL	CHI
Burdett, KS	DOD
Burgaw, NC	R
Burgettstown, PA	PIT
Burkburnett, TX	FWT
Burke, NY	OG
SD	RC
VA	ARL
Burkettsville, OH	CIN
Burkhart, OH	STU
Burleson, TX	FWT
Burley, ID	B
Burlingame, CA	SFR
Burlington, CO	COS
IA	DAV
KS	KCK
KY	COV
MA	BO
NC	R
ND	BIS
NJ	TR
VT	BUR
WA	SEA
WI	MIL
Burnet, TX	AUS
Burney, CA	SAC
Burnham, IL	CHI
Burns, KS	WCH
OR	BAK
Burnstad, ND	FAR
Burnsville, MN	STP
Burr Ridge, IL	JOL
Burt Lake, MI	GAY
Burton, MI	LAN

OH	PRM
Burtonsville, MD	WDC
Burwell, NE	GI
Bushkill, PA	SCR
Bushnell, FL	ORL
IL	PEO
Bushton, KS	WCH
Bushwood, MD	WDC
Butler, AL	MOB
MN	SCL
MO	KC
NJ	PAT
PA	PBR
PA	PIT
TN	KNX
WI	MIL
Butte, MT	HEL
NE	OM
Butternut, WI	SUP
Buttonwillow, CA	FRS
Buttonwood, PA	SCR
Buxton, NC	R
Buzzards Bay, MA	FR
Byers, CO	DEN
Byesville, OH	STU
Byron, CA	OAK
IL	RCK
MN	WIN
WI	MIL
Byron Center, MI	GR
MI	KAL
Cabery, IL	JOL
Cable, WI	SUP
Cabo Rojo, PR	MGZ
Cabot, PA	PIT
Cadet, MO	STL
Cadillac, MI	GAY
Cadiz, KY	OWN
OH	STU
Cadogan, PA	GBG
Cadott, WI	LC
Cadyville, NY	OG
Caguas, PR	CGS
Cahokia, IL	BEL
Cairo, IL	BEL
NY	ALB
Calais, ME	PRT
Caldwell, ID	B
KS	WCH
NJ	NEW
OH	STU
TX	AUS
Caledonia, MI	GR
MN	WIN
NY	ROC
WI	MIL
Calexico, CA	SD
Calhan, CO	COS
Calhoun, GA	ATL
KY	OWN
Caliente, NV	LAV
Califon, NJ	MET
California, KY	COV
MO	JC
PA	PIT
Calimesa, CA	SB
Calipatria, CA	SD
Calistoga, CA	SR
Callahan, FL	STA
Callaway, MN	CR
Callicoon, NY	NY
Calmar, IA	DUB
Calumet, MI	MAR
OK	OKL
PA	GBG
Calumet City, IL	CHI
Calumet Park, IL	CHI
Calvary, KY	L
Calvert, TX	AUS
Calvert City, KY	OWN
Camanche, IA	DAV
Camarillo, CA	LA
CA	SD
Camas, WA	SEA
Cambria, CA	MRY
Cambria Heights, NY	BRK
Cambridge, MA	BO
MD	WIL
MN	SCL
NE	LIN
NY	ALB
OH	STU
VT	BUR
WI	MAD
Cambridge City, IN	IND
Cambridge Springs, PA	E
Camden, AL	MOB
AR	LR
ME	PRT
MS	JKS
NJ	CAM

NY	SY
OH	CIN
SC	CHR
TN	MEM
WV	WH
Camdenton, MO	JC
Cameron, LA	LKC
MO	KC
TX	AUS
WI	SUP
WV	WH
Camillus, NY	SY
Camp Douglas, WI	LC
Camp Grove, IL	PEO
Camp Hill, PA	HBG
Camp Point, IL	SFD
Camp Springs, KY	COV
MD	WDC
Camp Verde, AZ	PHX
Campbell, CA	SJ
NE	LIN
OH	PBR
OH	Y
Campbellsport, WI	MIL
Campbellsville, KY	L
Campti, LA	ALX
Campus, IL	PEO
Camuy, PR	ARE
Canaan, CT	HRT
VT	BUR
Canadensis, PA	SCR
Canadian, TX	AMA
Canajoharie, NY	ALB
Canal Fulton, OH	Y
Canandaigua, NY	ROC
Canaseraga, NY	BUF
Canastota, NY	SY
Canby, MN	NU
OR	P
Candia, NH	MAN
Cando, ND	FAR
Caney, KS	WCH
Canfield, OH	Y
Canisteo, NY	ROC
Cankton, LA	LAF
Cannelburg, IN	EVN
Cannelton, IN	IND
Cannon Falls, MN	STP
Canoga Park, CA	LA
Canon City, CO	PBL
Canonsburg, PA	PBR
PA	PIT
Canovanas, PR	SJN
Canterbury, CT	NOR
Canton, GA	ATL
IL	PEO
MA	BO
MI	DET
MN	WIN
MO	JC
MS	JKS
NY	OG
OH	ROM
OH	SJP
OH	Y
PA	SCR
SD	SFS
Cantonment, FL	PT
Canutillo, TX	ELP
Canyon, TX	AMA
Canyon Country, CA	LA
Canyon Lake, TX	SAT
Capac, MI	DET
Capaldo, KS	WCH
Cape Charles, VA	RIC
Cape Coral, FL	VEN
Cape Elizabeth, ME	PRT
Cape Girardeau, MO	SPC
Cape May, NJ	CAM
Cape May Court House, NJ	CAM
Cape May Point, NJ	CAM
Cape Vincent, NY	OG
Capistrano Beach, CA	ORG
Capital Plaza, MD	WDC
Capitola, CA	MRY
Capulin, CO	PBL
Carbondale, IL	BEL
PA	SCR
Cardale, PA	GBG
Cardington, OH	COL
Carefree, AZ	PHX
Carencro, LA	LAF
Carey, OH	TOL
Caribou, ME	PRT
Carle Place, NY	RVC
Carleton, MI	DET
Carlin, NV	RNO
Carlinville, IL	SFD
Carlisle, AR	LR
IA	DM
KY	LEX

MA	BO
OH	STU
PA	HBG
Carlsbad, CA	SD
NM	LSC
TX	SAN
Carlton, MN	DUL
Carlyle, IL	BEL
Carmel, CA	MRY
IN	LFT
NY	NY
Carmel Valley, CA	MRY
Carmi, IL	BEL
Carmichael, CA	SAC
Carmichaels, PA	PIT
Carnegie, PA	PIT
PA	SJP
Carneys Point, NJ	CAM
Caro, MI	SAG
Carol Stream, IL	JOL
Carolina, PR	SJN
RI	PRO
Carolina Beach, NC	R
Carpentersville, IL	RCK
Carpinteria, CA	LA
Carrboro, NC	R
Carrington, ND	FAR
Carrizo Springs, TX	SAT
Carrizozo, NM	LSC
Carroll, IA	SC
Carrollton, GA	ATL
IL	SFD
KY	COV
MI	SAG
MO	KC
OH	STU
TX	DAL
TX	FWT
Carrolltown, PA	ALT
Carson, CA	LA
ND	BIS
Carson City, MI	GR
NV	RNO
Carter Lake, IA	DM
Carteret, NJ	MET
NJ	PHU
NJ	PSC
Cartersville, GA	ATL
Carterville, IL	BEL
Carthage, IL	PEO
MO	SPC
MS	JKS
NY	OG
TX	TYL
Carthagena, OH	CIN
Caruthersville, MO	SPC
Carver, MA	BO
MN	STP
Carverton, PA	SCR
Cary, IL	RCK
NC	PSC
NC	R
Casa Grande, AZ	TUC
Cascade, CO	COS
IA	DUB
NH	MAN
WI	MIL
Casco, ME	PRT
WI	GB
Caseville, MI	SAG
Casey, IA	DM
IL	SFD
Caseyville, IL	BEL
Cashion, AZ	PHX
Cashmere, WA	YAK
Cashton, WI	LC
Casper, WY	CHY
Caspian, MI	MAR
Cass City, MI	SAG
Cass Lake, MN	DUL
Cassadaga, NY	BUF
Cassandra, PA	ALT
Cassel, WI	LC
Casselberry, FL	ORL
Cassella, OH	CIN
Casselton, ND	FAR
Cassopolis, MI	KAL
Cassville, WI	MAD
Castaner, PR	PCE
Castine, ME	PRT
Castle Grove, IA	DUB
Castle Hayne, NC	R
Castle Rock, CO	COS
WA	SEA
Castle Shannon, PA	PIT
Castleton, KS	WCH
NY	ALB
VT	BUR
Castleton-on-Hudson, NY	ALB
Castlewood, SD	SFS
Castro Valley, CA	OAK

Castroville, CA	MRY
TX	SAT
Catahoula, LA	LAF
Catano, PR	SJN
Catasauqua, PA	ALN
Catawba, WI	SUP
Catawissa, MO	STL
Catharine, KS	SAL
Cathedral City, CA	SB
Cato, NY	ROC
Catonsville, MD	BAL
Catskill, NY	ALB
Cattaraugus, NY	BUF
Cavalier, ND	FAR
Cavour, SD	SFS
Cawker City, KS	SAL
Cayey, PR	CGS
Cayucos, CA	MRY
Cayuga, ND	FAR
NY	ROC
Cazenovia, NY	SY
WI	LC
Cecil, OH	TOL
PA	PIT
WI	GB
Cecilia, KY	L
LA	LAF
Cedar, MI	GAY
MN	STP
Cedar City, UT	SLC
Cedar Falls, IA	DUB
Cedar Grove, IN	IND
NJ	NEW
WI	MIL
Cedar Knolls, NJ	PAT
Cedar Lake, IN	GRY
MN	STP
Cedar Rapids, IA	DUB
NE	OM
Cedar Vale, KS	WCH
Cedarburg, WI	MIL
Cedarhurst, NY	RVC
Cedartown, GA	ATL
Cedarville, NJ	CAM
Ceiba, PR	CGS
Celestine, IN	EVN
Celina, OH	CIN
Center, CO	PBL
ND	BIS
TX	TYL
Center Harbor, NH	MAN
Center Moriches, NY	RVC
Center Ossipee, NH	MAN
Center Ridge, AR	LR
Center Square, PA	PH
Center Township, PA	PIT
Center Valley, PA	ALN
Centereach, NY	RVC
Centerline, MI	DET
Centerport, NY	BRK
NY	RVC
Centerville, IA	DAV
LA	LAF
MA	FR
MN	STP
MO	STL
MT	GF
NY	NY
OH	CIN
SD	SFS
TN	NSH
Central City, IA	DUB
KY	OWN
NE	OM
PA	ALT
Central Falls, RI	NTN
RI	PRO
Central Islip, NY	RVC
Central Point, OR	P
Central Square, NY	SY
Centralia, IL	BEL
MO	JC
PA	HBG
PA	PHU
WA	SEA
Centreville, IL	BEL
MD	WIL
Centuria, WI	SUP
Ceres, CA	STO
Cerrillos, NM	SFE
Cestohowa, TX	SAT
Chacahoula, LA	HT
Chackbay, LA	HT
Chadds Ford, PA	PH
Chadron, NE	GI
Chadwicks, NY	SY
Chaffee, MO	SPC
Chagrin Falls, OH	CLV
Chalan Kanoa Village, MP	CHK
Chalan Pago, GU	AGN
Chalfont, PA	PH

Chalmette, LA	NO
Chama, NM	SFE
Chamberino, NM	LSC
Chamberlain, SD	SFS
Chambers Island, WI	GB
Chambersburg, PA	HBG
Chamblee, GA	ATL
Chamois, MO	JC
Champaign, IL	PEO
Champion, MI	MAR
OH	Y
WI	GB
Champlain, NY	OG
Chancellorsville, VA	ARL
Chandler, AZ	PHX
OK	OKL
Chandlerville, IL	SFD
Chanhassen, MN	STP
Channahon, IL	JOL
Channelview, TX	GAL
Channing, MI	MAR
TX	AMA
Chantilly, VA	ARL
Chanute, KS	WCH
Chapel Hill, NC	R
Chapel Point, MD	WDC
Chapin, SC	CHR
Chapman, KS	SAL
Chappaqua, NY	NY
Chapparal, NM	LSC
Chappell, NE	GI
Chappell Hill, TX	AUS
Chaptico, MD	WDC
Chardon, OH	CLV
Charenton, LA	LAF
Chariton, IA	DM
Charleroi, PA	PBR
PA	PIT
Charles City, IA	DUB
Charles Town, WV	WH
Charlesburg, WI	GB
Charleston, AR	LR
IL	SFD
MO	SPC
MS	JKS
SC	CHR
WV	WH
Charlestown, IN	IND
MA	BO
NH	MAN
WI	GB
Charlevoix, MI	GAY
Charlotte, IA	DAV
MI	LAN
NC	CHL
TX	SAT
VT	BUR
Charlottesville, VA	RIC
Charlton City, MA	WOR
Charter Oak, IA	SC
Chase, KS	WCH
WI	GB
Chaska, MN	STP
Chasm Falls, NY	OG
Chassell, MI	MAR
Chastang, AL	MOB
Chataignier, LA	LAF
Chatawa, MS	JKS
Chateaugay, NY	OG
Chatfield, MN	WIN
Chatham, IL	SFD
MA	FR
NJ	PAT
NY	ALB
Chatham Township, NJ	PAT
Chatom, AL	MOB
Chatsworth, CA	LA
IL	PEO
Chattahoochee, FL	PT
Chattanooga, TN	KNX
Chaumont, NY	OG
Chauncey, OH	STU
Chauvin, LA	HT
Chazy, NY	OG
Cheat Lake, WV	WH
Chebanse, IL	JOL
Cheboygan, MI	GAY
Cheektowaga, NY	BUF
Chefornak, AK	FBK
Chehalis, WA	SEA
Chelan, WA	YAK
Chelmsford, MA	BO
Chelsea, IA	DUB
MA	BO
MI	LAN
NY	NY
SD	SFS
WI	SUP
Cheltenham, PA	PH
Chenango Forks, NY	SY
Cheney, NE	LIN
WA	SPK
Cheneyville, LA	ALX
Chenoa, IL	PEO
Chepachet, RI	PRO
Cheraw, SC	CHR
Cherokee, IA	SC
KS	WCH
NC	CHL
OK	OKL
Cherokee Village, AR	LR
Cherry, IL	PEO
Cherry Creek, NY	BUF
Cherry Hill, NJ	CAM
NJ	PHU
Cherry Mound, IA	DUB
Cherry Valley, CA	SB
NY	ALB
Cherryvale, KS	WCH
Chesaning, MI	SAG
Chesapeake, OH	STU
VA	RIC
Chesapeake City, MD	PHU
Cheshire, CT	HRT
MA	SPR
Chest Springs, PA	ALT
Chester, CT	NOR
IA	DUB
IL	BEL
MT	GF
NJ	PAT
NY	NY
PA	PH
PA	PHU
SC	CHR
VT	BUR
WV	WH
Chester Heights, PA	PH
Chester, Kent Island, MD	WIL
Chesterfield, MO	STL
Chesterland, OH	CLV
OH	ROM
Chesterton, IN	GRY
Chestertown, MD	WIL
NY	ALB
Chestnut Hill, MA	BO
Chetek, WI	SUP
Chetopa, KS	WCH
Chevak, AK	FBK
Cheverly, MD	WDC
Chevy Chase, MD	WDC
Chewelah, WA	SPK
Cheyenne, WY	CHY
Cheyenne Wells, CO	COS
Chicago, IL	CHI
IL	EST
IL	LIT
IL	PRM
IL	ROM
IL	STN
Chicago Heights, IL	CHI
Chicago Ridge, IL	CHI
Chichiltah, NM	GLP
Chickasaw, AL	MOB
OH	CIN
Chickasha, OK	OKL
Chico, CA	SAC
Chicopee, KS	WCH
MA	SPR
Chicora, PA	PIT
Chiefland, FL	STA
Childress, TX	AMA
Childs, MD	WIL
Chili, WI	LC
Chillicothe, IL	PEO
MO	KC
OH	COL
Chillum, MD	WDC
Chiloquin, OR	BAK
Chilton, WI	GB
Chimayo, NM	SFE
China, IN	IND
TX	BEA
China Springs, TX	AUS
Chincoteague, VA	RIC
Chinle, AZ	GLP
Chino, CA	SB
Chino Hills, CA	SB
Chinook, MT	GF
Chipley, FL	PT
Chippewa Falls, WI	LC
Chippewa Lake, OH	CLV
Chippewa Township, PA	PIT
Chisholm, MN	DUL
Chittenango, NY	SY
Chittenden, VT	BUR
Chokio, MN	SCL
Choteau, MT	HEL
Chowchilla, CA	FRS
Chrisney, IN	EVN
Christiansburg, VA	RIC
Christiansted, VI	STV
Christopher, IL	BEL
Christoval, TX	SAN
Chubbuck, ID	B
Chuckatuck, VA	RIC
Chula Vista, CA	SD
Church Point, LA	LAF
Church Rock, NM	GLP
Churchill Borough, PA	PIT
Churchtown, OH	STU
Churchville, IA	DM
NY	ROC
Churdan, IA	SC
Churubusco, IN	FTW
NY	OG
Chuuk, FM	CI
Ciales, PR	ARE
Cibecue, AZ	GLP
Cicero, IL	CHI
IN	LFT
NY	SY
Cidra, PR	CGS
Cimarron, NM	SFE
Cincinnati, OH	CIN
OH	OLL
Cinnaminson, NJ	TR
Circle, MT	GF
Circleville, OH	COL
Cisco, TX	FWT
Cistern, TX	VIC
Citronelle, AL	MOB
Citrus Heights, CA	SAC
Citrus Springs, FL	SP
Claflin, KS	DOD
Clairton, PA	PBR
PA	PIT
Clam Lake, WI	SUP
Clara City, MN	NU
Clare, IA	SC
MI	SAG
Claremont, CA	LA
MN	WIN
NH	MAN
Claremore, OK	TLS
Clarence, MO	JC
NY	BUF
PA	ALT
PA	PBR
Clarence Center, NY	BUF
Clarendon, TX	AMA
Clarendon Hills, IL	JOL
Clarinda, IA	DM
Clarion, IA	DUB
PA	E
Clarissa, MN	SCL
Clark, NJ	NEW
SD	SFS
Clark Mills, NY	SY
Clarkesville, GA	ATL
Clarkfield, MN	NU
Clarklake, MI	LAN
Clarks, NE	OM
Clarks Green, PA	SCR
Clarks Mills, WI	GB
Clarks Summit, PA	PSC
PA	SCR
Clarksburg, CA	SAC
WV	WH
Clarksdale, MS	JKS
Clarkson, KY	OWN
NE	OM
Clarkston, MI	DET
WA	SPK
Clarksville, AR	LR
IN	IND
MD	BAL
PA	PIT
TN	NSH
TX	TYL
VA	RIC
Claudell, KS	SAL
Clawson, MI	DET
Claxton, GA	SAV
Clay Center, KS	SAL
Claymont, DE	WIL
Clayton, MO	STL
NJ	CAM
NM	SFE
NY	OG
WA	SPK
Clayville, NY	SY
Cle Elum, WA	YAK
Clear Creek, IA	DAV
Clear Lake, IA	DUB
IN	FTW
MN	SCL
SD	SFS
WI	SUP
Clearfield, PA	E
SD	RC
Clearlake, CA	SR
Clearwater, FL	SP
MN	STP
Cleburne, TX	FWT
Clements, MN	NU
Clementsville, KY	L
Clemmons, NC	CHL
Clemson, SC	CHR
Clermont, FL	ORL
IA	DUB
Clermont Harbor, MS	BLX
Cleveland, MN	STP
MS	JKS
NY	SY
OH	CLV
OH	OLL
OH	PRM
OH	ROM
OH	SJP
OK	TLS
TN	KNX
TX	BEA
WI	GB
Cleveland Heights, OH	CLV
Clewiston, FL	VEN
Cliffside Park, NJ	NEW
NJ	NTN
Clifton, AZ	TUC
IL	JOL
KS	SAL
NJ	PAT
TX	FWT
VA	ARL
Clifton Forge, VA	RIC
Clifton Heights, PA	PH
PA	PHU
Clifton Park, NY	ALB
Clifton Springs, NY	ROC
Clint, TX	ELP
Clinton, AR	LR
CT	NOR
IA	DAV
IL	PEO
IN	IND
KY	OWN
MA	WOR
MD	WDC
MI	LAN
MO	KC
MS	JKS
NC	R
NJ	MET
NY	SY
OH	CLV
OK	OKL
SC	CHR
TN	KNX
WI	MAD
Clinton Heights, NY	ALB
Clinton Township, MI	DET
Clinton Twp., MI	DET
Clintonville, WI	GB
Clintwood, VA	RIC
Clio, MI	LAN
Clonmel, KS	WCH
Clontarf, MN	NU
Cloquet, MN	DUL
Closter, NJ	NEW
Cloutierville, LA	ALX
Clover Bottom, MO	STL
Cloverdale, CA	SR
OH	TOL
Cloverport, KY	OWN
Clovis, CA	FRS
NM	SFE
Clute, TX	GAL
Clutier, IA	DUB
Clyde, KS	SAL
MO	KC
NY	ROC
OH	TOL
Clyman, WI	MIL
Clymer, PA	GBG
PA	PBR
Coachella, CA	SB
Coal City, IL	JOL
Coal Run, PA	PBR
Coal Township, PA	HBG
Coal Valley, IL	PEO
Coaldale, PA	ALN
PA	PSC
Coalgate, OK	TLS
Coalinga, CA	FRS
Coalport, PA	E
Coalton, WV	WH
Coamo, PR	PCE
Coates, MN	STP
Coatesville, PA	PH
PA	PSC
Cobden, IL	BEL
Cobleskill, NY	ALB
Cockeysville, MD	BAL
Cocoa, FL	ORL

Cocoa Beach, FL	ORL
Coconut Creek, FL	MIA
FL	PSC
Coconut Grove, FL	MIA
Cody, WY	CHY
Coeur D'Alene, ID	B
Coffeen, IL	SFD
Coffeyville, KS	WCH
Coffman, MO	STL
Coggon, IA	DUB
Cogswell, ND	FAR
Cohasset, MA	BO
Cohocton, NY	ROC
Cohoes, NY	ALB
NY	STF
Colbert, WA	SPK
Colby, KS	SAL
WI	LC
Colchester, CT	NOR
CT	STF
VT	BUR
Cold Spring, KY	COV
MN	SCL
Cold Spring-on-Hudson, NY	NY
Cold Springs, MN	SCL
Colden, NY	BUF
Coldwater, MI	KAL
OH	CIN
Colebrook, NH	MAN
Coleman, MI	SAG
TX	SAN
WI	GB
Colerain, OH	STU
Coleraine, MN	DUL
Coleridge, NE	OM
Colesburg, IA	DUB
KY	L
Colesville, PA	ALN
Colfax, CA	SAC
IA	DAV
IL	PEO
LA	ALX
WA	SPK
College Park, MD	WDC
College Point, NY	BRK
College Station, TX	AUS
Collegeville, MN	SCL
PA	PH
Colleyville, TX	FWT
Collingdale, PA	PH
Collings Lakes, NJ	CAM
Collingswood, NJ	CAM
Collins Center, NY	BUF
Collinsville, CT	HRT
IL	SFD
OK	TLS
Collyer, KS	SAL
Colma, CA	SFR
Colman, SD	SFS
Colo, IA	DUB
Cologne, MN	STP
Colome, SD	RC
Colon, NE	LIN
Colona, IL	PEO
Colonia, NJ	MET
NJ	NEW
Colonia, Yap, FM	CI
Colonial Beach, VA	ARL
Colonial Heights, VA	RIC
Colonie, NY	ALB
The Colony, TX	FWT
Colorado City, TX	SAN
Colorado Springs, CO	COS
CO	VNN
Colstrip, MT	GF
Colton, CA	SB
NY	OG
WA	SPK
Colts Neck, NJ	TR
Columbia, CT	NOR
IL	BEL
KY	L
MD	BAL
MO	JC
MS	BLX
PA	HBG
SC	CHR
TN	NSH
VA	RIC
Columbia City, IN	FTW
Columbia Falls, MT	HEL
Columbia Heights, MN	STP
Columbia Station, OH	CLV
Columbiana, OH	Y
Columbus, GA	SAV
IN	IND
KS	WCH
MI	DET
MS	JKS
MT	GF
NE	OM
OH	COL
OH	NTN
OH	OLL
OH	PRM
TX	VIC
WI	MAD
Columbus Grove, OH	TOL
Columbus Junction, IA	DAV
Colusa, CA	SAC
Colver, PA	ALT
Colville, WA	SPK
Colwich, KS	WCH
Comanche, TX	FWT
Combined Locks, WI	GB
Comerio, PR	CGS
Comfort, TX	SAT
Comfrey, MN	NU
Commack, NY	RVC
Commerce, TX	DAL
Commerce City, CO	DEN
Compton, CA	LA
Conception, MO	KC
Conception Junction, MO	KC
Concho, AZ	GLP
Concord, CA	OAK
MA	BO
MI	LAN
NC	CHL
NH	MAN
Concord Hill, MO	STL
Concord Twp., OH	CLV
Concord Village, MO	STL
Concordia, KS	SAL
Conde, SD	SFS
Condon, OR	BAK
Conejos, CO	PBL
Conemaugh, PA	ALT
PA	PBR
Conewago Township, PA	HBG
Congers, NY	NY
Conifer, CO	DEN
Conklin, MI	GR
Conneaut, OH	Y
Conneaut Lake, PA	E
Conneautville, PA	E
Connell, WA	SPK
Connellsville, PA	GBG
Connersville, IN	IND
Conrad, MT	HEL
Conroe, TX	GAL
Conshohocken, PA	PH
Constable, NY	OG
Constableville, NY	OG
Constance, NE	OM
Continental, OH	TOL
Convent, LA	BR
Convent Station, NJ	PAT
Converse, TX	SAT
Conway, AK	LR
AR	LR
MI	GAY
MO	SPC
ND	FAR
PA	PIT
SC	CHR
Conway Springs, KS	WCH
Conyers, GA	ATL
Conyngham, PA	SCR
Cook, MN	DUL
Cookeville, TN	NSH
Cooks, MI	MAR
Cooks Valley, WI	LC
Coolidge, AZ	TUC
Coon Rapids, IA	SC
MN	STP
Coon Valley, WI	LC
Coopersburg, PA	ALN
Cooperstown, ND	FAR
NY	ALB
WI	GB
Coopersville, MI	GR
NY	OG
Coos Bay, OR	P
Copake Falls, NY	ALB
Copemish, MI	GAY
Copenhagen, NY	OG
Copiague, NY	RVC
Coplay, PA	ALN
Copley, OH	CLV
Coppell, TX	DAL
Copperas Cove, TX	AUS
Copperhill, TN	KNX
Copperopolis, CA	STO
Copperton, UT	SLC
Coquille, OR	P
Coral, PA	GBG
Coral Gables, FL	MIA
Coral Springs, FL	MIA
Coram, NY	RVC
Coraopolis, PA	PIT
Corbin, KY	LEX
Corcoran, CA	FRS
MN	STP
Cordele, GA	SAV
Cordova, AK	ANC
TN	MEM
Corfu, NY	BUF
Corinth, MS	JKS
NY	ALB
Cornelius, OR	P
Cornell, WI	LC
Corning, CA	SAC
IA	DM
KS	KCK
NY	ROC
OH	COL
Cornucopia, WI	SUP
Cornwall, NY	NY
PA	HBG
Cornwall Bridge, CT	HRT
Cornwall-on-Hudson, NY	NY
Corona, CA	SB
Coronado, CA	SD
Corozal, PR	ARE
Corozal-Padilla, PR	ARE
Corozal-Palmarito, PR	ARE
Corozal-Palos Blancos, PR	ARE
Corpus Christi, TX	CC
TX	SY
Corrales, NM	SFE
Corralitos, CA	MRY
Corrigan, TX	BEA
Corry, PA	E
Corsicana, TX	DAL
Cortaro, AZ	TUC
Cortez, CO	PBL
Cortland, NE	LIN
NY	SY
OH	Y
Cortlandt Manor, NY	NY
Corvallis, OR	P
Corwith, IA	DUB
Corydon, IA	DM
IN	IND
Cosgrove, IA	DAV
Coshocton, OH	COL
Costa Mesa, CA	ORG
Cotati, CA	SR
Coteau, LA	LAF
Coteau Holmes, LA	LAF
Coto Laurel, PR	PCE
Cottage Grove, MN	STP
OR	P
WI	MAD
Cottleville, MO	STL
Cottonport, LA	ALX
Cottonwood, AZ	PHX
ID	B
MN	NU
Cotulla, TX	SAT
Coudersport, PA	E
Coulee Dam, WA	SPK
Coulterville, IL	BEL
Council, ID	B
Council Bluffs, IA	DM
Council Grove, KS	WCH
Country Club Hills, IL	CHI
Countryside, IL	CHI
Coupon, PA	ALT
Courtenay, ND	FAR
Coventry, CT	NOR
RI	PRO
Covina, CA	LA
Covington, GA	ATL
IN	LFT
KY	COV
LA	NO
OH	CIN
TN	MEM
VA	RIC
Cow Island, LA	LAF
Coweta, OK	TLS
Cowiche, WA	YAK
Coxsackie, NY	ALB
Coylesville, PA	PIT
Cozad, NE	GI
Crabtree, PA	GBG
Crafton, PA	PIT
Craig, AK	JUN
CO	DEN
Cranberry Prairie, OH	CIN
Cranberry Township, PA	PIT
Cranbury, NJ	MET
Crandon, WI	GB
Crane, TX	SAN
Cranford, NJ	NEW
Cranston, RI	PRO
Crawford, NE	GI
Crawfordsville, IN	LFT
Creighton, NE	OM
PA	PIT
Creole, LA	LKC
Cresaptown, MD	BAL
Crescent, NY	ALB
OH	STU
Crescent City, CA	SR
FL	STA
Crescent Lake, WI	SUP
Crescent Springs, KY	COV
Cresco, IA	DUB
PA	SCR
Cresskill, NJ	NEW
Cresson, PA	ALT
Crested Butte, CO	PBL
Crestline, CA	SB
OH	TOL
Creston, IA	DM
Crestone, CO	PBL
Crestview, FL	PT
Crestwood, IL	CHI
KY	L
MO	STL
NY	NY
Crete, IL	JOL
NE	LIN
Creve Coeur, IL	PEO
MO	STL
Crewe, VA	RIC
Crivitz, WI	GB
Crocker, MO	JC
Crockett, CA	OAK
TX	TYL
Crofton, MD	BAL
NE	OM
Croghan, NY	OG
Cromwell, CT	NOR
Crookston, MN	CR
Crooksville, OH	COL
Crosby, MN	DUL
ND	BIS
TX	GAL
Cross Plains, WI	MAD
Cross Village, MI	GAY
Crossett, AR	LR
Crossingsville, PA	E
Crosslake, MN	DUL
Crossville, TN	KNX
Croswell, MI	SAG
Croton Falls, NY	NY
Croton-on-Hudson, NY	NY
Crow Agency, MT	GF
Crow Hill, ND	FAR
Crowell, TX	FWT
Crowley, LA	LAF
TX	FWT
Crown, PA	E
Crown Butte, ND	BIS
Crown Point, IN	GRY
LA	NO
NY	OG
Crownpoint, NM	GLP
Croydon, PA	PH
Crozet, VA	RIC
Cruz Bay, VI	STV
Crystal, MN	STP
ND	FAR
Crystal City, MO	STL
TX	SAT
Crystal Falls, MI	MAR
Crystal Lake, IL	RCK
Crystal River, FL	SP
Crystal Springs, MS	JKS
Cuba, KS	SAL
MO	JC
NM	GLP
NY	BUF
OH	TOL
Cuba City, WI	MAD
Cudahy, CA	LA
WI	MIL
Cuero, TX	VIC
Culbertson, MT	GF
Culebra, PR	CGS
Cullman, AL	BIR
Cullom, IL	PEO
Culpeper, VA	ARL
Culver, IN	FTW
Culver City, CA	LA
Culvertown, KY	L
Cumberland, IA	DM
KY	LEX
MD	BAL
RI	PRO
WI	SUP
Cumbola, PA	ALN
Cumming, GA	ATL
IA	DM
Cunningham, KS	WCH
Cupertino, CA	SJ
Curdsville, KY	OWN
Curlew, WA	SPK
Currie, MN	WIN
Curtis, NE	LIN

Curtis Bay, MD	PHU
Curwensville, PA	E
Cushing, OK	TLS
Cusick, WA	SPK
Custar, OH	TOL
Custer, MI	GR
SD	RC
WI	LC
Cut Bank, MT	HEL
Cutchogue, NY	RVC
Cutler, CA	FRS
Cut-Off, LA	HT
Cuyahoga Falls, OH	CLV
Cuyahoga Heights, OH	CLV
Cyclone, TX	AUS
Cygnet, OH	TOL
Cynthiana, KY	COV
Cypress, CA	ORG
Czestochowa, WI	LC
D'Hanis, TX	SAT
Dacada, WI	MIL
Dade City, FL	SP
Daggett, MI	MAR
Daguscahonda, PA	E
Dahlgren, IL	BEL
Dahlonega, GA	ATL
Daigle, ME	PRT
Daingerfield, TX	TYL
Dakota, MN	WIN
Dale, IN	EVN
Dale City, VA	ARL
Dalhart, TX	AMA
Dallas, OR	P
PA	SCR
TX	DAL
Dallastown, PA	HBG
The Dalles, OR	BAK
Dalton, GA	ATL
MA	SPR
PA	SCR
Dalton City, IL	SFD
Daly City, CA	SFR
Dalzell, IL	PEO
Damar, KS	SAL
Damascus, MD	WDC
Damiansville, IL	BEL
Damon, TX	GAL
Dana Point, CA	ORG
Danbury, CT	BGP
CT	NTN
CT	PSC
CT	SAM
IA	SC
TX	GAL
WI	SUP
Dane, WI	MAD
Dania, FL	MIA
Danielson, CT	NOR
Dannemora, NY	OG
Dansville, NY	ROC
Dante, SD	SFS
Danvers, MA	BO
MN	NU
Danville, CA	OAK
IL	PEO
IN	IND
KS	WCH
KY	LEX
OH	COL
PA	HBG
VA	RIC
Daphne, AL	MOB
Darboy, WI	GB
Darby, PA	PH
Dardanelle, AR	LR
Dardenne, MO	STL
Darien, CT	BGP
IL	JOL
Darien Center, NY	BUF
Darlington, NJ	NEW
PA	PIT
WI	MAD
Darnestown, MD	WDC
Darrow, LA	BR
Darwin, MN	NU
Dauby, WI	SUP
Dauphin, PA	HBG
Dauphin Island, AL	MOB
Davenport, CA	MRY
IA	DAV
WA	SPK
Davey, NE	LIN
David City, NE	LIN
Davidsonville, MD	BAL
Davidsville, PA	ALT
Davie, FL	MIA
Davis, CA	SAC
Davis Park, NY	RVC
Davison, MI	LAN
Dawson, MN	NU
NE	LIN
Dawson Springs, KY	OWN
Dayton, IA	SC
KY	COV
MN	STP
NV	RNO
NY	BUF
OH	CIN
OH	OLL
OH	PRM
TN	KNX
TX	BEA
WA	SPK
WY	CHY
Daytona Beach, FL	ORL
Dayville, CT	NOR
Dazey, ND	FAR
De Forest, WI	MAD
De Funiak Springs, FL	PT
De Graff, MN	NU
De Kalb Junction, NY	OG
De Land, FL	ORL
De Leon, TX	FWT
De Motte, IN	LFT
De Pere, WI	GB
De Queen, AR	LR
De Quincy, LA	LKC
De Ridder, LA	LKC
De Smet, SD	SFS
De Soto, MO	STL
WI	LC
De Witt, MI	LAN
Deadwood, SD	RC
Deal, NJ	TR
Dearborn, MI	DET
MI	ROM
MI	STN
Dearborn Heights, MI	DET
MI	STN
DeBary, FL	ORL
Decatur, AL	BIR
GA	ATL
IL	SFD
IN	FTW
MI	KAL
TX	FWT
Decherd, TN	NSH
Decorah, IA	DUB
Dededo, GU	AGN
Dedham, IA	SC
MA	BO
Deep River, CT	NOR
Deephaven, MN	STP
Deer Lodge, MT	HEL
Deer Park, NY	RVC
TX	GAL
WA	SPK
Deer River, MN	DUL
Deerfield, IL	CHI
KS	DOD
MI	LAN
MN	WIN
Deerfield Beach, FL	MIA
Deferiet, NY	OG
Defiance, IA	DM
OH	TOL
DeKalb, IL	RCK
Del Mar, CA	SD
Del Norte, CO	PBL
Del Rey, CA	FRS
Del Rio, TX	SAT
Delair, NJ	CAM
Delancey, PA	E
Delano, CA	FRS
MN	STP
Delanson, NY	ALB
Delavan, IL	PEO
MN	WIN
WI	MIL
Delaware, OH	COL
Delaware City, DE	WIL
Delcambre, LA	LAF
Delevan, NY	BUF
Delhi, IA	DUB
NY	ALB
Delia, KS	KCK
DeLisle, MS	BLX
Dell Rapids, SD	SFS
Delmar, IA	DAV
NY	ALB
Delmont, PA	GBG
Delphi, IN	LFT
PA	PH
Delphos, KS	SAL
OH	TOL
Delran, NJ	TR
Delray Beach, FL	NTN
FL	PMB
Delta, CO	PBL
Delta Junction, AK	FBK
Delton, MI	KAL
Deltona, FL	ORL
Demarest, NJ	NEW
Deming, NM	LSC
Demopolis, AL	BIR
Denham Springs, LA	BR
Denison, IA	SC
TX	DAL
Denmark, WI	GB
Dennison, OH	COL
Densmore, KS	SAL
Dent, MN	SCL
Denton, NE	LIN
TX	FWT
Denver, CO	DEN
CO	OLL
CO	STN
CO	VNN
Denver City, TX	LUB
Denville, NJ	PAT
Depew, NY	BUF
Deposit, NY	SY
Deptford, NJ	CAM
Depue, IL	PEO
Derby, CT	HRT
KS	WCH
NY	BUF
Derby Line, VT	BUR
Derry, NH	MAN
PA	GBG
Derwood, MD	WDC
Des Allemands, LA	NO
Des Moines, IA	DM
WA	SEA
Des Peres, MO	STL
Des Plaines, IL	CHI
Descanso, CA	SD
Desert Hot Springs, CA	SB
Deshler, OH	TOL
DeSmet, ID	B
Desoto, TX	DAL
Destin, FL	PT
Destrehan, LA	NO
DeTour, MI	MAR
Detroit, MI	ARM
MI	DET
MI	EST
MI	OLL
MI	PRM
MI	ROM
MI	STN
Detroit Lakes, MN	CR
Deville, LA	ALX
Devils Lake, ND	FAR
Devine, TX	SAT
Devon, PA	PH
Dewey, OK	TLS
DeWitt, IA	DAV
Dewitt, NY	SY
Dexter, ME	PRT
MI	LAN
MO	SPC
NM	LSC
Diamond, LA	NO
Diamond Bar, CA	LA
Diboll, TX	TYL
Dickey, ND	FAR
Dickeyville, WI	MAD
Dickinson, ND	BIS
TX	GAL
Dickson, TN	NSH
Dickson City, PA	SCR
Dieterich, IL	SFD
Dighton, KS	DOD
MA	FR
Dike, IA	DUB
Dilley, TX	SAT
Dillingham, AK	ANC
Dillon, MT	HEL
SC	CHR
Dillonvale, OH	STU
Dilly, WI	LC
Dilworth, MN	CR
Dime Box, TX	AUS
Dimmitt, TX	AMA
Dimock, SD	SFS
Dimondale, MI	LAN
Dinuba, CA	FRS
Dinwiddie County, VA	RIC
Dittmer, MO	STL
Divernon, IL	SFD
Dix Hills, NY	RVC
Dixon, CA	SAC
IL	RCK
MO	JC
NM	SFE
Dobbs Ferry, NY	NY
Dobie, WI	SUP
Dodge, NE	OM
Dodge Center, MN	WIN
Dodge City, KS	DOD
Dodgeville, IA	DAV
WI	MAD
Dodson Prairie, TX	FWT
Doland, SD	SFS
Dolgeville, NY	ALB
Dolton, IL	CHI
Dominican Republic, VA	ARL
Dona Ana, NM	LSC
Donaldson, IN	FTW
Donaldsonville, LA	BR
Donegal, PA	GBG
Doniphan, KS	KCK
MO	SPC
NE	LIN
Donna, TX	BWN
Donnelly, MN	SCL
Donora, PA	PBR
PA	PIT
Dorado, PR	SJN
Dorchester, IA	DUB
MA	BO
WI	LC
Dorothy, MN	CR
Dorr, MI	KAL
Dorrance, KS	SAL
PA	SCR
Dorville, GA	ATL
Dos Palos, CA	FRS
Dothan, AL	MOB
Dotyville, WI	MIL
Dougherty, IA	DUB
Douglas, AZ	TUC
GA	SAV
MI	KAL
WY	CHY
Douglas Co., NE	OM
Douglaston, NY	BRK
Douglasville, GA	ATL
Dousman, WI	MIL
Dover, DE	WIL
IN	IND
MA	BO
NH	MAN
NH	SAM
NJ	PAT
OH	COL
TN	NSH
Dover Plains, NY	NY
Dover-Foxcroft, ME	PRT
Dow City, IA	SC
Dowagiac, MI	KAL
Downers Grove, IL	JOL
Downey, CA	LA
Downieville, CA	SAC
Downingtown, PA	PH
Downs, IL	PEO
KS	SAL
Doylesburg, PA	HBG
Doylestown, OH	CLV
PA	PH
PA	PSC
WI	MAD
Dracut, MA	BO
Drake, ND	FAR
Drayton, ND	FAR
Dresden, OH	COL
Drexel Hill, PA	PH
Dripping Springs, TX	AUS
Drummond, MT	HEL
Drums, PA	SCR
Dryden, MI	DET
NY	ROC
Drywood, WI	LC
Du Bois, PA	E
PA	PBR
Du Quoin, IL	BEL
Duarte, CA	LA
Dublin, CA	OAK
GA	SAV
OH	COL
TX	FWT
Dublon, FM	CI
Dubois, IL	BEL
IN	EVN
Dubuque, IA	DUB
KS	DOD
Dudley, MA	WOR
PA	ALT
Due West, SC	CHR
Duelm, MN	SCL
Dufur, OR	BAK
Duluth, GA	ATL
MN	DUL
Dumas, TX	AMA
Dumont, IA	DUB
MN	SCL
NJ	NEW
Dunbar, PA	GBG
WV	WH
Duncan, IA	DUB
NE	OM
OK	OKL
SD	SFS

Duncan Mills, CA	SR
Duncansville, PA	ALT
Duncanville, TX	DAL
Duncombe, IA	SC
Dundee, IL	RCK
MI	DET
MN	WIN
Dunedin, FL	SP
Dunellen, NJ	MET
NJ	PSC
Dungannon, OH	Y
Dunkirk, IN	LFT
MD	BAL
MD	WDC
NY	BUF
Dunlap, IA	DM
IL	PEO
Dunlo, PA	ALT
PA	PBR
Dunmore, PA	PSC
PA	SCR
Dunn, NC	R
Dunnellon, FL	ORL
Dunnington, IN	LFT
Dunseith, ND	FAR
Dunsmuir, CA	SAC
Dunwoody, GA	ATL
Dupo, IL	BEL
Dupont, LA	ALX
PA	SCR
Duquesne, PA	PBR
PA	PIT
Duralde, LA	LAF
Durand, IL	RCK
MI	LAN
WI	LC
Durango, CO	PBL
Durant, OK	TLS
Durham, CT	NOR
NC	R
NH	MAN
Durhamville, NY	SY
Durward's Glen, WI	MAD
Duryea, PA	SCR
Dushore, PA	SCR
Duson, LA	LAF
Dutton, MT	HEL
Dutzow, MO	STL
Duxbury, MA	BO
Dwight, IL	PEO
NE	LIN
Dyckesville, WI	GB
Dyer, IN	GRY
Dyersburg, TN	MEM
Dyersville, IA	DUB
Dysart, IA	DUB
Eagan, MN	STP
Eagle, CO	DEN
ID	B
WI	MIL
Eagle Butte, SD	RC
Eagle Center, IA	DUB
Eagle Grove, IA	DUB
Eagle Lake, ME	PRT
TX	VIC
Eagle Pass, TX	SAT
Eagle River, AK	ANC
WI	SUP
Eagle Township, IL	PEO
Earl Park, IN	LFT
Earlimart, CA	FRS
Earling, IA	DM
Earlington, KY	OWN
Earlville, IA	DUB
IL	PEO
Early, IA	SC
Earth City, MO	STL
East Alton, IL	SFD
East Arcade, NY	BUF
East Aurora, NY	BUF
East Bay, NY	ROC
East Berlin, CT	HRT
East Bernard, TX	VIC
East Bethany, NY	BUF
East Bloomfield, NY	ROC
East Boston, MA	BO
East Brady, PA	E
East Bridgewater, MA	BO
East Bristol, WI	MAD
East Brookfield, MA	WOR
East Brunswick, NJ	MET
NJ	PSC
East Carbon, UT	SLC
East Carbon City, UT	SLC
East Chain, MN	WIN
East Chicago, IN	GRY
IN	PRM
IN	ROM
East Cleveland, OH	CLV
East Dorset, VT	BUR
East Douglas, MA	WOR
East Dubuque, IL	RCK
East Eden, NY	BUF
East Elmhurst, NY	BRK
East Falmouth, MA	FR
East Freetown, MA	FR
East Gary, IN	GRY
East Goshen, PA	PH
East Grand Forks, MN	CR
East Greenbush, NY	ALB
East Greenville, PA	PH
East Greenwich, RI	PRO
East Hampton, CT	NOR
NY	RVC
East Hanover, NJ	NEW
NJ	PAT
East Hartford, CT	HRT
East Haven, CT	HRT
East Helena, MT	HEL
East Islip, NY	RVC
East Jordan, MI	GAY
East Kingston, NY	NY
East Lansdowne, PA	PH
East Lansing, MI	LAN
East Liverpool, OH	Y
East Longmeadow, MA	SPR
East Lyme, CT	NOR
East McKeesport, PA	PIT
East Meadow, NY	RVC
East Millinocket, ME	PRT
East Millstone, NJ	MET
East Moline, IL	PEO
East Newark, NJ	NEW
East Northport, NY	RVC
East Orange, NJ	NEW
East Otto, NY	BUF
East Palestine, OH	Y
East Palo Alto, CA	SFR
East Patchogue, NY	RVC
East Pembroke, NY	BUF
East Peoria, IL	PEO
East Pittsburgh, PA	PBR
PA	PIT
East Pleasant Plain, IA	DAV
East Providence, RI	PRO
East Rochester, NY	ROC
East Rockaway, NY	RVC
East Rutherford, NJ	NEW
East St. Louis, IL	BEL
East Stroudsburg, PA	SCR
East Syracuse, NY	SY
East Taunton, MA	FR
East Tawas, MI	GAY
East Templeton, MA	WOR
East Troy, WI	MIL
East Vandergrift, PA	GBG
East Walpole, MA	BO
East Wenatchee, WA	YAK
East Windsor, CT	HRT
Easthampton, MA	SPR
Eastlake, OH	CLV
Eastland, TX	FWT
Eastman, WI	LC
Easton, CA	FRS
CT	BGP
KS	KCK
MD	WIL
MN	WIN
MO	KC
PA	ALN
PA	SAM
Eastpointe, MI	DET
Eastport, ME	PRT
NY	RVC
Eaton, OH	CIN
WI	GB
Eaton Rapids, MI	LAN
Eatonton, GA	ATL
Eatontown, NJ	TR
Eau Claire, WI	LC
Eau Galle, WI	LC
Ebensburg, PA	ALT
Ebeye, MH	MI
Echo, LA	ALX
Ecorse, MI	DET
Edcouch, TX	BWN
Eddystone, PA	PH
Eddyville, IA	DAV
KY	OWN
Eden, NC	CHL
NY	BUF
SD	SFS
TX	SAN
WI	MIL
Eden Prairie, MN	STP
Eden Valley, MN	NU
MN	SCL
Edenton, NC	R
Edgar, WI	LC
Edgard, LA	NO
Edgartown, MA	FR
Edgefield, SC	CHR
Edgeley, ND	FAR
Edgemont, SD	RC
Edgerton, KS	KCK
OH	TOL
WI	MAD
Edgewater, MD	BAL
NJ	NEW
Edgewood, IA	DUB
IL	SFD
KY	COV
MD	BAL
Edina, MN	STP
MO	JC
Edinboro, PA	E
Edinburg, TX	BWN
Edinburgh, IN	IND
Edison, NJ	MET
NJ	PSC
Edisto Beach, SC	CHR
Edmond, OK	OKL
Edmonds, WA	SEA
Edmonton, KY	L
Edmore, MI	GR
Edna, TX	VIC
Edson, WI	LC
Edwards, CO	DEN
NY	OG
Edwardsburg, MI	KAL
Edwardsville, IL	SFD
PA	PHU
PA	SCR
Effingham, IL	SFD
KS	KCK
Ege, IN	FTW
Egg Harbor, WI	GB
Egg Harbor City, NJ	CAM
Eggertsville, NY	BUF
Egypt, OH	CIN
Ehrenfeld, PA	ALT
El Cajon, CA	EST
CA	SD
El Campo, TX	VIC
El Centro, CA	SD
El Cerrito, CA	OAK
El Dorado, AR	LR
KS	WCH
El Dorado Hills, CA	SAC
El Dorado Springs, MO	SPC
El Mirage, AZ	PHX
El Monte, CA	LA
CA	OLL
El Paso, IL	PEO
TX	ELP
TX	OLL
El Reno, OK	OKL
El Rito, NM	SFE
El Segundo, CA	LA
CA	NTN
El Sobrante, CA	OAK
El Toro, CA	ORG
Eland, WI	GB
Elba, MN	WIN
NY	BUF
WI	MIL
Elberon, NJ	TR
Elberta, AL	MOB
Elbow Lake, MN	SCL
Elburn, IL	RCK
Elcho, WI	GB
Eldon, IA	DAV
MO	JC
Eldora, IA	DUB
Eldorado, IL	BEL
TX	SAN
WI	MIL
Eldred, PA	E
Eldridge, IA	DAV
Electra, TX	FWT
Elgin, IL	RCK
NE	OM
OR	BAK
TX	AUS
Elizabeth, IL	RCK
MN	SCL
NJ	NEW
NJ	PHU
NJ	PSC
PA	PIT
Elizabeth City, NC	R
Elizabethton, TN	KNX
Elizabethtown, IL	BEL
KY	L
NY	OG
PA	HBG
Elk, TX	AUS
Elk City, OK	OKL
Elk Grove, CA	SAC
Elk Grove Village, IL	CHI
Elk Mound, WI	LC
Elk Point, SD	SFS
Elk Rapids, MI	GAY
Elk River, MN	SCL
Elkader, IA	DUB
Elkhart, IA	DM
IL	PEO
IN	FTW
KS	DOD
Elkhart Lake, WI	MIL
Elkhorn, NE	OM
WI	MIL
Elkins, WV	WH
Elkins Park, PA	PH
Elkland, PA	SCR
Elko, NV	RNO
Elkton, FL	STA
KY	OWN
MD	WIL
SD	SFS
VA	RIC
Elkview, WV	WH
Ellenburg, NY	OG
Ellenburg Center, NY	OG
Ellendale, MN	WIN
ND	FAR
Ellengowan, PA	ALN
Ellensburg, WA	YAK
Ellenville, NY	NY
Ellicott City, MD	BAL
Ellicottville, NY	BUF
Ellington, CT	NOR
MO	SPC
Ellinwood, KS	DOD
Ellis, KS	SAL
Ellis Grove, IL	BEL
Ellisville, MO	STL
MS	BLX
Ellsworth, KS	SAL
ME	PRT
MN	WIN
PA	PIT
WI	LC
Ellwood City, PA	PIT
Elm Creek, NE	GI
Elm Grove, WI	MIL
Elma, IA	DUB
NY	BUF
WA	SEA
Elmdale, MN	SCL
Elmendorf, TX	SAT
Elmer, NJ	CAM
Elmhurst, IL	JOL
NY	BRK
PA	LIT
PA	SCR
Elmira, MI	GAY
NY	ROC
Elmira Heights, NY	ROC
NY	STF
Elmo, KS	SAL
Elmont, NY	RVC
Elmora, PA	ALT
Elmsford, NY	NY
Elmwood, IL	PEO
WI	LC
Elmwood Park, IL	CHI
NJ	NEW
Elon College, NC	R
Eloy, AZ	TUC
Elrama, PA	PIT
Elrosa, MN	SCL
Elroy, WI	LC
Elsa, TX	BWN
Elsberry, MO	STL
Elsmere, DE	WIL
Elton, LA	LKC
Eltopia, WA	SPK
Elverson, PA	PH
Elwood, IN	LFT
Ely, MN	DUL
NV	LAV
Elyria, NE	GI
OH	CLV
Elyria Township, OH	CLV
Elysburg, PA	HBG
Elysian, MN	STP
Emeigh, PA	ALT
Emerald, KS	KCK
Emerson, NE	OM
NJ	NEW
Emery, SD	SFS
Emeryville, CA	OAK
Emily, MN	DUL
Emlenton, PA	E
Emmaus, PA	ALN
Emmetsburg, IA	SC
Emmett, ID	B
KS	KCK
MI	DET
Emmitsburg, MD	BAL
Emmonak, AK	FBK
Empire, MI	GAY
Emporia, KS	KCK

VA	RIC
Emporium, PA	E
Emsworth, PA	PIT
Encinal, TX	CC
Encinitas, CA	SD
Encino, CA	LA
Enderlin, ND	FAR
Enders Island, CT	NOR
Endicott, NY	PSC
NY	SY
Endwell, NY	SY
Enfield, CT	HRT
IL	BEL
NH	MAN
Engadine, MI	MAR
Engelberg, AR	LR
Englewood, CO	DEN
FL	VEN
NJ	NEW
OH	CIN
Englewood Cliffs, NJ	NEW
Englishtown, NJ	TR
Enhaut, PA	HBG
Enid, OK	OKL
Eni-mwahn, FM	CI
Ennis, TX	DAL
Enochsburg, IN	IND
Enola, PA	HBG
Enosburg Falls, VT	BUR
Ensenada, PR	PCE
Enterprise, AL	MOB
OR	BAK
Enumclaw, WA	SEA
Ephraim, UT	SLC
Ephrata, PA	HBG
WA	YAK
Epiphany, SD	SFS
Epping, NH	MAN
Epworth, IA	DUB
Equality, IL	BEL
Erath, LA	LAF
Erie, CO	DEN
KS	WCH
MI	DET
PA	E
PA	PBR
Erin, WI	SUP
Erlanger, KY	COV
Ernest, PA	GBG
PA	PBR
Esbon, KS	SAL
Escalon, CA	STO
Escanaba, MI	MAR
Escobares, TX	BWN
Escondido, CA	SD
Eskridge, KS	KCK
Esmond, ND	FAR
Esopus, NY	NY
Espanola, NM	SFE
Essex, CT	NOR
MA	BO
NY	OG
Essex Center, VT	BUR
Essex Junction, VT	BUR
Essexville, MI	SAG
Essington, PA	PH
Estacada, OR	P
Estate Elizabeth, VI	STV
Estate Tutu, VI	STV
Estelline, SD	SFS
Estes Park, CO	DEN
Estherville, IA	SC
Ethan, SD	SFS
Etna, PA	PIT
Ettrick, WI	LC
Euclid, MN	CR
OH	CLV
OH	PRM
Eudora, KS	KCK
Eufaula, AL	MOB
Eugene, OR	P
Eunice, LA	LAF
Eureka, CA	SR
IL	PEO
KS	WCH
MO	STL
MT	HEL
NV	RNO
SD	SFS
UT	SLC
Eureka Springs, AR	LR
Eustis, FL	ORL
Eutaw, AL	BIR
Evangeline, LA	LAF
Evans City, PA	PIT
Evans Mills, NY	OG
Evansdale, IA	DUB
Evanston, IL	CHI
WY	CHY
Evansville, IL	BEL
IN	EVN
WI	MAD
Evart, MI	GR
Eveleth, MN	DUL
Everett, MA	BO
PA	ALT
WA	SEA
Evergreen, CO	DEN
LA	ALX
Evergreen Park, IL	CHI
Everson, PA	GBG
Evesham Township, NJ	TR
Ewa, HI	HON
Ewa Beach, HI	HON
Ewen, MI	MAR
Ewing, MO	JC
NE	OM
Excelsior Springs, MO	KC
Excelsior, Lake Minnetonka, MN	STP
Exeter, CA	FRS
NE	LIN
NH	MAN
PA	SCR
Exira, IA	DM
Export, PA	GBG
Exton, PA	PH
Eynon, PA	SCR
Eyota, MN	WIN
Fabens, TX	ELP
Fair Haven, NJ	TR
VT	BUR
Fair Lawn, NJ	NEW
Fair Oaks, CA	SAC
Fairbank, IA	DUB
Fairbanks, AK	FBK
Fairbault, MN	STP
Fairborn, OH	CIN
Fairburn, GA	ATL
Fairbury, IL	PEO
NE	LIN
Fairchance, PA	GBG
Fairchild, WI	LC
Fairdale, KY	L
Fairfax, CA	SFR
DE	WIL
IA	DUB
MN	NU
OK	TLS
SD	RC
VA	ARL
VT	BUR
Fairfield, AL	BIR
CA	SAC
CT	BGP
IA	DAV
IL	BEL
KY	L
ME	PRT
MT	HEL
ND	STN
NJ	NEW
OH	CIN
PA	HBG
TX	TYL
VT	BUR
Fairfield Bay, AR	LR
Fairfield Glade, TN	KNX
Fairhaven, MA	FR
Fairhope, AL	MOB
Fairlawn, OH	CLV
OH	OLL
Fairless Hills, PA	PH
Fairmont, MN	WIN
WV	WH
Fairmont City, IL	BEL
Fairmount, ND	FAR
NY	SY
Fairmount Springs, PA	SCR
Fairpoint, OH	STU
Fairport, NY	ROC
Fairport Harbor, OH	CLV
OH	PRM
Fairview, NJ	NEW
PA	E
TN	NSH
WI	LC
Fairview Heights, IL	BEL
Fairview Park, OH	CLV
OH	PRM
Faith, SD	RC
Fajardo, PR	CGS
Falconer, NY	BUF
Falfurrias, TX	CC
Fall Creek, WI	LC
Fall River, MA	FR
MA	SAM
MA	STF
Fallbrook, CA	SD
Fallentimber, PA	ALT
Fallon, NV	RNO
Falls, PA	SCR
Falls Church, VA	ARL
Falls City, NE	LIN
TX	SAT
Falls Creek, PA	E
Fallsington, PA	PH
Fallston, MD	BAL
Falmouth, KY	COV
MA	FR
ME	PRT
Falun, MN	CR
Fancher, WI	LC
Fancy Farm, KY	OWN
Fannett, TX	BEA
Far Hills, NJ	MET
Far Rockaway, NY	BRK
Fargo, ND	FAR
Faribault, MN	STP
Farley, IA	DUB
Farmer, SD	SFS
Farmer City, IL	PEO
Farmersville, CA	FRS
IL	SFD
Farming, MN	SCL
Farmingdale, NJ	TR
NY	BRK
NY	RVC
Farmington, CT	HRT
IA	DAV
IL	PEO
ME	PRT
MI	DET
MN	STP
MO	STL
NH	MAN
NM	GLP
PA	GBG
WI	MIL
WI	SUP
WV	WH
Farmington Hills, MI	DET
MI	OLD
Farmingville, NY	RVC
Farmville, NC	R
VA	RIC
Farnham, NY	BUF
Farrell, PA	E
Farwell, NE	GI
Fatima, OH	STU
Faulkner, MD	WDC
Faulkton, SD	SFS
Faxon Township, MN	NU
Fayette, AL	BIR
IA	DUB
MO	JC
MS	JKS
OH	TOL
Fayette City, PA	GBG
Fayetteville, AR	LR
GA	ATL
IL	BEL
NC	R
NC	SAM
NY	SY
OH	CIN
TN	NSH
TX	AUS
Feasterville, PA	PH
Federal Way, WA	SEA
Feeding Hills, MA	SPR
Fefan, FM	CI
Felicity, OH	CIN
Fellsmere, FL	PMB
Felton, CA	MRY
Fennimore, WI	MAD
Fenton, LA	LKC
MI	LAN
MO	STL
Ferdinand, ID	B
IN	EVN
Fergus Falls, MN	SCL
Ferguson, MO	STL
Fernandina Beach, FL	STA
Ferndale, CA	SR
MI	DET
WA	SEA
Fernley, NV	RNO
Ferriday, LA	ALX
Ferris, TX	DAL
Fertile, MN	CR
Fessenden, ND	FAR
Festina, IA	DUB
Festus, MO	STL
Fidelity, KS	KCK
Fieldon, IL	SFD
Fife Lake, MI	GAY
Fifield, WI	SUP
Fifth Ward, LA	ALX
Fillmore, CA	LA
IA	DUB
NY	BUF
Fincastle, VA	RIC
Findlay, OH	TOL
Fingal, ND	FAR
Finley, KY	L
ND	FAR
Finleyville, PA	PIT
Firebaugh, CA	FRS
Fish Creek, WI	GB
Fish Lake, IN	GRY
Fisher, MN	CR
Fishers, IN	LFT
Fishers Island, NY	NOR
Fisherville, MI	SAG
Fishkill, NY	NY
Fiskdale, MA	WOR
Fitchburg, MA	WOR
Flagler Beach, FL	STA
Flagstaff, AZ	PHX
Flaherty, KY	L
Flambeau, WI	SUP
Flanders, NJ	PAT
NJ	PSC
Flandreau, SD	SFS
Flasher, ND	BIS
Flat Rock, MI	DET
Flatonia, TX	VIC
Fleming, NY	ROC
Flemingsburg, KY	COV
Flemington, NJ	MET
Flensburg, MN	SCL
Flint, MI	LAN
MI	OLL
MI	STN
Flint Hill, MO	STL
Flintville, WI	GB
Floodwood, MN	DUL
Flora, IL	BEL
Flora Vista, NM	GLP
Floral Park, NY	RVC
Florence, AL	BIR
AZ	TUC
CO	PBL
KS	WCH
KY	COV
NJ	TR
NY	SY
OR	P
SC	CHR
SD	SFS
WI	GB
Floresville, TX	SAT
Florham Park, NJ	PAT
Florian, MN	CR
Florida, NY	NY
PR	ARE
Florissant, LA	NO
MO	STL
Flossmoor, IL	CHI
Flourtown, PA	PH
Floydada, TX	LUB
Flush, KS	KCK
Flushing, MI	LAN
MI	PRM
NY	BRK
OH	STU
Foley, AL	MOB
MN	SCL
Folk, MO	JC
Follansbee, WV	WH
Folsom, CA	SAC
LA	NO
PA	PH
Fond du Lac, WI	MIL
Fonda, IA	SC
NY	ALB
Fontana, CA	SB
CA	VNN
WI	MIL
Footedale, PA	GBG
Footville, WI	MAD
Forbes Road, PA	GBG
Force, PA	E
Ford, WA	SPK
Ford City, PA	GBG
PA	SJP
Fords, NJ	MET
Fordsville, KY	OWN
Fordyce, AR	LR
NE	OM
Forest, MS	JKS
Forest City, IA	DUB
MN	NU
NC	CHL
PA	PSC
PA	SCR
Forest Grove, OR	P
Forest Hill, LA	ALX
Forest Hills, NY	BRK
PA	PIT
Forest Lake, MN	STP
Forest Park, IL	CHI
Forestburgh, NY	NY
Foreston, MN	SCL

Forestport, NY	SY
Forestville, CT	HRT
MD	WDC
NY	BUF
Forked River, NJ	TR
Forks, WA	SEA
Forman, ND	FAR
Forney, TX	DAL
Forrest City, AR	LR
Forsyth, MO	SPC
MT	GF
Fort Ann, NY	ALB
Fort Ashby, WV	WH
Fort Atkinson, IA	DUB
WI	MAD
Fort Bend Co., TX	GAL
Fort Benton, MT	GF
Fort Berthold Reservation, ND	BIS
Fort Bragg, CA	SR
Fort Branch, IN	EVN
Fort Calhoun, NE	OM
Fort Collins, CO	DEN
Fort Covington, NY	OG
Fort Davis, TX	ELP
Fort Defiance, AZ	GLP
Fort Dodge, IA	SC
Fort Edward, NY	ALB
Fort Fairfield, ME	PRT
Fort Hancock, TX	ELP
Fort Jennings, OH	TOL
Fort Jones, CA	SAC
Fort Kent, ME	PRT
Fort Lauderdale, FL	MIA
Fort Leavenworth, KS	KCK
Fort Lee, NJ	NEW
Fort Loramie, OH	CIN
Fort Lupton, CO	DEN
Fort Madison, IA	DAV
Fort Mitchell, KY	COV
Fort Monroe, VA	RIC
Fort Morgan, CO	DEN
Fort Myers, FL	VEN
Fort Myers Beach, FL	VEN
Fort Oglethorpe, GA	ATL
Fort Pierce, FL	PMB
FL	PSC
Fort Pierre, SD	RC
Fort Plain, NY	ALB
Fort Recovery, OH	CIN
Fort Riley, KS	SAL
Fort Scott, KS	WCH
Fort Shaw, MT	GF
Fort Smith, AK	LR
AR	LR
Fort Stockton, TX	SAN
Fort Sumner, NM	SFE
Fort Thomas, KY	COV
Fort Thompson, SD	SFS
Fort Totten, ND	FAR
Fort Totten Reservation, ND	FAR
Fort Walton Beach, FL	PT
Fort Washington, MD	WDC
PA	PH
Fort Wayne, IN	FTW
Fort Wingate, NM	GLP
Fort Worth, TX	FWT
Fort Yates, ND	BIS
Fortuna, CA	SR
Fortville, IN	IND
Forty Fort, PA	SCR
Fosston, MN	CR
Foster, RI	PRO
Foster City, CA	SFR
Fostoria, OH	TOL
Fountain, CO	COS
FL	PT
MN	WIN
Fountain City, WI	LC
Fountain Hill, PA	ALN
Fountain Hills, AZ	PHX
Fountain Valley, CA	ORG
Four Corners, LA	LAF
Fowler, CA	FRS
IN	LFT
KS	DOD
MI	LAN
Fowlerville, MI	LAN
Fox Chase Manor, PA	PH
PA	PHU
Fox Lake, IL	CHI
WI	MIL
Fox Point, WI	MIL
Foxboro, MA	BO
Foxholm, ND	BIS
Foxhome, MN	SCL
Frackville, PA	ALN
PA	PHU
Framingham, MA	BO
Framingham Centre, MA	BO
Francesville, IN	LFT
Francis Creek, WI	GB
Frankenmuth, MI	SAG
Frankenstein, MO	JC
Frankfort, IL	JOL
IN	LFT
KS	KCK
KY	LEX
MI	GAY
NY	ALB
SD	SFS
Franklin, IL	SFD
IN	IND
KY	OWN
LA	LAF
MA	BO
MN	NU
NC	CHL
NH	MAN
NJ	PAT
OH	CIN
PA	E
TN	NSH
VA	RIC
WI	MIL
WV	WH
Franklin Lakes, NJ	NEW
Franklin Park, IL	CHI
Franklin Park Borough, PA	PIT
Franklin Square, NY	RVC
Franklinton, LA	NO
Franklinville, NJ	CAM
NY	BUF
Fraser, MI	DET
Frazee, MN	CR
Frederic, WI	SUP
Frederick, CO	DEN
MD	BAL
OK	OKL
Fredericksburg, TX	SAT
VA	ARL
Fredericktown, MO	SPC
PA	PIT
Frederiksted, VI	STV
Fredonia, KS	WCH
NY	BUF
WI	MIL
Free Soil, MI	GR
Freeburg, IL	BEL
MO	JC
Freedom, PA	PIT
WI	GB
Freehold, NJ	TR
Freeland, MI	SAG
PA	PSC
PA	SCR
Freeport, FL	PT
IL	RCK
MN	SCL
NY	RVC
OH	STU
PA	GBG
TX	GAL
Freer, TX	CC
Frelsburg, TX	VIC
Fremont, CA	NTN
CA	OAK
MI	GR
NE	OM
OH	TOL
Fremont Center, IL	CHI
French Creek, NY	BUF
French Lick, IN	IND
French Settlement, LA	BR
Frenchburg, KY	LEX
Frenchtown, IN	IND
MT	HEL
OH	CIN
OH	TOL
PA	E
Frenchville, ME	PRT
PA	E
Frenstat, TX	AUS
Fresh Meadows, NY	BRK
NY	STF
Fresno, CA	FRS
CA	VNN
Frewsburg, NY	BUF
Friday Harbor, WA	SEA
Fridley, MN	STP
Fried, ND	FAR
Friend, NE	LIN
Friendship, NY	BUF
Friendsville, PA	SCR
Friendswood, TX	GAL
Friona, TX	AMA
Front Royal, VA	ARL
VA	WDC
Frontenac, KS	WCH
MN	STP
MO	STL
Frostburg, MD	BAL
Fruita, CO	PBL
Fryburg, OH	CIN
PA	E
Frydek, TX	GAL
Fulda, IN	IND
MN	WIN
ND	FAR
OH	STU
Fullerton, CA	NTN
CA	OLL
CA	ORG
ND	FAR
NE	OM
Fulton, IL	RCK
KS	WCH
KY	OWN
MD	BAL
MO	JC
MS	JKS
NY	SY
Fuquay-Varina, NC	R
Gackle, ND	FAR
Gadsden, AL	BIR
Gaffney, SC	CHR
Gagetown, MI	SAG
Gagil, FM	CI
Gahanna, OH	COL
Gaines, MI	LAN
Gainesville, FL	STA
GA	ATL
TX	FWT
Gaithersburg, MD	WDC
Galena, AK	FBK
IL	RCK
KS	WCH
MD	WIL
Galena Park, TX	GAL
Gales Ferry, CT	NOR
Galesburg, IL	PEO
Galesville, WI	LC
Galeton, PA	E
Galion, OH	TOL
Gallatin, TN	NSH
Galliano, LA	HT
Gallipolis, OH	STU
Gallitzin, PA	ALT
Galloway, WI	LC
Gallup, NM	GLP
Galt, CA	SAC
Galva, IL	PEO
Galveston, TX	GAL
Ganado, AZ	GLP
TX	VIC
Gap, PA	PH
Garapan Village, District 11, MP	CHK
Garber, IA	DUB
Garberville, CA	SR
Garden, MI	MAR
Garden City, KS	DOD
MI	DET
NY	RVC
SC	CHR
Garden Grove, CA	ORG
Garden Plain, KS	WCH
Garden Valley, ID	B
Gardena, CA	LA
Gardendale, AL	BIR
Gardenville, MO	STL
Gardiner, ME	PRT
NY	NY
Gardner, CO	PBL
KS	KCK
MA	WOR
Gardnerville, NV	RNO
Garfield, NJ	NEW
NM	LSC
Garfield Heights, OH	CLV
Garfield Park, DE	WIL
Garland, TX	DAL
Garnavillo, IA	DUB
Garner, IA	DUB
NC	R
Garnerville, NY	NY
Garnett, KS	KCK
Garretson, SD	SFS
Garrett, IN	FTW
Garrett Park, MD	WDC
Garrettsville, OH	Y
Garrison, MN	DUL
ND	BIS
NY	NY
Garryowen, IA	DUB
SD	SFS
Garwin, IA	DUB
Garwood, NJ	NEW
Gary, IN	GRY
SD	SFS
WV	WH
Gary-New Duluth, MN	DUL
Garyville, LA	NO
Gas City, IN	LFT
Gasport, NY	BUF
Gassaway, WV	WH
Gastonia, NC	CHL
Gate City, VA	RIC
Gates Mills, OH	CLV
Gatesville, TX	AUS
Gatlinburg, TN	KNX
Gautier, MS	BLX
Gaylord, MI	GAY
MN	NU
Gays Mills, WI	LC
Geddes, SD	SFS
Genesee, ID	B
Genesee Depot, WI	MIL
Geneseo, IL	PEO
ND	FAR
NY	ROC
Geneva, IA	DUB
IL	RCK
IN	FTW
MN	WIN
NE	LIN
NY	ROC
OH	Y
Genoa, IL	RCK
NE	OM
OH	TOL
WI	LC
Gentilly, MN	CR
George West, TX	CC
Georgetown, CA	SAC
CT	BGP
DE	WIL
IA	DAV
IL	PEO
KY	LEX
MA	BO
MN	CR
OH	CIN
SC	CHR
TX	AUS
WI	SUP
Georgiaville, RI	PRO
Gering, NE	GI
Germantown, IL	BEL
MD	WDC
NY	ALB
OH	CIN
TN	MEM
WI	LC
WI	MIL
Gervais, OR	P
Gettysburg, PA	HBG
SD	SFS
Getzville, NY	BUF
Gheens, LA	HT
Ghent, MN	NU
WV	WH
Gibbon, MN	NU
Gibbsboro, NJ	CAM
Gibbstown, NJ	CAM
Gibraltar, MI	DET
Gibson, LA	HT
Gibson City, IL	JOL
Gibsonburg, OH	TOL
Gibsonia, PA	PIT
Giddings, TX	AUS
Gig Harbor, WA	SEA
Gila Bend, AZ	PHX
Gilbert, AZ	PHX
AZ	VNN
IA	DUB
MN	DUL
Gilbertville, IA	DUB
MA	WOR
Gildehaus, MO	STL
Gilford, NH	MAN
Gillespie, IL	SFD
Gillett, WI	GB
Gillette, WY	CHY
Gills Pier, MI	GAY
Gilman, IL	JOL
MN	SCL
VT	BUR
WI	SUP
Gilmanton Iron Works, NH	MAN
Gilmore City, IA	SC
Gilroy, CA	SJ
Girard, IL	SFD
KS	WCH
OH	Y
PA	E
PA	PBR
Girardville, PA	ALN
Glade Mills, PA	PIT
Gladstone, MI	MAR
MO	KC
NJ	PAT
Gladwin, MI	SAG
Gladwyne, PA	PH
Glandorf, OH	TOL
Glasco, KS	SAL

NY	NY
Glasgow, KY	L
MO	JC
MT	GF
Glasgow Village, MO	STL
Glassboro, NJ	CAM
Glassport, PA	PIT
Glastonbury, CT	HRT
CT	STF
Glen Allen, VA	RIC
Glen Burnie, MD	BAL
Glen Campbell, PA	GBG
Glen Carbon, IL	SFD
Glen Cove, NY	RVC
NY	STF
Glen Dale, WV	WH
Glen Ellyn, IL	JOL
Glen Falls, NY	ALB
Glen Head, NY	RVC
Glen Lyon, PA	PHU
PA	SCR
Glen Owen, MO	STL
Glen Rock, NJ	NEW
Glen Rose, TX	FWT
Glen Spey, NY	STF
Glen Ullin, ND	BIS
Glenbeulah, WI	MIL
Glenburn, ND	BIS
Glencoe, MN	NU
MO	STL
Glendale, AZ	PHX
CA	ARM
CA	LA
CO	DEN
NY	BRK
Glendale Heights, IL	JOL
Glendive, MT	GF
Glendora, CA	LA
Glenfield, NY	OG
Glenmoore, PA	PH
Glenmora, LA	ALX
Glenmore, WI	GB
Glennallen, AK	ANC
Glennie, MI	GAY
Glennonville, MO	SPC
Glenns Ferry, ID	B
Glenolden, PA	PH
Glenrock, WY	CHY
Glens Falls, NY	ALB
Glenshaw, PA	PIT
Glenside, PA	PH
Glenview, IL	CHI
Glenville, NY	ALB
WV	WH
Glenwood, IA	DM
IL	CHI
MN	SCL
Glenwood City, WI	SUP
Glenwood Springs, CO	DEN
Glidden, WI	SUP
Globe, AZ	TUC
Gloucester, MA	BO
NJ	CAM
VA	RIC
Glouster, OH	STU
Gloversville, NY	ALB
Gloverville, SC	CHR
Glyndon, MD	BAL
Glynwood, OH	CIN
GMF, GU	AGN
Gobles, MI	KAL
Godfrey, IL	SFD
Goetzville, MI	MAR
Goffstown, NH	MAN
Gold Hill, OR	P
Golden, CO	DEN
Golden Gate, FL	VEN
Golden Meadow, LA	HT
Golden Valley, MN	STP
Goldendale, WA	YAK
Goldenrod, FL	ORL
Goldsboro, NC	R
Goldthwaite, TX	AUS
Goleta, CA	LA
Goliad, TX	VIC
Gonic, NH	MAN
Gonzales, CA	MRY
LA	BR
TX	SAT
Good Hart, MI	GAY
Good Thunder, MN	WIN
Gooding, ID	B
Goodland, IN	LFT
KS	SAL
Goodman, WI	GB
Goodrich, IL	JOL
MI	LAN
Goodridge, MN	CR
Goodyear, AZ	PHX
Goose Creek, SC	CHR
Gordon, NE	GI
PA	ALN
WI	SUP
Gordonsville, VA	ARL
Gorham, KS	SAL
ME	PRT
NH	MAN
Goshen, CA	FRS
CT	HRT
IN	FTW
KY	L
MA	SPR
NY	NY
Gouldsboro, PA	SCR
Gouverneur, NY	OG
Gowanda, NY	BUF
Graceville, MN	NU
Graettinger, IA	SC
Graford, TX	FWT
Grafton, IL	SFD
MA	WOR
ND	FAR
NE	LIN
NY	ALB
OH	CLV
WI	MIL
WV	WH
Graham, TX	FWT
Grainfield, KS	SAL
Grambling, LA	SHP
Gramercy, LA	BR
Grampian, PA	E
Granada Hills, CA	LA
Granbury, TX	FWT
Granby, CT	HRT
MA	SPR
Grand Bay, AL	MOB
Grand Blanc, MI	LAN
Grand Caillou, LA	HT
Grand Canyon, AZ	PHX
Grand Chain, IL	BEL
Grand Chenier, LA	LKC
Grand Coteau, LA	LAF
Grand Coulee, WA	YAK
Grand Forks, ND	FAR
Grand Haven, MI	GR
Grand Island, NE	GI
NY	BUF
Grand Isle, LA	HT
ME	PRT
Grand Junction, CO	PBL
IA	SC
Grand Lake, CO	DEN
Grand Ledge, MI	LAN
Grand Marais, MI	MAR
MN	DUL
Grand Meadow, MN	WIN
Grand Mound, IA	DAV
Grand Prairie, LA	LAF
TX	DAL
Grand Rapids, MI	GR
MI	STN
MN	DUL
Grand River, IA	DM
Grand Rivers, KY	OWN
Grand Ronde, OR	P
Grand Terrace, CA	SB
Grandview, ID	B
MO	KC
WA	YAK
Grandville, MI	GR
Granger, IA	DM
IN	FTW
TX	AUS
WA	YAK
Grangeville, ID	B
Granite City, IL	SFD
Granite Falls, MN	NU
Graniteville, VT	BUR
Grant, NE	LIN
Grant Town, WV	WH
Grantfork, IL	SFD
Grants, NM	GLP
Grants Pass, OR	P
Grantsburg, WI	SUP
Grants-Milan, NM	GLP
Grantsville, MD	BAL
Grantwood, MO	STL
Granville, IA	SC
IL	PEO
ND	FAR
NY	ALB
NY	PSC
OH	COL
Grapevine, TX	FWT
Grass Lake, MI	LAN
Grass Valley, CA	SAC
Gratiot, WI	MAD
Gray, ME	PRT
Grayling, MI	GAY
Graymoor, NY	NY
Grayslake, IL	CHI
Grayson, KY	LEX
Grayson Springs, KY	OWN
Great Barrington, MA	SPR
Great Bend, KS	DOD
PA	SCR
Great Falls, MT	GF
VA	ARL
Great Meadows, NJ	MET
NJ	PHU
Great Mills, MD	WDC
Great Neck, NY	RVC
Greater Cincinnati, OH	CIN
Greeley, CO	DEN
IA	DUB
KS	KCK
NE	GI
Green, OH	CLV
Green Bay, WI	GB
Green Cove Springs, FL	STA
Green Creek, IL	SFD
Green Island, NY	ALB
Green Isle, MN	NU
Green Lake, WI	MAD
Green Pond, NJ	PAT
Green River, WY	CHY
Green Springs, OH	TOL
Green Tree, PA	PIT
Green Valley, AZ	TUC
MN	NU
Greenbelt, MD	WDC
Greenbrae, CA	SFR
Greenburgh, NY	NY
Greenbush, KS	WCH
MN	CR
Greencastle, IN	IND
PA	HBG
Greencreek, ID	B
Greendale, WI	MIL
Greene, IA	DUB
NY	SY
Greeneville, TN	KNX
Greenfield, CA	MRY
IA	DM
IL	SFD
IN	IND
MA	SPR
OH	CIN
WI	MIL
Greenfield Center, NY	ALB
Greenlawn, NY	RVC
Greenleaf, KS	SAL
MN	NU
WI	GB
Greenport, NY	RVC
Greensboro, GA	ATL
NC	CHL
Greensboro Bend, VT	BUR
Greensburg, IN	IND
KS	DOD
KY	L
PA	GBG
PA	PBR
Greenup, IL	SFD
Greenville, AL	MOB
DE	WIL
IL	SFD
ME	PRT
MI	GR
MS	JKS
NC	R
NH	MAN
NY	ALB
OH	CIN
PA	E
RI	PRO
SC	CHR
TX	DAL
WI	GB
Greenwald, MN	SCL
Greenwell Springs, LA	BR
Greenwich, CT	BGP
NY	ALB
Greenwood, IN	IND
MS	JKS
SC	CHR
WI	LC
Greenwood Lake, NY	NY
Greer, SC	CHR
Gregory, SD	RC
TX	CC
Grenada, MS	JKS
Grenora, ND	BIS
Grenville, SD	SFS
Gresham, OR	P
WI	GB
Gretna, LA	NO
NE	OM
Grey Eagle, MN	SCL
Greybull, WY	CHY
Gridley, CA	SAC
Griffin, GA	ATL
Griffith, IN	GRY
Griggsville, IL	SFD
Grindstone, PA	GBG
Grinnell, IA	DAV
KS	SAL
Griswold, IA	DM
Groom, TX	AMA
Grosse Ile, MI	DET
Grosse Pointe, MI	DET
Grosse Pointe Farms, MI	DET
Grosse Pointe Park, MI	DET
Grosse Tete, LA	BR
Groton, CT	NOR
MA	BO
NY	ROC
SD	SFS
Grove, OK	TLS
Grove City, FL	VEN
OH	COL
PA	E
Grove Hill, AL	MOB
Groveland, MA	BO
Groveport, OH	COL
Grover, SD	SFS
Groves, TX	BEA
Groveton, NH	MAN
Grulla, TX	BWN
Grundy Center, IA	DUB
Gruver, TX	AMA
Grygla, MN	CR
Guadalupe, AZ	PHX
CA	LA
Guanica, PR	PCE
Guasti, CA	SB
Guayama, PR	PCE
Guayanilla, PR	PCE
Guaynabo, PR	SJN
Guckeen, MN	WIN
Guerneville, CA	SR
Guernsey, WY	CHY
Gueydan, LA	LAF
Guilderland, NY	ALB
Guilford, CT	HRT
Gulf Breeze, FL	PT
Gulf Shores, AL	MOB
Gulfport, FL	SP
MS	BLX
Gull Lake, MI	KAL
Gun Barrel City, TX	TYL
Gunnison, CO	PBL
Guntersville, AL	BIR
Gurabo, PR	CGS
Gurnee, IL	CHI
Gustine, CA	FRS
Guthrie, KY	OWN
OK	OKL
Guthrie Center, IA	DM
Guttenberg, IA	DUB
NJ	NEW
Guymon, OK	OKL
Gwinn, MI	MAR
Gwinner, ND	FAR
Gwynedd Valley, PA	PH
Gypsum, KS	SAL
Hacienda Heights, CA	LA
Hackberry, LA	LKC
Hackensack, NJ	NEW
Hackettstown, NJ	MET
Haddon Heights, NJ	CAM
Haddon Township, NJ	CAM
Haddonfield, NJ	CAM
Hadley, MA	SPR
Hagaman, IL	SFD
NY	ALB
Hagerman, ID	B
Hagerstown, MD	BAL
Hague, ND	BIS
NY	ALB
Hahnville, LA	NO
Haiku, HI	HON
Hailey, ID	B
Haines, AK	JUN
Haines City, FL	ORL
Haines Falls, NY	ALB
Hainesport, NJ	TR
Hainesville, NJ	PAT
Halbur, IA	SC
Halder, WI	LC
Hale, MI	GAY
Hale Center, TX	LUB
Haledon, NJ	PAT
Hales Corners, WI	MIL
Half Moon Bay, CA	SFR
Halifax, MA	BO
Hallandale, FL	MIA
Hallettsville, TX	VIC
Halliday, ND	BIS
Hallock, MN	CR
Hallowell, ME	PRT
Halstad, MN	CR
Halstead, KS	WCH

Ham Lake, MN	STP
Hamburg, AR	LR
IA	DM
IN	IND
MI	LAN
NJ	PAT
NY	BUF
PA	ALN
Hamden, CT	HRT
Hamel, MN	STP
Hamilton, AL	BIR
GA	SAV
KS	WCH
MA	BO
MO	KC
MT	HEL
NY	SY
OH	CIN
TX	AUS
Hamilton Square, NJ	TR
Hamler, OH	TOL
Hamlet, IN	GRY
NC	CHL
Hamlin, ME	PRT
NY	ROC
Hammond, IN	GRY
IN	NTN
LA	BR
MN	WIN
NY	OG
WI	SUP
Hammondsport, NY	ROC
Hammondsville, OH	STU
Hammonton, NJ	CAM
Hampden, MA	SPR
ME	PRT
Hampshire, IL	RCK
Hampstead, NC	R
NH	MAN
Hampton, CT	NOR
IA	DUB
MN	STP
NH	MAN
NJ	MET
VA	RIC
Hampton Bays, NY	RVC
Hampton Beach, NH	MAN
Hamptonburgh, NY	STF
Hamptonville, NC	CHL
Hamtramck, MI	DET
MI	STN
Hana, HI	HON
Hancock, MD	BAL
MI	MAR
NY	ALB
Hancock Township, MN	STP
Hanford, CA	FRS
Hankinson, ND	FAR
Hannah, MI	GAY
Hannastown, PA	PBR
Hannibal, MO	JC
NY	SY
Hanover, IA	DUB
IL	RCK
KS	SAL
MA	BO
NH	MAN
PA	HBG
Hanover Park, IL	CHI
Hansboro, ND	FAR
Hanson, MA	BO
Hanston, KS	DOD
Hapeville, GA	ATL
Happy, TX	AMA
Harahan, LA	NO
Harbor Beach, MI	SAG
Harbor Springs, MI	GAY
Harborcreek, PA	E
Hardin, IL	SFD
MT	GF
Harding, MN	SCL
PA	SCR
Hardinsburg, KY	OWN
Hardwick, VT	BUR
Harietta, MI	GAY
Harker Heights, TX	AUS
Harlan, IA	DM
KY	LEX
Harleigh, PA	SCR
Harlingen, TX	BWN
Harlowton, MT	HEL
Harmarville, PA	PIT
Harmon, IL	RCK
Harmony, MN	WIN
Harper, IA	DAV
KS	WCH
TX	SAT
rper Woods, MI	DET
pers Ferry, IA	DUB
VV	WH
h, OK	OKL
Harriettsville, OH	STU
Harriman, NY	NY
TN	KNX
Harrington, WA	SPK
Harrington Park, NJ	NEW
Harris Hill, NY	BUF
Harrisburg, IL	BEL
PA	HBG
PA	PSC
Harrison, AR	LR
MI	SAG
NJ	NEW
NY	NY
WI	SUP
Harrison City, PA	GBG
Harrison Twp., MI	DET
Harrisonburg, VA	RIC
Harrisonville, MO	KC
Harrisville, MI	GAY
NH	MAN
NY	OG
RI	PRO
WV	WH
Harrodsburg, KY	LEX
Harrold, SD	SFS
Harsens Island, MI	DET
Hart, MI	GR
Hartford, AR	LR
CT	HRT
CT	STF
KS	KCK
KY	OWN
MI	KAL
SD	SFS
WI	MIL
Hartford City, IN	LFT
Hartington, NE	OM
Hartland, IL	RCK
MI	LAN
WI	MIL
Hartline, WA	YAK
Hartsdale, NY	NY
Hartshorne, OK	TLS
Hartsville, SC	CHR
Hartwell, GA	ATL
Harvard, IL	RCK
MA	WOR
NE	LIN
Harvey, IL	CHI
LA	NO
ND	FAR
Harvey Cedars, NJ	TR
Harveys Lake, PA	SCR
Harwick, PA	PIT
Harwinton, CT	HRT
Harwood Heights, IL	CHI
Hasbrouck Heights, NJ	NEW
Haskell, NJ	PAT
Hassan Township, MN	STP
Hastings, MI	KAL
MN	STP
NE	LIN
PA	ALT
Hastings-on-Hudson, NY	NY
Hatboro, PA	PH
Hatch, NM	LSC
Hatfield, MA	SPR
PA	PH
Hathaway Manor, MO	STL
Hatillo, PR	ARE
Hatley, WI	LC
Hato Rey, PR	SJN
Hattiesburg, MS	BLX
Haubstadt, IN	EVN
Haugen, WI	SUP
Hauppauge, NY	RVC
Havana, IL	PEO
Havelock, NC	R
Haverford, PA	PH
Haverhill, IA	DUB
MA	BO
Haverstraw, NY	NY
Havertown, PA	PH
Havre, MT	GF
Havre de Grace, MD	BAL
Hawaiian Gardens, CA	LA
Hawarden, IA	SC
Hawesville, KY	OWN
Hawi, HI	HON
Hawk Point, MO	STL
Hawk Run, PA	PBR
Hawkeye, IA	DUB
Hawkins, WI	SUP
Hawley, MN	CR
PA	SCR
Haworth, NJ	NEW
Hawthorne, CA	LA
NJ	PAT
NV	RNO
NY	NY
Hayden, AZ	TUC
Haydenville, MA	SPR
Hayesville, NC	CHL
Hayfield, MN	WIN
Hayneville, AL	MOB
Hays, KS	SAL
MT	GF
Haysville, KS	WCH
Hayward, CA	OAK
WI	SUP
Hazard, KY	LEX
Hazel Crest, IL	CHI
Hazel Green, WI	MAD
Hazel Park, MI	DET
Hazelton, ND	BIS
Hazelwood, MN	STP
MO	STL
Hazen, ND	BIS
Hazlehurst, GA	SAV
Hazlet, NJ	TR
Hazleton, IA	DUB
PA	PHU
PA	PSC
PA	SCR
Healdsburg, CA	SR
Healy, AK	FBK
Hearne, TX	AUS
Heart Butte, MT	HEL
Heath, OH	COL
Hebbronville, TX	CC
Hebron, CT	NOR
IN	GRY
ND	BIS
NE	LIN
Hecker, IL	BEL
Heckscherville, PA	ALN
Hecla, SD	SFS
Hector, MN	NU
Heffron, WI	LC
Hegbert, MN	NU
Heidelberg, MN	STP
Heilwood, PA	GBG
Helena, AR	LR
MI	SAG
MT	HEL
Helenwood, TN	KNX
Hellertown, PA	ALN
Helmetta, NJ	MET
Helmville, MT	HEL
Helotes, TX	SAT
Helper, UT	SLC
Hemet, CA	SB
Hemingford, NE	GI
Hemlock, MI	SAG
Hempstead, NY	RVC
NY	STF
TX	GAL
Henderson, KY	OWN
LA	LAF
MN	NU
NC	R
NV	LAV
TX	TYL
Hendersonville, NC	CHL
TN	NSH
Hennepin, IL	PEO
Hennessey, OK	OKL
Henniker, NH	MAN
Henning, MN	SCL
Henrietta, NY	ROC
TX	FWT
Henry, IL	PEO
LA	LAF
SD	SFS
Henryetta, OK	TLS
Henryville, IN	IND
Henshaw, KY	OWN
Heppner, OR	BAK
Herculaneum, MO	STL
Hereford, TX	AMA
Herington, KS	SAL
Herkimer, NY	ALB
Herman, MN	SCL
PA	PIT
Hermann, MO	JC
Hermansville, MI	MAR
Herminie, PA	GBG
PA	PBR
Hermiston, OR	BAK
Hermitage, MO	JC
PA	E
PA	PBR
Hermosa, SD	RC
Hermosa Beach, CA	LA
Hernando, MS	JKS
Herndon, KS	SAL
VA	ARL
Heron Bay, AL	MOB
Heron Lake, MN	WIN
Herreid, SD	SFS
Herrin, IL	BEL
Herron, MI	GAY
Herscher, IL	JOL
Hershey, PA	HBG
Hesperia, CA	SB
Hessen Cassel, IN	FTW
Hessmer, LA	ALX
Hettinger, ND	BIS
Heun, NE	OM
Heuvelton, NY	OG
Hewitt, NJ	PAT
WI	LC
Hewlett, NY	RVC
Hialeah, FL	MIA
Hialeah Gardens, FL	MIA
Hiawatha, IA	DUB
KS	KCK
Hibbing, MN	DUL
Hickman, KY	OWN
Hickory, MD	BAL
NC	CHL
Hickory Hills, IL	CHI
Hicksville, NY	RVC
OH	TOL
Hidalgo, TX	BWN
Higganum, CT	NOR
Higgins Lake, MI	GAY
Higginsville, MO	KC
High Bridge, NJ	MET
High Hill, TX	VIC
High Point, NC	CHL
High Ridge, MO	STL
High Springs, FL	STA
Highbridge, WI	SUP
Highgate Center, VT	BUR
Highland, CA	SB
IL	SFD
IN	GRY
MI	DET
NY	NY
WI	MAD
Highland Beach, FL	PMB
Highland Falls, NY	NY
Highland Heights, KY	COV
OH	CLV
Highland Lakes, NJ	PAT
Highland Mills, NY	NY
Highland Park, IL	CHI
MI	DET
NJ	MET
PA	PH
Highland Springs, VA	RIC
Highlands, NJ	TR
TX	GAL
Highlands Ranch, CO	COS
Highmore, SD	SFS
Hightstown, NJ	TR
Highwood, IL	CHI
Hilbert, WI	GB
Hill City, KS	SAL
MN	DUL
SD	RC
Hillcrest Heights, MD	WDC
Hilliard, OH	COL
Hillje, TX	VIC
Hillman, MI	GAY
MN	DUL
MN	SCL
Hills, IA	DAV
Hillsboro, IL	SFD
MO	STL
ND	FAR
OH	CIN
OR	P
TX	FWT
WI	LC
Hillsborough, NC	R
NH	MAN
NJ	MET
Hillsborough Township, NJ	PSC
Hillsdale, MI	LAN
NJ	NEW
Hillside, IL	CHI
IL	OLL
NJ	NEW
NJ	PHU
Hillsville, PA	PIT
Hilltop, MD	WDC
Hilltown, PA	PH
Hilmar, CA	FRS
Hilo, HI	HON
Hilton, NY	ROC
Hilton Head Island, SC	CHR
Hinckley, MN	DUL
NY	SY
OH	CLV
Hinesburg, VT	BUR
Hinesville, GA	SAV
Hingham, MA	BO
Hinsdale, IL	JOL
MA	SPR
NH	MAN
NY	BUF

Hinton, WV	WH
Hirlingen, MO	KC
Hitchcock, TX	GAL
Hoban Heights, PA	SCR
Hobart, IN	GRY
Hobbs, NM	LSC
Hobe Sound, FL	PMB
Hoboken, NJ	NEW
Hobson, TX	SAT
Hockessin, DE	WIL
Hodge, LA	SHP
Hodgenville, KY	L
Hofa Park, WI	GB
Hoffman Estates, IL	CHI
Hogansburg, NY	OG
Hohenwald, TN	NSH
Hohokus, NJ	NEW
Hoisington, KS	DOD
Hokah, MN	WIN
Holbrook, AZ	GLP
IA	DAV
MA	BO
NY	RVC
Holden, MO	KC
WV	WH
Holdenville, OK	TLS
Holdingford, MN	SCL
Holdrege, NE	LIN
Holgate, OH	TOL
Holiday, FL	SP
Holiday Park, PA	PIT
Holland, MI	GR
NY	BUF
PA	LIT
PA	PH
Holland Patent, NY	SY
Hollandale, WI	MAD
Hollandtown, WI	GB
Holley, NY	BUF
Hollidaysburg, PA	ALT
Hollister, CA	MRY
Holliston, MA	BO
Holloway, MN	NU
Holly, CO	PBL
MI	DET
Holly Springs, MS	JKS
Hollywood, CA	LA
FL	MIA
MD	WDC
Holmdel, NJ	TR
Holmen, WI	LC
Holmes Beach, FL	VEN
Holstein, IA	SC
Holton, KS	KCK
Holts Summit, MO	JC
Holtville, CA	SD
Holualoa, HI	HON
Holy Cross, AK	FBK
IA	DUB
KY	L
WI	MIL
Holy Hill, WI	MIL
Holy Trinity, AL	MOB
Holyoke, CO	DEN
MA	SPR
Holyrood, KS	SAL
Homedale, ID	B
Homer, AK	ANC
NY	SY
Homer City, PA	PBR
Homestead, FL	MIA
PA	PIT
Hometown, IL	CHI
Homewood, IL	CHI
Homosassa, FL	SP
Honaunau, HI	HON
Hondo, TX	SAT
Honeoye, NY	ROC
Honeoye Falls, NY	ROC
Honesdale, PA	SCR
Honey Brook, PA	PH
Honokaa, HI	HON
Honolulu, HI	HON
Hood River, OR	BAK
Hooksett, NH	MAN
Hoonah, AK	JUN
Hoopa, CA	SR
Hooper, NE	OM
Hooper Bay, AK	FBK
Hoopeston, IL	PEO
Hooppole, IL	PEO
Hoosick Falls, NY	ALB
Hooversville, PA	ALT
Hopatcong, NJ	PAT
Hope, AR	LR
KS	SAL
ND	FAR
Hope Mills, NC	R
Hope Valley, RI	PRO
Hopedale, MA	WOR
OH	STU

Hopewell, NJ	TR
VA	RIC
Hopewell Junction, NY	NY
Hopewell Township, PA	PIT
Hopkins, MN	STP
Hopkins Park, IL	JOL
Hopkinsville, KY	OWN
Hopkinton, IA	DUB
MA	BO
NY	OG
Hoquiam, WA	SEA
Horicon, WI	MIL
Horizon City, TX	ELP
Hormigueros, PR	MGZ
Hornell, NY	ROC
Hornick, IA	SC
Horseheads, NY	ROC
Horseshoe Bay, TX	AUS
Horseshoe Bend, AR	LR
ID	B
Horsham, PA	PH
Horton, KS	KCK
Hortonville, WI	GB
Hoschton, GA	ATL
Hosmer, SD	SFS
Hospers, IA	SC
Hostyn, TX	VIC
Hostyn Hill, TX	AUS
Hot Springs, AR	LR
NC	CHL
SD	RC
VA	RIC
Hot Springs National Park, AR	LR
Hot Springs Village, AR	LR
Houck, AZ	GLP
Houghton, IA	DAV
MI	MAR
Houghton Lake, MI	GAY
Houlton, ME	PRT
Houma, LA	HT
Housatonic, MA	SPR
House Springs, MO	STL
Houseville, NY	OG
Houston, MN	WIN
MO	SPC
TX	GAL
TX	OLL
TX	PBR
TX	STN
Houtzdale, PA	E
Hoven, SD	SFS
Howard, SD	SFS
WI	GB
Howard City, MI	GR
Howardstown, KY	L
Howell, MI	LAN
Howell Township, NJ	TR
Howells, NE	OM
Howes, SD	RC
Howland, ME	PRT
Hoxie, KS	SAL
Hoyt Lakes, MN	DUL
Hubbard, OH	Y
Hubbardston, MI	GR
Hubbell, MI	MAR
Hubertus, WI	MIL
Hudson, FL	SP
MA	BO
MI	LAN
NH	MAN
NY	ALB
NY	STF
OH	CLV
PA	SCR
WI	SUP
Hudson Falls, NY	ALB
Huff, ND	BIS
Huffman, TX	GAL
Hughestown, PA	SCR
Hughson, CA	STO
Hugo, MN	STP
OK	TLS
Hugoton, KS	DOD
Hull, MA	BO
Humacao, PR	CGS
Humacao Playa, PR	CGS
Humble, TX	GAL
Humboldt, IA	SC
KS	WCH
SD	SFS
TN	MEM
WI	GB
Hume, IL	SFD
Humphrey, NE	OM
NY	BUF
Hungerford, TX	VIC
Hunt Valley, MD	BAL
Hunter, ND	FAR
NY	STF
Huntimer, SD	SFS
Huntingburg, IN	EVN

Huntingdon, PA	ALT
TN	MEM
Huntingdon Valley, PA	PH
Huntington, CT	BGP
IN	FTW
MA	SPR
NY	RVC
WV	WH
Huntington Beach, CA	ORG
Huntington Park, CA	LA
Huntington Station, NY	RVC
Huntingtown, MD	WDC
Huntley, IL	RCK
Huntsville, AL	BIR
AR	LR
OH	CIN
TX	GAL
UT	SLC
Hurdsfield, ND	FAR
Hurley, NM	LSC
NY	NY
WI	SUP
Huron, CA	FRS
OH	TOL
SD	SFS
Hurricane, WV	WH
Hurt, VA	RIC
Hurtsboro, AL	MOB
Hutchinson, KS	WCH
MN	NU
Huttonsville, WV	WH
Hyannis, MA	FR
Hyattsville, MD	WDC
Hyde Park, NY	NY
VT	BUR
Hydes, MD	BAL
Ida, MI	DET
Ida Grove, IA	SC
Idabel, OK	TLS
Idaho City, ID	B
Idaho Falls, ID	B
Idaho Springs, CO	DEN
Idalou, TX	LUB
Idyllwild, CA	SB
Idylwilde, SD	SFS
Ignacio, CO	PBL
Ilasco, MO	JC
Iliff, CO	DEN
Ilion, NY	ALB
Illiopolis, IL	SFD
Imlay City, MI	DET
Immaculata, PA	PH
Immokalee, FL	VEN
Imogene, IA	DM
Imperial, CA	SD
MO	STL
NE	LIN
PA	PIT
Inarajan, GU	AGN
Inchelium, WA	SPK
Incline Village, NV	RNO
Independence, IA	DUB
KS	WCH
KY	COV
LA	BR
MO	KC
OH	CLV
OR	P
WI	LC
Indialantic, FL	ORL
Indian Creek, MO	JC
WI	LC
Indian Grove, MO	JC
Indian Head, MD	WDC
Indian Island, ME	PRT
Indian Lake, NY	OG
Indian River, MI	GAY
Indian Rocks Beach, FL	SP
Indian Township, ME	PRT
Indiana, PA	GBG
Indiana Harbor Co., IN	PRM
Indianapolis, IN	IND
IN	PRM
Indianola, IA	DM
MS	JKS
NE	LIN
Indiantown, FL	PMB
Indio, CA	SB
Industry, PA	PIT
Inez, TX	VIC
Ingalls, KS	DOD
Ingleside, IL	CHI
TX	CC
Inglewood, CA	LA
Ingram, PA	PIT
Inkerman, PA	SCR
Inkster, MI	DET
Inlet, NY	OG
Ino, WI	SUP
Institute, WI	GB
Interlachen, FL	STA

Interlaken, NY	ROC
International Falls, MN	DUL
Inver Grove Heights, MN	STP
Inverness, FL	SP
IL	CHI
Inwood, NY	RVC
WV	WH
Iola, KS	WCH
Iona, MN	WIN
Ione, CA	SAC
OR	BAK
WA	SPK
Ionia, IA	DUB
MI	GR
Iota, LA	LAF
Iowa, LA	LKC
Iowa City, IA	DAV
Iowa Falls, IA	DUB
Iowa Park, TX	FWT
Ipswich, MA	BO
SD	SFS
Ireland, IN	EVN
Irish Settlement, IA	DM
Iron Mountain, MI	MAR
Iron River, MI	MAR
WI	SUP
Irons, MI	GR
Ironton, MO	SPC
OH	STU
Ironwood, MI	MAR
Iroquois, SD	SFS
Irvine, CA	ORG
KY	LEX
Irving, TX	DAL
TX	PBR
Irvington, KY	OWN
NJ	NEW
Irvington-on-the-Hudson, NY	NY
Irwin, IL	JOL
PA	GBG
Irwindale, CA	LA
Isaar, WI	GB
Isabela, PR	ARE
Isanti, MN	SCL
Iselin, NJ	MET
PA	GBG
Ishpeming, MI	MAR
Island Falls, ME	PRT
Island Grove, IL	SFD
Island Park, NY	RVC
Island Pond, VT	BUR
Isle Brevelle, LA	ALX
Isle La Motte, VT	BUR
Isleta, NM	SFE
Isleton, CA	SAC
Islip, NY	RVC
Islip Terrace, NY	RVC
Issaquah, WA	SEA
Issue, MD	WDC
Itasca, IL	JOL
Ithaca, MI	SAG
NY	ROC
Ivanhoe, MN	NU
Ivesdale, IL	PEO
Jackman, ME	PRT
Jacksboro, TN	KNX
TX	FWT
Jackson, CA	SAC
GA	ATL
KY	LEX
MI	LAN
MN	WIN
MO	SPC
MS	JKS
NE	OM
NJ	TR
OH	COL
PA	SCR
TN	MEM
WY	CHY
Jacksonport, WI	GB
Jacksonville, AL	BIR
AR	LR
FL	OLD
FL	PSC
FL	STA
IL	SFD
NC	R
TX	TYL
Jacksonville Beach, FL	STA
Jacob's Prairie, MN	SCL
Jacumba, CA	SD
Jaffrey, NH	MAN
Jal, NM	LSC
Jamaica, IA	DM
NY	BRK
Jamaica Estates, NY	BRK
Jamaica Plain, MA	BO
MA	SAM
Jamesburg, NJ	MET
Jamestown, KS	SAL

KY	L
ND	FAR
NY	BUF
OH	CIN
RI	PRO
Jamesville, NY	SY
Jamison, PA	PH
Jamul, CA	SD
Janesville, MN	WIN
WI	MAD
Jarrell, TX	AUS
Jasonville, IN	EVN
Jasper, AL	BIR
IN	EVN
MN	WIN
TX	BEA
Java Center, NY	BUF
Jay, ME	PRT
Jayuya, PR	PCE
Jeanerette, LA	LAF
Jeannette, PA	GBG
PA	SJP
Jeffers, MN	WIN
Jefferson, IA	SC
LA	NO
MA	WOR
NC	CHL
OH	Y
SD	SFS
TX	TYL
WI	MAD
Jefferson Boro, PA	PIT
Jefferson City, MO	JC
TN	KNX
Jeffersontown, KY	L
Jeffersonville, IN	IND
NY	NY
Jellico, KY	LEX
TN	KNX
Jemez Pueblo, NM	SFE
Jemez Springs, NM	SFE
Jena, LA	ALX
Jenison, MI	GR
Jenkins, KY	LEX
Jenkintown, PA	PH
PA	PHU
Jennings, LA	LKC
MO	STL
Jensen Beach, FL	PMB
Jericho, WI	GB
Jermyn, PA	SCR
Jerome, AZ	PHX
ID	B
PA	PBR
Jersey City, NJ	NEW
NJ	PHU
NJ	PSC
Jersey Shore, PA	SCR
Jerseyville, IL	SFD
Jessenland, MN	NU
Jessie, ND	FAR
Jessup, MD	BAL
PA	PSC
PA	SCR
Jesup, GA	SAV
IA	DUB
Jetmore, KS	DOD
Jewell, IA	DUB
Jewett, OH	STU
Jewett City, CT	NOR
Jim Falls, WI	LC
Jim Thorpe, PA	ALN
Joanna, SC	CHR
Joelton, TN	NSH
Johannesburg, MI	GAY
John Day, OR	BAK
Johns Island, SC	CHR
Johnsburg, IL	RCK
MN	WIN
WI	MIL
Johnson, KS	DOD
Johnson City, NY	STF
NY	SY
TN	KNX
Johnsonburg, PA	E
Johnsonville, NY	ALB
Johnston, IA	DM
RI	PRO
Johnston City, IL	BEL
Johnstown, CO	DEN
NY	ALB
OH	COL
PA	ALT
PA	PBR
PA	SJP
Joliet, IL	JOL
IL	PRM
Jolon, CA	MRY
Jones, OK	OKL
Jonesboro, AR	LR
GA	ATL

Jonesborough, TN	KNX
Jonesburg, MO	JC
Joplin, MO	SPC
Joppa, MD	BAL
Jordan, MN	STP
NY	SY
OR	P
Jordan Valley, OR	BAK
Josephville, MO	STL
Joshua Tree, CA	SB
Jourdanton, TX	SAT
Juana Diaz, PR	PCE
Judice, LA	LAF
Julesburg, CO	DEN
Julian, CA	SD
Jump River, WI	SUP
Juncos, PR	CGS
Junction, OH	TOL
TX	SAN
Junction City, KS	SAL
OH	COL
OR	P
WI	LC
Juneau, AK	JUN
WI	MIL
Juno Beach, FL	PMB
Jupiter, FL	PMB
Justice, IL	CHI
Kadoka, SD	RC
Kahoka, MO	JC
Kahuku, HI	HON
Kahului, HI	HON
Kailua, HI	HON
Kalaheo, HI	HON
Kalamazoo, MI	KAL
Kalaupapa, HI	HON
Kalida, OH	TOL
Kalispell, MT	HEL
Kalkaska, MI	GAY
Kaltag, AK	FBK
Kamiah, ID	B
Kampsville, IL	SFD
Kamuela, HI	HON
Kanab, UT	SLC
Kandiyohi, MN	NU
Kane, PA	E
Kaneohe, HI	HON
Kankakee, IL	JOL
Kanopolis, KS	SAL
Kansas, OH	TOL
Kansas City, KS	KCK
MO	KC
Kansas City North, MO	KC
Kansasville, WI	MIL
Kapaa, HI	HON
Kaplan, LA	LAF
Karlsruhe, ND	FAR
Karnes City, TX	SAT
Kaskaskia, IL	BEL
Kasson, MN	WIN
Katonah, NY	NY
Katy, TX	GAL
Kaufman, TX	DAL
Kaukauna, WI	GB
Kaunakakai, HI	HON
Kawkawlin, MI	SAG
Kayenta, AZ	GLP
Keams Canyon, AZ	GLP
Keansburg, NJ	TR
Kearney, MO	KC
NE	GI
Kearneysville, WV	WH
Kearns, UT	SLC
Kearny, AZ	TUC
NJ	NEW
Keaukaha, Hilo, HI	HON
Keene, NH	MAN
NY	OG
Keeseville, NY	OG
Keewatin, MN	DUL
Keizer, OR	P
Kekaha, HI	HON
Kelayres, PA	ALN
Keller, TX	FWT
WA	SPK
Kelley's Island, OH	TOL
Kelliher, MN	CR
Kellnersville, WI	GB
Kellogg, ID	B
MN	WIN
Kelly, KS	KCK
Kelso, MO	SPC
WA	SEA
Kemmerer, WY	CHY
Kenai, AK	ANC
Kendall, NY	BUF
WI	LC
Kendall Park, NJ	MET
Kendallville, IN	FTW
Kenedy, TX	SAT
Kenel, SD	RC

Kenesaw, NE	LIN
Kenilworth, NJ	NEW
Kenmare, ND	BIS
Kenmore, NY	BUF
NY	STF
Kennebec, SD	RC
Kennebunk, ME	PRT
Kennebunkport, ME	PRT
ME	SP
Kennedy Township, PA	PIT
Kenner, LA	NO
Kennesaw, GA	ATL
Kennett, MO	SPC
Kennett Square, PA	PH
Kennewick, WA	YAK
Kenosha, WI	MIL
Kensal, ND	FAR
Kensington, CA	OAK
CT	HRT
MD	WDC
MN	SCL
Kent, CT	HRT
MN	SCL
OH	Y
PA	GBG
WA	SEA
Kentfield, CA	SFR
Kentfield-Greenbrae, CA	SFR
Kentland, IN	LFT
Kenton, KY	COV
OH	COL
Kenton Hills, KY	COV
Kenyon, MN	STP
Keokuk, IA	DAV
Keota, IA	DAV
Kerhonkson, NY	STF
Kerman, CA	FRS
Kermit, TX	ELP
Kernersville, NC	CHL
Kerrville, TX	SAT
Kersey, PA	E
Keshena, WI	GB
Keswick, IA	DAV
Ketchikan, AK	JUN
Kettle Falls, WA	SPK
Keuterville, ID	B
Kew Gardens, NY	BRK
Kewanee, IL	PEO
Kewanna, IN	LFT
Kewaskum, WI	MIL
Kewaunee, WI	GB
Key Biscayne, FL	MIA
Key Largo, FL	MIA
Key West, FL	MIA
IA	DUB
Keyesville, WI	LC
Keyport, NJ	TR
Keyser, WV	WH
Keystone Heights, FL	STA
Kickapoo, IL	PEO
Kiel, WI	GB
Kieler, WI	MAD
Kihei, HI	HON
Kilgore, TX	TYL
Kilkenny, MN	STP
Kill Devil Hills, NC	R
Killdeer, ND	BIS
Killeen, TX	AUS
Killingworth, CT	NOR
Kilmarnock, VA	ARL
Kiln, MS	BLX
Kimball, MN	SCL
NE	GI
SD	SFS
Kimberling City, MO	SPC
Kimberly, WI	GB
Kimberton, PA	PH
Kimeo, KS	SAL
Kimmswick, MO	STL
Kincaid, IL	SFD
Kinde, MI	SAG
Kinder, LA	LKC
Kindred, ND	FAR
King, WI	GB
King City, CA	MRY
King Ferry, NY	ROC
King of Prussia, PA	PH
Kingfisher, OK	OKL
Kingman, AZ	PHX
KS	WCH
Kings Park, NY	RVC
Kingsburg, CA	FRS
Kingsford, MI	MAR
Kingsford Heights, IN	GRY
Kingsland, TX	AUS
Kingsley, IA	SC
Kingsport, TN	KNX
Kingston, MA	BO
NY	NY
PA	PSC
PA	SCR

RI	PRO
Kingstree, SC	CHR
Kingsville, OH	Y
TX	CC
Kingwood, TX	GAL
WV	WH
Kinloch, MO	STL
Kinmundy, IL	BEL
Kinnelon, NJ	PAT
Kinross, IA	DAV
Kinsley, KS	DOD
Kinsman, IL	JOL
OH	Y
Kinston, NC	R
Kintyre, ND	FAR
Kiowa, KS	DOD
Kirby, OH	TOL
TX	SAT
Kirkland, WA	SEA
Kirksville, MO	JC
Kirkwood, MO	STL
NY	SY
Kirtland, OH	CLV
Kissimmee, FL	ORL
Kitii, FM	CI
Kittanning, PA	GBG
Kittery, ME	PRT
Klacking Creek, MI	GAY
Klamath Falls, OR	BAK
Kleinwood, LA	ALX
Klondike, WI	GB
Kloten, WI	GB
Knapp Creek, NY	BUF
Knights Landing, CA	SAC
Knightstown, IN	IND
Knottsville, KY	OWN
Knowlton, WI	LC
Knox, IN	GRY
ND	FAR
Knox City, TX	FWT
Knoxville, IA	DAV
TN	KNX
Kodiak, AK	ANC
Koerth, TX	VIC
Kohler, WI	MIL
Kokomo, IN	LFT
Koloa, HI	HON
Kolonia, FM	CI
Konawa, OK	OKL
Koppel, PA	PIT
Korona, FL	STA
Koror, FM	CI
Kosciusko, MS	JKS
Kosciuszko, TX	SAT
Kossuth, WI	GB
Kotlik, AK	FBK
Kotzebue, AK	FBK
Kountze, TX	BEA
Kouts, IN	GRY
Kovar, TX	AUS
Koyukuk, AK	FBK
Kraemer, LA	HT
Krakow, MO	STL
NE	OM
WI	GB
Kranzburg, SD	SFS
Krebs, OK	TLS
Kremmling, CO	DEN
Krok, WI	GB
Krotz Springs, LA	LAF
Kula, HI	HON
Kulpmont, PA	HBG
Kutztown, PA	ALN
Kwajalein, MH	MI
Kyle, SD	RC
TX	AUS
L'Anse, MI	MAR
La Canada Flintridge, CA	LA
La Crescent, MN	WIN
La Crescenta, CA	ARM
CA	LA
La Crosse, WI	LC
La Feria, TX	BWN
La Grande, OR	BAK
La Grange, IL	CHI
TX	AUS
La Grange Park, IL	CHI
La Habra, CA	ORG
La Jolla, CA	SD
La Joya, NM	SFE
TX	BWN
La Junta, CO	PBL
La Marque, TX	GAL
La Mesa, CA	SD
NM	LSC
La Mirada, CA	LA
La Motte, IA	DUB
La Moure, ND	FAR
La Pine, OR	BAK
La Place, LA	NO
La Plata, MD	WDC

La Porte, IN	GRY
TX	GAL
La Porte City, IA	DUB
La Pryor, TX	SAT
La Puente, CA	LA
La Quinta, CA	SB
La Rue, OH	COL
La Salle, IL	PEO
La Verne, CA	LA
La Vernia, TX	SAT
Labadieville, LA	BR
LaBelle, FL	VEN
Lac du Flambeau, WI	SUP
LaCenter, KY	OWN
Lacey, WA	SEA
Lackawanna, NY	BUF
NY	STF
Lacombe, LA	NO
Lacon, IL	PEO
Lacona, IA	DM
NY	SY
Laconia, NH	MAN
LaConner, WA	SEA
LaCoste, TX	SAT
LaCrosse, KS	DOD
Lacrosse, WA	SPK
Lacy, WA	VNN
LaCygne, KS	KCK
Ladd, IL	PEO
Ladue, MO	STL
Lady Lake, FL	ORL
Ladysmith, VA	RIC
WI	SUP
Lafargeville, NY	OG
Lafayette, CA	OAK
CO	DEN
IN	LFT
LA	LAF
LA	OLL
MN	NU
NJ	PAT
NY	SY
OR	P
TN	NSH
Lafayette Hill, PA	PH
Lafferty, OH	STU
Lafitte, LA	NO
Laflin, PA	SCR
LaFollette, TN	KNX
Lago Vista, TX	AUS
LaGrange, GA	ATL
IN	FTW
KY	L
TX	AUS
LaGrange Park, IL	CHI
Lagro, IN	FTW
Laguna, NM	GLP
Laguna Beach, CA	ORG
Laguna Hills, CA	ORG
Laguna Niguel, CA	ORG
Lagunitas, CA	SFR
Lahaina, HI	HON
Laingsburg, MI	LAN
Lajas, PR	MGZ
Lake Andes, SD	SFS
Lake Ariel, PA	SCR
Lake Arrowhead, CA	SB
Lake Arthur, LA	LKC
Lake Benton, MN	NU
Lake Charles, LA	LKC
Lake City, FL	STA
IA	SC
MI	GAY
MN	WIN
SC	CHR
SD	SFS
TN	KNX
Lake Clear, NY	OG
Lake Crystal, MN	WIN
Lake Dallas, TX	FWT
Lake Elmo, MN	STP
Lake Elsinore, CA	SB
Lake Eunice Township, MN	CR
Lake Five, WI	MIL
Lake Forest, CA	ORG
IL	CHI
Lake Geneva, WI	MIL
Lake George, NY	ALB
Lake Harmony, PA	ALN
Lake Havasu City, AZ	PHX
Lake Henry, MN	SCL
Lake Hopatcong, NJ	PAT
Lake Itasca, MN	CR
Lake Jackson, TX	GAL
Lake Katrine, NY	NY
Lake Leelanau, MI	GAY
Lake Lillian, MN	NU
Lake Linden, MI	MAR
Lake Luzerne, NY	ALB
Lake Mills, IA	DUB
WI	MAD

Lake Milton, OH	Y
Lake Nebagamon, WI	SUP
Lake Odessa, MI	GR
Lake Orion, MI	DET
Lake Oswego, OR	P
Lake Ozark, MO	JC
Lake Park, MN	CR
Lake Placid, FL	VEN
NY	OG
Lake Pleasant, NY	OG
Lake Providence, LA	SHP
Lake Reno, MN	SCL
Lake Ridge, VA	ARL
Lake Ronkonkoma, NY	RVC
Lake St. Croix Beach, MN	STP
Lake St. Louis, MO	STL
Lake San Marcos, CA	SD
Lake Silkworth, PA	SCR
Lake Station, IN	GRY
Lake Tamarisk, CA	SB
Lake Tomahawk, WI	SUP
Lake View, NY	BUF
Lake Villa, IL	CHI
Lake Village, AR	LR
IN	LFT
Lake Wales, FL	ORL
Lake Williams, ND	FAR
Lake Wilson, MN	WIN
Lake Winola, PA	SCR
Lake Worth, FL	PMB
FL	PSC
Lake Zurich, IL	CHI
Lakefield, MN	WIN
Lakehurst, NJ	TR
Lakeland, FL	ORL
GA	SAV
LA	BR
NY	SY
Lakeport, CA	SR
MI	DET
NH	MAN
Lakeside, CA	SD
Lakeview, MI	GR
OR	BAK
Lakeville, CT	HRT
IN	FTW
MA	BO
MN	STP
Lakewood, CA	LA
CO	DEN
NJ	TR
NY	BUF
OH	CLV
OH	PRM
WI	GB
Lakewood Club, MI	GR
Lakin, KS	DOD
Lakota, ND	FAR
Lamar, AR	LR
CO	PBL
MO	SPC
Lamberton, MN	NU
Lambertville, NJ	MET
Lame Deer, MT	GF
Lamesa, TX	LUB
Lamoille, MN	WIN
Lamont, CA	FRS
IA	DUB
LaMotte, IA	DUB
Lampasas, TX	AUS
Lanai City, HI	HON
Lanark, WI	LC
Lanark Village, FL	PT
Lancaster, CA	LA
KY	LEX
MA	WOR
MN	CR
NH	MAN
NY	BUF
NY	STF
OH	COL
PA	HBG
SC	CHR
TX	DAL
WI	MAD
Lancing, TN	KNX
Land O'Lakes, FL	SP
Landeck, OH	TOL
Lander, WY	CHY
Landisville, NJ	CAM
Land-O'-Lakes, WI	SUP
Landover Hills, MD	WDC
Lanesboro, MA	SPR
MN	WIN
Lanesville, IN	IND
Lanett, AL	BIR
Langdon, ND	FAR
Langford, NY	BUF
Langhorne, PA	PH
PA	PHU
Langlade, WI	GB

Langley, OK	TLS
WA	SEA
Lanham, MD	WDC
Lanham-Seabrook, MD	WDC
Lankin, ND	FAR
Lansdale, PA	PH
PA	PHU
Lansdowne, MD	BAL
PA	PH
Lansford, PA	ALN
PA	PSC
Lansford-Summit Hill, PA	ALN
Lansing, IA	DUB
IL	CHI
KS	KCK
MI	LAN
MI	NTN
NY	ROC
Lantana, FL	PMB
Laona, WI	GB
Lapeer, KS	KCK
MI	DET
LaPointe, WI	SUP
Laporte, MN	CR
Lapwai, ID	B
Laramie, WY	CHY
Larchmont, NY	NY
Larchwood, IA	SC
Laredo, TX	CC
Lares, PR	ARE
Largo, FL	SP
MD	WDC
Larimore, ND	FAR
Larks Lake, MI	GAY
Larkspur, CA	SFR
Larksville, PA	SCR
Larned, KS	DOD
Larose, LA	HT
Las Animas, CO	PBL
Las Cruces, NM	LSC
NM	VNN
Las Marias, PR	MGZ
Las Piedras, PR	CGS
Las Vegas, NM	SFE
NV	LAV
NV	OLL
NV	VNN
Lastrup, MN	SCL
Latham, NY	ALB
Latium, TX	AUS
Laton, CA	FRS
Latrobe, PA	GBG
PA	SJP
Lattimer Mines, PA	SCR
Laughlin, NV	LAV
LaUnion, NM	LSC
Laurel, MD	BAL
MD	WDC
MS	BLX
MT	GF
NE	OM
Laurence Harbor, NJ	MET
Laurens, IA	SC
Laurie, MO	JC
Laurinburg, NC	R
Lavallette, NJ	TR
Laveen, AZ	PHX
Laverock, PA	PH
Lawler, IA	DUB
Lawrence, KS	KCK
MA	BO
MA	NTN
MA	SAM
NE	LIN
PA	PIT
Lawrenceburg, IN	IND
KY	LEX
TN	NSH
Lawrenceton, MO	STL
Lawrenceville, GA	ATL
IL	BEL
NJ	TR
Lawtell, LA	LAF
Lawton, OK	OKL
Layton, UT	SLC
Le Center, MN	STP
Le Claire-Princeton, IA	DAV
Le Mars, IA	SC
Le Roy, MN	WIN
NY	BUF
WI	MIL
Le Sueur, MN	STP
Lead, SD	RC
Leadore, ID	B
Leadville, CO	COS
League City, TX	GAL
Leander, TX	AUS
Leavenworth, KS	KCK
MN	NU
WA	YAK
Leawood, KS	KCK

Lebanon, CT	NOR
IL	BEL
IN	LFT
KY	L
MO	SPC
NH	MAN
OH	CIN
OR	P
PA	HBG
TN	NSH
Lebanon Junction, KY	L
Lebanon Township, WI	GB
Lebeau, LA	LAF
Lecanto, FL	SP
Leckrone, PA	GBG
Lecompte, LA	ALX
Ledyard, IA	SC
Lee, IL	RCK
MA	SPR
Lee Center, NY	SY
Lee's Summit, MO	KC
Leechburg, PA	GBG
Leeds, AL	BIR
MA	SPR
ND	FAR
Leesburg, FL	ORL
VA	ARL
Leesville, LA	ALX
Leetonia, OH	Y
Lefor, ND	BIS
Leggett, CA	SR
Lehigh Acres, FL	VEN
Lehighton, PA	ALN
Leicester, MA	WOR
NY	ROC
Leigh, NE	OM
Leipsic, OH	TOL
Leisenring, PA	GBG
PA	PBR
Leisure City, FL	MIA
Leitchfield, KY	OWN
Leland, MS	JKS
Lemay, MO	STL
Lemhi, ID	B
Lemmon, SD	RC
Lemon Grove, CA	SD
Lemont, IL	CHI
IL	LIT
Lemoore, CA	FRS
Lena, IL	RCK
WI	GB
Lenexa, KS	KCK
Lenni, PA	PH
Lennox, SD	SFS
Lenoir, NC	CHL
Lenoir City, TN	KNX
Lenox, IA	DM
MA	SPR
Lenox Dale, MA	SPR
Leo, MN	CR
Leola, SD	SFS
Leominster, MA	WOR
Leon, IA	DM
Leon Springs, TX	SAT
Leonardtown, MD	WDC
Leone, AS	SPP
Leonia, NJ	NEW
Leonore, IL	PEO
Leonville, LA	LAF
Leopold, IN	IND
MO	SPC
Leopolis, WI	GB
Leoti, KS	DOD
Leoville, KS	SAL
Lepua, AS	SPP
Lepuapua, AS	SPP
Leroy, LA	LAF
ND	FAR
LeRoy, NY	BUF
Leslie, MI	LAN
Lester Prairie, MN	NU
Lesterville, SD	SFS
Letcher, SD	SFS
Levelland, TX	LUB
Levittown, NY	RVC
PA	PH
PA	PSC
Lewis Center, OH	COL
Lewis Run, PA	E
Lewisburg, PA	HBG
TN	NSH
Lewisport, KY	OWN
Lewiston, ID	B
ME	PRT
MI	GAY
MN	WIN
NY	BUF
Lewistown, IL	PEO
MT	GF
PA	HBG
Lewisville, TX	FWT

TX	OLL
Lexington, KY	LEX
MA	ARM
MA	BO
MI	SAG
MN	STP
MO	KC
MS	JKS
NC	CHL
NE	GI
OH	TOL
SC	CHR
TN	MEM
TX	AUS
VA	RIC
Lexington Park, MD	WDC
Libby, MT	HEL
Liberal, KS	DOD
Liberty, IL	SFD
IN	IND
KS	WCH
MO	KC
NY	NY
OH	TOL
TN	NSH
TX	BEA
Liberty Boro, PA	PIT
Libertytown, MD	BAL
Libertyville, IL	CHI
Library, PA	PIT
Lidderdale, IA	SC
Lidgerwood, ND	FAR
Liebenthal, KS	DOD
Liftwood, DE	WIL
Lighthouse Point, FL	MIA
Ligonier, IN	FTW
PA	GBG
Liguori, MO	STL
Lihue, HI	HON
Lilburn, GA	ATL
Lillian, AL	MOB
Lillis, KS	KCK
Lilly, PA	ALT
Lillyville, IL	SFD
Lily, SD	SFS
Lima, NY	ROC
OH	TOL
WI	LC
WI	MIL
Lime Ridge, WI	MAD
Limeport, PA	ALN
Limerick, ME	PRT
Limestone, ME	PRT
NY	BUF
Limon, CO	COS
Lincoln, CA	SAC
IL	PEO
KS	SAL
MA	BO
ME	PRT
NE	LIN
NE	STN
NH	MAN
RI	PRO
WI	GB
Lincoln City, OR	P
Lincoln Park, MI	DET
NJ	PAT
Lincolndale, NY	NY
Lincolnton, NC	CHL
Lincroft, NJ	TR
Lind, WA	SPK
Linden, CA	STO
NJ	NEW
NJ	PSC
Lindenhurst, NY	RVC
Lindenwold, NJ	CAM
Lindsay, CA	FRS
NE	OM
TX	FWT
Lindsborg, KS	WCH
Lindstrom, MN	STP
Linesville, PA	E
Linfield, PA	PH
Linn, MO	JC
Lino Lakes, MN	STP
Linthicum Heights, MD	BAL
Linton, IN	EVN
ND	BIS
Linwood, MA	WOR
MI	SAG
NJ	CAM
PA	PH
Lisbon, ME	PRT
ND	FAR
NH	MAN
NY	OG
OH	Y
Lisbon Falls, ME	PRT
Lisle, IL	JOL
Lismore, MN	WIN
Litchfield, CT	HRT
IL	SFD
MN	NU
OH	CLV
Litchfield Park, AZ	PHX
Lithia Springs, GA	ATL
Lithonia, GA	ATL
Lititz, PA	HBG
Litomysl, MN	WIN
Little Canada, MN	STP
Little Chute, WI	GB
Little Compton, RI	PRO
Little Falls, MN	SCL
NJ	PAT
NY	ALB
NY	STF
Little Ferry, NJ	NEW
Little Kohler, WI	MIL
Little Meadows, PA	SCR
Little River, KS	WCH
Little Rock, AR	LR
Little Suamico, WI	GB
Little Turkey, IA	DUB
Little Valley, NY	BUF
Little York, NJ	MET
Littlefield, TX	LUB
Littlefork, MN	DUL
Littlestown, PA	HBG
Littleton, CO	DEN
MA	BO
NH	MAN
Live Oak, FL	STA
Lively Grove, IL	BEL
Livermore, CA	OAK
IA	SC
KY	OWN
Liverpool, NY	SY
Livingston, AL	BIR
CA	FRS
IL	SFD
KY	LEX
MT	GF
NJ	NEW
TX	BEA
Livingston Manor, NY	NY
Livonia, LA	BR
MI	DET
MI	PRM
NY	ROC
Livonia Center, NY	ROC
Llano, TX	AUS
Lock Haven, PA	ALT
Lockbourne, OH	COL
Lockeford, CA	STO
Lockhart, TX	AUS
Lockport, IL	JOL
LA	HT
NY	BUF
Lockport South, IL	JOL
Locust Gap, PA	HBG
Locustdale, PA	HBG
Lodge Grass, MT	GF
Lodi, CA	STO
NJ	NEW
OH	CLV
WI	MAD
Logan, IA	DM
KS	SAL
OH	COL
UT	SLC
WV	WH
Logansport, IN	LFT
Lohrville, IA	SC
Loiza, PR	SJN
Loma, NE	LIN
Loma Linda, CA	SB
Lombard, IL	JOL
Lometa, TX	AUS
Lomice, ND	FAR
Lomira, WI	MIL
Lomita, CA	LA
Lompoc, CA	LA
Lonaconing, MD	BAL
London, KY	LEX
OH	COL
Londonderry, NH	MAN
Lone Pine, CA	FRS
Lone Rock, WI	LC
Lone Tree, IA	DAV
Lonedell, MO	STL
Long Beach, CA	LA
CA	ORG
MS	BLX
NY	RVC
Long Branch, NJ	TR
Long Grove, IA	DAV
Long Island City, NY	BRK
NY	NY
NY	STF
Long Lake, MN	STP
NY	OG
WI	GB
Long Prairie, MN	SCL
Long Valley, NJ	PAT
Longboat Key, FL	VEN
Longmeadow, MA	SPR
Longmont, CO	DEN
Longport, NJ	CAM
Longview, TX	TYL
WA	SEA
Longville, MN	DUL
Longwood, FL	ORL
Lonsdale, MN	STP
Loogootee, IN	EVN
Lookout Mountain, GA	ATL
Loomis, CA	SAC
Loose Creek, MO	JC
Lopez, PA	PSC
Lorain, OH	CLV
OH	PRM
OH	ROM
OH	SJP
Lords Valley, PA	SCR
Lordsburg, NM	LSC
Lore City, OH	STU
Loreauville, LA	LAF
Loretto, IL	PEO
KY	L
MN	STP
PA	ALT
TN	NSH
Los Alamitos, CA	ORG
Los Alamos, NM	SFE
Los Altos, CA	SJ
Los Altos Hills, CA	SJ
Los Angeles, CA	ARM
CA	LA
CA	OLL
CA	SB
CA	SFR
CA	STN
Los Banos, CA	FRS
Los Fresnos, TX	BWN
Los Gatos, CA	MRY
CA	SJ
Los Lunas, NM	SFE
Los Nietos, CA	LA
Los Ojos, NM	SFE
Los Osos, CA	MRY
Losoya, TX	SAT
Lost Creek, PA	ALN
Lost Lake, WI	MIL
Lost Nation, IA	DAV
Lostant, IL	PEO
Lott, TX	AUS
Loudonville, NY	ALB
OH	CLV
Louisa, KY	LEX
LA	LAF
Louisburg, KS	KCK
Louisiana, MO	JC
Louisville, CO	DEN
KY	L
KY	OLL
MS	JKS
NY	OG
OH	Y
Loup City, NE	GI
Lourdes, IA	DUB
Loveland, CO	DEN
OH	CIN
Lovell, WY	CHY
Lovelock, NV	RNO
Loves Park, IL	RCK
Lovilia, IA	DAV
Loving, NM	LSC
Lovington, IL	SFD
NM	LSC
Lowell, IN	GRY
MA	BO
MI	GR
OH	STU
Lowellville, OH	Y
Lower Brule, SD	RC
Lower Burrell, PA	GBG
Lower Makefield, PA	PH
Lowville, NY	OG
Loyal, WI	LC
Lubbock, TX	LUB
Lubec, ME	PRT
Lubeck, WV	WH
Lublin, WI	SUP
Lucan, MN	NU
Lucerne, IN	LFT
Lucerne Valley, CA	SB
Lucernemines, PA	GBG
Lucinda, PA	E
Ludington, MI	GR
Ludlow, KY	COV
MA	SPR
MA	STF
VT	BUR
Luebbering, MO	STL
Lufkin, TX	TYL
Lukachukai, AZ	GLP
Lukunor, FM	CI
Luling, LA	NO
TX	AUS
Lumberton, MS	BLX
NC	R
NM	GLP
TX	BEA
Lunenburg, MA	WOR
Luquillo, PR	SJN
Luray, VA	ARL
Lusk, WY	CHY
Lutherville, MD	BAL
Luverne, MN	WIN
Luxemburg, IA	DUB
MN	SCL
WI	GB
Luzerne, PA	SCR
Lycurgus, IA	DUB
Lydia, LA	LAF
Lyford, TX	BWN
Lykens, PA	HBG
Lyle, MN	WIN
Lyman, ME	PRT
Lynbrook, NY	RVC
Lynch, KY	LEX
NE	OM
Lynchburg, VA	RIC
Lynden, WA	SEA
Lyndhurst, NJ	NEW
OH	CLV
Lyndon Station, WI	LC
Lyndonville, NY	BUF
VT	BUR
Lyndora, PA	PBR
PA	PIT
PA	SJP
Lynn, MA	BO
Lynnfield, MA	BO
Lynnwood, WA	SEA
Lynwood, CA	LA
Lyon Mountain, NY	OG
Lyons, IL	CHI
KS	WCH
NE	OM
NY	ROC
OH	TOL
WI	MIL
Lyons Point, LA	LAF
Lytle, TX	SAT
Mabel, MN	WIN
Mabton, WA	YAK
Macclenny, FL	STA
Macdona, TX	SAT
Macedon, NY	ROC
Macedonia, OH	CLV
Machias, ME	PRT
NY	BUF
Mackinac Island, MI	MAR
Mackinaw City, MI	GAY
Mackville, WI	GB
Macomb, IL	PEO
MI	DET
Macon, GA	SAV
IL	SFD
MO	JC
Madawaska, ME	PRT
Maddock, ND	FAR
Madelia, MN	WIN
Madera, CA	FRS
Madison, AL	BIR
CT	HRT
FL	PT
IL	SFD
IL	STN
IN	IND
KS	WCH
ME	PRT
MN	NU
MS	JKS
MT	HEL
NE	OM
NJ	PAT
OH	CLV
SD	SFS
TN	NSH
VA	ARL
WI	MAD
WV	WH
Madison Heights, MI	DET
Madison Lake, MN	WIN
Madisonville, KY	OWN
LA	NO
TN	KNX
TX	GAL
Madonnaville, IL	BEL
Madras, OR	BAK
Madrid, IA	SC
NY	OG

Magee, MS	JKS
Maggie Valley, NC	CHL
Magna, UT	SLC
Magnolia, NJ	CAM
TX	GAL
Magnolia Springs, AL	MOB
Mahanoy City, PA	ALN
PA	PHU
PA	PSC
Mahanoy Plane, PA	ALN
Mahnomen, MN	CR
Mahomet, IL	PEO
Mahopac, NY	NY
Mahtomedi, MN	STP
Mahwah, NJ	NEW
NJ	PSC
Maina, GU	AGN
Maine, MN	SCL
NY	SY
Maizeville, PA	ALN
PA	PHU
Majuro, MH	MI
Makakilo, HI	HON
Makawao, HI	HON
Malaeloa, AS	SPP
Malaga, NJ	CAM
Malden, MA	BO
MO	SPC
Malibu, CA	LA
Mallard, IA	SC
Mallet, LA	LAF
Malojlo, GU	AGN
Malone, NY	OG
Maloy, IA	DM
Malta, MT	GF
Malvern, AR	LR
OH	STU
PA	PH
Malverne, NY	RVC
Mamaroneck, NY	NY
Mammoth, AZ	TUC
Mammoth Lakes, CA	STO
Mamou, LA	LAF
Man, WV	WH
Manalapan, NJ	TR
Manannah, MN	NU
Manasquan, NJ	TR
Manassas, VA	ARL
VA	PHU
Manati, PR	ARE
Manawa, WI	GB
Mancelona, MI	GAY
Manchaug, MA	WOR
Manchester, CT	HRT
IA	DUB
KY	LEX
MA	BO
MD	BAL
MI	LAN
MI	LIT
MO	STL
NH	MAN
NH	NTN
NH	STF
OH	CIN
PA	PIT
WA	SEA
Manchester Center, VT	BUR
Mancos, CO	PBL
Mandan, ND	BIS
Mandaree, ND	BIS
Manderson, SD	RC
Mandeville, LA	NO
Mangilao, GU	AGN
Mangum, OK	OKL
Manhasset, NY	RVC
Manhattan, IL	JOL
KS	SAL
Manhattan Beach, CA	LA
Manheim, PA	HBG
Manilla, IA	SC
Manistee, MI	GAY
Manistique, MI	MAR
Manito Station, WA	SPK
Manitou Beach, MI	LAN
Manitowish Waters, WI	SUP
Manitowoc, WI	GB
WI	MIL
Mankato, KS	SAL
MN	WIN
Manley, NE	LIN
Manlius, NY	SY
Manly, IA	DUB
Manning, IA	SC
Mannington, WV	WH
Manoa, PA	PH
Manor, TX	AUS
Manorhaven, NY	RVC
Manorville, NY	RVC
Mansfield, LA	SHP
MA	FR
MO	SPC
OH	TOL
PA	SCR
TX	FWT
Manson, IA	SC
Mansura, LA	ALX
Mantador, ND	FAR
Manteca, CA	STO
Manteno, IL	JOL
Manton, MI	GAY
Mantua, NJ	CAM
OH	Y
Manvel, ND	FAR
TX	GAL
Manville, NJ	MET
NJ	PHU
RI	PRO
Many, LA	SHP
Maple City, MI	GAY
Maple Glen, PA	PH
Maple Grove, MI	SAG
MN	STP
WI	GB
Maple Heights, OH	CLV
Maple Lake, MN	STP
Maple Mount, KY	OWN
Maple Park, IL	RCK
Maple River, IA	SC
Maple Shade, NJ	CAM
NJ	TR
Mapleton, IA	SC
MI	GAY
MN	WIN
WI	MIL
Mapleville, RI	PRO
Maplewood, MN	STP
MO	STL
NJ	NEW
WI	GB
Maquoketa, IA	DUB
Marak, TX	AUS
Marana, AZ	TUC
Marathon, FL	MIA
NY	SY
Marathon City, WI	LC
Marble, MN	DUL
Marble Falls, TX	AUS
Marblehead, MA	BO
OH	PRM
OH	TOL
Marbury, AL	MOB
Marceline, MO	JC
Marcellus, NY	SY
Marchand, WI	GB
Marco Island, FL	VEN
Marcus, IA	SC
Marcus Hook, PA	PH
Marengo, IA	DAV
IL	RCK
Marfa, TX	ELP
Margaretville, NY	ALB
Margate, FL	MIA
NJ	CAM
Marguerite, PA	GBG
Maria Stein, OH	CIN
Mariah Hill, IN	EVN
Marianna, FL	PT
Maricao, PR	MGZ
Marienthal, KS	DOD
Marietta, GA	ATL
OH	STU
PA	HBG
Marina, CA	MRY
Marina Del Rey, CA	LA
Marine, IL	SFD
Marine City, MI	DET
Marine on St. Croix, MN	STP
Marinette, WI	GB
Maringouin, LA	BR
Marion, AL	BIR
IA	DUB
IL	BEL
IN	LFT
KS	WCH
KY	OWN
MA	FR
MI	GR
ND	FAR
NY	ROC
OH	COL
SD	SFS
VA	RIC
WI	GB
Marion Heights, PA	HBG
PA	PHU
Marionville, MO	SPC
Mariposa, CA	FRS
Markesan, WI	MAD
Markham, IL	CHI
Marks, MS	JKS
Marksville, LA	ALX
Marlboro, MA	BO
NJ	PHU
NJ	TR
NY	NY
VT	BUR
Marlborough, CT	HRT
NH	MAN
Marlette, MI	SAG
Marlin, TX	AUS
Marlinton, WV	WH
Marlton, NJ	TR
Marmora, NJ	CAM
Marne, MI	GR
Marquette, MI	MAR
Marrero, LA	NO
Marriottsville, MD	BAL
Mars, PA	PIT
Mars Hill, ME	PRT
NC	CHL
Marseilles, IL	PEO
Marshall, AK	FBK
IL	SFD
MI	KAL
MN	NU
MO	JC
TX	TYL
WI	MAD
Marshalltown, IA	DUB
Marshfield, MA	BO
MO	SPC
VT	BUR
WI	LC
Martin, KY	LEX
SD	RC
TN	MEM
Martindale, TX	AUS
Martinez, CA	OAK
TX	SAT
Martins Creek, PA	ALN
Martins Ferry, OH	STU
Martinsburg, MO	JC
WV	WH
Martinsville, IN	IND
NJ	MET
VA	RIC
WI	MAD
Martinton, IL	JOL
Marty, SD	SFS
Marvin, SD	SFS
Mary Esther, FL	PT
Mary's Home, MO	JC
Marydale, IL	BEL
Marydel, MD	WIL
Marygrove, OH	TOL
Maryhill, IA	SC
Maryknoll, NY	NY
Maryland Heights, MO	STL
Marylhurst, OR	P
Marysburg, MN	STP
Marysdale, OH	TOL
Marystown, MN	STP
Marysville, CA	SAC
KS	KCK
MI	DET
OH	COL
PA	HBG
WA	SEA
Marytown, WI	MIL
Maryville, IL	SFD
MO	KC
Marywood, OH	TOL
Masaryktown, FL	SP
Mascoutah, IL	BEL
Mashpee, MA	FR
Mason, MI	LAN
OH	CIN
TX	AUS
Mason City, IA	DUB
Masontown, PA	GBG
WV	WH
Masonville, IA	DUB
Massapequa, NY	RVC
Massapequa Park, NY	NY
NY	RVC
Massena, IA	DM
NY	OG
Massillon, OH	Y
Mastic Beach, NY	RVC
Masury, OH	Y
Matamoras, PA	SCR
Matawan, NJ	PSC
NJ	TR
Matherville, IL	PEO
Mathews, VA	RIC
Mathis, TX	CC
Mattapoisett, MA	FR
Mattawa, WA	YAK
Mattawan, MI	KAL
Mattese, MO	STL
Matteson, IL	CHI
Mattoon, IL	SFD
WI	GB
Mattydale, NY	SY
Mauldin, SC	CHR
Maumee, OH	TOL
Maunabo, PR	CGS
Maurepas, LA	BR
Maurice, LA	LAF
Mauriceville, TX	BEA
Mauston, WI	LC
Maximo, OH	Y
Maxwell, CA	SAC
PA	GBG
May's Lick, KY	COV
Mayaguez, PR	MGZ
Maybee, MI	DET
Maybrook, NY	NY
Mayetta, KS	KCK
Mayfield, KY	OWN
PA	SCR
SD	SFS
Mayhew Lake, MN	SCL
Maynard, MA	BO
OH	STU
Mays Landing, NJ	CAM
Maysel, WV	WH
Maysville, KY	COV
Maytown, IL	RCK
Mayville, MI	SAG
ND	FAR
NY	BUF
WI	MIL
Maywood, CA	LA
IL	CHI
NJ	NEW
Mazeppa, MN	WIN
Mazomanie, WI	MAD
McAdoo, PA	ALN
PA	PHU
PA	PSC
McAfee, NJ	PAT
McAlester, OK	TLS
McAllen, TX	BWN
McBain, MI	GAY
McCall, ID	B
McCamey, TX	SAN
McCartyville, OH	CIN
McCloud, CA	SAC
McClusky, ND	FAR
McComb, MS	JKS
McConchie, MD	WDC
McConnellsburg, PA	ALT
McConnelsville, OH	STU
McCook, NE	LIN
TX	BWN
McCool Junction, NE	LIN
McCracken, KS	DOD
McDonald, OH	Y
PA	PIT
McDonough, GA	ATL
McDowell, KS	SAL
McEwen, TN	NSH
McFarland, CA	FRS
WI	MAD
McGehee, AR	LR
McGrath, AK	FBK
McGregor, IA	DUB
MN	DUL
MN	STP
TX	AUS
McHenry, IL	RCK
ND	FAR
McIntire, IA	DUB
McIntosh, SD	RC
McKean, PA	E
McKees Rocks, PA	PBR
PA	PIT
PA	SJP
McKeesport, PA	PBR
PA	PIT
PA	ROM
PA	SJP
McKenzie Bridge, OR	P
McKinleyville, CA	SR
McKinney, TX	DAL
McLaughlin, SD	RC
McLean, VA	ARL
VA	NTN
McLeansboro, IL	BEL
McLoud, OK	OKL
McMechen, WV	WH
McMinnville, OR	P
TN	NSH
McNair, TX	GAL
McNary, AZ	GLP
McPherson, KS	WCH
McQuady, KY	OWN
McRae, GA	SAV
McSherrystown, PA	HBG
Mead, NE	LIN
Meade, KS	DOD
Meadowbrook, PA	PH

Meadowlands, PA	PIT
Meadville, PA	E
Mecca, CA	SB
Mechanic Falls, ME	PRT
Mechanicsburg, OH	CIN
PA	HBG
Mechanicsville, IA	DAV
MD	WDC
VA	RIC
Mechanicville, NY	ALB
Medart, FL	PT
Medaryville, IN	LFT
Medfield, MA	BO
Medford, MA	BO
MN	WIN
NJ	TR
NY	RVC
OK	OKL
OR	P
WI	SUP
Media, PA	PH
Medical Lake, WA	SPK
Medicine Lodge, KS	DOD
Medina, ND	FAR
NY	BUF
OH	CLV
Medley's Neck, MD	WDC
Medora, IL	SFD
Medway, MA	BO
Meeker, CO	DEN
Megargel, TX	FWT
Mehlville, MO	STL
Meire Grove, MN	SCL
Melbourne, FL	ORL
KY	COV
Melbourne Beach, FL	ORL
Melcher, IA	DAV
Mellen, WI	SUP
Mellette, SD	SFS
Melrose, IA	DAV
MA	BO
MN	SCL
WI	LC
Melrose Park, IL	CHI
Melville, LA	LAF
NY	RVC
Melvindale, MI	DET
Memphis, MI	DET
MO	JC
TN	MEM
TX	AMA
Mena, AR	LR
Menahga, MN	SCL
Menands, NY	ALB
Menard, TX	SAN
Menasha, WI	GB
Mendham, NJ	PAT
Mendocino, CA	SR
Mendon, IL	SFD
MA	WOR
MI	KAL
NY	ROC
Mendota, CA	FRS
IL	PEO
MN	STP
Mendota Heights, MN	STP
Menlo Park, CA	OAK
CA	SFR
CA	SJ
Menoken, ND	BIS
Menominee, IL	RCK
MI	MAR
NE	OM
Menomonee Falls, WI	MIL
Menomonie, WI	LC
Mentor, MN	CR
OH	CLV
Mentor-on-the-Lake, OH	PRM
Mentz, TX	VIC
Meppen, IL	SFD
Mequon, WI	MIL
Meraux, LA	NO
Merced, CA	FRS
Mercedes, TX	BWN
Mercer, PA	E
WI	SUP
Mercer Island, WA	SEA
Merchantville, NJ	CAM
Meredith, KS	SAL
NH	MAN
Meriden, CT	HRT
CT	PSC
KS	KCK
Meridian, ID	B
MS	JKS
PA	PIT
Merion, PA	PH
Merion Station, PA	PH
Merizo, GU	AGN
Mermentau, LA	LAF
Merrick, NY	RVC

Merrill, IA	SC
MI	SAG
OR	BAK
WI	SUP
Merrillville, IN	GRY
IN	PRM
Merrimac, MA	BO
Merrimack, NH	MAN
Merritt Island, FL	ORL
Mesa, AZ	PHX
ID	B
Mescalero, NM	LSC
Meshoppen, PA	SCR
Mesilla, NM	LSC
Mesilla Park, NM	LSC
Meta, MO	JC
Metairie, LA	NO
Metaline Falls, WA	SPK
Metamora, IL	PEO
Methuen, MA	BO
MA	NTN
Metlakatla, AK	JUN
Metropolis, IL	BEL
Metuchen, NJ	MET
Metz, MI	GAY
Mexia, TX	AUS
Mexico, ME	PRT
MO	JC
NY	SY
Mexico Beach, FL	PT
Meyer, IA	DUB
Meyersdale, PA	ALT
Meyersville, TX	VIC
Miami, AZ	TUC
FL	MIA
FL	NTN
FL	PSC
FL	SAM
FL	SJP
OK	TLS
Miami Beach, FL	MIA
Miami Lakes, FL	MIA
Miami Shores, FL	MIA
Miami Springs, FL	MIA
Miamisburg, OH	CIN
Michael, IL	SFD
Michigan, ND	FAR
Michigan Center, MI	LAN
Michigan City, IN	GRY
Middle Lake, MN	NU
Middle Ridge, WI	LC
Middle River, MN	CR
Middle Village, NY	BRK
Middleboro, MA	BO
Middlebranch, OH	Y
Middleburg, FL	STA
VA	ARL
Middleburg Heights, OH	CLV
Middleburgh, NY	ALB
Middlebury, CT	HRT
VT	BUR
Middlefield, CT	NOR
OH	CLV
Middleport, NY	BUF
PA	PHU
Middlesboro, KY	LEX
Middlesex, NJ	MET
Middlesex County, VA	RIC
Middleton, MA	BO
WI	MAD
Middletown, CA	SR
CT	NOR
DE	WIL
MD	BAL
NJ	TR
NY	NY
NY	STF
OH	CIN
PA	HBG
RI	PRO
Middletown Springs, VT	BUR
Midland, MD	BAL
MI	SAG
PA	PIT
TX	SAN
Midland Park, NJ	NEW
Midlothian, IL	CHI
Midvale, UT	SLC
Midway City, CA	ORG
Miesville, MN	STP
Mifflintown, PA	HBG
Mikado, MI	GAY
Milaca, MN	SCL
Milan, IL	PEO
IN	IND
MI	LAN
MO	JC
NM	GLP
OH	TOL
TN	MEM
WI	LC

Milbank, SD	SFS
Mildred, PA	SCR
Miles, TX	SAN
Miles City, MT	GF
Milford, CT	HRT
DE	WIL
IA	SC
IN	FTW
MA	WOR
MI	DET
NH	MAN
NJ	MET
OH	CIN
PA	SCR
UT	SLC
Mililani Town, HI	HON
Mill Creek, WI	LC
Mill Valley, CA	SFR
Milladore, WI	LC
Millbrae, CA	OLL
CA	SFR
Millbrook, AL	MOB
NY	NY
Millbury, MA	WOR
Milledgeville, GA	ATL
Millen, GA	SAV
Miller, SD	SFS
Miller City, OH	TOL
Miller Heights, PA	ALN
Millers Falls, MA	SPR
Millersburg, OH	COL
PA	HBG
Millersville, MD	BAL
OH	TOL
PA	HBG
Millerville, MN	SCL
Millhousen, IN	IND
Millinocket, ME	PRT
Millis, MA	BO
Millstadt, IL	BEL
Milltown, NJ	MET
Millvale, PA	PIT
Millville, MA	WOR
NJ	CAM
NJ	PHU
OH	CIN
Millwood, MO	STL
Milmont Park, PA	PH
Milnor, ND	FAR
Milpitas, CA	SJ
Milroy, MN	NU
Milton, FL	PT
LA	LAF
MA	BO
ND	FAR
NY	NY
PA	HBG
VT	BUR
WI	MAD
Milton Freewater, OR	BAK
Miltonsburg, OH	STU
Miltonvale, KS	SAL
Milwaukee, WI	MIL
WI	NTN
WI	STN
Milwaukie, OR	P
Mims, FL	ORL
Minden, LA	SHP
NE	LIN
Mineola, NY	RVC
Mineral, VA	RIC
Mineral City, OH	COL
Mineral Point, WI	MAD
Mineral Ridge, OH	Y
Mineral Wells, TX	FWT
Minersville, PA	ALN
PA	PHU
PA	PSC
Minerva, OH	STU
Minetto, NY	SY
Mineville, NY	OG
Mingo Junction, OH	PBR
OH	STU
Minneapolis, KS	SAL
MN	OLL
MN	PRM
MN	STN
MN	STP
Minneiska, MN	WIN
Minneota, MN	NU
Minnesota City, MN	WIN
Minnesota Lake, MN	WIN
Minnetonka, MN	STP
Minnewaukan, ND	FAR
Minoa, NY	SY
Minocqua, WI	SUP
Minong, WI	SUP
Minonk, IL	PEO
Minooka, IL	JOL
Minot, ND	BIS
Minotola, NJ	CAM

Minster, OH	CIN
Minto, ND	FAR
Minturn, CO	DEN
Mio, MI	GAY
Miramar, FL	MIA
Mire, LA	LAF
Miriam, MI	GR
Mishawaka, IN	FTW
IN	LFT
IN	STN
Mishicot, WI	GB
Misquamicut, RI	PRO
Mission, KS	KCK
SD	RC
TX	BWN
Mission Hills, CA	LA
CA	ROM
Mission San Jose, CA	OAK
Mission Viejo, CA	ORG
Missoula, MT	HEL
Missouri City, TX	GAL
Missouri Valley, IA	DM
Mitchell, IN	IND
NE	GI
SD	SFS
WI	MIL
Mitchellville, MD	WDC
Moab, UT	SLC
Moberly, MO	JC
Mobile, AL	MOB
Mobridge, SD	SFS
Moca, PR	MGZ
Mocanaqua, PA	SCR
Mocksville, NC	CHL
Modesto, CA	STO
Modoc, IL	BEL
Moen, FM	CI
Mohall, ND	BIS
Mohawk, MI	MAR
NY	ALB
Mohnton, PA	ALN
Mojave, CA	FRS
Mokane, MO	JC
Mokena, IL	JOL
Molalla, OR	P
Moline, IL	PEO
KS	WCH
Momence, IL	JOL
Mon Luis Island, AL	MOB
Monaca, PA	PIT
Monahans, TX	ELP
Monarch, MT	GF
Monches, WI	MIL
Moncks Corner, SC	CHR
Mondamin, IA	DM
Mondovi, WI	LC
Monee, IL	JOL
Monessen, PA	GBG
PA	PBR
Moneta, VA	RIC
Monett, MO	SPC
Mongmong, GU	AGN
Monmouth, IL	PEO
Monmouth Beach, NJ	TR
Monmouth Junction, NJ	MET
Monona, IA	DUB
Monongah, WV	WH
Monongahela, PA	PBR
PA	PIT
Monroe, CT	BGP
GA	ATL
LA	SHP
MI	DET
NC	CHL
NY	NY
OH	CIN
OR	P
WA	SEA
WI	MAD
Monroe City, MO	JC
Monroe-Duvall, WA	SEA
Monroeville, AL	MOB
IN	FTW
OH	TOL
PA	PBR
PA	PIT
Monrovia, CA	LA
Monsey, NY	NY
Monson, MA	SPR
Mont Clare, PA	PSC
Montague, MI	GR
NJ	PAT
TX	FWT
Montauk, NY	RVC
Montclair, CA	SB
NJ	NEW
Montdale, PA	SCR
Monte Vista, CO	PBL
Montebello, CA	LA
Montecito, CA	LA
Montegut, LA	HT

Montello, WI	MAD
Monterey, CA	MRY
IN	LFT
NE	OM
Monterey Park, CA	LA
Montevallo, AL	BIR
Montevideo, MN	NU
Montezuma, IN	IND
NY	ROC
OH	CIN
Montfort, WI	MAD
Montgomery, AL	MOB
IN	EVN
MN	STP
NY	NY
WV	WH
Montgomery Center, VT	BUR
Montgomery City, MO	JC
Monti, IA	DUB
Monticello, AR	LR
FL	PT
IA	DUB
IL	PEO
IN	LFT
KY	LEX
MN	STP
NY	NY
UT	SLC
Montoursville, PA	SCR
Montpelier, IN	LFT
OH	TOL
VA	RIC
VT	BUR
WI	GB
Montreal, WI	SUP
Montrose, CA	ARM
CA	LA
CO	PBL
IA	DAV
IL	SFD
MI	LAN
MO	KC
NY	NY
PA	SCR
SD	SFS
Montvale, NJ	NEW
Montville, CT	NOR
NJ	PAT
Monument, CO	COS
Moodus, CT	NOR
Moody, TX	AUS
Mooers, NY	OG
Mooers Forks, NY	OG
Moon Township, PA	PIT
Moonachie, NJ	NEW
Mooney Creek, KS	KCK
Moore, OK	OKL
Moore Haven, FL	VEN
Moorefield, WV	WH
Moorestown, NJ	TR
Mooresville, IN	IND
NC	CHL
Mooreton, ND	FAR
Moorhead, MN	CR
Moorland, IA	SC
Moorpark, CA	LA
Moose Lake, MN	DUL
Moosup, CT	NOR
Moquah, WI	SUP
Mora, MN	SCL
NM	SFE
Moraga, CA	OAK
Moran, MI	MAR
MN	SCL
Moravia, NY	ROC
Moreauville, LA	ALX
Morehead, KY	LEX
Morehead City, NC	R
Morenci, AZ	TUC
Moreno Valley, CA	SB
Morgan, MN	NU
TX	FWT
Morgan City, LA	HT
Morgan Hill, CA	SJ
Morganfield, KY	OWN
Morganton, NC	CHL
Morgantown, KY	OWN
WV	PBR
WV	WH
Morganza, LA	BR
MD	WDC
Morges, OH	STU
Moriarty, NM	SFE
Morongo Valley, CA	SB
Morovis, PR	ARE
Morrice, MI	LAN
Morrill, MN	SCL
Morrilton, AR	LR
Morris, IL	JOL
IN	IND
MN	SCL

NY	ALB
Morris Plains, NJ	PAT
Morrisdale, PA	E
Morrison, IL	RCK
MO	JC
Morrison Bluff, AR	LR
Morrisonville, IL	SFD
NY	OG
Morristown, NJ	PAT
NY	OG
SD	RC
TN	KNX
Morrisville, NY	SY
PA	PH
VT	BUR
Morro Bay, CA	MRY
Morrow, LA	LAF
OH	CIN
Morrowville, KS	SAL
Morse, LA	LAF
Morse Bluff, NE	LIN
Morton, IL	PEO
MN	NU
PA	PH
TX	LUB
WA	SEA
Morton Grove, IL	CHI
Moscow, ID	B
PA	PHU
PA	SCR
TN	MEM
Moselle, MO	STL
Moses Lake, WA	YAK
Mosinee, WI	LC
Moss Beach, CA	SFR
Moss Bluff, LA	LKC
Moss Point, MS	BLX
Motley, MN	SCL
Mott, ND	BIS
Moulton, AL	BIR
TX	VIC
Moultrie, GA	SAV
Mound, MN	STP
Mound Bayou, MS	JKS
Mound City, IL	BEL
KS	KCK
Moundsville, WV	WH
Mt. Airy, NC	CHL
Mt. Angel, OR	P
Mount Arlington, NJ	PAT
Mt. Ayr, IA	DM
Mount Calvary, WI	MIL
Mount Carbon, PA	ALN
Mount Carmel, IA	SC
IL	BEL
Mt. Carmel, IN	LFT
Mount Carmel, ND	FAR
OH	CIN
PA	HBG
PA	PHU
Mount Carroll, IL	RCK
Mount Clemens, MI	DET
Mount Dora, FL	ORL
Mount Ephraim, NJ	CAM
Mount Holly, NJ	TR
Mount Hope, NJ	PAT
Mount Horeb, WI	MAD
Mount Jewett, PA	E
Mount Joy, PA	HBG
Mt. Kisco, NY	NY
Mount Laurel, NJ	TR
Mt. Lebanon, PA	PIT
Mount Morris, MI	LAN
NY	ROC
Mount Olive, IL	SFD
Mount Orab, OH	CIN
Mount Pleasant, IA	DAV
MI	SAG
PA	GBG
TX	TYL
Mt. Pleasant, VI	STV
Mount Pocono, PA	SCR
Mt. Prospect, IL	CHI
Mount Rainier, MD	WDC
Mount Repose, OH	CIN
Mount Saint Francis, IN	IND
Mount St. Macrina, PA	PBR
Mount Savage, MD	BAL
Mount Shasta, CA	SAC
Mount Sinai, NY	RVC
Mount Sterling, IL	SFD
Mt. Sterling, KY	LEX
Mount Union, PA	ALT
Mount Vernon, AL	MOB
IA	DUB
IL	BEL
IN	EVN
KS	WCH
Mt. Vernon, KY	LEX
Mount Vernon, MO	SPC
Mt. Vernon, NY	NY

OH	COL
Mount Vernon, SD	SFS
WA	SEA
Mount Washington, KY	L
Mt. Zion, IL	SFD
Mountain City, TN	KNX
Mountain Grove, MO	SPC
Mountain Home, AR	LR
ID	B
TX	SAT
Mountain Home Air Force Base, ID	B
Mountain Lakes, NJ	PAT
Mountain View, CA	SFR
CA	SJ
HI	HON
MO	SPC
Mountain Village, AK	FBK
Mountainair, NM	SFE
Mountainside, NJ	NEW
Mountaintop, PA	SCR
Mountlake Terrace, WA	SEA
Moville, IA	SC
Mowata, LA	LAF
Moweaqua, IL	SFD
Moxee City, WA	YAK
Muenster, TX	FWT
Mukwonago, WI	MIL
Mulberry, KS	WCH
Muleshoe, TX	LUB
Mullen, NE	GI
Mullens, WV	WH
Mullica Hill, NJ	CAM
Mulvane, KS	WCH
Muncie, IN	LFT
Muncy, PA	SCR
Mundelein, IL	CHI
Munden, KS	SAL
Mundys Corner, PA	ALT
Munger, MI	SAG
Munhall, PA	PBR
PA	PIT
Munich, ND	FAR
Munising, MI	MAR
Munjor, KS	SAL
Munnsville, NY	SY
Munster, IN	GRY
IN	PRM
IN	STN
Murdo, SD	RC
Murdock, FL	VEN
MN	NU
Murfreesboro, TN	NSH
Murphy, NC	CHL
Murphy Village, SC	CHR
Murphysboro, IL	BEL
Murray, KY	OWN
UT	OLL
UT	SLC
Murrayville, IL	SFD
Murrietta, CA	SB
Murrysville, PA	GBG
Muscatine, IA	DAV
Muscoda, WI	MAD
Muse, PA	PIT
Muskegan, MI	GR
Muskego, WI	MIL
Muskegon, MI	GR
Muskegon Heights, MI	GR
Muskogee, OK	TLS
Mustang, OK	OKL
Myerstown, PA	HBG
Myrtle Beach, SC	CHR
Myrtle Creek, OR	P
Mystic, CT	NOR
IA	DAV
Naalehu, HI	HON
Nabob, WI	MIL
Naches, WA	YAK
Nacogdoches, TX	TYL
Nada, TX	VIC
Nadeau, MI	MAR
Naguabo, PR	CGS
Nahant, MA	BO
Nahma, MI	MAR
Nampa, ID	B
Namur, WI	GB
Nanakuli, HI	HON
Nanticoke, PA	PHU
PA	PSC
PA	SCR
Nantucket, MA	FR
Nanty-Glo, PA	ALT
PA	PBR
Nanuet, NY	NY
Napa, CA	SR
Napanee, IN	FTW
Naperville, IL	JOL
Naples, FL	VEN
NY	ROC
Napoleon, IN	IND
ND	FAR

OH	TOL
Napoleonville, LA	BR
Napperville, IL	JOL
Naranja, FL	MIA
Naranjito, PR	CGS
Narberth, PA	PH
Narragansett, RI	PRO
Narrowsburg, NY	NY
Nashotah, WI	MIL
Nashua, IA	DUB
NH	MAN
Nashville, IL	BEL
IN	IND
TN	NSH
Nashwauk, MN	DUL
Nasonville, RI	PRO
Nassau, MN	NU
NY	ALB
Nassau Bay, TX	GAL
Natchez, LA	ALX
MS	JKS
Natchitoches, LA	ALX
Natick, MA	BO
National City, CA	SD
National Park, NJ	CAM
Natrona, PA	PIT
Natrona Heights, PA	PIT
Naugatuck, CT	HRT
WV	WH
Nauvoo, IL	PEO
Navajo, NM	GLP
Navarino, WI	GB
Navarre, FL	PT
OH	Y
Navasota, TX	GAL
Navilleton, IN	IND
Naytahwaush, MN	CR
Nazareth, KY	L
MI	KAL
PA	ALN
TX	AMA
Nebish, MN	CR
Nebraska City, NE	LIN
Necedah, WI	LC
Neche, ND	FAR
Nederland, TX	BEA
Needham, MA	BO
Needles, CA	SB
Needville, TX	GAL
Neenah, WI	GB
Neepwukos, Chuuk, FM	CI
Neffs, OH	STU
Negaunee, MI	MAR
Neier, MO	STL
Neillsville, WI	LC
Nekoma, ND	FAR
Nekoosa, WI	LC
Neligh, NE	OM
Nelsonville, OH	STU
Nemacolin, PA	PIT
Nemar, FM	CI
Nenana, AK	FBK
Nenno, WI	MIL
Neodesha, KS	WCH
Neoga, IL	SFD
Neola, IA	DM
Neopit, WI	GB
Neosho, MO	SPC
WI	MIL
Neptune, IA	SC
NJ	TR
Nerinx, KY	L
Nesbit, MS	JKS
Nesconset, NY	RVC
Neshannock, PA	PIT
Neshkoro, WI	MAD
Nespelem, WA	SPK
Nesquehoning, PA	ALN
PA	PSC
Ness City, KS	DOD
Netcong, NJ	PAT
Neva, WI	GB
Nevada, IA	DUB
MO	KC
Nevada City, CA	SAC
Nevis, MN	CR
New Albany, IN	IND
MS	JKS
OH	COL
New Albin, IA	DUB
New Alexandria, PA	GBG
PA	SJP
New Almelo, KS	SAL
New Alsace, IN	IND
New Athens, IL	BEL
New Auburn, WI	LC
New Baden, IL	BEL
New Baltimore, MI	DET
PA	ALT
New Bavaria, OH	TOL
New Bedford, MA	FR

MA	SAM
PA	PIT
New Berlin, IL	SFD
NY	SY
WI	MIL
New Bern, NC	R
New Bethlehem, PA	E
New Bloomfield, PA	HBG
New Bohemia, VA	RIC
New Boston, IN	EVN
MI	DET
NH	MAN
OH	COL
TX	TYL
New Braunfels, TX	SAT
New Bremen, OH	CIN
New Brighton, MN	STP
PA	PIT
New Britain, CT	HRT
CT	PSC
CT	STF
New Brunswick, NJ	MET
NJ	PHU
NJ	PSC
New Buffalo, MI	KAL
New Canaan, CT	BGP
New Caney, TX	GAL
New Carlisle, IN	FTW
OH	CIN
New Castle, DE	WIL
IN	IND
PA	PIT
PA	SAM
New Chicago, IN	GRY
New City, NY	NY
New Cleveland, OH	TOL
New Cumberland, PA	HBG
WV	WH
New Cuyama, CA	LA
New Derry, PA	GBG
New Effington, SD	SFS
New Egypt, NJ	TR
New England, ND	BIS
New Fairfield, CT	BGP
New Florence, PA	GBG
New Franken, WI	GB
New Freedom, PA	HBG
New Garden Township, PA	PH
New Hamburg, MO	SPC
New Hampton, IA	DUB
New Harmony, IN	EVN
New Hartford, CT	HRT
NY	SY
New Haven, CT	HRT
CT	STF
IA	DUB
IN	FTW
KY	L
MI	DET
MO	STL
New Holland, PA	HBG
New Holstein, WI	GB
New Hope, KY	L
MN	STP
PA	PH
New Hradec, ND	BIS
New Hyde Park, NY	RVC
New Iberia, LA	LAF
New Ipswich, NH	MAN
New Kensington, PA	GBG
PA	SJP
New Lebanon, NY	ALB
New Lenox, IL	JOL
New Lexington, OH	COL
New Lisbon, WI	LC
New London, CT	NOR
NH	MAN
NY	SY
OH	TOL
WI	GB
New Madrid, MO	SPC
New Marion, IN	IND
New Market, MN	STP
New Martinsville, WV	WH
New Melle, MO	STL
New Melleray, IA	DUB
New Miami, OH	CIN
New Middletown, IN	IND
OH	Y
New Milford, CT	HRT
NJ	NEW
New Monmouth, NJ	TR
New Munich, MN	SCL
New Munster, WI	MIL
New Orleans, LA	NO
New Oxford, PA	HBG
New Paltz, NY	NY
New Paris, OH	CIN
New Philadelphia, OH	COL
PA	ALN
New Plymouth, ID	B
New Port Richey, FL	PSC
FL	SP
New Post, WI	SUP
New Prague, MN	STP
New Providence, NJ	NEW
New Richland, MN	WIN
New Richmond, OH	CIN
WI	SUP
New Riegel, OH	TOL
New Ringgold, PA	ALN
New Roads, LA	BR
New Rochelle, NY	NY
New Rockford, ND	FAR
New Salem, ND	BIS
PA	GBG
PA	PBR
New Smyrna Beach, FL	ORL
New Taiton, TX	VIC
New Town, ND	BIS
New Trier, MN	STP
New Ulm, MN	NU
New Underwood, SD	RC
New Vernon, NJ	PAT
New Vienna, IA	DUB
OH	CIN
New Village, NJ	MET
New Washington, OH	TOL
New Waverly, TX	GAL
New Windsor, NY	NY
New York, NY	ARM
NY	NTN
NY	NY
NY	PSC
NY	ROC
NY	STF
New York Mills, NY	SY
Newark, CA	OAK
DE	WIL
NJ	NEW
NJ	OLD
NJ	PHU
NJ	PSC
NY	ROC
OH	COL
Newark Valley, NY	ROC
Newaygo, MI	GR
Newberg, OR	P
Newberry, MI	MAR
SC	CHR
Newberry Springs, CA	VNN
Newburg, WI	MIL
Newburgh, IN	EVN
NY	NY
Newbury, OH	CLV
Newbury Park, CA	LA
Newburyport, MA	BO
Newcastle, ME	PRT
NE	OM
WY	CHY
Newcomb, NY	OG
TN	KNX
Newcomerstown, OH	COL
Newell, SD	RC
Newfane, NY	BUF
Newfield, NJ	CAM
Newhall, IA	DUB
Newington, CT	HRT
Newkirk, OK	OKL
Newman, CA	STO
Newmarket, NH	MAN
Newnan, GA	ATL
Newport, AR	LR
IA	DAV
KY	COV
MD	WDC
MI	DET
NH	MAN
NY	ALB
OH	CIN
OR	P
RI	PRO
TN	KNX
VT	BUR
WA	SPK
Newport Beach, CA	ORG
Newport News, VA	RIC
Newry, PA	ALT
Newtok, AK	FBK
Newton, IA	DAV
IL	SFD
KS	WCH
MA	BO
MA	NTN
NC	CHL
NH	MAN
NJ	PAT
Newton Falls, OH	PBR
OH	Y
Newton Grove, NC	R
Newtown, CT	BGP
PA	ALN
PA	PH
Newtown Square, PA	PH
PA	SAM
Newtowne, MD	WDC
Nezperce, ID	B
Niagara, WI	GB
Niagara Falls, NY	BUF
NY	STF
Niagara University, NY	BUF
Niantic, CT	NOR
IL	SFD
Niceville, FL	PT
Nicholasville, KY	LEX
Nichols, IA	DAV
Nicholson, PA	SCR
Nicktown, PA	ALT
Nicollet, MN	NU
Nicoma Park, OK	OKL
Nightmute, AK	FBK
Niles, IL	CHI
KS	SAL
MI	KAL
OH	Y
Nine Mile, MI	SAG
Nipomo, CA	MRY
Niskayuna, NY	ALB
Nitro, WV	WH
Nix Settlement, IN	FTW
Nixon, TX	SAT
Noble, LA	SHP
Noblesville, IN	LFT
Nocona, TX	FWT
Nogales, AZ	TUC
Nokomis, IL	SFD
Nolan Settlement, IA	DAV
Nome, AK	FBK
Norbeck, MD	WDC
Norco, CA	SB
LA	NO
Norcross, GA	ATL
Norfolk, CT	HRT
MA	BO
NE	OM
NY	OG
VA	RIC
Norge, VA	RIC
Normal, IL	PEO
Norman, OK	OKL
WI	GB
Normandy, MO	STL
Normandy Beach, NJ	TR
Norridge, IL	CHI
Norris, SD	RC
TN	KNX
Norristown, PA	PH
North Adams, MA	SPR
North Andover, MA	BO
North Arlington, NJ	NEW
North Arm, IL	SFD
North Attleboro, MA	FR
North Auburn, OH	TOL
North Augusta, SC	CHR
North Aurora, IL	RCK
North Baltimore, OH	TOL
North Bangor, NY	OG
North Bay, NY	SY
North Beach, MD	WDC
North Bend, NE	OM
OR	P
North Bennington, VT	BUR
North Bergen, NJ	NEW
North Bethesda, MD	WDC
North Branch, MI	DET
MN	STP
North Branford, CT	HRT
North Brookfield, MA	SAM
MA	WOR
North Brunswick, NJ	MET
North Buena Vista, IA	DUB
North Caldwell, NJ	NEW
North Canton, OH	Y
North Cape May, NJ	CAM
North Chicago, IL	CHI
North Chili, NY	ROC
North Collins, NY	BUF
North Conway, NH	MAN
North Creek, NY	ALB
OH	TOL
WI	LC
North Dartmouth, MA	FR
North Dighton, MA	FR
North East, PA	E
North Easton, MA	FR
North English, IA	DAV
North Evans, NY	BUF
North Falmouth, MA	FR
North Fond du Lac, WI	MIL
North Fort Myers, FL	PSC
North Grafton, MA	WOR
North Greenbush, NY	ALB
North Grosvenordale, CT	NOR
North Guilford, CT	HRT
North Haledon, NJ	PAT
North Haven, CT	HRT
North Highlands, CA	SAC
North Hills, CA	LA
North Hills-Gibsonia, PA	PBR
North Hollywood, CA	EST
CA	LA
CA	NTN
CA	OLD
North Huntingdon, PA	GBG
PA	PBR
North Jackson, OH	OLL
OH	Y
North Java, NY	BUF
North Judson, IN	GRY
North Kingstown, RI	PRO
North Kinsley, KS	DOD
North Lake, WI	MIL
North Las Vegas, NV	LAV
North Lauderdale, FL	MIA
North Lawrence, NY	OG
North Lewisburg, OH	CIN
North Lima, OH	Y
North Little Rock, AR	LR
North Manchester, IN	FTW
North Mankato, MN	NU
North Merrick, NY	RVC
North Miami, FL	MIA
North Miami Beach, FL	MIA
North Muskegon, MI	GR
North Myrtle Beach, SC	CHR
North Oakland, PA	PIT
North Olmsted, OH	CLV
North Oxford, MA	WOR
North Palm Beach, FL	PMB
North Plainfield, NJ	MET
NJ	TR
North Plains, OR	P
North Platte, NE	GI
North Pole, AK	FBK
North Port, FL	SJP
FL	VEN
MI	GAY
North Prairie, MN	SCL
North Providence, RI	PRO
North Reading, MA	BO
North Ridgeville, OH	CLV
North Riverside, IL	CHI
North Rochester, PA	PIT
North Royalton, OH	CLV
OH	PRM
North St. Paul, MN	STP
North Scituate, RI	PRO
North Smithfield, RI	PRO
North Stamford, CT	BGP
North Star, OH	CIN
North Stonington, CT	NOR
North Stratford, NH	MAN
North Syracuse, NY	SY
North Tarrytown, NY	NY
North Tiverton, RI	PRO
North Tonawanda, NY	BUF
North Topsail Beach, NC	R
North Troy, VT	BUR
North Vassalboro, ME	PRT
North Vernon, IN	IND
North Wales, PA	PH
North Walpole, NH	MAN
North Washington, IA	DUB
North Wilkesboro, NC	CHL
Northampton, MA	SPR
PA	ALN
PA	PHU
Northboro, MA	WOR
Northbridge, MA	WOR
Northbrook, IL	CHI
Northeast Harbor, ME	PRT
Northeim, WI	GB
Northfield, IL	CHI
MA	SPR
MN	STP
NJ	CAM
OH	CLV
VT	BUR
Northford, CT	HRT
Northglenn, CO	DEN
Northhampton, PA	ALN
Northlake, IL	CHI
IL	NTN
Northome, MN	DUL
Northport, NY	RVC
WA	SPK
Northridge, CA	LA
Northumberland, PA	HBG
Northvale, NJ	NEW
Northville, MI	DET
NY	ALB
Northwood, OH	PRM
Norton, KS	SAL
MA	FR

OH	CLV
VA	RIC
Nortonville, KS	KCK
ND	FAR
Norwalk, CA	LA
CT	BGP
OH	TOL
WI	LC
Norway, IA	DUB
ME	PRT
MI	MAR
Norwell, MA	BO
Norwich, CT	NOR
NY	SY
Norwood, MA	BO
MN	STP
NJ	NEW
NY	OG
PA	PH
Notre Dame, IN	FTW
Novato, CA	SFR
Novi, MI	DET
Nulato, AK	FBK
Nunda, NY	ROC
Nutley, NJ	NEW
Nyack, NY	NY
Nyssa, OR	BAK
O'Donnell, TX	LUB
O'Fallon, IL	BEL
MO	STL
O'Hara Township, PA	PIT
O'Neill, NE	OM
Oak Bluffs, MA	FR
Oak Brook, IL	JOL
Oak Creek, CO	DEN
WI	MIL
Oak Forest, IL	CHI
IN	IND
Oak Grove, KY	OWN
LA	SHP
Oak Harbor, OH	TOL
WA	SEA
Oak Hill, WV	WH
Oak Lawn, IL	CHI
Oak Park, CA	LA
IL	CHI
MI	DET
MI	EST
Oak Ridge, MN	WIN
NJ	PAT
TN	KNX
Oak Ridge-Milton, NJ	PAT
Oakbrook Terrace, IL	JOL
Oakdale, CA	STO
CT	NOR
LA	LKC
MN	STP
NY	RVC
PA	PIT
Oakes, ND	FAR
Oakesdale, WA	SPK
Oakfield, NY	BUF
WI	MIL
Oakland, CA	NTN
CA	OAK
MD	BAL
ME	PRT
NJ	NEW
Oakland City, IN	EVN
Oakley, CA	OAK
KS	SAL
MI	SAG
Oaklyn, NJ	CAM
Oakmont, PA	PIT
Oakridge, OR	P
Oakville, CA	SR
CT	HRT
MO	STL
Oakwood, ND	FAR
Oberlin, KS	SAL
LA	LKC
OH	CLV
Obernburg, NY	NY
Oblong, IL	SFD
Ocala, FL	ORL
Occidental, CA	SR
Occum, CT	NOR
Ocean Beach, NY	RVC
Ocean City, MD	WIL
NJ	CAM
Ocean Shores, WA	SEA
Ocean Springs, MS	BLX
Oceanside, CA	SD
NY	RVC
Oconee, IL	SFD
Oconomowoc, WI	MIL
Oconto, WI	GB
Oconto Falls, WI	GB
Odanah, WI	SUP
Odebolt, IA	SC
Odell, IL	PEO

Odem, TX	CC
Odenton, MD	BAL
Odessa, MO	KC
NY	ROC
TX	SAN
WA	SPK
Odin, KS	DOD
Oelwein, IA	DUB
Offerle, KS	DOD
Ogallala, NE	GI
Ogden, IA	SC
KS	SAL
UT	SLC
Ogdensburg, NJ	PAT
NY	OG
Ogema, MN	CR
Ogilvie, MN	SCL
Oglala, SD	RC
Oglesby, IL	PEO
Ogletown, DE	WIL
Ohio, IL	PEO
Oil City, PA	E
Oildale, CA	FRS
Ojai, CA	LA
Okanogan-Omak, WA	SPK
Okarche, OK	OKL
Okauchee, WI	MIL
Okawville, IL	BEL
Okeechobee, FL	PMB
Okeene, OK	OKL
Okemos, MI	LAN
Oklahoma City, OK	OKL
Oklee, MN	CR
Okmulgee, OK	TLS
Olathe, KS	KCK
Olcott, NY	BUF
Old Bridge, NJ	MET
Old Brookville, NY	RVC
Old Fields, WV	WH
Old Forge, NY	OG
PA	PSC
PA	SCR
Old Hickory, TN	NSH
Old Lyme, CT	NOR
Old Mines, MO	STL
Old Monroe, MO	STL
Old Orchard Beach, ME	PRT
Old Saybrook, CT	NOR
Old Tappan, NJ	NEW
Old Town, ME	PRT
Old Washington-on-the Brazos, TX	AUS
Old Westbury, NY	RVC
Oldenburg, IN	IND
Oldham, SD	SFS
Olean, NE	OM
NY	BUF
NY	PSC
NY	SAM
Olema, CA	SFR
Olfen, TX	SAN
Olga, ND	FAR
Olive Branch, MS	JKS
Olive Hill, KY	LEX
Olivia, MN	NU
Olmitz, KS	DOD
Olmsted Falls, OH	CLV
Olmstedville, NY	OG
Olney, IL	BEL
MD	WDC
TX	FWT
Olpe, KS	KCK
Olympia, WA	SEA
Olympia Fields, IL	CHI
Olyphant, PA	PHU
PA	SCR
Omaha, NE	OM
NE	STN
Omak, WA	SPK
Omer, MI	PRM
Omro, WI	GB
Ona, WV	WH
Onaga, KS	KCK
Onaka, SD	SFS
Onalaska, WI	LC
Onamia, MN	SCL
Onawa, IA	SC
Onaway, MI	GAY
Oneida, NY	SY
WI	GB
Oneida Township, WI	GB
Onekama, MI	GAY
Oneonta, AL	BIR
NY	ALB
Onida, SD	SFS
Onley, VA	RIC
Onondaga Hill, NY	SY
Onset, MA	FR
Onsted, MI	DET
Ontario, CA	SB
NY	ROC

OR	BAK
Ontonagon, MI	MAR
Opa Locka, FL	MIA
Opelika, AL	MOB
Opelousas, LA	LAF
Opole, MN	SCL
Oquossoc, ME	PRT
Oradell, NJ	NEW
Oran, MO	SPC
Orange, CA	ORG
CT	HRT
MA	SPR
NJ	NEW
TX	BEA
VA	ARL
Orange Beach, AL	MOB
Orange Cove, CA	FRS
Orange Grove, TX	CC
Orange Park, FL	STA
Orange Village, OH	CLV
Orangeburg, NY	NY
SC	CHR
Orangefield, TX	BEA
Orangevale, CA	SAC
Orchard Lake, MI	DET
Orchard Park, NY	BUF
Ord, NE	GI
Ordot, GU	AGN
Oreana, ID	B
Orefield, PA	ALN
Oregon, IL	RCK
OH	TOL
WI	MAD
Oregon City, OR	P
Oreland, PA	PH
Orient, IA	DM
SD	SFS
Orinda, CA	OAK
Orion, IL	PEO
Orion Township, MI	DET
Oriska, ND	FAR
Oriskany, NY	SY
Oriskany Falls, NY	SY
Orland, CA	SAC
ME	PRT
Orland Hills, IL	CHI
Orland Park, IL	CHI
Orlando, FL	ORL
FL	PSC
FL	SAM
FL	STA
Orleans, MA	FR
NE	LIN
VT	BUR
Ormond Beach, FL	ORL
FL	PSC
Orocovis, PR	ARE
Orofino, ID	B
Orono, ME	PRT
Oroville, CA	SAC
WA	SPK
Orr, MN	DUL
Orrin, ND	FAR
Orrville, AL	MOB
OH	CLV
Ortonville, MI	DET
MN	NU
Orwell, OH	Y
VT	BUR
Orwigsburg, PA	ALN
Osage, IA	DUB
Osage Bend, MO	JC
Osage City, KS	KCK
Osakis, MN	SCL
Osawatomie, KS	KCK
Osborne, KS	SAL
Osceola, AR	LR
IA	DM
NE	LIN
WI	SUP
Osceola Mills, PA	E
Oscoda, MI	GAY
Osgood, IN	IND
OH	CIN
Oshkosh, WI	GB
Oskaloosa, IA	DAV
Oslo, MN	CR
Osman, WI	GB
Osmond, NE	OM
Osnabrock, ND	FAR
Osseo, MN	STP
Ossian, IA	DUB
Ossineke, MI	GAY
Ossining, NY	NY
Ost, KS	WCH
Osterville, MA	FR
Oswego, IL	JOL
KS	WCH
NY	SY
Othello, WA	SPK
Otis, IN	GRY

Otis Orchards, WA	SPK
Otisville, MI	LAN
NY	NY
Otsego, MI	KAL
Ottawa, IL	PEO
KS	KCK
OH	TOL
Ottenheim, KY	LEX
Otter Creek, IA	DUB
Otter River, MA	WOR
Otterbein, IN	LFT
Ottoville, OH	TOL
Ottsville, PA	PH
Ottumwa, IA	DAV
Otway, OH	COL
Ouray, CO	PBL
Overbrook, PA	PH
PA	PIT
Overgaard, AZ	GLP
Overland, MO	STL
Overland Park, KS	KCK
Overton, NV	LAV
Ovid, MI	LAN
NY	ROC
Owasso, OK	TLS
Owatonna, MN	WIN
Owego, NY	ROC
Owen, WI	LC
Owensboro, KY	OWN
Owensville, MD	BAL
MO	JC
OH	CIN
Owingsville, KY	LEX
Owosso, MI	LAN
Oxford, CT	HRT
IA	DAV
IN	LFT
KS	WCH
MA	WOR
MI	DET
MS	JKS
NJ	MET
NY	SY
OH	CIN
PA	PH
Oxford Junction, IA	DUB
Oxnard, CA	LA
Oxon Hill, MD	WDC
Oyens, IA	SC
Oyster Bay, NY	RVC
Ozark, AL	MOB
AR	LR
MO	SPC
Ozona, TX	SAN
Ozone Park, (1954)	STF
NY	BRK
Ozora, MO	STL
Pacific, MO	STL
Pacific City, OR	P
Pacific Grove, CA	MRY
Pacific Palisades, CA	LA
Pacifica, CA	SFR
Pacoima, CA	LA
Paden City, WV	WH
Paderborn, IL	BEL
Padua, MN	SCL
Paducah, KY	OWN
Paeonian Springs, VA	ARL
Page, AZ	GLP
ND	FAR
Pagedale, MO	STL
Pago Pago, AS	SPP
Pagosa Springs, CO	PBL
Pahala, HI	HON
Pahoa, HI	HON
Pahokee, FL	PMB
Pahrump, NV	LAV
Paia, HI	HON
Paincourtville, LA	BR
Painesville, OH	CLV
Painted Post, NY	ROC
Paintsville, KY	LEX
Paisley, OR	BAK
Pala, CA	SD
Pala Indian Missions, CA	SD
Palacios, TX	VIC
Palatine, IL	CHI
IL	STN
Palatka, FL	STA
Palau, PW	CI
Palenville, NY	ALB
Palestine, TX	TYL
Palikir, FM	CI
Palisades Park, NJ	NEW
Palm Bay, FL	ORL
Palm Beach, FL	PMB
Palm Beach Gardens, FL	PMB
Palm City, FL	PMB
Palm Coast, FL	STA
Palm Desert, CA	SB
Palm Harbor, FL	SP

Palm Springs, CA	SB
CA	VNN
Palmdale, CA	LA
Palmer, AK	ANC
MA	SPR
PA	GBG
PR	SJN
Palmerton, PA	ALN
PA	PHU
PA	PSC
Palmerton-Slatington, PA	ALN
Palmetto, FL	VEN
Palms, MI	SAG
Palmyra, IL	SFD
MO	JC
NE	LIN
NY	ROC
PA	HBG
VA	RIC
WI	MAD
Palo Alto, CA	SJ
Palo Cedro, CA	SAC
Palos Heights, IL	CHI
Palos Hills, IL	CHI
Palos Park, IL	CHI
IL	STN
Pampa, TX	AMA
Pana, IL	SFD
Panama, IA	DM
IL	SFD
Panama City, FL	PT
Panama City Beach, FL	PT
Panhandle, TX	AMA
Panna Maria, TX	SAT
Panora, IA	DM
Panorama City, CA	LA
Paola, KS	KCK
Paoli, IN	IND
PA	PH
Paonia, CO	PBL
Papaaloa, HI	HON
Papaikou, HI	HON
Papillion, NE	OM
Paradis, LA	NO
Paradise, CA	SAC
Paradox, NY	ALB
Paragould, AR	LR
Paramount, CA	LA
Paramus, NJ	NEW
Parana, Brazil	CHI
Parchment, MI	KAL
Pardeesville, PA	SCR
Pardeeville, WI	MAD
Paris, AR	LR
IL	SFD
KY	LEX
TN	MEM
TX	TYL
WI	MIL
Parish, NY	SY
Parisville, MI	SAG
Park, KS	SAL
Park City, UT	SLC
Park Falls, WI	SUP
Park Forest, IL	CHI
IL	JOL
Park Hills, MO	STL
Park Rapids, MN	CR
Park Ridge, IL	CHI
NJ	NEW
Park River, ND	FAR
Parker, AZ	TUC
CO	COS
PA	GBG
SD	SFS
Parkers Prairie, MN	SCL
Parkersburg, IA	DUB
WV	WH
Parkesburg, PA	PH
Parkland, FL	MIA
Parkman, OH	CLV
Parks, LA	LAF
Parkston, SD	SFS
Parkton, MD	BAL
Parkville, MO	KC
Parlier, CA	FRS
Parlin, NJ	MET
Parma, ID	B
OH	CLV
OH	PRM
OH	SJP
Parma Heights, OH	CLV
Parmelee, SD	RC
Parnell, IA	DAV
MI	GR
MO	KC
Parrish, FL	VEN
Parshall, ND	BIS
Parsippany, NJ	PAT
Parsons, KS	WCH
Pasadena, CA	LA
MD	BAL
TX	GAL
Pascagoula, MS	BLX
Pasco, WA	SPK
Pascoag, RI	PRO
Paso Robles, CA	MRY
Pass Christian, MS	BLX
Passaic, NJ	PAT
NJ	PHU
NJ	PSC
Patagonia, AZ	TUC
Pataskala, OH	COL
Patchogue, NY	RVC
Paterson, NJ	ARM
NJ	PAT
Patillas, PR	PCE
Patterson, CA	STO
LA	LAF
NY	NY
Pattison Park, WI	SUP
Pattison/Brookshire, TX	GAL
Patton, PA	ALT
PA	PBR
Paul, NE	LIN
Paulding, MS	JKS
OH	TOL
Paulina, LA	BR
Pauls Valley, OK	OKL
Paulsboro, NJ	CAM
Pavilion, NY	BUF
Paw Paw, MI	KAL
Pawcatuck, CT	NOR
Pawhuska, OK	TLS
Pawleys Island, SC	CHR
Pawling, NY	NY
Pawnee, IL	SFD
OK	TLS
Pawtucket, RI	PRO
RI	SAM
Paxico, KS	KCK
Paxton, IL	JOL
MA	WOR
Payette, ID	B
Payne, OH	TOL
Paynesville, MN	SCL
Payneville, KY	L
Payson, AZ	TUC
UT	SLC
Pe Ell, WA	SEA
Peabody, MA	BO
Peace Dale, RI	PRO
Peachtree City, GA	ATL
Peaks Island, ME	PRT
Peapack, NJ	MET
Pearisburg, VA	RIC
Pearl, MI	KAL
MS	JKS
Pearl City, HI	HON
Pearl Lake, MN	SCL
Pearl River, LA	NO
NY	NY
Pearland, TX	GAL
Pearlington, MS	BLX
Pearsall, TX	SAT
Pecatonica, IL	RCK
Peckville, PA	SCR
Pecos, NM	SFE
TX	ELP
Peebles, OH	CIN
Peekskill, NY	NY
NY	PSC
Peetz, CO	DEN
Pekin, IL	PEO
Pelham, NH	MAN
NY	NY
Pelham Manor, NY	NY
Pelican Lake, WI	SUP
Pelican Rapids, MN	SCL
Pell City, AL	BIR
Pell Lake, WI	MIL
Pella, IA	DAV
Pellston, MI	GAY
Pembina, ND	FAR
Pembine, WI	GB
Pembroke, MA	BO
Pembroke Pines, FL	MIA
Pen Argyl, PA	ALN
Pena Blanca, NM	SFE
Penacook, NH	MAN
Penasco, NM	SFE
Pence, WI	SUP
Pender, NE	OM
Pendleton, NY	BUF
OR	BAK
Penelope, TX	FWT
Penfield, IL	PEO
NY	ROC
Peninsula, OH	CLV
Penn, ND	FAR
PA	GBG
Penn Hills, PA	PIT
Penn Valley, PA	PH
Penn Yan, NY	ROC
Penndel, PA	PH
Penngrove, CA	SR
Pennington, MN	CR
NJ	TR
Pennington Gap, VA	RIC
Penns Grove, NJ	CAM
Penns Valley, PA	ALT
Pennsauken, NJ	CAM
Pennsville, NJ	CAM
Pensacola, FL	PT
Pensacola Beach, FL	PT
Penuelas, PR	PCE
Peonia, KY	OWN
Peoria, AZ	PHX
IL	OLL
IL	PEO
Peosta, IA	DUB
Peotone, IL	JOL
Peplin, WI	LC
Pepper Pike, OH	CLV
Pepperell, MA	BO
Pequannock, NJ	PAT
Pequot Lakes, MN	DUL
Peralta, NM	SFE
Perezville-Tamuning, GU	AGN
Perham, MN	SCL
Perkins, MI	MAR
Perkinston, MS	BLX
Perris, CA	SB
Perronville, MI	MAR
Perry, FL	PT
GA	SAV
IA	DM
KS	KCK
ME	PRT
MO	JC
NY	BUF
OH	CLV
OK	OKL
Perryopolis, PA	GBG
PA	PBR
Perrysburg, NY	BUF
OH	TOL
Perrysville, PA	PIT
Perryton, TX	AMA
Perryville, MD	WIL
MO	STL
Perth Amboy, NJ	MET
NJ	PHU
NJ	PSC
Peru, IL	PEO
IN	LFT
NY	OG
OH	TOL
Peshabestown, MI	GAY
Peshtigo, WI	GB
Pesotum, IL	PEO
Petaluma, CA	SFR
CA	SR
Peterborough, NH	MAN
Peters Township, PA	PIT
Petersburg, AK	JUN
IA	DUB
IL	SFD
IN	EVN
NE	OM
TX	LUB
VA	RIC
WV	WH
Petersham, MA	SAM
MA	WOR
Peterstown, IL	PEO
Petersville, IA	DAV
Petoskey, MI	GAY
Pevely, MO	STL
Pewamo, MI	GR
Pewaukee, WI	MIL
Pewee Valley, KY	L
Pfeifer, KS	SAL
Pflugerville, TX	AUS
Pharr, TX	BWN
Phelan, CA	SB
Phelps, NY	ROC
WI	SUP
Phenix City, AL	MOB
Philadelphia, MS	JKS
PA	ARM
PA	PH
PA	PHU
PA	PSC
PA	SAM
Philip, SD	RC
Philippi, WV	OLL
WV	WH
Philipsburg, MT	HEL
PA	ALT
Phillips, WI	SUP
Phillipsburg, KS	SAL
NJ	MET
NJ	PSC
Philmont, NY	ALB
Philo, CA	SR
IL	PEO
Philothea, OH	CIN
Philpot, KY	OWN
Phlox, WI	GB
Phoenicia, NY	NY
Phoenix, AZ	NTN
AZ	OLL
AZ	PHX
AZ	STN
AZ	VNN
NY	SY
Phoenixville, PA	PH
PA	PHU
Picayune, MS	BLX
Pickens, SC	CHR
Pickerington, OH	COL
Pico Rivera, CA	LA
Piedmont, CA	OAK
MO	SPC
Piedmont-Black Hawk, SD	RC
Pierce, NE	OM
Pierce City, MO	SPC
Pierceton, IN	FTW
Piermont, NY	NY
Pierre, SD	SFS
Pierre Part, LA	BR
Pierron, IL	SFD
Pier-Willow, WI	SUP
Pierz, MN	SCL
Piffard, NY	ROC
Pigeon, MI	SAG
Pikesville, MD	BAL
Pikeville, KY	LEX
Pilot Grove, MO	JC
Pilot Knob, MO	SPC
Pilot Point, TX	FWT
Pilot Rock, OR	BAK
Pilot Station, AK	FBK
Pilsen, KS	WCH
Pin Oak, TX	AUS
Pinckney, MI	LAN
Pinckneyville, IL	BEL
Pinconning, MI	SAG
Pine Apple, AL	MOB
Pine Bluff, AR	LR
WI	MAD
Pine Bluffs, WY	CHY
Pine Bush, NY	NY
Pine City, MN	DUL
NY	ROC
Pine Creek, WI	LC
Pine Grove, OH	STU
WI	GB
Pine Hill, NJ	CAM
Pine Island, MN	STP
NY	NY
Pine Lawn, MO	STL
Pine Plains, NY	NY
Pine Prairie, LA	LAF
Pine Ridge, SD	RC
Pine River, MN	DUL
Pinedale, WY	CHY
Pinehaven, NM	GLP
Pinehurst, NC	R
Pinellas Park, FL	SP
Pinetop, AZ	GLP
Pineville, LA	ALX
MS	BLX
WV	WH
Piney Fork, OH	STU
Pingree, ND	FAR
Pinnebog, MI	SAG
Pinole, CA	OAK
Pinon, AZ	GLP
Piopolis, IL	BEL
Piper City, IL	JOL
Pipestone, MN	WIN
Piqua, KS	WCH
OH	CIN
Pirtleville, AZ	TUC
Piscataway, MD	WDC
NJ	MET
Pisek, ND	FAR
Pismo Beach, CA	MRY
Pitcairn, PA	PIT
Piti, GU	AGN
Pitman, NJ	CAM
Pittsburg, CA	OAK
KS	WCH
TX	TYL
Pittsburgh, PA	PBR
PA	PIT
PA	SAM
PA	SJP
Pittsfield, IL	SFD
MA	SPR
MA	STF
ME	PRT

NH	MAN
Pittsford, NY	ROC
VT	BUR
Pittsgrove, NJ	CAM
Pittston, PA	PSC
PA	SCR
Pittstown, NJ	MET
NY	ALB
Pittsville, WI	LC
Placentia, CA	ORG
Placerville, CA	SAC
Placid, IA	DUB
Plain, WI	MAD
Plain City, OH	COL
Plainfield, CT	NOR
IL	JOL
IN	IND
NJ	NEW
WI	GB
Plains, KS	DOD
MT	HEL
PA	SCR
Plainsboro, NJ	MET
Plainview, MN	WIN
NE	OM
NY	RVC
TX	LUB
Plainville, CT	HRT
KS	SAL
MA	BO
Plaisance, LA	LAF
Plaistow, NH	MAN
Planada, CA	FRS
Plankinton, SD	SFS
Plano, IL	JOL
TX	DAL
Plant City, FL	SP
Plantation, FL	MIA
Plantersville, TX	GAL
Plantsville, CT	HRT
Plaquemine, LA	BR
Plateau, AL	MOB
Platte, SD	SFS
Platte Center, NE	OM
Plattekill, NY	NY
Plattenville, LA	BR
Platteville, CO	DEN
WI	MAD
Plattsburg, MO	KC
Plattsburgh, NY	OG
Plattsmouth, NE	LIN
Plaucheville, LA	ALX
Playa De Ponce, PR	PCE
Playa Del Rey, CA	LA
Playa Ponce, PR	PCE
Pleasant City, OH	PBR
Pleasant Hill, CA	OAK
Pleasant Hills, PA	PIT
Pleasant Mount, PA	SCR
Pleasant Point, ME	PRT
Pleasant Valley, NY	NY
Pleasanton, CA	OAK
NE	GI
TX	SAT
Pleasantville, NJ	CAM
NY	NY
Pleasure Ridge Park, KY	L
Plentywood, MT	GF
Plover, WI	LC
Plum, TX	VIC
Plum City, WI	LC
Plummer, MN	CR
Plymouth, IA	DUB
IN	FTW
MA	BO
MI	DET
MI	NTN
MN	STP
NC	R
NH	MAN
OH	TOL
PA	PHU
PA	SCR
WI	MIL
Plymouth Rock, IA	DUB
Pocahontas, AR	LR
IA	SC
IL	SFD
VA	RIC
Pocantico Hills, NY	NY
Pocasset, MA	FR
Pocatello, ID	B
Pocomoke City, MD	WIL
Pocono Pines, PA	SCR
Pohnpei, FM	CI
Poinciana, FL	ORL
Point Arena, CA	SR
Point Judith, RI	PRO
Point Lookout, NY	RVC
Point Marion, PA	GBG
Point Pleasant, NJ	TR
WV	WH
Point Pleasant Beach, NJ	TR
Point Richmond, CA	OAK
Pointe a la Hache, LA	NO
Pointe-Aux-Chenes, LA	HT
Pojoaque, NM	SFE
Poland, OH	Y
Pollock Pines, CA	SAC
Polo, IL	RCK
SD	SFS
Polonia, WI	LC
Polson, MT	HEL
Pomeroy, IA	SC
OH	STU
WA	SPK
Pomfret, CT	NOR
MD	WDC
Pomona, CA	LA
NJ	CAM
Pompano Beach, FL	MIA
Pompey, NY	SY
Pompton Lakes, NJ	PAT
Pompton Plains, NJ	PAT
Ponca, NE	OM
Ponca City, OK	OKL
Ponce, PR	PCE
Ponchatoula, LA	BR
LA	NO
Pond Settlement, IL	BEL
Poniatowski, WI	LC
Ponsford, MN	CR
Ponte Vedra Beach, FL	STA
Pontiac, IL	PEO
MI	DET
Poolesville, MD	WDC
Poplar, MT	GF
Poplar Bluff, MO	SPC
Poplar Springs, MD	BAL
Poquonock, CT	HRT
Poroupino, SD	RC
Port Allegany, PA	E
Port Allen, LA	BR
Port Angeles, WA	SEA
Port Aransas, TX	CC
Port Arthur, TX	BEA
Port Austin, MI	SAG
Port Barre, LA	LAF
Port Bolivar, TX	GAL
Port Carbon, PA	ALN
Port Charlotte, FL	VEN
Port Chester, NY	NY
Port Clinton, OH	TOL
Port Edwards, WI	LC
Port Ewen, NY	NY
Port Gibson, MS	JKS
Port Henry, NY	OG
Port Hudson, MO	STL
Port Huron, MI	DET
Port Isabel, TX	BWN
Port Jefferson, NY	RVC
Port Jervis, NY	NY
Port Lavaca, TX	VIC
Port Leyden, NY	OG
Port Murray, NJ	MET
Port Neches, TX	BEA
Port Orange, FL	ORL
Port Orchard, WA	SEA
Port Reading, NJ	MET
Port Richey, FL	SP
Port St. Joe, FL	PT
Port St. Lucie, FL	PMB
Port Sanilac, MI	SAG
Port Sulphur, LA	NO
Port Tobacco, MD	WDC
Port Townsend, WA	SEA
Port Vue, PA	PIT
Port Washington, NY	RVC
WI	MIL
Port Wentworth, GA	SAV
Portage, IN	GRY
MI	KAL
PA	ALT
PA	PBR
WI	MAD
Portage Des Sioux, MO	STL
Portageville, MO	SPC
NY	BUF
Portales, NM	SFE
Porterville, CA	FRS
Portland, CT	NOR
IN	LFT
ME	PRT
MI	GR
OR	OLL
OR	P
OR	VNN
TX	CC
Portola, CA	SAC
Portola Valley, CA	SFR
Portsmouth, IA	DM
NH	MAN
OH	COL
RI	PRO
VA	RIC
Portville, NY	BUF
Posen, IL	BEL
IL	CHI
MI	GAY
Poseyville, IN	EVN
Post, TX	LUB
Post Falls, ID	B
Postville, IA	DUB
Poteau, OK	TLS
Poteet, TX	SAT
Poth, TX	SAT
Potlatch, ID	B
Potomac, MD	WDC
Potosi, MO	STL
Potsdam, NY	OG
Pottstown, PA	PH
PA	PHU
PA	PSC
Pottsville, PA	ALN
Poughkeepsie, NY	NY
Poulsbo, WA	SEA
Poultney, VT	BUR
Poway, CA	SD
Powell, OH	COL
WY	CHY
Powhatan, LA	ALX
VA	RIC
WV	WH
Powhatan Point, OH	STU
Poy Sippi, WI	GB
Poynette, WI	MAD
Praga, MI	GAY
Prague, NE	LIN
OK	OKL
Praha, TX	VIC
Prairie du Chien, WI	LC
Prairie du Rocher, IL	BEL
Prairie du Sac, WI	MAD
Prairie View, TX	GAL
Prairie Village, KS	KCK
Prairieburg, IA	DUB
Prairieville, LA	BR
Pratt, KS	DOD
Prattville, AL	MOB
Premont, TX	CC
Prentice, WI	SUP
Prescott, AZ	PHX
MI	GAY
WI	LC
Prescott Valley, AZ	PHX
Presho, SD	RC
Presidio, TX	ELP
Presque Isle, ME	PRT
WI	SUP
Preston, CT	NOR
IA	DUB
MN	WIN
Prestonsburg, KY	LEX
Price, UT	SLC
Prichard, AL	MOB
Priest River, ID	B
Primos, PA	PH
Prince Frederick, MD	WDC
Princess Anne, MD	WIL
Princeton, IL	PEO
IN	EVN
KY	OWN
MA	WOR
MN	SCL
NJ	TR
OH	CIN
WI	MAD
WV	WH
Princeville, IL	PEO
Prineville, OR	BAK
Prior Lake, MN	STP
Proctor, MN	DUL
VT	BUR
Progreso, TX	BWN
Prophetstown, IL	RCK
Prospect, CT	HRT
PA	PIT
Prospect Heights, IL	CHI
Prospect Park, NJ	PAT
PA	PH
Prosser, WA	YAK
Protivin, IA	DUB
Providence, KY	OWN
OH	TOL
RI	PRO
Provincetown, MA	FR
Provo, UT	SLC
Prudenville, MI	GAY
Pryor, MT	GF
OK	TLS
Pueblo, CO	PBL
Puerta De Tierra, PR	SJN
Pukwana, SD	SFS
Pulaski, NY	SY
TN	NSH
WI	GB
Pulaskifield, MO	SPC
Pullman, WA	SPK
Puluwat, FM	CI
Punta Gorda, FL	VEN
Punxsutawney, PA	E
PA	PBR
Purcell, KS	KCK
OK	OKL
Purcellville, VA	ARL
Purchase, NY	NY
Put-In-Bay, OH	TOL
Putnam, CT	LIT
CT	NOR
IL	LIT
Putney, VT	BUR
Puyallup, WA	SEA
Pylesville, MD	BAL
Quaker Hill, CT	NOR
Quakertown, PA	PH
Quanah, TX	FWT
Quarryville, PA	HBG
Quebradillas, PR	ARE
Queens, NY	BRK
Queens Village, NY	BRK
Queensbury, NY	ALB
Quemado, NM	GLP
Questa, NM	SFE
Quincy, CA	SAC
FL	PT
IL	SFD
MA	BO
WA	YAK
Quinebaug, CT	NOR
Quinnesec, MI	MAR
Quinque, VA	RIC
Quinton, VA	RIC
Raceland, LA	HT
Racine, WI	MIL
Radcliff, KY	L
Raddle, IL	BEL
Radford, VA	RIC
Radisson, WI	SUP
Radnor, PA	ARM
PA	PH
Radom, IL	BEL
Raeford, NC	R
Raeville, NE	OM
Rahway, NJ	NEW
NJ	PSC
Rainelle, WV	WH
Rainier, OR	P
Raleigh, NC	R
ND	BIS
Ralls, TX	LUB
Ralston, NE	OM
Rambin, LA	SHP
Ramey, PA	E
PA	SJP
Ramona, CA	SD
SD	SFS
Ramsay, MI	MAR
Ramsey, IL	SFD
NJ	NEW
NJ	PHU
Ranchito, TX	BWN
Rancho Cordova, CA	SAC
Rancho Cucamonga, CA	SB
Rancho Dominguez, CA	LA
Rancho Palos Verdes, CA	LA
Rancho Santa Fe, CA	SD
Rancho Santa Margarita, CA	ORG
Ranchos De Taos, NM	SFE
Randall, MN	SCL
Randallstown, MD	BAL
Randolph, MA	BO
NE	OM
NJ	PAT
NY	BUF
VT	BUR
WI	MIL
Randolph Township, OH	Y
Random Lake, WI	MIL
Rangely, CO	DEN
Ranger, TX	FWT
Rankin, PA	PBR
PA	PIT
Ranshaw, PA	HBG
Ransom, IL	PEO
KS	DOD
Ransomville, NY	BUF
Rantoul, IL	PEO
Rapid City, SD	RC
Rapid River, MI	MAR
Rapids City, IL	PEO
Rapson, MI	SAG
Raquette Lake, NY	OG
Raritan, IL	PEO
NJ	MET

Ratcliff, AR	LR
Rathbun, IA	DAV
Rathdrum, ID	B
Raton, NM	SFE
Ravena, NY	ALB
Ravenna, KY	LEX
MI	GR
NE	GI
OH	Y
Ravenswood, WV	WH
Rawlins, WY	CHY
Raymond, IA	DUB
IL	SFD
LA	LKC
MN	NU
MS	JKS
NJ	CAM
WA	SEA
Raymondville, NY	OG
TX	BWN
Rayne, LA	LAF
Raynham, MA	FR
Raytown, MO	KC
Rayville, LA	SHP
Raywick, KY	L
Raywood, TX	BEA
Reading, KS	KCK
MA	BO
PA	ALN
PA	PHU
Readsboro, VT	BUR
Reardan, WA	SPK
Red Bank, NJ	TR
Red Bluff, CA	SAC
Red Brush, IN	EVN
Red Bud, IL	BEL
Red Cliff, WI	SUP
Red Cloud, NE	LIN
Red Feathers Lakes, CO	DEN
Red Hook, NY	NY
Red Lake, MN	CR
Red Lake Falls, MN	CR
Red Lodge, MT	GF
Red Oak, IA	DM
Red Wing, MN	STP
Redding, CA	SAC
CT	BGP
Redfield, SD	SFS
Redford, MI	DET
NY	OG
Redford Township, MI	DET
Redgranite, WI	GB
Redland, OR	P
Redlands, CA	SB
CA	VNN
Redmond, OR	BAK
WA	SEA
Redondo Beach, CA	LA
Redwood, NY	OG
Redwood City, CA	SFR
Redwood Falls, MN	NU
Redwood Valley, CA	STN
Reed, KY	OWN
OH	TOL
Reed City, MI	GR
Reedley, CA	FRS
Reedsburg, WI	MAD
Reedsport, OR	P
Reedsville/Maple Grove, WI	GB
Reese, MI	SAG
Reeseville, WI	MIL
Refugio, TX	CC
Regal, MN	NU
Regent, ND	BIS
Rego Park, NY	BRK
Rehoboth, DE	WIL
Reidsville, NC	CHL
Reinbeck, IA	DUB
Reliance, SD	RC
Remington, IN	LFT
Remsen, IA	SC
Remus, MI	GR
Renault, IL	BEL
Reno, NV	RNO
Renovo, PA	ALT
Rensselaer, IN	LFT
NY	ALB
Renton, PA	PIT
WA	SEA
Renville, MN	NU
Republic, MI	MAR
MO	SPC
OH	TOL
PA	GBG
WA	SPK
Reseda, CA	LA
Reserve, LA	NO
WI	SUP
Reserve Township, PA	PIT
Reston, VA	ARL
Revere, MA	BO
Revillo, SD	SFS
Revloc, PA	ALT
PA	SJP
Rexville, NY	ROC
Reynolds, IN	LFT
ND	FAR
Reynoldsburg, OH	COL
Reynoldsville, PA	E
Rhine, OH	CIN
Rhinebeck, NY	NY
Rhineland, MO	JC
TX	FWT
Rhinelander, WI	SUP
Rhodelia, KY	L
Rhodell, WV	WH
Rialto, CA	SB
Rib Lake, WI	SUP
Ribera, NM	SFE
Rice, MN	SCL
Rice Lake, WI	SUP
Riceville, IA	DUB
Rich Fountain, MO	JC
Richard, LA	LAF
Richardson, TX	DAL
Richardton, ND	BIS
Richboro, PA	PH
Richeyville, PA	PIT
Richfield, MN	STP
OH	CLV
UT	SLC
WI	MIL
Richfield Center, OH	TOL
Richfield Springs, NY	ALB
Richford, VT	BUR
Richland, IA	DAV
MO	JC
NJ	CAM
WA	YAK
Richland Center, WI	LC
Richland Township, PA	PIT
Richlands, VA	RIC
Richmond, CA	OAK
IA	DAV
IL	RCK
IN	IND
KS	KCK
KY	LEX
ME	PRT
MI	DET
MN	SCL
MO	KC
OH	STU
TX	GAL
VA	PHU
VA	RIC
VA	SAM
VT	BUR
Richmond Heights, MO	STL
Richmond Hill, GA	SAV
Richwood, TX	GAL
WV	WH
Richwoods, MO	STL
Rickardsville, IA	DUB
Ridge, MD	WDC
Ridge Manor, FL	SP
Ridgecrest, CA	FRS
Ridgefield, CT	BGP
NJ	NEW
Ridgefield Park, NJ	NEW
Ridgeland, SC	CHR
Ridgeley, WV	WH
Ridgely, MD	WIL
Ridgeville, SC	CHR
Ridgeway, WI	MAD
Ridgewood, NJ	NEW
NY	BRK
Ridgway, IL	BEL
PA	E
Ridley Park, PA	PH
Riegelsville, PA	PH
Riegelwood, NC	R
Rifle, CO	DEN
Riggsville, MI	GAY
Rincon, PR	MGZ
Rindge, NH	MAN
Ringtown, PA	ALN
Ringwood, NJ	PAT
Rio Grande, NJ	CAM
OH	STU
PR	SJN
Rio Grande City, TX	BWN
Rio Hondo, TX	BWN
Rio Piedras, PR	SJN
Rio Rancho, NM	SFE
Rio Rico, AZ	TUC
Rio Vista, CA	SAC
Ripley, OH	CIN
Ripon, WI	MIL
Rising Sun, WI	LC
Rittman, OH	CLV
Ritzville, WA	SPK
River Aux Vases, MO	STL
River Edge, NJ	NEW
River Falls, WI	SUP
River Forest, IL	CHI
River Grove, IL	CHI
River Ridge, LA	NO
River Rouge, MI	DET
River Vale, NJ	NEW
Riverbank, CA	STO
Riverdale, CA	FRS
IL	CHI
MD	WDC
NY	NY
Riverhead, NY	RVC
NY	STF
Riverside, CA	SB
CT	BGP
IA	DAV
IL	CHI
NJ	TR
RI	PRO
Riverton, IL	SFD
NJ	TR
WY	CHY
Riverview, FL	SP
MI	DET
Riverview Gardens, MO	STL
Riviera Beach, FL	PMB
Roanoke, AL	BIR
IL	PEO
IN	FTW
VA	RIC
VA	SAM
Roanoke Rapids, NC	R
Roaring Creek, PA	HBG
Roaring Spring, PA	ALT
Robbinsdale, MN	STP
Robert's Cove, LA	LAF
Robertsdale, AL	MOB
Robesonia, PA	ALN
Robinson, IL	SFD
Robinson Township, PA	PIT
Robinsonville, WI	GB
Robstown, TX	CC
Rochdale, MA	WOR
Rochelle, IL	RCK
Rochelle Park, NJ	NEW
Rochester, IL	SFD
IN	LFT
MA	BO
MI	DET
MN	WIN
NH	MAN
NY	NTN
NY	ROC
NY	STF
PA	PIT
Rochester Hills, MI	DET
Rock Creek, OH	Y
Rock Falls, IL	RCK
WI	LC
Rock Hill, SC	CHR
Rock Island, IL	PEO
Rock Lake, ND	FAR
PA	SCR
Rock Rapids, IA	SC
Rock Springs, WY	CHY
Rock Valley, IA	SC
Rockaway, NJ	PAT
NY	BRK
OR	P
Rockaway Beach, NY	BRK
Rockaway Park, NY	BRK
Rockaway Point, NY	BRK
Rockaway Township, NJ	PAT
Rockdale, IL	JOL
TX	AUS
Rockford, IA	DUB
IL	RCK
MI	GR
OH	CIN
WA	SPK
Rockland, MA	BO
ME	PRT
MI	MAR
Rockledge, FL	ORL
Rocklin, CA	SAC
Rockne, TX	AUS
Rockport, IN	EVN
MA	BO
TX	CC
Rocksprings, TX	SAT
Rockville, CT	NOR
IN	IND
MD	WDC
MN	SCL
VA	RIC
Rockville Centre, NY	BRK
NY	RVC
Rockwall, TX	DAL
Rockwell, IA	DUB
Rockwell City, IA	SC
Rockwood, MI	DET
Rocky Ford, CO	PBL
Rocky Hill, CT	HRT
Rocky Mount, NC	R
VA	RIC
Rocky Point, NY	RVC
Rocky River, OH	CLV
Rodeo, CA	OAK
Roebling, NJ	PSC
NJ	ROM
NJ	TR
Roeland Park, KS	KCK
Rogers, AR	LR
CT	NOR
MN	STP
TX	AUS
Rogers City, MI	GAY
Rogersville, TN	KNX
Roggen, CO	DEN
Rohnert Park, CA	SR
Rohrerstown, PA	HBG
Rolesville, NC	R
Rolette, ND	FAR
Rolfe, IA	SC
Rolla, MO	JC
ND	FAR
Rolling Ground, WI	LC
Rolling Hills, CA	LA
Rolling Meadows, IL	CHI
Rolling Prairie, IN	GRY
Rollingstone, MN	WIN
Rollinsford, NH	MAN
Roma, TX	BWN
Rome, GA	ATL
KY	OWN
NY	STF
NY	SY
Rome City, IN	FTW
Romeo, MI	DET
Romeoville, IL	JOL
Romney, WV	WH
Romulus, MI	DET
Ronan, MT	HEL
Ronceverte, WV	WH
Ronkonkoma, NY	RVC
Roosevelt, NY	RVC
UT	SLC
Rootstown, OH	Y
Rosalia, WA	SPK
Rosario, PR	MGZ
Rosaryville, MD	WDC
Rosati, MO	JC
Roscoe, MN	SCL
PA	PIT
SD	SFS
Roscommon, MI	GAY
Rose Creek, MN	WIN
Roseau, MN	CR
Rosebud, SD	RC
TX	AUS
Roseburg, OR	P
Rosebush, MI	SAG
Rosedale, MS	JKS
Roseland, NE	LIN
NJ	NEW
Roselle, IA	SC
IL	JOL
NJ	NEW
Roselle Park, NJ	NEW
Rosemead, CA	LA
Rosemont, PA	PH
Rosemont-Des Plaines, IL	CHI
Rosemount, MN	STP
Rosen, MN	NU
Rosenberg, TX	GAL
Rosencrans, IL	CHI
Rosendale, NY	NY
Rosenhayn, NJ	CAM
Roseto, PA	ALN
Roseville, CA	SAC
IA	DUB
MI	DET
MN	STP
Rosholt, SD	SFS
WI	LC
Rosiere, NY	OG
WI	GB
Roslyn, NY	RVC
PA	PH
WA	YAK
Rosman, NC	CHL
Ross Township, PA	PIT
Rossford, OH	SJP
OH	TOL
Rossiter, PA	GBG
Rossville, KS	KCK
Rostraver, PA	GBG
Roswell, GA	ATL
GA	PSC
NM	LSC

OH	COL
Rotan, TX	LUB
Rothbury, MI	GR
Rothschild, WI	LC
Rotterdam, NY	ALB
Rotterdam Junction, NY	ALB
Round Lake, IL	CHI
Round Rock, TX	AUS
Roundup, MT	GF
Rouses Point, NY	OG
Rouseville, PA	E
Rowena, TX	SAN
Rowland Heights, CA	LA
Rowlett, TX	DAL
Rowley, IA	DUB
MA	BO
Roxboro, NC	R
Roxbury, WI	MAD
Roy, NM	SFE
OR	P
Royal, IA	SC
PA	SCR
Royal City, WA	YAK
Royal Oak, MI	DET
Royal Palm Beach, FL	PMB
Royalton, IL	BEL
MN	SCL
Royersford, PA	PH
Rozellville, WI	LC
Rubicon, WI	MIL
Ruby, AK	FBK
Rudolph, WI	LC
Rudyard, MI	MAR
Rugby, ND	FAR
Ruidoso, NM	LSC
Rulo, NE	LIN
Ruma, IL	BEL
Rumford, ME	PRT
RI	PRO
Rumson, NJ	TR
Runge, TX	SAT
Runnemede, NJ	CAM
Running Springs, CA	SB
Rupert, ID	B
Rush, NY	ROC
Rush City, MN	STP
Rush Lake, MN	SCL
Rushford, MN	WIN
NY	BUF
Rushville, IL	PEO
IN	IND
Ruskin, FL	SP
Russell, KS	SAL
MA	SPR
Russells Point, OH	CIN
Russellton, PA	PIT
Russellville, AL	BIR
AR	LR
KY	OWN
MO	JC
Russia, OH	CIN
Ruston, LA	SHP
Ruth, MI	SAG
Rutherford, NJ	NEW
NJ	PHU
Ruthven, IA	SC
Rutland, IL	PEO
MA	SAM
MA	WOR
VT	BUR
Rutten, ND	FAR
Ryan, IA	DUB
MI	SAG
Rydal, PA	PH
Rye, CO	PBL
NY	NY
Rye Beach, NH	MAN
Rynella, LA	LAF
Sabana Grande, PR	MGZ
Sabattus, ME	PRT
Sabetha, KS	KCK
Sabin, MN	CR
Sabinal, TX	SAT
Sabula, IA	DUB
Sac City, IA	SC
Sackets Harbor, NY	OG
Saco, ME	PRT
Sacramento, CA	NTN
CA	SAC
CA	VNN
Saddle Brook, NJ	NEW
Saddle River, NJ	NEW
Saddle River Borough, NJ	NEW
Safety Harbor, FL	SP
Safford, AZ	TUC
Sag Harbor, NY	RVC
Sagamore, PA	GBG
PA	PBR
Saginaw, MI	SAG
St. Agatha, ME	PRT
St. Albans, ME	PRT
VT	BUR
WV	WH
St. Albans Bay, VT	BUR
St. Amant, LA	BR
St. Ann, MO	STL
St. Anna, MN	SCL
WI	GB
St. Anne, IL	JOL
IN	IND
St. Ansgar, IA	DUB
St. Anthony, IA	DUB
ID	B
IN	EVN
MN	SCL
MO	JC
ND	BIS
OH	CIN
St. Antonio, TX	FWT
St. Augusta, MN	SCL
St. Augustine, FL	STA
IL	PEO
PA	ALT
St. Augustine Shores, FL	STA
St. Benedict, IA	SC
KS	KCK
LA	NO
MN	STP
OR	P
St. Bernard, IN	EVN
LA	NO
St. Bonaventure, NY	BUF
St. Boniface, PA	ALT
St. Bonifacius, MN	STP
St. Catharine, KY	L
St. Catherine, IA	DUB
St. Cecilia, IA	DUB
St. Charles, IL	RCK
MI	SAG
MN	WIN
MO	STL
NE	OM
St. Clair, MI	DET
MN	WIN
MO	STL
Saint Clair, PA	ALN
St. Clair, PA	PHU
PA	PSC
St. Clair Shores, MI	DET
St. Clairsville, OH	STU
St. Clement, MO	JC
St. Cloud, FL	ORL
MN	SCL
WI	MIL
St. Columbans, NE	OM
St. Croix, IN	IND
VI	STV
St. David, AZ	TUC
St. Denis, IN	IND
St. Donatus, IA	DUB
St. Edward, NE	OM
St. Elizabeth, MO	JC
St. Elmo, IL	SFD
St. Francis, KS	SAL
KY	L
ME	PRT
MN	SCL
SD	RC
WI	MIL
St. Francisville, IL	BEL
LA	BR
St. Gabriel, LA	BR
St. George, IL	JOL
UT	SLC
WI	MIL
St. Hedwig, TX	SAT
St. Helen, MI	GAY
Saint Helena, CA	SR
St. Helena, NE	OM
St. Helena Island, SC	CHR
St. Helens, OR	P
St. Henry, IN	EVN
MN	STP
OH	CIN
St. Ignace, MI	MAR
St. Ignatius, MT	HEL
St. Inigoes, MD	WDC
St. Jacob, IL	SFD
St. James, IN	EVN
LA	BR
MI	GAY
MN	WIN
MO	JC
NE	OM
NY	RVC
St. Joe, WI	MIL
Saint John, IN	GRY
St. John, KS	DOD
KY	L
ME	PRT
ND	FAR
NE	OM
TX	VIC
WA	SPK
WI	GB
St. Johns, AZ	GLP
MI	LAN
St. Johnsbury, VT	BUR
St. Johnsville, NY	ALB
St. Joseph, FL	SP
IA	SC
IN	EVN
IN	IND
KS	SAL
KY	L
KY	OWN
LA	ALX
MI	KAL
MN	SCL
MO	KC
MO	STN
OH	CIN
Saint Joseph, TN	NSH
St. Joseph Hill, IN	IND
Saint Joseph Ridge, WI	LC
St. Joseph Settlement, WV	WH
St. Kilian, MN	WIN
WI	MIL
St. Lawrence, PA	ALT
TX	SAN
WI	MIL
St. Leo, FL	SP
KS	WCH
MN	NU
St. Leon, IN	IND
St. Libory, IL	BEL
NE	GI
St. Louis, KS	KCK
MI	SAG
MO	JC
MO	OLL
MO	PRM
MO	STL
MO	STN
OR	P
St. Louis County, MO	STL
St. Louis Park, MN	STP
St. Lucas, IA	DUB
Saint Maries, ID	B
St. Mark, IN	IND
St. Mark's, KS	WCH
St. Martin, IN	EVN
MN	SCL
Saint Martin, OH	CIN
St. Martins, MO	JC
WI	MIL
St. Martinville, LA	LAF
St. Mary, IN	EVN
KS	DOD
KY	L
St. Mary's, MO	STL
St. Mary's City, MD	WDC
Saint Mary's Ridge, WI	LC
St. Mary-of-the-Knobs, IN	IND
St. Mary-of-the-Rock, IN	IND
St. Mary-of-the-Woods, IN	IND
St. Marys, AK	FBK
GA	SAV
IA	DM
KS	KCK
OH	CIN
PA	E
WV	WH
St. Mathias, MN	DUL
St. Maurice, IN	IND
St. Meinrad, IN	IND
St. Michael, AK	FBK
IN	EVN
MN	STP
ND	BIS
ND	FAR
PA	ALT
WI	MIL
St. Michael's Ridge, OH	TOL
St. Michaels, AZ	GLP
St. Nazianz, WI	GB
St. Nicholas, IN	IND
MN	SCL
St. Paris, OH	CIN
St. Patrick, IN	EVN
KS	KCK
MO	JC
OH	CIN
St. Paul, IA	DAV
IN	IND
KS	WCH
KY	OWN
MN	OLL
MN	STN
MN	STP
MO	STL
NE	GI
OR	P
VA	RIC
St. Paul Park, MN	STP
St. Pete Beach, FL	SP
St. Peter, IN	IND
KS	SAL
MN	NU
WI	MIL
St. Peters, MO	STL
St. Petersburg, FL	MIA
FL	PSC
FL	SJP
FL	SP
FL	STA
St. Philip, IN	EVN
St. Pius, IN	IND
Saint Regis Falls, NY	OG
St. Rosa, MN	SCL
St. Rose, IL	BEL
LA	NO
OH	CIN
St. Sebastian, IL	BEL
OH	CIN
St. Simons Island, GA	SAV
St. Stephen, MN	SCL
OH	TOL
St. Stephens, WY	CHY
St. Theresa, IA	DUB
St. Thomas, KY	L
MN	STP
MO	JC
ND	FAR
VI	STV
St. Vincent, AR	LR
St. Vincent de Paul, IN	IND
St. Wendel, IN	EVN
MN	SCL
St. Wendelin, OH	CIN
St. Xavier, MT	GF
Saipan, MP	CHK
Salado, TX	AUS
Salamanca, NY	BUF
Salem, IL	BEL
IN	IND
MA	BO
MA	STF
MO	SPC
NH	MAN
NJ	CAM
NY	ALB
OH	Y
OR	P
SD	SFS
VA	RIC
WV	WH
Salem Twp., OH	TOL
Salida, CO	COS
Salina, KS	SAL
Salinas, CA	MRY
PR	PCE
Saline, MI	LAN
Salineville, OH	Y
Salisbury, MA	BO
MD	WIL
MO	JC
NC	CHL
Salix, IA	SC
Sallisaw, OK	TLS
Salmon, ID	B
Salt Lake City, UT	SLC
UT	VNN
Saltaire, NY	RVC
Saltsburg, PA	GBG
Samuels, KY	L
San Andreas, CA	STO
San Angelo, TX	SAN
San Anselmo, CA	SFR
San Antonio, FL	SP
TX	CLV
TX	FAR
TX	OLL
TX	PBR
TX	SAT
San Antonio Village, MP	CHK
San Benito, TX	BWN
San Bernardino, CA	NTN
CA	SB
San Bruno, CA	SFR
San Carlos, AZ	TUC
CA	SFR
TX	BWN
San Clemente, CA	ORG
San Diego, CA	NTN
CA	OLD
CA	OLL
CA	SD
CA	STN
CA	VNN
TX	CC
San Dimas, CA	LA
San Elizario, TX	ELP
San Fernando, CA	LA

San Fidel, NM	GLP
San Francisco, CA	SD
CA	SFR
CA	STN
San Gabriel, CA	LA
San German, PR	MGZ
San Isidro, TX	BWN
San Jacinto, CA	SB
San Jose, CA	EST
CA	SJ
San Jose Village, MP	CHK
San Jose-Palo Alto, CA	VNN
San Juan, PR	SJN
TX	BWN
San Juan Bautista, CA	MRY
San Juan Capistrano, CA	ORG
San Juan Pueblo, NM	SFE
San Leandro, CA	OAK
San Lorenzo, CA	OAK
PR	CGS
San Luis, CO	PBL
San Luis Obispo, CA	MRY
CA	VNN
San Luis Rey, CA	SD
San Manuel, AZ	TUC
San Marcos, CA	SD
TX	AUS
San Marino, CA	LA
San Mateo, CA	SFR
CA	VNN
NM	GLP
San Miguel, CA	MRY
NM	LSC
San Pablo, CA	OAK
San Pedro, CA	LA
San Pierre, IN	GRY
San Rafael, CA	SFR
NM	GLP
San Ramon, CA	OAK
San Roque Village	CHK
San Saba, TX	AUS
San Sebastian, PR	MGZ
San Vicente Village, MP	CHK
San Ysidro, CA	SD
Sanborn, IA	SC
MN	NU
ND	FAR
WI	SUP
Sanbornville, NH	MAN
Sand Lake, MI	GR
Sand Springs, IA	DUB
OK	TLS
Sanderson, TX	SAN
Sandia, TX	CC
Sandoval, IL	BEL
Sandpoint, ID	B
Sandstone, MN	DUL
Sandusky, MI	SAG
OH	TOL
Sandwich, IL	RCK
MA	FR
Sandy, OR	P
UT	SLC
Sandy Hook, KY	LEX
Sanford, FL	ORL
ME	PRT
MI	SAG
NC	R
Sanger, CA	FRS
Sanibel, FL	VEN
Sanitaria Springs, NY	SY
Santa Ana, CA	ORG
Santa Barbara, CA	LA
Santa Clara, CA	SJ
CA	STN
NM	LSC
Santa Clarita, CA	LA
Santa Claus, IN	EVN
Santa Cruz, CA	MRY
NM	SFE
Santa Fe, NM	SFE
Santa Fe Springs, CA	LA
Santa Isabel, PR	PCE
Santa Margarita, CA	MRY
Santa Maria, CA	LA
Santa Monica, CA	LA
Santa Paula, CA	LA
Santa Rita, GU	AGN
Santa Rosa, CA	SR
NM	SFE
TX	BWN
Santa Rosa Beach, FL	PT
Santa Ynez, CA	LA
Santa Ysabel, CA	SD
Santa Ysabel Indian Missions, CA	SD
Santee, CA	SD
Santurce, PR	SJN
Sappington, MO	STL
Sapulpa, OK	TLS
Saranac, MI	GR
Saranac Lake, NY	OG

Sarasota, FL	VEN
Saratoga, CA	SJ
NY	ALB
WY	CHY
Saratoga Springs, NY	ALB
Sarcoxie, MO	SPC
Sardinia, NY	BUF
OH	CIN
Sardis, OH	STU
Sarita, TX	CC
Sarona, WI	SUP
Sarpy Co., NE	OM
Sartell, MN	SCL
Satanta, KS	DOD
Satin, TX	AUS
Saugerties, NY	NY
Saugus, MA	BO
Sauk Centre, MN	SCL
Sauk City, WI	MAD
Sauk Rapids, MN	SCL
Sauk Village, IL	CHI
Saukville, WI	MIL
Sault Sainte Marie, MI	MAR
Sausalito, CA	SFR
Savage, MN	STP
Savanna, IL	RCK
Savannah, GA	SAV
MO	KC
TN	MEM
Saxon, WI	SUP
Saxonville, MA	BO
Sayner, WI	SUP
Sayre, PA	PHU
PA	SCR
Sayreville, NJ	MET
Sayville, NY	RVC
Scales Mound, IL	RCK
Scammon, KS	WCH
Scammon Bay, AK	FBK
Scappoose, OR	P
Scarborough, ME	PRT
NY	NY
Scarsdale, NY	NY
Schaffer, MI	MAR
Schaghticoke, NY	ALB
Schaller, IA	SC
Schaumburg, IL	CHI
Scheller, IL	BEL
Schenectady, NY	ALB
Schererville, IN	GRY
Schertz, TX	SAT
Schiller Park, IL	CHI
Schley, IA	DUB
Schnellville, IN	EVN
Schoenchen, KS	SAL
Schoharie, NY	ALB
School Hill, WI	GB
Schooley's Mountain, NJ	PAT
Schriever, LA	HT
Schroon Lake, NY	OG
Schulenburg, TX	VIC
Schulte, KS	WCH
Schuyler, NE	OM
Schuylerville, NY	ALB
Schuylkill Haven, PA	ALN
Scio, OR	P
Sciota, NY	OG
Scipio, KS	KCK
Scipio Center, NY	ROC
Scituate, MA	BO
Scobey, MT	GF
Scotch Plains, NJ	NEW
Scotia, CA	SR
NY	ALB
Scotland, SD	SFS
TX	FWT
Scott, LA	LAF
Scott City, KS	DOD
MO	SPC
Scott Township, PA	PIT
Scottdale, PA	GBG
PA	PBR
Scotts Valley, CA	MRY
Scottsbluff, NE	GI
Scottsboro, AL	BIR
Scottsburg, IN	IND
Scottsdale, AZ	EST
AZ	PHX
Scottsville, KY	OWN
NY	ROC
VA	RIC
Scottville, MI	GR
Scoventry, PA	PH
Scranton, AR	LR
IA	SC
KS	KCK
PA	NTN
PA	PHU
PA	PSC
PA	SAM
PA	SCR

Sea Cliff, NY	BRK
NY	RVC
Sea Girt, NJ	TR
Sea Isle City, NJ	CAM
Seabrook, NH	MAN
Seaford, DE	WIL
NY	RVC
Seaforth, MN	NU
Seahurst, WA	SEA
Seal Beach, CA	ORG
Sealy, TX	GAL
Searcy, AR	LR
Searles, MN	NU
Seaside, CA	MRY
OR	P
Seaside Heights, NJ	TR
Seaside Park, NJ	TR
Seat Pleasant, MD	WDC
Seattle, WA	SEA
WA	VNN
Seaview, WA	SEA
Sebastian, FL	PMB
Sebastopol, CA	SR
Sebewaing, MI	SAG
Seboyeta, NM	GLP
Sebree, KY	OWN
Sebring, FL	VEN
OH	Y
Secane, PA	PH
Secaucus, NJ	NEW
Secretary, MD	WIL
Security, CO	COS
Sedalia, CO	COS
MO	JC
Sedan, KS	WCH
MN	SCL
Sedona, AZ	PHX
Sedro Woolley, WA	SEA
Seekonk, MA	FR
Seelyville, IN	IND
Seffner, FL	SP
Seguin, KS	SAL
TX	SAT
Seinwar, FM	CI
Selah, WA	YAK
Selby, SD	SFS
Selden, KS	SAL
NY	RVC
Selfridge, ND	BIS
Seligman, AZ	PHX
Selinsgrove, PA	HBG
Sellersburg, IN	IND
Sellersville, PA	PH
Selma, AL	MOB
CA	FRS
TX	SAT
Selmer, TN	MEM
Selz, ND	FAR
Seminole, FL	SP
OK	OKL
TX	LUB
Semmes, AL	MOB
Senatobia, MS	JKS
Seneca, IL	PEO
KS	KCK
MO	SPC
SD	SFS
WI	LC
Seneca Falls, NY	ROC
Sentinel Butte, ND	BIS
Sepulveda, CA	LA
Sequim, WA	SEA
Sereno, MO	STL
Sesser, IL	BEL
Setauket, NY	RVC
Severn, MD	BAL
Severna Park, MD	BAL
Seville-Creston, OH	CLV
Seward, AK	ANC
KS	DOD
NE	LIN
PA	GBG
Sewickley, PA	PIT
Seymour, CT	HRT
IL	PEO
IN	IND
TN	KNX
TX	FWT
WI	GB
WI	MAD
Shade Gap, PA	ALT
Shady Cove, OR	P
Shadyside, OH	STU
Shafter, CA	FRS
Shaker Heights, OH	CLV
Shakopee, MN	STP
Shallotte, NC	R
Shallowater, TX	LUB
Shamokin, PA	HBG
PA	PHU
Shandon, OH	CIN

Shannon, IL	RCK
Sharon, CT	HRT
KS	DOD
MA	BO
PA	E
PA	ROM
WI	MIL
Sharon Hill, PA	PH
Sharon Springs, KS	SAL
Sharpsburg, OH	CIN
PA	PIT
Sharpsville, PA	E
Shavertown, PA	SCR
Shaw, MS	JKS
OR	P
Shaw Island, WA	SEA
Shawano, WI	GB
Shawnee, KS	KCK
OH	COL
OK	OKL
Shawneetown, IL	BEL
Sheboygan, WI	MIL
Sheboygan Falls, WI	MIL
Sheffield, IL	PEO
MA	SPR
OH	CLV
PA	E
PA	PBR
Sheffield Lake, OH	CLV
Shelbina, MO	JC
Shelburne, VT	BUR
Shelburne Falls, MA	SPR
Shelby, IN	GRY
MI	GR
MS	JKS
MT	HEL
NC	CHL
NE	LIN
OH	TOL
Shelby Twp., MI	DET
Shelbyville, IL	SFD
IN	IND
KY	L
TN	NSH
Sheldon, IA	SC
ND	FAR
NY	BUF
WI	SUP
Sheldon Springs, VT	BUR
Shell Knob, MO	SPC
Shell Lake, WI	SUP
Shell Rock, IA	DUB
Shelter Island, NY	RVC
Shelter Island Heights, NY	RVC
Shelton, CT	BGP
WA	SEA
Shenandoah, IA	DM
PA	ALN
PA	PHU
Shepherd, MI	SAG
Shepherdstown, WV	WH
Shepherdsville, KY	L
Sheppton, PA	ALN
PA	PSC
Sherborn, MA	BO
Sherburn, MN	WIN
Sherburne, NY	SY
VT	BUR
Sheridan, AR	LR
NY	BUF
OR	P
WY	CHY
Sherman, CT	BGP
IL	SFD
NY	BUF
TX	DAL
Sherman Oaks, CA	LA
Sherrill, IA	DUB
NY	SY
Sherwood, OR	P
Sherwood Park, DE	WIL
Sherwood/St. John, WI	GB
Shevlin, MN	CR
Shields, MI	SAG
Shieldsville, MN	STP
Shillington, PA	ALN
Shiloh, IL	BEL
Shiner, TX	VIC
Shinglehouse, PA	E
Shinnston, WV	WH
Shiocton, WI	GB
Shipman, IL	SFD
Shippensburg, PA	HBG
Shiprock, NM	GLP
Shiremanstown, PA	HBG
Shirley, MA	BO
Shoal Creek, AR	LR
Shoals, IN	EVN
Shohola, PA	SCR
Shoreham, NY	RVC
Shoreview, MN	STP

Shorewood, WI	MIL
Short Hills, NJ	NEW
Shortsville, NY	ROC
Shoshone, ID	B
Show Low, AZ	GLP
Shreveport, LA	SHP
Shrewsbury, MA	WOR
MO	STL
Shrub Oak, NY	NY
Shullsburg, WI	MAD
Shumway, IL	SFD
Siberia, IN	IND
Sibley, IA	SC
Sicklerville, NJ	CAM
Sidney, MT	GF
NE	GI
NY	ALB
OH	CIN
Sierra Blanca, TX	ELP
Sierra Madre, CA	LA
Sierra Vista, AZ	TUC
Sigel, IL	SFD
SD	SFS
WI	LC
Signal Mountain, TN	KNX
Sigourney, IA	DAV
Sikeston, MO	SPC
Siler City, NC	R
Siloam Springs, AR	LR
Silsbee, TX	BEA
Silver Bay, MN	DUL
Silver City, NM	LSC
Silver Creek, MI	KAL
NE	OM
NY	BUF
Silver Lake, MN	NU
MO	STL
Silver Spring, MD	BAL
MD	PHU
MD	WDC
Silver Springs, NY	BUF
Silver Springs Shores, FL	ORL
Silverado, CA	ORG
Silverton, CO	PBL
OR	P
Silvis, IL	PEO
Simi, CA	LA
Simi Valley, CA	LA
Simmesport, LA	ALX
Simpson, PA	PHU
PA	SCR
Simpsonville, SC	CHR
Simsbury, CT	HRT
Sinajana, GU	AGN
Sinclair, ME	PRT
Sinclairville, NY	BUF
Sinking Spring, PA	ALN
Sinsinawa, WI	MAD
Sinton, TX	CC
Sioux City, IA	SC
Sioux Falls, SD	SFS
Sioux Rapids, IA	SC
Sisseton, SD	SFS
Sister Bay, WI	GB
Sisters, OR	BAK
Sistersville, WV	WH
Sitka, AK	JUN
Siverado, CA	ORG
Skagway, AK	JUN
Skaneateles, NY	SY
Skiatook, OK	TLS
Skiatoon, OK	TLS
Skidmore, TX	CC
Skidway Lake, MI	GAY
Skillman, NJ	MET
Skokie, IL	CHI
Skowhegan, ME	PRT
Slater, MO	JC
Slatersville, RI	PRO
Slatington, PA	ALN
Slaton, TX	LUB
Slayton, MN	WIN
Sleepy Eye, MN	NU
Slickville, PA	GBG
Slidell, LA	NO
Slinger, WI	MIL
Slingerlands, NY	ALB
Slippery Rock, PA	PIT
Sloan, NY	BUF
Sloatsburg, NY	NY
NY	STF
Slovak, AR	LR
Slovan, WI	GB
Smethport, PA	E
Smiley, TX	SAT
Smith Center, KS	SAL
Smithfield, NC	R
OH	STU
RI	PRO
VA	RIC
Smithton, IL	BEL

PA	GBG
Smithtown, NY	PSC
NY	RVC
Smithville, MO	KC
TN	NSH
TX	AUS
Smock, PA	GBG
Smyrna, DE	WIL
GA	ATL
TN	NSH
Sneedville, TN	KNX
Snellville, GA	ATL
Snohomish, WA	SEA
Snoqualmie, WA	SEA
Snow Shoe, PA	ALT
Snowflake, AZ	GLP
Snowmass, CO	DEN
Snyder, NE	OM
NY	BUF
TX	LUB
Sobieski, MN	SCL
WI	GB
Soboba Indian Reservation, CA	SB
Socorro, NM	SFE
Soda Springs, ID	B
Sodus, NY	ROC
Sokens, FM	CI
Solana Beach, CA	SD
Soldotna, AK	ANC
Soledad, CA	MRY
Solomon, AZ	TUC
KS	SAL
Solomons, MD	WDC
Solon, IA	DAV
OH	CLV
OH	PRM
OH	SJP
Solon Springs, WI	SUP
Solvang, CA	LA
Solvay, NY	SY
Somerdale, NJ	CAM
Somers, NY	NY
Somers Point, NJ	CAM
Somerset, KY	LEX
MA	FR
NJ	MET
NJ	PSC
NJ	SAM
OH	COL
PA	ALT
TX	SAT
WI	SUP
Somersville, CT	NOR
Somersworth, NH	MAN
Somerton, AZ	TUC
Somerville, MA	BO
NJ	MET
TN	MEM
TX	AUS
Somonauk, IL	RCK
Songsong Village, MP	CHK
Sonoita, AZ	TUC
Sonoma, CA	SR
Sonora, CA	STO
TX	SAN
Soquel, CA	MRY
Sorgho, KY	OWN
Sorrento, LA	BR
Sound Beach, NY	RVC
Sour Lake, TX	BEA
South Amboy, NJ	MET
South Amherst, OH	CLV
South Ashburnham, MA	WOR
South Barre, MA	WOR
South Beloit, IL	RCK
South Bend, IN	FTW
IN	NTN
South Berwick, ME	PRT
South Boston, VA	RIC
South Bound Brook, NJ	MET
South Branch, WI	GB
South Burlington, VT	BUR
South Charleston, OH	CIN
WV	WH
South Coventry, PA	PH
South Dartmouth, MA	FR
South Dayton, NY	BUF
South Deerfield, MA	SPR
MA	STF
South Easton, MA	FR
South El Monte, CA	LA
South Euclid, OH	CLV
South Fork, PA	ALT
PA	PBR
South Gate, CA	LA
South Glastonbury, CT	HRT
South Glens Falls, NY	ALB
South Grafton, MA	WOR
South Hadley, MA	PSC
MA	SPR
South Haven, MI	KAL

South Heart, ND	BIS
South Hero, VT	BUR
South Hill, VA	RIC
South Holland, IL	CHI
South Houston, TX	GAL
South Huntington, NY	RVC
South Kingston, RI	PRO
South Kortright, NY	ALB
South Lake Tahoe, CA	SAC
South Lyon, MI	DET
South Mantoloking, NJ	TR
South Meriden, CT	HRT
South Milwaukee, WI	MIL
South Mountain, PA	HBG
South Onondaga, NY	SY
South Orange, NJ	NEW
South Park Township, PA	PIT
South Pasadena, CA	LA
South Pittsburg, TN	KNX
South Plainfield, NJ	MET
South Portland, ME	PRT
South Range, MI	MAR
South River, NJ	MET
South St. Paul, MN	STP
South San Francisco, CA	SFR
South Sioux City, NE	OM
South Union, KY	OWN
South Waverly, PA	SCR
South Williamsport, PA	SCR
South Wilmington, IL	JOL
South Windsor, CT	HRT
South Yarmouth, MA	FR
Southampton, NY	RVC
PA	PH
Southborough, MA	WOR
Southbridge, MA	WOR
Southbury, CT	HRT
Southeastern Portage County, WI	LC
Southern Pines, NC	R
Southfield, MI	DET
MI	EST
Southgate, KY	COV
MI	DET
Southhaven, MS	JKS
Southington, CT	HRT
Southold, NY	RVC
Southport, NC	R
Southwick, MA	SPR
Spalding, MI	MAR
NE	GI
Spangler, PA	ALT
Spanish Lake, MO	STL
Sparkill, NY	NY
Sparks, MD	BAL
NV	RNO
Sparta, IL	BEL
MI	GR
NJ	PAT
TN	NSH
WI	LC
Spartanburg, SC	CHR
Spaulding-City Point, WI	LC
Spearfish, SD	RC
Spearman, TX	AMA
Spearville, KS	DOD
Speigletown, NY	ALB
Spencer, IA	SC
IN	IND
MA	WOR
NE	OM
OH	CLV
SD	SFS
WI	LC
WV	WH
Spencerport, NY	ROC
Spencerville, OH	TOL
Spicer, MN	NU
Spillville, IA	DUB
Spirit Lake, IA	SC
Splendora, TX	GAL
Spokane, WA	SPK
WA	VNN
Spooner, WI	SUP
Spotswood, NJ	MET
Spotsylvania, VA	ARL
Sprague, WA	SPK
Spreckels, CA	MRY
Spring, TX	GAL
Spring Branch, TX	SAT
Spring City, PA	PH
Spring Green, WI	MAD
Spring Grove, IL	RCK
PA	HBG
Spring Hill, FL	SJP
FL	SP
MN	SCL
MO	KCK
Spring House, PA	PH
Spring Lake, MI	GR
NJ	TR
Spring Valley, CA	SD

IL	PEO
MN	WIN
NY	NY
NY	STF
WI	LC
Springbrook, IA	DUB
NY	BUF
Springdale, AR	LR
PA	PIT
WA	SPK
Springer, NM	SFE
Springerville, AZ	GLP
Springfield, CO	PBL
IL	SFD
KY	L
MA	SAM
MA	SPR
MN	NU
MO	SPC
NE	OM
NJ	NEW
OH	CIN
OR	P
OR	STN
PA	PH
SD	SFS
TN	NSH
VA	ARL
VT	BUR
WI	LC
Springfield Gardens, NY	BRK
Springvale, ME	PRT
WI	MIL
Springville, IA	DUB
NY	BUF
Spruce, WI	GB
Spruce Pine, NC	CHL
Spur, TX	LUB
Stacyville, IA	DUB
Stafford, VA	ARL
Stafford Springs, CT	NOR
Stamford, CT	BGP
CT	STF
NY	ALB
TX	LUB
Stamps, AR	LR
Stanberry, MO	KC
Standing Rock, SD	RC
Standish, ME	PRT
MI	SAG
Stanford, MT	GF
Stangelville, WI	GB
Stanley, KY	OWN
ND	BIS
NY	ROC
WI	LC
Stanton, CA	ORG
MI	GR
NE	OM
TX	SAN
WI	SUP
Stanwood, WA	SEA
Staples, MN	SCL
Stapleton, NE	GI
Star City, AR	LR
IN	LFT
WV	WH
Star Lake, NY	OG
Starford, PA	GBG
Stark, WI	GB
Starke, FL	STA
Starkville, MS	JKS
Starkweather, ND	FAR
Starlight, IN	IND
State Center, IA	DUB
State College, PA	ALT
Staten Island, NY	NY
NY	SAM
NY	STF
Statesboro, GA	SAV
Statesville, NC	CHL
Staunton, IL	SFD
VA	RIC
Stayton, OR	P
Ste. Genevieve, MO	STL
Ste. Marie, IL	SFD
Stead, NV	RNO
Steamboat Springs, CO	DEN
Stebbins, AK	FBK
Steele, ND	FAR
Steelton, PA	HBG
Steelville, MO	JC
Steger, IL	CHI
IL	JOL
Steinauer, NE	LIN
Stella Niagara, NY	BUF
Stephan, SD	SFS
Stephen, MN	CR
Stephenson, MI	MAR
Stephensville, WI	GB
Stephenville, TX	FWT

Sterling, CO	DEN
IL	RCK
MA	WOR
OK	OKL
VA	ARL
Sterling Heights, MI	DET
MI	PRM
Stetsonville, WI	SUP
Steubenville, OH	NTN
OH	STU
Stevens Point, WI	LC
Stevenson, MD	BAL
Stevensville, MT	HEL
Stewart, MN	NU
Stewartville, MN	WIN
Stickney, IL	CHI
SD	SFS
Stiles, WI	GB
Still River, MA	WOR
Stillwater, MN	STP
NY	ALB
OK	TLS
Stirling, NJ	PAT
Stirum, ND	FAR
Stockbridge, MA	SPR
WI	GB
Stockdale, TX	SAT
Stockholm, ME	PRT
NJ	PAT
Stockton, CA	OLL
CA	STO
CA	VNN
IL	RCK
KS	SAL
Stone Harbor, NJ	CAM
Stone Lake, WI	SUP
Stone Mountain, GA	ATL
Stone Park, IL	CHI
Stoneboro, PA	E
Stonefort, IL	BEL
Stoneham, CO	DEN
MA	BO
Stonelick, OH	CIN
Stonewall, TX	SAT
Stonewood, WV	WH
Stonington, CT	NOR
IL	SFD
ME	PRT
Stony Point, NY	NY
TX	AUS
Storm Lake, IA	SC
Storrs, CT	NOR
Stottville, NY	ALB
Stoughton, MA	BO
WI	MAD
Stow, MA	BO
OH	CLV
Stowe, PA	PH
VT	BUR
Strafford, PA	PH
Strandquist, MN	CR
Strasburg, ND	BIS
OH	COL
Stratford, CT	BGP
NJ	CAM
TX	AMA
WI	LC
Stratton, CO	COS
Strawberry Point, IA	DUB
Strawn, TX	FWT
Streamwood, IL	CHI
Streator, IL	PEO
Streetsboro, OH	Y
Strickland, WI	SUP
String Prairie, IA	DAV
TX	AUS
Stringtown, IL	BEL
Strong City, KS	WCH
Strongsville, OH	CLV
Stroudsburg, PA	SCR
Struble, IA	SC
Struthers, OH	Y
Stryker, OH	TOL
Strykersville, NY	BUF
Stuart, FL	PMB
IA	DM
NE	OM
Studio City, CA	LA
Sturgeon Bay, WI	GB
Sturgis, KY	OWN
MI	KAL
SD	RC
Sturtevant, WI	MIL
Stuttgart, AR	LR
Stuyvesant, NY	ALB
Stuyvesant Falls, NY	ALB
Suamico, WI	GB
Subiaco, AR	LR
Sublette, IL	RCK
Sublimity, OR	P
Succasunna, NJ	PAT

Sudbury, MA	BO
Suffern, NY	NY
Suffield, CT	HRT
Suffolk, VA	RIC
Sugar Camp, WI	SUP
Sugar Creek, IA	DAV
MO	KC
MO	PRM
Sugar Grove, OH	COL
Sugar Island, MI	MAR
Sugar Land, TX	GAL
Sugar Notch, PA	SCR
Sugarloaf, PA	PSC
Suitland, MD	WDC
Sulligent, AL	BIR
Sullivan, IL	SFD
IN	EVN
MO	STL
WI	MAD
Sulphur, LA	LKC
OK	OKL
Sulphur Springs, TX	TYL
Summerfield, KS	KCK
Summerhill, PA	ALT
Summersville, WV	WH
Summerton, SC	CHR
Summerville, SC	CHR
Summit, IL	CHI
NJ	NEW
NY	ALB
WI	LC
Summit Hill, PA	ALN
Summitville, OH	Y
Sumner, IA	DUB
WA	SEA
Sumter, SC	CHR
Sun City, AZ	PHX
CA	SB
Sun City Center, FL	SP
Sun City West, AZ	PHX
Sun Lakes, AZ	PHX
Sun Prairie, WI	MAD
Sun Valley, CA	LA
ID	B
NV	RNO
Sunbury, OH	COL
PA	HBG
Suncook, NH	MAN
Sunfish, KY	OWN
Sunland, CA	LA
Sunland Park, NM	LSC
Sunny Hills, FL	PT
Sunnyside, WA	YAK
Sunnyvale, CA	SJ
Sunrise, FL	MIA
Sunset Hills, MO	STL
Sunsites, AZ	TUC
Superior, AZ	TUC
NE	LIN
WI	SUP
Suring, WI	GB
Susanville, CA	SAC
Susquehanna, PA	SCR
Sussex, NJ	PAT
Sutersville, PA	GBG
Sutherland, IA	SC
NE	GI
Sutherlin, OR	P
Sutter Creek, CA	SAC
Sutton, MA	WOR
NE	LIN
Suttons Bay, MI	GAY
Swainsboro, GA	SAV
Swainton, NJ	CAM
NJ	PH
NJ	TR
Swampscott, MA	BO
Swan Lake, MN	NU
MT	HEL
Swan Valley, MT	HEL
Swannanoa, NC	CHL
Swansboro, NC	R
Swansea, MA	FR
Swanton, OH	TOL
VT	BUR
Swanville, MN	SCL
Swarthmore, PA	PH
Swartswood, NJ	PAT
Swartz Creek, MI	LAN
Swedesboro, NJ	CAM
Swedesburg, PA	PH
Sweeny, TX	GAL
Sweet Home, OR	P
TX	VIC
Sweetwater, TX	SAN
Swissvale, PA	PIT
Switzerland, FL	STA
Swormville, NY	BUF
Swoyersville, PA	PSC
PA	SCR
Sybertsville, PA	PHU

PA	PSC
Sycamore, IL	RCK
OH	TOL
Sykeston, ND	FAR
Sykesville, MD	BAL
PA	E
PA	PBR
Sylacauga, AL	BIR
Sylmar, CA	LA
Sylva, NC	CHL
Sylvania, GA	SAV
OH	TOL
Sylvia, IA	DUB
Syosset, NY	RVC
Syracuse, IN	FTW
KS	DOD
NE	LIN
NY	STF
NY	SY
Tabb, VA	RIC
Taberg, NY	SY
Tabernacle, NJ	TR
Tabor, MN	CR
SD	SFS
Tacoma, WA	SEA
Taft, CA	FRS
TX	CC
Taftville, CT	NOR
Tahlequah, OK	TLS
Tahoe City, CA	SAC
Tai, GU	AGN
Takoma Park, MD	WDC
Talkeetna, AK	ANC
Talladega, AL	BIR
Tallahassee, FL	PT
Tallassee, AL	MOB
Tallmadge, OH	CLV
Tallulah, LA	ALX
Talofofo, GU	AGN
Tamaqua, PA	ALN
Tamarac, FL	MIA
Tamaroa, IL	BEL
Tama-Toledo, IA	DUB
Tamoroi, FM	CI
Tampa, FL	SP
KS	WCH
Tampico, IL	RCK
Tamuning, GU	AGN
Tanana, AK	FBK
Tanapag Village, MP	CHK
Taneytown, MD	BAL
Tangipahoa, LA	BR
Tannersville, PA	SCR
Taos, MO	JC
NM	SFE
Tappahannock, VA	RIC
Tappan, NY	NY
Tappan Lake, OH	STU
Tappen, ND	FAR
Tarboro, NC	R
Tarentum, PA	PBR
PA	PIT
Tariffville, CT	HRT
Tarkio, MO	KC
Tarnov, NE	OM
Tarpon Springs, FL	SP
Tarrytown, NY	NY
Taunton, MA	FR
MN	NU
Tavernier, FL	MIA
Tawas City, MI	GAY
Taycheedah, WI	MIL
Taylor, MI	DET
MI	PRM
PA	PSC
PA	SCR
TX	AUS
Taylor Mill, KY	COV
Taylors, SC	CHR
Taylors Falls, MN	STP
Taylorsville, UT	SLC
Taylorville, IL	SFD
Tazewell, TN	KNX
VA	RIC
Tea, SD	SFS
Teaneck, NJ	NEW
Techny, IL	CHI
Tecumseh, MI	LAN
NE	LIN
Tehachapi, CA	FRS
Tekamah, NE	OM
Tekoa, WA	SPK
Tell City, IN	IND
Teller, AK	FBK
Telluride, CO	PBL
Temecula, CA	NTN
CA	SB
Tempe, AZ	PHX
Temperance, MI	DET
Temperanceville, OH	STU
Temple, TX	AUS

Temple City, CA	LA
Temple Hill, IA	DUB
Temple Terrace, FL	SP
Templeton, IA	SC
Tenafly, NJ	NEW
Tennessee Ridge, TN	NSH
Tennyson-Potosi, WI	MAD
Tequesta, FL	PMB
Terre Haute, IN	IND
Terrebonne, MN	CR
Terrell, TX	DAL
Terrytown, LA	NO
Terryville, CT	HRT
CT	STF
Teutopolis, IL	SFD
Tewksbury, MA	BO
Texarkana, AR	LR
TX	TYL
Texas City, TX	GAL
Thatcher, AZ	TUC
Theilman, MN	WIN
Theresa, WI	MIL
Theriot, LA	HT
Thermal, CA	SB
Thermopolis, WY	CHY
Thibodaux, LA	HT
Thief River Falls, MN	CR
Thiensville, WI	MIL
Thiry Daems, WI	GB
Thomas, WV	WH
Thomasboro, IL	PEO
Thomaston, CT	HRT
Thomasville, GA	SAV
NC	CHL
Thompson, CT	LIT
CT	NOR
ND	FAR
OH	CLV
WI	MIL
Thompson Falls, MT	HEL
Thomson, GA	ATL
Thoreau, NM	GLP
Thorndike, MA	SPR
ME	PRT
Thornwood, NY	NY
Thorp, WI	LC
Thousand Oaks, CA	LA
Thousand Palms, CA	SB
Three Bridges, NJ	MET
Three Forks, MT	HEL
Three Lakes, WI	SUP
Three Oaks, MI	KAL
Three Rivers, CA	FRS
MA	SPR
MI	KAL
TX	CC
Throckmorton, TX	FWT
Throop, PA	SCR
Thunderbolt, GA	SAV
Thurmont, MD	BAL
Tiburon, CA	SFR
Tickfaw, LA	BR
Ticonderoga, NY	OG
Tidioute, PA	E
Tierra Amarilla, NM	SFE
Tiff, MO	STL
Tiffin, OH	TOL
Tifton, GA	SAV
Tigard, OR	P
Tiger Point, FL	PT
Tigerton, WI	GB
Tijeras, NM	SFE
Tilden, NE	OM
WI	LC
Tillamook, OR	P
Tillman's Corner, AL	MOB
Tilton, NH	MAN
Tiltonsville, OH	STU
Timber Lake, SD	RC
Timken, KS	DOD
Timonium, MD	BAL
Tinaja, NM	GLP
Tinley Park, IL	CHI
Tintah, MN	SCL
Tioga, LA	ALX
ND	BIS
Tipp City, OH	CIN
Tipton, CA	FRS
IA	DAV
IL	BEL
IN	LFT
KS	SAL
MO	JC
Tisch Mills, WI	GB
Tiskilwa, IL	PEO
Titusville, FL	ORL
PA	E
Tiverton, RI	PRO
Tivoli, NY	NY
TX	CC
Toa Alta, PR	SJN

Toa Baja, PR	SJN
Tobyhanna, PA	SCR
Toccoa, GA	ATL
Todd's Mill, IL	BEL
Tohatchi, NM	GLP
Tokio, ND	FAR
Toksook Bay, AK	FBK
Tol, Chuuk, FM	CI
Toledo, OH	TOL
WA	SEA
Tolland, CT	NOR
Tolleson, AZ	PHX
Tolna, ND	FAR
Tolono, IL	PEO
Toluca, IL	PEO
Tomah, WI	LC
Tomahawk, WI	SUP
Tomales, CA	SFR
Tomball, TX	GAL
Tombstone, AZ	TUC
Tome, NM	SFE
Tomil, FM	CI
Tompkinsville, KY	L
Toms River, NJ	PHU
NJ	PSC
NJ	TR
Tonasket, WA	SPK
Tonawanda, NY	BUF
Tonet, WI	GB
Tonganoxie, KS	KCK
Tonkawa, OK	OKL
Tonopah, NV	LAV
Tontitown, AR	LR
Tony, WI	SUP
Tooele, UT	SLC
Topawa, AZ	TUC
Topeka, KS	KCK
Toppenish, WA	YAK
Topsfield, MA	BO
Toronto, IA	DAV
OH	PBR
OH	STU
Torrance, CA	LA
Torrington, CT	HRT
CT	SAM
WY	CHY
Torun, WI	LC
Toto, GU	AGN
Totowa, NJ	PAT
Totowa Borough, NJ	PAT
Tours, TX	AUS
Towanda, PA	SCR
Tower, MN	DUL
Tower City, PA	ALN
Town and Country, MO	STL
Town of Gates, NY	SY
Towner, ND	FAR
Townsend, MA	BO
MT	HEL
TN	KNX
Towson, MD	BAL
Trabuco Canyon, CA	ORG
Tracy, CA	STO
MN	NU
Traer, IA	DUB
Trafford, PA	GBG
Tranquillity, CA	FRS
Trappist, KY	L
Trauger, PA	GBG
PA	PBR
Traverse City, MI	GAY
Tremont, PA	ALN
Trempealeau, WI	LC
Trenary, MI	MAR
Trenton, IL	BEL
MI	DET
MO	KC
NE	LIN
NJ	PHU
NJ	PSC
NJ	ROM
NJ	TR
OH	CIN
Tres Pinos, CA	MRY
Tresckow, PA	ALN
Trevorton, PA	HBG
Triangle, VA	ARL
Tribes Hill, NY	ALB
Tribune, KS	DOD
Trimont, MN	WIN
Trinidad, CO	PBL
Trinity, TX	TYL
Tripp, SD	SFS
Trona, CA	SB
Trooper, PA	PH
Trout River, NY	OG
Troy, AL	MOB
IL	SFD
IN	IND
KS	KCK
MI	DET
MI	EST
MO	STL
NH	MAN
NY	ALB
NY	SAM
NY	STF
OH	CIN
VT	BUR
Truckee, CA	SAC
Trujillo Alto, PR	SJN
Truman, MN	WIN
Trumansburg, NY	ROC
Trumbull, CT	BGP
CT	PSC
Truro, MA	FR
Trussville, AL	BIR
Truth or Consequences, NM	LSC
Truxton, NY	SY
Tryon, NC	CHL
Tualatin, OR	P
Tuba City, AZ	GLP
Tubac, AZ	TUC
Tuckahoe, NY	NY
Tuckerton, NJ	TR
Tucson, AZ	STN
AZ	TUC
AZ	VNN
Tucumcari, NM	SFE
Tujunga, CA	LA
Tukwila, WA	SEA
Tulare, CA	FRS
Tularosa, NM	LSC
Tulelake, CA	SAC
Tulia, TX	AMA
Tullahoma, TN	NSH
Tully, NY	SY
Tulsa, OK	TLS
Tum Tum, WA	SPK
Tumon Bay, GU	AGN
Tumwater, WA	SEA
Tunkhannock, PA	SCR
Tunnuk, Chuuk, FM	CI
Tununak, AK	FBK
Tupelo, MS	JKS
Tupper Lake, NY	OG
Tupper Plains, OH	STU
Turlock, CA	EST
CA	STO
Turners Falls, MA	SPR
Turtle Creek, PA	PIT
Turtle Lake, WI	SUP
Turtle Mountain Reservation, ND	FAR
Turton, SD	SFS
Tuscaloosa, AL	BIR
Tuscarora, PA	ALN
Tuscola, IL	SFD
Tuscumbia, AL	BIR
Tuskegee Institute, AL	MOB
Tustin, CA	ORG
CA	SB
Tutwiler, MS	JKS
Tuxedo, NY	NY
Twain Harte, CA	STO
Twenty Mile Stand, OH	CIN
Twentynine Palms, CA	SB
Twin Falls, ID	B
Twin Lakes, MN	WIN
WI	MIL
Twin Rocks, PA	ALT
Twin Valley, MN	CR
Twinsburg, OH	CLV
Twisp, WA	SPK
Two Harbors, MN	DUL
Two Inlets, MN	CR
Two Rivers, WI	GB
Tybee Island, GA	SAV
Tyler, MN	NU
TX	TYL
Tyndall, SD	SFS
Tyngsboro, MA	BO
Tyringham, MA	SPR
Tyrone, PA	ALT
Ubly, MI	SAG
Udot, FM	CI
Uh, FM	CI
Uhland, TX	AUS
Ukiah, CA	SR
Ulithi and Neighboring Islands, FM	CI
Ullin, IL	BEL
Ulul, FM	CI
Ulysses, KS	DOD
NE	LIN
Umatac, GU	AGN
Umbarger, TX	AMA
Unadilla, NY	ALB
Unalakleet, AK	FBK
Uncasville, CT	NOR
Underhill Center, VT	BUR
Underwood, ND	BIS
Union, KY	COV
MO	STL
NJ	NEW
OR	BAK
SC	CHR
Union Beach, NJ	TR
Union Center, WI	LC
Union City, CA	OAK
CT	HRT
IN	LFT
NJ	NEW
OK	OKL
PA	E
TN	MEM
Union Grove, WI	MIL
Union Grove-Gladewater, TX	TYL
Union Hill, MN	STP
Union Springs, NY	ROC
Uniondale, NY	RVC
Uniontown, KY	OWN
OH	Y
PA	GBG
PA	PBR
PA	SAM
WA	SPK
Unionville, CT	HRT
United, PA	GBG
Unity, PA	PIT
Universal, IN	IND
University City, MO	STL
University Heights, OH	CLV
University Park, MD	WDC
PA	ALT
Upland, CA	SB
Upper Darby, PA	PH
Upper Frenchville, ME	PRT
Upper Gwynedd, PA	PH
Upper Marlboro, MD	BAL
MD	WDC
Upper Montclair, NJ	NEW
Upper Saddle River, NJ	NEW
Upper St. Clair, PA	PBR
PA	PIT
Upper Sandusky, OH	TOL
Upsala, MN	SCL
Upton, MA	WOR
Urbana, IA	DUB
IL	PEO
MD	BAL
OH	CIN
Urbandale, IA	DM
Urbank, MN	SCL
Ushers, NY	ALB
Usk, WA	SPK
Utica, IL	PEO
MI	DET
NY	NTN
NY	SAM
NY	STF
NY	SY
OH	COL
Utuado, PR	ARE
Uvalde, TX	SAT
Uxbridge, MA	WOR
Vacaville, CA	SAC
Vacherie, LA	BR
Vail, AZ	TUC
CO	DEN
IA	SC
Valatie, NY	ALB
Valdez, AK	ANC
Valdosta, GA	SAV
Vale, NC	CHL
OR	BAK
Valentine, NE	GI
Valeria, IA	DAV
Valhalla, NY	NY
Valier, MT	HEL
Valinda, CA	LA
Vallejo, CA	SAC
Valley, NE	OM
WA	SPK
Valley Center, CA	SD
Valley City, ND	FAR
OH	CLV
Valley Falls, KS	KCK
RI	PRO
Valley Forge, PA	PH
Valley Lee, MD	WDC
Valley Park, MO	STL
Valley Station, KY	L
Valley Stream, NY	RVC
Valley View, TX	FWT
Valmeyer, IL	BEL
Valparaiso, IN	GRY
NE	LIN
Valrico, FL	SP
Valyermo, CA	LA
Van Buren, AR	LR
ME	PRT
Van Etten, NY	ROC
Van Horn, TX	ELP
Van Horne, IA	DUB
Van Nuys, CA	LA
CA	VNN
Van Wert, OH	TOL
Vanceburg, KY	COV
Vancleave, MS	BLX
Vancouver, WA	SEA
Vandalia, IL	SFD
MO	JC
NY	BUF
OH	CIN
Vanderbilt, MI	GAY
TX	VIC
Vandergrift, PA	GBG
Varina, IA	SC
Varysburg, NY	BUF
Vashon, WA	SEA
Vassar, MI	SAG
Vattman, TX	CC
Vaughn, NM	SFE
Veblen, SD	SFS
Vega, TX	AMA
Vega-Alta, PR	ARE
Vega-Baja, PR	ARE
Velva, ND	FAR
Veneta, OR	P
Venice, CA	LA
FL	VEN
IL	SFD
Ventnor, NJ	CAM
PA	PH
Ventura, CA	LA
Vera Cruz, OH	CIN
Verboort, OR	P
Verdigre, NE	OM
Vergennes, VT	BUR
Vermilion, OH	TOL
Vermillion, MN	STP
SD	SFS
Vernal, UT	SLC
Verndale, MN	SCL
Vernon, CA	LA
CT	NOR
NY	SY
TX	FWT
Vernon Center, MN	WIN
Vernon Hills, IL	CHI
Vernonia, OR	P
Vero Beach, FL	PMB
Verona, MO	SPC
ND	FAR
NJ	NEW
NY	SY
PA	PIT
WI	MAD
Verplanck, NY	NY
Versailles, KY	LEX
OH	CIN
PA	PIT
Veseleyville, ND	FAR
Veseli, MN	STP
Vesper, WI	LC
Vesta, MN	NU
Vestal, NY	SY
Vevay, IN	IND
Vicksburg, MI	KAL
MS	JKS
Victor, IA	DAV
NY	ROC
Victoria, KS	SAL
MN	STP
TX	VIC
Victorville, CA	SB
Vidalia, GA	SAV
LA	ALX
Vidor, TX	BEA
Vienna, IL	BEL
MO	JC
OH	Y
VA	ARL
WV	WH
Vieques, PR	CGS
Villa Grove, IL	SFD
Villa Hills, KY	COV
Villa Maria, PA	PIT
Villa Nova, IA	DAV
Villa Park, IL	JOL
Villa Ridge, IL	BEL
Villalba, PR	PCE
Villanova, PA	PH
Villanueva, NM	SFE
Villard, MN	SCL
Villas, NJ	CAM
Ville Platte, LA	LAF
Villisca, IA	DM
Vina, CA	SAC
Vincennes, IN	EVN
Vincent, KS	SAL
OH	STU
Vine Grove, KY	L
Vineland, CO	PBL
MN	SCL

NJ	CAM
Vineyard Haven, MA	FR
Vining, IA	DUB
Vinita, OK	TLS
Vinita Park, MO	STL
Vinton, IA	DUB
LA	LKC
Violet, LA	NO
TX	CC
Virden, IL	SFD
Virgil, IL	RCK
Virginia, IL	SFD
MN	DUL
Virginia Beach, VA	RIC
Virginia City, NV	RNO
Viroqua, WI	LC
Visalia, CA	FRS
Vista, CA	SD
Vivian, LA	SHP
Vodnany, SD	SFS
Volga, IA	DUB
Volo, IL	CHI
Voluntown, CT	NOR
Von Ormy, TX	SAT
Voorheesville, NY	ALB
Vredenburgh, AL	MOB
Vulcan, MI	MAR
Wabash, IN	FTW
Wabasha, MN	WIN
Wabasso, MN	NU
Wabeno, WI	GB
Waco, TX	AUS
Waconia, MN	STP
Waddington, NY	OG
Wadena, MN	SCL
Wading River, NY	RVC
Wadsworth, IL	CHI
OH	CLV
Waggaman, LA	NO
Wagner, SD	SFS
WI	GB
Wagon Mound, NM	SFE
Wagoner, OK	TLS
Wahiawa, HI	HON
Wahkon, MN	SCL
Wahoo, NE	LIN
Wahpeton, ND	FAR
Waialua, HI	HON
Waianae, HI	HON
Waihee, HI	HON
Waikane, HI	HON
Wailuku, HI	HON
Waimanalo, HI	HON
Wainwright, OH	COL
Waipahu, HI	HON
Waite Park, MN	SCL
Waitsburg, WA	SPK
Waitsfield, VT	BUR
Wake Forest, NC	R
WaKeeney, KS	SAL
Wakefield, MA	BO
MI	MAR
RI	PRO
Wakeman, OH	TOL
Wakonda, SD	SFS
Walbridge, OH	TOL
Walden, CO	DEN
NY	NY
Waldorf, MD	WDC
MN	WIN
Waldport, OR	P
Waldron, AR	LR
Wales, ND	FAR
Walford, IA	DUB
Walhain, WI	GB
Walhalla, ND	FAR
Walker, IA	DUB
KS	SAL
MN	DUL
Walkersville, MD	BAL
Walkerton, IN	FTW
Walkerville, MT	HEL
Wall, PA	PBR
SD	RC
TX	SAN
Wall Lake, IA	SC
Walla Walla, WA	SPK
WA	VNN
Wallace, ID	B
KS	SAL
NE	LIN
Wallagrass, ME	PRT
Walled Lake, MI	DET
Wallingford, CT	HRT
PA	PH
VT	BUR
Wallington, NJ	NEW
Wallis, TX	GAL
Walls, MS	JKS
Walnut, CA	LA
IA	DM

IL	PEO
KS	WCH
Walnut Creek, CA	OAK
Walnut Grove, CA	SAC
MN	NU
Walnut Ridge, AR	LR
Walpole, MA	BO
Walsenburg, CO	PBL
Walsh, IL	BEL
WI	GB
Walston, PA	E
Walterboro, SC	CHR
Walters, OK	OKL
Waltham, MA	BO
Walthill, NE	OM
Walton, IL	RCK
KY	COV
NY	ALB
Wamego, KS	KCK
Wampum, PA	PIT
Wanamie, PA	SCR
Wanatah, IN	GRY
Wanblee, SD	RC
Wanda, MN	NU
Wantagh, NY	RVC
Wapakoneta, OH	CIN
Wapato, WA	YAK
Wapella, IL	PEO
Wapello, IA	DAV
Wappingers Falls, NY	NY
War, WV	WH
Ward, SC	CHR
Ward Springs, MN	SCL
Warden, WA	YAK
Wardsville, MO	JC
Ware, MA	SPR
Wareham, MA	FR
Warminster, PA	PH
Warner, NH	MAN
Warner Robins, GA	SAV
Warners, NY	SY
Warren, IL	RCK
MA	WOR
MI	DET
MI	NTN
MI	STN
MN	CR
NJ	MET
OH	PBR
OH	Y
PA	E
RI	PRO
Warrens, WI	LC
Warrensburg, MO	KC
NY	ALB
Warrensville Heights, OH	CLV
Warrenton, MO	STL
VA	ARL
Warrenville, CT	NOR
IL	JOL
Warrington, PA	PH
PA	PHU
Warroad, MN	CR
Warsaw, IL	PEO
IN	FTW
KY	COV
MO	JC
ND	FAR
NY	BUF
Warson Woods, MO	STL
Warwick, NY	NY
RI	PRO
Wasco, CA	FRS
OR	BAK
Waseca, MN	WIN
Washburn, IL	PEO
WI	SUP
Washington, DC	NY
DC	PHU
DC	SAM
DC	WDC
GA	ATL
IA	DAV
IL	PEO
IN	EVN
KS	SAL
LA	LAF
MI	DET
MO	STL
NC	R
NJ	MET
PA	PIT
VT	BUR
Washington Court House, OH	COL
Washington Crossing, NJ	TR
Washington Depot, CT	HRT
Washington Park, IL	BEL
Washington Township, NJ	CAM
NJ	NEW
Washingtonville, NY	NY
Washtunca, WA	SPK

Wasilla, AK	ANC
Wassaic, NY	NY
Watauga, SD	RC
Watchung, NJ	MET
Water Mill, NY	RVC
Waterbury, CT	HRT
CT	SAM
VT	BUR
Waterflow, NM	GLP
Waterford, CT	NOR
CT	NTN
MI	DET
NJ	CAM
NY	ALB
PA	E
WI	MIL
Waterloo, IA	DUB
IL	BEL
IN	FTW
KS	WCH
NY	ROC
WI	MAD
Watersmeet, MI	MAR
Watertown, CT	HRT
MA	BO
MN	STP
NY	OG
SD	SFS
WI	MAD
Waterville, KS	KCK
ME	PRT
ME	SAM
MN	STP
NY	SY
WA	YAK
Watervliet, MI	KAL
NY	ALB
NY	STF
Watford City, ND	BIS
Wathena, KS	KCK
Watkins, IA	DUB
MN	NU
Watkins Glen, NY	ROC
Watonga, OK	OKL
Watseka, IL	JOL
Watsonville, CA	MRY
Wattenberg, CO	DEN
Waubay, SD	SFS
Waubun, MN	CR
Wauchula, FL	VEN
Waucoma, IA	DUB
Wauconda, IL	CHI
Waukee, IA	DM
Waukegan, IL	CHI
Waukesha, WI	MIL
Waukon, IA	DUB
Waumandee, WI	LC
Waunakee, WI	MAD
Waupaca, WI	GB
Waupun, WI	MIL
Wauregan, CT	NOR
Wausau, WI	LC
Wausaukee, WI	GB
Wauseon, OH	TOL
Wautoma, WI	GB
Wauwatosa, WI	MIL
Wauzeka, WI	LC
Waveland, MS	BLX
Waverly, IA	DUB
IL	SFD
KS	KCK
KY	OWN
MN	STP
NE	LIN
NY	ROC
OH	COL
SD	SFS
Wax, KY	OWN
Waxahachie, TX	DAL
Waycross, GA	SAV
Wayland, MA	BO
MI	KAL
NY	ROC
Waymart, PA	SCR
Wayne, IL	JOL
MI	DET
NE	OM
NJ	PAT
PA	PH
WI	MIL
WV	WH
Waynesboro, GA	SAV
MS	BLX
PA	HBG
TN	NSH
VA	RIC
Waynesburg, OH	Y
PA	PIT
Waynesville, MO	JC
NC	CHL
OH	CIN

Wayside, NJ	TR
Wayzata, MN	STP
Wea, KS	KCK
Weare Twp., MI	GR
Weatherford, OK	OKL
TX	FWT
Weatherly, PA	ALN
Weaverville, CA	SAC
Webb City, MO	SPC
Webster, MA	WOR
NY	ROC
SD	SFS
WI	SUP
Webster City, IA	DUB
Webster Groves, MO	STL
Webster Springs, WV	WH
Wedron, IL	PEO
Weed, CA	SAC
Weedsport, NY	ROC
Weehawken, NJ	NEW
Weeno, Chuuk, FM	CI
Weimar, TX	VIC
Weiner, AR	LR
Weingarten, MO	STL
Weir, KS	WCH
Weirton, WV	PBR
WV	WH
Weiser, ID	B
Welch, WV	WH
Weldona, CO	DEN
Weller, IA	DAV
Wellesley, MA	BO
Wellfleet, MA	FR
Wellington, FL	PMB
KS	WCH
OH	CLV
SD	SFS
TX	AMA
Wellman, IA	DAV
Wellpinit, WA	SPK
Wells, ME	PRT
MI	MAR
MN	WIN
NY	OG
Wellsboro, PA	SCR
Wellsburg, WV	WH
Wellston, MO	STL
OH	COL
Wellsville, MO	JC
NY	BUF
OH	Y
Welsh, LA	LKC
Welton, IA	DAV
Wenatchee, WA	YAK
Wendelin, IL	BEL
Wendell, ID	B
NC	R
Wenham, MA	BO
Wenona, IL	PEO
Wentzville, MO	STL
Wernersville, PA	ALN
Weslaco, TX	BWN
Wesley, IA	SC
Wesley Hills, NY	NY
Wessington, SD	SFS
Wessington Springs, SD	SFS
West, TX	AUS
West Albany, MN	WIN
West Aliquippa, PA	PIT
West Allis, WI	MIL
West Alton, MO	STL
West Babylon, NY	RVC
West Bangor, PA	ALN
West Barnstable, MA	FR
West Bend, IA	SC
WI	MIL
West Bethesda, MD	WDC
West Bloomfield, MI	DET
MI	EST
West Boylston, MA	WOR
West Branch, IA	DAV
MI	GAY
West Brattleboro, VT	LIT
West Bridgewater, MA	BO
West Brookfield, MA	WOR
West Brooklyn, IL	RCK
West Burke, VT	STF
West Burlington, IA	DAV
West Chazy, NY	OG
West Chester, OH	CIN
PA	PH
West Chicago, IL	JOL
West Clarksville, NY	BUF
West Collingswood, NJ	CAM
West Concord, MN	WIN
West Conshohocken, PA	PH
West Covina, CA	LA
West Des Moines, IA	DM
West Duluth, MN	DUL
West Easton, PA	PHU
West Falls, NY	BUF

West Fargo, ND	FAR
West Frankfort, IL	BEL
West Franklin, NH	MAN
West Greenwich, RI	PRO
West Grove, PA	PH
West Hartford, CT	HRT
West Harwich, MA	FR
West Haven, CT	HRT
West Haverstraw, NY	NY
West Hazleton, PA	SCR
West Hempstead, NY	RVC
West Hollywood, CA	LA
FL	MIA
West Hurley-Woodstock, NY	NY
West Hyattsville, MD	WDC
West Islip, NY	RVC
NY	STF
West Jefferson, OH	COL
West Jordan, UT	SLC
West Kewaunee, WI	GB
West Lafayette, IN	LFT
West Lake Forest, IL	CHI
West Lebanon, NH	MAN
West Leechburg, PA	SJP
West Leyden, NY	OG
West Liberty, IA	DAV
KY	LEX
WV	WH
West Long Branch, NJ	TR
West Memphis, AR	LR
West Middlesex, PA	E
West Mifflin, PA	PIT
West Milford Township, NJ	PAT
West Milton, OH	CIN
West Mineral, KS	WCH
West Monroe, LA	SHP
West New York, NJ	NEW
West Newbury, MA	BO
West Newton, PA	GBG
West Newton Township, MN	NU
West Nyack, NY	NY
West Orange, NJ	NEW
West Overland, MO	STL
West Palm Beach, FL	PMB
FL	SAM
West Park, NY	NY
West Paterson, NJ	NTN
NJ	PAT
West Peoria, IL	PEO
West Pittsburg, PA	PIT
West Pittston, PA	SCR
West Plains, MO	SPC
West Point, IA	DAV
MS	JKS
NE	OM
NY	NY
VA	RIC
West Portsmouth, OH	COL
West Reading, PA	ALN
West Redding, CT	BGP
West Roxbury, MA	BO
West Rutland, VT	BUR
West Sacramento, CA	SAC
West St. Paul, MN	STP
West Salem, OH	CLV
WI	LC
West Salisbury, PA	ALT
West Seneca, NY	BUF
West Simsbury, CT	HRT
West Springfield, MA	SPR
West Stewartstown, NH	MAN
West Stockbridge, MA	SPR
West Sunbury, PA	PIT
West Swanzey, NH	MAN
West Taghkanic, NY	ALB
West Terre Haute, IN	IND
West Union, IA	DUB
MN	SCL
OH	CIN
WV	WH
West Valley, NY	BUF
West Valley City, UT	SLC
West View, PA	PIT
West Warren, MA	WOR
West Warwick, RI	PRO
West Willington, CT	NOR
West Windsor, NJ	TR
West Winfield, NY	ALB
West Wyoming, PA	SCR
West Yellowstone, MT	HEL
Westboro, WI	SUP
Westborough, MA	WOR
Westbrook, CT	NOR
ME	PRT
MN	WIN
Westbury, NY	PSC
NY	RVC
Westchester, IL	CHI
Westcliffe, CO	PBL
Westend, WA	SPK
Westerly, RI	PRO

Western Springs, IL	CHI
Westernport, MD	BAL
Westerville, OH	COL
Westfield, IN	LFT
MA	SPR
NJ	NEW
NY	BUF
VT	BUR
Westford, MA	BO
Westhampton Beach, NY	RVC
Westhope, ND	FAR
Westlake, LA	LKC
OH	CLV
Westlake Village, CA	LA
Westland, MI	DET
Westminster, CA	ORG
CO	DEN
MA	WOR
MD	BAL
Westmont, IL	JOL
NJ	CAM
Westmorland, CA	SD
Weston, CT	BGP
IA	DM
MA	BO
MO	KC
NE	LIN
PA	SCR
VT	BUR
WI	LC
WV	WH
Westover, WV	WH
Westphalia, IA	DM
KS	KCK
MI	LAN
MO	JC
TX	AUS
Westport, CT	BGP
MA	FR
NY	OG
SD	SFS
WI	MAD
Westtown, PA	PH
Westville, IL	PEO
NJ	CAM
Westville Grove, NJ	CAM
Westwego, LA	NO
Westwood, CA	SAC
MA	BO
NJ	NEW
Wethersfield, CT	HRT
Wetmore, KS	KCK
Wewahitchka, FL	PT
Wewoka, OK	OKL
Wexford, IA	DUB
PA	PIT
Weyauwega, WI	GB
Weyerhauser, WI	SUP
Weymouth, MA	BO
Wharton, TX	VIC
What Cheer, IA	DAV
Wheat Ridge, CO	DEN
Wheatfield, IN	LFT
Wheatland, IA	DAV
WY	CHY
Wheaton, IL	JOL
KS	KCK
MD	WDC
MN	SCL
Wheelersburg, OH	COL
Wheeling, IL	CHI
WV	OLL
WV	SJP
WV	WH
Whippany, NJ	PAT
NJ	PHU
Whistler, AL	MOB
White, SD	SFS
White Bear Lake, MN	STP
White Castle, LA	BR
White Cloud, MI	GR
White Cypress, MS	BLX
White Deer, TX	AMA
White Earth, MN	CR
White Hall, IL	SFD
White Haven, PA	SCR
White Lake, MI	DET
SD	SFS
WI	GB
White Mills, KY	L
PA	SCR
White Oak Boro, PA	PIT
White Pigeon, MI	KAL
White Pine, MI	MAR
White Plains, NY	NY
NY	PSC
White River, SD	RC
White River Junction, VT	BUR
White Salmon, WA	YAK
White Sulphur Springs, MT	HEL
WV	WH

White Swan, WA	YAK
Whitefield, ME	PRT
NH	MAN
Whitefish, MT	HEL
Whitefish Bay, WI	MIL
Whitehall, MT	HEL
NY	ALB
PA	ALN
PA	PIT
WI	LC
Whitehouse, OH	TOL
TX	TYL
Whitehouse Station, NJ	MET
Whitelaw, WI	GB
Whiteriver, AZ	GLP
Whitesboro, NY	SY
Whitestone, NY	BRK
Whitesville, KY	OWN
NY	BUF
WV	WH
Whitethorn, CA	SR
Whiteville, NC	R
Whitewater, CO	PBL
WI	MIL
Whiting, IN	GRY
IN	PRM
NJ	TR
Whitinsville, MA	WOR
Whitley City, KY	LEX
Whitman, MA	BO
Whitney, PA	GBG
Whitney Point, NY	SY
Whittemore, IA	SC
MI	GAY
Whittier, CA	LA
Whittlesey, WI	SUP
Wichita, KS	WCH
Wichita Falls, TX	FWT
Wickatunk, NJ	TR
Wickenburg, AZ	PHX
Wickford, RI	PRO
Wickliffe, OH	CLV
Wien, MO	JC
Wiggins, CO	DEN
MS	BLX
Wilber, NE	LIN
Wilberforce, OH	CIN
Wilbraham, MA	SPR
Wilbur, WA	SPK
Wilcox, PA	E
Wild Rice, ND	FAR
Wilder, KY	COV
Wildwood, NJ	CAM
PA	PIT
Wildwood Crest, NJ	CAM
Wilkes-Barre, PA	PHU
PA	PSC
PA	SAM
PA	SCR
Wilkinsburg, PA	PIT
Willacoochee, GA	SAV
Willard, OH	TOL
WI	LC
Willcox, AZ	TUC
Willey, IA	SC
Williams, AZ	PHX
IA	DUB
MN	CR
Williamsburg, IA	DAV
KY	LEX
OH	CIN
PA	ALT
VA	PSC
VA	RIC
Williamson, WV	WH
Williamsport, MD	BAL
PA	SCR
Williamston, MI	LAN
NC	R
Williamstown, KY	COV
MA	SPR
NJ	CAM
NJ	PHU
PA	HBG
PA	PSC
Williamsville, NY	BUF
NY	SAM
Willimantic, CT	NOR
CT	STF
Willingboro, NJ	TR
Williston, FL	STA
ND	BIS
VT	BUR
VT	SAM
Williston Park, NY	RVC
Willisville, IL	BEL
Willits, CA	SR
Willmar, MN	NU
Willoughby, OH	CLV
Willoughby Hills, OH	CLV
Willow City, ND	FAR

Willow Grove, PA	PH
Willow Lake, SD	SFS
Willow River, MN	DUL
Willow Springs, IL	CHI
MO	SPC
Willowburn, PA	PH
Willowdale, KS	WCH
Willowick, OH	CLV
Willows, CA	SAC
Willsboro, NY	OG
Wilmerding, PA	PIT
PA	SJP
Wilmette, IL	CHI
Wilmington, CA	LA
DE	PHU
DE	WIL
IL	JOL
MA	BO
NC	R
OH	CIN
VT	BUR
Wilmington Manor, DE	WIL
Wilmont, MN	WIN
Wilmore, PA	ALT
Wilmot, MI	SAG
SD	SFS
WI	MIL
Wilno, MN	NU
Wilson, KS	SAL
MN	WIN
NC	R
NY	BUF
WI	LC
WI	SUP
Wilsonville, IL	SFD
OR	P
Wilton, CT	BGP
IA	DAV
ME	PRT
MN	CR
ND	BIS
ND	STN
NH	MAN
WI	LC
Wilton Center, IL	JOL
Wimberley, TX	AUS
Wimbledon, ND	FAR
Winamac, IN	LFT
Winburne, PA	E
Winchendon, MA	WOR
Winchester, IL	SFD
IN	LFT
KY	LEX
MA	BO
NH	MAN
VA	ARL
Winchester Center, CT	HRT
Wind Lake, WI	MIL
Windber, PA	ALT
PA	PBR
Windham, CT	NOR
ME	PRT
NH	MAN
NY	ALB
OH	Y
Windom, MN	WIN
Windsor, CA	SR
CO	DEN
CT	HRT
ND	FAR
NY	SY
VT	BUR
Windsor Locks, CT	HRT
Windthorst, KS	DOD
TX	FWT
Winfield, AL	BIR
IL	JOL
KS	WCH
Winlock, WA	SEA
Winnebago, MN	WIN
NE	OM
Winneconne, WI	GB
Winnemucca, NV	RNO
Winner, SD	RC
Winnetka, IL	CHI
Winnfield, LA	ALX
Winnie, TX	BEA
Winnsboro, LA	ALX
Winona, MN	WIN
Winooski, VT	BUR
Winslow, AR	LR
AZ	GLP
ME	PRT
Winsted, CT	HRT
MN	NU
Winston-Salem, NC	CHL
Winter, WI	SUP
Winter Garden, FL	ORL
Winter Haven, FL	ORL
Winter Park, CO	DEN
FL	ORL

Winter Springs, FL	ORL
Winterhaven, CA	SD
Winterport, ME	PRT
Winters, CA	SAC
TX	SAN
Winterset, IA	DM
Wintersville, OH	STU
Winthrop, IA	DUB
MA	BO
ME	PRT
MN	NU
Wireton, PA	PIT
Wisconsin Dells, WI	MAD
Wisconsin Rapids, WI	LC
Wishek, ND	FAR
Wisner, NE	OM
Withamsville, OH	CIN
Witherbee, NY	OG
Witt, IL	SFD
Wittenberg, WI	GB
Woburn, MA	BO
Woden, IA	DUB
Wofford Heights, CA	FRS
Wolcott, CT	HRT
NY	ROC
Woleai and Neighboring Islands, FM	CI
Wolf Point, MT	GF
Wolfeboro, NH	MAN
Wolfforth, TX	LUB
Wonder Lake, IL	RCK
Wonewoc, WI	LC
Wood Dale, IL	JOL
Wood River, IL	SFD
NE	GI
Woodbine, IA	DM
NJ	CAM
NJ	PHU
Woodbourne, NY	NY
Woodbridge, CT	HRT
NJ	MET
VA	ARL
Woodburn, OR	P
Woodbury, CT	HRT
NJ	CAM
NY	RVC
Woodbury Heights, NJ	CAM
Woodcliff Lake, NJ	NEW
Woodcrest, DE	WIL
Woodhaven, MI	DET
Woodhull, IL	PEO
WI	MIL
Woodlake, CA	FRS
Woodland, CA	SAC
ME	PRT
WA	SEA
WI	MIL
Woodland Hills, CA	LA
Woodland Park, CO	COS
The Woodlands, TX	GAL
Woodlawn, NY	BUF
VA	RIC
Woodlynne, NJ	CAM
Woodmont, CT	HRT
Woodridge, IL	JOL
Wood-Ridge, NJ	NEW
Woodrow, TX	LUB
Woodruff, WI	SUP
Woods Hole, MA	FR
Woodsboro, TX	CC
Woodsfield, OH	STU
Woodside, CA	SFR
Woodson Terrace, MO	STL
Woodstock, CT	NOR
IL	RCK
MD	BAL
MN	WIN
VA	ARL
VT	BUR
Woodstown, NJ	CAM
Woodsville, NH	MAN
Woodville, FL	PT
MS	JKS
TX	BEA
Woodward, IA	DM
IA	SC
OK	OKL
Woonsocket, RI	NTN
RI	PRO
RI	STF
SD	SFS
Wooster, OH	CLV
Worcester, MA	NTN
MA	SAM
MA	WOR
NY	ALB
Worland, WY	CHY
Worth, IL	CHI
Worthing, SD	SFS
Worthington, IA	DUB
MN	WIN
OH	STU
Wrangell, AK	JUN
Wray, CO	DEN
Wrentham, MA	BO
Wright, KS	DOD
Wright Township, MI	GR
Wrightstown, WI	GB
Wrightsville Beach, NC	R
Wrightwood, CA	SB
Wuerzburg, WI	LC
Wurtsboro, NY	NY
Wyalusing, PA	SCR
Wyandanch, NY	RVC
Wyandotte, MI	DET
Wyckoff, NJ	NEW
Wykoff, MN	WIN
Wylie, TX	DAL
Wymore, NE	LIN
Wynantskill, NY	ALB
Wyncote, PA	PH
Wyndmere, ND	FAR
Wyndmoor, PA	PH
Wynne, AR	LR
Wynnewood, PA	PH
Wynot, NE	OM
Wyoming, DE	WIL
IL	PEO
PA	SCR
Wytheville, VA	RIC
Xenia, OH	CIN
Yabucoa, PR	CGS
Yakima, WA	YAK
Yakutat, AK	JUN
Yale, MI	DET
Yalesville, CT	HRT
Yamhill, OR	P
Yankton, SD	SFS
Yardley, PA	PH
Yarmouth, ME	PRT
Yates Center, KS	WCH
Yatesboro, PA	GBG
Yauco, PR	PCE
Yazoo City, MS	JKS
Yeadon, PA	PH
Yellow Springs, OH	CIN
Yelm, WA	SEA
Yerington, NV	RNO
Yigo, GU	AGN
Yoakum, TX	VIC
Yoder, IN	FTW
Yona, GU	AGN
Yonges Island, SC	CHR
Yonkers, NY	NTN
NY	NY
NY	PSC
NY	STF
Yorba Linda, CA	ORG
York, NE	LIN
PA	HBG
SC	CHR
York Harbor, ME	PRT
York Haven, PA	HBG
Yorktown, TX	VIC
VA	RIC
Yorktown Heights, NY	NY
Yorkville, IN	IND
NY	SY
OH	STU
Yosemite National Park, CA	FRS
Youngstown, NY	BUF
OH	OLL
OH	PBR
OH	ROM
OH	SJP
OH	Y
PA	GBG
Youngsville, LA	LAF
NY	NY
PA	E
Youngwood, PA	GBG
Yountville, CA	SR
Ypsilanti, MI	LAN
Yreka, CA	SAC
Yuba, WI	LC
Yuba City, CA	SAC
Yucaipa, CA	SB
Yucca Valley, CA	SB
Yukon, OK	OKL
PA	GBG
Yulan, NY	NY
Yuma, AZ	TUC
CO	DEN
Zachary, LA	BR
Zaleski, OH	COL
Zanesville, OH	COL
OH	NTN
Zapata, TX	CC
Zearing, IA	DUB
Zeeland, ND	FAR
Zeigler, IL	BEL
Zelienople, PA	PIT
Zell, MO	STL
SD	SFS
Zenda, KS	WCH
Zephyr Cove, NV	RNO
Zephyrhills, FL	SP
Zillah, WA	YAK
Zilwaukee, MI	SAG
Zimmerman, MN	SCL
Zion-Beach Park, IL	CHI
Zionsville, IN	LFT
Zumbrota, MN	STP
Zuni, NM	GLP
Zurich, KS	SAL
Zwolle, LA	SHP

The United States Embassy to the Holy See

ESTABLISHED UNITED STATES EMBASSY TO THE HOLY SEE JANUARY 10, 1984.

Address: Via Delle Terme Deciane, 26 00153 Rome, Italy. Tel: 011-39-6-4674-3425; Fax: 011-39-6-575-8346.
APO Address: U.S. Embassy to the Holy See, PSC 59, Box 66, APO AE 09624.

UNITED STATES AMBASSADOR TO THE HOLY SEE

His Excellency
The Honorable

RAYMOND L. FLYNN

Born in Boston, Massachusetts, July 22, 1939; graduated Providence College 1963; Masters Degree in Education, Harvard University, 1981; Public Service includes four terms in the Massachusetts Legislature (1971-1978) as South Boston/Dorchester State Representative; three terms on the Boston City Council, 1978-1983; three terms as the 46th Mayor of Boston (1983-1993); President of the United States Conference of Mayors; nominated Ambassador to the Holy See, March 1989; married to Catherine Flynn (nee Coyne); and father of six children.

Former Ambassadors to the Holy See:

The Honorable WILLIAM A. WILSON	1984-1986.
The Honorable FRANK SHAKESPEARE	1986-1989.
The Honorable THOMAS P. MELADY	1989-1993.

The Catholic Church in the United States

The organizational structure of the Catholic Church in the United States consists of 33 Provinces with as many Archdioceses (Metropolitan Sees); 148 Suffragan Sees (Dioceses); The Military Archdiocese; four Eastern-Rite jurisdictions immediately subject to the Holy See in Rome. The Eparchies of St. Maron (Maronites), Newton (Melkites), St. Thomas the Apostle of Detroit (Chaldeans) and St. George Martyr of Canton, Ohio (Romanians). Each of these jurisdictions is under the direction of an Archbishop and Bishop called an Ordinary, who has apostolic responsibility and authority for the pastoral service of the people in his care.

The structure includes the territorial episcopal conference known as the National Conference of Catholic Bishops. In and through this body, which is strictly ecclesiastical and has defined juridical authority, the Bishops exercise their collegiate pastorate over the Church in the entire country.

Related to the NCCB is the United States Catholic Conference, a civil corporation and operational secretariat through which the Bishops, in cooperation with other members of the Church, act on a wider-than-ecclesiastical scale for the good of the Church and society in the United States.

The following is a list of the thirteen regions in the United States and provinces within those regions.

Region I: Includes the states of Maine, Vermont, New Hampshire, Massachusetts, Rhode Island, and Connecticut. Provinces of Boston and Hartford; Eparchy of Stamford and Eparchy for Melkites.

Region II: Includes the state of New York. Province of New York and Eparchy of St. Maron.

Region III: Includes the states of New Jersey and Pennsylvania. Provinces of Newark and Philadelphia; Archeparchy of Philadelphia, Ukrainian Archeparchy of Pittsburgh, Byzantine Eparchy of Passaic, and Apostolic Exarchate for Armenians.

Region IV: Includes the states of Delaware, District of Columbia, Florida, Georgia, Maryland, North Carolina, South Carolina, Virgin Islands, Virginia and West Virginia. Provinces of Atlanta, Baltimore, Miami, Washington, and the Military Archdiocese.

Region V: Includes the states of Alabama, Kentucky, Louisiana, Mississippi and Tennessee. Provinces of Louisville, Mobile and New Orleans.

Region VI: Includes the states of Michigan and Ohio. Provinces of Cincinnati, Detroit; Eparchy of Parma, Apostolic Exarchate for Chaldeans, and Apostolic Exarchate for Romanians.

Region VII: Includes the states of Illinois, Indiana and Wisconsin. Provinces of Chicago, Indianapolis, Milwaukee; Eparchy of St. Nicholas in Chicago-Ukrainian.

Region VIII: Includes the states of Minnesota, North Dakota and South Dakota. Provinces of St. Paul and Minneapolis.

Region IX: Includes the states of Kansas, Missouri and Nebraska. Provinces of Dubuque, Kansas City in Kansas, Omaha and St. Louis.

Region X: Includes the states of Arkansas, Oklahoma and Texas (excluding El Paso). Provinces of Oklahoma City and San Antonio.

Region XI: Includes the states of California, Hawaii and Nevada. Provinces of Los Angeles and San Francisco (excluding Salt Lake City); Eparchy of Van Nuys.

Region XII: Includes the states of Alaska, Idaho, Montana, Oregon and Washington. Provinces of Anchorage, Portland and Seattle.

Region XIII: Includes the states of Utah, Arizona, New Mexico, Colorado and Wyoming. Provinces of Denver, Santa Fe, part of San Francisco, Salt Lake City, and El Paso.

Please refer to individual Diocesan and Archdiocesan listing for complete and detailed information. The following list does not include the retired Archbishops or retired Bishops.

PROVINCE OF ANCHORAGE

Includes the State of Alaska.

Archdiocese of Anchorage, AK.—Most Rev. Francis T. Hurley, Archbishop of Anchorage.

Diocese of Fairbanks, AK.—Most Rev. Michael Kaniecki, S.J., Bishop of Fairbanks.

Diocese of Juneau, AK.—Most Rev. Michael Warfel.

PROVINCE OF ATLANTA

Includes the States of Georgia, North Carolina and South Carolina.

Archdiocese of Atlanta, GA.—Most Rev. John F. Donoghue, Archbishop of Atlanta.

Diocese of Charleston, SC.—Most Rev. David B. Thompson, Bishop of Charleston.

Diocese of Charlotte, NC.—Most Rev. William G. Curlin, Bishop of Charlotte.

Diocese of Raleigh, NC.—Most Rev. F. Joseph Gossman, Bishop of Raleigh.

Diocese of Savannah, GA.—Most Rev. John K. Boland, Bishop of Savannah.

PROVINCE OF BALTIMORE

Includes the States of Maryland (except Montgomery, Prince Charles, St. Mary's, Calvert and Charles Counties), Delaware, Virginia and West Virginia.

Archdiocese of Baltimore, MD.—His Eminence William Cardinal Keeler, Archbishop of Baltimore. Most Rev. William Newmann, Auxiliary Bishop. Most Rev. P. Francis Murphy, Auxiliary Bishop.

Diocese of Arlington, VA.—Most Rev. John R. Keating, Bishop of Arlington.

Diocese of Richmond, VA.—Most Rev. Walter F. Sullivan, Bishop of Richmond.

Diocese of Wheeling-Charleston, WV.—Most Rev. Bernard W. Schmitt, Bishop of Wheeling-Charleston.

Diocese of Wilmington, DE.—Most Rev. Michael A. Saltarelli, Bishop of Wilmington.

PROVINCE OF BOSTON

Includes the States of Maine, New Hampshire, Vermont and Massachusetts.

Archdiocese of Boston, MA.—His Eminence Bernard Cardinal Law, Archbishop of Boston. Most Rev. John P. Boles, Auxiliary Bishop. Most Rev. John R. McNamara, Auxiliary Bishop. Most Rev. John B. McCormack, Auxiliary Bishop. Most Rev. William F. Murphy, Auxiliary Bishop. Most Rev. Francis X. Irwin, Auxiliary Bishop. Most Rev. Emilio Allue, S.D.B.

Diocese of Burlington, VT.—Kenneth A. Angell, Bishop of Burlington.

Diocese of Fall River, MA.—Most Rev. Sean P. O'Malley, O.F.M.Cap., Bishop of Fall River.

Diocese of Manchester, NH.—Most Rev. Leo E. O'Neil, Bishop of Manchester. Most Rev. Francis J. Christian, Auxiliary Bishop.

Diocese of Portland, ME.—Most Rev. Joseph Gerry, O.S.B., Bishop of Portland. Most Rev. Amedee Wilfrid Proulx, Auxiliary Bishop. Most Rev. Michael R. Cote, Auxiliary Bishop.

Diocese of Springfield, MA.—Most Rev. Thomas L. Dupre, Bishop of Springfield.

Diocese of Worcester, MA.—Most Rev. Daniel P. Reilly, Bishop of Worcester. Most Rev. George Rueger, Auxiliary Bishop.

PROVINCE OF CHICAGO

Includes the State of Illinois.

Archdiocese of Chicago, IL.—Vacant See. Most Rev. Most Rev. John R. Gorman, Auxiliary Bishop. Most Rev. Thad J. Jakubowski, Auxiliary Bishop. Most Rev. Raymond E. Goedert, Auxiliary Bishop. Most Rev. Gerald F. Kicanas, Auxiliary Bishop. Most Rev. Edwin M. Conway, Auxiliary Bishop. Most Rev. George V. Murry, S.J., Auxiliary Bishop. Most Rev. John R. Manz, Auxiliary Bishop.

Diocese of Belleville, IL.—Most Rev. Wilton D. Gregory, Bishop of Belleville.

Diocese of Joliet, IL.—Most Rev. Joseph L. Imesch, Bishop of Joliet. Most Rev. Roger L. Kaffer, Auxiliary Bishop.

Diocese of Peoria, IL.—Most Rev. John J. Myers, Bishop of Peoria.

Diocese of Rockford, IL.—Most Rev. Thomas G. Doran, Bishop of Rockford.

Diocese of Springfield, IL.—Most Rev. Daniel L. Ryan, Bishop of Springfield.

PROVINCE OF CINCINNATI

Includes the State of Ohio.

Archdiocese of Cincinnati, OH.—Most Rev. Daniel E. Pilarczyk, Archbishop of Cincinnati. Most Rev. Carl K. Moeddel, Auxiliary Bishop.

Diocese of Cleveland, OH.—Most Rev. Anthony M. Pilla, Bishop of Cleveland. Most Rev. A. Edward Pevec, Auxiliary Bishop. Most Rev. Alexander James Quinn, Auxiliary Bishop.

Diocese of Columbus, OH.—Most Rev. James A. Griffin, Bishop of Columbus.

Diocese of Steubenville, OH.—Most Rev. Gilbert I. Sheldon, Bishop of Steubenville.

Diocese of Toledo, OH.—Most Rev. James R. Hoffman, Bishop of Toledo. Most Rev. Robert Donnelly, Auxiliary Bishop.

Diocese of Youngstown, OH.—Most Rev. Thomas J. Tobin, Bishop of Youngstown.

PROVINCE OF DENVER

Includes the States of Colorado and Wyoming.

Archdiocese of Denver, CO.—Most Rev. Charles J. Chaput, O.F.M.Cap., Archbishop of Denver.

Diocese of Cheyenne, WY.—Most Rev. Joseph Hart, Bishop of Cheyenne.

Diocese of Colorado Springs, CO.—Most Rev. Richard C. Hanifen, Bishop of Colorado Springs.

Diocese of Pueblo, CO.—Most Rev Arthur N. Tafoya, Bishop of Pueblo.

PROVINCE OF DETROIT

Includes the State of Michigan.

Archdiocese of Detroit, MI.—His Eminence Adam Cardinal Maida, Archbishop of Detroit. Most Rev. Thomas J. Gumbleton, Auxiliary Bishop. Most Rev. Moses B. Anderson, S.S.E., Auxiliary Bishop. Most Rev. Dale J. Melczek, Auxiliary Bishop. Most Rev. Kevin M. Britt, Auxiliary Bishop. Most Rev. Bernard J. Harrington, Auxiliary Bishop. Most Rev. John C. Nienstedt, Auxiliary Bishop. Most Rev. Allen H. Vigneron, Auxiliary Bishop.

Diocese of Gaylord, MI.—Most Rev. Patrick R. Cooney, Bishop of Gaylord.

Diocese of Grand Rapids, MI.—Most Rev. Robert J. Rose, Bishop of Grand Rapids. Most Rev. Joseph C. McKinney, Auxiliary Bishop.

Diocese of Kalamazoo, MI.—Vacant See.

Diocese of Lansing, MI.—Most Rev. Carl F. Mengeling, Bishop of Lansing.

Diocese of Marquette, MI.—Most Rev. James H. Garland, Bishop of Marquette.

Diocese of Saginaw, MI.—Most Rev. Kenneth E. Untener, Bishop of Saginaw.

PROVINCE OF DUBUQUE

Includes the State of Iowa.

Archdiocese of Dubuque, IA.—Most Rev. Jerome G. Hanus, O.S.B., Archbishop of Dubuque.

Diocese of Davenport, IA.—Most Rev. William E. Franklin, Bishop of Davenport.

Diocese of Des Moines, IA.—Most Rev. Joseph L. Charron, C.P.P.S., Bishop of Des Moines.

Diocese of Sioux City, IA.—Most Rev. Lawrence Soens, Bishop of Sioux City.

PROVINCE OF HARTFORD

Includes the States of Connecticut and Rhode Island.

Archdiocese of Hartford, CT.—Most Rev. Daniel A. Cronin, Archbishop of Hartford. Most Rev. Peter A. Rosazza, Auxiliary Bishop.

Diocese of Bridgeport, CT.—Most Rev. Edward M. Egan, Bishop of Bridgeport.

Diocese of Norwich, CT.—Most Rev. Daniel A. Hart, Bishop of Norwich.

Diocese of Providence, RI.—Most Rev. Louis E. Gelineau, Bishop of Providence. Most Rev. Robert E. Mulvee, Coadjutor Bishop of Providence.

PROVINCE OF INDIANAPOLIS

Includes the State of Indiana.

Archdiocese of Indianapolis, IN.—Most Rev. Daniel M. Buechlein, O.S.B., Archbishop of Indianapolis.

Diocese of Evansville, IN.—Most Rev. Gerald A. Gettelfinger, Bishop of Evansville.

Diocese of Fort Wayne-South Bend, IN.—Most Rev. John D'Arcy, Bishop of Fort Wayne-South Bend. Most Rev. John R. Sheets, S.J., Auxiliary Bishop.

Diocese of Gary, IN.—Most Rev. Dale J. Melczek, Bishop of Gary.

Diocese of Lafayette in Indiana, IN.—Most Rev. William Higi, Bishop of Lafayette in Indiana.

PROVINCE OF KANSAS CITY, KANSAS

Includes the State of Kansas.

Archdiocese of Kansas City, KS.—Most Rev. James P. Keleher, Archbishop of Kansas City.

Diocese of Dodge City, KS.—Most Rev. Stanley Schlarman, Bishop of Dodge City.

Diocese of Salina, KS.—Most Rev. George K. Fitzsimons, Bishop of Salina.

Diocese of Wichita, KS.—Most Rev. Eugene J. Gerber, Bishop of Wichita.

PROVINCE OF LOS ANGELES

Includes Southern California and Central California.

Archdiocese of Los Angeles, CA.—His Eminence Roger Cardinal Mahony, Archbishop of Los Angeles. Most Rev. Stephen E. Blaire, Auxiliary Bishop. Most Rev. Thomas J. Curry, Auxiliary Bishop. Most Rev. Joseph M. Sartoris, Auxiliary Bishop. Most Rev. Gabino Zavala, Auxiliary Bishop.

Diocese of Fresno, CA.—Most Rev. John T. Steinbock, Bishop of Fresno.

Diocese of Monterey, CA.—Most Rev. Sylvester D. Ryan, Bishop of Monterey.

Diocese of Orange, CA.—Most Rev. Norman F. McFarland, Bishop of Orange. Most Rev. Michael P. Driscoll, Auxiliary Bishop.

Diocese of San Bernardino, CA.—Most Rev. Gerald R. Barnes, Bishop of San Bernardino.

Diocese of San Diego, CA.—Most Rev. Robert Brom, Bishop of San Diego. Most Rev. Gilbert Chavez, Auxiliary Bishop.

PROVINCE OF LOUISVILLE

Includes the States of Kentucky and Tennessee.

Archdiocese of Louisville, KY.—Most Rev. Thomas C. Kelly, O.P., Archbishop of Louisville.

Diocese of Covington, KY.—Most Rev. Robert W. Muench, Bishop of Covington.

Diocese of Knoxville, TN.—Most Rev. Anthony J. O'Connell, Bishop of Knoxville.

Diocese of Lexington, KY.—Most Rev. J. Kendrick Williams, Bishop of Lexington.

Diocese of Memphis, TN.—Most Rev. J. Terry Steib, S.V.D., Bishop of Memphis.

Diocese of Nashville, TN.—Most Rev. Edward U. Kmiec, Bishop of Nashville.

Diocese of Owensboro, KY.—Most Rev. John J. McRaith, Bishop of Owensboro.

PROVINCE OF MIAMI

Includes the State of Florida.

Archdiocese of Miami, FL.—Most Rev. John C. Favalora, Archbishop of Miami. Most Rev. Agustin A. Roman, Auxiliary Bishop.

Diocese of Orlando, FL.—Most Rev. Norbert Dorsey, C.P., Bishop of Orlando.

Diocese of Palm Beach, FL.—Most Rev. J. Keith Symons, Bishop of Palm Beach.

Diocese of Pensacola-Tallahassee, FL.—Most Rev. John Ricard, S.S.J., Bishop of Pensacola-Tallahassee.

Diocese of St. Augustine, FL.—Most Rev. John J. Snyder, Bishop of St. Augustine.

Diocese of St. Petersburg, FL.—Most Rev. Robert N. Lynch, Bishop of St. Petersburg.

Diocese of Venice, FL.—Most Rev. John J. Nevins, Bishop of Venice.

PROVINCE OF MILWAUKEE

Includes the State of Wisconsin.

Archdiocese of Milwaukee, WI.—Most Rev. Rembert G. Weakland, O.S.B., Archbishop of Milwaukee. Most Rev. Richard J. Sklba, Auxiliary Bishop.

Diocese of Green Bay, WI.—Most Rev. Robert Banks, Bishop of Green Bay. Most Rev. Robert F. Morneau, Auxiliary Bishop.

Diocese of La Crosse, WI.—Most Rev. Raymond L. Burke, Bishop of La Crosse.

Diocese of Madison, WI.—Most Rev. William H. Bullock, Bishop of Madison. Most Rev. George O. Wirz, Auxiliary Bishop.

Diocese of Superior, WI.—Most Rev. Raphael M. Fliss, Bishop of Superior.

PROVINCE OF MOBILE

Includes the states of Alabama and Mississippi.

Archdiocese of Mobile, AL.—Most Rev. Oscar H. Lipscomb, Archbishop of Mobile.

Diocese of Birmingham, AL.—Most Rev. David E. Foley, Bishop of Birmingham.

Diocese of Biloxi, MS.—Most Rev. Joseph L. Howze, Bishop of Biloxi.

Diocese of Jackson MS.—Most Rev. William R. Houck, Bishop of Jackson.

PROVINCE OF NEWARK

Includes the State of New Jersey.

Archdiocese of Newark, NJ.—Most Rev. Theodore McCarrick, Archbishop of Newark. Most Rev. Dominic A. Marconi, Auxiliary Bishop. Most Rev. David Arias, O.A.R., Auxiliary Bishop. Most Rev. Michael A. Saltarelli, Auxiliary Bishop. Most Rev. Charles J. McDonnell, Auxiliary Bishop. Most Rev. Nicholas A. DiMarzio, Auxiliary Bishop.

Diocese of Camden, NJ.—Most Rev. James T. McHugh, Bishop of Camden.

Diocese of Metuchen, NJ.—Most Rev. Edward Hughes, Bishop of Metuchen.

Diocese of Paterson, NJ.—Most Rev. Frank J. Rodimer, Bishop of Paterson.

Diocese of Trenton, NJ.—Most Rev. John C. Reiss, Bishop of Trenton. Most Rev. John M. Smith, Coadjutor Bishop of Trenton.

PROVINCE OF NEW ORLEANS

Includes the State of Louisiana.

Archdiocese of New Orleans, LA.—Most Rev. Francis B. Schulte, Archbishop of New Orleans. Most Rev. Robert W. Muench, Auxiliary Bishop. Most Rev. Dominic Carmon, Auxiliary Bishop. Most Rev. Gregory M. Aymond, Auxiliary Bishop.

Diocese of Alexandria, LA.—Most Rev. Sam Jacobs, Bishop of Alexandria.

Diocese of Baton Rouge, LA.—Most Rev. Alfred C. Hughes, Bishop of Baton Rouge.

Diocese of Houma-Thibodaux, LA.—Most Rev. Michael C. Jarrell.

Diocese of Lafayette, LA.—Most Rev. Edward J. O'Donnell, Bishop of Lafayette.

Diocese of Lake Charles, LA.—Most Rev. Jude Speyrer, Bishop of Lake Charles.

Diocese of Shreveport, LA. (1986)—Most Rev. William Friend, Bishop of Shreveport.

PROVINCE OF NEW YORK

Includes the State of New York.

Archdiocese of New York, NY.—His Eminence John Cardinal O'Connor, Archbishop of New York. Most Rev. James P. Mahoney, Auxiliary Bishop. Most Rev. Anthony F. Mestice, Auxiliary Bishop. Most Rev. Francisco Garmendia, Auxiliary Bishop. Most Rev. Austin B. Vaughan, Auxiliary Bishop. Most Rev. William J. McCormack, Auxiliary Bishop. Most Rev. Patrick J. Sheridan, Auxiliary Bishop. Most Rev. Edwin F. O'Brien.

Diocese of Albany, NY.—Most Rev. Howard J. Hubbard, Bishop of Albany.

Diocese of Brooklyn, NY.—Most Rev. Thomas Daily, Bishop of Brooklyn. Most Rev. Joseph M. Sullivan, Auxiliary Bishop. Most Rev. Rene A. Valero, Auxiliary Bishop. Most Rev. Ignatius Catanello, Auxiliary Bishop. Most Rev. Gerald M. Barbarito, Auxiliary Bishop.

Diocese of Buffalo, NY.—Most Rev. Henry J. Mansell, Bishop of Buffalo. Most Rev. Edward M. Grosz, Auxiliary Bishop.

Diocese of Ogdensburg, NY.—Most Rev. Paul S. Loverde, Bishop of Ogdensburg.

Diocese of Rochester, NY.—Most Rev. Matthew H. Clark, Bishop of Rochester.

Diocese of Rockville Centre, NY.—Most Rev. John R. McGann, Bishop of Rockville Centre. Most Rev. James J. Daly, Auxiliary Bishop. Most Rev. John C. Dunne, Auxiliary Bishop. Most Rev. Emil A. Wcela, Auxiliary Bishop.

Diocese of Syracuse, NY.—Most Rev. James M. Moynihan, Bishop of Syracuse. Most Rev. Thomas J. Costello, Auxiliary Bishop.

PROVINCE OF OKLAHOMA CITY

Includes States of Arkansas and Oklahoma.

Archdiocese of Oklahoma City, OK.—Most Rev. Eusebius J. Beltran, Archbishop of Oklahoma City.

Diocese of Little Rock, AR.—Most Rev. Andrew J. McDonald, Bishop of Little Rock.

Diocese of Tulsa, OK.—Most Rev. Edward J. Slattery, Bishop of Tulsa.

PROVINCE OF OMAHA

Includes the State of Nebraska.

Archdiocese of Omaha, NE.—Most Rev. Elden F. Curtiss, Archbishop of Omaha.

Diocese of Grand Island, NE.—Most Rev. Lawrence J. McNamara, Bishop of Grand Island.

Diocese of Lincoln, NE.—Most Rev. Fabian W. Bruskewitz, Bishop of Lincoln.

PROVINCE OF PHILADELPHIA

Includes the State of Pennsylvania.

Archdiocese of Philadelphia, PA.—His Eminence Anthony Cardinal Bevilacqua, Archbishop of Philadelphia. Most Rev. Martin N. Lohmuller, Auxiliary Bishop. Most Rev. Louis A. DeSimone, Auxiliary Bishop. Most Rev. Edward P. Cullen, Auxiliary Bishop. Most Rev. Robert P. Maginnis, Auxiliary Bishop. Most Rev. Joseph F. Martino, Auxiliary Bishop.

Diocese of Allentown, PA.—Most Rev. Thomas J. Welsh, Bishop of Allentown.

Diocese of Altoona-Johnstown, PA.—Most Rev. Joseph V. Adamec, Bishop of Altoona-Johnstown.

Diocese of Erie, PA.—Most Rev. Donald W. Trautman, Bishop of Erie.

Diocese of Greensburg, PA.—Most Rev. Anthony G. Bosco, Bishop of Greensburg.

Diocese of Harrisburg, PA.—Most Rev. Nicholas Dattilo, Bishop of Harrisburg.

Diocese of Pittsburgh, PA.—Most Rev. Donald W. Wuerl, Bishop of Pittsburgh. Most Rev. William J. Winter, Auxiliary Bishop. Most Rev. David A. Zubik, Auxiliary Bishop.

Diocese of Scranton, PA.—Most Rev. James C. Timlin, Bishop of Scranton. Most Rev. Francis DiLorenzo, Auxiliary Bishop. Most Rev. John M. Dougherty, Auxiliary Bishop.

PROVINCE OF PORTLAND IN OREGON

Includes the States of Oregon, Idaho and Montana.

Archdiocese of Portland, OR.—Most Rev. Francis E. George, O.M.I., Archbishop of Portland in Oregon. Most Rev. Kenneth D. Steiner, Auxiliary Bishop.

Diocese of Baker, OR.—Most Rev. Thomas J. Connolly, Bishop of Baker.

Diocese of Boise, ID.—Most Rev. Tod D. Brown, Bishop of Boise.

Diocese of Great Falls-Billings, MT.—Most Rev. Anthony M. Milone, Bishop of Great Falls-Billings.

Diocese of Helena, MT.—Most Rev. Alexander J. Brunett, Bishop of Helena.

PROVINCE OF ST. LOUIS

Includes the State of Missouri.

Archdiocese of St. Louis, MO.—Most Rev. Justin F. Regali, Archbishop of St. Louis. Most Rev. Edward K. Braxton, Auxiliary Bishop.

Diocese of Jefferson City, MO.—Most Rev. Michael F. McAuliffe, Bishop of Jefferson City.

Diocese of Kansas City-St. Joseph, MO.—Most Rev. Raymond J. Boland, Bishop of Kansas City-St. Joseph.

Diocese of Springfield-Cape Girardeau, MO.—Most Rev. John J. Leibrecht, Bishop of Springfield-Cape Girardeau.

PROVINCE OF ST. PAUL AND MINNEAPOLIS

Includes the States of Minnesota, South Dakota and North Dakota.

Archdiocese of St. Paul and Minneapolis, MN.—Most Rev. Harry J. Flynn, Archbishop of St. Paul and Minneapolis. Most Rev. Lawrence H. Welsh, Auxiliary Bishop.

Diocese of Bismarck, ND.—Most Rev. Paul A. Zipfel, Bishop of Bismarck.

Diocese of Crookston, MN.—Most Rev. Victor H. Balke, Bishop of Crookston.

Diocese of DULUTH, MN.—Most Rev. Roger L. Schwietz, O.M.I., Bishop of Duluth.
Diocese of FARGO, ND.—Most Rev. James Sullivan, Bishop of Fargo.
Diocese of NEW ULM, MN.—Most Rev. Raymond A. Lucker, Bishop of New Ulm.
Diocese of RAPID CITY, SD.—Vacant See.
Diocese of ST. CLOUD, MN.—Most Rev. John F. Kinney, Bishop of St. Cloud.
Diocese of SIOUX FALLS, SD.—Most Rev. Robert J. Carlson, Bishop of Sioux Falls.
Diocese of WINONA, MN.—Most Rev. John Vlazny, Bishop of Winona.

PROVINCE OF SAN ANTONIO

Includes the State of Texas.
Archdiocese of SAN ANTONIO, TX.—Most Rev. Patrick F. Flores, Archbishop of San Antonio. Most Rev. Joseph A. Galante, Auxiliary Bishop.
Diocese of AMARILLO, TX.—
Most Rev. John W. Yanta, Bishop of Amarillo.
Diocese of AUSTIN, TX.—Most Rev. John E. McCarthy, Bishop of Austin.
Diocese of BEAUMONT, TX.—Most Rev. Joseph A. Galante, Bishop of Beaumont.
Diocese of BROWNSVILLE, TX.—Most Rev. Raymundo J. Pena, Bishop of Brownsville.
Diocese of CORPUS CHRISTI, TX.—Most Rev. Rene Gracida, Bishop of Corpus Christi. Most Rev. Roberto O. Gonzalez, O.F.M., Coadjutor Bishop of Corpus Christi.
Diocese of DALLAS, TX.—Most Rev. Charles V. Grahmann, Bishop of Dallas.
Diocese of EL PASO, TX.—Most Rev. Amando Ochoa, Bishop of El Paso.
Diocese of FORT WORTH, TX.—Most Rev. Joseph P. Delaney, Bishop of Fort Worth.
Diocese of GALVESTON-HOUSTON, TX.—Most Rev. Joseph A. Fiorenza, Bishop of Galveston-Houston. Most Rev. Curtis Guillory, Auxiliary Bishop. Most Rev. James A. Tamayo, Auxiliary Bishop.
Diocese of LUBBOCK, TX.—Most Rev. Placido Rodriguez, C.M.F., Bishop of Lubbock.
Diocese of SAN ANGELO, TX.—Most Rev. Michael Pfeifer, O.M.I., Bishop of San Angelo.
Diocese of TYLER, TX.—Most Rev. Edmond Carmody, Bishop of Tyler.
Diocese of VICTORIA, TX.—Most Rev. David E. Fellhauer, Bishop of Victoria.

PROVINCE OF SAN FRANCISCO

Includes Northern California and the States of Nevada, Utah and Hawaii.
Archdiocese of SAN FRANCISCO, CA.—Most Rev. William J. Levada, Archbishop of San Francisco. Most Rev. Patrick J. McGrath, Auxiliary Bishop.
Diocese of HONOLULU, HI.—Most Rev. Francis X. DiLorenzo, Bishop of Honolulu.
Diocese of LAS VEGAS, NV.—Most Rev. Daniel F. Walsh, Bishop of Las Vegas.
Diocese of OAKLAND, CA.—Most Rev. John S. Cummins, Bishop of Oakland.
Diocese of RENO, NV.—Most Rev. Phillip F. Straling, Bishop of Reno.
Diocese of SACRAMENTO, CA.—Most Rev. William K. Weigand, Bishop of Sacramento.
Diocese of SALT LAKE CITY, UT.—Most Rev. George H. Niederauer, Bishop of Salt Lake City.
Diocese of SAN JOSE, CA.—Most Rev. Pierre DuMaine, Bishop of San Jose.
Diocese of SANTA ROSA, CA.—Most Rev. G. Patrick Zieman, Bishop of Santa Rosa.
Diocese of STOCKTON, CA.—Most Rev. Donald Montrose, Bishop of Stockton.

PROVINCE OF SANTA FE

Includes the States of New Mexico, and Arizona.
Archdiocese of SANTA FE, NM.—Most Rev. Michael Sheehan, Archbishop of Santa Fe.
Diocese of GALLUP, NM.—Most Rev. Donald E. Pelotte, S.S.S., Bishop of Gallup.
Diocese of LAS CRUCES, NM.—Most Rev. Ricardo Ramirez, C.S.B., Bishop of Las Cruces.
Diocese of PHOENIX, AZ.—Most Rev. Thomas J. O'Brien, Bishop of Phoenix.
Diocese of TUCSON, AZ.—Most Rev. Manuel D. Moreno, Bishop of Tucson.

PROVINCE OF SEATTLE

Includes the State of Washington.
Archdiocese of SEATTLE, WA.—Most Rev. Thomas J. Murphy, Archbishop of Seattle.
Diocese of SPOKANE, WA.—Most Rev. William S. Skylstad, Bishop of Spokane.
Diocese of YAKIMA, WA.—Most Rev. Carlos Sevilla, S.J., Bishop of Yakima.

PROVINCE OF WASHINGTON

Includes the District of Columbia, and Montgomery, Prince Georges, Charles, Calvert and St. Mary's Counties in Maryland, also Virgin Islands.
Archdiocese of WASHINGTON, DC.—His Eminence James Cardinal Hickey, Archbishop of Washington. Most Rev. Alvaro Corrada, Auxiliary Bishop. Most Rev. Leonard Olivier, S.V.D., Auxiliary Bishop. Most Rev. William E. Lori, Auxiliary Bishop.
Diocese of ST. THOMAS, V.I.—Most Rev. Elliot G. Thomas, Bishop of St. Thomas, Virgin Islands.
MILITARY ARCHDIOCESE—Most Rev. Joseph T. Dimino, Archbishop for the Military Services. Most Rev. Francis X. Roque, Auxiliary Bishop. Most Rev. John G. Nolan, Auxiliary Bishop. Most Rev. Joseph J. Madera, M.Sp.S., Auxiliary Bishop. Most Rev. John J. Glynn, Auxiliary Bishop.

EASTERN CATHOLIC JURISDICTIONS

ANTIOCHENE TRADITION

MARONITE RITE—
Diocese of SAINT MARON OF BROOKLYN—Most Rev. Hector Doueihi, Bishop St. Maron.
Diocese of OUR LADY OF LEBANON—Most Rev. John Chedid, Bishop of Our Lady of Lebanon.

ARMENIAN TRADITION

ARMENIAN CATHOLIC EXARCHATE OF U.S.A. AND CANADA—Most Rev. Hovhannes Tertzakian, O.M.Ven., Apostolic Exarch for the Armenians.

CHALDEAN TRADITION

Eparchy of ST. THOMAS THE APOSTLE—Most Rev. Ibrahim Ibrahim, Eparch of St. Thomas the Apostle.

CONSTANTINOPOLITAN TRADITION

MELKITE - GREEK RITE—
Diocese of NEWTON—Most Rev. John A. Elya, B.S., Bishop of Newton. Most Rev. Nicholas J. Samra, Auxiliary Bishop.
ROMANIAN RITE—
Diocese of ST. GEORGE'S IN CANTON—Most Rev. John M. Botean, Eparch of St. George's in Canton.
RUTHENIAN RITE—
Metropolitan Archdiocese of PITTSBURGH—Most Rev. Judson M. Procyk, Archbishop of Pittsburgh Byzantine Rite.
Diocese of PARMA—Most Rev. Basil Schott,*o.f.m.*, Bishop of Parma
Diocese of PASSAIC—Most Rev. Andrew Pataki, Bishop of Passaic.
Diocese of VAN NUYS—Most Rev. George M. Kuzma, Bishop of Van Nuys.
RUSSIAN RITE—
Two parishes
UKRAINIAN RITE—
Metropolitan Archdiocese of PHILADELPHIA—Most Rev. Stephan Sulyk, Archbishop of Philadelphia. Most Rev. Walter Paska, Auxiliary Bishop.
Diocese of ST. JOSAPHAT IN PARMA—Most Rev. Robert Moskal, Bishop of St. Josaphat in Parma.
Diocese of ST. NICHOLAS—Most Rev. Michael Wiwchar, C.S.S.R., Bishop of St. Nicholas in Chicago.
Diocese of STAMFORD—Most Rev. Basil Losten, Bishop of Stamford.
SYRIAN RITE—
Diocese of OUR LADY OF DELIVERANCE OF NEWARK—Most Rev. Joseph Younan, Bishop of Our Lady of Deliverance.

AN ALPHABETICAL LIST OF THE

Cardinals, Archbishops, Bishops, Archabbots & Abbots of the United States

CARDINALS

His Eminence Luis Cardinal Aponte Martinez, Archbishop of San Juan, P.O. Box S-1967, San Juan, PR 00903
His Eminence William Cardinal Baum, Prefect of Sacred Congregation for Catholic Education, Piazza Pio XII Vatican City State
His Eminence Anthony Cardinal Bevilacqua, Archbishop of Philadelphia, 222 N. 17th St., Philadelphia, PA 19103.
His Eminence John Cardinal Carberry, Retired Archbishop of Archdiocese of St. Louis, 4445 Lindell Blvd., St. Louis, MO 63108
His Eminence James Cardinal Hickey, Archbishop of Washington DC, P.O. Box 29260, Washington, DC 20017
His Eminence William Cardinal Keeler, Archbishop of Baltimore, 320 Cathedral St., Baltimore, MD 21201
His Eminence Bernard Cardinal Law, Archbishop of Boston, 2101 Commonwealth Ave., Boston, MA 02135
His Eminence Adam Cardinal Maida, Archbishop of Detroit, 1234 Washington Blvd., Detroit, MI 48226
His Eminence Roger Cardinal Mahony, Archbishop of Los Angeles, 3424 Wilshire Blvd., Los Angeles, CA 90010-2241
His Eminence John Cardinal O'Connor, Archbishop of New York, 452 Madison Ave., New York, NY 10022
His Eminence Edmund Cardinal Szoka, Pres. Prefecture for Economic Affairs of the Holy See, Vatican City State

ARCHBISHOPS

His Excellency,
The Most Reverend

Apuron, Anthony Sablan, *o.f.m.cap.*, Archbishop of Agana, Cuesta San Ramon Agana, Guam 96910.
Beltran, Eusebius J., Archbishop of Oklahoma City, P.O. Box 32180, Oklahoma City, OK 73123.
Borders, William D., Retired Archbishop of Baltimore, 320 Cathedral St., Baltimore, MD 21201.
Buechlein, Daniel, *o.s.b.*, Archbishop of Indianapolis, 1400 N. Meridian St., P.O. Box 1410, Indianapolis, IN 46206.
Chaput, Charles J., *o.f.m.cap.*, Archbishop of Denver.
Cronin, Daniel A., Archbishop of Hartford, 134 Farmington Ave., Hartford, CT 06105.
Curtiss, Elden F., Archbishop of Omaha, 100 N. 62nd St., Omaha, NE 68132-2795.
Dimino, Joseph T., Archbishop of Military Services, P.O. Box 4469, Washington, DC 20017-04692.
Donoghue, John F., Archbishop of Atlanta, 680 W. Peachtree St., N.W., Atlanta, GA 30308.
Favalora, John C., Archbishop of Miami, 9401 Biscayne Blvd., Miami Shore, FL 33138.
Flores, Patrick F., Archbishop of San Antonio, 2600 W. Woodlawn Ave., San Antonio, TX 78228.
Flynn, Harry J., Archbishop of St. Paul and Minneapolis, 226 Summit Ave., St. Paul, MN 55102.
Foley, John P., Archbishop, President of the Pontifical Council for Social Communications, 00120 Vatican City State Europe.
George, Francis E., *o.m.i.*, Archbishop of Portland in Oregon, 2838 E. Burnside St., Portland, OR 97214-1895.
Gerety, Peter Leo, Retired Archbishop of Newark, 31 Mulberry St., Newark, NJ 07102.
Hannan, Philip M., Retired Archbishop of New Orleans, 2929 S. Carrollton Ave., New Orleans, LA 70118-4301.
Hanus, Jerome, *o.s.b.*, Archbishop of Dubuque, 1229 Mt. Loretto Ave., P.O. Box 479, Dubuque, IA 52004-0479.
Hunthausen, Raymond G., Retired Archbishop of Seattle, 910 Marion St., Seattle, WA 98104.
Hurley, Francis T., Archbishop of Anchorage, P.O. Box 2239, Anchorage, AK 99510.
Keleher, James P., Archbishop of Kansas City, Kansas, 12615 Parallel Parkway, Kansas City, KS 66109.
Kelly, Thomas, *o.p.*, Archbishop of Louisville, 212 E. College St., Louisville, KY 40201.
Kucera, Daniel W., *o.s.b.*, Retired Archbishop of Dubuque, 13952 E. Marina Dr. -#612, Aurora, CO 80014.
Levada, William J., Archbishop of San Francisco, 445 Church St., San Francisco, CA 94114.
Lipscomb, Oscar H., Archbishop of Mobile, 400 Government St., Mobile, AL 36633.
Marcinkus, Paul C., Working Outside Chicago Archdiocese, Vatican City State, Europe.
Marino, Eugene A., *s.s.j.*, Former Archbishop of Atlanta, Salesian Province House, 148 Main St., New Rochelle, NY 10802.
McCarrick, Theodore E. Archbishop of Newark, 171 Clifton Ave., P.O. Box 9500, Newark, NJ 07104-9500.
McCarthy, Edward A., Retired Archbishop of Miami, 2900 S.W. 87th Ave., Miami, FL 33138.

His Excellency,
The Most Reverend

McDonough, Thomas J., Retired Archbishop of Louisville, St. Francis Country Home, 1412 Lansdowne Ave., Darby, PA 19023.
Murphy, Thomas J., Archbishop of Seattle, 910 Marion, Seattle, WA 98104.
Pilarczyk, Daniel E., Archbishop of Cincinnati, 100 E. 8th St., Cincinnati, OH 45202.
Power, Cornelius M., Retired Archbishop of Portland in Oregon, 2838 E. Burnside St., Portland, OR 97214.
Procyk, Judson M., Archbishop of Pittsburgh Byzantine, 66 Riverview Ave., Pittsburgh, PA 15214.
Quinn, John R., Retired Archbishop of San Francisco, 322 Middlefield Rd., Menlo Park, CA 94025.
Rigali, Justin F., Archbishop of St. Louis, 4445 Lindell Blvd., St. Louis, MO 63108.
Roach, John R., Retired Archbishop of St. Paul-Minneapolis, 226 Summit Ave., St. Paul, MN 55102.
Ryan, Joseph T., Retired Archbishop of the Military Services, Our Lady of Hope Residence, 1 Jeannine Jugan Ln., Latham, NY 12110.
Salatka, Charles A., Retired Archbishop of Oklahoma City, Box 23205, Oklahoma City, OK 73123.
Sanchez, Robert F., Former Archbishop of Santa Fe, Catholic Center, St. Joseph's Pl., N.W., Albuquerque, NM 87120.
Schleck, Charles A., *c.s.c.*, Titular Archbishop of Africa, Congregation for Evangelization, Palazzo di Propaganda Fide, Piazza di Spagna 48, 00187 Rome, Italy.
Schulte, Francis B., Archbishop of New Orleans, 7887 Walmsley Ave., New Orleans, LA 70125-3496.
Sheehan, Daniel E., Retired Archbishop of Omaha, 10412 Pacific St., Omaha, NE 68114.
Sheehan, Michael J., Archbishop of Santa Fe, Catholic Center, 4000 Saint Joseph's Place, N.W., Albuquerque, NM 87120.
Stafford, J. Francis, President - Pontifical Council for the Laity, Piazza San Calisto 16, Vatican City State, Europe 00120.
Strecker, Ignatius J., Retired Archbishop of Kansas City in Kansas, 12615 Parallel Pkwy., Kansas City, KS 66109.
Sulyk, Stephen, Archbishop of Philadelphia Ukrainian, 827 N. Franklin St., Philadelphia, PA 19123.
Weakland, Rembert G., *o.s.b.* Archbishop of Milwaukee, 3501 S. Lake Dr., St. Francis, WI 53235-3703.

BISHOPS

His Excellency,
The Most Reverend

Abramowicz, Alfred L., Retired Auxiliary Bishop of Chicago, 6101 S. 75th Ave., Summit-Argo, IL 60501.
Adamec, Joseph V., Bishop of Altoona-Johnstown, 126 Logan Blvd., Hollidaysburg, PA 16648.
Ahern, Patrick V., Retired Auxiliary Bishop of New York, St. Thomas More, 65 E. 89th St., New York, NY 10128.
Allue, Emilio, *s.d.b.*, Auxiliary Bishop of Boston, 558 South Ave., Weston, MA 02193-2699.
Anderson, Moses B., *s.s.e.*, Auxiliary Bishop of Detroit, 14155 Abingdon Rd., Detroit, MI 48227.

His Excellency,
The Most Reverend

Angell, Kenneth A., Bishop of Burlington, 351 North Avenue, Burlington, VT 05401-2999.
Arias, David, *o.a.r.*, Auxiliary Bishop of Newark, St. Joseph of the Palisade Rectory, 6401 Palisade Ave., West New York, NJ 07093.
Arzube, Juan, Retired Auxiliary Bishop of Los Angeles, Sacred Heart Church, 2889 N. Lincoln Ave., Altadena, CA 91001.
Aymond, Gregory M., Auxiliary Bishop of New Orleans, 2901 S. Carrollton Ave., New Orleans, LA 70118.
Balke, Victor, Bishop of Crookston, 1200 Memorial Dr., Crookston, MN 56716.
Baltakis, Paul A., *o.f.m.*, Titular Bishop of Egara & Lithuanian Catholics, 361 Highland Blvd., Brooklyn, NY 11207.
Banks, Robert J., Bishop of Green Bay, 1910 S. Webster Ave., Green Bay, WI 54301.
Barbarito, Gerald, Auxiliary Bishop of Brooklyn, 1956 Batchelder St., Brooklyn, NY 11229.
Barnes, Gerald R., Bishop of San Bernardino, 1201 E. Highland Ave., San Bernardino, CA 92405.
Begley, Michael J., Retired Bishop of Charlotte, 3104 Stone Orchard Pl., Charlotte, NC 28209.
Blaire, Stephen E., Auxiliary Bishop of Los Angeles, 2636 S. Mansfield Ave., Los Angeles, CA 90016-3512.
Boland, J. Kevin, Bishop of Savannah, 601 E. Liberty St., Savannah, GA 31401.
Boland, Raymond J., Bishop of Kansas City-St. Joseph, P.O. Box 419037, Kansas City, MO 64141-6037.
Boles, John P., Auxiliary Bishop of Boston, 307 Bowdoin St., Dorchester, MA 02122.
Bosco, Anthony G., Bishop of Greensburg, 723 E. Pittsburgh St., Greensburg, PA 15601.
Botean, John M., Bishop of Romanian-rite St. George's in Canton, 1121 44th St., N.E., Canton, OH 44714
Boudreaux, Warren L., Retired Bishop of Houma-Thibodaux, 233 Rienzi Dr., Thimodaux, LA 70301.
Braxton, Edward K., Auxiliary Bishop of St. Louis, 4445 Lindell Blvd., St. Louis, MO 63108-2497.
Breitenbeck, Joseph M., Retired Bishop of Grand Rapids, 660 Burton St., S.E. Grand Rapids, MI 49507.
Britt, Kevin M., Auxiliary Bishop of Detroit, 1234 Washington Blvd., Detroit, MI 48226.
Broderick, Edwin B., Former Bishop of Albany, 900 Park Ave., New York, NY 10021.
Brom, Robert H., Bishop of San Diego, P.O. Box 85728, San Diego, CA 92186-5728.
Brown, Tod D., Bishop of Boise, 303 Federal Way, Boise, ID 83705-5925.
Brunett, Alexander J., Bishop of Helena, P.O. Box 1729, 515 North Ewing, Helena, MT 59624.
Bruskewitz, Fabian W., Bishop of Lincoln, 5301 A Street, Lincoln, NE 68510.
Brzana, Stanislaus J., Retired Bishop of Ogdensburg, P.O. Box 369, Ogdensburg, NY 13669.
Bullock, William H., Bishop of Madison, 15 E. Wilson St., Madison, WI 53701.
Burke, Raymond L., Bishop of La Crosse, 3710 East Avenue, S., Box 4004, La Crosse, WI 54602-4004.
Buswell, Charles A., Retired Bishop of Pueblo, 13 Tartan Ln., Pueblo, CO 81003.
Camacho, Tomas A., Bishop of Chalan Kanoa, Our Lady of Mt. Carmel, P.O. Box 745, Saipan, CM 96950.

His Excellency,
The Most Reverend

Carlson, Robert J., Bishop of Sioux Falls, 3100 West 41 St., Sioux Falls, SD 57117.
Carmody, Edmond, Bishop of Tyler, 1015 East Southeast Loop 323, Tyler TX 75701-9663.
Carmon, Dominic, *s.v.d.,* Auxiliary Bishop of New Orleans, 5500 Paris Ave., New Orleans, LA 70122-2699.
Casiano-Vargas, Ulises, Bishop of Mayaguez, P.O. Box 2272, Mayaguez, PR 00708.
Catanello, Ignatius, Auxiliary Bishop of Brooklyn
Charron, Joseph J., *c.pp.s.,* Bishop of of Des Moines, P.O. Box 1816, 601 Grand Ave., Des Moines, IA 50306-5071.
Chavez, Gilbert E., Auxiliary Bishop of San Diego, 2020 Alaquinas Dr., San Ysidro, CA 92073.
Chedid, John, Bishop of Our Lady of Lebanon of Los Angeles, 333 S. San Vicente Blvd., Los Angeles, CA 90048.
Clark, Matthew H., Bishop of Rochester, 1150 Buffalo Rd., Rochester, NY 14624.
Clinch, Harry A., Retired Bishop of Monterey, 3400 Paul Sweet Rd., #C-119, Santa Cruz, CA 95065.
Connolly, Thomas J., Bishop of Baker, P.O. Box 5999, Bend, OR 97708.
Conway, Edwin M., Auxiliary Bishop of Chicago, 126 N. Des Plaines St., Chicago, IL 60661-2357.
Christian, Francis J., Auxiliary Bishop of Manchester, St. Joseph Cathedral, 145 Lowell St., Manchester, NH 03105.
Cooney, Patrick R., Bishop of Gaylord, 1665 M-32 West, Seton Building, Gaylord, MI 49735.
Corrada, Alvaro, *s.j.,* Auxiliary Bishop of Washington, 826 Wayne Ave., Silver Spring, MD 20910.
Costello, Thomas J., Auxiliary Bishop of Syracuse, P.O. Box 511, Syracuse, NY 13201.
Cote, Michael R., Auxiliary Bishop of Portland in Maine, 510 Ocean Ave., P.O. Box 11559, Portland, OR 04104-7559.
Crowley, Joseph R., Retired Auxiliary Bishop of Fort Wayne-South Bend, 1701 Miami St., South Bend, IN 46613.
Cullen, Edward P., Auxiliary Bishop of Philadelphia, 222 N. 17th St., Philadelphia, PA 19103.
Cummins, John S., Bishop of Oakland, 634 21st St., Oakland, CA 94612.
Curlin, William G., Bishop of Charlotte, P.O. Box 36776, Charlotte, NC 28236.
Curry, Thomas J., Auxiliary Bishop of Los Angeles, Santa Barbara Pastoral Region, 3240 Calle Pinon, Santa Barbara, CA 93105.
Curtis, Walter W., Retired Bishop of Bridgeport, 128 Strawberry Hill Ave., Stamford, CT 06904.
Daily, Thomas V., Bishop of Brooklyn, P.O. Box C, Brooklyn, NY 11202.
Daly, James J., Former Auxiliary Bishop of Rockville Centre, 25 Lanes End, Blue Point, NY 11715.
D'Antonio, Nicholas, *o.f.m.,* Retired Vicar for Latin American Apostolate, Archdiocese of New Orleans, 1221 Mandeville St., New Orleans, LA 70117-8498.
D'Arcy, John M., Bishop of Fort Wayne-South Bend, P.O. Box 390, Fort Wayne, IN 46801.
Dattilo, Nicholas, Bishop of Harrisburg, 4800 Union Deposit Rd., P.O. Box 2153, Harrisburg, PA 17105.
Delaney, Joseph P., Bishop of Fort Worth, 800 West Loop 820 South, Fort Worth, TX 76108.
DeSimone, Louis A., Auxiliary Bishop of Philadelphia, 2422 S. 17th St., Philadelphia, PA 19145.
DiMarzio, Nicholas A., Auxiliary Bishop of Newark, 1160 Raymond Blvd., Newark, NJ 07102-4105.
DiLorenzo, Francis X., Bishop of Honolulu, 1184 Bishop St., Honolulu, HI 96813.
Donnelly, Robert, Auxiliary Bishop of Toledo, 2544 Parkwood Ave., Toledo, OH 43610.
Donovan, Paul V., Retired Bishop of Kalamazoo, 238 Falkirk, Kalamazoo, MI 49006.
Doran, Thomas G., Bishop of Rockford, 1245 North Court St., Rockford, IL 61103.
Dorsey, Norbert L., *c.p.,* Bishop of Orlando, 421 E. Robinson, P.O. Box 1800, Orlando, FL 32802-1800.
Doueihi, Hector, Bishop of the Maronite Eparchy of St. Maron of Brooklyn, Our Lady of Lebanon Cathedral, 113 Remsen St., Brooklyn, NY 11201.
Dougherty, John M., Auxiliary Bishop of Scranton, 300 Wyoming Ave., Scranton, PA 18503.
Driscoll, Michael P., Auxiliary Bishop of Orange, 2811 E. Villa Real Dr., Orange, CA 92867.
Dudick, Michael J., Retired Bishop of Passaic, 32 Lakeview Trail, Sugarloaf, PA 18249-1043.
Dudley, Paul V., Retired Bishop of Sioux Falls, Church of St. Dominic, 116 North Linden, Northfield, MN 55057-1435.
DuMaine, R. Pierre, Bishop of San Jose, 900 Lafayette St., Suite 301, Santa Clara, CA 95050-4966.
Dunne, John C., Auxiliary Bishop of Rockville Centre, P.O. Box 39, Farmingdale, NY 11735-0039.
Dupre, Thomas L., Bishop of Springfield, P.O. Box 1730, Springfield, MA 01105.

His Excellency,
The Most Reverend

Egan, Edward M., Bishop of Bridgeport, Office, 238 Jewett Ave., Bridgeport, CT 06606-2892.
Elya, John A. *b.s.o.,* Eparch of Newton, 19 Dartmouth St., West Newton, MA 02165.
Federal, Joseph Lennox, Retired Bishop of Salt Lake City, 27 C St., Salt Lake City, UT 84111.
Fellhauer, David E., Bishop of Victoria, P.O. Box 4070, Victoria, TX 77903.
Ferrario, Joseph A., Retired Bishop of Honolulu, 45 N. Kalaheo Ave., Kailua, HI 96734.
Fiorenza, Joseph A., Bishop of Galveston-Houston, 1700 San Jacinto, Houston, TX 77002.
Fitzpatrick, John J., Retired Bishop of Brownsville, P.O. Box 2279, Brownsville, TX 78522-2279.
Fitzsimons, George K., Bishop of Salina, P.O. Box 980, Salina, KS 67402-0980.
Flanagan, Bernard J., Retired Bishop of Worcester, Vianney House, 222 June St., Worcester, MA 01602.
Fliss, Raphael M., Bishop of Superior, Gitchinadji Dr., P.O. Box 969, Superior, WI 54880.
Foley, David E., Bishop of Birmingham, P.O. Box 12047, Birmingham, AL 35202-2047.
Forst, Marion F., Retired Bishop of Dodge City, St. Joseph Care Center, 759 Vermont Ave., Kansas City, KS 66101-3470.
Francis, Joseph A., *s.v.d.,* Retired Auxiliary Bishop of Newark, Claridge House II, 2 Claridge Dr.-Apt. 1FW, Verona, NJ 07044.
Franklin, William E., Bishop of Davenport, 2761 Scott St., Davenport, IA 52803.
Franzetta, Benedict C., Retired Auxiliary Bishop of Youngstown, 144 W. Wood St., Youngstown, OH 44503.
Freking, Frederick W., Retired Bishop of La Crosse, 3524 East Ave., Apt. 7-B, La Crosse, WI 54601.
Frey, Gerard L., Retired Bishop of Lafayette, P.O. Drawer 3387, Lafayette, LA 70502.
Friend, William B., Bishop of Shreveport, 2104 Chase Crossing, Shreveport, LA 71118.
Galante, Joseph A., Bishop of Beaumont, 6550 Lexinton - Apt. 259, Beaumont, TX 77706.
Garland, James H., Bishop of Marquette, 300 Rock St., P.O. Box 550, Marquette, MI 49855.
Garmendia, Francis, Auxiliary Bishop of New York, St. Thomas Aquinas, 1900 Crotona Parkway, Bronx, NY 10460.
Garner, Robert F., Retired Auxiliary Bishop of Newark, 311 Prospect St., Midland Park, NJ 07432.
Gaughan, Norbert F., Retired Bishop of Gary, 180 West Joliet Rd., Valparaiso, IN 46383.
Gelineau, Louis E., Bishop of Providence, One Cathedral Square, Providence, RI 02903.
Gendron, Odore J., Retired Bishop of Manchester, St. Joseph Cathedral Rectory, 145 Lowell St., Manchester, NH 03104-6135.
Gerber, Eugene J., Bishop of Wichita, 307 E. Central Ave., Wichita, KS 67202.
Gerry, Joseph J., *o.s.b.,* Bishop of Portland (in Maine), 510 Ocean Ave., Portland, ME 04101.
Gettelfinger, Gerald A., Bishop of Evansville, 3980 Woodcastle, Evansville, IN 47711.
Glynn, John J., Auxiliary Bishop of the Military Services, P.O. Box 4469, Washington, DC 20017-0469.
Goedert, Raymond E., Archdiocesan Admin. & Auxiliary Bishop of Chicago, P.O. Box 1979, Chicago, IL 60690.
González, Roberto O., *o.f.m.,*Coadjutor Bishop of Corpus Christi, 4109 Ocean Dr., Corpus Christi, TX 78411.
Gorman, John R., Auxiliary Bishop of Chicago, 2330 W. 118th St., Chicago, IL 60643.
Gossman, F. Joseph, Bishop of Raleigh, 1601 Westbridge Ct., Raleigh, NC 27606.
Gottwald, George J., Retired Auxiliary Bishop of St. Louis, c-o General Delivery, Valles Mines, MO 63087.
Gracida, Rene H., Bishop of Corpus Christi, 620 Lipan St., Corpus Christi, TX 78403-2620.
Grady, Thomas J., Retired Bishop of Orlando, P.O. Box 1800, Orlando, FL 32802-1800.
Graham, John J., Retired Auxiliary Bishop of Philadelphia, 9172 New Falls Rd., Fallsington, PA 19054-1899.
Grahmann, Charles V., Bishop of Dallas, 3725 Blackburn, P.O. Box 190507, Dallas, TX 75219.
Gregory, Wilton D., Bishop of Belleville, 222 South Third St., Belleville, IL 62220.
Griffin, James A., Bishop of Columbus, 198 E. Broad St., Columbus, OH 43215.
Grosz, Edward M., Auxiliary Bishop of Buffalo, St. Stanislaus Kostka Parish, 2437 Niagara St., Niagara Falls, NY 14303-1925.
Guillory, Curtis J., Auxiliary Bishop of Galveston-Houston, 1700 San Jacinto St., Houston, TX 77001.

His Excellency,
The Most Reverend

Gumbleton, Thomas J., Auxiliary Bishop of Detroit, 4860 15th St., Detroit, MI 48208.
Ham, J. Richard, *m.m.,* Retired Auxiliary Bishop of St. Paul-Minneapolis, St. Teresa's Residence, Maryknoll Headquarters, Ossining, NY 10545.
Hanifen, Richard C., Bishop of Colorado Springs, 29 West Kiowa St., Colorado Springs, CO 80903-1498.
Harrington, Bernard J., Auxiliary Bishop of Detroit, 1315 N. Woodward Ave., Bloomfield Hills, MI 48304.
Harrington, Timothy J., Retired Bishop of Worcester, 30 Julio Dr., #105, Shrewsbury, MA 01545.
Harrison, Frank J., Retired Bishop of Syracuse, 6655 Kirkville Rd., East Syracuse, NY 13057.
Hart, Daniel A., Bishop of Norwich, 201 Broadway, P.O. Box 587, Norwich, CT 06360.
Hart, Joseph H., Bishop of Cheyenne, Box 468, Cheyenne, WY 82001.
Head, Edward D., Retired Bishop of Buffalo, 77 Oakland Place, Buffalo, NY 14222.
Herrmann, Edward J., Retired Bishop of Columbus, St. Raphael Home, 1550 Roxbury Rd., Columbus, OH 43212.
Hickey, Dennis W., Retired Auxiliary Bishop of Rochester, 415 Ames St., Rochester, NY 14611.
Higi, William L., Bishop of Lafayette in Indiana, 610 Lingle Ave., Lafayette, IN 47902.
Hoffman, James R., Bishop of Toledo, 2544 Parkwood Ave., OH 43610.
Hogan, James J., Retired Bishop of Altoona-Johnstown, 126 Logan Blvd., Hollidaysburg, PA 16648.
Hogan, Joseph L., Retired Bishop of Rochester, 4199 East Avenue, Rochester, NY 14618.
Houck, William R., Bishop of Jackson, Mailing Address: P.O. Box 2248, Jackson, MS 39225.
Howze, Joseph L., Bishop of Biloxi, P.O. Box 1189, Biloxi, MS 39533.
Hubbard, Howard J., Bishop of Albany, 125 Eagle St., Albany, NY 12203.
Hughes, Alfred C., Bishop of Baton Rouge, 1800 South Acadian Thruway, P.O. Box 2028, Baton Rouge LA 70821-2028.
Hughes, Edward T., Bishop of Metuchen, 10 Library Pl., Metuchen, NJ 08840.
Hughes, William A., Retired Bishop of Covington, Catheral Basilica of the Assumption, 1140 Madison Ave., Covington, KY 41011-3116.
Hurley, Mark J., Former Bishop of Santa Rosa, 273 Ulloa St., San Francisco, CA 94127.
Ibrahim, Ibrahim, Bishop-Eparch to St. Thomas the Apostle, 25585 Berg Rd., Southfield, MI 48034.
Imesch, Joseph L., Bishop of Joliet, 425 Summit St., Joliet, IL 60435.
Irwin, Francis X., Auxiliary Bishop of Boston, 2 Gardner St., Peabody, MA 01960-1896.
Jacobs, Sam, Bishop of Alexandria, P.O. Box 7417, Alexandria, LA 71306.
Jakubowski, Thad J., Auxiliary Bishop of Chicago, 6002 W. Berteau Ave., Chicago, IL 60634-7720.
Jarrell, Charles Michael, Bishop of Houma Thibodaux
Kaffer, Roger L., Auxiliary Bishop of Joliet, 425 Summit St., Joliet, IL 60435.
Kaniecki, Michael J., *s.j.,* Bishop of Fairbanks, 1316 Peger Rd., Fairbanks, AK 99709.
Keating, John R., Bishop of Arlington, 4600 N. Carlin Springs Rd., Arlington, VA 22203.
Kicanas, Gerald F., Auxiliary Bishop of Chicago, 200 N. Milwaukee, Suite 200, Libertyville, IL 60048-2250.
Kinney, John F., Bishop of St. Cloud, 214 Third Ave., South, Box 1248, St. Cloud, MN 56302-1248.
Kmiec, Edward U., Bishop of Nashville, 2400 Twenty-First Ave., South, Nashville, TN 37212.
Koester, Charles R., Retired Auxiliary Bishop of St. Louis.
Krawczak, Arthur H., Retired Auxiliary Bishop of Detroit, Marywood Nursing Center, 36975 Five Mile Rd., Livonia, MI 48154.
Kuzma, George M., Bishop of Van Nuys, Byzantine Catholic Eparchy of Van Nuys, 8131 North 16th St., Phoenix, AZ 85020.
Larkin, W. Thomas, Retired Bishop of St. Petersburg, P.O. Box 40200, St. Petersburg, FL 33743.
Leibrecht, John J., Bishop of Springfield-Cape Girardeau, The Catholic Center, 601 S. Jefferson, Springfield, MO 65806-3143.
Lessard, Raymond W., Retired Bishop of Savannah, St. Vincent de Paul Seminary, 10701 S. Military Trail, Boynton Beach, FL 33436-4899.
Lohmuller, Martin N., Retired Auxiliary Bishop of Philadelphia, Villa Maria House of Studies, King Rd., Immaculate, PA 19345.
Lori, William E., Auxiliary Bishop of Washington, 5001 Eastern Ave., (P.O. Box 29260) Washington, DC 20017.
Losten, Basil, Bishop of Stamford, 14 Peveril Rd., Stamford, CT 06902-3019

His Excellency,
The Most Reverend

Lotocky, Innocent, *o.s.b.m.*, Retired Bishop of St. Nicholas in Chicago, 2245 W. Rice St., Chicago, IL 60622.
Loverde, Paul S., Bishop of Ogdensburg, P.O. Box 369, 622 Washington St., Ogdensburg, NY 13669.
Lucker, Raymond A., Bishop of New Ulm, 1400 Sixth North St., New Ulm, MN 56073-2099.
Lynch, George E., Retired Auxiliary Bishop of Raleigh, P.O. Box 130, Bronx, NY 10470-0130.
Lynch, Robert N., Bishop of St. Petersburg, P.O. Box 40200, St. Petersburg, FL 33743.
Lyne, Timothy J., Retired Auxiliary Bishop of Chicago, 730 N. Wabash, Chicago, IL 60611.
Madera, Joseph J., *m.sp.s.*, Auxiliary Bishop of Military Services, P.O. Box 4469, Washington, DC 20017-0469.
Maguire, Joseph F., Retired Bishop of Springfield, 68 Elliot St., Springfield, MA 01101.
Maginnis, Robert P., Auxiliary Bishop of Philadelphia, St. Colman Rectory, 11 Simpson Rd., Ardmore, PA 19003-2812.
Mahoney, James P., Retired Auxiliary Bishop of New York, St. Peter's Rectory, 424 Violet Ave., Poughkeepsie, NY 12601.
Malone, James W., Retired Bishop of Youngstown, 144 W. Wood St., Youngstown, OH 44503.
Maloney, Charles G., Retired Auxiliary Bishop of Louisville, P.O. Box 1073, Louisville, KY 40201.
Mansell, Henry J., Bishop of Buffalo, 795 Main St., Buffalo, NY 14203.
Manz, John R., Auxiliary Bishop of Chicago, 1820 S. Leavitt St., Chicago, IL 60608.
Marconi, Dominic A., Auxiliary Bishop of Newark, P.O. Box 1246, Linden, NJ 07036.
Markiewicz, Alfred John, Bishop of Kalamazoo, 215 N. Westnedge Ave., Kalamazoo, MI 49007-3760.
Martino, Joseph F., Auxiliary Bishop of Phildelphia, St. Charles Borromeo Seminary, Overbrook, 100 E. Wynnewood Rd., Wynnewood, PA 19096.
Matthiesen, Leroy T., Retired Bishop of Amarillo, P.O. Box 5644, Amarillo, TX 79117.
McAuliffe, Michael F., Bishop of Jefferson City, Bishop's House, P.O. Box 417, Jefferson City, MO 65102.
McCarthy, John E., Bishop of Austin, P.O. Box 13327, Austin, TX 78711.
McCormack, John B., Auxiliary Bishop of Boston, 236 Pleasant St., Weymouth, MA 02190.
McCormack, William J., Auxiliary Bishop of New York, 142 E. 29th St., New York, NY 10016.
McDonald, Andrew J., Bishop of Little Rock, P.O. Box 7239, Little Rock, AR 72217.
McDonnell, Charles J., Auxiliary Bishop of Newark, 31 Mulberry St., Newark, NJ 07102.
McDowell, John B., Retired Auxiliary Bishop of Pittsburgh, 1817 Red Coach Rd., Allison Park, PA 15101.
McFarland, Norman F., Bishop of Orange, Marywood Center, 2811 E. Villa Real Dr., Orange, CA 92867.
McGann, John R., Bishop of Rockville Centre, 29 Quealy Place, Rockville Centre, NY 11570.
McGrath, Patrick J., Auxiliary Bishop of San Francisco, 445 Church St., San Francisco, CA 94114.
McHugh, James T., Bishop of Camden, Marywood, 1600 Peter Cheeseman Rd., P.O. Box 577, Blackwood, NJ 08012.
McKinney, Joseph C., Auxiliary Bishop of Grand Rapids, 654 Davis, N.W., Grand Rapids, MI 49504.
McLaughlin, Bernard J., Retired Auxiliary Bishop of Buffalo, 204 Knoche Rd., Tonawand, NY 14150.
McManus, William E., Retired Bishop of Fort Wayne-South Bend, 409 S. SeeGwun, Mt. Prospect, IL 60056.
McNamara, John R., Auxiliary Bishop of Boston, 70 Lawrence St., Lowell, MA 01852.
McNamara, Lawrence J., Bishop of Grand Island, P.O. Box 1531, Grand Island, NE 68802.
McRaith, John J., Bishop of Owensboro, 501 W. Fifth St., Owensboro, KY 42301.
Melczek, Dale J., Bishop of Gary, 9292 Broadway, Merrillville, IN 46410.
Mengeling, Carl F., Bishop of Lansing, 300 West Ottawa St., Lansing, MI 48933.
Mestice, Anthony F., Auxiliary Bishop of New York, Resurrection, 910 Post Rd., Rye, NY 10580.
Michaels, James E., *s.s.c.*, Resigned Auxiliary Bishop of Wheeling-Charleston, P.O. Box 606, Berryville, VA 22611.
Mikloshazy, Attila, *s.j.*, Bishop to Hungarians, St. Augustine's Seminary, 2661 Kingston Rd., Scarborough, Ontario, Canada, M1M 1M3.
Milone, Anthony M., Bishop of Great Falls-Billings, 3208 2nd Ave., S., Great Falls, MT 59405.
Moeddel, Carl K., Auxiliary Bishop of Cincinnati, 100 East 8th St., Cincinnati, OH 45202.
Montrose, Donald, Bishop of Stockton, 1105 N. Lincoln St., Stockton, CA 95204-0237.

His Excellency,
The Most Reverend

Moreno, Manuel D., Bishop of Tucson, 192 S. Stone Ave., Tucson, AZ 85702.
Morneau, Robert F., Auxiliary Bishop of Green Bay, 1910 S. Webster, P.O. Box 23066, Green Bay, WI 54305-3066.
Moskal, Robert M., Bishop of St. Josaphat in Parma, 5720 State Rd., Parma, OH 44134.
Moynihan, James M., Bishop of Syracuse, 240 East Onondaga St. -P.O. Box 511, Syracuse, NY 13201.
Muench, Robert W., Bishop of Covington, P.O. Box 18548, Erlanger, KY 41018.
Mulvee, Robert E., Coadjutor Bishop of Providence, One Cathedral Sq., Providence, RI 02903.
Murphy, Michael J., Retired Bishop of Erie, 130 E. Fourth St., Erie, PA 16507.
Murphy, P. Francis, Auxiliary Bishop of Baltimore, 320 Cathedral St., Baltimore, MD 21201.
Murphy, William F., Auxiliary Bishop of Boston, 2121 Commonwealth Ave., Brighton, MA 02135.
Murry, George V., *s.j.*, Auxiliary Bishop of Chicago, Box 733, South Holland, IL 60473-0733.
Myers, John Joseph, Bishop of Peoria, 607 N.E. Madison, Peoria, IL 61603.
Nevins, John J., Bishop of Venice, P.O. Box 2006, Venice, FL 34284.
Newman, William C., Auxiliary Bishop of Baltimore, 5300 N. Charles St., Baltimore, MD 21210.
Neylon, Martin J., *s.j.*, Retired Bishop of The Caroline Islands, P.O. Box 250, Truk, Caroline Islands 96942.
Niederauer, George H., Bishop of Salt Lake City, 27 C St., Salt Lake City, UT 84103.
Niedergeses, James D., Retired Bishop of Nashville, 2400 Twenty-First Ave., South, Nashville, TN 37212.
Nienstedt, John C., Auxiliary Bishop of Detroit, 1234 WashingtonBlvd., Detroit, MI 48226.
Nolan, John Gavin, Auxiliary Bishop of the Military Services, 962 Wayne Ave., Silver Spring, MD 20910.
Ochoa, Armando, Bishop of El Paso, 499 St. Matthews St., El Paso TX 79907.
O'Brien, Edwin F., Auxiliary Bishop of New York, St. Joseph's Seminary, Dunwoodie, Yonkers, NY 10704.
O'Brien, Thomas J., Bishop of Phoenix, 48 E. Wagon Wheel Dr., Phoenix, AZ 85020.
O'Connell, Anthony J., Bishop of Knoxville, 805 Northshore Dr., Knoxville, TN 37919-7551.
O'Donnell, Edward J., Bishop of Lafayette, P.O. Box Drawer 3387, Lafayette, LA 70502.
O'Keefe, Gerald, Former Bishop of Davenport, 2706 N. Gaines St., Davenport, IA 52804-1998.
O'Keefe, Joseph T., Retired Bishop of Syracuse, 214 North State St., Syracuse, NY 13201.
O'Leary, Edward C., Retired Bishop of Portland (in Maine), 510 Ocean Ave., Portland, ME 04102.
Olivier, Leonard J., *s.v.d.*, Auxiliary Bishop of Washington, 3340 St. Peter's Dr., Waldorf, MD 20601-2359.
O'Malley, Sean, *o.f.m.cap.*, Bishop of Fall River, Box 2577, Fall River, MA 02722.
O'Neil, Leo Edward, Bishop of Manchester, 657 North River Rd., Manchester, NH 03104.
O'Neill, Arthur J., Retired Bishop of Rockford, 1245 North Court St., Rockford, IL 61103.
O'Rourke, Edward W., Retired Bishop of Peoria, St. Augustine Manor, 1301 N.E. Glendale, Peoria, IL 61603.
Ottenweller, Albert H., Retired Bishop of Steubenville, 609 North Seventh St., Steubenville, OH 43952.
Paschang, John L., Retired Bishop of Grand Island, St. Joseph's Home, 320 E. Decatur St., West Point, NE 68788.
Paska, Walter, Auxiliary Bishop of Philadelphia Ukraine, 827 N. Franklin St., Philadelphia, PA 19123.
Pataki, Andrew, Bishop of Passaic of the Ruthenians, 445 Lackawanna Ave., West Paterson, NJ 07424.
Paul, John J., Retired Bishop of La Crosse, P.O. Box 69, La Crosse, WI 54601.
Pelotte, Donald, *s.s.s.*, Bishop of Gallup, 711 S. Puerco Drive, Gallup, NM 87301.
Pena, Raymundo J., Bishop of Brownsville, 1910 E. Elizabeth St., Brownsville, TX 78522-2279.
Pevec, A. Edward, Auxiliary Bishop of Cleveland, 28700 Euclid Ave., Wickliffe, OH 44092.
Pfeifer, Michael D., *o.m.i.*, Bishop of San Angelo, 116 S. Oakes, San Angelo, TX 75902.
Pilla, Anthony M., Bishop of Cleveland, 1027 Superior Ave., Cleveland, OH 44114.
Popp, Bernard F., Retired Auxiliary Bishop of San Antonio, 4535 Lord Rd., San Antonio, TX 78220-3543.
Povish, Kenneth J., Retired Bishop of Lansing, 401-A East Madison St., DeWitt, MI 48820.
Pursley, Leo A., Retired Bishop of Fort Wayne-South Bend, 2 Northway Dr., Huntington, IN 46750.

His Excellency,
The Most Reverend

Puscas, Vasile Louis, Former Apostolic Eparch of St. George Martyr in Canton for Romanian-Byzantine Catholics, 609 N. Lincoln Ave., Aurora, IL 60505-2112.
Quinn, A. James, Auxiliary Bishop of Cleveland, 2500 Elyria Ave., Lorain, OH 44055.
Quinn, Francis A., Retired Bishop of Sacramento, 8840 East 22nd St., Tucson, AZ 85710.
Ramirez, Ricardo, *c.s.b.*, Bishop of Las Cruces, 1280 Med Park Dr., Las Cruces, NM 88005.
Reilly, Daniel P., Bishop of Worcester, 49 Elm St., Worcester, MA 01609.
Reiss, John C., Bishop of Trenton, 701 Lawrence Rd., Trenton, NJ 08648.
Ricard, John H., *s.s.j.*, Bishop of Pensacola-Tallahassee.

Riley, Lawrence J., Retired Auxiliary Bishop of Boston, 43 Maple St., Hyde
Park, Boston, MA 02136.
Rivera, Enrique Hernandez, Bishop of Caguas, P.O. Box 8698, Caguas, PR 00626.
Rivera, Hector M., Auxiliary Bishop of San Juan, P.O. Box S-1967, San Juan, PR 00603.
Rodimer, Frank J., Bishop of Paterson, 178 Derrom Ave., Paterson, NJ 07504.
Rodriguez, Miguel, *c.ss.r*, Retired Bishop of Arecibo, Calle Comercio 32, P.O. Box 238, Aguadilla, PR 00605-0238.
Rodriguez, Placido, *c.m.f.*, Bishop of Lubbock, P.O. Box 98700 - 4620 4th St., Lubbock, TX 79416.
Roque, Francis X., Auxiliary Bishop Military Services, P.O. Box 4469, Washington, DC 20017-0469.
Roman, Agustin A., Auxiliary Bishop of Miami, 9401 Biscayne Blvd., Miami Shores, FL 33138.
Rosazza, Peter A., Auxiliary Bishop of Hartford, 1450 Chapel St., New Haven, CT 06511.
Rose, Robert J., Bishop of Grand Rapids, 660 Burton St., S.E., Grand Rapids, MI 49507.
Rueger, George E., Auxiliary Bishop of Worcester, 2 High Ridge Rd., Worcester, MA 01602.
Ryan, Daniel L., Bishop of Springfield in Illinois, P.O. Box 1667, Springfield, IL 62705.
Ryan, Sylvester D., Bishop of Monterey, 580 Fremont St., P.O. Box 2048, Monterey, CA 93942-2048.
Saltarelli, Michael A., Bishop of Wilmington, 1925 Delaware Ave., Suite 1-A, Wilmington, DE 19806.
Samo, Amando, Auxiliary Bishop of The Caroline Islands. P.O. Box 250, Truk, Caroline Islands FSM 96942.
Samra, Nicholas J., Auxiliary Bishop of Newton, 8525 Cole St., Warren, MI 48093.
Santana, Hermin Negron, Auxiliary Bishop of San Juan, Calle 6, D-9 Urb. Royal Town, Bayamon, PR 00956.
Sartoris, Joseph M., Auxiliary Bishop of Los Angeles, San Pedro Pastoral Region, 3555 St. Pancratius Plc., Lakewood, CA 90712-1416.
Scanlan, John J., Retired Bishop of Honolulu, Nazareth House, 245 Nova Albion Way, San Rafael, CA 94903.
Schad, James L., Retired Auxiliary Bishop of Camden, Neumann House - St. Mary's Home, Suite 102, 1730 Kresson Rd., Cherry Hill, NJ 08003.
Schlarman, Stanley G., Bishop of Dodge City, 910 Central Ave., P.O. Box 0137, Dodge City, KS 67801-0137.
Schmitt, Bernard W., Bishop of Wheeling-Charleston, 1300 Byron St., Box 230, Wheeling, WV 26003.
Schmitt, Mark F., Retired Bishop of Marquette, HC01 Box 159, Marquette, MI 49855.
Schoenherr, Walter J., Retired Auxiliary Bishop of Detroit, 14465 Levan Rd.- Apt. A, Livonia, MI 48154-5022.
Schuster, Eldon B., Retired Bishop of Great Falls, 1325 Smelter Ave., Black Eagle, Great Falls, MT 59414.
Schwietz, Roger L., *o.m.i.*, Bishop of Duluth, 2830 E. 4th St., Duluth, MN 55812.
Schott, Basil, *o.f.m.*, Bishop of Parma of the Ruthenians
Setian, Nerses M., Former Apostolate Exarch for the Armenian Catholics, c/o Our Lady Queen of Martyrs Church, 1327 Pleasant Ave., Los Angeles, CA 90033.
Sevilla, Carlos, *s.j.*, Bishop of Yakima.
Sheets, John R., *s.j.*, Auxiliary Bishop of Ft. Wayne-South Bend, St. Matthew Cathedral, 1701 Miami St., South Bend, IN 46613.
Sheldon, Gilbert I., Bishop of Steubenville, P.O. Box 969, Steubenville, OH 43952.
Sheridan, Patrick J., Auxiliary Bishop of New York, 452 Madison Ave., New York, NY 10022.
Sklba, Richard J., Auxiliary Bishop of Milwaukee, 2491 N. Murray Ave., Milwaukee, WI 53211.
Skylstad, William S., Bishop of Spokane, W. 1023 Riverside Ave., Spokane, WA 99201.
Slattery, Edward J., Bishop of Tulsa, P.O. Box 2009, Tulsa, OK 74101.

His Excellency,
The Most Reverend

Smith, John M., Coadjutor Bishop of Trenton, 701 Lawrenceville Rd., Trenton, NJ 08638.
Snyder, John J., Bishop of St. Augustine, 35 Treasury St., St. Augustine, FL 32084.
Soens, Lawrence D., Bishop of Sioux City, P.O. Box 3379, Sioux City, IA 51102-1437.
Speltz, George H., Retired Bishop of St. Cloud, Box 1248, St. Cloud, MN 56301.
Speyrer, Jude, Bishop of Lake Charles, P.O. Box 3223, Lake Charles, LA 70602.
Steib, James Terry, *s.v.d.*, Bishop of Memphis, The Catholic Center, P.O. Box 341669, Memphis, TN 38184-1669.
Steinbock, John T., Bishop of Fresno, 1550 N. Fresno St., Fresno, CA 93703-3788.
Steiner, Kenneth D., Auxiliary Bishop of Portland in Oregon, 501-N.W. 25th St., Corvalis, OR 97330.
Straling, Phillip F., Bishop of Reno, P.O. Box 1211, Reno, NV 89504-1211.
Sullivan, James S., Bishop of Fargo, Box 1750, Fargo, ND 58107.
Sullivan, John J., Retired Bishop of Kansas City-St. Joseph, 1236 West 66th St., Kansas City, MO 64114.
Sullivan, Joseph M., Auxiliary Bishop of Brooklyn, 256 Clinton Ave., Brooklyn, NY 11205.
Sullivan, Walter F., Bishop of Richmond, 800 Cathedral Place, Richmond, VA 23220.
Surinach-Carreras, Ricardo, Auxiliary Bishop of Ponce, P.O. Box 205, Ponce, PR 00731.
Symons, J. Keith, Bishop of Palm Beach, 9995 N. Military Trail (P.O. Box 109650), Palm Beach Gardens, FL 33410-9650.
Tafoya, Arthur N., Bishop of Pueblo, 1001 N. Grand Ave., Pueblo, CO 81003.
Tamayo, James A., Auxiliary Bishop of Galveston-Houston, 1700 San Jacinto, Houston, TX 77002-8291.
Tawil, Joseph, Retired Eparch of Newton, 19 Dartmouth St., West Newton, MA 02165.
Tertzakian, Hovhannes, *O.M.Ven.*, Apostolic Exarch for Armenian Catholics in the United States and Canada, 110 E 12th St., New York, NY 10003-5395.
Thomas, Elliot G., Bishop of St. Thomas, in the Virgin Islands, P.O. Box 1825, Charlotte Amalie, VI 00803.
Thompson, David B., Bishop of Charleston, 119 Broad St., Charleston, SC 29401.
Timlin, James C., Bishop of Scranton, 300 Wyoming Ave., Scranton, PA 18503.
Tobin, Thomas J., Bishop of Youngstown, 144 W. Wood St., Youngstown, OH 44503.
Torres, Juan Fremiot, Bishop of Ponce, P.O. Box 205, Ponce, PR 00732.
Trautman, Donald W., Bishop of Erie, 205 West 9th St., Erie, PA 16501.
Tschoepe, Thomas, Retired Bishop of Dallas, 3915 Lemmon Ave, Box 19507, Dallas, TX 75219.
Txertudi, Inaki Mallona, *c.p.*, 206 Dr. Salas St. - Box 616, Arecibo, PR 00613-0616.
Untener, Kenneth E., Bishop of Saginaw, 5800 Weiss St., Saginaw, MI 48603.
Valero, Rene, Auxiliary Bishop of Brooklyn, 34-43 93rd St., Jackson Heights, NY 11372.
Vaughan, Austin B., Auxiliary Bishop of New York, St. Mary, 180 South St., Newburgh, NY 12550.
Vigneron, Allen H., Auxiliary Bishop of Detroit, Sacred Heart Major Seminary, 2701 Chicago Blvd., Detroit, MI 48206.
Vlazny, John G., Bishop of Winona, P.O. Box 588, Winona, MN 55987.
Walsh, Daniel F., Bishop of Las Vegas, P.O. Box 18316, Las Vegas, NV 89114.
Walsh, Nicolas E., Bishop Emeritus of Yakima, 6770 E. Carondelet Dr., Tucson, AZ 85710.
Ward, John J., Former Auxiliary Bishop of Los Angeles, 3424 Wilshire Blvd., Los Angeles, CA 90010-2241
Warfel, Michael, Bishop of Juneau, 419 6th St., Suite 200, Juneau, AK 99801.
Watters, Loras J., Retired Bishop of Winona, 618 Forest, Apt. D., Pacific Grove, CA 93950.
Wcela, Emil A., Auxiliary Bishop of Rockville Centre, Eastern Vicariate, P.O. Box 780, Riverhead, NY 11901.
Weigand, William K., Bishop of Sacramento, Pastoral Center, 2110 Broadway, Sacramento CA 95818-2541.
Weitzel, John Quinn, *m.m.*, Bishop of Samoa-Pago Pago, Fatuoaiga P.O. Box 596, Pago Pago, American Samoa 967.
Welsh, Lawrence H., Auxiliary Bishop of St. Paul-Minneapolis, 226 Summit Ave., St. Paul, MN 55102.
Welsh, Thomas J., Bishop of Allentown, 202 North 17th St., P.O. Box F. Allentown, PA 18105.
Whelan, Robert L., *s.j.*, Retired Bishop of Fairbanks, Regis Community, 1107 N. Astor, Spokane, WA 99202.
Williams, James Kendrick, Bishop of Lexington, 1310 Leestown Rd., P.O. Box 12350, Lexington, KY 40582-2350.
Winter, William J., Auxiliary Bishop of Pittsburgh, Sacred Heart Church, 310 Shady Ave., Pittsburgh, PA 15206-4389.
Wirz, George O., Auxiliary Bishop of Madison, 404 E. Main St., Madison, WI 53703.
Wiwchar, Michael, *c.s.s.r.*, Bishop of St. Nicholas in Chicago for Ukrainians, 224 W. Rice St., Chicago, IL 60622.
Wuerl, Donald W., Bishop of Pittsburgh, 111 Blvd. of the Allies, Pittsburgh, PA 15222-1618.
Wycislo, Aloysius J., Retired Bishop of Green Bay, 1910 S. Webster, P.O. Box 23835, Green Bay, WI 54305-3825.
Yanta, John W., Bishop of Amarillo.
Younan, Joseph,, Bishop of Our Lady of Deliverance of Newark of the Syrians, P.O. Box 8366, Union City, NJ 07087-8262.
Zayek, Francis M., Former Eparch (Bishop) of St. Maron of Brooklyn, 294 Howard Ave., P.O. Box 010-360, Staten Island, NY 10301.
Zavala, Gabino, Auxiliary Bishop of Los Angeles, San Gabriel Pastoral Region, 16009 East Cypress Ave., Irwindale, CA 91706-2122
Ziemann, G. Patrick, Bishop of Santa Rosa, 547 B St., P.O. Box 1297, Santa Rosa, CA 95402.
Zipfel, Paul A., Bishop of Bismarck.

OTHER HIERARCHY RESIDING IN THE UNITED STATES

Comber, John W., *m.m.*, Former Superior & Bishop of Maryknoll, 141 E 43rd St., New York, NY 10017.
Cotey, Arnold R., *s.d.s.*, Former Bishop of Nachingwea, 3140 Hwy K, Random Lake WI 53075.
DePalma, Joseph A., *s.c.j.* Former Bishop of De Aar, South Africa, Sacred Heart Residence, 6701 82nd Ave., N., Pinellas Park, FL 34665.
Durning, Dennis V., *c.s.sp.*, Bishop Emeritus of Arusha Tanzania, East Africa, Holy Ghost Provincialate, 6230 Brush Run Rd., Bethel Park, PA 15102.
Dempsey, Michael J., *o.p.*, 3005 W. 29th Ave., Denver, CO 80211.
Glennie, Ignatius T., *s.j.*, Retired Bishop from the Missions, Mary-Joseph Residence for the Elderly, 4201 Woodland Dr., New Orleans, LA 70131.
Kung, Ignatius Cardinal, Our Lady Queen of the Clergy Home, 128 Strawberry Hill Ave., Stamford, CT 06904.
Kupfer, William F., *m.m.*, Former Bishop of Taichung, Taiwan, Annunciation Rectory, 410 Walnut St., Williamsport, PA 17701.
Nolker, Bernard J., *c.ss.r.*, Retired Bishop of Paranagua Brazil, 600 S. Conkling St., Baltimore, MD 21224.
Pearce, George H., *s.m.*, Former Archbishop of Suva, 30 Fenner St., Providence, RI 02903.
Reilly, Thomas, *c.ss.r.*, Retired Bishop of San Juan de la Maguana, Dominican Republic, 1545 Tremont St., Roxbury, MA 02120.
Schlotterback, Edward J., *o.s.f.s.*, Retired Bishop of Keetmanschoop-Namibia, The Salesianum, 1801 N. Broom St., Wilmington, DE 19802.
Schmidt, Firmin, *o.f.m.cap.*, Former Bishop of Papua, New Guinea, c/o Diocese of Salina, 103 N. Ninth, Salina, KS 67402-0980.
Secondo, Louis J., *t.o.r.*, St. Anthony, 124 Maple Ave., Johnstown, PA 15901.
Veigle, Adriano J., *t.o.r.*, Retired Bishop of Borba, Brazil, Mount Assisi Monastery, Loretto, PA 15940.

U.S. (MISSIONARY) (ARCH)BISHOPS SERVING IN FOREIGN COUNTRIES

Adams, Edward J., Archbishop Apostolic Nuncio in Bangladesh.
Boyle, Paul M., *c.p.*, Apostolic Vicar of Mandeville, Jamaica, West Indies.
Brown, Charles A.,*m.m.*, Auxiliary Bishop of Santa Cruz, Arzobispado, Casilla 25, Calle Ingavi 49, Santa Cruz, Bolivia.
Dion, George E., *o.m.i.*, Retired Bishop of Jolo, Oblates of Notre Dame Motherhouse, Sinsuat Ave., 9600 Cotabato City, Philippines.
Lambert, Francis Roland, *s.m.*, Bishop of Port-Vila, Eveche, B.P. 59, Port-Vila, Vanuatu.
McGarry, Urban E., *t.o.r.*, Bishop of Bhagalpur, Chancery Office: Nawab Colony, P.O. Box 61, Bhagalpur 812001, Bihar, India.
McNaughton, William J., *m.m.*, Bishop of Inchon, 3 Tap Tong, P.O. Box 19, Chung Ku, Inchon 400-600, Korea.
Smith, Philip Francis, *m.m.*, Archbishop of Cotabato, Residence, P.O. Box 186, Sinsuat Ave., Cotabato City 9600, Philippines.

ARCHABBOTS

The Right Reverend
Donovan, Egbert, *o.s.b.*, Retired. St. Vincent Archabbey, Latrobe, PA 15650.
Knaebel, Bonaventure, *o.s.b.*, Resigned. St. Meinrad Archabbey, St. Meinrad, IN 47577.
Maher, Paul R., *o.s.b.*, St. Vincent Archabbey, Latrobe, PA 15650.
Nowicki, Douglas R., *o.s.b.*, St. Vincent Archabbey, Latrobe, PA 15650.
Reilly, Lambert, *o.s.b.*, St. Meinrad Archabbey, St. Meinrad, IN 47577.

ABBOTS

Abdo, Michael, *o.c.s.o.*, St. Benedict Monastery, 1012 Monastery Rd., Snowmass, CO 81654.
Anderson, Hugh R., *o.s.b.*, St. Procopius Abbey, 5601 College Rd., Lisle, IL 60532.
Balsavich, Marion E., *o.s.b.*, Retired. St. Bede Abbey, Peru, IL 61354.
Bamberger, John E., *o.c.s.o.*, Abbey of Genesee, Piffard, NY 14533.
Bataille, Vincent, *o.s.b.*, Marmion Abbey, Butterfield Rd., Aurora, IL 60504.
Benedict, Francis, *o.s.b.*, St. Andrew's Abbey, 31001 N. Valyermo Rd., Valyermo, CA 93563.
Benkert, Gerald, *o.s.b.*, Resigned. Marmion Abbey, Butterfield Rd., Aurora, IL 60504.
Berndt, Alan, *o.s.b.*, Retired. Blue Cloud Abbey, P.O. Box 98, Marvin, SD 57252.
Berning, Philip, *o.s.b.*, Retired. St. Gregory Abbey, Shawnee, OK 74801.
Bock, David R., *o.c.s.o.*, Retired. New Melleray Abbey, 6500 Melleray Circle, Peosta, IA 52068.
Boultwood, Alban, *o.s.b.*, St. Anselm Abbey, 4501 S. Dakota Ave., N.E., Washington, DC 20017.
Bowman, Marion, *o.s.b.*, Retired. St. Leo Abbey, St. Leo, FL 33574.
Boyle, Joseph, *o.s.b.*, St. Benedict Monastery, 1012 Monastery Rd., Snowmass, CO 81654.
Buergler, Luke, *o.s.b.*, Corpus Christi Abbey, HCR #2, Box 6300, Sandia, TX 78383.
Burne, Martin J., *o.s.b.*, Retired. St. Mary Abbey, Delbarton, Mendham Rd., Morristown, NJ 07960.
Burnett, Oscar, *o.s.b.*, Belmont Abbey, 100 Belmont - Mount Holly Rd., Belmont, NC 28012-2795.
Burns, Flavian, *o.c.s.o.*, Abbey of Our Lady of the Holy Cross, Rt. 2, Box 3870, Berryville, VA 22611.
Campbell, Edward C., *o.s.b.*, Retired. Glastonbury Abbey, 16 Hull St., Hingham, MA 02043.
Carr, Christian Aidan, *o.c.s.o.*, Retired. Our Lady of Mepkin Abbey, HC 69, Box 800, Moncks Corner, SC 29461. Serving as chaplain in Africa.
Cassell, Leonard G., *o.s.b.*, Retired. St. Mary Abbey, Delbarton, Mendham Rd., Morristown, NJ 07960.
Chassagne, M. Anthony, *o.c.s.o.*, Retired. Abbey of Our Lady of Mepkin, HC 69, Box 800, Moncks Corner, SC 29461.
Clark, Victor J., *o.s.b.*, St. Bernard Abbey, 1600 St. Bernard Dr., Cullman, AL 35055.
Clarke, Brian H., *o.s.b.*, St. Mary Abbey, Delbarton, Mendham Rd., Morristown, NJ 07960.
Coggin, Walter A., *o.s.b.*, Retired. Belmont Abbey, 100 Belmont - Mount Holly Rd., Belmont, NC 28012-2795.
Cole, Edwin J., *o.s.b.*, St. Anselm Church, 530 S. Mason Rd., St. Louis, MO 63141.
Connor, James, *o.c.s.o.*, Assumption Abbey, Rte 5 - Box 1056, Ava, MO 65660.
Coppersmith, Anselm, *o.s.b.*, Retired. Conception Abbey, Conception, MO 64433.
Coriston, Charles V., *o.s.b.*, Resigned. St. Paul Abbey, Newton, NJ 07860.
Corpus, Roger, *o.s.b.*, St. Bede Abbey, Peru, IL 61354.
Cyr, David J., *o.s.b.*, Marmion Abbey, Butterfield Rd., Aurora, IL 60504.
Dagher, George, *b.s.o.*, American Headquarters, 30 East St., Methuen, MA 01844.
Davis, Thomas X., *o.c.s.o.*, Our Lady of New Clairvaux Abbey, P.O. Box 80, Vina, CA 96092.
De Wane, Thomas E., *o.praem.*, St. Norbert Abbey, 1016 N. Broadway, De Pere, WI 54115-2697.
Dimitrijevich, Nicholas, Our Lady of the Valley, P.O. Box 419, Gloverville, SC 29828.
Dreaper, Hilary, *o.s.b.*, St. Bernard Abbey, 1600 St. Bernard Dr., Cullman, AL 35055.

Dzikowicz, Justin E., *o.s.b.*, St. Paul Abbey, Newton, NJ 07860.
Eberle, Peter, *o.s.b.*, Mount Angel Abbey, St. Benedict, OR 97373.
Ehringer, Claude, *o.s.b.*, Prince of Peace Abbey, Oceanside, CA 92054.
Eidenschink, John, *o.s.b.*, Chaplain. Mother of Mercy Nursing Home & Retirement Center, Albany, MN 56307.
Farkasfalvy, Denis, *o.cist.*, Abbey of Our Lady of Dallas, 1 Cistercian Rd., Irving, TX 75039.
Flaherty, Malachy, *o.c.s.o.*, Abbey of Our Lady of the Holy Trinity, 1250 S. 9500 E., Huntsville, UT 84317.
Freeman, Brendan J., *o.c.s.o.*, Abbey of Our Lady of New Melleray, 6500 Melleray Circle, Peosta, IA 52068.
Fuez, Blaise J. *o.cist.*, Our Lady of Spring Bank Abbey, Rt. 3, Box 211, Sparta, WI 54656.
Galvin, Anselm, *o.s.b.*, Resigned, Mt. Angel Abbey, St. Benedict, OR 97373.
Garber, Andrew V., *o.s.b.*, Resigned. St. Benedict Abbey, Benet Lake, WI 53102.
Geraets, David, *o.s.b.*, Our Lady of Guadalupe Abbey, Pecos, NM 87552.
Gibbs, Gabriel, *o.s.b.*, St. Benedict Abbey, 252 Still River Rd., P.O. Box 67, Still River (Harvard), MA 01467.
Gries, Roger, *o.s.b.*, St. Andrew Abbey, 10510 Buckeye Rd., Cleveland, OH 44104.
Harrison, Cyprian, *o.c.s.o.*, Assumption Abbey, Rt. 5, Box 1056, Ava, MO 65608.
Hartman, Thomas F., *o.s.b.*, Retired. St. Benedict Abbey, Atchison, KS 66002.
Havlik, Thomas J., *o.s.b.*, St. Procopius Abbey, 5601 College Rd., Lisle, IL 60532.
Heidgen, Warren J., *o.s.b.*, Retired. Holy Cross Abbey, P.O. Box 1510, Canon City, CO 81215-1510.
Hess, Gilbert, *o.s.b.*, Retired. Blue Cloud Abbey, P.O. Box 98, Marvin, SD 57251.
Hillenbrand, Thomas, *o.s.b.*, Blue Cloud Abbey, P.O. Box 98, Marvin, SD 57251.
Hinches, Augustine J., *o.s.b.*, Resigned. St. Paul Abbey, Newton, NJ 07860.
Hoenig, Alfred, *o.s.b.*, Retired. Corpus Christi Abbey, HCR No. 2, P.O. Box 6300, Sandia, TX 78383.
Johnson, Bernard, *o.c.s.o.*, Retired. Monastery of the Holy Spirit, 2625 Hwy 212 S.W., Conyers, GA 30208.
Jones, James, *o.s.b.*, Retired. St. Gabriel Archangel, 4737 N. Cleveland Ave., Kansas City, MO 64117.
Keating, Thomas, *o.c.s.o.*, Contemplative Outreach, Chrysalis House, 21 Ball Rd., Warwick, NY 10990.
Kelly, Timothy, *o.s.b.*, St. John's Abbey, Collegeville, MN 56321.
Kelly, Timothy, *o.c.s.o.*, Abbey of Gethsemani, Trappist, KY 40051.
Kerndt, James J., *o.c.s.o.*, Retired. New Melleray Abbey, 6500 Melleray Circle, Dubuque, IA 52068.
Killeen, Sylvester M., *o.praem.*, Retired. St. Norbert Abbey, 1016 N. Broadway, De Pere, WI 54115-2697.
Kline, Francis, *o.c.s.o.*, Our Lady of Mepkin Abbey, HC 69, Box 800, Moncks Corner, SC 29461.
Kodell, Jerome, *o.s.b.*, New Subiaco Abbey, Subiaco, AR 72865.
Koehler, Ralph, *o.s.b.*, Retired. St. Benedict Abbey, Atchison, KS 66002.
Lawrence, Philip, *o.s.b.*, Monastery of Christ in the Desert, Abiquiu, NM 87510.
Leavy, Matthew, *o.s.b.*, St. Anselm Abbey, Manchester, NH 03102.
Logan, John M., *o.praem.*, Daylesford Abbey, 220 S. Valley Rd., Paoli, PA 19301.
Luykx, Boniface, Holy Transfiguration Monastery, 17001 Tomki Rd., Redwood Valley, CA 95470.
Mackin, Benjamin T., *o.praem.*, Retired, St. Norbert Abbey, 1016 N. Broadway, De Pere, WI 54115-2697.
Massoth, Charles, *o.s.b.*, St. Gregory Abbey, Shawnee, OK 74801.
Matter, Robert, *o.c.s.o.*, Retired. Assumption Abbey, Rt. 5, Box 1056, Ava, MO 65608.
McCarthy, Gerald, *o.s.b.*, Resigned. St. Anselm Abbey, Manchester, NH 03102.
McCorkell, Edward, *o.c.s.o.*, Retired. Abbey of Our Lady of the Holy Cross, Rt. 2, Box 3870, Berryville, VA 22611.
Macrae, Maurus, *o.s.b.*, Mt. Angel Abbey, St. Benedict, OR 97373.
McDermott, Benedict, *o.s.b.*, Mary Mother of Church Abbey, 304 N. Sheppard St., Richmond, VA 23221.
McGonigle, Kevin, *o.s.b.*, Retired. Conception Abbey, Conception, MO 64433.
McVeigh, Bernard, *o.c.s.o.*, Our Lady of Guadalupe Abbey, Lafayette, OR 97127.
Moore, Augustine J., *o.c.s.o.*, Retired. Monastery of the Holy Spirit, 2625 Hwy. 213 S.W., Conyers, GA 30208.
Moore, Patrick, *o.s.b.*, Assumption Abbey, P.O. Box A, Richardton, ND 58652.
Morcone, Nicholas J., *o.s.b.*, Glastonbury Abbey, 16 Hull St., Hingham, MA 02043.
Neitzel, John E., *o.praem.*, Retired. Daylesford Abbey, 220 S. Valley Rd., Paoli, PA 19301.
O'Connor, Philip J., *o.c.s.o.*, Retired. New Melleray Abbey, 6500 Melleray Circle, Peosta, IA 52068.
Odenbrett, Stephen, *o.s.b.*, Our Lady of Guadalupe Abbey, Pecos, NM 87552.
Parcher, Adrian, *o.s.b.*, Retired. St. Martin's Abbey, 5300 Pacific Ave. S.E., Lacey, WA 98503.
Parker, Ladislaus K., *o.praem.*, St. Michael Abbey, 1042 Star Rt., Orange, CA 92667.
Purcell, Owen, *o.s.b.*, St. Benedict Abbey, Atchison, KS 66002.
Quinkert, Denis, *o.s.b.*, Blue Cloud Abbey, P.O. Box 98, Marvin, SD 57251.
Rausch, Conrad, *o.s.b.*, Retired. St. Martin's Abbey, 5300 Pacific Ave. S.E., Lacey, WA 98503.
Regan, Patrick, *o.s.b.*, St. Joseph Abbey, St. Benedict, LA 70457.
Rigby, Luke, *o.s.b.*, Abbey of St. Mary and St. Louis, 500 S. Mason Rd., St. Louis, MO 63141.
Roberts, Augustine, *o.c.s.o.*, St. Joseph Abbey, Spencer, MA 01562.
Rodriguez-Santiago, Jose M., *o.s.b.*, Abbey of San Antonio, Box 729, Humacao, PR 00661.
Roettger, Gregory J., *o.s.b.*, Retired. St. Bernard Abbey, 1600 St. Bernard Dr., Cullman, AL 35055.
Rooney, Marcel, *o.s.b.*, Conception Abbey, Conception, MO 64433.
Roth, Neal G., *o.s.b.*, St. Martin's Abbey, 5300 Pacific Ave. S.E., Lacey, WA 98503.
Ryska, Leo M., *o.s.b.*, St. Benedict's Abbey and Retreat Center, Benet Lake, WI 53102.
Schoofs, Robert, *o.s.b.*, St. Benedict Abbey, Benet Lake, WI 53102.
Serna, Dom Mark, *o.s.b.*, Abbey of St. Gregory, Cory's Ln., Portsmouth, RI 02871.
Shea, Aidan, *o.s.b.*, St. Anselm Abbey, 4501 S. Dakota, N.E., Washington, DC 20017.
Shelton, Patrick, *o.s.b.*, St. Leo Abbey, St. Leo, FL 33574.
Skluzacek, Valentine, *o.s.b.*, St. Procopius Abbey, 5601 College Rd., Lisle, IL 60532.
Skutecky, Paschal, *o.c.s.o.*, Retired. St. Joseph Abbey, Spencer, MA 01562.
Spillane, M. Emmanuel, *o.c.s.o.*, Retired. Abbey of Our Lady of the Trinity, 1250 S. 9500 E. Huntsville, UT 84317.
Stark, Matthew, *o.s.b.*, Abbey of St. Gregory the Great, Portsmouth, RI 02871.
Tremel, Jerome G., *o.praem.*,Admin.- Daylesford Abbey Norbertine Canonry, 220 S. Valley Rd., Paoli, PA 19301-1900.
Valvano, Melvin J., *o.s.b.*, Newark Abbey, 528 Dr. Martin Luther King Jr. Blvd., Newark, NJ 07102.
Veilleux, Armand J., *o.s.c.o.*, Monastery of the Holy Spirit, 2625 Hwy. 213 S.W., Conyers, GA 30208.
Vollmer, Edward J., *o.s.b.*, Retired. Holy Cross Abbey, P.O. Box 1510, Canon City, CO 81215-1510.
Vorderlandwehr, Adrian R., *o.s.b.*, Retired. St. Gregory Abbey, Shawnee, OK 74801.
Wagner, Lawrence, *o.s.b.*, Retired. Assumption Abbey, P.O. Box A, Richardton, ND 58652.
Walsh, Raphael, *o.s.b.*, Mt. Michael Abbey, Elkhorn, NE 68022.
Wechter, David L., *o.s.c.o.*, Retired. New Melleray Abbey, 6500 Melleray Circle, Peosta, IA 52068.
Wendt, Gregory F. Monastery of the Exaltation of the Most Holy Cross, 12425 Sunset Dr., Miami, FL 33183.
West, Robert, *o.s.b.*, Retired. Assumption Abbey, P.O. Box A, Richardton, ND 58652.
Wiseman, James, *o.s.b.*, Resigned. St. Anselm Abbey, 4501 S. Dakota Ave., N.E., Washington, DC 20017.
Wolff, Theodore, *o.s.b.* Mount Michael Abbey, Elkhorn, NE 68022.

A LIST OF CARDINALS IN THE UNITED STATES IN THE ORDER OF THEIR SENIORITY

CARDINALS

His Eminence John Cardinal Carberry, St. Louis
His Eminence Luis Cardinal Aponte Martinez, San Juan
His Eminence William Cardinal Baum, Vatican City State
His Eminence Bernard Cardinal Law, Boston
His Eminence John Cardinal O'Connor, New York
His Eminence James Cardinal Hickey, Washington
His Eminence Edmund Cardinal Szoka, Vatican City State
His Eminence Roger Cardinal Mahony, Los Angeles
His Eminence Anthony Cardinal Bevilacqua, Philadelphia
His Eminence William Cardinal Keeler, Baltimore
His Eminence Adam Cardinal Maida, Detroit

A CHRONOLOGICAL LIST OF CARDINAL, ARCHBISHOP & BISHOP ACTIVITY BY YEAR

1947

Bishops

McDonough, Thomas J., Appointed March 10, Ordained May 26, 1938. Auxiliary Bishop of St. Augustine.

1950

Bishops

Pursley, Leo A., Appointed July 22, Ordained June 11, 1927. Auxiliary Bishop of Fort Wayne-South Bend.

1951

Bishops

Federal, Joseph Lennox, Appointed Feb. 5, Ordained Dec. 8, 1934. Auxiliary Bishop of Salt Lake City.
Paschang, John L., Appointed July 28, Ordained June 12, 1921. Retired Bishop of Grand Island.

1953

Bishops

Flanagan, Bernard J., Appointed Sept. 1, Ordained Dec 8, 1931. Bishop of Norwich.

1954

Bishops

Maloney, Charles G., Appointed Dec. 30, Ordained Dec. 8, 1937. Retired Auxiliary Bishop of Louisville.
Scanlan, John J., Appointed July 8, Ordained June 22, 1930. Auxiliary Bishop of Honolulu.

1956

Bishops

Carberry, John J., Appointed May 3, Ordained July 28, 1929. Coadjutor Lafayette in Indiana.
Clinch, Harry A., Appointed Dec. 5, Ordained June 6, 1936. Auxiliary Bishop of Monterey-Fresno.
Hannan, Philip M., Appointed June 16, Ordained Dec. 8, 1939. Auxiliary Bishop of Washington.
Helmsing, Charles H., Appointed Aug. 24, Ordained June 10, 1933. Bishop of Springfield-Cape Girardeau.

1957

Bishops

Carberry, John J., Succeeded to See Nov. 20. Bishop of Lafayette in Indiana.
Curtis, Walter W., Appointed June 27, Ordained Dec. 8, 1937. Auxiliary Bishop of Newark.
Freking, Frederick W., Appointed Oct. 10, Ordained July 31, 1938. Bishop of Salina.
McDonough, Thomas J., Appointed Jan. 2, Ordained May 26, 1938. Auxiliary Bishop of Savannah.
Pursley, Leo A., Appointed Feb. 26. Retired Bishop of Fort Wayne-South Bend.

1958

Bishops

Federal, Joseph L., Appointed May 8, Ordained Dec. 8, 1934. Coadjutor of Salt Lake City.

1959

Bishops

Buswell, Charles A., Appointed Aug. 8, Ordained July 9, 1939. Retired Bishop of Pueblo.
Flanagan, Bernard J., Appointed April 12, Ordained Dec. 8, 1931. Retired Bishop of Worcester.
Hogan, James J., Appointed Nov. 27, Ordained Dec. 8, 1937. Auxiliary Bishop of Trenton.

1960

Bishops

Aponte Martinez, Luis, Appointed July 23, Ordained April 10, 1950. Auxiliary of Ponce.
Federal, Joseph L., Succeeded to See March 31. Retired Bishop of Salt Lake City.
Forst, Marion F., Appointed Jan. 2, Ordained June 10, 1934. Former Bishop of Dodge City.
Malone, James W., Appointed Jan. 2, Ordained May 26, 1945. Auxiliary Bishop of Youngstown.
McDonough, Thomas J., Appointed March 2, Ordained May 26, 1938. Bishop of Savannah.
Wycislo, Aloysius J., Appointed Oct. 17, Ordained April 7, 1934. Auxiliary Bishop of Chicago.

1961

Archbishops

Bishops

Curtis, Walter W., Appointed Sept. 23, Ordained Dec. 8, 1937. Retired Bishop of Bridgeport.
Gottwald, George J., Appointed June 20, Ordained June 9, 1940. Retired Auxiliary Bishop of St. Louis.
O'Keefe, Gerald, Appointed May 5, Ordained Jan. 29, 1944. Auxiliary Bishop of St. Paul.
Salatka, Charles A., Appointed Dec. 9, Ordained Feb. 24, 1945. Auxiliary Bishop of Grand Rapids.
Schuster, Eldon B., Appointed Oct. 30, Ordained May 27, 1937. Titular Bishop of Amblada.

1962

Archbishops

Bishops

Boudreaux, Warren L., Appointed May 19, Ordained May 30, 1942. Auxiliary Bishop of Lafayette.
Helmsing, Charles H. Appointed Jan. 27, Ordained June 10, 1933. Retired Bishop of Kansas City-St. Joseph.
Hunthausen, Raymond G., Appointed July 8, Ordained June 1, 1946. Bishop of Helena.
Reh, Francis F., Appointed June 4, Ordained Dec. 8, 1935. Bishop of Charleston.
Strecker, Ignatius J., Appointed April 7, Ordained Dec. 19, 1942. Bishop of Springfield-Cape Girardeau.
Zayek, Francis M., Appointed May 30, Ordained March 17, 1946. Titular Bishop of Callinicum.

1963

Bishops

Aponte Martinez, Luis, Appointed Nov. 18, Ordained April 10, 1950. Coadjutor Bishop of Ponce.
D'Antonio, Nicholas, Appointed Dec. 31, Ordained June 7, 1942. Bishop of Olancho, Honduras.
Graham, John J., Appointed Nov. 25, Ordained Feb. 26, 1938. Retired Auxiliary
Bishop of Philadelphia.
Speltz, George H., Appointed Feb. 13, Ordained June 2, 1940. Auxiliary Bishop of Winona.
Ward, John J., Appointed Oct. 16, Ordained May 4, 1946. Auxiliary Bishop of Los Angeles.

1964

Archbishops

Aponte Martinez, Luis, Appointed Nov. 11, Ordained April 10, 1950. Archbishop of San Juan.

Bishops

Brzana, Stanislaus J., Appointed May 24, Ordained June 7, 1941. Auxiliary Bishop of Buffalo.
Freking, Frederick W., Appointed Dec. 30, Ordained July 31, 1938. Retired Bishop of La Crosse.
Reh, Francis F., Appointed Sept. 5, Ordained Dec. 8, 1935. Titular Bishop of Macinna & Rector of North American College Rome.
Sheehan, Daniel E., Appointed Jan. 4, Ordained May 23, 1942. Auxiliary Bishop of Omaha.
Torres, Juan Fremiot, Appointed Nov. 4, Ordained April 10, 1950. Bishop of Ponce.

1965

Archbishops

Hannan, Philip M., Appointed Sept. 29, Ordained Dec. 8, 1939. Retired Archbishop of New Orleans.

Bishops

Breitenbeck, Joseph M., Appointed Oct. 18, Ordained May 30, 1942. Auxiliary Bishop of Detroit.
Carberry, John J., Appointed Jan. 16, Ordained July 28, 1929. Bishop of Columbus.
McCarthy, Edward A., Appointed April 21, Ordained May 29, 1943. Auxiliary Bishop of Cincinnati.
Watters, Loras J., Appointed June 23, Ordained June 7, 1941. Auxiliary Bishop of Dubuque.

1966

Archbishops

Ryan, Joseph T., Appointed Feb. 7, Ordained June 3, 1939. Archbishop of Anchorage.

Bishops

Gerety, Peter L., Appointed March 4, Ordained June 29, 1939. Coadjutor Bishop of Portland (in Maine).
Herrmann, Edward J., Appointed March 4, Ordained June 12, 1947. Auxiliary Bishop of Washington.

Hogan, James J., Appointed May 23, Ordained Dec. 8, 1937. Retired Bishop of Altoona-Johnstown.
Malone, James W., Appointed Jan. 22, Ordained May 26, 1945. Apostolic Administrator of Youngstown.
Michaels, James, *s.s.c.*, Appointed Feb. 15, Ordained Dec. 21, 1951. Resigned Auxiliary Bishop of Wheeling-Charleston.
McDowell, John B., Appointed July 18, Ordained Nov. 4, 1945. Auxiliary Bishop of Pittsburgh.
O'Keefe, Gerald F., Appointed Oct. 20, Ordained Jan. 29, 1944. Bishop of Davenport.
Schad, James L., Appointed Oct. 18, Ordained April 10, 1943. Auxiliary Bishop of Camden.
Speltz, George H., Appointed April 4, Ordained June 2, 1940. Coadjutor Bishop of St. Cloud.
Tschoepe, Thomas, Appointed Jan. 12, Ordained May 30, 1943. Retired Bishop of Dallas.

1967

Archbishops

McDonough, Thomas J., Appointed March 1, Ordained May 26, 1938. Retired Archbishop of Louisville.

Bishops

Broderick, Edwin B., Appointed March 4, Ordained May 30, 1942. Auxiliary Bishop of New York.
Clinch, Harry A., Appointed Dec. 14, Ordained June 6, 1936. Retired Bishop of Monterey.
Frey, Gerard L., Appointed May 31, Ordained April 2, 1938. Bishop of Savannah.
Gerety, Peter L., Appointed Feb. 18, Ordained June 29, 1939. Apostolic Administrator of Portland (in Maine).
Grady, Thomas J., Appointed June 21, Ordained April 23, 1938. Auxiliary Bishop of Chicago.
Ham, J. Richard *m.m.*, Appointed Nov. 28, Ordained June 12, 1948. Auxiliary Bishop of Guatemala.
Hickey, James A., Appointed April 14, Ordained June 15, 1946. Auxiliary Bishop of Saginaw.
Hurley, Mark J., Appointed Oct. 12, Ordained Sept. 23, 1944. Auxiliary Bishop of San Francisco.
McManus, William E., Appointed June 21, Ordained April 15, 1939. Auxiliary Bishop of Chicago.
Quinn, John R., Appointed Oct. 21, Ordained July 19, 1953. Auxiliary Bishop of San Diego.
Reiss, John C., Appointed Oct. 21, Ordained May 31, 1947. Auxiliary Bishop of Trenton.
Scanlon, John J., Appointed Nov. 10, Ordained June 22, 1930. Apostolic Administrator of Honolulu.
Schuster, Eldon B., Appointed Dec. 2; Ordained May 27, 1937. Retired Bishop of Great Falls.
Whelan, Robert L., *s.j.*, Appointed Dec. 6, Ordained June 17, 1944. Coadjutor Bishop of Fairbanks.

1968

Archbishop

Carberry, John J., Appointed Feb. 17, Ordained July 28, 1929. Retired Archbishop of St. Louis.

Bishops

Abramowicz, Alfred L., Appointed May 8, Ordained May 1, 1943. Auxiliary Bishop of Chicago.
Borders, William D., Appointed May 8, Ordained May 18, 1940. Bishop of Arlington.
Brzana, Stanislaus J., Appointed Oct. 22, Ordained June 7, 1941. Bishop of Ogdensburg.
Cronin, Daniel A., Appointed June 10, Ordained Dec. 20, 1952. Auxiliary Bishop of Boston.
Dudick, Michael J., Appointed Aug. 21, Ordained Nov. 13, 1945. Bishop of Passaic.
Fitzpatrick, John J., Appointed June 24, Ordained Dec 13, 1942. Auxiliary Bishop of Miami.
Gossman, F. Joseph, Appointed July 15, Ordained Dec. 17, 1955. Auxiliary Bishop of Baltimore.
Gumbleton, Thomas J., Appointed March 8, Ordained June 2, 1956. Auxiliary Bishop of Detroit.
Harrington, Timothy J., Appointed April 2, Ordained Jan. 19, 1946. Auxiliary Bishop of Worcester.
Hickey, Dennis W., Appointed Jan. 10, Ordained June 7, 1941. Retired Auxiliary Bishop of Rochester.
Malone, James W., Succeeded to See May 2. Bishop of Youngstown.
McKinney, Joseph C., Appointed July 24, Ordained Dec. 20, 1953. Auxiliary Bishop of Grand Rapids.
McLaughlin, Bernard J., Appointed Dec. 28, Ordained Dec. 21, 1935. Retired Auxiliary Bishop of Buffalo.
O'Neill, Arthur J., Appointed Aug. 19, Ordained March 27, 1943. Bishop of Rockford.
Reh, Francis F., Appointed Dec. 18, Ordained Dec. 8, 1935. Retired Bishop of Saginaw.
Salatka, Charles A., Appointed Jan. 10, Ordained Feb. 24, 1945. Bishop of Marquette.
Scanlon, John J., Succeeded to See March 6; Retired Bishop of Honolulu.
Schoenherr, Walter J., Appointed March 8; Ordained Oct. 27, 1945. Auxiliary Bishop of Detroit.
Shea, Robert L., *s.j.*, Succeeded to See Nov. 30; Retired Bishop of Fairbanks.
Speltz, George H., Succeeded to See Jan. 31; Retired Bishop of St. Cloud.
Wycislo, Aloysius J., Appointed March 8; Ordained April 7, 1934. Retired Bishop of Green Bay.

1969

Cardinals

Carberry, John Cardinal, Created April 28; Retired Archbishop of St. Louis.

Archbishops

Sheehan, Daniel E., Appointed June 11, Ordained May 23, 1942. Archbishop of Omaha.
Strecker, Ignatius J., Appointed Sept. 10, Ordained Dec 19, 1942. Archbishop of Kansas City in Kansas.

Bishops

Breitenbeck, Joseph, Appointed Oct. 15, Ordained May 30, 1942. Retired Bishop of Grand Rapids.
Broderick, Edwin B., Appointed March 19, Ordained May 30, 1942. Former Bishop of Albany.
Gerety, Peter L., Succeeded to See Sept. 15. Bishop of Portland (in Maine).
Hogan, Joseph L., Appointed Oct. 15, Ordained June 6, 1942. Retired Bishop of Rochester.
Hurley, Mark J., Appointed Nov. 4, Ordained Sept. 23, 1944. Resigned Bishop of Santa Rosa.
Lynch, George E., Appointed Oct. 20, Ordained May 29, 1943. Retired Auxiliary Bishop of Raleigh.
McAuliffe, Michael F., Appointed July 2, Ordained May 31, 1945. Bishop of Jefferson City.
McCarthy, Edward A., Appointed Aug. 25, Ordained May 29, 1943. Bishop of Phoenix.
Neylon, Martin J., *s.j.*, Appointed Oct. 2, Ordained June 18, 1950. Titular Bishop of Libertina.
Power, Cornelius M., Appointed Feb. 5, Ordained June 3, 1939. Bishop of Yakima.
Tawil, Joseph E., Appointed Oct. 29, Ordained July 20, 1936. Apostolic Exarch of Newton.
Tshoepe, Thomas, Appointed Aug. 27, Ordained May 30, 1943. Retired Bishop of Dallas.
Watters, Loras J., Appointed Jan. 8, Ordained June 7, 1941. Retired Bishop of Winona.

1970

Bishops

Ahern, Patrick V., Appointed Feb. 3, Ordained Jan. 27, 1945. Auxiliary Bishop of New York.
Baum, William, Appointed Feb. 18, Ordained May 12, 1951. Bishop of Springfield-Cape Girardeau.
Bosco, Anthony G., Appointed May 14, Ordained June 7, 1952. Auxiliary Bishop of Pittsburgh.
Cronin, Daniel A., Appointed Oct. 30, Ordained Dec. 20, 1952. Bishop of Fall River.
Flores, Patrick F., Appointed March 18, Ordained May 26, 1956. Auxiliary Bishop of San Antonio.
Head, Edward D., Appointed Jan. 27, Ordained Jan. 27, 1945. Auxiliary Bishop of New York.
Hurley, Francis T., Appointed Feb. 4, Ordained June 16, 1951. Auxiliary Bishop of Juneau.
Lohmuller, Martin N., Appointed Feb. 11, Ordained June 3, 1944. Auxiliary Bishop of Philadelphia.
McFarland, Norman F., Appointed June 5, Ordained June 15, 1946. Auxiliary Bishop of San Francisco.
McGann, John R., Appointed Nov. 12, Ordained June 3, 1950. Auxiliary Bishop of Rockville Centre.
O'Leary, Edward C., Appointed Nov. 17, Ordained June 15, 1946. Auxiliary Bishop of Portland (in Maine).
Povish, Kenneth J., Appointed July 28, Ordained June 3, 1950. Bishop of Crookston.
Schmitt, Mark F., Appointed May 5, Ordained May 22, 1948. Auxiliary Bishop of Green Bay.
Sullivan, Walter F., Appointed Oct. 20, Ordained May 9, 1953. Auxiliary Bishop of Richmond.
Welsh, Thomas J. Appointed Feb. 18, Ordained May 30, 1946. Auxiliary Bishop of Philadelphia.

1971

Bishops

Arzube, Juan, Appointed Feb. 9, Ordained May 5, 1954. Auxiliary Bishop of Los Angeles.
Begley, Michael J., Appointed Nov. 30, Ordained May 26, 1934. Retired Bishop of Charlotte.
Boudreaux, Warren L., Appointed June 4, Ordained May 30, 1942. Bishop of Beaumont.
Connolly, Thomas J., Appointed May 4, Ordained April 8, 1947. Bishop of Baker.
Crowley, Joseph R., Appointed June 16, Ordained May 1, 1953. Retired Auxiliary Bishop of Fort Wayne-South Bend.
Donovan, Paul V., Appointed June 15, Ordained May 20, 1950. Bishop of Kalamazoo.
Fitzpatrick, John J., Appointed April 21, Ordained Dec. 13, 1942. Retired Bishop of Brownsville.
Gelineau, Louis E., Appointed Dec 6, Ordained June 5, 1954. Bishop of Providence.
Gracida, Rene H., Appointed Dec. 6, Ordained May 23, 1959. Auxiliary Bishop of Miami.
Harrison, Frank J., Appointed March 1, Ordained June 4, 1937. Auxiliary Bishop of Syracuse.
Hurley, Francis T., Appointed July 20, Ordained June 16, 1951. Bishop of Juneau.
Koester, Charles R., Appointed Jan. 5, Ordained Dec. 20, 1941. Retired Auxiliary Bishop of St. Louis.
Losten, Basil, Appointed March 15, Ordained June 10, 1957. Auxiliary Bishop of Philadelphia Ukrainian.
Lucker, Raymond A., Appointed July 12, Ordained June 7, 1952. Auxiliary Bishop of St. Paul-Minneapolis.
Maguire, Joseph F., Appointed Dec. 1, Ordained June 29, 1945. Auxiliary Bishop of Boston.
Neylon, Martin J., *s.j.*, Appointed Sept. 20, Ordained June 18, 1950. Vicar Apostolic of The Carolines-Marshalls.
O'Rourke, Edward W., Appointed May 24, Ordained May 28, 1944. Retired Bishop of Peoria.
Riley, Lawrence J., Appointed Dec. 7, Ordained Sept. 21, 1940. Retired Auxiliary Bishop of Boston.
Roach, John R., Appointed July 12, Ordained June 8, 1946. Auxiliary Bishop of St. Paul-Minneapolis.
Szoka, Edmund, Appointed June 15, Ordained June 5, 1954. Bishop of Gaylord.
Zayek, Francis M., Appointed Nov. 11, Ordained March 17, 1946. Eparch of St. Maron.

1972

Archbishops

Quinn, John R., Appointed Dec. 13; Ordained July 19, 1953. Archbishop of Oklahoma City.

Bishops

Frey, Gerard L., Appointed Nov. 7, Ordained April 2, 1938. Retired Bishop of Lafayette.
Howze, Joseph L., Appointed Nov. 8, Ordained May 7, 1959. Auxiliary Bishop of Jackson.
Mahoney, James P., Appointed July 25, Ordained May 19, 1951. Auxiliary Bishop of New York.
McDonald, Andrew J., Appointed July 4, Ordained May 8, 1948. Bishop of Little Rock.
Snyder, John J., Appointed Dec. 19, Ordained June 9, 1951. Auxiliary Bishop of Brooklyn.
Sullivan, James S., Appointed July 25, Ordained June 4, 1955. Auxiliary Bishop of Lansing.
Sullivan, John J., Appointed July 25, Ordained Sept. 23, 1944. Bishop of Grand Island.

1973

Cardinals

Aponte Martinez, Luis Cardinal, Created March 5. Archbishop of San Juan.

Archbishops

Baum, William, Appointed May 9, Ordained May 12, 1951. Archbishop of Washington.

Bishops

Head, Edward D., Appointed Jan. 17, Ordained Jan. 27, 1945. Bishop of Buffalo.
Herrmann, Edward J., Appointed June 26, Ordained June 12, 1947. Retired Bishop and Apostolic Administrator of Columbus.
Imesch, Joseph L., Appointed Feb. 8, Ordained Dec. 16, 1956. Auxiliary Bishop of Detroit.
Krawczak, Arthur H., Appointed Feb. 8, Ordained May 18, 1940. Retired Auxiliary Bishop of Detroit.
Law, Bernard, Appointed Oct. 22, Ordained May 21, 1961. Bishop of Springfield-Cape Girardeau.
Lessard, Raymond W., Appointed March 5, Ordained Dec. 16, 1956. Bishop of Savannah.
Mestice, Anthony F., Appointed March 5, Ordained June 4, 1949. Auxiliary Bishop of New York.
Sullivan, Walter F., Appointed April 30, Ordained May 9, 1953. Apostolic Administrator of Richmond.

1974

Archbishops

Borders, William D., Appointed March 25; Ordained May 18, 1940. Retired Archbishop of Baltimore.
Gerety, Peter Leo, Appointed April 2, Ordained June 29, 1939. Retired Archbishop of Newark.
Power, Cornelius M., Appointed Jan. 22; Ordained June 3, 1939. Retired Archbishop of Portland in Oregon.
Sanchez, Robert F., Appointed June 1; Ordained Dec. 20, 1959. Archbishop of Santa Fe.

Bishops

Angell, Kenneth A., Appointed Aug. 9, Ordained May 26, 1956. Auxiliary Bishop of Providence.
Chavez, Gilbert E., Appointed April 19, Ordained March 19, 1960. Auxiliary Bishop of San Diego.
Cummins, John S., Appointed Feb. 26, Ordained Jan. 24, 1953. Auxiliary Bishop of Sacramento.
Daily, Thomas V., Appointed Dec. 31, Ordained Jan. 10, 1952. Auxiliary Bishop of Boston.
D'Arcy, John M., Appointed Dec. 31, Ordained Feb. 2, 1957. Auxiliary Bishop of Boston.
Gendron, Odore J., Appointed Dec. 12, Ordained May 31, 1947. Retired Bishop of Manchester.
Grady, Thomas J., Appointed Nov. 9, Ordained April 23, 1938. Retired Bishop of Arlington.
Hanifen, Richard C., Appointed July 6, 1974. Ordained June 6, 1959. Auxiliary Bishop of Denver.
Hickey, James A., Appointed June 4, Ordained June 15, 1946. Bishop of Cleveland.
Hughes, William A., Appointed July 23, Ordained April 6, 1946. Auxiliary Bishop of Youngstown.
Marino, Eugene, *s.s.j.*, Appointed July 15, Ordained June 6, 1962. Auxiliary Bishop of Washington.
McFarland, Norman F., Appointed Dec. 6, Ordained June 15, 1946. Apostolic Administrator of Reno-Las Vegas.
O'Leary, Edward C., Appointed Dec. 4, Ordained June 15, 1946. Retired Bishop of Portland (in Maine).
Ottenweller, Albert H., Appointed April 17, Ordained June 19, 1943. Auxiliary Bishop of Toledo.
Pilarczyk, Daniel E., Appointed Nov. 12, Ordained Dec. 20, 1959. Auxiliary Bishop of Cincinnati.
Rodriguez, Miguel, *c.ss.r.*, Appointed Jan. 21, Ordained June 22, 1958. Retired Bishop of Arecibo.
Sullivan, Walter F., Succeeded to See June 6. Bishop of Richmond.
Walsh, Nicolas E., Appointed Sept. 5, Ordained June 6, 1942. Bishop of Yakima.
Welsh, Thomas J., Appointed June 4. Bishop of Arlington.

1975

Archbishops

Hunthausen, Raymond G., Appointed Feb. 25, Ordained June 1, 1946. Archbishop of Seattle.
Roach, John R., Appointed May 21, Ordained June 8, 1946. Archbishop of St. Paul-Minneapolis.
Ryan, Joseph T., Appointed Oct. 24, Ordained June 3, 1939. Coadjutor Archbishop to the Military Vicar.

Bishops

Fitzsimons, George K., Appointed May 27, Ordained March 18, 1961. Auxiliary Bishop of Kansas City-St. Joseph.
Gaughan, Norbert F., Appointed April 2, Ordained Nov. 4, 1945. Auxiliary Bishop of Greensburg.
Gracida, Rene H., Appointed Oct. 1, Ordained May 23, 1959. Bishop of Pensacola-Tallahassee.
Gossman, F. Joseph, Appointed April 8, Ordained Dec. 17, 1955. Bishop of Raleigh.
Lucker, Raymond A., Appointed Dec. 23, Ordained June 7, 1952. Bishop of New Ulm.
Mahony, Roger M., Appointed Jan. 7, Ordained May 1, 1962. Auxiliary Bishop of Fresno.
Niedergeses, James D., Appointed April 8, Ordained May 20, 1944. Bishop of Nashville.
Povish, Kenneth J., Appointed Oct. 21, Ordained June 3, 1950. Bishop of Lansing.
Reilly, Daniel P., Appointed June 17, Ordained May 30, 1953. Bishop of Norwich.
Surinach Carreras, Ricardo, Appointed May 26, Ordained April 13, 1957. Auxiliary Bishop of Ponce.

1976

Cardinals

Baum, William Cardinal, Created May 24. Prefect of Sacred Congregation for Catholic Education, Vatican.

Archbishops

Hurley, Francis T., Appointed May 4, Ordained June 16, 1951. Archbishop of Anchorage.
McCarthy, Edward A., Appointed Sept. 17, Ordained May 29, 1943. Coadjutor Archbishop of Miami.

Bishops

Balke, Victor, Appointed July 7, Ordained May 24, 1958. Bishop of Crookston.
Broderick, Edwin B., Appointed June 3. Exec. Dir. Catholic Relief Services.
Casiano-Vargas, Ulises, Appointed March 4, Ordained May 30, 1967. Bishop of Mayaguez.
Curtiss, Elden F., Appointed March 4, Ordained May 24, 1958. Bishop of Helena.
Dudley, Paul V., Appointed Nov. 16, Ordained June 2, 1951. Auxiliary Bishop of St. Paul-Minneapolis.
Forst, Marion F., Appointed Oct. 16, Ordained June 10, 1934. Retired Auxiliary Bishop of Kansas City in Kansas.
Francis, Joseph, *s.v.d.*, Appointed May 3, Ordained Oct 7, 1950. Auxiliary Bishop of Newark.
Garner, Robert F., Appointed May 3, Ordained June 15, 1946. Auxiliary Bishop of Newark.
Gerber, Eugene J., Appointed Oct. 16, Ordained May 19, 1959. Bishop of Dodge City.
Harrison, Frank J., Appointed Nov. 16, Ordained June 4, 1937. Retired Bishop of Syracuse.
Hart, Daniel A., Appointed Aug. 30, Ordained Feb. 2, 1953. Auxiliary Bishop of Boston.
Hart, Joseph H., Appointed July 1, Ordained May 1, 1956. Bishop of Cheyenne.
Hughes, Edward T., Appointed June 14, Ordained May 31, 1947. Auxiliary Bishop of Philadelphia.
Kinney, John F., Appointed Nov. 16, Ordained Feb. 2, 1963. Auxiliary Bishop of St. Paul-Minneapolis.
Losten, Basil H., Appointed June 8, Ordained June 10, 1957. Apostolic Administrator Philadelphia Ukrainian.
Maguire, Joseph F., Appointed April 3, Ordained June 29, 1945. Coadjutor Bishop of Springfield.
Marconi, Dominic A., Appointed May 3, Ordained May 30, 1953. Auxiliary Bishop of Newark.
McFarland, Norman F., Appointed Feb. 10, Ordained June 15, 1946. Bishop of Reno-Las Vegas.
McGann, John R., Appointed May 3, Ordained June 3, 1950. Bishop of Rockville Centre.
McManus, William E., Appointed Aug. 31, Ordained April 15, 1939. Bishop of Fort Wayne-South Bend.
Moreno, Manuel D., Appointed Dec. 20, Ordained April 25, 1961. Auxiliary Bishop of Los Angeles.
Murphy, Michael J., Appointed April 20, Ordained Feb. 28, 1942. Auxiliary Bishop of Cleveland.
Murphy, P. Francis, Appointed Jan. 27, Ordained Dec. 20, 1958. Auxiliary Bishop of Baltimore.
Pena, Raymundo, Appointed Oct. 16, Ordained May 25, 1957. Auxiliary Bishop of San Antonio.
Sheldon, Gilbert I., Appointed April 20, Ordained Feb. 28, 1953. Auxiliary Bishop of Cleveland.
Stafford, J. Francis, Appointed Jan. 27, Ordained Dec. 15, 1957. Auxiliary Bishop of Baltimore.
Tawil, Joseph, Appointed July 15, Ordained July 20, 1936. Eparch Emeritus of Newton.
Timlin, James C., Appointed Aug. 3, Ordained July 16, 1951. Auxiliary Bishop of Scranton.
Walsh, Nicolas, Appointed Aug. 10, Ordained June 6, 1942. Retired Auxiliary Bishop of Seattle.

1977

Archbishops

McCarthy, Edward A., Succeeded to See July 26. Archbishop of Miami.
Quinn, John R., Appointed Feb. 22, Ordained July 19, 1953. Archbishop of San Francisco.
Salatka, Charles A., Appointed Sept. 27, Ordained Feb. 24, 1945. Archbishop of Oklahoma City.
Weakland, Rembert, *o.s.b.*, Appointed Sept. 20, Ordained June 24, 1951.
Archbishop of Milwaukee.

Bishops

Boudreaux, Warren L., Appointed June 5, Ordained May 30, 1942. Bishop of Houma-Thibodaux.
Cummins, John S., Appointed May 3, Ordained Jan. 24, 1953. Bishop of Oakland.
Daly, James J., Appointed Feb. 28; Ordained May 22, 1948. Auxiliary Bishop of Rockville Centre.
D'Antonio, Nicholas, *o.f.m.*, Appointed Aug. 22. Retired Vicar for Spanish-speaking, New Orleans.
Ferrario, Joseph A., Appointed Nov. 8, Ordained May 19, 1951. Auxiliary Bishop of Honolulu.
Garmendia, Francis, Appointed May 24, Ordained June 28, 1947. Auxiliary Bishop of New York.
Howze, Joseph L., Appointed March 1, Ordained May 7, 1959. Bishop of Biloxi.
Hubbard, Howard J., Appointed Feb. 1, Ordained Dec. 18, 1963. Bishop of Albany.
Kelly, Thomas C., *o.p.*, Appointed July 12, Ordained June 5, 1958. Auxiliary Bishop of Washington.
Kucera, Daniel W., *o.s.b.*, Appointed June 6, Ordained May 26, 1949. Auxiliary Bishop of Joliet.
Losten, Basil H., Appointed Sept. 20, Ordained June 10, 1957. Bishop of Stamford.
Maguire, Joseph F., Succeeded to See Nov. 4. Bishop of Springfield.
McCarrick, Theodore E., Appointed May 24, Ordained May 31, 1958. Auxiliary Bishop of New York.
Mulvee, Robert E., Appointed Feb. 15, Ordained June 30, 1957. Auxiliary Bishop of Manchester.
Ottenweller, Albert H., Appointed Oct. 11, Ordained June 19, 1943. Retired Bishop of Steubenville.
Paul, John J., Appointed May 17, Ordained Jan. 24, 1943. Titular Bishop of Lambese.
Rodimer, Frank J., Appointed Dec. 13, Ordained May 19, 1951. Bishop of Paterson.
Skylstad, William, Appointed Feb. 22, Ordained May 21, 1960. Bishop of Yakima.
Steiner, Kenneth, Appointed Dec. 6, Ordained May 19, 1962. Auxiliary Bishop of Portland in Oregon.
Sullivan, John J., Appointed June 27, Ordained Sept. 23, 1944. Bishop of Kansas City-St. Joseph.
Vaughan, Austin B., Appointed May 24, Ordained Dec. 8, 1956. Auxiliary Bishop of New York.
Wirz, George O., Appointed Dec. 20, Ordained May 31, 1952. Auxiliary Bishop of Madison.

1978

Bishops

Beltran, Eusebius J., Appointed Feb. 28, Ordained May 14, 1960. Bishop of Tulsa.
Costello, Thomas J., Appointed Jan. 10, Ordained June 5, 1954. Auxiliary Bishop of Syracuse.
Dudley, Paul V., Appointed Sept. 26, Ordained June 2, 1951. Bishop of Sioux Falls.
DuMaine, R. Pierre, Appointed April 28, Ordained June 5, 1957. Auxiliary Bishop of San Francisco.
Flores, Patrick F., Appointed April 4, Ordained May 26, 1956. Bishop of El Paso.
Hoffman, James R., Appointed April 18, Ordained July 28, 1957. Auxiliary Bishop of Toledo.
McNamara, Lawrence J., Appointed Jan. 10, Ordained May 30, 1953. Bishop of Grand Island.
Morneau, Robert F., Appointed Dec. 19, Ordained May 28, 1966. Auxiliary Bishop of Green Bay.
Murphy, Michael J., Appointed Nov. 28, Ordained Feb. 28, 1942. Coadjutor Bishop of Erie.
Murphy, Thomas J., Appointed July 5, Ordained April 12, 1958. Bishop of Great Falls.
Quinn, Francis A., Appointed April 28, Ordained June 15, 1946. Auxiliary Bishop of San Francisco.
Rosazza, Peter A., Appointed Feb. 28, Ordained June 29, 1961. Auxiliary Bishop of Hartford.
Schmitt, Mark F., Appointed March 21, Ordained May 22, 1948. Bishop of Marquette.
Straling, Phillip F., Appointed July 18, Ordained March 19, 1959. Bishop of San Bernardino.
Welsh, Lawrence H., Appointed Nov. 7, Ordained May 26, 1962. Retired Bishop of Spokane.

1979

Archbishops

Flores, Patrick F., Appointed Aug. 28; Ordained May 26, 1956. Archbishop of San Antonio.

Bishops

Clark, Matthew H., Appointed May 2, Ordained Dec. 19, 1962. Bishop of Rochester.
Fiorenza, Joseph A., Appointed Sept. 4, Ordained May 29, 1954. Bishop of San Angelo.
Fliss, Raphael M., Appointed Nov. 6, Ordained May 26, 1956. Coadjutor Bishop of Superior.
Friend, William B., Appointed Aug. 31, Ordained May 7, 1959. Auxiliary Bishop of Alexandria-Shreveport.
Griffin, James A., Appointed June 30, Ordained May 28, 1960. Auxiliary Bishop of Cleveland.
Houck, William R., Appointed March 28, Ordained May 19, 1951. Auxiliary Bishop of Jackson.
Hughes, William A., Appointed April 13, Ordained April 6, 1946. Bishop of Covington.
Imesch, Joseph L., Appointed June 30, Ordained Dec. 16, 1956. Bishop of Joliet.
Keeler, William H., Appointed July 24, Ordained July 17, 1955. Auxiliary Bishop of Harrisburg.
Larkin, W. Thomas, Appointed April 24, Ordained May 15, 1947. Retired Bishop of St. Petersburg.
Madera, Joseph J., *m.sp.s.*, Appointed Dec. 18, Ordained June 15, 1957. Coadjutor Bishop of Fresno.
McCarthy, John E., Appointed Jan. 23, Ordained May 26, 1956. Auxiliary Bishop of Galveston-Houston.
Nevins, John J., Appointed Feb. 6, Ordained June 6, 1959. Auxiliary Bishop of Miami.
Neylon, Martin J., *s.j.*, Appointed May 3, Ordained June 18, 1950. Bishop of The Carolines-Marshalls.
O'Connor, John J., Appointed April 24, Ordained Dec. 15, 1945. Auxiliary Bishop of Military Vicariate.
Pilla, Anthony M., Appointed June 30, Ordained May 23, 1959. Auxiliary Bishop of Cleveland.
Quinn, Francis A., Appointed Dec. 18, Ordained June 15, 1946. Bishop of Sacramento.
Rivera, Enrique Hernandez, Appointed June 11, Ordained June 8, 1968. Auxiliary Bishop of San Juan.
Rivera, Hector M., Appointed June 11, Ordained June 12, 1966. Auxiliary Bishop of San Juan.
Roman, Agustin A., Appointed Feb. 6, Ordained July 5, 1959. Auxiliary Bishop of Miami.
Schlarman, Stanley G., Appointed March 13, Ordained July 13, 1958. Auxiliary Bishop of Belleville.
Sklba, Richard J., Appointed Nov. 6, Ordained Dec. 20, 1959. Auxiliary Bishop of Milwaukee.

Snyder, John J., Appointed Oct. 2, Ordained June 9, 1951. Bishop of St. Augustine.

1980

Archbishops

Hickey, James A., Appointed June 17; Ordained June 15, 1946. Archbishop of Washington.
Lipscomb, Oscar H., Appointed July 29; Ordained July 15, 1956. Archbishop of Mobile.
Sulyk, Stephen, Appointed Dec. 29; Archbishop of Philadelphia Ukrainian.

Bishops

Bevilacqua, Anthony, Appointed Oct. 7, Ordained June 11, 1949. Auxiliary Bishop of Brooklyn.
Bullock, William H., Appointed June 3, Ordained June 7, 1952. Auxiliary Bishop of St. Paul-Minneapolis.
Chedid, John, Appointed Oct. 28, Ordained Dec. 21, 1951. Auxiliary Bishop of St. Maron.
Franzetta, Benedict C., Appointed July 29, Ordained April 29, 1950. Auxiliary Bishop of Youngstown.
Ham, J. Richard, *m.m.*, Appointed Oct. 7, Ordained June 12, 1948. Retired Auxiliary Bishop of St. Paul-Minneapolis.
Hoffman, James R., Appointed Dec. 16, Ordained July 28, 1957. Bishop of Toledo.
Kucera, Daniel W., *o.s.b.*, Appointed March 11, Ordained May 26, 1949. Bishop of Salina.
Madera, Joseph J., *m.sp.s.*, Succeeded to See July 1. Bishop of Fresno.
Mahony, Roger M., Appointed Feb. 26, Ordained May 1, 1962. Bishop of Stockton.
Matthiesen, Leroy T., Appointed March 25, Ordained March 10, 1946. Bishop of Amarillo.
O'Neil, Leo Edward, Appointed June 3, Ordained June 4, 1955. Auxiliary Bishop of Springfield.
Pena, Raymundo J., Appointed April 29, Ordained May 25, 1957. Bishop of El Paso.
Pilla, Anthony M., Appointed Nov. 18, Ordained May 23, 1959. Bishop of Cleveland.
Reiss, John C., Appointed March 4, Ordained May 31, 1947. Bishop of Trenton.
Speyrer, Jude, Appointed Jan. 29, Ordained July 25, 1953. Bishop of Lake Charles.
Sullivan, Joseph M., Appointed Oct. 7, Ordained June 2, 1956. Auxiliary Bishop of Brooklyn.
Tafoya, Arthur N., Appointed July 1, Ordained May 12, 1962. Bishop of Pueblo.
Untener, Kenneth E., Appointed Oct. 4, Ordained June 1, 1963. Bishop of Saginaw.
Valero, Rene, Appointed Oct. 7, Ordained June 2, 1956. Auxiliary Bishop of Brooklyn.
Weigand, William K., Appointed Sept. 3, Ordained May 25, 1963. Bishop of Salt Lake City.

1981

Archbishops

Kelly, Thomas C., *o.p.*, Appointed Dec. 29, Ordained June 5, 1958. Archbishop of Louisville.
Marcinkus, Paul C., Appointed Sept. 26, Ordained May 3,1947. Titular Archbishop of Orta, Vatican City State.
Szoka, Edmund C., Appointed March 28, Ordained June 5, 1954. Emeritus Archbishop of Detroit.

Bishops

Delaney, Joseph P., Appointed July 10, Ordained Dec. 18, 1960. Bishop of Fort Worth.
DeSimone, Louis A., Appointed June 27, Ordained May 10, 1952. Auxiliary Bishop of Philadelphia.
Dumaine, Pierre, Appointed Jan. 27, Ordained June 5, 1957. Bishop of San Jose.
Grahmann, Charles V., Appointed June 30, Ordained March 17, 1956. Auxiliary Bishop of San Antonio.
Hughes, Alfred C., Appointed July 21, Ordained Dec. 15, 1957. Auxiliary Bishop of Boston.
Lotocky, Innocent, *o.s.b.m.*, Appointed Jan. 29, Ordained Nov. 24, 1940. Bishop of St. Nicholas Chicago.
McCarrick, Theodore E., Appointed Nov. 24. Bishop of Metuchen.
Milone, Anthony M., Appointed Nov. 10, Ordained Dec. 15, 1957. Auxiliary Bishop of Omaha.
Moskal, Robert M., Appointed Aug. 3, Ordained March 25, 1963. Auxiliary Bishop of Philadelphia Ukrainian.
O'Brien, Thomas J., Appointed Nov. 24. Ordained May 7, 1961. Bishop of Phoenix.
Ramirez, Ricardo, *c.s.b.*, Appointed Oct. 27, Ordained Dec. 10, 1966. Auxiliary Bishop of San Antonio.
Rivera, Enrique Hernandez, Appointed Feb. 13, Ordained June 8, 1968. Bishop of Caguas.
Rose, Robert J., Appointed Oct. 13, Ordained Dec. 21, 1955. Bishop of Gaylord.
Ryan, Daniel L., Appointed Aug. 14, Ordained May 3, 1956. Auxiliary Bishop of Joliet.
Santana, Hermin Negron, Appointed June 30, Ordained May 30, 1969. Auxiliary Bishop of San Juan.
Schulte, Francis B., Appointed June 27, Ordained May 10, 1952. Auxiliary Bishop of Philadelphia.
Setian, Nerses Mikael, Appointed July 3, Ordained April 13, 1941. Bishop of Armenian Catholic Exarchate of U.S.A. and Canada.
Symons, J. Keith, Appointed Jan. 16, Ordained May 18, 1958. Auxiliary Bishop of St. Petersburg.
Walsh, Daniel F., Appointed June 30, Ordained March 30, 1963. Auxiliary Bishop of San Francisco.

1982

Archbishops

Pilarczyk, Daniel E., Appointed Nov 2, Ordained Dec. 20, 1959. Archbishop of Cincinnati.
Zayek, Francis M., Appointed Dec. 22, Ordained March 17, 1946. Archbishop of St. Maron, Brooklyn.

Bishops

Anderson, Moses B., *s.s.e.*, Appointed Dec. 3, Ordained May 30, 1958. Auxiliary Bishop of Detroit.
Cooney, Patrick, R., Appointed Dec. 7, Ordained Dec. 20, 1959. Auxiliary Bishop of Detroit.
Ferrario, Joseph A., Appointed May 13, Ordained May 13, 1951. Bishop of Honolulu.
Friend, William B., Appointed Nov. 23. Bishop of Alexandria-Shreveport.
Gerber, Eugene J., Appointed Nov. 23, Ordained May 19, 1959. Bishop of Wichita.
Grahmann, Charles V., Appointed April 14, Ordained March 17, 1956. Bishop of Victoria.
Kinney, John F., Appointed June 28, Ordained Feb. 2, 1963. Bishop of Bismarck.
Kmiec, Edward V., Appointed Aug. 26, Ordained Dec. 20, 1961. Auxiliary Bishop of Trenton.
McRaith, John J., Appointed Oct. 23, Ordained Feb. 21, 1960. Bishop of Owensboro.
Melczek, Dale J., Appointed Dec. 3, Ordained June 6, 1964. Auxiliary Bishop of Detroit.
Moreno, Manuel D., Appointed Jan. 12, Ordained April 25, 1961. Bishop of Tucson.
Murphy, Michael J., Succeeded to See July 16. Bishop of Erie.
O'Keefe, Joseph T., Appointed July 3, Ordained April 17, 1948. Auxiliary Bishop of New York.
Pevec, Edward A., Appointed April 13, Ordained April 29, 1950. Auxiliary Bishop of Cleveland.
Puscas, Louis, Appointed Dec. 4, Ordained May 14, 1942. Eparch of Romanian Diocese of Canton.
Ramirez, Ricardo, *c.s.b.*, Appointed Aug. 31, Ordained Dec. 10, 1966. Bishop of Las Cruces.
Stafford, J. Francis, Appointed Nov. 16, Ordained Dec. 15, 1957. Bishop of Memphis.

1983

Archbishops

Kucera, Daniel, Appointed Dec. 20. Archbishop of Dubuque.

Bishops

Apuron, Anthony, *o.f.m.cap.*, Appointed Dec. 8. Auxiliary Bishop of Agana.
Arias, David, *o.a.r.*, Appointed Jan. 25. Auxiliary Bishop of Newark.
Bevilacqua, Anthony, Appointed Oct. 7. Bishop of Pittsburgh.
Brom, Robert, Appointed March 25. Bishop of Duluth.
Carlson, Robert, Appointed Nov. 22. Auxiliary Bishop of St. Paul-Minneapolis.
Dimino, Joseph, Appointed March 29. Auxiliary Bishop of Military Services.
Gracida, Rene, Appointed May 19. Bishop of Corpus Christi.
Gregory, Wilton, Appointed Oct. 31. Auxiliary Bishop of Chicago.
Griffin, James, Appointed Feb. 7. Bishop of Columbus.
Hanifen, Richard, Appointed Nov. 10. Bishop of Colorado Springs.
Harrington, Timothy, Appointed Sept. 6. Bishop of Worcester.
Keating, John R., Appointed June 7. Bishop of Arlington.
Keeler, William, Appointed Nov. 10. Bishop of Harrisburg.
Levada, William, Appointed March 29. Auxiliary Bishop of Los Angeles.
Lyne, Timothy, Appointed Oct. 31. Auxiliary Bishop of Chicago.
Maida, Adam, Appointed Nov. 8. Bishop of Green Bay.
Montrose, Donald, Appointed March 25. Auxiliary Bishop of Los Angeles.
Moskal, Robert, Appointed Dec. 5. Bishop of St. Josaphat in Parma.
O'Connor, John, Appointed May 10. Bishop of Scranton.
O'Donnell, Edward, Appointed Dec. 6. Auxiliary Bishop of St. Louis.
Pataki, Andrew, Appointed May 30. Auxiliary Bishop of Passaic.
Paul, John J., Appointed Oct. 18. Bishop of LaCrosse.
Popp, Bernard, Appointed June 7. Auxiliary Bishop of San Antonio.
Quinn, A. James, Appointed Oct. 14. Auxiliary Bishop of Cleveland.
Rodriguez, Placido, *c.m.f.*, Appointed Oct. 31. Auxiliary Bishop of Chicago.
Roque, Francis, Appointed March 29. Auxiliary Bishop of Military Services.
Ryan, Daniel, Appointed Nov. 22. Bishop of Springfield in Illinois.
Schlarmann, Stanley, Appointed March 1. Bishop of Dodge City.
Sheehan, Michael, Appointed March 29. Bishop of Lubbock.
Soens, Lawrence, Appointed June 15. Bishop of Sioux City.
Steib, J. Terry, *s.v.d.*, Appointed Dec. 6. Auxiliary Bishop of St. Louis.
Symons, J. Keith, Appointed Sept. 29. Bishop of Pensacola-Tallahassee.
Vlazny, John, Appointed Oct. 31. Auxiliary Bishop of Chicago.
Welsh, Thomas, Appointed Feb. 8. Bishop of Allentown.

1984

Archbishops

Foley, John, Appointed April 9; Archbishop to the Pontifical Commission for Social Communication.
Law, Bernard, Appointed Jan. 24; Archbishop of Boston.
O'Connor, John J., Appointed Jan. 31; Archbishop of New York.

Bishops

Baltakis, Paul, Appointed June 1. Bishop for the Lithuanian Apostolate.
Camacho, Tomas A., Appointed Nov. 8. Bishop of Chalan Kanoa.
Daily, Thomas, Appointed July 17. Bishop of Palm Beach.
Donnelly, Robert, Appointed March 20. Auxiliary Bishop of Toledo.
Donoghue, John, Appointed Nov. 6. Bishop of Charlotte.
Fiorenza, Joseph, Appointed Dec. 18. Bishop of Galveston-Houston.
Fitzsimons, George, Appointed March 22. Bishop of Salina.
Garland, James, Appointed June 25. Auxiliary Bishop of Cincinnati.
Gaughan, Norbert, Appointed July 9. Bishop of Gary.
Higi, William, Appointed April 7. Bishop of Lafayette in Indiana.
Houck, William, Appointed April 24. Bishop of Jackson.
Kaniecki, Michael, *s.j.*, Appointed March 8. Coadjutor Bishop of Fairbanks.
Keleher, James, Appointed Oct. 23. Bishop of Belleville.
Leibrecht, John, Appointed Oct. 23. Bishop of Springfield-Cape Girardeau.
Nevins, John, Appointed July 17. Bishop of Venice.
Newman, William, Appointed July 2. Auxiliary Bishop of Baltimore.
O'Malley, Sean, *o.f.m.cap.*, Appointed May 30. Coadjutor Bishop of St. Thomas Virgin Islands.
Pataki, Andrew, Appointed June 19. Bishop of Parma.
Ricard, John, *s.s.j.*, Appointed May 29. Auxiliary Bishop of Baltimore.
Steinbock, John, Appointed May 29. Auxiliary Bishop of Orange.
Timlin, James, Appointed April 24. Bishop of Scranton.
Williams, J. Kendrick, Appointed April 15. Auxiliary Bishop of Covington.

1985

Cardinals

Law, Bernard Cardinal, Created May 25; Archbishop of Boston.
O'Connor, John Cardinal, Created May 25; Archbishop of New York.
Mahony, Roger, Appointed July 16; Archbishop of Los Angeles.

Archbishops

Ryan, Joseph T., Succeeded to See March 16, Retired Archbishop to the Military Services.

Bishops

Apuron, Anthony S., *o.f.m.cap.*, Appointed Oct. 27. Apostolic Administrator of Agana.

Banks, Robert J., Appointed June 26. Auxiliary Bishop of Boston.
Corrada, Alvaro, *s.j.*, Appointed Aug. 4. Auxiliary Bishop of Washington.
D'Arcy, John M., Appointed Feb. 26. Bishop of Fort Wayne-South Bend.
Egan, Edward M., Appointed April 1. Auxiliary Bishop of New York.
Fliss, Raphael M., Succeeded to See June 27. Bishop of Superior.
Ibrahim, Ibrahim, Appointed Sept. 14. Eparch of St. Thomas the Apostle.
Kaffer, Roger L., Appointed April 25. Auxiliary Bishop of Joliet.
Kaniecki, Michael J., *s.j.*, Succeeded to See July 28. Bishop of Fairbanks.
McCarthy, John E., Appointed Dec. 24. Bishop of Austin.
Montrose, Donald, Appointed Dec. 19. Bishop of Stockton.
Mulvee, Robert E., Appointed Feb. 16. Bishop of Wilmington.
O'Malley, Sean, *o.f.m.cap.*, Succeeded to See Oct. 16. Bishop of St. Thomas in the Virgin Islands.
Pfeifer, Michael, *o.m.i.*, Appointed July 26. Bishop of San Angelo.
Schulte, Francis B., Appointed June 4. Bishop of Wheeling-Charleston.
Sullivan, James S., Appointed April 2. Bishop of Fargo.
Trautman, Donald W., Appointed Feb. 27. Auxiliary Bishop of Buffalo.
Wuerl, Donald, Appointed Dec. 3. Auxiliary Bishop of Seattle.

1986

Archbishops

Apuron, Anthony S., *o.f.m.cap.*, Succeeded to See May 11; Archbishop of Agana.
Levada, William J., Appointed July 1; Archbishop of Portland in Oregon.
McCarrick, Theodore, Appointed June 1; Archbishop of Newark.
Stafford, J. Francis, Appointed June 3; Archbishop of Denver.

Bishops

Dorsey, Norbert, *c.p.*, Appointed Jan. 10. Auxiliary Bishop of Miami.
Elya, John A., *b.s.o.*, Appointed April 2. Auxiliary Bishop of Newton.
Favalora, John C., Appointed June 16. Bishop of Alexandria.
Flynn, Harry, Appointed April 19. Coadjutor Bishop of Lafayette.
Foley, David, Appointed May 3. Auxiliary Bishop of Richmond.
Friend, William, Appointed June 1. Bishop of Shreveport.
Gerry, Joseph, *o.s.b.*, Appointed April 21. Auxiliary Bishop of Manchester.
Hughes, Edward, Appointed Dec. 11. Bishop of Metuchen.
Kuzma, George M., Appointed Nov. 11. Auxiliary Bishop of Passaic.
Markiewicz, Alfred, Appointed July 7. Auxiliary Bishop of Rockville Centre.
McCormack, William J., Appointed Dec. 23. Auxiliary Bishop of New York.
McFarland, Norman F., Appointed Dec. 29. Bishop of Orange.
Ochoa, Armando, Appointed Dec. 29. Auxiliary Bishop of Los Angeles.
Pelotte, Donald E., *s.s.s.*, Appointed Feb. 24. Coadjutor Bishop of Gallup.
Watters, Loras J., Appointed Oct. 14. Apostolic Administrator of Winona.
Weitzel, John Q., *m.m.*, Appointed Oct. 29. Bishop of Samoa-Pago Pago.
Ziemann, G. Patrick, Appointed Dec. 29. Auxiliary Bishop of Los Angeles.

1987

Archbishops

Murphy, Thomas J., Appointed May 26; Coadjutor Archbishop of Seattle.

Bishops

Adamec, Joseph V., Appointed March 12. Bishop of Altoona-Johnstown.
Bosco, Anthony G., Appointed April 14. Bishop of Greensburg.
Buechlein, Daniel, *o.s.b.*, Appointed Jan. 20. Bishop of Memphis.
Bullock, William, Appointed Feb. 10. Bishop of Des Moines.
Franklin, William, Appointed Jan. 29. Auxiliary Bishop of Dubuque.
Guillory, Curtis, Appointed Dec. 29. Auxiliary Bishop of Galveston-Houston.
Hanus, Jerome, *o.s.b.*, Appointed July 6. Bishop of St. Cloud.
McHugh, James T., Appointed Nov. 20. Auxiliary Bishop of Newark.
Milone, Anthony G., Appointed Dec. 14. Bishop of Great Falls-Billings.
Myers, John J., Appointed July 14. Coadjutor Bishop of Peoria.
Nolan, John G., Appointed Dec. 14. Auxiliary Bishop of the Military Services.
O'Keefe, Joseph T., Appointed June 16. Bishop of Syracuse.
Rueger, George, Appointed Jan. 19. Auxiliary Bishop of Worcester.
Samo, Amando, Appointed May 10. Auxiliary Bishop of The Carolines-Marshalls.
Smith, John M., Appointed Dec. 1. Auxiliary Bishop of Newark.
Steinbock, John, Appointed March 31. Bishop of Santa Rosa.
Vlazny, John, Appointed May 19. Bishop of Winona.
Walsh, Daniel F., Appointed June 9. Bishop of Reno-Las Vegas.

1988

Cardinals

Hickey, James Cardinal, Created June 29; Archbishop of Washington.
Szoka, Edmund Cardinal, Created June 29; Pres. Prefecture for Economic Affairs of the Holy See, Vatican.

Archbishops

Bevilacqua, Anthony J., Appointed Feb. 11; Archbishop of Philadelphia.
Marino, Eugene A., Appointed March 14; Resigned Archbishop of Atlanta.
Schulte, Francis B., Appointed Dec. 13; Archbishop of New Orleans.

Bishops

Boland, Raymond J., Appointed Feb. 2. Bishop of Birmingham.
Brown, Tod D., Appointed Dec. 27. Bishop of Boise.
Carmody, Edmond, Appointed Nov. 8. Auxiliary Bishop of San Antonio.
Chaput, Charles, *o.f.m.cap.*, Appointed April 11. Bishop of Rapid City.
Curlin, William G., Appointed Dec. 20. Auxiliary Bishop of Washington.
DiLorenzo, Francis, Appointed Jan. 26. Auxiliary Bishop of Scranton.
Dunne, John C., Appointed Oct. 21. Auxiliary Bishop of Rockville Centre.
Egan, Edward, Appointed Nov. 8. Bishop of Bridgeport.
Gerry, Joseph, *o.s.b.*, Appointed Dec. 27. Bishop of Portland (in Maine).
Gonzalez, Roberto, *o.f.m.*, Appointed July 19. Auxiliary Bishop of Boston.
Gorman, John R., Appointed Feb. 16. Auxiliary Bishop of Chicago.
Jakubowski, Thaddeus J., Appointed Feb. 16. Auxiliary Bishop of Chicago.
Loverde, Paul S., Appointed Feb. 3. Auxiliary Bishop of Hartford.
McGrath, Patrick, Appointed Dec. 6. Auxiliary Bishop of San Francisco.
O'Connell, Anthony J., Appointed June 7. Bishop of Knoxville.
Olivier, Leonard J., *s.v.d.*, Appointed Dec. 20. Auxiliary Bishop of Washington.
Schmitt, Bernard W., Appointed May 31. Auxiliary Bishop of Wheeling-Charleston.
Sevilla, Carlos A., *s.j.*, Appointed Dec. 6. Auxiliary Bishop of San Francisco.
Wcela, Emil A., Appointed Oct. 21. Auxiliary Bishop of Rockville Centre.
Williams, J. Kendrick, Appointed March 2. Bishop of Lexington.
Winter, William J., Appointed Dec. 27. Auxiliary Bishop of Pittsburgh.
Wuerl, Donald, Appointed Feb. 11. Bishop of Pittsburgh.

1989

Archbishops

Keeler, William, Appointed April 6. Archbishop of Baltimore.

Bishops

Brom, Robert, Appointed April 22. Coadjutor Bishop of San Diego.
Charron, Joseph, *c.pp.s.*, Appointed Nov. 6. Auxiliary Bishop of St. Paul-Minneapolis.
Cooney, Patrick, Appointed Nov. 21. Bishop of Gaylord.
Datillo, Nicholas, Appointed Nov. 21. Bishop of Harrisburg.
Driscoll, Michael P., Appointed Dec. 19. Auxiliary Bishop of Orange.
Favalora, John, Appointed March 7. Bishop of St. Petersburg.
Flynn, Harry J., Succeeded to the See May 13. Bishop of Lafayette.
Gettelfinger, Gerald A., Appointed March 11. Bishop of Evansville.
Grahmann, Charles V., Appointed Dec. 18. Coadjutor Bishop of Dallas.
Grosz, Edward, Appointed Nov. 22. Auxiliary Bishop of Buffalo.
Jacobs, Sam, Appointed July 1. Bishop of Alexandria.
McHugh, James T., Appointed May 13. Bishop of Camden.
Mikloshazy, Attila, *s.j.*, Appointed Aug. 12. Bishop for the Apostolate to the Hungarians.
O'Neil, Leo, Appointed Oct. 17. Coadjutor Bishop of Manchester.
Rose, Robert J., Appointed July 11. Bishop of Grand Rapids.
Samra, Nicholas J., Appointed June 29. Auxiliary Bishop of Newton.
Schmitt, Bernard W., Appointed March 30. Bishop of Wheeling-Charleston.
Schwietz, Roger L., *o.m.i.*, Appointed Dec. 12. Bishop of Duluth.
Thompson, David B., Appointed May 9. Coadjutor Bishop of Charleston.
Zipfel, Paul A., Appointed May 16. Auxiliary Bishop of St. Louis.

1990

Archbishops

Maida, Adam J., Appointed June 11. Archbishop of Detroit.

Bishops

Banks, Robert J., Appointed Oct. 16. Bishop of Green Bay.
Blaire, Stephen E., Appointed Feb. 17. Auxiliary Bishop of Los Angeles.
Brom, Robert H., Succeeded to the See July 10. Bishop of San Diego.
Daily, Thomas V., Appointed Feb. 20. Bishop of Brooklyn.
Dorsey, Norbert M., *c.p.*, Appointed March 20. Bishop of Orlando.
Dupre, Thomas L., Appointed April 19. Auxiliary Bishop of Springfield in Massachusetts.
Fellhauer, David E., Appointed April 19. Bishop of Victoria.
George, Francis E., *o.m.i.*, Appointed July 10. Bishop of Yakima.
Grahmann, Charles V., Succeeded to See July 14. Bishop of Dallas.
Kuzma, George M., Appointed Oct. 23. Bishop of Van Nuys.
Muench, Robert W., Appointed May 8. Auxiliary Bishop of New Orleans.
Myers, John J., Succeeded to See Jan. 23. Bishop of Peoria.
O'Neil, Leo E., Succeeded to See June 12. Bishop of Manchester.
Pelotte, Donald E., *s.s.s.*, Succeeded to See March 20. Bishop of Gallup.
Ryan, Sylvester D., Appointed Feb. 17. Auxiliary Bishop of Los Angeles.
Saltarelli, Michael A., Appointed June 12. Auxiliary Bishop of Newark.
Sheridan, Patrick J., Appointed Dec. 12. Auxiliary Bishop of New York.
Skylstad, William S., Appointed April 17. Bishop of Spokane.
Symons, J. Keith, Appointed June 2. Bishop of Palm Beach.
Thompson, David B., Succeeded to See Feb. 22. Bishop of Charleston.
Trautman, Donald W., Appointed July 16. Bishop of Erie.

1991

Cardinals

Bevilacqua, Anthony Cardinal, Created June 28; Archbishop of Philadelphia.
Mahony, Roger Cardinal, Created June 28; Archbishop of Los Angeles.

Archbishops

Cronin, Daniel A., Appointed Dec. 9; Archbishop of Hartford.
Dimino, Joseph T., Succeeded to the See June 21; Archbishop of the Military Services.
Murphy, Thomas J., Succeeded to the See Aug. 21; Archbishop of Seattle.

Bishops

Glynn, John J., Appointed Dec. 10. Auxiliary Bishop of the Military Services.
Goedert, Raymond E., Appointed July 8. Auxiliary Bishop of Chicago.
Madera, Joseph J., *m.sp.s.*, Appointed May 28. Auxiliary Bishop of the Military Services.
Sheets, John R., *s.j.*, Appointed May 14. Auxiliary Bishop of Fort Wayne-South Bend.
Smith, John M., Appointed June 24. Bishop of Pensacola-Tallahassee.
Steinbock, John T., Appointed October 15. Bishop of Santa Rosa.
Welsh, Lawrence H., Appointed November 8. Auxiliary Bishop of St. Paul-Minneapolis.

1992

Archbishops

Beltran, Eusebius J., Appointed November 24; Archbishop of Oklahoma City, from Bishop of Tulsa.
Buechlein, Daniel M., *o.s.b.*, Appointed July 14; Archbishop of Indianapolis, from Bishop of Memphis.

Bishops

Angell, Kenneth A., Appointed October 10, Bishop of Burlington, from Auxiliary Bishop of Providence.
Barnes, Gerald R., Appointed January 28, Auxiliary Bishop of San Bernardino.
Boles, John P., Appointed April 14 Auxiliary Bishop of Boston.
Bruskewitz, Fabian W., Appointed March 24, Bishop of Lincoln.
Carmody, Edmond, Appointed March 24, Bishop of Tyler, from Auxiliary Bishop of San Antonio.
Carmon, Dominic, *s.v.d.*, Appointed December 16, Auxiliary Bishop of New Orleans.
Galante, Joseph A., Appointed October 13, Auxiliary Bishop of San Antonio.
Garland, James H., Appointed October 10, Bishop of Marquette, from Auxiliary Bishop of Cincinnati.
Jarrell, Michael Charles, Appointed December 29, Bishop of Houma-Thibodaux.
Kmiec, Edward Urban, Appointed October 13, Bishop of Nashville, from Auxiliary Bishop of Trenton.
McNamara, John R., Appointed April 14, Auxiliary Bishop of Boston.
Mansell, Henry J., Appointed November 24, Auxiliary Bishop of New York.
O'Malley, Sean P., *o.f.m.cap.*, Appointed July 16, Bishop of Fall River, from Bishop of St. Thomas Virgin Islands.
Paska, Walter, Appointed January 26, Auxiliary Bishop of Philadelphia Ukrainian.
Ryan, Sylvester D., Appointed January 21, Bishop of Monterey, from Auxiliary Bishop of Los Angeles.
Sheldon, Gilbert I., Appointed January 28, Bishop of Steubenville, from Auxiliary Bishop of Cleveland.
Tobin, Thomas J., Appointed November 3, Auxiliary Bishop of Pittsburgh.
Ziemann, G. Patrick, Appointed July 14, Bishop of Santa Rosa, from Auxiliary Bishop of Los Angeles.

1993

Archbishops

Curtiss, Elden F., Appointed May 4, Archbishop of Omaha, from Bishop of Helena.
Donoghue, John F., Appointed June 22, Archbishop of Atlanta, Bishop of Charlotte.
Keleher, James P., transferred Sept. 8, Archbishop of Kansas City in Kansas, from Bishop of Belleville.
Sheehan, Michael J., Appointed April 6, Archbishop of Santa Fe.

Bishops

Boland, Raymond J., Appointed June 22, Bishop of Kansas City St. Joseph, from Bishop of Birmingham.
Britt, Kevin M., Appointed November 23, Auxiliary Bishop of Detroit.
Bullock, William H., Appointed April 13, Bishop of Madison, from Bishop of Des Moines.
Charron, Joseph J., *c.pp.s.* Appointed November 12, Bishop of Des Moines, from Auxiliary Bishop of St. Paul and Minneapolis.
Elya, John A., *b.s.o.* Appointed December 7, Bishop of Newton from Auxiliary Bishop of Newton.
Franklin, William E., Appointed November 12, Bishop of Davenport, from Auxiliary Bishop of Dubuque.
Gregory, Wilton, Appointed December 29, Bishop of Belleville from Auxiliary Bishop of Chicago.
Harrington, Bernard J., Appointed November 23, Auxiliary Bishop of Detroit.
Hughes, Alfred C., Appointed September 7, Bishop of Baton Rouge, from Auxiliary Bishop of Boston.
Loverde, Paul S., Appointed November 11, Bishop of Ogdensburg, from Auxiliary Bishop of Hartford.
Moeddel, Carl K., Appointed June 15, Auxiliary Bishop of Cincinnati.
Slattery, Edward J., Appointed November 11, Bishop of Tulsa.
Steib, James Terry, *s.v.d.* Appointed March 23, Bishop of Memphis, from Auxiliary Bishop of St. Louis.
Tamayo, James A., Appointed January 26, Auxiliary Bishop of Galveston-Houston.
Thomas, Elliot G., Appointed October 10, Bishop of St. Thomas, Virgin Islands.
Weigand, William K., Appointed November 3, Bishop of Sacramento from Bishop of Salt Lake City.
Wiwchar, Michael, *c.ss.r.* Appointed July 15, Bishop of St. Nicholas in Chicago for Ukrainians.

1994

Cardinals

Keeler, William Cardinal, Created November 26; Archbishop of Baltimore.
Maida, Adam Cardinal, Created November 26; Archbishop of Detroit.

Archbishops

Favalora, John C., Appointed November 3, Archbishop of Miami.
Flynn, Harry J., Appointed February 2, Coadjutor Archbishop of St. Paul-Minneapolis.
Hanus, Jerome, *o.s.b.* Appointed August 23, Coadjutor Archbishop of Dubuque.
Procyk, Judson M., Appointed November 15, Archbishop of Pittsburgh Byzantine.
Rigali, Justin F., Appointed January 25, Archbishop of St. Louis.

Bishops

Barbarito, Gerald, Appointed June 28, Auxiliary Bishop of Brooklyn.
Brunett, Alexander J., Appointed April 19, Bishop of Helena.
Burke, Raymond L., Appointed December 10, Bishop of La Crosse.
Carlson, Robert J., Appointed January 13, Bishop Coadjutor of Sioux Falls, from Auxiliary Bishop of St. Paul-Minneapolis.
Catanello, Ignatius, Appointed June 28, Auxiliary Bishop of Brooklyn.
Chedid, John G., Appointed March 1, First Bishop of Our Lady of Lebanon in Los Angeles, from Auxiliary Bishop of St. Maron of Brooklyn.
Cullen, Edward P., Appointed February 8, Auxiliary Bishop of Philadelphia.
Curlin, William G., Appointed February 22, Bishop of Charlotte, from Auxiliary Bishop of Washington.
Curry, Thomas J., Appointed February 8, Auxiliary Bishop of Los Angeles.
Doran, Thomas G., Appointed April 19, Bishop of Rockford.
DiLorenzo, Francis X., Appointed October 4, Bishop of Honolulu.
Foley, David E., Appointed March 22, Bishop of Birmingham, from Auxiliary Bishop of Richmond.
Galante, Joseph A., Appointed April 5, Bishop of Beaumont, from Auxiliary Bishop of San Antonio.
Markiewicz, Alfred J., Appointed November 22, Bishop of Kalamazoo.
McDonnell, Charles J., Appointed March 15, Auxiliary Bishop of Newark.
Niederauer, George H., Appointed November 3, Bishop of Salt Lake City.
O'Donnell, Edward J., Appointed November 8, Bishop of Lafayette (Louisiana).
Reilly, Daniel P., Appointed October 27, Bishop of Worcester.
Rodriguez, Placido, *c.m.f.*, Appointed April 5, Bishop of Lubbock, from Auxiliary Bishop of Chicago.
Sartoris, Joseph M., Appointed February 8, Auxiliary Bishop of Los Angeles.
Yanta, John W., Appointed October 27, Auxiliary of San Antonio.
Zavala, Gabino, Appointed February 8, Auxiliary Bishop of Los Angeles.

1995

Archbishops

Flynn, Harry J., Appointed September 8, from Coadjutor to Archbishop of St. Paul-Minneapolis.
Hanus, Jerome G., O.S.B., Succeeding as Archbishop of Dubuque from status of Coadjutor.
Levada, William J., Succeeding as Archbishop of San Francisco December 1995.

Bishops

Barnes, Gerald R., Appointed December 28, 1995, Bishop of San Bernardino, from Auxiliary of same Diocese.
Boland, J. Kevin, Appointed February 7, 1995, Bishop of Savannah.
Braxton, Edward K., Appointed March 28, Auxiliary Bishop of St. Louis.
Carlson, Robert J., Succeeding as Bishop of Sioux Falls in March, from status of Coadjutor.
Conway, Edwin M., Appointed January 24, Auxiliary Bishop of Chicago.
Cote, Michael R., Appointed May 9, Auxiliary Bishop of Portland in Maine.
Dougherty, John M., Appointed February 7, 1995, Auxiliary Bishop of Scranton.
Dupre, Thomas L., Appointed March 14, Bishop of Springfield, from Auxiliary Bishop of Springfield.
Gonzalez, Roberto O., O.F.M., Appointed May 16, Coadjutor Bishop of Corpus Chrisit, from Auxiliary Bishop of Boston.
Hart, Daniel A., Appointed September 12, Bishop of Norwich, from Auxiliary Bishop of Boston.
Kicanas, Gerald F., Appointed January 24, Auxiliary Bishop of Chicago.
Kinney, John F., Appointed May 8, Bishop of St. Cloud from Bishop of Bismarck.
Lori, William E., Appointed February 27, Auxiliary Bishop of Washington.
Lynch, Robert N., Appointed Bishop of St. Petersburg December 4, 1995.
McCormack, John B., Appointed November Auxiliary Bishop of Boston.
Mansell, Henry J., Appointed April 18, effective June 12, Bishop of Buffalo, from Auxiliary Bishop of New York.
Melczek, Dale J., named Coadjutor Bishop of Gary November 9.
Mengeling, Carl F., Appointed November Bishop of Lansing.
Moynihan, James M., Appointed April 29, effective May 29, Bishop of Syracuse.
Mulvee, Robert Edward, Appointed February 7, Coadjutor Bishop of Providence from Bishop of Wilmington.
Murphy, William F., Appointed November Auxiliary Bishop of Boston.
Murry, George V., *s.j.* Appointed January 24, Auxiliary Bishop of Chicago.
Pataki, Andrew, Appointed Bishop of Passaic November, from Bishop of Parma.
Pena, Raymundo J., Appointed May 23, Bishop of Brownsville, from Bishop of El Paso.
Saltarelli, Michael A., Apponted Bishop of Wilmington, from Auxiliary of Newark.
Smith, John M., named Coadjutor of Trenton from Bishop of Pensacola-Tallahassee.
Straling, Phillip F., Appointed March 21, Bishop of Reno, from former Bishop of San Bernadino.
Tertzakian, Hovhannes, *o.m.ven.*, Appointed January 6, effective April 29, Apostolic Exarch for Armenian Catholics in the United States and Canada.
Tobin, Thomas J., Appointed Bishop of Youngstown, from Auxiliary of Pittsburg.
Walsh, Daniel F., Appointed March 21, Bishop of Las Vegas, formerly Bishop of Reno-Las Vegas.

1996

Archbishops

George, Francis, *o.m.i.*, Appointed Archbishop of Portland in Oregon from Bishop of Yakima.

Bishops

Allue, Emilio, *s.d.b.*, Appointed Auxiliary Bishop of Boston July 24.
Aymond, Gregory M., Appointed Auxiliary Bishop of New Orleans November 19.
Botean, John Michael, Appointed Bishop of Romanian Catholic Diocese of St. George in Canton.
DiMarzio, Nicholas A., Appointed Auxiliary Bishop of Newark September.
Doueihi, Hector, Appointed Bishop of St. Maron of Brooklyn.
Irwin, Francis X., Appointed Auxiliary Bishop of Boston July 24.
O'Brien, Edwin, Appointed Auxiliary Bishop of New York.
Manz, John R., Appointed Auxiliary Bishop of Chicago January 23.
Maginnis, Robert P., Appointed Auxiliary Bishop of Philadelphia January 23.
Martino, Joseph F., Appointed Auxiliary Bishop of Philadelphia, January 23.
Muench, Robert W., Bishop of Covington from Auxiliary Bishop of New Orleans.
Nienstedt, John C., Appointed Auxiliary Bishop of Detroit June 11.
Ochoa, Armando, Appointed Bishop of El Paso from Auxiliary Bishop of Los Angeles.
Sevilla, Carlos A., *s.j.* Appointed Bishop of Yakima from Auxiliary Bishop of San Francisco December 31.
Schott, Basil, *o.f.m.*, Bishop of Parma (Ruthenians).

Steiner, Kenneth, Appointed Auxiliary Bishop of Portland in Oregon.
Vigneron, Allen H., Appointed Auxiliary Bishop of Detroit June 11.
Warfel, Michael, Appointed Bishop of Juneau November 19.
Younan, Joseph, Appointed Bishop of Our Lady of Deliverance of Newark.
Zipfel, Paul A., Appointed Bishop of Bismarck from Auxiliary Bishop of Saint Louis December 31.

1997

Archbishops

Chaput, Charles J., *o.f.m.cap.*, appointed Archbishop of Denver February 18, 1997, from Bishop of Rapid City.

Bishops

Ricard, John H., *s.s.j.*, appointed Bishop of Pensacola-Tallahassee January
Yanta, John W., appointed Bishop of Amarillo, from Auxiliary of San Antonio in January.
Zubik, David A., appointed Auxiliary Bishop of Pittsburgh February 18, 1997.

National Conference of Catholic Bishops

Address—3211 Fourth St., Washington, DC 20017-1194. Tel: 202-541-3000.

The National Conference of Catholic Bishops (NCCB) is a canonical entity operating in accordance with the Conciliar Decree *Christus Dominus*. Its purpose is to foster the Church's mission by providing the Bishops of the United States of America with an opportunity to exchange views and insights of prudence and experience and to exercise in a joint manner their pastoral office. (cf. *Christus Dominus*, # 38). The NCCB is the successor to the Annual Meeting of the Bishops of the United States, approved in the brief "Communes" issued by Pope Benedict XV, April 10, 1919 and in a special letter of Pius XI issued on August 10, 1927. The present NCCB statutes with some slight amendment are those originally approved by the Sacred Consistorial Congregation in a decree issued on June 22, 1922.

The National Conference of Catholic Bishops is composed of every Bishop, residential or titular, who serves the Church in the United States, its territories or possessions. Each Bishop has an active and passive voice in the Conference. Under certain conditions, enunciated in conciliar legislation, the National Conference of Catholic Bishops can initiate actions that are juridically binding on all the bishops of the country.

The National Conference of Catholic Bishops is presided over by a president who is elected by the general membership. Other officers of the organization are a vice president, secretary, treasurer and general secretary. The National Conference of Catholic Bishops is a distinct entity from the United States Catholic Conference. Its relationship to the USCC is that of a sponsoring organization.

NCCB OFFICES AND COMMITTEES

I. Officers

President—Bishop Anthony M. Pilla
Vice President—Bishop Joseph A. Fiorenza
Treasurer—Bishop Robert J. Banks
Secretary—Archbishop Harry J. Flynn

II. NCCB General Secretariat

General Secretary—Rev. Msgr. Dennis M. Schnurr
Associate General Secretary—Sr. Sharon A. Euart, R.S.M.
Associate General Secretary—Rev. Msgr. William P. Fay
Associate General Secretary—Rev. Msgr. Paul D. Theroux
Assistant General Secretary—Mr. Bruce E. Egnew

III. Staff Offices

Finance—Mr. Kenneth Korotky, Dir.
Accounting—Ms. Jennifer McGowan
General Counsel—Mr. Mark E. Chopko
Associate General Counsel—Ms. Deirdre A. Halloran
Associate General Counsel—Mr. John A. Liekweg
General Services—Mr. Douglas Cissel, Dir.
Printing & Mailing Services—Mr. Mark J. Bowen, Dir.
Government Liaison—Mr. Frank J. Monahan, Dir.
Human Resources—Mr. Thomas J. Meehan, Dir.
Library Services—Mr. Guy Wilson,Dir.
Management Information Systems—Mr. William Kissane, Dir.
Office of Public and Promotion Services—Mr. Richard W. Daw, Dir.

NCCB COMMITTEES

I. Executive Level

Administrative Committee

Chairman—Bishop Anthony M. Pilla
Members— Anthony Cardinal Bevilacqua (Region III)
James Cardinal Hickey
Bernard Cardinal Law
Archbishop Daniel A. Cronin (Region I)
Archbishop John C. Favalora (Region IX)
Archbishop Harry J. Flynn
Archbishop Jerome G. Hanus, O.S.B.
Archbishop Thomas C. Kelly, O.P. (Region V)
Archbishop Theodore E. McCarrick
Archbishop Daniel E. Pilarczyk
Archbishop Justin F. Rigali (Region IX)
Archbishop Francis B. Schulte
Archbishop Michael J. Sheehan
Bishop Victor H. Balke
Bishop Robert J. Banks
Bishop Gerald R. Barnes
Bishop Alexander J. Brunett
Bishop Matthew H. Clark (Region II)
Bishop Thomas J. Costello
Bishop John S. Cummins
Bishop John C. Dunne
Bishop Edward M. Egan
Bishop David E. Fellhauer
Bishop Joseph A. Fiorenza
Bishop Joseph A. Galante
Bishop William R. Houck
Bishop Joseph L. Imesch
Bishop John R. Keating, (Region IV)
Bishop John F. Kinney
Bishop Edward U. Kmiec
Bishop Paul S. Loverde
Bishop Henry J. Mansell
Bishop Anthony M. Milone (Region XII)
Bishop Robert F. Morneau
Bishop George V. Murry,S.J.
Bishop John J. Myers (Region VII)
Bishop Thomas J. O'Brien
Bishop Sean P. O'Malley, O.F.M.Cap.
Bishop Armando X. Ochoa (Region XIII)
Bishop Andrew Pataki
Bishop Raymundo J. Pena
Bishop A. Edward Pevec (Region VI)
Bishop Richardo Ramirez
Bishop John H. Ricard, S.S.J.
Bishop Frank J. Rodimer
Bishop Placido Rodriquez, C.M.F.
Bishop Roger L. Schwietz (Region VIII)
Bishop William S. Skylstad
Bishop Edward J. Slattery (Region X)
Bishop James A. Tamayo
Bishop Daniel F. Walsh (Region XI)
Bishop G. Patrick Ziemann
Bishop Paul A. Zipfel

Executive Committee

Chairman—Bishop Anthony M. Pilla
Members—Bishop Joseph A. Fiorenza, Vice Pres.
Bishop Robert J. Banks, Treas.
Archbishop Harry J. Flynn, Sec.
Staff—Rev. Msgr. Dennis Schnurr

Committee on Budget and Finance

Chairman—Bishop Robert J. Banks
Members—Bishop David E. Fellhauer
Bishop John H. Ricard, S.S.J.
Bishop Daniel F. Walsh
Rev. Msgr. Dennis Schnurr
Staff—Mr. Kenneth Korotky

Committee on Personnel

Chairman—Bishop Joseph A. Fiorenza
Members—Bishop Joseph L. Imesch
Bishop Henry J. Mansell
Rev. Msgr. Dennis Schnurr
Staff—Mr. Bruce E. Egnew

Committee on Priorities and Plans

Chairman—Bishop Anthony M. Pilla
Vice-President—Bishop Joseph A. Fiorenza
Treasurer—Bishop Robert J. Banks
Past President—William Cardinal Keeler
Members—Bishop Henry J. Mansell
Rev. Msgr. Dennis Schnurr
Staff—Sr. Sharon A. Euart, R.S.M.

SubCommittee on the Millennium

Chairman—Bishop Joseph A. Fiorenza
Members—Archbishop Oscar H. Lipscomb
Bishop Stephen E. Blaire
Bishop Tod D. Brown
Bishop Wilton D. Gregory
Bishop William C. Newman
Bishop Armando X. Ochoa
Bishop John G. Vlazny
Staff—Mr. Paul Henderson,Exec. Dir.
Ms. Emily Davis,Project Assistant

II. General Membership Level

Standing Committees

African American Catholics

Chairman—Bishop George V. Murry, S.J.
Members—Archbishop Thomas C. Kelly, O.P.
Bishop Joseph A. Galante
Bishop Michael A. Saltarelli
Bishop J. Terry Steib, S.V.D.
Bishop David B. Thompson
Consultants—James Cardinal Hickey
William Cardinal Keeler
Bishop Joseph A. Francis, S.V.D.
Bishop Curtis J. Guillory, S.V.D.
Secretariat—Ms. Beverly A. Carroll, Exec. Dir.

American Board of Catholic Missions

Chairman—Bishop Victor H. Balke
Members—Archbishop Francis E. George, O.M.I.
Bishop William R. Houck
Bishop John H. Ricard, S.S.J.
Bishop Arthur N. Tafoya
Bishop J. Kendrick Williams
Consultants—Archbishop Michael J. Sheehan
Bishop Thomas V. Daily
Bishop J. Keith Symons
Staff—Dr. David M. Byers, Ph.D., Exec. Dir.
Mrs. Patricia D. Boman, Special Asst.
Ms. Mary Mencarini Campbell, Exec. Asst.

American College Louvain

Chairman—Bishop Frank J. Rodimer
Members by Region—
Region I Bishop Louis E. Gelineau
Region II Bishop Matthew H. Clark
Region III Bishop Frank J. Rodimer
Region IV Bishop Joseph J. Madera, M.Sp.S.
Region V Bishop Jude Speyrer
Region VI Bishop Allen H. Vigneron
Region VII Bishop Gerald A. Gettelfinger
Region VIII Bishop James S. Sullivan
Region IX Bishop Lawrence J. McNamara
Region X Bishop Leroy T. Matthiesen
Region XI Bishop Michael P. Driscoll
Region XII Archbishop Francis George, O.M.I.
Region XIII Bishop Thomas J. O'Brien
Staff—Very Rev. David E. Windsor

Bishops' Welfare Emergency Relief

Chairman—Bishop Anthony M. Pilla
Members—Administrative Committee Members

Boundaries of Dioceses and Provinces

Chairman—Bishop Anthony M. Pilla
Members by Region—Region I Bishop Michael R. Cote
Region II Bishop Thomas V. Daily
Region III Bishop Dominic A. Marconi
Region IV Archbishop John F. Donoghue
Region V Archbishop Francis B. Schulte
Region VI Bishop Moses B. Anderson, S.S.E.
Region VII Bishop Raymond E. Goedert
Region VIII Bishop Victor Balke
Region IX Bishop Joseph L. Charron, C.P.P.S.
Region X Bishop James A. Tamayo
Region XI Bishop John T. Steinbock
Region XII Bishop Thomas J. Connolly
Region XIII Bishop Donald E. Pelotte, S.S.S.
Staff—Rev. Msgr. Dennis M. Schnurr

Canonical Affairs

Chairman—Bishop David E. Fellhauer
Members—Archbishop Thomas C. Kelly, O.P.
Bishop Raymond L. Burke
Bishop Michael R. Cote
Bishop Thomas G. Doran
Bishop Raymond E. Goedert
Bishop John J. Myers
Advisors —Adam Cardinal Maida
Bishop Joseph A. Galante
Staff—Sr. Sharon A. Euart, R.S.M.

Church in Latin America

Chairman—Bishop Raymundo J. Pena

Members—Archbishop Eusebias J. Beltran
Archbishop Francis E. George, O.M.I.
Archbishop James P. Keleher
Bishop Sean O'Malley, O.F.M.Cap.
Bishop J. Keith Symons
Bishop William K. Weigand
Consultants—Bishop Thomas V. Daily
Bishop Roberto O. Gonzalez, O.F.M.
Staff—Rev. James J. Ronan, Exec. Dir.

Diaconate

Chairman—Bishop Edward U. Kmiec
Members—Bishop Dominic Carmons, S.V.D.
Bishop Howard J. Hubbard
Bishop William E. Lori
Bishop Thomas J. O'Brien
Bishop Frank J. Rodimer
Bishop Rene A. Valero
Consultants—Rev. Msgr. William A. Varvaro Rev. Kevin W. Irwin
Staff—Deacon John Pistone, Exec. Dir.

Doctrine

Chairman— Archbishop Daniel E. Pilarczyk
Members— Archbishop William J. Levada
Archbishop Francis E. George, O.M.I.
Bishop Francis X. DiLorenzo
Bishop Wilton D. Gregory
Bishop Richard J. Sklba
Consultants—Rev. Avery Dulles, S.J.
Robin Darling Young, Ph.D.
Staff—Rev. J. Augustine DiNoia, O.P., Exec. Dir.
Ms. Siobhan M. Verbeek, Assoc. Dir.

Ecumenical and Interreligious Affairs

Chairman—Bishop Alexander J. Brunett
Members—William Cardinal Keeler
Archbishop Rembert G. Weakland, O.S.B.
Bishop Joseph J. Gerry, O.S.B.
Bishop Donald E. Pelotte, S.S.S.
Bishop Placido Rodriguez, C.M.F.
Bishop Nicholas J. Samra
Bishop William S. Skylstad
Bishop John J. Snyder
Bishop J. Kendrick Williams
Consultants—John Cardinal O'Connor
Bishop John S. Cummins
Bishop Howard J. Hubbard
Bishop George V. Murry, S.J.
Bishop James C. Timlin
Moderator—William Cardinal Keeler
Bishop Joseph Gerry, O.S.B.
Staff—Rev. John F. Hotchkin, Exec. Dir.
John Borelli, Ph.D., Assoc. Dir.
Eugene Fisher, Ph.D., Assoc. Dir.
Bro. Jeffrey Gros, F.S.C., Assoc. Dir.
Rev. Ronald G. Roberson, C.S.P., Assoc. Dir.

Evangelization

Chairman—Archbishop Michael J. Sheehan
Members—Anthony Cardinal Bevilacqua
Bishop Stephen E. Blaire
Bishop Sam G. Jacobs
Bishop Raymond A. Lucker
Bishop Joseph F. Martino
Bishop Daniel F. Walsh
Staff—Dr. David M. Byers, Exec. Dir.
Rev. John E. Hurley, C.S.P., Assoc. Dir.

Hispanic Affairs

Chairman—Bishop Gerald R. Barnes
Members—Bishop Emilio Allue, S.D.B.
Bishop Curtis J. Guillory S.V.D.
Bishop James R. Hoffman
Bishop Ricardo Ramirez, C.S.B.
Bishop Placido Rodriguez, C.M.F.
Bishop Agustin A. Roman
Bishop Carlos A. Sevilla, S.J.
Bishop Gabino Zavala
Consultants—Archbishop Patrick F. Flores
Bishop David Arias, O.A.R.
Bishop Juan A. Arzube
Bishop Gilbert E. Chavez
Bishop Alvaro Corrada del Rio, S.J.
Bishop Francisco Garmendia
Bishop Roberto O. Gonzalez, O.F.M.
Bishop Rene H. Gracida
Bishop Joseph J. Madera, M.Sp.S.
Bishop George H. Niederauer
Bishop Armando X. Ochoa
Bishop Raymundo J. Pena
Bishop Arthur N. Tafoya
Bishop James A. Tamayo
Bishop Rene A. Valero
Rev. Msgr. Lorenzo Albacete
Sr. Maria Elena Gonzalez, R.S.M.
Mr. Gonzalo Saldana
Staff—Mr. Ronaldo M. Cruz, Exec. Dir.

Laity

Chairman—Bishop G. Patrick Ziemann
Members—Archbishop Harry J. Flynn
Bishop Joseph P. Delaney
Bishop Gerald F. Kicanas
Bishop Manuel D. Moreno
Bishop Roger L. Schwietz, O.M.I.
Bishop Phillip F. Straling
Staff—Mrs. Dolores Leckey, Exec. Dir.
H. Richard McCord, Ed.D., Assoc. Dir.
Ms. Sheila Garcia, Asst. Dir.
Ms. Ana Villamil, Asst. Dir.
Sr. Amy Hoey, R.S.M., Project Coord.

Lay Ministry SubCommittee

Chairman—Bishop Phillip F. Straling
Members—Bishop Tod D. Brown
Bishop John C. Dunne
Bishop Bernard J. Harrington
Bishop James R. Hoffman
Bishop Edward U. Kmiec
Bishop Armando X. Ochoa
Bishop Emil A. Wcela
Advisors—Zoila Diaz, D.Min.
Dr. Zeni Fox
Rev. Msgr. Phil Murnion

SubCommittee on Youth

Chairman—Bishop Roger L. Schwietz,O.M.I.
Members—(Unannounced at time of publication)
Staff—Ms. Ana Villamil, Asst. Dir.

Liturgy

Chairman—Archbishop Jerome Hanus, O.S.B.
Members—Archbishop Justin F. Rigali
Archbishop Rembert G. Weakland, O.S.B.
Bishop Gerald F. Kicanas
Bishop Leonard J. Olivier, S.V.D.
Bishop Sylvester D. Ryan
Bishop Emil A. Wcela
Consultants—Roger Cardinal Mahony
Archbishop Daniel E. Pilarczyk
Bishop Roberto Gonzalez, O.F.M.
Bishop Frank J. Rodimer
Staff—Rev. James P. Moroney, Exec. Dir.
Sr. Ann F. Rehrauer, Assoc. Dir.

Marriage and Family Life

Chairman—Bishop Thomas J. O'Brien
Members—Archbishop Elden F. Curtiss
Bishop John F. Kinney
Bishop Carl K. Moeddel
Bishop Richard J. Sklba
Bishop John M. Smith
Bishop John W. Yanta
Staff—Mrs. Dolores R. Leckey, Exec. Dir.
H. Richard McCord, Ed.D., Assoc. Dir.

Migration

Chairman—Bishop John S. Cummins
Members—Adam Cardinal Maida
Archbishop John C. Favalora
Bishop George V. Murry, S.J.
Bishop Peter A. Rosazza
Bishop John W. Yanta
Bishop Gabino Zavata
Consultants—Archbishop Theodore E. McCarrick
Archbishop Francis B. Schulte
Bishop R. Pierre DuMaine
Bishop John A. Elya, B.S.O.
Bishop Joseph L. Howze
Bishop James C. Timlin
Staff—Mr. John Swenson, Exec. Dir.

Missions

Chairman—Bishop Sean P. O'Malley, O.F.M.Cap.
Members—Archbishop Francis George, O.M.I.
Archbishop William J. Levada
Bishop William E. Lori
Bishop Robert E. Mulvee
Bishop Edward J. Slattery
Bishop Elliott G. Thomas
Consultant—Bishop William J. McCormack
Staff—Dr. David M. Byers, Ph.D., Exec. Dir.
Mrs. Patricia D. Bowman, Special Asst.

North American College Rome

Chairman—James Cardinal Hickey
Members—Region I Bishop Edward M. Egan
Region II Bishop Paul S. Loverde
Region III Bishop Donald W. Wuerl
Region IV James Cardinal Hickey
Region V Archbishop Oscar H. Lipscomb
Region VI Bishop Joseph C. McKinney
Region VII Bishop Thomas G. Doran
Region VIII Bishop John G. Vlazny
Region IX Bishop Fabian W. Bruskewitz
Region X Bishop Joseph A. Galante
Region XI Bishop Robert M. Brom
Region XII Bishop Tod D. Brown
Region XIII Archbishop Michael J. Sheehan
Staff—Rev. Msgr. William P. Fay

Pastoral Practices

Chairman—Bishop Joseph L. Imesch
Members—Bishop Gerald R. Barnes
Bishop Stephen E. Blaire
Bishop J. Kevin Boland
Bishop Robert W. Donnelly
Bishop Stanley G. Schlarman
Bishop Emil A. Wcela
Staff—Rev. J. Augustine DiNoia, O.P., Exec. Dir.
Ms. Siobhan M. Verbee, Assoc. Dir.

Priestly Formation

Chairman—Archbishop John C. Favalora
Members—Bishop Curtis J. Guillory, S.V.D.
Bishop Gerald F. Kicanas
Bishop Robert W. Muench
Bishop Edwin F. O'Brien
Bishop John G. Vlazny
Bishop Gabino Zavala
Advisor—Bishop Norbert M. Dorsey, C.P.
Bishop Donald W. Wuerl
Staff—Rev. Timothy Reker, Exec.Dir.

Priestly Life and Ministry

Chairman—Bishop Robert F. Morneau
Members—Archbishop Michael J. Sheehan
Bishop Edward P. Cullen
Bishop Bernard J. Harrington
Bishop John F. Kinney
Bishop Edward J. Slattery
Bishop David B. Thompson
Advisors—Bishop William G. Curlin
Bishop—James A. Tamayo
Staff—Rev. Thomas R. Bevan, Exec. Dir.

Pro-Life Activities

Chairman—Bernard Cardinal Law
Members—William Cardinal Keeler
Adam Cardinal Maida
Archbishop Daniel Buechlein, O.S.B.
Bishop Roberto O. Gonzalez, O.F.M.
Bishop James T. McHugh
Bishop Andrew Pataki
Bishop John H. Ricard, S.S.J.
Bishop William K. Weigand
Consultants—Anthony Cardinal Bevilacqua
James Cardinal Hickey
Roger Cardinal Mahony
John Cardinal O'Connor
Archbishop Joseph T. Dimino
Archbishop John C. Favalora
Archbishop Charles J. Chaput, O.F.M.Cap.
Mr. Virgil Dechant
Ms. Frances X. Hogan, Esq.
Staff—Ms. Gail P. Quinn, Exec. Dir.
Ms. Helen Alvare, Dir. Information & Planning
Mr. Richard Doerflinger, Assoc. Dir. Policy Devel.
Mrs. Susan Wills, Asst. Dir. Programming
Ms. Theresa Notare, Spec. Asst. Natural Family Planning

Relationship Between Eastern and Latin Catholic Churches

Chairman—Bishop Andrew Pataki
Members—Bishop Gerald Barbarito
Bishop Kevin M. Britt
Bishop Ibrahim N. Ibrahim
Bishop Basil H. Losten
Bishop James M. Moynihan
Bishop Nicholas J. Samra
Bishop Joseph Younan
Staff—Rev. Msgr. William P. Fay

Religious Life and Ministry

Chairman—Bishop Joseph A. Galante
Members—Archbishop Francis George, O.M.I.
Bishop John C. Dunne
Bishop Carlos A. Sevilla, S.J.
Bishop John G. Vlazny
Staff—Rev. Msgr. Dennis M. Schnurr
Sr. Sharon A. Euart, R.S.M.

Science and Human Values

Chairman—Bishop Edward M. Egan
Members—Archbishop Daniel A. Cronin
Bishop Edward K. Braxton

Bishop John S. Cummins
Bishop Francis X. DiLorenzo
Bishop R. Pierre DuMaine
Bishop William E. Lori
Consultants—Bishop John C. Dunne
Bishop William B. Friend
Staff—Dr. David M. Byers, Ph.D., Exec. Dir.

Selection of Bishops

Chairman—Bishop Anthony M. Pilla
Members—Region I Bishop Michael R. Cote
Region II Bishop Thomas V. Daily
Region III Bishop Dominic A. Marconi
Region IV Archbishop John F. Donoghue
Region V Archbishop Francis B. Schulte
Region VI Bishop Moses B. Anderson, S.S.E.
Region VII Bishop Raymond E. Goedert
Region VIII Bishop Victor Balke
Region IX Bishop Joseph L. Charron, C.P.P.S.
Region X Bishop James A. Tamayo
Region XI Bishop John T. Steinbock
Region XII Bishop Thomas J. Connolly
Region XIII Bishop Donald E. Pelotte, S.S.S.
Staff—Rev. Msgr. Dennis M. Schnurr

Vocations

Chairman—Bishop Paul S. Loverde
Members—Bishop Kevin M. Britt
Bishop John J. McRaith
Bishop John J. Myers
Bishop Roger L. Schwietz, O.M.I.
Bishop Daniel F. Walsh
Bishop Gabino Zavala
Consultants—Bishop Robert J. Carlson
Bishop John J. Glynn
Bishop Donald E. Pelotte, S.S.S.
Bishop J. Terry Steib, S.V.D.
Sr. Catherine Bertrand, S.S.N.D.
Mrs. Dorothy Foss
Staff—Rev. Timothy Reker, Exec. Dir.

Women in Society and in the Church

Chairman—Bishop John C. Dunne
Members—Bishop F. Joseph Gossman
Bishop Richard C. Hanifen
Bishop Howard J. Hubbard
Bishop George V. Murry, S.J.
Bishop William C. Newman
Bishop Gabino Zavala
Advisors—Ms. Mary Ann Dantuono
Ms. Joan M. Finucci
Ms. Kathleen Henricks
Sr. Lynn Jarrell
Ms. Joan F. Neal
Staff—Mrs. Dolores R. Leckey, Exec. Dir.
Ms. Sheila Garcia, Asst. Dir.

AD HOC COMMITTEES

1999 Special Assembly

Chairman—Bishop Robert N. Lynch
Members—Archbishop Francis E. George, O.M.I.
Bishop Gerald R. Barnes
Bishop Joseph P. Delaney
Bishop Howard J. Hubbard
Bishop Robert E. Mulvee
Bishop George V. Murry, S.J.
Bishop John M. Smith
Staff—Sr. Sharon Euart, R.S.M.

Aid to the Church in Central and Eastern Europe

Chairman—Adam Cardinal Maida
Members—Archbishop Patrick F. Flores
Bishop Joseph V. Adamec
Bishop Paul A. Baltakis, O.F.M.
Bishop Basil H. Losten
Bishop Dale J. Melczek
Bishop Daniel P. Reilly
Staff—Rev. Msgr. R. George Sarauskas, Exec. Dir.
Mr. James H. O'Beirne, Deputy Dir.
Ms. Margit Serenyi, Assoc. Dir.

Bishops' Life and Ministry

Chairman—Bishop William Skylstad
Members—Archbishop William S. Skylstad
Bishop Francis X. DiLorenzo
Bishop Joseph A. Francis, S.V.D.
Bishop Joseph F. Maguire
Bishop Robert E. Mulvee
Bishop Ricardo Ramirez, C.S.B.
Bishop Thomas J. Tobin
Bishop Lawrence H. Welsh
Staff—Rev. Msgr. Paul D. Theroux

Catholic Charismatic Renewal

Chairman—Bishop Sam G. Jacobs
Members—Archbishop Harry J. Flynn
Archbishop George H. Pearce, S.M.
Bishop Francisco Garmendia
Bishop Edward T. Hughes
Bishop Raymond A. Lucker
Bishop Joseph C. McKinney
Bishop Donald W. Montrose
Bishop Kenneth J. Povish
Bishop Patrick G. Ziemann
Staff—Sr. Sharon A. Euart, R.S.M.

Economic Concerns of the Holy See

Chairman—Archbishop James P. Keleher
Members—James Cardinal Hickey
Bernard Cardinal Law
Archbishop Daniel A. Cronin
Archbishop Theodore E. McCarrick
Archbishop Justin F. Rigali
Archbishop Francis B. Schulte
Bishop Robert J. Banks
Bishop Edward M. Egan
Bishop Joseph A. Fiorenza
Bishop Henry J. Mansell
Bishop Thomas J. O'Brien
Bishop Edward J. Slattery
Staff—Rev. Msgr. Paul D. Theroux

Forum on the Principles of Translation

Chairman—Archbishop Jerome G. Hanus, O.S.B.
Members—Archbishop Justin F. Rigali
Bishop Victor Balke
Bishop Alexander J. Brunett
Bishop Joseph J. Gerry, O.S.B.
Staff—Sr. Ann Rehrauer, O.S.F.

Health Care Issues and the Church

Chairman—Bishop Donald W. Wuerl
Members—Archbishop Daniel E. Pilarczyk
Archbishop Justin F. Rigali
Bishop Henry J. Mansell
Bishop Joseph M. Sullivan
Consultants—Bishop James W. Malone
Staff—Rev. J. Augustine DiNoia, O.P. , Exec. Dir.

Mission and Structure of the NCCB

Chairman—(Unannounced at time of publication)
Members—Bernard Cardinal Law
Roger Cardinal Mahony
Archbishop William J. Levada
Archbishop Oscar H. Lipscomb
Archbishop Rembert G. Weakland, O.S.B.
Bishop Joseph A. Fiorenza
Bishop James W. Malone
Bishop Donald W. Wuerl
Staff—Sr. Sharon Euart, R.S.M.

Native American Catholics

Chairman—Bishop Donald E. Pelotte, S.S.S.
Members—Archbishop Charles J. Chaput, O.F.M.Cap.
Bishop Alexander J. Brunett
Bishop Michael J. Kaniecki, S.J.
Bishop Anthony M. Milone
Staff—Rev. Msgr. William P. Fay

Nomination of Conference Offices

Chairman—Bishop Dale J. Melczek
Members—Region I Bishop Thomas L. Dupre
Region II Bishop Thomas J. Costello
Region III Bishop Nicholas C. Dattilo
Region IV Bishop William Lori
Region V Bishop William B. Friend
Region VI Bishop A. James Quinn
Region VII Bishop Dale J. Melczek
Region VIII Bishop Robert J. Carlson
Region IX Bishop Lawrence D. Soens
Region X Archbishop Eusebias J. Beltran
Region XI Bishop Gabino Zavala
Region XII Bishop Michael J. Kaniecki, S.J.
Region XIII Bishop George H. Niederauer
Staff—Sr. Sharon A. Euart, R.S.M.

Oversee the Use of the Catechism

Chairman—Archbishop Daniel M. Buechlein
Members—Bernard Cardinal Law
Archbishop Francis George, O.M.I.
Archbishop William Levada
Bishop Alfred C. Hughes
Bishop Donald W. Wuerl
Staff—Rev. John E. Pollard, Exec. Dir.
Rev. Thomas D. DeVries, Coord.-Assessment & Research

Review of Scripture Translations

Chairman—Bishop Richard J. Sklba
Members—Bishop Edward K. Braxton
Bishop Donald W. Trautman
Bishop Emil A. Wcela
Staff—Rev. J. Augustine DiNoia, O.P., Exec. Dir.
Ms. Siobhan M. Verbeek, Assoc. Dir.

Shrines

Chairman—Archbishop James P. Keleher
Members—Archbishop Charles J. Chaput, O.F.M.Cap.
Archbishop Francis George, O.M.I.
Bishop John J. Myers
Bishop Sean O'Malley, O.F.M.Cap.
Staff—Rev. Msgr. Anthony Czarnecki

Stewardship

Chairman—Archbishop Thomas J. Murphy
Members—Archbishop James P. Keleher
Bishop Eugene J. Gerber
Bishop James R. Hoffman
Bishop Joseph L. Imesch
Bishop John J. McRaith
Bishop Sylvester Ryan
Staff—Rev. Msgr. Paul D. Theroux

United States Catholic Conference

Address—*3211 Fourth St., N.E., Washington, DC 20017-1194. Tel: 202-541-3000.*

The United States Catholic Conference (USCC) is a civil entity of the American Catholic Bishops assisting them in their service to the Church in the United States of America by uniting the People of God where voluntary, collective action on a broad diocesan level is needed. The USCC provides an organizational structure and the resources needed to insure coordination, cooperation, and assistance in the public, educational, and social concerns of the Church at the national, regional, state, interdiocesan and, as appropriate, diocesan levels.

I. Officers

President—Bishop ANTHONY M. PILLA
Vice President—Bishop JOSEPH A. FIORENZA
Treasurer—Bishop ROBERT J. BANKS
Secretary—Archbishop HARRY J. FLYNN

II. NCCB General Secretariat

General Secretary—Rev. Msgr. DENNIS M. SCHNURR
Associate General Secretary—Sr. SHARON A. EUART, R.S.M.
Associate General Secretary—Rev. Msgr. WILLIAM P. FAY
Associate General Secretary—Rev. Msgr. PAUL D. THEROUX
Assistant General Secretary—Mr. BRUCE E. EGNEW

III. Staff Offices

Finance—Mr. KENNETH KOROTKY, Dir.
Accounting—Ms. JENNIFER McGOWAN, Dir.
General Counsel—Mr. MARK E. CHOPKO
Associate General Counsel—Ms. DEIRDRE A. HALLORAN
Associate General Counsel—Mr. JOHN A. LIEKWEG
General Services—Mr. DOUGLAS CISSEL, Dir.
Printing & Mailing Services—Mr. MARK J. BOWEN, Dir.
Government Liaison—Mr. FRANK J. MONAHAN, Dir.
Human Resources—Mr. THOMAS J. MEEHAN, Dir.
Library Services—Mr. GUY WILSON, Dir.
Management Information Systems—Mr. WILLIAM KISSANE, Dir.
Office of Public & Promotional Services—Mr. RICHARD W. DAW, Dir.

USCC COMMITTEES

EXECUTIVE LEVEL

Administrative Board

Chairman—Bishop ANTHONY M. PILLA
Members—
ANTHONY CARDINAL BEVILACQUA (Region III); JAMES CARDINAL HICKEY; BERNARD CARDINAL LAW; Archbishop DANIEL A. CRONIN (Region I); Archbishop JOHN C. FAVALORA; Archbishop HARRY J. FLYNN; Archbishop JEROME G. HANUS, O.S.B.; Archbishop THOMAS C. KELLY, O.P.; Archbishop THEODORE E. McCARRICK; Archbishop DANIEL E. PILARCZYK; Archbishop JUSTIN F. RIGALI, (Region IX); Archbishop FRANCIS B. SCHULTE; Archbishop MICHAEL J. SHEEHAN; Bishop VICTOR H. BALKE; Bishop ROBERT J. BANKS; Bishop GERALD R. BARNES; Bishop ALEXANDER J. BRUNETT; Bishop MATTHEW H. CLARK (Region II); Bishop THOMAS J. COSTELLO; Bishop JOHN S. CUMMINS; Bishop JOHN C. DUNNE; Bishop EDWARD M. EGAN; Bishop DAVID E. FELLHAUER; Bishop JOSEPH A. FIORENZA; Bishop JOSEPH A. GALANTE; Bishop WILLIAM R. HOUCK; Bishop JOSEPH L. IMESCH; Bishop JOHN R. KEATING (Region IV); Bishop JOHN F. KINNEY; Bishop EDWARD U. KMIEC; Bishop PAUL S. LOVERDE; Bishop HENRY J. MANSELL; Bishop ANTHONY M. MILONE (Region XII); Bishop ROBERT F. MORNEAU; Bishop GEORGE V. MURRY, S.J.; Bishop JOHN J. MYERS (Region XII); Bishop THOMAS J. O'BRIEN; Bishop SEAN P. O'MALLEY, O.F.M.Cap.; Bishop ARMANDO X. OCHOA (Region XIII); Bishop ANDREW PATAKI; Bishop RAYMUNDO J. PENA; Bishop A. EDWARD PEVEC (Region VI); Bishop RICARDO RAMIREZ, C.S.B.; Bishop JOHN H. RICARD, S.S.J.; Bishop FRANK J. RODIMER; Bishop PLACIDO RODRIQUEZ, C.M.F.; Bishop ROGER L. SCHWIETZ (Region VIII); Bishop WILLIAM S. SKYLSTAD; Bishop EDWARD J. SLATTERY (Region X); Bishop JAMES A. TAMAYO; Bishop DANIEL F. WALSH (Region XI); Bishop G. PATRICK ZIEMANN; Bishop PAUL A. ZIPFEL
Regional Alternates—
Bishop JOHN R. McNAMARA (Region I); Bishop JAMES M. MOYNIHAN (Region II); Bishop CHARLES J. MC DONNELL (Region III); Bishop WILLIAM E. LORI (Region IV); Bishop JUDE SPEYRER (Region V); Bishop BERNARD J. HARRINGTON (Region VI); Vacant - (Region VII); Bishop JOHN F. KINNEY (Region VIII); Bishop EDWARD K. BRAXTON (Region IX); Bishop CHARLES V. GRAHMANN (Region X); Bishop WILLIWM K. WEIGAND (Region XI); Archbishop FRANCIS GEORGE, O.M.I. (Region XII); Bishop GEORGE H. NIEDERAUER (Region XIII)

Executive Committee

Chairman—Bishop ANTHONY M. PILLA
Members—Bishop JOSEPH A. FIORENZA, Vice Pres.; Bishop ROBERT J. BANKS, Treas.; Archbishop HARRY J. FLYNN, Sec.
Members—BERNARD CARDINAL LAW
Staff—Rev. Msgr. DENNIS M. SCHNURR

Committee on Budget and Finance

Chairman—Bishop ROBERT J. BANKS
Members—Bishop DAVID E. FELLHAUER; Bishop JOHN H. RICARD, S.S.J.; Bishop DANIEL F. WALSH; Rev. Msgr. DENNIS M. SCHNURR
Staff—Mr. KENNETH KOROTKY

Committee on Personnel

Chairman—Bishop JOSEPH A. FIORENZA
Members—Bishop JOSEPH L. IMESCH; Bishop HENRY J. MANSELL; Rev. Msgr. DENNIS M. SCHNURR
Staff—Mr. BRUCE E. EGNEW

Committee on Priorities and Plans

Chairman—Bishop ANTHONY A. PILLA.
Vice President—Bishop JOSEPH A. FIORENZA
Treasurer—Bishop ROBERT J. BANK
Past President—WILLIAM CARDINAL KEELER
Members—Bishop HENRY J. MANSELL; Rev. Msgr. Dennis M. Schnurr
Staff—Sr. SHARON A. EUART, R.S.M.

DEPARTMENTAL LEVEL

Campaign for Human Development

Chairman—Bishop RICARDO RAMIREZ, C.S.B.
Members—Bishop STEPHEN E. BLAIRE; Bishop HOWARD J. HUBBARD; Bishop GEORGE V. MURRY, S.J.; Bishop PLACIDO RODRIGUEZ, C.M.F.; Bishop BERNARD W. SCHMITT; Bishop JOHN J. SNYDER; Bishop PAUL A. ZIPFEL; Mr. JOHN A. CARLISI; Ms. MAUREEN GEDDES; Mr. J. GIBBS MACVEIGH; Sr. PEG MALONEY, R.S.M.; Dr. WILLIAM A. MASON; Ms. KERRY A. ROBINSON; Sr. CONSUELO TOVAR, D.C.
Staff—Rev. ROBERT J. VITILLO, Exec. Dir.; Mr. TIMOTHY COLLINS, Deputy Exec. Dir.; Mr. DOUGLAS M. LAWSON, Assoc. Dir.- Field Operations; Ms. BARBARA STEPHENSON, Assoc. Dir.- Communications

COMMUNICATIONS

Chairman—Bishop THOMAS J. COSTELLO
Members—Sr. CAROL HOVERMAN, O.S.F.; Mr. FRANK MOROCK; Bishop MICHAEL R. COTE; Bishop WILLIAM E. FRANKLIN; Bishop JOSEPH A. GALANTE; Bishop ROBERTO O. GONZALEZ, O.F.M.; Bishop ROBERT N. LYNCH; Bishop LAWRENCE J. McNAMARA; Bishop CARL K. MOEDDEL; Bishop EDWIN F. O'BRIEN; Bishop PAUL A. ZIPFEL; Sr. MARIA DE LA C. AYMES, S.H.; Mr. GERALD D'AVOLIO; Mr. CHRISTOPHER GUNTY; Mr. GREG ERLANDSON; Mr. WILLIAM G. HALPIN; Dr. MARTI TOMAS IZRAL; Rev. PAUL A. SOUKUP, S.J.; Mrs. MARILYN VYDRA; Mr. JOSEPH ZWILLING
Consultant—WILLIAM CARDINAL KEELER
Staff—Rev. Msgr. FRANCIS J. MANISCALCO, Dir. for Communications; Mr. RAMON E. RODRIGUEZ, Dir. Catholic Communication Campaign; Mr. HENRY HERX, Dir. Film and Broadcasting; Mr. THOMAS N. LORSUNG, Dir. & Editor-in-Chief Catholic News Service.

DOMESTIC POLICY

Chairman—Bishop WILLIAM S. SKYLSTAD
Members—Archbishop JOHN F. DONOGHUE; Bishop JAMES W. MALONE; Bishop JOHN J. McRAITH; Bishop EDWARD O'DONNELL; Bishop JOHN RICARD, S.S.J.; Bishop CARLOS A. SEVILLA, S.J.; Bishop JOSEPH M. SULLIVAN; Mr. W. SHEPHERDSON ABELL; Rev. DENNIS J. DEASE; Mr. ROGER LYONS; Sr. MARY ROCH ROCKLAGE, R.S.M.; Ms. MILDRED SHANLEY; Mr. JOHN SWEENEY
Observers—Bro. DAVID ANDREWS, C.S.C.; Mr. J. MARK BRINKMOELLER; Ms. BEVERLY CARROLL; Mr. TIM COLLINS; Mr. JOHN E. CURLEY, Jr.; Mr. RONALDO CRUZ; Rev. JOHN HUEBSCHER; Mr. JOHN HUEBSCHER; Rev. FRED KAMMER, S.J.; Ms. ANNETTE KANE

Department of Social Development and World Peace

Sec.-Social Development & World Peace—Mr. JOHN CARR
Outreach Coord.—Mr. RICHARD FOWLER

Office of Domestic Social Development

Director—Ms. NANCY WISDO
Advisor-Health & Welfare Issues—Ms. PATRICIA KING
Advisor-Food, Agriculture & Rural Devel.—Mr.DANIELMISLEH
Advisor-Urban & Economic Issues—Mr. THOMAS SHELLABUGER

EDUCATION

Chairman—Archbishop FRANCIS B. SCHULTE
Members—Bishop EDWARD K. BRAXTON; Bishop EDWARD M. EGAN; Bishop BERNARD J. HARRINGTON; Bishop WILLIAM E. LORI; Bishop HENRY J. MANSELL; Bishop G. PATRICK ZIEMAN; Sr. JOAN CURTIN, C.N.D.; Rev. RICHARD M. JACOBS, O.S.A., Ph.D.; Sr. DOMENICA ROCCHIO, S.C.; Dr. ELAINE SCHUSTER
Staff—Rev. Msgr. THOMAS J. McDADE

Advisory Committee on Public Policy and Catholic Schools

Chairman—Archbishop FRANCIS B. SCHULTE
Members—BishopHENRY J. MANNSELL; Sr. MONICA KOSTIELNEY; Dr. MICHAEL McCARRON; Sr. DALE McDONALD; Dr. JEROME PORATH; Dr. ELAINE SCHUSTER; Mr.GEORGE SOLANA; Dr. LEONARD DEFIORE (NCEA)
At Large—Rev. PHILIP CRIBBEN; Sr. DOMINICA ROCCHIO, S.C.
Staff—Rev. Msgr. THOMAS J. McDADE; Rev. WILLIAM DAVIS, O.S.F.S.

Committee of Bishops and Catholic College and Univeristy Presidents

Chairman—Archbishop FRANCIS B. SCHULTE
Members—Bishop JOHN P. BOLES; Bishop IGNATIUS A. CATANELLO; Bishop JOHN M. D'ARCY; Bishop ROBERT N. LYNCH; Bishop GEORGE H. NIEDERAUER.
Presidents—Sr. BARBARA DOHERTY, S.P., (St. Mary's of the Woods, IN); Sr. BRIGID DRISCOLL, R.S.H.M., (Marymount College, Tarrytown, NY); Bro. PATRICK ELLIS, F.S.C., (The Catholic University of America, Washington, DC); Sr. MAUREEN FAY, O.P., (Detroit-Mercy University, Detroit, MI); Rev. PAUL L. LOCATELLI, S.J., (Santa Clara University, Santa Clara, CA); Rev. JOSEPH O'HARE, (Fordham University, New York, NY); Bro. DIETRICH REINHART, O.S.B., (St. John's University, New York, NY)
Representatives—Rev. CHARLES H. HAGAN, Higher Education and Campus Ministry; Dr. MONIKA HELLWIG, Exec. Dir., Association of Catholic Colleges and Universities
Staff—Rev. Msgr. THOMAS J. McDADE, Sec. for Education

SAPIENTIA CHRISTIANA

Chairman—Bishop JOHN P. BOLES
Members—Bishop DONALD W. TRAUTMAN; Bishop DONALD W. WUERL
Staff—Rev. CHARLES H. HAGAN, Rep.-Higher Education & Campus Ministry; Rev. Msgr. THOMAS J. McDADE, Sec. for Education

USCC Department of Education

Secretary for Education—Rev. Msgr. THOMAS J. McDADE

Representative for Catholic Schools and Federal Assistance—Rev. William Davis, O.S.F.S.
Representative for Higher Education and Campus Ministry—Rev. Charles H. Hagan
Representative for Catechesis and Multicultural Concerns—Sr. Elaine McCarron, S.C.N.
Representative for Catechesis and Leadership Development—Sr. Maureen Shaughnessy
Representative for Catholic School Parent Associations—Mr. Raymond J. Burnell

COMMITTEE ON INTERNATIONAL POLICY

Chairman—Archbishop Theodore E. McCarrick; *Members*—Adam Cardinal Maida; Bishop John S. Cummins; Bishop John J. Glynn; Bishop Wilton D. Gregory; Bishop James A. Griffin; Bishop William F. Murphy; Bishop Donald W. Wuerl; Bishop Ricardo Ramirez, C.S.B.; Bishop James A. Tamayo; Mr. James Bishop; Mr. Eugene Theroux, Esq.
Observers—Mr. J. Mark Brinkmoeller; Mr. Ken Hackett; Rev. Ted Keating, S.M.; Rev. Msgr. Robert L. Stern; Mr. John Swenson

Department of Social Development and World Peace

Secretary for Social Development and World Peace—Mr. John L. Carr
Outreach Coordinator—Mr. Richard Fowler

Office of International Justice and Peace

Director for International Justice and Peace—Rev. Drew Christiansen, S.J.
Policy Advisor, International Economic Affairs—Ms. Barbara Kohnen
Policy Advisor, Latin American, Caribbean, and Asian Affairs—Mr. Thomas Quigley
Policy Advisor, African Affairs—Mr. Kevin James Lee
Policy Advisor, Europe and Security Policies—Mr. Gerard F. Powers
Manager, Environmental Justice Project—Mr. Walter Grazer

SUBCOMMITTEE ON CATECHESIS

Chairman—Bishop G. Patrick Ziemann
Members—Bishop Edward K. Braxton; Dr. Maria de los Angeles Garcia; Dr. Mary Anne Boyarski; Sr. Joan Curtin, C.N.D.; Sr. Catherine Dooley, O.P.; Rev. Alfred McBride
Staff—Rev. Msgr. Thomas J. McDade, Sec. for Education; Sr. Elaine McCarron, S.C.N., Rep.- Catechesis and Multicultural Concerns; Sr. Maureen Shaughnessy, S.C., Rep.-Catechesis and Leadership Development

NATIONAL ADVISORY COUNCIL

Officers—Ms. Kathleen Dyer, Chm. (Fulton, NY); Mrs. Helen Boettcher, Chm.-Elect (Evansville, IN); Ms. Rita Wray, Sec. (Brandon, MS)
Members—Bishop Matthew H. Clark; Bishop George V. Murry, S.J.; Bishop G. Patrick Ziemamm; Bishop James A. Tamayo; Rev. John E. MacInnis; Rev. Richard G. Mohr; Rev. Martin M. Muller; Rev. Joseph Naumann; Rev. Lawrence J. O'Keefe; Rev. Msgr. Edward R. Sacks; Rev. Msgr. Donald Webber; Rev. Bernard Smith; Bro. Kevin Smith, O.F.S.; Sr. Theresa Kelly, F.M.A.; Sr. Mary Mollison, C.S.A.; Sr. Sean Peters, C.S.J.
Regional Representatives—
Region I: Mr. Matthew T. Boyle; Mrs. Lois E. McKinney
Region II: Mr. Joseph P. Schramm; Ms. Dolores B. Grierny
Region III: Mr. J. Brian Benestad; Mrs. Rita Martin
Region IV: Rev. Mr. Curtiss P. Todd; Ms. Mary M. Jeffcoat
Region V: Dr. Peter Pavlov, D.D.S.; Mrs. Rita Wray
Region VI: Mr. Kenneth Shepard; Mrs. Adele G. Salerno
Region VII: Mr. Joseph A. Russo; Mrs. Helen Boettcher
Region VIII: Mr. Justin W. Gullekson; Mrs. Elizabeth Mohr
Region IX: Mr. William B. Guyol; Mrs. Rhonda M. Lohkamp
Region X: Mr. Philip Verhalen; Mrs. Anne C. Dierks
Region XI: Mr. Justin K. Kwak; Mrs. Sharon Seitz
Region XII: Mr. Mario M. Villanueva; Mrs. Katherine Bishop
Region XIII: Mr. Antonio Gonzalez, Ph.D.; Mrs. Rachel Pineda
Members—Bishop Patrick R. Cooney; Bishop Joseph F. Martino; Deacon Ronald R. Ealey; Mrs. Graciela Contreras; Mrs. D. Phyllis DeCory; Ms. Kathleen Dyer; Sr. Teresa Gomez, H.M.S.S.; Ms. Carolyn C. Jenkins; Mr. Andrew Lyke, Jr.; Mr. Timothy D. McCauley; Bro. Donald Mouton, F.S.C.; Mrs. Nedra R. Robinson; Mrs. Olga Seim; Mr. Kenneth Wang; Rev. Msgr.Donald F. Zimmerman
Staff—Rev. Msgr. Paul D. Theroux

RELATED ORGANIZATIONS

*** Catholic Legal Immigration Network, Inc. (CLINIC)—**
Theological College, National Office, 401 Michigan Ave. N.E., First Flr., Washington, DC 20017. Tel: 202-635-2556; Fax: 202-635-2649.
Staff—Mr. John Swenson, Pres. & C.E.O.; Mr. Donald Kerwin, Vice Pres. & C.O.O.; Bishop George V. Murry, S.J., Treas.; Rev. Msgr. Dennis M. Schnurr, Sec.
Catholic Legal Immigration Network, Inc. (CLINIC) Board of Directors—
Chairman—Bishop John S. Cummins
Members—Adam Cardinal Maida; Archbishop John C. Favalora; Bishop Peter A. Rosazza; Bishop John W. Yanta; Bishop Gabino Zavala; Ms. Jane Golden Belford, Esq.; Judge James Belson; Mr. Edward L. Quinn
CLINIC was incorporated in 1988 as a non-profit tax-exempt subsidiary of the National Conference of Catholic Bishops. It is a unique legal services corporation charged with the mandate to serve as a national support and resource center and to assist diocesan programs in the provision of immigration services to their indigent and low-income clients, regardless of race, nationality, ethnicity, political or religious beliefs.

Catholic Relief Services—
World Headquarters: 209 W. Fayette St., Baltimore, MD 21201. Tel: 410-625-2220; Fax: 410-685-1635. Each diocese has a local CRS representative, listed in this book. Mr. Kenneth F. Hackett, Exec. Dir.
Catholic Relief Services Board of Directors—
Chairman—Bishop John H. Ricard, S.S.J.
Members—Archbishop Michael J. Sheehan; Bishop Joseph L. Imesch; Bishop John F. Kinney; Bishop Lawrence J. McNamara; Bishop Dale J. Melczek; Bishop Robert F. Morneau; Bishop Anthony J. O'Connell; Bishop Sean P. O'Malley, O.F.M.Cap.; Bishop Donald E. Pelotte, S.S.S.; Bishop William S. Skylstad; Bishop John M. Smith; Rev. Msgr. Dennis M. Schnurr

Catholic Relief Services-USCC The official overseas relief and development agency of U.S. Catholics; it is a separately incorporated organization of the U.S. Catholic Conference.

CRS was founded in 1943 by the bishops of the United States to assist the poor and disadvantaged outside this country.

CRS maintains programs and projects in 80 countries around the world. Help is given to all those in need regardless of race, creed or political affiliation.

In addition to its highly acclaimed disaster relief work, CRS carries on development and nutrition programs throughout the developing world. These include health projects, school feeding programs, agricultural development, water resource management, income-generating projects, and community promotion and are designed to help people help themselves and to raise the standard of living not only of the individual but of families and entire communities.

CRS operations are funded, in part, from the proceeds of an annual collection - American Bishops Overseas Appeal (also known as the Bishop's Welfare Emergency Fund) - held during the Lenten season in more than 18,000 Catholic churches in the U.S. - Support is also received from Operation Rice Bowl, a Lenten program of prayer, fasting, and almsgiving, and from individuals, church and school groups, foundations and corporations. Assistance from the federal government takes several forms: food available under Title II of Public Law 480; defrayment of ocean freight costs on U.S. government-donated foods and relief supplies generated by CRS itself; grants for some emergency operations.

Videos, education kits, posters, brochures, newsletters, and information on planned giving programs, including wills/bequests, and annuities, are available upon request.

In the year ending Dec. 31, 1994, the CRS global program in 80 countries had a total value of 300 milion dollars.

CTNA Telecommunications, Inc.—
3211 Fourth St. N.E., Washington, DC 20017-1194. Tel: 202-541-3200. Rev. Msgr. Francis J. Maniscalco, President; Rev. Msgr. William P. Fay, Chairman, Board of Directors.

National Religious Retirement Office—
3211 Fourth St., N.E., Washington, DC 20017-1194. Tel: 202-541-3215. Sr. Janet Roesener, C.S.J., Dir.

NATIONAL ORGANIZATIONS

Listing in this category is not related to classification under Canon Law as a public juridic person.

American Catholic Correctional Chaplains Association—
1717 N.E. Ninth St., Ste. 123, Gainesville, FL 32609. Most Rev. J. Kendrick Williams, D.D., Episcopal Advisor; Bro. Peter Donohue, C.F.X., Pres.; Rev. Mark Santo, Vice Pres.; Sr. Dorothea Murphy, R.S.M., Sec.; Rev. John Wilkinson, O.M.I., Treas.

The Board of Directors include the Episcopal Advisor, Elected Officers, Regional Vice Presidents, and Past Presidents. Address all Communications to the President or Secretary.

A non-profit organization for the purposes of unifying and implementing the Church's corrective and rehabilative efforts for the spiritual welfare of persons committed to the Catholic Chaplains' care, and to foster a Catholic approach to the problems and study of the correctional field in accord with the principles of Sacred Scriptures, Catholic philosophy and theology. Affiliated with the Social Development and World Peace Department, U.S. Catholic Conference, Inc., American Correctional Association, American Correctional Chaplains Association, National Council on Crime and Delinquency and Catholic University of America, it was established with approval of the American Bishops. Grants USCC recognized certification to qualified members.

Publications: *The Chap-lett.*

American Catholic Historical Association (1919)—
The Catholic University of America, Washington, DC 20064. Uta-Renate Blumenthal, Pres.; Rev. Msgr. Robert Trisco, Sec. & Treas.

A membership organization, founded to promote the study of church history understood in the broad sense and to assist American Catholics and other members in all fields of history.

The American College of the Roman Catholic Church of the United States—North American College (1859)—
Mailing Address: P.O. Box 29260, Washington, DC 20017-0260. His Eminence James Cardinal Hickey, Chm.; Very Rev. Timothy M. Dolan, Rector, 00120, Vatican City, Europe. Mr. Patrick W. Kennedy, Dir. Office for Devel. & Public Rels., Forrestal Village, 116 Village Blvd., Ste. 200, Princeton, NJ 08540-5799. Tel: 609-951-2209; Fax: 609-520-1702.

The College is owned and operated by the Bishops of the United States and is incorporated under the laws of the State of Maryland.

Association of Catholic Diocesan Archivists—
711 W. Monroe St., Chicago, IL 60661. Tel: 312-831-0711; Fax: 312-831-0610. Rev. Msgr. Francis J. Weber, Pres.; Mr. Charles Nolan, Vice Pres.; Sr. Catherine Louise LaCoste, C.S.J., Sec.

The Association of Catholic Diocesan Archivists was established in 1979 and is committed to the active promotion of professionalism in the management of diocesan archives in the United States.

Catholic Association of Teachers of Homiletics (CATH)—
Weston School of Theology, 3 Phillips Pl., Cambridge, MA 02138. Tel: 617-492-1960; Fax: 617-492-5833. Officers: Rev. Thomas A. Kane, C.S.P., Pres.; Rev. Daniel E. Harris, C.M., Sec. & Treas.

Catholic Campus Ministry Association—
Executive Office: 300 College Park Ave., Dayton, OH 45469-2515. Tel: 513-229-4648; Fax: 513-229-4024. Donald R. McCrabb, Exec. Dir.

Founded in 1969 by campus ministers, the association promotes the mission of the Church in higher education and implements the 1985 Pastoral Letter on Campus Ministry through educational programs and services, leadership, the development of cooperative relationships with other organizations and development activities. Membership is open to individuals interested in campus ministry.

Publications: *Crossroads, the Association Newsletter; The Catholic Campus, Ministry Directory; The Journal of The Catholic Campus Ministry Association.*

Catholic Charities USA—

1731 King St., Ste. 200, Alexandria, VA 22314. Tel: 703-549-1390; Fax: 703-549-1656. Most Rev. Joseph M. Sullivan, Episcopal Liaison; Rev. Timothy Hogan, Chm.; Rev. Fred Kammer, S.J., Pres.

Catholic Charities USA is a national network of more than 1,200 agencies and institutions as well as thousands of concerned individuals who are dedicated to serving the most vulnerable members of American society. The nation's largest network of private, independent social service organizations aims to support families, strengthen communities, and reduce poverty.

Diocesan Catholic Charities agencies provide shelter, food, counseling and a host of other services to children, teen parents, adults, and the elderly. The services are offered to people of all religious, national, racial, social, and economic backgrounds. Each year, millions of people turn to Catholic Charities for everything from a hot meal at a soup kitchen to a new family through adoption.

The organization was founded in 1910 as the National Conference of Catholic Charities by the Most Rev. Thomas J. Shahan and Rt. Rev. Msgr. William J. Kerby in cooperation with lay leaders of the Society of St. Vincent de Paul. Today the network has several hundred thousand volunteers and staff members who provide services to people in need, advocate for justice in social structures, and call the entire Church and other people of good will to do the same.

Catholic Charities USA serves members through national and regional meetings and networking, training, literature, and social policy advocacy on the national level. It is commissioned by the U.S. Catholic Conference to represent the Catholic community when disasters strike in the United States. Catholic Charities USA's president represents North America before Caritas Internationalis, the international conference of Catholic Charities, and thus maintains contact with the Catholic Charities Movement throughout the world.

Publications: quarterly membership magazine, *Charities U.S.A.*, biannual, *Directory of Catholic Charities, Agencies and Organizations; Annual, Survey* of Catholic Charities services nationwide; annual report; and various books, pamphlets and studies.

The Catholic Communications Foundation (CCF)—

P.O. Box 374, Pawling, NY 12564. Tel: 203-746-6685. The Catholic Communications Foundation was established and is supported by Catholic Fraternal Benefit Societies. Its mission is to assist the communications apostolates of the Catholic Church in the United States, with particular emphasis at the diocesan level. The Foundation awards religious communications training scholarships; Most Rev. Anthony G. Bosco, Chm.; Most Rev. Daniel A. Cronin, Pres.; Bernard J. Lengerman, Exec. Vice Pres.; James R. Bastis, Sec.

The Catholic Health Association of the United States (1915)—

Headquarters, 4455 Woodson Rd., St. Louis, MO 63134. Tel: 314-427-2500; Fax: 314-427-0029. 1875 Eye St. N.W., Ste. 1000, Washington, DC 20006-5409. Tel: 202-296-3993; Fax: 202-296-3997. John E. Curley, Jr., Pres. & CEO; William J. Cox, Exec. Vice Pres.; Timothy J. Eckels, Sr. Vice Pres. Planning & Policy Devel.; Sr. Jean deBlois, C.S.J., Vice. Pres., Mission, Ethics & Pastoral Svcs.; Rev. Joseph W. Kukura, Vice Pres. Church Rels.; David J. Sauer, Vice Pres. Admin. Svcs.; Brian F. Camey, Chief Financial Officer; J. Fred Caesar, Dir. Media Svcs.; Jack Bresch, Congressional & Exec. Liaison; Joanne Elden Beale, Co.-Dir. Sponsor Svcs.; Peter M. Leibold, Gen. Counsel; Bro. Peter Campbell, C.F.X., Vice Pres. Sponsor Svcs.

The Catholic Health Association of the United States is the national leadership organization of more than 1,200 Catholic healthcare sponsors, systems, facilities, and related organizations and services. Founded in 1915, CHA enables its members to accomplish collectively what they could not achieve individually. The association participates in the life of the Church by advancing the healthcare ministry and by asserting leadership within the Church and the rest of society through programs of advocacy, facilitation, and education. Presents Achievement Citation Award. Sponsors continuing education for healthcare personnel. Conducts surveys; compiles statistics. Divisions: Government Services; Administrative Services; IDN Services; Ministry Services; and Information Services.

Publications: 6 times-year, *Health Progress,* bimonthly, *Catholic Health World,* annual, *Guidebook of Catholic Health Care Facilities,* booklets, books & audio-visual on healthcare, Church-related subjects, CHA's Web Site, *CHA Online,* can be found at http:\\www.chausa.org.

Catholic Kolping Society of America (1849)—

P.O. Box 46252, Chicago, IL 60646-0252. (Please direct all correspondence to the National Secretary, Cheryl Boyle.) Cheryl Boyle, Natl. Sec.

The Society was founded by Rev. Adolph Kolping in Cologne, Germany, and established in the United States in 1856. The Catholic Kolping Society of America is a part of the world-wide Kolping movement and belongs to the International Kolping Society. There are 13 branches in principal cities of the United States with a combined membership of approximately 2,500. The membership is open to men and women of all ages. The Society's mission statement reads: We, the members of the Catholic Kolping Society of America, extend the vision of our founder, Blessed Adolph Kolping, by promoting the development of the individual and family; we foster a sense of belonging and friendship through our program of spiritual, educational, charitable and social activities.

Catholic Network Of Volunteer Service—

4121 Harewood Rd., N.E., Washington, DC 20017. Tel: 202-529-1100; 800-543-5046; Fax: 202-526-1094. Most Rev. Joseph A. Francis, S.V.D., Episcopal Advisor; James G. Lindsay, Exec. Dir. *National Office Team:* Phyllis Scaringe; Mary Ellen Moore; Jean Newell; Deborah F. McArdle; Jennifer L. Schumacher; Jack Dunne; Kent Cheng.

The Catholic Network of Volunteer Service promotes, recruits and refers volunteers to missions in the United States and overseas. We represent over 180 faith-based volunteer programs worldwide and work with the U.S. dioceses, religious communities and the private sector to determine their needs for help. The Catholic Network of Volunteer Services (CNVS) is committed to the goal that every Catholic man and woman be invited to consider a period of service in the missions, as a vital and important manifestation of the baptismal call of all Catholic people to missionary life. Currently, 5,500 men and women are serving in CNVS member mission programs offering their gifts and abilities in full-time service to people in need and living their Catholic faith more fully than many had imagined possible. These volunteers are serving domestically for a summer, six months, a year or more, and they are serving internationally for two or more years at a time. They are single and married, recent college graduates and early retirees, doctors and teachers, parish ministers and social workers, community organizers, computer operators, legal aides and more. Gatherings: Annual Conference; Formation Workshops, Training Seminars.

Publications: annual, cir. 70,000, *The Response,* biweekly, *How Can I Help?,* quarterly, *Mission Handbook. Awards:* The Father George Mader Award, given annually to honor organizations and individuals who promote the value of lay mission service. Previous recipients include the Missionary Cenacle Volunteers; the Catholic Church Extension Society; the Bureau of Catholic Indian Missions, the American Board of Catholic Missions; in 1992, the Year of the Woman, five women: Mrs. Erica John; Mrs. John McShane; Mrs. Susan Keane; Ms. Frances LaFollette; and Mrs. Elizabeth Christine Fojtu; the CNVS Episcopal Advisor, Bishop Joseph Francis, S.V.D. (retired); Sr. Ellen Cavanaugh, R.S.M., who served as the CNVS Executive Director from 1987-94; the University of Notre Dame and Villanova University for exemplary student, staff, and alumni programs.

The Catholic Theological Society of America—

Creighton University, 2500 California Plaza, Omaha, NE 68178-0116. Tel: 402-280-2505; Fax: 402-280-2502. William Thompson, Pres., Pittsburgh, PA, Mary Ann Donovan, Pres.-Elect, Berkeley, CA, Robert Schreiter, Vice Pres., Chicago, IL, Mary Ann Hinsdale, Sec., Worcester, MA, Roger McGrath, Treas., Baltimore, MD, Elizabeth Johnson, Past Pres., Bronx, NY. Board Members: Mary Ellen Sheehan, Toronto, Terrence Tilley, Dayton, OH, Susan Secker, Seattle, WA, Jeffrey Gros, Washington, DC, Joan Miller, Exec. Sec., Omaha, NE, Judith Dwyer, Editor of Proceedings, Staten Island, NY.

An association of professional theologians. Its purpose is to promote studies and research in theology within the Roman Catholic tradition, to relate theological science to current problems, and to foster a more effective theological education by providing a forum for an exchange of views among theologians and with scholars in other disciplines.

The Center For Human Development (1972)—

National Office: St. Joseph Abbey, Spencer, MA 01562. Tel: 508-885-8720.

The Center for Human Development is established to provide service and support to the people of God. To achieve this end, the Center designs and administers programs to foster the holistic spiritual growth and development of clergy, religious and laity.

Conference of Diocesan Coordinators of Health Affairs—

417 N. Main St., Davenport, IA 52801. Tel: 319-322-3303. Rev. James Conroy, Chm.

Membership in this Conference is by direct appointment and authority from the Ordinary of the appointee and gives members an opportunity of maintaining mutually helpful relationships with the Catholic Health Association, with one another, and with all religious, professional and governmental organizations in the health and hospital field.

The Conference of Major Religious Superiors of Men's Institutes of the United States, Inc.—

8808 Cameron St., Silver Spring, MD 20910. Tel: 301-588-4030; Fax: 301-587-4575. Rev. Steven Henrich, O.S.C., Exec. Dir.; Rev. Joseph Levesque, C.M., Pres.; Bro. Stephen Glodek, S.M., Vice Pres.; Bro. John Klein, F.M.S., Pres.-Elect; Rev. Mark Curesky, O.F.M.Conv., Sec. & Treas.

An association of the major superiors of religious communities and institutes of men for the purpose of promoting the spiritual and apostolic welfare of priests and brothers.

The Confraternity of Christian Doctrine, Inc.—

3211 Fourth St. N.E., Washington, DC 20017. Tel: 202-541-3098. Mary Sperry, Permissions Mgr.

The Confraternity is a distinct entity, separately incorporated and directed by a Board of Trustees from the United States Catholic Conference of Bishops. The purpose of the Corporation is to foster and promote the teachings of Christ as understood and handed down by the Roman Catholic Church. To this end it licenses religious and spiritual literature especially the Lectionary for Mass and the New American Bible, a translation made from the original languages in accordance with the papal encylical "Divino Afflante Spiritu" of Pope Pius XII and a revision of the New Testament and the Revised Psalms of the New American Bible.

Council of Major Superiors of Women Religious in the United States of America—

4200 Harewood Rd. N.E., P.O. Box 4467, Washington, DC 20017-0467. Tel: 202-832-2575; Fax: 202-832-6325. Mother Mary Bernard Nettle, L.S.P., Chm.

A canonically erected conference of Major Superiors of women's religious communities established in 1992 to promote mutual support among them and to foster coordination and cooperation with the Bishops' conference and individual Bishops, under the governance of the Holy See.

Federation of Diocesan Liturgical Commissions—

National Office, 401 Michigan Ave. N.E., P.O. Box 29039, Washington, DC 20017. Tel: 202-635-6990. Rev. Michael Spillane, Exec. Dir.; Rev. Edward J. Hislop, Chm.; Ms. Anne Grycz, Vice Chm.; Ms. Mary Ann Wittgen, Treas.; Rev. Joseph Fata, Delegate-at-Large; Ms. Carolyn Lassek, Delegate-at-Large.

The FDLC is a voluntary association of all diocesan liturgical commissions/offices from the United States. Two members of each diocesan liturgical commission/office serve as diocesan representatives to the FDLC. From this membership are elected 24 representatives (two from each of the 12 episcopal regions) to serve as the National Board of Directors. The day-to-day activities of the FDLC are directed by the Executive Director. The FDLC relates closely to the Bishops because its membership consists of their appointees. The Federation serves the Bishops and local commissions in matters of ongoing liturgical renewal. It also serves through education and other coordinated services requested by individual commissions or through consultation and voting at national meetings. The FDLC is organized and operated exclusively for religious and educational purposes.

Diocesan Fiscal Management Conference—

National Office, 3225 Pickle Rd., Oregon, OH 43616-4099. Tel: 419-693-0465. Most Rev. Donald W. Trautman, S.T.D., S.S.L., Episcopal Moderator; Rev. Robert J. Yeager, Ed.D., Exec. Dir.; Barbara

WOODBURY, Pres.; DAVID MALANOWSKI, Vice Pres.; DAVID CASTILLEJA, Sec. & Treas.

Mindful of their special ministry in the Roman Catholic Church as the extension of the Diocesan Bishop in fiscal matters, the members of the DFMC unite to be of service to the Church in the ministry of fiscal management.

In particular, this organization promotes the spiritual growth of its members; promotes financial and administrative knowledge and expertise in service to the local and national Church; facilitates the free exchange of ideas and information, and serves as a liaison among the fiscal managers of the Dioceses and Archdioceses of the Church.

Instituto de Liturgia Hispana—

P.O. Box 29387, Washington, DC 20017-0387. Tel: 202-319-6450; Fax: 202-319-6449. Rev. RAUL GOMEZ, S.D.S., Pres.; Ms. SYLVIA SANCHEZ, Vice Pres.; Mrs. MARIA PEREZ RUDISILL, Sec.; Rev. RUDY VELA, S.M., Treas.; Sr. DORIS MARY TUREK, S.S.N.D., Exec. Dir.

The Instituto is a national organization committed to meeting the liturgical needs of Hispanic Catholic communities. Its aim is to study, reflect and celebrate more authentically our Catholic faith from the perspective of our religious traditions and in the light of the teachings of the Church. Its members cooperate and assist in national, regional, diocesan, and parish groups with regard to Hispanic liturgical needs and concerns. They give lectures, publish in Spanish and in bilingual editions, and translate liturgical materials. Membership is open to all persons and institutions interested in liturgy. Committees: Art and Environment, Music, Popular Religiosity, Sacraments and Sacramentals, and Texts. The Instituto sponsors a national conference every two years on liturgical topics. The members meet annually.

International Catholic Migration Commission (ICMC) & ICMC, Inc.—

ICMC, Inc. Headquarters, 1319 F St. N.W., Washington, DC 20004. MICHAEL WHITELEY, Pres.; Dr. ANDRE VAN CHAU, Sec. Gen.

Provides technical assistance and coordination in area of service to migrants and refugees. Nonprofit New York Corporation.

Jesuit Conference, Inc.—

1616 P St., N.W., Washington, DC 20036-1405. Tel: 202-462-0400; Fax: 202-328-9212. Rev. DANIEL C. McDONALD, S.J., Exec. Sec. & Treas.

Ladies of Charity of the United States of America (LCUSA).—

910 Carnoustie Dr., Kansas City, MS 64145-1250. Mrs. JOHN E. HOAG, Pres.; Most Rev. PAUL ZIPFEL, Episcopal Chm. Spiritual Advisors: Revs. FRED KAMMER, S.J.; RICHARD GIELOW.

LCUSA Service Center, Ladies of Charity in the United States of America, whose 35,000 members give personal service to the needy, sick (especially the poor sick), underprivileged, handicapped and elderly, and also assist the clergy in pastoral care. They also strive for social justice. LCUSA encourages activities of the current Associations and promotes the organization of new Associations. The Board of Directors is the governing body of LCUSA. Organizational information is provided to members and Bishops through its official publication "Servicette," published four times annually and through contact with the President. National Biennial Meetings are held in even-numbered years in conjunction with Catholic Charities USA with whom LCUSA affiliates and Regional Meetings are held in alternate years. They also affiliate with the Association of International Charities of St. Vincent de Paul (AIC). Ladies of Charity was founded in 1617 by St. Vincent de Paul and has continued in existence longer than any other church-oriented volunteer group of lay persons. They work closely with the Daughters of Charity.

Leadership Conference of Women Religious in the United States of America—

Office, 8808 Cameron St., Silver Spring, MD 20910. Tel: 301-588-4955; Fax: 301-587-4575. Sr. MARGARET CAFFERTY, P.B.V.M., Exec. Dir.; Sr. NANCY SCHRECK, O.S.F., Past Pres.; ANNE MUNLEY, I.H.M., Pres.; MARY WASKOWIAK, R.S.M., Vice Pres.; Sr. MARY ANN GSCHWIND, F.S.P.A., Sec.; Sr. JUDITH ANN KARAM, C.S.A., Treas.

An association of the major superiors of Religious Communities of Women for the purpose of promoting the spiritual and apostolic welfare of the Sisterhoods of the United States.

Lithuanian Roman Catholic Federation of America—

4545 W. 63rd St., Chicago, IL 60629. Tel: 312-585-9500. Most Rev. PAULIUS BALTAKIS, O.F.M., Episcopal Advisor; Rev. Msgr. JOSEPH PRUNSKIS, Spiritual Advisor; SAULIUS V. KUPRYS, Pres., 150 S. Wacker Dr., Ste. 1050, Chicago, IL 60606. Tel: 312-346-5275; 708-243-0416; Fax: 312-346-5640; 708-243-0418.

A not-for-profit corporation founded in 1906 in Wilkes-Barre, PA, to promote and coordinate religious, educational and charitable activities among Lithuanian American Catholics, their organizations, institutions, religious communities, and parishes (for detailed information regarding religious institutions please refer to the Apostolate for Lithuanians).

Mariological Society of America (1949)—

Secretariat: Marian Library, University of Dayton, Dayton, OH 45469-1390. Tel: 937-229-4294; Fax: 937-229-4590. Rev. THOMAS A. THOMPSON, S.M., Exec. Sec.; Most Rev. AUSTIN B. VAUGHAN, Episcopal Chm.

The objects and purposes of this organization are to promote interest and research in the theology of the Virgin Mary. Membership is not limited to professional theologians. Annual convention in late May or early June.

The Mexican American Cultural Center (1972)—

3019 West French Pl., San Antonio, TX 78228. Tel: 210-732-2156. Most Rev. PATRICK F. FLORES, Chm.; Sr. MARIA ELENA GONZALEZ, R.S.M., Pres.

The Mexican American Cultural Center (MACC) is a National Catholic Institute for Pastoral Leadership and Language Studies for Hispanic ministry. MACC researches and responds to the religious and social needs of the Hispanic community in light of the Gospel and the social teachings of the Roman Hispanic community in light of the Gospel and the social teachings of the Roman Catholic Church. MACC programs include:

Hispanic Pastoral Ministry: A program that offers a creative response to the need for preparation for U.S. Hispanic ministry. Dates: January-April (in English) and September-December (in Spanish). *Mini-Pastoral:* An intense three-week preparation to meet the challenges of U.S. Hispanic ministry. Dates: January (in English), June (in English), July (in Spanish), and August (in English). Intensive Pastoral Spanish: A language program that concentrates on the needs of persons engaged in Hispanic ministry. *Intensive Pastoral English* for those whose first language is other than English; Cooperative Seminary Program, Masters degree in cooperation with Universities throughout the United States; Summer Workshops and Weeks of Study.

By Request, MACC faculty members serve dioceses, parishes and other groups by offering courses and workshops throughout the United States.

National Apostolate with People with Mental Retardation (1968)—

Mailing Address, 4516 30th Street, N.W., Washington, DC 20008. Tel: 800-736-1280; Fax: 202-686-6716. Dr. MICHELA M. PERRONE, Exec. Dir.

Established in 1968 to promote the full participation and inclusion of Catholics with mental retardation in the life of their church community.

Publications: quarterly journal; newsletter; pamphlets; training materials.

The National Association of Religious Brothers—

National Office, 1337 W. Ohio St., Chicago, IL 60622-6490. Tel: 312-829-8525; Fax: 312-829-8915. Bros. THOMAS J. SULLIVAN, F.S.C., Pres.; ROBERT FITZSIMMONS, C.F.C., Vice Pres.; AQUIN GAUTHIER, S.C., Treas.; GERALD MEEGAN, S.D.B., Pres.-Elect; Sr. EMILY WOLLSCHLAGER, S.S.N.D., Exec. Sec.; Bro. DENNIS WERMERT, S.C., Sec.

The National Association of Religious Brothers is a membership organization of brothers from all religious orders in the U.S., Canada and around the world.

Publications: bi-monthly, *Brothers.*

National Assembly of Religious Women (NARW)—

National Office, 529 S. Wabash, Rm. 404, Chicago, IL 60605. Tel: 312-663-1980; Fax: 312-663-9161. Sr. JUDITH VAUGHAN, C.S.J., Natl. Coord.

A grassroots organization of Catholic women with a commitment to work inclusively for systemic change. NARW members commit themselves to a Ministry of Justice by the continuous use of their organized power for the liberation of all peoples from oppression; to work actively to promote respect for and dignity of all, and to ensure effective participation of people in decisions which affect their own lives. Their challenging and supportive action is based on Gospel values. NARW publishes books, periodicals, and other educational materials; sponsors training conferences and workshops; and collaborates with groups addressing similar issues, particularly but not exclusively, those of justice for women in society, the Church and the world.

National Association of African American Catholic Deacons, Inc.—

4323 Chaplin St. N.E., Washington, DC 20019. Tel: 202-575-1296; Fax: 202-678-3325. Deacon JOHN P. STEWART, Pres.

National Association of Catholic Chaplains—

National Office, 3501 South Lake Dr., Milwaukee, WI 53207. Tel: 414-483-4898. Most Rev. THOMAS KELLY, O.P., Episcopal Advisor; Sr. MONICA LUCAS, S.C., Pres.; Rev. STEPHEN R. RYAN, O.S.M., Pres.-Elect; Rev. JOSEPH J. DRISCOLL, Exec. Dir.

The purpose of this organization is to assist priests, religious, and lay institutional and parish professionals to attain the realization of progressively higher ideals and professional competency for ministry in specialized works and settings. Membership includes those who minister to the sick and dying, the mentally retarded, the aged, the incarcerated and confined; the families of the above and all who are a part of the faith and/or service communities in which the members serve in both public and private institutions. Certification as Chaplain and Supervisor is granted. Continuing education programs are presented on a national and a regional basis. The regions are coterminus with the Bishops' regions. Local associations are also encouraged.

Publications: 10 times-year, journal-newsletter, *Vision.*

The National Association of Catholic Family Life Ministers—

Univ. of Dayton, 300 College Park, Dayton, OH 45469-1415. KAY RYAN, C.S.J., Pres.; PAT McCARTHY, Sec.

The National Association of Church Personnel Administrators (NACPA)—

Headquarters, 100 E. Eighth St., Cincinnati, OH 45202. Tel: 513-421-3134; Fax: 513-421-3085. Rev. KEVIN J. SPIESS, Pres.; Sr. ANN WHITE, S.L., Exec. Dir.

The National Association of Church Personnel Administrators (NACPA) is a membership association of lay, religious and clergy Personnel Directors, Assistant Directors, and Personnel Board Members serving dioceses, religious congregations and other church-related institutions. The purpose of the Association is to identify skills and competencies for human resource managers, develop personnel systems which integrate management and pastoral values, and advocate standards of just treatment for Church Personnel.

National Association of Deacon Organizations—

4410 89th St., Kenosha, WI 53142. Tel: 414-694-9143. Deacon RON LESJAK, Pres.

National Association of Diocesan Directors of Campus Ministry—

6 Madbury Rd.-P.O. Box 620, Durham, NH 03824-0620. Tel: 603-862-1310. Rev. FREDERICK J. PENNETT, Jr., Pres.

National Association of Diocesan Ecumenical Officers (NADEO)—

462 N. Taylor, St. Louis, MO 63108. Tel: 314-531-9700; Fax: 314-531-2269. Rev. VINCENT A. HEIER, Pres.; Mrs. GARLAND POHL, Vice Pres.; Rev. LAWRENCE J. McNEIL, Treas.; Deacon THOMAS McGOWAN, Sec.

The purposes of NADEO are to stimulate an exchange of ideas, experiences and evaluations among the ecumenical officers of the (Arch)Dioceses in union with Rome; to promote programs which further the work of Christian unity and of interreligious cooperation; and to cooperate with the Bishops' Committee for Ecumenical and Interreligious Affairs of the National Conference of Catholic Bishops, and with other ecumenical and interreligious agencies.

Publications: quarterly Newsletter; annual booklets on various ecumenical topics, *Handbook for Catholic Ecumenical Officers.*

National Association of the Holy Name Society (1970)—

Office of Communications, P.O. Box 1292, Baltimore, MD 21281-2012. Most Rev. MICHAEL A. SALTARELLI, Episcopal Moderator, Newark, NJ; Rev. THOMAS DZURENDA, National Spiritual Dir., Metuchen, NJ, AARON X. GILYARD, Pres., New Orleans, LA, FELIX AD SABLAD, Newsletter Editor, San Francisco, CA; Deacon STEPHEN ANDRUSSIAN, Supply Officer, Minersville, PA.

Association of parochial and diocesan Holy Name units of the International Society, established to promote reverence for the Divine Name of Jesus and for the sanctification of its members through spiritual and social action programs.

National Association of Pastoral Musicians—
National Office, 225 Sheridan St. N.W., Washington, DC 20011. Tel: 202-723-5800; Fax: 202-723-2262. Rev. Virgil C. Funk, Exec. Dir.

A national membership organization for the improvement of music within the parish, with special emphasis on liturgical music. Membership includes parish musicians and parish clergy simultaneously, with a unique interest in the practical issues facing the practicing musician and parish clergy.

Publications: six times a year with membership, *Pastoral Music,* bi-monthly with membership, *Pastoral Music Notebook.*

Services: NPM Conventions—national and regional gatherings for clergy and musicians. Director of Music Ministries Division (DMMD)—division for members who are full-time, salaried music staff in a parish or diocese and have responsibility for managing the overall liturgical music program. NPM-ME—division for music educators working in Catholic schools. NPM Hotline assists musicians seeking positions, and parishes looking for musicians. Resources for Association members are issued under the name, NPM Publications. NPM Board and NPM Council: Dr. J. Michael McMahon, Chm. The Association has Sections for Clergy, Choir Directors, Organists, Cantors, Seminary Music Educators, Military Musicians, Campus Ministers, Young Musicians, Hispanic Musicians and Musicians serving African-American parishes. The NPM Council provides committee leadership in each of these areas. National Training programs: annually, for Choir Directors, Organists, Guitarists and Cantors with emphasis on developing musical skills, leadership abilities and ministerial skills.

National Association of Diaconate Directors (1977)—
National Office, 1337 W. Ohio St., Chicago, IL 60622. Tel: 312-226-4033; Fax: 312-829-8915. Deacon Thomas C. Welch, Exec. Dir.; Rev. Msgr. Joseph Roth, Pres.; Deacon Maury Reed, Pres.-Elect.

Directors, vicars of deacons, and others responsible for the formation of candidates and the ongoing growth and development of deacons in the U.S. Promotes communication and facilitates the exchange of information and resources among members. Seeks to develop professional expertise among members through research, dialogue, formation and self-evaluation procedures. Proposes ways and means for effective implementation of solutions to national and regional issues relating to the diaconate. Maintains library on related issues.

National Black Catholic Clergy Caucus—
Office, 343 N. Walnut St., P.O. Box 1088, Opelousas, LA 70571-1088. Tel: 318-942-2481; Fax: 318-942-9201. Rev. Albert J. McKnight, C.S.Sp., Exec. Dir.

National Catholic Cemetery Conference—
National Office, 710 North River Rd., Des Plaines, IL 60016. Tel: 708-824-8131. Mr. Leo A. Droste, Exec. Dir.; Most Rev. G. Patrick Ziemann, D.D., Episcopal Moderator.

The Conference is an organization of Diocesan Directors of Cemeteries and parish cemetery administrators from throughout the United States and Canada. Guided by the principle: "That burial of the dead is one of the Corporal Works of Mercy," the Conference promotes high standards of Catholic cemetery management, development, operation and maintenance consistent with Christian service to the Catholic community; and fosters and promotes the religious, charitable and educational interests of Catholic cemeteries and the people they serve.

Publications: monthly magazine, *Catholic Cemetery,* various booklets on cemetery management & evaluation service; funeral liturgy at the cemetery. Annual Convention.

National Catholic Conference of Airport Chaplains (NCCAC)—
Mailing Address: Chicago O'Hare International Airport, P.O. Box 66353, Chicago, IL 60666-0353. Tel: 312-686-2636; Fax: 312-686-0130. Rev. John A. Jamnicky, Pres., (Chicago O'Hare Intl. Airport); Rev. Edward B. Hemkens, Vice Pres., (St. Louis Lambert Intl. Airport); Deacon Ben Wenning, Sec., (Charlotte/Douglas Intl. Airport); Rev. James T. Devine, Treas., (New York John F. Kennedy Intl. Airport); Most Rev. James C. Timlin, Bishop of Scranton, Episcopal Liaison.

This Conference provides support and communication for all Catholics performing pastoral ministry to airport & airline workers, and travelers; in affiliation with the Bishop's Committee on Migration of the National Conference of Catholic Bishops.

National Catholic Conference for Seafarers—
545 Savannah Ave., Port Arthur, TX 77640. Tel: 409-985-9661; Fax: 409-985-9691. Rev. Sinclair Oubre, Pres.; Mrs. Karen Lai, Vice Pres.; Bro. Hugh Maguire, Sec.; Col. Jack Booth, Treas.

An association of Chaplains, Seafarers and laity serving in the pastoral care of seafarers in the ports of the U.S. in affiliation with the Apostleship of the Sea in the United States.

National Catholic Committee on Scouting Executive Committee (1934)—
1325 W. Walnut Hill Lane, P.O. Box 152079, Irving, TX 75015-2079; Fax: 972-580-2502. Most Rev. Robert Carlson, Bishop of Sioux Falls, SD, Episcopal Advisor; Robert Runnels, Jr., Chm., (Merriam, KS), Thomas T. Nishikubo, Vice Chm., (Gardena, CA), Edward Gargiulo, Vice Chm., (Wilmington, DE), David Peavy, Vice Chm., (Houston, TX), Al Feliksa, Vice Chm., (St. Ignace, MI), Jack Deckenbach, Vice Chm., (Minneapolis, MN), Eleanore P. Starr, Admin. Sec., (Irving, TX); Revs. Randy Cuevas, Natl. Chap., (Donaldsonville, LA), Roger Gaulin, Assoc. Chap., (Colchester, CT), Leo LeBlanc, Past Natl. Chap., (Manchester, NH).

A voluntary organization of clergy and laymen, members include a chaplain and lay chairman from all of the dioceses in the United States Conferences. It serves as an advisory committee to the Boy Scouts of America. It has the responsibility of promoting and guiding cooperative contracts between the proper authorities of the Catholic Church in the United States and the Boy Scouts of America.

National Catholic Conference for Total Stewardship, Inc. (NCCTS)—
Mailing Address, 1633 N. Cleveland Ave., Chicago, IL 60614. Tel: 773-363-8046; 800-572-CCLO (2250); Fax: 773-363-2123. Rev. Francis A. Novak, C.SS.R., Pres.; Margaret Ann Filipovich, Admin. Asst.

The goal of this organization is to provide parishes and dioceses with a Total Stewardship Process called THE CHRISTIAN CELEBRATION OF LIFE (CCL), an integrated, comprehensive, systematically carried out formation of laity and clergy in Evangelization, Discipleship and Stewardship. The NCCTS achieves its goal by conducting Schools of Evangelization in dioceses and parishes and on the Internet for clergy, religious and laity and by working with them to implement the CCL in the local church. Implementation takes place on three levels: 1) Information on the CCL for in-place *Leadership,* clergy and laity; 2)Formation in the CCL for both parish leadership and newly recruited lay leaders called the *Matrix and Associate Matrices* (Small Faith Communities); 3) Transformation of church-going people into responsible Stewards of their Gifts, who reach out to non-church-going people by Home Visitation and Evangelization to build up the faith community. Transformation climaxes with *Stewardship of Eucharist* in order to deepen belief in and love of the Holy Eucharist, the fountain and summit of holiness. Under the title *Giving in Thanksgiving,* tithing is introduced as an "act of worship" within the liturgy. The CCL is also a perfect instrument for implementing the Holy Father's universal plan of preparation of the Church for the Great Jubilee Year 2000.

National Catholic Council on Alcoholism and Related Drug Problems, Inc.—
Headquarters, 1550 Hendrickson St., Brooklyn, NY 11234-3514. Tel: 718-951-7177; Fax: 718-951-7233. Rev. Msgr. Kieran Martin, Sec. & Treas.; His Eminence Anthony Cardinal Bevilacqua, Episcopal Moderator.

N.C.C.A. is an agency of the Church which is dedicated to the promotion of adequate treatment for all clergy, men and women religious, and laity who are suffering from alcoholism and other drug dependencies. N.C.C.A. also provides educational programs, especially through and an annual symposium and publication of the Blue Book, to reach all those engaged in pastoral ministry and (or) education concerning the problems associated with the use, misuse and abuse of alcohol and other drugs in our society.

National Catholic Development Conference (1968)—
86 Front St., Hempstead, NY 11550. Tel: 516-481-6000. Rev. Charles F. Shelby, C.M., Pres.; Mr. William J. Nixon, Vice Pres.; Ms. Carmelita Linden, Sec.; Sr. Ladonna Kassmeyer, F.S.P.A., Treas.; Mr. George T. Holloway, Exec. Dir.

Members include religious orders, colleges, high schools, hospitals, Catholic social service organizations and other institutions engaged in raising funds to support their activities. The function of the NCDC is to assist its members in developing effective, professional, ethical methods of raising funds. Members of the NCDC have subscribed to a code of ethics called Precepts of Stewardship. The national office serves as a center of information, issues special interest bulletins, conducts an annual conference and numerous seminars, workshops and regional meetings, maintains a library, follows and reports on legislative matters, conducts a special public information program, Giving is an Act of Faith, and maintains relations with a number of associations and organizations in related fields.

Publications: monthly newsletter, *Dimensions,* monthly, *Fund Raising Forum,* monthly, *The Member Exchange* (devoted to the methodology and theology of fund raising and stewardship), frequently issued, *Monitor* on postal, regulatory and tax issues; *NCDC Bibliography Of Fund Raising And Philanthropy; Nonprofit Postal Situation Facts,* quarterly, *A Guide for Preparing a Statement of Accountability.*

National Catholic Educational Association (1904)—
National Headquarters, 1077-30th St. N.W., Ste. 100, Washington, DC 20007. Tel: 202-337-6232; Fax: 202-333-6706. Most Rev. John J. Leibrecht, D.D., Chm.; Dr. Leonard DeFiore, Pres.

The National Catholic Educational Association (NCEA) has been providing leadership and service to American Catholic educators since 1904. NCEA's institutional and individual memberships represent Catholic education at all levels and in a variety of settings: preschools, elementary and secondary schools, parish catechetical/religious education programs, diocesan offices, colleges, universities and seminaries. The Association advances the educational and catechetical mission of the Church; provides leadership and service to its members; articulates the contribution of Catholic education to the Church and society; proclaims the uniqueness of Catholic schools; advocates recognition of and support for Catholic education in parish, school, college and university communities; enhances and supports leadership among the members; and fosters local, national and international collaboration

National Catholic Office for the Deaf (1971)—
NCOD Office, 7202 Buchanan St., Landover Hills, MD 20784-2236. Tel: 301-577-1684 (Voice); 301-577-4184 (TTY only); Fax: 301-577-1690. Nora Letourneau, Exec. Dir.

The NCOD, established by the Catholic pastoral workers of the deaf in 1971 at Trinity College, Washington, DC is devoted to coordinating the Church's pastoral ministry to deaf and hard-of-hearing persons at the national level; developing special liturgies, catechetical texts and materials; organizing workshops, leadership programs, cursillos and marriage encounters, and national and regional pastoral workers meetings; coordinating a training program for ministers with the deaf; and serving as an information and referral center for all those involved in this special ministry as well as members of the deaf community and their families. Policy is established by a board of directors elected by the members.

Publications: pastoral journal, *Vision,* newsletter for members, *RADAR.*

National Catholic Office for Persons with Disabilities (NCPD) (1982)—
P.O. Box 29113, Washington, DC 20017. Tel: 202-529-2933 (TT-voice); Fax: 202-529-4678. Mary Jane Owen, Exec. Dir.; Sr. Bernadette Downes, C.I.J., Chm.

Established to implement the Bishops' Statement on ministry with persons with disabilites. Prime concern is the establishment of Diocesan offices, support and education of newly appointed personnel, collaborating with other national Catholic organizations relative to the need for inclusion of disability perspectives in their programs, and advocacy in religious and secular concerns. Provides training, national conferences, resources, in cooperation with other national organizations concerned with ministry in the area of disabilities.

National Catholic Rural Life Conference—
National Headquarters, 4625 Beaver Ave., Des Moines, IA 50310-2199. Tel: 515-270-2634; Fax: 515-270-9447. Bro. David G. Andrews, Esq., C.S.C., Exec. Dir.; Most Rev. Raymond Burke, Bishop of La-Crosse, Pres. of the Bd. of Directors of the National Catholic Rural Life Conference.

The National Catholic Rural Life Conference is a membership organization grounded in a spiritual tradition which brings together the Church, care for creation and care for community. The NCRLC fosters programs of direct service and systemic change. As an educator in the faith, the NCRLC seeks to relate religion to the rural world; develops support services for rural pastoral ministers; serves as a prophetic voice and as a catalyst and convener for social justice.

National Catholic Stewardship Council, Inc.—
National Office, 1275 K St. N.W., Ste. 980, Washington, DC 20005. Tel: 202-289-1093; Fax: 202-682-9018. Most Rev. James P. Keleher, S.T.D., Archbishop of Kansas City, KS, Episcopal Moderator; Mr. Matthew R. Paratore, Natl. Dir.

The Stewardship Council promotes the concept of holistic Christian stewardship. It serves dioceses, parishes, professional firms, religious congregations, Catholic colleges/universities and Catholic associations from the U.S., Canada and the Caribbean through its seminars, summer institute, publications and annual international annual conference. It encourages the growing professionalism of diocesan development procedures and programs directed toward improving the long-term growth of diocesan funds. It also fosters the development of parish-centered stewardship programs aimed at increasing monies and personal service on the basis of the principles of stewardship as outlined in the 1992 NCCB Pastoral Letter: *Stewardship: A Disciple's Response.*

Publications: newsletter, *Commitment,* journal, *Resource,* publications available for parish and diocesan use through, Liturgical Press; *Stewardship Kit, For a complete list of services and publications contact the National Office. Membership information available on request.*

National Catholic Student Coalition (1988)—
Campus Ministry Center, 344 N. Prairie St., Whitewater, WI 53190. Tel: 414-473-5555. Rev. James Goodman, Admin.

The National Catholic Student Coalition (NCSC) is a national coalition of Catholic student communities in institutes of higher education. The coalition provides a platform for Catholic students to reflect, speak, and act on issues within the university, the Church and society. The NCSC promotes the development of campus ministry and Catholic lay and religious leaders for the Church and society. The NCSC is a member of the International Movement of Catholic Students. Membership is open to groups or individuals associated with Catholic student groups in higher education. The NCSC holds an annual leadership conference.

Publications: *The Catholic Collegian.*

The National Center for Urban Ethnic Affairs (1971)—
National Office, P.O. Box 20, Cardinal Station, Washington, DC 20064. Tel: 202-232-3600; 635-5128. Dr. John A. Kromkowski, Pres.; Rev. George F. McLean, Sec.; Rev. Msgr. Salvatore Polizzi, Chm.; Ruth Dee, Treas.

"The great task incumbent on all men of good will is to restore the relations of the human family in truth, in justice, in love, and in freedom." (Pope John XXIII, *Peace on Earth.*) The independent program of this non-profit organization has evolved from the efforts initiated by the former Task Force on Urban Problems of the United States Catholic Conference. Its aims and purposes are to continue the expression of the Catholic Church's concern for the problems facing our urban society. NCUEA promotes the celebration of cultural pluralism in America and bridges the gaps between groups of various ethnic and cultural traditions. The Center disseminates information, conducts research, develops and supports programs concerned with ethnic Americans and urban society. The Center in association with various community and church groups develops workshops, conferences and programs related to the quality of human life, national priorities and the development of an urban mission strategy. The Center is also associated with public and private agencies in developing urban economic, social, and intercultural programs, etc.

The National Conference of Catechetical Leadership (NCCL)—
3021 Fourth St. N.E., Washington, DC 20017-1102. Tel: 202-636-3826; Fax: 202-832-2712. Most Rev. Sylvester Ryan, Episcopal Moderator; Dr. Carole Eipers, Pres.; Mr. Neil Parent, Exec. Dir.

A voluntary organization composed of diocesan catechetical personnel, including vicars and secretaries of education, catechetical office directors and staff; academics specializing in religious education; representatives of diocesan parish DRE organizations and various associate and affiliated members, including publishers of catechetical texts. The Conference operates on three levels: national, regional and provincial. The purpose of the Conference is to assist its members in their roles as leaders in the Church's catechetical ministry through networking, resource development, research, training, consultation and advocacy. The Conference is also committed to collaboration with other national groups concerned with catechesis/religious education.

National Council for Catholic Evangelization (1983)—
905 E. 166th St., P.O. Box 1260, South Holland, 60473-2420 22111. Tel: 1-800-786-NCCE. Rev. Carl Tenhundfeld, Pres., Houston, TX; Ms. Gloria Clark, Vice Pres., Lafayette, LA; Sr. Louise Alff, F.M.D.C., Sec., Buffalo, NY; Bro. Douglas Zlatis, C.F.C., Treas., Lisle, IL; Mr. John Simon, Exec. Dir., South Holland, IL; Most Rev. John G. Vlazny, Episcopal Liaison, Winona, MN.

Established at the request of the Bishops' Committee on Evangelization, NCCE is an independent membership association which brings together (Arch)Dioceses, organizations, religious congregations, parishes and individuals to promote evangelization as the primary and essential mission of the Church. NCCE sponsors an Annual Conference and Evangelization Training Workshops and Seminars.

Publications: ten issues a year, *Newsletter; Resource Review.* Resources: printed materials, audio and video tapes. Memberships are available to (Arch)Dioceses, religious congregations, organizations, parishes and individuals.

National Council of the Catholic Men—
4712 Randolph Dr., Annandale, VA 22003. Mr. William Sandweg, Pres.

The NCCM, a federation of Catholic organizations of men, has pioneered in promoting parish councils and diocesan renewal. Through its affiliation with the National Council of Catholic Laity, NCCM provides programs of information and action, national conferences, leadership training, information services and a medium through which Catholic men may be heard nationally on matters of common interest.

National Council of Catholic Women—
1275 K St. N.W., Ste. 975, Washington, DC 20005. Tel: 202-682-0334; Fax: 202-682-0338. Joan McGrath, Pres.; Annette Kane, Exec. Dir.

The NCCW is a federation of Catholic women's organizations in the United States, numbering 7,000 local, diocesan and national organizations. It programs through its six commissions, Church, Family Concerns, Community Concerns, International Concerns, Legislation and Organization. The program of the Council is furthered through leadership training institutes and national conventions.

Publications: bimonthly, *Catholic Woman.*

National Federation of Catholic Physicians' Guilds (1932)—
850 Elm Grove Rd., Elm Grove, WI 53122. Tel: 414-784-3435; Fax: 414-782-8788. *Officers* 1996-1997: Michael V. Rock, M.D., Pres., Paradise Valley, AZ, Paul A. Byrne, M.D., Pres.-Elect, Toledo, OH, Richard A. Watson, M.D., Vice Pres., Mountainside, NJ, Michael R. Aiello, M.D., Sec., Rochester, NY, Charles P. Prezzia M.D., Treas., Holland, OH; Most. Rev. Edwin O'Brien, S.T.D. D.D., Episcopal Advisor, Yonkers, NY, Robert H. Herzog, Exec. Dir.; Michael J. Herzog, Asst. Dir.

Directors:

Region I: John A. Roque, M.D., 1997, Saunderstown, RI, E. Joanne Angelo, M.D., 1998, Cambridge, MA.

Region II: Michael R. Aiello, M.D., 1997, Rochester, NY, Alfred W. Murphy, M.D., 1998, White Plains, NY.

Region III: Larry Lyons, M.D., 1997, N. Huntington, PA, John D. Lane, M.D., 1998, Philadelphia, PA.

Region IV: Dennis M. Doody, M.D., 1997, Columbus, OH, Felino Barnes, M.D., 1998, Zanesville, OH.

Region V: Robert J. Saxer, M.D., 1997, Ft. Walton Beach, FL, Patrick Mongan, M.D., 1998, Augusta, GA.

Region VI: Albert E. Gunn, M.D., 1997, Houston, TX.

Region VII: Donald J. Mehan, M.D., 1997, St. Louis, MO, Patrick D. Guinan, M.D., 1998, Chicago, IL.

Region VIII: John I. Lane, M.D., 1998, Great Falls, MT.

Region IX: Robert Hurt, M.D., 1997, Phoenix, AZ, William A. Brophy, M.D., 1998, Phoenix, AZ.

Region X: Thomas M. Goodwin, M.D., 1997, Monrovia, CA, Stephen G. Watson, M.D., 1998, Van Nuys, CA.

Military Guild: Richard A. Watson, M.D., 1998, Mountainside, NJ. Upholding the principles of the Catholic faith and morality as related to the science and practice of medicine.

National Federation for Catholic Youth Ministry, Inc. (NFCYM) (1981)—
3700-A Oakview Terr. N.E., Washington, DC 20017-2591. Tel: 202-636-3825. Rev. Leonard C. Wenke, Exec. Dir.; Ms. Charlotte McCorquodale, Chm.; Ms. Kathleen Carver, Assoc. Dir.; Ms. Therese Brown, Assoc. Dir.; Ruby Mikell, Admin. Asst.; Jane Parvis, Sec.

A membership association of diocesan youth offices, founded after a reorganization of the USCC Department of Education and the National CYO Federation (now defunct). The stated purpose is "In light of the Gospel message, the Federation will foster the development of youth ministry in the United States to, with, by, and for youth." Members of the Federation work through diocesan, regional and national structures to provide national leadership, support and direction for adults and youth in youth ministry. The biennial National Conference on Catholic Youth Ministry (a conference for adults working with youth); the biennial National Catholic Youth Conference (for teenagers and their adult chaperones); the writing and distributing of resource booklets for parish workers; religious recognitions for Catholic Girl Scouts/Camp Fire; position papers on current topics and issues in youth ministry; and regional and diocesan consultations.

The National Federation of Spiritual Directors—
St. John's Seminary, 127 Lake St., Brighton, MA 02135; Fax: 617-787-2336. Rev. George P. Evans, Pres.

A federation of persons charged with the responsibility of spiritual formation in high school seminaries, college seminaries, novitiates, theologates, and houses of formation in the United States.

National Foundation for Catholic Youth—
3700-A Oakview Terr., Washington, DC 20017. Tel: 202-636-3825. Rev. Leonard Wenke, Exec. Dir.; Most Rev. Robert Carlson, Pres. of Board; His Eminence John Cardinal O'Connor, Honorary Chm.

National Office for Black Catholics (1972)—
The Paulist Center, 3025 Fourth St. N.E., Washington, DC 20017. Tel: 202-635-1778. Walter T. Hubbard, Exec. Dir.

The National Office for Black Catholics, organized in 1970, is a central agency with the general purpose of promoting active and full participation by Black Catholics in the Church and of making more effective the presence and ministry of the Church in the Black community. Its operations support the aspirations of Black Catholics for objectives that include: representation and voice among Bishops and other leaders of the Church; promotion of vocations to the priesthood and religious life; sponsorship of programs of evangelization, pastoral ministry, education and liturgy on national and regional levels; recognition of Black heritage in liturgy, community life, theology and education; and establishment of an Institute for Leadership Training Formation and Development.

National Organization for Continuing Education of Roman Catholic Clergy, Inc.—
1337 W. Ohio St., Chicago, IL 60622-6490. Tel: 312-226-1890; Fax: 312-829-8915. Rev. Francis S. Tebbe, O.F.M., Pres.; Bro. Paul J. Murray, C.F.X., Exec. Dir.

A professional organization of those involved in the continuing education/formation of priests in the Catholic Church. Dioceses and religious communities in the U.S. are full members. Institutions and organizations that are concerned with continuing education/formation of priests are associate members. Dioceses and provinces outside the U.S. may be associate members. NOCERCC was founded in 1973 through the efforts of the National Federation of Priests Councils. It is governed by a Board of Directors that involves a president elected by the membership, elected members from the 13 NCCB Regions and two elected religious members. Its services include an Annual Convention, training for new and experienced directors, regional meetings, consultations and service to regional and interdiocesan programs.

Publications: bimonthly, *NewsNotes, Book of Sabbaticals,* other resource publications.

National Pastoral Center for the Chinese Apostolate, Inc.—
234 Fairview Ave., Paramus, NJ 07652. Tel: 201-634-0709; Fax: 201-634-0801. Rev. Joseph Chiang, Dir.

National Pastoral Life Center—
Headquarters, 18 Bleeker St., New York, NY 10012-2404. Tel: 212-431-7825; Fax: 212-274-9786. Rev. Philip J. Murnion, Dir.; Ms. Karen Sue Smith, Editorial Dir.; Donna Ciangio, O.P., Project Dir.

The Center is an information, training, and consulting resource for diocesan and parish leader The Center works with bishops and diocesan directors as consultants for diocesan evaluation and reorganization and conducts and staffs educational and training programs for pastors and others in ministry. It also sponsors pastoral ministry conventions, conducts pastoral research, and serves as a resource and referral center for church ministers.

Publications: magazine and, *Church,* Center Papers and other publications.

The Papal Foundation.

Office, 222 North 17th St., Philadelphia, PA 19103. Tel: 215-587-2491. Rev. Msgr. Thomas J. Benestad, Exec. Dir.; Mr. Thomas Moran, Dir. of Devel. Board of Trustees; John Cardinal O'Connor, Chm.; Anthony Cardinal Bevilacqua, Vice Chm.; John Cardinal Carberry; Bernard Cardinal Law; James Cardinal Hickey; Roger Cardinal Mahony; William Cardinal Keeler; Adam Cardinal Maida. Trustees: Most Rev. Theodore E. McCarrick, Pres.; Most Rev. Francis B. Schulte; Most Rev. Thomas V. Daily; Mr. Arthur Birtcher; Mr. Geoffrey T. Boisi; Mr. John Brennan; Mr. William F. Connell; Mr. Thomas J. Flatley; Mr. E. F. Hansen; Mr. Frank J. Lynch; Mr. William A. McIntosh; Mr. Thomas S. Monaghan; Mr. Robert J. Morrissey; Mr. Frank Pasquerilla; Mr. Gerald A. Rauenhorst; Mr. John Saeman; Mr. Francis J. Sehn; Mr. Daniel J. Donohue, Trustee Emeritus.

The Parish Evaluation Project—

O'Hare Lake Office Plaza, 2200 E. Devon, Ste. 283, Des Plaines, IL 60018. Tel: 847-297-2080; Fax: 847-297-2107. Co-Dirs.: Rev. Thomas P. Sweetser, S.J.; Ms. Margie A. Tomlinson; Ms. Mary Beth Vogel, Assoc. Dir. The Parish Evaluation Project is a non-profit organization under the laws of Illinois, whose purpose is to provide religious and educational services to Catholic parishes in the United States in the areas of surveying, needs assessment, leadership skills, goal setting, evaluation techniques, staff development, pastoral council formation and other resources helpful in parish planning and renewal.

Pax Christi U.S.A., National Catholic Peace Movement.

532 W. 8th St., Erie, PA 16502-1343. Tel: 814-453-4955; Fax: 814-452-4784. Mr. Etienne de'Jonghe, Intl. Sec.; Most Rev. Walter F. Sullivan, Pres.; Mary Carter-Warren, Chm.; Colleen McHenry-Connell, Treas.; Most Rev. Thomas J. Gumbleton; Matthew Smith; Ligory Fernandes; Margaret Gaffney; Eirik Frederick-Harteis; Sheila Marie Tobbe; Tom Cordaro. Pax Christi has as its primary objective to work with all people for peace for all humankind, always witnessing to the peace of Christ. The Movement springs from a gospel vision of peace. It asks its members to ground their peacemaking in prayer, study and action on the message of Jesus. Pax Christi keeps as its priorities the Christian vision of spirituality, nonviolence and peacemaking, disarmament, demilitarization, reconciliation with justice, human rights and global restoration, and economic and interracial justice in the United States.

Publications: quarterly newspaper and peace education materials.

Religious Formation Conference—

National Office, 8820 Cameron St., Silver Spring, MD 20910. Tel: 301-588-4938; Fax: 301-585-7649. Sr. Jane Finnerty, O.S.U., Exec. Dir.; Sr. Clare D'Auris, O.S.F., Assoc. Dir. Board Co-Chm.: Sr. Dorothy Batto, C.C.V.I.; Rev. Nick Waseline, O.S.F.S. An association of women and men Religious engaged in Initial and On- going Formation ministry in their Communities. The Conference, through its National Office and Regional Conferences, seeks to be a forum for exchange and a center for communication and the sharing of resources.

Retreats International, Inc.—

National Office, Box 1067, Notre Dame, IN 46556. Tel: 219-631-5320; Fax: 219-631-6968. Rev. Thomas W. Gedeon, S.J., Dir.; Most Rev. Robert Morneau, Bishop Advisor; Mr. Larry Novakowski, Pres.; Sr. Mary Elizabeth Imler, O.S.F., Vice Pres.; Mr. Kevin DePrey, Sec. & Treas. Trustees: Sr. Catherine Cahill, O.S.F.; Ms. Geri Eitter; Sr. Sheila McEvoy, S.N.J.M.; Ms. Nancy Golen; Rev. Ted Haag, O.F.M. Created in 1928 under the guidance of the Archbishops and Bishops of the United States. The national headquarters for information and all phases of the retreat movement in the United States.

The Slovak Catholic Federation (1911)—

134 S. Washington St., P.O. Box 348, Wilkes-Barre, PA 18701. Tel: 717-823-4168. Rev. Msgr. Thomas V. Banick, Pres.; Most Rev. Joseph V. Adamec, Episcopal Advisor; Rev. Edward A. Slosarcik, Spiritual Dir.; Mr. Tibor T. Kovalovsky, Sec. & Treas.

Founded by Father Joseph Murgas at Wilkes-Barre, Pennsylvania as a non-profit corporation to promote and coordinate religious activities among Slovak Catholic fraternal societies, religious communities, and Slovak ethnic parishes in their effort to address themselves to the pastoral needs of Slovak Catholics in the United States and Canada.

UNDA-USA National Catholic Association for Communicators—

National Office, 901 Irving Ave., Dayton, OH 45409-2316. Tel: 937-229-2303; Fax: 937-229-2300. Mr. Frank Morock, Pres.; Mr. David Maloney, 1st Vice Pres.; Sr. Rose Pacatte, 2nd Vice Pres.; Marilyn Vydra, Treas.; Rev. James Gardiner, S.A., Sec.

UNDA-USA, the national Catholic association of communicators, includes more than 400 individual and organizational members: diocesan directors of communications, professional broadcasters, editors of regional and national publications, educators, religious community communications personnel, directors of closed-circuit educational television (ITFS) systems and staffs, and syndicators of national Catholic radio and television programs. UNDA-USA has on its Board of Directors representatives of local, regional and national Catholic communications agencies, including the Catholic Television Network (dioceses having ITFS systems), the Association of Catholic Television and Radio Syndicators and the U.S. Catholic Conference Department of Communications. UNDA-USA, organized in 1972 as successor to the Catholic Broadcasters Association (CBA), is a member of the international Catholic association for radio and television known as UNDA International (the Latin word for "Wave," symbolic of air waves of communication). UNDA-USA is dependent on annual individual and organizational membership fees for its operating expenses. Principal activities of UNDA-USA: annual General Assembly for all members, consisting of professional communication sessions; previews and ministry-related activities; annual Gabriel Awards for excellence in broadcasting on local and national levels.

Publications: quarterly newsletter, *White papers.*

The USCC Commission on Certification and Accreditation—

3501 S. Lake Dr., P.O. Box 07058, Milwaukee, WI 53207-0058. Tel: 414-486-0139; Fax: 414-489-0006. Stephanie Y. Mitchem, Board Chm.; Sr. Kay L. Sheskaitis, I.H.M., Exec. Dir.

Accredits post-secondary programs that offer pastoral formation or education for persons preparing for ministry. These programs may be offered or sponsored by colleges, dioceses, health institutions, retreat centers, universities, or other institutions that are authorized to conduct post- secondary programs and whose programs are in compliance with the USCC/CCA standards, accreditation policies, and procedures established by the Commission. The Commission also approves certification standards for national organizations of specialized ministers and certification procedures of dioceses utilizing the Commission-certification standards of national organizations and procedures established by the Commission. Certification procedures approved by the Commission authorize the certification of specialized ministers in the name of the USCC.

United States Catholic Mission Association—

3029 Fourth St. N.E., Washington, DC 20017. Tel: 202-832-3112; Fax: 202-832-3688. Mr. William Morton, Pres.; Sr. Rosanne Rustemeyer, S.S.N.D., Exec. Dir.

The USCMA was juridically established September 1, 1981. Its members include U.S. missioners, mission organizations, diocesan mission offices, and others concerned about the mission of the Church and global solidarity. The Association seeks to help missioners to stay up-to-date on mission and world trends, to promote greater global awareness, sensibility, and solidarity in the U.S., and periodically to be a voice for U.S. missioners speaking out in defense of the poor and oppressed throughout the world. USCMA activities include a national conference and regional seminars that highlight specific mission themes and issues, liaison and cooperation with missionary bodies of other Christian churches, and training programs and refresher courses for departing and returning missionaries. The USCMA is responsible for gathering statistical data on the U.S. missionary personnel, which is published bi-annually.

Publications: bimonthly newsletter, *Mission Update,* reports, *U.S. Catholic Missionary Statistics,* and education programs on mission and global awareness.

NATIONAL ORGANIZATIONS WITH INDIVIDUAL I.R.S. RULINGS

The Beginning Experience—

International Ministry Center, 1209 Washington Blvd., Detroit, MI 48226. Tel: 313-965-5110; Fax: 313-965-5557. Most Rev. A. Edward Pevec, Episcopal Moderator; Timothy Bauer, Pres.; Kathleen Murphy, Vice Pres.; Eugenia Tarantino, Sec. & Treas.

The Beginning Experience is a copyrighted weekend program to help divorced, separated and widowed persons, as well as their families, work through the trauma of the loss of their spouse and make a new beginning in life. The program was designed by and for Catholics and has its roots in sound Catholic tradition and the sacramental life of the Church. True to the ecumenical spirit in the Church since Vatican II, it has been open to persons of all faiths from the beginning. The BE Weekend was originated in 1974 by Sr. Josephine Stewart of Fort Worth, TX. It has spread throughout the United States as well as other countries. Trained teams make the Beginning Experience Weekend available on a regular basis. It also serves as an informational and materials resource for the establishment of support groups to minister to the needs of the divorced, separated and widowed and their families at various points in their growth process.

Canon Law Society of America—

Catholic University, Washington, DC 20064. Tel: 202-269-3491; Fax: 202-319-5719. Rev. Patrick J. Cogan, S.A., Exec. Coord.; Sr. Lynn Jarrell, O.S.U., Pres., San Francisco, CA; Very Rev. Lawrence DiNardo, Vice Pres., Pittsburgh, PA; Rev. Paul Counce, Sec., Baton Rouge, LA; Rev. Msgr. Robert Deely, Treas., Boston, MA.

A membership association of Bishops, Clergy, Religious and Laity for the purpose of promoting research and professional collaboration in the area of Ecclesiastical Law.

Catholic Coalition on Preaching, Inc.—

University of Notre Dame, 1201 Hesburgh Library, Notre Dame, IN 46556. Tel: 219-631-5328. Rev. Eugene F. Lauer, Pres.

Catholic Engaged Encounter, Inc.—

5 Tara Dr., Pittsburgh, PA 15209. Tel: 412-487-5116. Mr. Dave Florijan; Mrs. Millie Florijan.

Catholic Library Association—

461 W. Lancaster Ave., Haverford, PA 19041. Tel: 215-649-5250. Bro. Paul J. Osterdorf, Pres. Tel: 507-457-6935.

The Catholic Mutual Relief Society of America—

4223 Center St., Omaha, NE 68105. Tel: 402-551-8765. Mr. Donald E. Ruth, Pres. & CEO; Mr. Joseph T. Beveridge, Exec. Vice Pres. & Chief Oper. Officer.

The Catholic Relief Insurance Company of America—

4223 Center St., Omaha, NE 68105. Tel: 402-551-8765. Mr. Donald E. Ruth, Pres. & CEO; Mr. Joseph T. Beveridge, Exec. Vice Pres. & Chief Oper. Officer.

Conference for Pastoral Planning and Council Development—

625 Cleveland St., Clearwater, FL 34615. Tel: 813-461-5000; Fax: 813-462-6037. Robert Burke, Chm.; Mr. Arthur X. Deegan, II, Exec Dir.

National Association for Lay Ministry (NALM)—

National Office, 5420 S. Cornell Ave., Ste. 103, Chicago, IL 60615-5604. Tel: 773-241-6050; Fax: 773-241-6061. Sr. Louise Bond, S.N.J.M., Exec. Dir. Executive Board; Barbara L. Castellano, Chair; Tom Germanson, Sec. & Treas.; Dennis Beeman; Catherine Crino; Kathleen Heffern; Marti Jewell; Graziano Marcheschi; John Reid.

NALM is a professional organization that supports, educates and advocates for lay ministers and promotes the development of lay ministry in the Catholic Church. In accomplishing its mission, NALM is committed to: 1) the Gospel; 2) working for justice; 3) upholding the dignity of each person; 4) ongoing conversion of persons and structures; 5) collaboration in ministry and participative Church leadership; 6) on-going dialogue and consultation with national groups.

Publications: bimonthly, *Lay Ministry; National Competency-Based Standards for Pastoral, Ministers, Pastoral Associates, Parish Life Coordinators;*

No Turning Back: A Lay Perspective on Ministry in the Catholic Church of the United States; Focus Group Study of Career/Volunteer Lay Ministers Annual Conference—1997 "Ministry: Holy People Walking on Holy Ground" will focus on the Church's responsibility to care for the earth. Research and Networking.

National Catholic Conference for Interracial Justice NCCIJ (1959)—
Office, 1200 Varnum St., N.E., Washington, DC 20017-1102. Tel: 202-529-6480; Fax: 202-526-1262. Co-Chm.: Most Rev. Charles J. Chaput, O.F.M.; Hon. Lindy Boggs; Deacon Joseph M. Conrad, Jr., Exec. Dir.
Established to implement the teaching of the Catholic Church on cultural and racial justice and to promote the church's vision of multicultural, multiracial understanding, mutual respect and collaboration.

National Catholic Risk Retention Group, Inc.—
National Office, 1500 N. Woodward Ave., Ste. 209, P.O. Box 864, Bloomfield Hills, MI 48303-0864. Tel: 810-642-6676; Fax: 810-642-6412. Most Rev. Raymond J. Boland, Episcopal Moderator; Mr. Henry P. Devlin, Mng. Dir.; Rev. Kevin C. McCoy, Chmn. Bd.; Mr. William H. Hinkes, Pres.; Mr. Joseph Frank, Vice. Pres.; Rev. Jay C. Haskin, Sec.; Mrs. Maryellen Connor, Treas.
The Company is wholly owned by 45 Catholic Dioceses and The Christian Brothers Risk Pooling Trust. It underwrites excess liability insurance for Diocese and other Church organizations listed in the Kenedy Directory. Coverage is always subject to a minimum self-insured retention or underlying coverage of $250,000. Maximum limits of coverage available are $5 million. The company has the capability to underwrite insurance in all states, Territories and Possessions of the U.S.

National Catholic Young Adult Ministry Association, Inc.—
3700-A Oakview Terr. N.E., Washington, DC 20017-2591. Tel: 202-636-3825; Fax: 202-526-7544. James J. Breen, Pres. Tel: 617-783-4505.

National Conference of Diocesan Vocation Directors (1962)—
National Office, P.O. Box 1570, Little River, SC 29566. Tel: 803-280-7191. Revs. Michael Kuse, Pres.; Robert Flagg, Vice Pres.; Sr. Mary Jo Kirt, O.S.F.S.C., Sec.-Treas. Members at Large: Revs. William Kubacki; Carlos Velazquez; Mrs. Dorothy Foss, Exec. Dir.
This Conference serves as a resource-service to the personnel of vocation offices in dioceses associated with the USCC-NCCB. Besides direct service to its membership, this Conference also represents them to various related organizations and offers personal and ministerial support to the staffs of these diocesan vocation office members. The Conference is a member organization of the National Coalition for Church Vocations and represents members to the NCCB Committee on Vocations.
Publications: five times a year, *Newsletter,* documents of interest. Meetings annually for Regional Conferences and a National Convention.

The National Federation of Priests' Councils (1968)—
National Office, 1337 W. Ohio, Chicago, IL 60622. Tel: 312-226-3334; Fax: 312-829-8915. Rev. Donald Wolf, Pres.; Bro. Bernard F. Stratman, S.M., Exec. Dir.
The NFPC was organized to promote priestly fraternity by facilitating communication among priests' councils, to provide a forum for priests to discuss pastoral matters, to enable priests' councils to speak with a common voice, to promote and collaborate on programs of pastoral research, to further the spiritual renewal of priestly life, to collaborate with national lay and religious groups in ways that promote renewal in the Church, to collaborate with the NCCB in addressing the needs of the Church in the U.S.A., to encourage priests' councils to promote justice in light of the social teachings of the Church, and to participate in developing a national and universal perspective of church and ministry.
The NFPC represents 109 priests' councils, priests' associations and religious communities. Elected delegates of member councils meet annually to set policy, and a national executive board meets regularly to carry out the work of the NFPC, assisted by standing committees. Member councils represent approximately 26,000 priests.
Publications: quarterly newsletter, *Touchstone,* bimonthly, *NFPC Update,* books; occasional papers and studies concerned with various aspects, of ministry, the ministerial priesthood and the spiritual renewal of priests.

National Institute for the Word of God—
Headquarters, 487 Michigan Ave. N.E., Washington, DC 20017. Tel: 202-529-0001. Episcopal Advisory Board: Most Rev. John R. Quinn; Most Rev. John L. May; Most Rev. David E. Foley; Most Rev. Juan A. Arzube; Most Rev. William G. Connare; Most Rev. Rene H. Gracida; Most Rev. James W. Malone; Most Rev. Francis R. Shea. Staff: Rev. John Burke, O.P., Exec. Dir.; Mr. William H. Graham, Assoc. Dir.; Mr. Robert W. McChesney, Jr., Sec.; Very Rev. Joseph P. Allen, O.P., Treas. Councilors; James R. Dimond, Jr.; Mary C. Graham; Michael A. Graham; Rev. Thomas M. Kalita; Francis Litz; Joseph A. Taney; Janet Waters; Rev. John Farren, O.P.; Carol McCarty; Kay McDonald.
The Institute is an unaffiliated nonprofit organization incorporated under the laws of the District of Columbia, whose purpose is to promote, support, conduct and assist in any way whatsoever educational, liturgical, and remedial programs and activities, public and private, through the use of any and all media, to further effective communication of the revealed word of God, as the primary pastoral work of the Church. Ongoing efforts include the dissemination of scriptural, theological and pastoral aids such as books, films and tape albums, and the conducting of parish missions, conferences and retreats for clergy and laity.

National Service Committee of the Catholic Charismatic Renewal of the United States Inc.—
P.O. Box 628, Locust Grove, VA 22508-0628. Rev. Patsy Iaquinta, Chm.; Mr. Walter Matthews, Dir.
Our focus is to foster baptism in the Holy Spirit in the life of the Church in the United States and throughout the world, to broaden and deepen the understanding that baptism in the Holy Spirit is the Christian inheritance of all, and to strengthen the Catholic Charismatic Renewal. The National Service Committee has established and supported numerous programs to help further our mission. Some of the activities and programs include the establishment of Chariscenter USA, which serves as the national headquarters for our committee. The NSC offers a national newsletter, a Prayer Group directory and leadership training materials as well as an annual national conference, outreach to youth and youth ministers, and evangelization training. The NSC has supported the International Catholic Charismatic Renewal Office in Rome.

North American Pastoral Center for Czech Catholics—
c/o St. Norbert Catholic Church, 300 E. Taft Ave., Orange, CA 92865-4388. Tel: 714-998-0251; Fax: 714-637-0201. Rev. Msgr. Peter Esterka, Pres.

The North American Forum on the Catechumenate—
3033 Fourth St., N.E., Washington, DC 20017-1102. Tel: 202-529-9493; Fax: 202-529-9497. Thomas H. Morris, Exec. Dir.
The North American Forum on the Catechumenate is an international network committed to the implementation of the Order of Christian Initiation of Adults. The work of FORUM is overseen by a Board of Directors of 5 elected representatives. A variety of institutes are offered in co-sponsorship with a hosting diocese to serve the local Church. FORUM networks with other national groups, promotes research into issues raised by Christian Initiation (including outreach to the inactive through a process of Re-Membering Church), and provides a quarterly newsletter which focuses on the impact of Christian Initiation on the Church as well as key issues related to its implementation.

Worldwide Marriage Encounter (1969)—
National Office, 2210 E. Highland Ave., Ste. 106, San Bernardino, CA 92404. Tel: 909-863-9963; Fax: 909-863-9986. Most Rev. G. Patrick Ziemann, D.D., Episcopal Moderator. Secretariat Team: Rev. Richard O'Brien, C.M.; Dennis Battaglia; Alynn Battaglia.
Organized to foster a program of Christian information to instruct married couples in the means to find God's plan and matrimony in their lives, for their own spiritual development and the betterment of all humankind; and to develop, foster and disseminate an adult catechesis supporting, furthering and building upon such instruction. Worldwide Marriage Encounter offers the marriage encounter weekend experience in 150 dioceses in the United States as well as in 88 foreign countries. In the United States over 1,500,000 couples and over 5,000 priests and bishops have experienced the Worldwide weekend.
Publications: quarterly, *Matrimony - A Sign of Our Church.*

Catholic Committee for Refugees & Children—
3211 Fourth St. N.E., Washington, DC 20017-1194; Fax: 202-541-3399. Mr. John Swenson, Pres.
In operation since January 4, 1937, and incorporated since 1954, the Catholic Committee for Refugees and Children was founded to counsel and cooperate with European refugees during and after World War II. Since that time its mission has been expanded to include service to refugees worldwide. It has a special mandate from the bishops concerning its work with children through international child welfare, child care or placement, international adoption, and the coordination of services to refugee minors.

National Association of State Catholic Conference Directors

An Association of the Directors of the State Catholic Conference, organized in 1968 to facilitate and encourage the exchange of information among its members pertaining to the activities, programs and organization of the Conferences. A State Catholic Conference is a Church agency composed of the dioceses within a state to provide for the coordination of the public policy concerns of the Church. Thus a Conference of the Church communicates with state government, other Church Agencies, non-Catholic churches and secular agencies. Bishops, priests, religious and lay persons are involved in the work of the State Conferences. *National Association:* NCCB-USCC, 3211 4th St., N.E., Washington, DC 20017-1194.

ARIZONA

Arizona Catholic Conference.
400 E. Monroe St., Phoenix, AZ 85004-2376. Tel: 602-257-0030; Fax: 602-258-3425.
Chairman—Bishop THOMAS J. O'BRIEN.
Executive Director—Rev. Msgr. EDWARD J. RYLE, M.A., M.S.W.

CALIFORNIA

California Catholic Conference.
Cathedral Square, 1010 11th St., Suite 200, Sacramento, CA 95814. Tel: 916-443-4851; Fax: 916-443-5629; E-mail: cacathcon@aol.com.
President—Bishop JOHN S. CUMMINS.
Vice President—Bishop SYLVESTER D. RYAN.
Secretary-Treasurer—Bishop MICHAEL P. DRISCOLL.
Executive Director—Rev. Msgr. E. JAMES PETERSEN.
Director of Catholic Charities of California, Inc.—Mr. RICHARD MOCKLER.
Associate Director for Public Policy—Mr. DAVID A. POLLARD.
Associate Director for Hispanic Affairs—Rev. ALEJANDRO CASTILLO, S.V.D.
Associate Director for Communications—Mrs. CAROL HOGAN.
Associate Director for Education—Mr. ROBERT TEEGARDEN.
Associate Director for Finances—Mr. RICHARD STRAWN.
General Counsel—Mr. RAYMOND LEONARDINI, Esq.

COLORADO

Colorado Catholic Conference.
200 Josephine, Denver, CO 80206. Tel: 303-388-4411; Fax: 303-388-5786.
Executive Director—Mr. JAMES P. TATTEN.

CONNECTICUT

Connecticut Catholic Conference.
134 Farmington Avenue, Hartford, CT 06105. Tel: 203-524-7882; Fax: 203-525-0750.
President and Chairman of the Board—Archbishop DANIEL A. CRONIN.
Secretary—Bishop EDWARD M. EGAN.
Executive Director—Rev. THOMAS J. BARRY, J.C.L.

FLORIDA

Florida Catholic Conference.
P.O. Box 1638, Tallahassee, FL 32302. Tel: 904-222-3803; Fax: 904-681-9548.
President—Archbishop JOHN CLEMENT FAVALORA.
Executive Director—D. MICHAEL MCCARRON, Ph.D.

GEORGIA

Georgia Catholic Conference.
Office Building, 3200 Deans Bridge Rd., Augusta, GA 30906. Tel: 404-798-1719; Fax: 706-798-6037.
Executive Director—Mr. CHEATHAM E. HODGES, Jr.

HAWAII

Hawaii Catholic Conference.
St. Stephen Diocesan Center, 6301 Pali Hwy., Kaneohe, HI 96744-5298. Tel: 808-263-8844, ext. 548; Fax: 808-261-7022; E-mail: 73377.1027@compuserve.com.
Executive Director—Rev. MARC R. ALEXANDER, S.T.D.

ILLINOIS

Catholic Conference of Illinois.
500 North Clark St., Chicago, IL 60610. Tel: 312-467-4375. and 200 Broadway, Springfield, IL 62701. Tel: 217-528-9200.
Chairman—JOSEPH CARDINAL BERNARDIN.
Executive Director—Mr. DOUG DELANEY.
Associate Directors—JURA S. SCHARF; JOAN L. MCKINNEY.

INDIANA

Indiana Catholic Conference.
1400 N. Meridian St., P.O. Box 1410, Indianapolis, IN 46206. Tel: 317-236-1455; Fax: 317-236-1456.
General Chairman—Archbishop DANIEL M. BUECHLEIN, O.S.B., D.D.
Executive Chairman—Bishop WILLIAM L. HIGI, D.D.
Executive Director—Dr. M. DESMOND RYAN, Ph.D.

IOWA

Iowa Catholic Conference.
505 5th Ave., Ste. 818, Des Moines, IA 50309-2392. Tel: 515-243-6256; Fax: 515-243-6257.
President—Archbishop JEROME HANUS, O.S.B.
Vice President—Bishop LAWRENCE D. SOENS.
Secretary-Treasurer—Bishop JOSEPH CHARRON, C.PP.S.
Executive Director—TIMOTHY MCCARTHY.

KANSAS

Kansas Catholic Conference.
6301 Antioch, Merriam, KS 66202. Tel: 913-722-6633.
Chairman—Archbishop JAMES P. KELEHER.
Executive Director—Mr. ROBERT RUNNELS, JR.
Program Coordinator—Mrs. BEATRICE SWOOPES.

KENTUCKY

Catholic Conference of Kentucky.
1042 Burlington Ln., Frankfort, KY 40601. Tel: 502-875-4345; Fax: 502-875-2841.
Chairman—Archbishop THOMAS C. KELLY, O.P.
Executive Director—Mrs. JANE J. CHILES.

LOUISIANA

Louisiana Catholic Conference.
3423 Hundred Oaks Ave., Baton Rouge, LA 70808. Tel: 504-344-7120; Fax: 504-383-9591.
Chairman—Archbishop FRANCIS B. SCHULTE.
Executive Director—Mr. KIRBY J. DUCOTE.
Assistant Director for Administrative Services—Mrs. BARBARA BOVARD.

MARYLAND

Maryland Catholic Conference.
188 Duke of Gloucester St., Annapolis, MD 21401-2515. Tel: 410-269-1155.
Chairman—WILLIAM CARDINAL KEELER.
Executive Director—RICHARD J. DOWLING.

MASSACHUSETTS

Massachusetts Catholic Conference.
55 Franklin St., Boston, MA 02110. Tel: 617-574-0771.
Executive Director—Mr. GERALD D. D'AVOLIO.

MICHIGAN

Michigan Catholic Conference.
505 N. Capitol Ave., Lansing, MI 48933. Tel: 517-372-9310; Fax: 517-372-3940.
Chairman—His Eminence ADAM CARDINAL MAIDA.
President & CEO—Sr. MONICA KOSTIELNEY, R.S.M.
Secretary-Treasurer—Most Rev. PATRICK R. COONEY.

MINNESOTA

Minnesota Catholic Conference.
475 University Ave., W., Suite B, St. Paul, MN 55103-1996. Tel: 612-227-8777; Fax: 612-227-2675.
President—Archbishop HARRY J. FLYNN.
Vice President—Bishop RAYMOND A. LUCKER.
Secretary/Treasurer—Bishop ROGER L. SCHWIETZ, O.M.I.
Executive Director—Rev. DAVID F. MCCAULEY.
Education Department Director—Mr. THOMAS J. PEARSON.
Social Concerns Director—Mr. TIMOTHY J. RUDNICKI.

MISSOURI

Missouri Catholic Conference.
600 Clark Ave., P.O. Box 1022, Jefferson City, MO 65102. Tel: 573-635-7239; Fax: 573-635-7431.
General Chairman—Archbishop JUSTIN RIGALI.
Executive Chairman—Bishop MICHAEL MCAULIFFE.
General Counsel Executive Director—LOUIS C. DEFEO, JR.
Assistant Director—MIKE HOEY.
Administrative Assistant—JOSETTA M. FORCK.

MONTANA

Montana Catholic Conference.
P.O. Box 1708, Helena, MT 59624. Tel: 406-442-5761; Fax: 406-442-9047.
President—JEREMIAH LOWNEY.
Vice President—Vacant.
Treasurer—Mr. EDWARD WAMBOLT.
Executive Director—Mrs. SHARON HOFF.

NEBRASKA

Nebraska Catholic Conference.
215 Centennial Mall South, Ste. 410, Lincoln, NE 68508-1890. Tel: 402-477-7517.
President—Archbishop ELDIN FRANCIS CURTISS.
Vice President—Bishop FABIAN W. BRUSKEWITZ.
Secretary-Treasurer—Bishop LAWRENCE J. MCNAMARA.
Executive Director—JAMES R. CUNNINGHAM.

NEW JERSEY

New Jersey Catholic Conference.
211 N. Warren St., Trenton, NJ 08618. Tel: 609-599-2110.
President—Archbishop THEODORE E. MCCARRICK.
Executive Director—WILLIAM F. BOLAN, JR. J.D.

NEW YORK

New York State Catholic Conference.
465 State St., Albany, NY 12203. Tel: 518-434-6195.
President—JOHN CARDINAL O'CONNOR.
Vice President—Bishop JOHN R. MCGANN.
Treasurer—Bishop THOMAS V. DAILY.
Chairman—Public Policy Committee—Bishop HOWARD J. HUBBARD.
Executive Director—JOHN M. KERRY.

NORTH DAKOTA

North Dakota Catholic Conference.
227 W. Broadway, Suite 2, Bismarck, ND 58501. Tel: 701-223-2519; Fax: 701-223-6075.
President—Bishop JAMES S. SULLIVAN.
Secretary-Treasurer—Bro. BASIL ATWELL, O.S.B.
Executive Director—CHRISTOPHER T. DODSON.

OHIO

Catholic Conference of Ohio.
35 E. Gay St., Columbus, OH 43215. Tel: 614-224-7147.
President—Archbishop DANIEL E. PILARCZYK.
Vice President—Bishop ANTHONY M. PILLA.
Secretary-Treasurer—Bishop JAMES A. GRIFFIN.
Executive Director—TIMOTHY V. LUCKHAUPT.

OREGON

Oregon Catholic Conference.
2838 E. Burnside St., Portland, OR 97214. Tel: 503-233-8387; Fax: 503-235-2630.
President—Archbishop FRANCIS E. GEORGE, O.M.I.
Vice President—Bishop THOMAS J. CONNOLLY.
Secretary-Treasurer—Very Rev. GREGORY MOYS.
General Counsel & Executive Director—Mr. ROBERT J. CASTAGNA.

PENNSYLVANIA

Pennsylvania Catholic Conference.
223 North St., P.O. Box 2835, Harrisburg, PA 17105. Tel: 717-238-9613; Fax: 717-238-1473.
Chairman—Anthony Cardinal Bevilacqua.
President—Bishop Nicholas C. Dattilo.
Vice President—Rev. Msgr. George B. Flinn.
Secretary—Rev. Msgr. Joseph E. Kurtz.
Interim Executive Director—Mr. Francis J. Viglietta.
Treasurer—Rev. Msgr. Michael E. Servinsky.

TEXAS

Texas Catholic Conference.
1625 Rutherford Ln., Bldg. D, Austin, TX 78754-5105. Tel: 512-339-9882.
Chairman—Archbishop Patrick F. Flores.
Executive Director—Bro. Richard Daly, C.S.C.
Associate Director—Rev. Msgr. William L. Broussard.
Associate Director for Education—Mr. George Solana.
Director, Volunteers for Education and Socical Services—Mrs. Barbara Price.
Director of Evangelization—Rev. John Duffy, C.S.P.
Director, Catholic Archives of Texas—Mrs. Kinga Perzynska.

WASHINGTON

Washington State Catholic Conference.
419 Occidental Ave., S. #608, Seattle, WA 98104. Tel: 206-382-4821; Fax: 206-382-4822.
President—Archbishop Thomas J. Murphy.
Vice President—Bishop William S. Skylstad.
Executive Director—Mr. Edward E. Dolejsi.
Associate Director—Sister Sharon Park, O.P.
Administrative Assistant—Ms. Evelyn Tangalin.

WEST VIRGINIA

West Virginia State Catholic Conference.
1300 Byron St., P.O. Box 230, Wheeling, WV 26003.
Director—Rev. John R. Gallagher.

WISCONSIN

Wisconsin Catholic Conference.
30 W. Mifflin St., Room 302, Madison, WI 53703-2579. Tel: 608-257-0004; Fax: 608-257-0376.
Chairman—Archbishop Rembert G. Weakland, O.S.B.
Vice Chairman—Bishop William H. Bullock.
Executive Director—John A. Huebscher.
Associate Director—Sharon L. Schmeling.

Diocese of Albany

(Dioecesis Albanensis)

Most Reverend

HOWARD J. HUBBARD, D.D.

Bishop of Albany; ordained December 18, 1963; appointed February 1, 1977; ordained and installed March 27, 1977. *Res., 125 Eagle St., Albany, NY, 12202.* Tel.: 518-462-3804.

Chancery Office: Pastoral Center, 40 N. Main Ave., Albany, NY, 12203. Tel.: 518-453-6600; Fax: 518-453-6795.

ESTABLISHED APRIL 23, 1847.

Square Miles 10,419.

(Incorporated by a special act of the Legislature of the State of New York, April 12, 1941, with the title "The Roman Catholic Diocese of Albany, New York.")

Comprises the entire Counties of Albany, Columbia, Delaware, Fulton, Green, Montgomery, Otsego, Rensselaer, Saratoga, Schenectady, Schoharie, Warren and Washington and that part of Herkimer and Hamilton Counties, south of the northern line of the townships of Ohio and Russia, as existing in 1872 in the State of New York.

For legal titles of parishes and diocesan institutions, consult the Chancery Office.

STATISTICAL OVERVIEW

Personnel	
Bishop	1
Retired Bishops	1
Priests: Diocesan Active in Diocese	238
Priests: Active Outside Diocese	8
Priests: Diocesan in Foreign Missions	1
Priests: Retired, Sick or Absent	77
Number of Diocesan Priests	324
Religious Priests in Diocese	128
Ordinations:	
Diocesan Priests	3
Transitional Deacons	2
Permanent Deacons	4
Permanent Deacons in Diocese	91
Total Brothers	86
Total Sisters	980
Parishes	
Parishes	188
With Resident Pastor:	
Resident Diocesan Priests	145
Resident Religious Priests	18
Without Resident Pastor:	
Administered by Priests	9
Administered by Women Religious	2
Missions	37
Closed Parishes	1
Professional Ministry Personnel:	
Brothers	2
Sisters	42
Lay Ministers	31
Welfare	
Catholic Hospitals	4
Total Assisted	560,000
Health Care Centers	10
Total Assisted	42,000
Homes for the Aged	8
Total Assisted	15,000
Day Care and Extended Day Care Centers	7
Total Assisted	89
Specialized Homes	12
Total Assisted	1,140
Special Centers for Social Services	22
Total Assisted	149,260
Residential Care of Disabled	7
Total Assisted	200
Other Institutions	7
Total Assisted	720
Educational	
Diocesan Students in Other Seminaries	15
Total Seminarians	15
Colleges and Universities	4
Total Students	4,550
High Schools, Diocesan and Parish	4
Total Students	1,923
High Schools, Private	3
Total Students	1,183
Elementary Schools, Diocesan and Parish	37
Total Students	9,328
Elementary Schools, Private	2
Total Students	418
Non-residential Schools for the Disabled	1
Total Students	50
Catechesis/Religious Education:	
High School Students	8,237
Elementary Students	22,653
Total Students Under Catholic Instruction	48,357
Teachers in the Diocese:	
Priests	6
Brothers	19
Sisters	86
Lay Teachers	817
Vital Statistics	
Receptions into the Church:	
Infant Baptism Totals	6,017
Adult Baptism Totals	353
Received into Full Communion	205
First Communions	5,249
Confirmations	3,264
Marriages:	
Catholic	1,539
Interfaith	546
Total Marriages	2,085
Deaths	4,844
Total Catholic Population	403,403
Total Population	1,315,414

Former Bishops—His Eminence JOHN CARDINAL MCCLOSKEY, D.D., appt. Bishop of Axiere and Coadjutor to the Bishop of New York, Nov. 21, 1843; cons. March 10, 1844; transferred to Albany, May 21, 1847; promoted to New York, May 6, 1864; created Cardinal Priest of the Holy Roman Church, March 15, 1875, under the title Sanctae Mariae supra Minervam; died Oct. 10, 1885.—Rt. Rev. JOHN J. CONROY, appt. Bishop July 7, 1865; cons. Oct. 15, 1865; resigned Oct. 16, 1877; transferred to the See of Curium, March 22, 1878; died Nov. 20, 1895.—Rt. Rev. Msgr. FRANCIS MCNEIRNY, D.D., appt. Bishop of Rhesina and Coadjutor to the Bishop of Albany, Dec. 22, 1871; cons. April 21, 1872; appt. Administrator of the Diocese of Albany, Jan. 18, 1874: Bishop of Albany, by right of succession, Oct. 16, 1877; died Jan. 2, 1894.—Rt. Rev. Msgr. THOMAS M. A. BURKE, D.D., preconized May 18, 1894; cons. July 1, 1894; died Jan 20, 1915.—Rt. Rev. Msgr. THOMAS F. CUSACK, D.D., cons. Titular Bishop of Themiscyra and Auxiliary to the Archbishop of New York. April 25, 1904; transferred to Albany, July 5, 1915; died July 12, 1918.—Most Rev. EDMUND F. GIBBONS, D.D., appt. Bishop, Feb. 1, 1919; cons. March 25, 1919; resigned Nov. 10, 1954; transferred to See of Verbe; died June 19, 1964.—Most Rev. WILLIAM A. SCULLY, D.D., appt. Coadjutor Bishop "cum jure successionis," Aug. 21, 1945; cons. Oct. 24, 1945; succeeded to See, Nov. 10, 1954; died Jan 5, 1969.—Most Rev. EDWIN B. BRODERICK, D.D., appt. Titular Bishop of Tizica and Auxiliary of New York, March 8, 1967; cons. April 21, 1967; transferred Albany, March 19, 1969; resigned June 2, 1976; appt. Exec. Dir. Catholic Relief Services, June 3, 1976; retired September, 1985.

Chancery Office—Pastoral Center, 40 N. Main Ave., Albany, 12203. Tel: 518-453-6600; Fax: 518-453-6793. Office Hours: Mon.-Fri. 8:30-4:30.

Vicars General—Rev. LEO P. O'BRIEN, *900 Madison Ave., Albany, 12208.* Tel: 518-489-5408. Rev. MICHAEL A. FARANO, *2 Fairview Rd., Loudonville, 12211.* Rev. Msgr. JAMES G. HART, Vicar General Emeritus, *391 Delaware Ave., Albany, 12209.*

Chancellors—Pastoral Center, 40 N. Main Ave., Albany, 12203. Rev. GEOFFREY BURKE, Chancellor, Personnel & Public Information. Tel: 518-453-6612. Mr. JOHN FEENEY, Chancellor, Finance & Admin. Tel: 518-453-6612. Sr. KATHLEEN TURLEY, R.S.M., Chancellor, Planning & Pastoral Svcs. Tel: 518-453-6661.

Comptroller—RICHARD FARRELL, *40 N. Main Ave., Albany, 12203.* Tel: 518-453-6640.

Insurance Office—RONALD WATERS, Dir., *40 N. Main Ave., Albany, 12203.* Tel: 518-453-6790.

Office of Human Resources—JOHN COSGROVE, Dir., *40 N. Main Ave., Albany, 12203.* Tel: 518-453-6635. FRANK DUCHARME, Human Resource Assoc. Tel: 518-453-4461. MARY JO HELNARSKI, Personnel Asst. Tel: 518-453-6635. Sr. NOLA BRUNNNER, Spec. Projects. Tel: 518-453-6662.

Pastoral Planning—Sr. KATHLEEN TURLEY, R.S.M., Dir., *40 N. Main Ave., Albany, 12203.* Tel: 518-453-6661.

Archivist—Sr. MARY BERCHMANS MAHONEY, R.S.M., *40 N. Main Ave., Albany, 12203.* Tel: 518-453-6633.

Office of Canonical Services—40 N. Main Ave., Albany, 12203. Tel: 518-453-6620. Office Hours: 8:30-4:30 (By appointment only).

Vicar Judicial—Rev. JAMES I. DONLON, J.C.D.

Adjutant Vicar Judicial—Rev. PETER J. SULLIVAN, III, J.C.L.

Judges—Revs. THOMAS BERARDI; DAVID BERBERIAN; ANTHONY C. DIACETIS; ALMERICO F. DICERBO; JAMES I. DONLON; PETER J. SULLIVAN, III; STANISLAUS J. SWIERZOWSKI; BERNARD TURNER; Sr. MARY ANN HAYES.

Defender of the Marriage Bond in First Instance—Rev. JOSEPH S. AMATO.

Promoter of Justice—Sr. MARY ANN HAYES, C.S.J.

Advocates—Revs. THOMAS KRUPA; THOMAS BERARDI; JAMES LEFEBVRE; JOSEPH O'BRIEN; JOHN MOYNA; ARTHUR BECKER; FRANK GILCHRIST.

Bishop's Delegate for Marriage Dispensations—Revs. JAMES I. DONLON, J.C.D.; PETER J. SULLIVAN, III, J.C.L.

Secretary to the Tribunal—ANN COYLE.

Notaries—ANN COYLE; JOANNNE MONAHAN; BETTE DONNELLY; MARTHA MCEWAN.

Inter Diocesan Tribunal for the Province of NY—

(Second Instance Appeal Court), Rev. Msgr WALTER F. KENNY, Vicar Judicial; Sr. AILEEN KELLY, Admin. and Chief Exec. Sec., *1011 First Ave., New York, 10022-4190.* Tel: 212-371-1000.

Presbyteral Council—Most Rev. HOWARD J. HUBBARD, Pres.; Revs. KENNETH DOYLE, Chm.; PATRICK BUTLER, Sec.; MARTIN FISHER, Vice Chm.; JOHN MEDWID; BRIAN RAICHE; PETER PAGONES; CHRISTOPHER DRENNAN, O.S.A.; JOSEPH O'BRIEN; DONALD CZELUSNIAK; JAMES DALY; JOHN MEALEY,Bishop's Staff (Non-Voting): Rev. Msgr. JAMES G. HART; Revs. LEO P. O'BRIEN; MICHAEL A. FARANO; RANDALL P. PATTERSON; JAMES I. DONLON; Mr. RICHARD N. FARRELL.

Diocesan Board of Consultors—Revs. MARTIN FISHER; JOHN MEDWID; CHRISTOPHER DRENNAN, O.S.A.; PATRICK BUTLER; DONALD CZELUSNIAK; KENNETH DOYLE; BRIAN RAICHE; JOSEPH O'BRIEN; DAVID MICKIEWICZ; PETER PAGONES; JAMES DALY; JOHN MEALEY; MICHAEL A. FARANO, Sec. JAMES I. DONLON, Canonical Consultant to the Board.

Deans—Albany Co.—City: Rev. ROBERT J. HOHENSTEIN, V.F.; *Northern: Rev.* LAWRENCE MCTAVEY, V.F.; *Suburban: Rev.* JAMES DALEY, V.F.; *Colombia: Rev.* THOMAS M. POWERS, V.F.; *Delaware: Rev.* ROBERT PURCELL, V.F.; *Fulton: Rev.* JOSEPH BARKER, V.F.; *Greene: Rev.* JEREMIAH NUNAN, V.F.; *Herkimer: Rev.* JOSEPH BENINTENDE; *Montgomery: Rev.* JAMES GULLEY; *Otsego: Rev.* PAUL ROMAN; *Rensselaer Co.—Northern: Rev.* DONALD OPHALS; *Southern: Rev.* J. JOSEPH DELANEY; *Saratoga: Rev.* ANTHONY DIACETIS; *Schenectady Co.: Rev.* JOHN PROVOST; *Schoharie: Rev.* THOMAS BERARDI; *Warren: Rev.* JOSEPH ANSELMENT; *Washington: Rev.* EDWARD C. PRATT.

Diocesan Offices and Directors

All Diocesan Offices and Directors are located at The Pastoral Center, 40 N. Main Ave., Albany, 12203. Tel: 518-453-6600; Fax: 518-453-6793 unless otherwise indicated.

Office of Real Property—NOEL OLSEN, Dir. Tel: 518-453-6623.

Receptionist—Ms. SUZANNE SECOR; Ms. ZOE BOPP; Ms. PEG GILBRIDE.

Administrative Review Board (Due Process)—Rev. DAVID BERBERIAN, Chm. Tel: 518-453-6620.

Apostleship of Prayer—Rev. JOHN J. PARET, S.J., *Auriesville, 12016.* Tel: 518-853-3153.

Korean Catholic Apostolate—Rev. PIUS BIO JUNG, *10 Lodge St., Albany, 12207.*

Bishop's Appeal—JOHN MANNING, Dir. Tel: 518-453-6680.

Black Apostolate—Rev. KOFI NTSIFUL-AMISSAH, Admin., *St. George's Church, 50 Thornton St., Albany, 12206.* Tel: 518-462-9604.

Campus Ministry—Sr. MAUREEN O'LEARY, F.S.P., Diocesan Dir., *SUNY at Albany, P.O. Box 22225, Albany, 12222.* Tel: 518-489-8573.

Cemeteries—Rev. ROBERT BUCKLEY, Diocesan Dir., *St. Agnes Cemetery, 48 Cemetery Ave., Menands, Albany, 12204.* Tel: 518-432-4953., *Res., 18 Pearl St., Schuylerville, 12871.* RICHARD TOUCHETTE, Exec. Dir.

Censores Librorum—Rev. JOHN R. ROOS, J.C.D.

Catholic Office for Motion Pictures—Rev. ANTHONY D. GULLEY, Diocesan Dir., *Res., 607 Central Ave., Albany, 12205.* Tel: 518-482-3375.

Architecture and Building Commission—Rev. THOMAS PHELAN, Chm. CAROL FITZGERALD, Coord. Tel: 518-453-6622.

Communications Commission—Rev. GEOFFREY BURKE, Public Information Officer. Tel: 518-453-6612. ROBERT J. MURPHY, Dir. Media Operations & Devel. Tel: 518-453-6690.

Cursillos in Christianity Diocese of Albany—Rev. CHRISTOPHER J. DRENNEN, O.S.A., *Assumption/St. Paul, 52 William St., P.O. Box 308, Mechanicville, 12118.* Tel: 518-664-6196.

Diocesan Service Committee for Charismatic Renewal—Rev. MARTIN FISHER, *62 Warren St., Glen Falls, 12801.* Tel: 518-792-0989. JAMES B. RYAN, Communications, *707 Pleasantview Ave., Scotia, 12302.*

Diocesan Stewardship Office—JOHN MANNING. Tel: 518-453-6680.

Department of Information Resources—JERRY WEISGRAU, Dir. Tel: 518-453-6685; Fax: 518-453-6779.

Catholic Charities of Diocese of Albany, Inc.; St. Vincent's Child Care Society, Inc.—Sr. MAUREEN JOYCE, R.S.M., Exec. Dir. & Sec. to the Bishop for Health and Social Svcs. Tel: 518-453-6650; Fax: 518-453-6792. Sr. MAUREEN JOYCE, R.S.M., Sec., St. Vincent's Child Care Society, Inc. RICHARD MARINI, Chief Financial Officer; Sr. PEG SULLIVAN, R.S.M., Assoc. Exec. Dir. WILLIAM J. PRZYLUCKI, Assoc. Exec. Dir. KAREN DEHAIS, Assoc. Exec. Dir. ALBERT TURO, Assoc. Exec. Dir., Catholic Relief Svcs., Disaster Relief Svcs. & Staff; JAMES J. MCCORMACK, Ph.D., Health Care Coord.

Catholic Family Service Agencies—CATHERINE NICHOLS BERMAN, Dir., Albany Catholic Family and Community Svcs., *100 Slingerland St., Albany, 12202.* Tel: 518-426-3511. AGNES DONLON, Dir., Catholic Charities of Colombia & Greene Counties, *431 E. Allen St., Hudson, 12534.* Tel: 518-828-8660. JOHN NASSO, Dir., Catholic Family & Community Svcs., Fulton Co., *208 W. State St., Johnstown, 12095.* Tel: 518-762-8313. Vacant, Catholic Charities of Colombia & Greene Counties, 19 S. Jefferson Ave., Catskill, 12414. Tel: 518-943-1462. Vacant, Catholic Family & Community Svcs., Herkimer Co., 61 West St., Ilion, 13357. Tel: 315-894-9917. JOSEPH WALKER, Dir., Catholic Charities, Delaware & Otsego Cos., 9-11 S. Main St., Oneonta, 13820. Tel: 607-432-0061. Sr. CHARLA COMMINS, Dir., Catholic Family and Community Svcs., Saratoga Co., *142 Regent St., Saratoga, 12866.* Tel: 518-587-5000. JOHN D. STEELE, Dir., Schenectady Catholic Family and Community Svcs., *818 Union St., Schenectady, 12308.* Tel: 518-372-5667. THOMAS MAYER, Dir., Family and Community Svcs., Schoharie Co., *41 W. Main St., Cobleskill, 12043.* Tel: 518-234-3541. LINDA BONESTEEL, Dir., Catholic Charities, Northern Albany & Rensselaer Cos., *1400 Eighth Ave., Watervliet, 12189.* Tel: 518-272-4964. Sr. CHARLA COMMINS, C.S.J., Dir., Catholic Charities, Warren & Washington Cos., *35 Broad St., Glens Falls, 12801.* Tel: 518-793-6212.

Other Agencies and Commissions—Sr. SERENA BRANSON, D.C., Staff, Commission on Aging, *40 N. Main Ave., Albany, 12203.* Tel: 518-453-6650. BARBARA DITOMMASO, Dir., Commission on Peace & Justice, *40 N. Main Ave., Albany, 12203.* Tel: 518-453-6650. Vacant; Staff, Task Force on Chemical Dependency, *40 N. Main Ave., Albany, 12203.* Tel: 518-453-6650. MARTHA HAASE, Dir., Caregivers Program, *100 Slingerland St., Albany, 12202.* Tel: 518-449-2001. Sr. MARY ANN LOGIUDICE, R.S.M., Dir., Community Maternity Svcs., *27 N. Main Ave., Albany, 12203.* Tel: 518-482-8836. GARY SIEGEL, Dir., Catholic Charities Developmental Disabilities Svcs., *15 Avis Dr., Latham, 12210.* Tel: 518-482-8904. ROBERT SAHM, Dir., Catholic Charities Housing, *40 N. Main Ave., Albany, 12203.* Tel: 518-453-6650. JAMES MCCAFFREY, Dir., Inter-County Home Care, *100 Slingerland St., Albany, 12203.* Tel: 518-432-0089. VICKY PELINSKI, Dir., Masterson Child Devel. Center, *50 Philip St., Albany, 12207.* Tel: 518-434-8585. DENISE KIRKLEY-CAIN, Dir., Neighborhood Community Centre, *340 1st St., Albany, 12206.* Tel: 518-465-5408. Sr. CLAUDETTE HARRIS, C.S.J., Dir., Sunnyside Center, *P.O. Box 1410, Troy, 12181.* Tel: 518-274-5986. PETER NAPOLITANO, Dir., St. Charles Lwanga Center, *115 Grand St., Albany, 12202.* Tel: 518-465-4973. Sr. ANNE TRANELLI, C.S.J., Dir., Hispanic Outreach Svcs., *40 N. Main Ave., Albany, 12203.* Tel: 518-453-6655. KAREN LAQUIDARA-DICKINSON, Dir., HIV/AIDS Svcs., *40 N. Main Ave., Albany, 12203.* Tel: 518-453-6650.

Campaign for Human Development—ALBERT TURO. Tel: 518-453-6650.

Catholic Relief Services—See Catholic Charities of the Diocese of Albany.

Disaster Relief Services—See Catholic Charities of the Diocese of Albany.

Health and Hospitals Office—Sr. MAUREEN JOYCE, Bishop's Rep. Tel: 518-453-6650.

Catholic Women's Service League—LORI J. TANGREDI, Pres., *c/o LaSalle, 391 Western Ave., Albany, 12203.* Tel: 518-426-8202.

Ladies of Charity—ANNA O'CONNOR, *17 Edgewood Ave., Albany, 12203.* Tel: 518-489-4259.

Society of St. Vincent de Paul—EDWARD NARE, Diocesan Central Council Pres., *202 S. Ballston Ave., Scotia, 12302.* Tel: 518-374-2548. EMMET J. LYNCH, Pres. Emeritus; Rev. RICHARD DOWNS, Spiritual Dir., *12 Rosemont St., Albany, 12203.* Tel: 518-489-8197.

Consultation Center of the Diocese of Albany—A non-profit Mental Health Center, which provides quality professional psychological counseling services and educational programs in the area of mental health, to individuals and groups.

Office—Rev. ANTHONY J. CHIARAMONTE, Ph.D., Dir.; Sr. MARY FRANCES BECK, S.N.J.M., Admin. Dir.; Rev. JOHN J. MALECKI, Ph.D., Psychologist; KATHLEEN STIFFEN, Sec., *790 Lancaster St., Albany, 12203.* Tel: 518-489-4431.

Psychological Counseling—Provides individual therapy, psychological testing, and consultative services to individuals and groups in matters calling for psychological expertise.

Group Therapy—Provides a variety of different kinds of therapy groups.

Educational Programs—Offers lectures and workshops in the area of mental health and personal growth. The Center also offers specialized workshops and training programs to meet the needs of various groups.

Counseling for Laity—Sr. ANNE BRYAN SMOLLIN, C.S.J., Ph.D., Exec. Dir. ETTA JONES, Admin. Asst., *40 N. Main Ave., Albany, 12203.* Tel: 518-453-6625. Provides individual and group psychological counseling-therapy by certified trained therapists. The staff provides services for the Young Married program and assessments for second marriages. Consultation and training programs are offered upon request.

Diocesan Pastoral Council—PATRICIA MOUSAW, Staff; FRANK MASON, Chm. PAT BARR, Vice Chm. Tel: 518-453-6661.

Ecumenical and Interreligious Affairs of the Roman Catholic Diocese of Albany, Commission for—Sr. MAUREEN O'LEARY F.S.P.; AUDREY HUGHES; Deacons WILLIAM GAFFNEY; EARLE FLATT; Sr. JOAN NOLAN, O.P.; JOAN HOLMAN; JOAN LIPSCOMB; Revs. JOSEPH MANEROWSKI; JOHN MEALEY; THOMAS PHELAN; Ms. PATRICIA CREWELL; Ms. MARGE MILANESE; Sr. MARY GEN SMYTHE, R.C.S.J.; JOAN DUNHAM; Sr. ELIZABETH HOYE, R.S.C.J.; FRANK M. PELL; Revs. MAURICE DROWN; JAMES KANE, Dir.; Mrs. MARY JO HELNARSKI, Sec. Tel: 518-453-6660.

"The Evangelist"—Diocesan Newspaper *Albany Catholic Press Assoc., Inc.*, JAMES P. BREIG, Editor. Tel: 518-453-6688.

Family Life Office—Sr. KAY RYAN, C.S.J., Dir.; Assoc. Dirs.: Sr. MARY MORIARTY; PAT LEDERMAN, Respect Life; KAREN FONTANELLI, Admin. Asst.; LIZ KIRK, Sec. Tel: 518-453-6677. Family Perspective; Respect Life; Marriage Preparation; Marriage & Family Enrichment; Catholic Singles; Ministry to the Divorced, Separated, Widowed, Remarried and Bereaved, Young Adult Ministry.

Natural Family Planning—HELENE WALLINGFORD, *315 S. Manning Blvd., Albany, 12208.* Tel: 518-525-1388.

Hispanic Apostolate—Rev. MICHAEL HOGAN, Coord., *801 Stanley St., Schenectady, 12307.* Tel: 518-377-8559; 346-0261.

Holy Name Societies—Rev. WILLIAM W. CRANDALL, Dir., *St. Joseph Rectory, 181 Main St., Worcester, 12197.* Tel: 607-397-9373.

Initial & Ongoing Formation—Rev. THOMAS POWERS, Dir., Continuing Education of Clergy and Ministry to Priests Program. Tel: 518-453-6670. ELIZABETH ROWE, Formation for Ministry Program. Tel: 518-453-6670. Rev. JOHN MOLYN, Dir., Vocations & Diaconate Formation Program. Tel: 518-453-6670.

Legion of Mary—Deacon WILLIAM J. BRETT, *197 Woodbridge Ct., Voorheesville, 12186.*

Office of Religious Education—JEANNE SCHREMPF, Diocesan Dir.; CHRISTOPHER WEBER, Assoc. Dir., Catechist Formation; CATHY ANN LAVENDER, Assoc. Dir., Persons with Developmental Disabilities; Sr. ANNA TANTSITS, I.H.M., Assoc. Dir., Adult Faith Formation; MARY HARRISON, Assoc. Dir., Youth Ministry; JOYCE SOLIMINI, Assoc. Dir., Children and Adolescents.

Permanent Diaconate Office—Co-Directors: Deacons FRANK LUKOVITS; TIMOTHY MCAULIFFE. Tel: 518-453-6670.

Catholic Foundation—Most Rev. HOWARD J. HUBBARD; JOHN MANNING, Exec. Dir. Tel: 518-453-6680.

Priests Personnel Board—Revs. GEOFFREY BURKE, Chm. RICHARD CARLINO; KENNETH DOYLE; JOHN BRADLEY; JAMES LEFEBVRE; WILLIAM JILLISKY.

Priests Retirement Board—Revs. GEOFFREY BURKE, Chm. MARTIN FISHER; JOSEPH E. ANSELMENT; JOHN T. PROVOST; MORRIS R. DWYER; MICHAEL A. FARANO; EDWARD C. PRATT; RANDALL PATTERSON; Rev. Msgr. HOWARD MANNY; Rev. Msgr. JAMES G. HART; Mr. RICHARD FARRELL. Tel: 518-453-6670.

Priests' Retirement Plan—Rev. GEOFFREY BURKE, Chancellor.

Propagation of the Faith-Pontifical Society—Revs. PAUL P. TARTAGLIA, Dir.; JAMES M. MACKEY, Asst. Dir. Tel: 518-453-6675.

Schools: Diocesan School Board—ALBERT J. BROWN, JR. Tel: 518-453-6666.

Diocesan School Office—Sr. ANN MCCARTHY, C.S.J., Supt. of Schools. Tel: 518-453-6666. THOMAS FITZGERALD, Asst. Supt., Admin. Svcs.; NANCY MACHOLD, Dir. Devel.; MARY BRYAN, Asst. Supt., Instructional Svcs.; CURTIS A. MCEWAN, Business Mgr.; SAL CARBONE, Coord. Special Projects - Asbestos; STEPHEN PARTISANO, Coord., Special Projects-Mandated Svcs.

Scouting—Rev. JOSEPH SCHUCK, Diocesan Chap., *c/o Gilead House of Prayer, R.D. 1, P.O. Box 54, Unadilla, 13849-9771.* Tel: 607-369-2317.

Vicar for Religious—Sr. NOLA BRUNNER, C.S.J. Tel: 518-453-6662. Rev. JOHN ROOS, Asst. Vicar, *Res., St. Mary Rectory, 31 Elm St., Cooperstown, 13326.* Tel: 607-547-2213.

Vocations and Vocation Awareness Program—Rev. JOHN MOLYN, Diocesan Dir. Tel: 518-453-6670.

CLERGY, PARISHES, MISSIONS AND PAROCHIAL SCHOOLS

CITY OF ALBANY
(Albany County)

1—CATHEDRAL OF THE IMMACULATE CONCEPTION, Rev. William Pape, Rector; Deacon Arthur H. Egan. In res., Most Rev. Howard J. Hubbard Tel: 518-462-3804; Revs. Peter J. Sullivan, III Tel: 518-465-7244; Dennis P. Murphy.
Rectory Office: 125 Eagle St., 12202. Tel: 518-463-4447; Fax: 518-436-5177.
Religious Education Office—Tel: 518-436-7918.
Cathedral Social Services—Tel: 518-463-2279.
Convent—93 Park Ave., 12202. Tel: 518-436-7697. Sisters 13.

2—ST. JOHN-ST. ANN, Rev. John Kirwin.
Office: 157 Franklin St., 12202. Tel: 518-472-9091; Fax: 518-427-5983.

3—BLESSED SACRAMENT, Revs. John J. Bradley; Anthony Ligato; Sr. Ann Rose, C.S.J., Pastoral Assoc.; Deacon William Fitzgerald. In res., Rev. Anthony D. Gulley.
Res., 607 Central Ave., 12206. Tel: 518-482-3375.
School—605 Central Ave., 12206. Tel: 518-438-5854. Sr. Jane Somerville, Prin.
Sisters of Mercy 1; Lay Teachers 18; Students 240.

4—ST. CASIMIR (Polish). Attended by Our Lady of Angels. Rev. Alvin Somerville, O.F.M., Admin. In res., Revs. Frank O'Connor; Frank Gilchrist.
Res., 324 Sheridan Ave., 12206. Tel: 518-463-7147.
School—Tel: 518-434-4264. Arthur Farrington, Prin.
Sisters of the Resurrection 3; Lay Teachers 14; Students 290.
Convent—315 Sheridan Ave., 12206. Tel: 518-463-5440.

5—ST. CATHERINE OF SIENA, Rev. Kennth Doyle; Deacon Gerald Ladouceur. In res., Revs. John A. Keefe; Joseph Romano; John Yanas.
Res., 40 Collins Pl., 12208. Tel: 518-489-3204; Fax: 518-482-3721.
School—35 Hurst Ave., 12208. Tel: 518-439-3111. Theresa L. Ewell, Prin.
Lay Teachers 17; Students 245.

6—ST. GEORGE (Lithuanian), Rev. Kofi Amissah, Admin. & Dir. Black Apostolate.
Res., 50 Thornton St., 12206. Tel: 518-463-3585.

7—CHURCH OF THE HOLY CROSS, Revs. Daniel J. Maher; Peter Sullivan; Sr. Helen Charles, Spiritual Growth Coord.
Res., 12 Rosemont St., 12203. Tel: 518-489-8197.
School—Rosement St., 12203. Tel: 518-438-0066. Sr. Mary Ellen Owens, Prin.
Sisters 1; Lay Teachers 16; Students 291.

8—ST. JAMES, Rev. Dominic Ingemie. In res., Rev. Msgr. James B. Hart; Rev. Anthony Sidoti, Pastor Emeritus.
Res., 391 Delaware Ave., 12209. Tel: 518-434-4028.
School—50 Summit Ave., 12209. Tel: 518-465-1973. Sr. Katherine Arseneau, C.S.J., Prin.
Sisters 8; Lay Teachers 12; Students 202.
Convent—58 Summit Ave., 12209. Tel: 518-449-7993.
Mission—Albany, Albany Co., Child's Hospital & Eden Park Nursing Home.

9—ST. JOSEPH,
Parish Office: 12 St. Joseph Ter., 12210.

10—ST. MARGARET MARY, Rev. Thomas H. Chevalier; Deacons Richard D. Cioppa; J. Neil Hook. In res., Revs. Raymond Dlugos, O.S.A.; John Fitzpatrick.
Parish Office: 1168 Western Ave., 12203. Tel: 518-482-4497.

11—ST. MARY, Rev. James Lefebvre; Deacon George Witko. In res., Revs. Lloyd Rebeyro; Pius-Bio Jung.
Res., 10 Lodge St., 12207. Tel: 518-462-4254; Fax: 518-462-4255.
Chapel—111 Washington Ave., 12203.

12—OUR LADY OF ANGELS, Revs. Alvin Somerville, O.F.M.Conv., Guardian; Germain Williams, O.F.M.Conv.; Evan Bucci, O.F.M.Conv. In res., Revs. Rufino Maloney, O.F.M.Conv.; Salvatore Pantano, O.F.M.Conv.; Evan Roche, O.F.M.; Bro. Leo Merriman, O.F.M.Conv.
Res., 183 Central Ave., 12206. Tel: 518-463-3262; Fax: 518-463-3264. [CEM]

13—OUR LADY HELP OF CHRISTIANS (German), Very Rev. Robert J. Hohenstein, V.F.
Res., 74 Second Ave., 12202. Tel: 518-463-7338; 434-4868. [CEM]

14—ST. PATRICK, Rev. Francis A. O'Connor.
Office: 283 Central Ave., 12206. Tel: 518-465-3685.

15—SACRED HEART OF JESUS, Revs. Thomas J. Hayes, Admin.; Michael Mai Tran, C.M.C.
Res., 31 Walter St., 12204. Tel: 518-463-3286.

16—ST. TERESA OF AVILA, Rev. John H. Mealey; Deacon Raymond Sullivan. In res., Revs. John L. Close; John L. Jones, (Retired).
Res., 435 New Scotland Ave., 12208. Tel: 518-438-7851.
Schools—(Grades PreK-5) 433 New Scotland Ave., 12208. Tel: 518-438-5268; Fax: 518-482-3745.; (Grades 6-8) 8 Hollywood Ave., 12208. Tel: 518-482-3736. Sr. Patricia Houlihan, R.S.M., Prin.
Sisters of Mercy 4; Lay Teachers 10; Students 215.
Convent—401 New Scotland Ave., 12208. Tel: 518-482-8901.
Mission—Albany, Albany Co., Albany Medical Center.

17—ST. VINCENT DE PAUL, Rev. Leo P. O'Brien; Deacon William Gaffney.
Parish Office: 900 Madison Ave., 12208. Tel: 518-489-5408; Fax: 518-489-5474.
Res., 599 Hudson Ave., 12203. Tel: 518-489-0563.

OUTSIDE THE CITY OF ALBANY

Altamont, Albany Co., St. Lucy, Rev. Charles P. Lockwood; Sr. Mary Lou Liptak, R.S.M., Pastoral Assoc.
Res., 109 Grand St., 12009. Tel: 518-861-8770.
Mission—Berne, Albany Co., St. Bernadette, 1763 Helderberg Trail, Berne, 12023. Tel: 518-872-1131.

Amsterdam, Montgomery Co.,

1—ST. CASIMIR, (Lithuanian), Rev. Joseph J. Grabys. In res., Rev. Frank Gilchrest, (Retired).
Res., 260 E. Main St., 12010. Tel: 518-842-5481. [CEM]

2—ST. JOHN THE BAPTIST, (Polish), Rev. Stanislaus J. Swierzowski.
Res., 40 Van Derveer St., 12010. Tel: 518-842-6851. [CEM]

3—ST. JOSEPH-ST. MICHAEL-OUR LADY OF MOUNT CARMEL. Canonically merged parishes in 1980. Rev. Lawrence J. Decker.
Mailing Address: P.O. Box 699, 12010.
Office: 39 St. John St. & 58 Grove St., 12010. Tel: 518-843-3250; Fax: 518-453-4070.
Res., 35 St. John St., 12010. Tel: 518-843-3250.

4—ST. JOSEPH. Canonically merged in 1980 into St. Joseph-St. Michael-Our Lady of Mount Carmel. All inquiries should be directed to the listed address, 39 St. John St. & 58 Grove St., Amsterdam, NY 12010.

5—ST. MICHAEL THE ARCHANGEL. Canonically merged in 1980 into St. Joseph-St. Michael-Our Lady of Mount Carmel. All inquiries should be directed to the listed address, 39 St. John St. & 58 Grove St., Amsterdam, NY 12010.

6—OUR LADY OF MT. CARMEL, (Italian). Canonically merged in 1980 into St. Joseph-St. Michael-Our Lady of Mount Carmel. All inquiries should be directed to the listed address, 39 St. John St. & 58 Grove St., Amsterdam, NY 12010.

7—ST. MARY, Rev. James Gulley. In res., Rev. Msgr. Edward R. Glavin, Pastor Emeritus.
Res., 156 E. Main St., 12010. Tel: 518-842-4500. [CEM]
School—St. Mary Institute, Upper Church St., 12010.
Sisters 2; Lay Teachers 19; Students 456.

8—ST. STANISLAUS, (Polish), Revs. Walter Czechowicz; Edward Sipperly.
Res., 73 Reid St., 12010. Tel: 518-842-2771. [CEM]
School—42-44 Cornell St., 12010. Tel: 518-842-6710. Sr. M. Bernice, C.S.S.F., Prin.
Felician Sisters 3; Lay Teachers 7; Students 212.
Convent—46 Cornell St., 12010. Tel: 518-842-2621.

Athens, Greene Co., St. Patrick, Rev. Richard J. Doyle.
Res., 19 N. Franklin St., 12015. Tel: 518-945-1656.

Averill Park, Rensselaer Co., St. Henry, Rev. Peter N. Pagones; Deacons Frank Lukovits; John W. Novak; Robert Pasquarelli.
Res., Crystal Lake Rd., P.O. Box 550, 12018. Tel: 518-674-3818. [CEM 2]

Ballston Lake, Saratoga Co., Our Lady of Grace, Rev. Anthony C. Diacetis.
Res., 73 Midline Rd., 12019. Tel: 518-399-5713.

Ballston Spa, Saratoga Co., St. Mary, Rev. John French.
Res., 167 Milton Ave., 12020. Tel: 518-885-7411; Fax: 518-885-6863. [CEM]
School—40 Thompson St., 12020. Tel: 518-885-7300. Sr. Annette M. Allard, C.S.J., Prin.
Sisters 2; Lay Teachers 8; Students 143.

Berlin, Rensselaer Co., Sacred Heart, Rev. James Barry Lonergan.
Res., P.O. Box 243, Main St., 12022. Tel: 518-658-2780.
Mission—Stephentown, St. Joseph. [CEM]

Bolton Landing, Warren Co., Blessed Sacrament, Rev. Peter G. Young.
Res., Goodman Ave., P.O. Box 266, 12814. Tel: 518-644-3861. [CEM]

Broadalbin, Fulton Co., St. Joseph, Rev. Timothy Mangan, S.S.S.
Res., 7 North St., 12025. Tel: 518-883-3774; Fax: 518-883-3774.
Mission—Galway, St. Mary. [CEM]

Cairo, Greene Co., Sacred Heart, Revs. Jeremiah Nunan; Sean McMahon. In res., Rev. John F. Mallon.
Res., Mountain Ave., 12413. Tel: 518-622-3319.
Missions—Acra, St. Edmund; Cairo, Greene Co., Alphonsus Manor Rest; East Durham, St. Mary.

Cambridge, Washington Co., St. Patrick, Revs. Joseph J. Getz, O.S.A.; Roger Hanouille, O.S.A.
Res., 17 S. Park St., 12816-1248. Tel: 518-677-2757. [CEM]

Canajoharie, Montgomery Co., St. Peter's and Paul's, Rev. William J. Gaffigan.
Res., 100 Cliff St., 13317-1199. Tel: 518-673-3333. [CEM]

Castleton-on-Hudson, Rensselaer Co., Sacred Heart, Rev. Thomas J. Krupa.
Res., 3 Catholic Way, 12033-1526. Tel: 518-732-2155; Fax: 518-732-4906. [CEM]
Missions—Schodack Landing, Assumption of B.V.M.; Schodack Landing, Shrine of St. Jude.

Catskill, Greene Co., St. Patrick, Revs. John J. Murphy; John Medwid, Assoc.
Res., 157 Bridge St., 12414. Tel: 518-943-3150.
School—80 Woodland Ave., 12414. Tel: 518-943-2952.
Franciscan Sisters of Allegany 1; Lay Teachers 10; Students 188.
Convent—82 Woodland Ave., 12414. Tel: 518-943-5341.
Missions—Leeds, St. Bridget; Smith's Landing, St. Mary's, 6104 Rte. 9W, Smith's Landing, 12415.

Chatham, Columbia Co., St. James, Rev. Gary Paul Gelfenbien; Deacon Peter Trawinski.
Res., 129 Hudson Ave., 12037. Tel: 518-392-4991.

Cherry Valley, Otsego Co., St. Thomas the Apostle, Rev. Santino Titta.
Res., 24 Maple Ave., 13320. Tel: 607-264-3779.
Mission—Springfield Center, Blessed Sacrament.

Chestertown, Warren Co., St. John the Baptist, Rev. Joseph O'Brien, Admin.
Res., Riverside Dr., P.O. Box 471, 12817. Tel: 518-494-2617.

Clifton Park, Saratoga Co., St. Edward the Confessor, Revs. John L. Cairns; John R. Lanese; Deacons Jerry Grigaitis; Walter MacKinnon.
Office: Tel: 518-371-7372; Fax: 518-371-1206.
Res., 21 Hemlock Dr., 12065-4845. Tel: 518-371-9595.

Clinton Heights, Rensselaer Co., St. Mary, Rev. J. Joseph Delaney. In res., Rev. Gary Mercure.
Res., 163 Columbia Tpke., Rensselaer, 12144. Tel: 518-449-2232; Fax: 518-449-2234.
School—Tel: 518-449-2498. Sr. Patricia Lynch, R.S.M., Supr.
Lay Teachers 16; Students 249.

Cobleskill, Schoharie Co., St. Vincent de Paul, Rev. Thomas F. Berardi; Deacon Gary Surman.
Res., One Washington Heights, 12043. Tel: 518-234-2892. [CEM]
Mission—Sharon Springs, St. Mary.

Cohoes, Albany Co.,

1—ST. AGNES-ST. PATRICK, Rev. Arthur J. Becker; Deacons Owen South; Albert Schrempf.
Office: 49 Johnston Ave., 12047. Tel: 518-237-6091.
Res., 122 Vliet Blvd., 12047-1842. Tel: 518-237-2373; Fax: 518-238-9427.
School—Cohoes Consolidated Catholic Schools. See separate listing.

2—ST. BERNARD, Revs. Lawrence G. McTavey; Marc L. Touchette; Deacon Walter MacKinnon; Sr. Margaret Totten, C.S.J., Pastoral Assoc.
Res., P.O. Box 137, 107 Canvass St., 12047. Tel: 518-237-2721; Fax: 518-237-7980.

3—ST. JOSEPH, (French), Rev. Joseph S. Robitaille.
Res., 65 Congress St., 12047. Tel: 518-237-4241. [CEM]
School—Cohoes Consolidated Catholic Schools. See separate listing.

4—ST. MARIE, Rev. Arthur J. Becker; Deacons Owen South; Albert Schrempf.
Res., 122 Vliet Blvd., 12047. Tel: 518-237-2373; Fax: 518-238-9427.
School—Cohoes Consolidated Catholic Schools. See separate listing.

5—ST. MICHAEL, (Polish), Rev. Richard W. Dybas.
Res., 36 Page Ave., 12047. Tel: 518-237-5151. [CEM]

6—ST. RITA-SACRED HEART, Rev. John Facci, S.A.C.
Res., 50 St. Rita Ln., 12047. Tel: 518-237-4444.
Mission—Cohoes, Sacred Heart of Jesus.

Colonie, Albany Co., Our Lady of Mercy, Rev. John F. Waldron.

Res., Colonie Towers, Bldg. No. 2, 422 Sand Creek Rd., Albany, 12205. Tel: 518-459-2608.
Parish Center: 26 Wilson Ave., Albany, 12205. Tel: 518-459-1272.

St. Clare, Rev. Michael T. Schmitt; Deacon George Nahm. In res., Rev. Michael Miller.
Res., 1947 Central Ave., 12205-4299. Tel: 518-456-3112; Fax: 518-456-1072.

Cooperstown, Otsego Co., St. Mary, Rev. John R. Roos.
Res., 31 Elm St., 13326. Tel: 607-547-2213. [CEM 2]

Copake Falls, Columbia Co., St. Bridget, Rev. Peter Russo; Deacon Martin Stosiek.
Res., 8074 State Rte. 22, 12517. Tel: 518-329-4711. [CEM]

Corinth, Saratoga Co., Immaculate Conception, Rev. Owen F. Shanley.
Res., 409 Palmer Ave., 12822. Tel: 518-654-2113. [CEM]

Coxsackie, Greene Co., St. Mary, Rev. John L. Moyna.
Res., 80 Mansion St., 12051. Tel: 518-731-8800; Fax: 518-731-8505. [CEM]

Crescent, Saratoga Co., St. Mary, Rev. Richard Broderick; Deacon Richard Wahl.
Parish Center: 86 Church Hill Rd., Waterford, 12188. Tel: 518-371-9632; Fax: 518-371-7235.

Delanson, Schenectady Co., Our Lady of Fatima, Rev. John Connolly.
Res., 1735 Alexander Rd., P.O. Box 219, 12053. Tel: 518-895-2788.

Delhi, Delaware Co., St. Peter, Rev. Joseph Manerowski.
Res., 8 Franklin St., P.O. Box 71, 13753. Tel: 607-746-2503.

Delmar, Albany Co., St. Thomas the Apostle, Revs. James D. Daley; James J. Walsh; Deacon Alfred Manzella.
Res., 35 Adams Pl., 12054. Tel: 518-439-4951; Fax: 518-439-0108.
School—42 Adams Pl., 12054. Tel: 518-439-5573. Sr. Mary Frederick Coyne, S.N.J.M., Prin.
Lay Teachers 18; Students 287.

Dolgeville, Herkimer Co., St. Joseph, Rev. Leo F. Potvin; Deacon Peter Manno.
Res., 31 N. Helmer Ave., 13329. Tel: 315-429-8338. [CEM 2]

East Greenbush, Rensselaer Co., Holy Spirit, Rev. George G. St. John; Deacons William Dringus; Cyril Lavin. In res., Rev. Joseph M. Siniskey.
Res., 667 Columbia Tpke., 12061. Tel: 518-477-7925.
School—Highland Dr., 12061. Tel: 518-477-5739; Fax: 518-477-5743. Sr. Maureen Moffitt, C.S.J., Prin.
Sisters 1; Lay Teachers 17; Students 246.

Fonda, Montgomery Co., St. Cecilia, Rev. Patrick Gallagher, O.F.M.Conv. In res., Rev. Ronald Schultz, O.F.M.Conv.
Res., 26 Broadway, P.O. Box 837, 12068. Tel: 518-853-4195. [CEM]

Fort Ann, Washington Co., St. Ann, Rev. Robert J. Donnelly.
Res., 10 George St., P.O. Box 226, 12827. Tel: 518-639-5218.
Mission—South Hartford, St. Philip.

Fort Edward, Washington Co., St. Joseph, Rev. James Rosoh; Deacon Donald Webster. In res., Rev. Edward N. Leroux.
Mailing Address: P.O. Box 347, 12828.
Res., 164 Broadway, 12828. Tel: 518-747-5117; Fax: 518-747-3444.

Fort Plain, Montgomery Co., St. James, Rev. Kenneth J. Swain.
Parish Office: Tel: 518-993-3822.
Res., 119 Reid St., P.O. Box 287, 13339-0287. Tel: 518-993-5523.

Frankfort, Herkimer Co., Our Lady Queen of Apostles (1995), Rev. O. Robert DeMartinis.
Res., 414 Frankfort St., 13340. Tel: 315-894-2025; 894-2360; Fax: 315-894-2025.

St. Mary. Merged with SS. Peter & Paul, Frankfort, to form Our Lady Queen of Apostles, Frankfort, Jan. 8, 1995.

SS. Peter & Paul. Merged with St. Mary, Frankfort, to form Our Lady Queen of Apostles, Frankfort, Jan. 8, 1995.

Germantown, Columbia Co., Resurrection, Rev. Theodore Gerken.
Res., 9 Church Ave., P.O. Box 96, 12526. Tel: 518-537-6136. [CEM]
Mission—Linlithgo, Nativity of Our Lord.

Glens Falls, Warren Co., St. Alphonsus, Rev. Robert W. Powhida; Deacon William F. Bazinet.
Res., 35 Broad St., P.O. Box 2088, 12801. Tel: 518-792-1574; Fax: 518-792-6056. [CEM]
School—Merged with St. Mary's Academy to form St Mary's/St. Alphonsus Regional School. Tel: 518-792-1574; Fax: 518-792-6056.

St. Mary, Revs. Martin Fisher; Thomas Holmes; Deacon F. David Powers. In res., Rev. Mark Haight.
Res., 62 Warren St., 12801. Tel: 518-792-0989; Fax: 518-792-0251.
School—St. Mary's/St. Alphonsus Regional School, Tel: 518-792-3178; Fax: 518-792-6056.

Glenville, Schenectady Co., Immaculate Conception, Revs. J. Thomas Connery; R. Mansfield Starks, Pastor Emeritus; Jerome Gingras, O.F.M.Conv.; Deacons August Van Patten; Michael Melanson.
Res., 400 Saratoga Rd., 12302. Tel: 518-399-9168; Fax: 518-384-3278.

Gloversville, Fulton Co., St. Mary. Canonically merged with Our Lady of Mount Carmel in 1990. See St. Mary of Mount Carmel.

St. Mary of Mt. Carmel. Consolidated from Our Lady of Mount Carmel and St. Mary in 1990. Rev. Donald Czelusniak.
Res., 149 S. Main St., 12078. Tel: 518-725-3143.
Mission—Caroga Lake, St. Barbara.

Sacred Heart, Rev. Thomas Boyle, Admin.
Res., 189 Kingsboro Ave., 12078. Tel: 518-725-9375.

Grafton, Rensselaer Co., St. John Francis Regis, Sr. Mary Kenan McGowan, R.S.M., Admin.; Rev. Kenneth Gregory, Sacramental Min.
Mailing Address: P.O. Box 234, 12082. Tel: 518-279-4943.

Granville, Washington Co., Roman Catholic Community of Granville. Consolidated St. Mary's, All Saints, and Our Lady of Mount Carmel. Rev. Thomas Zelker.
Res., 23 Bulkley Ave., 12832. Tel: 518-642-1262.
Parish Center: All Saints House, Morrison Ave., 12832.

St. Mary. Closed. For inquiries for parish records contact the Chancery.

Greenfield Center, Saratoga Co., St. Joseph, Rev. John Weyand; Deacon Arthur Turcott.
Res., 3159 Rte. 9N, P.O. Box 168, 12833. Tel: 518-893-7680.
Mission—Rock City Falls, St. Paul, Tel: 518-885-4877.

Green Island, Albany Co., St. Joseph, Rev. Donald Kelly.
Res., 131 George St., 12183. Tel: 518-273-3552; Fax: 518-273-3978.

Greenville, Greene Co., St. John the Baptist, Rev. William M. Bauer.
Mailing Address: P.O. Box 340, 12083.
Office: R.D. No. 2, Box 2, 12083. Tel: 518-966-8317.
Mission—Crystal Lake.

Greenwich, Washington Co., St. Joseph, Revs. David J. Kelley, O.S.A.; Joseph D. Keffer, O.S.A.; Deacon Herbert Howley.
Res., 36 Bleecker St., 12834. Tel: 518-692-2159.

Guilderland, Albany Co., Christ the King, Revs. Patrick J. Butler; Mark Allman; Deacons Timothy McAuliffe; Joseph Markham.
Res., 20 Sumpter Ave., Albany, 12203. Tel: 518-456-1644; Fax: 518-456-4696.
School—Tel: 518-456-5400. Mr. Thomas F. Gould, Prin.
Lay Teachers 14; Students 190.

St. Madeleine Sophie, Revs. James Belogi; Desmond Rossi; Sr. Frances Mesley, R.S.M., Pastoral Assoc.; Deacons Earle Flatt; Gary Beck.
Res., 3500 Carman Rd., Schenectady, 12303. Tel: 518-355-0421.
School—3510 Carman Rd., Schenectady, 12303. Tel: 518-355-3080. Miss Teresa Kovarovic, Prin.
Lay Teachers 13; Students 236.
Convent—3514 Carman Rd., Schenectady, 12303. Tel: 518-355-8052.

Hagaman, Montgomery Co., St. Stephen, Rev. Ronald Matulewicz.
Res., 51 Pawling, 12086. Tel: 518-843-2951. [CEM]

Hague, Warren Co., Blessed Sacrament, Rev. Joseph O'Brien, Admin.
Res., Hague Rd., P.O. Box 529, 12836. Tel: 518-494-2617.
Mission—Brant Lake, Warren Co., St. Teresa.

Haines Falls, Greene Co., Immaculate Conception, Rev. Anthony Motta.
Res., Mountain House Rd., 12436. Tel: 518-589-5577. [CEM]
Missions—Elka Park, Greene Co., St. Francis de Sales; Lexington, St. Francis de Sales; Hunter, Greene Co., St. Mary of the Mountains; Haines Falls, Greene Co., Wayside Shrine.

Hancock, Delaware Co., St. Paul the Apostle, Rev. James Cribbs.
Res., 60 W. Main St., 13783. Tel: 607-637-2571. [CEM 2]

Herkimer, Herkimer Co., St. Anthony-St. Joseph, Rev. Robert Shinos; Sr. Patricia Woolheater, C.S.J., Pastoral Assoc.
Res., 228 S. Main St., 13350. Tel: 315-866-2892; 866-6373 (Parish Office).

St. Francis de Sales, Rev. Peter J. Nabozny.
Res., 25 Park Pl. S., 13350. Tel: 315-866-4282.
School—220 Henry St., 13350. Tel: 315-866-4831. Sr. Rosalie Kelly, C.S.J., Prin.
Sisters of St. Joseph of Carondolet 5; Lay Teachers 7; Students 195.
Convent—One Park Pl., 13350. Tel: 315-866-4492.

Hoosick Falls, Rensselaer Co., Immaculate Conception, Revs. John J. Sheridan, O.S.A.; Daniel Menihane, O.S.A.
Res., Box 343, 67 Main St., 12090. Tel: 518-686-5064; Fax: 518-686-5064. [CEM]
School—St. Mary Academy, 4 Parsons Ave., 12090. Tel: 518-686-4314. Mrs. Ann M. Donovan, Prin.
Lay Teachers 15; Students 163.

Hudson, Columbia Co., Church of St. Mary. Canonically merged with Our Lady of Mount Carmel and Our Lady of Perpetual Help-Sacred Heart in 1991. Rev. Winston L. Bath. In res., Rev. Edward F. Cantwell.
Mailing Address: P.O. Box 323, 12534.
Res., 429 E. Allen St., 12534. Tel: 518-828-1334; Fax: 518-828-2783.

Our Lady of Mt. Carmel. Canonically merged with Church of St. Mary in 1991. All inquiries should be directed to P.O. Box 323, Hudson, NY 12534. Tel: 518-828-1334.

Our Lady of Perpetual Help-Sacred Heart (Polish). Canonically merged with Church of St. Mary in 1991. All inquiries should be directed to P.O. Box 323, Hudson, NY 12534. Tel: 518-828-1334.

Hudson Falls, Washington Co., Church of St. Mary's/St. Paul's (Sandy Hill). The Roman Catholic Community of Hudson Falls/Kingsbury. Revs. Edward C. Pratt; Leo L. Marcil; Deacon Frank Herlihy.
Res., 11 Wall St., 12839. Tel: 518-747-4823. [CEM]

Immaculate Heart of Mary (Sandy Hill) (French). Canonically merged with St. Paul, Hudson Falls. Now called Church of St. Mary's/St. Paul's, Roman Catholic Community of Hudson Falls/Kingsbury.

St. Paul (Sandy Hill) (French). Canonically merged with Immaculate Heart of Mary parish, Hudson Falls. Now called Church of St. Mary's/St. Paul's, Roman Catholic Community of Hudson Falls/Kingsbury.

Ilion, Herkimer Co., Annunciation, Rev. Joseph Benintende.
Res., 109 West St., 13357. Tel: 315-894-3766; Fax: 315-894-1550. [CEM]

Johnsonville, Rensselaer Co., St. Monica's Church, Rev. Bernard Turner.
Res., St. Monica's Rectory, 16 St. Monica Ln., 12094. Tel: 518-753-4003; Fax: 518-752-4003.

Johnstown, Fulton Co., St. Anthony (Slovak), Rev. Francis Dunbar.
Res., 4 Nicholas St., 12095. Tel: 518-762-8176. [CEM]

Immaculate Conception (Italian), Rev. Joseph F. DiMaggio.
Res., One Warren St., 12095. Tel: 518-762-3272.

St. Patrick, Rev. Joseph F. Barker.
Res., 205 Glebe St., 12095. Tel: 518-762-8775. [CEM]

Lake George, Warren Co., Sacred Heart, Revs. Paul Cox; James I. Donlon.
Res., 50 Mohican St., 12845. Tel: 518-668-2046; Fax: 518-668-4377.
Mission—Queensbury, Our Lady of the Assumption, Tel: 518-668-2046.

Lake Luzerne, Warren Co., Holy Infancy, Rev. Charles A. Gaffigan.
Res., 323 Lake Ave., 12846. Tel: 518-696-2625. [JC]

Latham, Albany Co., Our Lady of the Assumption, Revs. John J. Hardiman; David L. Tressic; Deacon Robert Rucinski.
Res., 498 Watervliet-Shaker Rd., 12110. Tel: 518-785-0234.

St. Ambrose, Revs. Francis J. DuBois; John Bertolucci. In res., Rev. George Phillips.
Res., 347 Old Loudon Rd., 12110. Tel: 518-785-1351; Fax: 518-785-8370.
School—Tel: 518-785-6453. Sr. Mary Catherine, P.B.V.M., Prin.
Sisters 11; Lay Teachers 9; Students 293.

Little Falls, Herkimer Co.,

1—St. Joseph. Consolidated with St. Mary and Sacred Heart to form Holy Family Parish, Little Falls.

2—St. Mary. Consolidated with St. Joseph and Sacred Heart to form Holy Family Parish, Little Falls.

3—Sacred Heart, (Polish). Consolidated with St. Joseph and St. Mary to form Holy Family Parish, Little Falls.

4—Holy Family, Rev. Charles R. Celeste; Sr. Marilyn Hayes, C.S.J., Pastoral Assoc.
Office: 763 E. Main St., 13365. Tel: 315-823-3410; 823-2110; Fax: 315-823-2701. [CEM]

Loudonville, Albany Co., St. Pius X, Revs. Michael A. Farano, V.G.; Thomas Konopka.
Res., 2 Fairview Rd., 12211. Tel: 518-462-1336; Fax: 518-462-1338.
School—Upper Loudon Rd., 12211. Tel: 518-465-4539. Nicholas Audi, Prin.
Sisters 3; Lay Teachers 19; Students 316.
Convent—Upper Loudon Rd., 12211. Tel: 518-449-1658.

St. Francis de Sales (1972), Revs. David E. Noone; Christopher Welch.
Church & Offices: One Maria Dr., 12211. Tel: 518-489-8386; Fax: 518-489-6910.
Res., 15 Exchange St., Albany, 12205. Tel: 518-489-8386.
Old Church—15 Exchange St., Albany, 12205.

Margaretville, Delaware Co., Sacred Heart, Rev. Robert H. Purcell, V.F.
Res., Academy St., 12455. Tel: 914-586-2665.
Missions—Andes, St. Ann; Roxbury, Our Lady of Good Counsel.

Mechanicville, Saratoga Co., Assumption-St. Paul, Revs. Christopher J. Drennen, O.S.A.; Francis X. Gallogly, O.S.A. In res., Rev. Anthony J. Tomasulo, O.S.A.; Deacon Arthur Canary.
Res., P.O. Box 308, 12118. Tel: 518-664-6196; Fax: 518-664-6782.
Convent—77 Viall Ave., 12118. Tel: 518-664-4053. Sisters of St. Joseph

Menands, Albany Co., Church of St. Joan of Arc, Rev. William F. Jillisky; Deacon Andy Cohen. In res., Rev. Msgr. Joseph Conway.
Parish Office & Res.: 76 Menand Rd., 12204. Tel: 518-463-0378; 462-2496.

Middleburgh, Schoharie Co., St. Catherine, Rev. James E. Clark, Admin.
Res., 24 Wells Ave., 12122. Tel: 518-827-5132; Fax: 518-827-7873.

Mohawk, Herkimer Co., Blessed Sacrament, Rev. James Steuer.
Res., 54 E. Main St., 13407. Tel: 315-866-1752.

Morris, Otsego Co., Holy Cross, Rev. Morris R. Dwyer.
Res., 43 W. Main St., P.O. Box 118, 13808. Tel: 607-263-5143.
Mission—Edmeston, Nativity of B.V.M.

Nassau, Rensselaer Co., St. Mary, Rev. Antone Kandrac, O.F.M.Conv.; Deacon John Skelly.
Res., 26 Church St., P.O. Box 435, 12123. Tel: 518-766-2701. [CEM]

New Lebanon, Columbia Co., Immaculate Conception, Rev. Joseph Halloran.
Church—Church and Shrine of Our Lady of Lourdes, U.S. Rte. 20, 12125. Tel: 518-794-7651; 766-5651. [CEM]

Newport, Herkimer Co., St. John the Baptist, Rev. Leo Potvin.
Res., Main St., Box 475, 13416. Tel: 315-845-8017.
Mission—Middleville, St. Mary of the Assumption. [CEM]

North Creek, Warren Co., St. James, Rev. Joseph O'Brien.
Res., Main St., 12853. Tel: 518-251-2518. [CEM]
Mission—Pottersville, St. Pius X.

Northville, Fulton Co., St. Francis of Assisi, Rev. Augustine Kapinus, O.F.M.Conv.
Mailing Address: P.O. Box 126, 12134.
Res., 501 Bridge St., 12134. Tel: 518-863-4736.

Oneonta, Otsego Co., St. Mary, Revs. Paul A. Roman; Brian Raiche; Mrs. Diane Beuerman, Pastoral Ministry; Susan Nesbitt, Campus Ministry.
Res., 39 Walnut St., 13820. Tel: 607-432-3920. [CEM]
School—38 Walnut St., 13820. Tel: 607-432-1450. Sr. Mary Christopher Comproski, C.R., Prin.
Religious 2; Lay Teachers 13; Students 219.
Convent—10 Irving Pl., 13820. Tel: 607-433-2220.

Palenville, Greene Co., Sacred Heart, Rev. Paul R. Guido, O.F.M.
Mailing Address: Box 40, Rte. 32 A, 12463. Tel: 518-678-9937.

Philmont, Columbia Co., Sacred Heart, Rev. Raymond Ethier, Admin.
Res., 141 Main St., 12565. Tel: 518-672-4655. [CEM]
Mission—Philmont, Pine Haven Home.

Pittstown, Rensselaer Co., St. George, Revs. John J. Sheridan, O.S.A.; Daniel J. Menihane, O.S.A.
Res., Immaculate Conception Friary, Box 343, Main St., Hoosick Falls, 12090.
Mission—Grafton, Rensselaer Co., St. John Francis Regis.

Queensbury, Warren Co., Our Lady of the Annunciation, Revs. Joseph Anselment; James Rosch.
Res., 448 Aviation Rd., 12804. Tel: 518-793-9677; Fax: 518-793-9678.

Ravena, Albany Co., St. Patrick, Rev. Vincent J. Ciotoli.
Res., 21 Main St., 12143. Tel: 518-756-3145. [CEM]

Rensselaer, Rensselaer Co., St. John, Rev. Joseph Cotugno, Admin. In res., Rev. Thomas Hiney. Pastoral Assocs.: Sr. M. Anastasia, R.S.M.; Sr. M. Andre, R.S.M.
Res., 50 Herrick St., 12144. Tel: 518-465-2209. [CEM]
Parish Office: P.O. Box 256, 12144. Tel: 518-465-0482.
Convent—20 Lawrence St., 12144. Tel: 518-465-1514. Sr. M. Kathleen Turley, R.S.M., Coord. Sisters 21.

St. Joseph (1915), Rev. R. Adam Forno, Admin.
Office: 1620 Third St., 12144. Tel: 518-463-4401; Fax: 518-463-3194.
School—St. Joseph-St. John, 1641 Third St., 12144. Tel: 518-465-1151. Sr. Kathleen Pritty R.S.M., Prin.
Lay Teachers 16; Students 155.
Catechesis/Religious Programs—Students 165.

Richfield Springs, Otsego Co., St. Joseph, Rev. Francis E. Husselbeck.
Res., 35 Canadarago St., 13439-0791. Tel: 315-858-1682. [CEM]

Rotterdam, Schenectady Co., St. Gabriel the Archangel, Rev. Leo F. Markert; Deacon Kenneth Baechel.
Res., 3040 Hamburg St., Schenectady, 12303. Tel: 518-355-6600.

Rotterdam Junction, Schenectady Co., St. Margaret of Cortona, Rev. Denis J. Brennan.
Res., 2 Putnam St., P.O. Box 60, 12150. Tel: 518-887-5288.

St. Johnsville, Montgomery Co., St. Patrick, Rev. Pascal A. Iannotti.
Res., 30 Center St., 13452. Tel: 518-568-7418.

Salem, Washington Co., Holy Cross, Rev. Liam Condon.
Res., 26 N. Main St., 12865. Tel: 518-854-7626. [CEM]
Mission—Cossayuna Lake.

Saratoga Springs, Saratoga Co., St. Clement, Revs. James O'Blaney, C.SS.R.; James Cannon, C.SS.R.; Pierce Kenny, C.SS.R.; Arthur Tuttle, C.SS.R. Pastoral Assocs.: Sr. Carolyn Krebs, O.P.; Deacon Larry Willette.
Res., 231 Lake Ave., 12866. Tel: 518-584-6122; Fax: 518-584-2644.
School—Lake Ave., 12866. Tel: 518-584-7350. Michael Dillon, Prin.
Lay Teachers 27; Students 406.
Chapel—Gansevoort, St. Therese, Tel: 518-587-3180. Deacon Danny Boyd.

St. Peter, Rev. Robert J. LeFevre Tel: 518-584-6113; Deacon William Hewitt.
Res., 241 S. Broadway, 12866. Tel: 518-584-2375. [CEM]

Schaghticoke, Rensselaer Co., St. John the Baptist, Rev. Anthony J. Tomasulo, O.S.A.; Deacon Walter Rehder.
Mailing Address: P.O. Box 300, 12154.
Res., 52 William St., Mechanicville, 12118. Tel: 518-753-4554. [CEM]
Mission—Valley Falls, Our Lady of Good Counsel.

Schenectady, Schenectady Co.,

1—CHURCH OF ST. ADALBERT, (Polish), Rev. Carl A. Urban; Sr. Bernadette Filter, C.R., Pastoral Assoc. for Elderly.
Res., 550 Lansing St., 12303-1195. Tel: 518-346-4204; Fax: 518-346-0348. [CEM]

2—ST. ANTHONY, (Italian), Revs. Richard Carlino; Anthony DeFranco, Pastor Emeritus; Sr. Maria Rose Querini, M.P.V., Pastoral Assoc.; Deacon August DiDonna.
Parish Office: 331 Seward Pl., 12305. Tel: 518-374-4591; Fax: 518-374-4592.
School—1840 Van Vranken Ave., 12305. Tel: 518-372-5961. Sr. Elisa Brasili, M.P.V., Prin.
Venerini Sisters 3; Lay Teachers 8; Students 149.
Convent—1834 Van Vranken Ave., 12305. Tel: 518-346-2060.

3—SACRED HEART-ST. COLUMBA, Rev. Michael Hogan; Mr. George Vielkind, Admin. Pastoral Assocs.: Sr. Rosemary Endres, C.S.J.; Sr. Joseph Andrew Dunham, C.S.J., Coord. of Food Pantry; Sr. Norina Mastro, M.P.V.; Sr. M. Therese Van de Mosselaer, I.C.M., Parish Visitor; Judy Fitzner-Atchinson, Artist-in-Residence.
Res., 801 Stanley St., 12307. Tel: 518-377-8559; 346-0261; Fax: 518-393-9265.

4—SS. CYRIL AND METHODIUS. Closed. For inquiries for parish records contact Our Lady of Mount Carmel, Schenectady.

5—ST. HELEN, Rev. James J. Kane.
Res., 1803 Union St., 12309. Tel: 518-346-6137; Fax: 518-346-5390.
School—1801 Union St., 12309. Tel: 518-382-8225; Fax: 518-382-2226. Sr. Anne Marie, P.B.V.M., Prin.
Sisters of Presentation 4; Lay Teachers 14; Students 248.
Convent—40 Ray St., 12309. Tel: 518-374-7055.

6—HOLY CROSS, Rev. John T. Provost.
Res., 19 N. College St., 12305. Tel: 518-374-1551.

7—IMMACULATE CONCEPTION, Rev. L. Edward Deimeke.
Res., 523 Thompson St., 12306. Tel: 518-382-0451.
School—520 Bradt St., 12306. Tel: 518-377-7470; Fax: 518-370-1089. Marjorie Edgar, Prin.
Lay Teachers 12; Students 225.

8—ST. JOHN THE BAPTIST, Rev. John Peter Rosson.
Res., 427 Franklin St., 12305. Tel: 518-374-9148. [CEM]

9—ST. JOHN THE EVANGELIST, Revs. John T. Provost; George Fleming; Deacon Frank Schickel. In res., Revs. Anthony DeFranco; Anthony Curran.
Res., 802 Union St., 12308. Tel: 518-377-9607; Fax: 518-374-4663.
Office: 816 Union St., 12308. Tel: 518-372-3381.
School—806 Union St., 12308. Tel: 518-393-5331. Marie Keenan, Prin.
Lay Teachers 14; Students 270.

10—ST. JOSEPH, (German), Rev. Bernard J. Gustas. In res., Rev. Joseph P. Biondino.
Res., 225 Lafayette St., 12305. Tel: 518-374-4466. [CEM 2]

11—ST. LUKE, Rev. Msgr. Howard F. Manny, Pastor Emeritus; Rev. Dominic Isopo.
Res., 1241 State St., 12304. Tel: 518-346-3405; Fax: 518-346-3406.
School—1252 Albany St., 12304. Tel: 518-377-7330; Fax: 518-377-7330. Sr. Ann Christi Brink, C.S.J., Prin.
Sisters of St. Joseph of Carondelet 7; Lay Teachers 7; Students 192.
Convent—1252 Albany St., 12304. Tel: 518-372-2182.
Mission—Schenectady, Schenectady Co., St. Teresa Carmelite Monastery, 428 Duane Ave., 12304.

12—ST. MARY, (Polish), Rev. John T. Provost. In res., Rev. Michael Zakens.
Res., 828 Eastern Ave., 12308. Tel: 518-374-2423;. [CEM]

13—OUR LADY OF THE ASSUMPTION, Revs. Richard A. Carlino; John Kostek.
Res., 3034 Ford Ave., 12306. Tel: 518-346-4926.

14—OUR LADY OF FATIMA, Rev. Alan D. Jupin.
Res., 2216 Rosa Rd., 12309. Tel: 518-370-3136.

15—OUR LADY OF MT. CARMEL, (Italian), Rev. Joseph A. Mancuso.
Res., 1255 Pleasant St., 12303. Tel: 518-393-4109; Fax: 518-393-4100.
School—1274 Pleasant St., 12303. Tel: 518-372-0336. Sr. Elizabeth Calello, M.P.F., Prin.
Religious Teachers Filippini 2; Lay Teachers 15; Students 197.
Convent—1383 Pleasant St., 12303. Tel: 518-393-6702.

16—ST. PAUL THE APOSTLE, Revs. George W. Brucker; Joseph A. McKay; Deacon Robert H. Stanton. In res., Rev. Kenneth J. Tunny.
Res., 2777 Albany St., 12304. Tel: 518-377-8886; Fax: 518-377-8886.
School—16 Van Zandt St., 12304. Tel: 518-377-0506. Mr. Claude Palczak, Prin.
Lay Teachers 8; Students 212.

17—ST. THOMAS THE APOSTLE, Rev. William J. Kelleher.
Res., 1228 Sixth Ave., 12303. Tel: 518-370-2066.

Schoharie, Schoharie Co., St. Joseph, Rev. Kenneth Tunny, Sacramental Min.; Sr. Joan Curley, C.S.J., Pastoral Admin.
Res., P.O. Box 514, 12157. Tel: 518-295-8923.

Schuylerville, Saratoga Co., Notre Dame-Visitation, Rev. Robert L. Buckley.
Res., 18 Pearl St., 12871. Tel: 518-695-3391; Fax: 518-695-4651. [CEM 2]
Convent—127 Pearl St., 12871. Tel: 518-695-3318.

Visitation of the Blessed Virgin Mary. Closed. For inquiries for parish records contact Notre Dame de Lourdes Parish, Schuylerville.

Scotia, Schenectady Co., St. Joseph, Rev. Ronald A. Menty; Deacons Robert R. Brady; John P. Crane.
Res., 231 Second St., 12302. Tel: 518-346-4960.
Parish Center: 45 MacArthur Dr., 12302. Tel: 518-346-2316.

Sidney, Delaware Co., Sacred Heart, Revs. Gordon Polenz; Joseph J. Schuck; Deacons Thomas E. Luby; Michael R. Donnell.
Res., 15 Liberty St., 13838. Tel: 607-563-1591.
Convent—24 1/2 Grand St., 13838. Tel: 607-563-3301.
Missions—Unadilla, Otsego Co., St. Ambrose; Franklin, Delaware Co., St. Paul.

South Glens Falls, Saratoga Co., St. Michael the Archangel, Revs. Robert Nugent; M. Curtis Hughes, Pastor Emeritus.
Res., 80 Saratoga Ave., 12803. Tel: 518-792-5859.

South Kortright, Delaware Co., Church of the Most Precious Blood of Jesus, Rev. John R. Burns; Deacon George D. Sheehan.

Res., Main St., P.O. Box 186, 13842-0186. Tel: 607-538-9309.
Mission—Davenport Center, Delaware Co., Chapel of St. Theresa the Little Flower.

Speigletown, Rensselaer Co., St. Bonaventure, Rev. Salvatore A. Rodino.
Res., Hillview Dr., Troy, 12182. Tel: 518-235-0337.

Stamford, Delaware Co., Sacred Heart, Rev. Joseph S. Cebula.
Res., 27 Harper St., P.O. Box 38, 12167. Tel: 607-652-7170. [CEM]
Mission—Grand Gorge, Delaware Co., St. Philip Neri.

Stillwater, Saratoga Co., St. Peter the Apostle, Rev. James O'Neill.
Res., 271 N. Hudson Ave., 12170. Tel: 518-664-3354. [CEM]
Mission—Saratoga Lake, Saratoga Co., St. Isaac Jogues. (Summer).

Stottville, Columbia Co., Holy Family, Rev. William H. Kennedy.
Res., 2824 Atlantic Ave., 12172. Tel: 518-828-1889; Fax: 518-822-9238.

Stuyvesant, Columbia Co., Nativity of the Blessed Virgin Mary, Rev. Joseph Falletta.
Church—1820 Rte. 9, 12173. Tel: 518-799-5411.

Stuyvesant Falls, Columbia Co., St. Mary, Rev. Joseph Faletta.
Church—1820 Rte. 9, Stuyvesant, 12173. Tel: 518-799-5411; Fax: 518-799-3144.

Summit, Schoharie Co., St. Anna, Rev. Edward Golding, Admin.
Res., Main St., P.O. Box 124, 12175. Tel: 518-287-1553.
Missions—Camp Summit, N.Y.S. Correctional Facility; Camp Summit, S.U.N.Y. Cobleskill College.

Tribes Hill, Montgomery Co., Sacred Heart, Rev. Conrad Somerville, O.F.M.Conv.
Res., Box 264 Third Ave., 12177. Tel: 518-829-7301.

Troy, Rensselaer Co.,

1—St. Anthony of Padua, (Italian), Revs. Isaac J. Calicchio, O.F.M.; Louis M. Pintye, O.F.M.; Bro. James Welch, III; Deacon Gerald Christiano.
Res., Friary, 28 State St., 12180. Tel: 518-273-8622.
Center—107 Fourth St., Tel: 518-273-8351.

2—St. Augustine, Revs. Thomas J. Meehan, O.S.A.; Joseph Keffer, O.S.A.; Bro. Joseph T. Spindler, O.S.A., Pastoral Assoc.
Res., 25 115th St., 12182. Tel: 518-235-3861; Fax: 518-233-0284.
School—525 Fourth Ave., 12182. Tel: 518-235-7287. Ms. Elizabeth Allard, Prin.
Sisters of St. Joseph 1; Lay Teachers 14; Students 182.
Convent—523 Fourth Ave., 12182. Tel: 518-235-5959.

3—St. Francis de Sales, Rev. Donald J. Ophals. In res., Rev. John Lysogorski.
Res., 316 Congress St., 12180. Tel: 518-274-4232.

4—Holy Trinity, (Polish), Rev. Romaeus Cooney, O.Carm., Admin.
Mailing Address: St. Joseph's Priory, 416 Third St., 12180. Tel: 518-274-6720.

5—St. Joseph, Revs. Albert Pavlik, O.Carm.; Romaeus Cooney, O.Carm.; Vincent McDonald, O.Carm.
Res., 416 Third St., 12180. Tel: 518-274-6720; Fax: 518-272-6503. [CEM]

6—St. Lawrence. Closed. For inquiries for parish records contact St. Joseph Parish, Troy.

7—St. Mary, Rev. Harry Donaghy; Deacon Joseph Dillon.
Res., 331 Fourth St., 12180. Tel: 518-272-5820.

8—St. Michael the Archangel, Rev. James M. Mackey; Deacons Frank Yankowski; John Skelly.
Res., 26 Bridle Pl., East Greenbush, 12061. Tel: 518-477-5656.
Church—175 Williams Rd., 12180. Tel: 518-283-6110; Fax: 518-283-3938.
Missions—North Greenbush, Rensselaer Co., Van Rensselaer Manor, County Welfare Home; Troy, Rensselaer Co., Hallmark Nursing Home.

9—Our Lady of Victory, Rev. Randall P. Patterson. In res., Revs. David Berberian; Gregory Weider.
Res., 55 N. Lake Ave., 12180. Tel: 518-273-7609; 273-7602 (Office); Fax: 518-273-0310.
School—451 Marshland Ct., 12180. Tel: 518-274-6202.
Lay Teachers 15; Students 155.

10—St. Patrick, Revs. Thomas J. Kelly; Cyril F. Pereira.
Res., 3027 Sixth Ave., 12180. Tel: 518-272-4666.
School—762 River St., 12180. Tel: 518-274-6502.
Sisters 2; Lay Teachers 5; Students 141.
Convent—139 Fifth Ave., 12180. Tel: 518-274-6768.

11—St. Paul the Apostle, Rev. James McNerney.
Res., 138 Twelfth St., 12180. Tel: 518-274-4083.

12—St. Peter, Rev. Thomas K. Flanigan.
Res., 2310 Fifth Ave., 12180. Tel: 518-272-2750. [CEM]

13—Sacred Heart, Revs. James Vaughan; James Howard.
Res., 310 Spring Ave., 12180. Tel: 518-274-1363; Fax: 518-274-8720.
School—308 Spring Ave., 12180. Tel: 518-274-3655; Fax: 518-274-8270. Susan Holland, Prin.
Sisters 3; Lay Teachers 21; Students 318.

14—St. Williams, Rev. Joseph E. Keyrouze.
Res., 1010 Madison Ave., 12180. Tel: 518-273-1680.

Ushers, Saratoga Co., Corpus Christi, Rev. Edward Fitzpatrick; Deacons Michael Sheppeck; John Tierney.
Res., 10 Southwood Dr., Ballston Lake, 12019. Tel: 518-877-8503; 877-8506 (Office); Fax: 518-877-8506.

Valatie, Columbia Co., St. John the Baptist, Rev. Thomas M. Powers.
Res., 1025 Kinderhook St., 12184. Tel: 518-758-9401; Fax: 518-758-9409. [CEM]

Voorheesville, Albany Co., St. Matthew, Rev. Arthur A. Toole.
Res., 31 Mountain View St., 12186. Tel: 518-765-2805; Fax: 518-765-3701.

Walton, Delaware Co., St. John the Baptist, Rev. Eugene F. Willis; Deacon George Sheehan.
Mailing Address: P.O. Box 315, 13856.
Res., 15 Benton Ave., 13856-0315. Tel: 607-865-4720.
Mission—Downsville, Delaware Co., Holy Family.

Warrensburg, Warren Co., St. Cecilia, Rev. Nellis J. Tremblay.
Res., 99 Main St., 12885. Tel: 518-623-3021; Fax: 518-623-3021. [CEM]

Waterford, Saratoga Co., St. Anne, Rev. John Riley.
Res., 75 Grace St., 12188. Tel: 518-237-5211.
St. Mary of the Assumption, Revs. Marshall J. Halphen, O.S.A.; John J. Byrnes, O.S.A.; J. Riley Havener, O.S.A. In res., Rev. W. Howard McGraw, O.S.A.
Res., 119 Broad St., 12188-2397. Tel: 518-237-3131; Fax: 518-237-9625. [CEM]
School—Waterford Central Catholic School, 12 Sixth St., 12188. Tel: 518-237-0652. Sr. Geraldine Corkrey, C.S.J., Prin.
Lay Teachers 16; Students 258.

Watervliet, Albany Co.,

1—St. Brigid, Rev. Joseph Busch. In res., Rev. Timothy Harrison.
Res., 695 Fifth Ave., 12189. Tel: 518-273-2913.
School—(Regional) 700 Fifth Ave., 12189. Tel: 518-273-3321; Fax: 518-273-9355. Patricia Eldridge, Prin.
Sisters 4; Lay Teachers 20; Students 314.
Convent—709 Fourth Ave., 12189. Tel: 518-273-4022.

2—Immaculate Conception, (Polish), Rev. Paul J. Antos. In res., Rev. Boleslaus M. Watroba, Pastor Emeritus.
Res., 2420 Seventh Ave., 12189. Tel: 518-273-3173. [CEM]
Convent—2425 Seventh Ave., 12189. Tel: 518-273-4423.

3—Our Lady of Mt. Carmel, (Italian), Revs. Emery Parillo, O.F.M.; Bonaventure Bionda, O.F.M.
Res., 410 23rd St., 12189. Tel: 518-273-2932.

4—St. Patrick, Rev. Erwin H. Schweigardt. In res., Rev. James I. Donlon.
Res., 515 19th St., Box 388, 12189. Tel: 518-273-2971; Fax: 518-273-2972.

5—Sacred Heart of Mary, Rev. John J. Rooney.
Res., 1511 Sixth Ave., 12189. Tel: 518-273-6252.

West Taghkanic, Holy Cross, Rev. Peter V. Kranch.
Res., 880 Rte. 82, Elizaville, 12523. Tel: 518-851-7577.

West Winfield, Herkimer Co., St. Joseph, Rev. Terence P. Healy; Deacon Richard Brown.
Res., 305 W. Main St., P.O. Box 360, 13491-0360. Tel: 315-822-3191. [CEM]

Whitehall, Washington Co., Notre Dame des Victoires, Rev. George C. Gagnon.
Res., 9 Wheeler Ave., 12887. Tel: 518-499-1656.
Our Lady of Angels, Rev. William Esmond.
Res., 2 Boardman St., 12887. Tel: 518-499-1597. [CEM]

Windham, Greene Co., St. Theresa of Child Jesus, Revs. Donald E. Doyle; John G. O'Grady.
Res., Main St., 12496. Tel: 518-734-3352.
Mission—Ashland, St. Joseph's Chapel.

Worcester, Otsego Co., St. Joseph, Rev. William W. Crandall.
Res., 181 Main St., 12197. Tel: 607-397-9373.
Mission—Schenevus, Otsego Co., St. Mary. [CEM]

Wynantskill, Rensselaer Co., St. Jude the Apostle, Rev. John J. Varno; Deacon G. Timothy Dorsey.
Res., 6 Schuyler Ct., P.O. Box 347, 12198. Tel: 518-283-1162.
School—Brookside Ave., 12198. Tel: 518-283-0333. Mrs. Marcia Rosenfield, Admin.
Sisters 2; Lay Teachers 12; Students 190.

Chaplains of Public Institutions

Albany. *Albany County Jail*. Rev. Richard Shaw, Rensselaer, Schenectady.
Albany County Nursing Home. Rev. Rufino Maloney, O.F.M.Conv.; Sr. Anne Marie Peterson, R.G.S., Chap.; Deacon Frank Schickel, Chap.
Albany Medical Center Hospital. Revs. David Mickiewicz; Kenneth Gregory; John Lysogorski; John Bertolucci; Sr. Lucille Theroux, Chap.
Capital District Psychiatric Center. Rev. James Joslin.
Memorial Hospital. Rev. John T. Kelly; Sr. Frances Markham, R.G.S., Chap.; Deacon Cyril Lavin, Chap.
University Heights Nursing Home. Sr. Jane Carr, R.S.M., Chap.
Veterans' Administration Hospital. Rev. John Minkler.

Comstock. *Great Meadows Correctional Institution*. Rev. James Hayes.

Coxsackie. *Coxsackie Correctional Facility*. Revs. William Kennedy; John Moyna.
Greene County Correctional Institution. Rev. Joseph Romano.

Glens Falls. *Glens Falls Hospital*. Chaplains: Rev. Mark Haight; Sr. Helen LeClerc, C.S.J.

Schenectady. *Ellis Hospital*. Rev. Martin DeRose; Sr. June Baker, O.P., Chap.; Deacons George Nahm, Chap.; August Van Patten, Chap.
Schenectady County Nursing Home. Sr. Elizabeth Hunter, R.S.C.J., Chap.
Silver Haven Nursing Home. Deacon Earle Flatt, Chap.

Troy. *Leonard Hospital*. Deacon Gerald Christiano, Chap.
Samaritan Hospital. Rev. Gregory Weider.
Van Rensselaer Manor. Deacon John Skelly, Chap.

Wilton. *Mount McGregor Correctional Facility*. Rev. Richard Severson.
Wilton Developmental Center Tel: 518-584-3110. Rev. Gerald D. Kampfer.

Special Assignment:
Reverend Fathers—
Amissah, Kofi, Black Apostolate, 50 Thornton St., Albany, NY 12206
Burke, Geoffrey, 40 N. Main Ave., Albany, NY 12203
Cantwell, Edward F., 428 E. Allen St., Hudson, NY 12534
Chiaramonte, Anthony, Consultation Center, 790 Lancaster St., Albany, NY 12203
Close, John L., Computer Services, Pastoral Center, St. Teresa, Albany
DeGiovine, Christopher, College of St. Rose, 432 Western Ave., Albany, NY 12203
DeRose, Martin, 2166D Daisy Ln., Schenectady, NY 12309
Donlon, James I., Judicial Vicar, Tribunal, Pastoral Center
Dworak, Joseph, 427 Guy Park Ave., Amsterdam, NY 12010
Farano, Michael A., Vicar Gen., 2 Fairview Rd., Loudonville, NY 12211
Fitzpatrick, Edward J., c/o Priests' Personnel, 40 N. Main Ave., Albany, NY
Fitzpatrick, John, c/o Priests' Personnel Board, 40 N. Main Ave., Albany, NY 12203
Gagnon, George C., 138 12th St., Troy, NY 12180
Gregory, Kenneth, Chap., Albany Medical Center, Albany, NY 12208
Gulley, Anthony D., 607 Central Ave., Albany, NY 12206
Hayes, James, 23 Bulkley Ave., Granville, NY 12832
Hiney, Thomas J., 50 Herrick St., Rensselaer, NY 12144
Hogan, Michael, Hispanic Apostolate, 801 Stanley St., Schenectady, NY 12307
Holmes, Thomas, 122 Vliet Blvd., Cohoes, NY 12047
Joslin, James R., 1086 Regent St., Schenectady, NY 12308
Kacerguis, Edward, 2008 19th St., Troy, NY 12181
Kampher, Gerald D., Sonoma Pt., Loon Lake, Chestertown, NY 12817
Kane, James, Dir., Pastoral Center, Ecumenical & Interreligious Affairs
Kelly, James, 204 S. Boulder Hwy., Henderson, NV 89015
Kelly, John T., 600 N. Blvd., Albany, NY 12010
Kirwin, John, One Ichabod Ln., Albany, NY 12211
Leskovar, Richard J., 600 McClellan St., Schenectady, NY 12304
Lysogorski, John, AIDS Ministries/Albany Med., 39 Grandview Dr., Latham, NY 12110

Maione, Anthony, Saratoga Catholic Central High, 247 S. Broadway, Saratoga Springs, NY 12866
Malecki, John, Consultation Ctr., 790 Lancaster St., Albany, NY 12203
Marbury, Cabell, 99 Slingerland St., Albany, NY 12202
McCloskey, Francis, Copake Falls, NY 12517
Mickiewicz, David, Chaplain, Albany Medical Hospital, New Scotland Ave., Albany, NY 12208
Minkler, John, V.A. Hospital, Albany, NY 12208
Molyn, John, Dir., Vocations, Pastoral Center
O'Brien, Leo P., Vicar Gen., 900 Madison Ave., Albany, NY 12208
Pereira, Cyril F., 3027 Sixth Ave., Troy, NY 12180
Piechocki, Raymond, R.D. 3, Amsterdam, NY 12010
Pius, Jung Bio, Korean Apostolate, 10 Lodge St., Albany, NY 12207-2196
Powers, Thomas, Continuing Education for Clergy, Pastoral Center
Romano, Joseph, 40 Collins Pl., Albany, NY 12208
Rosson, John, 39 Walnut St., Oneonta, NY 13820
Severson, Richard, P.O. Box 2264, Wilton, NY 12866
Shaw, Richard, 312 Hoosick St., Troy, NY 12180
Smith, Paul, 37 Parkwood St. E., Albany, NY 12203
Sullivan, Peter J., III, Adjutant Vicar Judicial Tribunal, Pastoral Center
Tartaglia, Paul, Propagation of Faith, Pastoral Center
Testa, Richard, 512 Third Ave., Troy, NY 12182
Tunny, Kenneth J., P.O. Box 550, Averill Park, NY 12018
Turner, Bernard, P.O. Box 6673, Albany, NY 12206
Vosko, Richard, 4611 Foxwood Dr., Clifton Park, NY 12605
Weider, Gregory, Chaplain Samaritan Hospital, Troy, NY 12180
Yanas, John, 40 Collins Pl., Albany, NY 12208

On Duty Outside the Diocese:
Reverend Fathers—
Allie, Stanley J., Sacred Heart Church, 1201 Bogard Rd., Wasilla, AK 99654-6523
Bentley, David, Custody of St. Francis, P.O. Box 20111, Kitwe, Zambia
Casey, Liam C., St. Francis Hospital, 114 Woodland St., Hartford, CT 06105
Cioppa, Philip, Exec. Dir., NW Regional Office for Hispanic Affairs, 920 S. 6th St., Sunnyside, WA 98944
Fragomeni, Richard, 5401 S. Cornell Ave., Chicago, IL 60615-5698
Kelly, James, P.O. Box 977, McGill, NY 89318
Murphy, Dennis, 15 Hawthorne St., Cambridge, MA 02138
Nusbaum, Daniel C., Mt. St. Mary College, Emmitsburg, MD 21727
O'Grady, John F., Barry University, 11300 N.E. Second Ave., Miami, FL 33161
Pilson, Paul, 224 W. 24th St., New York, NY 10011
Polewczak, Michael, Holy Trinity Parish, 2202 Riverbank Dr., P.O. Box 1207, Orangeburg, MD 29116
Redmond, Paul, Mt. St. Mary College, Emmitsburg, MD 21727
Ryan, Patrick
Testa, David, Holy Spirit Monastery, Franciscan University, Steubenville, OH 43952-6701

Military Chaplains:
Reverend Fathers—
Estabrook, Joseph, CDR, CHC, USN, 5902 Mount Eagle Dr., Alexandria, VA 22303
Lonergan, James B., HHC V Corps Command Chaplain, CMR 420 Box 1616, APO AE 09063
Minkler, John, Chaplain's Office, V.A. Hospital, Holland Ave., Albany, NY 12208
Rutherford, Donald L., 826 Kiln Ln., Hinesville, GA 31313

Unassigned:
Reverend Fathers—
Cronin, Brian
Gorman, William
Murphy, Dennis

Retired:
Reverend Monsignors—
Conway, Joseph P., Our Lady of Hope Residence, 1 Jeanne Jugan Ln., Latham, NY 12110
Glavin, Edward R., 156 Main St., Amsterdam, NY 12010
Hart, James G., 391 Delaware Ave., Albany, NY 12209
Jones, John L., St. Teresa's Rectory, 435 New Scotland Ave., Albany, NY 12208-2397
Manny, Howard F., St. Luke's Rectory, 1241 State St., Schenectady, NY 12304
Reverend Fathers—
Ahern, Bernard, 4418 Poppy Tree Ln., Jacksonville, FL 32223
Amato, Joseph, St. Martha's Church, 200 Orange Ave., P.O. Box 1706, Sarasota, FL 34230-1706
Ashline, Alfred, 808 Sixth Ave., Watervliet, NY 12189
Baniak, Walter, 540 Second St., Troy, NY 12180
Batkiewicz, Joseph J., Teresian House, 200 Washington Ave. Ext., Albany, NY 12203-5894
Blazquez, Marcelo, 63 Ormond St., Albany, NY 12203
Bondi, Paul, 167 Milton Ave., Balton Spa, NY 12020
Caldara, John N., 3025 Myrtle Ave., Schenectady, NY 12306
Campagnone, Nicholas, Wesley Health Care Center, 131 Lawrence St., Hathorn Residence, Room 117, Saratoga Springs, NY 12866
Cekovsky, Andrew B., Mt. St. Vincent Home, Holy Family Rd., Holyoke, MA 01040
Ciani, Francis P., 49 Warwick Rd., Elmont, NY 11003
Ciulek, Joseph, One Gorski St., Amsterdam, NY 12010
Clemente, Michael, 11570 - 64th Ter. N., Seminola, FL 34642
Clune, Gerald F., 9466 Navajo Tr., Morongo Valley, CA 92256
Colburn, Harold, Our Lady of Mercy Life Center, 2240 Western Ave., Guilderland, NY 12084
Collins, William, Villa Mary Immaculate, 301 Hackett Blvd., Albany, NY 12208
Cyvas, Matthew, 555 68th Ave., St. Petersburg Beach, FL 33706
D'Agostino, Joseph, 6 Bircher Ave., Poughkeepsie, NY 12601
De Caprio, John, 105 Florida Ave., Amsterdam, NY 12010
De Pasquale, Daniel, CDR, 2750 Blarrita Ct., Ponte Vedra Beach, FL 32802
DeFranco, Anthony, 802 Union St., Schenectady, NY 12308
Delos, Bernard M., 4044 N.W. 19th St., G 109, Lauderhill, FL 33313
Di Cerbo, Almerico F., McAuley Residence, 308 S. Manning Blvd., Albany, NY 12208
Donnelly, Elmer, Teresian House, 200 Washington Ave. Ext., Albany, NY 12203-5894
Douglas, Louis, 600 Woods Rd., Germantown, NY 12526
Downs, Richard J., 77 Crescent Dr., Albany, NY 12208
French, John F., Dutch Village, 1 CR Van Rensselaer House, Menands, NY 12204
Girzone, Joseph, 8 Leesome Ln., Altamont, NY 12209
Guillaume, Lionel A., 131 George St., Green Island, NY 12183
Halpin, Raymond J., 12 Van Buren Ave., East Greenbush, NY 12061
Hughes, M. Curtis, 80 Saratoga Ave., South Glens Falls, NY 12801
Jonaitis, Peter, 189 Kingsboro Ave., Gloversville, NY 12078
Keefe, John A., 40 Collins Pl., Albany, NY 12208
Keefe, John W., Our Lady of Hope, 1 Jeanne Jugan Ln., Latham, NY 12110
Keeshan, Paul
Kelly, Donald, St. Mary's Rectory, 156 E. Main St., Amsterdam, NY 12010
Kelly, Joseph Anthony, Our Lady of Hope Residence, 1 Jeanne Jugan Ln., Latham, NY 12110
Klementowicz, Chester, 30 William St., Amsterdam, NY 12010
Konisky, Edward, 64 Parkwin Dr., Delmar, NY 12054
Lamanna, Alfred, The Prospect Inn, 20 N. Prospect St., Apt. J, Herkimer, NY 13350
Lemoyne, William, 29 Burgoyne St., Schuylerville, NY 12871
Lerox, Edward, P.O. Box 347, Fort Edward, NY 12828
Lynch, Patrick J., P.O. Box 68, Lans Sta., Troy, NY 12182
Malin, Peter, 8104 San Bernardine Dr., Port Richey, FL 34688
Mallon, John F., St. Mary's Rectory, P.O. Box 351, East Durham, NY 12423-0223
Marcil, Leo, 11 Wall St., Hudson Falls, NY 12839
McManus, Edward, Mercy Life Center, 2240 Western Ave., Guilderland, NY 12084
McNamara, John, Our Lady of Hope Residence, 1 Jeanne Jugan Ln., Latham, NY 12110
Morrill, Giles, c/o Nolan, 106 Fairlawn Ave., Albany, NY 12203
Mulcahy, Howard J., McAuley Residence, 308 S. Manning Blvd., Albany, NY 12208
Mulhall, J. Gregory, Our Lady of Hope, 1 Jeanne Jugan Ln., Lathan, NY 12110
Mullen, Francis, 103 Madison St., Troy, NY 12180
Nowak, Vincent A., King Park Apt., 125 Bldg. B., 4025 N. Federal Hwy., Ft. Lauderdale, FL 33308
Nowakowski, Francis M., c/o Stanley Zima, 17 Sixth St., Yorkville, NY 13495
O'Connor, Stephen, 26 Irving St., Albany, NY 12202
O'Grady, John G., Box 123, Windham, NY 12496
Petit, Roland, 1850 St. Joseph Blvd., E. #1, Montreal, Quebec H2H 1C7 Canada
Phillips, George, 347 Old Loudon Rd., Latham, NY 12110
Powers, John J., 1471 Greenwood Ave., Palo Alto, CA 94301
Prichard, James F., Mary McClellan Nursing Home, Cambridge, NY 12816
Ryan, Edward, P.O. Box 277, Stamford, NY 12094
Sidoti, Anthony, 496 Delaware Ave., Albany, NY 12209
Sinisky, Joseph, 667 Columbia Tpke., East Greenbush, NY 12061
Sise, John, 64 Pioneer St., Apt. C., Box 293, Cooperstown, NY 13346
Smith, Peter H., Teresian House, Washington Ave. Ext, Albany, NY 12203
Starks, R. Mansfield, 400 Saratoga Rd., Scotia, NY 12302
Stone, Carl, P.O. Box Owlshead, Owlshead, NY 12969
Szarek, Joseph, St. Mary's Woodland Village, Upper Tibbits Ave., Troy, NY 12180
Tartaglia, Paul, 465 State St., Albany, NY 12203
Vail, Thomas, 76 Moreland St., Little Falls, NY 13365
Watroba, Boleslaus M., 2420 Seventh Ave., Watervliet, NY 12189
Whalen, John P., 1614 Pacham Rd., Silver Spring, MD 20903

Permanent Deacons:
Baechel, Kenneth, St. Gabriel, Rotterdam & Office of Prayer and Worship
Bazinet, William, St. Alphonsus, Glens Falls
Beck, Gary, Dioc. AIDS Task Force, St. Madeleine Sophie, Guilderland
Beckman, Martin L., Outside Diocese
Beuerman, David, St. Mary's, Cooperstown
Bickmore, Henry, Sacred Heart and Chancery, Albany
Boyd, Danny S., St. Therese Mission, Gansevoort
Brady, Robert, Glendale Nursing Home & St. Joseph, Scotia
Brett, William, Chap., Our Lady of Mercy Center, Guilderland; Legion of Mary
Brown, Richard, St. Joseph, West Winfield
Canary, Arthur, Assumption-St. Paul, Mechanicville
Chambers, Frank, Annunciation, Ilion
Christiano, Gerald, St. Anthony & Leonard Hospital, Troy
Cioppa, Richard, St. Margaret Mary, Albany
Cohen, Andrew, Office of Prayer & Worship & St. Joan of Arc, Menands
Crane, John, ARC Homes & St. Joseph, Scotia
Culkin, John J., Sr., Outside Diocese
Desormeaux, David, Leave of Absence
Devine, Patrick, Holy Cross, Albany
Didonna, August, Dioc. Formation Team, St. Anthony, Schenectady
Dillon, Joseph, St. Mary's, Troy
Donnell, Michael, Sacred Heart, Sidney
Dringus, William, Holy Spirit Church, East Greenbush
Eagan, Arthur, Cathedral and Cathedral Social Services, Albany
Fitzgerald, William, Blessed Sacrament, Albany
Flatt, Earle, St. Madeleine Sophie & Hallmark Nursing Home, Rotterdam
Gaffney, William, St. Vincent de Paul, Albany
Gallipeo, Paul, St. Mary, Glens Falls
Gaul, William H., Jr., St. Joseph's Church, Greenwich; Diocesan Office of Scouting
Gil, Joseph, St. Vincent de Paul, Albany and Hispanic Outreach Services
Glennon, Dr. John E., Health Care Advocate for HIV/AIDS, Great Meadow Correctional Facility; St. Mary's, Granville
Gorman, William A., St. Helen's, Schenectady
Grigaitis, Jerry, St. Edward the Confessor, Clifton Park
Hall, Charles R., St. John the Baptist, Greenville
Herlihy, Frank, St. Mary, Glens Falls; St. Mary's/St. Paul's, Hudson Falls
Hewitt, William, St. Peter's, Saratoga
Hook, J. Neil, St. Margaret Mary, Albany
Howley, Herbert J., St. Joseph's, Greenwich
Hyland, Arnold K., Leave of Absence
Kratz, Russell J., Educational/Sacramental Preparation, St. John's/St. Ann's, Albany
Ladouceur, Gerald, St. Catherine of Siena, Albany
Lavin, Cyril, Holy Spirit, East Greenbush & Memorial Hospital
Luby, Thomas T., Rural Ministry, Sacred Heart, Sidney
Lukovits, Frank, St. Henry, Averill Park & Dir. Deacon Personnel

MacKinnon, Walter, St. Edward, Clifton Park; St. Bernard's, Cohoes
Manno, Peter, St. Joseph's, Dolgeville
Manzella, Alfred R., St. Thomas, Delmar
Markham, Joseph, Christ the King, Albany
McAuliffe, Timothy, Christ the King, Westmere & Permanent Diaconate Office
McGarry, Frank, Leave of Absence
McNamara, Eugene, Outside Diocese
Melanson, Michael, Immaculate Conception, Glenville
Monscko, Walter G., St. John the Baptist, Chestertown
Nahm, George H., St. Clare's, Colonie
Neurohr, Helmut N., St. Ambrose, Latham
Novak, John W., St. Henry, Averill Park
O'Connell, Thomas, Outside Diocese
O'Neill, Charles, St. Mary's, Hudson
Pasquarelli, Robert, St. Henry's, Averill Park
Powers, David F., St. Mary's, Glen Falls
Pudney, E. Jack, Leave of Absence
Raup, Konrad, St. Patrick's, Ravena
Rehder, Walter, St. John the Baptist, Schaghticoke
Robert, Joseph, Outside Diocese
Roemer, Paul W., St. Patrick's, Catskill
Rucinski, Robert, Our Lady of the Assumption, Latham; Family Life Office
Salamone, Samuel, Our Lady Queen of Apostles, Frankfort
Schickel, Frank, St. John the Baptist, Schenectady; Ann Lee Home
Schrempf, Albert G., St. Marie & St. Patrick's, Cohoes; St. Thomas, Delmar
Sedelmeir, Peter, St. John the Baptist, Greenville
Sheehan, George D., Rural Preaching, Delaware County
Sheppeck, Michael, Corpus Christi, Ushers
Skelly, John, St. Mary, Nassau & Van Rensselaer Manor Nursing Home
Solar, Richard, St. Anthony, Johnstown
South, Owen D., St. Agnes/St. Patrick/St. Marie, Cohoes
Stalter, William, Outside Diocese
Stanton, Robert, St. Paul the Apostle, Schenectady & Family Life Commission
Stosiek, Martin, St. Bridget, Copake Falls; Rural Affairs Coord., Diocese of Albany
Sullivan, Raymond, St. Teresa of Avila, Albany
Surman, Dr. Gary, St. Vincent, Cobleskill
Szarejko, Walter, St John the Baptist, Newport
Tierney, John, Corpus Christi, Ushers; County and State Prison
Trawinski, Peter, St. James, Chatham
Turcotte, Arthur W., St. Paul's, Rock City Falls
Vaillancourt, Leonard, St. Peter Hospital, Albany; St. Joseph, Rensselaer
VanPatten, August, Immaculate Conception, Glenville
Wahl, Richard, St. Mary, Crescent
Webster, Donald, St. Joseph, Fort Edward
Whalen, Charles, Outside Diocese
Willette, Lawrence, St. Clement, Saratoga Springs
Witko, George, St. Mary, Albany
Yankowski, Frank, Eden Park Nursing Home & St. Michael, Troy

INSTITUTIONS LOCATED IN THE DIOCESE

[A] SEMINARIES, RELIGIOUS OR SCHOLASTICATES

ALTAMONT. *LaSalette Shrine and Seminary*, Leesome Ln., P.O. Box 680, 12009-0680. Tel: 518-861-8159. Rev. Joseph Horgan, M.S., Dir.; Bros. Raymond J. Aubin, M.S., Assoc. Dir.; G. Peter Collins, M.S., Treasurer.
Corporate Titles: Missionaries of Our Lady of LaSalette, Inc., Altamont, NY; LaSalette Seminary, Altamont, NY.

CATSKILL. *St. Anthony Friary*, P.O. Box 487, Harrison St., 12414. Tel: 518-943-3451. Order of Friars Minor. Revs. Owen Angeloni, O.F.M., Guardian; Francis Solanus DeLorenzo, O.F.M., Vicar; Frederick Fusco, O.F.M.; Gregory Palma, O.F.M.; Bros. John Golisano, O.F.M.; Lawrence Stumpo, O.F.M.

RENSSELAER. *Conventual Franciscan Friars*. Immaculate Conception Province, Provincialate, Office of the Treasurer, P.O. Box 629, 12144. Tel: 518-472-1016; Fax: 518-472-1013. (Corporate Name: Order Minor Conventuals). 517 Washington Ave., 12144. Friars Minor Conventual. Very Revs. Giles Van Wormer, O.F.M.Conv., Minister Prov.; Jude De Angelo, O.F.M.Conv., Vicar Prov.; Rev. Anthony Kall, O.F.M.Conv., Treas.; Mr. Peter Sheehan, Dir. of Finance, Friary Wing. Tel: 518-463-2261. Retreat Wing. Tel: 518-434-8200. Franciscan Center. Tel: 518-434-8200. Revs. Anthony Kall, O.F.M.Conv., Guardian & Dir.; Thomas Crimmins, O.F.M.Conv., Assoc. Dir.; Simon Mohr, O.F.M.Conv., Asst. Dir. & Vicar. In res., Revs. Owen Bennett, O.F.M.Conv.; Andrew Ehlinger, O.F.M.Conv.; Angelus Netzer, O.F.M.Conv.; Ambrose Hojsik, O.F.M.Conv.; Kirk Holland, O.F.M.Conv.; Michael Taylor, Teacher; Nicholas Weiss, O.F.M.Conv.; Bros. Robert Lynch, O.F.M.Conv., Procurator; Andre Picotte, O.F.M.Conv., Dir. of Cemeteries; Nicholas Lorson, O.F.M.Conv., Hospitality. Priests 10; Brothers 3. Our Lady of Mercy Life Center, Guilderland. Rev. Paul Galka, O.F.M.Conv.
Priests of the Province serving outside the U.S.: Rev. Jobe Abbass, O.F.M.Conv., Via del Serafico 1, 00142. Rev. Julian Zambanini, O.F.M.Conv., Via del Serafico 1, 00142. Rev. Donato Cocciardi, O.F.M.Conv., Via del Serafico 1, 00142. Rev. Roman Ondecko, O.F.M.Conv.

[B] COLLEGES AND UNIVERSITIES

ALBANY. *The College of Saint Rose*, 432 Western Ave., 12203. Tel: 518-454-5111; 800-657-8556; Fax: 518-458-5447.
For a complete listing, refer to the Colleges and Universities section.
Maria College, 700 New Scotland Ave., 12208.
For a complete listing, refer to the Colleges and Universities section.
St. Bernard's Institute at Albany, 40 N. Main St., 12203. Tel: 518-453-6760.
For a complete listing, refer to the Colleges and Universities section.

LOUDONVILLE. *Siena College*, 12211. Tel: 518-783-2300.
For a complete listing, refer to the Colleges and Universities section.

[C] HIGH SCHOOLS, DIOCESAN

ALBANY. *Bishop Maginn High School*, 99 Slingerland St., 12202. Mr. Joseph Grasso, Prin.; Rev. Cabell B. Marbury, Vice Prin. Priests 1; Sisters 7; Lay Teachers 27; Students 452.

AMSTERDAM. *Bishop Scully High School*, Upper Church St., 12010. Tel: 518-842-4100.

GLENS FALLS. *St. Mary-St. Alphonsus Regional Catholic School*, 10-12 Church St., 12801. Tel: 518-792-3178. Mr. Jack Callery, Prin. Pastors: Revs. Martin Fisher; Robert Powhida. Lay Teachers 21; Students 281.

SARATOGA SPRINGS. *Saratoga Central Catholic High School*. (Grades 7-12), 247 South Broadway, 12866. Tel: 518-587-7070; Fax: 518-587-0678. Mr. Edwin Hammond, Jr., Prin. Lay Teachers 23; Students 274.

SCHENECTADY. *Notre Dame-Bishop Gibbons School*. (Coed Grades 7-12), 2600 Albany St., 12304. Tel: 518-393-3131. Conducted by the Congregation of Christian Brothers. Brothers 4; Sisters 2; Lay Teachers 31; Students 450.

TROY. *Catholic Central High School*. (Grades 7-12), 625 Seventh Ave., 12182. Tel: 518-235-7100; Fax: 518-237-1796. Sr. Carolyn Schanz, C.S.J., Pres.; Rev. William D. Turnbull, Prin. Priests 1; Sisters 7; Lay Teachers 45; Students 750.

[D] HIGH SCHOOLS, PRIVATE

ALBANY. *Academy of the Holy Names Upper, Middle and Lower Schools*, 1073 New Scotland Rd., 12208. Tel: 518-438-7895. Sr. Constance Casey, S.N.J.M., Pres. (PreK-12); Ms. Mary Anne Vigliante, Prin. (Grades 9-12); Sr. Virginia Dunn, S.N.J.M., Prin. (Grades PreK-8); Rev. Paul Smith. Sisters 8; Lay Teachers 47; Students 467.
Christian Brothers' Academy, De La Salle Rd., 12208. Tel: 518-462-5447. Brothers of the Christian Schools. Bro. James Stolz, F.S.C., Prin. JROTC College Prep. Program. Brothers 9; Lay Teachers 33; Students 400.
The Doane Stuart School. (Grades PreK-12). Ecumenical Day School. Coed., 12202. Religious of the Sacred Heart and the Episcopal Diocese of Albany. Faculty 26; Students 217.
Mercy High, Private School for Girls, 310 S. Manning Blvd., 12208. Tel: 518-482-1110.

TROY. *LaSalle Institute*, 174 Williams Rd., 12180. Tel: 518-283-2500; Fax: 518-283-6265. Brothers of the Christian Schools. Bro. James Romond, F.S.C., Prin. Brothers 13; Lay Teachers 44; Students 565.

[E] ELEMENTARY SCHOOLS, PRIVATE

LOUDONVILLE. *Saint Gregory's School*, 121 Old Niskayuna Rd., 12211-1399. Tel: 518-785-6621. Michael O'Donoghue, Headmaster. An independent Catholic day school for boys staffed by laity (PreK-8). Girls admitted in Pre-K and Kindergarten classes. Lay Teachers 23; Students 205.

[F] CONSOLIDATED ELEMENTARY SCHOOLS

ALBANY. *Cathedral Academy*, 75 Park Ave., 12202. Tel: 518-449-5232.

COHOES. *Cohoes Catholic School*, One St. Marie's Ln., 12047. Tel: 518-235-5202. Sr. Sandra Tripp, C.S.J., Prin. Convent, 5 Wilson Way, 12047. Tel: 518-237-1457.

WATERFORD. *Waterford Central Catholic School*. (Grades K-8), 12 Sixth St., 12188. Tel: 518-237-0652. Sr. Geraldine Corkrey, C.S.J., Prin. Lay Teachers 17; Students 258.

[G] RESIDENTIAL INSTITUTIONS FOR CHILDREN & ADOLESCENTS

ALBANY. *LaSalle School, Inc.*, 391 Western Ave., 12203. Tel: 518-242-4731; Fax: 518-242-4747.
For a complete listing, refer to the Special Care Facilities section.
Saint Anne Institute, 160 N. Main Ave., 12206. Tel: 518-437-6500.
For a complete listing, refer to the Special Care Facilities section.
Saint Catherine's Center for Children, 40 N. Main Ave., 12203. Tel: 518-453-6700; Fax: 518-453-6712.
For a complete listing, refer to the Special Care Facilities section.

ALTAMONT. *Bernard & Caroline Cobb Memorial School*, (1962), 12009. Tel: 518-861-6446.
For a complete listing, refer to the Special Care Facilities section.

WATERVLIET. *St. Colman's Home*, 12189. Tel: 518-273-4911; Fax: 518-273-3312.
For a complete listing, refer to the Special Care Facilities section.

[H] GENERAL HOSPITALS

ALBANY. *Mercycare Corporation*, 315 S. Manning Blvd., 12208. Tel: 518-454-1084; Fax: 518-454-1520.
For a complete listing, refer to the Hospitals section.
Mercycare Corporation, St. Peter's Hospital, 315 S. Manning Blvd., 12208. Tel: 518-454-1540.
For a complete listing, refer to the Hospitals section.

AMSTERDAM. *St. Mary's Hospital*, 427 Guy Park Ave., 12010. Tel: 518-842-1900.
For a complete listing, refer to the Hospitals section.

SCHENECTADY. *St. Clare's Holding Company, Inc.*, 600 McClellan St., 12304.
For a complete listing, refer to the Hospitals section.
St. Clare's Hospital, 600 McClellan St., 12304. Tel: 518-382-2000.
For a complete listing, refer to the Hospitals section.

TROY. *Seton Health System, Inc.*, 1300 Massachusetts Ave., 12180. Tel: 518-272-5000.
For a complete listing, refer to the Hospitals section.

[I] SERVICES FOR ELDERLY

ALBANY. *SMILE, Independent Living Services, Inc. at Catholic Charities*, 100 Slingerland St., 12202. Tel: 518-432-0089. James McCaffrey, Dir.

[J] NURSING AND AGED HOMES

ALBANY. *Teresian House*, (1974) Washington Ave. Ext., 12203. Tel: 518-456-2000.
For a complete listing, refer to the Special Care Facilities section.
Villa Mary Immaculate, 301 Hackett Blvd., 12208. Tel: 518-482-3363.
For a complete listing, refer to the Special Care Facilities section.

AMSTERDAM. *Mt. Loretto Nursing Home*, 302 Swart Hill Rd., 12010. Tel: 518-842-6790; Fax: 518-843-5993.
For a complete listing, refer to the Special Care Facilities section.

CASTLETON. *Resurrection Nursing Home*, 12033. Tel: 518-732-7617; Fax: 518-732-4211.
For a complete listing, refer to the Special Care Facilities section.

CATSKILL. *St. Joseph's Villa*, 38 Prospect Ave., 12414. Tel: 518-943-5701.
For a complete listing, refer to the Special Care Facilities section.

LATHAM. *Our Lady of Hope Residence*. Little Sisters of the Poor, Jeanne Jugan Ln., 12110. Tel: 518-785-4551.
For a complete listing, refer to the Special Care Facilities section.

TROY. *St. Mary's Woodland Village, Inc.*, Upper Tibbits Ave., 12180. Tel: 518-273-2040.
For a complete listing, refer to the Special Care Facilities section.

[K] APARTMENTS FOR ELDERLY

ALBANY. *Bishop Broderick Apartments Housing Development Fund Co., Inc.*, 50 Prescott St., 12205. Tel: 518-869-7441; Fax: 518-869-0443.
For a complete listing, refer to the Special Care Facilities section.
C.S.C. Housing Development Fund Co., Inc., dba Sanderson Court Senior Apts. 6 Carondelet Dr. Watervliet, 12189. Tel: 518-436-0156; 782-1123; Fax: 518-782-1125.

For a complete listing, refer to the Special Care Facilities section.

DePaul Management Corp., 41 N. Main Ave., 12203. Tel: 518-459-0183; Fax: 518-459-0202.
For a complete listing, refer to the Special Care Facilities section.

St. Vincent Apartments Housing Development Fund Co., Inc., 475 Yates St., 12208. Tel: 518-482-8915; Fax: 518-489-1220.
For a complete listing, refer to the Special Care Facilities section.

CLIFTON PARK. *Halfmoon Housing Development Fund Co., Inc. dba Bishop Hubbard Senior Apartments / De Paul Management Corp.*, 54 Katherine Dr., 12065. Tel: 518-383-2705.
For a complete listing, refer to the Special Care Facilities section.

NORTH GREENBUSH. *S.J. Housing Development Fund Company, Inc. dba St. Jude's Apartments.* 50 Dana Ave. Wynantskill, 12198. Tel: 518-283-5690; Fax: 518-283-5893.
For a complete listing, refer to the Special Care Facilities section.

RENSSELAER. *East Greenbush Housing Development Fund Co., Inc. dba Branson Manor Senior Apartment*, 3 Grandview Dr., 12144. Tel: 518-283-8280; Fax: 518-283-8292.
For a complete listing, refer to the Special Care Facilities section.

SLINGERLANDS. *Marie-Rose Manor HDFCI*, 100 Marquis Dr., 12159 Fax: 518-459-0204.
For a complete listing, refer to the Special Care Facilities section.

WATERVLIET. *Delatour Housing*, 2 Carondelet Dr., 12189. Tel: 518-783-0444; Fax: 518-783-0456.
For a complete listing, refer to the Special Care Facilities section.

Italian-American Housing Development Fund Co., Inc. dba Cabrini Acers Senior Apts., 4 Carondelet Dr., 12189. Tel: 518-785-0050; Fax: 518-785-0110.
For a complete listing, refer to the Special Care Facilities section.

[L] MONASTERIES AND RESIDENCES OF PRIESTS AND BROTHERS

ALBANY. *Vincentian Fathers Residence*, 110 Menands Rd., 12204-1499. Tel: 518-433-1003. Revs. John A. Doyle, C.M., Supr.; Stephen J. India, C.M.; James E. Smith, C.M., Dir. of Daughters of Charity. Priests 3.

LAKE GEORGE. *St. Mary of the Lake*, P.O. Box 31, 12845. Tel: 518-668-5594. Rev. Robert T. Scott, Dir. Summer retreat of the Paulist Fathers.

RENSSELAER. *Franciscan Mission House*, Washington Ave., 12144. Tel: 518-465-0062. Promotion Center for Order's Missions. Bro. James Amrhein, O.F.M.Conv., Dir.

Provincialate, Immaculate Conception Friary - Order of Friars Minor Conventual (1872). (Immaculate Conception Province), P.O. Box 629, 12144. Tel: 518-472-1000. Very Revs. Giles Van Wormer, O.F.M.Conv., Min. Prov.; Jude DeAngelo, O.F.M.Conv., Vicar Prov. & Sec.; Bros. Stephen Merrigan, O.F.M.Conv., Teacher; Michael Snyder, O.F.M.Conv., Vocation Dir. & Guardian.
(Corporate Name: Order Minor Conventuals, Inc.). Very Rev. Giles Van Wormer, O.F.M.Conv., Pres.; Rev. Alvin Somerville, O.F.M.Conv., Vice Pres.; Very Rev. Anthony Kall, O.F.M.Conv., Treas.; Rev. Jude DeAngelo, O.F.M.Conv., Sec.

SARATOGA SPRINGS. *St. John Neumann Residence*, 233 Lake Ave., 12866. Tel: 518-584-7500. Redemptorist Priests and Brothers of the Baltimore Province. Revs. Joseph Austin; John R. Connell, C.SS.R.; Joseph Coughlin; James Ferris; Joseph Oberle; James King; Alfred C. Rush, C.SS.R.; Thomas F. O'Toole, C.SS.R.; Arthur Finn, C.SS.R.; Owen Rice; Thomas Egan, C.SS.R.; Richard Knappik, C.SS.R.; Simon J. Glasl, C.SS.R.; John Guiniven, C.SS.R.; Luke Doheny; Carl J. Langhirt, C.S.S.R.; James May; Joseph Oberle, C.S.S.R.; Maurice McDonald, C.S.S.R.; James Lacey; Joseph Noll, C.S.S.R.; Charles Fehrenbach; James Ferris, C.S.S.R.; Joseph Austin, C.S.S.R.; Edward Tardiff, C.S.S.R.; Adam Otterbein, C.S.S.R.; Bros. Richard Driscoll, C.S.S.R.; Augustine Fritsch, C.S.S.R.; Barnabas Hipkins; Anthony Strella, C.S.S.R.

VALATIE. *St. Joseph.* Residence for retired Holy Cross Brothers and Priests. 495 Maple Ln., 12184. Tel: 518-784-9481; Fax: 518-784-9494. Bros. Richard Kiniry, Supr. & Dir.; John Thorton, C.S.C., Admin.; Rev. Gregory Roy, S.J., Chap.

[M] CONVENTS AND RESIDENCES FOR SISTERS

ALBANY. *Convent of Mercy*, 310 S. Manning Blvd., 12208. Tel: 518-437-3000; Fax: 518-437-3030. Motherhouse of Sisters of Mercy. Sr. Rosemary Sgroi, R.S.M., Pres.; Sr. Arlene Boyd, R.S.M., V.P. Internal Affairs; Sr. Marilyn Murray, V.P. Corporate Affairs. Sisters 181.

Convent of the Sacred Heart, Kenwood, 799 S. Pearl St., 12202. Tel: 518-465-3341. Convent and Retirement Center for Religious of the Sacred Heart. Sr. Elizabeth Sherman, R.S.C.J., Area Dir.; Sr. Joan Inglis, R.S.C.J., Admin. of Kenwood Campus & Coord. of the Pax Christi Community; Rev. Christopher DeGiovine, Chap.
(Corporate Name: Female Academy of the Sacred Heart of Albany). Sisters 75.

Franciscan House, Mill Hill Sisters. Regional House, 1006 Madison Ave., 12208. Tel: 518-482-1991. Sr. Judith Dever, F.M.S.J. Sisters 5.

Franciscan Sisters of Mary, 4 Katherine St., 12801-5102. Tel: 518-761-0976.

Holy Name, Province Center, 1061 New Scotland Ave., 12208-1198. Tel: 518-489-5469; Fax: 518-489-5804.
(Corporate Name: Sisters of the Holy Names of Jesus and Mary of the New York Province, Inc.).

Academy of the Holy Names of New York, 1075 New Scotland Ave., 12208. Tel: 518-489-2559.

CASTLETON-ON-HUDSON. *Provincial House, Juniorate and Novitiate of the Sisters of Resurrection*, Mount St. Joseph, 35 Boltwood Ave., 12033. Tel: 518-732-2226; Fax: 518-732-2898. Sr. Jeanne Marie Harla, Prov. Sup.; Sr. M. Krystyna, C.R., Local Supr.; Sr. Dolores Palermo, C.R., Dir. Novices. Sisters 20. 34 Boltwood Ave. Tel: 518-732-7831.

CLIFTON PARK. *Sisters of Charity of St. Louis Convent*, 6 Secada Dr., 12065-5005. Tel: 518-371-0247; Fax: 518-371-1206. Sr. Louise Marceau, S.C.S.L., Vocation & Formation Dir.; Sr. Georgette Royer, S.C.S.L., Regional Treas.

GERMANTOWN. *St. Teresa's Motherhouse*, Avila on the Hudson, 600 Woods Rd., 12526-5617. Tel: 518-537-5000. Motherhouse and Novitiate. Carmelite Sisters for the Aged and Infirm. Mother M. Suzanne, O.Carm., Supr. Gen.; Rev. Joseph E. Finch, Chap. Sisters 28; Novices 1.

Postulation Office. Mother M. Angeline Teresa, O.Carm., Servant of God; Rev. Mario Esposito; Sr. M. Gabriel, O.Carm., Coord. of the Cause.

GLEN FALLS. *Franciscan Sisters of Mary*, 4 Katherine St., 12801-5102. Tel: 518-761-0976.

LATHAM. *Congregation of Notre Dame*, Rose Garden Ct., Bldg. 5, Apt. 14, Sparrowbrush Rd., 12110.

Provincial House of the Sisters of St. Joseph of Carondelet (Albany Province), 12110. Tel: 518-783-3500. Sr. Sean C. Peters, C.S.J., Prov. Dir.; Rev. Geoffrey D. Burke, Chap. Sisters 614.

MENANDS. *De Paul Provincial House.* (Corporate Name: Daughters of Charity of St. Vincent de Paul, N.E. Prov.), 96 Menands Rd., 12204. Tel: 518-462-5593. Sr. Louise Gallahue, D.C., Prov. Sup.; Rev. James E. Smith, Prov. Dir.

SCHENECTADY. *Monastery of St. Teresa of Jesus of Discalced Carmelites*, 428 Duane Ave., 12304. Mother Elia of the Trinity, O.C.D., Prioress. Professed Sisters 12; Novices 1; Postulants 2.

WATERVLIET. *St. Colman's Convent*, 12189. Tel: 518-273-4911; Fax: 518-273-3312. Motherhouse and Novitiate of Sisters of the Presentation of the B.V.M. Mother M. Carmel, P.B.V.M., Mother Gen.; Rev. John A. Molyn, Chap.

[N] TEEN CENTER

GUILDERLAND. *Innovative Teen Services, Inc.*, 2333A Western Ave., 12084.

[O] HOUSES OF PRAYER AND RETREAT HOUSES

ALBANY. *Abba House of Prayer.* A nonprofit corporation. 647 Western Ave., 12203. Tel: 518-438-8320.

AURIESVILLE. *Gonzaga Jesuit Community*, 12016. Tel: 518-853-3383; 829-7400. Rev. Edward L. Guth, S.J., Supr.; Bros. Paul C. Acer, S.J.; John T. Gibbons, S.J.; Edward J. Lawniczak, S.J. Priests 2; Brothers 5.

Jesuit Retreat House for Priests, Religious and Lay People, 12016. Tel: 518-853-4496; Fax: 518-853-3051. Revs. John G. Marzolf, S.J., Supr. & Dir.; Joseph A. Cavanaugh, S.J.; William B. Cogan, S.J.; Thomas E. Brady, S.J.; James J. McGinley, S.J.; Vincent M. McNally, S.J.; Louis A. Mounteer, S.J.; William P. Poorten, S.J.; Bros. Theodore C. Bender, S.J.; Paul C. Acer, S.J.; John T. Gibbons, S.J.; Edward G. Lawniczak, S.J. Priests 8; Brothers 4.

Shrine of Our Lady of Martyrs, 12016. Tel: 518-853-3033. National Shrine of the Jesuit Martyrs of North America. Revs. John G. Marzolf, S.J.; John J. Paret, S.J., Asst. Dir. & Vice-Postulator Cause of Kateri Tekakwitha; John M. Doolan, S.J.

CHESTERTOWN. *The Priory*, 12817. Tel: 518-494-3733. Sr. Constance M. Messitt, C.S.J., Dir.; Sr. Francis Anne Gilchrist, C.S.J., Co-Dir.

FONDA. *Blessed Kateri Retreat House*, Rte. 5, P.O. Box 627, 12068. Tel: 518-853-3646; Fax: 518-853-3371. Rev. Kevin Kenny, O.F.M.Conv., Dir.; Bro. Kenneth H. Lucas, O.F.M.Conv., Assoc. Shrine Dir.

GLENS FALLS. *Wellsprings.* A program for Christian Ministers. 93 Maple St., 12801. Tel: 518-792-3183; Fax: 518-792-3184. A four-month holistic enrichment sabbatical program for men and women serving in the church. Sr. Margaret Picha, S.S.N.D., Dir.; Michael Laratonda, F.M.S., Assoc. Dir.

PARADOX. *Pyramid Life Center.* Corporation name: Albany Catholic Youth Association, Inc., 12858. Tel: 518-585-7545. Summer, fall and winter retreat house, located at Pyramid Lake.

SCHENECTADY. *Dominican Spiritual Life Center.* Corporation Name: Dominican Congregation of St. Catherine De Ricci. 1945 Union St., 12309. Tel: 518-393-4169. Jeanne Qualters, Admin. Residence Facilities for 45; Non-resident Facilities for 90 to 100.

STILLWATER. *Still Point House of Prayer*, Rte. 423, Box 53, 12170. Tel: 518-587-4967. House of Prayer operated by The Community of Still Point, Inc. Yearround hermitages, retreats, sabbaticals, holistic and interfaith programs. Sr. M. Sylvia Alicia Rosell, O.P., Dir.

UNADILLA. *Gilead, Inc.*, R.D. 1, Box 54, 13849. Eucharistic Community.

VALATIE. *St. Joseph Spiritual Life Center*, 495 Maple Ln., 12184. Tel: 518-784-9481.

[P] SHELTER FOR WOMEN

ALBANY. *Arbor House*, 302 Western Ave., 12203. Tel: 518-489-6030.
For a complete listing, refer to the Special Care Facilities section.

[Q] YOUTH TREATMENT FACILITIES

ALBANY. *Hospitality House Therapeutic Community Inc.*, 271 Central Ave., 12206. Tel: 518-434-6468. A private, not-for-profit, residential treatment program for young people, 16 to 30 years old, with a history of drug and/or substance abuse.

[R] SHRINES

FONDA. *The National Shrine of Blessed Kateri Tekakwitha and Friary*, P.O. Box 627, 12068. Tel: 518-853-3646; Fax: 518-853-3371. Rev. Kevin Kenny, O.F.M.Conv., Shrine Dir. & Guardian; Bro. Kenneth Lucas, O.F.M.Conv., Assoc. Dir.

[S] CAMPUS MINISTRY

ALBANY. *New York State University at Albany.* (Albany Collegiate Interfaith Center, Inc.) with offices at SUNYA. Box 22225, 12222. Tel: 518-489-8573; Fax: 518-489-8573. Sr. Maureen O'Leary, F.S.P., Chap.

COBLESKILL. *State University of New York College of Agricultural & Technology at Cobleskill*, Main St., P.O. Box 124, 12175. Rev. Edward Golding.

DELHI. *State University of New York College of Agricultural & Technology at Delhi*, St. Peter Rectory, 8 Franklin St., 13753. Tel: 607-746-2503. Rev. Joseph Manerowski.

GLENS FALLS. *Adirondack Community College*, Annunciation, 12804. Tel: 518-793-9677. Rev. Gary Mercure.

HUDSON. *Columbia-Greene Community College*, P.O. Box 1000, 12534. Tel: 518-828-4181.

LOUDONVILLE. *Siena College*, 12211. Tel: 518-783-2332. Rev. Francis X. Gunn, O.F.M., Dir. Campus Ministry. Assoc. Campus Ministers: Revs. Kevin Daly, O.F.M.; Michael J. Harlan, O.F.M., Assoc. Campus Min.; Charlotte Tabor, Protestant Min.; Ms. Claire Morgan, Vol. Coord.; Ms. Judy Dougherty, Sec.

ONEONTA. *New York State University at Oneonta and Hartwick College.* Corporate Title: Oneonta Newman Foundation. Newman House, 77 Spruce St., 13820. Tel: 607-432-4400. Susan Resbitt, Campus Min. Tel: 607-432-4400; Sidney Levine, Pres. of Foundation, Bd. of Dir.; Rev. Brian Raiche, Sacramental Min.; Tracie Jones, Sec.

SARATOGA. *Skidmore College*, Broadway, 12866. Tel: 584-5000, Ext. 2175. Rev. Ronald J. Boccieri, M.M.

SCHENECTADY. *Union College, Catholic Campus Ministry*, 12308. Tel: 518-388-6087. Mr. Thomas J. Frieberg, Chap. Religious Programs Office of Union College, the College Center.

TROY. *Hudson Valley Community College*, 80 Vandenburgh Ave., 12180. Tel: 518-270-7168. Sr. Rosemary Ann Cuneo, C.R., Campus Min.

Rensselaer Polytechnic Institute. Office of the Resident Catholic Chaplain, 217 Rensselaer Union, 12180. Tel: 518-276-6518. Rev. Edward Kacerguis, Chap.; Catherine A. Waibel, Chap.

The Rensselaer Newman Foundation, 217 Rensselaer Union, 12180. Michael Duffy, Pres.

University Parish of Christ Sun of Justice. Rev. Thomas Phelan, Chapel & Cultural Center, 2008 19th St., 12180. Tel: 518-274-7793. William McQuiston, Dir.

Russell Sage College, Campus Ministry Office, Rm. #304 Student Center, 12180. Tel: 518-271-4507. Sr. Rosemary Cuneo, C.R.

[T] MISCELLANEOUS LISTINGS

ALBANY. *Birthright of Albany*, 586 Central Ave., 12206.

Tel: 518-438-2978. Diane Koster, Dir.

Burke Community Service Corp., Inc., 40 N. Main Ave., 12203. Tel: 518-453-6600.

Diocesan HIV/AIDS Ministries, 40 N. Main Ave., 12203. Tel: 518-453-6650, Ext. 485; Fax: 518-453-6792. Rev. Bernard R. Turner, Dir.

Emmaus House. Albany Catholic Worker Community, 35 N. Main Ave., 12203.

The Family Rosary Worldwide Office. Sponsored by Congregation of Holy Cross (Eastern Prov.). (Corporate Name: The Family Rosary, Inc.), 4 Pine West Plaza, 12205-5520. Tel: 518-452-3082; Fax: 518-452-3956. Revs. Robert de Leon, C.S.C., National Dir.; Hugh W. Cleary, C.S.C., Prov.; Leo Polselli, C.S.C., Pres. (On Leave); John P. Phelan, C.S.C., Pres. (Interim); Mr. Robert Klein, Vice Pres., Finance & Admin.

Crusade for Family Prayer, Inc. Sponsored by Congregation of Holy Cross (Eastern Prov.). Revs. Hugh W. Cleary, C.S.C., Prov.; Leo Polselli, C.S.C., Pres. (On Leave); John P. Phelan, C.S.C., Pres. (Interim); Mr. Robert P. Klein, Vice Pres., Finance & Admin.

The Foundation of the Roman Catholic Diocese of Albany, New York, Inc., 40 N. Main Ave., 12203. Tel: 518-453-6680; Fax: 518-453-6793. Mr. Jack Manning, Dir.

LaSalle Albany, Inc., De La Salle Rd., 12208. Bros. Michael Corry, F.S.C., Chm.; Stephen McCabe, F.S.C., Vice Chm.; E. James Stolz, F.S.C., Sec.

McCloskey Community Service Corporation, 40 N. Main Ave., 12203. Tel: 518-453-6683. Phyllis Hathaway, Exec. Dir.

New York State Catholic Conference, 465 State St., 12203. Tel: 518-434-6195; Fax: 518-434-9796. John M. Kerry, Exec. Dir.

New York State Catholic Healthcare Council, 465 State St., 12203. Tel: 518-434-8293. Richard N. McDevitt, Exec. Sec.

New York State Council of Catholic Charities Directors, 465 State St., 12203. Tel: 518-434-3482. Joseph Buttigieg, Exec. Sec.

New York State Council of Catholic School Superintendents. New York State Council of Diocesan Directors of Religious Education. 465 State St., 12203. Tel: 518-434-6195. James D. Cultrara, Exec. Sec.

Sisters of the Holy Names of Jesus and Mary. Community Support Charitable Trust. 1061 New Scotland Ave., 12208-1198; Fax: 518-489-5804.

Support Fund Trust of the Province of St. Thomas of Villanova, c/o 40 N. Main Ave., 12203.

CASTLETON-ON-HUDSON. *C.C.M. of Schodack, Inc.*, 92 S. Main St., 12033.

COHOES. *Apostolate for the Suffering*, c/o St. Rita Rectory, 50 St. Rita Pl., 12047. Tel: 518-237-4444. Rev. Mario Pacini, S.A.C.

GERMANTOWN. *Oneness in Peace Spiritual Center*, 49 Main St., 12526. Tel: 518-537-5678. Co-Directors: Sr. Vergilia Jim, O.S.F.; Claire Langie.

NISKAYUNA. *Villa Fusco Adult & Child Day Care Center*, 955 Balltown Rd., 12309. Tel: 518-377-1613. Sr. Josephine Alderuccio, D.C.P.B., Supr. Daughters of Charity of the Most Precious Blood. Capacity 10.

RENSSELAER. *Order of Friars Minor Conventual Immaculate Conception Province Charitable Trust*. (Established 1990), P.O. Box 629, 12144. Tel: 518-432-6623. Rev. Anthony Kall, O.F.M.Conv., Trustee.

SCHENECTADY. *St. Luke's Guild*, c/o St. Clare Hospital, 600 McClellan St., 12304. Tel: 518-347-5760. Paul Brisson, M.D., Pres.

Secular Order of Discalced Carmelites, 428 Duane Ave., 12304-2691. Ms. Mary Therese Thouin, Pres.

TROY. *Catholic School Administrators' Association of New York State*, 406 Fulton St., Ste. 512, 12180. Tel: 518-273-1205; Fax: 518-273-1206. Sr. Mary Anne Brawley, D.C., Exec. Dir.; Sr. Carol Cimino, S.S.J., Assoc. Dir.

[U] SUMMER CAMPS

ALBANY. *Camp Scully*, 100 Slingerland St., 12202. Tel: 518-426-3511; 283-1617 (Snyders Lake). Summer Address, 24 Camp Scully Way, Wynantskill, 12198. A program of Albany Catholic Family and Community Services. Summer Residential Camp for children 7-14. Under direction of Catholic Charities of the Diocese of Albany. Financed by local Youth Bureaus, the Albany Catholic Diocese, USDA Summer Program and by contributions. Capacity 110 per week for 7 weeks.

TROY. *Troy CYO Day Camp*, Box 867, 237 Fourth St., 12180. Tel: 518-274-2630. Sponsored by Troy Youth Organization, Inc. for Boys and Girls, ages 5-12 yrs. Raymond R. Piscitelli, Exec. Dir.; Mara A. Wager, Prog. Dir.; Jeanne Mailloux, Exec. Sec.

RELIGIOUS INSTITUTES OF MEN REPRESENTED IN THE DIOCESE

For further details refer to the corresponding bracketed number in the Religious Institutes of Men or Women section.

[0140]—*The Augustinians*.—O.S.A.
[0330]—*Brothers of the Christian Schools*. (New York Prov.).—F.S.C.
[0600]—*Brothers of the Congregation of Holy Cross*. (Eastern Prov.).—C.S.C.
[0270]—*Carmelite Fathers & Brothers*.—O.Carm.
[0310]—*Congregation of Christian Brothers*. (Eastern US).—C.F.C.
[0220]—*Congregation of the Blessed Sacrament*.—S.S.S.
[1330]—*Congregation of the Mission*. (Eastern Prov.).—C.M.
[0480]—*Conventual Franciscans*. (Prov. of Immaculate Conception).—O.F.M.Conv.
[0520]—*Franciscan Friars*. (Most Holy Name Prov.).—O.F.M.
[0690]—*Jesuit Fathers and Brothers*. (New York Prov.).—S.J.
[0720]—*The Missionaries of Our Lady of La Salette*. (Prov. of Our Lady of Seven Dolors).—M.S.
[1030]—*Paulist Fathers*. (New York).—C.S.P.
[0610]—*Priests of the Congregation of Holy Cross*. (Eastern Prov.).—C.S.C.
[1070]—*Redemptorist Fathers*. (Baltimore Prov.).—C.SS.R.
[0990]—*Society of the Catholic Apostolate*.—S.A.C.

RELIGIOUS INSTITUTES OF WOMEN REPRESENTED IN THE DIOCESE

[0330]—*Carmelite Sisters for the Aged and Infirm*.—O.Carm.
[0760]—*Daughters of Charity of St. Vincent de Paul*.—D.C.
[0740]—*Daughters of Charity of the Most Precious Blood*.—D.C.P.B.
[0420]—*Discalced Carmelite Nuns*.—O.C.D.
[1070-11]—*Dominican Sisters - Congregation of Our Lady of the Rosary*.—O.P.
[1070-17]—*Dominican Sisters - Congregation of St. Catherine de Ricci*.—O.P.
[1070-22]—*Dominican Sisters - Congregation of St. Catherine of Siena*.—O.P.
[1070-05]—*Dominican Sisters - Congregation of the Holy Cross*.—O.P.
[1170]—*Felician Sisters*.—C.S.S.F.
[1180]—*Franciscan Sisters of Allegany, New York*.—O.S.F.
[1415]—*Franciscan Sisters of Mary*.—F.S.M.
[1425]—*Franciscan Sisters of Peace*.—F.S.P.
[1190]—*Franciscan Sisters of the Atonement*.—S.A.
[2340]—*Little Sisters of the Poor*.—L.S.P.
[1410]—*Mill Hill Sisters (Franciscan Missionaries of St. Joseph)*.—F.M.S.J.
[2070]—*Religious of the Holy Union of the Sacred Hearts*.—S.U.S.C.
[3430]—*Religious Teachers Filippini*.—M.P.F.
[4180]—*Religious Venerini Sisters*.—M.P.V.
[2970]—*School Sisters of Notre Dame*.—S.S.N.D.
[2575]—*Sisters of Mercy of the Americas*. (Albany).—R.S.M.
[1660]—*Sisters of St. Francis of the Providence of God*.—O.S.F.
[3840]—*Sisters of St. Joseph of Carondelet*.—C.S.J.
[0150]—*Sisters of the Assumption*.—S.A.S.V.
[2980]—*Sisters of the Congregation de Notre Dame*.—C.N.D.
[1990]—*Sisters of the Holy Names of Jesus and Mary*.—S.N.J.M.
[3320]—*Sisters of the Presentation of the B.V.M.*.—P.B.V.M.
[3480]—*Sisters of the Resurrection*.—C.R.
[1490]—*Sisters of the Third Franciscan Order*.—O.S.F.
[4070]—*Society of the Sacred Heart*.—R.S.C.J.

DIOCESAN CEMETERIES

COHOES. *St. Agnes Cemetery*, St. Agnes Hwy., 12047. Tel: 518-463-0134.

GLENVILLE. *St. Anthony Cemetery*, Glenridge Rd., 12325. Tel: 518-374-5319.

MENANDS. *St. Agnes Cemetery*, 48 Cemetery Ave. Tel: 518-463-0134.

ROTTERDAM. *Holy Cross Cemetery*. Tel: 518-374-5319.

SCHENECTADY. *Most Holy Redeemer Cemetery*, 2501 Troy Rd.

St. Cyril & St. Methodius Cemetery. Tel: 518-374-5319.

TROY. *St. Jean Baptiste Cemetery*, 968 Spring Ave., 12180. Tel: 518-272-0931.

St. John Cemetery. Tel: 518-272-0931.

St. Mary's Cemetery of Troy, Inc., Brunswick Rd., 12180. Tel: 518-272-0931.

WATERVLIET. *St. Patrick Cemetery*, Troy Rd., 12189. Tel: 518-463-0134.

NECROLOGY

† Prusko, Edwin, (Retired). —Died May 7, 1996.
† Tessier, Henri, (Retired). —Died May 4, 1996.

Diocese of Alexandria

(Dioecesis Alexandrina in Louisiana)

Most Reverend

SAM G. JACOBS, D.D.

Bishop of Alexandria; ordained June 6, 1964; appointed Bishop of Alexandria July 1, 1989; ordained and installed August 24, 1989. *Mailing Address: P.O. Box 7417, Alexandria, LA, 71306.*

Chancery Office: 4400 Coliseum Blvd., P.O. Box 7417, Alexandria, LA, 71306. Tel.: 318-445-2401; Fax: 318-448-6121.

ERECTED AS DIOCESE OF NATCHITOCHES JULY 29, 1853.

Square Miles 22,212.

TRANSFERRED TO ALEXANDRIA AUGUST 6, 1910 AND BECAME DIOCESE OF ALEXANDRIA.

REDESIGNATED DIOCESE OF ALEXANDRIA-SHREVEPORT ON JANUARY 12, 1977; SPLIT, FORMING TWO DIOCESES, THE DIOCESE OF ALEXANDRIA AND THE DIOCESE OF SHREVEPORT AS OF JUNE 16, 1986.

Square Miles ll,116.

Comprises the counties (parishes) of Rapides, Avoyelles, Concordia, Catahoula, LaSalle, Grant, Natchitoches, Vernon, Tensas, Caldwell, Winn, Franklin and Madison.

For legal titles of parishes and diocesan institutions, consult the Chancery Office.

STATISTICAL OVERVIEW

Personnel	
Bishop	1
Priests: Diocesan Active in Diocese	37
Priests: Active Outside Diocese	5
Priests: Retired, Sick or Absent	22
Number of Diocesan Priests	64
Religious Priests in Diocese	15
Extern Priests in Diocese	6
Ordinations:	
Diocesan Priests	3
Transitional Deacons	3
Permanent Deacons in Diocese	7
Total Brothers	3
Total Sisters	69
Parishes	
Parishes	48
With Resident Pastor:	
Resident Diocesan Priests	31
Resident Religious Priests	9
Without Resident Pastor:	
Administered by Priests	7
Administered by Women Religious	1
Missions	23
Pastoral Centers	1

Professional Ministry Personnel:	
Brothers	1
Sisters	7
Lay Ministers	17
Welfare	
Catholic Hospitals	1
Total Assisted	73,946
Health Care Centers	1
Total Assisted	400
Homes for the Aged	2
Total Assisted	164
Special Centers for Social Services	16
Total Assisted	125,150
Residential Care of Disabled	1
Total Assisted	152
Educational	
Diocesan Students in Other Seminaries	11
Total Seminarians	11
High Schools, Diocesan and Parish	3
Total Students	514
Elementary Schools, Diocesan and Parish	9
Total Students	2,635

Catechesis/Religious Education:	
High School Students	1,541
Elementary Students	3,044
Total Students Under Catholic Instruction	7,745
Teachers in the Diocese:	
Brothers	2
Sisters	19
Lay Teachers	194
Vital Statistics	
Receptions into the Church:	
Infant Baptism Totals	751
Adult Baptism Totals	97
Received into Full Communion	131
First Communions	753
Confirmations	546
Marriages:	
Catholic	166
Interfaith	115
Total Marriages	281
Deaths	638
Total Catholic Population	48,050
Total Population	393,880

Former Bishops—Rt. Rev. AUGUSTUS M. MARTIN, cons. Nov. 30, 1853; died Sept. 29, 1875.—Rt. Rev. FRANCIS XAVIER LERAY, cons. Bishop of Natchitoches, April 22, 1877; named Bishop of Janopolis, Coadjutor of New Orleans, and Administrator of Natchitoches, Oct. 23, 1879; promoted to the See of New Orleans, Dec., 1883; died Sept. 23, 1887.—Rt. Rev. ANTHONY DURIER, D.D., cons. March 19, 1885; died Feb. 28, 1904.—Most Rev. CORNELIUS VAN DE VEN, cons. Nov. 30, 1904 made assistant at the Pontifical Throne, Nov. 12, 1929; died May 8, 1932.—Most Rev. DANIEL FRANCIS DESMOND, D.D., cons. Bishop of Alexandria Jan. 5, 1933; died Sept. 11, 1945.—Most Rev. CHARLES P. GRECO, D.D., cons. Feb. 25, 1946; retired May 22, 1973; died Jan. 20, 1987.—Most Rev. LAWRENCE P. GRAVES, D.D., J.C.L., cons. April 25, 1969; retired July 20, 1982; died Jan. 15, 1994.—Most Rev. WILLIAM B. FRIEND, D.D., ord. Aug. 31, 1979; installed Bishop of Alexandria-Shreveport Jan. 11, 1983 then after Diocese of Alexandria-Shreveport was split into two dioceses June 16, 1986; installed Bishop of Shreveport July 30, 1986.—Most Rev. JOHN C. FAVALORA, D.D., ord. December 20, 1961; appt. Bishop of Alexandria June 16, 1986; ord. and installed July 29, 1986; installed Bishop of St. Petersburg May 16, 1989; installed Archbishop of Miami Dec. 20, 1994.

Vicar General—Rev. Msgr. RONALD C. HOPPE, *P.O. Box 7417, Alexandria, 71306.* Tel: 318-445-2401.

Chancery Office—4400 Coliseum Blvd., P.O. Box 7417, Alexandria, 71306. Tel: 318-445-2401; Fax: 318-448-6121. Office Hours: Mon.-Fri. 8-12 & 1-4:30.

Moderator of the Curia—Rev. Msgr. RONALD C. HOPPE, V.G.

Chancellor—Rev. Msgr. JOSEPH M. SUSI.

Ecclesiastical Notaries—Rev. Msgr. JOSEPH M. SUSI; Ms. DEBORAH DEOROSAN; Mrs. PATRICIA LACAZE; Mrs. ETTA OHRT; Mrs. PATRICIA THOMAS.

Diocesan Tribunal—P.O. Box 7417, Alexandria, 71306. Tel: 318-445-2401.

Judicial Vicar—Rev. BRUCE MILLER, J.C.L.

Judges—Most Rev. SAM G. JACOBS; Rev. BRUCE MILLER, J.C.L.

Defenders of the Bond and Promoters of Justice—Rev. JAMES A. FERGUSON, J.C.L.

Chief Auditors—Mrs. PATRICIA THOMAS.

College of Consultors—Rev. Msgr. RONALD C. HOPPE, V.G.; Rev. Msgr. JOSEPH M. SUSI; Rev. Msgr. STEVE J. TESTA, V.F.; Revs. JAMES A. FERGUSON, J.C.L.; GERARD M. FOLEY, V.F.; KENNETH J. ROY, V.F.; D. MATHEW WOOLLETT; BERNARD L. ZAGST, V.F.

Finance Council—Mr. ROBERT CHAPPUIS; Mr. WILLIAM HAMLIN; Mr. TODD MARYE; Mr. FINLEY PONTHIE; Mr. GUS VOLTZ, JR.; Rev. Msgr. HENRY F. BECKERS; Rev. Msgr. RONALD C. HOPPE, V.G.

Priests Council—Revs. KENNETH J. ROY, V.F., Chm. JAMES A. FERGUSON, J.C.L., Vice Chm. SCOTT CHEMINO, Sec.-Treas.; Rev. Msgr. RONALD C. HOPPE, V.G.; Rev. Msgr. JOSEPH M. SUSI; Rev. Msgr. STEVE J. TESTA, V.F.; Revs. GERARD FOLEY, V.F.; D. MATHEW WOOLLETT, V.F.; BERNARD L. ZAGST, V.F.; BRUCE MILLER, J.C.L.; AUGUST THOMPSON; SHELDON L. ROY; JOSEPH F. PELLETTIERI, C.SS.R.; JACOB THOMAS; KENNETH J. MICHIELS.

Retirement Board—Rev. Msgr. FREDERICK J. LYONS; Rev. Msgr. JOSEPH M. SUSI; Rev. Msgr. JOHN M. TIMMERMANS; Judge ROBERT P. JACKSON; Mr. ROBERT W. DVORAK.

Rural Deans—Rev. Msgr STEVE J. TESTA, V.F.; Revs. KENNETH J. ROY, V.F.; GERARD M. FOLEY, V.F.; BERNARD L. ZAGST, V.F.

The Catholic Foundation of North-Central Louisiana, Inc.—P.O. Box 8021, Alexandria, 71306. Tel: 318-487-9222. JOSEPH L. HEBERT, Pres.-Treas.; Mrs. BETTY CHOP, Corp. Sec. *Board of Directors:* Mr. GRAHAM KRAMER, Chm.; Rev. Msgr. FREDERICK J. LYONS, Vice Chm.; Rev. Msgr. HENRY F. BECKERS; Mr. SCOTT O. BRAME; Mr. MARION J. CHANEY; Mr. ROBERT E. CHAPPUIS; Rev. S. SCOTT CHEMINO; Mr. STEVEN W. COOK; Mr. JAMES CURLEY; Mr. LEO P. DOBARD, JR.; Mr. HENRY KINBERGER; Rev. Msgr. J. CARSON LACAZE; Mr. JOSEPH MCGINTY, JR.; JOSEPH T. SIMMS, JR.

Diocesan Offices and Directors

Archivist—Rev. Msgr. JOSEPH M. SUSI, *4400 Coliseum Blvd., P.O. Box 7417, Alexandria, 71306-0417.* Tel: 318-445-2401.

Black Affairs—Rev. AUGUST THOMPSON, Vicar, *900 Daspit St., Alexandria, 71302.* Tel: 318-445-6700.

Business Affairs—Mr. DAVID BROOK, Dir., *4400 Coliseum Blvd., P.O. Box 7417, Alexandria, 71306-0417.* Tel: 318-445-2401.

Campaign for Human Development—Sr. JOHN MARTIN EBROM, C.D.P., Dir., *4400 Coliseum Blvd., P.O. Box 7417, Alexandria, 71306-0417.* Tel: 318-445-2401.

Campus Ministry—Rev. EDWIN RODRIGUEZ-HERNANDEZ, Dir., *LSU-A, 8700 Hwy. 71-S, Alexandria, 71302-9633.* Tel: 318-473-6494.

Catholic Community Services—Sr. JOHN MARTIN EBROM, C.D.P., Dir., *4400 Coliseum Blvd., P.O. Box 7417, Alexandria, 71306-0417.* Tel: 318-445-2401.

Catholic Relief Services—Sr. JOHN MARTIN EBROM, C.D.P., Dir., *4400 Coliseum Blvd., P.O. Box 7417, Alexandria, 71306-0417.* Tel: 318-445-2401.

Cemeteries—Rev. Msgr. JOHN M. TIMMERMANS, Coord., *238 Mon Borde St., Moreauville, 71355.* Tel: 318-985-1774.

Charismatic Movement—Rev. H. GERALD BORDELON, Diocesan Liaison, *401 21st St., Alexandria, 71301.* Tel: 318-445-3693.

Church Financial Development—Mrs. ANN MASDEN, Dir., *4400 Coliseum Blvd., P.O. Box 7417, Alexandria, 71301.* Tel: 318-445-2401.

Church Vocations Board—Most Rev. SAM G. JACOBS; Revs. EDWIN RODRIGUEZ-HERNANDEZ; SHELDON L. ROY; KENNETH J. MICHIELS; GEORGE KROSFIELD; Mr. TOMMY RIGMAIDEN; Ms. GAIL BRODNAX; Sr. OLIVE BORDELON, C.C.V.I.

Clergy and Religious—Rev. SAMUEL J. POLIZZI, Vicar, *P.O. Box 7417, Alexandria, 71306-0417.* Tel: 318-445-2401.

Communications—Mr. AL NASSIF, Print Media; Mrs. ANN MASDEN, Electronic Media, *4400 Coliseum Blvd., P.O. Box 7417, Alexandria, 71306-0417.* Tel: 318-445-2401.

Continuing Formation of the Clergy—Rev. H. GERALD BORDELON, Dir., *401 21st St., Alexandria, 71301.* Tel: 318-445-3693.

Ecumenical—Rev. S. SCOTT CHEMINO, Liaison, *P.O. Box 8, Plaucheville, 71362.* Tel: 318-922-3131.

Eucharistic League, Priests—Rev. Msgr. JOSEPH M. SUSI, Dir., *4400 Coliseum Blvd., P.O. Drawer 7417, Alexandria, 71306-0417.* Tel: 318-445-2401.

Evangelization—Rev. JOSE A. ROBLES-SANCHEZ, Dir., *207 S. Washington St., Marksville, 71351.* Tel: 318-253-5610.

Family Life Ministry—Sr. JOHN MARTIN EBROM, C.D.P., Dir., *4400 Coliseum Blvd., P.O. Box 7417, Alexandria, 71306-0417.* Tel: 318-445-2401.

Fiscal Management—Mr. DAVID BROOK, Dir. Business Affairs, *4400 Coliseum Blvd., P.O. Box 7417, Alexandria, 71306-0417.* Tel: 318-445-2401.

Hispanic Apostolate—Rev. PEDRO J. SIERRA-POSADA, *4400 Coliseum Blvd., P.O. Box 7417, Alexandria, 71306-0417.* Tel: 318-445-2401.

Holy Childhood Association—Rev. Msgr. STEVE J. TESTA, V.F., Dir., *4400 Coliseum Blvd., P.O. Box 7417, Alexandria, 71306-0417.* Tel: 318-445-2401.

Liturgy Committee—Rev. KENNETH MATHEWS, *626 Fourth St., Alexandria, 71301.* Tel: 318-445-1451.

Maryhill Renewal Center—Sr. RUTHANN WILLIAMS, O.P., *600 Maryhill Rd., Pineville, 71360.* Tel: 318-640-1378.

Newspaper "The Church Today"—Mr. AL NASSIF, Editor, *4400 Coliseum Blvd., P.O. Box 7417, Alexandria, 71306-0417.* Tel: 318-445-2401.

Permanent Deacons—Rev. D. MATHEW WOOLLETT, *P.O. Box 3009, Pineville, 71361-3009.* Tel: 318-445-2496.

Personnel/Property Management—Mr. DANNY GUILLORY, Dir., *P.O. Box 7417, Alexandria, 71306-0417.* Tel: 318-445-2401.

Print Media—(The Church Today and Digest of the News)—Mr. AL NASSIF, Dir. and Editor, *4400 Coliseum Blvd., P.O. Box 7417, Alexandria, 71306-0417.* Tel: 318-445-2401.

Propagation of the Faith and Foreign Mission Education—Rev. Msgr. STEVE J. TESTA, Dir., *4400 Coliseum Blvd., P.O. Box 7417, Alexandria, 71306-0417.* Tel: 318-445-2401.

Public Affairs—Mrs. ANN MASDEN, Dir., *4400 Coliseum Blvd., P.O. Box 7417, Alexandria, 71306-0417.* Tel: 318-445-0417.

Religious, Coordinator for—Bro. ANDRE M. LUCIA, F.S.E., *P.O. Box 25, Plaucheville, 71362.* Tel: 318-922-3630.

Religious Education—Mrs. MARY J. MCDONALD, Dir., *4400 Coliseum Blvd., P.O. Box 7417, Alexandria, 71306-0417.* Tel: 318-445-2401.

Renew—Mr. TOM WEBB, Dir., *4400 Coliseum Blvd., P.O. Box 7417, Alexandria, 71306-0417.* Tel: 318-445-2401.

Rural Life Ministry—Rev. JAMES ROY, Coord., *P.O. Box 66, Hessmer, Alexandria, 71341.* Tel: 318-563-4550.

Schools—Sr. MARICE ELVEKROG, S.S.N.D., Supt., *4400 Coliseum Blvd., P.O. Box 7417, Alexandria, 71306-0417.* Tel: 318-445-2401.

Scouting—Rev. CHARLES MORGAN, Area 5 Chap., *1712 West St., Winnsboro, 71295.* Tel: 318-435-5658. Rev. DANIEL P. O'CONNOR, Diocesan and Attakapas Council Chap., *P.O. Drawer 7056, Alexandria, 71306-0417.* Tel: 318-445-7120.

Seminarians—Rev. EDWIN RODRIGUEZ-HERNANDEZ, Dir., *P.O. Box 7056, Alexandria, 71306-0417.* Tel: 318-445-7120.

Social Ministry—Sr. JOHN MARTIN EBROM, C.D.P., Admin., *4400 Coliseum Blvd., P.O. Box 7417, Alexandria, 71306-0417.* Tel: 318-445-2401.

School Food Service—Mrs. DEBORAH M. PAYNE, C.N.P., Supvr., *4400 Coliseum Blvd., P.O. Box 7417, Alexandria, 71306-0417.* Tel: 318-445-2485.

The Beginning Experience—Rev. BRUCE MILLER, J.C.L., *4400 Coliseum Blvd., P.O. Box 7417, Alexandria, 71306-0417.* Tel: 318-445-2401.

Vocations Recruitment—Rev. EDWIN RODRIGUEZ-HERNANDEZ, Dir., *P.O. Box 7056, Alexandria, 71306-0417.* Tel: 318-445-7120.

Youth Ministry—Mr. WARREN DUNGEN, Dir., *4400 Coliseum Blvd., P.O. Box 7417, Alexandria, 71306-0417.* Tel: 318-445-2401.

CLERGY, PARISHES, MISSIONS AND PAROCHIAL SCHOOLS

CITY OF ALEXANDRIA (Rapides Parish)

1—ST. FRANCIS XAVIER CATHEDRAL (1834), Rev. Kenneth M. Mathews, Rector. In res., Rev. Pedro J. Sierra-Posada (Colombia).
Res., 626 Fourth St., 71301. Tel: 318-445-1451; Fax: 318-445-0204.

2—OUR LADY OF PROMPT SUCCOR (1947), Revs. H. Gerald Bordelon; Michael Craig Scott. In res., Revs. Edwin Rodriguez-Hernandez; Thomas M. Jezak.
Res., 401 21st St., 71301. Tel: 318-445-3693; Fax: 318-445-8471.
School—Sisters of Divine Providence 2; Lay Teachers 26; Students 516.

3—ST. FRANCES XAVIER CABRINI (1947), Rev. Msgr. Ronald C. Hoppe, V.G.
Office: 2211 E. Texas Ave., P.O. Box 5004, 71301. Tel: 318-445-4588; Fax: 318-443-7156.
Res., 2012 Wedgewood Ave., 71301. Tel: 318-487-4413; Fax: 318-443-7156.
School—Sisters of Charity of the Incarnate Word 1; Lay Teachers 22; Students 293.

4—ST. JAMES MEMORIAL (1911), Rev. August L. Thompson.
Mailing Address: 900 Daspit St., 71302. Tel: 318-445-6700; Fax: 318-445-9826.
Church—714 Winn St., 71301. Tel: 318-487-9512.
Convent—Tel: 318-473-8601.
Handmaids of the Holy Child Jesus 3.

5—ST. JULIANA (1959), Rev. August L. Thompson.
Res., 900 Daspit St., 71302. Tel: 318-445-6700; Fax: 318-445-9826.

6—ST. RITA (1940), Revs. Bruce Miller, J.C.L.; Stephen J. Brandow.
Res., 214 N. 17th St., P.O. Box 7056, 71306-0056. Tel: 318-445-7120; Fax: 318-448-0704.
School—Sisters 3; Lay Teachers 18; Students 191.

OUTSIDE THE CITY OF ALEXANDRIA

Belledeau, Avoyelles Parish, St. Martin of Tours (1950), Rev. Timothy R. Marceau, O.S.B.
Res., 1981 Hwy. 114, Hessmer, 71341. Tel: 318-563-4533. [CEM]

Bordelonville, Avoyelles Parish, St. Peter (1903), Rev. Vincent Manuel, S.A.C. (India).
Res., P.O. Box 31, 71320. Tel: 318-997-2151. [CEM]

Boyce, Rapides Parish, St. Margaret (1936), Rev. Bernard L. Zagst, V.F.
Res., P.O. Box 367, 71409. Tel: 318-793-8811. [CEM]
Missions—Flatwoods, St. Cyril; Gorum, St. Margaret Mary.

Brouillette, Avoyelles Parish, St. Genevieve (1953), Rev. Morson Ravi Livingston, S.A.C. (India).
Res., 4052 Hwy. 452, Marksville, 71351. Tel: 318-253-9237. [CEM]

Bunkie, Avoyelles Parish, St. Anthony of Padua (1904), Rev. Msgr. Steve J. Testa, V.F.
Res., 409 St. John St., P.O. Box 719, 71322. Tel: 318-346-7274; Fax: 318-346-7275. [CEM]
School—Daughters of Divine Providence 1; Lay Teachers 11; Students 281.

Campti, Natchitoches Parish, Nativity of The Blessed Virgin Mary (1831), Rev. Jacob Thomas, S.A.C. (India); Deacons John Foster; Robert Daspit.
Res., 119 Tally St., P.O. Box 439, 71411. Tel: 318-476-2116. [CEM 3]
Missions—Trichel, St. Joseph; Black Lake, Our Lady of the Holy Rosary.

Cheneyville, Rapides Parish, St. Joseph (1966), Rev. Msgr. Julius G. Walle.
Res., P.O. Box 446, 71325. Tel: 318-279-2394. [CEM]

Cloutierville, Natchitoches Parish, St. John the Baptist (1816), Rev. Daniel Corkery.
Res., P.O. Box 40, 71416. Tel: 318-379-2231. [CEM]
Missions—Emmanuel, Holy Rosary; Monet Ferry, Holy Family.

Colfax, Grant Parish, St. Joseph (1897), Rev. James A. Foster.
Res., 801 Third St., P.O. Box 243, 71417. Tel: 318-627-5442.
Mission—Montgomery, St. Patrick, P.O. Box 243, 71417.

Cottonport, Avoyelles Parish, St. Mary Assumption (1889), Rev. William B. Provosty.
Res., P.O. Box 1123, 71327. Tel: 318-876-3681. [CEM 3]
School—Sisters 1; Lay Teachers 9; Students 222.

Deville, Rapides Parish, St. John the Baptist (1942), Rev. Joseph F. Pellettieri, C.SS.R.
Res., P.O. Box 7, 71328. Tel: 318-466-5587; Fax: 318-466-5265. [CEM 2]
Missions—Kolin, Sts. Francis and Anne; Effie, St. Winifred.

Dupont, Avoyelles Parish, Immaculate Conception (1945), Rev. Abraham Kallarackal, C.M.I. (India); Deacon Norman Gremillion.
Res., P.O. Box 385, 71329. Tel: 318-922-3243. [CEM]

Echo, Rapides Parish, St. Francis de Sales (1894), Rev. Ferreolus D'Cruz (India).
Res., P.O. Box 37, 71330. Tel: 318-563-4530. [CEM]

Evergreen, Avoyelles Parish, Little Flower (1928), Rev. Harvey J. Fortier.
Res., P.O. Box 20, 71333. Tel: 318-346-2840. [CEM]
Mission—Goudeau, St. Charles.

Ferriday, Concordia Parish, St. Patrick (1952), Revs. Paul Kunnumpuram, M.S.F.S. (India); Anthony Dharmaraj, M.S.F.S. (India).
Res., P.O. Box 369, 71334. Tel: 318-757-3834. [JC]
Mission—Jonesville, St. Gerard, P.O. Box 863, Jonesville, 71343. Tel: 318-339-6143.

Fifth Ward, Avoyelles Parish, Our Lady of Lourdes (1948), Rev. Daniel P. O'Connor.
Res., 1315 Eggbend Rd., 71351. Tel: 318-253-9936. [CEM 4]
Mission—Moncla, St. John the Baptist.

Glenmora, Rapides Parish, St. Louis (1941), Rev. Msgr. Ronald C. Hoppe, V.G.; Revs. Thomas Jezak; Pedro J. Sierra-Posada (Colombia). In res., Sr. Marie T. Brogan, S.S.N.D., Parish Life Coord.
Res., 826 8th St., P.O. Box 636, 71433. Tel: 318-748-8324. [CEM]
Missions—Elmer, St. Peter; Sieper, St. Jude.

Hessmer, Avoyelles Parish, St. Alphonsus (1898), Rev. James Roy.
Res., P.O. Box 66, 71341. Tel: 318-563-4550. [CEM]

Isle Brevelle, Natchitoches Parish, St. Augustine's (1856), Rev. Victor P. Vead.
Res., 2262 Highway 484, Natchez, 71456. Tel: 318-379-2521. [CEM]
Convent—Tel: 318-379-2325.
Sisters of Divine Providence 2.
Missions—Bermuda, St. Charles; Old River, St. Anne.

Jena, LaSalle Parish, St. Mary (1949), Rev. John H. Cunningham.
Mailing Address: Second St., P.O. Box 669, Pollock, 71467. Tel: 318-765-3798.
Mission—Fishville, St. Edward, P.O. Box 669, Pollock, 71467.

Kleinwood, Avoyelles Parish, St. Michael (1964), Rev. Vincent Manuel, S.A.C. (India).
Res., P.O. Box 31, Bordelonville, 71320. Tel: 318-997-2151. [CEM]

Lecompte, Rapides Parish, St. Martin (1860), Rev. Terry E. Allen.
Res., P.O. Box 459, 71346. Tel: 318-776-9480; Fax: 318-776-9485.
Mission—Woodworth, Mary, Mother of Jesus.

Leesville, Vernon Parish, St. Michael (1946), Rev. Angelo Messina.
Res., 604 S. Fifth St., P.O. Box 240, 71496. Tel: 318-239-2656.

Mansura, Avoyelles Parish, Our Lady of Prompt Succor (1937), Revs. Kenneth J. Michiels; James Moran, C.O.
Res., Escude St., P.O. Box 67, 71350. Tel: 318-964-2654.

St. Paul the Apostle (1796), Rev. Russell J. Lemoine.
Res., P.O. Box 130, 71350. Tel: 318-964-2921. [CEM]

Marksville, Avoyelles Parish, Holy Ghost (1919), Revs. Kenneth J. Michiels; James Moran, C.O.
Res., 121 S. Preston St., 71351. Tel: 318-253-7131. [CEM 2]
Mission—Hickory Hill, St. Richard.

St. Joseph's (1869), Revs. James A. Ferguson, J.C.L.; Jose' A. Robles-Sanchez (Puerto Rico).
Res., 303 S. Washington, 71351. Tel: 318-253-5610; 253-7561 (Office). [CEM 2]

Moreauville, Avoyelles Parish, Our Lady of Sorrows (1944), Rev. Joseph E. Montalbano.

Res., 9986 Bayou Des Glaise St., 71355. Tel: 318-985-2774. [CEM]

Sacred Heart (1860), Rev. Joseph E. Montalbano.
Res., 9986 Bayou Des Glaise St., 71355. Tel: 318-985-2774. [CEM]
School—Sisters of Our Lady of Sorrows 4; Lay Teachers 16; Students 252.

Natchitoches, Natchitoches Parish, Holy Cross (1968), Rev. Sheldon L. Roy.
Res., 129 Second St., P.O. Box 211, Nachitoches, 71458-0211. Tel: 318-352-2615; Fax: 318-352-8989.
Mission—Spanish Lake, St. Anne. [CEM]

Immaculate Conception (1728), Revs. Kenneth J. Roy, V.F.; David Jude Braquet.
Res., 145 Church St., P.O. Box 13, Nachitoches, 71458. Tel: 318-352-3422. [CEM]
School—St. Mary, (Grades PreK-8) 1101 E. Fifth St., P.O. Box 2070, 71458-0013.
Sisters of Notre Dame 1; Lay Teachers 14; Students 229.
High School—Lay Teachers 21; Students 186.

St. Anthony (1935), Rev. Julian Wrobel, C.S.Sp.
Res., 911 Fifth St., P.O. Box 432, Nachitoches, 71457. Tel: 318-352-2559. [JC]

Pineville, Rapides Parish, Sacred Heart (1933), Rev. D. Mathew Woollett.
Res., 600 Lakeview, P.O. Drawer 3009, 71361-3009. Tel: 318-445-2496.

Plaucheville, Avoyelles Parish, Mater Dolorosa (1879), Revs. Stephen Scott Chemino; John W. Andries.
Res., P.O. Box 8, 71362. Tel: 318-922-3131. [CEM]
School—Brothers of the Holy Eucharist 2; Marianites of the Holy Cross 2; Lay Teachers 11; Students 365.
High School—Sisters 1; Brothers 1; Lay Teachers 6; Students 103.

Powhatan, Natchitoches Parish, St. Francis (1952), Revs. Kenneth J. Roy; David J. Braquet.
Mailing Address: P.O. Box 13, Natchitoches, 71458-0013. Tel: 318-352-3422. [JC]
P.O. Box 211, Natchitoches, 71458. Tel: 318-352-2615.

St. Joseph, Tensas Parish, St. Joseph (1940), Rev. Antony Aelavanthara (India).
Res., P.O. Box 198, 71366. Tel: 318-766-3565. [CEM]
Mission—Waterproof, St. Francis of Assisi, P.O. Box 198, 71366.

Simmesport, Avoyelles Parish, Christ the King (1935), Rev. George Krosfield (India).
Res., P.O. Box 186, 71369. Tel: 318-941-2381. [CEM]

Tallulah, Madison Parish, St. Edward (1936), Rev. Msgr. Patrick J. Murphy.
Res., Hwy. 80 E., P.O. Box 1308, 71282. Tel: 318-574-1677.

Tioga, Rapides Parish, Immaculate Heart of Mary (1971), Rev. Gerard M. Foley, V.F.
Res., P.O. Box 687, 71477. Tel: 318-640-5314; 640-9446 (Office).

Vidalia, Concordia Parish, Our Lady of Lourdes (1887), Revs. Paul Kunnumpuram, M.S.F.S. (India); Antony Dhamaraj, M.S.F.S. (India).
Res., 503 Texas St., P.O. Box 460, 71373. Tel: 318-336-5450. [JC]

Winnfield, Winn Parish, Our Lady of Lourdes (1988), Rev. B. Stanley Abeysekera (India).
Res., 772 Country Club Rd., 71483. Tel: 318-628-2561.
Mission—Olla, St. William, P.O. Box 1412, 71483.

Winnsboro, Franklin Parish, St. Mary (1945), Rev. Charles J. Morgan.
Res., 1712 West St., 71295. Tel: 318-435-5658.
Mission—Columbia, St. John, 1712 West St., 71295.

Chaplains of Public Institutions

PINEVILLE. *Central Louisiana State Hospital* W. Shamrock Ave., P.O. Box 5031, 71361. Tel: 318-484-6357; 484-6352. Revs. Joseph S. Hasieber; Timothy Marceaux, O.S.B.

Special Assignment:
Reverend Monsignors—
Susi, Joseph M., Chancellor

On Duty Outside the Diocese:
Reverend Monsignors—
Bordelon, Roland, USCC Relief Services, New York, NY
Reverend Fathers—
Matthews, Ron, Christ the King Church, Bossier City, LA
Smith, Paul, Holy Angels School, Chicago, IL
Viviano, Nino, St. Michael Church, Clearwater, FL

Military Chaplains:
Reverend Fathers—
Fey, Thomas J., U.S.A.F.

Absent on Leave:
Reverend Fathers—
Deevy, Edward

Retired:
Reverend Monsignors—
Anderson, Marcel
Beckers, Henry F.
Early, Thomas C.
Lyons, Frederick J.
Susi, Joseph M.
Timmermans, John
Wakeman, John J.
Walle, Julius G.
Reverend Fathers—
Cloutier, Wilbur G.
Cumella, Anthony N.
Deasy, Edward
Engelen, R. J.
Gagnard, Louis
Glasnovic, Serafin
Horacek, Mark
Robitaille, Yves
Ryan, John
Van-Hoorn, Leo
Villaverde, Antonio E.
Voorhies, Louis

Permanent Deacons:
Daigrepont, William, Avoyelles Prison Ministry
Daspit, Robert A., Jr., St. Joseph, Trichel
Foster, John, Our Lady of the Rosary, Black Lake
Giaco, Vincent, Chap., Rapides Regional Medical Center
Gremillion, Norman, Immaculate Conception, Dupont
Jones, Charles A., (Retired)
Peltier, Joseph

INSTITUTIONS LOCATED IN THE DIOCESE

[A] HIGH SCHOOLS, DIOCESAN

ALEXANDRIA. *Holy Savior Menard Central*, 4603 Coliseum Blvd., 71303. Tel: 318-445-8233; Fax: 318-448-8170. Junior & High School. Mr. Ronald Lemoine, Prin. Sisters 1; Lay Teachers 28; Students 355.

[B] ELEMENTARY SCHOOLS, INTERPAROCHIAL

MARKSVILLE. *Marksville Catholic School*, 320 E. Mark St., 71351. Tel: 318-253-6932; 253-7440. Sr. Jean Martinez, S.S.F., Prin. Sisters of the Holy Family 3; Lay Teachers 12; Students 156.

[C] GENERAL HOSPITALS

ALEXANDRIA. *St. Frances Cabrini Hospital*, 3330 Masonic Dr., 71301. Tel: 318-487-1122.
For a complete listing, refer to the Hospitals section.

[D] PROTECTIVE INSTITUTIONS

ALEXANDRIA. *St. Mary's Residential Training School, Inc.*, P.O. Box Drawer 7768, 71306. Tel: 318-445-6443; Fax: 318-449-8520.
For a complete listing, refer to the Special Care Facilities section.

FOREST HILL. *Our Lady of Guadalupe Mission*, 10 Butter Cemetery Rd., 71430.
For a complete listing, refer to the Special Care Facilities section.

[E] HOMES FOR AGED

ALEXANDRIA. *Our Lady's Manor, Inc.*, 402 Monroe St., 71301. Tel: 318-473-2560.
For a complete listing, refer to the Special Care Facilities section.

MOREAUVILLE. *St. John's Village*, 116 Beridon St., 71355-3004. Tel: 318-985-2948.
For a complete listing, refer to the Special Care Facilities section.

[F] RESIDENCES OF PRIESTS AND BROTHERS

NATCHITOCHES. *Holy Ghost Fathers Home, Maison Brothier*, 911 Second St., 71457. Tel: 318-357-7940. Revs. John A. Burns, C.S.Sp.; Anthony F. Frommholz, C.S.Sp.; William J. McElroy, C.S.Sp.; Henry J. Planinsek, C.S.Sp.

PLAUCHEVILLE. *Brothers of the Holy Eucharist*, P.O. Box 25, 71362. Tel: 318-922-3630. Bro. Andre M. Lucia, F.S.E., Supr. Brothers 3.

[G] CONVENTS AND RESIDENCES FOR SISTERS

ALEXANDRIA. *Congregation of the Franciscan*, 4615 Coliseum Blvd., 71303. Tel: 318-449-9522. Religious of Our Lady of Refuge (Guadalajara, Mexico). Sisters 3.
Congregation of the Marianites of Holy Cross, St. Rita Convent, 1717 Ashley St., 71301. Tel: 318-448-8001. Sisters 2.
Congregation of the Sisters of Charity of the Incarnate Word, St. Francis Cabrini Hospital Convent, 3330 Masonic Dr., 71301. Tel: 318-443-5520. Sisters 11.
Disciples of the Lord Jesus Christ, 4609 Coliseum Blvd., 71303. Sisters 3.
Sisters of Divine Providence of San Antonio, Texas, Our Lady of Prompt Succor Convent, 580 Chester St., 71301. Tel: 318-442-3315. Sisters 8.
Sisters of Our Lady of Sorrows, St. Mary's Convent, P.O. Box 7768, 71306. Tel: 318-445-6461. Sisters 8.
The Sisters of the Handmaids of the Holy Child Jesus (of Nigeria, Africa), 332 Avoyelles Drive, 71302. Tel: 318-473-8601. Sisters 3.

BUNKIE. *Daughters of Divine Providence*, St. Anthony Convent, 114 Knoll St., 71322. Tel: 318-346-4481. Sisters 3.

COTTONPORT. *Congregation of the Marianites of Holy Cross*, Holy Cross Convent, P.O. Box 1062, 71327-1062. Tel: 318-876-3794. Sisters 3.

GLENMORA. *School Sisters of Notre Dame*, Miryam House, P.O. Box 636, 71433. Tel: 318-748-8324. Sisters 2.

MARKSVILLE. *Congregation of the Sisters of the Holy Family*, Holy Ghost Convent, 304 E. Mark St., 71351. Tel: 318-253-7440. Sisters 4.

MOREAUVILLE. *Sisters of Our Lady of Sorrows*, Sacred Heart Convent, P.O. Box 179, 71355. Tel: 318-985-2772. Sisters 5.

NATCHEZ. *Sisters of Divine Providence*, 2242 Highway 484, 71456. Tel: 318-379-2325. Sisters 2.

NATCHITOCHES. *School Sisters of Notre Dame*, 938 E. Fifth St., 71457. Tel: 318-352-4829.

[H] RETREAT HOUSES

PINEVILLE. *Maryhill Renewal Center*, 600 Maryhill Rd., 71360. Tel: 318-640-1378; Fax: 318-640-8604. Sr. Ruthann Williams, O.P., Exec. Dir.; Sr. B. DeRouen, O.Carm., Spirituality Coord.

[I] CATHOLIC COMMUNITY SERVICES

ALEXANDRIA. *Catholic Community Services*, 4400 Coliseum Blvd., P.O. Box 7417, 71306. Tel: 318-445-2401. Sr. John Martin Ebrom, C.D.P., Dir.

[J] NEWMAN CENTERS

ALEXANDRIA. *Louisiana State University at Alexandria*, Catholic Student Center, 8100 Hwy. 71-S, 71302-9633. Tel: 318-473-6494. Rev. Edwin Rodriguez-Hernandez, Dir.

NATCHITOCHES. *Northwestern State University*, Catholic Student Center, 129 Second St., P.O. Box 211, 71458. Tel: 318-352-2615. Rev. Sheldon L. Roy, Chap.

RELIGIOUS INSTITUTES OF MEN REPRESENTED IN THE DIOCESE

For further details refer to the corresponding bracketed number in the Religious Institutes of Men or Women section.

[0200]—*Benedictine Monks.* (Lisle, IL).—O.S.B.

[0620]—*Brothers of the Holy Eucharist.*—F.S.E.

[0275]—*Carmelites of Mary Immaculate.*—C.M.I.

[0520]—*Franciscan Friars.* (Sacred Heart Prov.).—O.F.M.

[0650]—*Holy Ghost Fathers.* (Western Prov.).—C.S.Sp.

[]—*Missionaries of St. Francis de Sales (of India).*—M.S.F.S.

[0860]—*Missionhurst Congregation of the Immaculate Heart of Mary.*—C.I.C.M.

[0950]—*Oratorians.*—C.O.

[1070]—*Redemptorist Fathers.*—C.Ss.R.

[0990]—*Society of the Catholic Apostolate.*—S.A.C.

RELIGIOUS INSTITUTES OF WOMEN REPRESENTED IN THE DIOCESE

[0400]—*Congregation of Our Lady of Mount Carmel.*—O.Carm.

[2410]—*Congregation of the Marianites of Holy Cross.* (Louisiana Prov.).—M.S.C.

[0470]—*Congregation of the Sisters of Charity of the Incarnate Word.*—C.C.V.I.

[1950]—*Congregation of the Sisters of the Holy Family.*—S.S.F.

[0800]—*Daughters of Divine Providence.*—F.D.P.

[0965]—*Disciples of the Lord Jesus Christ.*—D.L.J.C.

[1070-05]—*Dominican Sisters.*—O.P.

[]—*Handmaids of the Holy Child Jesus (of Nigeria, Africa).*—H.H.C.J.

[2970]—*School Sisters of Notre Dame.*—S.S.N.D.

[1010]—*Sisters of Divine Providence of San Antonio, Texas.*—C.D.P.

[3120]—*Sisters of Our Lady of Sorrows.*—O.L.S.

[4070]—*Society of the Sacred Heart.*—R.S.C.J.

DIOCESAN CEMETERIES

PINEVILLE. *Maryhill Cemetery for Clergy.*

NECROLOGY

† Conway, Rev. Msgr. Paul E., (Retired). —Died Jan. 15, 1996.

† Maguire, Bernard F., (Retired). —Died April 10, 1996.

† Scallan, Rev. Msgr. Belton A., (Retired). —Died Aug. 7, 1996.

Diocese of Allentown

(Dioecesis Alanopolitana)

Most Reverend

THOMAS J. WELSH, D.D., J.C.D.

Bishop of Allentown; ordained May 30, 1946; appointed Titular Bishop of Scattery Island and Auxiliary Bishop of Philadelphia on February 18, 1970; consecrated April 2, 1970; appointed as First Bishop of Arlington on June 4, 1974; installed on August 13, 1974; appointed Bishop of Allentown February 8, 1983; installed Second Bishop of Allentown on March 21, 1983. *Mailing Address: Chancery Office, 202 N. 17th St., P.O. Box F, Allentown, PA, 18105.*

Chancery Office: 202 N. 17th St., P.O. Box F, Allentown, PA, 18105. Tel.: 610-437-0755; Fax: 610-433-7822.

ESTABLISHED JANUARY 28, 1961.

Square Miles 2,773.

Comprises the Counties of Berks, Carbon, Lehigh, Northampton and Schuylkill in the State of Pennsylvania.

STATISTICAL OVERVIEW

Personnel	
Bishop	1
Priests: Diocesan Active in Diocese	210
Priests: Active Outside Diocese	11
Priests: Diocesan in Foreign Missions	1
Priests: Retired, Sick or Absent	28
Number of Diocesan Priests	250
Religious Priests in Diocese	81
Extern Priests in Diocese	4
Ordinations:	
Diocesan Priests	4
Transitional Deacons	3
Permanent Deacons in Diocese	84
Total Brothers	11
Total Sisters	690
Parishes	
Parishes	153
With Resident Pastor:	
Resident Diocesan Priests	127
Resident Religious Priests	5
Without Resident Pastor:	
Administered by Priests	21
Missions	13
Welfare	
Catholic Hospitals	3
Total Assisted	632,592
Homes for the Aged	11
Total Assisted	587
Day Care and Extended Day Care Centers	49
Total Assisted	1,980
Specialized Homes	10
Total Assisted	454
Special Centers for Social Services	14
Total Assisted	78,872
Residential Care of Disabled	2
Total Assisted	25
Other Institutions	1
Total Assisted	1,641
Educational	
Diocesan Students in Other Seminaries	31
Total Seminarians	31
Colleges and Universities	2
Total Students	3,001
High Schools, Diocesan and Parish	9
Total Students	4,129
Elementary Schools, Diocesan and Parish	54
Total Students	14,288
Elementary Schools, Private	1
Total Students	13
Non-residential Schools for the Disabled	3
Total Students	128
Catechesis/Religious Education:	
High School Students	2,364
Elementary Students	16,336
Total Students Under Catholic Instruction	40,290
Teachers in the Diocese:	
Priests	22
Sisters	100
Lay Teachers	817
Vital Statistics	
Receptions into the Church:	
Infant Baptism Totals	3,960
Adult Baptism Totals	193
Received into Full Communion	358
Confirmations	3,259
Marriages:	
Catholic	865
Interfaith	633
Total Marriages	1,498
Deaths	3,130
Total Catholic Population	258,527
Total Population	1,084,189

Former Bishops—Most Rev. JOSEPH MCSHEA, appt. Titular Bishop of Mina and Auxiliary Bishop of Philadelphia Feb. 9, 1952; cons. March 19, 1952; appt. Bishop of Allentown Feb. 15, 1961; installed April 11, 1961; retired Feb. 8, 1983; died Nov. 28, 1991.

Moderator of the Curia—Rev. Msgr. ANTHONY D. MUNTONE, P.A., V.G., S.T.L.

Vicar General—Rev. Msgr. ANTHONY D. MUNTONE, P.A., V.G., S.T.L.

Chancellor—Rev. Msgr. JOSEPH M. WHALEN, S.T.L.

Vice Chancellor—Rev. Msgr. EDWARD J. COYLE, Th.M., M.A.

Office of Vicar General and Chancery Office—202 N. 17th St., P.O. Box F, Allentown, 18105. Tel: 610-437-0755; Fax: 610-433-7822.

Canonical Consultant—Rev. Msgr. DAVID J. MORRISON, J.C.D., M.A., Diocesan Tribunal, *219 N. 18th St., Allentown, 18104.* Tel: 610-434-3200.

Secretary to the Bishop—Rev. Msgr. EDWARD J. COYLE, Th.M., M.A., *Bishop's Office, 202 N. 17th St., P.O. Box F, Allentown, 18105.* Tel: 610-437-0755.

Director of Information—Deacon JOHN W. MURPHY, JR., *Office of Information, 2141 Downyflake Ln., Allentown, 18103-4724.* Tel: 610-797-3845; Fax: 610-797-3941.

Assistant to the Diocesan Director for Radio and Television—BRIAN MULVIHILL, *"The A.D. Times", 2141 Downyflake Ln., Allentown, 18103-4724.* Tel: 610-797-3330.

Diocesan Financial Secretary—Rev. Msgr. JOHN J. MARTIN; RONALD J. JACOBS, M.B.A., Admin. Asst.; Rev. Msgr. WILLIAM F. BAVER, Th.M., Admin. Asst., *Diocesan Office, 1729 Turner St., P.O. Box F, Allentown, 18105.* Tel: 610-435-9527.

Vicar for Religious—Rev. Msgr. THOMAS E. HOBAN, *415 S. Sixth St., Emmaus, 18094.*

Diocesan Tribunal—219 N. 18th St., Allentown, 18104. Tel: 610-434-3200.

Judicial Vicar—Rev. Msgr. RONALD W. GAINER, M.Div., J.C.L.

Judges—Rev. Msgr. DAVID J. MORRISON, J.C.D.; Revs. JOSEPH J. MORRELL, M.Ed., J.C.L.; JAMES J. WARD, M.Div.; JOHN PAUL, M.S.C., S.T.L., J.C.D.

Promoter of Justice—Rev. DAVID J. KOZAK, J.C.L.

Defenders of the Bond—Revs. DAVID J. KOZAK, J.C.L.; MICHAEL S. LAWRENCE, M.Div.; ALFRED A. SCHLERT, J.C.L.

Secretary—Deacon EUGENE J. WYRWA.

Advocates—Revs. JAMES J. BURDESS; EDWARD R. DOMIN, M.A.; VICTOR F. FINELLI, Th.M.; DAVID C. LIEBNER, M.Div.; FRANCIS P. STRAKA; ROBERT G. COFENAS, Ed.D.; DAVID J. LOEPER, M.A.; EDWARD J. O'CONNOR, M.Th., M.S.W.; EDWARD S. ZEMANIK, M.Div., B.A.; Rev. Msgr. STANLEY T. SOSNOWSKI, M.Div.; Deacon JOHN D. CUMMINGS.

Notaries—JUDY CHUSS; PATRICIA ECHTERNACH; DIANE SELDOMRIDGE; COLETTE SNYDER.

Special Services—Deacon JAMES R. DUNCAN, Ed.D.

Diocesan Offices and Directors

Allentown Catholic Communications, Inc.—Most Rev. THOMAS J. WELSH, D.D., J.C.D., Pres.; Rev. Msgr. JOHN J. MARTIN, Treas., *202 N. 17th St., P.O. Box F, Allentown, 18105.* Tel: 610-437-0755.

Apostolate for the Spanish Speaking—Rev. ROBERT J. BISZEK, Diocesan Dir., *Holy Infancy Rectory, 312 E. Fourth St., Bethlehem, 18015.* Tel: 610-866-1121. Regional Directors: Berks Co.: Rev. CHARLES A. MARCIANO; Deacons LEOPOLDO ALVARADO; JESUS CENTENO; FRANCISCO COLON; JULIO COLON; FERNANDO TORRES; MARIANO TORRES, Lehigh Co.: Rev. Msgr. JOSEPH R. SOBIESIAK; Deacons JAIME DEJESUS; JOSE GONZALEZ; VICTOR QUILES, Northampton Co.: Rev. ROBERT J. BISZEK; Deacons RAFAEL CUEVAS; ROBERT DEJESUS; ALFONSO SOLIS; EDISON MORALES; NICASIO RODRIGUEZ; RODOBERTO MATOS.

Bishop's Annual Appeal—Rev. Msgr. EDWARD R. SACKS, M.Ed., Vicar Devel., *P.O. Box F, Allentown, 18105.* Tel: 610-797-6657.

Books, Censor of—Rev. Msgr. JAMES J. MULLIGAN, S.T.L., *300 Cherryville Rd., Northampton, 18067.* Tel: 610-262-1885.

Building Committee—Rev. Msgr. RICHARD J. LOEPER, M.A., Chm., *417 Carlton Ave., Bethlehem, 18015.* Tel: 610-867-9382.

Campus Ministry—Rev. LARRY J. HESS, M.A., Dir., *Newman Assocation for Kutztown University, 15207 Kutztown Rd., Kutztown, 19530.* Tel: 610-683-8380.

Catechumenate Office—CAROLE CHUK, Dir., *P.O. Box 20607, 2145 Madison Ave., Lehigh Valley, 18002-0607.* Tel: 610-866-4919.

Catholic Charities—Rev. Msgr. JOSEPH E. KURTZ, Dir., *2141 Downyflake Ln., Allentown, 18103-4774.* Tel: 610-791-3888.

Catholic Charities, Appeal Office—Rev. Msgr. EDWARD R. SACKS, M.Ed., Diocesan Dir., *P.O. Box F, Allentown, 18105.* Tel: 610-797-6657.

Catholic Housing Corporations—Rev. Msgr. DENNIS A.

RIGNEY, Pres. & Chief Exec. RONALD G. DELORENZO, Dir. of Housing, *1200 Spring St., Bethlehem, 18018.* Tel: 610-865-5595; Fax: 610-865-5866.

Catholic Social Agency-Family Life Bureau—Rev. Msgr. JOHN B. MCCANN, S.T.L., Dir.; Deacon BERNARD M. WISSER, *2141 Downyflake Ln., Allentown, 18103-4774.* Tel: 610-791-3888.

Catholic Youth Organization—(See Youth Ministry).

Cemeteries Office—Rev. Msgr. WILLIAM F. BAVER, Dir., *1729 Turner St., P.O. Box F, Allentown, 18105.* Tel: 610-435-9527.

Christian Doctrine, Confraternity of—BARBARA A. PENGITORE, Dir.; RITANNE PURSEL, Asst. Dir., *Dewberry & Madison Aves., P.O. Box 20607, Lehigh Valley, 18002-0607.* Regional Directors: Lehigh Co.: Rev. JAMES J. BURDESS; Berks Co.: Rev. RICHARD H. CLEMENT; Carbon Co.: Rev. STEPHEN J. HALABURA; Northampton Co.: Rev. STEPHEN J. RADOCHA; South Schuylkill Co.: Rev. EDWARD J. O'CONNOR; North Schuylkill Co.: Rev. ROBERT J. KUZMANN.

Council of Priests/Diocesan Consultors—202 N. 17th St., P.O. Box F, Allentown, 18105. Tel: 610-437-0755.

Consultors—Rev. Msgr. ANTHONY D. MUNTONE, P.A., V.G., S.T.L.; Rev. Msgr. JOSEPH M. WHALEN; Rev. Msgr. RICHARD J. LOEPER, M.A.; Rev. Msgr. FRANCIS X. BARRETT; Rev. Msgr. WILLIAM E. HANDGES; Rev. Msgr. JOHN P. MURPHY; Rev. Msgr. JOHN J. MARTIN; Rev. Msgr. ALFRED R. OTT; Rev. Msgr. FRANCIS J. ZAVODNY; Rev. Msgr. GERALD E. GOBITAS; Rev. LADISLAUS J. DUDEK.

Ex Officio Members—Rev. Msgr. EDWARD R. SACKS, V.F.; Rev. Msgr. JAMES A. TRESTON, V.F.; Rev. Msgr. ALFRED R. OTT, V.F.; Rev. Msgr. WILLIAM E. JONES, V.F.; Rev. Msgr. JOHN G. CHIZMAR, V.F.; Rev. Msgr. DENNIS A. RIGNEY; Rev. Msgr. THOMAS E. HOBAN; Rev. Msgr. JOSEPH E. KURTZ; Rev. Msgr. WALTER T. SCHEAFFER; Rev. Msgr. JOHN B. MCCANN; Rev. ROBERT J. BISZEK; Rev. LARRY J. HESS.

Elected Members—Rev. Msgr. ROBERT M. FORST; Revs. JOHN A. AUCHTER; JOSEPH D. HULKO; JOHN M. GIBBONS; EDWARD J. DONAHUE; RONALD C. BOCIAN; FRANCIS J. FOX; JOHN J. PAUL, M.S.C.; GABRIEL M. PATIL, C.R.S.P.

Appointed Members—Rev. Msgr. JOSEPH P.T. SMITH; Rev. Msgr. WILLIAM E. HANDGES; Rev. Msgr. JOHN P. MURPHY.

Committee on Ecumenism—Rev. ROBERT C. QUINN, Chm., *St. Columbkill, 200 Indian Spring Rd., Boyertown, 19512-2008.* Tel: 610-367-2371. Revs. BERNARD O'CONNOR, O.S.F.S., Ph.D.; EDWIN J. SANDERS, S.J.

Department of Education—Rev. Msgr. WALTER T. SCHEAFFER, M.Ed., Vicar for Education; Dr. JAMES J. CUSIMANO, ESQ., Supt.; Rev. JOHN S. MRAZ, M.A., Asst. Supt. Education; BARBARA A. PENGITORE, Dir. Religious Education; Asst. Dir. Religious Education; RITANNE PURSEL. Asst. Supts. Elementary Education: MARIANNE C. WHELAN; Sr. EILEEN DOROTHY MAGUIRE, I.H.M.; JOHN CLARK, Asst. Secondary Education; SUZANNE M. MELLO, Media Librarian, *Dewberry & Madison Aves., P.O. Box 20607, Lehigh Valley, 18002-0607.* Tel: 610-866-0581.

Deposit and Loan Fund-Diocesan Review Board—Rev. Msgr. JOHN J. MARTIN, Chm.; Rev. Msgr. JOSEPH P. DOOLEY; Rev. Msgr. FELIX A. LOSITO; Rev. Msgr. FRANCIS J. ZAVODNY; Rev. MICHAEL J. STONE; BERNARDINE STANZ; EDWARD A. HARTMAN, JR., *1729 Turner St., P.O. Box F, Allentown, 18105.* Tel: 610-435-9527.

Diocesan Board of Education—Voting Members: Mr. MICHAEL DEPAUL, Pres.; Mrs. ROSE YAVULLA, Vice Pres. PATRICIA AGGER; Dr. DWIGHT R. DAVIS; JOSEPH DOUGHERTY; Rev. DAVID W. KARNS, M.Div.; MARK LIEBERMAN; Rev. ROBERT J. MCCONAGHY, M.Th.; JOHN MORGANELLI, Esq.; Rev. Msgr. JOSEPH R. SOBIESIAK, Th.M.; Rev. MICHAEL J. STONE; Mrs. MARGARET M. SURDOVAL; Rev. VINCENT P. YORK,Non-voting Member: JAMES J. CUSIMANO, Esq. Non-voting Consultants: ELIZABETH BULAH; Sr. PATRICIA CULLEN, S.S.J.; Rev. Msgr. JOHN J. MARTIN, M.Div.; Rev. Msgr. ANTHONY D. MUNTONE, P.A., V.G., S.T.L.; RITA PURSEL; Rev. WILLIAM N. SEIFERT, M.Div. Executive Secretary: JAMES J. CUSIMANO, ESQ.

Diocesan Development Office—Rev. Msgr. EDWARD R. SACKS, M.Ed., Vicar Devel. PAUL W. ZAMBO, Dir. FRANK C. GODINO, Dir. School Devel. ROBERT DESILVER, Dir. Planned Giving, *P.O. Box F, Allentown, 18105.* Tel: 610-797-9691.

Diocesan Director of Programs for Priestly Life and Ministry—Rev. Msgr. JAMES J. MULLIGAN, S.T.L., *Mary Immaculate Seminary, Northampton, 18067.* Tel: 610-262-1885.

Diocesan Financial Office Annex—RONALD J. JACOBS, Admin. Asst.; JOHN A. MILISITS, Insurance Coord.; CAROLE A. SARMIR, Benefits Admin., *2222 S. 12th St., Suite D, Allentown, 18103-5648.* Tel: 610-797-2811.

Diocesan Health Affairs—Rev. Msgr. JOSEPH E. KURTZ, M.Div L.S.W., Coord., *2141 Downyflake Ln., Allentown, 18103-4774.* Tel: 610-791-3888; Fax: 610-791-1878.

Diocesan Newspaper—

"The A.D. Times"—The Allentown Diocese in the Year of Our Lord, Deacon JOHN W. MURPHY, JR., Editor; JILL M. CARAVAN, Mng. Editor; PAULINE PARK-FINNEGAN, Production & Design Editor, *2141 Downyflake Ln., Allentown, 18103-4724.* Tel: 610-797-3330.

Diocesan Pastoral Planning Committee—Rev. Msgr. EDWARD R. SACKS, M.Ed., Chm., *3219 Santee Rd., Bethlehem, 18017.* Tel: 610-867-8409.

Diocesan Textbook Review Committee—Vacant.

Directory—Deacon JOHN W. MURPHY, JR., Editor, *"The A.D. Times," 2141 Downyflake Ln., Allentown, 18103-4724.* Tel: 610-797-3845.

Family Life Bureau—(See Catholic Social Agency).

Finance Committee—Rev. Msgr. ANTHONY D. MUNTONE, P.A., V.G., S.T.L., Bishop's Delegate, *202 N. 17th St., P.O. Box F, Allentown, 18105.* Tel: 610-437-0755. Very Rev. DANIEL G. GAMBET, O.S.F.S.; Sr. FRANCIS ANNE HARPER, O.S.F.; CARL FEICHTEL; JOHN HORRIGAN, JR.; MARIANNE S. LAVELLE, ESQ.; BERNARD F. MULLIGAN; Rev. Msgr. ALFRED R. OTT; THOMAS F. TRAUD, ESQ.; ALBERT BOVA.

Forward with Christ Allocation Committee—Rev. Msgr. WILLIAM E. HANDGES, Chm., *900 Washington St., Easton, 18042.* Tel: 610-253-7188. Rev. Msgr. RICHARD J. LOEPER, M.A.; Sr. FRANCIS BISLAND, C.P.S.; Sr. MARY ANNE BEDNAR, I.H.M.; PAUL DOMALAKES, Esq.; FRANCIS HARTNETT; FRANK C. GODINO, M.P.A.

High School Budget Boards—Allentown Central Catholic High School: Rev. Msgr. JOSEPH R. SOBIESIAK; Rev. Msgr. JOHN P. MURPHY; Rev. Msgr. THOMAS E. HOBAN; Rev. Msgr. FRANCIS J. ZAVODNY. Bethlehem Catholic High School: Rev. Msgr. RICHARD J. LOEPER; Rev. Msgr. JAMES J. MCHALE; Rev. Msgr. RAYMOND F. MERMAN. Cardinal Brennan High School: Rev. ROBERT J. POTTS; Rev. Msgr. JAMES C. BECHTEL; WILLIAM H. CARTER; Rev. ANTHONY P. MONGIELLO. Holy Name High School: Rev. Msgr. JAMES A. TRESTON; Rev. DAVID C. GILLIS; JAMES J. REICHERT, M.Div.; Rev. FRANCIS T. GILLESPIE. Marian Catholic High School: Rev. JOSEPH L. GREMBOCKI; Rev. Msgr. JOHN G. CHIZMAR; Revs. THOMAS A. DERZACK; WILLIAM T. CAMPION. Nativity B.V.M. High School. Rev. DANIEL J. YENUSHOSKY; Rev. Msgr. WILLIAM E. JONES; Revs. FRANCIS P. SCHOENAUER; MICHAEL J. STONE. Notre Dame High School: Rev. Msgr. WILLIAM E. HANDGES; Rev. THOMAS J. KING; Rev. Msgr. EDWARD R. SACKS, M.Ed.; Rev. Msgr. GERALD E. GOBITAS, Pius X High School: Rev. Msgr. JOSEPH P. DOOLEY; Rev. Msgr. CHARLES T. MOSS; Revs. JAMES G. PRIOR, C.M.; RICHARD A. SCHWARE, M.Div. Reading Central Catholic High School: Rev. Msgr. JOSEPH P.T. SMITH; Rev. Msgr. FRANCIS X. BARRETT; Rev. MICHAEL J. BRIGGMAN; Rev. Msgr. FELIX A. LOSITO.

Liturgical Commission—Rev. Msgr. EDWARD J. COYLE, Th.M., Chm., *Bishop's Office, 202 N. 17th St., P.O. Box F, Allentown, 18105.* Tel: 610-437-0755. Revs. FRANCIS J. BARANSKY, M.Div.; EDMUND J. BRENNAN, M.Div.; CAROLE C. CHUK; Rev. THOMAS A. DERZACK, M.Div.; ALETHA FASSI; RITA FERRONE; Revs. ERIC J. GRUBER, M.Div.; JOHN A. HANLEY, O.S.F.S.; MARTIN F. KERN, M.Div.; Rev. EDWARD J. O'CONNOR; TERESA RODGERS; Deacon BERNARD J. SALABSKY; Rev. WILLIAM N. SEIFERT; Sr. REGINA STUPAK, I.H.M.

National Shrine of the Immaculate Conception—Rev. Msgr. JOHN G. CHIZMAR, Chm. Diocesan Pilgrimage Committee, *180 W. Broadway, Jim Thorpe, 18229.* Tel: 717-325-2791.

Nurses, Council of Catholic—Rev. Msgr. DENNIS A. RIGNEY, M.Div., A.C.S.W., N.H.A., Dir., *1200 Spring St., Bethlehem, 18018.* Tel: 610-865-5595. Regional Directors: Revs. JOSEPH A. ROCK, Lehigh Co. & Northampton Co.; WALTER J. HALL, South Schuylkill Co.; WILLIAM H. CARTER, North Schuylkill Co.; VINCENT I. CRONIN, Carbon Co.

Permanent Diaconate, Office of the—Rev. Msgr. JAMES J. MULLIGAN, S.T.L., Dir.; Deacon FRANCIS J. COSGROVE, Assoc. Dir., *P.O. Box 20607, Dewberry & Madison Aves., Lehigh Valley, 18002-0607.* Tel: 610-866-0581.

Project H.E.A.D.—Diocesan Golden Age Clubs, Rev. Msgr. DENNIS A. RIGNEY, M.Div., L.S.W., A.C.S.W., N.H.A., Dir., *1200 Spring St., Bethlehem, 18018.* Tel: 610-865-5595. Regional Directors: Rev. ROBERT J. REED, Lehigh Co.; Rev. FRANCIS T. GILLESPIE, Berks Co.; Rev. Msgr. WILLIAM E. HANDGES, Northampton Co.; Rev. STEPHEN J. HALABURA, Carbon Co.; Rev. Msgr. ANTHONY F. WASSEL, Schuylkill Co.

Pro-Life Office—Rev. Msgr. STEPHEN T. FORISH, M.Div., Diocesan Dir.; Revs. GREGORY J. TAUBER, Asst. Dir.; RONALD P. BOWMAN, Asst. Dir.; JOHN J. GRABISH, Spanish Apostolate, *1135 Stefko Blvd., Bethlehem, 18017.* Tel: 610-691-0380; Fax: 610-691-0403.

Recruitment Committee for Encouraging Vocations to the Priesthood and Religious Life—Rev. WILLIAM F. GLOSSER, Chm., *900 W. Market St., Orwigsburg, 17961.* Tel: 717-366-1405.

Saint Francis Center—Deacon ALEX L. MAGGITTI, Dir., *900 W. Market St., Orwigsburg, 17961.* Tel: 717-366-1016.

Dept. of Youth Ministry and Youth and Adult Retreats—Tel: 717-366-1405.

Catholic Social Agency—Tel: 717-366-1403; 1404.

Holy Family Health Care—Tel: 717-366-0990.

Holy Family Residence—Tel: 717-366-2912.

St. Francis Adult Day Care Center—Tel: 717-366-2924.

Scouting—(See Youth Ministry).

Social Action Bureau—MARY ANN HAMMER, Exec. Dir., *2141 Downyflake Ln., Allentown, 18104-4774.* Tel: 610-791-3888. Advisory Board: JOHN B. SYLVESTER, Chm.; ANNE CHILES, Vice-Chm.; BARBARA PENGITORE, Sec.; ELBA APONTE; FLORA BECKER; DAVID BOWEN; Rev. WILLIAM H. CARTER, M.Div.; LYDIA DASILVA; KIRK DAVIS; Sr. MIRIAM DENIS, S.S.J.; MARY BETH DOUGHERTY; Rev. ANTHONY M. DROUNCHECK; JOSEPHINE GARCIA; JOSEPHINE HOZZA; DENNIS KEAN, M.D.; Rev. Msgr. FELIX A. LOSITO; TERRY QUAIN; JAMES A. RITTER, Esq.; Deacon DANIEL METZKER; Mrs. DANIEL METZKER; Sr. ST. GREGORY, S.S.J.; BRUCE VIECHNICKI, M.D.; Deacon LUIS R. VISOT, M.D.; Rev. GEORGE R. WINNE. Staff: MARY ANN HAMMER, Exec. Dir.; ROBIN DURSO, Sec./Bookkeeper; Rev. JOHN M. GIBBONS, M.Div.; MARY-ANN HARTZELL.

Social Services, Council of—Rev. Msgr. JOSEPH E. KURTZ, M.Div., A.C.S.W., Exec. Sec. & Moderator, *2141 Downyflake Ln., Allentown, 18104-4774.* Tel: 610-791-3888. Member Agencies: Catholic Social Agency; Department for the Aged; Diocesan Liaison for Ministry to the Elderly; Family Life Bureau; Holy Family Home Health Care; Holy Family Manor, Inc.; Pro-Life Office; Social Action Bureau; Spanish Apostolate.

Family Life Review Committee—Rev. JOHN S. MRAZ, Chm., *P.O. Box 20607, Lehigh Valley, 18002-0607.* Tel: 610-866-0581.

Vicars Forane—Carbon Co.: Rev. Msgr. JOHN G. CHIZMAR, V.F.; Lehigh Co.: Rev. Msgr. ALFRED R. OTT, V.F.; Berks Co.: Rev. Msgr. JAMES A. TRESTON, V.F.; Northampton Co.: Rev. Msgr. EDWARD R. SACKS, V.F.; South Schuylkill Co.: Rev. Msgr. WILLIAM E. JONES, V.F.; North Schuylkill Co.: Vacant.

Vocations and Priestly Formation Committee—Rev. RONALD V. JANKAITIS, Chm., *St. Casimir Rectory, 441 S. Nichols St., St. Clair, 17970.* Tel: 717-429-2400. Revs. JOHN A. AUCHTER; ROBERT J. BISZEK; DONALD W. CIENIEWICZ, M.Div.; Rev. Msgr. EDWARD J. COYLE; Rev. Msgr. JOHN P. MURPHY; Revs. MICHAEL J. STONE; Rev. Msgr. ROBERT J. WARGO.

Vocations Apostolate—Rev. Msgr. ROBERT J. WARGO, Dir.; Rev. Msgr. EDWARD J. COYLE, Asst. Dir., *202 N. 17th St., P.O. Box F, Allentown, 18105.* Tel: 610-437-0755. Regional Directors: Lehigh Co.: Rev. ERIC A. ARNOUT; Berks Co.: Rev. RICHARD H. CLEMENT; Carbon Co.: Rev. THOMAS A. DERZACK; Northampton Co.: Rev. FRANCIS A. NAVE; North Schuylkill Co.: Rev. EDWARD J. ESSIG; South Schuylkill Co.: BERNARD A. FLANAGAN; For Hispanics: Rev. GEORGE R. WINNE.

Women Religious, Commission for—Sr. MARTINA REVAK, O.S.B., Pres., *St. Ann Convent, 526 Fairview St., Emmaus, 18049.* Tel: 610-965-6818.

Youth Ministry, Department of—Rev. WILLIAM F. GLOSSER, M.A., Dir. LYNN PAPA, Retreat Coord.; MARY ELLEN JOHNS, Retreats & Young Adult Ministry; Rev. JOSEPH L. GREMBOCKI, Scouting Coord.; EDWARD TRAY, C.Y.O. Coord.; DENISE RYAN, Sec., *St. Francis Center, 900 W. Market St., Orwigsburg, 17961.* Tel: 717-366-1405. Regional Directors: Lehigh Co.: Rev. MARTIN F. KERN; Berks Co.: Rev. CHRISTOPHER L. WAKEFIELD; Carbon Co.: Rev. JAMES J. WARD; Northampton Co.: Rev. MICHAEL A. METRO; North Schuylkill Co.: Rev. DAVID J. KOZAK; South Schuylkill Co.: Rev. EDWARD J. O'CONNOR; Berks Co. for Spanish: Rev. JOHN M. GIBBONS. High School Directors: Revs. GEORGE R. WINNE, Allentown Central Catholic; WILLIAM N. SEIFERT, Bethlehem Catholic; ANTHONY P. MONGIELLO, Cardinal Brennan; THOMAS J. DRSULAK, Holy Name; DONALD J. SCHAIBLE, Marian Catholic; BERNARD A. FLANAGAN, Nativity; ALFRED A. SCHLERT, Notre Dame; PATRICK H. LAMB, Reading Central Catholic; WAYNE E. KILLIAN, Saint Pius X. C.Y.O. Regional Directors: Carbon Co. and East Schuylkill Co.: Rev. JOHN G. HILFERTY; Berks Co.: Rev. RICHARD C. BRENSINGER; Lehigh Co.: Rev. ROBERT J. GEORGE; Mid-Schuylkill Co.: Rev. ANTHONY P. MONGIELLO; Northampton Co.: Rev. EDWARD R. DOMIN; West Schuylkill Co.: Rev. ERIC J. GRUBER. Catholic Scouting Area Chaplains: Minsi Trails Council: Carbon Co.: Rev. ROBERT J. MCCONAGHY; Lehigh Co.: Rev. VICTOR F. FINELLI; Northampton Co.: Rev. FRANCIS A. NAVE. Hawk Mountain Council Co-Chairpersons: ELIZABETH PAOLINI; ANNE MARIE HALCOVAGE, Berks Co.: Rev. MICHAEL E. AHRENSFIELD; North Schuylkill Co. Area: Rev. VICTOR J. ANSELMI; South Schuylkill

Co. Area: Rev. EDWARD J. O'CONNOR. Scouting (Girls): CAROLE YEAGER. Camp-Fire Inc.: ELIZABETH PAOLINI.

Affiliated Organizations

Apostleship of Prayer—Very Rev. EUGENE W. JUNG, M.S.C., Dir., *55 Rothermel St., Reading, 19605.* Tel: 610-929-2025.

American Catholic Overseas Aid Fund—Rev. RICHARD J. FORD, Diocesan Dir., *3121 Kutztown Rd., Reading, 19605.* Tel: 610-921-2729. Regional Directors: Lehigh Co.: Rev. Msgr. WILLIAM F. BAVER, Th.M.; Northampton Co.: Rev. DAVID J. LOEPER, M.A.; North Schuylkill Co.: Rev. FRANCIS M. GRUNDOWSKI; South Schuylkill Co.: Rev. JAMES R. BRADY.

Beginning Experience—Rev. Msgr. RONALD W. GAINER, Diocesan Spiritual Dir., *4102 S. Church St., Whitehall, 18052.* Tel: 610-262-9315.

Catholic Daughters of the Americas—KAY ELLEN KUCHINSKY, Diocese Committee Chm., *127 "A" St., Girardville, 17935.*

Charismatic Renewal—Rev. LARRY J. HESS, Bishop's Liaison, *Newman Association, 15207 Kutztown Rd., Kutztown, 19530.* Tel: 610-683-8380.

Courage—Rev. BERNARD J. EZAKI, Dir., *1861 Catasauqua Rd., Bethlehem, 18018.* Tel: 610-866-8938.

Cursillo Movement—Rev. ROBERT J. REED, Dir., *SS. Simon & Jude Rectory, 730 W. Broad St., Bethlehem, 18018.* Tel: 610-866-5582.

Dayspring Homes, Inc.—Sr. FRANCIS BISLAND, C.P.S., Dir. A program providing residential settings for adult persons with mental retardation. *Corporate Address: P.O. Box 172, Shillington, 19607.* Tel: 610-777-1624.

Holy Childhood Association—Rev. Msgr. JOHN P. MURPHY, Dir., *1040 Flexer Ave., Allentown, 18103.* Tel: 610-433-7413.

Holy Name Societies—Deacon STEPHAN ANDRUSISIAN, Dir., *516 N. Front St., Minersville, 17954.* Tel: 717-544-5339. Regional Directors: North Schuylkill Co.: Deacon JOHN A. SETLOCK; Northampton Co.: Rev. THOMAS J. KING; South Schuylkill Co.: Deacon STEPHEN ANDRUSISIAN; Carbon Co.: Rev. BRUNO M. TUCCI.

Legion of Mary—ELIZABETH PAOLINI, *414 Douglass St., Reading, 19601.*

Magnificat House—4530 Vera Cruz Rd., Center Valley, 18034. Tel: 610-797-1950.

Marriage Encounter—Rev. ROBERT A. DRESSLER, *33 Fourth St., P.O. Box G, Kelayres, 18231-0070.* Tel: 717-929-3670.

National Society for Shut-Ins—Rev. Msgr. FELIX A. LOSITO, Natl. Dir., *237 Franklin St., Reading, 19602.* Tel: 610-374-2930. MICHAEL SHEIDY, Pres.

Operation Rice Bowl—Rev. Msgr. JOHN P. MURPHY, Dir., *1040 Flexer Ave., Allentown, 18103.* Tel: 610-433-7413.

Priests' Eucharistic League—Rev. Msgr. THOMAS E. HOBAN, Dir., *415 S. Sixth St., Emmaus, 18049.* Tel: 610-965-2426.

Propagation of the Faith—Rev. Msgr. JOHN P. MURPHY, Dir., *1040 Flexer Ave., Allentown, 18103.* Tel: 610-433-7413.

Saint Vincent de Paul—Rev. Msgr. JOHN B. MCCANN, S.T.L., L.S.W., Spiritual Advisor; EDWARD BUTLER, Diocesan Council Pres., *2141 Downyflake Ln., Allentown, 18103-4774.* Tel: 610-791-3888.

Serra Clubs—Forks of the Delaware Serra, Rev. JOSEPH A. SHEEHAN; JANET DEBELLIS, Pres., *2211 Stocker Mill Rd., Easton, 18045.* Serra Club of Allentown, Rev. Msgr. ALFRED R. OTT, Chap.; MARGARET A. FRENSKY, Pres., *3037 Imperial Dr., Allentown, 18103.* Reading Serra, Rev. JAMES J. REICHERT, Chap.; LEROY S. MAIORANA, M.D., Pres., *1512 Rose Virginia Rd., Reading, 19610.* Serra Club of Bethlehem, Rev. Msgr. ROBERT F. KOZEL, Chap.; ANTHONY F. ORTWEIN, Pres., *755 Johnston Dr., Bethlehem, 18017.*

CLERGY, PARISHES, MISSIONS AND PAROCHIAL SCHOOLS

CITY OF ALLENTOWN
(Lehigh County)

1—CATHEDRAL OF ST. CATHARINE OF SIENA (1919), Rev. Msgr. Alfred R. Ott, V.F.; Revs. David C. Liebner; David L. James; Deacons Ralph Jaccodine; Joseph V. Salvo.
Res., 1825 Turner St., 18104. Tel: 610-433-6461; Fax: 610-433-5452.
School—(Grades K-8) 210 N. 18th St., 18104. Tel: 610-434-8981; Fax: 610-437-4951. Mrs. H. Jacqueline Greco, Prin.
Lay Teachers 27; Students 651.
Catechesis/Religious Programs—Tel: 610-432-7655. Sr. Elizabeth Agnes, S.S.J., D.R.E.
Students 131.
Convent—215 N. 18th St., 18104. Tel: 610-434-9824.

2—ST. FRANCIS OF ASSISI (1928), Rev. Msgr. Dennis A. Rigney; Rev. Joseph McGarr; Deacons Alexander L. Maggitti, Sr.; Arthur L. Chin-Fatt. In res., Rev. Joseph J. Morrell.
Res., 801 N. 11th St., 18102. Tel: 610-434-8770; Fax: 610-434-6972.
School—(Grades PreK-8) 1035 Washington St., 18102. Tel: 610-435-0364.
Sisters of St. Francis of Philadelphia 2; Lay Teachers 17; Students 321.
Parish Center—1028 W. Cedar St., 18102. Tel: 610-433-6102.
Catechesis/Religious Programs—Tel: 610-434-8299.
Students 150.

3—IMMACULATE CONCEPTION. (Declared National Shrine of Our Lady of Guadalupe, Mother of the Americas 1974). Rev. Harold F. Dagle; Deacon Brian J. Monahan. In res., Rev. Msgr. John B. McCann.
Res., 501 Ridge Ave., 18102. Tel: 610-433-4404. [CEM]
School—Holy Spirit Regional Catholic Elementary School, Allentown. See separate listing.
Convent—508 Ridge Ave., 18102. Tel: 610-432-0838.

4—ST. JOHN THE BAPTIST (Slovak), Rev. Msgr. Francis J. Zavodny; Rev. Andrew Sroba.
Res., 924 N. Front St., 18102. Tel: 610-432-0034. [CEM]
School—Holy Spirit Regional Catholic Elementary School, Allentown. See separate listing.
Convent—920 N. Front St., 18102. Tel: 610-434-1471.

5—OUR LADY HELP OF CHRISTIANS (1927), Revs. Stephen L. Maco, Admin.; Robert G. Cofenas; Deacon Charles Coyle.
Res., 444 N. Jasper St., 18103. Tel: 610-432-9384.
School—934 Hanover Ave., 18103. Tel: 610-433-1592.
Sisters of Christian Charity 2; Lay Teachers 8; Students 221.
Catechesis/Religious Programs—Students 54.
Convent—922 Hanover Ave., 18103. Tel: 610-433-4915.

6—OUR LADY OF MT. CARMEL (Italian), Rev. Msgr. Joseph R. Sobiesiak; Deacon Dominick F. Amedeo.
Res., 177 Chew St., 18102. Tel: 610-437-6949. [CEM]
School—Sacred Heart Regional Catholic Elementary School, Allentown. See separate listing.

7—ST. PAUL (1928), Rev. Msgr. Robert M. Forst; Revs. Francis J. Fromholzer; Luigi Palmieri; Deacon Daniel A. Thomson. In res., Rev. Michael S. Lawrence.
Res., 920 S. Second St., 18103. Tel: 610-797-9733.
Church—Second St. & Susquehanna St., 18103.
School—(Grades K-8) Third St. & Susquehanna St., 18103. Tel: 610-797-5321. Sr. Ruth Hennessy, R.S.M., Prin.
Sisters of Mercy 1; Lay Teachers 12; Students 285.
Catechesis/Religious Programs—Students 150.
Convent—311 W. Susquehanna St., 18103. Tel: 610-797-8533.

8—SS. PETER AND PAUL (Polish), Rev. Ladislaus J. Dudek.
Res., 1065 Fullerton Ave., 18102. Tel: 610-432-2252.
School—Holy Spirit Regional Catholic Elementary School, Allentown. See separate listing.

9—SACRED HEART OF JESUS (1869) (German-Spanish), Rev. Msgr. Joseph R. Sobiesiak; Rev. Martin F. Kern; Deacons Jaime de Jesus; Victor M. Quiles; Jose Gonzalez; Dominic Amadeo. In res., Rev. George R. Winne.
Res., 336 N. Fourth St., 18102. Tel: 610-434-5171; Fax: 610-434-2441.
School—(Grades PreK-8) 321 N. Fourth St., 18102. Tel: 610-437-3031. James Krupka, Prin.
Lay Teachers 10; Students 216.
High School—Tel: 610-437-4601. James Hodrick, Prin.
Catechesis/Religious Programs—Parish Center, 417 Pine St., 18102. Tel: 610-434-5171; Fax: 610-434-2441. Sr. Regina Rosaii, D.R.E.
Students 363.

10—ST. STEPHEN OF HUNGARY (1915) (Hungarian), Rev. Msgr. William F. Baver, Th.M.
Res., 510 Union St., 18101-2307. Tel: 610-439-0111; Fax: 610-439-6048.
School—Sacred Heart Regional Catholic Elementary School, Allentown. See separate listing.

11—ST. THOMAS MORE (1966), Rev. Msgr. John P. Murphy; Rev. Eric R. Arnout, Jr.; Deacons James R. Duncan; Robert J. Tyson. In res., Rev. John S. Mraz.
Res., 1040 Flexer Ave., 18103. Tel: 610-433-7413; Fax: 610-433-2308.
School—Tel: 610-432-0396; Fax: 610-432-1395.
Bernardine Sisters 4; Lay Teachers 28; Students 610.
Catechesis/Religious Programs—Tel: 610-437-3491.
Students 573.
Convent—992 Flexer Ave., 18103. Tel: 610-437-9520.

OUTSIDE CITY OF ALLENTOWN

Ashland, Schuylkill Co., St. Joseph (1856), Rev. Floyd Caesar; Deacon Robert McManus. In res., Rev. Frans J. Berkhout.
Res., 1100 Walnut St., 17921. Tel: 717-875-1521. [CEM]
School—Immaculate Heart Regional Catholic Elementary School, Girardville. See separate listing.
Catechesis/Religious Programs—Students 52.
Convent—1123 Walnut St., 17921. Tel: 717-875-3553.

St. Mauritius (1856) (German), Rev. Floyd Caesar; Deacon Robert McManus. In res., Rev. Frans J. Berkhout.
Res., 802 Pine St., 17921. Tel: 717-875-2990. [CEM]
School—Immaculate Heart Regional Catholic Elementary School, Girardville. See separate listing.
Mission—Lavelle, Schuylkill Co., St. Elizabeth, Lavelle, 17943.

Bally, Berks Co., Most Blessed Sacrament (1741), Rev. Michael J. Briggman; Deacon Thomas J. Murphy.
Res., 610 Pine St., Box C, 19503. Tel: 610-845-2460; Fax: 610-845-2660. [CEM]
School—St. Francis Academy, Bally. See separate listing.
Catechesis/Religious Programs—Barbara A. Seaman, D.R.E.
Students 179.

Bangor, Northampton Co., Our Lady of Good Counsel (1915), Revs. John B. Fitzgerald, C.M.; Emerick J. Hydo, C.M.; Daniel E. Donovan, (Retired).
Res., 436 S. Second St., 18013. Tel: 610-588-5445; Fax: 610-588-5445. [CEM]
School—Our Lady of Mt. Carmel Regional Catholic Elementary School, Roseto. See separate listing.
Catechesis/Religious Programs—Elizabeth Thompson, D.R.E.
Students 112.
Mission—Portland, Northampton Co., St. Vincent de Paul, Church St., Portland, 18351.

Barnesville, Schuylkill Co., St. Richard (1950), Rev. Paul G. Puza.
Res., Park Crest, R.R. 2, Box 221, 18214-9747. Tel: 717-467-2315; Fax: 717-467-3803.
Catechesis/Religious Programs—Tel: 717-668-2812. Michelle Pyrsda, D.R.E.
Students 56.

Bath, Northampton Co., Sacred Heart (1920), Rev. Msgr. James J. McHale; Rev. Francis A. Nave.
Res., 210 E. Northampton St., 18014. Tel: 610-837-7874; Fax: 610-837-4570. [CEM]
School—(Grades PreK-8) 115 Washington St., 18014. Tel: 610-837-6391. Patricia A. Wertman, Prin.
Lay Teachers 9; Students 177.
Catechesis/Religious Programs—Mrs. Helen Browne, D.R.E.
Students 275.

Beaver Meadows, Carbon Co., St. Mary (1841), Rev. John J. Duminiak.
Res., 121 Berwick St., P.O. Box 235, 18216. Tel: 717-455-2613; Fax: 717-455-3125. [CEM]
Catechesis/Religious Programs—Students 48.

Berlinsville, Northampton Co., St. Nicholas, Rev. Edward W. McElduff.
Res., 1152 Oak Rd., Walnutport, 18088. Tel: 610-767-3148.
School—St. John Neumann Regional Catholic Elementary School, Palmerton-Slatington. See separate listing.

Bethlehem, Northampton Co.,

1—ST. ANNE, (1929), Rev. Msgr. Robert F. Kozel; Revs. Michael A. Metro; William R. Dermott; Deacons John D. Cummings; Richard G. Scrak; Sr. Kathleen Mackerer, S.S.J., Pastoral Assoc. In res., Rev. Stephen L. Maco.
Res., 450 Washington Ave., 18017. Tel: 610-867-5039; Fax: 610-882-4094.
School—(Grades PreK-8) Easton Ave. & Hickory St., 18017. Tel: 610-868-4182. Sr. Mary Jane Daily, S.S.J., Prin.
Sisters of St. Joseph 1; Lay Teachers 20; Students 425.
Catechesis/Religious Programs—Tel: 610-868-7514.
Students 186.

Convent—434 Washington Ave., 18017. Tel: 610-866-2752.

2—SS. CYRIL AND METHODIUS, (1891) (Slovak), Rev. Msgr. Michael J. Chaback, S.T.D.; Deacon Frank J. Danyi, Jr.
Res., 617 Pierce St., 18015. Tel: 610-866-3391; Fax: 610-866-6490. [CEM]
School—(Grades PreK-8) 551 Thomas St. & Pierce St., 18015. Tel: 610-866-0422. Mrs. Joan M. West, Prin.
Lay Teachers 11; Students 178.
Catechesis/Religious Programs—Students 20.
Convent—520 Buchanan St., 18015. Tel: 610-866-0275.

3—HOLY GHOST, (1871) (German), Rev. Msgr. Richard J. Loeper; Deacon Franklin J. Chiles. In res., Rev. Ai Ba Do (Vietnam).
Res., 417 Carlton Ave., 18015. Tel: 610-867-9382; Fax: 610-867-6839. [CEM]
School—Holy Child Regional Catholic Elementary School, Bethlehem. See separate listing.
Convent—427 Carlton Ave., 18015. Tel: 610-867-3364.

4—HOLY INFANCY, Rev. Msgr. James M. Butler; Deacons Edison Morales; Alfonso D. Solis; Nicasio Rodriguez; Rafael Cuevas. In res., Revs. Robert J. Biszek; Jose Dos Santos (Portugal).
Res., 312 E. Fourth St., 18015. Tel: 610-866-1121. [CEM]
School—(Grades PreK-8) 202 E. Fourth St., 18015. Tel: 610-868-2621. Sr. Joyce Valese, Prin.
Sisters of St. Joseph 4; Lay Teachers 8; Students 285.
Catechesis/Religious Programs—Stephanie Rivera, D.R.E.
Students 132.
Convents—202 E. Fourth St., 18015. Tel: 610-867-7384. Poor Sisters of St. Joseph; Casa Belen, 305 E. Fourth St., 18015. Tel: 610-867-4030.

5—ST. JOHN CAPISTRANO, (1903) (Hungarian), Rev. Edward C. Bolez.
Res., 910 E. Fourth St., 18015. Tel: 610-866-2714.
School—SS. Cyril and Methodius Regional Catholic Elementary School, Bethlehem. See separate listing.

6—ST. JOSEPH, (Slovenian), Rev. Robert Galinac, O.F.M.
Res., 416 E. Fifth St., 18015. Tel: 610-866-4102.
School—SS. Cyril and Methodius Regional Catholic Elementary School, Bethlehem. See separate listing.

7—NOTRE DAME OF BETHLEHEM, Lehigh Co., (1954), Rev. Msgr. Joseph E. Kurtz, M.Div.,L.S.W.; Revs. Paul Rothermel; Richard W. Campo; Deacons Lemuel Von Leer; Richard Sewald. In res., Rev. Bernard J. Ezaki.
Res., 1861 Catasauqua Rd., 18018-1298. Tel: 610-866-4371; Fax: 610-866-9065.
School—(Grades K-8) 1835 Catasauqua Rd., 18018. Tel: 610-866-2231. Sr. Patricia A. Cullen, S.S.J., Prin.
Sisters of St. Joseph 1; Lay Teachers 19; Students 421.
Catechesis/Religious Programs—Tel: 610-866-1418. Mrs. Marianne Grello, D.R.E.
Students 330.
Convent—1823 Catasauqua Rd., 18018. Tel: 610-866-4310.

8—OUR LADY OF PERPETUAL HELP, (1963), Rev. Msgr. Edward R. Sacks; Rev. John A. Frink; Deacon Bernard J. Salabsky, Jr. In res., Rev. Msgr. David J. Morrison.
Res., 3219 Santee Rd., 18017. Tel: 610-867-8409; Fax: 610-867-4870.
School—3221 Santee Rd., 18017. Tel: 610-868-6570; Fax: 610-868-7941.
Lay Teachers 11; Students 310.
Catechesis/Religious Programs—
Students 486.

9—OUR LADY OF POMPEII, (1902) (Italian), Rev. Msgr. Paul B. della Picca.
Res., 826 E. Fourth St., 18015. Tel: 610-691-0719; Fax: 610-691-0719.
School—SS. Cyril and Methodius Regional Catholic Elementary School, Bethlehem. See separate listing. Tel: 610-866-0042.

10—SS. SIMON AND JUDE, Lehigh Co., (1917), Revs. Robert J. Reed; David J. Loeper. In res., Rev. William N. Seifert.
Res., 730 W. Broad St., 18018. Tel: 610-866-5582; Fax: 610-866-2992.
School—(Grades K-8) 6th & North St., 18018. Tel: 610-867-9530. Sr. Lisa Ann Golden, I.H.M., Prin.
Sisters of the Immaculate Heart of Mary 5; Lay Teachers 7; Students 215.
Catechesis/Religious Programs—Tel: 610-861-7507. Mrs. Rose Seifert, D.R.E.
Students 245.
Convent—714 W. Broad St., 18018. Tel: 610-867-9546.

11—ST. STANISLAUS, (1906) (Polish), Rev. Frederick Przydzial.
Res., 429 Hayes St., 18015. Tel: 610-867-9323.
School—SS. Cyril and Methodius Regional Catholic Elementary School, Bethlehem. See separate listing.

Birdsboro, Berks Co., Immaculate Conception, Rev. Joseph A. Barnes; Deacon Lawrence J. Fessler.
Res., 640 Main St., 19508. Tel: 610-582-2411. [CEM]
School—St. Catharine of Siena Regional Catholic Elementary School, Birdsboro. See separate listing.

Boyertown, Berks Co., St. Columbkill (1921), Revs. Robert C. Quinn; Philip F. Rodgers.
Res., 200 Indian Spring Rd., 19512. Tel: 610-367-2371; Fax: 610-369-0242.
School—St. Francis Academy, Bally. See separate listing. Tel: 610-845-7364.
Catechesis/Religious Programs—Tel: 610-367-2371; Fax: 610-369-0242. D.R.E.: Sr. Nancy Kramer, S.S.J.; Constance Boyer.
Students 701.

Branchdale, Schuylkill Co., St. Mary Star of the Sea (1886), Rev. Edward J. O'Connor, M.Th., M.S.W.
Res., State Rd., 17923. Tel: 717-544-2592. [CEM]
School—Good Shepherd Regional Catholic Elementary School, Minersville. See separate listing. Tel: 717-544-3766.

Brockton, Schuylkill Co., St. Bartholomew (1846), Rev. Francis M. Grundowski.
Res., 214 Green St., Box 292, 17925. Tel: 717-668-1500. [CEM]
School—St. Jerome Regional Catholic Elementary, Tamaqua. See separate listing.

Catasauqua, Northampton Co., St. Andrew (1902), Rev. Stephen J. Radocha.
Mailing Address: 2174 Lincoln Ave., Northampton, 18067. Tel: 610-262-2559; Fax: 610-262-1613. [CEM]
Church—Third St. & Cypress St., North Catasauqua, 18032. Tel: 610-264-0612.
School—Our Lady of Hungary Regional Catholic Elementary School, Northampton. See separate listing.

Annunciation B.V.M. - St. Mary's, Lehigh Co., (1857) (German), Revs. John S. Mraz; Thomas M. Courtney.
Res., 122 Union St., 18032. Tel: 610-264-0332; Fax: 610-266-7133. [CEM]
Catechesis/Religious Programs—Tel: 610-264-9383.
Students 251.

St. Lawrence (Lehigh Co.) (1858), Rev. Joseph J. Campion. In res., Rev. Msgr. Francis C. Revak.
Res., 1001 Second St., 18032. Tel: 610-264-1972; Fax: 610-264-2105. [CEM]

Coaldale, Schuylkill Co., SS. Cyril and Methodius (1920) (Slovak), Rev. Francis J. Baransky.
Res., 41 E. Ruddle St., 18218. Tel: 717-645-4647. [CEM]
School—St. Michael Regional Catholic Elementary School, Lansford. See separate listing.

St. John the Baptist (1914) (Lithuanian), Rev. Francis J. Baransky.
Res., 41 E. Ruddle St., 18218. Tel: 717-645-4647. [JC]
School—St. Michael Regional Catholic Elementary School, Lansford. See separate listing.

St. Mary of the Assumption (1892), Rev. Francis J. Baransky.
Res., 41 E. Ruddle St., 18218. Tel: 717-645-4647. [JC]
School—St. Michael Regional Catholic Elementary School, Lansford. See separate listing.
Convent—231 Second St., 18218. Tel: 717-645-2310.

Colesville, Lehigh Co., Assumption B.V.M. (1927), Rev. Msgr. John J. Martin; Rev. James Finnegan, O.S.F.S.; Patricia Herbst, Pastoral Min.; Deacon Bernard M. Wisser.
Res., 4101 Old Bethlehem Pike, Bethlehem, 18015. Tel: 610-867-7424; Fax: 610-865-3021.
School—St. Michael the Archangel Regional Catholic Elementary School, Colesville-Limeport. See separate listing.
Catechesis/Religious Programs—Tel: 610-867-7424. D.R.E.: Christina M. Bigatel; Gina Kelechava.
Students 180.

Coplay, Lehigh Co., St. Peter (1927) (Austrian-Hungarian), Rev. Paul L. Bader; Deacon Michael J. Laroche. In res., Rev. Stephen F.X. Flynn, M.Ed.
Res., 4 S. Fifth St., 18037. Tel: 610-262-2417; Fax: 610-262-0211. [CEM]
School—Christ the King Regional Catholic Elementary School, Coplay, Whitehall. See separate listing. Tel: 610-262-5822.
Catechesis/Religious Programs—Tel: 610-262-2417. Deacon Michale J. Laroche, D.R.E.
Students 70.

Cumbola, Schuylkill Co., St. Anthony of Padua (1907) (Polish), Rev. Ronald C. Bocian.
Res., Market St., 17930. Tel: 717-277-0064. [CEM]
School—Holy Cross Regional Catholic Elementary School, New Philadelphia. See separate listing.

Easton, Northampton Co.,

1—ST. ANTHONY OF PADUA, (1909) (Italian), Rev. Msgr. William E. Handges; Revs. Edward S. Zemanik; Joseph D. Hulko; Deacon Charles A. DeBellis.
Res., 900 Washington St., 18042. Tel: 610-253-7188; Fax: 610-253-6184. [CEM]
School—Easton Catholic School, Easton. See separate listing. Tel: 610-252-1393; Fax: 610-253-6184.
Catechesis/Religious Programs—Tel: 610-253-7188; Fax: 610-253-6184. Mrs. Karen Donato, D.R.E.
Students 220.
Convent—770 Washington St., 18042. Tel: 610-258-7792.
Chapel—South Easton, St. Mary's.
Nursery School—138 E. Nesquehoning St., 18042. Tel: 610-242-4033.

2—ST. BERNARD, (1829), Revs. John J. Grabish; William J. Nahn; Deacons Henry Fleck, Jr.; Thomas C. Reichard. In res., Rev. Thomas J. Kessler.
Res., 132 S. Fifth St., 18042. Tel: 610-252-7381; Fax: 610-252-6757. [CEM][JC]
School—Easton Catholic School, Easton. See separate listing.
Catechesis/Religious Programs—Tel: 610-258-4548. Patricia Pierson, D.R.E.
Students 247.
Parish Center—123 S. Sixth St., 18042. Tel: 610-252-4387.

3—ST. JANE FRANCES DE CHANTAL, (1925), Rev. Msgr. Gerald Gobitas; Revs. John F. Sheridan; Edward Domin; Deacon Robert W. Rodgers.
Res., 1918 Washington Blvd., 18042. Tel: 610-253-3553; Fax: 610-253-5711. [JC]
Church—19th St. & Washington Blvd., 18042.
School—(Grades PreK-8) 1946 Washington Blvd., 18042. Tel: 610-253-8442.
Sisters of the Immaculate Heart of Mary 7; Lay Teachers 17; Students 514.
Catechesis/Religious Programs—Tel: 610-253-7794.
Students 470.
Convent—Tel: 610-253-4912.

4—ST. JOSEPH, (1852), Rev. Joseph A. Sheehan.
Res., 129 Davis St., 18042-6295. Tel: 610-252-0242. [CEM 2]
School—Easton Catholic School, Easton. See separate listing.
Catechesis/Religious Programs—Fax: 610-253-7558.
Students 78.

5—ST. MICHAEL, (1915) (Lithuanian), Rev. John J. Grabish; Deacons Thomas C. Reichard; Henry Fleck, Jr.
Res., 132 S. Fifth, 18042. Tel: 610-252-7381; Fax: 610-252-6757. [CEM]
School—Easton Catholic School, Easton. See separate listing.
Catechesis/Religious Programs—Students 78.

Ellengowan, Schuylkill Co., St. Aidan. Closed. Parish from November 1919 to July 9, 1948. Records at the Annunciation B.V.M. Church, Shenandoah.

Emmaus, Lehigh Co., St. Ann (1931), Rev. Msgr. Thomas E. Hoban; Revs. Robert P. George; Edmund J. Brennan; Deacon Richard B. Close.
Res., 415 S. Sixth St., 18049. Tel: 610-965-2426; Fax: 610-967-1099. [CEM]
School—(Grades PreK-8) 570 Wood St., 18049. Tel: 610-965-9220. Loretta Chapin, Prin.
Sisters 2; Lay Teachers 10; Students 325.
Catechesis/Religious Programs—Tel: 610-965-6888. Angela Faidley, D.R.E.
Students 540.
Convent—526 Fairview St., 18049. Tel: 610-965-6818.

Fountain Hill, Lehigh Co., St. Ursula (Bethlehem P.O.), Revs. Vincent P. York; Peter Jurcik; Joseph K. Kweder.
Res., 1300 Broadway, Bethlehem, 18015. Tel: 610-867-5122.
School—Holy Child Regional Catholic Elementary School, Bethlehem. See separate listing.

Frackville, Schuylkill Co., St. Ann (1924) (Polish), Rev. Dominik P. Kolota, M.Ed.; Deacon John A. Setlock.
Res., 7 S. Broad Mountain Ave., 17931. Tel: 717-874-0842; Fax: 717-874-2265.
School—Holy Family Regional Catholic Elementary School, Frackville. See separate listing. Tel: 717-874-0285.

Annunciation B.V.M. (1917) (Lithuanian), Rev. Dominik P. Kolota, M.Ed.; Deacon John A. Setlock. In res., Rev. David Kozak, J.C.L.
Res., 7 S. Broad Mountain Ave., 17931. Tel: 717-874-0842; Fax: 717-874-2265. [CEM]
School—Holy Family Regional Catholic Elementary School, Frackville. See separate listing. Tel:

717-874-0285.
Convent—25 S. Broad Mountain Ave., 17931. Tel: 717-874-0351.
St. Joseph (1909). St. Joseph's, Frackville administers over Our Lady of Siluva Parish, Maizeville. Rev. Albert J. Byrne; Deacon Joseph Burda.
Res., 14 N. Nice St., 17931. Tel: 717-874-0610; Fax: 717-874-0969. [CEM]
School—Holy Family Regional Catholic Elementary School, Frackville. See separate listing. Tel: 717-874-1921.
Catechesis / Religious Programs—Tel: 714-874-0610 7.
Students 169.

Girardville, Schuylkill Co., St. Joseph (1870), Rev. Anthony P. Mongiello.
Res., 211 W. Main St., 17935. Tel: 717-276-6239; Fax: 717-276-1444. [CEM]
School—Immaculate Heart Regional Catholic Elementary School, Girardville. See separate listing.
Catechesis / Religious Programs—Students 285.
St. Vincent de Paul (1907) (Lithuanian), Rev. David M. Liebner.
Res., 260 N. Second St., 17935. Tel: 717-276-6033. [CEM]
School—Immaculate Heart Regional Catholic Elementary School, Girardville. See separate listing.

Gordon, Schuylkill Co., Our Lady of Good Counsel (1922), Rev. James C. Bechtel.
Res., 220 W. Biddle St., 17936. Tel: 717-875-0774; Fax: 717-875-2443.
School—Immaculate Heart Regional Catholic Elementary School, Girardville. See separate listing. Tel: 717-276-6568.

Hamburg, Berks Co., St. Mary (1854), Rev. Joseph M. Braudis; Deacon Henry G. Gordon.
Res., 766 State St., 19526. Tel: 610-562-7657; Fax: 610-562-0379. [CEM]
Catechesis / Religious Programs—Parish Hall, 501 State St., 19526. Tel: 610-562-8110. Sr. Michele Fisher, C.S.F.N., D.R.E.
Students 246.
Station—Hamburg State School and Hospital, Tel: 610-562-6063.

Heckscherville, Schuylkill Co., St. Kieran, Rev. Walter J. Hall.
Res., R.D. No. 2, Box 2401, Pottsville, 17901. Tel: 717-544-4857. [CEM]
School—St. Elizabeth Ann Seton Regional Catholic Elementary School, Minersville. See separate listing.
Mission—Buck Run.

Hellertown, Northampton Co., St. Theresa of the Child Jesus, Rev. Msgr. Raymond F. Merman; Rev. Francis P. Straka.
Res., 1408 Easton Rd., 18055. Tel: 610-838-7045.
School—(Grades PreK-8) 300 Leonard St., 18055. Tel: 610-838-8161. Sr. Roseann Velas, O.S.F., Prin. Sisters of the Third Order of St. Francis 5; Lay Teachers 13; Students 244.
Catechesis / Religious Programs—Sr. S. M. Electa Barlok, O.S.F., D.R.E.
Students 141.
Convent—255 Wilson Ave., 18055. Tel: 610-838-7645.

Jim Thorpe, Carbon Co., Immaculate Conception, Rev. Msgr. John G. Chizmar, V.F.
Res., 180 W. Broadway, 18229. Tel: 717-325-2791. [CEM]
School—St. Joseph Regional Academy, Jim Thorpe. See separate listing.
St. Joseph (1871), Rev. John G. Hilferty.
Res., 526 North St., 18229. Tel: 717-325-3731; Fax: 717-325-2523. [CEM]
School—St. Joseph Regional Academy, Jim Thorpe. See separate listing. Tel: 717-325-3186.
Catechesis / Religious Programs—Tel: 717-722-0259; Fax: 717-325-2523.
Students 130.
Convent—27 W. Sixth St., 18229. Tel: 717-325-2212.

Kelayres, Schuylkill Co., Immaculate Conception (1899) (Italian), Rev. Robert A. Dressler.
Res., 33 Fourth St., P.O. Box G, 18231-0070. Tel: 717-929-3670. [CEM]
School—McAdoo Regional Catholic Elementary School, McAdoo. See separate listing.
Catechesis / Religious Programs—Students 35.

Kutztown, Berks Co., St. Mary (1919), Rev. Msgr. Walter T. Scheaffer.
Res., 236 E. Main St., 19530. Tel: 610-683-7443; 683-0740 (Church); Fax: 610-683-7625.
Catechesis / Religious Programs—Rose St. & Grimley St., 19530. Tel: 610-683-3797.
Students 361.

Lake Harmony, Carbon Co., St. Peter the Fisherman (1989), Rev. John A. Auchter.
Res., 27 Fawn Ct., P.O. Box 237, 18624. Tel: 717-722-2034; Fax: 717-722-2034.
Catechesis / Religious Programs—Students 155.

Lansford, Carbon Co., St. Ann, Rev. Stephen J. Halabura.
Res., 8 E. Bertsch St., 18232. Tel: 717-645-2575.
School—Our Lady of the Valley Regional Catholic Elementary School, Lansford-Summit Hill. See separate listing.
Convent—30 E. Bertsch St., 18232. Tel: 717-645-2750.
St. Michael (Slovak), Rev. Thomas A. Derzack.
Res., 124 E. Abbott St., 18232. Tel: 717-645-2282. [CEM]
School—St. Michael Regional Catholic Elementary School, Lansford. See separate listing.
Convent—124 E. Water St., 18232. Tel: 717-645-2484.
SS. Peter and Paul (Polish). Attended by St. Ann's Church. Rev. Stephen J. Halabura.
Mailing Address: 8 E. Bertsch St., 18232.
Church—225 W. Phillip St., Coaldale, 18218. Tel: 717-645-7605. [CEM]
School—St. Michael Regional Catholic Elementary School, Lansford. See separate listing.

Lehighton, Carbon Co., SS. Peter and Paul (1885), Rev. Robert J. McConaghy; Deacon William J. Wagner.
Res., 260 N. Third St., 18235-1595. Tel: 610-377-3690; Fax: 610-377-8881. [CEM]
School—307 Coal St., 18235. Tel: 610-377-4466. Mrs. Antoinette Collier, M.A., Prin.
Lay Teachers 6; Students 123.
Catechesis / Religious Programs—Students 105.

Limeport, Lehigh Co., St. Joseph (1926), Rev. Thomas R. Buckley.
Res., 5050 St. Joseph's Rd., 18060. Tel: 610-965-2877; Fax: 610-965-8317. [CEM]
School—St. Michael the Archangel Regional Catholic Elementary School, Colesville-Limeport. See separate listing. Tel: 610-965-4441; Fax: 610-965-1030.
Catechesis / Religious Programs—Students 221.

Lost Creek, Schuylkill Co., St. Mary Magdalen (1879), Rev. William H. Carter. In res., Rev. Charles J. Dene.
Res., P.O. Box 73, 17946. Tel: 717-462-1916. [JC]
School—Father Walter J. Ciszek Elementary School, Shenandoah. See separate listing. Tel: 717-462-9666.

McAdoo, Schuylkill Co.,
1—St. Kunegunda, (Polish), Rev. Joseph L. Grembocki.
Res., 36 E. Washington St., 18237. Tel: 717-929-2341; Fax: 717-929-2158. [CEM]
School—McAdoo Regional Catholic Elementary School, McAdoo. See separate listing. Tel: 717-929-1442.
2—St. Mary, (1893) (Slovak), Rev. Joseph Martinkovic (Slovakia).
Res., 101 E. Grant St., 18237. Tel: 717-929-1061. [CEM]
School—McAdoo Regional Catholic Elementary School, McAdoo. See separate listing.
3—St. Patrick, (1869) (Irish), Rev. David W. Karns.
Res., 17 N. Cleveland St., 18237. Tel: 717-929-1073. [CEM]
School—McAdoo Regional Catholic Elementary School, McAdoo. See separate listing. Tel: 717-929-1442.
4—St. Stephen of Hungary, (Hungarian). Attended by St. Kunegunda, McAdoo, 36 E. Washington St., 18237.

Mahanoy City, Schuylkill Co.,
1—Assumption B.V.M., (1892) (Slovak), Rev. William J. Maslar.
Res., 728 W. Centre St., 17948. Tel: 717-773-1990. [CEM]
School—Mahanoy City Regional Catholic Elementary School, Mahanoy City. See separate listing.
2—St. Canicus, (1862), Rev. William T. Campion; Deacon Ted Koval. In res., Rev. Robert J. Kuzmann.
Res., 22 S. Catawissa St., 17948. Tel: 717-773-0550; Fax: 717-775-0668. [CEM]
School—Mahanoy City Regional Catholic Elementary School, Mahanoy City. See separate listing.
3—St. Casimir, (1883) (Polish), Rev. Lawrence J. Bukaty.
Res., 113 S. Catawissa St., 17948. Tel: 717-773-2461. [CEM]
School—Mahanoy City Regional Catholic Elementary School, Mahanoy City. See separate listing. Tel: 717-773-2668.
Convent—300 W. Maple St., 17948. Tel: 717-773-1797.
4—St. Fidelis, (1863) (German), Rev. William T. Campion; Deacon Ted Koval. In res., Rev. Robert J. Kuzmann.
Res., 22 S. Catawissa St., 17948. Tel: 717-773-2850; Fax: 717-773-0668. [CEM]
School—Mahanoy City Regional Catholic Elementary School, Mahanoy City. See separate listing.
5—St. Joseph, (Lithuanian), Rev. Msgr. Anthony F. Wassel.
Res., 614 W. Mahanoy Ave., 17948. Tel: 717-773-2771. [CEM]
School—Mahanoy City Regional Catholic Elementary School, Mahanoy City. See separate listing.
6—Sacred Heart, (Italian), Rev. William J. Maslar.
Res., 728 W. Centre St., 17948. Tel: 717-773-1990. [CEM]
School—Mahanoy City Regional Catholic Elementary School, Mahanoy City. See separate listing.

Mahanoy Plane, Schuylkill Co., Holy Rosary. Closed. 1988. Parish records at St. Joseph's Church, Girardville.

Maizeville, Schuylkill Co., Our Lady of Siluva (Gilberton P.O.) (1907) (Lithuanian). (Formerly St. Louis). Rev. Albert J. Byrne.
Res., c/o 14 N. Nice St., Frackville, 17931. Tel: 717-874-0610; Fax: 717-874-0969. [CEM]

Martins Creek, Northampton Co., St. Rocco (1937), Rev. Msgr. Joseph P. Dooley.
Res., Box 421, 18063-0010. Tel: 610-258-9059; Fax: 610-258-4780.
School—Immaculate Conception Regional Catholic Elementary School, Pen-Argyl. See separate listing. Tel: 610-863-4816.
Catechesis / Religious Programs—Tel: 610-258-9059.
Students 72.

Miller Heights, Northampton Co., Sacred Heart of Jesus (1936), Rev. Thomas J. King; Deacon Hugh E. McShane. In res., Rev. James E. Sweeney.
Res., 1817 First St., Bethlehem, 18017. Tel: 610-865-5042; Fax: 610-865-1912.
School—(Grades K-8). Tel: 610-867-0221; Fax: 610-867-8351. Dr. Robert LaFrankie, Prin.
Lay Teachers 11; Students 274.
Catechesis / Religious Programs—Students 196.

Minersville, Schuylkill Co.,
1—St. Barbara, (1913) (Italian), Rev. Daniel J. Yenushosky; Deacon Cyril Roth.
Res., 320 Spruce St., 17954. Tel: 717-544-2234; Fax: 717-544-5043. [CEM]
School—Holy Redeemer Regional Catholic Elementary School, Minersville. No longer Holy Redeemer Regional Catholic Elementary School. Merged to form Good Shepherd Regional School, Minersville. See separate listing.
2—St. Francis of Assisi, (1895) (Lithuanian), Rev. Daniel J. Yenushosky; Deacon Cyril Roth.
Res., 320 Spruce St., 17954. Tel: 717-544-2234; Fax: 717-544-5043. [CEM]
School—Good Shepherd Regional School, (Grades PreK-3). No longer Holy Redeemer Regional Catholic Elementary School. Merged to form Good Shepherd Regional School, Minersville. 538 Sunbury St., 17954. Tel: 717-544-4560.
(Grades 4-8) 301 St. Francis St., 17954. Tel: 717-544-3766. Ms. Rosalie Novack, Prin.
Catechesis / Religious Programs—Tel: 717-544-2016. Sr. Catherine Therese, S.S.J., D.R.E.
Students 37.
Convent—300 Oak St., 17954. Tel: 717-544-4534. Sisters of St. Casimir
3—Our Lady of Mount Carmel, (1855) (German), Rev. John W. Bambrick.
Res., 519 School St., 17954. Tel: 717-544-2031; Fax: 717-544-4978. [CEM]
School—Good Shepherd Regional School, (Grades PreK-3) 538 Sunbury St., 17954. Tel: 717-544-4560. (Grades 4-8) 301 St. Francis St., 17954. Tel: 717-544-3766. Ms. Rosalie Novack, Prin.
Catechesis / Religious Programs—Students 350.
4—St. Stanislaus Kostka, (1905) (Polish), Rev. Leo J. Maletz.
Res., 139 Spruce St., 17954. Tel: 717-544-2211; Fax: 717-544-2317. [CEM 2]
School—Good Shepherd Regional School, (Grades PreK-3) 538 Sunbury St., 17954. Tel: 717-544-4560. (Grades 4-8) 301 St. Francis St., 17954. Tel: 717-544-3766. Ms. Rosalie Novack, Prin.
Catechesis / Religious Programs—Tel: 717-544-4360:2016.
Students 71.
5—St. Vincent de Paul, (1842), Rev. Msgr. John S. Campbell.
Res., 541 Sunbury St., 17954. Tel: 717-544-4741; Fax: 717-544-4742. [CEM 2]
School—Good Shepherd Regional Catholic School, Minersville. See separate listing under Regional Catholic Elementary Schools, Diocesan.
Catechesis / Religious Programs—Students 295.
Convent—534 Sunbury St., 17954. Tel: 717-544-2016. Sisters of St. Joseph

Mohnton, Berks Co., St. Benedict's (1955), Rev. Dennis T. Hartgen.
Res., R.D. 1, Box 1346, 19540. Tel: 610-856-1006; Fax: 610-856-1035.
School—LaSalle Academy, Shillington. See separate listing.
Catechesis / Religious Programs—Tel: 610-370-0199; 856-5146; Fax: 610-856-1035. Ms. Valerie

Christo, D.R.E.
Students 175.

Mount Carbon, Schuylkill Co., St. Francis de Sales (Pottsville P.O.), Rev. Edward B. Connolly.
Res., 49 Main St., Pottsville, 17901. Tel: 717-622-8270.
School—All Saints Regional Catholic Elementary School, Pottsville. See separate listing.

Nazareth, Northampton Co., Holy Family (1908), Revs. Norbert Weber, M.S.C.; John Schweikert, M.S.C.; Deacon Michael P. McGouldrick.
Res., 23 Forest Dr., 18064. Tel: 610-759-0870; Fax: 610-759-8507. [CEM 2]
School—(Grades PreK-8) 17 Convent Ave., 18064. Tel: 610-759-5642. Ms. Barbara Amabile, Prin.
Lay Teachers 18; Students 310.
Catechesis/Religious Programs—Tel: 610-759-7467. D.R.E.: Jeanine Breault; Eileen Boligitz.
Students 489.

Nesquehoning, Carbon Co., Immaculate Conception of B.V.M. (1914) (Slovak), Rev. Bruno M. Tucci.
Res., 15 E. Garibaldi Ave., 18240. Tel: 717-669-6321; Fax: 717-669-9440.
School—Our Lady of the Valley Regional Catholic Elementary School, Lansford-Summit Hill. See separate listing.

Our Lady of Mount Carmel (1913) (Italian), Rev. Bruno M. Tucci. In res., Rev. Donald J. Schaible.
Res., 15 E. Garibaldi Ave., 18240. Tel: 717-669-6321; Fax: 717-669-9440. [CEM]
School—Our Lady of the Valley Regional Catholic Elementary School, Lansford-Summit Hill. See separate listing.

Sacred Heart (1887), Revs. Paul P. Welkie, Pastor Emeritus; Edward W. Coleman.
Res., 81 W. High St., 18240. Tel: 717-669-9008; Fax: 717-669-5091. [CEM]
School—Our Lady of the Valley Regional Catholic Elementary School, Lansford-Summit Hill. See separate listing. Tel: 717-645-4700.

New Philadelphia, Schuylkill Co., Holy Family (1866), Rev. William J. O'Donnell.
Res., 99 Valley St., 17959. Tel: 717-277-6800. [CEM]
School—Holy Cross Regional Catholic Elementary School, New Philadelphia. See separate listing. Tel: 717-277-0197.

Sacred Heart (Lithuanian), Rev. James J. Lofton.
Res., 41 Clay St., 17959. Tel: 717-277-6815. [CEM]
School—Holy Cross Regional Catholic Elementary School, New Philadelphia. See separate listing.
Convent—47 Wiggan St., 17959. Tel: 717-277-6820.
Mission—Middleport, Immaculate Heart of Mary Chapel.

Newtown, Schuylkill Co., Sacred Heart (1896) (German), Rev. Edward J. O'Connor, M.Th., M.S.W.
Res., State Rd., Branchdale, 17923. Tel: 717-544-2592. [CEM]
School—Good Shepherd Regional School, (Grades PreK-3) 538 Sunbury St., Minersville, 17954. Tel: 717-544-4560.
(Grades 4-8) 301 St. Francis St., Minersville, 17954. Tel: 717-544-3766. Ms. Rosalie Novack, Prin.

Northampton, Northampton Co., Assumption of the Blessed Virgin Mary (1922), Rev. Stephen J. Radocha.
Res., 2174 Lincoln Ave., 18067. Tel: 610-262-2559; Fax: 610-262-1613. [CEM]
School—Our Lady of Hungary Regional Catholic Elementary School, Northampton. See separate listing.
Catechesis/Religious Programs—22nd & Washington Ave., 18067. Tel: 610-262-7343. Sr. Lorraine Molchanow, M.S.C., D.R.E.
Students 189.

St. Michael (1914) (Polish), Rev. John J. Pavlosky.
Res., 829 Main St., 18067. Tel: 610-262-2472; Fax: 610-262-2472. [JC]
School—Our Lady of Hungary Regional Catholic Elementary School, Northampton. See separate listing.

Our Lady of Hungary (German-Magyar), Revs. Edwin V. Schwartz; John J. L. Little. In res., Rev. Msgr. James J. Mulligan.
Res., 1324 Newport Ave., 18067. Tel: 610-262-2227. [CEM]
School—Our Lady of Hungary Regional Catholic Elementary School, Northampton. See separate listing.
Convent—1314 Newport Ave., 18067. Tel: 610-262-2427.

Orefield, Lehigh Co., St. Joseph The Worker (1948), Rev. Msgr. Robert J. Wargo; Rev. James J. Burdess; Sr. Mary Kathryn Quinn, S.S.J., Pastoral Assoc.; Deacons Daniel F. Metzker; Martin L. Koy; Charles A. Coyle. In res., Rev. Edward J. Donahue.
Res., 1879 Applewood Dr., 18069-9507. Tel: 610-395-2876; Fax: 610-395-2616.
Catechesis/Religious Programs—Tel: 610-395-7221. Mrs. Patricia Johnson, D.R.E.
Students 900.

Palmerton, Carbon Co., Sacred Heart (1908), Rev. Vincent I. Cronin; Deacons William P. Pitts; Andrew J. Mihalik.
Res., 243 Lafayette Ave., 18071-1597. Tel: 610-826-2335; Fax: 610-826-5360. [CEM]
School—St. John Neumann Regional Catholic Elementary School, Palmerton-Slatington. See separate listing.
Annex—252 Lafayette Ave., 18071. Tel: 610-826-2849.
Mission—Bowmanstown, Holy Cross.

Pen Argyl, Northampton Co., St. Elizabeth of Hungary (1929), Rev. Richard A. Schware. In res., Rev. Wayne E. Killian, M.A.
Res., 300 W. Babbitt Ave., P.O. Box 126, 18072. Tel: 610-863-4777. [CEM]
School—Immaculate Conception Regional Catholic Elementary School, Pen Argyl. See separate listing.
Catechesis/Religious Programs—Students 179.
Convent—111-115 Lobb Ave., 18072. Tel: 610-863-9214.
Mission—Wind Gap, Northampton Co., St. Joseph, Lehigh Ave. & Genoga Ave., 18072.

Port Carbon, Schuylkill Co., St. Stephen, Rev. John J. McNamara.
Res., 218 Valley St., 17965. Tel: 717-622-6600. [CEM]
School—214 Valley St., 17965.
Sisters of the Immaculate Heart of Mary 3; Lay Teachers 7; Students 183.
Convent—Tel: 717-622-1461.

Pottsville, Schuylkill Co.,

1—St. John the Baptist, (1841) (German), Rev. Gregory J. Tauber; Sr. Barbara J. Wojnicki, C.S.N.F., Pastoral Assoc.; Deacon Luis R. Visot.
Res., 913 Mahantongo St., 17901. Tel: 717-622-5470; Fax: 717-622-4589. [CEM 3]
School—All Saints Regional Catholic Elementary School, Pottsville. See separate listing.
Catechesis/Religious Programs—Lucilla Kochol, D.R.E.
Students 281.

2—St. Joseph, (Italian), Rev. Edward B. Connolly.
Res., 321 W. Howard Ave., 17901. Tel: 717-622-3081. [CEM]
School—All Saints Regional Catholic Elementary School, Pottsville. See separate listing.

3—Mary Queen of Peace, (1920), Rev. James J. Mihalak; Deacon Stephen Andrusisian.
Res., 728 N. Centre St., 17901. Tel: 717-622-7004; Fax: 717-622-4287.
School—All Saints Regional Catholic Elementary School, Pottsville. See separate listing. Tel: 717-622-0106.
Catechesis/Religious Programs—Peterine Wojcik, D.R.E.
Students 135.

4—St. Patrick, (1827), Rev. Msgr. William E. Jones, V.F.; Revs. Edward J. Essig, M.Div.; Frederick F. Sattler, M.Div. In res., Rev. Ronald P. Bowman.
Res., 319 Mahantongo St., 17901. Tel: 717-622-1802; Fax: 717-622-2593. [CEM]
Catechesis/Religious Programs—Students 244.
Convent—825 Mahantongo St., 17901. Tel: 717-622-0203.
Chapel—St. John Neumann, 2051 W. Norwegian St., 17901.

Reading, Berks Co.,

1—St. Anthony, (Lithuanian). Attended by St. Peter, 322 S. Fifth St., 16902. Tel.: 610-372-9652.

2—St. Anthony of Padua, (1914) (Polish), Rev. Richard E. Nachajski; Sr. Mary Joy Wasnesky, O.S.F., Pastoral Assoc.
Res., 501 Summit Ave., 19611. Tel: 610-374-1539; Fax: 610-374-0263.
School—LaSalle Academy & Early Childhood Center, Shillington. See separate listing.
Catechesis/Religious Programs—Students 63.
Convent—234 Grace St., 19611. Tel: 610-372-8578.

3—St. Catharine of Siena, (1925), Rev. Msgr. Joseph P.T. Smith; Revs. Anthony M. Drouncheck; Richard H. Clement; Deacons George J. Faller; Richard A. Horst. In res., Rev. Paul L. Rothermel.
Res., 2427 Perkiomen Ave., 19606. Tel: 610-779-4005; Fax: 610-779-0859.
Church—4975 Boyertown Pike, 19606. Tel: 610-779-4090.
School—St. Catharine of Siena Regional Catholic Elementary School, Reading. See separate listing. Tel: 610-779-5810.
Catechesis/Religious Programs—Tel: 610-779-5810.
Students 440.
Convent—2328 Perkiomen Ave., 19606. Tel: 610-779-5583.

4—SS. Cyril and Methodius, (1895) (Slovak), Rev. Charles S. Sperlak; Deacon John J. Allison.
Res., 449 S. Sixth St., 19602. Tel: 610-373-0627.
Convent—502 S. Sixth St., 19602. Tel: 610-375-8001.

5—Holy Guardian Angels, (1929), Rev. Msgr. Francis X. Barrett; Revs. Kevin P. Gallagher; Richard J. Ford.
Res., 3121 Kutztown Rd., 19605. Tel: 610-921-2729; Fax: 610-921-8886.
School—(Grades PreK-8) 3125 Kutztown Rd., 19605. Tel: 610-929-4124. Mr. Philip Fromuth, Prin.
Lay Teachers 10; Students 301.
Catechesis/Religious Programs—Sr. Kathleen White, M.S.C., D.R.E.
Students 322.
Mission—Temple, Berks Co., St. Anthony, 8th & Columbus, Temple, 19560.

6—Holy Rosary, (1904) (Italian), Rev. Msgr. Felix A. Losito; Rev. Andrew A. Ulincey, P.A.; Deacon Lawrence A. Dudeck.
Res., 237 Franklin St., 19602. Tel: 610-373-5579; Fax: 610-372-0130.
School—Cabrini Academy, (Grades PreK-8) 240 Franklin St., 19602. Tel: 610-374-8483.
Sisters 6; Lay Teachers 9; Students 300.
Catechesis/Religious Programs—Students 102.
Convent—234 Franklin St., 19602. Tel: 610-375-9072.
Mission—Reading, Berks Co., Holy Rosary Chapel, Schuylkill Ave., 19601. Tel: 610-376-4383.

7—St. Joseph, (1891), Revs. Thomas D. Baddick; Thomas G. Shanfelt; Deacon Peter LaFata.
Res., 1018 N. Eighth St., 19604. Tel: 610-376-2976; Fax: 610-376-2825.
School—(Grades K-8) 1040 N. Eighth St., 19604. Tel: 610-374-2951. Sr. Eileen Therese Gillespie, Prin.
Sisters of the Immaculate Heart of Mary 3; Lay Teachers 7; Students 185.
Catechesis/Religious Programs—Students 80.
Convent—Tel: 610-372-1302.

8—St. Margaret, (1920), Revs. Francis T. Gillespie; Ronald J. Yarrosh; Michael E. Ahrensfield; Deacon John P. Konopelski.
Res., 925 Centre Ave., 19601. Tel: 610-376-2919.
School—(Grades K-8) 233 Spring St., 19601. Tel: 610-375-1882. Sr. Diane Licordare, Prin.
Servants of Immaculate Heart of Mary 2; Lay Teachers 9; Students 238.
Catechesis/Religious Programs—William Davis, D.R.E.
Students 217.
Convent—233 Spring St., 19601. Tel: 610-372-1302.

9—St. Mary, (1888) (Polish), Rev. Leo S. Stajkowski. In res., Rev. Donald W. Cieniewicz.
Res., 250 S. 12th St., 19602. Tel: 610-376-6321; Fax: 610-376-1378. [CEM]
School—1200 Spruce St., 19602. Tel: 610-375-9311; Fax: 610-375-1298.
Lay Teachers 12; Students 140.

10—St. Paul, (1860), Rev. Msgr. John P. Seitzinger; Rev. Theodore S. Macunas.
Mailing Address: P.O. Box 13455, 19612-3455. Tel: 610-372-1531; Fax: 610-372-7478.
Res., 151 N. Ninth St., 19601. [CEM]

11—St. Peter, (1752) (Spanish American), Revs. Charles A. Marciano; John M. Gibbons; Deacons Jesus Centeno; Mariano Torres; Francisco Colon; Julio Colon; Fernando L. Torres; Leopoldo Alvarado. In res., Rev. Thomas J. Orsulak.
Res., 322 S. Fifth St., 19602. Tel: 610-372-9652; Fax: 610-374-3351. [CEM]
School—218 S. Fifth St., 19602. Tel: 610-374-2447.
Sisters of the Immaculate Heart of Mary 5; Lay Teachers 7; Students 224.
Catechesis/Religious Programs—Students 210.
Convent—Tel: 610-373-6185.

Ringtown, Schuylkill Co., St. Mary (1923), Rev. Victor J. Anselmi.
Res., 86 N. Center St., 17967. Tel: 717-889-3850. [CEM]
School—Father Walter J. Ciszek Elementary School, Shenandoah. See separate listing.
Catechesis/Religious Programs—Students 62.

Robesonia, Berks Co., St. Francis de Sales (1982), Rev. James P. Byrne, O.S.F.S.; Deacon Leonard F. Cain; Sr. Carolyn Ackerman, M.S.C., Pastoral Assoc.
Res., 321 N. Church St., 19551. Tel: 610-693-5851; Fax: 610-693-5852.
Catechesis/Religious Programs—Students 195.

Roseto, Northampton Co., Our Lady of Mt. Carmel (1897) (Italian), Revs. George E. Krock, C.M.; James G. Prior, C.M. In res., Rev. Daniel Renaldo, C.M.
Res., P.O. Box 422, 18013. Tel: 610-588-2183. [CEM 2]
School—Our Lady of Mt. Carmel Regional Catholic Elementary School, Roseto. See separate listing. Tel: 610-588-2629.
Catechesis/Religious Programs—Students 342.

Convent—80 Ridge St., 18013. Tel: 610-588-2906.

Saint Clair, Schuylkill Co.,

1—St. Boniface, (1854) (German), Rev. Francis P. Schoenauer.
Res., 250 E. Hancock St., 17970. Tel: 717-429-0701; Fax: 717-429-0630. [CEM]
School—St. Stephen Regional Catholic School, Port Carbon. See separate listing. Tel: 717-622-3063; Fax: 717-622-3689.

2—St. Casimir, (Lithuanian), Rev. Ronald V. Jankaitis.
Res., 441 S. Nichols St., 17970. Tel: 717-429-2400. [CEM]
School—Saint Clair Regional Catholic Elementary School, Saint Clair. See separate listing.

3—Immaculate Conception, (1905) (Slovak), Rev. Paul E. Masiar.
Res., Caroline Ave., Diener's Hill, 17970-1361. Tel: 717-429-1315; Fax: 717-429-0369. [CEM]

4—St. Mary, (1864), Rev. Francis P. Schoenauer; Deacon John F. Pogash. In res., Rev. Bernard A. Flanagan.
Res., 250 E. Hancock St., 17970. Tel: 717-429-0701; Fax: 717-424-0630. [CEM 2]
School—St. Stephen Regional Catholic School, Port Carbon. See separate listing. Tel: 717-622-3063; Fax: 717-622-3689.
Catechesis/Religious Programs—Tel: 717-429-1621.
Students 150.

5—SS. Peter and Paul, (1918) (Polish), Rev. Francis P. Schoenauer.
Res., 216 N. Mill St., 17970. Tel: 717-429-0370; Fax: 717-429-0630. [CEM]
School—St. Stephen Regional Catholic School, Port Carbon. See separate listing. Tel: 717-622-3063; Fax: 717-622-3689.

Schuylkill Haven, Schuylkill Co., St. Ambrose (1851), Revs. Michael J. Stone; Eric J. Gruber. In res., Rev. William F. Glosser.
Res., 201 Randel St., 17972. Tel: 717-385-1031; Fax: 717-385-1035. [CEM]
School—(Grades PreK-8) 302 Randel St., 17972. Tel: 717-385-2377. Mary Lou Casserly, Prin.
Lay Teachers 10; Students 203.
Catechesis/Religious Programs—Sr. Dolorita C.S.F.N., D.R.E.
Students 355.
Station—Schuylkill County Hospital and Home for Aged.

Shenandoah, Schuylkill Co.,

1—Annunciation, (1870), Revs. William H. Carter; James F. Gaffney.
Res., 218 W. Cherry St., 17976. Tel: 717-462-1916. [CEM]
School—Father Walter J. Ciszek Elementary School, Shenandoah. See separate listing. Tel: 717-462-9666.
Convent—229 W. Cherry St., 17976. Tel: 717-462-1024.

2—St. Casimir, (Polish), Rev. Edward W. Sarzynski.
Res., 108 W. Cherry St., 17976. Tel: 717-462-1968. [CEM]
School—St. Casimir-St. Stanislaus Regional Catholic Elementary School, Shenandoah. See separate listing.
Convent—233 N. Jardin St., 17976. Tel: 717-462-0877.

3—St. George, (1891) (Lithuanian), Revs. Robert J. Potts; Ronald J. Oranczak.
Res., 129 S. Jardin St., 17976. Tel: 717-462-1989; Fax: 717-462-1980. [CEM 5]
School—Father Walter J. Ciszek Elementary School, Shenandoah. See separate listing.

4—Holy Family, (1870-1934). Closed. Records kept at Annunciation Church, Shenandoah.

5—Our Lady of Mt. Carmel, (1914) (Italian), Revs. Robert J. Potts; Ronald J. Oranczak.
Res., 129 S. Jardin St., 17976. Tel: 717-462-1989; Fax: 717-462-1980. [CEM]
School—Father Walter J. Ciszek Elementary School, Shenandoah. See separate listing.

6—St. Stanislaus, (Polish), Rev. Edward W. Sarzynski.
Res., 108 W. Cherry St., 17976. Tel: 717-462-1968. [CEM]
School—Father Walter J. Ciszek Elementary School, Shenandoah. See separate listing.

7—St. Stephen, (1899) (Slovak), Rev. Victor J. Anselmi.
Res., 18 E. Oak St., 17976. Tel: 717-462-0331. [CEM]
School—Father Walter J. Ciszek Elementary School, Shenandoah. See separate listing. Tel: 717-462-9666.

Sheppton, Schuylkill Co., St. Joseph (1894), Rev. Raymond P. Slezak.
Res., E. Oak St., 18248. Tel: 717-384-4102; Fax: 717-384-4757. [CEM]
Mission—Oneida, Schuykill, St. John the Baptist, P.O. Box 118, 18248.

Shillington, Berks Co., St. John Baptist de la Salle (1948), Rev. Msgr. Thomas J. Birch, Pastor Emeritus; Rev. David C. Gillis; Deacon Sylvester F. Simchick; Rev. Christopher L. Wakefield. In res., Rev. Robert T. Finlan, Jr.
Res., 400 Holland St., 19607. Tel: 610-777-1697; Fax: 610-777-4468.
School—LaSalle Academy, Shillington. See separate listing.
Catechesis/Religious Programs—Bernadette H. Yohn, D.R.E.
Students 348.

Sinking Spring, Berks Co., St. Ignatius Loyola (1965), Rev. Msgr. James A. Treston, V.F.; Revs. Richard C. Brensinger; Francis J. McNelis; Deacons John A. Coffin; John W. Murphy, Jr.
Res., 2810 St. Alban's Dr., 19608-1028. Tel: 610-678-3767; Fax: 610-678-4483.
School—(Grades PreK-8). Tel: 610-678-0111; Fax: 610-670-5795. Mrs. Janice Bayerle, Prin.
Sisters of the Third Order of St. Francis 2; Lay Teachers 27; Students 606.
Catechesis/Religious Programs—2710 St. Alban's Dr., Reading, 19609. Tel: 610-678-0676.
Students 522.
Convent—2601 St. Alban's Dr., West Lawn, 19609. Tel: 610-678-2769.

Slatington, Lehigh Co., Assumption B.V.M. (1883). Unassigned.
Res., 633 W. Washington St., 18080. Tel: 610-767-2214; Fax: 610-767-2702. [CEM]
School—St. John Neumann Regional Catholic Elementary School, Palmerton-Slatington. See separate listing. Tel: 610-767-2935.
Catechesis/Religious Programs—Students 91.

Summit Hill, Carbon Co., St. Joseph (1850), Rev. James J. Ward; Sr. Mary Florence, R.S.M., Pastoral Assoc.; Deacon Andrew J. Mihalik, Jr.
Res., 118 N. Market St., 18250. Tel: 717-645-2664. [CEM]
School—Our Lady of the Valley Regional Catholic Elementary School, Lansford-Summit Hill. See separate listing.
Catechesis/Religious Programs—Students 107.

St. Stanislaus (1924) (Polish), Rev. James J. Ward; Sr. Mary Florence, R.S.M., Pastoral Assoc.; Deacon Andrew J. Mihalik, Jr.
Res., 118 N. Market St., 18250. Tel: 717-645-3037.
School—Our Lady of the Valley Regional Catholic Elementary School, Lansford-Summit Hill. See separate listing.

Tamaqua, Schuylkill Co., St. Jerome (1833), Revs. Robert R. Fagan; Henry E. Strassner. In res., Rev. Donald J. Schaible.
Res., 266 W. Broad St., 18252. Tel: 717-668-2301; Fax: 717-668-4406.
School—250 W. Broad St., 18252. Tel: 717-668-2757.
Sisters of the Immaculate Heart of Mary 3; Lay Teachers 8; Students 215.
Catechesis/Religious Programs—Tel: 717-668-4416.
Students 211.
Convent—Tel: 717-668-2730.
Mission—Coaldale, Schuylkill Co., St. Patrick (Seek), Miner St., Coaldale, 18218. [CEM][JC 2]

SS. Peter and Paul (1911) (Lithuanian), Rev. William J. Linkchorst.
Res., 307 Pine St., 18252. Tel: 717-668-1150. [CEM]

Tower City, Schuylkill Co., SS. Peter and Paul (1896), Rev. Francis J. Opps.
Res., 825 E. Grand Ave., 17980. Tel: 717-647-9472.
School—St. Elizabeth Ann Seton Regional Catholic Elementary School, Minersville. See separate listing.
Catechesis/Religious Programs—Students 97.

Tremont, Schuylkill Co., Immaculate Conception (1853), Rev. James R. Brady; Deacon William Ahrensfield.
Res., 113 Clay St., P.O. Box 35, 17981. Tel: 717-695-3648. [CEM]
School—Good Shepherd Regional School, (Grades PreK-3) 538 Sunbury St., Minersville, 17954. Tel: 717-544-4560.
(Grades 4-8) 301 St. Francis St., Minersville, 17954. Tel: 717-544-3766. Ms. Rosalie Novack, Prin.
Catechesis/Religious Programs—Margaret Stine, D.R.E.
Students 113.

Tresckow, Carbon Co., St. Bartholomew (Italian), Rev. John L. Ondic.
Res., 49 E. Maple St., P.O. Box 238, 18254-0238. Tel: 717-455-0922.
School—McAdoo Regional Catholic Elementary School, McAdoo. See separate listing.

St. Michael, Rev. John Ondic.
Res., 18 S. Chestnut St., 18254. Tel: 717-454-2802. [CEM]
School—McAdoo Regional Catholic Elementary School, McAdoo. See separate listing.

Tuscarora, Schuylkill Co., St. Bertha (1922), Rev. Francis M. Grundowski; Deacon Leo F. Keenan.
Res., 214 Green St., Brockton, 17925. Tel: 717-668-1500. [CEM]
Church—710 Broad St., P.O. Box 245, 17982. Tel: 717-668-4465.
School—St. Jerome Regional Catholic Elementary School, Tamaqua. See separate listing.

Weatherly, Carbon Co., St. Nicholas (1874), Rev. William J. Onushco; Deacon Raymond W. Wilkinson.
Res., 318 Plane St., 18255. Tel: 717-427-4123; Fax: 717-427-4615. [CEM 2][JC]
School—McAdoo Regional Catholic Elementary School, McAdoo. See separate listing. Tel: 717-929-1442.
Catechesis/Religious Programs—Students 83.
Station—Weatherwood, Carbon County District Home, Tel: 717-427-8683.

West Bangor, Northampton Co., St. Roch (1937), Rev. Msgr. Charles T. Moss. In res., Rev. Joseph A. DeSantis.
Res., 1141 Verona Dr., Pen Argyl, 18072. Tel: 610-863-9055; Fax: 610-863-5971. [CEM]
School—Immaculate Conception Regional Catholic Elementary School, Pen Argyl. See separate listing.

West Reading, Berks Co., Sacred Heart (1917) (German), Revs. James J. Reichert; Joseph J. Whalen; David J. Fick; E. Jerry Yoder, Admin.; Deacon William R. Kase.
Res., Lakeview Dr. and Cherry St., P.O. Box 6217, Reading, 19610. Tel: 610-372-4010; Fax: 610-372-4926.
School—701 Franklin St., 19611. Tel: 610-373-3316. Dr. Richard Flannery, Prin.
Lay Teachers 11; Students 181.
Catechesis/Religious Programs—Tel: 610-374-5430. Valerie Christo, D.R.E.
Students 231.

Whitehall, Lehigh Co., Holy Trinity (1928), Rev. Msgr. Ronald W. Gainer; Rev. Msgr. Stanley T. Sosnowski; Deacon Eugene J. Wyrwa.
Res., 4102 S. Church St., 18052. Tel: 610-262-9315.
School—Christ the King Regional Catholic Elementary School, Coplay, Whitehall. See separate listing.
Catechesis/Religious Programs—Mrs. Carole C. Chuk, D.R.E.
Students 262.

St. Elizabeth (1941), Rev. Msgr. Anthony D. Muntone, V.G.; Rev. Victor F. Finelli; Deacon Alexander L. Maggitti, Sr. In res., Rev. James M. Torpey.
Res., 618 Fullerton Ave., 18052. Tel: 610-266-0695; Fax: 610-266-1548.
School—(Grades PreK-8) 431 Pershing Blvd., 18052. Tel: 610-264-0143. Sr. Helen Ann Sharkey, R.S.M., Prin.
Sisters of Mercy 1; Lay Teachers 11; Students 264.
Catechesis/Religious Programs—Mrs. Carol O'Connor, D.R.E.
Students 175.

St. John the Baptist (1927), Rev. Francis J. Schuster, K.H.S.
Res., 3024 S. Ruch St., 18052. Tel: 610-262-2260. [CEM]
School—Christ the King Regional Catholic Elementary School, Coplay, Whitehall. See separate listing.
Catechesis/Religious Programs—Tel: 610-262-4177. Sr. Mary Dolora, D.R.E.
Students 75.

Chaplains of Public Institutions

Allentown. *Good Shepherd Home*. (St. Paul).
Lehigh County Prison. (Sacred Heart).
Lehigh Valley Hospital at 17th St. (St. Catharine of Siena).
Lehigh Valley Hospital at Cedar Crest. (St. Thomas More). Rev. Joseph P. Becker, O.S.F.S.; Deacon Richard B. Close.
Liberty Nursing Center. (St. Catharine of Siena).
Luthercrest. (St. Joseph, Orefield).
Osteopathic Hospital. (St. Catharine of Siena).
Phoebe Devitt Home. (St. Catharine of Siena).
State Hospital. (Our Lady Help of Christians).
Westminster Village. (Our Lady Help of Christians).

Ashland. *Ashland State Hospital*. Administered by St. Mauritius, Ashland; St. Joseph, Ashland; St. Joseph, Girardville; St. Vincent de Paul, Girardville.

Bethlehem. *Leader Nursing & Rehab Centers*. (Notre Dame of Bethlehem).

Lutheran Manor. (Notre Dame of Bethlehem).
Muhlenberg Medical Center. (Notre Dame of Bethlehem).
Muhlenberg Rehab Center. (Notre Dame of Bethlehem).
COALDALE. *Coaldale State Hospital*. Administered by SS. Cyril & Methodius, Coaldale; St. Michael, Lansford; St. Stanislaus, Summit Hill; SS. Peter and Paul, Lansford. Rev. Paul E. Masiar.
EASTON. *Easton Hospital*. (Priests of Easton Area).
Northampton County Prison. (St. Bernard). Deacon Robert W. Rodgers.
FOUNTAIN HILL. *Cedarbrook*. (Lehigh County Home) St. Ursula.
FRACKVILLE. *State Prison*. Rev. Ronald P. Bowman.
HAMBURG. *Hamburg State School and Hospital*. (St. Mary).
LEHIGHTON. *Gnaden Huetten Memorial Hospital*. (SS. Peter and Paul).
Gnaden Huetten Nursing Home. (SS. Peter & Paul).
Mahoning Valley Nursing Home. (SS. Peter & Paul).
MINERSVILLE. *FCI-Schuylkill, Federal Correctional Institute*. Rev. Charles J. Dene.
NAZARETH. *Gracedale*. (Northampton County Home) Holy Family. Deacon Michael P. McGouldrick.
NEW TRIPOLI. *Zimmerman Country Homestead*. (St. Joseph, Orefield).
ORWIGSBURG. *Orwigsburg Manor*. (St. Ambrose, Schuylkill Haven).
PALMERTON. *Palmerton Hospital*. (Sacred Heart).
PINEBROOK. *Personal Care Center*. (St. Ambrose, Schuylkill).
POTTSVILLE. *Leader Nursing Home*. (Mary, Queen of Peace).
Pottsville Hospital and Warne Clinic. Sr. Marjorie S.S.J., Chap.
Schuylkill County Prison. (Mary, Queen of Peace).
READING. *Community Hospital*. (St. Peter).
Reading Hospital. (Sacred Heart). Deacon John P. Konopelski.
SCHUYLKILL HAVEN. *Rest Haven County Home*. (St. Ambrose).
TREXLERTOWN. *Mosser Nursing Home*. (St. Joseph, Orefield).
WEATHERWOOD. *Carbon County District Home*. (St. Nicholas, Weatherly).
WERNERSVILLE. *Berks County Prison*. (St. Ignatius Loyola, Reading; St. Joseph, Reading; St. Peter, Reading).
Berksheim. (Berks County Home; St. Ignatius Loyola, Reading).
State Hospital. Deacons Richard A. Horst; John J. Allison.
WESCOSVILLE. *Lehigh County Home*. (Cedarbrook) St. Catharine of Siena, Allentown.

Special Assignment:
Reverend Fathers—
Coyle, Edward J., Bishop's Residence, 2920 Chew St., Allentown, PA 18104

On Duty Outside the Diocese:
Reverend Monsignors—
Bartkus, Algimantas A., Pontificio Collegio Lituano, Via Casal Monferrato, Rome, 00182 Italy
Benestad, Thomas J., The Papal Foundation, 222 N. 17th St., Philadelphia, PA 19103
Callaghan, Aloysius R., Moderator of the Curia & Chancellor, Archdiocese for the Military Services, P.O. Box 4469, Washington, DC 20017-0469
Klinger, Nevin J., Congregation for Divine Worship and Discipline of the Sacraments, Piazza Pio XII, 10, Rome, 00193 Italy
Reverend Fathers—
Baker, William T., Casilla 919, Santa Cruz, Bolivia
Beers, John Michael, S.S.L., Ph.D., Mt. St. Mary's Seminary, Emmitsburg, MD 21727-7797
Donahue, Edward J., Bishop Moore High School, 3901 Edgewater Dr., Orlando, FL 32804
Fanti, Joseph J.
Henry, Donald H., St. John the Evangelist, 10631 Regent Circle, Naples, FL 33942

Military Chaplains:
Reverend Fathers—
Connolly, James M., Dept. of the Navy, Religious Ministries Dept., U.S.S. Enterprise (CVN65), FPO AE 09543-2810
Czartorynski, David F., PSC 88 Box 2076, APO, AE, NJ 09821
Thomas, James J., Chap. Major USAF, PSC 78, Box 3384, APO, AP 96326-3384

Graduate Studies:
Reverend Fathers—
Baker, Andrew R., Casa Santa Maria Via dell' Umilta, 30, Roma, 00187 Italia

Unassigned:
Reverend Fathers—
Bender, Thomas J.
Conte, John P.
Czaus, Joseph C.
Galko, Joseph
Kean, Joseph H.
Kerestus, Thomas J.
Soderlund, David

Retired:
Reverend Monsignors—
Birch, Thomas J., 1315 Penn Forest Streams, Jim Thorpe, PA, PA 18229
Coll, Robert J., P.O. Box 1363, Marco, FL 34145
Messaros, Michael F., Fairways at Brookside, 2866 Whitemarsh Pl., Macungie, PA 18062
Reverend Fathers—
Carr, James M., Holy Family Villa, 1325 Prospect Ave., Bethlehem, PA 18018
Carroll, Joseph D., Holy Family Villa, 1325 Prospect Ave., Bethlehem, PA 18018
Edwards, Thomas L., Precious Blood Convent, P.O. Box 97, Reading, PA 19607
Flynn, Stephen F.X., St. Peter Rectory, 4 S. Fifth St., Coplay, PA 18037
Fox, Francis J., 331 Florida Ave., Whitehall, PA 18052
Graff, Edward R., P.O. Box 47, Silverton, TX 79257
Horan, Thomas A., 125 E. Main St., Girardville, PA 17935
Jones, William P., Holy Family Villa, 1325 Prospect Ave., Bethlehem, PA 18018
Luszczak, Francis J., 735 N. Kearney St., Allentown, PA 18103
McKenna, F. Charles, Holy Family Villa, 1325 Prospect Ave., Bethlehem, PA 18018
McNulty, Charles L., Holy Family Villa, 1325 Prospect Ave., Bethlehem, PA 18018
Nave, Francis R., Holy Family Villa, 1325 Prospect Ave., Bethlehem, PA 18018
Paskowicz, Marian, 611 Caroline Dr., Norristown, PA 19401
Rapczynski, Joseph B., Holy Family Villa, 1325 Prospect Ave., Bethlehem, PA 18018
Romagno, Michael, Holy Family Manor, 1200 Spring St., Bethlehem, PA 18018
Sverchek, Michael P., 70 W. Juniper St., Box 301, Hazleton, PA 18201
Sweeney, James E., 1817 First St., Miller Heights, PA 18017
Vandergeest, Peter J., 1008 Hemlock Pl., Huntington Valley, PA 19006
Welkie, Paul P., Lake Hauto, R.R.1 Lake Dr., P.O. Box 34, Nesquehoning, PA 18240-0034

Permanent Deacons:
Ahrensfield, William L., Immaculate Conception, Tremont
Allison, John J., Wernersville State Hospital & SS. Cyril and Methodius, Reading
Alvarado, Leopoldo, Spanish Apostolate, Berks County & St. Peter, Reading
Amedeo, Dominick F., Sacred Heart & Our Lady of Mt. Carmel, Allentown
Andrusisian, Stephen, Mary, Queen of Peace, Pottsville
Bankos, Gregory J., Assumption B.V.M., Northampton, St. Andrew, Catasauqua, & Pro-Life Office, Bethlehem
Bogusky, Joseph H., Annunciation B.V.M., Catasauqua
Buragino, Joseph G., St. Ursula, Bethlehem
Burda, Joseph R., St. Joseph, Frackville
Cain, Leonard, St. Francis de Sales, Robesonia
Centeno, Jesus, Spanish Apostolate, Berks Co. & St. Peter, Reading
Chiles, Franklin J., Holy Ghost, Bethlehem
Chin-Fatt, Arthur L., St. Francis of Assisi, Allentown
Close, Richard B., Lehigh Valley Hospital Center, Allentown & St. Ann, Emmaus
Coffin, John A., St. Ignatius Loyola, Sinking Spring
Colon, Francisco, Hispanic Apostolate, Berks Co. & St. Peter, Reading
Colon, Julio, Hispanic Apostolate, Berks Co. & St. Peter, Reading
Cosgrove, Francis J., Office of the Permanent Diaconate & St. Anne, Bethlehem
Costa, Joseph J., Our Lady of Siluva, Gilberton
Coyle, Charles A., Our Lady Help of Christians, Allentown
Cuevas, Rafael, Spanish Apostolate, Lehigh Co. & Holy Infancy, Bethlehem
Cummings, John D., Tribunal, Allentown
Danyi, Frank J., SS. Cyril and Methodius, Bethlehem
de Bellis, Charles A., St. Anthony of Padua, Easton
de Jesus, Jaime, Hispanic Apostolate, Lehigh Co. & Sacred Heart of Jesus, Allentown
de Jesus, Roberto, Spanish Apostolate, Northampton County & Holy Infancy, Bethlehem
Dudeck, Larry, Holy Rosary, Reading
Duncan, James R., Diocesan Tribunal & St. Thomas More, Allentown
Faller, George J., St. Catharine of Siena, Mt. Penn
Fessler, Lawrence J., Immaculate Conception, Birdsboro
Fleck, Henry, Jr., St. Bernard, Easton
Giltrap, James F., St. Joseph, Limeport
Godiska, Joseph F., Our Lady of Hungary, Northampton
Gonzalez, Jose, Spanish Apostolate, Lehigh Co. & Sacred Heart, Allentown
Gordon, Henry G., St. Mary, Hamburg
Gousie, Joseph N., Sr., St. Joseph, Reading
Horst, Richard A., St. Catharine of Siena, Reading & Wernersville State Hospital, Wernersville
Hunkele, Thomas H., Precious Blood Convent, Shillington
Jaccodine, Ralph J., St. Catharine of Siena, Allentown
Kase, William R., Holy Name High School, Reading & Sacred Heart, West Reading
Keenan, Leo F., Jr., St. Bertha, Tuscarora & St. Bartholomew, Brockton
Konopelski, John P., Reading Hospital & St. Margaret, Reading
Koval, Edward P., State Correctional Facility, Frackville & St. Canicus and St. Fidelis, Mahanoy City
Koy, Martin L., St. Joseph the Worker, Orefield
Lafata, Peter M., St. Joseph, Reading
Laroche, Michael J., St. Peter, Coplay
Maggitti, Alexander L., Sr., St. Elizabeth, Whitehall & St. Francis Center, Orwigsburg
Matos, Rodoberto, Spanish Apostolate, Northampton Co. & Holy Infancy, Bethlehem; St. Bernard, Easton
McGouldirck, Michael P., Gracedale County Home & Holy Family, Nazareth
McManus, Robert J., St. Mauritius & St. Joseph, Ashland
McShane, Hugh E., Sacred Heart, Miller Heights
Metzker, Daniel F., Cathedral, Allentown
Mihalik, Andrew J., Jr., Sacred Heart, Bath
Monahan, Brian, Immaculate Conception, Allentown
Morales, Edison, Hispanic Apostolate, Northampton Co. & Holy Infancy, Bethlehem
Murphy, John W., Jr., St. Ignatius Loyola, Sinking Spring; "The A.D. Times," Allentown
Murphy, Thomas J., Most Blessed Sacrament, Bally
Musalavage, Clement A., St. Patrick, Pottsville
Pitts, William P., Sacred Heart, Palmerton
Pogash, John F., SS. Peter and Paul, St. Clair
Quiles, Victor M., Hispanic Apostolate, Lehigh Co. & Sacred Heart of Jesus, Allentown
Reichard, Thomas C., St. Bernard & St. Michael, Easton
Rodgers, Robert W., Northampton County Prison, Easton & St. Jane Frances de Chantal, Wilson Borough
Rodriguez, Nicasio, Spanish Apostolate, Northampton Co. & Holy Infancy, Bethlehem
Roos, Carl J.
Roth, Cyril A., St. Barbara & St. Francis of Assisi, Minersville
Salabsky, Bernard J., Jr., Our Lady of Perpetual Help, Bethlehem
Scrak, Richard G., Catholic Social Agency, Ecumenical Soup Kitchen, Allentown & St. Anne, Bethlehem
Setlock, John A., Annunciation & St. Ann, Frackville
Sewald, Richard T., Notre Dame of Bethlehem, Bethlehem
Simchick, Sylvester, St. John Baptist de la Salle, Shillington
Solis, Alfonso D., Hispanic Apostolate, Northampton Co. & Holy Infancy, Bethlehem
Thomson, Daniel, Good Shepherd Home and Rehabilitation Hospital & St. Paul, Allentown
Torres, Fernando L., Hispanic Apostolate, Berks Co. & St. Peter, Reading
Torres, Mariano, Spanish Apostolate, Berks Co. & St. Peter, Reading
Tyson, Robert J., St. Thomas More, Allentown
Visot, Luis R., St. John the Baptist, Pottsville
VonLeer, Lemuel, Catholic Social Agency, Allentown & Notre Dame, Bethlehem
Wagner, William J., S.S. Peter and Paul, Lehighton
Wilkinson, Raymond, St. Nicholas, Weatherly
Wisser, Bernard M., Family Life Bureau & Assumption B.V.M., Colesville
Wyrwa, Eugene, Holy Trinity, Whitehall

INSTITUTIONS LOCATED IN THE DIOCESE

[A] SEMINARIES, RELIGIOUS OR SCHOLASTICATES

CENTER VALLEY. *Missionaries of the Sacred Heart*, 3300 Station Ave., P.O. Box 9, 18034-0009. Tel: 610-282-1415; Fax: 610-282-0610. Revs. Anthony Ripp, M.S.C., Supr.; Raymond Costello, M.S.C.; Jacob Welle, M.S.C.; E. Michael Camilli, M.S.C.; Michael Vasti, M.S.C.; Stephen Geusic, M.S.C.; Bro. Lawrence Viele.

NORTHAMPTON. *Mary Immaculate Seminary*, 300 Cherryville Rd., Box 27, 18067-0027. Tel: 610-262-7866; Fax: 610-262-6766. Conducted: by the Archdiocese of Philadelphia as a seminary for the Spirituality Year Program for the seminarians and for the ongoing formation of priests, and as a house of prayer and retreat for priests, religious, and laity. Rev. Msgr. Michael J. Chaback, S.T.D., Faculty; Revs. Peter J. Welsh, M.Div., Ph.D., Assoc.; Thomas M. Mullin, M.Div., M.A., S.S.L., Dir. for Continuing Formation of Diocesan Priests, Spirituality Year Program. Tel: 610-262-9674. Rev. John M. Savinski, M.Div., M.A., Dir., Vincentian Community in Residence. Tel: 610-262-7530; 262-7589; Fax: 610-262-7490. Bro. John P. McErlean, F.S.C., Retreat Admin. In res., Revs. William W. Sheldon, C.M., S.T.L., Supr.; Joseph P. McClain, C.M., S.T.D., Asst.; John G. Nugent, C.M., J.C.D., Treas.

WERNERSVILLE. *Novitiate of St. Isaac Jogues*, 19565. Tel: 610-678-8085; Fax: 610-678-8747. Very Rev. William F. Gavin, S.J., Rector; Rev. John T. McCaslin, S.J., Admin.; Mr. Joseph Rodolff, Treas. In res., Revs. George A. Aschenbrenner, S.J.; John P. Barron, S.J.; Frederick A. Brew, S.J.; Ralph C. Campbell, S.J.; Joseph A. Cawley, S.J.; William F. Graham, S.J.; Joseph B. Hanzely, S.J.; Harold J. Hocking, S.J.; Thomas J. Kuller, S.J.; Thomas J. Linsky, S.J.; Clarence A. Martin, S.J.; Robert J. McAllister, S.J.; Burton Proctor, S.J.; Edwin J. Sanders, S.J.; William E. Schaffner; D. Gilbert Sweeney, S.J.; Edward J. Tinney, S.J.; Francis A. Wallner, S.J.; Robert J. Whalen, S.J.; George S. Williams, S.J.; John J. Keenan, S.J.; Richard W. Norman, S.J.; Eugene J. Power, S.J. Brothers 4.

[B] COLLEGES AND UNIVERSITIES

CENTER VALLEY. *Allentown College of St. Francis de Sales*, 2755 Station Ave., 18034-9568. Tel: 610-282-1100.
For a complete listing, refer to the Colleges and Universities section.

READING. *Alvernia College*, 19607. Tel: 610-796-8200; Fax: 610-796-8324.
For a complete listing, refer to the Colleges and Universities section.

[C] HIGH SCHOOLS, DIOCESAN

ALLENTOWN. *Allentown Central Catholic High School*, 301 N. Fourth St., 18102-3098. Tel: 610-437-4601. Rev. Msgr. Joseph R. Sobiesiak, Dir.; Mr. James M. Hodrick, M.Ed., Prin.; Mr. William F. Tielman, Vice Prin.; Rev. Msgr. Francis C. Revak; Revs. Peter J. Hosak, (Byzantine); Gregory R. Karpyn; John A. Krivak; George R. Winne. Priests 5; Sisters 3; Lay Teachers 45; Students 906.

ASHLAND. *Cardinal Brennan Jr./Sr. High School*, R.D. 2, 17921. Tel: 717-874-3921. Rev. Frans Berkhout, Prin.; Mr. Daniel T. Demczko, Vice Prin.; Revs. David J. Kozak; Anthony Mongiello, Dir. of Spiritual Activities; James Betchel; Lawrence Bukaty. Lay Teachers 16; Students 268.

BANGOR. *Pius X High School*, 580 Third Ave., 18013-1399. Tel: 610-588-3291. Mr. Leonard D. Litzi, Jr., Prin.; Revs. Joseph A. DeSantis, Asst. Prin.; Wayne E. Killian, Dir. Spiritual Activities. Priests 2; Lay Teachers 17; Students 272.

BETHLEHEM. *Bethlehem Catholic High School*, 2133 Madison Ave., 18017-4699. Tel: 610-866-0791. Founded as two-year commercial high school, 1897. Founded as four-year comprehensive high school, 1925. Mr. Richard B. Culver, M.Ed., Prin.; Sr. Marjorie Keenan, S.S.J., Vice Prin.; Mr. Michael R. McCauley, Admin. Asst.; Mr. Richard F. Mazza, Dir. Studies; Revs. William N. Seifert, Dir. Spiritual Activities; Stephen L. Maco; Bernard J. Ezaki. Sisters of St. Joseph 5; Lay Teachers 41; Students 845.

EASTON. *Notre Dame High School*, 3417 Church Rd., 18042. Tel: 610-868-1431. Mr. Joseph R. Kramer, Prin.; Revs. Thomas J. Kessler; Alfred A. Schlert. Priests 2; Sisters 6; Lay Teachers 28; Students 491.

POTTSVILLE. *Nativity B.V.M. High School*, Lawtons Hill, 17901. Tel: 717-622-8110. Revs. Ronald C. Bocian, Prin.; Bernard A. Flanagan; Ronald V. Jankaitis. Sisters 6; Lay Teachers 18; Students 306.

READING. *Holy Name High School*, 955 E. Wyomissing Blvd., 19611. Tel: 610-374-8361. Sr. Joseph Eleanor Murphy, I.H.M., Prin.; Deacon William R. Kase, Vice Prin.; Revs. Thomas J. Orsulak, Dir. of Spiritual Activities; Robert T. Finlan. Priests 2; Brothers 1; Sisters 3; Lay Teachers 24; Students 354.
Reading Central Catholic High School (Monsignor Bornemann Memorial), 1400 Hill Rd., 19602-1499. Tel: 610-373-4178. Mr. Vincent T. Shemanski, Prin.; Revs. Donald W. Cieniewicz, Vice Prin.; Paul L. Rothermel; Patrick H. Lamb. Priests 2; Sisters 11; Lay Teachers 20; Administrators 2; Students 452.

TAMAQUA. *Marian Catholic High School*, R.D. 4, Box 446, 18252. Tel: 717-467-3335; Fax: 717-467-0186. Mr. John P. Malarkey, Prin.; Revs. Robert J. Kuzmann, Vice Prin.; Donald J. Schaible, Dir. Spiritual Activities; Paul G. Puza. Priests 2; Servants of the Immaculate Heart of Mary 2; Lay Teachers 27; Students 410.

[D] REGIONAL CATHOLIC ELEMENTARY SCHOOLS, DIOCESAN

ALLENTOWN. *Holy Spirit School*. Serving St. John the Baptist, Immaculate Conception, SS. Peter and Paul, Allentown. Primary School (Grades PreK-3), Front St. & Bridge St., 18102. Tel: 610-820-0220. Middle School (Grades 4-8), 508 Ridge Ave., 18102. Tel: 610-434-4044. Sr. Catherine Ortwein, S.S.J., Prin. Tel: 610-434-4044. Enrollment 225 (Grades PreK-8).
Sacred Heart School, 325 N. Fourth St., 18102. Tel: 610-437-3031. Mr. James Krupka, Prin. Lay Teachers 9; Students 211.
Serving Sacred Heart, Our Lady of Mt. Carmel, St. Stephen, Allentown.

BALLY. *St. Francis Academy*, 668 Pine St., 19503. Tel: 610-845-7364. Deacon Thomas J. Murphy, Prin. Lay Teachers 10; Students 250.
Serving Most Blessed Sacrament, Bally, and St. Columbkill, Boyertown.

BETHLEHEM. *Holy Child School*. (Grades K-8), 1301 Sioux St., 18015. Tel: 610-865-0861. Sr. Marie John Holland, O.S.F., Prin. Sisters 1; Lay Teachers 9; Students 233.
Serving Holy Ghost, St. Ursula, Bethlehem.
St. Michael the Archangel School. Primary Bldg. & Main Office. (Grades K-4), St. Joseph's Rd., Limeport, 18060. Tel: 610-965-4441. Middle School. (Grades PreK & 5-8), 4121 Old Bethlehem Pike, 18015. Tel: 610-867-8422. Carol Sonon, Prin. Priests 2; Lay Teachers 14; Students 328.
Serving Assumption B.V.M., Colesville; St. Joseph, Limeport.
SS. Cyril and Methodius Regional Catholic Elementary School. (Grades PreK-8), 551 Thomas St., 18015. Tel: 610-866-0042. Mrs. Joan M. West, Prin. Lay Teachers 10; Students 162.
Serving SS. Cyril and Methodius, St. Joseph, St. John Capistrano, Our Lady of Pompeii, St. Stanislaus.

COPLAY. *Christ the King School*, Primary Bldg., 3008 Ruch St., 18052. Tel: 610-262-4177. Middle Bldg., 22 S. Fifth St., 18037. Tel: 610-262-5822. Miss Anna C. Oleszczuk, Prin. Lay Teachers 12; Students 342.
Preschool, 40 S. Fifth St., 18037. Tel: 610-262-4064.
Serving St. Peter, Coplay; St. John the Baptist, Whitehall; Holy Trinity, Egypt.

EASTON. *Easton Catholic Elementary School*. (Grades K-3), Primary Bldg., 283 W. St. Joseph St., 18042. Tel: 610-253-0651. Middle Bldg. (Grades 4-8), 841 Washington St., 18042. Tel: 610-252-1393. Mary Frances Haluska, Prin. Lay Teachers 12; Students 204.
Serving St. Anthony, St. Joseph, St. Michael, St. Bernard.

FRACKVILLE. *Holy Family School*. (Grades PreK-6), 29 S. Broad Mountain Ave., 17931. Tel: 717-874-0285. Mr. Paul T. Coombe, Prin. Sisters 1; Lay Teachers 6; Students 146.
Serving Annunciation, B.V.M., St. Joseph, St. Ann.

GIRARDVILLE. *Immaculate Heart Elementary School*. (Grades PreK-8), Main St. & Richard St., 17935. Tel: 717-276-6568. Sr. Helene Joseph Kollar, I.H.M., Prin. Religious 2; Lay Teachers 8; Students 229.
Serving St. Joseph, St. Mauritius, Ashland; St. Joseph, St. Vincent, Girardville; Our Lady of Good Counsel, Gordon.

JIM THORPE. *St. Joseph Regional Academy*. (Grades K-8), Sixth St. & School St., 18229. Tel: 717-325-3186. Sr. Maria Electa Schulz, S.C.C., Prin. Sisters 2; Lay Teachers 9; Students 208.
Serving St. Joseph, Immaculate Conception and St. Peter the Fisherman.

LANSFORD. *St. Michael School*. (Grades PreK-8), 123 E. Water St., 18232. Tel: 717-645-7170. Miss Susan M. Klinger, Prin. Students 225.
Serving St. Michael, SS. Peter and Paul, Lansford; SS. Cyril and Methodius, St. John the Baptist, St. Mary of the Assumption, Coaldale.

LANSFORD-SUMMIT HILL. *Our Lady of the Valley School*. (Grades K-4), 118 W. Ludlow St., 18250. Tel: 717-645-4700. (Grades 5-8), 30 E. Bertsch St., 18232. Tel: 717-645-7101. Sr. Katharine M. McGee, I.H.M., Prin. Sisters 2; Lay Teachers 7; Students 170.
Serving St. Joseph, St. Stanislaus, Summit Hill; St. Ann, Lansford; Immaculate Conception, Our Lady of Mt. Carmel, Sacred Heart, Nesquehoning.

MAHANOY CITY. *Mahanoy City Catholic Elementary School*. (Grades K-8), S. Catawissa St. & Pine St., 17948. Tel: 717-773-2668. Sr. Anna Mae, O.S.F., Prin. Religious 2; Lay Teachers 7; Students 93.
Serving Assumption B.V.M., Sacred Heart, St. Canicus, St. Casimir, St. Fidelis, St. Joseph, Our Lady of Silva, St. Richard, and St. Mary Byzantine.

MCADOO. *McAdoo Catholic Elementary School*. (Grades K-8), 35 N. Cleveland St., 18237. Tel: 717-929-1442. Sr. Anne Francine Windle, I.H.M., Prin. Sisters 3; Lay Teachers 9; Students 199.
Serving St. Patrick, St. Kunegunda, St. Mary, McAdoo; St. Bartholomew, St. Michael, Tresckow; Immaculate Conception, Kelayres; St. Nicholas, Weatherly; St. Mary, Beaver Meadows.

MINERSVILLE. *Good Shepherd Regional School*. (Grades PreK-3). Holy Redeemer Elementary School. Consolidated with St. Elizabeth Ann Seton to form Good Shepherd Regional School. 538 Sunbury St., 17954. Tel: 717-544-4360. (Grades 4-8), 301 Heffner St., 17954. Tel: 717-544-3766. Ms. Rosalie Novack, Prin. Sisters 1; Lay Teachers 11; Students 238.
Serving St. Kieran, Heckscherville; St. Mary, Star of the Sea, Branchdale; Sacred Heart, Newtown; Immaculate Conception, Tremont; SS. Peter and Paul, Tower City; St. Barbara, St. Francis of Assisi, St. Stanislaus Kostka, St. Vincent de Paul, Our Lady of Mt. Carmel, Minersville.

NEW PHILADELPHIA. *Holy Cross Elementary School*. (Grades K-8), Clay St. & Wiggan St., 17959. Tel: 717-277-0197. Mrs. Dolores Bartashus, Prin. Lay Teachers 6; Students 84.
Serving Holy Family, Sacred Heart, New Philadelphia; St. Anthony, Cumbola.

NORTHAMPTON. *Our Lady of Hungary Regional School*, 1300 Newport Ave., 18067. Tel: 610-262-9171. Mrs. Barbara J. Sullivan, M.Ed., Prin. Sisters 3; Lay Teachers 16; Students 375.
Serving Our Lady of Hungary, Assumption B.V.M., St. Michael, Northampton; St. Lawrence and St. Andrew, Catasauqua.

PALMERTON-SLATINGTON. *St. John Neumann Regional School*. (Grades K-3), 641-645 W. Washington St., Slatington, 18080. Tel: 610-767-2935. (Grades 4-8), 259 Lafayette Ave., Palmerton, 18071. Tel: 610-826-2354. Mrs. Mary Ellen Chuss-Mirro, M.Ed., Prin. Lay Teachers 9; Students 168.
Serving St. Nicholas, Berlinsville; Sacred Heart, Palmerton; Assumption B.V.M., Slatington.

PEN ARGYL. *Immaculate Conception School*. (Grades K-6), Babbitt Ave. & Heller Ave., 18072. Tel: 610-863-4816. Sr. Maria Evelyn, O.P., Prin. Sisters 7; Lay Teachers 2; Students 163.
Serving St. Elizabeth, Pen Argyl; St. Rocco, Martins Creek; St. Roch, West Bangor.

PORT CARBON. *St. Stephen Regional School*. (Grades PreK-8), 214 Valley St., 17965. Tel: 717-622-3063. Sr. Mary Anne Hoesle, I.H.M., Prin. Sisters 4; Lay Teachers 9; Students 196.
Serving the following parishes: St. Stephen, Port Carbon, St. Mary, Immaculate Conception, St. Casimir, Ss. Peter & Paul, St. Boniface, St. Clair.

POTTSVILLE. *All Saints Elementary School*. (Grades K-8), 112 S. Seventh St., 17901. Tel: 717-622-0106; 622-1765. Sr. Sharon McCarthy, S.S.J., Prin.
Serving St. Patrick; St. John the Baptist; Mary, Queen of Peace; St. Joseph;and St. Francis. Sisters 1; Lay Teachers 18; Students 285.
Little Saints Preschool, 2051 W. Norwegian St., 17901. Tel: 717-622-1073. Sr. M. Leonore, S.S.J., Dir. Sisters 1; Lay Teachers 1; Students 60.
Serving the Pottsville area.

READING. *St. Catharine of Siena School*, 2330 Perkiomen Ave., 19606. Tel: 610-779-5810. Sr. Maria Patris, I.H.M., Prin. Sisters 4; Lay Teachers 20; Students 537.
Serving St. Catharine of Siena, Reading, and Immaculate Conception, Birdsboro.

ROSETO. *Our Lady of Mt. Carmel School*, 80 Ridge St., 18013. Tel: 610-588-2629. Dorothy Ruggiero, Prin. Lay Teachers 10; Students 228.
Serving Our Lady of Mt. Carmel, Roseto, and Our Lady of Good Counsel, Bangor.

SHENANDOAH. *Father Walter J. Ciszek Elementary School*. (Grades PreK-6), 233 W. Cherry St., 17976. Tel: 717-462-9666. Sr. Barbara Ann Browne, I.H.M., Prin. Sisters 1; Lay Teachers 11; Students 291.
Serving Annunciation, St. Casimir, St. George, Our Lady of Mt. Carmel, St. Stanislaus, St. Stephen, Shenandoah; St. Mary Magdalen, Lost Creek; St. Mary, Ringtown.

SHILLINGTON. *La Salle Academy and Early Childhood Center.* (Grades PreK-8), 440 Holland St., 19607. Tel: 610-777-7392. Miss Geraldine M. Williams, M.Ed., Prin. Sisters 1; Lay Teachers 22; Students 401.
Serving St. John Baptist de La Salle, Shillington; St. Benedict, Plowville; St. Anthony, Millmont.

SINKING SPRING. *St. Ignatius Loyola School.* (Grades PreK-8), 2700 St. Alban's Dr., 19609. Tel: 610-678-0111. Mrs. Janice E. Bayerle, Prin. Sisters 2; Lay Teachers 27; Students 609.
Serving St. Ignatius Loyola, Sinking Spring; St. Francis de Sales, Robesonia.

TAMAQUA. *St. Jerome Regional School*, 250 W. Broad St., 18252. Tel: 717-668-2757. Sr. Honora Marie Johnston, I.H.M., Prin. Sisters 3; Lay Teachers 8; Students 221.
Serving St. Jerome, SS. Peter and Paul, Tamaqua; St. Bartholomew, Brockton; St. Bertha, Tuscarora.

WHITEHALL. *St. Elizabeth School*, 433 Pershing Blvd., 18052. Tel: 610-264-0143. Sr. Helen Ann Sharkey, R.S.M., Prin. Lay Teachers 10; Students 261.
Serving St. Elizabeth, Whitehall; Annunciation, Catasauqua.

[E] SPECIAL SCHOOLS

ALLENTOWN. *Mercy Special Learning Center*, 830 S. Woodward St., 18103. Tel: 610-797-8242. Sr. Janice Marie Johnson, R.S.M., Prin. Ages: Newborn to 21. Sisters of Mercy 1; Lay Teachers 8; Students 85.

BETHLEHEM. *St. Francis Academy Kindergarten*, Monocracy Manor, 395 Bridle Path Rd., 18017. Tel: 610-866-5030. Sr. Carol Ann Papp, O.S.F., Prin. Sisters 1; Students 16.
St. Francis Day Care, Monocracy Manner, 395 Bridle Path Rd., 18017. Tel: 610-866-5030. Sr. Carol Ann Papp, O.S.F., Dir. Sisters 4; Lay Staff 7; Students 70.

POTTSVILLE. *St. Joseph Center*, 2075 W. Norwegian St., 17901. Tel: 717-622-4638. Sr. Grace Christi, S.S.J., Prin. Lay Teachers 4; Students 34.

READING. *Alvernia Montessori School.* (Grades PreK-K), Mt. Alvernia, 19607. Tel: 610-775-0250; Fax: 610-777-6029. Sr. Ann Marie Coll, Dir. Sisters 4; Students 65.
John Paul II Center for Special Learning, 450 S. Sixth St., 19602. Tel: 610-373-5687. Lawrence P. O'Donnell, Prin. Lay Teachers 3; Students 16.

WHITEHALL. *National LEARNING CLUB Ministry*, Two Maryland Cir.-120, 18052. Tel: 610-437-4463; Fax: 610-437-8843. Outside-of-school education ministry for "at-risk" youth. Students 550.

[F] CATHOLIC CHARITIES AND SOCIAL AGENCIES

ALLENTOWN. *Catholic Social Agency-Catholic Charities Administrative Office*, 2141 Downyflake Ln., 18103-4774. Tel: 610-791-3888. Rev. Msgr. Joseph E. Kurtz, L.S.W., M.S.W., Diocesan Dir. of Catholic Charities; Rev. Msgr. John B. McCann, L.S.W., S.T.L., Exec. Dir. of Catholic Social Agency.
Branch Offices:
Branch Office, 928 Union Blvd., 18103. Tel: 610-435-1541. (For Lehigh and Northampton Cos.).
Adult Outreach Center, 310 E. Mahanoy Ave., Mahanoy City, 17948. Tel: 717-773-2010.
St. Francis Center, 900 W. Market St., Orwigsburg, 17961. Tel: 717-366-1403. (For Schuylkill and Carbon Cos.).
Operation Plus, 913 Howard Ave., Pottsville, 17901. Tel: 717-622-6010. Day Treatment Center and Partial Hospitalization for Adolescents.
Berks County Branch Office, 2147 Perkiomen Ave., Reading, 19606. Tel: 610-370-3378.
Pastoral Visitor, 218 W. Cherry St., Shenandoah, 17976. Tel: 717-462-1154.
Pregnancy Crisis Center. (24-Hour Hotline). Bangor. Tel: 717-897-6060. Easton. Tel: 610-253-3373. Pen Argyl. Tel: 610-588-8400. Parish-Based Counseling Centers: Our Lady of Mt. Carmel, Bangor; Sacred Heart, Palmerton; St. Fidelis, Mahanoy City; St. Joseph, Summit Hill; St. Columbkill, Boyertown.

[G] GENERAL HOSPITALS

ALLENTOWN. *Sacred Heart Hospital*, 421 Chew St., 18102-3490. Tel: 610-776-4500.
For a complete listing, refer to the Hospitals section.

POTTSVILLE. *Good Samaritan Regional Medical Center*, 700 E. Norwegian St., 17901. Tel: 717-621-4000; Fax: 717-622-7950.
For a complete listing, refer to the Hospitals section.

READING. *Bornemann Health Corporation*, c/o Saint Joseph Hospital, 12th St. & Walnut St., P.O. Box 316, 19603. Tel: 610-378-2300.
For a complete listing, refer to the Hospitals section.
Saint Joseph Medical Center, 215 N. 12th St., P.O. Box 316, 19603. Tel: 610-378-2000.
For a complete listing, refer to the Hospitals section.

[H] SKILLED NURSING FACILITIES

BETHLEHEM. *Holy Family Manor*, 1200 Spring St., 18018. Tel: 610-865-5595; Fax: 610-865-5866.
For a complete listing, refer to the Special Care Facilities section.

ORWIGSBURG. *Holy Family Home Health and Hospice Care*, Schuylkill County and Admin. Office, 900 W. Market St., 17961. Tel: 717-366-0990; 800-726-8761.
For a complete listing, refer to the Special Care Facilities section.

[I] HOMES AND SERVICES FOR THE ELDERLY AND CONVALESCENT

BETHLEHEM. *Grace Mansion Personal Care Residence of Holy Manor*, 1200 Spring St., 18018. Tel: 610-865-6748.
For a complete listing, refer to the Special Care Facilities section.
Holy Family Adult Day Care, 1200 Spring St., 18018. Tel: 610-865-5595.
For a complete listing, refer to the Special Care Facilities section.
Holy Family Apartments, 330-338 13th Ave., 18018. Tel: 610-866-4603.
For a complete listing, refer to the Special Care Facilities section.
Trexler Pavilion, Personal Care Residence of Holy Family Manor, 1220 Prospect Ave., 18018. Tel: 610-868-7776.
For a complete listing, refer to the Special Care Facilities section.

EASTON. *Antonian Towers*, 2405 Hillside Ave., 18042. Tel: 610-258-2033.
For a complete listing, refer to the Special Care Facilities section.

NEW PHILADELPHIA. *Holy Family Apartments*, Valley St. & Clay St., 17959. Tel: 717-429-0699.
For a complete listing, refer to the Special Care Facilities section.

ORWIGSBURG. *Holy Family Adult Day Care at St. Francis Center*, 900 W. Market St., 17961. Tel: 717-366-2924.
For a complete listing, refer to the Special Care Facilities section.
Holy Family Residence, 900 W. Market St., 17961. Tel: 717-366-2912.
For a complete listing, refer to the Special Care Facilities section.

POTTSVILLE. *Queen of Peace Apartments*, 777 Water St., 17901. Tel: 717-628-4504.
For a complete listing, refer to the Special Care Facilities section.

READING. *Queen of Angels Apartment*, 22 Rothermel St., Hyde Park, 19605. Tel: 610-921-3115.
For a complete listing, refer to the Special Care Facilities section.

SAINT CLAIR. *Neumann Apartments*, 25 N. Nichols St., 17970. Tel: 717-429-0699.
For a complete listing, refer to the Special Care Facilities section.

[J] HOMES FOR PRIESTS

BETHLEHEM. *Holy Family Villa*, 1325 Prospect Ave., 18018. Tel: 610-694-0395. Rev. Msgr. Dennis A. Rigney, M.Div., L.S.W., A.C.S.W., Diocesan Dir. In res., Revs. James M. Carr; Joseph D. Carroll; William P. Jones; Joseph H. Kean; Thomas J. Kerestus; F. Charles McKenna; Charles L. McNulty; Francis R. Nave; Joseph B. Rapczynski; Joseph A. Rock, Chap.; Rev. Msgr. Joseph M. Whalen, Chancellor; Revs. William J. Shields; Albert T. Cervella.

[K] MONASTERIES AND RESIDENCES OF PRIESTS AND BROTHERS

BETHLEHEM. *The Barnabite Fathers Barnabite Spiritual Center*, R.D. 1, 4301 Hecktown Rd., 18017. Tel: 610-691-8648; 8649. Revs. Anthony M. Bianco, C.R.S.P., M.A., Local Supr. & Moderator of Spiritual Center; Gabriel M. Patil, C.R.S.P., M.A., S.T.L., S.S.L., Theology College Professor, Provincial Vicar & House Treasurer; Peter M. Calabrese, C.R.S.P., Seminarian, (Rome, Italy); Dick M. Delzingaro, C.R.S.P., Local Vicar & House Sec.

CENTER VALLEY. *Oblates of St. Francis de Sales*, Wills Hall, 2755 Station Ave., 18034-9568. Tel: 610-282-3300. In res., Very Rev. Bernard F. O'Connor, O.S.F.S., Ph.D., Supr.; Revs. Joseph P. Becker, O.S.F.S., M.A.; Thomas F. Dailey, O.S.F.S., S.T.D.; Bernard F. Donahue, O.S.F.S., Ph.D.; James P. Finnegan, O.S.F.S., S.T.D.; Daniel G. Gambet, O.S.F.S., Ph.D.; John A. Hanley, O.S.F.S., M.R.E.; John F. Harvey, O.S.F.S., S.T.D.; Peter J. Leonard, O.S.F.S., Ph.D.; A. Robert McGilvray, O.S.F.S., Ph.D.; John F. McGinley, O.S.F.S., M.Ed.; Alexander T. Pocetto, O.S.F.S., Ph.D.; Gerard H. Schubert, O.S.F.S., Ph.D.; Robert M. Rutledge, O.S.F.S. Total in Residence 14.

EASTON. *St. Francis Friary*, 3908 Chipman Rd., 18045. Tel: 610-258-3053; Fax: 610-258-2412. Franciscan Vice Province of the Holy Savior. Revs. William Reisteter, O.F.M., Dir. of Retreat Development; Michael Lenz, O.F.M., Guardian; Roland Maruscak, O.F.M.; Bros. Michael Dubec, O.F.M.; Edward Skutka, O.F.M. Total in Residence 5. Brothers 2.

NEW RINGGOLD. *Cistercian Conventual Priory, St. Mary's Priory*, R.D. 1, Box 206, 17960. Tel: 717-943-2645. Very Rev. Luke Anderson, S.O.Cist., Th.M., Ph.D., Prior; Revs. Hugh Montague, S.O.Cist., M.A., Th.M.; Alphonsus Lachapelle, S.O.Cist., M.A., Th.M. Fathers 3.

NORTHHAMPTON. *Vincentian Community*, Mary Immaculate Seminary, 300 Cherryville Rd., 18067-0027. Tel: 610-262-7530; 262-7530; Fax: 610-262-7490. Revs. William W. Sheldon, C.M., S.T.L., Supr.; Joseph P. McClain, C.M., S.T.D., Assis.; John G. Nugent, C.M., J.C.D., Treas.

READING. *Missionaries of the Sacred Heart*, 55 Rothermel St., 19605-2680. Tel: 610-929-2025; Fax: 610-929-4397. Very Rev. John J. Paul, M.S.C., Supr.; Revs. Philip DeRea, M.S.C.; Joseph W. Gaspar, M.S.C.; William Gies, M.S.C.; Eugene Jung, M.S.C.; Robert Tobolski, M.S.C.; Lawrence H. Wildonger, M.S.C.; Philip Yandrisevits, M.S.C.; Bros. Edward Baker, M.S.C.; Richars Kuhl, M.S.C.; Warren Perrotto, M.S.C.

[L] CONVENTS AND RESIDENCES OF SISTERS

ALLENTOWN. *Missionary Sisters of the Most Sacred Heart of Jesus*, 425 Pine St., 18102. Tel: 610-776-4855. Staff Sacred Heart Hospital. Sr. M. Adella Lukae, M.S.C., Supr. Sisters 5.
Villa Maria Convent, 303 N. Sixth St., 18102. Tel: 610-433-3567. Faculty house of Sisters, Servants of the Immaculate Heart of Mary, who teach at Allentown Central Catholic High School and staff Centro Parroquial Sacred Heart Parish. Sr. Helene Thomas, I.H.M., Supr. Clergy of Sacred Heart Parish, Chap., Tel: 610-434-5171 (Rectory at Sacred Heart). Sisters 5.

BETHLEHEM. *Casa Belen*, 305 E. Fourth St., 18015. Tel: 610-867-4030. Sr. Marta Munoz, P.S.S.J., Supr. Residence of the Poor Sisters of St. Joseph who minister to the Spanish speaking people of the area. Sisters 3.
Monocacy Manor, 395 Bridle Path Rd., 18017. Tel: 610-866-2597. Provincialate and Novitiate of the School Sisters of the Third Order Regular of St. Francis (Bethlehem Prov.). Sr. Mary Xavier Bomberger, O.S.F., Prov. Supr. Professed Sisters 25; Retreat Center Total Staff 8.
St. Joseph Convent, 2133 Madison Ave., 18017-4699. Tel: 610-865-4691. Sisters of St. Joseph. Sr. Marie Natalie Sommer, S.S.J., Supr. Sisters 16.

COOPERSBURG. *Carmelite Monastery*. St. Therese of the Child Jesus and St. Mary Magdalen de Pazzi, St. Therese's Valley. 3551 Lanark Rd., 18036. Tel: 610-797-3721. Carmelite Nuns of the Ancient Observance. Mother Joseph Marie, O.Carm., Prioress; Rev. Michael S. Lawrence, Chap. Professed Nuns 13.

MAHANOY CITY. *St. Joseph Convent*, 536 W. South St., 17948. Tel: 717-773-1420. Missionaries of Charity. Sisters 4.

NESQUEHONING. *Our Lady of Perpetual Help House of Prayer*, 140 W. Mill St., 18240. Tel: 717-669-9858. Sister Servants of the Immaculate Heart of Mary. Sr. Katharine McCormack, I.H.M., Supr. Sisters 4.

PEN ARGYL. *Dominican Daughters of the Immaculate Mother*, 115 Lobb Ave., 18072. Sr. Maria Felisa, O.P., Supr. Sisters 7.

POTTSVILLE. *Sisters House*, 700 E. Norwegian St., 17901. Tel: 717-621-4000; 621-4651. Res. of the Daughters of Charity of St. Vincent de Paul, Northeast Province, who staff Good Samaritan Regional Medical Center and Nativity High School. Sr. Andrea Miller, D.C., Supr. Priests 1; Sisters 14.

READING. *Alvernia College Convent*, 19607. Tel: 610-796-8331. Residence for Bernardine Sisters on college faculty. Sr. M. Pacelli, Local Min. Tel: 610-796-8329.
Daughters of Divine Zeal, Inc., 1526 Hill Rd., 19602. Tel: 610-375-1738; 375-9072; Fax: 610-375-2188. Sr. Gesulmina Micali, F.D.Z., Supr. Sisters 6.
House of Nazareth (Casa Nazaret), 532 Spruce St., 19602. Tel: 610-378-1947. Sr. Maria Gonzalez, Supr. Residence of the Poor Sisters of St. Joseph who work in Spanish Apostolate of Berks County. Sisters 3.
MSC Province Center, 2811 Moyers Ln., 19605. Tel: 610-929-5944. Sr. Marie Clark, M.S.C., Prov. Sisters 3.
Neumann Convent Sisters of St. Francis of Philadelphia (Glen Riddle). Mailing Address: P.O. Box 978, 19603. Tel: 610-374-4974. Sisters 12.
Our Lady of the Assumption Convent, 1500 Eckert Ave., 19602. Tel: 610-373-8203. Faculty House of Sisters of Christian Charity, teaching in Central Catholic High School. Sr. Karen Miller, S.C.C., Supr. Sisters 7.

Sacred Heart Convent, Mt. Alvernia, 460 St. Bernardine St., 19607-1737. Tel: 610-777-6111; Fax: 610-777-6029. Residence for Bernardine Sisters of Third Order of St. Francis. Sr. Mary Maxine, O.S.F., Admin. Tel: 610-777-7221; Sr. Marietta, Local Min.; Rev. Patrick H. Lamb, O.F.M., Chap.
Montessori School. Total Staff 4.
U.S. Province Offices. Total Staff 9. Professed Sisters 37.

St. Clare Convent, 465 St. Bernardine St., 19607. Tel: 610-777-4590. Bernardine Franciscan Sisters. Sr. Claude Marie Jablonski, O.S.F., Local Min. Sisters 2; Candidates 2.

St. Joseph Villa, 464 Bernardine St., 19607. Tel: 610-777-5556. Home of the Retired Bernardine Sisters of the Third Order of St. Francis. Sr. M. Lorentia, O.S.F., Admin.; Sr. Anna, O.S.F., Supr.; Rev. Robert Reece, O.S.F.S., Chap. Sisters 110.

St. Michael Convent, 19605. Tel: 610-929-5751. Missionary Sisters of the Sacred Heart of Jesus. Sr. Theresa Lepera, M.S.C., Coord., Motherhouse Community; Sr. Joanne Leblanc, M.S.C., Coord., Motherhouse Community; Sr. Rita Ehrmann, M.S.C., Coord., Retirement Center Community; Sr. Kathleen White, M.S.C., Coord., Linckens Center Community.
Attended by M.S.C. Fathers from Sacred Heart Monastery, Hyde Park. Professed Sisters 90.

Sisters of St. Francis Residence, 502 S. Sixth St., 19602. Tel: 610-375-8001. Convent of the Sisters of St. Francis of Philadelphia who are on the staffs at Central Catholic High School, SS. Cyril and Methodius Parish, and St. Joseph Hospital. Sisters 5.

SHILLINGTON. *Precious Blood Convent*, P.O. Box 97, 19607. Tel: 610-777-1624; Fax: 610-777-3359. Novitiate of the Missionary Sisters of the Precious Blood. Sr. M. Francis Bisland, C.P.S., Supr. Sisters 29.

WHITEHALL. *Sisters for Christian Community*, Two Maryland Cir.-120, 18052. Sisters 2.

[M] RETREAT HOUSES

BETHLEHEM. *St. Francis Center for Renewal (Monocacy Manor)*, 395 Bridle Path Rd., 18017. Tel: 610-867-8890. School Sisters of St. Francis. Sr. M. Anita Kuchera, O.S.F., Dir. Weekend retreats (68) and days of recollection (150); retreats for men and women, marriage encounter; engaged encounters; parish retreats; workshops; youth groups; weekends; privately directed retreats; private retreats. Total Staff 5.

EASTON. *St. Francis Retreat House*, 3918 Chipman Rd., 18045. Tel: 610-258-3053. Rev. William Reisterer, O.F.M., Dir. of Retreat Development. Houses of Religious Men: Total in Residence 5; Total Staff 7; Retreat Centers: Total in Residence 5; Total Staff 10. Retreatants 80.

NORTHHAMPTON. *Mary Immaculate Seminary*, 300 Cherryville Rd., 18067-0027. Tel: 610-262-7866; Fax: 610-262-6766. Bro. John P. McErlean, F.S.C., Admin.

ORWIGSBURG. *St. Francis Center*, 900 W. Market St., 17961. Tel: 717-366-1016. Deacon Alex L. Maggitti, Dir.
Adult & Youth Retreats. Tel: 717-366-1405. Retreat Centers Total Staff 6. Overnight retreats, day retreats, weekend retreats and workshops.
Other Diocesan Agencies with Facilities in the St. Francis Center:
Catholic Social Agency. (Branch Office). Tel: 717-366-1403. Sr. Miriam Denis, S.S.J., M.B.A.
Department of Youth Ministry. Tel: 717-366-1405. Rev. William F. Glosser, M.A.
Holy Family Adult Day Care. Tel: 717-366-2924. Mrs. Linda Herb, Dir. Total Assisted Average 25/Day; Total Staff 5.
Holy Family Home Health Care. Tel: 717-366-0990. Mrs. Arlene Mongrain, R.N., B.S., Exec. Dir.
Holy Family Residence. Tel: 717-366-2912. Mr. James Polaski, Admin.

SHILLINGTON. *Mariawald Renewal Center-Precious Blood Convent*. 1094 Welsh Rd., P.O. Box 97, Reading, 19607. Tel: 610-777-0135; Fax: 610-777-3359. For women, men and mixed groups. Sr. M. Francis Bisland, C.P.S., Supr.; Sr. Theresa Bringazi, C.P.S., Dir. Total Staff 6; Total in Residence 2.

[N] CENTERS FOR SPIRITUAL GROWTH

WERNERSVILLE. *Jesuit Center for Spiritual Growth*, 19565. Tel: 610-678-8085; Fax: 610-678-8747. Revs. George A. Aschenbrenner, S.J., Dir.; John P. Barron, S.J.; George S. Williams, S.J.; Sr. Susan Bowers, I.H.M.; Sr. Bernadette Duross, R.S.M.; Sr. Maria McCoy, S.S.J.; Sr. Barbara Weigand, I.H.M.; Bro. Renatus Foldenauer, C.S.C. Directed retreats, programs in prayer, discernment, psychology and spirituality.

[O] NEWMAN CENTERS

KUTZTOWN. *Christopher House*, 15207 Kutztown Rd., 19530. Tel: 610-683-8380. Rev. Larry J. Hess, Diocesan Dir., Campus Ministry.
Albright College (Reading), St. Margaret Rectory, 925 Centre St., Reading, 19601. Tel: 610-376-2919. Rev. Ronald J. Yarrosh, M.S.
Allentown College of St. Francis de Sales (Center Valley), 2755 Station Ave., Center Valley, 18034-9568. Rev. John Hanley, O.S.F.S. Tel: 610-282-1100 Ext. 1389.
Alvernia College, Dept. of Campus Ministry, Mt. Alvernia, Reading, 19607. Tel: 610-796-8300. Mr. Bob Shearn.
Cedar Crest College (Allentown), Catholic Chaplaincy Center, 2400 Chew St., Allentown, 18104-5586. Tel: 610-821-3122. Rev. John A. Krivak, Ed.D.
Kutztown University (Kutztown), Christopher House, 15207 Kutztown Rd., 19530. Tel: 610-683-8380. Rev. Larry J. Hess, M.A.
Lafayette College (Easton), 119 McCartney St., Easton, 18042-7647. Tel: 610-253-5044. Rev. William F. Walsh, O.S.F.S.
Lehigh University (Bethlehem), Newman Center at Lehigh University #41, 661 Taylor St., Bethlehem, 18015-3107. Tel: 610-758-4148; 866-0581. Rev. Alfred A. Schlert, J.C.L.
Moravian College (Bethlehem), Koinonia House, 1130 Monocacy St., Bethlehem, 18018-6650. Tel: 610-861-3936. Rev. William F. Walsh, O.S.F.S.
Muhlenberg College (Allentown), Catholic Chaplaincy Center, 2400 Chew St., Allentown, 18104-5586. Tel: 610-821-3122. Rev. John A. Krivak, Ed.D.
Penn State University (Sinking Spring), St. Ignatius Loyola, 2810 St. Alban Dr., Sinking Spring, 19608. Tel: 610-678-3767.
Penn State University (Schuylkill Haven Center, Schuylkill Haven), St. Ambrose Rectory, 201 Randel St., Schuylkill Haven, 17972. Tel: 717-385-1031. Rev. Eric Gruber.

RELIGIOUS INSTITUTES OF MEN REPRESENTED IN THE DIOCESE

For further details refer to the corresponding bracketed number in the Religious Institutes of Men or Women section.

[]—*Cistercian Monks of the Strict Observance*.—S.O.Cist.
[0160]—*Clerics Regular of St. Paul*. (Bernabite Fathers).—C.R.S.P.
[1330]—*Congregation of the Mission*. (Eastern Prov.).—C.M.
[0520]—*Franciscan Friars*. (Custody of the Most Holy Savior; Croatian Custody of the Holy Family).—O.F.M.
[0690]—*Jesuit Fathers and Brothers*. (Maryland Prov.).—S.J.
[1110]—*Missionaries of the Sacred Heart*. (U.S. Prov.).—M.S.C.
[0860]—*Missionhurst Congregation of the Immaculate Heart of Mary*.—C.I.C.M.
[0920]—*Oblates of St. Francis De Sales*.—O.S.F.S.

RELIGIOUS INSTITUTES OF WOMEN REPRESENTED IN THE DIOCESE

[0120]—*Angelic Sisters of St. Paul*.—A.S.S.P.
[1810]—*Bernardine Sisters of the Third Order of St. Francis*.—O.S.F.
[0320]—*Carmelite Nuns of the Ancient Observance*.—O.Carm.
[0760]—*Daughters of Charity of St. Vincent de Paul*.—D.C.
[0795]—*Daughters of Divine Zeal*.—F.D.Z.
[1065]—*Dominican Daughters of the Immaculate Mother*.—O.P.
[2575]—*Institute of the Sisters of Mercy of the Americas*. (Merion, PA).—R.S.M.
[2710]—*Missionaries of Charity*.—M.C.
[2800]—*Missionary Sisters of the Most Sacred Heart of Jesus of Hiltrup*.—M.S.C.
[2850]—*Missionary Sisters of the Precious Blood*.—C.P.S.
[3240]—*Poor Sisters of Jesus Crucified and the Sorrowful Mother*.—C.J.C.
[3250]—*Poor Sisters of St. Joseph*.—P.S.S.J.
[1700]—*School Sisters of the Third Order of St. Francis*. (Bethlehem, PA).—O.S.F.
[0660]—*Sisters of Christian Charity*.—S.C.C.
[3780]—*Sisters of Saints Cyril and Methodius*.—SS.C.M.
[3700]—*Sisters of St. Benedict*.—O.S.B.
[3740]—*Sisters of St. Casimir*.—S.S.C.
[1650]—*Sisters of St. Francis of Philadelphia*.—O.S.F.
[3830]—*Sisters of St. Joseph*.—S.S.J.
[2170]—*Sisters, Servants of the Immaculate Heart of Mary*.—I.H.M.

DIOCESAN CEMETERIES

ALLENTOWN. *Resurrection*, 547 N. Krocks Rd., 18106. Tel: 610-395-3819.

BETHLEHEM. *Holy Saviour*, 857 E. Langhorne Ave., 18017. Tel: 610-866-2372.

NECROLOGY

† Courtney, Thomas M., (Retired). —Died Aug. 26, 1996.
† Dick, C. Norbert, (Retired). —Died Feb. 7, 1996.
† Loeper, Frederick J., (Retired). —Died Aug. 31, 1996.
† Neverauskas, Rev. Msgr. Joseph A., (Retired). —Died Jan. 13, 1996.
† Sabas, John Paul, (Retired). —Died July 18, 1996.

Diocese of Altoona-Johnstown

(Dioecesis Altunensis-Johnstoniensis)

Most Reverend

JOSEPH V. ADAMEC, D.D., S.T.L.

Bishop of Altoona-Johnstown; ordained July 3, 1960; appointed Bishop of Altoona-Johnstown March 17, 1987; ordained and installed May 20, 1987. *Mailing Address: Chancery Office, 126 Logan Blvd., Hollidaysburg, PA, 16648.*

Most Reverend

JAMES J. HOGAN, D.D.

Retired Bishop of Altoona-Johnstown; ordained December 8, 1937; appointed Titular Bishop of Philomelium and Auxiliary of Trenton November 27, 1959; consecrated February 25, 1960; appointed to the See of Altoona-Johnstown May 23, 1966; installed July 6, 1966; retired October 17, 1986. *Office: 126 Logan Blvd., Hollidaysburg, PA, 16648.*

ESTABLISHED DIOCESE OF ALTOONA, MAY 27, 1901.

REDESIGNATED DIOCESE OF ALTOONA-JOHNSTOWN, OCTOBER 9, 1957.

Square Miles 6,674.

Comprises the Counties of Bedford, Blair, Cambria, Centre, Clinton, Fulton, Huntingdon and Somerset in the State of Pennsylvania.

For legal titles of parishes and diocesan institutions, consult the Chancery Office.

The Chancery: 126 Logan Blvd., Hollidaysburg, PA, 16648. Tel.: 814-695-5579; Fax: 814-695-8894.

STATISTICAL OVERVIEW

Personnel	
Bishop	1
Retired Bishops	1
Priests: Diocesan Active in Diocese	112
Priests: Active Outside Diocese	6
Priests: Retired, Sick or Absent	40
Number of Diocesan Priests	158
Religious Priests in Diocese	65
Ordinations:	
Diocesan Priests	2
Religious Priests	1
Transitional Deacons	3
Permanent Deacons	2
Permanent Deacons in Diocese	16
Total Brothers	4
Total Sisters	155
Parishes	
Parishes	113
With Resident Pastor:	
Resident Diocesan Priests	86
Resident Religious Priests	13
Without Resident Pastor:	
Administered by Priests	14
Missions	5
Welfare	
Catholic Hospitals	2
Total Assisted	204,995
Homes for the Aged	3
Total Assisted	230
Special Centers for Social Services	2
Total Assisted	43,844
Educational	
Diocesan Students in Other Seminaries	11
Total Seminarians	11
Colleges and Universities	2
Total Students	6,083
High Schools, Diocesan and Parish	3
Total Students	1,230
Elementary Schools, Diocesan and Parish	31
Total Students	5,336
Catechesis/Religious Education:	
High School Students	4,807
Elementary Students	8,803
Total Students Under Catholic Instruction	26,270
Teachers in the Diocese:	
Priests	6
Brothers	1
Sisters	29
Lay Teachers	707
Vital Statistics	
Receptions into the Church:	
Infant Baptism Totals	1,627
Adult Baptism Totals	127
Received into Full Communion	207
First Communions	1,922
Confirmations	1,810
Marriages:	
Catholic	520
Interfaith	351
Total Marriages	871
Deaths	1,563
Total Catholic Population	114,914
Total Population	649,961

Former Bishops—Rt. Rev. EUGENE A. GARVEY, D.D., ord. Sept. 22, 1869; cons. Sept. 8, 1901; died Oct. 22, 1920.—Most Rev. JOHN JOSEPH MCCORT, D.D., ord. Oct. 14, 1883; cons. Titular Bishop of Azotus and Auxiliary to the Archbishop of Philadelphia, Sept. 17, 1912; appt. Coadjutor cum jure successionis to the Bishop of Altoona, Jan. 27, 1920; appt. Bishop of Altoona, Oct. 22, 1920; appt. Assistant at the Pontifical Throne, Oct. 5, 1933; died April 21, 1936.—Most Rev. RICHARD T. GUILFOYLE, D.D., ord. June 2, 1917; appt. Aug. 8, 1936; cons. Nov. 30, 1936; died June 10, 1957.—Most Rev. HOWARD J. CARROLL, D.D., ord. April 2, 1927; appt. Dec. 5, 1957; cons. Jan. 2, 1958; died March 21, 1960.—Most Rev. J. CARROLL MCCORMICK, D.D., ord. July 10, 1932; cons. April 20, 1947; appt. June 25, 1960; transferred to See of Scranton March 4, 1966; retired Feb. 15, 1983; died Nov. 2, 1996.—Most Rev. JAMES J. HOGAN, D.D., ord. Dec. 8, 1937; appt. Titular Bishop of Philomelium and Auxiliary of Trenton, Nov. 27, 1959; cons. Feb. 25, 1960; appt. to the See of Altoona-Johnstown May 23, 1966; retired Oct. 17, 1986.

Diocesan Officials

Bishop—Most Rev. JOSEPH V. ADAMEC, D.D., S.T.L., *126 Logan Blvd., Hollidaysburg, 16648.* Tel: 814-695-5579.

Secretary to the Bishop—Rev. Msgr. DENNIS R. BOGGS, *126 Logan Blvd., Hollidaysburg, 16648.* Tel: 814-695-5579.

Retired Bishop—Most Rev. JAMES J. HOGAN, D.D., J.C.D., *126 Logan Blvd., Hollidaysburg, 16648.* Tel: 814-696-0278.

Vicars General—Rev. Msgr. STANLEY B. CARSON, V.G., Admin. (Secretariats), *126 Logan Blvd., Hollidaysburg, 16648.* Tel: 814-695-5579; 943-8553 (Res.).; Rev. Msgr. GEORGE B. FLINN, V.G., S.T.L., Pastoral Life and Ministry, *126 Logan Blvd., Hollidaysburg, 16648.* Tel: 814-695-5579; 536-0117 (Res.).

Judicial Vicar—Rev. Msgr. MICHAEL E. SERVINSKY, S.T.L., J.C.L., *126 Logan Blvd., Hollidaysburg, 16648.* Tel: 814-695-5579; 943-8464 (Res.).

Bishop's Delegate for Religious—Sr. MARY ANN DILLON, R.S.M., Ph.D., *Our Lady of the Alleghenies Convent, 538 Main St., Lilly, 15938.* Tel: 814-886-2534 (Res.).

Vicars Forane

Allegheny—Rev. Msgr. JOHN R. SASWAY, V.F.
Altoona—Very Rev. PAUL E. TURNBULL, V.F.
Barnesboro—Very Rev. CHARLES F. BODZIAK, V.F.
Cambria—Very Rev. CHARLES M. AMERSHEK, V.F.
Clinton-Centre—Very Rev. D. TIMOTHY GRIMME, V.F.
Ebensburg—Rev. Msgr. JOHN J. LITTLE, V.F.
Huntingdon-Blair—Rev. Msgr. DAVID A. LOCKARD, V.F.
Johnstown—Rev. Msgr. JOSEPH R. KINIRY, P.A., V.F.
Prince Gallitzin—Rev. Msgr. THOMAS J. MAHER, V.F.
Southern—Rev. Msgr. SAMUEL J. TOMASELLI, V.F.
Windber—Rev. Msgr. IGNATIUS C. WADAS, V.F.

Secretariats

CHANCERY—Rev. Msgr. DENNIS R. BOGGS, Sec., *126 Logan Blvd., Hollidaysburg, 16648.* Tel: 814-695-5579; Fax: 814-695-8894. Office Hours: Mon.-Fri. 9-4:30. Closed Holy Days.

Catholic Register—Rev. TIMOTHY P. STEIN, Editor. Tel: 814-695-7563; Fax: 814-695-7517.

Ecumenical Minister—Rev. HAROLD N. BILLER. Tel: 814-539-2186.

Information Officers—Rev. Msgr. DENNIS R. BOGGS; Rev. TIMOTHY P. STEIN. Tel: 814-695-5579.

Interfaith Minister—Rev. Msgr. ROY F. KLINE. Tel: 814-695-2337.

EVANGELIZATION—Sr. CHARMAINE GRILLIOT, C.PP.S., M.A., Sec., *126A Logan Blvd., Hollidaysburg, 16648.* Tel: 814-695-5579.

Education—Sr. CHARMAINE GRILLIOT, C.PP.S., M.A., Dir. Tel: 814-695-5579.

Youth/Campus Ministry—ROBERT SHERWIN. Tel: 814-695-5579.

Catholic Scouting—Rev. JOSEPH ORR. Tel: 717-485-3723.

MINISTERIAL & LEADERSHIP—Rev. ROBERT C. MAZUR, Sec., *124 Logan Blvd., Hollidaysburg, 16648.* Tel: 814-695-5579.

Christian Initiation—Sr. BARBARA BETTWY, C.C.W. Tel: 814-695-5579.
Diaconal Formation—Deacon JOHN J. CONCANNON. Tel: 814-695-5579.
Lay Ministries—HAROLD HORELL. Tel: 814-695-5579.
Liturgy & Worship—Rev. ROBERT C. MAZUR, Dir. Tel: 814-695-5579.
Ongoing Formation of the Clergy—Rev. ROBERT J. KELLY. Tel: 814-695-5579.
Pastoral Centers—Sr. MARJORIE MCGUIRE, C.C.W. Tel: 814-247-9954.
Propagation of the Faith—Rev. ROBERT J. KELLY. Tel: 814-695-5579.
Vocation—Rev. MICHAEL A. BECKER. Tel: 814-695-5579.

PASTORAL SERVICES—Rev. Msgr. ROBERT J. SALY, Sec., *1300 12th Ave., P.O. Box 1349, Altoona, 16603.* Tel: 814-944-9388.
Catholic Social Services—Rev. Msgr. ROBERT J. SALY. Tel: 814-944-9388.
Family Life Ministries—Sr. MARILYN WELCH, C.C.W. Tel: 814-472-5333.
Peace & Justice Commission—Mr. CHARLES LEIDEN. Tel: 814-946-9291.
Priests' Residence - Dmitri Manor—Rev. Msgr. ROBERT J. SALY. Tel: 814-944-9388.

TEMPORALITIES—LARRY R. SUTTON, Sec., *126 Logan Blvd., Hollidaysburg, 16648.* Tel: 814-695-5579.
Building Commission—Mr. JERRY KINIRY. Tel: 814-288-2663.
Building & Grounds—ERNEST ENEDY. Tel: 814-695-5579.
Comptroller—HERMAN NAGLE. Tel: 814-695-5579.
Computer Systems—RONALD MULDOON. Tel: 814-695-5579.
Cemetery Commission—Rev. RICHARD D. CLARK. Tel: 814-536-4622.
Development Office—JAMES EDWARDS. Tel: 814-695-5579.
Diocesan Shrines—LARRY R. SUTTON. Tel: 814-695-5579.
Financial & Legal—LARRY R. SUTTON, Dir. Tel: 814-695-5579.

Diocesan Offices

Building Commission—Mr. JERRY KINIRY. Tel: 814-288-2663.
Campus Ministry—(For further details regarding Campus Ministries please refer to Institutions Located in the Diocese.).
Catholic Social Service—Rev. Msgr. ROBERT J. SALY, Dir. JOHN R. PRICHARD, M.S.W., A.C.S.W., Asst. Dir.; Sr. CAROL JEAN CZYRNIK, Intake Worker, *1300 12th Ave., P.O. Box 1349, Altoona, 16603.* Tel: 814-944-9388.
Johnstown Offices—232 Walnut St., 2nd Flr., Johnstown, 15901. Tel: 814-535-6538.
State College Offices—276 W. Hamilton Ave., P.O. Box 680, State College, 16801. Tel: 814-238-4937.
"The Catholic Register"—Rev. TIMOTHY P. STEIN, Editor, *P.O. Box 413, Hollidaysburg, 16648.* Tel: 814-695-7563.
Cemetery Commission—Rev. RICHARD D. CLARK, *Sacred Heart Rectory, 219 Oak St., Conemaugh, 15909.* Tel: 814-536-4622.
Chancery—Rev. Msgr. DENNIS R. BOGGS, Chancellor. Tel: 814-695-5579; Fax: 814-695-8894.
Christian Initiation—Sr. BARBARA BETTWY, C.C.W., *126A Logan Blvd., Hollidaysburg, 16648.* Tel: 814-695-5579.
Computer Systems—RONALD MULDOON. Tel: 814-695-5579.
Comptroller—HERMAN NAGLE. Tel: 814-695-5579.
Development Office—JAMES EDWARDS, *P.O. Box 409, Hollidaysburg, 16648.* Tel: 814-696-4389.
Diaconal Formation—Deacon JOHN J. CONCANNON, *124 Logan Blvd., Hollidaysburg, 16648.* Tel: 814-695-5579.
Diocesan Shrines—LARRY R. SUTTON, *126 Logan Blvd., Hollidaysburg, 16648.* Tel: 814-695-5579.
Education—Sr. CHARMAINE GRILLIOT, C.PP.S., M.A., Dir., *126A Logan Blvd., Hollidaysburg, 16648.* Tel: 814-695-5579. Asst. Directors: CHARLEEN BLUM, Religious Ed.; Sr. MARK PLESCHER, C.S.A., Elementary; ROBERT SHERWIN, Campus/Youth Ministry.
Ecumenical Minister—Rev. HAROLD N. BILLER, *609 Park Ave., Johnstown, 15902.* Tel: 814-539-2186.
Family Life Office—Sr. MARILYN WELCH, C.C.W., Dir., *1116 N. Center St., P.O. Box 565, Ebensburg, 15931.* Tel: 814-472-5333. SUSAN STITH, Prog. Coord. *Divorced / Separated & Bereaved Ministries; Parent & Marriage Preparation Ministries.* Programs: *Persons with Disabilities Ministry; Natural Family Planning; Respect Life.*
Finance Council—FRANK PASQUERILLA.
Finance Office—LARRY R. SUTTON, Dir., *126 Logan Blvd., Hollidaysburg, 16648.* Tel: 814-695-5579.
Holy Childhood Association—Rev. ROBERT J. KELLY, Dir., *124 Logan Blvd., Hollidaysburg, 16648.* Tel: 814-695-5579.
Information Office—Rev. Msgr. DENNIS R. BOGGS; Rev. TIMOTHY P. STEIN, *126 Logan Blvd., Hollidaysburg, 16648.* Tel: 814-695-5579.
Interfaith Minister—Rev. Msgr. ROY KLINE, *P.O. Box 88, Duncansville, 16635.* Tel: 814-695-2337.
Lay Ministries—HAROLD HORELL, *124 Logan Blvd., Hollidaysburg, 16648.* Tel: 814-695-5579.
Liturgical Commission—Sr. KAREN GRUSECK, C.C.W., *741 Railroad St., Johnstown, 15901.* Tel: 814-539-2113.
Liturgy & Worship—Rev. ROBERT C. MAZUR, *124 Logan Blvd., Hollidaysburg, 16648.* Tel: 814-695-5579.
Mission - Carmelite Community of the Word—110 S. Third St., McConnellsburg, 17233. Tel: 717-485-5917.
Ongoing Formation Clergy—Rev. ROBERT J. KELLY, Dir., *124 Logan Blvd., Hollidaysburg, 16648.* Tel: 814-695-5579.
Pastoral Centers—
Altoona—Sr. KAREN ELIZABETH DUDDY, Dir., *1304 13th Ave., Altoona, 16601.* Tel: 814-942-7661.
Johnstown—Sr. MARTHA BURBULLA, Dir., *741 Railroad St., Johnstown, 15901.* Tel: 814-535-7005.
Permanent Deacons—Deacon JOHN J. CONCANNON, *124 Logan Blvd., Hollidasyburg, 16648.* Tel: 814-695-5579.
Peace & Justice Commission—Mr. CHARLES LEIDEN, *306 Coleridge Ave., Altoona, 16602.* Tel: 814-946-9291.
Presbyteral Council—Rev. GEORGE D. KOHARCHIK, Chm., *509 Caldwell Ave., Portage, 15946.* Tel: 814-736-4279.
Priests' Personnel Board—Rev. Msgr. GEORGE B. FLINN, V.G., S.T.L., *126 Logan Blvd., Hollidaysburg, 16648.* Tel: 814-695-5579.
Priests' Residence - Dmitri Manor—Rev. Msgr. ROBERT J. SALY, Dir., *St. Mary's Lane, Hollidaysburg, 16648.* Tel: 814-944-9338.
Retreat & Conference Center—St. John the Baptist Retreat Center, P.O. Box 10, New Baltimore, 15553. Tel: 814-733-2210.
Scouting—Rev. JOSEPH ORR, *303 Lincoln Way E., McConnellsburg, 17233.* Tel: 717-485-3723.
Self Insurance Program—JOSEPH WATT, *Gallagher Bassett Insurance - Berkshire Center, Ste. 302, Greensburg, 15601.* Tel: 800-831-3247.
Society for the Propagation of the Faith—Rev. ROBERT J. KELLY, Dir., *124 Logan Blvd., Hollidaysburg, 16648.* Tel: 814-695-5579.
St. Vincent de Paul Society—PAUL MCCONNELL, Pres.; Deacon JOHN E. SROKA, Exec. Dir., *566 Vine St., Johnstown, 15901.* Tel: 814-535-4357.
Tribunal Office—Rev. Msgr. MICHAEL E. SERVINSKY, S.T.L., J.C.L., *126 Logan Blvd., Hollidaysburg, 16648.* Tel: 814-695-5579.
Vocation Office—Rev. MICHAEL A. BECKER, *124 Logan Blvd., Hollidaysburg, 16648.* Tel: 814-695-5579.

CLERGY, PARISHES, MISSIONS AND PAROCHIAL SCHOOLS

CITY OF ALTOONA
(Blair County)

1—CATHEDRAL OF THE BLESSED SACRAMENT (1851), Revs. Robert C. Mazur; George M. Gulash; John J. Slovikovski; Rev. Msgr. Thomas E. Madden, P.A., (Retired); Deacon James F. Leap.
Res., 1331 13th Ave., P.O. Box 33, 16603. Tel: 814-944-4603.
School—See Elementary Diocesan Schools under Institutions Located in the Diocese. Tel: 814-943-7423; Fax: 814-949-4794. Mrs. Jennifer Long, Prin.
Catechesis / Religious Programs—Tel: 814-943-7423. Mrs. Jeanne Thompson, D.R.E.
Students 189.

2—IMMACULATE CONCEPTION (1860). (St. Mary's). Revs. Robert G. Neugebauer; Robert P. Reese. In res., Rev. Sean K. Code.
Res., 1405 Fifth Ave., 16602. Tel: 814-942-2416. [CEM]
School—1400 Fourth Ave., 16602. Tel: 814-944-1250; Fax: 814-942-0894.
Lay Teachers 11; Students 192.
Catechesis / Religious Programs—Sr. Julia Zilka, V.S.C., D.R.E.
Students 192.

3—ST. MARK'S (1889), Rev. Msgr. Robert J. Saly; Rev. Henry Stange.
Res., 416 Sixth Ave., 16602. Tel: 814-942-0364.
Catechesis / Religious Programs—Students 102.
Chapel—Valley View Home for the Aged, Tel: 814-944-0845.

4—SACRED HEART (1890), Rev. Msgr. Stanley B. Carson, V.G. In res., Rev. Leo A. Lynch.
Res., 511 20th St., 16602. Tel: 814-943-8553; Fax: 814-943-1556.
Formation Center—2009 Sixth Ave., 16602. Tel: 814-944-3922.
Catechesis / Religious Programs—Students 153.

5—HOLY ROSARY (1901), Revs. Carl A. Spishak; Edward J. Dabcosky.
Res., 900 Fourth St.-Juniata, 16601. Tel: 814-944-6676.
Catechesis / Religious Programs—Tel: 814-944-7709. Mrs. Shirley A. Mercer, D.R.E.
Students 131.

6—OUR LADY OF FATIMA (1995) (Irish-Polish), Rev. Anthony J. Pollack.
Res., 2010 12th Ave., 16601. Tel: 814-942-0371. [CEM]
School—McNelis Catholic. See Elementary Diocesan Schools under Institutions Located in the Diocese. Tel: 814-943-7423.
Catechesis / Religious Programs—1304 13th Ave., 16603. Tel: 814-943-7423.
Students 62.

7—OUR LADY OF MT. CARMEL (1905) (Italian), Revs. Giles A. Schinelli, T.O.R.; Terrence T. Smith, T.O.R.; Louis J. Secondo, T.O.R. In res., Rev. Alan Polimine, T.O.R., (Retired).
Res., 806 11th St., 16602. Tel: 814-942-8501; Fax: 814-944-2208.
School—1012 Eighth Ave., 16602. Tel: 814-943-5931; Fax: 814-942-5787. Sr. Mary Kevin, Prin. & D.R.E.
Franciscan Sisters of the Immaculate Conception 1; Lay Teachers 10; Students 200.
Catechesis / Religious Programs—Students 140.
Convent—Tel: 814-942-8964.
Mission—Pleasant Valley, Blair Co., Our Lady of the Assumption, (1925) 15 1/2 Pierce St., Pleasant Valley, 16602.

8—ST. LEO THE GREAT (1911). Merged with SS. Peter & Paul to form Our Lady of Fatima, Altoona.
School—McNelis Catholic. See Elementary Diocesan Schools under Institutions Located in the Diocese. Tel: 814-943-7423.

9—SS. PETER AND PAUL (1911) (Polish). Merged with St. Leo the Great to form Our Lady of Fatima, Altoona.
School—McNelis Catholic. See Elementary Diocesan Schools under Institutions Located in the Diocese. Tel: 814-943-7423.

10—ST. JOHN THE EVANGELIST (1921), Very Rev. Paul E. Turnbull, V.F.; Deacon Gene Neral.
Res., 309 Lotz Ave., Lakemont, Altoona, 16602. Tel: 814-942-5503; Fax: 814-942-4514.
School—Tel: 814-943-4966. Lois Werfel, Prin.
Lay Teachers 7; Students 91.
Catechesis / Religious Programs—Ms. Joan Price, D.R.E.
Students 263.

11—OUR LADY OF LOURDES (1923), Revs. Robert C. Hall; John J. Neugebauer; Edward L. Eckenrod.
Res., 2716 Broad Ave., 16601. Tel: 814-943-6185.
School—2713 W. Chestnut Ave., 16601. Tel: 814-942-3421. Mrs. Catherine M. DiSabato, Prin.
Lay Teachers 10; Students 162.
Catechesis / Religious Programs—Students 65.

12—ST. ROSE OF LIMA (1924), Revs. Michael A. Becker; Dennis J. Braman. In res., Rev. Robert J. Kelly.
Res., 5514 Roselawn Ave., 16602. Tel: 814-944-8509.
School—5519 Sixth Ave., 16602. Tel: 814-942-7835; Fax: 814-942-1095. Patricia Ronan, Prin.
Lay Teachers 11; Students 232.
Catechesis / Religious Programs—D.R.E.: Viola Bettwy; Barbara Jean Daly Horell.
Students 242.

13—ST. THERESE OF THE CHILD JESUS (1927), Rev. Msgr. Anthony B. Little; Rev. Allen P. Zeth.
Church & Rectory: 2329 Fourth St., 16601-3632. Tel: 814-942-4479.
Res., 205 27th Ave., 16601. Tel: 814-943-4844.
School—424 Wopsononock Ave., 16601. Tel: 814-944-3751. Linda Truesdell, Prin.; Andrew Callaghan, D.R.E.
Religious 1; Lay Teachers 8; Students 123.
Catechesis / Religious Programs—Students 133.

CITY OF JOHNSTOWN
(Cambria County)

1—ST. JOHN GUALBERT CATHEDRAL (1835), Rev. Msgr. George B. Flinn, V.G., Rector; Revs. John F. Brezovec; Alan E. Thomas; Clarence S. Bridges; Deacon John J. Concannon.
Res., P.O. Box 807, 117 Clinton St., 15907. Tel:

814-536-0117; Fax: 814-535-6771. [CEM 2]
School—Central Catholic Elementary. See Elementary Diocesan Schools under Institutions Located in the Diocese. Tel: 814-536-1532.
Catechesis/Religious Programs—124 Maple Ave., 15901.
Students 63.

2—St. Joseph's (1852) (German). Merged with Our Lady of Mercy to form St. John Gualbert Cathedral, Johnstown.
School—Central Catholic Elementary. See Elementary Diocesan Schools under Institutions Located in the Diocese. Tel: 814-536-1532.

3—Immaculate Conception (1859) (German), Rev. Andrew C. Stanko.
Res., 308 Broad St., 15906. Tel: 814-535-4407. [CEM]
School—West End Catholic. See Elementary Diocesan Schools under Institutions Located in the Diocese. Tel: 814-536-4722.

4—St. Columba's (1888), Rev. Benjamin Dykas.
Res., 916 Broad St., 15906. Tel: 814-535-1627. [CEM]
School—West End Catholic. See Elementary Diocesan Schools under Institutions Located in the Diocese. Tel: 814-536-4722.

5—St. Stephen, First King of Hungary (1891) (Slovak), Rev. Lawrence L. Lacovic.
Res., 414 Fourth Ave., 15906. Tel: 814-539-6334. [CEM]
School—West End Catholic. See Elementary Diocesan Schools under Institutions Located in the Diocese. Tel: 814-536-4722.
Catechesis/Religious Programs—Students 75.

6—St. Rochus (1900) (Croatian), Rev. Charles M. Amershek, Jr., V.F.; Sr. Patricia Milko, C.D.P., Pastoral Min.
Res., 314 Eighth Ave., 15906. Tel: 814-539-1520; Fax: 814-539-8845. [CEM]
School—West End Catholic. See Elementary Diocesan Schools under Institutions Located in the Diocese. Tel: 814-536-4722.
Catechesis/Religious Programs—Tel: 814-535-5409. Theresa Marcus, D.R.E.
Students 178.

7—St. Casimir's (1902) (Polish), Rev. John J. Marshall Tel: 814-536-8534; Rev. Msgr. Casimir B. Ossowski, Pastor Emeritus.
Res., 501 Power St., 15906. Tel: 814-535-2139. [CEM]
School—West End Catholic. See Elementary Diocesan Schools under Institutions Located in the Diocese. Tel: 814-536-4722.
Catechesis/Religious Programs—Students 82.

8—St. Patrick's (1904), Rev. Harold N. Biller; Deacon Leo A. Kist, P.D.
Res., 609 Park Ave., 15902. Tel: 814-539-2186.
School—617 Park Ave., 15902. Tel: 814-535-2926. Sr. Mary Magdaline Wagner, Prin.
Sisters of St. Joseph 2; Lay Teachers 7; Students 189.
Catechesis/Religious Programs—Students 43.

9—St. Emerich's (1905) (Hungarian), Rev. John J. Marshall.
Res., 501 Power St., 15906. Tel: 814-535-2139. [CEM]
School—West End Catholic. See Elementary Diocesan Schools under Institutions Located in the Diocese. Tel: 814-536-4722.

10—St. Anthony's (1905) (Italian), Revs. Patrick Seelman, T.O.R.; Leonard Blostic, T.O.R.; Bro. Stephen Baker, T.O.R.
Res., 124 Maple Ave., 15901. Tel: 814-535-4228. [CEM]
School—Central Catholic Elementary. See Elementary Diocesan Schools under Institutions Located in the Diocese. Tel: 814-536-1532.
Catechesis/Religious Programs—Students 168.

11—St. Michael's (1910) (German), Revs. Andrew C. Stanko; Donald Dusza; John J. Byrnes.
Res., 180 Gilbert St., 15906. Tel: 814-535-7646.

12—SS. Peter and Paul's (1918) (Slovak), Rev. Christopher Panagoplos, T.O.R.
Res., 218 Maple Ave., 15901. Tel: 814-535-1133. [CEM]
School—Central Catholic Elementary. See Elementary Diocesan Schools under Institutions Located in the Diocese. Tel: 814-536-1532.

13—Our Mother of Sorrows (1920), Rev. Msgr. Thomas K. Mabon; Revs. Donald W. Dusza; John D. Byrnes.
Res., 407 Tioga St., 15905. Tel: 814-535-7646; Fax: 814-536-7850.
School—430 Tioga St., 15905. Tel: 814-539-5315. Mr. John Skubak, Prin.
Lay Teachers 21; Students 393.
Catechesis/Religious Programs—Tel: 814-255-1264. Mrs. Karen Fink, D.R.E.
Students 149.

14—Our Lady of Mercy (1921). Merged with St. Joseph to form St. John Gualbert Cathedral, Johnstown.
School—Central Catholic Elementary. See Elementary Diocesan Schools under Institutions Located in the Diocese. Tel: 814-536-1532.

15—St. Francis of Assisi (1922) (Slovak), Rev. Francis P. Balestino.
Res., 120 Barron Ave., 15906. Tel: 814-539-1632. [CEM]
School—West End Catholic. See Elementary Diocesan Schools under Institutions Located in the Diocese.
Catechesis/Religious Programs—Students 91.

16—Visitation of the B.V.M. (1927), Rev. Martin A. Cingle; Deacon John E. Sroka. In res., 1428 Coventry Ct., 15905. Tel: 814-255-4973 Rev. Bernard Grattan, Hospital Chap.
Res., 1127 McKinley Ave., 15905. Tel: 814-536-6110.
Catechesis/Religious Programs—Tel: 814-536-6110.
Students 54.

17—St. Therese of the Child Jesus (1929) (Slovenian), Revs. Bernard Karmanocky, O.F.M.; Raphael Stragisher, O.F.M., (Retired); Bonaventure Borgola, O.F.M., (Retired).
Res., 536 Decker Ave., 15906. Tel: 814-539-7633. [CEM]
School—West End Catholic. See Elementary Diocesan Schools under Institutions Located in the Diocese. Tel: 814-536-4472.
Mission—Moxham, Cambria Co., St. Anne's, (1935) 533 Woodland Ave., Moxham, 15902. Tel: 814-539-7633.
Catechesis/Religious Programs—Students 50.

18—St. Clement's (1956), Rev. William E. Rosenbaum.
Res., 114 Lindberg Ave., 15905. Tel: 814-255-4422.
School—110 Lindberg Ave., 15905. Tel: 814-255-1964. A. Ernest Papinchak, Prin.
Lay Teachers 10; Students 153.
Catechesis/Religious Programs—Ms. Mary Drager, D.R.E.
Students 212.

19—St. Andrew's (1956), Revs. Barry J. Baroni; Joseph D. Maurizio; Deacon Herman J. Lux.
Res., 1621 Ferndale Ave., 15905. Tel: 814-288-4324; Fax: 814-288-6750.
School—1629 Ferndale Ave., 15905. Tel: 814-288-1854.
Lay Teachers 10; Students 170.
Catechesis/Religious Programs—Students 126.

20—St. Gregory's (1919), Rev. Msgr. Daniel J. O'Neill.
Res., 120 Boltz St., 15902. Tel: 814-536-6818.
Catechesis/Religious Programs—Students 99.

21—St. Barnabas (1954) (Slovenian), Rev. Daniel J. O'Neill.
Res., 120 Boltz St., 15902. Tel: 814-536-6818. [CEM]

22—St. Benedict's (1930), Rev. Msgr. Joseph R. Kiniry, P.A., V.F.; Revs. James M. Dugan; David S. Peles.
Res., 2310 Bedford St., 15904. Tel: 814-266-9718.
School—2306 Bedford St., 15904. Tel: 814-266-3837; Fax: 814-266-7718. Gerald Brown, Prin.
Lay Teachers 29; Students 503.
Catechesis/Religious Programs—Tel: 814-266-2105. Diane Redvay, D.R.E.
Students 406.

OUTSIDE THE CITIES OF ALTOONA AND JOHNSTOWN

Acosta, Somerset Co., St. John the Baptist's (1912). Merged with St. Joseph, Boswell, and St. Stanislaus, Boswell, to form All Saints Church, Boswell.

Ashville, Cambria Co., St. Thomas Aquinas (1889), Rev. James F. Bunn.
Res., 16613. Tel: 814-944-5615; 674-5416. [CEM]
Catechesis/Religious Programs—Mrs. Ann Bilko, D.R.E.
Students 111.

Bakerton, Cambria Co., Sacred Heart (1904). Merged with St. Patrick, Spangler, to form St. Jude, Elmora. Rev. David J. Arseneault.
Res., 1274 Deveaux St., Elmora, 15737. Tel: 814-948-9241. [CEM]
Catechesis/Religious Programs—Students 47.
Mission—Spangler, St. Jude Chapel, 15775.

Barnesboro, Cambria Co.,

1—St. John the Baptist's, (1896) (Slovak), Rev. Gerard M. Connolly, T.O.R.
Res., 811 Chestnut Ave., 15714. Tel: 814-948-6842. [CEM]
School—Northern Cambria Catholic, Nicktown. See Elementary Diocesan Schools under Institutions Located in the Diocese. Tel: 814-948-8900.
Catechesis/Religious Programs—Tel: 814-948-8391. Rita Switzler, D.R.E.
Students 66.

2—St. Stanislaus Kostka, (1906) (Polish), Very Rev. Charles F. Bodziak, V.F.
Res., 3805 Bigler Ave., 15714. Tel: 814-948-8582. [CEM]
School—Northern Cambria Catholic, Nicktown. See Elementary Diocesan Schools under Institutions Located in the Diocese. Tel: 814-948-8900.
Catechesis/Religious Programs—Tel: 814-948-9226. Valerie Hood, D.R.E.
Students 84.

3—Our Lady of Mt. Carmel, (1908) (Italian), Rev. Gerard M. Connolly, T.O.R.
Res., 606 Philadelphia Ave., 15714. Tel: 814-948-8391. [CEM]
Catechesis/Religious Programs—Rita Switzler, D.R.E.
Students 136.

4—Christ the King, (1993), Very Rev. Charles F. Bodziak, V.F.
Res., 1104 Maple Ave., 15714. Tel: 814-948-8582.
Catechesis/Religious Programs—Tel: 814-948-9226.
Students 64.

Beans Cove, Bedford Co., Seven Dolors B.V.M. (1878), Rev. Msgr. Charles D. Rager.
Mailing Address: R.D. 3, Box 158-B, Clearville, 15535. Tel: 814-696-7480.
Res., St. Mary's Ln., 4 Apt., Hollidaysburg, 16648. Tel: 814-696-7480. [CEM]

Beaverdale, Cambria Co., St. Joseph's (1904) (Slovak). Merged with St. Agnes, Beaverdale, and Corpus Christi, Dunlo, to form Holy Spirit Church, Beaverdale. Rev. Nicholas J. Mancini.
St. Agnes (1909). Merged with St. Joseph, Beaverdale, and Corpus Christi, Dunlo, to form Holy Spirit Church, Beaverdale. Rev. Nicholas J. Mancini.
Holy Spirit (1995),
Mailing Address: 727 Cameron Ave., P.O. Box 616, 15921. Tel: 814-487-5633. [CEM 2]
Catechesis/Religious Programs—Students 99.

Bedford, Bedford Co., St. Thomas (1816), Rev. John C. Vago.
Res., 215 E. Penn St., 15522. Tel: 814-623-5526. [CEM 2]
School—129 W. Penn St., 15522. Tel: 814-623-8873. Joyce Wityk, Prin.
Lay Teachers 9; Students 81.
Catechesis/Religious Programs—Tel: 814-652-5028. Mrs. Jane Cunard, D.R.E.
Students 185.

Bellefonte, Centre Co., St. John the Evangelist's (1828), Very Rev. D. Timothy Grimme; Rev. James M. Foster.
Res., 134 E. Bishop St., 16823. Tel: 814-355-3134; Fax: 814-355-4820. [CEM 2]
School—(Grades PreK-7) 116 E. Bishop St., 16823. Tel: 814-355-7859. Mrs. Carol Gouty, Prin.
Lay Teachers 11; Students 197.
Catechesis/Religious Programs—Students 246.

Bellwood, Blair Co., St. Joseph's (1890), Rev. David H. Roesch.
Res., 623 E. Third St., 16617. Tel: 814-742-7075.
Catechesis/Religious Programs—Tel: 814-742-8373.
Students 122.

Boswell, All Saints (1995), Rev. Blase Wegierski, O.F.M.Conv.
Res., 325 Quemahoning St., 15531. Tel: 814-629-5551. [CEM 3]
Catechesis/Religious Programs—Students 157.
St. Stanislaus, Somerset Co., (1901) (Polish). Merged with St. John the Baptist, Acosta, and St. Joseph, Boswell, to form All Saints Church, Boswell. Rev. Blase Wegierski, O.F.M.Conv.
Res., 325 Quemahoning St., 15531. Tel: 814-629-5551. [CEM 3]
Catechesis/Religious Programs—Tel: 814-629-5551.
Students 157.

Carrolltown, Cambria Co., St. Benedict's (1840), Revs. Blane Resko, O.S.B.; Kieran Rodgers, O.S.B.
Res., 15722. Tel: 814-344-6548. [CEM]
School—119 S. Benedict St., 15722. Tel: 814-344-6512. Sr. Theresa Nelen, Prin.
Lay Teachers 7; Students 106.
Catechesis/Religious Programs—Tel: 814-674-5786. Bonnie Westrick, D.R.E.
Students 259.

Cassandra, Cambria Co., St. Agnes (1909), Rev. Robert L. Ruston.
Res., P.O. Box 56, 15925. Tel: 814-736-8314.

Central City, Somerset Co., Sacred Heart (1914) (Polish), Rev. Msgr. Ignatius C. Wadas, V.F.
Res., 738 Sunshine Ave., 15926. Tel: 814-754-5224. [CEM]
Catechesis/Religious Programs—Students 49.
St. John the Baptist (1917) (Slovak), Rev. Msgr. Ignatius C. Wadas, V.F.

Res., 164 Wheeler St., 15926. Tel: 814-754-5224. [CEM]
Catechesis/Religious Programs—Students 56.

Chest Springs, Cambria Co., St. Monica's (1859), Rev. Timothy P. Stein.
Res., 3037 Colonel Drake Hwy., 16624. Tel: 814-674-3712. [CEM]
Catechesis/Religious Programs—Students 100.

Clarence, Centre Co., St. Michael's (1900) (Slovak), Rev. Sylvester J. Bendzella.
Res., 102 Church St., 16829. Tel: 814-387-6762. [CEM]
Catechesis/Religious Programs—Students 110.

Colver, Cambria Co., Holy Family (1912) (Polish), Rev. James B. Coveney.
Res., 562 Fifth St., 15927. Tel: 814-748-7054. [CEM]
Catechesis/Religious Programs—Tel: 814-748-7593. Louise Lambie, D.R.E.
Students 113.

Conemaugh, Cambria Co., Sacred Heart (1902), Rev. Richard D. Clark.
Res., 219 Oak St., 15909. Tel: 814-536-4622. [CEM]
Catechesis/Religious Programs—Students 105.

Assumption of B.V.M. (1910) (Polish), Rev. Bernard F. Grega.
Res., 340 Second St., 15909. Tel: 814-535-2250. [CEM]
Catechesis/Religious Programs—335 Second St., 15909. Tel: 814-539-5203.
Students 65.

Coupon, Cambria Co., St. Joseph's (1855), Rev. Msgr. Michael E. Servinsky.
Res., 16629. Tel: 814-943-8464. [CEM 2]
Catechesis/Religious Programs—Students 46.

Cresson, Cambria Co., St. Aloysius (1838), Rev. William E. Mullen.
Res., 7911 Admiral Peary Hwy., 16630. Tel: 814-886-2235. [CEM]
School—All Saints Catholic. See Elementary Diocesan Schools under Institutions Located in the Diocese. Tel: 814-886-7942.
Catechesis/Religious Programs—Tel: 814-886-2669. Margaret H. Eberhart, D.R.E.
Students 225.

St. Francis Xavier (1908), Rev. David W. Cronauer; Deacon Michael Condor. In res., Rev. George J. Valko.
Res., 211 Powell Ave., 16630. Tel: 814-886-2374. [CEM]
School—All Saints Catholic. See Elementary Diocesan Schools under Institutions Located in the Diocese. Tel: 814-886-7942.
Catechesis/Religious Programs—Tel: 814-886-2374. Mrs. Janet Rickens, D.R.E.
Students 143.

Davidsville, Somerset Co., St. Anne (1911), Rev. Conrad M. Salach, O.F.M.Conv.
Mailing Address: P.O. Box 500, Woodstown Rd., 15928. Tel: 814-479-2664. [CEM]
Catechesis/Religious Programs—Students 129.

Dudley, Huntingdon Co., Immaculate Conception (1856), Rev. Patrick R. Leahey.
Res., P.O. Box 188, 16634. Tel: 814-635-2919. [CEM]
Catechesis/Religious Programs—Students 59.

Duncansville, Blair Co., St. Catherine of Siena (1963), Rev. Msgr. Roy F. Kline.
Res., 49 Woodland Terr., 16635. Tel: 814-695-2337.
Catechesis/Religious Programs—P.O. Box 88, 16635. Tel: 814-696-0616. D.R.E.: Debra Terchanik; Sr. Barbara Bettwy.
Students 147.

Dunlo, Cambria Co., Corpus Christi (1903). Merged with St. Agnes, Beaverdale, and St. Joseph, Beaverdale, to form Holy Spirit Church, Beaverdale. Rev. Nicholas J. Mancini.

Ebensburg, Cambria Co., Holy Name (1816), Rev. Msgr. Arnold L. Gaus; Rev. Walter J. Moll. In res., Rev. Msgr. Faber J. Malloy.
Res., 500 N. Julian St., 15931. Tel: 814-472-7244; Fax: 814-472-7249. [CEM]
School—Tel: 814-472-8817. Sr. Christine Hill, C.S.J., Prin.
Sisters 2; Lay Teachers 20; Students 399.
Catechesis/Religious Programs—Sr. Nancy Spence, C.C.W., D.R.E.
Students 561.

Ehrenfeld, Cambria Co., Our Lady of Mt. Carmel (1892). Merged with St. James, South Fork, and St. Anthony's, South Fork, to form Most Holy Trinity, South Fork.

Elmora, St. Jude (1995), Rev. David J. Arseneault.
Res., 1274 Deveaux St., P.O. Box 10, 15737. Tel: 814-948-9241. [CEM]
Catechesis/Religious Programs—Students 82.
Mission—Spangler, St. Jude Chapel, 15775.

Emeigh, Cambria Co., Most Precious Blood. See Christ the King, Barnesboro.

Everett, Bedford Co., St. John the Evangelist (1971), Rev. Angelo J. Patti.
Res., 161 E. First Ave., 15537. Tel: 814-652-5854.
Church—163 E. First Ave., 15537.
Catechesis/Religious Programs—Students 57.

Fallentimber, Cambria Co., St. Mary Magdalen's (Frugality) (1889). Merged with St. Richard's Mission, Blandburg, to form St. Joan of Arc Church, Fallentimber. Rev. James F. Bunn.
Res., 692 Glendale Valley Blvd., 16639. Tel: 814-943-5437.
Catechesis/Religious Programs—Students 57.

St. Joan of Arc (1995), Rev. James F. Bunn.
Res., 692 Glendale Valley Blvd., 16639. Tel: 814-943-5437.
Catechesis/Religious Programs—Tel: 814-941-3440. Mrs. Mary Lou Coloussy, D.R.E.
Students 58.

Gallitzin, Cambria Co., St. Patrick's (1850), Rev. Bernard A. Przybocki.
Res., 811 Church St., 16641. Tel: 814-886-7941. [CEM]
School—825 Church St., 11641. Tel: 814-886-8772. Mrs. Helen Saylor, Prin.
Lay Teachers 8; Students 114.
Catechesis/Religious Programs—Students 142.

Our Lady of Czestochowa (1903) (Polish), Rev. Msgr. Bernard A. Przybocki.
Res., 811 Church St., 16641. Tel: 814-886-4203. [CEM]
Catechesis/Religious Programs—Tel: 814-886-8772.
Students 63.

Hastings, Cambria Co., St. Bernard (1890), Rev. Joachim R. Fatora, O.S.B. In res., Rev. Germain L. Lieb, O.S.B.
Res., P.O. Box 497, 16646. Tel: 814-247-6558. [CEM]
School—Tel: 814-247-6322. Sr. Florine Madigan, I.H.M., Prin.
Sisters of Immaculate Heart of Mary 2; Lay Teachers 9; Students 110.
Catechesis/Religious Programs—Tel: 814-674-5841. Mrs. Aileen Ropp, D.R.E.
Students 171.
Mission—St. Boniface, Cambria Co., St. Boniface Chapel, 16675.

Hollidaysburg, Blair Co., St. Mary's (1841), Revs. John J. Palko; John A. Tiernan.
Res., 312 Clark St., P.O. Box 317, 16648. Tel: 814-695-0622; Fax: 814-696-9609. [CEM 2]
School—Hollidaysburg Consolidated Catholic Elementary. See Elementary Diocesan Schools under Institutions Located in the Diocese.
Catechesis/Religious Programs—Tel: 814-695-5678. Mrs. Connie Curfman, D.R.E.
Students 251.

St. Michael's (1862), Rev. Clement Gardner.
Res., 301 Spruce St., 16648. Tel: 814-695-0912. [CEM]
School—Hollidaysburg Consolidated Catholic Elementary. See Elementary Diocesan Schools under Institutions Located in the Diocese. Tel: 814-695-6112; Fax: 814-695-1215.
Catechesis/Religious Programs—Tel: 814-695-6972. James G. Burke, D.R.E.
Students 237.

Hooversville, Somerset Co., Holy Family (1911), Rev. Romulus Roslowski, O.F.M. Conv.
Res., 15936. Tel: 814-798-2933; Fax: 814-798-8601. [CEM]
Catechesis/Religious Programs—Students 75.

Huntingdon, Huntingdon Co., Most Holy Trinity (1826), Rev. Msgr. David A. Lockard, V.F.
Res., 524 Mifflin St., 16652. Tel: 814-643-0160; Fax: 814-643-0160. [CEM]
Catechesis/Religious Programs—Students 194.

Lilly, Cambria Co., St. Brigid's (1883). Merged with Our Lady of Mount Carmel, Lilly, to form Our Lady of the Alleghenies, Lilly. Rev. Msgr. John R. Sasway.
Res., 608 Main St., 15938. Tel: 814-866-2504. [CEM]
Catechesis/Religious Programs—Tel: 814-886-2161. Barbara Pysher, D.R.E.
Students 172.

Our Lady of Mt. Carmel (1910) (Polish). Merged with St. Brigid, Lilly, to form Our Lady of the Alleghenies, Lilly. Rev. Msgr. John R. Sasway.
Res., 608 Main St., 15938. Tel: 814-886-2504. [CEM]
Catechesis/Religious Programs—Students 92.

Our Lady of the Alleghenies (1995), Rev. Msgr. John R. Sasway.
Res., 608 Main St., 15938. Tel: 814-886-2504. [CEM]
Catechesis/Religious Programs—Tel: 814-886-2161.
Students 217.

Lock Haven, Clinton Co., Immaculate Conception (1852), Rev. James F. Crookston.
Res., 310 W. Water St., 17745. Tel: 717-748-4535; Fax: 717-748-8252. [CEM]
School—Lock Haven Catholic School, Tel: 717-748-7252. Sr. Mary Joan Gibson, O.P., Prin.
Sisters of Sinsinawa Dominicans 3; Lay Teachers 18; Students 201.
Catechesis/Religious Programs—Tel: 717-748-4828.
Students 116.

St. Agnes (1873), Rev. Neil R. Dadey.
Res., 3 E. Walnut St., 17745. Tel: 717-748-4594. [CEM]
School—Lock Haven Catholic School. See Immaculate Conception for details. Tel: 717-742-7252.
Catechesis/Religious Programs—Tel: 717-748-4282.
Students 84.

Loretto, Cambria Co., St. Michael's (1799), Very Rev. Msgr. Thomas J. Maher, V.F.
Res., 15940. Tel: 814-472-8551. [CEM]
School—Tel: 814-472-9117. Sr. Elizabeth Ann Brody, R.S.M., Prin.
Lay Teachers 9; Students 102.
Catechesis/Religious Programs—Tel: 814-472-2332. D.R.E.: Sr. Miriam Rita, R.S.M., (Elementary); Betty Seymour, (High School & Conf.), Tel: 717-472-6279.
Students 260.

McConnellsburg, Fulton Co., St. Stephen's (1962), Rev. Joseph T. Orr.
Res., 303 Lincoln Way E., 17233. Tel: 717-485-3723.

Meyersdale, Somerset Co., SS. Philip and James (1850), Rev. Raymond E. Karr; Rev. Msgr. Timothy J. Swope, Admin.
Res., 247 High St., 15552. Tel: 814-634-8150. [CEM 2]
Catechesis/Religious Programs—Students 90.
Mission—MacDonaldton, Somerset Co., St. Gregory, (1907) 247 High St., 15552. Tel: 814-634-8150.

Mount Union, Huntingdon Co., St. Catherine's (1912), Rev. Elwood F. Figurelle.
Res., 205 W. Market St., 17066. Tel: 814-542-4582. [CEM]
Catechesis/Religious Programs—Students 47.

Mundys Corner, Cambria Co., St. John Vianney's (1950), Rev. Paul M. Robine.
Res., 3513 William Penn Ave., Johnstown, 15909. Tel: 814-322-4789.
Catechesis/Religious Programs—Tel: 814-322-1109. Ms. Mary Ellen Broad, D.R.E.
Students 174.

Nanty-Glo, Cambria Co., St. Mary's (1902), Rev. Msgr. John J. Little, V.F.; Deacon Thomas M. Buige.
Res., 1020 Caroline St., 15943. Tel: 814-749-9103. [CEM]
School—1005 Caroline St., 15943. Tel: 814-749-9031. Mrs. Rosemary Conzo, Prin.
Sisters of St. Agnes 2; Lay Teachers 9; Students 119.
Catechesis/Religious Programs—Mrs. Patricia LaMantia, D.R.E.
Students 129.

New Baltimore, Somerset Co., St. John the Baptist (1829), Rev. Mark S. Begly.
Res., 15553. Tel: 814-733-2210; Fax: 814-733-2966. [CEM]
Catechesis/Religious Programs—Students 86.

Newry, Blair Co., St. Patrick's (1816), Rev. William A. Rosensteel; Rev. Msgr. Harold Burkardt.
Res., P.O. Box 398, 16665. Tel: 814-695-3413. [CEM 2]
School—Tel: 814-695-3819. Sr. Pauline Kastoski, C.C.W., Prin.
Sisters 2; Lay Teachers 8; Students 116.
Catechesis/Religious Programs—Tel: 814-695-3819. Mrs. Linda Guiffre, D.R.E.
Students 106.

Nicktown, Cambria Co., St. Nicholas (1861), Rev. Claude W. Pollak, O.S.B.
Res., 15762. Tel: 814-948-9614. [CEM]
School—Northern Cambria Catholic. See Elementary Diocesan Schools under Institutions Located in the Diocese. Tel: 814-948-8900; Fax: 814-948-8720.
Catechesis/Religious Programs—Tel: 814-948-8900. Nancy McKee, D.R.E.
Students 143.

Patton, Cambria Co., Our Lady of Perpetual Help (1892). Merged with St. George, Patton, and St. Lawrence to form Queen of Peace, Patton. Revs. Joseph Gerg, O.S.B.; Robert Roche, O.S.B.
Res., 907 Sixth Ave., 16668. Tel: 814-674-8983. [CEM]
Catechesis/Religious Programs—Tel: 814-674-8938. D.R.E.: Michelle Kirk; Rita Horne.
Students 239.

Queen of Peace (1995), Revs. Joseph Gerg, O.S.B.; Robert Roche, O.S.B.

Res., 907 Sixth Ave., 16668. Tel: 814-674-8983; Fax: 814-674-8805. [CEM]
Catechesis / Religious Programs—Tel: 814-674-5591. Joanne VanOrmer, D.R.E.
Students 232.

St. George (1907) (Slovak). Merged with Our Lady of Perpetual Help, Patton, and St. Lawrence to form Queen of Peace, Patton.

Penns Valley, Centre Co., Blessed Kateri Tekakwitha (1986), Rev. William S. Crouse.
Res., R.D. No. 1, Box 245A, Spring Mills, 16875. Tel: 814-422-8983.
Catechesis / Religious Programs—Students 95.

Philipsburg, Centre Co., SS. Peter and Paul (1868), Rev. Msgr. Philip P. Saylor.
Res., 400 S. Fourth St., 16866. Tel: 814-342-1700; Fax: 814-342-5480. [CEM]
Catechesis / Religious Programs—William J. Slother, Jr., D.R.E.
Students 222.

Portage, Cambria Co.,

1—ST. JOSEPH'S, (1898), Rev. George D. Koharchik.
Res., 509 Caldwell Ave., 15946. Tel: 814-736-4279; Fax: 814-736-4764.
School—Tel: 814-736-4033.
Lay Teachers 7; Students 65. Principals: Mrs. Teresa Koenigberg; Mrs. Deborah Boyko.
Catechesis / Religious Programs—Mary E. Heinrich, D.R.E.
Students 210.

2—SACRED HEART, (1909) (Polish), Rev. Ronald V. Osinski.
Res., 601 Mountain Ave., 15946. Tel: 814-736-4239. [CEM]
School—812 Orchard St., 15946. Tel: 814-736-3588. Sr. Margaret Mary, S.S.C.J., Prin.
Pre-School & Kindergarten Students 29.
Convent—803 Orchard St., 15946. Tel: 814-736-3875.
Catechesis / Religious Programs—Students 182.

3—ASSUMPTION B.V.M., (1907) (Slovak), Rev. Ronald V. Osinski.
Res., 806 Hammers St., 15946. Tel: 814-736-9770. [CEM]
Catechesis / Religious Programs—Tel: 814-736-3588.
Students 182.

4—ST. JOHN THE BAPTIST, (1923) (Hungarian), Rev. Ronald B. Yogus.
Res., 900 Johnson Ave., 15946. Tel: 814-736-9747. [CEM]

Renovo, Clinton Co., St. Joseph's (1869), Rev. Donald E. Boslett.
Res., 925 Huron Ave., 17764. Tel: 717-923-0172. [CEM 2]
Catechesis / Religious Programs—Vicky A. Penton, D.R.E.
Students 157.

Revloc, Cambria Co., Most Holy Redeemer (1920), Rev. William J. Kovach.
Res., 553 Cambria Ave., 15948. Tel: 814-472-7928.

Roaring Spring, Blair Co., St. Thomas More (1969), Rev. Msgr. William E. Schultz.
Res., 825 Williams St., 16673. Tel: 814-224-4522.
Catechesis / Religious Programs—Students 90.

St. Augustine, Cambria Co., St. Augustine (1847), Rev. Joseph W. Fleming.
Res., 803 St. Augustine Rd., Dysart, 16636. Tel: 814-674-8550. [CEM]
Catechesis / Religious Programs—Students 155.

St. Boniface, Cambria Co., St. Boniface Chapel (1859). Merged to form St. Bernard, Hastings.

St. Lawrence, Cambria Co., St. Lawrence's (1853). Merged with Our Lady of Perpetual Help, Patton, and St. George, Patton, to form Queen of Peace, Patton. Rev. Joseph Gerg, O.S.B.
Res., 907 Sixth Ave., Patton, 16668. Tel: 814-674-8983; Fax: 814-674-8805. [CEM]

St. Michael, Cambria Co., St. Michael's (1913), Rev. John P. Ellias.
Res., Box 103, 15951. Tel: 814-495-9640. [CEM]
Catechesis / Religious Programs—Students 212.

Shade Gap, Huntingdon Co., St. Mary's (1840), Rev. David R. Becker.
Res., Shade Gap, H.C. 62, Box 696, 17255. Tel: 814-447-3172. [CEM 2]

Snow Shoe, Centre Co., St. Mary's (1865) (Irish), Rev. Sylvester J. Bendzella.
Res., 522 Fourth St., 16874. Tel: 814-387-6793. [CEM]

Somerset, Somerset Co., St. Peter's (1920), Rev. Msgr. Samuel J. Tomaselli; Deacon Frederick F. Weaver. In res., Rev. Joseph Mazurkiewicz.
Res., 433 W. Church St., 15501. Tel: 814-443-6574; Fax: 814-445-7766. [CEM]
School—Tel: 814-445-6662. Mrs. Susan Dudley, Prin.
Lay Teachers 6; Students 119.
Catechesis / Religious Programs—Tel: 814-443-6574.
Students 363.

St. Peter in Chains (1995),
Mailing Address: S.C.I.-Somerset, 1590 Walters Mill Rd., 15501-0001. Tel: 814-443-8100.

South Fork, Cambria Co., Most Holy Trinity (1995), Rev. Louis J. Mulvehill.
Res., 550 Main St., 15956. Tel: 814-495-4419. [CEM]
Catechesis / Religious Programs—Tel: 814-495-4028. Mrs. Betty Rosmus, D.R.E.
Students 82.

St. Anthony's (1905) (Polish). Merged with St. James, South Fork, and Our Lady of Mt. Carmel, Ehrenfeld, to form Most Holy Trinity, South Fork.

St. James (1906). Merged with St. Anthony, South Fork, and Our Lady of Mt. Carmel, Ehrenfeld, to form Most Holy Trinity, South Fork. Rev. Louis J. Mulvehill.
Res., 550 Main St., 15956. Tel: 814-495-4419. [CEM]
Catechesis / Religious Programs—Tel: 814-495-4028. Mrs. Betty Rosmus, D.R.E.
Students 82.

Spangler, Cambria Co., Holy Cross (1893), Rev. David J. Arseneault.
Res., 2410 Campbell Ave., P.O. Box 507, 15775-0507. Tel: 814-948-8043. [CEM]
Catechesis / Religious Programs—Students 121.

St. Patrick's (1902). Merged with Sacred Heart, Bakerton, to form St. Jude, Elmora. Rev. David J. Arseneault.
Res., 15775. Tel: 814-948-9241. [CEM]

State College, Centre Co., Good Shepherd (1989), Rev. Philip M. Bender.
Res., 867 Gray's Woods Blvd., P.O. Box 8186, 16803. Tel: 814-238-7463.
Church—Tel: 814-238-2110.
Catechesis / Religious Programs—Dorothy Kardohely, D.R.E.
Students 311.

Our Lady of Victory (1908), Revs. Martin Dugan McCamley; Anthony Petracca; James D. Zatalava; Leo F. Arnone.
Res., 820 Westerly Pkwy., 16801. Tel: 814-237-7832; Fax: 814-237-6709.
School—Tel: 814-238-1592. Kathleen Hershbine, Prin.
Lay Teachers 16; Students 318.
Pre School—Tel: 814-238-6616.
Lay Teachers 2; Students 61.
Catechesis / Religious Programs—Tel: 814-234-3315. Steve Kretschmer, D.R.E.
Students 546.

Summerhill, Cambria Co., St. John (1903), Rev. Daniel C. Wolfel, O.S.B.
Res., 538 Main St., P.O. Box 248, 15958. Tel: 814-495-5241. [CEM]
Mission—New Germany, Cambria Co., Immaculate Conception, (1855) 1640 New Germany Rd., P.O. Box 248, 15958.
Catechesis / Religious Programs—Students 252.

Twin Rocks, Cambria Co., St. Charles (1917). Merged with Immaculate Conception Mission, Vintondale, to form SS. Timothy & Mark Parish, Twin Rocks. Rev. Matthew E. Misurda.
Res., 116 Church St., P.O. Box 275, 15960. Tel: 814-749-9331. [CEM]
Catechesis / Religious Programs—Diane Clark, D.R.E.
Students 55.
Mission—Vintondale, Cambria Co., Immaculate Conception, (1900).

SS. Timothy & Mark (1995),
Mailing Address: P.O. Box 275, 15960. Tel: 814-749-9331.

Tyrone, Blair Co., St. Matthew's (1853), Rev. Norman P. Imgrund.
Res., 406 W. 11th St., 16686. Tel: 814-684-1480. [CEM]
School—1107 Cameron Ave., 16686. Tel: 814-684-3510. Mrs. Kathleen Bechdel, Prin.
Lay Teachers 5; Students 84.
Catechesis / Religious Programs—Tel: 814-684-4808. Teresa Jeffries, D.R.E.
Students 159.

West Salisbury, Somerset Co., St. Michael's (1887), Rev. Bernard L. White.
Res., 15565. Tel: 814-662-2958. [CEM 2]
Mission—Pocahontas, Somerset Co., St. Mary's, (1906) P.O. Box 31, 15565. Tel: 814-662-2958.
Catechesis / Religious Programs—Students 61.

Williamsburg, Blair Co., St. Joseph (1861), Rev. Dennis M. Kurdziel.
Res., 628 W. First St., 16693. Tel: 814-832-2137. [CEM 2]
Catechesis / Religious Programs—Students 70.

Wilmore, Cambria Co., St. Bartholomew's (1840), Rev. Robert L. Ruston.
Res., P.O. Box 96, 15962. Tel: 814-495-5360; 736-8314. [CEM]
Catechesis / Religious Programs—Tel: 814-495-5360.
Students 120.

Windber, Somerset Co.,

1—ST. JOHN CANTIUS, (1898) (Polish), Rev. Leonard E. Voytek.
Res., 605 Graham Ave., 15963-1398. Tel: 814-467-7191. [CEM]
Catechesis / Religious Programs—D.R.E.: Paul Banjak, (High School), Tel: 814-467-8443; Sr. Evangelista Stronmier, (Elementary), Tel: 814-467-9670.
Students 169.

2—SS. CYRIL AND METHODIUS, (1906) (Slovak), Rev. James H. Conrad, S.T.L.
Res., 604 Graham Ave., 15963. Tel: 814-467-7042. [CEM 2]
Catechesis / Religious Programs—600 Graham Ave., 15963. Tel: 814-467-9670.
Students 73.

3—ST. ANTHONY OF PADUA, (1908) (Italian), Very Rev. William Santre, T.O.R.; Revs. Adrian Tirpak, T.O.R.; Mark Reifel, T.O.R.; Deacon Joseph R. Dalla Valle.
Res., 2201 Graham Ave., 15963. Tel: 814-467-7292. [CEM]
School—St. Benedict School, Tel: 814-266-3837.
Students 16.
Catechesis / Religious Programs—Tel: 814-467-9670;467-8443. Sr. Evangelista R.S.M., D.R.E.
Students 211.

4—ST. MARY'S, (1914) (Hungarian), Rev. Leonard E. Voytek.
Res., 605 Graham Ave., 15963-1398. Tel: 814-467-7191. [CEM]
Catechesis / Religious Programs—D.R.E.: Sr. Evangelista Stronmier, (Elementary), Tel: 814-467-9670; Paul Banjak, (High School), Tel: 814-467-8443.
Students 55.

5—HOLY CHILD JESUS, (1921) (Irish), Rev. Charles F. Leonardis.
Res., 913 Graham Ave., 15963. Tel: 814-467-7097. [JC]
Catechesis / Religious Programs—Students 53.

Chaplains of Public Institutions

ALTOONA. *Altoona Hospital.* Howard Ave. & Seventh St., 16601. Tel: 814-946-2011; 942-2416 (Res.). Chaplains: Revs. Donald E. Boslett; Clarence S. Bridges; James M. Foster.

Veterans Medical Center. 2907 Pleasant Valley Blvd., 16602. Tel: 814-943-8164. Rev. Edward J. Dabcosky, Chap.

JOHNSTOWN. *Lee Hospital.* 320 Main St., 15901. Tel: 814-533-0123; 536-0117 (Res.). Chaplains: Revs. John F. Brezovec; Christopher Panagoplos, T.O.R.

Memorial Hospital. Franklin St., 15905. Tel: 814-533-9000; 536-0117 (Res.). Chaplains: Revs. John F. Brezovec; Christopher Panagoplos, T.O.R.

BELLEFONTE. *State Correctional Institution.* Our Lady of the Mount, Box A, 16823. Tel: 814-355-4874; 422-8983 (Res.). Rev. William S. Crouse.

CRESSON. *State Correctional Institution.* Drawer A, 16630. Tel: 814-886-8181; 736-9497 (Res.). Rev. Ronald B. Yogus, Chap.

EBENSBURG. *Laurel Crest Manor.* Vacant. P.O. Box 360, 15931. Tel: 814-472-8100.

HUNTINGDON. *State Correctional Institution.* St. Dismas, Drawer R, 16652. Tel: 814-643-2400; 447-3172 (Res.). Rev. David R. Becker.

LORETTO. *Federal Correctional Institution.* P.O. Box 1000, 15940. Tel: 814-472-4140; 472-9363 (Res.). Sr. Mary Ann Palko, C.C.W., Chap.

SMITHFIELD. *State Correctional Institution.* 1120 Pike St., Huntingdon, 16652. Tel: 814-643-6520; 643-0160 (Res.). Rev. Dennis Kurdziel, Chap.

SOMERSET. *State Correctional Institution.* St. Peter in Chains, 1590 Walters Mill Rd., 15510. Tel: 814-443-8100; 443-6574 (Res.). Rev. Joseph Mazurkiewicz.

On Special Assignment:
Reverend Monsignors—
Boggs, Dennis R., Chancellor and Sec. to the Bishop, 126 Logan Blvd., Hollidaysburg, PA 16648
Reverend Fathers—
Radasky, Robert M., 215 Robinson Ave., Johnstown, PA 15905

On Duty Outside the Diocese:
Reverend Monsignors—
Lenz, Paul A., Black and Indian Mission Office, 2021 H St., N.W., Washington, DC 20006. Tel: 202-331-8542
Reverend Fathers—
Anselmi, Albert

Military Chaplains:
Reverend Fathers—
Gergel, Stephen J., U.S. Navy
Gomulka, Eugene T., U.S. Navy
Legarski, Anthony J., U.S. Navy

Absent on Leave:
Reverend Fathers—
Christiana, Nicholas M.
Karr, Raymond E.
Mascherino, Alphonse
Norcavage, Albert R.

Retired:
Reverend Monsignors—
Ackerson, Francis A.
Beiter, Lambert M., 224 Main St., Conemaugh, PA
Burkardt, Harold J., 5509 5th Ave., Altoona, PA 16602
Fleming, Joseph H., 14408 Gallagher Rd., Delray Beach, FL 33484. Tel: 407-498-7646
Fleming, Patrick V., FL 33484. Tel: 407-498-7646
Gorney, Francis L., 105 Pine St., Natrona, PA 15065. Tel: 412-224-5644
Greinader, Linford F., 455 Finch St., Apt. 2, Johnstown, PA 15905. Tel: 814-255-7812
Lafferty, John J., 1123 23rd Ave., Altoona, PA 16601. Tel: 814-943-7221
Madden, Thomas E., P.O. Box 33, Altoona, PA 16603
Malloy, Faber J., Bishop's Liaison, 500 N. Julian St., Ebensburg, PA 15931
McCaa, Francis B., 311 Lincoln Dr., Martinsburg, WV 25401
O'Toole, Anthony J., 6 St. Mary's Ln., Hollidaysburg, PA 16648
O'Toole, Joseph M., 7 St. Mary's Ln., Hollidaysburg, PA 16648
Ossowski, Casimir B., 511 Power St., Johnston, PA 15906. Tel: 814-536-8534
Panza, Paul D., P.A., Dmitri Manor, 1 St. Mary's Ln., Holidaysburg, PA 16648
Pier, Joseph, 1776 Clapboard Run Rd., Johnstown, PA 15904
Rager, Charles D., 4 St. Mary's Ln., Hollidaysburg, PA 16648
Walsh, Richard J., 1254 Lincoln Ave., P.O. Box 197, Tyrone, PA 16686. Tel: 814-684-2505
Reverend Fathers—
Bender, Joseph J., 72 Clover Dr., Holidaysburg, PA 16648
Boyle, John J., P.O. Box 159, Mill Hall, PA 17751
Crosser, Raymond G., P.O. Box 433, Bedford, PA 15522
Greiner, Kenneth A., REAR 319 Cherry Ave., Altoona, PA 16601
Inman, Leonard T., Garvey Manor, 128 Logan Blvd., Hollidaysburg, PA 16648
Joly, Henry L., P.O. Box 705, Holidaysburg, PA 16648
Knapik, Andrew G., P.O. Box 111, Bellefonte, PA 16823
Mattiello, Lucian C., 121 E. 25th Ave., Altoona, PA 16601
Michaels, Emmett T., Box 94, Accomac, VA 23301
Myers, Regis F., 10 St. Mary's Ln., Holidaysburg, PA 16648
Orlando, John V., Garvey Manor Nursing Home, 128 Logan Blvd., Hollidaysburg, PA 16648
Ream, Gerard J., 351 Habicht St., Johnstown, PA 15906
Strittmatter, J. Joseph, St. Mary's Ln., Box 8, Hollidaysburg, PA 16648
Thomas, Paul, 1681 Eckenrode Mill Rd., Patton, PA 16668
Wolf, Benedict L., 1034 Lydia St., Louisville, KY 40217
Zywicki, Francis S., Garvey Manor, 128 Logan Blvd., Hollidaysburg, PA 16648

Permanent Deacons:
Buige, Thomas M., St. Mary, Nanty Glo
Cammarata, Samuel M., Holy Spirit, Beaverdale
Cassidy, Joseph A., (Retired)
Concannon, John, St. John Gualbert, Johnstown
Condor, Michael, Jr., St. Francis Xavier, Cresson
Dalla Valle, Joseph R., St. Anthony, Windber
Janisko, Thaddeus J., St. John Cantius/St. Mary, Windber
Kist, Leo A., St. Patrick, Johnstown
Lapinski, David C., Our Lady of Victory, State College
Leap, James F., Blessed Sacrament Cathedral, Altoona
Lux, Herman J., St. Andrew, Johnstown
Neral, Gene, St. John the Evangelist, Lakemont
Rzewnicki, Philipe, St. Rose of Lima, Altoona
Sroka, John, Visitation, Johnstown
Tiernan, John A., St. Mary, Holidaysburg
Weaver, Frederick F., St. Peter, Somerset

INSTITUTIONS LOCATED IN THE DIOCESE

[A] COLLEGES AND UNIVERSITIES (NON-DIOCESAN)

CRESSON. *Mount Aloysius College*, 7373 Admiral Peary Hwy., 16630. Tel: 814-886-4131.
For a complete listing, refer to the Colleges and Universities section.

LORETTO. *St. Francis College*, P.O. Box 600, 15940-0600. Tel: 814-472-3000.
For a complete listing, refer to the Colleges and Universities section.

[B] HIGH SCHOOLS, DIOCESAN

ALTOONA. *Bishop Guilfoyle High School*, 2400 Pleasant Valley Blvd., 16602. Tel: 814-944-4014; Fax: 814-944-8695. Joseph E. Macharola, Prin.; Sr. Beverly Hmel, I.H.M., Asst. Prin.; Rev. Sean K. Code, Chap. Sisters 4; Lay Teachers 25; Students 376.

JOHNSTOWN. *Bishop McCort High School*, 25 Osborne St., 15905. Tel: 814-536-8991; Fax: 814-535-4118. Mr. William H. Rushin, Prin.; Revs. John Byrnes; Matthew Misurda; Bro. Steve Baker, T.O.R. Sisters 2; Lay Teachers 29; Students 507.

EBENSBURG. *Bishop Carroll High School*, 15931. Tel: 814-472-7500; Fax: 814-472-8020. Mr. Charles J. Koren, Prin.; Rev. Alan E. Thomas, Chap. Priests 1; Sisters 1; Lay Teachers 22; Students 347.

[C] ELEMENTARY DIOCESAN SCHOOLS

ALTOONA. *McNelis Catholic School*. (Grades K-6). Located at the Cathedral of the Blessed Sacrament. 1304 13th Ave., 16603. Tel: 814-943-7423. Mrs. Jennifer Long, Prin.
Consolidation of the following parishes: Cathedral of the Blessed Sacrament; Our Lady of Fatima. Sisters 1; Lay Teachers 7; Students 154.

JOHNSTOWN. *Central Catholic Elementary School*. (Grades K-8), 751 Railroad St., 15901. Tel: 814-536-1532. Mrs. Lois Ryan, Prin.
Consolidation of the following parishes: St. Anthony; St. John Gualbert; Ss. Peter & Paul. Lay Teachers 9; Students 151.
West End Catholic School. (Grades K-8), 317 Power St., 15906. Tel: 814-536-4722. Mr. Louis Bennese, Prin.
Consolidation of the following parishes: St. Casimir; St. Columba; St. Emerich; St. Francis of Assisi; Immaculate Conception; St. Rochus; St. Stephen; St. Therese. Sisters 1; Lay Teachers 10; Students 191.

CRESSON. *All Saints Catholic School*. (Grades K-8), 220 Powell Ave., 16630. Tel: 814-886-7942. Mrs. Susan Glass, Prin.
Merger of the following parishes: St. Francis Xavier; St. Aloysius; St. Agnes; Our Lady of the Alleghenies. Sisters 1; Lay Teachers 8; Students 135.

HOLLIDAYSBURG. *Hollidaysburg Consolidated Catholic Elementary School*. (Grades PreK-8), Spruce & Wayne Sts., P.O. Box 599, 16648. Tel: 814-695-6112. Mr. Edward DiSabato, Prin.
Consolidation of the following parishes: St. Michael's; St. Mary's. Lay Teachers 10; Students 160.

NICKTOWN. *Northern Cambria Catholic School*, P.O. Box 249, Rte. 271S, 15762. Tel: 814-948-8900. Sr. Jane Mary Prostko, C.S.S.F., Prin.
Consolidation of the following parishes: Holy Cross; Our Lady of Mount Carmel; St. John the Baptist; St. Nicholas; St. Jude; Christ the King; St. Stanislaus. Sisters 2; Lay Teachers 8; Students 133.

[D] GENERAL HOSPITALS (NON-DIOCESAN)

ALTOONA. *Mercy Regional Health System*, 2500 Seventh Ave., 16602. Tel: 814-944-1681.
For a complete listing, refer to the Hospitals section.

JOHNSTOWN. *Good Samaritan Medical Center*, 1020 Franklin St., 15905. Tel: 814-533-1000; 533-1410; Fax: 814-533-1819.
For a complete listing, refer to the Hospitals section.

[E] HOMES FOR AGED (NON-DIOCESAN)

HOLLIDAYSBURG. *Garvey Manor*, Logan Blvd., 16648. Tel: 814-695-5571.
For a complete listing, refer to the Special Care Facilities section.
St. Leonard's Home, Inc., 601 N. Montgomery St., 16648. Tel: 814-695-9581; Fax: 814-695-2606.
For a complete listing, refer to the Special Care Facilities section.

(DIOCESAN)

HOLLIDAYSBURG. *Dmitri Manor Priests' Residence*, St. Mary's Ln., 16648.
For a complete listing, refer to the Special Care Facilities section.

[F] MONASTERIES AND RESIDENCES OF PRIESTS AND BROTHERS (NON-DIOCESAN)

HOLLIDAYSBURG. *St. Joseph Friary*, 501-503 Walnut St., 16648. Tel: 814-695-5802. Bro. Bernard Dougherty, T.O.R., Supr.; Very Rev. Canon Aloysius Hankinson, T.O.R.; Revs. Stephen C. Waldruff, T.O.R.; Kenneth C. LaPan, T.O.R.; Domenic R. Aversa, T.O.R.; Cletus A. Adams, T.O.R.; Adalbert Wolski, T.O.R.

LORETTO. *Mount Assisi Monastery*, P.O. Box 40, 15940. Revs. Marianus D. Lieb, T.O.R.; Damian L. Noel, T.O.R.; Bro. Mark McBride, T.O.R., House Econome & Prov. Econome; Revs. Ronald Bodenschatz, T.O.R.; Thomas Edwards, T.O.R., Vicar Min.; John J. Wilger, T.O.R.; Vincent R. Negherbon; Thomas G. Bourque, Local Min. Tel: 814-472-5324 ext. 302; Bros. Callistus Gerardi, T.O.R.; Bernard J. Nicolosi, T.O.R.; Damien W. Koehler, T.O.R. Priests 7; Brothers in Solemn Vows 4.
St. Bonaventure Friary, P.O. Box 155, 15940. Tel: 814-472-9422. Revs. Christopher J. Dobson, T.O.R., Dir. Novices & Supr.; Bernard F. Tickerhoof, T.O.R., Dir. Vocations & Dir. Postulants. Priests 2; Novices 2; Postulants 6.
St. Francis Friary, Third Order Regular of St. Francis of Penance. Province of the Most Sacred Heart of Jesus., 15940. Tel: 814-472-3331. Revs. Christian R. Oravec, T.O.R., Pres., St. Francis College; Joseph Chancler, T.O.R.; Bede Hines, T.O.R.; Emil Resconich, T.O.R.; Jude Ventiquattro, T.O.R.; Oliver Herbert, T.O.R.; Carl A. Szura, T.O.R.; James Morman, T.O.R.; Thomas Carapella, T.O.R.; Fabian McNichol, T.O.R.; Andre Strittmatter, T.O.R.

NEWRY. *St. Bernardine Monastery*, P.O. Box 208, 16665. Tel: 814-695-3992; 695-8991. Revs. Frank Scornaienchi, T.O.R., Vicar & Dir. Devel. & Mass Assoc.; James Cox, T.O.R.; Reginald Krakovsky, T.O.R.; Eugene Kubina, T.O.R., Local Min. & Provincial Treas.; Camillus Angle, T.O.R.; Kenneth La Pan, T.O.R. Priests 6.
Novitiate of the Immaculate Conception Province of the T.O.R. of St. Francis. Franciscan Development Office, P.O. Box 139, Hollidaysburg, 16648. Tel: 814-695-3802; Fax: 814-695-1611. Province Treasurer's Office, P.O. Box 117, Hollidaysburg, 16648. Tel: 814-696-3321; Fax: 814-695-1611.

[G] CONVENTS AND RESIDENCES FOR SISTERS (NON-DIOCESAN)

ALTOONA. *Carmelite Community of the Word*, Ss. Peter & Paul Convent, 1906 19th St., 16601. Tel: 814-942-5747. Total in Residence 4.
Carmelite Community of the Word Motherhouse and Diocesan Pastoral Center, 1304 13th Ave., 16601. Tel: 814-943-0088; 944-9070. Sr. Martha Burbulla, C.C.W., General Admin. Total in Residence 5.
Our Lady of Perpetual Help Convent, 601 Sixth Ave. Juniata, 16601. Tel: 814-942-3819. Sisters, Servants of the Immaculate Heart of Mary. Total in Residence 2; Total Staff 2.
Sisters of Charity, 2011 Second Ave., 16602. Tel: 814-942-8601. Total in Residence 3.

JOHNSTOWN. *Carmelite Community of the Word*, St. Joseph's Convent, 741 Railroad St., 15901. Tel: 814-535-7118. Total in Residence 4.
Sisters of Mercy, Mercy Convent, 972 Fritz St., 15905. Tel: 814-536-2610. Sr. Vincent de Paul Gibbon, R.S.M., Coord.

CRESSON. *McAuley Hall*, 4 College Dr., 16630-1900. Tel: 814-886-4159. Institute of the Sisters of Mercy of the Americas (Silver Spring, MD). Sr. Ruth Hollen, R.S.M., Coord. Professed Sisters 21.
Sisters Servants of the Sacred Heart, Provincial House, 866 Cambria St., 16630-1713. Tel: 814-886-4223. Sr. Theresa Marie, S.S.C.J., Provincial Sup.
Personal Care Home. Total in Residence 18; Total Staff 7.

EBENSBURG. *Carmelite Community of the Word*, St. Therese Convent, 218 W. Lloyd St., 15931. Tel: 814-472-9457. Total in Residence 2.
Family Life Office, 786 Ben Franklin Hwy., P.O. Box 565, 15931. Tel: 814-472-5333. Total in Residence 2.
Mount St. Ann Retreat House and Novitiate, P.O. Box 328, 15931. Tel: 814-472-9354. Sisters of St. Ann. Sr. Melany Pereira, S.S.A., Supr. Total In Residence 4.

GALLITZIN. *Little Sisters of Jesus*, 347 Tunnel Hill St., 16641. Tel: 814-886-4679. Total in Residence 3.

HASTINGS. *Carmelite Community of the Word*. (Novitiate), Our Lady of Grace Convent, 197 Harvey St., P.O. Box 669, 16646. Tel: 814-247-9954; 247-9956. Total in Residence 3.

LORETTO. *Carmel of St. Therese of Lisieux Monastery*, P.O. Box 57, 15940. Tel: 814-472-8620. Mother Teresa of Jesus, O.C.D., Prioress. Discalced Carmelite Nuns. Nuns with Solemn Vows 8; Extern Professed 1; Novices 2.

Our Lady of Loretto, Box 36, 15940. Tel: 814-886-5798. Sisters of Mercy. Total in Residence 5.

MCCONNELLSBURG. *Carmelite Community of the Word*, Fulton County Mission, 110 S. Third St., 17223. Tel: 717-485-5917; 485-5863. Total in Residence 2. Total in Residence 2.

PORTAGE. *Sisters Servants of the Sacred Heart Novitiate*, Sacred Heart Novitiate, 1872 Munster Rd., 15946. Tel: 814-886-7785. Sr. Jacinta Miryam, S.S.C.J., Novice Mistress.

[H] CAMPUS MINISTRY

HUNTINGDON. *Juniata College*, 17th & Moore St., 16648. Tel: 814-641-3361 (Office). Rev. Allen P. Zeth, Chaplain; Cheryl Carson, Campus Min.; Allen Machielson, Campus Min.

Lock Haven University (Lock Haven), Newman Center, 445 W. Main St., Lock Haven, 17745. Tel: 717-748-8592. Chaplains: Rev. Neil Dadey; Ms. Theresa Miller.

Mt. Aloysius Jr. College (Cresson), Wm. Penn Hwy., Cresson, 16630. Tel: 814-886-4131. Sr. Benedict Joseph Watters, R.S.M., M.S., Dir.; Rev. George J. Valko, M.A., M.Div., Chap.

Penn State University - Altoona Campus, 3000 Ivyside Park, Altoona, 16601. Tel: 814-949-5000; 949-5835 (Office). Rev. Allen P. Zeth, Chaplain.

St. Francis College (Loretto), Loretto, 15940. Tel: 814-472-7000. Campus Ministers: Revs. Carl Szura, T.O.R., Campus Min. Tel: 814-472-3390 (Office); Jude Ventiquattro, T.O.R., Campus Min. Tel: 814-472-3391 (Office); Thomas Carapella, T.O.R.

University of Pittsburgh at Johnstown, 450 Schoolhouse Rd., Johnstown, 15904. Tel: 814-266-9662, Ext. 336. Rev. Daniel J. O'Neill; Sr. Virginia DeWan, SS.C.M.

[I] NEWMAN CENTERS
(NON-DIOCESAN)

UNIVERSITY PARK. *Penn State Catholic Community*, 207A Helen Eakin Eisenhower Chapel, 16802. Tel: 814-865-4281. Campus Ministers: Revs. Conan E. Feigh, O.S.B.; Frederick Byrne, O.S.B.; Leo F. Arnone. Total in Residence 2; Total Staff 6. Catholic Students attending Penn State University 10,000.

[J] MISCELLANEOUS LISTINGS
(NON-DIOCESAN)

BEDFORD. *St. Mary's House of Greater Solitude*, Passionist Community, R.D. 1, Box 276, 15522. Tel: 814-623-1796; Fax: 814-623-2457. Revs. Silvan Rouse, C.P., Supr.; Malachy McGill, C.P.; Howard Chirdon, C.P.; Cletus Dawson, C.P.; David Wilkie, C.P.

LORETTO. *Prince Gallitzin Chapel House (Diocesan)*. Mailing Address: 124 Logan Blvd., Hollidaysburg, 16648. Tel: 814-695-5579.

The Society for the Propagation of the Faith & Holy Childhood Assn. Tel: 814-695-5579. Rev. Robert J. Kelly, Dir.

NEW BALTIMORE. *St. John The Baptist Retreat Center*, P.O. Box 10, 15553. Total in Residence 1; Total Staff 7.

RELIGIOUS INSTITUTES OF MEN REPRESENTED IN THE DIOCESE

For further details refer to the corresponding bracketed number in the Religious Institutes of Men or Women section.

[0200]—*Benedictine Monks*.—O.S.B.
[0470]—*The Capuchin Friars*.—O.F.M.Cap.
[1000]—*Congregation of the Passion*.—C.P.
[0480]—*Conventual Franciscans*. (St. Anthony of Padua Prov.).—O.F.M.Conv.
[0520]—*Franciscan Friars*.—O.F.M.
[0560]—*Third Order Regular of Saint Francis*. (Provs. of Sacred Heart, Immaculate Conception).—T.O.R.

RELIGIOUS INSTITUTES OF WOMEN REPRESENTED IN THE DIOCESE

[0100]—*Adorers of the Blood of Christ*.—A.S.C.
[0315]—*Carmelite Community of the Word*.—C.C.W.
[0330]—*Carmelite Sisters for the Aged and Infirm*.—O.Carm.
[3710]—*Congregation of the Sisters of Saint Agnes*.—C.S.A.
[0420]—*Discalced Carmelite Nuns*.—O.C.D.
[1070-03]—*Dominican Sisters*.—O.P.
[1170]—*Felician Sisters*.—C.S.S.F.
[2330]—*Little Sisters of Jesus*.—L.S.J.
[3630]—*Servants of the Most Sacred Heart of Jesus*.—S.S.C.J.
[0570]—*Sisters of Charity of Seton Hill, Greensburg, Pennsylvania*.—S.C.
[2575]—*Sisters of Mercy of the Americas*.—R.S.M. (Dallas Regional Community).
[1620]—*Sisters of Saint Francis of Millvale, Pennsylvania*.—O.S.F.
[3780]—*Sisters of Ss. Cyril and Methodius*.—SS.C.M.
[3718]—*Sisters of St. Ann*. (Italy).—S.S.A.
[3830]—*Sisters of St. Joseph*.—C.S.J.
[1970]—*Sisters of the Holy Family of Nazareth*.—C.S.F.N.
[3260]—*Sisters of the Precious Blood (Ohio)*.—C.PP.S.
[2160]—*Sisters, Servants of the Immaculate Heart of Mary*. (Scranton, PA).—I.H.M.
[4160]—*Vincentian Sisters of Charity*.—V.S.C.

NECROLOGY

† Conti, Rev. Msgr. Richard E, Johnstown, PA St. Gregory. —Died May 10, 1996.
† Giltinan, William P., (Medical Leave). —Died Dec. 21, 1995.
† McGovern, William H., (Retired). —Died Dec. 29, 1995.
† Skupien, James F, Bellwood, PA St. Joseph. —Died Feb. 11, 1996.

Diocese of Amarillo

(Dioecesis Amarillensis)

Most Reverend

JOHN W. YANTA, D.D.

Bishop of Amarillo; ordained March 17, 1956; appointed Titular Bishop of Naratcata and Auxiliary Bishop of San Antonio October 27, 1994; consecrated December 30, 1994; appointed Bishop of Amarillo January 21, 1997.

Most Reverend

LEROY T. MATTHIESEN, D.D., M.A., LITT.D.

Retired Bishop of Amarillo; ordained March 10, 1946; appointed March 25, 1980; ordained May 30, 1980; retired January 21, 1997. *Mailing Address: P.O. Box 5644, Amarillo, TX, 79117-5664.*

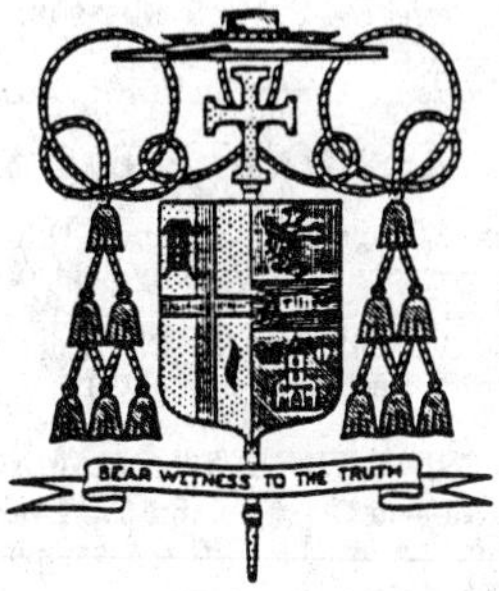

ERECTED A DIOCESE BY POPE PIUS XI, AUGUST 25, 1926.

Square Miles Approximately 25,800.

Comprises that part of the State of Texas known as the Panhandle, and extending thence southward; bounded on the east by Oklahoma, and by the eastern county line of Childress and by the southern lines Childress, Hall, Briscoe, Swisher, Castro and Parmer Counties; the western boundary is the New Mexico state line from the southern line of Parmer County, Texas, northward to the northwestern corner of the Panhandle of Texas. There are 26 counties.

For legal titles of parishes and diocesan institutions, consult the Chancery Office.

Diocesan Pastoral Center: 1800 N. Spring St., P.O. Box 5644, Amarillo, TX, 79117-5644. Tel.: 806-383-2243; Fax: 806-383-8452.

STATISTICAL OVERVIEW

Personnel	
Bishop	1
Retired Bishops	1
Priests: Diocesan Active in Diocese	43
Priests: Active Outside Diocese	7
Priests: Retired, Sick or Absent	15
Number of Diocesan Priests	65
Religious Priests in Diocese	8
Extern Priests in Diocese	3
Ordinations:	
Diocesan Priests	2
Permanent Deacons in Diocese	45
Total Brothers	1
Total Sisters	143
Parishes	
Parishes	35
With Resident Pastor:	
Resident Diocesan Priests	26
Resident Religious Priests	5
Without Resident Pastor:	
Administered by Priests	3
Administered by Permanent Deacons	3
Completely Vacant	2
New Parishes Created	1
Professional Ministry Personnel:	
Sisters	4
Lay Ministers	6
Welfare	
Catholic Hospitals	1
Total Assisted	8,000
Health Care Centers	1
Total Assisted	720
Homes for the Aged	1
Total Assisted	56
Day Care and Extended Day Care Centers	8
Total Assisted	300
Specialized Homes	2
Total Assisted	550
Special Centers for Social Services	4
Total Assisted	35,000
Other Institutions	1
Total Assisted	3
Educational	
Diocesan Students in Other Seminaries	12
Total Seminarians	12
High Schools, Diocesan and Parish	1
Total Students	131
Elementary Schools, Diocesan and Parish	8
Total Students	911
Catechesis/Religious Education:	
High School Students	2,204
Elementary Students	3,853
Total Students Under Catholic Instruction	7,111
Teachers in the Diocese:	
Sisters	14
Lay Teachers	76
Vital Statistics	
Receptions into the Church:	
Infant Baptism Totals	1,014
Adult Baptism Totals	84
Received into Full Communion	106
First Communions	1,589
Confirmations	1,589
Marriages:	
Catholic	193
Interfaith	76
Total Marriages	269
Deaths	280
Total Catholic Population	52,431
Total Population	386,574

Former Bishops—Most Rev. RUDOLPH ALOYSIUS GERKEN, D.D., ord. June 10, 1917; cons. April 26, 1927; installed Bishop of Amarillo, April 28, 1927; elevated to the Metropolitan See of Santa Fe, NM, June 2, 1933; died March 2, 1943.—Most Rev. ROBERT E. LUCEY, ord. May 14, 1916; cons. May 1, 1934; installed May 16, 1934; elevated to the Metropolitan See of San Antonio, Jan. 22, 1941.—Most Rev. LAURENCE J. FITZSIMON, D.D., ord. May 17, 1921; cons. Oct. 22, 1941; installed Nov. 5, 1941; died July 2, 1958.—Most Rev. JOHN L. MORKOVSKY, appt. Auxiliary of Amarillo, Dec. 22, 1955; named Bishop of Amarillo, Aug. 18, 1958; transferred as Coadjutor Bishop of Galveston-Houston *"cum jure successionis"*, April 16, 1963.—Most Rev. LAWRENCE M. DEFALCO, D.D., ord. June 11, 1942; appt. April 16, 1963; cons. May 30, 1963; installed June 13, 1963; retired Aug. 28, 1979; died Sept. 22, 1979.—Most Rev. LEROY T. MATTHIESEN, D.D., M.A., LITT.D, ord. March 10, 1946; appt. March 25, 1980; ord. Bishop, May 30, 1980; retired Jan. 21, 1997.

Diocesan Officials

Diocesan Pastoral Center—1800 N. Spring St., P.O. Box 5644, Amarillo, 79117-5644. Tel: 806-383-2243; Fax: 806-383-8452.

Vicar General—Rev. Msgr. JAMES C. GURZYNSKI, J.C.L.

Diocesan Tribunal—

Judicial Vicar—Rev. Msgr. JAMES C. GURZYNSKI, J.C.L.

Defender of the Bond—Rev. Msgr. HAROLD WALDOW.

Advocates—Rev. Msgr. JOSEPH TASH; Rev. Msgr. HAROLD WALDOW; Revs. MICHAEL COLWELL; PHU PHAN, J.C.L.

Notaries—Mrs. MADOLYN GUTIERREZ; Ms. SUSAN GARNER.

Chancellor—Ms. MARY LOUISE VIGIL.

Diocesan Advisory Councils

Presbyteral Council—Revs. RAYMOND CROSIER; JOSE E. GOMEZ; Rev. Msgr. ORVILLE R. BLUM; Rev. Msgr. HAROLD WALDOW; Revs. JOHN VALDEZ; NEAL DEE; JOHN SALAZAR; GREG MAYERS, C.S.S.R.; Rev. Msgr. JAMES C. GURZYNSKI, J.C.L.

College of Consultors—Revs. JOSEPH BIXENMAN; NEAL DEE; JOHN SALAZAR; Rev. Msgr. JAMES C. GURZYNSKI; Rev. Msgr. KEVIN HAND; Rev. Msgr. FRANCIS A. SMYER; Rev. Msgr. JOSEPH TASH.

Diocesan Pastoral Council—LEO LENERS; LAURENCE WALKER; PAULA BREEDING.; THERESA LOPEZ; BRENDA SAUCEDO; MARGIE LONG; MARIA NEAL; ELODIA BRAVO; VENTURA RAMOS; AMPARO BECERRA; GEORGIA SCIACA; ANITA SUMNER; GLORIA MARTIN; MATILDA BACA; BETTY KOELZER; DOROTHY SCHERLEN; Deacon JOE SCHWERTNER.

Vocation Team—Rev. Msgr. ORVILLE BLUM, *St. Anthony's Church, 115 N. 25 Mile Rd., Hereford, 79045.* Rev. KENNETH KELLER, *St. Mary's Church, 1200 S. Washington, Amarillo, 79102.* Rev. Msgr. NORBERT C. KUEHLER, *St. John's Church, 201 St. John's Rd., Borger, 79007.* Rev. GUILLERMO MORALES, *Immaculate Conception Church, Dimmitt;* Sr. JOANN ALEGRE, F.M.I., *St. Francis Convent, 4301 N.E. 18th Ave., Amarillo, 79107.*

Deacon Advisory Council—Deacon BLAINE WESTLAKE, Coord.; Revs. GUILLERMO MORALES; JOHN DALTON; PATRICK HOFFMAN; Deacons TIMOTHY REID; RICHARD RILEY; BILL DORSEY; Mrs. FRANCES DORSEY; MADOLYN GUTIERREZ.

Diocesan Departments

Youth and Young Adult Ministry—Deacon JESSIE GUERRERO, Dir.

Office for the Catholic Schools—Sr. CORNELIA MARIE KNEZEK, S.S.C.J., Supt.

Christian Formation Commission—CHARLOTTE PAETZOLD, Coord., *St. Anthony's Church, 115 N. 25 Mile Rd., Hereford, 79045.* Tel: 806-364-0969.
Department of Communications—CHRIS ALBRACHT, Dir. Information & Editor "West Texas Catholic."
Department of Finances and Ecclesiastical Properties—Fiscal Manager—BEN R. SMART.
Director of Administrative Services—PATSY GRAHAM.
Office of Development and Stewardship—NANCY KOONS, Dir., *P.O. Box 1011, Canyon, 79015.* Tel: 806-655-2556.
United Catholic Appeal—NANCY KOONS.

General Auxiliary Pastoral Services

Diocesan Attorney—FREDERICK J. GRIFFIN, *504 S. Polk, Amarillo, 79101.*
Vicar for Canonical Affairs—(see Tribunal).
Coalition for Catholic Social Services - CCSS—Rev. KEN KELLER, Chm.
Catholic Historical Society—EDITH DANILE, Pres.
Diocesan Liturgical Commission—Rev. PHILIP LINDLEY, Chm.
Rural Life Director—Rev. JERRY STEIN.
Holy Childhood Association—Rev. Msgr. RICHARD F. VAUGHAN.
Propagation of the Faith—Rev. Msgr. RICHARD F. VAUGHAN.
Office of Worship—Rev. PATRICK CARATHERS, Dir.
Rite of Christian Initiation of Adults—CAROL SALDANA, Dir.

Auxiliary Pastoral Services for the Laity

Institute for Pastoral Ministry—Rev. ROBERT BUSCH, Dir., *2610 4th Ave., Canyon, 79015.* Tel: 806-655-4345. THERESA UNRUH, Asst. to Dir.
Diocesan Council of Catholic Women—Rev. Msgr. FRANCIS A. SMYER, Moderator, *1200 S. Washington, Amarillo, 79102.*
Engaged Encounter—Directors: BLAIN WESTLAKE; LOUISE WESTLAKE. Contact Couple: JENNY BALLARD; AGNES BALLARD. Tel: 806-353-0907.
Beginning Experience—BECKY SONDERSON. Tel: 806-364-5813.
Catholic Student Center at West Texas A & M University—Rev. ROBERT BUSCH, Dir.-Chap., *2614 Fourth Ave., Canyon, 79015.* Tel: 806-655-4345.
Scouting—Deacon JESSIE GUERRERO, *1200 S. Washington, Amarillo, 79102.*
Serra Club—DAVID DZIK, Pres.
Natural Family Planning—Certified Teaching Couples: GERALD MARNELL; DENISE MARNELL, *Rte. 5, Box 117-A, Hereford, 79045.* JOHN BRADICICH; CALEY BRADICICH.

Auxiliary Pastoral Services for Clergy and Religious

Vicar for Priests—Rev. Msgr. RICHARD F. VAUGHAN.
Vicar for Religious—Sr. HELEN ANN COLLIER, C.C.V.I., *St. Anthony's Hospital, 200 N.W. Seventh St., Amarillo, 79176-0001.* Tel:
Office for the Permanent Diaconate—Deacon BLAINE WESTLAKE, Coord.
Continuing Education of Clergy—Rev. Msgr. JAMES C. GURZYNSKI.
Priests' Retirement—PATSY GRAHAM.

CLERGY, PARISHES, MISSIONS AND PAROCHIAL SCHOOLS

CITY OF AMARILLO (Potter County)

1—SACRED HEART CATHEDRAL. Closed. This parish ceased to exist 1/19/75. For inquiries contact the Diocese of Amarillo: P.O. Box 5644, Amarillo, TX 79117-5644. Tel: 806-383-2243.

2—ST. LAURENCE CATHEDRAL, Revs. Patrick Hoffman; Arulfo Gradillas, C.S.Sp.; Deacon Leo Ramos.
Res., 2300 N. Spring St., 79107. Tel: 806-383-2261.
Kindergarten & Child Development Center—Sisters 3; Lay Teachers 17; Students 120.
Catechesis/Religious Programs—Students 397.

3—BLESSED SACRAMENT, Rev. Phillip Lindley; Deacon Mark Seidlitz.
Res., 4112 S.E. 25th St., 79103. Tel: 806-374-1132.
Catechesis/Religious Programs—Carolina Searcy, D.R.E.
Students 120.

4—OUR LADY OF GUADALUPE, Rev. John Valdez; Deacon Hector Gallegos.
Res., 1210 E. 11th Ave., 79102. Tel: 806-372-1128.
School—See Elementary Schools, City-Wide under Institutions Located in the Diocese.
Catechesis/Religious Programs—Martha Loza, D.R.E.
Students 460.

5—OUR LADY OF VIETNAM, Revs. Aloysius Tran Ngoc Thoai, C.M.C.; Polycarp Ducthllan, C.M.C. Pastoral Assocs.: John Baptist Phan Van Chac; Joseph Le Van Canh.
Res., 1800 N. Spring Rd., 79107. Tel: 806-383-0467.

6—ST. FRANCIS, Rev. Ted Podson, Sch.P.
Res., 5005 Klinke Rd., 79107-9628. Tel: 806-335-1872.
Catechesis/Religious Programs—Evelyn Detten, D.R.E.
Students 31.

7—ST. HYACINTH'S, Revs. Pat Carathers; Bert Horvath; Sr. Pauline Brorman, O.S.F., Pastoral Assoc. & D.R.E.
Res., 4500 W. Hills Tr., 79106. Tel: 806-358-1351; Fax: 806-467-1708.
Catechesis/Religious Programs—Students 80.

8—ST. JOSEPH'S, Rev. Neal Dee; Deacons James R. Ambs; Richard Riley; Bill Jordon; Robert Smith.
Res., 4122 Bonham St., 79110. Tel: 806-355-5622; Fax: 806-355-5622.
School—See Elementary Schools, City-Wide under Institutions Located in the Diocese.
St. Joseph Day Care Center—4108 Bonham, 79110. Tel: 806-353-7043.
Students 86.
Catechesis/Religious Programs—Mrs. Rosie Sisneros, D.R.E.
Students 219.

9—ST. MARTIN DE PORRES MISSION, Rev. Francis R. Crowe, O.P.
Res., 1501 N. Adams, P.O. Box 1951, 79105. Tel: 806-376-8871.

10—ST. MARY'S, Rev. Msgr. Francis A. Smyer; Revs. William Brashears; Ken Keller.
Res., 1200 Washington St., 79102. Tel: 806-376-7204; Fax: 806-376-4314.
School—See Elementary Schools, City-Wide under Institutions Located in the Diocese.
Catechesis/Religious Programs—Cindy Luginbill, D.R.E.
Students 426.

11—ST. THOMAS THE APOSTLE, Rev. Msgr. Joseph T. Tash; Deacons Terry Pevehouse; Timothy Reid; Blain Westlake. In res., Rev. Robert Busch.
Res., 4100 Coulter Dr., 79109. Tel: 806-358-2461; Fax: 806-358-2529.
Catechesis/Religious Programs—D.R.E.: Bernice Noggler, (Grades PreK-5); Amy Reid, (Grades 6-12).
Students 632.
Mission—Amarillo, Potter Co., Laotian Catholic Community. Rev. Phu Phan, J.C.L.

OUTSIDE THE CITY OF AMARILLO

Borger, Hutchinson Co., St. John the Evangelist, Rev. Msgr. Norbert Kuehler; Rev. Jose Gomez; Deacon Zeferino Villarreal.
Res., 201 St. John's Rd., 79007. Tel: 806-274-7064.
School—Linda Wright, Dir. Sisters 2; Lay Teachers 3; Students 23.
Catechesis/Religious Programs—Cathy Gregory, D.R.E.
Students 245.
Convent—Tel: 806-274-6504.
Mission—Stinnett, St. Ann's.

Bovina, Parmer Co., St. Ann's, Rev. Ed Kieran; Deacon Zeferino Villarreal.
Res., Box 657, 79009. Tel: 806-238-1511.
Catechesis/Religious Programs—Nancy Schwertner, D.R.E.
Students 158.

Canadian, Hemphill Co., Sacred Heart, Revs. Joe Bixenman; James McGhee; Deacon Jose Jesus Gutierrez.
Res., 721 Main, P.O. Box 786, 79014. Tel: 806-323-9705.

Canyon, Randall Co., St. Ann's, Rev. Phu T. Phan; Deacons Jerry Grossman; August Hesse, III; Mauro Hernandes; Gabriel Rivas.
Mailing Address: P.O. Box 59, 79015.
Res., 38th St. at Conner Dr., 79015. Tel: 806-655-3302; Fax: 806-655-3384.
Catechesis/Religious Programs—Carol Sanford, D.R.E.
Students 275.

Childress, Childress Co., Holy Angels, Rev. Dennis Boylan.
Res., 308 Ave. B, S.W., P.O. Box 608, 79201. Tel: 817-937-3946; Fax: 817-937-3946.
Catechesis/Religious Programs—Students 37.

Clarendon, Donley Co., St. Mary's, Rev. Ted Podson, Sch.P.; Deacon Bill Dorsey.
Res., 815 McClelland St., P.O. Drawer C, 79226. Tel: 806-874-3910.

Dalhart, Dallam Co., St. Anthony's, Rev. Dale Guidry; Deacon Javier Cruz.
Res., 411 Texas Blvd., Box 1029, 79022. Tel: 806-249-4128; Fax: 806-249-4637.
School—1302 Oak St., 79022. Tel: 806-249-2390. Mrs. Sandra Kelso, Prin.
School Sisters of the Third Order of St. Francis 2; Lay Teachers 3; Students 77.
Mission—Texline, St. Mary's. Deacon Ronald Hein.

Dimmitt, Castro Co., Immaculate Conception, Rev. Guillermo Morales; Deacons Joseph Ortega; John Nino; Hose Velo.
Res., 710 W. Halsell St., 79027. Tel: 806-647-4219 (Church); 647-0105 (Office).
Catechesis/Religious Programs—Mary Helen Flores, D.R.E.
Students 700.
Mission—Hart, St. John Nepomucene. Deacon Roberto Gonzales.

Dumas, Moore Co., SS. Peter and Paul, Rev. Richard D. Scully; Deacons Joseph Schwertner; Jessie Ruiz; Vacilio Anaya.
Res., Box 503, 79029. Tel: 806-935-5002.
Catechesis/Religious Programs—D.R.E.: Wanda Brooks; Ann Easterling.
Students 300.
Missions—Sunray, Christ the King. Deacon Wayne Norrell.; Cactus, Our Lady of Guadalupe.

Friona, Parmer Co., St. Teresa of Jesus, Rev. Edward Sweeney; Deacons Zeferino Villarreal; Raymond Solano.
Res., HCR 2, Box 1A, P.O. Box 381, 79035-0381. Tel: 806-247-2871; Fax: 806-247-2871.
Catechesis/Religious Programs—Lesa Echavarria, D.R.E.
Students 186.

Groom, Carson Co., Immaculate Heart of Mary, Rev. Raymond Crosier.
Res., 411 Ware Ave., P.O. Box 130, 79039. Tel: 806-248-7584. [CEM]
Catechesis/Religious Programs—Students 96.

Gruver, Cristo Redentor, Rev. Scott Raef; Deacon Jesus Favela.
Res., 603 Main St., P.O. Box 238, 79040. Tel: 806-733-5236.
Catechesis/Religious Programs—Elena Salazar, D.R.E.
Students 51.

Happy, Swisher Co., Holy Name of Jesus, Revs. Jerry Stein; John Hickey; Deacon Amadeo Perez.
Res., 317 W. Main, P.O. Box 128, 79042. Tel: 806-558-2871. [CEM]
Catechesis/Religious Programs—Students 35.

Hereford, Deaf Smith Co., St. Anthony's, Rev. Msgr. Orville Blum; Deacon Jon E. Cloud; Charlotte Paetzold, Pastoral Assoc.
Res., 115 N. 25 Mile Ave., 79045. Tel: 806-364-6150; 364-6152.
School—120 W. Park Ave., 79045. Tel: 806-364-1952. Ann Lueb, Prin.
Franciscan Sisters of Mary Immaculate 3; Lay Teachers 11; Students 163.
Catechesis/Religious Programs—Students 192.
Convent—114 Sunset, 79045. Tel: 806-364-3344.
San Jose, Rev. Domingo Castillo; Deacons Esteban Castillo; Emilio Fuentes; Vicente Garcia; Jessie Guerrero, Pastoral Assoc.
Res., 735 Brevard, 79045. Tel: 806-364-5053; Fax: 806-364-2880.
Preschool—.
Catechesis/Religious Programs—Domingo St., 79045. Tel: 806-364-4365.
Students 374.

Memphis, Hall Co., Sacred Heart, Rev. Ramiro Trejo, O.F.M.Cap.
Mailing Address: 213 N. Third St., P.O. Box 239, 79245. Tel: 806-259-2178.
Catechesis/Religious Programs—Mrs. Juanita Garza, D.R.E.
Students 43.

Nazareth, Castro Co., Holy Family, Revs. Jerry Stein; John Hickey; Deacons Jerome Brockman; Alfonse Mauer.
Res., 210 St. Joseph, P.O. Box 100, 79063. Tel: 806-945-2616.
Catechesis/Religious Programs—Gladys Fortenberry, D.R.E.
Students 193.

Pampa, Gray Co., St. Vincent de Paul, Revs. Joseph E. Bixenman; Rosendo Herrera; Sr. Nancy Dragotta, S.C.S.J.A., Pastoral Assoc.; Deacons Tony Campos; Daniel Rose.
Res., 810 W. 23rd St., 79065. Tel: 806-665-8933.
School—2300 N. Hobart, 79065.
Lay Teachers 10; Students 110.
Catechesis/Religious Programs—Students 204.

Panhandle, Carson Co., St. Theresa, Rev. Gary Sides.
Res., P.O. Box 366, 79068. Tel: 806-537-3677.
Catechesis/Religious Programs—Mother M. Valentina, D.R.E.

Students 131.

Perryton, Ochiltree Co., Immaculate Conception, Rev. Rex F. Nicholl.
Res., 1000 S.W. Fifth Ave., 79070. Tel: 806-435-3802.
Catechesis/Religious Programs—Daryla Allred, D.R.E.
Students 225.
Mission—Booker, St. Peter.

Spearman, Hansford Co., Sacred Heart, Rev. Scott Raef.
Res., 1109 Townsend, P.O. Box 127, 79081. Tel: 806-659-2166; Fax: 806-659-1042.
Catechesis/Religious Programs—David & Lisa Link, D.R.E.
Students 130.

Stratford, Sherman Co., St. Joseph's, Rev. David Contreras; Deacon Willie Artho.
Mailing Address: Box 28, 79084. Tel: 806-396-5687.
Catechesis/Religious Programs—Johnny Garza, D.R.E.
Students 70.

Tulia, Swisher Co., Church of the Holy Spirit, Rev. John Salazar-Jimenez. Pastoral Assocs.: Mary Lou Moreno; Ventura Ramos.
Res., 513 S. Austin, P.O. Box 25, 79088. Tel: 806-995-3191; Fax: 806-995-3286.
Catechesis/Religious Programs—Martha Rocha, D.R.E.
Students 225.
Missions—Silverton, Briscoe Co., Our Lady of Loreto, P.O. Box 47, Silverton, 79257. Rev. Ed Graff, Parochial Admin.; Kress, Swisher Co., St. Paul's, P.O. Box 231, Kress, 79052. Ampara Becerra, Pastoral Assoc.
Station—Quitaque.

Umbarger, Randall Co., St. Mary's, Rev. James Hutzler.
Res., P.O. Box 105, 79091. Tel: 806-499-3531. [CEM]
Catechesis/Religious Programs—Karen Frimel, D.R.E.
Students 100.

Vega, Oldham Co., Immaculate Conception, Revs. Patrick Carathers; Bert Horvath.
Res., P.O. Box 250, 79092. Tel: 806-267-2343.
Catechesis/Religious Programs—Dolores Broman, D.R.E.
Students 88.

Wellington, Collingsworth Co., Our Mother of Mercy, Rev. Ramario Trejo, O.F.M.Cap.
Church—1108 Floydada, P.O. Box 686, 79095.
Mission—Shamrock, St. Patrick. Rev. Cal Stalter, Admin.

White Deer, Carson Co., Sacred Heart, Rev. Msgr. Kevin Hand.
Res., Box 427, 79097. Tel: 806-883-4781.
Catechesis/Religious Programs—D.R.E.: Manuel Visil; Delfina Vigil.
Students 81.

Absent on Leave:
Reverend Fathers—
Alvarez, Xavier
Jaramillo, Peter
Madrigal, Hector
Rosolen, Emil
Sherry, Brendan
Wood, Michael

On Duty Outside the Diocese:
Reverend Fathers—
Afenugo, Emmanuel
Birkenfeld, Darryl
Colwell, Michael
Greka, David
Kieferle, Norbert
Malnar, Matthew
Meza, Arturo

Military Chaplains:
Reverend Fathers—
Otto, Peter B., U.S. Air Force

Retired:
Reverend Monsignors—
Corcoran, Clifton J., P.O. Box 1179, Panhandle, TX 79068
Erpen, B. A., 318 S.E. Fifth, Tulia, TX 79088
Morsch, Peter, 1410 Peoria Dr., Slaton, TX 79364
Sonderman, James W., P.O. Box 1179, Panhandle, TX 79068
Reverend Fathers—
Carlson, J. Arnold, St. Mary's, Drawer C, Clarendon, TX 79226-2003
Chen, Raphael, 9170 Graham, Cypress, CA 90630
Choong, Norbert, 6303 Butte Ave., New Port Richey, FL 34653
Pawlak, Ed, 5431 Denise Ave., Orlando, FL 32810-3609
Stortz, Mario, Rte. 1, Box 174, Tulia, TX 79088

Permanent Deacons:
Ambs, James R., St. Joseph's Church, Amarillo
Anaya, Vacilio, Sts. Peter and Paul Church, Dumas
Artho, Kenneth, Inactive
Artho, Willie F., St. Joseph's Church, Stratford
Blunt, Orvel Ray, On Leave
Brockman, Jerome, Holy Family Church, Nazareth
Campos, Tony, St. Vincente de Paul Church, Pampa
Castillo, Esteban, On Leave
Cloud, Jonny E., St. Anthony Church, Hereford
Dorsey, Bill, St. Mary's Church, Clarendon
Frausto, Joseph, Inactive
Fuentes, Emilio, Sr., San Jose Church, Hereford
Gallegos, Hector, Our Lady of Guadalupe Church, Amarillo
Garcia, Vicente H., San Jose Church, Hereford
Gonzales, Roberto, St. John Nepomucene Church, Hart
Grossman, Jerry, St. Ann's Church, Canyon
Guerrero, Jesse, San Jose Church, Hereford
Gutierrez, Jose Jesus, Sacred Heart Church, Canadian
Gutierrez, Robert, On Leave
Hein, Ronald, St. Anthony's Church, Dalhart
Hernandez, Mauro, St. Ann's Church, Canyon
Hesse, August, III, St. Ann's Church, Canyon
Jimenez, Aeferino, St. John's Church, Borger
Jordan, Bill, St. Joseph's Church, Amarillo
Keller, Robert C., Diocese of Galveston-Houston
Maurer, Alfons A., Holy Family Church, Nazareth
Nino, John, Immaculate Conception Church, Dimmitt
Norrell, Wayne, Christ the King Church, Sunray
Ortega, Joseph, Immaculate Conception Church, Dimmitt
Perez, Amadeo, Holy Name Church, Happy
Pevehouse, Terry, St. Thomas the Apostle Church, Amarillo
Ramos, Leo, St. Laurence Cathedral, Amarillo
Reid, Timothy, St. Thomas Church, Amarillo
Riley, Richard D., St. Joseph's Church, Amarillo
Rivas, Gabriel, St. Ann's Church, Canyon
Rose, Daniel, St. Vincente de Paul Church, Pampa
Ruiz, Jesse P., SS. Peter & Paul Church, Dumas
Schwertner, Joseph A., SS. Peter & Paul Church, Dumas
Seidlitz, Mark, Blessed Sacrament Church, Amarillo
Smith, Robert, St. Joseph's Church, Amarillo
Solano, Raymond, St. Theresa's Church, Friona
Stewart, Arthur Gerald, (Retired)
Thiele, William E., Sick Leave
Valdez, Pete, Blessed Sacrament Church, Amarillo
Velo, Joe, Immaculate Conception Church, Dimmitt
Villarreal, Zeferino, St. Ann's Church, Bovina
Westlake, Blain, St. Thomas Church, Amarillo

INSTITUTIONS LOCATED IN THE DIOCESE

[A] HIGH SCHOOLS, CITY-WIDE

AMARILLO. *Alamo Catholic High School and Amarillo Catholic Middle School.* (Coed), 4114 S. Bonham, 79110-1113. Tel: 806-355-9637; 356-0550. Darla Mueller, Prin., 4110 S. Bonham, 79110-1113. High School. Sisters 2; Lay Teachers 15; Students 61.
Middle School. Sisters 2; Lay Teachers 12; Students 70.

[B] ELEMENTARY SCHOOLS, CITY-WIDE

AMARILLO. *Our Lady of Guadalupe School,* 1103 S. Houston, 79102. Tel: 806-372-2629. Allison Cobb, Prin. Lay Teachers 3; Students 52. 1108 S. Houston, 79102.
St. Joseph's School, 4118 Bonham St., 79110. Tel: 806-359-1604. Mrs. Betty Keller, Prin. Sisters 1; Lay Teachers 12; Students 91.
St. Laurence Cathedral School, 2300-B N. Spring St., 79107. Tel: 806-383-2261. Esther Ford, Prin. Sisters 1; Lay Teachers 3; Students 52.
St. Mary School, 1200 S. Washington, 79102. Davlyn Duesterhaus, Prin. Sisters 2; Lay Teachers 21; Students 283.

[C] CATHOLIC CHILDREN'S DEVELOPMENT CENTERS

AMARILLO. *Amarillo Catholic Children's Development Centers.*
St. Joseph Campus, 4108 Bonham St., P.O. Box 19726, 79114. Tel: 806-383-4411. Theresa Pigott, Dir. Sisters 1; Teachers 2; Caregivers 11; Students 95.
St. Laurence Campus, 2300-B N. Spring St., 79107. Tel: 806-383-4411. Theresa Pigott, Dir. Sisters 1; Lay Teachers 2; Students 100.
Our Lady of Guadalupe Campus, 1108 S. Houston, 79102. Tel: 806-372-2629. Theresa Hamilton, Dir. Students 30.
St. Mary's Montessori School, 1200 S. Washington, 79102. Tel: 806-376-9155. Roe Fitzsimmons, Dir.

[D] HOMES FOR THE AGED

PANHANDLE. *St. Ann's Nursing Home,* P.O. Box 1179, 79068. Tel: 806-537-3194.
For a complete listing, refer to the Special Care Facilities section.
St. Joseph's Home for Retired Priests, P.O. Box 1179, 79068.
For a complete listing, refer to the Special Care Facilities section.

[E] COALITION OF CATHOLIC SOCIAL SERVICES

AMARILLO.
**Catholic Family Service, Inc.*, 200 S. Tyler, 79102. Tel: 806-376-4571; Fax: 806-345-7911. Al Bednorz, Dir.
Morning Star Hostel and Mark Schupp Center, 2501 W. Sixth, 79102. Tel: 806-371-0373. Rev. Terence Burke, Dir.
**Downtown Women's Center and Abba House, Inc.*, P.O. Box 1985, 79105. Tel: 806-372-3625. Sr. Mary Virginia Clarke, D.C., Dir.
**Another Chance Houses, Inc.*, 209 S. Jackson, 79101. Tel: 806-372-3344. Dale Botts, Dir.

[F] GENERAL HOSPITALS

*AMARILLO. *St. Anthony's Hospital,* 200 N.W. Seventh St., P.O. Box 950, 79176. Tel: 806-376-4411.
For a complete listing, refer to the Hospitals section.

[G] SPECIAL HOSPITALS

AMARILLO. *St. Anthony's Hospice and Life Enrichment Center,* 600 N. Tyler, P.O. Box 950, 79176. Tel: 806-378-6777; Fax: 806-378-5031.
For a complete listing, refer to the Hospitals section.

[H] RETREAT HOUSE

AMARILLO. *Bishop DeFalco Retreat Center,* 2100 N. Spring St., 79107. Tel: 806-383-1811; Fax: 806-383-6919. The Redemptorist Fathers. Rev. Gregory Mayers, C.SS.R., Dir. Retreat Staff: Rev. Pat Hawk, C.SS.R.; Bro. Michael Rhodes, C.SS.R.
Bishop DeFalco Retreat Center Foundation.

[I] MONASTERIES AND RESIDENCES OF PRIESTS AND BROTHERS

AMARILLO. *Redemptorists Fathers,* 2100 N. Spring St., 79107. Tel: 806-383-1811. Priests 2; Brothers 1.

[J] CONVENTS AND RESIDENCES FOR SISTERS

AMARILLO. *Daughters of Charity of St. Vincent de Paul,* 1104 S. Washington, 79102. Tel: 806-734-7812. Sisters 3.
Madres Clarisas Capuchinas, Capuchin Nuns of St. Clare, 4201 N.E. 18th Ave., 79107.
Convent of the Blessed Sacrament and Our Lady of Guadalupe. Mother Rocio Hernandez, O.S.C., Abbess. Professed Nuns 12; Apostulants 1.
St. Francis Convent, Novitiate and U.S. Provincial House, 4301 N.E. 18th, 79107. Tel: 806-383-5769. Franciscan Sisters of Mary Immaculate of the Third Order of St. Francis. Sr. Mary Magdalene Baca, F.M.I., Prov. Supr.; Rev. Bert Horvath, Chap. Sisters 47.
St. Francis Mission Community, O.S.F., LaVerna Convent, 203 S. Avondale, 79106. Tel: 806-352-2981. Sr. Celine Thames, O.S.F., Mission Community Coord. Sisters 5. St. Clare Convent, 5407 W. 15th, 79106. Tel: 806-359-4110. Sisters 3.
St. Martin's Convent, 1507 N. Adams St., P.O. Box 5398, 79117. Tel: 806-373-6024. Sisters of Charity of St. Jeanne Antide.
Sisters of St. Joseph-St. Benedict's Convent, 4122 Bonham, 79110. Tel: 806-352-0106. Sisters of St. Benedict. Sisters 2.

BORGER. *St. John's Convent,* 201 St. John's Rd., 79007. Tel: 806-274-6504. Franciscan Sisters of Mary Immaculate. Sisters 3.

CANYON. *St. Benedict's Monastery,* 2100 Fifth Ave., 79015. Tel: 806-655-9317. Sr. Mary Hawkins, O.S.B., Supr. Sisters 5.

CHANNING. *Disciples of the Lord Jesus Christ.* Mailing Address: Emmanuel Prayer Town, Motherhouse and Retreat Center, P.O. Box 17, 79018-0017. Tel: 806-534-2312. House of Prayer (Mission House), 4609 Coliseum Blvd., Alexandria, LA, 71303. Sr. Bernadette Beamsley, Supr. Gen.; Rev. John Dalton, Chap. Members 42.

DALHART. *St. Anthony's Convent,* 1301 Oak Ave., 79022.

Tel: 806-249-2390. School Sisters of St. Francis. Sisters 5.

HEREFORD. *St. Anthony's Convent*, 114 Sunset Dr., 79045. Tel: 806-364-3344. Franciscan Sisters of Mary Immaculate. Sisters 3.

PANHANDLE. *Sancta Maria Convent (North American Region and Novitiate)*, P.O. Box 906, 79068-0906. Tel: 806-537-3182. School Sisters of the Third Order of St. Francis. Mother Bernadette Black, Regl. Supr. Sisters 20.

[K] CAMPUS MINISTRY

CANYON. *Catholic Student Center at West Texas A & M University*, 2610 Fourth Ave., 79015. Tel: 806-655-4345. Rev. Robert Busch, Chap. & Dir.

[L] MISCELLANEOUS LISTINGS

AMARILLO. *Amarillo Catholic Education Foundation*, 1800 N. Spring St., 79107. Tel: 806-383-2243; Fax: 806-383-8452.

Amarillo Catholic School System, 1800 N. Spring St., 79109. Tel: 806-383-2243; Fax: 806-383-8452.

Amarillo Scholarship Endowment and Assistance Fund, 1800 N. Spring St., 79107. Tel: 806-383-2243; Fax: 806-383-8452.

Engaged Encounter, 3600 Torre, 79109. Tel: 806-352-2607. Directors: Blain Westlake; Louise Westlake. Contact Couple: Jenny Ballard. Tel: 806-353-0907; Agnes Ballard.

Marriage Encounter, 1800 N. Spring, 79107. Rev. Arnulfo Gradillas, C.S.Sp., Dir.

RELIGIOUS INSTITUTES OF MEN REPRESENTED IN THE DIOCESE

For further details refer to the corresponding bracketed number in the Religious Institutes of Men or Women section.

[]—*Congregation of Mother Coredemptrix.*—C.M.C.

[0430]—*Order of Preachers-Dominicans.*—O.P.

[1070]—*Redemptorist Fathers.* (New Orleans Vice Prov.).—C.SS.R.

RELIGIOUS INSTITUTES OF WOMEN REPRESENTED IN THE DIOCESE

[0230]—*Benedictine Sisters of Pontifical Jurisdiction.* (Little Rock, AR).—O.S.B.

[0460]—*Congregation of the Sisters of Charity of the Incarnate Word.*—C.C.V.I.

[0760]—*Daughters of Charity of St. Vincent De Paul.*—D.C.

[0965]—*Disciples of the Lord Jesus Christ.*—D.L.J.C.

[1500]—*Franciscan Sisters of Mary Immaculate of the Third Order of St. Francis of Assisi.*—F.M.I.

[]—*Franciscan Sisters of Perpetual Adoration.*—F.F.P.A.

[]—*St. Clare Capuchin Sisters.*—C.P.C.

[1695]—*School Sisters of the Third Order of St. Francis, Panhandle, Texas.*—O.S.F.

[0600]—*Sisters of St. Jeanne Antide.*—S.C.S.J.A.

[3670]—*Sisters of the Sacred Heart of Jesus of St. Jacut.*—S.S.C.J.

[1705]—*Sisters of the Third Order of St. Francis of Assisi.*—O.S.F.

NECROLOGY

† Crocchiola, Rev. Msgr. Stanley, (Retired). —Died Feb. 6, 1996.

† DiBenedetto, Rev. Msgr. Peter Paul, Amarillo, TX St. Hyacinth's. —Died Nov. 28, 1995.

Archdiocese of Anchorage

(Archidioecesis Ancoragiensis)

Most Reverend

FRANCIS T. HURLEY, D.D.

Archbishop of Anchorage; ordained June 16, 1951; appointed Titular Bishop of Daimlaig and Auxiliary of Juneau February 4, 1970; consecrated March 19, 1970; appointed Bishop of Juneau July 20, 1971; installed September 8, 1971; appointed Archbishop of Anchorage May 4, 1976; installed July 8, 1976.

ESTABLISHED FEBRUARY 9, 1966.

Comprises the Third Judicial Division of Alaska.

Square Miles 138,985.

For legal titles of parishes and archdiocesan institutions, consult the Chancery Office.

Chancery Office: 225 Cordova St., Anchorage, AK, 99501. Tel.: 907-258-7898; Fax: 907-279-3885.

STATISTICAL OVERVIEW

Personnel	
Archbishop	1
Priests: Active Outside Diocese	13
Priests: Diocesan in Foreign Missions	1
Priests: Retired, Sick or Absent	5
Number of Diocesan Priests	19
Religious Priests in Diocese	12
Extern Priests in Diocese	7
Ordinations:	
Diocesan Priests	1
Permanent Deacons in Diocese	12
Total Brothers	1
Total Sisters	47
Parishes	
Parishes	20
With Resident Pastor:	
Resident Diocesan Priests	12
Resident Religious Priests	2
Without Resident Pastor:	
Administered by Women Religious	4
Administered by Lay People	1
Administered by Pastoral Teams, etc.	1
Missions	8
Professional Ministry Personnel:	
Sisters	8
Lay Ministers	14
Welfare	
Catholic Hospitals	1
Total Assisted	287,000
Health Care Centers	1
Total Assisted	380
Homes for the Aged	1
Total Assisted	89
Special Centers for Social Services	4
Total Assisted	27,697
Educational	
Diocesan Students in Other Seminaries	3
Total Seminarians	3
High Schools, Private	1
Total Students	40
Elementary Schools, Diocesan and Parish	2
Total Students	379
Elementary Schools, Private	1
Total Students	140
Catechesis/Religious Education:	
High School Students	1,067
Elementary Students	2,932
Total Students Under Catholic Instruction	4,561
Teachers in the Diocese:	
Sisters	3
Lay Teachers	43
Vital Statistics	
Receptions into the Church:	
Infant Baptism Totals	538
Adult Baptism Totals	60
Received into Full Communion	97
First Communions	545
Confirmations	341
Marriages:	
Catholic	64
Interfaith	71
Total Marriages	135
Deaths	132
Total Catholic Population	27,019
Total Population	373,019

Former Bishop—Most Rev. JOSEPH T. RYAN, D.D., Archbishop of Anchorage; ord. June 3, 1939; cons. March 25, 1966; installed April 14, 1966; transferred as Coadjutor Military Vicar of U.S. Armed Forces, Dec. 13, 1975; appt. First Archbishop of the Archdiocese for the Military Services, U.S.A., March 16, 1985.

Vicar General—Rev. STEVEN C. MOORE.

Chancery Office—225 Cordova St., Anchorage, 99501. Tel: 907-258-7898; Fax: 907-279-3885.

Chancellor—Vacant.

Assistant to Archbishop—Rev. TIMOTHY M. CROWLEY.

Secretary to Archbishop—JOANN WHITE.

Office of Stewardship/Development—Mr. JAMES CALDAROLA.

Tribunal—225 Cordova St., Box 102239, Anchorage, 99510-2239. Tel: 907-258-7898.

Judicial Vicar—Rev. J. MICHAEL HORNICK, S.T.B., J.C.L.

Defenders of the Bond—Deacon WILLIAM FINNEGAN, J.C.L.; MIRIAM DONOHUE.

Advocate for Respondents—Sr. MAUREEN MCPARTLAND, O.P.

Notaries—MIRIAM DONOHUE; EILEEN T. KRAMER.

Diocesan Consultors—Rev. Msgr. FRANCIS A. COWGILL; Revs. STEVEN C. MOORE, Ex-officio; ALFRED W. GIEBEL; LEO DESSO; LASALLE HALLISSEY, O.P.; RICHARD D. TERO; MICHAEL W. WARFEL; DANIEL J. HEBERT.

Representatives for Pastoral Adminstrators—Sr. MARIE ANN BRENT, S.H.F.; Sr. JOYCE ROSS, R.S.M.

Archdiocesan Offices and Directors

Apostleship of the Sea—Port Chaplains: Anchorage: SALLY BOSTWICK, Cordova: Sr. PEGGY GLYNN, O.P., Kodiak: Rev. FRED BUGARIN, Seward: Rev. RICHARD STRASS, C.SS.R.

A.R.E.A./RENEW Coordinator—KATHY BISHOP, *c/o Chancery Office.*

Campaign for Human Development—Rev. ERNEST H. MUELLERLEILE, Dir., *8147 Medellin Cir., Anchorage, 99507.* Tel: 907-349-3910.

Catholic Social Services—SUZANNE GOODRICH, Exec. Dir., *225 Cordova St., Anchorage, 99501.* Tel: 907-277-2554; Fax: 907-279-3885.

Board Members—DAVID GOTTSTEIN; JAMES PALMER; Rabbi HARRY ROSENFELD; Mr. CHRIS SWALLING; Mr. DONALD STONEBURNER; Mr. JOE MORAN; FRAN MARGARGER; SUSAN ELLIOTT; BEN BARRERA; REGINA DEFRANCISCO; LISA MURKOWSKI.

Communications—Bro. CHARLES MCBRIDE, C.S.C., *c/o Chancery Office.*

Hispanic Ministry—c/o Our Lady of Guadalupe Parish, 3900 Wisconsin St., Anchorage, 99517.

Korean Ministry—Sr. MARIE BEDA KIM, S.P.C.; Sr. SHIN IN-JA (LUCIA), S.P.C.; Sr. MYEONG SEON (CLAIRE) SEONG, S.P.C., *St. Anthony's Parish, 825 S. Klevin St., Anchorage, 99508.* Tel: 907-337-5307.

Lay Leadership Formation—Sr. ELLEN CALLAGHAN, O.S.F., Coord., *c/o Chancery Office.*

Native Ministry—THERESA "TINY" DEVLIN, *c/o Chancery Office.*

Office of Finance—c/o Chancery Office.

Pastoral Associates—Rev. LEROY CLEMENTICH, C.S.C., Coord., *c/o Chancery Office.*

Permanent Diaconate—Rev. TIMOTHY M. CROWLEY, *c/o Chancery Office.*

Propagation of the Faith—JAMES CALDAROLA, *c/o Chancery Office.*

Retreats—Rev. VINCENT BEUZER, S.J., Dir., *Holy Spirit Retreat House, 10980 Hillside Dr., Anchorage, 99516.* Tel: 907-346-2343.

Superintendent of Schools—Sr. DIANE BARDOL, G.N.S.H., *St. Mary's School, 2932 Mill Bay Rd., Kodiak, 99615.* Tel: 907-486-3513.

Vocations—c/o Chancery Office.

Youth—Vacant, *c/o Chancery Office.*

CLERGY, PARISHES, MISSIONS AND PAROCHIAL SCHOOLS

CITY OF ANCHORAGE

1—HOLY FAMILY CATHEDRAL, Revs. LaSalle Hallissey, O.P.; John Adams, O.P.; Deacon Felix Maguire, Pastoral Assoc. In res., Rev. Urban M. Bates, O.P.

Mailing Address: 800 W. 5th Ave., 99501-2093. Tel: 907-276-3455; Fax: 907-258-9785. [JC]

Catechesis/Religious Programs—Mrs. Jo Brosamer, D.R.E. Students 257.

2—ST. ANTHONY, Rev. Msgr. Francis A. Cowgill; Rev. Leo A. Walsh, Jr.; Deacon Theodore W. Greene, Pastoral Assoc.

Res., 825 S. Klevin St., 99508-2698. Tel: 907-333-5544; Fax: 907-338-3864.

Catechesis/Religious Programs—Students 260.

3—ST. BENEDICT, Rev. Alfred W. Giebel; Deacon Ray W. Allor.

Res., 8110 Jewel Lake Rd., 99502. Tel: 907-243-2195; Fax: 907-243-0088.

Catechesis/Religious Programs—Students 395.

4—ST. ELIZABETH ANN SETON, Revs. Daniel J. Hebert; Scott Medlock; Sr. Loretta Luecke, C.PP.S., Pastoral Assoc.; Deacon Kenneth Donohue.

Res., 2901 E. Huffman Rd., 99516. Tel: 907-345-4466; Fax: 907-345-6361.
Catechesis/Religious Programs—Connie Ripley, D.R.E.
Students 804.

5—HOLY CROSS, Rev. Ernest H. Muellerleile; Sr. Joan Oberle, C.PP.S., Pastoral Assoc.; Deacon William Finnegan.
Res., 8147 Medellin Cir., 99507. Tel: 907-349-3910; Fax: 907-349-3910.
Catechesis/Religious Programs—Mrs. Peggy Snyder, D.R.E.
Students 170.

6—OUR LADY OF GUADALUPE, Rev. Msgr. John A. Lunney, Pastor Emeritus; Revs. Michael Warfel; Art Lopilato, S.J.; Sr. Kathleen O'Hara, R.S.M., Pastoral Assoc. In res., Rev. Timothy Crowley (LAN).
Res., 3900 Wisconsin St., 99517. Tel: 907-248-2000; Fax: 907-245-1600.
Guadalupe Centre—Tel: 907-243-2657.
Catechesis/Religious Programs—Mrs. Carol Akers, D.R.E.
Students 101.

7—ST. PAUL MIKI. Closed. For inquiries for parish records contact St. Elizabeth Ann Seton Parish, Anchorage.

8—ST. PATRICK, Very Rev. Steven C. Moore, V.G.
Res., 2111 Muldoon Rd., 99504-3699. Tel: 907-337-1538; Fax: 907-337-5460.
Catechesis/Religious Programs—Martha Rogers, D.R.E.
Students 135.

OUTSIDE THE CITY OF ANCHORAGE

Cordova, St. Joseph, Sr. Peggy Glynn, O.P., Pastoral Admin.
Res., 220 Adams Ave., P.O. Box 79, 99574. Tel: 907-424-3637; Fax: 907-424-3637.

Dillingham, Holy Rosary, Rev. James F. Kelley.
Res., P.O. Box 810, 99576. Tel: 907-842-5581.
Missions—Naknek, St. Theresa, P.O.Box 73, Naknek, 99633. Tel: 907-246-6652; Unalaska, St. Christopher, P.O. Box 405, Unalaska, 99685. Tel: 907-581-4022; Fax: 907-581-4022. Sr. Peggy Griffin, O.P., Pastoral Admin.
Stations—Chignik Lagoon; Chignik Lake; Clarks Point; Cold Bay; Ekwok; Igiugig; Iliamna; King Salmon; Levelock; Manokotak; Naknek; New Stuyohok; Sand Point; South Naknek; Togiak; Alexander; Ekuk; Port Moller; New Koliganek; Ivanof Bay.

Eagle River, St. Andrew, Rev. Leo C. Desso; Sr. Camilla Menting, S.S.S.F., Pastoral Assoc. & D.R.E.; Deacon James Hostman.
Res., 16601 Artillery Rd., 99577. Tel: 907-694-2170; Fax: 907-694-1385.
Catechesis/Religious Programs—Students 551.

Glennallen, Holy Family, Mrs. Tami Jindra, Pastoral Admin.
Res., P.O. Box 126, 99588. Tel: 907-822-3442; Fax: 907-822-3442.
Station—Kenny Lake.

Homer, St. John the Baptist. Unassigned.
Res., 238 Jenny Ln., 99603. Tel: 907-235-8436; Fax: 907-235-8436.
Missions—Seldovia, St. James the Apostle, Tel: 907-234-7478; Ninilchik, St. Peter, Box 290, Ninilchik, 99639. Tel: 907-567-3490.
Catechesis/Religious Programs—Mrs. Gloria Stuart, D.R.E.
Students 90.

Kenai, Our Lady of the Angels, Sr. Joyce Ross, R.S.M., Admin.; Sr. Joan Barina, M.M.S., Pastoral Assoc.
Res., 225 S. Spruce Rd., 99611. Tel: 907-283-4555; Fax: 907-283-4555.
Catechesis/Religious Programs—Kathleen Moore, D.R.E.
Students 98.

Kodiak, St. Mary's of Kodiak and the Islands, Rev. Fred Bugarin; Mrs. Delores Ossowski, Pastoral Assoc.
Res., 2934 Mill Bay Rd., 99615. Tel: 907-486-5411.
School—Tel: 907-486-3513. Sr. Diane Bardol, G.N.S.H., Prin. & D.R.E.
Sisters 3; Lay Teachers 15; Students 205.
Catechesis/Religious Programs—Students 91.

Palmer, St. Michael, Rev. David Cowden.
Res., 432 E. Fireweed Ave., 99645. Tel: 907-745-3229; Fax: 907-746-7040.
Catechesis/Religious Programs—Mrs. Joanne Rousculp, D.R.E.
Students 220.

Seward, Sacred Heart, Rev. Richard Strass, C.Ss.R.
Res., 409 Fifth Ave., P.O. Box 207, 99664. Tel: 907-224-5414; Fax: 907-224-5093.
Catechesis/Religious Programs—Mrs. Diane Elhard, D.R.E.
Students 80.
Mission—Cooper Landing, St. John Neumann Church, P.O. Box 737, Cooper Landing, 99572. Tel: 907-595-1300.

Soldotna, Our Lady of Perpetual Help, Rev. Richard D. Tero.
Res., 222 Redoubt Ave., 99669. Tel: 907-262-4749; Fax: 907-262-4749.
Catechesis/Religious Programs—Marlys Verba, D.R.E.
Students 250.

Talkeetna, St. Bernard. Unassigned.
Res., P.O. Box 510, 99676. Tel: 907-733-2442.
Missions—Trapper Creek, St. Philip Benizi, Trapper Creek, 99683; Willow, St. Christopher, Willow, 99688.

Valdez, St. Francis Xavier, Sr. Marie Ann Brent, S.H.F., Pastoral Admin.
Res., 341 Pioneer Dr., P.O. Box 908, 99686. Tel: 907-835-4556; Fax: 907-835-4556.
Catechesis/Religious Programs—Sandy Crump, D.R.E.
Students 78.

Wasilla, Sacred Heart, Rev. Stanley J. Allie (ALB); Kathleen Agoff, Pastoral Assoc. & D.R.E.
Res., 1201 Bogard Rd., 99654-6523. Tel: 907-376-5087; Fax: 907-373-1156.
Catechesis/Religious Programs—Students 180.
Mission—Big Lake, Our Lady of the Lake, P.O. Box 520769, Big Lake, 99652-0769. Tel: 907-892-6492; Fax: 907-892-6497. Deacon Louis Hoffman, Admin.

On Duty Outside Archdiocese:
Reverend Fathers—
Abele, Alan Carl
Means, David (STL), Magadan, Russia
Shields, Michael, Magadan, Russia

Retired:
Reverend Monsignors—
Murphy, Francis A., P.O. Box 1625, Cuba, NM 87013
Reverend Fathers—
Daley, Neil, 100 4th Ave., Shalimar, FL 32579
Houck, Peter, 4611 Kupreanof St., Anchorage, AK 99507
Lunney, John A., 3900 Wisconsin St., Anchorage, AK 99517
Marx, John, 2200 First Ave. N., Apt. 208, Seattle, WA 98109
Power, Thomas E., 415 Maplewood Cir., Greer, SC 29651

Permanent Deacons:
Albert, Merle, Milan, NH
Allor, Raymond W., Anchorage
Donohue, Kenneth, St. Elizabeth Ann Seton, Anchorage
Foreman, Dennis, Anchorage
Gnerich, Otto, Anchorage
Greene, Theodore, St. Anthony Church, Anchorage
Hoffman, Louis, Our Lady of the Lake, Big Lake
Hostman, James, St. Andrew, Eagle River
Larroque, Robert, Port Angeles, WA
Maguire, Felix M., Cathedral, Anchorage
Rivera, Manuel, Laguna Hills, CA

INSTITUTIONS LOCATED IN THE ARCHDIOCESE

[A] GRADE SCHOOLS, PAROCHIAL

ANCHORAGE. *St. Elizabeth Ann Seton School*, 2901 E. Huffman Rd., 99516. Tel: 907-345-3712. Mr. John Fleming, Prin. Lay Teachers 9; Students 174.

KODIAK. *St. Mary's*, 2932 Mill Bay Rd., 99615. Tel: 907-486-3513. Sr. Diane Bardol, G.N.S.H., Prin. Sisters 3; Lay Teachers 15; Students 205.

[B] PRIVATE SCHOOLS

ANCHORAGE. *Holy Rosary Academy*, 1010 W. Fireweed Ln., 99503. Tel: 907-276-5822; Fax: 907-258-1055. Mr. Jim Hickel, Headmaster.
Lumen Christi Jr./Sr. High School, 750 E. Fireweed Ln., 99503. Tel: 907-272-7692; Fax: 907-272-7641. Mrs. Pat Wagner, Acting Prin.

[C] GENERAL HOSPITALS

ANCHORAGE. *Providence Alaska Foundation*, 3200 Providence Dr., P.O. Box 196604, 99519. Tel: 907-261-3600; Fax: 907-261-3048.
For a complete listing, refer to the Hospitals section.
Providence Alaska Medical Center, 3200 Providence Dr., P.O. Box 196604, 99519. Tel: 907-562-2211; Fax: 907-261-3041.
For a complete listing, refer to the Hospitals section.

[D] NURSING HOME

ANCHORAGE. *Providence Extended Care Center*, 4900 Eagle St., 99503. Tel: 907-562-2281.
For a complete listing, refer to the Special Care Facilities section.

[E] HOMES FOR AGED

*ANCHORAGE. *Mary Conrad Center*, 9100 Centennial Dr., 99504. Tel: 907-333-8100; Fax: 907-338-6789.
For a complete listing, refer to the Special Care Facilities section.

[F] CATHOLIC SOCIAL SERVICES

ANCHORAGE. *Brother Francis Shelter*, 1021 E. Third Ave., 99501. Tel: 907-277-1731. Hillary Morgan, Dir. Overnight Shelter for homeless men and women.
Brother Francis Shelter, 411 Cedar St., P.O. Box 3421, Kodiak, 99615. Tel: 907-486-5610. Monte Hawver, Dir.
Catholic Social Services Center, Administrative Office, 225 Cordova St., Bldg. B, 99501. Tel: 907-277-2554. Ms. Suzanne Goodrich, Exec. Dir., Catholic Social Services Center, 3710 E. 20th Ave., 99508. Tel: 907-258-2673. Sr. Kathy Radich, O.S.F., Dir., Bishop Whelan Family Support & Counseling; Mr. Edward Cordova, Dir., Immigration & Refugee Svcs.; Sr. Karen Yesh, S.M.A.H., Dir., Pregnancy Support Svcs.; Elaine Stoneburner, Dir., Adoption Svcs.; Karleen Jackson, Dir., Beyond Shelter Prog., St. Francis House; Lynn Caswell, Dir., Special Needs Respite Prog.
Clare House, 420 W. 54th Ave., 99518. Tel: 907-563-4545. Cheryl Sheldon, Dir. Temporary shelter for homeless women and women with children.
McAuley Manor, 3015 Yale Dr., 99508. Ms. Cheryl Sheldon, Dir. Residence for homeless teenage girls.

[G] MONASTERIES AND RESIDENCES OF PRIESTS AND BROTHERS

ANCHORAGE. *Fathers and Brothers of Holy Cross*, Guadalupe Arms, 3007 W. 34th Ave., No. 3, 99517. Tel: 907-248-6809 (Fathers); 248-5176 (Brothers). Rev. LeRoy Clementich, C.S.C.; Bro. Charles P. McBride, C.S.C.
Holy Spirit Retreat House, 10980 Hillside Dr., 99516. Tel: 907-346-2343; Fax: 907-346-2140. Revs. Vincent J. Beuzer, S.J.; J. Michael Hornick; William T. Burke, S.J.
Jesuit House, 1500 Birchwood, 99508. Tel: 907-279-4389. Revs. Rene Astruc, S.J.; Art Lopilato, S.J.; Paul B. Macke, S.J. Alaska Region of OR Prov.
Jesuit Residence, 237 E. 3rd Ave. #1, 99501. Tel: 907-277-5933. Rev. Thomas Gallagher, S.J.

[H] CONVENTS AND RESIDENCES FOR SISTERS

ANCHORAGE. *Convent of Mercy*, 2627 Redwood St., 99508. Tel: 907-258-7802. Sisters 2.
Daughters of St. Paul, 750 W. 5th Ave., 99501. Tel: 907-272-8183; Fax: 907-272-3753. Sisters 2.
Guadalupe Arms, 3007 W. 34th Ave., 99517. Tel: 907-248-9881. Priests 1; Brothers 1; Sisters 1.
Little Sisters of Jesus, 1280 E. 17th #318, 99501. Tel: 907-272-0799. 3713 Alexander Ave., 99508. Tel: 907-258-6655. Sisters 3. Sisters 1.
Marian House Apartments, 3005 W. 34th Ave., 99517. Priests 1; Sisters 2.
Mary's House, 3424 E. 15th Ave., 99508. Tel: 907-276-4921. Dominican Sisters of Sinsinawa 2.
Providence Alaska Medical Center, 3200 Providence Dr., P.O. Box 196604, 99519. Tel: 907-562-2211. Sisters of Providence in Washington 2.
Sisters of Perpetual Adoration, 2645 E. 72nd Ave., 99507. Tel: 907-344-3330. Mother Maria de las Victorias Amezcua, A.P., Supr. Sisters 7.
Sisters of St. Francis, 324 N. Klevin St., 99508. Tel: 907-279-6226. Sisters 3.
Sisters of St. Joseph of Peace, 1441 E. 17th Ave., #16, 99501. 355 Donna Dr. #19, 99504.
Sisters of St. Paul de Chartres, 825 S. Klevin St., 99508. Tel: 907-258-3273. Sisters 3.

EAGLE RIVER. *School Sisters of St. Francis*, 16601 Artillery Rd., 99577. Tel: 907-694-8087.

KENAI. *Kenai Convent*, 1122 Walnut St., 99611. Tel: 907-283-6466. Sisters 2.

KODIAK. *St. Mary's Convent*, 2932 Mill Bay Rd., 99615. Tel: 907-486-5214. Sisters 4.

[I] RETREAT HOUSES

ANCHORAGE. *Holy Spirit Retreat House*, 10980 Hillside Dr., 99516. Tel: 907-346-2343; Fax: 907-346-2140. Rev. Vincent J. Beuzer, S.J., Dir.

[J] CAMPS

ANCHORAGE. *St. Theresa's Camp*. Sept-May: 225 Cordova St., 99501. Tel: 907-258-7898. June-Sept: Box 3144, 99669. Tel: 907-262-4215. Archdiocesan summer camp for boys and girls.

[K] MISCELLANEOUS

ANCHORAGE. *Covenant House Alaska*, 609 F St., 99501.

Tel: 907-272-1255. Ms. Deirdre Phayer, Exec. Dir. Crisis center for homeless and runaway youth.

Pauline Books & Media, 750 W. 5th Ave., 99501. Tel: 907-272-8183. Operated by the Daughters of St. Paul.

St. Vincent de Paul Society, Holy Family Cathedral, 800 W. 6th Ave., 99501. Tel: 907-276-3455.

RELIGIOUS INSTITUTES OF MEN REPRESENTED IN THE ARCHDIOCESE

For further details refer to the corresponding bracketed number in the Religious Institutes of Men or Women section.

[0600]—*Brothers of the Congregation of Holy Cross.*—C.S.C.

[0690]—*Jesuit Fathers and Brothers.* (Oregon Prov.).—S.J.

[0780]—*Marist Fathers.* (Boston Prov.).—S.M.

[0430]—*Order of Preachers-Dominicans.* (Oakland Prov.).—O.P.

[1070]—*Redemptorist Fathers.* (Oakland Prov.).—C.Ss.R.

RELIGIOUS INSTITUTES OF WOMEN REPRESENTED IN THE ARCHDIOCESE

[1070-03]—*Dominican Sisters.*—O.P.

[1840]—*Grey Nuns of the Sacred Heart.*—G.N.S.H.

[2575]—*Institute of the Sisters of Mercy of the Americas.* (Albany, NY; Merion, PA; Providence, RI).—R.S.M.

[2330]—*Little Sisters of Jesus.*—L.S.J.

[2490]—*Medical Mission Sisters.*—M.M.S.

[2690]—*Missionary Catechists of Divine Providence.*—M.C.D.P.

[3190]—*Nuns of Perpetual Adoration of the Blessed Sacrament.* (Mexico).—A.P.

[0950]—*Pious Society Daughters of St. Paul.* (Boston).—F.S.P.

[1680]—*School Sisters of St. Francis.*—O.S.F.

[3350]—*Sisters of Providence.*—S.P.

[1650]—*Sisters of St. Francis of Philadelphia.*—O.S.F.

[1570]—*Sisters of St. Francis of the Holy Family, Dubuque, IA.*—O.S.F.

[3890]—*Sisters of St. Joseph of Peace.* (Bellevue).—C.S.J.P.

[3980]—*Sisters of St. Paul de Chartres, South Korea.*—S.P.C.

[1960]—*Sisters of the Holy Family.*—S.H.F.

[1990]—*Sisters of the Holy Names of Jesus and Mary.*—S.N.J.M.

[3270]—*Sisters of the Most Precious Blood.* (O'Fallon, MO).—C.PP.S.

[4110]—*Ursuline Nuns.*—O.S.U.

NECROLOGY

(No Deaths)

Diocese of Arlington

(Dioecesis Arlingtonensis)

Most Reverend

JOHN R. KEATING

Bishop of Arlington; ordained December 20, 1958; appointed Bishop of Arlington June 7, 1983; consecrated and installed as Second Bishop of Arlington August 4, 1983. *Res., 4600 N. Carlin Springs Rd., Arlington, VA, 22203.*

ESTABLISHED AUGUST 13, 1974.

Square Miles 6,541.

Comprises the following 21 Counties in Northern Virginia: Arlington, Clarke, Culpeper, Fairfax, Fauquier, Frederick, King George, Lancaster, Loudoun, Madison, Northumberland, Orange, Page, Prince William, Rappahannock, Richmond, Shenandoah, Spotsylvania, Stafford, Warren and Westmoreland and the 7 independent cities of Alexandria, Fairfax City, Falls Church, Fredericksburg, Manassas, Manassas Park and Winchester.

For legal titles of parishes and diocesan institutions, consult the Chancery Office.

The Chancery: Ste. 704, 200 N. Glebe Rd., Arlington, VA, 22203. Tel.: 703-841-2500; Fax: 703-524-5028.

STATISTICAL OVERVIEW

Personnel	
Bishop	1
Priests: Diocesan Active in Diocese	116
Priests: Active Outside Diocese	8
Priests: Diocesan in Foreign Missions	2
Priests: Retired, Sick or Absent	17
Number of Diocesan Priests	143
Religious Priests in Diocese	74
Extern Priests in Diocese	15
Ordinations:	
Diocesan Priests	13
Transitional Deacons	1
Permanent Deacons in Diocese	55
Total Brothers	17
Total Sisters	218
Parishes	
Parishes	62
With Resident Pastor:	
Resident Diocesan Priests	51
Resident Religious Priests	11
Without Resident Pastor:	
Missions	6
New Parishes Created	2
Welfare	
Special Centers for Social Services	7
Total Assisted	30,981
Educational	
Diocesan Students in Other Seminaries	35
Seminaries, Religious	1
Total Seminarians	35
Colleges and Universities	2
Total Students	3,035
High Schools, Diocesan and Parish	3
Total Students	3,293
High Schools, Private	1
Total Students	156
Elementary Schools, Diocesan and Parish	31
Total Students	11,788
Elementary Schools, Private	2
Total Students	528
Non-residential Schools for the Disabled	1
Total Students	55
Catechesis/Religious Education:	
High School Students	9,230
Elementary Students	16,900
Total Students Under Catholic Instruction	44,965
Teachers in the Diocese:	
Priests	7
Scholastics	3
Brothers	1
Sisters	69
Lay Teachers	837
Vital Statistics	
Receptions into the Church:	
Infant Baptism Totals	5,194
Adult Baptism Totals	1,967
First Communions	5,839
Confirmations	4,566
Marriages:	
Catholic	1,026
Interfaith	848
Total Marriages	1,874
Deaths	1,253
Total Catholic Population	311,351
Total Population	2,115,700

Former Bishop—Most Rev. THOMAS J. WELSH, D.D., J.C.D., appt. Titular Bishop of Scattery Island and Auxiliary Bishop of Philadelphia on Feb. 18, 1970; cons. April 2, 1970; appt. as 1st Bishop of Arlington on June 4, 1974; installed on Aug. 13, 1974; transferred to the See of Allentown, Feb. 8, 1983.

The Chancery

The Chancery—Ste. 704, 200 N. Glebe Rd., Arlington, 22203. Tel: 703-841-2500; Fax: 703-524-5028. Office Hours: Mon.-Fri. 8:30-4:30. Address all official business to this office.

Vicar General—Rev. Msgr. R. ROY COSBY, V.G., *905 Park Ave., Falls Church, 22046.* Tel: 703-532-8815.

Chancellor and Moderator of the Curia—Rev. ROBERT J. RIPPY, J.C.L., *The Chancery, 200 N. Glebe Rd., Ste. 704, Arlington, 22203.* Tel: 703-841-2508.

Diocesan Fiscal Manager—SUSAN D. HANDLON, Fiscal Mgr., *200 N. Glebe Rd., Ste. 704.* Tel: 703-841-2577.

Director of Diocesan Charities—Rev. JOHN T. O'HARA, M.S.W., *Ste. 704.* Tel: 703-841-2500.

Deans—Rev. Msgr. JOHN P. HANNAN, V.F.; Rev. Msgr. R. ROY COSBY, V.F.; Rev. Msgr. JOHN T. CILINSKI, V.F.; Revs. WILLIAM F. RUEHL, V.F.; JOHN J. HUGHES, V.F.

Vicar for The Permanent Diaconate—Rev. ROBERT J. RIPPY, J.C.L., The Chancery. Tel: 703-841-2508; 684-9261 (Res.).

Vicar for Women Religious—Rev. GERVASE CAIN, T.O.R., *Our Lady of the Valley, 200 Collins Ave., P.O. Box 462, Luray, 22835.* Tel: 540-743-4919.

The Tribunal

The Tribunal—Ste. 620, 200 N. Glebe Rd., Arlington, 22203. Tel: 703-841-2555.

Judicial Vicar—Rev. MARK S. MEALEY, O.S.F.S., J.C.D., Ph.D.

Diocesan Judges—Revs. ROBERT C. BROOKS; J. STEWART CULKIN, M.A.; JOHN C. CREGAN; HORACE H. GRINNELL; HILARY HAYDEN, O.S.B., S.T.L.; PATRICK HOLROYD; EUGENIO J. HOYOS, C.S.V.; MARK S. MEALY, O.S.F.S., J.C.D., Ph.D.; WILLIAM J. RUHL, O.S.F.S., S.T.D.; WILLIAM B. SCHARDT, J.C.L.; JAMES A. VERRECCHIA; LEO J. ZONNEVELD, C.I.C.M., Ph.D., V.F.

Defenders of the Bond—Revs. ROBERT E. AVELLA, M.A.; ROBERT C. CILINSKI; Rev. Msgr. R. ROY COSBY, M.A., V.G.; Rev. PAUL F. DELADURANTAYE, S.T.L.; Sr. PATRICK MARIE DOHERTY, I.H.M.; Revs. DANIEL E. HAMILTON; THOMAS J. LEHNING, S.T.L., Ph.D.; DAVID MARTIN, C.S.S., M.A.; FRANCISCO D. MENDEZ; DANIEL L. MODE; LEE R. ROOS; DAVID H. WHITESTONE, J.C.L.; PETER W. NASSETTA; Deacon CHARLES A. COUTU.

Advocates—Revs. DONALD C. GREENHALGH; JOHN H. MELMER; JOHN D. Kelly; STEPHEN F. LEVA; CHARLES W. MERKLE; JAMES R. GOULD.

Notaries—Revs. JAMES S. BARKETT; PAUL A. BERGHOUT; VINCENT P. BORK; CHRISTIAN T. CONNELLY; JOHN C. DE CELLES; ROBERT J. DEMARTINO; DENIS M. DONAHUE; ALEXANDER R. DRUMMOND; RONALD S. ESCALANTE; WILHELM J. ETTNER; PAUL M. EVERSOLE; KEVIN P. GALLAGHER; DANIEL N. GEE; RONALD J. GRIPSHOVER, JR.; RICHARD M. GUEST; EDWARD C. HATHAWAY; MICHAEL C. KELLY; DENNIS J. KLEINMANN; KEVIN J. LARSEN; CHRISTOPHER J. MOULD; RICHARD A. MULLINS; CHRISTOPHER S. MURPHY; J. KEVIN O'KEEFE; CARROLL L. OUBRE; FRANCIS P. PEFFLEY; JOHN P. PETERSON; JERRY J. POKORSKY; MARCUS A. POLLARD; DAVID C. RAHN; SEAN K. ROUSSEAU; PAUL D. SCALIA; TERRY W. SPECHT; TERRENCE R. STAPLES; MICHAEL G. TAYLOR; EDWIN T. TEWES; THOMAS C. VANDER WOUDE; LAWRENCE M. VIOLETTE; JERRY A. WOOTEN; JOHN ZIEGLER; MATTHEW H. ZUBERBUELER.

Diocesan Offices

Diocesan Offices—Unless otherwise noted, all offices are located at, 200 N. Glebe Rd., Arlington, 22203.

Accounting Office—CLARE FARISS, Mgr., *Ste. 602.* Tel: 703-841-2582.

Archives—Sr. MARY ARTHUR, I.H.M., *80 N. Glebe Rd.* Tel: 703-524-2122.

Arlington Catholic Herald, Inc.—MICHAEL F. FLACH, Editor & Gen. Mgr., *Ste. 607, Arlington.* Tel: 703-841-2590.

Audio-Visual—MAGGIE O'CONNOR, Coord., *Ste. 608.* Tel: 703-841-2530.

Campaign for Human Development—Rev. JOHN T. O'HARA, M.S.W., Diocesan Dir., *3838 Cathedral Ln., Arlington, 22203.* Tel: 703-841-2531.

Campus Ministry—Rev. JAMES R. GOULD, Bishop's Liaison, *Ste. 619.* Tel: 703-841-2514.

Catholic Charities of the Diocese of Arlington—Rev. JOHN T. O'HARA, M.S.W., Exec. Dir. MICHAEL J. O'ROURKE, Assoc. Dir. Admin. ELIANA V. TURINA, Asst. to the Exec. Dir., *3838 N. Cathedral Ln., Arlington, 22203.* Tel: 703-841-2544.

Catholic Charities Fredericksburg Office—612 Lafayette Blvd., Ste. 50, Fredericksburg, 22401.

Catholic Charities Winchester Office—1011 Berryville Ave., Ste. 1, Winchester, 22601.

Children's Services—PATRICIA MUDD, Prog. Dir., *5294 Lyngate Ct., Burke, 22015.* Tel: 703-425-0100.

Christ House—ROSE MARIE LAROCCA, Prog. Dir., *131 S. West St., Alexandria, 22314.* Tel: 703-549-8644.

Communications—TANIA HINDERT, Prog. Dir., *3838 Cathedral Ln., Arlington, 22203.* Tel: 703-841-2531.

Elderly Services—CAROL AUGUSTINE, Prog. Dir., *St.*

Martin de Porres Senior Center, 4650 Taney Ave., Alexandria, 22304. Tel: 703-751-2766.
Emergency Assistance—131 S. West St., Alexandria, 22314. Tel: 703-548-4227.
Family Services—DAVID CAVANAUGH, M.S.W., Prog. Dir., *3838 N. Cathedral Ln., Arlington, 22203.* Tel: 703-841-2531.
Fredericksburg Office—DIANN KELLISON, M.S.W., Prog. Dir., *612 Lafayette Blvd., Ste. 50, Fredericksburg, 22401.* Tel: 540-371-1124.
Parish Outreach—BERNADETTE TRAVERS, *3838 N. Cathedral Ln., Arlington, 22203.* Tel: 703-841-2531.
Prison Ministry—RAYMOND O'BRIEN, *3838 N. Cathedral Ln., Arlington, 22203.* Tel: 703-841-2531.
Services with Disabled Persons—HARRY BURKE, Prog. Dir., *3838 N. Cathedral Ln., Arlington, 22203.* Tel: 703-841-2531.
Winchester Office—LORETTA DUNN, Prog. Dir., *1011 Berryville Ave., Ste. 1, Winchester, 22601.* Tel: 540-667-7940.
Catholic Education, Office of Catechetics—Rev. PAUL F. DELADURANTAYE, Sec. for Religious Education, *Ste. 703.* Tel: 703-841-2554. MAGGIE O'CONNOR, Coord., Audio-Visual Materials. Tel: 703-841-2530. ELAINE BICKEL, Master Catechist Training Prog. Tel: 703-430-1755. Mrs. M. PROVIE RYDSTROM, Coord.-Pastoral Ministry for the Hearing Impaired. Tel: 703-978-7997 (V-TTD). NADINE HALLUMS, Dir., Special Religious Education (SPRED). Tel: 703-569-2428.
Office of Catholic Schools—Dr. TIMOTHY J. MCNIFF, Supt. of Schools. Tel: 703-841-2519. Sr. PATRICIA HELENE EARL, I.H.M., Asst. Supt. for Secondary Education & Proffessional Educational Personnel. Tel: 703-841-2519. Sr. KARL ANN HOMBERG, S.S.J., Asst. Supt. for Elementary Education. Tel: 703-841-2519.
Catholic Mutual Relief Society of America—RICHARD DUFFEY, *Ste. 613.* Tel: 703-841-2503.
Catholic Relief Services—Rev. JOHN T. O'HARA, M.S.W., Dir., *3838 N. Cathedral Ln., Arlington, 22203.* Tel: 703-841-2531.
Central Purchasing—JOAN CANAN, Purchasing Agent, *Ste. 618.* Tel: 703-841-2571.
Communications Office—CONCHITA VALLECILLO, Coord., *Ste. 617.* Tel: 703-841-2517.
Computer Operations Systems—WILFREDO MALDONADO, Coord., *Ste. 606.* Tel: 703-841-2585.
Construction Management, Office of—Ste. 625. Tel: 703-841-2572. PETER B. FISHER, Supvr. Construction; PAUL E. MAY, Supvr. Construction.
Development Office—TODD SMITH, Mgr., *Ste. 617.* Tel: 703-841-2570.
Ecumenical Affairs—Rev. Msgr. R. ROY COSBY, Coord., *St. James, Falls Church.* Tel: 703-532-8815; 8816.
Employee Benefits—LINDA HENNESSEY, Mgr., *Ste. 611.* Tel: 703-841-2588.
Family Life Office—Deacon ROGER T. OSTROM, Dir., *Ste. 700.* Tel: 703-841-2550.
Liturgy, Office of Sacred—Rev. DOMINIC P. IRACE, Dir. Tel: 703-841-2587. RICHARD GIBALA, Chm., Diocesan Music Committee. Tel: 703-476-1697.
Permanent Diaconate—Rev. ROBERT J. RIPPY, J.C.L., *Ste. 704.* Tel: 703-841-2508.
Propagation of the Faith—Rev. DONALD C. GREENHALGH, Dir., *St. Mary of Sorrows, 5222 Sideburn Rd., Fairfax, 22032.* Tel: 703-978-4141.
Spanish Apostolate—Rev. OVIDIO PECHARROMAN, Dir., *80 N. Glebe Rd., Arlington, 22203.* Tel: 703-524-2122.
Hogar Hispano of the Diocese of Arlington, Inc.—CLAIRE CHERKASKY-HACKETT, Dir., *2300 S. 9th St., Ste. 305, Arlington, 22204.* Tel: 703-979-1705.
Office of Resettlement—DAVID HERRMANN, Refugee Program Coord., *80 N. Glebe Rd., Arlington, 22203.* Tel: 703-524-2130.
Vocations, Office of—Revs. JAMES R. GOULD, Dir. OVIDIO PECHARROMAN, Coord. Spanish Speaking Vocations, *Ste. 619.* Tel: 703-841-2514.
Youth Activities, Office of—Rev. CHARLES C. MCCOART, Dir., *Ste. 623.* Tel: 703-841-2559.
Scouting & Camp Fire, Diocesan Committee on—GENE WICHMANN, Chm., *7313 Mizzen Pl., Burke, 22015.* Tel: 703-455-3539.

Consultative Bodies

Clergy Personnel Board—Rev. FRANKLIN M. MCAFEE, Chm., *St. Lawrence, Alexandria.* Tel: 703-971-4378.
Diaconal Council—Deacon NICHOLAS J. LADUCA, Chm. Tel: 703-350-4460.
Diocesan Consultors—Rev. Msgr. JOHN P. HANNAN; Rev. Msgr. JAMES W. MCMURTRIE; Rev. Msgr. JOHN T. CILINSKI; Rev. Msgr. R. ROY COSBY; Revs. FRANK J. READY; ROBERT J. RIPPY; LEO J. ZONNEVELD, C.I.C.M.
Diocesan Finance Committee—Most Rev. JOHN R. KEATING, Chm.; Rev. LEO J. ZONNEVELD, C.I.C.M., Vice Chm. Tel: 540-825-8945. Rev. DANIEL J. MAHER, Sec. Tel: 202-526-8300.
Diocesan School Board—MOLLIE ROY, Chm. Tel: 703-250-9121.
Priests' Council—Most Rev. JOHN R. KEATING, Pres. Tel: 703-841-2500. Rev. ROBERT E. AVELLA, Vice Pres. Tel: 703-273-5369.
Religious Education Committee—ROSE WAKEHAM, *St. Luke, McLean.* Tel: 703-356-8419.
Sisters' Council—Sr. DOROTHY MENNIS, R.C., Pres., *The Cenacle House, Great Falls.* Tel: 703-759-6901. Sr. CARLA PRZYBILLA, O.S.F., Vice Pres., *New Life Center, Middleburg.* Tel: 540-687-3809; 800-982-6216.

CLERGY, PARISHES, MISSIONS AND PAROCHIAL SCHOOLS

COUNTY OF ARLINGTON

1—CATHEDRAL OF ST. THOMAS MORE (1938), Revs. Dominic P. Irace, Rector; Christian T. Connelly; Deacons Samuel M. Taub, Jr.; Claudio F. Benedi. In res., Rev. Paul F. deLadurantaye.
Res., 3901 Cathedral Ln., 22203. Tel: 703-525-1300; 525-0450; Fax: 703-528-5760.
School—105 N. Thomas St., 22203. Tel: 703-528-6781. Sr. Carmel Regina Shields, I.H.M., Prin. Sisters Servants of the Immaculate Heart of Mary 1; Lay Teachers 21; Students 424.
Catechesis/Religious Programs—Tel: 703-528-7104. Sr. Maria Angelica I.H.M., D.R.E. Students 281.

2—ST. AGNES (1936), Revs. James R. Gould; Wilhelm J. Ettner. In res., Rev. Msgr. Thomas P. Scannell; Revs. Curtis L. Clark; Paul G. Onyango.
Res., 1914 N. Randolph St., 22207. Tel: 703-525-1166; Fax: 703-243-2840.
School—2024 N. Randolph St., 22207. Tel: 703-527-5423; Fax: 703-527-6325. Ms. Sheila Tomlinson, Prin.
Sisters 2; Lay Teachers 18; Students 321.
Catechesis/Religious Programs—Tel: 703-522-7045. Sr. Mary Margaret Ann Schlather, S.N.D., D.R.E.
Students 345.

3—ST. ANN (1947), Revs. William B. Schardt; Stephen F. Leva; Rev. Msgr. Thomas J. Cassidy; Deacons Eduardo Ramirez; William J. Donovan.
Res., 5312 10th St., N., 22205. Tel: 703-528-6276; Fax: 703-522-4758.
School—980 N. Frederick St., 22205. Tel: 703-525-7599; Fax: 703-525-2687. Mrs. Marlene Tennier, Prin.
Sisters of Notre Dame of Cleveland, Ohio 3; Lay Teachers 18; Students 235.
Catechesis/Religious Programs—Tel: 703-524-8377. Sr. Theresa Sullivan, S.N.D., D.R.E.
Students 227.
Convent—5307 N. Fairfax Dr., 22205. Tel: 703-525-8395.

4—ST. CHARLES BORROMEO (1909), Revs. Gerard Creedon; Francisco Mendez de Dios (Spain); Deacon John B. Mallon. In res., Rev. Lee W. Gross.
Res., 3304 N. Washington Blvd., 22201. Tel: 703-527-5500.
School—Tel: 703-527-0608; Fax: 703-527-3402. Sr. Benedict Kesock, O.S.B., Prin.
Sisters of St. Benedict 1; Lay Teachers 14; Students 237.
Catechesis/Religious Programs—Mrs. Judy Marchese, D.R.E.
Students 216.

5—HOLY MARTYRS OF VIETNAM (1979) (Vietnamese), Rev. John T.B. Trong; Deacon Pham Minh Kien, D.R.E. In res., Rev. Anthony Hoang Minh Thu.
Res., 915 S. Wakefield St., 22204. Tel: 703-553-0370; Fax: 703-553-4326.
Catechesis/Religious Programs—Tel: 703-553-4326.
Students 375.

6—OUR LADY OF LOURDES (1946), Rev. John T. O'Hara. Pastoral Assocs.: Revs. Robert A. Lange; Robert J. Rippy; Deacon James F. Ambury.
Res., 830 S. 23rd St., 22202. Tel: 703-684-9261; 684-9211; Fax: 703-684-6342.

7—OUR LADY, QUEEN OF PEACE (1947), Revs. Jeffrey T. Duaime, C.S.Sp.; Edward J. Kelly, C.S.Sp.; Deacon Eugene D. Betit.
Res., 2700 S. 19th St., 22204. Tel: 703-979-5580; Fax: 703-979-5590.
Catechesis/Religious Programs—Students 92.

OUTSIDE THE COUNTY OF ARLINGTON

Alexandria

1—BLESSED SACRAMENT (1946), Revs. John C. Cregan; John C. De Celles; Tarsicio Buitrago (Columbia); Charles W. Merkle, III; Deacon Francisco R. Soutuyo.
Church—1427 W. Braddock Rd., 22302. Tel: 703-998-6100; Fax: 703-671-3219.
Res., 1407 W. Braddock Rd., 22302. Tel: 703-578-4707.
School—Tel: 703-998-4170. Maureen Dowling, Prin. Sisters of the Holy Cross 1; Lay Teachers 17; Students 355.
Catechesis/Religious Programs—Patrica Wheatley, D.R.E.
Students 450.

2—GOOD SHEPHERD (1965), Revs. George J. Griffin; Charles C. McCoart, Jr.; Deacons Lawrence B. Henry, Jr.; Thomas G. White. In res., Rev. Francisco Cristancho.
Church & Mailing Address—8710 Mount Vernon Hwy., 22309. Tel: 703-780-4055; Fax: 703-360-5385.
Res., 3321 Wessynton Way, 22309.
Catechesis/Religious Programs—Judi Ryerse, D.R.E.
Students 530.

3—QUEEN OF APOSTLES (1963), Revs. William P. Saunders; Kevin O'Keefe; Tran Dinh Nhi; Franz Howscher, C.I.C.M.
Res., 4329 Sano St., 22312. Tel: 703-354-8711; Fax: 703-354-0766.
School—4409 Sano St., 22312. Tel: 703-354-0714; Fax: 703-354-1820. C. Douglas Workman, Prin.
Lay Teachers 16; Students 270.
Catechesis/Religious Programs—Tel: 703-354-4360. D.R.E.: Philip Girardi; Sally Girardi.
Students 150.

4—ST. JOSEPH'S (1915), Rev. John A. Carroll, S.S.J.; Deacon George L'Heureux.
Res., 711 N. Columbus St., 22314. Tel: 703-836-3725.
Catechesis/Religious Programs—Mrs. Wilma Anderson, D.R.E.
Students 80.

5—ST. LAWRENCE (Franconia) (1967), Revs. Franklyn M. McAfee; John Ziegler; Ronald Escalante; Deacons Joseph L. Bosch; Walter E. Classen; Joseph Benin; Joseph L. Bosch.
Res., 6222 Franconia Rd., 22310. Tel: 703-971-4378; Fax: 703-313-0971.
Catechesis/Religious Programs—Tel: 703-971-8541. Deacon Anthony Barrasso, D.R.E.
Students 400.

6—ST. LOUIS (1949), Revs. Richard J. Ley; David A. Whitestone; Marcus A. Pollard; Deacon Paul J. Plaisance. In res., Rev. Robert I. Bradley, S.J.
Res., 2907 Popkins Ln., 22306. Tel: 703-765-4421; Fax: 703-765-4571.
School—2901 Popkins Ln., 22306. Tel: 703-768-7732; Fax: 703-768-3836. Mrs. Noreen M. Gilmour, Prin.
Lay Teachers 22; Students 450.
Catechesis/Religious Programs—Tel: 703-765-6600. Deacon Paul J. Plaisance, M.R.E., D.R.E.
Students 433.

7—ST. MARY'S (1795), Revs. Stanley J. Krempa; Christopher Murphy; Carroll L. Oubre; Dr. Betty McLaughlin, Pastoral Assoc.
Res., 310 Duke St., 22314. Tel: 703-549-3603; 836-4100; Fax: 703-549-3605. [CEM]
School—400 Green St., 22314. Tel: 703-549-1646; Fax: 703-519-0840. Mrs. Mary F. Davis, Prin.
Sisters 2; Lay Teachers 29; Students 616.
Catechesis/Religious Programs—Tel: 703-548-6833. Sr. Bernadette Snearinger, C.S.C., D.R.E.
Students 192.
Convent—309 S. Royal St., 22314. Tel: 703-548-3545. Sisters of the Holy Cross

8—ST. RITA'S (1914), Revs. Clarence N. Watkins; Kevin Walsh.
Res., 3815 Russell Rd., 22305. Tel: 703-836-1640.
School—231 W. Glebe Rd., 22305. Tel: 703-548-1888. Sr. Catherine Michael Fee, S.S.J., Prin.
Sisters of St. Joseph 3; Lay Teachers 12; Students 210.
Catechesis/Religious Programs—Tel: 703-836-1940.
Students 121.

Annandale, Fairfax Co., Holy Spirit (1964), Revs. Frank J. Ready; Jerry Pokorsky; Joseph J. Clark. In res., Rev. Msgr. Francis L. Bradican, V.F., (Retired).
Res., 5121 Woodland Way, 22003. Tel: 703-978-8074; Fax: 703-978-9671.
School—8800 Braddock Rd., 22003. Tel: 703-978-7117; Fax: 703-978-7438. Mrs. Deborah Mohney, Prin.
Lay Teachers 27; Students 492.
Catechesis/Religious Programs—Tel: 703-978-8925. Mrs. Margaret Whitehead, D.R.E.
Students 825.

St. Ambrose (1996), Revs. Mark A. Pilon; Lawrence Violette; Deacon Roger T. Ostrom.

Res., 3901 Woodburn Rd., 22003. Tel: 703-280-4400.
School—St. Ambrose.
Lay Teachers 12; Students 214.
Catechesis/Religious Programs—Tel: 703-280-1122. Patrice Connolly, D.R.E.
Students 175.

St. Michael's (1953), Rev. Msgr. Edward P. Browne; Revs. Richard A. Mullins; Stefan P. Starzynski; Deacons Joseph W. Stasiak; Robert E. deLadurantaye. In res., Rev. J. Eugene Poirier, S.J.
Res., 7401 St. Michael's Ln., 22003. Tel: 703-256-7822; Fax: 703-256-0446.
School—7421 St. Michael's Ln., 22003. Tel: 703-256-1222. Sr. Dorothy Mayer, I.H.M., Prin.
Servants of the Immaculate Heart of Mary 7; Lay Teachers 24; Students 490.
Catechesis/Religious Programs—Tel: 703-941-9403. Mrs. Ann Buckreis, D.R.E.
Students 415.

Ashburn, St. Theresa (1991), Rev. Msgr. James W. McMurtrie; Rev. David P. Meng.
Mailing Address: P.O. Box 526, 20146-0526. Tel: 703-729-2287.
Rectory—4331 Dovetail Pl., 20147. Tel: 703-729-9036.
Church—21370 St. Theresa Ln., 20147. Tel: 703-729-2287.
Catechesis/Religious Programs—Tel: 703-729-3714. Mrs. Denise Pope, D.R.E.
Students 655.

Burke, Fairfax Co., Church of the Nativity (W. Springfield) (1973), Revs. Richard B. Martin; Christopher J. Mould; Sr. Vicky Bartkowski, Pastoral Min.
Mailing Address: 6400 Nativity Ln., 22015. Tel: 703-455-2400; Fax: 703-455-6832.
Res., 9523 Lyra Ct., 22015. Tel: 703-913-2306.
Catechesis/Religious Programs—Tel: 703-455-0372. D.R.E.: Sr. Donatella Merulla; Sr. Mary Attilia Todaro.
Students 1,364.

Chancellorsville, Spotsylvania Co., St. Patrick's (1983), Revs. Philip S. Majka; John P. Peterson; Deacons David Conroy; David J. Geary.
Res., 8200 Robert E. Lee Dr., Spotsylvania, 22553. Tel: 540-582-5252; Fax: 540-582-8639.
Church—9151 Ely's Ford Rd., Fredericksburg, 22407.
School—Tel: 540-786-2277. Mrs. Patricia Marcus, Prin.
Lay Teachers 8; Students 135.
Catechesis/Religious Programs—Mrs. Corita O'Brien, D.R.E.
Students 470.
Convent—8208 Robert E. Lee Dr., Spotsylvania, 22553. Tel: 540-582-2653. Daughters of Charity of St. Vincent de Paul (Emmitsburg, MD). Sr. Carol, Supr.
Sisters 4.
Mission—Spotsylvania, Spotsylvania Co., St. Matthew, 8200 Robert E. Lee Dr., Spotsylvania, 22553. Tel: 540-582-5575.

Chantilly, Fairfax Co., St. Timothy (1969), Revs. Cornelius O'Brien; John W. Rea, (Retired); Matthew H. Zuberbueler; Alexander Drummond; Deacons David E. Conroy; William J. Pyrek.
Res., 13807 Poplar Tree Rd., 20151. Tel: 703-378-7461; 378-7646; Fax: 703-378-7552.
School—13809 Poplar Tree Rd., 20151. Tel: 703-378-6932; Fax: 703-378-1273. Mrs. Marilyn Valatka, Prin.
Lay Teachers 28; Students 629.
Catechesis/Religious Programs—Tel: 703-378-9143. Maria Garvey, D.R.E.
Students 1,227.

Clifton, Fairfax Co., St. Andrew the Apostle (1989), Rev. Msgr. John P. Hannan, V.F.; Revs. Edward C. Hathaway; Robert J DeMartino. In res., Rev. Julius J. Ciliniski, (Retired).
Res., 6720 Union Mill Rd., 20124. Tel: 703-817-1770.
School—Tel: 703-817-1774. Mrs. Cherie Geide, Prin.
Lay Teachers 15; Students 253.
Catechesis/Religious Programs—Tel: 703-817-1773. Mrs. Maura Rush, D.R.E.
Students 1,282.

St. Claire of Assisi. Unassigned.
Res., 12049 Henderson Rd., 20124.

Colonial Beach, Westmoreland Co., St. Elizabeth (1916), Revs. William J. Schopps; William Aitcheson (RNO); Deacons Robert Baker; Edward Cleary; Gerry Melvin.
Res., 11 Irving Ave. S., P.O. Box 275, 22443. Tel: 804-224-7221; Fax: 804-224-7221. [JC]
Catechesis/Religious Programs—Rev. William J. Schopps, D.R.E.
Students 185.
Mission—King George, King George Co., St. Anthony's, P.O. Box 275, 22443. [CEM]
Chaplaincy—Naval Surface Weapons Center, Dahlgren, Tel: 540-653-8297; Fax: 540-653-7278.

Culpeper, Culpeper Co., Precious Blood (1880), Rev. Leo J. Zonneveld, C.I.C.M.
Res., 114 E. Edmondson St., 22701. Tel: 540-825-8945; Fax: 540-825-8987.
Catechesis/Religious Programs—Tel: 540-825-1339. Miss Kathleen Holter, D.R.E.
Students 293.
Mission—Washington, Rappahannock Co., St. Peter, P.O. Box 27, Washington, 22747. Tel: 540-675-3432. Rev. Clarence M. Trinkle.

Dale City, Prince William Co., Holy Family (1970), Revs. Joseph P. Biniek; James S. Barkett; J. Armando Avellaneda, P., M.Ss.A. (Columbia); Andrew W. Krafcik, (Retired); Deacons Charles A. Coutu; Gerald J. Moore; Richard L. Demers.
Res., 14160 Ferndale Rd., 22193. Tel: 703-670-8161; Fax: 703-670-8323.
School—Bibiana Quiamba, Dir. Lay Teachers 5; Students 95.
Catechesis/Religious Programs—Tel: 703-670-3137. Jan Clark.
Students 1,062.

Fairfax, Fairfax Co., St. Leo's (1957), Revs. Robert E. Avella; David C. Rahn; Sean K. Rousseau.
Res., 3700 Old Lee Hwy., 22030. Tel: 703-273-5369; Fax: 703-273-2371.
School—3704 Old Lee Hwy., 22030. Tel: 703-273-1211; Fax: 703-273-6913. Mrs. Diane Drews, Prin.
Lay Teachers 25; Students 575.
Catechesis/Religious Programs—Tel: 703-273-4868.
Students 473.
Station—Fairfax Nursing Home, Tel: 703-273-7705.

St. Mary of Sorrows (1858), Revs. Donald C. Greenhalgh; Terry W. Specht; Terrence R. Staples; Deacons John M. Ligon; Nicholas LaDuca.
Parish Center: 5222 Sideburn Rd., 22032. Tel: 703-978-4141; Fax: 703-978-2568.
Historic Church—5612 Ox Rd., Fairfax Station, 22039.
Res., 11112 Fairfax Station Rd., Fairfax Station, 22039. Tel: 703-978-4146. [CEM]
Catechesis/Religious Programs—Maureen Kelly, D.R.E.
Students 1,222.

St. Paul Chung,
Res., 4712 Rippling Pond Dr., 22033. Tel: 703-968-3010; Fax: 703-968-3013.

Falls Church, Fairfax Co., St. Anthony's (1952), Revs. Horace H. Grinnell; Jose E. Hoyos; Dennis M. Donahue; Ben M. Opara (Nigeria); Deacons Robert Curtin; Mario Mendoza.
Res., 3305 Glen Carlyn Rd., 22041. Tel: 703-820-7111; Fax: 703-379-9195.
Catechesis/Religious Programs—Tel: 703-820-2158. Mary Lou Miller, D.R.E.
Students 880.

St. James (1892), Revs. R. Roy Cosby; Paul L. Dudzinski; Michael D. Kelly; Deacons James A. Fishenden; Thomas M. Bello. In res., Rev. Peter W. Nassetta.
Res., 905 Park Ave., 22046. Tel: 703-532-8815. [CEM]
School—Tel: 703-533-1182; Fax: 703-532-8316. Sr. Janet Regina, I.H.M., Prin. & Supr.
Servants of the Immaculate Heart of Mary 7; Lay Teachers 25; Students 569.
Catechesis/Religious Programs—Tel: 703-532-4344. Sr. Michele I.H.M., D.R.E.
Students 380.
Convent—101 N. Spring St., 22046. Tel: 703-532-2388.

St. Philip (1963), Revs. Joseph J. Loftus; M. Paul Richardson; Deacon Wilson Korpi. In res., Rev. Ovidio Pecharroman.
Res., 7500 St. Philip's Ct., 22042. Tel: 703-573-3808; Fax: 703-560-2832.
Catechesis/Religious Programs—Tel: 703-573-1899; Fax: 703-573-6832. Ms. Charlotte Egnot, D.R.E.
Students 232.

Fredericksburg, Spotsylvania Co., St. Mary (1858), Revs. Christopher M. Buckner; Michael T. Orlowsky; John Edwin Thayer Tewes.
Res., 1009 Stafford Ave., 22401-5418. Tel: 540-373-6491; 373-6663; Fax: 540-371-0251.
Catechesis/Religious Programs—Tel: 540-373-7770.
Students 915.

Front Royal, Warren Co., St. John the Baptist (1884), Rev. William F. Ruehl; Deacon Paul J. Rees, (Retired).
Res., 123 W. Main St., 22630. Tel: 540-635-3780; Fax: 540-635-2683.
Catechesis/Religious Programs—Tel: 540-635-9493. Dr. Eleanor Kelly, D.R.E.
Students 198.

Gordonsville, Orange Co., St. Mark's, Rev. David L. Martin, Admin.
Res., 317 Main St., P.O. Box 124, 22942. Tel: 540-832-3062.

Great Falls, Fairfax Co., St. Catherine of Siena (1979), Revs. Jerome Fasano; Thomas Vander Woude.
Mailing Address: 1020 Springvale Rd., 22066. Tel: 703-759-4350; Fax: 703-759-3753.
Catechesis/Religious Programs—Tel: 703-759-3530. Mrs. Evanne Hoyt, D.R.E.
Students 711.

Herndon, Fairfax Co., St. Joseph (1955), Revs. David Bonarrigo, T.O.R.; Terrance Adams, T.O.R.; Christopher Dobson, T.O.R.; Deacon James A. Sheehan.
Res., 750 Peachtree St., 20170. Tel: 703-437-3737; Fax: 703-437-8745.
School—Tel: 703-437-3014. Mrs. Joan Cargill, Prin.
Lay Teachers 22; Students 522.
Catechesis/Religious Programs—Tel: 703-481-0788. Bro. Dennis Snyder, T.O.R., D.R.E.
Students 1,076.

Kilmarnock, Lancaster Co., St. Francis de Sales (1966), Rev. James C. Bruse; Sr. Elizabeth Mary Allard, M.S.B.T., Pastoral Assoc.
Res., 151 Church St., P.O. Box 759, 22482-0759. Tel: 804-435-1511. [CEM]
Catechesis/Religious Programs—Students 75.
Mission—Hague, Westmoreland Co., St.Paul, 22482-0759. Tel: 804-435-0568.

Lake Ridge, Prince William Co., St. Elizabeth Seton (1976), Revs. Daniel E. Hamilton; Ronald J. Gripshover, Jr.; Deacons Emil P. Myskowski; W. Vincent Einsmann.
Mailing Address: 12805 Valleywood Dr., 22192. Tel: 703-690-1493; Fax: 703-494-1995.
Res., 12805A Valleywood Dr., 22192. Tel: 703-690-1493; Fax: 703-494-1995.
Catechesis/Religious Programs—Tel: 703-494-3966. Jackie Ezersky, D.R.E.
Students 1,011.

Leesburg, Loudoun Co., St. John the Apostle (1926), Revs. Robert C. Brooks; Jerry A. Wooton.
Mailing Address: 101 Oakcrest Manor Dr., N.E., 20176-2221. Tel: 703-777-1317; Fax: 703-771-9016. [CEM]
Res., 302 N. King St., 22075.
Catechesis/Religious Programs—Mrs. Judy A. Joyce, D.R.E.
Students 381.

Luray, Page Co., Our Lady of the Valley (1954), Revs. Gervase Cain, T.O.R.; Andrew Draper, T.O.R.
Mailing Address: 200 Collins Ave., P.O. Box 462, 22835. Tel: 703-743-4919.
Catechesis/Religious Programs—Students 42.

McLean, Fairfax Co., St. John's (1913), Revs. Jerome R. Daly; James R. Haley. In res., Rev. Daniel L. Mode.
Res., 6420 Linway Ter., 22101. Tel: 703-356-7916; Fax: 703-356-4517.
School—6422 Linway Ter., 22101. Tel: 703-356-7554. Mrs. Christine Wells, Prin.
Lay Teachers 16; Students 297.
Catechesis/Religious Programs—Tel: 703-356-5275; Fax: 703-448-3811. Mrs. Olivia McFadden, D.R.E.
Students 292.

St. Luke's (1961), Revs. Martin McGuill; John D. Kelly. In res., Rev. Leo R. Roos.
Res., 7001 Georgetown Pike, 22101. Tel: 703-356-7481; 356-1255.
School—7005 Georgetown Pike, 22101. Tel: 703-356-1508. Margaret Cahill, Prin.
Lay Teachers 21; Students 240.
Catechesis/Religious Programs—Tel: 703-356-8419. Rose Wakeham, D.R.E.
Students 516.

Madison, Madison Co., Our Lady of the Blue Ridge (1974), Rev. John F. Morel, C.I.C.M.
Res., H.C.R. 4, Box 28, 22727. Tel: 540-948-4144.
Catechesis/Religious Programs—Mr. Bill Daley, D.R.E.
Students 60.

Manassas, Prince William Co., All Saints (1929), Revs. James A. Verrecchia; John J. Riley; Paul A. Berehout; Daniel N. Gee; Deacons John W. Eberlein; Richard O'Connell.
Res., 9300 Stonewall Rd., 20110. Tel: 703-368-4500; Fax: 703-257-9299.

School—9294 Stonewall Rd., 20110. Tel: 703-368-4400; Fax: 703-361-8573. Mr. David E. Conroy, Jr., Prin.
Lay Teachers 23; Students 436.
Catechesis/Religious Programs—Tel: 703-361-7850. Mrs. Maryann Riley, D.R.E.
Students 1,101.

Sacred Heart (1984), Revs. Thomas J. Lehning; Andrew W.P. Krafcik; William J. Erbacher.
Res., 6258 Terrapin Dr., 22111. Tel: 703-791-5131.
Church—12975 Purcell Rd., 22111-3217. Tel: 703-590-0030; Fax: 703-590-0141. [CEM]
Catechesis/Religious Programs—Students 282.

Middleburg, Loudoun Co., St. Stephen the Martyr (1975), Rev. James D. Muldowney.
Res., Route 748, P.O. Box 474, 22117. Tel: 703-687-6433. [JC]
Catechesis/Religious Programs—Students 96.

Orange, Orange Co., St. John's (1946), Rev. David L. Martin (ARL).
Res., 108 W. Nelson St., P.O. Box 350, 22960. Tel: 703-672-4933; Fax: 703-672-7416.
Catechesis/Religious Programs—Tel: 540-672-4969. Leigh Ann Faulconer.
Students 45.

Purcellville, Loudoun Co., St. Francis de Sales (1967), Revs. Martin A. Schratz, O.F.M.Cap.; Anthony R. Giudice, O.F.M.Cap.
Res., 37730 St. Francis Ct., 20132. Tel: 540-338-6381; Fax: 540-338-6431.
Catechesis/Religious Programs—Students 395.

Reston, Fairfax Co., St. John Neumann (1979), Revs. Robert A. Brown, O.S.F.S.; James M. Turner, O.S.F.S.; William N. Dougherty, O.S.F.S. In res., Rev. Michael C. Connolly, O.S.F.S.; Most Rev. Lewis S. Fiorelli, O.S.F.S.
Res., 11900 Lawyers Rd., 22091. Tel: 703-860-8510; Fax: 703-860-2136.
Catechesis/Religious Programs—Tel: 703-860-2815. D.R.E.: Susan Merkel Hayden; Corinne Butera; Rick Thier.
Students 1,428.

St. Thomas a Becket (1970), Rev. Patrick Holroyd.
Res., 1421 Wiehle Ave., 20190. Tel: 703-437-7113.
Catechesis/Religious Programs—Maureen Riddel, D.R.E.
Students 405.

Springfield, Fairfax Co., St. Bernadette's (1959), Revs. John J. Hughes; Kevin Larsen; Paul D. Scalia.
Res., 7600 Old Keene Mill Rd., 22152-2022. Tel: 703-451-8576; Fax: 703-451-6893.
School—7602 Old Keene Mill Rd., 22152-2099. Tel: 703-451-8696. Mrs. Catherine M. Gilbride, Prin.
Priests 2; Lay Teachers 22; Students 515.
Catechesis/Religious Programs—Tel: 703-569-0512.
Students 1,209.

Stafford, Fairfax Co., St. William of York (1971), Revs. Gerald Weymes; Richard Guest; Deacons Richard P. Smith; Donald K. McKaskill. In res., Rev. Anthony Pinizotto, O.S.F.S.
Mailing Address: P.O. Box 116, 22555. Tel: 540-659-1102; Fax: 540-659-5637.
Res., 3130 Jefferson Davis Hwy., 22554. Tel: 540-659-9190.
Catechesis/Religious Programs—Tel: 540-659-5705. Mrs. Martha Sallette, D.R.E.
Students 690.

Sterling, Loudoun Co., Christ the Redeemer (1972), Revs. C. Donald Howard, S.A.; Robert E. Langone, S.A.; Deacon Joseph Singer.
Res., 512 N. York Rd., 20164. Tel: 703-430-1686.
Church—46833 Harry Byrd Hwy., 20164. Tel: 703-430-0811; Fax: 703-430-1590.
Catechesis/Religious Programs—Tel: 703-430-0813. Mrs. Marie Kordes, D.R.E.
Students 950.

Triangle, Prince William Co., St. Francis of Assisi (1957), Revs. John F. O'Connor, O.F.M.; Robert Menard, O.F.M.; Joseph V. Kiernan, O.F.M.
Res., 18825 Fuller Heights Rd., 22172. Tel: 703-221-4575.
Church—Tel: 703-221-4044; Fax: 703-221-3246.
School—Tel: 703-221-3868. Dr. Tricia Barber, Prin.
Lay Teachers 16; Students 347.
Catechesis/Religious Programs—Tel: 703-221-4978. Mrs. Margaret Bruni, D.R.E.
Students 800.

Vienna, Fairfax Co., Our Lady of Good Counsel (1956), Revs. Raymond G. Collins, O.S.F.S.; John M. O'Neill, O.S.F.S.; Angelo F. Maraldo, O.S.F.S.; Deacon Leonard P. Malinowski. In res., Revs. Mark Mealey, O.S.F.S.; Edward Corcoran, O.S.F.S., (Retired).
Office: Box 97, 22183. Tel: 703-938-2828; Fax: 703-938-2416.
Res., 8601 Wolftrap Rd., 22182.
School—Tel: 703-938-3600. Sr. Ann McGreevy, O.S.B., Prin.
Benedictine Sisters of Virginia 2; Lay Teachers 23; Students 535.
Catechesis/Religious Programs—Tel: 703-938-2553; Fax: 703-255-1543. Ms. Patricia Jones, D.R.E.
Students 308.

St. Mark's (1965), Revs. J. Stewart Culkin; Mark E. Moretti; John H. Melner; Deacon Lawrence L. Ziemianski.
Res., 9970 Vale Rd., 22181. Tel: 703-281-9100; Fax: 703-281-0675.
Catechesis/Religious Programs—Tel: 703-938-1948. Sue Long, D.R.E.
Students 822.

Warrenton, Fauquier Co., St. John the Evangelist (1874), Revs. Michael J. Bazan; Michael G. Taylor; Deacons W. Bernard Ragan, Jr.; Richard A. Cronican.
Res., 271 Winchester St., 22186. Tel: 540-347-2922; Fax: 540-347-1274.
School—111 King St., 22186. Tel: 540-347-2458; Fax: 540-349-8007. Elizabeth Roach, Prin.
Sisters of Notre Dame 1; Lay Teachers 9; Students 247.
Catechesis/Religious Programs—Sr. Mary Donna Yost, S.N.D., D.R.E.
Students 502.
Convent—279 Winchester St., 22186. Tel: 540-347-2191.

Winchester, Frederick Co., Sacred Heart of Jesus (1870), Revs. Daniel S. Spychala; Dennis W. Kleinmann; Deacon Edward L. Christianson.
Res., 1717 Amherst St., 22601-2806. Tel: 540-662-5858; Fax: 540-667-6156. [CEM]
School—1713 Amherst St., 22601-2800. Tel: 703-662-7177. Ms. Mariette L. Zucchi, Prin.
School Sisters of Notre Dame 3; Lay Teachers 13; Students 204.
Catechesis/Religious Programs—Tel: 703-665-1975. Mr. Thomas L. McFadden, D.R.E.
Students 450.
Mission—Berryville, Clark Co.

Woodbridge, Prince William Co., Our Lady of Angels (1959), Rev. Msgr. John T. Cilinski; Revs. Francis J. Peffley; Paul M. Eversole; Deacons Danny E. Johnson; Richard L. Burrell; Jose I. Pardo; John Mosimann.
Res., 13752 Mary's Way, 22191. Tel: 703-494-2444; 494-5015; Fax: 703-494-0005.
Catechesis/Religious Programs—Tel: 703-494-3696; Fax: 703-494-3605. Kathleen Fridley, D.R.E.
Students 651.

Woodstock, Shenandoah Co., St. John Bosco (1888), Rev. Robert L. Ruskamp.
Res., 315 N. Main St., 22664. Tel: 540-459-4448.
Catechesis/Religious Programs—Students 130.
Day Care Center—Foundry St., 22664. Tel: 703-459-3321.
Teachers 5; Students 40.
Mission—Basye, Shenandoah Co., Our Lady of the Shenandoah, Basye, 22810. Tel: 703-459-4448.

DIOCESAN MISSION PARISH

Dominican Republic, San Francisco de Asis, Banica, Rev. Donald J. Rooney.
San Jose, Pedro Santana, Rev. Patrick L. Posey.

Special Assignment:
Reverend Fathers—
Cilinski, Robert C., George Mason University, Fairfax

On Duty Outside the Diocese:
Reverend Fathers—
Clark, Curtis L., Jr., St. Charles Borromeo Seminary, Overbrook, PA
Gross, Lee W., Mount St. Mary's Seminary, Emmitsburg, MD
Maher, Daniel J., Basilica of the National Shrine of the Immaculate Conception, Washington, DC
Posey, Patrick L., St. Francis of Assisi Parish, Banica, Dominican Republic
Reverend Fathers—
Rooney, Donald J., Dominican Republic

Military Chaplains:
Reverend Fathers—
Albertson, Eric, Capt., APO, AE

Retired:
Reverend Monsignors—
Bradican, Francis L., Holy Spirit, Annandale
Burke, Richard J., Cathedral of St. Thomas More, Arlington
Hendrick, Frank J., Pinehurst, NC
Scannell, Thomas P., St. Agnes, Arlington
Reverend Fathers—
Cilinski, Julius, St. Andrew the Apostle
Dair, Richard J., Fairfax
Gerloff, Charles W., Virginia Beach
Hammond, Henry E., Dumfries
Kollar, Edmund, Lecanto, FL
Krafcik, Andrew W.P., Holy Family, Dale City
McLean, Edward J., Little Sisters of the Poor, Washington, DC
Rea, John W., Sacred Heart of Jesus, Winchester
Slivonik, Stanley, Lovettsville
Snella, Adolph A., Little Sisters of the Poor, Richmond

Permanent Deacons:
Ambury, James F., Our Lady of Lourdes, Arlington
Arquette, Lester K., Leave of Absence
Bayne, James L., Leave of Absence
Bello, Thomas M., St. James, Falls Church
Benedi, Claudio F., Cathedral of St. Thomas More, Arlington
Benin, Joseph G., St. Lawrence, Alexandria
Betit, Eugene D., Our Lady Queen of Peace, Arlington
Bidon, Patrick J., St. Paul, Colorado Springs, CO
Bosch, Joseph L., St. Lawrence, Alexandria
Braun, Richard L., Leave of Absence
Brodeur, Harold H., St. John, Atlantic Beach, FL
Burrell, Richard L., Our Lady of Angels, Woodbridge
Canonica, Donald A., St. Mary, Opelika, AL
Christianson, Edward L., Sacred Heart, Winchester
Classen, Walter E., St. Lawrence, Alexandria
Conroy, David E., St. Timothy, Chantilly
Coutu, Charles A., Holy Family, Dale City
Curtin, Robert J., St. Anthony, Falls Church
De Ladurantaye, Robert E., St. Michael, Annandale
Demers, Richard L., Holy Family, Dale City
Donovan, William J., St. Ann, Arlington
Dunn, Darryl A., St. Mark, Westminster, CO
Eberlein, John W., All Saints, Manassas
Einsmann, W. Vincent, St. Elizabeth Ann Seton, Lake Ridge
Fishenden, James A., St. James, Falls Church
Frank, John L., Leave of Absence
Galvez, Rene A., Leave of Absence
George, Paul J., Leave of Absence
Harding, Stanley L., Military Retirement Home, Fort Belvoir
Henry, Lawrence B., Good Shepherd, Alexandria
Johnson, Danny E., Our Lady of Angels, Woodbridge
Kenski, Frank G., Our Lady of Good Counsel, Marysville, PA
Korpi, Wilson I., St. Philip, Falls Church
La Duca, Nicholas J., St. Mary of Sorrows, Fairfax
Lee, Jea Duck, Leave of Absence
Lee, Paul, St. Paul Chung, Fairfax
Ligon, Jack M., St. Mary of Sorrows, Fairfax
Malinowski, Leonard P., Our Lady of Good Counsel, Vienna
Mallon, John B., St. Charles Borromeo, Arlington
Melvin, Gerald A., Leave of Absence
Mendoza, Mario L., St. Anthony, Falls Church
Moore, Gerald J., Holy Family, Dale City
Myskowski, Emil P., St. Elizabeth Ann Seton, Lake Ridge
Nickle, Dennis E., Leave of Absence
O'Connell, Richard T., All Saints, Manassas
Ostrom, Roger T., St. Ambrose, Annandale
Pardo, Jose I., Our Lady of Angels, Woodbridge
Pham, Kien Minh, Holy Martyrs of Vietnam, Arlington
Pivarnik, William D., Immaculate Conception, Hendersonville, NC
Prien, Richard K., St. Francis of Xavier, Carbondale, IL
Pyrek, William J., St. Timothy, Chantilly
Ragan, W. Bernard, St. John the Evangelist, Warrenton
Ramirez, Eduardo A., St. Ann, Arlington
Rees, Paul J., Leave of Absence
Resendes, Daniel F., Vice Chancellor, Sacred Heart Cathedral, Gallup, NM
Sheehan, James A., St. Joseph, Herndon
Singer, Joseph R., Christ the Redeemer, Sterling
Smith, Richard P., St. William of York, Stafford
Soutuyo, Francisco R., Blessed Sacrament, Alexandria
Stasiak, Joseph W., St. Michael, Annandale
Taub, Samuel M., Cathedral of St. Thomas More, Arlington
Tiernan, James V., Leave of Absence
Vivaldi, Noel, St. Philip, Falls Church
White, Thomas G., Good Shepherd, Alexandria
Wilbur, Carl A., Catholic Chapel, National Institute of Health
Wolter, Thomas W., St. Francis of Assisi, Triangle

INSTITUTIONS LOCATED IN THE DIOCESE

[A] COLLEGES AND UNIVERSITIES

ARLINGTON. *Marymount University*, 2807 N. Glebe Rd., 22207. Tel: 703-522-5600.
For a complete listing, refer to the Colleges and Universities section.

FRONT ROYAL. *Christendom College*. Tel: 540-636-2900.
For a complete listing, refer to the Colleges and Universities section.

[B] CATECHETICAL INSTITUTE

ARLINGTON. *Notre Dame Institute for Catechetics*, 4407 Sano St., 22312. Tel: 703-658-4304. Rev. William P. Saunders, Ph.D., Pres.; Sr. M. Timothy Prokes, F.S.E., Ph.D., Dean of Students; Sr. Mary St. Mark, I.H.M., Dean Summer School; Luther P. Niehoff, Registrar & Treas.; Valerie A. Brown, Dir. Devel. Students 230.

[C] CORRESPONDENCE SCHOOL

PAEONIAN SPRINGS. *The Catholic Distance University*, 39959 Catoctin Ridge St., 20129-0178. Tel: 504-882-3737; Fax: 504-882-3654. Accredited Catechetical Institute for Adults; Catechetical Diploma; Continuing Education; and Optional College credit, Masters in Religious Studies. All programs through distance learning. Marianne Evans Mount, Exec. Dir.

[D] HIGH SCHOOLS, DIOCESAN

ARLINGTON. *Bishop Denis J. O'Connell High School*, 6600 Little Falls Rd. and Underwood St., 22213. Tel: 703-237-1400. Mr. Alward V. Burch, Prin. Assistant Principals: Sr. Marie laReine, I.H.M.; Mr. John Gutter; Richard J. Martin; Rev. Daniel L. Mode, Spiritual Dir.; Mr. Thomas McNichol, Guidance Dir. Sisters Servants of the Immaculate Heart of Mary 11; Lay Teachers 86; Students 1,400.

ALEXANDRIA. *Bishop Ireton High School*, 201 Cambridge Rd., 22314. Tel: 703-751-7606. (See separate listing for Oblates of St. Francis de Sales Residence). Rev. William J. Metzger, O.S.F.S., M.A., Prin.; Very Rev. Michael J. McCue, O.S.F.S., M.A., Supr.; Revs. John J. Dolan, O.S.F.S., M.Div.; John J. Muzdakis, O.S.F.S., B.S.; Manning C. Moore, O.S.F.S., M.A.; Mr. Michael Robinson. Oblates of St. Francis de Sales 5; Brothers 1; Sisters 2; Lay Teachers 47; Students 775.

FAIRFAX. *Paul VI High School*, 10675 Lee Hwy., 22030. Tel: 703-352-0925. Rev. John W. Lyle, O.S.F.S., Prin. Asst. Principals: Mr. David DiPippa; Mrs. Joan Grossel; Mrs. Marie Powell; Revs. Matthew J. Hillyard, O.S.F.S.; Michael Cavanaugh, O.S.F.S. Oblates of St.Francis de sales 3; Lay Teachers 80; Students 1,120.

[E] HIGH SCHOOLS, PRIVATE

MIDDLEBURG. *Notre Dame Academy, Middleburg, VA.* (Coed High School), 35321 Notre Dame Ln., 22117. Tel: 540-687-5581; Fax: 540-687-3103. Sr. Cecilia Liberatore, S.N.D., Head of School. Sisters of Notre Dame 7; Lay Teachers 16; Students 158.

[F] ELEMENTARY SCHOOLS, PRIVATE

BRISTOW. *Linton Hall.* (Coed), 9535 Linton Hall Rd., 22013. Tel: 703-368-3157. Sr. Glenna Smith, O.S.B., Prin. Benedictine Sisters of Virginia 9; Lay Teachers 15; Students 175.

FREDERICKSBURG. *Montfort Academy, Inc.* (Grades K-8), 700 Sunken Rd., 22401. Tel: 703-373-9478. Sr. Joan Rohan, D.W., Prin. Daughters of Wisdom 2; Lay Teachers 22; Students 355.

[G] INTERPAROCHIAL SCHOOLS

FALLS CHURCH. *Corpus Christi School.* (Grades 1-8), 3301 Glen Carlyn Rd., 22041. Tel: 703-820-7450. Sponsoring parishes: St. Anthony and St. Philip. Mr. George Chiplock, Prin. Lay Teachers 22; Students 450.

WOODBRIDGE. *Aquinas School.* (Grades K-8), 13750 Mary's Way, 22191. Tel: 703-491-4447.
Sponsoring parishes: Our Lady of Angels, Woodbridge; Holy Family, Dale City; St. Elizabeth Ann Seton, Lake Ridge; and Sacred Heart, Manassas. Sr. Mary Anne, O.P., Prin. Dominican Sisters, Congregation of St. Cecilia 4; Lay Teachers 25; Students 542.

[H] DAY CARE AND CHILD LEARNING CENTERS

ARLINGTON. *Holy Martyrs of Vietnam Church Child Enrichment Day Care Center.* (Children 2-5 years), 915 S. Wakefield St., 22204. Tel: 703-920-1049. Mrs. T. Mai Nguyen. Lay Teachers 5; Students 40.

ALEXANDRIA. *Blessed Sacrament Grade School and Early Childhood Center.* (Grades PreK-8). (Children 3-14 years), 1417 W. Braddock Rd., 22302. Tel: 703-998-4170. Ms. Maureen Dowling, Prin. Lay Teachers 23; Students 360.

St. Gabriel's, 4319 Sano St., 22312. Tel: 703-354-0395. Poor Sisters of St. Joseph (Buenos Aires). Sr. Margarita Quintero, P.S.S.J., Supr. Sisters 8; Students 90.

FALLS CHURCH. *Corpus Christi Early Childhood Center.* (Children 3-5 years), 7506 St. Philip's Ct., 22042. Tel: 703-573-4570. Mr. George Chiplock, Prin.; Mrs. Monique T. Myers, Dir.; Mrs. Mary Stevens, Daycare Dir. Sponsoring Parishes: St. Anthony and St. Philip. Lay Teachers 8; Students 184.

St. Joseph's Day Nursery & Kindergarten, 203 N. Spring St., 22046. Tel: 703-533-8441. Servants of St. Joseph (Salamanca, Spain). Sr. Jacinta Salazar, S.S.J., Dir. Sisters 3; Lay Teachers 7; Students 80.

[I] SCHOOLS FOR EXCEPTIONAL CHILDREN

ARLINGTON. *St. Coletta School*, 3130 Lee Hwy., 22201-4208. Tel: 703-525-4433. Ms. Sharon Raimo, Prin. School for mentally retarded, multi-handicapped children. Students 5 years old through adulthood. Sisters 1; Teachers 7; Teacher Aides 20; Speech Pathologists 3; Physical Therapists 2; Occupational Therapists 2; Music Therapists 1; Religion Instructors 1; Psychologists 1; Vocational Coordinators/Employment Specialists 1; Students 60. Individualized supported employment program for disabled adults.

FALLS CHURCH. *Seton Centers, Inc.*, 115 Hillwood Ave., 22046. Tel: 703-533-7670. Elementary & High School Programs. School for children with learning disabilities. Mary K. Doherty, Exec. Dir. Teachers 6; Students 70.

[J] MONASTERIES AND RESIDENCES OF PRIESTS AND BROTHERS

ARLINGTON. *Missionary Servants of the Most Holy Trinity, S.T.*, 1215 N. Scott St., 22209-3097. Tel: 703-276-8646; Fax: 703-522-2656. Generalate of the Missionary Servants of the Most Holy Trinity. Revs. Domingo Rodriguez, S.T., Gen. Custodian; Jesus Rivera, S.T., Gen. Councilor & Vicar for Spanish-speaking Personnel & Apostolates; John McSpiritt, S.T., Gen. Councilor & Vicar for Personnel; Bro. Hilary Mettes, S.T., Sec. Gen. Legal Titles: *Missionary Servants Charitable Trust*; *Father Judge Charitable Trust.*

Missionhurst, C.I.C.M.-Central House and Provincialate, 4651 N. 25th St., 22207. Tel: 703-528-3800; Fax: 703-528-5355. Congregation of the Immaculate Heart of Mary foreign and home missions. Legal Titles: *American I.H.M. Province, Inc.*; *Immaculate Heart Missions, Inc.*; *Missionhurst, Inc.* Revs. Joseph Lapauw, C.I.C.M., Prov. Supr.; Paul DeWolf, C.I.C.M., Rector; Leo Zonneveld, C.I.C.M., Prov. Treas. & Dir. Devel.; Louis Tysmans, C.I.C.M., Dir. Prog. Svcs. & Asst. Editor of Missionhurst Magazine; Bill Wyndaele, C.I.C.M., Editor of Missionhurst Magazine & Dir. Mission Ctr.; His Eminence Jan Cardinal Schotte, C.I.C.M.; Revs. Howard Picard, C.I.C.M.; Albert VanNuffelen, C.I.C.M.; Francis Loos, C.I.C.M.; Roger Van Cauwenburgh, C.I.C.M.; Joseph Dewaele, C.I.C.M.; John Van de Paer, C.I.C.M.; Frank Holscher, C.I.C.M.; Jerome Meersman, C.I.C.M.; Albert De Crits, C.I.C.M.; Charles Denys, C.I.C.M.; Marcel Van Thillo, C.I.C.M.; Joseph Smits, C.I.C.M.; Bros. Raymond Vanloo, C.I.C.M., Promotion Board; Miguel Portuondo, C.I.C.M.

ALEXANDRIA. *Oblates of St. Francis de Sales Residence*, 101 Cambridge Rd., 22314. Tel: 703-751-7606. (See separate listing for Bishop Ireton High School regarding staff.). Revs. Michael McCue, O.S.F.S., Supr.; John Dolan, O.S.F.S.; William J. Metzger, O.S.F.S.; Manning C. Moore, O.S.F.S.; John J. Muzdakis, O.S.F.S.; Bro. Edward Ogden, O.S.F.S.

BERRYVILLE. *Cistercian Abbey of Our Lady of the Holy Cross*, Rte. 2, Box 3870, 22611-9526. Tel: 540-955-1425. Order of Cistercians of the Strict Observance (Trappist). Rt. Revs. Flavian Burns, O.C.S.O., Chap., Our Lady of the Angels, Crozet; Edward McCorkell, O.C.S.O., Retired Abbot; Revs. Edmund Flynn, O.C.S.O., Treas.; Paschal Balkan, O.C.S.O.; Andrew Gries, O.C.S.O.; Rt. Rev. Mark Delery, O.C.S.O., Retreat House Counsellor and Retired Abbot; Revs. Maurice Flood, O.C.S.O.; Robert Barnes, O.C.S.O.; Joseph Wittstock, O.C.S.O., Prior and Vocation Dir.; James Orthmann, O.C.S.O., Novice Master; Malachy Marrion, O.C.S.O.; Bros. Benedict Simmonds, O.C.S.O., Supr.; Stephen Maguire, O.C.S.O., Guest Master. Community 29; Leave of Absence 2; Residents 27; Priests 12; Solemnly Professed Non-priest Monks 8; Novices 3; Temporarily Professed 3; Postulants 1.

FAIRFAX. *Oblates of St. Francis de Sales Residence.* (See separate listing for Paul VI High School.), 10600 Cedar Ave., 22030. Tel: 703-273-8067. Very Rev. Michael Cavanaugh, O.S.F.S., Supr.; Revs. John W. Lyle, O.S.F.S.; Matthew J. Hillard, O.S.F.S.

FALLS CHURCH. *Missionhurst-C.I.C.M.*, 3425 Annandale Rd., 22042. Tel: 703-560-0766. Revs. Louis Tysmans, C.I.C.M., Supr.; Robert Timperman, C.I.C.M.; Albert Verbeke, C.I.C.M.

WINCHESTER. *Sacred Heart Friary*, Box 825, 22604. Tel: 540-869-1599. Third Order Regular of St. Francis. Revs. Patrick Boland, T.O.R.; Martin Brohead, T.O.R.; Marion Deck, T.O.R.; Bonaventure Kiley, T.O.R.; Francis McKinney, T.O.R.; Samuel Tiesi, T.O.R.; Christopher Petrosky, T.O.R.; James Cleary, T.O.R.; Bros. Richard Gates, T.O.R., Local Min.; Stephen Liebal, T.O.R.; Stan Prenatt, T.O.R.; Dominic Barkovich, T.O.R.; John Paul McMahon, T.O.R.; Finbar Gallagher, T.O.R.; Norman McNelis, T.O.R. Professed Brothers 5.

[K] CONVENTS AND RESIDENCES FOR SISTERS

ARLINGTON. *Religious of the Sacred Heart of Mary*, 2807 N. Glebe Rd., 22207. Tel: 703-284-1495. Sr. Catherine Browne, R.S.H.M., Coord. Sisters 12.

Sisters Servants of the Immaculate Heart of Mary, 6600 Little Falls Rd., 22213. Tel: 703-237-1410. Teachers at Bishop O'Connell High School. Sr. Mary Theresa McBride; Sr. Mary Lynn; Sr. St. Kathleen Blaston; Sr. Charles B. Harvey; Sr. Mary Raphael Hafner; Sr. Marie la Reine Spain; Sr. Joanna McKelvey; Sr. Maureen Chistopher Dusterhoff; Sr. Rose Harlan; Sr. Janice Urbanec; Sr. Ingrid Schwerkart; Sr. Susan Cronin. Sisters 12.

ALEXANDRIA. *Poor Clare Monastery of Mary, Mother of the Church*, 2505 Stonehedge Dr., 22306. Tel: 703-768-4918. Observing the Primitive Rule of St. Clare. Solemnly Professed 11; Junior Professed 4; Novices 1.

St. Gabriel's Convent, 4319 Sano St., 22312. Tel: 703-354-0395. Sr. Margarita Quintero, P.S.S.J., Supr. Poor Sisters of St. Joseph's Buenos Aires Regional House and Novitiate 8.

Sisters of the Holy Cross, 5582 First Statesman Ln., 22312. Tel: 703-658-9519. Legal Title: *Sisters of the Holy Cross, Inc.* Sisters 2.

BRISTOW. *St. Benedict Monastery*, 9535 Linton Hall Rd., 20136-1217. Tel: 703-361-0106. Sr. Cecilia Dwyer, O.S.B., Prioress. Tel: 703-368-4848; Rev. Mark Broski, O.S.B., Chap. Tel: 703-335-2195. Professed Sisters 41; Sisters in Temporary Commitment 1; Sisters Resident at Motherhouse 38.

FALLS CHURCH. *Holy Family House Convent, S.S.J.*, 3438 Charles St., 22041. Tel: 703-820-9785. Sisters 4.

Servants of St. Joseph Convent, 203 N. Spring St., 22046. Tel: 703-533-8441. Sr. Carmen Guerrero, S.S.J., Supr. Tel: 703-534-9549; Sr. Prudencia Gonzalo, S.S.J.; Sr. Josefina Laguno, S.S.J.; Sr. Jacinta Salazar, S.S.J.; Sr. Agustina Temprano, S.S.J. Sisters 5.

GREAT FALLS. *Sisters of the Cenacle*, 1033 Riva Ridge Dr., 22066. Tel: 703-759-6901. Religious of the Cenacle 2.

SPOTSYLVANIA. *Daughters of Charity of St. Vincent de Paul*, St. Matthew's House, 8208 Robert E. Lee Dr., 22553-3504. Tel: 540-582-2653. Sisters 4.

WOODBRIDGE. *Dominican Sisters Convent.* (Congregation of St. Cecilia), 2655 Falmouth Ct., 22192. Tel: 703-494-4488. Dominican Sisters. Sr. Mary Anne, O.P., Prin., Supr. Sisters 4.

[L] RETREAT HOUSES

BERRYVILLE. *Retreat House, Holy Cross Abbey*, Rte. 2, Box 3870, 22611. Tel: 540-955-3124. Retreat Masters: Rt. Rev. Mark Delery, O.C.S.O., Retreat Dir.; Rev. Maurice Flood, O.C.S.O.; Bro. Stephen Maguire, O.C.S.O., Guest Master.

MCLEAN. *Dominican Retreat.* Accommodations for 41 persons. 7103 Old Dominion Dr., 22101. Tel: 703-356-4243. Dominican Sisters of St. Catherine De Ricci. Sr. Bartholomew VanDusky, O.P., Coord. Sisters 5.

[M] CAMPUS MINISTRY

FAIRFAX. *George Mason University, Catholic Campus Ministry House*, 4521 Roberts Rd., 22032. Tel: 703-425-0022. Rev. Robert C. Cilinski, Chap. & Dir. Campus Ministry.

St. Robert Bellarmine Chapel. Catholic Campus Ministry. George Mason University, 4515 Roberts Rd., 22032. Tel: 703-425-0022. Rev. Robert Cilinski; Ms. Michelle Miller, Assoc. Campus Min.; Dr. Elaine Rendler, Dir. Liturgical Music.

[N] MISCELLANEOUS

ARLINGTON. *Youth Apostles Institute, An Association of Christian Faithful.* 1600 Carlin Ln., McLean, 22101-4100. Tel: 703-556-0914.

ALEXANDRIA. *St. Paul Book and Media Center (Daughters of St. Paul)*, 1025 King St., 22314. Tel: 703-549-3806; 683-1741 (Convent). Sr. Joan Paula Arruda,

F.S.P., Supr. Missionary Sisters of the Communications Media.

BROAD RUN. *National Association of Catholic Home Educators (NACHE)*, 6102 Saints Hill Ln., 20137. Tel: 703-349-4314. Mr. Bill Bales, Pres.

FRONT ROYAL. *Seton Home Study School*, 1350 Progress Dr., 22630. Tel: 540-636-9990. Dr. Mary K. Clark, Dir.

SPOTSYLVANIA. *St. Francis Catholic Worker West*, 9631 Peppertree Rd., 22553. Tel: 540-972-3218. Mr. John Mahoney.

STAFFORD. *American Life League, Inc.*, P.O. Box 1350, 22555. Tel: 540-659-4171. Mrs. Judie Brown, Pres.

VIENNA. *Mount Tabor Society, Inc.*, 2363 Hunter Mill Rd., 22181. Tel: 703-938-2564. A House of Prayer and Christian Community. Rev. Paul G. Wynants, C.I.C.M., Dir.

WOODBRIDGE. *Apostolate for Family Consecration*, St. Damien Center, 1410 Harrison St., 22191-2215. Tel: 703-491-6544. Jerome F. Coniker, Exec. Dir.

RELIGIOUS INSTITUTES OF MEN REPRESENTED IN THE DIOCESE

For further details refer to the corresponding bracketed number in the Religious Institutes of Men or Women section.

[0470]—*The Capuchin Friars.* (New Jersey Prov. of the Stigmata).—O.F.M.Cap.

[0350]—*Cistercians Order of the Strict Observance.* (Trappists).—O.C.S.O.

[0520]—*Franciscan Friars.* (Holy Name Prov.).—O.F.M.

[0650]—*Holy Ghost Fathers.*—C.S.Sp.

[0690]—*Jesuit Fathers and Brothers.*—S.J.

[0840]—*Missionary Servants of the Most Holy Trinity.*—S.T.

[0860]—*Missionhurst Congregation of the Immaculate Heart of Mary.*—C.I.C.M.

[0920]—*Oblates of St. Francis de Sales.* (Wilmington-Philadelphia Prov.).—O.S.F.S.

[0700]—*St. Joseph's Society of the Sacred Heart.* (Baltimore, MD).—S.S.J.

[0560]—*Third Order Regular of Saint Francis.* (Sacred Heart Prov.).—T.O.R.

RELIGIOUS INSTITUTES OF WOMEN REPRESENTED IN THE DIOCESE

[0230]—*Benedictine Sisters.* (Erie, PA).—O.S.B.

[0230]—*Benedictine Sisters.* (South Dakota).—O.S.B.

[0230]—*Benedictine Sisters.* (Virginia).—O.S.B.

[3110]—*Congregation of Our Lady of the Retreat in the Cenacle.*—R.C.

[1920]—*Congregation of the Sisters of the Holy Cross.*—C.S.C.

[0760]—*Daughters of Charity of St. Vincent de Paul.* (Emmitsburg Province).—D.C.

[0960]—*Daughters of Wisdom.*—D.W.

[1070-17]—*Dominican Sisters Congregation of St. Catherine deRicci.*—O.P.

[1070-07]—*Dominican Sisters Congregation of St. Cecilia.*—O.P.

[1070-21]—*Dominican Sisters of the Congregation of the Most Holy Trinity.*—O.P.

[1880]—*Handmaidens of Reparation of the Sacred Heart of Jesus.*—A.R.

[2790]—*Missionary Servants of the Most Blessed Trinity.*—M.S.B.T.

[3760]—*Order of St. Clare (Cloistered).*—P.C.C.

[0950]—*Pious Society of Daughters of St. Paul.*—F.S.P.

[3250]—*Poor Sisters of St. Joseph.*—P.S.S.J.

[3465]—*Religious of the Sacred Heart of Mary.* (Eastern North Amer. Prov.).—R.S.H.M.

[2970]—*School Sisters of Notre Dame.*—S.S.N.D.

[3595]—*Servants of St. Joseph.*—S.S.J.

[3830]—*Sister of St. Joseph.* Philadelphia.—S.S.J.

[2990]—*Sisters of Notre Dame.*—S.N.D.

[1650]—*Sisters of St. Francis of Philadelphia.*—O.S.F.

[2170]—*Sisters, Servants of the Immaculate Heart of Mary.*—I.H.M.

NECROLOGY

† Casey, Thomas A, Fairfax, VA St. Mary of Sorrows. —Died Feb. 29, 1996.

Archdiocese of Atlanta

(Archidioecesis Atlantensis)

Most Reverend

JOHN FRANCIS DONOGHUE, D.D.

Archbishop of Atlanta; ordained June 4, 1955; appointed Bishop of Charlotte November 6, 1984; appointed Archbishop of Atlanta June 22, 1993; installed August 18, 1993.

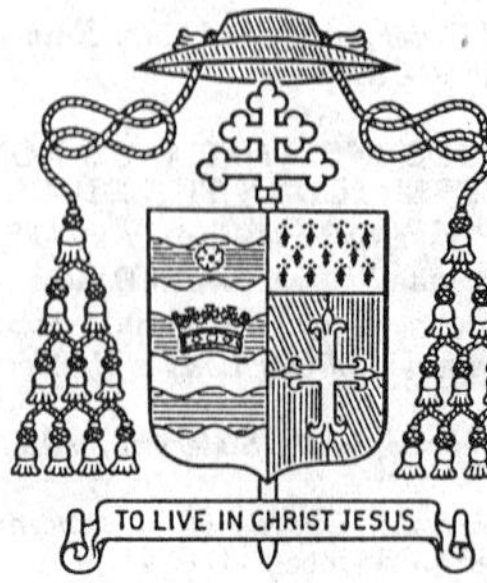

Catholic Center Archdiocese of Atlanta: 680 W. Peachtree St., N.W., Atlanta, GA, 30308.

Web site address: http://www.archatl.com/

ESTABLISHED JULY 2, 1956.

CANONICALLY ERECTED NOVEMBER 8, 1956.

CREATED AN ARCHDIOCESE FEBRUARY 21, 1962.

Square Miles 21,445.

Comprises the 69 Counties in the northern part of the State of Georgia, north of and including the following counties: Lincoln, McDuffie, Warren, Hancock, Baldwin, Putnam, Jasper, Monroe, Upson, Meriwether and Troup.

PATRONS OF THE ARCHDIOCESE: I. Our Blessed Lady under the title of the Immaculate Heart of Mary; II. Saint Pius X.

For legal titles of parishes and archdiocesan institutions, consult the Archbishop's Office.

STATISTICAL OVERVIEW

Personnel	
Archbishop	1
Retired Archbishops	1
Abbots	1
Retired Abbots	1
Priests: Diocesan Active in Diocese	103
Priests: Active Outside Diocese	9
Priests: Retired, Sick or Absent	5
Number of Diocesan Priests	117
Religious Priests in Diocese	94
Extern Priests in Diocese	5
Ordinations:	
Diocesan Priests	11
Transitional Deacons	7
Permanent Deacons in Diocese	105
Total Brothers	1
Total Sisters	125
Parishes	
Parishes	69
With Resident Pastor:	
Resident Diocesan Priests	54
Resident Religious Priests	15
Without Resident Pastor:	
Missions	22
Pastoral Centers	2
New Parishes Created	1
Professional Ministry Personnel:	
Sisters	15
Lay Ministers	97
Welfare	
Catholic Hospitals	2
Total Assisted	226,691
Health Care Centers	2
Total Assisted	262
Homes for the Aged	3
Total Assisted	100
Day Care and Extended Day Care Centers	1
Total Assisted	55
Specialized Homes	1
Total Assisted	48
Special Centers for Social Services	5
Total Assisted	37,430
Educational	
Diocesan Students in Other Seminaries	64
Total Seminarians	64
High Schools, Diocesan and Parish	1
Total Students	1,010
High Schools, Private	1
Total Students	1,025
Elementary Schools, Diocesan and Parish	13
Total Students	4,617
Elementary Schools, Private	2
Total Students	195
Catechesis/Religious Education:	
High School Students	3,882
Elementary Students	24,194
Total Students Under Catholic Instruction	34,987
Teachers in the Diocese:	
Priests	6
Brothers	1
Sisters	7
Lay Teachers	383
Vital Statistics	
Receptions into the Church:	
Infant Baptism Totals	5,539
Adult Baptism Totals	494
Received into Full Communion	932
First Communions	4,468
Confirmations	3,419
Marriages:	
Catholic	872
Interfaith	758
Total Marriages	1,630
Deaths	888
Total Catholic Population	256,049
Total Population	4,712,254

Former Bishops—Most Rev. FRANCIS E. HYLAND, D.D., J.C.D., appt. Titular Bishop of Gomphi and Auxiliary Bishop of Savannah-Atlanta, Oct. 15, 1949; cons. Dec. 21, 1949; First Bishop of Atlanta, July 17, 1956; installed on Nov. 8, 1956; resigned and appointed Titular Bishop of Bisica, Oct. 11, 1961; died Jan. 31, 1968.—Most Rev. PAUL J. HALLINAN, D.D., appt. Bishop of Charleston, Sept. 9, 1958; cons. Oct. 28, 1958; elevated to the Archiepiscopal dignity, Feb. 21, 1962; installed First Archbishop of Atlanta, March 29, 1962; died March 27, 1968.—Most Rev. JOSEPH L. BERNARDIN, D.D., appt. Auxiliary of Atlanta, March 9, 1966; cons. April 26, 1966; appt. Gen. Sec. U.S.C.C., April 5, 1968.—Most Rev. THOMAS A. DONNELLAN, appt. Bishop of Ogdensburg, March 4, 1964; cons. April 9, 1964; appt. to Atlanta, May 29, 1968; installed July 16, 1968; died Oct. 15, 1987.—Most Rev. EUGENE A. MARINO, S.S.J., D.D., appt. Auxiliary of Washington, July 15, 1974; appt. Archbishop of Atlanta, March 14, 1988; installed May 5, 1988; resigned July 10, 1990.—Most Rev. JAMES P. LYKE, O.F.M., Ph.D., appt. Auxiliary Bishop of Cleveland and Titular Bishop of Fornos Maggiore, June 30, 1979; cons. Aug. 1, 1979; appt. Apostolic Administrator Archdiocese of Atlanta, July 10, 1990; appt. Archbishop of Archdiocese of Atlanta, April 30, 1991; installed June 24, 1991 Palium conferred June 29, 1991; died Dec. 27, 1992.

Moderator of Religious—Sr. MARY BETH BERES, *P.O. Box 29548, Atlanta, 30359.*

Vicar for Clergy—Rev. Msgr. HENRY C. GRACZ.

Associate Vicar for Clergy—Rev. RICHARD MORROW.

Archdiocesan Offices and Directors

Catholic Center Archdiocese of Atlanta—680 W. Peachtree St., N.W., Atlanta, 30308.

Catholic Information—Tel: 404-888-7801.

Archbishop's Office—Tel: 404-888-7804; Fax: 404-885-7494.

Vicar General—Rev. Msgr. EDWARD J. DILLON, J.C.D.

Chancellor—Rev. MARK W. LACEY. Tel: 404-888-7804. ANNO HARDAGE. Tel: 404-888-7804.

Secretariat for Finance & Administration—Tel: 404-888-7808. MICHAEL J. MCNAMARA, Sec. & Chief Financial Officer.

Secretariat for Education—Tel: 404-888-7833. BERTHA MARTIN, Sec. Education.

Continuing Education in Ministry—Rev. MARK W. LACEY. Tel: 404-888-7804.

Secretariat for Catholic Charities—Mr. CARROLL STERNE, Dir. Tel: 404-881-6571. See separate listing for detailed information.

Office for Black Catholic Ministry—Tel: 404-888-7843. HOWARD BROWN, Dept. Head (Secretariat Supvr. & Chancellor).

Office Of Communications—Tel: 404-888-7832; Fax: 404-888-7849. GRETCHEN KEISER, Dir. (Secretariat Supvr. & Chancellor).

"The Georgia Bulletin"—GRETCHEN KEISER, Editor.

Media Relations—Rev. Msgr. PETER A. DORA. Tel: 706-548-6332; Fax: 706-354-1783.

Metropolitan Tribunal—

Judicial Vicar—Rev. Msgr. LOUIS NAUGHTON, J.C.L., S.T.B., M.A.

Court Administrator—Deacon WHITNEY F. ROBICHAUX, B.S., M.A., M.P.S.

Auditor—Sr. FRANCES WHITMAN, G.N.S.H., M.A.

Archdiocesan Judges—Rev. STEPHEN T. CHURCHWELL, J.C.D., M.Div.; Rev. Msgr. EDWARD J. DILLON, J.C.D.; Rev. DAVID P. TALLEY, J.C.L., M.Div., B.A., M.S.W.

Defender of the Bond—Rt. Rev. DOM BERNARD M. JOHNSON, O.C.S.O., J.C.L.; Mr. ROBERT J. KAMPINE, J.C.L., S.T.B., B.A.; Mr. ROBERT G. WESSELMANN, J.C.L., S.T.L.

Notaries—Mrs. BERNICE H. EVERETT; Ms. ROBERTA I. SIEGWALD; Ms. JEAN M. SMITH.

Court of Appeals-Province of Atlanta—Tel: 404-888-7813; Fax: 404-885-7494.

Judicial Vicar—Very Rev. PAUL J. HACHEY, S.M., J.C.D.

Administrator—Sr. MARIE BREITENBECK, O.P., J.C.D.

Defenders of the Bond—Rev. Msgr. PETER A. DORA, M.Div.; Revs. JOHN R. HENLEY, M.Div.; DANIEL J. MCCORMICK, B.A.

Judges—Sr. MARIE BREITENBECK, O.P. J.C.D.; Revs. GREGORY D. GOOLSBY, M.Div.; ALBERT J. JOWDY, M.Div.; Rev. Msgr. R. DONALD KIERNAN, P.A., D.P.A.; Revs. JAMES A. MICELI, M.Div.; RICHARD B. MORROW, B.A.; Rev. Msgr. MICHAEL J. REGAN, J.C.D.; Revs. PAUL H. REYNOLDS; JAMES A. SCHILLINGER, S.T.L.

Notary—DOROTHY WESSELMANN, M.S.Ed.

Promoter of Justice—Rev. DANIEL J. MCCORMICK, B.A.

Office of Vocations—Rev. Msgr. DONALD A. KENNY, Dir. Tel: 770-422-5633.

Office for Permanent Diaconate—Deacons ALFRED MITCHELL, Dir. (Secretariat Supvr./Chancellor); LORIS SINANIAN, Dir. of Formation.

Office for Pro-Life—PEGGY SINANIAN, Dir. (Secretariat Supvr. & Chancellor).

Office of Family Concerns—Tel: 404-888-7819. MARY ELLEN HUGHES, Dir. (Secretariat Supvr./Catholic Charities).

Office of Hispanic Apostolate—Tel: 404-888-7839. Mr. GONZALO SALDANA, Dir. (Secretariat Supvr. & Chancellor).

Development Office—

Director—ANNO HARDAGE. Tel: 404-888-7804.

Director of the Archdiocesan Annual Appeal and Archdiocesan Stewardship—ANNO HARDAGE.

Archives—ANTHONY R. DEES. Tel: 404-888-7802.

Other Archdiocesan Offices

AACCW—DIEDRA HOLLER, *680 W. Peachtree St., N.W., Atlanta, 30308-1984.* Tel: 770-469-4123. Rev. PAUL W. BERNY, Spiritual Moderator. Tel: 404-885-7200.

Apostleship of Prayer—Rev. VINCENT R. MALATESTA, S.J., *Ignatius House, 6700 Riverside Dr., N.W., Atlanta, 30328.* Tel: 404-255-0503.

Girl and Boy Scouts—Deacon BRUCE C. PUBLICOVER, *P.O. Box 78, Woodstock, 30188.* Tel: 770-591-9200.

Cana Conferences—MARY ELLEN HUGHES, *680 W. Peachtree St., N.W., Atlanta, 30308.* Tel: 404-888-7819.

Consultors—Rev. Msgr. EDWARD J. DILLON,Very Rev. Deans and Vicar for Clergy, Presbyteral Council Pres. & Chancellor.

Cursillo—Sr. MARGARET MCANOY, I.H.M., Dir., *680 W. Peachtree St., N.W., Atlanta, 30308.* Tel: 404-885-7413.

Deans—Northeast Metro: Very Rev. JAMES J. FENNESSY, V.F., Northwest Metro: Very Rev. PAUL H. REYNOLDS, V.F., South Metro: Very Rev. FRANK J. GIUSTA, V.F., Northeast Rural: Very Rev. WALTER J. FOLEY, V.F., Northwest Rural: Very Rev. JOSEPH G. AQUINO, M.S., V.F., South Rural: Very Rev. LEO P. HERBERT, V.F.

Georgia Catholic Conference—CHEATHAM E. HODGES, JR., Exec. Sec., *Office Bldg., 3200 Deans Bridge Rd., Augusta, 30906.* Tel: 706-798-1719.

Campus Ministry—Rev. MARK W. LACEY, *680 W. Peachtree St., N.W., Atlanta, 30308.* Tel: 404-888-7804.

Council of Priests—Rev. Msgr. HENRY C. GRACZ, *P.O. Box 32, McDonough, 30253.*

Atlanta Conference of Sisters—Sr. MARY-BETH BERES, O.P., *P.O. Box 29548, Atlanta, 30359.* Tel: 404-325-3664.

Archdiocesan Councils, Boards, Commissions, and Committees

Councils—

Hispanic Pastoral Council—MARGARET PORTILLO-BELL, *134 Prince Ave., Athens, 30601.* Tel: 706-548-3897.

Boards—

Clergy Personnel Board—Most Rev. JOHN F. DONOHUE; Rev. Msgr. EDWARD J. DILLON, V.G.; Rev. Msgr. DONALD KIERNAN, P.A.; Rev. Msgr. DONALD A. KENNY; Revs. MARK W. LACEY, Dir. Personnel; PAUL REYNOLDS; STEWART WILBER.

Education—BERTHA MARTIN, Chm. & Sec. Education, *680 W. Peachtree St., N.W., Atlanta, 30308.* Tel: 404-888-7833.

Social Services—CARROLL P. STERNE, Sec. Catholic Charities, *680 W. Peachtree St., N.W., Atlanta, 30308.* Tel: 404-881-6571.

Clergy Retirement—Rev. Msgr. R. DONALD KIERNAN, P.A., *2443 Mt.Vernon Rd., Dunwoody, 30338.* Tel: 404-393-3255.

Commissions—

Liturgical—Rev. Msgr. LOUIS NAUGHTON, Sec., *680 W. Peachtree St., N.W., Atlanta, 30308.* Tel: 404-888-7815.

CLERGY, PARISHES, MISSIONS AND PAROCHIAL SCHOOLS

CITY OF ATLANTA
(Fulton County)

1—CATHEDRAL OF CHRIST THE KING (1936), Rev. Msgr. Thomas Kenny, Rector; Revs. Martin Ralph Kalu; Richard B. Morrow; Richard Young; James Harrison; Deacons Richard Narey; Whitney Robichaux. In res., Rev. Msgr. Louis Naughton.
Res., 2699 Peachtree Rd., N.E., 30305. Tel: 404-233-2145; Fax: 404-233-9711.
School—46 Peachtree Way, 30305. Tel: 404-233-0383; Fax: 404-266-0704. Mrs. Peggy Warner, Prin.
Lay Teachers 30; Students 505.
Catechesis/Religious Programs—Tel: 404-237-0564; Fax: 404-233-4984.
Students 447.

2—HOLY CROSS (1964), Revs. Paul Fogarty; Larry P. Niese; Alvaro D. Avendano; Peter Duc Vu; Deacons Frank Coughlin; Lou Hettel; Bill Jindrich; Sam Mure; Cece Reimer; Dick Suever; Tom Silvestri.
Res., 3175 Hathaway Ct., 30341. Tel: 770-939-3501; Fax: 770-723-7013.
Catechesis/Religious Programs—Tel: 770-934-5757.
Students 475.

3—HOLY SPIRIT (1964), Rev. Msgr. Edward J. Dillon, V.G.; Revs. Adam Z. Ozimek; Thomas Hennessy; Deacon Thomas Shuler.
Church & Res.: 4465 Northside Dr., N.W., 30327. Tel: 404-252-4513; Fax: 404-252-1162.
Catechesis/Religious Programs—Tel: 404-252-2764.
Students 416.

4—IMMACULATE HEART OF MARY (1958), Revs. Richard A. Kieran; James H. Sexstone; Carlos Carreras, S.J.; Jose D. Gonzalez-Florez; Deacons James Stewart; Arturo Jimenez; Thomas McGrane.
Res., 2855 Briarcliff Rd., N.E., 30329. Tel: 404-636-1418; Fax: 404-636-4394.
School—Tel: 404-636-4488; Fax: 404-636-1853. Mrs. Margo A. Wolke, Prin.
Lay Teachers 28; Students 480.
Catechesis/Religious Programs—Tel: 404-321-3175.
Students 285.
Mission—Doraville, Dekalb Co., Our Lady of the Americas, 5918 New Peachtree Rd., Doraville, 30340. Tel: 404-454-8437.

5—MOST BLESSED SACRAMENT (1960), Rev. Bruce W. Wilkinson.
Res., 1926 Austin Rd., S.W., 30331-4805. Tel: 404-349-0176; Fax: 404-349-0178.
Church—2971 Butner Rd. S.W., 30331.

6—OUR LADY OF THE ASSUMPTION (1951), Revs. Andrew McCormack, S.M.; Lawrence Schmuhl, S.M.; Eugene Hughes, S.M.; Deacons Douglas Anderson; Bill Bevacqua; Robert Gresher; Michael O'Brien; William Pond; John Shell.
Office: 1350 Hearst Dr., N.E., 30319. Tel: 404-261-7181; Fax: 404-364-1913.
Res., 1406 Hearst Dr., N.E., 30319. Tel: 404-261-1909.
School—1320 Hearst Dr., N.E., 30319. Tel: 404-364-1902; Fax: 404-364-1914. Mrs. Joan Tiernan, Prin.
Lay Teachers 28; Students 500.
Catechesis/Religious Programs—Tel: 404-364-1905; Fax: 404-364-1913.
Students 150.
Chapels—Marist School, Tel: 404-457-7201; Fax: 404-457-8402; St. Joseph's Hospital, Tel: 404-851-7001; Fax: 404-851-5901; Sisters of Mercy Convent at St. Joseph's Hospital, Tel: 404-255-6427.

7—OUR LADY OF LOURDES (1911), Rev. Frank Giusta. Pastoral Assocs.: Deacons Homer Woods; Thomas Zaworski.
Res., 25 Boulevard, N.E., 30312. Tel: 404-522-6776; Fax: 404-222-0202.
School—29 Boulevard, N.E., 30312. Tel: 404-581-0643.
Lay Teachers 15; Students 107.
Catechesis/Religious Programs—Students 122.

8—SACRED HEART OF JESUS (1890), Revs. Stephen T. Churchwell; Carlos Rocha-Sosa; Deacons Wayne D. Smith; Loris Sinanian. In res., Rev. Msgr. Walter J. Donovan, (Retired).
Res., 353 Peachtree St., N.E., 30308. Tel: 404-522-6800; Fax: 404-524-5440.

9—ST. ANTHONY OF PADUA, Rev. Hugh Marren; Deacon Joseph Barker. In res., Rev. John C.K. Fallon.
Res., 951 Ralph David Abernathy Blvd., S.W., 30310. Tel: 404-758-8861.
School—953 Ralph David Abernathy Blvd., S.W., 30310.
Sisters of St. Joseph of Carondelet 2; Lay Teachers 13; Students 130.
Child Care Center—.
Lay Teachers 10; Students 62.

10—ST. JUDE (1960), Rev. Msgr. Daniel J. O'Connor; Revs. Michael P. Hogan; Victor J. Reyes; William M. Hickey.
Res., 7171 Glenridge Dr. N.E., 30328. Tel: 770-394-3896; Fax: 770-399-7866.
School—Tel: 770-394-2880; Fax: 770-804-9248.
Lay Teachers 36; Students 508.
Catechesis/Religious Programs—Tel: 770-394-4588.
Students 396.

11—ST. PAUL OF THE CROSS (1954) (African American), Revs. Melvin Shorter, C.P.; Michael Greene, C.P.; Deacons Joseph P. Goolsby; Hilliard M. Lee, Jr.; Leon Allain; Benjamin Petty, (Retired). In res., Rev. Joseph A. Fahy, C.P.
Res., 551 Harwell Rd. N.W., 30318. Tel: 404-696-6704; Fax: 404-696-4735.
Catechesis/Religious Programs—Students 50.

12—SHRINE OF THE IMMACULATE CONCEPTION (1848), Revs. John S. Adamski; Alan M. Dillmann; Norberto Mateus (Columbia); T.J. Meehan; Deacon William Payne.
Res., 48 Martin Luther King, Jr. Dr., S.W., 30303-3599. Tel: 404-521-1866.
Mission—Atlanta, Fulton Co., San Felipe de Jesus Catholic Mission, 402 McDonough Blvd., S.E., 30315. Tel: 404-627-0821.

OUTSIDE CITY OF ATLANTA

Alpharetta, Fulton Co., St. Thomas Aquinas (1972), Revs. Albert W. Jowdy; John R. Anderson; Daniel Toof; Deacons William W. Keeling; Edmund LaHouse; Donald N. Nadeau; John Strachan.
Res., 535 Rucker Rd., 30201. Tel: 770-475-4501; Fax: 770-772-0355.
Catechesis/Religious Programs—Tel: 770-475-4508.
Students 1,675.

Athens, Clarke Co., St. Joseph's (1873), Rev. Msgr. Peter A. Dora; Rev. Joseph Chaloux; Deacons Don Marchildon; Bill Lakin; Jim Gaudin.
Res., 134 Prince Ave., 30610. Tel: 706-548-6332; Fax: 706-354-1783.
School—Tel: 706-543-1621. Sr. Teresa Ballisty, I.H.M., Prin.
Servants of the Immaculate Heart of Mary 3; Missionary Sisters of the Sacred Heart 1; Lay Teachers 21; Students 362.
Catechesis/Religious Programs—Tel: 706-548-5487.
Students 359.
Chapels—St. Mary's Hospital, Tel: 706-548-7581; Catholic Student Center, Tel: 706-543-2293; University of Georgia.

Blairsville, Union Co., St. Francis of Assisi (1966), Rev. Ronald G. Fuchs, Jr.; Sr. Rosemary Wickham, O.S.F., Pastoral Assoc.; Deacons Robert O'Neill; Lawrence Casey.
Res., 2839 Young Harris Hwy., 30512. Tel: 706-745-6400; Fax: 706-745-1468.
Catechesis/Religious Programs—Students 93.
Mission—Cleveland, Union Co., St. Paul the Apostle, 1397 Helen Hwy., Cleveland, 30528. Tel: 706-865-4474; Fax: 706-219-3009. Deacon Daniel Bradach.

Blue Ridge, Fannin Co., St. Anthony's (1976), Rev. Brendan Doyle.
Res., P.O. Box 1448, 30513. Tel: 706-632-5970; Fax: 706-632-2120.
Mission—Ellijay, Good Samaritan Mission, (1982).

Buford, Gwinnett Co., Prince of Peace (1975), Rev. James P. Adams; Deacon Michael R. Jones.
Mailing Address: P.O. Box 591, 30518-0591. Tel: 404-945-2244 (Office); 945-0200 (Rectory); Fax: 770-945-4599.
Res., 4300 S. Lee St., 30518-0591. Tel: 770-945-0200.
Catechesis/Religious Programs—Tel: 770-945-2244.
Students 550.

Calhoun, Gordon Co., St. Clements (1958), Rev. Leo B. Cummings, M.S.
Mailing Address: P.O. Box 1301, 30703-1301.
Res., 102 Greenbriar Cir., 30703. Tel: 706-625-0375; Fax: 706-625-5219.

Canton, Cherokee Co., St. Michael the Archangel, Rev. Cornelius Fitzgerald.
Res., 115 Jay Ln., 30115. Tel: 770-345-0183.
Our Lady of LaSalette (1984), Revs. Neil G. Jones, M.S.; Denis Kolumber, M.S.
Res., 2942 Sam Nelson Rd., P.O. Box 1146, 30114. Tel: 770-479-8923; Fax: 770-479-8923.
Catechesis/Religious Programs—Students 172.
Mission—Jasper, Pickens Co., Our Lady of the Mountains, P.O. Box 248, Jasper, 30143. Tel: 706-692-3078.

Carrollton, Carroll Co., Church of Our Lady of Perpetual Help (1962), Rev. Msgr. Michael J. Regan, (Retired); Rev. John P. Farrelly; Deacon David Higgins.
Res., 210 Old Center Point Rd., 30117. Tel: 770-832-8977; Fax: 770-832-1666. [CEM]
Newman Center West Georgia College—Rev. Msgr. Michael J. Regan, J.C.D., Catholic Campus Min.
Catechesis/Religious Programs—Students 200.

Cartersville, Bartow Co., St. Francis of Assisi (1969), Rev. Joseph G. Aquino, M.S.; Bro. Robert Russell, M.S.
850 Douthit Ferry Rd., P.O. Box 2048, 30120. Tel:

770-382-4549.
Res., 57 Pine Grove Rd., 30120.
Catechesis/Religious Programs—Students 172.

Cedartown, Polk Co., St. Bernadette's (1941), Rev. Patrick J. Kingery.
Res., 101 S. College St., 30125. Tel: 770-748-1517; Fax: 770-748-1568.
Catechesis/Religious Programs—Students 55.

Clarkesville, Habersham Co., St. Mark's (1964), Rev. Luis Zarama; Deacon John F. Thompson.
Res., Rte. 4, Box 4822, 30523. Tel: 706-754-4518.
Church—Rte. 5, Box 5058, 30523-9542. Tel: 706-754-6504.
Mission—Clayton, Rabun Co., St. Helena's, Box 534, Clayton, 30525. Tel: 706-782-5152. Deacon M. Robert Mulligan.
Station—Lee Arrendale Correctional Institute, Alto, Tel: 706-776-4700.

Conyers, Rockdale Co., St. Pius X Catholic (1974), Revs. John C. Kieran; Charles J. Kerscher, (Retired); Paul D. Williams, Jr.
Res., 2621 Hwy. 20, S.E., 30208. Tel: 770-483-3660; Fax: 770-483-7006.
Catechesis/Religious Programs—Tel: 770-929-1017.
Students 797.

Covington, Newton Co., St. Augustine Church (1959), Rev. Michael J. Redden; Deacon Herbert C. Berding.
Res., 11524 Hwy. 278 E., 30209. Tel: 404-787-0685; Fax: 404-787-0871.
Catechesis/Religious Programs—Students 62.
Mission—Madison, Morgan Co., St. James, 562 Vine St., Madison, 30650. Tel: 706-342-9661.

Cumming, Forsyth Co., Good Shepherd (1975), Rev. Peter J. Rau.
Church—3740 Holtzclaw Rd., 30131. Tel: 770-887-9861; Fax: 770-887-9861.
Catechesis/Religious Programs—Tel: 770-781-5378.
Students 344.

Dahlonega, Lumpkin Co., St. Luke Catholic (1960), Rev. Edward A. Danneker.
Catholic Center—75 Park St. N., 30533. Tel: 706-864-4779; Fax: 706-864-2568.
Res., 215 N. Park St., 30533.
Catechesis/Religious Programs—Students 68.
Mission—Dawsonville, Dawson Co., Christ Redeemer, P.O. Box 506, Dawsonville, 30534. Tel: 706-265-1361.
Station—Dahlonega, North Georgia College (Newman Club).

Dalton, Whitfield Co., St. Joseph's (1941), Rev. Daniel Stack; Sr. Santa Basilio, M.A.G.; Sr. Delfina Maravilla, M.A.G.
Res., 623 S. Thornton Ave., 30720. Tel: 706-278-3107; Fax: 706-278-6902.
Catechesis/Religious Programs—Students 425.

Decatur, DeKalb Co., Sts. Peter and Paul (1959), Rev. Richard P. Wise; Deacons Jerry Lett; Alfred Mitchell; J. Eugene Whitmeyer.
Res., 2372 Collier Dr., 30032. Tel: 404-241-5862; Fax: 404-241-5839.
School—2560 Tilson Rd., 30032. Tel: 404-241-3063; Fax: 404-241-4382. Sr. Mary Jane McDonnell, I.H.M., Prin.
Sister Servants of the Immaculate Heart of Mary 3; Lay Teachers 12; Students 163.
Catechesis/Religious Programs—Sr. Carol Tenerovich, C.D.P., D.R.E.
Students 181.

St. Thomas More (1949), Revs. Patrick F. Mulhern; Balappa Selvaraj; Ms. Ann Dugan, Pastoral Assoc. In res., Rev. Joseph Peacock, (Retired).
Res., 624 W. Ponce de Leon Ave., 30030. Tel: 404-378-4588; Fax: 404-378-0506.
School—Tel: 404-373-8456; Fax: 404-377-8554. Dr. Thomas Collins, Prin.
Sisters Notre Dame de Namur 3; Lay Teachers 25; Students 468.
Catechesis/Religious Programs—Students 196.
Convent—636 W. Ponce de Leon Ave., 30030. Tel: 404-378-6119.

Douglasville, Douglas Co., St. Theresa (1985), Rev. Stewart A. Wilber.
Res., 3194 S. Elizabeth Dr., 30135.
Church—4401 Prestley Mill Rd., 30135. Tel: 770-489-7115; Fax: 770-489-4873.
Catechesis/Religious Programs—Tel: 770-942-9765.
Students 300.

Duluth, Fulton, St. Benedict (1987), Rev. Msgr. Terry W. Young; Revs. Gregory D. Goolsby; Daniel J. Fleming; Deacons John Stroop; William Monahan; Walker P. King; William Lange.
Office: 11045 Parsons Rd., 30155. Tel: 770-442-5903; Fax: 770-442-0744.
Res., 11230 Surrey Park Tr., 30155. Tel: 770-664-5099.
Catechesis/Religious Programs—Students 1,784.
Mission—Duluth, Gwinnett Co., St. Monica, 1925 Peach Bluff Dr., 30155. Tel: 770-495-9201; Fax: 770-495-9216. In res., Rev. Gregory D. Goolsby.

Dunwoody, DeKalb Co., All Saints Catholic (1977), Rev. Msgr. R. Donald Kiernan, P.A.; Revs. Daniel J. McCormick; David M. Dye; W. Joseph Corbett; Deacon Raymond F. Egan.
Res., 2443 Mount Vernon Rd., 30338-3099. Tel: 770-393-3255; Fax: 770-913-0140.
Catechesis/Religious Programs—Students 703.
Mission—Norcross, Gwinnett Co., Mary, Our Queen, 5875 Peachtree Industrial Blvd., Ste. 260, Norcross, 30092. Tel: 770-416-0002; Fax: 770-416-1846.

Eatonton, Putnam Co., Christ Our Savior Mission (1993). (Independent).
Res., 307 S. Walnut St., Greensboro, 30642. Tel: 706-453-7292; 485-0102 (Eatonton); Fax: 706-453-7095. Rev. Serge E. Ward.

Fairburn, Fulton Co., St. Matthew's (1979), Rev. Leo C. Holleran, M.S.
Res., 104 W. Campbellton St., P.O. Box 158, 30213. Tel: 770-964-5804; Fax: 770-964-1228.
Catechesis/Religious Programs—Students 174.

Fayetteville, Fayette Co., St. Gabriel (1993), Rev. Paul W. Berny; Deacons Al C. McHugh; I. Carl McBride; T.C. Meuninck.
Office: 135 Antioch Rd., 30215-5702. Tel: 770-461-0492; Fax: 770-461-0374.
Catechesis/Religious Programs—Tel: 770-461-0493.
Students 302.

Fort Oglethorpe, Catoosa Co., St. Gerard's (1947), Rev. Timothy M. Hepburn.
Res., 415 LaFayette Rd., P.O. Box 2217, 30742. Tel: 706-861-9410; Fax: 706-866-0574.
Catechesis/Religious Programs—Students 64.

Gainesville, Hall Co., St. Michael's (1945), Revs. William G. Hoffman; Jorge Christancho; Deacons Felix Cosme; Michael Kennedy.
Office: 1440 Pearce Cir., 30501. Tel: 770-534-3338; 536-1603 (Rectory); Fax: 770-535-2440.
Catechesis/Religious Programs—Students 368.

Greensboro, Greene Co., Christ Our King Parish (1992). (Independent). Rev. Serge E. Ward.
Res., 307 S. Walnut St., 30642. Tel: 706-453-7292; Fax: 706-453-7095.
Mission—Eatonton, Christ Our Savior.

Griffin, Spalding Co., Sacred Heart (1941), Revs. John L. Smyth, C.SS.R.; James E. McGonagle, C.SS.R.; Thomas Burke, C.SS.R.; Deacons James Hedderman, (Retired); Felix Marrero; Stanley T. Prawdzik. In res., Rev. Jerome Chavarriq, C.SS.R.
Res., 1323 MacArthur Dr., 30223. Tel: 770-227-2378; Fax: 770-227-6440.
Catechesis/Religious Programs—Tel: 770-227-2898.
Students 163.
Missions—Thomaston, Upson Co., St. John the Baptist, P.O. Box 897, Thomaston, 30286. Tel: 706-647-9993; Barnesville, Lamar Co., St. Ann, Hwy. 341, Barnesville, 30204. Tel: 706-358-0635.
Chapel—Redemptorist Fathers Residence, Tel: 404-227-0541.
Station—Forsyth.

Hapeville, Fulton Co., St. John the Evangelist (1950), Rev. Vincent J. Douglass, C.Ss.R.; Deacons Richard Beckman; Henry Akers; Michael K. Mobley. In res., Rev. Msgr. Francis Pham Van Phuong (Vietnam).
Mailing Address: 230 Arnold St., 30354-1530. Tel: 404-768-5647 (Church); Fax: 404-767-6416.
School—Tel: 404-767-4312; Fax: 404-767-0359.
Lay Teachers 16; Students 269.
Catechesis/Religious Programs—Tel: 404-767-5877. Mrs. Barbara Nichols, D.R.E.
Students 155.
Mission—Forest Park, Fulton Co., Our Lady of Vietnam, 4265 Thurman Rd., Forest Park, 30050. Tel: 404-361-3741. Rev. Msgr. Francis Pham Van Phuong, Admin.

Hartwell, Hart Co., Sacred Heart of Jesus (1977), Rev. Walter W. Foley.
Res., 1009 Benson St., 30643. Tel: 404-376-4112; Fax: 404-376-1695.
Catechesis/Religious Programs—Students 85.

Jonesboro, Clayton Co., St. Philip Benizi (1965), Revs. Gregory J. Hartmayer, O.F.M.Conv.; Edwin Mendez; John A. Koziol, O.F.M.Conv.; Deacons Matias A. Casal; Joseph C. Anzalone; William F. McCarthy.
Res., 591 Flint River Rd., 30236-3452. Tel: 770-478-0178; Fax: 770-471-2079.
Catechesis/Religious Programs—Tel: 770-471-2881. Mary M. Mauldin, D.R.E.
Students 750.

Kennesaw, Cobb Co., St. Catherine of Siena (1981), Revs. Terence Kane; Greg Benassu; Deacons Pat O'Connor; David Rauth; Martin Lampe.
Res., 1620 Overlook Ct., 30144. Tel: 770-419-9112.
Church—1618 Ben King Rd., N.W., 30144. Tel: 770-428-7139; Fax: 770-428-0131.
Catechesis/Religious Programs—Tel: 770-428-7440. D.R.E.: Rita Bek; Catherine Hackney; Lisa Bohn; Maureen Ingalls.
Students 1,280.

LaGrange, Troup Co., St. Peter's (1936), Rev. John M. Murphy.
Res., 200 LaFayette Pkwy., 30241. Tel: 706-884-0445 (Rectory); 884-4224 (Church); Fax: 706-884-1624.
Catechesis/Religious Programs—Students 180.
Mission—Warm Springs, Meriwether Co., St. Elizabeth Seton, P.O. Box 638, Warm Springs, 31830. Tel: 706-846-5223.

Lawrenceville, Gwinnett Co., St. Lawrence (1971), Revs. Anthony T. Curran; Christopher Williamson; Deacons Richard Johnson; Walter T. Bedard, Sr.
Res., 319 Grayson Hwy., 30245. Tel: 770-963-8992; Fax: 770-963-1710.
Catechesis/Religious Programs—Tel: 770-962-2765. Matthew Robaszkiewicz, D.R.E.
Students 930.

St. Marguerite D'Youville (1995), Rev. Donald R. Caron.
Res., Hwy. 29 at Huff Rd., P.O. Box 464335, 30246. Tel: 770-513-4109; Fax: 770-513-1731.
Catechesis/Religious Programs—Students 400.

Lilburn, Gwinnett Co., St. John Neumann (1977), Revs. James J. Fennessy; Michael J. Campbell; Patrick H. Donaghey; Craig David; Deacons Rafael Cintron; Evelio Garcia; Jim O'Brien; Gary Womack; Larry French.
Res., 801 Tom Smith Rd., 30247. Tel: 770-923-6633; 923-6909; Fax: 770-381-7856.
School—(Grades K-8). (Regional). Tel: 404-381-0557; Fax: 404-381-0276. Sr. Mary Margaret O'Hara, G.N.S.H., Prin.
Sisters 1; Lay Teachers 35; Students 575.
Catechesis/Religious Programs—Students 1,404.
Mission—Lilburn, Gwinnet Co., St. Stephen the Martyr, 30247. Tel: 770-925-2736.

Lithia Springs, Douglas Co., St. John Vianney (1958), Revs. David Stachurski, O.F.M.Conv.; Carl Zdancewicz, O.F.M.Conv.; Deacon William Lyday. In res., Rev. Linus DeSantis, O.F.M.Conv.
Mailing Address: 1920 Skyview Dr., 30057. Tel: 770-941-2807; Fax: 770-941-5821.
Catechesis/Religious Programs—Students 299.
Mission—Dallas, Paulding Co., St. Vincent de Paul, 680 W. Memorial Dr., Dallas, 30132.

Lithonia, DeKalb Co., Christ Our Hope (1984), Rev. Austin Fogarty.
Res., 1786 Wellborn Rd., 30058. Tel: 770-482-5017; Fax: 770-482-9476.
Catechesis/Religious Programs—Tel: 770-482-5894.
Students 120.

Lookout Mountain, Walker Co., Our Lady of the Mount (1947), Rev. Francis X. Richardson.
Res., 1227 Scenic Hwy., P.O. Box 214, 30750. Tel: 706-820-0680; Fax: 706-820-2797. [JC]
Catechesis/Religious Programs—Students 97.

McDonough, Henry Co., St. James The Apostle (1979), Rev. Msgr. Henry C. Gracz; Rev. John T. Howren; Deacons Robert Rich; Robert Readdy.
Res., Georgia Hwy. 155, P.O. Box 32, 30253. Tel: 770-957-5441; Fax: 770-957-0383.
Catechesis/Religious Programs—Tel: 770-957-2990.
Students 435.
Mission—Jackson, Butts Co., St. Mary's, P.O. Box 901, Jackson, 30233. Tel: 770-775-4162; Fax: 770-775-4162.

Marietta, Cobb Co.,

1—HOLY FAMILY, (1973), Revs. Edward Thein; Timothy A. Gadziala; Juan de la Cruz; Deacons Paul Dietz; Al Gallagher.
Res., 3401 Lower Roswell Rd., 30068. Tel: 770-973-0038; Fax: 770-578-0475.
Catechesis/Religious Programs—Tel: 770-973-7400. Theresa Johnson, D.R.E.
Students 685.

2—CHURCH OF ST. ANN, (1978), Revs. Robert Susann, M.S.; Ron Gagne, M.S.; Joseph Nolan, M.S.; James P. Hurley, M.S.; Deacons Edmund Grabowy; J. Nicholas Morning.

Res., 4905 Roswell Rd., N.E., 30062. Tel: 770-998-1373; Fax: 770-993-3022.
Catechesis/Religious Programs—Tel: 770-998-0444.
Students 2,300.

3—St. Joseph, (1952), Rev. Msgr. Donald A. Kenny; Revs. Paul A. Burke; William M. Williams; Deacons Thomas Shaver; Michael Esper.
Res., 87 Lacy St., N.W., 30060. Tel: 770-422-5633; Fax: 770-422-1148.
School—Tel: 770-428-3328; Fax: 770-424-2960. Sr. Patricia Baber, R.S.M., Prin.
Lay Teachers 24; Students 489.
Catechesis/Religious Programs—Tel: 770-428-1833. Linda Hughey, D.R.E.
Students 780.

4—Church of the Transfiguration, (1977), Revs. Patrick A. Bishop; Joseph E. Morris; Sr. Barbara Baker, M.H.S.H., Pastoral Assoc.; Deacon Bruce Publicover.
Res., 1815 Blackwell Rd., N.E., 30066-2911. Tel: 770-977-1442; Fax: 770-578-1415.
Catechesis/Religious Programs—Tel: 770-973-8600; Fax: 770-973-1270. Rick Fehrenbach, D.R.E.
Students 1,136.

Milledgeville, Baldwin Co., Sacred Heart of Jesus (1850), Rev. Michael L. McWhorter.
Res., 110 N. Jefferson St., P.O. Box 754, 31061. Tel: 912-452-2421.
Chapel—Milledgeville, Central State Hospital.

Monroe, Walton Co., St. Anna's (1951), Rev. John R. Henley; Deacon Jerry F. Connell.
Res., 836 E. Spring St., 30655. Tel: 770-267-7637. [JC]
Catechesis/Religious Programs—Students 84.

Newnan, Coweta Co., St. George's (1952), Rev. Leo P. Herbert; Deacons Ben Gross; John Myers.
Res., 771 Roscoe Rd., 30263. Tel: 770-253-0512; Fax: 770-251-2053. [JC]
Catechesis/Religious Programs—Tel: 770-254-9933.
Students 357.

Norcross, Gwinnett Co., Saint Patrick's (1968), Revs. Martin J. Kopchik, M.S.F.S.; Joseph Mendes, M.S.F.S.; Joseph Mullakkara, M.S.F.S.; Deacons Jose Narvaez; Rigoberto Santiago; Bob Tipton.
Res., 2140 Beaver Ruin Rd., 30071. Tel: 770-446-2041.
Church—Beaver Ruin Rd., 30071. Tel: 770-448-2028; Fax: 770-448-7046.
Catechesis/Religious Programs—Tel: 770-448-6386.
Students 511.

Peachtree City, Fayette Co., Holy Trinity Catholic (1972), Revs. Francis G. McNamee; John P. Walsh; Deacons Don Kelsey; Anthony F. Cuomo.
Res., 101 Walt Banks Rd., P.O. Box 2121, 30269. Tel: 770-487-7672; Fax: 770-486-9152.
Catechesis/Religious Programs—Tel: 770-487-0175. Mary Ann Cox, D.R.E.
Students 1,150.

Rome, Floyd Co., St. Mary's (1930), Rev. James A. Miceli; Deacon Ronald A. Comeau.
Res., 911 N. Broad St., 30161. Tel: 706-295-7014.
School—401 E. 7th St., 30161. Tel: 404-234-4953. Ms. Susan Odle, Prin.
Lay Teachers 16; Students 183.
Catechesis/Religious Programs—Students 214.

Roswell, Fulton Co., St. Andrew (1981), Revs. Paul H. Reynolds; William Keen; Robert Smith; John C. Druding.
Res., 115 River Lake Ct., 30075. Tel: 404-552-0485; Fax: 404-641-8564 (Office).
Catechesis/Religious Programs—Tel: 404-641-0261.
Students 970.

Smyrna, Cobb Co., St. Thomas the Apostle (1966), Revs. James Caffery, M.S.; Daniel Bradley, M.S.
Res., 4300 King Springs Rd., 30082. Tel: 770-432-8579; Fax: 770-432-8570.
Catechesis/Religious Programs—Tel: 770-432-5296.
Students 384.

Snellville, Gwinnett Co., St. Oliver Plunkett (1978), Revs. Thomas J. Carroll, M.S.; Michael J. Flanagan, M.S.; Clifford Hasler, M.S.; Deacon Michael Cappoza.
Res., 1318 Summit Chase Dr., 30278. Tel: 770-979-0318; Fax: 770-985-6590.
Church—3200 Brooks Dr., 30278. Tel: 770-979-2500; Fax: 770-985-6590.
Catechesis/Religious Programs—Tel: 770-978-6751.
Students 1,005.
Mission—Winder, Barrow Co., St. Matthew, c/o St. Oliver Plunkett, 30278.

Stone Mountain, DeKalb Co., Corpus Christi (1971), Revs. Gregory D. Kenny, C.M.F.; Ronald Stua, C.M.F.; Severino Lopez, C.M.F.; Deacon Will MacDonald.
Res., 600 Mountain View Dr., 30083. Tel: 770-469-0395; Fax: 770-469-6822. [JC]
Catechesis/Religious Programs—Tel: 770-469-0597.
Students 417.

Thomson, McDuffie Co., Queen of Angels (1955), Rev. Edward O'Connor.
Res., 1326 Washington Rd., 30824. Tel: 706-595-2913.
Catechesis/Religious Programs—Students 70.

Toccoa, Stephens Co., St. Mary's (1956), Rev. Paul A. Flood (Ireland).
Res., 6388 Rothell Rd. Ext., 30577. Tel: 706-886-2819. [JC]
Catechesis/Religious Programs—Students 57.
Mission—Commerce, Jackson Co., St. Catherine Laboure, 708 State St., Commerce, 30529. Tel: 706-335-2622.

Washington, Wilkes Co., St. Joseph's (1840), Rev. G. Philip Ryan.
Res., P.O. Box 632, U.S. Hwy. 78, 30673. Tel: 706-678-2110; Fax: 706-678-3353. [CEM]
Missions—Elberton, Elbert Co., St. Mary's, Forest Ave., Elberton, 30635.; Sharon, Talifero Co., Purification.

Chaplains of Public Institutions

Atlanta. *Atlanta Veterans Administration Hospital*. Rev. Thad B. Rudd, Chap.
Dobbins Air Force Base. Vacant. 94 AW/HC, 1311 Patrol Rd., Dobbins Air Force Base, 30069-5003. Tel: 404-919-4955; 4956.
Fort McPherson. Office of the Garrison Chaplain, Vacant. Bldg. 51, Fort McPherson, 30330-5000. Tel: 404-752-2616. Office of the FORSCOM Chap., 6 W. Staff Row, 30310. Tel: 404-755-1487. Rev. Kenneth A. Seifried.
U.S. Penitentiary 601 McDonough Blvd., S.E., 30315. Rev. John C.K. Fallon.

Special or Other (Arch)Diocesan Assignment:
Reverend Monsignors—
Kenny, Donald A., Vocations Dir.

On Duty Outside the Archdiocese:
Reverend Fathers—
Atkins, James P., Monastery of Our Savior, 711 North St., Steubenville, OH 43952
Kinast, Robert L., P.O. Box 86035, Maderia Beach, FL 33738-6035
McBrearity, Gerald D., Society of St. Sulpice, 5408 Roland Ave., Baltimore, MD 21210
Patterson, David L., Diocese of Savannah, GA
Sanches, Joseph A., Diocese of Nashville, TN
Scherer, James F., Diocese of Charlotte, NC
Talley, David P., Pontifical, North American College, Rome, Italy
Woods, Michael A., Diocese of Knoxville, TN

Military Chaplains:
Reverend Fathers—
McCormick, Patrick J., PSC 816, FPO AE 09612

Retired:
Reverend Monsignors—
Regan, Michael J.
Reverend Fathers—
Calhoun, William
Donovan, Walter J., Sacred Heart Church, 353 Peachtree St., Atlanta, GA 30308
O'Shea, John J., Cathedral of Christ the King, Atlanta
Peacock, Joseph
Ware, Joseph F., St. Francis Cabrini, 11500 Middleground Rd., Savannah, GA 31419

Permanent Deacons:
Akers, Henry
Allain, Leon G.
Anderson, Douglas J.
Angelich, George D.
Anzalone, Joseph C.
Anzalone, Joseph S.
Appel, Charles M.
Barker, Joseph J.
Bathea, Val
Beckman, Richard F.
Bedard, Walter T.
Berding, Herbert C.
Bevacqua, Bill J.
Bradach, Daniel D.
Briesch, Forrest R.
Capozza, Michael A.
Casal, Matias A.
Cintron, Rafael
Comeau, Ronald A.
Connell, Jerry F.
Coughlin, Frank F.
Cuomo, Anthony F.
DeSandre, Bart R.
Dietz, Paul E.
Easterwood, James M.
Egan, Raymond F.
French, Lawrence E.
Gallagher, Alexander S.
Galvis, Enrique L.
Garcia-Carreras, Evelio
Gaudin, James M., Jr.
Goolsby, Joseph B.
Gourgues, Harold W., Jr.
Grabowy, Edmund M.
Gresher, Robert C.
Gross, Benedict
Hedderman, James J., Sr., (Retired)
Henrich, Robert A.
Hettel, Louis A.
Higgins, David J.
Jansen, John C.
Jimenez, Arthuo P.
Jindrich, William L.
Johnson, Richard M.
Jones, Michael R.
Keeling, William W.
Keen, William
Kelsey, Donald A.
King, Walker P.
Kirksey, Timothy K.
Korte, Jerry R.
La House, Edmund J.
Lakin, William P.
Lampe, Martin J.
Lange, William G.
Lee, Hilliard M., Jr.
Lett, Jerry M.
Leverett, Winston A., (Retired)
Lyday, Kevin W., Inactive
Lyday, William E.
Mac Donald, Will
Mackin, Thomas F.
Marchildon, Donald W.
Marrero, Felix
Martorell, Gerardo G.
Mc Carthy, Kevin J.
Mc Grane, Thomas J.
Mc Hugh, Al C.
McCarthy, William F.
Meuninck, Tilton C.
Miller, Paul M., (Retired)
Mitchell, Alfred
Mobley, Michael K.
Moenk, Jean R., (Retired)
Morning, J. Nicholas
Mulligan, M. Robert
Mure, Samuel M.
Nadeau, Donald N.
Narey, Richard D.
Narvaez, Jose A.
O'Brien, James M.
O'Brien, Michael J.
O'Connor, D. Patrick
Payne, William E., Jr.
Petty, Benjamin R., (Retired)
Pond, Billy
Prawdzik, Stanley T.
Publicover, Bruce C.
Rauth, David W.
Readdy, Robert G.
Reimer, Cecil R.
Rich, Robert M.
Robichaux, Whitney F., Jr.
Rusmisel, William O.
Sambrone, Fred J., Jr.
Shaver, Thomas R.
Shell, John B.
Shoemaker, John W.
Shuler, Thomas B.
Silvestri, Thomas D.
Sinanian, Loris R.
Smith, Robert B.
Smith, Wayne D.
Stagg, James A.
Stewart, James M.
Stives, Edward C.
Stone, James E.
Strachan, John S.
Stroop, John
Suever, Richard M.
Thompson, John F.
Timme, William G., (Retired)
Tolcher, Richard P.
Weeks, Jim G.
Whitmeyer, J. Eugene
Womack, Gary D.
Woods, Homer, Sr.
Zaworski, Thomas E.

INSTITUTIONS LOCATED IN THE ARCHDIOCESE

[A] SEMINARIES, RELIGIOUS OR SCHOLASTICATES

ATLANTA. *Aquinas Center of Theology at Emory University*, 1703 Clifton Rd., F-5, 30329. Tel: 404-727-8860; Fax: 404-727-8862. Dr. P. Lyndon Reynolds, Dir.

[B] HIGH SCHOOLS, ARCHDIOCESAN

ATLANTA. *St. Pius X Catholic High School*. (Coed), 2674 Johnson Rd., N.E., 30345. Tel: 404-636-3023. Mr. Donald T. Sasso. Priests 2; Sisters 1; Lay Teachers 75; Students 1,010.

[C] HIGH SCHOOLS, PRIVATE

ATLANTA. *Marist School*. (Grades 7-12), 3790 Ashford-Dunwoody, N.E., 30319-1899. Tel: 770-457-7201; 451-1316 (Res.); Fax: 770-457-8402. A Private Catholic School. College Preparatory Day School conducted by The Marists. Corporate Title: Marist School, Inc. Mr. Michael F. Maher, Headmaster; Revs. Francis J. Kissel, S.M., Dir. Admissions; Ralph F. Olek, S.M., Supr.; James L. Hartnett, S.M., Pres.; Ronald J. Nikodem, S.M., Campus Pastor; Bro. Timothy McCoy, S.M. In res., Revs. Thomas Gilroy, S.M., (Retired); James M. Cummings, S.M., (Retired); Paul J. Hachey, S.M., Metropolitan Tribunal; Thomas D. O'Donnell, S.M., (Retired); Charles Pfab, S.M., (Retired). Priests 10; Lay Faculty 95; Students 1,025.

[D] ELEMENTARY SCHOOLS, PRIVATE

ATLANTA. *Archbishop Thomas A. Donnellan School*, 4820 Long Island Dr., 30342-2570. Tel: 404-255-0900; Fax: 404-255-0914. Sr. Dawn Gear, G.N.S.H., Prin. Lay Teachers 11; Students 86.

[E] RESIDENTIAL TREATMENT CENTER AND DAY SCHOOL

ATLANTA. *Village of St. Joseph*. (Children & Adolescents, Ages 11-16), 2969 Butner Rd., S.W., 30331. Tel: 404-349-2400. Charles L. Bright, M.A.Ed. Lay Teachers 5; Students 48.

[F] CATHOLIC SOCIAL SERVICES

Departmental Agencies

ATLANTA. *Catholic Social Services, Inc.*, 680 W. Peachtree St., N.W., 30308-1984. Tel: 404-881-6571. Pam Buckmaster, Exec. Dir.; Walt Denero, CSS Chm. Bd.

Counseling Services, Crisis Pregnancy & Adoption, Immigration Services, Multicultural Services & Parish Social Ministry. Branch Offices outside the city of Atlanta.

Rural Social Services, 1480 Bettis Tribble Gap Rd., P.O. Box 507, Cumming, 30130. Tel: 404-887-1098. Dolores Mitchell, Prog. Dir.

CCS Athens, 134 Prince Ave., 30601. Tel: 706-548-9421. Margaret Portillo Bell, Prog. Dir.

Village of St. Joseph, Inc., 2969 Butner Rd. S.W., 30331. Tel: 404-349-2400. Charles I. Bright, M.A.Ed., Dir. Residential Child Care for Emotionally Disturbed Children.

Catholic Personal Care Homes, Inc., 3409 Washington Rd., S.W., 30344. Tel: 404-669-0143. Sr. Helen Mick, Dir., Marian Manor, 2801 Briarcliff Rd. N.E., 30329. Tel: 404-982-0606. St. Thomas Manor, 3409 Washington Rd. S.W., 30329. Tel: 404-669-0143. St. Teresa Manor, 227 Medical Way, 30329. Tel: 404-996-8707.

Catholic Housing Initiatives, Inc., 680 W. Peachtree St. N.W., 30308-1984. Tel: 404-881-6571. Mary Lou Scruggs, Asst. Dir.

Catholic Retirement Facilities, Inc. Carroll Sterne, Pres. Total Assisted 37,578; Total Staff 221.

[G] GENERAL HOSPITALS

ATLANTA. *Saint Joseph's Hospital of Atlanta, Inc.*, 5665 Peachtree Dunwoody Rd., N.E., 30342. Tel: 404-851-7001.

For a complete listing, refer to the Hospitals section.

ATHENS. *St. Mary's Hospital*, 1230 Baxter St., 30606-3791. Tel: 706-354-3033; Fax: 706-354-3197.

For a complete listing, refer to the Hospitals section.

[H] SPECIAL HOSPITALS

ATLANTA. *Our Lady of Perpetual Help Home*, 760 Washington St. S.W., 30315. Tel: 404-688-9515.

For a complete listing, refer to the Special Care Facilities section.

Saint Joseph's Mercy Care Services, 60 Eleventh St., 30309-3970. Tel: 404-249-8600.

For a complete listing, refer to the Special Care Facilities section.

[I] MONASTERIES AND RESIDENCES OF PRIESTS

CONYERS. *The Monastery of the Holy Spirit*, 2625 Hwy. 212 S.W., 30208. Tel: 770-483-8705; Fax: 770-760-0989. Rt. Revs. Dom Bernard Johnson, O.C.S.O.; Augustine J. Moore, O.C.S.O., Retired Abbot; Bro. Mark Dohle, O.C.S.O., Prior; Revs. Methodius Telnack, O.C.S.O., Procurator; Clarence J. Biggers, O.C.S.O.; Edmund H. Brand, O.C.S.O.; Malachy Corley, O.C.S.O.; Cyprian E. Carew, O.C.S.O.; Philip R. Dehner, O.C.S.O.; Anthony Delisi, O.C.S.O., Prior; Richard Donarski, O.C.S.O.; Alberic Farbolin, O.C.S.O., Deacon & Novice Master; Corentine J. Finnegan, O.C.S.O.; Jerome J. Hickey, O.C.S.O.; Francis X. Kavanagh, O.C.S.O.; Luke C. Kot, O.C.S.O.; John M. O'Brien, O.C.S.O.; Robert L. Pearson, O.C.S.O.; Eduardo Rodriguez, O.C.S.O.; Thomas F. Skonny, O.C.S.O.; Thomas F. Smith, O.C.S.O.; Francis Michael Stiteler, O.C.S.O.; Lawrence Swartz, O.C.S.O.; Joachim Tierney, O.C.S.O.; Matt G. Torpey, O.C.S.O.; Damian C. Turk, O.C.S.O.; Joseph F. Tynan, O.C.S.O.; Charles Felix Zell, O.C.S.O.; Gerard Gross, C.SS.R.

Located Elsewhere: Revs. Dom Armand Veilleux, O.C.S.O Italy, Generalate; Patrick Duffy, O.C.S.O.; George J. Evans, O.C.S.O., V.A. Hospital, San Antonio, TX; Edward T. Morley, O.C.S.O.; Manuel Rodriguez, Cistercian Monastery in Merida, Venezuela. Priests 33; Professed Brothers 16; Novices 5.

DUNWOODY. *Legionaries of Christ*, 225 Lack Land Ct., 30350-5076. Tel: 770-394-2158; Fax: 770-393-3688. Revs. John Hopkins, L.C., Supr.; Dean Stasell, L.C., Promotion, Retreats.

[J] CONVENTS AND RESIDENCES OF SISTERS

ATLANTA. *Missionaries of Charity*, 995 St. Charles Ave., N.E., 30306-4211. Tel: 404-892-5111. Sr. M. Marlene, M.C., Supr. Sisters 4; Total Assisted 60.

CHAMBLEE. *Missionary Sisters of the Sacred Heart "ad Gentes"*, 3152 Terramar Dr., 30341. Tel: 770-934-8939. To serve the Hispanic community. Sr. Beatriz Taneco, M.A.G., Supr., Atlanta Community. Sisters 5.

GAINESVILLE. *Adrian Dominican Sisters, Mid-Atlantic Mission Chapter*, 5735 Dawsonville Hwy., 30506-3889. Tel: 770-844-1370; Fax: 770-844-1371. Sr. Mary Kathryn Cliatt, O.P., Chapter Prioress.

SNELLVILLE. *Monastery of the Visitation* (Maryfield), 2055 Ridgedale Dr., 30278. Tel: 770-972-1060. Strictly cloistered contemplative Office of First Federation. Private retreats for women, no more than 3 at a time. Mother Mary Jozefa Kowalewski, V.H.M., Pres. First Federation of the Visitation & Supr. of MD; Rev. Michael P. Hogan, Chap. U.S. Professed Sisters 13; Novices 3.

[K] RETREAT HOUSES

ATLANTA. *Ignatius House*, 6700 Riverside Dr., N.W., 30328. Tel: 404-255-0503. Revs. James C. Babb, S.J., Assoc. Dir.; Vincent R. Malatesta, S.J., Assoc. Dir.; John L. Vessels, S.J., Dir.

Maisha House of Prayer, Inc., 392 Glen Iris Dr., N.E., 30308. Tel: 404-688-8040. Total in Residence 2; Total Staff 2.

GAINESVILLE. *Cedar Hill Enrichment Center, Inc.*, 5735 Dawsonville Hwy., 30506. Tel: 770-887-0051. Sr. June Racicot, O.P., Dir.

HOSCHTON. *Sisters of the Cenacle*, 5913 Jackson Trail Rd., 30548. Tel: 706-654-3460. Congregation of Our Lady of the Retreat in the Cenacle.

Retreat Ministry, Spiritual Development Programs, Spiritual Direction, and Other Forms of Spiritual Ministry. Sisters 3.

[L] CAMPUS MINISTRY CENTERS

ATLANTA. *Campus Ministry*, 680 W. Peachtree St., N.W., 30308. Tel: 404-888-7804. Rev. Mark W. Lacey.

Atlanta University Complex, 165 James P. Brawley Dr., N.W., 30314-3518. Tel: 404-524-0511. Rev. Edward Branch.

Berry College. St. John Vianney Catholic Church, 1920 Skyview Dr., Lithia Springs, 30057. Tel: 770-745-5445. Rev. Linus De Santis, O.F.M.Conv.

Emory University, Agnes Scott College, 1753 N. Decatur Rd., N.E., 30307. Tel: 404-636-7237. Rev. James Schillinger.

Georgia Institute of Technology, 172 4th St., N.W., 30313. Tel: 404-892-6759. Rev. Mario Di Lella, O.F.M.

Oglethorpe University. 4484 Peachtree Rd., N.E., 30319. Tel: 404-261-1441. Our Lady of the Assumption Catholic Church, 1350 Hearst Dr., N.E., 30319. Tel: 404-261-7181. Rev. Andrew McCormack, S.M.

Catholic Student Center - University of Georgia. (Athens), 1344 S. Lumpkin St., Athens, 30605. Tel: 706-543-2293. Rev. Steven J. Pavignano, O.F.M., Dir.

West Georgia College. (Carrollton), Church of Our Lady of Perpetual Help, Center Point Rd., Rte. 5, Box 100, Carrollton, 30117. Tel: 706-832-8977. Rev. Msgr. Michael Regan.

North Georgia College. (Dahlonega). St. Luke the Evangelist Church, 301 Hawkins St., Dahlonega, 30533. Tel: 706-864-2568. Rev. Edward Danneker.

Dalton Junior College. (Dalton). Church of St. Joseph, 623 S. Thornton Ave., Dalton, 30720. Tel: 706-278-3107. Rev. Daniel Stack.

Brenau College. (Gainesville), 440 Pearce Cir., N.E., Gainesville, 30501-2457. Tel: 706-534-3338. Rev. William G. Hoffman.

Kennesaw State University. (Kennesaw). St. John Vianney, 1920 Skyview Dr., Lithia Springs, 30057. Tel: 770-745-5445. Rev. Linus De Santis, O.F.M.Conv.

LaGrange Jr. College. (LaGrange), 200 LaFayette Pkwy., LaGrange, 30240. Tel: 706-884-4224. Rev. John C. Kieran.

Georgia College. (Milledgeville), 345 Glenhaven Dr., Milledgeville, 31061. Tel: 706-452-8628. Rev. John P. Farrelly.

Shorter College. (Rome). St. Mary's Church, 911 N. Broad St., Rome, 30161. Tel: 706-295-7014. Rev. James A. Miceli.

Dekalb Community College. (Stone Mountain). Corpus Christi Church, 600 Mountain View Dr., Stone Mountain, 30083. Tel: 770-469-0395. Rev. Gregory D. Kenny, C.M.F.

[M] MISCELLANEOUS LISTINGS

ATLANTA. *Atlanta Particular Council, St. Vincent de Paul Society, Inc.*, 26 Third St., N.W., 30308. Tel: 404-874-7014; 874-7140; 874-6990. Ms. Sheila Bissonnette, Exec. Dir. Total Assisted 12,000; Total Staff 10.

Carlow College Bicentennial Fund, Inc., 680 W. Peachtree St., N.W., 30308. Tel: 708-888-7804. Rev. Msgr. Edward J. Dillon, Contact Person.

The Catholic Charismatic Renewal in Atlanta. Rev. Timothy M. Hepburn.

Catholic Foundation of North Georgia, Inc., 680 W. Peachtree St., N.W., 30308-1984. Tel: 404-888-7837.

Good Shepherd Services. (Incorporated as Good Shepherd Corporation).

Good Shepherd Counseling Center, 2855 Briarcliff Rd., N.E., 30329. Tel: 404-636-0712; Fax: 770-908-8777.

Good Shepherd Outreach Center, 2426 Shallowford Ter., Chamblee, 30341. Tel: 770-455-9379; Fax: 770-908-8777. Sr. Mary Brigid Lawlor, Pres. Sisters 4.

National Catholic Association of Diocesan Directors for Hispanic Ministry, Inc., 680 W. Peachtree St., N.W., 30308.

Saint Joseph's Health System, Inc., 5671 Peachtree Dunwoody Rd., Ste. 700, 30342. Tel: 404-851-5700. Ronald P. Hogan, Pres. & CEO; Sr. Jane Gerety, R.S.M., Senior Vice Pres. for Sponsorship.

Sponsorship. Holding Company Sponsored by Sisters of Mercy of Americas, Baltimore Regional Community, which operates: Saint Joseph's Hospital of Atlanta, Inc.; Saint Joseph's Mercy Foundation, Inc.; Saint Joseph's Mercy Care Services, Inc.; and Saint Joseph's Service Corporation.

Saint Joseph's Mercy Foundation, 5671 Peachtree Dunwoody Rd., Ste. 700, 30342. Tel: 404-851-5710. Ted D. Bayley, Pres.

Serra Club #120, Dis. 18. Metro Atlanta, 680 W. Peachtree St., N.W., 30308. James N. Gillen, Pres.

Serra Club #684, Dis. 18. North Metro Atlanta, 680 W. Peachtree St., N.W., 30308. Joseph J. Krygiel, Pres.

ALPHARETTA. *St. Francis de Sales Latin Mass Community - Pastoral Center*, 3400 Old Alabama Rd., 30202-5525. Tel: 770-442-2511. Rev. Mark F. Fischer, F.S.S.P.

DORVILLE. *Korean Martyrs Pastoral Center*, 6003 Buford Hwy., N.E., 30340. Tel: 770-455-1380. Rev. Msgr. Donald Kiernan, Admin.

DUNWOODY. *Pinecrest Academy*, c/o Dunwoody Mail Sta., 2482 Jett Ferry Rd., #680, A-7, 30338. Tel: 770-901-9799.

GAINESVILLE. *Southern Dominican Ministries, Inc.*, 5735 Dawsonville Hwy., 30506.

JACKSON. *Magnificat - Joyful Visitation Chapter, Inc.*, 198 Harris Rd., 30233. Tel: 770-775-3783; 504-8703. Olga Myers, Coord.

RELIGIOUS INSTITUTES OF MEN REPRESENTED IN THE ARCHDIOCESE

For further details refer to the corresponding bracketed number in the Religious Institutes of Men or Women section.

[0350]—*Cistercians Order of the Strict Observance-Trappists*.—O.C.S.O.

[0360]—*Claretian Missionaries*. (Eastern Province).—C.M.F.

[1000]—*Congregation of the Passion*. (Prov. of St. Paul of the Cross).—C.P.

[0480]—*Conventual Franciscans.* (Prov. of St. Anthony of Padua, Baltimore).—O.F.M.Conv.
[0520]—*Franciscan Friars.* (Prov. of the Most Holy Name of Jesus).—O.F.M.
[0570]—*Glenmary Home Missioners.*
[0690]—*Jesuit Fathers and Brothers.* (New Orleans Prov.).—S.J.
[0730]—*Legionaries of Christ.*—L.C.
[0780]—*Marist Fathers.* (Washington Prov.).—S.M.
[0720]—*The Missionaries of Our Lady of La Salette.*—M.S.
[]—*Missionaries of St. Francis de Sales.* (Annecy, France).—M.S.F.S.
[1065]—*The Priestly Fraternity of St. Peter.*—F.S.S.P.
[1070]—*Redemptorist Fathers.* (Baltimore Prov.).—C.SS.R.

RELIGIOUS INSTITUTES OF WOMEN REPRESENTED IN THE ARCHDIOCESE

[3110]—*Congregation of Our Lady of the Retreat in the Cenacle.*—R.C.
[1070-13]—*Dominican Sisters (Adrian, MI).*—O.P.
[1070-03]—*Dominican Sisters (Sinsinawa, WI).*—O.P.
[1070-23]—*Dominican Sisters of St. Rose of Lima (Hawthorne, NY).*—O.P.
[1370]—*The Franciscan Missionaries of Mary.*—F.M.M.
[1840]—*Grey Nuns of the Sacred Heart.*—G.N.S.H.
[1870]—*Handmaids of the Sacred Heart of Jesus.*—A.C.J.
[2575]—*Institute of the Sisters of Mercy of the Americas.* (Merion, PA; Rochester, NY; Baltimore, MD).—R.S.M.
[2720]—*Mission Helpers of the Sacred Heart.*—M.H.S.H.
[2710]—*Missionaries of Charity.*—M.C.
[2800]—*Missionary Sisters of the Most Sacred Heart of Jesus of Hiltrup.*—M.S.C.
[]—*Missionary Sisters of the Sacred Heart.* (Mexico).—M.A.G.
[]—*Religious Franciscan Sisters of Our Lady of Refuge.*—R.F.R.
[2970]—*School Sisters of Notre Dame.*—S.S.N.D.
[]—*Sisters for Christian Community.*—S.F.C.C.
[0650]—*Sisters of Charity of St. Vincent de Paul.* New York.—S.C.
[0430]—*Sisters of Charity of the Blessed Virgin Mary.*—B.V.M.
[0990]—*Sisters of Divine Providence.*—C.D.P.
[2360]—*Sisters of Loretto.*—S.L.
[3000]—*Sisters of Notre Dame de Namur.*—S.N.D.deN.
[1580]—*Sisters of St. Francis (Sylvania, OH).*—O.S.F.
[1570]—*Sisters of St. Francis of the Holy Family.*—O.S.F.
[3830-01]—*Sisters of St. Joseph.*—C.S.J.
[3840]—*Sisters of St. Joseph of Carondelet.*—C.S.J.
[3830-15]—*Sisters of St. Joseph of Concordia.*—C.S.J.
[0260]—*Sisters of the Blessed Sacrament for Indians and Colored People.*—S.B.S.
[1830]—*The Sisters of the Good Shepherd.*—R.G.S.
[1990]—*Sisters of the Holy Names of Jesus and Mary.*—S.N.J.M.
[4190]—*Sisters of the Visitation.*—V.H.M.
[2170]—*Sisters, Servants of the Immaculate Heart of Mary.*—I.H.M.
[2150]—*Sisters, Servants of the Immaculate Heart of Mary.*—I.H.M.
[]—*Ursuline of Brown County.*—O.S.U.

ARCHDIOCESAN CEMETERIES

ATLANTA. *Washington.*

NECROLOGY

(No Deaths)

Diocese of Austin

(Dioecesis Austiniensis)

Most Reverend

JOHN E. MCCARTHY, D.D.

Bishop of Austin; ordained May 26, 1956; appointed Titular Bishop of Padena and Auxiliary Bishop of Galveston-Houston January 23, 1979; consecrated March 14, 1979; appointed Bishop of Austin December 24, 1985; installed February 25, 1986. *Office: P.O. Box 13327, Austin, TX, 78711.*

ERECTED 1948.

Square Miles 19,511.

Comprises the Counties of Mills, Hamilton, San Saba, Lampasas, Coryell, McLennan, Limestone, Bell, Falls, Robertson, Mason, Llano, Burnet, Williamson, Milam, Brazos, Blanco, Travis, Bastrop, Lee, Burleson, Washington, Hays, Caldwell and the part of Fayette County north of the Colorado River in the State of Texas.

For legal titles of parishes and diocesan institutions, consult the Chancery Office.

Chancery Office: 1600 N. Congress Ave., P.O. Box 13327, Austin, TX, 78711. Tel.: 512-476-4888; Fax: 512-469-9537.

STATISTICAL OVERVIEW

Personnel	
Priests: Diocesan Active in Diocese	120
Priests: Active Outside Diocese	6
Priests: Retired, Sick or Absent	11
Number of Diocesan Priests	137
Religious Priests in Diocese	56
Extern Priests in Diocese	6
Ordinations:	
Diocesan Priests	3
Permanent Deacons in Diocese	104
Total Brothers	41
Total Sisters	122
Parishes	
Parishes	91
With Resident Pastor:	
Resident Diocesan Priests	72
Resident Religious Priests	19
Without Resident Pastor:	
Administered by Permanent Deacons	11
Administered by Lay People	1
Missions	45
New Parishes Created	1
Professional Ministry Personnel:	
Brothers	1
Sisters	9
Lay Ministers	62
Welfare	
Catholic Hospitals	4
Total Assisted	70,360
Health Care Centers	3
Total Assisted	82,000
Homes for the Aged	2
Total Assisted	650
Residential Care of Children	1
Total Assisted	250
Day Care and Extended Day Care Centers	3
Total Assisted	190
Specialized Homes	1
Total Assisted	187
Special Centers for Social Services	1
Total Assisted	140
Residential Care of Disabled	1
Total Assisted	9,900
Educational	
Diocesan Students in Other Seminaries	15
Total Seminarians	15
Colleges and Universities	1
Total Students	3,050
High Schools, Diocesan and Parish	2
Total Students	242
High Schools, Private	1
Total Students	345
Elementary Schools, Diocesan and Parish	15
Total Students	3,484
Elementary Schools, Private	1
Total Students	39
Catechesis/Religious Education:	
High School Students	5,333
Elementary Students	19,874
Total Students Under Catholic Instruction	32,382
Teachers in the Diocese:	
Priests	7
Brothers	1
Sisters	19
Lay Teachers	356
Vital Statistics	
Receptions into the Church:	
Infant Baptism Totals	5,540
Adult Baptism Totals	692
Received into Full Communion	464
First Communions	4,708
Confirmations	3,532
Marriages:	
Catholic	1,133
Interfaith	484
Total Marriages	1,617
Deaths	1,547
Total Catholic Population	212,182
Total Population	1,638,245

Former Bishops—Most Rev. LOUIS J. REICHER, D.D., ord. Dec. 6, 1918; appt. first Bishop of Austin Nov. 29, 1947; cons. April 14, 1948; died Feb. 23, 1984.—Most Rev. VINCENT M. HARRIS, D.D., ord. March 19, 1938; appt. Bishop of Beaumont July 4, 1966; cons. Sept. 28, 1966; transferred to Austin April 21, 1971; succeeded to the See Nov. 16, 1971; retired Feb. 25, 1986; died March 31, 1988.

Vicar-General—Rev. Msgr. EDWARD C. MATOCHA, P.A.

Moderator of the Curia—Rev. Msgr. DONALD J. FRUGE, J.C.D.

Chancery Office—1600 N. Congress Ave., P.O. Box 13327, Austin, 78711. Tel: 512-476-4888; Fax: 512-469-9537. Office Hours: Mon.-Fri. 8:30-5.

Deans—Austin: Rev. ELMER HOLTMAN, Central Austin: Rev. Msgr. LONNIE REYES, North Austin: Rev. ELMER HOLTMAN, South Austin: Rev. JOHN KORCSMAR, C.S.C., Brazos Valley: Rev. JOHN MCCAFFREY, Southern: Rev. EDWARD DOKUPIL, Temple: Rev. WILLIAM DONAHUE, C.S.C., Northern: Rev. ANGELO BERTINI, Eastern: Rev. Msgr. RALPH BRENNAN, Central: Rev. LONNIE URBAN, Western: Rev. EDWIN KADZIELAWSKI, C.S.C.

Presbyteral Council—Rev. Msgr. EDWARD MATOCHA; Rev. Msgr. FRED BOMAR; Rev. Msgr. EDWARD JORDAN; Rev. Msgr. BEN MAZURKIEWICZ; Rev. Msgr. LOUIS WOZNIAK; Revs. LARRY COVINGTON; WILLIAM DONAHUE, C.S.C.; KIRBY GARNER; VICTOR GOERTZ; OLIVER JOHNSON; JOHN KORCSMAR, C.S.C.; JOSEPH MARTORELL, T.O.R.; JAMES MCCABE, C.S.P.; LONNIE URBAN; DEAN WILHELM; PATRICK ZUREK.

Consultors—Rev. Msgr. FRED BOMAR; Rev. Msgr. LONNIE REYES; Rev. Msgr. MARK DEERING; Rev. Msgr. HARRY MAZURKIEWICS; Revs. KIRBY GARNER; ALBERT RUIZ.

Diocesan Tribunal—1625 Rutherford Ln., Austin, 78754. Tel: 512-832-0313; Fax: 512-832-0316. Direct all inquiries concerning marriage and dispensations to this address.

Judicial Vicar—Rev. DAVID-MARIA A. JAEGER, O.F.M. J.C.D.

Diocesan Judges—Rev. Msgr. DONALD J. FRUGE, J.C.D.; Revs. VICTOR GOERTZ, J.C.D.; JOZEF MUSIOL, S.D.S., J.C.D.; PHILLIP HILL, J.C.D.

Defenders of the Bond—Rev. Msgr. EDWARD C. MATOCHA; Rev. KIRBY GARNER; TAMMY EDGERLY, J.C.L.

Assistant—Ms. GEORGIA LOVETT.

Assessor—Rev. GILES AMARASKERA.

Notaries—Ms. GEORGIA LOVETT; PEGGY LEAZER; CHARLES COLLINS; Rev. GILES AMARASKERA.

Advocates—Any priest or deacon approved for ministry in the diocese.

Procurators at the Tribunal—Deacons W. J. HAM; LARRY HANSEN; ROBERT EMBRY.

Finance Office—Rev. Msgr. DONALD J. FRUGE, J.C.D., Finance Officer; PATRICIA RUSSELL, Business Mgr., *P.O. Box 13327, Austin, 78711.* Tel: 512-476-4888; Fax: 512-469-9537.

Finance Council—Rev. Msgr. DONALD J. FRUGE, J.C.D.; DON E. COX; SWITZER DEASON; CAMPBELL MCGINNIS; PATRICIA RUSSELL; PHILIP JOSEPH; ROBERT GREENWOOD; JIM SMOLIK; CATHERINE GHIGLIERI.

Archives—KINGA PERZYNSKA, Archivist, *P.O. Box 13124, Austin, 78711-3124.* Tel: 512-476-6296; Fax: 512-476-3715.

Black Ministry—Mr. JOHNNY DORSEY, Dir., *P.O. Box 13327, Austin, 78711.* Tel: 512-388-1320; 472-3741.

Building Commission—Rev. Msgr. EDWARD C. MATOCHA, *P.O. Box 13327, Austin, 78711.* Tel: 512-476-4888; Fax: 512-469-9537.

Campaign for Human Development—Rev. JOHN KORCSMAR, C.S.C., *1111 Montopolis Dr., Austin, 78741.* Tel: 512-385-4333.

Campus Ministry—Rev. ALBERT PALERMO, Dir., *St. Albert the Great, 12041 Bittern Hollow, Austin, 78758.* Tel: 512-837-7825.

Catholic Charities—Rev. JIM EVANS, Dir., *P.O. Box 13327, Austin, 78711-3327.* Tel: 512-476-4888; Fax: 512-469-9537.

Catholic Schools Office—Sr. THECLA CAIN, O.S.F., Supt., *1625 Rutherford Ln., Austin, 78754.* Tel: 512-873-7771; Fax: 512-873-8338.

Catholic Services Appeal—LEANN POWERS, Dir., *P.O. Box 13327, Austin, 78711.* Tel: 512-476-4888; Fax: 512-469-9537.

"Catholic Spirit"—HELEN OSMAN, Editor, *P.O. Box 13327, Austin, 78711.* Tel: 512-476-4888; Fax: 512-469-9537.

Catholic Youth Ministry Office—Sr. MARY LOU BARBA, M.C.D.P., Dir., *1625 Rutherford Ln., Austin, 78754.* Tel: 512-873-7771; Fax: 512-873-8338.

Cemeteries—Rev. Msgr. JOHN MALINOWSKI, *2541 E. By-Pass, College Station, 77845.* Tel: 409-693-6994.
Charismatic Renewal—JESSE MARTINEZ, Dir., *1104 Turtle Creek, Austin, 78745.* Tel: 512-447-8977.
Communications—HELEN OSMAN, Dir., *P.O. Box 13327, Austin, 78711.* Tel: 512-476-4888.
Continuing Education Priests—Rev. ELMER HOLTMAN, *10205 R.R. 620 N., Austin, 78726.* Tel: 512-258-1161.
Council of Catholic Women—EUNICE WASHA, Pres.
Cursillo—Our Lady of Guadalupe Cursillo Center, Jarrell. Tel: 512-746-2041. Spanish: LOUIS RUIZ, Pres., *3201 Shady Hill, Temple, 76502.* Tel: 817-773-5905. English: MARGARET CAMACHO, *1505 Haskell, Austin, 78702.* Tel: 512-478-1719. Young Adults: Deacon WILLIE CORTEZ, *1816 E. Sixth St., Austin, 78762.* Tel: 512-322-0632.
Deaf Ministry—Sr. DENISE MARIE HACKETT, C.S.C., Dir., *St. Ignatius Church, 2309 Euclid St., Austin, 78704.* Tel: 512-444-5330.
Diaconate—Deacon JEROME KLEMENT, Dir., *St. Luke's, 2807 Oakdale, Temple, 76502.* Tel: 817-773-1561.
Diocesan Pastoral Center—Sr. MARY LOU BARBA, M.C.D.P., Dir., *1625 Rutherford Ln., Austin, 78754.* Tel: 512-873-7771; Fax: 512-873-8338.
Diocesan Social Concerns—Rev. JAMES L. EVANS, Dir., *P.O. Box 13327, Austin, 78711.* Tel: 512-476-4888; Fax: 512-469-9537.
Ecumenism—Rev. CHARLES L. COVINGTON, Dir., *St. Louis Church, 7601 Burnet Rd., Austin, 78757.* Tel: 512-454-0384.
Evangelization—Sr. MARY LOU BARBA, M.C.D.P., *1625 Rutherford Ln., Austin, 78754.* Tel: 512-873-7771; Fax: 512-873-8338.
Family Life Office—Vacant.
Health Care—Rev. Msgr. WILLIAM BROUSSARD, Dir., *3001 S. Congress Ave., Austin, 78704.* Tel: 512-447-9949.
Historical Commission—CHARLES HRNCIR, Dir., *7007 Bent Oak Cir., Austin, 78749.* Tel: 512-892-3704.
Holy Childhood—Bro. THEO FLYNN, C.S.C., *3001 S. Congress Ave., Austin, 78704.* Tel: 512-442-4534.
Criminal Justice Ministry—Deacon E. GENERES (DOOTS) DUFOUR, Dir., *P.O. Box 13327, Austin, 78711.* Tel: 512-476-4888.
Knights of Columbus—Rev. Msgr. EDWARD RABROKER, Moderator, *P.O. Box 608, Granger, 76530.* Tel: 512-859-2223.
Lifeline—THERESA WARE, Dir., *2026 Guadalupe St., Austin, 78705.* Tel: 512-477-1092.
Ministry Programs Office—Sr. MARY LOU BARBA, M.C.D.P., Dir., *1625 Rutherford Ln., Austin, 78754.* Tel: 512-873-7771; Fax: 512-873-8338.
Mission Council—Rev. LOUIS PAVLICEK, Chm., *St. Luke's, 2807 Oakdale, Temple, 76502.* Tel: 817-773-4541; Fax: 817-774-7044.
Natural Family Planning—Co-Dirs.: RANDY MCCASLIN; NANCY MCCASLIN, *2026 Guadalupe St., Austin, 78705.* Tel: 512-474-2757.
Office of Hispanic Ministry—Rev. ALBERT RUIZ, *2903 E. Rancier Ave., Kileen, 76543-3522.* Tel: 817-634-7878.
Parish Social Ministries—CHRIS ATTAL, Coord., *2811 E. Second, Austin, 78702.* Tel: 512-323-4921; Fax: 512-323-4929.
Pastoral Care—Rev. RICHARD TIJERINA, *203 E. 10th St., Austin, 78701.* Tel: 512-476-6182.
Propagation of the Faith—Bro. THEO FLYNN, C.S.C., *3001 S. Congress Ave., Austin, 78704.* Tel: 512-442-4534.
Religious Education Office—Sr. MARY LOU BARBA, M.C.D.P., Dir., *1625 Rutherford Ln., Austin, 78754.* Tel: 512-873-7771; Fax: 512-873-8338.
Respect Life—ANN BIERSCHENK, *1803 Chincoteague, Round Rock, 78681.* Tel: 512-255-8435.
Rural Life—Rev. Msgr. EDWARD RABROKER, *P.O. Box 608, Granger, 76530.* Tel: 512-859-2223.
Serra Clubs—Rev. WALT CARR, Chap.-Austin; Rev. EDWARD KARASEK, Chap.-Waco.
Special Collections—LEANN POWERS, Dir., *P.O. Box 13327, Austin, 78711.* Tel: 512-476-4888; Fax: 512-469-9537.
Stewardship—LEANN POWERS, Dir., *P.O. Box 13327, Austin, 78711-3327.* Tel: 512-476-4888; Fax: 512-476-5341.
Synod Implementation Office—PAT STANKUS, Dir., *Cedarbrake Renewal Center, P.O. Box 58, Belton, 76513-0058.* Tel: 817-780-2436; Fax: 817-780-2684.
Vicar for Religious—Sr. MARIE ANDRE WALSH, I.H.M., *3001 S. Congress Ave., Austin, 78704.* Tel: 512-448-8617.
Vocations—Rev. PATRICK ZUREK, Dir., *101 Westlake Dr., Austin, 78746.* Tel: 512-328-3220. LYNN JOHNSON, Sec. Tel: 512-873-7771.
Worship Office & Liturgical Commission—Sr. LOIS PAHA, O.P., Dir., *1625 Rutherford Ln., Austin, 78754.* Tel: 512-873-7771; Fax: 512-873-8338.

Miscellaneous

Charitable Trusts—
Father Bernard C. Goertz Scholarship Trust Fund—Sacred Heart Church, Rte. 1, Box 108, Bastrop, 78602.
John J. Kearns Memorial Charitable Trust Fund—P.O. Box 5040, Waco, 78708.
Clerical Endowment Fund—Rev. Msgr. HARRY MAZURKIEWICZ, *Sacred Heart Church, P.O. Box 548, LaGrange, 78945.* Tel: 409-968-3430.
Sts. Cyril & Methodius School Endowment—Rev. Msgr. EDWARD RABROKER, *Sts. Cyril & Methodius, P.O. Box 201, Granger, 76530.*
Clergy Medical and Retirement Trust of the Diocese of Austin and the Diocese of Austin Pension Plan Committee—Most Rev. JOHN E. MCCARTHY, Chm., Diocesan Presbyteral Council.
Seton Fund of the Daughters of Charity of St. Vincent De Paul—ALLAN SHIVERS, JR., Chm., *1201 W. 38th St., Austin, 78705.*
St. Joseph's Foundation of Bryan—MILTON L. DARE, Exec., *2801 Franciscan Dr., Bryan, 77802.* Tel: 409-774-4087.
St. Jude Foundation, Inc.—1306 N. Park, Brenham, 77833.
Children's Hospital Foundation of Austin—1201 W. 38th St., Austin, 78705-1056. Tel: 512-480-1243; Fax: 512-480-1220. Mr. GENE ATTAL, Vice Pres.

CLERGY, PARISHES, MISSIONS AND PAROCHIAL SCHOOLS

CITY OF AUSTIN
(Travis County)

1—ST. MARY'S CATHEDRAL (1852), Very Rev. Gregory G. Perez, Rector. Pastoral Assocs.: Rev. Jerry A. Smith; Rev. Msgr. Edward C. Matocha, P.A., Rector Emeritus; Rev. Richard Tijerina; Deacon Willie Cortez.
Res., 203 E. 10th St., 78701. Tel: 512-476-6182; Fax: 512-476-8799.
School—Tel: 512-476-1480; Fax: 512-476-9968. Cecilia Abbott, Prin.
Lay Teachers 20; Students 226.
Catechesis/Religious Programs—Tel: 512-476-4801. Mary Cortez, D.R.E.
Students 280.

2—ST. ALBERT THE GREAT (1987), Rev. Albert A. Palermo; Deacon Jesse Ramsey.
Office: 12041 Bittern Hollow, 78758. Tel: 512-837-7825; Fax: 512-834-2377.
Res., 1104 Huntridge Cir., 78758. Tel: 512-339-1104. [CEM]
Catechesis/Religious Programs—Students 308.

3—CRISTO REY (1950) (Hispanic), Rev. Lawrence Mattingly, O.F.M.Conv.; Bro. Kerry Guillory, O.F.M.Conv.; Deacons Lupe Medrano; John Ojeda.
Res., 2110 E. 2nd St., 78702. Tel: 512-474-6376; Fax: 512-474-8417.
Catechesis/Religious Programs—Tel: 512-477-1099. Sr. Irene Tapia, F.M.A., D.R.E.
Students 570.

4—HOLY CROSS (1936) (African American), Revs. George Artis, S.V.D.; Isidore Ndagizimana.
Res., 1610 E. 11th St., 78702. Tel: 512-472-3741; Fax: 512-472-3783.
Catechesis/Religious Programs—Tel: 512-292-4376. D.R.E.: Ms. Cynthia Olivier; Mr. Regius Guillory.
Students 68.

5—HOLY VIETNAMESE MARTYRS (1990) (Vietnamese), Rev. Joe Van Anh Nguyen.
Res., 1107 E. Yager Ln., 78753. Tel: 512-834-8483.
Catechesis/Religious Programs—Tel: 512-836-6632.
Students 140.

6—OUR LADY OF GUADALUPE (1907), Rev. William Elliott, O.M.I. In res., Deacons Salvador Hernandez; Mario Renteria.
Res., 1206 E. 9th St., 78702. Tel: 512-478-7955.
Catechesis/Religious Programs—Students 310.

7—EMMAUS CATHOLIC CHURCH (1996), Rev. Msgr. Richard McCabe.
Res., 2203 Lakeway Blvd., 78734. Tel: 512-261-5958. [CEM]

8—NUESTRA SENORA DE DOLORES (1952) (Hispanic), Rev. John S. Korcsmar, C.S.C.
Res., 1111 Montopolis Dr., 78741. Tel: 512-385-4333; Fax: 512-385-6116.
Catechesis/Religious Programs—Sr. Rose Moreno, D.R.E.
Students 440.
Convent—(Spain). Tel: 512-385-5090. Hijas De La Misericordia.
Sisters 3.

9—SACRED HEART (1958), Rev. Robert Becker; Deacons Roger Behr; James Fuller; Bill Vela; Rob Embry. In res., Rev. Robert Bradley, S.J.
Res., 5909 Reicher Dr., 78723. Tel: 512-926-2552; Fax: 512-926-5138.
School—Tel: 512-926-0687. Sr. Mary Jean Olsovsky, Prin.
Sisters of St. Dominic 1; Lay Teachers 17; Students 218.
Catechesis/Religious Programs—Tel: 512-926-2116. Angelica Mishoe, D.R.E.
Students 435.
Convent—5911 Reicher Dr., 78723. Tel: 512-926-0687.

10—SANTA BARBARA (1991) (Hispanic), Rev. Bernard Goertz; Mr. Joe Arellano, Admin.
Mailing Address: 13713 FM 969, 78724. Tel: 512-276-7718.

11—ST. AUSTIN'S (1908), Revs. James F. McCabe, C.S.P.; Augustus McGuire, C.S.P.; Thomas Clerkin, C.S.P. Pastoral Assocs.: Barbara Budde; Sr. Sharon Groetsh, D.C. In res., Revs. Bernard Campbell, C.S.P.; John Duffy, C.S.P.; Patrick Hensy, C.S.P.; Robert Michele, C.S.P.; Edward Philip O'Hern, C.S.P.
Res., 2026 Guadalupe St., 78705. Tel: 512-477-9471; Fax: 512-477-9430.
School—1911 San Antonio St., 78705. Tel: 512-577-3751; Fax: 512-477-3079. Paula Harris, Prin.
Lay Teachers 21; Students 240.
Catechesis/Religious Programs—Michael Guerra, D.R.E.
Students 240.

12—ST. CATHERINE OF SIENA (1979), Revs. Oliver F. Johnson; Harry F. Dean, Jr.; Deacon W. J. Ham.
Church—4800 Convict Hill Rd., 78749. Tel: 512-892-2420; Fax: 512-892-0488.
Res., 4916 Flaming Oak, 78749. Tel: 512-892-1799.
Catechesis/Religious Programs—Tel: 512-892-2426. Richard Phillips, D.R.E.
Students 1,184.

13—ST. IGNATIUS MARTYR (1937), Revs. Barry Cabell, C.S.C.; Harold G. Zink, C.S.C.; Harold Essling, C.S.C.; Jeffrey Allison, C.S.C.; Deacons James T. Graham; Patrick Murray. In res., Rev. John T. Payne, C.S.C.
Res., 2309 Euclid Ave., 78704. Tel: 512-442-3602; Fax: 512-442-3529.
School—Tel: 512-442-8547. Mr. Rob Lewis, Prin.
Lay Teachers 14; Students 250.
Catechesis/Religious Programs—Tel: 512-442-8586. D.R.E.: Kathy Cole; Sr. Judith Hallock, C.S.C.; Sr. Denise Hackett, C.S.C.; Sr. Agnes Murray, I.H.M.
Students 268.

14—ST. JOHN NEUMANN (1984), Revs. Edward Milton Maddox; Richard Reginald Hudson; Patrick J. Zurek; Giles Amaraseka (Sri Lanka); Deacons Douglas Morris; D. Mark Hamlet.
Office: 101 Westlake Dr., 78746. Tel: 512-328-3220.
Res., 105 Reveille Rd., 78746. Tel: 512-328-6544.
Catechesis/Religious Programs—102 Westlake Dr., 78746. Tel: 512-328-8856; Fax: 512-328-3226.
Students 683.

15—ST. JULIA (1957), Rev. Msgr. Lonnie C. Reyes.
Res., 3010 Lyons Rd., 78702. Tel: 512-926-4186; Fax: 512-926-8821.
Catechesis/Religious Programs—Tel: 512-928-3381. Sr. Jane Mary Sanchez, F.M.A., D.R.E.
Students 629.
Convent—747 Cherico St., 78702. Tel: 512-385-9122. Salesian Sisters of St. John Bosco.
Sisters 3. Daughters of Mary Help of Christian.

16—ST. LOUIS (1952), Revs. Larry Covington; Rafael Clancy; David Konderla; Deacons Richard Hudson; Alfred Peschka; Jess Ramsey. In res., Rev. David Jaeger.
Res., 7601 Burnet Rd., 78757. Tel: 512-454-0384; Fax: 512-454-2010.
School—Tel: 512-454-0384, Ext. 242. Marsha Solana, Prin.
Sisters 1; Lay Teachers 27; Students 469.
Catechesis/Religious Programs—Tel: 512-454-0384, Ext. 225. D.R.E.: Betty Danner, Childhood Ministries; Rene Biediger, Youth Ministries; Charles Balsam, Adult Ministries.
Students 617.

17—ST. MARGARET OF SCOTLAND (1984), Rev. Joseph H. Frazer.
Mailing Address: 2435 Oak Crest Ave., 78704. Tel: 512-444-7587.

18—ST. PAUL'S (1989) (Hispanic), Rev. Paul F. McCallum.
Res., 10000 David Moore Rd., 78748. Tel: 512-280-4460; Fax: 512-280-7219.
Catechesis/Religious Programs—Tel: 512-280-5777; Fax: 512-280-7219. Joyce Gerold, D.R.E.
Students 620.

19—ST. PETER THE APOSTLE (1962), Rev. Msgr. Fred Bomar.
Res., P.O. Box 17575, 4600 E. Ben White Blvd., 78760. Tel: 512-442-0655.
Catechesis/Religious Programs—Tel: 512-444-7477.
Students 203.

20—ST. THERESA (1968), Rev. Msgr. Edward F. Jordan; Rev. Greg Romanski, C.S.P.; Deacons Clarence Hansen; Ray James.
Res., 4311 Small Dr., 78731. Tel: 512-451-5121; Fax: 512-453-6824.
School—(Grades PreK-6). Tel: 512-451-7105; Fax: 512-451-8808. William S. Davidson, Prin.
Lay Teachers 16; Students 238.
Catechesis/Religious Programs—Tel: 512-451-2940; Fax: 512-453-6824. Rosemary Edwards, D.R.E.
Students 804.

21—ST. THOMAS MORE (1978), Revs. Elmer E. Holtman; Steven P. Ryan, S.J.; Deacons Peter Schwab; Thomas Mallinger.
Office: 10205 Ranch Rd., 620 N., 78726. Tel: 512-258-1161; Fax: 512-258-8812.
Catechesis/Religious Programs—Tel: 512-258-1944. Mary Osborn, D.R.E.
Students 1,350.

22—ST. THOMAS MORE CHAPEL (1958),
Chancery Building: 1600 N. Congress Ave., 78701. Tel: 512-476-4888.

23—ST. VINCENT DE PAUL (1995), Rev. Daniel Garcia.
Res., 13007 Partridge Bend, 78729. Tel: 512-918-8356; Fax: 512-918-0598. [CEM]
Catechesis/Religious Programs—Students 196.

24—SAN FRANCISCO (1941) (Hispanic), Rev. James R. Martin, C.S.C.; Deacon Richard Duecker.
Res., 9110 Hwy. 183 S., 78747. Tel: 512-243-1404.
Catechesis/Religious Programs—Tel: 512-243-1899. Sr. Jacinta Amengual, F.H.M., D.R.E.
Students 309.
Mission—Stony Point, Bastrop Co., No. 42 & 43 Stony Point Del Valle, 78617. Tel: 512-247-2476.

25—SAN JOSE (1939) (Hispanic), Revs. Kirby D. Garner; Joel McNeil; Deacons George Joseph, Jr.; John Rivera; Enrique Saenz; Alfredo Vasquez.
Res., 2435 Oak Crest, 78704. Tel: 512-444-7587; Fax: 512-443-1212.
Catechesis/Religious Programs—Tel: 512-444-4664. Anna Singleton, D.R.E.
Students 995.

OUTSIDE CITY OF AUSTIN

Andice, Williamson Co., Santa Rosa (1937), Rev. Walt Carr.
Mailing Address: c/o St. Helen Catholic Church, 2700 E. University Ave., Georgetown, 78626-9803. Tel: 817-793-2047.

Bastrop, Bastrop Co., Ascension (1911), Rev. Edward J. Dokupil.
Res., P.O. Drawer W, 78602. Tel: 512-321-2452.
Catechesis/Religious Programs—Tel: 512-321-5511. Laura Wymer, D.R.E.
Students 334.

Belton, Bell Co., Christ the King (1969), Rev. Rock I. Vaz, S.J.; Deacon William Shoemake.
Res., 310 E. 24th Ave., 76513. Tel: 817-939-0806.
Catechesis/Religious Programs—Students 300.

Betram, Burnet Co., Holy Cross (1941) (Hispanic). Attended by Our Mother of Sorrows, Burnet. Rev. Joseph DeVliegher, C.S.C.; Deacon Joe Ruiz.
Mailing Address: P.O. Box 94, 78605. Tel: 512-756-4410.
Catechesis/Religious Programs—Students 155.

Blanco, Blanco Co., St. Ferdinand's (1940), Rev. James Harnan, M.S.C.
Res., Rte. 1, Box 1, 78606. Tel: 210-833-5227. [CEM]
Catechesis/Religious Programs—Tel: 210-833-5227. Mrs. Shirley Cole, D.R.E.
Students 100.
Missions—Johnson City, Blanco Co., Good Shepherd, P.O. Box 528, Johnson City, 78636. Tel: 210-868-0370; Twin Sisters, Blanco Co., Our Lady Help of Christians, 78606.

Bremond, Robertson Co., St. Mary's (1879), Rev. Jozef Musiol.
Res., Rte. 1, Box 58, 76629. Tel: 817-746-7789. [CEM]
Catechesis/Religious Programs—Tel: 817-746-7789.
Students 112.
Convent—Rte. 1, Box 57, 76629. Tel: 816-746-7788.

Brenham, Washington Co., St. Mary of the Immaculate Conception (1870), Rev. Msgr. Ralph A. Brennan; Deacon Bill Januszewski.
Res., 701 Church St., 77833. Tel: 409-836-4441. [CEM]
Catechesis/Religious Programs—Tel: 409-830-8331.
Students 455.
Mission—Old Washington, Washington Co., Blessed Virgin Mary, (1849) 77833.
Mailing Address: c/o St. Mary's of the Immaculate Conception, 701 Church St., 77833.

Bryan, Brazos Co., St. Joseph's (1873), Rev. John McCaffrey; Deacons Switzer Deason; Ray Sis; Gilbert Wilson; Abraham Orozco; Gary Nelson.
Res., 600 E. 26th St., 77803. Tel: 409-822-2721; Fax: 409-779-3120. [CEM 2]
School—Tel: 409-822-6641. Mr. Mark Reinberg, Elementary Prin.; Mrs. Susan Nelson, Junior High Prin.
Lay Teachers 36; Students 418.
Catechesis/Religious Programs—Tel: 409-822-6643. Becky Luza, D.R.E.
Students 530.

St. Anthony's (1896) (Italian), Rev. Steven Kana.
Res., 306 S. Parker, 77803. Tel: 409-823-8145; Fax: 409-823-6001. [JC]
Mission—Caldwell, San Salvador.
Catechesis/Religious Programs—Tel: 409-822-3700.
Students 420.

Santa Teresa's (1940), Rev. Victor G. Robles; Deacon Louis Garcia.
Res., 1212 Lucky, 77803. Tel: 409-822-2932; Fax: 409-822-6957.
Catechesis/Religious Programs—Nickie Rodriguez, D.R.E.
Students 466.

Buda, Hays Co., Santa Cruz (1941) (Hispanic), Rev. Richard Teall, C.S.C.
Res., P.O. Box 187, 78610. Tel: 512-295-2034.
Catechesis/Religious Programs—Tel: 512-295-4818. Cathryn Green, D.R.E.
Students 201.

Cyclone, Bell Co., St. Joseph's (1902) (Czech-German), Rev. Leonard Leddy.
Mailing Address: 20120 FM 485, Burlington, 76519. Tel: 817-985-2280.
Res., Farm Rd. 485, Tel: 817-985-2280. [CEM 2]
Catechesis/Religious Programs—1201 S. St. Joseph Rd. #400, Burlington, 76519. Tel: 817-985-2257.
Students 48.
Mission—Marak, Milam Co., Ss. Cyril & Methodius, FM 485, Burlington, 76519. Tel: 817-985-2280.

Burnet, Burnet Co., Our Mother of Sorrows (1941) (Hispanic), Rev. Joseph DeVliegher, C.S.C.; Deacon Eugene Montag.
Res., 507 Buchanan Dr., 78611-2304. Tel: 512-756-4410.
Catechesis/Religious Programs—Tel: 512-756-2323.
Students 165.
Mission—Bertram, Burnet Co., Holy Cross, P.O. Box 90, Bertram, 78611. Tel: 512-355-2972. Deacon Jose Ruiz.

Caldwell, Burleson Co., St. Mary's (1895) (Hispanic), Rev. Dimitrij Colankin; Deacon John Young.
Res., 509 N. Thomas, 77836. Tel: 409-567-3667. [CEM]
Catechesis/Religious Programs—Students 238.

Calvert, Robertson Co., St. Mary (1876) (Hispanic). Attended by St. Mary's Church, Hearne. Rev. Gregory McLaughlin; Deacon Luis Doriocourt.

Cameron, Milam Co., St. Monica's (1883), Rev. Thomas J. Hanus; Deacon Juan Garza.
Res., P.O. Box 673, 76520. Tel: 817-697-2107. [CEM]
Church—306 S. Nolan, 76520.
Catechesis/Religious Programs—Tel: 817-697-4544. Sr. Jeanette McCarthy, P.B.V.M., D.R.E.
Students 280.

Chappell Hill, Washington Co., St. Stanislaus (1889) (Polish), Rev. Eugene Sheherd.
Res., P.O. Box 179, 77426. Tel: 409-836-3030; Fax: 409-836-7170. [CEM]
Catechesis/Religious Programs—Diane Curry, D.R.E.
Students 67.

China Springs, Mclennan Co., St. Philip. (Mission Parish). Deacon James Weynand, Pastoral Admin.
Res., P.O. Box 327, 76633. Tel: 817-836-4321.

College Station, Brazos Co., St. Mary's (1926), Revs. Michael J. Sis; Dean E. Wilhelm; Deacon Bill Scott, Jr.
Res., 103 Nagle St., 77840. Tel: 409-846-5717; Fax: 409-846-4493.

St. Thomas Aquinas (1982), Rev. Samuel L. Hose. In res., Rev. Msgr. John C. Malinowski.
Res., 2541 East By-Pass, 77845. Tel: 409-696-3284; 693-6994 (Office); Fax: 409-693-0284.
Catechesis/Religious Programs—Tel: 409-693-7551. Becky Slovak, D.R.E.
Students 543.

Copperas Cove, Coryell Co., Holy Family (1963), Rev. William H. Donahue, C.S.C.; Rev. Msgr. John Frizelle.
Res., 1001 Georgetown Rd., 76522. Tel: 817-547-3735.
Catechesis/Religious Programs—Leslie Noel, D.R.E.
Students 455.

Dime Box, Lee Co., St. Joseph's (1902), Rev. Msgr. Emilian Foltyn.
Res., Rte. 1, Box 5A, 77853. Tel: 409-884-3100. [CEM]

Dripping Springs, Hays Co., St. Martin de Porres (1974), Rev. James L. Evans.
Mailing Address: P.O. Box 1062, 78620. Tel: 512-894-0774.
Catechesis/Religious Programs—Tel: 512-894-0212. Mary Carder, D.R.E.
Students 175.

Elgin, Bastrop Co., Sacred Heart (1908), Rev. John G. Boiko; Deacon Larry Dunne.
Res., 302 W. 11th St., 78621. Tel: 512-281-3536. [JC]
Catechesis/Religious Programs—Tel: 512-285-9543. Paula Bramlett, D.R.E.
Students 315.

Elk, McLennon Co., St. Joseph's (1925). Attended by St. Martin, Tours.
Mailing Address: Rte. 2, Box 209-A, West, 76691. Tel: 817-822-1145. [CEM]
Res., 301 St. Martins Church Rd., West, 76691.
Catechesis/Religious Programs—Mary Mann, D.R.E.
Students 66.

Fayetteville, Fayette Co., St. John's (1872) (Czech), Rev. Msgr. Benedict J. Mazurkiewicz.
Res., P.O. Box 57, 78940. Tel: 409-378-2277. [CEM]
Catechesis/Religious Programs—Sr. Euphrosine Honc, D.R.E.
Students 140.
Convent—Tel: 409-378-2275. Sisters of Divine Providence
Missions—Hostyn Hill, Fayette Co., St. Mary's, 78940.; Warrenton, Fayette Co., St. Martin's, 78940.

Frenstat, Burleson Co., Holy Rosary (1888). Attended by St. Ann's, Somerville. Rev. Robert P. Herald.
Mailing Address: P.O. Box 99, Somerville, 77879. Tel: 409-596-1966. [CEM]

Gatesville, Coryell Co., Our Lady of Lourdes (1946), Rev. Hilario Guajardo; Deacon Victor Beltran.
Res., 1108 W. Main St., 76528-1123. Tel: 817-865-6710.
Catechesis/Religious Programs—Rita Cloud, D.R.E.
Students 100.

Georgetown, Williamson Co., St. Helen's (1932), Rev. Msgr. Louis J. Wozniak; Rev. Walter F. Carr; Deacons Roger Collins; Juan C. Gonzalez, Jr.; Victor Droll.
Res., 2700 E. University Ave., 78626. Tel: 512-863-3041.
Catechesis/Religious Programs—Maria Kaesberg, D.R.E.
Students 609.
Mission—Andice, Santa Rosa.

Giddings, Lee Co., St. Margaret (1944) (German-Hispanic), Rev. David M. Leibham; Deacon Edward J. Hoefling.
Res., 500 S. Grimes, 78942. Tel: 409-542-3380. [JC]
Catechesis/Religious Programs—Students 200.
Mission—Pin Oak, Bastrop Co., St. Mary's, 78942.

Goldthwaite, Mills Co., St. Peter's (1885). Attended by St. Mary's, San Saba. Rev. Earl M. Hedberg.
Res., P.O. Box 352, 76844. Tel: 817-386-5513; 915-648-3732. [JC]
Catechesis/Religious Programs—Students 40.

Granger, Williamson Co., SS. Cyril and Methodius (1891), Rev. Msgr. Edward Rabroker.
Res., 300 W. Davilla, P.O. Box 608, 76530. Tel: 512-859-2223. [CEM 2]
School—Tel: 512-859-2927. Jim Byfield, Prin.
Lay Teachers 9; Students 88.
Catechesis/Religious Programs—Tel: 512-859-2224. D.R.E.: Marie Haida; Irene Cavanaugh; Cara Finn.
Students 250.

Hamilton, Hamilton Co., St. Thomas (1965) (Hispanic), Deacon James L. Gallagher, Admin.
Res., 905 N. Nicholson Ave., Rte. 1, Box 305, 76531. Tel: 817-386-5513. [JC]

Harker Heights, Bell Co., St. Paul Chong Hasang (1986), Rev. Richard O'Rourke, M.S.C. (Ireland).
Res., 1000 E. FM Rd. 2410, 76548. Tel: 817-698-4110; 698-4338; Fax: 817-698-4110.
Catechesis/Religious Programs—Ms. Olga Touchet, D.R.E.
Students 92.

Hearne, Robertson Co., St. Mary's (1872) (Italian & Mexican-American), Rev. Gregory McLaughlin.

Res., 402 W. First St., 77859. Tel: 409-279-2233. [CEM]
Catechesis/Religious Programs—Ada Sifuentes, D.R.E.
Students 274.
Mission—Calvert, Robertson Co., St. Mary, 77859.

Horseshoe Bay, Burnet Co, St. Paul the Apostle (1982), Rev. Robert T. Scott, C.S.P.
Res., P.O. Box 8019, 78657. Tel: 512-598-8342.
Catechesis/Religious Programs—Students 55.

Hostyn Hill, Fayette Co., St. Mary's (1855) (Czech). Attended by St. John's, Fayetteville.
Mailing Address: P.O. Box 57, Fayetteville, 78940. Tel: 409-378-2277. [CEM]

Jarrell, Williamson Co., Holy Trinity (1889) (Czech & German), Rev. Msgr. Arthur Michalka.
Res., Rte. 1, Box 63, 76537. Tel: 512-863-3020. [CEM]
Catechesis/Religious Programs—Lousie Straka, D.R.E.
Students 100.

Killeen, Bell Co., St. Joseph's (1954), Revs. Walter J. Matus; Albert Ruiz; Deacons Lyman Fansler; George Shieldes. In res., Rev. Charles E. Van Winkle, C.S.C.
Res., 2903 E. Rancier Ave., 76543. Tel: 817-634-7878; 634-7844; Fax: 817-634-1224.
School—(Grades PreK-5). Tel: 817-634-7272.
Lay Teachers 10; Students 120.
Catechesis/Religious Programs—Tel: 817-634-7878.
Students 369.

Kingsland, Llano Co., St. Charles Borromeo (1965), Rev. Joseph Mitrano, C.S.B.; Deacon Dr. George Lillard.
Mailing Address: P.O. Box 1748, 78639. Tel: 915-388-3742.
Res., 1927 Hwy. 1431, 78639.
Mission—Sunrise Beach, Burnet Co., Our Lady of the Lake.

Kovar, Bastrop Co., Sts. Peter and Paul (1909). Attended by St. Paul's, Smithville. Rev. Henry Heese.
Res., 204 Mills St., Smithville, 78957. Tel: 512-237-2179. [CEM 2]

Kyle, Hays Co., St. Anthony Marie De Claret (1909) (Hispanic), Rev. Howard Goertz; Deacons Richard Duecker; John Peca; John Lawrence; Joe Flores.
Res., 801 N. Burleson St., P.O. Box 268, 78640. Tel: 512-268-5312; 268-5311 (Office).
Catechesis/Religious Programs—Tel: 512-268-5311; Fax: 512-268-5311.
Students 540.

Lago Vista, Travis Co., St. Mary, Our Lady of the Lake (1970), Rev. Msgr. Joseph J. Schmitt.
Res., 6502 Avenida Ann, 78645. Tel: 512-267-1336; Fax: 512-267-2649.
Catechesis/Religious Programs—Tel: 512-267-2644.
Students 77.

La Grange, Fayette Co., Sacred Heart of Jesus (1886), Rev. Msgr. Harry C. Mazurkiewicz.
Res., Box 548, 78945. Tel: 409-968-3430; Fax: 409-968-5740. [JC]
School—Tel: 409-968-3223. Elmer Faykus, Prin.
Lay Teachers 16; Students 184.
Catechesis/Religious Programs—Sr. Elizabeth Agnes Gabriel, C.V.I., D.R.E.
Students 192.

Lampasas, Lampasas Co., St. Mary's (1885), Rev. Msgr. William C. Kinlough; Deacon Carlos Jasso.
Res., P.O. Box 866, 76550-0866. Tel: 512-556-5544.
Catechesis/Religious Programs—Tel: 512-556-6203. Sr. Mary Szabo, D.R.E.
Students 124.
Mission—Lometa, Lampasas Co., Good Shepherd Catholic Church, (1927).

Latium, Washington Co., Sacred Heart (1872) (Polish & Czech). Attended by St. Mary's, Brenham.
701 Church St., Brenham, 77833. Tel: 409-836-4441. [CEM]

Leander, Williamson Co., St. Yoo Peter Catholic Church, Rev. San Yil Lee.
Res., P.O. Box 1476, 78646.
St. Margaret Mary (1942), Rev. William Benish; Deacon Allen Desorcie.
Res., P.O. Box 2410, Cedar Park, 78630-2410. Tel: 512-259-3126; Fax: 512-259-9658.
Catechesis/Religious Programs—Therese Sternenberg, D.R.E.
Students 315.

Lexington, Lee Co., Holy Family (1990). Mission of St. Joseph, Rockdale. Rev. Victor Mathias.

Llano, Llano Co., Holy Trinity (1890). Attended by St. Joseph's Church, Mason. Rev. Karel Fink.
Mailing Address: P.O. Box 673, 78643. Tel: 915-247-4481. [JC]
Catechesis/Religious Programs—Susan Hagar, D.R.E.
Students 88.
Mission—Mason, Box 1572, Mason, 76856.

Lockhart, Caldwell Co., St. Mary's (1887), Rev. Adam Martinez; Deacons Guadalupe Aguilar; William Long; William Haywood.
Res., 205 W. Pecan, 78644. Tel: 512-398-4649; 376-3634; Fax: 512-398-2285. [CEM]
Catechesis/Religious Programs—Tel: 512-398-3506. Eva Mendez, D.R.E.
Students 518.

Lometa, Lampasas Co., Good Shepherd (1927). Attended by St. Mary's, Lampasas. Rev. Msgr. William C. Kinlough.
Mailing Address: P.O. Box 866, Lampasas, 76550-0866. Tel: 512-556-5544.
500 W. Main St., 76853.

Lott, Falls Co., Sacred Heart (1906), Rev. E. Peter Royal.
Res., P.O. Box 371, Marlin, 76661. Tel: 817-883-2016. [CEM]

Luling, Caldwell Co., St. John the Evangelist (1879), Rev. Jesse Euresti.
Res., 500 E. Travis St., 78648. Tel: 210-875-5354. [CEM]
Catechesis/Religious Programs—Tel: 210-875-3901. Sr. Mary Frances Bartsch, O.L.V.M., D.R.E.
Students 238.

Manor, Travis Co., St. Joseph's (1876) (Hispanic), Rev. Robert Mahoney.
Mailing Address: P.O. Box 389, 78653. Tel: 512-272-4004. [JC]
Catechesis/Religious Programs—Students 107.

Marak, Milam Co., SS. Cyril and Methodius (1903). Attended from St. Joseph's, Burlington. Rev. Leonard Leddy.
Rte. 1, Box 62, Burlington, 76519. Tel: 817-985-2280.
Church—Tel: 817-697-4861.
Catechesis/Religious Programs—Tel: 817-697-4459.
Students 25.

Marble Falls, Burnet Co., St. John the Evangelist (1961), Rev. Edwin J. Kadzielawski, C.S.C.
Church—105 Hwy. 1431 E., 78654. Tel: 512-693-5134.
Catechesis/Religious Programs—Students 57.

Marlin, Falls Co., St. Joseph's (1876), Rev. E. Peter Royal; Deacon Julian Tyboroski.
Res., Box 371, 76661. Tel: 817-883-2016.
Catechesis/Religious Programs—Gene Wilkey, D.R.E.
Students 213.
Mission—Marlin, Falls Co., Sacred Heart, 76661.

Martindale, Caldwell Co., Immaculate Heart of Mary (1908). Attended by St. John the Evangelist, San Marcos. Rev. Jose L. Sanchez, C.M.F.
Mailing Address: P.O. Box 117, 78655. Tel: 512-357-6573.
Catechesis/Religious Programs—Frances S. Castillo, D.R.E.
Students 169.

Mason, Mason Co., St. Joseph's (1873) (Hispanic), Rev. Karel Fink.
Res., P.O. Box 1572, 76856. Tel: 915-347-6932. [CEM]
Catechesis/Religious Programs—Della Moneyhon, D.R.E.
Students 80.
Mission—Llano, Holy Trinity Church.

McGregor, McLennan Co., St. Eugene (1958) (Hispanic), Rev. George C. George.
Res., 207 N. Johnson Dr., 76657. Tel: 817-840-3174.
Catechesis/Religious Programs—Tel: 817-666-0021.
Students 124.
Mission—Moody, McLennan Co., Our Lady of San Juan, 207 N. Johnson Dr., 76657.

Mexia, Limestone Co., St. Mary's (1886), Rev. Scott Mikkelson.
Mailing Address: 506 E. Sumpter, 76667. [JC]
Res., 606 N. Bonham, 76667. Tel: 817-562-3619.
Catechesis/Religious Programs—Students 115.

Moody, McLennan Co., Our Lady of San Juan (1991) (Hispanic). Attended by Mission of St. Eugene, McGregor. Rev. George S. Chengazhacheril; Deacon Weldon Bowling, Admin.
207 N. Johnson Dr., McGregor, 76657. Tel: 817-840-3174.
Catechesis/Religious Programs—Tel: 817-853-9011.
Students 55.

Old Washington-on-the Brazos, Washington Co., Blessed Virgin Mary (1849) (African American). Attended by St. Mary's Church, Brenham. Rev. Leonard Cornelius, O.F.M.; Deacon Raymond Sis.
701 Church St., Brenham, 77833. Tel: 409-836-4441. [CEM]

Pflugerville, Travis Co., St. Elizabeth (1932), Revs. Tom Frank; Kevin Rai; Deacons Roy Hubbard; Victor Droll; Marc Washburne.
Mailing Address: P.O. Box 524, 78691-0524. Tel: 512-251-9838.
Res., 304 S. 8th St., Tel: 512-251-9866.
Catechesis/Religious Programs—Students 475.

Pin Oak, Bastrop Co., St. Mary's (1866) (German). Attended by St. Margaret's, Giddings.
500 S. Grimes, Giddings, 78942. Tel: 409-542-3380. [CEM]

Rockdale, Milam Co., St. Joseph's (1880), Rev. Victor Mathias.
Church—P.O. Box 548, 76567. Tel: 512-446-2049.
Res., 521 E. Davilla St., 76567. Tel: 512-446-2196.
Catechesis/Religious Programs—Carol Janak, D.R.E.
Students 190.
Mission—Lexington, Lee Co., Holy Family, P.O. Box 541, Lexington, 78947. Tel: 409-773-2244.

Rockne, Bastrop Co., Sacred Heart (1876), Rev. Msgr. Clyde Holtman; Deacon Roger Muehr.
Res., Rte. 1, Box 108, Bastrop, 78602. Tel: 512-321-7991. [CEM]
Catechesis/Religious Programs—Jeanease Friske, D.R.E.
Students 200.
Mission—String Prairie, Assumption of the Blessed Virgin Mary. [CEM]

Rogers, Bell Co., St. Matthew (1991), Rev. Ricardo Aguilar; Deacon Juan Garza, Admin.
Mailing Address: P.O. Box 366, 76569.
103 E. Gulf St., 76569. Tel: 817-642-3450.

Rosebud, Falls Co., St. Ann's (1915), Rev. Thaddeus Tabak, S.D.S. (Poland).
Res., P.O. Drawer 85, Burlington, 76519. Tel: 817-869-2525. [CEM]
Catechesis/Religious Programs—Tel: 817-583-4624.
Students 126.
Mission—Burlington, Milam Co., St. Michael's, (1879) P.O. Box 85, Burlington, 76519.

Round Rock, Williamson Co., St. William's (1956), Revs. Don Loftin; Jairo Lopez; Beverly Collin, Pastoral Assoc.; Deacons Concho Castillo; Juan Gonzalez, Jr.; Jim Moat. In res., Bro. Luke M. Baldwin, M.M.
Office: 1000 McNeil Rd., 78681. Tel: 512-255-4473; Fax: 512-255-8126.
Res., 1700 St. William's St., 78681. Tel: 512-255-3825.
Catechesis/Religious Programs—Tel: 512-255-9118.
Students 1,038.

Salado, Bell Co., St. Stephen's (1989), Deacon John Petter, Pastoral Admin.
Mailing Address: P.O. Box 662, 76571. Tel: 817-947-8037.
Res., Holy Trinity Church, Holland Rd. off IH 35, 76751.
Catechesis/Religious Programs—Tel: 817-947-0114. Robert Michalewicz, D.R.E.
Students 70.

San Marcos, Hays Co., St. John the Evangelist (1883), Revs. Brian Culley, C.M.F.; Henry Luna, C.M.F. Pastoral Assocs.: Sr. Teresa Cruz, M.C.M., Youth Min.; Sr. Juliana Soto, M.C.M.; Mr. Michael Philen, Pastoral Assoc.; Deacons Lalo Duran; Domingo Vargas. In res., Revs. Art Gramaje, C.M.F., Campus Min.; Paul Keller, C.M.F.
Res., 624 E. Hopkins, 78666. Tel: 512-353-8969.
Catechesis/Religious Programs—Tel: 512-353-5065. Sr. Socorro Lozoya, M.C.M., D.R.E.
Students 1,000.
Convent—964 Field St., 78666. Tel: 512-396-5333.
Missions—San Marcos, Hays Co., Guadalupe Chapel, Corner of Roosevelt & Churchill, 78666.; Uhland, Hays Co., St. Michael's, 80 S. Old Spanish Tr., Uhland, 78640. Tel: 512-398-7475. Deacon Lalo Duran, Pastoral Coord.; Martindale, Caldwell Co., Immaculate Heart of Mary, P.O. Box 117, Martindale, 78655. Tel: 512-357-6573.

San Saba, San Saba Co., St. Mary's (1967) (Hispanic), Rev. Earl M. Hedberg.
Church—P.O. Box 415, 76877. Tel: 915-372-3679.
Catechesis/Religious Programs—Tani Menchaca, D.R.E.
Students 62.
Mission—Lampass Co., Izoro.

Satin, Satin Falls Co., Santa Rita Shrine (1921) (Hispanic). Attended by St. Francis, Waco. Rev. Jose A. Martorell, T.O.R.
301 Jefferson Ave., Waco, 76701. Tel: 817-752-8434; Fax: 817-752-2415.

Smithville, Bastrop Co., St. Paul the Apostle (1896), Rev. Henry Heese; Deacon Cleofas Cruz.
Res., 204 Mills St., 78957. Tel: 512-237-2179.
Catechesis/Religious Programs—Students 163.

Somerville, Burleson Co., St. Ann's (1954), Rev. Joel D. McNeil.

Res., P.O. Box 99, 77879. Tel: 409-596-1966.
Catechesis/Religious Programs—Tel: 409-596-1494. Sr. M. John, D.R.E.
Students 57.
Mission—Frenstat, Burleson Co., Holy Rosary, 77879.

Stony Point, Travis Co., Father Joel Atwood Catholic Community Center (1987). Attended by St. Anthony, Kyle. Rev. Howard Goertz; Deacon Richard Duecker, Pastoral Admin.
Mailing Address: 9110 Hwy. 183 S., Austin, 78745. Tel: 512-243-1404.
Res., No. 22 & 43 Stoney Point Dr., Del Valle, 78617.

String Prairie, Bastrop Co., St. Mary's of the Assumption (1876) (German). Attended by Sacred Heart, Rockne. Rev. Msgr. Clyde Holtman.
Rte. 1, Box 108, Bastrop, 78602. Tel: 512-839-4580. [CEM]

Taylor, Williamson Co., St. Mary's (1877), Rev. Lonnie A. Urban.
Res., 408 Washburn St., 76574. Tel: 512-352-2175; Fax: 512-365-1431. [CEM]
School—Tel: 512-352-2313. Sr. Carita Ulm, O.P., Prin.
Sisters 4; Lay Teachers 19; Students 221.
Catechesis/Religious Programs—Tel: 512-352-2133. Mrs. Belinda Ozuna, D.R.E.
Students 455.
Convent—317 E. 4th St., 76574. Tel: 512-352-2144.
Our Lady of Guadalupe (1914) (Hispanic), Rev. Pedro Garcia; Deacon Gumisindo Gonzales.
Res., 113 Dickey St., 76574. Tel: 512-365-2380; Fax: 512-365-1733. [CEM]
Catechesis/Religious Programs—Students 350.

Temple, Bell Co., St. Mary's (1883), Revs. Le-Mihn Pham; Steven Nesrsta; Deacons Don Burleson; John Petter.
Res., 1018 S. 7th St., 76504. Tel: 817-773-4541; Fax: 817-774-7044. [JC]
School—Tel: 817-778-8141. Loris Edwards, Prin.
Lay Teachers 20; Students 239.
Catechesis/Religious Programs—Tel: 817-773-1980. Barbara Burleson, D.R.E.
Students 384.
Rectory—1004 S. 7th St., 76504. Tel: 817-773-3238.
St. Luke's (1969), Revs. Louis Paulicek; Steve Kana; Deacons Jerome J. Klement; Bill Smetana.
Res., 2807 Oakdale, 76502. Tel: 817-773-1561; Fax: 817-773-4623. [JC]
Catechesis/Religious Programs—Tel: 817-773-2330.
Students 413.
Our Lady of Guadalupe (1952) (Hispanic), Rev. Ricardo Aguilar.
Res., 708 S. 6th St., 76504. Tel: 817-773-6779; Fax: 817-773-2699.
Catechesis/Religious Programs—Students 280.

Tours, McLennan Co., St. Martin (1870) (German-Czech), Rev. Isidore Rozycki.
Res., 301 St. Martin's Church Rd., West, 76691-2135. Tel: 817-822-1145. [CEM]
Catechesis/Religious Programs—Tel: 817-822-1026. Dorothy Middleton, D.R.E.
Students 190.
Mission—Elk, McLennon Co., St. Joseph.

Uhland, Hays Co., St. Michael's (1924). Attended by St. John's, San Marcos. Rev. Brian Culley, C.M.F.; Deacon Lalo Duran, Pastoral Coord.
Mailing Address: 624 E. Hopkins St., San Marcos, 78666.
Res., 80 Old Spanish Tr., 78640. Tel: 512-398-7475.
Catechesis/Religious Programs—Mrs. Trina Alvarez, D.R.E.
Students 60.

Waco, McLennan Co.,

1—Sacred Heart, (1957) (Spanish), Rev. Lawrence Soler, T.O.R.
Res., 2621 Bagby Ave., 76711. Tel: 817-756-2656.
Catechesis/Religious Programs—Tel: 817-756-2390.
Students 400.

2—St. Francis on the Brazos, (1924) (Hispanic), Revs. Jose A. Martorell, T.O.R.; Anthony P. Ferrer, T.O.R.; Anselmo Mondragon, T.O.R.; Deacon Jessie Garza.
Res., 301 Jefferson Ave., 76701. Tel: 817-752-8434; Fax: 817-752-2415. [JC]
School—Tel: 817-753-5565; Fax: 817-753-6816. Sr. Barbara Herrera, Prin.
Sisters 4; Lay Teachers 5; Students 140.
Nursery & Kindergarten—612 N. 3rd St., 76701.
Catechesis/Religious Programs—Tel: 817-752-1159.
Students 610.
Convent—612 N. 3rd St., 76701. Tel: 817-753-5565.
Mission—Satin, Satin Falls Co., Santa Rita.

3—St. Jerome, (1982), Rev. William C. Brooks.
Res., 9820 Chapel Rd., 76712. Tel: 817-666-2120; Fax: 817-666-7722.
Catechesis/Religious Programs—Tel: 817-666-3555; Fax: 817-666-2120. D.R.E.: Nancy Coker; Pam Kosarek.
Students 570.

4—St. John the Baptist, (1953) (African American), Deacons Alton Hithe, Pastoral Admin.; Joseph A. Weynand.
Res., 1312 Dallas St., P.O. Box 585, 76704-0585. Tel: 817-753-6742.
Catechesis/Religious Programs—Students 981.
Mission—Waco.

5—St. Joseph, (Bellmead) (1950), Rev. Timothy V. Vaverek. In res., Rev. James O'Connor.
Res., 1011 Boston St., 76705. Tel: 817-799-2531.
Catechesis/Religious Programs—Tel: 817-799-6646. Brenda Fetsch, D.R.E.
Students 200.

6—St. Louis, (1964), Rev. Msgr. Mark Deering. In res., Revs. Leo A. Baysinger, S.D.B.; Martin Rabbitte, M.S.C.
Res., 2001 N. 25th St., P.O. Box 5040, 76708. Tel: 817-754-1221.
School—Tel: 817-754-2041. John Vasek, Prin.
Lay Teachers 22; Students 330.
Catechesis/Religious Programs—Sally Rue, D.R.E.
Students 126.

7—St. Mary of the Assumption, (1870), Rev. Angelo Bertini; Deacon Sidney Prewitt.
Res., 1401 Washington Ave., 76701. Tel: 817-753-0146; Fax: 817-753-5100. [JC]
School—Tel: 817-754-1622; Fax: 817-756-6365. Sr. M. Kenneth Regan, C.S.C., Prin.
Sisters 1; Lay Teachers 14; Students 156.
Catechesis/Religious Programs—Sr. Virginia Dunker, D.C., D.R.E.
Students 115.
Convent—224 N. 14th St., 76701. Tel: 817-756-0548.

West, McLennan Co., Assumption (1892) (Czech), Revs. Edward Karasek; Melvin Dornak.
Res., P.O. Box 276, 76691. Tel: 817-826-3705. [CEM]
School—Tel: 817-826-5991; Fax: 817-826-5996. Joe Gough, Prin.
Lay Teachers 10; Students 142.
Catechesis/Religious Programs—Mrs. Pam Urbanovsky, D.R.E.
Students 366.

Westphalia, Falls Co., Visitation (1883), Rev. Reinhold Schmitt, C.M.M.
Res., Rte. 2, Box 53A, Lott, 76656. Tel: 817-584-4983. [CEM]
Catechesis/Religious Programs—Tel: 817-584-4407. Edna Spivey, D.R.E.
Students 135.

Wimberley, Hays Co., St. Mary (1956), Rev. Everett Trebtoske; Deacon John C. Maher.
Res., 14711 Ranch Rd. 12, 78676. Tel: 512-847-9181 (Church); Fax: 512-847-5573. [CEM]
Catechesis/Religious Programs—Diane Whitten, D.R.E.
Students 98.

Chaplains of Public Institutions

Austin. *Brackenridge Hospital.* Rev. Richard Tijerina.
Brown School 2309 Euclid St., 78704. Tel: 512-442-3602. Rev. Barry Cabell, C.S.C.
St. David's Hospital. 2010 Guadalupe, 78705. Tel: 512-477-9471. Rev. Robert Michele, C.S.P.
School for the Blind. 7601 Burnet Rd., 78757. Tel: 512-454-0384. Rev. Larry Covington.
School for the Deaf. 2309 Euclid St., 78704. Tel: 512-442-3602. Rev. Barry Cabell, C.S.C.
State Hospital. 4110 Guadalupe, 78751. Tel: 512-419-2573. Sr. Ruth Steiner, S.M.I.C.
State School. 2010 Guadalupe, 78705. Tel: 512-477-9471. Rev. James McCabe.

Bastrop. *Federal Correctional Institute.* P.O. Box 730, 78602. Rev. Emmett N. Faber (LC).

Gatesville. *State School for Boys.* P.O. Box 665, 76528. Deacon James Gallagher, Chap.

Giddings. *State School.* P.O. Box 600, 78942. Tel: 409-542-3686. Rev. Peter McCabe.

Marlin. *V.A. Hospital.* P.O. Box 371, 76661. Rev. Peter Royal.

Mexia. *State School.* 606 N. Bonham, 76667. Tel: 817-562-3619. Rev. Scott Mikkelson.

Temple. *V.A. Hospital.* 1901 S. First St., 76501. Rev. Harry Bilski.

Waco. *V.A. Hospital.* Memorial Dr., 76703. Rev. Thomas J. Niemira.

Special Assignments:
Reverend Monsignors—
Fruge, Donald J. (GAL), Finance Officer
Matocha, Edward C., Vicar General
Reverend Fathers—
Goertz, Bernard C., Rte. 2, Box 129, Cedar Creek, TX 78612
Goertz, Victor, Cedarbrake Renewal Center, P.O. Box 58, Belton, TX 76513

On Duty Outside the Diocese:
Reverend Monsignors—
Chatham, Donald, #12 the Lindens, 222 Kew Rd., Richmond, Surrey TW93LL England
Elmer, Charles, North American College, 00120 Vatican State Europe
Reverend Fathers—
Chalupa, Fred, Diocese of Galveston-Houston, P.O. Box 907, Houston, TX 77001
Chamberlain, Thomas, Parroquia de San Isidro Labrador, Hidalgo 204, Apdo. 24, Arteaga, Coahuila C.P. 25350 Mexico
Herald, Robert P., Texas Department of Corrections, Office of the Catholic Chaplain, Ellis Unit I, Rte. 6, Huntsville, TX 77343
Jenkins, Ronnie, Divine Word College, 1025 Michigan Ave. N.E., Washington, D.C. 20017-1895
Kinel, Robert, St. Joseph Seminary, 1200 Varnum St. N.E., Washington, D.C. 20017
Mahoney, Bernard, 1722 Chippendale, Houston, TX 77108
Mulvey, Michael, Scuoia Sarcerdotale, via S. Francesco 4, Vivaio, C.P. 72, Incisa Valdarno (F1) 50064 Italy
Perez, Greg, Holy Trinity Seminary, P.O. Box 140309, Irving, TX 75014
Strieder, Leon, St. Mary's Seminary, 9845 Memorial Dr., Houston, TX 77024
Willemsen, Andrew J., Eindhovenseweg 32, 5524 AR Steensel, Netherlands

---

Military Chaplains:
Reverend Fathers—
Moss, Donald, Naval Chaplain's School, Mailing Address: Code PO 705, NAVAIR WPNSTA, 521 Ninth St., Port Mugo, CA 93042

Absent on Sick Leave:
Reverend Monsignors—
Miller, Frank, Rte. 2, Box 46-E, Abbott, TX 76621

Retired:
Reverend Monsignors—
Frizelle, John D., 1108 W. Main St., Gatesville, TX 76528-1123. Tel: 817-865-6710
Fuchs, Robert A., Rte. 2, Box 48A, Rosebud, TX 76570
Fuchs, Sylvester, Lost Prairie Villa, 9901 FM Rd. 2086, Temple, TX 76501-3528
Stram, Gideon, Rte. 1, Box 138-N, Jarrell, TX 76537. Tel: 512-746-2028
Tydlacka, George, 874 Burleson-Manor Rd., Manor, TX 78653
Widacki, Roman, 400 Austin Ave., #1102, Waco, TX 76703
Reverend Fathers—
Collins, Robert, 3003 Maplelawn Cir., Austin, TX 78723
Conrad, Stanley, Niepokalanow-Teresin, 96-515 K, Sochaczew, Poland
Guttenberger, Xavier, RBJ, 21 Waller #906, Austin, TX 78702. Tel: 512-478-7277
Hand, Chester, Jr., 400 Austin Ave., Waco, TX 76703
Herledan, John, Box 702, Georgetown, TX 78627
Lazek, Aleck, The Regis, No. 533, 400 Austin Ave., Waco, TX 76703
Tzanakas, George M., 1433 Williams St., Apt. 206, Denver, CO 80218

Permanent Deacons:
Adam, Klaus, Ft. Hood Cath. Comm., Killeen
Aguilar, Guadalupe, St. Mary's, Lockhart
Barkley, Roy, St. Joseph's, Manor
Behr, Roger L., Sacred Heart, Austin
Beltran, Victor, Hughes Unit, Gatesville
Berg, James R.
Bowling, Weldon, St. Paul, Chong Hasanh
Burleson, Don, St. Mary's, Temple
Castillo, Concepcion, St. Williams, Round Rock
Cepak, Benny, St. Joseph's, Bellmead
Cochrane, Lee
Collins, Roger, St. Helen's, Georgetown
Cortez, Willie, Our Lady's Youth Center, Austin; St. Mary's, Austin
Crochet, Larry, St. John the Evangelist, Marble Falls
Crowley, Joe, Our Lady's, Maronite, Austin
Cruz, Cleofas, Sts. Peter and Paul, Smithville
Deason, Switzer, St. Joseph's, Bryan
Desorcie, Allen, St. Vincent de Paul, Austin
Doriocourt, Luis, St. Mary's, Hearne
Droll, Victor, St. Helen's, Georgetown
Duecker, Richard, Fr. Joel Atwood, Stoney Point
Dufour, E. Generes, Diocesan Prison Ministry
Dunne, Larry, Sacred Heart, Elgin
Duran, Everardo S., St. Michael's, Uhland

Elliott, Gregg, Ben Taub Hospital
Embry, Rob, St. Margaret of Scotland, Austin
Fansler, Lyman C., St. Joseph's, Killeen
Flores, Joe, St. Anthony's, Kyle
Foreman, Boyce A., Lakeway, Austin
Fuller, James, Sacred Heart, Austin
Gallagher, James, St. Thomas, Hamilton
Garcia, Louis, Santa Teresa, Bryan
Garza, Jessie, St. Francis of the Brazos, Waco
Garza, Juan, St. Matthew's, Rogers
Gonzales, Gumisindo, Our Lady of Guadalupe, Taylor
Gonzalez, John, St. William, Round Rock
Graham, James, St. Ignatius Martyr, Austin
Ham, W. J., St. Catherine of Siena, Austin
Hamlet, Mark, St. John Neuman, Austin
Hansen, Clarence, St. Theresa's, Austin
Haywood, Daryl, St. Mary's, Lockhart
Hernandez, Salvador, Our Lady of Guadalupe, Austin
Hithe, Alton, St. John's, Waco
Hoefling, Ed, St. Margaret, Giddings
Hubbard, Roy, St. Elizabeth's, Pflugerville
Hudson, Richard, St. Louis, Austin
Jacobs, James A., (Retired)
James, Ray, St. Theresa's, Austin
Januszewski, Bill, St. Mary's, Brenham
Jasso, Carlos, St. Mary's, Lampasas
Joseph, George, San Jose, Austin
Kennedy, Pat, St. Albert, Austin
Kim, Peter, St. Mary's, Austin
Klement, Jerome, St. Luke's, Temple
Krotzer, Philip, St. Martin de Porres, Dripping Springs
Larner, Richard, St. Paul's, Austin
Lawrence, John, St. Anthony's, Kyle
Lilliard, George, St. Charles, Kingsland
Long, Bill, St. Mary's, Lockhart
Maddox, Edward, Assumption, San Antonio
Maher, John, St. Mary's, Wimberly
Mallinger, Thomas, St. Thomas More, Austin
Martinez, Jesse, Apache Shores, Austin
Medrano, Guadalupe, Cristo Rey, Austin
Menchaca, Richard, St. Mary's, San Saba
Moat, Jim, St. Williams, Round Rock
Montag, Eugene J., Our Mother of Sorrows, Burnet
Montalvo, Manuel, San Jisidro Labrador, Arteaga, Coahuila, Mexico
Morris, Douglas, St. John Neumann, Austin
Muehr, Roger, Sacred Heart, Rockne
Murray, Patrick, St. Ignatius, Austin
Murrell, Jack, Good Shepherd, Johnson City
Nelson, Gary, St. Joseph's, Bryan
Nira, Oswaldo, St. Peter the Apostle, Austin
Ojeda, Johnny, Cristo Rey, Austin
Orozco, Abraham
Peca, John M., St. Anthony's, Kyle
Peschka, Alfred, St. Louis, Austin
Petter, John, St. Mary's, Temple
Pfuntner, Jordan, St. Mary's & Baylor Catholic Comm., Waco
Potter, Joseph, St. Eugene, McGregor
Prewitt, Sidney, St. Mary's, Waco
Ramsey, Jesse, St. Louis, Austin
Renteria, Mario, Our Lady of Guadalupe, Austin
Reyna, Frank, St. Francis of Assisi, Frisco
Reynolds, Joseph, St. Anne's, Somerville
Rivera, John, San Jose, Austin
Ruiz, Joe, Holy Cross, Bertram
Saenz, Enrique, San Jose, Austin
Schwab, Peter, St. Thomas Moore, Austin
Scott, Bill, St. Mary's, College Station
Shieldes, George, St. Joseph's, Killeen
Shoemaker, William, Christ the King, Belton
Sis, Ray, St. Joseph's, Bryan
Smetana, Bill, St. Luke's, Temple
Solarzano, Eraclio, St. John the Evangelist, Marble Falls
Terry, Frank, St. Ferdinand, Blanco
Tyborowski, Julian, St. Joseph's, Marlin
Valeriano, Oscar, Christ the King, Belton
Vargas, Domingo, St. John's, San Marcos
Vasquez, Alfredo, San Jose, Austin
Vela, William, Sacred Heart, Austin
Washburne, Marc, St. Elizabeth, Pflugerville
Weilert, Otto, Diocesan Pastoral Center
Weynand, Joe, St. John's, Waco
Wilson, Gilbert, St. Joseph's, Bryan
Young, John, St. Mary's, Caldwell

INSTITUTIONS LOCATED IN THE DIOCESE

[A] COLLEGES AND UNIVERSITIES

AUSTIN. *Brothers of the Congregation of the Holy Cross*, (1881) St. Edward's University, 3001 S. Congress Ave., 78704. Tel: 512-448-8400.
For a complete listing, refer to the Colleges and Universities section.

[B] HIGH SCHOOL, DIOCESAN

WACO. *Reicher Catholic High School*, 2102 N. 23rd St., 76708. Rev. Leo A. Baysinger, S.D.B., Prin. Priests 1; Sisters 3; Lay Teachers 17; Students 216.

[C] HIGH SCHOOL, PRIVATE

AUSTIN. *St. Michaels's Catholic Academy*, 3000 Barton Creek Blvd., 78735. Tel: 512-328-2323. Rev. Joel M. Konzen, S.M., Prin. Schoenstatt Sisters of Mary 1; Lay Teachers 40; Students 345.

[D] ELEMENTARY SCHOOL, PRIVATE

AUSTIN. *Dominican Academy*. (Grades K-3), 12475 Trail Driver, 78737. Tel: 512-288-4266. Sr. Leona Castle, O.P.; Sr. Benita Kelly, O.P. Sisters 2; Lay Teachers 2; Students 36.

[E] MATERNITY AND ADOPTION PROGRAM

AUSTIN. *Marywood Children & Family Services*, 510 W. 26th St., 78705. Tel: 512-472-9251; Fax: 512-472-4829. Total in Residence 38; Staff 35. Daughters of Charity of St. Vincent de Paul 1; Capacity 35.

[F] GENERAL HOSPITALS

AUSTIN. *Seton East Community Health Center*, 2811 E. Second St., 78702. Tel: 512-323-4930.
For a complete listing, refer to the Hospitals section.
Seton Medical Center, 1201 W. 38th St., 78705. Tel: 512-323-1000.
For a complete listing, refer to the Hospitals section.
Seton Northwest Hospital, 1113 Research Blvd., 78759. Tel: 512-795-1000.
For a complete listing, refer to the Hospitals section.
Seton South Community Health Center, 3706 S. First St., 78704. Tel: 512-323-4940.
For a complete listing, refer to the Hospitals section.

BRENHAM. *Trinity Community Medical Center of Brenham*, 700 Medical Pkwy., 77833. Tel: 409-836-6173.
For a complete listing, refer to the Hospitals section.

BRYAN. *Burleson Lease Corp. Inc./dba Burleson St. Joseph Health Center*, 2801 Franciscan Dr., 77802. Tel: 409-776-2464.
For a complete listing, refer to the Hospitals section.
Burleson-St. Joseph Services Corp., 2801 Franciscan Dr., 77802. Tel: 409-776-3777.
For a complete listing, refer to the Hospitals section.
St. Joseph Hospital and Health Center of Bryan, Inc., 2801 Franciscan Dr., 77802. Tel: 409-776-3777.
For a complete listing, refer to the Hospitals section.

WACO. *Providence Health Center*, 6901 Medical Pkwy., P.O. Box 2589, 76702-2589. Tel: 817-751-4763.
For a complete listing, refer to the Hospitals section.

[G] SPECIAL HOSPITAL

WACO. *DePaul Center*, 301 Londonderry Dr., 76712. Tel: 817-776-5970; 1-800-777-5043.
For a complete listing, refer to the Special Care Facilities section.

[H] MONASTERIES AND RESIDENCES OF PRIESTS AND BROTHERS

AUSTIN. *Brother Andre House*, 2113 Brackenridge St., 78704. Tel: 512-462-3540; Fax: 512-416-1216. Bro. Thomas G. Krieter, C.S.C.
Brothers of the Congregation of Holy Cross, Brother John Baptist Province Center, c/o St. Edward's University, No. 1046, 78704. Tel: 512-442-7856; Fax: 512-444-3133. Bros. Donald Blauvelt, C.S.C., Prov. Supr.; Matthew Lyons, C.S.C., Asst. Provincial; Harold Ehlinger, C.S.C., Steward; Richard Critz, C.S.C., Sec.; Stanley Culotte, C.S.C., Councilor; Richard Daly, C.S.C., Councilor; Stephen Walsh, C.S.C., Coucilor; Mel Keil, C.S.C., Asst. Steward; Carl Smith, C.S.C., Admin. Asst.; Donald Dufour, C.S.C., Staff Asst. Total in province 130.
Congregation of Holy Cross - Southern Province, Provincial Office, 2111 Brackenridge St., 78704. Tel: 512-443-3886; Fax: 512-416-1216. Revs. John R. Birkmeyer, C.S.C., (Retired); Jeremiah R. Buttomer, C.S.C., (Retired); Leonard J. Collins, C.S.C., Prov.; Joseph DeVliegher, C.S.C.; Joseph F. Houser, C.S.C., (Retired); Joseph M. Kmiecik, C.S.C., (Retired); Joseph M. Moyer, C.S.C.; Paul B. Rankin, C.S.C., (Retired); Joseph W. Rehage, (Retired); O. Fred Underwood, C.S.C.; Charles E. Van Winkle, C.S.C.; Allen L. Cormier, C.S.C., (Retired); Leon J. Boarman, C.S.C., (Retired); Bro. Thomas G. Krieter, C.S.C., Prov. Steward.
Dominican Fathers, 2502 Comburg Castle Way, 78748-5258. Tel: 512-282-3908; Fax: 512-280-9011. Revs. James A. McDonough, O.P., Supr.; Neal Wise, O.P. Tel: 512-448-8455, 2421 Oak Crest, 78704. Tel: 512-444-7614. Rev. Ralph Rogawski, O.P., 3001 S. Congress, 78704. Tel: 512-442-4534. Rev. Eduardo Gabriel, O.P.
Jesuit Fathers and Brothers, St. Thomas More Church, 10205 R.R. 620, 78726. Tel: 512-258-1161. Revs. Steven Ryan, S.J.; Gerard Steckler, S.J.; Rocky Vaz, S.J.
Moreau House, St. Edward University #1069, 3001 S. Congress, 78704. Tel: 512-448-8595. Bros. Lawrence Atkinson, C.S.C., Dir.; Edwin Reggio, C.S.C.; James Kane, C.S.C.; Howard Metz, C.S.C.
St. Edward's University, 3001 S. Congress Ave., Box 1041, 78704. Tel: 512-443-3732. Revs. John Collet, O.M.I.; William Davis, O.M.I.; Emmanuel Kawanguzi, St. Joseph Hall.
St. Joseph Hall. St. Edward University, 3001 S. Congress Ave., 78704. Tel: 512-442-4534; Fax: 512-442-0589. Bro. Joseph Harris, C.S.C., Supr. In res., Revs. Joseph Rehage, C.S.C.; Emmanuel Kawanguzi (Uganda); Eduardo Gabriel, O.P.; Leon Boarman, C.S.C. Total in Residence 29; Brothers 25.
Steiner Lodge Retreat, 3117 Westlake Dr., 78746. Tel: 512-328-0459.

BRENHAM. *Order of Friars Minor*, St. Francis Friary, 9539 FM 2193, 77833. Tel: 409-830-1554. Rev. Leonard Cornelius, O.F.M. Total in Residence 8.

WACO. *Salesians of Don Bosco*, Reicher High School, 2102 N. 23rd St., 76708. Tel: 817-752-8349. Rev. Leo A. Baysinger, S.D.B.

[I] CONVENTS AND RESIDENCES FOR SISTERS

AUSTIN. *Adrian Dominican Sisters*, 1943 Dapplegrey Ln., 78727-4590. Tel: 512-834-9620.
Daughters of Charity of St. Vincent De Paul, 1018 W. 31st St., 78705. Tel: 512-453-9655. Sisters 11. 5803 Fairlane Dr., 78757. Tel: 512-452-8980. Sisters 2. Other Address: 3404 Medical Pkwy., 78705. Tel: 512-323-4906. Sisters 4.
Daughters of Mary Help of Christians (Salesian Sisters of St. John Bosco), St. Mary Mazzarello Convent, 747 Cherico, 78702. Tel: 512-385-9122. Sr. Irene Tapia, F.M.A. Sisters 3.
Dominican Sisters of Houston, 5911 Reicher Dr., 78723. Tel: 512-926-0687. Sr. Mary Jean Olsovsky; Sr. Leona Castle, O.P.; Sr. Benita Kelly, O.P., Other address: 12507 A Traildriver, 78737. Sr. Carol Wagner, O.P.; Sr. Steven Zawacki, O.P., Sisters 5. Other Address: 12505 B Traildriver, 78737.
Franciscan Sisters Daughters of Mercy (Hermanas Franciscanas Hijas de la Misericordia), Dolores Convent, 1111 Montopolis Dr., 78741. Tel: 512-385-5090. Sisters 4. Other Address: 612 N. 3rd St., Waco, 76701. Tel: 817-753-6816. Sisters 5.
Missionary Cathechists of Divine Providence, 1943 Dopplegrey Ln., 78727. Tel: 512-837-7562; 873-7771. Sr. Mary Lou Barba, M.C.D.P., 2301-A Metcalf St., 78741. Tel: 512-448-2430; 444-7477. Sr. Maria Guadalupe Castaneda, M.C.D.P.
Missionary Sisters of the Immaculate Conception of the Mother of God, 4211-B Shoalwood, 78756. Tel: 512-451-2890. Sisters 2.
School Sisters of Notre Dame, S.S.N.D., 1625 Rutherford Ln., Bldg. D, 78754-5105. Sr. Carla Marie Lusch, S.S.N.D.
Secular Institute of Schoenstatt Sisters of Mary, 12022 Ladrido Ln., 78727-6034. Tel: 512-343-2559. Total in Residence 3.
Sinsinawa Dominican Sisters, 11700 Metric Blvd #903, 78758-3215. Tel: 512-836-6424. Sr. Helen Raycraft, O.P.; Sr. Guadalupe Soria, O.P., 2421 Oakcrest Ave., 78704. Tel: 512-444-7614. Sisters 3.
Sisters of Divine Providence, 3308A Dunleigh, 78745. Tel: 512-280-5976. Sisters 3.
Sisters of Notre Dame de Namur, 3111 Parker Ln. #261, 78741. Tel: 512-462-9342. 1615 Redwood Dr., Harker Heights, 76543. Sr. Donna M. Jurick, S.N.D.deN., 1615 Redwood Dr., Harker Heights, 76543. Tel: 817-690-1518. Sr. Margaret Hunt, S.N.D.deN.; Sr. Estelle Kessling, S.N.D.deN. Sisters 3.
Sisters of St. Francis of Dubuque, 1943 Dopplegrey Ln., 78727-4590. Tel: 512-834-9793.
Sisters of the Holy Cross, La Casa Convent, 2213 Euclid Ave., 78704. Tel: 512-441-6693.
Sisters of the Holy Cross, Our Lady of Victory Convent, 2215 Euclid Ave., 78704. Tel: 512-441-2927. Sisters 3. Loretto Convent, 2301 East Side Dr., 78704-5214. Tel: 512-441-3850. Sisters 2. Other Address: 2213 Euclid Ave., 78704-5125. Tel: 512-441-6693.
Rebekah Baines Johnson Center, 21 Waller St., 78702.
Sisters of the Holy Cross, Loretto Convent, 2301 East Side Dr., 78704. Tel: 512-441-3850.
Sisters, Servants of the Immaculate Heart of Mary, 3300 Parker Ln., #134, 78741. Tel: 512-447-1335; Fax: 512-448-8492. Sr. Marie Andre Walsh, I.H.M., Contact Person, 3300 Parker Ln., #230, 78741. Tel: 512-326-8239. 3001 S. Congress, #1030, 78704. Tel: 512-442-5295. 1508 South Port #229, 78704. Tel: 512-442-1124. 5508 N. Hwy 317, Belton, 76513. Tel: 817-780-1739. 4101 W. Adams St. #423, Temple, 76501. Tel: 817-771-1048.

BREMOND. *Felician Sisters*, St. Mary's Convent, Rte. 1, Box 57, 76629. Tel: 817-746-7788. Sisters 2.

BRENHAM. *Monastery of St. Clare*, 9300 Hwy. 105, 77833.

Tel: 409-836-2444; Fax: 409-836-9652. Rev. Leonard Cornelius, O.F.M., Chap. Sisters 8. Res., Rte. 2, Box 280, 77833. Tel: 409-830-1554. Sr. Mary Angela Chandler, O.S.C., Abbess.

Sisters of St. Francis of Our Lady of Lourdes (O.S.F.), Trinity Medical Center, 700 Medical Pkwy., 77833. Tel: 512-836-9481. Sisters 3.

BRYAN. *Sisters of St. Francis of Our Lady of Lourdes*, 2801 Franciscan Dr., 77802. Tel: 409-776-2381. Sisters 7.

CAMERON. *Sisters of the Presentation of the Blessed Virgin Mary*, P.O. Box 673, 76520. Tel: 817-697-2107.

FAYETTEVILLE. *Sisters of Divine Providence*, St. John's Convent, Rte. 1, Box 99A, 78940. Tel: 409-378-2275.

LA GRANGE. *Sisters of the Incarnate Word and Blessed Sacrament*, Sacred Heart Convent, 580 Pearl St., 78945. Tel: 409-968-6574.

LAMPASAS. *Sisters of St. John Bosco*, St. Mary Convent, Box 864, 76550. Tel: 512-556-6203. Total in Residence 2.

LULING. *Our Lady of Victory Missionary Sisters*, 500 E. Travis, 78648. Tel: 512-875-5354.

SAN MARCOS. *Cordi-Marian Sisters*, 964 Field St., St. Anthony Claret Mission House, 78666. Tel: 512-396-5333. Sisters 4.

SOMERVILLE. *Missionary Ecumenical*, P.O. Box 367, 77879. Tel: 409-595-1494. Total in Residence 3.

TAYLOR. *Dominican Sisters of Houston*, St. Mary Convent, 317 E. Fourth St., 76574. Tel: 512-352-2144. Sisters 4.

Sisters of St. John Bosco, St. John's Convent, 1101 Symes, 76574. Tel: 512-352-2802.

WACO. *Congregation of the Sisters of the Incarnate Word, C.C.V.I.*, P.O. Box 2589, 76702-2589. Sr. Rosemary Burke, C.C.V.I.

Daughters of Charity of St. Vincent De Paul, 2416 Colcord, 76707. Tel: 817-753-3817; 753-4629. Sisters 5. 213 Bonham Dr., 76643. Tel: 817-666-0611. Sisters 4.

Franciscan Sisters Daughters of Mercy. (Franciscanas Hijas de la Misericordia), 612 N. Third St., 76701. Tel: 817-753-5565. Sisters 5. Sisters 5.

Sisters of Charity of the Incarnate Word, 717 Cardinal, 76712. Tel: 817-776-2707; Fax: 817-754-0133. Sisters 3.

Sisters of the Holy Cross, St. Mary's Convent, 224 N. 14th St., 76701. Tel: 817-756-0548.

[J] HOMES FOR THE AGED

WACO. *The Regis Retirement Home and St. Elizabeth Nursing Home*, 400 Austin Ave., P.O. Box 1909, 76703. Tel: 817-756-5441; Fax: 817-754-0133.

For a complete listing, refer to the Special Care Facilities section.

[K] MISSION CENTERS

SOMERVILLE. *St. Ann Mission Center*, P.O. Box 367, 77879. Missionary Ecumenical. Sr. M. John Della Morte, M.E., Supr. Kindergarten Students 20; Total Staff 3.

WACO. *St. Francis Mission Center*, 612 N. Third St., 76701. Tel: 817-753-5565. Franciscan Sisters Daughters of Mercy. Sr. Catherine Vallespir, F.H.M., Supr. Catechetical and Social Work, Kindergarten; Sr. Barbara Herrera, F.H.M., Supr. Total Staff 12. Sisters 5.

[L] RENEWAL CENTERS

BELTON. *Cedarbrake Renewal Center*, P.O. Box 58, 76513-0058. Tel: 817-780-2436; Fax: 817-780-2684. Sr. Jean Burbo, I.H.M., Dir. Total in Residence 3; Total Staff 9.

[M] NEWMAN APOSTOLATE

AUSTIN. *University Catholic Center*, 2010 University Ave., 78705. Tel: 512-476-7351; Fax: 512-476-7377. Serving the Catholic community at the University of Texas. Rev. Patrick E. Hensy, C.S.P., Dir. Campus Ministers: Rev. Bernard Campbell, C.S.P.; Elaine Morin, M.A.; Dana Campbell, L.M.S.W., Admin.; Sr. Margaret Andre, C.S.C., Liturgist.

BRENHAM. *Blinn College Catholic Student Union*, Blinn College, 77833. For Catholic students attending Blinn Jr. College. Rev. Msgr. Ralph A. Brennan; Mr. Daniel Schiller, Sponsor. Tel: 409-830-4417; Deacon William Januszewski, Campus Minister. Tel: 409-836-9329.

COLLEGE STATION. *St. Mary's Catholic Center*, 103 Nagle St., 77840. Tel: 409-846-5717. Campus ministry at Texas A & M University. Revs. Michael J. Sis; Dean E. Wilhelm; Deacon Bill Scott, Jr. Total in Residence 2; Total Staff 9.

SAN MARCOS. *Catholic Student Center*, 100 Concho St., 78666. Tel: 512-392-5925; Fax: 512-392-5922. Catholic Students attending Southwest Texas State University. Rev. Art Gramaje, C.M.F.

WACO. *Catholic Student Center at Baylor University*, 821 Speight Ave., P.O. Box 6060, 76706-6060. Tel: 817-757-0636. For Catholic students attending Baylor University. Mr. Mervyn S. Pacheco, Dir., 304 Stead Dr., 76705. Tel: 817-799-5064.

[N] MISCELLANEOUS

AUSTIN. *Association of Catholic Chaplains of Texas*, 3001 S. Congress, 78704. Tel: 512-447-4132.

Brothers of Holy Cross, South-West Province, Charitable Trust, 3001 S. Congress Ave., #1046, 78704. Tel: 512-442-7856; Fax: 512-444-3133.
Trustees: Bros. Richard Daly, C.S.C.; Harold Ehlinger, C.S.C., Chm.; Ralph Kuder, C.S.C.; William Nick, C.S.C.

Catholic Archives of Texas, N. Congress & W. 16th St., P.O. Box 13124, 78711-3124. Tel: 512-476-6296; Fax: 512-476-3715. Kinga L. Perzynska, Archivist; Susan Eason, Archives Asst. Historical collection of the Church in the Southwest and Texas from 1519.

Catholic Family Fraternal of Texas. KJZT, P.O. Box 1884, 78767-1844. Tel: 512-444-9586. Mrs. Geraldine Nekuza, Pres.; Loretta Shal, Vice Pres.

Catholic Southwest, 1625 Rutherford Ln., Bldg. D, 78754-5105. Patrick Foley, Ph.D., Editor; Jesus F. de la Teja, Ph.D., Mng. Editor.

Children's Hospital Foundation of Austin, 1201 W. 38th St., 78705-1056. Tel: 512-480-1243; Fax: 512-480-1220. Ms. Martha St. Romain, Contact Person.

Juan Diego Missionary Society, Inc., P.O. Box 6067, 78762. Elias and Christina Limon, Directors.

Ladies of Charity, 510 W. 26th St., 78705. Affiliated with the Ladies of Charity of the United States of America (LCSUA). Other Addresses: P.O. Drawer W, Bastrop, 78602. 104 Shannon Ln., Georgetown, 78628. 1005A S. Ann Blvd., Harker Heights, 76548. 2203 Lakeway Blvd., 78734. P.O. Box 23323, Waco, 76702-3302. Thrift stores are operated by the Ladies of Charity Associations in Austin, Bastrop, Harker Heights, Lakeway and Waco.

National Christ Child Society, 503 Vale St., 78746. Merlie Morales, Contact Person.

North Central Catholic School Corp., 13729 Research Blvd., #610-147, 78750. Tel: 512-219-8914. Ms. Jan McCall, Pres.

Our Lady's Family Center, 1815 E. Sixth St., P.O. Box 6453, 78762. Tel: 512-322-0632. Deacon Willie J. Cortez, Dir. Patients Assisted 200; Total Staff 2.

Road to Emmaus (Catholic Home for Girls of all Faith), 5407 Musket Ridge, 78759. Tel: 512-502-0765. Joe & Dee Benante, Founders. Directors: Terri Nira; L. Hollingsworth; R. DeLuna.

The Seton Cove - A Spirituality Center, 3708 Crawford St., 78705. Total Staff 5.

Society of St. Vincent de Paul, 6503 Wolfcreek Pass, 78749-1825. Tel: 512-288-3370; Fax: 512-288-1926. Rev. Paul McCallum, Spiritual Advisor; Raymond DuPont, Pres.; Frederick L. Gale, Vice Pres.; Jeannine DuPont, Treasurer; Mary Johnson, Secretary; Bobby L. Sherry, Dir.

Texas Catholic Conference, 1625 Rutherford Ln., Bldg. D, 78754-5105. Tel: 512-339-9882. Bro. Richard Daly, C.S.C., Exec. Dir.

Texas Catholic Historical Society, c/o Texas Catholic Conference,1625 Rutherford Ln. Bldg. D, 78704-5105. Roy Barkley, Ph.D., Pres.

Texas Conference of Catholic Health Facilities, 1625 Rutherford Ln., Bldg. D, 78754-5105. Tel: 512-339-1157; Fax: 512-339-8670. Rev. Msgr. William L. Broussard, Exec. Dir.

Trustees: Bros. Richard Daly, C.S.C.; Harold Ehlinger, C.S.C., Chm.; Ralph Kuder, C.S.C.; William Nick, C.S.C.

VESS, Volunteers for Educational and Social Services, 1625 Rutherford Ln., Bldg. D, 78754-5105. Tel: 512-339-7123; 1-800-771-5677. Barbara Price, Dir.

LAGRANGE. *Catholic Union of Texas*, KJT, P.O. Box 297, 78945. Tel: 409-968-5877; Fax: 409-968-5823. Elo J. Goerig, Pres. KJT NEWS, official publication.

RELIGIOUS INSTITUTES OF MEN REPRESENTED IN THE DIOCESE

For further details refer to the corresponding bracketed number in the Religious Institutes of Men or Women section.

[0170]—*Basilian Fathers.* (Galveston-Houston, TX).—C.S.B.

[0600]—*Brothers of the Congregation of Holy Cross.* (Southwest Province).—C.S.C.

[0360]—*Claretian Missionaries.* (South Pasadena, CA).—C.M.F.

[0750]—*Congregation of Marian Hill Missionaries.* (Dearborn Heights, MI).—C.M.M.

[0480]—*Conventual Franciscans.* (Las Cruces, NM).—O.F.M.Conv.

[0520]—*Franciscan Friars.* (Cincinnati Prov.).—O.F.M.

[0690]—*Jesuit Fathers and Brothers.* (Los Gatos, CA; Portland, OR).—S.J.

[0780]—*Marist Fathers.* (Washington, DC).—S.M.

[0910]—*Oblates of Mary Immaculate.* (San Antonio, TX).—O.M.I.

[0430]—*Order of Preachers-Dominicans.* (New Orleans, LA).—O.P.

[1030]—*Paulist Fathers.* (Scarsdale, NY).—C.S.P.

[0610]—*Priests of the Congregation of Holy Cross.* (Southern Prov.).—C.S.C.

[1190]—*Salesians of Don Bosco.* (San Francisco Prov.).—S.D.B.

[1200]—*Society of the Divine Savior.* (Milwaukee, WI).—S.D.S.

[0560]—*Third Order Regular of Saint Francis.* (Waco, TX).—T.O.R.

RELIGIOUS INSTITUTES OF WOMEN REPRESENTED IN THE DIOCESE

[2190]—*Congregation of the Incarnate Word and Blessed Sacrament.* (Houston, TX).—C.V.I.

[0470]—*Congregation of the Sisters of Charity of the Incarnate Word.* (Houston, Texas).—C.C.V.I.

[0460]—*Congregation of the Sisters of Charity of the Incarnate Word.* (San Antonio, TX).—C.C.V.I.

[1920]—*Congregation of the Sisters of the Holy Cross.* (Notre Dame, IN).—C.S.C.

[]—*Cordi-Marian Sisters.* (San Antonio, TX).—M.C.M.

[0760]—*Daughters of Charity of St. Vincent de Paul.* (St. Louis, MO).—D.C.

[0850]—*Daughters of Mary Help of Christian.* (San Antonio, TX).—F.M.A.

[1070-13]—*Dominican Sisters.* (Adrian, MI).—O.P.

[1070-19]—*Dominican Sisters.* (Houston, TX).—O.P.

[1070-03]—*Dominican Sisters.* (Sinsinawa, WI).—O.P.

[1170]—*Felician Sisters.* (Rio Rancho, NM).—C.S.S.F.

[1235]—*Franciscan Sisters Daughters of Our Lady of Mercy (Franciscanas Hijas de la Misericordia).* (U.S. delegation: Waco, TX).—F.H.M.

[2690]—*Missionary Catechists of Divine Providence.* (San Antonio, Texas).—M.C.D.P.

[]—*Missionary Ecumenical.* (Rome, Italy).—M.E.

[2760]—*Missionary Sisters of the Immaculate Conception of the Mother of God.* (Paterson, NJ).—S.M.I.C.

[3760]—*Order of St. Clare.* (Brenham, TX).—O.S.C.

[3130]—*Our Lady of Victory Missionary Sisters.* (Huntington, IN).—O.L.V.M.

[2970]—*School Sisters of Notre Dame.* (St. Louis, MO).—S.S.N.D.

[]—*Secular Institute of Schoenstatt Sisters of Mary.* (Southern Prov., Rockport, TX).—I.S.S.M.

[1010]—*Sisters of Divine Providence.* (San Antonio, TX).—C.D.P.

[3000]—*Sisters of Notre Dame de Namur.* (Cincinnati, OH).—S.N.D.deN.

[1530]—*Sisters of St. Francis of the Congregation of Our Lady of Lourdes.* (Sylvania, OH).—O.S.F.

[1570]—*Sisters of St. Francis of the Holy Family.* (Dubuque, IA).—O.S.F.

[]—*Sisters of St. John Bosco.* (Taylor, TX).—S.J.B.

[3320]—*Sisters of the Presentation of the Blessed Virgin Mary.* (Dubuque, IA).—(P.B.V.M.).

[2150]—*Sisters, Servants of the Immaculate Heart of Mary.* (Monroe, MI).—I.H.M.

NECROLOGY

† Krol, Michael, (Retired). —Died Sept. 18, 1996.

Diocese of Baker

(Dioecesis Bakeriensis)

Most Reverend

THOMAS J. CONNOLLY, D.D., J.C.D.

Bishop of Baker; ordained April 8, 1947; appointed May 4, 1971; consecrated June 30, 1971. *Res., P.O. Box 5999, Bend, OR, 97708.*

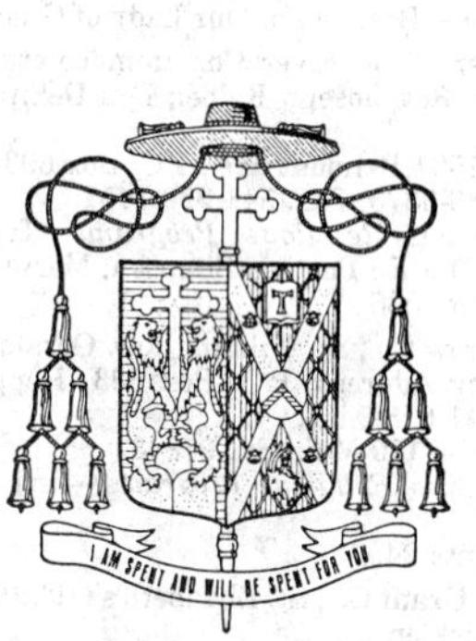

ESTABLISHED JUNE 19, 1903.

Square Miles 66,826.

Comprises the counties of Baker, Crook, Deschutes, Gilliam, Grant, Harney, Hood River, Jefferson, Klamath, Lake, Malheur, Morrow, Sherman, Umatilla, Union, Wallowa, Wasco and Wheeler in the State of Oregon.

For legal titles of parishes and diocesan institutions, consult the Chancery Office.

Diocesan Pastoral Office: P.O. Box 5999, Bend, OR, 97708. Tel.: 541-388-4004; Fax: 541-388-2566.

E-mail address: kentpunt@bendnet.com

STATISTICAL OVERVIEW

Personnel	
Bishop	1
Priests: Diocesan Active in Diocese	23
Priests: Active Outside Diocese	2
Priests: Diocesan in Foreign Missions	1
Priests: Retired, Sick or Absent	12
Number of Diocesan Priests	38
Religious Priests in Diocese	9
Ordinations:	
Diocesan Priests	1
Permanent Deacons in Diocese	5
Total Sisters	34
Parishes	
Parishes	35
With Resident Pastor:	
Resident Diocesan Priests	23
Resident Religious Priests	6
Without Resident Pastor:	
Administered by Priests	7
Missions	29
Professional Ministry Personnel:	
Sisters	7
Lay Ministers	17
Welfare	
Catholic Hospitals	4
Total Assisted	225,140
Homes for the Aged	1
Total Assisted	140
Day Care and Extended Day Care Centers	3
Total Assisted	155
Educational	
Diocesan Students in Other Seminaries	5
Total Seminarians	5
Elementary Schools, Diocesan and Parish	3
Total Students	615
Catechesis/Religious Education:	
High School Students	984
Elementary Students	2,119
Total Students Under Catholic Instruction	3,723
Teachers in the Diocese:	
Sisters	5
Lay Teachers	34
Vital Statistics	
Receptions into the Church:	
Infant Baptism Totals	876
Adult Baptism Totals	142
Received into Full Communion	115
First Communions	751
Confirmations	353
Marriages:	
Catholic	131
Interfaith	79
Total Marriages	210
Deaths	298
Total Catholic Population	31,794
Total Population	406,800

Former Bishops—Rt. Rev. CHARLES J. O'REILLY, D.D., ord. June 29, 1890; appt. June 24, 1903; cons. Bishop of Baker City, Aug. 25, 1903; transferred to the See of Lincoln March 20, 1918; died Feb. 4, 1923.—Most Rev. LEO F. FAHEY, D.D., ord. May 29, 1926; appt. Titular Bishop of Ipsus and Coadjutor "cum jure successionis" March 13, 1948; cons. May 26, 1948; died March 31, 1950.—Most Rev. JOSEPH F. MCGRATH, D.D., assistant at the Pontifical Throne, Bishop of Baker City; ord. Dec. 21, 1895; appt. Dec. 21, 1918; cons. March 25, 1919; died April 12, 1950.—Most Rev. FRANCIS P. LEIPZIG, D.D., ord. April 14, 1920; appt. Bishop of Baker July 18, 1950; cons. Sept. 12, 1950; retired May 4, 1971; died Jan. 17, 1981.

Vicar General—Rev. Msgr. MATTHEW M. CROTTY.

Chancellor and Secretary to the Bishop—MARY ANN DAVIS.

Diocesan Pastoral Office—Mailing Address: P.O. Box 5999, Bend, 97708. Tel: 541-388-4004; Fax: 541-388-2566. *911 S.E. Armour, Bend, 97702.* All applications for dispensations, faculties, etc., and all correspondence should be addressed: The Chancery Office.

Receptionist and Secretary—VIRGINIA MOHR.

Diocesan Tribunal—Tel: 541-388-4010.

Judicial Vicar and Chief Judge—Very Rev. W. THOMAS FAUCHER, J.C.L.

Arbitration-Conciliation—Vacant.

Judge—Rev. Msgr. MATTHEW M. CROTTY, J.C.D.

Defender of the Bond and Promoter of Justice—Rev. MATTHEW PU, J.C.D.

Second Instance Defender of the Bond—Rev. LEO F. WECKERLE, J.C.L.

Coordinatior and Notary—DOLORES FRIBERG.

Diocesan Senate and Board of Consultors—Council of Priests and Diocesan Consultors. Most Rev. THOMAS J. CONNOLLY, Pres., Ex Officio; Rev. JOSEPH KELBEL, Chm.; Revs. FRANKLIN BUCKMAN; DENNIS J. STRACHOTA; CHARLES V. DREISBACK; JAMES RADLOFF; RICHARD O. FISCHER; ROBERT GREINER; Rev. Msgr. MATTHEW M. CROTTY, V.G.

Personnel Board—Revs. RAYMOND M. HOPP; LEO F. WECKERLE; CHARLES V. DREISBACH.

Deans—Central: Rev. ROBERT SIMARD, Eastern: Rev. RAYMOND JARBOE, Northern: Rev. DENNIS STRACHOTA, Southern: Rev. CHARLES V. DREISBACH, Western: Rev. JOSEPH A. KELBEL.

Diocesan Offices and Directors

Board of Education—Most Rev. THOMAS J. CONNOLLY; Revs. RONALD E. MAAG; EVANGELIST KELLY, O.F.M.Cap.; W. RAYMOND JARBOE,Principals of Schools and Representatives from each Parish School Board.

Building Committee—Rev. Msgr. MATTHEW M. CROTTY; Revs. ROBERT E. SIMARD; RONALD E. MAAG.

Campus Ministry Apostolate—Rev. W. RAYMOND JARBOE, *829 S.W. Second Ave., Ontario, 97914.* Tel: 541-889-8469.

Catholic Services—MARGUERITE REED, *2605 Second St., Baker City, 97814.* Tel: 541-523-2902.

Church Property, Administration of—Most Rev. THOMAS J. CONNOLLY, D.D., Pres.; Rev. Msgr. MATTHEW M. CROTTY, Sec.

DeSales Program of Adult Education—Direct Inquiries to:Tel: 800-488-0488. Direct Orders to: *St. Anthony Messenger Press, 1615 Republic St., Cincinnati, OH, 45210;* Fax: 513-241-1197.

Diocesan Attorney—Vacant.

Diocesan Development Office—KENT PUNTENNEY, Dir., *P.O. Box 5999, Bend, 97708.* Tel: 541-388-4004.

Diocesan Finance Minister—MARY ANN DAVIS, Pastoral Office; KENT PUNTENNEY, Accountant.

Diocesan Financial Board—Rev. CHARLES V. DREISBACH; JAMES V. HURLEY; DAVID F. LINDLEY; JOSEPH LACASSE.

Diocesan Pastoral Council—BOB ASHLEY, Chm.; Most Rev. THOMAS J. CONNOLLY, Pres. TONY BOCCHI, Vice Pres. JAMES ROSETTI, Sec. ROBERT ILOSKY, Treas. and Exec. Sec. Delegates from each Congregation of Sisters; delegates from each parish; and ex officio members.

Diocesan Superintendent of Schools—Sr. MARY CATHERINE PERKINS, O.P., *P.O. Box 5999, Bend, 97708.* Tel: 541-385-1865.

Director of Campaign for Human Development—Rev. RONALD E. MAAG, *St. Peter Church, P.O. Box 41, The Dalles, 97058.* Tel: 541-296-2026.

Director of Catholic Hospitals—Rev. TODD UNGER, *P.O. Box 786, Madras, 97741.* Tel: 541-475-2936.

Friends of the Catholic University of America—Rev. Msgr. WILLIAM S. STONE, *2633 S.W. Obsidian, No. 52, Redmond, 97756.* Tel: 541-548-6123.

Health and Retirement Board—Most Rev. THOMAS J. CONNOLLY, D.D., Pres.; Rev. Msgr. WILLIAM S. STONE, Chm.; Rev. TODD UNGER, Sec.-Treas.; Revs. FRANKLIN BUCKMAN; RAYMOND HOPP; Rev. Msgr. BERNARD A. KEATING.

Historian—Vacant.

Liturgical Commission—Rev. MICHAEL G. MILES, *P.O. Box 29, Lakeview, 97630.* Tel: 541-947-2741.

Natural Family Planning—PATRICIA PUNTENNEY, Dir., *P.O. Box 5999, Bend, 97708.* Tel: 541-383-8928; 388-4004.

Office of Faith Development and Ministry—Most Rev. THOMAS J. CONNOLLY, D.D., J.C.D., Chm. Directors: KEVIN SAUNDERS; DIANE SAUNDERS, *P.O. Box 9250, Bend, 97708. 911 S.E. Armour, Bend, 97702.* Tel: 541-388-3991.

Adult Education—Sr. M. CATHERINE PERKINS, O.P., Dir. Tel: 541-385-1865.

Office of Hispanic Ministry—Sr. MARIE VIANNEY BILGRIEN, Dir., *P.O. Box 823, Madras, 97741.* Tel: 541-475-2564.

Priests' Continuing Education Committee—Most Rev. THOMAS J. CONNOLLY; Revs. DENNIS J. STRACHOTA, Chm. ROBERT GREINER; ROBERT C. IRWIN; JOSEPH KELBEL; KENNETH MORTON.

Priests' Eucharistic League—Rev. JOHN BAUMGARTNER, Dir.

Propagation of the Faith—Vacant.

R.C.I.A. Office—Rev. DENNIS STRACHOTA, Dir., *800 S.E. Court Ave., Pendleton, 97801.* Tel: 541-276-3615.

Respect for Life Committee—KENT PUNTENNEY, Dir.

Diocesan Scout Director—TED YAROSH, *5160 S. Etna St., Klamath Falls, 97603.* Tel: 541-882-4611.

Vocations—Rev. RONALD E. MAAG, *St. Peter Church, P.O. Box 41, The Dalles, 97058.* Tel: 541-296-2026.

CLERGY, PARISHES, MISSIONS AND PAROCHIAL SCHOOLS

BAKER CITY
(County of Baker)

1—CATHEDRAL OF ST. FRANCIS DE SALES (1871), Rev. James P. Logan, Rector. Pastoral Assocs.: Carole Watt; Michelle Curtis; Mary Margaret Hansen; Lisa Ward, Parish Coord.
Res., 2235 First St., 97814. Tel: 541-523-4521; 523-6244. [CEM]
Catechesis/Religious Programs—Tamara Skidmore, D.R.E.
Students 145.
Missions—Halfway, St. Therese; Unity, St. Joseph's; North Powder, St. Anthony.

OUTSIDE BAKER CITY

Arlington, Gilliam Co., St. Francis (1931), Rev. Richard O. Fischer.
Mailing Address: P.O. Box 485, Condon, 97823. Tel: 541-384-5271.

Bend, Deschutes Co., St. Francis of Assisi (1904), Revs. Evangelist Kelly, O.F.M.Cap.; Michael Walsh, O.F.M.Cap.; Fintan Whelan, O.F.M.Cap.; Brian McKenna, O.F.M.Cap.; Sr. Patricia Rayburn, O.S.F., Pastoral Assoc.; Deacon Bob Walling.
Res., 409 N.W. Franklin, 97701. Tel: 541-382-3631; Fax: 541-385-8879.
School—(Grades PreK-7) 720 Bond St., 97701. Tel: 541-382-4701. Sr. Kathleen Cordes, S.H.C.J., Prin.
Lay Teachers 20; Students 255.
Day Care—.
Students 50.
Catechesis/Religious Programs—Tel: 541-382-3731.
Students 250.

Burns, Harney Co., Holy Family (1899), Rev. Matthew C. Pu, Admin.
Res., 685 N. Fairview Ave., 97720. Tel: 541-573-2613.
Catechesis/Religious Programs—620 N. Egan Ave., 97720. Tel: 541-573-1147. Mary Lemos, D.R.E.
Students 145.
Missions—Drewsey, Our Lady of Loretto; Crane, St. Thomas.

Chiloquin, Klamath Co., Our Lady of Mt. Carmel (1927), Rev. Ronald J. Warren.
Res., 503 W. Chocktoot, P.O. Box 396, 97624. Tel: 541-783-2411.
Catechesis/Religious Programs—Students 23.
Mission—Bly, St. James the Apostle.

Condon, Gilliam Co., St. John's (1925), Rev. Richard O. Fischer.
Res., P.O. Box 485, 97823. Tel: 541-384-5271.
Catechesis/Religious Programs—Students 58.
Mission—Fossil, St. Catherine.

Dufur, Wasco Co., St. Alphonsus (1911), Rev. Anselm Fister, O.S.B., Admin.
Res., P.O. Box 395, 97021. Tel: 541-467-2580.
Mission—Maupin, St. Mary's.

Elgin, Union Co., St. Mary (1966). Attended by Our Lady of the Valley, La Grande. Deacon Joseph Garlitz.
Res., P.O. Box 97, 97827. Tel: 541-437-8101.
Catechesis/Religious Programs—Sharon Woody, D.R.E.
Students 31.

Enterprise, Wallowa Co., St. Katherine's (1923), Rev. C.H. Gillan, Admin.
Res., 301 E. Garfield St., P.O. Box 370, 97828. Tel: 541-426-3043.
Parish Office: Tel: 541-426-4008.
Catechesis/Religious Programs—Vonnie Pottenger, D.R.E.
Students 81.
Mission—Wallowa, St. Pius X.

Heppner, Morrow Co., St. Patrick's (1887), Rev. Gerald W. Condon.
Res., 525 Gale St., P.O. Box 633, 97836. Tel: 541-676-9462.
Catechesis/Religious Programs—Linda Kenny, D.R.E.
Students 45.

Hermiston, Umatilla Co., Our Lady of Angels (1910), Rev. Francisco Vallejos; Kay Edwards, Parish Admin.
Res., 565 Hermiston Ave., 97838. Tel: 541-567-5812; Fax: 541-564-0933.
Catechesis/Religious Programs—Tel: 541-567-3825. Kay Stull, D.R.E.
Students 325.
Mission—Boardman, Our Lady of Guadalupe.

Hood River, Hood River Co., Immaculate Conception (1906), Rev. Joseph Kelbel; Lou DeSitter, Pastoral Assoc.
Res., 1501 Belmont Ave., P.O. Box 693, 97031. Tel: 541-386-3373; Fax: 541-386-1451. [CEM]
Catechesis/Religious Programs—Tel: 541-386-2527. D.R.E.: Patricia Simpson; Maria Ramirez.
Students 336.

Ione, Morrow Co., St. William, Rev. Gerald W. Condon.
Mailing Address: P.O. Box 633, Heppner, 97836. Tel: 541-676-9462.
Church—110 Main St., 97843.
Catechesis/Religious Programs—Jeri Mc Elligott, D.R.E.
Students 24.

John Day, Grant Co., St. Elizabeth's (1939), Rev. Robert Van Sickler.
Res., 111 S.W. 2nd St., P.O. Box 189, 97845. Tel: 541-575-1459.
Catechesis/Religious Programs—Mary Ann Vidourek, D.R.E.
Students 11.
Missions—Monument, St. Ann; Seneca, St. Charles; Longcreek, St. Katherine.

Jordan Valley, Malheur Co., St. Bernard's (1915), Rev. Lawrence Kearney, Admin.
Res., P.O. Box 186, 97910. Tel: 541-586-2266.
Catechesis/Religious Programs—Lily Garrard, D.R.E.
Students 21.
Mission—Arock, Holy Family.

Klamath Falls, Klamath Co., Sacred Heart (1904), Rev. Charles V. Dreisbach; Deacon P. Kenneth Morton, Pastoral Assoc.
Res., 815 High St., 97601. Tel: 541-884-4566; Fax: 541-882-0472.
Catechesis/Religious Programs—Tel: 541-882-4864. Vicki Bauer, D.R.E.
Students 204.

St. Pius Xth (1957), Rev. Franklin J. Buckman (ORG) Admin. Pastoral Ministers: Karen Marie Bickett; Sharon Roberts.
Res., 4880 Bristol Ave., 97603. Tel: 541-884-4242. [CEM]
Catechesis/Religious Programs—Tel: 541-882-7593. Deacon Jim Roy, D.R.E.
Students 180.

La Grande, Union Co., Our Lady of the Valley (1914). (Under the title of the Immaculate Conception). Rev. Louis Henry Albrecht; Margaret Irish, Admin.
Res., 1101 4th St., P.O. Box L, 97850. Tel: 541-963-0006; 963-7341 (Parish).
Catechesis/Religious Programs—Charlene Storoe, D.R.E.
Students 106.

La Pine, Deschutes Co., Holy Redeemer (1983), Rev. James A. Radloff.
Res., P.O. Box 299, 97739. Tel: 541-536-3571.
Catechesis/Religious Programs—Students 48.
Missions—Gilchrist, Our Lady of the Snows; Christmas Valley, Holy Family.
Station—Sun River.

Lakeview, Lake Co., St. Patrick's (1912), Rev. Raymond Hopp.
Res., 12 G St. N., P.O. Drawer 29, 97630. Tel: 541-947-2741; Fax: 541-947-2756.
Catechesis/Religious Programs—185 S. G St., Tel: 541-947-3875.
Students 90.
Missions—Adel, St. Richard; Plush, St. Thomas; Paisley, St. John the Apostle.

Madras, Jefferson Co., St. Patrick's (1955), Rev. Todd J. Unger.
Res., 341 S.W. J St., P.O. Box 786, 97741. Tel: 541-475-2936; Fax: 541-475-2444.
Catechesis/Religious Programs—Tel: 541-475-2444. D.R.E.: Barbara Manning; Elouise Kirsch.
Students 205.
Mission—Warm Springs, Jefferson Co., Blessed Kateri Tekakwitha. (Indian Reservation) P.O. Box 764, Warm Springs, 97761. Tel: 541-553-1235. Sr. Pauline Igoe, O.P., Dir. Native American Affairs.

Merrill, Klamath Co., St. Augustine (1939), Rev. Michael Miles.
Res., 905 E. Front St., P.O. Box 340, 97633. Tel: 541-798-5823.
Catechesis/Religious Programs—Mrs. Roger Nelson, D.R.E.
Students 125.
Mission—Bonanza, St. Frances Cabrini, Tel: 541-545-6602.

Milton Freewater, Umatilla Co., St. Francis of Assisi (1940), Rev. Richard Saksons, O.Praem.
Res., 925 Vining, 97862. Tel: 541-938-5436; Fax: 541-938-7721.
Catechesis/Religious Programs—Students 34.
Mission—Athena, Sacred Heart.

Nyssa, Malheur Co., St. Bridget of Kildare (1951), Rev. Robert M. Greiner.
Res., 504 Locust, 97913-3235. Tel: 541-372-3133.
Catechesis/Religious Programs—Students 140.
Mission—Adrian, Our Lady of Guadalupe. 2nd St. & Owyhee St.

Ontario, Malheur Co., Blessed Sacrament (1911), Rev. W. Raymond Jarboe. Pastoral Assocs.: Mrs. Francis A. Schaffer; Sr. Mary Ellen Robinson S.N.J.M.
Res., 829 S.W. Second Ave., 97914-2695. Tel: 541-889-8469; Fax: 541-889-8483.
School—Saint Peter, (Grades K-7) 98 S.W. Ninth St., 97914. Tel: 541-889-7363; Fax: 541-889-2852. Sr. Linda Riggers, S.N.J.M., Prin.
Lay Teachers 8; Students 140.
Catechesis/Religious Programs—Tel: 541-889-8404. D.R.E.: Maria Reed; Tim Cables.
Students 220.
Mission—Huntington, St. Joachim. [CEM]

Paisley, Lake Co., St. John the Apostle. Reverted to a mission of Lakeview, St. Patrick Parish.

Pendleton, Umatilla Co., St. Andrew's Indian Mission (1847), Rev. Michael J. Fitzpatrick, S.J. Pastoral Assocs.: Diana Littlejohn; Faydeena Luke.
Res., Rte. 1, Box 515, 97801. Tel: 541-276-6155. [CEM]
Catechesis/Religious Programs—Tel: 541-276-0767. Lillian Moses, D.R.E.
Students 38.

St. Mary's (1902), Revs. Dennis Strachota; Robert C. Irwin.
Res., 800 S.E. Court Ave., 97801. Tel: 541-276-3615; Fax: 541-276-7484. [CEM]
Catechesis/Religious Programs—Tel: 541-276-6163. Mrs. Darlene Ledbetter, D.R.E.
Students 250.

Pilot Rock, Umatilla Co., St. Helen (1930). Attended by St. Mary's, Pendleton.
Res., 740 S.W. Birch, P.O. Box V, 97868. Tel: 541-443-3151.
Catechesis/Religious Programs—Students 38.

Prineville, Crook Co., St. Joseph's (1943), Rev. Robert E. Simard.
Res., 150 E. First, P.O. Box 338, 97754. Tel: 541-447-6475.
Catechesis/Religious Programs—200 E. First St., P.O. Box 721, 97754. Tel: 541-447-1227. D.R.E.: Krista Lucas; Sheryl Denfeld; Denise Vargas.
Students 116.

Redmond, Deschutes Co., St. Thomas (1941), Rev. Leo F. Weckerle.
Res., 526 S. 12th, P.O. Box 247, 97756. Tel: 541-923-3390; Fax: 541-548-6630.
Catechesis/Religious Programs—535 S. 11th St., 97756. Tel: 541-923-0597. Mary Lehnertz, D.R.E.
Students 165.

Sisters, Deschutes Co., St. Edward (1984), Rev. W. Thomas Faucher.
Res., 68817 Trinity Way, P.O. Box 489, 97759-0489. Tel: 541-549-0751; 549-9391.
Catechesis/Religious Programs—Richard Engstrom, D.R.E.
Students 54.

The Dalles, Wasco Co., St. Peter's (1848), Rev. Ronald E. Maag.
Res., 1222 W. 10th St., P.O. Box 41, 97058. Tel: 541-296-2026; Fax: 541-296-8634. [CEM]
School—St. Mary, (Grades PreK-7) 1112 Cherry Heights Rd., Tel: 541-296-6004. Stephanie Ritchie, Prin.
Lay Teachers 13; Students 220.
Catechesis/Religious Programs—1111 W. 10th, P.O. Box 41, 97058. Tel: 541-296-3610. Allen Zaugg, D.R.E.
Students 20.

Union, Union Co., Sacred Heart (1905). Attended by Our Lady of the Valley, La Grande.
Church—340 S. 10th St., P.O. Box 473, 97883. Tel: 541-562-6285.

Catechesis/Religious Programs—Willard Bertrand, D.R.E.
Students 34.

Vale, Malheur Co., St. Patrick's (1946), Rev. Lawrence C. Bower.
Res., P.O. Box J, 97918. Tel: 541-473-3906.
Catechesis/Religious Programs—Tel: 541-473-3848. D.R.E.: Audrey Erstrom; Jim Arritola.
Students 65.
Mission—Juntura, St. Charles.
Station—Harper, St. John the Beloved.

Wasco, Sherman Co., St. Mary's (1954), Rev. Anselm Fister, O.S.B.
Res., 807 Barnett St., P.O. Box 14, 97065. Tel: 541-442-5496.
Catechesis/Religious Programs—D.R.E.: Sandy MacNab; Mary Anne MacNab.
Students 53.
Missions—Antelope, St. Mary's; Grass Valley, St. John the Baptist.

Chaplains of Public Institutions

PENDLETON. *Eastern Oregon Correctional Institution.* Vacant.

Eastern Oregon State Hospital. Vacant. St. Mary, 800 S.E. Court, 97801.

Special Assignment:
Reverend Monsignors—
Crotty, Matthew M., Vicar Gen., 1011 S.E. 15th, #31, Bend, OR 97702

On Duty Outside the Diocese:
Reverend Fathers—
Hickie, J. Noel, Sacred Heart General Hospital, 1305 Willagillespie Rd., Eugene, OR 97401
Kiely, Cornelius, Iglesia La Immaculada Concepcion, Puerto Lopez, Manabi, Ecuador
Reeves, Joseph, 12223 N.W. Cornell Rd., Apt. 306, Portland, OR 97229

Absent on Leave:
Reverend Fathers—
Holmes, Dennis
Kirby, Larry Joseph

Retired:
Reverend Monsignors—
Beard, Raymond, P.O. Box 57, Athena, OR 97813
Keating, Bernard A., P.O. Box 861, Redmond, OR 97756
Phelan, John F., 26 Cedarwood Ave., Laughboy, Co. Kilkenney, Ireland
Stone, William S., 2633 S.W. Obsidian, #52, Redmond, OR 97756

Reverend Fathers—
Baumgartner, John, St. Elizabeth Nursing Home, 3985 Midway Dr., Baker City, OR 97814
Collins, Timothy, Pendleton House, Avondale House, Kilrush Rd., Ennis, Co. Clare, Ireland
Conway, Richard J., 950 Pomona, #166, The Dalles, OR 97058
Cribbin, Austin J., 220 Newcastle Rd., Klamath Falls, OR 97601
Fisher, A. J., 1200 W. Dimond #14105, Anchorage, AK 99515
Quigley, Martin J., 533 Ayres Rd., The Dalles, OR 97058
Scanlon, Thomas R., P.O. Box 695, The Dalles, OR 97058

INSTITUTIONS LOCATED IN THE DIOCESE

[A] GENERAL HOSPITALS

BAKER CITY. *St. Elizabeth Health Services, Inc.*, 3325 Pocahontas Rd., 97814. Tel: 541-523-6461.
For a complete listing, refer to the Hospitals section.

BEND. *St. Charles Medical Center*, 2500 N.E. Neff Rd., 97701. Tel: 541-382-4321; Fax: 541-388-7723.
For a complete listing, refer to the Hospitals section.

ONTARIO. *Holy Rosary Medical Center*, 351 S.W. Ninth St., 97914. Tel: 541-889-5331; Fax: 541-889-7642.
For a complete listing, refer to the Hospitals section.

PENDLETON. *St. Anthony Hospital*, 1601 S.E. Court Ave., 97801. Tel: 541-276-5121.
For a complete listing, refer to the Hospitals section.

[B] HOMES FOR AGED

BAKER CITY. *St. Elizabeth Health Care Center*, 3985 Midway Dr., 97814. Tel: 541-523-4452; Fax: 541-523-8151.
For a complete listing, refer to the Special Care Facilities section.

[C] CONVENTS & RESIDENCES FOR SISTERS

BAKER CITY. *St. Clare Convent*, 3030 A St., 97814. Tel: 541-523-6770. Sisters 2.

LA PINE. *Solitary Hermitesses.* (Hermit Colony), 97739. Members 2.

[D] MISCELLANEOUS

BEND. *Saint Vincent de Paul Society - District Council of Central Oregon*, P.O. Box 1011, 97709. Tel: 541-389-3325. Wes Colbo, Pres.; Judy Mackel, Exec. Dir. Tel: 541-389-5117.
Bend Social Services Conference. Tel: 541-389-6643.

THE DALLES. *Saint Vincent de Paul Society - The Dalles Conference*, P.O. Box 41, 97058. Tel: 541-298-1315. David Lutgens, Pres.

LA PINE. *La Pine Conference*, P.O. Box 1008, 97739. Tel: 541-536-1956. Arlene Mura, Pres.

PRINEVILLE. *Saint Vincent de Paul Society - Prineville Conference*, 990 S.E. 2nd St., 97754. Tel: 541-447-4565. John Stolitz, Pres.

REDMOND. *Saint Vincent de Paul Society - Redmond Conference*, 1114 S.W. Evergreen, 97756. Tel: 541-923-5264. Yvonne Light, Pres.

RELIGIOUS INSTITUTES OF MEN REPRESENTED IN THE DIOCESE

For futher details refer to the corresponding bracketed number in the Religious Institutes of Men or Women section.

[0200]—*Benedictine Monks.* (Benet Hills, CA).—O.S.B.
[0900]—*Canons Regular of Premontre, England.*—O. Praem.
[0470]—*The Capuchin Friars.*—O.F.M.Cap.
[0690]—*Jesuit Fathers and Brothers.* (California, Oregon Provs.).—S.J.
[0430]—*Order of Preachers (Dominicans).*—O.P.

RELIGIOUS INSTITUTES OF WOMEN REPRESENTED IN THE DIOCESE

[1070-25]—*Dominican Sisters of Kenosha, WI.*—O.P.
[1070-03]—*Dominican Sisters of Sinsinawa, WI.*—O.P.
[1070-20]—*Dominican Sisters of St. Thomas Aquinas.*—O.P.
[2470]—*Maryknoll Sisters of St. Dominic.*—M.M.
[2970]—*School Sisters of Notre Dame.*—S.S.N.D.
[3000]—*Sisters of Notre Dame de Namur.*—S.N.D.deN.
[1630]—*Sisters of St. Francis of Penance and Christian Charity.*—O.S.F.
[1650]—*Sisters of St. Francis of Philadelphia.*—O.S.F.
[3830]—*Sisters of St. Joseph.*—C.S.J.
[3960]—*Sisters of St. Mary of Oregon.*—S.S.M.O.
[1990]—*Sisters of the Holy Names of Jesus and Mary.*—S.N.J.M.
[4060]—*Society of the Holy Child Jesus.*—S.H.C.J.

NECROLOGY

(No Deaths)

Archdiocese of Baltimore

(Archidioecesis Baltimorensis)

His Eminence

WILLIAM CARDINAL KEELER, D.D. J.C.D.

Archbishop of Baltimore; ordained July 17, 1955; appointed Titular Bishop of Ulcinium and Auxiliary Bishop of Harrisburg July 24, 1979; ordained Bishop September 21, 1979; appointed Bishop of Harrisburg November 10, 1983; installed January 4, 1984; appointed Archbishop of Baltimore April 6, 1989; installed as Fourteenth Archbishop of Baltimore May 23, 1989; created Cardinal Priest November 26, 1994. *Office: 320 Cathedral St., Baltimore, MD, 21201.* Tel.: 410-547-5437.

Most Reverend

WILLIAM DONALD BORDERS, D.D.

Retired Archbishop of Baltimore; ordained May 18, 1940; appointed Bishop of Orlando May 2, 1968; consecrated June 14, 1968; appointed Archbishop of Baltimore March 25, 1974; installed June 26, 1974; retired April 6, 1989. *Office: 320 Cathedral St., Baltimore, MD, 21201.* Tel.: 410-547-5439.

Most Reverend

P. FRANCIS MURPHY, D.D., V.G.

Auxiliary Bishop of Baltimore, Western Vicar and Titular Bishop of Tacarata; ordained December 20, 1958; ordained Bishop February 29, 1976. *Office: 320 Cathedral St., Baltimore, MD, 21201.* Tel.: 410-547-5447.

Most Reverend

WILLIAM C. NEWMAN, D.D., V.G.

Auxiliary Bishop of Baltimore, Eastern Vicar and Titular Bishop of Numluli; ordained May 29, 1954; ordained Bishop July 2, 1984. *Office: 320 Cathedral St., Baltimore, MD, 21201.* Tel.: 410-547-5438. *Res., 5300 N. Charles St., Baltimore, MD*

ESTABLISHED A DIOCESE NOVEMBER 6, 1789; ESTABLISHED AN ARCHDIOCESE APRIL 8, 1808.

Square Miles 4,801.

Comprises the City of Baltimore and Allegany, Anne Arundel, Baltimore, Carroll, Frederick, Garrett, Harford, Howard and Washington Counties.

By a Decree of the Sacred Congregation of the Propaganda, July 19, 1858, approved by His Holiness, Pius IX, July 25, 1858, "Prerogative of Place" was conferred on the Archdiocese of Baltimore. By the explicit words of said decree of the Holy See, the Archbishop of Baltimore takes precedence over all Archbishops of the United States (not Cardinals) in Councils, gatherings and meetings of whatever kind of the Hierarchy (in concillis, coetibus et comitiis quibuscumque) regardless of the seniority of other Archbishops in promotion or ordination. Decree signed by Cardinal Barnabo, August 15, 1858.

For legal titles of parishes and archdiocesan institutions, consult the Chancery Office.

Chancery Office: 320 Cathedral St., Baltimore, MD, 21201. Tel.: 410-547-5446.

Web site address: http://www.archbalt.org

E-mail address: facts@archbalt.org

STATISTICAL OVERVIEW

Personnel	
Cardinal	1
Retired Archbishops	1
Auxiliary Bishops	2
Priests: Diocesan Active in Diocese	203
Priests: Active Outside Diocese	8
Priests: Retired, Sick or Absent	77
Number of Diocesan Priests	288
Religious Priests in Diocese	257
Extern Priests in Diocese	8
Ordinations:	
Diocesan Priests	4
Transitional Deacons	1
Permanent Deacons	18
Permanent Deacons in Diocese	166
Total Brothers	121
Total Sisters	1,332
Parishes	
Parishes	154
With Resident Pastor:	
Resident Diocesan Priests	106
Resident Religious Priests	30
Without Resident Pastor:	
Administered by Priests	13
Administered by Women Religious	5
Missions	8
Pastoral Centers	3
New Parishes Created	1
Professional Ministry Personnel:	
Brothers	2
Sisters	70
Lay Ministers	131
Welfare	
Catholic Hospitals	5
Total Assisted	915,205
Homes for the Aged	17
Total Assisted	1,898
Residential Care of Children	2
Total Assisted	251
Day Care and Extended Day Care Centers	10
Total Assisted	1,544
Specialized Homes	6
Total Assisted	1,258
Special Centers for Social Services	29
Total Assisted	749,497
Residential Care of Disabled	4
Total Assisted	787
Educational	
Seminaries, Diocesan	2
Students from This Diocese	18
Students from Other Diocese	261
Diocesan Students in Other Seminaries	10
Total Seminarians	28
Colleges and Universities	3
Total Students	11,365
High Schools, Diocesan and Parish	9
Total Students	3,563
High Schools, Private	13
Total Students	7,020
Elementary Schools, Diocesan and Parish	68
Total Students	23,292
Elementary Schools, Private	6
Total Students	1,105
Non-residential Schools for the Disabled	2
Total Students	232
Catechesis/Religious Education:	
High School Students	4,742
Elementary Students	36,623
Total Students Under Catholic Instruction	87,970
Teachers in the Diocese:	
Priests	60
Brothers	22
Sisters	129
Lay Teachers	2,269
Vital Statistics	
Receptions into the Church:	
Infant Baptism Totals	8,435
Adult Baptism Totals	692
Received into Full Communion	1,261
First Communions	8,211
Confirmations	5,176
Marriages:	
Catholic	1,764
Interfaith	1,162
Total Marriages	2,926
Deaths	5,248
Total Catholic Population	480,152
Total Population	2,862,671

Former Bishops—Most Rev. JOHN CARROLL, D.D., cons. August 15, 1790; Archbishop, April 8, 1808; died Dec. 3, 1815.—Most Rev. LEONARD NEALE, D.D., cons. Coadjutor, Dec. 7, 1800; acceded Dec. 3, 1815; died June 18, 1817.—Most Rev. AMBROSE MARECHAL, S.S., D.D., cons. Dec. 14, 1817; died Jan. 29, 1828.—Most Rev. JAMES WHITFIELD, D.D., cons. May 25, 1828; died Oct. 19, 1834.—Most Rev. SAMUEL ECCLESTON, S.S., D.D., cons. Sept. 14, 1834; died April 22, 1851.—Most Rev. FRANCIS PATRICK KENRICK, D.D., cons. June 6, 1830; Coadjutor Bishop of Philadelphia; promoted to Aug. 19, 1851; died July 8, 1863.—Most Rev. MARTIN JOHN SPALDING, D.D., cons. Sept. 10, 1848; Coadjutor Bishop of Louisville; promoted to May 6, 1864; died Feb. 7, 1872.—Most Rev. JAMES ROOSEVELT BAYLEY, D.D., cons. Oct. 30, 1853; Bishop of Newark; promoted to July 30, 1872; died Oct. 3, 1877.—His Eminence JAMES CARDINAL GIBBONS, cons. Vicar Apostolic of North Carolina, Aug. 16, 1868; transferred to See of Richmond, July 30, 1872; promoted to See of Baltimore, Oct. 3, 1877; created Cardinal Priest of S. Maria in Trastevere, June 7, 1886; died March 24, 1921.—Most Rev. MICHAEL J. CURLEY, D.D., cons. Bishop of St. Augustine, June 30, 1914; promoted to Aug. 10, 1921; died May 16, 1947.—Most Rev. FRANCIS P. KEOUGH, D.D., cons. Bishop of Providence, May 22, 1934; promoted to Nov. 29, 1947; died Dec. 8, 1961.—His Eminence LAWRENCE CARDINAL SHEHAN, cons. Auxiliary Bishop of Baltimore, Dec. 12, 1945; transferred to Diocese of Bridgeport, Aug. 25, 1953; appt. Coadjutor Archbishop of Baltimore, July 10, 1961; acceded Dec. 8, 1961; created

Cardinal Priest of S. Clemente, Feb. 22, 1965; retired March 25, 1974; died Aug. 26, 1984.—Most Rev. WILLIAM DONALD BORDERS, D.D., appt. Bishop of Orlando, May 2, 1968; cons. June 14, 1968; promoted to March 25, 1974; installed June 26, 1974; retired April 6, 1989.

Vicars General—Most Rev. P. FRANCIS MURPHY, D.D., V.G.; Most Rev. WILLIAM C. NEWMAN, D.D., V.G.; Most Rev. JOHN H. RICARD, S.S.J., Ph.D., V.G.; Rev. Msgr. W. FRANCIS MALOOLY, V.G.

Archbishop, Office of the—Rev. JOHN B. WARD, Sec. to the Cardinal. Tel: 410-547-5303., *320 Cathedral St., Baltimore, 21201.* Tel: 410-547-5437.

Chancery Office—320 Cathedral St., Baltimore, 21201. Tel: 410-547-5446. Office Hours: Mon.-Fri. 9-5; Closed holidays.

Chancellor—Rev. Msgr. W. FRANCIS MALOOLY, V.G.; Rev. Msgr. JEREMIAH F. KENNEY, Vice Chancellor; Rev. JOHN B. WARD, Asst. Chancellor.

Consultors—Most Rev. P. FRANCIS MURPHY; Most Rev. WILLIAM C. NEWMAN; Most Rev. JOHN H. RICARD; Rev. Msgr. PAUL G. COOK; Rev. Msgr. ROBERT ARMSTRONG; Rev. Msgr. W. FRANCIS MALOOLY; Rev. Msgr. JAMES MCGOVERN; Rev. Msgr. G. MICHAEL SCHLEUPNER; Rev. Msgr. EDWARD F. STAUB; Rev. Msgr. VICTOR GALEONE; Rev. JOHN T. WIELEBSKI.

Eastern Vicar, Office of the—Most Rev. WILLIAM C. NEWMAN, D.D., V.G., Vicar; Sr. EDITHANN KANE, S.N.D., Admin. Asst., *320 Cathedral St., Baltimore, 21201.* Tel: 410-547-5438.

Ecclesiastical Court in Equity—

Chief Judge and Moderator—Rev. Msgr. JEREMIAH F. KENNEY, J.V.

Judges in Equity—Honorables WILSON K. BARNES; J. HAROLD GRADY; JAMES A. PERROTT; ROBERT A. WATTS.

Interdiocesan Tribunal of Appeals of the Province of Baltimore—320 Cathedral St., Baltimore, 21201. Tel: 410-576-6924.

Judicial Vicar—Rev. Msgr. JEREMIAH F. KENNEY, J.V.

Interdiocesan Judges—Rev. Msgr. JOHN P. HANNAN; Rev. Msgr. PAUL J. SCHIERSE; Revs. FREDERICK P. ANNIE; EDMUND F. CARROLL, T.O.R.; WILLIAM J. DALE; EMIL DOBOSZ; FREDERICK J. FEUSAHRENS; GEORGE J. GRIFFIN; CHRISTIAN J. HAYDINGER; CHARLES A. KELLY; MARK R. LANE; JOHN S. LEDFORD; CHRISTOPHER P. MOORE; WILLIAM J. NOLTE; EUGENE S. OSTROWSKI; Rev. Msgr. JOSEPH REBMAN; Revs. RICHARD A. REISSMANN; JOHN E. RIDGELL; THOMAS F. SHREVE; J. ANTHONY WARNER; EUGENE J. WEBER; Deacon ROBERT GRAHAM.

Defenders of the Bond—Rt. Rev. BENEDICT MCDERMOTT, O.S.B.; Revs. CHARLES DILLINGHAM; ROBERT S. EMBILE; JAMES F. KAUFFMAN; RICHARD T. MOONEY; GILBERT J. SEITZ, JR.; JOHN B. WARD; GERALD T. WEYMES.

Notaries—Rev. KEVIN GALLAGHER; JOANNE D'SURNEY; BETTY I. HICKMAN; JOANN KUBASKO; JEANNETTE LINDNER.

Metropolitan Tribunal—320 Cathedral St., Baltimore, 21201. Tel: 410-576-6920.

Cardinal's Delegate for Tribunal Canonical Administration—Rev. Msgr. JEREMIAH F. KENNEY, J.V.

Judicial Vicar—Rev. Msgr. G. MICHAEL SCHLEUPNER.

Adjutant Judicial Vicar—Rev. WILLIAM A. COLLINS.

Judges—Revs. JAMES A. BRENNAN, S.S.; MICHAEL J. CARRION; JAMES J. DITILLO, S.J.; THOMAS J. GOLUEKE; Deacons RAY BRITT; HARRY ST. A. O'NEILL.

Defenders of the Bond—Rev. Msgr. ROBERT A. ARMSTRONG; Rev. WILLIAM Q. SIMMS; LUCY LEE.

Promoter of Justice—Rev. Msgr. JOHN H. MCCALL.

Advocates and Procurators—Revs. BERNARD BAK; MICHAEL J. CALLAGHAN; PATRICK CARRION; E. JOSEPH COTE; RICHARD E. CRAMBLITT; MARTIN E. FEILD; WILLIAM FOLEY; JAMES HANNON; ROBERT HARTNETT; C. LOU MARTIN; EDWARD MILLER; KEVIN MUELLER; G. EUGENE NICKOL; MITCHELL ROZANSKI; RICHARD W. WOY; Deacons JOHN ABELL; NICHOLAS FEURER; PATRICK GOLES; HERMAN GRABENSTEIN; JOHN MCKENNA; ROBERT LEHR; JOHN MARTELLE; WILLIAM NAIRN; STANLEY G. PIET; GERALD RAIBLE; JOHN J. RAFTER; FRANK RONGIONE; WALTER SHIPLEY; DANIEL STRETMATER; FREDDY WENDT; Sr. KATHERINE BELL, R.S.M.; Sr. REGINA BURGAN, S.S.N.D.; Sr. AGNESINE CONNORS, S.S.N.D.; Sr. MARIETTA CULHANE, O.S.F.; Sr. CAROL CZYZEWSKI, F.S.S.J.; Sr. FRANCES DEMARCO, R.S.M.; Sr. JOAN BASTRESS, I.H.M.; Sr. SUSAN ENGEL, M.H.S.H.; Sr. JOYCE HOLDEN, M.H.S.H.; Sr. ELIZABETH KANE, O.S.F.; Sr. PATRICIA MCALPIN, O.S.F.; Sr. JOAN MINELLA, S.S.N.D.; Sr. NANCY STILES, S.U.S.C.; MARY JOYCE BLESSING; ROBERT NICHOLSON; JOHN SAUER; JOHN KUTZ.

Notaries—PATRICIA FREUND; CHRISTINA MAKOWIECKI.

Receptionist—CLARA JULIAO.

Urban Vicar, Office of the—Most Rev. JOHN H. RICARD, S.S.J., D.D., V.G., Ph.D., Vicar, *320 Cathedral St., Baltimore, 21201.* Tel: 410-547-5452.

Western Vicar, Office of the—Most Rev. P. FRANCIS MURPHY, D.D., V.G., Vicar; Sr. DOLORES TODD, S.S.N.D., *320 Cathedral St., Baltimore, 21201.* Tel: 410-547-5447.

Archdiocesan Offices and Directors

African-American Ministries, Archdiocesan Office of—THERESE WILSON FAVORS, Dir., *320 Cathedral St., Baltimore, 21201.* Tel: 410-625-8472.

Apostleship of Prayer—Rev. WILLIAM M. J. DRISCOLL, S.J., Dir., *Loyola College, 4501 N. Charles St., Baltimore, 21210.* Tel: 410-323-1010.

Archdiocesan Committee on Alcoholism—Rev. Msgr. A. THOMAS BAUMGARTNER, Chm., *8801 Harford Rd., Baltimore, 21234.*

Archdiocesan Directory—SUSAN M. SEILER, Editor, *320 Cathedral St., Baltimore, 21201.* Tel: 410-547-5311. Official directory of the Archdiocese of Baltimore. Published annually by *The Catholic Review.* 25 dollars per copy.

Archdiocesan Gay-Lesbian Outreach (AGLO)—Rev. JOSEPH HUGHES, Coord., *2034 Park Ave., Baltimore, 21217.* Tel: 410-728-2638.

Archdiocesan Pastoral Council—(See Pastoral Council Archdiocesan).

Archives-Archivist—Rev. PAUL THOMAS, *320 Cathedral St., Baltimore, 21201.* Tel: 410-547-5443 (By appointment).

Associated Catholic Charities, Inc.—HAROLD A. SMITH, Exec. Dir., *320 Cathedral St., Baltimore, 21201.* Tel: 410-547-5495; Fax: 410-752-7260.

Division of Family and Children's Services—ANGELO BOER, Dir., *320 Cathedral St., Baltimore, 21201.* Tel: 410-547-5540.

Christopher Place—709 E. Eager St., Baltimore, 21202. Tel: 410-576-0066.

My Sister's Place—123 W. Mulberry St., Baltimore, 21201. Tel: 410-727-3523.

Our Daily Bread—411 Cathedral St., Baltimore, 21201. Tel: 410-659-4000.

Sarah's House—2013 20th St., Fort Meade, 20755. Tel: 410-551-7722.

Division of Children's Services—JACK RUSINKO, Dir., *2300 Dulaney Valley Rd., Lutherville-Timonium, 21093.* Tel: 410-252-4700.

Gallagher Services—2520 Pot Spring Rd., Timonium, 21093. Tel: 410-252-4005.

St. Vincent's Center—2600 Pot Spring Center, Timonium, 21093. Tel: 410-252-4000.

Villa Maria—2300 Dulaney Valley Rd., Timonium, 21093. Tel: 410-252-4700.

Villa Louise—DePaul Building, 900 S. Caton Ave., Baltimore, 21229. Tel: 410-368-2060.

Division of Housing Services—DALE MCARDLE, Dir., *320 Cathedral St., Baltimore, 21201.* Tel: 410-547-5544.

Division of Services to the Aging and Long-Term Care—REBECCA GALLOWAY, Dir., *St. Elizabeth's Nursing Home, 3320 Benson Ave., Baltimore, 21229.* Tel: 410-646-6502.

Jenkins Memorial, Inc.—1000 S. Caton Ave., Baltimore, 21229. Tel: 410-644-7100.

Stella Maris Hospice—2300 Dulaney Valley Rd., Towson, 21204. Tel: 410-252-4500. *Institutional Corporations Merged into Association:* St. Leo Italian Orphan Asylum; Dolan Childrens Aid Society; St. Patrick's Orphanage; St. Vincent's Infant Asylum; St. Anthony's Orphan Asylum in Baltimore City; St. Mary's Female Orphan Asylum of Baltimore (St. Mary's Villa); St. James Home for Boys of Baltimore City; St. Mary's Industrial School for Boys; Schmidt's Orphan Home, Inc.; Christopher Place; My Sister's Place; Our Daily Bread; Sarah's House.

Boy Scouts—(See Catholic Youth Activities).

Campaign For Human Development, Archdiocese of Baltimore, Inc.—Rev. Msgr. WILLIAM F. BURKE, Dir., *320 Cathedral St., Baltimore, 21201.* Tel: 410-235-5136; 547-5446.

Campus Ministry (Newman Apostolate)—Rev. ROBERT E. ALBRIGHT, Dir., *7909 York Rd., Baltimore, 21204.* Tel: 410-828-0622.

The Cathedral Foundation, Inc.—His Eminence WILLIAM H. KEELER, D.D., J.C.D., Pres.; Rev. Msgr. THOMAS J. DONELLAN, Vice Pres. Publishers of *The Catholic Review* and *Official Archdiocesan Directory. P.O. Box 777, Baltimore, 21203.* Tel: 410-547-5380.

Catholic Center Operations, Div. of—LOUIS WILLETT, Facilities Mgr., *320 Cathedral St., Baltimore, 21201.* Tel: 410-547-5312.

Catholic Charity Fund, Inc.—320 Cathedral St., Baltimore, 21201.

Catholic Education Ministries, Department of—RONALD J. VALENTI, Ph.D., Sec., *320 Cathedral St., Baltimore, 21201.* Tel: 410-547-5383.

Catholic Relief Services—MARY D'AMBROGI, Archdiocesan Dir., *320 Cathedral St., Baltimore, 21201.* Tel: 410-547-5323.

"The Catholic Review"—His Eminence WILLIAM H. KEELER, D.D., J.C.D., Publisher; DANIEL L. MEDINGER, Assoc. Publisher/Editor; JILL JASUTA, Mng. Editor, *320 Cathedral St., P.O. Box 777, Baltimore, 21203.* Tel: 410-547-5380. Newspaper of the Archdiocese of Baltimore. Established 1913. Published every Wednesday by the Cathedral Foundation, Inc.

Catholic Schools Division—Dr. RONALD J. VALENTI, Supt., *320 Cathedral St., Catholic Center, Baltimore, 21201.* Tel: 410-547-5384.

Catholic Students Mission Crusade—See Propagation of the Faith.

Cemeteries, Office of—4300 Old Frederick Rd., Baltimore, 21229. Tel: 410-566-7770.

Censor Librorum—Rev. Msgr. CARROLL E. SATTERFIELD, S.T.D., *College of Notre Dame of Maryland, 4701 N. Charles St., Baltimore, 21210.*

Commission for Ecumenical and Inter-Religious Affairs—Rev. RICHARD H. TILLMAN, Chm., *10431 Twin Rivers Rd., Columbia, 21044.* Tel: 410-964-1425.

Controller, Division of the—PAUL J. AYD, C.P.A., Controller, *320 Cathedral St., Baltimore, 21201.* Tel: 410-547-5300.

Facilities Management, Division of—LOUIS F. BAIRD, Dir.; LOUIS WILLETT, Facilities Mgr.; ROSE MCNALLY, Assoc. Dir., *320 Cathedral St., Baltimore, 21201.* Tel: 410-547-5366.

Family Life, Office of—Ms. CAROL J. PACIONE, Dir., *320 Cathedral St., Baltimore, 21201.* Tel: 410-547-5422; Fax: 410-347-7896.

Financial Administration, Board of—Rev. Msgr. G. MICHAEL SCHLEUPNER, Chm., *320 Cathedral St., Baltimore, 21201.*

Fiscal Services—PAUL J. AYD, Dir. & Controller, *320 Cathedral St., Baltimore, 21201.* Tel: 410-547-5300.

Fund Development, Department of—THOMAS J. SONNI, Exec. Dir.; GEORGE E. REED, III, Sr. Devel. Officer; JANIS M. PECK, Devel. Assoc.; LYNN BOERI, DP Spec., *320 Cathedral St., Baltimore, 21201.* Tel: 410-547-5356.

Holy Childhood Association—Rev. Msgr. VICTOR GALEONE, Dir., *320 Cathedral St., Baltimore, 21201.*

Human Resources Development, Department of—SHEILA KELLY, Sec., *320 Cathedral St., Baltimore, 21201.* Tel: 410-547-5556.

Human Resources Services, Division of—MICHELLY MERRICK, Dir., *320 Cathedral St., Baltimore, 21201.* Tel: 410-547-5448.

Information Systems, Division of—JAMES B. TUCKER, Dir., *320 Cathedral St., Baltimore, 21201.* Tel: 410-547-5305.

Insurance, Division of—PETRA PHELPS, Dir., *320 Cathedral St., Baltimore, 21201.* Tel: 410-547-5551; Fax: 410-783-5993.

Insurance Committee—WILLIAM FRANEY, Chm.; PETRA PHELPS, Sec., *320 Cathedral St., Baltimore, 21201.* Tel: 410-547-5317.

Lay Employees Retirement Board—JANE MCGEEHAN, Chm.; PETRA PHELPS, Sec., *320 Cathedral St., Baltimore, 21201.* Tel: 410-547-5317.

League of the Little Flower—Rev. Msgr. PAUL G. COOK, Dir., *320 Cathedral St., Baltimore, 21201.* Tel: 410-547-5361.

Archdiocesan RENEW Office—WILLIAM JOHNSTON, Dir., *320 Cathedral St., Baltimore, 21201.* Tel: 410-547-5404.

Management Services, Department of—Rev. Msgr. G. MICHAEL SCHLEUPNER, Sec., *320 Cathedral St., Baltimore, 21201.* Tel: 410-547-5591.

Maryland Catholic Conference—RICHARD J. DOWLING, ESQ., Exec. Dir., *188 Duke of Gloucester St., Annapolis, 21401.* Tel: 410-269-1155 (Bal.); 301-261-1979 (Wash.); Fax: 410-269-1790.

Pastoral Personnel Services, Division of—Revs. RICHARD WOY, Dir.; J. BRUCE JARBOE, Assoc. Dir.; Ms. MARTHA SHETLER, Admin. Asst., *320 Cathedral St., Baltimore, 21201.* Tel: 410-547-5427.

Pastoral Council, Archdiocesan—320 Cathedral St., Baltimore, 21201. Tel: 410-547-5455.

Permanent Deacon Formation Program—Rev. RICHARD WOY, Dir., *320 Cathedral St., Baltimore, 21201.* Tel: 410-547-5557.

Planning and Council Services, Division of—Sr. ROSALIE MURPHY, Dir. GERIANNE SAVAGE, Consultant Collegial Svcs. JOSEPH S. NADOLNY, JR., Archdiocesan Information Coord. Tel: 410-547-5455.

Priests Council—Rev. Msgr. JOSEPH LUCA; Rev. Msgr. ROBERT PASSARELLI; Rev. Msgr. THOMAS J. TEWES; Rev. Msgr. ARTHUR VALENZANO; Revs. LLOYD AIKEN; WILLIAM AU; DOMENIC CIERI; JAMES CONN, S.J.; DONALD FEST, S.S.J.; GERARD FRANCIK; JOHN FILIPELLI, S.S.J.; DONALD GRZYMSKI, O.F.M.Conv.; ROBERT LENTZ; KEVIN SCHENNING; ALFRED E. SMITH; DONALD STERLING; JOHN WIELEBSKI, *320 Cathedral St., Baltimore, 21201.* Tel: 410-547-5455.

Ex-Officio—His Eminence WILLIAM H. KEELER, D.D., J.C.D.; Most Rev. P. FRANCIS MURPHY; Most Rev.

WILLIAM C. NEWMAN; Most Rev. JOHN H. RICARD, S.S.J.; Rev. Msgr. ROBERT ARMSTRONG; Rev. Msgr. PAUL COOK; Rev. Msgr. G. MICHAEL SCHLEUPNER; Rev. Msgr. W. FRANCIS MALOOLY; Rev. Msgr. EDWARD STAUB; Rev. Msgr. JAMES O. MCGOVERN; Rev. Msgr. VICTOR GALEONE; Rev. JOHN T. WIELEBSKI.

Priest Personnel Board—Rev. Msgr. VICTOR GALEONE, Chm.; Rev. Msgr. ARTHUR VALENZANO, Vice Chm.; Rev. Msgr. JOHN MCCALL; Rev. Msgr. JOSEPH LUCA; Rev. Msgr. JAMES MCGOVERN; Rev. Msgr. ROBERT PASSARELLI; Revs. WILLIAM AU; RICHARD BOZZELLI; WILLIAM FRANKIN; WAYNE FUNK; MITCHELL ROZANSKI.

Propagation of the Faith, Home and Foreign Mission Society—His Eminence WILLIAM H. KEELER, D.D., J.C.D., Gen. Dir.; Rev. Msgr. VICTOR GALEONE, Dir., *320 Cathedral St., Baltimore, 21201.* Tel: 410-547-5323.

Public Relations Office—320 Cathedral St., Baltimore, 21201. Tel: 410-547-5379. WILLIAM BLAUL, Dir.

Religious Education, Division of—JAMES J. DEBOY, Dir., *320 Cathedral St., Baltimore, 21201.* Tel: 410-547-5403; Fax: 410-347-7896.

Senior Priests Retirement Board—Rev. Msgr. JAMES MCGOVERN, Chm.; PETRA PHELPS, Sec., *320 Cathedral St., Baltimore, 21201.* Tel: 410-547-5317.

Urban Affairs, Archdiocesan Office—320 Cathedral St., Baltimore, 21201. Tel: 410-547-5486.

St. Vincent de Paul Society—Baltimore Council: His Eminence WILLIAM H. KEELER, D.D., Honorary Pres.; Rev. Msgr. JEREMIAH F. KENNEY, Spiritual Dir. MICHAEL F. ARMETTA, Pres. JOHN J. SCHIAVONE, Exec. Dir., *320 Cathedral St., Baltimore, 21201.* Tel: 410-547-5377.

Vocation Office—Rev. JAMES BARKER, Dir. Tel: 410-547-5426.

Youth Ministry, Office of—MARK PACIONE, Dir., *320 Cathedral St., Baltimore, 21201.* Tel: 410-547-5372; Fax: 410-347-7896.

CLERGY, PARISHES, MISSIONS AND PAROCHIAL SCHOOLS

METROPOLITAN BALTIMORE
(Baltimore City and Baltimore County)

1—CATHEDRAL OF MARY OUR QUEEN (1954), Rev. Msgr. Robert A. Armstrong, Rector; Revs. Thomas Ryan; Lawrence Waudby. In res., Most Rev. William C. Newman, D.D.; Rev. Joseph F. Breighner.
Res., 5300 N. Charles St., 21210-2023. Tel: 410-433-8800; Fax: 410-433-4909.
School—111 Amberly Way, 21210. Tel: 410-433-6204; Fax: 410-433-7678. Sr. Eileen Weisman, S.S.N.D., Prin.
Lay Teachers 25; Students 444.
Catechesis/Religious Programs—115 Amberly Way, 21210. Tel: 410-435-1921.
Students 312.
Parish & Family Ministry—115 Amberly Way, 21210. Tel: 410-532-5269. Mrs. Sharon Buono, Dir.

2—BASILICA OF THE NATIONAL SHRINE OF THE ASSUMPTION OF THE BLESSED VIRGIN MARY (1806). (Co-Cathedral). Corporate Title: The Trustees of the Catholic Cathedral Church of Baltimore (The Basilica); Basilica of the Assumption Historic Trust, Inc. Established for the Preservation of the Basilica as a National Landmark of American Architecture. Cathedral & Mulberry St. Rev. Msgr. James V. Hobbs, Rector; Deacon Robert Oliver.
The Cardinal's Residence: 408 N. Charles St., 21201. Tel: 410-727-3566; Fax: 410-539-0407. His Eminence William Keeler, D.D., J.C.D.; Rev. Msgr. James V. Hobbs, Rector; Parish Office: 408 N. Charles St., 21201. Tel: 410-727-3565.

3—ST. AGNES (Catonsville) (1852), Rev. Msgr. Francis W. Fortenbaugh, Pastor Emeritus; Rev. Msgr. Victor B. Galeone; Rev. William M. Mannion.
Res., 5422 Old Frederick Rd., 21229. Tel: 410-744-2900; Fax: 410-744-8304. [CEM]
School—603 St. Agnes Ln., 21229. Tel: 410-747-4070; Fax: 410-747-0138. Sr. Anne Mary Smith, I.H.M., Prin.
Sisters of the Immaculate Heart of Mary 5; Lay Teachers 21; Students 499.
Catechesis/Religious Programs—Tel: 410-747-9073. Sr. Patricia Anne Huesman, S.S.N.D., D.R.E.
Students 197.

4—THE NEW ALL SAINTS (1912) (African American), Rev. Donald A. Sterling; Deacons Paul D. Shelton; Malcolm Thompson.
Res., 4408 Liberty Heights Ave., 21207. Tel: 410-542-0445; Fax: 410-542-8852.
School—(Grades 4-8) 3510 Eldorado Ave., 21207. Tel: 410-664-9433. Dr. Phyllis Douglass, Prin.
Lay Teachers 6; Students 155.

5—ST. ALPHONSUS (1845) (Lithuanian), Revs. Thomas Bauernfeind, S.T.L.,J.C.L., Rector; John P. Barbernitz, Pastor Emeritus; Casimir A. Pugevicius, M.A., S.T.L.
Res., 114 W. Saratoga St., 21201. Tel: 410-685-6090; Fax: 410-244-1670.
School—125 W. Saratoga St., 21201. Tel: 410-837-7310; Fax: 410-837-6948.
Lay Teachers 13; Students 200.

6—ST. AMBROSE (1907), Pastoral Ministry: Rev. John Pfannenstiel, O.F.M.Cap.; Deacon Watson Fulton.
Res., 4502 Park Heights Ave., 21215. Tel: 410-367-9918; Fax: 410-542-6056.
School—Rosa Parks Elementary School, 4506 Park Heights Ave., 21215. Tel: 410-664-2373.
Lay Teachers 13; Students 228.
Outreach Center—3445 Park Heights Ave., 21215. Tel: 410-225-0870. Sr. Charmaine Krohe, S.S.N.D., Dir.

7—ST. ANDREW. Closed 1974. Parish records available at the Chancery. Tel: 410-547-5446.

8—ST. ANN (1873) (African American). Merged with St. Wenceslaus, Baltimore.
Res., 528 E. 22nd St., 21218. Tel: 410-235-8169; Fax: 410-675-5746. Deacon James E. Bee; Sr. Jeanne Barasha, S.S.N.D., Pastoral Admin.

9—ANNUNCIATION (1968), Rev. William P. Foley; Sr. Susan Engel, M.H.S.H., Pastoral Assoc.; Deacon Frederick Schoennagel, Jr. In res., Rev. Gregory Bennet.
Res., 5212 McCormick Ave., 21206. Tel: 410-866-4020; Fax: 410-866-2754.
Catechesis/Religious Programs—Tel: 410-866-4706.
Students 185.

10—ST. ANTHONY OF PADUA (1884). Merged with Most Precious Blood. Revs. C. Lou Martin; Raymond Lee Harris; William F. Spacek. In res., Revs. John Lombardi; Casimir Pugevicius.
Res., 4414 Frankford Ave., 21206. Tel: 410-488-0400; Fax: 410-488-2433.
School—4410 Frankford Ave., 21206. Tel: 410-488-4848; Fax: 410-325-3766. Mrs. Mary Jo Hutson, Prin.
Lay Teachers 17; Students 367.

11—ASCENSION (Halethorpe) (1913), Rev. Manuel R. Roman; Rev. Msgr. Gerard W. Spraker, Pastor Emeritus; Revs. Conan H. Timoney; Basil Stockmeyer, C.P.; Sr. Mary Catherine Lewandowski, O.S.F., Pastoral Assoc.
Res., 4603 Poplar Ave., 21227. Tel: 410-242-2292; Fax: 410-242-6807.
School—(Grades PreK-8). Tel: 410-242-2020. Ms. Rita Ann Swift, M.S., Prin.
Sisters 1; Lay Teachers 13; Students 187.
Catechesis/Religious Programs—Students 166.

12—ST. ATHANASIUS (1891) (Polish), Rev. Timothy B. Klunk.
Res., 4708 Prudence St., Curtis Bay, 21226. Tel: 410-355-5740; Fax: 410-355-8122.

13—ST. AUGUSTINE (Elkridge) (1844), Rev. Gerard J. Bowen. In res., Rev. Msgr. Chester J. Mieczchowski.
Res., 5976 Old Washington Rd., 21227. Tel: 410-796-1520; Fax: 410-796-8172. [CEM]
School—5990 Old Washington Rd., 21227. Tel: 410-796-3040. Sr. Rita Dorn, S.S.N.D, Prin.
School Sisters of Notre Dame 4; Lay Teachers 9; Students 260.
Catechesis/Religious Programs—Tel: 410-796-8150.
Students 325.

14—ST. BARNABAS. Closed 1931. Parish records available at St. Pius V Church. Tel: 410-523-1930.

15—ST. BENEDICT (1893), Rt. Rev. Paschal A. Morlino, O.S.B. Pastoral Assocs.: Sr. Mary Anna Wilkes, S.S.N.D.; Sr. Beatrice Wise, D.C. In res., Revs. Robert Reed; Avelino Garcia.
Res., 2612 Wilkens Ave., 21223. Tel: 410-947-4988; Fax: 410-947-6009.

16—ST. BERNARD (Korean), Rev. Joseph Y. Kim; Deacon Charles Cook.
Res., 928 Gorsuch Ave., 21218. Tel: 410-235-9513; 467-6474.
Holy Spirit Middle School—932 Gorsuch Ave., 21218. Tel: 410-889-0679.
School Sisters of Notre Dame 2; Lay Teachers 12; Students 218.

17—ST. BERNARDINE (1928) (African American), Rev. Edward M. Miller; Deacons Phillip W. Harcum; Charles Knight.
Res., 3812 Edmondson Ave., 21229. Tel: 410-362-8664; Fax: 410-945-0459.
Catechesis/Religious Programs—Tel: 410-362-8978.
Students 200.

18—BLESSED SACRAMENT CHURCH (1911), Rev. P. Edward Kenny, Jr.; Mr. John Prenger, Pastoral Assoc.
Res., 4103 Old York Rd., 21218. Tel: 410-323-0424; Fax: 410-323-4478.

19—ST. BRIGID (1854), Rev. Joseph G. Bochenek.
Res., 911 S. Ellwood Ave., 21224. Tel: 410-563-1717.
School—Bishop John Newmann. See separate listing.

20—ST. CASIMIR (1902), Revs. Bernard Dudek, O.F.M.Conv.; Bernard Kuczborski, O.F.M.Conv.; Timothy Zientek, O.F.M.Conv.
Res., 2736 O'Donnell St., 21224. Tel: 410-276-1981; Fax: 410-732-7436.
School—Father Kolbe Interparochial School. See separate listing.

21—ST. CECILIA (1902) (African American), Rev. Sylvester Peterka, C.M.; Deacon Thomas A. Wilson.
Res., 3300 Clifton Ave., 21216. Tel: 410-624-3600; Fax: 410-945-0157.

22—ST. CHARLES BORROMEO (Pikesville) (1848), Rev. E. Joseph Cote; Deacon Raymond Bullinger; Sr. M. Martha Geipe, S.S.N.D., Pastoral Min.; Sr. Marylita Friia, S.S.N.D., D.R.E.
Res., 101 Church Ln., 21208. Tel: 410-486-5400; Fax: 410-486-5421. [CEM]

23—CHRIST THE KING (Dundalk) (1956), Rev. Richard P. Wojciechowski.
Res., 335 Sollers Point Rd., 21222. Tel: 410-288-3629.

24—ST. CLARE (Essex) (1956), Revs. Michael W. Carrion; Dale M. Picarella; Deacon Fred Miller.
Res., 714 Myrth Ave., 21221-4898. Tel: 410-687-6011; Fax: 410-687-3054.
School—Tel: 410-687-7787. Sr. Kathleen Jancuk, S.S.N.D., Prin.
Sisters 3; Lay Teachers 17; Students 244.
Catechesis/Religious Programs—Tel: 410-686-7693.
Students 235.

25—ST. CLEMENT (Lansdowne) (1891), Revs. Steven P. Girard; Joseph A. Kenney, Pastor Emeritus; Deacons Norman E. Colson; John I. McKenna; Hugh H. Mills; Thomas J. Yannuzzi.
Res., 2700 Washington Ave., 21227. Tel: 410-242-1025.
School—Mrs. Mary Garmer, Acting Prin. Lay Teachers 9; Students 162.

26—ST. CLEMENT MARY HOFBAUER (Rosedale) (1925), Revs. Richard Florek, O.F.M.Conv.; Timothy Kulbicki, O.F.M.Conv.; Santo Cricchio, O.F.M.Conv.; Deacons Nicholas Feurer, Pastoral Min.; Walter Shipley; Francis Zeiler.
Res., 1220 Chesaco Ave., 21237. Tel: 410-686-6188; Fax: 410-686-6198.
School—Tel: 410-686-3316. Sr. Michael Kathleen, O.S.F., Prin.
Sisters of St. Francis of Philadelphia 4; Lay Teachers 23; Students 443.
Catechesis/Religious Programs—Tel: 410-391-5028. Sr. Maura Walsh, M.H.S.H., Directress.
Students 150.

27—CORPUS CHRISTI (1881), Sr. Jane Coyle, M.M.S., Pastoral Dir.; Sr. Marge Schnellinger, M.M., Pastoral Assoc.; Deacon Frank Hodges.
Res., 110 W. Lafayette Ave., 21217. Tel: 410-523-4161; Fax: 410-523-5745.

28—ST. DOMINIC (1906), Revs. George Loskarn; Matthew Smith.
Res., 5310 Harford Rd., 21214. Tel: 410-426-0354.
School—Patricia Larkin, Prin. Lay Teachers 15; Students 256.

29—ST. EDWARD (1880), Rev. Maurice J. Blackwell; Deacons Earl Smith; Joseph Neale; Carl A. Anderson.
Res., 901 Poplar Grove St., 21216. Tel: 410-362-2000.

30—ST. ELIZABETH OF HUNGARY (1895), Rev. Christopher P. Moore.
Office: 2 N. Belnord Ave., 21224. Tel: 410-675-8260; Fax: 410-558-0028.
Res., 2638 E. Baltimore St., 21224. Tel: 410-675-7771.
School—35 N. Lakewood Ave., 21224. Tel: 410-276-6344. Mr. Richard Gatto, Prin.
Lay Teachers 15; Students 200.

31—FOURTEEN HOLY MARTYRS. Closed 1964. Parish records available at St. Martin Church. Tel: 410-947-1242.

32—ST. FRANCIS OF ASSISI (1927), Rev. Msgr. William F. Burke; Rev. Joseph Bonadio, S.S.; Sr. Katherine Bell, R.S.M., Pastoral Assoc.
Res., 3615 Harford Rd., 21218. Tel: 410-235-5136; 235-1371; Fax: 410-467-9503.
School—3617 Harford Rd., 21218. Tel: 410-467-1683.
Sisters of St. Joseph 1; School Sisters of Notre Dame 1; Lay Teachers 21; Students 337.
Catechesis/Religious Programs—Students 61.

33—St. Francis Xavier, Rev. William L. Norvel, S.S.J.; Deacons Russell Matthews; Charles Mercer. In res., Most Rev. John H. Ricard, S.S.J.
Res., 1501 E. Oliver St., 21213. Tel: 410-727-3103; 3104.

34—St. Gregory the Great (1883) (African American), Rev. Damien Nalepa.
Res., 1507 N. Smallwood St., 21216. Tel: 410-669-1233.
Church—1542 Gilmor St., 21217. Tel: 410-523-0061; Fax: 410-669-1385.

35—Holy Cross (1858) (German), Rev. Mitchell T. Rozanski. In res., Rev. Msgr. John L. Reinsfelder.
Res., 110 E. West St., 21230. Tel: 410-752-8498; Fax: 410-685-0692. [CEM]
School—Catholic Community School of South Baltimore. See separate listing. Tel: 410-685-6155.

36—Holy Rosary (1887) (Polish), Revs. Ronald Pytel; James Miles; Francis Okroy, S.Ch.; Sr. Mary Valenta, C.S.S.F., Pastoral Assoc. In res., Rev. Tomasz Kozub, S.Ch.
Res., 408 S. Chester St., 21231. Tel: 410-732-3960. [CEM]
School—420 Chester St., 21231. Tel: 410-276-0073. Lay Teachers 6; Students 80.

37—St. Ignatius (1856), Rev. William J. Watters, S.J. In res., Revs. Francis P. Ernest, S.J.; Patricio Fernandes, S.J.
Res., 740 N. Calvert St., 21202. Tel: 410-727-3848; Fax: 410-727-1573.
Church—Jesuit Community of St. Ignatius Parish, 102 E. Madison St., 21202. Tel: 410-727-3848.
St. Ignatius Social Services Self-Help—Tel: 410-625-4509. Francine Warden, Dir.

38—Immaculate Conception (1850), Rev. Sylvester Peterka, C.M.; Bro. William Stover, C.M.
Res., 1512 Druid Hill Ave., 21217. Tel: 410-523-0809.

39—Immaculate Conception (Towson) (1883), Rev. Msgr. Edward J. Lynch; Revs. Charles L. Lafferty; John J. Abraham; James D. Profitt; Salvatore J. Livigni.
Res., 200 Ware Ave., 21204. Tel: 410-823-6175; Fax: 410-823-3936. [CEM]
School—(Grades PreK-8). Tel: 410-337-5222. Mrs. Marie Ann Cote, Prin.
Sisters of St. Francis 3; Lay Teachers 21; Students 479.
High School—Towson Catholic, 114 Ware Ave., 21204. Tel: 410-823-8400; Fax: 410-823-8404. Dr. Andrew H. Dotterweich, Prin.
Lay Teachers 20; Students 205.
Catechesis/Religious Programs—School of Religion, 701 Baltimore Ave., 21204. Tel: 410-821-8287. Ms. Lisa E. Padian, Dir.
Students 182.
Convent—112 Ware Ave., 21204. Tel: 410-823-3470.

40—Immaculate Heart of Mary (Baynesville) (1948), Revs. Joseph McManus; Michael J. Jendrek; Deacons Jack Martin; Ken Pivec; Charles Hiebler. In res., Rev. John Ward.
Res., 8501 Loch Raven Blvd., 21286. Tel: 410-668-7935; Fax: 410-661-6560.
School—Tel: 410-668-8466. Mrs. Wilma Short, Prin.
Sisters of Mercy 3; Lay Teachers 23; Students 439.
Catechesis/Religious Programs—Tel: 410-661-3820.
Students 427.

41—St. Isaac Jogues (1968), Rev. Martin Hammond; Rev. Msgr. James J. Cronin, Pastor Emeritus; Rev. M. Shawn Mahon; Deacons James R. Kent; Arthur L. Micozzi; James Westwater.
Church Office—9215 Old Harford Rd., 21234. Tel: 410-661-4888; Fax: 410-882-1484.
Res., 9400 Old Harford Rd., 21234. Tel: 410-661-4883.
Catechesis/Religious Programs—Tel: 410-665-2561.
Students 725.

42—St. James and St. John. Closed 1986. Parish records available at the Chancery. Tel: 410-547-5446.
School—Queen of Peace Elementary Cluster. See separate listing.

43—St. John German Catholic Church. Closed 1841. Original records, stored at The Catholic Center, are available to researchers on microfilm at the Maryland State Archives in Annapolis.

44—St. John The Evangelist. Closed 1966. Parish records available at the Chancery. Tel: 410-547-5446.

45—St. Joseph. Closed 1962. Parish records available at Holy Cross Rectory. Tel: 410-752-8498.

46—St. Jerome (1887), Rev. Msgr. Arthur Bastress; Sr. Joan Bastress, I.H.M., Pastoral Assoc.; Deacon Gerald Anthony Roberts.
Res., 775 W. Hamburg St., 21230. Tel: 410-727-0430.
School & Social Hall—765 W. Hamburg St., 21230. Tel: 410-539-2429.

47—St. Joseph (Fullerton) (1850) (German), Rev. Msgr. George B. Moeller; Revs. Simon Obeng-Kyeremeh; Paul Sparklin; Stephen R. Sutton; Deacons William DeAngelis; Vincent Perticone; Charles Baynes; William Albaugh.
Res., 8420 Belair Rd., 21236. Tel: 410-256-1630; Fax: 410-529-2990. [CEM]
School—Tel: 410-256-8026. Mrs. Joyce Thaler, Prin.
Sisters of St. Francis of Philadelphia 2; Lay Teachers 27; Students 523.
Catechesis/Religious Programs—Tel: 410-256-8235.
Students 923.

48—St. Joseph Passionist Monastery Parish (1868), Rev. Gregory Paul, C.P., Admin.
Res., 251 S. Morley St., 21229. Tel: 410-566-0877; Fax: 410-233-4974.
School—Madonna Catholic School, 3601 Old Frederick Rd., 21229. Tel: 410-624-5088. Dr. Gretchen Styles, Prin.
Lay Teachers 14; Students 340.

49—St. Jude Shrine (1873) (Italian), Revs. Louis Micca, S.A.C.; Louis J. Phillips, S.A.C.
Res., 308 N. Paca St., P.O. Box 2437, 21203. Tel: 410-685-6026; 685-3497; Fax: 410-244-5728.
St. Jude Shrine Corp.—Tel: 410-685-6026.

50—St. Katharine of Sienna. Closed 1986. Parish records available at St. Wenceslaus Church. Tel: 410-675-7304.

51—St. Lawrence (1962), Rev. Michael T. Buttner, Adm.; Deacons John J. Codd; Paul T. Mann. In res., Rev. Richard Woy.
Res., 5801 Security Blvd., 21207. Tel: 410-298-8888; Fax: 410-298-8544.
School—John Paul Regional Catholic School. See separate listing.

52—St. Leo (1881) (Italian), Rev. Oreste Pandola. In res., Rev. Flavian Bonifazi, S.A.C.
Res., 227 S. Exeter St., 21202. Tel: 410-675-7275; Fax: 410-675-8291.
School—Father Kolbe Interparochial. See separate listing.

53—Little Flower, Shrine of (1926), Revs. Michael J. Orchik; Richard Bozzelli.
Res., 2854 Brendan Ave., 21213. Tel: 410-483-1700; Fax: 410-488-6482.
School—(Grades PreK-8). Tel: 410-488-1483. Mr. George L. Logue, Prin.
Sisters of St. Francis of Philadelphia 2; Lay Teachers 13; Students 292.

54—St. Luke (Edgemere) (1888), Rev. Joseph S. Lizor, Jr.
Res., 7517 N. Point Rd., 21219-1499. Tel: 410-477-5200; Fax: 410-477-5996.
School—Our Lady of Hope/St. Luke's School, 8003 N. Boundary Rd., 21222. Tel: 410-288-2793; Fax: 410-282-9361.

55—St. Mark (Cantonsville) (1888), Rev. Ross A. LaPorta; Rev. Msgr. Henry F. Zerhusen; Rev. Ronald Zoubek; Sr. Kathleen Martin, M.H.S.H., Pastoral Assoc.
Res., 27 Melvin Ave., 21228. Tel: 410-744-6560; Fax: 410-747-3182.
School—Tel: 410-747-6613; Fax: 410-747-3188. Sr. Raymond Lorenzen, S.S.N.D., Prin.
Lay Teachers 29; Students 532.
Catechesis/Religious Programs—Tel: 410-788-6211.
Students 458.

56—St. Martin (1865), Rev. John D. Harvey, O.F.M.Cap.; Deacon Kevin Thompson, O.F.M.Cap. Pastoral Assocs.: Sr. Teresa Ann Walsh, D.C.; Sr. Eleanor Casey, D.C.
Res., 31 N. Fulton Ave., 21223. Tel: 410-947-1242; Fax: 410-542-6056.

57—St. Mary of the Assumption (1849), Rev. P. Edward Kenny; Deacon Miguel Sainz. In res., Deacon Rochus Hoat.
Res., 5502 York Rd., 21212. Tel: 410-435-5900.
School—Ms. Denise Wallace, Prin. Lay Teachers 18; Students 235.

58—St. Mary, Star of the Sea (1868), Rev. Mitchell T. Rozanski.
Res., 1419 Riverside Ave., 21230. Tel: 410-685-2255.
School—Catholic Community School of South Baltimore. See separate listing. Tel: 410-685-6155; Fax: 410-685-0692.
Convent—1410 Riverside Ave., 21230. Tel: 410-752-4344. Sisters of St. Joseph

59—St. Matthew (1949), Rev. Joseph R. Muth.
Res., 5401 Loch Raven Blvd., 21239. Tel: 410-433-2300; Fax: 410-433-5263.
School—Cardinal Shehan School. See separate listing.

60—St. Michael (Broadway) (1852) (Hispanic). Merged with St. Patrick. Revs. John P. Lavin, C.SS.R., Supr.; Andrew Carr, C.SS.R.; Deacons Rafael Villagaray; Pablo Osorio; Richard Novak.
Res., 7 S. Wolfe St., 21231. Tel: 410-276-1646; Fax: 410-522-0789.
School—Bishop John Neuman School. See separate listing.

61—St. Michael (Overlea) (1914), Revs. Christopher M. Carney; John F. Lesnick; J. James Purvey. In res., Rev. James M. Barker.
Res., 2 Willow Ave., 21206. Tel: 410-665-4200; Fax: 410-665-4024.
School—Tel: 410-668-8797; Fax: 410-668-8797. Sr. Patricia Shea, S.S.N.D., Prin.
Lay Teachers 18; Students 432.

62—St. Mildred Church. Closed 1967. Parish records available at Our Lady of Hope Rectory. Tel: 410-284-6600.

63—St. Monica. Closed 1959. Parish records available at the Chancery. Tel: 410-547-5446.

64—Most Precious Blood, Community of (1948). Merged with St. Anthony of Padua. Rev. C. Lou Martin; Sr. Marie Mack, S.S.N.D., Pastoral Assoc.
Office: 5010 Bowleys Ln., 21206. Tel: 410-488-7771. [CEM]

65—Our Lady of the Angels Catholic Community (Catonsville) (1993), Rev. Leo J. Larrivee, S.S.; Sr. Mary Pierre Newman, S.S.N.D.; Sr. Victoria Kessler, S.S.N.D., Pastoral Assoc.
Mailing Address: 711 Maiden Choice Ln., Catonsville, 21228. Tel: 410-247-4779; Fax: 410-737-8826.

66—Our Lady of Fatima (1951), Revs. Henry E. Sattler, C.SS.R.; Lawrence E. Lover, C.SS.R.; Richard K. Poetzel, C.SS.R.; Sr. Loretta Cornell, M.H.S.H., Pastoral Assoc.; Deacon Alphonse Bankard, III. In res., Rev. Peter Chin, C.SS.R. Missionaries: Rev. Gerard Chylko, C.SS.R.
Res., 6420 E. Pratt St., 21224. Tel: 410-633-9393; Fax: 410-631-7239.
School—Tel: 410-633-5882.
School Sisters of Notre Dame 3; Lay Teachers 13; Students 278.
Catechesis/Religious Programs—Tel: 410-633-6256.
Students 112.

67—Our Lady of Good Counsel (1889), Rev. David G. Smith.
Office: 1532 E. Fort Ave., 21230. Tel: 410-752-0205; Fax: 410-576-0929.
School—Catholic Community School of South Baltimore. See separate listing.

68—Our Lady of Hope, Rev. Msgr. Thomas J. Tewes; Revs. Charles H. Young, Jr., Pastor Emeritus; Paul G. Witthauer; Samuel V. Young, Jr.
Res., 1727 Lynch Rd., 21222. Tel: 410-284-6600; Fax: 410-282-9361.
School—(Grades PreK-18) 8003 N. Boundary Rd., 21222. Tel: 410-288-2793.
School Sisters of Notre Dame 4; Lay Teachers 20; Students 326.
Catechesis/Religious Programs—8003 N. Boundary Rd., Tel: 410-282-3120; Fax: 410-282-9361.
Students 425.

69—Our Lady of Lourdes. Closed 1995. Parish records available at The New All Saints Church. Tel: 410-542-0445.

70—Our Lady of Mount Carmel (Middle River) (1887), Revs. Robert L. Hartnett; David Kruse. Pastoral Assocs.: Sr. Betty Kane, O.S.F.; Deacon Daniel R. Kopczyk.
Res., 1704 Eastern Ave., 21221. Tel: 410-686-4972.
School—1702 Eastern Ave., 21221. Tel: 410-686-0859; Fax: 410-686-4916. Mrs. Kathleen Sipes, Prin.
Sisters of St. Francis of Philadelphia 4; Lay Teachers 28; Students 455.
High School—1706 Eastern Ave., 21221. Tel: 410-686-1023. Mrs. Kathleen Sipes, Prin.
Sisters 3; Lay Teachers 23; Students 147.
Catechesis/Religious Programs—Tel: 410-686-9016; Fax: 410-574-8785.
Students 676.

71—Our Lady of Perpetual Help (1936), Rev. Robert F. Lentz.
Res., 6950 Dogwood Rd., 21244-2697. Tel: 410-944-2106; Fax: 410-944-7409.
School—John Paul Regional Catholic School. See separate listing.

72—Our Lady of Pompei (1924), Rev. Louis Esposito; Deacon Thom Kuhl.
Res., 3600 Claremont St., 21224. Tel: 410-675-7790.
School—201 S. Conkling St., 21224. Tel: 410-276-6534. Ms. Angela Rebbert, Prin.
Lay Teachers 10; Students 192.
High School—Tel: 410-276-4503. Mr. Christopher Russo, Prin.
Priests 1; Lay Teachers 7; Students 109.

73—Our Lady of Sorrows. Closed 1935. Parish records available at Holy Cross Rectory. Tel: 410-752-8498.

74—OUR LADY, QUEEN OF PEACE (1953), Revs. Thomas A. Hagendorf, O.Praem.; Salvatore H. Cuccia, O.Praem.; Deacon George Jenkins.
Res., 10003 Bird River Rd., 21220. Tel: 410-686-3085; Fax: 410-687-1916.
School—10001 Bird River Rd., 21220. Tel: 410-687-8513; Fax: 410-687-1916. Ms. Cynthia Stewart, Prin.; Mr. Richard Brotzman, Asst. Prin.
Lay Teachers 18; Students 221.

75—OUR LADY OF VICTORY (Arbutus) (1952), Revs. William F. Franken; John Kelmartin, Pastor Emeritus; Deacon William Jauquet. In res., Rev. Michael Callaghan.
Res., 4414 Wilkens Ave., 21229. Tel: 410-242-0131; Fax: 410-242-6963.
School—Tel: 410-242-3688; Fax: 410-242-8867. Thomas E. Riddle, Prin.; Deborah Reese, Assis. Prin.
Sisters 4; Lay Teachers 19; Students 491.

76—ST. PATRICK (Broadway) (1792). Twinned with St. Michael (Wolfe St.) 1995. Rev. John P. Lavin, C.SS.R., Supr.
Res., 7 S. Wolfe St., 21231. Tel: 410-276-1646; Fax: 410-522-0789.

77—ST. PAUL'S CATHOLIC CHURCH. Closed. Parish records available at St. Francis Xavier. Tel: 410-727-3103.

78—ST. PETER THE APOSTLE (1842), Rev. Msgr. Arthur Bastress. In res., Rev. Robert Reed.
Res., 848 Hollins St., 21201. Tel: 410-685-5044.

79—ST. PETER CLAVER (1888) (African American), Most Rev. Roger J. Caesar, S.S.J.; Rev. Henry Harper, S.S.J.
Res., 1546 N. Fremont Ave., 21217. Tel: 410-669-0512; Fax: 410-383-8227.
School—Father Charles A. Hall Lower School, (Grades K-3) Carey St., 21217. Tel: 410-225-7555.
Sisters 1; Lay Teachers 7; Students 167.
Convent—1526 N. Fremont Ave., 21217. Tel: 410-383-1288.

80—SS. PHILIP AND JAMES (1897), Rev. William A. Au; Rev. Msgr. John J. Duggan, Pastor Emeritus.
Res., 2801 N. Charles St., 21218. Tel: 410-235-2294; Fax: 410-243-5262.

81—ST. PIUS V (1878) (African American), Rev. John C. Crotty, S.S.J.; Deacon Clifford Lonesome.
Res., 521 N. Schroeder St., 21223. Tel: 410-523-1930; Fax: 410-523-8164.

82—ST. PIUS X (1958), Revs. Thomas J. Golueke; Louis M. Reitz, S.S.; Ms. Ann La Rocque, Pastoral Assoc.; Mrs. Pat Howlett, Admin.
Res., 6428 York Rd., 21212. Tel: 410-377-7440; Fax: 410-377-2651.
School—6432 York Rd., 21212. Tel: 410-377-9738. Martha Pierorazio, Prin.
School Sisters of Notre Dame 2; Lay Teachers 25; Students 451.
Catechesis/Religious Programs—Tel: 410-377-0722. Mrs. Pinky Howard, D.R.E.
Students 309.

83—ST. RITA (1922), Rev. William J. Remmel, S.D.S.
Res., 2903 Dunleer Rd., 21222. Tel: 410-284-0388; Fax: 410-284-3998.
School—2905 Dunleer Rd., 21222. Tel: 410-284-3580. Sr. Mary Mark Carnes, I.H.M., Prin.
Sisters of the Immaculate Heart of Mary 2; Lay Teachers 12; Students 212.
Catechesis/Religious Programs—Tel: 410-284-7355.
Students 196.

84—ST. ROSE OF LIMA (1913), Rev. Joseph M. O'Meara. Pastoral Assocs.: Sr. Kathleen White, O.S.B.; Sr. Mary Fennell, S.N.D. In res., Rev. Msgr. Jeremiah Kenney.
Res., 3803 4th St., 21225. Tel: 410-355-8515; 8516; Fax: 410-355-1938.
School—Tel: 410-355-1050; Fax: 410-355-2804. Jane Towery, Prin.
Lay Teachers 16; Students 250.

85—SACRED HEART OF JESUS (1873), Revs. Thomas B. Loftus, C.SS.R.; Joseph Freund, C.SS.R.; William Harbison, C.SS.R.; Deacon Leo Nuedling. In res., Revs. Gerard Kurech; John Farrell, C.SS.R.; Henry V. Sattler; Bro. Raphael Rock, C.SS.R.
Res., 600 S. Conkling St., 21224-4294. Tel: 410-342-4336; Fax: 410-522-2022. [CEM]
School—Bishop John Neumann School. See separate listing.
Missions—Baltimore, Baltimore Co., Holy Redeemer Chapel, 800 S. Oldham St., 21224. Tel: 410-342-0151; Baltimore, Baltimore Co., St. Gerard's Chapel, Cardiff & Gusryan St., 21224. Tel: 410-633-9515.

86—SACRED HEART OF MARY (1925), Revs. Richard E. Parks; Leo Warczynski, Pastor Emeritus. In res., Rev. Charles R. Klein; Deacon Albert Chesnavage.
Res., 6736 Youngstown Ave., 21222-1087. Tel: 410-633-2828; Fax: 410-633-0349. [CEM]
School—6726 Youngstown Ave., 21222. Tel: 410-633-7040. Sr. M. Philomena, C.S.F.N., Prin.
Sisters of Holy Family of Nazareth 4; Lay Teachers 18; Students 267.
Convent—Tel: 410-633-3355; Fax: 410-633-2318.
Catechesis/Religious Programs—Students 267.

87—SHRINE OF THE SACRED HEART (Mt. Washington) (1867), Rev. Richard E. Cramblitt; Rev. Msgr. E. Melville Taylor, Pastor Emeritus; Sr. Mary Margaret Savage, S.S.J., Pastoral Assoc. In res., Rev. Msgr. G. Michael Schleupner.
Res., 1701 Regent Rd., 21209. Tel: 410-466-6884; 6885; Fax: 410-664-0523.
School—5800 Smith Ave., 21209. Tel: 410-542-7406; Fax: 410-664-1463. John Moran, Prin.
Sisters of Mercy 2; Lay Teachers 16; Students 221.
Catechesis/Religious Programs—Students 152.

88—ST. STANISLAUS KOSTKA (1880) (Polish), Rev. Maurice Piszczatowski, O.F.M.Conv. In res., Revs. Andrew Kasak, O.F.M.Conv.; Matthew Kotkowski, O.F.M.Conv.; Bro. Roland Warner, O.F.M.Conv.
Res., 700 S. Ann St., 21231. Tel: 410-276-2849. [CEM]
School—Father Kolbe Interparochial. See separate listing.

89—ST. THOMAS AQUINAS (1867), Rev. James Farmer. In res., Revs. George Restrepo, S.J.; Blair Raum; William Simms.
Res., 1008 W. 37th St., 21211. Tel: 410-366-4488.
School—Community School of the Holy Spirit, (Grades K-5) 3710 Roland Ave., 21211. Tel: 410-889-4618.
School Sisters of Notre Dame 3; Lay Teachers 8; Students 179.
Catechesis/Religious Programs—Fax: 410-366-8352.
Students 153.

90—ST. THOMAS MORE (1961), Rev. John P. Cunningham; Deacons James Mann, Jr.; Michael McCoy. In res., Rev. Msgr. Francis Malooly.
Res., 6237 Laurelton Ave., 21214. Tel: 410-254-1544.
Office—6806 McClean Blvd., 21234.
Parish Center—6806 McClean Blvd., 21234. Tel: 410-444-6500; Fax: 410-444-6502.
School—Cardinal Shehan School. See separate listing.

91—ST. URSULA (Parkville) (1937), Rev. Msgr. A. Thomas Baumgartner; Revs. Gerald Hynes, C.P.; Robert C. Jones, C.SS.R.; Rev. Msgr. Myles McGowan, Pastor Emeritus; Sr. Anne Mooney, S.S.N.D., Pastoral Min.; Deacons Robert Keenan; Frank Rongione, Sr.; Harry St. A. O'Neil.
Res., 8801 Harford Rd., 21234. Tel: 410-665-2111; Fax: 410-665-0758.
School—8900 Harford Rd., 21234. Tel: 410-665-3533; Fax: 410-661-1620. Sr. Joan Kelly, S.N.D., Prin.
Sisters of Notre Dame de Namur 1; Benedictine 1; Lay Teachers 35; Students 755.
Catechesis/Religious Programs—Tel: 410-655-4106.
Students 450.

92—ST. VERONICA (1945) (African American), Rev. Donald M. Fest, S.S.J.; Deacons Williard Pinkney; Alexander Smith.
Res., 806 Cherry Hill Rd., 21225. Tel: 410-355-7466; Fax: 410-355-7741.

93—ST. VINCENT DE PAUL (1840), Rev. Richard T. Lawrence. In res., Rev. Charles J. Canterna.
Res., 120 N. Front St., 21202. Tel: 410-962-5078; Fax: 410-962-8427. [CEM]
St. Vincent de Paul Church Historic Trust, Inc.—.
Jonestown Planning Council, Inc.—.

94—ST. WENCESLAUS (1870) (Bohemian), Revs. Michael Sergi, C.SS.R.; John McLaughlin, C.SS.R.; Patrick Magnier, C.SS.R.; Scott Bailey, C.SS.R.; Bros. Vincent Hoerner, C.SS.R.; Martin de Porres Smith, C.SS.R. In res., Rev. George Deimel, C.SS.R.
Res., 2111 Ashland Ave., 21205. Tel: 410-675-7304; Fax: 410-675-5746.
School—Queen of Peace Elementary Cluster. See separate listing.
Father George A. Wichland Center—Redemptorist Food Center, 901 E. Eager St. at Valley St., 21202. Tel: 410-625-0553. Rev. John McLoughlin, C.Ss.R., Dir.; Mrs. Deborah Barnes, Program Dir.

95—ST. WILLIAM OF YORK (1914), Rev. Martin H. Demek; Deacons Donald Miller; Daniel Spytkowski.
Res., 600 Cooks Ln., 21229. Tel: 410-566-2140; Fax: 410-362-5475.
School—Tel: 410-945-1442.
Sisters 2; Lay Teachers 17; Students 235.

OUTSIDE METROPOLITAN BALTIMORE

Aberdeen, Harford Co., St. Joan of Arc (1920), Rev. Kevin T. Schenning; Deacons William Vaughan; George LeFevre; Sr. Regina DeAngelis, S.S.F., Pastoral Assoc. In res., Rev. Msgr. James J. Cronin.
Office: 222 S. Law St., 21001. Tel: 410-272-4535; 575-6909; Fax: 410-272-9025.
Res., 257 S. Law St., 21001.
School—Tel: 410-272-1387. Sr. Ann Therese, S.S.C., Prin.
Sisters of St. Casimir 2; Lay Teachers 16; Students 211.

Abingdon, Harford Co., St. Francis de Sales (1866), Rev. Thomas L. Phillips; Deacon Richard Stine. In res., Rev. Gilbert Seitz.
Res., 1450 Abingdon Rd., 21009. Tel: 410-676-5119; 679-4555; Fax: 410-679-4555. [CEM]
Catechesis/Religious Programs—Tel: 410-676-3354.
Students 444.

Annapolis, Anne Arundel Co., St. Andrew by the Bay (Cape St. Claire) (1981), Revs. Jay O'Connor; James Kiesel; Deacons R. Paul Woofter; James C. Monaghan, Jr.
Parish Center—701 College Pkwy., 21401. Tel: 410-974-4366; Fax: 410-974-4339.
Catechesis/Religious Programs—Students 620.

St. Mary (1853), Revs. Thomas Siconolfi, C.SS.R.; John Sodomora, C.SS.R.; Eric Hoog, C.SS.R.; Patrick Flynn, C.SS.R.; John G. Tizio, C.SS.R.; Deacons John L. Wilson; Leroy S. Moore; Anthony F. Norcio. In res., Revs. Bernard Baumgartner, C.SS.R.; Francis X. Murphy, C.SS.R.; Henry O'Meara, C.SS.R.
Res., 109 Duke of Gloucester St., 21401. Tel: 410-263-2397; 269-6092; Fax: 410-263-3027. [CEM]
School—Tel: 410-269-0568; 263-2869.
School Sisters of Notre Dame 1; Lay Teachers 22; Students 940.
High School—109 Duke of Gloucester St., 21401. Tel: 410-263-3294.
School Sisters of Notre Dame 2; Lay Teachers 26; Students 576.
Convent—4 Shipwright St., 21401. Tel: 410-269-0568.
School Sisters of Notre Dame 5.

Bel Air, Harford Co., St. Margaret (1905), Revs. Francis X. Callahan; Frank C. McFadden; Thomas R. Malia; Deacons Paul Ciesla; Patrick Goles; J. Donald MacKnew.
Res., 141 Hickory Ave., 21014. Tel: 410-879-2670; Fax: 410-879-2518.
School—205 Hickory Ave., 21014. Tel: 410-879-1113. Ms. Amelia Mike, Prin.
Lay Teachers 29; Students 553.
Catechesis/Religious Programs—Tel: 410-838-4224.
Students 1,387.

Bradshaw, Baltimore Co., St. Stephen (1863), Revs. Lawrence F. Kolson; John A. Messina; Deacons Gilbert Hartlieb; Robert Schott; Frank R. Laws. In res., Rev. John J. Kandathinkara, V.C. (India).
Res., 8030 Bradshaw Rd., 21021. Tel: 410-592-7071; Fax: 410-592-6803. [CEM]
School—8028 Bradshaw Rd., 21021. Tel: 410-592-7617; Fax: 410-592-7330. Mrs. Helena K. Scher, Prin.
Lay Teachers 18; Students 312.
Catechesis/Religious Programs—Tel: 410-592-8666. Sr. Angela DeFontes, O.S.F., D.R.E.
Students 496.

Brunswick, Frederick Co., St. Francis of Assisi (1895), Revs. Lawrence Gesy; Peter M. Hiltz, Pastor Emeritus.
Res., 113 First Ave., 21716. Tel: 301-834-9185; Fax: 301-834-4162. [CEM]
Mission—Petersville, Frederick Co., St. Mary's.

Buckeystown, Frederick Co., St. Joseph-on-Carrollton Manor (1811), Rev. Paul P. Iaia; Deacon Robert M. Balderas.
Mailing Address: P.O. Box 33, 21717. Tel: 301-663-0907; Fax: 301-663-6525.
Res., 5843 Manor Woods Rd., Frederick, 21703. [CEM]
Catechesis/Religious Programs—Students 164.

Clarksville, Howard Co., St. Louis (1855), Rev. Msgr. Joseph L. Luca; Revs. Jeffrey Dauses; Andrew Aaron; Sr. Louann Sciubba, S.N.D., Pastoral Assoc.; Deacons Donald Parker; Daniel Stretmater; Verdan Wiedel; Lawrence Teixeira.
Res., 21029. Tel: 410-531-6040; Fax: 410-531-6191. [CEM]
School—Tel: 410-531-6664. Ms. Terry Prevosto, Prin.
Sisters 1; Lay Teachers 30; Students 423.
Catechesis/Religious Programs—Tel: 410-531-6688. D.R.E.: Mrs. Gloria Sauter; Mrs. Rhonda Milauskas.
Students 1272.

Cockeysville, Baltimore Co., St. Joseph (1852), Rev. Msgr. Paul G. Cook; Revs. Bernard Bak; Kevin A. Mueller; Sr. Judith Zeiler, M.H.S.H., Pastoral Assoc.; Deacon Edward Sulivan.
Res., 101 Church Ln., 21030. Tel: 410-666-1619; Fax: 410-628-2956. [CEM]
School—Tel: 410-666-0393; Fax: 410-628-6814. Sr.

Anne O'Donnell, R.S.M., Prin.
Sisters of Mercy of the Americas 2; Lay Teachers 24; Students 450.
Catechesis/Religious Programs—40 Church Ln., 21030. Tel: 410-666-8840.
Students 666.

Columbia, Howard Co., St. John the Evangelist (1967), Rev. Richard H. Tillman; Deacons George Martin; George McAndrews. In res., Rev. Michael A. Murphy.
Res., 21044.
Interfaith Centers—(Wilde Lake) 10431 Twin Rivers Rd., 21044. Tel: 410-964-1425; Fax: 410-730-9253.
(Oakland Mills) 5885 Robert Oliver Pl., 21045. Tel: 410-964-1434; Fax: 410-740-9323.
Catechesis/Religious Programs—Students 767.

Cresaptown, Allegany Co., St. Ambrose (1886), Rev. Robert E. McCreary, O.F.M.Cap.; Ms. Margaret Gaughan, Pastoral Assoc.
Res., P.O. Box 5130, 21505-5130. Tel: 301-729-2790; Fax: 301-729-2436. [CEM]

Crofton, Anne Arundel Co., St. Elizabeth Ann Seton (1976), Rev. Edward C. Connelly; Sr. Joan Bunty, O.S.F., Pastoral Assoc.; Deacon Frederick Seibold.
Office: 1800 Seton Dr., 21114. Tel: 410-721-5770; Fax: 410-721-5508. [CEM]
Catechesis/Religious Programs—Tel: 410-721-5774.
Students 612.
School—Arthur Slade Regional Catholic School. See separate listing.

Cumberland, Allegany Co., St. Mary (1900) (Italian), Rev. Milton A. Hipsley; Bro. James T. Kirkpatrick, F.S.C., Pastoral Asst.; Deacon David A. Conley.
Res., 300 E. Oldtown Rd., 21502. Tel: 301-777-2990; Fax: 301-777-1108. [CEM]
School—St. John Neumann. See separate listing.

St. Patrick (1790) (Irish), Rev. Frank J. Brauer, Admin.; Deacons Gerald A. Raible; Paul H. Dignan, Sr.; Loren Mooney; Francis L. Werner, Jr.
Res., 201 N. Centre St., 21502. Tel: 301-777-1750; Fax: 301-777-2669. [CEM]
School—St. John Neumann. See separate listing.

SS. Peter and Paul (1848) (German), Revs. Vance Pastorius, O.F.M.Cap.; Vernon Busch, O.F.M.Cap.; Bro. Michael Masich, O.F.M.Cap.; Deacon Herman Grabenstein.
Res., 125 Fayette St., 21502. Tel: 301-777-3131; Fax: 301-759-3568. [CEM]
School—St. John Neumann. See separate listing.

Davidsonville, Anne Arundel Co., Holy Family (1929), Rev. Joseph F. Barr; Deacon Robert Graham.
Res., P.O. Box 130, 21035-0130. Tel: 410-269-0586; 261-7399; Fax: 410-798-5315.
Catechesis/Religious Programs—Tel: 410-798-5680.
Students 467.

Edgewater, Anne Arundel Co., Our Lady of Perpetual Help (1976). Unassigned.
Res., 515 Loch Haven Rd., 21037. Tel: 410-956-2883; 798-5161; Fax: 410-798-0076; 269-5553.
Catechesis/Religious Programs—Mary Ellen Fisher, D.R.E.
Students 233.

Edgewood, Harford Co., Prince of Peace (1977), Rev. Stephen D. Gosnell.
Res., 2600 Willoughby Beach Rd., 21040. Tel: 410-679-5912; 679-8778.

Ellicott City, Howard Co., Our Lady of Perpetual Help (1892), Rev. Richard E. Smith; Sr. Mary McFadden, S.N.D., Pastoral Assoc. In res., Rev. John Hodgson, C.SS.R. (Australia).
Res., 4795 Ilchester Rd., 21043. Tel: 410-747-4334; Fax: 410-747-4399. [CEM]
School—Tel: 410-744-4251; Fax: 410-788-5210.
Xaverian Brother 1; Lay Teachers 12; Students 261.
Catechesis/Religious Programs—Tel: 410-455-0399.
Students 950.

Resurrection (1974), Revs. James O. McGovern; Donald J. Parson. Pastoral Assocs.: Ruth A. Puls; Donald S. Henderson; Linda M. Keedy; Amy McClain; Deacon Ray Britt. In res., Rev. Bryan J. Hehir.
Office: 3175 Paulskirk Dr., 21042. Tel: 410-461-9111; Fax: 410-461-9419.
School—Resurrection/St. Paul, Tel: 410-465-8746. Ms. Lynn Leaf, Prin.
Lay Teachers 23; Students 339.
Catechesis/Religious Programs—Tel: 410-461-9111, Ext. 221.
Students 1091.

St. Paul (1838), Rev. Thomas J. Donaghy.
Res., 3755 St. Paul St., 21043. Tel: 410-465-1670; Fax: 410-313-8851. [CEM]

Emmitsburg, Frederick Co., St. Anthony Shrine (1805), Rev. Leo R. Tittler; Sr. Carol C. Czyzewski, F.S.S.J., Pastoral Assoc., Tel: 301-271-7300; Sr. Mary Jan Nasiadka, F.S.S.J., Pastoral Admin., Tel: 301-271-7300.
Res., 16150 St. Anthony Rd., 21727. Tel: 301-447-2367; Fax: 301-447-6318. [CEM]

St. Joseph (1793), Revs. Michael J. Kennedy, C.M., Admin.; William P. Goff, C.M.; Joseph R. Wright, C.M.
Res., 47 DePaul St., 21727. Tel: 301-447-2326; Fax: 301-447-3579. [CEM]

Fallston, Harford Co., St. Mark (1887), Rev. Msgr. John H. McCall; Rev. Edward Hemler; Sr. Kathleen Garrity, O.S.F., Pastoral Assoc.; Deacons T. Russell Gibson; Charles Hicks.
Res., 812 Reckord Rd., 21047. Tel: 410-879-9110; 877-9750; Fax: 410-877-9750.
Catechesis/Religious Programs—Tel: 410-879-1706; 877-1692.
Students 589.

Frederick, Frederick Co., St. John the Evangelist (1763), Revs. Wayne G. Funk; J. Kevin Farmer; Rev. Msgr. Edward V. Echle, Pastor Emeritus; Deacons Daniel C. Roff; James F. Casey; John L. Manley; J. Michael Zusi.
Res., 116 E. Second St., 21701. Tel: 301-662-8288; Fax: 301-698-1832. [CEM]
School—St. John Regional Catholic School. See separate listing.
Catechesis/Religious Programs—Tel: 410-662-8495.
Students 778.

Frostburg, Allegany Co., St. Michael (1850), Rev. Paul A. Byrnes; Deacons Bertrand O. Michael; Lou Concordia.
Res., 44 E. Main St., P.O. Box 402, 21532. Tel: 301-689-6767; Fax: 301-689-6411. [CEM]
School—Tel: 301-689-2155.
Lay Teachers 12; Students 185.

Fulton, Howard Co., St. Francis of Assisi Mission (1988), Rev. Dennis P. Diehl.
Office: 11445 Rte. 216, 20759. Tel: 410-792-0470; Fax: 410-792-0472.
Res., 10681 Glen Hannah Dr., Laurel, 20723. Tel: 410-880-3068.
Catechesis/Religious Programs—Students 359.

Glen Burnie, Anne Arundel Co., Church of the Crucifixion (Marley) (1972), Rev. Brendan T. Carr, M.A.; Sr. Marlene Cunningham, S.N.D., Pastoral Assoc.
Res., 100 Scott Ave., 21060. Tel: 410-768-4880; Fax: 410-768-5025.
School—Arthur Slade Regional Catholic School. See separate listing.

Church of the Good Shepherd (1972), Revs. John L. Kelly; Joseph V. Messer, (Retired).
Res., 1451 Furnace Rd., 21060. Tel: 410-761-4607; Fax: 410-761-6019.
School—Arthur Slade Regional Catholic School. See separate listing.
Catechesis/Religious Programs—Students 150.

Holy Trinity (1931), Revs. G. Eugene Nickol; Raymond Martin; Deacons LeRoy Beimel; John Boscoe; Edward Gardner; Robert Herzog.
Res., 7436 Baltimore-Annapolis Blvd., 21061. Tel: 410-766-1213.
Parish Center—126 Dorsey Rd., 21061. Tel: 410-766-5070; Fax: 410-760-6738.
School—Arthur Slade Regional Catholic School. See separate listing.
Catechesis/Religious Programs—Tel: 410-766-5070; Fax: 410-760-6738. Joseph Goggin, D.R.E.
Students 1186.

Glyndon, Baltimore Co., Sacred Heart (1873), Revs. Lloyd E. Aiken; John T. Wielebski; Christopher J. Whatley; James J. Ditillo, S.J.; Deacon James A. Ryan.
Res., 65 Sacred Heart Ln., 21071. Tel: 410-833-1696; Fax: 410-833-2676.
School—Tel: 410-833-0857. Mr. Steven M. Johnson, Prin.; Anne H. Price, Asst. Prin.
Lay Teachers 40; Students 620.
Catechesis/Religious Programs—Tel: 410-833-8515.
Students 540.

Grantsville, Northern Garrett Co., St. Ann (1976), Revs. David T. Lawlor; William R. Craig.
Res., 12814 New Germany Rd., 21536. Tel: 301-895-5877; Fax: 301-895-4353.

Hagerstown, Washington Co., St. Ann (1966), Revs. Edward W. Manalis; Andrew Mohl; Deacons William Nairn; Richard Kunkel.
Res., 1010 Oak Hill Ave., 21742. Tel: 301-791-2727; Fax: 301-733-6218.
Church—1525 Oak Hill Ave., 21742. Tel: 301-733-0410; Fax: 301-733-6218.
Catechesis/Religious Programs—Tel: 301-733-0411.
Students 479.

St. Joseph, Half Way (1951), Rev. Kloman F. Riggie.
Res., 17628 Virginia Ave., 21740. Tel: 301-797-9435; 797-9445; Fax: 301-797-2490.

St. Mary (1790), Rev. George A. Limmer; Rev. Msgr. Robert S. Passarelli, Pastor Emeritus; Rev. John N. Fullen.
Res., 224 W. Washington St., 21740. Tel: 301-739-0390; Fax: 301-739-7082.
School—Tel: 301-733-1184.
School Sisters of Notre Dame 3; Lay Teachers 15; Students 292.
Mission—Boonsboro, Washington Co., St. James, 224 W. Washington St., 21740. Tel: 410-432-2887.

Hancock, Washington Co., St. Peter's (1834), Rev. George W. Glick.
Res., 16 E. High St., 21750. Tel: 301-678-6339; Fax: 301-678-7578. [CEM]
Mission—Little Orleans, Allegany Co., St. Patrick's, (1860) 12517 St Patrick Rd. S.E., Little Orleans, 21766.
Mailing Address: 16 E. High St., 21750.

Havre de Grace, Harford Co., St. Patrick's (1847), Rev. Paul J. Henry. In res., Rev. William G. Hisky.
Res., 615 Congress Ave., 21078. Tel: 410-939-2525; 575-6741; Fax: 410-575-6490. [CEM]
Catechesis/Religious Programs—Tel: 410-939-2547.
Students 173.

Hickory, Harford Co., St. Ignatius (1792), Revs. Kenneth Farabaugh; William Dawson, S.J.; Deacons Robert Lehr; Ralph Trautwein; Sr. Marjorie Gallagher, S.N.D., Pastoral Assoc.
Res., 533 E. Jarrettsville Rd., Forest Hill, 21050. Tel: 410-879-1926; Fax: 410-879-1352. [CEM]
Catechesis/Religious Programs—Students 1,008.

Hunt Valley, Baltimore Co., St. Francis Xavier (1988), Rev. Msgr. Thomas J. Donellan.
Mailing Address: Ste. LL1, Exec. Plaza I, 11350 McCormick Rd., 21031. Tel: 410-785-0356; Fax: 410-785-1628.
Res., Hampton House, Apt. 515, 204 E. Joppa Rd., Towson, 21286. Tel: 410-938-8860.

Hydes, Baltimore Co., St. John the Evangelist (1822), Revs. Martin R. Strempeck; Charles M. Wible; Deacon J. Donald Murray.
Res., 13305 Long Green Pike, 21082. Tel: 410-592-6206; Fax: 410-817-4432. [CEM]
School—Tel: 410-592-6206, Ext. 120; Fax: 410-817-4548. Mrs. Genevieve Delcher, Prin.
School Sisters of Notre Dame 3; Lay Teachers 27; Students 352.
Catechesis/Religious Programs—Tel: 410-592-6206, Ext. 107.
Students 774.

Jessup, Anne Arundel Co., St. Lawrence (1866), Rev. William J. Axe, O.SS.T. In res., Rev. Stanley W. DeBoe, O.SS.T.
Res., 7669 Clark Rd., Hanover, 21076. Tel: 410-799-1970; Fax: 410-799-4425. [CEM]
Catechesis/Religious Programs—St. Lawrence School of Religion, P.O. Box 1188, 20794. Tel: 410-799-7790.
Students 129.

Joppa, Harford Co., Church of the Holy Spirit (1963), Rev. Joseph C. Simmons.
Res., 540 Joppa Farm Rd., 21085. Tel: 410-679-2191.
Office: Tel: 410-679-0377; Fax: 410-679-2874.
Catechesis/Religious Programs—Students 205.

Laurel, Anne Arundel Co., Resurrection of Our Lord (1968), Rev. Joseph F. Kitko; Deacon John N. Parrish; Sr. Ann E. Hartnett, S.S.N.D., Pastoral Assoc.
Res., 8402 Brock Bridge Rd., 20724. Tel: 410-792-7982; Fax: 410-792-8337.
Catechesis/Religious Programs—Students 216.

Libertytown, Frederick Co., St. Peter (1821), Rev. John Dietzenbach; Deacons Michael Misulia; James Wright.
Res., 9201 A Church St., Box 278, 21762. Tel: 301-898-5111; 898-9069; Fax: 301-898-4011. [CEM]
Catechesis/Religious Programs—Tel: 301-898-0783; Fax: 301-898-5111.
Students 650.

Linthicum Heights, Anne Arundel Co., St. Philip Neri (1964), Rev. Msgr. Francis X. Zorbach; Rev. John L. Lippold; Deacon Robert Keeley.
Res., 6405 S. Orchard Rd., 21090-2628. Tel: 410-859-0571; Fax: 410-859-5047.
School—6401 Orchard Rd., 21090. Tel: 410-859-1212. Teresa Baker, Prin.
Lay Teachers 22; Students 580.
Catechesis/Religious Programs—Tel: 410-859-0249.
Students 400.

Lonaconing, Allegany Co., St. Mary of the Annunciation (1865), Sr. Marietta Culhane, O.S.F., Pastoral Life Dir.
Res., 16102 St. Mary Ter., 21539. Tel: 301-463-2514; Fax: 301-463-6729. [CEM]

Manchester, Carroll Co., St. Bartholomew (1865), Rev. Michael Roach.

Res., 2940 Park Ave., P.O. Box 448, 21102-0448. Tel: 410-239-8207; Fax: 410-239-3216. [CEM]
Parish Center—3071 Park Ave., 21102. Tel: 410-239-8881.
Catechesis/Religious Programs—Students 465.

Middletown, Frederick Co., Holy Family Catholic Community (1986), Rev. John Charles Moore; Deacon P. Gregory Rausch.
Res., 3240 Old National Pike, 21769. Tel: 301-473-4800; Fax: 301-371-6810.
Catechesis/Religious Programs—Students 350.

Midland, Allegany Co., St. Joseph (1891) (Irish), Sr. Joan Maenner, Pastoral Life Dir.
Mailing Address: P.O. Box 1, 21542. Tel: 301-777-7060; Fax: 301-463-6729. [CEM]

Millersville, Anne Arundel Co., Our Lady of the Fields (1902), Revs. John J. Auer; Thomas Gills; Deacons James L. Awalt; Anthony Grillo; Dennis Hayden; Edward Stoops; Albert Kosla; G. William Walker.
Res., 1069 Cecil Ave., 21108. Tel: 410-923-3133; 987-1551; Fax: 410-987-9723. [CEM]
School—Arthur Slade Regional Catholic School. See separate listing.
Catechesis/Religious Programs—Tel: 410-923-2195.
Students 577.

Mount Savage, Allegany Co., St. Patrick (1863), Revs. David T. Lawlor, Admin.; John J. Mackey, Pastor Emeritus; William R. Craig.
Mailing Address: P.O. Box 577, 21545. Tel: 301-264-3521; Fax: 301-264-3603. [CEM]
Shipping Address:—15706 Church St., 21545.

Oakland, Garrett Co., St. Peter the Apostle (1852), Rev. F. Richard Spencer; Deacon James L. Comfort, Sr.
Res., 208 S. Fourth St., P.O. Box 186, 21550. Tel: 301-334-2202; Fax: 301-334-9006.
Mission—Kitzmiller, Garrett Co., Immaculate Conception, P.O. Box 186, 21550.

Odenton, Anne Arundel Co., St. Joseph (1924), Revs. John B. Harrison, C.SS.R.; Francis A. Poux, C.SS.R.; Modesto Martinez Navarro, T.C. (Hispanic); Guillermo Casa Ferrer, T.C. (Hispanic); Deacon Richard C. Swann.
Mailing Address: P.O. Box 172, 21113-0172.
Res., 1283 Odenton Rd., 21113. Tel: 410-551-9238; Fax: 410-674-4761.
School—Arthur Slade Regional Catholic School. See separate listing.

Owensville, Anne Arundel Co., Our Lady of Sorrows (1866), Rev. Mark Logue.
Res., 101 Owensville Rd., West River, 20778. Tel: 410-867-2059 (Local); 269-6803 (Baltimore); Fax: 410-867-8276. [CEM]

Parkton, Baltimore Co., Our Lady of Grace (1974), Rev. Msgr. Nicholas P. Amato.
Res., 425 Everett Rd., P.O. Box 517, Monkton, 21111. Tel: 410-329-2102.
Parish Center—18310 Middletown Rd., P.O. Box 360, 21120. Tel: 410-329-6826.

Pasadena, Anne Arundel Co., St. Jane Frances de Chantal (Riviera Beach) (1946), Revs. F. Dennis Tinder; Robert A. DiMattei; James Reusing; Deacon Fred Wendt.
Res., 8499 Virginia Ave., 21122. Tel: 410-255-4646; Fax: 410-437-5191.
School—Tel: 410-255-4750. Ronald Burinski, Prin. School Sisters of Notre Dame 4; Lay Teachers 28; Students 540.
Catechesis/Religious Programs—Tel: 410-437-4727.
Students 626.

Our Lady of the Chesapeake (1979), Rev. Brian M. Rafferty.
Church—8325 Ventnor Rd., 21122. Tel: 410-255-3677; Fax: 410-437-7527.
Catechesis/Religious Programs—Tel: 410-255-3677; Fax: 410-437-7527.
Students 100.

Poplar Springs, Howard Co., St. Michael (1879), Rev. Michael Ruane; Deacons William Fallon; Gary Fulmer.
Res., 1200 St. Michael's Rd., Mt. Airy P.O., 21771. Tel: 410-489-4211; 442-2845; Fax: 410-442-1486. [CEM]
Parish Center—Tel: 410-489-7667; 442-1717; 442-1486; Fax: 410-442-1486.
Catechesis/Religious Programs—Tel: 410-489-2979.
Students 750.

Pylesville, Harford Co., St. Mary (1855), Rev. A. Henry Kunkel, III; Deacons Simon Driesen; John R. Simpson.
Res., 1021 St. Mary's Rd., 21132. Tel: 410-452-5166; 879-4015; Fax: 410-452-8493. [CEM]
Catechesis/Religious Programs—Tel: 410-838-7471.
Students 497.

Randallstown, Baltimore Co., Holy Family (1876), Revs. Edward J. Bayer; Walter J. McGovern; William A. Collins; Deacon Richard Montalto.
Res., 9533 Liberty Rd., 21133. Tel: 410-521-3883. [CEM]
Office: Tel: 410-922-3800; Fax: 410-922-3804.
School—Tel: 410-922-3677; Fax: 410-521-9764. Helen Roby, Prin.
Sisters 1; Lay Teachers 16; Students 239.
Catechesis/Religious Programs—9531 Liberty Rd., 21133. Tel: 410-922-2805.
Students 158.

Severn, Anne Arundel Co., St. Bernadette (1969), Rev. Domenic L. Cieri.
Res., 801 Stevenson Rd., 21144. Tel: 410-969-2783; Fax: 410-969-2789.
School—Arthur Slade Regional Catholic School. See separate listing.
Catechesis/Religious Programs—Tel: 410-969-2786.
Students 361.

Severna Park, Anne Arundel Co., St. John the Evangelist (1959), Rev. Msgr. Edward F. Staub; Revs. Joseph J. Cosgrove; Richard B. Hilgartner, Jr.; Deacons John Naughton, (Retired); Dean Lopata.
Res., 689 Ritchie Hwy., S.E., 21146. Tel: 410-647-4884; Fax: 410-544-3047.
School—Tel: 410-647-2283; Fax: 410-431-5438. Sr. Linda Larsen, S.S.J., Prin.
Sisters of St. Joseph, Chestnut Hill 4; Lay Teachers 38; Students 600.
Catechesis/Religious Programs—Tel: 410-647-4892.
Students 685.
Convent—Tel: 410-647-2041.

Sykesville, Carroll Co., St. Joseph (1868), Revs. Patrick J. Tonry, S.M.; Paul A. Reich, S.M.; Terence P. Weik, S.M.
Office: 915 Liberty Rd., Eldersburg, 21784. Tel: 410-795-7838; Fax: 410-795-7516.
Res., 7620 Mellor Ave., P.O. Box 384, 21784. Tel: 410-795-2722. [CEM]
Catechesis/Religious Programs—Students 997.

Taneytown, Carroll Co., St. Joseph (1797), Revs. Martin Eugene Feild; Paul F. Dolan, Pastor Emeritus; Deacon Darrell W. Smith.
Res., 44 Frederick St., 21787. Tel: 410-756-2500; Fax: 410-756-1260. [CEM]
Catechesis/Religious Programs—Students 157.

Thurmont, Frederick Co., Our Lady of Mount Carmel (1856), Rev. Leo R. Tittler; Sr. Carol C. Czyzewski, F.S.S.J., Pastoral Assoc., Tel: 301-271-7300; Sr. Mary Jan Nasiadka, F.S.S.J., Pastoral Min., Tel: 301-271-7300.
Office—16150 St. Anthony Rd., Emmitsburg, 21727. Tel: 301-447-2367; Fax: 301-447-3618.
Res., 18 Altamont Ave., 21788. Tel: 301-271-7300. [CEM]

Timonium, Baltimore Co., Church of the Nativity (1968), Rev. Michael J. White; Rev. Msgr. Charles F. Meisel, Pastor Emeritus; Rev. John J. Jicha.
Office: 20 E. Ridgely Rd., 21093. Tel: 410-252-6080; Fax: 410-252-2657.
Res., Tel: 410-252-0345.
Catechesis/Religious Programs—Kathleen P. Mclhinney, D.R.E.
Students 504.

Urbana, Frederick Co., St. Ignatius Loyola (1879), Rev. Thomas Polk.
Res., 3523 Urban Pike, Frederick, 21704. Tel: 301-865-5783.
Office: 3523 Urbana Pike, 21701. Tel: 301-695-8845; Fax: 301-695-0259.
Church—R.R. 80, Fingerboard Rd.
Catechesis/Religious Programs—Tel: 301-695-8879.
Students 302.

Walkersville, Frederick Co., St. Timothy (1980), Rev. Richard J. Murphy.
Res., 200 Glade Blvd., 21793. Tel: 301-845-8028; Fax: 301-845-0332.
Catechesis/Religious Programs—Tel: 301-845-8025.
Students 257.

Westernport, Allegany Co., St. Peter (1851), Rev. James W. Hannon.
Res., 127 Church St., 21562. Tel: 301-359-3055. [CEM]
School—Lay Teachers 4; Students 69.
Mission—Barton, St. Gabriel.

Westminster, Carroll Co., St. John (1789), Revs. Arthur Valenzano; John Dobranski; Isaac Karoor; Robert E. Morey; Deacons John Coster; Robert Malinowski.
Res., 43 Monroe St., 21157. Tel: 410-848-4744; 876-2248; Fax: 410-857-1519. [CEM]
School—Tel: 410-848-7455.
School Sisters of Notre Dame 2; Lay Teachers 19; Students 415.
Catechesis/Religious Programs—Tel: 410-848-8443.
Students 1,625.

Williamsport, Washington Co., St. Augustine, Rev. Alfred E. Smith; Deacon Andrew Komarinski.
Res., 32 E. Potomac St., 21795. Tel: 301-223-7959.
Mission—Clear Spring, St. Michael.

Woodstock, Baltimore Co., St. Alphonsus Rodriguez (1869), Rev. Joseph R. Lerch, S.J.
Res., 10800 Old Court Rd., 21163. Tel: 410-461-5267; Fax: 410-750-7286. [CEM]
Catechesis/Religious Programs—Students 201.

Chaplains of Public Institutions

BALTIMORE. *Baltimore City Correctional Center, Baltimore Pre-Release Unit.* Vacant.
Baltimore City Jail. Rev. Damien Nalepa, Chap.
Baltimore City Jail, Women's Detention Center. Sr. Margaret Costello, S.S.J., Chap.
Carroll County Detention Center. John Shetler, Lay Coord.
Charles H. Hickey School. Deacon Russell Matthews, Chap.
Church Hospital. Covered on rotating basis by St. Casimir, St. Elizabeth, St. Michael (Wolfe St.), Sacred Heart of Jesus, St. Brigid, St. Wenceslaus, Holy Rosary and St. Stanislaus parish staff.
Dismas House. Rev. Joseph R. Wenderoth, Chap.
Francis Scott Key Medical Center. Staffed by Our Lady of Fatima Parish.
Franklin Square Hospital. Rev. E. Gerard Huesman; Deacons Nicholas F. Feurer; Daniel R. Kopczyk; Walter Shipley.
Greater Baltimore Medical Center. Rev. Salvatore Livigni.
Harbor Hospital. Covered on rotating basis by Holy Cross, St. Mary Star of the Sea, Our Lady of Good Counsel, St. Veronica, St. Rose and St. Athanasius parish staff.
Johns Hopkins Medical Institutions. Rev. Alphonse G. Rose.
Maryland Correctional Adjustment Center. Rev. Charles J. Canterna, Chap.
Maryland Penitentiary. Deacon Americus Roy.
Rosewood State Hospital. Vacant.
Spring Grove Center Hospital. Rev. F. Philip Vogel, S.D.S.
University of Maryland Hospital. Revs. Lawrence Schulmeister, O.F.M.; William H. O'Brien.
Veterans Hospital, Baltimore. Rev. Conan H. Timoney, C.P., Chap.
Veterans Hospital, Fort Howard. Rev. Conan H. Timoney, C.P., Chap.

CROWNSVILLE. *Crownsville Hospital Center.* Staffed by St. Mary's Parish, Annapolis.

HAGERSTOWN. *Maryland Correctional Institution.* Sr. Dolores Chepiga, S.S.J.
Maryland Correctional Training Center. Sr. Dolores Chepiga, S.S.J.
Roxbury Correctional Institution. Sr. Dolores Chepiga, S.S.J.

JESSUP. *Brockbridge Pre-Release Unit.* Vacant.
Maryland Correctional Institution. Mary Dunn, Lay Coord.
Maryland Correctional Institution for Women. Jim Sanders, Lay Coord.
Maryland House of Correction & Annex. Rev. Jeffrey Carlsen, Chap.
Patuxent Institute. Al Ennulat, Lay Coord.
Perkins Hospital. Al Ennulat, Lay Coord.

SYKESVILLE. *Springfield Hospital Center.* Rev. Stanley Janaites, Chap.; Deacon George C. Wachter, Chap.
Sykesville Laundry Facility. Bryan Masterson, Lay Coord.; Richard Horwitt, Lay Coord.

Special Assignment:
Reverend Monsignors—
Kenney, Jeremiah F., Tribunal, 320 Cathedral St., Baltimore, MD 21201
Malooly, Francis W., Chancellor, 320 Cathedral St., Baltimore, MD 21201
Schleupner, G. Michael, Sec., Dept. of Mgmt. Svcs.
Reverend Fathers—
Abrahams, John, Chap., Perry Point VA Medical Center
Albright, Robert, Campus Ministry, Towson, MD 21204
Barker, James, Vocation Dir., 320 Cathedral St., Baltimore, MD 21201
Bergquist, Patrick, Missionary Work, Fairbanks, AK
Bevan, Thomas R., Exec. Dir. Secretariat of Priestly Life & Ministry Committee NCCB, Washington, DC
Bonderenko, Thomas, Admin. Shelter & Food Programs, A.C.C.
Breighner, Joseph F.
Byrne, Glenn, St. Anthony Church, Allston, MA 02134
Canterna, Charles J., Chap., Baltimore City Jail & Maryland Penitentiary
Carey, David M., Special Ministry

Carlsen, Jeffrey, Chap., Maryland House of Correction & Annex
Carrion, Patrick, Interim Pastoral Admin.
Chase, Raymond, Gallagher Center
Collins, William A., Tribunal, 320 Cathedral St., Baltimore, MD 21201
Collopy, John C., Dir. Senior & Retired Priests
Delclos, John L., 320 Cathedral St., Baltimore, MD 21201
Francik, Gerard, Chap., Mt. St. Mary's College, Emmitsburg
Hawkins, Robert, Chap., St. Martin Home for Aged
Hendricks, Edward, Campus Minister, Frostburg, MD
Janaitcs, Stanley, Chap., Springfield Hospital
Jarboe, J. Bruce, Assoc. Dir., Pastoral Personnel Serv.
Johnson, Lawrence, Chap., Cardinal Sheehan Center
Lobert, Richard, Teaching
Lombardi, John, St. Elizabeth Home for Nursing Care, Baltimore
Lupico, Samuel J., Chap., St. Joseph Hospital, Baltimore
Madden, Denis J., Ecumenical Inst., P.O. Box 19556, Jerusalem, Israel
Martin, Joseph C., S.S., 103 Foxridge Dr., Havre de Grace, MD 21078
O'Brien, William, Chap., Shock Trauma Unit, 715 Druid Hill Ave., Baltimore, MD 21201
Raum, Blair, Dir., Project Rachel
Riepe, Charles, Chap., John Hopkins Univ., Newman Apostolate, Baltimore, MD
Rose, Alphonse, Chap., John Hopkins Hospital, Baltimore, MD
Simms, William, Archdiocesan Tribunal, 320 Cathedral St., Baltimore, MD 21201
Snouffer, Philip T., Div. of Information Systems, 320 Cathedral St., Baltimore, MD 21201
Spillane, Michael, Washington, DC
Thomas, Paul, Archdiocesan Archivist
Ward, John B., Sec. to Cardinal & Defender of the Bond, Interdiocesan Tribunal of Appeals
Wenderoth, Joseph
Woy, Richard, Dir., Pastoral Personnel Svcs.

On Duty Outside the Archdiocese:
Reverend Fathers—
Hisky, William, Perrypoint V.A. Medical Ctr., 5288 E. Pulaski Hwy., Perryville, MD 21903
Hoffman, David, Immaculate Heart Hermitage, Big Sur, CA
Obrimski, Paul G.
Warman, William C.

Educational Sabbatical:
Reverend Fathers—
Boisvert, Keith W.
Byrne, Glenn
Frazier, Lawrence K.
Pietropaoli, David

Military Chaplains:
Reverend Fathers—
Carter, John T., U.S.N.
Cummings, Carl
Fitzgerald, John L., CHC, U.S.N.
Hill, Edward T., U.S.N.
Wilson, Stuart T., U.S.N.
Zeller, Leonard H., U.S.A.F.

Absent on Leave:
Reverend Monsignors—
Kinsella, John
Reverend Fathers—
Cooper, Craig D.
DePetris, Joseph J.
Dowdy, James H.
Hart, J. Joseph, Jr.
Hirt, William
Le Fevre, Francis J.
Losemann, Heinrich J., Jr.
Maskell, A. Joseph
Wade, Michael J.

Awaiting Assignment:
Reverend Fathers—
Holthaus, Paul

Unassigned:
Reverend Fathers—
Cox, Brian M.
Toohey, Jerome

Retired:
Reverend Monsignors—
Bozel, Robert A., St. Elizabeth Hall M-201, 2300 Dulaney Valley Rd., Baltimore, MD 21204
Bradley, Joseph P., 116 W. University Pkwy., Apt. 710, Baltimore, MD 21210
Broderick, Gerard W., Rich-Mar Apts., 3-J Trolod Ct., Owings Mills, MD 21117
Cronin, James J., St. Joan of Arc, 257 S. Law St., Aberdeen, MD 21001
Echle, Edward V., St. Catherine Nursing Home, Emmitsburg, MD 21727
Fortenbaugh, Francis W., St. Agnes Rectory, 5422 Old Frederick Rd., Baltimore, MD 21228
Kenny, Simon E., St. John Hall, Long Crandon, 2300 Dulaney Valley Rd., Baltimore, MD 21204
Linn, Francis J., St. John Hall, Long Crandon, 2300 Dulaney Valley Rd., Baltimore, MD 21204
McGowan, Myles, 3 Baratra Ct., Apt. 204, Timonium, MD 21093
Meisel, Charles F., St. Elizabeth Hall, Apt. W 301, 2300 Dulaney Valley Rd., Baltimore, MD 21204
Mieczkowski, Chester J., St. Augustine Rectory, 5976 Old Washington Rd., Elkridge, MD 21227
Passarelli, Robert S., 27 First St., Frostburg, MD 21532
Phillips, Hugh J., Mount St. Mary's College, Emmitsburg, MD 21727
Reinsfelder, John L., Holy Cross Rectory, 110 E. West St., Baltimore, MD 21230
Satterfield, Carroll E., 363 Homeland Southway, Apt. 1, Baltimore, MD 21212
Sauerwein, Anthony L., 8215 Evergreen Ave., Baltimore, MD 21234
Scarff, Stanley J., St. John Hall, Long Crandon, 2300 Dulaney Valley Rd., Baltimore, MD 21204
Schwalenberg, Martin, 8465 Meadow Ln., Riviera Beach, MD 21122
Spraker, Gerard W., St. Martin Home, 601 Maiden Choice Ln., Baltimore, MD 21228
Taylor, E. Melville, St. John Hall, long Crandon, 2300 Dulaney Valley Rd., Baltimore, MD 21204
Reverend Fathers—
Altmann, George, 32 Carrolls Tract Rd., Fairfield, PA 17320
Barbernitz, John P., 7915 Elmhurst Ave., Baltimore, MD 21237
Begley, Patrick J., Locust House, Apt. 502, 30 Locust St., Westminster, MD 21157
Bowling, Frederick T., Carlyle Apts., 500 W. University Pkwy., Baltimore, MD 21210
Boyle, Howard, Anchorage Tower #301, 2515 Boston St., Baltimore, MD 21224
Buettner, George, 600 Light St., Apt. 351, Baltimore, MD 21230
Byrd, Thomas J., Mount St. Mary's Seminary, Emmitsburg, MD 21727
Carney, John, College Lanes Apts., #801-J, Salisbury, MD 21801
Coady, Edward L., 1221 First St., 8A, Jacksonville, FL 32250-6446
Collopy, John C., St. John Hall, Long Crandon, 2300 Dulaney Valley Rd., Baltimore, MD 21204
Coyne, Patrick J., St. Croix House, 106 E. West St., Baltimore, MD 21230
Dolan, Paul F., St. John Hall, Long Crandon, 2300 Dulaney Valley Rd., Baltimore, MD 21204
Fannon, Thomas J., St. Elizabeth Hall F210, 2300 Dulaney Valley Rd., Baltimore, MD 21204
FitzGerald, William, St. Brigid Rectory, 2 North Belnord Ave., Baltimore, MD 21224
Gallagher, Joseph J., 3838 Roland Ave., #1302, Baltimore, MD 21211
Gies, Norman J., 2453 Brazilia Dr., Apt. 21, Clearwater, FL 21163
Hiltz, Peter M., 10816 Davis Ave., Woodstock, MD 21163
Hoat, Rochus Vu Dinh, St. Mary Rectory, 5502 York Rd., Baltimore, MD 21212
Hopkins, Robert, 941 Bishop Walsh Rd., Cumberland, MD 21502
Hughes, Joseph B., 2034 Park Ave., Baltimore, MD 21217
Kaczkowski, Leon, Stella Maris Hospice, 2300 Dulaney Valley Rd., Baltimore, MD 21204
Kaiser, Joseph A., St. John Hall, Long Crandon, 2300 Dulaney Valley Rd., Baltimore, MD 21204
Kelmartin, John J., 9050 Waltham Woods Rd., Apt. C, Baltimore, MD 21234
Kenney, Joseph A., Stella Maris Hospice, 2300 Dulaney Valley Rd., Baltimore, MD 21204
Klein, Charles, Sacred Heart of Mary, 6736 Youngstown Ave., Baltimore, MD 21222
Krach, Joseph W., 805 Union Ave., Baltimore, MD 21211
La Porta, Gerald, 95 Broadway, Frostburg, MD 21532
Melycher, Stephen D., 5613 Patrick Henry Dr., Baltimore, MD 21225
Messer, Joseph V., Good Shepherd Rectory, 1451 Furnace Ave., Glen Burnie, MD 21061
Moody, William, 86 Mt. Pleasant St., Frostburg, MD 21532
Muller, Kennard, 9417 Perglen Rd., Baltimore, MD 21236
Muller, Myles, St. Elizabeth Hall M101, 2300 Dulaney Valley Rd., Baltimore, MD 21204
Paulits, Walter J., 7853 Americana Circle, Apt. 102, Glen burnie, MD 21061
Peterson, Casimir, 3601 Greenway, Apt. 704, Baltimore, MD 21218
Pugevicues, Casimir, St. Anthony Rectory, 4414 Frankford Ave., Baltimore, MD 21206
Quinn, Charles H., St. John Hall, Long Crandon, 2300 Dulaney Valley Rd., Baltimore, MD 21204
Reed, Robert A., St. Benedict Rectory, 2612 Wilkens Ave., Baltimore, MD 21223
Sargus, Edward T., Lawn Acres, 420 S. 57 St., Hollywood, FL 33023
Shaum, David, Mount St. Mary's College, P.O. Box 246, Emmitsburg, MD 21727
Stroup, Edmund F., 36 E. Drumbred Rd., Villas, NJ 08251
Tierney, John J., St. John Hall, Long Crandon, 2300 Dulaney Valley Rd., Baltimore, MD 21204
Warczynski, Leon, 3316 Beverly Rd., Baltimore, MD 21214
West, Gerald, Franciscan Sisters of Baltimore Generalate, 3725 Ellerslie Ave., Baltimore, MD 21218
Wisniewski, Theodore, 5709 Magie St., Baltimore, MD 21225

Permanent Deacons:
Abell, John H., Jr., Our Lady of Sorrows, Owensville
Albaugh, William S., St. Joseph, Fullerton
Anderson, Carl A., St. Edward, Baltimore
Antczak, George, St. Jerome, Baltimore
Awalt, James L., Our Lady of the Fields, Millersville
Bankard, Alphonse, Our Lady of Fatima, Baltimore
Baranoski, Melvin L., (Retired)
Battee, James W., St. Elizabeth, Baltimore
Baynes, Charles A., St. Joseph, Fullerton
Bee, James E., St. Ann, Baltimore
Beimel, Leory W., Holy Trinity, Glen Burnie
Berg, James R., Austin, TX
Bielik, Stanley W., Leave of Absence
Bisser, John, St. Clement, Lansdowne
Boscoe, John, Holy Trinity, Glen Burnie
Briscoe, John, St. Peter Claver
Britt, Ray, Resurrection, Ellicott City
Bullinger, Raymond A., St. Charles, Pikesville
Carpenter, Harry G., St. William of York, Baltimore
Casey, J. Faherty, St. John, Frederick
Chesnavage, Albert W., Sacred Heart of Mary, Baltimore
Ciesla, Paul R., St. Margaret, Bel Air
Clyde, Harry, Leave of Absence
Codd, John J., Sr., St. Lawrence, Baltimore
Colson, Norman E., St. Clement, Lansdowne
Comfort, James L., Sr., St. Peter the Apostle, Oakland
Concordia, Louis, St. Michael, Frostburg
Conley, David, St. Mary, Cumberland
Cook, Charles E., St. Bernard, Baltimore
Coster, John E., St. John, Westminster
Crawford, Raymond C., Our Lady of Perpetual Help, Ilchester
Davis, Henry, St. Michael, Overlea
DeAngelis, William J., St. Joseph, Fullerton
Derouaux, Bert, (Retired)
Dignan, Paul H., St. Patrick, Cumberland
Driesen, Simon, St. Mary, Pylesville
Dunn, Eugene C., Leave of Absence
Evans, George T., St. Rita, Baltimore
Fallon, William L., St. Michael, Poplar Springs
Feehley, Gerard P., St. Elizabeth, Baltimore
Feurer, Nicholas E., St. Clement and Franklin Square Hospital, Rosedale
Firlie, Joseph P., Leave of Absence
Fulmer, Gary Lee, St. Michael, Poplar Springs
Fulton, Watson, Jr., St. Ambrose, Baltimore
Gardner, Edward L., Sr., Holy Trinity, Glen Burnie
Gervasoni, Thomas R., Leave of Absence
Gibson, T. Russell, St. Mark, Fallston
Goles, Patrick J., St. Margaret, Bel Air
Grabenstein, Herman J., SS. Peter & Paul, Cumberland
Graham, Robert L., Holy Family, Davidsonville
Gramling, John C., Immaculate Conception, Towson
Grape, William F., (Retired)
Grillo, Anthony, Our Lady of the Fields, Millersville
Gross, Theodore C., (Retired)
Hacker, Robert, Church Home and Hospital, Baltimore
Handlir, James F., Leave of Absence
Harcum, Philip W., St. Bernardine, Baltimore
Hargrove, David, Leave of Absence
Harris, Jhan M., St. Veronica, Baltimore
Hartlieb, Gilbert J., St. Stephen, Bradshaw
Hayden, Dennis L., Our Lady of the Fields, Millersville
Hicks, Charles, St. Mark, Fallston
Hiebler, Charles H., Jr., Immaculate Heart of Mary, Baltimore

Hodges, Frank P., Corpus Christi, Baltimore
Jakowski, Chester J., SS. Philip & James, Baltimore
Jauquet, William, Our Lady of Victory, Baltimore
Jenkins, George, Our Lady Queen of Peace, Baltimore
Jensen, Joseph E., Permanent Diaconate Program and Justice and Peace Commission
Johe, Richard, (Retired)
Joseph, Bernard K., Leave of Absence
Justice, John T., Leave of Absence
Kalb, John L., Jr., (Retired)
Keating, Joseph J., (Retired)
Keeley, Robert L., St. Philip Neri, Linthicum Heights
Keenan, Robert G., St. Ursula, Baltimore
Kempf, William J., Jr., Unassigned
Kent, James R., Sr., St. Isaac Jogues, Baltimore
Knight, Charles, St. Bernardine, Baltimore
Komarinski, Andrew, (Retired)
Kopczyk, Daniel R., Our Lady of Mt. Carmel and Franklin Square Hospital, Baltimore
Kosla, Albert F., Our Lady of the Fields, Millersville
Kruger, Charles R., Jr., St. Bartholomew, Manchester
Krysiak, Joseph C., St. Anthony Padua and Most Precious Blood, Baltimore
Kucharczyk, John, Holy Rosary, Baltimore
Kuhl, Thomas, Our Lady of Pompei, Baltimore
Kunkel, Richard, St. Ann, Hagerstown
Landers, Joseph T., St. Anthony, Baltimore
Langbehn, Eugene, St. Joseph, Sykesville
Latrick, Donald P., Holy Family Ukrainian Catholic Church
Laws, Francis R., St. Stephen, Bradshaw
LeFevre, George F., St. Joan of Arc, Aberdeen
Lehr, Robert I., St. Ignatius, Hickory
Lind, Michael R., Leave of Absence
Lindeman, H. Richard, Leave of Absence
Lonesome, Clifford, St. Pius V, Baltimore
Lopata, Dean M., St. John, Severna Park
Lynne, Robert O., Holy Cross, Baltimore
MacKnew, J. Donald, St. Margaret, Bel Air
Malinowski, Robert, St. John, Westminster
Manley, John L., St. John, Frederick
Mann, James L., Sr., St. Thomas More, Baltimore
Mann, Paul T., St. Lawrence, Woodlawn
Maranto, Anthony S., St. Dominic, Baltimore
Martelle, John T., St. Rita and Church Hospital, Dundalk
Martin, George W., St. John, Columbia
Martin, John, Immaculate Heart of Mary, Baltimore
Matthews, Russell, St. Francis Xavier and Maryland Training School for Boys, Baltimore
Matthews, Wayne, Holy Family, Middletown
McAndrews, George F., St. John, Columbia
McCoy, Michael, St. Thomas More, Baltimore
McKenna, John I., St. Clement, Lansdowne
Mercer, Charles S., St. Francis Xavier, Baltimore
Michael, Bertrand O., St. Michael, Frostburg
Micozzi, Arthur L., St. Isaac Jogues, Baltimore
Miller, Donald, St. William of York, Baltimore
Miller, Eugene, Jr., St. Margaret, Bel Air
Miller, Ferdinand G., St. Clare, Essex
Mills, Hugh, Jr., St. Clement, Lansdowne
Misulia, Michael, St. Peter, Libertytown
Monaghan, James, St. Andrew by the Bay, Cape St. Claire
Montalto, Richard W.
Mooney, Loren, St. Patrick, Cumberland
Moore, LeRoy S., St. Mary, Annapolis
Moritz, Francis X., (Retired)
Morris, Richard F., St. Elizabeth of Hungary, Baltimore
Murphy, Lawrence, Resurrection, Laurel
Murray, Donald, St. Ignatius, Hickory
Nairn, William P., St. Ann, Hagerstown
Naughton, John F., St. John, Severna Park
Neale, Joseph L., St. Edward, Baltimore
Norcio, Anthony F., St. Mary, Annapolis
Novak, Richard D., St. Patrick and Church Home Hospital, Baltimore
Nuedling, Leo, Sacred Heart of Jesus, Baltimore
O'Keefe, Francis G., Leave of Absence
O'Neill, Harry St. A., St. Ursula, Baltimore
Oliver, Robert W., Basilica of the Assumption, Baltimore
Opalka, Klaus O., Leave of Absence
Osorio-Carmona, Pablo E., Spanish Ministry
Parrish, John N., Church of Resurrection, Laurel
Perticone, Vincent, Jr., St. Joseph, Fullerton
Piet, Stanley G., (Retired)
Pinkney, Willard A., Jr., St. Veronica, Baltimore
Pivec, J. Kenneth, Immaculate Heart of Mary, Baltimore
Provenza, Vincent, SS. Philip and James, Baltimore
Rafter, John J., Jr., St. John, Hydes
Raible, Gerald A., St. Patrick, Cumberland
Rausch, Paul G., Holy Family, Middletown
Reinsfelder, Edward, St. Michael, Frostburg
Resh, Michael K., St. Anthony, Baltimore
Roberts, Gerald A., Univ. of Maryland Hospital And St. Jerome, Baltimore
Roff, Daniel, St. John the Evangelist, Frederick
Rongione, Frank, St. Ursula, Baltimore
Rose, Alan, Prison Ministry
Roy, Americus M., (Retired)
Ryan, James A., Sacred Heart,Glyndon
Sainz, Miguel E., St. Mary and Spanish Apostolate, Govans
Schoennagel, Frederick, Annunciation, Baltimore
Schott, Robert G., St. Stephen, Bradshaw
Schultz, Joseph L., St. Anthony, Baltimore
Seibold, Frederick, St. Elizabeth Ann Seton, Crofton
Shelton, Paul D., All Saints, Baltimore
Shipley, Walter R., Jr., St. Clement, Rosedale
Siarkowski, Henry L., Shrine of the Little Flower, Baltimore
Simpson, John R., St. Mary, Pylesville
Smith, Alexander, St. Veronica, Baltimore
Smith, Darrell, St. Joseph, Taneytown
Smith, Earl A., St. Edward, Baltimore
Smith, Walton, St. Francis Xavier, Baltimore
Spytkowski, Daniel, St. William of York, Baltimore
Stine, Richard J., St. Francis de Sales, Abingdon
Stoops, Edward, Our Lady of the Fields, Millersville
Stretmater, Daniel, Jr., St. Louis, Clarksville
Sullivan, Edward C., St. Joseph, Cockeysville
Swann, C. Richard, St. Joseph, Odenton
Swanson, James V., St. Michael, Frostburg
Szuchnicki, Alexander P., (Retired)
Teixeira, Lawrence, St. Louis, Clarksville
Thompson, Malcolm, Our Lady of Lourdes, Baltimore
Trautwein, Ralph, St. Ignatius, Hickory
Vassie, Frederick
Vaughan, William E., St. Joan of Arc, Aberdeen
Villagaray, Rafael F., Hispanic Ministry
Wachter, George C., Springfield Hospital Center, Sykesville
Walker, George W., Jr., Our Lady of the Fields, Millersville
Warner, Anthony, Leave of Absence
Wendt, Fred, American Embassy, London
Werner, Francis L., St. Patrick, Cumberland
Westwater, James, St. Isaac Jogues, Baltimore
Wiedel, Verdaw P., St. Louis, Clarksville
Wilson, John L., St. Mary, Annapolis
Wilson, Thomas A., St. Cecilia, Baltimore
Wise, Stanley L., St. Joseph, Taneytown
Woofter, R. Paul, St. Andrew by the Bay, Cape St. Claire
Wright, James, Hospice of Frederick Co.
Yannuzzi, Thomas J., St. Clement, Lansdowne
Yorkshire, Thomas X., St. Gregory, Baltimore
Zeiler, Francis, St. Clement, Rosedale

INSTITUTIONS LOCATED IN THE ARCHDIOCESE

[A] SEMINARIES, ARCHDIOCESAN

BALTIMORE. *St. Mary's Seminary and University*, 5400 Roland Ave., 21210. Tel: 410-323-3200; Fax: 410-323-3554. Legal Title: *St. Mary's Seminary and University*. His Eminence William Cardinal Keeler, D.D., J.C.D., Archbishop of Baltimore, Chancellor, Chm. Board of Trustees.
Officers of the Administration: Revs. Robert F. Leavitt, S.S., S.T.D., Pres.-Rector; Roger E. McGrath, S.S., Ph.D., Vice Rector; James J. Conn, S.J., J.D., J.C.D., Dean, School of Theology; John W. Bowen, S.S., Alumni News Editor; Mr. Richard G. Childs, Treas.; Michael J. Gorman, Ph.D., Dean, Ecumenical Institute of Theology; Sr. Mary Hennessey, R.C., M.A., Dir. Field Education; Mrs. Christa R. Klein, Ph.D., Dean, Center for Continuing Formation; Mrs. Kathleen P. Mignini, Business Mgr.; Mrs. Susan A. Lemmon, Registrar, School of Theology & Ecumenical Institute of Theology; Ms. Priscilla Y. Gordon, Financial Aid Officer; Mr. David P. Siemsen, Dir., Library Svcs.; Mrs. Elizabeth L. Visconage, Dir., Institutional Advancement.
Faculty: Revs. Michael L. Barre, S.S., S.T.L., Ph.D.; Thomas J. Burke, O.SS.T., S.T.M.; E. Michael Camilli, M.S.C., S.T.B., S.T.L.; James J. Conn, S.J., M.A., M.Div., J.C.D., J.D; Michael J. Gorman, M.Div., Ph.D.; Sr. Mary Hennessey, r.c., M.A.; Mrs. Tina Lamberti, M.Ed.; Patricia A. Lamoureux, Ph.D.; Revs. Philip S. Keane, S.S., S.T.D.; Robert F. Leavitt, S.S., S.T.D.; Patrick J. Madden, M.A., M.Div., Ph.D.; Roger E. McGrath, S.T.L., Ph.D.; David M. Mellott, S.T.L.; David O'Leary, M.Ed., S.T.L.; Daniel M. Ruff, S.J., M.A., M.Div., S.T.M.; David D. Thayer, S.S., S.T.M., S.T.L., Ph.D.; Mr. David P. Siemsen, M.L.S.
Adjunct Academic Faculty: Mr. Peter Culman, B.A.; Ms. Sylvia P. Moore, B.S.; Mr. Kenneth D. Hines, M.A., S.T.B., Ph.L.; Mrs. Mary E. Hines, M.A., Ph.D.; Revs. Peter A. Lyons, T.O.R., S.T.L., Ph.D.; William W. Rich, M.A., M.Div.; Thomas R. Ulshafer, S.S., S.T.L., Ph.D. Visiting Professors: Rev. John J. Long, S.J., Ph.L., S.T.L., S.E.O.L.; Very Rev. Lawrence B. Terrien, S.S., S.T.L., S.T.D. Diocesan Seminarians 67; Diocesan Seminarians on Pastoral Leave 5; Others Studying 7; Priests 17; Sisters 1; Lay Teachers 9. Ecumenical Institute of Theology, 5400 Roland Ave., 21210. Tel: 410-323-1463. Michael J. Gorman, M.Div., Ph.D. Students 182.

EMMITSBURG. *Mount St. Mary's Seminary*, 21727-7797. Tel: 301-447-5295; Fax: 301-447-5636. Legal Title: *An integral part of corporation known as Mount St. Mary's College and Seminary*.
Administration: His Eminence William Cardinal Keeler, Chancellor and Chm. of Seminary Committee; Rev. Msgr. Kenneth W. Roeltgen, S.T.M. (WDC), Rector; Revs. Leonard G. Obloy, S.S.L (CLV), Vice Rector; Kevin C. Rhoades, S.T.L., J.C.L. (HBG), (Admisions); J. Daniel Mindling, O.F.M.Cap., S.T.D., Academic Dean; Lee W. Gross, M.Div. (ARL), Dean of Students; Edward M. Gaffney, O.P., S.T.B., Dir. Spiritual Formation; Russell E. Smith, S.T.D. (RIC), Coord., Pre-Theology Prog.; Sr. Paula Jean Miller, F.S.E., S.T.D., Coord. of Pastoral Field Educ./Seminary Planning & Research; Mrs. Rosemary S. Mick, Registrar & Admin. Asst.
Full Time Faculty: Rev. Msgr. Paul J. Langsfeld, S.T.D. (WDC); Rev. Msgr. Kenneth W. Roeltgen, S.T.M. (WDC); Revs. J. Michael Beers, Ph.D., S.S.L. (ALN); Edward M. Gaffney, O.P., S.T.B.; Lee W. Gross, M.Div. (ARL); Donald F. Haggerty, S.T.D. (NY); Frederick M. Jelly, O.P., S.T.D., S.T.L., (Sabbatical); J. Daniel Mindling, O.F.M.Cap., S.T.D.; Leonard J. Obloy, S.S.L.; Kevin C. Rhoades, S.T.L., J.C.L. (HBG); Russell E. Smith, S.T.D. (RIC); Robert V. Zylla, O.S.C., S.T.L.; Sr. Joan Gormley, P.V.M.I., Ph.D.; Sr. Paula Jean Miller, F.S.E., S.T.D.; Dr. Pamela Jackson, Ph.D.
Part Time Faculty: Rev. Michael J. Roach, M.A. (BAL); Dr. Herbert W. Stroup, Ph.D.; Mr. Frederick J. Ziegler, M.S.Mus.; Sr. Ann Miriam Gallagher, R.S.M., Ph.D.; Dr. Carol L. Houghton, S.T.D., J.C.D. Priests 13; Sisters 3; Lay Teachers 4; Lay Administrators 1; Support Staff 2; Total Staff 23; Diocesan Seminarians 207; Religious Seminarians 1; Others 9; Total Enrollment 217.

[B] SEMINARIES, RELIGIOUS OR SCHOLASTICATES

ELLICOTT CITY. *Friary of St. Joseph Cupertino*, 12290 Folly Quarter Rd., 21042-1499. Tel: 410-988-9822. Companions of St. Anthony. Tel: 410-988-9833. Secular Franciscans. Tel: 410-988-9855. Conventual Franciscan Friars. Revs. Bart Karwacki, O.F.M.Conv., Guardian; James Elliot, O.F.M.Conv., Vicar; Rick Deptula, O.F.M.Conv.; Bros. Thaddeus Grzankowski, O.F.M.Conv.; Richard O'Hanlon, O.F.M.Conv.; Augustine Kelly, O.F.M.Conv.; Daniel Geary, O.F.M.Conv.; Revs. Jude Winkler, O.F.M.Conv.; Romuald Meograssi, O.F.M.Conv.

[C] COLLEGES AND UNIVERSITIES

BALTIMORE. *College of Notre Dame of Maryland*, 4701 N. Charles St., 21210. Tel: 410-435-0100.
For a complete listing, refer to the Colleges and Universities section.
**Loyola College*, 4501 N. Charles St., 21210. Tel: 410-617-2000.
For a complete listing, refer to the Colleges and Universities section.

EMMITSBURG. *Mount Saint Mary's College*, (1808), 21727. Tel: 301-447-6122.
For a complete listing, refer to the Colleges and Universities section.

[D] HIGH SCHOOLS, PRIVATE

BALTIMORE. *Archbishop Curley High School*, 3701 Sinclair Ln., 21213. Tel: 410-485-5000; Fax: 410-483-2545.
Administered by Order of Friars Minor Conventual, St. Anthony of Padua Province (USA). Revs. Donald Grzymski, O.F.M.Conv., Pres. & Guardian; Michael Heine, O.F.M.Conv.; Thomas E. Walsh, O.F.M.Conv., Vicar; Michael Zielke, O.F.M.Conv.; Ignatius M. Piatek, O.F.M.Conv.; Michael Martin, O.F.M.Conv., Prin.; Conrad Miller, O.F.M.Conv.; Bro. Christian Katusz, O.F.M.Conv.; Friar Vincent Rubino, O.F.M.Conv. Priests 7; Brothers 1; Friars 1; Sisters 1; Lay Teachers 34; Students 575; Total Staff 61.
Calvert Hall College, 8102 La Salle Rd., 21286. Tel: 410-825-4266.
Conducted by the Brothers of the Christian Schools (F.S.C.). Bros. Kevin Strong, F.S.C., Pres.; Kevin Stanton, F.S.C., Prin.; Mr. Louis Heidrick, Asst.

Prin. Academic Affairs; Mr. Charles Stembler, Asst. Prin. Student Affairs. Brothers 14; Sisters 1; Lay Teachers 69; Students 1,098.

Cardinal Gibbons School for Boys (1962). (Grades 6-12), 3225 Wilkens Ave., 21229-4286. Tel: 410-644-1770. Mr. Philip J. Forte, Prin. Lay Teachers 21; Students 236.

The Catholic High School of Baltimore, 2800 Edison Hwy., 21213. Tel: 410-732-6200. Sisters of St. Francis of Philadelphia. Sisters 8; Lay Teachers 31; Students 405; Total Staff 54.

Institute of Notre Dame (1847), 901 Aisquith St., 21202. Tel: 410-522-7800. Legal Title: *Institute of Notre Dame, Inc.* Mary Fitzgerald, S.S.N.D., Prin. Sisters 8; Lay Employees 43; Counselors 2; Students 424.

Loyola High School, P.O. Box 6819, 21285-6819. Tel: 410-823-0601. Revs. James F. McAndrews, S.J., Pres.; J. Gregory Quinn, S.J., Rector; Joseph M. Alminde, S.J.; Michael J. Kuchera, S.J.; Henry Erhart, S.J., Chap.; Lloyd D. George, S.J.; Gregory C. Hartley, S.J.; Robert B. Cullen, S.J.; Bros. Joseph M. Bonello, S.J., Minister; Darrell J. Burns, S.J., Chap.; Dr. Donald Urbancic, Headmaster; Mr. John T. Butler. Priests 8; Brothers 2; Scholastics 4; Lay Teachers 70; Students 855.

Mercy High School, 1300 E. Northern Pkwy., 21239. Tel: 410-433-8880. Sisters of Mercy of the Americas. Sr. Carol E. Wheeler, R.S.M., Prin. Sisters 6; Lay Teachers 40; Students 514; Total Staff 77.

Mount de Sales Academy, 700 Academy Rd., 21228. Tel: 410-744-8498. Sr. Helen Marie Glaser, O.P., Headmistress. Sisters 7; Lay Teachers 25; Students 340.

Mt. St. Joseph College High School, 4403 Frederick Ave., 21229. Tel: 410-644-3300. Xaverian Brothers. Mr. Charles L. Reiter, Ph.D., Pres.; Mr. Barry J. Fitzpatrick, Prin. Brothers 3; Lay Teachers 70; Students 1,058; Total Staff 142.

St. Frances Academy. (Coed), 501 E. Chase St., 21202. Tel: 410-539-5794. Oblate Sisters of Providence. Sr. John Francis Schilling, O.S.P., Pres. & Prin.; Bro. Brian Henderson, F.S.C., Asst. Prin.; Mrs. Judy Treadwell, Dir. Guidance; Mr. Freddie Lee, Dean of Students. Brothers 4; Sisters 7; Lay Teachers 10; Students 240.

The Seton Keough High School, 1201 Caton Ave., 21227. Tel: 410-646-4444. Sr. Marie Danielle Amspacher, S.S.N.D., Pres.; Sr. Joan Elias, G.N.S.H., Prin.; Ms. Mary Bridget Byrnes, Asst. Prin. Sisters 10; Lay Teachers 42; Students 495.

BEL AIR. *The John Carroll School*, 703 Churchville Rd., 21014. Tel: 410-879-2480; Fax: 410-836-8514. Mrs. Carol R. Goldbeck, Prin.; Mrs. Marellen Mayers, Campus Min. Priests 1; Sisters of St. Joseph Chestnut Hill 8; Sisters of Notre Dame 1; Lay Teachers 42; Students 682; Total Staff 105.

BROOKLANDVILLE. *Maryvale Preparatory School*. (Grades 6-12). (Girls), 21022. Tel: 410-252-3366. Sr. Shawn Marie Maguire, S.N.D., Prin. Sisters of Notre Dame de Namur 3; Lay Teachers 33; Students 270; Total Staff 53.

CUMBERLAND. *Bishop Walsh Middle-High School*. (Grades 6-12), 700 Bishop Walsh Rd., 21502. Tel: 301-724-5360. Brothers of the Christian Schools, School Sisters of Notre Dame, Ursuline Sisters of Louisville. Bro. Kevin Dalmasse, F.S.C., Prin. Brothers 8; Sisters 3; Lay Teachers 23; Students 315.

FREDERICK. *St. John's Literary Institution at Prospect Hall* (1841). (Grades 9-12). (Coed), 889 Butterfly Ln., 21703. Tel: 301-662-4210. Mr. Thomas J. Peri, Headmaster; Mr. Thomas Farrell, Prin. Priests 1; Lay Teachers 22; Students 225; Total Staff 35.

HAGERSTOWN. *St. Maria Goretti High School*. (Coed), 1535 Oak Hill Ave., 21742. Tel: 301-739-4266; Fax: 301-739-4261. Sr. Susan Albert, S.S.N.D., Prin. School Sisters of Notre Dame 2; Lay Teachers 20; Students 253.

SEVERN. *Archbishop Spalding High School*, 8080 New Cut Rd., 21144. Tel: 410-969-9105. Barbara H. Schwitzer, Prin.; Rev. Michael Callaghan, Chap. Priests 1; Lay Teachers 50; Students 846.

TOWSON. *Notre Dame Preparatory School*. (Grades 6-12), 815 Hampton Ln., 21286. Tel: 410-825-6202. Legal Title: *Notre Dame Preparatory School, Inc.* Sr. Helen Marie, S.S.N.D., Headmistress. Sisters 7; Lay Teachers 77; Students 637.

[E] ELEMENTARY SCHOOLS, PRIVATE

ELLICOTT CITY. *Trinity School*, 4985 Ilchester Rd., 21041. Tel: 410-744-1524. Sr. Catherine Phelps, Prin. Sisters of Notre Dame de Namur 2; Lay Teachers 24; Students 394.

EMMITSBURG. *Mother Seton School*, 100 Creamery Rd., 21727. Tel: 301-447-3161. Sr. Mary Catherine Conway, Prin. Daughters of Charity of St. Vincent de Paul 5; Lay Teachers 22; Students 329.

FREDERICK. *Academy of the Visitation*, 200 E. 2nd St., 21701. Tel: 301-662-3322; 662-2814. Dr. Bernadette Emerson, Prin. Sisters of the Visitation 5; Lay Teachers 12; Students 172.

WOODSTOCK. *Woodmont Academy*. (Grades K-8), 10817 Davis Ave., 21163. Tel: 410-203-0619; Fax: 410-465-9162. Miss Denise Folz, Prin. Lay Teachers 10; Students 90.

[F] ELEMENTARY SCHOOLS, REGIONAL & COMMUNITY

BALTIMORE. *Bishop John Neumann School*. (Grades PreK-8), 3500 Foster Ave., 21224. Tel: 410-675-6271; Fax: 410-522-2022. Miss Katherine Davis, Prin. Sisters 1; Lay Teachers 18; Students 270.

Cardinal Shehan School, 5407 Loch Raven Blvd., 21239. Tel: 410-433-2775.
Serving the St. Matthew and St. Thomas More Parishes. Sr. Mary Vandergeest, O.S.F., Prin. Lay Teachers 19; Sisters 1; Total Staff 21; Students 405.

Catholic Community School of South Baltimore. (Grades PreK-8), 300 E.Gittings St., 21230. Tel: 410-685-6155; Fax: 410-685-0692. Sr. Josephann Wagoner, S.S.N.D., Prin. Sisters 3; Lay Teachers 10; Students 230. Res. Sisters of St. Joseph, 1410 Riverside Ave., 21230-4695. Tel: 410-752-4344.
Consolidation of the following parishes: Holy Cross; Our Lady of Good Counsel; St. Mary, Star of the Sea.

Father Kolbe Interparochial School, 1035 S. Kenwood Ave., 21224. Tel: 401-342-2681.
Serving the parishes of St. Casimir, St. Leo and St. Stanislaus. Sr. Barbara Ann Brzeczko, F.S.S.J., Prin. Franciscan Sisters of St. Joseph 2; Lay Teachers 10; Students 195.

John Paul Regional Catholic School, Inc. (Grades 1-8), 6946 Dogwood Rd., 21244. Tel: 410-944-0367. Ms. Mary Frey, Prin., (Grades PreK-K), 5801 Security Blvd., 21207. Tel: 410-265-7454. Mrs. Joann Callahan, Dir. Lay Teachers 28; Students 390.

Mother Seton Academy, 724 S. Ann St., 21231. Tel: 410-563-2833. Sr. Mary Bader, D.C., Prin. Innovative Middle School for Inner City Youth. Sisters 8; Brothers 2; Lay Volunteers 2; Students 58.

Queen of Peace Elementary Cluster, St. James and St. John School. (Grades PreK-5), 1010 Somerset St., 21202. Tel: 410-342-3222. Ms. Lauanah King-Cassell, Prin. Sisters 1; Lay Teachers 9; Students 240.

St. Katherine of Sienna School, 1201 N. Rose St., 21213. Tel: 410-327-4738. Mr. Kevin Parson, Prin. Lay Teachers 10; Students 240.

St. Ignatius Loyola Academy, 740 N. Calvert St., 21202. Tel: 410-539-8268. Revs. William J. Watters, S.J., Pres.; Jeffrey R. Sindler. Middle School for underprivileged boys. Students 60.

CUMBERLAND. *St. John Neumann School*. (Grades K-5), Fayette St. & Smallwood St., 21502. Tel: 301-724-4055. Sr. Dolores Hudson, O.S.U., Prin. Sisters 2; Lay Teachers 20; Students 334.
Bishop Walsh Middle-High School. (See listing under High Schools, Private).

FREDERICK. *St. John Regional Catholic School*. (Grades K-8), 114 E. Second St., 21701. Tel: 301-662-7024. Ms. Janet L. Jensen, Prin. Lay Teachers 26; Students 515.

GLEN BURNIE. *Arthur Slade Regional Catholic School*, 120 Dorsey Rd., 21061. Tel: 410-766-7130.
Serving Glen Burnie, Millersville, Odenton, Crofton and Severn Parishes. Mrs. Janice McIntosh, Prin. Lay Teachers 37; Students 870.

[G] SPECIAL EDUCATION

BALTIMORE. *St. Elizabeth School*, 801 Argonne Dr., 21218. Tel: 410-889-5054. Christine Manlove, Ed.D., Prin. Franciscan Sisters of Baltimore 4; Lay Teachers 22; Aides 24; Children 115.

St. Francis School for Special Education, 3725 Ellerslie Ave., 21218. Tel: 410-235-3378.

St. Peter's Adult Learning Center, 13 S. Poppleton St., 21201. Tel: 410-685-7340. Program for developmentally disabled persons. Sr. Katherine Nueslein, R.S.M., Dir. Sisters 1; Lay Teachers 4; Students 25.

TIMONIUM. *Villa Maria School*, 2300 Dulaney Valley Rd., 21093. Tel: 410-252-6343; Fax: 410-560-1347. John M. Pumphrey, Dir. of Education. Non-public (Level V and VI) special education for children with emotional disabilities, ages 6-13. Lay Teachers 22; Teacher Aides 18; Children 112.

[H] CHILD CARE CENTERS

BALTIMORE. *Good Shepherd Center*, 4100 Maple Ave., 21227. Tel: 410-247-2770. Legal Titles: *House of the Good Shepherd; Sisters of the Good Shepherd, A Corporation*. Sr. Mary Rosaria Baxter, R.G.S., Admin.; Sr. Mary Catherine Massei, R.G.S., Supr.
Residential psychiatric treatment for adolescent girls. Sisters 6; Capacity 105; Residents 80.

St. Frances Outreach Center, 1026 Brentwood Ave., 21202. Tel: 410-539-1903. Sr. Brenda Motte, O.S.P., Dir. Total Assisted 30 Families; Total Staff 3.

Sisters Servants of Mary Immaculate Day Nursery & Convent, 100-104 S. Patterson Park Ave., 21231. Tel: 410-276-2630. Sr. Grazyna Rybus, Supr. Total Assisted 75.

Villa Louise Family Resource Center, St. Agnes Hospital, DePaul Bldg., 900 Caton Ave., 21229. Tel: 410-368-2060. Bon Secours Hospital, 2000 W. Baltimore St. Tel: 410-362-3168. Ms. Ellen Warnock-Eckhart, Div. Dir., ACC. Total Staff 9; Total Assisted 150.

TIMONIUM. *Francis X. Gallagher Services*, 2520 Pot Spring Rd., 21093. Tel: 410-252-4005. Mark J. Schulz, Admin.
Residential day habilitation and medical day programs for the developmentally disabled. Priests 1; Residential Capacity 189; Day Capacity 232; Total Assisted 182; Total Staff 34.

St. Vincent's Center, 2600 Pot Spring Rd., 21093. Tel: 410-252-4000; Fax: 410-561-8109. John D. Rusinko, Dir. Children's Continuum of ACC. Residential Treatment Center for children, ages 18 mos.-12 years that are emotionally disturbed, abused, & neglected. Residents 70.

Villa Maria, A Residential Treatment Center, 2300 Dulaney Valley Rd., 21093. Tel: 410-252-4700; Fax: 410-252-3040. Mark Greenberg, Admin.; Rev. Raymond Chase, Chap. Children 80; Intensive Treatment Units 6.

[I] GENERAL HOSPITALS

BALTIMORE. *Bon Secours Baltimore Health System, Inc.*, 2000 W. Baltimore St., 21223. Tel: 410-362-3000.
For a complete listing, refer to the Hospitals section.

Mercy Medical Center, Inc., 301 St. Paul Pl., 21202. Tel: 410-332-9000; Fax: 410-783-5993.
For a complete listing, refer to the Hospitals section.

St. Agnes HealthCare, Inc., 900 Caton Ave., 21229-5299. Tel: 410-368-6000.
For a complete listing, refer to the Hospitals section.

St. Joseph Medical Center, 7620 York Rd., 21204. Tel: 410-337-1000; Fax: 410-337-1017.
For a complete listing, refer to the Hospitals section.

CUMBERLAND. *Sacred Heart Hospital*, 900 Seton Dr., 21502. Tel: 301-759-4200.
For a complete listing, refer to the Hospitals section.

[J] NURSING HOMES (SKILLED)

BALTIMORE. *St. Elizabeth Home for Nursing Care*, 3320 Benson Ave., 21227-1088. Tel: 410-644-7100; Fax: 410-644-2154.
For a complete listing, refer to the Special Care Facilities section.

ELLICOTT CITY. *Bon Secours Nursing Care Center, Inc.*, 3000 N. Ridge Rd., 21043. Tel: 410-461-6660; Fax: 410-461-6695.
For a complete listing, refer to the Special Care Facilities section.

[K] HOMES FOR AGED

BALTIMORE. *The Cardinal Shehan Center, Inc.*, 2300 Dulaney Valley Rd. Towson, 21204. Tel: 410-252-4500; Fax: 410-628-8095.
For a complete listing, refer to the Special Care Facilities section.

St. Charles Villa, 603 Maiden Choice Ln., 21228. Tel: 410-747-1211.
For a complete listing, refer to the Special Care Facilities section.

St. Joseph's Nursing Home, 1222 Tugwell Dr., 21228. Tel: 410-747-0026; Fax: 410-747-0386.
For a complete listing, refer to the Special Care Facilities section.

St. Martin's Home for Aged, Little Sisters of the Poor, 601 Maiden Choice Ln., 21228. Tel: 410-744-9367.
For a complete listing, refer to the Special Care Facilities section.

Stella Maris Operating Corporation, 2300 Dulaney Valley Rd., 21204. Tel: 410-252-4500.
For a complete listing, refer to the Special Care Facilities section.

[L] RETREAT HOUSES FOR MEN, WOMEN AND YOUTH

BALTIMORE. *Holy Trinity Spiritual Center*, 8400 Park Heights Ave., P.O. Box 5719, 21282. Tel: 410-486-5171. Rev. Timothy Murphy, O.SS.T., Guest Master Spirituality Center. Total Assisted 1,027; Total Staff 2; Total in Residence 10.

St. Mary's Spiritual Center, 600 N. Paca St., 21201-1995. Tel: 410-728-6464. Rev. John E. McMurry, S.S., Dir.

ADAMSTOWN. *Christian Brothers Spiritual Center*, 2535 Buckeystown Pike, 21710. Tel: 301-874-5180. Bro. Richard W. Breese, F.S.C., Admin. Brothers 3.

CATONSVILLE. *Our Lady of Guadalupe Renewal Center*, 10 Sharonwood Ct., 21228. Tel: 410-788-8821. Sr. Anne Colette Potthast, S.N.D., Dir. Total in Residence 2; Total Staff 2; Pastoral Team 14.

EMMITSBURG. *Seton Retreat Center*, 333 S. Seton Ave., 21727. Tel: 301-447-3121. Daughters of Charity. Sr. Irene Kraus, D.C., Dir.

MARRIOTTSVILLE. *Bon Secours Spiritual Center*, 21104-1301. Tel: 410-442-1320. Sisters of Bon Secours. Sr. Carol Marozzi, S.S.J., Dir. Total Staff 23.

SPARKS. *Msgr. Clare J. O'Dwyer Retreat House*, 15523 York Rd., 21152. Tel: 410-472-2400. Revs. John E. O'Brien, Dir.; John J. Thornsberry.

[M] MONASTERIES AND RESIDENCES OF PRIESTS AND BROTHERS

BALTIMORE. *Ferdinand Wheeler House*, 3048 Guilford Ave., 21218. Tel: 410-338-1296. Revs. James R. Stormes, S.J., Supr.; Theodore E.A. Brady, S.J.; James R. Conroy, S.J.; Francis R. Carmody, S.J.; Charles P. Costello, S.J.; Todd Harrison, S.J.; Thomas P. Gaunt, S.J.; Mark F. Horak, S.J.; Bro. James Horan, S.J. Priests 8; Brothers 1.

Holy Trinity Monastery, Prov. Admin. & Spiritual Center, 8400 Upper Park Heights Ave., P.O. Box 5742, 21282. Tel: 410-486-5171; Fax: 410-486-0614. Office, 8400 Upper Park Heights Ave., P.O. Box 5719, 21208-0742. Tel: 410-486-5764. In res., Revs. John Dorn, O.SS.T., Min. Prov.; Charles J. Flood, O.SS.T., Min. Conventual, Prov. Sec. & Treas.; Albert Anuszewski, O.SS.T., Vocation Dir.; Timothy Murphy, O.SS.T., Dir. Spiritual Center; Edward Wagner, O.S.S.T., Chap.; Bernard Harding, (Retired); Bros. Eric Beardsley, O.SS.T.; Christopher Doyle, O.SS.T.; Daniel Montemarano, O.SS.T.; Francis Scullion. Priests 6; Brothers 4.

Assigned But Serving Elsewhere: Revs. Luke Mennella, O.SS.T., General Council, The Trinitarians, Via Massimi, 114C, Rome, Italy, 00136; Joseph C. Gidaro, O.SS.T., General Sec., St. Brigid Church, 119 Ave. B, NY, NY 10009; Aaron M. Dowdell, O.SS.T., St. Brigid Church, 119 Ave. B, NY, NY 10009; Jose T. Narlaly, O.SS.T., Holy Trinity Ashram-Laloor, P.O. Aranattuka, Trichur, Kerala State, India, 680026; Damon Geiger, O.SS.T., P.B. No. 2911 Third Main Rd., Jayanagar East Byrasandra, Bangalore 560 011; Eric T. Burdt, O.SS.T., Christian Brothers High School, 5900 Walnut Grove Rd., Memphis, TN, 38120-2104. Rev. Italo Gasbarri, O.SS.T., 439 Hall Ave., Perth Amboy, NJ, 08861-2501. Rev. Donald Hayden, O.SS.T., SS. Cyril & Methodius Church, 125 Half Hollow Rd., Deer Park, NY, 11729-1288. Rev. Armond Iavarone, O.SS.T., St. Joseph's Church, 333 Sneden Pl. W., Spring Valley, NY, 10977-3943. Rev. Weston J. Lamb, O.SS.T., 4250 South 5th, Apt. 2, Terre Haute, IN, 47805-4253. Rev. August Pinci, O.SS.T., The Trinitarians, Via Massimi, 114C, Rome, Italy, 00136. Rev. Alberto Edgardo Rodrigues, O.SS.T., Holy Name of Jesus Church, 345 S. Military Trail, West Palm Beach, FL, 33415-2807. Bro. Ervin J. Wegscheid, O.SS.T., 213 Argonaut, #146, El Paso, TX, 79912-6052. The Trinitarian Community, 8636 Trail View Dr., Ellicott City, 21043. In res., Revs. Thomas J. Burke, O.SS.T.; Damian Anuszewski, O.SS.T.; William J. Moorman, O.SS.T., The Trinitarian Community, 8612 Laverne Dr., Adelphi, 20783. In res., Revs. Claude Gravel, O.SS.T.; Lawrence Hernandez, O.SS.T.; William Sullivan, O.SS.T.

Redeemer House, 1401 Battery Ave., 21230-4603. Tel: 410-576-9565. In res., Bros. Richard J. Micka, Prog. Dir.; David Nash, Treas. Brothers 2; Total Staff 2.

Immaculate Heart of Mary Friary, 4220 Erdman Ave., 21213. Tel: 410-485-5511; Fax: 410-483-2545. Residence of Franciscan Friars, O.F.M.Conv., conducting Archbishop Curley High School. Rev. Conrad Miller, O.F.M.Conv.; Bro. Christian Katusz, O.F.M.Conv., Procurator; Revs. Michael Martin, O.F.M.Conv.; Michael Heine, O.F.M.Conv.; Michael Zielke, O.F.M.Conv.; Ignatius M. Piatek, O.F.M.Conv.; Donald Grzymski, O.F.M.Conv., Pres. & Guardian; Thomas Walsh, O.F.M.Conv., Vicar; Friar Vincent Rubino, O.F.M.Conv. Priests 7; Brothers 1; Friars 1.

Jesuit Community of Loyola College, Inc., Loyola College, 4501 N. Charles St., 21210-2699. Tel: 410-617-2000. Revs. Patrick F. Earl, S.J., Rector; Ronald J. Anton; Timothy B. Brown; John L. Brunett; Edwin H. Convey; William M. Davish; Michael D. French; C. Kevin Gillespie; Edgar Graham; John H. Gray; Frank R. Haig; Robert K. Judge; Joseph M. Kennedy; William K. McGroarty; Daniel J. McGuire; Francis G. McManamin; Francis J. Nash; Harold E. Ridley; Joseph S. Rossi; Peter F. Ryan; William P. Ryan; James F. Salmon; William J. Sneck; Joseph A. Sobierajski; Paul Sun. Total in Residence 25.

Jesuit Fathers and Brothers Maryland Provincial Curia, 5704 Roland Ave., 21210. Tel: 410-532-1400; Fax: 410-532-1419. Legal Title: *Corporation of the Roman Catholic Clergymen*. Very Rev. James R. Stormes, S.J.; Revs. James A. Casciotti, S.J., Supr., Sec.; James F. Salmon, S.J., Treas.; James J. Conn, S.J., Dir. Communications; John P. McGinty, S.J., Min.; Thomas P. Gaunt, S.J., Asst. for Formation and Studies; David G. Allen, S.J.; Vincent C. Curtin, S.J.; James H. Donahoe, S.J.; Thomas R. Fitzgerald, S.J.; Hugh A. Kennedy, S.J., Asst. Sec.; James J. Ditillo, S.J.; Francis X. Knott, S.J.; Liborio J. LaMartina, S.J., Asst.Res. Archivist; William F. Lamm, S.J., Asst. Treas. & Asst. Sec.; Thomas P. Martin, S.J., Asst. Treas.; Francis X. Metzbower, S.J.; Thomas E. Peacock, S.J.; T. Donald Rinfret, S.J., Dir. of Jesuit Seminary and Mission Bureau. Total in Residence 17. Military Chaplains: Revs. E. Paul Betowski, S.J., White Sands Missile Range, NM; Paul J. Shaughnessy, S.J., PSC 559, Box 5148, FPO AP, Okinawa, Japan, 96377-5148.

Priests of the Province Serving Abroad: Rev. George V. Coyne, S.J., Specola Vaticana, Vatican City State, Italy. Rev. Harry F. Geib, S.J., Peter Faber Residence, 28 Brookvale Ave., Belfast BT14 6BW, Northern Ireland. Rev. Philip J. Rosato, S.J., Collegio S. Roberto Bellarmino, Via de Seminario 120, Rome, Italy, 00186. Rev. J. Allan Loftus, S.J., 200 Shakespeare Dr. #1001, Waterloo, Canada, N2L 6C1. Rev. John F. Martin, S.J., 95 St. Joseph St., Toronto, Canada, M5S 2R9. Rev. Dominic W. Maruca, S.J., Pont Univ. Greg, Piazza della Pilotta 4, Rome, Italy, 00187. Rev. Thomas M. McCoog, S.J., 114 Mount St., London, United Kingdom, W1Y 6A4. Rev. Daniel R. Sweeney, S.J., St. Edmund's College, Cambridge CB3 0BN, England. Rev. Jon J. O'Brien, S.J., North American College, Via del Gianicolo, Vatican City State, Italy, 00128.

Priests of the Province Serving Elsewhere: Rev. John J. Cecero, S.J., 1414 Whitney Ave., Apt. E-3, Hamden, CT, 06517-2444. Rev. William A. Dawson, S.J., St. Ignatius Church, 533 E. Jarrettsville Rd., Forest Hill, 21050. Rev. Bernard J. Dooley, S.J., 302-A Sea Oats Dr., Juno Beach, FL, 33408. Rev. Bernard G. Filmyer, S.J., 9784 Guisante Ter., San Diego, CA, 92124. Rev. Gerald J. McGlone, S.J., 1607 Cable St., San Diego, CA, 92107-3313. Rev. Joseph C. Sands, S.J., 66 Witherspoon St. #176, Princeton, NJ, 08542. Rev. George B. Wilson, S.J., 5824 Rhode Island Ave. No. 2, Cincinatti, OH, 45237.

On Leave: Revs. Joseph F. Curran, S.J.; Daniel C. Doherty, S.J.; Michael J. Maruca, S.J.; Andrew J. Novotney, S.J.; Clayton A. Railey, S.J.; Christopher J. Whatley, S.J.; Francis X. Winters, S.J.

Marianist Community, 738 S. Beechfield Ave., 21229. Tel: 410-242-5159. Rev. Paul A. Reich, S.M., Dir.; Bros. Jesse O'Neill, S.M.; Francis Schroepfer. Priests 1; Brothers 2; Total in Residence 3; Total Staff 3.

Marianists Community (New York Province), Marianist Provincial House, 4301 Roland Ave., 21210-2793. Tel: 410-366-1300; Fax: 410-889-5743. Rev. George J. Cerniglia, S.M., Asst. Prov.; Bros. Stephen M. Glodek, S.M., Prov.; Francis Mullan, S.M.; Frank O'Donnell, S.M., Dir. Education; Rev. John D. Pawlos, S.M.; Bros. Paul Quinn, S.M.; William Tarrant, F.S.M. Priests 2; Brothers 5; Total in Residence 82. Priests living elsewhere: Rev. Daniel F. Doyle, S.M., 4921 Lincoln St., Hollywood, FL, 33021. Tel: 954-964-1026.

Pallottine Center for Apostolic Causes, 512 W. Saratoga St., 21201. Tel: 410-685-3063; Fax: 410-234-1459. Promotional Center for St. Jude Shrine. Legal Title: *St. Jude Shrine-Pallottine Missions; Pallottine Center for Apostolic Causes, Inc.* Co-Directors: Revs. Peter T. Sticco, S.A.C.; Oreste Pandola, S.A.C.

St. Charles Villa, 603 Maiden Choice Ln., 21228. Tel: 410-747-1211. Home for Retired Sulpicians conducted by the Little Sisters of the Poor. Revs. William T. O'Keeffe, S.S. (CLV), Dir. & Supr.; Raymond F. Hesler, S.S. (ALB), Assoc. Dir.; Lawrence A. Bender, S.S. (WDC); John W. Bowen, S.S. (BAL); James H. Brennan, S.S. (BAL); Frederick V. Chudzinski, S.S. (TOL); Charles P. Dillon, S.S. (TOL); Claude H. Dukehart, S.S. (BAL); Vincent M. Eaton, S.S. (RIC); Andrew A. Forster, S.S. (DET); James J. Healy, S.S. (MAN); William J. Lee, S.S. (CLV); William S. Morris, S.S. (NY); William A. Thielemann, S.S. (WIL); John A. Ward, S.S. (DET); J. Paul Welch, S.S. (SEA); Joseph L. White, S.S. (BAL). Priests 17.

St. Joseph Society of the Sacred Heart House of Central Administration, 1130 N. Calvert St., 21202. Tel: 410-727-3386. Very Revs. Robert M. Kearns, S.S.J., Supr. Gen.; Edward J. Chiffriller, S.S.J., Vicar Gen.; Roger J. Caesar, S.S.J., Consultor Gen.; Peter E. Hogan, S.S.J., Archivist; Revs. Peter J. Kenney, S.S.J., Historian and Asst. Archivist; Joseph L. Waters, S.S.J., Historian; Mrs. Bernice Jones, Asst. Archivist; Revs. Edward J. Gartner, S.S.J., Dir., Promotional Fund-raising; Eugene P. McManus, S.S.J., Dir. Public Rels.; Edward J. Mullowney, S.S.J., Treas. and Rector; Earle A. Newman, S.S.J.; Joseph C. Verrett, S.S.J., Editor, The Josephite Harvest; Robert E. McCall, S.S.J., Dir. Josephite Evangelization; John F. Byrne, S.S.J., Asst. to Admin. Priests 12. Retired: Revs. John J. Conlon, S.S.J.; N. Wilfrid DesRosiers, S.S.J.; Francis H. Fallon, S.S.J.; Dominic A. Marchese, S.S.J.; Ralph R. Ransom, S.S.J.; Joseph R. Murphy, S.S.J.; Paul A. Ortner, S.S.J.; W. Dayton Salisbury, S.S.J.; James P. Schappert, S.S.J.

St. Joseph's Manor. (Josephite Fathers), 911 W. Lake Ave., 21210. Tel: 410-323-3829. Rectors: Very Rev. Jeremiah D. Brady, S.S.J.; Revs. James F. Didas, S.S.J.; John J. Rawlins, S.S.J.; Daniel H. Cassidy, S.S.J.; Arthur T. Colbert, S.S.J.; John F. Byrne, S.S.J.; George F. O'Dea, S.S.J.; Thomas J. Fitzgerald, S.S.J.; Bartholomew F. Hines, S.S.J.; Rupert A. MacDonald, S.S.J.; Robert E. McCall, S.S.J.; Eugene J. McKenna, S.S.J.; Robert J. O'Connell, S.S.J.; Calvin F. Sinclair, S.S.J.; Bro. Andrew Hogya, S.S.J. Priests 15; Brothers 1.

St. Joseph's Passionist Community, 251 S. Morley St., 21229. Tel: 410-566-3750. Congregation of the Most Holy Cross and Passion of Our Lord Jesus Christ. Revs. Basil Stockmeyer, C.P.; Simon Wood, C.P.; Eustace McDonald, C.P.; Daniel Free, C.P.; Gregory Paul, C.P. Priests 5.

Sulpician Provincial House. (Associated Sulpicians of the United States), 5408 Roland Ave., 21210. Tel: 410-323-5070; Fax: 410-433-6524. Very Rev. Gerald L. Brown, S.S., U.S. Prov. of the Society of St. Sulpice; Revs. Thomas R. Ulshafer, S.S., Prov. Sec.; Melvin C. Blanchette, S.S., Dir. Formation and Personnel Svcs. & Dir. Discernment, Admissions; Multicultural Studies and Programs; Louis M. Reitz, S.S., Prov. Treas.; Mr. Joseph M. Reynolds, Exec. Asst. to Prov., Operations Mgr.

Members and Candidates on Individual Assignments: Rev. Joseph J. Bonadio, S.S., St. Francis of Assisi Church, 3615 Harford Rd., 21218-3196. Rev. William E. Hartgen, S.S., 634 E. St., N.E., Washington, DC, 20002. Rev. Joseph C. Martin, S.S., 800 Tydings Dr., Havre De Grace, 21078-2100. Rev. Robert P. Waznak, S.S., 5 Buttercharm Ct., Silver Spring, 20905-5738. Rev. John J. Kselman, S.S., 7 Kirkland Rd., Cambridge, MA, 02138-3012. Rev. Addison G. Wright, S.S., 24 Killian Ave., Trumbull, CT, 06611-4118. Rev. Thomas Doyle, S.S., 1248 Brentwood Pointe, Brentwood, TN, 37027-2945. Rev. Edward J. Frazer, S.S., St. Dominic's Major Seminary, P.O. Box 320-191 Woodlands, Lusaka, Zambia, Central Africa, 157101. Rev. J. Michael Strange, S.S., St. Augustine's Major Seminary, P.O. Box 81011, Kabwe, Zambia, Central Africa, 157101. Rev. Cale J. Crowley, S.S., Rector, Emmaus Spirituality Center, P.O. Box 32-0084 Woodlands, Lusaka, Zambia, Central Africa, 157101. Rev. John L. Bitterman, S.S., Emmaus Spirituality Center, P.O. Box 32-0084, Woodlands, Lusaka, Zambia, Central Africa, 157101. Rev. Gerald V. Lardner, Emmaus Spirituality Center, P.O. Box 32-0084, Woodlands, Lusaka, Zambia, Central Africa, 157101. Rev. M. Stephen Barrett, S.S., 10910 Olde Woods Way, Columbia, 21044. Rev. Martin Duc Tran, Casa Santa Maria dell'Umilta, Via dell'Umilta 30, Rome, Italy, 00187. Rev. Kenneth J. Martin, S.S., Our Lady of Victory Rectory, 4835 MacArthur Blvd., Washington, DC, 20007-1592. Rev. Ronald S. Ochylski, S.S., Calle Canillas 40, #1 Drcha., Madrid, Spain, 28002. Rev. Anthony Perez, S.S., Parkstraat 108-5D/54, Leuven, Belgium, 3000.

ADAMSTOWN. *Christian Brothers Provincialate*, P.O. Box 29, 21710. Tel: 301-874-5188; Fax: 301-847-5674. Legal Title: *Christian Brothers of Frederick, Inc.* Brothers of the Christians Schools, Baltimore Province. Bros. Benedict Oliver, F.S.C., Prov.; Timothy J. Froelich, F.S.C., Dir. Finance; Robert I. Schieler, F.S.C., Asst. Prov.; Martin J. Fahey, F.S.C., Admin. Asst. Brothers 4; Total in Residence 212; Total Staff 7.

ANNAPOLIS. *Saint Mary Rectory*, 109 Duke of Gloucester St., 21401. Tel: 410-263-2396. Residence of the Redemptorist Fathers and Brothers. Very Rev. Thomas Siconolfi, C.SS.R., Pastor; Revs. Patrick Flynn, C.SS.R.; John Sodomora, C.SS.R.; John Tizio, C.SS.R. In res., Revs. Bernard Baumgartner, C.SS.R.; Henry O'Meara, C.SS.R.; Francis X. Murphy, C.SS.R.

CUMBERLAND. *SS. Peter and Paul Friary*, 125 Fayette St., 21502. Tel: 301-777-3131; 301-777-3137. Legal Title: *Province of St. Augustine of the Capuchin Order*. Revs. Vance Pastorius, O.F.M.Cap., Guardian and Pastor; Vernon Busch, O.F.M.Cap., Vicar & Assoc. Pastor; Roberto McCreary, O.F.M.Cap., Pastor, St. Ambrose, Cresaptown; Bro. Michael Masich, O.F.M.Cap. Priests 3; Brothers 1.

ELLICOTT CITY. *Order of Friars Minor Conventual*, 12300 Folly Quarter Rd., 21042-1419. Tel: 410-531-9200; Fax: 410-531-4881. Very Revs. Mark L. Curesky, O.F.M.Conv., Min. Prov.; Thomas Reist, O.F.M.Conv., Vicar Prov.; Revs. Vincent Gluc, O.F.M.Conv., Sec.; Martin Kobos, O.F.M.Conv., Dir. Devel. (Franciscan Devel. Office); Bro. Brian Newbigging, O.F.M.Conv. On Assignment Outside the U.S.A.: Very Revs. Joachin Giermek, O.F.M.Conv.; Matteo Luo, O.F.M.Conv.; Rev. Martin Breski, O.F.M.Conv.; Bro. Joseph Wood, O.F.M.Conv., Curia Generale dei Frati Minori Conventualli, Piazza Ss. Apostoli 51, Rome, Italy, 00187. Rev. George Maslar, O.F.M.Conv., Piazza Inferiore di S Francesco, 06082 Assisi Santuario (PG). Rev. Donald Kos, O.F.M.Conv., Convento S. Antonio Baccelli, 56, Via del Serafico,

1, Rome, Italy, 00153. Rev. Bernard Przewozny, O.F.M.Conv., Seraphicum, Via del Serafico, 1, Rome, Italy, 00142. Rev. Jerome Lukaszewski, O.F.M.Conv., St. Francis of Assisi Friary Nagata-Cho, 19-1 NAZE SHI, Kagoshima-Ken 850, Japan. Rev. Ron Roll, O.F.M.Conv., Central America, Apartado 5311, Tegucigalpa, DC, Honduras. Rev. Vincent Lachendro, O.F.M.Conv., Immaculata Retreat House Metro Manila, Novaliches Post Office, P.O. Box 186, Quezon City, Phillipines, 1147. Rev. Dominic Slemba, O.F.M.Conv., St. Francis of Assisi Friary, P.O. Box 238, Ghana, West Africa. Rev. Giles Zakowicz, O.F.M.Conv., St. Francis of Assisi Friary, P.O. Box 238, Ghana, West Africa. Rev. Paul Marut, O.F.M.Conv., P.O. Box 3, Achimota, Accra, Ghana, West Africa. Rev. Nicholas Swiatek, O.F.M. Conv., Seibo No Kishi Friary, Hongochi-cho 196, Nagasaki, Japan. Bro. Mitchell Sawicki, O.F.M.Conv., St. Bonaventure Friary, P.O. Box 3, Ghana, West Africa. Rev. Henry Karwel, O.F.M.Conv., St. Mary's Parish, 60 South St., Ware, MA 01082-1619. Rev. Daniel Pietrzak, O.F.M.Conv., St. Joseph Cupertino Friary, 10 Dimar Ct., Dingley, Victoria, Australia, 3172.

Individual Assignment Within the U.S.A.: Rev. Thomas Gwozdz, O.F.M.Conv., (Retired), Pope John Paul II Center, 33 Lincoln Ave., Danbury, CT, 06810. Rev. Peter Bucki, O.F.M.Conv., (Retired); Bro. Aloysius Stanczak, O.F.M.Conv., (Retired), 50 Pulaski St., New Britain, CT, 06053. Rev. Paul Zabicki, (Retired), St. Joseph's SNC/Morris Hall, 1 Bishop's Dr., Lawrenceville, NJ, 08648. Rev. Felician Plichta, O.F.M.Conv., Corpus Christi Rectory, 324 Quaker Meeting House Rd., East Sandwich, MA, 02537-0384. Rev. Roger Haas, O.F.M.Conv., Christ the King Seminary, P.O. Box 607, East Aurora, NY, 14052-0607. Rev. Paul Duzinski, O.F.M.Conv., Sts. Mary and Joseph Home, 4291 Richmond Rd. - #102, Cleveland, OH, 44122-6103. Rev. Clement Jarnot, O.F.M.Conv., St. Mary of Czetochova Parish, 79 S. Main St., Middletown, CT, 06457-3606. Rev. Luke Dyjak, O.F.M.Conv., (Retired), Little Sisters of the Poor, 2100 S. Western Ave., San Pedro, CA, 97032. Rev. Patrick Rolak, O.F.M.Conv., (Retired), Sacred Heart Home, 4520 Ransom Rd., Clarence, NY, 14031. Rev. Ronald Sermak, O.F.M.Conv., Chaplain's Office, 5286 South Park Ave., Hamburg, NY, 14075-1596. Total in Residence 195.

St. Joseph Cupertino Friary, Friars Minor Conventual of St. Francis of Assisi, 12290 Folly Quarter Rd., 21042-1419. Tel: 410-988-9822.

Corporate Title: Franciscan Fathers Minor Conventuals of MD, Inc. Secular Franciscans. Tel: 410-988-9855. Revs. Bart Karwacki, O.F.M.Conv., Guardian & Prov. Spiritual Asst. for Secular Franciscan Order; James Elliott, O.F.M.Conv., Vicar; Rick Deptula, O.F.M.Conv.; Augustine M. Kelly, O.F.M.Conv.; Ted Grzankowski, O.F.M.Conv.; Richard Thomas O'Hanlon, O.F.M.Conv.; Romuald Meograssi, O.F.M.Conv.; Jude Winkler, O.F.M.Conv.; Bro. Daniel Geary, O.F.M.Conv.

Xaverian Brothers Provincialate, 10318 B Baltimore National Pike, 21042-2191. Tel: 410-750-2850; Fax: 410-465-4220. Bros. Richard Murphy, C.F.X., Prov.; John Olson, C.F.X., Assoc. Dir. Xaverian Sponsored Schools & Prov. Treas.; Cornelius Hubbuch, C.F.X., Dir. Staff Formation; Henry Marino, C.F.X., Devel. Dir.

Legal Titles and Schools Sponsored: Xaverian Brothers Community Support Trust Fund; American Central Province of the Xaverian Brothers, Inc.; St. Mary's-Ryken High School, Inc.; Our Lady of Good Counsel High School, Inc.; St. Xavier High School, Inc.; Xaverian High School, Inc.; Holy Family High School, Inc.; Mt. St. Joseph High School, Inc.; Xaverian Brothers Auxiliary; St. Michael's High School Alumni Association; Nazareth Regional High School, Inc.

EMMITSBURG. *Vincentian House*. Revs. Michael J. Kennedy, C.M., Admin.; William P. Goff, C.M.; Louis B. Storms, C.M., Asst. Supr. & Chap.; John J. Lawlor, C.M., Dir., Daughters of Charity; John W. Carven, C.M., Chap.; John F. King, C.M., Chap.; Joseph R. Wright, C.M. Priests 6.

[N] CONVENTS AND RESIDENCES FOR SISTERS

BALTIMORE. *Carmelite Monsatery*, 1318 Dulaney Valley Rd., 21286-1399. Tel: 410-823-7415. Discalced Carmelite Nuns. Sr. Veronica Emmick, Prioress. Professed Sisters 15; Novices 1.

Chesapeake Province of the Sisters of Notre Dame de Namur, Provincial Offices, 305 Cable St., 21210-2511. Tel: 410-243-1993; Fax: 410-243-2279. Administrative Team: Sr. Agnes Rose McNally, S.N.D.deN.; Sr. Mary Margaret Pignone, S.N.D-.deN. Sisters in Province 83; Sisters in Diocese 31.

Daughters of Charity, 900 Caton Ave., 21229. Total in Residence 14.

Franciscan Sisters of Baltimore-General Motherhouse and Novitiate, 3725 Ellerslie Ave., 21218. Tel: 410-235-0139; Fax: 410-243-2569. Legal Titles: *Franciscan Sisters of Baltimore City; Declaration of Trust of the Franciscan Sisters of Baltimore, Inc*. Sr. Ritamary Tan, O.S.F., Gen. Supr.; Rev. Gerald West, Chap. Sisters 50.

Little Sisters of Jesus-Regional Residence, 400 N. Streeper St., 21224. Tel: 327-7863. Sr. Cathy Wright, Regl. Supr. Sisters 4.

Little Sisters of the Poor-Provincial Residence, 601 Maiden Choice Ln., 21228-3698. Tel: 410-744-9367. Sr. Mary Bernard Du St. Esprit, L.S.P., Prov.; Sr. Marguerite, L.S.P., Supr.; Rev. Robert Hawkins. Sisters 21; Total Assisted 106; Total Staff 130.

Mission Helper Center, 1001 W. Joppa Rd., 21204-3787. Tel: 410-823-8585; Fax: 410-825-6355. Sr. Catharine Dages, Pres.; Sr. Carol Ann Gray, Gen. Treas.; Sr. Natalie DeLuca, Asst.; Sr. Ruth Catherine Trauger, Mgr. Sisters 30; Sisters in Diocese 55.

Mission Helpers of the Sacred Heart-Our Lady of Pompei Convent, 225 S. Conkling St., 21224. Tel: 410-675-6034. Sisters 3.

Missionaries of Charity, Gift of Hope Convent, 818 N. Collington Ave., 21205. Tel: 410-732-6056. Sr. M. Pietra, M.C., Supr. Sisters 4; Total Assisted 277; Total Staff 8.

Our Lady of Mt. Providence Convent-Motherhouse, 701 Gun Rd., 21227. Tel: 410-242-8500; Fax: 410-242-4963. Oblate Sisters of Providence. Sisters in the Motherhouse 74; Sisters in the Diocese 84; Total in Residence 125; Total Assisted 60; Total Staff 48.

Attended by Sulpician Fathers and Josephite Fathers.

The School Sisters of Notre Dame in the City of Baltimore (Baltimore Prov.), 6401 N. Charles St., 21212. Tel: 410-377-7774. Sr. Jane Burke, S.S.N.D., Prov. Leader; Rev. David M. Carey, Chap. Sisters 100; Novices 2; Postulants 2; Sisters in Province 430; Sisters in Diocese 308.

Sisters of Mercy, P.O. Box 11448, 21239. Tel: 410-435-4400. Sisters of Mercy of the Americas, Baltimore Regional Community. Sr. Margaret Beatty, R.S.M., Pres. Sisters in Community 251; Sisters in Diocese 125.

Sisters of St. Francis of Philadelphia. Congregational Office - Our Lady of Angels, 609 S. Convent Rd., Aston, PA, 19014. Tel: 215-459-4125. Convents in the Diocese: Shrine of the Little Flower Convent, 2851 Kentucky Ave., 21213. Tel: 410-483-3484. Our Lady of Mt. Carmel Convent, 1706 Eastern Ave., 21221. St. Clement Convent, 1212 Chesaco Ave., 21237. Tel: 410-687-4433. St. Elizabeth Convent, 128 N. Linwood Ave., 21224. Tel: 410-675-1301. St. Joseph Convent, 8418 Belair Rd., 21236. Tel: 410-256-8596. St. Joseph Hospital Convent, 7620 York Rd., 21204. Tel: 410-337-1100. St. Mary of the Angels Convent, 2810 Edison Hwy., 21213. Tel: 410-732-3171. St. Peter Claver Convent, 1526 N. Fremont Ave., 21217. Tel: 410-383-1288. St. Stephen Convent, 8020 Bradshaw Rd., P.O. Box 62, Bradshaw, 21021-0062. Tel: 410-592-9433. Immaculate Conception Convent, 112 Ware Ave., Towson, 21204. Tel: 410-823-3470. Bethany House, 2618 Erdman Ave., 21213. Tel: 410-235-4767. St. Joseph Convent, Box 1, Midland, 21542. Tel: 301-463-2248. Franciscan Residence, 2602 Fleet St., 21224. Tel: 410-276-5099. St. Anthony Convent, 4500 Frankford Ave., 21206. Tel: 410-488-0054. St. Anthony Convent Annex, 4500 Frankford Ave., 21206. Tel: 410-488-0162. Sisters of St. Francis, 34 Acorn Cir. #202, 21286. Tel: 410-832-1858. St. Clement I Convent, 135 First Ave., 21227. Tel: 410-247-2145. Sisters of St. Francis, 806D Cinnamon Ridge Pl., Cockeysville, 21030. Tel: 410-683-1427. Sisters of St. Francis, 3675 College Ave., Ellicott, 21043. Tel: 410-418-8823. St. Mark Convent, 800 Old Fallston Rd., Fallston, 21047. Tel: 410-879-3702. Genesis House, 9 Skidmore Ct., Towson, 21204. Tel: 410-296-8071. Sisters of St. Francis, 10336 "K" Malcolm Cir., Cockeysville, 21030. Tel: 410-683-9459.

Sisters of the Good Shepherd, 4100 Maple Ave., 21227-4099. Tel: 410-247-2770. Sr. Mary Catherine Massei, R.G.S., Supr. Sisters 17.

Sisters of the Good Shepherd-St. Joseph Residence, 4100 Maple Ave., 21227. Tel: 410-247-3898; 247-2770, Ext. 232; Fax: 410-242-5890. Infirmary and Retirement Center for Washington Province. Sisters 25.

Sisters of the Holy Cross, Holy Cross Place, 3813 Edmondson Ave., 21229. Tel: 410-566-8967.

Sisters of the Visitation-Stella Maris Hospice, 2300 Dulaney Valley Rd., 21204. Legal Title: *Visitation Monasteries, Inc*. Total in Residence 13.

Sisters Servants of Mary Immaculate, Inc. Convent and Novitiate. 1220 Tugwell Dr., 21228. Tel: 410-747-1353; Fax: 410-747-0386. Sr. Bernadetta Kozyra, Prov.; Rev. Joseph Sielski, M.I.C., Chap., Sisters Servants of Mary Immaculate Day Nursery & Convent, 100-104 S. Patterson Park Ave., 21231. Tel: 410-276-2630. Sr. Grazyna Rybus, Supr. Sisters 14; Total Assisted 60; Total in Residence 25; Total Staff 12.

The Villa, 6806 Bellona Ave., 21212-1299. Tel: 410-377-2450; Fax: 410-377-2501. Mrs. Martha Coleman, Admin. Convent for Retired Sisters of Mercy and Mission Helpers of the Sacred Heart. Legal Title: *Joint Retirement Convent, Inc.-The Villa*. Sisters 70.

EMMITSBURG. *Daughters of Charity of St. Vincent de Paul, Emmitsburg Province*, 21727. Tel: 301-447-3121. (St. Joseph's Provincial House). Legal Title: *Sisters of Charity of St. Joseph's, Emmitsburg, MD*. Sr. Virginia Ann Brooks, D.C., Prov. Sisters at Provincial House 50; Sisters in Diocese 182; Sisters in Province 299.

Villa St. Michael-St. Joseph's Provincial House, 333 S. Seton Ave., 21727-9299. Tel: 301-447-3121. Home of Daughters of Charity of St. Vincent de Paul. Sr. Virginia Cotter, D.C., Admin. Sisters 106.

FREDERICK. *Visitation Monastery of Frederick, MD*, 200 E. Second St., 21701. Tel: 301-662-3322. Mother Marguerite Therese Leary, V.H.M., Supr. Cloistered Community with Apostolate of Teaching (Grades PreK-8). Sisters 6.

LUTHERVILLE. *Emmanuel Monastery*, 2229 W. Joppa Rd., 21093. Tel: 410-821-5792. Benedictine Sisters of Baltimore.

Ministering in Education, Pastoral Ministry, Retreats and Spiritual Direction, Social Services, Justice Ministry, Hospice Chaplaincy, and Christian and Jewish Studies. Sisters 15.

MARRIOTTSVILLE. *Sisters of Bon Secours, C.B.S., Provincial House*, 21104. Tel: 410-442-1333; Fax: 410-442-1394. Sr. Anne Marie Mack, Pres. Retired Sisters 14; Total in Residence 49; Total Staff 53.

STEVENSON. *Maryland Province Center*, 1531 Greenspring Valley Rd., 21153. Tel: 410-486-5599. Maryland Province of the Sisters of Notre Dame de Namur. Legal Titles: *Baltimore Province of the Sisters of Notre Dame de Namur, Inc.*; *Trinity School, Inc.*; *Maryvale Preparatory School, Inc.*; *Academy of Notre Dame de Namur, Inc.*; *Sisters of Notre Dame de Namur, Maryland Province, Charitable Trust*.

Additional Projects Sponsored: Maryland Province Center of Stevenson, MD; Villa Julie at Seven Oaks of Stevenson, MD; Julie Billiart Residence of Washington, DC.

Additional Projects Co-Sponsored: The Development Office, a joint project of the Maryland Chesapeake & Notre Dame Base Communities Provinces; Directors: Srs. Alice Gillen, Catharine Lafferty, Ann Patricia May, Elizabeth Lebano. Sr. Bernadette Glodek, Prov. Moderator; Sr. Jeanne McGlone, Prov. Leadership; Sr. Patricia Loome, Prov. Leadership. Sisters in Province 160; Sisters in Diocese 70; Total in Residence 25; Total Staff 11.

Villa Julie at Seven Oaks, 1531 Greenspring Valley Rd., 21153. Tel: 410-486-6946. Assisted Living Home for Sisters of Notre Dame and Staff Residence. Sisters 25.

St. Catherine Nursing Home, 331 S. Seton Ave., Emmitsburg, 21727. Tel: 301-447-3121. Sisters of Notre Dame 12.

Stella Maris, 2300 Dulaney Valley Rd., Baltimore, 21204. Tel: 410-461-6695. Sisters of Notre Dame 5.

[O] NEWMAN CENTERS

BALTIMORE. *Archdiocesan Office-Newman Center*, 7909 York Rd., 21204. Tel: 410-828-0622. Rev. Robert E. Albright, Archdiocesan Dir.

Johns Hopkins University, Newman House, 2941 N. Charles St., 21218. Tel: 410-243-7066. Rev. Charles K. Riepe.

Morgan State College, St. Matthew Church, 5401 Loch Raven Blvd., 21239. Tel: 410-433-2300.

Towson State University, Newman Center, 7909 York Rd., 21204. Tel: 410-828-0622. Rev. Robert E. Albright, Dir.

University of Maryland-Baltimore County, 5401 Wilkens Ave., 21228. Tel: 410-828-0622.

Hood College, St. John Church, Rosemont Ave., Frederick, 21701. Tel: 301-662-8288.

Frostburg State College, Osborne Center, 130 S. Broadway, Frostburg, 21532. Tel: 301-689-5041. Rev. Edward S. Hendricks.

Western Maryland College. Contact St. John Church, Westminster, 21157. Tel: 410-848-4744.

[P] FOUNDATIONS, FUNDS & TRUSTS

BALTIMORE. *Bon Secours Baltimore Health Corp., Inc.*, 400 Millington Ave., 21223. Tel: 410-566-0701.

Bon Secours Housing, Inc.

Bon Secours Housing II, Inc.

Bon Secours Facilities, Inc.

Bon Secours of Maryland Foundation, Inc.

Chancery Office. For further information contact the Secretary of Management Services. Also see Miscellaneous Section for additional listings. 320 Cathedral St., 21201. Tel: 410-547-5444.

Archbishop of Baltimore Annual Appeal Trust.

Archdiocesan Health Plan Trust Fund Agreement.
**Backbone Housing, Inc.*
Basilica of the Assumption Historic Trust, Inc.
The Bethany Community, Inc.
Catholic Charities of Central Maryland, Inc.
The Catholic Housing, Inc.
Cemetery Continuing Care Trust. St. Patrick's Havre de Grace, Cemetery Continuing Care Trust; Holy Cross Cemetery Continuing Care Trust; St. Joseph, Fullerton, Cemetery-Continuing Care Trust Agreement; St. Mary of the Assumption, Govans, Cemetery Continuing Care Trust; St. Mary's, Pylesville Cemetery, Continuing Care Trust.
The Children's Fund, Inc.
Christian Brothers Community Support Charitable Trust.
Corpus Christi Jenkins Memorial Trust, Inc.
Dart, Inc.
Friends of Villa Maria, Inc.
Franciscan Sisters of Baltimore, Inc., Trust.
The Gallagher Family Fund, 320 Cathedral St., 21201.
G S Health, Inc.
G S Health Endowment, Inc.
**G S Housing, Inc.*
G S Properties, Inc.
Gallagher Services Auxiliary, Inc.
Jenkins Apartments, Inc.
Jenkins Housing, Inc.
John Carroll Foundation of the Roman Catholic Archdiocese of Baltimore.
John Paul II Regional School, Inc.
St. Joseph's Texas, School Endowment Trust.
Marian House, Inc.
The Marion Burk Knott Scholarship Fund, Educational Trust.
Maryvale Educational Fund, Inc.
Mercy Primary Care Group, Inc.
The National Black Catholic Congress, Inc.
Neumann Early Childhood Center, Inc.
Our Lady of Good Counsel Historic Trust, Inc.
Prime E.A.P., Inc.
St. Agnes Clinical Practice Group, Inc.
St. Francis Housing Corporation.
St. Gregory the Great Housing Committee, Inc.
St. Agnes Hospital Foundation, Inc.
St. Jerome Housing Corporation, Inc.
St. John Neuwmann Regional School, Inc.
St. Jude Shrine Corporation.
St. Martha's Housing, Inc.
St. Mary's Housing, Inc.
St. Peter's Cemetery Restoration Fund, Inc.
St. Peter's, Westernport, School Endowment Trust.
St. Pius V Housing Committee, Inc.
St. Vincent's Child Care Center, Inc.
St. Vincent De Paul Historic Trust, Inc.
Sacred Heart Community Health Services, Inc.
Sacred Heart Foundation, Inc.
Sacred Heart Hospital of the Sisters of Charity, Inc.
School Sisters of Notre Dame in the City of Baltimore Charitable Trust, Inc.
Seton Regional Foundation, Inc.
Seton Regional Health System, Inc.
Sisters of Notre Dame de Namur Charitable Trusts.
Sisters of Notre Dame de Namur, Maryland Province, Charitable Trust.
Women's Auxiliary Board.

MARRIOTTSVILLE. *Bon Secours Health System, Inc.*, 1505 Marriottsville Rd., 21104. Tel: 410-442-5511.
Bon Secours, Inc., 1525 Marriottsville Rd., 21104. Tel: 410-442-1333.
Bon Secours Providers, Inc.

[Q] MISCELLANEOUS

BALTIMORE. *Alhambra, International Order of,* Supreme Headquarters, 4200 Leeds Ave., 21229. Non-profit organization dedicated to assisting the developmentally disabled.
Apostles in the Marketplace (A.I.M.), 320 Cathedral St., 21201.
Apostleship of the Sea, 1532 E. Fort Ave., 21230. Tel: 410-752-0205. Rev. David Smith, Port Chap.
**Cardijn Associates, Inc.*, 1806 Lancaster St., 21231. Tel: 410-563-3190. Ms. Nancy Lee Conrad, Sec.
Carmelite Communities Assoc., 1318 Dulaney Valley Rd., 21286-1399.
The Caroline Center, 900 Somerset St., 21202. Tel: 410-563-1303. Legal Title: *The Caroline Freiss Center, Inc.* Sr. Kathleen Feeley, S.S.N.D., Dir. Total Staff 2. Employment counseling center for women.
Cathedral Library, 5200 N. Charles St., 21210. Tel: 410-433-6769. Elizabeth Howard, Library Chm. Staffed by the Catholic Evidence League.
Catholic Alumni Club, P.O. Box 1492, 21203.
Catholic Community at Relay, 5025 Cedar Ave., 21227. Tel: 410-247-4033. Rev. Mark F. Horak, S.J.
Catholic Daughters of the Americas, 6433 Gilmore Ave., 21207. Tel: 410-265-5481. Rev. Henry J. Hughes, State Chap.; Most Rev. William Newman, Clergy Consultant; Mrs. Lucretia Coates, State Regent.
Catholic Deaf of Baltimore, Lower Chapel, Shrine of the Little Flower, 2854 Brendan Ave., 21213.
Catholic Evidence League, 5200 N. Charles St., 21210.
Catholic Fraternity. Incorporated 1910. 951 Rosedale Ave., 21237. Tel: 410-687-8787.
Catholic Relief Services, U.S.C.C. World Headquarters, 209 W. Fayette St., 21201. Tel: 410-625-2220.
Catholic War Veterans, Inc., Linden Ave. & Highview Ave., 21227. Tel: 410-247-4936. Rev. Conan H. Timoney, State Chap.
Christlife, Inc., 518 Stamford Rd., 21229. Tel: 410-566-2658; Fax: 410-525-2322. Mr. Dave Nodar, Pres.
Cursillo Movement, 320 Cathedral St., 21201. Tel: 410-922-3800. Rev. Edward J. Bayer, Spiritual Dir. Tel: 410-686-6188.
Daughters of Charity National Health System East, Inc., 1302 Concourse Dr., 21090. Tel: 410-850-9000. James E. Small, Regional Exec.
Dismas House East, 1415 N. Caroline St., 21213. Tel: 410-539-2520. Rev. Joseph R. Wenderoth, Exec. Dir. Non-Sectarian-Use Diocesan Property. Rehabilitation center under contract to the Maryland Division of Corrections to provide inmate svcs. Total Staff 18; Total in Residence 45.
Dismas House West, 105 S. Mount St., 21223. Tel: 410-566-9400. Rev. Joseph R. Wenderoth, Exec. Dir. Non-Sectarian. Rehabilitation center under contract to the Maryland Division of Corrections to provide inmate svcs. Total Staff 22; Total in Residence 45.
Efharisto Studio, Inc., 5130 N. Franklintown Rd., 21207-6598. Tel: 410-448-1711; Fax: 410-448-3259. Sr. Stephana Toomey, O.P., Pres.
Services to advance the Roman Catholic religion by charitable, religious, and educational efforts in pursuing a nonprofit ministry of preaching by developing colorful worship areas and art forms to communicate visual meditations and services for the liturgy.
Food for Thought, Inc., 1625 E. Baltimore, 21231. Tel: 410-563-0081. Sr. Mary Ann Hartnett, S.S.N.D., Dir. Tutorial program for children & adult literacy.
Francis House, Inc., 2226 Maryland Ave., 21218-5625. Tel: 410-235-2588; Fax: 410-243-6125. Sr. Patricia McAlpin, O.S.F., Director. Total in Residence 8; Total Staff 2.
Franciscan Center, 2212 Maryland Ave., 21218. Tel: 410-467-5340. Franciscan Sisters of Baltimore. Total Assisted 150,000; Total Staff 18.
Holy Name Society, 320 Cathedral St., 21201. Rev. Msgr. Jeremiah Kenney, Archdiocesan Dir.
Ignatian Lay Volunteer Corps, 3048 Guilford Ave., 21218. Tel: 410-366-8364. Revs. James R. Conroy, S.J., Dir.; Charles P. Costello, S.J., Asst. Dir.
International Federation of Catholic Alumnae, Maryland Chapter, 1000 E. Joppa Rd. #202, 21286-5622. Tel: 410-337-8864. Sr. M. Dominic Karwacki, R.S.M., Governor. Total Staff 98. Benefits & other fund raising activities are held to accumulate funds which are rewarded to members catholic schools in the archdiocese, for scholarships & financial assistance to students.
Jesuit Educational Association of Maryland, Inc., 5704 Roland Ave., 21210. Tel: 410-532-1400; Fax: 410-532-1419. Rev. Allen P. Novotny, S.J., Pres.
Jesuit Jamshedpur Mission Society, Inc. Merged with Jesuit Seminary Guild & Jesuit Mission Bureau, Baltimore, MD. 14 W. Cold Spring Ln., #116, 21210-2631. Tel: 410-433-1782. Rev. Joseph M. Kennedy, S.J., Dir.
Jesuit Seminary Guild & Jesuit Mission Bureau, Maryland Province, Inc., 14 W. Cold Spring Ln. #116, 21210-2631. Tel: 410-435-7090. Revs. T. Donald Rinfret, S.J., Dir.; Richard J. Colgan, S.J., Assoc. Dir.; Francis R. Carmody, S.J., Assoc. Dir.; Joseph M. Kennedy, S.J., Assoc. Dir.
Johns Hopkins Hospital Apostolate. Revs. Alphonse G. Rose; Theodore M. Wisniewski.
Chaplain's Office, Johns Hopkins Medical Center, 600 N. Wolfe St., 21287-4170. Tel: 410-955-5842; Fax: 410-550-6765.
Ladies of Charity, 320 Cathedral St., 21201. Tel: 410-426-0880. Rev. Msgr. Victor B. Galeone, Spiritual Dir.; Mrs. Mary M. Panzer, Pres.
Legion of Mary, 320 Cathedral St., 21201. Tel: 410-465-1355. Rev. Patrick Magnier, C.SS.R., Spiritual Dir.; Mr. Jim Saboe, Pres.
Baltimore Regional Senatus, principal council for states of Maryland, Delaware, West Virginia, Virginia, North Carolina and District of Columbia.
Marianist Conference, 4301 Roland Ave., 21210. Tel: 410-366-1300. Rev. George J. Cerniglia, S.M., Pres.
Maryland Catholic Health Care Consortium, Inc., Holy Cross Hospital of Silver Spring, Inc., 1500 Forest Glen Rd., 20910.
Mercy Home Health Services, Inc., 102 E. Pleasant St., 21202. Ms. Maryann Yentzer, Admin.
Mission Helper Productions, Inc. (video production studio), 1001 W. Joppa Rd., 21204-3787. Tel: 410-823-8585, Ext. 240. Sr. Anne Guinan, M.H.S.H., Contact Person.
Mother Seton House on Paca Street, Inc., 600 N. Paca St., 21201. Tel: 410-523-3443; 825-7272.
Mount Providence Child Development Center, 701 Gun Rd., 21227. Tel: 410-247-0449. Oblate Sisters of Providence. Sr. Mary Concetta Melton, O.S.P., Dir. Sisters 2; Students 80; Total Assisted 9; Total Staff 21.
Mount Providence Reading Center, 701 Gun Rd., 21227. Tel: 410-247-0448; 242-8500. Oblate Sisters of Providence. Sr. M. Constance Fenwick, O.S.P., Dir. Students 112; Total Assisted 112; Total Staff 10.
Parish Social Ministry Outreach, 1512 Druid Hill Ave., 21217. Tel: 410-523-3256.
Immaculate Conception Parish, Baltimore. Sr. Genevieve Noonan, D.C., Staff.
Radio Mass of Baltimore, Inc., St. Ignatius Church, 740 N. Calvert St., 21202. Tel: 410-539-7812. Rev. William J. Watters, S.J., Dir.
Mass is broadcast every Sunday morning from Chapel of Mercy Medical Center at 9:30 A.M., WBGR, 860 AM Radio Dial.
Manresa of Baltimore. Sr. Marie Carmel Galligan, Dir.
Reparation Society of the Immaculate Heart of Mary, 3601 Greenway, Apt. 704, 21218-2450. Rev. Casimir M. Peterson, S.T.L., J.C.D., Dir.
St. Agnes Clinical Practice Group, Inc. (inactive at this time), 900 S. Caton Ave., 21229. Tel: 410-368-6000. Robert E. Pezzoli, Pres.
St. Frances Educational Center, 501 E. Chase St., 21202. Tel: 410-685-2650. Sr. Barbara Spears, O.S.P., Dir.
St. Thomas More Society of Maryland. The local branch of the National Society of Catholic Lawyers. 320 Cathedral St., 21201. Tel: 410-426-3000. Anthony R. Mignini, Esq., Pres.
St. Veronica's Headstart Center, 2920 Joseph Ave., 21225. Tel: 410-354-0220. Sr. Loretta Rosendale, S.S.N.D., Dir. Children (3-4) 358.
SS. Matthew and Thomas More Religious Education and Youth Ministry Center, Inc., 6806 McClean Blvd., 21234. Tel: 410-444-4563.
Serra Club, 320 Cathedral St., 21201. Tel: 410-547-5426. Rev. James Barker, Chap.
Trinitarian Counseling Services, Inc., 8400 Park Heights Ave., P.O. Box 5719, 21282. Tel: 410-476-5764. Rev. Thomas J. Burke, O.SS.T., Dir. Total Assisted 238; Total Staff 2.
Veteran Mission Crusade, Archdiocesan, 320 Cathedral St., 21201.
Vietnamese Catholic Community at Baltimore (VC-CAB), 8515 Philadelphia Rd., 21237. Tel: 410-780-3149. Rev. John the Baptist Thong, Chap.
Woodlawn Catholic Faith Center, Inc., 5801 Security Blvd., 21207. Tel: 410-298-8956. Ennio Mastroianni, Dir. Provide total religious education programs for St. Lawrence and Our Lady of Perpetual Help parishes in Woodlawn, MD.

CUMBERLAND. *Catholic Education Ministries of Western Maryland.* Bishop Walsh Middle/High School, 700 Bishop Walsh Rd., 21502. Tel: 301-777-9082; Fax: 301-722-6114. Margaret Meyers, Area Coord.
Neumann Early Childhood Center, Inc., 209 N. Centre St., 21502. Tel: 301-777-1166. Mrs. G. Louise Elliott, Dir. Total Assisted 126; Total Staff 12.

DUNKIRK. *Family of the Americas Foundation, Inc.*, P.O. Box 1170, 20754-1170. Tel: 301-627-3346; 800-443-3395; Fax: 301-627-0847.
E-mail: FAF@idsonline.com

ELLICOTT CITY. *Conventual Franciscan Friars, St. Anthony of Padua Province,* 12300 Folly Quarter Rd., 21042. Tel: 410-531-9200; Fax: 410-531-4881. Legal Title: *Order of Friars Minor Conventual, St. Anthony of Padua Province, U.S.A., Inc.; Franciscan Minor Conventuals of Maryland, Inc. of Ellicott City, MD.; The Franciscan Fathers, Minor Conventuals, of St. Stanislaus Church of Baltimore City, Inc.; Franciscan Friars, St. Anthony of Padua Province, Education Fund, Inc.; Franciscan Friars, St. Anthony of Padua Province, Fund for the Aged and Infirm Friars, Inc.; St. Francis of Assisi Community, Inc., Companions of St. Anthony; St. Stanislaus Cemetery, Inc.* Total in Residence 195.

EMMITSBURG. *National Shrine of St. Elizabeth Ann Seton,* 333 S. Seton Ave., 21727. Tel: 301-447-6606. Sr. Cecilia Rose, D.C., Admin.
Seton Center, Inc., 16840 S. Seton Ave., 21727. Tel: 301-447-6102. Social Service; Day Care; Outreach; Thrift Shop. Daughters of Charity. Sr. Mary Beard, D.C., Admin. Total Assisted 16,941; Total Staff 34.

LANSDOWNE.
**Coursey Station Apartments, Inc.*, 200 First Ave., 21227. Tel: 410-242-6167. Carolyn Peoples, Dir. Operations.

MARRIOTTSVILLE. *Bon Secours Health System, Inc.*, 1505 Marriottsville Rd., 21104. Tel: 410-442-5511. Sr. Anne M. Lutz, C.B.S., Vice Pres., Mission; John Fitzgerald, CEO and Pres.

PASADENA. *Mary's Center,* P.O. Box 1804, 21123-1804.

Tel: 410-761-8082. Pregnancy Support Services. Anne Fitzsimmons, Dir. Total Assisted 707; Total Staff 25.

PIKESVILLE. *St. Charles House, Inc.*, 11 Church Ln., 21208. Tel: 410-484-6125. Carolyn Peoples, Dir.

SILVER SPRING. *Christian Life Community Regional Information Center*, 201 E. Wayne Ave., 20901. Tel: 301-495-2969; Fax: 301-495-7318. Mr. Fred C. Leone, Reg. Rep.

UPPER MARLBORO. *Knights of Columbus*, 9305 Southmoor Ct., 20772. Tel: 301-856-2158. Rev. James A. Finan, State Chap.; John J. Glynn, State Deputy.

WESTMINSTER. *Dominican Pastoral Counseling Center*, 187 E. Main St., 21157. Tel: 410-876-8315. Sr. Dolores A. Pfeiffer, O.P., M.A., M.S., Dir. Total Assisted 330 (Counseling Hrs.); Total Staff 1.

RELIGIOUS INSTITUTES OF MEN REPRESENTED IN THE ARCHDIOCESE

For further details refer to the corresponding bracketed number in the Religious Institutes of Men or Women Section.

[0200]—*Benedictine Monks (Latrobe, PA)*.—O.S.B.

[1350]—*Brothers of St. Francis Xavier*.—C.F.X.

[0330]—*Brothers of the Christian Schools*. (Baltimore Prov.).—F.S.C.

[0470]—*The Capuchin Friars*. (Prov. of St. Augustine).—O.F.M.Cap.

[1330]—*Congregation of the Mission*. (Eastern Prov.).—C.M.

[1000]—*Congregation of the Passion*. (Prov. of St. Paul of the Cross).—C.P.

[0480]—*Conventual Franciscans*. (Buffalo, NY).—O.F.M.Conv.

[0690]—*Jesuit Fathers and Brothers*. (Maryland Prov.).—S.J.

[0430]—*Order of Preachers-Dominicans*.—O.P.

[1310]—*Order of the Most Holy Trinity, Immaculate Heart of Mary Province*.—O.SS.T.

[1030]—*Paulist Fathers*.—C.S.P.

[1070]—*Redemptorist Fathers*. (Baltimore Prov.).—C.SS.R.

[0700]—*St. Joseph's Society of the Sacred Heart*.—S.S.J.

[1260]—*Society of Christ*.—S.Ch.

[0760]—*Society of Mary*.—S.M.

[0990]—*Society of the Catholic Apostolate*. (Immaculate Conception Prov.).—S.A.C.

[1200]—*Society of the Divine Saviour*.—S.D.S.

RELIGIOUS INSTITUTES OF WOMEN REPRESENTED IN THE ARCHDIOCESE

[0230]—*Benedictine Sisters of Pontifical Jurisdiction*. (Baltimore).—O.S.B.

[0270]—*Congregation of Bon Secours*.—C.B.S.

[1920]—*Congregation of the Sisters of the Holy Cross*.—C.S.C.

[0760]—*Daughters of Charity of St. Vincent de Paul*.—D.C.

[0960]—*Daughters of Wisdom*.—D.W.

[0420]—*Discalced Carmelite Nuns*.—O.C.D.

[1070-03]—*Dominican Sisters*.—O.P.

[1070-07]—*Dominican Sisters*.—O.P.

[1070-13]—*Dominican Sisters*.—O.P.

[1170]—*Felician Sisters*.—C.S.S.F.

[1330]—*Franciscan Missionary Sisters of Assisi*.—F.M.S.A.

[1200]—*Franciscan Sisters of Baltimore*.—O.S.F.

[1470]—*Franciscan Sisters of St. Joseph*.—F.S.S.J.

[2575]—*Institute of the Sisters of the Mercy of the Americas*.—R.S.M.

[2330]—*Little Sisters of Jesus*.

[2340]—*Little Sisters of the Poor*.—L.S.P.

[2720]—*Mission Helpers of the Sacred Heart*.—M.H.S.H.

[3040]—*Oblate Sisters of Providence*.—O.S.P.

[2070]—*Religious of the Holy Union of the Sacred Hearts*.—S.U.S.C.

[3430]—*Religious Teachers Filippini*.—M.P.F.

[2970]—*School Sisters of Notre Dame*.—S.S.N.D.

[0570]—*Sisters of Charity of Seton Hill, Greensburg, Pennsylvania*.—S.C.

[0990]—*Sisters of Divine Providence*.—C.D.P.

[3000]—*Sisters of Notre Dame de Namur*.—S.N.D.deN.

[3360]—*Sisters of Providence of Saint Mary-of-the-Woods, Indiana*.—S.P.

[3740]—*Sisters of St. Casimir*. (Chicago, IL).—S.S.C.

[1650]—*Sisters of St. Francis of Philadelphia*.—O.S.F.

[3830]—*Sisters of St. Joseph*.—C.S.J.

[1030]—*Sisters of the Divine Savior*.—S.D.S.

[1830]—*Sisters of the Good Shepherd*. (Washington Prov.).—R.G.S.

[1970]—*Sisters of the Holy Family of Nazareth*.—C.S.F.N.

[3610]—*Sisters Servants of Mary Immaculate*.—S.S.M.I.

[2150]—*Sisters, Servants of the Immaculate Heart of Mary*.—I.H.M.

[2160]—*Sisters, Servants of the Immaculate Heart of Mary*.—I.H.M.

[4120]—*Ursuline Nuns, of the Congregation of Paris*.—O.S.U.

[4190]—*Visitation Nuns*.—V.H.M.

ARCHDIOCESAN CEMETERIES

BALTIMORE. *New Cathedral*.

NECROLOGY

† Dohony, Rev. Msgr. Nicholas, (Retired). —Died May 25, 1996.

† Dorsch, Rev. Msgr. David, (Retired). —Died July 2, 1996.

† Duggan, Rev. Msgr. John J., (Retired). —Died March 28, 1996.

† Hlavac, Wencelaus M., (Retired). —Died April 30, 1996.

† Mackey, John J., (Retired). —Died July 6, 1996.

† Mullen, Rev. Msgr. Timothy M., (Retired). —Died March 11, 1996.

† Mylin, Edwin B., (Retired). —Died Dec. 31, 1995.

Diocese of Baton Rouge

(Dioecesis Rubribaculensis)

Most Reverend

ALFRED C. HUGHES, S.T.D.

Bishop of Baton Rouge; ordained December 15, 1957; appointed Auxiliary Bishop of Boston and Titular Bishop of Massimiana in Bizacena July 21, 1981; ordained Bishop September 14, 1981; promoted to Baton Rouge September 7, 1993; installed Fourth Bishop of Baton Rouge November 4, 1993. *Res., P.O. Box 2028, Baton Rouge, LA, 70821-2028.* Tel.: 504-387-0561; Fax: 504-336-8789.

ESTABLISHED JULY 20, 1961.

Square Miles 5,513.

Comprises the civil parishes (counties) of Ascension, Assumption, East Baton Rouge, West Baton Rouge, Iberville, Pointe Coupee, East Feliciana, West Feliciana, St. Helena, Tangipahoa, Livingston and St. James in the State of Louisiana.

For legal titles of parishes and diocesan institutions, consult the Chancery Office.

Chancery Office: Catholic Life Center, 1800 S. Acadian Thruway, P.O. Box 2028, Baton Rouge, LA, 70821-2028. Tel.: 504-387-0561; Fax: 504-336-8789.

Web site address: http://www.diobr.org

E-mail address: 104072.1446@compuserve.com

STATISTICAL OVERVIEW

Personnel	
Retired Archbishops	1
Priests: Diocesan Active in Diocese	68
Priests: Active Outside Diocese	4
Priests: Retired, Sick or Absent	21
Number of Diocesan Priests	93
Religious Priests in Diocese	47
Extern Priests in Diocese	8
Ordinations:	
Religious Priests	1
Permanent Deacons	2
Permanent Deacons in Diocese	27
Total Brothers	15
Total Sisters	120
Parishes	
Parishes	70
With Resident Pastor:	
Resident Diocesan Priests	52
Resident Religious Priests	14
Without Resident Pastor:	
Administered by Priests	3
Administered by Lay People	1
Professional Ministry Personnel:	
Brothers	2
Sisters	18
Lay Ministers	65
Welfare	
Catholic Hospitals	1
Total Assisted	230,000
Homes for the Aged	5
Total Assisted	657
Specialized Homes	4
Total Assisted	152
Special Centers for Social Services	6
Total Assisted	104,733
Educational	
Diocesan Students in Other Seminaries	7
Total Seminarians	7
Colleges and Universities	1
Total Students	869
High Schools, Diocesan and Parish	6
Total Students	2,482
High Schools, Private	2
Total Students	1,532
Elementary Schools, Diocesan and Parish	26
Total Students	12,562
Catechesis/Religious Education:	
High School Students	11,260
Elementary Students	5,101
Total Students Under Catholic Instruction	33,813
Teachers in the Diocese:	
Priests	1
Brothers	4
Sisters	22
Lay Teachers	874
Vital Statistics	
Receptions into the Church:	
Infant Baptism Totals	2,985
Adult Baptism Totals	264
Received into Full Communion	406
First Communions	2,849
Confirmations	2,506
Marriages:	
Catholic	799
Interfaith	393
Total Marriages	1,192
Deaths	1,750
Total Catholic Population	218,576
Total Population	798,343

Former Bishops—Most Rev. ROBERT E. TRACY, D.D., appt. Titular Bishop of Sergentza and Auxiliary of Lafayette March 18, 1959; cons. May 19, 1959; appt. first Bishop of Baton Rouge Aug. 10, 1961; retired March 21, 1974; died April 4, 1980.—Most Rev. JOSEPH V. SULLIVAN, S.T.D., appt. Titular Bishop of Tagamuta and Auxiliary to the Bishop of Kansas City-St. Joseph March 3, 1967; cons. April 3, 1967; appt. Second Bishop of Baton Rouge August 5, 1974; died September 4, 1982.—Most Rev. STANLEY JOSEPH OTT, S.T.D., appt. Titular Bishop of Nicives and Auxiliary Bishop of New Orleans May 24, 1976; cons. June 29, 1976; appt. Third Bishop of Baton Rouge January 18, 1983; died November 28, 1992.

Vicar General & Moderator of the Curia—Very Rev. JOHN CARVILLE, S.T.D., V.G.

Chancery Office—Catholic Life Center, 1800 S. Acadian Thruway, P.O. Box 2028, Baton Rouge, 70821-2028. Tel: 504-387-0561; Fax: 504-336-8789. Office Hours: Mon.-Fri. 8:30-4:30.

Chancellor—Rev. Msgr. ROBERT H. BERGGREEN.

Vice-Chancellors—Very Rev. PAUL D. COUNCE, J.C.L., M.C.L.; Rev. MARTIN A. HERNANDEZ, J.C.L., M.C.L.

Diocesan Tribunal—Catholic Life Center, 1800 S. Acadian Thruway, P.O. Box 1087, Baton Rouge, 70821-1087. Tel: 504-387-0561; Fax: 504-336-8789.

Judicial Vicar—Very Rev. PAUL D. COUNCE, J.C.L., M.C.L.

Promotor of Justice—Rev. VINCENT J. DUFRESNE, S.T.L., J.C.L.

Judges—Rev. Msgr. WILLIAM L. GREENE; Rev. Msgr. GERALD M. LEFEBVRE, V.F.; Rev. MARTIN A. HERNANDEZ, J.C.L., M.C.L.; Very Revs. FRANK M. UTER, V.F.; MICHAEL J. MORONEY, V.F.; Revs. M. JEFFREY BAYHI; DEAN J. MARTIN, J.C.L.

Defenders of the Bond—Revs. DAVID A. VAVASSEUR; THOMAS P. DUHE; MARK A. ALISE, S.T.L.; VINCENT J. DUFRESNE, S.T.L., J.C.L.; THAN N. VU, S.T.L.; SHELTON J. FABRE; J. MARK MAGGIO; GERARD R. MARTIN.

Notaries—Mrs. JO ZGANJAR; PATRICIA F. SONIAT.

Diocesan Pro-Vicar—

Pro-Vicar for Women Religious—Sr. DIANNE HEINRICH, C.D.P.

College of Consultors—Very Rev. JOHN CARVILLE, S.T.D., V.G.; Rev. Msgr. ROBERT H. BERGGREEN; Very Rev. MICHAEL J. MORONEY, V.F.; Rev. GERARD F. YOUNG; Very Rev. HENRY C. VAVASSEUR; Rev. WILLIAM L. NORVEL, S.S.J.

Diocesan Corporation (The Roman Catholic Church of the Diocese of Baton Rouge)—Most Rev. ALFRED C. HUGHES, S.T.D.; Very Rev. JOHN CARVILLE, S.T.D., V.G., Vice Pres.; Rev. Msgr. ROBERT H. BERGGREEN, Sec.; Mr. J. ERROL GAUTREAU, Treas.

Diocesan Offices and Directors

Apostleship of Prayer—Rev. Msgr. JOHN A. WEBER, *5445 Government St., #105, Baton Rouge, 70806-6003.* Tel: 504-925-9431; Fax: 504-928-3284.

Apostolate to the Deaf—WILLIAM G. DUGAS, Dir., *2585 Brightside Ln., Baton Rouge, 70820-3504.* Tel: 504-766-9320; 769-0223; Fax: 504-766-9320.

Archives—Mrs. UNA DAIGRE, Archivist, *P.O. Box 2028, Baton Rouge, 70821-2028.* Tel: 504-387-0561.

Black Catholics—Rev. SHELTON J. FABRE, *412 North St., Baton Rouge, 70802-5496.* Tel: 504-387-5928; Fax: 504-387-5929.

Campus Ministry—Rev. PATRICK J. MASCARELLA, *P.O. Box 25131, Baton Rouge, 70894-5131.* Tel: 504-383-1574; Fax: 504-344-1920.

Catholic Charismatic Renewal Office—Rev. HENRY W. GAUTREAU, *2121 N. Sherwood Forest Dr., Baton Rouge, 70815-1998.* Tel: 504-275-7280; Fax: 504-275-5845.

Catholic Community Services—DEBORAH A. ROE, M.S.W., Exec. Dir., Office: *1800 S. Acadian Thruway, P.O. Box 1668, Baton Rouge, 70821-1668.* Tel: 504-336-8770; Fax: 504-336-8745.

Catholic Social Services Dept.—JANICE SAPP, M.S.W., *4884 Constitution Ave., Suite 1-B, Baton Rouge, 70808-3326.* Tel: 504-927-4930; Fax: 504-927-9246.

Social Responsibility Dept.—DONNA BROUSSARD SEGURA.

Family Life Dept.—Dr. TOM C. ABEL, Dir., Office: *Catholic Life Center, 1800 S. Acadian Thruway, P.O. Box 1668, Baton Rouge, 70821-1668.* Tel: 504-336-8770; 387-0561; Fax: 504-336-8745.

Cemeteries—Very Rev. FRANK M. UTER, V.F., *412 North St., Baton Rouge, 70802-5496.* Tel: 504-387-5928; Fax: 504-387-5929.

Ecumenical Affairs—Very Rev. MICHAEL J. MORONEY, V.F., *445 Marquette Ave., Baton Rouge, 70806-4497.*

Tel: 504-926-1883; Fax: 504-923-0448.

Communications—Deacon ROBERT FURLOW, *P.O. Box 2028, Baton Rouge, 70821-2028.* Tel: 504-387-0561; 383-0880; Fax: 504-383-0924.

Continuing Formation for the Clergy—Rev. PATRICK J. MASCARELLA, Dir., *P.O. Box 25131, Baton Rouge, 70894-5131.* Tel: 504-383-1574; Fax: 504-344-1920.

Development—MARK BLANCHARD, Dir., *P.O. Box 2028, Baton Rouge, 70821-2028.* Tel: 504-336-8790; Fax: 504-336-8710.

Evangelization—Rev. Msgr. WILLIAM L. GREENE, Dir., *P.O. Box 2028, Baton Rouge, 70821-2028.* Tel: 504-387-0561; Fax: 504-336-8710.

Finance—Mr. J. ERROL GAUTREAU, Sec. for Finance & Fiscal Officer, *P.O. Box 2028, Baton Rouge, 70821-2028.* Tel: 504-387-0561; Fax: 504-336-8789.

Christian Formation—BETTY BOURGEOIS, *P.O. Box 2028, Baton Rouge, 70821-2028.* Tel: 504-336-8760; Fax: 504-336-8765.

Hispanic Apostolate—Rev. GILBERT WALKER, C.M., Dir., *2585 Brightside Ln., Baton Rouge, 70820-3504.* Tel: 504-766-9320; Fax: 504-766-8973.

Newspaper "The Catholic Commentator"—LAURA G. DEAVERS, Exec. Editor and Gen. Mgr., Office: *Catholic Life Center, 1800 S. Acadian Thruway, Baton Rouge, 70821-1668., Mailing Address: P.O. Drawer 14746, Baton Rouge, 70898-4746.* Tel: 504-387-0983; Fax: 504-336-8710.

Pastoral Planning—Rev. PATRICK J. MASCARELLA, Dir., *P.O. Box 25131, Baton Rouge, 70894-5131.* Tel: 504-383-1574; Fax: 504-344-1920.

Permanent Diaconate Office—Rev. Dr. WARREN D. FORTENBERRY, Dir., *P.O. Box 411, Holden, 70744-0411.* Tel: 504-567-3271; Fax: 504-567-2031.

Presbyteral Council—Rev. MARK A. ALISE, S.T.L.; Rev. Msgr. ROBERT H. BERGGREEN; Rev. JULES A. BRUNET; Very Rev. JOHN CARVILLE, S.T.D., V.G.; Revs. DEAN J. MARTIN, J.C.L.; ROBERT F. STINE; Very Rev. PAUL D. COUNCE, J.C.L.; Rev. ERIC V. GYAN; Very Rev. MICHAEL J. MORONEY, V.F.; Revs. HUNG V. NGUYEN; WILLIAM L. NORVEL, S.S.J.; N. JOHN NUTTER; MANSUETO P. PALANG, S.V.D.; ROBERT U. PERRY, O.P.; MARIANO J. RIZZUTO, S.M.; Very Rev. HENRY C. VAVASSEUR; Revs. GILBERT WALKER, C.M.; GERARD F. YOUNG.

Propagation of the Faith and Association of Holy Childhood—Rev. N. JOHN NUTTER, Dir., *P.O. Box 2028, Baton Rouge, 70821-2028.* Tel: 504-387-0561; Fax: 504-336-8789.

Religious Education—Vacant, *Catholic Life Center, P.O. Box 2028, Baton Rouge, 70821-2028.* Tel: 504-336-8730; Fax: 504-336-8731.

Catholic Schools—Sr. MARY MICHAELINE GREEN, O.P., Supt. Asst. Supts.: Dr. JUDY H. ARMSTRONG, Ph.D.; Mrs. THAIS T. JOHNSON, *Catholic Life Center, P.O. Box 2028, Baton Rouge, 70821-2028.* Tel: 504-336-8735; Fax: 504-336-8711.

Scouting—Rev. DUANE L. BREAUX, Chm., *P.O. Box 190, Pierre Part, 70339-0190.* Tel: 504-252-6008; Fax: 504-252-8011.

Separated and Divorced—Rev. FRED YOUNGS, Dir., *5657 Thomas Rd., Baton Rouge, 70811-7356.* Tel: 504-775-8850; Fax: 504-775-7072.

Sierra Clubs—Very Rev. FRANK M. UTER, V.F., Spiritual Advisor, *412 North St., Baton Rouge, 70802-5496.* Tel: 504-387-5928; Fax: 504-387-5929. Rev. CAYE A. NELSON, *7853 Broker Ave., Baton Rouge, 70817-6002.* Tel: 504-752-6230; Fax: 504-756-5014.

Vietnamese Apostolate—Rev. HUNG VIET NGUYEN, Dir., *2580 Tecumseh St., Baton Rouge, 70805-7999.* Tel: 504-357-4787; Fax: 504-355-9794.

Vocations—Rev. M. JEFFREY BAYHI, Dir.; Sr. DIANNE HEINRICH, C.D.P., Assoc. Dir., *P.O. Box 2028, Baton Rouge, 70821-2028.* Tel: 504-387-0561; Fax: 504-336-8731.

Women, Council of Catholic—Rev. MARK A. ALISE, S.T.L., *348 W. Main St., New Roads, 70760-3587.* Tel: 504-638-9665; Fax: 504-638-6346.

Worship, Office of—Rev. THOMAS C. RANZINO, Dir., *P.O. Box 2028, Baton Rouge, 70821-2028.* Tel: 504-387-0561; Fax: 504-336-8789.

Youth Ministry—CHARLES JUMONVILLE, Dir., *P.O. Box 2028, Baton Rouge, 70821-2028.* Tel: 504-336-8751; Fax: 504-336-8765.

CLERGY, PARISHES, MISSIONS AND PAROCHIAL SCHOOLS

CITY OF BATON ROUGE
(East Baton Rouge Parish)

1—ST. JOSEPH CATHEDRAL (1792), Very Rev. Frank M. Uter, V.F.; Deacons Robert Furlow; James Wax.
Res., 412 North St., 70802-5496. Tel: 504-387-5928; Fax: 504-387-5929.

2—ST. AGNES (1917), Rev. Msgr. Robert H. Berggreen. In res., Rev. M. Jeffrey Bayhi.
Res., 749 East Blvd., 70802-6398. Tel: 504-383-4127; Fax: 504-383-4154.

3—ST. ALOYSIUS (1955), Revs. Hubert J. Brou; Gregory J. Daigle.
Mailing Address: 2025 Stuart Ave., 70808-3998. Tel: 504-343-6657; Fax: 504-344-6847.
School—Tel: 504-383-3871; Fax: 504-383-4500. Mr. John L. Bennett, Prin.
Daughters of Jesus 3; Lay Teachers 45; Students 866.

4—ST. ANTHONY OF PADUA (1920), Rev. Hung Viet Nguyen, I.C.M., (Vietnam) Admin. In res., Rev. Dominic Chinh Pham, I.C.M. (Vietnam).
Res., 2580 Tecumseh St., 70805-7999. Tel: 504-357-4800; Fax: 504-355-9794.

5—ST. CHARLES BORROMEO (1964), Rev. Chris M. Haydel; Deacon Brent Duplessis.
Res., 3852 E. Brookstown Dr., 70805-4791. Tel: 504-356-2527; Fax: 504-356-2528.

6—CHRIST THE KING (1980), Revs. Patrick J. Mascarella; Garland T. Belsome.
Mailing Address: P.O. Box 25131, 70894-5131.
Res., Highland Rd. & Dalrymple Dr., 70894. Tel: 504-344-8595; 383-1574; Fax: 504-344-1920.

7—ST. FRANCIS DE SALES PARISH (1979). (Center for Hearing Impaired). Mr. William G. Dugas, Exec. Dir.; Rev. Paul Cabrita, S.M., Chap.
Res., 2585 Brightside Dr., 70820-3504. Tel: 504-766-9320; 769-0223 (Voice/TDD); Fax: 504-766-9320.

8—ST. FRANCIS XAVIER (1918), Revs. Michael Sarah-Buckman, S.S.J.; Francis J. Schroeder, S.S.J.
Res., 1143 11th St., 70802-4997. Tel: 504-383-3479; Fax: 504-343-4259.
School—(Grades PreK-8). Tel: 504-387-6639. Mrs. Lorina Turner, Prin.
Sisters of the Holy Family 2; Lay Teachers 14; Students 302.

9—ST. GEORGE (1908), Revs. Thomas C. Ranzino; Rubin R. Paliathayil; Deacons Albert Ellis; Guy E. Decker.
Office: 7808 St. George Dr., 70809-4699. Tel: 504-293-2212; Fax: 504-291-8063. [CEM]
School—7880 St. George Dr., 70809-4699. Tel: 504-293-1298. Mrs. Ann Bertsch, Prin.
Lay Teachers 35; Students 801.

10—ST. GERARD MAJELLA (1944), Rev. Timothy Kerner, C.SS.R. In res., Rev. Henry F. Porten, C.SS.R.
Res., 3808 Gerard St., 70805-2834. Tel: 504-355-2553; Fax: 504-356-7472.
School—3655 St. Gerard Ave., 70805-2898. Tel: 504-355-1437. Mr. Lee Faucette, Prin.
Lay Teachers 20; Students 287.

11—IMMACULATE CONCEPTION (1958), Rev. Hilton L. Rivet, S.J. In res., Rev. Francis R. Brou, S.J.
Res., 1565 Curtis St., P.O. Box 74273, 70874-4273. Tel: 504-775-7067.

12—ST. JEAN VIANNEY (1975), Revs. Donald V. Blanchard; Keun-Soo Lee, Ph.D.; Deacon Thomas M. Robinson.
Res., 16166 S. Harrell's Ferry Rd., 70816-3199. Tel: 504-753-7950; Fax: 504-753-7965.
School—(Grades K-8) 16266 S. Harrell's Ferry Rd., 70816. Tel: 504-751-1831; Fax: 504-752-8774. Mr. Mike Lucia, Prin.
Lay Teachers 23; Students 454.
Preschool—Tel: 504-752-5356. Ms. Kathy Simoneaux, Dir.
Lay Teachers 17; Students 131.

13—ST. JUDE THE APOSTLE (1966), Revs. Michael J. Collins; Myles J. Kearney.
Res., 9150 Highland Rd., 70810-4096. Tel: 504-766-2431; Fax: 504-766-0722.
School—(Grades PreK-8). Tel: 504-769-2344; Fax: 504-769-3290. Mrs. Joy Wagener, Prin.
Lay Teachers 31; Students 663.

14—ST. LOUIS, KING OF FRANCE (1966), Revs. Maynard E. Hurst; Henry W. Gautreau.
Res., 2121 N. Sherwood Forest Dr., 70815-1998. Tel: 504-275-7280; Fax: 504-275-5845.
School—(Grades K-8) 2311 N. Sherwood Forest Dr., 70815-1997. Tel: 504-273-3932; Fax: 504-273-3978. Mrs. Karen Weilbacher, Prin.
Lay Teachers 32; Students 505.
Early Learning Center—Tel: 504-272-6438; Fax: 504-275-5845. Diane Blouin, Dir.
Lay Teachers 9; Students 100.

15—MOST BLESSED SACRAMENT (1979), Revs. Gerard F. Young; Caye A. Nelson.
Res., 7853 Broker Ave., 70817-6002. Tel: 504-752-6230; Fax: 504-756-5014.
School—(Grades K-8). Tel: 504-751-0273.
Lay Teachers 26; Students 560.

16—OUR LADY OF MERCY (1947), Very Rev. Michael J. Moroney, V.F.; Revs. Edgar J. Tiblier, S.J.; Victor G. Messina; Deacon Eugene Allen.
Office: 445 Marquette Ave., 70806-4497. Tel: 504-926-1883; Fax: 504-923-0448.
Res., 450 Marquette Ave., 70806-4497. Tel: 504-927-7106.
School—400 Marquette Ave., 70806-4498. Tel: 504-924-1054; Fax: 504-923-2201. Mrs. Carolyn Guidry, Prin.
Lay Teachers 38; Students 798.

17—ST. PATRICK (1974), Rev. Than N. Vu, S.T.L.; Deacon J. Peter Walsh.
Res., 12424 Brogdon Ln., 70816-4801. Tel: 504-753-5750; Fax: 504-756-9636.

18—ST. PAUL THE APOSTLE (1960), Rev. Joseph I. Guidry, S.V.D.
Res., 3912 Gus Young Ave., 70802-1727. Tel: 504-383-2537.

19—ST. PIUS X (1963), Rev. Jon C. Koehler.
Res., 6380 Hooper Rd., 70811-2499. Tel: 504-357-5935; Fax: 504-357-6005.

20—SACRED HEART OF JESUS (1928), Rev. Kenneth A. Smith. In res., Rev. Msgr. Donald J. Songy; Rev. Francis V. Ferrier, S.J.
Res., 2250 Main St., 70802-3198. Tel: 504-387-6671; Fax: 504-387-6672.
School—Tel: 504-383-7481; Fax: 504-383-1810. Sr. Patricia Sullivan, C.S.J., Prin.
Sisters of St. Joseph 1; Lay Teachers 31; Students 468.

21—ST. THOMAS MORE (1959), Very Rev. John Carville, S.T.D., V.G.; Rev. Gerard R. Martin. Pastoral Assocs: Sr. Jane Louise Arbour, C.S.J.; Sr. Dianne Heinrich, C.D.P.; Deacon Clayton Hollier.
Office: 11441 Goodwood Blvd., 70815-6299. Tel: 504-275-3940; Fax: 504-275-1407.
School—Tel: 504-275-2820; Fax: 504-275-0376. Sr. Mila Sones, C.S.J., Prin.
Sisters of St. Joseph of Medaille 1; Lay Teachers 50; Students 1,047.
Preschool—Tel: 504-272-3477; Fax: 504-272-0468. Ms. Angie Ducote, Dir.
Lay Teachers 15; Students 134.

OUTSIDE THE CITY OF BATON ROUGE

Albany, Livingston Parish, St. Margaret Queen of Scotland (1910), Rev. Msgr. Leo Guillot; Deacon Warren Fortenberry.
Res., P.O. Box 100, 70711-0100. Tel: 504-567-3573; Fax: 504-567-2031. [CEM]

Amite, Tangipahoa Parish, St. Helena (1868), Rev. N. John Nutter.
Res., P.O. Box 685, 70422-0685. Tel: 504-748-9057; Fax: 504-748-9094.

Baker, East Baton Rouge Parish, St. Isidore the Farmer (1958), Rev. Fred Youngs; Deacon Bruno Rizzo. In res., Rev. David A. Vavasseur.
Res., 5657 Thomas Rd., Baton Rouge, 70811-7356. Tel: 504-775-8850 (Office); Fax: 504-775-7072.
School—Tel: 504-775-3336; Fax: 504-775-3351.
Lay Teachers 23; Students 468.

Bayou Pigeon, Iberville Parish, St. Joan of Arc (1965), Rev. Joseph M. Camilleri.
Res., 39315 Hwy. 75, Plaquemine, 70764-9629. Tel: 504-545-8213; Fax: 504-545-2456.

Belle Rose, Assumption Parish, St. Jules (1912), Rev. Mansueto P. Palang.
Res., P.O. Box 38, 70341-0038. Tel: 504-473-8569; Fax: 504-473-2950. [CEM 2]

Brusly, West Baton Rouge Parish, St. John the Baptist (1835), Rev. Eric V. Gyan.
Res., P.O. Box 248, 70719-0248. Tel: 504-749-2189; 687-8363; Fax: 504-749-1921.

Convent, St. James Parish, St. Michael the Archangel (1812), Rev. Mariano J. Rizzuto, S.M.; Deacon Alfred Adams, Sr. In res., Rev. Albert Hebert, S.M.
Res., P.O. Box 65, 70723-0065. Tel: 504-562-3211; Fax: 504-562-3211. [CEM]

Darrow, Ascension Parish, St. Anthony of Padua (1962), Very Rev. James Martone, V.F.
Res., P.O. Box 151, 70725-0151. Tel: 504-473-9327; Fax: 504-473-0927.

Denham Springs, Livingston Parish, Immaculate Conception (1960), Revs. Cleo J. Milano, S.T.L.; David R. Johnson (PIT).
Mailing Address: P.O. Box 1609, 70727-1609.
Res., 865 Hatchell Ln., 70726. Tel: 504-665-5359; Fax: 504-665-4422.

Donaldsonville, Ascension Parish, Ascension of Our Lord Jesus Christ (1772), Rev. Randy M. Cuevas, S.T.L. In res., Rev. Joseph Goss, O.P.
Res., P.O. Box 508, 70346-0508. Tel: 504-473-3176; Fax: 504-473-3256. [CEM]

St. Catherine of Siena (1924), Rev. Walter A. Cerbin, S.S.J. In res., Rev. Martin F. Kenney, S.S.J.
Res., P.O. Box 428, 70346-0428. Tel: 504-473-8350; Fax: 504-473-9978.

St. Francis of Assisi (1884), Rev. Michael A. Galea.
Res., 818 W. Tenth St., 70346-9191. Tel: 504-473-8302; Fax: 504-474-0348. [CEM]

French Settlement, Livingston Parish, St. Joseph

(1849), Rev. James A. Kinkead; Deacon James A. Little.
Res., 15710 Louisiana Hwy. 16, 70733-9802. Tel: 504-698-3110. [CEM]

Gonzales, Ascension Parish, St. Theresa of Avila (1918), Revs. Philip F. Spano; Joseph Thai-Doan Nguyen.
Res., 1022 N. Burnside Ave., 70737-2551. Tel: 504-647-6588; Fax: 504-647-2223.
School—212 E. New River St., 70737-2499. Tel: 504-647-2803; Fax: 504-647-7814. Mr. Jay L. Sullivan, Prin.
Sisters 4; Lay Teachers 26; Students 603.
St. Mark (1973), Rev. Herculan F.X. DeMaria, O.F.M.Cap.
Res., 42021 Hwy. 621, 70737-9354. Tel: 504-647-8461; Fax: 504-647-5125.

Gramercy, St. James Parish, Most Sacred Heart of Jesus (1961), Rev. Edward F. Fuss, S.M. In res., Rev. Paul Cabrita, S.M.
Res., P.O. Box 1501, 70052-1501. Tel: 504-869-5324; Fax: 504-869-5325.

Greenwell Springs, East Baton Rouge Parish, St. Alphonsus Liguori (1962), Revs. Thomas P. Duhe; Stephen J. Hymel; Deacon J. Phillip BeJeaux.
Res., 14040 Greenwell Springs Rd., 70739-9182. Tel: 504-261-4650; Fax: 504-261-5650.
School—Tel: 504-261-5299; Fax: 504-262-1139. Sr. Mary Esther Hulin, C.S.J., Prin.
Lay Teachers 33; Students 683.

Grosse Tete, Iberville Parish, St. Joseph (1904), Rev. Shelton J. Fabre.
Res., P.O. Box 8, 70740-0008. Tel: 504-648-2420; Fax: 504-648-2506.

Hammond, Tangipahoa Parish, Holy Ghost (1902), Revs. Robert U. Perry, O.P.; Justin R. Kauchak, O.P.; Deacon Wallace Gainey, Jr.
Res., P.O. Box 1797, 70404-1797. Tel: 504-345-3360; Fax: 504-542-4191.
School—506 N. Magnolia St., 70401-2598. Tel: 504-345-0977. Mrs. Peggy Sharkey, Prin.
Lay Teachers 36; Students 713.

Independence, Tangipahoa Parish, Mater Dolorosa (1908), Rev. Dean J. Martin, J.C.L.; Deacon Bennett Flattman.
Res., P.O. Box 349, 70443-0349. Tel: 504-878-9639; Fax: 504-878-6260.
School—P.O. Box 380, 70443-0380. Tel: 504-878-4295; Fax: 504-878-4888. Ms. Joyce Nixon, Prin.
Lay Teachers 14; Students 211.

Labadieville, Assumption Parish, St. Philomena (1847), Rev. Vincent J. Dufresne, S.T.L., J.C.L.
Res., P.O. Box 11, 70372-0011. Tel: 504-526-4247; Fax: 504-526-4128. [CEM]
School—120 Convent St., 70732-9760. Tel: 504-526-8508; Fax: 504-526-4128. Mr. Roland J. Cheramie, Prin.
Lay Teachers 11; Students 186.

Lakeland, Pointe Coupee Parish, Immaculate Conception (1859), Rev. Matthew P. Lorrain.
Res., P.O. Box 158, 70752-0158. Tel: 504-627-5124; Fax: 504-627-5125. [CEM 2]

Livonia, Pointe Coupee Parish, St. Frances Xavier Cabrini (1955), Rev. David E. Allen.
Res., P.O. Box 128, 70755-0128. Tel: 504-637-2396; Fax: 504-637-2390.

Maringouin, Iberville Parish, Immaculate Heart of Mary (1964), Rev. Shelton J. Fabre.
Res., 11140 Hwy. 77, 70757-9703. Tel: 504-625-2438; Fax: 504-625-3513. [CEM]

Maurepas, Livingston Parish, St. Stephen Martyr (1964), Rev. Msgr. Gerald M. Lefebvre, V.F.
Res., 22494 Hwy. 22, 70449-5321. Tel: 504-695-6310; Fax: 504-695-6039.

Morganza, Pointe Coupee Parish, St. Ann (1729), Rev. Louis T. Oubre.
Res., P.O. Box 128, 70759-0128. Tel: 504-694-3781; Fax: 504-694-3711. [CEM 2]

Napoleonville, Assumption Parish, St. Anne (1874), Very Rev. Gerald H. Burns, V.F.
Res., P.O. Box 99, 70390-0090. Tel: 504-369-6656; Fax: 504-369-9718. [CEM 2]
St. Benedict the Moor, Rev. Joseph C. Rodney, S.S.J.
Res., P.O. Box 218, 70390-0218. Tel: 504-369-7225; Fax: 504-369-2772. [CEM 2]

New Roads, Pointe Coupee Parish, St. Augustine (1923), Rev. Richard T. Sadlier, S.S.J.; Sr. Celeste Barret, S.H.Sp., Pastoral Assoc. In res., Rev. Philip Tarallo, S.S.J.; Deacon Norman Christophe.
Res., P.O. Box 548, 70760-0548. Tel: 504-638-7553.
St. Mary of False River (1865), Rev. Michael J. Schatzle, C.S.S.R. In res., Rev. J. Joel LeBauve.
Res., 348 W. Main St., 70760-3587. Tel: 504-638-9665; Fax: 504-638-6346. [CEM 2]

Paincourtville, Assumption Parish, St. Elizabeth (1840), Rev. Juan Ramon Vega (San Salvador).
Mailing Address: P.O. Box 1, 70391-0001.
Res., 6057 St. Elizabeth St., 70391. Tel: 504-369-7398; Fax: 504-369-9892. [CEM]

Paulina, St. James Parish, St. Joseph (1900), Rev. Joseph J. McLaughlin, S.M.; Bro. Matthew F. Wade, S.M., Pastoral Min.
Res., P.O. Box 129, 70763-0129. Tel: 504-869-5751; Fax: 504-869-4166. [CEM]

Pierre Part, Assumption Parish, St. Joseph the Worker (1858), Rev. Duane L. Breaux.
Res., P.O. Box 190, 70339-0190. Tel: 504-252-6008; Fax: 504-252-8011. [CEM 2]

Plaquemine, Iberville Parish, St. Clement of Rome (1964), Very Rev. Jerome A. Dugas, V.F.; Rev. Michael Jung, O.S.B.; Sr. Cecile Poitras, S.S.J., Pastoral Assoc.
Res., 58725 St. Clement Ave., 70764-3535. Tel: 504-687-3337; 687-1227; 336-9584; Fax: 504-687-3658.
St. John the Evangelist (1850), Rev. Eugene R. Engels.
Res., 57810 Plaquemine St., 70764-2538. Tel: 504-687-2402; Fax: 504-687-1587. [CEM]

Plattenville, Assumption Parish, Assumption of the Blessed Virgin Mary (1793), Very Rev. Gerald H. Burns, V.F.
Mailing Address: P.O. Box 99, Napoleonville, 70390-0099. Tel: 504-369-6656; Fax: 504-369-9718. [CEM]

Ponchatoula, Tangipahoa Parish, St. Joseph (1875), Revs. Richard R. Archer, O.P.; Robert Bordenkircher, O.P.; Deacons Milton Schanzbach; Larry Melancon.
Res., P.O. Box 368, 70454-0368. Tel: 504-386-3749; Fax: 504-386-4188. [CEM]
School—(Grades K-8) 175 N. Eighth St., 70454-3306. Tel: 504-386-6421. Mrs. Sherlyne Meissner, Prin.
Lay Teachers 15; Students 255.

Port Allen, West Baton Rouge Parish, Holy Family (1920), Rev. Henry C. Vavasseur.
Res., P.O. Box 290, 70767-0290. Tel: 504-383-1838; Fax: 504-383-1839.
School—(Grades K-8) 335 N. Jefferson Ave., 70767-2798. Tel: 504-344-4100; Fax: 504-344-1928. Sr. Joel Miller, M.S.C., Prin.
Marianites of Holy Cross 1; Lay Teachers 33; Students 508.
Preschool—415 N. Jefferson Ave., 70767-2727. Tel: 504-343-6541. Diane Harkins, Dir.
Lay Teachers 5; Students 58.

Prairieville, Ascension Parish, St. John the Evangelist (1919), Revs. Martin A. Hernandez, J.C.L., M.C.L.; Adrian C. Pere; Deacon Reese Wiggins.
Res., 15208 Hwy. 73, 70769-3507. Tel: 504-673-8307; Fax: 504-673-8680.

St. Amant, Ascension Parish, Holy Rosary (1905), Rev. Robert F. Stine; Sr. Mary John Hotard, C.S.J., Pastoral Assoc.
Res., 44450 Hwy. 429, 70774-4597. Tel: 504-647-5321; Fax: 504-647-5322. [CEM 2]

St. Francisville, West Feliciana Parish, Our Lady of Mount Carmel (1874), Rev. Msgr. William L. Greene.
Res., P.O. Box 67, 70775-0067. Tel: 504-635-3630; Fax: 504-383-5219.
Chapel—Angola State Penitentiary, Tel: 504-655-4411, Ext. 2028.

St. Gabriel, Iberville Parish, St. Gabriel (1769), Rev. Robert G. Marcell; Deacon Vernon J. Melancon.
Res., 3625 Hwy. 75, 70776-9411. Tel: 504-642-8441; Fax: 504-642-8491.

St. James, St. James Parish, St. James (1757), Rev. Howard B. Hall; Deacon Henry Zeringue.
Res., 6613 Hwy. 18, 70086-9054. Tel: 504-265-4210; Fax: 504-265-4210. [CEM]

Sorrento, Ascension Parish, St. Anne (1963), Very Rev. James Martone, V.F.; Deacon Jerry Braud.
Res., P.O. Box 8, 70778-0008. Tel: 504-675-8126; Fax: 504-675-6150.

Tickfaw, Tangipahoa Parish, Our Lady of Pompeii (1973), Rev. Ceslaus Prazan, O.P.
Res., P.O. Box 276, 70466-0276. Tel: 504-345-8957; Fax: 504-542-1585.

Vacherie, St. James Parish, Our Lady of Peace (1864), Rev. Clarence J. Waguespack; Deacon Steven J. Becnel.
Res., 13281 Hwy. 644, 70090-9716. Tel: 504-265-3953; Fax: 504-265-2507. [CEM]
St. Philip (1873), Rev. David M. Chauvin; Deacon Francis Waguespack.
Res., 1175 Hwy. 18, 70090-9527. Tel: 504-265-4085; Fax: 504-265-9348. [CEM]

White Castle, Iberville Parish, Our Lady of Prompt Succor (1899), Rev. Jules A. Brunet.
Res., P.O. Box 249, 70788-0249. Tel: 504-545-3635; Fax: 504-545-8615. [CEM 2]
School—32625 Bowie St., 70788-2698. Tel: 504-545-3302; Fax: 504-545-8615. Mrs. Cassie Bourgeois, Prin.
Lay Teachers 11; Students 153.

Zachary, East Baton Rouge Parish, St. John the Baptist (1964), Rev. Kenneth W. Laird.
Res., 4727 McHugh Dr., 70791-3935. Tel: 504-654-5778; Fax: 504-654-5796.

Chaplains of Public Institutions

BATON ROUGE. *Baton Rouge General Medical Center.* P.O. Box 3611, 70821-3611. Tel: 504-387-7000. Rev. Michael Jung, O.S.B., Chap.
East Baton Rouge Parish Prison. Deacon Bruno Rizzo, Chap., Res., 2577 South St., Baker, 70714-3235. Tel: 504-775-3325.
Nursing Homes not under Catholic auspices. Rev. Peter D. Crifasi, Chap., Res., 6824 Ozark St., 70805-6248. Tel: 504-336-8708; 357-9562. Rev. David A. Vavasseur, Res., 5657 Thomas Rd., 70811-7356. Tel: 504-775-0978.
Woman's Hospital. Rev. Myles J. Kearney, Chap., Res., 9150 Highland Rd., 70810-4096. Tel: 504-766-2431; Fax: 504-769-3290.

ANGOLA. *Louisiana State Penitentiary.* St. Augustine Chapel. Rev. J. Joel Labauve, Mailing Address: P.O. Box 428, 70712-0428. Tel: 504-655-4411; 655-3243.

CARVILLE. *National Hansen's Disease Center.* Gillis Long Memorial Hospital. Rev. Reynolds Garland, O.F.M., Chap., 5445 Point Clair Rd., 70721-9607. Tel: 504-642-5533.

JACKSON. *East Feliciana Chronic Disease Hospital and Rehabilitation Center.* Rev. J. Daniel Walsh, C.S.C., Chap., P.O. Box 438, 70748-0438.

ST. GABRIEL. *Hunt Correctional Institute.* Deacon Guy E. Decker, Mailing Address: P.O. Box 174, 70776-0174. Tel: 504-642-3306.

Special Assignment:
Reverend Fathers—
Counce, Paul D., J.C.L., M.C.L., Diocesan Tribunal, P.O. Box 1087, Baton Rouge, LA 70821-1087. Tel: 504-337-0561; 504-383-4370; Fax: 504-336-8789
McCue, Will, S.C., 855 Hearthstone Dr., Baton Rouge, LA 70806-5599. Tel: 504-383-0381
Seynaeve, Jaak, M.Afr., S.T.D., 2187 Olive St., Baton Rouge, LA 70806-6621. Tel: 504-336-9867
Walsh, Miles D., S.T.L., North American College, Vatican City, 00120 Rome. Tel: 011-39-6-684-9384-7; Fax: 011-39-6-686-7561

On Duty Outside the Diocese:
Reverend Fathers—
Landry, Clyde B., 911-A Country Club Dr., Rio Rancho, NM 87124. Tel: 505-892-9853
Smolley, Robert J., St. Basil Seminary, 195 Glenbrook Rd., Stamford, CT 06902-3099. Tel: 203-324-4578; Fax: 203-357-7681

On Leave:
Reverend Fathers—
Alise, Mark A., S.T.L.
DeBenedetto, David J.
Gensler, George D.
Maggio, J. Mark
Shore, Ray

Military Chaplains:
Reverend Fathers—
Rodriguez, Aloysius M.

Retired:
Reverend Monsignors—
Frey, Andrew F., P.O. Box 2458, Bay St. Louis, MS 39521-2458. Tel: 601-467-4382; Fax: 601-466-6477
Sanchez, Carlos, Southside Gardens, 4604 Perkins Rd., Baton Rouge, LA 70808-3037. Tel: 504-925-2930
Songy, Donald J., 2250 Main St., Baton Rouge, LA 70802-3198. Tel: 504-387-6671; Fax: 504-387-6672
Weber, John A., 5445 Government St., #105, Baton Rouge, LA 70806-6003. Tel: 504-925-9431; Fax: 504-928-3284
Reverend Fathers—
Braud, Edmond P., 41358 Bayou Narcisse Rd., Gonzales, LA 70737-1385. Tel: 504-644-2032
Caballero, Lloyd C., 24546 Louand Dr., Lacombe, LA 70445-9801. Tel: 504-626-7765; Fax: 504-626-7765
Clement, James P., 655 North St., #1404, Baton Rouge, LA 70802-5421. Tel: 504-343-5637; Fax: 504-383-0850
Faschan, Matthew, 9108 LA Hwy. 19, Slaughter, LA 70777-9801
Hewson, William J., 24546 Louand Dr., Lacombe, LA 70445-9801. Tel: 504-626-7765; Fax: 504-626-7765
Ibanez, Rodolfo, Domingo Sautu, 15, Murguia, Alava 01130 Spain
Kersey, Walter L., 1035 Belmont Ave., Apt. 1205, Victoria, BC V8S 3T5 Canada. Tel: 503-276-3615

McDonald, A. John, 333 Lee Dr., #134, Baton Rouge, LA 70808-4974. Tel: 504-767-8237
Merino, Zenon R., Jaenar 2, Madrid 33, Spain
Rocheleau, Raymond, 338 W. University Blvd., Tucson, AZ 85705-1084
Ruiz, Adolfo, Hurtado de Amezaga, 22 1, 48008 Bilbao, Vizcaya, Spain
Termini, Mario, 38860 LA Hwy. 75, Plaquemine, LA 70764-7729. Tel: 504-545-8213

Permanent Deacons:
Adams, Alfred P., St. Michael the Archangel, Convent
Allen, Eugene F., Our Lady of Mercy Church, Baton Rouge
Becnel, Steven J., Our Lady of Peace Church, Vacherie
BeJeaux, J. Phillip, St. Alphonsus Liguori Church, Greenwell Springs
Braud, Jerry W., St. Anne Church, Sorrento
Bustillo, Carlos, (Retired)
Decker, Guy E., Hunt Correctional Institute, St. Gabriel
Duplessis, W. Brent, St. Charles Borromeo, Baton Rouge
Ellis, Albert R., Jr., St. George Church, Baton Rouge
Flattmann, Bennett W., Mater Dolorosa Church, Independence
Fortenberry, Warren D., Diocesan Permanent Diaconate Office and St. Margaret, Albany
Furlow, Robert E., Jr., Diocesan Communications Office and St. Joseph Cathedral, Baton Rouge
Gainey, Wallace L., Jr., Holy Ghost, Hammond
Hollier, Clayton A., St. Thomas More Church, Baton Rouge
Lacoste, Ronald J., On Leave
Little, James A., St. Joseph Church, French Settlement
Melancon, Larry, St. Joseph Church, Ponchatoula
Melancon, Vernon J., St. Gabriel Church, St. Gabriel
Rizzo, Bruno, St. Isidore the Farmer Church, Baker
Robinson, Thomas H., St. Jean Vianney Church, Baton Rouge
Schanzbach, Dr. Milton, St. Joseph Church, Ponchatoula
Waguespack, Francis, Jr., St. Philip Church, Vacherie
Walsh, J. Peter, St. Patrick Church, Baton Rouge
Wax, James E., St. Joseph Cathedral, Baton Rouge
Wiggins, Reese, St. John the Evangelist, Prairieville
Zeringue, Henry J., St. James Church, St. James

INSTITUTIONS LOCATED IN THE DIOCESE

[A] COLLEGES AND UNIVERSITIES

BATON ROUGE. *Our Lady of the Lake College*, 5345 Brittany Dr., 70808-4398. Tel: 504-768-1710; Fax: 504-768-1726.
For a complete listing, refer to the Colleges and Universities section.

[B] DIOCESAN HIGH SCHOOLS, INTERPAROCHIAL

BATON ROUGE. *Bishop Joseph V. Sullivan Diocesan Regional Catholic High School*. Mailing Address: P.O. Box 86110, 70879-6110. 17521 Monitor Ave., 70817-2640. Mr. Joseph M. Scimeca, Prin. Sisters 1; Lay Teachers 53; Students 693.
Redemptorist High School, 4000 St. Gerard Ave., 70805-2999. Tel: 504-357-0936; Fax: 504-356-7882. Mr. John C. Fabre, Prin. Lay Teachers 45; Students 623.
Serving parishes in Baton Rouge, Baker, Brusly, Denham Springs, Greenwell Springs, Lakeland, New Roads, Gonzales, Port Allen, St. Gabriel, Zachary, Plaquemine and Maringouin.

DONALDSONVILLE. *Ascension Catholic Interparochial High School*, 311 St. Vincent St., 70346-2697. Mr. Larry Dugas, Prin. Lay Teachers 18; Students 200.
Serving parishes in Donaldsonville, St. James, Belle Rose, Vacherie, White Castle, Darrow, Gonzales, Convent, Paincourtville and Plattenville.

NEW ROADS. *Catholic High School of Pointe Coupee*, 504 Fourth St., 70760-3499. Tel: 504-638-3469. Mr. Kirk J. Guidry, Prin. Lay Teachers 27; Students 414.
Serving parishes in Lakeland, Livonia, Morganza, New Roads and Maringouin.

PLAQUEMINE. *St. John Interparochial High School*, 24250 Regina St., 70764-3598. Tel: 504-687-3056; Fax: 504-687-3658. Mrs. Ruth Larpenteur, Admin.; Mrs. Brenda L. Fremin, Prin. Lay Teachers 21; Students 270.
Serving parishes in Plaquemine, Brusly, Port Allen, Grosse Tete and White Castle.

TANGIPAHOA. *St. Thomas Aquinas Regional Catholic High School*, 14520 Voss Dr., 70401-9801. Tel: 504-542-7662; Fax: 504-542-4010. Dominican Sisters, Springfield, IL. Sr. Philip Neri Crawford, O.P., Prin. Sisters 3; Lay Teachers 21; Students 264.

[C] HIGH SCHOOLS, PRIVATE

BATON ROUGE. *Catholic High School*, 855 Hearthstone Dr., 70806-5599. Tel: 504-383-0397; Fax: 504-383-0381. Dr. Gregory Brandao, Prin. Brothers of the Sacred Heart 5; Lay Teachers 59; Boys 814.
St. Joseph's Academy, 3015 Broussard St., 70808-1198. Tel: 504-383-7207. Sr. Judith Brun, C.S.J., Prin. Sisters of St. Joseph 4; Lay Teachers 60; Girls 718.

[D] DIOCESAN ELEMENTARY SCHOOLS, INTERPAROCHIAL

DONALDSONVILLE. *Ascension Catholic Interparochial School*, 311 St. Vincent St., 70346-3499. Tel: 504-473-9227. Mr. Larry Dugas, Admin. Lay Teachers 20; Students 362.
Serving parishes in Donaldsonville, St. James, Belle Rose, Vacherie, White Castle, Darrow, Gonzales, Convent, Paulina, Paincourtville, and Plattenville.

NEW ROADS. *Catholic Elementary School of Pointe Coupee*, 304 Napoleon St., 70760-3527. Tel: 504-638-9313; Fax: 504-638-6471. Dr. Jacqueline C. Lewis, Prin. Sisters of St. Joseph 2; Lay Teachers 21; Students 540.
Serving parishes in Lakeland, Livonia, Morganza, New Roads and Maringouin.

PAINCOURTVILLE. *St. Elizabeth Interparochial*. (Grades PreK-8), P.O. Drawer M, 70391-0420. Tel: 504-369-7402. Mr. Richard N. Prejeant, Prin. Lay Teachers 10; Students 210.
Serving parishes in Belle Rose, Bertrandville, Napoleonville, Paincourtville, Pierre Part, and Plattenville.

PAULINA. *St. Peter Chanel Interparochial School*, P.O. Box 159, 70763-0159. Tel: 504-869-5778; Fax: 504-869-4166. Mr. Earl Mannina, Prin. Lay Teachers 25; Students 375.
Serving parishes in Paulina, Gramercy and Convent.

PLAQUEMINE. *St. John Interparochial Elementary/ Middle School*, 58645 St. Clement Ave., 70764-3599. Ruth H. Larpenteur, Prin. Lay Teachers 27; Students 526.
Serving parishes in Plaquemine, Brusly, Grosse Tete, White Castle, Baton Rouge, Belle Rose, St. Gabriel, Maringouin, Bayou Pigeon, Port Allen, Gonzales and Paincourtville.

[E] SCHOOL, EXCEPTIONAL CHILDREN

BATON ROUGE. *Department of Special Education*. Guardian Angels Center (7-14 yrs.) and Redemptorist Center (15-21 yrs.). P.O. Box 2028, 70821-2028. Tel: 504-383-3066. Mrs. Gail Campo, Admin. Housed on St. Gerard Elementary Campus and at Redemptorist High School. Teachers 6; Speech Therapist 1; Students 39.

[F] GENERAL HOSPITALS

BATON ROUGE. *Our Lady of the Lake Regional Medical Center*, 5000 Hennessy Blvd., 70808-4398. Tel: 504-765-6565; Fax: 504-766-5645.
For a complete listing, refer to the Hospitals section.

[G] HOMES AND SPECIAL CARE FACILITIES

BATON ROUGE. *Assisi Homes, Inc., of Our Lady of the Lake Medical Center*, 5000 Hennessy Blvd., 70808-4398. Tel: 504-765-6565.
For a complete listing, refer to the Special Care Facilities section.
Ollie Steele Burden Manor, 4250 Essen Ln., 70809-2196. Tel: 504-926-0091; Fax: 504-926-4937.
For a complete listing, refer to the Special Care Facilities section.

[H] MONASTERIES AND RESIDENCES OF PRIESTS OR BROTHERS

BATON ROUGE. *Brothers of the Sacred Heart*, 855 Hearthstone Dr., 70806-5599. Tel: 504-383-7117. Bro. Francis David, S.C., Dir. Brothers 8.
Franciscan Residence, 4155 Essen Ln. #2, 70809-2115. Tel: 504-924-3836. Revs. Emmeran Frank, O.F.M.; Marcellus Moorman, O.F.M.; Anthony Walter, O.F.M.
Incarnational Consecration Mission. (Vietnamese Assoc.), 2305 Choctaw Dr., 70805-7999. Tel: 504-357-1204. Revs. Hung Viet Nguyen, I.C.M., Dir.; Joseph Lien To, I.C.M.; Dominic Khoai Nguyen, I.C.M.; Dominic Chinh Pham, I.C.M.
The Redemptorist Education and Formation, P.O. Box 53900, 70892-3900. Tel: 504-355-2600; Fax: 504-355-6200. Rev. Robert A. Ruhnke, C.SS.R.
Redemptorist Fathers Vice Provincialate. Mailing Address: P.O. Box 53900, 70892-3900. Tel: 504-355-2600; Fax: 504-355-6200. Very Rev. Monroe G. Perrier, C.Ss.R., Vice Prov.; Rev. Samuel C. Maranto, C.Ss.R., Vice Prov. Consultor, Local Supr. & Archivist; Bros. Charles E. Fucik, C.Ss.R., Vice Prov. Treas.; Steven E. Fruge, C.Ss.R., Admin. Asst.; Clement J. Furno, C.Ss.R., Asst. Archivist & Librarian. In res., Rev. Eugene J. Staub, C.Ss.R. Priests 5.
Priests of Vice Province in Residences not listed elsewhere: Revs. Carl A. Schindler, C.Ss.R., Chap., U.S. Army Reserve; John C. Vargas, C.Ss.R., Redemptorist Generalate, Rome; Robert O. Curry, C.Ss.R.

[I] CONVENTS AND RESIDENCES FOR SISTERS

BATON ROUGE. *Baton Rouge / Southwest Regional Office*, 555 St. Tammany St., Ste. C, 70806-6064. Tel: 504-927-6778. Sr. Carolyn Brady, C.S.J., Development Dir.
Maryville Novitiate and Provincial House, P.O. Box 80376, 70898-0376. North American Province, 4200 Essen Ln., 70809-2196. Tel: 504-927-7481; 926-1627. Sr. Brendan Mary Ronayne, O.S.F., Prov. Supr.; Sr. Helen Cahill, O.S.F., Formation Dir.; Rev. Marcellus Moorman, O.F.M., Chap. Temporary Professed 2; Final Vows 14.
St. Joseph Convent, 3080 Kleinert Ave., 70806-6899. Tel: 504-344-1517. Sr. Ursula Harelson, C.S.J., Local Coord. Sisters of St. Joseph 14.

TICKFAW. *Our Lady Queen Contemplative Monastery*, 50352 Antioch Rd., 70466-9747. Tel: 504-345-2630. Benedictine Nuns. Very Rev. Mary Herbert Walsh, O.S.B., Prioress; Revs. Marion C. Walsh, O.S.B. (IND), Chap.; Frederick P. Walsh, O.S.B. (IND), (Retired); Joachim E. Walsh, O.S.B. (IND), (Retired). Nuns 8.

[J] RETREAT HOUSES

BATON ROUGE. *Bishop Robert E. Tracy Center*. Mailing Address: P.O. Box 2028, 70821-2028. Tel: 504-336-8750. 3300 Hundred Oaks Ave., 70808-1599. Mr. Charles Jumonville, Admin.

CONVENT. *Manresa, House of Retreats*, Office, P.O. Box 89, 70723-0089. Tel: 504-562-3596; 800-782-9431; Fax: 504-562-3147. Revs. A. Patrick Phillips, S.J., Dir.; Thomas J. Cronin, S.J., Asst. Dir.; Anthony Ostini, S.J., Asst. Dir.; Hacker J. Fagot, S.J., Asst. Dir.; Edward J. Romagosa, S.J., Asst. Dir.

PONCHATOULA. *Rosaryville / Spirit Life Center*, 39003 Rosaryville Rd., 70454-9580. Tel: 504-294-5039; 800-627-9183; Fax: 504-294-3510. Sr. M. Edmund Gibson, O.P., Dir.; Rev. William J. Aldridge, O.P., Chap. Dominican Sisters 4.

[K] CAMPUS MINISTRY

BATON ROUGE. *Christ the King Parish and Catholic Student Center*, Louisiana State University, P.O. Box 25131, 70894-5131. Tel: 504-344-8595; 504-383-1574; Fax: 504-344-1920. Revs. Patrick J. Mascarella; Garland T. Belsome, Highland Rd. & Dalrymple Dr., 70894. Total Catholic Students 14,500.
Martin Luther King, Jr. Student Center, St. Joseph Chapel, Southern University, 586 Harding Blvd., 70807-5301. Tel: 504-775-8691; 775-1301; Fax: 504-775-7067. Rev. Francis Brou, S.J., Chap.-Dir. Total Catholic Students 3,270.

HAMMOND. *St. Albert the Great Catholic Center*, 409 W. Dakota St., 70401-2597. Tel: 504-345-7206; Fax: 504-345-7223. Serving Southeastern Louisiana University. Rev. Sean O. Sheehy, Ed.D., Dir. Total Students 14,000.

[L] MISCELLANEOUS

BATON ROUGE. *Bishop Stanley J. Ott Shelter*. Mailing Address: P.O. Box 127, 70821-0127. Tel: 504-356-9854. Mr. Michael Acaldo, Exec. Dir.
Catholic-Presbyterian Apts., Inc., 655 North St., 70802-5420. Tel: 504-383-5551. Mr. Gordon D. McDowell, Exec. Dir.
FMOL Health Systems, Inc., 4200 Essen Ln., 70809-2196. Tel: 504-923-2701; 926-0708. Mr. John J. Finan, Jr., Pres.
Joseph Homes, Incorporated, P.O. Box 1668, 70821-1668. Tel: 504-387-0561; Fax: 504-336-8789. Ms. Deborah Roe, M.S.W., Contact Person.
Life America, Inc., 646 College Hill Dr., 70808. Dr. John S. Baker, Jr., Pres.
MAGNIFICAT-Baton Rouge Chapter, 4307 Lake Lawrence Cir., 70816-4423. Tel: 504-291-2550. A Ministry to Catholic Women. Mrs. Carol Dazzio, Coord.
Myriam's House, Inc., 1141 W. Chimes St., 70802-8532. Tel: 504-383-3349. Sr. Lydia Champagne, C.S.J., Pres.; Mrs. Myria Andre-Martin, Admin.

Sisters of St. Joseph. Facility for homeless women, providing temporary housing, assistance with job placement and other needed services.

Queen of Peace Home and Soup Kitchen, 749 East Blvd., 70802-6399. Tel: 504-383-4127. Missionaries of Charity.

St. Michael's Home. (Vietnamese Assoc.), 2305 Choctaw Dr., 70805-7999. Rev. Hung Viet Nguyen, I.C.M., Dir. Tel: 504-357-1204.

St. Vincent DePaul Dining Room. Mailing Address: P.O. Box 127, 70821-0127. Tel: 504-383-7439. Mr. Michael J. Acaldo, Exec. Dir.

St. Vincent DePaul Store. Mailing Address: P.O. Box 127, 70821-0127. Tel: 504-356-5158. Mr. Al St. Pierre, Mgr. Tel: 504-357-9073; Mr. Michael J. Acaldo, Exec. Dir. Tel: 504-356-9854.

Sisters of St. Joseph - St. Paul Center, 3920 Gus Young Ave., 70802-1727. Tel: 504-344-8590. Sr. Kathleen Bahlinger, C.S.J., Dir.

**St. Vincent DePaul Community Pharmacy, Inc.* Mailing Address: P.O. Box 127, 70827. Tel: 504-383-7450. Mr. Michael J. Acaldo, Exec. Dir.

Unwed Mothers Home, 715 East Blvd., 70802-6399. Tel: 504-343-2138. Missionaries of Charity.

[M] FOUNDATIONS, FUNDS AND TRUSTS

BATON ROUGE. *Baton Rouge Chancery Office.* Mailing Address: P.O. Box 2028, 70821-2028. 1800 S. Acadian Thruway, 70808-1698. Tel: 504-387-0561; Fax: 504-336-8789.

Ascension Catholic Interparochial School Endowment Fund, Donaldsonville.
Bishop Stanley J. Ott Works of Mercy Trust.
Diocese of Baton Rouge Clergy Retirement Plan.
Diocese of Baton Rouge Lay Retirement Plan.
Diocese of Baton Rouge Trust Fund.
Nim Pecquet Holy Family School Foundation.
Our Lady of Perpetual Help Trust.
Pamphile and Mabyn Donaldson Trust for St. Louis King of France Church.
Pointe Coupee Catholic Interparochial School Endowment Fund, New Roads.
Sacred Heart Parish Endowment Fund.
St. Aloysius School Endowment Fund.
St. Joseph Cathedral Cemetery Fund.
St. Joseph Cathedral Trust.
St. Theresa of Avila Catholic School Educational Foundation, Gonzales.
St. Thomas More School Endowment Trust.
Sherri Lyn Shaffer Trust for St. Thomas More Church.
Veritas Foundation, Hammond.
Vocational Development Fund of the Brothers of the Sacred Heart, Inc., 720 Hearthstone Dr., 70806-5599. Tel: 504-338-0034; Fax: 504-336-0505. Bro. Will McCue, S.C., Pres.
CHS Foundation, 855 Hearthstone Dr., 70806-5599. Tel: 504-389-0978; Fax: 504-389-0983. Bro. Aquin Gauthier, S.C., Pres.
Our Lady of the Lake Foundation, 5000 Hennessy Blvd., 70808-9907. Tel: 504-765-5000.

RELIGIOUS INSTITUTES OF MEN REPRESENTED IN THE DIOCESE

For further details refer to the corresponding bracketed number in the Religious Institutes of Men or Women section.

[0200]—*Benedictine Monks.* (St. Meinrad Archabbey).—O.S.B.
[0200]—*Benedictine Monks.* (St. Joseph Abbey, St. Benedict, LA).—O.S.B.
[1100]—*Brothers of the Sacred Heart.* (New Orleans Prov.).—S.C.
[0470]—*The Capuchin Friars.*—O.F.M.Cap.
[1070]—*Congregation of the Most Holy Redeemer-Redemptorists.* (New Orleans Vice Prov.) C.Ss.R.
[0520]—*Franciscan Friars.* (Prov. of St. John the Baptist).—O.F.M.
[0850]—*Missionaries of Africa.*—M.Afr.
[0430]—*Order of Preachers-Dominicans.* (Prov. of St. Martin de Porres).—O.P.
[0610]—*Priests of the Congregation of Holy Cross.* (Southern Prov.).—C.S.C.
[0700]—*St. Joseph's Society of the Sacred Heart-Josephites.*—S.S.J.
[0690]—*Society of Jesus.* (New Orleans Prov.).—S.J.
[0760]—*Society of Mary-Marists.* (American Prov.).—S.M.
[0420]—*Society of the Divine Word.* (Southern Prov.).—S.V.D.

RELIGIOUS INSTITUTES OF WOMEN REPRESENTED IN THE DIOCESE

[0233]—*Benedictine Nuns.*—O.S.B.
[0400]—*Congregation of Our Lady of Mt. Carmel*—O.Carm.
[0760]—*Daughters of Charity of St. Vincent de Paul.* (West Central Prov.).—D.C.
[0840]—*Daughters of Jesus.*—F.I.
[1070-08]—*Dominican Sisters.*—O.P.
[1070-10]—*Dominican Sisters.*—O.P.
[1140]—*Eucharistic Missionaries of St. Dominic.*
[1380]—*Franciscan Missionaries of Our Lady.*—O.S.F.
[2410]—*Marianites of Holy Cross.*—M.S.C.
[2710]—*Missionaries of Charity.*—M.C.
[1070-03]—*Sinsinawa Dominican Congregation of the Most Holy Rosary.*—O.P.
[0500]—*Sisters of Charity of Nazareth.* (Southern Region).—S.C.N.
[0990]—*Sisters of Divine Providence.*—C.D.P.
[2570]—*Sisters of Mercy of Philadephia.*—R.S.M.
[2630]—*Sisters of Mercy of the Holy Cross.*—S.C.S.C.
[3880]—*Sisters of St. Joseph of Medaille.*—C.S.J.
[3830-16]—*Sisters of St. Joseph of Springfield, Mont Marie.*—S.S.J.
[1950]—*Sisters of the Holy Family.*—S.S.F.
[2940]—*Sisters of the Most Holy Sacrament.*—M.H.S.
[4070]—*Society of the Sacred Heart.*—R.S.C.J.

NECROLOGY

(No Deaths)

Diocese of Beaumont

(Dioecesis Bellomontensis)

Most Reverend

JOSEPH A. GALANTE, D.D., J.C.D.

Bishop of Beaumont; ordained May 16, 1964; appointed Titular Bishop of Equilum and Auxiliary Bishop of San Antonio October 13, 1992; consecrated December 11, 1992; appointed Bishop of Beaumont April 5, 1994; installed May 9, 1994. *Res., 6550 Lexington, Apt. 259, Beaumont, TX, 77706.* Tel.: 409-860-9410. All official communications should be addressed to the Pastoral Office: *P.O. Box 3948, Beaumont, TX, 77704-3948.* Tel.: 409-838-0451.

ESTABLISHED SEPTEMBER 29, 1966.

Square Miles 7,878.

Comprises the counties of Chambers, Hardin, Jasper, Jefferson, Liberty, Newton, Orange, Polk and Tyler.

For legal titles of parishes and diocesan institutions, consult the Diocesan Pastoral Office.

Diocesan Pastoral Office: 703 Archie St., P.O. Box 3948, Beaumont, TX, 77704-3948. Tel.: 409-838-0451; Fax: 409-838-4511.

E-mail address: dioofbmt@sat.net

STATISTICAL OVERVIEW

Personnel	
Bishop	1
Priests: Diocesan Active in Diocese	36
Priests: Active Outside Diocese	6
Priests: Retired, Sick or Absent	13
Number of Diocesan Priests	55
Religious Priests in Diocese	25
Extern Priests in Diocese	2
Ordinations:	
Diocesan Priests	1
Transitional Deacons	2
Permanent Deacons in Diocese	30
Total Brothers	3
Total Sisters	62
Parishes	
Parishes	43
With Resident Pastor:	
Resident Diocesan Priests	25
Resident Religious Priests	16
Without Resident Pastor:	
Administered by Priests	2
Missions	10
Pastoral Centers	2
Professional Ministry Personnel:	
Brothers	1
Sisters	47
Lay Ministers	48
Welfare	
Catholic Hospitals	2
Total Assisted	419,753
Specialized Homes	1
Total Assisted	8
Special Centers for Social Services	1
Total Assisted	54,000
Educational	
Diocesan Students in Other Seminaries	10
Total Seminarians	10
High Schools, Diocesan and Parish	1
Total Students	685
Elementary Schools, Diocesan and Parish	7
Total Students	1,610
Catechesis/Religious Education:	
High School Students	2,180
Elementary Students	7,088
Total Students Under Catholic Instruction	11,573
Teachers in the Diocese:	
Brothers	1
Sisters	14
Lay Teachers	151
Vital Statistics	
Receptions into the Church:	
Infant Baptism Totals	1,380
Adult Baptism Totals	139
Received into Full Communion	242
First Communions	1,369
Confirmations	1,630
Marriages:	
Catholic	210
Interfaith	185
Total Marriages	395
Deaths	804
Total Catholic Population	85,906
Total Population	561,605

Former Bishops—Most Rev. VINCENT M. HARRIS, D.D., ord. March 19, 1938; appt. Bishop of Beaumont, July 4, 1966; cons. Sept. 28, 1966; installed as First Bishop of Beaumont, Sept. 29, 1966; appt. Titular Bishop of Rotaria and Coadjutor with right of succession to the Bishop of Austin, TX, April 21, 1971; succeeded to See as Second Bishop of Austin, November 16, 1971; died March 31, 1988.—Most Rev. WARREN L. BOUDREAUX, J.C.D., D.D., ord. May 30, 1942; appt. Titular Bishop of Calynda and Auxiliary Bishop of Lafayette, LA, May 19, 1962; cons. July 25, 1962; appt. second Bishop of Beaumont, June 4, 1971; installed August 25, 1971; appt. first Bishop of Houma-Thibodaux, March 2, 1977; installed as first Bishop of Houma-Thibodaux, June 5, 1977.—Most Rev. BERNARD J. GANTER, D.D., ord. May 22, 1952; appt. first Bishop of Tulsa, Dec. 19, 1972; cons. and installed, Feb. 7, 1973; appt. third Bishop of Beaumont, Oct. 3, 1977; installed Dec. 13, 1977; died Oct. 9, 1993.

Vicar General & Moderator of the Curia—Very Rev. MICHAEL A. JAMAIL, J.C.D., Ed.D., *P.O. Box 3948, Beaumont, 77704-3948.* Tel: 409-838-0451; 835-9902 (Res.); Fax: 409-838-4511.

Episcopal Vicars—Central Vicariate: Rev. Msgr. FRANCIS H. BURLTON, *Our Lady of the Assumption, 4445 Ave. A, Beaumont, 77705.* Eastern Vicariate: Very Rev. FRANCIS X. CONROY, *St. Francis of Assisi, 4300 Meeks Dr., Orange, 77632.* Northern Vicariate: Very Rev. RONALD B. FOSHAGE, M.S., *St. Michael, P.O. Box 239, Jasper, 75951.* Southern Vicariate: Very Rev. DON GOLASINSKI, *Immaculate Conception Church, P.O. Box 967, Groves, 77619.* Western Vicariate: Very Rev. PATRICK A. TURNER, *St. Louis Church, Rte. 1, Box 354, Winnie, 77665.*

Consultors, Diocesan College of—Rev. Msgr. M. N. ENDERLE; Revs. DAN MALAIN; RONALD FOSHAGE, M.S.; FRANCIS CONROY; T. R. BLANCO, O.S.A.; BENNIE J. PATILLO; MICHAEL A. JAMAIL; FRANK PADUCH; AUGUST PUCAR; WILLIAM MANGER.

Diocesan Pastoral Office—703 Archie St., P.O. Box 3948, Beaumont, 77704-3948. Tel: 409-838-0451; Fax: 409-838-4511. Office Hours: Mon.-Fri. 8:30-5.

Chancellor—Sr. ESTHER DUNEGAN, I.W.B.S., J.C.L., *Diocesan Pastoral Office, P.O. Box 3948, Beaumont, 77704-3948.* Tel: 409-838-0451; Fax: 409-838-4511.

Chief Financial Officer/Controller—RUSSELL J. CHIMENO, C.P.A., *Diocesan Pastoral Office, P.O. Box 3948, Beaumont, 77704-3948.* Tel: 409-838-0451; Fax: 409-838-4511.

Tribunal—703 Archie St., P.O. Box 3948, Beaumont, 77704-3948. Tel: 409-838-0451; Fax: 409-838-4511.

Judicial Vicar—Rev. LUONG QUANG TRAN, M.A., J.C.L.

Collegiate Judge of the Tribunal—Sr. ESTHER DUNEGAN, I.W.B.S., J.C.L.

Pro-Synodal Judges—Rev. Msgr. KENNETH R. GREIG; Rev. Msgr. SIDNEY J. MARCEAUX, J.C.D.; Revs. BENNIE J. PATILLO, M.Ed.; ARTHUR MORGAN, J.C.L.

Promotor of Justice—Rev. Msgr. FRANCIS H. BURLTON, S.T.L.

Defenders of Bond—Revs. MICHAEL A. JAMAIL, J.C.D., Ed.D., V.G.; SINCLAIR OUBRE, J.C.B., J.C.L. (Cand.).

Auditors—All priests and deacons serving the diocese, "ad causam".

Psychologists for the Tribunal—RAY COXE, Ph.D.; Very Rev. MICHAEL A. JAMAIL, J.C.D., Ed.D., V.G.; Rev. PATRICK BRADY, M.A., C.H.

Secretary-Notary—MARILYN PRICE.

Censor Librorum—Rev. Msgr. FRANCIS H. BURLTON, S.T.L.

Diocesan Officers and Directors

Apostleship of the Sea—Beaumont Port: Rev. SINCLAIR OUBRE, *3503 Gulfway Dr., Port Arthur, 77642.*

African-American Catholic Commission, Diocesan—WILLIAM JAMES CARTER, Chm., *5298 15th St., Port Arthur, 77642.*

Boy Scouts—Rev. NOLAN GOUTHIER, *St. Henry Parish, P.O. Box 427, Bridge City, 77611-0427.*

Building Commission, Diocesan—Rev. S. J. CULOTTA, Chm., *5075 Bigner Rd., Beaumont, 77708.*

Campus Ministry—TOMMY CHATLOSH, Dir., *P.O. Box 10095, Beaumont, 77710.* Tel: 409-835-3972.

Catholic Charities—Sr. CATHERINE PARENT, C.D.P., Dir. RON GOUGENHEIM, Dir. Devel., *Mailing Address: P.O. Box 829, Beaumont, 77704-0829. 1297 Calder St., Beaumont, 77704.* Tel: 409-832-7994; Fax: 409-833-9706.

Catholic Clerical Student Fund—P.O. Box 3948, Beaumont, 77704.

Catholic Education, Dept. of—Sr. EVELINA BELFIORE, O.P., M.Th., M.R.E., Dir. and Supt. of Schools; Sr. CAROL SHIVELY, O.S.U., Assoc. Supt., *P.O. Box 3948, Beaumont, 77704.* Tel: 409-838-0451; Fax: 409-838-4511.

Catholic Women, Council of—Rev. Msgr. GEORGE F. RABROKER, Moderator, *Our Lady of Assumption Church, 4445 Ave. A, Beaumont, 77705.*

Charismatic Prayer Renewal—Rev. WILLIAM MANGER, Group Liaison, *St. Anne Church, P.O. Box 3429, Beaumont, 77704-3429.*

Communication, Information & Diocesan Press—Rev.

JAMES VANDERHOLT, Exec. Dir., *1019 Colorado, Beaumont, 77705*. Tel: 409-832-3944; Fax: 409-832-4129., *P.O. Box 3948, Beaumont, 77704-3948.*

Continuing Education of Religious and Clergy, Office of—Rev. JAMES VANDERHOLT, Dir., *P.O. Box 967, Groves, 77619-0967.*

Diaconate, Permanent Diaconate—Rev. JEREMIAH MCGRATH, Vicar, *St. Anthony Cathedral, P.O. Box 3309, Beaumont, 77704-3309.* Tel: 409-833-6433; Fax: 409-833-6688. Deacon JOSEPH SCHEURICH, Dir., *310 Summerwood St., Beaumont, 77706.* Tel: 409-892-6990; Fax: 409-896-5230.

Diocesan Development & Stewardship, Office of—ANNE STEINMAN, C.P.A., Dir., *P.O. Box 3948, Beaumont, 77704.* Tel: 409-838-0451; Fax: 409-838-4511.

Hispanic Ministry, Diocesan Office of—Sr. PILAR DALMAU, A.C.J., *P.O. Box 3948, Beaumont, 77704-3948.* Tel: 409-838-0451; Fax: 409-838-4511.

Holy Childhood—Ms. ANNE STEINMAN, *P.O. Box 3948, Beaumont, 77704-3948.* Tel: 409-838-0451; Fax: 409-838-4511.

Master of Ceremonies, Diocesan—Rev. PATRICK A. TURNER.

Office of Worship; Liturgical Commission; R.C.I.A. Commission—Rev. PATRICK A. TURNER, Dir., *P.O. Box 3948, Beaumont, 77704-3948.*

Diocesan Choir—ROSALIND SANCHEZ, Dir., *P.O. Box 3948, Beaumont, 77704.* Tel: 409-838-0451.

Priests' Personnel Board—Rev. DON GOLASINSKI, Chm., *P.O. Box 3948, Beaumont, 77704-3948.*

Priests' Retirement Committee—*P.O. Box 3948, Beaumont, 77704-3948.*

Propagation of the Faith; Mission Coop—Ms. ANNE STEINMAN, *P.O. Box 3948, Beaumont, 77704-3948.* Tel: 409-838-0451; Fax: 409-838-4511.

Family Life Office & Respect Life Liaison—JOSIE CURTIS, *4930 Gulfway Dr., Pt. Arthur, 77642.* Tel: 409-983-4586.

Parish Social Ministry, Office of—Sr. MARY BORDELON, C.D.P., Dir., *4930 Gulfway Dr., Pt. Arthur, 77642.* Tel: 409-983-4586; Fax: 409-983-2306.

School Board, Diocesan—GRACIE SLOVAK, Pres., *P.O. Box 3948, Beaumont, 77704.*

Synod Office—Sr. MARILYN VOLLMER, S.S.M., Dir., *P.O. Box 3948, Beaumont, 77704-3948.* Tel: 409-838-0451; Fax: 409-838-4511.

Vocations—Rev. Msgr. JOHN DISTEFANO, Dir.; Very Rev. MICHAEL A. JAMAIL, Dir. of Seminarians, *P.O. Box 10095 L.U.S., Beaumont, 77710.* Tel: 409-835-5037.

Women Religious, Vicar For—Sr. JULIE MARIE GRIEG, O.P., Vicar, *9920 N. Major Dr., Beaumont, 77713.* Tel: 409-899-5617; Fax: 409-899-3161.

Youth Ministry, Catholic—TOMMY CHATLOSH, Dir., *P.O. Box 10095 L.U.S., Beaumont, 77710.* Tel: 409-835-3972.

CLERGY, PARISHES, MISSIONS AND PAROCHIAL SCHOOLS

CITY OF BEAUMONT
(Jefferson County)

1—ST. ANTHONY CATHEDRAL (1879), Rev. Jeremiah McGrath; Deacon Harry Davis. In res., Rev. Delphyn Meeks.
Res., 700 Jefferson St., P.O. Box 3309, 77704-3309. Tel: 409-833-6433; Fax: 409-833-6688.
School—Holy Cross Brothers 1; Sisters 2; Lay Teachers 8; Students 262.

2—ST. ANNE (1937), Revs. William Manger; Earl Mudd; Deacon Joseph Scheurich. In res., Rev. Michael A. Jamail.
Res., Calder Ave. & 11th, P.O. Box 3429, 77704-3429. Tel: 409-832-9963; Fax: 409-832-9964.
School—(Formerly St. Anne Tri-Parish School). Lay Teachers 41; Students 673.

3—BLESSED SACRAMENT (1915) (African American), Rev. Rodney J. Armstrong, S.S.J. In res., Rev. Dan Bastianelli, S.S.J.
Res., 780 Porter St., 77701-7198. Tel: 409-833-6089; Fax: 409-833-6091.

4—CRISTO REY (1951) (Hispanic), Rev. Luis Urriza, O.S.A. In res., Rev. Juan A. Garcia, F.M.M.
Res., 767 Ave. A, 77701. Tel: 409-835-7788; Fax: 409-835-7788.

5—ST. JOSEPH (1905) (Italian-Vietnamese), Rev. Khanh Ho.
Res., 1115 Orange St., 77701-4392. Tel: 409-835-5662; Fax: 409-832-7717.

6—OUR LADY OF THE ASSUMPTION (1951), Rev. Msgr. Francis H. Burlton. In res., Rev. Msgr. George F. Rabroker.
Res., 4445 Ave. A, 77705-4998. Tel: 409-835-5343; Fax: 409-835-5344.
School—1345 Woodrow St., 77705. Tel: 409-835-2651.
Dominican Sisters 1; Lay Teachers 11; Students 110.

7—OUR MOTHER OF MERCY (1952) (African American), Revs. Ray Bomberger, S.S.J.; John Raphael, S.S.J. In res., Rev. Henry Offer, S.S.J.
Res., 3390 Sarah St., 77705-3098. Tel: 409-842-5533; Fax: 409-842-4710.
School—Sisters 2; Lay Teachers 6; Students 86.
Convent—3380 Sarah St., Tel: 409-842-2940. Sisters of the Holy Spirit and Mary Immaculate

8—ST. PIUS X (1954), Revs. Salvador J. Culotta; John Colbert; Deacon Robert Gros.
Res., 5075 Bigner Rd. at East Lucas, 77708-5299. Tel: 409-892-3316; Fax: 409-892-8916.

9—ST. JUDE THADDEUS (1978), Revs. Richard DeStefano; John Hughes; Deacon Dow Wynn.
Res., 6825 Gladys, 77706-3239. Tel: 409-866-5088; Fax: 409-866-1866.

OUTSIDE THE CITY OF BEAUMONT

Ames, Liberty Co., Our Mother of Mercy (1903) (African American), Rev. Paul Ngozichukwu Ofoha, M.S.P.
Res., R.R. 2, Box 264, Liberty, 77575-9610. Tel: 409-336-3004; Fax: 409-336-3004. [CEM]

Anahuac, Chambers Co., Our Lady of Light (1938), Rev. Louis J. Villarreal, O.M.I.; Deacon E. R. LeBlanc.
Res., Rte. 2, Box 1-F, 77514-9001. Tel: 409-267-3158; Fax: 409-267-3158.
Mission—Mont Belvieu, Chambers Co., Holy Trinity, (1991) 7419 Lone Oak Dr., Baytown, 77521-4915. Tel: 713-383-2294; Fax: 713-383-7407.

Bridge City, Orange Co., St. Henry (1948), Rev. Nolan Gouthier; Deacon Hazen Kenney.
Mailing Address: P.O.Box 427, 77611-0427.
Res., 475 W. Round Bunch Rd., 77611-2448. Tel: 409-735-2422; Fax: 409-738-2158.

China, Jefferson Co., Our Lady of Sorrows (1918), Rev. Joseph Stratman.
Res., P.O. Box 38, 77613-0038. Tel: 409-752-3571; Fax: 409-752-5134. [CEM]

Cleveland, Liberty Co., St. Mary (1950), Rev. Michael Dwyer, M.S.C.; Deacon Bill Rudolph.
Res., P.O. Box 816, 77328-0816. Tel: 713-592-2985; Fax: 713-592-7247.

Corrigan, Polk Co., St. Martin de Porres Mission (1971), Rev. Roger Thibodeaux, Admin.; Deacon Rudy Cockburn.
Res., 1200 Asia Rd., 75939-9766. Tel: 409-398-2807 (Parish Center).

Dayton, Liberty Co., St. Joseph the Worker (1945), Revs. James Vanderholt, Admin.; Joseph Anithottom, C.M.I.; Deacon Wilbert Wycliff.
Res., P.O. Box 640, 77535-0640. Tel: 409-258-5735; Fax: 409-258-7220. [CEM]
Mission—Eastgate, Liberty Co., St. Ann, (1918).

Fannett, Jefferson Co., St. Mary (1964), Rev. Clement M. Iglesias.
Res., 9894 Gilbert Rd., Beaumont, 77705-9696. Tel: 409-794-2548; Fax: 409-794-3411.
Mission—Cheek, St. Martin de Porres.

Groves, Jefferson Co., Immaculate Conception (1928), Rev. Donald J. Golasinski. In res., Rev. James Vanderholt.
Res., 6250 Washington, P.O. Box 967, 77619-0967. Tel: 409-962-0255; Fax: 409-963-3464.
St. Peter the Apostle (1972), Rev. Msgr. Kenneth R. Greig. In res., Rev. Msgr. M.N. Enderle.
Res., 2049 Taft Ave., 77619-4953. Tel: 409-962-8365; Fax: 409-962-8365.

Jasper, Jasper Co., St. Michael (1951), Revs. Ronald Foshage, M.S.; Thomas J. Huhn, M.S.; Deacon David Luther.
Res., P.O. Box 239, 75951-0239. Tel: 409-384-2447; Fax: 409-384-2447.
Missions—Kirbyville, Our Lady of La Salette, (1948); Rayburn, St. Raymond, (1970).
Station—Toledo Village.

Kountze, Hardin Co., Holy Spirit Mission (1986), Rev. Paul Sumler, Admin.
Res., Hwy. 326, P.O. Box 1454, 77625-1454. Tel: 409-246-4457 (Office); Fax: 409-246-4623.

Liberty, Liberty Co., Immaculate Conception (1756), Revs. August Pucar; Michael Hinken, S.O.L.T.; Deacon Luther Wells.
Res., 411 Milam, 77575-4730. Tel: 409-336-3318; Fax: 409-336-7268. [CEM]

Livingston, Polk Co., St. Joseph, Revs. Roger Thibodeaux, Admin.; Juan Maravilla-Vigil, F.M.M. (Guatamala); Deacon Rudy Cockburn.
Res., P.O. Box 930, TX 77351-0930. Tel: 409-967-4657; 967-8385 (Church).
Mission—Corrigan, Polk Co., St. Martin de Porres, Corrigan, 75939.

Lumberton, Hardin Co., Infant Jesus (1948), Rev. Paul E. Sumler.
Res., Box 8126, LRS, 77657-0126. Tel: 409-755-1734; Fax: 409-755-2833.

Mauriceville, Orange Co., St. Maurice (1966), Rev. Louis DeLarue.
Res., R.R. 12, Box 1335, Orange, 77632-9812. Tel: 409-745-4060; Fax: 409-745-4272.

Nederland, Jefferson Co., St. Charles Borromeo (1923), Rev. Dan Malain; Deacons Vernon Drummond; Dallas Broussard. In res., Rev. Luong Quang Tran.
Res., 211 Hardy Ave., 77627-7399. Tel: 409-722-3413; Fax: 409-722-2020.

Orange, Orange Co., St. Mary (1880), Rev. Msgr. Marvin F. Enderle; Deacons Melvin Payne; Eddie Blankenstein.
Res., 912 W. Cherry St., 77630-5017. Tel: 409-883-2883; Fax: 409-883-3547. [CEM]
School—2600 Bob Hall Rd., 77630-2418. Tel: 409-883-8913.
Sisters 3; Lay Teachers 20; Students 379.
St. Therese (1924) (African American), Rev. Henry McKay, M.S.; Deacon Julian Richard.
Res., 1409 N. Sixth St., 77630-3927. Tel: 409-883-3783.
St. Francis of Assisi (1978), Rev. Francis X. Conroy; Deacons Harvey Dubois; Stronnie McBride.
Church—4300 Meeks Dr., 77632-4508. Tel: 409-883-9153; Fax: 409-883-9154.

Orangefield, Orange Co., St. Helen (1938), Rev. Arthur Morgan (LSC) Admin.; Deacons Morris Smith; Glen Hebert.
Res., P.O. Box 360, 77639-0360. Tel: 409-735-2200 (Office); Fax: 409-735-7786.

Port Arthur, Jefferson Co.,

1—OUR LADY OF GUADALUPE, (1927) (Hispanic), Rev. Telesforo R. Blanco, O.S.A.; Deacon Roy Garcia.
Res., 3648 S. Sgt. Lucian Adams Dr., 77642-6100. Tel: 409-962-6777; Fax: 409-963-0669.

2—QUEEN OF VIETNAM, (1977) (Vietnamese), Revs. Mark Nguyen Thanh Huynh, C.M.C.; Martin Tran Van Ban, C.M.C.
Res., 801 Ninth Ave., 77642-3329. Tel: 409-983-7676; Fax: 409-982-1212.
Convent—1148 Ninth Ave., 77642. Tel: 409-985-5102.
Dominican Sisters 5.

3—SACRED HEART, (1915) (African American), Rev. Anthony Ekanem, M.S.P.
Res., 920 Washington Ave., 77640-4923. Tel: 409-985-5104; Fax: 409-985-5104.

4—ST. CATHERINE OF SIENA, (1954), Rev. Joseph J. Romero; Deacon Jim Gard.
Res., 3706 Woodrow Dr., 77642-2320. Tel: 409-962-5715; Fax: 409-962-4775. [CEM]
School—Dominican Sisters 2; Lay Teachers 25; Students 268.

5—ST. JAMES, Revs. Sinclair Dubre; Socorro D. Rosario. In res., Rev. Msgr. Martin Bordages.
Res., 3503 Gulfway Dr., 77642-3693. Tel: 409-985-8865; Fax: 409-985-3847.
Mission—Sabine Pass, St. Paul.

6—ST. JOHN, (1951) (African American), Rev. Francis J. McCarthy, S.S.J.; Deacon W. B. Goudeau.
Res., 620 53rd St., 77640-2351. Tel: 409-985-8010; Fax: 409-833-6091.

7—ST. JOSEPH, (1951), Rev. D. Stephen McCrate.
Res., 4600 Procter St., 77642-1365. Tel: 409-982-6409; Fax: 409-983-5383.

8—ST. MARY, (1903) (African American), Rev. George Kalapurra, C.M.I.; Deacon Roy Cormier, Sr.
Office: 545 Savannah Ave., P.O. Box 1387, 77640-6026. Tel: 409-985-9661; Fax: 409-985-9691.

9—ST. THERESE THE LITTLE FLOWER OF JESUS, (1928), Rev. Fawaz Ayoub; Deacon Jimmy Bourgeois.
Res., 6412 Garnet Ave., 77640-1308. Tel: 409-736-1536; Fax: 409-736-1537.

Port Neches, Jefferson Co., St. Elizabeth (1922), Rev. Bennie J. Patillo.
Res., 2006 Nall St., 77651-3714. Tel: 409-727-8874; Fax: 409-727-8875.

Raywood, Liberty Co., Sacred Heart (1952) (African American), Rev. John J. McBrearty, S.S.J.
Res., P.O. Box 429, 77582. Tel: 409-587-4631. [CEM]

Silsbee, Hardin Co., St. Mark the Evangelist (1940), Rev. Charles Sellers, O.M.I.; Deacon Nolen Landry.
Res., 905 N. Ninth St., 77656. Tel: 409-385-4498; 385-5631; Fax: 409-385-6882.
Mission—Buna, Jasper Co., St. Francis of Assisi, P.O. Box 1688, Buna, 77612. Tel: 409-994-3456; Fax: 409-994-2923.

Sour Lake, Hardin Co., Our Lady of Victory (1906). (Independent Mission). Rev. Frank Paduch, Admin.
Res., 442 Barkley St., P.O. Box 1359, 77659. Tel: 409-287-3287; Fax: 409-287-3287.

Vidor, Orange Co., Our Lady of Lourdes (1938), Rev. Severiano Fernandez, O.S.A.
Res., 1600 N. Main, 77662. Tel: 409-769-2865; Fax: 409-769-2865.

Winnie, Chambers Co., St. Louis (1947), Rev. Patrick A. Turner.
Res., Rte. 1, Box 354, 77665-9711. Tel: 409-296-4200; Fax: 409-296-9715.

Woodville, Tyler Co., Our Lady of the Pines (1950), Rev. Roger Thibodeaux; Deacon Paul Rachal.
Res., P.O. Box 2029, 75979-2029. Tel: 409-283-5367; Fax: 409-283-5367.

Chaplains of Public Institutions

BEAUMONT. *Baptist Hospital.* Rev. William Richardson, S.S.J.
Columbia Beaumont Hospital. Rev. William Richardson, S.S.J.

Prisons

BEAUMONT. *Larry Gist State Jail.* Deacon Harry Davis, Chap.
Mark Stiles Unit, TDCJ. Deacon Alfred J. O'Brien, Chap.

DAYTON. *Plane State Jail.* Ms. Glory Siller, Chap.

LIVINGSTON. *Terrell Unit.* Deacon John Stanley, Chap.

Special Assignment:
Reverend Fathers—
Badeaux, Kevin
Daleo, Joseph
Engle, James C.
McClintock, Jim

On Duty Outside the Diocese:
Reverend Fathers—
DeFrancisco, Joseph, St. Ambrose Univ., Davenport, IA

Military Chaplains:
Reverend Monsignors—
Marceaux, Sidney J., Chap. Col., U.S.A., #3 Couchman St., Fort Bragg, NC 28307
Reverend Fathers—
Beck, Robert P., Chap. Capt., U.S.A.F., PSC 94, Box 3044, APO, AE 09824

Absent On Leave:
Reverend Fathers—
Courville, James
Deeter, Timothy
Leger, Steven
Phelan, Thomas
Sumler, Kevin

Retired:
Reverend Monsignors—
Bordages, Martin
Enderle, Martin N.
Fee, Paul A.
O'Connell, Patrick
Rabroker, George F.
Reverend Fathers—
DiStefano, John
Hanafin, William
Montondon, Walter

Permanent Deacons:
Blankenstein, Ed, St. Mary, Orange
Bourgeois, Jimmy, St. Therese, Little Flower, Port Arthur
Broussard, Dallas, St. Charles, Nederland
Cockburn, Rudy, St. Martin de Porres, Corrigan
Cormier, Roy, Sr., St. Mary, Port Arthur
Davis, Harry, St. Anthony Cathedral & Larry Gist State Jail, TDCJ, Beaumont
Drummond, Vernon, St. Charles Borromeo, Nederland
Dubois, Harvey, St. Francis, Orange
Garcia, Roy, Our Lady of Guadalupe, Port Arthur
Gard, Jim, St. Catherine of Siena, Port Arthur
Goudeau, W. B., St. John, Port Arthur
Gros, Robert, St. Pius X, Beaumont
Hebert, Glen, St. Helen, Orangefield
Kenny, Hazen, St. Henry, Bridge City
Landry, Nolen, St. Mark the Evangelist, Silsbee
LeBlanc, E. R., Holy Trinity Mission, Mont Belvieu
Luther, David, St. Michael, Jasper
McBride, Stronnie, St. Francis of Assisi and Southeast Texas Hospice, Orange
McKinney, Tom (GAL), TDCJ, Anacostacita
O'Brien, Alfred J., Mark Stiles Unit, TDCJ, Beaumont
Payne, Melvin, St. Mary, Orange
Rachal, Paul, Our Lady of the Pines, Woodville
Richard, Julian, St. Therese, Orange
Rudolph, William, St. Mary, Cleveland
Scheurich, Joseph, St. Anne and Dir. of Permanent Diaconate, Beaumont
Smith, Morris, St. Helen, Orangefield
Stanley, John, TDCJ, Terrell Unit, Livingston
Wells, Luther, Immaculate Conception, Liberty
Wycliff, Wilbert, St. Joseph the Worker, Dayton
Wynn, Dow, St. Jude Thaddeus, Beaumont

INSTITUTIONS LOCATED IN THE DIOCESE

[A] HIGH SCHOOLS, DIOCESAN

BEAUMONT. *Monsignor Kelly Catholic High School,* 5950 Kelly Dr., 77707. Tel: 409-866-2351. Dr. Mary Gagne, Prin. Sisters 2; Lay Teachers 55; Students 685.

[B] ELEMENTARY SCHOOLS, DIOCESAN

PORT ARTHUR, TX. *Sr. Thea Bowman Academy.* (Formerly Central Catholic Parochial School), 4604 Procter St., 77642. Tel: 409-982-4140. Juanita Odom, Prin. Dominican Sisters 2; Lay Teachers 15; Students 105.

[C] GENERAL HOSPITALS

BEAUMONT. *St. Elizabeth Hospital of Beaumont,* 2830 Calder Ave., P.O. Box 5405, 77726-5405. Tel: 409-892-7171.
For a complete listing, refer to the Hospitals section.

PORT ARTHUR. *St. Mary Hospital,* 3600 Gates Blvd., P.O. Box 3696, 77643. Tel: 409-985-7431; Fax: 409-985-9404.
For a complete listing, refer to the Hospitals section.

[D] MONASTERIES AND RESIDENCES OF PRIESTS AND BROTHERS

BEAUMONT. *Holy Cross Brothers Residence,* 2520 Liberty, 77702-1912. Tel: 409-835-1699.

[E] NEWMAN CENTERS

BEAUMONT. *Lamar University-Catholic Student Center,* 1010 E. Virginia, P.O. Box 10095, 77710. Tel: 409-835-3972. Mr. Tommy Chatlosh, Dir.; Rev. Nolan Gouthier, Chap.

[F] RETREAT CENTERS

BEAUMONT. *Holy Family Retreat Center,* 9920 N. Major Dr., 77713-9316. Tel: 409-899-5617; Fax: 409-899-3161. Sr. Julie Greig, O.P., M.A., Dir.; Sr. Carletta LaCour, O.P., B.A., Asst. Dir.

[G] MISCELLANEOUS

BEAUMONT. *Assumption School Foundation,* 1345 Woodrow, 77705. Jack Leggett, Prin.
Diocese of Beaumont School Foundation, Inc., P.O. Box 3948, 77704-3948. Sr. Evelina Belfiore, O.P., Sec. & Treas.
The Garth House, 1895 McFaddin, 77701-1622. Tel: 409-838-9084. Lanis McWilliams, Dir. The Mickey Mehaffy Children's Advocacy Program.
Monsignor Kelly Catholic High School Foundation, Inc., 5950 Kelly Dr., 77707. Camille Mouton, Dir.
Our Mother of Mercy School Foundation, 3380 Sarah St., 77705.
Primary Care Clinic, P.O. Box 5405, 77726-5405.
Rev. Herman Vincent Scholarship Fund. 211 Hardy, Nederland, 77627. Rev. Dan Malain, Admin.
St. Anne's Catholic School Foundation, 375 N. 11th St., 77702.
St. Anthony Cathedral School Foundation, 850 Forsythe St., 77701-2890. Sr. Ann Middlebrooks, S.E.C., Prin.
St. Thomas More Society of Southeast Texas, P.O. Box 467, 77704. Mr. Richard Clarkson, Pres.; Rev. Luong Quang Tran, Chap.

ORANGE. *The Hamlet,* P.O. Box 626, 77631-0626. A residential facility for persons with AIDS. Pat Bowman, Dir.
St. Mary School Foundation, 912 Cherry, 77630.

PORT ARTHUR. *Hospitality Center, Inc.,* 4928 Gulfway Dr., 77642. Tel: 409-982-4842. Jim O'Brien, Dir.
St. Catherine School Foundation, 3840 Woodrow Dr., 77642.
St. Mary Hospital Foundation of Port Arthur, P.O. Box 3696, 77643. Brenda Drago, Exec. Dir.

RELIGIOUS INSTITUTES OF MEN REPRESENTED IN THE DIOCESE

For further details refer to the corresponding bracketed number in the Religious Institutes of Men or Women section.

[0140]—*The Augustinians.* (Prov. of Castile, Spain).—O.S.A.
[0600]—*Brothers of the Congregation of Holy Cross.* (Midwest Prov.).—C.S.C.
[0275]—*Carmelites of Mary Immaculate.* (India).—C.M.I.
[]—*Congregation of the Mother Coredemptrix.* (Missouri).—C.M.C.
[0720]—*The Missionaries of Our Lady of La Salette.* (Prov. of Mary Queen).—M.S.
[]—*Missionaries of St. Paul.*—M.S.P.
[1110]—*Missionaries of the Sacred Heart.*—M.S.C.
[0910]—*Oblates of Mary Immaculate.* (Southern Prov.).—O.M.I.
[0700]—*St. Joseph's Society of the Sacred Heart.* (Baltimore).—S.S.J.
[0975]—*Society of Our Lady of the Most Holy Trinity.* (Texas).—S.O.L.T.

RELIGIOUS INSTITUTES OF WOMEN REPRESENTED IN THE DIOCESE

[0100]—*Adorers of the Blood of Christ.* (Prov. of Wichita).—A.S.C.
[2190]—*Congregation of the Incarnate Word and Blessed Sacrament.* (Houston, TX).—C.V.I.
[0470]—*Congregation of the Sisters of Charity of the Incarnate Word.* (Houston, TX).—C.C.V.I.
[1070-03]—*Dominican Sisters.*—O.P.
[1070-19]—*Dominican Sisters.*—O.P.
[1140]—*Eucharistic Missionaries of St. Dominic.* (New Orleans).—O.P.
[1870]—*The Handmaids of the Sacred Heart of Jesus.* (U.S. Prov.).—A.C.J.
[1010]—*Sisters of Divine Providence.* (San Antonio).—C.D.P.
[]—*Sisters of the Eucharistic Covenant.*—S.E.C.
[2050]—*Sisters of the Holy Spirit and Mary Immaculate.*—S.H.Sp.
[2200]—*Sisters of the Incarnate Word and Blessed Sacrament.* (Victoria).—I.W.B.S.
[2205]—*Sisters of the Incarnate Word and Blessed Sacrament.* (Corpus Christi).—I.W.B.S.
[4100]—*Sisters of the Sorrowful Mother.* (U.S./Caribbean Prov.).—S.S.M.
[4120]—*Ursuline Nuns of the Congregation of Paris.* (St. Martin, OH).—O.S.U.
[]—*Vietnamese Dominican Sisters.* (Houston).—O.P.

NECROLOGY

† Bollich, Ronald, (Retired). —Died Aug. 7, 1996.
† Tortorice, John, (Retired). —Died May 7, 1996.

Diocese of Belleville

(Dioecesis Bellevillensis)

Most Reverend

WILTON D. GREGORY, S.L.D.

Bishop of Belleville; ordained May 9, 1973; appointed Auxiliary Bishop of Chicago and Titular Bishop of Oliva October 31, 1983; consecrated December 13, 1983; appointed Bishop of Belleville December 29, 1993; installed February 10, 1994. *Mailing Address: Chancery Office, 222 S. Third St., Belleville, IL, 62220.* Tel.: 618-277-8181.

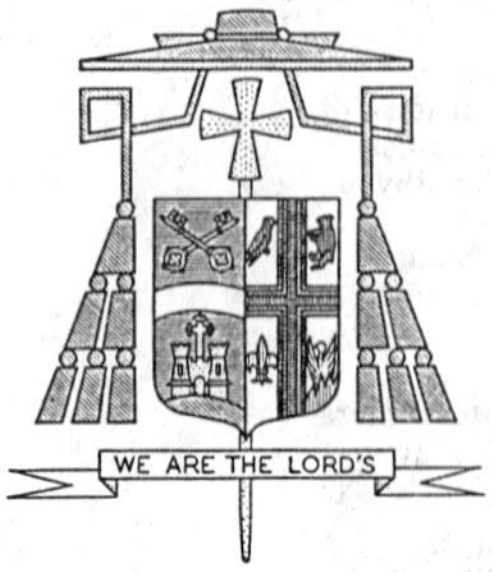

ERECTED JANUARY 7, 1887.

Square Miles 11,678.

Comprises Illinois south of the northern limits of the counties of St. Clair, Clinton, Marion, Clay, Richland and Lawrence.

For legal titles of parishes and diocesan institutions, consult the Chancery Office.

Chancery Office: 222 S. Third St., Belleville, IL, 62220-1985. Tel.: 618-277-8181; 397-1279; Fax: 618-277-0387.

STATISTICAL OVERVIEW

Personnel	
Bishop	1
Priests: Diocesan Active in Diocese	98
Priests: Active Outside Diocese	5
Priests: Retired, Sick or Absent	45
Number of Diocesan Priests	148
Religious Priests in Diocese	45
Extern Priests in Diocese	1
Ordinations:	
Diocesan Priests	3
Transitional Deacons	1
Permanent Deacons in Diocese	25
Total Brothers	10
Total Sisters	263
Parishes	
Parishes	128
With Resident Pastor:	
Resident Diocesan Priests	89
Resident Religious Priests	5
Without Resident Pastor:	
Administered by Priests	31
Administered by Permanent Deacons	2
Administered by Lay People	1
Missions	1
Pastoral Centers	7
Welfare	
Catholic Hospitals	7
Total Assisted	354,669
Homes for the Aged	4
Total Assisted	376
Day Care and Extended Day Care Centers	4
Total Assisted	550
Specialized Homes	1
Total Assisted	268
Special Centers for Social Services	3
Total Assisted	43,856
Educational	
Diocesan Students in Other Seminaries	13
Total Seminarians	13
Colleges and Universities	1
Total Students	632
High Schools, Diocesan and Parish	3
Total Students	1,641
Elementary Schools, Diocesan and Parish	39
Total Students	7,574
Catechesis/Religious Education:	
High School Students	1,286
Elementary Students	7,174
Total Students Under Catholic Instruction	18,307
Teachers in the Diocese:	
Sisters	12
Lay Teachers	382
Vital Statistics	
Receptions into the Church:	
Infant Baptism Totals	1,655
Adult Baptism Totals	280
Received into Full Communion	251
First Communions	1,901
Confirmations	2,102
Marriages:	
Catholic	370
Interfaith	363
Total Marriages	733
Deaths	1,267
Total Catholic Population	109,985
Total Population	855,010

Former Bishops—Most Rev. JOHN JANSSEN, D.D., ord. Nov. 19, 1858; cons. April 25, 1888; died July 2, 1913.—Most Rev. HENRY J. ALTHOFF, D.D., ord. July 26, 1902; appt. Dec. 4, 1913; cons. Feb. 24, 1914; died July 3, 1947.—Most Rev. ALBERT R. ZUROWESTE, D.D., ord. June 8, 1924; appt. Nov. 29, 1947; cons. Jan. 29, 1948; retired Sept. 3, 1976; died March 28, 1987.—Most Rev. WILLIAM M. COSGROVE, D.D., ord. Dec. 18, 1943; Auxiliary Bishop of Cleveland June 19, 1968; cons. Sept. 3, 1968; appt. Bishop of Belleville Sept. 3, 1976; installed Oct. 28, 1976; retired May 19, 1981; died Dec. 11, 1992.—Most Rev. JOHN N. WURM, S.T.D., Ph.D., ord. April 3, 1954; Auxiliary Bishop of St. Louis June 25, 1976; cons. Aug. 17, 1976; appt. Bishop of Belleville Sept. 19, 1981; installed Nov. 4, 1981; died April 27, 1984.—Most Rev. JAMES P. KELEHER, S.T.D., M.ED., ord. April 12, 1958; appt. Bishop of Belleville Oct. 23, 1984; cons. Dec. 11, 1984; transferred to Kansas City, KS Sept. 8, 1993.

Diocese of Belleville Chancery Office—222 S. Third St., Belleville, 62220-1985. Tel: 618-277-8181; 397-1279; Fax: 618-277-0387.

Diocesan Pastoral Center—2620 Lebanon Ave., Belleville, 62221. Tel: 618-235-9601; Fax: 618-235-7416.

Vicar General—Very Rev. JAMES E. MARGASON, J.C.L., M.Div.

Moderator of the Curia—Very Rev. JAMES E. MARGASON, J.C.L., M.Div., V.G.

Chancellor—Rev. KENNETH J. YORK, J.C.L.

Vice-Chancellor—DAVID R. SPOTANSKI.

Secretary to the Bishop—Sr. JOYCE ANN BERKEL, S.S.N.D.

Chief Fiscal Officer—PHILIP W. BUETTNER.

Archivist—Sr. MARY KENAN WOLF, S.S.N.D., *220 W. Lincoln St., Belleville, 62220.* Tel: 618-234-3157.

Diocesan Tribunal—Diocesan Pastoral Center, 2620 Lebanon Ave., Belleville, 62221. Tel: 618-235-9601. Address all rogatory commissions to the Chancellor at the Chancery Office.

Judicial Vicar—Rev. EDWARD F. SCHAEFER, J.C.L.

Adjutant Judicial Vicar—Rev. PAUL R. WIENHOFF, J.C.L.

Judges—Revs. PAUL R. WIENHOFF, J.C.L.; EDWARD F. SCHAEFER, J.C.L.; Rev. Msgr. HARRY J. JEROME, J.C.L., S.T.L.

Promotor Justitiae—Rev. Msgr. BERNARD O. SULLIVAN, J.C.D.

Defensores Vinculi—Rev. EDWARD J. STOKES, S.J., J.C.D.

Advocates—Revs. JOHN T. MYLER; KENNETH J. YORK, J.C.L.

Notaries—RENEE QUIRIN; JACQUELINE MATT.

Diocesan Consultors—Very Rev. JAMES E. MARGASON, J.C.L., M.Div., V.G.; Revs. THEODORE J. BAUMANN; JAMES A. BLAZINE; VINCENT A. HASELHORST; WILLIAM J. HITPAS; JAMES M. NALL; PATRICK N. PETER; CARL E. SCHERRER; EUGENE H. WOJCIK.

Diocesan Deans—Belleville Deanery: Very Rev. JAMES A. BLAZINE, V.F.; East St. Louis Deanery: Very Rev. JAMES T. LONG, V.F.; East Deanery: Very Rev. MELVIN B. VANDELOO, V.F.; North Central Deanery: Very Rev. THEODORE J. BAUMANN, V.F.; West Deanery: Very Rev. DENNIS R. SCHAEFER, V.F.; South Deanery: Very Rev. JAMES A. BUERSTER, V.F.

Diocesan Finance Council—JEFF RENNER, Chm.; Very Rev. JAMES E. MARGASON, J.C.L., M.Div., V.G.; PHILIP W. BUETTNER; J. ROY DEE, III; JACK GUNDLACH; VERNON KOVARIK; IRENE KRUSE; Revs. THOMAS MILLER; STEPHEN RUDOLPHI; JACKIE SETTLES; JOHN SMITH; JAY TEBBE.

Building Commission, Chancery Office—Rev. JEROME D. HARTLEIN, Chm. WILLIAM JOHNSON.

Campaign for Human Development—Rev. J. CLYDE GROGAN, Dir., *771 Vogel Pl., East St. Louis, 62205.* Tel: 618-874-5025.

Catholic Social Service—PETER CERNEKA, III, Dir., Office: *617 S. Belt W., Belleville, 62220.* Tel: 618-277-9200, Branch Offices: *201 E. Main St., Carbondale, 62901.* Tel: 618-351-0743, *4230 Lincolnshire Dr., Mt. Vernon, 62864.* Tel: 618-244-0344, *120 W. Fifth St., P.O. Box 23, Mt. Carmel, 62863.* Tel: 618-263-3863, *535 N. First St., Breese, 62230.* Tel: 618-526-2267, *Newman Center, 715 S. Washington St., Carbondale, 62901.* Tel: 618-549-1018.

Catholic Urban Programs—JOSEPH P. HUBBARD, Coord., *771 Vogel Pl., East St. Louis, 62205.* Tel: 618-398-5616.

Holy Angels Shelter—1410 N. 36th St., East St. Louis, 62205. Tel: 618-874-4079. PATRICIA LEWIS, Dir.

Griffin Center—2630 Lincoln Ave., East St. Louis, 62204. Tel: 618-874-2500. Sr. JULIA HUISKAMP, D.C., Dir.

Griffin Center Sites:—De Shields Center: *1235 McCasland, East St. Louis, 62201.* Tel: 618-874-0637. Roosevelt Center: *400 Bunkum Rd., East St. Louis.* Tel: 618-271-9859. ORR-Weathers Center: *1400 Missouri Ave., D-1 Bldg., East St. Louis, 62201.* Tel: 618-875-0535.

Family Center—705 Summit, East St. Louis, 62201. Tel: 618-875-7295. Sr. CAROL LEHMKUHL, O.P.

St. Regis Center After School Program—3500 Market St., East St. Louis, 62207. GLENDA DREW, Dir., After School Prog.

C.Y.O.—COLETTE KENNETT, Dir.; Rev. BERNARD C.

GOEDDE, JR., Spiritual Moderator; JAMES KEIM, Athletic Dir., *Diocesan Pastoral Center.*
Cemeteries—Rev. Msgr. LEONARD A. BAUER, Dir., *Chancery Office.*
Clergymen's Aid Society—Very Rev. THEODORE J. BAUMANN, V.F., Pres., *Box 176, Bartelso, 62218.* Tel: 618-765-2162.
Conciliation and Arbitration Board—THOMAS E. PRICE, Chm., *740 Market St., Mt. Carmel, 62863.* Tel: 618-263-6591.
Council of Women Religious—Sr. HELEN MOORE, A.S.C., Pres., *1036 Rutledge, Belleville, 62221.* Tel: 618-235-5486.
Diocesan Development Office—MARTIN LIEFELD, *Chancery Office.*
Diocesan Liturgical Commission—Rev. EDWARD F. SCHAEFER, J.C.L., *Diocesan Pastoral Center.*
Diocesan Outreach Apostolate—Serving Alexander and Pulaski Counties. Daystar Community Program, *909 Washington Ave., Cairo, 62914.* Tel: 618-734-0178. Sr. MARY JOAN TRIPPEL, P.H.J.C., Dir., *Res., Mary Katherine Convent, 725 22nd St., Cairo, 62914.* Tel: 618-734-0778.
Diaconate, Office of Permanent—Rev. ROBERT B. FLANNERY, Dir. Assoc. Directors: Rev. EDWIN H. HUSTEDDE; Deacon PETER CERNEKA, *Diocesan Pastoral Center.*
Diocesan Council of Catholic Women—Rev. ALBERT L. JEROME, Diocesan Moderator, *Box 332, Nashville, 62263.* Tel: 618-327-3232. JOSEPHINE FITCH, Pres., *Diocesan Pastoral Center.*
Ecumenical and Interreligious Affairs—Rev. JAMES R. DOUGHERTY, Dir., *133 N. Elm St., Centralia, 62801.* Tel: 618-532-6291.
Formation of Priests—Rev. JAMES R. DEITERS, Chm., *205 W. Third St., O'Fallon, 62269.* Tel: 618-632-3562.
Office of Education—THOMAS H. POSNANSKI, Dir., *Diocesan Pastoral Center.*
Department of Elementary Education—Sr. PATRICIA DELANEY, S.S.N.D., Dir.
Religious Education and Catechesis—MARK MARKULY, Assoc. Dir.
Diocesan Board of Education—MARTHA O'MALLEY, Pres., *44 Glenview Dr., Belleville, 62203.*
Guatemala Mission Society—VIRGINIA KOCH, Chm., *One Park Ln., Centralia, 62801.* Tel: 618-532-6291.
Hispanic Ministry—Carbondale Area: Rev. FEDERICO HIGUERA, *1101 Centennial St., Box 237, Cobden, 62920.* Tel: 618-893-2276. Fairmont City Area: Sr. ROSALIE GUTIERREZ, P.H.J.C., *2728 N. 42nd St., Fairmont City, 62201.* Tel: 618-271-0360.
Holy Childhood Association—Rev. KENNETH J. YORK, Dir., *Chancery.*
Hospitals—Rev. DENNIS F. VOSS, Delegate, *St. Elizabeth Hospital, 211 S. 3rd St., Belleville, 62220.* Tel: 618-234-2120.
Insurance Commission—PHILIP W. BUETTNER, Dir., *Chancery Office.*
Catholic Mutual Group—WILLIAM P. JOHNSON, Claims/Risk Mgr., *Diocesan Pastoral Center.* Tel: 618-233-1090.
Ministry Formation—IRENE DILL, Dir., *Diocesan Pastoral Center.*
Natural Family Planning—*Catholic Social Services, 617 S. Belt W., Belleville, 62220-2414.* Tel: 618-277-9200.
Newman Center—JOHN SCARANO, Diocesan Dir. & Campus Min., *715 S. Washington St., Carbondale, 62901.* Tel: 618-529-3311. Rev. CECIL PICKERT, O.Carm., Campus Min.
Newman Auxiliary—JOYCE WOLF, Pres., *110 Becky Dr., Waterloo, 62298.* Tel: 618-939-8978.
Newspaper, "The Messenger"—RAPHAEL H. MIDDEKE, Mng. Editor, *Diocesan Pastoral Center.*
Office of Planning—DAVID R. SPOTANSKI, Dir., *Chancery Office.*
Ondessonk, Camp—Diocese of Belleville, Department of Outdoor Education: PATRICK R. HIGGINS, Exec. Dir., *Ozark, 62972.* Tel: 618-695-2489; Fax: 618-695-3593.
Priest Personnel Board—Very Rev. THEODORE J. BAUMANN, V.F., Chm., *Chancery Office.*
Priests Organizations—
Confraternity of Catholic Clergy—Vacant.
Southern Illinois Association of Priests—Co-Chm: Revs. WALTER M. BARR; GEORGE A. MAUCK, *1171 Jefferson, Carlyle, 62231.* Tel: 618-594-2225.
Pro-Life Office—ANN POLKA, Chm., *Diocesan Pastoral Center.*
Propagation of the Faith—Rev. KENNETH J. YORK, J.C.L., Dir., *Chancery.*
Review Board—MARGIE MENSEN, L.C.S.W.- M.S.W., Admin., *220 W. Lincoln St., #407, Belleville, 62220.* Tel: 618-236-1812.
Rural Life Conference—Rev. JOSEPH A. LAWLER, Dir., *R.R. 3-Piopolis, McLeansboro, 62859.* Tel: 618-648-2490.
St. Vincent DePaul Society—RAY BERKEL, Admin., *3718 State St., East St. Louis, 62205.* Tel: 618-397-3113.
Sick and Aged (Ministry)—Rev. EUGENE J. NEFF, Dir., *Diocesan Pastoral Center.* Tel: 618-235-9991.
Vocation Office—Rev. KENNETH J. SCHAEFER, Dir., *Diocesan Pastoral Center.*
Worship, Office of—DENISE ANDERSON, *Diocesan Pastoral Center.*

CLERGY, PARISHES, MISSIONS AND PAROCHIAL SCHOOLS

CITY OF BELLEVILLE
(St. Clair County)

1—CATHEDRAL OF ST. PETER, Revs. Eugene H. Wojcik, Rector; Steven F. Poole; Deacons Robert Becker; Joseph Stock. In res., Rev. Edward J. Stokes, S.J.
Res., 200 W. Harrison, 62220. Tel: 618-234-1166. [CEM]
School—Cathedral School, 200 S. Second St., 62220. Tel: 618-233-6414. Sr. Deanne Stratmann, S.S.N.D., Prin.
School Sisters of Notre Dame 3; Lay Teachers 21; Students 336.
Catechesis/Religious Programs—Sr. Theresa Markus, S.S.N.D., D.R.E.
Students 160.
Convent—300 S. Second St., 62220.

2—BLESSED SACRAMENT, Rev. Marvin C. Volk, Pastor.
Res., 8707 W. Main St., 62223. Tel: 618-397-2287; Fax: 618-397-2269.
School—8801 W. Main St., 62223. Tel: 618-397-1111; Fax: 618-397-8431. Ms. Claire Hatch, Prin.
School Sisters of Notre Dame 1; Lay Teachers 12; Students 200.
Catechesis/Religious Programs—Students 60.
Convent—8901 W. Main St., 62233.

3—OUR LADY QUEEN OF PEACE, Rev. John W. McEvilly.
Res., 5923 N. Belt W., 62223. Tel: 618-234-6196; Fax: 618-234-6217.
School—5915 N. Belt W., 62223. Tel: 618-234-1206. Mrs. Jane Spreng, Prin.
Lay Teachers 18; Students 307.
Catechesis/Religious Programs—Students 60.

4—ST. AUGUSTINE OF CANTERBURY, Rev. Andrew J. Knopik.
Res., 1910 W. Belle, 62223. Tel: 618-233-3813.
School—1900 Canterbury Dr., 62223. Tel: 618-234-4958. Dr. Kay Bennett, Prin.
Lay Teachers 18; Students 240.
Catechesis/Religious Programs—Students 107.

5—ST. HENRY, Rev. Bernard L. Voss. In res., Rev. James S. Orumpakkat, C.M.I.
Res., 5315 W. Main St., 62223. Tel: 618-233-2423.
School—5303 W. Main St., 62223. Tel: 618-234-6061. Mr. Ronald Karcher, Prin.
Lay Teachers 10; Students 125.

6—ST. LUKE, Rev. James E. Margason, V.G., J.C.L.; Sr. Grace Marie Mueller, S.S.N.D., Pastoral Assoc., Tel: 618-236-1839; Deacon Peter Cerneka.
Res., 301 N. Church St., 62220. Tel: 618-236-1124.
Catechesis/Religious Programs—Students 82.

7—ST. MARY, Very Rev. James A. Blazine, V.F.
Res., 1706 W. Main St., 62226. Tel: 618-233-2391; Fax: 618-233-9201.
School—1722 W. Main St., 62226. Tel: 618-234-2476; Fax: 618-234-7736.
Lay Teachers 11; Students 237.
Catechesis/Religious Programs—Sr. Mary Catherine Clark, A.S.C., D.R.E.
Students 99.

8—ST. TERESA OF THE CHILD JESUS. (Little Flower). Revs. Donald W. Eichenseer, Admin.; Robert D. Gore, Pastor.
Res., 1201 Lebanon Ave., 62221. Tel: 618-233-3500; Fax: 618-233-9703.
School—1108 Lebanon Ave., 62221. Tel: 618-235-4066. Mr. Leo Hodapp, Prin.
Lay Teachers 18; Students 346.
Catechesis/Religious Programs—Fax: 618-235-7930.
Students 155.

9—CHAPEL OF ST. JOHN CHILDREN'S HOME. Unassigned. Mailing Address:s 2620 Lebanon Ave., 62221. [CEM]
Chancery Office, 222 S. Third St., 62220. Tel: 618-277-8181. Rev. Msgr. James E. Margason, J.C.L.
Convent—Tel: 618-277-9699. Sisters, Poor Handmaids of Jesus Christ.

OUTSIDE THE CITY OF BELLEVILLE

Albers, Clinton Co., St. Bernard, Rev. Leo S. Reinhardt.
Res., 62215. Tel: 618-248-5112. [CEM]
Catechesis/Religious Programs—Mrs. Norma Jansen, D.R.E.
Students 150.

Anna, Union Co., St. Mary, Rev. Thomas W. Miller; Sr. Joan Backes, S.S.N.D., Pastoral Assoc. & D.R.E.
Res., 402 Freeman, 62906. Tel: 618-833-5835; 833-3131.
Catechesis/Religious Programs—Tel: 618-833-3131.
Students 130.

Ava, Jackson Co., St. Elizabeth, Rev. Leo J. Hayes.
Res., 606 W. George St., P.O. Box 157, 62907. Tel: 618-426-3321.

Aviston, Clinton Co., St. Francis of Assisi, Rev. Daniel L. Friedman; Deacon Gerald E. Stockman.
Res., 251 S. Clinton, Box 93, 62216. Tel: 618-228-7219; Fax: 618-228-7320. [CEM]
Catechesis/Religious Programs—Tel: 618-228-7245.
Students 235.

Bartelso, Clinton Co., St. Cecilia, Very Rev. Theodore J. Baumann, V.F.
Res., 304 S. Washington St., P.O. Box 176, 62218. Tel: 618-765-2162; Fax: 618-765-2264.
Catechesis/Religious Programs—Fax: 618-765-2163. Sr. Mary Benedict Hayden, A.S.C., D.R.E.
Students 188.

Beaver Prairie, Clinton Co., St. Felicitas. Attended by Marydale.
Mailing Address: 18021 Marydale Rd., Carlyle, 62231. Tel: 618-594-3266. [CEM]

Beckemeyer, Clinton Co., St. Anthony, Very Rev. Richard J. Weidert, Pastor; Rev. James A. Voelker.
Res., P.O. Box 305, 62219. Tel: 618-227-8236. [CEM]
Catechesis/Religious Programs—Students 75.

Benton, Franklin Co., St. Joseph, Rev. Donald J. Lenzini.
Res., 506 W. Main, 62812. Tel: 618-438-9941. [CEM]
Catechesis/Religious Programs—Students 69.

Breese, Clinton Co., St. Augustine, Rev. Melvin B. Haas.
Res., 525 S. Third St., P.O. Box 67, 62230. Tel: 618-526-4362.
Catechesis/Religious Programs—Students 38.
St. Dominic, Rev. Patrick N. Peter.
Res., 480 N. Second St., 62230. Tel: 618-526-7746; Fax: 618-526-7755. [CEM]
Catechesis/Religious Programs—Mrs. Rill Anthony, D.R.E.
Students 117.

Bridgeport, Lawrence Co., Immaculate Conception. Attended by St. Lawrence, Lawrenceville.
1006 Collins, Lawrenceville, 62439. Tel: 618-943-5255. [CEM]

Cahokia, St. Clair Co., Holy Family, Rev. John T. Myler, D.Min.
Res., 116 Church St., 62206. Tel: 618-337-4548; Fax: 618-332-1699. [CEM 3]
School—Tel: 618-337-2880. Vincent Schmidt, Prin.
Lay Teachers 9; Students 206.
St. Catherine Laboure, Rev. John Patrick Day, C.P.
Res., 913 Rome Ln., 62206. Tel: 618-337-4173; Fax: 618-337-1231.
School—1820 Jerome Ln., 62208. Tel: 618-337-4448; Fax: 618-337-1231.
Lay Teachers 9; Students 158.
Day Care—1826 Jerome Ln., 62208. Tel: 618-337-3555.

Cairo, Alexander Co., St. Patrick, Rev. Jerome D. Fortenberry, C.M.
Res., 312 Ninth St., 62914. Tel: 618-734-2061. [CEM]
School—St. Joseph, Tel: 618-734-4182. Louis Fortenberry, Prin.
98105.

Carbondale, Jackson Co., St. Francis Xavier, Rev. Carl E. Scherrer. In res., Bro. John Monzyk, C.P.; Deacon Richard Prien.
Res., 303 S. Poplar St., 62901. Tel: 618-457-4556; Fax: 618-457-7368.
Catechesis/Religious Programs—Toni Intravaia, D.R.E.
Students 211.

Carlyle, Clinton Co., St. Mary. (Immaculate Conception). Rev. George A. Mauck.
Res., 12th St. & Jefferson St., Box 179, 62231. Tel: 618-594-2225; Fax: 618-594-4638. [CEM]
Catechesis/Religious Programs—Tel: 618-594-2863. Sr. Mary Dietz, S.S.N.D., D.R.E.
Students 252.

Carmi, White Co., St. Polycarp, Rev. Stephen A. Rudolphi.

Res., 209 S. Fourth St., P.O. Box 56, 62821. Tel: 618-382-7732. [CEM]
Catechesis/Religious Programs—Students 56.

Carterville, Williamson Co., Church of the Holy Spirit. Attended by Our Lady of Mount Carmel, Herrin.
316 W. Monroe St., Herrin, 62948. Tel: 618-942-3114; Fax: 618-942-3114.
Catechesis/Religious Programs—Tel: 618-985-5059.
Students 76.

Caseyville, St. Clair Co., St. Stephen, Rev. Thomas D. Flach; Deacon Julius Gasawski.
Res., 901 S. Main St., P.O. Box 458, 62232. Tel: 618-397-0666; Fax: 618-397-4430.

Centralia, Marion Co., St. Mary, Rev. James R. Dougherty.
Res., 424 E. Broadway, 62801. Tel: 618-532-6291; Fax: 618-532-4758. [CEM]
Church Office: 424 E. Broadway, 62801.
School—Mrs. Jeanette Shaw, Prin. Lay Teachers 7; Students 124.
Catechesis/Religious Programs—Mrs. Dolores Sanders, D.R.E.
Students 90.

Centreville, St. Clair Co., Immaculate Conception, Rev. Elmar Mauer, O.M.I.; Bro. Edward Driggins, O.M.I., Pastoral Assoc.
Res., 6210 Church Rd., 62207. Tel: 618-337-5682; 337-7493; Fax: 618-337-7493. [CEM]

Chester, Randolph Co., St. Mary Help of Christians, Very Rev. Dennis R. Schaefer, V.F.
Res., 911 Swanwick St., 62233. Tel: 618-826-2444. [CEM]
School—Tel: 618-826-3120. Lorna Gibbar, Prin.
Sisters 1; Lay Teachers 11; Students 159.
Catechesis/Religious Programs—Tel: 618-826-2526. Sr. Catherine Schmiz, A.S.C., D.R.E.
Students 45.

Christopher, Franklin Co., St. Andrew, Rev. Walter M. Barr.
Res., 412 E. Washington St., 62822. Tel: 618-724-4114. [CEM]
Catechesis/Religious Programs—Elaine Polbinski, D.R.E.
Students 76.

Cobden, Union Co., St. Joseph, Rev. Federico Higuera; Deacons Garth Gillan; Patrick Patterson.
Res., 101 Centennial St., P.O. Box 237, 62920. Tel: 618-893-2276. [CEM]
Catechesis/Religious Programs—Tel: 618-893-2368.
Students 62.

Columbia, Monroe Co., Immaculate Conception of the B.V.M., Rev. Stephen J. Humphrey; Sr. Lorraine DeFabbo, O.S.F., Pastoral Assoc.; Deacons John DuPrey; Linus Horcher; Leo A. Weilbacher.
Res., 117 E. Madison, 62236. Tel: 618-281-5105. [CEM]
School—Tel: 618-281-5358; 281-5353. Michael Kish, Prin.
Lay Teachers 18; Students 364.
Catechesis/Religious Programs—Students 121.

Coulterville, Randolph Co., St. Anthony. Attended by St. Anthony, Lively Grove.
6101 St. Anthony Church Rd., Oakdale, 62268. Tel: 618-824-6271.

Dahlgren, Hamilton Co., St. John Nepomucene, Rev. E. Alan Ruppert.
Main St., Box H, 62828. Tel: 618-736-2879; 643-3552. [CEM]
Res., 103 N. Hancock, McLeansboro, 62859.
Catechesis/Religious Programs—Rita Rapp, D.R.E.
Students 60.

Damiansville, Clinton Co., St. Damian, Rev. Leo S. Reinhardt, Pastor.
Res., One W. Main St., 62215. Tel: 618-248-5134. [CEM]
Catechesis/Religious Programs—Students 99.

Dubois, Washington Co., St. Charles Borromeo, Rev. Daniel J. Jurek.
Res., P.O. Box 6, 62831. Tel: 618-787-2781. [CEM]
School—Tel: 618-787-2722. Mrs. Charlotte Pestka, Prin.
Lay Teachers 5; Students 37.

Dupo, St. Clair Co., Sacred Heart of Jesus, Rev. Paul R. Wienhoff.
Res., 100 S. 3rd St., 62239. Tel: 618-286-3224.
Catechesis/Religious Programs—Tel: 618-286-4373.
Students 39.

Du Quoin, Perry Co., Sacred Heart of Jesus, Rev. Richard L. Daly.
Res., 17 N. Walnut St., 62832. Tel: 618-542-3423. [CEM]
School—Tel: 618-542-2335. William Daters, Prin.
Lay Teachers 8; Students 103.
Catechesis/Religious Programs—Students 35.

East St. Louis, St. Clair Co.,

1—Immaculate Conception, (Lithuanian). Unassigned.
1509 Baugh Ave., 62205. Tel: 618-874-0162.

2—St. John Francis Regis. Attended by St. Patrick, East St. Louis.
Tel: 618-874-5025.

3—St. Joseph, Revs. Robert J. Luchi, S.J.; Robert L. Sullivan, S.J.
Res., 408 Columbia Pl., 62205. Tel: 618-274-0655.
Catechesis/Religious Programs—Nicole Younge, D.R.E.
Students 20.

4—St. Patrick, Rev. James Clyde Grogan. In res., Rev. James A. Voelker.
Res., 771 Vogel Pl., 62205. Tel: 618-874-5025; Fax: 618-274-4659. [CEM]
Catechesis/Religious Programs—Students 29.

5—St. Philip, Rev. James A. Voelker, Pastor.
Res., 771 Vogel Pl., 62205. Tel: 618-271-6168. [CEM]
Church—8313 Church Ln., 62203. Tel: 618-397-1860.

Eldorado, Saline Co., St. Mary, Rev. Donald E. Abell.
Res., 1158 N. 2nd St., 62930. Tel: 618-273-6947. [CEM]
Catechesis/Religious Programs—Students 104.

Elizabethtown, Hardin Co., St. Joseph, Rev. Joseph L. Trapp, Admin.
Res., 185E 350N. Rd., Rte. 1, P.O. Box 140, 62931-9711. Tel: 618-285-3332. [CEM]
Catechesis/Religious Programs—Students 45.

Ellis Grove, Randolph Co., Divine Maternity of the B.V.M., Deacon Omer E. DuBois.
Res., 7362 Shawneetown Trail, 62241. Tel: 618-859-3541.

Enfield, White Co., St. Patrick, Rev. Michael Maughan, S.M.A.
Res., Rte. 2, 62835. Tel: 618-963-2013. [CEM]

Equality, Gallatin Co., St. Joseph, Rev. Msgr. Charles A. NeBel, Admin.
Mailing Address: P.O. Box 99, 62934. Tel: 618-276-4252.
Res., P.O. Box 190, Ridgway, 62979. Tel: 618-272-7059. [CEM]

Evansville, Randolph Co., St. Boniface, Rev. Joseph C. Rascher; Sr. Diane Marie Turner, S.S.N.D., Pastoral Assoc.
Res., 1003 Olive St., 62242. Tel: 618-853-4453; Fax: 618-853-4453. [CEM]
Catechesis/Religious Programs—Students 39.

Fairfield, Wayne Co., St. Edward,
Res., 300 N.W. 5th St., 62837. Tel: 618-847-7931.
Catechesis/Religious Programs—Jean Hadfield, D.R.E.
Students 50.

Fairmont City, St. Clair Co., Holy Rosary, Rev. David M. Wilke, Pastor.
Res., 2716 N. 42nd St., 62201. Tel: 618-274-3486; Fax: 618-274-1814.
School—Tel: 618-271-8600. Mrs. Shirley Kurre, Prin.
Lay Teachers 6; Students 95.

Fairview Heights, St. Clair Co., Our Lady of the Assumption, Rev. James H. Jansen; Deacon Dennis C. Rickert.
Res., 9950 Bunkum Rd., 62208. Tel: 618-397-0121.
Catechesis/Religious Programs—Students 75.

St. Albert the Great, Very Rev. James T. Long, V.F.; Deacons David Bigham; James P. Duff.
Res., 15 E. Lincoln Hwy., 62208. Tel: 618-632-5334; Fax: 618-632-0903.
School—Tel: 618-632-4937. Sr. Mary Jane Nowakowski, O.S.F., Prin.
Sisters 3; Lay Teachers 14; Students 235.
Catechesis/Religious Programs—Tel: 618-632-8577. Robert Bigham, D.R.E.
Students 190.

Fayetteville, St. Clair Co., St. Pancratius, Very Rev. James A. Blazine, V.F.; Deacon George Munie.
Res., 2213 N. 2nd St., 62258. Tel: 618-677-2717. [CEM]

Flora, Clay Co., St. Stephen, Rev. Hyacinth Mazuchowski.
Res., 812 N. Main St., 62839. Tel: 618-662-6261. [CEM]
Catechesis/Religious Programs—Students 72.

Freeburg, St. Clair Co., St. Joseph, Rev. Henry J. Fischer.
Res., 9 N. Alton St., 62243. Tel: 618-539-3209. [CEM]
School—Tel: 618-539-3930. Sr. Cynthia Weber, S.S.N.D., Prin.
Sisters 2; Lay Teachers 8; Students 140.
Catechesis/Religious Programs—Tel: 618-539-3209.
Students 123.

Germantown, Clinton Co., St. Boniface, Rev. Vincent A. Haselhorst.
Res., 402 Munster St., Box 280, 62245. Tel: 618-523-4271. [CEM]
Catechesis/Religious Programs—Students 278.

Grand Chain, Pulaski Co., St. Catherine. Attended by Immaculate Conception-St. Mary, Mound City. Sr. Nancy Flamm, S.S.N.D., Pastoral Assoc.
517 N. Walnut St., Box 67, Mound City, 62963. Tel: 618-748-9113. [CEM]

Harrisburg, Saline Co., St. Mary, Rev. John E. Stallings; Margaret Bickett, Pastoral Assoc.; Deacon Carl J. Hauptmann.
Res., 2000 W. Poplar St., 62946. Tel: 618-253-7408. [CEM]
Catechesis/Religious Programs—Tel: 618-252-7874.
Students 83.

Hecker, Monroe Co., St. Augustine of Canterbury, Rev. Ralph L. Haas.
Res., P.O. Box 126, 62248. Tel: 618-473-2217; Fax: 618-473-9141. [CEM]
School—Tel: 618-473-2678; Fax: 618-473-9141. Lydia Dudzik, Prin.
Lay Teachers 6; Students 45.

Herrin, Williamson Co., Our Lady of Mount Carmel, Revs. Kenneth J. Schaefer; Brian Barker.
Res., 316 W. Monroe St., 62948. Tel: 618-942-3114; Fax: 618-942-3114. [CEM]
School—Tel: 618-942-4484. Mrs. Christine Hill, Prin.
Lay Teachers 11; Students 246.
Catechesis/Religious Programs—Students 55.

Johnston City, Williamson Co., St. Paul, Rev. Msgr. Paulin J. Dobkowski.
Res., 1103 Washington St., 62951. Tel: 618-983-5073.
Catechesis/Religious Programs—Rev. Msgr. Paulin J. Dobkowski, D.R.E.
Students 44.

Kaskaskia, Randolph Co., Immaculate Conception. (Independent Mission).
Mailing Address:St. Mary's, MO 63673.

Kinmundy, Marion Co., St. Elizabeth Ann Seton. Attended by St. Theresa of Avila, Salem.
719 Markland St., Salem, 62881. Tel: 618-548-0899.

Lawrenceville, Lawrence Co., St. Lawrence, Rev. C. Ray Schultz.
Res., 1006 Collins, 62439. Tel: 618-943-5255. [JC]
Catechesis/Religious Programs—Students 62.

Lebanon, St. Clair Co., St. Joseph, Revs. James E. Margason; Eugene J. Neff; Mrs. Brenda Pehle, Parish Life Coord.
Res., 901 N. Alton St., 62254. Tel: 618-537-2575. [CEM]
Catechesis/Religious Programs—Students 120.

Lively Grove, Washington Co., St. Anthony, Rev. Dean Braun.
Res., 6101 St. Anthony Church Rd., Oakdale, 62268. Tel: 618-824-6271. [CEM]
Catechesis/Religious Programs—Tel: 618-824-9212.
Students 68.

Madonnaville, Monroe Co., Immaculate Conception. Attended by St. Mary, Valmeyer.
101 S. Meyer St., Valmeyer, 62295.; Tel: 618-939-6618; 618-935-2247.

Marion, Williamson Co., St. Joseph, Rev. Richard G. Mohr.
Res., 600 N. Russell St., P.O. Box 1679, 62959. Tel: 618-993-3194; Fax: 618-997-9391.
Catechesis/Religious Programs—Tel: 618-997-9046. Sr. Anastasia Wehner, S.S.N.D., D.R.E.
Students 233.

Marydale, Clinton Co., St. Teresa of Avila, Rev. Jerome W. Feldmann.
Res., 18021 Marydale Rd., Carlyle, 62231. Tel: 618-594-3266.
Catechesis/Religious Programs—Tel: 618-594-4298. John Hempen, D.R.E.
Students 117.

Mascoutah, St. Clair Co., Holy Childhood of Jesus, Rev. Jerome D. Hartlein.
Res., 104 N. Independence St., P.O. Box 160, 62258. Tel: 618-566-2958. [CEM]
School—Tel: 618-566-2922. Diana Roberts, Prin.
Sisters 1; Lay Teachers 16; Students 228.
Catechesis/Religious Programs—Tel: 618-566-2922. Sr. Frances McDonagh, O.S.U., D.R.E.
Students 138.

McLeansboro, Hamilton Co., St. Clement, Rev. E. Alan Ruppert.
Res., 601 E. Market, 62859. Tel: 618-643-3552. [CEM]
Catechesis/Religious Programs—Tel: 618-643-3628. D.R.E.: Robin Hylton; Kathy Smith.
Students 72.

Metropolis, Massac Co., St. Rose of Lima, Rev. Joseph L. Trapp.

Res., 315 E. Third St., 62960-2229. Tel: 618-524-9006.
Catechesis/Religious Programs—Office:, 405 E. Third St., 62960. Tel: 618-524-8202. Marjorie J. Hawes, D.R.E.
Students 57.

Millstadt, St. Clair Co., St. James, Rev. Bernard C. Goedde, Jr.
Res., 405 W. Madison St., 62260. Tel: 618-476-3513. [CEM]
School—Tel: 618-476-3510. Sr. Barbara Hudock, A.S.C., Prin.
Sisters 3; Lay Teachers 7; Students 191.
Catechesis/Religious Programs—Students 105.

Modoc, Randolph Co., St. Leo, Rev. John J. Joyce, Admin.
Res., #1 Pioneer Ln., Red Bud, 62278. Tel: 618-282-3176. [CEM]

Mound City, Pulaski Co., Church of the Immaculate Conception-St. Mary, Rev. William P. McGhee; Sr. Nancy Flamm, S.S.N.D., Pastoral Assoc.
Res., 517 N. Walnut St., Box 67, 62963. Tel: 618-748-9113. [CEM]

Mount Carmel, Wabash Co., St. Mary, Rev. William J. Rowe.
Res., 125 W. Fifth St., 62863. Tel: 618-262-5337. [CEM]
School—Tel: 618-263-3183.
Lay Teachers 12; Students 203.
Catechesis/Religious Programs—Students 86.

Mount Vernon, Jefferson Co., St. Mary, Very Rev. Melvin B. Vandeloo, V.F.
Res., 115 N. 14th St., 62864. Tel: 618-244-1559; Fax: 618-242-5365. [CEM]
School—Tel: 618-242-5353; Fax: 618-242-5365. Sr. Susan Cunningham, Prin.
Lay Teachers 7; Students 91.
Catechesis/Religious Programs—Students 285.

Murphysboro, Jackson Co., St. Andrew, Very Rev. James A. Buerster, V.F.; Deacon Michael Dougherty (JOL).
Res., 724 Mulberry St., 62966. Tel: 618-687-2012; Fax: 618-687-2012. [CEM]
School—Tel: 618-687-2013; Fax: 618-684-4969. Marilyn Johnson, Prin.
Lay Teachers 12; Students 179.
Catechesis/Religious Programs—Tel: 618-684-6364. Mrs. Patti Wagnitz, D.R.E.
Students 127.

Nashville, Washington Co., St. Ann, Rev. Albert L. Jerome.
Res., 631 S. Mill St., 62263. Tel: 618-327-3232. [CEM]
School—Tel: 618-327-8741. Sr. Barbara Habing, S.S.N.D., Prin.
Sisters 1; Lay Teachers 7; Students 91.
Catechesis/Religious Programs—Tel: 618-327-3232.
Students 94.
Convent—695 S. Mill St., 62263. Tel: 618-327-3771.

New Athens, St. Clair Co., St. Agatha, Rev. David M. Darin.
Res., 205 S. Market St., 62264. Tel: 618-475-2331.
School—Tel: 618-475-2170. Sr. Annette M. Kaba, O.S.F., Prin.
Lay Teachers 4; Students 67.
Catechesis/Religious Programs—Students 90.

New Baden, Clinton Co., St. George, Rev. Thomas M. Barrett.
Res., 200 N. 3rd St., 62265. Tel: 618-588-4323. [CEM]
Catechesis/Religious Programs—Tel: 618-588-3504.
Students 176.

O'Fallon, St. Clair Co., St. Clare, Rev. James E. Deiters.
Res., 205 W. 3rd St., 62269. Tel: 618-632-3562; Fax: 618-632-9036. [CEM]
School—214 W. 3rd St., 62269. Tel: 618-632-6327.
Lay Teachers 24; Students 431.
Catechesis/Religious Programs—Tel: 618-632-4281. Mrs. Martha Tasker, D.R.E.
Students 340.

St. Nicholas, Rev. William J. Hitpas; Deacon Richard H. Olson.
Res., 900 N. Smiley, 62269. Tel: 618-632-1797.
Catechesis/Religious Programs—Tel: 618-632-1007. Barbara Furdek, D.R.E.
Students 240.

Okawville, Washington Co., St. Barbara, Rev. Msgr. Angelo J. Lombardo.
Res., 305 N. Front St., 62271. Tel: 618-243-6236. [CEM]
Catechesis/Religious Programs—Tel: 618-243-6236.
Students 113.

Olney, Richland Co., St. Joseph, Revs. Jerry E. Wirth; Gerald R. Hechenberger.
Res., 215 S. Elliott St., 62450. Tel: 618-392-8181; Fax: 618-395-8500. [CEM]
School—Tel: 618-395-8500; Fax: 618-395-8500. Carol Steinman, Prin.
Lay Teachers 12; Students 229.
Catechesis/Religious Programs—Students 75.

Paderborn, St. Clair Co., St. Michael, Rev. Joseph D. Hansmann.
Res., 4576 Buss Branch Rd., Waterloo, 62298. Tel: 618-473-2798. [CEM]
Catechesis/Religious Programs—Jackie Billings, D.R.E.
Students 70.

Pinckneyville, Perry Co., St. Bruno, Rev. John L. Venegoni.
Res., 204 W. Gordon Ave., P.O. Box 205, 62274. Tel: 618-357-5510; Fax: 618-357-6050. [CEM]
School—Tel: 618-357-8276; Fax: 618-357-6425. Sr. Janet McCann, A.S.C., Prin.
Sisters 2; Lay Teachers 8; Students 144.
Catechesis/Religious Programs—Marcia Hagene, D.R.E.
Students 82.

Piopolis, Hamilton Co., St. John the Baptist, Rev. Joseph A. Lawler.
Res., Rte. 3, P.O. Box 170, McLeansboro, 62859. Tel: 618-648-2490. [CEM]
Catechesis/Religious Programs—Jewell Wilson, D.R.E.
Students 63.

Pond Settlement, Gallatin Co., St. Patrick. Attended by St. Mary, Shawneetown.
P.O. Box 579, Shawneetown, 62984. Tel: 618-269-3318.

Posen, Washington Co., Our Lady of Perpetual Help, Rev. James R. Van Oss.
Res., 19824 Posen Rd., Nashville, 62263. Tel: 618-327-3556. [CEM]

Prairie du Rocher, Randolph Co., St. Joseph, Rev. Albert E. Kreher.
Res., 802 Middle St., 62277. Tel: 618-284-3314. [CEM]
Catechesis/Religious Programs—Students 101.

Raddle, Jackson Co., St. Ann. Attended by St. Elizabeth, Ava.
606 W. George St., P.O. Box 157, Ava, 62907. Tel: 618-426-3321.

Radom, Washington Co., St. Michael, Rev. Jerome H. Hibner.
Res., 52 S. Third St., 62876. Tel: 618-485-2265. [CEM]
School—Tel: 618-485-6461. Mrs. Mary Czerniejewski, Prin.
Lay Teachers 4; Students 66.
Catechesis/Religious Programs—Students 66.

Red Bud, Randolph Co., St. John the Baptist, Rev. Thomas Stout.
Res., 515 Locust St., 62278. Tel: 618-282-3222. [CEM]
School—Tel: 618-282-3215. Sr. Louise O'Connor, S.S.N.D., Prin.
School Sisters of Notre Dame 2; Lay Teachers 8; Students 207.
Catechesis/Religious Programs—Students 75.

Renault, Monroe Co., Our Lady of Good Counsel, Rev. Roger R. Karban, Admin.
Res., P.O. Box 98, 62279. Tel: 618-458-7710. [CEM]

Ridgway, Gallatin Co., St. Joseph, Rev. Msgr. Charles A. Nebel, Admin.
Res., P.O. Box 190, 62979. Tel: 618-272-7059. [CEM]
Catechesis/Religious Programs—Tel: 618-272-7455.
Students 105.

Royalton, Franklin Co., St. Aloysius, Rev. Peter Hsu.
Res., Pecan St., P.O. Box 100, 62983. Tel: 618-984-2146. [CEM]
Catechesis/Religious Programs—Students 16.

Ruma, Randolph Co., St. Patrick, Rev. John J. Joyce, Admin.
Res., #1 Pioneer Ln., Red Bud, 62278. Tel: 618-282-3176. [CEM]
Catechesis/Religious Programs—Students 22.

St. Francisville, Lawrence Co., St. Francis Xavier. Attended by St. Lawrence.
1006 Collins St., Lawrenceville, 62439. [CEM]

St. Libory, St. Clair Co., St. Liborius, Rev. Jose Ancheril.
Res., P.O. Box 331, 62282. Tel: 618-768-4921. [CEM]
Catechesis/Religious Programs—Tel: 618-768-4992. Donna Dressler, D.R.E.
Students 115.

St. Rose, Clinton Co., St. Rose, Rev. Edward F. Schaefer.
Res., 18010 St. Rose Rd., 62230-2506. Tel: 618-526-4118; Fax: 618-526-0004. [CEM]
Catechesis/Religious Programs—Tel: 618-526-4886. Sr. Justina Schaefer, A.S.C., D.R.E.
Students 300.

St. Sebastian, Wabash Co., St. Sebastian. Attended by St. Edward, Fairfield.
300 N.W. Fifth St., Fairfield, 62837. Tel: 618-847-7931. [CEM]

Salem, Marion Co., St. Theresa of Avila, Rev. Jon O'Guinn.
Res., 719 Markland St., 62881. Tel: 618-548-0899. [CEM]
School—Sr. Ruth Chausse, S.S.N.D., Prin. School Sisters of Notre Dame 1; Lay Teachers 6; Students 82.
Catechesis/Religious Programs—Students 70.

Sandoval, Marion Co., St. Lawrence, Rev. Charles W. Tuttle.
Church—311 W.M St., P.O. Box 278, 62882. Tel: 618-247-3300. [CEM]
Res., P.O. Box 189, Breese, 62230. Tel: 618-594-2131.
Catechesis/Religious Programs—Students 67.

Scheller, Jefferson Co., St. Barbara. Attended by St. Michael, Radom.
Res., 62883. Tel: 618-279-7207.

Sesser, Franklin Co., St. Mary, Rev. Louis A. Koehr.
Res., 100 N. Poplar St.; P.O. Box 568, 62884. Tel: 618-625-5053.
Catechesis/Religious Programs—Students 32.

Shawneetown, Gallatin Co., St. Mary, Rev. Henry Ray Engelhart.
Res., P.O. Box 579, 62984. Tel: 618-269-3318. [CEM]
Catechesis/Religious Programs—Students 50.

Shiloh, St. Clair Co., Corpus Christi, Rev. Gerald C. Miriani.
Res., 206 Rasp St., O'Fallon, 62269. Tel: 618-632-5631.
Catechesis/Religious Programs—Tel: 618-632-7614.
Students 67.

Smithton, St. Clair Co., St. John the Baptist, Rev. Kenneth J. York, J.C.L.
Res., 10 S. Lincoln St., 62285-1614. Tel: 618-234-2068; Fax: 618-234-0179. [CEM]
School—Tel: 618-233-0581. Stephen Boyer, Prin.
Lay Teachers 7; Students 102.

Sparta, Randolph Co., Our Lady of Lourdes, Rev. William F. Rensing; Deacon J. Richard Downen.
Res., 611 W. Broadway, 62286. Tel: 618-443-2811.
Catechesis/Religious Programs—Tel: 618-443-2878. Lila Lehnherr, D.R.E.
Students 136.

Stonefort, Williamson Co., St. Francis de Sales. Attended by St. Paul, Vienna.
2020 State Rte. 146E., Vienna, 62995. Tel: 618-658-4501.

Stringtown, Richland Co., St. Joseph. Attended by St. Joseph, Olney.
215 S. Elliott St., Olney, 62450. Tel: 618-392-6711; Fax: 618-395-8500. [CEM]
Catechesis/Religious Programs—Tel: 618-395-2862. Barbara Ochs, D.R.E.
Students 56.

Tamaroa, Perry Co., Immaculate Conception, Rev. Daniel J. Jurek.
Res., R.R. 2, Box 91, 62888. Tel: 618-496-5867.
Catechesis/Religious Programs—Students 57.

Tipton, Monroe Co., St. Patrick, Rev. Gary P. Gummersheimer.
Res., 5675 LL Rd., Waterloo, 62298. Tel: 618-458-6875. [CEM]

Todd's Mill, Perry Co., St. Mary Magdalen, Rev. James R. Van Oss.
Res., R.R. 3, Nashville, 62263. Tel: 618-336-5414. [CEM]

Trenton, Clinton Co., St. Mary, Rev. Robert B. Flannery; Sr. Angela J. Schrage, A.S.C., Pastoral Assoc. & D.R.E.; Deacon John P. Dilley.
Res., 215 W. Kentucky St., 62293. Tel: 618-224-9335; Fax: 618-224-9346. [CEM]
Catechesis/Religious Programs—Students 187.

Ullin, Pulaski Co., Our Lady of Fatima. Attended by St. Mary, Mound City. Sr. Nancy Flamm, S.S.N.D., Pastoral Assoc.
517 N. Walnut St., Box 67, Mound City, 62963. Tel: 618-748-9113. [CEM]

Valmeyer, Monroe Co., Seven Dolors of the B.V.M., Rev. Edwin H. Hustedde.
Res., 101 Meyer Dr., P.O. Box 206, 62295. Tel: 618-939-6618; Fax: 618-935-2247.
Catechesis/Religious Programs—Tel: 618-935-2521. Mrs. Carol Sondag, D.R.E.
Students 67.

Vienna, Johnson Co., St. Paul, Rev. Edward Balestrieri, Admin.
Res., 2020 State Rte. 146E., 62995. Tel: 618-658-4501.

Catechesis/Religious Programs—Students 40.

Walsh, Randolph Co., St. Pius. Attended by St. Boniface, Evansville. Sr. Diane Marie Turner, S.S.N.D., Pastoral Assoc.
P.O. Box 32, 62297. Tel: 618-853-4404.
Catechesis/Religious Programs—Students 35.

Washington Park, St. Clair Co., St. Martin of Tours, Rev. James A. Yoelker.
Res., 771 Vogel Pl., East St. Louis, 62205. Tel: 618-874-0713; 271-6168.

Waterloo, Monroe Co., SS. Peter and Paul, Rev. Francis L. Seyer.
Res., 204 W. Mill St., 62298. Tel: 618-939-6426. [CEM]
School—Tel: 618-939-7217. Mrs. Ruth Rosenhauer, Prin.
Lay Teachers 21; Students 340.
Catechesis/Religious Programs—Lucille Ohms, D.R.E.
Students 240.

Wendelin, Clay Co., Holy Cross, Rev. David L. Braun.
Res., P.O. Star Rte., Newton, 62448. Tel: 618-752-5671. [CEM]
Catechesis/Religious Programs—Students 202.

West Frankfort, Franklin Co., St. John the Baptist, Rev. John A. Baggio.
Res., 703 E. Main St., 62896. Tel: 618-932-2828. [CEM]
School—Tel: 618-937-2017. Sr. Lucia Pinski, O.S.F., Prin.
Franciscan Sisters of Our Lady of Perpetual Help 2; Lay Teachers 5; Students 80.
Catechesis/Religious Programs—Kathy Heim, D.R.E.
Students 21.

Willisville, Perry Co., St. Joseph. Attended by St. Elizabeth, Ava.
606 George St., P.O. Box 157, Ava, 62907. Tel: 618-426-3321. [CEM]
Catechesis/Religious Programs—Students 24.

Zeigler, Franklin Co., Sacred Heart. Attended by St. Aloysius, Royalton.
Pecan St., P.O. Box 100, Royalton, 62983. Tel: 618-984-2146.
Catechesis/Religious Programs—Students 16.

Sacramental Records Located In Chancery Archives:

1—St. John's Orphanage, Belleville.
2—Holy Angels Church, East St. Louis.
3—Sacred Heart Church, East St. Louis.
4—St. Adalbert Church, East St. Louis.
5—SS. Cyril and Methodius Church, East St. Louis.
6—St. Elizabeth Church, East St. Louis.
7—St. Henry Church, East St. Louis.
8—St. Mary Church, East St. Louis.
9—St. Thomas Church, Millstadt.
10—St. Augustine Church, East St. Louis.
11—St. Joseph Church, Wetaug.

Chaplains of Correctional Institutions and State Hospitals

Anna. *Anna State Hospital*. Attended from St. Mary Church, Anna. Thomas W. Miller, Chap., Tel: 618-833-5835.

Centralia. *Centralia Correctional Center*. Vacant. P.O. Box 1266, 62801.

Chester. *Chester Mental Health Center.* P.O. Box 31, 62233. Tel: 618-826-4571. 310 N. Main St., Hecker, 62248. Tel: 618-473-2217. Rev. Ralph L. Haas, Chap.

Harrisburg. *Illinois Youth Center*. Vacant. P.O. Box 300, 62946.

Marion. *Federal Maximum Security Prison*. P.O. Box 2000, 62959. Deacon Pat Patterson, Chap., Tel: 618-964-1441.
Veterans Hospital. Attended from St. Joseph, Marion. Vacant.

Menard. *Menard Correctional Center.* P.O. Box 711, 62259. Rev. Leo J. Hayes, Chap., Tel: 618-826-5071.
Menard Psychiatric Center Box 56, 62259. Tel: 618-826-4593. Rev. Joseph C. Rascher, Chap.

Vienna. *Dixon Springs Work Camp*. Vacant. 62995.
Shawnee Correctional Center. Box 400, 62995. Rev. Thomas W. Miller, Chap.
Vienna Correctional Center. Attended from Anna. Rev. Thomas W. Miller, Chap., Tel: 618-833-5835.

Military Chaplains:
Reverend Fathers—
Gegotek, Tadeusz, U.S.N.
Voelker, David A., U.S.A.F.

Special Assignment:
Reverend Fathers—
Frerker, Jack W., Lacey, WA
Geller, Charles H., Fort Stockton, TX
Nall, James M., Rome, IL
Stec, Mark D.

Leave of Absence:
Reverend Monsignors—
Schwaegel, Joseph R.
Reverend Fathers—
Chlopecki, Robert J.
Crook, David G.
Harbaugh, Paul E.
Kownacki, Raymond F.
Linnemann, Eugene C.
Peterson, Louis P.
Sebescak, Gary
Unverferth, Steven R.
Vonnahmen, Robert J.
Witte, D. Steven

Retired:
Reverend Monsignors—
Driscoll, Maurice F., 228 River Bend Dr., Mobile, AL 36605-3198
Drone, Raphael E., Ch. Col. U.S.A.F., 5723 Worchester Dr., Montgomery, AL 36116
Dunn, Meinrad M., Hincke Residence for Priests, 2620 Lebanon Ave., Belleville, IL 62221
Fellner, John V.
Kuhl, Urban B., Hincke Residence for Priests, 2620 Lebanon Ave., Belleville, IL 62221
McCormick, James R., Hincke Residence for Priests, 2620 Lebanon Ave., Belleville, IL 62221
Nebel, Charles A., Hincke Residence for Priests, 2620 Lebanon Ave., Belleville, IL 62221
Sullivan, Bernard O., 222 S. Third St., Belleville, IL 62220
Reverend Fathers—
Arentsen, Edwin F., Sense Residence, 2620 Lebanon Ave., Belleville, IL 62221
Arnold, J. Ralph, Hincke Residence for Priests, 2620 Lebanon Ave., Belleville, IL 62221
Bertsche, Conrad J., 6451 Fairlynn Blvd., Yorba Linda, CA 92686
Brandmeyer, William H., 126 Pullen Blvd., Centralia, IL 62801
Bungay, Eugene L., Hincke Residence for Priests, 2620 Lebanon Ave., Belleville, IL 62221
Dollar, Robert J., 222 S. Third St., Belleville, IL 62220
Gasiunas, John, Shore Plaza Bldg., Apt. 215, 1893 Shore Dr., South Pasadena, FL 33707
Hays, Joseph C., Sense Residence, 2620 Lebanon Ave., Belleville, IL 62221
Hentschel, Cletus B., 5315 W. Main St., Belleville, IL 62223
Iffert, Wilbert J., 147 Juniper Dr., Oak Grove Terrace, Mount Vernon, IL 62864
Kastner, Edwin H., 222 S. Third St., Belleville, IL 62220
Kopff, Herbert C., 4419 Taft, St. Louis, MO 63116
Kribs, Charles R., Jefferson Town Homes, 2686 Elkhill Dr., St. Louis, MO 63125
Lopardo, Vito R., Hincke Residence for Priests, 2620 Lebanon Ave., Belleville, IL 62221
MacPherson, Walter E., 222 S. Third St., Belleville, IL 62220
Malec, Raymond S., Hincke Residence for Priests, 2620 Lebanon Ave., Belleville, IL 62221
Meskenas, Vincent A., St. Isidore Church, 222 Clark Ave., Yuba City, CA 95991
Misho, Lloyd P., Sense Residence, 2620 Lebanon Ave., Belleville, IL 62221
Mueller, Joseph P., Hincke Residence for Priests, 2620 Lebanon Ave., Belleville, IL 62221
Perjak, Edmond J., 210 Pelham Rd., Pier 1, Apt. 108-B, Fort Walton Beach, FL 32547
Podrasky, Michael P., 1500 Hardy St., Eldorado, IL 62930
Ratermann, Jerome B., 222 S. Third St., Belleville, IL 62220
Reeb, Edward J., 1427 Evergreen Ln., Columbia, IL 62236
Ruggles, John J., P.O. Box 271, Okawville, IL 62271
Stauder, Paul W., Hincke Residence for Priests, 2620 Lebanon Ave., Belleville, IL 62221
Thoon Kuzhy, Joseph, 782 State St. B, Chester, IL 62233

Permanent Deacons:
Becker, Robert H.
Bigham, David J.
Cerneka, Peter
Dilley, John P.
Dougherty, Michael
Downen, J. Richard
DuBois, Omer E.
Duff, James P.
DuPrey, John L.
Gasawski, Julius S., (Retired)
Gillan, Garth J.
Hauptmann, Carl J.
Horcher, Linus H.
Igel, Joseph H., (Retired)
Kirchgraber, Robert B., (Retired)
Kronenberger, Ken, Leave of Absence
Munie, George J.
Olson, Richard H.
Patterson, Pat
Prien, Richard K.
Rickert, Dennis
Stock, Joseph E.
Stockmann, Gerald E.
Theis, Francis D., Leave of Absence
Weilbacher, L. Arthur, Jr.

INSTITUTIONS LOCATED IN THE DIOCESE

[A] COLLEGES AND UNIVERSITIES

Cahokia. *Parks College of Saint Louis University*, 62206. *For a complete listing, refer to the Colleges and Universities section.*

[B] HIGH SCHOOLS, DIOCESAN

Belleville. *Althoff Catholic High School*, 5401 W. Main St., 62223. Tel: 618-235-1100. Sr. Jan Renz, A.S.C., Prin. Sisters 2; Lay Teachers 50; Students 755.

Breese. *Mater Dei High School*, 900 N. Mater Dei Dr., 62230. Tel: 618-526-7216. Central Catholic High School for Clinton Co. Curt L. Winter, Prin.; Sr. Virginia Kampwerth, P.H.J.C., Asst. Prin., Academics; Dennis Litteken, Asst. Prin., Student Affairs; Rev. Charles W. Tuttle. Sisters 3; Lay Teachers 41; Students 571.

Waterloo. *Gibault Catholic High School*, 501 Columbia Ave., 62298. Tel: 618-939-3883. Mr. Daniel J. Brueggeman, Prin.; Revs. Edwin H. Hustedde, Dir. of Devel.; Gary P. Gummersheimer; Roger R. Karban. Priests 3; Adorers of the Blood of Christ 1; Lay Teachers 20; Students 315.

[C] ELEMENTARY SCHOOLS

Breese. *All Saints Academy*. (Grades PreK-8), 295 N. Clinton St., 62230. Tel: 618-526-4323. Consolidated schools of Saint Augustine, Saint Dominic parishes, Breese, IL, and St. Anthony Parish, Beckemeyer, IL. Co-Principals: Alice Gardner; Kelly Koishor. Sisters 1; Lay Teachers 23; Students 490.

East St. Louis. *Sister Thea Bowman Catholic School*, 8213 Church Ln., 62203. Tel: 618-397-0316. Mr. Richard Williams, Prin.; Cynthia Rivera, Asst. Prin. Sisters 2; Lay Teachers 13; Students 273.

Fairview Heights. *Elizabeth Ann Seton Catholic School*, 9940 Bunkum Rd., 62208. Tel: 618-398-3011. Consolidated schools of St. Stephen Parish, Caseyville, IL, and Our Lady of the Assumption Parish, Fairview Heights, IL. Sr. Patricia Gravemann, S.S.N.D., Prin. Sisters 2; Lay Teachers 10; Students 212.

[D] DAY CARE CENTERS

Belleville. *Don Bosco Home Children's Center*, 300 N. Church St., 62220. Tel: 618-277-7055. Michele Dain, Dir.
St. Henry Day Care Center, 5301 W. Main St., 62223. Tel: 618-233-3454. Coordinators: Judy Shovlin; Linda Moyer. Children 107.
St. John Children's Home, 2620 Lebanon Ave., 62221. Very Rev. James E. Margason, V.G., Chancery Office, 222 S. Third St., 62220. Tel: 618-277-8181.
St. John Day Care Center, 2620 Lebanon Ave., 62221. Tel: 618-235-6717. Pamela Buettner, Dir. Lay Women 11; Children 76.

East St. Louis. *Catholic Day Care Center*, 617 Summit Ave., 62201. Tel: 618-874-7178. Nursery and Kindergarten. Conducted by the Cordi-Marian Sisters. Sr. Gema Juarez, M.C.M., Dir.; Sr. Henrietta Torres, M.C.M., Supr., 2417 Ridge Ave., 62205. Tel: 618-875-1447. Sisters 3; Lay Teachers 14; Children 100.

[E] GENERAL HOSPITALS

Belleville. *St. Elizabeth Hospital*, 211 S. Third St., 62222. Tel: 618-234-2120; Fax: 618-234-4391.
For a complete listing, refer to the Hospitals section.

Breese. *St. Joseph Hospital*, 9515 Holy Cross Ln., 62230. Tel: 618-526-4511.
For a complete listing, refer to the Hospitals section.

Centralia. *St. Mary's Hospital*, 400 N. Pleasant Ave., 62801. Tel: 618-532-6731.
For a complete listing, refer to the Hospitals section.

East St. Louis. *St. Mary's Hospital*, 129 N. 8th St., 62201. Tel: 618-274-1900.
For a complete listing, refer to the Hospitals section.

Mount Vernon. *Good Samaritan Regional Health Center*, 605 N. 12th St., 62864. Tel: 618-242-4600.
For a complete listing, refer to the Hospitals section.

MURPHYSBORO. *St. Joseph Memorial Hospital*, 800 N. Second St., P.O. Box 580, 62966. Tel: 618-684-3156.
For a complete listing, refer to the Hospitals section.

RED BUD. *St. Clement Health Services*, One St. Clement Blvd., 62278. Tel: 618-282-3831; Fax: 618-282-6101.
For a complete listing, refer to the Hospitals section.

[F] HOMES FOR SENIOR CITIZENS

BELLEVILLE. *Charles and Bertha Hincke Residence for Priests and Sense Residence*, 2620 Lebanon Ave., 62221. Tel: 618-234-5722.
For a complete listing, refer to the Special Care Facilities section.

Meredith Memorial Home, 16 S. Illinois St., 62220. Tel: 618-233-8780.
For a complete listing, refer to the Special Care Facilities section.

Our Lady of the Snows Apartment Community Retirement Home, 9500 W. Illinois Hwy. 15, 62223. Tel: 618-397-6700.
For a complete listing, refer to the Special Care Facilities section.

RED BUD. *Maria Care Center*, 350 W. South First St., 62278. Tel: 618-282-3891.
For a complete listing, refer to the Special Care Facilities section.

[G] MONASTERIES AND RESIDENCES OF PRIESTS AND BROTHERS

BELLEVILLE. *Missionary Oblates of Mary Immaculate - St. Henry's Oblate Residence*, 200 N. 60th St., 62223. Tel: 618-233-2991. Revs. Michael S. Deis, O.M.I., Supr. Oblate Community; Robert Aaron, O.M.I.; Ronald Carignan, O.M.I.; Andrew Chalkey, O.M.I.; Michael Clark, O.M.I.; Rene DuFour, O.M.I.; John Ettensohn, O.M.I.; Vincent Fitzgerald, O.M.I.; Eugene Glaub, O.M.I.; Joseph Knoeber, O.M.I.; Lon Konold, O.M.I.; Robert Morin, O.M.I.; James E. Taylor, O.M.I.; Stephen Wessel, O.M.I.; Bro. David Schell, O.M.I. Priests 14; Brothers 3.

Shrine of Our Lady of the Snows, 442 S. DeMazenod Dr., 62223. Tel: 618-397-6700. Missionary Oblates of Mary Immaculate. Revs. William P. Clark, O.M.I., Dir.; Clarence Zachman, O.M.I., Supr.; Floyd Boeckman, O.M.I.; Gabriel Biondolillo, O.M.I.; Zygmunt Dzierzek, O.M.I.; Boniface Wittenbrink, O.M.I.; Robert Braun, O.M.I.; Robert Eimer, O.M.I.

[H] CONVENTS AND RESIDENCES FOR SISTERS

BELLEVILLE. *Hospital Sisters of St. Francis*, 1036 Rutledge Dr., 62221. Tel: 618-235-5486. Sisters 4.

Hospital Sisters of St. Francis, 1000 Royal Heights Rd., Apt. 58, 62223. Tel: 618-233-1687. Sisters 2.

Motherhouse and Novitiate of Ursuline Sisters of Belleville, 1026 N. Douglas Ave., 62220-4198. Tel: 618-235-3444; 233-5010. Sr. Dorothy Helbling, O.S.U., Community Leader. Total Membership of Congregation 14.

Poor Clare Monastery of Our Lady of Mercy, 300 N. 60th St., 62223. Tel: 618-235-4407. Mother Mary Therese, P.C.C., Abbess; Rev. James S. Orumpakkatt, C.M.I., Chap. Tel: 618-233-6378. Sisters 8.

CAIRO. *Mary Katherine Convent, Poor Handmaids of Jesus Christ*, 725 22nd St., 62914. Tel: 618-734-0778. Sisters 3.

EAST ST. LOUIS. *St. Mary Convent, Poor Handmaids of Jesus Christ*, 5727 Warren St., 62204. Tel: 618-875-7570. Sisters 2.

MOUNT VERNON. *Franciscan Sisters of Mary Convent*, 4235 Lincolnshire Dr., #3-C, 62864-2164. Tel: 618-244-3091. Sisters 2.

RUMA. *Provincial House, Adorers of the Blood of Christ, Province of Ruma*, 2 Pioneer Ln., 62278. Tel: 618-282-3848. Sr. Margaret Mary Kopish, A.S.C., Prov. Supr.; Sr. Bernice Klostermann, A.S.C., Local Admin.; Rev. John J. Joyce, Chap. Sisters 84; Total Membership of the Province 208.

[I] RETREAT HOUSES

BELLEVILLE. *Retreat and Renewal Center*, 700 N. 66th St., 62223-3949. Tel: 618-397-0584. Bro. William Johnson, O.M.I., Team Moderator; Revs. James Donovan, O.M.I.; Roger Schoenhofen, O.M.I.; David Kraus, O.M.I.; Wayne Like, O.M.I.; Bro. Victor Capek, O.M.I.

[J] NEWMAN CENTERS

CARBONDALE. *The Newman Center*, Southern Illinois University, 715 S. Washington, 62901. Tel: 618-529-3311. Mr. John Scarano, Diocesan Dir.; Rev. Cecil Pickert, O.Carm., Campus Min.

[K] MISCELLANEOUS LISTINGS

BELLEVILLE. *Althoff Catholic High School Educational Endowment Trust*, 5401 W. Main St., 62223. Tel: 618-235-1100. Sr. Jan Renz, A.S.C., Contact Person.

Ancient Order of Hibernians. 6616 Itaska, St. Louis, MO, 63109. Tel: 314-353-6351. William Dillon, Pres.

Ancient Order of Hibernians (LAOH). 9773 Holy Cross Rd., Fairview Heights, 62208. Tel: 618-397-0451. Betty Martz, Pres.

Catholic Committee on Scouting of the Diocese of Belleville. 19824 Posen Rd., Nashville, 62263. Tel: 618-336-5414. Rev. James R. Van Oss, Chap.

Catholic Daughters of the Americas. 429 S. Elm St., Centralia, 62801. Tel: 618-532-8352. Miss Mercedes Campbell, Diocesan Chm.

Catholic Knights and Ladies of Illinois, 2021 Mascoutah Ave., 62220. Tel: 618-233-0286.

Catholic War Veterans, Hincke Residence for Priests, 2620 Lebanon Ave., 62221. Tel: 618-257-1584. Rev. Msgr. Urban B. Kuhl, Chap.

Cursillos in Christianity. Belleville Diocese, 1025 Spotsylvania, New Athens, 62264. Tel: 618-475-3438. Bob Emge, Lay Dir.

Engaged Encounter, 221 S. 17th St., 62223. Tel: 618-277-1652. Gerry Bach, Coord.; Ann Bach, Co-ord.

Health Care Endowment Fund of the Reverend Oblate Fathers, 726 Community Dr., 62223. Tel: 618-397-6700.
Oblate Fathers and Trustees. D. Robert McCardle, Admin. & Contact Person. Legal Title: *Health Care Endowment Fund of the Reverend Oblate Fathers at the Shrine of Our Lady of the Snows*.

Missionary Association of Mary Immaculate-Mission Oblates of Mary Immaculate. Serving the missions of the Missionary Oblates, the National Shrine of Our Lady of the Snows, and the Tekakwitha Indian Missions. 9840 N. DeMazenod Dr., 62223-1160. Tel: 618-398-4848. Rev. Louis B. Studel, O.M.I., Dir.; Mr. William J. Nixon, Exec. Dir.; Mr. William P. O'Connor, Dir. Planned Giving. Planned Giving Associates: Revs. Floyd B. Boeckman, O.M.I.; James E. Taylor, O.M.I.; Mrs. Rosalee Cavataio.

Oblate Preaching Team, 200 N. 60th St., 62223. Tel: 618-233-2991. Specializing in Parish Missions. Revs. John Ettensohn, O.M.I., Dir.; Robert Morin, O.M.I.; Lon Konold, O.M.I.; Robert Aaron, O.M.I.

Our Lady of the Snows Layman's Association, 9500 W. Illinois Hwy. 15, 62223. Tel: 618-397-6700. Mr. Dennis Bielke, Pres.; Rev. William P. Clark, O.M.I., Spiritual Mod.

Radio Information Service for Blind and Print Handicapped, 9500 W. State Rte. 15, 62223. Tel: 618-397-6700, Ext. 2221; Fax: 618-398-6549. Closed Circuit Radio for the blind and print handicapped. Mr. Joseph E. Kasperek, Exec. Dir.

St. Francis Thrift Shop, 800 E. Main St., 62220. Tel: 618-233-6998. Mrs. Catherine Heap, Mgr.

Scott Air Force Base, Scott AFB Chapel, 375 AW/HC, 320 J St., Bldg. 1620, 62225-5256. Tel: 618-256-3303. Revs. Terence J. Figel, O.M.I., Lt. Col., Senior Catholic Chap.; Hilarion Mikalofsky (MIL), Major, Chap.; James R. Dixon (NO), Lt. Col.

Secular Franciscan Order, 200 W. Harrison, 62220. Tel: 618-234-1166. St. Peter Fraternity.

Serra Club of St. Clair County, P.O. Box 23017, Dutch Hallow Sta., 62223. Tel: 618-234-2773. Chaplains: Rev. Msgr. Leonard A. Bauer, 16 S. Illinois St., 62220. Rev. Bernard L. Voss, 5315 W. Main St., 62223. Tel: 618-233-2423.

TEC (Teens Encounter Christ), 2620 Lebanon Ave., 62221.

Victorious Missionaries, 9500 W. State Rte. 15, 62223. Tel: 618-397-6700 (Voice/TDD), Ext. 2281. Spiritual Support Network for people with disabilities. Bro. Francis Sullivan, O.M.I., Natl. Dir.

Western Catholic Union, Br. No. 59, 405 Southgate, 62223. Tel: 618-277-2892. Mr. Marion Mueth, Pres.

Worldwide Marriage Encounter, 8116 Circle Dr., 62223. Tel: 618-398-1614. Executive Couple: Dave & Carol Daly.

BREESE. *Daughters of Isabella*. Precious Blood Circle #718, 248 W. Elm, Aviston, 62216. Tel: 618-228-7372. Miss Amelia Wesselmann, Diocesan Chairperson.

CARLYLE. *Carlyle Priest Center*. Contact the Chancery, Tel: 618-277-8181. R.R. 3, 62231.

DAHLGREN. *Couple to Couple League*. 4934 Itaska, St. Louis, MO, 63109. Tel: 314-481-1908. John & Vicki Wiese.

EAST ST. LOUIS. *St. Mary Hospital of East St. Louis, Illinois Volunteers*, 129 N. 8th St., 62201. Tel: 618-274-1900. Richard Mark, Pres. & CEO.

St. Mary's Hospital Health Foundation, 129 N. 8th St., 62201.

O'FALLON. *ASC Health Services*, 6 Eagle Center, Ste. 4, 62269. Tel: 618-632-1284. Sr. Mary Louise Degenhart, A.S.C., Exec. Dir.

RED BUD. *Senior Adorers*, 2 Pioneer Ln., 62278. Tel: 618-282-3848. Sr. Irene McGrath, A.S.C., Pres.

RUMA. *World Apostolate of Fatima, The Blue Army, U.S.A.*, 105 W. Mill St., 62278. Tel: 618-282-4108. Mr. Roger Mathews, Pres.

INCORPORATED CEMETERIES

BELLEVILLE. *Green Mount Catholic Cemetery of the Cathedral Congregation of Belleville*.

BREESE. *St. Dominic Roman Catholic Cemetery of Breese*.

EAST ST. LOUIS. *Holy Cross Cemetery of St. Henry Roman Catholic Church of East St. Louis*.

Mount Carmel Cemetery of St. Patrick Roman Catholic Church.

FAIRVIEW HEIGHTS. *St. Adalbert Association (An Illinois Religious Corporation)*.

O'FALLON. *Mount Calvary Cemetery of St. Clare Roman Catholic Congregation*.

VILLA RIDGE. *Calvary Cemetery of St. Patrick Roman Catholic Church of Cairo*.

NECROLOGY

† Calhoun, James R., (Retired). —Died May 26, 1996.
† Jones, Fred B., (Retired). —Died March 12, 1996.
† Keating, Robert J., (Retired). —Died Sept. 26, 1996.
† Maziarz, Emil J., (Retired). —Died Sept. 24, 1996.

Diocese of Biloxi

(Dioecesis Biloxiiensis)

Most Reverend

JOSEPH LAWSON HOWZE, D.D.

Bishop of Biloxi; ordained May 7, 1959; appointed Titular Bishop of Maxita and Auxiliary of Natchez-Jackson November 8, 1972; ordained Bishop January 28, 1973; appointed Bishop of Biloxi March 1, 1977; installed June 6, 1977. *Mailing Address: P.O. Box 1189, Biloxi, MS, 39533.*

Legal Title: "Catholic Diocese of Biloxi".

ESTABLISHED MARCH 1, 1977.

Square Miles 9,653.

Comprises 17 counties in southern Mississippi: Jackson, Harrison, Hancock, George, Stone, Pearl River, Greene, Perry, Forrest, Lamar, Marion, Walthall, Wayne, Jones, Covington, Jefferson Davis and Lawrence.

For legal titles of parishes and diocesan institutions, consult the Chancery Office.

Chancery Office: 120 Reynoir St., P.O. Box 1189, Biloxi, MS, 39533. Tel.: 601-374-0222; Fax: 601-435-7949.

STATISTICAL OVERVIEW

Personnel	
Bishop	1
Priests: Diocesan Active in Diocese	42
Priests: Active Outside Diocese	1
Priests: Retired, Sick or Absent	13
Number of Diocesan Priests	56
Religious Priests in Diocese	27
Extern Priests in Diocese	8
Ordinations:	
Permanent Deacons in Diocese	19
Total Brothers	33
Total Sisters	59
Parishes	
Parishes	44
With Resident Pastor:	
Resident Diocesan Priests	35
Resident Religious Priests	7
Without Resident Pastor:	
Administered by Priests	2
Missions	12
Professional Ministry Personnel:	
Sisters	10
Lay Ministers	4
Welfare	
Homes for the Aged	7
Total Assisted	637
Special Centers for Social Services	6
Total Assisted	81,224
Other Institutions	1
Educational	
Diocesan Students in Other Seminaries	7
Total Seminarians	7
High Schools, Diocesan and Parish	4
Total Students	1,204
High Schools, Private	1
Total Students	599
Elementary Schools, Diocesan and Parish	14
Total Students	2,245
Catechesis/Religious Education:	
High School Students	2,481
Elementary Students	3,890
Total Students Under Catholic Instruction	10,426
Teachers in the Diocese:	
Priests	1
Sisters	17
Lay Teachers	278
Vital Statistics	
Receptions into the Church:	
Infant Baptism Totals	772
Adult Baptism Totals	586
Received into Full Communion	135
First Communions	1,168
Confirmations	564
Marriages:	
Catholic	174
Interfaith	189
Total Marriages	363
Deaths	688
Total Catholic Population	64,556
Total Population	705,163

Office of the Bishop—*120 Reynoir St., P.O. Box 1189, Biloxi, 39533.* Tel: 601-374-0220.

Vicar General—Rev. Msgr. ANDREW MURRAY, J.C.L., *120 Reynoir St., P.O. Box 1189, Biloxi, 39533.* Tel: 601-374-0222.

Chancery Office—*120 Reynoir St., P.O. Box 1189, Biloxi, 39533.* Tel: 601-374-0222; Fax: 601-435-7949. Office Hours: Mon.-Fri. 8:30-5 All Offices are at this address unless otherwise noted.

Chancellor—Rev. Msgr. ANDREW MURRAY, J.C.L. Tel: 601-374-0222.

Vice Chancellor—Rev. JOHN R. MCGRATH, J.C.L. Tel: 601-374-0226.

Office for Planning and Development—Deacon ROBERTO JIMENEZ, Dir. Tel: 601-374-2009.

Marriage Tribunal—

Judicial Vicar—Rev. JOHN R. MCGRATH, J.C.L. Tel: 601-374-0226. Rev. Msgr. ANDREW MURRAY, J.C.L., Adjutant. Tel: 601-374-0222.

Promotor of Justice—Rev. Msgr. JAMES J. HANNON, J.C.D.

Defenders of the Bond—Rev. Msgr. RONALD P. HERZOG; Rev. Msgr. JAMES P. MCGOUGH, J.C.D.; Rev. THOMAS CONWAY; Deacon GEORGE SORENSEN.

Pro-Synodal Judges—Rev. Msgr. JAMES J. HANNON, J.C.D.; Rev. Msgr. JAMES P. MCGOUGH, J.C.D.; Rev. Msgr. MICHAEL THORNTON, J.C.L.; Rev. JAMES B. TAYLOR.

Advocates—Revs. LOUIS LOHAN; PATRICK MOCKLER.

Deans—West Coast Deanery: Rev. Msgr. RONALD P. HERZOG; Central Coast Deanery: Rev. Msgr. JAMES P. MCGOUGH, J.C.D.; East Central Coast Deanery: Rev. Msgr. JAMES M. RUSSELL; East Coast Deanery: Rev. GERARD M. CLEARY; Northern Deanery: Rev. THOMAS CONWAY.

Diocesan Attorney—KEVIN J. NECAISE, *P.O. Box 636, Gulfport, 39502.* Tel: 601-864-4345.

Department of Administration and Finance Comptroller—DANIEL R. BLAKE; MARJORIE GILL, Chief Accountant. Tel: 601-374-0224.

Diocesan Risk Management for Property and Medical—Mr. A. J. SCARDINO, Contact Person. Tel: 601-374-0222; 452-3014.

Catholic Foundation of the Diocese of Biloxi, Inc.—Deacon ROBERTO JIMENEZ, Exec. Dir. Tel: 601-374-2009.

Mission Office—Rev. Msgr. JAMES M. RUSSELL. Tel: 601-374-1717. Rev. Msgr. ANDREW MURRAY. Tel: 601-374-0222.

Department of Communications—

"Gulf Pine Catholic Newspaper"—Rev. Msgr. JAMES M. RUSSELL, Dir. SHIRLEY HENDERSON, Editor. Tel: 601-374-8318.

Radio & Television—SHIRLEY HENDERSON. Tel: 601-374-8318.

Department of Education—

Office of Superintendent of Catholic Schools—Sr. JOANNE COZZI, D.C. Tel: 601-374-0440; 374-0229., *Res., 3900 16th St., Gulfport, 39501.* Tel: 601-863-2159.

Office of Resource Center—Sr. JOANNE COZZI, D.C., Dir.; Sr. ROSEMARY EICH, C.H.M., Coord. Tel: 601-374-0440.

Office of Special Education—Sr. JOANNE COZZI, D.C.

Office of Religious Education—Sr. JANE WALKER, O.P., Dir., *Res., 164 E. Beach Blvd., Apt. 201, Gulfport, 39507.* Tel: 601-863-6263.

Office of Youth Ministry—BRAGG MOORE, Dir. Tel: 601-436-6046.

Catholic Boy Scouts—ERNEST J. FALGO, JR., *3511 Magnolia St., Pascagoula, 39567.* Tel: 601-762-8174.

Campus Ministry—Rev. MICHAEL TRACEY, Dir., *3117 W. Fourth St., Hattiesburg, 39401.* Tel: 601-264-5192.

Priests' Continuing Education and Retreat Programs—Co-Dirs.: Revs. GREGORY M. BARRAS, *8343 Woolmarket Rd., Biloxi, 39532.* Tel: 601-392-7500. KENNETH RAMON-LANDRY, *833 West Sixth, Laurel, 39440.* Tel: 601-426-3473.

Ecumenical & Interreligious Affairs—Sr. JANE WALKER, O.P., Contact Person. Tel: 601-374-0229.

Liturgy, Office of—Rev. Msgr. RONALD P. HERZOG, Dir., *P.O. Box 548, Pass Christian, 39571.* Tel: 601-452-4686.

Department of Social and Community Services—*120 Reynoir St., P.O. Box 1457, Biloxi, 39533.* Tel: 601-374-8316. All offices at this address unless otherwise noted. Legal Title: Catholic Social and Community Services, Inc. Sr. REBECCA RUTKOWSKI, A.C.S.W., Exec. Dir.

Hattiesburg Regional Office—*208 S. 25th Ave., Hattiesburg, 39401.* Tel: 601-545-1616. VICKI TAYLOR, L.M.S.W., Dir. POLLY SUMRALL, Office Mgr.

Pascagoula Regional Office—*3512 Magnolia St., Pascagoula, 39567-3113.* Tel: 601-769-8283.

Council of the St. Vincent de Paul Society—Sr. REBECCA RUTKOWSKI, A.C.S.W., Facilitator. Tel: 601-374-8316. Dr. PETER PAVLOV, Pres. Tel: 601-875-5230.

Counseling Services—DENNIS CENAC, L.S.W.; APRIL PIERCE, L.P.C., N.C.C. L.S.W.

Adoption Services—BRENDA STILES, L.S.W., *2204 24th Ave., Gulfport.* Tel: 601-864-7917.

Emergency Assistance—Sr. KATHERINE FENNELL, P.B.V.M., M.A.; DELANE KRAUSE; DIANNE PURSER, *870 Nativity Dr., Biloxi, 39533.* Tel: 601-432-0045; 800-851-3702. JANNIE GREENE FUNCHESS, *208 S. 25th Ave., Hattiesburg, 39401.* Tel: 601-545-1616.

Morning Star Pregnancy Care Center—(Unplanned pregnancy services); NANCY LOFTUS, Maternity Caseworker; ANN RIVERA, Office Mgr., *2204 24th Ave., Gulfport.* Tel: 601-864-4221; 800-570-LOVE.

Respect Life Office—BETH RILEY, Dir. Tel: 601-374-8316.

12 Baskets Food Banking—SHIRLEY HEGGINS, Dir. Tel: 601-374-6884.

Refugee Resettlement—Mrs. MAGDA LELEAUX, Dir., *870 Nativity Dr., Biloxi, 39530.* Tel: 601-374-6507.

Family Life Office—Tel: 601-374-8316.

Catholic Charities Housing Association of Biloxi, Inc.

Santa Maria Retirement Apartments; Villa Maria Retirement Apartments—Most Rev. JOSEPH L. HOWZE, D.D., Pres. Tel: 601-374-0220. Sr. REBECCA RUTKOWSKI, A.C.S.W., Contact Person. Tel: 601-374-8316.

Samaritan Housing, Inc.—Most Rev. JOSEPH L. HOWZE, D.D., Pres. Tel: 601-374-0220. Sr. REBECCA RUTKOWSKI, A.C.S.W., Contact Person. Tel: 601-374-8316.

Notre Dame de la Mer, Inc.—Most Rev. JOSEPH L. HOWZE, D.D., Pres. Tel: 601-374-0220. Sr. REBECCA RUTKOWSKI, A.C.S.W. Tel: 601-374-8316.

Gabriel Manor, Inc.—Most Rev. JOSEPH L. HOWZE, D.D., Pres. Tel: 601-374-0220. Sr. REBECCA RUTKOWSKI, A.C.S.W. Tel: 601-374-8316.

Caritas Manor, Inc.—Most Rev. JOSEPH L. HOWZE, D.D., Pres. Tel: 601-374-0220. Sr. REBECCA RUTKOWSKI, A.C.S.W. Tel: 601-374-8316.

Carlow Manor—Most Rev. JOSEPH L. HOWZE, D.D., Pres. Tel: 601-374-0220. Sr. REBECCA RUTKOWSKI, A.C.S.W. Tel: 601-374-8316.

Gabriel Manor II, Inc.—Most Rev. JOSEPH L. HOWZE, D.D., Pres. Tel: 601-374-8316. Sr. REBECCA RUTKOWSKI, A.C.S.W. Tel: 601-374-8316.

Apostleship of the Sea—Deacon CHARLES L. WALKER; HAROLD SEAMEN, JR.

Vietnamese Apostolate—Rev. DOMINIC PHAN, *St. Michael Church, P.O. Box 523, Biloxi, 39533.* Tel: 601-435-5578.

Prison Apostolate—Deacon VICTOR BAGLIONI, Dir. Tel: 601-475-5437. Jackson County Jails: Deacon THOMAS MILLER. Harrison County Jails: Tel: 601-388-5467. South Mississippi Correctional Facility: Rev. REMIGIUS A. KOZAK. Tel: 601-735-9420.

Diocesan Boards and Committees—

Association of Priests (Diocese of Biloxi and Jackson)—Most Rev. JOSEPH L. HOWZE, D.D., Bishop of Biloxi & Co-Chm.; Most Rev. WILLIAM R. HOUCK, Bishop of Jackson & Co-Chm.; Rev. Msgr. NOEL FOLEY, Pres.; Rev. Msgr. RONALD HERZOG, Sec. & Treas. Trustees: Rev. Msgr. MICHAEL THORNTON; Revs. THOMAS CONWAY; KENT BOWLES; THOMAS McGING.

Building and Real Estate Committee—Rev. Msgr. FRANCIS FARRELL, Chm. LEONARD COLLINS; EDWARD CRAIG; WILLIAM H. CRAIG; H. F. FOUNTAIN, JR.; GERALD HOPKINS; GERALD PORCHE; MARK SEYMOUR; BOB SLAUGHTER.

Catholic Foundation-Diocese of Biloxi—Most Rev. JOSEPH L. HOWZE, D.D., Pres.; Rev. Msgr. ANDREW MURRAY, Vice Pres.; Deacon ROBERTO JIMENEZ, Exec. Dir.; Dr. HARRY SCHMIDT, JR., Chm. CHARLES HEWES; JOSEPH HUDSON; TED LONGO; DAVID LORD; ALFRED PARKER; MICHAEL PELA; ROBERT TUCEI.

Catholic Housing Board—Most Rev. JOSEPH L. HOWZE, D.D., Pres.; Sr. REBECCA RUTKOWSKI, A.C.S.W., Chm.; Rev. Msgr. ANDREW MURRAY; Rev. BERNARD FARRELL; DANIEL R. BLAKE; SALVADOR DOMINO; MICHAEL FOX; GERALD HOPKINS.

Council of Religious—Sr. JANE WALKER, O.P., Pres., *P.O. Box 1189, Biloxi, 39533.* Tel: 601-374-0229.

Diocesan Counsultors—Rev. Msgr. RONALD P. HERZOG; Rev. Msgr. JAMES P. McGOUGH, J.C.D.; Rev. Msgr. ANDREW MURRAY; Rev. Msgr. JAMES M. RUSSELL; Revs. THOMAS CONWAY; GERARD M. CLEARY.

Finance Council—Most Rev. JOSEPH L. HOWZE, D.D.; WILLIAM PENEGUY, Chm.; Rev. Msgr. FRANCIS FARRELL; Rev. Msgr. ANDREW MURRAY; RAYMOND HUDACHEK; JOSEPH P. HUDSON; DAVID L. LORD; STEVE MONTAGNET; JOHN P. MYERS; A. J.M. OUSTALET, JR.; DAVID A. TRUETEL.

Insurance Committee—Most Rev. JOSEPH L. HOWZE, D.D.; Dr. LANNY ACOSTA; Sr. JOANNE COZZI, D.C.; Rev. Msgr. RONALD P. HERZOG; Sr. MARY JO MIKE; Dr. MATTHEW F. McNULTY, JR., Sc.D.; Sr. REBECCA RUTKOWSKI, A.C.S.W.; STEVE MONTAGNET; Rev. Msgr. ANDREW MURRAY. Advisors: DANIEL R. BLAKE; A. J. SCARDINO, JR.

Mission Board—Most Rev. JOSEPH L. HOWZE, D.D.; Rev. Msgr. ANDREW MURRAY; Rev. Msgr. JAMES M. RUSSELL.

Personnel Board—Rev. Msgr. FRANCIS FARRELL; Rev. Msgr. JOSEPH MERCIER; Rev. Msgr. ANDREW MURRAY; Rev. Msgr. JAMES M. RUSSELL; Rev. Msgr. MICHAEL THORNTON; Rev. KENNETH RAMON-LANDRY.

Presbyteral Council—Most Rev. JOSEPH L. HOWZE, D.D., Pres.; Revs. DENNIS CARVER; GERARD M. CLEARY; BERNARD FARRELL; Rev. Msgr. RONALD P. HERZOG; Rev. WILLIAM KELLY, S.V.D.; Revs. LOUIS LOHAN; ANTONE LYNCH; Rev. Msgr. JAMES P. McGOUGH, J.C.D.; Revs. JOHN McGRATH; THOMAS CONWAY; CUTHBERT O'CONNELL; Rev. Msgr. ANDREW MURRAY; Rev. KENNETH RAMON-LANDRY; Rev. Msgr. JAMES M. RUSSELL; Rev. ROBERT SULLIVAN, S.S.J.; Rev. Msgr. MICHAEL THORNTON.

Vocations Committee—Most Rev. JOSEPH L. HOWZE, D.D.; Rev. Msgr. JOSEPH MERCIER; Revs. I. ANTHONY ARGUELLES; LOUIS LOHAN; GREGORY M. BARRAS.

Miscellaneous Apostolates—

Campaign for Human Development—Rev. IVAN J. WEIS, Dir., *27074 St. Matthew Church Rd., Perkinson, 39573.*

Catholic Relief Services—Sr. REBECCA RUTKOWSKI, A.C.S.W., *P.O. Box 1457, Biloxi, 39533.*

Catholic University, Friends of—Rev. Msgr. ANDREW MURRAY, *P.O. Box 1189, Biloxi, 39533.*

Charismatic Renewal—Rev. GEORGE KITCHIN, Dir., *4900 Riley Rd., Ocean Springs, 39564.*

Cursillo and Retreats—Rev. DENNIS CARVER, *14595 Vidalia Rd., Pass Christian, 39571.* Tel: 601-255-7560.

Deaf and Disabled, Office of the—Sr. DOLORES COLEMAN, D.C., Dir., *de l'Epee Deaf Center, Inc., 1450 North St., Gulfport, 39507., Mailing Address: P.O. Box 6918, Gulfport, 39506-6918.* Tel: 601-897-2280 (Voice-TDD); Fax: 601-897-2462.

Latin American Apostolate—Mission-Saltillo, Mexico, co-sponsored with Diocese of Jackson. Rev. PATRICK QUINN, C.P., *Suc. "A" Apdo. 509, Saltillo, Coah., Mexico, C.P., 25000.*

Legion of Mary—Deacon VICTOR A. BAGLIONI, *3855 Riverpine Dr., Moss Point, 39563.*

Permanent Diaconate Program—Deacon MARTIN FINNEGAN, Dir., *5715 Belle Fountain Dr., Ocean Springs, 39564.* Assoc. Directors: Deacons VICTOR BAGLIONI, (Formation); THOMAS LEBLANC, (Continuing Education & Formation).

Pontifical Association of the Holy Childhood—Rev. Msgr. JAMES M. RUSSELL, Dir., *P.O. Box 367, Biloxi, 39533.*

Propagation of the Faith—Rev. Msgr. JAMES M. RUSSELL, Dir., *P.O. Box 367, Biloxi, 39533.*

Vocations—Rev. Msgr. JAMES M. RUSSELL, Dir., *P.O. Box 367, Biloxi, 39533.* Tel: 601-374-1717.

CLERGY, PARISHES, MISSIONS AND PAROCHIAL SCHOOLS

CITY OF BILOXI
(Harrison County)

1—CATHEDRAL OF THE NATIVITY OF THE BLESSED VIRGIN MARY (1843), Rev. Msgr. James M. Russell, Rector; Rev. Manuel Leon Bosarge, IV; Deacons Rene J. Moniot; Roberto M. Jimenez; Ray DeRosier; Sr. Mary Riordan, R.S.M., Pastoral Assoc. & D.R.E.
Res., 870 Howard Ave., P.O. Box 367, 39533. Tel: 601-374-1717; Fax: 601-374-1773.
School—(Grades K-6). Tel: 601-432-2269. Sr. Mary Jo Mike, O.S.F., Prin.
Nativity 1; Lay Teachers 19; Students 419.
Catechesis/Religious Programs—Students 222.

2—OUR LADY OF FATIMA (1957), Rev. Msgr. Francis Farrell.
Res., 2090 Pass Rd., 39531. Tel: 601-388-3887.
School—(Grades PreK-6) 320 Jim Money Rd., 39531. Tel: 601-388-3609. Sr. Mary Ann Peltier, M.S.C., Prin.
Lay Teachers 16; Students 226.
Catechesis/Religious Programs—Tel: 601-388-5737. Sr. Lynda Rink, D.R.E.
Students 150.

3—OUR MOTHER OF SORROWS (1914) (African American), Rev. Peter O. Quinn (JKS).
Res., 803 Division St., 39530. Tel: 601-436-6503.

4—SACRED HEART (1921), Rev. Patrick M. McDermott. In res., Rev. Denis Harlow; Rev. Msgr. Andrew Murray.
Res., 10446 Le Moyne Blvd., 39532. Tel: 601-392-4526.
School—(Grades PreK-6). Tel: 601-392-4180. Sr. Joan Landry, R.S.M., Prin.
Sisters of Mercy 4; Lay Teachers 8; Students 185.
Catechesis/Religious Programs—Tel: 601-392-4180. Sr. Julia Marie Burke, R.S.M., D.R.E.
Students 582.

5—ST. JOHN (1922), Rev. I. Anthony Arguelles.
Res., 724 Bradford St., 39530. Tel: 601-374-0116; 0117.
Catechesis/Religious Programs—Tel: 601-374-1717.
Students 70.

6—ST. LOUIS (1957), Rev. I. Anthony Arguelles. In res., Rev. Msgr. Kevin Bambrick.
Res., 425 Division St., P.O. Box 212, 39533. Tel: 601-432-7735.

7—ST. MARY (1973), Rev. Greg Barras; Deacon Al Stockert.
Res., 8343 Woolmarket Rd., 39532. Tel: 601-392-7500.
Catechesis/Religious Programs—Students 160.

8—ST. MICHAEL (1917), Revs. Patrick O'Shaughnessy; Dominic Phan, Dir. Vietnamese Apostolate.
Res., 177 First St., P.O. Box 523, 39533. Tel: 601-435-5578.

OUTSIDE THE CITY OF BILOXI

Bassfield, Jefferson Davis Co., St. Peter (1904) (Irish), Rev. Cuthbert O'Connell, Admin.; Deacon Robert Everard.
Res., P.O. Box 10, 39421. Tel: 601-943-5104. [CEM 2][JC 2]
Catechesis/Religious Programs—Tel: 601-943-6259. Mrs. Mary E. Coulter, D.R.E.
Students 119.
Missions—Carson, Jefferson Davis Co., St. Elizabeth; Prentiss, Jefferson Davis Co., St. Mary's.

Bay St. Louis, Hancock Co., Our Lady of the Gulf (1847), Revs. Peter F. Mockler; Lee Bosarge. In res., Rev. John T. O'Brien, (Retired).
Res., 228 S. Beach Blvd., P.O. Box 208, 39520-0208. Tel: 601-467-6509; Fax: 601-467-6509. [CEM]
School—Bay St. Louis Catholic Elementary, (Grades PreK-6). Tel: 601-467-5158. Mrs. Myrna Jordan, Prin.
Lay Teachers 15; Students 335.
High School—Tel: 601-467-7048. Sr. Donella Hartman, Prin.
Sisters 3; Lay Teachers 16; Students 274.
Catechesis/Religious Programs—Students 224.

St. Rose De Lima (1926) (African American), Rev. A. Francis Theriault, S.V.D.
Res., 301 S. Necaise Ave., 39520. Tel: 601-467-7347.
Catechesis/Religious Programs—Tel: 601-466-2769. Mrs. Joan Thomas, D.R.E.
Students 91.

Clermont Harbor, Hancock Co., St. Ann (1915), Rev. John J. Kelly.
Res., 5858 Lower Bay Rd., P.O. Box 1037, Lakeshore, 39558-1037. Tel: 601-467-4746.
Catechesis/Religious Programs—Anna Medley, D.R.E.
Students 125.
Mission—Lakeshore, Hancock Co., St. John.

Columbia, Marion Co., Most Holy Trinity (1959), Rev. Tommy Conway.
Res., 1429 N. Park Ave., 39429. Tel: 601-736-3136.
Catechesis/Religious Programs—Tel: 601-736-8787. D.R.E.: Sharon Rogers, (Holy Trinity); Betty Smet, (St. Paul the Apostle).
Students 84.
Mission—Tylertown, Walthall Co., St. Paul the Apostle, 702 Union Rd., Tylertown, 39667. Tel: 601-876-6422.

DeLisle, Harrison Co., The Catholic Church in DeLisle (1874), Rev. Walter O'Donnell, S.T.; Bro. Senan Gallagher, S.T., Pastoral Assoc.
Res., 25220 St. Stephen Rd., 39571. Tel: 601-255-1294.
Catechesis/Religious Programs—Students 175.
Missions—Dubuisson, Harrison Co., St. Ann, Vidalia Rd., 39571.; Rotten Bayou, Harrison Co., St. William, Edwin Ladner Rd., 39571.

Gautier, Jackson Co., St. Mary (1968), Rev. Michael Kelleher; Deacon Patrick Houghton.
Res., 809 De La Pointe Rd., P.O. Box 151, 39553. Tel: 601-497-2364.
Catechesis/Religious Programs—Bonnie Bond, D.R.E.
Students 134.

Gulfport, Harrison Co.,

1—ST. ANN, (1939), Rev. Fintan J. Kilmurray.
Res., 23529 Hwy. 53, 39503. Tel: 601-832-2560.
Catechesis/Religious Programs—Tel: 601-831-9452. Robert Earl Lizana, D.R.E.
Students 21.
Mission—Delmas Dedeaux, Harrison Co., Our Lady of Chartres.

2—ST. JAMES, (1898), Rev. Msgr. James P. McGough; Rev. Todd Dominick Fullam; Deacon John R. Henderson.
Res., 366 Cowan Rd., P.O. Box 7267, 39506. Tel: 601-896-6059; Fax: 601-896-6095. [CEM]
School—(Grades PreK-6). Tel: 601-896-6631; Fax: 601-896-6638. Mrs. Susie Bass, Prin.
Sisters of Mercy (Ennis, Ireland) 4; Lay Teachers 7; Students 205.
Catechesis/Religious Programs—Tel: 601-896-4579. Mrs. Mary Beth Sweeney, D.R.E.
Students 151.

3—ST. JOHN THE EVANGELIST, (1900), Rev. Thomas White. In res., Rev. Clement Kovacsik, S.T.
Res., 2414 17th St., P.O. Box 970, 39501. Tel: 601-864-2272.
School—(Grades PreK-6). Tel: 601-863-1606; Fax: 601-863-9677. Patty Zupko, Prin.

Presentation Sisters 1; Lay Teachers 17; Students 299.
High School—Tel: 601-863-8343; Fax: 601-864-2788. Lanny Acosta, Prin.
Lay Teachers 26; Students 451.
Catechesis/Religious Programs—D.R.E.: Sr. Lelia O'Sullivan; Kimberly Goodson.
Students 25.

4—ST. JOSEPH CATHOLIC CHURCH, (Northwood Hills) (1966), Rev. Antone J. Lynch; Deacon Jack Hunter.
Res., 12290 DePew Rd., 39503. Tel: 601-832-1166.
Catechesis/Religious Programs—Tel: 601-832-1166. Mr. Gerard Scheuermann, D.R.E.
Students 215.

5—ST. THERESE, (1932) (African American), Rev. Robert W. Sullivan, S.S.J.
Res., 3521 19th St., 39501. Tel: 601-863-0624.
Catechesis/Religious Programs—Tel: 601-863-7719. Judy Lombard Whitfield, D.R.E.
Students 106.

Hattiesburg, Forrest Co., Holy Rosary (1949), Rev. William Vollor.
Res., 900 Dabbs St., 39401. Tel: 601-584-6528.

Sacred Heart (1900), Rev. George Murphy.
Res., 313 Walnut St., P.O. Box 1027, 39401. Tel: 601-583-9404.
School—(Grades PreK-6). Tel: 601-583-8683; Fax: 601-582-2470. Sr. Sharon Friedrich, M.S.C., Prin.
Sisters 1; Lay Teachers 8; Students 187.
Catechesis/Religious Programs—Tel: 601-583-9404. Mrs. Wanda Scheuermann, D.R.E.
Students 318.

St. Thomas Aquinas (1968). (University of Southern Mississippi-Student Parish). Rev. Michael J. Tracey.
Res., 3117 W. Fourth St., 39401. Tel: 601-264-5192; Fax: 601-264-0834.
Catechesis/Religious Programs—Tel: 601-261-9627. Mary Coghlan, D.R.E.
Students 141.
Station—Danforth Chapel, U.S.M. (University of Southern Mississippi-Student Parish). Sr. Annette Seymour, R.S.M., Campus Min.

Kiln, Hancock Co., Annunciation (1869), Rev. Henry McInerney; Deacon Lucien Moragas.
Res., P.O. Box 97, 39556. Tel: 601-255-1800.
Catechesis/Religious Programs—Tel: 601-255-1869. Ms. Jean Bruneau, D.R.E.
Students 150.

Laurel, Jones Co., Immaculate Conception (1887), Rev. Kenneth Ramon-Landry; Deacon Milce Nance, Pastoral Assoc.; Mrs. Suzie Middleton, Youth Min.
Res., 833 W. Sixth St., 39440. Tel: 601-426-3473.
School—(Grades PreK-6). Tel: 601-428-0129. Sr. Jacqueline Tarrant, R.S.M., Prin.
Religious 1; Lay Teachers 12; Students 158.
Catechesis/Religious Programs—Tel: 601-426-3473.
Students 111.
Convent—610 N. Eighth Ave., 39440. Tel: 601-426-2610.

Long Beach, Harrison Co., St. Thomas the Apostle (1903), Rev. Louis Lohan; Sr. Mary Anne O'Brien, Pastoral Assoc.; Deacon Bob Jones.
Res., 720 E. Beach Blvd., 39560. Tel: 601-863-1610; Fax: 601-868-6068.
School—(Grades PreK-6). Tel: 601-863-6876. Mrs. J. B. Pike, Prin.
Lay Teachers 8; Students 130.
Catechesis/Religious Programs—Tel: 601-868-3774. Sr. Consilio Buckley, D.R.E.
Students 520.

Lumberton, Lamar Co., Our Lady of Perpetual Help (1922), Rev. Clark Bearden; Mrs. Katie Murphy, Pastoral Assoc.
Res., 379 W. Seneca Rd., 39455-9519. Tel: 601-796-3051 (Office); 769-3053 (Rectory). [CEM]
Catechesis/Religious Programs—Students 88.
Mission—Poplarville, Pearl River Co., St. Joseph, P.O. Box 202, Poplarville, 39470. Tel: 601-795-4471.

Moss Point, Jackson Co., St. Joseph (1950), Rev. Patrick E. Hayes; Deacons Victor A. Baglioni; Emery E. Elder.
Res., 4114 First St., P.O. Box 8549, 39562-8549. Tel: 601-475-0777; Fax: 601-475-3672.
Catechesis/Religious Programs—D.R.E.: Mrs. Triss Elder, (St. Joseph), Tel: 601-475-3449; Mrs. Rhonda Boudreaux, (St. Ann), Tel: 601-588-6736.
Students 112.
Mission—Hurley, Jackson Co., St. Ann, P.O. Box 8549, 39562-8549.

Ocean Springs, Jackson Co., St. Alphonsus (1860), Revs. Bernard Farrell; Anthony Doan Tran; Deacon Thomas Miller.
Res., 502 Jackson Ave., 39564. Tel: 601-875-5419.
School—(Grades PreK-6). Tel: 601-875-5329; Fax: 601-875-3458. Sherrie McAllister, Prin.
Lay Teachers 17; Students 235.
Catechesis/Religious Programs—Tel: 601-872-2652. Sr. Eileen Lowney, D.R.E.
Students 357.

St. Elizabeth Ann Seton (1975), Rev. George Kitchin; Deacon Martin Finnegan.
Res., 4900 Riley Rd., 39564. Tel: 601-875-0654.
Catechesis/Religious Programs—Students 256.

Pascagoula, Jackson Co., Our Lady of Victories (1855), Rev. Gerard Cleary.
Res., 510 Convent St., P.O. Box 368, 39568. Tel: 601-762-1653.
Catechesis/Religious Programs—Virginia L. Delmas, D.R.E.
Students 199.

Sacred Heart (1963), Rev. Msgr. Michael J. Thornton; Sr. Audrey Mae Kihnemann, S.S.N.D., Pastoral Assoc.; Deacon Warren Goff. In res., Rev. James B. Taylor, (Retired).
Mailing Address: P.O. Box 2190, 39569. Tel: 601-762-1837.
Res., 3702 Quinn Dr., 39581. Tel: 601-762-1837.
School—Resurrection School-Elementary, (Grades PreK, 3-5) 3704 Quinn Dr., 39581-2356. Tel: 601-762-7207; Fax: 601-762-0611. Jean Pisors, Prin.
Lay Teachers 15; Students 277.
Catechesis/Religious Programs—Tel: 601-769-9242. Mrs. Suzanne Williams, D.R.E.
Students 125.

St. Peter the Apostle (1907), Rev. David P. Frueh, S.S.J.
Res., 1715 Telephone Rd., P.O. Box 876, 39567. Tel: 601-762-1759; Fax: 601-762-1759.
School—(Grades K-6). Tel: 601-762-3766. Sr. Bernadette McNamara, S.H.Sp., Prin.
Servants of the Holy Spirit 3; Lay Teachers 8; Students 99.
Catechesis/Religious Programs—Tel: 601-762-1759. Mrs. Edna Fields, D.R.E.
Students 137.

Pass Christian, Harrison Co., Our Mother of Mercy (1911) (African American), Rev. Joseph M. Calamari, S.S.J.
Res., 222 E. Railroad Ave., 39571. Tel: 601-452-4514. [JC]
Catechesis/Religious Programs—Students 106.
Convent—251 Saucier Ave., P.O. Box 157, 39571.

Sacred Heart (Dedeaux) (1967), Rev. Dennis Carver.
Res., 14595 Vidalia Rd., 39571. Tel: 601-255-7453; Fax: 601-255-7560.
Catechesis/Religious Programs—Students 157.
Station—Cursillo Center, Tel: 601-255-7560. Sr. Florence Young, M.S.B.T., Pastoral Assoc.
Students 157.

St. Paul (Dedeaux) (1847), Rev. Msgr. Ronald P. Herzog; Deacon George Sorensen, (Retired). In res., Rev. John R. McGrath.
Res., 140 E. Beach Blvd., P.O. Box 548, 39571. Tel: 601-452-4686; Fax: 601-452-5488. [CEM]
School—(Grades PreK-6). Tel: 601-452-7359. Sr. Kathleen Curtin, R.S.M., Prin.
Religious Teachers 1; Lay Teachers 12; Students 194.
Catechesis/Religious Programs—Students 56.

Pearlington, Hancock Co., St. Joseph (1939), Rev. Dominic Cangemi, S.T., Ph.D.
Mailing Address: P.O. Box 39, 39572. Tel: 601-533-7968. [JC]

Picayune, Pearl River Co., St. Charles Borromeo (1950), Rev. John Noone; Deacon Harold Gaule.
Res., 321 Juniper St., 39466. Tel: 601-798-4779; Fax: 601-798-4779.
Catechesis/Religious Programs—Dorothy Ducote, D.R.E.
Students 277.

Pineville, Harrison Co., Our Lady of Lourdes (Pass Christian) (1973), Rev. James O'Bryan, S.T.
Mailing Address: P.O. Box 508, Pass Christian, 39571. Tel: 601-452-7132.
Res., 22342 Evangeline Rd., Pass Christian, 39571. Tel: 601-452-7132.

Vancleave, Jackson Co., Catholic Church of the Holy Spirit (1980), Rev. Frank Scott, Admin.
Res., P.O. Box 5032, 39564. Tel: 601-826-4256.
Catechesis/Religious Programs—Students 181.
Mission—Latimer, Jackson Co., Christ the King, 10601 Daisy Vestry, Latimer, 39565. Tel: 601-392-0340.

Waveland, Hancock Co., St. Clare (1919), Rev. Noel Fannon.
Res., 236 S. Beach Blvd., P.O. Box 500, 39576. Tel: 601-467-9275.
School—Ms. Harriet Bellone, Prin. Lay Teachers 8; Students 201.
Catechesis/Religious Programs—Mrs. Andrew Scafidi, D.R.E.
Students 150.

Waynesboro, Wayne Co., St. Bernadette (1977), Rev. Ken Ramon Landry.
Res., 401 Mississippi Dr., 39367. Tel: 601-735-9420. [JC]
Catechesis/Religious Programs—Students 14.
Mission—Leakesville, Holy Trinity.

White Cypress, Hancock Co., St. Matthew the Apostle (1982), Rev. Ivan Weis.
Res., 27074 St. Matthew Church Rd., Perkinston, 39573. Tel: 601-255-7720.
Catechesis/Religious Programs—Students 180.

Wiggins, Stone Co., St. Francis Xavier (1961), Rev. Patrick J. Mockler.
Res., 1200 Hwy. 26 E., P.O. Box 566, 39577. Tel: 601-928-2182; Fax: 601-928-2182.
Church—Tel: 601-947-9756.
Catechesis/Religious Programs—Students 85.
Mission—Lucedale, St. Lucy, CB6308, Lucedale, 39452. Tel: 601-947-9968.
Station—Perkinston Junior College.

Chaplains of Public Institutions

BILOXI. *Biloxi Regional Hospital, Gulf Coast Community Hospital*. Rev. Denis Harlow.
Keesler Airforce Base. Vacant.
V.A. Center. Rev. Frank Popeleski; Rev. Msgr. Francis Farrell.

COLUMBIA. *Industrial and Training School*. Rev. Thomas Conway.

GULFPORT. *Naval Const. Bn. Center*. Vacant.
U.S. Naval Home. Rev. Clement Kovascik, S.T.
V.A. Hospital. Rev. Frank Popeleski.

HATTIESBURG. *University of Southern Mississippi*. Rev. Michael J. Tracey.

LEAKESVILLE. *South Mississippi Correctional Institution*. Rev. Remiquius A. Kozak.

Special Assignment:
Reverend Fathers—
Dilettuso, Joseph, Veterans Affairs Hospital, Biloxi, MS 39531

Military Chaplains:
Reverend Fathers—
Higginbotham, Robert, U.S.A.F.

Retired:
Reverend Monsignors—
Bambrick, Kevin
Hannon, James J.
Johnson, Gregory
Mercier, Joseph
Reverend Fathers—
Filipich, Nicholas
Izral, John
Kavanagh, Morgan
O'Brien, John
Taylor, James B.

Permanent Deacons:
Baglioni, Victor A., St. Joseph, Moss Point
DesRosier, Raymond
Elder, Emery, St. Joseph, Moss Point
Everard, Robert, St. Peter the Apostle, Bassfield
Finnegan, Martin, St. Elizabeth Seton, Ocean Springs
Gaule, Harold, St. Charles Borromeo, Picayune
Goff, Warren P., Sr., Sacred Heart, Pascagoula
Henderson, John R., St. James, Gulfport
Houghton, Patrick, St. Mary, Gautier
Hunter, Jack
Jimenez, Roberto, Nativity B.V.M. Cathedral, Biloxi
Jones, Bob, St. Thomas, Long Beach
LeBlanc, Tom, St. Francis Xavier, Wiggins
Miller, Thomas M.
Moniot, Rene Joseph, Nativity of the Blessed Virgin Mary, Biloxi
Moragas, Lucien F., Jr., Annunciation, Kiln
Sorensen, George
Stockert, Al, St. Mary, Woolmarket
Walker, Charles L., St. John the Evangelist, Gulfport

INSTITUTIONS LOCATED IN THE DIOCESE

[A] SEMINARIES, RELIGIOUS OR SCHOLASTICATES

BAY ST. LOUIS. *St. Augustine's*, 199 Seminary Dr., 39520. Tel: 601-467-6414; Fax: 601-466-4393. The Society of the Divine Word. Retreat Center. Tel: 601-467-9837. Very Rev. Michael Sucharski, S.V.D., Rector; Bro. Richard Chambers, S.V.D., Fin. Admin.; Rev. William Kelley, S.V.D., Retreat Dir., Media Production Center. Tel: 601-467-1097. Rev. James Pawlicki, S.V.D., Dir. Media Production Center. In res., Revs. John Kersten, S.V.D.; Arthur Winters, S.V.D.; Francis Drzaic, S.V.D.; Stephen Schuler,

S.V.D.; Joseph Simon, S.V.D.; William Halvey, S.V.D.; John LaBauve, S.V.D.; Thaddeus Boucrees, S.V.D.; Pete Smits, S.V.D. Priests 11. Bros. Joachim Brignac, S.V.D.; Paul Lengyel, S.V.D.; Lawrence Morton, S.V.D.; Stillfried Wahl, S.V.D.; Jim Heeb, S.V.D.; Mike Decker, S.V.D. Brothers 7.

[B] HIGH SCHOOLS, INTERPAROCHIAL

BILOXI. *Mercy Cross Inter-Parochial High School.* (Coed), 390 Crusader Dr., 39530. Tel: 601-374-4145; Fax: 601-374-8119. Martha Watjus, Ed.D., Prin. Lay Teachers 27; Students 340.

BAY ST. LOUIS. *Our Lady's Academy.* (Grades 7-12). (Girls), 222 S. Beach Blvd., 39520-4320. Tel: 601-467-7048; Fax: 601-467-1666. Sr. Mary Donella Hartman, R.S.M., Prin. Sisters of Mercy 3; Lay Teachers 19; Students 257.

GULFPORT. *St. John Inter-Parochial High School.* (Coed), 620 Pass Rd., 39501-6494. Tel: 601-863-8141; Fax: 601-864-2788. Dr. Lanny J. Acosta, Prin. Lay Teachers 29; Students 450.

PASCAGOULA. *Resurrection School-Jr. / Sr. School.* (Coed), P.O. Box 1267, Watts & Magnolia, 39568. Sr. Richard Marie Burke, S.S.N.D., Prin. Religious 2; Lay Teachers 18; Students 198.

[C] HIGH SCHOOLS AND ELEMENTARY SCHOOLS, DIOCESAN

BAY ST. LOUIS. *St. Stanislaus College,* P.O. Box 8001, 39521-8001. Tel: 601-467-9057; Fax: 601-466-2972. Boys boarding and day school, secondary and elementary. Brothers of the Sacred Heart. Bros. Donnan Berry, S.C., Pres.; Ronald Talbot, S.C., Prin.; Noel Lemmon, S.C., Dir. Admissions. Brothers 29; Lay Teachers 46; Students 625.

[D] HOUSING FOR THE ELDERLY

BILOXI. *Gabriel Manor,* 2321 Atkinson Rd., 39531. Tel: 601-388-1013.
For a complete listing, refer to the Special Care Facilities section.

Santa Maria Retirement Apartments, 674 Beach, 39530. Tel: 601-432-1289.
For a complete listing, refer to the Special Care Facilities section.

BAY ST. LOUIS. *Notre Dame de la Mer Retirement Apartments,* 292 Hwy. 90, 39520. Tel: 601-467-2885; Fax: 601-466-6300.
For a complete listing, refer to the Special Care Facilities section.

OCEAN SPRINGS. *Samaritan House,* 642 Jackson Ave., 39564.
For a complete listing, refer to the Special Care Facilities section.

Villa Maria Retirement Apartments, 921 Porter Ave., 39564. Tel: 601-875-8811.
For a complete listing, refer to the Special Care Facilities section.

[E] MONASTERIES AND RESIDENCES OF PRIESTS AND BROTHERS

BILOXI. *St. John Neumann Residence,* 1044 Beach Blvd., 39530. Tel: 601-374-1800. Redemptorists. Revs. Matthew J. Kerschen, C.Ss.R., Supr.; Albert Babin, C.Ss.R.; Warren Drinkwater, C.Ss.R.; Joseph Elworthy, C.Ss.R.; John A. Hensgen, C.Ss.R.; Edward C. Cosgrove, C.Ss.R.; Reinhard Stump, C.Ss.R.; Earl Toups, C.Ss.R.

BAY ST. LOUIS. *Media Production Center "In A Word,"* 199 Seminary Dr., 39520. Tel: 601-467-1097; Fax: 601-466-4393. Rev. James Pawlicki, S.V.D., Dir. & Editor.

Saint Stanislaus Community, 304 S. Beach Blvd., P.O. Box 8001, 39521-8001. Tel: 601-466-3419; 466-3411. Brothers of the Sacred Heart. Bro. Xavier Werneth, S.C., Dir. Total in Residence 24.

Southern Province of St. Augustine - Provincial Residence, 201 Ruella Ave., 39520. Tel: 601-467-4322; Fax: 601-466-5618. Society of the Divine Word. Very Rev. Clifton Labbe, S.V.D., Prov.; Rev. Thomas James, S.V.D., Prov.; Bro. Richard Chambers, S.V.D., Treas.

Province Development Office.

WAVELAND. *Brothers of the Sacred Heart,* 126 Bienville St., 39576. Tel: 601-463-0282. Bro. Adrian Gaudin, S.C., Dir. Total in Residence 5.

[F] CONVENTS AND RESIDENCES FOR SISTERS

BILOXI. *Congregation of Humility of Mary,* 126 Reynoir St., Apt. No. 2, 39530. Sr. Rose Mary Eich, C.H.M.

Daughters of Our Lady of the Holy Rosary. (Vietnamese), Presentation Convent, 424 Division St., 39530. Tel: 601-374-6105. Sisters 3; Total Staff 3.

Our Lady of Fatima Convent, 314 Jim Money Rd., 39531. Tel: 601-388-8912. Marianite of Holy Cross 1; Sisters of the Living Word 1; Total Staff 2.

Sisters of Mercy Convent, 11454 Spring Ln., 39532. Tel: 601-392-2575. Sr. M. Aimee Starks, R.S.M., Contact Person. Religious Sisters of Mercy of the Americas 5.

GULFPORT. *Daughters of Charity Residence,* 3900 16th St., 39501. Tel: 601-863-2159. Daughters of Charity 2.

Eucharistic Missionaries of St. Dominic, 164 E. Beach Blvd., Apt. 201, 39507. Tel: 601-863-6263. Other Address: Seashore Manor, 1450 Beach Blvd., Apt. 221, Biloxi, 39530. Tel: 601-432-8698. Sr. Catherine Marie Drawe, O.P., Pres.

Sisters of Mercy - St. James Convent, 366 Cowan Rd., 39507. Tel: 601-896-3277. Sisters of Mercy of the Americas. Sr. Susan Carr, R.S.M.; Sr. Anna Quinlan, R.S.M.; Sr. Eileen Lowney, R.S.M. Sisters of Mercy (Ireland) 2. Other Addresses: 15 Lafayette Pl., 39507. Tel: 601-896-5598. Sr. Rita Murray, R.S.M.; Sr. Rose Fennesy, R.S.M.; Sr. Kathleen Byrne, R.S.M. Sisters 3. 2805 Oakridge Cir., 39507. Tel: 601-896-6302. Sr. Mary Riordan, R.S.M.; Sr. Kathleen Curtin, R.S.M.; Sr. Therese O'Connor, R.S.M.; Sr. Teresa McNamara, R.S.M. Sisters 4.

HATTIESBURG. *Sisters For Christian Community,* #4 North Ln., 39402. Tel: 601-264-9307.

LONG BEACH. *Congregation of the Holy Rosary.* (Vietnamese), 1102 E. Beach Blvd., 39560. Tel: 601-864-5291. Sisters 2; Aspirants 12.

Presentation Convent, 18091 Commission Rd., 39560. Tel: 601-864-8418. Union of the Sisters of the Presentation of the Blessed Virgin Mary.

PASCAGOULA. *Emmaus Community,* 5507 LeMans Cir., 39581. Tel: 601-762-8401. School Sisters of Notre Dame 2.

St. Peter the Apostle Convent, 1703 Telephone Rd., 39567. Sisters of the Holy Spirit and Mary Immaculate Consensus Community Sisters 3; Total Staff 10; Total in Residence 3.

PASS CHRISTIAN. *Sacred Heart Cenacle,* 14595 Vidalia Rd., 39571. Tel: 601-255-3991.

WAVELAND. *St. Clare Convent,* 234 S. Beach Blvd., 39576. Tel: 601-467-7071.

[G] NEWMAN CENTERS

ELLISVILLE. *Jones Junior College.* c/o Immaculate Conception Church, 833 W. Sixth St., Laurel, 39440. Rev. Kenneth Ramon-Landry, Chap.

GAUTIER. *Jackson County Junior College,* 10601 Daisy Ventry Rd., 39564.

GULFPORT. *Mississippi Gulf Coast Community College,* Courthouse Road Station, 39507.

HATTIESBURG. *University of Southern Mississippi,* St. Thomas Aquinas Chapel, 3117 W. Fourth St., 39401. Rev. Michael J. Tracey, Chap.

LONG BEACH. *University of Southern Mississippi, Gulf Park,* 630 E. Beach, 39560. Rev. Louis Lohan, Chap.

LUMBERTON. *Pearl River Junior College, St. Joseph Catholic Center,* 379 W. Seneca Rd., 39455-9519. Tel: 601-796-3051. Rev. Clark Bearden, Chap.

PERKINSTON. *Perkinston Junior College.* Mailing Address: P.O. Box 566, 39577. Rev. Patrick Mockler, Chap.

[H] MISCELLANEOUS

BILOXI. *Gabriel Manor II, Inc.,* c/o The Catholic Diocese of Biloxi, P.O. Box 1189, 39533. Tel: 601-374-8316; 374-0220. Most Rev. Joseph Lawson Howze, D.D., Pres.; Sr. Rebecca Rutkowski, A.C.S.W., Contact Person.

BAY ST. LOUIS. *SSC Progression Corporation,* 304 S. Beach Blvd., 39520. Tel: 601-466-3401. Patricia A. Modenbach, Pres.

Camp Stanislaus. Tel: 601-466-3418. Bro. Lee Barker, Pres.

RELIGIOUS INSTITUTES OF MEN REPRESENTED IN THE DIOCESE

For further details refer to the corresponding bracketed number in the Religious Institutes of Men or Women section.

[1100]—*Brothers of the Sacred Heart.*—S.C.
[1330]—*Congregation of the Mission (Southern Prov.).*—C.M.
[0840]—*Missionary Servants of the Most Holy Trinity.*—S.T.
[1070]—*Redemptorist Fathers.*—C.Ss.R.
[0700]—*St. Joseph's Society of the Sacred Heart.*—S.S.J.
[0420]—*Society of the Divine Word.*—S.V.D.

RELIGIOUS INSTITUTES OF WOMEN REPRESENTED IN THE DIOCESE

[2100]—*Congregation of the Humility of Mary.*—C.H.M.
[2410]—*Congregation of the Marianites of Holy Cross.*—M.S.C.
[1920]—*Congregation of the Sisters of the Holy Cross.*—C.S.C.
[0760]—*Daughters of Charity of St. Vincent de Paul.*—D.C.
[]—*Daughters of Our Lady of the Holy Rosary.*—F.M.S.R.
[1070-11]—*Dominican Sisters.*—O.P.
[1140]—*Eucharistic Missionaries of St. Dominic.*—O.P.
[2575]—*Institute of the Sisters of Mercy of the Americas.*—R.S.M.
[2790]—*Missionary Servants of the Most Blessed Trinity.*—M.S.B.T.
[3530]—*Missionary Sisters Servants of the Holy Spirit.*—S.Sp.S.
[3280]—*Presentation of the Blessed Virgin Mary Sisters.*—P.B.V.M.
[3450]—*Religious of Jesus-Mary.*—R.J.M.
[2970]—*School Sisters of Notre Dame.*—S.S.N.D.
[]—*Sisters for Christian Community.*—S.F.C.C.
[0430]—*Sisters of Charity of the Blessed Virgin Mary.*—B.V.M.
[2560]—*Sisters of Mercy (Killaloe).*
[1510]—*Sisters of St. Francis.*—O.S.F.
[2040]—*Sisters of the Holy Spirit.*—S.H.S.
[2350]—*Sisters of the Living Word.*—S.L.W.
[2940]—*Sisters of the Most Holy Sacrament.*—M.H.S.

NECROLOGY

(No Deaths)

Diocese of Birmingham

(Dioecesis Birminghamiensis)

Most Reverend

DAVID E. FOLEY, D.D.

Bishop of Birmingham; ordained May 26, 1956; appointed Titular Bishop of Ottaba and Auxiliary Bishop of Richmond May 3, 1986; consecrated June 27, 1986; appointed Bishop of Birmingham 1994; consecrated and installed May 13, 1994.

Chancery Office: St. Thomas Catholic Life Center, P.O. Box 12047, Birmingham, AL, 35202-2047. Tel.: 205-838-8322; Fax: 205-836-1910.

E-mail address: Chancery@bhmdiocese.org

ESTABLISHED JUNE 28, 1969.

Square Miles 28,091.

Comprises the Counties of North Alabama in an irregular line between the Counties (west to east) of Sumter and Choctaw and following the base of the following Counties: Marengo, Perry, Chilton, Coosa, Tallapoosa and Chambers or comprising the Counties of: Bibb, Blount, Calhoun, Chambers, Cherokee, Chilton, Clay, Clebourne, Colbert, Coosa, Cullman, DeKalb, Etowah, Fayette, Franklin, Greene, Hale, Jackson, Jefferson, Lamar, Lauderdale, Lawrence, Limestone, Madison, Marengo, Marion, Marshall, Morgan, Perry, P.ickens, Randolph, St. Clair, Shelby, Sumter, Talladega, Tallapoosa, Tuscaloosa, Walker and Winston.

Legal Title: *The Catholic Bishop of Birmingham in Alabama, a Corporation Sole.*

For legal titles of institutions, consult the Chancery Office.

STATISTICAL OVERVIEW

Personnel	
Bishop	1
Abbots	1
Retired Abbots	3
Priests: Diocesan Active in Diocese	49
Priests: Active Outside Diocese	2
Priests: Diocesan in Foreign Missions	2
Priests: Retired, Sick or Absent	12
Number of Diocesan Priests	65
Religious Priests in Diocese	49
Ordinations:	
Transitional Deacons	1
Permanent Deacons in Diocese	24
Total Brothers	31
Total Sisters	171
Parishes	
Parishes	62
With Resident Pastor:	
Resident Diocesan Priests	40
Resident Religious Priests	15
Without Resident Pastor:	
Administered by Priests	4
Administered by Permanent Deacons	2
Administered by Lay People	2
Missions	13
Professional Ministry Personnel:	
Brothers	2
Sisters	18
Lay Ministers	51
Welfare	
Catholic Hospitals	1
Total Assisted	119,158
Health Care Centers	2
Total Assisted	893,390
Special Centers for Social Services	12
Total Assisted	66,474
Educational	
Diocesan Students in Other Seminaries	10
Total Seminarians	10
High Schools, Diocesan and Parish	3
Total Students	1,043
High Schools, Private	2
Total Students	300
Elementary Schools, Diocesan and Parish	20
Total Students	4,907
Elementary Schools, Private	1
Total Students	190
Non-residential Schools for the Disabled	1
Total Students	143
Catechesis/Religious Education:	
High School Students	1,763
Elementary Students	6,003
Total Students Under Catholic Instruction	14,359
Teachers in the Diocese:	
Priests	7
Scholastics	1
Sisters	22
Lay Teachers	395
Vital Statistics	
Receptions into the Church:	
Infant Baptism Totals	1,210
Adult Baptism Totals	180
Received into Full Communion	445
First Communions	1,159
Confirmations	1,002
Marriages:	
Catholic	180
Interfaith	225
Total Marriages	405
Deaths	495
Total Catholic Population	68,979
Total Population	2,682,886

Former Bishops—Most Rev. JOSEPH G. VATH, ord. June 7, 1941; appt. Auxiliary Bishop of Mobile-Birmingham March 25, 1966; cons. May 26, 1966; transferred to the Diocese of Birmingham Dec. 9, 1969; died July 14, 1987.—Most Rev. RAYMOND J. BOLAND, D.D., ord. June 16, 1957; appt. Bishop of Birmingham Feb. 2, 1988; cons. March 25, 1988; transferred to Kansas City-St. Joseph Sept. 9, 1993.—Most Rev. DAVID E. FOLEY, D.D., ord. May 26, 1956; appt. Titular Bishop of Ottaba and Auxiliary Bishop of Richmond, May 3, 1986; cons. June 27, 1986; appt. Bishop of Birmingham in Alabama, March 22, 1994; installed May 13, 1994.

Chancery Office—P.O. Box 12047, Birmingham, 35202-2047. St. Thomas Catholic Life Center, *8131 Fourth Ave. S., Birmingham, 35206.* Tel: 205-838-8322; Fax: 205-836-1910. Address all Diocesan Correspondence to the above Post Office Box unless otherwise indicated. Telephones listed below.

Office of the Bishop—Tel: 205-838-8318. PEGGY SELIG, Sec.

Chancellor—Sr. MARY FRANCES LOFTIN, D.C. Tel: 205-833-0175. GERRY NABORS, Sec.

Priests' Council—Most Rev. DAVID E. FOLEY, D.D., Pres.; Rev. EDWIN DILL, S.T., Moderator. Tel: 334-289-2767. Members: Rev. Msgr. MICHAEL SEXTON, V.G.; Revs. GREGORY BITTNER; KEVIN COOKE; JOSEPH CULOTTA; RAYMOND DUNMYER; BRIAN EGAN, V.F.; JOHN FALLON, V.F.; THOMAS KELLY; RAYMOND MURRIN; FRANK MUSCOLINO; PHILIP O'KENNEDY; JOHN OWEN; PAUL ROHLING.

Diocesan College of Consultors—Rev. Msgr. MICHAEL SEXTON, V.G.; Revs. GREGORY BITTNER; JOSEPH CULOTTA; RAYMOND DUNMYER; BRIAN EGAN, V.F.; JOHN FALLON, V.F.; FRANK MUSCOLINO; PAUL ROHLING.

Diocesan College of Vicars—Rev. Msgr. MICHAEL SEXTON, Vicar General-Vicar for Northwest Deanery. Tel: 205-764-3303. Revs. GREGORY BITTNER, Judicial Vicar. Tel: 205-838-8307. PAUL ROHLING, Vicar for Clergy. Tel: 205-871-1153. FRANK MUSCOLINO, Vicar for Vocations. Tel: 205-933-2500. BRIAN EGAN, Vicar for Admin.-Vicar for East Birmingham Deanery. Tel: 205-838-8309. JOHN IGOE, Vicar for West Birmingham Deanery. Tel: 205-838-8305. PATRICK SULLIVAN, Vicar for Central Birmingham Deanery. Tel: 205-822-4480. LOUIS GIARDINO, Vicar for Northeast Deanery. Tel: 205-881-4781. JOHN FALLON, Vicar for Southwest Deanery. Tel: 205-553-9733. RICHARD DONOHOE, Vicar for Southeast Deanery. Tel: 205-237-3011.

Diocesan Pastoral Council—Most Rev. DAVID E. FOLEY, D.D., Pres.; Sr. MARY FRANCES LOFTIN, D.C., Moderator Members include lay representatives of the Diocesan Deaneries, four Vicars for Deaneries, four religious and a staff representative.

Diocesan Finance Council—Most Rev. DAVID E. FOLEY, D.D., Pres.; Rev. BRIAN EGAN, V.F., Vicar for Admin. THOMAS CURTIN, Chm. Members: Rev. GREGORY BITTNER; GREG CLARK; JOHN DEWITT, C.P.A.; J. ROBERT DOODY; RAY G. DYER, JR., C.P.A.; MICHAEL L. PATTERSON; MARY ELLEN PETERS; ANDREW RUCKS; PAT RUMORE; YOLANDA N. SULLIVAN, C.P.A.; Sr. MARY FRANCES LOFTIN, Ex-Officio. Staff Members: JOHN ANSON, Finance Officer.

Tribunal—Rev. GREGORY T. BITTNER, J.C.L., Judicial Vicar. Tel: 205-838-8307; 838-8320. CYWILLA FABIJANIC, Sec.-Notary-Case Mgt. Trial Advocates: Revs. TIMOTHY BURNS; KEVIN COOKE.

Judges—Sr. MARILYN VASSALLO, C.S.J., J.C.L.; Revs. RICHARD DONOHOE; LOUIS GIARDINO.

Defenders of the Bond—Revs. BRIAN EGAN; PAUL ROHLING; Sr. LYNN MCKENZIE, O.S.B., J.C.L.,Please address all Rogatory Commissions to the Office of the Tribunal, *St. Thomas Catholic Life Center.* Tel: 205-838-8307.

Catholic Social Services—KEVIN BURNS, Board Pres. Tel: 205-324-1600.

Catholic Family Services—VIOLA LAWRENCE, Dir., *2164 11th Ave. S., Birmingham, 35205.* Tel: 205-324-6561.

Catholic Family Services Offices—LAURA DINWIDDLE, Dir., *1010 Church St., Huntsville, 35804.* Tel: 205-536-0073. Dr. TOM COOK, Supvr., *733 37th St. E., Tuscaloosa, 35405.* Tel: 205-553-9045.

Catholic Centers of Concern—Birmingham; Anniston; Gadsden; Hamilton; Huntsville; Eutaw; Winfield; Sulligent; Fayette.

Apostolate to the Aged—AL GERMANN, *369 Midwood Ave., Birmingham, 35228.* Tel: 205-923-7108.

Engaged Encounter—PAM DIPIAZZA; ANTHONY DIPIAZZA, *1932 Crossvine Rd., Birmingham, 35244.* Tel: 205-987-0977.

Natural Family Planning—HAROLD GRAY; CATHY GRAY, *613 Bienville Ln., Birmingham, 35213.* Tel: 205-879-2042.

Department of Education—FRANK X. SAVAGE, Dir.,

Catholic Education & Lifelong Learning.
Catholic Schools Office—EILEEN MOORE, Supt. Tel: 205-838-8303.
Religious Education Office—Sr. FRANCES M. LENDLE, S.D.S., Dir. Tel: 205-838-8312.
Apostolate with Mentally Retarded Persons—Rev. PATRICK CULLEN; Sr. MARY VERNON GENTLE, R.S.M., *The Nazareth House, 2120 Third Ave. N., Birmingham, 35202.* Tel: 205-251-1279 (Voice or TDD).
Catholic Youth Ministry—LAURIE DELGATTO, Dir. Tel: 205-838-8301.
Campus Ministry—Rev. RAYMOND DUNMYER, Dir., *St. Francis University Parish, 811 Fifth Ave., Tuscaloosa, 35401.* Tel: 205-758-5672.
Catholic Scouting—LAURIE DELGATTO, Dir. Tel: 205-838-8301.
Toy Bowl Association—MICHAEL CAMMARATA, Dir., *222 73rd St., N., Birmingham.* Tel: 205-838-2112.
Board of Education—JOHN KEARNEY, Chm. Tel: 205-942-1100 (Office); 979-4928 (Res.).
Finance Office and Administration—
Diocesan Finance Officer—JOHN ANSON. Tel: 205-833-0173.
Diocesan Development and Annual Catholic Charities Appeal, Campaign for Human Development, and *Catholic Relief Services*—Rev. BRIAN EGAN, Dir. Tel: 205-838-8309.
Office of Pastoral Services—
Beginning Experience—HELEN BOWERS. Tel: 205-802-6216; 969-8509 (Voice Mail).
Children's Beginning Experience—JEANNETTE CAMPISI, *c/o St. Peter Church, 2061 Patton Chapel Rd., Bham, 35216.* Tel: 205-822-4480.
Cursillo Program—Directors: DICK SWEENEY; JANE SWEENEY. Tel: 205-987-8038.
Hispanic Ministries—BRENDA BULLOCK, Dir. Tel: 205-838-8306.
Lay Ministries Program—Sr. MARIE LEONARD, O.S.B., Dir. Tel: 205-838-8300.
Marriage Encounter—DEL FISHER; NANCY FISHER. Tel: 205-556-6471.
Office of Black Ministry—OLIVIA HILL, Dir. Tel: 205-838-8313.
Peace and Justice Commission—Tel: 205-838-8306. JANE SWEENEY, Sec.
Pro-Life Activities—Rev. JOHN IGOE, Dir. Tel: 205-838-8305.
Propagation of the Faith and Holy Childhood—Rev. RAYMOND MURRIN, Dir. RUTH CARMELLO, Asst. Dir. Tel: 205-838-8306.
Serra Club of Birmingham—RICHARD C. SWEENEY, Pres. Tel: 205-987-8038.
Vocations Office—Rev. FRANK MUSCOLINO, Dir. Tel: 205-933-2500.
"One Voice"—Diocesan weekly; Rev. JOHN IGOE, Editor. Tel: 205-838-8305. MARY ALICE CROCKETT, Editorial Asst. SAMUEL A. CIULLA, Advertising; ANN LANZI, Circulation, *The Birmingham Catholic Press, Inc., P.O. Box 10822, Birmingham, 35202.* Tel: 205-838-8305; Fax: 205-838-8319.
Council of Religious—Sr. ROSE SEVENICH, O.S.F., Chm., *420A Elder Oaks Way, Birmingham, 35209.* Tel: 205-870-1791.
Diocesan Council of Catholic Women—FRANCES WIDEMAN, Pres., *106 Lockerbie Cir., Birmingham, 35223.* Tel: 205-428-9559.
Priests' Retirement Fund—Rev. JOSEPH UNDERWOOD, Chm., *6520 Court K, Birmingham, 35228.* Tel: 205-925-8239.

CLERGY, PARISHES, MISSIONS AND PAROCHIAL SCHOOLS

CITY OF BIRMINGHAM
(Jefferson County)

1—ST. PAUL'S CATHEDRAL (1871), Rev. Patrick P. Cullen; Deacon Hugh O'Brien. In res., Most Rev. David E. Foley, D.D.; Rev. Desmond Regan.
Mailing Address: P.O. Box 10044, 35202. Tel: 205-251-1279; Fax: 205-251-1284.
Res., 2120 Third Ave. N., 35203.
School—Tel: 205-251-9345. Ann Mason, Prin.
Lay Teachers 17; Students 242.

2—ST. ANTHONY'S (1900). Closed. For inquiries for parish records contact St. Paul Cathedral, Birmingham.

3—ST. BARNABAS (1908), Rev. Eugene O'Connor. In res., Rev. Edward P. Walsh.
Mailing Address: P.O. Box 610304, 35261.
Res., 7921 First Ave. N., 35206. Tel: 205-833-0334; 833-5695.
School—7901 First Ave. N., 35206. Tel: 205-836-5385. Olga R. Veit, Prin.
Lay Teachers 13; Students 230.
Mailing Address: P.O. Box 610347, 35261.
Catechesis/Religious Programs—Tel: 205-836-4567. Rosemary Gagliano, D.R.E.
Students 26.

4—ST. BERNARD'S (Inglenook) (1928), Rev. Brian J. Egan.
Res., 3814 37th Ave., N., 35217. Tel: 205-841-2019.

5—BLESSED SACRAMENT (1910), Rev. Matthew F. Brennan. In res., Rev. Charles V. Cross.
Res., 1460 Pearson Ave., S.W., P.O. Box 110006, 35211. Tel: 205-785-9840.

6—ST. FRANCIS XAVIER (1953), Revs. Paul Rohling; Andrew Sullivan; Sr. Jane Bishop, O.S.B., Pastoral Min.; Deacon George Mickwee.
Res., P.O. Box 130669, 35213. Tel: 205-871-1153; Fax: 205-871-9831.
School—Tel: 205-871-1687. Sr. Judith Dianne McGowan, R.S.M., Prin.
Sisters 1; Lay Teachers 13; Students 237.
Catechesis/Religious Programs—Tel: 205-871-1153; Fax: 205-871-1153. Sr. Therese Francis Walker, M.S.B.T., D.R.E.
Students 276.

7—HOLY FAMILY (1938) (African American), Revs. Robert Crossmeyer, C.P.; Thaddeus Tamm, C.P.; E. John Hilgert, C.P.; Deacon Benjamin Jett.
Res., 1910 19th St., 35218. Tel: 205-780-3440; Fax: 205-780-5272.
School—1916 19th St., Ensley, 35218. Tel: 205-785-5858. Sr. M. DePorres Collier, C.S.S.F., Prin.
Sisters 2; Lay Teachers 14; Students 300.
Catechesis/Religious Programs—Students 490.
Mission—Fairfield, Jefferson Co., St. Mary's.

8—HOLY ROSARY (Gate City) (1889), Revs. Daniel Rauzi, S.D.B.; James Naughton, S.D.B.; Peter Malloy, S.D.B.; Bro. Charles Todel, S.D.B.
Mailing Address: P.O. Box 321576, 35232. Tel: 205-595-0652; Fax: 205-595-3091.
Res., 7414 Georgia Rd. S., 35212.

9—ST. JOHN BOSCO (1973), Rev. James Naughton, S.D.B. In res., Rev. Sean Rooney, S.D.B.
Mailing Address: P.O. Box 321576, 35232. Tel: 205-595-1009; Fax: 205-595-3091.
Res., 5224 First Ave., N., 35212.

10—ST. JOSEPH'S (1921) (Italian), Rev. John T. Igoe; Deacon Al Germann.
Res., 3020 Avenue K, 35218. Tel: 205-781-4612.
School—Tel: 205-787-9711; Fax: 205-787-9839. Dr. John Douglass, Prin.
Sisters of the Presentation 2; Lay Teachers 10; Students 141.
Convent—1100-31st St., 35218. Tel: 205-787-1517.

11—KOREAN CATHOLIC COMMUNITY, ST. LUKE HWANG, Rev. John Sung Kyu Kim.
Res., 2513 Mountain Lodge Cir., 35216. Tel: 205-823-6511.

12—ST. MARGARET'S. Closed. 1986. For inquiries for parish records contact Blessed Sacrament Parish, Birmingham.

13—ST. MARK'S (1904), Rev. Crescenzio DeFazio.
Res., 1010 16th Ave., W., P.O. Box 310058, 35231. Tel: 205-251-7875.

14—OUR LADY OF FATIMA (1905), Rev. John J. O'Rourke, S.S.J.; Deacons Andrew Andrews; Willie Moore.
Res., 708 First St., S., 35205. Tel: 205-322-1205.
School—630 First St. S., 35205. Tel: 205-251-8395. Sr. M. Ann Christine, S.N.D., Prin.
Sisters of Notre Dame of Covington, KY 4; Lay Teachers 9; Students 150.
Catechesis/Religious Programs—Tel: 205-251-8395. Sr. Mary Carleta, S.N.D., D.R.E.
Students 92.

15—OUR LADY OF LOURDES (1959), Rev. Andrew Kennedy.
Res., 980 Huffman Rd., 35215.
Office: Tel: 205-836-2274.
Catechesis/Religious Programs—D.R.E.: Robin Barron; Vonda Gordon.
Students 185.

16—OUR LADY OF SORROWS (1887), Revs. Martin M. Muller; Thomas M. Kelly. In res., Rev. Paschal Ferlisi, O.S.B.
Mailing Address: P.O. Box 59447, 35259. Tel: 205-871-8121; Fax: 205-871-8180.
Res., (Homewood) 1728 Oxmoor Rd., 35209.
School—Tel: 205-879-3237; Fax: 205-879-9332. Mrs. Deborah White, Prin.
Lay Teachers 30; Students 444.
Catechesis/Religious Programs—Tel: 205-871-1431. D.R.E.: Patricia Higuera; Barbara Bess.
Students 446.

17—OUR LADY OF THE VALLEY (1974) (Asian-Spanish), Revs. Michael MacMahon; Michael J. White, Pastor Emeritus.
Res., 5514 Double Oak Ln., 35242. Tel: 205-991-6288; Fax: 205-991-5181.
Church—Tel: 205-991-5488; Fax: 205-991-5181.
School—Tel: 205-991-5692; Fax: 205-991-1251. Mrs. Sandra Roden, Prin.
Lay Teachers 19; Students 310.
Catechesis/Religious Programs—Tel: 205-991-5489; Fax: 205-991-5181. Phyllis Schifanella, D.R.E.
Students 397.

18—OUR LADY QUEEN OF THE UNIVERSE (1955) (African American), Rev. Vernon Huguley.
Res., 961 Center St., N., 35204. Tel: 205-328-7729; Fax: 205-328-7703.
Mission—Collegeville, Jefferson Co., Sacred Heart.

19—ST. PATRICK'S (1983), Rev. Raymond J. Murrin; Sr. Joan Harrington, C.S.J., Pastoral Min. & D.R.E.; Deacon Daniel Whitaker.
Res., 301 Shamrock Tr., Adamsville, 35005. Tel: 205-674-1426; 798-5326; 791-2931; Fax: 205-798-5330.
Catechesis/Religious Programs—Tel: 205-798-5326; Fax: 205-798-5330.
Students 143.

20—ST. PETER THE APOSTLE (1962), Revs. Patrick J. Sullivan; Robert J. Sullivan; Sr. Virginia Rohling, O.S.B., Pastoral Assoc.; Deacon Dr. Sam Anzalone.
Res., 2061 Patton Chapel Rd., 35216. Tel: 205-822-4480; Fax: 205-822-4534.
Catechesis/Religious Programs—Tel: 205-823-6324; Fax: 205-822-4534. Dr. Rebecca Sullivan.
Students 565.

21—PRINCE OF PEACE (1984), Rev. Jerry Deasy; Deacons Frank Iovino; John Ferguson.
Mailing Address: P.O. Box 26209, 35226.
Church—4600 Moss Creek Blvd., Hoover, 35226. Tel: 205-822-9125; Fax: 205-822-9127.
Res., 614 Valley St., 35226. Tel: 205-979-7776.
Catechesis/Religious Programs—Tel: 205-822-9125; Fax: 205-822-9127. Kathleen Dunne, D.R.E.
Students 386.

22—SACRED HEART (1955) (African American), Rev. Vernon Huguley.
Church—3401 27th Ct. N., 35207. Tel: 205-252-8909.

23—ST. STANISLAUS (1914), Rev. Timothy Hill.
Mailing Address: 904 Indiana St., 35224. Tel: 205-785-9625.

24—ST. STEPHEN UNIVERSITY PARISH (1990), Rev. Frank J. Muscolino; Sr. Mary Ann O'Brien, D.C., Pastoral Assoc.
Res., 1515 12th Ave. S., 35205. Tel: 205-933-2500; Fax: 205-939-1500.

25—ST. THERESA'S. Closed. For inquiries for parish records contact St. Paul's Cathedral, Birmingham.

OUTSIDE THE CITY OF BIRMINGHAM

Alexander City, Tallapoosa Co., St. John the Apostle (1948), Rev. John J. Nicholas, C.M.
Res., 454 N. Central St., 35010. Tel: 205-234-3631.
Catechesis/Religious Programs—Tel: 205-329-2592. Martha Rodriguez, D.R.E.
Students 54.

Anniston, Calhoun Co., Sacred Heart of Jesus (1885), Rev. Richard E. Donohoe; Deacon William Taffee.
Res., 1024 Quintard Ave., P.O. Box 639, 36201. Tel: 205-237-3011; Fax: 205-237-2615.
School—1821 McCall Dr., 36207. Tel: 205-237-4231. Ms. Robin Woolsey, Prin.
Lay Teachers 10; Students 172.
Catechesis/Religious Programs—Tel: 205-237-3011; Fax: 205-237-2615. Mary Zielinski, D.R.E.
Students 106.
All Saints. Unassigned. Contact Naurrese Phillips 205-237-0128.
Res., 1104 W. 15th St., 36204. Tel: 205-237-9230.

Ashland, Catholic Community of Ashland, Rev. John Nicholas, C.M., Agent of the Bishop, Tel: 205-234-3631.
Mailing Address: P.O. Box 295, 36251. Tel: 205-354-2923; Fax: 205-354-4237.
Res., 454 N. Central Ave., Alexander City, 35010.
Mrs. Rosanne Gaither, Community Coord.; Res., 35450 Hwy. 775, 36251.

Athens, Limestone Co., St. Paul's, Rev. Joseph C. Allen.
Mailing Address: P.O. Box 998, 35612.
Res., 1900 Hwy. 72 W., 35611. Tel: 205-232-4191.
Catechesis/Religious Programs—Tel: 205-232-4191. Mrs. Sharon Prohaska, D.R.E.
Students 160.

Bessemer, Jefferson Co., St. Aloysius Church (1886), Rev. Liam Sullivan.
Res., 204 Westwood Dr., 35023. Tel: 205-424-2984.
School—Tel: 205-425-0045; Fax: 205-425-0046. Mrs. Lisa Corona, Prin.
Lay Teachers 12; Students 191.
Catechesis/Religious Programs—Mrs. Donna Duchock, D.R.E.
Students 90.
St. Francis of Assisi (1940) (African American), Rev. Noel Danielewicz, O.F.M.Conv.; Bro. John Obara, O.F.M.Conv.

Res., 2400 Seventh Ave. N., 35020. Tel: 205-425-0984.
School—2410 Seventh Ave. N., 35020. Tel: 205-428-1684; Fax: 205-428-1684. Sr. Maria Dina, M.C., Prin.
Consolata Missionary Sister 1; Franciscan Friars 2; Lay Teachers 7; Students 150.

Cullman, Cullman Co., Sacred Heart (1877) (German), Revs. Kevin D. McGrath, O.S.B.; Leo Carter, O.S.B.; Deacon William Roberson.
Res., 217 Second St. S.E., P.O. Box 1085, 35056. Tel: 205-734-3730; Fax: 205-734-3476. [CEM]
School—Tel: 205-734-4563; Fax: 205-734-3476. Sr. Mary Jude Clark, O.S.B., Prin.
Order of St. Benedict 4; Lay Teachers 9; Students 223.
Catechesis/Religious Programs—Tel: 205-734-3730; Fax: 205-734-3476. Mary Merritt, D.R.E. Students 125.
Mission—Hanceville, Cullman Co., St. Boniface, P.O. Box 1085, 35056. Tel: 205-734-3730; Fax: 205-734-3476. [CEM]

Decatur, Morgan Co., St. Ann's (1870), Rev. Joseph Culotta; Sr. Janet Marie Flemming, O.S.B., Pastoral Assoc.
Res., 250 Johnston St. S.E., 35601. Tel: 205-353-2667; Fax: 205-353-8994. [JC]
School—Tel: 205-353-6543. Sr. Lois Justen, O.S.F., Prin.
Lay Teachers 11; Students 211.
Catechesis/Religious Programs—Tel: 205-353-2667; Fax: 205-353-8994. Barbara Romei, D.R.E. Students 228.
Mission—Hartselle, Morgan Co., Holy Family, P.O. Box 783, Hartselle, 35640. Tel: 205-773-5701.

Demopolis, Marengo Co., St. Leo (1936), Rev. Edwin Dill, S.T.
Res., 307 Main Ave., P.O. Box 937, 36732. Tel: 205-289-2767.
Mission—Greensboro, Hale Co., Our Lady of Lourdes.

Eutaw, Greene Co., St. Mary (1948) (African American). Administered by West Alabama Mission. Rev. David Buchanan, Dir.
Tel: 205-553-2200.

Fairfield, Jefferson Co., St. Mary (1943), Rev. E. John Hilgert, C.P.
Church—6101 Dr. Martin Luther King Dr., 35064. Tel: 205-923-0202.
School—6124 Myron Massey Blvd., 35064. Tel: 205-923-5161; Fax: 205-923-5166. Mary Collins, Prin.
Lay Teachers 11; Students 248.

Florence, Lauderdale Co., St. Joseph's (1898), Rev. Msgr. Michael Sexton, V.G.
Res., 1111 E. College St., 35630. Tel: 205-764-3303; Fax: 205-718-0208.
School—Tel: 205-766-1923; 766-1955; Fax: 205-718-0208. Susan B. Halfman, Prin.
Lay Teachers 19; Students 255.
Catechesis/Religious Programs—Tel: 205-757-5038; Fax: 205-247-7018. Kelli Gaputis, D.R.E. Students 116.

St. Michael (1873), Rt. Rev. Victor J. Clark, O.S.B.
Res., Rte. 11, Box 48, 35630. Tel: 205-764-1885. [CEM]
Catechesis/Religious Programs—D.R.E.: Karen Holden, (High School); Melanie Stumpe, (Elementary).
Students 54.

Gadsden, Etowah Co., St. James (1912), Rev. Kevin Cooke.
Mailing Address: P.O. Box 38, 35902.
Res., 225 Carleen St., 35901. Tel: 205-546-2975; Fax: 205-546-2930.
Church—622 Chestnut St., 35901. Tel: 205-546-2975; Fax: 205-546-2930.
School—Tel: 205-546-0132. Sr. M. Cecilia MacDermott, O.S.B., Prin.
Lay Teachers 11; Students 170.
Catechesis/Religious Programs—Judy Ritter, D.R.E. Students 126.
Mission—Fort Payne, DeKalb Co., Our Lady of the Valley, P.O. Box 1446, Fort Payne, 35967. Tel: 205-845-4774.

St. Martin de Porres. Closed. For inquiries for parish records contact St. James, Gadsden.

Gardendale, Jefferson Co., St. Elizabeth Ann Seton (1976), Rev. Ray W. Keiser.
Mailing Address: 334 Main St., 35071. Tel: 205-631-9398.
Res., 105 Powell Dr., P.O. Box 1027, 35071. Tel: 205-631-8582. [CEM]
Catechesis/Religious Programs—Sam Dunne, D.R.E.
Students 105.
Mission—Warrior, Jefferson Co., St. Henry, 211 5th St., Warrior, 35180. Tel: 205-647-7738.

Guntersville, Marshall Co., St. William's (1952), Rev. Paul J. Donnelly.
Res., 929 Gunter Ave., 35976. Tel: 205-582-4964; 582-4245 (Office).
Catechesis/Religious Programs—Ms. Darice Perreault, D.R.E.
Students 100.

Huntsville, Madison Co.,

1—Good Shepherd, (1981), Rev. Philip N. O'Kennedy; Sr. Deborah Kennedy, R.S.M., Pastoral Assoc.; Deacons Ron Puent; Helmut Sassenfeld.
Res., P.O. Box 4447, 35815-4447. Tel: 205-882-1844; Fax: 205-882-1841.
Catechesis/Religious Programs—Tel: 205-822-1844. Katherine Maxwell, D.R.E.
Students 503.

2—St. Mary of the Visitation, (1861), Revs. William M. Kelly, S.D.S.; Dominic Giles, S.D.S.
Res., 222 N. Jefferson St., 35801. Tel: 205-536-6349; Fax: 205-536-6349.
Catechesis/Religious Programs—Tel: 205-536-6760. Mrs. Evelyn Jaap, D.R.E.
Students 79.

3—St. Joseph's, (1952), Revs. Gregory Coulthard, S.D.S.; Robert Wagner, S.D.S.
Res., 2300 Beasley Ave., N.W., 35816. Tel: 205-534-8459; Fax: 205-534-8450.
School—Holy Family School, 205-539-5221. Ms. Susan McGraw, Prin.
Religious 1; Sisters of the Divine Savior 3; Lay Teachers 17; Students 267.
Catechesis/Religious Programs—Tel: 205-534-1310. Carmen Amato, D.R.E.
Students 110.

4—Holy Spirit, (1965), Revs. Louis Giardino; Sean Paris Merino; Deacon Lee Roy Hoekenschnieder, Sr.; Bro. Benedict Stoegbauer, S.D.S.
Res., 625 Airport Rd., 35802. Tel: 205-881-4781.
School—Tel: 205-881-4852; Fax: 205-881-4904. Mr. James Bell, Prin.
Lay Teachers 21; Students 306.
Catechesis/Religious Programs—Tel: 205-881-0345. Sr. Janice Rooney, S.N.D., D.R.E.
Students 355.

5—Our Lady Queen of the Universe, (1965), Rev. Timothy L. Burns.
Mailing Address: P.O. Box 3268, 35810.
Res., 3701 Grizzard, 35810. Tel: 205-852-0788; Fax: 205-852-0788.
Church—2421 Shady Lane Dr., N.W., 35810.
Catechesis/Religious Programs—Susan Turner, D.R.E.
Students 172.

Jacksonville, Calhoun Co., St. Charles (1964), Rev. William Lucas.
Church—308 Seventh St. N.E., 36265. Tel: 205-435-3238.
Res., 400 Seventh St. N.E., 36265. Tel: 205-435-1307.
Catechesis/Religious Programs—Marcia Anzur, D.R.E.
Students 109.
Mission—Piedmont, Calhoun Co., St. Joachim, 308 7th St. N.E., 36265.

Jasper, Walker Co., St. Cecilia (1964), Rev. Albert Fisher.
Res., P.O. Box 3638, 35502. Tel: 205-384-4800.
Catechesis/Religious Programs—Tel: 205-384-4800. Becky Romano, D.R.E.
Students 85.
Mission—Haleyville, Winston Co., Our Lady of Guadalupe, P.O. Box 3638, 35502. Tel: 205-486-9691. Sr. Catherine Concannon, S.S.N.D., Pastoral Min.

Lanett, Chambers Co., Holy Family (1915), Rev. Martin McGeough, C.M.
Res., 705 N. Third Ave., 36863-0325. Tel: 334-644-4405; Fax: 334-644-4405.
Catechesis/Religious Programs—Deacon Donald Canonica, D.R.E.
Students 45.
Mission—Roanoke, Randolph Co., Immaculate Conception, Tel: 205-863-4418.

Leeds, Jefferson Co., St. Theresa's (1951), Rev. Peter T. MacCarthy.
Res., P.O. Box 525, 35094. Tel: 205-699-8534. [CEM]

Livingston, Sumter Co., St. Francis of Assisi (1972). Administered by West Alabama Missions. Rev. David Buchanan, Dir.
Res., P.O. Box RR, 35470. Tel: 205-652-7742.

Madison, Madison Co., St. John the Baptist (1973), Rev. Patrick Murphy; Deacons Dan Laurita; Darrell Diem; Terry Thompson, Pastoral Asst. & D.R.E.
Res., 1055 Hughes Rd., 35758. Tel: 205-722-0130; Fax: 205-722-0303.
School—1057 Hughes Rd., 35758. Tel: 205-722-0772. Tommy Bridges, Prin.
Lay Teachers 8; Students 130.
Catechesis/Religious Programs—Tel: 205-722-8590.
Students 495.

Marion, Perry Co., Marion Military Institute, Rev. Charles McNeice, S.S.E.
Res., Washington St., 36756. Tel: 334-874-8931.

Montevallo, Shelby Co., St. Thomas the Apostle (1951), Rev. Raymond Remke; Sr. Pat Hinton, O.S.F., Pastoral Assoc.
Res., 80 St. Thomas Way, 35115. Tel: 205-663-3936; Fax: 205-663-3929.
Catechesis/Religious Programs—Students 255.
Mailing Address: 80 St. Thomas Way, 35115. Tel: 205-663-3936; Fax: 205-663-3929.
Mission—Clanton, Chilton Co., Church of the Resurrection, P.O. Box 735, Clanton, 35046. Tel: 205-755-5498. Sr. Veronica Ryan, O.S.B., Pastoral Coord.

Moulton, Lawrence Co., Resurrection Catholic Chapel (1993), Deacon Bob Laremore, Pastoral Coord.
Res., 7363 Alabama Hwy. 33, 35650. Tel: 205-292-3333.

Oneonta, Blount Co., Corpus Christi (1983), Deacon Al Girodo, Admin.
Church—Rte. 3, P.O. Box 751, 35121. Tel: 205-625-6078.

Pell City, St. Clair Co., Our Lady of the Lake (1969), Rev. Gregory T. Bittner.
Mailing Address: Hwy. 231 S., P.O. Box 388, 35125.
Res., 117 Ingram Lane, Cropwell, 35054. Tel: 205-525-4711; 525-5161 (Church); Fax: 205-991-6312.
Catechesis/Religious Programs—Students 42.
Mission—Childersburg, Talladega Co., Holy Name of Jesus, 4th St. N.W., Childersburg, 35044.

Roanoke, Randolph Co., The Vincentian Mission of East Central Alabama, Rev. Francis W. Sacks, C.M., Dir.
Mailing Address: P.O. Box 645, 36274-0645. Tel: 334-863-4418; Fax: 334-863-4418.

Russellville, Franklin Co., Good Shepherd Church (1973), Rev. Robert A. Dalton; Bro. Thomas Kelly, Pastoral Assoc.
Res., 1700 N. Jackson Ave., P.O. Box 630, 35653. Tel: 205-332-4861. [JC]

Scottsboro, Jackson Co., St. Jude (1971), Rev. Camillus W. Blazek; Deacon Jerome P. Raispis.
Res., P.O. Box 971, 35768. Tel: 205-259-2520.
Catechesis/Religious Programs—Tel: 205-574-6156. Carol Miller, D.R.E.
Students 49.

Sylacauga, Talladega Co., St. Jude (1947), Rev. Henry McDaid, Admin.
Res., 306 W. Bay St., P.O. Box 111, 35150. Tel: 205-245-7741.
Catechesis/Religious Programs—Students 44.

Talladega, Talladega Co., St. Francis of Assisi (1951), Rev. Henry A. McDaid.
Res., 722 S. East St., P.O. Box 1142, 35160. Tel: 205-362-5372; Fax: 205-362-5372.
Catechesis/Religious Programs—Students 58.

Trussville, Jefferson Co., Holy Infant of Prague (1941), Rev. Patrick O'Donoghue. Pastoral Ministers: Sr. Marie Carolyn Cutcliff, R.S.M., D.R.E.; Mrs. Terry Pruet; Deacon Ed Pruet. In res., Rev. John Owens.
Res., 215 Hewitt St., P.O. Box 43, 35173. Tel: 205-655-2541.
Catechesis/Religious Programs—Tel: 205-655-3002.
Students 275.

Tuscaloosa, Tuscaloosa Co., Holy Spirit (1961), Revs. John Fallon; David Buchanan, Dir.
Res., 733 37th St. E., 35405. Tel: 205-553-9733; Fax: 205-554-0136.
School—711 37th St., 35405. Tel: 205-553-9630. Ana MacCrone, Prin.
Lay Teachers 27; Students 530.
Catechesis/Religious Programs—Students 230.
Missions—Tuscaloosa, Tuscaloosa Co., St. John, 8th & Lurleen Wallace Blvd., 35401. Tel: 205-553-9733; Reform, Dickens Co., St. Robert. Administered by West Alabama Mission. Hwy. 17 S., Reform, 35481. Tel: 205-375-8141.

St. Francis of Assisi University Parish (1929), Rev. Raymond A. Dunmyer; Ms. Molly Campbell, Campus Co-Min.
Res., 811 Fifth Ave., 35401. Tel: 205-758-5672; Fax: 205-758-5673.
Catechesis/Religious Programs—Nancy Woodbury, D.R.E.
Students 137.

Tuscumbia, Colbert Co., Our Lady of the Shoals (1869), Rev. Patrick J. Tierney.
Res., 1103 E. Third St., 35674. Tel: 205-383-7207; 381-2699. [CEM]
Church—200 N. East Commons, 35674. Tel: 205-383-7207.
Catechesis/Religious Programs—Carolyn Wilson, D.R.E.
Students 86.

Winfield, Marion Co., Holy Spirit (1965), Rev. Gerald

Peterson, Glmy. Pastoral Ministers: Tel: 205-487-2331. Sr. Catherine Concannon, S.S.N.D.; Sr. Mary Burke, S.S.N.D.
Res., Meadowbrook Dr., Rte. 2, Box 277, 35594. Tel: 205-487-4307.
Catechesis/Religious Programs—Students 34.
Mission—Fayette, Fayette Co., Holy Family, 423 19th St. N.W., Fayette, 35555. Tel: 205-932-6242.

On Duty Outside the Diocese:
Reverend Monsignors—
Marino, Joseph, Apostolic Nunciature, 9 Anifwoshe St., Victoria Island, P.O. Box 2470, Lagos, Nigeria
Reverend Fathers—
Appel, George, Caixa Postal 1103, Belem Para, 66-017-970 Brazil
Klauck, Michael, Holy Innocents Catholic Church, 4923 Odell St., St. Louis, MO 63139. Tel: 314-776-6440 (Office); 314-990-9860 (Home)
Reynolds, Jeffrie S., Notre Dame Seminary, 2901 S. Carrollton Ave., New Orleans, LA 70118. Tel: 504-866-7426

Absent on Leave:
Reverend Fathers—
Cairns, Thomas
Summitt, James A.
Ventura, John

Retired:
Reverend Fathers—
Bauler, Robert J., P.O. Box 7460, Laguna Beach, FL 32407
Bordenca, Charles, P.O. Box 933, Fairhope, AL 36533
Finneran, Michael, 6224 Lake Lugano, Jacksonville, FL 32256
Inkel, Roland, 130 Moss Ln., River Ridge, LA 70123. Tel: 504-737-4368
Kula, Joseph, P.O. Box 685, Gulfshores, AL 36547
Mulvaney, James J., 1321 Santa Maria, Lady Lake, FL 32159. Tel: 904-750-4284
O'Sullivan, Robert, 1500 S.W. 66th Ave., Boca Raton, FL 33428. Tel: 407-488-6147
Owen, John J., P.O. Box 259, Trussville, AL 35173. Tel: 205-655-9092
Regan, Desmond, Cathedral of St. Paul, P.O. Box 10044, Birmingham, AL 35202. Tel: 205-251-1279
Sheehan, J. Peter, 653 S.E. Lakeview Dr., Sebring, FL 33870. Tel: 813-471-0378
Thorsen, Henry, 700 Connell Dr., Pensacola, FL 32507. Tel: 904-469-0919
Underwood, Joseph, 6520 Court K, Birmingham, AL. Tel: 205-925-8329

Permanent Deacons:
Andrews, Andy, Our Lady of Fatima, Birmingham
Anzalone, Sam, St. Peter the Apostle, Birmingham
Canonica, Donald, Holy Family, Lanett
Caporiccio, Richard C., Our Lady of the Valley, Birmingham
Diem, Darrell, St. John the Baptist, Madison
Ferguson, John, Prince of Peace, Birmingham
Germann, Aloysius A., St. Joseph, Birmingham
Girodo, Albert, Admin., Corpus Christi Church, Oneonta
Hoekenschnieder, Lee Roy, Holy Spirit, Huntsville
Iovino, Frank, Prince of Peace, Birmingham
Jett, Benjamin, Holy Family, Birmingham
Joly, Walter Jerome, On Leave
Kelly, Alfred, (Retired)
Laremore, Robert, Glen Mary Ministries, Moulton
Laurita, Dan, St. John the Baptist, Madison
Mickwee, George, St. Francis Xavier, Birmingham
Moore, William, Our Lady of Fatima, Birmingham
O'Brien, Hugh A., Cathedral of St. Paul, Birmingham
Pruett, Ed, Holy Infant of Prague, Trussville
Puent, Ron, Good Shepherd, Huntsville
Raispis, Jerome P., St. Jude, Scottsboro
Roberson, William, Sacred Heart, Cullman
Sassenfeld, Helmut, Good Shepherd, Huntsville
Taffee, William Francis, Jr., Sacred Heart of Jesus, Anniston
Whitaker, Dan, St. Patrick, Adamsville; St. Cecilia, Jasper
Zieverink, Edward Walter, Jr., Cathedral of St. Paul, Birmingham

INSTITUTIONS LOCATED IN THE DIOCESE

[A] HIGH SCHOOLS, DIOCESAN

BIRMINGHAM. *John Carroll High School*, 300 Lakeshore Pkwy., P.O. Box 19907, 35219. Tel: 205-940-2400; Fax: 205-940-2400. Mr. Lee W. Fisher, Prin.; Revs. Thomas Kelly; Andrew Sullivan; Robert J. Sullivan; Peter V. Malloy, S.D.B. Priests 4; Sisters 1; Lay Teachers 61; Students 943.

HUNTSVILLE. *Catholic High School*, 4810 Bradford Dr., 35805. Tel: 205-430-1760; Fax: 205-430-1766. Ms. Alice I. Hession, Prin. Lay Teachers 6; Students 37.

TUSCALOOSA. *Holy Spirit High School*, 711 37th St., E., 35405. Tel: 205-553-5606; Fax: 205-556-7103. Mr. Michael Burke, Prin. Lay Teachers 12; Students 64.

[B] HIGH SCHOOLS, PRIVATE

BIRMINGHAM. *Holy Family High School*, 2001 19th St., 35218. Tel: 205-787-9937. Passionist Community of Chicago, IL. Mrs. Phyllis Jones, Prin. Sisters 1; Lay Teachers 8; Deacons 1; Students 190.

CULLMAN. *St. Bernard Preparatory School, Inc.*, 101 St. Bernard Dr., 35055. Tel: 205-739-6682; Fax: 205-734-2925. Revs. Marcus J. Voss, O.S.B., Pres.; Joel W. Martin, O.S.B., Headmaster. Priests 1; Sisters 1; Brothers 1; Lay Teachers 15; Students 110.

[C] ELEMENTARY SCHOOLS, PRIVATE

BIRMINGHAM. *St. Rose of Lima Academy*. (Grades K-8), 1401 S. 22nd St., 35219. Tel: 205-933-0549; Fax: 205-933-0501. Sr. Mary George, O.P., Prin. Dominican Sisters of Nashville, TN. Sisters 6; Lay Teachers 14; Students 190.

[D] GENERAL HOSPITALS

BIRMINGHAM. *St. Vincent's Hospital*, P.O. Box 12407, 35202-2407. Tel: 205-939-7000.
For a complete listing, refer to the Hospitals section.
Seton Health Corporation of North Alabama, P.O. Box 12407, 35202-2407. Tel: 205-458-4040.
For a complete listing, refer to the Hospitals section.

[E] MONASTERIES AND RESIDENCES OF PRIESTS AND BROTHERS

BIRMINGHAM. *Franciscan Missionaries of the Eternal Word, A Public Association of the Christian Faithful*, 5821 Old Leeds Rd., 35210. Tel: 205-956-6455. Revs. Joseph M. Wolfe, M.F.V.A., Father Guardian; John Mary Klobuchar, M.F.V.A.; Augustine Mary Hedderman, M.F.V.A. Professed 16 (3 Priests; 13 Brothers); Novices 4; Total in Residence 20.

CULLMAN. *St. Bernard Abbey*. (Corporate Title: Benedictine Society of Alabama, Inc.), 1600 St. Bernard Dr., 35055. Tel: 205-734-8291; Fax: 205-734-2925. Rt. Revs. Cletus D. Meagher, O.S.B., Abbot; Victor J. Clark, O.S.B., Retired Abbot; Hilary B. Dreaper, O.S.B., Retired Abbot; Gregory J. Roettger, O.S.B., J.U.D., Retired Abbot; Very Rev. Edward P. Markley, O.S.B., Prior; Revs. Eric D. Guthrie, O.S.B., Subprior; Thomas J. Schnurr, O.S.B.; Paul G. Koehler, O.S.B.; Mark C. Mages, O.S.B.; Michael T. Morgan, O.S.B.; George J. Salem, O.S.B.; Charles J. Reiner, O.S.B.; Bernard J. Patterson, O.S.B.; Leo J. Carter, O.S.B.; Roger R.S. Lott, O.S.B.; Thomas J. O'Connor, O.S.B.; Ignatius B. Kane, O.S.B.; Howard R. Moussier, O.S.B.; Marcus J. Voss, O.S.B.; Paschal A. Ferlisi, O.S.B.; Kevin D. McGrath, O.S.B.; Jose Ramon Mascareno, O.S.B.; M. Lawrence Bouchea, O.S.B.; Joel W. Martin, O.S.B. Total Priests of Abbey 24; Brothers 13.

[F] CONVENTS AND RESIDENCES OF SISTERS

BIRMINGHAM. *Our Lady of the Angels Monastery, Inc.*, 5817 Old Leeds Rd., 35210. Tel: 205-956-5987; Fax: 205-956-5696. Mother M. Angelica, P.C.P.A., Abbess & Pres. Poor Clare Nuns of Perpetual Adoration. Sisters 31; Novices 5; Postulants 3; 50 Members of the Lay Missionaries of the Eternal Word. Properties owned or sponsored: Eternal Word Television Network, Inc. (EWTN); WEWN Shortwave Network. Legal Titles: *Eternal Word Television Network, Inc. (EWTN); WEWN Shortwave Network; AM/FM Radio; Journey Into Scripture Publishing.* Global television, radio, and book apostolates.
Sister Servants of the Eternal Word, A Public Association of the Christian Faithful, 3721 Belmont Rd., 35210. Tel: 205-951-2486. Mother Mary Gabriel, Supr. Sisters in Residence 8.

CULLMAN. *Sacred Heart Monastery*, P.O. Box 488, 35056. Tel: 205-734-4622; 734-2199. Sr. Treva Heinberg, O.S.B., Prioress. Benedictine Sisters. Professed Sisters 67.

[G] DIOCESAN SOCIAL SERVICE

BIRMINGHAM. *Catholic Center of Concern*. (Div. of Catholic Charities), 712 Fourth Ct., W., 35204. Tel: 205-786-4388. Sr. Cecilia Clara Zamboni, M.C. Total Staff 5; Total Assisted 32,000. Consolata Missionary Sisters.
Catholic Family Services, 2164 11th Ave., S., 35205. Tel: 205-324-6561; Fax: 205-323-0475. Total Staff 6; Total Assisted 1,073.

ANNISTON. *All Saints Interfaith Center of Concern*, 1029 W. 15th St., 36201. Tel: 205-236-7793. Sr. Mary Roy, D.H.S., Dir. Tel: 205-546-5337. Total Staff 1; Total Assisted 16,492.

EUTAW. *Consolata Apostolate*, 331 Boligee St., P.O. Box 538, 35462. Tel: 205-372-3497. Sr. Mary Carmen Velasco, M.C. Total Staff 3; Total Assisted 1,858.

FAYETTE. *Christian Center of Concern*. Mailing Address: P.O. Box 466, 35555. 631 First St., N.W., 35555. Tel: 205-932-3218. Shelia Gant, Dir. Staff 10; Total Assisted 2,602.

GADSDEN. *Catholic Center of Concern*, P.O. Box 94, 35902. M. J., Heiberger, Acting Dir. Total Assisted 5,000.

HAMILTON. *Christian Center of Concern*, P.O. Box 973, 35570. Tel: 205-921-3470. Sonja Leonelli, Dir.

HUNTSVILLE. *Catholic Center of Concern*, 1010 Church St., N.W., P.O. Box 745, 35804. Tel: 205-536-0041. Cindy M. Whalen, L.B.S.W., Dir. Total Assisted 2,828.
Catholic Family Services, 1010 Church St., N.W., P.O. Box 745, 35804. Tel: 205-536-0073; Fax: 205-534-3141. Laura Dinwiddie, Supvr. Total Served 603.

SULLIGENT. *Christian Center of Concern*, P.O. Box 1154, 35584. Tel: 205-698-7197. Martha Richards, Dir. Staff 6; Total Assisted 249.

TUSCALOOSA. *Catholic Family Services*, 733 37th St., E., 35405. Tel: 205-553-9046. Dr. Thomas Cook, Supvr. Total Serviced 356.

WINFIELD. *Christian Center of Concern*, 119 Main St., 35594. Tel: 205-487-6230. Marie Weeks, Dir.

[H] CAMPUS MINISTRY

BIRMINGHAM. *St. Stephen University Parish*, Catholic Campus Center, 1515 12th Ave. S., 35205. Tel: 205-933-2500. Rev. Frank J. Muscolino.

FLORENCE. *University of North Alabama*, St. Joseph's Church, 1111 E. College St., 35630. Tel: 205-764-3303. Rev. Msgr. Michael Sexton.

JACKSONVILLE. *Jacksonville State University*, St. Charles Church, 308 Seventh St., N.E., 36265. Tel: 205-435-3238. Rev. William Lucas. Total Staff 2; Total in Program 25.

MONTEVALLO. *University of Montevallo*, St. Thomas the Apostle Catholic Campus Ministry, 80 St. Thomas Way, 35115. Tel: 205-665-7379. Rev. Raymond J. Remke.

TALLADEGA. *Talladega College Catholic Campus Ministry*, St. Francis of Assisi, P.O. Box 1142, 35160. Rev. Henry A. McDaid.

TUSCALOOSA. *Diocesan Campus Ministry Office*, St. Francis University Parish, 811 Fifth Ave., 35401. Tel: 205-758-5672. Rev. Raymond A. Dunmyer, Dir. Total Staff 1; Total in Residence 1.
University of Alabama in Tuscaloosa, St. Francis University Parish, 811 Fifth Ave., 35401. Tel: 205-758-5672. Campus Ministers: Rev. Raymond A. Dunmyer; Ms. Molly Campbell. Total Staff 2; Total in Residence 1.

[I] MISCELLANEOUS LISTINGS

BIRMINGHAM. *Agape Institute of St. Teresa of Jesus*, 3528 Deerfield Dr., 35226. Bob and Rita Tevebaugh, Co-Founders; Rev. Paul Rohling, Mod. Members 23.
Catholic Horizons, Inc., 2828 Crestwood Blvd., 35210. Tel: 205-956-1053. Sue M. Dominick, Advisory Board Pres. Diocesan book, gift, & information center.
Catholic Housing of Birmingham, Inc., P.O. Box 12047, 35202. Tel: 205-838-8309. 8131 Fourth Ave., S., 35206. Albert H. Rohling, Pres.; Rev. Brian Egan, Vice Pres. & Sec.
Congregation of the Passion: Holy Family Community, Inc. (House of Religious Men), 1910 19th St., 35218. Tel: 205-780-3440. Corporation for Holy Family Church, and Holy Family Elementary, Birmingham, and St. Mary's Church, Fairfield.
Contemplative Outreach Birmingham. Sacred Heart Monastery, P.O. Box 488, Cullman, 35056. Tel: 205-734-4622. Sr. Mary McGehee, O.S.B., Coord.; Aloysius Golden, Area Contact Person. Tel: 205-592-3930.
Holy Family Educational Foundation, 1910 19th St., 35218. Tel: 205-780-3440.
Holy Name of Jesus Hospital Trust. (Senior Citizen Housing), c/o First Alabama Bank, P.O. Box 10247, 35202. Tel: 205-326-7219; Fax: 205-326-7052. Sidney O. Roebuck, Jr., Trustee, Vice Pres. & Senior Trust Officer, First Alabama Bank. Total Assisted 109.
John Carroll Education Foundation, P.O. Box 12047, 35202.
Magnificat: Mary, Woman of Faith Chapter, 1341 Forest Ridge Ct., 35226. Tel: 205-941-0144.
Our Lady of Sorrows Educational School Foundation, 1728 Oxmoor Rd., 35209. Tel: 205-871-8121.
Our Lady of the Valley Educational Foundation, 5514 Double Oak Ln., 35242. Tel: 205-991-5488; Fax: 205-991-5181.
St. Barnabas Regional School Educational Foundation, 7901 First Ave. N., 35206. Tel: 205-833-0334.

St. Francis Xavier Catholic School Education Foundation, P.O. Box 130669, 35213. Tel: 205-871-1153. Sr. Judith Dianne McGowan, R.S.M., Prin. & Contact Person.

St. Paul Cathedral School Education Foundation, P.O. Box 370104, 35237. Tel: 205-251-9345.

St. Peter's Endowment Foundation, 2061 Patton Chapel Rd., 35216. Mrs. Tillie Barnhill, Dir.

Villa Maria, 500 82nd St., S., 35206. Tel: 205-836-7839. Sr. Mary Cecilia Schlebecker, D.C., Admin. Total Staff 7; Total in Residence 65.

ANNISTON. *Gertrude C. Luther, M.D. Charitable Trust*, 1821 McCall Dr., 36207. Tel: 205-237-4231.

Sacred Heart of Jesus Charitable Trust, 1821 McCall Dr., 36207. Tel: 205-237-4231.

BESSEMER. *St. Aloysius Educational Foundation*, P.O. Box 1570, 35021. Total Assisted Monthly 171.

CULLMAN. *Benedictine Manor Retirement Home, Inc.*, 200 Janeway Dr., 35055. Tel: 205-739-2853. Sr. Margaret Mary Fisher, O.S.B.; Sr. Mary Adrian McLean, O.S.B. Sisters 2; Resident Capacity 40-50.

Benedictine Spirituality and Conference Center, P.O. Box 488, 35056. Tel: 205-734-8302. Sr. Eleanor Harrison, O.S.B., Dir. Beds 72; Total Staff 5.

DECATUR. *St. Ann's Educational Foundation*, 240 Johnson St. S.E., 35601. Rev. Joseph Culotta.

FLORENCE. *St. Joseph School Foundation, Florence*, 115 Plum St., 35630.

GADSDEN. *St. James Educational Foundation*, 700 Albert Rains Blvd., 35901. Total Staff 1; Total Assisted 22.

HUNTSVILLE. *Holy Family Regional School Foundation*, 2300 Beasley Ave., 35816-4004. Total Staff 23; Total Assisted 260.

Holy Spirit Regional School Foundation, 625 Airport Rd., 35802. Tel: 205-881-4781.

Society of St. Vincent de Paul, P.O. Box 16070, 35802.

MADISON. *St. John's Educational Foundation*, 1055 Hughes Rd., 35758. Tel: 205-722-0130. Rev. Patrick J. Murphy, Contact Person.

TUSCALOOSA. *Holy Spirit School of Tuscaloosa Endowment Foundation*, 711 37th St., E., 35405. Total Staff 14; Students 96.

RELIGIOUS INSTITUTES OF MEN REPRESENTED IN THE DIOCESE

For further details refer to the corresponding bracketed number in the Religious Institutes of Men or Women section.

[0200]—*Benedictine Monks*.—O.S.B.

[1350]—*Brothers of St. Francis Xavier*.—C.F.X.

[1330]—*Congregation of the Mission*. (Eastern Prov.).—C.M.

[1000]—*Congregation of the Passion*.—C.P.

[0480]—*Conventual Franciscans*. (Prov. of St. Anthony of Padua).—O.F.M.Conv.

[]—*Franciscan Missionaries of the Eternal Word*.—M.F.V.A.

[0570]—*Glenmary Home Missioners*. (Cincinnati, OH).

[0840]—*Missionary Servants of the Most Holy Trinity*.—S.T.

[0700]—*St. Joseph's Society of the Sacred Heart*. (Baltimore, MD).—S.S.J.

[1190]—*Salesians of Don Bosco*.—S.D.B.

[1200]—*Society of the Divine Savior*.—S.D.S.

RELIGIOUS INSTITUTES OF WOMEN REPRESENTED IN THE DIOCESE

[0230]—*Benedictine Sisters of Pontifical Jurisdiction*.—O.S.B.

[0720]—*Consolata Missionary Sisters*.—M.C.

[0760]—*Daughters of Charity of St. Vincent de Paul*.—D.C.

[0820]—*Daughters of the Holy Spirit*.—D.H.S.

[1070-03]—*Dominican Sisters*. (Adrian, MI).—O.P.

[1070-07]—*Dominican Sisters*. (Nashville, TN).—O.P.

[1070-13]—*Dominican Sisters*. (Sinsinawa, WI).—O.P.

[1170]—*Felician Sisters*.—C.S.S.F.

[2790]—*Missionary Servants of the Most Blessed Trinity*.—M.S.B.T.

[3210]—*Poor Clares of Perpetual Adoration*.—P.C.P.A.

[0850]—*Salisian Sisters, Daughters of Mary, Help of Christians (Salisian Sisters)*.—F.M.A.

[2970]—*School Sisters of Notre Dame*.—S.S.N.D.

[]—*Sister Servants of the Eternal Word*.—S.S.E.W.

[2575]—*Sisters of Mercy of the Americas*.—R.S.M.

[2990]—*Sisters of Notre Dame*.—S.N.D.

[3000]—*Sisters of Notre Dame de Namur*.—S.N.D.deN.

[1705]—*The Sisters of St. Francis of Assisi*.—O.S.F.

[3840]—*Sisters of St. Joseph of Carondelet*.—C.S.J.

[1030]—*Sisters of the Divine Savior*.—S.D.S.

[2110]—*Sisters of the Humility of Mary*.—H.M.

[3320]—*Sisters of the Presentation of the B.V.M.*.—P.B.V.M.

[2150]—*Sisters, Servants of the Immaculate Heart of Mary*.—I.H.M.

[4048]—*Society of Sisters Faithful Companions of Jesus*.—F.C.J.

[4120-03]—*Ursuline Nuns of the Congregation of Paris*.—O.S.U.

[4190]—*Visitation Nuns*.—V.H.M.

NECROLOGY

† Fox, John, (Retired). —Died Oct. 1, 1996.

† Jones, William, (Retired). —Died Oct. 30, 1996.

† O'Reilly, James, (Retired). —Died May 5, 1996.

† Wade, Rev. Msgr. Francis J., (Retired). —Died Oct. 21, 1996.

Diocese of Bismarck

(Dioecesis Bismarckiensis)

Most Reverend

PAUL A. ZIPFEL, D.D.

Bishop of Bismarck; ordained March 18, 1961; appointed Titular Bishop of Walla Walla and Auxiliary Bishop of St. Louis May 16, 1989; consecrated June 29, 1989; appointed Bishop of Bismarck December 31, 1996; installed February 20, 1997.

ESTABLISHED DECEMBER 31, 1909.

Square Miles 34,268.

Comprises the Counties of Adams, Billings, Bowman, Burke, Burleigh, Divide, Dunn, Emmons, Golden Valley, Grant, Hettinger, McKenzie, McLean, Mercer, Morton, Mountrail, Oliver, Renville, Sioux, Slope, Stark, Ward and Williams in the State of North Dakota.

For legal titles of parishes and diocesan institutions, consult the Chancery Office.

Chancery Office: 420 Raymond St., Box 1575, Bismarck, ND, 58502-1575. Tel.: 701-223-1347; Fax: 701-223-3693.

STATISTICAL OVERVIEW

Personnel	
Bishop	1
Abbots	1
Retired Abbots	2
Priests: Diocesan Active in Diocese	49
Priests: Active Outside Diocese	5
Priests: Retired, Sick or Absent	14
Number of Diocesan Priests	68
Religious Priests in Diocese	28
Extern Priests in Diocese	4
Ordinations:	
Diocesan Priests	1
Transitional Deacons	2
Permanent Deacons in Diocese	51
Total Brothers	23
Total Sisters	169
Parishes	
Parishes	65
With Resident Pastor:	
Resident Diocesan Priests	46
Resident Religious Priests	8
Without Resident Pastor:	
Administered by Priests	10
Administered by Permanent Deacons	1
Missions	39
Professional Ministry Personnel:	
Brothers	2
Sisters	9
Lay Ministers	42
Welfare	
Catholic Hospitals	6
Total Assisted	279,028
Homes for the Aged	4
Total Assisted	437
Specialized Homes	1
Total Assisted	90
Other Institutions	1
Total Assisted	6
Educational	
Diocesan Students in Other Seminaries	20
Students Religious	1
Total Seminarians	21
Colleges and Universities	1
Total Students	2,016
High Schools, Diocesan and Parish	3
Total Students	1,334
Elementary Schools, Diocesan and Parish	16
Total Students	2,157
Catechesis/Religious Education:	
High School Students	3,319
Elementary Students	7,081
Total Students Under Catholic Instruction	15,928
Teachers in the Diocese:	
Priests	6
Brothers	1
Sisters	27
Lay Teachers	290
Vital Statistics	
Receptions into the Church:	
Infant Baptism Totals	1,153
Adult Baptism Totals	113
Received into Full Communion	114
First Communions	1,380
Confirmations	1,071
Marriages:	
Catholic	353
Interfaith	186
Total Marriages	539
Deaths	669
Total Catholic Population	66,425
Total Population	253,552

Former Bishops—Most Rev. VINCENT DE PAUL WEHRLE, O.S.B., D.D., appt. Bishop of Bismarck, April 9, 1910; cons. May 19, 1910; retired Dec. 11, 1939; named Titular Bishop of Teos by Pope Pius XII; died Nov. 2, 1941.—Most Rev. VINCENT J. RYAN, D.D., LL.D., appt. March 19, 1940; cons. May 28, 1940; died Nov. 10, 1951.—Most Rev. LAMBERT A. HOCH, D.D., L.L.D., appt. Jan. 23, 1952; cons. March 25, 1952; transferred to Diocese of Sioux Falls, Dec. 5, 1956; died June 27, 1990.—Most Rev. HILARY B. HACKER, D.D., appt. Bishop, Dec. 29, 1956; retired June 28, 1982; died Nov. 6, 1990.—Most Rev. JOHN F. KINNEY, D.D., J.C.D., appt. June 28, 1982 Episcopal Ord. Jan. 25, 1977; installed Aug. 23, 1982; transferred to Diocese of St. Cloud, July 6, 1995.

Administrator of Diocese of Bismarck—Rev. Msgr. GERALD J. WALSH, *P.O. Box 1575, Bismarck, 58502-1575.*

Vicar General—Vacant.

Chancery Office—420 Raymond St., Box 1575, Bismarck, 58502-1575. Tel: 701-223-1347; Fax: 701-223-3693.

Chancellor—Sr. JOANNE GRAHAM, O.S.B., J.C.L.

Center for Pastoral Ministry Office—520 N. Washington St., P.O. Box 1137, Bismarck, 58502-1137. Tel: 701-222-3035.

Diocesan Tribunal—520 N. Washington St., P.O. Box 1137, Bismarck, 58502-1137. Tel: 701-222-3035.

Judicial Vicar—Rev. DAVID L. ZIMMER, J.C.L.

Defensor Vinculi—Revs. LEONARD A. ECKROTH; GENE LINDEMANN, J.C.L.

Pro-Synodal Judges—Revs. THEODORE F. GUSTIN; GEORGE A. DUKART; ROBERT H. KIPPLEY; MARVIN J. KLEMMER; BRUCE D. KREBS; THOMAS E. KRAMER; MICHAEL T. KRANK; ALBERT R. LEARY; EDWIN P. WEHNER.

Procurator/Advocates—ROSE BALL; RUTH MOERICKE.

Notaries—Sr. JOANNE GRAHAM, O.S.B., J.C.L.; TAMMY J. MUNSON; ROSE BALL.

Censor Librorum—Sr. JOANNE GRAHAM, O.S.B., J.C.L., *Box 1575, Bismarck, 58502-1575.*

College of Consultors—Rev. Msgr. GERALD J. WALSH, Admin.; Revs. THOMAS E. KRAMER; JEROME G. KAUTZMAN; LEONARD A. ECKROTH; ALBERT R. LEARY; CHRIS B. WALTER; DENNIS R. SCHAFER; EDWARD F. KORTE; MARVIN J. KLEMMER; EDWIN P. WEHNER; KENNETH G. PHILLIPS; JOHN G. GUTHRIE; Rt. Rev. PATRICK MOORE, O.S.B.

Diocesan Corporate Board—Rev. Msgr. GERALD J. WALSH, Pres.; Vacant, Vice Pres.; Revs. PETER KRAMER; THEODORE F. GUSTIN; Sr. JOANNE GRAHAM, O.S.B., J.C.L.; DWIGHT C.H. KAUTZMANN, Legal Counsel; JEFFRY TESCHER, Agent of Record.

Diocesan Finance Council—Rev. Msgr. GERALD J. WALSH, Admin.; Revs. MARVIN J. KLEMMER, Chm. PETER KRAMER; THEODORE F. GUSTIN; Mr. WILLIAM HETH; THOMAS STOCKERT; TERRY DAFFINRUD; MIKE SCHWINDT; MARVIN HEINERT; JEFFRY TESCHER; Sr. JOANNE GRAHAM, O.S.B., J.C.L.; RON SCHATZ.

Due Process Service—Sr. JOANNE GRAHAM, O.S.B., J.C.L.

Presbyteral Council—Vacant.

Pastoral Council—Vacant.

Parish Priest Consultors—Vacant.

Diocesan Offices and Directors

Archives—KENNETH SMALL, *Box 1137, Bismarck, 58502-1137.* Tel: 701-222-3035.

Boy Scouts—KEN ROETHLER, Chm., *1210 N. 18th St., Bismarck, 58501.*

Campaign For Human Development—Sr. JOANNE GRAHAM, O.S.B., J.C.L., Dir., *P.O. Box 1575, Bismarck, 58502-1575.* Tel: 701-223-1347.

Catholic Family Service—ROGER SCHWINGHAMMER, Exec. Dir., *2537 University Dr. S., Fargo, 58103.* Tel: 701-235-4457. Other Locations: *1223 S. 12th, Bismarck, 58504.* Tel: 701-255-1793. Sr. LOIS BYRNE, P.B.V.M., *400-22nd Ave., N.W., Minot, 58701.* Tel: 701-852-2854. SUE DOKKEN.

Catholic Relief—Sr. JOANNE GRAHAM, O.S.B., J.C.L., Dir., *P.O. Box 1575, Bismarck, 58502-1575.* Tel: 701-223-1347.

Office of Vocations—Rev. Msgr. GERALD J. WALSH, *P.O. Box 1137, Bismarck, 58502-1137.* Tel: 701-222-3035.

Vicar for Presbyters—Rev. Msgr. GERALD J. WALSH, *P.O. Box 1137, Bismarck, 58502-1137.* Tel: 701-222-3035.

Office of Worship—Vacant, *Box 1137, Bismarck, 58501.* Tel: 701-222-3035.

Continuing Education for Clergy—P.O. Box 1137, Bismarck, 58502-1137. Tel: 701-222-3035.

Ecumenism—Rev. MARVIN J. KLEMMER, *1902 S. Third St., Bismarck, 58504.* Tel: 701-223-3606.

Health Care Commission—Sr. JOANNE GRAHAM, O.S.B., J.C.L., *P.O. Box 1575, Bismarck, 58502-1575.* Tel: 701-223-1347.

Holy Childhood—Sr. JOANNE GRAHAM, O.S.B., J.C.L., Dir., *P.O. Box 1575, Bismarck, 58502-1575.* Tel: 701-223-1347.

Newspaper—"Dakota Catholic Action," MARGE GROSZ,

Editor, *P.O. Box 1137, Bismarck, 58502-1137.* Tel: 701-222-3035.

North Dakota Catholic Conference—CHRISTOPHER DODSON, *227 W. Broadway, Ste. 2, Bismarck, 58501.* Tel: 701-223-2519.

Pastoral Planning—Sr. JOANNE GRAHAM, O.S.B., J.C.L., Dir., *P.O. Box 1137, Bismarck, 58502-1137.* Tel: 701-223-1347.

Permanent Diaconate Office—Rev. THEODORE F. GUSTIN, Vicar for Deacons; Deacons STEPHEN B. MAYS, Dir. ALVIN W. SCHWINDT, Dir., Formation Prog. Permanent Diaconate, *P.O. Box 1137, Bismarck, 58502-1137.* Tel: 701-222-3035.

Priests' Benefit Association—Revs. C. ROBERT KAVANEY; WILLIAM J. FAHNLANDER; JAMES B. BRAATEN; DAVID MORMAN; WILLIAM RUSHFORD.

Priests' Personnel Board—Rev. ALBERT R. LEARY, Chm.; Rev. Msgr. GERALD J. WALSH; Revs. DENNIS R. SCHAFER; BRUCE D. KREBS; NORMAN J. DUKART.

Propagation of the Faith—Sr. JOANNE GRAHAM, O.S.B., J.C.L., *P.O. Box 1575, Bismarck, 58502-1575.* Tel: 701-223-1347.

Communications Office—Rev. JOHN J. OWENS, *P.O. Box 1137, Bismarck, 58502-1137.* Tel: 701-222-3035; Fax: 701-673-3178.

Office of Catechesis—Vacant, *Box 1137, Bismarck, 58502-1137.* Tel: 701-222-3035.

Pro-Life—Rev. JOHN J. OWENS, *P.O. Box 1137, Bismarck, 58502-1137.* Tel: 701-222-3035; Fax: 701-673-3178.

Office of Education—ROMAN WEILER, Dir., *P.O. Box 1137, Bismarck, 58502-1137.* Tel: 701-222-3035.

Social Concerns—ANNETTA SUTTON, Dir., *Box 1137, Bismarck, 58502-1137.* Tel: 701-222-3035.

Stewardship and Resource Development Office—RONALD SCHATZ, Dir., *Box 1137, Bismarck, 58502-1137.* Tel: 701-222-3035.

Directors for Office of Religious—Rev. DANIEL MALONEY, O.S.B., *Annunciation Priory, 7520 University Dr., Bismarck, 58504-9653.* Tel: 701-255-1520. Sr. JOANNE GRAHAM, O.S.B., J.C.L., *P.O. Box 1575, Bismarck, 58502-1575.* Tel: 701-223-1347.

Youth Ministry—KENNETH H. ROSHAU, Dir., *Box 1137, Bismarck, 58502-1137.* Tel: 701-222-3035.

Search Program—KENNETH H. ROSHAU, *Box 1137, Bismarck, 58502-1137.* Tel: 701-222-3035.

CLERGY, PARISHES, MISSIONS AND PAROCHIAL SCHOOLS

CITY OF BISMARCK
(Burleigh County)

1—CATHEDRAL OF THE HOLY SPIRIT (1947), Revs. Thomas E. Kramer; Thomas J. Richter; Deacons Wilfred Wolf; Ralph von Reuden.
Res., 519 Raymond St., 58501. Tel: 701-223-1033; Fax: 701-223-1438. [JC]
School—Tel: 701-223-5484. Elizabeth Gross, Prin. Sisters of St. Benedict 2; Lay Teachers 17; Students 262.
Catechesis/Religious Programs—Tel: 701-222-2259. Helen Poling, D.R.E.
Students 353.

2—ASCENSION (1974), Rev. Marvin J. Klemmer; Deacons John Lamontagne; Ray Grabar; Al Schwindt; Larry Dorrheim.
Res., 1905 S. Third St., 58504. Tel: 701-223-3606.
Catechesis/Religious Programs—Tel: 701-258-5692. Marie Krous-Gabel, D.R.E.
Students 716.

3—CORPUS CHRISTI (1964), Rev. Stephen R. Zastoupil; Sr. Ivo Schoch, Pastoral Assoc.; Deacons Lynn Clancy; Harry M. Deichert; Joseph J. Mathern; Rex McDowell; LeRoy M. Kuss; James V. Ressler; Robert Schuller; John Tharaldsen; Duane J. Koble, Admin.
Res., 1919 N. Second St., 58501. Tel: 701-255-4600; Fax: 701-255-4616. [JC]
Catechesis/Religious Programs—Tel: 701-255-3104; Fax: 701-255-4616. D.R.E.: Patricia Clark; Mary Kay Vetter; Patrick Hall.
Students 969.

4—ST. ANNE (1957), Rev. Edwin P. Wehner; Betty E. Greff, Pastoral Assoc.; Deacons Alvin Schmitz; Kasper Greff.
Res., 1321 Braman Ave., 58501. Tel: 701-223-1549.
School—(Grades PreK-8). Tel: 701-223-3373. Mrs. Darlene Reinarts, Prin.
Lay Teachers 13; Students 257.
Catechesis/Religious Programs—Tel: 701-224-0847. Mrs. Frances I. Roehrich, D.R.E.
Students 498.

5—ST. MARY (1877), Rev. Charles A. Heidt; Steve Braus, Admin.; Sr. Patricia Schap, O.S.B., Pastoral Min.; Deacons Kenneth Klein; Morris Martin; Tony Dworshak.
Res., 806 E. Broadway, 58501. Tel: 701-223-5562. [JC]
School—Tel: 701-223-0225. Winnifred Pratt, Prin.
Lay Teachers 13; Students 206.
Catechesis/Religious Programs—Students 135.

OUTSIDE THE CITY OF BISMARCK

Beach, Golden Valley Co., St. John the Baptist (1909), Rev. David G. Morman; Deacons Samuel Larson; Donald Nistler; James Wosepka.
Res., Box 337, 58621. Tel: 701-872-4153; Fax: 701-872-4695. [CEM 2]
Catechesis/Religious Programs—Tel: 701-872-4153; Fax: 701-872-4695. Carla Steffen, D.R.E.
Students 203.
Mission—Golva, Golden Valley Co., St. Mary, P.O. Box 337, 58621. Tel: 701-872-4153. [CEM 3]

Belfield, Stark Co., St. Bernard (1910), Rev. John G. Guthrie; Deacon Albert Hibl.
Res., P.O. Box 38, 58622. Tel: 701-575-4295. [CEM]
School—Tel: 701-575-4868. Rebecca K. Lutz, Prin.
Lay Teachers 3; Students 37.
Catechesis/Religious Programs—Tel: 701-575-4099. D.R.E.: Diane Procive; Pam Evoniuk, (Elementary); Cathy Cerkoney, (High School).
Students 152.
Mission—Medora, Billings Co., St. Mary, Box 11, Medora, 58645. Tel: 701-623-4450.

Beulah, Mercer Co., St. Joseph (1915) (German-Russian), Revs. Edwin Volk; James E. Reardon.
Res., P.O. Box 146, 58523. Tel: 701-873-5397. [CEM]
Catechesis/Religious Programs—Tel: 701-873-5006; 873-5622. Julie Knodel, D.R.E.
Students 301.

Bowbells, Burke Co., St. Joseph (1905) (German-Scandinavian), Rev. George Uralikunnel (India); Deacon Edmund Morgel.
Res., P.O. Box 339, 58721. Tel: 701-377-2611.
Catechesis/Religious Programs—Tel: 701-377-2766. D.R.E.: Clarice Corey; Mary Hawbaker.
Students 26.
Mission—Portal, Burke Co., St. John the Baptist, Portal, 58772. Tel: 701-926-4621. [CEM]

Bowman, Bowman Co., St. Charles (1910), Rev. Charles Zins.
Res., 58623. Tel: 701-523-5292. [CEM]
Catechesis/Religious Programs—Tel: 701-523-5415. D.R.E.: Jon Tuhy, (Grades 1-12).
Students 123.
Missions—Rhame, Bowman Co., St. Mel, P.O. Box 709, 58623. Tel: 701-523-5292; Marmarth, Slope Co., Immaculate Heart of Mary, P.O. Box 709, 58623.

Burlington, Ward Co., St. Francis of Assisi. Closed. For inquiries for parish records contact the Chancery. (Quasi-Parish).

Carson, Grant Co., St. Theresa the Child Jesus (1920), Rev. Kenneth G. Phillips.
Res., 421 Court St., Flasher, 58535-7216. Tel: 701-597-3570; 597-3228. [JC]
Catechesis/Religious Programs—Tel: 701-597-3228.
Students 53.

Center, Oliver Co., St. Martin (1916), Rev. Austin A. Vetter.
Res., P.O. Box 2766, 58530. Tel: 701-794-3329. [CEM][JC 2]
Catechesis/Religious Programs—Tel: 201-794-3191. D.R.E.: Judith McNulty; Alice Henderscheid.
Students 125.

Crosby, Divide Co., St. Patrick (1917), Rev. Ed Korte.
Res., P.O. Box 89, 58730. Tel: 701-965-6537. [CEM 3][JC 2]
Catechesis/Religious Programs—Tel: 701-965-6537.
Students 73.
Mission—Noonan, Divide Co., St. Luke, 304 Main St., Noonan, 58765. Tel: 701-965-6537.

Crown Butte, Morton Co., St. Vincent (1896), Deacon Robert Olson; Loretta Olson, Pastoral Assoc. & D.R.E.
Mailing Address: Rte. 1, Box 78, Mandan, 58554.
Res., 1703 1/2 N.E. Second, Mandan, 58554. Tel: 701-663-2544. [CEM]
Catechesis/Religious Programs—Students 26.

Dickinson, Stark Co.,

1—QUEEN OF PEACE CHURCH, (1973), Rev. Jerome G. Kautzman.
Office: 725 12th St. W., 58601-3516. Tel: 701-225-2134; 225-2991 (Res.). [JC]
Catechesis/Religious Programs—Tel: 701-225-2134. Dickie Jo Boespflug, D.R.E.
Students 244.

2—ST. JOSEPH, (1902) (German-Russian), Rev. C. Robert Kavaney; Deacon Ralph Stockert.
Res., 240 E. Broadway, 58601. Tel: 701-225-2222.
School—Tel: 701-225-6162.
Sisters 3; Lay Teachers 7; Students 100.
Catechesis/Religious Programs—Tel: 701-225-2222. Marlene Reisenauer, D.R.E.
Students 245.

3—ST. PATRICK, (1885), Rev. George A. Dukart; Sr. Stephanie Dolyniuk, O.S.B., Pastoral Assoc.; Deacons Joe Kappel; Anton Wanner.
Res., 229 Third Ave. W., 58601. Tel: 701-225-2012; Fax: 701-225-2012.
School—Tel: 701-225-8094. Sr. Richarde Marie Wolf, S.S.N.D., Prin.
Sisters 2; Lay Teachers 10; Students 186.
Catechesis/Religious Programs—Tel: 701-225-8831. Mary Agostini, D.R.E.
Students 121.

4—ST. PIUS. Closed. For inquiries for parish records contact St. Joseph, Dickinson.

5—ST. WENCESLAUS, (1912), Rev. Peter L. Kramer; Deacons Eugene F. Morman; Raymond Jilek.
Res., 525 Third St. E., 58601. Tel: 701-225-3972.
School—Tel: 701-225-9463. Sr. Therese Collinson, Prin.
Lay Teachers 9; Students 190.
Catechesis/Religious Programs—Tel: 701-225-3972. Gini Zent, D.R.E.
Students 324.

Flasher, Morton Co., St. Lawrence (1912), Rev. Kenneth G. Phillips.
Res., 421 Court St., 58535-7216. Tel: 701-597-3570; 597-3228. [CEM]
Catechesis/Religious Programs—Tel: 701-597-3228.
Students 147.

Fort Yates, Sioux Co., St. Peter - Catholic Indian Mission (1878). (Standing Rock Indian Reservation). Revs. Casimir Paluck, O.S.B.; Leonard SauelKoul, O.S.B.
Res., P.O. Box 394, 58538. Tel: 701-854-3473; Fax: 701-854-3474. [CEM]
School—St. Bernard Mission School, Tel: 701-854-7413. Sr. Paulette Pass, S.S.N.D., Prin.
Sisters 5; Lay Teachers 3; Students 103.
Catechesis/Religious Programs—Tel: 701-854-7413. Sr. Irene Dohmen, S.S.N.D., D.R.E.
Students 55.
Missions—Cannon Ball, Sioux Co., St. Elizabeth, P.O. Box 394, 58538. Tel: 701-854-3473. [CEM]
Porcupine, Sioux Co., St. James. [CEM]

Foxholm, Ward Co., St. Mary, Rev. Paul D. Becker.
Res., R.R. 1, P.O. Box 124, 58718. Tel: 701-852-8575. [CEM]
Catechesis/Religious Programs—Tel: 701-468-5648.
Students 148.
Mission—Berthold, Ward Co., St. Ann, Berthold, 58718. Tel: 701-453-3660.

Garrison, McLean Co., St. Nicholas (1905), Rev. Gene E. Lindemann, J.C.L.
Res., 235 Second St. N.E., P.O. Box 870, 58540. Tel: 701-463-2327. [CEM]
Catechesis/Religious Programs—Tel: 701-337-2296. Jane Krausert, D.R.E.
Students 116.
Mission—Max, McClean Co., Immaculate Conception, P.O. Box 295, Max, 58759.

Glenburn, Renville Co., St. Philomena (1948) (German-Scandinavian), Rev. Jacob Konath.
Res., 302 Raymond St., Box 68, 58740. Tel: 701-362-7571; Fax: 701-362-7571. [CEM]
Catechesis/Religious Programs—Tel: 701-362-7437. Dianne Henson, D.R.E.
Students 53.
Mission—Lansford, Bottineau Co., St. John, Rt. 2, Box 3, Lansford, 58750. Tel: 701-784-5421.

Glen Ullin, Morton Co., Sacred Heart of Jesus (1883) (German-Russian), Rev. Claude Seeberger, O.S.B.
Res., Box 609, 58631. Tel: 701-348-3518. [CEM 2]
Catechesis/Religious Programs—Tel: 701-348-3527. Mrs. Kathy Schirado, D.R.E.
Students 147.
Mission—Glen Ullin, Grant Co., St. Joseph, 58631-0609.

Grenora, Williams Co., St. Boniface, Rev. Raymond A. Aydt.
Church—P.O. Box 37, 58845. Tel: 701-694-3743.
Res., 118 Fifth St., W., Williston, 58801. Tel: 701-572-6732. [JC]
Catechesis/Religious Programs—Peggy Degele, D.R.E.
Students 17.

Hague, Emmons Co., St. Mary (1890), Rev. Leonard A. Eckroth.
Church—P.O. Box 156, 58542. Tel: 701-336-7119.
Res., Box 322, Strasburg, 58573. Tel: 701-336-2603; 336-7172. [CEM 2]

Catechesis/Religious Programs—Tel: 701-336-7102. Sr. Rose Schwab, S.S.N.D., D.R.E.
Students 30.

Halliday, Dunn Co., St. Paul (1952). (Quasi-Parish). Rev. Gerald Ruelle, O.S.B.
Res., P.O. Box 299, Killdeer, 58640. Tel: 701-764-5357. [CEM][JC]
Catechesis/Religious Programs—Tel: 701-938-4504. D.R.E.: Vickie Clarys; Deacon Edward J. Ziman; Herman Dukart.
Students 57.

Hazelton, Emmons Co., St. Paul (1905), Revs. Jeffrey A. Zwack; Mathew Arackal (India); Deacon Kenneth Wolbaum.
Res., P.O. Box 758, Linton, 58552. Tel: 701-254-4588.
Catechesis/Religious Programs—Tel: 701-782-6281. Charlotte Beastrom, D.R.E.
Students 69.
Mission—Braddock, Emmons Co., St. Katherine, P.O. Box 758, Linton, 58552. Tel: 701-254-4588. [CEM 2]

Hazen, Mercer Co., St. Martin (1914), Rev. James E. Reardon.
Res., P.O. Box 387, 58545. Tel: 701-748-2121. [CEM]
Catechesis/Religious Programs—Tel: 701-748-2121. D.R.E.: Peg Rahn; LuAnn Woeste.
Students 226.

Hebron, Morton Co., St. Ann (1906) (German), Rev. Francis dos Remedios, O.S.B.
Res., P.O. Box 12, 58638. Tel: 701-878-4658. [CEM 3]
Catechesis/Religious Programs—Tel: 701-878-4658. Harvey Tibor, D.R.E.
Students 92.
Mission—Haymarsh, Morton Co., St. Clement, P.O. Box 12, 58638.

Hettinger, Adams Co., Holy Trinity (1916), Rev. Bruce Krebs.
Res., 405 3rd St. N., 58639. Tel: 701-567-2772. [JC]
Catechesis/Religious Programs—Grace Meier, D.R.E.
Students 113.
Missions—Reeder, Adams Co., Sacred Heart, 405-3rd St. N., 58639. Tel: 701-853-2920; Scranton, Bowman Co., Sacred Heart, 405-3rd St. N., 58639. Tel: 701-275-8778.

Huff, Morton Co., St. Martin, Rev. Albert R. Leary.
Res., HCR 1, Box 330, 58537-9628. Tel: 701-667-2022. [CEM]
Catechesis/Religious Programs—HCR 1, Box 5, Fort Rice, 58554. Bonnie Miller, D.R.E.
Students 10.

Kenmare, Ward Co., St. Agnes (1901), Rev. Kenneth Wald, Admin.
Res., P.O. Box 488, 58746. Tel: 701-385-4311. [CEM]
Catechesis/Religious Programs—Tel: 701-386-2403. Evan and Deb Zeltinger, D.R.E.
Students 112.
Mission—Donnybrook, Ward Co., St. Anthony, Donnybrook, 58734. [CEM]

Killdeer, Dunn Co., St. Joseph (1917), Rev. Gerald Ruelle, O.S.B.; Deacon Edward J. Ziman.
Res., P.O. Box 299, 58640. Tel: 701-764-5357. [CEM][JC 2]
Catechesis/Religious Programs—Tel: 701-548-8068. Candice Benz, D.R.E.
Students 119.

Lefor, Stark Co., St. Elizabeth (1898), Rev. Lawrence L. Wagner, O.S.B.
Res., P.O. Box 218, 58641. Tel: 701-225-3375. [CEM][JC 3]
Catechesis/Religious Programs—Rev. Lawrence Wagner, O.S.B., D.R.E.
Students 35.
Mission—Gladstone, Stark Co., St. Thomas the Apostle, Gladstone, 58630.

Linton, Emmons Co., St. Anthony (1909), Revs. Jeffrey Zwack; Mathew Arackal, M.C.B.S. (India); Deacon Martin Schumacher.
Res., Box 758, 58552. Tel: 701-254-4588. [CEM]
Catechesis/Religious Programs—Tel: 701-254-4646. Diane Wangler, D.R.E.
Students 187.

Mandan, Morton Co., Christ the King (1957), Rev. Albert R. Leary; Deacons Ward Johnson; Emil Riehl. In res., Revs. William Fahnlander; Hugo L. Blotsky, O.S.B.
Res., 505-10th Ave., N.W., 58554-2599. Tel: 701-663-8842; Fax: 701-667-1730. [CEM]
School—Tel: 701-663-6200; Fax: 701-667-1730. Rev. Albert Leary, Prin.
Lay Teachers 13; Students 147.
Catechesis/Religious Programs—Tel: 701-663-8842; Fax: 701-667-1730. Julie Schatz, D.R.E.
Students 185.

St. Joseph (1881), Rev. Robert E. Feeney; Deacon Peter Hoffman.
Res., 108 Third St. N.E., P.O. Box 603, 58554. Tel: 701-663-9562. [CEM]
School—(Grades K-6). Tel: 701-663-9563; Fax: 701-663-0183.
Lay Teachers 10; Students 135.
Catechesis/Religious Programs—Kasper Greff, D.R.E.
Students 238.

Spirit of Life (1978), Rev. Cyprian T. Meier; Deacon David Vaughn.
Mailing Address: Box 247, 58554. Tel: 701-663-1660; Fax: 701-667-2021.
Res., 801 First St. S.E., 58554. Tel: 701-663-1660; Fax: 701-667-2021.
Catechesis/Religious Programs—Jim Fritzhuspen, D.R.E.
Students 330.

Mandaree, Dunn Co., St. Anthony (Native American), Rev. Stephen Kranz, O.S.B.; Bro. Bernard Vogel, O.S.B., Pastoral Assoc.
Res., HCO 2, Box 27, 58757. Tel: 701-759-3412. [CEM]
Catechesis/Religious Programs—Students 241.
Missions—Twin Buttes, Dunn Co., St. Joseph, 58757. Tel: 701-759-3412; White Shield, McLean Co., Sacred Heart, 58757.

Menoken, Burleigh Co., St. Hildegard (1949), Rev. John J. Owens.
Res., 17200 Hwy. 10, 58558-9604. Tel: 701-673-3177; Fax: 701-673-3178.
Catechesis/Religious Programs—Tel: 701-673-3177; Fax: 701-673-3178. Janice Aberle, D.R.E.
Students 74.
Mission—Driscoll, Burleigh Co., St. Anthony, 17200 Highway 10, 58558-9604. Tel: 701-673-3177; Fax: 701-673-3178.

Minot, Ward Co.,

1—Minot Air Force Base Chapel, (1954), Rev. Kerry M. Abbott, O.F.M.Conv.
Res., 5 BW/HC, 230 Missile Ave., 58705-5003. Tel: 701-723-2456; Fax: 701-723-3052.
Catechesis/Religious Programs—Tel: 701-723-2456.
Students 219.

2—Our Lady of Grace, (1959), Rev. Robert H. Kippley.
Res., 715 16th Ave., S.W., 58701. Tel: 701-839-6834; Fax: 701-838-5929.
Catechesis/Religious Programs—Tel: 701-839-6834. D.R.E.: Darlene Demars, (Grades K-6); Joan Aftem, (Grades 7-12).
Students 410.

3—St. John the Apostle, (1961), Rev. Henry W. Schneider; Deacon M. Stephen Mays.
Res., 109-25th St. N.W., 58701. Tel: 701-839-7076. [JC]
Catechesis/Religious Programs—Tel: 701-839-4076. Mrs. William Brock, D.R.E.
Students 261.

4—St. Leo, (1886) (German), Rev. Chris B. Walter.
Res., 305 First St. S.E., 58701. Tel: 701-838-1026.
Catechesis/Religious Programs—Tel: 701-838-1026. Rosie Workman, D.R.E.
Students 359.

5—St. Theresa, the Little Flower, (1954), Rev. Paul L. Cervinski.
Res., 800 University Ave., W., 58703. Tel: 701-838-1520; Fax: 701-839-8567. [JC]
School—See separate listing under Institutions Located in the Diocese. Tel: 701-839-5882; Fax: 701-839-8567.
Catechesis/Religious Programs—D.R.E.: Sr. Angela Korte, O.S.F., Pastoral Assis.; Mary Wolfe.
Students 141.

Mohall, Renville Co., St. Jerome (1906), Rev. James B. Braaten.
Res., 307 E. Main St., 58761. Tel: 701-756-6601. [CEM]
Catechesis/Religious Programs—Tel: 701-756-6601.
Students 117.
Mission—Sherwood, Renville Co., St. James, Mohall, 58761. Tel: 701-756-6601.

Mott, Hettinger Co., St. Vincent de Paul (1907), Rev. Dennis R. Schafer; Deacon Ervin Schneider.
Res., 408 Iowa Ave., 58646. Tel: 701-824-2651. [CEM]
School—Tel: 701-824-2651.
Lay Teachers 4; Students 36.
Catechesis/Religious Programs—Mary Jo Fries, D.R.E.
Students 122.
Mission—New Leipzig, Grant Co., St. John the Baptist, New Leipzig, 58562. Tel: 701-824-2651; Fax: 701-824-2651.

New England, Hettinger Co., St. Mary (1910), Rev. Patrick A. Schumacher, S.T.L.
Res., 437 Main Ave., P.O. Box 369, 58647. Tel: 701-579-4312; Fax: 701-579-4312.
School—Tel: 701-579-4481.
Sisters 2; Lay Teachers 4; Students 20.
Catechesis/Religious Programs—Tel: 701-579-4811.
Students 110.
Mission—Amidon, Slope Co., SS. Peter & Paul, P.O. Box 369, 58647. Tel: 701-579-4312; Fax: 701-579-4312. [CEM]

New Hradec, Dunn Co., SS. Peter and Paul (1898) (Czech), Rev. Wilfrid Splonskowski, O.S.B.
Res., Box 35-B, 58648. Tel: 701-225-2644. [CEM]
Catechesis/Religious Programs—Tel: 701-225-2644.
Students 43.
Mission—Gladstone, Dunn Co., St. Philip, P.O. Box 72, Gladstone, 58630. [CEM]

New Salem, Morton Co., St. Pius V (1912), Rev. David L. Zimmer.
Res., P.O. Box C, 58563. Tel: 701-843-7144. [CEM]
Catechesis/Religious Programs—Tel: 701-843-7061. Mary Lou Klemisch, D.R.E.
Students 152.
Mission—Almont, Morton Co., St. Mary, Queen of Peace, Almont, 58520.

New Town, Mountrail Co., St. Anthony (1954), Rev. John P. O'Leary.
Res., P.O. Box 715, 58763. Tel: 701-627-4423. [CEM 4][JC]
Catechesis/Religious Programs—Tel: 701-627-4912. Mary Bangen, D.R.E.
Students 108.

Parshall, Mountrail Co., St. Bridget (1917), Rev. Thomas P. Sullivan.
Res., 12 First St., N.W., Box 519, 58770-0519. Tel: 701-862-3484. [JC 3]
Catechesis/Religious Programs—Tel: 701-862-3484. Claudia Schneider, D.R.E.
Students 39.
Missions—Plaza, Mountrail Co., Sacred Heart, 58770-0519. Tel: 701-862-3484; Makoti, Ward Co., St. Elizabeth, 58770-0519.

Raleigh, Grant Co., St. Gertrude (1913), Rev. Kenneth G. Phillips.
Res., 421 Court St., Flasher, 58535-7216. Tel: 701-597-3570; 597-3228. [CEM]
Catechesis/Religious Programs—Tel: 701-597-3228.
Students 35.

Regent, Hettinger Co., St. Henry (1913), Rev. Michael T. Krank.
Res., P.O. Box 155, 58650-0155. Tel: 701-563-4595. [JC]
Catechesis/Religious Programs—Tel: 701-563-4543. D.R.E.: Karen Kouba; Cindy Krauter.
Students 67.

Richardton, Stark Co., St. Mary (1895), Rev. Brian Wangler, O.S.B.
Res., P.O. Box A, 58652. Tel: 701-974-3569. [CEM]
School—Tel: 701-974-3674. Deborah Bohn, Prin.
Lay Teachers 5; Students 70.
Catechesis/Religious Programs—Marilyn Metz, D.R.E. (Grades K-11).
Students 141.
Mission—Richardton, Stark Co., St. Stephen, Box A, 58652. Tel: 701-974-3332.

St. Anthony, Morton Co., St. Anthony (1897) (German-Russian), Rev. Florian Fairbanks, O.S.B.
Res., P.O. Box 45, 58566. Tel: 701-445-7373. [CEM]
Catechesis/Religious Programs—Tel: 701-445-7373.
Students 76.

St. Michael, Emmons Co., St. Michael's. Closed. For inquiries for parish records contact the Chancery.

Selfridge, Sioux Co., St. Philomena (1919) (German-Russian), Rev. Casimir A. Paluck.
Res., Box 85, 58568. Fax: 701-854-3474. [CEM]
Catechesis/Religious Programs—David Volk, D.R.E.
Students 46.
Mission—Solen, Sioux Co., Sacred Heart, 58568.

South Heart, Stark Co., St. Mary (1923), Rev. Jacob Schumacher.
Res., P.O. Box 189, 58655. Tel: 701-677-5886. [CEM]
Catechesis/Religious Programs—Tel: 701-677-5886.
Students 103.

Stanley, Mountrail Co., Queen of the Most Holy Rosary (1908), Rev. Vincent Chembakassery.
Res., P.O. Box 159, 58784. Tel: 701-628-2323. [CEM][JC]
Catechesis/Religious Programs—Betty Leith, D.R.E.
Students 165.
Mission—Powers Lake, Burke Co., St. James, 8334 Hwy. 50, Powers Lake, 58773. Tel: 701-464-5771. [JC]

Strasburg, Emmons Co., Sts. Peter and Paul (1889) (German-Russian), Rev. Leonard A. Eckroth.

Res., Box 322, 58573. Tel: 701-336-2603; 336-7172. [CEM]
Catechesis/Religious Programs—Tel: 701-336-7102. Sr. Rose Schwab, S.S.N.D., D.R.E. Students 137.
Mission—Rural Linton, Emmons Co., St. Michael's, P.O. Box 322, 58573-0322. Tel: 701-336-7172.

Tioga, Williams Co., St. Thomas (1914), Rev. Thomas Dignan.
Res., P.O. Box 667, 58852. Tel: 701-664-2445. [CEM][JC]
Catechesis/Religious Programs—Students 83.
Mission—Ray, Williams Co., St. Michael, Ray, 58849. Tel: 701-568-2252.

Underwood, McLean Co., St. Bonaventure (1913), Rev. James W. Ryan.
Res., P.O. Box 700, 58576. Tel: 701-442-5229.
Catechesis/Religious Programs—Tel: 701-442-3412. Students 112.
Mission—Turtle Lake, McLean Co., St. Catherine, Main St., Turtle Lake, 58575. Tel: 701-488-9289. [CEM][JC]

Watford City, McKenzie Co., Epiphany (1915), Rev. John M. Pfeifer.
Res., P.O. Box 670, 58854. Tel: 701-842-3505.
Catechesis/Religious Programs—Tel: 701-842-3791. Kathy Johnson, D.R.E. Students 172.
Missions—Alexander, McKenzie Co., Our Lady of Consolation, R.R. 1, Box 58, Alexander, 58831. Tel: 701-586-3720; Grassy Butte, McKenzie Co., St. Peter Canisius, 58854.

Williston, Williams Co., St. Joseph (1901), Revs. Norman J. Dukart; Thomas Pittappilly (India).
Res., 124 Sixth St. W., P.O. Box K, 58802. Tel: 701-572-6731. [JC]
School—Tel: 701-572-6384. Pamela Lambert, Prin. Lay Teachers 15; Students 141.
Catechesis/Religious Programs—Tel: 701-572-0201. Ida Kirchmeier, D.R.E. Students 550.
Mission—Trenton, Williams Co., St. John the Baptist, P.O. Box K, 58802. Tel: 701-572-6731.

Wilton, McLean Co., Sacred Heart (1908), Rev. Theodore F. Gustin.
Res., P.O. Box 128, 58579. Tel: 701-734-6384. [JC]
Catechesis/Religious Programs—Tel: 701-734-8136. Kathy Clausen, D.R.E. Students 186.
Missions—Washburn, McLean Co., St. Edwin, P.O.Box 65, Washburn, 58577. Tel: 701-462-3340; Wing, Burleigh Co., St. Ignatius, P.O. Box 128, Wilton, 58477.

INDIAN MISSIONS

Fort Berthold Reservation, Sacred Heart Indian Mission. (Ree, Gros Venture and Mandan).
Res., St. Anthony, R.R. 12, Box 27, Mandaree, 58701. Tel: 701-759-3412. Rev. Stephen Kranz, O.S.B.

Chaplains of Public Institutions

BISMARCK. *Bismarck State College,* Schafer St., 58501. Tel: 701-224-5400. Deacon John Lamontagne, Chap.
North Dakota State Penitentiary, 2905 Winnipeg Dr., 58501. Tel: 701-258-7566. Deacon John Tharaldsen.
North Dakota Youth Correctional Center, 215 E. Arbor, Apt. 308C, 58504. Tel: 701-224-1302. Deacon Morris E. Martin.

Special Assignment:
Reverend Monsignors—
Walsh, Gerald J., P.O. Box 1575, Bismarck, ND 58502-1575

On Duty Outside the Diocese:
Reverend Fathers—
Allen, Joseph A., Diocese of Pensacola-Tallahassee, FL
Deichert, Joseph, 442 13th St., Box 53006, Dover A.F.B., DE 19902-0113
Hill, Donald, Chap., Army National Guard, Washington, DC
Kuss, Allen R., U.S. Navy
Tuxbury, James C., Franciscan Friars, 141 Main St., Buzzards Bay, MA 02532
Wehner, Eugene C., Franciscan Friars, 5345 S. University Ave., Chicago, IL 60615

Graduate Studies:
Reverend Fathers—
Brown, Phillip J., North American College, Rome

Retired:
Reverend Fathers—
Adkins, Joseph H., 1020 N. 26th St., Bismarck, ND 58501
Backes, Charles H., 1020 N. 26th St., Bismarck, ND 58501
Backes, Hugo G., 1050 N. 28th St., Bismarck, ND 58501-3193
Bova, Eugene R., 360 Pinon Rd., Bailey, CO 80421
Brydl, Ladislaus C., 1020 N. 26th St., Bismarck, ND 58501
Cook, Blaine, 7500 University Dr., Bismarck, ND 58504
Fahnlander, William J., 505 10th Ave. N.W., Mandan, ND 58554-0047
Flavin, Daniel F., Fox Ridge Apartments, Bldg. 176, Marshfield, MA 02050
Frank, Eugene G., 1021 N. 26th St., Bismarck, ND 58501
Kuhn, John H., 1020 N. 26th St., Bismarck, ND 58501
Rushford, William A., 1020 N. 26th St., Bismarck, ND 58501
Spain, P. Arnold, 2881 B Warwick Loop, Bismarck, ND 58504

Permanent Deacons:
Barone, Daniel, St. Anthony, New Town
Berg, Melvin J., (Retired)
Clancy, Lynn, Corpus Christi, Bismarck
Cunningham, Patrick M., Little Flower, Minot
Dean, Dennis L., St. John, Lansford
Deichert, Harry M., Corpus Christi, Bismarck
Dorrheim, Larry L., Ascension, Bismarck
DuKart, Herman, St. Joseph, Killdeer
Dworshak, Anton T., St. Mary, Bismarck
Grabar, Ray A., Ascension, Bismarck
Greff, Kasper N., St. Anne, Bismarck
Harmon, Steve M., Bismarck
Hibl, Albert W., St. Bernard, Belfield
Hoffman, Peter, St. Joseph, Mandan
Jilek, Raymond, St. Wenceslaus, Dickinson
Johnson, Ed J., Sr., United Tribes Chapel, Bismarck
Johnson, Ward A., Christ the King, Mandan
Kappel, Joseph, St. Patrick, Dickinson
Kilzer, Werner J., (Retired)
Klein, Kenneth M., St. Mary, Bismarck
Knopik, Martin, (Retired)
Kordonowy, Leonard J., Ukranian Church of St. Demetrius, Fairfield
Kuss, Leroy M., Corpus Christi, Bismarck
Lamontagne, John H., Ascension, Bismarck
Larson, Samuel, St. John the Baptist, Beach
Martin, Morris E., St. Mary, Bismarck
Mathern, Joseph J., Corpus Christi, Bismarck
Mays, Stephen B., St. John, Minot
McDowall, Rexford R., Corpus Christi, Bismarck
Morgel, Edmund D., St. John the Baptist, Portal
Morman, Eugene F., St. Wenceslaus, Dickinson
Nistler, Donald R., St. Mary, Golva
Nistler, James A., Kenya, East Africa
Olson, Robert C., St. Vincent De Paul, Crown Butte
Piasecki, Stanley T., (Retired)
Ressler, James V., Corpus Christi, Bismarck
Riehl, Emil J., Christ the King, Mandan
Schmitz, Alvin R., St. Anne, Bismarck
Schneider, Ervin H., St. Vincent de Paul, Mott
Schuller, Robert P., Corpus Christi, Bismarck
Schumacher, Martin, St. Anthony, Linton
Schwindt, Alvin W., Ascension, Bismarck
Stockert, Ralph F., St. Joseph, Dickinson
Tharaldsen, John, Corpus Christi, Bismarck
Vaughn, David L., Spirit of Life, Mandan
Von Ruden, Ralph, Cathedral of the Holy Spirit, Bismarck
Wanner, Anton, Jr., St. Patrick, Dickinson
Wolbaum, Kenneth J., St. Katherine, Braddock
Wolf, Wilfred P., Cathedral of the Holy Spirit, Bismarck
Wosepka, James, St. John the Baptist, Beach
Ziman, Edward J., St. Joseph, Killdeer; St. Paul, Halliday

INSTITUTIONS LOCATED IN THE DIOCESE

[A] SEMINARIES, RELIGIOUS OR SCHOLASTICATES

RICHARDTON. *Assumption Abbey,* P.O. Box A, 58652. Tel: 701-974-3315; Fax: 701-974-3317. Rt. Revs. Patrick Moore, O.S.B., Abbot; Lawrence Wagner, O.S.B., Retired Abbot; Robert West, O.S.B., Retired Abbot; Very Rev. Valerian Odermann, O.S.B., Prior; Revs. Thomas Wordekemper, O.S.B., Subprior; David Wolf, O.S.B., Business Mgr.; Florian Fairbanks, O.S.B.; Eugene Hornstein, O.S.B.; Claude Seeberger, O.S.B.; Gerald Ruelle, O.S.B.; Wilfrid J. Splonskowski, O.S.B.; Raymond Dietlein, O.S.B.; Richard Wilhelmi, O.S.B.; John Odermann, O.S.B. (FAR); Stephen Kranz, O.S.B.; Damian Dietlein, O.S.B. (IND); Raphael Stovik, O.S.B.; Sebastian Schmidt, O.S.B., (Overseas); Denis Fournier, O.S.B.; Francis Wehri, O.S.B., (Overseas); Terrence Kardong, O.S.B.; Victor Feser, O.S.B.; Odo Muggli, O.S.B.; Daniel Maloney, O.S.B.; Brian Wangler, O.S.B.; Philip Vanderlin, O.S.B., (Overseas); Francis dos Remedios, O.S.B.; Carlos Suarez, O.S.B., (Overseas); Julian Nix, O.S.B.; Hugo L. Blotsky, O.S.B.; Efraim Villegas, O.S.B., (Overseas); Boniface Muggli, O.S.B.; Gonzalo Blanco, O.S.B., (Overseas). Priests 33; Brothers 25.

[B] COLLEGES AND UNIVERSITIES

BISMARCK. *University of Mary,* 7500 University Dr., 58504-9652. Tel: 701-255-7500.
For a complete listing, refer to the Colleges and Universities section.

[C] HIGH SCHOOLS, INTERPAROCHIAL AND PARISH

BISMARCK. *St. Mary Central High School,* 1025 N. Second St., 58501. Tel: 701-223-4113. Les Kramer, Supt.; Cheryl Kalberer, Prin. Sisters 1; Lay Teachers 30; Students 485.

DICKINSON. *Trinity High School,* 8th & 10th St., P.O. Box 1177, 58602-1177. Tel: 701-225-6081. Steve Brannan, Supt.; Walter Beseler, Prin. Sisters 1; Lay Teachers 19; Students 427.

MINOT. *Bishop Ryan High School,* 316 11th Ave. N.W., 58701. Tel: 701-852-4004. Don Bunce, Supt.; Patrick McNally, Prin. Lay Teachers 26; Students 416.

[D] GENERAL HOSPITALS

BISMARCK. *St. Alexius Medical Center,* P.O. Box 5510, 58502. Tel: 701-224-7000; Fax: 701-224-7284.
For a complete listing, refer to the Hospitals section.

DICKINSON. *St. Joseph's Hospital and Health Center,* 30 W. Seventh St., 58601. Tel: 701-225-7271.
For a complete listing, refer to the Hospitals section.

GARRISON. *Garrison Memorial Hospital,* P.O. Box 39, 58540. Tel: 701-463-2275.
For a complete listing, refer to the Hospitals section.

*KENMARE. *Kenmare Community Hospital,* P.O. Box 697, 58746. Tel: 701-385-4296.
For a complete listing, refer to the Hospitals section.

MINOT. *St. Joseph's Hospital dba UniMed Medical Center,* Attn: Administration, P.O. Box 5001, 58702. Tel: 701-857-2000; Fax: 701-839-8947.
For a complete listing, refer to the Hospitals section.
UniMed Medical Center Foundation, 3rd St. S.E. & Burdick Expwy., 58701. Tel: 701-857-2070.
For a complete listing, refer to the Hospitals section.

WILLISTON. *Mercy Hospital,* 1301 15th Ave. W., 58801. Tel: 701-774-7400; Fax: 701-774-7409.
For a complete listing, refer to the Hospitals section.
Mercy Medical Center, 1301 15th Ave., W., 58801. Tel: 701-774-7401.
For a complete listing, refer to the Hospitals section.
Mercy Medical Foundation, 1301 15th Ave., W., 58801. Tel: 701-774-7404.
For a complete listing, refer to the Hospitals section.
Mercy Recovery Center, 1301 15th Ave. W., 58801. Tel: 701-774-7409; Fax: 701-774-7479.
For a complete listing, refer to the Hospitals section.

[E] SPECIAL CARE FACILITIES

DICKINSON. *St. Benedict's Health Center,* 851 Fourth Ave. E., 58601. Tel: 701-225-5138; Fax: 701-225-3947. Operated by Benedictine Health System Long Term Care, Inc. Kevin Greff, Admin. Bed Capacity 175; Total Staff 230; Total Assisted 175.

GARRISON. *Garrison Nursing Center,* Eastern Acres, P.O. Box 219, 58540. Tel: 701-463-2226; Fax: 701-463-2650. Operated by Benedictine Health System Long Term Care, Inc. Mark Seibold, Admin. Bed Capacity 71; Total Staff 72; Total Assisted 71.

[F] PROTECTIVE INSTITUTIONS

SENTINEL BUTTE. *Home on the Range,* HC 1, Box 41, 58654. Tel: 701-872-3745; Fax: 701-872-3748.
For a complete listing, refer to the Special Care Facilities section.

[G] HOMES FOR AGED

BISMARCK. *Emmaus Place,* 1020 N. 26th St., 58501. Tel: 701-258-2618.
For a complete listing, refer to the Special Care Facilities section.
Marillac Manor, 1016 N. 28th St., 58501. Tel: 701-258-8702; Fax: 701-223-3127.
For a complete listing, refer to the Special Care Facilities section.
St. Vincent's Care Center, 1021 N. 26 St., 58501-3199. Tel: 701-223-6888.
For a complete listing, refer to the Special Care

Facilities section.

[H] CONVENTS AND RESIDENCES FOR SISTERS

BISMARCK. *Annunciation Priory*, 7520 University Dr., 58504-9653. Tel: 701-255-1520. Sr. Susan Berger, O.S.B., Prioress; Rev. Daniel Maloney, O.S.B., Res. Chap. Motherhouse and Novitiate of the Benedictine Sisters, B.M.V. Professed Sisters 102.

RICHARDTON. *Sacred Heart Monastery*, P.O. Box 364, 58652. Tel: 701-974-2121. Sr. Paula Larson, O.S.B., Prioress. Motherhouse and Novitiate of the Sisters of the Order of St. Benedict. Professed Sisters 40.

[I] NEWMAN CENTERS

DICKINSON. *Catholic Student Center*, 238 Eighth Ave., W., 58601. Tel: 701-225-6210. Louise A. Oleson, Dir. Total Staff 1.

MINOT. *Catholic Student Center*, 409 University Ave., N.W., 58703-2212. Tel: 701-838-2815. Louise A. Oleson, Dir. Total Staff 1.

[J] MISCELLANEOUS

DICKINSON. *Subiaco Manor*, 2441 10th Ave., W., 58601. Tel: 701225-4220.

Sponsored by the Benedictine Sisters of Sacred Heart Monastery in Richardton. Sr. Renee Branigan, O.S.B., Res. Mgr.

MINOT. *Minot Catholic Schools Corporation*, 316 11th Ave., N.W., 58703-2299. Tel: 701-852-4004; Fax: 701-839-4651. Don Bunce, Supt.

Bishop Ryan High School, 316 11th Ave., N.W., 58703-2299. Tel: 701-852-4004; Fax: 701-839-4651. Patrick McNally, Prin. Lay Teachers 26; Students 416.

Little Flower School, 800 University Ave., W., 58703. Tel: 701-839-5882; Fax: 701-839-8567. Diane Zander, Prin. Lay Teachers 10; Students 136.

St. Leo's School, 305 First St., S.E., 58701. Tel: 701-838-2597. Gerry Champion, Prin. Lay Teachers 12; Students 149.

RICHARDTON. *Sacred Heart Benedictine Foundation*, P.O. Box 364, 58652-0364.

RELIGIOUS INSTITUTES OF MEN REPRESENTED IN THE DIOCESE

For further details refer to the corresponding bracketed number in the Religious Institutes of Men or Women section.

[0200]—*Benedictine Monks*. (Richardton, ND) .—O.S.B.

[]—*Missionary Congregation of the Blessed Sacrament*. (Kerala, India).—M.C.B.S.

[1200]—*Society of the Divine Savior*. (Milwaukee, WI).—S.D.S.

RELIGIOUS INSTITUTES OF WOMEN REPRESENTED IN THE DIOCESE

[0230]—*Benedictine Sisters of Pontifical Jurisdiction*. (Bismarck; Richardton, ND; Watertown, SD; Yankton, SD; Duluth).—O.S.B.

[2970]—*School Sisters of Notre Dame*. (Mankato Prov.).—S.S.N.D.

[0990]—*Sisters of Divine Providence*. (Allison Park, PA).—C.D.P.

[2630]—*Sisters of Mercy of the Holy Cross*. (Merrill, WI).—S.C.S.C.

[2475]—*Sisters of Mercy of the Union*. (Omaha, NE).—R.S.M.

[1630]—*Sisters of St. Francis of Penance and Christian Charity*. (Denver, CO).—O.S.F.

[3320]—*Sisters of the Presentation of the Blessed Virgin Mary*. (Fargo, ND; Aberdeen, SD).—P.B.V.M.

NECROLOGY

† Lukach, John P., New Town, ND, Church of St. Anthony. —Died Jan. 31, 1996.

Diocese of Boise

(Dioecesis Xylopolitana)

Most Reverend

TOD DAVID BROWN

Bishop of Boise; ordained May 1, 1963; appointed December 27, 1988; Episcopal Ordination April 3, 1989. *Res., 303 Federal Way, Boise, ID, 83705-5925.*

ESTABLISHED AS A VICARIATE-APOSTOLIC MARCH 3, 1868.

ERECTED A DIOCESE BY HIS HOLINESS POPE LEO XIII, AUGUST 26, 1893.

Square Miles 84,290.

Legal Title: "Roman Catholic Diocese of Boise."

Comprises the State of Idaho, with a Total Population of 1,163,000.

For legal titles of parishes and diocesan institutions, consult the Chancery Office.

Chancery Office: 303 Federal Way, Boise, ID, 83705-5925. Tel.: 208-342-1311; Fax: 208-342-0224.

STATISTICAL OVERVIEW

Personnel	
Bishop	1
Priests: Diocesan Active in Diocese	58
Priests: Active Outside Diocese	8
Priests: Diocesan in Foreign Missions	2
Priests: Retired, Sick or Absent	27
Number of Diocesan Priests	95
Religious Priests in Diocese	16
Extern Priests in Diocese	4
Ordinations:	
Diocesan Priests	1
Permanent Deacons in Diocese	30
Total Brothers	8
Total Sisters	121
Parishes	
Parishes	73
With Resident Pastor:	
Resident Diocesan Priests	57
Resident Religious Priests	4
Without Resident Pastor:	
Administered by Priests	11
Administered by Women Religious	1
Missions	40
Closed Parishes	1
Professional Ministry Personnel:	
Brothers	1
Sisters	8
Lay Ministers	27
Welfare	
Catholic Hospitals	5
Total Assisted	485,821
Day Care and Extended Day Care Centers	4
Total Assisted	135
Special Centers for Social Services	12
Total Assisted	51,116
Educational	
Diocesan Students in Other Seminaries	10
Total Seminarians	10
High Schools, Diocesan and Parish	1
Total Students	713
Elementary Schools, Diocesan and Parish	13
Total Students	2,388
Catechesis/Religious Education:	
High School Students	2,787
Elementary Students	6,595
Total Students Under Catholic Instruction	12,493
Teachers in the Diocese:	
Sisters	5
Lay Teachers	152
Vital Statistics	
Receptions into the Church:	
Infant Baptism Totals	2,579
Adult Baptism Totals	202
Received into Full Communion	261
First Communions	1,913
Confirmations	1,014
Marriages:	
Catholic	342
Interfaith	234
Total Marriages	576
Deaths	671
Total Catholic Population	116,500
Total Population	1,163,000

Former Bishops—Rt. Rev. LOUIS LOOTENS, D.D., appt. first Vicar-Apostolic of Idaho, March 3, 1868; cons. Bishop of Castabala, Aug. 9, 1868; resigned July 16, 1876; died Jan. 13, 1898.—Rt. Rev. ALPHONSE JOSEPH GLORIEUX, D.D., appt. second Vicar-Apostolic of Idaho, Feb. 27, 1885; cons. Titular Bishop of Apolonia, April 19, 1885; appt. first Bishop of the Diocese of Boise, Aug. 26, 1893; died Aug. 25, 1917.—Rt. Rev. DANIEL MARY GORMAN, D.D. LL.D., cons. May 1, 1918; died June 9, 1927.—Most Rev. EDWARD JOSEPH KELLY, D.D., cons. March 6, 1928; died April 21, 1956.—Most Rev. JAMES J. BYRNE, D.D., S.T.D., ord. June 3, 1933; appt. Titular Bishop of Etenna and Auxiliary of St. Paul, July 2, 1947; cons. July 2, 1947; transferred to Boise June 16, 1956; appt. Archbishop of Dubuque, March 19, 1962; retired Aug. 23, 1983; died Aug. 2, 1996.—Most Rev. SYLVESTER WILLIAM TREINEN, D.D., ord. June 11, 1946; appt. May 19, 1962; cons. July 25, 1962; retired Aug. 17, 1988; died Sept. 30, 1996.

Vicar General/Moderator of the Curia—Rev. Msgr. DENNIS G. FALK, V.G.

Vicar for Religious—Rev. Msgr. DENNIS G. FALK, V.G.

Vicar for Administration—Rev. Msgr. DENNIS G. FALK, V.G.

Office of Multi-Cultural/Ethnic Ministry—Rev. MARCELLUS FERNANDEZ, Interim Dir., *303 Federal Way, Boise, 83705-5925.* Tel: 208-342-1311.

Chancery Office—303 Federal Way, Boise, 83705-5925. Tel: 208-342-1311; Fax: 208-342-0224.

Chancellor—Deacon JAMES BOWEN.

Notaries—LODICE GRANT; RUTH V. GRAFF.

Diocesan Tribunal—303 Federal Way, Boise, 83705-5925. Tel: 208-344-1344; Fax: 208-342-0224. (Direct all correspondence here.).

Director—Dr. DIANE L. BARR.

Judicial Vicar—Very Rev. JOSEPH F. MCDONALD, III, J.C.L.

Vice Judicial Vicar—Rev. GERALD J. FUNKE.

Promotor of Justice—Dr. DIANE L. BARR.

Notaries—Rev. Msgr. DENNIS G. FALK, V.G.; Deacon JAMES E. BOWEN; Dr. DIANE L. BARR; RUTH GRAFF; KATHRYN HARRIMAN; THERESA WEBSTER.

Judges—Revs. JOHN W. MORGAN; WILLIAM C. CROWLEY; WILLIAM DOHMAN; SIMEON VAN DE VOORD, O.S.B.; SEAN CAULFIELD; Very Rev. JOSEPH MCDONALD, III, J.C.L.; Rev. GERALD FUNKE.

Defenders of the Bond—Dr. DIANE L. BARR; Sr. BERNICE WESSELS, O.S.B.

Consultors—Rev. Msgr. DENNIS G. FALK; Very Revs. GERALD DYE, V.F.; WILLIAM CROWLEY, V.F.; ROGER LACHANCE, V.F.; ANDREW SCHUMACHER, V.U.; JOHN MORGAN, V.F.; TIMOTHY O'TOOLE, V.F.; Revs. JOHN KOELSCH; ALFRED PUCCINELLI, S.M.; JOSEPH SCHMIDT; MICHAEL ST. MARIE; ENRIQUE TERRIQUEZ.

Deans—Northern Deanery: Very Rev. ROGER LACHANCE, V.F., North Central Deanery: Very Rev. WILLIAM CROWLEY, V.F., Western Deanery: Very Rev. GERALD DYE, V.F., West Central Deanery: Very Rev. ANDREW SCHUMACHER, V.U., Southern Deanery: Very Rev. JOHN MORGAN, V.F., Eastern Deanery: Very Rev. TIMOTHY O'TOOLE, V.F.

Presbyteral Council—Rev. Msgr. DENNIS G. FALK; Very Revs. GERALD DYE, V.F.; ROGER LACHANCE, V.F.; WILLIAM CROWLEY, V.F.; ANDREW SCHUMACHER, V.U.; JOHN MORGAN, V.F.; TIMOTHY O'TOOLE, V.F.; Revs. JOHN KOELSCH; ALFRED PUCCINELLI, S.M.; JOSEPH SCHMIDT; MICHAEL ST. MARIE; ENRIQUE TERRIQUEZ.

Priest Personnel Board—Most Rev. TOD D. BROWN; Rev. Msgr. DENNIS G. FALK, V.G.; Revs. HENRY CARMONA; JOHN KOELSCH; ROGER LACHANCE; TIMOTHY RITCHEY; ANDREW SCHUMACHER; DENNIS WASSMUTH; JOHN WORSTER.

Finance Council—Most Rev. TOD D. BROWN; Rev. Msgr. DENNIS G. FALK, V.G., Chm. LARRY HELLHAKE; Rev. Msgr. RAYMOND PEPLINSKI, P.A.; STANLEY WELSH; JAMES BRUCE; SUSAN COPPLE; T. STEVE JOYCE; RANDY STEINER, Finance Office Consultant.

Building Committee—Deacon JAMES BOWEN; Rev. Msgr. RAYMOND PEPLINSKI, P.A.; CHARLES HUMMEL; MARILYN SCANLAN; DAVID DAVIES.

Priest Retirement Committee—Rev. Msgr. DENNIS G. FALK, V.G.; Revs. JOHN KOELSCH; MORSE LATER, Chm.; JOHN MORGAN; DENNIS WASSMUTH; RICHARD HALDANE, *7225 Cascade Dr., Boise, 83704.* Tel: 208-376-1940.

Diocesan Offices and Directors

Apostleship of Prayer—Vacant.

Bureau of Information—"Idaho Catholic Register," 303 Federal Way, Boise, 83705-5925.

Campaign for Human Development—Deacon JAMES E. BOWEN, *303 Federal Way, Boise, 83705-5925.*

Catholic Communications Center—Vacant.

Catholic Relief Services—Rev. Msgr. DENNIS G. FALK, V.G., *303 Federal Way, Boise, 83705-5925.*

Catholic Scouts—Rev. ROGER LACHANCE, Chap., *St. Pius X, 625 E. Haycraft, Coeur d'Alene, 83814.* Tel: 208-765-5108.

Catholic Daughters of the Americas—BONNIE MCDOWELL, State Regent, *1146 N. 15th St., Coeur d'Alene, 83814.* Tel: 208-664-4888.

Catholic Elementary Schools—Dr. ROBERT FONTAINE, Supt., *303 Federal Way, Boise, 83705-5925.*

Catholic Hospitals—Rev. MARK R. SCHMACHER, *St. Augustine's Catholic Center, P.O. Box 3457 University Sta., Moscow, 83843.* Tel: 208-882-4613.

Catholic Liturgical Commission—Most Rev. TOD D. BROWN; JOHN ANNEN; MARCIA BECKMAN; DELINDA FEHRINGER; LARRY HARRISON; Bro. ERNEST MORASCI, S.M.; MARY HERSLEY; MILDRED TILLOTSON; Deacon RALPH PIERCE; Sr. CECILE MARIE UHLORN, O.S.B., *303 Federal Way, Boise, 83705.* Tel: 208-342-1311.

Censor Librorum—Rev. ANDREW SCHUMACHER, *2612 W. State St., Boise, 83702.*

Charismatic Renewal—Rev. ROBB KELLER, *152 7th Ave. E., Twin Falls, 83301.*

Priest Retirement Plan—Direct Inquiries to the Chancery, *303 Federal Way, Boise, 83705.*

Cursillo Movement—Rev. JOHN KOELSCH, Spiritual Dir., *P.O. Box 5127, Boise, 83705.* Rev. MAURICIO MEDINA, Hispanic Dir., *584 W. Sexton, Blackfoot, 83221.*

Development/Stewardship Office—Rev. DONALD J. RIFFLE.

Ecumenical Commission—Rev. JOHN KOELSCH, *P.O. Box 5127, Boise, 83705.*

Education Ministries Office—Dr. ROBERT FONTAINE, Dir. CHERYL MCCRORIE, Administrative Asst., *303 Federal Way, Boise, 83705.* Tel: 208-342-1311.

Supt. of Schools—Dr. ROBERT FONTAINE.

Children's Catechesis,—Sr. CLARISSA GOECKNER, O.S.B.

Youth Ministry—DIANE LIND.

Adult Education—Sr. ARLENE ELLIS, S.S.C.

Resource Center—CAROL MEADOWS.

Eucharistic League—Rev. Msgr. DENNIS G. FALK, V.G.

Vitality Project—DORIS MURPHY.

Family Life—Vacant.

Finance Officer—RANDY STEINER.

Idaho Council of Catholic Women—GLADYS ESQUIAEL, Pres., *P.O. Box 835, Burley, 83318.*

Knights of Columbus—WILLIAM A. SHAMION, State Deputy, *12857 Hartford Ave., Orofino, 83544.* Rev. GEORGE L. KING, State Chap.

Legislative Liaison—TIMOTHY BRENNAN.

Campus Ministry—Sr. DAVID HARTSE, O.S.U., *1915 University Dr., Boise, 83706.*

Newspaper—"Idaho Catholic Register"; Most Rev. TOD BROWN, Publisher; COLETTE COWMAN, Exec. Editor; LEONARD GEORGE, Advertising/Business/Circulation; BARBARA HAMILTON, Artist/Library/Production, *303 Federal Way, Boise, 83705.* Tel: 208-342-1311.

Deacons, Director—Deacon RICHARD BONNEY, *11 Stanford, Pocatello, 83201.* Tel: 208-233-4661.

Deacon Council President—Deacon JAMES KELLY, *1323 Johnson St., Boise, 83705.* Tel: 208-343-9619.

Deacon Formation Director—Sr. GRAYCE ROSS, S.N.J.M., *4450 N. Five Mile Rd., Boise, 83713.* Tel: 208-376-5787.

Prison Ministry—ALFREDO CORTEZ, *P.O. Box 413, Parma, 83660.* Tel: 208-722-7545.

Propagation of Faith—Rev. Msgr. DENNIS G. FALK, V.G., *303 Federal Way, Boise, 83705.*

Respect Life Program—Deacon RALPH FLAGER, Dir., *5152 Burlington Dr., Boise, 83704.* Tel: 208-375-2459.

St. Vincent de Paul Society—Rev. ANDREW SCHUMACHER, Diocesan Spiritual Dir., *2612 W. State St., Boise, 83702.* Tel: 208-344-2597. Deacon JAMES E. BOWEN, Diocesan Dir., *303 Federal Way, Boise, 83705.* Tel: 208-342-1311.

Vocations Awareness—Rev. RONALD COOK, Dir., *P.O. Box 626, Bohl, 83316.* Tel: 208-543-5136.

CLERGY, PARISHES, MISSIONS AND PAROCHIAL SCHOOLS

CITY OF BOISE
(Ada County)

1—CATHEDRAL OF ST. JOHN THE EVANGELIST, Revs. Donald J. Riffle; Simeon Van De Voord, O.S.B.; Deacons Ken Hiner; Richard Henning.
Res., 804 N. 9th St., 83702. Tel: 208-342-3511; 3512.
School—St. Joseph's School. Mrs. Kathleen Giles, Prin.
Lay Teachers 13; Students 280.
Catechesis/Religious Programs—Linda Bratnober, D.R.E.
Students 304.

2—ST. MARK'S, Revs. John F. Donoghue; Jairo Restrepo; Deacons Ralph Pierce; James Bowen.
Res., 7503 Northview St., 83704. Tel: 208-375-6651; Fax: 208-375-3211.
School—Dan Maloney, Prin. Lay Teachers 8; Students 245.
Catechesis/Religious Programs—Students 533.

3—ST. MARY'S, Rev. Andrew J. Schumacher; Sr. Angela Uhlhorn, O.S.B., Pastoral Assoc.
Res., 2612 W. State St., 83702. Tel: 208-344-2597; Fax: 208-342-9337.
School—2620 W. State St., 83702. Tel: 208-342-7476; Fax: 208-342-7477. Marcia Beckman, Prin., Tel: 208-342-7476; Fax: 208-342-7477.
Lay Teachers 11; Students 240.
Catechesis/Religious Programs—Terry Jung, D.R.E.
Students 180.

4—OUR LADY OF THE ROSARY, Rev. Dennis Wassmuth; Deacons Gene Halstrom; Michael Dessert.
Res., 1500 E. Wright, 83706. Tel: 208-343-9041.
Catechesis/Religious Programs—Rosie Skoro, D.R.E.
Students 210.

5—RISEN CHRIST CATHOLIC COMMUNITY, Rev. Joseph da Silva; Deacon Michael Eisenbeiss.
Res., 11511 W. Lake Hazel Rd., 83709. Tel: 208-362-6584.
Catechesis/Religious Programs—Students 222.

6—SACRED HEART, Rev. John W. Koelsch; Deacons Alan Shaber; James Kelly.
Office: 811 S. Latah St., P.O. Box 5127, 83705. Fax: 208-344-8312.
Res., 3902 Camas St., 83705. Tel: 208-344-8311.
School—3901 Cassia St., 83705. Tel: 208-344-9738. John Loffer, Prin.
Sisters 1; Lay Teachers 12; Students 252.
Catechesis/Religious Programs—Deborah Fischer, D.R.E.
Students 123.

7—ST. PAUL'S. Closed. See Our Lady of the Rosary, Boise for details.

OUTSIDE THE CITY OF BOISE

Aberdeen, Bingham Co., Blessed Sacrament, Rev. B. Ernest Anderson.
Res., Hwy. 39 & S. 4th W., P.O. Drawer C, 83210. Tel: 208-397-4028.
Catechesis/Religious Programs—Aren Schanh, D.R.E.
Students 107.

American Falls, Power Co., St. Mary, Rev. B. Ernest Anderson; Deacon Francis X. McNamara.
Mailing Address: P.O. Box 117, 83211. Tel: 208-226-5217.
Catechesis/Religious Programs—Kathy Barkdull, D.R.E.
Students 121.

Arco, Butte Co., St. Ann's. See St. Charles, Salmon for details.

Blackfoot, Bingham Co., St. Bernard's, Rev. Mauricio Medina, Admin.
Res., 584 W. Sexton St., 83221. Tel: 208-785-1935; Fax: 208-785-1935.
Catechesis/Religious Programs—Sharon Cathrae, D.R.E.
Students 85.
Station—Pingree, St. John's.

Bonners Ferry, Boundary Co., St. Ann's, Rev. Gordon Taylor.
Res., El Paso & Lincoln, P.O. Box 58, 83805. Tel: 208-267-2852; Fax: 208-267-5612.
Catechesis/Religious Programs—Anette Sturmans, D.R.E.
Students 67.
Station—St. Michael's Indian Station.

Buhl, Twin Falls Co., Immaculate Conception, Rev. Ronald Cook.
Res., 1701 Poplar, Box 626, 83316. Tel: 208-543-5136.
Catechesis/Religious Programs—Christine Welch, D.R.E.
Students 133.
Station—Hagerman, St. Catherine's.

Burley, Cassia Co., St. Theresa, Rev. Juan Maria Garatea.
Res., 1550 Oakley, Box 1223, 83318. Tel: 208-678-5453.
Catechesis/Religious Programs—Dorothy Gagnon, D.R.E.
Students 139.

Caldwell, Canyon Co., St. Mary, Revs. Enrique Terriquez; Charles Foltz.
Office: 616 Dearborn, P.O. Box 399, 83606. Tel: 208-459-3653; Fax: 208-459-3653.
Catechesis/Religious Programs—Students 405.
Station—Marsing, Good Shepherd.

Chubbuck, Bannock Co., St. Paul's, Rev. James E. Rodenspiel.
Res., 831 Todd St., Box 5367, 83202. Tel: 208-237-7167; Fax: 208-237-2724.
Church—820 W. Chubbuck, 83202.
Catechesis/Religious Programs—Theresa Owen, D.R.E.
Students 68.
Station—Blessed Kateri Tekakwitha Chapel, Sheepskin Rd., Fort Hall, 83203.

Coeur D'Alene, Kootenai Co., St. Pius X, Rev. Roger LaChance; Deacon Gary McSwain.
Office: 625 E. Haycraft, 83814.
Res., 2804 N. 6th St., 83814. Tel: 208-765-5108; Fax: 208-664-5325.
Catechesis/Religious Programs—D.R.E.: Sr. Roberta Lamanna, S.N.J.M.; Sr. Rosemary Thielman, S.N.J.M.
Students 400.

St. Thomas, Revs. Michael Logan, C.SS.R.; George Rassley, C.SS.R.; Robert Simon, C.SS.R.; Bro. Dennis Lee, C.SS.R., Pastoral Assoc.
Res., 919 Indiana Ave., 83814. Tel: 208-664-9259.
Catechesis/Religious Programs—Carol White, D.R.E.
Students 123.

Cottonwood, Idaho Co., St. Mary's, Rev. Joseph Muha.
Mailing Address: P.O. Box 425, 83522-0425. Tel: 208-962-3214.
Res., 503 Garrett St., 83522. Tel: 208-962-3111.
Catechesis/Religious Programs—Mary Jane Arnzen, D.R.E.
Students 165.

Council, Adams Co., St. Jude, Rev. Leonard MacMillan.
Res., 501 Cross Rd., P.O. Box 821, McCall, 83638. Tel: 208-634-5474.

DeSmet, Benewah Co., Sacred Heart, Revs. Thomas Connolly, S.J.; Joseph L. Dersinner, S.J.; Sr. Dolores Ellwart, S.P., Pastoral Assoc.
Res., Box 306, 83824. Tel: 208-274-5871.
Stations—Plummer, Our Lady of Perpetual Help; Worley, St. Michael's.

Eagle, Ada Co., St. Matthew, Rev. Phillip Mark Finley; Deacon Ralph Flager.
Res., 500 N. Eagle Rd., P.O. Box 296, 83616. Tel: 208-939-6801.
Catechesis/Religious Programs—Margery Rabdau, D.R.E.
Students 120.

Emmett, Gem Co., Sacred Heart, Rev. David Riffle.
Res., 211 E. First, 83617. Tel: 208-365-4320.
Catechesis/Religious Programs—Students 135.
Stations—Horseshoe Bend, Our Lady Queen of Angels; Garden Valley, St. Jude.

Ferdinand, Idaho Co., Assumption, Rev. Canisius Hayes, S.T., Admin.
Mailing Address: P.O. Box 112, 83526. Tel: 208-962-5220.
Catechesis/Religious Programs—Mary Jane Arnzen, D.R.E.
Students 42.

Garden Valley, Boise Co., St. Jude's. See Sacred Heart, Emmett for details.

Genesee, Latah Co., St. Mary, Rev. Robert Finucane.
Res., 138 N. Jackson, P.O. Box 36, 83832. Tel: 208-285-1218.
Catechesis/Religious Programs—Eric Bennett, D.R.E.
Students 38.

Glenns Ferry, Elmore Co., Our Lady of Limerick, Revs. Raul R. Covarrubias, Admin.; Eugene Esch, O.S.B.
Res., 113 W. Arthur St., Box 216, 83623. Tel: 208-366-7721.
Catechesis/Religious Programs—Dixie Black, D.R.E.
Students 80.

Gooding, Gooding Co., St. Elizabeth's, Rev. Michael St. Marie.
Res., 1515 California St., Box 147, 83330. Tel: 208-934-5634.
Catechesis/Religious Programs—Christine Arkoosh, D.R.E.
Students 115.
Station—Wendell, St. Anthony's.

Grandview, Owyhee Co., St. Henry. See Our Lady of Good Counsel, Mountain Home for details.

Grangeville, Idaho Co., SS. Peter and Paul, Rev. William Dohman, J.C.L.
Res., 318 S. B St., 83530. Tel: 208-983-0403.
School—Tel: 208-983-2182. Rev. William Dohman, Acting Prin.
Lay Teachers 4; Students 70.
Catechesis/Religious Programs—Students 77.
Stations—Riggins, St. Jerome's; Elk City, Elk City Catholic Community.

Greencreek, Idaho Co., St. Anthony's, Rev. Canisius Hayes, S.T., Admin.
Res., Rte. 1, Box 90, 83533. Tel: 208-962-3565.
Catechesis/Religious Programs—Mary Jane Arnzen, D.R.E.
Students 73.

Hagerman, Gooding Co., St. Catherine's. See Immaculate Conception, Buhl for details.

Hailey, Blaine Co., St. Charles Borromeo, Revs. John W. Morgan, Admin.; Thomas F. Keller; Deacon Bill Mallory, (Retired).
Res., 311 S. 1st. Ave. E, Box 789, 83333. Tel: 208-788-3024; Fax: 208-788-0726.
Catechesis/Religious Programs—Students 124.
Stations—Fairfield, Immaculate Conception; Carey.

Homedale, Owyhee Co., St. Hubert, Rev. Donald D. Fraser.
Res., 115 E. Owyhee St., Box 186, 83628. Tel: 208-337-3153.
Catechesis/Religious Programs—Lynne Tiddens, D.R.E.
Students 140.
Station—Silver City, Our Lady of Tears.

Horseshoe Bend, Boise Co., Our Lady Queen of Angels. Closed. See Sacred Heart, Emmett for details.

Idaho City, Boise Co., St. Joseph's, Rev. Morse A. Later, Admin.
Res., 7225 Cascade Dr., Boise, 83704. Tel: 208-376-1940.

Idaho Falls, Bonneville Co., Holy Rosary, Revs. Gerald J. Funke; Calvin Blankinship, Jr.; Deacon Richard Kelso. In res., Rev. Nondier Zuleta.
Res., 228 Ninth St., Box 50899, 83405. Tel: 208-522-4366; Fax: 208-523-3827.
Office: 145 Ninth St., 83404.
School—161 Ninth St., 83404. Tel: 208-522-7781. Ellen Close, Prin.
Lay Teachers 9; Students 241.
Catechesis/Religious Programs—Denise Echiverri, D.R.E.
Students 600.
Stations—Roberts, St Anthony's; Mud Lake, St. Ann's.

Christ the King, Rev. Timothy L. O'Toole; Deacon James Goettsche.
Res., 1690 E. 17th St., 83404. Tel: 208-529-8170; Fax: 208-528-9164.
Catechesis/Religious Programs—Susan Clark, D.R.E.
Students 214.
Station—Shelley, Our Lady of Guadalupe.

Jerome, Jerome Co., St. Jerome's, Rev. Jesus Camacho; Deacon William Last.
Res., 216 2nd Ave. E., Box 169, 83338. Tel: 208-324-8794.
Catechesis/Religious Programs—Theresa May, D.R.E.
Students 225.

Kamiah, Lewis Co., St. Catherine's of Siena, Rev. George L. King.
Res., 407 7th St., Box 685, 83536. Tel: 208-935-2130; Fax: 208-935-2484.
Catechesis/Religious Programs—Students 35.
Station—Pierce, Our Lady of Woodland.

Kellogg, Shoshone Co., St. Rita's, Rev. Mel Sprute; Deacon Walt Jackson.
Res., 27 Kellogg Ave., 83837-2626. Tel: 208-784-7361.

Keuterville, Idaho Co., Holy Cross. Merged with St. Mary's, Cottonwood.

Lapwai, Nez Perce Co., Sacred Heart, Rev. James R. Wilson, Admin.
Res., 2015 13th Ave., P.O. Box 157, Lewiston, 83501. Tel: 208-843-2562; 743-6101; Fax: 208-743-5301.

Leadore, Lemhi Co., St. Joseph's Mission. See St. Charles, Salmon for details.

Lewiston, Nez Perce Co., St. Stanislaus, Rev. Sean Caulfield; Sr. Margie Schmidt, O.S.B., Pastoral Assoc.
Res., 633 5th Ave., 83501. Tel: 208-743-7331; Fax: 208-746-7134.
School—Tri-Parish School. Marcia Ney, Prin.
Sisters 1; Lay Teachers 6; Students 167.
Catechesis/Religious Programs—Students 80.

Our Lady of Lourdes, Rev. James R. Wilson.
Church & Res.—2015 13th Ave., 83501. Tel: 208-743-3238; 743-6101 (Church); Fax: 208-743-5301.
Catechesis/Religious Programs—Students 156.

St. James, Rev. William C. Crowley.
Office: 1519 Ripon Ave., 83501. Tel: 208-743-8231; Fax: 208-798-8407.
Catechesis/Religious Programs—Students 155.

McCall, Valley Co., Our Lady of the Lake, Rev. Len MacMillan; Deacon William Petzak.
Res., 501 Cross Rd., Box 821, 83638. Tel: 208-634-5474.
Stations—Cascade, St. John the Baptist; Council, St. Jude The Apostle.

Meridian, Ada Co., Holy Spirit, Rev. Timothy M. Ritchey.
Res., 828 W. Cherry Ln., Box 708, 83680. Tel: 208-888-1182; Fax: 208-884-1800.
Catechesis/Religious Programs—Jan Siron, D.R.E.
Students 214.

Moscow, Latah Co., St. Mary's, Rev. Joseph F. Schmidt.
Res., 618 E. First St., Box 9106, 83843. Tel: 208-882-4813.
School—412 N. Monroe, 83843. Tel: 208-882-2121. Sr. Margaret Johnson, O.S.U., Prin.
Lay Teachers 8; Students 166.
Kindergarten & Preschool, St. Rose—Owned by the Ursuline Nuns, affiliated with St. Mary's School. 412 N. Howard, 83843. Tel: 208-882-4014.
Catechesis/Religious Programs—Students 130.

St. Augustine's. (Catholic Center). Rev. Mark Schumacher; Deacon Verne Geidl.
Res., 628 Deakin St., Box 3457 University Sta., 83843. Tel: 208-882-4613.

Mountain Home Air Force Base, Elmore Co., St. Mary's, Rev. Richard P. Novotny, Chap.
Res., 366 Wing/HC, 420 Gunfighter Ave., 83648. Tel: 208-828-6417; Fax: 208-828-4570.

Mountain Home, Elmore Co., Our Lady of Good Counsel, Rev. Raul R. Covarrubias.
Res., 115 N. 4th St. E., Box 310, 83647. Tel: 208-587-3046; Fax: 208-587-6373.
Catechesis/Religious Programs—Barbara Faneuf, D.R.E.
Students 231.
Stations—Bruneau, St. Bridget; Grandview, St. Henry's.

Nampa, Canyon Co., St. Paul's, Revs. Alfred H. Puccinelli, S.M.; Paul Mathews, S.M.; Bros. Ernie Morasci, S.M.; Joseph Grima, S.M.; Rev. Thomas Kirk Clemens, S.M., (Retired).
Res., 1515 8th St. S., 83651. Tel: 208-466-7031; Fax: 208-467-6485.
School—Tel: 208-467-3601. Thomas Antonoplos, Prin.
Sisters 1; Lay Teachers 8; Students 181.
Catechesis/Religious Programs—Students 202.
Station—Melba, St. Joseph.

Our Lady of Guadalupe Parish, Rev. Carlos Perez, Admin.
Res., 1203 Seventh St. N., 83687. Tel: 208-467-6798; 467-5438; Fax: 208-467-6798.
Catechesis/Religious Programs—Hortencia Lemus, D.R.E.
Students 110.
Station—Oreana, Queen of Heaven.

New Plymouth, Payette Co., St. Aloysius, Rev. Gerald B. Dye; Sr. Mary Louise Deroin, C.S.C., Pastoral Assoc.
Res., 217 W. Elm, P.O. Box 377, 83655. Tel: 208-278-5802.
Catechesis/Religious Programs—Students 67.

Nezperce, Lewis Co., Holy Trinity, Rev. Kenneth Arnzen.
Res., 506 Willow St., Box 65, 83543. Tel: 208-937-2300.
Catechesis/Religious Programs—Students 57.

Oreana, Owyhee Co., Queen of Heaven. See Our Lady of Guadalupe, Nampa for details.

Orofino, Clearwater Co., St. Theresa's, Rev. George L. King.
Res., 446 Brown Ave., Box 1169, 83544. Tel: 208-476-5121.
Catechesis/Religious Programs—Students 43.

Parma, Canyon Co., Sacred Hearts of Jesus and Mary, Rev. Donald D. Fraser, Admin.
Mailing Address: P.O. Box 777, 83660.
Res., 101 E. Owyhee St., P.O. Box 186, Homedale, 83628. Tel: 208-337-3153.
Catechesis/Religious Programs—Students 88.

Payette, Payette Co., Holy Family, Rev. Gerald B. Dye, Admin.; Sr. Mary Louise Deroin, C.S.C., Pastoral Assoc.
Res., 1212 First Ave. S., P.O. Box 818, 83661. Tel: 208-642-2261.
Catechesis/Religious Programs—Students 55.

Pocatello, Bannock Co., St. Joseph's, Rev. Steven Rukavina.
Res., 455 N. Hays, P.O. Box 757, 83204. Tel: 208-232-1470; Fax: 208-232-0586.
Catechesis/Religious Programs—Kathryn Brokaw, D.R.E.
Students 85.

St. Anthony's, Very Rev. Joseph McDonald, III, Admin.; Deacon Mel Hardy.
Res., 524 N. 7th Ave., Box 4188, 83205. Tel: 208-232-1196; Fax: 208-234-1624.
School—540 N. 7th Ave., 83205. Tel: 208-232-5763. Andy Marincic, Prin.
Lay Teachers 8; Students 171.
Catechesis/Religious Programs—Ann Hysell, D.R.E.
Students 160.

St. John's Community, Very Rev. Joseph McDonald, III; Deacon Richard Bonney.
Res., 920 E. Lovejoy St., I.S.U., Box 8129, 83209. Tel: 208-233-0880; Fax: 208-233-5745.

Post Falls, Kootenai Co., St. George's, Rev. William Gould.
Res., 2004 N. William St., Box 10, 83854-0010. Tel: 208-773-4715.
Catechesis/Religious Programs—Valerie Clapper, D.R.E.
Students 151.

Potlatch, Latah Co., St. Mary's, Rev. Mark R. Schumacher, Admin.
Res., 628 Deakin Ave., Box 3457 University Sta., Moscow, 83843. Tel: 208-882-4613.

Priest River, Bonner Co., St. Catherine's, Rev. Dennis Day; Sr. Jane Kelly, S.N.J.M., Admin.
Res., 206 Summit Blvd., Box 445, 83856. Tel: 208-448-2127.
Catechesis/Religious Programs—Students 16.
Station—Priest Lake, St. Blanche.

Rathdrum, Kootenai Co., St. Stanislaus, Rev. Michael S. Scarcello.
Res., W. 3500 Scarcello Rd., 83858. Tel: 208-687-0788.
Catechesis/Religious Programs—D.R.E.: Mr. Paul Franz; Mrs. Beth Franz.
Students 80.
Station—Spirit Lake, St. Joseph's.

Rupert, Minidoka Co., St. Nicholas, Rev. Henry Carmona; Deacon Pete Rodriquez.
Res., 802 F St., Box 115, 83350. Tel: 208-436-3781.
School—P.O. Box 26, 83350. Tel: 208-436-6320. Sandee Schwan Nelson, Prin.
Lay Teachers 5; Students 145.
Catechesis/Religious Programs—Angelita Ortega, D.R.E.
Students 206.

St. Anthony, Fremont Co., Mary Immaculate, Rev. Paul H. Wander.
Res., 328 W. First N., Box 527, 83445. Tel: 208-624-7459.
Catechesis/Religious Programs—Mrs. Jeanne Fischer, D.R.E.
Students 90.
Stations—Rexburg, St. Patrick's; Driggs, Good Shepherd; Island Park, Chapel of the Pines.

Saint Maries, Benewah Co., St. Mary's, Rev. William Taylor.
Res., 921 Jefferson St., Box 335, 83861. Tel: 208-245-2977.
Catechesis/Religious Programs—Kelly Pugh, D.R.E.
Students 80.
Station—Harrison, Our Lady of Perpetual Help.

Salmon, Lemhi Co., St. Charles, Revs. Richard S. Haldane; Anthony DiLoreto; Peter Bourne.
Res., 505 Hope Ave., 83467. Tel: 208-756-2432.
Catechesis/Religious Programs—Mary Vander Schaaf, D.R.E.
Students 150.
Stations—Leadore, St. Joseph; Arco, St. Ann; Challis, St. Louise; Mackay, St. Barbara.

Sandpoint, Bonner Co., St. Joseph's, Rev. Dennis C. Day; Deacon Ralph Arndt, (Retired).
Res., 621 Oak St., P.O. Box 279, 83864-0279. Tel: 208-263-3720; Fax: 208-265-4974.
Catechesis/Religious Programs—Irene Sundquist, D.R.E.
Students 175.
Station—Clark Fork, Sacred Heart.

Shoshone, Lincoln Co., St. Peter's, Rev. Michael St. Marie; Deacon Dee Aslett.
Res., 215 W. B St., Box 336, 83352. Tel: 208-886-2002; 934-5634; Fax: 208-886-2030.
Catechesis/Religious Programs—Students 26.

Soda Springs, Caribou Co., St. Mary's, Rev. John Worster.
Res., 99 W. Center, 83276. Tel: 208-547-3200.
Stations—Montpelier, Blessed Sacrament; Malad City, St. Paul's; Preston, St. Peter's; Lava Hot Springs, Our Lady of Lourdes.

Sun Valley, Blaine Co., Our Lady of the Snows, Rev. John W. Morgan.
Res., Sun Valley Rd., Box 1650, 83353. Tel: 208-622-3432; Fax: 208-622-4348.
Catechesis/Religious Programs—Pam Ritzau, D.R.E.
Students 89.
Station—Stanley. (Summer).

Twin Falls, Twin Falls Co., St. Edward's, Rev. Robb Keller; Deacons John McKinley; Lloyd LeClair; Robert Sass.
Res., 152 7th Ave., E., 83301-6319. Tel: 208-733-3907; Fax: 208-733-3935.
School—Tel: 208-734-3872. Margaret Peck, Prin.
Lay Teachers 9; Students 167.
Catechesis/Religious Programs—Jean Thompson, D.R.E.
Students 275.

Our Lady of Guadalupe, Rev. Thomas Loucks.
Res., 630 Falls Ave., 83301-3300. Tel: 208-734-2327; 734-4145; Fax: 208-734-4145.

Wallace, Shoshone Co., St. Alphonsus, Rev. Mel Sprute; Deacon Walt Jackson.
Res., 214 Pine St., Box 970, 83873. Tel: 208-752-3551.
Station—Mullan, St. Michael's.

Weiser, Washington Co., St. Agnes, Rev. Xavier Aresseril; Deacon Francis Wander.
Res., 214 E. Liberty, P.O. Box 87, 83672. Tel: 208-549-0088.
Catechesis/Religious Programs—Leslie Moser, D.R.E.
Students 112.
Station—Cambridge, Holy Rosary.

Wendell, Gooding Co., St. Anthony's. See St. Elizabeth's, Gooding for details.

Chaplains of Public Institutions

BOISE. *Chateau de Boise Retirement Center.* 7250 Poplar St., 83704. Tel: 208-372-0257. Rev. Patrick Russell.

Elks Rehabilitation. Attended by St. John Cathedral, 804 N. 9th St., Boise, ID, 83702. Tel: 208-342-3511. Vacant. 204 Fort Pl., 83702.

St. Luke's Medical Center. Attended by St. John Cathedral, 804 N. 9th St., Boise, ID, 83702. Tel: 208-342-3511. Vacant. 190 E. Bannock, 83712.

VA Hospital. Attended by St. John Cathedral, 804 N. 9th St., Boise, ID, 83702. Tel: 208-342-3511. Vacant. 5th St. & Fort St., 83401.

COTTONWOOD. *Monastery of St. Gertrude.* HC 3 Box 121, 83522. Tel: 208-962-3574. Rev. Liam Davitt.

On Special Assignment:
Reverend Monsignors—
Falk, Dennis G., Vicar Gen. & Moderator of the Curia

On Duty Outside the Diocese:
Reverend Fathers—
Dennis, Patrick, FCI Tucson, 8901 S. Wilmot Rd., Tucson, AZ 85706
Dolan, Raymond, Box 217-MH Station, Staten Island, NY 10303
Faucher, W. Thomas, St. Edward's, 68817 Trinity Way, P.O. Box 489, Sisters, OR 97759
Harlow, Francis G., 177 107th N.E., Ste 1019, Bellevue, WA 98004
Jaramillo, Oscar, Parroquia San Marcos, A.A. 5109, Cali, Valle Columbia, S.A.
Pu, Matthew, Holy Family, 685 N. Fairview, Burns, OR 97720
Segatta, Bruno, Gonzaga in Florence, Palazzo Antinori No. 3, Florence, Italy
Stravinskas, Peter, 15 E. 26th St., Bayonne, NJ 07105
Wekerle, Ronald, Parroquia San Marcos, A.A. 5109, Cali, Valle Columbia, S.A.

Absent on Sick Leave:
Reverend Fathers—
Legerski, John

Leave of Absence:
Reverend Fathers—
Mathes, Thomas

Retired:
Reverend Monsignors—
Hallissey, James T., Galena Ct., Box 370, Mountain Home, ID 83647
Hughes, Nicholas V., Rosemount, Kilkenny, Co. Johnston, Ireland Ireland
Later, Morse, 7225 Cascade Dr., Boise, ID 83704
Peplinski, Raymond J., P.A., 322 S. Manville St., Boise, ID 83705
Simmons, Donald W., 2612 E. 44th St., Spokane, WA 99223
Reverend Fathers—
Carroll, William, 569 Fairview Dr., Hamilton, MT 59840
Daws, Dominic, 215 W. Heyburn Ave., Twin Falls, ID 83301
Dodds, Perry W., P.O. Box 264, Twin Falls, ID 83303
Dodgson, William, 2852 N. Rosedale, Boise, ID 83704
Dulberg, Albert V., Box 943, Post Falls, ID 83854
Gebhardt, Joseph M., 3060 S.E. Stark St., Portland, OR 97214
Grant, Robert H., One Haven Dr., Andover, MA 01810
Hebert, Francis, Rte. 2, Box 2018, Heppner, OR 97836
Hughes, Martin F., Rosemount, Kilkenny, Co. Johnston, Ireland Ireland
Lustig, Victor Joseph, Rte. 1, Box 109A, Cottonwood, ID 83522
McGoldrick, John T., 106 N. 12th St., #4C, Payette, ID 83661
McNeill, Malachy, 6 Dublin Rd., Drogheda, Co. Louth, Ireland
O'Donovan, Timothy John, Box 266, Hope, ID 83836
O'Sullivan, John, 700 E. Fairview, #116, Meridian, ID 83642
Peterson, Francis A., 107 20th Ave. S., Nampa, ID 83651
Riffle, Douglas H., P.O. Box 456, Meridian, ID 83642
Shimmaly, Edward E., P.O. Box 148, Eagle, ID 83616
Shinnick, James F., 1520 N. Fillmore, Jerome, ID 83338
Spegele, Michael A., P.O Box 23, Keuterville, ID 83538
Steinhoff, Henry, P.O. Box 626, Eureka, MT 59917
Waldmann, Robert J., P.O. Box 112, Ferdinand, ID 83526

Permanent Deacons:
Arndt, Ralph, (Retired)
Aslett, Devon H., St. Peter, Shoshone
Bonney, Richard James, II, St. John's, Pocatello
Bowen, James E., St. Mark, Boise
Dessert, Michael, Our Lady of the Rosary, Boise
Eisenbeiss, Michael, Risen Christ Catholic Community, Boise
Flager, Ralph, St. Matthew, Eagle
Geidl, Verne, St. Augustine Catholic Center, Moscow
Goettsche, James, Christ the King, Idaho Falls
Halstrom, Eugene, Our Lady of the Rosary, Boise
Hardy, Melvin, St. Anthony's, Pocatello
Henning, Richard, St. John Cathedral, Boise
Hiner, Kenneth, St. John Cathedral, Boise
Jackson, Walter, St. Alphonsus, Wallace
Kelly, James, Sacred Heart, Boise
Kelso, Richard, Holy Rosary, Idaho Falls
Kreilcamp, Ben, (Retired)
Last, William, St. Jerome, Jerome
Le Clair, Lloyd, St. Edward, Twin Falls
Mallory, William, (Retired)
McKinley, John D., Jr., St. Edward, Twin Falls
McNamara, Francis, St. Mary, American Falls
McSwain, Gary, St. Pius X, Coeur d'Alene
Petzak, William, Our Lady of the Lake, McCall
Pierce, Ralph, St. Mark, Boise
Rodriguez, Pete, St. Nicholas, Rupert
Sass, Robert, St. Edward, Twin Falls
Shaber, Alan, Sacred Heart, Boise
Solbrig, Charles W., Idaho Falls
Wander, Francis, St. Agnes, Weiser

INSTITUTIONS LOCATED IN THE DIOCESE

[A] HIGH SCHOOLS, INTER-PAROCHIAL

BOISE. *Bishop Kelly High School,* 7009 Franklin Rd., 83709-0998. Tel: 208-375-6010; Fax: 208-375-3626. Dr. David Lachiondo, Prin. Lay Teachers 46; Students 712.

COEUR D'ALENE. *Holy Family Catholic School of Coeur d'Alene,* 406 N. Tenth, 83814. Tel: 208-765-4327. Barbara Dettlaff, Prin. Lay Teachers 3; Students 62.

[B] GENERAL HOSPITALS

BOISE. *St. Alphonsus Regional Medical Center, Inc.,* 1055 N. Curtis Rd., 83706. Tel: 208-378-2121.
For a complete listing, refer to the Hospitals section.

COTTONWOOD. *St. Mary's Hospital,* 83522. Tel: 208-962-3251; Fax: 208-962-3722.
For a complete listing, refer to the Hospitals section.

JEROME. *St. Benedict Family Medical Center,* 709 N. Lincoln, 83338. Tel: 208-324-4301.
For a complete listing, refer to the Hospitals section.

LEWISTON. *St. Joseph Regional Medical Center,* 415 6th St., P.O. Box 816, 83501. Tel: 208-743-2511.
For a complete listing, refer to the Hospitals section.

NAMPA. *Mercy Medical Center,* 1512 12th Avenue Rd., 83686. Tel: 208-467-1171.
For a complete listing, refer to the Hospitals section.

[C] MONASTERIES AND RESIDENCES OF PRIESTS AND BROTHERS

JEROME. *Ascension Priory,* 541 East, 100 South, 83338. Tel: 208-324-2377. Order of St. Benedict. Revs. Boniface Lautz, O.S.B., Prior; Meinrad Schallberger, O.S.B., Subprior; Jude Anderson, O.S.B.; Andrew Baumgartner, O.S.B.; Hugh Feiss, O.S.B.; Joel Kehoe, O.S.B.; Joseph Wood, O.S.B.; Eugene Esch, O.S.B.; Simeon VanDeVoord, O.S.B.; Bros. Sylvester Sonnen, O.S.B.; Tobiah Urrutia, O.S.B.; Kevin McMullen, O.S.B.; Inigo Echanove, O.S.B.

LEMHI. *Hermitage of St. Joseph,* Box 37, 83465. Hermits of Mt. Carmel. Rev. Peter Bourne, H.M.C., Prior; Bro. Maurice Mansfield, H.M.C.

[D] CONVENTS AND RESIDENCES OF SISTERS

BOISE. *St. Alphonsus Regional Medical Center Convent-Sisters of Holy Cross,* 2480 N. Westminster Ln., 83704. Tel: 208-367-2121. 8650 W. Rifleman St., Apt. D104, 83704. Tel: 208-323-0019. 217 W. Elm St., P.O. Box 377, New Plymouth, 83655. Tel: 208-278-5802. Legal Title: *Sisters of the Holy Cross, Inc.* Sisters 5.

COTTONWOOD. *Monastery of St. Gertrude, Motherhouse and Novitiate,* HC3 Box 121, 83522-9408. Tel: 208-962-3224; Fax: 208-962-7212. Sr. Mary Kay Henry, O.S.B., Prioress; Sr. Barbara Jean Glodowski, O.S.B., Subprioress. Sisters of St. Benedict 90.

MESA. *Marymount Hermitage, Inc., Hermit Sisters of Mary,* 2150 Hermitage Ln., 83643. Tel: 208-256-4354 (msg. only). Sr. Rebecca Mary Bonnell, H.S.M., Supr. Sisters 2.

[E] RETREAT HOUSES

BOISE. *Nazareth,* 4450 N. Five Mile Rd., 83713. Tel: 208-375-2932; Fax: 208-376-5787. Sr. Grayce E. Ross, S.N.J.M., Exec. Dir.; Board of Directors: Mr. James Ballantyne; Mr. Cornelius O'Keefe; Mrs. Greta Pate; Rev. Joseph DaSilva.

[F] CAMPUS MINISTRY

BOISE. *Boise State University, St. Paul's Catholic Center,* 1915 University Dr., 83706. Tel: 208-343-2128. Sr. David Hartse, O.S.J., Dir.

CALDWELL. *Albertson's College of Idaho,* c/o St. Mary, 616 Dearborn, Box 399, 83606. Rev. Enrique Terriquez.

COEUR D'ALENE. *North Idaho College,* St Pius X, 625 E. Haycraft, 83814. Tel: 208-765-5108. Rev. Roger LaChance.

LEWISTON. *Lewis and Clark State College,* St. Stanislaus, 633 5th Ave., 83501. Tel: 208-743-7331. Rev. Sean Caulfield.

MOSCOW. *University of Idaho, St. Augustine Catholic Center,* 628 Deakin, Box 3457, University Sta., 83843. Tel: 208-882-4613. Rev. Mark Schumacher.

POCATELLO. *Idaho State University, St. John's Community,* 920 E. Lovejoy, I.S.U. Box 8129, 83209. Tel: 208-233-0880; Fax: 208-233-5745. Rev. Joseph F. McDonald, III, Campus Min.

TWIN FALLS. *College of Southern Idaho.* Attended by Our Lady of Guadalupe, Twin Falls. 630 Falls Ave., P.O. Box 203, 83303. Tel: 208-734-2327. Rev. Thomas J. Loucks.

[G] MISCELLANEOUS

BOISE. *St. Francis of Assisi Conference, St. Vincent de Paul,* 6464 W. State St., 83703. Tel: 208-853-4921; Fax: 208-853-4935. Charles Nilles, Exec. Dir.

St. Vincent de Paul Society. St. John's Conference. 3717 Ticonderoga, 83706. Tel: 208-344-0702. Margo Henning, Pres.

BLACKFOOT. *St. Vincent de Paul Thrift Store,* 206 S. Spruce, 83221. Tel: 208-785-0353; 785-0423. Charles Belnap, Pres.

CALDWELL. *Society of St. Vincent de Paul,* 3719 E. Cleveland Blvd., 83605. Tel: 208-454-2132. Jerry Phillips, Store Mgr.

COEUR D'ALENE. *St. Vincent de Paul Store.* St. Thomas Conference. 108 E. Walnut, 83814. Tel: 208-664-3095; Fax: 208-664-1772. Lynn Peterson, Mgr.

IDAHO FALLS. *St. Vincent de Paul Society,* 184 First St., 83404. Tel: 208-528-9979. Jack Crane, Mgr.

KELLOGG. *Society of St. Vincent de Paul,* 104 E. Riverside, 83837. Tel: 208-783-5551. Jim Koskimaki, Conference Pres.; Terry Davis, Mgr.

LEWISTON. *Lewis and Clark District Council of St. Vincent de Paul,* 3138 5th St., 83501. Tel: 208-746-7860. Collen Stevens, Pres.; Kathie McConnell, Store Mgr.

MERIDIAN. *St. Vincent Thrift Store,* 213 E. First St., 83642. Tel: 208-888-9101. Charles Nilles, Exec. Dir.

MOUNTAIN HOME. *Our Lady of Good Counsel Conference, St. Vincent de Paul Society,* 115 N. 4th East St., 83647. Tel: 208-587-3046. Monique Drauszewski, Pres.

NAMPA. *Mercy Housing Idaho, Inc.,* 1512 12th Avenue Rd., 83686. Tel: 208-463-5858; Fax: 208-463-5859. Christina Martel, Pres.
Mercy Properties II, Inc.
Mercy Affordable Housing, Inc.
Mercy Housing Idaho Properties, Inc.
Mercy Twin Falls, Inc.
Mercy Moscow, Inc., 1512 12th Avenue Rd., 83686. Tel: 208-463-5858; Fax: 208-463-5859. Christina Martel, Pres.
Mercy Southeast Idaho, Inc., 1512 12th Avenue Rd., 83686. Tel: 208-463-5858; Fax: 208-463-5859. Christina Martel, Pres.

POCATELLO. *Port Neuf Valley (St. Vincent de Paul),* P.O. Box 2553, 83206-2553. Tel: 208-233-2555. Geraldine Cde Baca, Store Mgr.

TWIN FALLS. *Catholic Social Services, Inc. (St. Vincent de Paul),* 244 Main Ave. S., 83301. Tel: 208-734-9143. Mary Nutting, Pres.; Rick Mesaros, Store Mgr.

RELIGIOUS INSTITUTES OF MEN REPRESENTED IN THE DIOCESE

For further details refer to the corresponding bracketed number in the Religious Institutes of Men or Women section.

[0200]—*Benedictine Monks.* (Oregon).—O.S.B.

[0690]—*Jesuit Fathers.* (Oregon Prov.).—S.J.

[]—*Misionary Oblates.*—O.M.I.

[0840]—*Missionary Servants of the Most Holy Trinity.*—S.T.

[1070]—*Redemptorist Fathers.*—C.SS.R.

[0760]—*Society of Mary.* (San Francisco Western Prov.).—S.M.

RELIGIOUS INSTITUTES OF WOMEN REPRESENTED IN THE DIOCESE

[0230]—*Benedictine Sisters of Pontifical Jurisdiction.*—O.S.B.

[1920]—*Congregation of the Sisters of the Holy Cross.*—C.S.C.

[1780]—*Congregation of the Sisters of the Third Order of St. Francis of Perpetual Adoration.*—F.S.P.A.

[1070-21]—*Dominican Sisters.*—O.P.

[]—*Hermit Sisters of Mary.*—H.S.M.

[1250]—*Institute of the Franciscan Sisters of the Eucharist.*—F.S.E.

[2575]—*Institute of the Sisters of Mercy of the Americas.*—R.S.M.

[3340]—*Sisters of Providence.*—S.P.

[3830]—*Sisters of St. Joseph.*—C.S.J.

[1990]—*Sisters of the Holy Names.*—S.N.J.M.

[]—*Society of Sisters of the Church.*—S.S.C.

[4110]—*Ursuline Nuns.* (Western Prov.).—O.S.U.

NECROLOGY

✠ Treinen, Most Rev. Sylvester William, (Retired). —Died Sept. 30, 1996.

Archdiocese of Boston

(Archidioecesis Bostoniensis)

Most Reverend

LAWRENCE J. RILEY, D.D., S.T.D., LL.D.

Auxiliary Bishop Emeritus of Boston and Titular Bishop of Daimlaig; ordained September 21, 1940; appointed December 7, 1971; ordained Bishop February 2, 1972. *Res., 43 Maple St., Hyde Park, MA, 02136.*

Most Reverend

JOHN R. McNAMARA, D.D.

Auxiliary Bishop of Boston and Titular Bishop of Risinium; ordained January 10, 1952; appointed April 14, 1992; ordained Bishop May 21, 1992. *Res., 220 Pawtucket St., Lowell, MA, 01854. Office: 70 Lawrence St., Lowell, MA, 01852.*

Most Reverend

JOHN P. BOLES, D.D., ED.D.

Auxiliary Bishop of Boston and Titular Bishop of Nova Sparsa; ordained February 2, 1955; appointed April 14, 1992; ordained Bishop May 21, 1992. *Res., 2223 Dorchester Ave., Dorchester, MA, 02124. Office: 307 Bowdoin St., Dorchester, MA, 02122.*

Most Reverend

JOHN B. McCORMACK

Auxiliary Bishop of Boston and Titular Bishop of Cerbali; ordained February 2, 1960; appointed November 21, 1995; ordained Bishop December 27, 1995.

His Eminence

BERNARD CARDINAL LAW, D.D.

Archbishop of Boston; ordained May 21, 1961; appointed Bishop of Springfield-Cape Girardeau October 22, 1973; ordained Bishop December 5, 1973; promoted Boston January 24, 1984; installed March 23, 1984; Created Cardinal Priest, May 25, 1985. *Res., 2101 Commonwealth Ave., Boston, MA, 02135.*

Chancery Office: 2121 Commonwealth Ave., Brighton, MA, 02135. Tel.: 617-254-0100; Fax: 617-783-4564.

Web site address: http://www.rcab.org

Most Reverend

WILLIAM F. MURPHY

Auxiliary Bishop of Boston and Titular Bishop of Saia Maggiore; ordained December 14, 1964; appointed November 21, 1995; ordained Bishop December 27, 1995.

Most Reverend

FRANCIS XAVIER IRWIN

Auxiliary Bishop of Boston and Titular Bishop of Ubaza; ordained February 2, 1960; appointed July 24, 1996; ordained Bishop September 17, 1996.

Most Reverend

EMILIO S. ALLUE, S.D.B.

Auxiliary Bishop of Boston and Titular Bishop of Croe; ordained December 22, 1996; appointed July 24, 1996; ordained Bishop September 17, 1996.

ERECTED APRIL 8, 1808.

CREATED AN ARCHBISHOPRIC 1875.

Square Miles 2,465.

Comprises the Counties of Essex, Middlesex, Suffolk, Norfolk and Plymouth in the State of Massachusetts, the towns of Mattapoisett, Marion and Wareham excepted.

For legal titles of parishes and archdiocesan institutions, consult the Chancery Office.

STATISTICAL OVERVIEW

Personnel	
Cardinal	1
Auxiliary Bishops	6
Retired Bishops	1
Abbots	1
Priests: Diocesan Active in Diocese	633
Priests: Active Outside Diocese	69
Priests: Retired, Sick or Absent	275
Number of Diocesan Priests	977
Religious Priests in Diocese	752
Extern Priests in Diocese	22
Ordinations:	
Diocesan Priests	10
Permanent Deacons	17
Permanent Deacons in Diocese	187
Total Brothers	183
Total Sisters	3,154
Parishes	
Parishes	394
With Resident Pastor:	
Resident Diocesan Priests	355
Resident Religious Priests	33
Without Resident Pastor:	
Administered by Priests	6
Professional Ministry Personnel:	
Sisters	76
Lay Ministers	47
Welfare	
Catholic Hospitals	8
Total Assisted	79,676
Residential Care of Children	2
Total Assisted	469
Day Care and Extended Day Care Centers	9
Total Assisted	1,917
Specialized Homes	18
Total Assisted	1,630
Special Centers for Social Services	45
Total Assisted	136,651
Residential Care of Disabled	5
Total Assisted	168
Other Institutions	3
Total Assisted	22,906
Educational	
Seminaries, Diocesan	3
Students from This Diocese	59
Students from Other Diocese	108
Seminaries, Religious	3
Students Religious	167
Total Seminarians	226
Colleges and Universities	9
Total Students	21,657
High Schools, Diocesan and Parish	17
Total Students	5,209
High Schools, Private	19
Total Students	9,749
Elementary Schools, Diocesan and Parish	119
Total Students	35,674
Elementary Schools, Private	11
Total Students	2,686
Catechesis/Religious Education:	
High School Students	28,859
Elementary Students	122,350
Total Students Under Catholic Instruction	226,410
Teachers in the Diocese:	
Priests	24
Brothers	37
Sisters	369
Lay Teachers	2,866
Vital Statistics	
Receptions into the Church:	
Infant Baptism Totals	26,728
Adult Baptism Totals	3,346
Received into Full Communion	316
First Communions	22,970
Confirmations	13,273
Marriages:	
Catholic	7,385
Interfaith	1,988
Total Marriages	9,373
Deaths	18,952
Total Catholic Population	2,024,039
Total Population	3,793,058

Former Bishops—Most Rev. JOHN LEFEVRE DE CHEVERUS, ord. Dec. 18, 1790; appt. first Bishop of Boston, Apr. 8, 1808; cons. Nov. 1, 1810; transferred to Montauban, Jan. 15, 1823, thence to Bordeaux, Oct. 2, 1826; appt. Cardinal Archbishop of Bordeaux, Oct. 2, 1826; died July 19, 1836.—Most Rev. BENEDICT J. FENWICK, S.J., ord. June 11, 1808; appt. second Bishop of Boston, May 10, 1825; cons. Nov. 1, 1825; died Aug. 11, 1846.—Most Rev. JOHN BERNARD FITZPATRICK, ord. June 13, 1840; appt. Titular Bishop of Callipolis and Coadjutor of Boston, Nov. 21, 1843; cons. March 24, 1844; appt. third Bishop of Boston, Aug. 11, 1846; died Feb. 13, 1866.—Most Rev. JOHN JOSEPH WILLIAMS, D.D., ord. May 17, 1845; appt. Titular Bishop of Tripolis and Coadjutor of Boston, Jan. 8, 1866; appt. fourth Bishop of Boston, March 11, 1866; created first Archbishop of Boston, Feb. 12, 1875; died Aug. 30, 1907.—His Eminence WILLIAM CARDINAL O'CONNELL, ord. June 7, 1884; appt. third Bishop of Portland, Maine, Feb. 8, 1901; cons. May 19, 1901; appt. Titular Archbishop of Constantia and Coadjutor with right of succession to the Archbishop of Boston, Feb. 8, 1906; appt. fifth Bishop and second Archbishop of Boston, April 30, 1907; created Cardinal, Nov. 27, 1911; died April 22, 1944.—His Eminence RICHARD CARDINAL CUSHING, ord. May 26, 1921; appt. Titular Bishop of Mela and Auxiliary of Boston, June 10, 1939; cons. June 29, 1939; appt. sixth Bishop and third Archbishop of Boston, Sept. 25, 1944; created and proclaimed Cardinal Priest under the title of St. Susanna in the Consistory of December 15, 1958; died Nov. 2, 1970.—His Eminence HUMBERTO CARDINAL MEDEIROS, ord. June 15, 1946; appt. second Bishop of Brownsville, April 14, 1966; cons. June 9, 1966; appt. seventh Bishop and fourth Archbishop of Boston, Sept. 8, 1970; created and proclaimed Cardinal Priest under the title of St. Susanna in the Consistory of March 5, 1973; died Sept. 17, 1983.

Regional Bishops—Central Region: Most Rev. JOHN P. BOLES, D.D., Ed.D., Bishop's Office: *307 Bowdoin St., Dorchester, 02122-2245.* Tel: 617-436-3113; Fax: 617-436-7619. South Region: Most Rev. JOHN B. MCCORMACK, D.D., M.S.W., Bishop's Office: *236 Pleasant St., Weymouth, 02190-2599.* Tel: 617-337-4413; Fax: 617-337-3625. Merrimack Region: Most Rev. JOHN R. MCNAMARA, D.D., Bishop's Office: *70*

Lawrence St., Lowell, 01852-2697. Tel: 508-459-4082; Fax: 508-452-5584. West Region: Most Rev. EMILIO S. ALLUE, D.D., S.T.B., S.T.L., Ph.D., Bishop's Office: *558 South Ave., Weston, 02193.* Tel: 617-647-4179; Fax: 617-894-4262. North Region: Most Rev. FRANCIS X. IRWIN, D.D., A.S.C.W., Bishop's Office: *55 Lynn Shore Dr., Lynn, 01902.* Tel: 617-592-7633.

Vicars General—Most Rev. JOHN R. MCNAMARA, D.D.; Most Rev. JOHN P. BOLES, D.D.; Most Rev. JOHN B. MCCORMACK, D.D.; Most Rev. FRANCIS X. IRWIN; Most Rev. EMILIO S. ALLUE, S.D.B.; Most Rev. WILLIAM F. MURPHY.

Vicars—CENTRAL REGION: Vicariate I: Very Rev. CHARLES J. BOURQUE, V.F., *Our Lady of Lourdes Rectory, Jamaica Plain.* Tel: 617-524-0434. Vicariate II: Very Rev. THOMAS CONWAY, V.F., *St. Margaret Rectory, Dorchester.* Tel: 617-436-5327. Vicariate III: Very Rev. ALBERT J. SALLESE, V.F., *Sacred Heart Rectory, East Boston.* Tel: 617-567-5776. Vicariate IV: Very Rev. PETER J. CASEY, V.F., *St. Ann Rectory, Somerville.* Tel: 617-625-1904. *SOUTH REGION: Brockton Vicariate: Very Rev.* JOSEPH F. MANNING, V.F., *Our Lady of Lourdes Rectory, Brockton.* Tel: 508-586-4715. Norwood Vicariate:; Vacant, *Blessed Sacrament Rectory, Walpole.* Tel: 508-668-4700. Plymouth Vicariate: Very Rev. JOHN MARK HANNON, V.F., *St. Joseph the Worker Rectory, Hanson.* Tel: 617-293-3581. Quincy Vicariate: Very Rev. DANIEL M. GRAHAM, V.F., *St. Joseph Rectory, Quincy.* Tel: 617-472-6321. Weymouth Vicariate: Very Rev. JAMES J. RAFFERTY, V.F., *St. Paul Rectory, Hingham.* Tel: 617-749-0587. *WEST REGION: Framingham Vicariate: Very Rev.* FRANCIS V. STRAHAN, V.F., *St. Bridget Rectory, Framingham.* Tel: 508-875-5959. Marlboro Vicariate: Very Rev. ROBERT D. TYRRELL, V.F., *St. Julia Rectory, Weston.* Tel: 617-899-2611. Natick Vicariate: Very Rev. JOSEPH G. LIND, V.F., *St. Paul Rectory, Wellesley.* Tel: 617-235-1060. Newton Vicariate: Very Rev. ROBERT FICHTNER, V.F., *St. Patrick Rectory, Watertown.* Tel: 617-926-9680. *MERRIMACK REGION: Chelmsford Vicariate: Very Rev.* EDWARD P. GEARY, V.F., *St. Anne, Littleton.* Tel: 508-486-4100. Concord Vicariate: Very Rev. MARK S. SHEEHAN, V.F., *St. Michael Rectory, Bedford.* Tel: 617-275-6318. Haverhill Vicariate: Very Rev. EMILE GUILMETTE, S.M., V.F., *St. Joseph Rectory, Haverhill.* Tel: 508-372-7721. Lawrence Vicariate: Very Rev. GEORGE F. CARLSON, V.F., *St. Patrick Rectory, Lawrence.* Tel: 508-683-9416. Lowell Vicariate: Very Rev. JOHN W. HANELY, O.M.I., V.F., *Sacred Heart Rectory, Lowell.* Tel: 508-453-3962. *NORTH REGION: Gloucester Vicariate: Very Rev.* JOHN E. FARRELL, V.F., *Our Lady of the Assumption Rectory, Lynnfield.* Tel: 617-598-4313. Medford Vicariate: Very Rev. FRANCIS E. DALEY, V.F., *St. James the Apostle Rectory, Arlington.* Tel: 617-643-0636. Salem Vicariate: Rev. Msgr. JOHN P. MCDONOUGH, V.F., *St. John the Baptist Rectory, Peabody.* Tel: 508-531-0002. Stoneham Vicariate: Very Rev. VINCENT P. MELLONE, V.F., *St. Barbara Rectory, Woburn.* Tel: 617-933-4130.

Presbyteral Council—His Eminence BERNARD CARDINAL LAW, Pres.; Rev. RICHARD G. LENNON, Moderator. Membership: Most Rev. LAWRENCE J. RILEY; Most Rev. JOHN R. MCNAMARA; Most Rev. JOHN P. BOLES; Most Rev. WILLIAM F. MURPHY; Most Rev. JOHN B. MCCORMACK; Most Rev. FRANCIS X. IRWIN; Most Rev. EMILIO S. ALLUE, S.D.B.; Revs. ANDREW R. ALBERT, S.M.; FRANCISCO ANZOATEGUI, S.X.; ROBERT BOUFFIER, S.M.; EPHREM VU KIEM CUNG, C.M.C.; PETER V. CONLEY; ALBERT J. CONTONS; Rev. Msgr. ROBERT P. DEELEY; Revs. BRENNAN R. EGAN, O.F.M.; GEORGE P. EVANS; JOHN E. FARRELL; GERALD J. FITZGERALD; EDWARD P. GEARY; PETER G. GORI, O.S.A.; JAMES J. HARRINGTON; MICHAEL J. KALLOCK, C.S.P.; Rev. Msgr. FRANCIS D. KELLY; Revs. JOHN F. LEONARD; JAMES D. LYONS; RICHARD J. MALONE; Rev. Msgr. JOHN P. MCDONOUGH; Rev. Msgr. TIMOTHY J. MORAN, S.T.D.; Revs. JOHN F. MULLOY, JR.; FREDERICK J. MURPHY; JAMES O'BRIEN, S.S.C.; EDWARD M. O'FLAHERTY, S.J.; JOHN J. PHILBIN; PAUL A. PHINN; PRIMO PISCITELLO, O.F.M.; JOSEPH K. RAEKE; JOSEPH M. ROSSI; JOHN E. SASSANI; KEVIN M. SEPE; GREGORY SHORT, O.M.V.; JOHN P. SPENCER, S.J.; EUGENE P. SULLIVAN; VINCENT P. VON EUW; LEO WETZEL, O.M.I.

Finance Council—His Eminence BERNARD CARDINAL LAW, Pres. Membership: Most. Rev. WILLIAM F. MURPHY; REGINA E. CAINES; WILLIAM F. CONNELL; JOHN CUNNINGHAM; THOMAS FLATLEY; Sr. THERESE HIGGINS, C.S.J.; JOHN KANEB; PETER S. LYNCH; WILLIAM MCCALL; ROBERT MORRISSEY; GILES MOSHER, JR.; JOHN E. MCNIECE; GERALD T. REILLY; ANTONIO J. TAMBONE; HELEN VALERIO.

Archdiocesan College of Consultors—Most Rev. LAWRENCE J. RILEY; Most Rev. JOHN R. MCNAMARA; Most Rev. JOHN P. BOLES; Most Rev. WILLIAM F. MURPHY; Most Rev. JOHN B. MCCORMACK; Most Rev. FRANCIS X. IRWIN; Most Rev. EMILIO S. ALLUE, S.D.B.; Revs. PETER G. GORI, O.S.A., J.C.D.; JOHN F. LEONARD; JOHN F. MULLOY, JR.

Vicar General and Moderator of the Curia—Most Rev. WILLIAM F. MURPHY, S.T.D., *2121 Commonwealth Ave., Brighton, 02135.* Tel: 617-254-0100; Fax: 617-783-2947.

Assistant to the Moderator of the Curia for Administrative Affairs—Rev. THOMAS J. DALY.

Assistant to the Moderator of the Curia for Canonical Affairs—Rev. RICHARD G. LENNON.

Office of Development—ROBERT X. CHANDLER, *2121 Commonwealth Ave., Brighton, 02135.* Tel: 617-254-0100; Fax: 617-783-6366.

Office of Planning and Research—Rev. ROBERT MCMILLAN, S.J., *2121 Commonwealth Ave., Brighton, 02135.* Tel: 617-254-0100; Fax: 617-254-6209.

Office of Propagation of the Faith—Rev. Msgr. ANDREW F. CONNELL, *49 Franklin St., Boston, 02110.* Tel: 617-542-1776; Fax: 617-542-1778.

Office of Holy Childhood Association—Rev. Msgr. ANDREW F. CONNELL, *49 Franklin St., Boston, 02110.* Tel: 617-542-1771; Fax: 617-542-1778.

Society of St. Peter the Apostle—Rev. Msgr. ANDREW F. CONNELL, *49 Franklin St., Boston, 02110.* Tel: 617-542-1771; Fax: 617-542-1778.

Synod Office—Rev. THOMAS J. DALY, Exec. Dir., *2121 Commonwealth Ave., Brighton, 02135.* Tel: 617-254-0100.

Cabinet Secretaries

Secretary for Pastoral Services—Rev. PAUL B. O'BRIEN, *2121 Commonwealth Ave., Brighton, 02135.* Tel: 617-254-0100; Fax: 617-254-6209.

Secretary for Education—Rev. RICHARD J. MALONE, *One Lake St., Brighton, 02135.* Tel: 617-254-4425; Fax: 617-782-0213.

Secretary for Community Relations—JOHN B. WALSH, *2121 Commonwealth Ave., Brighton, 02135.* Tel: 617-254-0100; Fax: 617-782-8358.

Secretary for Social Services—Dr. JOSEPH DOOLIN, *49 Franklin St., Boston, 02110.* Tel: 617-482-5440; Fax: 617-451-0337.

Secretary for Health Care Services—MICHAEL F. COLLINS, M.D., *736 Cambridge St., Brighton, 02135-2997.* Tel: 617-789-2500; Fax: 617-789-2124.

Secretary for Ministerial Personnel—Rev. PAUL E. MICELI, *2121 Commonwealth Ave., Brighton, 02135.* Tel: 617-254-0100; Fax: 617-783-2947.

Delegate for Religious—Sr. ROBERTA MARIE BROWN, C.S.J., *2121 Commonwealth Ave., Boston, 02135-3173.* Tel: 617-254-0100; Fax: 617-783-2947.

Secretary for Central Services—GERALD T. REILLY, C.P.A., *2121 Commonwealth Ave., Brighton, 02135;* Fax: 617-783-4564.

Chancery Office—2121 Commonwealth Ave., Brighton, 02135. Tel: 617-254-0100; Fax: 617-783-4564. Office Hours: Mon.-Fri. 9-5.

Chancellor—GERALD T. REILLY.

Archivist—ROBERT JOHNSON-LALLY. Tel: 617-254-1000; Fax: 617-783-5642.

Secretaries to the Cardinal and Master of Ceremonies—Rev. Msgr. PAUL B. MCINERNY; Revs. MICHAEL W. MACEWEN; RICHARD C. LENNON, Asst. Master of Ceremonies.

Metropolitan Tribunal—One Lake St., Brighton, 02135. Tel: 617-254-9150; Fax: 617-783-2423. Office Hours: Mon.-Fri. 9-5.

Judicial Vicar—Rev. Msgr. ROBERT P. DEELEY, J.C.D.

Associate Judicial Vicar—Rev. MICHAEL S. FOSTER, J.C.D.

Promotor of Justice—Rev. RICHARD G. CUNNINGHAM, J.C.D.

Defender of the Bond—Rev. JAMES G. BURKE, J.C.L.

Secretary to the Tribunal—Sr. MARY L. WALSH, S.N.D., M.A.

Diocesan Judges—Revs. DAVID P. BAILEY, J.C.L.; JAMES G. BURKE, J.C.L.; RODNEY J. COPP, J.C.L.; RICHARD G. CUNNINGHAM, J.C.D.; Rev. Msgr. ROBERT P. DEELEY, J.C.D.; Rev. MICHAEL S. FOSTER, J.C.D.; Rev. Msgr. PAUL B. MCINERNY, J.C.L.; Rev. JAMES A. O'DONOHOE, J.C.D.; Sr. MARGARET L. SULLIVAN, C.S.J., J.C.L.

Judge Auditor—Rev. JAMES W. DEADDER, S.T.D., Ph.D., J.D.

Court Advocates—Revs. PETER G. GORI, O.S.A., J.C.D.; JOSEPH M. HENNESSEY, J.C.L.

Advocates—Revs. JOSEPH A. ANTONELLIS; JAMES J. BARRY; ROBERT BRAUNREUTHER, S.J.; MICHAEL J. BOVA CONTI; JOHN E. BUCKLEY; RICHARD A. BUNTEL; JAMES M. CARROLL; PETER J. CASEY; DISMAS CENTRELLA, O.F.M.; HENRY G. CHAMBERS; WILLIAM D. COUGHLIN; JOHN A. DOOHER; PAUL J. FINEGAN; PAUL R. E. FRANCIS, J.C.B., S.T.D.; MICHAEL HARKINS; GEORGE G. HOGAN; FRANCIS H. KELLEY; THOMAS A. KOPP; JAMES F. LANERGAN; VICTOR C. LAVOIE; JOHN F. LEONARD; ANTONIO MEDEIROS; BRIAN F. MANNING; LEONARD T. MCGRATH; DENNIS J. NASON; PETER J. O'HARA, A.C.S.W.; JAMES E. O'LEARY; LEONARD F. O'MALLEY; GERALD J. OSTERMAN; PETER F. QUINN; THOMAS J. REILLY; FRANK J. SILVA; MARTIN J. WALSH; THOMAS J. WALSH; ROBERT A. WARD.

Psychological Consultants—Family Counseling & Guidance Centers, Inc., NEIL J. CRONIN, L.I.C.S.W., Clinical Dir. JOSEPH DOHERTY, Ed.D.; CHARLES J. FERRO, M.Ed.; MARGARET L. HAGER, L.I.C.S.W.; THOMAS F. HIGGINS, Ed.D.; CHARLES H. HOGAN, Psy.D.; FRANCIS J. KELLY, L.I.C.S.W., M.S.W.; HELEN O'MEARA, L.I.C.S.W.; CLAIRE O'ROURKE; MICHAEL ST. CLAIR, M.A., Ph.D.; JOSEPH LIFTIK, Ph.D.; THOMAS H. KELLEY, Ph.D.; KERNAN T. MANION, M.D.; PAUL MCCORMICK, M.Div., Ph.D.; A. EUGENE NEWMAN, Ph.D.; DANIEL J. QUINN, L.I.C.S.W.

Ecclesiastical Notary—LAURA M. CELLUCCI; M. CONNIE MURPHY.

Provincial Tribunal

Tribunal of Boston Province-Regional Matrimonial Appeal Court—2121 Commonwealth Ave., Brighton, 02135. Tel: 617-254-2772; Fax: 617-562-1104.

Judicial Vicar—Rev. DAVID P. BAILEY, J.C.L.

Associate Judicial Vicars and Defenders of the Bond—Most Rev. BERNARD J. FLANAGAN, S.T.L., J.C.D.; Rev. Msgr. DONALD J. GILBERT, JR.; Rev. Msgr. ROGER VIAU, J.C.D.; Rev. HENRY G. BOWEN, S.T.L., J.C.D.; Rev. Msgr. ROBERT P. DEELEY, J.C.D.; Revs. JAY T. MADDOCK, J.C.L.; PAUL F. STEFANKO, J.C.L.

Promoter of Justice—Rev. HENRY G. BOWEN, S.T.L., J.C.D.

Judges—(Boston); Revs. DAVID P. BAILEY, J.C.L.; DENNIS J. BURNS, J.C.D.; Rev. Msgr. ROBERT P. DEELEY, J.C.D.; Rev. MICHAEL S. FOSTER, J.C.D.; Rev. Msgr. PAUL B. MCINERNY, J.C.L.; Revs. JAMES A. O'DONOHOE, J.C.D., (Burlington): Revs. BERNARD F. DEPEAUX, S.T.B., M.A.; WALTER D. MILLER, J.C.D., (Fall River): Rev. Msgr. THOMAS J. HARRINGTON; Revs. GERARD HEBERT, J.C.L.; MARK R. HESSION, J.C.L.; THOMAS E. MCGLYNN, J.C.L.; Rev. JAY T. MADDOCK, J.C.L., (Manchester): Rev. Msgr. RAYMOND O. BLAIR, S.T.L., J.C.D.; Rev. Msgr. NORMAN P. BOLDUC, J.C.L.; Rev. Msgr. PAUL L. BOUCHARD, S.T.L., M.A., J.C.L.; Revs. FRANCIS L. DEMERS, O.M.I., J.C.D.; Rev. Msgr. DONALD J. GILBERT, J.C.L.; Sr. LOUISE TESSIER, P.M., J.C.L.; Rev. MICHAEL A. HENCHAL, J.C.L., (Portland): Rev. Msgr. RAYMOND F. BEGIN, J.C.D.; Rev. Msgr. VINCENT A. TATARCZUK, S.T.L., J.C.D.; Revs. JOSEPH J. KOURY, S.J., J.C.D.; MARK P. NOLETTE, J.C.L.; PAUL F. STEFANKO, J.C.L.; Sr. CLAUDIA BARBRE, R.S.M., J.C.L.; Sr. RITA-MAE BISSONNETTE, R.S.R., J.C.L.; Sr. ANN KEEVAN, C.S.J., J.C.D.; GEORGE G. PAVLOFF, J.C.D., (Springfield): Rev. Msgr. JOHN F. HARRINGTON, J.C.L.; Rev. Msgr. JOSEPH I. JOHNSON, J.C.D.; Rev. Msgr. ROGER VIAU, J.C.D.; Revs. HENRY KARWEL, O.F.M.Conv., J.C.L.; DANIEL P. LISTON, J.C.L.; JOHN P. MCDONAGH, J.C.L.; JOHN J. SHEA, S.T.L., J.C.D.; JOHN L. SULLIVAN, J.C.L.; ROBERT W. THRASHER, J.C.D., (Worchester): Most Rev. BERNARD J. FLANAGAN, S.T.L., J.C.D.; Revs. HENRY G. BOWEN, S.T.L., J.C.D.; BRIAN R. CORMIER, J.C.L.; PAUL T. O'CONNELL, J.C.D.; F. STEPHEN PEDONE.

Seminaries—

Pope John XXIII National Seminary—Rev. Msgr. FRANCIS D. KELLY, S.T.D., Rector, *558 South St., Weston, 02193.* Tel: 617-899-5500; Fax: 617-899-9057.

St. John's Seminary School of Theology—Rev. Msgr. TIMOTHY J. MORAN, S.T.D., Rector, *Lake St., Brighton, 02135.* Tel: 617-254-2610; Fax: 617-787-2336.

St. John's Seminary College of Liberal Arts—Rev. ROBERT W. FLAGG, S.T.L., Dean, *197 Foster St., Brighton, 02135.* Tel: 617-254-2610; Fax: 617-787-2336.

Continuing Education and Spiritual Enrichment of Priests—Rev. JOHN E. MACINNIS, *5 Lake St., Brighton, 02135.* Tel: 617-254-2610.

Pastoral Services

Pastoral Services—Rev. PAUL B. O'BRIEN, Cabinet Sec., *2121 Commonwealth Ave., Brighton, 02135.* Tel: 617-254-0100.

Black Catholics, Office for—MEYER CHAMBERS, *2121 Commonwealth Ave., Brighton, 02135.* Tel: 617-254-0100; Fax: 617-783-5642.

Charismatic Renewal—DAVID THORP, *20 Pond St., Waltham, 02154.* Tel: 617-891-3592; Fax: 617-891-3593.

Cursillo—Rev. ROBERT W. FLAGG, *St. John's Seminary, 127 Lake St., Brighton, 02135.* Tel: 617-254-2610.

Deaf Apostolate—Rev. MICHAEL J. MEDAS, *2121 Commonwealth Ave., Boston, 02135.* Tel: 617-254-0100.

Ethnic Apostolates—Rev. JOSEPH COGO, C.S., Coord., *Sacred Heart Parish, 12 North Square, Boston, 02113.* Tel: 617-523-5638. Sr. PEGGY LOFTUS, S.N.D.; Sr. CHARLOTTE KANE, S.N.D., *2121 Commonwealth Ave., Brighton, 02135.* Tel: 617-254-0100; Fax: 617-783-5642.

Asian Indian Apostolate—Rev. THOMAS D'SOUZA. Tel: 617-631-3443.

Brazilian Apostolate—Rev. ROBERT BOUFFIER, S.M. Tel: 617-354-5008.

Cambodian Apostolate—Rev. ANTHONY GIANG NGUYEN. Tel: 617-889-2774. Sr. PEGGY CUMMINS, S.N.D. Tel: 508-454-7663.

Cameroon Apostolate—Sr. MARILYN GIGNAC. Tel: 508-458-8862.

Cape Verdean Apostolate—Rev. PIO GOTTIN, O.F.M.Cap. Tel: 617-445-7645.

Chinese Apostolate (Mandarin)—Rev. DENIS R. COMO, S.J. Tel: 617-482-2949.

Croatian Apostolate—JOYCE GALANTIC. Tel: 617-484-2619.

Ethiopian/Eritrean Apostolate—Rev. HABTAMARIAN KETEMA. Tel: 617-289-1234.

Laotion Apostolate—Sr. EILEEN BURNS, S.N.D. Tel: 508-599-7750.

Filipino Apostolate—Rev. JOHN COSS, F.M.S.I. Tel: 508-879-6711.

French Apostolate—*Office for Ethnic Apostolates.* Tel: 617-254-0100.

Ghanaian Apostolate—Rev. PETER AYOROGO. Tel: 617-325-1404.

German Apostolate—Rev. FREDERICK J. MURPHY. Tel: 617-542-5682.

Haitian Apostolate—Rev. JOHN MORIN, O.M.I. Tel: 617-298-0080.

Hmong Apostolate—PAULE VERDET. Tel: 617-965-2499.

Irish Apostolate—Rev. DANIEL FINN. Tel: 617-288-2367.

Italian Apostolate—Rev. PRIMO PISCITELLO, O.F.M. Tel: 617-523-2110.

Japanese Apostolate—Sr. FEDRE TANNO, P.D.D.M. Tel: 617-482-0978.

Khmhu Laotian Apostolate—Rev. JOHN FAGAN, S.J. Tel: 617-445-1524.

Korean Apostolate—Rev. PAUL RI. Tel: 617-899-9947. Dr. KYU KIM. Tel: 508-835-6947.

Liberian Apostolate—Rev. JAMES CALLAHAN, S.M.A. Tel: 617-329-4774.

Lithuanian Apostolate—Rev. ALBERT CONTONS. Tel: 617-268-0353.

Nigerian Apostolate—Rev. GERALD OSTERMAN. Tel: 617-442-1431.

Polish Apostolate—Rev. Msgr. STANISLAUS SYPEK. Tel: 617-361-0565.

Portuguese Apostolate—Rev. JOSE S. FERREIRA. Tel: 617-547-5593.

Rwanda Apostolate—Rev. BASILE BAZINE. Tel: 617-229-6884.

Ugandan Apostolate—Dr. ALOYSIUS LUGIRA. Tel: 617-729-9245.

Vietnamese Apostolate—Rev. EPHREM VU KIEM CUNG, C.M.C. Tel: 617-265-2479.

Zaire Apostolate—Rev. BASILE BAZINE. Tel: 617-229-6884.

Family Life Apostolate—MARY ALICE BREINLINGER, *2121 Commonwealth Ave., Brighton, 02135.* Tel: 617-783-2451; Fax: 617-783-5642.

Health Care Ministry, Office for—KELLY L. DUNN, *St. Elizabeth's Hospital, 736 Cambridge St., Brighton, 02135.* Tel: 617-789-2456; Fax: 617-789-2573.

Hispanic Apostolate, Office for the—Mrs. MARISOL GOMEZ-ARROYO, Dir., *2121 Commonwealth Ave., Brighton, 02135.* Tel: 617-254-0100; Fax: 617-357-5858.

Holy Name Society—Rev. JOHN MCLAUGHLIN, *25 Arlington St., Somerville, 02145.* Tel: 617-625-0029.

Juvenile Court Chaplain—Rev. JAMES F. FRATUS, *601 Broadway, Chelsea, 02150.* Tel: 617-889-2774.

League of Catholic Women—Rev. MARTIN CONNOR, Spiritual Dir., *St. John's Seminary, 127 Lake St., Brighton, 02135.* Tel: 617-254-2610; Fax: 617-783-2336.

Legion of Mary—Rev. ALFRED PUCCINI, *12 Thacher St., Malden, 02148.* Tel: 617-322-6142.

Liturgical Commission—Rev. SEAN M. MCCARTHY, Chm. Tel: 617-769-2522.

Marian Devotions Coordinator—Rev. WILLIAM R. CARROLL, *24 Medford St., Arlington, 02174.* Tel: 617-648-0220; Fax: 617-643-8955.

Pilgrimages, Coordinator of—Rev. WALTER H. CUENIN, *573 Washington St., Newton, 02158.* Tel: 617-527-7560; Fax: 617-527-1338.

Prison Ministry Office—Deacon WALTER J. MILES, JR., Dir., *253 Watertown St., Newton, 02158.* Tel: 617-244-7544.

Seaport of Boston—Waterfront Chapel, Rev. PHILIP LAPLANTE, S.M., *27 Isabella St., Boston, 02116.* Tel: 617-482-5495; Fax: 617-268-8100.

Spiritual Development, Office of—Rev. JOHN E. SASSANI, *2121 Commonwealth Ave., Brighton, 02135.* Tel: 617-254-1040; Fax: 617-254-6469.

Worship, Office for—Rev. JAMES F. FIELD, *2121 Commonwealth Ave., Brighton, 02135.* Tel: 617-254-0100; Fax: 617-894-4262.

Young Adult Ministry, Office for—JAMES J. BREEN, *2121 Commonwealth Ave., Brighton, 02135.* Tel: 617-254-0100; 783-4505; Fax: 617-783-5642.

Youth Ministry, Office for—Rev. THOMAS A. DUNNE, S.D.B., *139 Crescent St., West Quincy, 02169.* Tel: 617-472-0333; Fax: 617-479-6298.

Education

Education—Rev. RICHARD J. MALONE, Cabinet Sec., *One Lake St., Brighton, 02135-3800.* Tel: 617-782-0690; Fax: 617-782-0213.

Campus Ministry—Sr. KATHLEEN CROWLEY, S.C.H., Dir., *68 St. Stephen St., Boston, 02115.* Tel: 617-266-2635; Fax: 617-266-6148.

Office of Religious Education—Rev. RICHARD J. MALONE, Dir., *One Lake St., Brighton, 02135.* Tel: 617-254-4425; Fax: 617-782-0213.

Catholic School Office—Sr. ANN DOMINIC ROACH, O.P., Supt., Schools, *2200 Dorchester Ave., Boston, 02124-5607.* Tel: 617-298-6555; Fax: 617-298-6622.

Social Services

Social Services—Dr. JOSEPH DOOLIN, Ph.D., Cabinet Sec., *49 Franklin St., Boston, 02110.* Tel: 617-482-5440; Fax: 617-451-0337.

Catholic Charitable Bureau of the Archdiocese of Boston, Inc.—Dr. JOSEPH DOOLIN, *49 Franklin St., Boston, 02110.* Tel: 617-482-5440; Fax: 617-482-2429.

Catholic Relief Services—Dr. JOSEPH DOOLIN, *49 Franklin St., Boston, 02110.* Tel: 617-482-5440; Fax: 617-482-2429.

Life Resources, Inc.—ROBERT M. TURILLO, *199 State St., 5th Fl., Boston, 02109.* Tel: 617-227-8766.

Office of AIDS Ministry—Sr. ZITA FLEMING, C.S.J., *49 Franklin St., Boston, 02110.* Tel: 617-482-5440; Fax: 617-482-2429.

Office of Pro-Life Activities—BARBARA THORP, *159 Washington St., Brighton, 02135.* Tel: 617-783-5410; Fax: 617-787-7797.

Society of St. Vincent de Paul—ALBERT CROCKER, Coord., *1280 Washington St., Boston, 02118.* Tel: 617-542-0883.

Nazareth, Inc.—JOAN KILDAY PULEO, *19 St. Joseph St., Jamaica Plain, 02130.* Tel: 617-522-4040.

St. Ann's Home, Inc.—Dr. PATRICK T. VILLANI, *100A Haverhill St., Methuen, 01844.* Tel: 508-682-5276.

Health Care Services

Caritas Christi Health Care System—MICHAEL F. COLLINS, M.D., Pres./C.E.O., *736 Cambridge St., Brighton, 02135-2997.* Tel: 617-789-2500; Fax: 617-789-2124. - Holy Family Hospital, Inc., Methuen - St. Elizabeth's Medical Center, Brighton - St. John of God Hospital, Brighton - Good Samaritan Hospice, Inc., Brighton - Good Samaritan Medical Center, Inc., Brockton & Stoughton - Caritas Christi Support Services, Inc., Boston - Holy Family Hospital Foundation, Inc., Methuen - Valley Regional Health System, Inc., Methuen - Valley Regional Support Services, Inc., Methuen - Metropolitan Boston Dialysis Center, Waltham Archdiocesan Liaison with all other Catholic Hospitals in the Archdiocese - The Carney Hospital, Boston - Franciscan Children's Hospital & Rehabilitation Center, Boston - Sancta Maria Hospital, Cambridge - Youville Hospital, Cambridge - Bethany Hospital, Framingham - Saints Memorial Medical Center, Inc., Lowell.

Nurses, Archdiocesan Council of—Rev. J. JOSEPH KIERCE, *35 Virginia St., Dorchester, 02125.* Tel: 617-436-2777.

Community Relations

Community Relations—JOHN B. WALSH, Cabinet Sec. Tel: 617-254-0100; Fax: 617-562-1104.

Labor Guild—Rev. EDWARD F. BOYLE, S.J., Dir., *883 Hancock St., Quincy, 02170.* Tel: 617-786-1822; Fax: 617-472-2486.

Planning Office for Urban Affairs—Rev. MICHAEL F. GRODEN, Dir., *185 Devonshire St., Boston, 02110.* Tel: 617-350-8885; Fax: 617-350-8889.

Boston Catholic Directory—Rev. PETER V. CONLEY, Editor; Rev. ROBERT M. O'GRADY, Asst. to the Editor, *49 Franklin St., Boston, 02110.* Tel: 617-542-8393; Fax: 617-452-9547.

Campaign for Human Development—Rev. WILLIAM F. JOY, *St. Angela Parish, 1548 Blue Hill Ave., Boston, 02126.* Tel: 617-298-0080; Fax: 617-298-2388.

Office of Communications—JOHN WALSH, Dir., *2121 Commonwealth Ave., Brighton, 02135-2947.* Tel: 617-254-0100; Fax: 617-562-1104.

Ecumenical and Interreligious Affairs—Rev. EDWARD M. O'FLAHERTY, S.J., Dir., *2121 Commonwealth Ave., Brighton, 02135.* Tel: 617-254-0100; Fax: 617-562-1104.

Liasion for Catholic-Jewish Relations—Rev. JOHN P. MCGINTY, *St. Theresa of Avila Parish, 10 St. Theresa St., Boston, 02132.* Tel: 617-325-1300; Fax: 617-325-0380.

Mass Catholic Conference—GERALD D'AVOLIO, Exec. Dir., *49 Franklin St., Boston, 02110-1304.* Tel: 617-574-0771; Fax: 617-574-9227.

The Pilot—Revs. PETER V. CONLEY, Editor in Chief; ROBERT M. O'GRADY, Asst. to the Editor, *49 Franklin St., Boston, 02110-1381.* Tel: 617-482-4316; Fax: 617-482-5647.

Radio Apostolate—Rev. ROBERT P. REED, Dir., *St. Matthew Rectory, 33 Stanton St., Boston, 02124.* Tel: 617-436-3590.

Office of Social Justice—Rev. WILLIAM P. JOY, Dir., *St. Angela Parish, 1548 Blue Hill Ave., Boston, 02126.* Tel: 617-298-0080; Fax: 617-298-2388.

TV Apostolate—Rev. FRANCIS T. MCFARLAND, *55 Chapel St., P.O. Box 9109, Newton, 02158-9109.* Tel: 617-965-0050; Fax: 617-965-6587. *Boston Catholic Television Center, Inc.*

Ministerial Personnel

Ministerial Personnel—Rev. PAUL E. MICELI, Cabinet Sec., Delegate to the Archbishop. Co-Delegates: Sr. RITA MCCARTHY, C.S.J.; Rev. JOHN A. DOOHER. Tel: 617-254-0100; Fax: 617-783-2947.

Clergy Personnel Office—Revs. JAMES J. MCCARTHY; WILLIAM F. MURPHY, *One Lake St., Brighton, 02135.* Tel: 617-254-2085; Fax: 617-254-8407.

Delegate for Religious—Sr. ROBERTA MARIE BROWN, C.S.J., *2121 Commonwealth Ave., Brighton, 02135.* Tel: 617-254-0100; Fax: 617-783-2947.

Office of Pastoral Ministries—BARBARA A. SHINE, Dir.; Sr. DOROTHEA MASURET, C.S.J., *One Lake St., Brighton, 02135.* Tel: 617-782-6675; Fax: 617-254-8407.

Pastoral Support for Priests—Rev. EDWARD M. O'FLAHERTY, S.J., *5 Lake St., Brighton, 02135.* Tel: 617-254-2610.

Office of Senior Priests—Rev. Msgr. JAMES E. TIERNEY, Dir., *Regina Cleri, 60 Wm. Cardinal O'Connell Way, Boston, 02114.* Tel: 617-523-1861; Fax: 617-720-0585.

Permanent Diaconate Program—Deacon DONOGHUE, Dir.; Rev. JOSE CORRAL, S.J., Assoc. Dir. for Hispanic Deacons; Sr. CLARE O'KEEFE, S.C.H., Asst. Dir., *774 Boylston St., Chestnut Hill, 02167.* Tel: 617-730-8477; Fax: 617-783-3330.

Priests Recovery Program—Rev. ROBERT P. BEALE, Dir., *287 Highland St., Milton, 02186.* Tel: 617-696-0593.

Regina Cleri, Inc.—Rev. Msgr. JAMES E. TIERNEY, *60 Wm. Cardinal O'Connell Way, Boston, 02114.* Tel: 617-523-1861; Fax: 617-720-0585.

Society of St. James the Apostle—Rev. GABRIEL TROY, *24 Clark St., Boston, 02109.* Tel: 617-742-4715; Fax: 617-723-7389.

Vocation Information Center—Rev. ROBERT W. FLAGG, *127 Lake St., Brighton, 02135.* Tel: 617-254-2610; Fax: 617-787-2336.

Sisters Senate—Sr. MARY RITA GRADY, C.S.J., *72 Cresent Ave., Newton, 02159.* Tel: 617-630-9057.

Lay Volunteer Program—PATRICK MARCHAN, *Pallotti Center, 159 Washington St., Brighton, 02135.* Tel: 617-783-3924.

Central Services - Chancery

Central Services—GERALD T. REILLY, C.P.A., Cabinet Sec. & Chancellor. Tel: 617-254-0100; Fax: 617-783-4564.

Cemeteries—DONALD F. KENNEY, *175 Broadway, Malden, 02148.* Tel: 617-322-6300; Fax: 617-332-3801.

Office for Volunteers—Mrs. ANN LALLY, *2121 Commonwealth Ave., Brighton, 02135.* Tel: 617-254-0100; Fax: 617-783-4564.

CLERGY, PARISHES, MISSIONS AND PAROCHIAL SCHOOLS

BOSTON

(Suffolk County)

1—CATHEDRAL OF THE HOLY CROSS (1788), Rev. Frederick J. Murphy, Rector; Rev. Msgr. William H. Roche; Deacons Luis Casillas; Andres Rosa. Pastoral Assocs.: Sr. M. Celeste Burgos, M.H.S.H.; Sr. Mary Madeline Gallagher, M.H.S.H. In res., Bro. Steven B. Wang, F.M.S.

Res., 75 Union Park St., 02118. Tel: 617-542-5682.

School—Tel: 617-422-0042.

Sisters 3; Lay Teachers 7; Students 191.

2—ST. ADALBERT (1913) (Polish), Rev. Msgr. Stanislaus T. Sypek. In res., Rev. Thaddeus A. Saja.

Res., 1450 River St., Hyde Park, 02136-2150. Tel: 617-361-0565; Fax: 617-361-0565.

3—ALL SAINTS (1894). Closed. Parochial records at St. Joseph Parish, Roxbury.

4—ST. AMBROSE (1914), Rev. Vincent P. Von Euw. In

res., Rev. John Raymaker, C.I.C.M.
Res., 240 Adams St., Dorchester, 02122-1380. Tel: 617-265-5302; Fax: 617-265-0886.
School—Tel: 617-825-9400.
Sisters 5; Lay Teachers 9; Students 250.

5—St. Andrew (1918), Revs. Richard J. Mehm; Robert E. O'Brien.
Res., 40 Walk Hill St., Forest Hills, 02130-4196. Tel: 617-522-1222; Fax: 617-522-0489.
School—Tel: 617-524-7733.
Sisters 6; Lay Teachers 3; Students 226.

6—St. Angela (1907), Revs. John Morin, O.M.I.; William Joy. Pastoral Assocs.: Sr. Maria Charles Norton, C.S.J.; Sr. Paula Coelho, S.U.S.C.
Res., 1548 Blue Hill Ave., Mattapan, 02126. Tel: 617-298-0080; Fax: 617-298-2388.
School—Tel: 617-296-1161.
Lay Teachers 7; Students 222.

7—St. Ann (1945), Rev. Paul E. Kilroy. Pastoral Assocs.: Sr. Rosemary Mulvihill, R.S.M.; Sr. Mary Walsh, S.U.
Tel: 617-266-2635.

8—St. Ann (1889), Revs. Walter E. Keymont; John E. Sheridan. In res., Rev. Joseph Hennessey.
Res., 243 Neponset Ave., Dorchester, 02122-3239. Tel: 617-825-6180; Fax: 617-825-7869.
School—Tel: 617-825-6262.
Religious 5; Lay Teachers 12; Students 328.

9—St. Anne (1919), Rev. William F. Joyce.
Res., 79 W. Milton St., Readville, 02136-1929. Tel: 617-361-3443; Fax: 617-361-6690.
School—Tel: 617-361-3563.
Lay Teachers 11; Students 225; Religious 1.

10—Annunciation Cathedral (1908) (Melkite-Greek Catholic), Rt. Rev. Edward G. Kakaty, Rector; Deacon Paul Lawler.
Res., 7 V.F.W. Pkwy., Roslindale, 02131-1098. Tel: 617-323-5242; Fax: 617-325-2662.

11—St. Anthony (1896), Revs. Daniel P. Hegarty; Robert Bouffier, S.M. (Brazil); Glen F. Byrne; Ralph Gwale.
Res., 43 Holton St., Allston, 02134-1397. Tel: 617-782-0775; Fax: 617-782-2008.
School—Tel: 617-782-7170.
Lay Teachers 8; Students 119.

12—St. Augustine (1868), Revs. Thomas J. McDonnell; Philip Harrigan, S.J.
Res., 9 F St., South Boston, 02127-2898. Tel: 617-268-1230; Fax: 617-269-2233.
School—Tel: 617-269-2233.
Sisters 2; Lay Teachers 9; Students 249.

13—Basilica of Our Lady of Perpetual Help (1868), Very Rev. John J. Hennessy, C.SS.R., Rector; Revs. Vincent J. Kelly, C.SS.R.; Lawrence J. Buckley, C.SS.R.; John Devin, C.SS.R.; William Harbison, C.SS.R.; Michael Hopkins, C.SS.R.; John Furey, C.SS.R.; Joseph Adamec, C.SS.R.; Joseph E. Manton, C.SS.R.; Edward McDonough, C.SS.R.; John E. Doherty, C.SS.R.; Philip Cabasino, C.SS.R.; George C. Gardner, C.SS.R.; Alex Ortiz, C.SS.R.; John Ryan, C.SS.R.; George W. Drew, C.SS.R.; John Anderson, C.SS.R.; Richard Moran, C.SS.R. Pastoral Assocs.: Sr. Elaine O'Donnell, S.S.N.D.; Sr. Vincent Ferrea, C.S.J.
Res., 1545 Tremont St., Roxbury, 02120-2996. Tel: 617-445-2600; Fax: 617-445-1857.
School——(Grades 1-6). Tel: 617-442-2660.
Sisters 4; Lay Teachers 3; Students 152.

14—Blessed Sacrament (1891), Rev. Michael F. McLellan; Deacon Luciano Herrera.
Res., 365 Centre St., Jamaica Plain, 02130-1240. Tel: 617-522-0650; Fax: 617-983-1407.
School—Tel: 617-522-1870.
Sisters 2; Lay Teachers 7; Students 198.

15—St. Brendan (1929), Rev. James H. Lane; Deacons Thomas F. Egan; James B. Little; Sr. Lillian McDonald, C.S.J., Pastoral Assoc.
Res., 15 Rita Rd., Dorchester, 02124. Tel: 617-436-0310; Fax: 617-436-1386.
School—Tel: 617-282-3388.
Sisters 2; Lay Teachers 9; Students 245.

16—St. Brigid (1908), Revs. John P. Culloty; Joseph S. McCarthy.
Res., 841 E. Broadway, South Boston, 02127-2397. Tel: 617-268-2122; Fax: 617-268-2666.
School—Tel: 617-268-2326.
Sisters 2; Lay Teachers 7; Students 275.

17—St. Catherine of Siena (1887), Rev. James DiPerri.
Res., 49 Vine St., Charlestown, 02129. Tel: 617-242-1750; Fax: 617-242-1899.
School—Tel: 617-242-0169.
Lay Teachers 8; Students 161.

18—St. Cecilia (1888), Rev. Michael F. Groden. In res., Revs. Thomas Grenham, S.P.S.; Peter Walsh, C.S.C.
Res., 30 St. Cecilia St., 02115-3132. Tel: 617-536-4548; Fax: 617-536-1781.

19—St. Christopher (1956), Rev. George A. Carrigg, Admin.
Res., 263 Mt. Vernon St., Dorchester, 02125-3182. Tel: 617-436-7273; Fax: 617-436-7273.

20—Christ The King (1940) (Catholic Ukrainian), Rev. Jaroslav Nalysnyk, Admin.
Res., 146 Forest Hills St., Jamaica Plain, 02130. Tel: 617-522-9720.

21—St. Columbkille (1871), Revs. Richard J. Shmaruk; James J. O'Rourke; Deacon Eddy Montes. In res., Rev. Carney E. Gavin.
Res., 321 Market St., Brighton, 02135-2199. Tel: 617-782-5126; 782-5774; Fax: 617-782-7283.
School—Tel: 617-254-3110.
Sisters 2; Lay Teachers 6; Students 200.

22—St. Francis de Sales-St. Philip (1867), Rev. Thomas F. Clark, S.J. Pastoral Assocs.: Sr. Mary Hart, R.G.S.; Mr. James Atkins; Mr. Tipp Harris. In res., Rev. Robert G. McMillan, S.J.
Res., One Warwick St., Roxbury, 02120-2415. Tel: 617-445-8915; Fax: 617-445-6522.

23—St. Francis de Sales (1859), Rev. Daniel J. Mahoney. In res., Rev. John J. Mullen, S.J.
Res., 303 Bunker Hill St., Charlestown, 02129-1826. Tel: 617-242-0147; Fax: 617-242-3026.

24—St. Gabriel's (1934), Rev. Justinian Manning, C.P. In res., Rev. Brendan Breen, C.P.
Res., 139 Washington St., Brighton, 02135-4325. Tel: 617-254-6582; Fax: 617-783-1766.

25—Gate of Heaven (1862), Revs. Alexander J. Keenan; Anthony J. Medairos; A. Paul White; Deacon Richard C. Martin, Sr.
Res., 606 E. 4th St., South Boston, 02127-3092. Tel: 617-268-3344; Fax: 617-269-4299.
School—Tel: 617-268-8431.
Sisters 3; Lay Teachers 17; Students 483.

26—St. Gregory (1863), Revs. Paul T. Ryan; James M. Larner; John F. O'Donnell. In res., Most Rev. John P. Boles.
Res., 2223 Dorchester Ave., Dorchester, 02124. Tel: 617-298-2460; Fax: 617-298-9232.
School—Tel: 617-296-1210.
Sisters 2; Lay Teachers 8; Students 495.

27—Holy Family (1995), Rev. William C. Francis; Deacon Francisco Guerrios; Sr. Rita Brereton, S.S.N.D., Pastoral Assoc. In res., Revs. Jose C. Corral, S.J.; J. Joseph Kierce.
Mailing Address: One Lingard St., Dorchester, 02125-2732. Tel: 617-445-9553; Fax: 617-445-2417.
School—516 Columbia Rd., Dorchester, 02125. Tel: 617-825-3883.

28—Holy Name (1927), Revs. Paul Rouse; William F. Murphy; Richard J. Malone.
Res., 1689 Centre St., West Roxbury, 02132-1292. Tel: 617-325-4865; Fax: 617-327-6122.
School—Tel: 617-325-9338.
Sisters 10; Lay Teachers 19; Students 639.

29—Holy Trinity (1844) (German), Rev. Hugh H. O'Regan, Admin.
Res., 140 Shawmut Ave., 02118-2227. Tel: 617-426-6142; Fax: 617-426-6142.

30—Immaculate Conception Church (1858). (Jesuit Urban Center). Revs. John P. Spencer, S.J.; James M. Shaughnessy, S.J.; Sr. Jeanette Normandin, S.S.A., Pastoral Assoc.
Res., 775 Harrison Ave., 02118. Tel: 617-536-8440.

31—St. James the Greater in Chinatown (1854), Revs. Hugh H. O'Regan; Daniel J. McCarthy, SS.CC.; Roberg Pollis. In res., Rev. Joseph J. Baggetta.
Mailing Address: G.M.F., P.O. Box 1538, 02205. Tel: 617-542-5044; 542-8489.
Res., 135 Harrison Ave., 02111.

32—St. John-St. Hugh (1901), Rev. Gerald J. Osterman. In res., Rev. Anthony Oyeyipo.
Church—517 Blue Hill Ave., Roxbury, 02121.
Res., 26 Lawrence Ave., Dorchester, 02121. Tel: 617-442-1431; Fax: 617-442-2965.

33—St. John Baptist (1921) (Portuguese), Rev. Albert J. Sallese, V.F., Admin.; Sr. Judi Clemens, S.N.D., Pastoral Assoc.
Res., 303 Paris St., East Boston, 02128. Tel: 617-567-5776; Fax: 617-567-3042.

34—St. John Chrysostom (1952), Revs. Paul A. Phinn; Charles B. Flaherty, S.S.C.; Sr. Maureen Taaffe, S.C.N., Pastoral Assoc.
Res., 4740 Washington St., West Roxbury, 02132-2199. Tel: 617-323-4410; Fax: 617-323-0423.

35—St. Joseph (1862), Rev. Gerald L. Bucke. In res., Rev. Philip McGaugh.
Res., 68 Cardinal O'Connell Way, 02114. Tel: 617-523-4342; Fax: 617-523-8459.

36—St. Joseph (1845), Revs. Walter J. Waldron; Russell W.M. Best, Jr. Pastoral Assocs.: Sr. Gerard Ndagano, I.H.M.R.; Sr. Marie Mullane, R.C.
Res., 85 Regent St., Roxbury, 02119-1990. Tel: 617-442-0900; Fax: 617-442-0900.
School—18 Hulbert St., Roxbury, 02119. Tel: 617-442-2675.
Lay Teachers 9; Students 159; Religious 1.

37—St. Joseph-St. Lazarus (1891), Rev. Richard P. McLaughlin.
Res., 59 Ashley St., East Boston, 02128. Tel: 617-569-0406; Fax: 617-569-8212.

38—St. Joseph (1938), Revs. William H. McLaughlin; John M. Toomey.
Res., 21 Chapel Rd., Hyde Park, 02136. Tel: 617-361-1314; Fax: 617-364-7129.

39—St. Kevin (1945). Closed. Merged with St. Paul to form Holy Family Parish, Dorchester.

40—St. Lazarus (1892). See St. Joseph Parish, now known as St. Joseph-St. Lazarus.

41—St. Leo (1902), Rev. Leandre Jeannot; Deacon Aubert Lauture.
Res., 177 Harvard St., P.O. Box 307, Dorchester, 02124-0307. Tel: 617-436-1445; Fax: 617-436-1445.

42—St. Leonard of Port Maurice (1873) (Italian), Revs. Michael Nappo, O.F.M.; Richard Passeri, O.F.M.; Dismas Centrella, O.F.M.
Res., 14 N. Bennet St., 02113. Tel: 617-523-2110.
Chapel—St. Mary, 150 Endicott St., 02113. Tel: 617-523-2110.

43—St. Margaret (1893), Very Rev. Thomas D. Conway, V.F.; Rev. Stephen P. Zukas; Sr. Catherine Therese Barrett, S.C.H., Pastoral Assoc.
Res., 800 Columbia Rd., Dorchester, 02125-1750. Tel: 617-436-2190; Fax: 617-282-5428.
School—Tel: 617-282-5621.
Sisters of Charity 8; Lay Teachers 9; Students 316.
High School—Msgr. Ryan Memorial High School, Tel: 617-282-2818.
Sisters 7; Lay Teachers 1; Girls 227.

44—St. Mark (1905), Revs. Daniel J. Finn; John J. Connolly, Jr. In res., Revs. John J. Jennings; Timothy J. O'Sullivan.
Res., 20 Roseland St., Dorchester, 02124. Tel: 617-825-2852; Fax: 617-825-0514.
School—Tel: 617-282-2577.
Sisters 7; Lay Teachers 15; Students 512.

45—St. Mary. See St. Leonard of Port Maurice for details.

46—St. Mary (1828), Rev. James B. Canniff.
Res., One Monument Sq., Charlestown, 02129-3499. Tel: 617-242-4664; Fax: 617-242-0016.

47—St. Mary of the Angels (1904), Rev. John E. Fagan, S.J.; Sr. Katherine McGrath, S.C.H, Pastoral Assoc.
Res., 377 Walnut Ave., Roxbury, 02119. Tel: 617-445-1524; Fax: 617-442-6455.

48—St. Mary, Star of the Sea (1864), Rev. Robert R. Kennedy.
Res., 63 Moore St., East Boston, 02128-1547. Tel: 617-567-0056; Fax: 617-569-8440.
School—Tel: 617-567-6609.
Lay Teachers 10; Students 266.

49—St. Matthew (1900), Revs. Robert Reed; Francis C. O'Brien; Sr. Mary Damien Powers, O.S.M., Pastoral Assoc.
Res., 33 Stanton St., Dorchester, 02124-3716. Tel: 617-436-3590; Fax: 617-822-0407.
School—Tel: 617-825-7955.
Sisters 2; Lay Teachers 10; Students 247.

50—St. Monica (1907), Rev. Thomas J. Reilly.
Res., 70 Devine Way, South Boston, 02127-3536. Tel: 617-269-6760; Fax: 617-269-3654.

51—Most Holy Redeemer (1844), Revs. Robert F. Hennessey; James B. Clarke; Deacon Antonio M. Perea.
Res., 65 London St., East Boston, 02128-1924. Tel: 617-567-3227; Fax: 617-569-6950. Member Central Catholic School of East Boston.

52—Most Precious Blood (1880), Rev. Daniel J. Cavanaugh; Most Rev. Lawrence J. Riley. In res., Rev. Msgr. John D. Day.
Res., 43 Maple St., Hyde Park, 02136-2738. Tel: 617-364-9500; Fax: 617-364-2590.
School—Tel: 617-361-2162.
Sisters 2; Lay Teachers 6; Students 187.

53—Our Lady of the Assumption (1869), Revs. Adelard J. Gagnon; Giuseppe Vescera, C.P.
Res., 404 Sumner St., East Boston, 02128. Tel: 617-567-1223; Fax: 617-561-6319. Member East Boston Central Catholic School Consortium.

54—Our Lady of the Cedars of Lebanon (1893) (Maronite), Chorbishop Joseph F. Lahoud; Deacon Nicholas Nashawaty.
Res., 61 Rockwood St., Jamaica Plain, 02130. Tel: 617-522-0225; Fax: 617-522-0194.

55—Our Lady of Czestochowa (1893) (Polish), Revs. Piotr Kleszcz, O.F.M.Conv.; Andrew Sujka, O.F.M.Conv. In res., Revs. Stephen Majewski, O.F.M.Conv.; Wladyslav Matejek, O.F.M. Conv.; Germaine Kopaczynski, O.F.M. Conv.
Res., 655 Dorchester Ave., South Boston, 02127-3551. Tel: 617-268-4355; Fax: 617-268-4599.
School—Tel: 617-268-3766.

Felician Sisters 3; Lay Teachers 6; Students 202.
Convent—666 Dorchester Ave., 02127.

56—OUR LADY OF LOURDES (1908), Very Rev. Charles J. Bourque, V.F.; Deacon Leonard F. De Coste. In res., Rev. Michael F. McLellan.
Res., 46 Brookside Ave., Jamaica Plain, 02130-2370. Tel: 617-524-0434; Fax: 617-524-1888.
School—Tel: 617-524-6136.
Sisters 3; Lay Teachers 8; Students 220.

57—OUR LADY OF MT. CARMEL (1905) (Italian), Revs. Francis de Sales Paolo, O.F.M.; Kenneth Garofalo, O.F.M. In res., Revs. Aubert Marie Picardi, O.F.M.; Donald D'Ippolito, O.F.M.; Bro. Stephen Colangelo, O.F.M.
Res., 128 Gove St., East Boston, 02128. Tel: 617-567-3215; Fax: 617-569-0552. Member East Boston Central Catholic School.

58—OUR LADY OF THE PRESENTATION (1909), Rev. William F. Salmon.
Res., 676 Washington St., Brighton, 02135-1612. Tel: 617-782-6260; 6261; Fax: 617-782-3303.
School—Tel: 617-782-8670.
Sisters 1; Lay Teachers 9; Students 226.

59—OUR LADY OF VICTORIES (1880) (French), Revs. Andrew R. Albert, S.M.; Roger J. Bourgea, S.M.; Armand Thibault, S.M.; Tito Cruz, S.M.; Albert DiIanni, S.M.; Very Rev. Joseph Hindelang, S.M., Prov.; Revs. Lucien Chasse, S.M.; Rudolph Deziel, S.M.; Philip Laplante, S.M.; Viotri Vuatana, S.M.; Bros. Gregory Theriault, S.M.; Jude Roy, S.M.; Roland Bernier, S.M.
Res., 27 Isabella St., 02117. Tel: 617-426-4448.

60—ST. PATRICK (1836), Revs. Walter J. Waldron; Russell W. Best. Pastoral Assocs.: Sr. Mary Andreas, S.B.S.; Sr. Immaculada Silva; Sr. M. Matthias Gallagher, S.B.S.; Sr. Mary Hurley, S.B.S.; Sr. Maria Macedo; Sr. Mary Thomasine Twomey, M.S.B.T.; Sr. Luisa Vasconcelos; Sr. Domingas Baptista; Revs. Pio Gottin, O.F.M.Cap.; Paolino Pina, O.F.M.Cap.; Bernardo Vaschetto, O.F.M.Cap.; Terence J. Moran.
Res., 10 Magazine St., Roxbury, 02119-2797. Tel: 617-445-7645; Fax: 617-445-6166.
School—Tel: 617-427-3881.
Sisters 2; Lay Teachers 14; Students 349.

61—ST. PAUL (1907). Closed. Merged with St. Kevin to form Holy Family Parish, Dorchester.

62—ST. PETER (1872), Revs. John L. Doyle; Andrew Nguyen, C.M.C.; Hilary Nguyen Haikhana; Ephrem Vu Khiem Cung, C.M.C.; Deacon Jesus Ortiz; Sr. Sally McLaughlin, S.C.H., Pastoral Assoc.; Sr. Glenna Connors, S.C.H., Pastoral Assoc.
Res., 309 Bowdoin St., Dorchester, 02122-1834. Tel: 617-265-1132; Fax: 617-265-0463.
School—Tel: 617-282-8573.
Sisters 3; Lay Teachers 5; Students 210.

63—ST. PETER (1904) (Lithuanian), Rev. Albert J. Contons.
Res., 50 Orton-Marotta Way, South Boston, 02127-2006. Tel: 617-268-0353; Fax: 617-268-2588.
School—Tel: 617-268-0750.
Sisters 3; Lay Teachers 8; Students 260.

64—SS. PETER AND PAUL (1844). Closed. See St. Vincent de Paul, South Boston.

65—ST. PHILIP. Closed. See St. Francis de Sales-St. Philip, Roxbury.

66—ST. RICHARD. Closed. Parochial records at St. Joseph's Parish, Roxbury.

67—SACRED HEART (1888) (Italian), Rev. Joseph A. Cogo, C.S. In res., Revs. Mario Tardivo, C.S.; Peter Bortolazzo, C.S.; Deacon Mario Lopriore.
Res., 12 North Sq., 02113-2498. Tel: 617-523-5638; Fax: 617-227-4552.
School—St. John's School, Tel: 617-227-3143.
Lay Teachers 11; Students 171.

68—SACRED HEART (1873), Very Rev. Albert J. Sallese, V.F.; Rev. Thomas J. Stanton.
Res., 303 Paris St., East Boston, 02128-3063. Tel: 617-567-5776; Fax: 617-567-3042.
School—Member East Boston Catholic School Consortium.
Sisters 1; Brothers 3; Lay Teachers 8; Students 229.

69—SACRED HEART (1893), Revs. Francis H. Kelley; Leon F. Beauvais; John J. Graham; Sr. Virginia Bobrowsky, S.S.N.D., Pastoral Assoc. In res., Revs. Robert E. Maguire, S.J.; Peter Arroygo.
Res., 169 Cummins Hwy., Roslindale, 02131-3739. Tel: 617-325-3322; Fax: 617-325-2145.
School—Tel: 617-323-2500.
Sisters 2; Lay Teachers 15; Students 464.

70—ST. STEPHEN (1843), Revs. Gabriel Troy; Milton Eggerling; Patrick Cleary.
Res., 24 Clark St., 02109. Tel: 617-523-1230; Fax: 617-723-7389.

71—ST. THERESA (1895), Revs. William M. Helmick; John P. McGinty; Robert J. Sullivan. In res., Rev. Raymond F. Helmick, S.J.
Res., 10 St. Theresa Ave., West Roxbury, 02132-3499. Tel: 617-325-1300; Fax: 617-325-0380.
School—Tel: 617-323-1050.
Sisters 2; Lay Teachers 20; Students 589.

72—ST. THOMAS AQUINAS (1869), Revs. John E. Thomas; Paul Bolduc. In res., Sr. Jeanne Marie Gribaudo, C.S.J.
Res., 97 South St., Jamaica Plain, 02130-3899. Tel: 617-524-0240; Fax: 617-524-1840.

73—ST. VINCENT DE PAUL (1872), Rev. Richard F. Cannon. In res., Rev. Msgr. Andrew F. Connell; Sr. Catherine Panetta, S.N.D.
Res., 55 W. Broadway, South Boston, 02127. Tel: 617-268-0710; Fax: 617-268-1277.

74—ST. WILLIAM (1909), Revs. Daniel J. Riley; John J. Unni; Joseph Chinh Nguyen; Deacon Stanley Pugsley.
Res., 1048 Dorchester Ave., Dorchester, 02125-1750. Tel: 617-265-0100; Fax: 617-265-5464.
School—Tel: 617-265-7110.
Lay Teachers 9; Students 193.

OUTSIDE THE CITY OF BOSTON

Abington, Plymouth Co., St. Bridget (1863), Revs. Allan L.W. Butler; Louis R. Palmieri; Deacon Thomas H. Hanlon; Sr. Jane Sellmayer, S.U.S.C., Pastoral Assoc.
Res., 455 Plymouth St., 02351-1841. Tel: 617-878-0900; Fax: 617-878-6566.
School—Tel: 617-878-8482.
Lay Teachers 11; Students 249.

St. Nicholas (1964), Revs. Mark V. Carr; Robert B. Costello.
Res., 127 N. Quincy St., West Abington, 02351-1073. Tel: 617-857-2461; 2462; Fax: 617-857-2923.

Acton, Middlesex Co., St. Elizabeth of Hungary (1945), Revs. Robert J. Boyle; James J. Daley; Edmond L Parker; Peggy Lauzon, Pastoral Assoc.; Deacons Alexander J. Patrick; Eugene Counihan; Howard P. Hardin.
Res., 89 Arlington St., West Acton, 01720. Tel: 508-263-4305; Fax: 508-263-9014.

Amesbury, Essex Co., St. Joseph (1866), In res., Rev. John D. Silk.
Res., 9 Sparhawk St., 01913. Tel: 508-388-0160.

Sacred Heart (1903) (French), Team Ministry: Revs. Robert E. Casey; Thomas J. Buckley; Deacon Richard R. Bowley; Hilde Champion, Pastoral Assoc.
Res., 9 Sparhawk St., 01913. Tel: 508-388-0330; Fax: 508-388-1451.

Andover, Essex Co., St. Augustine (1866), Revs. Alfred J. Ellis, O.S.A.; Richard L. Foley, O.S.A.; Terence Highland, O.S.A.; Deacon John J. Capomaccio. In res., Revs. Fritz J. Cerullo, O.S.A.; George R. Morgan, O.S.A.
Res., 43 Essex St., 01810-3779. Tel: 508-475-0050; Fax: 508-475-3078. [CEM]
School—Tel: 508-475-2414.
Sisters 2; Lay Teachers 21; Students 405.
Mission—Ballardville, St. Joseph's, (1881).

St. Robert Bellarmine (1961), Rev. Arthur J. Driscoll; Deacon Thomas Raymond; Mrs. Betty Pendergast, Pastoral Assoc.
Res., 198 Haggetts Pond Rd., 01810. Tel: 508-683-8922; Fax: 508-689-8878.

Arlington, Middlesex Co.,

1—ST. AGNES, (1872), Revs. Brian M. Flatley; William R. Carroll; Charles E. Herlihy; Charles McGanhey; Sr. Margaret Lowell, C.S.J., Pastoral Assoc.; Deacon Francis A. Mendoza. In res., Revs. Philip B. Earley; Ronald Lawson.
Res., 24 Medford St., 02174. Tel: 617-648-0220; Fax: 617-643-7883.
School—Tel: 617-643-9031.
Religious 1; Lay Teachers 20; Students 426.
High School—Tel: 617-646-7770; Fax: 617-648-8345.
Religious 5; Lay Teachers 24; Students 628.

2—ST. CAMILLUS, (1950), Rev. James E. O'Leary.
Res., 1175 Concord Tpke., 02174-7298. Tel: 617-643-3132; Fax: 617-643-8228.

3—ST. JAMES THE APOSTLE, (1914), Very Rev. Francis E. Daley, V.F. In res., Revs. Kenneth McAskill; Robert F. McAuliffe.
Res., 22 Appleton St., 02174-5900. Tel: 617-643-0636; Fax: 617-643-7488.

4—ST. JEROME, (1934), Rev. James L. Publicover.
Res., 201 Lake St., 02174-0298. Tel: 617-648-2506; Fax: 617-648-2126.

Ashland, Middlesex Co., St. Cecilia (1885), Revs. Paul F. Mulligan; Carlos C. Kim. In res., Rev. Darius Sleszynski.
Res., 54 Esty St., 01721-2126. Tel: 508-881-1107; Fax: 508-881-8606.

Avon, Norfolk Co., St. Michael (1908), Rev. John W. McElroy.
Res., 87 N. Main St., 02322-1286. Tel: 508-586-7210; Fax: 508-586-7211.

Ayer, Middlesex Co., St. Mary (1858), Rev. Richard Gosselin. In res., Rev. John J. Fallon.
Res., 31 Shirley St., 01432-1295. Tel: 508-772-2414; Fax: 508-772-2414.

Bedford, Middlesex Co., St. Michael (1931), Very Rev. Mark S. Sheehan, V.F.; Revs. Henry W. Gagnon; William P. Smith. In res., Rev. Joseph P. Robinson.
Res., 90 Concord Rd., 01730-1596. Tel: 617-275-6318; Fax: 617-271-9879.

Bellingham, Norfolk Co., Assumption (1927), Rev. Leo E. Martel; Deacon Bertrand H. Guerin. In res., Rev. Daniel J. Gilmartin.
Res., 370 Pulaski Blvd., 02019. Tel: 508-883-8226; Fax: 508-883-1713.

St. Blaise (1962), Rev. James H. Connolly; Phyllis Calvey, Pastoral Assoc.
Res., 1158 S. Main St., 02019-1597. Tel: 508-966-1258; Fax: 508-966-0310.

St. Brendan (1945), Rev. David J. Mullen.
Res., 384 Hartford Ave., 02019. Tel: 508-966-0260; Fax: 508-966-4404.

Belmont, Middlesex Co., St. Joseph (1900), Revs. William C. Burckhart; Timothy J. Harrison. In res., Rev. Richard R. Santerre.
Res., 345 Waverley St., 02178-2418. Tel: 617-484-0279; Fax: 617-489-5445.

St. Luke (1919), Rev. Msgr. Roger J. Brady; Sr. Ernestine Quealy, C.S.J., Pastoral Assoc.
Res., 132 Lexington St., 02178-1239. Tel: 617-484-1996; Fax: 617-484-7831.

Our Lady of Mercy (1926), Rev. James J. McGowan.
Res., 15 Lawndale St., 02178-3451. Tel: 617-489-1160; Fax: 617-489-9682.

Beverly, Essex Co., St. John the Evangelist (1955), Revs. George J. Butera; Joseph Keville; Sr. Agnes Therrien, S.S.C.H., Pastoral Assoc.; Deacon Tomas Sanchez.
Res., 552 Cabot St., 01915. Tel: 508-922-5542; Fax: 508-921-4563.
School—Tel: 508-922-0048.
Sisters 1; Lay Teachers 8; Students 157.

St. Mary Star of the Sea (1870), Revs. Richard G. Johnson; Richard C. Beaulieu; James J. Foley; Deacon Joseph Kasenenko. Pastoral Assocs.: Sr. Marian Patrice, S.N.D.; Sr. Bernadette Mary, S.N.D.
Res., 253 Cabot St., 01915-4597. Tel: 508-922-0113; Fax: 508-922-8501.
School—Tel: 508-927-3259.
Sisters 4; Lay Teachers 6; Students 212.

St. Margaret (1905), Rev. Cyril J. Conroy; Sr. Elizabeth O'Connor, S.N.D., Pastoral Assoc.
Res., 672 Hale St., 01915-. Tel: 508-927-0069; Fax: 508-922-9359.

Billerica, Middlesex Co., St. Andrew (1868), Rev. Joseph C. Wilson. In res., Rev. Francis L. Gallagher.
Res., 45 Talbot Ave., 01862-1414. Tel: 508-663-3624; Fax: 508-670-1433.

St. Mary (1937), Revs. Edward M. McMahon; Lawrence J. O'Toole, S.J.; Deacon Allan R. Shanahan.
Res., 796 Boston Rd., 01821. Tel: 508-663-2215; Fax: 508-663-0127.

St. Theresa (1945), Revs. Eugene D. Tully; Mark J. Coiro; John J. McCormick; Deacon Thomas F. Mullins.
Res., 80 Concord Rd., 01821. Tel: 508-663-8816; Fax: 508-663-0577.

Braintree, Norfolk Co., St. Clare (1959), Revs. William B. O'Connor; Charles E. Salamone; Deacon John J. McDonough.
Res., 1244 Liberty St., 02184-8299. Tel: 617-848-7480; Fax: 617-356-8380.

St. Francis of Assisi (1903), Revs. Richard P. Crowley; Charles I. Sheehy; William H. Mullin. In res., Rev. Paul J. Tivnan.
Res., 856 Washington St., South Braintree, 02184-6464. Tel: 617-843-1332; Fax: 617-848-0976.
School—Tel: 617-848-0842.
Lay Teachers 8; Students 193.

St. Thomas More (1938), Revs. Cornelius J. Mullaney; Joseph M. Rossi.
Res., 8 Hawthorn Rd., P.O. Box 330, 02184-0330. Tel: 617-843-1980; Fax: 617-843-7110.

Bridgewater, Plymouth Co., St. Thomas Aquinas (1853), Revs. Michael J. Regan; Thomas H. Maguire; Edward J. McLaughlin.
Res., 103 Center St., 02324-1397. Tel: 508-697-9528; Fax: 508-279-1859.

Brockton, Plymouth Co.,

1—ST. CASIMIR, (1898) (Lithuanian), Rev. John P. Prusaitis.
Res., 21 Sawtell Ave., 02402. Tel: 508-586-2226; Fax: 508-559-2761.
School—Tel: 508-587-7367.
Sisters 1; Lay Teachers 5; Students 176.

2—ST. COLMAN OF CLOYNE, (1910), Revs. John E. Schatzel; James A. Flavin; Deacon Henry Welch.

Res., 42 Wendell Ave., 02402-3191. Tel: 508-586-1575; Fax: 508-586-9393.

3—St. Edward, (1897), Revs. Robert N. Kelleher; William M. Walsh; Sr. Mary Lou McCarthy, C.S.J., Pastoral Assoc.
Res., 71 E. Main St., 02401-2461. Tel: 508-586-6491; Fax: 508-587-1796.
School—Tel: 508-583-6231.
Lay Teachers 9; Students 238.

4—St. Margaret, (1902), Revs. Joseph F. Donovan; Thomas D. Reynolds; William J. McConnell.
Res., P.O. Box 3025, 917 Montello St., 02404-6657. Tel: 508-586-1295; Fax: 508-586-8443.

5—Our Lady of Lourdes, (1931), Very Rev. Joseph H. Manning, V.F.; Rev. David C. Murphy. In res., Rev. Francis G. Goss.
Res., 439 West St., 02401-4899. Tel: 508-586-4715; Fax: 508-584-6257.

6—Our Lady of Ostrobrama, (1914) (Polish), Rev. Msgr. John B. Missa.
Res., 696 N. Main St., 02401-2444. Tel: 508-586-4270; Fax: 508-586-7507.

7—St. Patrick, (1856), Rev. Francis J. Cloherty; Rev. Msgr. Joseph A. Gaudet; Sr. Jane Elizabeth O'Connell, S.C.N., Pastoral Assoc. In res., Rev. Paul L. Moritz.
Res., 335 Main St., 02401-5396. Tel: 508-586-4840; Fax: 508-941-0639.

8—Sacred Heart, (1891) (French), Revs. Thomas A. Kopp; Jean Marx Pierre-Louis.
Res., 235 Court St., 02402-4698. Tel: 508-586-1740; Fax: 508-584-8553.
School—Tel: 508-588-4481.
Sisters 3; Lay Teachers 6; Students 228.

9—St. Theresa, (Maronite), Rev. Msgr. David M. George.
Mailing Address: P.O. Box 2567, 02405. Tel: 508-586-1428; Fax: 508-587-8139.
Res., 10 Lebanon St., 02401.

Brookline, Norfolk Co.,

1—St. Aidan, (1911), Rev. Leonard A. Coppenrath. In res., Rev. James H. Coffey.
Res., 158 Pleasant St., 02146-3149. Tel: 617-277-0799; Fax: 617-277-3922.

2—Infant Jesus, (1938), Rev. Peter V. Conley, Admin.
Res., 6 Woodcliff Rd., Chestnut Hill, 02167-3719. Tel: 617-469-0234; Fax: 617-469-0234.

3—St. Lawrence, (1898), Rev. Paul B. O'Brien, Admin.; Deacon John J. Mannion. In res., Rev. Nathan Munsch, O.S.B.
Res., 774 Boylston St., Chestnut Hill, 02167-2501. Tel: 617-566-3131; Fax: 617-738-3330.

4—St. Mary of the Assumption, (1852), Revs. Jack Ahern; Joseph F. Scorzello; Deacon Richard F. Radford, Jr. In res., Revs. Richard G. Lennon; Joseph P. Trainor, M.M.
Res., 5 Linden Pl., 02146-7311. Tel: 617-734-0444; Fax: 617-734-3001.
School—Tel: 617-566-7184.
Sisters 1; Lay Teachers 10; Students 185.

Burlington, Middlesex Co., St. Margaret (1945), Revs. John R. Crispo; John E. Buckley. In res., Rev. Basile Bazina.
Res., 111 Winn St., 01803-3124. Tel: 617-272-3111; Fax: 617-272-9204.

St. Malachy (1964), Rev. Leonard F. O'Malley; Deacon B. Richard McLaughlin; Mr. Ken Meltz, Pastoral Assoc. In res., Rev. John O'Brien, C.P.
Res., 99 Bedford St., 01803. Tel: 617-272-5111; Fax: 617-270-9407.

Cambridge, Middlesex Co.,

1—St. Anthony, (1902) (Portuguese), Revs. Jose S. Ferreira; Walter A. Carreiro.
Res., 400 Cardinal Medeiros Ave., 02141. Tel: 617-547-5593; Fax: 617-547-1505.

2—Blessed Sacrament, (1905), Rev. Paul W. Hurley.
Res., 189 Pearl St., 02139-4087. Tel: 617-547-1669; Fax: 617-547-3220.

3—St. Francis of Assisi, (1917) (Italian), Revs. Norbert DeAmato, O.F.M.; Lucius Annese, O.F.M.; Zravko Kujundzija.
Res., 42 Sciarappa St., 02141-1204. Tel: 617-876-6754; Fax: 617-876-6753.

4—St. Hedwig, (1907) (Polish). Closed. For inquiries for parish records contact the Chancery.

5—Holy Cross, (1920) (Armenian), Rev. Rafael Andonian, C.M.Vd.
Res., 100 Mt. Auburn St., P.O. Box 15, 02238-0015. Tel: 617-547-2122; Fax: 617-547-2122.

6—Immaculate Conception, (1910) (Lithuanian), Rev. Simeon W. Saulenas. In res., Rev. Clement Kasinskas, C.P.
Res., 432 Windsor St., 02141-1343. Tel: 617-547-1623; Fax: 617-547-0336.

7—Immaculate Conception, (1926), Rev. Arthur F. Wright; Sr. Phyllis O'Callagahn, C.S.J., Pastoral Assoc. In res., Rev. W. James Nyhan.
Res., 45 Alewife Brook Pkwy., 02140-1098. Tel: 617-547-3456; Fax: 617-354-8052.

8—St. John the Evangelist, (1893), Revs. Charles E. Collins; William J. Minigan; Francis P. Ready.
Res., 2254 Massachusetts Ave., 02140-1891. Tel: 617-547-4880; Fax: 617-441-8028.
School—Tel: 617-876-3589. Miss Marian Burns, Prin.
Lay Teachers 10; Students 198.

9—St. Mary of the Annunciation, (1867), Revs. John D. Crowley; Alfred Monsalue. In res., Rev. Andres G. Nino, O.S.A.; Sr. Edna Molloy, S.N.D., Pastoral Assoc.
Res., 134 Norfolk St., 02139-1805. Tel: 617-547-0120; Fax: 617-547-0232.

10—Our Lady of Pity, (1892) (French), Revs. Ronald A. Lajoie, S.M.; Guy Cyr, S.M. In res., Rev. Anthony Charest, S.M.; Deacon Alfred Geneus.
Res., 35 Middlesex St., 02140. Tel: 617-547-2037; Fax: 617-547-3037.

11—St. Patrick, (1908). Closed. For sacramental records contact Sacred Heart of Jesus, Cambridge.

12—St. Paul, (1875), Rev. Msgr. Dennis F. Sheehan; Rev. James W. Savage. In res., Rev. George S. Salzmann, O.S.F.S.
Res., 29 Mt. Auburn St., 02138. Tel: 617-491-8400; Fax: 617-354-7092.
School—Tel: 617-868-8658.
Sisters 2; Lay Teachers 4; Students 49.

13—St. Peter, (1848), Rev. William D. Walsh. In res., Rev. Richard Powers.
Res., 31 Buckingham St., 02138-2297. Tel: 617-547-4235; Fax: 617-547-1525.
School—Tel: 617-547-0101.
Sisters 5; Lay Teachers 7; Students 201.

14—Sacred Heart of Jesus, (1842), Rev. John P. Tackney. In res., Revs. David G. Bonfiglio; Paul Miceli.
Res., 49 Sixth St., 02141-1594. Tel: 617-547-0399; Fax: 617-441-8648.

Canton, Norfolk Co., St. Gerard Majella (1960), Revs. Bernard P. McLaughlin; Paul F. Curran; Sr. Christiana Cronin, C.S.J.
Res., 1860 Washington St., 02021-1642. Tel: 617-828-3420; Fax: 617-828-2520.

St. John the Evangelist (1861), Very Rev. James L. McCune, V.F.; Revs. Raymond P. Kiley; Wilfrid L. Pied; Deacon Edward M. Quigley. In res., Rev. Thomas H. Maguire.
Res., 700 Washington St., 02021-3036. Tel: 617-828-0090; Fax: 617-828-2480.
School—Tel: 617-828-2130.
Sisters 1; Lay Teachers 11; Students 256.

Carlisle, Middlesex Co., St. Irene (1960), Rev. Thomas P. Donohoe; Donald M. Nicholson, Pastoral Assoc. In res., Rev. Terence Langley, S.C.J.; Deacon Dean Bulpett.
Res., 187 East St., 01741. Tel: 508-369-3940; Fax: 508-287-1440.

Carver, Plymouth Co., Our Lady of Lourdes (1950), Rev. Edward L. Gallagher; Sr. Elizabeth Brabazon, C.S.J., Pastoral Assoc.
Res., 192 Center St., P.O. Box 68, 02355-0068. Tel: 508-866-4491; Fax: 508-866-5588.

Chelmsford, Middlesex Co., St. John the Evangelist (1893), Revs. Richard J. Craig; John W. Gentleman; Deacon Joseph A. Donnelly; Joyce Wholey, Pastoral Assoc.
Res., 115 Middlesex St., 01863-2037. Tel: 508-251-8571; Fax: 508-251-7873.

St. Mary (1931), Revs. Joseph P. Smyth; Paul J. Finegan; Michael J. Harkins; Deacon Robert W. Dzuris.
Res., 25 North Rd., 01824-2767. Tel: 508-256-2374; Fax: 508-256-0122.

Chelsea, Suffolk Co.,

1—Our Lady of the Assumption, (1907) (French), Rev. James F. Fratus, Admin.
Res., 55 Clark Ave., 02150-2530. Tel: 617-889-2045; Fax: 617-884-3404.
School—Tel: 617-884-5194.
Lay Teachers 9; Students 151.

2—St. Rose, (1849), Revs. James F. Fratus; Francis X. Mawn; Anthony Giang Nguyen; Deacon Robert Carr. Pastoral Assocs.: Sr. Sergia M.S.S.H.; Sr. Pasquala Tejada, M.S.S.H.; Sr. Josepha M.S.S.H.
Res., 601 Broadway, 02150-2998. Tel: 617-889-2774; Fax: 617-889-2854.
School—Tel: 617-884-2626.
Sisters 8; Lay Teachers 10; Students 423.

3—St. Stanislaus, (1905) (Polish), Revs. Andrezj Grelak; Walter Matejek, O.F.M.Conv.
Res., 163 Chestnut St., 02150. Tel: 617-889-0261; Fax: 617-889-2967.

4—Our Lady of Grace (1913), Rev. James J. Barry; Sr. Margaret Holleran, S.S.C.; Deacon Leo A. Martin, Pastoral Assoc.
Res., 59 Nichols St., 02150. Tel: 617-884-0030; Fax: 617-884-0957.
School—Tel: 617-387-8034.
Lay Teachers 7; Students 147.

Cohasset, Norfolk Co., St. Anthony (1873), Rev. John R. Mulvehill.
Res., 129 S. Main St., 02025-2006. Tel: 617-383-0219; Fax: 617-383-2988.

Concord, Middlesex Co., St. Bernard (1863), Rev. John A. Murray; Deacons Alfred Murphy; Robert Kramisch. In res., Rev. Thomas Culley, S.J.
Res., 70 Monument Sq., 01742. Tel: 508-369-3778; Fax: 508-371-3346.

Our Lady Help of Christians (1907), Rev. Austin H. Fleming; Deacon Charles Clough.
Res., 1404 Main St., 01742-2937. Tel: 508-369-2810; Fax: 508-371-0853.

Danvers, Essex Co., St. Mary of the Annunciation (1871), Revs. Gerard L. Dorgan; Mark O'Connell; Richard F. Ahearn; Kenneth Nielson.
Res., 24 Conant St., 01923-2988. Tel: 508-774-0340; Fax: 508-774-9407.

St. Richard (1963), Revs. Charles J. Higgins; Edward Doughty; Deacon David Shrader.
Res., 90 Forest St., 01923. Tel: 508-774-7575; Fax: 508-774-9543.

St. Alphonsus (1917), Rev. Robert W. Kirchmeyer; Robert Tufts, Pastoral Assoc. In res., Rev. Edward D. Cowhig.
Res., 488 Elliott St., Beverly, 01915-2399. Tel: 508-922-1240; Fax: 508-922-8614.

Dedham, Norfolk Co., St. Mary (1866), Revs. John J. Dooher; Christopher J. Hickey. In res., Revs. Edward J. Banks, S.J.; John H. Curley, S.J.
Res., 420 High St., 02026-2892. Tel: 617-326-0550; Fax: 617-326-1809.

St. Susanna (1960), Rev. Terence P. Curley. In res., Rev. Kenneth Gandolfo.
Res., 262 Needham St., 02026-0033. Tel: 617-329-9575; Fax: 617-329-5966.

Dover, Norfolk Co., Most Precious Blood (1959), Rev. Joseph P. Fratic.
Res., 30 Center St., P.O. Box 33, 02030-0033. Tel: 508-785-0305; Fax: 508-785-0432.

Dracut, Middlesex Co., St. Francis (1963), Rev. Brian P. Kiely.
Res., 110 Percy St., 01826. Tel: 508-452-6611; Fax: 508-452-0772.

St. Mary of the Assumption (1909), Rev. Lucien H. Loiselle.
Res., 1868 Lakeview Ave., 01826. Tel: 508-957-3214; Fax: 508-957-7883.

St. Therese (1927) (French), Revs. Lawrence J. Chane; Robert E. Bergeron.
Res., 1340 Lakeview Ave., 01826-3499. Tel: 508-957-0322; Fax: 508-957-5266.

Duxbury, Plymouth Co., Holy Family (1945), Rev. Msgr. William F. Glynn; Rev. Joseph K. Raeke; Deacon Arthur J. Keefe.
Church—601 Tremont St., 02332-4450. Tel: 617-934-5055; Fax: 617-934-5796.

East Bridgewater, Plymouth Co., St. John (1902), Rev. John W. Corcoran; Deacons Leo J. Donoghue; Lee A. Beatrice; Brendan Fitzgerald, Pastoral Assoc.
Res., 210 Central St., 02333-1913. Tel: 508-378-4207; Fax: 508-378-7317.

Essex, Essex Co., St. John the Baptist (1931), Rev. Thomas W. Buckley.
Res., 52 Main St., 01929. Tel: 508-768-6284; Fax: 508-768-2533.

Everett, Middlesex Co.,

1—St. Anthony, (1927) (Italian), Rev. Camillo Lando, C.S.; Deacon Thomas W. Marchant.
Res., 38 Oakes St., 02149. Tel: 617-387-0310; Fax: 617-387-1229.
School—Tel: 617-389-2448.
Sisters 2; Lay Teachers 8; Students 213.

2—Immaculate Conception, (1885), Revs. Edmond J. Sviokla; Joseph L. Crehan, S.S.C.; Keith LeBlanc.
Res., 489 Broadway, 02149. Tel: 617-389-5660; 5661.
School—Tel: 617-387-8304.
Sisters 3; Lay Teachers 9; Students 270.

3—St. Joseph, (1912), Rev. Philip J. DesRosiers.
Res., 195 Bucknam St., 02149-1297. Tel: 617-387-3343; Fax: 617-389-4733.

4—St. Therese, (1927), Rev. Msgr. William J. Forster; Rev. Roger C. Cormier.
Res., 20 Gledhill Ave., 02149-4605. Tel: 617-389-0412; Fax: 617-387-0052.

Foxboro, Norfolk Co., St. Mary (1859), Revs. Richard L. Casey; Stephen J. Madden; Ms. Lenore Danesco, Pastoral Assoc. In res., Rev. John J. Hever.
Res., 83 Central St., 02035. Tel: 508-543-7726.

Framingham, Middlesex Co.,

1—St. Bridget, (1878), Very Rev. Francis V. Strahan, V.F.; Rev. Leroy E. Owens; Mrs. Elizabeth Mingolelli, Pastoral Assoc.

Res., 15 Wheeler Ave., 01702-2902. Tel: 508-875-5959; Fax: 508-875-1270.
School—Tel: 508-875-0181.
Lay Teachers 14; Students 242.

2—St. George, (Saxonville) (1847), Revs. Francis E. O'Brien; Albert C. Hughes; Sr. Ann Marie McAndrews, Pastoral Assoc.; Deacon Neil F. Lacey.
Res., 74 School St., Framingham (Saxonville), 01701. Tel: 508-877-5130; Fax: 508-877-3080.

3—St. Jeremiah, (1958), Revs. William J. O'Connor; Robert W. Murray.
Res., 41 Brook St., 01701-3996. Tel: 508-877-1428; Fax: 508-788-1592.

4—St. Stephen, (1883), Revs. Albert H. Stankard; George F. Emerson; Sr. Beverly Good, Pastoral Assoc.; Deacons Guy Spiri; Pedro Torres. In res., Rev. Emilio S. Allue.
Res., 221 Concord St., 01702. Tel: 508-875-4788; Fax: 508-875-2577.

5—St. Tarcisius, (1907) (Italian), Revs. Joseph A. Scopa, C.S.; Roque R. Pattussi, C.S.
Res., 35 Cedar St., 01701-6950. Tel: 508-875-8623; Fax: 508-875-6358.
School—Tel: 508-872-8188.

Franklin, Norfolk Co., St. Mary (1877), Revs. Thomas J. Walsh; D. George Spagnolia; David F. Ziomek. In res., Rev. Francis W. Beksha.
Res., Church Sq., 02038-1896. Tel: 508-528-0020; Fax: 508-528-0020.

Georgetown, Essex Co., St. Mary (1870), Rev. Frederick J. Collins. In res., Rev. Gerald B. Horgan.
Res., 94 Andover St., P.O. Box 396, 01833. Tel: 508-352-2024; Fax: 508-352-5513.

Gloucester, Essex Co.,

1—St. Ann, (1855), Revs. Frederick Guthrie; James J. O'Driscoll; Deacon Richard Gindel.
Res., 60 Prospect St., 01930. Tel: 508-283-0054; Fax: 508-283-5313.
School—Tel: 508-283-3455.
Sisters 3; Lay Teachers 6; Students 185.
Mission—Magnolia, St. Joseph's Chapel.

2—Our Lady of Good Voyage, (1889) (Portuguese), Rev. Eugene L. Alves.
Res., 142 Prospect St., 01930-3797. Tel: 508-283-1490; Fax: 508-283-0787.

3—St. Peter, (1928), Rev. Thomas J. Fleming.
Res., One Brightside Ave., East Gloucester, 01930-3299. Tel: 508-283-0874; Fax: 508-283-8223.
Chapel—Eastern Point, St. Anthony's-by-the-Sea.

4—Sacred Heart, (1946), Rev. Myron F. Bullock.
Res., 5 High St., 01930-1113. Tel: 508-283-4457; Fax: 508-281-7279.

Groton, Middlesex Co., St. James (1945), Rev. John T. Atwater; Ella Kingsley, Pastoral Assoc.
Res., 29 Old Orchard Rd., P.O. Box 186, West Groton, 01472-0186. Tel: 508-448-5513; Fax: 508-448-9308.
Sacred Heart (1907), Rev. John T. Atwater; Ella Kingsley, Pastoral Assoc.
Res., 271 Main St., P.O. Box 259, 01450. Tel: 508-448-6633; Fax: 508-448-2732.

Groveland, Essex Co., St. Patrick (1946), Rev. Robert H. Gosselin.
Res., 728 Salem St., South Groveland, 01834. Tel: 508-372-6044; Fax: 508-374-9006.

Halifax, Plymouth Co., Our Lady of the Lake (1945), Revs. Paul G. McPartland; Charles D. Logue; Deacon John L. LaFargue.
Res., P.O. Box 35, 580 Monponsett St., 02338-0035. Tel: 617-293-7971; Fax: 617-293-7969.

Hamilton, Essex Co., St. Paul (1922), Rev. Louis D. Bourgeois.
Res., 50 Union St., South Hamilton, 01982-2118. Tel: 508-468-2337; Fax: 508-468-6538.

Hanover, Plymouth Co., St. Mary of the Sacred Heart (1907), Revs. Henry F. Doherty; Bruce G. Flanagan. In res., Rev. John P. Mahoney.
Res., 392 Hanover St., 02339-2215. Tel: 617-826-4303; Fax: 617-826-5203.

Hanson, Plymouth Co., St. Joseph the Worker (1956), Revs. John Mark Hannon; Paul Kevin Hurley.
Res., One Maquan St., 02341-0714. Tel: 617-293-3581; Fax: 617-294-1052.

Haverhill, Essex Co.,

1—St. George, (1961), Rev. James M. Broderick.
Res., 440 Washington St., 01832-5243. Tel: 508-374-8853; Fax: 508-469-0790.

2—St. James, (1859), Revs. Frederick R. McGowan; Edward L. King; Robert D. Smith; Charles J. Higgins.
Res., 6 Cottage St., 01830-4999. Tel: 508-372-8537; Fax: 508-373-1505.

3—St. John the Baptist, (1955), Rev. Frederick E. Sweeney.
Res., 110 Lincoln Ave., 01830. Tel: 508-372-2780; Fax: 508-469-0947.

4—St. Joseph's, (1876) (French), Revs. Emile Guilmette, S.M.; Julian Rondeau, S.M.; Robert Graham, S.M.; Bro. Leonard Haley, S.M., Pastoral Assoc.
Res., 120 Bellevue Ave., 01832. Tel: 508-372-7721; Fax: 508-372-2085.
School—Tel: 508-521-4256.
Sisters 3; Lay Teachers 13; Students 279.

5—St. Michael, (1910) (Polish), Rev. Stanley Wladyka, O.F.M.Conv.
Res., 71 High St., 01832-5496. Tel: 508-372-0023; Fax: 508-521-0544.

6—St. Rita, (1932), Rev. James M. Carroll; Sr. Mildred Malone, C.S.J., Pastoral Assoc.
Res., 61 Temple St., 01832-5499. Tel: 508-372-2513; Fax: 508-374-2477.

7—Sacred Hearts, (1908), Revs. Marc A. Piche; James T. Kelly; Deacon Robert J. Gaudreau; Mrs. Eileen Snow, Pastoral Assoc.
Res., 48 Chestnut St., Bradford, 01835-7446. Tel: 508-373-1281; Fax: 508-374-3043.
School—Tel: 508-372-5451.
Sisters 1; Lay Teachers 9; Students 247.

Hingham, Plymouth Co., St. Paul (1871), Revs. James F. Rafferty; Albert M. Fareta; Deacons John W. McHugh; John B. Halloran, Jr.; Sr. Eleanor Ballantine, Pastoral Assoc.
Res., 147 North St., 02043-7894. Tel: 617-749-0587; Fax: 617-749-8053.
School—18 Fearing Rd., 02043. Tel: 617-749-2407.
Lay Teachers 9; Students 253; Religious 1.
Resurrection of Our Lord and Saviour Jesus Christ (1957), Rev. Arthur M. Calter; Deacon Charles E. Sullivan. In res., Rev. Robert C. Bryson.
Res., 1057 Main St., 02043-1497. Tel: 617-749-3577; Fax: 617-740-0689.

Holbrook, Norfolk Co., St. Joseph (1887), Revs. Paul L. Clougherty; John J. Stagnaro.
Res., 153 S. Franklin St., 02343. Tel: 617-767-0605; Fax: 617-767-2563.
School—143 S. Franklin St., 02343. Tel: 617-767-1544.
Sisters 2; Lay Teachers 14; Students 290.

Holliston, Middlesex Co., St. Mary (1870), Revs. William J. Haley; Mark A. Mahoney; Deacons Martin Breinlinger; Philip Caruso.
Res., 8 Church St., 01746-1741. Tel: 508-429-4427; Fax: 508-429-3324.

Hopkinton, Middlesex Co., St. John the Evangelist (1866), Revs. James F. Degnan; Joseph Diem.
Res., 25 Main St., 01748. Tel: 508-435-3313.

Hudson, Middlesex Co., Christ the King (1927), Rev. Leo R. Mahoney.
Res., 12 Florence St., 01749-2098. Tel: 508-562-7662; Fax: 508-562-9762.
St. Michael (1870), Revs. Thomas M. Curran; Richard M. O'Brien.
Res., 20 High St., 01749-2391. Tel: 508-562-2552; Fax: 508-568-1761.
School—Tel: 508-562-2917.
Lay Teachers 8; Students 119.
High School—Hudson Catholic, Tel: 508-562-6701.

Hull, Plymouth Co., St. Mary of the Assumption (1938), Revs. William G. Williams; Joseph M. White; Deacon Edward L. Doyle.
Res., 58 Nantasket Ave., 02045. Tel: 617-925-0680; Fax: 617-925-0685.

Ipswich, Essex Co., St. Joseph (1889), Rev. Lawrence E. Wetterholm.
Res., One Pineswamp Rd., 01938-2909. Tel: 508-356-3944; Fax: 508-356-9592.
Sacred Heart (1908) (Polish), Rev. Joseph S. Lukas.
Res., 26 Topsfield Rd., 01938-2024. Tel: 508-356-2212; Fax: 508-356-2212.
St. Stanislaus (1910) (French), Rev. Lawrence F. Wetterholm, Admin.
Res., Tel: 508-356-3944; Fax: 508-356-9592.

Kingston, Plymouth Co., St. Joseph (1908), Rev. Msgr. Robert W. McNeill; Deacon William Nagle.
Res., 268 Main St., 02364-1922. Tel: 617-585-6679; Fax: 617-585-7104.

Lakeville, Plymouth Co., Saints Martha and Mary (1958), Rev. Daniel F. Moran. In res., Rev. Thomas J. Mooney.
Res., 354 Bedford St., 02347-2107. Tel: 508-947-2107; Fax: 508-947-6543.

Lawrence, Essex Co.,

1—St. Anne. Closed. For sacramental records contact Sacred Heart, Lawrence.

2—St. Anthony, (1903) (Maronite), Rev. James T. Khoury (SAM); Deacon Allen Ramey; Subdeacons Abraham Abdulla; Tony Saab.
Res., 145 Amesbury St., 01841-3400. Tel: 508-685-7233.

3—Assumption of the Blessed Virgin Mary, (1887) (Spanish), Rev. Vincent E. Daily.
Res., 216 Lawrence St., 01841-1715. Tel: 508-683-1069; Fax: 508-686-4677.

4—St. Augustine, (1935), Rev. Peter G. Gori, O.S.A.; Sr. Monica Madden, S.N.D., Pastoral Assoc.; Deacon Edward J. Grimley.
Res., 124 Ames St., 01841. Tel: 508-686-0727; Fax: 508-686-1988.
School—Tel: 508-682-9761.
Sisters of Notre Dame de Namur 1; Lay Teachers 9; Students 226.

5—St. Francis, (1903) (Lithuanian), Rev. Richard J. Brady.
Res., 94 Bradford St., 01840-1003. Tel: 508-687-7356; Fax: 508-687-6480.

6—Holy Rosary, (1904) (Italian), Revs. Dennis M. McGowan, O.S.A.; Thomas J. Casey, O.S.A.
Res., 35 Essex St., 01840-1797. Tel: 508-685-1711; Fax: 508-687-9047.

7—Holy Trinity, (1905) (Polish), Revs. Daniel Fink, O.F.M.Conv.; Jan Hernik, O.F.M.Conv.; Valerian Czywil, O.F.M.Conv.
Res., 30 Trinity St., 01841. Tel: 508-688-7226; Fax: 508-681-5356.
School—Tel: 508-686-3007.
Sisters 2; Lay Teachers 7; Students 231.

8—St. Joseph, (1902) (Melkite-Greek), Rev. Joseph Thomas, B.S.O.; Deacons Bryan McNeill; John Marmillan.
Res., 241 Hampshire St., 01841. Tel: 508-682-8152; Fax: 508-685-0275.

9—St. Mary Immaculate Conception, (1848), Revs. Russell A. Ortega, O.S.A., Admin.; Jorge A. Reyes, O.S.A.; Arthur G. O'Rourke, O.S.A.; Deacon Murphy Steven; Carlos Urbina, Pastoral Assoc.
Res., 300 Haverhill St., 01840-3698. Tel: 508-685-1111; Fax: 508-686-5555.
School—Tel: 508-685-2091.
Sisters 2; Lay Teachers 8; Students 171.

10—St. Patrick, (1872), Very Rev. George F. Carlson, V.F.; Revs. Kenneth N. German; Stephen S. Donohoe; Lawrence J. Doyle; Sr. Mary O'Connor, S.S.N.D., Pastoral Assoc.; Deacon Paul V. Specht.
Res., 118 S. Broadway, 01843-1427. Tel: 508-683-9416; Fax: 508-681-5808.
School—101 Parker St., 01843. Tel: 508-683-5822.
Sisters 6; Lay Teachers 11; Students 440.

11—SS. Peter and Paul, (1907) (Portuguese), Rev. Albert A. Sylvia; Deacon Richard A. Rocha.
Res., 125 Chestnut St., 01841-3844. Tel: 508-681-9080; Fax: 508-687-4112.

12—Sacred Heart, (1905) (French), Revs. Gerard A. Demers, S.M.; Raymond Fournier, S.M.; Laurence Ross, S.M.; Clifton W. Moors, S.M.; Deacon Gerard E. Gagne.
Res., 321 S. Broadway, 01843-2691. Tel: 508-686-7921; Fax: 508-686-5687.
School—Tel: 508-682-8935.
Sisters 1; Lay Teachers 13; Students 289.

Lexington, Middlesex Co., St. Brigid (1931), Revs. Eugene P. Curtin; David P. O'Donnell; Francine Edwards, Pastoral Assoc.; Deacon William H. Wildes. In res., Rev. Msgr. Robert P. Deeley.
Res., 2001 Massachusetts Ave., 02173. Tel: 617-862-0335; Fax: 617-862-1409.
Sacred Heart (1931), Revs. Arnold F. Coletti; Patrick Tarrant; Sr. Jean Ackerman, O.P., Pastoral Assoc.; Deacon Anthony Rizzuto.
Res., 21 Follen Rd., 02173-5921. Tel: 617-862-4646; Fax: 617-863-5614.

Lincoln, Middlesex Co., St. Joseph (1945), Rev. Lawrence J. Drennan.
Res., 142 Lincoln Rd., Box 234, 01773-0234. Tel: 617-259-8364; Fax: 617-259-3332.

Littleton, Middlesex Co., St. Anne (1945), Very Rev. Edward P. Geary, V.F.; Rev. James G. Burke.
Res., 75 King St., Box 2246, 01460-3246. Tel: 508-486-4100; Fax: 508-952-6303.

Lowell, Middlesex Co.,

1—St. Anthony, (1901) (Portuguese), Rev. Francis M. Glynn. In res., Rev. Antonio Madeiros.
Res., 893 Central St., 01852-3407. Tel: 508-452-1506; Fax: 508-458-9662.

2—Holy Trinity, (1904) (Polish), Rev. Jon C. Martin.
Res., 340 High St., 01852. Tel: 508-452-2564; Fax: 508-452-4679.
School—St. Stanislaus, Tel: 508-453-2360.
Sisters 2; Lay Teachers 6; Students 224.

3—Immaculate Conception, (1869), Revs. John J. Savage, O.M.I.; John J. Lyons, O.M.I.; John F. McHugh, O.M.I.; Francis X. Gorham, O.M.I.; John J. Hogan, O.M.I.; Donald O'Brien, O.M.I. In res., Rev. Lawrence P. Deery, O.M.I.; Bro. Francis Lenehan, O.M.I.
Res., 3 Fayette St., 01852-1298. Tel: 508-458-1474; Fax: 508-446-0790.
School—Tel: 508-454-5339.
Sisters 1; Lay Teachers 8; Students 175.

4—Sainte Jeanne d'Arc, (1922), Revs. Roger E. Lamoureux, O.M.I.; Donald Lozier, O.M.I.; Anatole Lessard, O.M.I.

Res., 129 Fourth Ave., 01854-2904. Tel: 508-458-6316; Fax: 508-970-2299.
School—Tel: 508-453-4114.
Sisters 2; Lay Teachers 18; Students 466.

5—ST. JEAN BAPTISTE. Closed. For sacramental records contact St. Louis de France, Lowell.

6—ST. JOSEPH, (1908) (Lithuanian), Rev. Leonard T. McGrath; Sr. Claire Couillard, S.A.S.V.
Res., 151 Rogers St., 01852. Tel: 508-452-5992; Fax: 508-446-0249.

7—ST. LOUIS DE FRANCE, (1904) (French), Team Ministry: Revs. Leonard E. Pelletier, Mod.; John E. Gallagher.
Res., 221 W. Sixth St., 01850. Tel: 508-454-0496; Fax: 508-446-7992.
School—Tel: 508-458-7594.
Sisters 5; Lay Teachers 6; Students 275.

8—ST. MARGARET, (1910), Revs. Joseph A. Ruggeri; John F. Walsh; Deacon Barry Lloyd.
Res., 374 Stevens St., 01851-3695. Tel: 508-454-5143; Fax: 508-458-8472. [CEM]
School—Tel: 508-453-8491.
Sisters 1; Lay Teachers 19; Students 430.

9—ST. MARIE, (1931), Rev. Paul W. Beauregard, O.M.I.; Deacon Daniel A. Dunn.
Res., 80 Chamberlain St., 01852-5523. Tel: 508-453-2134; Fax: 508-446-0324.

10—ST. MICHAEL, (1883), Revs. Robert E. Nee; Albert J. Capone; Deacon John S. McGrail. Pastoral Assocs.: Sr. Charles Francis, O.P.; Sr. Rose Frances, O.P.
Res., 543 Bridge St., 01850. Tel: 508-459-0713; Fax: 508-453-1123.
School—Lay Teachers 9; Students 260.

11—NOTRE DAME DE LOURDES, (1908) (French), Rev. James P. Robichaud, O.M.I. Pastoral Assocs.: Carmen Coughlan; Jeanne C. Pinard. In res., Rev. Robert G. Levesque, O.M.I.; Bro. Andrew W. Sonsenig.
Res., 101 Smith St., 01851-2698. Tel: 508-459-2339; Fax: 508-446-0838.

12—NUESTRA SENORA DEL CARMEN 1990, (1990), Revs. James Loiacono, O.M.I.; Terrence E. O'Connell, O.M.I. In res., Revs. George Protopapas, O.M.I.; Thomas G. Coughlin, O.M.I.
Res., 725 Merrimack St., 01854-3978. Tel: 508-459-7829; Fax: 508-446-0442.

13—ST. PATRICK, (1831), Revs. Arthur M. Coyle; Anthony Giang Nguyen; Deacon Peter An Ros.
Res., 282 Suffolk St., 01854-4297. Tel: 508-459-0561; Fax: 508-446-0266.
School—Tel: 508-458-4232.
Sisters 2; Lay Teachers 8; Students 231.

14—ST. PETER, (1841). Closed. For inquiries for parish records contact Sacred Heart, Lowell.

15—SHRINE OF ST. RITA, (1910), Revs. Daniel M. Magni; Paul R. Soper.
Res., 158 Mammoth Rd., 01854. Tel: 508-452-4812; Fax: 508-459-8969.

16—SACRED HEART, (1884), Very Rev. John W. Hanley, O.M.I., V.F.; Rev. Leo Wetzel, O.M.I.; Sr. Joan Gregoire, S.N.D. In res., Rev. Gerald Forkin, O.M.I.
Res., 159 Moore St., 01852-5099. Tel: 508-453-3962; Fax: 508-454-3466.
School—Tel: 508-453-4751.
Sisters 1; Lay Teachers 8; Students 255.

Lynn, Essex Co.,

1—HOLY FAMILY, (1922) (Italian), Rev. Gregory Mercurio, Admin.
Res., 26 Bessom St., East Lynn, 01902-1205. Tel: 617-599-7200; Fax: 617-599-7201.

2—ST. JEAN BAPTISTE, (1886) (French), Rev. David J. Bartley; Sr. Estelle Grenier, S.A.S.V., Pastoral Assoc.; Deacon Richard W. Cordeau.
Res., 7 Endicott St., 01902-4005. Tel: 617-592-4246; Fax: 617-598-9930.

3—ST. JOSEPH, (1874), Rev. James E. Gaudreau.
Res., 40 Green St., 01902-2999. Tel: 617-599-7040; Fax: 617-598-7439.
Convent—Sisters of St. Joseph 2.

4—ST. MARY, (1862), Revs. Paul V. Garrity; Michael M. Ferraro; Charles J. Hughes; Lamartine Petit-Monsieur; Timothy Kearney; Deacon Timothy F. Dempsey; Sr. Eileen Burns, S.N.D., Pastoral Assoc.
Res., 8 S. Common St., 01902-4489. Tel: 617-598-4907; Fax: 617-599-2088.
High School—Tel: 617-595-7885.
Lay Teachers 16; Students 291.

5—ST. MICHAEL, (1906) (Polish), Rev. Kazimierz Zastawny.
Res., 567 Summer St., 01905-2011. Tel: 617-593-4584; Fax: 617-599-7547.

6—ST. PATRICK, (1906), Rev. Paul V. Garrity; Sr. Eileen Burns, S.N.D., Pastoral Assoc.
Res., 12 Orchard St., 01905. Tel: 617-599-7750; Fax: 617-599-2201.

7—ST. PIUS THE FIFTH, (1912), Team Ministry: Revs. Edward T. Malone; Robert J. Deehan; Scott Euvrad; Deacon Edward Elibero. In res., Rev. Msgr. Peter F. Hart.
Res., 215 Maple St., 01904-2799. Tel: 617-595-7487; Fax: 617-595-7270.
School—Tel: 617-593-8292.
Sisters 2; Lay Teachers 8; Students 540.

8—SACRED HEART, (1894), Revs. Jerome F. Gillespie; Oscar J. Pratt; Deacon John Hardy.
Res., 571 Boston St., 01905-2160. Tel: 617-593-8047; Fax: 617-599-4040.
School—Tel: 617-592-7581.
Sisters 1; Lay Teachers 8; Students 261.

Lynnfield, Essex Co., Our Lady of the Assumption (1937), Very Rev. John E. Farrell, V.F.; Rev. Kevin J. O'Leary.
Res., 17 Grove St., 01940-1446. Tel: 617-598-4313; Fax: 617-598-0055.
School—Sisters 1; Lay Teachers 16; Students 457.

St. Maria Goretti (1960), Rev. J. Michael Lawlor. In res., Rev. John J. Stagnaro.
Res., 112 Chestnut St., 01940. Tel: 617-334-2367.

Malden, Middlesex Co.,

1—IMMACULATE CONCEPTION, (1854), Revs. Frank J. Silva; John M. Sullivan; Henry T. Ronan; Michael Parise; Peter J. Murphy. Pastoral Assocs.: Sr. Laetitia Campbell, O.P.; Sr. Julienn E. Sullivan, S.N.D.
Res., 10 Fellsway E., 02148. Tel: 617-324-4941; Fax: 617-397-8571.
School—Tel: 617-322-0129.
Sisters 3; Lay Teachers 14; Students 426.

2—ST. JOSEPH, (1902), Revs. John A. Daley; Richard T. Bakker; Sr. Deborah Daigle, Pastoral Assoc.
Res., 790 Salem St., 02148. Tel: 617-324-0402; Fax: 617-324-1790.

3—SACRED HEARTS, (1890), Revs. Daniel J. Hickey; Martin J. Walsh, Jr.
Res., 297 Main St., 02148. Tel: 617-324-0728.
School—Tel: 617-324-6584.
Sisters 2; Lay Teachers 17; Students 463.

4—ST. PETER, (1972) (Italian), Rev. Alfred V. Puccini. In res., Rev. John U. Paris.
Res., 12 Thacher St., 02148. Tel: 617-322-6142; Fax: 617-321-6169.

Manchester, Essex Co., Sacred Heart (1905), Rev. James J. Harrington.
Res., 62 School St., 01944. Tel: 508-526-1263; Fax: 508-526-4335.

Marblehead, Essex Co., Our Lady, Star of the Sea (1859), Revs. Dennis J. Burns; Joseph R. Foster.
Res., 85 Atlantic Ave., 01945-3036. Tel: 617-631-0086; Fax: 617-631-5668.

Marlboro, Middlesex Co.,

1—ST. ANN, (1921) (Italian), Revs. G. Michael Bercik, O.F.M.; Richard Donovan, O.F.M.; Bro. Damien Johnson, O.F.M.
Res., 466 Lincoln St., 01752-3036. Tel: 508-485-1968; Fax: 508-481-7255.

2—IMMACULATE CONCEPTION, (1854), Revs. Paul J. McLaughlin; J. Garret Thompson; Deacon Douglas Peltak. In res., Rev. Geraldo Ildeo Franco.
Res., 17 Washington Ct., 01752. Tel: 508-485-0016; Fax: 508-480-9644.
School—Tel: 508-460-3400.
Lay Teachers 14; Students 257.

3—ST. MARY, (1870) (French), Revs. Laurier J. Martineau; Lionel P. Ouellette.
Res., 26 Broad St., 01752-4098. Tel: 508-485-0390; Fax: 508-480-9835.

4—ST. MATTHIAS, (1963), Rev. John R. Lizio; Deacon Robert I. Hoaglund.
Res., 409 Hemenway St., 01752-6710. Tel: 508-460-9255; Fax: 508-480-8801.

Marshfield, Plymouth Co., St. Ann's by the Sea (1945), Revs. Edward T. Serena; Stephen M. Healy.
Res., 591 Ocean St. P.O. Box 2607, Ocean Bluffs (Marshfield), 02065. Tel: 617-834-4953; Fax: 617-834-7472.

St. Christine (1945), Revs. Francis A. Regan; Vincent P. Doolan. Pastoral Assocs.: Mary Doolan; Barbara MacRae.
Res., Rte. 3A, P.O. Box 274, Marshfield Hills, 02051-0274. Tel: 617-834-6003; Fax: 617-834-0671.
Mission—Humarock, St. Theresa's.

Our Lady of the Assumption (1949), Rev. Donald P. Clifford.
Res., 40 Canal St., P.O. Box 368, Green Harbor, 02041-0368. Tel: 617-834-6252; Fax: 617-834-5694.

Maynard, Middlesex Co., St. Bridget (1881), Revs. Kenneth Quinn; Michael A.J. Alfano; Deacon John Pepi.
Res., One Percival St., 01754-1699. Tel: 508-897-2171; Fax: 508-897-5358.

St. Casimir (1912) (Polish), Rev. Louis S. Bilicky.
Res., 253 Main St., 01754. Tel: 508-897-2403; Fax: 508-897-1258.

Medfield, Norfolk Co., St. Edward the Confessor (1892), Rev. Kevin J. Crowley; Sr. Mary Jane Sullivan, R.S.C.J., Pastoral Assoc.
Res., 133 Spring St., P.O. Box 336, 02052-0003. Tel: 508-359-2633; Fax: 508-359-1846.

Medford, Middlesex Co.,

1—ST. FRANCIS OF ASSISI, (1921), Revs. Brian McMahon; Paul Coughlin; Sr. Marie Ridge, S.N.D., Pastoral Assoc.; Deacon Henry A. Mariani.
Res., 441 Fellsway W., 02155. Tel: 617-396-3400; Fax: 617-396-3254.
School—Tel: 617-395-9170.
Sisters 4; Lay Teachers 12; Students 347.

2—ST. JAMES, (1919), Rev. Paul R. Franz; Deacon Arthur F. Rogers, Jr.
Res., 779 Fellsway, 02155-4953. Tel: 617-396-0025; Fax: 617-396-2161.

3—ST. JOSEPH, (1883), Team Ministry: Revs. Robert J. Fountain; Patrick McLaughlin; Patrick J. McLaughlin; Deacon Robert Amerault; Mrs. Kathy Mitchell, Pastoral Assoc. In res., Rev. Francis T. McFarland.
Res., 114 High St., 02155-3882. Tel: 617-396-3860; Fax: 617-391-2919.
School—Tel: 617-396-3636.
Sisters 5; Lay Teachers 14; Students 342.

4—ST. RAPHAEL, (1905), Revs. Dennis T. Nason; Mark G. Derrane. In res., Rev. Charles T. Duggan, Senior Priest.
Res., 38 Boston Ave., West Medford, 02155-6722. Tel: 617-488-5444; Fax: 617-483-3375.
School—Sisters of St. Joseph 2; Lay Teachers 11; Students 283.

5—SACRED HEART, (1937), Rev. Robert J. Doherty. In res., Rev. Anthony J. Vasatauro.
Res., 51 Winthrop St., 02155-5324. Tel: 617-396-2232; Fax: 617-396-3731.

Medway, Norfolk Co., St. Joseph (1885), Revs. William M. MacKenzie; Clyde H. Chetwynd.
Res., 2 Barber St., Box 557, Village Station, 02053508-533-1236. Tel: 617-533-6500.

Melrose, Middlesex Co., Incarnation (1958), Team Ministry: Revs. David F. Delaney; Lawrence E. Pratt; Deacon John W. Wise.
Res., 429 Upham St., 02176-3233. Tel: 617-662-8844; 662-9340; Fax: 617-662-6653.

St. Mary of the Annunciation (1894), Rev. John J. Ronaghan; Rev. Msgr. Alfonso G. Palladino; Rev. David P. Callahan.
Res., 46 Myrtle St., 02176-3898. Tel: 617-665-0152; Fax: 617-665-2750.
School—4 Myrtle St., 02176. Tel: 617-665-5037.
Lay Teachers 10; Students 198.

Merrimac, Essex Co., Nativity (1891), Rev. Henry M. Cunney.
Res., 4 Green St., 01860. Tel: 508-346-8604; Fax: 508-346-9970.

Methuen, Essex Co.,

1—ST. LUCY, (1958), Revs. Angelo P. Loscocco; Thomas E. Keyes; Deacon Leonard B. Albis.
Res., 254 Merrimack St., 01844. Tel: 508-686-3311.

2—ST. MONICA, (1917), Revs. Richard P. Little; Robert G. Buckley; Robert W. Conole.
Res., 231 Broadway, 01844-3067. Tel: 508-683-1193; Fax: 508-686-0249.
School—Tel: 508-686-1801.
Sisters 4; Lay Teachers 12; Students 522.

3—OUR LADY OF MOUNT CARMEL, (1937), Revs. Andre Gosselin, S.M.; John Meade, S.M.; Roland Lacasse, S.M.
Res., 78 Union St., 01844-3699. Tel: 508-682-9160; 685-6290; Fax: 508-725-6099.
School—Tel: 508-688-3040.
Sisters 1; Lay Teachers 9; Students 221.

4—ST. THERESA, (1936) (French), Revs. Walter Gaudreau, S.M.; Leo Bourdeau, S.M. In res., Rev. Irenee DuPerry, S.M.
Res., 22 Plymouth St., 01844-4299. Tel: 508-686-3984; Fax: 508-686-8300.

Middleboro, Plymouth Co., Sacred Heart (1885), Rev. Ronald G. Calhoun. In res., Rev. John J. Philbin.
Res., 340 Center St., 02346. Tel: 508-947-0444; Fax: 508-947-2364.

Middleton, Essex Co., St. Agnes (1945), Very Rev. Samuel J. Lombard, V.F.; Deacon John M. Bresnahan; Janine Bowes, Pastoral Assoc.
Res., 22 Boston St., 01949-2199. Tel: 508-774-1958; Fax: 508-774-1964.

Millis, Norfolk Co., St. Thomas the Apostle (1937), Rev. Henry C. Chambers.
Res., 111 Exchange St., 02054-9998. Tel: 508-376-2621; Fax: 508-376-4308.

Milton, Norfolk Co.,

1—ST. AGATHA, (1922), Revs. Francis X. Turke; Robert J. Bowers; Sr. Rita MacDonald, S.C.H., Pastoral Assoc.; Deacon Daniel F. Sullivan. In res., Rev. Charles E. Anadore, Senior Priest.
Res., 432 Adams St., 02186-4399. Tel: 617-698-2439; 698-2507; Fax: 617-698-1517.

School—Tel: 617-696-3548.
Sisters 2; Lay Teachers 15; Students 377.

2—St. Elizabeth, (1946), Revs. Gilbert S. Phinn; William R. Coen; Vincent E. Daily; Sr. Regina Harrington, C.S.J., Pastoral Assoc.; Deacon Joseph MacDonald.
Res., 350 Reedsdale Rd., 02186. Tel: 617-696-6688; Fax: 617-698-4864.

3—St. Mary of the Hills, (1931), Rev. Thomas C. Foley; Deacon John P. Connor, Jr.
Res., 29 St. Mary's Rd., 02186-2024. Tel: 617-696-0120; Fax: 617-696-7044.
School—Tel: 617-698-2464.
Sisters 2; Lay Teachers 14; Students 307.

4—St. Pius Tenth, (1954), Rev. David M. Burke.
Res., 865 Brush Hill Rd., 02186-1299. Tel: 617-333-0401; Fax: 617-333-0191.

Nahant, Essex Co., St. Thomas Aquinas (1902), Rev. George D. Vartzelis.
Res., 248 Nahant Rd., 01908. Tel: 617-581-0023; Fax: 617-598-8860.

Natick, Middlesex Co., St. Linus (1950), Rev. J. Robert Giggi.
Res., 119 Hartford St., 01760-6092. Tel: 508-653-5505; Fax: 508-655-4577.

St. Patrick (1856), Revs. Daniel F. Twomey; Nicholas C. Ciccone, Jr.
Res., 44 E. Central St., 01760-4639. Tel: 508-653-1093; Fax: 508-650-2922.

Sacred Heart (1891), Rev. Thomas F. Murray. In res., Rev. William J. Donlon, Senior Priest.
Res., 19 Eliot St., 01760-6092. Tel: 508-653-5113; Fax: 508-653-3051.

Needham, Norfolk Co., St. Bartholomew (1952), Revs. Francis D. Garrity; Henry J. Meade; Rev. Msgr. John F. Lawlor.
Res., 1180 Greendale Ave., 02192-4700. Tel: 617-444-3434; Fax: 617-449-7550.

St. Joseph (1917), Revs. James J. Haddad; John W. Delaney; Deacon William J. McCarty. In res., Rev. Francis J. McGann.
Res., 1382 Highland Ave., 02192-2694. Tel: 617-444-0245; Fax: 617-444-7713.
School—Tel: 617-444-4459.
Sisters 1; Lay Teachers 18; Students 411.

Newburyport, Essex Co., Immaculate Conception (1848), Revs. Robert L. Connors; Kevin P. Horrigan; Deacon Milton E. Connelly, Jr.; Sr. Ellen Julie Flanagan, S.N.D., Pastoral Assoc.
Res., 7 Court St., 01950-2502. Tel: 508-462-2724; Fax: 508-463-6989.
School—Tel: 508-465-7780.
Sisters 2; Lay Teachers 7; Students 198.
Mission—Plum Island, St. James.

St. Louis de Gonzague (1902) (French), Rev. Robert G. Labrie; Deborah Bartlett, Pastoral Assoc.
Res., 17 Federal St., 01950-2899. Tel: 508-465-7333; Fax: 508-463-8938.

Newton, Middlesex Co.,

1—St. Bernard, (1876), Revs. Gerard D. Barry; Stephen J. Malloy; Sr. Diane Vallerio, Pastoral Assoc. In res., Rev. Francis M. Conroy.
Res., 1529 Washington St., West Newton, 02165-4419. Tel: 617-244-0608; Fax: 617-332-4951.

2—Corpus Christi, (1922), Rev. Joseph F. McGlone; Sr. Anne Marie Ralph, S.N.D., Pastoral Assoc. In res., Rev. Vincent H. Poirier.
Res., 45 Ash St., Newton (Auburndale), 02166. Tel: 617-244-9110; Fax: 617-558-7515.

3—St. Ignatius, (1926), Revs. Robert F. VerEecke, S.J.; James F. Morgan, S.J.; Joseph E. O'Connor, S.J.; James A. Benson, S.J.; James Mattaliano, S.J.
Res., 28 Commonwealth Ave., Newton (Chestnut Hill), 02167-3849. Tel: 617-332-1104; Fax: 617-244-0488.

4—St. John the Evangelist, (1911), Rev. Walter H. Cuenin; Deacon Robert N. Johnson. Pastoral Assocs.: Sr. Marie LaBollita, S.C.; Mary Ellen Cocks; Thomas Leahy. In res., Rev. Msgr. Michael Foster; Revs. John E. Sassani; Michael Medas.
Res., 253 Watertown St., 02158-1494. Tel: 617-527-7560; Fax: 617-527-1338.

5—Mary Immaculate of Lourdes, (1870), Rev. Stephen E. Koen. In res., Rev. James Fitzmaurice, O.F.M.
Res., 270 Elliot St., Newton-Upper Falls, 02164-203. Tel: 617-244-0558; Fax: 617-965-4815.

6—Our Lady Help of Christians, (1878), Rev. Walter H. Cuenin; Deacon Robert Johnson. Pastoral Assocs.: Mr. Thomas Leahy; Marie Labollita; Mary Ellen Cocks. In res., Revs. Paul E. Kilroy; Francis P. O'Brien; Peter Wolf.
Res., 573 Washington St., 02158-1494. Tel: 617-527-7560; Fax: 617-527-1338.
High School—Trinity Catholic High School Interparish, Tel: 617-244-1841.
Sisters 2; Lay Teachers 10; Students 152.

7—St. Philip Neri, (1934), Rev. Charles J. McCoy.
Res., 1518 Beacon St., Newton (Waban), 02168-1530. Tel: 617-244-0590; Fax: 617-558-7522.

8—Sacred Heart, (1890), Rev. John J. Connelly.
Res., 1321 Centre St., 02159-2496. Tel: 617-969-2248; Fax: 617-965-7515.

Norfolk, Norfolk Co., St. Jude (1949), Rev. Robert M. Connor.
Res., 86 Main St., Box 305, 02056-0305. Tel: 508-528-0170; Fax: 508-528-1470.

North Andover, Essex Co., St. Michael (1900), Revs. Paul T. Keyes; George C. Hogan; Michael C Randone.
Res., 196 Main St., 01845-2598. Tel: 508-686-4050; Fax: 508-606-5408.
School—Tel: 508-686-1862.
Sisters 8; Lay Teachers 8; Students 153.

North Reading, Middlesex Co., St. Theresa (1945), Revs. Thomas M. Gillespie; Paul L. Ring; Deacon Alfred Balestracci; Marjorie Hedley, Pastoral Assoc.
Res., 63 Winter St., 01864-2264. Tel: 508-664-3412; Fax: 508-276-0034.

Norwell, Plymouth Co., St. Helen (1950), Rev. Richard J. Smith.
Res., 383 Washington St., 02061-2009. Tel: 617-659-2993; Fax: 617-659-7861.

Norwood, Norfolk Co.,

1—St. Catherine of Siena, (1890), Revs. Arthur A. Brown; Emile R. Boutin; James P. Braley; Sr. Frances Sears, C.S.J., Pastoral Assoc.
Res., 547 Washington St., 02062-0547. Tel: 617-762-6080; Fax: 617-256-9312.
School—Tel: 617-769-5354.
Sisters 1; Lay Teachers 20; Students 472.

2—St. George, (1912) (Lithuanian), Rev. William L. Wolkovich.
Res., 36 St. George Ave., 02062-4420. Tel: 617-762-0979; Fax: 617-762-6389.

3—St. Peter, (1918) (Polish), Rev. Richard P. Waswewski.
Res., 27 St. Joseph Ave., 02062-4310. Tel: 617-762-0852; Fax: 617-769-7326.

4—St. Timothy, (1963), Revs. Richard Butler; Sean M. McCarthy. In res., Rev. James A. Field.
Res., 650 Nichols St., 02062. Tel: 617-769-2522; Fax: 617-769-9362.

Peabody, Essex Co.,

1—St. Adelaide, (1962), Revs. Robert H. Blute; John C. Chaisson; Deacon Anthony Juliano.
Res., 17 Bow St., 01960-3427. Tel: 508-535-1985; Fax: 508-535-4845.

2—St. Ann, (1937), Rev. Wallace E. Blackwood; Deacon Martin J. Walsh.
Res., 136 Lynn St., 01960-6432. Tel: 508-531-1480; Fax: 508-531-6683.

3—St. John the Baptist, (1874), Rev. Msgr. John P. McDonough, V.F.; Revs. Robert M. Blaney; Francisco Anzoategui, S.X.; Rev. Msgr. Francis G. O'Sullivan; Rev. Clifton M Thuma; Sr. Nancy Rowen, S.N.D., Pastoral Assoc.
Res., 17 Chestnut St., 01960-5480. Tel: 508-531-0002; Fax: 508-531-5199.
School—Tel: 508-531-0444.
Sisters 5; Lay Teachers 5; Students 578.

4—St. Joseph, (1927), Rev. John Sutton. In res., Most Rev. Francis X. Irwin, Aux. Bishop of Boston.
Res., 2 Gardner St., 01960-1896. Tel: 508-531-0087; Fax: 508-531-5312.

5—Our Lady of Fatima, (1965),
Res., 35 Newcastle Rd., 01960. Tel: 508-532-0272; Fax: 508-977-2991.

Pembroke, Plymouth Co., St. Thecla (1964), Revs. James F. Mahoney; James E. Robertson.
Res., 145 Washington St., 02358-0587. Tel: 617-826-9786; Fax: 617-826-3484.

Pepperell, Middlesex Co., St. Joseph (1870), Rev. Robert J. Butler; Sr. Roberta Rzeznik, S.N.D., Pastoral Assoc.
Res., 28 Tarbell St., Box 1486, 01463-3486. Tel: 508-433-5737; Fax: 508-433-9566.

Plainville, Norfolk Co., St. Martha (1953), Rev. Vincent R. Maffei. In res., Rev. John E. Jusseaume.
Res., 227 South St., P.O. Box 1745, 02762-1745. Tel: 508-699-8543; Fax: 508-699-6677.

Plymouth, Plymouth Co.,

1—Blessed Kateri Tekakwitha, (1982), Rev. William T. Kremmell; Deacon Edward F. Creutz.
Res., 126 S. Meadow Rd., 02360-4740. Tel: 508-747-1568; Fax: 508-747-0616.

2—St. Bonaventure, (1950), Very Rev. William F. Kenneally, V.F.; Rev. Donald A. Sherpenski, S.J.; Deacon Charles H. Bower.
Res., 807 State Rd., P.O. Box 996, Plymouth (Manomet), 02345-0996. Tel: 508-224-3636; Fax: 508-224-5889.
Mission—White Horse Beach, St. Catherine's Chapel.

3—St. Mary, (1915), Revs. Francis A. O'Hara; James F. Lanergan.
Res., 313 Court St., 02360-4336. Tel: 508-746-0426; Fax: 508-747-5886.

4—St. Peter, (1876), Revs. Paul F. Bailey; John J. Shea.
Res., 81 Court St., 02360-3886. Tel: 508-746-0663; Fax: 508-747-1071.

Quincy, Norfolk Co.,

1—St. Ann, (1922), Revs. Thomas F. Keane; Gerard V. Dever.
Res., 757 Hancock St., Quincy (Wollaston), 02170-2761. Tel: 617-479-5400; Fax: 617-479-0955.
School—St. Ann's Rd., 02170. Tel: 617-471-9071.
Sisters 4; Lay Teachers 8; Students 176.

2—St. Boniface, (1956), Rev. Richard S. DeVeer.
Res., 26 Shed St., 02169-5923. Tel: 617-479-9200; Fax: 617-479-5766.

3—St. John the Baptist, (1863), Revs. Peter F. Quinn; Richard S. Moran, C.SS.R.; Gerard Petringa; Deacon Joseph A. Papile. In res., Revs. Theodore L. Fortier, A.A.; William R. McCarthy.
Res., 21 Gay St., 02169-6602. Tel: 617-773-1021; Fax: 617-773-5608.

4—St. Joseph, (1917), Revs. Robert J. Monagle; Daniel J. Riley; Deacon John F. Jennette.
Res., 556 Washington St., 02169-7216. Tel: 617-472-6321; Fax: 617-471-8849.
School—Tel: 617-773-8080.
Sisters 3; Lay Teachers 9; Students 234.

5—St. Mary, (1840), Revs. Ronald L. Bourgault; John M. Rowan.
Res., 115 Crescent St., 02169. Tel: 617-773-0120; Fax: 617-786-9199.
School—Tel: 617-773-5237.
Lay Teachers 10; Students 226.

6—Most Blessed Sacrament, (1915), Revs. William J. English; John P. Carroll; Deacon Paul G. Markey.
Res., 1000 Sea St., 02169. Tel: 617-773-0233; Fax: 617-471-7143.

7—Our Lady of Good Counsel, (1938), Rev. James F. Curtin; Sr. Barbara Higgins, S.C., Pastoral Assoc.
Res., 227 Sea St., 02169-2537. Tel: 617-472-1408; Fax: 617-847-3958.

8—Sacred Heart, (1903), Revs. John W. O'Brien; David P. White; Deacon John D. Salenius. In res., Rev. James F. Hawker.
Res., 386 Hancock St., 02171-2414. Tel: 617-328-8666; Fax: 617-773-2522.
School—Tel: 617-328-3830.
Sisters 5; Lay Teachers 16; Students 479.

9—Star of the Sea, (1945), Rev. Daniel J. Crowley.
Res., 107 Bellevue Rd., N. Quincy, 02171. Tel: 617-328-0866; Fax: 617-328-8457.

Randolph, Norfolk Co., St. Bernadette (1937), Revs. Richard C. Conway; Joseph Skyva; Deacon John J. Ego.
Res., 1026 N. Main St., 02368-3099. Tel: 617-963-1327; Fax: 617-963-0198.

St. Mary (1851), Revs. Richard L. Harrington; Kevin M. Sepe; Deacon James Eames.
Res., 211 N. Main St., 02368. Tel: 617-963-4141; Fax: 617-963-0884.

Reading, Middlesex Co., St. Agnes (1904), Revs. Arthur C. Flynn; Thomas J. Powers; Deacon Jack H. Fenton; Carol A. Gaudette, Pastoral Assoc.
Res., 186 Woburn St., 01867-3599. Tel: 617-944-0490; Fax: 617-944-4409.

St. Athanasius (1961), Revs. Francis C. O'Hare; Richard T. Conway; Sr. Jean Delaney, O.P., Pastoral Assoc.
Res., 306 Haverhill St., 01867-1898. Tel: 617-944-0330; Fax: 617-944-1266.

Revere, Suffolk Co.,

1—St. Anthony of Padua, (1906) (Italian), Revs. F. Dominic Menna; Anthony J. Rebeiro; Deacon Joseph Belmonte.
Res., 250 Revere St., 02151-4618. Tel: 617-289-1234; Fax: 617-284-7123.

2—Immaculate Conception, (1888), Revs. Joseph A. Antonellis; Ronald A. Barker; Deacons Francis M. Gaffney; Frederick G. Guarante.
Res., 22 Lowe St., 02151-3125. Tel: 617-289-0735; Fax: 617-286-1124.
School—Tel: 617-284-0519.
Sisters 3; Lay Teachers 6; Students 269.

3—St. John Vianney, (1950), Rev. Francis B. Leonard.
Res., 7 Harrington Ave., 02151. Tel: 617-289-5268.

4—St. Mary of the Assumption, (1947), Rev. William L. Butler.
Res., 670 Washington Ave., 02151. Tel: 617-284-5252.

5—Our Lady of Lourdes, (1905), Rev. Vincent J. Gianni.
Res., One Endicott Ave., Beachmont, 02151. Tel: 617-284-0234.

6—St. Theresa, (1937), Rev. Edward J. Gaudette.
Res., 500 Revere St., 02151-1536. Tel: 617-289-2404; Fax: 617-286-9256.

Rochester, Plymouth Co., St. Rose of Lima, Rev. John P. Lyons.
Res., 282 Vaughan Hill Rd., Box 40, 02770-0040. Tel: 508-763-2244; Fax: 508-763-9877.

Rockland, Plymouth Co., Holy Family (1882), Revs. James F. Hickey; John J. Walsh, S.J.; Sr. Ann Conway, C.S.J., Pastoral Assoc. In res., Rev. Henry F. Barry, Senior Priest.
Res., 403 Union St., 02370-1799. Tel: 617-878-0160; Fax: 617-871-6389.
School—Tel: 617-878-1154.
Religious 3; Lay Teachers 14; Students 315.

Rockport, Essex Co., St. Joachim (1870), Rev. Ronald J. Gariboldi; Deacon William F.X. Kane.
Res., 9 Broadway Ave., 01966. Tel: 508-546-6756; Fax: 508-546-2272.

Rowley, Essex Co., St. Mary (1945), Rev. James D. Lyons; Ms. Lynn Annen, Pastoral Assoc.; Deacon Daniel E. McCarthy.
Res., Main St., 01969-0737. Tel: 508-948-3344; Fax: 508-948-3356.

Salem, Essex Co.,

1—St. Anne, (1901) (French), Rev. George J. Dufour; Deacon Lewis Warren.
Res., 292 Jefferson Ave., 01970-2895. Tel: 508-744-1930; Fax: 508-745-1190.

2—Immaculate Conception, (1826), Revs. Daniel J. Doyle; Timothy J. Murphy.
Res., 15 Hawthorne Blvd., 01970-3709. Tel: 508-745-6303; Fax: 508-744-4382.

3—St. James, (1850), Revs. John F. Leonard; Francis J. Ritchie. In res., Rev. Maurice V. Connolly; Deacon George L'Ialien.
Res., 161 Federal St., 01970-3297. Tel: 508-745-9060; Fax: 508-745-4229.

4—St. John the Baptist, (1903) (Polish), Rev. Stanley Parsieniczyk (Poland).
Res., 28 St. Peter St., 01970. Tel: 508-744-1278; Fax: 508-744-2093.

5—St. John the Baptist Ukrainian Catholic, (1918) (Ukrainian), Rev. James Morris.
Res., Bridge and Lemon St., Box 208, 01970-0208. Tel: 508-745-3151; Fax: 508-745-3151.

6—St. Joseph, (1873) (French), Revs. Lawrence J. Rondeau; James D. Foley; Deacon Norman P. LaPointe.
Res., 135 Lafayette St., 01970-5099. Tel: 508-744-0095; Fax: 508-744-3312.
School—Tel: 508-744-4773.
Sisters 4; Lay Teachers 6; Students 232.

7—St. Mary's Italian Church, (1918) (Italian), Rev. Edward M. Keohan, Admin.
Res., 56 Margin St., 01970. Tel: 508-744-0631; 745-9740; Fax: 508-744-4620.

8—St. Thomas the Apostle, (1927), Rev. Daniel J. Sheehan; Deacon John M. Barton.
Res., One Margin St., Peabody P.O., 01960-1999. Tel: 508-531-0224; Fax: 508-531-6517.

Salisbury, Essex Co., Star of the Sea (1947), Rev. Thomas B. Morgan.
Res., 28 Beach Rd., 01950-2007. Tel: 508-465-3334; Fax: 508-465-5524.

Saugus, Essex Co., Blessed Sacrament (1917), Revs. John F. Mulloy; Gerald J. Foley; Paul Flammia; Sr. Mary O'Rourke, C.S.J., Pastoral Assoc.
Res., 14 Summer St., 01906-2189. Tel: 617-233-2497; Fax: 617-231-5569.
St. Margaret (1949), Rev. George E. Morin.
Res., 431 Lincoln Ave., 01906-3917. Tel: 617-233-1040; Fax: 617-233-7135.

Scituate, Plymouth Co., St. Frances Xavier Cabrini (1960), Rev. James M. Gibbons.
Res., 78 Mann Hill Rd., North Scituate, 02066-2117. Tel: 617-545-4585; Fax: 617-545-4249.
St. Mary of the Nativity (1921), Rev. Msgr. Eugene P. McNamara; Rev. Stirling B. MacDonald; Mrs. Joanne Curry, Pastoral Assoc.
Res., One Kent St., 02066-4215. Tel: 617-545-3335; Fax: 617-545-6538.

Sharon, Norfolk Co., Our Lady of Sorrows (1906), Rev. Robert W. Bullock; Deacon Michael Iwanowicz.
Res., 59 Cottage St., 02067-2132. Tel: 617-784-2265; Fax: 617-784-2540.

Sherborn, Middlesex Co., St. Theresa (1945), Rev. David P. Bailey.
Res., 24 S. Main St., P.O. Box 176, 01770. Tel: 508-653-6253; Fax: 508-651-1318.

Shirley, Middlesex Co., St. Anthony (1905), Rev. Edmond Derosier; Deacon Raymond Gagnon.
Res., 14 Phoenix St., P.O. Box 595, 01464-0595. Tel: 508-425-4588; Fax: 508-425-2033.

Somerville, Middlesex Co.,

1—St. Ann, (1881), Very Rev. Peter J. Casey, V.F.; Rev. Steven Poitras; Deacon Lawrence J. Bloom; Sr. Margaret Stinson, C.S.J., Pastoral Assoc. In res., Rev. John Sawick, C.S.S.P.
Res., 399 Medford St., 02145-3899. Tel: 617-625-1904; Fax: 617-625-7043.
School—Tel: 617-625-1108.
Sisters 4; Lay Teachers 6; Students 235.

2—St. Anthony, (1915) (Italian), Revs. Vincent Monaco, C.S.; John Bocciarelli, C.S.; Marcos daSilva.
Res., 12 Properzi Way, 02143-3226. Tel: 617-625-4530; Fax: 617-625-2457.
School—Tel: 617-623-0995.
Sisters 5; Lay Teachers 5; Students 204.

3—St. Benedict, (1911), Revs. John E. McLaughlin; David A. Doucet; Joachim Martinez, S.J.
Res., 25 Arlington St., 02145-3342. Tel: 617-625-0029; Fax: 617-666-5944.
School—Tel: 617-628-7775.
Sisters 5; Lay Teachers 4; Students 196.

4—St. Catherine of Genoa, (1891), Revs. Brian F. Manning; Kevin G. Toomey; Robert A. Ward; Sr. Mary Nagle, C.S.J., Pastoral Assoc. In res., Rev. Richard J. Malone.
Res., 179 Summer St., 02143-2596. Tel: 617-666-2087; Fax: 617-666-5470.
School—Tel: 617-666-9116.
Sisters 2; Lay Teachers 9; Students 225.

5—St. Clement, (1912), Revs. Dennis A. Dever; John McLaughlin; Michael Oruche (Nigeria).
Res., 71 Warner St., West Somerville, 02144-1399. Tel: 617-625-0122; Fax: 617-628-7767.
School—Tel: 617-625-3459.
Sisters of St. Joseph 2; Lay Teachers 17; Students 421.
High School—Sisters 2; Lay Teachers 3; Students 196.

6—Patronage of St. Joseph, (1869), Revs. Henry J. Jennings; Stephen Brennick; Deacon John F. Cabral. In res., Revs. John P. Kelly, Senior Priest; Thomas P. Halleran, S.V.D.
Res., 264 Washington St., 02143-3313. Tel: 617-666-4140; Fax: 617-628-0557.

7—St. Polycarp, (1927), Rev. Robert M. Doyle; Timothy McGonigle, Pastoral Assoc.
Res., 100 Temple St., 02145. Tel: 617-625-3322; Fax: 617-625-3322.

Stoneham, Middlesex Co., St. Patrick (1868), Revs. William T. Schmidt; Thomas P. Rossi; Scott B. Hendricks; Mark J. Riley. Pastoral Assocs.: Sr. Neonilla Barrett, C.S.J.; Sr. Marylou A. Cassidy, C.S.J.; Deacons John R. Turner; Cyril T. O'Neil.
Res., 9 Pomeworth St., 02180-2025. Tel: 617-438-0960; Fax: 617-438-6809.
School—Tel: 617-438-2593.
Lay Teachers 10; Students 223.

Stoughton, Norfolk Co., Immaculate Conception (1872), Revs. Joseph P. McDermott; Joseph K. Fagan; Deacon Francis X. Heffernan.
Res., 122 Canton St., 02072-2271. Tel: 617-344-2073; Fax: 617-344-2979.
St. James (1962), Rev. William Scanlon. In res., Deacon Joseph G. Arsenault.
Res., 560 Page St., 02072. Tel: 617-344-9121; Fax: 617-341-9323.
Our Lady of the Rosary (1958), Rev. Maurice J. O'Connor; Deacon Eugene V. Stenstrom.
Res., 39 South St., 02072-3705. Tel: 617-341-6110; Fax: 617-344-3306.

Stow, Middlesex Co., St. Isidore (1961), Rev. Robert P. Soucy; Shirley Ormsby, Pastoral Assoc.; Deacon Charles A. Cornell.
Res., 429 Great Rd., Box 279, 01775-1101. Tel: 508-897-2710; Fax: 508-461-0577.

Sudbury, Middlesex Co., St. Anselm (1963), Rev. Very James Bertelli; Sr. Jacqueline Oulette, S.S.C.H., Pastoral Assoc.
Res., 100 Landham Rd., 01776-0916. Tel: 508-443-8981; Fax: 508-443-7032.
Our Lady of Fatima (1955), Revs. Michael J. Bova Conte; Michael J. Doyle; Deacon Walter J. Miles.
Res., 160 Concord Rd., P.O. Box 916, 01776-0916. Tel: 508-443-2647; Fax: 508-443-6264.

Swampscott, Essex Co., St. John the Evangelist (1907), Revs. Joseph T. Sheehy; David C. Michael.
Res., 174 Humphrey St., 01907-2512. Tel: 617-593-2544; Fax: 617-593-3616.

Tewksbury, Middlesex Co., St. William (1935), Revs. Gerald Flater, O.M.I.; Martin Walsh, O.M.I.; George Knab, O.M.I.; Deacon William Emerson. In res., Rev. Edward Lowney, O.M.I.
Mailing Address: 1268 Main St., Ste. 161, 01876. Tel: 508-851-7331.
Res., 1351 Main St., 01876-2098. Tel: 508-851-7331; Fax: 508-858-0544.

Topsfield, Essex Co., St. Rose of Lima (1945), Rev. Richard A. Driscoll; Deacon Ronald Gagne.
Res., 17 Prospect St., P.O. Box 258, 01983-0458. Tel: 508-887-5505; Fax: 508-887-8201.

Townsend, Middlesex Co., St. John (1945), Rev. Peter J. O'Hara.
Res., One School St., P.O. Box 533, 01469-0523. Tel: 508-597-2291; Fax: 508-597-3401.

Tyngsborough, Middlesex Co., St. Mary Magdalen (1959), Revs. John G. Kiley; Ronald L. St. Pierre; Deacon Everett F. Penney, Jr.
Res., 93 Lakeview Ave., P.O. Box 100, Tyngsboro, 01879. Tel: 508-649-7315; Fax: 508-649-3796.

Wakefield, Middlesex Co., St. Florence (1947), Revs. H. Joseph Murphy; Michael J. Higgins.
Res., 49 Butler Ave., 01880-5125. Tel: 617-245-2711; Fax: 617-245-4512.
St. Joseph (1854), Revs. Michael J. Steele; Lawrence J. Burns, M.M.; Paul T. Clifford.
Res., 173 Albion St., 01880-3296. Tel: 617-245-5770; Fax: 617-246-2423.
School—Tel: 617-245-2081.
Sisters 1; Lay Teachers 7; Students 167.
Most Blessed Sacrament (1931), Revs. William D. Coughlin; Thomas P. MacLeod.
Res., 11 Grove St., 01880-4222. Tel: 617-245-2080; Fax: 617-245-7981.

Walpole, Norfolk Co., Blessed Sacrament (1874), Revs. Timothy J. Kelleher; Joseph D. Flynn; Christopher J. Kirwan, Jr.; Sr. Anne O'Brien, C.S.J., Pastoral Assoc.
Res., 10 Diamond St., 02081-3408. Tel: 508-668-4700; Fax: 508-668-3554.
School—Tel: 508-668-2336.
Sisters 3; Lay Teachers 17; Students 433.
St. Mary (1931), Rev. William J. Burns.
Res., 176 Washington St., Box 131, East Walpole, 02032-0131. Tel: 508-668-4974; Fax: 508-668-3083.

Waltham, Middlesex Co.,

1—St. Charles Borromeo, (1909), Rev. Daniel E. Flaherty; Deacon James C. Callahan.
Res., 51 Hall St., 02154-5217. Tel: 617-893-0330; Fax: 617-893-2060.

2—St. Joseph, (1894) (French), Rev. Roger N. Jacques; Deacon Albert J. Aucoin.
Res., 519 Main St., 02154-5524. Tel: 617-893-3185; Fax: 617-893-9681.

3—St. Jude, (1949), Rev. Robert J. Waldron; Deacon Alfred E. Santosuosso.
Res., 147 Main St., 02154-6622. Tel: 617-893-3100; Fax: 617-893-6635.
School—Tel: 617-899-3644.
Sisters 2; Lay Teachers 8; Students 199.

4—St. Mary, (1839), Revs. Wendell Verrill; Lawrence E. Novello; Henry M. Adeyanju; Deacons Francisco Alicea; Teodoro Camacho.
Res., 133 School St., 02154. Tel: 617-891-1730; Fax: 617-642-0604.

5—Our Lady, Comforter of the Afflicted, (1930), Revs. Joseph F. Byrne; Kenneth A. LeBlanc; Deacon William E. MacKenzie.
Res., 857 Trapelo Rd., 02154. Tel: 617-894-3481; Fax: 617-894-0021.
School—Tel: 617-899-0353.
Lay Teachers 8; Students 180.

6—Sacred Heart, (1922), Rev. Gregory J. Hoppough, C.S.S. In res., Rev. Pius C.W. Murray, C.S.S.
Res., 311 River St., 02154. Tel: 617-899-0469; Fax: 617-899-0081.

Watertown, Middlesex Co., St. Patrick (1847), Very Rev. Robert C. Fichtner, V.F.; Rev. James M. Mahoney; Deacon Leo F. LaBrache. In res., Rev. Rodney J. Copp.
Res., 25 Chestnut St., 02172-2337. Tel: 617-926-9680; Fax: 617-926-3715.
Sacred Heart (1893), Revs. Paul H. McEntee; Joseph L. Curran; Sr. Estellyn Ganley, C.S.J., Pastoral Assoc. In res., Rev. Robert M. O'Grady.
Res., 770 Mt. Auburn St., 02172-1567. Tel: 617-924-9110; Fax: 617-926-3341.
St. Theresa of the Child Jesus (1927), Rev. John J. Nichols.
Res., 248 School St., 02172-1495. Tel: 617-924-3222; Fax: 617-923-0380.

Wayland, Middlesex Co., St. Ann (1945), Rev. Patrick J. Kelly.
Res., 124 Cochituate Rd., 01778-2610. Tel: 508-358-2985; Fax: 508-358-3415.
St. Zepherin (Cochituate Village) (1889), Rev. Paul W. Berube.
Res., 99 Main St., Cochituate Village, 01778-4936. Tel: 508-653-8013; Fax: 508-655-6948.

Wellesley, Norfolk Co., St. James the Great (1950), Very Rev. Timothy J. Shea, V.F.; Sr. Arline Stringer, S.C.H., Pastoral Assoc.
Res., 900 Worcester St., 02181. Tel: 617-237-1160; Fax: 617-237-0497.
St. John the Evangelist (1890), Revs. Thomas F. Powers; Bryan Mahoney; Sr. Evelyn Ronan, S.N.D., Pastoral Assoc. In res., Rev. Msgr. William F. Murphy.
Res., 9 Glen Rd., 02181. Tel: 617-235-0045; Fax: 617-235-6990.
School—Tel: 617-235-0300.
Sisters 2; Lay Teachers 5; Students 187.
St. Paul (1922), Revs. Joseph G. Lind; Bryan K. Parrish.

Res., 502 Washington St., 02181-5907. Tel: 617-235-1060; Fax: 617-235-4620.
School—Tel: 617-235-1510.
Sisters 3; Lay Teachers 7; Students 134.

West Bridgewater, Plymouth Co., St. Ann (1938), Rev. Edward C. McDonagh.
Res., 103 N. Main St., P.O. Box 427, 02379-0427. Tel: 508-586-4880; Fax: 508-588-0239.

Westford, Middlesex Co., St. Catherine (1922), Revs. Daniel F. Cronin; Joseph P. LaRaia; William M. Sullivan; Deacon Russell Morey.
Res., 107 N. Main St., 01886-1219. Tel: 508-692-6353; Fax: 508-392-0644.

West Newbury, Essex Co., St. Ann (1945), Rev. Laurence E. Kelley.
Res., 46 Maple St., P.O. Box 237, 01985. Tel: 508-363-2303; Fax: 508-363-2046.

Weston, Middlesex Co., St. Julia (1919), Rev. Robert D. Tyrell; Susan Bayard, Pastoral Assoc.
Res., 374 Boston Post Rd., 02193. Tel: 617-899-2611; Fax: 617-899-8046.

Westwood, Norfolk Co., St. Margaret Mary (1931), Rev. T. Joseph Moynihan; Deacons Joseph Holderried; Joseph M. Messina.
Res., 845 High St., P.O. Box 386, 02090-0386. Tel: 617-326-1071; Fax: 617-329-1879.

St. Denis (1949), Revs. Frederick J. Murray; John Kelley; Deacons Joseph L. Delaney; Joseph I. Crowley, Jr.
Res., 157 Washington St., 02090-1336. Tel: 617-326-5858; Fax: 617-326-1232.

Weymouth, Norfolk Co.,

1—St. Albert the Great, (1950), Rev. Laurence Borges; Deacon Herbert W. Crosby; Sr. Catherine O'Brien, S.N.D. In res., Rev. Msgr. Robert J. Powers; Rev. Raymond Benoit.
Res., 1130 Washington St., East Weymouth, 02189-1997. Tel: 617-337-8778; Fax: 617-335-5850.

2—St. Francis Xavier, (1851), Revs. Eugene P. Sullivan; Charles J. Murphy; Deacon Joseph Vitello.
Res., 261 Pleasant St., South Weymouth, 02190-2507. Tel: 617-337-2171; Fax: 617-331-4192.
School—Pleasant St., 02190. Tel: 617-335-6868.
Religious 2; Lay Teachers 5; Students 172.

3—Immaculate Conception, (1879), Revs. Peter T. Martocchio; Thomas C. Healy. Pastoral Assocs.: Mrs. Mary Fox; Sr. Florita Rodman, C.D.P.; Deacon Josep T. Nickley. In res., Rev. William F. Murphy.
Res., 1199 Commercial St., East Weymouth, 02189. Tel: 617-337-0380.

4—St. Jerome, (1928), Revs. Thomas F. Wyndham; Gerard J. Pineau; Deacon Michael Hickey.
Res., 632 Bridge St., North Weymouth, 02191-1845. Tel: 617-335-2038; Fax: 617-340-7165.
School—Tel: 617-335-1235.
Sisters 1; Lay Teachers 9; Students 234.

5—Sacred Heart, (1871), Revs. Paul V. MacDonald; Brian J. McHugh; Deacon Henry Welch.
Res., 55 Commercial St., 02188-2688. Tel: 617-337-6333.
School—Tel: 617-335-6010.
Sisters 2; Lay Teachers 7; Students 165.

Whitman, Plymouth Co., Holy Ghost (1897), Rev. Henry P. Boivin; Deacon Gerald F. Ryan.
Res., 518 Washington St., 02382. Tel: 617-447-4421; Fax: 617-447-1375.

Wilmington, Middlesex Co., St. Dorothy (1954), Revs. Rickard J. O'Donovan; Donald Abbott.
Res., 11 Harnden St., 01887-3519. Tel: 508-658-3550; Fax: 508-658-2006.

St. Thomas of Villanova (1919), Revs. Robert M. Browne; Edward F. Sherry; Deacon Clifford D. King; Paul Merullo, Pastoral Assoc.
Res., 126 Middlesex Ave., P.O. Box 397, 01887-2723. Tel: 508-658-4665; Fax: 508-658-4670.

Winchester, Middlesex Co., St. Eulalia (1966), Revs. Victor Lavoie; James L. Laughlin; Sr. Rose Marie Lipke, C.D.P, Pastoral Assoc.
Res., 50 Ridge St., 01890. Tel: 617-729-8220; Fax: 617-729-0919.

Immaculate Conception (1931), Rev. Thomas J. Naughton.
Res., 1004 Main St., 01890-1929. Tel: 617-729-1858; Fax: 617-721-5329.

St. Mary (1876), Revs. Richard C. Messina; Paul G. Kelley; Thomas S. Foley; Mr. Salvatore Caraviello, Pastoral Assoc.
Res., 158 Washington St., 01890. Tel: 617-729-0055; Fax: 617-721-6542.
School—Lay Teachers 7; Students 144.

Winthrop, Suffolk Co., Holy Rosary (1953), Rev. Thomas DiLorenzo, Admin.
Res., 993 Shirley St., 02152-2535. Tel: 617-846-1210; Fax: 617-539-4402.

St. John the Evangelist (1907), Rev. Paul Sullivan; Sr. Jane Lannaccone, S.P., Pastoral Assoc.; Rev. Gregory J. Mercurio, O.F.M.
Res., 320 Winthrop St., 02152. Tel: 617-846-7400; Fax: 617-539-0627.

Woburn, Middlesex Co.,

1—St. Anthony, (1945), Revs. Leo X. Lynch; Hubert E. Desmond.
Res., 80 Elm St., 01801-1855. Tel: 617-933-1323; Fax: 617-937-3233.

2—St. Barbara, (1954), Very Rev. Vincent P. Mellone, V.F.; Revs. Thomas C. Boudreau; Edward G. Carroll; Deacon William E. Kerns.
Res., 138 Cambridge Rd., 01801-4772. Tel: 617-933-4130; Fax: 617-932-2536.

3—St. Charles, (1862), Revs. Paul S. Sughrue; Wayne Belschner; Deacon Philip Hardcastle.
Res., 280 Main St., 01801-3294. Tel: 617-933-0300; Fax: 617-932-7581.
School—Tel: 617-935-4635.
Lay Teachers 19; Students 315.

4—St. Joseph, (1906), Rev. Harold E. LeBlanc.
Res., 22 Central St., 01801. Tel: 617-938-0473; Fax: 617-938-7818.

Wrentham, Norfolk Co., St. Mary (1928), Rev. John G. Connolly; Deacon Kenneth W. Oles. In res., Rev. John E. Fernz.
Res., 130 South St., P.O. Box 326, 02093-0326. Tel: 508-384-3373; Fax: 508-384-5747.

Chaplains of Public Institutions

Brighton. *Health Care Ministry.* Our Lady's Hall, St. Elizabeth Hospital, 736 Cambridge St., 02135. Tel: 617-789-2457; Fax: 617-789-2573. Mrs. Kelly L. Dunn, Dir.

Hospitals

Boston. *Addison Gilbert Hospital.* Attended by St. Ann, Gloucester. Tel: 508-283-0054.
Amesbury Hospital. Attended by Sacred Heart, Amesbury. Tel: 508-388-0330.
AMI Westwood Lodge Hospital. Attended by St. Margaret Mary, Westwood. Tel: 617-326-1071.
Anna Jacques Hospital. Attended by Immaculate Conception, Newburyport. Tel: 508-462-2724.
The Arbour Hospital. Very Rev. Charles Bourque Tel: 617-524-0434.
Atlanticare Medical Center. Deacon Lawrence R. McManus Tel: 617-598-5100.
Baldpate Hospital. Attended by St. Mary, Georgetown. Tel: 508-352-2024.
Beth Israel Hospital. Rev. John R. Carroll Tel: 617-735-2000.
Bethany Hospital. Sr. Catherine Melly, C.S.J.; Rev. Francis J. O'Neil, S.J. Tel: 508-872-6750.
Beverly Hospital. Sr. Bernadette Mary McGrath, S.N.D.; John Carley Tel: 508-922-3000.
Boston City Hospital. Ms. Carmela D'Elia; Sr. Claire Hayes, C.D.P. Tel: 617-593-5336,
Boston Speciality and Rehabilitation Hospital, Rev. Antonio L. Andrade Tel: 617-298-2460.
Bournewood Hospital. Attended by Infant Jesus, Chestnut Hill. Tel: 617-469-0234.
Braintree Hospital. Attended by St. Francis of Assisi, Braintree. Tel: 617-843-1332.
Brigham and Women's Hospital. Revs. Francis T. Ziotkowski, C.S.C.; George P. Winchester, S.J. Tel: 617-732-5500.
Brockton Hospital. Rev. Francis L. MacFarland, C.S.C.; Ms. Frances McCarthy Tel: 508-941-7000.
Cambridge Hospital. Revs. Maurice Meade; David G. Bonfiglio Tel: 617-498-1000.
Carney Hospital. Rev. John J. Ronaghan; Sr. Rita Burkhart, D.C.; Sr. Kathleen Simpson, D.C.; Sr. Louise F. Maccia, D.C.; Sr. Thecla Robinson, D.C.; Rev. John Fernz Tel: 617-296-4000.
Charles River Hospital. Attended by St. Paul, Wellesley. Tel: 617-235-1060.
Children's Hospital. Rev. George C. Gardner, C.SS.R.; Deacon Joseph I. Crowley, Jr. Tel: 617-735-6000.
Cranberry Specialty Hospital. Attended by Sacred Heart, Middleboro. Tel: 508-947-0444.
Dana Farber Cancer Institute. Rev. John E. Doherty, C.SS.R. Tel: 617-732-3000.
Deaconess Hospital. Revs. Paul Bolduc; Paul Tivnan Tel: 617-243-6000.
Emerson Hospital. Ms. Gloria Clough Tel: 508-369-1400.
Faulkner Hospital. Deacon Leonard F. DeCosta Tel: 617-522-5800.
Franciscan Children's Hospital. Sr. Helen Mary McGonagle, C.S.J.; Sr. Doris McShane, F.M.M.; Sr. Marceline Valasquez, F.M.M.; Rev. Canisius Hazlett, C.P. Tel: 617-254-3800.
Glover Memorial Hospital. Attended by St. Joseph, Needham. Tel: 617-444-0245.
Good Samaritan Medical Center. Rev. John J. Murphy, C.S.C.; Sr. Helen Glidden, S.C.N.; Sr. Margaret Crowley, S.C.N., Cushing Campus: Tel: 617-296-4000. Goddard Campus: Tel: 617-344-5100.
Hahnemann Hospital. Attended by St. Gabriel, Brighton. Tel: 617-254-6582.
Haverhill Municipal Hale Hospital. Attended by St. John the Baptist, Haverhill. Tel: 508-372-2780.
Hebrew Memorial Hospital. Attended by Sacred Heart, Roslindale. Tel: 617-325-3322.
Holy Family Hospital Medical Center. Rev. Francis Murphy; Sr. Anne Doherty, C.B.S. Tel: 508-687-1051 Ext. 2005.
Hunt Memorial Hospital. Attended by St. Mary, Danvers. Tel: 508-774-0340.
Jewish Memorial Hospital. Attended by St. Joseph, Roxbury. Tel: 617-442-0900.
Jordan Hospital. Attended by St. Peter, Plymouth. Tel: 508-746-0663.
Josiah B. Thomas Hospital. Attended by St. John the Baptist, Peabody. Tel: 508-531-0002.
Lahey Clinic. Rev. Victor LaVoie; Sr. Irene M. Hache, R.C.E. Tel: 617-273-5100.
Lakeville State Hospital. Attended by St. Martha and Mary, Lakeville. Tel: 508-947-2107.
Lawrence F. Quigley Memorial Hospital. Rev. Lawrence F. Sullivan Tel: 617-884-5660.
Lawrence General Hospital. Revs. Thomas C. Kenny, O.S.A.; George Morgan, O.S.A.; Bro. Frank Grimaldi, O.F.M. Tel: 508-883-4000.
Lawrence Memorial Hospital. Sr. Mary Siena Kennedy, S.M.S.M. Tel: 617-396-9250.
Lemuel Shattuck Hospital. Rev. Leonard J. Tighe; Sr. Elizabeth Harnett, S.C.N.J. Tel: 617-522-8110 Ext. 463.
Lowell General Hospital. Sr. Eileen Auger, C.S.C. Tel: 508-937-6000.
Malden Hospital. Sr. Ann Marie Barry, S.C.H. Tel: 617-322-7560.
Marlborough Hospital. Sr. Jeannette Gonthier, S.S.Ch. Tel: 485-0016.
Massachusetts Eye & Ear Infirmary. (Same as Massachusetts General Hospital).
Massachusetts General Hospital. Sr. Sheila Hammond, R.S.C.J.; Revs. David Cavanagh; Philip E. McGaugh; James R. O.Connell, O.F.M.; Rudo Deziel, S.M. Tel: 617-726-2222.
Massachusetts Hospital School. Rev. William R. Coen Tel: 617-828-3420.
Massachusetts Mental Health Center. Rev. Philip A. Cabasino, C.SS.R. Tel: 617-734-1300.
Massachusetts Respiratory Hospital. Vacant.
McLean Hospital. Rev. Joseph Murphy Tel: 617-855-2000.
Medfield State Hospital. Rev. John J. Hever Tel: 508-359-7312.
Melrose-Wakefield Hospital. Sr. Marie T. Mahoney, S.P. Tel: 617-979-3000.
Metro West Medical Center. Framingham Campus: Revs. Albert F. McMahon, O.F.M.; Robert Champagn, S.M.; Sr. Gabriella O'Connell, C.S.J.; Elizabeth Mingoletti Tel: 508-879-7111, Leonard Morse Campus: Attended by St. Patrick, Natick. Tel: 508-653-1093.
Middlesex County Hospital. Attended by Our Lady, Comforter of the Afflicted, Waltham. Tel: 617-894-3481.
Milton Medical Center. Attended by St. Elizabeth, Milton. Tel: 617-696-6688.
Mount Auburn Hospital. Revs. Maurice Meade; David G. Bonfiglio Tel: 617-492-3500.
Nashoba Community Hospital. Attended by St. Mary, Ayer. Tel: 508-772-2414.
New England Baptist Hospital. Rev. John J. Ryan, C.SS.R. Tel: 617-783-5800.
New England Medical Center. Sr. Claire Walsh, M.H.S.H., Dir.; Revs. James Shaughnessey, S.J.; Daniel McCarthy, SS.CC. Tel: 617-965-5000.
New England Memorial. Attended by St. Patrick, Stoneham. Tel: 617-438-0960.
New England Rehabilitation Hospital. Attended by St. Barbara, Woburn. Tel: 617-933-4130.
New England Sinai Hospital. Attended by St. James, Stoughton. Tel: 617-344-9121.
Newton-Wellesley Hospital. Rev. Daniel J. Cavanaugh Tel: 617-243-6000.
North Shore Medical Center. North Shore Children's Hospital, Tel: 508-745-2100. Salem Hospital, Tel: 508-741-1200. Shaughnessy Rehabilitation Hospital, Tel: 508-744-1930. Rev. Edward Keohan.
Norwood Hospital. Sr. Barbara Lavin, O.P.; Bro. Daniel J. Elliott, C.F.X. Tel: 617-769-4000.
Plymouth County Hospital. Attended by St. Joseph the Worker, Hanson. Tel: 617-293-3581.
Quincy Hospital. Rev. Theodore L. Fortier, A.A.
St. Elizabeth's Medical Center. Revs. Phillip M. Conroy; John H. Curley; Sr. Ivan Cadigan, C.S.J.; Sr. Virginia Murray, C.S.J.; Sr. Margaret Sheehan, C.S.J.; Sr. Nora O'Connell, S.N.D.; Sr. Louise Murray, C.S.J.; Deacon Patrick Guerrini.
St. John of God Hospital. Rev. Joseph Coleman; Sr. Alicia Brennan, D.C. Tel: 617-277-5750.
St. Margaret's Center for Women and Infants. Martha Sullivan Tel: 617-789-3045.

Saints Memorial Medical Center.
St. John's Campus, Sr. Catherine O'Brien, C.S.J.; Revs. John J. Hogan, O.M.I.; Francis Gorham, O.M.I. Tel: 508-458-1411,
St. Joseph's Campus, Sr. Doris Brouillette, S.C.O.; Rev. Romeo J. Murphy, O.M.I.; Sr. Rina Brunetti, P.M.; Ms. Patricia Hardy Tel: 508-453-1761.
Shriners Hospital. Attended by St. Joseph, Boston. Tel: 617-523-4342.
Somerville Hospital. Deacon John Cabral Tel: 617-666-4400.
South Shore Hospital. Rev. Phillip McGaugh Tel: 617-340-8000.
Southwood Community Hospital. Attended by St. Jude, Norfolk. Tel: 508-528-0170.
Spaulding Rehabilitation Hospital. Sr. Mary Samson, S.H.C.J.; Rev. William Doyle, S.J. Tel: 617-720-6400.
Symmes Hospital. Attended by St. Charles, Woburn. Tel: 617-933-0300.
Tewksbury Hospital. Rev. Edward Lowney, O.M.I. Tel: 617-851-7321.
University Hospital. Rev. Roger J. Bourgea, S.M. Tel: 617-638-6850.
V.A. Medical Centers. Bedford: Revs. Aidan J. Walsh; Joseph P. Robinson; Philip A. Cabasino, C.SS.R.; Ronald Lawson; Deacon John W. Watson Tel: 617-275-7500, Brockton-West Roxbury: Revs. Austin Nagle, SS.CC.; Yvon Dubois, A.A.; Patrick McShane; Henry P. Nichols Tel: 508-583-4500, Jamaica Plain: Revs. John F.X. Fallon; Roger A. Sinclair; Phillip Salois Tel: 617-232-9500.
Walter E. Fernald School. Rev. William T. Leonard; Deacon Eugene Counihan Tel: 617-894-3600.
Waltham-Weston Hospital & Medical Center. Rev. James Cunningham, C.S.S. Tel: 617-647-6202.
Whidden Memorial Hospital. Attended by Our Lady of Grace, Chelsea. Tel: 617-884-0030.
Winthrop Hospital. Attended by St. John the Evangelist, Winthrop. Tel: 617-846-7400.
Wrentham State School. Rev. John Fernz Tel: 508-384-3114.
Youville Hospital. Ms. Anne Cody; Rev. Patrick Terrant; Mr. Ernest Boyer; Ms. Patricia Kennedy; Margaret Klacik; Julianne Bousquet Tel: 617-876-4344.

Prison Ministry

WALTHAM. *Coordinator of Prison Ministry,* 681 Main St., Room 16, 02154. Tel: 617-894-3811.
M.C.I. Bridgewater, Rev. James F. Lanergan Tel: 617-727-7672,
M.C.I. Bay State Correctional Center, Mrs. Patricia Barrett-Dunn Tel: 617-727-8474,
M.C.I. Old Colony Correctional Center, Deacon Robert W. Alence Tel: 617-727-3400,
M.C.I. Southeastern Correctional Center, Deacon Robert P. Amerault Tel: 617-727-0288,
M.C.I. Concord, Rev. Thomas P. Forry Tel: 617-727-1950,
M.C.I. Framingham, Sr. Maureen Clark, C.S.J. Tel: 617-727-5056,
M.C.I. Norfolk, Rev. Robert Rivard, F.M.S.I. Tel: 508-879-6711; Deacon Gerard P. Rooney, Asst.; Sr. Kathleen Donovan, O.S.F. Tel: 508-376-8262; Ms. Ruth Raichle Tel: 508-376-8262,
M.C.I. Plymouth, Deacon John L. LaFargue Tel: 617-727-6938,
M.C.I. Pondville, Mrs. Elizabeth Slaney Tel: 617-727-5203,
M.C.I. Shirley, Deacon Carroll H. Taylor Tel: 508-425-4341 Ext. 3818; Rev. John Kilmartin, F.D.P., Asst., Tel: 508-792-7580,
M.C.I. Cedar Junction, Deacon John J. Mannion Tel: 617-727-1686.

County Prisons (House of Correction and Jails)

BOSTON. *Guild of Our Lady of Ransom.* Archdiocese of Boston. Vacant.
Juvenile Court Chaplains. Rev. James F. Fratus, Coord., Tel: 617-889-2774.
Juvenile Detention and Treatment Facilities. Department of Youth Services, Roslindale. Rev. Joseph J. Baggetta, Chap., Tel: 617-288-9100 Ext. 218.
ESSEX COUNTY. *Essex County Correctional Facility, Middleton.* Rev. Jon C. Martin Tel: 508-750-1900.
MIDDLESEX COUNTY. *East Cambridge and Billerica.* Rev. Msgr. Francis Rossiter Tel: 617-523-1861; Deacon Harold E. Killam Tel: 617-494-4410.
NORFOLK COUNTY. *Dedham.* Rev. Robert P. Beale Tel: 617-329-6730.
PLYMOUTH COUNTY. *Plymouth.* Deacons Charles Bower Tel: 508-868-5521; Edward Creutz Tel: 508-748-3540.
SUFFOLK COUNTY. *Boston-Nashua Street Jail.* Rev. John J. Mullen, S.J. Tel: 617-894-3199.
South Bay House of Correction. Rev. George T. Williams, S.J. Tel: 617-536-8440 Ext. 305.

On Special or Other Diocesan Assignment:
Reverend Fathers—
Daly, Thomas J., Exec. Dir. Synod Office & Asst. to the Moderator of the Curia. Tel: 617-254-0100
DePietro, Arthur J., Juvenile Court Chap.
DiFruscio, John A., 105 Charles St. #535, Boston, MA 02114
Fitzpatrick, John P., Dir., Catholic Guild for the Deaf. Tel: 508-875-3617
Flagg, Robert W., Dir. Vocations. Tel: 617-254-2610
Flatley, Brian M., Asst. to the Sec. for Minsterial Personnel & Archbishop's Delegate. Tel: 617-254-0100
Gavin, Carney E., Harvard University Faculty
Keane, John F., Emergency Response Group
King, Philip J., Boston College Faculty
MacEwen, Michael W., Sec. to the Cardinal. Tel: 617-782-2544
Mansfield, John L., Emergency Response Group, c/o Clergy Personnel Office, Brighton, MA 02135. Tel: 617-254-2085
McCarthy, James J., Dir. Clergy Personnel. Tel: 617-254-2085
McCoy, Charles J.
McInerny, Paul B., Sec. to the Cardinal. Tel: 617-782-2544
McQuade, Richard E.
Miceli, Paul W., Sec. Ministerial Personnel. Tel: 617-254-0100
Murphy, Francis J., Boston College Faculty
O'Donohoe, James A., Boston College Faculty
Plourde, Raymond C., Convent Chap. Tel: 508-682-9391
Ryan, Frederick J., Vice Chancellor. Tel: 617-254-0100
Sawyer, Lucien A., O.M.I.
Stagnaro, John J.

On Duty Outside the Archdiocese:
(For further information contact Tel: 617-254-2085.)
Reverend Monsignors—
Abbruzzese, John A.
Edyvean, Walter J.
McManus, Frederick R., Provost, Catholic University, Washington, DC
Reverend Fathers—
Brown, Francis E.
Donahue, Richard
Driscoll, Joseph J., Natl. Assoc. of Catholic Chaplains, 3501 S. Lake Dr., P.O. Box 07473, Milwaukee, WI 53207-0473
Fay, William P.
Flanagan, James
Galvin, John P., Catholic University, Washington, DC
Gavin, Carney E.
Hawker, James F.
Hehir, J. Bryan, Washington, DC
Kelley, Edward J.
Kennedy, Arthur L., St. Thomas College, St. Paul, MN
King, Philip
Kramer, George C.
McMahon, Gerard T.
McNeil, John R.
McRae, Cornelius
O'Donohue, James A.
O'Leary, David M.
Oliveira, Joel D., Lend Lease, Providence, RI
Regan, John J., Lend Lease, Phoenix, AZ
Ronan, James J.
Sullivan, Brendan J.

Military & VA Chaplains:
Reverend Fathers—
Bourke, Charles E., Jr., Capt., Chief of Chaplain's Office, Department of the Navy, Washington, DC 20350-2000
Butler, Timothy A., Capt., U.S. Air Force, 7750 Culebra Rd., #3310, San Antonio, TX 78251
Condon, Edwin D., Jr., CDR, CHC, USN, Department of the Navy, Chief of Naval Education and Training, Naval Air Sta., Pensacola, FL 32508-5100
Crowley, Francis J., VA Medical Center, 830 Chalkstone Ave., Providence, RI 02908-4799
Cuddy, William F., Jr., CHC, USNR, Command Religious Ministries Dept., 1653 Morris St., Norfolk, VA 23511-2895
DeAngelis, Mark J.
Deeley, Kevin J.
Devine, William D., Lt., CHC, USN, Chaplains Office, U.S.S. Wasp (LHD-1), FPO, AE 09556-1660
Girardin, Peter T., Office of the Chaplain, 6342 Teal Run Dr., Houston, TX 77035
Kennedy, William M., Lt., CHC, USNR, HQ Co. 4th Marines (Chaplain), Unit 35970, FPO, AP 96002-5970
Linehan, Stephen J.
Moran, James F., CDR, CHC, USNR, Chaplains Office, H & HS BN (Code C053), Quantico, VA 22134-5010
Nichols, Henry P., Ch. (Lt. Col), Brockton/West Roxbury, Veteran Affairs Medical Center, 940 Belmont St., Brockton, MS 02401
Pucciarelli, George W., CDR, CHC, USN, Headquarters USMC/Atlantic (MarForLant) (CODE REL), Norfolk, VA 23515
Raux, Redmond
Robinson, Joseph P., Edith Nourse Rogers Memorial Veterans Hospital, c/o Chaplain Svc., 200 Springs Rd., Bedford, MA 01730
Rock, Stephen B., CDR, CHC, USN, Chaplains Office Sigonella, PSC 824 Box #305, FPO, AE 09627-0824
Russo, Lawrence J., LCDR, CHC, USNR, Office of the Chaplain, U.S. Naval Support Activity, PSC 810, Box 14, FPO, AE 09619-1014

Graduate Studies:
Reverend Fathers—
Congdon, Robert J.
Guarino, R. Michael
Kelly, William T.
O'Brien, Paul B.
Russell, Paul F.

Priestly Renewal:
Reverend Fathers—
Fraser, Gerald C.
Ryan, Frederick

Society of St. James the Apostle:
(For further information contact Tel: 617-742-4715.)
Reverend Fathers—
Cleary, Patrick J.
Domurat, Thomas S.
Fairbairn, Frank E.
Flynn, George R.
Grimes, John J.
Kirke, Eugene K.
Martin, Joseph I.
Masciarelli, Rudolph
McCarthy, J. Joseph
McManus, Paul G.
O'Meara, Gerard J.
O'Sullivan, Raymond
Oates, Thomas F.
Pashby, John J.
Pearsall, William T.
Stanley, Charles R.
Sullivan, John L.
Thomas, Robert W.
Troy, Gabriel
Tynan, Desmond

Awaiting Assignment:
Reverend Fathers—
Barr, Frederick L.
Bogusz, Joseph G.
Buchette, Anthony L.
Buntel, Richard A.
Connell, John K.
Curran, Richard G.
Delay, Donald R.
Dolan, Patrick J.
Donahue, Daniel J.
Driscoll, Nicholas J.
Fallon, John F.X.
Gale, Robert
German, Kenneth N.
Hickey, Gerlad J.
Jezowski, Anthony C.
Josoma, Stephen S.
Keefe, Dennis A.
Kelley, Arnold E.
Kelly, Thomas P.
Lockey, Paul E.
Manning, Paul F.
Mason, Albert M.
McAuliffe, Robert J.
McCabe, Edward D.
McNamara, Michael J.
McQuade, Richard E.
Mowatt, John J.
O'Sullivan, Eugene
Picardi, John J.
Power, James F.
Tivnan, Paul J.
Uftring, Richard A.
Whelan, Thomas J.

Absent on Leave:
Reverend Fathers—
Bouton, Thomas F.
Divine, Kevin J.
Gomes, Ronald A.
McCarthy, Paul R.
Montague, James G.

Purdy, Robert M.
Schiavone, Christopher F.

Absent on Sick Leave:
Reverend Fathers—
Arens, John F.
Balcom, Gary E.
Butler, James P.
Conte, Denis A.
Coyne, Ronald D.
Curley, John H.
DiFruscio, John A.
Dufour, Louis C.
Fay, Robert D.
Frost, Peter J.
Geoghan, John J.
Goulet, Raymond O.
Hession, James J.
Kearney, Michael J.
Kinsella, Charles R.
Lawson, Harold F.
Mahan, Paul J.
Matte, Richard O.
Meskell, David B.
Morris, John S.
Morrisette, Robert H.
Motherway, Thomas F.
Mullin, Jay M.
Paquin, Ronald H.
Pollis, Robert G.
Rosenkranz, George J.
Rossi, Thomas P.
Santerre, Richard R.
Tourigney, Ernest E.
Wilson, James L., Jr.

Permanent Disability:
Reverend Fathers—
Barrett, Robert E.
Bowab, Michael L.
Brennan, James F.
Driscoll, Walter L.
Finn, Alfred E.
Foley, John T.
Jansonis, Alphonse B.
Kerivan, William C.
McGrade, Kevin M.
O'Hearn, Paul V.
Reardon, Arthur L., St. Joseph Home, 321 Centre St., Dorchester, MA 02122
Rothwell, Joseph T.
Sullivan, James L.
Tolland, Cyril E.
Weber, Charles P.

Retired:
(For further information contact Tel: 617-523-1861.)
Reverend Monsignors—
Abucewicz, John A.
Alves, Joseph T., 229 Adams St., Milton, MA 02186
Carroll, John P., Regina Cleri, 60 Wm. Cardinal O'Connell Way, Boston, MA 02114
Collins, Russell J.
Day, John D., Most Precious Blood, 43 Maple St., Hyde Park, MA 02136
Finnegan, Thomas J.
Granville, William A., St. Thomas Aquinas, Bridgewater
Hart, Peter F., St. Pius V Rectory, 215 Maple St., Lynn, MA 01904
Hyland, Charles H., St. Therese Rectory, 20 Gledhill Ave., Everett, MA 02149
Kearney, Philip J., Regina Cleri, 60 Wm. Cardinal O'Connell Way, Boston, MA 02114
Keilty, John P., Regina Cleri, 60 Wm. Cardinal O'Connell Way, Boston, MA 02114
Keohane, Mark H., 37 Pelton St., West Roxbury, MA 02132
Lawler, John F.
Low, Albert W., Regina Cleri, 60 Wm. Cardinal O'Connell Way, Boston, MA 02114
McCarthy, Charles W.
McGann, Francis J.
McManus, Paul J., St. Paul the Apostle Church, P.O. Box N-8187, Nassau, Bahamas
Moritz, Paul L., St. Patrick Rectory, 335 Main St., Brockton, MA 02401
Novello, Russell R., Mailing Address: 190 Sherman Rd., Chestnut Hill, MA 02167
O'Sullivan, Francis G.
Palladino, Alfonso G., St. Mary of the Annunciation, 46 Myrtle St., Melrose, MA 02176
Roche, William H.
Rossiter, Francis, Regina Cleri, 60 Wm. Cardinal O'Connell Way, Boston, MA 02114
Sennott, Robert J.
Shea, William B.
Sheehan, John J.
Sullivan, Timothy E., 180 Laurel Dr., Needham, MA 02192
Reverend Fathers—
Abracinskas, Albert C., 231 Thatcher St., Brockton, MA 02402
Anadore, Charles E., St. Agatha, 432 Adams St., Milton, MA 02186
Anderson, William R., 43 Shore Dr., Plymouth, MA 02360
Aubut, Charles E., 84 Lilley Ave., Lowell, MA 01850
Baltrushunas, Anthony P., 496 E. Broadway, South Boston, MA 02127
Barrett, Daniel J.
Barry, Henry F., Holy Family Rectory, 403 Union St., Rockland, MA 02370
Beksha, Francis W., St. Mary Rectory, Church Square, Franklin, MA 02038
Bernatonis, John F., P.O. Box 314, East Wareham, MA 02538
Berube, John J., 137 Pleasant St., P.O. Box 364, Marshfield Hills, MA 02051
Bonfilgio, David G.
Boucher, Clarence R., 2 Ropes St., Salem, MA 01970
Boyle, J. Leo
Brennan, Gerard M.
Broderick, John A., Regina Cleri, 60 Wm. Cardinal O'Connell Way, Boston, MA 02114
Brudzynski, Peter F.
Bryson, Robert C.
Buckley, Frederick J.
Buckley, John K.
Burke, Leonard J.
Burns, John F., 30 Colonial Ave., Waltham, MA 02154
Campbell, William W.
Carr, John F., 10525 Audie Brook Dr., 7 Hills the Linx, Spring Hill, FL 34606
Casey, Walter E.
Cedrone, Laurence C.
Cintolo, Antonio A., St. Anselm Rectory, 100 Landham Rd., Sudbury, MA 01776
Clifford, Donald G., Summer Res., 8 Rainbow Pond Dr., Walpole, MA 02081
Coen, William R.
Coffey, James H., St. Aidan Rectory, 158 Pleasant St., Brookline, MA 02146
Collins, Joseph I., Regina Cleri, 60 Wm. Cardinal O'Connell Way, Boston, MA 02114
Commane, William J.
Connick, Alfred J.
Connolly, Maurice V.
Connor, John E., Summer Res., 57 Maureen Rd., P.O. Box 153, Centerville, MA 02632
Cormier, Leo G.
Cowhig, Edward D.
Creighton, Gerard E., 50 Hall St., Dennis, MA 02638
Dacier, Gerard A.
Daley, Joseph D., 63 Winslow St., P.O. Box 1455, Marshfield, MA 02050
Daly, James J., 22 Bradfield Ave., Roslindale, MA 02131
Daniele, Anthony J.
Delaney, Francis H.
Dempsy, Thomas F., Medford Farms, Rte. 4, Box 42, Goffstown, NH 03045
Donelin, John M., Immaculate Conception, 1199 Commercial St., East Weymouth, MA 02189
Donlon, William J., Sacred Heart Rectory, 19 Elliot St., Natick, MA 01760
Donovan, John L.
Doocey, Michael F.
Doonan, John A., P.O. Box 282, Dover, DE 19903-0282
Downey, Joseph J.
Doyle, Lawrence J., St. Patrick, 118 S. Broadway, Lawrence, MA 01843
Duggan, Charles T., c/o Murphy, 20 Lakeview Dr., Lynnfield, MA 01940
Duquette, Delphis O., 45 Linnaean St. Apt. 1F, Cambridge, MA 02138
Edwards, John G., 200 Ledgewood Dr., Apt. 406, Stoneham, MA 02180
Fallon, John J., St. Mary, 31 Shirley St., Ayer, MA 01432
Finnegan, John T.
Flynn, John H.
Flynn, Robert G., c/o Cronin, 8 Hearthstone Dr., Medfield, MA 02052
Foley, John E., St. Bernard Rectory, 1529 Washington St., Newton, MA 02165
Foley, John I., Regina Cleri, 60 Wm. Cardinal O'Connell Way, Boston, MA 02114
Foley, John J.
Francis, Paul R.
Gallagher, Francis L., St. Andrew, 45 Talbot Ave., North Billerica, MA 01862
Gillis, Edward F., 73 Broadreach Apts. #141, North Weymouth, MA 02191
Gilmartin, Daniel J.
Goss, Francis G., Our Lady of Lourdes Rectory, 439 West St., Brockton, MA 02401
Grant, Frederick A.
Greaney, Francis M.
Guarcello, Russell V., 157 Livoli Ave., Braintree, MA 02184
Guerette, William J.
Guiney, John E., Morse Rd., South Royalston, Athol, MA 01331
Hane, Howard S.
Hanlon, John R., 44 Village St., Medway, MA 02053
Hart, James P., St. Joseph Home, 321 Centre St., Dorchester, MA 02122
Hogan, Cornelius J., Regina Cleri, 60 Wm. Cardinal O'Connell Way, Boston, MA 02114
Horgan, Gerald B., St. Mary Rectory, P.O. Box 396, Georgetown, MA 01822
Janiunas, Albin F.
Jennings, John J., St. Mark Rectory, 20 Roseland St., Dorchester, MA 02124
Johnson, Harold J., Regina Cleri, 60 Wm. Cardinal O'Connell Way, Boston, 02114
Joyal, Rene J
Jusseaume, John E.
Keeley, John A., P.O. Box 231444, Encinitas, CA 92323-1444
Kelley, Paul G.
Kelly, John P., St. Joseph, 264 Washington St., Somerville, MA 02143
Kierce, J. Joseph, St. Kevin, 35 Virginia St., Dorchester, MA 02125
Lambert, Raymond P.
Langley, Joseph W., 19 Sunset Rd., Arlington, MA 02174
Laurano, Anthony J.
Lawler, John T., St. Joseph, 3675 Amberly Cir. #C103, Naples, FL 33962
Leonard, Clyde A.
Linehan, William J., Regina Cleri, 60 Wm. Cardinal O'Connell Way, Boston, MA 02114
Lucey, William F.
Lucid, Vincent F.
Lynch, Daniel G., 27 Victoria Heights Rd., Hyde Park, MA 02136
Maguire, John J., Regina Cleri, 60 Wm. Cardinal O'Connell Way, Boston, MA 02114
Mahoney, John P., St. Mary of the Sacred Heart, 392 Hanover St., Hanover, MA 02339. Tel: 617-826-4303
Masciarelli, Rudolph, Apartado 18 - 1025 Miraflores, Lima, Peru
McAndrews, Walter J., P.O. Box 542, Amesbury, MA 01913
McAskill, Kenneth F.
McCarthy, William R.
McConville, Philip G.J., Box 648, Dennis, MA 02638
McDonald, James T.
McGann, Gerard J., P.O. Box 900, East Sandwich, MA 02537-0900
McNulty, Joseph P., 94 Alma Rd., Falmouth, MA 02540
Meade, Henry J.
Meade, Maurice P.
Medeiros, Antonio S.
Meffan, Robert V.
Minigan, Frederick J., Regina Cleri, 60 William Cardinal O'Connell Way, Boston, MA 02114
Mooney, Thomas J., Sts. Martha & Mary, 354 Bedford St., Lakeville, MA 02347
Morgan, William H., 51 Atlantic Rd., Gloucester, MA 01930
Moriarty, Thomas W., Regina Cleri, 60 William Cardinal O'Connell Way, Boston, MA 02114
Mosley, Francis J., Regina Cleri, 60 Wm. Cardinal O'Connell Way, Boston, MA 02114
Mottau, Robert S.
Moynihan, Paul V.
Mulkern, John F., 141 Essex St., Bldg. A-Apt. #8, Saugus, MA 01906
Murphy, Kenneth B.
Murphy, Lawrence F.
Naguszewski, Edward B., 11 Peatfield St., Ipswich, MA 01938
Navien, Thomas A., Regina Cleri, 60 Wm. Cardinal O'Connell Way, Boston, MA 02114
Noonan, William J., Regina Cleri, 60 William Cardinal O'Connell Way, Boston, MA 02114
O'Brien, Frederick W., 68 Suomi Rd., P.O. Box 54, Pembroke, MA 02359
O'Brien, Robert E.
O'Leary, Adrian P., 7 Westbourne St., Roslindale, MA 02131
O'Leary, Arthur P.
Palmieri, John A., 5113 Yearling Ln., Jacksonville, FL 32210
Pearsall, Ernest P., Regina Cleri, 60 Wm. Cardinal O'Connel Way, Boston, MA 02114
Perron, Richard J., 419 Lafayette St., Salem, MA 01970
Philbin, John J., Sacred Heart, 340 Center St., Middleborough, MA 02346
Pied, Wilfred L.

Piscitelli, Vincent J., 98 Second St., Medford, MA 02155
Powers, Richard J.
Ready, Francis P., St. John the Evangelist Rectory, 2254 Massachusetts Ave., Cambridge, MA 02140
Reilly, Joseph L., 1000 Paradise Rd., Apt. W1K, Swampscott, MA 01907
Riley, James H.
Riordan, Daniel F., St. Joseph's Manor, 215 Thatcher St., Brockton, MA 02402
Roche, Allan E., 9 Seabrook Village, Seabrook, NH 03874
Rogers, James M., c/o Viano, 536 Fisher St., Walpole, MA 02081
Ronan, Henry T.
Ryan, Joseph E., 64 Garden St., Milton, MA 02186
Rynne, Paul P.
Saja, Thaddeus A.
Saunders, John A., 140 Cabot St., Milton, MA 02186
Segadelli, Joseph D., St. Patrick Manor, 863 Central St., Framingham, MA 01701
Shakalis, Peter A.
Shanley, Paul R.
Sheehy, Charles I., St. Francis of Assisi Rectory, 856 Washington St., Braintree, MA 02184
Silk, John D.
Silva, John F., 465 Winsor St., Ludlow, MA 01056
Slejzer, Ferdinand E., St. John the Baptist Rectory, 28 St. Peter St., Salem, MA 01970
Stocklosa, J. Walter, 36 Trull Ln., Lowell, MA 01853
Sullivan, Francis P., St. Patrick's Manor, 863 Central St., Framingham, MA 01701
Sullivan, Michael D., Regina Cleri, 60 Wm. Cardinal O'Connell Way, Boston, MA 02114
Sullivan, William P., Regina Cleri, 60 Wm. Cardinal O'Connell Way, Boston, MA 02114
Svirskas, Joseph J., 419 Washington St., Haverhill, MA 01832
Toland, Paul L.
Vasaturo, Anthony J., St. Thomas Aquinas, Jamaica Plain, MA
Veneto, Joseph P., 8 Thistle Ave., Milton, MA 02186
White, John J.
Whittier, James E.
Williams, George J., Regina Cleri, 60 Wm. Cardinal O'Connell Way, Boston, MA 02114
Zuromskis, John D., 21346 St. Andrew Blvd, P.O. Box 150, Boca Raton, FL 33433

Permanent Deacons:
Albis, Leonard B., St. Lucy, Methuen
Alicea, Francisco, St. Mary, Waltham
Amerault, Robert P., St. Joseph, Medford
Arsenault, Joseph G., St. James, Stoughton
Aucoin, Albert J., St. Joseph, Waltham
Balestracci, Alfred, St. Theresa, North Reading
Barton, John M., St. Thomas, Peabody
Beatrice, Lee A., St. John, East Bridgewater
Belmonte, Joseph A., St. Anthony, Revere
Bloom, Laurence J., St. Ann, Somerville
Bower, Charles H., St. Bonaventure, Manomet
Bowley, Richard R., Sacred Heart, Amesbury
Breinlinger, Martin, St. Mary's, Holliston
Bresnahan, John M., St. Agnes, Middleton
Bulpett, Dean C., St. Irene, Carlisle
Cabral, John F., Somerville Hospital
Callahan, James C., St. Charles Borromeo, Waltham
Camacho, Teodoro, St. Mary, Waltham
Canoua, Joseph A., St. Anthony, Cohasset
Capomaccio, John J., Sick Leave
Caruso, Philip M., St. Mary, Holliston
Casillas, Luis, Cathedral of the Holy Cross, Boston
Chevarley, Joseph W., Senior Deacon
Chisholm, Finley H., St. Joseph, Lynn
Clough, Charles I., Our Lady Help of Christians, Concord
Connelly, Milton E., Jr., Immaculate Conception, Newburyport
Connor, John P., St. Mary, Milton
Cordeau, Richard W., St. Jean Baptiste, Lynn
Cornell, Charles A., St. Isidore, Stowe
Counihan, Eugene A., Fernald School, Naltham
Creutz, Edward F., Blessed Kateri Tekakwitha, Plymouth
Crosby, Herbert W., St. Albert the Great, Weymouth
Crowley, Joseph I, Jr., Children's Hospital, Boston
Crump, James M., St. Patrick, Natick
D'Ambrosio, Francis A., M.D., Senior Deacon, Unassigned
Dacey, Dennis J., Sick Leave
DeCoste, Leonard F., Our Lady of Lourdes, Jamaica Plain
Delaney, Joseph L., St. Denis, Westwood
Dempsey, Timothy F., St. Mary, Lynn
Diotalevi, Augustus J., St. Tarcisius, Framingham
Donnelly, Joseph A., St. John, Chelmsford
Donoghue, Leo J., St. John, East Bridgewater
Doyle, Edward L., St. Mary of the Assumption, Hull
Dunn, Daniel A., St. Marie, Lowell
Dzuris, Robert W., St. Mary, Chelmsford
Eames, James H., St. Mary, Randolph
Egan, Thomas F., St. Brendan, Dorchester
Ego, John J., St. Bernadette, Randolph
Elibero, Edward P., St. Pius V, Lynn
Emerson, William R., St. William, Tewksbury
Farguheson, Wood Rowe, St. Joseph, Salem
Fenton, Jack H., St. Agnes, Reading
Gaffney, Francis M., Immaculate Conception, Revere
Gagne, Gerard E., Sacred Heart, Lawrence
Gagne, Ronald D., St. Rose of Lima, Topsfield
Gagnon, Raymond A., St. Anthony, Shirley
Gardyna, Henry A., Sick Leave
Gaudreau, Robert J., Sacred Hearts, Haverhill
Geneus, Alfred J., Our Lady of Pity, Cambridge
Gindel, Richard W., St. Ann, Gloucester
Goldy, Andrew J., St. Clement, Somerville
Grimley, Edward J., St. Augustine, Lawrence
Guerin, Bertrand H., Assumption, Bellingham
Guerrini, Patrick E., St. Elizabeth's Hospital, Brighton
Guerrios, Francisco, Holy Family, Dorchester
Guillet, Andre, Jesuit Urban Center, Boston
Hackett, Robert T., Most Blessed Sacrament, Wakefield
Halloran, John B., St. Paul, Hingham
Hanlon, Thomas H., St. Bridget, Abington
Hardcastle, Philip P., St. Charles, Woburn
Hardin, Howard P., St. Elizabeth of Hungary, Acton
Hardy, Gerard J., St. Louis, Lowell
Hardy, John W., Sacred Heart, Lynn
Harrison, John D., St. Mary-Immaculate Conception, Lawrence
Heffernan, Francis X., Immaculate Conception, Stoughton
Herrera, Luciano, Blessed Sacrament, Jamaica
Hickey, Charles M., St. Jerome, Weymouth
Hoaglund, Robert, St. Matthias, Marlboro
Holderried, Joseph E., St. Margaret Mary, Westwood
Iwanowicz, Michael A., Our Lady of Sorrows, Sharon
James, William H., St. Paul, Hamilton
Jennette, John F., St. Joseph, Quincy
Johnson, Robert N., St. John the Evangelist, Newton
Juliano, Anthony J., St. Adelaide, Peabody
Kaelin, Gerard J., Leave of Absence
Kane, William F.X., St. Joachim, Rockport
Kasenenko, Joseph S., St. Mary Star of the Sea, Beverly
Keefe, Arthur J., Holy Family, Duxbury
Kerns, William E., St. Barbara, Woburn
Killam, Harold E., Prison Ministry
King, Clifford D., St. Thomas, Wilmington
Kramich, Robert A., St. Bernard, Concord
L'Italien, George G., St. James, Salem
LaBrache, Leo F., St. Patrick, Watertown
Lacey, Neil F., St. George, Framingham
LaFargue, John L., Our Lady of the Lake, Halifax
LaPointe, Norman P., St. Joseph, Salem
Lauture, Aubert, St. Leo, Dorchester
Leavitt, James P., Hanscom Air Force Base, Bedford
LePage, Donald E., Senior Deacon, Unassigned
Leslie, Charles O., Holy Name, West Roxbury
Little, James B., St. Brendan, Dorchester
Lloyd, Barry V., St. Margaret, Lowell
LoPriore, Mario, Sacred Heart, Boston
MacDonald, Joseph P., St. Elizabeth, Milton
Machicado, Hernan, Senior Deacon, Unassigned
MacKenzie, William E., Our Lady, Waltham
Mandoza, Francis A., St. Agnes, Arlington
Mannion, John J., M.C.I. Cedar Junction, Walpole
Marchant, Thomas W., St. Anthony, Everett
Mariani, Henry A., St. Francis of Assisi, Medford
Markey, Paul G., Most Blessed Sacrament, Quincy
Martin, Leo A., Our Lady, Chelsea
Martin, Richard C., Sr., Gate of Heaven, South Boston
Martinez, Orlando, Asunsion, Lawrence
McCarthy, Daniel E., St. Mary, Rowley
McCarthy, John P., Unassigned
McCarty, William J., St. Joseph, Needham
McDavitt, Thomas S., Regl. Bishop's Office (South)
McDonough, John J., St. Clare, Braintree
McGrail, John S., St. Michael, Lowell
McHugh, John W., St. Paul, Hingham
McLaughlin, Richard B., St. Malachy, Burlington
McManus, Lawrence R., St. Joseph, Lynn
Menz, John R., St. Boniface, Quincy
Messina, Joseph M., St. Margaret Mary, Westwood
Miles, Walter J., Jr., M.C.I., Concord
Mills, Chester P., Unassigned
Montes, Edward M., St. Columbkille, Brighton
Morey, Russell W., St. Catherine, Westford
Mullins, Thomas F., St. Theresa, Billerica
Murphy, Alfred I., St. Bernard, Concord
Murphy, Steven J., St. Mary, Lawrence
Nagle, William V., St. Joseph, Kingston
Naveo, Jose, Asunsion, Lawrence
Nickley, Joseph T., Jr., Immaculate Conception, Weymouth
O'Neil, Cyril T., St. Patrick, Stoneham
Oles, Kenneth W., St. Mary, Wrentham
Ortiz, Jesus M., St. Peter, Dorchester
Papile, Joseph A., St. John, Quincy
Patrick, Alexander J., Jr., St. Elizabeth of Hungary, Acton
Peltak, Douglas P., Immaculate Conception, Marlboro
Penney, Edward F., Jr., St. Mary Magdalene, Tyngsboro
Pepe, John W., St. Bridget, Maynard
Perea, Antonio M., Most Holy Redeemer, East Boston
Pugsley, Stanley G., St. William, Dorchester
Quigley, Edward M., Senior Deacon, Unassigned
Quiles, Jesus, St. Patrick, Roxbury
Radford, Richard F., Jr., St. Mary, Brookline
Ramey, Allan A., St. Anthony, Lawrence
Ramrath, Joseph R., St. Anselm, Sudbury
Raymond, Thomas W., St. Robert Bellarmine, Andover
Rivera, Louis, St. Rose, Chelsea
Rivera, Valentin, St. John, Peabody
Rizzuto, Anthony P., Sacred Heart, Lexington
Rocha, Richard H., St. Peter & Paul, Lawrence
Rogers, Arthur F., Jr., St. James, Medford
Rooney, Gerard P., Senior Deacon, Unassigned
Ros, Peter An, St. Patrick, Lowell
Rosa, Andres, Cathedral of the Holy Cross, Boston
Ryan, Gerald P., Holy Ghost, Whitman
Ryan, John G., Senior Deacon
Salenius, John D., Sacred Heart, Quincy
Sanchez, Tomas E., St. John the Evangelist, Beverly
Santosuosso, Alfred E., St. Jude, Waltham
Shanahan, Allan R., St. Mary, Billerica
Shrader, David J., St. Richard, Danvers
Sicuso, Anthony C., Leave of Absence
Specht, Paul V., St. Patrick, Lawrence
Spiri, Guy J., St. Stephen, Framingham
Stenstrom, Eugene, Our Lady, Stoughton
Sullivan, Charles E., Resurrection, Hingham
Sullivan, Daniel F., St. Agatha, Milton
Taylor, Carroll H., Prison Ministry
Torres, Pedro L., St. Joseph, Framingham
Turner, J. Robert, St. Patrick, Stoneham
Valeri, Frank A., St. Peter, Malden
Vitello, Joseph V., St. Francis Xavier, Weymouth
Walsh, Martin J., St. Ann, Peabody
Warren, Lewis F., St. Anne, Salem
Watson, John W., Jr., Veterans Medical Center, Bedford
Welch, Henry M., St. Colman, Brockton
Whipple, John E., Our Lady, Marblehead
Wildes, William H., Senior Deacon, Unassigned
Wise, John W., Incarnation, Melrose
Yanikoski, Florian F., Senior Deacon

INSTITUTIONS LOCATED IN THE ARCHDIOCESE

[A] SEMINARIES, ARCHDIOCESAN

BOSTON. *St. John's Seminary.* College of Liberal Arts, 197 Foster St., Brighton, 02135. Tel: 617-254-2610. Rev. Robert W. Flagg, M.Div., M.S., S.T.L., Dean of College & Admissions; John J. Clabeaux, Ph.D., Academic Dean; Revs. Thomas F. Nestor, Ph.D., Dean of Students; George P. Evans, S.T.D., Spiritual Formation; Richard M. Erikson, Ph.D., Pastoral Formation; Mark L. Noonan, Ph.D.; Romanus Cessario, O.P.; Thomas T. Howard, Ph.D.; Deborah DeChiara-Quenzer, Ph.D.; Jeffrey Hause, Ph.D.; Tracey Stark, Ph.D. Priests 5; Lay Teachers 5; Students 35.

St. John's Seminary School of Theology. 127 Lake St., Brighton, 02135. Tel: 617-254-2610. Rev. Msgr. Timothy J. Moran, J.C.L., S.T.D., Rector; Revs. Martin P. Connor, S.T.L.; Laurence W. McGrath, M.S., M.A.; John L. Sullivan, S.S.L.; Walter J. Woods, S.T.D.; Robert E. Sullivan, Ph.D.; George P. Evans, M.Div., S.T.D.; Stephen E. Salocks, S.S.L.; Richard G. Cunningham, J.C.D.; Robin C. Ryan, C.P., Ph.D.; John P. McGinty, S.T.D.; John E. MacInnis, S.T.D.; Paul E. Ritt, S.T.D.; Thomas E. Nestor, Ph.D.; William B. Palardy, Ph.D.

WESTON. *Pope John XXIII National Seminary,* 558 South Ave., 02193. Tel: 617-899-5500; Fax: 617-899-9057. Rev. Msgr. Francis D. Kelly, S.T.L., Ph.D., Rector & Pres.; Revs. Paul P. Gilmartin, S.J., S.T.L., S.T.D.; James W. De Adder, Ph.D., S.T.D.; Alfred McBride, O.Praem., Ph.D.; Charles J. Healey, S.J.,

S.T.L., S.T.D.; James Massa, Ph.D., Coord.; Paul M. Parker, M.A., S.T.L.; Peter Uglietto, S.T.D.; Sr. Rose Clarisse Gadoury, S.S.A., M.A., M.Div. A Major National Seminary open to men over thirty studying for the diocesan and religious priesthood. Students 65.

[B] SEMINARIES, RELIGIOUS OR SCHOLASTICATES

BOSTON. *Oblate Provincialate*, 2 Ipswich St., 02215-3607. Tel: 617-536-7471; 536-4141; Fax: 617-536-7016. St. Ignatius Province of the Oblates of the Virgin Mary, Inc. Rev. Timothy Gallagher, O.M.V., Prov.; Bro. Luigi Falbo, O.M.V., Prov. Treas. Priests of the Province on Special Assignment:
Chile: Revs. Clifford Graham, O.M.V.; Roberto Jakanovich, O.M.V.
Italy: Revs. Vincenzo Antolini, O.M.V.; Thomas Haake, O.M.V.; Gerald Wright, O.M.V.
U.S.A.: Revs. Frank Cinque, O.M.V.; Thomas Cinque, O.M.V.; Placido Ferracino, O.M.V.; John Ferrara, O.M.V.; Stephen McAndrew, O.M.V.; James Montanaro, O.M.V.; Bruce Williamson, O.M.V.

Our Lady of Grace Seminary, 1105 Boylston St., 02215-3660. Tel: 617-266-5999; Fax: 617-247-7576. St. Ignatius Province of the Oblates of the Virgin Mary, Inc. Revs. Peter Gruver, O.M.V., Formator; Gregory Staab, O.M.V., Dir. of Novices; Bro. David N. Beauregard, O.M.V., Prefect of Studies. Students 7; Novices 3.

BRIGHTON. *Oblate Seminary Residence*, 62 Kirkwood Rd., 02135-5157. Tel: 617-787-0008. Bro. Richard Cote, O.M.I., Dir.

CAMBRIDGE. *Weston Jesuit School of Theology*, 3 Phillips Pl., 02138. Tel: 617-492-1960. Revs. Robert E. Manning, S.J., Pres.; Brian O. McDermott, S.J., Dean. Legal Title: *Weston College Corporation*. Priests 15; Sisters 3; Brothers 1; Lay Teachers 7; Students 253.

DANVERS. *Xavier Center*. House of Formation. 21 Spring St., 01923. Tel: 508-777-1326. American Northeastern Province of the Brothers of St. Francis Xavier (Xaverian Brothers). Bro. John D. Hamilton, C.F.X., Dir. Brothers Professed 3.

FRAMINGHAM. *Sylva Maria*, 567 Salem End Rd., 01701. Tel: 508-879-7667. Motherhouse and Novitiate of the Sons of Mary Missionary Society. Revs. John Murphy, F.M.S.I.; John Coss, F.M.S.I.; Henry Cicale, F.M.S.I.; Robert Rivard, F.M.S.I.; Joseph Saulnier, F.M.S.I.; Henry Branagan, F.M.S.I.; John Wallace, F.M.S.I. Priests 7; Brothers 5.

HAVERHILL. *Sons of Divine Providence School for Exceptional Boys* (Bradford), Groveland Rd., P.O. Box 205, 01835. Tel: 508-373-0461. Rev. Gino Marchesani, F.D.P.

[C] COLLEGES AND UNIVERSITIES

BOSTON. *Emmanuel College*, 400 The Fenway, 02115. Tel: 617-277-9340; 735-9825.
For a complete listing, refer to the Colleges and Universities section.

*CHESTNUT HILL. *Boston College*, 02167. Tel: 617-552-8000.
For a complete listing, refer to the Colleges and Universities section.

NORTH ANDOVER. *Merrimack College*, 01845. Tel: 508-683-7111; 837-5000.
For a complete listing, refer to the Colleges and Universities section.

WESTON. *Regis College*, Wellesley St., 02193. Tel: 617-893-1820.
For a complete listing, refer to the Colleges and Universities section.

[D] HIGH SCHOOLS, DIOCESAN

BOSTON. *Cathedral High School*, 74 Union Park St., 02118. Tel: 617-542-2325. Mary Kay Brady, Prin. Brothers 1; Sisters 7; Lay Teachers 20; Students 260.

Notre Dame Education Center. (Adults), 50 W. Broadway, 02127. Tel: 617-268-1912; Fax: 617-268-1912. Sisters of Notre Dame de Namur. Sr. Maria Delaney, Dir. Sisters 15; Adults 350; Total Staff 21.

St. Clare High School, 190 Cummins Hwy., 02131. Tel: 617-323-0966. Sr. Karen Hokanson, S.N.D., Prin. Sisters 10; Lay Teachers 12; Students 205.

BRAINTREE. *Archbishop Williams' High School*, 80 Independence Ave., 02184. Tel: 843-3636. Mary Ellen Barnes, Prin.; Rev. John M. Capuci, Chap. Priests 1; Sisters 4; Lay Teachers 36; Students 525.

BRIGHTON. *Archdiocesan Central High Schools, Inc.*, 2121 Commonwealth Ave., 02135. His Eminence Bernard Cardinal Law; Most Rev. John P. Boles; Rev. Robert J. Boyle; Paul R. Gauron, Esq.; Dorothy H. Jodice, Sec. Educ.; Sr. Ann Dominic Roach, O.P.; Sr. Blaithin Sullivan, C.S.J.

BROCKTON. *Cardinal Spellman High School*, 738 Court St., 02402. Tel: 508-583-6875; Fax: 508-580-1977. Sisters of St. Joseph. Sr. Thomasine Knowlton, C.S.J., Prin. Priests 1; Sisters 4; Lay Teachers 25; Students 490.

CAMBRIDGE. *Matignon High School*, One Matignon Rd., 02140. Tel: 617-876-1212. Mr. Gary R. LeFave, Prin.; Ms. Kathleen Fraser, Asst. Prin.; Rev. Vincent P. Doolan, Chap. College Preparatory. Religious 3; Lay Teachers 38; Students 600.

North Cambridge Catholic High School, 40 Norris St., 02140. Tel: 617-876-6068. Sr. Ellen Powers, C.S.J., Prin. Sisters 5; Lay Teachers 12; Students 180.

EVERETT. *Pope John XXIII Central High School*, 888 Broadway, 02149. Tel: 617-389-0240. Sr. Kristin Hokanson, S.N.D., Prin. Sisters 4; Lay Teachers 22; Students 400.

FRAMINGHAM. *Marian High School*, 273 Union Ave., 01701. Tel: 508-875-7646; Fax: 508-875-0838. Bro. Paul R. Alves, SS.CC., Prin.; Rev. Robert W. Murray. Priests 1; Brothers 1; Sisters 3; Lay Teachers 21; Students 301.

PEABODY. *Bishop Fenwick High School*, 99 Margin St., 01960. Tel: 508-531-8200; Fax: 508-532-9053. Robert McNamara, Prin.; Rev. John V. Sutton, Chap. Religious 8; Brothers 1; Lay Teachers 53; Students 890.

[E] HIGH SCHOOLS, PRIVATE

BOSTON. *Boston College High School & Jesuit Community*. 150 Morrissey Blvd., Dorchester, 02125. Tel: 617-436-3900; Fax: 617-282-7503. Revs. Joseph R. Fahey, S.J., Pres.; Philip A. Pusateri, S.J., Rector; Joseph T. Bennett, S.J.; Edward F. Boyle, S.J.; James P. Carr, S.J.; Terrence P. Devino, S.J.; Francis O. Hagerty, S.J.; William J. Hamilton, S.J.; Philip K. Harrigan, S.J.; James J. Hosie, S.J.; Daniel C. Lewis, S.J.; Thomas J. C. Kelly, S.J.; John L. Mahoney, S.J.; Joaquin Martinez-Mari, S.J. (Bolivia); James W. O'Neil, S.J.; Francis J. O'Neill, S.J.; Joseph P. O'Neill, S.J.; Clement L. Pelletier, S.J.; Ignatius F. Pennisi, S.J.; Leo E. Pollard, S.J.; Donald A. Sherpenski, S.J.; George A. Duffy, S.J.; Robert M. Hanlon, S.J.; Peter D. Hickey, S.J.; Stephen F. Dawber, S.J.; Joseph R. Laughlin, S.J.; Jose C. Corral, S.J. (Castilla); John Joseph Walsh, S.J.; Robert J. Higgins, S.J.; Bros. Cornelius C. Murphy, S.J.; Donald J. Murray, S.J.; Pedro O. Carrasquillo, S.J., Scholastic. Religious 32; Lay Teachers 66; Students 1,120. Jesuit Community. Tel: 617-929-9423; Fax: 617-929-9459.

Catholic Memorial High School and Lower School. (Grades 7-12). 235 Baker St., West Roxbury, 02132-4395. Tel: 617-323-7333; Fax: 617-325-0888. Congregation of Christian Brothers. Bro. John B. Flaherty, C.F.C., Pres.; Mr. Luke Nawrocki, Prin.; Rev. Robert J. Cordery, Chap. Priests 1; Brothers 10; Lay Teachers 43; Boys 707.

Don Bosco Preparatory School of Technology, 300 Tremont St., 02116. Tel: 617-426-9457. Rev. Richard J. McCormick, S.D.B., Dir.; Mr. Barry Hynes, Headmaster; Mr. John Moran, Prin.; Revs. Angelo Bongiorno, S.D.B.; James Heuser, S.D.B., Vice Dir.; James Mulloy, S.D.B.; Thomas Dunne, S.D.B.; Emil Fardellone, S.D.B. In res., Rev. Mario Carpanese, S.D.B.; Bros. William Hanna; Frank Tilton. Priests 7; Brothers 2; Lay Teachers 20; Boys 300.

Savio Preparatory High School. 145 Byron St., East Boston, 02128. Tel: 617-567-2710. Dr. Edward J. Gotgart, Exec. Dir.; Dr. Richard K. Chrystal, Prin. A college preparatory school. Lay Teachers 23; Students 340.

BRIGHTON. *Mt. St. Joseph Academy*, 617 Cambridge St., 02135. Tel: 617-254-8383 (School Office); 783-4747 (Guidance Office). Sponsored by Sisters of St. Joseph of Boston. Sr. Mary L. Murphy, C.S.J., Prin. Sisters 4; Lay Teachers 17; Girls 300.

DANVERS. *St. John's Preparatory School*, 01923. Tel: 508-774-1050; Fax: 508-774-5069. Day Students. Bro. William Drinan, C.F.X., Headmaster. Brothers 6; Lay Teachers 72; Boys 1,024.

DEDHAM. *Ursuline Academy*. (Grades 7-12), 85 Lowder St., 02026-4299. Tel: 617-326-6161. Sr. Mercedes Videira, O.S.U., Prin. Operated by Ursuline Convent. Ursuline Nuns. College Prep School for Girls (Grades 7-12). Sisters 9; Lay Teachers 38; Girls 357.

HINGHAM. *Notre Dame Academy*, 1073 Main St., 02043. Tel: 617-749-5930; 749-4727. Total Staff 70; Girls 550.

KINGSTON. *Sacred Heart High School*, 399 Bishops Hwy., 02364. Tel: 617-585-7511. Mrs. Susan Krastin, H.S. Prin.; Mr. John F. Enos, Junior High Prin. Religious 11; Lay Teachers 36; Students 554.

LAWRENCE. *Central Catholic High School of Lawrence, Inc.*, 300 Hampshire St., 01841. Tel: 508-682-0260. Bro. Richard J. Carey, F.M.S., Prin. Conducted by the Marist Brothers of the Schools. Religious 8; Lay Teachers 46; Boys 870.

LOWELL. *Lowell Catholic High School, Inc.*, 530 Stevens St., 01851. Tel: 508-452-1794. Mr. Edward J. Quinn. Brothers 1; Sisters 2; Lay Teachers 16; Students 280.

MALDEN. *Malden Catholic High School*, 99 Crystal St., 02148. Tel: 617-322-3098; Fax: 617-397-0573. Xaverian Brothers. Bro. Richard Cook, C.F.X., Headmaster.; Lay Teachers 30; Boys 548.

METHUEN. *Presentation of Mary Academy*, 209 Lawrence St., 01844. Tel: 508-682-9391; Fax: 508-975-3595. Sisters of the Presentation of Mary. Sr. Rose Marie Dupre, Prin. Sisters 3; Lay Teachers 14; Total Staff 37; Girls 241.

MILTON. *Fontbonne Academy*, 930 Brook Rd., 02186. Tel: 617-696-3241. Sr. Marilyn McGoldrick, Pres. Sisters of St. Joseph 6; Lay Teachers 37; Students 500.

NEEDHAM. *St. Sebastian's Country Day School, Inc.*, 1191 Greendale Ave., 02192. Tel: 617-449-5200; Fax: 617-449-5630. Mr. William L. Burke, III, Headmaster; Revs. John F. Arens; John U. Paris. Priests 2; Lay Teachers 45; Boys 315.

NEWTON. *Country Day School of the Sacred Heart*. (Grades 5-12), 785 Centre St., 02158. Tel: 617-244-4246. Sr. Barbara Rogers, R.S.C.J., Prin. Legal Title: *Boston Academy of the Sacred Heart*. Religious of the Sacred Heart 1; Lay Teachers 30; Girls 210.

Mount Alvernia High School, 790 Centre St., 02158. Tel: 617-964-5643 (Convent); 969-2260 (School). Missionary Franciscan Sisters of the Immaculate Conception. Sr. Suzanne Fondini, O.S.F., Prin. Sisters 10; Lay Teachers 18; Girls 254.

READING. *Austin Preparatory School*, 101 Willow St., 01867. Tel: 617-944-4900. Paul J. Moran, Headmaster; Revs. John D. Harrington (England); Kenneth Healey, S.M.; James Morris. Priests 3; Sisters 1; Brothers 1; Lay Teachers 35; Students 564.

TYNGSBORO. *Academy of Notre Dame*, 01879. Tel: 508-649-7611. Sr. Maureen Marr, S.N.D., Prin. Sisters of Notre Dame de Namur 4; Faculty 34; Girls 261.

WAKEFIELD. *Our Lady of Nazareth Academy*, 14 Winship Dr., 01880. Tel: 617-245-5210. Sisters of Charity of Nazareth. Mrs. Molly Kelley, Prin. Lay Teachers 18; Girls 178.

WESTWOOD. *Xaverian Brothers High School*, 800 Clapboardtree St., 02090. Tel: 617-326-6392. Xaverian Brothers. Bro. Daniel Skala, C.F.X., Headmaster. Priests 1; Brothers 3; Lay Teachers 51; Boys 730.

[F] ELEMENTARY SCHOOLS, DIOCESAN

DANVERS. *St. Mary of the Annunciation School*, 14 Otis St., 01923. Tel: 508-774-0307. Mrs. Constance Morency, M.Ed., Prin. (Grades K-8 & Extended Day Care). Sisters of Notre Dame de Namur 1; Lay Teachers 29; Students 527.

[G] MONTESSORI SCHOOLS

HAVERHILL. *The Merrimack Montessori School*, 55 Saltonstall Rd., 01830. Tel: 508-374-6103. Juliet Nagle, Dir. (For boys and girls aged 3-5). Sisters 2; Lay Teachers 4; Students 125.

MARLBORO. *The St. Anne Montessori School*, 720 Boston Post Rd., 01752. Tel: 508-485-3791. Sr. Doreen Scott, S.S.A., Dir. (For boys and girls aged 3-5). Religious 2; Lay Teachers 2; Students 72.

NEWTON. *Walnut Park Montessori School*, 47 Walnut Park, 02158. Tel: 617-969-9208. Heywot Yawand-Wossen, Dir. Religious 5; Lay Teachers 3; Students 141.

WENHAM. *Notre Dame Children's Class*, 74 Grapevine Rd., 01984. Tel: 508-468-1340. Sr. Barbara Beauchamp, S.N.D., Dir.; Sr. Susan Raymo, S.N.D., Co-Dir. Religious 2; Lay Teachers 4; Primary Class 31; Preschool Students 48.

[H] ELEMENTARY SCHOOLS, PRIVATE

BOSTON. *Lt. Joseph P. Kennedy, Jr., Memorial School*. (Under the patronage of Our Lady of Czestochowa.). 17 Hale St., Hyde Park, 02136. Tel: 617-364-4975; 361-1726. Bernardine Sisters of the Third Order of St. Francis of Mass., Inc. Sr. Joanne Helen Grejdus, O.S.F., Prin.; Sr. M. Theresine Jablonski, O.S.F., Clerk-Treas. Sisters 6; Lay Teachers 4; Students 230.

Nativity Preparatory School. (Grades 5-8). 30 Raynor Cir., Roxbury, 02120. Tel: 617-442-1993. Legal Title: *Nativity-Boston, Inc.* Revs. Raymond J. Callahan, S.J., Exec. Dir.; Alfred J. Hicks, S.J., Prin.; William J. Cullen, S.J. A Jesuit Middle School. Priests 3; Lay Teachers 11; Boys 61.

BRAINTREE. *St. Coletta Day School, Inc.*, 85 Washington St., 02184. Tel: 617-848-6250; Fax: 617-848-0640. Day School for multiply handicapped, developmentally delayed children, ages 4-22 years. Legal Title: *Braintree St. Coletta Day School*. Sisters of St. Francis of Assisi 2; Lay Teachers 33; Students 74.

DORCHESTER. *Mother Caroline Academy*. (Grades 5-8), 35 Bird St., 02125. Tel: 617-288-3300. School Sisters of Notre Dame. Sr. Mary Dooley, S.S.N.D., Exec. Dir.; Sr. Frances Butler, S.S.N.D., Prin.; Sr. Barbara Dewey, S.S.N.D., Admin. Legal Title: *Mother Caroline Academy for Girls, Inc.* Students 60; Sisters 3; Lay Teachers 10.

GLOUCESTER. *St. Mel Independent Day School*, 12 Edgemoor Rd., 01930. Tel: 508-283-1700. Sr. Catherine Mary Albright, O.P., Prin. Sisters 2; Lay Teachers 7; Students 89.

GROTON. *Country Day School of the Holy Union*, 14 Main St., Box 993, 01450. Tel: 508-448-5646. Sr. Lucille Guay, S.U.S.C., Prin. Sisters of the Holy Union 2; Lay Teachers 8; Students 210.

HANOVER. *Cardinal Cushing School and Training Center, Inc.*, 400 Washington St., 02339. Tel: 617-826-6371. Dr. Henry W. Perrin, Jr., Dir. Sisters 9; Lay Staff 250; Students 140.

KINGSTON. *Sacred Heart Elementary School*. (Day School), 329 Bishops Hwy., 02364. Tel: 617-585-2114. Sr. Jeanne Morris, C.D.P., Prin. (Grades 1-6). Sisters of Divine Providence 8; Lay Teachers 17; Students 444.

Sacred Heart Pre-Primary School, 363 Bishops Hwy., 02364-2035. Tel: 617-585-3545. Sr. Angela, C.D.P., Dir. Religious 1; Lay Teachers 3; Students 62.

LOWELL. *Franco-American Private School*, 357 Pawtucket St., 01854. Tel: 508-458-0308. Sr. Lorraine Richard, S.C.Q., Prin. Religious 1; Lay Teachers 16; Students 369.

MARLBORO. *Our Lady Preschool Learning Center*, 197 Pleasant St., 01752. Tel: 481-0654. Sr. Debra Bow, S.S.Ch., Dir. Religious 1; Students 80 (ages 3-5).

MILTON. *Jeanne d'Arc Convent*, 55 Parkwood Dr., 02186. Tel: 617-698-8265; 698-8266. Religious of Christian Education. Sisters 7.

NEWTON. *Jackson School Elementary*. (Grades 1-6), 200 Jackson Rd., 02158-1428. Tel: 617-969-1537. Mrs. Susan G. Niden, Prin. Sisters 12; Lay Teachers 15; Students 198.

Mount Alvernia Academy. (Grades N-6). 20 Manet Rd., Chestnut Hill, 02167. Tel: 617-527-7540. Missionary Franciscan Sisters 7; Lay Teachers 29; Students 308. Convent School. Tel: 617-527-7540. Sr. Irene Laurence, O.S.F., Prin. Convent. Tel: 617-244-3696.

TYNGSBORO. *Academy of Notre Dame at Tyngsboro*, 180 Middlesex Rd., 01879. Tel: 508-649-7611. Sr. Marcia Billings, S.N.D., Prin. Sisters of Notre Dame de Namur 3; Lay Teachers 28; Students 454.

[I] SPECIAL SCHOOLS

BOSTON. *Emmanuel House Kindergarten*, 11 Newcomb St., 02118. Tel: 617-445-2037; Fax: 617-445-2479. Community Based Agency of Catholic Charitable Bureau of Archdiocese of Boston, Inc. Sr. Mary Helena Sproul, Dir. Franciscan Sisters of the Atonement 4; Lay Teachers 4; Students 44.

Laboure College, Inc., 2120 Dorchester Ave., 02124. Tel: 617-296-8300; Fax: 617-296-7947. Sr. Clarisse Correia, D.C., Pres. Two year college for nursing and allied health. Associate member of the Daughters of Charity Health System. Priests 2; Sisters 6; Lay Teachers 60; Students 600.

METHUEN. *St. Ann's Home Special Needs School*, 100 A. Haverhill St., 01844. Patrick Villani, Ph.D., Exec. Dir. Lay Teachers 35; Students 130.

MILTON. *Aquinas College at Milton*. Degree-Granting Programs. 303 Adams St., 02186-4296. Tel: 617-696-3100. Dr. Mary Huegel, Pres. Sisters 7; Students 255.

NEWTON. *Aquinas College at Newton*, 15 Walnut Park, 02158. Tel: 617-969-4400. Sisters of St. Joseph. Sr. Marian Batho, Pres. A Two Year College. Students 225.

PEABODY. *Holy Childhood Nursery & Kindergarten*, 5 Wheatland St., 01960. Tel: 508-531-4733. Sr. Bernadette Zaccardi, Supr.; Sr. M. Joan Melei, O.Carm., Co-Dir. Sisters 7; Lay Teachers 6; Students 100.

RANDOLPH. *The Boston School Serving Deaf & Aphasic Children*, 800 N. Main St., 02368. Tel: 617-963-8150. Sr. Bernadette Kenney, C.S.J., Exec. Dir. Sisters of St. Joseph. Lay Teachers 14; Students 68.

SWAMPSCOTT. *Marian Court College*, Little's Point Rd., 01907. Tel: 617-595-6768; Fax: 617-595-3560. Sr. Joanne Bibeau, R.S.M., Pres. Sisters 5; Lay Staff 44; Students 225.

WATERTOWN. *Rosary Academy Learning Center*, 2 Rosary Dr., 02172. Tel: 617-923-1935. Preschool & Day Care. Sr. Rosaire, O.P., Dir. Sisters of St. Dominic (St. Catherine, KY). Sisters 3; Lay Teachers 7; Students 70.

[J] CATHOLIC CHARITIES

BOSTON. *Catholic Charitable Bureau of the Archdiocese of Boston, Inc.*, Central Office, 49 Franklin St., 02110. Tel: 617-482-5440; Fax: 617-451-0337. Dr. Joseph Doolin, Pres. Multi-Service Agency. Total Clients served 126,345.

[K] FAMILY COUNSELING AND GUIDANCE CENTERS

BOSTON. *Family Counseling and Guidance Centers*. A Division of Catholic Charities. Admin. Headquarters, 49 Franklin St., 02110. Tel: 617-482-4355. Mr. Jack E. Mazzotti, III, M.A, Clinic Admin.
Local Clinics:
Metropolitan Boston, 49 Franklin St., 02110. Tel: 617-542-0903.
South Shore Braintree, 40 Independence Ave., Braintree, 02184. Tel: 617-848-7840.
West Area-Framingham, 350 Worcester Rd., Framingham, 01701. Tel: 508-875-0648.
North Shore-Danvers, 6 State Rd., Danvers, 01923. Tel: 508-774-6820.
Plymouth County-Marshfield, 475 School, Marshfield, 02050. Tel: 617-837-1133.

QUINCY. *The Good Shepherd: Maria Droste Services*, 1354 Hancock St., Suite 209, 02169. Tel: 617-471-5686. Sr. Joanne Westwater, Exec. Dir. Legal Title: *Madonna Hall*. Total Staff 4; Volunteers 14; Total Assisted 300.

[L] SOCIETY OF ST. VINCENT DE PAUL

BOSTON. *Society of St. Vincent DePaul, Central Office*, 1280 Washington St., 02118. Tel: 617-542-0883. Mr. Albert N. Crocker, Exec. Dir.

[M] CHILD CARE AGENCIES

BOSTON. *The Laboure Center/Catholic Charities*, 371 & 376 W. Fourth St., 02127. Tel: 617-268-9670. Daughters of Charity of St. Vincent de Paul. Sr. Maryadele Robinson, D.C., Dir., Laboure Center; Mrs. Margaret Kelly, Dir. Early Childhood Services (includes Infant-Toddler, Preschool, Child Care, Special Needs). Sisters 1; Lay Teachers 12; Students 80.

BRIGHTON. *Nazareth Group Home*, 192 Foster St., 02135. Tel: 617-787-4324. Community based group residence (ages 6-12). Capacity 6.

JAMAICA PLAIN. *Nazareth Day Care*. (3 mos.-6 yrs.), 19 St. Joseph St., 02130. Tel: 617-522-4040. Legal Title: *Nazareth*. Capacity 79; Total Staff 16.

Nazareth Family Center, 19 St. Joseph St., 02130. Tel: 617-522-4040. Joan Kilday Puleo, Agency Pres. Total Assisted 97; Total Staff 28.

METHUEN. *St. Ann's Home, Inc.*, 100A Haverhill St., 01844. Tel: 508-682-5276. Patrick T. Villani, Ph.D., Dir.; Mrs. Sharon Cutter, Business Mgr. School. Children 130. Residential Treatment Center: Children 85. Total in Residence 85; Total Staff 175.

[N] SETTLEMENT HOUSES

BOSTON. *Chinese Catholic Pastoral Center*, 78 Tyler St., 02111-1831. Tel: 617-482-2949. Total Assisted 70; Total Staff 2.

El Centro Del Cardenal/Catholic Charities, 76 Union Park St., 02118. Tel: 617-542-9292; Fax: 617-542-6912. Ms. Elisabeth Zweig-Snippe.

Emmanuel House/Catholic Charities - Community Social Service Center, 11 Newcomb St., 02118. Tel: 617-445-2037; Fax: 617-445-2479. Sr. Mary Helena Sproul, S.A., Exec. Dir. Community Based Agency of Catholic Charitable Bureau of Archdiocese of Boston, Inc.
Various Adult Programs-Multi-Service. Franciscan Sisters of the Atonement 4; Total Assisted 764; Total Staff 7.

Haitian Multi-Service Center/Catholic Charitable Bureau of Boston. 12 Bicknell St., Dorchester, 02121. Tel: 617-436-2848. Mr. Jean Marc Jean-Baptiste, Dir. Education and outreach, day care, counseling and advocacy.

Salesian Boys & Girls Club. (Central Unit), 189 Paris St., 02128. Tel: 567-0508. (Orient Heights Unit), 145-150 Bryon St. Salesians of St. John Bosco. Revs. Mark Hyde, S.D.B., Exec. Dir.; Augustine Baek, S.D.B., Asst. Exec. Dir.; Mr. David Ferraro, Fin. Admin. & Dir. Oper.; Revs. Richard Cressman, S.D.B., Chap.; Jack Janko, S.D.B.; Terence O'Donnell, S.D.B.; Bros. John Robert Metell, S.D.B.; George Sheehan, S.D.B. Total Assisted 3,000; Total Staff 20.

HULL. *Children's Vacation House/Catholic Charities*, 138 Edgewater Rd., 02045. Tel: 617-925-0710. Conducted by the Catholic Charitable Bureau of Boston. Children 300.

[O] GUIDANCE CENTERS

BOSTON. *Alpha-Omega*, Four Omega Way, P.O. Box 922, 01460. Tel: 508-486-8919; Fax: 508-486-3990. A long term residence for 17 adolescent boys. James R. McKenna, Prog. Dir.

Life Resources, Inc., 199 State St., Fifth Floor, 02109; Fax: 617-523-1747. Mr. William J. Chiaradonna, L.I.C.S.W., B.C.D., Pres. Tel: 617-227-8766. Total in Residence 245; Total Staff 158; Total Assited 46.

St. Mary's Women and Infants Center, 90 Cushing Ave., 02125. Tel: 617-436-8600. For pregnant & parenting women & their children. Caritas Christi. Joyce Murphy, Pres. & CEO. Patients assisted annually 250; Total Staff 60.

BROCKTON. *Phaneuf Center*, 104 Market St., 02401. Tel: 508-584-0500. Coed emergency shelter for 9 adolescents.

Phaneuf Out-Patient, 792 N. Main St., 02401. Tel: 508-588-2882. Drug and alcohol outpatient counseling for all ages.

LAKEVILLE. *Bishop Joseph John Ruocco House*, 22 Highland Rd., 02347. Tel: 508-947-2823. Mr. Stephen Folino, Dir. Long term residential group home for 17 male adolescents. To provide comprehensive life skill services to residents and their families.

[P] INFORMATION - CONFERENCE CENTERS

BOSTON. *Archdiocesan Information Center*, Boston Catholic Directory, 49 Franklin St., 02110. Tel: 617-542-8393. Rev. Peter V. Conley, Editor. Assistants to the Editor: Rev. Robert M. O'Grady; Sr. Mary Ellen Sweney, S.N.D.; Sr. Theresa Cunningham, S.N.D.; Mrs. Anita Sweet.

Paulist Center, 5 Park St., 02108. Tel: 617-742-4460. Revs. Stanley F. MacNevin, C.S.P., Supr.; Joseph T. Griffin, C.S.P.; Walter J. Sullivan, C.S.P.; Thomas J. Holanhaw, C.S.P.; Harold Foye, C.S.P.; Robert J. Sadowski, C.S.P.; Francis M. Sweeney, C.S.P.; John P. Campbell, C.S.P.; Michael J. Kallock, C.S.P.; Edward J. McDonald, C.S.P.; Charles E. Cunniff, C.S.P.; Richard J. Colgan, C.S.P. Total in Residence 12; Total Staff 4.

ANDOVER. *Franciscan Center*, 475 River Rd., 01810. Tel: 508-851-3391. Order of Friars Minor. Rev. John D. Bavaro, O.F.M., Dir.; Guardian, Retreat Team. Retreat Team: Revs. Roland Petinge, O.F.M., Vicar; John C. DiMauro, O.F.M.; Robert J. Caprio, O.F.M.; Bros. Gabriel Aceto, O.F.M.; Chris Meyers, O.F.M.; Sr. Lorraine Pianka, S.S.N.D.; Mrs. Mildred Sheehan, Sec.; Jerrie Lou Buffo; Eileen Bowes; Gayle Jaskal; Margaret McCarthy; Joanna Howorth. Total in Residence 9; Total Staff 12.

BROCKTON. *Chapel of Our Savior-Catholic Pastoral and Information Center*, 475 Westgate Dr., 02401. Tel: 508-583-8357. Revs. Boniface Riedmann, S.A.; Joseph DiMauro, S.A.; Malcolm Martin, S.A.; Bros. Louis Marek, S.A.; John Poncia, S.A., Dir. Priests 3; Brothers 2.

PEABODY. *Catholic Information Center*, North Shore Shopping Center, 01960. Tel: 508-531-6145. Revs. Ferdinand T. Schaefer, O.Carm., Dir.; Kilian Healy, O.Carm.; Alan N. Crowley, O.Carm.; Peter Thomas Sherry, O.Carm.; Henry D. Goodwin, O.Carm.; Mark A. Dittami, O.Carm.; Lloyd Wiegele, O.Carm.; Thomas Hakala, O.Carm. Priests 8; Brothers 2.

[Q] GENERAL HOSPITALS

BOSTON. *Carney Hospital*, 2100 Dorchester Ave., 02124. Tel: 617-296-4000.
For a complete listing, refer to the Hospitals section.

BRIGHTON. *St. Elizabeth's Hospital of Boston*, 736 Cambridge St., 02135. Tel: 617-789-3000.
For a complete listing, refer to the Hospitals section.

BROCKTON. *Good Samaritan Medical Center*, 235 N. Pearl St., 02401. Tel: 508-427-3000; 427-3151.
For a complete listing, refer to the Hospitals section.

LOWELL. *Saints Memorial Health System, Inc.*. P.O. Box 30, 01852. Tel: 508-458-1411; Fax: 508-458-8369.
For a complete listing, refer to the Hospitals section.

METHUEN. *Holy Family Hospital and Medical Center*, 70 East St., 01844-4597. Tel: 508-687-0151.
For a complete listing, refer to the Hospitals section.

[R] SPECIAL HOSPITALS

BOSTON. *Franciscan Children's Hospital and Rehabilitation Center*. General Pediatrics, Rehabilitation and Special Education, 30 Warren St. Brighton, 02135. Tel: 617-254-3800.
For a complete listing, refer to the Special Care Facilities section.

BRIGHTON. *St. John of God Hospital*, 296 Allston St., 02146. Tel: 617-277-5750.
For a complete listing, refer to the Special Care Facilities section.

*CAMBRIDGE. *Youville Hospital & Rehabilitation Center, Inc.*, 1575 Cambridge St., 02138-4398. Tel: 617-876-4344.
For a complete listing, refer to the Special Care Facilities section.

METHUEN. *Holy Family Hospital Men's Guild*, 70 East St., 01844.
For a complete listing, refer to the Special Care Facilities section.

[S] SOCIAL SERVICES

BOSTON. *The Laboure Center/Catholic Charities*, 371 & 376 W. Fourth St., 02127. Tel: 617-268-9670. Sr. Maryadele Robinson, D.C., Dir. Certified Home Health Services, Elderly Social Services, Early Childhood Services, Adult Day Health Program, Substance Abuse and Mental Health Counseling, Family Intervention Services, Emergency Assistance, Afterschool Programs, and Support Groups. Daughters of Charity of St. Vincent de Paul 5.

DORCHESTER. *Little Sisters of the Assumption, Family Health Service, Inc. (Project Hope)*, 45 Magnolia St.,

02125. Tel: 617-442-1880; Fax: 617-442-1356. A community based shelter for homeless families offering food pantry, education, and community organizing programs to neighborhood. Total Assisted 24; Staff 10; Sisters 5.

LEXINGTON. *Grey Nuns' Adult Day Health Center, Inc.*, 10 Pelham Rd., 02173. Sr. Dorothy Cooper, S.G.M., Prov. Supvr.

[T] PROTECTIVE INSTITUTIONS

BOSTON. *St. Mary's Women and Infants Center.* 90 Cushing Ave. Dorchester, 02125.
For a complete listing, refer to the Special Care Facilities section.

MARLBORO. *Madonna Hall*, Cushing Hill Dr., 01752. Tel: 508-485-8610.
For a complete listing, refer to the Special Care Facilities section.

[U] HOMES FOR AGED-RESIDENTS & NURSING

BOSTON. *Don Orione Nursing Home.* 111 Orient Ave. East Boston, 02128. Tel: 617-569-2100.
For a complete listing, refer to the Special Care Facilities section.

Marian Manor, (1954). 130 Dorchester St. South Boston, 02127. Tel: 617-268-3333.
For a complete listing, refer to the Special Care Facilities section.

St. Joseph Nursing Care Center. 321 Centre St. Dorchester, 02122. Tel: 617-825-6320; Fax: 617-825-7410.
For a complete listing, refer to the Special Care Facilities section.

BROCKTON. *St. Joseph Manor Nursing & Extended Care Facility*, 215 Thatcher St., 02402-3999. Tel: 508-583-5834; Fax: 508-583-8551.
For a complete listing, refer to the Special Care Facilities section.

*CAMBRIDGE. *Youville Healthcare Center, Inc.*, 1575 Cambridge St., 02138-4398. Tel: 617-876-4344.
For a complete listing, refer to the Special Care Facilities section.

FRAMINGHAM. *Carmel Terrace*, 933 Central St., 01701. Tel: 508-788-8000.
For a complete listing, refer to the Special Care Facilities section.

St. Patrick's Manor, Inc., 863 Central St., 01701. Tel: 508-879-8000; Fax: 508-626-1604.
For a complete listing, refer to the Special Care Facilities section.

*LAWRENCE. *M.I. Adult Day Health Center, Inc.*, 189 Maple St., 01841. Tel: 508-682-7575.
For a complete listing, refer to the Special Care Facilities section.

M.I. Nursing-Restorative Center, Inc., 172 Lawrence St., 01841. Tel: 508-685-6321.
For a complete listing, refer to the Special Care Facilities section.

M.I. Residential Community II, Inc., 191 Maple St., 01841. Tel: 508-682-7575.
For a complete listing, refer to the Special Care Facilities section.

M.I. Residential Community III, Inc., 193 Maple St., 01841. Tel: 508-682-7575.
For a complete listing, refer to the Special Care Facilities section.

M.I. Residential Community, Inc., 189 Maple St., 01841. Tel: 508-682-7575.
For a complete listing, refer to the Special Care Facilities section.

**M.I. Transportation, Inc.*, 189 Maple St., 01841. Tel: 508-682-7575.
For a complete listing, refer to the Special Care Facilities section.

LOWELL. *D'Youville Manor*, 981 Varnum Ave., 01854. Tel: 508-454-5681.
For a complete listing, refer to the Special Care Facilities section.

MARLBORO. *Marie Esther Health Center, Inc.*, 720 Boston Post Rd., 01752. Tel: 508-485-3791.
For a complete listing, refer to the Special Care Facilities section.

SOMERVILLE. *Jeanne Jugan Pavilion*, 190 Highland Ave., 02143.
For a complete listing, refer to the Special Care Facilities section.

Jeanne Jugan Residence, 186 Highland Ave., 02143. Tel: 617-776-4420; Fax: 617-623-0707.
For a complete listing, refer to the Special Care Facilities section.

WALTHAM. *Maristhill Nursing Home*, 66 Newton St., 02154. Tel: 617-893-0240.
For a complete listing, refer to the Special Care Facilities section.

[V] PERSONAL PRELATURES

CAMBRIDGE. *Opus Dei, Prelature of the Holy Cross and Opus Dei*, 25 Follen St., 02138. Tel: 617-354-3204. Revs. Salvador M. Ferigle; John C. Agnew. Legal Title: *The Work of God, Inc.*

CHESTNUT HILL. *Opus Dei*, 481 Hammond St., 02167. Tel: 617-738-7348. Revs. David Cavanagh; Richard W. Rieman; Alvaro Silva; Raphael Caamano.

[W] MONASTERIES AND RESIDENCES OF PRIESTS AND BROTHERS

BOSTON. *Arrupe House*, 35 Creighton St., 02130. Tel: 617-524-9328. Revs. James A. Gillon, S.J., Supr. & Novice Dir.; Walter M. Abbott, S.J.; Terrence Devino, S.J. Priests 3; Novices 6.

Divine Word Missionaries, 184 Beacon St., 02116. Tel: 617-267-5143. Divine Word Missionaries. Revs. Donald P. Mulrenan, S.V.D., Supr. & Mission Dir.; Joseph Connolly, S.V.D., Asst. Mission Dir. In res., Revs. William Kane, S.V.D.; Donald Skerry, S.V.D.

Jesuit Urban Center & Immaculate Conception Community, 775 Harrison Ave., 02118-2311. Tel: 617-536-8440; Fax: 617-536-2142. Revs. David I. Donovan, S.J., Supr.; Charles B. Connolly, S.J., Minister and Treas.; Denis R. Como, S.J.; John R. d'Anjou, S.J.; Jon D. Fuller, S.J.; Thomas J. Gallagher, S.J.; Thomas F. Hussey, S.J.; Robert E. Linsay, S.J.; James M. Shaughnessy, S.J.; Simon E. Smith, S.J.; George P. Winchester, S.J.

Little Brothers of St. Francis, 785-789 Parker St., 02120. Tel: 617-442-2556. Bro. James Curran, L.B.S.F., Guardian. Regional Fraternity and Novitiate. Legal Title: *Little Brothers of St. Francis Franciscan Fraternity of Peace and Love.* Brothers 3; Novices 1; Postulants 2.

Loyola House, 300 Newbury St., 02115. Tel: 617-267-1008. The Society of Jesus. Revs. Aram J. Berard, S.J.; Joseph J. Bruce, S.J.; Thomas F. Clark, S.J.; Herbert J. Cleary, S.J.; John T. Crabb, S.J.; Charles G. Crowley, S.J.; William J. Cullen, S.J.; William F. Doyle, S.J.; John E. Fagan, S.J.; William G. Guindon, S.J.; Robert F. Hoey, S.J.; Norman H. Houle, S.J.; William D. Ibach, S.J.; Joseph F. Keaney, S.J.; William J. Larkin, S.J.; Paul T. Lucey, S.J.; Robert G. McMillan, S.J.; George S. Mahan, S.J.; Jose A. Mesa, S.J.; William L. Mulligan, S.J.; Edward J. Murawski, S.J.; John P. Murray, S.J.; George W. Nolan, S.J., Supr.; Joseph P. Murray, S.J.; James T. Sheehan, S.J.; S. Jin-yeul Song, S.J.; Alfred O. Winshman, S.J.; Bros. Paul J. Geysen, S.J.; James J. Moran, S.J.; Austin J. Burns, S.J. Priests 27; Brothers 3; Total in Residence 30; Total Staff 5.

Marist Fathers and Brothers Provincial House, 27 Isabella St., 02116-5216. Tel: 617-426-5297; 426-4448; Fax: 617-482-1570. Very Rev. Joseph Hindelang, S.M., Prov.; Rev. Michael McElhinny, S.M., Vicar Prov.
Priests of the Province Not Listed Elsewhere: Rev. William Foley, S.M., (Retired Army Chaplain-Leave of Absence), 31 Fillmore Ct., Satellite Beach, FL, 32937. Rev. Armand Thibault, S.M., 27 Isabella St., 02116-5216. Rev. Robert Poirier, S.M., Rocky Creek Village, 8614 Shell Dr., Tampa, FL, 33615-1439. Rev. Frank Reitter, S.M., 3007 W. 34th Ave., Apt. 1, Anchorage, AK, 99517-2257. Rev. Faustino Cruz, S.M., 28 Colborne Rd., Apt. 14, Brighton, 02135.

Marist Fathers Lourdes Residence, 698 Beacon St., 02215. Tel: 617-262-2271. Revs. Gerard Caron, S.M., Dir.; Michael Pavlick, S.M.; Paul H. Pepin, S.M.; J. Armand Robichaud, S.M. Priests 4.

Marist Fathers of Our Lady of Victories (Boston Prov.), 27 Isabella St., 02116. Tel: 617-426-4448. Revs. Andrew Albert, S.M.; Roger J. Bourgea, S.M.; Lucien Chasse, S.M.; Joseph Hindelang, S.M.; Albert DiIanni, S.M.; Philip Laplante, S.M.; Rudolph Deziel, S.M.; Vitori Buatava, S.M.; Armand Thibault, S.M.; Bros. Roland Bernier, S.M.; Jude Roy, S.M.; Gregory Theriault, S.M. Priests 9; Brothers 3; Sisters 5.

Ministry of the Word. Revs. Philip O'Shea, O.F.M.; John Anglin, O.F.M.; James Fitzmaurice, O.F.M.; Bro. Robert Frazzetta, O.F.M.

Paulist Fathers Residence, 5 Park St., 02108-4897. Tel: 617-742-4460. Revs. Stanley F. MacNevin, C.S.P., Supr.; John P. Campbell, C.S.P.; Charles E. Cunniff, C.S.P.; Harold J. Foye, C.S.P.; Joseph T. Griffin, C.S.P.; Thomas P. Holahan, C.S.P.; Michael J. Kallock, C.S.P., Dir.; William D. Larkin, C.S.P.; Charles A. Martin, C.S.P.; Gilbert S. Martinex, C.S.P.; Edward J. McDonald, C.S.P.; Robert J. Sadowski, C.S.P.; Walter J. Sullivan, C.S.P.; Francis M. Sweeney, C.S.P. Total in Residence 14; Total Staff 3.

St. Christopher Friary, 18 N. Bennet St., Box 230, 02113. Tel: 617-742-4190. Revs. Primo P. Piscitello, O.F.M., Guardian; Francis DeSales Paolo, O.F.M.; Regis Gallo, O.F.M.; Friars Michael Ciryak, O.F.M.; Michael DellaPenna, O.F.M.; Vit Fiala, O.F.M.; Michael MacInnis, O.F.M.; Richard Martignetti, O.F.M.; Christopher Meyers, O.F.M.; Juniper O'Connor, O.F.M.; Edwin Paniagua, O.F.M.; Lawrence Parent, O.F.M.; Thomas Washburn, O.F.M.; James Welch, O.F.M. Priests 4; Brothers 11.

The Society of Jesus of New England-Provincial Offices, 771 Harrison Ave., 02118-2311. Tel: 617-266-7233; Fax: 617-536-8074. Revs. William A. Barry, S.J., Prov.; Robert J. Levens, S.J., Socius to Prov., Asst. for Social Justice Issues, & Pastoral Ministries; Thomas J. Gibbons, S.J., Asst. for Prov. Finances; James F. LaFontaine, S.J., Asst. for Formation & Secondary Educ.; Martin P. MacDonnell, S.J., Asst. for Intl. Ministries; William C. Russell, S.J., Asst. for Devel. & Vocation Dir.
Priests of Province on Special Assignment: Revs. Albert A. Agresti, S.J.; George S. Albert, S.J.; Brian E. Albino, S.J.; Robert J. Araujo, S.J.; Edward J. Banks, S.J.; John J. Begley, S.J.; Richard D. Bertrand, S.J.; B. Jeffrey Blangiardi, S.J.; Stephen J. Bonian, S.J.; John V. Borgo, S.J.; David G. Boulton, S.J.; James M. Bowler, S.J.; Richard P. Boyle, S.J.; James F. Bresnahan, S.J.; Scott N. Brodeur, S.J.; Joseph J. Bruce, S.J.; Francis C. Buck, S.J.; Robert R. Burke, S.J.; John J. Caskin, S.J.; Gregory C. Chisholm, S.J.; Thomas F. Clark, S.J.; Michael J. Connolly, S.J.; William J. Connolly, S.J.; Neal J. DeStefano, S.J.; Joseph D. Devlin, S.J.; Michael J. Doody, S.J.; Robert R. Dorin, S.J.; Robert F. Drinan, S.J.; Raymond V. Dunn, S.J.; John E. Fagan, S.J.; Michael A. Fahey, S.J.; Peter J. Fennessy, S.J.; Gerald F. Finnegan, S.J.; James J. Fleming, S.J.; William B. Foley, S.J.; Anthony J. Forte, S.J.; Francois Gick, S.J.; Paul P. Gilmartin, S.J.; Julio Giulietti, S.J.; John D. Golenski, S.J.; Donald F. Grady, S.J.; William J. Hamilton, S.J.; John B. Handrahan, S.J.; Robert M. Hanlon, S.J.; John A. Hanrahan, S.J.; Paul F. Harman, S.J.; Philip K. Harrigan, S.J.; Charles J. Healey, S.J.; Daniel P. Jamros, S.J.; John J. Karwin, S.J.; James M. Keegan, S.J.; Charles F. Kelley, S.J.; William J. Kennedy, S.J.; Philip S. Kiley, S.J.; Michael J. Kossak, S.J.; James M. Krupa, S.J.; Kenneth G. Loftus, S.J.; Daniel J. Lusch, S.J.; Frederic A. Maples, S.J.; Thomas J. Massaro, S.J.; Richard B. McCafferty, S.J.; Martin F. McCarthy, S.J.; Michael C. McFarland, S.J.; Peter R. McGrath, S.J.; John P. McIntyre, S.J.; Frederick G. McLeod, S.J.; Francis J. McManus, S.J.; Robert G. McMillan, S.J.; Ronald A. Mercier, S.J.; Daniel M. Merrigan, S.J.; Perard C. Monestime, S.J.; Francis J. Moy, S.J.; Joseph E. Mullen, S.J.; John F. Mullin, S.J.; George R. Murphy, S.J.; Frederick J. O'Brien, S.J.; Thomas P. O'Malley, S.J.; Francis J. O'Neill, S.J.; Eugene F. Orteneau, S.J.; Lawrence J. O'Toole, S.J.; James M. Palmigiano, S.J.; Arthur H. Pare, S.J.; Ernest F. Passero, S.J.; James F.X. Pratt, S.J.; William J. Raftery, S.J.; Richard W. Rousseau, S.J.; Gregory R. Roy, S.J.; Solomon I. Sara, S.J.; Francis X. Sarjeant, S.J.; Thomas J. Savage, S.J.; Andrew J. Scopp, S.J.; James M. Shea, S.J.; John F.X. Sheehan, S.J.; Myles N. Sheehan, S.J.; Donald A.J. Sherpenski, S.J.; Edward J. Small, S.J.; Walter J. Smith, S.J.; Paul M. Sullivan, S.J.; Robert J. Sullivan, S.J.; John E. Surette, S.J.; Paul J. Tabor, S.J.; Robert F. Taft, S.J.; David O. Travers, S.J.; James F. Walsh, S.J.; John Joseph Walsh, S.J.; Terrance G. Walsh, S.J.; Ronald E. Wozniak, S.J.
Chaplains: Revs. Robert L. Keane, S.J.; Lawrence C. Smith, S.J., Res. Ignatius House, 771 Harrison Ave, 02118-2311. Revs. Robert J. Levens, S.J., Sup.; William A. Barry, S.J.; Raymond J. Callahan, S.J.; Thomas J. Gibbons, S.J.; Alfred J. Hicks, S.J.; Walter J. Kane, S.J.; Paul C. Kenney, S.J.; James F. Lafontaine, S.J.; Bros. Edward P. Babinski, S.J.; H. Francis Cluff, S.J.; James P. McDavitt, S.J. Priests 8; Brothers 3.

The Society of St. James the Apostle, Inc., 24 Clark St., 02109. Tel: 617-742-4715. Revs. Gabriel Troy, Dir.; Patrick Cleary (England); Milton Eggerling (OAK); Joseph Shields (PH).
Founded by His Eminence Richard Cardinal Cushing, in 1958 to recruit Priest volunteers for South America. See American Foreign Missions Section for Diocesan Priests serving in Latin America.

ANDOVER. *St. Francis Friary*, 459 River Rd., 01810. Tel: 508-851-3391. Revs. Roland Petinge, O.F.M., Vicar, Retreat Team; John D. Bavaro, O.F.M., Dir., Guardian, Retreat Team; John C. DiMauro, O.F.M., Retreat Team; Gabriel Aceto, O.F.M.; Chris Myers, O.F.M.; Robert J. Caprio, O.F.M., Retreat Team; Mario Julian, O.F.M.; Dennis Wheatley, O.F.M.; Deacon Charles Gingerich, O.F.M. Total in Residence 9; Total Staff 12.

BRIGHTON. *Assumptionist Center*, 330 Market St., 02135. Tel: 617-783-0400. Very Rev. John L. Franck, A.A., Prov. Supr.; Bro. Stephen Goguen, A.A., Prov. Treas., Supr.; Revs. Ernest Fortin, A.A.; Joseph Richard, A.A.; Yvon Dubois, A.A.; George Tavard, A.A.; Deacons Mark Brown, A.A.; Jerome Lively, A.A.; Jeff Pearce, A.A.
Assumption Guild, Inc.: Rev. Richard E. Richards, A.A., Dir.
Attached to Province: Rev. Gregory Boisvert, A.A., Cathedral of the Sacred Heart, 711 Northshore Dr., Knoxville, TN, 37919. Rev. Theodore L. Fortier, A.A., St. John, 21 Gay St., Quincy, 02169. Rev. Anselm Morrison, A.A., Immaculate Conception, 98 Summer St., Portsmouth, NH, 03801. Rev. John

Martin, A.A., 229 W. 14th St., New York, NY, 10011. Serving Abroad: Rev. Francisco Dominguez, A.A., Parroquia Emperatriz de America, Mercaderes 99, 03900 Mexico D.F., Mexico. Rev. Norman Meiklejohn, A.A., P.O. Box 57, Moscow, Russia, 121248. Rev. Gary Perron, A.A., Parroquia Emperatriz de America, Mercaderes 99, 03900 Mexico D.F., Mexico. Rev. Camillus Thibault, A.A., Parroquia de la Emperatriz, Mercaderes 99, Mexico D.F., Mexico. Rev. Roger Tougas, A.A., Montmartre Canadien, 1676 Chemin, St. Louis, Quebec, QUE GIS 165, Canada. Rev. Robert Fortin, A.A., St. Peter in Gallicantu, P.O. Box 31653, 91316 Jerusalem, Israel. Rev. Leo Brassard, A.A., 836-24 Naebang Dong, Sogu, Korea, 502-250. Revs. Luc Martel, A.A.; Richard Brunelle, A.A., Assumptionist Community, P.O. Box 58488, Nairobi, Kenya.

Special Situations: Revs. John Martin, A.A.; Dennis Gallagher, A.A.; Edward Pepka, A.A.

Carmelite Monastery, 166 Foster St., 02135-3902. Tel: 617-787-5056; Fax: 617-783-1396. Discalced Carmelite Friars. Revs. Giles Dzuban, O.C.D.; Emmanuel Sullivan, O.C.D.; Anthony Haglof, O.C.D.; Vincent Bowes, O.C.D.; Paul Tremantozzi, O.C.D.; Lawrence Sullivan, O.C.D.; Albert Bourke, O.C.D.; Michael Dodd, O.C.D.; Salvatore Sciurba, O.C.D.; Stephen-Joseph Ross, O.C.D.; Benedict Bishop, O.C.D. Priests 11; Brothers 1; Total in Residence 14.

St. Bonaventure Friary, Franciscan Friars, 284 Foster St., 02135. Tel: 617-254-2447. Bro. Gabriel Aceto, O.F.M., Guardian; Revs. Valerian Faugno, O.F.M., Vicar, Proc., FMU Prom.; John B. Frisoli, O.F.M.; Albert McMahon, Framingham Union Hospital. Priests 3; Brothers 1.

St. Gabriel's Passionist Community, 139 Washington St., 02135-4235. Tel: 617-254-6582; 254-8512. The Congregation of the Passion (The Passionists). Rev. Justinian Manning, C.P., Supr. Pastor. In res., Rev. Brendan Breen, C.P. Priests 2.

St. Gabriel's Residence, 201 Washington St., 02135. Tel: 617-787-0859. The Congregation of the Passion (The Passionists). Revs. Canisius W. Hazlett, C.P.; Daniel J. Hunt, C.P.; Marcellus R. White, C.P. Priests 3.

BROCKTON. *Chapel of Our Saviour*, 475 Westgate Dr., 02401. Tel: 508-583-8357. Franciscan Friars of the Atonement. Revs. Boniface Riedmann, S.A.; Joseph Di Mauro, S.A.; Malcolm Martin, S.A.; Bros. John Poncia, S.A., Dir.; Louis Marek, S.A. Priests 3; Brothers 2.

CAMBRIDGE. *Faber House*, 42 Kirkland St., 02138. Tel: 617-497-5564. Revs. Thomas Brodie, O.P. (Ireland); Kevin Burke, S.J. (Missouri); Neil Decker, S.J. (New England); Kenneth J. Hughes, S.J. (New England), House Coord.; Robert Kaslyn, S.J. (New York); Nicholas King, S.J. (Great Britain); Peter Knott, S.J. (Great Britain); Bruno Lautenschlager, S.J. (Switzerland); Dionysius Rasquinha, S.J. (Delhi); William Russel, S.J. (New England); Hae-Wuk Ryu, S.J. (Korea); Bros. Robert Schneider, S.J. (CHI); Thomas Williams, S.J. (Maryland); Christopher Daignault, S.S.E., Scholastics. Residence for Jesuit Priests and Scholastics.

Our Lady of Mercy Marist Novitiate, 15 Notre Dame Ave., 02140-2598. Tel: 617-354-6214. Revs. Philip Parent, S.M., Supr.; Michael McElhinny, S.M., Novice Dir.; Robert Langlois, S.M., Staff. Novices 3.

Weston Jesuit Community, 20 Sumner Rd., 02138. Tel: 617-547-3742. Rev. John J. O'Donnell, S.J., Rector.

Residences of Priests: Rev. Richard J. Clifford, S.J., 7 Kirkland Rd., 02138. Tel: 617-661-4155. Rev. William J. Connolly, S.J., 2240 Massachusetts Ave., 02140. Tel: 617-547-4122. Rev. Neil F. Decker, S.J., 42 Kirkland St., 02138. Tel: 617-497-6621. Rev. Frank J. Devine, S.J., 15 Hawthorn St., 02138. Tel: 617-497-6621. Rev. Peter E. Fink, S.J., 6 Sumner Rd., 02138. Tel: 617-547-5310. Rev. Daniel J. Harrington, S.J., 12 Linnaean St., 02138. Tel: 617-547-0931. Rev. Stanley B. Marrow, S.J., 3 Phillips Pl., 02138. Tel: 617-492-1960. Rev. Brian O. McDermott, S.J., 7 Kirkland Rd., 02138. Tel: 617-661-4155. Rev. James Keenan, S.J., 10 Martin St., 02138. Tel: 617-491-2155. Rev. John W. O'Malley, S.J., 10 Martin St., 02138. Tel: 617-491-2155. Rev. John R. Sachs, S.J., 6 Sumner Rd., 02136. Tel: 617-547-5310. Rev. Edward V. Vacek, S.J., 40 Kirkland St., 02138. Tel: 617-868-6568. Rev. Roger D. Haight, S.J., 7 Kirkland Rd., 02138. Tel: 617-661-4155. Rev. Robert Kaslyn, S.J., 42 Kirkland St., 02138. Tel: 617-497-5564. Rev. John J. Kselman, S.S., 7 Kirkland Rd., 02138. Tel: 617-661-4155. Rev. Kenneth J. Hughes, S.J., 42 Kirkland St., 02138. Tel: 617-497-5565. Rev. Kevin F. Burke, S.J., 42 Kirkland St., 02138. Tel: 617-497-5564. Rev. George L. Drury, S.J., 15 Hawthorn St., 02138. Tel: 617-497-0164. Rev. Robert E. Manning, S.J., 7 Kirkland Rd., 02138. Rev. Robert Scholla, S.J., 15 Avon St., 02138. Rev. William C. Russell, S.J., 42 Kirkland St., 02138. Priests 38; Brothers 3; Scholastics 71.

CHESTNUT HILL. *The Jesuit Community at Boston College*, 02167. Tel: 617-552-8200. Very Rev. Joseph A. Appleyard, S.J., Rector; Revs. James M. Collins, S.J., Admin. & Treas. & Asst. Rector; Francis J. Nicholson, S.J., Asst. Rector; Edward M. O'Flaherty, S.J., Asst. Rector; R. Bentley Anderson, S.J. (New Orleans); Ronald Anderson, S.J.; Felipe Bacalso, S.J. (Philippines/China); J. Robert Barth, S.J. (New York); James W. Bernauer, S.J. (New York); Stanley J. Bezuszka, S.J.; Richard Blake, S.J. (NY); Jeyarah Boniface, S.J. (India); Robert J. Braunreuther, S.J.; Thomas Brennan, S.J. (Wisconsin); Michael Buckley, S.J. (California); Claudio Burgaleta, S.J. (New York); Edward R. Callahan, S.J.; Robert Caro, S.J. (San Francisco); John F. Caulfield, S.J.; Richard T. Cleary, S.J.; Francis X. Clooney, S.J. (New York); John J.L. Collins, S.J.; Walter Conlan, S.J. (New England); Joseph J. Connor, S.J.; Paul Crowley, S.J. (California); Robert J. Daly, S.J.; John F. Devane, S.J.; John A. Dinneen, S.J. (New York); Charles F. Donovan, S.J.; Joseph P. Duffy, S.J.; William Dynch, S.J. (Maryland); Theodore Dziak, S.J.; Harvey D. Egan, S.J.; Joseph Fallon, S.J.; Wellington Fernando, S.J. (India); Robert Farrell, S.J.; Joseph F. X. Flanagan, S.J.; Thomas F. Fleming, S.J.; Joseph D. Gauthier, S.J.; David H. Gill, S.J. (New England); Paul P. Gilmartin, S.J.; Joseph A. Glavin, S.J.; Howard Gray, S.J. (Detroit); Thomas J. Grey, S.J.; Gary Gurtler, S.J. (New York); Edward J. Hanrahan, S.J.; Charles J. Healey, S.J.; Raymond G. Helmick, S.J.; Frank Herrmann, S.J. (New York); David Hollenbach, S.J. (Maryland); John W. Howard, S.J.; John Izzo, S.J. (California); T. Frank Kennedy, S.J.; Telesphore Kerketta, S.J. (India); Kevin Kersten, S.J. (Korea); William Leahy, S.J. (Wisconsin); William J. Larkin, S.J.; William J. Leonard, S.J.; Francis Liuima, S.J. (Lithuania); Daniel J. Lusch, S.J.; Arthur A. MacGillivray, S.J.; Francis C. Mackin, S.J.; Arthur R. Madigan, S.J. (New York); James B. Malley, S.J.; Paul Manwelo, S.J. (Africa); Douglas Marcouiller, S.J. (New England); James Mattaliano, S.J. (New England); Richard A. McGowan, S.J. (Maryland); William McInnes, S.J. (New England); William W. Meissner, S.J. (New York); William McNichols, S.J. (Missouri); Paul A. Messer, S.J.; Francis P. Molloy, S.J.; J. Donald Monan, S.J. (New York), Pres.; Franco Mormando, S.J. (New England); Bruce Morrill, S.J. (New England); Frederick L. Moriarty, S.J.; John F. Mullin, S.J.; Paul A. Nash, S.J.; William B. Neenan, S.J. (Wisconsin); Edward H. Nowlan, S.J.; Gerard C. O'Brien, S.J.; James C. O'Brien, S.J. (New England); Joseph O'Keefe, S.J.; Cyril Opeil, S.J. (Maryland); John Paris, S.J.; Frank J. Parker, S.J.; Donald J. Plocke, S.J.; Joseph F. Quane, S.J.; William J. Richardson, S.J. (New York); Herminio Rico, S.J. (Portugal); James W. Ring, S.J.; Jesse Rodriguez, S.J. (New Orleans); Patrick J. Ryan, S.J.; Stephen J. Sanford, S.J. (New England); John Savard, S.J. (New England); Joop Schopman, S.J. (Netherlands); James W. Skehan, S.J.; John Spencer, S.J. (New England); Francis A. Sullivan, S.J.; Francis W. Sweeney, S.J.; Ronald K. Tacelli, S.J.; Felix F. Talbot, S.J.; Charles B. Toomey, S.J.; Benedict Triatmoko, S.J. (Indonesia); Joao J. Vila-Cha, S.J. (Portugal/Lusitania); Andrea Vincini, S.J. (Italy); Francis W. Vye, S.J.; Gerard Walmsley, S.J. (Great Britain); John R. Willis, S.J.; James A. Woods, S.J.; Dennis J. Yesalonia, S.J.; Michael Zampelli, S.J. (Maryland).

COHASSET. *Bellarmine House*, 150 Howard Gleason Rd., 02025. Tel: 617-383-0723. Rev. James M. Collins, S.J., Admin. (Summer Res. for Jesuits of New England Prov.).

DANVERS. *Xavier Center*, 21 Spring St., 01923. Tel: 508-777-1326. American Northeastern Province of The Brothers of St. Francis Xavier (Xaverian Brothers). Bro. John D. Hamilton, C.F.X., Dir. of Formation, House of Formation. Brothers Professed 3.

DEDHAM. *African Mission House and African Cultural Center*. Society of African Missions, Inc., 337-389 Common St., 02026. Tel: 617-326-3288; 326-4670. Revs. Thomas E. Hayden, S.M.A.; Paul Alrutz, S.M.A.; James F. Callahan, S.M.A.; Francis B. Gillis, S.M.A.; James B. Hill, S.M.A.; Michael J. Rooney, S.M.A.; John P. Sweeney, S.M.A. Priests 7.

DOVER. *St. Stephen Priory*, 20 Glen St., Box 370, 02030. Tel: 508-785-0124; Fax: 508-785-1020. Revs. Michael DeTemple, O.P.; Thomas C. McGowan, O.P.; E. Henry Gallagher, O.P.; Michael E. Stock, O.P.; Richard A. Fleck, O.P.; Charles C. Cavalconte, O.P.; Norman A. Haddad, O.P., Prior; Stephen D. Ryan, O.P.; Bro. Patrick Foley, O.P. Spiritual Life Center and Retreat Center. Priests 8; Religious Brother 1.

DUXBURY. *Society of the Divine Word*, 121 Parks St., P.O. Box M, 02331. Tel: 617-585-2460. Revs. Edward Dudink, S.V.D.; John J. Bergin, S.V.D.; Edward Tuohy, S.V.D.; Robert Mallonee, S.V.D.; Robert Jones, S.V.D.; Bros. Kevin Diederich, S.V.D.; Donald Champagne, S.V.D. Priests 5; Brothers 2.

EAST WALPOLE. *Maryknoll Department of Development*, 80 Emerson Rd., 02032-1349. Tel: 508-668-6831. Revs. Fernand L. Gosselin, M.M.; Leo F. McCarthy, M.M.; Alfred Keane, M.M.; Gerald E. Kelly, M.M., Dir.

HINGHAM. *Glastonbury Abbey*, 16 Hull St., 02043. Tel: 617-749-2155; Fax: 617-749-6236. Rt. Revs. Nicholas J. Morcone, O.S.B., Abbot; Edward C. Campbell, O.S.B., Retired Abbot; Very Rev. Timothy J. Joyce, Prior; Revs. Andrew M. Quillen; Paul J. Evich, O.S.B.; Gerald T. Leibenguth, O.S.B.; Richard J. Bourgeois, O.S.B.; Thomas J. O'Connor; Bros. David K. Coakley, O.S.B.; James Crowley, O.S.B.; Daniel F. Walters, O.S.B. Priests 8; Brothers 3. Retreat Center. Benedictine Monks. Capacity 29. Lincoln School Apartments for the Elderly.

HOLLISTON. *Xaverian Missionaries*, Mission Education Center, 101 Summer St., P.O. Box 5857, 01746-5857. Tel: 508-429-2144. Revs. Robert S. Maloney, S.X., Supr.; Dominic Calarco, S.X.; Tony Lalli, S.X.; Francisco J. Anzoategui, S.X.; Aniello Salicone, S.X.; Paolo Gobbo. Priests 5.

IPSWICH. *Missionaries of Our Lady of LaSalette Corp*. National Shrine of Our Lady of LaSalette. Formation Res., 251 Topsfield Rd., 01938-1195. Tel: 508-356-3151. Revs. John R. Dolan; Victor W. Chaupetta; Bros. Robert J. Bellivean, M.S.; Anthony Casso., M.S. Priests 2; Brothers 2; Total in Residence 4; Total Staff 9.

LAWRENCE. *Marist Brothers Residence*, 12 Sheridan St., 01841. Tel: 508-682-1163. Bros. William Lambert, F.M.S., Dir.; C. Vincent Dinnean, F.M.S.; Ernest Beland, F.M.S.; John McDonagh, F.M.S.; Emil Denworth, F.M.S.; Brice Byczynski, F.M.S.; Richard Carey, F.M.S. Brothers 7.

LOWELL. *Missionary Oblates of Mary Immaculate*, 27 Kirk St., 01852. Tel: 508-937-9594. Andre Garin Retirement Residence. Bro. Charles Gilbert, Dir. Tel: 508-441-1245; Revs. Roland Couture, Asst. Dir.; Lionel Desjardins; George Dupont; Paul Marquis; George Rivard.

Missionary Oblates of Mary Immaculate, 285 Andover St., 01852. Tel: 508-441-0649. St. Eugene House. Revs. Charles Breault, O.M.I.; Herve Gagnon, O.M.I.; Lucien Richard, O.M.I.; Francis Demers, O.M.I., Preaching Team. Total in Residence 12; Total Staff 6.

LYNN. *Franciscan Community (Province of Immaculate Conception)*, 38 Michigan Ave., 01902. Tel: 617-592-7396; Fax: 617-593-8805. Revs. Alfonse Ferreira, O.F.M., Procurator & Guardian; Bede Ferrara, O.F.M.

"The Listening Place", 36 Michigan Ave., 01902. Rev. Alfonse Ferreira, O.F.M., Dir.; Sr. Jane Hogan, O.S.F., Assoc. Dir.

MILTON. *House of Theological Studies and Provincialate*, 65 Fr. Carney Dr., 02186. Tel: 617-698-6785. Congregation of the Oblates of the Virgin Mary. Revs. Timothy Gallagher, O.M.V., Prov.; David Beauregard, O.M.V. Priests 3; Scholastics 6.

Xaverian Brothers Provincialate, 704 Brush Hill Rd., 02186. Tel: 617-333-0970. Bros. Bartholomew Varden, C.F.X.; Alois O'Toole, C.F.X.; John Dagwell, C.F.X.; Edward Keefe, C.F.X.; Sebastian Barresi, C.F.X. Brothers 5; Total in Residence 5.

QUINCY. *St. Columban's Foreign Mission Society*, 310 Adams St., 02169. Tel: 472-1494. Rev. John S. Roche, S.S.C., P.O. Box 227, Humarock, 02047. Rev. Edward A. Roberts, S.S.C., 20 Frisbie Rd., Marshfield, 02050. Rev. James O'Brien, Supr., 310 Adams St., 02169. Rev. Michael Breen, S.S.C., 310 Adams St., 02169. Rev. Charles B. Flaherty, S.S.C., St. John Chrystostom, 4750 Washington St., West Roxbury, 02132. Rev. Michael F. Cody, S.S.C., 310 Adams St., 02169. Rev. George V. Herrgott, S.S.C., 78 Tyler St., Boston, 02111. Rev. Joseph L. Crehan, S.S.C., Immaculate Conception, 487 Broadway, Everett, 02149. Rev. Francis J. Keaney, S.S.C. (Philippines), 22 Border St., Winchester, 01890. Priests 8.

TEWKSBURY. *Oblate Fathers-Oblate World/Missionary Association of Mary Immaculate*, 486 Chandler St., Box 680, 01876. Rev. Thomas J. Reddy, O.M.I., Editor & Prov. Dir.

Oblate Fathers-Office of the Provincial Treasurer, 486 Chandler St., Box 419, 01876; Fax: 508-858-3661. Rev. Patrick Hollywood, O.M.I., Prov. Treas. Legal Title: *Society of Oblate Fathers for Missions Among the Poor*.

WALTHAM. *Stigmatine Fathers & Brothers Provincial House*, 554 Lexington St., 02154. Tel: 617-894-7713. Very Rev. Robert S. White, C.S.S., Prov. Supr.; Revs. John Ceresatto, C.S.S. (Thailand); Anthony Corigliano, C.S.S.; Charles Dolan, C.S.S. (Thailand); Ferdinando Ronconi, C.S.S. (Thailand); Donald Toner, C.S.S. (Brazil); Richard Woodarek, C.S.S. (Thailand); John Ford, C.S.S. (Brazil); Carmen Russo, C.S.S.

Stigmatine House. Bertoni Hall, 554 Lexington, 02154. Tel: 617-899-6525. Revs. David F. Gallagher, C.S.S.; Francis L. Keefe, C.S.S.; Gerald Goggin, C.S.S.;

Anthony Penna, C.S.S.; Donald Higgins, C.S.S.; Joseph Flood, C.S.S.; Nicholas Spagnolo, C.S.S.

WESTON. *Campion Center*, 319 Concord Rd., 02193. Tel: 617-894-0751; Fax: 617-894-5864. Revs. Ronald J. Amiot, S.J., Rector; Edward J. Banks, S.J.; David G. Boulton, S.J.; John F. Broderick, S.J.; Harry J. Cain, S.J.; Joseph H. Casey, S.J.; Ned H. Cassem, S.J.; Lawrence E. Corcoran, S.J.; John J. Diskin, S.J.; Robert G. Doherty, S.J.; Thomas P. Donovan, S.J.; Robert T. Ferrick, S.J.; John F. Foley, S.J.; Gabriel Ghirlando, S.J. (Malta); Francis J. Griffin, S.J.; Joseph I. Holland, S.J.; Philip S. Kiley, S.J.; Robert E. Maguire, S.J.; John J. Mandile, S.J.; James P. McCaffrey, S.J.; Paul T. McCarty, S.J.; John J. McGrath, S.J.; John J. Mullen, S.J.; George B. Murray, S.J.; Lawrence J. O'Toole, S.J.; Anthony R. Picariello, S.J.; William J. Sheehan, S.J.; Thomas J. Spillane, S.J.; Patrick A. Sullivan, S.J.; John J. Tucker, S.J.; Wilfred J. Vigeant, S.J.; E. Corbett Walsh, S.J.; James P. Walsh, S.J.; Harry A. Williamson, S.J.; Bros. Vincent M. Brennan, S.J.; Edward L. Niziolek, S.J.; Italo A. Parnoff, S.J. Legal Title: *Campion Residence & Renewal Center, Inc.* Priests 76; Brothers 7.

Campion Health Center, Inc., 319 Concord Rd., 02193. Tel: 617-894-0751. Revs. William J. Raftery, S.J., Rector; Frederick J. Adelmann, S.J.; George F. Barry, S.J.; James H. Barry, S.J.; Richard M. Brackett, S.J.; Eugene C. Brissette, S.J.; Henry J. Butler, S.J.; Maurice L. Buttimer, S.J.; Francis F. Callahan, S.J.; Richard J. Coakley, S.J.; Joseph J. Connor, S.J.; Hubert F. Cunniff, S.J.; Ralph B. Delaney, S.J.; Joseph A. Devenny, S.J.; William J. Duffy, S.J.; Peter T. Farrelly, S.J.; Joseph G. Fennell, S.J.; Francis J. Gilday, S.J.; Frederick A. Harkins, S.J.; Henry A. Jurewich, S.J.; Gerald A. Kinsella, S.J.; Laurence C. Langguth, S.J.; Joseph A. Martus, S.J.; George V. McCabe, S.J.; Raymond E. McCluskey, S.J.; Thomas F. McDermott, S.J.; Nicholas J. McNeil, S.J.; James L. Monks, S.J.; William F. O'Connor, S.J.; Richard F. Olson, S.J.; Francis J. Osborne, S.J.; Joseph A. Paquet, S.J.; Michael G. Pierce, S.J.; William J. Power, S.J.; James E. Powers, S.J.; Joseph F. Quane, S.J.; Martin E. Ryan, S.J.; Daniel J. Shine, S.J.; Laurence J. Skelly, S.J.; John W. Sullivan, S.J.; John J. Walsh, S.J.; William H. Weeks, S.J.; Bros. Robert J. Clifford, S.J.; Joseph A. Garneau, S.J.; Edgar J. LeBlanc, S.J.; Anthony A. Somers, S.J.

[X] CONVENTS AND RESIDENCES FOR SISTERS

BOSTON. *Cardinal's Residence*. 2101 Commonwealth Ave., Brighton, 02135. Tel: 617-782-2101; Fax: 617-782-8358. Sisters of St. Joan of Arc of Quebec 4.

Columban Sisters. 73 Mapleton St., Brighton, 02135. Tel: 617-782-5683. Sr. Corona Colleary, Regl. Coord. Professed Sisters 7. Legal Title: *Missionary Sisters of Saint Columban*.

Daughters of St. Paul Inc. 50 St. Paul's Ave., Jamaica Plain, 02130. Tel: 617-522-8911. Prov. Community 6; Perpetually Professed Sisters 54; Temporary Professed 10; Novices 6; Initial Formation 3. Legal Title: *Daughters of St. Paul, Inc. Novitiate, Juniorate, Provincialate Headquarters, and Technical Apostolate Center for U.S.*

Pauline Book & Media Center, 885 Providence Hwy., Dedham, 02026. Tel: 617-326-5385.

Franciscan Missionary Sisters for Africa. (USA Headquarters and only house.). Serving in Uganda, Kenya, Zambia, Ethiopia, Zimbabwe, And South Africa. Completely a Missionary congregation. 172 Foster St., Box 35095, Brighton, 02135. Tel: 617-254-4343; Fax: 617-787-8007. Sisters 7.

Franciscan Monastery of St. Clare, The, 920 Centre St., 02130. Tel: 617-524-1760. Franciscan Poor Clare Nuns.

Solemn Vows. Cloistered Solemnly Professed 23; Extern Sisters 2.

Immaculate Conception Convent. 120 Orient Ave., East Boston, 02128. Tel: 617-569-2100; Fax: 508-521-6711. Little Missionary Sisters of Charity. Sr. Mary Bertilla, Supr. Sisters 3.

Little Sisters of the Assumption Convent. 65 Magnolia St., Dorchester, 02125. Tel: 617-442-9411; Fax: 617-442-2590. Legal Title: *Little Sisters of the Assumption Family Health Services, Inc., dba Project Hope, Co-Opportunity, Inc.* 45 Magnolia St., Dorchester, 02125. Tel: 617-442-1880. Sisters 6.

Monastery of Discalced Carmelites. 61 Mt. Pleasant Ave., Roxbury, 02119. Tel: 617-442-1411. Cloistered. Sr. Mary Teresa, O.C.D., Prioress. Professed 8.

Motherhouse of the Sisters of St. Joseph of Boston. 637 Cambridge St., Brighton, 02135. Tel: 617-746-2020. Sr. Kathleen McCluskey, C.S.J., Pres. Sisters 82.

Sacred Heart Convent. Mission Helpers of the Sacred Heart. Legal Title: *Institute of Mission Helpers*. 286 Shawmut Ave., 02118-1613. Tel: 617-542-1143. Sisters 2.

St. Theresa House. 50 Brown Ave., Roslindale, 02131. Tel: 617-323-4644. Sr. Mary. Little Missionaries (A Pious Society) 1; Sisters 1; Lay Associates 12.

Sister Disciples of the Divine Master, Convent and Eucharistic Center, 43 West St., 02111. Tel: 482-0978; 423-2629. Sr. M. Lucille Van Hoogmoed, P.D.D.M., Supr. Sisters 10.

Sisters of Notre Dame de Namur (Boston Province Offices). Mailing Address: 351 Broadway, Everett, 02149. Legal Title: *The Boston Province of the Sisters of Notre Dame de Namur, Inc.*

Sisters of Notre Dame de Namur Generalate Office of the General Treas., 400 The Fenway, 02115. Tel: 617-738-4547; Fax: 617-566-6068. Sr. Anne Mary Donovan, S.N.D.

Casa Generalizia di Suore di Nostra Signora di Namur. (Generalate). Via Raffaello Sardiello, 20, Rome, Italy, 00165. Tel: 39-6-818-5678. Sr. Ellen Gielty, S.N.D.deN., Gen. Mod.

Sisters of the Good Shepherd. 35 Tyndale St., Roslindale, 02131. Tel: 617-469-2492. Sisters 3.

Sisters of the Holy Cross. 19 Elgin St., West Roxbury, 02132. Tel: 617-469-3636. Sr. Madonna Murphy, C.S.C., Coord.

ANDOVER. *Monastery of St. Clare*, 460 River Rd., 01810-4260. Tel: 508-851-6743. Poor Clare Nuns. Sr. Therese La Croix, O.S.C., Abbess. Cloistered Solemnly Professed 14; Extern Perpetually Professed 2.

ARLINGTON. *Religious of Christian Education, Inc.*, 14 Bailey Rd., 02174. Tel: 617-643-3032. Sr. Martha Brigham, R.C.E., Prov. Provincial House; Total in Residence 2.

BRADFORD. *Sacred Hearts Convent*, 48 S. Chestnut St., 10835. Tel: 508-521-6867. Sr. Marie Gerarda Lirette, Supr. Servants of the Immaculate Heart of Mary. Good Shepherd Sisters of Quebec 5.

BROCKTON. *Our Lady of Sorrows Convent*, 261 Thatcher St., 02402-3997. Tel: 508-588-5070. Sr. Celestine Stakutis, C.J.C., Supr. Gen. Poor Sisters of Jesus Crucified and the Sorrowful Mother. Sisters 33.

CAMBRIDGE. *Franciscan Missionaries of Mary*, 16 Lancaster St., 02140. Tel: 617-868-8036. Sr. Mary Petrosky, F.M.M., Prov., 3305 Wallace Ave., Bronx, NY, 10467-6599. Sr. Thesesa Conway, F.M.M., Coord.; Sr. Nancy Cabrol, F.M.M.; Sr. Mary Griffin, F.M.M.; Sr. Katherine Hower, F.M.M.; Sr. Maeda Sumiko, F.M.M.; Sr. Doris McShane, F.M.M.; Sr. Anne Richards, F.M.M.; Sr. Margarida Tavares, F.M.M.; Sr. Patricia Murphy, F.M.M.; Sr. Helen Luing, F.M.M.; Sr. Pauline Williams, F.M.M.; Sr. Cecilia Yeh Pao-Kuie, F.M.M.

Sancta Maria Convent, 799 Concord Ave., 02238. Tel: 617-868-2200, Ext. 2950.

CHELSEA. *Don Guanella Center, Inc., Daughters of St. Mary of Providence*, 37 Nichols St., 02150. Tel: 617-889-0179. Sr. Florine Licavoli, D.S.M.P., Dir. of Center; Sr. Arlene Riccio, Family Support Respite for Developmentally Handicapped Ladies (Ages 10-65). Families 70; Total Staff 22. Sisters 2.

DANVERS. *Discalced Carmelite Monastery*, 15 Mt. Carmel Rd., 01923-3796. Tel: 508-774-3008. Mother Michael of Christ the King, O.C.D., Prioress. Professed Nuns 15; Novices 1; Postulants 1.

DEDHAM. *Ursuline Convent*, 65 Lowder St., 02026-4205. Tel: 617-326-3158. Sr. Dorothy Doyle, O.S.U., Prioress. Sisters 15.

Ursuline Provincialate, 45 Lowder St., 02026-4200. Tel: 617-326-6219. Sr. Dorothy Doyle, O.S.U., Prov. Ursulines of the Roman Union, Northeastern Province 66.

EAST BOSTON. *Little Missionary Sisters of Charity, Immaculate Conception Convent*, 120 Orient Ave., 02128. Tel: 617-569-2100. Sr. Mary Gladys, Supr., Mailing Address: Little Missionary Sisters of Charity, Inc., 120 Orient Ave., 02128. Sisters 4.

EVERETT. *Pope John XXIII Convent*, 888 Broadway, 02149. Sr. Marjarita, Coord. Sisters 3.

FRAMINGHAM. *Fontbonne Hall*, 85 Bethany Rd., 01702. Tel: 508-879-1295. Sr. Maureen Doherty, C.S.J., Admin.; Sr. Rena Foley, C.S.J., Pastoral Min.; Rev. Henry Bourgeois, C.S.C., Chap. Professed Sisters 82.

GROTON. *Sisters of the Holy Union Provincial House*, Main St., Box 993, 01450. Tel: 508-448-6049. Sr. Alice Arsenault, S.U.S.C., Prov. Supr. Sisters 7.

IPSWICH. *Sisters of Notre Dame de Namur (Provincial Residence)*, 30 Jeffrey's Neck Rd., 01938-1310. Tel: 508-356-4381; Fax: 508-356-9759. Sr. Catherine Owens, S.N.D., Prov. Supr. Legal Title: *Notre Dame Training School, Inc.* Sisters 93; Total Staff 15.

KINGSTON. *Provincial Residence, Sisters of Divine Providence*, Our Lady of Divine Providence Province, 363 Bishops Hwy., 02364. Tel: 617-585-7707. Sr. Claudia Ward, C.D.P., Prov.

LEXINGTON. *Congregation of Armenian Catholic Sisters of Immaculate Conception, Inc.*, 6 Eliot Rd., 02173. Tel: 617-863-5962. Sr. Veronica Achikian. Sisters 3.

Grey Nuns Provincial House, 10 Pelham Rd., 02173-5799. Tel: 617-862-4700; Fax: 617-861-9641. Headquarters (U.S.A. Province) of the Sisters of Charity of Montreal. "Grey Nuns". General Administration, 138 Rue Saint-Pierre, Montreal, Canada, PQ H2Y 2L7. Sr. June Ketterer, S.G.M., Prov. Supr.; Rev. Robert P. Deeley, Chap. In res., Rev. James O'Donohoe. Sisters 38.

LOWELL. *Convent of the Holy Union Retirement Home*, 142 Chestnut St., 01852. Tel: 508-458-8862. Sisters of the Holy Union. Sr. Pauline LaRoche, S.U.S.C.; Sr. Marilyn Gignac, S.U.S.C. Sisters 31.

Notre Dame Development Fund, Inc., 88 11th St., 01850. Tel: 508-970-0531. Sr. Janice Waters, S.N.D., Pres.; Mrs. Claire Lawlor, Devel. Dir.

St. Joseph Provincial House, 975 Varnum Ave., 01854. Tel: 508-453-4993. Sisters of Charity of Ottawa (Grey Nuns of the Cross). Sr. Gabrielle Jean, S.C.O., Prov. Supr. Sisters 26.

LYNN. *St. Chretienne Novitiate*, 30 Basset St., 01902. Tel: 617-593-1014. Sr. Lisette Michaud, S.S.Ch. Sisters 4.

MARLBORO. *Mary Martha House Convent*, 326 W. Hill Rd., 01752. Tel: 508-481-6272. Sr. Patricia Bassett, S.S.A., Coord. Sisters of St. Anne 4.

Sisters of St. Anne, Provincialate, 720 Boston Post Rd., 01752. Tel: 508-481-4934; Fax: 508-481-4934. Headquarters of American Province. Sisters 166.

Community of the Sisters of Saint Anne. St. Anne Convent, 720 Boston Post Rd., 01752. Tel: 508-485-3791. Sisters 50.

Sisters of Ste. Chretienne, 197 Pleasant St., 01752-1169. Tel: 508-485-0740. Sr. Rachel Gonthier, S.S.Ch., Local Coord. House of Retirement. Sisters 40.

Sisters of Ste. Chretienne, 207 Pleasant St., 01752. Sr. Yvette Campbell, S.S.Ch., Local Coord. Sisters 5.

Sisters of the Good Shepherd. 406 Hemenway St., 01752. Tel: 508-485-0970. Superiors: Sr. Lillian Masse, R.G.S. Sisters 32.

METHUEN. *Our Lady of Mount Carmel Convent*, 82 Union St., 01844. Tel: 508-682-4833. Sr. Fernande Marquis, Supr. Servants of the Immaculate Heart of Mary. Good Shepherd Sisters of Quebec 6.

Provincial House, 209 Lawrence St., 01844. Tel: 508-687-1369. Sr. Aline Plante, Prov. Supr. Presentation of Mary. Sisters 172.

MIDDLEBORO. *Sacred Heart Convent*, 40 Oak St., 02346. Tel: 508-947-4333. Daughters of the Charity of the Sacred Heart of Jesus, F.C.S.C.J.

MILTON. *Franciscan Sisters of the Immaculate Conception, St. Mary of the Hills*, 260 Brook Rd., 02186. Sr. Rita Murray, O.S.F., Supr. School. St. Mary of the Hills. (Grades K-8).

NEWTON. *Franciscan Sisters of the Immaculate Conception, St. Francis Community*, 790 Centre St., 02158; Fax: 617-964-6338. Sisters 7.

Immaculate Conception Provincialate, 790 Centre St., 02158. Tel: 617-527-1004; Fax: 617-527-2528. Missionary Franciscan Sisters of the Immaculate Conception. Sr. M. Michele Craig, M.F.I.C. Total in Residence 5; Total Staff 3.

Mt. Alvernia Convent, 790 Centre St., 02158-2529. Tel: 617-969-4766; Fax: 617-527-2528. Sisters 38.

PLAINVILLE. *Jesus and Mary Mission Center*, 92 School St., 02762-2033. Tel: 508-699-4427. Sr. Michelle Authier, R.J.M., Admin. Total in Residence 17.

QUINCY. *Boston Province, Sisters of Charity of St. Vincent de Paul. (Halifax)*. (Boston Branch office). 26 Phipps St., 02169; Fax: 617-773-4794. Sr. Esther Plefka, Congregational Councillor.

Sisters of Charity of Nazareth Regional House, 169 Fenno St., 02170. Tel: 617-479-4909. Sr. Gwen McMahon, S.C.N., Regional. Legal Title: *Nazareth Literary and Benevolent Institution*.

SALEM. *St. Chretienne Convent*, 12 Pope St., 01970. Tel: 508-744-1228. Sisters 3.

SCITUATE. *Sisters of St. Anne*, 3 Tilden Rd., 02066. Tel: 617-545-8214. Sisters 2.

SOMERVILLE. *Medical Missionaries of Mary, Inc.*, Somerville House, 179 Highland Ave., 02143. Tel: 617-666-3223. Congregation of the Medical Missionaries of Mary Motherhouse, Beechgrove, Drogheda, Ireland. Professed Sisters 7.

WALTHAM. *Marist Missionary Sisters*. Legal Title: *Missionary Sisters of the Society of Mary, Inc., S.M.S.M.* Provincial Offices, 349 Grove St., 02154. Tel: 617-893-0149. Sr. Rosalie Warpeha, S.M.S.M., Prov., Residence for Senior Sisters, 62 Newton St. Tel: 617-893-3960. Sisters 42.

Other Local Communities: 60 Newton St., 02154. Tel: 617-899-1837. Sisters 3. 21 Beech St., Belmont, 02178. Tel: 617-489-3587. Sisters 7. 4 Craig St., Framingham, 02107. Tel: 617-877-7371. Sisters 2. 357 Grove St., 02154. Tel: 617-899-3839. Sisters 9. 20 Bartlett Ave., Arlington, 02174. Tel: 617-648-4341. Sisters 7.

WATERTOWN. *Rosary Manor*, One Rosary Dr., 02172. Tel: 617-924-1717. Sr. Mary Esther Owens, O.P., Coord. Total in Residence 40; Total Staff 2.

WAYLAND. *Emmanuel House*, Sisters of St. Anne, 17

Forty Acres Dr., 01778. Tel: 508-358-4033. Sisters 7.

WELLESLEY. *Elizabeth Seton Residence, Inc.*, 125 Oakland St., 02181; Fax: 617-431-2589. Nursing Home. 84 bed skilled nursing-Medicare/Medicaid certified. Accredited by Joint Commission on Accreditation of Healthcare Organizations(JCAHO). Sr. Blanche LaRose, S.C., Admin. Sisters of Charity of St. Vincent de Paul, Halifax, Nova Scotia, Canada.

Mount Saint Vincent, 125 Oakland St., 02181. Tel: 617-237-2161; Fax: 617-237-8152. Sisters of Charity of St. Vincent de Paul. Residence for Retired Sisters. Sisters 85.

Elizabeth Seton Residence, Health Care Facility. Sisters 42.

WEST ROXBURY, 19 Elgin St., 02132. Tel: 617-469-3636. Sr. Madonna Murphy, C.S.C., Coord.

WRENTHAM. *Mount St. Mary's Abbey*, 300 Arnold St., 02093. Tel: 508-528-1282. Legal Title: *The Cistercians of the Strict Observance in Massachusetts, Inc.* The Cistercian Nuns of the Strict Observance (Trappistines). Mother M. Agnes Day, O.C.S.O., Abbess. Professed Sisters 45.

St. Chretienne Provincialate, 297 Arnold St., 02093-1798. Tel: 508-384-8066; 384-7841. Sisters of St. Chretienne. Sr. Suzanne Beaudoin, S.S.Ch. Sisters 4; Total in Residence 4.

[Y] RETREAT HOUSES

ANDOVER. *Franciscan Center - Retreat House*, 459 River Rd., 01810. Tel: 508-851-3391. Order of Friars Minor. Revs. John D. Bavaro, O.F.M., Dir.; Guardian, Retreat Team; Roland Petinge, O.F.M., Vicar, Retreat Team; John C. DiMauro, O.F.M., Retreat Team; Robert J. Caprio, O.F.M., Retreat Team; Sr. Lorraine Pianka, S.S.N.D.; Bros. Gabriel Aceto, O.F.M.; Chris Meyers, O.F.M.; Mrs. Mildred Sheehan, Sec. Youth Ministry: Eileen Bowes; Gayle Jaskel; Joanna Howorth. Total in Residence 9; Total Staff 12.

BILLERICA. *St. Thecla's Retreat House*, 77 Dudley Rd., 01821. Tel: 508-667-5580. Daughters of St. Paul.

BRADFORD. *Don Orione Center*, Old Groveland Rd., P.O. Box 205, 01835. Tel: 508-373-0461. Rev. Gino Marchesani, F.D.P., Dir.

COHASSET. *Retreat Center*, 339 Jerusalem Rd., 02025. Tel: 617-383-6029; 383-6024. Sisters of St. Joseph 3.

DEDHAM. *Boston Cenacle Society*, 25 Avery St., 02026-2804. Tel: 617-326-1393. Sisters of the Congregation of Our Lady of the Retreat in the Cenacle. Sr. Helen Harber, R.C., Contact Person; Sr. Marian Hahm, R.C., Prov. Liaison. Professed Sisters 13.

DOVER. *St. Stephen Priory Spiritual Life Center*, 20 Glen St., Box 370, 02030-0370. Tel: 508-785-0124; Fax: 508-785-1020. Revs. Norman Haddad, O.P., Prior; Richard A. Fleck, O.P., Subprior. Co-Directors of Retreat & Renewal: Rev. Michael DeTemple, O.P.; Sr. Maureen Casey, S.N.D. Dominican Priests 8; Religious Brother 1; Total in Residence 12.

DUXBURY. *Miramar Retreat Center*, 121 Parks St., P.O. Box M, 02331. Tel: 617-585-2460. Rev. Robert M. Jones, Rector. Total in Residence 7; Total Staff 17.

FRAMINGHAM CENTRE. *The Marist House*, 518 Pleasant St., 01701. Tel: 508-879-1620. Revs. Raymond J. Arsenault, S.M., Supr.; Guy Lebel, S.M.; Peter D'Ambrosia, S.M., Retreat Dir.; Fernard J. Gallant, S.M.; George Szal, S.M.; Robert E. Champagne, S.M.; Dolor Ginchereau, S.M.; Henry Rancourt, S.M.; Raymond Boulanger, S.M.; Donald Gagne, S.M. Total in Residence 13; Total Staff 6.

GLOUCESTER. *Eastern Point Retreat House*, Gonzaga Hall, 37 Niles Pond Rd., 01930. Tel: 508-283-0013. Revs. William G. Devine, S.J., Supr. & Dir.; Joseph B. McHugh, S.J.; Gerard R. McKeon, S.J.; John B. Kerdiejus, S.J.; Bro. William J. Spokesfield, S.J. Priests 4; Brothers 1; Sisters 1.

IPSWICH. *LaSalette Retreat House at Newman Hall*, 251 Topsfield Rd., 01938. Tel: 508-356-3151. Revs. Hector O. LaChapelle, Dir.; Phil M. Negley, M.S., Dir. Shrine Ministries; Ms. Tensi Boylan, Admin. Asst.

Sacred Heart Retreat Center, Rte. 1A, P.O. Box 567, 01938. Tel: 508-356-3838. Salesians of St. John Bosco. Revs. Gerard Pellegrino, S.D.B., Retreat Dir.; Denis Kelleher, S.D.B.; Joseph Doran, S.D.B.; Bros. Peter Bersezio, S.D.B.; Alfred Flatoff, S.D.B. Priests 3; Lay Brothers 2; Total in Residence 5; Total Staff 7.

SCITUATE. *Foyer of Charity*, 74 Hollett St., 02066. Tel: 617-545-1080. Rev. Matthew Bradley, Dir. Total in Residence 2; Total Staff 6.

WALTHAM. *Espousal Retreat House and Conference Center*, 554 Lexington St., 02154. Tel: 617-647-0033. Stigmatine Fathers and Brothers. Weekend and Weekly Retreats, Days-Evenings of Recollection. Rev. Robert Masciocchi, C.S.S. Total in Residence 1; Total Staff 6.

WESTON. *Campion Renewal Center*, 319 Concord Rd., 02193. Tel: 617-894-3199. Revs. Joseph F. McHugh, S.J., Dir; Ronald J. Amiot, Rector; Robert G. Dougherty, S.J.; John F. Foley, S.J.; William J. Sheehan, S.J., Dir.; James P. Walsh, S.J., Staff. Total in Residence 6; Total Staff 8.

[Z] RETIREMENT RESIDENCES FOR PRIESTS AND BROTHERS

BOSTON. *Regina Cleri, Inc.*, 60 William Cardinal O'Connell Way, 02114. Tel: 617-523-1861. Rev. Msgr. James E. Tierney, Dir.; Rev. John J. Geoghan, Asst. Dir. Residence for Retired Archdiocesan Priests. Priests 41; Sisters 2.

Saint Anthony Residence, 103 Arch St., 02110-1102. Tel: 617-542-6454; 6455.
(For Retired Franciscan Friars). Revs. Robert Lynch, O.F.M.; David Fleming, O.F.M.; Jerome Kelly, O.F.M.; Lawrence Kidder, O.F.M.; Amadeus Burke, O.F.M.; Gordon A. Murphy, O.F.M.; Cormac Dungan, O.F.M.; Fabian Joyce, O.F.M.; Martin L. McCormack, O.F.M.; Cornelius F. Kelly, O.F.M.; Urban A. Cain, O.F.M.; Stephen M. Walsh, O.F.M.; Francis B. Carroll, O.F.M.; Kenan Morris, O.F.M.; Frank Waywood, O.F.M., Vicar; Remy A. Goudreau, O.F.M.; Bros. Hyacinth Wenz, O.F.M.; Albert Aldrich, O.F.M., Vicar; Agapitus Rothmann, O.F.M. Total in Residence 21.

LAWRENCE. *Marist Brothers*, 26 Leeds Ter., 01843. Tel: 508-686-7411. Bros. Kenneth Hogan, F.M.S.; Peter Chanel Arel, F.M.S.; Eugene Birmingham, F.M.S.; Joseph DiBenedetto, F.M.S.; Richard La Rose, F.M.S.; Jerry Dowsky, F.M.S.; Daniel Cronin, F.M.S. Brothers 6.

TEWKSBURY. *Immaculate Heart of Mary Novitiate-Infirmary*, 486 Chandler St., P.O. Box 419, 01876. Tel: 508-851-7258. Revs. F. William Denzel, O.M.I.; William J. Kirwin, O.M.I.; Patrick M. Linehan, O.M.I.; Patrick J. Hollywood, O.M.I., Supr.; Salvatore Costa, O.M.I.; Robert F. Kilroy, O.M.I.; Francis D. Flanagan, O.M.I.; Thomas D. Manning, O.M.I.; Francis P. McCartin, O.M.I.; Joseph O. Stack, O.M.I.; Thomas F. Walsh, O.M.I.; Thomas J. Reddy, O.M.I.; Francis X. McCarron, O.M.I.; Joseph C. Wild, O.M.I.; George P. Buckley, O.M.I.; George Waggett, O.M.I.; Joseph A. Ryan, O.M.I.; Patrick F. Healy, O.M.I.; William Keohane, O.M.I.; John Tracy, O.M.I.; Francis Campbell, O.M.I.; Joseph Murphy, O.M.I.; Bros. Earl Wetzel, O.M.I.; Patrick O'Neil; Francis Linehan. Priests 23; Brothers 3.

WALTHAM. *Stigmatine Fathers and Brothers*, St. Joseph's Hall, 554 Lexington St., 02154. Tel: 617-647-0005; 0006. Rev. Richard Ahern, C.S.S., Tel: 617-894-7125. Rev. James Cunningham, C.S.S., Chap. Waltham Hospital; Bros. John E. Fowler, C.S.S.; David L. Gallagher, C.S.S.; Daniel Egan, C.S.S.; Richard Spencer, C.S.S.; Revs. Rocco Leotilo, C.S.S.; Paul Merrill, C.S.S.; Ettore Canzano, C.S.S.; Charles Egan, C.S.S.; Gerald Goggin, C.S.S.; Henry Linse, C.S.S.; Robert Masciocchi, C.S.S., Reservoir Nursing Home, 1841 Trapelo Rd., 02154. Rev. George Ecker, C.S.S., Mont Marie Health Care Center. Priests 16; Brothers 4.

[AA] RESIDENCES FOR MEN AND WOMEN

BOSTON. *Our Lady of the Way Residence*. 60-80 Pond St., Jamaica Plain, 02130. Tel: 617-524-1640. Oblate Sisters of the Most Holy Redeemer. Residence young women. (students, workers, travelers). Sisters 3; Residents 25.

Our Lady's Guild House, 20 Charlesgate W., 02215. Tel: 617-536-3000. Andrea Beall, Admin. Daughters of Mary of the Immaculate Conception 2. Attended by Oblate Sisters of the Virgin Mary. Residents 126.

St. Helena House, 89 Union Park St., 02118. Tel: 617-426-2922; Fax: 617-542-3460. Seniors, low income & disabled persons. Kay Gillespie, Property Mgr. Residents 89.

[BB] PUBLIC ORATORIES AND CHAPELS

BOSTON. *Chapel of Our Lady of Lourdes*, 698 Beacon St., 02215. Tel: 617-536-2761. Marist Fathers. Marist Fathers Residence. Tel: 617-262-2271. Revs. Gerard Caron, S.M., Dir.; Michael Pavlick, S.M.; Paul H. Pepin, S.M.; J. Armand Robichaud, S.M. Priests 4.

Chapel of the Holy Spirit, Paulist Center, 5 Park St., 02108. Tel: 617-742-4460. Paulist Fathers. Revs. Michael J. Kallock, C.S.P., Dir.; Richard J. Colgan, C.S.P.

Madonna Queen Shrine. 111 Orient Ave., East Boston, 02128. Tel: 617-569-2100. Don Orione Fathers. Rev. John Kilmartin, F.D.P., Rector.

Our Lady of Good Voyage Chapel, 65 Northern Ave., 02110. Tel: 617-268-0710. Revs. John A. Dooher, Admin.; Philip La Plante, S.M., Chap. to Seaport, Sts. Peter & Paul Rectory, 02127.

St. Anthony Shrine, 100 Arch St., P.O. Box 2278, 02107-2278. Tel: 617-542-6440; Fax: 617-542-4225. Revs. Kevin J. Mullen, O.F.M., Guardian & Rector; Brice A. Leavins, O.F.M., Vice Rector; William Beaudin, O.F.M.; Giles Bello, O.F.M.; Vincent Carroll, O.F.M.; Stephen Doyle, O.F.M.; Aidan Duffy, O.F.M.; Michael Feeney, O.F.M.; Lawrence D. Ford, O.F.M.; Fergus Healey, O.F.M.; Wilfrid Hept, O.F.M.; Hugh Hines, O.F.M.; John P. Hogan, O.F.M.; Philip Lavere, O.F.M.; Patrick Leary, O.F.M.; Raymond Mann, O.F.M.; Gerald T. McCaffrey, O.F.M.; Myron McCormick, O.F.M.; Donan McGovern, O.F.M; Emeric Meier, O.F.M.; Carmel Miotke, O.F.M.; Khoa Nguyen, O.F.M.; Samuel O'Connor, O.F.M.; Zachary O'Friel, O.F.M.; Colin O'Rourke, O.F.M.; Charles Rowley, O.F.M.; Cyril Seaman, O.F.M.; Mark Smith, O.F.M.; Flavian Tobin, O.F.M.; Dac Tran, O.F.M.; Alexander Wyse, O.F.M. Priests 31; Brothers 12.

St. Clement's Archdiocesan Eucharistic Shrine, 1105 Boylston St., 02215-3660. Tel: 617-266-5999; Fax: 617-247-7576. St. Ignatius Province of the Oblates of the Virgin Mary. Rev. Peter Grover, O.M.V., Dir. of Shrine. Priests 1.

St. Francis Chapel, Prudential Center Plaza, 800 Boylston St., #21, 02199. Tel: 617-437-7117. St. Ignatius Province of the Oblates of the Virgin Mary. Revs. James Nibler, O.M.V., Dir.; Thomas Carzon, O.M.V.; Robert Lowrey, O.M.V.; William G. Mullen, O.M.V. Priests 4.

St. Thomas More Chapel, 49 Franklin St., 02110. Tel: 617-482-4324. Rev. Msgr. Andrew F. Connell, K.J.

BROCKTON. *Chapel of Our Saviour*, 475 Westgate Dr., 02401. Tel: 508-583-8357. Revs. Malcolm Martin, S.A.; Boniface Riedmann, S.A.; Joseph Di Mauro, S.A.; Bros. John M. Poncia, S.A., Dir.; Louis Marek, S.A. Priests 3; Brothers 2.

EAST BOSTON. *Our Lady of the Airways Chapel*, Logan Airport, 02128. Tel: 617-567-2800; Fax: 617-569-6950. Rev. Robert F. Hennessey, Res. Most Holy Redeemer Rectory, 65 London St., Boston, 02128. Tel: 617-567-3227.

HOLLISTON. *Our Lady of Fatima Shrine*, 101 Summer St., P.O. Box 5857, 01746-5857. Tel: 508-429-2144. Xaverian Missionaries. Rev. Tony Lalli, S.X., Dir.

IPSWICH. *National Shrine of Our Lady of La Salette*, 251 Topsfield Rd., 01938-1195. Tel: 508-356-3151. Rev. John R. Dolan, M.S., Dir. Total in Residence 4; Total Staff 9.

PEABODY. *St. Theresa Carmelite Chapel*, North Shore Shopping Center, 01960. Tel: 508-531-6145. Revs. Ferdinand T. Schaefer, O.Carm., Supr. & Dir.; Kilian Healy, O.Carm., Supr.; Alan Crowley, O.Carm.; Peter Thomas Sherry, O.Carm.; Lloyd Wiegele, O.Carm. Priests 5.

[CC] CAMPUS MINISTRY

BOSTON. *Emmanuel College Campus Ministry*, 400 The Fenway, 02115. Tel: 617-735-9777. Sr. Patricia McSharry, S.N.D.

Newman House Catholic Center at Boston University, 211 Bay State Rd., 02215. Tel: 617-353-3632. Rev. Charles E. Cunniff, C.S.P.; Dr. Jane M. LaMarche, D.Min.

St. Ann's University Parish. (Serving Northeastern Univ. and the Fenway Colleges). Catholic Student Center, 68 St. Stephen St., 02115. Tel: 617-266-2635; Fax: 617-266-9015. Rev. Paul E. Kilroy, Campus Min., Northeastern Univ. Pastoral Assocs. - Campus Ministers: Sr. Rosemary Mulvihill, R.S.M., Northeastern Univ.; Sr. Mary Walsh, S.U., Emerson College.

BRIDGEWATER. *Bridgewater State College Catholic Center*, 122 Park Ave., 02324. Tel: 508-697-2402. Campus Ministers: Rev. John P. Kearns; Sr. Anne Marie O'Shea, S.C.N.

CAMBRIDGE. *Harvard-Radcliffe Catholic Student Center*, 20 Arrow St., 02138. Tel: 617-868-6585. Revs. J. Bryan Hehir; George S. Salzmann, O.S.F.S.; Jacqueline L. Landry; Joan Travers.

Massachusetts Institute of Technology Catholic Community, 40 Massachusetts Ave., W-11, 02139. Tel: 617-253-2981. Rev. Thomas J. Holahan, C.S.P.; Sr. Mary Karen Powers, R.S.M. Total Staff 2.

CHESTNUT HILL. *Boston College University Chaplaincy*, McElroy 215, 02167. Tel: 617-552-3475. Rev. Richard T. Cleary, S.J. Total in Residence 3; Total Staff 9.

DORCHESTER. *University of Massachusetts at Boston Campus Ministry*, Harbor Campus, 02125. Tel: 617-287-5839. Rev. Richard F. Chancy; Mrs. Aldona Lingertat.

FRAMINGHAM. *Framingham State College Campus Ministry*, 100 State St., 01701. Tel: 508-626-4609, Ext. 280. Rev. Vincent H. Poirier.

LOWELL. *The Catholic Center U Mass, Lowell*, 52 Colonial Ave., 01854. Tel: 508-454-0151. Rev. Paul Soper; Mrs. Maura Caples. Total in Residence 6; Total Staff 2.

MEDFORD. *Tufts University Catholic Center*, 58 Winthrop St., 02155. Tel: 617-391-7272. Rev. Michael J. Hunt, C.S.P.

MILTON. *Aquinas College at Milton Campus Ministry*, 303 Adams St., 02186. Tel: 617-696-3100. Sr. Helen Callahan, C.S.J.

NEWTON. *Aquinas College at Newton Campus Ministry*,

15 Walnut Park, 02158. Tel: 617-969-4400. Sr. Ellen Doyle, S.C.N., Campus Min. Total Assisted 45; Total Staff 3.

NORTH ANDOVER. *Merrimack College Campus Ministry Center*, 303 Gildea Hall, 01845. Tel: 508-837-5450. Sr. Elaine Polcari, S.S.N.D., Dir. Campus Ministers: Revs. Joseph L. Farrell, O.S.A.; Scott C. Ness, O.S.A.

SALEM. *Salem State College, Catholic Campus Ministry*, 352 Lafayette St., 01970. Tel: 508-741-6074. Rev. Mark O'Connell; Sr. Kathleen Crowley, S.C.; Magdalena Bennasar.

WALTHAM. *Bentley College Campus Ministry*, 175 Forest St., 02154-4705. Tel: 617-891-2194.

Brandeis University Campus Ministry, M.S. U5, 02154. Tel: 617-736-3574. Rev. Joseph Marshall, S.M.

WELLESLEY. *Babson College Campus Ministry*, 9 Glen Rd., 02181. Tel: 617-235-1200. Sr. Frances Sheehey, O.S.F., Campus Coord.

Wellesley College Campus Ministry, 02181. Tel: 617-235-0320, Ext. 2688. Rev. Vincent H. Poirier.

WESTON. *Regis College Office of Campus Ministry*, 235 Wellesley St., 02193. Tel: 617-768-7027, Ext. 2087. Sr. Mildred Crowley, S.C., Dir.; Joan Collupy, Campus Min.

[DD] FOUNDATIONS, FUNDS & TRUSTS

BOSTON. *The Archdiocese of Boston Self-Insurance Group, Inc.* 2121 Commonwealth Ave., Brighton, 02135.

Chancery Office. 2121 Commonwealth Ave., Brighton, 02135. Tel: 617-254-0100. Also see Miscellaneous Section for additional listings.

The Cardinal Medeiros Trust.

Cardinal Cushing General Hospital Foundation, Brockton.

The Carney Hospital Foundation, Inc., 2100 Dorchester Ave., 02124. Tel: 617-296-1788. J. Barry Driscoll, Pres.; Paul J. Kingston, Vice Pres.; Daniel J. McDevitt, Sec.; William F. Henderson, Exec. Dir.

**Catholic Schools Foundation, Inc.* (Formerly St. Anthony's Scholarship Fund, Inc.).

Clergy Benefit Trust. Most Rev. William F. Murphy, Sec.

Clergy Fund Society.

Clergy Medical-Hospitalization Trust.

Clergy Retirement-Disability Trust.

Family Counseling Endowment Fund, Inc., One Bromfield St., 02108. Tel: 617-482-4355.

Marist Capital Trust Fund. c/o Financial Admin., The Missionary Sisters of the Society of Mary, Inc., 349 Grove St., Waltham, 02154. Tel: 617-893-0149. Sr. Virginia Fornasa, S.M.S.M., Trustee; John E. McCormack.

Metropolitan Boston Dialysis Center, Inc., 125 Technology Dr., Bldg. 1, Ste. 5, Waltham, 02154. Tel: 617-893-8544.

Mission Promotion..Missionary Sisters of the Society of Mary. c/o Mission Promoter, 13 Pelham Rd., Lexington, 02173. Tel: 617-861-6116.

Roman Catholic Archdiocese of Boston Health Benefit Trust. Mr. David W. Smith, Admin.

Roman Catholic Archdiocese of Boston Insurance Trust. Benefit Office, Mr. David W. Smith, Admin.

Roman Catholic Archdiocese of Boston Pension Trust. Benefit Office, Mr. David W. Smith, Admin.

Roman Catholic Archdiocese of Boston Long Term Disability Trust. Mr. David W. Smith, Admin.

Roman Catholic Archdiocese of Boston Common Investment Fund.

Roman Catholic Archdiocese of Boston Fixed Income Investment Fund.

St. Charles Borromeo Educational Foundation, Inc.

Sacred Heart Trust Fund, c/o Society of Jesus, Trustee, 761 Harrison Ave., 02118. Tel: 617-536-5604. Bro. H. Francis Cluff, S.J.

St. Elizabeth's Hospital Foundation, Inc., 159 Washington St., Brighton, 02135.

Valley Regional Health Care Foundation, Inc.

Catholic Foundation of the Archdiocese of Boston, 2121 Commonwealth Ave., Brighton, 02135. Mr. John A. McNeice, Jr., Pres.

The Xaverian Brothers Northeastern Community Support Charitable Trust Fund, 704 Brush Hill Rd., Milton, 02186.

Benefit Trust for Non-Incardinated Priests. Legal Title: *Benefit Trust for Non-Incardinated Priest Duly Assigned for Service in the Archdiocese of Boston.*

BRIGHTON. *Clergy Assistance Trust*, 2121 Commonwealth Ave., 02135.

FRAMINGHAM. *Senior Religious Trust Fund of Marist Fathers of Boston*, 518 Pleasant St., 01701-2898.

HANOVER. *St. Coletta's of Massachusetts, Inc.*, 405 Washington St., 02339. Tel: 617-826-6371. Mr. John W. Shyne, Jr., Pres. & CEO.

IPSWICH. *Blin Charitable Trust*, 30 Jeffrey's Neck Rd., 01938; Fax: 508-356-9759. Sisters of Notre Dame de Namur.

LOWELL. *Saints Memorial Medical Center Foundation*, P.O. Box 367, 01853-0367. Tel: 508-934-8334; Fax: 508-934-8252. Thom Clark, Pres. & CEO; Kevin E. Coughlin, Vice Pres. & Exec. Dir.

METHUEN. *Holy Family Hospital Foundation, Inc.*, 70 East St., 01844-4597. Tel: 508-687-0151. Mrs. Noreen V. Mallen, Ex. Dir.

NEEDHAM. *St. Joseph's Parish School Fund, Inc., Needham*, 1382 Highland Ave., 02192. Mr. James S. DiStasio, Treas.

TEWKSBURY. *The Society of Oblate Fathers Continuing Support Fund*, c/o the Society of Oblate Fathers for Missions Among the Poor, 486 Chandler St., 01876; Fax: 508-858-3661. Rev. William Sheehan, O.M.I., Prov.

The Society of Oblate Fathers for Missions Among the Poor Formation Charitable Trust, 486 Chandler St., P.O. Box 419, 01876; Fax: 508-858-3661. Rev. William Sheehan, O.M.I., Prov.

[EE] LIFE RESOURCES

BRAINTREE.

**Pilgrim Center*, 140 Adams St., P.O. Box 850907, 02184-0907. Tel: 617-848-5510. Students 40.

[FF] MISCELLANEOUS

BOSTON. *Caritas Christi - A Catholic Health Care System.* 736 Cambridge St., Brighton, 02135. Tel: 617-789-2500. Michael F. Collins, M.D., Pres. & CEO.

Caritas Christi Support Services, Inc.

C.C. Medical Associates, Inc.

Caritas Christi Diagnostic Support Services, Inc.

Valley Regional Health Care System, Inc.

Valley Regional Support Services, Inc.

St. Elizabeth's Realty Corporation.

Metropolitan Boston Dialysis Center.

Good Samaritan Hospice.

The Catholic Lawyers Guild of the Archdiocese of Boston, Inc., One Union St., 02108. Tel: 617-523-2640. Hon. Joseph R. Nolan, Pres.

Equestrian Order of the Holy Sepulchre of Jerusalem. Northeastern Lieutenancy, 12 Kenilworth Rd., Milton, 02186. Mr. George T. Ryan, KGCHS Lt.; Most Rev. Odore J. Gendron, KC HS Chancellor.

League of Catholic Women of the Archdiocese of Boston. 127 Lake St., Brighton, 02135. Tel: 617-254-2610. Mrs. Joseph Cullinan, Pres.; Rev. Martin P. Connor, Spiritual Dir.

Lourdes Bureau, 698 Beacon St., 02215. Tel: 617-536-2761. Marist Fathers. Official Representatives in America for the Shrine of Lourdes, France.

Medaille Corporation, 637 Cambridge St., 02135. Tel: 617-746-2020. Sr. Kathleen McCluskey, C.S.J., Pres.; Sr. Frances Wool, C.S.J., Treas.

MI Management, Inc. Zero Bennington St., Lawrence, 01841. Tel: 508-685-6321; Fax: 508-975-0050. Thomas L. Lucas, Pres. & CEO. Sisters of Charity Montreal (Grey Nuns) 3.

Ministry of Evangelization and Catechesis, 286 Shawmut Ave., 02118-1613. Tel: 617-542-1143. Legal Title: *Institute of Mission Helpers.* Mission Helpers of the Sacred Heart. Sr. M. Celeste Burgos, M.H.S.H., Local Coord. & Contact Person.

National Catholic Group Purchasing Association, Inc. 580 Washington St., Newton, 02158. Tel: 617-965-4343; Fax: 617-965-5430. Mr. Richard J. Wasilauskas, Pres.

Pine Street Inn, 444 Harrison Ave., 02118. Tel: 617-482-4944. Shelter for homeless men and women. Erik Payne Butler, Pres.

Propagation of the Faith and Holy Childhood Association & Society of St. Peter the Apostle, 49 Franklin St., 02110. Tel: 617-542-1776; Fax: 617-542-1778. Rev. Msgr. Andrew F. Connell, Dir.

St. Francis Charities, 2121 Commonwealth Ave., 02135.

Spiritearth, Inc., 771 Harrison Ave., 02118-2311. Tel: 617-266-7233. Total in Residence 3.

BRAINTREE. *Our Lady of Kazan Russian Greek Catholic Mission.* Byzantine Slavonic Rite. Records at St. Peter & Paul Rectory, Braintree. St. Peter & Paul Rectory, 55 W. Broadway, South Boston, 02127. Tel: 617-268-8100. Rev. John A. Dooher, The Cambridge Center for the Study of Faith and Culture, Inc., 2101 Commonwealth Ave., Brighton, 02135. Tel: 617-323-3999. Sr. Madonna Murphy, C.S.C., Pres., St. Vincent Pallotti Center for Apostolic Development of Boston, Inc., 159 Washington St., Brighton, 02135. Tel: 617-783-3924; Fax: 617-787-7797. Ms. Carolyn C. Thompson, Dir.

Pope John Center, 186 Forbes Rd., 02184-2612. Tel: 617-848-6965; Fax: 617-849-1309. Revs. John M. Haas, Ph.D., S.T.L., Pres.; Germain Kopaczynski, O.F.M.Conv., Ph.D., S.T.D., Dir. Education; Peter J. Cataldo, Ph.D., Dir. of Research; Daniel Maher, Dir. Publication; Leila Harrington Little, Dir. Development; Rev. Albert S. Moraczewski, O.P., Ph.D., Pres. Emeritus, Distinguished Scholar in Residence.

BRIGHTON. *The Christian Institute for the Study of Human Sexuality*, 127 Lake St., 02135-3898. Tel: 617-562-0766; Fax: 617-562-0668. Rev. James J. Gill, S.J., M.D., Dir.

The Jesuit Educational Center for Human Development, 127 Lake St., 02135-3898. Tel: 617-562-0766; Fax: 617-562-0668. Rev. James J. Gill, S.J., M.D., Dir.

CAMBRIDGE. *Notre Dame Mission Volunteer Corporation*, 203 Erie St., 02134. Branch Office: 403 Markland Ave., Baltimore, MD, 21212. Tel: 410-532-6864.

Sancta Maria Nursing Facility, 799 Concord Ave., 02138. Tel: 617-868-2200. Daughters of Mary of the Immaculate Conception. Sr. Mary Mark, D.M., Admin. In-Patients/Residents 141; Bed Capacity 141; Sisters 4.

**The Youville House, Inc.*, 1575 Cambridge St., 02138-4398. Tel: 617-876-4344. Mr. T. Richard Quigley, Pres. & CEO; Sr. Therese Capistran, S.G.M., Vice Pres. Mission Effectiveness. Chaplains: Revs. William Mulligan, S.J.; Neil F. Decker, S.J.; Ms. Patricia Kennedy, Dir. of Pastoral Care Services; Ms. Elizabeth Walsh.

Member of Youville Lifecare, Inc. Priests 2; Sisters of Charity (Grey Nuns) 3; Assisted Living Units 95.

**Youville Lifecare, Inc.*, 1575 Cambridge St., 02138-4398. Tel: 617-876-4344. Mr. T. Richard Quigley, Pres. & CEO; Sr. Therese Capistran, S.G.M., Vice Pres. Mission Effectiveness.

Member of Covenant Health Systems, Lexington, MA. Total Staff 221.

DEDHAM. *St. Paulene Book and Media Center*, 885 Providence Hwy., Rte. 1, 02026. Tel: 617-326-5385. Pious Society, Daughters of St. Paul (Missionary Sisters of the Media of Social Communication).

FRAMINGHAM. *Bethany Health Care Center, Inc.*, 97 Bethany Rd., 01701. Tel: 508-872-6750; Fax: 508-875-5425. Skilled Nursing Facility and Health Clinic. Congregation of Sisters of St. Joseph of Boston. Rev. Francis J. O'Neil, S.J., Chap. Bed Capacity 101. Legal Title: *Bethany Health Care Center, Inc.* Bethany Hill School, Inc., 89 Bethany Rd., 01701.

IPSWICH. *Cuvilly Arts and Earth Center, Inc.*, 10 Jeffrey Neck Rd., 01938. Tel: 508-356-4288. Sr. Catherine Owens, S.N.D., Pres. Total Assisted 85; Total Staff 7.

LEXINGTON. *Covenant Health Systems, Inc.*, 420 Bedford St., 02173. Tel: 617-862-4700. David R. Lincoln, Pres. & CEO.

LOWELL. *Oblate Ministry Development Service*, 27 Kirk St., P.O. Box 1401, 01853-1401. Tel: 508-459-1637. Rev. Adhemar Deveau, O.M.I. Legal Title: *Oblate Ministry Development Service.*

Pro Maria Committee, 22 Second Ave., 01854-2808. Tel: 508-453-5281. Miss Doris M. Poisson, Sec.

MALDEN. *Xaverian Brothers Province Development Office.* (Corporate Title: American Northeastern Province of Xaverian Brothers, Inc. and Working Boy's Home), 99 Crystal St., 02148-5994. Tel: 617-324-8099. Bro. Edward Rice, C.F.X.

METHUEN. *Holy Family Hospital Men's Guild*, 70 East St., 01844-4597. Tel: 508-687-0151, Ext. 2304.

Valley Regional Health System, Inc., 70 East St., 01844-4597. Tel: 508-687-0151.

Holy Family Hospital, Inc.

Holy Family Hospital Foundation, Inc.

Valley Regional Support Services, Inc.

NEWTON. *Focolare Movement*, Women's Branch, 189 Jackson Rd., 02158-1427. Tel: 617-965-4879. Total in Residence 5.

The Ministry Development Center for Women Religious, Inc., 15 Walnut Park, Rm. 208, 02158. Tel: 617-964-3230; Fax: 617-796-7933. Sr. Peggy Nichols, C.S.J., Exec. Dir. Total Assisted 300.

RELIGIOUS INSTITUTES OF MEN REPRESENTED IN THE ARCHDIOCESE

For further details refer to the corresponding bracketed number in the Religious Institutes of Men or Women section.

[0130]—*Assumptionists.*—A.A.

[1040]—*The Augustinians.* (Villanova, PA).—O.S.A.

[0200]—*Benedictine Monks.*—O.S.B.

[1350]—*Brothers of St. Francis Xavier.*—C.F.X.

[0330]—*Brothers of the Christian Schools.* (Long Island, New England Provs.).—F.S.C.

[0470]—*The Capuchin Friars.* (Prov. of Mary).—O.F.M.Cap.

[0270]—*Carmelite Fathers & Brothers.* (Prov. of Most Pure Heart of Mary).—O.Carm.

[0310]—*Congregation of Christian Brothers.* (Eastern Prov.).—C.F.C.

[1210]—*Congregation of the Missionaries of St. Charles.*—C.S.

[1000]—*Congregation of the Passion.* (St. Paul of the Cross Prov.).—C.P.

[1140]—*Congregation of the Sacred Hearts of Jesus and Mary.*—SS.CC.

[0480]—*Conventual Franciscans.* (Buffalo, NY).—O.F.M.Conv.

[0260]—*Discalced Carmelite Friars.*—O.C.D.

[0520]—*Franciscan Friars.* (Assumption of B.V.M., Holy Name, Immaculate Conception Provs.).—O.F.M.
[0530]—*Franciscan Friars of the Atonement.*—S.A.
[0670]—*Hospitaller Brothers of St. John of God.*—O.H.
[0690]—*Jesuit Fathers and Brother.* (New England Prov.).—S.J.
[0770]—*The Marist Brothers.* (Poughkeepsie, NJ).—F.M.S.
[0780]—*Marist Fathers.* (Boston Prov.).—S.M.
[0800]—*Maryknoll.*—M.M.
[]—*Mekhitarist Fathers.*—C.M.Vd.
[0720]—*The Missionaries of Our Lady of La Salette.* (Eastern Prov.).—M.S.
[0910]—*Oblates of Mary Immaculate.* (Eastern, St. John the Baptist Provs.).—O.M.I.
[0430]—*Order of Preachers-Dominicans.* (Prov. of St. Joseph).—O.P.
[1030]—*Paulist Fathers.*—C.S.P.
[0610]—*Priests of the Congregation of Holy Cross.* (Eastern Prov.).—C.S.C.
[1070]—*Redemptorist Fathers.* (Baltimore Prov.).—C.SS.R.
[1190]—*Salesians of Don Bosco.* (Prov. of St. Philip).—S.D.B.
[0110]—*Society of African Missions.*—S.M.A.
[0420]—*Society of Divine Word.* (Sacred Heart Prov.).—S.V.D.
[0850]—*Society of Missionaries of Africa.*—M.Afr.
[0370]—*Society of St. Columban.* (American Region).—S.S.C.
[0410]—*Sons of Divine Providence.*—F.D.P.
[1270]—*Sons of Mary Missionary Society.*—F.M.S.I.
[1280]—*Stigmatine Fathers and Brothers.* (Rome, Italy).—C.S.S.
[1360]—*Xaverian Missionary Fathers.*—S.X.

RELIGIOUS INSTITUTES OF WOMEN REPRESENTED IN THE ARCHDIOCESE

[0330]—*Carmelite Sisters for the Aged and Infirm.*—O.Carm.
[0670]—*Cistercian Nuns of the Strict Observance.*—O.C.S.O.
[0270]—*Congregation of Bon Secours.*—C.B.S.
[3110]—*Congregation of Our lady of the Retreat in the Cenacle.*—R.C.
[]—*Congregation of the Armenian Catholic Sisters of the Immaculate Conception, Inc..*
[1920]—*Congregation of the Sisters of the Holy Cross.*—C.S.C.
[0760]—*Daughters of Charity of St. Vincent de Paul.*—D.C.
[0860]—*Daughters of Mary of the Immaculate Conception.*—C.M.
[0420]—*Discalced Carmelite Nuns.*—O.C.D.
[1070-01]—*Dominican Sisters.*—O.P.
[1070-03]—*Dominican Sisters.*—O.P.
[1070-13]—*Dominican Sisters.*—O.P.
[1170]—*Felician Sisters.*—C.S.S.F.
[1370]—*Franciscan Missionaries of Mary.*—F.M.M.
[1320]—*Franciscan Missionary Sisters for Africa.* (Co. Louth, Ireland).—O.S.F.
[1180]—*Franciscan Sisters of Allegany, New York.*—O.S.F.
[1470]—*Franciscan Sisters of St. Joseph.*—F.S.S.J.
[1840]—*Grey Nuns of the Sacred Heart.*—G.N.S.H.
[0410]—*Institute of the Sisters of Our Lady of Mt. Carmel.*—O.Carm.
[2290]—*Little Missionary Sisters of Charity.*—L.M.S.C.
[2310]—*Little Sisters of the Assumption.*—L.S.A.
[2320]—*Little Sisters of the Holy Family.*—P.S.S.F.
[2340]—*Little Sisters of the Poor.*—L.S.P.
[2420]—*Marist Missionary Sisters-Missionary Sisters of the Society of Mary.*—S.M.S.M.
[2470]—*Maryknoll Sisters of St. Dominic.*—M.M.
[2480]—*Medical Missionaries of Mary.*—M.M.M.
[1360]—*Missionary Franciscan Sisters of the Immaculate Conception.*—O.S.F.
[2790]—*Missionary Servants of the Most Blessed Trinity.*—M.S.B.T.
[2880]—*Missionary Sisters of St. Columban.*—S.S.C.
[2800]—*Missionary Sisters of the Most Sacred Heart of Jesus of Hiltrup.*—M.S.C.
[3030]—*Oblates of the Most Holy Redeemer.*—O.SS.R.
[3760]—*Order of St. Clare.*—O.S.C.
[0950]—*Pious Society Daughters of St. Paul.*—D.S.P.
[3240]—*Poor Sisters of Jesus Crucified and the Sorrowful Mother.*—C.J.C.
[3410]—*Religious of Christian Education.*—R.C.E.
[2070]—*Religious of the Holy Union of the Sacred Hearts.*—S.U.S.C.
[2970]—*School Sisters of Notre Dame.*—S.S.N.D.
[3550]—*Servants of the Immaculate Heart of Mary.*—S.C.I.M.
[0980]—*Sisters Disciples of the Divine Master.*—P.D.D.M.
[0490]—*Sisters of Charity of Montreal-Grey Nuns.*—S.G.M.
[0500]—*Sisters of Charity of Nazareth.*—S.C.N.
[0560]—*Sisters of Charity of Quebec-Grey Nuns.*—S.C.Q.
[0590]—*Sisters of Charity of Saint Elizabeth, Convent Station.*—S.C.
[0640]—*Sisters of Charity of St. Vincent de Paul, Halifax.*—S.C.
[0540]—*Sisters of Charity, At Ottawa-Grey Nuns of the Cross.*—S.C.O.
[0990]—*Sisters of Divine Providence.*—C.D.P.
[2580]—*Sisters of Mercy of the Union in the United States of America.*—R.S.M.
[3000]—*Sisters of Notre Dame de Namur.*—S.N.D.deN.
[3360]—*Sisters of Providence of Saint Mary-Of-The-Woods, Indiana.*—S.P.
[3950]—*Sisters of Saint Mary of Namur.*—S.S.M.N.
[3720]—*Sisters of St. Anne.*—S.S.A.
[3750]—*Sisters of St. Chretienne.*—S.S.Ch.
[1650]—*Sisters of St. Francis of Philadelphia.*—O.S.F.
[3830]—*Sisters of St. Joseph.*—C.S.J.
[3815]—*Sisters of Ste. Jeanne D'Arc.*—S.J.A.
[0150]—*Sisters of the Assumption B.V.*—S.A.S.V.
[1830]—*Sisters of the Good Shepherd.*—R.G.S.
[3310]—*Sisters of the Presentation of Mary.*—P.M.
[1490]—*Sisters of the Third Franciscan Order.*—O.S.F.
[1705]—*Sisters of the Third Order of St. Francis of Assisi.*—O.S.F.
[4060]—*Society of the Holy Child Jesus.*—S.H.C.J.
[4070]—*Society of the Sacred Heart.*—R.S.C.J.
[4110]—*Ursuline Nuns.* (Eastern Prov.).—O.S.U.

ARCHDIOCESAN CEMETERIES

BOSTON. *Diocesan Office.* 175 Broadway, Malden, 02148. Mr. D. F. Kenney, Dir.
ARLINGTON. *St. Paul.*
BEVERLY. *St. Mary.*
CAMBRIDGE. *North Cambridge Catholic.*
CHARLESTOWN. *St. Francis de Sales.*
HAVERHILL. *St. James, St. Joseph & St. Patrick.*
LOWELL. *St. Patrick.*
LYNN. *St. Mary, St. Joseph & St. Jean Baptiste.*
MALDEN. *Holy Cross & St. Mary.*
MARBLEHEAD. *Star of the Sea.*
SALEM. *St. Mary.*
SAXONVILLE. *St. George.*
STONEHAM. *St. Patrick.*
WALTHAM. *Calvary.*
WATERTOWN. *Mount Auburn & St. Patrick.*
WOBURN. *Calvary.*

NECROLOGY

† Bergeron, Arthur I., Groton, MA, St. James. —Died Oct. 25, 1996.
† Casey, Thomas F., Braintree, MA, St. Clare. —Died July 20, 1995.
† Connors, Francis J., Needham, MA, St. Joseph. —Died Oct. 7, 1996.
† Davis, Rev. Msgr. Russell H., Wellesley, MA, St. Paul. —Died Sept. 26, 1995.
† Dewey, Rev. Msgr. Charles F., Dedham, MA, St. Mary. —Died Sept. 15, 1996.
† Feeney, John T., Newton, MA, Corpus Christi. —Died Aug. 22, 1996.
† Flynn, William C., Rockland, MA, Holy Family. —Died Nov. 25, 1995.
† Gallivan, A. Paul, Braintree, MA, St. Clare. —Died Oct. 16, 1995.
† Gough, Joseph F., Sudbury, MA, Our Lady of Fatima. —Died Dec. 10, 1995.
† Hardiman, Francis J., Saugus, MA, Blessed Sacrament. —Died April 15, 1996.
† Heery, Cornelius J., Quincy, MA, Sacred Heart. —Died Jan. 12, 1996.
† Hobbs, Frederick J., Wayland, MA, St. Zepherin. —Died April 11, 1995.
† Howatt, William F., Revere, MA, Our Lady of Lourdes. —Died Sept. 1, 1995.
† Julien, Rene E., Shirley, MA, St. Anthony. —Died May 3, 1996.
† Keating, Rev. Msgr. James J., (Retired). —Died Nov. 15, 1995.
† Keohane, John J., Cohasset, MA, St. Anthony. —Died May 31, 1996.
† King, Edward F., Concord, MA, Our Lady Help of Christians. —Died Dec. 27, 1995.
† Neill, Rev. Msgr. Christopher C., Woburn, MA, St. Charles. —Died Dec. 4, 1995.
† Pitaro, Rev. Msgr. Mimie B., Stoughton, MA, Immaculate Conception. —Died Sept. 3, 1995.
† Rittenhouse, David A., Cambridge, MA, Blessed Sacrament. —Died Sept. 17, 1996.
† Sexton, Rev. Msgr. Francis J., Brookline, MA, St. Mary. —Died Aug. 25, 1996.
† Tucke, Charles L., (Retired). —Died Dec. 2, 1995.

Diocese of Bridgeport

(Dioecesis Bridgeportensis)

Most Reverend

EDWARD M. EGAN, J.C.D., D.D.

Bishop of Bridgeport; ordained December 15, 1957; appointed Titular Bishop of Allegheny and Auxiliary Bishop of New York April 1, 1985; consecrated May 22, 1985; appointed Bishop of Bridgeport November 8, 1988; installed December 14, 1988. *Office: The Catholic Center, 238 Jewett Ave., Bridgeport, CT, 06606-2892.* Tel.: 203-372-4301.

Most Reverend

WALTER W. CURTIS, S.T.D., D.D.

Retired Bishop of Bridgeport; ordained December 8, 1937; appointed Titular Bishop of Bisica in Tunis and Auxiliary Bishop of Newark June 27, 1957; consecrated September 24, 1957; appointed Bishop of Bridgeport September 23, 1961; installed November 20, 1961; retired June 28, 1988. *Res., Queen of the Clergy Home, 128 Strawberry Hill Ave., Stamford, CT, 06904.* Tel.: 203-353-2250.

ESTABLISHED AUGUST 6, 1953.

Square Miles 633.

Corporate Title: *The Bridgeport Roman Catholic Diocesan Corporation.*

Comprises all of Fairfield County in the State of Connecticut.

For legal titles of parishes and diocesan institutions, consult the Chancery at The Catholic Center.

Chancery: The Catholic Center, 238 Jewett Ave., Bridgeport, CT, 06606-2892. Tel.: 203-372-4301; Fax: 203-371-8698.

STATISTICAL OVERVIEW

Personnel	
Bishop	1
Retired Bishops	1
Priests: Diocesan Active in Diocese	196
Priests: Active Outside Diocese	14
Priests: Diocesan in Foreign Missions	2
Priests: Retired, Sick or Absent	46
Number of Diocesan Priests	258
Religious Priests in Diocese	82
Extern Priests in Diocese	9
Ordinations:	
Diocesan Priests	6
Transitional Deacons	5
Permanent Deacons	4
Permanent Deacons in Diocese	77
Total Brothers	2
Total Sisters	523
Parishes	
Parishes	88
With Resident Pastor:	
Resident Diocesan Priests	84
Resident Religious Priests	4
Without Resident Pastor:	
Missions	2
Professional Ministry Personnel:	
Brothers	1
Sisters	32
Lay Ministers	81
Welfare	
Catholic Hospitals	2
Total Assisted	200,000
Homes for the Aged	4
Total Assisted	708
Day Care and Extended Day Care Centers	21
Total Assisted	340
Specialized Homes	13
Total Assisted	41
Special Centers for Social Services	20
Total Assisted	13,675
Other Institutions	1
Total Assisted	15
Educational	
Seminaries, Diocesan	1
Students from This Diocese	21
Diocesan Students in Other Seminaries	24
Total Seminarians	45
Colleges and Universities	3
Total Students	10,868
High Schools, Diocesan and Parish	5
Total Students	2,448
High Schools, Private	3
Total Students	989
Elementary Schools, Diocesan and Parish	32
Total Students	9,682
Elementary Schools, Private	2
Total Students	419
Catechesis/Religious Education:	
High School Students	3,257
Elementary Students	26,423
Total Students Under Catholic Instruction	54,131
Teachers in the Diocese:	
Priests	17
Brothers	2
Sisters	46
Lay Teachers	699
Vital Statistics	
Receptions into the Church:	
Infant Baptism Totals	6,090
Adult Baptism Totals	202
Received into Full Communion	157
First Communions	5,425
Confirmations	3,741
Marriages:	
Catholic	2,067
Interfaith	466
Total Marriages	2,533
Deaths	3,526
Total Catholic Population	359,455
Total Population	830,728

Former Bishops—His Eminence LAWRENCE J. CARDINAL SHEHAN, D.D., ord. Dec. 23, 1922; cons. Dec. 12, 1945 as Auxiliary Bishop of Baltimore; installed as first Bishop of Bridgeport, Dec. 1, 1953; transferred to Archdiocese of Baltimore, July 10, 1961; created Cardinal, Feb. 22, 1965; died Aug. 26, 1984.—Most Rev. WALTER W. CURTIS, S.T.D., ord. Dec. 8 1937; appt. Auxiliary Bishop of Newark and Titular Bishop of Bisica in Tunis; cons. Sept. 24, 1957; appt. Bishop of Bridgeport, Sept. 23, 1961; installed Nov. 20, 1961; retired June 28, 1988.

Vicar General—Rev. Msgr. WILLIAM J. SCHEYD, P.A., *238 Jewett Ave., Bridgeport, 06606-2892.*

Chancery—The Catholic Center, 238 Jewett Ave., Bridgeport, 06606-2892. Tel: 203-372-4301; Fax: 203-371-8698. Office Hours: Sept.-June Mon.-Fri. 9-5; July-Aug. 9-4.

Chancellor—Rev. Msgr. THOMAS J. DRISCOLL, *Catholic Center, 238 Jewett Ave., Bridgeport, 06606-2892.* Tel: 203-372-4301.

Assistant Chancellor & Secretary to the Bishop—Rev. MICHAEL K. JONES.

Episcopal Vicar for Clergy and Religious—Rev. Msgr. LAURENCE R. BRONKIEWICZ, S.T.D.

Episcopal Vicar for Hispanics—Rev. Msgr. ANICETO VILLAMIDE.

Finance Officer—BERNARD E. REIDY, M.B.A., K.C.S.G.

Judicial Vicar—Rev. JERALD A. DOYLE, Ph.D., J.C.D.

Diocesan Tribunal—The Catholic Center, 238 Jewett Ave., Bridgeport, 06606-2892. Tel: 203-372-4301.

Judges—Rev. Msgr. WILLIAM A. GENUARIO, P.A., J.C.D.; Rev. Msgr. THOMAS J. DRISCOLL; Rev. Msgr. JEAN C. TETREAULT; Rev. Msgr. J. JAMES CUNEO, J.C.D.; Revs. GEORGE D. BIRGE; MICHAEL A. BOCCACCIO; JOHN B. HOSSAN; ALBERT W. WATTS, J.C.L.; JOSEPH K. PARAMPATH, J.C.D.; ALBERT W. MCGOLDRICK, J.C.L.; MICHAEL R. MOYNIHAN, J.C.L.

Defenders of the Bond—Revs. RICHARD F. FUTIE, J.C.D.; WILLIAM F. VERRILLI; PAUL D. GRIFFIN.

Notaries—MARY A. MOLLOY; MARIE PECYLAK.

Promotor of Justice—Rev. G. FRANTZ DESRUISSEAUX, J.C.L.

Diocesan General Counsel—MICHAEL T. DOLAN, ESQ.

Diocesan Censors—Rev. Msgr. THOMAS J. DRISCOLL; Rev. CHRISTOPHER J. WALSH.

Diocesan Consultors—Rev. Msgr. LAURENCE R. BRONKIEWICZ; Rev. Msgr. THOMAS J. DRISCOLL; Rev. Msgr. JOSEPH D. POTTER; Rev. Msgr. BERNARD S. SCANLON; Rev. Msgr. JOHN C. SANDERS; Rev. Msgr. WILLIAM J. SCHEYD, P.A., V.G.; Rev. Msgr. EDWARD R. SURWILO; Rev. Msgr. ANICETO VILLAMIDE; Rev. Msgr. KEVIN W. WALLIN; Revs. JERALD A. DOYLE; MICHAEL C. PALMER.

Presbyteral Council—Most Rev. EDWARD M. EGAN, Chm.; Rev. Msgr. LAURENCE R. BRONKIEWICZ; Rev. JERALD A. DOYLE; Rev. Msgr. WILLIAM J. SCHEYD, P.A., V.G., Vice Chm.; Rev. Msgr. BERNARD S. SCANLON; Rev.

Msgr. MARTIN P. RYAN; Rev. Msgr. ANICETO VILLAMIDE; Rev. Msgr. KEVIN W. WALLIN; Rev. Msgr. THOMAS J. DRISCOLL; Rev. Msgr. NICHOLAS V. GRIECO; Rev. Msgr. BLASE M. GINTOLI; Revs. MATTHEW BERNELLI; EDWIN F. BURKE; GEORGE D. BIRGE; MICHAEL F. DOGALI; ERNEST T. ESPOSITO; FRANCIS T. HOFFMAN; WILLIAM KENNEDY, S.J.; DAVID C. LEOPOLD; WILLIAM R. MOYNIHAN; WALTER C. ORLONSKI; ROBERT G. POHLEY; JOSEPH A. PRINCE; MICHAEL K. JONES; ANDREW G. VARGA; ROBERT E. WEISS; INNOCENT C. KURKOWSKI, O.F.M.Conv.

Pastoral Council—Most Rev. EDWARD EGAN, J.C.D.; Rev. Msgr. WILLIAM J. SCHEYD, P.A., V.G.; Rev. G. FRANTZ DESRUISSEAUX; Rev. Msgr. ANICETO VILLAMIDE; Deacons DANIEL J. IANNIELLO; JOHN J. MORANSKI; Mr. TIMOTHY DEVINE; Sr. CHRISTINE KILEY, A.S.C.J.; Sr. MADELINE MCADAM, S.N.D.; THOMAS MULLIGAN, JR., ESQ.; ROBERT SALVESTRINI; HELEN F. CARROLL; NANCY DOLAN; Dr. ROMELEE A. HOWARD, K.S.G.; EILEEN HOWARD; Mrs. ROLAND J. WILSON, JR.; ISRAEL CORTES; MARY LOUISE SAMEDO; FRANK J. CARROLL; STEFAN GAWEL; MARIE WALSH; NICHOLAS PAVIA; ANNE CHATLOS; EMILIO ALICEA; ADRIANA MOLINA; Rev. MICHAEL K. JONES.

Finance Council—Most Rev. EDWARD M. EGAN; Rev. Msgr. WILLIAM J. SCHEYD, P.A., V.G.; Rev. Msgr. THOMAS J. DRISCOLL; Mr. DIGBY W. BARRIOS; EDWARD P. LYONS; WILLIAM G. MALONEY, K.M., K.H.S., K.C.S.G.; DONALD T. STUDLEY, C.P.A.; BERNARD E. REIDY, M.B.A., K.C.S.G.; GEORGE TAYLOR; WILLIAM TOTTON.

Parochial Examiners—Rev. Msgr. LOUIS A. DEPROFIO; Rev. Msgr. JOHN E. GILMARTIN; Rev. Msgr. JOSEPH D. POTTER; Rev. Msgr. JOHN F. JAZOWSKI; Rev. Msgr. BARTHOLOMEW J. LAURELLO; Revs. MICHAEL C. PALMER; JOSEPH A. SULLIVAN; Rev. Msgr. ANICETO VILLAMIDE.

Territorial Vicars—Vicariate I (Stamford, Darien, Glenbrook, Greenwich, Byram, Riverside): Rev. ROBERT G. POHLEY, Vicar, *Sacred Heart Rectory, 37 Schuyler Ave., Stamford, 06902.* Tel: 203-324-9544. Vicariate II (Norwalk, New Canaan, Wilton, Weston, Westport): Rev. EDWIN T. BURKE, Vicar, *St. Ladislaus Rectory, 25 Cliff St., South Norwalk, 06856.* Tel: 203-866-1867. Vicariate III (Fairfield, Easton, West Bridgeport): Rev. Msgr. BLASE M. GINTOLI, Vicar, *Assumption Rectory, 545 Stratfield Rd., Fairfield, 06432.* Tel: 203-333-9065. Vicariate IV (East Bridgeport, Stratford, Trumbull, Monroe, Shelton): Rev. ROBERT E. WEISS, Vicar, *St. Joseph Rectory, 50 Fairmont Pl., Shelton, 06484.* Tel: 203-924-8611. Vicariate V (Bethel, Brookfield, Danbury, Georgetown, Newtown, New Fairfield, Redding, Ridgefield, Sherman): Rev. Msgr. MARTIN P. RYAN, *St. Edward Rectory, 3 Macbean Dr., P.O. Box 8866, New Fairfield, 06812.* Tel: 203-746-2200.

Ministry for Clergy and Religious—Rev. Msgr. LAURENCE R. BRONKIEWICZ, S.T.D., Episcopal Vicar & Dir. Clergy Personnel.

The Catholic Center—238 Jewett Ave., Bridgeport, 06606. Tel: 203-372-4301.

Finance Office—Business Office; BERNARD E. REIDY, M.B.A., K.C.S.G., Finance Officer; JOSEPH E. TANGREDI, JR., Controller; JOHN P. ROONEY, Dir., Parish Accounting and Finance, *The Catholic Center, 238 Jewett Ave., Bridgeport, 06606-2892.* Tel: 203-372-4301.

Members of the Clergy Personnel Committee—Rev. Msgr. STANLEY B. ROUSSEAU, Chm.; Rev. KEVIN T. ROYAL; Rev. Msgr. PETER P. DORA.

Office for the Continuing Education of Clergy—Rev. Msgr. LAURENCE R. BRONKIEWICZ, S.T.D., Dir.

Office of Vocations—Rev. STEPHEN M. DIGIOVANNI, H.E.D., Dir., *St. John Fisher Residence, 894 Newfield Ave., Stamford, 06905.* Tel: 203-322-5331.

Office of the Permanent Diaconate—Deacons ANTHONY J. DETJE, Dir., Formation; RICHARD STENBERG, Dir., Continuing Education; Rev. Msgr. LAURENCE R. BRONKIEWICZ, S.T.D., Spiritual Dir., Formation, *The Catholic Center, 238 Jewett Ave., Bridgeport, 06606-2892.* Tel: 203-372-4301.

Office for Ecumenical and Interreligious Affairs—Rev. KEVIN T. ROYAL, Dir., *St. John Fisher Residence, 894 Newfield Ave., Stamford, 06905.* Tel: 203-322-5331.

Office of Liturgy—Rev. Msgr. KEVIN W. WALLIN, Dir., *The Catholic Center, 238 Jewett Ave., Bridgeport, 06606-2892.* Tel: 203-372-4301.

Diocesan Commission on the Liturgy—Rev. ANDREW G. VARGA, D.Min., Chm., *Res., St. Joseph, 159 Whisconier Rd., P.O. Box 5072, Brookfield Center, 06804.* Tel: 203-775-1035.

Pastoral Planning—Rev. Msgr. THOMAS J. DRISCOLL, *238 Jewett Ave., Bridgeport, 06606-2892.* Tel: 203-372-4301.

Catechesis, Office for—Mrs. LOIS E. MCKINNEY, Dir., *The Catholic Center, 238 Jewett Ave., Bridgeport, 06606-2892.* Tel: 203-372-4301.

Catechist Formation—OLIVE S. GREENE, Asst. Dir.
Special Services—K. JANE KRESSER, Asst. Dir.
Catechumenate—ELIZABETH GIGLIO, Asst. Dir.
Youth Services—JOHN P. CAMPBELL, Asst. Dir.
Catholic Scouts—Deacon JOSEPH MELITA, Dir.

Office for Education—ARMAND R. FABBRI, Dir. & Supt., Schools; Sr. JOHN VIANNEY ZULLO, S.S.N.D., Asst. Dir., Elementary Education; Rev. Msgr. FRANK C. WISSEL, Pres., Diocesan Secondary Schools, *238 Jewett Ave., Bridgeport, 06606-2892.* Tel: 203-372-4301. WILLIAM J. ADAMS, Coord., Federal-State Programs, *238 Jewett Ave., Bridgeport, 06606.* Tel: 203-576-7944.

Special Education—Sr. ELEACE KING, I.H.M., Ed.D., Dir., *The Catholic Center, 238 Jewett Ave., Bridgeport, 06606-2892.* Tel: 203-372-4301, Ext. 330. THERESA DEPASCALE, Coord., Ministry to the Deaf. Tel: 203-372-4782 (TTY).

Apostolate for the Deaf—Rev. PETER A. DEMARCO, Moderator, *St. Teresa Rectory, 5302 Main St., Trumbull, 06611.* Tel: 203-261-3672; 459-0484 (TTY).

Catholic Charities of Fairfield County, Inc.—BRIAN A. CRONIN, A.C.S.W., C.I.S.W., Exec. Dir. DAVID J. FABRIZI, Comptroller, *Catholic Center, 238 Jewett Ave., Bridgeport, 06606-2892.* Tel: 203-372-4301, Ext. 379; 564; Fax: 203-372-5045.

Diocesan Offices and Directors

Ethnic and Cultural Services—Deacon JOSEPH J. FARLEY, Sec., *238 Jewett Ave., Bridgeport, 06606-2892.* Tel: 203-372-4301.

Aging, Diocesan Task Force—EDIE CASSIDY, Chm., *238 Jewett Ave., Bridgeport, 06606-2892.* Tel: 203-372-4301.

Archives—Rev. Msgr. JOHN V. HORGAN, Archivist, *238 Jewett Ave., Bridgeport, 06606-2892.* Tel: 203-372-4301.

African Americans, Apostolate of—Rev. Msgr. JOHN C. SANDERS, Dir., *St. Mary Rectory, 669 West Ave., Norwalk, 06850.* Tel: 203-866-5546.

Catholic Lawyers—Rev. Msgr. J. JAMES CUNEO, J.C.D., Spiritual Moderator; JAMES J. RUANE, ESQ., Coord., St. Thomas More Society of Fairfield Co., *238 Jewett Ave., Bridgeport, 06606-2892.* Tel: 203-372-4301.

Catholic Physicians Guild—Dr. THOMAS G. FLYNN, Coord., *39 Old Studio Rd., New Canaan, 06840.* Tel: 203-966-1959.

Catholic Women, Council of—Rev. MICHAEL R. MOYNIHAN, Diocesan Dir., *St. Michaels Rectory, 469 N. St., Greenwich, 06083.* Tel: 203-869-5421. CONSTANCE KERSTEN, Diocesan Pres., *5 Abigail Rd., Danbury, 06811.* Tel: 203-792-3043. District Spiritual Directors: Revs. ERNEST T. ESPOSITO, (Bridgeport): MARTIN S. IGOE, (Greenwich): EDWIN F. BURKE, (Norwalk): ROBERT G. POHLEY, (Stamford):

Cemeteries—BERNARD E. REIDY, M.B.A., K.C.S.G., Dir., *238 Jewett Ave., Bridgeport, 06606-2892.* Tel: 203-372-4301. LAWRENCE W. ARSZYLA, Mgr., *238 Jewett Ave., Bridgeport, 06606-2892.* Tel: 203-372-4301.

Charismatic Renewal—FRAN FRALEIGH, *238 Jewett Ave., Bridgeport, 06606-2892.* Tel: 203-372-4301.

Communications—Rev. CHRISTOPHER J. WALSH, Dir., *238 Jewett Ave., Bridgeport, 06606-2892.* Tel: 203-372-4301., *Res., St. John Fisher Residence, 894 Newfield Ave., Stamford, 06905.* Tel: 203-322-5331. Rev. MARK CONNOLLY, Diocesan Dir., Radio & Television, *10 Millbrook Rd. West, Stamford, 06902.* Tel: 203-348-7114.

Connecticut Catholic Conference—Rev. THOMAS J. BARRY, Exec. Dir., *134 Farmington Ave., Hartford, 06105.* Tel: 203-524-7882.

Cursillos of Fairfield County, Inc.—Rev. PAUL F. MERRY, Advisor for English Language, *Blessed Sacrament Church, 254 Wilmot Ave., Bridgeport, 06607.* Tel: 203-333-1202. Rev. Msgr. ANICETO VILLAMIDE, Advisor for Spanish Language, *St. Peter Rectory, 695 Colorado Ave., Bridgeport, 06605.* Tel: 203-366-5611.

Deaf, Apostolate for—Rev. PETER A. DEMARCO, Moderator, *Res., St. Teresa Rectory, 5301 Main St., Trumbull, 06611.* Tel: 203-261-3676; 459-0484 (TTY).

Development, Office of—JOHN G. BYRNE, Dir. Planned Giving; Rev. Msgr. KEVIN W. WALLIN, Dir. Inner City Foundation; Deacon RICHARD R. KOVACS, Dir., Annual Bishop's Appeal, *238 Jewett Ave., Bridgeport, 06606-2892.* Tel: 203-372-4301.

Fairfield Foundation of the Diocese of Bridgeport, Inc.—MICHELLE JONES DELMHORST, Pres. JOHN CROFFY, Exec. Dir., *238 Jewett Ave., Bridgeport, 06606-2892.* Tel: 203-372-4301.

Inner-City Foundation for Charity and Education—Rev. Msgr. KEVIN W. WALLIN, Exec. Dir., *238 Jewett Ave., Bridgeport, 06606-2892.* Tel: 203-372-4301.

Geriatrics Apostolate—Rev. DAVID H. KRAHEL, Chap. (Greenwich, Darien, Stamford), *Our Lady Star of the Sea Rectory, 1200 Shippan Ave., Stamford, 06902.* Tel: 203-324-4634.

Hispanic Apostolate, Episcopal Vicar for—Rev. Msgr. ANICETO VILLAMIDE, Vicar, *The Catholic Center, 238 Jewett Ave., Bridgeport, 06606-2892.* Tel: 203-372-4301.

Insurance Office—JOSEPH G. BURTON, Claims & Risk Mgr., *Catholic Mutual Group, 238 Jewett Ave., Bridgeport, 06606.* Tel: 203-371-8471.

Nurses, Council of Catholic—Rev. STEPHEN J. GLEESON, Dir., *St. Stephen's Rectory, 6949 Main St., Trumbull, 06611.* Tel: 203-268-6217; Fax: 203-268-9861.

Official Newspapers—*"The Fairfield County Catholic "*, (Monthly), Rev. CHRISTOPHER J. WALSH, Editor, *238 Jewett Ave., Bridgeport, 06606.* Tel: 203-372-4301., *"The Catholic Transcript"*, (Weekly), *785 Asylum Ave., Hartford, 06105.* Tel: 203-527-1175.

Pilgrimages, Office of Diocesan—Rev. Msgr. WILLIAM J. LOUGHLIN, *St. Thomas Rectory, 1719 Post Rd., Fairfield, 06430.* Tel: 203-255-1097.

Pontifical Association of the Holy Childhood—Rev. Msgr. BERNARD SCANLON, Dir. ELIZABETH SAULNIER, Coord. for Schools; R.E. Programs, *The Catholic Center, 238 Jewett Ave., Bridgeport, 06606-2892.* Tel: 203-372-4301.

Portuguese-Speaking People, Apostolate for—Rev. Msgr. CONSTANTINO R. CALDAS, Dir., *429 Huntington Rd., Bridgeport, 06608.* Tel: 203-333-7575.

Propagation of the Faith—Rev. ROBERT J. MATY, Dir., *The Catholic Center, 238 Jewett Ave., Bridgeport, 06606-2892.* Tel: 203-372-4301.

Boy Scouts and Girl Scouts—Deacon JOSEPH MELITA, Dir., *Catholic Center, 238 Jewett Ave., Bridgeport, 06606-2982.* Tel: 203-372-4301. Rev. STEPHEN J. BALINT, *Res., St. Ladislaus Rectory, 25 Cliff St., South Norwalk, 06854.* Tel: 203-866-1867.

Retired Priests—Rev. Msgr. BERNARD S. SCANLON, Dir., *Catholic Center, 238 Jewett Ave., Bridgeport, 06606-2892.* Tel: 203-372-4302.

CLERGY, PARISHES, MISSIONS AND PAROCHIAL SCHOOLS

CITY OF BRIDGEPORT
(Fairfield County)

1—ST. AUGUSTINE CATHEDRAL (1842), Rev. Msgr. Stanley B. Rousseau. In res., Rev. Martin J. Federici; Rev. Msgr. Kevin W. Wallin; Revs. Richard J. Gemza; Alphonsus Tran Van Dong; Sr. Antoinette Mongkolrutana, S.L.C., Vietnamese Pastoral Assoc., Tel: 203-333-0837; Deacon Timothy Sullivan.
Res., 359 Washington Ave., 06604. Tel: 203-368-6777.
School—See separate listing under Elementary Schools, Regional in the Institution section.
Catechesis/Religious Programs—Students 250.

2—ST. AMBROSE (1928), Revs. Dennis G. Bludnicki; Joan Marmolejo. In res., Rev. Nello A. Barachini, C.M.; Deacon James Volpe.
Res., 1596 Boston Ave., 06610. Tel: 203-333-1336.
School—See separate listing under Elementary Schools, Regional in the Institution section.
Stations—Augustana Homes; Success Park.

3—ST. ANDREW, Revs. J. Barry Furey; Carlos Rodrigues; Charles T. Carr; Deacons Roland Blier; Edward Hendricks.
Res., 435 Anton St., 06606. Tel: 203-374-6171.
School—See separate listing under Elementary Schools, Regional in the Institution section.
Catechesis/Religious Programs—Mrs. Jeanne Bisson, D.R.E.
Students 290.

4—ST. ANN'S (1922), Revs. Joseph J. Malloy; Gill C. Babeu; Sr. Phyllis Campoli, Pastoral Assoc. & Prin.; Deacon John J. Moranski.
Res., 481 Brewster St., 06605. Tel: 203-368-1607.
School—See separate listing under Elementary Schools, Regional in the Institution section.
Catechesis/Religious Programs—Tel: 203-334-5856.
Students 320.

5—ST. ANTHONY OF PADUA. Merged with St. Peter, Bridgeport. See separate listing.

6—BLESSED SACRAMENT, Rev. Paul F. Merry; Deacon Ricardo Martinez.
Res., 254 Wilmot Ave., 06607. Tel: 203-333-1202.

7—ST. CHARLES (1902), Rev. Msgr. Joseph D. Potter; Revs. Gustavo Adolfo Falla; Marcel St. Jean; Sr. Antoinette Mongkolrutana, S.L.C., Laotian Pastoral Assoc., Tel: 203-333-0837; Deacon Santos Garcia.
Res., 391 Ogden St., 06608. Tel: 203-333-2147.
Catechesis/Religious Programs—Tel: 203-576-1629. Sr. Ann Moles, S.S.N.D., D.R.E.
Students 537.

8—SS. CYRIL AND METHODIUS (1907) (Slovak), Rev. Joseph W. Pekar.
Res., 79 Church St., 06608. Tel: 203-333-7003.

9—ST. GEORGE'S, Rev. Jose Rebaque, S.A.C., Admin.,

Tel: 203-579-1653.
Res., 443 Park Ave., 06604. Tel: 203-335-1797.

10—HOLY ROSARY (Italian), Rev. Guido G. Montanaro; Deacon Daniel Ianniello. In res., Rev. James J. Midgley.
Res., 365 E. Washington Ave., 06608. Tel: 203-334-2447.

11—ST. JOHN NEPOMUCENE. Closed. For inquiries for parish records contact Holy Name of Jesus, Stratford.

12—ST. JOSEPH'S. Closed. May 23, 1988. For inquiries for parish records contact the Catholic Center.

13—ST. MARY'S (1857), Revs. Matthew Bernelli; Joseph J. Karcsinski.
Res., 25 Sherman St., 06608. Tel: 203-334-8811.

14—ST. MICHAEL THE ARCHANGEL (1989) (Polish), Revs. James Smyka, O.F.M.Conv.; Stefan Morawski, O.F.M.Conv. In res., Revs. Chester Kicia, O.F.M.Conv.; Marcel Sokalski.
Res., 310 Pulaski St., 06608. Tel: 203-334-1822.

15—OUR LADY OF FATIMA (1962) (Portugese), Rev. Msgr. Constantino R. Caldas; Revs. Joseph De Brito Alves (Portugal); Fernando Eurico Lages de Silva; Deacon Gabriel A. Pereira.
Res., 429 Huntington Rd., 06608. Tel: 203-333-7575.
Catechesis/Religious Programs—Students 332.

16—OUR LADY OF GOOD COUNSEL (1955), Rev. Martin J. Nikodem. In res., Rev. Msgr. Gregory M. Smith.
Res., 163 Ortega Ave., 06606. Tel: 203-372-3533.
Catechesis/Religious Programs—Virginia Mora, D.R.E.
Students 35.

17—ST. PATRICK CHURCH (1889), Rev. Msgr. Andrew G. Marus; Rev. Michael J. Bachman; Sr. Eleanore Studwell, Pastoral Assoc. In res., Rev. Eugene R. Szantyr; Deacon William J. Bissenden.
Res. and Business Office: 170 Thompson St., 06604. Tel: 203-335-0106.
Church—851 North Ave., 06606.
Catechesis/Religious Programs—Sandra Mihalek, D.R.E.
Students 105.
Stations—Connecticut State Correctional Institution; St. Vincent Medical Center; Barnett Multi Health Facility.

18—ST. PETER'S (1900), Rev. Msgr. Aniceto Villamide; Deacon Domingo Reveron. In res., Rev. Msgr. Francis C. Wissel; Revs. Jose Rebaque, S.A.C.; Joseph J. Saba.
Res., 695 Colorado Ave., 06605. Tel: 203-366-5611; Fax: 203-335-1924.
School—See separate listing under Elementary Schools, Regional in the Institution section.
Catechesis/Religious Programs—Tel: 203-334-5681. Sr. Mirta Cruz, D.R.E.
Students 250.

19—ST. RAPHAEL'S (Italian), Revs. Carducci S. D'Amico; Grazioso Artuso; Deacon Joseph Melita. In res., Rev. Michael A. D'Elia.
Res., 162 Oak St., 06604. Tel: 203-333-3161; Fax: 203-368-1727.
School—See separate listing under Elementary Schools, Regional in the Institution section.
Catechesis/Religious Programs—Students 338.
Convent—671 Oak St., 06604.
Chapel—St. Margaret's, 2539 Park Ave., 06604.

OUTSIDE THE CITY OF BRIDGEPORT

Bethel, Fairfield Co., St. Mary's (1882), Revs. Edward B. Karl; Albert D. Audette, Jr.; Francis T. Hoffmann; Deacon Robert Becker.
Res., 237 Greenwood Ave., P.O. Box 289, 06801. Tel: 203-744-5777; Fax: 203-744-3740. [CEM]
School—See separate listing under Elementary Schools, Regional in the Institution section.
Catechesis/Religious Programs—24 Dodgingtown Rd., 06801. Tel: 203-743-4557. Mary Amend, D.R.E.
Students 850.
Convent—24 Dodgingtown Rd., 06801. Tel: 203-743-6985.

Brookfield, Fairfield Co., St. Joseph's (1941), Revs. Andrew G. Varga; Russell A. Augustine; Deacons William Shaughnessy; Richard Kovacs.
Res., 159 Whisconier Rd., P.O. Box 5072, 06804. Tel: 203-775-1035.
School—See separate listing under Elementary Schools, Regional in the Institution section.
Catechesis/Religious Programs—Tel: 203-775-5806.
Students 450.

St. Marguerite Bourgeoys (1982), Revs. Robert A. Uzzilio; James J. Cole; Deacon Thomas E. Nelson.
Res., 138 Candlewood Lake Rd., 06804. Tel: 203-775-5117; Fax: 203-775-9254.
Catechesis/Religious Programs—Tel: 203-775-2644. Sr. Ann Marie Strileckis, C.N.D., D.R.E.
Students 265.

Danbury, Fairfield Co.,

1—ST. GREGORY'S, (1960), Revs. Angelo S. Arrando; John Stronkowski; Raymond M. Scherba; Deacons Robert Blankschen; William D. Murphy; Daniel N. Myott.
Res., 85 Great Plain Rd., 06811. Tel: 203-797-0222; Fax: 203-743-5464.
School—See separate listing under Elementary Schools, Regional in the Institution section.
Catechesis/Religious Programs—Tel: 203-743-5168. Mrs. Frances Britt, D.R.E.
Students 567.

2—IMMACULATE HEART OF MARY, (1980) (Portuguese), Rev. Antonio Carvalho de Azevedo, Admin.; Deacon Jose Rodrigues Cabral.
Res., 149 Deer Hill Ave., 06811. Tel: 203-797-1821.
Catechesis/Religious Programs—Students 160.

3—OUR LADY OF GUADALUPE, (Spanish), Rev. Frederick L. Saviane.
Res., 29 Golden Hill Rd., 06811-4629. Tel: 203-743-1021; Fax: 203-798-8143.

4—ST. JOSEPH'S, (1905), Revs. James D. Grosso; Lawrence F. Carew; Deacon David Vaughn. In res., Rev. Joseph V. Rossitto.
Res., 8 Robinson Ave., 06810. Tel: 203-748-8177; Fax: 203-748-8177.
School—See separate listing under Elementary Schools, Regional in the Institution section.
Catechesis/Religious Programs—Tel: 203-743-7754.
Students 327.

5—ST. PETER'S, (1851), Rev. Msgr. John J. Bumstead; Revs. Corey V. Piccinino; John Kallattil, V.C.; Douglas J. Tufaro; Gregg Daniel Mecca.
Res., 104 Main St., 06810. Tel: 203-743-2707.
School—See separate listing under Elementary Schools, Regional in the Institution section.
Catechesis/Religious Programs—Tel: 203-743-1048. Margaret Curran, D.R.E.
Students 260.

6—SACRED HEART, (1925) (Polish), Revs. Xavier Nawrocki, O.F.M.Conv.; Joseph Dorniak, O.F.M.Conv.; Adam Zajdel, O.F.M.Conv.; Deacon John F. Esterheld. In res., Revs. Gilbert Wdzieczny, O.F.M.Conv., Chap. Danbury Hospital; Robert Schlageter, O.F.M.Conv., Campus Min. West Connecticut Univ.
Res., 12 Cottage St., 06810. Tel: 203-748-9029; Fax: 203-748-9168.
School—See separate listing under Elementary Schools, Regional in the Institution section.
Catechesis/Religious Programs—Students 86.
Convent—46 Stone St., 06810. Tel: 203-743-6406.

Darien, Fairfield Co., St. John (1895), Revs. Michael Jude Fay; J. Bruce Lincon; Joseph Cervero; Deacon William K. Rowe. In res., Rev. Msgr. Joseph J. Kohut.
Res., 1986 Post Rd., 06820. Tel: 203-655-1145; Fax: 203-656-3571.
Catechesis/Religious Programs—Tel: 203-655-8020. John Cunningham, D.R.E.
Students 385.

St. Thomas More (1966), Revs. Edward J. Howley; Jeffrey A. Hudanish; Sr. Madeline McAdam, S.N.D., Pastoral Assoc.; Deacon Joseph Rowan.
Res., 384 Middlesex Rd., 06820. Tel: 203-655-3303; Fax: 203-655-8901.
Catechesis/Religious Programs—374 Middlesex Rd., 06820. Tel: 203-655-3077. Mrs. Zita O'Brian, D.R.E.
Lay Teachers 70; Students 665.
Convent—370 Middlesex Rd., 06820. Tel: 203-655-3580.
Sisters of Notre Dame de Namur 4.

Easton, Fairfield Co., Notre Dame of Easton (1956), Rev. Robert J. Hyl; Deacons Harold J. Lynch; Gerald F. Sabol. In res., Rev. Joseph K. Parampath.
Res., 640 Morehouse Rd., 06612. Tel: 203-268-5838.
Church—655 Morehouse Rd., 06612. Tel: 203-261-5596.
Catechesis/Religious Programs—Students 328.

Fairfield, Fairfield Co.,

1—ST. ANTHONY OF PADUA, (1927) (Polish), Revs. Innocent Kurkowski, O.F.M.Conv.; Edwin Agonis, O.F.M.Conv.
Res., 149 S. Pine Creek Rd., 06430. Tel: 203-259-0358.

2—ASSUMPTION, Rev. Msgr. Blase M. Gintoli; Revs. John P. Baran; Ernest T. Esposito; Deacons George I. Saulnier; Donald J. Ross, Jr.
Res., 545 Stratfield Rd., 06430. Tel: 203-333-9065.
School—See separate listing under Elementary Schools, Regional in the Institution section.
Catechesis/Religious Programs—Frank Macari, D.R.E.
Students 365.
Convent—605 Stratfield Rd., 06432.

3—ST. EMERY'S, (1932) (Hungarian). (United with St. Stephen's of Bridgeport). Revs. Robert Nemeth, O.F.M.; Emeric Szlezak, O.F.M.
Res., 838 King's Hwy., 06432. Tel: 203-334-0312; Fax: 203-579-9423.
Convent—105 Biro St., 06432. Tel: 203-334-3913.
Congregation of Notre Dame 3.

4—HOLY CROSS, (Slovenian), Revs. Louis M. Dytkowski, Admin.; Milan Dimic, S.D.B., Pastoral Assoc.; Deacon Kevin Moore.
Res., 750 Tahmore Dr., 06430. Tel: 203-372-4595; Fax: 203-372-4668.
Catechesis/Religious Programs—Students 156.

5—HOLY FAMILY, Revs. William D. Donovan; Peter J. Towsley; Mr. Gerald Cryan, Pastoral Min.
Res., 700 Old Stratfield Rd., 06430. Tel: 203-336-1835; Fax: 203-336-0342.
School—See separate listing under Elementary Schools, Regional in the Institution section.
Catechesis/Religious Programs—Sr. Monica Leonard, C.N.D., D.R.E.
Students 240.
Convent—70 Laurel St., 06432.

6—ST. PIUS X, (1955), Revs. Edward J. Scull; George Sankoorikal; Deacon Richard Stenberg.
Res., 834 Brookside Dr., 06430. Tel: 203-255-6134; Fax: 203-255-5232.
Catechesis/Religious Programs—Tel: 203-259-4800.
Students 518.

7—ST. THOMAS AQUINAS, (1876), Revs. Victor T. Martin; Alfred F. Pecaric; Michael K. Jones; William J. Loughlin.
Res., 1719 Post Rd., 06430. Tel: 203-255-1097. [CEM]
School—See separate listing under Elementary Schools, Regional in the Institution section.
Catechesis/Religious Programs—Tel: 203-255-1984. Sr. Catherine Jemapete, S.S.N.D., D.R.E.
Students 412.

Georgetown, Fairfield Co., Sacred Heart (1881), Rev. M. Joseph Joaquin.
Res., 30 Church St., Box 388, 06829. Tel: 203-544-8345.
Catechesis/Religious Programs—Tel: 203-544-8423.
Students 224.

Greenwich, Fairfield Co.,

1—ST. MARY'S, (1874), Rev. Msgr. Charles W. Stubbs; Revs. Francis F. Moy, S.J.; Michael Dogali; German Martinez, O.S.B., (Spain) Hispanic Ministry; Sr. Michael Marie Fitzpatrick, S.S.N.D., Pastoral Assoc.; Deacon Matthew T. Ashe.
Res., 178 Greenwich Ave., 06830. Tel: 203-869-9393; Fax: 203-869-1032.
Catechesis/Religious Programs—Tel: 203-869-9250. Stacey Filewicz-Ross, M.A., D.R.E.
Students 350.

2—ST. MICHAEL THE ARCHANGEL, (1963) (Korean), Revs. Michael Robert Moynihan; William J. Kennedy, S.J.; Mark Connolly.
Res., 469 North St., 06830. Tel: 203-869-5421; Fax: 203-869-0169.
Catechesis/Religious Programs—Sr. Cecilia Moloughney, D.R.E.
Students 385.
Mission—Banksville, Fairfield Co., St. Timothy's.

3—ST. PAUL'S, (1902), Revs. Joseph A. Sullivan; Roger F. McDonough.
Res., 84 Sherwood Ave., 06831. Tel: 203-531-8741.
Catechesis/Religious Programs—Tel: 203-531-4265; Fax: 203-532-1414. Sr. Margaret Hoban, D.R.E.
Students 150.

4—ST. ROCH, (1938) (Italian), Rev. Nicholas J. Calabro. In res., Rev. Bartholomew C. Salter, C.S.C.
Res., 10 St. Roch Ave., 06830. Tel: 203-869-4176.
Catechesis/Religious Programs—Harry Florentine, D.R.E.
Students 200.

5—ST. AGNES, Rev. Stephen J. DeLuca.
Res., 247 Stanwich Rd., 06830. Tel: 203-869-5396; Fax: 203-625-0596.
Catechesis/Religious Programs—Mrs. Linda Nardone, D.R.E.
Students 45.

6—SACRED HEART, (1990), Rev. Martin S. Igoe.
Res., 95 Henry St., 06830. Tel: 203-531-8730; Fax: 203-531-8794.
Catechesis/Religious Programs—Tel: 203-531-4772. Sr. Lucille Menard, S.A., D.R.E.
Students 269.

Huntington, Fairfield Co., St. Lawrence (1955), Rev. Msgr. Joseph M. Fitzgerald; Revs. Robert J. Crofut; Donald Guglielmi; Deacons James A. Brown; Joseph Filingeri.
Res., 505 Shelton Ave., 06484. Tel: 203-929-5355; Fax: 203-929-8939.
School—See separate listing under Elementary Schools, Regional in the Institution section.
Catechesis/Religious Programs—Tel: 203-929-8421. Mrs. Barbara Pekar, D.R.E.

Students 1,080.

Monroe, Fairfield Co., St. Jude (1974), Rev. Msgr. John B. Sabia; Rev. Matthew R. Mauriello.
Res., 707 Monroe Tpke., 06468. Tel: 203-261-6404.
School—See separate listing under Elementary Schools, Regional in the Institution section.
Catechesis/Religious Programs—Tel: 203-261-6788. Mrs. Jean Paul, D.R.E.
Students 980.

New Canaan, Fairfield Co., St. Aloysius, Rev. Msgr. J. Peter Cullen; Revs. Kevin T. Royal; Robert J. Valentine; Deacon John H. Tugman.
Res., 40 Maple St., 06840. Tel: 203-966-0020; Fax: 203-972-7691.
School—See separate listing under Elementary Schools, Regional in the Institution section.
Catechesis/Religious Programs—30 Maple St., 06840. Tel: 203-966-4555.
Students 635.

New Fairfield, Fairfield Co., St. Edward the Confessor (1954), Rev. Msgr. Martin P. Ryan; Revs. Mark E. Grimes; John Castaldo; Deacons Anthony J. Detje; Paul Pilkington; Henry Hein.
Res., P.O. Box 8866, 06812. Tel: 203-746-2200; Fax: 203-746-4856.
Catechesis/Religious Programs—Tel: 203-746-4270. Ms. Joan Marschall, D.R.E.
Students 1,083.

Newtown, Fairfield Co., St. Rose of Lima, Revs. George D. Birge; Lawrence A. Larson; Raja Bose; Rev. Msgr. Jean C. Tetreault; Deacons Kenneth P. Stroud; Charles C. Dietsch, III.
Res., 46 Church Hill Rd., 06470. Tel: 203-426-2572. [CEM]
School—See separate listing under Elementary Schools, Regional in the Institution section.
Catechesis/Religious Programs—Tel: 203-426-2333. Alice Kohler, D.R.E.
Students 940.

Norwalk, Fairfield Co.,

1—St. Jerome, (1960), Revs. David W. Blanchfield; Joseph Palacino.
Church—23 Half Mile Rd., 06851. Tel: 203-847-5349.
Catechesis/Religious Programs—Tel: 203-846-2111. Ann Simpson, D.R.E.
Students 460.

2—St. Joseph's, (South Norwalk) (1895), Revs. David W. Howell; Edgardo Gutierrez. In res., Rev. G. Frantz Desruisseaux; Deacon William O. Murphy.
Res., 85 S. Main St., P.O. Box 443, 06856. Tel: 203-838-4171.
Catechesis/Religious Programs—Tel: 203-866-1225. Sr. Patricia Wachter, S.S.N.D., D.R.E.
Students 255.
Convent—14 Chestnut St., 06854. Tel: 203-866-9452.

3—St. Ladislaus, (1907) (Hungarian), Rev. Edwin F. Burke. In res., Rev. Stephen J. Balint.
Res., 25 Cliff St., 06854. Tel: 203-866-1867; Fax: 203-866-7830.

4—St. Mary's, (1848), Rev. Alfred J. Bietighofer; Rev. Msgr. John C. Sanders.
Res., 669 West Ave., 06850. Tel: 203-866-5546.
Catechesis/Religious Programs—Tel: 203-866-7429. Mrs. Pam Arsenault, D.R.E.
Students 169.

5—St. Matthew, (1957), Revs. Walter C. Orlowski; Gregory J. Huminski; Deacon David M. Sochacki.
Res., 216 Scribner Ave., 06854. Tel: 203-838-3788.
Catechesis/Religious Programs—Tel: 203-838-0231. Kathleen B. Sochacki, D.R.E.
Students 368.

6—St. Philip, (1964), Revs. Michael A. Boccaccio; Albert G. Pinciaro, III.
Res., One Fr. Conlon Pl., 06851. Tel: 203-847-4549 (Office); Fax: 203-847-4148.
Catechesis/Religious Programs—Tel: 203-847-4286. Sr. Mary Ann McPartland, C.N.D., D.R.E.
Students 323.
Convent—23 France St., 06851. Tel: 203-847-1478.

7—St. Thomas the Apostle, (1935), Rev. Msgr. William J. Scheyd, P.A., V.G.; Revs. Michael F. Flynn; David A. Yocis; Richard Daniel Murphy.
Res., 203 East Ave., 06855. Tel: 203-866-3141.
Catechesis/Religious Programs—Tel: 203-866-1189. Dr. Lorraine DeLuca, D.R.E.
Students 252.
Convent—5 Prowitt St., 06855. Tel: 203-866-3738. Sisters of Congregation de Notre Dame

Redding, Fairfield Co., St. Patrick (1879), Rev. John B. Hossan; Deacon William C. Timmel.
Res., 169 Black Rock Tpke., P.O. Box 119, Redding Ridge, 06876. Tel: 203-938-2253.
Catechesis/Religious Programs—Tel: 203-938-2963. Barbara L. Clarke, D.R.E.
Students 196.

Ridgefield, Fairfield Co., St. Elizabeth Seton (1978), Rev. Joseph A. Prince; Deacons Bart Mauceri; Terence Grant.
Res., 520 Ridgebury Rd., 06877. Tel: 203-438-7292; Fax: 203-438-0600.
Catechesis/Religious Programs—Tel: 203-438-9707; Fax: 203-438-0600. Andrea Kennedy, D.R.E.
Students 700.

St. Mary's, Fairfield Co, (1882), Revs. Robert P. Morrissey; Thomas D. Nicastro, Jr.; Michael J. Madden.
Res., 183 High Ridge Ave., 06877. Tel: 203-438-6538; Fax: 203-438-1902. [CEM]
Catechesis/Religious Programs—Tel: 203-438-7335. Sr. Joan Brennan, D.R.E.
Students 1,121.

Riverside, Fairfield Co., St. Catherine of Siena (1913), Rev. Msgr. William A. Genuario, P.A.; Revs. Gilbert D'Souza; Robert A. Loftus; Deacons Renato Berzolla; Robert Henrey; Vincent Heidenreich; Rev. William F. Platt.
Res., 4 Riverside Ave., 06878. Tel: 203-637-3661.
Catechesis/Religious Programs—13 Riverside Ave., 06878. Tel: 203-637-4213. Barbara Glynn, D.R.E.
Students 606.

Shelton, Fairfield Co., St. Joseph's (1906), Revs. Robert E. Weiss; Paul G. Murphy; Deacon David Munson.
Res., 50 Fairmont Pl., 06484. Tel: 203-924-8611; Fax: 203-924-9446.
School—See separate listing under Elementary Schools, Regional in the Institution section.
Catechesis/Religious Programs—430 Coram Ave., 06484. Tel: 203-924-9677. Mrs. Francesca Scarpa, D.R.E.
Students 400.
Convent—420 Coram Ave., 06484. Tel: 203-924-1545. Sisters of St. Joseph Chambery

St. Margaret Mary (1963), Rev. Msgr. Thomas J. Whalen; Deacon Matthew Skurat.
Res., 380 Long Hill Ave., 06484. Tel: 203-924-4929.
Catechesis/Religious Programs—Tel: 203-924-2679. Mrs. Carol D'Amico, D.R.E.
Students 360.

Sherman, Fairfield Co., Holy Trinity (1985), Rev. David J. Riley.
Res., Rte. 37 & 39, P.O. Box 97, 06784. Tel: 203-354-1414.
Catechesis/Religious Programs—Tel: 203-354-1498. Ms. Ginny Verhoff, D.R.E.
Students 180.

Stamford, Fairfield Co.,

1—St. Benedict's, (Slovak), Rev. Vincent J. Veich. In res., Bro. Cletus Burke, O.S.F.
Res., One St. Benedict Cir., 06902. Tel: 203-327-7250; Fax: 203-327-7251.

2—St. Bridget, (1963), Rev. Msgr. John F. Jazowski.
Res., 278 Strawberry Hill Ave., 06902. Tel: 203-324-2910.
Catechesis/Religious Programs—Tel: 203-357-8157. Mrs. Rose Stearns, D.R.E.
Students 94.

3—St. Cecilia's, (1926), Revs. Roger J. Watts; William G. Carey.
Res., 1184 Newfield Ave., 06905. Tel: 203-322-1562; Fax: 203-968-1550.
School—See separate listing under Elementary Schools, Regional in the Institution section.

4—St. Clement's, (1928), Revs. Andre R. Dube; David W. Franklin.
Res., 535 Fairfield Ave., 06902. Tel: 203-348-4206; Fax: 203-316-8131.
Catechesis/Religious Programs—Students 108.

5—St. Gabriel, (1963), Rev. Robert A. Uzzilio; Deacon Loreto M. Buzzeo. In res., Rev. Brian M. Gray.
Res., 914 Newfield Ave., 06905. Tel: 203-322-7426; Fax: 203-968-6266.
School—See separate listing under Elementary Schools, Regional in the Institution section.
Catechesis/Religious Programs—Tel: 203-329-1978. Mrs. Madeleine Buzzeo, D.R.E.
Students 216.

6—Holy Name of Jesus, (1903) (Polish), Revs. Sherman W. Gray, Jr.; John F. Pikulski (Poland).
Res., 4 Pulaski St., 06902. Tel: 203-323-4967; Fax: 203-323-6403.
Catechesis/Religious Programs—Tel: 203-359-3618; Fax: 203-323-4546. Marian Karas, D.R.E.
Students 110.

Stamford Co., Fairfield, Holy Spirit (1962), Rev. Msgr. Normand A. Methe.
Res., 403 Scofieldtown Rd., Stamford, 06903. Tel: 203-322-3722; Fax: 203-322-0543.
School—See separate listing under Elementary Schools, Regional in the Institution section.
Catechesis/Religious Programs—Tel: 203-357-1094. Linda Dunn, D.R.E.
Students 139.

Stamford, Fairfield Co.,

1—St. John's, (1847), Revs. William A. Nagle; Michael F. Dogali; Robert E. Onze.
Res., 279 Atlantic St., 06901. Tel: 203-324-1553; Fax: 203-359-2660.
Catechesis/Religious Programs—Tel: 203-359-2052. Sr. Frances C.S.J., D.R.E.
Students 227.

2—St. Leo's, (1960), Rev. Msgr. Benedict F. Tighe; Rev. David W. Franklin; Deacon Joseph J. Farley.
Res., 24 Roxbury Rd., 06902. Tel: 203-322-1669; 329-8884.
Catechesis/Religious Programs—Tel: 203-348-0052. Mrs. Florence Gambino, D.R.E.
Students 500.

3—St. Mary's, (1907), Revs. Richard F. Futie; James A. McDevitt.
Res., 566 Elm St., 06902. Tel: 203-324-7321. Rev. Paul B. Lalic.
Catechesis/Religious Programs—Mr. Robert Kraus, D.R.E.
Students 251.

4—St. Maurice, (1935), Revs. Gerald T. Devore; Bernard A. Keefe.
Res., 358 Glenbrook Rd., 06906-2198. Tel: 203-324-3434; Fax: 203-964-8023.
Catechesis/Religious Programs—Tel: 203-348-8768; Fax: 203-964-8023. Margaret Borders, D.R.E.
Students 215.

5—Our Lady of Montserrat, (1984) (Spanish), Revs. Bernardo Rodriguez; Gregorio Raya; Deacon Ramon Isidro.
Res., 93 Hope St., 06906. Tel: 203-323-7379; Fax: 203-323-0798.
Catechesis/Religious Programs—Students 550.

6—Our Lady Star of the Sea, (1964), Rev. Msgr. Edward R. Surwilo; Deacons Edward R. Kovacs; John Mann. In res., Rev. David H. Krahel.
Res., 1200 Shippan Ave., 06902. Tel: 203-324-4634.
School—See separate listing under Elementary Schools, Regional in the Institution section.
Convent—1216 Shippan Ave., 06902. Tel: 203-359-1127.

7—Sacred Heart, (1920) (Italian), Revs. Robert G. Pohley; Jose Mendonca (Brazil); Robert J. Post, Ph.D.; Deacons Louis F. Howe; Fred Harrity.
Res., 37 Schuyler Ave., 06902. Tel: 203-324-9544; Fax: 203-324-9202.
School—See separate listing under Elementary Schools, Regional in the Institution section.
Catechesis/Religious Programs—Students 198.
Convent—21 Schuyler Ave., 06902. Tel: 203-323-3524.

Stratford, Fairfield Co.,

1—Holy Name of Jesus, (1923) (Slovak), Rev. Msgr. Peter P. Dora; Rev. Msgr. James J. Cuneo.
Res., 1950 Barnum Ave., 06497. Tel: 203-375-5815.
School—See separate listing under Elementary Schools, Regional in the Institution section.
Catechesis/Religious Programs—Students 298.
Convent—2 Mary Ave., 06497. Tel: 203-378-1203.

2—St. James, (1886), Revs. Thomas F. Lynch; Emidio O. Gregori; Daniel Kennelly; Darius J. Zielonka; Michael Patrick Lyons; Deacon John Barton. In res., Rev. Lawrence J. Carroll.
Res., 2110 Main St., 06497. Tel: 203-375-5887.
School—See separate listing under Elementary Schools, Regional in the Institution section.
Catechesis/Religious Programs—Kathleen Donnelly, D.R.E.
Students 535.

3—St. Mark's, (1960), Rev. Msgr. Lawrence J. McMahon; Rev. Stanley N. Koziol; Deacons T. Emmet Murray; F. Paul Kurmay; Andrew Dzujna.
Res., 500 Wigwam Ln., 06497. Tel: 203-377-0444; Fax: 203-378-7913.
School—See separate listing under Elementary Schools, Regional in the Institution section.
Catechesis/Religious Programs—Tel: 203-377-3158. Helen E. Bendyk, D.R.E.
Students 227.

4—Our Lady of Grace, (1954), Rev. Msgr. William F. Schultz; Rev. Donald L. Kloster, Pastoral Assoc. In res., Rev. Jerald A. Doyle.
Res., 497 Second Hill Ln., 06497. Tel: 203-377-0928.
Parish Center—375 Second Hill Ln., 06497. Tel: 203-375-2005.
Catechesis/Religious Programs—Susan Czaplicki, D.R.E.
Students 275.

5—Our Lady of Peace, Rev. Msgr. John E. Gilmartin. In res., Rev. Msgr. Thomas J. Driscoll.
Res., 230 Park Blvd., Lordship, 06497. Tel: 203-377-4863.
Catechesis/Religious Programs—Tel: 203-378-3053. Mrs. Mary Hoyt, D.R.E.
Students 140.

Trumbull, Fairfield Co.,

1—Christ the King, (1962), Revs. Bernard M. Dolan; Edward Small, S.J.

Res., 4700 Madison Ave., 06611. Tel: 203-268-8695.
Catechesis/Religious Programs—Tel: 203-261-2583.
Students 410.

2—St. Catherine of Siena, Rev. Msgr. Richard J. Shea; Revs. Michael Lawrence Dunn; Robert D. Karpinski.
Res., 200 Shelton Rd., 06611. Tel: 203-377-3133.
School—See separate listing under Elementary Schools, Regional in the Institution section.
Convent—19 Rosemond Ter., 06611.

3—St. Stephen, (1953), Rev. Stephen J. Gleeson; Deacons Gary Carpenter; Donald Brunetto; Michael Wolfer. In res., Revs. William F. Verrill; Edward A. Colohan, Pastoral Assoc.
Res., 6948 Main St., 06611. Tel: 203-268-6217; Fax: 203-268-9861.
Catechesis/Religious Programs—Tel: 203-268-6860. Sr. Beth McGlynn, S.S.N.D., D.R.E.
Students 488.

4—St. Theresa's, (1934), Rev. Msgr. Louis A. DeProfio; Revs. Walter J. Seekamp; Peter A. DeMarco; Robert J. Maty; Sr. Joan Flynn, R.S.M., Dir. Pastoral Min.; Deacon H. Paul Herman. In res., Rev. William F. Sangiovanni.
Res., 5301 Main St., 06611. Tel: 203-261-3676; Fax: 203-268-8723.
School—See separate listing under Elementary Schools, Regional in the Institution section.
Catechesis/Religious Programs—19 Rosemond Ter., 06611. Tel: 203-261-4706. Sr. Julia Bargiel, C.S.F.N., D.R.E.
Students 753.
Convent—Tel: 203-261-3848.
School Sisters of Notre Dame 8.

Weston, Fairfield Co., St. Francis of Assisi (1955), Rev. Msgr. Nicholas V. Grieco. In res., Rev. Joseph K. Parampath.
Res., 35 Norfield Rd, P.O. Box 1025, 06883. Tel: 203-227-1341; Fax: 203-226-1154.
Catechesis/Religious Programs—Tel: 203-226-9474.
Students 410.

Westport, Fairfield Co., Assumption (1876), Revs. Frank C. McGrath; David C. Leopold; Deacons Eugene P. Kamper; John S. Fay. In res., Rev. Msgr. Laurence R. Bronkiewicz.
Res., 98 Riverside Ave., 06880. Tel: 203-227-5161; Fax: 203-227-1206. [CEM]
Catechesis/Religious Programs—Tel: 203-226-5448. Sr. Maureen Fleming, D.R.E.
Students 278.

St. Luke (1957), Revs. Pierre A. Botton; Samuel V. Scott; Deacon Brian Kelly; Sr. Dorothy Choyce, Pastoral Assoc.
Res., 84 Long Lots Rd., 06880. Tel: 203-227-7245; Fax: 203-226-8063.
Catechesis/Religious Programs—Tel: 203-226-0729; Fax: 203-226-8063. Jane Ferreira, D.R.E.
Students 748.

Wilton, Fairfield Co., Our Lady of Fatima, Revs. Michael C. Palmer; John Kallatil; James Breen; Deacon Thomas K. Seith.
Res., 229 Danbury Rd., 06897. Tel: 203-762-3928; Fax: 203-834-1261.
School—See separate listing under Elementary Schools, Regional in the Institution section.
Catechesis/Religious Programs—Tel: 203-762-9080; Fax: 203-831-1261. Mrs. Kathleen Rooney, D.R.E.
Students 750.

Chaplains of Public Institutions

Bridgeport. *Bridgeport Community Correctional Facility.* 1106 North Ave., 06604. Tel: 203-579-6131. Deacon Carl M. Vecca Tel: 203-582-6477.
Bridgeport Health Care. 600 Bond St., 06610. Tel: 203-384-6400. Rev. Michael A. D'Elia.
Bridgeport Hospital. 267 Grant St., 06610. Tel: 203-384-3311. Revs. Eugene R. Szantyr, Assoc. Chap.; Nello A. Barachini.

Danbury. *Danbury Area Mental Health Authority.* 64 West St., 06810. Tel: 203-778-1640, Ext. 247. Rev. Arthur E. Norton, Assoc. Chap.
Danbury Hospital. 24 Hospital Ave., 06810. Tel: 203-797-7000. Revs. Gilbert Wdzieczny, O.F.M.Conv.; John F. Pikulski.
Federal Correctional Institution. 06811. Tel: 203-743-6471. Rev. James A. McDevitt, Chaplain; Sr. Anne Marie Raftery, O.S.F., Dir. of Pastoral Care.

Greenwich. *Greenwich Hospital.* 06830. Tel: 203-863-3000. Rev. James McIntyre, O.F.M.Cap.

Norwalk. *Norwalk Hospital.* 06856. Tel: 203-852-2000. Rev. Rufin Kuveikis, O.F.M.Cap.

Stamford. *Stamford Hospital.* 06902. Tel: 203-325-7584. Rev. Brian M. Gray.

On Duty Outside the Diocese:
Reverend Monsignors—
Cusack, Andrew T., Dir. National Institute for Clergy Formation, Seton Hall University, 400 S. Orange Ave., South Orange, NJ 07079
Millea, William V., Via della Nocetta 63, Rome, 00164 Italy
Reverend Fathers—
Barrett, M. Stephen, S.S., 10910 Olde Woods Way, Columbia, Maryland 21044
Green, Thomas J., Catholic University of America, Department of Canon Law, Washington, DC 20017
Holbrook, Harold M., Padres De Santiago Apostol, Casilla 1021, Oruro, Bolivia
Mitchell, John C., P.O. Box 701, Carmel, NY 10072
Moore, Joseph P., Society of St. John Vianney, 455 Washington St., Coventry, RI 02816
Posluszny, Francis, Parroquia San Juan Apostal, APTO 735, Chiclayo, Peru
Smolko, John F., Catholic University of America, 9808 Dale Dr., Upper Marlboro, MD 20870
Talar, Charles J.T., Alvernia College, Reading, PA
Terentieff, Robert J., Mount St. Mary College, Emmitsburg, MD 21727
Tracy, David W., University of Chicago, The Divinity School, 5521 S. University, Chicago, IL 60637

Graduate Studies:
Reverend Fathers—
Guglielmi, Donald A., Pontifical University of St. Thomas Aquinas, Rome

---

Military Chaplains:
Reverend Fathers—
Carey, William F., U.S. Army
Gay, James A., U.S. Navy
Thompson, William D., U.S. Air Force

Awaiting Assignment:
Reverend Fathers—
Julien, Jean Ridly

Leave of Absence:
Reverend Fathers—
Ahearn, Kieran T.
Biondino, Joseph P.
Carr, Charles T.
Federici, Martin J.
Yocis, David A.

Retired:
Reverend Monsignors—
Campagnone, Francis A.
Conroy, Walter R.
Curtis, Walter W.
Foley, Daniel J.
Guinan, Thomas P.
Hale, Harry L.
Halloran, Edward D.
Henahan, Thomas F.
Horgan, John V.
Kohut, Joseph J.
Laurello, Bartholomew J.
Lengen, James G.
Pranckus, Francis J.
Scanlon, Bernard S.
Sienkiewicz, Alfred J.
Tetreault, Jean C.
Reverend Fathers—
Brady, Philip W.
Caldas, Constantine R.
Coleman, W. Philip
Coyne, Edwin J.
Dennehy, Martin J.
Dennis, James J.
Dunn, Richard R.
Fernandez, Jose A.
Fonseca, John
Grise, J. Clifford
Hitchcock, Martin B.
Hribsek, Aloysius J.
Jazowski, John F.
Knurek, Dennis A.
Maglione, Joseph J.
Medinski, Francis J.
Monahan, Richard J.
Morrissey, Philip T.
Odie, John P.
Polinsky, John R.
Rarus, Boleslaus J.
Rossitto, Joseph V.
Suwinski, Leo S.
Usenza, Robert J.

Permanent Deacons:
Ashe, Matthew, St. Mary, Greenwich
Barton, Jack, St. James, Stratford
Becker, Robert, St. Mary, Bethel
Berzolla, Renato L., St. Catherine, Riverside
Bissenden, William J., St. Patrick, Bridgeport
Blankschen, Robert, St. Gregory, Danbury
Blier, Roland, St. Andrew, Bridgeport
Brown, James, St. Lawrence, Huntington
Brunetto, Donald W., St. Stephen, Trumbull
Buzzeo, Michael L., St. Gabriel, Stamford
Cabral, Jose R., Immaculate Heart of Mary, Danbury
Calabrese, Robert P., St. Anthony Maronite, Danbury
Carpenter, Gary E., St. Stephen, Trumbull
Chiappetta, Frank, St. Philip, Norwalk
Detje, Anthony, St. Edward the Confessor, New Fairfield
Dwyer, F. Robert, St. Joseph, Shelton
Dzujna, Andrew W., St. Mark, Stratford
Esterheld, John, Sacred Heart, Danbury
Farley, Joseph J., St. Leo, Stamford
Fay, John S., Assumption, Westport
Filingeri, Joseph, St. Lawrence, Huntington
Freibott, Thomas, Holy Name, Stratford
Garcia, Santos, Florida
Grant, Terence J., St. Elizabeth Seton, Ridgefield
Hammock, Ralph, St. Leo, Stamford
Harrity, Frederick A., Sacred Heart, Stamford
Heidenreich, Vincent, St. Catherine, Riverside
Hein, Henry R., St. Edward, New Fairfield
Hendricks, Edward R., St. Andrew, Bridgeport
Henrey, Robert, St. Catherine of Siena, Riverside
Herman, H. Paul, St. Teresa, Trumbull
Howe, Louis F., Sacred Heart, Stamford
Ianniello, Daniel, Holy Rosary, Bridgeport
Isidro, Ramon, Our Lady of Montserrat, Stamford
Kamper, Eugene P., Assumption, Westport
Kelly, Brian J., St. Luke, Westport
Kovacs, Edward, Our Lady Star of the Sea, Stamford
Kovacs, Richard, St. Joseph, Brookfield
Kurmay, Paul, St. Mark, Stratford
Lynch, Harold, Notre Dame, Easton
Mann, John J., Our Lady Star of the Sea, Stamford
Martinez, Ricardo, Blessed Sacrament, Bridgeport
Mauceri, Bartholomew, St. Elizabeth Seton, Ridgefield
Melita, Joseph, St. Raphael, Bridgeport
Moore, Kevin, Holy Cross, Fairfield
Moranski, John J., St. Ann, Bridgeport
Munson, David D., St. Joseph, Shelton
Murphy, William D., St. Gregory the Great, Danbury
Murphy, William O., St. Joseph, Norwalk
Murray, Emmet, St. Mark, Stratford
Myott, Daniel N., St. Gregory the Great, Danbury
Naiman, Donald, St. Gregory, Danbury
Nelson, Thomas E., Marguerite Bourgeoys, Brookfield
Pereira, Gabriel, Our Lady of Fatima, Bridgeport
Pilkington, Paul, St. Edward, New Fairfield
Reilly, Paul, St. Philip, Norwalk
Reveron, Domingo, St. Peter, Bridgeport
Ross, Donald J., Assumption, Fairfield
Ross, Norman, St. Mary, Ridgefield
Rowan, Joseph L., St. Thomas More, Darien
Rowe, William K., St. John, Darien
Sabol, Gerald, Notre Dame, Easton
Saulnier, George, Assumption, Fairfield
Saymon, Richard F., Leave of Absence
Seith, Thomas K., Our Lady of Fatima, Wilton
Shaughnessy, William, St. Joseph, Brookfield
Skurat, Matthew, St. Margaret Mary, Shelton
Sochacki, David, St. Matthew, Norwalk
Stenberg, S. Richard, St. Pius X, Fairfield
Stroud, Kenneth, St. Rose, Newtown
Sullivan, Timothy, St. Augustine Cathedral, Bridgeport
Timmel, William C., St. Patrick, Redding
Tugman, John H., St. Aloysius, New Canaan
Tupper, Paul, St. Clement, Stamford
Vaughn, David J., St. Joseph, Danbury
Volpe, James, St. Ambrose, Bridgeport
Wolfer, Michael K., St. Stephen, Trumbull

INSTITUTIONS LOCATED IN THE DIOCESE

[A] COLLEGES AND UNIVERSITIES

BRIDGEPORT. *St. Vincent's College*, 2800 Main St., 06606. Tel: 203-576-5235.
For a complete listing, refer to the Colleges and Universities section.

*FAIRFIELD. *Sacred Heart University*, 5151 Park Ave., 06432-1000. Tel: 203-371-7999.
For a complete listing, refer to the Colleges and Universities section.

**Fairfield University*, 1073 N. Benson Rd., 06430-5195. Tel: 203-254-4000.
For a complete listing, refer to the Colleges and Universities section.

[B] SPECIAL SCHOOLS, DIOCESAN

BRIDGEPORT. *Queen of Saints, The Catholic Center*, 238 Jewett Ave., 06606. Tel: 203-372-4301, Ext. 217. School of Religion and Spirituality and Retreat Facility.

[C] HIGH SCHOOLS, DIOCESAN

BRIDGEPORT. *Kolbe Teen Health Center*, 33 Calhoun Pl., 06604. Tel: 203-335-2554.
Kolbe-Cathedral High School, 33 Calhoun Pl., 06604. Tel: 203-335-2554. Mrs. Jo Anne Jakab, Prin.; Ms. Carol A. Jones, Asst. Prin.; Revs. Marcel Sokalski, O.F.M.Conv.; James J. Midgley, Spiritual Dir. Priests 2; Lay Teachers 19; Administrators 2; Students 281.

DANBURY. *Immaculate High School*, 73 Southern Blvd., 06810. Tel: 203-744-1510. Dr. Joseph Gerics, Prin.; Mr. Richard T. Stoops, Asst. Prin.; Rev. Corey V. Piccinino, Spiritual Dir. Priests 2; Sisters 1; Lay Teachers 26; Students 368.

FAIRFIELD. *Notre Dame Catholic High School*, 220 Jefferson St., 06432. Tel: 203-372-6521; Fax: 203-374-0387. Rev. William F. Sangiovanni, Prin.; Mr. Carl Philipp, Asst. Prin.; Rev. Lawrence J. Carroll, Asst. Prin. Priests 2; Sisters of Notre Dame de Namur 1; Lay Teachers 38; Students 610.

STAMFORD. *Trinity Catholic High School*. (Formerly Stamford Catholic High School), 926 Newfield Ave., 09605. Tel: 203-322-3401; Fax: 203-322-5330. Sr. Ritamary Schulz, A.S.C.J., Prin.; Bro. Cletus Burke, O.S.F., Asst. Prin.; Sr. Christine Kiley, A.S.C.J., Asst. Prin.; Mr. Robert D'Aquila, Dir. of Studies; Rev. Jeffrey Hudanish, Spiritual Dir.; Mr. Michael Roper, Dir. Guidance; Mr. Tracy Nichols, Athletic Dir.; Mrs. Susan Dougherty, Dir. Devel. & Alumni Rels.; Mrs. Mary D'Aquila, Volunteer Coord. Priests 1; Brothers 1; Sisters 3; Lay Teachers 30; Students 453. Records for Central Catholic High School, Norwich, and St. Mary's High School, Greenwich, located at Trinity.

TRUMBULL. *St. Joseph High School*, 2320 Huntington Tpke., 06611. Tel: 203-378-9378; Fax: 203-378-7306. Mr. Richard A. Bishop, Prin.; Rev. Raymond Petrucci, Vice Prin. for Institutional Advancement; Mrs. Joan M. Caliendo, Vice Prin. for Academic Affairs; Mrs. Susan L. Unger, Dir. of Guidance; Rev. Robert D. Karpinski, Spiritual Dir.; Mr. Vito M. Montelli, Dir. Athletics; Mr. Norman DeTullio, Dir. Devel.; Mrs. Kristen King, Coord. for Student Activities; Mr. Thomas Roach, Dean of Students; Mrs. Margaret Marino, Admissions Coord.; Sr. Marie E. Iannuccillo, Dir. of Campus Min. Priests 3; Sisters 4; Lay Teachers 45; Students 736.

[D] HIGH SCHOOLS, PRIVATE

FAIRFIELD. *Fairfield College Preparatory School*, N. Benson Rd., 06430. Tel: 203-254-4000; Fax: 203-254-4108. A preparatory day school for boys, established in 1942. Society of Jesus of New England. Very Rev. Aloysius P. Kelley, S.J., Pres.; Revs. Michael E. Boughton, S.J., Headmaster; Donald M. Barry, S.J.; Richard G. Cipolla; William J. Eagan, S.J.; George A. Gallarelli, S.J.; Walter R. Pelletier, S.J.; Ronald V. Perry, S.J.; Lawrence D. Ryan, S.J.; Martin G. Shaughnessy, S.J. Priests 10; Lay Teachers 46; Students 766.

GREENWICH. *Convent of the Sacred Heart, Religious of the Sacred Heart*, 1177 King St., 06831. Tel: 203-531-6500; Fax: 203-531-5206. Sr. Joan Magnetti, R.S.C.J., Headmistress.
Day School for girls (Grades PreK-12). Students 484.

STAMFORD. *Sacred Heart Academy*, 200 Strawberry Hill Ave., 06902. Tel: 203-323-3173. Sisters of St. Joseph. Sr. Jeanne Paulella, C.S.J., Prin. Sisters 4; Lay Teachers 15; Students 100.

[E] ELEMENTARY SCHOOLS, REGIONAL

BRIDGEPORT. *Catholic Elementary Schools-Region X*, St. Andrew Rectory, 435 Anton St., 06606. Tel: 203-333-1336. Mr. Richard Christensen, Business Mgr.
St. Ambrose. (Grades K-8), 461 Mill Hill Ave., 06610. Tel: 203-368-2835. Sr. Michael Marie Hartman, I.H.M., Prin.; Sr. Richard Mary Peters, I.H.M., Supr. Servants of the Immaculate of Mary 6; Lay Teachers 9; Students 326. St. Andrew. (Grades 1-8), 395 Anton St., 06606. Tel: 203-372-4819. Mr. Michael Fettig, Prin. Lay Teachers 9; Students 207. St. Ann. (Grades PreK-8), 521 Brewster St., 06605. Tel: 203-334-5856. Sr. Phyllis Campoli, C.S.J., Prin. Lay Teachers 14; Students 237. St. Augustine Cathedral. (Grades K-8), 63 Pequonnock St., 06604. Tel: 203-367-5896. Mrs. Barbara A. Coscio, Prin. Lay Teachers 11; Students 265. St. Peter. (Grades K-8), 659 Beechwood Ave., 06605. Tel: 203-333-2048. Miss Suzanna Zello, Prin. Sisters 3; Lay Teachers 6; Students 234. St. Raphael. (Grades PreK-8), 324 Frank St., 06604. Tel: 203-333-6818. Sr. Mary Anne Shurron, A.S.C.J., Prin. Apostles of the Sacred Heart 4; Lay Teachers 10; Students 330.

DANBURY. *Catholic Elementary Schools-Region IX*, St. Gregory, 3 Tammany Tr., 06811. Tel: 203-744-6248. Rev. David J. Riley, St. Mary. (Grades K-8), 24 Dodgingtown Rd., 06801. Tel: 203-744-2922. Sr. Anne McCarthy, S.S.N.D., Prin., St. Joseph. (Grades K-8), Rte. 133, 06804. Tel: 203-775-2774. Miss Mary Kathryn Deakin, Prin. Lay Teachers 10; Students 200. Sacred Heart. (Grades K-8), 17 Cottage St., 06810. Tel: 203-792-6194. Sr. M. Benilda Nadolski, F.S.S.J., Prin. Franciscan Sisters of St. Joseph 3; Lay Teachers 8; Students 227. St. Gregory the Great. (Grades K-8), 85 Great Plains Rd., 06811. Tel: 203-748-1217. Sr. Mary John O'Rourke, O.S.U., Prin. Lay Teachers 10; Students 236. St. Joseph. (Grades K-8), 370 Main St., 06810. Tel: 203-748-6615. Mrs. Susan C. Goethals, Prin. Lay Teachers 14; Students 314. St. Peter. (Grades PreK-8), 98 Main St., 06810. Tel: 203-748-2895. Mrs. Josephine P. Ferry, Prin. Sisters of Mercy 3; Lay Teachers 11; Students 226. St. Rose. (Grades K-8), 40 Church Hill Rd., Newtown, 06470. Tel: 203-426-5102. Mrs. Elizabeth M. Lynch, Prin. Lay Teachers 10; Students 237.

FAIRFIELD. *Catholic Elementary Schools-Region V*, Fairfield/Easton Regional Catholic School, Inc., 1719 Post Rd., 06430. Tel: 203-259-6735. Mrs. Jean Correa, Business Mgr., Holy Family. (Grades PreK-8), Edison Ave., 06430. Tel: 203-367-5409. Mrs. Mary McCormack. Lay Teachers 15; Students 265. Our Lady of the Assumption. (Grades K-8), 605 Stratfield Rd., 06432. Tel: 203-334-6271. Ms. Gerri Desio, Prin. Sisters of St. Dominic of Newburgh 1; Lay Teachers 15; Students 365. St. Thomas Aquinas. (Grades PreK-8), 118 Ruane St., 06430. Tel: 203-255-0556. Sr. Catherine Leonard, C.N.D., Prin. Congregation of Notre Dame 2; Lay Teachers 20; Students 445.

GREENWICH. *Catholic Elementary Schools-Region I*, Greenwich Catholic School, 471 North St., 06830. Tel: 203-869-4000; Fax: 203-869-3405. Mrs. Mary Flume, Business Mgr., Greenwich Catholic School. (Grades PreK-8), 471 North St., 06830. Tel: 203-869-4000. Mrs. Genevieve Madonna, Prin. Lay Teachers 30; Students 454.

NORWALK. *Catholic Elementary Schools-Region III*, All Saints Catholic School, 139 W. Rocks Rd., 06851. Tel: 203-847-3881. Mrs. Jean Nichols, Business Mgr., All Saints Catholic Elementary School. (Grades DayCare-8), 139 W. Rocks Rd., 06851. Tel: 203-847-3881. Sr. Catherine Sheehy, R.S.M., Prin. Lay Teachers 51; Sisters 3; Students 843.

SHELTON. *Catholic Elementary Schools-Region VIII*, St. Lawrence Rectory, 505 Shelton Ave., 06484. Tel: 203-926-8495. Mrs. Jo Ann Simpson, Business Mgr., St. Joseph. (Grades PreK-8), 430 Coram Ave., 06484. Tel: 203-924-4669. Sr. Ethel MacIlvain, C.S.J., Prin. Sisters of St. Joseph of Chambery 3; Lay Teachers 19; Students 361. St. Lawrence. (Grades PreK-8), 503 Shelton Ave., Huntington, 06484. Tel: 203-929-4422. Mrs. Kathleen Gosart, Prin. Sisters 1; Lay Teachers 13; Students 300.

STAMFORD. *Catholic Elementary Schools-Region II*, Catholic Regional School System, Inc., 926 Newfield Ave., P.O. Box 3127, 06905-0127. Tel: 203-968-2795. Mrs. Kathleen K. Carty, Business Mgr., St. Aloysius. (Grades K-8), 33 South Ave., New Canaan, 06840. Tel: 203-966-0786. Bro. James Timoney, C.F.C., Prin. Lay Teachers 12; Students 199. Holy Spirit. (Grades PreK-5), 403 Scofieldtown Rd., 06903. Tel: 203-329-1623. Sr. Marie Vianney Gallagher, S.S.N.D., Prin. Lay Teachers 8; Students 171. Our Lady Star of the Sea. (Grades K-5), 1170 Shippan Ave., 06902. Tel: 203-348-1155. Mrs. Gail Ryan, Prin. Ursuline Sisters 1; Lay Teachers 6; Students 161. Sacred Heart. (Grades K-8), One Schuyler Ave., 06902. Tel: 203-323-4844. Sr. Pietrina Mazzola, M.P.F., Prin. Religious Teachers Filippini 2; Lay Teachers 8; Students 175. St. Cecilia. (Grades PreK-6), 1186 Newfield Ave., 06905. Tel: 203-322-6505. Mrs. Joann Borchetta, Prin. Sisters 1; Lay Teachers 11; Students 331. St. Gabriel. (Grades 6-8), 948 Newfield Ave., 06905. Tel: 203-322-7383. Mr. Peter Borchetta, Prin. Lay Teachers 13; Students 260.

STRATFORD. *Catholic Elementary Schools-Region VI*, St. James School, One Monument Pl., 06497. Tel: 203-380-1990; Fax: 203-380-0749. Mrs. Natalia Zamachaj, Business Mgr., St. James. (Grades K-8), One Monument Pl., 06497. Tel: 203-375-5994. Mrs. Carolyn S. Potts, Prin.; Sr. Gloria Marie Kascak, S.S.C.M., Asst. Prin. Lay Teachers 31; Students 502. St. Mark. (Grades K-8), 500 Wigwam Ln., 06497. Tel: 203-375-4291. Mr. Phillip T. Adzima, Prin. Lay Teachers 14; Students 238.

TRUMBULL. *Catholic Elementary Schools-Region VII*, St. Catherine of Siena, 190 Shelton Rd., 06611. Tel: 203-375-1947. Sr. Anne Marie Dorff, St. Jude. (Grades PreK-8), 707 Monroe Tpke., Monroe, 06468. Tel: 203-261-3619. Sr. Dorothy Anne Novak, C.S.F.N., Prin. Sisters of the Holy Family of Nazareth 1; Lay Teachers 12; Students 296. St. Catherine of Siena. (Grades PreK-8), 190 Shelton Rd., 06611. Tel: 203-375-1947. Sr. Anne Marie Dorff, S.S.N.D., Prin. Lay Teachers 11; Students 319. St. Theresa. (Grades PreK-8), 55 Rosemond Ter., 06611. Tel: 203-268-3236. Mr. Edward C. Lovely, Prin. Sisters 1; Lay Teachers 12; Students 310.

WILTON. *Catholic Elementary Schools-Region IV*, Our Lady of Fatima School, 225 Danbury Rd., 06897. Tel: 203-762-8100. Mrs. Mary Gardiner, Business Mgr., Our Lady of Fatima. (Grades PreK-8), 225 Danbury Rd., 06897. Tel: 203-762-8100. Mrs. Mary Ann Bozzuti, Prin. Lay Teachers 18; Students 261.

[F] ELEMENTARY SCHOOLS, PRIVATE

GREENWICH. *Convent of the Sacred Heart*, 1177 King St., 06831. Tel: 203-531-6500; Fax: 203-531-5206. Sr. Joan Magnetti, R.S.C.J., Headmistress. Students 484.

STAMFORD. *Villa Maria Education Center*, 161 Sky Meadow Dr., 06903. Tel: 203-322-5886; Fax: 203-322-0228. Bernardine Sisters. School for Children with Learning Disabilities. Sr. Carol Ann, O.S.F., Admin. Students 60.

[G] CATHOLIC CHARITIES

BRIDGEPORT. *Catholic Charities of Fairfield County*, Catholic Center, 238 Jewett Ave., 06606-2892. Tel: 203-372-4301, Ext. 379; 564.
Adoption Program. China Identified Adoptions, Traditional Adoptions and Home Studies. 238 Jewett Ave., 06606. Tel: 203-372-4301 ext. 370. Anne Sters, Dir.
Catholic Family Services, Bridgeport, 238 Jewett Ave., 06606. Tel: 203-372-4301, Ext. 348. Michael Tintrup, A.C.S.W., L.C.S.W., District Exec. Dir.
Catholic Family Services, Danbury, 30 Main St., Suite 503, Danbury, 06810. Tel: 203-743-4412. Edward S. Laskowski, A.C.S.W., L.C.S.W., District Exec. Dir.
Catholic Family Services, Norwalk, 7 Chapel St., P.O. Box 2025, Norwalk, 06852. Tel: 203-838-2316. Carol Kwan, M.S.W., District Exec. Dir.
Catholic Family Services, Stamford, 30 Myano Ln., Stamford, 06902. Tel: 203-323-1105. Joan Pollack, A.C.S.W., L.C.S.W., District Exec. Dir.
Catholic Family Services Outreach Offices: 1986 Post Rd., Darien, 06820. Tel: 203-655-2169. 387 Main St., Ridgefield, 06877. Tel: 203-431-8170. 452 Howe Ave., Shelton, 06484. Tel: 203-924-9604. 80 Ferry Blvd., Stratford, 06497. Tel: 203-375-9553. 44 Old Ridgefield Rd., Wilton, 06897. Tel: 203-834-2076.
Houses of Hospitality:
New Covenant House of Hospitality (Yerwood Center), 90 Fairfield Ave., Stamford, 06904. Tel: 203-964-8228. Deacon Frank Chiappetta, Dir.
Thomas Merton Center, 43 Madison Ave., 06604. Tel: 203-367-9036. Mary Ann Furlong, R.N., Dir.
Family Life Ministry. Please call Rev. Ernest T. Esposito, Exec. Dir., Tel: 203-372-4301, Ext. 314, for the following programs: Ministry to Widows; Bereavement; Job Transition; Post-Abortion Support; Divorced and Separated; Marriage Profile; Marriage Preparation; Marriage Enrichment; and Family Enrichment. Diocesan Office, 238 Jewett Ave., 06606-2892. Tel: 203-372-4301, Ext. 320. Rev. Ernest T. Esposito, D.Min., Dir.
Family Life/Respect Life Catholic Center, 238 Jewett Ave., 06606-2892. Tel: 203-372-4301, Ext. 314.
Gary Crooks/St. Stephen's Emergency Food Center, 301 Bostwick Ave., 06605. Tel: 203-384-6904. Community Mental Health Support Services. Donna Teriney, M.P.A., Dir.
Mental Health Outreach: Danbury, Barrett House, 235 White St., Danbury, 06810. Tel: 203-794-0819. Sandy Harris, Dir. Case Management Program, 233 White St., Danbury, 06810. Tel: 203-748-0848. Sandy Cole, Supervisor.
Thresholds. (Shelter for Women & Children), 41 New St., Danbury, 06810. Tel: 203-792-8609. Sharon

Bien, Program Dir.
Nutrition and Aging Services, 30 Myano Ln., Stamford, 06902. Tel: 203-324-6175. Cindy Phelps, Dir.
Senior Citizen Outreach, 233 White St., Danbury, 06810. Tel: 203-743-4412. Mrs. Clare Hipp, B.A., Program Coord.
Social Action-Campaign for Human Needs, Catholic Relief Services.
Social Concern Ministries, Catholic Center, 238 Jewett Ave., 06606-2892. Tel: 203-372-4301, Ext. 386.
Social Issues Advocacy. Edie Cassidy, Dir. Health, Aging Issues. Tel: 203-372-4301, Ext. 394.
St. Joseph Residence for Mother and Child, 96 Catherine St., 06604. Tel: 203-366-0443. Kate Fox, Dir.
St. Joseph Center for Poor and Needy, Inc., 238 Jewett Ave., 06606. Tel: 203-372-4301 ext. 564. Brian A. Cronin, Exec. Dir.

[H] DAY NURSERIES

BRIDGEPORT. *Daughters of Charity of the Most Precious Blood Day Nursery*, 1490 North Ave., 06604. Tel: 203-334-7000. Sr. Theresa Tremblay, Dir.

STAMFORD. *Our Lady of Grace Day Nursery*, 635 Glenbrook Rd., 06906. Little Workers of the Sacred Hearts. Sr. Lillian Cairo, P.O.S.C., Supr.
Stepping Stones Preschool, Inc., Sacred Heart Academy, 200 Strawberry Hill Ave., 06902. Tel: 203-323-3173. Sisters of Saint Joseph.

[I] GENERAL HOSPITALS

BRIDGEPORT. *St. Vincent's Development Corporation*, 2800 Main St., 06606. Tel: 203-576-5459.
For a complete listing, refer to the Hospitals section.
St. Vincent's Health Services Corporation, 2800 Main St., 06606. Tel: 203-576-5455.
For a complete listing, refer to the Hospitals section.
St. Vincent's Medical Center, 2800 Main St., 06606. Tel: 203-576-6000.
For a complete listing, refer to the Hospitals section.
St. Vincent's Medical Center Foundation, 2800 Main St., 06606. Tel: 203-576-5451.
For a complete listing, refer to the Hospitals section.

STAMFORD. *St. Joseph Medical Center*. 128 Strawberry Hill Ave., 06904-1222. Tel: 203-353-2001.
For a complete listing, refer to the Hospitals section.
St. Joseph Medical Center Corporation, 128 Strawberry Hill, 06904-1222.
For a complete listing, refer to the Hospitals section.
St. Joseph Medical Center Foundation, Inc., 128 Strawberry Hill Ave., 06904.
For a complete listing, refer to the Hospitals section.

[J] SPECIAL HOSPITALS

BRIDGEPORT. *Bridgeport Diocesan Health Care Corporation*, 238 Jewett Ave., 06606. Tel: 203-372-4301.
For a complete listing, refer to the Special Care Facilities section.
St. Camillus Home Foundation, Inc., 238 Jewett Ave., 06606 Fax: 203-353-0550.
For a complete listing, refer to the Special Care Facilities section.

DANBURY. *The Pope John Paul II Center for Health Care, Inc.*, 33 Lincoln Ave., 06810. Tel: 203-797-9300.
For a complete listing, refer to the Special Care Facilities section.
The Pope John Paul II Foundation, Inc., 238 Jewett Ave., 06606.
For a complete listing, refer to the Special Care Facilities section.

STAMFORD. *St. Camillus Health Center*, 494 Elm St., 06902. Tel: 203-353-0550.
For a complete listing, refer to the Special Care Facilities section.

[K] HOMES FOR AGED

BRIDGEPORT. *Augustana Homes Bishop Curtis Homes - Danbury*, 238 Jewett Ave., 06606.
For a complete listing, refer to the Special Care Facilities section.
Augustana Homes/Bishop Curtis Homes, 525 Palisade Ave., 06610. Tel: 203-366-4333; Fax: 203-576-6790.
For a complete listing, refer to the Special Care Facilities section.
Augustana Homes/Bishop Curtis Homes, 230 Jewett Ave., 06606. Tel: 203-372-4301.
For a complete listing, refer to the Special Care Facilities section.
Roncalli Apartments, 430 Grant St., 06610. Tel: 203-384-9984.
For a complete listing, refer to the Special Care Facilities section.
Roncalli Charities Inc., 430 Grant St., 06610. Tel: 203-384-9984.
For a complete listing, refer to the Special Care Facilities section.

BETHEL. *Augustana Homes/Bishop Curtis Homes*, Simeon Rd., 06801. Tel: 203-743-2508.
For a complete listing, refer to the Special Care Facilities section.

FAIRFIELD. *Augustana Homes/Bishop Curtis Homes*, 1677 Post Rd., 06430.
For a complete listing, refer to the Special Care Facilities section.

RIVERSIDE. *Augustana Homes of Greenwich/Bishop Curtis Homes*, 1040 E. Putnam Ave., 06878.
For a complete listing, refer to the Special Care Facilities section.

STAMFORD. *Augustana Homes/Bishop Curtis Homes - Glenbrook*, 352 Glenbrook Rd., 06902. Tel: 203-576-0823.
For a complete listing, refer to the Special Care Facilities section.

TRUMBULL. *Carmel Ridge*, 6454 Main St., 06611. Tel: 203-261-2229.
For a complete listing, refer to the Special Care Facilities section.
St. Joseph's Housing Corporation, Teresian Towers & Carmel Ridge Estates, 6448 Main St., 06611. Tel: 203-261-2229.
For a complete listing, refer to the Special Care Facilities section.
St. Joseph's Manor, 6448 Main St., 06611. Tel: 203-268-6204; Fax: 203-268-5271.
For a complete listing, refer to the Special Care Facilities section.

[L] CONVALESCENT HOMES

NORWALK. *Notre Dame Convalescent Home*, 76 W. Rocks Rd., 06851. Tel: 203-847-5893.
For a complete listing, refer to the Special Care Facilities section.

[M] SOCIAL PROGRAMS

BRIDGEPORT. *Social Issues Advocate-Parish Social Concerns*, 238 Jewett Ave., 06606. Tel: 203-372-4301. Brian A. Cronin, Campaign for Human Development; Edith Cassidy, Social Concerns Coord.

[N] MONASTIC FOUNDATIONS

WEST REDDING. *The Benedictine Grange*, 06896. Tel: 203-938-3689. Rev. John B. Giuliani, Dir.
Mary House, Benedictine Grange Guest House. Tel: 203-938-9268. Gregory Hauck, Guest Master.

[O] RESIDENCES OF PRIESTS AND BROTHERS

BRIDGEPORT. *Provincial Offices of the Priests and Brothers of Holy Cross, Eastern Province*. (Province of Our Lady of Holy Cross), 835 Clinton Ave., 06604. Tel: 203-367-7252; Fax: 203-366-7886. Revs. Hugh W. Cleary, C.S.C., Prov.; Wilfred J. Raymond, Asst. Prov.; R. Bradley Beaupre, C.S.C., Treas., Holy Cross Novitiate, Marigreen Pines, Cascade, CO. Educational Institutions: King's College, Wilkes-Barre, PA, 18711. Stonehill College, North Easton, MA, 02356. Bishop McNamara High School, Forestville, MD, 20747. Rev. Robert E. de Leon, C.S.C, St. Vincent's Medical Center, 06606. Rev. Thaddeus S. Swertz, C.S.C, Mount St. John's School, Deep River, 06417-0415. Rev. Francis T. Zlotkowski, C.S.C, Brigham & Womens' Hospital, Boston, MA, 02115. Legal Title: *Congregation of Holy Cross - Eastern Province, Inc.*

FAIRFIELD. *The Fairfield Jesuit Community-Fairfield University*, 06430-5195. Tel: 203-256-1650. Revs. Charles H. Allen, S.J.; Francis R. Allen, S.J.; Donald M. Barry, S.J.; Dean P. Bechard, S.J.; James R. Blaetter, S.J.; John V. Borgo, S.J.; Michael G. Boughton, S.J.; Gerhard H. Bowering, S.J. (Germany); Vincent M. Burns, S.J.; Albert A. Cardoni, S.J.; William F. Carr, S.J.; Paul E. Carrier, S.J.; Richard D. Costello, S.J.; Joseph D. Devlin, S.J.; Anthony J. Eiardi, S.J.; John W. Elder, S.J.; George A. Gallarelli, S.J.; Andrew J. Garavel, S.J.; G. Simon Harak, S.J.; Kenneth J. Jorgensen, S.J.; Aloysius P. Kelley, S.J.; William J. Kennedy, S.J.; Johannes B. Hari Kustanto, S.J. (Indonesia); Victor F. Leeber, S.J.; Francis W. Lewis, S.J.; Donald D. Lynch, S.J.; Joseph F. MacDonnell, S.J.; James J. Mayzik, S.J.; Francis J. Moy, S.J.; Henry J. Murphy, S.J.; Thomas A. Murphy, S.J.; W. Laurence O'Neil, S.J.; Mark J. Burke, S.J.; John J. Cecero, S.J.; William J. Eagan, S.J.; Walter R. Pelletier, S.J.; Ronald V. Perry, S.J.; Francis T. Hannafey, S.J.; Francis J. McManus, S.J.; G. Paul Peterson, S.J.; Albert F. Reddy, S.J.; Thomas J. Regan, S.J.; Joseph L. Ryan, S.J.; Laurence D. Ryan, S.J.; Joseph J. Schad, S.J.; James P. Scull, S.J.; Martin G. Shaughnessy, S.J.; Edward J. Small, S.J.; Robert N. Sproule, S.J.; Richard J. Stanley, S.J.; Christopher W. Steck, S.J.; James G. Stinson, S.J.; Timothy E. Toohig, S.J., Rector; Maurice Wong, S.J.; Walter J. Young, S.J.

STAMFORD. *Lourdes Capuchin Chaplains Community*, 2 Rock Spring Rd., 06906. Tel: 203-348-5368. Revs. Bruce Quinn, O.F.M.Cap, Supr. & Coord. of Capuchin Hospital Chaplains; James McIntyre, O.F.M.Cap.; Rufin Kuveikis, O.F.M.Cap.
Our Lady Queen of the Clergy Home. Home for Retired Priests. 128 Strawberry Hill Ave., 06904. Rev. Msgr. Bernard S. Scanlon; Rev. Msgr. Walter R. Conroy; Rev. Msgr. James G. Lengen; His Eminence Ignatius Cardinal Kung; Rev. Msgr. John V. Horgan; Rev. Msgr. Edward D. Halloran; Rev. John P. Odie.
St. John Fisher Seminary Residence, 894 Newfield Ave., 06905. Tel: 203-322-5331; Fax: 203-461-9876. Revs. Stephen M. DiGiovanni, H.E.D., Rector; Kevin T. Royal, S.T.L., Vice-Rector; Christopher J. Walsh, Ph.D., Spiritual Dir.; Rev. Msgr. James C. Turro, S.T.L., S.S.L., A.M., Ph.D., Confessor.

[P] CONVENTS AND RESIDENCES FOR SISTERS

BRIDGEPORT. *Convent of Mary Immaculate, Missionary Sisters of the Blessed Sacrament and Mary Immaculate*. Prov. Headquarters. 1111 Wordin Ave., 06605. Tel: 203-334-5681. Sr. Presentacion Zabala, Provincial. Sisters 5. Assisting the Apostolate to Spanish-Speaking People.
Daughters of Charity of the Most Precious Blood Convent, 1482 North Ave., 06604. Tel: 203-334-7000.
Holy Spirit Convent, Daughters of the Holy Spirit, 50 Pequonnock St., 06604. Tel: 203-334-6926.
Staffing & ministry work in public health.
Sisters of the Company of the Savior, 820 Clinton Ave., 06604. Tel: 203-368-1875. Spanish-Speaking Apostolate. Mother Constanza Lopez, Supr.

GREENWICH. *Convent of the Sacred Heart, Religious of the Sacred Heart of Jesus*, 1177 King St., 06831. Tel: 203-531-0866.
Sacred Heart Convent, 38 Gold St., 06830. Tel: 203-531-8547. Franciscan Sisters of the Atonement 4.

MONROE. *Provincial House, Immaculate Heart of Mary Province, Sisters of the Holy Family of Nazareth, C.S.F.N.*, 1428 Monroe Tpke., 06468. Tel: 203-268-7646. Sr. M. Janice Kobierowski, C.S.F.N., Prov. Supr.; Rev. Raymond Petrucci, Chap. Professed 67.

NORWALK. *Regional House of Sisters of St. Thomas of Villanova*, 76 W. Rocks Rd., 06851. Tel: 203-847-2885. Mother Edmond, S.S.T.V., Supr. Notre Dame Convalescent Home; Rev. Albert W. Watts, Chap. Professed 5.

RIDGEFIELD. *Provincial House, Congregation de Notre Dame*, 223 W. Mountain Rd., 06877. Tel: 203-438-5282; Fax: 203-438-3150. Sr. Anne Leonard, C.N.D., Prov. Supr.; Sr. Alyn Larson, C.N.D., Supr., Local Community. Tel: 203-438-3115; Rev. Michael J. McCarthy, Chap.

STAMFORD. *Heart of Mary Convent (Residence for Bernardine Sisters)*, 163 Sky Meadow Dr., 06903. Tel: 203-322-5920. Sr. M. Dymphna Zakowski, O.S.F., Admin. Tel: 203-322-8721. Bernardine Sisters 12.
Villa Maria Education Center. Tel: 203-322-5886. School for children with learning disabilities (Grades 1-8). Sr. Carol Ann Nawracaj, O.S.F., Prin.
Monastery of St. Clare, 1954 Long Ridge Rd., 06903-3232. Tel: 203-329-2252. Sr. Mary Michael Bosseau, O.S.C., Abbess.
Our Lady of Grace Convent, 635 Glenbrook Rd., 06906. Tel: 203-348-5531. Motherhouse and Novitiate of Little Workers of Sacred Hearts. Sr. Lillian Cairo, P.O.S.C., Supr.
Sisters Minor of Mary Immaculate, Holy Name of Jesus Convent, 305 Washington Blvd., 06902. Sr. Theresa Marie Kovacs, S.S.M.I., Local Supr. Sisters 3.
St. Francis Villa Custody House, Immaculate Conception Custody, 138 Brushy Hill Rd., Danbury, 06810. Sr. Theresa Marie Kovacs, S.M.M.I., Custodian, Local Supr. and V.G. Sisters 3.
Villa Divino Amore Convent, Little Workers of the Sacred Hearts of Jesus & Mary, 117 Hope St., 06906. Tel: 203-324-2449. Sr. Giacinta Scaramuzzo, P.O.S.C., Supr.

WILTON. *Lourdes Health Care Center*, 345 Belden Hill Rd., 06897. Tel: 203-762-3318, Ext. 361. Rev. James Madden, C.S.C., Res. Chap.
School Sisters of Notre Dame Motherhouse (Northeastern Province), 345 Belden Hill Rd., 06897. Tel: 203-762-3318. Sr. Marie Jeannette Blatz, Prov. Supr.; Rev. James Madden, C.S.C., Res. Chap. Tel: 203-762-5156. Priests 1; Professed 154.

[Q] SECULAR INSTITUTES

BRIDGEPORT. *The Society of Our Lady of the Way*, 584 Capitol Ave., Apt. 6, 06606. A secular institute for women. Miss Margaret Gould, Unit Dir.; Rev. Timothy Curtin, S.J.

[R] FOUNDATIONS, TRUSTS AND FUNDS

BRIDGEPORT. *Fairfield Foundation of the Diocese of Bridgeport, Inc.*, 238 Jewett Ave., 06606-2892. Tel: 203-372-4301; Fax: 203-371-8698. Mrs. Michele H. Jones Delmhorst, Pres.; Mr. John Croffy, Exec. Dir.
Inner-City Foundation for Charity & Education, 238

Jewett Ave., 06606-2892. Tel: 203-372-4301. Rev. Msgr. Kevin W. Wallin, Exec. Dir.

[S] GUEST HOUSES

DARIEN. *Convent of St. Birgitta*, 06820. Tel: 203-655-1068. Sr. M. Sabina Kavanadi, O.SS.S., Supr.; Rev. Richard J. Cipolla, Chap.

[T] HOUSES OF STUDIES

BRIDGEPORT. *St. Peter's Parish, St. Maximillian Kolbe House of Studies*, 535 Colorado Ave., 06605. Tel: 203-335-4992. Rev. Msgr. Francis C. Wissel, Dir.; Ms. Carmen Serrano, Supr.

[U] RETREAT HOUSES

BRIDGEPORT. *The Urban Center of St. Charles Parish*, 1279 E. Main St., 06608. Tel: 203-366-4190. Luis Baeza, House Manager; Rev. Msgr. Joseph Potter, Consultant; Sr. Ann Moles, S.S.N.D., Consultants.

NORTH STAMFORD. *Villa Maria Retreat House*, 159 Sky Meadow Dr., 06903. Tel: 203-322-0107. Retreat house for men & women. Sr. M. Concetta Labenz, O.S.F., Admin.; Sr. Joanne Slanga, O.S.F., Retreat Team, Spiritual Direction, Directed Retreats, MBTI Reiki Master; Sr. Bernadine Grego, O.S.F., Retreat Team, Reiki Practicioner, Enneagram; Sr. Patricia Jamison, C.N.D., Program Dev. Dir., Spiritual Direction; Sr. Peggy Riordan, R.S.M., Program Dev. Dir., Spiritual Director, Reiki Practitioner; Rev. Aloysius Hribsek, Chap. Bernardine Franciscan Sisters 13.

[V] NEWMAN CENTERS

BRIDGEPORT. *Newman Centers*. Dr. Margaret A. Palliser, Dir. of Campus Ministry; Rev. Thomas M. McLernon, Campus Min.

Sacred Heart University (Fairfield), 5151 Park Ave., 06430. Tel: 203-371-7840. Rev. Robert Schlageter, O.F.M.Conv., Dir. Campus Ministry.

Western Connecticut State University (Danbury), P.O. Box 706, Danbury, 06813. Tel: 203-837-9225.

Fairfield University (Fairfield), N. Benson Rd., 06430. Tel: 203-255-4511. Revs. Paul Carrier, S.J.; Joseph J. Shad, S.J., Asst. Chap.; Richard J. Stanley, S.J., Asst. Chaplain; Mr. Robert W. Canter, S.J., Asst. Chaplain.

[W] MISCELLANEOUS LISTINGS

BRIDGEPORT. *Blessed Brother Andre Charitable Trust*, 835 Clinton Ave., 06604.

Cardinal Shehan Center, Inc., 1494 Main St., 06604. Tel: 203-336-4468. Mr. Terry O'Connor, Exec. Dir.

The Diocesan Cemetary Care Foundation, Inc., 238 Jewett Ave, 06606.

Faith in the Future Fund, Inc., 238 Jewett Ave., 06606.

Hispanic Social Ministries of Fairfield County, Inc., 238 Jewett Ave., 06606-9990. Rev. Msgr. Aniceto Villamide, Contact Person.

Needle Fund, Inc., 238 Jewett Ave., 06606.

The Queen's Daughters, c/o Sr. Therese, D.H.S., 50 Pequonnock St., 06604. Mrs. Josephine Faggella, Pres. Sponsoring agency for Holy Spirit Convent. Care of the sick and poor in their homes by Daughters of the Holy Spirit.

FAIRFIELD. *The Institute for Religious Education and Pastoral Studies (REAPS)*, Sacred Heart University, 5151 Park Ave., 06432-1000. Tel: 203-371-7843; 371-7867; Fax: 203-374-9968. Rev. Msgr. Gregory M. Smith, Ed.D., Dir.; Mrs. Carole Akers, M.A., Asst. to the Dir.; Deacon Daniel Ianniello, Dir. of Devel. & Grants; Mrs. Patricia Maurer, Coord. Admissions/Retention; Mrs. Catherine Brewer, Admin. Sec.

GREENWICH. *Clemons Productions, Inc.* (In association with That's The Spirit Productions, Inc.), P.O. Box 7466, 06836; Fax: 203-324-6915. Rev. Mark Connolly, Pres. Tel: 203-348-7114, Spirituality For Today.

RIDGEFIELD. *The St. Mary's Endowment Trust*, 183 High Ridge Ave., 06877.

SHELTON. *Fr. McKenna St. Vincent de Paul Shoppe*, 185 Canal St., 06484. Tel: 203-924-4817. Rev. Robert G. Pohley, Chap.; Barbara Samor, Dir. Store Managers: Mary Thomas; Sandie Bailie.

STAMFORD. *Stamford Catholic Library*, 14 Peveril Rd., 06902. Tel: 203-348-4422. Mr. Nicholas Cognetta, Pres.; Rev. Robert G. Pohley, Chap.; Mary Louise Flowers, Contact Person.

WILTON. *Caroline House, Inc.*, 345 Belden Hill Rd., 06897.

St. Benedict Guild, Cannondale Depot, 06897. Tel: 203-762-3633. Marion Najamy, Mgr.

RELIGIOUS INSTITUTES OF MEN REPRESENTED IN THE DIOCESE

For further details refer to the corresponding bracketed number in the Religious Institutes of Men or Women section.

[0200]—*Benedictine Monks*.—O.S.B.

[0470]—*The Capuchin Friars*. (Prov. of St. Mary).—O.F.M.Cap.

[0270]—*Carmelite Fathers & Brothers*. (St. Elias Prov. New York).—O.Carm.

[0480]—*Conventual Franciscans*. (St. Anthony of Padua Prov.).—O.F.M.Conv.

[0490]—*Franciscan Brothers of Brooklyn*.—O.S.F.

[0520]—*Franciscan Friars*. (Commissariat of St. Stephen).—O.F.M.

[0650]—*Holy Ghost Fathers*. (Irish Prov.).—C.S.Sp.

[0690]—*Jesuit Fathers and Brothers*. (New England Prov.).—S.J.

[0870]—*Montfort Missionaries*. (Haitian Prov.).—S.M.M.

[0610]—*Priests of the Congregation of Holy Cross*. (Prov. of Our Lady of Holy Cross).—C.S.C.

RELIGIOUS INSTITUTES OF WOMEN REPRESENTED IN THE DIOCESE

[0130]—*Apostles of the Sacred Heart of Jesus*.—A.S.C.J.

[1810]—*Bernardine Sisters of the Third Order of St. Francis*.—O.S.F.

[0280]—*Brigittine Sisters*.—O.SS.S.

[0330]—*Carmelite Sisters for the Aged and Infirm*.—O.Carm.

[0710]—*Company of the Savior*.—C.S.

[4030]—*Congregation of Sisters of St. Thomas of Villanova*.—S.S.T.V.

[0760]—*Daughters of Charity of St. Vincent de Paul*.—D.C.

[0740]—*Daughters of Charity of the Most Precious Blood*.

[0790]—*Daughters of Divine Charity*.—F.D.C.

[0820]—*Daughters of the Holy Spirit*.—D.H.S.

[0960]—*Daughters of Wisdom*.—D.W.

[1070]—*Dominican Sisters*.—O.P.

[1470]—*Franciscan Sisters of St. Joseph*.—F.S.S.J.

[1190]—*Franciscan Sisters of the Atonement*.—S.A.

[2575]—*Institute of the Sisters of Mercy of the Americas*.—R.S.M.

[2345]—*Little Workers of the Sacred Hearts of Jesus & Mary*.—P.O.S.C.

[2780]—*Missionary Sisters of the Most Blessed Sacrament*. (Spain).—M.SS.S.

[3430]—*Religious Teachers Filippini*.—M.P.F.

[2970]—*School Sisters of Notre Dame*.—S.S.N.D.

[]—*Sisters Minor of the Mary Immaculate*.—S.M.M.I.

[0590]—*Sisters of Charity of Saint Elizabeth, Convent Station*.—S.C.

[0620]—*Sisters of Charity of St. Louis*.—S.C.S.L.

[2990]—*Sisters of Notre Dame*.—S.N.D.

[3000]—*Sisters of Notre Dame de Namur*.—S.N.D.deN.

[3780]—*Sisters of Saints Cyril and Methodius*.—SS.C.M.

[3850]—*Sisters of St. Joseph of Chambery*.

[2980]—*Sisters of the Congregation de Notre Dame*.—C.N.D.

[1970]—*Sisters of the Holy Family of Nazareth*.—C.S.F.N.

[3480]—*Sisters of the Resurrection*. (Eastern Prov.).—C.R.

[2160]—*Sisters, Servants of the Immaculate Heart of Mary*.—I.H.M.

[4070]—*Society of the Sacred Heart*.—R.S.C.J.

[4130]—*Ursuline Sisters of the Congregation of Tildonk, Belgium*.—O.S.U.

DIOCESAN CEMETERIES

BRIDGEPORT. *St. Michael's*, 2205 Stratford Ave., 06497. Tel: 203-378-0404.

DANBURY. *St. Peter's*, Lake Ave. Exit, 06810. Tel: 203-743-9626.

GREENWICH. *Putnam*, 35 Parsonage Rd., 06830. Tel: 203-869-4828.

St. Mary's, 399 North St., 06830. Tel: 203-869-7026.

NEWTOWN. *Resurrection*, c/o St. Peter Cemetery, Lake Ave. Exit, 06810. Tel: 203-743-9626.

NORWALK. *St. John's & St. Mary's*, 223 Richards Ave., 06850. Tel: 203-838-4271.

STAMFORD. *Queen of Peace*, c/o St. John Cemetery, 25 Camp Ave., 06820. Tel: 203-322-0455.

St. John's, 25 Camp Ave., 06820. Tel: 203-322-0455.

TRUMBULL. *Gate of Heaven*, c/o St. Michael's, 2205 Stratford Ave., 06497. Tel: 203-378-0404.

WESTPORT. *Assumption Green Farms*, Kings Hwy., c/o St. John Cemetery, 223 Richards Ave., 06850. Tel: 203-838-4271.

NECROLOGY

† Bumstead, Rev. Msgr. John Joseph, Danbury, CT, St. Peter Parish. —Died June 20, 1996.

† Galla, Rev. Msgr. Francis George, Monroe, CT, Provincial House, Immaculate Heart of Mary Province, Sisters of the Holy Family of Nazareth. —Died Jan. 27, 1996.

† O'Malley, James Joseph, St. Rose Parish. —Died June 9, 1996.

† Torres-Frias, Rev. Msgr. Victor Joseph, (Retired). —Died Nov. 10, 1995.

Diocese of Brooklyn

(Dioecesis Bruklyniensis)

Most Reverend

THOMAS V. DAILY, D.D.

Sixth Bishop of Brooklyn; ordained January 10, 1952; appointed Auxiliary to the Archbishop of Boston and Titular Bishop of Bladia December 31, 1974; consecrated February 11, 1975; appointed First Bishop of Palm Beach July 17, 1984; appointed Sixth Bishop of Brooklyn February 20, 1990; took possession April 16, 1990; installed April 18, 1990. *Mailing Address: 75 Greene Ave., P.O. Box C, Brooklyn, NY, 11202.*

Chancery Office: 75 Greene Ave., P.O. Box C, Brooklyn, NY, 11202. Tel.: 718-399-5990; Fax: 718-399-5934.

Most Reverend

JOSEPH M. SULLIVAN, M.S.W., M.P.A., V.E.

Tenth Auxiliary to the Bishop of Brooklyn; ordained June 2, 1956; appointed Titular Bishop of Suliana October 7, 1980; episcopal ordination November 24, 1980. *Mailing Address: 378 Clermont Ave., Brooklyn, NY, 11238.*

Most Reverend

RENE A. VALERO, M.S.W.

Eleventh Auxiliary to the Bishop of Brooklyn; priestly ordination June 2, 1956; appointed Titular Bishop of Vicus Turris October 7, 1980; episcopal ordination November 24, 1980. *Res., 34-43 93rd St., Jackson Heights, NY, 11372.*

Most Reverend

IGNATIUS A. CATANELLO, PH.D.

Twelfth Auxiliary to the Bishop of Brooklyn; ordained May 28, 1966; appointed Titular Bishop of Deulto June 28, 1994; episcopal ordination August 22, 1994. *Res., 175-20 74th Ave., Flushing, NY, 11366.*

Most Reverend

GERALD M. BARBARITO, D.D., J.C.L.

Thirteenth Auxiliary to the Bishop of Brooklyn; ordained January 31, 1976; appointed Titular Bishop of Gisipa June 28, 1994; episcopal ordination August 22, 1994. *Mailing Address: 1956 Batchelder St., Brooklyn, NY, 11229.*

ESTABLISHED JULY 29, 1853.

Square Miles 179.25.

Comprises Kings and Queens Counties in the State of New York.

For legal titles of parishes and diocesan institutions, consult the Chancery Office. .

STATISTICAL OVERVIEW

Personnel	
Bishop	1
Auxiliary Bishops	4
Retired Bishops	1
Priests: Diocesan Active in Diocese	437
Priests: Active Outside Diocese	47
Priests: Diocesan in Foreign Missions	4
Priests: Retired, Sick or Absent	197
Number of Diocesan Priests	685
Religious Priests in Diocese	232
Extern Priests in Diocese	44
Ordinations:	
Diocesan Priests	2
Religious Priests	2
Transitional Deacons	7
Permanent Deacons in Diocese	164
Total Brothers	191
Total Sisters	1,572
Parishes	
Parishes	219
With Resident Pastor:	
Resident Diocesan Priests	189
Resident Religious Priests	23
Without Resident Pastor:	
Administered by Priests	7
Professional Ministry Personnel:	
Brothers	7
Sisters	199
Lay Ministers	167
Welfare	
Catholic Hospitals	4
Total Assisted	186,831
Health Care Centers	22
Total Assisted	1,251,643
Homes for the Aged	3
Total Assisted	600
Residential Care of Children	18
Total Assisted	8,500
Day Care and Extended Day Care Centers	15
Total Assisted	2,100
Specialized Homes	6
Total Assisted	526,713
Special Centers for Social Services	50
Total Assisted	38,000
Residential Care of Disabled	50
Total Assisted	1,630
Other Institutions	2,185
Total Assisted	3,187
Educational	
Seminaries, Diocesan	1
Students from This Diocese	16
Students from Other Diocese	1
Diocesan Students in Other Seminaries	33
Seminaries, Religious	2
Students Religious	16
Total Seminarians	65
Colleges and Universities	3
Total Students	20,739
High Schools, Diocesan and Parish	4
Total Students	1,933
High Schools, Private	18
Total Students	15,922
Elementary Schools, Diocesan and Parish	155
Total Students	55,067
Elementary Schools, Private	3
Total Students	509
Non-residential Schools for the Disabled	1
Total Students	91
Catechesis/Religious Education:	
High School Students	9,650
Elementary Students	46,000
Total Students Under Catholic Instruction	149,976
Teachers in the Diocese:	
Priests	10
Brothers	60
Sisters	310
Lay Teachers	3,065
Vital Statistics	
Receptions into the Church:	
Infant Baptism Totals	23,753
Adult Baptism Totals	835
Received into Full Communion	1,077
First Communions	15,456
Confirmations	11,779
Marriages:	
Catholic	4,604
Interfaith	480
Total Marriages	5,084
Deaths	12,744
Total Catholic Population	1,603,110
Total Population	4,207,649

Former Bishops—Rt. Rev. JOHN LOUGHLIN, D.D., First Bishop of Brooklyn; ord. Oct. 18, 1840; cons. Oct. 30, 1853; died Dec. 28, 1891.—Rt. Rev. CHARLES E. MCDONNELL, D.D., Second Bishop of Brooklyn; ord. May 19, 1878; cons. April 25, 1892; died Aug. 8, 1921.—Most Rev. THOMAS E. MOLLOY, D.D., Third Bishop of Brooklyn; ord. Sept. 19, 1908; cons. Second Auxiliary Bishop of Brooklyn, Oct. 3, 1920; appt. Bishop of Brooklyn, Nov. 21, 1921; installed Feb. 15, 1922; died Nov. 26, 1956.—Most Rev. BRYAN J. MCENTEGART, D.D., LL.D., Fourth Bishop of Brooklyn; ord. September 8, 1917; appt. Bishop of Ogdensburg, June 5, 1943; cons. August 3, 1943; appt. Rector of the Catholic University of America, Washington, DC, June 26, 1953; appt. Titular Bishop of Aradi, Aug. 19, 1953; appt. Bishop of Brooklyn, April 16, 1957; installed June 13, 1957; retired and appt. Titular Archbishop of Gabii, July 17, 1968; died Sept. 30, 1968.—Most Rev. FRANCIS J. MUGAVERO, D.D., Fifth Bishop of Brooklyn; ord. May 18, 1940; Bishop of Brooklyn; appt. July 15, 1968; cons. Sept. 12, 1968; installed Sept. 12, 1968; retired Feb. 20, 1990; died July 12, 1991.

Central Offices—75 Greene Ave., Brooklyn, 11238., Mailing Address: P.O. Box C, Brooklyn, 11202-3604. Tel: 718-399-5900. Office Hours: Mon.-Fri. 9-4:30.

Vicar General—Rev. Msgr. OTTO L. GARCIA, J.C.D., V.G., *75 Greene Ave., P.O. Box C, Brooklyn, 11202.* Tel: 718-399-5900.

Regional Bishop of Brooklyn West and Episcopal Vicar for Human Services—Most Rev. JOSEPH M. SULLIVAN, M.S.W., M.P.A., V.E., *191 Joralemon St., Brooklyn, 11201.* Tel: 718-722-6000.

Regional Bishop of Queens North and Episcopal Vicar for Elderly and Racial Concerns—Most Rev. RENE A. VALERO, M.S.W., V.E., *7200 Douglaston Pkwy., Douglaston, 11362.* Tel: 718-229-8001, Ext. 710; 700.

Regional Bishop of Queens South and Episcopal Vicar for Evangelization and Spiritual Development—Most Rev. IGNATIUS A. CANTANELLO, Ph.D., V.E., *St. John's University, St. John's Hall, Rm. 103, 8000 Utipia Pkwy., Jamaica, 11439.* Tel: 718-990-6161, Ext. 5490.

Regional Bishop of Brooklyn East and Episcopal Vicar for Ministry—Most Rev. GERALD M. BARBARITO, D.D., J.C.L., V.E., *1956 Batchelder St., Brooklyn, 11229.* Tel: 718-339-4639; Fax: 718-339-4587.

Episcopal Vicars-Territorial—Brooklyn West: Very Rev. RAYMOND F. CHAPPETTO, V.E., *St. Agatha, 702 48th St., Brooklyn, 11220.* Tel: 718-436-1080. Brooklyn East: Rev. Msgr. OCTAVIO CISNEROS, V.E., Curial Residence: *378 Clermont Ave., Brooklyn, 11238.* Tel: 718-638-0697. Queens South: Very Rev. DENIS M. HERRON, V.E., *Our Lady of Lourdes, 92-96 220th St., Queens Village, 11428.* Tel: 718-479-5111. Queens North: Rev. Msgr. ROBERT J. PAWSON, V.E., *Mary's Nativity, 46-02 Parson's Blvd., Flushing, 11355.* Tel: 718-359-5996.

Episcopal Vicar for Administration—Rev. Msgr. AUSTIN P. BENNETT, *75 Greene Ave., P.O. Box C, Brooklyn, 11202.* Tel: 718-399-5900.

Episcopal Vicar for Education—Rev. Msgr. VINCENT D. BREEN, *75 Greene Ave., P.O. Box C, Brooklyn, 11202.* Tel: 718-399-5900; Fax: 718-399-7224.

Chancery Office—75 Greene Ave., P.O. Box C., Brooklyn, 11202. Tel: 718-399-5990; Fax: 718-399-5934.

Chancellor—Rev. Msgr. OTTO L. GARCIA, J.C.D., V.G.

Vice-Chancellors—Revs. JOHN J. BROWN, S.T.L., J.C.L.; ANDREW J. VACCARI, J.C.L.

Diocesan Archivist—JOSEPH W. COEN, C.A., Mailing Address: *7200 Douglaston Pky., Douglaston, 11362.* Tel: 718-229-8001, Ext. 475.

Censors of Books—Rev. PETER I. VACCARI, S.T.L., *75 Greene Ave., P.O. Box C, Brooklyn, 11202.*

Secretary to the Diocesan Bishop—Rev. RALPH J. MARESCA, M.Div. Tel: 718-399-5970; Fax: 718-399-5975.

Masters of Ceremonies to Bishops—Bishop Daily—Rev. RALPH J. MARESCA, M.Div. *Bishop Sullivan*—Rev. Msgr. JOSEPH P. NAGLE; Revs. PATRICK J. FRAWLEY; MICHAEL J. HARDIMAN; MICHAEL A. CARRANO. *Bishop Valero*—Rev. Msgr. JAMES L. TAHANEY; Revs. JOHN F. BROGAN; JOHN COSTELLO; THOMAS V. DOYLE. *Bishop Catanello*—REVS. THOMAS G. CASERTA; JOSEPH T. HOLCOMB; GREGORY C. WIELUNSKI; ANDREW J. VACCARI. *Bishop Barbarito*—REVS. JOHN J. BROWN; VITO BUONANNO; JOSEPH R. GRIMALDI, J.C.L.; BRIAN P. DOWD.

Tribunal—7200 Douglaston Pkwy., Douglaston, 11362. Tel: 718-229-8131; Fax: 718-631-1339.

Officialis-Judicial Vicar—Rev. Msgr. EDWARD B. SCHARFENBERGER, S.T.L., J.C.L., J.D.

Vice Officiales-Associate Judicial Vicars—Revs. THOMAS CHENG, J.C.D., M.A.; GREGORY C. WIELUNSKI, J.C.D.; JOSEPH R. GRIMALDI, J.C.L.; HUGO BEDOYA, S.T.L., J.C.D.

Defenders of the Marriage Bond—Revs. JOHN J. BROWN, S.T.L., J.C.L.; ROBERT J. YOUNG, J.C.L.

Promoter of Justice—Rev. Msgr. WILLIAM A. VARVARO, P.A., S.T.D., J.C.D.

Attorneys and Counselors at Canon Law—Sr. M. JOSITA WALSH, R.S.M., M.A.; MARIA CHRISTINA PRINCE, M.A.; Sr. MARY PARRY, O.P., M.A.; Revs. JOHN D. CAPILLO, M.Div.; JOAQUIN SURAN, M.A., Ed.D., J.C.L.; THOMAS MACHALSKI, M.Div.; THOMAS F. LEACH, M.S.; SEAN G. OGLE, M.Div.; ANDREW J. VACCARI, J.C.L.; EDWARD G. BROPHY, M.Div.

Senior Priests, Episcopal Delegate for—Rev. JEFFREY T. DILLON, *7200 Douglaston Pkwy., Douglaston, 11362.* Tel: 718-229-8001, Ext. 411.

Religious, Episcopal Delegate for—Sr. JANE SCANLON, C.N.D., *75 Greene Ave., P.O. Box C, Brooklyn, 11202.* Tel: 718-399-5900.

The Brooklyn & Queens Asbestos Management Corp.—JAMES A. O'BRIEN, Exec. Dir., *7200 Douglaston Pkwy., Douglaston, 11362.* Tel: 718-229-8001, Ext. 320; 321.

Property Administration & Special Projects—Rev. WILLIAM F. KRLIS, Dir., *7200 Douglaston Pkwy., Douglaston, 11362.* Tel: 718-229-8001, Ext. 300; Fax: 718-631-1339.

Cemeteries—Rev. MICHAEL J. REID, Dir., *80-01 Metropolitan Ave., Middle Village, 11379.* Tel: 718-894-4888.

Development Office, Diocesan—Rev. Msgr. JOHN J. BRACKEN, Dir., *7200 Douglaston Pkwy., Douglaston, 11362.* Tel: 718-229-8001; Fax: 718-631-1339.

Education, Offices—(See Institutions Located in the Diocese for details).

Family Life Office—Rev. JOHN COSTELLO, S.T.L., Dir. ('89); Deacon LEON F. MILLER, Asst. Dir. for Hispanics, *7200 Douglaston Pkwy., Douglaston, 11362.* Tel: 718-229-8001, Ext. 342.

Finance, Diocesan Department of—Rev. Msgr. AUSTIN P. BENNETT, Dir.; Rev. THOMAS V. DOYLE, Asst.; Mr. FRANCIS W. GALLIGAN, Admin. JOSEPH MCCAFFREY, Admin., Special Projects, *75 Greene Ave., P.O. Box C, Brooklyn, 11202.* Tel: 718-399-5900; Fax: 718-399-5966.

Institutional Services—7200 Douglaston Pkwy., Douglaston, 11362. Tel: 718-229-8001, Ext. 100.

Liturgical Office—Rev. JOHN C. TOSI, Exec. Sec., *75 Greene Ave., P.O. Box C, Brooklyn, 11202.* Tel: 718-399-5980; Fax: 718-399-5930.

Mediation and Arbitration, Board of—Rev. Msgr. EDWARD J. BREEN, Exec. Sec., *Mailing Address: P.O. Box C, Brooklyn, 11202.*

Ministerial Development Program—Most Rev. GERALD M. BARBARITO, D.D., J.C.L., V.E., Dir., Newly Ordained & Ministry to Priests Programs, *1956 Batchelder St., Brooklyn, 11229.* Tel: 718-339-4639; Fax: 718-339-4587.

Newspaper "The Tablet"—Rev. ANTHONY S. DANNA, S.T.L., Assoc. Publisher; ED WILKINSON, Editor, *653 Hicks St., Brooklyn, 11231.* Tel: 718-858-3838.

Parish Service Corporation—Rev. Msgr. AUSTIN P. BENNETT, J.C.D., Dir. FLORENCE C. FLYNN, Admin., *75 Greene Ave., P.O. Box C, Brooklyn, 11202.* Tel: 718-399-5900.

Pension Office, Diocesan—Rev. THOMAS V. DOYLE, Dir. ANNMARIE FAHEY, Admin., *P.O. Box C, Brooklyn, 11202.* Tel: 718-399-5920; Fax: 718-399-5917.

Permanent Diaconate Program—Rev. Msgr. EDWARD V. WETTERER, Dir.; Deacon SALVATORE V. LICATA, Exec. Sec., *75 Greene Ave., P.O. Box C, Brooklyn, 11202.* Tel: 718-399-5900.

Personnel Office—Rev. Msgr. MARTIN P. BANNAN, Sec., Bishop for Clergy Personnel, *75 Greene Ave., P.O. Box C, Brooklyn, 11202.* Tel: 718-399-5941.

Assignment Board—The Secretary for Clergy Personnel, The Episcopal Vicars. Other members by appointment.

Personnel Board (Clergy)—Rev. Msgr. MARTIN P. BANNAN, Chm.

Propagation of the Faith—Rev. Msgr. JOHN J. CONDON, Dir., Office: *191 Joralemon St., P.O. Box 200, Brooklyn, 11202.* Tel: 718-875-4375.

Holy Childhood, Pontifical Association—Rev. Msgr. JOHN J. CONDON, Dir., *191 Joralemon St., P.O. Box 200, Brooklyn, 11202.*

Public Information Office—FRANK DEROSA, Dir., *75 Greene Ave., P.O. Box C, Brooklyn, 11202.* Tel: 718-399-5955; Fax: 718-399-5957.

Retirement Board (Priests)—Most Rev. RENE A. VALERO, M.S.W., V.E., Chm., *Mailing Address: 7200 Douglaston Pkwy., Douglaston, 11362.* Members: Rev. Msgr. AUSTIN P. BENNETT; Rev. Msgr. JOHN J. ANTONCIC; Rev. Msgr. MARTIN P. BANNAN; Rev. Msgr. OCTAVIO CISNEROS; Rev. Msgr. GEORGE T. DEAS; Rev. Msgr. GEORGE V. FOGARTY; Rev. Msgr. PETER V. KAIN; Revs. THOMAS F. BROSNAN; JOHN J. BROWN; JEFFREY T. DILLON; MICHAEL M. GREENE; PAUL V. JERVIS; MARCELLO J. LATONA; LEWIS H. MAYNARD; Mrs. PAT BRENNAN, R.N.; ANN C. CARROLL.

Vocations, Office of—Rev. MICHAEL G. TEDONE, Dir.; Sr. REGINA WILSON, I.H.M., Assoc. Dir., *75 Greene Ave., P.O. Box C, Brooklyn, 11202.* Tel: 718-399-5900.

Consultative Bodies

Presbyteral Council—Rev. Msgr. JOHN C. ANTONCIC, Exec. Sec.; Most Rev. JOSEPH M. SULLIVAN, M.S.W., M.P.A., V.E.; Most. Rev. RENE A. VALERO, M.S.W., V.E.; Most Rev. IGNATIUS A. CATANELLO, Ph.D., V.E.; Most Rev. GERALD M. BARBARITO, D.D., J.C.L., V.E.; Rev. Msgr. OTTO L. GARCIA, V.G.; Rev. Msgr. JOSEPH G. KONRAD, J.C.D.; Rev. Msgr. KEVIN B. NOONE; Rev. Msgr. MICHAEL J. PHILLIPS; Rev. Msgr. ED SCHARFENBERGER; Rev. Msgr. ANTHONY SHERMAN; Rev. Msgr. WILLIAM A. VARVARO; Very Rev. DENIS M. HERRON; Revs. THOMAS LEACH; DOMINICK CUTRONE; GUY A. MASSIE; PAUL W. JERVIS; JOHN BROWN; KEVIN MCBRIEN; SEAN G. OGLE, M.Div.; VICTOR ULTO, *75 Greene Ave., P.O. Box C, Brooklyn, 11202.*

Diocesan Budget Committee—Rev. Msgr. AUSTIN P. BENNETT, Chm.

Subcommittee for Schools—Rev. Msgr. VINCENT D. BREEN.

Subcommittee for Agencies—Rev. Msgr. JOHN J. BRACKEN.

Subcommittee for Parishes—Rev. RAYMOND W. KUTNER.

Diocesan Consultors—Rev. Msgr. OTTO L. GARCIA, J.C.D., V.G., Sec.; Most Rev. JOSEPH M. SULLIVAN, M.S.W., M.P.A., V.E.; Most Rev. RENE A. VALERO, M.S.W., V.E.; Most Rev. IGNATIUS A. CATANELLO, Ph.D., V.E.; Most Rev. GERALD M. BARBARITO, D.D., J.C.L., V.E.; Rev. Msgr. JAMES P. KING, P.A., V.G.; Rev. Msgr. KEVIN B. NOONE; Rev. Msgr. WILLIAM A. VARVARO; Revs. JOSEPH T. HOLCOMB; SEAN G. OGLE, M.Div., *75 Greene Ave., P.O. Box C, Brooklyn, 11202.*

Diocesan Pastoral Council—CARL DE FREITAS-POLLONAIS, Pres. DANIEL S. MURPHY, Liaison Officer,*6713 Ridge Blvd., Brooklyn, 11220.*

Brothers' Senate—Bro. LAWRENCE SEWARD, S.C., *71-06 31st Ave., East Elmhurst, 11370.* Tel: 718-898-9600.

Commissions and Offices for Pastoral Services

Alcoholism Committee—Rev. Msgr. KIERAN MARTIN, Chm., *1550 Hendrickson St., Brooklyn, 11234.* Tel: 718-951-7302; Fax: 718-951-7233.

Art and Architecture Commission—Revs. JOHN C. TOSI, Exec. Sec. THOMAS G. PETTEI; VITO BUONANNO; CHARLES CACCAVALE; THOMAS V. DOYLE; Sr. MARY JANE KELLY, O.P., Office: *75 Greene Ave., P.O. Box C, Brooklyn, 11202.*

Black Ministry, Office of—MADELINE ANDERSON, Exec. Dir., *666 Essex St., Brooklyn, 11238.* Tel: 718-257-2570; Fax: 718-272-5412.

Hispanic Ministry, Office of—Rev. JOHN F. BROGAN, Dir., *7200 Douglaston Pkwy., Douglaston, 11362.* Tel: 718-229-8001, Ext. 741.

Catholic Consultation Center—Rev. MICHAEL R. PARISI, Ph.D., Dir. Counselors: Sr. MAUREEN ASHE, C.S.J., C.S.W.; JUSTINE JOHNSON, B.S.N., M.S.; ELIZABETH GATELY, Certified Counselor; VINCENT FOLEY, Ph.D., Staff Psychologist; ANNE M. PALEY, M.D., Psychiatrist, *7200 Douglaston Pkwy., Douglaston, 11362.* Tel: 718-279-1700.

Catholic Charities—Most Rev. JOSEPH M. SULLIVAN, Episcopal Vicar, Human Svcs. and Sec., Bishop for Charities, *191 Joralemon St., Brooklyn, 11201.* Tel: 718-722-6000; Fax: 718-643-0522.

Catholic Migration and Refugee Office—(See Institutions located in the Diocese for details).

Catholic Migration Services, Inc.—Rev. RONALD T. MARINO, Dir. Tel: 718-236-3000.

Diocesan Institute of Languages—7200 Douglaston Pkwy., Douglaston, 11362. Tel: 718-229-8001.

Chaplains and Uniformed Services, Official—Police Department: Rev. Msgr. JOHN P. MCCULLAGH; Fire Department: Rev. JOHN DELENDICK; Sanitation Department: Rev. VINCENT J. TERMINE; BMT Holy Name Society: Rev. Msgr. WILLIAM J. FLOOD.

Diocesan Building Commission—Revs. WILLIAM F. KRLIS, Chm. VINCENT M. DALY; JAMES J. MUELLER, S.T.L.; Rev. Msgr. KEVIN B. NOONE; Rev. GARY P. ROGERS; FRANK GALLIGAN, Consultant, Mailing Address: *7200 Douglaston Pkwy., Douglaston, 11362.*

Diocesan Real Estate Board—Revs. RAYMOND W. KUTNER, Chm.; JOSEPH D. COLBERT; JOHN DELENDICK; WILLIAM F. KRLIS; Mr. JOHN TYNAN, Mailing Address: *34-43 93rd St., Jackson Heights, 11372.*

Diocesan Food Service—Rev. Msgr. VINCENT A. KEANE, Dir., *7200 Douglaston Pkwy., Douglaston, 11362.* Tel: 718-229-8001, Ext. 100.

Ecumenical and Interreligious Affairs, Diocesan Commission for—Rev. Msgr. MICHAEL J. CANTLEY, S.T.D., Exec. Sec.

Committee for Eastern Orthodox-Catholic Relations—Prof. THOMAS E. BIRD, Chm.

Committee for Christian Relations—Rev. Msgr. MICHAEL J. CANTLEY, S.T.D., Chm.

Committee for Catholic-Jewish Relations—Rev. GUY MASSIE, M.Div.

Catholic Muslim Dialogue—Rev. MICHAEL LYNCH, S.T.L., Chm.

Evangelization Commission—Members: JUNE BAKER; Dr. THOMAS BIRD; Rev. ROBERT BLAUVELT; Rev. JOHN BROGAN; JOSEPHINE CACHIA; Rev. Msgr. MICHAEL J. CANTLEY; Rev. Msgr. OCTAVIO CISNEROS; Sr. PATRICIA CONROY; Rev. JOHN COSTELLO; Rev. JOSEPH DIELE; Sr. BERNADETTE DOWNES; ROBERT FALLON; Rev. Msgr. EUGENE FELDHAUS; Rev. JOSEPH MALAGRECA; Sr. PATRICIA O'BRIEN; RON RIZZUTO; Rev. GUY SANSARICG; Rev. Msgr. EDWARD SCHARFENBERGER; Rev. Msgr. ANTHONY SHERMAN; Rev. JOHN TOSI; MARY WING. Office of Religious Education: Rev. MICHAEL CARRANO; Rev. JOSEPH GIBINO; Sr. ALICE MICHAEL; JOAN SOKOLL; Sr. EILEEN SWEENEY; Episcopal Liaison: Most Rev. IGNATIUS A. CATANELLO; Auxiliary Bishop of Brooklyn Chair: JOAN SNOW; Executive Sec.: Rev. DENNIS MCAULIFFE, Ph.D. Tel: 718-492-1800.

Home School Association—Rev. Msgr. THOMAS A. GRAHAM. Tel: 718-525-9099.

Liturgical Commission—Rev. Msgr. EDWARD J. BREEN; Rev. Msgr. OCTAVIO CISNEROS; Revs. JOHN F. BROGAN; JOSEPH R. GIBINO; MARTIN F. KIRBY; EDWARD L. MAURER; Sr. MARY JANE KELLY, O.P.; Sr. MARY ALICE PIIL, C.S.J.; Sr. JULIE UPTON, R.S.M.; Mrs. JOAN SNOW; BRIAN ZUAR; Rev. JOHN C. TOSI, Exec. Sec., Office: *75 Greene Ave., P.O. Box C, Brooklyn, 11202.* Tel: 718-399-5980.

Music Commission—BRIAN ZUAR; Revs. PETER D. GILLEN; SEAN G. OGLE; JOHN C. TOSI, Exec. Sec.; Mrs. JOSEPHINE SANGES; EDWARD BURKARD; STEVEN R. GIUSTO; CHARLES MALLIA; MERRY A. NADDEO, Ed.D.; JOSEPH B. SMITH; Mr. EMMANUEL BOLOGNA; TERESA BRYANT; ROBERT ZAPPULLA; Dr. FRANK RETZEL, Mailing Address: *7200 Douglaston Pkwy., Douglaston, 11362.* Tel: 718-229-8001.

Pastoral Care of the Sick Office—(See Institutions located in the Diocese for details).

Pastoral Communications, Office of—Rev. Msgr. MICHAEL J. DEMPSEY, Dir., *1712 10th Ave., Brooklyn, 11215.* Tel: 718-499-9705. Legal Title: *Trans Video Communications, Inc.*

Pastoral Institute, Continuing Education of Priests—Rev. MARTIN F. KIRBY, S.S.L., Dir., General Course and Special Programs, *7200 Douglaston Pkwy., Douglaston, 11362.* Tel: 718-631-4267.

Prison Ministries Office—(See Listing Under Catholic Charities).

Religious Education, Office of—Evangelization and Catholic Formation: JOAN M. SNOW, Diocesan Dir.;

Sr. EILEEN SWEENEY, O.S.F., Dir. Elementary Religious Educ.; JOAN R. SOKOLL, Dir. Rel. Educ., Elementary; Rev. MICHAEL A. CORRANO, Dir. Youth Min. & Adolescent Catechesis/Dir. College Campus Min.; Sr. ALICE MICHAEL, Dir. Rel. Educ., Cultural & Ethnic Groups/Coord. R.C.I.A.; Rev. JOSEPH R. GIBINO, Dir. Adult Rel. Educ.; Rev. DENNIS MCAULIFFE, Ph.D., Coord. Evangelization.

Respect Life Office—EVELYN AQUILA, Dir., *75 Greene Ave., P.O. Box C, Brooklyn, 11202.* Tel: 718-399-5900.

Synod, Office of the—Rev. MICHAEL J. HARDIMAN, Dir., Mailing Address: *7200 Douglaston Pkwy., Douglaston, 11362.* Tel: 718-229-8001, Ext. 736; Fax: 718-428-4574.

Apostolic Organizations

Catholic Youth Organization, Diocesan—MICHAEL ABERNETHY, Dir., *191 Joralemon St., Brooklyn, 11201.* Tel: 718-596-5500, Ext. 234. JUDY AGEE, Queens Co. Dir. Tel: 718-779-1600.

Charismatic Groups, Catholic—

Charismatic Renewal (English-speaking) of the Diocese of Brooklyn—JOSEPHINE CACHIA, Dir. JOSEPHINE MCNALLY, Sec., *240 Jay St., Brooklyn, 11201.* Tel: 718-260-9111; Fax: 718-260-9121.

Renouveau Charismatique of the Diocese of Brooklyn—(serving the Haitian Charismatics of the Diocese); Rev. JOSEPH MALAGRECA, Dir., *218-26 105th Ave., Queens Village, 11429.* Tel: 718-465-0124; Fax: 718-479-3548.

Renovacion Carismatica of the Diocese of Brooklyn—(serving the Hispanic Charismatics of the Diocese); Rev. JOSEPH MALAGRECA, Dir., *218-26 105th Ave., Queens Village, 11429.* Tel: 718-465-0124; Fax: 718-479-3548.

Confraternity of the Guard of Honor and Confraternity of the Holy Hour—Rev. Msgr. THOMAS F. CRIBBIN, Dir., *St. Joseph's Residence, 256 Clinton Ave., Brooklyn, 11205.*

Confraternity of the Precious Blood—Rev. Msgr. JOSEPH K. PARKS, Dir.; Rev. Msgr. EDWARD T. BURKE, Assoc. Dir., *5300 Fort Hamilton Pkwy., Brooklyn, 11219.* Tel: 718-436-1120.

Guilds—

Accountants—Rev. Msgr. WALTER C. MURPHY, Dir.

Catholic Cemetery Guild—Rev. MICHAEL J. REID, Moderator.

Lawyers—Rev. EDWARD B. SCHARFENBERGER, S.T.L., J.C.L., J.D., Kings Co.; Rev. Msgr. THOMAS F. DONOVAN, Queens Co.

Pharmacists—Rev. Msgr. ALFRED A. VARRIALE, Dir.

Physicians—Rev. Msgr. JOSEPH C. KONRAD, J.C.D., Kings Co. Chapter Moderator.

Teachers—Rev. Msgr. THOMAS F. NOONAN, M.S., Dir.

Holy Name Society—Rev. RAYMOND MCKIERNAN, Moderator.

Marriage Encounter—Coords.: BOB NOBBS; MELINDA NOBBS. Tel: 718-805-7232.

National Council of Catholic Women—CLAIRE DUNNE, Pres.; Rev. Msgr. LAWRENCE J. MCALISTER, Spiritual Dir., *35-60 158th St., Flushing, 11358.*

Legion of Mary—Rev. Msgr. VINCENT F. FULLAM, Dir.; Rev. Msgr. JOSEPH ROSA, Spanish Curia; Deacon JEAN BAPTISTE BOURSIQUOT, Haitian Curia; Revs. JOSEPH AMN, Korean Curia; ALFRED WEINLICH, Flushing Curia; CHARLES REPOLE, O.F.M.Cap., N.W. Queens Curia; JOSEPH MARRIN, C.SS.R., Bay Ridge Curia, *82-00 35th Ave., Jackson Heights, 11372.* Tel: 718-429-2333.

Nocturnal Adoration Society—Rev. Msgr. JOHN F. WILSON, *245 Prospect Park W., Brooklyn, 11215.*

Priests' Eucharistic League—Rev. Msgr. JOHN F. WILSON, *245 Prospect Park W., Brooklyn, 11215.*

Sodality Union—Vacant.

St. John's Priests Relief Society—Rev. Msgr. GEORGE M. SCHUSTER, Pres.; Rev. Msgr. WILLIAM A. VARVARO, Recording Sec.; Rev. Msgr. WILLIAM FLOOD, 1st Vice Pres.; Rev. RAYMOND STAFFORD, 2nd Vice Pres. and Acting Treas.; Rev. MATTHEW W. SHERIDAN, Fin. Sec., *66-05 79th Rd., Middle Village, 11379.* Tel: 718-326-1911.

CLERGY, PARISHES, MISSIONS AND PAROCHIAL SCHOOLS

CITY OF NEW YORK
BOROUGH OF BROOKLYN

1—THE CATHEDRAL-BASILICA OF ST. JAMES (Jay St. at Tillary), Rev. John C. Tosi. In res., Rev. Msgr. Otto L. Garcia, J.C.D.; Rev. Joseph R. Gibino.
Res., 250 Cathedral Pl., 11201. Tel: 718-852-4002; Fax: 718-852-9452.

2—ST. AGATHA'S, Revs. Paul R. Sanchez; Lewis H. Maynard; Sr. Ann Heavey, R.S.M., Pastoral Assoc.; Deacons George M. Tokarcsik; Richard Vermilyea; Juan R. Vargas. In res., Very Rev. Raymond F. Chappetto, V.E.
Res., 702 48th St., 11220. Tel: 718-436-1080; Fax: 718-436-8870.
School—736 48th St., 11220. Tel: 718-435-3137; Fax: 718-437-7505. Sr. Mary Davies, O.P., Prin.
Sisters of Mercy 3; Lay Teachers 8; Students 282.
Catechesis/Religious Programs—Peggy Horgan, D.R.E.
Students 310.

3—ST. AGNES, Revs. John Delendick; George Manchapilly, C.M.I.; Deacon Aurelio Pagan. In res., Rev. Msgr. Guy Puglisi.
Res., 417 Sackett St., 11231. Tel: 718-625-1717; Fax: 718-625-1929.

4—ALL SAINTS, Rev. Donald J. Kenna.
Res., 115 Throop Ave., 11206. Tel: 718-388-1951; Fax: 718-388-7712.
School—113 Throop Ave., 11206. Tel: 718-782-0569. Ms. Mary Ann Rys, Prin.
Lay Teachers 9; Students 158.

5—ST. ALPHONSUS. Merged 1976. Records at St. Anthony of Padua-St. Alphonsus.

6—ST. AMBROSE. Merged 1978. Records at Our Lady of Monserrate-St. Ambrose.

7—ST. ANDREW THE APOSTLE, Rev. Daniel S. Murphy; Deacons Gregory Dixon; William Wander.
Res., 6713 Ridge Blvd., 11220. Tel: 718-680-1010; Fax: 718-680-3160.
Catechesis/Religious Programs—6725 Ridge Blvd., 11220. Tel: 718-630-5856; Fax: 718-630-5856.
Students 170.

8—ST. ANN-ST. GEORGE, Rev. Joseph Diele; Mr. Richard Carter, Pastoral Assoc.
Res., 207 York St., 11201. Tel: 718-625-0794; Fax: 718-625-4986.

9—ANNUNCIATION OF THE BLESSED VIRGIN MARY, Rev. Vytautas A. Palubinskas.
Res., 259 N. Fifth St., 11211. Tel: 718-387-2111; Fax: 718-782-4459.

10—ST. ANSELM'S, Rev. Msgr. Michael J. Phillips; Revs. Charles McLaughlin; Michael C. Gribbon; Joseph Vu; Deacon Thomas Davis. In res., Rev. Herbert A. Travis.
Res., 356 82nd St., 11209. Tel: 718-238-2900; Fax: 718-238-2902.
School—357 83rd St., 11209. Sr. Eileen Mary McMahon, S.S.N.D., Prin.
Sisters of Notre Dame 6; Lay Teachers 22; Students 670.
Catechesis/Religious Programs—Sr. Anne Bernadette, M.S.B.T., D.R.E.
Students 200.
Missionary Cenacle—351 83rd St., 11209. Tel: 718-836-0957. Sr. Regina Corde, O.P., Pastoral Ministry, Tel: 718-836-0780; Sr. Mary Gilmore, O.P. Missionary Servants of the Most Blessed Trinity 3.

11—ST. ANTHONY OF PADUA-ST. ALPHONSUS, Revs. John H. Reilly; David P. Bertolotti; Alberto Farinango, O.P.; Bro. Richard O'Brien, C.S.C. In res., Rev. Msgr. Anthony F. Passarella, Pastor Emeritus.
Res., 862 Manhattan Ave., 11222. Tel: 718-383-3339; Fax: 718-383-6958.
School—725 Leonard St., 11222. Tel: 718-383-5860; Fax: 718-389-5953.
Lay Teachers 18; Students 355.
Catechesis/Religious Programs—Tel: 718-383-6935. Rose Accetta, Prin.
Students 300.

12—ASSUMPTION OF THE BLESSED VIRGIN MARY, Rev. Msgr. Joseph A. Funaro. In res., Revs. John Cremins; Michael A. Carrano.
Res., 64 Middagh St., 11201. Tel: 718-625-1161; Fax: 718-625-7223.

13—ST. ATHANASIUS, Revs. Fernando A. Ferrarese, M.Div.; John J. O'Connor, S.L.L.; Thaddeus J. Kazanecki, C.O. In res., Rev. Msgr. David T. Dougherty, Pastor Emeritus; Rev. Dennis McAuliffe.
Res., 2154 61st St., 11204. Tel: 718-236-0124; Fax: 718-236-4960.
School—6120 Bay Pkwy., 11204. Sr. Elizabeth Schroeder, C.S.J., Prin.
Lay Teachers 15; Students 280.
Catechesis/Religious Programs—Tel: 718-331-8811; Fax: 718-331-2582.
Students 383.
Convent—2201 62nd St., 11204. Tel: 718-236-2680.

14—ST. AUGUSTINE, Revs. Robert J. Whelan; James G. Hannan; Deacon Joseph Bichotte. In res., Rev. Bernard R. Bonnot (Y).
Res., 116 Sixth Ave., 11217. Tel: 718-783-3132; Fax: 718-638-4669.

15—ST. BARBARA, Rev. Msgr. John J. Powis; Rev. Francis Shannon. In res., Rev. Peter A. Mahoney.
Res., 138 Bleecker St., 11221. Tel: 718-452-3660; Fax: 718-452-1279.

16—ST. BENEDICT'S. Closed. For inquiries for parish records contact the Chancery.

17—ST. BERNARD. Closed. For inquiries for parish records contact the Chancery.

18—ST. BERNADETTE, Revs. Robert J. Romano, M.Div.; Eugene P. Coyle; Thomas Kallumady. In res., Rev. Msgr. Cosmo G. Saporito, Pastor Emeritus; Rev. Msgr. Santi J. Primavera, Pastor Emeritus; Rev. David Dettmer.
Res., 8201 13th Ave., 11228. Tel: 718-837-3400; Fax: 718-236-5883.
School—1313 83rd St., 11228. Tel: 718-236-1560.
Religious Teachers Filippini 3; Lay Teachers 12; Students 308.

19—ST. BERNARD'S, Revs. Vincent J. Gallo; Edward R. Stewart; Deacon Frank J. D'Accordo. In res., Rev. Msgr. Thomas C. Clancey, Pastor Emeritus; Rev. Robert J. Whelan.
Res., 2055 E. 69th St., 11234. Tel: 718-763-5533; Fax: 718-763-0224.
School—2030 E. 69th St., 11234. Tel: 718-241-6040; Fax: 718-241-7258. Linda Mele, Prin.
Lay Teachers 17; Students 322.
Catechesis/Religious Programs—Tel: 718-444-4674.
Students 311.

20—ST. BLAISE. Merged with St. Francis of Assisi in 1980. Records at St. Francis of Assisi-St. Blaise.

21—BLESSED SACRAMENT, Revs. John E. Mahoney; James F. Fitzpatrick. In res., Rev. Msgr. Raymond Rau; Rev. Anselm E. Onuoha (Nigeria).
Res., 198 Euclid Ave., 11208. Tel: 718-827-1200; Fax: 718-827-2422.
School—187 Euclid Ave., 11208. Tel: 718-235-4863. Catherine Marlowe, Prin.
Lay Teachers 12; Students 315.
Catechesis/Religious Programs—Tel: 718-277-3231. Sr. Catherine Thornton, O.P., D.R.E.
Students 500.

22—ST. BONIFACE, Very Rev. Dennis M. Corrado, C.O., Pastor & Provost, Brooklyn Oratory; Rev. Mark Lane, C.O., D.R.E. In res., Rev. Terence Gleason, C.O.; Bros. James Simon, C.O.; Joel Warden, C.O.
Res., 109 Willoughby St., 11201. Tel: 718-875-2096; Fax: 718-875-4678.

23—ST. BRENDAN'S, Rev. Msgr. James B. McMahon; Rev. Richard E. Long.
Res., 1525 E. 12th St., 11230. Tel: 718-339-2828; Fax: 718-339-5951.

24—ST. BRIGID, Rev. Msgr. James J. Kelly; Revs. Michael M. Greene; Jose Herrera; Vincente Sanchez; Deacon Philip J. Ehresmann. In res., Rev. John H. Wilkinson.
Res., 409 Linden St., 11237. Tel: 718-821-1690; Fax: 718-386-4302.
School—438 Grove St. E., 11237. Tel: 718-821-1477. Francine Guastello, Prin.
Sisters 1; Lay Teachers 10; Students 280.
Catechesis/Religious Programs—Tel: 718-821-6401. Sr. Patricia Neary, O.P., D.R.E.
Students 910.

25—ST. CASIMIR (Polish). Merged with Our Lady of Czestochowa in 1980. Records at Our Lady of Czestochowa-St. Casimir.

26—ST. CATHARINE OF ALEXANDRIA, Revs. John S. Wtulich; Robert M. Powers.
Res., 1119 41st St., 11218. Tel: 718-436-5917; Fax: 718-871-5140.
School—1053 41st St., 11219. Tel: 718-436-9721; Fax: 718-853-3347.
Sisters, Religious Sisters of the Sacred Heart of Mary 1; Lay Teachers 9; Students 285.
Catechesis/Religious Programs—Tel: 718-438-2613. Sr. Rosalind Picciano, C.S.J., D.R.E.
Students 396.

27—ST. CATHERINE OF GENOA, Rev. Gerald Dumont; Deacon Louis Guastella.
Res., 520 Linden Blvd., 11203. Tel: 718-282-7162; Fax: 718-282-5568.
School—870 Albany Ave., 11203. Tel: 718-284-1050; Fax: 718-284-3461. Patricia Maio, Co-Prin.; Mary Blanchard, Co-Prin.
Lay Teachers 19; Students 404.

28—ST. CECILIA, Revs. Kevin J. O'Donoghue; Richard W. Conlon; Deacons Nicholas J. Mazza; Carlos Valderama. In res., Rev. Joseph F. Buckley.
Res., 84 Herbert St., 11222. Tel: 718-389-0010; Fax: 718-389-5090.
School—Tel: 718-389-3161. Sr. Miriam Daniels, C.S.J., Prin.
Sisters 5; Lay Teachers 14; Students 485.
Catechesis/Religious Programs—1-15 Monitor St., 11222. Tel: 718-389-2546. Bro. Philip Zeller, F.S.C., D.R.E.
Students 160.

29—ST. CHARLES BORROMEO, Rev. Charles A. Kraus; Rev. Msgr. Charles E. Diviney, Pastor Emeritus; Bro. Becket Ryan, O.S.F.; Deacon John Flannery.
Res., 21 Sidney Pl., 11201. Tel: 718-625-1177; Fax: 718-624-1627.
School—23 Sidney Pl., 11201. Tel: 718-596-1362; Fax: 718-875-9471. Sr. Eileen McGuire, C.S.J., Prin.
Sisters of St. Joseph 1; Lay Teachers 13; Students 206.
Catechesis/Religious Programs—Students 70.

30—ST. COLUMBA, Revs. Edward J. Kiernan; Anthony C. Casey; Sr. Emily Masse, O.P., Pastoral Assoc.; Deacon Lawrence Coyle. In res., Rev. James P. Collins.
Res., 2245 Kimball St., 11234. Tel: 718-338-6265; Fax: 718-377-6440.
Catechesis/Religious Programs—Tel: 718-253-8840. Nancy Azzaro, D.R.E.
Students 229.

31—ST. COLUMBKILLE. Closed. Parochial records are at SS. Cyril and Methodius. Became Mission in 1939.

32—SS. CYRIL AND METHODIUS (Polish), Revs. Joseph Mietelski, C.M.; Stephen J. Minkiel, C.M.; Tadeusz Maciejewski, C.M.
Res., 119 Eagle St., 11222. Tel: 718-389-4424; Fax: 718-389-4191.
School—96 Dupont St., 11222. Tel: 718-389-4926.
Sisters of the Holy Family of Nazareth 1; Lay Teachers 9; Students 142.

33—ST. DOMINIC, Revs. Arthur Minichello; Italo Barozzi; Sr. Margaret Cavanagh, O.P., Pastoral Min.; Deacons Carlo V. Mellace; Dante Colandrea.
Res., 2001 Bay Ridge Pkwy., 11204. Tel: 718-259-4636; 4637; 4638; Fax: 718-259-3066.
Catechesis/Religious Programs—Sr. Mary Jane Rolston, O.P., D.R.E., Tel: 718-259-6383.
Students 690.

34—ST. EDMUND'S, Rev. Msgr. Thomas F. Noonan; Revs. Brian P. Dowd; Edward R. Kane.
Res., 2460 Ocean Ave., 11229. Tel: 718-743-0102; Fax: 718-891-7834.
School—1902 Avenue T, 11229. Tel: 718-648-9229. Patricia O'Connor, Prin.
Lay Teachers 18; Students 375.
High School—Denis Maloney Institute, 2474 Ocean Ave., 11229. Tel: 718-743-6100; Fax: 718-743-5243. Mr. John Lorenzetti, Prin.; Rev. Joseph G. Fonti, Chap.
Sisters 2; Lay Teachers 30; Students 506.
Catechesis/Religious Programs—Tel: 718-743-8107. Marie Graham, D.R.E.
Students 255.

35—ST. EDWARD. Merged with St. Michael Archangel in 1942. Parochial records are at St. Michael-St. Edward, 108 St. Edwards St., 11205.

36—ST. EPHREM'S, Revs. Robert A. Moore, Senior Priest; James King; Joseph Giordano, C.I.C.M.; Deacon Charles C. DiTargiani. In res., Rev. David J. Dettmer; Deacons Wilfred Malone; Wilfred Horne.
Res., 929 75th St., 11228. Tel: 718-833-1010; Fax: 718-921-5232.
School—Tel: 718-833-1440; Fax: 718-745-5301. Ms. Joanne LoFaso, Prin.
Sisters, Servants of the Immaculate Heart of Mary 4; Lay Teachers 17; Students 368.
Catechesis/Religious Programs—Tel: 718-745-7486. Diane Mosconi, D.R.E.
Students 311.
Convent—935 75th St., 11228. Tel: 718-833-1555.

37—EPIPHANY, Rev. Msgr. Matthew F. Foley; Deacon Angel Baez.
Res., 96 S. Ninth St., 11211. Tel: 718-387-6328; Fax: 718-387-2449.
Catechesis/Religious Programs—Students 90.
Arriba Juntos—Forward Together, Inc. Center—96 S. Ninth St., 11211. Tel: 718-384-2121.

38—ST. FINBAR'S, Revs. Anthony J. Failla; Luke Wei; Deacon Giovanni Rizzo.
Res., 138 Bay 20th St., 11214. Tel: 718-236-3312; Fax: 718-236-3750.
School—1825 Bath Ave., 11214. Tel: 718-256-0818. Sr. Mary Hyacinth, C.S.A.C., Prin.
Sisters of the Catholic Apostolate 4; Lay Teachers 13; Students 220.
Catechesis/Religious Programs—Tel: 718-837-3935. Sr. Ann Joachim, C.S.A.C., D.R.E.
Students 380.

39—ST. FORTUNATA, Revs. James W. Ryan; Freddy Cintron. In res., Rev. Charles F. Harth, Pastor Emeritus.
Res., 2609 Linden Blvd., 11208. Tel: 718-647-2632; Fax: 718-647-1321.
School—Sisters of the Catholic Apostolate. (Pallottine) 2635 Linden Blvd., 11208. Tel: 718-647-6440; Fax: 718-647-2166. Miss Marian J. Siconolfi, Prin.
Lay Teachers 10; Students 262.
Catechesis/Religious Programs—Rev. Freddy Cintron, D.R.E.
Students 215.

40—FOURTEEN HOLY MARTYRS. Merged with St. Martin of Tours in 1976. Records at St. Martin of Tours-Fourteen Holy Martyrs.

41—ST. FRANCES CABRINI, Rev. Emilio J. Salerno.
Res., 35 Bay 11th St., 11228. Tel: 718-236-9165; Fax: 718-331-8139.
School—21 Bay 11th St., 11228. Tel: 718-232-6700. Sr. Martin Marie Doran, O.P., Prin.
Sisters of St. Dominic 2; Lay Teachers 8; Students 338.
Catechesis/Religious Programs—Tel: 718-232-4228. Eileen Maguire, D.R.E.
Students 340.

42—ST. FRANCES CABRINI CHAPEL. Attended by Sacred Hearts of Jesus and Mary and St. Stephen, 108 Carroll St., 11231. Tel: 718-596-7750.

43—ST. FRANCES DE CHANTAL, Revs. Arthur D. Purcell; Jose George (India); Andriej Lukianiuk. In res., Rev. Michael J. Hunt, Pastor Emeritus.
Res., 1273 58th St., 11219. Tel: 718-436-6407; Fax: 718-854-2761.
Catechesis/Religious Programs—Lay Teachers 18; Students 320.

44—ST. FRANCIS IN THE FIELDS. Closed. For inquiries for parish records contact the Chancery.

45—ST. FRANCIS OF ASSISI-ST. BLAISE, Revs. Gerard G. Pelletier, S.M.; Omer St. Onge, S.M.; Sante Inselvini, S.M.
Res., Tel: 718-756-2015; Fax: 718-756-1773.
Church—1081 Nostrand Ave., 11225.
School—Tel: 718-778-1300. Sr. Theresa Scanlon, C.S.J., Prin.
Sisters 4; Lay Teachers 17; Students 460.
Catechesis/Religious Programs—Tel: 718-778-1302. Mrs. Gilbert Verna, D.R.E.
Students 350.

46—ST. FRANCIS OF PAOLA (Italian), Rev. Andrew R. Varano.
Res., 219 Conselyea St., 11211. Tel: 718-387-0256; Fax: 718-387-6344.
Catechesis/Religious Programs—Students 85.

47—ST. FRANCIS XAVIER, Revs. Edward P. Doran; Stephen Placa; Deacons John Franca; James Ramos. In res., Revs. William A. Smith; Paul W. Farin; Michael Perry.
Res., 225 Sixth Ave., 11215. Tel: 718-638-1880; Fax: 718-638-2839.
School—763 President St., 11215. Tel: 718-857-2559. Sr. Kathleen Sullivan, C.S.J., Prin.
Sisters of St. Joseph 3; Lay Teachers 15; Students 520.
Catechesis/Religious Programs—Tel: 718-857-2903. Sr. Helene Conway, D.R.E.
Students 195.

48—ST. GABRIEL THE ARCHANGEL, Rev. Carlos Walker (Argentina). In res., Rev. Eduardo Coll (Argentina).
Res., 749 Linwood St., 11208. Tel: 718-257-0612; Fax: 718-257-6076.
Catechesis/Religious Programs—666 Essex St., 11208. Tel: 718-649-0450.
Students 228.

49—ST. GEORGE. Merged with St. Ann in 1986. Records at St. Ann-St. George.

50—GOOD SHEPHERD, Rev. Msgr. Thomas F. Brady; Revs. Richard M. Lewkiewicz; James K. Cunningham. In res., Rev. Msgr. Robert E. Welsh, Pastor Emeritus; Rev. Garvey G. Meade.
Res., 1950 Batchelder St., 11229. Tel: 718-998-2800; Fax: 718-382-5428.
School—1943 Brown St., 11229. Tel: 718-339-2745. Sr. Patricia Hanvey, Prin.
Sisters of St. Dominic 1; Lay Teachers 20; Students 506.
Catechesis/Religious Programs—Tel: 718-375-0899; Fax: 718-645-4513.
Students 405.

51—ST. GREGORY THE GREAT, Rev. Gary P. Rogers; Deacons Roy N. George; Andres De Leon, Jr.
Res., 224 Brooklyn Ave., 11213-2505. Tel: 718-773-0100; Fax: 718-773-4198.
School—991 St. Johns Pl., 11213-2532. Tel: 718-774-3330; Fax: 718-774-3332.
Lay Teachers 15; Students 300.
Catechesis/Religious Programs—Tel: 718-773-0100. Julia Bramwell, D.R.E.
Students 150.

52—GUARDIAN ANGEL, Rev. Msgr. Perfecto Vazquez; Rev. John Prakasam (India); Deacon Anthony J. Russo.
Res., 2978 Ocean Pkwy., 11235. Tel: 718-266-1561; Fax: 718-372-1603.
Catechesis/Religious Programs—Tel: 718-372-1967. Ariene Ambert, D.R.E.
Students 222.

53—HOLY CROSS, Rev. Msgr. Rollin J. Darbouze.
Res., 2530 Church Ave., 11226. Tel: 718-469-5900; Fax: 718-469-5901.
School—Tel: 718-282-1710. Sr. Angela Patrice Murray, C.S.J., Prin.
Sisters of St. Joseph 2; Lay Teachers 13; Students 240.
Catechesis/Religious Programs—Tel: 718-941-5066.
Students 470.

54—HOLY FAMILY, Rev. Thomas E. Fox; Deacon Hector Montalvo. In res., Revs. Anankwah Danquah (Ghana); Leo Nitural.
Res., 205 14th St., 11215. Tel: 718-768-0736; Fax: 718-832-2879.
Catechesis/Religious Programs—Students 160.

55—HOLY FAMILY, Revs. John A. McShane; Paul Vazhapilly. In res., Rev. Msgr. Raphael A. Florido, Pastor Emeritus; Rev. Joseph Pelligrin (Sierra Leone).
Res., 9719 Flatlands Ave., 11236. Tel: 718-257-4423; Fax: 718-257-4806.
School—216 Conklin Ave., 11236. Tel: 718-257-2954. Mary Lou Reitz, Prin.
Lay Teachers 15; Students 301.
Catechesis/Religious Programs—Tel: 718-257-8016; Fax: 718-257-4806. Elizabeth Mathew, D.R.E.
Students 340.

56—HOLY FAMILY (Slovak), Rev. Sebastian Kochuparackal, C.M.I. (India).
Res., 21 Nassau Ave., 11222. Tel: 718-388-5145.

57—HOLY INNOCENTS, Revs. Joseph J. Weber; Alfred R. Guthrie; Roger A. Pierre; Deacon Antoine Felix. In res., Rev. Robert Hume, Pastor Emeritus.
Res., 279 E. 17th St., 11226. Tel: 718-469-9500; Fax: 718-941-4931.
School—249 E. 17th St., 11226. Tel: 718-282-5294. Sr. Mary Immaculate, R.S.M., Prin.
Sisters of Mercy 3; Lay Teachers 13; Students 307.
Catechesis/Religious Programs—Tel: 718-469-8159.
Students 407.

58—HOLY NAME, Revs. Dennis J. Farrell; Raymond McKiernan; Matthew Manalel; Deacon Abel Torres. In res., Rev. Msgr. John F. Wilson, Pastor Emeritus.
Res., 245 Prospect Park W., 11215. Tel: 718-768-3071; Fax: 718-369-2039.
School—241 Prospect Park W., 11215. Tel: 718-768-7629. Robert Hughes, Prin. & D.R.E.
Sisters of St. Joseph 2; Lay Teachers 13; Students 227.
Catechesis/Religious Programs—243 Prospect Park W., 11215. Tel: 718-768-7003; Fax: 718-369-2039.
Students 250.

59—HOLY ROSARY, Rev. William Smith.
Res., 141 Chauncey St., 11233. Tel: 718-493-8001; Fax: 718-493-8002.
School—Sr. Kathleen Appier, Prin.; Sr. Cheryl Hillig, Vice Prin. Sisters 3; Lay Teachers 13; Students 350.

60—HOLY SPIRIT, Revs. Jerome T. Jecewiz; Varghese Vadakethayil (India); Deacon Wilfredo Hernandez.
Res., 1712 45th St., 11204. Tel: 718-436-5565; Fax: 718-436-5586.
School—1668 46th St., 11204. Tel: 718-633-3959.
Sisters of St. Joseph 2; Lay Teachers 7; Students 160.
Convent—1679 47th St., 11204.

61—MOST HOLY TRINITY, Revs. Ross Syracuse, O.F.M.Conv.; Santo Cricchio, O.F.M.Conv.; Bro. Vincent Vivian, O.F.M.Conv., Pastoral Assoc.
Res., 138 Montrose Ave., 11206. Tel: 718-384-0215; Fax: 718-384-3030.
School—140 Montrose Ave., 11206. Tel: 718-384-1101. Sr. Joseph Maureen Zick, O.P., Prin.

62—ST. IGNATIUS, Revs. John R. Hyatt, S.J.; Steven Pugliese, S.J.; Alfredo S. Quevedo, S.J.; Deacons Berthal Beaubrun; Jean-Baptiste Boursiquot.
Res., 1101 Carroll St., 11225. Tel: 718-774-2102; Fax: 718-774-5821.
Catechesis/Religious Programs—Students 260.

63—IMMACULATE CONCEPTION OF THE BLESSED VIRGIN MARY, Revs. Robert P. Morales, Admin.; Dagoberto Noguera (Colombia).
Res., 72 Maujer St., 11206. Tel: 718-384-0765; Fax: 718-384-2898.
Catechesis/Religious Programs—Students 140.

64—IMMACULATE HEART OF MARY, Revs. Patrick J. McNelis; John E. Capillo; James L. Tahaney; Charles Fermeglia. In res., Revs. Edward T. O'Connor, Pastor Emeritus; Barry W. Frazzitta.
Res., 2805 Ft. Hamilton Pkwy., 11218. Tel: 718-871-1310; Fax: 718-633-1866.
School—3002 Ft. Hamilton Pkwy., 11218. Tel: 718-438-7873. Sr. Theresa Sweeney, Prin.
Sisters 2; Lay Teachers 15; Students 301.
Catechesis/Religious Programs—Joyce Checkett, D.R.E., Tel: 718-854-7326.
Students 260.

65—ST. JEROME'S, Rev. Guy Sansaricq; Deacons Anthony Arthur; Magloire Marcel.
Res., 2900 Newkirk Ave., 11226. Tel: 718-462-0223;

Fax: 718-462-7753.
School—465 E. 29th St., 11226. Tel: 718-462-0211; Fax: 718-462-1828. Ms. Linda Mele, Prin. & D.R.E.
Sisters of Mercy 2; Lay Teachers 16; Students 453.
Catechesis/Religious Programs—Paul Norman, D.R.E.
Students 465.

66—ST. JOHN THE BAPTIST, Revs. Stephen M. Grozio, C.M.; Joseph V. Agostino, C.M.; John P. Timlin, C.M., Supr. In res., Rev. Thomas S. Krafinski, C.M.; Bro. Joseph Tauraso, C.M.
Res., 75 Lewis Ave., 11206. Tel: 718-455-6864; Fax: 718-452-3738.
School—82 Lewis Ave., 11206. Tel: 718-453-1000; Fax: 718-453-1000. Sr. Mary Jane Raeihle, C.S.J., Prin.
Sisters 3; Lay Teachers 21; Students 539.
Catechesis/Religious Programs—Sr. Patricia Evanick, D.C., D.R.E.
Students 190.

67—ST. JOHN CANTIUS, Rev. John A. Gurrieri; Deacon Rafael Marte. Pastoral Assocs.: Sr. Mary Alice MacKenzie, S.C.; Sr. Rita Rompre. In res., Rev. Msgr. Walter C. Galuszka, Pastor Emeritus; Rev. James Sweeney.
Res., 479 New Jersey Ave., 11207. Tel: 718-342-2679; Fax: 718-342-4878.
School—Tel: 718-385-7494. Mrs. Margaret Otunba, Prin.
Lay Teachers 10; Students 205.
Catechesis/Religious Programs—Students 355.

68—ST. JOHN THE EVANGELIST, Rev. Carlos D. Valencia.
Res., 250 21st St., 11215. Tel: 718-768-3751; Fax: 718-768-4689.

69—ST. JOHN'S CHAPEL. Closed. For inquiries for parish records contact the Chancery.

70—ST. JOSEPH'S, Rev. Robert Vitaglione; Sr. Genevieve Delaney, Pastoral Assoc.
Res., 856 Pacific St., 11238. Tel: 718-783-4500.
Catechesis/Religious Programs—Students 135.

71—ST. JOSEPH PATRON OF THE UNIVERSAL CHURCH. (Scalabrini Fathers). Revs. Gianni Agostinelli, C.S.; Francisco Huguet; Jairo Alfonso, C.S.
Res., 185 Suydam St., 11221. Tel: 718-386-0175; Fax: 718-821-1726.
School—St. Frances Cabrini, 181 Suydam St., 11221. Tel: 718-386-9277. Miss Maria Crifasi, Prin.
Lay Teachers 11; Students 220.

72—SHRINE CHURCH OF ST. JUDE, Revs. Mateo J. Rizzo; Frank Caggiano; Deacon Arthur J. Cuccia.
Res., 1677 Canarsie Rd., 11236. Tel: 718-763-6300; Fax: 718-531-9655.
School—1696 Canarsie Rd., 11236. Tel: 718-241-5533.
Sisters 1; Lay Teachers 13; Students 300.
Catechesis/Religious Programs—Mr. Ronald Rizzuto, D.R.E.
Students 300.
Convent—(Amityville) 2195 Canarsie Rd., 11236. Sisters of St. Dominic

73—ST. LAURENCE, Rev. Steven A. Ferrari; Sr. Theresa Agliardi, R.S.M., Pastoral Assoc.
Res., 1020 Van Siclen Ave., 11207. Tel: 718-649-0545; Fax: 718-649-1606.
Catechesis/Religious Programs—Tel: 718-927-3310. Sr. Mary Jareth, D.R.E.
Students 248.
Convent—990 Van Siclen Ave., 11207. Tel: 718-272-2875.
Sisters of Mercy, Brooklyn 3.

74—ST. LEONARD OF PORT MAURICE. Closed 1978. Records at St. Joseph, Patron of the Universal Church.

75—ST. LOUIS. Closed. Became a Mission of St. Lucy in 1939. Parochial records are at St. Lucy-St. Patrick's, 285 Willoughby Ave., 11205. Tel: 718-622-8748; Fax: 718-622-6330.

76—ST. LUCY-ST. PATRICK, Rev. William A. Smith; Sr. Patricia DeMarco, O.P., Pastoral Assoc.; Deacon Jose Ramos.
Res., 285 Willoughby Ave., 11205. Tel: 718-622-8748; Fax: 718-622-6330.
Catechesis/Religious Programs—Students 175.

77—ST. MALACHY'S, Revs. Raymond J. Kelly; Maximo Leoz; Sr. Diane Carollo, M.S.B.T., Pastoral Assoc. In res., Rev. Joseph W. Denzer.
Res., 207 Hendrix St., 11207. Tel: 718-647-5900.
Catechesis/Religious Programs—Tel: 718-235-3562. Sr. Diane Carollo, M.S.B.T., D.R.E.
Students 335.

78—ST. MARGARET MARY, Rev. William J. McLoughlin.
Res., 215 Exeter St., Manhattan Beach, 11235. Tel: 718-743-1824; Fax: 718-743-0232.

79—ST. MARK'S, Rev. Msgr. Gerard J. Arella; Revs. Cyril J. Doody; Benedict Barszcz, S.A.C. (Poland). Pastoral Assocs.: Sr. Gloria Lepere, O.P.; Deacon Mark Seliga. In res., Rev. Joseph P. Quigley.
Res., 2609 E. 19th St., 11235. Tel: 718-891-3100; Fax: 718-891-9677.
Church—Ocean Ave. & Avenue Z, 11235.
School—2602 E. 19th St., 11235. Tel: 718-332-9604; Fax: 718-891-9677. Sr. Catherine Roche, O.P., Prin.
Sisters of St. Dominic 3; Lay Teachers 11; Students 297.
Catechesis/Religious Programs—Tel: 718-769-6311. Sr. Florence Symes, C.S.J., D.R.E.
Students 375.

80—ST. MARTIN OF TOURS-FOURTEEN HOLY MARTYRS, Rev. Joseph M. Hoffman. In res., Rev. John F. Brogan.
Res., 1288 Hancock St., 11221. Tel: 718-443-8484; Fax: 718-443-2968.
School—See St. Elizabeth Seton under Consolidated Elementary Schools in the Institutions located in the Diocese. Tel: 718-386-4050.
Catechesis/Religious Programs—Sr. Mary Tully, D.R.E.
Students 215.

81—ST. MARY MOTHER OF JESUS, Rev. Msgr. Rocco D. Villani; Revs. Gregory A. Stankus; Angelo A. Venuti. In res., Rev. Msgr. Vincent D. Breen.
Res., 2326 84th St., 11214. Tel: 718-372-4000; Fax: 718-372-4002.
School—8401 23rd Ave., 11214. Sr. Thomasine Stagnitta, C.S.J., Prin.
Sisters of St. Joseph 7; Lay Teachers 19; Students 562.
Catechesis/Religious Programs—Sr. Patricia Conroy, R.S.M., D.R.E.
Students 722.

82—ST. MARY OF THE ANGELS (Lithuanian). Closed 1981. Records at Annunciation Parish, Brooklyn.

83—MARY QUEEN OF HEAVEN, Revs. John A. Burns; Eugene J. Stoklie; Robert J. McConnin; Deacons Charles J. Smith; John Joseph Murphy.
Res., 1395 E. 56th St., 11234. Tel: 718-763-2330; Fax: 718-763-6592.
School—1326 E. 57th St., 11234. Tel: 718-763-2360.
Sisters 1; Lay Teachers 15; Students 204.
Catechesis/Religious Programs—Tel: 718-763-2590.
Students 515.

84—ST. MARY, STAR OF THE SEA, Revs. Thomas J. O'Rourke; Robert S. Lawsine; Deacon Francis X. Nelson. In res., Rev. Benjamin Sebastian (India).
Res., 467 Court St., 11231. Tel: 718-625-2270; Fax: 718-624-9017.

85—ST. MATTHEW'S, Rev. Edward J. Smith; Deacons Florencio Cruz; Dennis A. DaCosta; Herve Desdunes.
Res., 1123 Eastern Pkwy., 11213. Tel: 718-774-6747; Fax: 718-953-4895.
Catechesis/Religious Programs—Sr. Christine Scherer, D.W., D.R.E.
Students 850.
Social Action Coord.—Sr. Dolores Augustine, P.V.M.I.

86—ST. MICHAEL'S, Revs. Michael J. Brennan; Ricardo Raveneau. In res., Rev. Youssef Bochra Nasri.
Res., 352 42nd St., 11232. Tel: 718-768-6065; Fax: 718-768-3336.
School—4222 Fourth Ave., 11232. Tel: 718-768-3582. Sr. Margaret M. Ford, C.S.J., Prin.
Sisters of St. Joseph 1; Lay Teachers 8; Students 240.
Catechesis/Religious Programs—Sr. Helene Jakubowski, R.S.M., D.R.E.
Students 206.

87—ST. MICHAEL'S, Revs. Brendan P. Buckley, O.F.M.Cap.; Philip F. Fabiano, O.F.M.Cap.; Deacon Leon Miller. In res., Revs. George Dash, O.F.M.Cap.; Raphael Iannoni, O.F.M.Cap., Supr.; William Hugo, O.F.M.Cap.
Res., 225 Jerome St., 11207. Tel: 718-647-1818; Fax: 718-647-2384.
School—Tel: 718-277-6766.
Catechesis/Religious Programs—Tel: 718-647-1818.
Students 238.

88—ST. MICHAEL ARCHANGEL AND ST. EDWARD, Rev. John A. Thompson.
Res., 108 St. Edward's St., 11205. Tel: 718-625-3017; Fax: 718-625-2536.

89—NATIVITY OF OUR BLESSED LORD. Merged with St. Peter Claver in 1973. Records at St. Peter Claver Church.

90—ST. NICHOLAS, Rev. Pedro Nel Ossa.
Res., 26 Olive St., 11211. Tel: 718-388-1420; Fax: 718-388-9516.
School—287 Powers St., 11211. Tel: 718-388-7992. Sr. Joan Losson, O.P., Prin.
Sisters of St. Dominic 4; Lay Teachers 10; Students 203.
Convent—312 De Voe St., 11211.

91—OUR LADY OF ANGELS, Rev. Msgr. James M. Cavanagh; Revs. Kenneth J. Calder; Louis J. DeGaetano; Bartholemew Egan, C.S.Sp.; Deacons Michael J. Troy; Martin B. Mulroy.
Res., 7320 Fourth Ave., 11209. Tel: 718-836-7200; Fax: 718-238-2466.
School—Mrs. Dorothy La Mere, Prin. Lay Teachers 16; Students 304.
Catechesis/Religious Programs—Sr. Lucille Aliperti, C.S.J., D.R.E.
Students 373.

92—OUR LADY OF CHARITY, Rev. Edward J. Smith, Admin.
Res., 1669 Dean St., 11213. Tel: 718-774-5100; Fax: 718-778-3335.
Catechesis/Religious Programs—Fax: 718-778-3338. Ethel Ando-Menson, D.R.E.
Students 60.

93—OUR LADY OF CONSOLATION (Polish), Revs. Wlodzimierz Las, S.D.S., (Poland) Admin.; Tadeusz Majcher, S.D.S. (Poland); Wieslaw P. Strzadala, S.D.S. (Poland).
Res., 184 Metropolitan Ave., 11211. Tel: 718-388-1942; Fax: 718-388-8993.

94—OUR LADY OF CZESTOCHOWA-ST. CASIMIR (Polish), Revs. Peter W. Zendzian; Stephen J. Jozwicki; Witold Mroziewski. In res., Rev. Joseph A. Cestaro.
Res., 183 25th St., 11232. Tel: 718-768-5724; Fax: 718-768-4996.
School—169 25th St., 11232. Tel: 718-768-8182.
Lay Teachers 10; Students 117.

95—OUR LADY OF GOOD COUNSEL, Revs. Marc Fallon, C.S.C.; James E. Fenstermaker, C.S.C. In res., Rev. Jerome R. Lawyer, C.S.C.; Bro. Lewis E. Morrow, C.S.C.
Res., 915 Putnam Ave., 11221. Tel: 718-443-7211; Fax: 718-443-0121.
Catechesis/Religious Programs—Sr. Rosalina Garcia, C.C.V., D.R.E.
Students 98.

96—OUR LADY OF GRACE, Revs. Dominick F. Cutrone; Barry W. Frazzitta; James L. Tighe; Sr. Jane Talbot, Pastoral Min.
Res., 430 Avenue W, 11223. Tel: 718-627-2020; Fax: 718-336-8033.
School—385 Avenue W, 11223. Tel: 718-375-2081; Fax: 718-376-7685. Mrs. Monica Crowley, Prin.
Lay Teachers 19; Students 344.
Catechesis/Religious Programs—Tel: 718-375-0404; Fax: 718-376-7685. Linda Nacinovich, D.R.E.
Students 300.

97—OUR LADY OF GUADALUPE, Rev. Msgr. Kevin B. Noone; Revs. Francis Gillen; Anthony J. Acciarito; John C. Miller; Sr. Ann Elizabeth, O.P, Pastoral Assoc. In res., Rev. Msgr. Angelo Brugli, Pastor Emeritus.
Res., 7201 Fifteenth Ave., 11228. Tel: 718-236-8300; Fax: 718-236-8119.
School—1518 73rd St., 11228. Tel: 718-331-2070. Sr. Lora Bannon, O.P., Prin.
Sisters of St. Joseph 1; Lay Teachers 21; Students 640.
Catechesis/Religious Programs—Tel: 718-331-4003. Mrs. Suzanne O'Connor, D.R.E.
Students 375.

98—OUR LADY HELP OF CHRISTIANS, Revs. Anthony M. Rucando; Joseph D. Pasciuto. In res., Rev. Guy Massie.
Res., 1315 E. 28th St., 11210. Tel: 718-338-5242; Fax: 718-258-5341.
School—1340 E. 29th St., 11210. Tel: 718-377-1800; Fax: 718-377-6374. Mrs. Patricia O'Farrell, Prin.
Sisters of Charity 1; Lay Teachers 12; Students 180.
Catechesis/Religious Programs—Tel: 718-377-6932; Fax: 718-258-5341. Mary Macchiarola, D.R.E.
Students 120.

99—OUR LADY OF LORETO, Rev. Msgr. James A. Hunt, Admin.; Rev. Fredi Rosales; Sr. Immaculata Kennedy, O.S.F., Pastoral Assoc. & D.R.E.
Res., 124 Sackman St., 11233. Tel: 718-385-3740; Fax: 718-385-3446.

100—OUR LADY OF LOURDES, Rev. Frank Capellupo.
Res., 11 DeSales Pl., 11207. Tel: 718-452-2260.
School—2-12 Aberdeen St., 11207. Tel: 718-455-0037.
Lay Teachers 10; Students 204.

101—OUR LADY OF MERCY, Rev. James H. Sweeney.
Res., 680 Mother Gaston Blvd., 11212. Tel: 718-346-3166; Fax: 718-346-5776.
Catechesis/Religious Programs—Sr. Bernadette Sassone, D.W., D.R.E.
Students 250.

102—OUR LADY OF MERCY. Closed 1908. Second church at Schermerhorn & Bond closed April, Debevoise Place & DeKalb Ave. For inquiries for parish records contact the chancery.

103—OUR LADY OF MIRACLES, Revs. Thomas F. Leach; Steven J. Aguggia. In res., Revs. Gennaro M. Simonetti, Pastor Emeritus; Giovanna Piccioli, Pastoral Outreach.
Res., 757 E. 86th St., 11236. Tel: 718-257-2400; Fax: 718-257-4634.

School—Tel: 718-649-0271; Fax: 718-649-3113. Sr. Anna Desiderio, C.S.J., Prin.
Sisters 1; Lay Teachers 10; Students 390.
Catechesis/Religious Programs—Sr. Carmel Ann Sperti, D.R.E., Tel: 718-649-1006.
Students 300.

104—OUR LADY OF MONSERRATE-ST. AMBROSE, Revs. Jaime Pico, C.M.; Robin E. Rodriguez, C.M.
Res., 134 Vernon Ave., 11206. Tel: 718-388-5196; Fax: 718-388-5153.
Catechesis/Religious Programs—Mrs. Justina Velqzquez, D.R.E.
Students 173.

105—SHRINE OF OUR LADY OF MOUNT CARMEL (Italian), Rev. Msgr. David L. Cassato; Rev. Carmelo Gagliardi, O.F.M.Cap. Pastoral Assocs.: Giuditta Coccia, O.A., Italian Apostolate; John S. Fruner; Deacon Joseph Occhiuto.
Res., 275 N. Eighth St., 11211. Tel: 718-384-0223; Fax: 718-384-5838.
School—Mt. Carmel Academy, 10 Withers St., 11211. Tel: 718-782-1110. Sr. Helen Gulczynski, C.S.J., Prin.
Catechesis/Religious Programs—Students 135.

106—OUR LADY OF PEACE (Italian), Revs. Roderick A. Crispo, O.F.M.; Bruno Ciardiello, O.F.M.
Res., 522 Carroll St., 11215. Tel: 718-624-5122; Fax: 718-852-6149.
Convent—209 First St., 11215. Tel: 718-624-6720; Fax: 718-852-6149. Hermanas Franciscanas de la Immaculada

107—OUR LADY OF PERPETUAL HELP BASILICA, Very Rev. Kevin Moley, C.SS.R., Pastor & Rector; Revs. Norman S. Bennett, C.SS.R.; Joseph Buono, C.SS.R.; Edward Byrne, C.SS.R.; Martin Crowe, C.SS.R.; Edward Dunne, C.SS.R.; Sylvester E. Feeley, C.SS.R.; Thomas F. Hickey, C.SS.R.; Joseph A. Keenan, C.SS.R.; Francis P. McElroy, C.SS.R.; John McGuire, C.SS.R.; Thomas J. McLellan, C.SS.R.; Thomas J. Maher, C.SS.R.; Joseph Marron, C.SS.R.; John J. Travers, C.SS.R. Pastoral Assocs.: Sr. Bernard Loretto, C.S.J.; Sr. Noraleen Murphy, C.S.J.; Deacons Abdon Mejia (Peru); Eduviges Lopez; Jesus Soto. In res., Most Rev. Ronald Connors, C.SS.R., (Retired).
Res., 526-59th St., 11220. Tel: 718-492-9200; Fax: 718-439-8528.
School—Tel: 718-492-8067; Fax: 718-439-8081. Sr. Madeline Therese DiCarlo, C.S.J., Prin.
Sisters 5; Lay Teachers 15; Students 322.
High School—Tel: 718-492-5800; Fax: 718-492-2588. Sr. Mary Febronia, C.S.J., Prin.
Sisters 10; Lay Teachers 18; Students 235.
Catechesis/Religious Programs—584 60th St., 11220. Tel: 718-492-4019.
Students 410.

108—OUR LADY OF THE PRESENTATION, Rev. Msgr. James A. Hunt; Rev. Fredi A. Rosales; Sr. Ann Reyes, O.P., Pastoral Assoc.; Deacons Joseph Francois; Jaime Landron.
Res., 1661 St. Marks Ave., 11233. Tel: 718-345-2604; Fax: 718-345-4639.

109—OUR LADY OF REFUGE, Revs. Andrew L. Struzzieri; Augustin Almyr.
Res., 2020 Foster Ave., 11210. Tel: 718-434-2090; Fax: 718-859-7411.
School—1087 Ocean Ave., 11230. Tel: 718-434-4117.
Sisters of St. Dominic 2; Lay Teachers 21; Students 502.

110—OUR LADY OF THE ROSARY OF POMPEII, Revs. Frank Amato, S.A.C.; Anthony Lorento, S.A.C.; Michael Salerno, S.A.C.; Bro. William Sharkey, S.A.C.
Res., 225 Siegel St., 11206. Tel: 718-497-0614; Fax: 718-366-3236.

111—OUR LADY OF SOLACE, Rev. Albert Bellantonio; Deacon Dan J. Marley.
Res., 2866 W. 17th St., 11224. Tel: 718-266-1612; Fax: 718-946-3651.
School—2865 W. 19th St., 11224. Tel: 718-372-0997. Mr. Robert P. Thomas, Prin.
Lay Teachers 12; Students 228.
Catechesis/Religious Programs—Mr. Nelson Caraballo, D.R.E.
Students 259.

112—OUR LADY OF SORROWS. Merged with St. Leonard in 1942. Parochial records are at St. Joseph Patron of the Universal Church.

113—OUR LADY OF VICTORY, Revs. Martin J. Carter, S.A.; Martan Madison, S.A.
Res., 583 Throop Ave., 11216-2496. Tel: 718-574-5772; Fax: 718-919-2265.
Catechesis/Religious Programs—Students 100.

114—ST. PATRICK'S. Merged with St. Lucy's in 1974. Records at St. Lucy-St. Patrick's.

115—ST. PATRICK, Rev. Msgr. Fursey O'Toole; Revs. Martin Kull; Thomas Anastasio; Jamie J. Gigantiello; Sr. Jeanne Elaine, Pastoral Assoc. In res., Rev. Msgr. Joseph K. Parks, Pastor Emeritus; Rev. Msgr. Joseph T. Lahey; Deacon Charles Postler.
Res., 9511 Fourth Ave., 11209. Tel: 718-238-2600; Fax: 718-238-1508.
School—401 97th St., 11209. Tel: 718-833-0124; Fax: 718-238-6840. Mrs. Mary T. Biers, Prin.
Lay Teachers 18; Students 262.
Catechesis/Religious Programs—Miss Michelle Reid, D.R.E., Tel: 718-238-2600.
Students 262.

116—ST. PETER-ST. PAUL-OUR LADY OF PILAR, Revs. Gabriel D. Real, C.M., (Spain) Supr.; Astor L. Rodriguez, C.M., Pastoral Assoc.; Sr. Innocentia P. Lipari, M.S.B.T., Pastoral Svcs. In res., Revs. Jose Barcelo; Balduino Martinez, C.M. (Spain).
Res., 234 Congress St., 11201. Tel: 718-624-3425; Fax: 718-834-0380.
Catechesis/Religious Programs—Tel: 718-797-9262. Rev. Astor L. Rodriguez, C.M.
Lay Teachers 10; Students 250.

117—ST. PETER CLAVER, Rev. Patrick J. West.
Res., 29 Claver Pl., 11238. Tel: 718-622-4647; Fax: 718-622-3304.
Catechesis/Religious Programs—Students 70.

118—SS. PETER AND PAUL'S, Rev. Msgr. Agustin Ruiz. In res., Rev. Walter A. Mitchell.
Res., 71 S. Third St., 11211. Tel: 718-388-9576; Fax: 718-388-4735.
School—Tel: 718-388-1041. Sr. Teresa Chesnavage, Prin.
Lay Teachers 10; Students 224.
Catechesis/Religious Programs—Sr. Maria Monserrat.
Students 181.

119—MOST PRECIOUS BLOOD, Rev. Joseph Rosa.
Res., 70 Bay 47th St., 11214. Tel: 718-372-8022.
School—133-157 27th Ave., 11214. Tel: 718-373-7343.
Sisters 4; Lay Teachers 6; Students 215.
Catechesis/Religious Programs—Sr. M. DiLoretta, D.R.E.
Students 202.

120—QUEEN OF ALL SAINTS, Rev. Victor A. Ulto; Deacon Edward A. Aigbojie. In res., Revs. John J. Brown; Joseph Holcomb.
Res., 300 Vanderbilt Ave., 11205. Tel: 718-638-7625; 7626; Fax: 718-638-7393.
School—Lafayette & Vanderbilt Ave., 11205. Tel: 718-857-3114. Theresa Attianese, Prin.
Sisters 1; Lay Teachers 10; Students 240.
Catechesis/Religious Programs—Lay Teachers 13; Students 140.

121—REGINA PACIS VOTIVE SHRINE. Attended by St. Rosalia, 65 St. & 12th Ave.
1230 65th St., 11219. Tel: 718-236-0909; Fax: 718-236-5357.

122—RESURRECTION, Rev. Msgr. Francis J. Fahy; Rev. Msgr. Raymond R. Shevlin, Pastor Emeritus; Revs. Jerome J. Schmidt, Senior Priest; James T. O'Brien.
Res., 2325 Gerrittsen Ave., 11229. Tel: 718-743-7234; 7235.
School—2335 Gerrittsen Ave., 11229. Tel: 718-332-9806; Fax: 718-743-0152. Mrs. Susan Cappiello, Prin.
Sisters 1; Lay Teachers 10; Students 300.
Catechesis/Religious Programs—Tel: 718-891-0888; Fax: 718-743-0152. Mrs. Angela Parente, D.R.E.
Students 400.

123—RESURRECTION CATHOLIC COPTIC CHAPEL, Rev. Youssef Bochra Nasri, (Coptic Catholic Patriarchate).
Mailing Address: 352 42nd St., 11232. Tel: 718-965-0422.
Church—328 14th St., 11215. Tel: 718-499-6946.

124—ST. RITA'S, Rev. John T. Peyton; Deacon Ronald Ronacher.
Res., 275 Shepherd Ave., 11208. Tel: 718-647-4910; Fax: 718-827-2767.
School—280 Shepherd Ave., 11208. Tel: 718-647-6040. William Geasor, Prin.
Sisters 2; Lay Teachers 16; Students 525.
Catechesis/Religious Programs—Mrs. Annemarie Ronacher, D.R.E.
Students 345.

125—ST. ROCCO'S, Rev. Faustino Cordero. In res., Rev. George Ebejer.
Res., 216 27th St., 11232. Tel: 718-768-9798; Fax: 718-768-7742.
Catechesis/Religious Programs—Elsie De Jesus.
Students 144.

126—ST. ROSALIA-REGINA PACIS, Rev. Msgr. Dino M. Zeni; Revs. John Maduri; Edward A. Cassar; Deacon Joseph Cafiero. In res., Rev. Ronald T. Marino.
Res., 1230 65th St., 11219. Tel: 718-236-0909; Fax: 718-236-5357.
Center Regina Center, Inc.—1258 65th St., 11219. Tel: 718-232-4340.
School—1201 66th St., 11219. Tel: 718-236-8150. Mr. Vincent Tannacore, Prin.
Lay Teachers 15; Students 232.
Catechesis/Religious Programs—Tel: 718-331-5465. Mr. Vincent Tannacore, Dir.
Students 463.
Mission—Brooklyn, Regina Pacis Votive Shrine.

127—ST. ROSE OF LIMA, Revs. Joseph P. Byrns; Thomas B. Nohilly.
Res., 269 Parkville Ave., 11230. Tel: 718-434-8040; Fax: 718-421-4223.
School—259 Parkville Ave., 11230. Tel: 718-434-1739.
Sisters of St. Joseph 3; Lay Teachers 11; Students 211.
Catechesis/Religious Programs—Fax: 718-421-4213.
Students 140.

128—SACRED HEART, Rev. Msgr. Walter C. Murphy; Sr. Eileen Neary, R.S.M., Pastoral Assoc. & D.R.E.
Res., 41 Adelphi St., 11205. Tel: 718-625-5115; Fax: 718-625-2918.

129—SACRED HEART CHAPEL. Closed. 1996. For inquiries for parish records contact the Chancery.

130—SACRED HEART MISSION. Closed. 1942. For inquiries for parish records contact the Chancery.

131—SACRED HEARTS OF JESUS AND MARY AND ST. STEPHEN, Rev. Msgr. Anthony S. Danna; Sr. Barbara Leonardo, M.S.C., Pastoral Assoc. In res., Revs. Charles J. Mariani; Vincent La Rocca; Charles Nichols; Nicholas Polichnowski, T.O.R.
Res., 108 Carroll St., 11231. Tel: 718-596-7750; Fax: 718-260-9233.
School—Tel: 718-625-2267.
Lay Teachers 10; Students 160.
Chapel—St. Frances Cabrini Chapel, Degraw St., 11231.
Day Care Center—56 Strong Pl., 11231. Tel: 718-624-2993.

132—ST. SAVIOUR, Rev. Msgr. Joseph P. Nagle; Rev. Kaleem Umrahn; Deacon William Williamsen.
Res., 611 Eighth Ave., 11215. Tel: 718-768-4055; 768-7983; Fax: 718-768-4872.
School—701 Eighth Ave., 11215. Tel: 718-768-8000. Mr. James Flanagan, Prin.
Lay Teachers 21; Students 413.
High School—588 Sixth St., 11215. Tel: 718-768-4406; Fax: 718-369-2688. Sr. Valeria Belanger, S.S.N.D., Prin.
Students 300.
Catechesis/Religious Programs—Tel: 718-768-4980; Fax: 718-768-4980.
Students 65.

133—SS. SIMON AND JUDE, Revs. Edward A. Floretta; John G. Hauser; Christopher Pliauplis.
Res., 185 Van Sicklen St., 11223. Tel: 718-375-9600; Fax: 718-375-6642.
School—Tel: 718-449-1857.
Lay Teachers 13; Students 204.
Catechesis/Religious Programs—Tel: 718-372-0733.
Students 400.

134—ST. STANISLAUS KOSTKA, Revs. Roman Gorowski, C.M.; Stanislaw Miekina, C.M.; Joseph Lachowski, C.M.; Edmund Gutowski, C.M.; Joseph Wisniewski, C.M.; Andrzej R. Kopystynski, C.M. In res., Rev. Jan Urbaniak, C.M.
Res., 607 Humboldt St., 11222. Tel: 718-388-0170; Fax: 718-384-5290.
School—10 Newel St., 11222. Tel: 718-383-1970; Fax: 718-384-5290. Sr. M. Marita Ruppe, Prin.
Priests 7; Sisters of the Holy Family of Nazareth 6; Lay Teachers 19; Students 418.
Catechesis/Religious Programs—Tel: 718-388-0170.
Students 352.

135—ST. STANISLAUS MARTYR. Merged with Holy Family (14th St.) in 1979. Records at Holy Family, 14th St., between Sixth and Seventh Aves.

136—ST. STEPHEN. Merged with Sacred Hearts in 1941. Parochial records are at Sacred Hearts-St. Stephen Church, Carroll St.

137—ST. SYLVESTER, Revs. Thomas M. Haggerty; Raymond C. Gruhn. In res., Rev. Charles P. Vogel.
Res., 416 Grant Ave., 11208. Tel: 718-647-1995; Fax: 718-348-4035.
School—396 Grant Ave., 11208. Tel: 718-235-4729. Carmen Padin, Prin.
Lay Teachers 11; Students 257.
Catechesis/Religious Programs—Tel: 718-647-6810.
Students 257.

138—ST. TERESA OF AVILA, Rev. Philip Pizzo.
Res., 563 Sterling Pl., 11238. Tel: 718-622-6500; Fax: 718-622-2234.
School—Tel: 718-638-5884. Mrs. Eleanor R. Menna, Prin.
Lay Teachers 12; Students 275.
Catechesis/Religious Programs—Students 103.

139—ST. THERESE OF LISIEUX. (The Little Flower). Revs. William M. Hoppe; Jean-Miguel Auguste; Deacon Mauclair Simon.
Res., 1281 Troy Ave., 11203. Tel: 718-451-1500; Fax: 718-451-1502.
School—4410 Avenue D, 11203. Tel: 718-629-9330; Fax: 718-451-1671. Sr. Paulette Pollina, R.S.M., Prin.
Sisters of Mercy 3; Lay Teachers 18; Students 404.
Catechesis/Religious Programs—Tel: 718-451-1671. Frances McCormick, D.R.E.
Students 202.

140—ST. THOMAS AQUINAS, Revs. James D. Hess, O.Carm., Prior; James Sidoti, O.Carm.; Matthew Faulkner, O.Carm.; Stanislaus Lewinski.
Res., 249 Ninth St., 11215. Tel: 718-768-9471; Fax: 718-965-4022.
School—211 Eighth St., 11215. Tel: 718-768-9007.
Sisters 1; Lay Teachers 9; Students 240.
Catechesis/Religious Programs—Tel: 718-768-9219. Sr. Mary Parry, O.P., D.R.E.
Students 182.

141—ST. THOMAS AQUINAS, Rev. Msgr. Brian F. Callahan; Revs. Joseph G. Fonti; Thomas J. Lyons; Deacons James Kennedy; Heebong B. Nam. In res., Rev. Msgr. Kieran J. Martin; Sr. Carole Fitzpatrick, C.S.J.
Res., 1550 Hendrickson St., 11234. Tel: 718-253-4404; Fax: 718-951-7573.
School—1501 Hendrickson St., 11234. Tel: 718-377-0442; Fax: 718-377-0442. Sr. M. Alice Traynor, O.S.U., Prin.
Lay Teachers 21; Students 390.
Catechesis/Religious Programs—Tel: 718-338-3542. Rev. Joseph G. Fonti, D.R.E.
Students 479.

142—TRANSFIGURATION, Rev. Msgr. Bryan J. Karvelis; Deacon German Martinez.
Res., 263 Marcy Ave., 11211. Tel: 718-388-8773; Fax: 718-387-6052.
School—Tel: 718-388-1120. Sr. Mary Anne Ricioppo, Prin.
Sisters 2; Lay Teachers 7; Students 275.
Catechesis/Religious Programs—Students 336.
Southside Mission for Social Services—280 Marcy Ave., 11211. Tel: 718-388-3784. Carmen Calderon, Dir.

143—ST. VINCENT DE PAUL, Rev. Richard J. McCormack. In res., Rev. Msgr. John P. McCullagh; Rev. Justo Beltran (Philippines).
Res., 167 N. Sixth St., 11211. Tel: 718-388-4218.
School—Mrs. Eileen Ogoff, Prin. Religious 1; Lay Teachers 9; Students 176.
Catechesis/Religious Programs—Students 15.

144—ST. VINCENT FERRER, Revs. Coman V. Brady; Raymond J. Dundon, Pastor Emeritus; Anthony P. Mullen, C.S.Sp. (Ireland); Mrs. Mary Anne Muller, Pastoral Assoc.
Res., 1603 Brooklyn Ave., 11210-3495. Tel: 718-859-0041; Fax: 718-859-9032.
Church—E. 37th St. & Glenwood Rd., 11210.
School—Tel: 718-859-3505. Ms. Jean Guy, Prin.
Lay Teachers 13; Students 328.
Catechesis/Religious Programs—Mary Anne Muller, D.R.E.
Students 320.

145—VISITATION OF THE BLESSED VIRGIN MARY, Rev. Msgr. John E. Waldron.
Res., 98 Richards St., 11231. Tel: 718-624-1572; Fax: 718-722-7748.
Catechesis/Religious Programs—Sr. Marjorie McHugh, R.S.M., D.R.E.
Students 166.

BOROUGH AND COUNTY OF QUEENS

146—ST. ADALBERT, Revs. Timothy Pasek, O.F.M.Conv., Guardian; Gerard Maciejewski, O.F.M.Conv.; Paul Miskiewicz, O.F.M.Conv.; John Kryzyanski, O.F.M.Conv.; Bro. Hugh Dymski, O.F.M.Conv.
Res., 52-29 83rd St., Elmhurst, 11373. Tel: 718-639-0212; Fax: 718-651-1705.
School—52-17 83rd St., Elmhurst, 11373. Tel: 718-424-2376.
Sisters 2; Lay Teachers 18; Students 399.
Catechesis/Religious Programs—Tel: 718-446-8622. Mary Hellman, D.R.E.
Students 115.
Office for Pastoral Care of the Sick—Tel: 718-429-2005.

147—ST. ALOYSIUS, Revs. Eugene F. McGovern; Luke Pham Anh Du; Anthony V. Dell'Anno; Deacon Fabio Flaim; Sr. Noemi Valdes, S.M.R., Min. to Homebound.
Res., 382 Onderdonk Ave., Ridgewood, 11385. Tel: 718-821-0231; Fax: 718-628-7304.
School—360 Seneca Ave., Ridgewood, 11385. Tel: 718-821-7384. Sr. Naomi Varrone, O.P., Prin.
Sisters of St. Dominic 2; Lay Teachers 11; Students 254.
Catechesis/Religious Programs—Tel: 718-417-6327. Blanche Ciangiulli, D.R.E.
Students 96.
Pastoral Care Office—Tel: 718-963-7687.

148—AMERICAN MARTYRS, Revs. John F. Keppler; John J. Murray. In res., Rev. Anthony S. Ercolano.
Res., 79-43 Bell Blvd., Bayside, 11364. Tel: 718-464-4582; Fax: 718-464-5488.
School—216-15 Peck Ave., Bayside, 11364. Tel: 718-776-3779. Sr. Maureen Coyne, O.P., Prin.
Religious 1; Lay Teachers 12; Students 276.
Catechesis/Religious Programs—Mrs. Carol Cella, D.R.E.
Students 250.

149—ST. ANASTASIA, Rev. Msgr. Michael J. Cantley; Revs. John J. Gribbon; George J. Lutjen; Francis J. Mann.
Res., 45-14 245th St., Douglaston, 11362. Tel: 718-631-4454; Fax: 718-631-1774.
School—45-11 245th St., Douglaston, 11362. Mrs. Christina Teisch, Prin.
Lay Teachers 18; Students 306.
Catechesis/Religious Programs—Tel: 718-225-5191. Florence Rose, D.R.E.
Students 340.

150—ST. ANDREW AVELLINO, Rev. Msgr. James P. Grace, S.T.L.; Revs. Matthew J. Diamond; Gerard T. Walker; Wilfred E. Dewan, C.S.P. In res., Rev. Msgr. Lawrence J. McAlister, Pastor Emeritus; Rev. John J. Costello, S.T.L.
Res., 35-60 158th St., Flushing, 11358. Tel: 718-359-0417; Fax: 718-539-2830.
School—35-50 158th St., Flushing, 11358. Tel: 718-359-7887; Fax: 718-359-2295.
Lay Teachers 19; Students 382.
Catechesis/Religious Programs—Tel: 718-445-7012; Fax: 718-539-2830.
Students 270.

151—ST. ANN'S, Revs. George A. Pfundstein; Joseph N. Grisaitis.
Res., 142-30 58th Ave., Flushing, 11355. Tel: 718-886-3890; Fax: 718-358-4964.
School—142-25 58th Rd., Flushing, 11355. Tel: 718-463-1238. Mrs. Elizabeth Vecchio, Prin.
Sisters 2; Lay Teachers 16; Students 398.
Catechesis/Religious Programs—Tel: 718-359-8019; Fax: 718-358-4964. Sr. Joan Hackett, C.S.J., D.R.E.
Students 150.

152—ST. ANTHONY OF PADUA, Revs. James J. Mueller; Thomas Muthukattil (India); Deacon J. Edward Joesten.
Res., 133-25 128th St., South Ozone Park, 11420. Tel: 718-843-7410; 843-3356; Fax: 718-659-1478.
School—125-18 Rockaway Blvd., South Ozone Park, 11420. Tel: 718-641-0212; Fax: 718-641-8079. Sr. Julia Mary, S.S.N.D., Prin.
School Sisters of Notre Dame 2; Lay Teachers 10; Students 408.
Catechesis/Religious Programs—Tel: 718-848-1127. Marcella Slobodzian, D.R.E.
Students 100.

153—ASCENSION, Revs. Charles A. Bleilevens; Daniel G. Keohane. In res., Revs. Wisdom Akalefu; Peter Chidi Osuangwa.
Res., 86-13 55th Ave., Elmhurst, 11373. Tel: 718-335-2626; Fax: 718-335-4181.
School—86-37 53rd Ave., Elmhurst, 11373. Tel: 718-335-9755.
Sisters 3; Lay Teachers 10; Students 310.
Catechesis/Religious Programs—Sr. Barbara Ann Haran, C.S.J., D.R.E.
Students 80.
Convent—53-04 Seabury St., Elmhurst, 11373. Tel: 718-446-8352. Sisters of St. Joseph

154—ST. BARTHOLOMEW'S, Rev. Msgr. James E. Gotimer; Revs. John J. Garkowski; Roque Fernandes (India); Eugene Soriano (Philippines).
Res., 43-22 Ithaca St., Elmhurst, 11373. Tel: 718-424-5400; Fax: 718-899-5257.
School—44-15 Judge St., Elmhurst, 11373. Tel: 718-446-7575.
Sisters of St. Dominic 4; Lay Teachers 32; Students 702.
Catechesis/Religious Programs—Tel: 718-898-0096. James Thompson, D.R.E.
Students 600.

155—ST. BENEDICT JOSEPH LABRE, Rev. Msgr. John H. O'Brien; Rev. Kevin P. Cavalluzzi; Deacon Angel R. Rivera. In res., Rev. Msgr. Thomas W. Hendel; Rev. John J. Jurgensen; Rev. Msgr. John J. Condon.
Res., 94-40 118th St., Richmond Hill, 11419. Tel: 718-849-4048; Fax: 718-856-0732.
School—94-25 117th St., Richmond Hill, 11419. Tel: 718-441-6674.
Sisters 3; Lay Teachers 18; Students 535.
Convent—94-24 118th St., Richmond Hill, 11419. Tel: 718-849-5571.

156—ST. BENEDICT, THE MOOR, Rev. Paul C. Palmiotto.
Res., 171-17 110th Ave., Jamaica, 11433. Tel: 718-526-4018.
Catechesis/Religious Programs—Caroll Forbes, D.R.E.
Students 40.

157—BLESSED SACRAMENT, Revs. Raymond W. Kutner; Jesus Cuadros; Patrick G. Burns; Deacon Roberto J. Pouso. In res., Most Rev. Rene A. Valero.
Res., 34-43 93rd St., Jackson Heights, 11372. Tel: 718-639-3888; Fax: 718-478-5536.
School—34-20 94th St., Jackson Heights, 11372. Tel: 718-446-4449; Fax: 718-446-5366.
Grey Nuns of the Sacred Heart 5; Lay Teachers 18; Students 430.

158—BLESSED VIRGIN MARY, HELP OF CHRISTIANS, Rev. Donald M. Berran; Deacon Kevin Ryan. In res., Revs. Thomas M. Catania; Donagh O'Meara.
Res., 70-31 48th Ave., Woodside, 11377. Tel: 718-672-4848; Fax: 718-457-4055.
School—70-20 47th Ave., Woodside, 11377. Donna Schroder, Prin.
Lay Teachers 14; Students 251.
Catechesis/Religious Programs—Tel: 718-672-4784; Fax: 718-651-0445. Sheila Smith Gonzalez, D.R.E.
Students 204.

159—ST. BONAVENTURE'S, Rev. Paul Palmiotto; Sr. Susan Smolinski, S.C., Pastoral Assoc. & D.R.E.; Deacon Harry Coleman.
Res., 114-58 170th St., Jamaica, 11434. Tel: 718-526-0040; Fax: 718-526-4825.
Catechesis/Religious Programs—Students 85.

160—ST. CAMILLUS, Revs. James M. Dunne; William F. Sweeney.
Res., 99-15 Rockaway Beach Blvd., Rockaway Beach, 11694. Tel: 718-634-8229; Fax: 718-634-8353.
School—185 Beach & 99th St., Rockaway Beach, 11694. Tel: 718-634-5260. Sr. Francis Bernadette, Prin.
Sisters of St. Joseph 2; Lay Teachers 10; Students 200.
Catechesis/Religious Programs—Tel: 718-474-3101. Sr. St. Claude, D.R.E.
Students 135.

161—ST. CATHERINE OF SIENNA, Rev. John J. Amann; Deacons James Burrell; Luis Taylor.
Res., 118-22 Riverton St., St. Albans, 11412. Tel: 718-528-1220; Fax: 718-528-7907.
School—Tel: 718-528-1857. Sr. Barbara Kradick, O.P., Prin.
Sisters of St. Dominic 3; Lay Teachers 19; Students 469.
Catechesis/Religious Programs—Sr. Mary Tropeano, C.S.J., D.R.E.
Students 113.

162—CHRIST THE KING, Revs. George F. Zatarga; Francisco J. Ares; Deacons Winston M. Mayers; John P. Coffey.
Res., 145-39 Farmers Blvd., Springfield Gardens, 11434. Tel: 718-528-6010; Fax: 718-949-3255.
Catechesis/Religious Programs—Deacon John D. Coffey, D.R.E.
Students 143.

163—ST. CLARE, Rev. Msgr. James Cooney; Revs. Edward G. Brophy; Louis Uzoh.
Res., 137-35 Brookville Blvd., Rosedale, 11422. Tel: 718-341-1018; Fax: 718-276-2001.
School—137-25 Brookville Blvd., Rosedale, 11422. Tel: 718-528-7174. Mr. Anthony Danile, Prin.
Lay Teachers 20; Students 525.
Catechesis/Religious Programs—Tel: 718-527-6153. Richard Pipchinski, D.R.E.
Students 130.

164—ST. CLEMENT POPE, Rev. Edward J. Brenkert; Deacon Robert Nero.
Res., 141-11 123rd Ave., Jamaica, 11436. Tel: 718-529-0273; Fax: 718-529-3089.
School—Tel: 718-659-9011. Sr. Ave Regina Laffey, Prin.
Religious 2; Lay Teachers 14; Students 360.
Catechesis/Religious Programs—Students 127.

165—CORPUS CHRISTI, Rev. Msgr. Richard F. Dunn; Rev. George Berrios (Venezuela); Deacon John O'Neill.
Res., 31-30 61st St., Woodside, 11377. Tel: 718-278-8114; Fax: 718-278-3619.
School—31-29 60th St., Woodside, 11377. Tel: 718-721-2484. Lucetta Darragh, Prin.
Lay Teachers 13; Students 270.
Catechesis/Religious Programs—Tel: 718-721-2484.
Students 146.

166—ST. ELIZABETH'S, Revs. Edward A. Ryan; Michael S. Melendez. In res., Rev. Thomas D. Dolan.
Res., 94-20 85th St., Ozone Park, 11416. Tel: 718-296-4900; Fax: 718-296-1140.
School—Tel: 718-641-6990. Sr. Francis Marie Sheridan, R.S.M., Prin.
Lay Teachers 12; Students 350.
Catechesis/Religious Programs—Tel: 718-738-3294. Sr. Patricia Anglin, O.P., D.R.E.

Students 127.

167—ST. FIDELIS, Revs. James E. Devlin; Ronald M. D'Antonio; Sr. Helen Muhlbauer, O.P., Pastoral Min.; Sr. Angela DiPaola, A.D.; Deacon Theodore J. Van de Van. In res., Rev. Peter J. Seeger, Pastor Emeritus; Rev. Msgr. William J. Osborne, Pastor Emeritus.
Res., 123-06 14th Ave., College Point, 11356. Tel: 718-445-6164; Fax: 718-445-1623.
School—124-06 14th Ave., College Point, 11356. Tel: 718-539-2628. Sr. Joan Martin, O.P., Prin.
Sisters of St. Dominic 3; Lay Teachers 20; Students 501.
Catechesis/Religious Programs—Tel: 718-359-1249. Joan Colombo, D.R.E.
Students 420.

168—ST. FRANCIS OF ASSISI, Rev. Leonard F. Badia, Ph.D.; Deacons John Sucich; Savior Hili. In res., Rev. Msgr. Thomas P. Campbell, Pastoral Emeritus.
Res., 21-17 45 St., Long Island City, 11105. Tel: 718-728-7801; Fax: 718-728-7853.
School—21-18 46th St., Astoria, 11105. Tel: 718-726-9405. Barbara McArdle, Prin.
Lay Teachers 20; Students 340.
Catechesis/Religious Programs—Tel: 718-278-0259.
Students 250.

169—ST. FRANCIS DE SALES, Rev. Msgr. Martin T. Geraghty; Rev. Michael Whelan; Deacon Robert Hitter.
Res., 129-16 Rockaway Beach Blvd., Belle Harbor, 11694. Tel: 718-634-6464; Fax: 718-634-0716.
School—216 Beach & 130th St., Belle Harbor, 11694. Tel: 718-634-2775. Sr. Patricia Chelius, C.S.J., Prin.
Sisters of St. Joseph 4; Lay Teachers 17; Students 607.
Catechesis/Religious Programs—Tel: 718-945-6911. Sr. Margaret Murphy, C.S.J., D.R.E.
Students 348.

170—ST. GABRIEL, Rev. Robert F. Barclay. In res., Revs. Celestine Anyanwu (Nigeria); Robert Titone.
Res., 26-26 98th St., East Elmhurst, 11369. Tel: 718-639-0474; Fax: 718-639-2810.
School—26-25 97th St., East Elmhurst, 11369. Tel: 718-426-7170; Fax: 718-426-1741. Bro. Edward Shields, F.S.C., Prin.
Sisters 2; Brothers 1; Lay Teachers 13; Students 380.
Catechesis/Religious Programs—Tel: 718-426-9577.
Students 95.

171—ST. GENEVIEVE, Rev. John Cullinane.
Res., 6 Beach 178 St., Rockaway Point, 11697. Tel: 718-634-7276; Fax: 718-318-7905.
Catechesis/Religious Programs—Students 49.

172—ST. GERARD MAJELLA, Rev. Msgr. James F. Spengler; Deacon Guillermo Gomez. In res., Rev. Msgr. Eugene A. Feldhaus, Senior Priest.
Res., 188-16 91st Ave., Hollis, 11423. Tel: 718-468-6565; Fax: 718-468-3136.
School—Tel: 718-468-1166.
Sisters 1; Lay Teachers 11; Students 325.

173—ST. GERTRUDE, Rev. Brendan W. Downing; Deacon Alfred L. Whelan.
Res., 336 Beach 38th St., Far Rockaway, 11691. Tel: 718-327-5673.

174—ST. GREGORY THE GREAT, Revs. Joseph L. Cunningham, S.T.L.; Kevin F. McBrien, S.T.L.
Res., 242-20 88th Ave., Bellerose, 11426. Tel: 718-347-3707; Fax: 718-343-0926.
School—244-44 87th Ave., Bellerose, 11426. Tel: 718-343-5053; Fax: 718-347-1142. Sr. Mary Arline Hornidge, O.P., Prin.
Sisters 3; Lay Teachers 24; Students 514.
Catechesis/Religious Programs—Tel: 718-347-0525. Regina Joyce, D.R.E.
Students 350.
Convent—88-19 Cross Island Pkwy., Bellerose, 11426.

175—ST. HELEN, Rev. Msgr. Joseph C. Pfeiffer; Revs. Richard Bretone; Francis J. Hughes; Sr. Hannah Marie Cox, P.B.V.M., Pastoral Assoc.; Deacon Anthony Cusumano.
Res., 157-10 83 St., Howard Beach, 11414. Tel: 718-738-1616; Fax: 718-835-5144.
School—83-09 157th Ave., Howard Beach, 11414. Tel: 718-835-4155.
Religious 2; Lay Teachers 14; Students 387.
Catechesis/Religious Programs—Tel: 718-835-6216.
Students 455.

176—HOLY CHILD JESUS, Rev. Msgr. John J. Antoncic; Revs. John J. Boylan; Joseph Saxe; William F. Krlis; Deacons Sal Licata; Dean Tully.
Res., 111-11 86th Ave., Richmond Hill, 11418. Tel: 718-847-1860; Fax: 718-847-2696.
School—112-02 86th Ave., Richmond Hill, 11418. Tel: 718-849-3988.
Sisters of St. Joseph 2; Lay Teachers 20; Students 415.
Catechesis/Religious Programs—Tel: 718-849-8560. Sr. Catherine Bernadette, M.S.B.T., D.R.E.
Students 360.
Missionary Cenacle—8622 112th St., Richmond Hill, 11418. Missionary Servants of the Most Blessed Trinity.

177—HOLY CROSS (Polish), Rev. Msgr. John J. Strynkowski, S.T.D.; Revs. Andrzej Kurowski, S.A.C. (Poland); Ryszard Koper (Poland); Rev. Msgr. Edward A. Fus, Pastor Emeritus.
Res., 61-21 56th Rd., Maspeth, 11378-2498. Tel: 718-894-1387; Fax: 718-416-9245.
School—56-01 61st St., Maspeth, 11378-2499. Tel: 718-894-2356. Sr. Rose Thelma Meckowski, C.S.F.N., Prin.
Sisters 1; Lay Teachers 9; Students 287.

178—HOLY FAMILY, Rev. Msgr. Joseph L. Stafford; Revs. Louis D. Aufiero, Pastoral Assoc.; Thaddeus Abraham (India). In res., Rev. Edward M. Keane; Most Rev. Ignatius Catanello, D.D.
Res., 175-20 74th Ave., Flushing, 11366. Tel: 718-969-2448; Fax: 718-591-6166.
School—75th Ave. & 175th St., Flushing, 11366. Tel: 718-969-2124. Sr. Matthew Mary Gay, C.S.J., Prin.
Sisters of St. Joseph 5; Lay Teachers 17; Students 403.
Catechesis/Religious Programs—Tel: 718-591-6438. Barbara Makolin, D.R.E.
Students 330.

179—HOLY TRINITY, Revs. Marcello J. Latona; Joseph A. Pfaff, D.R.E.; James F. Fraser. In res., Rev. James E. Sullivan, Senior Priest.
Res., 14-51 143rd St., Whitestone, 11357. Tel: 718-746-7730; Fax: 718-767-1368.
School—Tel: 718-746-1479; Fax: 718-746-4793. Janet Hengl, Prin.
Lay Teachers 15; Students 188.
Catechesis/Religious Programs—Students 175.

180—IMMACULATE CONCEPTION, Revs. Thomas Joyce, C.P.; James Price, C.P.; Theophane Cooney, C.P.
Res., 86-45 Edgerton Blvd., Jamaica, 11432. Tel: 718-739-0880; Fax: 718-657-0543.
School—179-14 Dalny Rd., Jamaica, 11432. Tel: 718-739-5933. Dr. Charlene Jaffie, Prin.
Sisters of St. Joseph 6; Lay Teachers 16; Students 430.
Catechesis/Religious Programs—86-16 Midland Pkwy., Jamaica, 11432. Tel: 718-291-3080. Sr. Elizabeth Gildea, C.S.J., D.R.E.
Students 247.

181—IMMACULATE CONCEPTION, Rev. Msgr. Charles P. Boccio; Rev. James W. Bukofsky. In res., Revs. James D. Gajere (Nigeria); Leo V. Rosero (Philippines).
Res., 21-47 29th St., Long Island City, 11105. Tel: 718-728-1613; Fax: 718-956-9229.
School—21-63 29th St., Long Island City, 11105. Tel: 718-728-1969. Sr. Jeanne Stegmann, S.U.S.C., Prin.
Sisters 2; Lay Teachers 19; Students 415.
Catechesis/Religious Programs—Tel: 718-956-4494. Marylyn Crum, D.R.E.
Students 345.
Convent—21-60 31st St., Long Island City, 11105.

182—THE INCARNATION, Rev. Msgr. John F. Casey; Rev. Robert J. Armato; Deacons Thomas F. Rogers; Francois Innocent. In res., Rev. Msgr. Edward J. Nolan, Pastor Emeritus.
Res., 89-43 Francis Lewis Blvd., Queens Village, 11427. Tel: 718-465-8534; Fax: 718-465-3834.
School—89-15 Francis Lewis Blvd., Queens Village, 11427. Tel: 718-465-5066; Fax: 718-464-4128. Sr. Ellen Patrice, Prin.
Sisters of St. Dominic (Amityville) 7; Lay Teachers 16; Students 510.
Catechesis/Religious Programs—Tel: 718-776-8956. Sr. Kathleen Thomas, O.P., D.R.E.
Students 180.

183—SS. JOACHIM AND ANNE, Revs. Joseph P. Malagreca; John W. Byrnes.
Res., 218-26 105 Ave., Queens Village, 11429. Tel: 718-465-0124; Fax: 718-479-3548.
School—218-19 105th Ave., Queens Village, 11429. Tel: 718-465-2230. Linda Freebes, Prin.
Sisters of Notre Dame de Namur 1; Lay Teachers 20; Students 565.
Catechesis/Religious Programs—Teresa Rosero.
Students 339.
Convent—St. Boniface 621 Elmont Rd., Elmont, 11003.

184—ST. JOAN OF ARC, Revs. John A. McGuirl; Timothy J. Hirten; Stephen Valdazo; Alexander G. Abugel; Rev. Msgr. James F. Donegan, Pastor Emeritus.
Res., 82-00 35th Ave., Jackson Heights, 11372. Tel: 718-429-2333; Fax: 718-672-5881.
School—35-27 82nd St., Jackson Heights, 11372. Tel: 718-639-9020. Linda C. Kelly, Prin.
Grey Nuns of the Sacred Heart 1; Lay Teachers 24; Students 552.
Catechesis/Religious Programs—Tel: 718-478-5593.
Students 263.

185—ST. JOHN VIANNEY, Rev. George M. Nicholson; Rev. Msgr. Celsius Collini, Admin.; Deacon John McGreevey.
Res., 140-10 34th Ave., Flushing, 11354. Tel: 718-762-7920; Fax: 718-460-8032.
Catechesis/Religious Programs—Eileen Nesi, D.R.E.
Students 160.

186—ST. JOSAPHAT (Polish), Rev. Msgr. Arthur A. Demski; Rev. Francis P. Bien. In res., Rev. Martin J. Sullivan.
Res., 34-32 210th St., Bayside, 11361. Tel: 718-229-1663; Fax: 718-229-8018.

187—ST. JOSEPH (Polish), Revs. Krzysztof Bugno, S.D.S. (Poland); Andrzej Waszczenko, S.D.S. (Poland).
Res., 108-43 Sutphin Blvd., Jamaica, 11435. Tel: 718-739-4781; Fax: 718-658-5447.

188—ST. JOSEPH, Revs. George J. Ryan; Michael J. McGee; Anthony J. Sansone; Deacon Felipe J. Alvarez.
Res., 43-19 30th Ave., Long Island City, 11103. Tel: 718-278-1611; Fax: 718-956-3589.
School—28-46 44th St., Long Island City, 11103. Tel: 718-728-0724.
Sisters of St. Dominic 3; Lay Teachers 29; Students 560.
Catechesis/Religious Programs—Tel: 718-545-7338.
Students 425.

189—ST. KEVIN, Rev. James T. Smith; Rev. Msgr. George V. Fogarty, Pastor Emeritus; Revs. John P. Maloney; Charles B. Kehoe. In res., Revs. Michael Parlsi; Paul A. Wood.
Res., 45-21 194 St., Flushing, 11358. Tel: 718-357-8888; Fax: 718-357-3671.
School—45-50 195th St., Flushing, 11358. Tel: 718-357-8110.
Sisters of Mercy (Dallas, PA) 3; Lay Teachers 23; Students 510.
Catechesis/Religious Programs—Tel: 718-357-5317. Mrs. Laura Stroligo, D.R.E.
Students 310.

190—ST. LEO, Revs. Charles P. Keeney; Thomas Ahern; Sr. Joan S. Dawber, S.C., Pastoral Assoc.; Deacon Rafael Diaz.
Res., 104-05 49th Ave., Corona, 11368. Tel: 718-592-7569; Fax: 718-271-6726.
School—104-19 49th Ave., Corona, 11368. Tel: 718-592-7050.
Lay Teachers 18; Students 424.
Catechesis/Religious Programs—Tel: 718-699-8565.
Students 424.
Mission—Brooklyn, Queens Co., Our Lady of Mount Carmel, 103-56 52nd Ave., Corona, 11368. Tel: 718-592-7569.

191—ST. LUKE, Rev. Msgr. Nicholas J. Capua; Revs. Joaquin S. Longres; Joseph F. Wilson; Deacon Harry A. Svebel. In res., Rev. Msgr. James W. Asip; Rev. John J. McVernon.
Res., 16-34 Clintonville St., Whitestone, 11357. Tel: 718-746-8102; Fax: 718-746-3589.
School—16-01 150th Pl., Whitestone, 11357. Tel: 718-746-3833. Jean Howlett, Prin.
Sisters of St. Dominic 3; Lay Teachers 20; Students 324.
Catechesis/Religious Programs—Tel: 718-746-3409. Theresa Mulgrew Agrusa, D.R.E.
Students 500.

192—ST. MARGARET'S, Rev. Msgr. William A. Varvaro; Revs. Brian M. Keller; Christopher Marcynski; Deacon Vincent F. DeBiase. In res., Revs. Gregory Wielunski; William R. Dulaney; Joseph F. Daly.
Res., 66-05 79th Pl., Middle Village, 11379. Tel: 718-326-1911; Fax: 718-326-1883.
School—66-10 80th St., Middle Village, 11379. Sr. Bridget Olwell, O.S.U., Prin.
Sisters of St. Dominic 4; Lay Teachers 19; Students 503.
Catechesis/Religious Programs—Margaret Walter, D.R.E.
Students 468.

193—ST. MARGARET MARY, Rev. Edmund P. Brady. Pastoral Assocs.: Sr. Maryann McHugh, C.S.J.; Sr. Judy Fay, C.S.J.
Res., 9-18 27th Ave., Long Island City, 11102. Tel: 718-721-9020; Fax: 718-278-0998.
Catechesis/Religious Programs—Sr. Judy Fay, C.S.J., D.R.E.
Students 125.

194—ST. MARY, Rev. Raymond F. Schmidt.
Res., 10-08 49th Ave., Long Island City, 11101. Tel: 718-786-0705.

Catechesis/Religious Programs—Fax: 718-482-7115.
Students 63.

195—St. Mary Gate of Heaven, Revs. Matthew Considine, S.M.M.; Bernard Brault, S.M.M.; James Brady, S.M.M.; Bros. Paul Llorens, S.M.M.; Richard Politte, S.M.M.; Deacons Michael Squillante; Thomas Heaphy; Richard Gilligan.
Res., 101-25 104th St., Ozone Park, 11416. Tel: 718-847-5957; Fax: 718-846-6489.
School—104-06 101st Ave., Ozone Park, 11416. Tel: 718-846-0689. Patrick Scannell, Prin.
Sisters 1; Lay Teachers 26; Students 602.
Catechesis/Religious Programs—Tel: 718-849-9329. Sr. Anne Werner, D.W., D.R.E.
Students 311.

196—St. Mary Magdalene, Rev. John Maloney; Deacon Lee C. Williams; Sr. Marian Jagiello, S.C.
Res., 218-12 136th Ave., Springfield Gardens, 11413. Tel: 718-949-4311; Fax: 718-528-7208.

197—Mary's Nativity, Rev. Msgr. Edward J. Bottino; Rev. Gary Sommermeyer. In res., Rev. Msgr. Robert J. Pawson, V.E.; Rev. Joseph F. Wiseman.
Res., 46-02 Parsons Blvd., Flushing, 11355. Tel: 718-359-5996; Fax: 718-939-6737.
School—146-28 Jasmine Ave., Flushing, 11355. Tel: 718-359-1800. Sr. Margaret T. Maloney, C.S.J., Prin.
Sisters of St. Joseph 7; Lay Teachers 9; Students 267.
Catechesis/Religious Programs—Tel: 718-353-5961. Donna Marie Sticco, D.R.E.
Students 250.

198—St. Mary Star of the Sea, Revs. Sean Ogle; Anthony Hernandez; Rev. Msgr. James J. McKenna, Pastor Emeritus; Deacon Martin Waldron.
Res., 1920 New Haven Ave., Far Rockaway, 11691. Tel: 718-327-1133; Fax: 718-327-3276.
School—595 Beach & 19th St., Far Rockaway, 11691. Tel: 718-327-2242. Miss Angela Brucia, Prin.
Priests 3; Lay Teachers 14; Students 330.
Catechesis/Religious Programs—1920 New Haven Ave., Far Rockaway, 11691. Sr. Kathy Hickey, C.S.J., Rel. Educ. Coord.
Students 353.

199—St. Matthias, Rev. Msgr. Anthony F. Sherman; Revs. James J.M. Reynolds; Richard J. Beuther; Deacons Gerard Steffens; John Sands. In res., Rev. Msgr. Joseph G. Konrad.
Res., 58-15 Catalpa Ave., Ridgewood, 11385. Tel: 718-821-6447; 6448; 6449; Fax: 718-821-6876.
School—58-25 Catalpa Ave., Ridgewood, 11385. Tel: 718-381-8003. Sr. Serafine Della Croce, S.S.N.D., Prin.
Sisters of Notre Dame 6; Lay Teachers 9; Students 329.
Catechesis/Religious Programs—Tel: 718-386-1077. Mrs. Carol E. Powell, D.R.E.
Students 450.

200—St. Mel, Rev. George R. Cowan; Rev. Msgr. James P. King, Senior Priest; Rev. Ralph Barile (TR). In res., Rev. August J. Iantosca.
Res., 28-20 154th St., Flushing, 11354. Tel: 718-886-0201; 886-0881; Fax: 718-886-0882.
School—154-24 26th Ave., Flushing, 11354. Tel: 718-539-8211. Sr. Mary Spencer, O.P., Prin.
Sisters 5; Lay Teachers 15; Students 439.
Catechesis/Religious Programs—Tel: 718-461-9840. Marie Hayes, D.R.E.
Students 261.

201—St. Michael, Rev. Msgr. Edward V. Wetterer; Revs. Jose R. Aldegunde; John Mendonca; Deacon Elias Yepes.
Res., 136-76 41st Ave., Flushing, 11355. Tel: 718-961-0295; 961-0182; Fax: 718-961-1403.
School—136-58 41st Ave., Flushing, 11355. Tel: 718-961-0246. Sr. Miriam Blake, C.S.J., Prin.
Sisters of St. Joseph 3; Lay Teachers 19; Students 460.
Catechesis/Religious Programs—Mrs. Zilia Hirsch, Coord.
Students 446.

202—St. Monica (Jamaican). Closed. For inquiries for parish records contact the Chancery.

203—Most Precious Blood, Rev. Raymond W. Stafford; Rev. Msgr. George T. Voiland, (Retired); Revs. Michael J. McHugh; Anton Bozanic (Yugoslavia); Vincent F. Miceli. In res., Rev. Andrew Niccoli (Yugoslavia) (Retired).
Res., 32-23 36th St., Long Island City, 11106. Tel: 718-278-3337.
School—32-52 37th St., Long Island City, 11106. Mr. Anthony Biscione, Prin.
Sisters of St. Joseph 4; Lay Teachers 23; Students 580.
Catechesis/Religious Programs—Tel: 718-721-9850; Fax: 718-278-3089.
Students 225.
Convent—36-16 36th St., Long Island City, 11106.

204—Nativity of the Blessed Virgin Mary, Rev. Msgr. Robert J. Thelen; Revs. Angelo B. Pezzullo; Edward M. Kachurka; Deacon Andrew A. Marchello. In res., Rev. Msgr. Dominick J. Adessa, P.E., Senior Priest.
Res., 101-41 91st St., Ozone Park, 11416. Tel: 718-845-3691; Fax: 718-845-8978.
School—101-60 92nd St., Ozone Park, 11416. Tel: 718-845-3074. Sr. Marguerite Torre, O.S.U., Prin.
Sisters 2; Lay Teachers 14; Students 418.
Catechesis/Religious Programs—Tel: 718-845-1524. Michael Rosa, D.R.E.
Students 300.

205—St. Nicholas of Tolentine, Revs. William F. Waters, O.S.A.; Richard M. Nahman, O.S.A.; James Keating, O.S.A.; Deacon Lionel Knight.
Res., 150-75 Goethals Ave., Jamaica, 11432. Tel: 718-969-3226; Fax: 718-380-0345.
School—80-22 Parsons Blvd., Jamaica, 11432. Tel: 718-380-1900. Sr. Elizabeth McNeelan, S.C., Prin.
Sisters of Charity (Halifax) 4; Lay Teachers 18; Students 500.
Catechesis/Religious Programs—Tel: 718-591-6536. Sr. Agnes Moylan, O.P., D.R.E.
Students 170.

206—Our Lady of the Angelus, Rev. Msgr. John R. Dwyer; Rev. James Hughes; Deacon Edwin Cancel. In res., Rev. Msgr. William T. Hickey, Pastoral Emeritus; Rev. Vincent A. Brown.
Res., 63-63 98th St., Rego Park, 11374. Tel: 718-897-4444; Fax: 718-897-1453.
School—Tel: 718-896-7220. Sr. Marietta Joseph Mackin, S.C., Prin.
Sisters 2; Lay Teachers 10; Students 245.
Catechesis/Religious Programs—Tel: 718-896-4388; Fax: 718-897-1453. Sr. Jo Ann Schwarz, D.R.E.
Students 300.

207—Our Lady of the Blessed Sacrament, Rev. Msgr. George T. Deas; Revs. William J. Rueger; Thomas C. Machalski. In res., Rev. Msgr. Robert M. Harris; Rev. Richard R. Viladesau (RVC).
Res., 34-24 203rd St., Bayside, 11361. Tel: 718-229-5929.
School—34-45 202nd St., Bayside, 11361. Tel: 718-229-4434.
Sisters 1; Lay Teachers 21; Students 486.
Catechesis/Religious Programs—Mary Mullaney, D.R.E.
Students 270.

208—Our Lady of the Cenacle, Rev. Msgr. Cornelius T. Kneafsey; Revs. Peter De Sanctis; Pablo Sans. In res., Revs. James P. Bradley; Mathew Kulapurath, Hospital Chaplain.
Res., 136-06 87th Ave., Richmond Hill, 11418. Tel: 718-291-2540; Fax: 718-291-2541.
School—Tel: 718-657-6690. Katherine Massell, Prin.
Sisters of Charity (Halifax) 2; Lay Teachers 14; Students 401.
Catechesis/Religious Programs—Roberta Van Buskirk, D.R.E.
Sisters 1; Lay Teachers 2; Students 320.

209—Our Lady of China Chapel, Revs. Thomas Sung, C.S.J.B. (Taiwan); Xavier Cai, S.J. (China).
Res., 54-09 92nd St., Elmhurst, 11373. Tel: 718-699-1929; Fax: 718-271-3215.
School—Tel: 718-699-1929.
Catechesis/Religious Programs—Students 870.
Chinese School—Ming Yuan Chinese School, Tel: 718-271-3944; Fax: 718-271-3215. See Monasteries and Residences for Priests and Brothers for the Religious Community.

210—Our Lady of Fatima, Rev. Msgr. Edward J. Breen; Revs. Eugene F. Donnelly; James Zona. In res., Revs. Patrick J. Frawley; Francis J. Passenant.
Res., 25-02 80th St., Jackson Heights, 11370. Tel: 718-899-2801; Fax: 718-429-6404.
School—25-38 80th St., Jackson Heights, 11370. Tel: 718-429-7031. Mrs. Cassie Zelic, Prin.
Sisters 1; Lay Teachers 26; Students 730.
Convent—25-56 80th St., Jackson Heights, 11370. Tel: 718-446-7097.

211—Our Lady of Grace, Rev. Msgr. William Flood; Rev. Vito A. Buonanno, M.Div.; Deacons Joseph Campisi; Edward Mergler. In res., Rev. Francis J. Labita; Rev. Msgr. Francis J. Evans, Pastor Emeritus.
Res., 100-05 159th Ave., Howard Beach, 11414. Tel: 718-843-6218; Fax: 718-738-8208.
School—158-12 101st St., Howard Beach, 11414. Tel: 718-848-7440; Fax: 718-641-3464. Sr. Loretto Crowe, O.S.U., Prin.
Ursuline Sisters 1; Lay Teachers 14; Students 430.
Catechesis/Religious Programs—Tel: 718-835-2765. Sr. Ann Martha, O.P., D.R.E.
Sisters 2; Students 200.

212—Our Lady of Hope, Rev. Msgr. Nicholas W. Sivillo; Rev. Gaetano J. Sbordone. In res., Rev. Joseph R. Grimaldi, M.Div.; Rev. Msgr. Anthony J. Barretta; Deacon Robert F. Lavanco.
Res., 61-27 71st St., Middle Village, 11379. Tel: 718-429-5438; Fax: 718-429-2764.
School—Tel: 718-258-3535; Fax: 718-458-9031.
Sisters 6; Lay Teachers 26; Students 739.
Catechesis/Religious Programs—Tel: 718-335-8394.
Students 210.

213—Our Lady of Lourdes, Rev. Msgr. Peter V. Kain; Rev. Donald Kavanagh; Deacon Warren Winkler. In res., Revs. Denis Herron, V.E.; John A. McNeill.
Res., 92-96 220th St., Queens Village, 11428. Tel: 718-479-5111; Fax: 718-479-0826.
School—92-80 220th St., Queens Village, 11428. Tel: 718-464-1480. Sr. Josephine Barbiere, C.S.J., Prin.
Lay Teachers 24; Students 464.
Catechesis/Religious Programs—Tel: 718-740-4090. Joanne Russo, D.R.E.
Students 360.

214—Our Lady of Mercy, Rev. Msgr. Gerald J. Langelier; Rev. William A. With; Deacon Edward Smolinski. In res., Rev. Msgr. Edward B. Scharfenberger.
Res., 70-01 Kessel St., Forest Hills, 11375. Tel: 718-268-6143; Fax: 718-544-3764.
School—70-25 Kessel St., Forest Hills, 11375. Tel: 718-793-2086.
Sisters Servants of the Immaculate Heart of Mary 5; Lay Teachers 14; Students 299.

215—Our Lady of the Miraculous Medal, Rev. Msgr. George M. Schuster; Rev. Michael J. Lynch; Deacon Jerome Krebs. In res., Revs. William T. Davis; Andrew J. Vaccari.
Res., 62-81 60th Pl., Ridgewood, 11385. Tel: 718-366-3360; Fax: 718-456-0564.
School—Bleecker & 61st St., Ridgewood, 11385. Tel: 718-821-2221. Ms. Margaret A. Baxter, Prin.
Lay Teachers 14; Students 264.
Catechesis/Religious Programs—Tel: 718-456-3275. Mary Macciaroli, D.R.E.
Students 419.

216—Our Lady of Mount Carmel, Revs. Frank Lynch; Joseph Pham; Anthony Raso. In res., Revs. Edmund P. Brady; Raymond P. Roden.
Res., 23-25 Newtown Ave., Long Island City, 11102. Tel: 718-278-1834; Fax: 718-278-0998.
School—25-15 Newtown Ave., Long Island City, 11102. Tel: 718-728-8376. Ms. Angela Fazio, Prin.
Lay Teachers 14; Students 340.
Catechesis/Religious Programs—Tel: 718-545-7987.
Students 200.

217—Our Lady of Perpetual Help, Revs. Edward W. Richards; Brian P. Dowd; George Koyikara Antony (India). In res., Rev. James T. Devine.
Res., 111-50 115th St., South Ozone Park, 11420. Tel: 718-843-1212; Fax: 718-843-3554.
School—111-10 115th St., South Ozone Park, 11420. Tel: 718-843-4184; Fax: 718-323-2333. Margaret Mahon, Prin.
Lay Teachers 20; Students 436.
Catechesis/Religious Programs—Thomas Columbia, D.R.E.
Students 251.

218—Our Lady, Queen of Martyrs, Rev. Msgr. Thomas J. Gradilone; Revs. Daniel Weiscopf; Thomas P. Murtagh; Deacon Thomas McCarthy. In res., Rev. Msgr. Michael J. Dempsey.
Res., 110-06 Queens Blvd., Forest Hills, 11375. Tel: 718-268-6251.
School—Sisters 2; Lay Teachers 12; Students 325.
Convent—109-04 72 Rd., Forest Hills, 11375.

219—Our Lady of the Skies Chapel, Rev. James T. Devine, Admin.
Church—Kennedy International Airport, International Arrivals Bldg., Second Floor, Jamaica, 11430. Tel: 718-656-5348; Fax: 718-656-8162.

220—Our Lady of the Snows, Revs. James C. Tugwood; Casper Furnari; George J. Stack; Deacons Henry J. Smith; Arthur Candreva; Leonard Sclafani.
Res., 258-15 80th Ave., Floral Park, 11004. Tel: 718-347-6070; Fax: 718-343-3221.
School—79-33 258th St., Floral Park, 11004. Tel: 718-343-1346. Sr. Roberta Oberle, Prin.
Sisters of St. Joseph 2; Lay Teachers 15; Students 480.
Catechesis/Religious Programs—Tel: 718-347-3511.
Students 480.

221—Our Lady of Sorrows, Revs. Thomas J. Healy; Lawrence Gellel, S.J.; Manuel Ros; Deacon Orlando Pascal. In res., Rev. Constantine V. Pesaresi, Pastor Emeritus.
Res., 104-11 37th Ave., Corona, 11368. Tel: 718-424-7554; Fax: 718-424-4910.
School—35-33 104th St., Corona, 11368. Tel: 718-426-5517. Sr. Katherine Hanrahan, C.S.J., Prin.
Sisters of St. Joseph 2; Lay Teachers 19; Students 387.

Catechesis/Religious Programs—Tel: 718-397-5312. Deacon Elias Yepes, D.R.E.
Lay Teachers 60; Students 975.

222—ST. PANCRAS, Revs. Joseph D. Colbert; John J. Fullum.
Res., 72-22 68th St., Glendale, 11385. Tel: 718-821-2323; Fax: 718-417-8021.
School—Myrtle Ave. & 68th St., Glendale, 11385. Tel: 718-821-6721. Sr. Jane Creighton, O.P., Prin.
Lay Teachers 14; Students 382.
Catechesis/Religious Programs—Tel: 718-479-0590. Mary E. McIntyre, D.R.E.
Students 350.

223—ST. PASCAL BAYLON, Rev. Msgr. Robert R. McCourt. Pastoral Assocs.: Sr. Mary Walsh, C.S.J.; Sr. Bernadette Walsh, S.S.N.D. In res., Rev. John W. Maloney.
Res., 112-43 198th St., St. Albans, 11412. Tel: 718-468-3511; Fax: 718-479-2303.
Catechesis/Religious Programs—Students 158.

224—ST. PATRICK, Rev. Robert M. Robinson, Admin. In res., Rev. Jean-Pierre Ruiz, S.T.D.
Res., 39-38 29th St., Long Island City, 11101. Tel: 718-729-6060; Fax: 718-729-1276.
Catechesis/Religious Programs—Tel: 718-937-1239. Sr. Flora Marinelli, D.R.E.
Students 125.

225—ST. PAUL THE APOSTLE, Revs. Paul W. Jervis; Joaquin Suran (Argentina); Jose Sanchez (Philippines).
Res., 98-16 55 Ave., Corona, 11368. Tel: 718-271-1100.

226—ST. PAUL CHONG HA-SANG ROMAN CATHOLIC CHAPEL (Korean Apostolate), Revs. Joseph S. Ahn (Korea); Thomas F. Brosnan; Deacon Paul M. Chin. In res., Revs. Thomas U. Jung (Korea) (Retired); John Park; Bro. Thomas Burns, C.S.C., D.R.E.
Office: 32-15 Parsons Blvd., Flushing, 11354. Tel: 718-321-7676; Fax: 718-321-7005.
Convent—32-15 Parsons Blvd., Flushing, 11354. Olivetan Benedictine Sisters
Catechesis/Religious Programs—D.R.E.: Bro. Thomas Burns, C.S.C.; Sr. Bonifacio Ro, O.S.B.; Sr. Bona Lee, O.S.B.
Students 600.
St. Augustine Yu Chin-gil Chapel: 2115 61st St., Brooklyn, 11204. Rev. Thomas F. Brosnan.; Korean Martyrs Chapel: 35-20 Greenpoint Ave., Long Island City, 11101. Rev. Garino Kim (Korea).

227—ST. PIUS V, Rev. Richard J. Ahlemeyer.
Res., 106-12 Liverpool St., Jamaica, 11435. Tel: 718-739-3731; Fax: 718-739-7086.

228—ST. PIUS X, Rev. Msgr. Thomas A. Graham; Revs. James F. Marron; Joachim Fernando (Sri Lanka). In res., Rev. Denis M. Dore, (Retired).
Res., 148-10 249th St., Rosedale, 11422. Tel: 718-525-9099; Fax: 718-276-2467.
School—147-65 249th St., Rosedale, 11422. Tel: 718-525-7171. John Toomey, Prin.
Religious of the Sacred Heart of Mary 1; Lay Teachers 9; Students 272.
Catechesis/Religious Programs—Marianne Gratto, D.R.E.
Students 167.

229—PRESENTATION OF THE BLESSED VIRGIN MARY, Rev. Msgr. Thomas M. O'Brien; Rev. Stephen Lynch.
Res., 88-19 Parsons Blvd., Jamaica, 11432. Tel: 718-739-0241; Fax: 718-739-2753.
Providence House III—159-23 89th Ave., Jamaica, 11432. Tel: 718-739-1348.
School—Tel: 718-739-2003. Sr. Judith Flanagan, O.P., Prin.
Lay Teachers 13; Students 320.
Catechesis/Religious Programs—Tel: 718-526-4152.
Students 352.

230—QUEEN OF ANGELS, Revs. Matthew W. Sheridan; Charles Caccavale; Deacon Juan Calvo.
Res., 44-04 Skillman Ave., Long Island City, 11104. Tel: 718-392-0011; 0012; Fax: 718-472-2625.
School—41-12 44th St., Long Island City, 11104. Tel: 718-786-2990. Sr. Mary Dolores, R.S.M., Prin.
Sisters of Mercy 2; Lay Teachers 10; Students 200.
Catechesis/Religious Programs—Tel: 718-937-5174.
Students 200.

231—QUEEN OF PEACE, Rev. Ralph J. Caputo. In res., Rev. Msgr. Celsus Collini, Pastor Emeritus; Rev. John C. Reilly, Pastor Emeritus.
Res., 141-36 77th Ave., Flushing, 11367. Tel: 718-380-5031; Fax: 718-969-2025.
School—141-25 77th Rd., Flushing, 11367. Tel: 718-969-3640; Fax: 718-969-5640. Dr. Joan A. Mestecky, Prin.
Lay Teachers 10; Students 350.
Convent—Tel: 718-380-4293. Sisters of St. Dominic

232—ST. RAPHAEL, Rev. James I.J. Frost.
Res., 35-20 Greenpoint Ave., Long Island City, 11101. Tel: 718-729-8957; Fax: 718-729-5238.
School—48-25 37th St., Long Island City, 11101. Tel: 718-784-0482. Sr. Maureen Ahlemeyer, P.B.V.M., Prin.
Sisters of the Presentation 2; Lay Teachers 13; Students 300.
Catechesis/Religious Programs—Students 80.

233—RESURRECTION-ASCENSION, Rev. Msgr. Joseph P. Bynon; Revs. Robert W. Blauvelt; Salvatore Amato. In res., Rev. Msgr. John J. Bracken; Rev. James S. Musumeci.
Res., 61-11 85th St., Rego Park, 11374. Tel: 718-424-5212; Fax: 718-639-8679.
School—85-25 61st Rd., Rego Park, 11374. Tel: 718-426-4963. Sr. Margaret Sweeney, C.S.J., Prin.
Sisters 2; Lay Teachers 17; Students 380.
Catechesis/Religious Programs—Tel: 718-533-7898.
Students 120.

234—ST. RITA, Rev. Msgr. Joseph A. Nugent; Deacon Vincent Parisi. In res., Revs. Michael G. Tedone; John Ugochukwu-Awka (Nigeria).
Res., 36-25 11th St., Long Island City, 11106. Tel: 718-361-1884; Fax: 718-472-9362.
School—36-14 12th St., Long Island City, 11106. Tel: 718-729-1594. Mrs. Anne Schaefer, Prin.
Sisters of St. Joseph 1; Lay Teachers 9; Students 173.
Catechesis/Religious Programs—Fax: 718-472-9362.
Students 155.

235—ST. ROBERT BELLARMINE, Rev. Msgr. John B. Lavin; Revs. Christopher J. Turczany; Salvatore L. Capolarello.
Res., 56-15 213th St., Bayside, 11364. Tel: 718-229-6465; Fax: 718-229-8126.
School—56-10 214th St., Bayside, 11364. Sr. Mary Ann Carotenuto, C.S.J., Prin.
Sisters of St. Joseph 6; Lay Teachers 18; Students 398.
Catechesis/Religious Programs—Students 204.

236—ST. ROSE OF LIMA, Revs. Peter D. Gillen; Francis J. McGee; Christopher L. Coleman.
Res., 130 Beach 84th St., Rockaway Beach, 11693. Tel: 718-634-7394; Fax: 718-474-7489.
School—154 Beach 84th St., Rockaway Beach, 11693. Tel: 718-474-7079. Mrs. Theresa Anderson, Prin.
Sisters 2; Lay Teachers 8; Students 234.
Catechesis/Religious Programs—Tel: 718-945-4850. Ms. Antoinette Camarda, D.R.E.
Students 120.

237—SACRED HEART OF JESUS, Rev. Msgr. Thomas F. Donovan; Revs. Kenneth J. Hand; Noel Moynihan; Sr. Kathleen Masterson, Pastoral Min.
Res., 215-35 38th Ave., Bayside, 11361. Tel: 718-428-2200; Fax: 718-428-5840.
School—216-33 38th Ave., Bayside, 11361. Tel: 718-631-4804. Dennis J. Farrell, Prin.
Lay Teachers 25; Students 525.
Catechesis/Religious Programs—Tel: 718-631-1307. Mrs. Georgette Lyons, D.R.E.
Students 250.

238—SACRED HEART, Revs. Joseph M. Nolan; Jean-Augustin Francois; Felix Akpabio (Nigeria); Sr. Margaret Mary Igoe, O.P., Pastoral Assoc.; Sr. Carmelle Nerette; Deacons Paul Dorsinville; Roy Dudley.
Res., 115-58 222 St., Cambria Heights, 11411. Tel: 718-528-0577; Fax: 718-341-0253.
School—115-50 221st St., Cambria Heights, 11411. Tel: 718-527-0123.
Lay Teachers 24; Students 386.
Catechesis/Religious Programs—Elizabeth Wright, D.R.E.
Students 120.

239—SACRED HEART, Rev. Msgr. John F. Hartmann; Rev. James Stapleton, C.S.P.; Deacons John P. Dennehy; Arthur A. Candreua. In res., Rev. Romano Zanon.
Res., 83-17 78th Ave., East Glendale, 11385. Tel: 718-821-6434; Fax: 718-497-2881.
School—84-05 78th Ave., East Glendale, 11385. Tel: 718-456-6636.
Sisters of St. Dominic 1; Lay Teachers 19; Students 374.
Catechesis/Religious Programs—Tel: 718-386-5616.
Students 311.

240—ST. SEBASTIAN, Rev. Msgr. D. Joseph Finnerty; Revs. Kenneth J. Grande; Christopher Cashman; Sabino Estrada; Deacon Stephen Damato.
Res., 39-63 57th St., Woodside, 11377. Tel: 718-429-4442; Fax: 718-429-7581.
School—39-68 58th St., Woodside, 11377. Sr. Kathleen Michael, S.C.H., Prin.
Sisters of Charity (Halifax) 2; Lay Teachers 19; Students 462.
Catechesis/Religious Programs—39-66 58th St., Woodside, 11377. Tel: 718-899-3341. Sr. Dolores Ryan, C.S.J., D.R.E.
Students 498.

241—ST. STANISLAUS BISHOP AND MARTYR, Revs. James J. Meszaros; Andrzej Gorczyca; Francis C. Romanowski, Pastor Emeritus.
Res., 88-10 102nd Ave., Ozone Park, 11416. Tel: 718-845-6206; Fax: 718-843-6408.
School—90-01 101st Ave., Ozone Park, 11416. Sr. Francis Marie, C.S.F.N., Prin.
Sisters of the Holy Family of Nazareth 1; Lay Teachers 8; Students 200.
Catechesis/Religious Programs—Dorothy Bonowitz, D.R.E.
Students 130.

242—ST. STANISLAUS KOSTKA, Revs. Michael J. Walsh, S.T.D.; Edward L. Maurer; Joseph Palackal, C.M.I (India).
Res., 57-15 61st St., Maspeth, 11378. Tel: 718-326-2185; Fax: 718-416-2108.
School—61-17 Grand Ave., Maspeth, 11378. Tel: 718-326-1815.
Lay Teachers 20; Students 345.
Catechesis/Religious Programs—Students 180.

243—ST. TERESA, Rev. Msgr. Lawrence E. Hinch; Revs. Colm Campbell (Ireland); Adnel Burgos. In res., Rev. Hugo Bedoya, C.M. (Colombia).
Res., 50-20 45th St., Woodside, 11377. Tel: 718-784-2123; Fax: 718-706-6797.
School—50-15 44th St., Woodside, 11377. Tel: 718-784-0178. Martin C. Abruzzo, Prin.
Lay Teachers 15; Students 278.
Catechesis/Religious Programs—Tel: 718-937-4819.
Students 350.

244—ST. TERESA OF AVILA, Revs. Vincent M. Daly; James J. Krische; Deacon Ramon Smith.
Res., 109-26 130th St., South Ozone Park, 11420. Tel: 718-529-3587; Fax: 718-529-0324.
School—Ms. Loretta Rybacki, Prin. Lay Teachers 12; Students 329.
Catechesis/Religious Programs—Elaine L'Etoile, D.R.E.
Students 225.

245—ST. THOMAS APOSTLE, Rev. Msgr. Joseph A. Martusciello; Revs. Felice J. De Laura; Martin Elekwachi (Nigeria).
Res., 87-19 88th Ave., Woodhaven, 11421. Tel: 718-847-1353; Fax: 718-849-3776.
School—87-49 87th St., Woodhaven, 11421.
Sisters 1; Lay Teachers 16; Students 347.
Catechesis/Religious Programs—Tel: 718-441-8409. Lorraine Hissiger, D.R.E.
Students 497.

246—ST. THOMAS MORE-ST. EDMUND, Rev. Msgr. Michael J. Connelly; Rev. Hugh A. Byrne; Deacons Bernard M. Deschier; Richard G. Lee.
Res., 204-25 Rockaway Point Blvd., Rockaway Point, 11697. Tel: 718-634-6357; Fax: 718-634-7900.

247—TRANSFIGURATION (Lithuanian), Rev. James T. Rooney. In res., Rev. Msgr. Francis J. Bulovas, Pastor Emeritus.
Res., 64-14 Clinton Ave., Maspeth, 11378. Tel: 718-326-2236; Fax: 718-326-2249.

248—ST. VIRGILIUS (Noel Rd.), Rev. Charles H. White.
Res., 210 Noel Rd., Broad Channel, 11693-1091. Tel: 718-634-5680; Fax: 718-474-1538.
School—Tel: 718-634-6237. Martha A. Accordino, Prin.
Lay Teachers 9; Students 176.
Catechesis/Religious Programs—Students 60.

Chaplains of Public Institutions

BROOKLYN. *Brookdale Hospital Medical Center*. Vacant.
Brooklyn Correctional Facility. Rev. Walter Mitchell.
Brooklyn House of Detention. Rev. Walter Mitchell.
The Brooklyn-Caledonian Hospital. Rev. Barry Frazzitta.
Coney Island Hospital. Rev. Joseph P. Quigley.
Downstate Medical Center. Sr. Mary Donohue.
Kings County Hospital Center. Rev. Lucien Charlot; Sr. Patricia Murphy, C.S.J.
Kingsboro Psychiatric Center. Rev. Robert Frueh.
Long Island College Hospital. Vacant.
Lutheran Medical Center. Bro. Gerard Chylko, C.SS.R.; Rev. Francis P. McElroy, C.SS.R.
Maimonides Medical Center of Brooklyn. Sr. Mary Catherine Murphy, R.S.H.M.
Methodist Hospital. Sr. Therese Marie Camardella, C.S.J.
University Hospital of Brooklyn. Sr. Mary Donohue.
Veterans Administration Medical Center. Revs. Edward Finn, C.SS.R.; Robert J. Chalany, O.S.B.; Vito Tiboni; Robert Milde.
Victory Memorial Hospital. Bro. Lewis Morrow, C.S.C.
Woodhull Medical & Mental Health Center. Rev. Msgr. Felipe C. Diaz (Philippines); Sr. Claudia Paredes.
Wyckoff Heights Hospital. Rev. Justo R. Beltran Regado (Philippines).

QUEENS. *Bedford Hills Correctional Facility*. Sr. Elaine Roulet, C.S.J., Family Liaison & Dir. Children's Center.
Creedmoor Psychiatric Center. Revs. Paul Chenot, C.P.; August Iantosca.
Elmhurst General Hospital. Rev. Jose Sanchez (Philippines).
Flushing Hospital and Medical Center. Sr. Florence Dippold, C.S.J.
Jamaica Hospital - Trump Pavilion. Sr. Lorraine Liebold, O.P.
Long Island Jewish Hospital. Vacant.
N.Y. Hospital Medical Center of Queens. Sr. Mary Schutte, S.C.
Peninsula Hospital Center. Sr. Joanne Feulner, C.S.J.
Queens Hospital Center—Pastoral Care Office. Rev. Jose Cadusale (Philippines); Mrs. Alice Comperiati.
Queens House of Detention. Rev. John H. Wilkinson.
Queensboro Correctional Facility. Deacon Frank DeTucci.
Veterans Affairs Extended Care Center, St. Albans, NY. Revs. Joseph Gleeson; James T. Devine.
Western Queens Community Hospital. Sr. Frances Casteran, C.S.J.

Special Assignment:
Reverend Monsignors—
Reilly, Philip J., Chap., Monastery of the Precious Blood, 5400 Ft. Hamilton Pkwy., Brooklyn, NY 11219
Reverend Fathers—
Hardiman, Michael J., Office of the Synod, 7200 Douglaston Pkwy., Douglaston, NY 11362-1997
Maresca, Ralph J., Sec. to the Diocesan Bishop, 75 Greene Ave., P.O. Box C, Brooklyn, NY 11202
Massie, Guy A., Brooklyn College Newman Club, Our Lady Help of Christians, 1315 E. 28th St., Brooklyn, NY 11210
Parisi, Michael R., Catholic Consultation Center, 7200 Douglaston Pkwy., Rm. # 213, Douglaston, NY 11362
Reid, Michael R., Diocesan Dir., Catholic Cemeteries, Catholic Cemeteries, 137-35 Brookville Blvd., Rosedale, NY 11422
Tedone, Michael G., Dir. of Vocations, St. Rita, 36-26 11th St., Long Island City, NY 11106

Military Chaplains:
Reverend Monsignors—
Gilhooley, John P., (Retired), 1260 Stevens Ave., Arbutus, MD 21227
Reverend Fathers—
Boyd, James A., Chap. Dept., Naval Air Sta., Barbers Point, HI 96862-5050
Ceriello, Joseph A., NAB Chapel, Naval Amphibious Base, Little Creek, Norfolk, VA 23521
Dillon, James P., 1834 Tara Dr., Prattville, AL 36060
Leibold, James C., Office of the Base Chap., MCB, Camp 5.D. Butler, Butler, FPO AP 96373-5001
Leone, James M., 126 Laurelton Dr., P.O. Box 426, Mastic Beach, NY 11951
Mulkerin, Terrence J., Chaplain's Office, USCG Reserve Training Center, Yorktown, VA 23690-9761
Teahan, Timothy J., HHC 8th SPT GRP, CMR 426 Box 563, APO AE 09613
Vella, Joseph C., 1297B Redwood Dr., Grand Forks AFB, ND 58204

Released from Diocesan Assignment:
Reverend Monsignors—
Ecker, Robert J., 300 Second St., Coronado, CA 92118
LaRocca, Vincent R., 108 Carroll St., Brooklyn, NY 11231
Maksymowicz, John H., Apostolic Nunciature, 3339 Massachusetts Ave., N.W., Washington, DC 20008
Sarno, Robert J., Congregation for the Causes of Saints, Vatican City State 00120
White, Leo J., St. George's Cathedral House, Westminster Bridge Rd., London SE1 7HY, England
Reverend Fathers—
Bordeleau, Normand G., St. John the Baptist Rectory, P.O. Box 219, Suncook, NH 03275
Brennan, Edward C., Our Lady Queen of Martyrs, 110-06 Queens Blvd., Forest Hills, NY 11375
Catania, Thomas M., B.V.M. Help of Christians, 70-31 48th Ave., Woodside, NY 11377
Cremins, John J., Assumption, 64 Middagh St., Brooklyn, NY 11201
Curran, Michael J., Immaculate Conception Seminary, West Neck Rd.-Lloyd Harbor, Huntington, NY 11743
D'Albro, Thomas G., 62A Widmer Rd., Wappingers Falls, NY 12590
DaSilva, Joseph, Risen Christ Catholic Church, 11336 Valley Heights Cir., Boise, ID 83709
Diffley, Patrick J., 283 Paulette Dr., Newport News, VA 23602
Dunne, Richard J., Dept. of Veterans Affairs, P.O. Box 5474, Hampton, VA 23667
Finley, James F., Kath. Amerikanische Gemeinde, Huttenweig, 46, 14195 Berlin, Germany
Folchetti, John T., Christian Brothers Academy, 850 Newman Springs Rd., Lincroft, NJ 07738
Heerey, John J., St. John's, P.O. Box 207, Interlachen, FL 32148
Heffernan, James F., Chap., Veterans Admin. Medical Center, Northport, NY 11768
Heffernan, Thomas A., (Retired), 29A Upland Dr., E. Northport, NY 11731
Higuero, Francisco J., 2871 Troy Center Dr. South, Apt. 2005, Troy, MI 48084
Himes, Michael J., Department of Theology, Boston College, Chestnut Hill, MA 02167-3806
Johnston, John F., Oratory Prep School, One Beverly Rd., Summit, NJ 07901
Lanahan, William F., 11869 Washington Pl., Los Angeles, CA 90066
Lauder, Robert E., Cathedral Residence, 7200 Douglaston Pkwy., Douglaston, NY 11362
Longo, Robert M., Capuchin Franciscans, Our Lady of Guadalupe Friary, 319 36th St., P.O. Box 809, Union City, NJ 07087
LoPinto, Alfred P., 1450 N. D St., San Bernardino, CA 92405
Mahoney, Cornelius H., Immaculate Conception Seminary, W. Neck Rd.-Lloyd Harbor, Huntington, NY 11743
Mariano, John M., 1620 S. Ocean Blvd. (9N), Pompano Beach, FL 33062
Matonti, Charles, 175-20 Wexford Ter., Jamaica, NY 11432
McNicholas, Edward J., Bishop Mugavero Residence, 7200 Douglaston Pkwy., P.O. Box 630433, Little Neck, NY 11363-0433
McVernon, John J., 16-34 Clintonville St., Whitestone, NY 11357
Mulqueen, Joseph C., Apostolic Nunciature, 3339 Massachusetts Ave., N.W., Washington, DC 20008-3687
Nadine, Jerome E., St. Elizabeth Ann Seton Church, 18-11 Pueblo Vista Dr., Las Vegas, NV 89128
Passenant, Francis J., Our Lady of Fatima Church, 25-02 80th St., Jackson Heights, NY 11370
Paterno, Salvatore D., St. Mary, 42 Goshen Ave., Washingtonville, NY 10992
Penta, Leo J., c/o: Maryknoll, 6367 Overbrook Ave., Philadelphia, PA 19151
Pomilio, Matthew J., 175-20 Wexford Ter., Jamaica, NY 11432
Ruiz, Jean Pierre, St. Patrick Rectory, 39-38 29th St., Long Island City, NY 11101
Schuck, Joseph J., R.D. 1, Box 54, Unadilla, NY 13847-9771
Sears, William J., 1745 Padre Ln., Englewood, FL 34223
Smith, LeRoy J., Red Cottage, Chatham Center, NY 12184
Steinhauser, Kenneth B., Belmont Abbey College, Belmont, NC 28012
Steinhauser, Michael G., Toronto School of Theology, 47 Queen's Park, Crescent Park, Toronto, Ontario M55 2CS Canada
Tivenan, John J., Mercy Medical Center, 1512 12th Ave. Rd., Nampa, ID 83686
Trombetta, Paul N., 219 Old Oak Bucket Rd., Scituate, MA 02066
Upson, Michael G., Immaculate Conception Church, 445 Frederick Douglas St., Rochester, NY 14608
Vaccari, Peter I., Immaculate Conception Seminary, W. Neck Rd.-Lloyd Harbor, Huntington, NY 11743
Vendetti, Michael A., 94-26 Sutter Ave., Ozone Park, NY 11417
Vesey, John E., Casa del Clero, Apt. Postal # 1, Panajachel-Solola, Guatemala
Wulinski, Stanley F., 1701 N.E. 42nd St., Beacon Heights, FL 33064

Graduate Studies:
Reverend Fathers—
Swartvargher, Mark, North American College, Vatican City State, 00120 Italy

Absent on Sick Leave:
Reverend Monsignors—
Demski, Arthur A.
Reverend Fathers—
Abrams, John L.
Byrnes, Francis J., (Retired)
Cushing, Charles B., (Retired)
Denzer, Joseph W.
Early, William F.
Esposito, Joseph J.
Flynn, Francis J., (Retired)
Franco, Salvator V.
Grant, Matthew M.
Gural, Marion A., (Retired)
Kenny, Albert N., (Retired)
Malleck, Joseph L., (Retired)
Mangini, Charles M.
Milde, Robert F., (Retired)
Newell, John J.
Niemczyk, Joseph W.
O'Brien, David G.
O'Sullivan, John J.
Prochaski, Adam F.
Sabatos, Daniel C.
Salamone, Michael J.
Siedlecki, Aloysius M., (Retired)
Titore, Robert A.
Wildgruber, Francis C.

Absent on Leave:
Reverend Monsignors—
Manzo, Francis J.
Reverend Fathers—
Barbetta, Philip
Beliveau, Richard
Boyle, Victor J.
Brown, Charles L.
Ferraro, Romano J.
Ferro, Robert A.
Kozma, Raymond M.
Lazar, John E.
Liona, Kenneth J.
Mason, Edward J.
Merolla, George R.
Miller, Joseph A.
Morris, James J.
Morrow, Thomas O.
Peyton, Thomas
Piro, Gerald J.
Ryan, Barry
Sexton, Patrick D.
Visich, Eduard C.
Walsh, John F.
Wood, Paul F.

Retired:
Reverend Monsignors—
Adessa, Dominick J., 555 Albany Ave., Amityville, NY 11701
Asip, James W., 16-34 Clintonville St., Whitestone, NY 11357
Barretta, Anthony J., 61-27 71st St., Middle Village, NY 11379
Bednartz, August C., Cathedral Prep Seminary, 56-25 92nd St., Elmhurst, NY 11373
Bulovas, Francis J., 64 Clinton Ave., Brooklyn, NY
Burke, Edward J.T., Precious Blood Monastery, 5300 Fort Hamilton Pkwy., Brooklyn, NY 11219
Burke, William F., Bishop Mugavero Residence, 7200 Douglaston Pkwy., P.O. Box 433, Little Neck, NY 11363-0433
Campbell, Thomas P., 21-17 45th St., Long Island City, NY 11105
Clancy, Thomas C., 2055 E. 69th St., Brooklyn, NY 11234
Cosgrove, Henry P., Bishop Mugavero Residence, 7200 Douglaston Pkwy., P.O. Box 433, Little Neck, NY 11363-0433
Cribbin, Thomas F., 256 Clinton Ave., Brooklyn, NY 11205
D'Anca, Achille, 274 Beachway Dr., Palm Coast, FL 32137
Diviney, Charles E., 21 Sidney Pl., Brooklyn, NY 11201
Donegan, James F., St. Joan of Arc, 82-00 35th Ave., Jackson Heights, NY 11372
Feldhaus, Eugene A., 188-16 91st Ave., Hollis, NY 11423
Fitzpatrick, Franklin E., 91-18 86th Ave., Woodhaven, NY 11421
Flanagan, Thomas J., P.O. Box 804, Beatrice Ct., Hampton Bays, NY 11946
Florido, Raphael A., 9719 Flatlands Ave., Brooklyn, NY 11236
Fogarty, George V., Bishop Mugavero Residence, 7200 Douglaston Pkwy., P.O. Box 433, Little Neck, NY 11363-0433
Fus, Edward A., 43 Highpoint Dr., Kunkletown, PA 18058
Galuszka, Walter C., 479 New Jersey Ave., Brooklyn, NY 11207
Haggarty, James J., St. Pius, 1100 Woodside Rd., Redwood City, CA 94061
Haggerty, James J., St. Saviour, 611 Eighth Ave., Brooklyn, NY 11215
Hendel, Thomas W., 94-40 118th St., Richmond Hill, NY 11419
Hickey, William T., 63-63 98th St., Rego Park, NY 11374
Jolley, Edward W., Bishop Mugavero Residence, 7200 Douglaston Pkwy., P.O. Box 433, Little Neck, NY 11363-0433
Kean, John J., 1281 Troy Ave., Brooklyn, NY 11203
King, James P., 28-20 154th St., Flushing, NY 11354

Konrad, Joseph G., 5815 Catalpa Ave., Ridgewood, NY 11385
Lahey, Joseph T., 9511 Fourth Ave., Brooklyn, NY 11209
Landi, Andrew P., St. Stephen, 142 E. 29th St., New York, NY 10016
Martin, Kieran J., 1550 Hendrickson St., Brooklyn, NY 11234
McAlister, Lawrence J., 638 Rathbun Ave., Staten Island, NY 10312-2613
McKenna, James J., St. Mary Star of the Sea, 1920 New Haven Ave., Far Rockaway, NY 11691
Mooney, George A., 66-01 80th St., Middle Village, NY 11379
Mulhall, Francis X., Bishop Mugavero Residence, 7200 Douglaston Pkwy., Box 433, Little Neck, NY 11363-0433
Nolan, Edward J., 89-43 Francis Lewis Blvd., Queens Village, NY 11427
Osborne, William J., 9-41 120 St., College Point, NY 11356
Parks, Joseph K., St. Patrick, 9511 Fourth Ave., Brooklyn, NY 11209
Passarella, Anthony F., 862 Manhattan Ave., Brooklyn, NY 11222
Privitera, Santi J., Sts. Joachim and Ann Residence, 2720 Surf Ave., Brooklyn, NY 11224
Rodgers, William J., Queen of Peace Residence, 110-30 221st St., Queens Village, NY 11429
Sapporito, Cosmo G., St. Bernadette, 8201 13th Ave., Brooklyn, NY 11228
Shevlin, Raymond R., 2325 Gerritsen Ave., Brooklyn, NY 11229
Voiland, George T., 32-23 36th St., Long Island City, NY 11106
Welsh, Robert E., 199 River Rd., Nissequoque, NY 11780
Wilson, John F., 245 Prospect Park W., Brooklyn, NY 11215

Reverend Fathers—
Angles, Sebastian, 2601 Muscatello St., Orlando, FL 32821
Baltrucki, Leon S., 19 Wright St., Gardner, MA 01440
Bartley, William J., Holy Name, 245 Prospect Park W., Brooklyn, NY 11215
Bartruff, Louis B., Bishop Mugavero Residence, 7200 Douglaston Pkwy., P.O. Box 433, Little Neck, NY 11363-0433
Bihler, Joseph J., Queen of Peace Residence, 110-30 221st St., Queens Village, NY 11429
Blaeser, Alfred A., 1088 Lloyd St., Franklin Square, NY 11010
Borzaga, Rinaldo, Manhattan College, Riverdale, NY 10471
Brevetti, Adrian, c/o D. Valeriano Iole, Via S. Cosimato, 27, Mandela, Roma 00020 Italy
Brown, Vincent A., 63-63 98th St., Rego Park, NY 11374
Buckley, Joseph F., St. Cecilia, 84 Herbert St., Brooklyn, NY 11222
Buetow, Harold A., Bishop Mugavero Residence, 7200 Douglaston Pkwy., P.O. Box 433, Little Neck, NY 11363-0433
Byrnes, Francis J., P.O. Box 784, Welaka, FL 32193
Calderwood, Vincent T., 38 Duncan Dr., Morganville, NJ 07751
Conroy, Edward G., 98-10 103rd Ave., Ozone Park, NY 11417
Cronin, John F., Bishop Mugavero Residence, 7200 Douglaston Pkwy., P.O. Box 433, Little Neck, NY 11363-0433
D'Amato, James J., 1550 Hendrickson St., Brooklyn, NY 11234
Daly, Joseph F., 66-05 79th Pl., Middle Village, NY 11379
Davis, William J., 62-81 60th Pl., Ridgewood, NY 11385
Dennen, Gerard F., P.O. Box 2143, Pinehurst, NC 28374
Dolan, Thomas D., 94-20 85th St., Ozone Park, NY 11416
Donnelly, Eugene F., 25-02 80th St., Jackson Heights, NY 11370
Dore, Denis 4, 245-46 147th Dr., Rosedale, NY 11422
Dundon, Raymond J., St. Vincent Ferrer, 1603 Brooklyn Ave., Brooklyn, NY 11210
Duran, Ernesto, Santa Beatriz 269, Apt. 503, Santiago 9, Chile S.A.
Ebejer, George, 216 27th St., Brooklyn, NY 11232
Flynn, Francis J., Chancery Office (c/o Msgr. Otto L. Garcia), P.O. Box C, Brooklyn, NY 11202
Forsyth, George W., 2 Pheasant Ln., Lloyd Harbor, NY 11743
Giuliano, Louis A., 52-10 NW 53rd. Ave., Cocoanut Creek, FL 33073
Grillo, Anthony, R.R. 1, Box 1144, Beach Lake, PA 18405
Harth, Charles F., 2609 Linden Blvd., Brooklyn, NY 11208
Hogan, Edward P., 130 Oceanside, Rockaway Pt., NY 11697
Hughes, John F., Queen of Peace Residence, 110-30 221st St., Queens Village, NY 11429
Hume, Robert B., Holy Innocents, 279 E. 17th St., Brooklyn, NY 11226
Hunt, Michael J., Mugavero Geriatric Center, 155 Dean St., Brooklyn, NY 11217
Hyland, James G., (c/o Mrs. Fixter), 413 Salem Rd., Spring Lake, NJ 07762
Jurgensen, John W., 94-40 118th St., Richmond Hill, NY 11419
Kakizaki, John T., 99-15 Rockaway Beach Blvd., Rockaway Park, NY 11694
Keane, Joseph P., Two Pinetop Dr., Shirley, NY 11967
Kelly, Thomas F., 7320 Fourth Ave., Brooklyn, NY 11209
Kenny, Albert N., 273 78th St., Brooklyn, NY 11209
Kenny, Michael J., 17 Old Rte. 9W, Fort Montgomery, NY 10922
Kirrane, James A., St. Anthony of Pauda, 20 Cheshire Pl., Box 308, E. Northport, NY 11731
Klohr, Paul McC., Queen of Peace Residence, 110-30 221st St., Queens Village, NY 11429
Labita, Francis J., 100-05 159th St., Howard Beach, NY 11414
Lang, Henry A., 56-15 213th St., Bayside Hills, NY 11364
Lennon, Joseph L., 450 E. 20th St., 1B, New York, NY 10009
LoGatto, Rosario J., 2334 Sunset Dr., Escondido, CA 92025
Maceli, Anthony J., 6908 Stonesthrow Cir. N., St. Petersburg, FL 33710
Mankowski, Edmund A., R.R. 2, Box 319 Locust Dr. & Noyack Rd., Sag Harbor, NY 11963
Mannion, Thomas F., 415 Gauntlatt, P.O. Box 33, Gold Beach, OR 97444
Mariani, Charles J., 108 Carroll St., Brooklyn, NY 11231
McCarren, William J., 8000 Roma N.E., Albuquerque, NM 87108
McDermott, James P., 1600 N. Ocean Blvd., Apt. 408, Pompano Beach, FL 33062
McDermott, Joseph J., Mugavero Geriatric Center, 155 Dean St., Brooklyn, NY 11217
McElroy, Herbert, Holy Family Home, 1740 84th St., Brooklyn, NY 11214
McGee, Francis J., 130 Beach 84th St., Rockaway Beach, NY 11693
McGuirk, Raymond A., 279 E. 17th St., Brooklyn, NY 11226
McNeill, John A., Our Lady of Lourdes, 92-96 220th St., Queens Village, NY 11428
Melleck, Joseph L., 24 Steven St., Plainview, NY 11803
Milde, Robert F., Bishop Mugavero Residence, 7200 Douglaston Pkwy., P.O. Box 433, Little Neck, NY 11363-0433
Moore, Robert A., 929 Bay Ridge Pkwy., Brooklyn, NY 11228
Morgan, Raymond J., Bishop Mugavero Residence, 7200 Douglaston Pkwy., P.O. Box 433 7, Little Neck, NY 11363-0433
Mueller, Anthony E., 204-25 Rockaway Point Blvd., Rockaway Point, NY 11697
Mullen, Joseph A., 555 Albany Ave., Amityville, NY 11701
Nichols, Charles P., Sacred Hearts of Jesus & Mary - St. Steven, 108 Carroll St., Brooklyn, NY 11231
O'Connor, Edward T., 6255 S.E. Charleston Pl., Hobe Sound, FL 33455
O'Leary, William A., 215 Beach 216th St., Breezy Point, NY 11697
Oravecz, John F., Bishop Mugavero Residence, 7200 Douglaston Pkwy., P.O. Box 433, Little Neck, NY 11363-0433
Pakalniskis, John, Bishop Mugavero Residence, 7200 Douglaston Pkwy., P.O. Box 433, Little Neck, NY 11363-0433
Pesaresi, Constantine V., Our Lady of Sorrows, 104-11 37th Ave., Corona, NY 11368
Pikturna, Vytautas, 2800 Ocean Dr. B 6D, Riviera Beach, FL 33404
Pitkiewicz, Vincent, 789 Essex St., Brooklyn, NY 11208-4805
Powers, Anthony F., 124 Beaver Dr., Mastic Beach, NY 11951
Pullo, Francis S., Bishop Mugavero Residence, 7200 Douglaston Pkwy., P.O. Box 433, Little Neck, NY 11363-0433
Pupin, Vito A., Mugavero Geriatric Center, 155 Dean St., Brooklyn, NY 11217
Raila, Stanislaus, Bishop Mugavero Residence, 7200 Douglaston Pkwy., P.O. Box 433, Little Neck, NY 11363-0433
Rau, Raymond F., 198 Euclid Ave., Brooklyn, NY 11208
Reilly, John C., 141-36 77 Ave., Kew Gardens Hills, NY 11367
Rizzi, Salvatore, 126 Pond Rd., Woodbury, NY 11797
Romanowski, Francis C., St. Stanislaus, Bishop & Martyr, 88-10 102nd Ave., Ozone Park, NY 11416
Schmidt, Jerome J., 2325 Gerritson Ave., Brooklyn, NY 11229
Schwind, Donald F., 182 Monitor St., Brooklyn, NY 11222
Seeger, Francis J., P.O. Box 6678, Flushing, NY 11365
Seeger, Peter J., 123-06 14th Ave., College Point, NY 11356
Simonetti, Gennaro M., Our Lady of Miracles, 757 E. 86 St., Brooklyn, NY 11236
Stonebridge, John H., 83-17 78th Ave., East Glendale, NY 11385
Sullivan, James E., Most Holy Trinity, 14-51 143rd St., Whitestone, NY 11357
Travis, Herbert A., St. Anselm, 356 82nd St., Brooklyn, NY 11209
Tully, James J., 24 Brookway Dr., Greensboro, NC 27410
Vogel, Charles P., 416 Grant Ave., Brooklyn, NY 11208
Walsh, Michael J., 80 John St., Staten Island, NY 10302
Wang, Barnabas, Bishop Mugavero Residence, 7200 Douglaston Pkwy., Douglaston, NY 11362
Weinlich, Alfred J., St. Luke, 16-34 Clintonville St., Whitestone, NY 11357
Witterholt, Herbert M., 42-41 201 St., Bayside, NY 11361
Wolf, Matthias J., Bishop Mugavero Residence, 7200 Douglaston Pkwy., Douglaston, NY 11362
Yonson, Wenceslaus, 279 E. 17 St., Brooklyn, NY 11226

Permanent Deacons:
Aigbojie, Edward A., Queen of All Saints, Brooklyn
Almodovar, Ismael, Diocese of Orlando
Alvarez, Felipe J., St. Joseph, Long Island City
Arcand, Dennis A., Diocese of Savannah
Aris, Anthony J., Inactive
Arthur, Anthony H., St. Jerome, Brooklyn
Baez, Angel, Epiphany, Brooklyn
Beaubrun, Berthal, St. Ignatius, Brooklyn
Bichotte, Joseph, St. Augustine, Brooklyn
Boursiquot, Jean B., St. Ignatius, Brooklyn
Burrell, James, St. Catherine of Siena, St. Alban
Caceres, Ycelso, Inactive
Cafiero, Joseph D., St. Rosalia, Brooklyn
Cajiao, Henry, Diocese of St. Petersburg
Calvo, Juan, Queen of Angels, Long Island City
Campisi, Joseph, Our Lady Grace, Howard Beach
Cancel, Edwin, Our Lady of the Angelus, Rego Park
Candreva, Arthur, Sacred Heart, Glendale
Cardona, Ramon, Diocese of Mayaguez, PR
Cederroth, Charles J., Diocese of Trenton
Chin, Paul M., St. Paul Chong Ha-Sang Chapel, Flushing
Coffey, John P., Christ the King, Springfield Gardens
Colandrea, Dante, St. Dominic, Brooklyn
Coleman, Harry J., St. Bonaventure, Jamaica
Colon, James A., Unassigned
Colon, Rafael, Unassigned
Coyle, Lawrence J., St. Columba, Brooklyn
Coyle, Richard J., Unassigned
Cruz, Florencio, St. Matthew, Brooklyn
Cruz, Rafael, Archdiocese of Miami
Cuccia, Arthur J., St. Jude
Cusumano, Anthony P., St. Helen, Howard Beach
D'Accordo, Frank J., Saint Bernard, Brooklyn
Da Costa, Dennis A., St. Matthew, Brooklyn
Damato, Stephen T., St. Sebastian, Woodside
Davis, Thomas G., St. Anselm, Brooklyn
De Cola, Joseph P., Diocese of Palm Beach
De Tucci, Frank A., Catholic Charities Office for Prison Ministry
DeBiase, Vincent F., St. Margaret, Middle Village
DeLeon, Andres, St. Gregory the Great, Brooklyn
Dennehy, John P., Sacred Heart, East Glendale
Desdunes, Herve, St. Matthew, Brooklyn
Devaney, Thomas J., Immaculate Heart of Mary, Brooklyn
Diaz, Rafael A., St. Leo, Corona
DiTargiani, Charles C., St. Ephrem, Brooklyn
Dixon, Gregory D., St. Andrew the Apostle, Brooklyn
Dorsinville, Paul C., Sacred Heart, Cambria Heights
Dudley, Roy A., Sacred Heart, Cambria Heights
Earley, George G., Diocese of Rockville Centre
Ehresmann, Philip J., St. Brigid, Brooklyn
Felix, Antoine, Holy Innocents, Brooklyn
Flaim, Fabio, St. Aloysius, Ridgewood
Flannery, John A., St. Charles Borromeo, Brooklyn
Fogerty, James P., Diocese of Rockville Centre
Franca, John J., St. Francis Xavier, Brooklyn
Francis, John J., Pastoral Care of the Sick, Catholic Charities

Francois, Joseph K., Our Lady of the Presentation, Brooklyn
Fugelsang, Louis, Inactive
Gannon, John J., Unassigned
Garamella, Robert, Diocese of Rockville Centre
George, Roy N., St. Gregory the Great, Brooklyn
Germain, Moliere, St. Vincent Ferrer, Brooklyn
Giglio, John P., Unassigned
Gilligan, Richard J., St. Mary Gate of Heaven, Ozone Park
Gomez, Guillermo D., St. Gerard Majella, Hollis
Gonzalez, Rafael, Diocese of Orlando
Grace, James T., St. Stanislaus Kostka, Maspeth
Guastella, Louis J., St. Catherine of Genoa, Brooklyn
Heaphy, Thomas F., St. Mary Gate of Heaven, Ozone Park
Heinrich, Joseph, Office of Disabled Persons, Catholic Charities
Hernandez, Rafael, Diocese of Orlando
Hernandez, Wilfredo, Holy Spirit, Brooklyn
Hili, Saviour, St. Francis of Assisi, Long Island City
Hitter, Robert A., St. Francis de Sales, Belle Harbor
Horne, Wilfred N., Archdiocese for the Military Services, USA
Huckemeyer, Edward J., On Personal Leave
Innocent, Francois, Incarnation, Brooklyn
Joesten, F. Edward, St. Anthony of Padua, South Ozone Park
Johnson, Stanley D., Unassigned
Kennedy, James F., St. Thomas Aquinas, Brooklyn
Knight, Lionel A., St. Nicholas of Tolentine, Jamaica
Krebs, Jerome H., Our Lady Miraculous Medal, Brooklyn
Landron, Jaime, Our Lady of the Presentation, Brooklyn
Lavanco, Robert F., Our Lady of Hope, Middle Village
Lee, Richard G., St. Thomas More-St. Edmund, Rockaway Point
Licata, Salvatore V., Exec. Sec. Permanent Diaconate Office
Lima, Ramon, Unassigned
Lopez, Eduvigis, Our Lady of Perpetual Help, Brooklyn
Lopez, Hiram, Archdiocese of New York
Maldonado, Andres, Diocese of Ponce, PR
Malone, William F., St. Ephrem, Brooklyn
Marcel, Magloire, St. Jerome, Brooklyn
Marchello, Andrew A., Nativity of the Blessed Virgin Mary, Queens
Marley, Daniel J., Our Lady of Solace, Brooklyn
Marte, Rafael, St. John Cantius, Brooklyn
Martinez, German, Transfiguration, Brooklyn
Mayers, Winston M., Christ the King, Springfield Gardens
Mazza, Nicholas, St. Cecilia, Brooklyn
McCarthy, Thomas R., Our Lady Queen of Martyrs, Forest Hills
McGreevey, John F., St. John Vianney, Brooklyn
McGuire, Joseph P., St. Brendan, Brooklyn
Mejia, Abdon, Our Lady of Perpetual Help, South Ozone Park
Mellace, Carlo V., St. Dominic, Brooklyn
Mergler, Edward P., Our Lady of Grace, Howard Beach
Miller, Leon F., St. Michael, East New York
Montalvo, Hector, Holy Family, Brooklyn
Morales, Julio A., Diocese of Orlando
Mulroy, Martin B., Our Lady of Angels, Brooklyn
Murphy, John J., Mary Queen of Heaven, Brooklyn
Nero, Robert V., (Retired)
O'Neill, John P., Corpus Christi, Woodside
Occhiuto, Joseph J., Our Lady of Mt. Carmel, Williamsburg
Ortiz, Sergio, Unassigned
Pagan, Aurelio, St. Agnes, Brooklyn
Parisi, Vincent, St. Rita, Long Island City
Pascal, Orlando, Our Lady of Sorrows, Corona
Paul, Ernst, St. Rita, Brooklyn
Postler, Charles A., St. Patrick, Brooklyn
Pouso, Roberto J., Blessed Sacrament, Jackson Heights
Proce, Horatio A., Inactive
Ramirez, Manuel, Diocese of Scranton
Ramos, James, St. Francis Xavier, Brooklyn
Ramos, Jose A., St. Lucy-St. Patrick, Brooklyn
Ramos, Pedro, Diocese of Caguas, PR
Rivera, Angel R., St. Benedict Joseph Labre, Richmond Hill
Rivera, Hector R., Archdiocese of San Juan, PR
Rizzo, Giovanni A., St. Finbar, Brooklyn
Roberts, Lionel V., Released from Diocesan Assignment
Rogers, Thomas F., Incarnation, Queens Village
Ronacher, Ronald M., St. Rita, Brooklyn
Rosati, Frank J., Catholic Charities, Pastoral Care of the Sick
Ruiz, Jose D., Diocese of Ponce, PR
Russo, Anthony J., (Retired)
Ryan, Kevin F., Blessed Virgin Mary Help of Christians, Queens
Sands, John E., St. Matthias, Ridgewood
Sawney, Ira, Florida
Sclafani, Leonard A., St. Paul Center, Long Island City
Seliga, Mark A., St. Mark, Brooklyn
Simon, Mauclair, St. Therese of Lisieux, Brooklyn
Sinisi, Henry C., On Leave
Smith, Charles J., Mary Queen of Heaven, Brooklyn
Smith, Henry J., Our Lady of the Snows, North Floral Park
Smith, Ramon, St. Teresa of Avila, S. Ozone Park
Smolinski, Chester, (Retired)
Smolinski, Edward A., Our Lady of Mercy, Forest Hills
Soto, Jesus, Our Lady of Perpetual Help, Brooklyn
Squillante, Michael A., St. Mary Gate of Heaven, Ozone Park
Steffens, Gerard K., St. Matthias, Ridgewood
Sucich, John R., St. Francis of Assisi, Long Island City
Svebel, Harry A., St. Luke, Whitestone
Taylor, Luis C., St. Catherine of Sienna, St. Alban
Tierney, John A., Diocese of Albany
Tokarcsik, George M., St. Agatha, Brooklyn
Torres, Abel, Holy Name, Brooklyn
Troy, Michael J., Our Lady of Angels, Brooklyn
Tully, Dean T., Holy Child Jesus, Richmond Hill
Valderrana, Carlos, St. Cecilia, Brooklyn
Valle Valle, Esteban, Archdiocese of San Juan, PR
Van de Ven, Theodore J., St. Fidelis, College Point
Van Wassenhove, Raymond J., Diocese of Peoria
Vargas, Juan R., St. Agatha, Brooklyn
Vermilyea, Richard, St. Agatha, Brooklyn
Waldron, Martin T., St. Mary Star of the Sea, Far Rockaway
Wander, William H., St. Andrew the Apostle, Brooklyn
Whelan, Alfred L., St. Gertrude, Far Rockaway
Williams, Lee C., St. Mary Magdalene, Springfield Gardens
Williamsen, William, St. Saviour, Brooklyn
Winkler, Warren A., Our Lady of Lourdes, Queens Village
Yepes, Elias H., St. Michael, Flushing

INSTITUTIONS LOCATED IN THE DIOCESE

[A] PASTORAL CENTERS

DOUGLASTON. *Immaculate Conception Pastoral Center*, 7200 Douglaston Pkwy., 11362-1997. Tel: 718-229-8001. Rev. Msgr. Vincent A. Keane, Dir.; Mr. Thomas D. Flynn, Controller; Mr. John Campanelli, Bldgs. & Grounds; Mr. Thomas Powers, Athletic Center; Mr. Charles C. Lindner, Librarian; Brian Zuar, Performing Arts; James Austin, Food Svc. Mgr.

Offices Located at the Center include Cathedral Residence; Bishop Mugavero Residence; The Tribunal; Office of the Synod Institutional Svcs.; Bldg. & Property Office; Pastoral Institute; Regl. Bishop of Queens-N.; Office of the Archivist; Office of the Diocesan Dir. of Music; Diocesan Language Institute; Hispanic Ministry; Diocesan Devel.; Futures in Educ.; and Brooklyn-Queens Environmental Mgmt. Corp.: Catholic Medical Center, Emergency Svc. Institute, Catholic Consultation Center, and Family Life Ministry.

[B] SEMINARIES, DIOCESAN

DOUGLASTON. *Cathedral Residence of the Immaculate Conception*, 7200 Douglaston Pkwy., 11362. Tel: 718-229-8001. Residence for college level and post college level candidates for Priesthood. Rev. Msgr. Vincent A. Keane, M.A., Rector; Revs. Conrad R. Dietz, Ph.D., Academic Dean, Philosophy Prof.; Thomas G. Caserta, M.A., M.Div., Spiritual Dir.; Dennis D. Klein, Ph.D., Philosophy Prof. In res., Revs. Martin F. Kirby, M.A.; Robert E. Lauder, Ph.D. Priests 4; Lay Teachers 3; Seminarians 25.

ELMHURST. *Cathedral Preparatory Seminary of the Immaculate Conception*, 56-25 92nd St., 11373. Tel: 718-592-6800. Revs. Richard E. Marchese, Rector & Prin.; William R. Dulaney, Spiritual Dir.; Joseph Calise; Fred Marano. In res., Rev. Msgr. August C. Bednartz; Rev. Sofronio LoFranco. Priests 4; Sisters 2; Lay Teachers 16; Seminarians 225.

[C] SEMINARIES, RELIGIOUS

WHITESTONE. *St. Alphonsus Formation Residence*, 22-04 Parsons Blvd., 11357-3440. Tel: 718-321-1096; Fax: 718-321-1246. Very Rev. Peter E. Sousa, C.SS.R., Rector/Dir. of Formation; Revs. Paul J. Borowski, C.SS.R., Asst. Dir.; Edmund Faliskie, C.SS.R., Vocation Dir.; James J. Toulas, C.SS.R.; James W. Gilmour, C.SS.R.; Bro. George Armoogan, C.SS.R. Priests 5; Brothers 1; Students 9.

[D] COLLEGES AND UNIVERSITIES

*BROOKLYN. *St. Francis College*, 180 Remsen St., 11201. Tel: 718-522-2300.
For a complete listing, refer to the Colleges and Universities section.

**St. Joseph's College*, 245 Clinton Ave., 11205. Tel: 718-636-6800.
For a complete listing, refer to the Colleges and Universities section.

JAMAICA. *St. John's University*, 8000 Utopia Pkwy., 11439. Tel: 718-990-1924; Fax: 718-990-5886.
For a complete listing, refer to the Colleges and Universities section.

QUEENS AND STATEN ISLAND. *St. John's University*, (1870). Main Campus, 8000 Utopia Pkwy. Jamaica, 11439. Tel: 718-990-6161; Fax: 718-990-6555.
For a complete listing, refer to the Colleges and Universities section.

[E] CATHOLIC EDUCATION OFFICES

BROOKLYN. *Office of Religious Education: Evangelization and Catholic Formation*, 6025 6th Ave., 11220. Tel: 718-492-1800. Mrs. Joan M. Snow, Diocesan Dir.; Sr. Eileen Sweeney, Dir. of Elementary Rel. Educ.; Joan R. Sokoll, Dir. Elementary Rel. Educ.; Rev. Michael A. Carrano, Dir. Youth Ministry & Adolescent Catechesis, & Dir. College Campus Ministry; Sr. Alice Michael, S.U.S.C., Dir. Rel. Educ. for Cultural and Ethnic Groups; Revs. Joseph R. Gibino, Ph.D., Dir. of Adult Rel. Educ.; Dennis McAuliffe, Ph.D., Coord. for Evangelization.
Legal Titles & Corporations: Newman Apostolate, Inc.

Office of the Superintendent of Schools, 6025 Sixth Ave., 11220. Tel: 718-492-1800. Rev. Msgr. Guy J. Puglisi, Supt. of Schools; Mr. Robert A. Annucci, Deputy Supt. - Dir. Personnel; Mrs. Patricia Kelly-Stiles, Assoc. Supt. Prin. Personnel; Mrs. Mary Santos, Assoc. Supt. Prog. Mgmt.; Bro. Lawrence Boyle, O.S.F., Dist. Supt. - Brooklyn East Schools; Mr. Thomas Chadzutko, Dist. Supt. - Brooklyn West Schools; Sr. Ruth Cunningham, C.S.J., Dist. Supt. - Queens North Schools; Sr. Jane Ellis, I.H.M., Dist. Supt. - Queens South Schools; Sr. Sheila Conley, S.C., Dir. Curriculum; Sr. Margaret Schmit, O.P., Asst. Dir. Personnel; Miss June Stuart, Admin. Asst. Personnel; Mr. William E. Slow, Assoc. Supt., Special Ed.; Mr. Gilbert Ortiz, Exec. Dir. Prog. for the Devel. of Human Potential.

Diocese of Brooklyn Education Offices. Legal Titles & Corporations: Department of Education, Diocese of Brooklyn; Henry M. Hald High School Association; Saint John's Preparatory School, Brooklyn.

Campus Ministers and Ministry Centers. Revs. Guy Massie; Michael A. Perry, Pratt Institute; Paul A. Wood, Queen's College; Bros. John Reidy, C.F.C., Kingsboro Community College; Jeffrey Rederson, O.S.F., St. Francis College; Sr. Margaret Smith, C.I.J., Long Island University; Sr. Alice Danaher, O.P., Queensboro Community College.

[F] HIGH SCHOOLS, DIOCESAN

BROOKLYN. *Bishop Loughlin Memorial High School*, 357 Clermont Ave., 11238. Tel: 718-857-2700; Fax: 718-398-4227.
(Coed).
Legal Corp.: Henry M. Hald Assoc. Bro. James Bonilla, F.S.C., Prin.; Rev. Paul W. Farin, Chap. Brothers of the Christian Schools 7; Priests 1; Sisters 1; Lay Teachers 53; Students 925.

[G] HIGH SCHOOLS, PRIVATE

BROOKLYN. *Bishop Ford Central Catholic High School*, 500 19th St., 11215. Tel: 718-965-6400.
(Coed). Mr. James G. Mullaney, Prin.; Mr. Rocco V. Grella, Asst. Prin. Brothers 6; Sisters 4; Lay Teachers 43; Students 812.

Bishop Kearney, 2202 60th St., 11204-2599. Tel: 718-236-6363; Fax: 718-236-7784.
(Girls). Sr. Joan McAvoy, C.S.J., Prin.; Rev. James P. Collins, M.Div., Chap. Priests 2; Sisters of St. Joseph (Brentwood Community) 29; Sisters 2; Lay Teachers 53; Students 1,067.

Catherine McAuley, 710 E. 37th St., 11203. Tel: 718-462-7282; Fax: 718-462-7284.
(Girls). Sr. Peggy Lake, R.S.M., Prin.; Rev. John W. Maloney, Spiritual Dir. Sisters of Mercy 7; Lay Teachers 21; Students 300.

Fontbonne Hall, 9901 Shore Rd., 11209. Tel: 718-748-2244.
(Girls). Sr. Anne P. Clancy, C.S.J., Prin. Sisters of St. Joseph (Brentwood Community) 13; Lay Teachers 30; Students 516.

Nazareth Regional, 475 E. 57th St., 11203. Tel: 718-763-1100.
(Coed). Dr. Robert Muccigrosso, Ph.D., Prin. Sisters 1; Lay Teachers 30; Students 600.

St. Joseph, 80 Willoughby St., 11201. Tel: 718-624-3618; Fax: 718-723-3477.
(Girls). Sr. Eugenia Calabrese, C.S.J., Prin. Sisters of St. Joseph (Brentwood Community) 20; Lay Teachers 18; Students 300.
Xaverian, 7100 Shore Rd., 11209. Tel: 718-836-7100; Fax: 718-836-7114.
(Boys). Mr. Salvatore Ferrara, Pres.; Dr. Joseph Marino, Prin.; Mr. George Donnelly, Dir. of Devel.; Mr. Thomas Grenham, Asst. Prin. for Student Activities; Mr. Philip Crivelli, Asst. Prin. for Student Formation; Mr. Sigfried Heiles, Dir. of Alumni Affairs; Rev. David Dettmer, Chap. & Academic Dean. Priests 1; Xaverian Brothers 10; Lay Teachers 85; Students 1,325.

Queens

ASTORIA. *St. John Preparatory School*, 21-21 Crescent St., 11105-3398. Tel: 718-721-7200.
(Coed). Mr. William A. Higgins, Prin.; Rev. Raymond Roden, Spiritual Dir. Priests 2; Sisters 8; Lay Teachers 70; Students 1,335.
BRIARWOOD. *Archbishop Molloy*, 83-53 Manton St., 11435. Tel: 718-441-2100.
(Boys). Bro. Richard Van Houten, F.M.S., Prin. Brothers 22; Sisters 2; Lay Teachers 57; Students 1,525.
COLLEGE POINT. *St. Agnes Academic*, 13-20 124 St., 11356. Tel: 718-353-6276; Fax: 718-353-6068.
(Girls). Sr. Marguerite Warren, Prin. Sisters of St. Dominic (Amityville) 19; Lay Teachers 22; Students 452.
EAST ELMHURST. *Monsignor McClancy*, 71-06 31st Ave., 11370. Tel: 718-898-3800.
(Boys). Bro. Joseph Rocco, S.C., Prin. Brothers 11; Sisters 2; Lay Teachers 30; Boys 700.
FLUSHING. *Holy Cross*, 26-20 Francis Lewis Blvd., 11358. Tel: 718-886-7250.
(Boys). Bro. Stephen Lamendola, C.S.C., Pres.; Mr. Joseph Giannuzzi, Prin. Brothers of the Holy Cross 13; Sisters 1; Lay Teachers 50; Students 1,000.
FRESH MEADOWS. *St. Francis Preparatory School*, 6100 Francis Lewis Blvd., 11365. Tel: 718-423-8810.
(Coed). Bro. Leonard Conway, O.S.F., Prin.; Rev. Thomas G. Pettei, Chap. Priests 1; Franciscan Brothers 15; Sisters 24; Lay Teachers 110; Students 2,850.
JAMAICA. *Dominican Commercial*, 161-06 89th Ave., 11432. Tel: 718-739-2060.
(Girls). Sisters of St. Dominic (Amityville) 20; Lay Teachers/Staff 23; Students 315.
JAMAICA ESTATES. *The Mary Louis Academy (College Preparatory)*, 176-21 Wexford Ter., 11432. Tel: 718-297-2120.
(Girls). Sr. Joan Petito, C.S.J., Prin. Priests 1; Sisters of St. Joseph (Brentwood Community) 25; Sisters of St. Dominic (Amityville) 1; Sisters of Mercy (Brooklyn) 1; Lay Teachers 60; Students 909.
MIDDLE VILLAGE. *Christ the King*, 6802 Metropolitan Ave., 11379. Tel: 718-366-7400.
(Coed). Daughters of Wisdom. Mr. Hugh Kirwan, Prin.; Rev. Anthony S. Ercolano, Chap. Priests 1; Sisters 5; Lay Teachers 88; Students 1,815.
ROCKAWAY PARK. *Stella Maris*, Beach 112th St., 11694. Tel: 718-634-4994.
(Girls). Miss Geri Martinez, Prin. Sisters of St. Joseph (Brentwood) 8; Lay Teachers 42; Students 465.
Maura Clarke Coed Jr. High Program. (Grades 7-8). Sr. Jeanne Curley, C.S.J., Dir.

[H] HIGH SCHOOLS PAROCHIAL

BROOKLYN. *Denis Maloney Institute/St. Edmund Preparatory High School*, 2474 Ocean Ave., 11229. Tel: 718-743-6100; Fax: 718-743-5243.
(Coed). Mr. John P. Lorenzetti, Prin.; Sr. Barbara Doyle, C.S.J., Asst. Prin. Sisters 3; Lay Teachers 30; Students 500.
Our Lady of Perpetual Help, 550-59th St., 11220. Tel: 718-492-5800; 492-2588.
(Girls). Sr. Mary Febronia, C.S.J., Prin.; Ms. Patricia Conley, Asst. Prin. Priests 1; Sisters 11; Lay Teachers 22; Students 375.
St. Saviour, 588 6th St., 11215. Tel: 718-768-4406; Fax: 718-369-2688.
(Girls). Sr. Valeria Belanger, S.S.N.D., Prin.; Mrs. Margaret Bernstein, Asst. Prin. School Sisters of Notre Dame 6; Lay Teachers 20; Students 275.

[I] SPECIAL SCHOOLS

BROOKLYN. *Robert F. Kennedy Incentive Program*, 2635 Linden Blvd., 11208-4992. Tel: 718-235-0744.
(Coed). Bro. Adrian Fannon, O.S.F., Prin. Brothers 1; Lay Teachers 5; Students 64.
St. Francis de Sales School for the Deaf, 260 Eastern Pkwy., 11225. Tel: 718-636-4573; Fax: 718-636-4577. Infant through Elementary Grades. Edward McCormack, M.A., Supt. Sisters 5; Lay Teachers 55; Students 180.
SPRINGFIELD GARDENS. *Martin de Porres School*, 136-25 218th St., 11413-2226. Tel: 718-525-3414. Specialized day school for emotionally disturbed children, ages 7-21. Brothers 4; Sisters 1; Staff 52; Capacity 144.

[J] ELEMENTARY SCHOOLS PRIVATE

BROOKLYN. *St. Agnes Seminary*, 2221 Avenue R, 11229. Tel: 718-376-2756. Sr. Grace Eidt, C.S.J., Prin. Sisters of St. Joseph 2; School Sisters of Notre Dame 1; Lay Teachers 14; Students 177.
St. Angela Hall Academy, 290 Washington Ave., 11205. Tel: 718-622-6919.
Under supervision of Sisters of St. Joseph. Sisters 1; Lay Teachers 9; Students 125.
Visitation Academy, 8902 Ridge Blvd., 11209. Tel: 718-680-9452; Fax: 718-680-4441. Sisters of the Visitation 14; Lay Teachers 18; Girls 200.

[K] CONSOLIDATED ELEMENTARY SCHOOLS (REGIONAL)

BROOKLYN. *St. Elizabeth Seton*, 751 Knickerbocker Ave., 11221. Tel: 718-386-4050. Sr. Mary Tully, C.S.J., Prin. Sisters 3; Lay Teachers 14; Students 383.
St. Frances Cabrini, 181 Suydam St., 11221. Tel: 718-386-9277. Maria Crifasi, Prin. Lay Teachers 10; Students 222.
St. John Neumann, 237 Jerome St., 11207. Tel: 718-277-6766. Sr. Margaret Merritt, O.P., Prin. Sisters 1; Lay Teachers 16; Students 391.

[L] CATHOLIC CHARITIES

BROOKLYN. *Catholic Charities*, Central Office, 191 Joralemon St., 11201. Tel: 718-722-6000; Fax: 718-722-6096. Most Revs. Thomas V. Daily, D.D., Corp. Member; Joseph M. Sullivan, D.D., M.S., M.P.A., Exec. Vice Pres. & Episcopal Vicar for Human Svcs.; Mr. Thomas A. DeStefano, M.S.W., Exec. Dir.; Mr. Antonio M. Blanco, C.S.W., Assoc. Exec. Dir.; Rev. Msgr. Thomas F. Cribbin, Assoc. Exec. Dir.; Carlo de Rege, M.U.P., Assoc. Exec. Dir.; Robert Siebel, M.S.W., Asst. Exec. Dir.; Elise Gotimer, Esq., Dir. Legal Affairs; Sr. Frances Picone, R.S.M., Regl. Admin. Brooklyn South; Sr. Ellen Patricia Finn, O.P., Regl. Admin. Brooklyn North; Robert Marquez, Regl. Admin. Queens West; Robert Mundy, Regl. Admin. Queens East; Rev. Msgr. Joseph Funaro, Special Asst. to Exec. Dir.; Sr. Lorna Colin, C.S.J., Special Asst. to Exec. Dir.; Sr. Kathleen Newell, B.V.M., Special Asst. to Exec. Dir.; Joan M. Murphy, M.A., C.F.R.E., Dir. Public Affairs; Stephanie Raneri, M.A., Dir. Aging; Barbara Conley, M.S.W., Dir. Child Care; Sr. Bernadette Downes, C.I.J., Dir. Disabled Persons; Bro. Joseph Moloney, O.S.F., Dir. Disability Svcs.; Sharon Fox, M.S.W., Dir. Early Childhood Devel.; John Tynan, M.U.P., Dir. Housing; Gayle DeRienzis, M.S.W., Dir. Mental Health; Rev. James S. Musumeci, M.Div., Dir. Pastoral Care of the Sick and Prison Ministries; Rev. Msgr. Howard Basler, M.A., Dir. Social Action & Campaign for Human Devel.; Rosalyn Ferguson, M.S.W., Dir. Youth Svcs.; Robert Driscoll, Dir. Employee Rels.; Marie Meyer, Dir. Financial Affairs; Kenneth Haag, Dir. Financial Svcs., B.F.F.Y.; Kathleen Slattery, Deputy Dir. Fiscal Svcs., B.F.F.Y.; Joseph Gaspard, Dir. Office Svcs.; Frank Paterno, Dir. Computer Svcs.; Margaret Keaveney, Coord. Public Rels.
Aging Services:
Golden Age Clubs, 191 Joralemon St., 11201. Tel: 718-722-6022.
Human Services:
Center for Pregnant Women, 191 Joralemon St., 11201. Tel: 718-722-6200.
Family Centers:
Brooklyn North, 191 Joralemon St., 11201. Tel: 718-722-6002.
Brooklyn South, 2341 Coney Island Ave., 11235. Tel: 718-998-7321.
Queens West, 70-11 48th Ave., Woodside, 11377. Tel: 718-899-8493.
Queens East, 90-39 189th St., Hollis, 11423. Tel: 718-217-1238.
Services For Disabled Persons:
Deafness Services, 191 Joralemon St., 11201. Tel: 718-722-6214.
Office for Disabled Persons, 191 Joralemon St., 11201. Tel: 718-722-6235.
Comprehensive Human Services:
Builders for the Family and Youth of the Diocese of Brooklyn, Inc. Most Rev. Joseph M. Sullivan, Pres.; Mr. Thomas A. De Stefano, Vice Pres. Operations; Mr. Antonio M. Blanco, Vice Pres. Svcs.; Mr. Kenneth Haag, Exec. Sec.
B.F.F.Y. - Administration: Regional Office - Brooklyn North, 191 Joralemon St., 11201. Tel: 718-722-6050. Regional Office - Brooklyn South, 2341 Coney Island Ave., 11235. Tel: 718-788-8422. Regional Office - Queens East, 90-39 189th St., Hollis, 11423. Tel: 718-217-1440. Regional Office - Queens West, 70-11 48th Ave., Woodside, 11377. Tel: 718-899-8487.
Aging Services:
Alzheimers Adult Day Care, 157-16- 65th Ave., Flushing, 11357. Tel: 718-358-3541.
Bayside Senior Center, 221-15 Horace Harding Expwy., Bayside, 11364. Tel: 718-225-1144.
Bayside Senior Services, 45-50 195th St., Flushing, 11358. Tel: 718-357-4903.
Bensonhurst Senior Services Center, 1867 Bath Ave., 11241. Tel: 718-236-3205.
Catherine Sheridan Senior Center, 35-24 83rd St., Jackson Heights, 11372. Tel: 718-458-4600.
Narrows Senior Services Center, 7907 New Utrecht Ave., 11214. Tel: 718-256-1166.
Ozone Park Senior Center, 103-12 101st Ave., Ozone Park, 11420. Tel: 718-847-2100.
Peter J. Della Monica Center for Seniors, 23-56 Broadway, Astoria, 11106. Tel: 718-626-1500.
Richmond Hill Senior Center, 123-08 Jamaica Ave., Richmond Hill, 11418. Tel: 718-846-2511.
Sheepshead Bay Senior Services, 1215 Avenue O, 11230. Tel: 718-375-3377.
Southwest Queens Senior Services, 87-04 88th Ave., Woodhaven, 11421. Tel: 718-847-9200.
St. Charles Jubilee Center, 55 Pierrepont St., 11201. Tel: 718-855-0326.
St. Louis Senior Center, 230 Kingston Ave., 11213. Tel: 718-771-7945.
St. Mary's Senior Center, 10-15 49th Ave., Long Island City, 11101. Tel: 718-729-2688.
Steinway Senior Center, 20-43 Steinway St., Astoria, 11105. Tel: 718-728-8472.
Wakefield Senior Center, 135-45 Lefferts Blvd., South Ozone Park, 11420. Tel: 718-641-0454.
Woodhaven Senior Center, 61-20 Woodside Ave., Woodhaven, 11421. Tel: 718-849-4187.
Woodside Senior Assistance Center, 70-11 48th Ave., Woodside, 11377. Tel: 718-799-1234.
B.F.F.Y. - Child Care & Head Start Programs:
Coney Island Child Care Center, 2757 W. 33rd St., 11224. Tel: 718-946-8759.
Farragut Child Care Center, 32 Navy St., 11201. Tel: 718-875-7555.
J. Di Marco Child Care Center, 36-49 11th St., Long Island City, 11106. Tel: 718-786-1166.
J.F. Kennedy Child Care Center, 103-15 Farragut Rd., 11236. Tel: 718-272-8751.
John Oravecz Child Care Center, 25 Nassau Ave., 11222. Tel: 718-782-2727.
R.F. Kennedy Child Care Center, 741 Flushing Ave., 11206. Tel: 718-782-0766.
Vincent J. Caristo Child Care Center, 5901 13th Ave., 11219. Tel: 718-853-8300.
De Paul Head Start, 71 Lincoln Pl., 11215. Tel: 718-622-2060.
Madeline Jones Head Start, 3415 Neptune Ave., 11224. Tel: 718-266-5987.
Padre Kennedy Head Start, 288 Berry St., 11211. Tel: 718-387-3679.
St. Barbara's Head Start, 139 Menahan St., 11221. Tel: 718-443-9800.
St. Joseph's Head Start, 300 Vernon Ave., 11206. Tel: 718-455-5900.
St. Margaret Mary Head Start, 9-16 27th Ave., Long Island City, 11102. Tel: 718-721-8065.
Therese Cervini Head Start, 35-34 105th St., Corona, 11368. Tel: 718-478-7786.
St. Malachy Child Development Center, 220 Hendricks St., 11207. Tel: 718-277-0625.
St. Malachy Head Start, 220 Hendricks St., 11207. Tel: 718-277-0625.
B.F.F.Y. - Human Services:
Compeer, 165-15 88th Ave., Jamaica, 11432. Tel: 718-291-4848.
F.A.N. Program, 89-56 162nd St., Jamaica, 11432. Tel: 718-523-2220.
B.F.F.Y. - Mental Health Services:
Bethlehem CSS, 157 Graham Ave., 11211. Tel: 718-963-3958.
Bond Street Drop-in-Center, 39-41 Bond St., 11201. Tel: 718-935-0439.
Brooklyn Community Living, 2000 Flatbush Ave., 11234. Tel: 718-253-1366.
Corona - Elmhurst Clinic, 37-22 82 St., Jackson Heights, 11372. Tel: 718-779-1600.
Corona Elmhurst Community Support Systems, 37-22 82nd St. & 37-66 72nd St., Jackson Heights, 11372. Tel: 718-779-2803.
Flatbush Addiction Treatment Center, 1457-69 Flatbush Ave., 11234. Tel: 718-951-9009.
Flatlands Guidance Clinic, 2000 Flatbush Ave., 11234. Tel: 718-377-5755.
Glendale Child Guidance Center, 67-29 Myrtle Ave., Glendale, 11385. Tel: 718-456-7001.
Human Outreach Mobile Exc., 492-94 Pacific St., 11201. Tel: 718-875-5015.
Queens Homeless Outreach, 165-15 88th Ave., Jamaica, 11432. Tel: 718-297-4848.
Innovation Club, 80-45 Winchester Blvd., Queens Village, 11427. Tel: 718-468-4700.
Jamaica CSS - Cont. Treatment, 165-15 88th Ave., Jamaica, 11432. Tel: 718-291-4848.

Jamaica CSS - Queens Manor, 153-90 Rockaway Blvd., Jamaica, 11434. Tel: 718-527-2971.
Jamaica CSS - Whitman Home, 160-11 89th Ave., Jamaica, 11432. Tel: 718-291-7173.
Mobile Crisis Psych. Team, 327 Beach 19th St., Far Rockaway, 11694. Tel: 718-337-6800.
On-Site School Project, 67-13 Myrtle Ave., Glendale, 11385. Tel: 718-456-7001.
Partnership of Hope, 715 Dean St., 11238. Tel: 718-398-0409.
Queen Community Living Program, 35-24 83rd St., Jackson Heights, 11372. Tel: 718-639-0700.
Rockaway CSS - Central Manor, 1509 Central Ave., Far Rockaway, 11691. Tel: 718-471-7545.
Rockaway CSS - Surfside Manor, 95-04 Rockaway Beach Blvd., Rockaway Park. Tel: 718-471-7545.
Rockaway CSS - Screening Team, 13-19 Beach Channel Dr., Far Rockaway, 11691. Tel: 718-471-7586.
Rockaway Community Life Skills (Freedom Village), 13-29 Beach Channel Dr., Far Rockaway, 11691. Tel: 718-471-7545.
Rockaway Community Life Skills - Cont. Treatment, 13-19 Beach Channel Dr., Far Rockaway, 11691. Tel: 718-337-6850.
Rockaway Mental Health Services, 13-19 Beach Channel Dr., Far Rockaway, 11691. Tel: 718-337-6800.
Rose House (RCCA), 80-45 Winchester Blvd., Queens Village, 11427. Tel: 718-468-4700.
The Open Door, 2000 Flatbush Ave., 11234. Tel: 718-377-7757.
Woodside Senior Assistance Center, 61-20 Woodside Ave., Woodside, 11377. Tel: 718-799-1234.
Monica House, 161-01 89th Ave., Jamaica, 11432. Tel: 718-657-9027.
B.F.F.Y. - Prevention of Foster Care:
Coney Island Family Resource Center, 2201 Neptune Ave., 11224. Tel: 718-372-6400.
Family Support Center of East New York, 2635 Linden Blvd., 11208. Tel: 718-827-5700.
Jamaica Family & Youth Center, 120-09 141st. St., South Ozone Park, 11432. Tel: 718-738-2500.
B.F.F.Y. - Services for Disabled Persons:
Peter J. Connelly Residence, 15 Willow St., 11201. Tel: 718-625-5590.
Adessa House, 101-38 92 St., Ozone Park, 11416. Tel: 718-848-1940.
Alhambra Day Treatment Center, 11-29 Catherine St., 11211. Tel: 718-388-5900.
Caldwell House, 121-01 116th Ave., South Ozone Park, 11420. Tel: 718-845-1200.
Carmel Residence, 275 N. Eighth St., 11211. Tel: 718-388-6109.
Cribbin House, 218-20 104th Ave., Queens Village, 11429. Tel: 718-776-4190.
Dawson Manor, 94-17 84th St., Ozone Park, 11416. Tel: 718-296-1172.
Donald Savio Residence, 104-22 48th Ave., Corona, 11368. Tel: 718-699-7800.
Fitzpatrick Residence, 240 McKinley Ave., 11208. Tel: 718-647-7070.
Garfield Manor, 305 Garfield Pl., 11215. Tel: 718-622-2100.
Golden Residence, 225 Brooklyn Ave., 11213. Tel: 718-953-4444.
Graci Residence, 132-14 90th St., Ozone Park, 11416. Tel: 718-848-1970.
Helen Owen Carey Residence, 174 Java St., 11222. Tel: 718-383-2451.
McLees House, 112-16 200th St., St. Albans, 11412. Tel: 718-217-0285.
Mugavero Manor, 145-16 Farmers Blvd., Springfield Gardens, 11434. Tel: 718-217-0285.
Mulrooney Manor, 479 E. 29th St., 11226. Tel: 718-287-7553.
Senior F.U.N., 415 Bleeker St., 1121. Tel: 718-417-5316.
Sterling Residence, 152 Sterling St., 11225. Tel: 718-282-8045.
Straus Residence, 3730 Shore Pkwy., 11233. Tel: 718-769-8836.
Supportive Living Apartments, 243 Prospect Park W., 11215. Tel: 718-788-8422.
The Francis De Falco Dental Clinic, 11-29 Catherine St., 11211. Tel: 718-384-0303.
B.F.F.Y. - Services for Persons Living with AIDS:
Circle of Hope, 2341 Coney Island, 11235. Tel: 718-788-8422.
B.F.F.Y. - Youth Services:
N.E. Queens Young Parents, 41-06 163rd St., Flushing, 11358. Tel: 718-217-1238.
N.Q. Parenting Partnership, 70-11 48th Ave., Woodside, 11377. Tel: 718-899-8487.
Project Bridge, 144 Bleeker St., 11221. Tel: 718-455-4649.
Rainbow Workshops for Youth, 144 Bleeker St., 11221. Tel: 718-455-4649.
St. Mary's Youth Center, 10-08 49th Ave., Long Island City, 11101. Tel: 718-899-8487.
Project Reach Out - Youth In Rockaway, 336 Beach 38th St., Far Rockaway, 11691. Tel: 718-217-1238.
Work Experience Program, 191 Joralemon St., 11201. Tel: 718-596-5500.
Housing Development and Management Services:
Progress of Peoples Development Corporation. John Tynan, M.U.P.
Progress of Peoples Managment Corporation. Maureen McKeown, Dir., Housing Svcs.; Terri Mejillones, Dir. Fiscal Svcs.
Housing Corporations:
Bethlehem, 191 Joralemon St., 11201.
Bishop Boardman Apartments, HDFC, Inc., 191 Joralemon St., 11201.
Bishop Francis J. Mugavero, HDFC, Inc., 191 Joralemon St., 11201.
Sr. Lucian Apartments, HDFC, Inc., 191 Joralemon St., 11201.
Caring Communities, 191 Joralemon St., 11201.
Mary Star of the Sea Apartments, HFDC, Inc., 191 Joralemon St., 11201.
Catherine Sheridan Houses, 191 Joralemon St., 11201.
Pope John Paul II, HDFC, Inc., 191 Joralemon St., 11201.
Pierrepont Holding Corp., 191 Joralemon St., 11201.
Pierrepont Associates, 191 Joralemon St., 11201.
Pierrepont House for the Elderly, Inc., 191 Joralemon St., 11201.
Queens Rehab, 191 Joralemon St., 11201.
St. Brendans Apartments, HDFC, Inc., 191 Joralemon St., 11201.
Msgr. John O'Brien Apts., HDFC, Inc., 191 Joralemon St., 11201.
Msgr. Mullaney Apartments, 191 Joralemon St., 11201.
POP 55, 191 Joralemon St., 11201.
Five seventy two 572 Sterling Place, 191 Joralemon St., 11201.
Southside Apartments (General Partnership), 191 Joralemon St., 11201.
Southburg Apartments, 191 Joralemon St., 11201.
Whipple Lewis Apartments, Inc. (General Partnership), 191 Joralemon St., 11201.
Long Island City Senior House, 191 Joralemon St., 11201.
Willoughby-Classon Avenue, Ltd. Partnership, 191 Joralemon St., 11201.
Families Together, 191 Joralemon St., 11201.
Parkville, HDFC, 191 Joralemon St., 11201.
Holy Spirit/Rego Park, 191 Joralemon St., 11201.
One sixty one 161-01 89th Avenue Corp., 191 Joralemon St., 11201.
Our Lady of Fatima Apts., HDFC, Inc., 191 Joralemon St., 11201.
David Minkin Residence, HDFC, Inc., 191 Joralemon St., 11201.
Emmaus of the Diocese of Brooklyn, Inc., 191 Joralemon St., 11201.
Youth Development and Recreation:
Catholic Youth Organization of the Diocese of Brooklyn, Inc., 191 Joralemon St., 11201. Tel: 718-596-5500.
Nursing Home:
Ss. Joachim & Anne Residence, 2720 Surf Ave., 11224. Tel: 718-714-4800.
Home Care for the Sick:
Care at Home for the Diocese of Brooklyn, Inc., 6910 Fifth Ave., 11209. Tel: 718-238-4700.
Residences for Women:
Providence House, Inc., P.O. Box 210529. Tel: 718-455-0197. Sr. Marie Leniham, C.S.J., Exec. Dir., Providence House 1, 2518 Church Ave., 11226. Providence House 2, 172 Bainbridge St., 11233. Providence House 3, 159-23 89th Ave., Jamaica, 11432. Providence House 4, 89 Sickles Ave., New Rochelle, 10801. Providence House 5, 396 Lincoln Rd., 11225.
Community Centers:
Dr. White Community Center, 200 Gold St., 11201. Tel: 718-875-8801.
Bhrags, Inc., 1212 E. New York Ave., 11212. Tel: 718-778-5484. Sr. Rosemary McKenna, D.W., Exec. Dir.
Haitian Center, 1063 Winthrop St., 11212. Tel: 718-778-5485. Edouard Louis, Dir.
Other Affiliated Agencies:
Anthonian Hall, Inc. Thomas A. De Stefano, Treas.; Most Rev. Joseph M. Sullivan, Treas.; Rev. Msgr. Thomas F. Cribbin, Sec.
Catholic Guild for the Blind, Diocese of Brooklyn, Inc. Rev. Msgr. Thomas F. Cribbin.
Ecclesial Consultants, Inc., 191 Joralemon St., 11201. Tel: 718-596-5500.
A management service for Church agencies and organizations. Directors: Most Rev. Joseph M. Sullivan; Rev. Msgr. Emmet Fagan (RVC); Rev. Msgr. Charles J. Fahey (RVC).
Ferrini Welfare League, 98-21 101 Ave., Ozone Park, 11416. Tel: 718-845-0539.
Flowers with Care, Diocese of Brooklyn, Inc., 23-40 Astoria Blvd., Astoria, 11102. Tel: 718-726-9790.
Italian Board of Guardians, 1781 73 St., 11204. Tel: 718-232-4242. Rev. Anthony Failla, Mod.; Mrs. Angela R. Villanella, C.S.W., Dir. Social Svcs.; Mrs. Beatrice Rizzo, Exec. Sec.
Mary's Hall, Inc. Most Rev. Joseph M. Sullivan, Pres.
Society of St. Vincent de Paul in Diocese of Brooklyn, Central Office, 191 Joralemon St., 11201. Tel: 718-625-1400. Most Rev. Thomas V. Daily, D.D., Spiritual Advisor; Rev. Msgr. James W. Asip, Assoc. Spiritual Advisor; Mr. Joseph Martino, Pres., District Council of Kings, 191 Joralemon St., 11201. Tel: 718-625-1400. Rev. Raymond J. Kelly, S.T.L., Spiritual Advisor; Mr. Frank Mauro, Pres., District Council of Queens, 191 Joralemon St., 11201. Tel: 718-625-1400. Rev. Msgr. James W. Asip, Spiritual Advisor; Mr. Vito Buccaria, Pres.
Catholic Guild for the Blind, Diocese of Brooklyn, Inc. Rev. Msgr. Thomas F. Cribbin.
Bread & Life Soup Kitchen, 75 Lewis Ave., 11206. Tel: 718-574-0058. Rev. James Maher, Pres.

[M] NURSING SERVICES

BROOKLYN. *Nursing Sisters Home Visiting Service, Inc.*, Corporate Office, 310 Prospect Park W., 11215. Tel: 516-683-1370. Sr. Mary Nadine Casey, C.I.J., Pres.; Sr. Agnes Stumpf, C.I.J., Exec. Dir., Nursing Service Offices, Kings County, 310 Prospect Park W., 11215. Tel: 718-965-7339. Mrs. Elise Mattia, Supvr.

[N] HOSPITALS

JAMAICA. *Catholic Medical Center of Brooklyn & Queens*, 88-25 153rd St., 11432. Tel: 718-558-6900.
For a complete listing, refer to the Hospitals section.

[O] CHILD CARE AGENCIES

BROOKLYN. *The Angel Guardian Homes*, 6301 12th Ave., 11219. Tel: 718-232-1500; Fax: 718-232-0331. Ms. Sheila N. Pelan, Exec. Dir.
Foster Boarding Home and Adoption Services, 372 Clinton Ave., 11238. Tel: 718-638-7424. Adoption Service and Residence for Mother-Baby.
Preventive Programs, Fort Greene, 430 Myrtle Ave., 11205. Tel: 718-624-2100.
Family Support Center, 57 Willoughby St., 11201. Tel: 718-855-7778. Sisters 4; Students 750.
Catholic Child Care Society of the Diocese of Brooklyn, 540 Atlantic Ave., 11217. Tel: 718-797-6080; Fax: 718-797-6092. John J. Bennett, Jr., Pres.; Cecilia Rivera Healy, C.S.W., Exec. Dir.
Good Shepherd Services, 441 Fourth Ave., 11215. Tel: 718-788-0666. Sr. Paulette LoMonaco, R.G.S., Exec. Dir. Provides a comprehensive range of neighborhood family services to individuals & youth from the South Brooklyn community. Services include educational support, employment, counseling & crisis intervention, literacy, skills training & advocacy services to children & families as well as foster care & adoption & residences for teenagers.
HeartShare Human Services of New York, Roman Catholic Diocese of Brooklyn, 191 Joralemon St., 11201. Tel: 718-330-0600; Fax: 718-237-2550. William R. Guarinello, M.S., Pres. & CEO. Foster Boarding Home Program, Adoption Program, Family Service Centers. Programs for Developmentally Disabled: Group Homes, Supportive Apartments, Preschool Program (Early Childhood Centers), Respite/ Recreation Program, Day Treatment/Day Habilitation Programs, Services for People with HIV/AIDS, School-Based Beacon Program, Youth Services, Traditional Preschool Program.
HeartShare Human Services - Clinton Residence, 217 Clinton Ave., 11205. Tel: 718-638-2625.
HeartShare Human Services - Clermont Residence, 26 Clermont Ave., 11205. Tel: 718-834-9317.
HeartShare Human Services - Msgr. Thomas G. Hagerty Residence, 128 Montrose Ave., 11206. Tel: 718-387-3595.
HeartShare Human Services - Dr. Catherine White Residence, 175 Metropolitan Ave., 11211. Tel: 718-782-9104.
HeartShare Human Services - 54th Street Residence, 1966 54th St., 11204. Tel: 718-259-4432.
HeartShare Human Services - Antonetta Ferraro Residence, 603 Beach 19 St., Far Rockaway, 11691. Tel: 718-327-9000.
HeartShare Human Services - Thomas J. Cuite Residence, 50-36 45th St., Woodside, 11377. Tel: 718-786-3113.
HeartShare Human Services - 35th Avenue Residence, 172-07 35th Ave., Flushing, 11358. Tel: 718-961-7673.
HeartShare Human Services - Doonan-Drake Residence, 300 E. 18th St., 11226. Tel: 718-469-5000.
HeartShare Human Services - Hart Street Residence, 689 Hart St., 11221. Tel: 718-919-7477.
HeartShare Human Services - James and Kathleen Buckley Residence, 977-979 E. 92nd St., 11236. Tel: 718-272-1441.

HeartShare Human Services - Frances Aiello Day Treatment Center, 163 MacDonough St., 11206. Tel: 718-443-5071.

HeartShare Human Services - Eileen and William Lavin Day Treatment Center, 545 Broadway, 11206. Tel: 718-388-1665.

HeartShare Human Services - John and Lillian Sharkey, Sr. Residence, 60-12 56th St., Maspeth, 11378. Tel: 718-417-6846.

HeartShare Human Services - Harry Hoffman Day Treatment Center, 62-10 Northern Blvd., Woodside, 11377. Tel: 718-899-2752.

HeartShare Human Services - Matilda Raffa Cuomo First Step Early Childhood Center, 115-15 101st Ave., Richmond Hill, 11419. Tel: 718-441-5333.

HeartShare Human Services - Lefferts/Liberty Kiwanis First Step Early Childhood Center, 82-12 151st Ave., Howard Beach, 11414. Tel: 718-848-0300.

HeartShare Human Services - Russo First Step Early Childhood Center, 118-03 111th Ave., Richmond Hill, 11419. Tel: 718-805-7117.

HeartShare Human Services - Red Hook Family Services, 732 Henry St., 11231. Tel: 718-858-8387.

HeartShare Human Services - HIV/AIDS Scattered Site Housing Program, 221 Smith St., 11201. Tel: 718-596-3391.

HeartShare Human Services - South Brooklyn Family Services, 213 Smith St., 11201. Tel: 718-596-3391.

HeartShare Human Services - East Brooklyn Family Services, 3005 Glenwood Rd., 11210. Tel: 718-434-7900.

HeartShare Human Services - Bensonhurst Family Services, 138 Bay 20th St., 11214. Tel: 718-234-1717.

HeartShare Human Services - Surfside Beacon Program and Surfside Family Services, 2926 W. 30th St., 11214. Tel: 718-714-0103.

HeartShare Human Services - HIV/AIDS Community Follow-up Program, 2882 W. 15 St., 11224. Tel: 718-372-0580.

HeartShare Human Services - Preschool Center, 8515 Ridge Blvd., 11220. Tel: 718-238-4637.

HeartShare Human Services - Day Habilitation Program, 61-58 Springfield Blvd., Bayside, 11364. Tel: 718-287-0480. Total Assisted 3,000.

Little Flower Children's Services, 186 Remsen St., 11201. Tel: 718-260-8840. Rev. Msgr. John T. Fagan, M.S.W., Exec. Vice Pres.; Mary G. Ryder, Exec. Dir.; Sr. Agnese Palczynski, C.S.F.N., Supr. Foster Care, Adoption & Post Adoption Services, Services for Adult MR/DD clients; Residential Treatment Center, U.F.S.D., & Family Day Care at Wading River, NY; Teen Mothers & Infants in Foster Homes.

Mercy Home for Children, 310 Prospect Park W., 11215. Tel: 718-965-7342. Sr. Catherine Crumlish.

Under the supervision of the Sisters of Mercy. Six Intermediate Care Facilities (Residences) for adolescents & adults who are severely developmentally disabled: Visitation Residence; Harold Warren Residence; M. Vincent Haire Residence; Littlejohn Residence; Santulli Residence; Kevin Keating Residence. Sisters 10; Staff 176; Residents 72.

St. Francis Home for Boys, 132 Eagle St., 11222. Tel: 718-383-9870. Rev. Benedict J. Groeschel, C.F.R., Exec. Dir.; Mr. Joseph Campo, Dir. Residents 5.

St. Joseph Services for Children and Families, 540 Atlantic Ave., 11217. Tel: 718-858-8700. Cecilia Rivera Healy, C.S.W., Exec. Dir. Sisters of Charity of Mount St. Vincent, NY. Programs: Foster Boarding Homes, Group Homes, 24 Hour Emergency Foster Boarding Homes, Adoption Services, Williamsburgh Family Services, Bushwick Family Services, S.T.A.R.S. (Specialized Treatment & AIDS Related Services), Mother/Child Residential Program.

St. Vincent's Services, Inc. (Formerly St. Vincent's Home for Boys and St. Vincent's Hall, Inc.), 66 Boerum Pl., 11201. Tel: 718-522-3700; Fax: 718-875-8536. Rev. Msgr. Robert M. Harris, M.S.W., M.Phil, M.A., Pres. & CEO. Services include: Foster Boarding Homes, Group Homes, Adoption Services, Pediatric AIDS Program, Refugee Assistance Program, Enhanced Independent Living Program, Mental Health Services OutPatient Service, & Residences for the Developmentally Disabled. Sisters 6; Priests 2; Children 1,300.

ROCKAWAY PARK. *St. John's Residence and School for Boys*, 144-Beach 111 St., 11694. Tel: 718-945-2800. Bro. Thomas N. Trager, S.M., Exec. Dir. Conducted by the Brothers of Society of Mary (Marianists). Residential care for adolescent boys. Diagnostic Reception Centers, Non-Secure Detention/Independent Living Program. Brothers 8; Residents 100.

SEA CLIFF. *St. Christopher-Ottilie*, Park and Downing Aves., 11579. Tel: 516-671-1253; 718-895-8670; Fax: 516-671-2899. Mr. Robert J. McMahon, Exec. Dir.; Mary Hall, Dir. of Intake and Placement. Residential Treatment Center for the profoundly & severely mentally retarded, Intermediate Care Facilities, Group Homes for Adolescent Teenage Boys and Girls, Teen Mother-Child Residence Program, Homeless Program for Teenage Boys, Preventive Programs (3), EFBH Network, Unaccompanied Vietnamese Program, Supervised Independent Living Apartments, Therapeutic Foster Boarding Homes, Residential Treatment Facility, Article 81 School. Regular Foster Care Program for Mentally Retarded Individuals, Crisis Respite, Home & Community Based Waiver Services, Madonna Heights Services. Children 2,650.

[P] GROUP HOMES FOR RETARDED CHILDREN

SPRINGFIELD GARDENS. *Martin De Porres Group Homes*, 136-25 218th St., 11413.

For a complete listing, refer to the Special Care Facilities section.

[Q] SUMMER CAMPS AND DAY CAMPS

BROOKLYN. *Bishop McDonnell Camp*, c/o Society of St. Vincent De Paul, 191 Joralemon St., 11201. Tel: 718-625-1400. Joseph E. Collins, Dir. Day Outings for Senior Citizen Groups, Handicapped & Children from poor areas. Sponsored by the Society of St. Vincent de Paul Brooklyn Diocese.

CENTERPORT. *Camp Alvernia*, Prospect Rd., P.O. Box 301, 11721. Tel: 516-261-5730. Bro. Bryan Murphy, O.S.F., Dir.

Under the supervision of the Franciscan Brothers.

[R] RESIDENCES FOR THE AGED

BROOKLYN.

For a complete listing, refer to the Special Care Facilities section.

Bishop Francis J. Mugavero Center for Geriatric Care, Inc., 155 Dean St., 11217. Tel: 718-694-6700.

For a complete listing, refer to the Special Care Facilities section.

Holy Family Home, 1740 84th St., 11214. Tel: 718-232-3666.

For a complete listing, refer to the Special Care Facilities section.

SS. Joachim & Anne Residence, Inc., 2720 Surf Ave., 11224. Tel: 718-714-4800.

For a complete listing, refer to the Special Care Facilities section.

BAYSIDE. *Ozanam Hall of Queens Nursing Home, Inc.*, 42-41 201st St., 11361. Tel: 718-423-2000.

For a complete listing, refer to the Special Care Facilities section.

JAMAICA. *Msgr. James H. Fitzpatrick Pavilion for Skilled Nursing Care*, 152-11 89th Ave., 11432. Tel: 718-291-4300.

For a complete listing, refer to the Special Care Facilities section.

QUEENS VILLAGE. *Queen of Peace Residence*, 110-30 221st St., 11429. Tel: 718-464-1800.

For a complete listing, refer to the Special Care Facilities section.

[S] SETTLEMENT ASSOCIATIONS

GLENDALE. *Kolping Center*, 65-04 Myrtle Ave., 11385. Tel: 718-456-7727. Ms. Louise G. Conte, Pres. Legal Title: *Catholic Kolping Society (Katholischer Gesellen Verein) of Brooklyn, Inc.*

[T] CATHOLIC MIGRATION AND REFUGEE OFFICES

BROOKLYN. *Catholic Migration & Refugee Office, Catholic Migration Services, Inc.*, 1258 65th St., 11219. Tel: 718-236-3000; Fax: 718-256-9707. Rev. Ronald T. Marino, Dir. Apostolate Coordinators.

Brazilian Apostolate. Rev. Amarilho Checon, Coord.

Chinese Apostolate-Queens. Rev. Thomas Sung.

Chinese Apostolate-Brooklyn. Rev. John Tan.

Croation Apostolate. Rev. Anton Bozanic, Coord.

Filipino Apostolate. Rev. Eugene Soriano, Coord.

Haitian Apostolate. Rev. Guy Sansaricq, Coord.

Hispanic Ministry Office. Rev. John Brogan.

Indian Apostolate. Rev. Paul Vazhapilly, Coord.

Indonesian Apostolate. Rev. Alex Wijoyo, Coord.

Irish Apostolate. Rev. Colm Campbell, Coord.

Italian Apostolate. Rev. John Costello, Coord.

Korean Apostolate. Rev. Thomas F. Brosnan, Coord.

Knanaya Indian Apostolate. Rev. Joseph Saurimakel, Coord.

Pakistan Apostolate.

Portuguese Apostolate.

Polish Apostolate. Rev. Peter Zendzian, Coord.

Rumanian Apostolate.

Russian Apostolate. Rev. John Soles.

Vietnamese Apostolate. Rev. Luke Pham Anh Du, Coord.

West Indian Apostolate. Rev. Martin Carter, S.A., Coord.

Resources, Inc., 1258 65th St., 11219. Tel: 718-236-3000; Fax: 718-256-9707. Rev. Ronald T. Marino, Dir.

Catholic Immigrant Ministries, Inc., 1258 65th St., 11219. Rev. Ronald T. Marino, Dir.

Apostleship of the Sea. Stella Maris Center, 45 DeGraw St., 11231. Tel: 718-834-1234.

ASTORIA-LONG ISLAND CITY. *Regional Service Centers*, 23-40 Astoria Blvd., 11102. Tel: 718-728-2621. Immigration Counselors: Mr. Juan Fernandez; Mrs. Lidia Fernandez; Angela DiPaola; Ms. Deborah Maldonado, 1258-65th St., Borough Park, 11219. Tel: 718-236-3000. Mr. Frank J. Schorn, Attorney at Law; Rev. John J. Garkowski, Asst. Staff Attorney; Mrs. Carmen Gonzalez.

[U] MONASTERIES AND RESIDENCES OF PRIESTS AND BROTHERS

BROOKLYN. *Carmelites of Mary Immaculate, Inc.*, 21 Nassau Ave., 11222. Tel: 718-388-5145. Rev. Sebastian Kochupurackal, C.M.I. (India), Supr. & Regl. Coord.

Christian Brothers Residence, 367 Clermont Ave., 11238. Bros. James Bonilla, F.S.C., Prin.; Peter Bonventre, F.S.C.; James Brennan, F.S.C.; John Guasconi, F.S.C.; David Carroll, F.S.C.; Raphael Cecchini, F.S.C.; Richard Grieco, F.S.C.; Charles Guglielmo, F.S.C.; William Kemmerer, F.S.C.; John McMahon, F.S.C.; Frederick Del Antonio, F.S.C.; Philip Zeller, F.S.C., Dir. Brothers 12.

Curial Residence, 378 Clermont Ave., 11238. Tel: 718-638-0697. Most Rev. Joseph M. Sullivan, M.S.W., D.D.; Rev. Msgr. Austin P. Bennett, J.C.D.; Rev. Msgr. Octavio Cisneros, V.E.; Rev. Thomas Doyle.

Oratory of Saint Philip Neri, Congregation Pontifical Right, 109 Willoughby St., 11201. Tel: 718-875-2096. Very Rev. Dennis M. Corrado, C.O., Provost; Bros. James Simon, C.O.; Joel Warden, C.O.; Revs. Terence P. Gleeson, C.O.; Mark J. Lane, C.O. Priests 3; Brothers 2; Full Member Triennial Seminarian 1.

Our Lady of Good Counsel Residence, 7509 Shore Rd., 11209. Tel: 718-833-1900; Fax: 718-630-5666. Provincial Residence for Redemptorist Fathers and Brothers. Very Rev. George J. Keaveney, C.SS.R., Prov. Supr.; Revs. Patrick F. Woods, C.SS.R., Prov. Vicar; Albert R. Schreiber, C.SS.R., Sec. of Prov.; Francis J. O'Rourke, C.SS.R., Prov. Consultor; Francis P. Nelson, C.SS.R., Procurator; Gerard J. Knapp, C.SS.R., Asst. Procurator; Carl W. Hoegerl, C.SS.R., Prov. Archivist; Ruskin S. Piedra, C.SS.R.; Thomas Rochacewicz, C.SS.R. Priests 7; Brothers 2.

St. Casimir's Monastery, Printing Plant and Cultural Center, 361 Highland Blvd., 11207. Tel: 718-235-5962. Franciscan Fathers of the Lithuanian Province of St. Casimir. Most Rev. Paul Baltakis, O.F.M.; Revs. Francis Giedgaudas, O.F.M., Dir. Printery & Supr.; Cornelius Bucmys, O.F.M., Editor of Darbininkas "The Worker". Priests 1; Brothers 1.

St. Francis Monastery-Generalate Offices of Franciscan Brothers, 135 Remsen St., 11201-4212. Tel: 718-858-8217. Bros. Kevin Smith, O.S.F., Supr. Gen.; Jeffrey Pedersen, O.S.F., Vocation Dir.; Joseph Moloney, O.S.F., 1st Councillor; Edward Wesley, O.S.F., 2nd Councillor; Robert Smith, O.S.F., 3rd Councillor; Gabriel O'Brien, O.S.F., 4th Councillor; Timothy Walsh, O.S.F., Bus. Mgr.; Edwin Gill, O.S.F., Treas. Gen. Brothers 111.

St. John the Baptist Rectory, 75 Lewis Ave., 11206. Tel: 718-455-6864. Revs. Stephen M. Grozio, C.M., Pastor; Thomas S. Krafinski, C.M.; Joseph V. Agostino, C.M.; John P. Timlin, Supr.; Bro. Joseph Tauraso, C.M.

St. Joseph's Priest Residence, 256 Clinton Ave., 11205. Tel: 718-783-4989. Rev. Msgr. Thomas F. Cribbin; Rev. Msgr. Howard B. Basler, S.T.B., M.A.; Rev. Msgr. Martin Bannan, B.A., M.S.W.; Rev. Robert Frueh, M.S.

St. Michael's Friary, 225 Jerome St., 11207. Tel: 718-827-6990. Revs. Brendan P. Buckley, O.F.M.Cap., Pastor; Philip Fabiano, O.F.M.Cap., Parochial Vicar; Raphael Iannone, O.F.M.Cap., Supr. & Co-Dir. of Capuchin Postulancy Prog.; William Hugo, O.F.M.Cap., Friary Vicar & Co-Dir. of Capuchin Postulancy Prog. In res., George Dash, O.F.M.Cap., Prison Chap.; John Conway, O.F.M.Cap., Hospital Chap. Priests 5; Postulants 6; Brothers 1.

DOUGLASTON. *Bishop Mugavero Residence*, 7200 Douglaston Pkwy., 11362. Tel: 718-229-8001; Fax: 718-229-2658. Rev. Jeffry T. Dillon, Dir. In res., Rev. Msgr. Henry P. Cosgrove, (Retired); Rev. Msgr. Francis X. Mulhall; Rev. Msgr. George V. Fogarty; Rev. Msgr. Edward W. Jolley; Revs. Louis B. Bartruff; Harold A. Buetow; Harry M. Culkin; John F. Cronin; Thomas U. Jung; Raymond J. Morgan; Raymond A. McGuirk; John F. Oravecz; John L. Pakalniskis; Francis S. Pullo; Stanislaus Raila; Robert Young; Barnabas Wang.

Institutional Services Residence, 7200 Douglaston Pkwy., 11362; Fax: 718-279-3004. Rev. Msgr. Joseph P. Nagle, Dir.; Mr. Robert Rymers, Operations Mgr.

ELMHURST. *Congregation of St. John the Baptist of China*, 55-21 92nd St., 11373. Tel: 718-592-5981; Fax: 718-271-3215. Revs. Thomas Sung, C.S.J.B.

(Taiwan), Prior; Dehua Zhang, C.S.J.B.; Bro. Silvester Liang, C.S.J.B. Seminarians 3.

FOREST HILLS. *Augustinian Fathers-Province of Castile, Spain*, 111-41 77th Ave., 11375. Tel: 718-575-3546. Rev. Manuel J. Rodriguez, O.S.A.

JAMAICA. *Immaculate Conception Monastery*, 86-45 Edgerton Blvd., 11432. Tel: 718-739-6502; Fax: 718-657-0578. Very Rev. Justin Kerber, C.P., Rector; Revs. Stanislaus Wasek, C.P., Vice Rector; Giles Ahrens, C.P.; Lawrence Bellew, C.P., Chap.; Jerome Bracken, C.P.; Albert Catanzaro, C.P.; Paul Chenot, C.P., Chap.; Theophane Cooney, C.P., Asst. Pastor; Paul Joseph Fullam, C.P.; Mario Gallipoli, C.P.; Bernardine Grande, C.P.; Thomas Griffiths, C.P.; Joseph D. Guzinski, C.P.; Colman Haggerty, C.P., Econome; Arnold Horner, C.P.; Ernest Hotz, C.P.; Thomas Joyce, C.P., Pastor; Owen Lally, C.P.; Dominic Papa, C.P., Dir., Preaching Office; Albert Pellicane, C.P., Chap.; John Chrysostom Ryan, C.P.; Romuald Walsh, C.P.; Theodore Walsh, C.P.; Nicholas Zitz, C.P.; Neil Davin, C.P.; John Douglas, C.P.; Justin Garvey, C.P.; John R. Mescall, C.P.; John P. Moore, C.P.; Kenan Peters, C.P.; Claudio Piccinini, C.P.; James Price, C.P.; Lawrence Rywalt, C.P.; Robin Ryan, C.P., Retreat Dir.; Bros. Vincent Basile, C.P.; Philip Maggiulli, C.P.; Kenneth Pughe, C.P.; Angelo Sena, C.P.; John Jepsen, C.P. Priests 37; Brothers 6. Marist Brothers of Ulster County, 83-53 Manton St., 11435-1697.

Parsons Manor, 88-25 153rd St., 11432. Tel: 718-558-2000. Revs. John L. Kiernan; Daniel J. Sheehan; Romano J. Ferraro; Jose Cadusale (Philippines); James P. Sweeney.

Saint Charles House of Studies, 168-41 84th Ave., 11432. Tel: 718-526-3917. Rev. Peter P. Polo, C.S., Rector.

St. Vincent's House, 84-15 Kendrick Pl., 11432. Tel: 718-262-8265. Vincentian Fathers. Revs. James Kiernan, C.M.; Joseph Daly, C.M., Supr.; Joseph Foley, C.M.; John Freund, C.M.; Donald Harrington, C.M.; James Maher, C.M.; John McKenna, C.M.; Bernard Tracey, C.M.; Robert Vignola, C.M.

Vincentian Residence, St. John's University, 8000 Utopia Pkwy., 11439. Tel: 718-990-6744. Revs. Michael J. Carroll, C.M., Supr.; Peter Albano, C.M.; Henry M. Bradbury; Michael J. Callahan; Thomas Concagh, C.M.; Stephen Denig, C.M.; James Dorr, C.M.; Peter Goldbach, C.M.; Richard J. Kehoe; James Kelly, C.M.; John McDonnell, C.M.; James A. Morris; Michael F. Mullen, C.M.; John B. Murray, C.M.; David O'Connell, C.M.; Joseph M. O'Donnell, C.M.; Martin Peterson, C.M.; Thomas Prior, C.M.; Robert J. Rivard, C.M.; Kenneth Slattery, C.M.; Daniel J. Sullivan, C.M.; Robert J. Swain.

JAMAICA ESTATES. *Paulist Fathers - Generalate*, 86-11 Midland Pkwy., 11432. Tel: 718-291-5995.

KEW GARDENS. *St. Columbans Foreign Mission Society*, 118-32 80 Rd., 11415. Tel: 718-847-3700; Fax: 718-847-3702. Revs. Paul J. O'Rourke, S.S.C.; Patrick Meehan, S.S.C. Priests 2.

LONG ISLAND CITY. *Holy Ghost Fathers of Ireland*, 48-49 37th St., 11101. Tel: 718-729-5273; Fax: 718-279-6949. Very Rev. Vincent O'Connell, C.S.Sp., Prov. Delegate; Revs. Michael J. McCarthy, C.S.Sp.; Patrick Holohan, C.S.Sp.

OZONE PARK. *Montfort Missionaries Provincialate*, 101-18 104th St., 11416. Tel: 718-849-5885. Revs. Gerald J. Fitzsimmons, S.M.M., Prov. Supr.; Matthew J. Considine, S.M.M., Prov. Treas. Priests 2.
Priests of Province Serving Abroad: Revs. Frank Setzer, S.M.M.; Everett Brown, S.M.M.; Peter D'Abele, S.M.M., Chontales, Nicaragua; John Breslin, S.M.M., Dominican Republic.

QUEENS VILLAGE. *DePaul Residence*, 80-14 217th St., 11427. Revs. Richard J. Devine, C.M.; Stephen C. Bicsko, C.M.; John J. Conway, C.M.; John D. McElynn, C.M.

SPRINGFIELD GARDENS. *Martin De Porres Brothers Community*, 136-01 219th St., 11413. Tel: 718-978-7155; Fax: 718-525-0982.

[V] CONVENTS AND RESIDENCES FOR SISTERS

BROOKLYN. *Discalced Carmelite Nuns*, 745 St. John's Pl., 11216.

Franciscan Sisters of the Poor, Congregational Office, 133 Remsen St., 11201. Tel: 718-643-1919; Fax: 718-643-9710. Sr. Bernadette Sullivan, S.F.P., Congregational Min.

Franciscan Sisters of the Poor Health System, Inc.

Missionaries of Charity, Contemplative Our Lady of Lourdes Convent, 34 Aberdeen St., 11207. Tel: 718-443-2868. Sr. M. Maria, M.C., Supr. Sisters 6.

Monastery of the Sisters Adorers of the Precious Blood, 54th St. and Ft. Hamilton Pkwy., 11219. Sr. Margaret Mary, Supr.; Rev. Msgr. Joseph K. Parks, Dir. Confraternity of the Precious Blood; Rev. Msgr. Philip J. Reilly, Chap. In res., Rev. Msgr. Edward T. Burke. Sisters 18.

Monastery of the Visitation, 8902 Ridge Blvd., 11209. Tel: 718-745-5151; Fax: 718-680-4441. Marie Anatrella, Supr. Professed Sisters 22.

Motherhouse and Convent of Infant Jesus, 310 Prospect Park W., 11215. Tel: 718-965-7317. Sr. Mary Louise Kelly, C.I.J., Pres. Nursing Sisters of the Sick Poor-Congregation of the Infant Jesus. Sisters 20.

Motherhouse and Convent of the Sisters of Mercy of the Americas, Brooklyn Regional Community, 273 Willoughby Ave., 11205. Tel: 718-622-5840. Sr. Camille D'Arienzo, R.S.M., Pres. Sisters 29.

Nursing Sisters of the Sick Poor, St. Francis de Sales Convent, 218 76th St., 11209. Tel: 718-833-4343. Sisters 5.

Sisters of Sion Residence-Congregation of Our Lady of Sion, 349 Westminster Rd., 11218. Tel: 718-282-9043; Fax: 718-469-6977.

Sisters of the Good Shepherd, 348 Ninth St., 11215. Tel: 718-499-9212. Sisters 2. 420 E. 5th St., 11218. Tel: 718-851-4844. Provincial Office, 82-31 Dancaster Pl., Jamaica, 11432.

JAMAICA. *Provincialate of the Sisters of the Good Shepherd*, 82-31 Doncaster Pl., 11432. Tel: 718-380-3270; Fax: 718-591-9376. Legal Title: *Sisters of the Good Shepherd, Province of New York*. Sr. Helene Hayes, R.G.S.; Margaret Miley, Prov. Sec. Sisters 5.

Ursuline Provincial Administration Office, Glengarda, 81-15 Utopia Pkwy., 11432. Tel: 718-591-0681; Fax: 718-969-4275. Sr. Catherine Talia, O.S.U., Prov. Supr.

LONG ISLAND CITY. *Franciscan Sisters of Peace*, 35-22 30th St., 11106. Tel: 718-482-1243.

QUEENS VILLAGE. *Little Sisters of the Poor*, Provincial Residence, 110-30 221st St., 11429. Tel: 718-464-1800. Mother Genevieve Regina, L.S.P., Prov. Sisters 174; Fraternity Jeanne Jugan 4.

St. Ann's Novitiate, Little Sisters of the Poor, 110-39 Springfield Blvd., P.O. Box 280356, 11428. Tel: 718-464-4920; Fax: 718-479-3126. Sr. Mary Richard, L.S.P., Supr. & Mistress of Novices; Rev. Msgr. Thomas Clancy, Chap. Sisters 8; Novices 8; Postulants 7.

REGO PARK. *Blessed Trinity Missionary Cenacle*, 85-10 61 Rd., 11374. Tel: 718-424-7563. Parish Social Ministry, Ministry to the Handicapped, Elderly, Bereaved and Homebound. Missionary Servants of the Most Blessed Trinity 3.

RIDGEWOOD. *Convent of the Sisters of Mary Reparatrix*, 62-67 60 Pl., 11385. Tel: 718-456-4242. Sr. Patricia Mullen, S.M.R., Supr. Sisters 8.

ROCKAWAY PARK. *Stella Maris Convent, Sisters of St. Joseph*, 11694-2497. Sisters 15.

[W] EVANGELIZATION AND RENEWAL CENTERS

BROOKLYN. *Centro Evangelizacion San Vicente de Paul*, 118 Congress St., 11201. Tel: 718-624-5670. Revs. Jose Barcelo, C.M. (Spain), Dir. & Dir. of Cursillo Movement; Victor Dallo, C.M. (Spain); Baldvino Martinez, C.M. (Spain), Dir. of Jornada Movement.

ASTORIA. *St. Paul Center*, 21-35 Crescent St., 11105. Tel: 718-932-0752. Rev. Joseph T. Holcomb, Dir. Staff: Mrs. Carolyn Conides; Mr. Phil Crivelli; Mrs. Carmela Crivelli; Deacon Len Sclafani; Ms. Maureen Powers, Sec. Center for Lay Spirituality; American Cursillo in English; Christian Awakening.

FLUSHING. *Cenacle Center for Spiritual Renewal*, 154-27 Horace Harding Expwy., 11367. Tel: 718-463-2073. Sr. Mary F. Walsh, R.C., Contact Person.

JAMAICA. *Bishop Molloy Retreat House for Laymen*, 86-45 Edgerton Blvd., 11432. Tel: 718-739-1229. Passionist Fathers. Rev. Robin Ryan, C.P., Retreat Dir. Associates: Revs. John Patrick Moore, C.P.; Lawrence Ryalt, C.P.; Mr. John Moreno; Sr. Anna Maria Porzio, S.M.R.

[X] SECULAR INSTITUTES

BROOKLYN. *The Institute of Apostolic Oblates*, 730 E. 87th St., 11236. Tel: 718-649-0324; Fax: 718-272-5012. Giovanna Piccioli, Local Mod.

[Y] MISCELLANEOUS LISTINGS

BROOKLYN. *Bay Webster Corporation, Inc.*, 143 Bay 20th St., 11214. Mailing Address: 214 W. Maple Ave., Merchantville, NJ, 08109. Very Rev. Peter T. Sticco, S.A.C., Pres.

Bellerose Senior Housing Development Fund Company, Inc., 191 Joralemon St., 11201.

Bethlehem Community Housing Development Fund Company, Inc., 191 Joralemon St., 11201.

Caring Communities Associates Housing Development Fund Company, Inc., 191 Joralemon St., 11201.

Clermont Residence, 26 Clermont Ave., 11205. Tel: 718-834-9317; Fax: 718-834-9364. Miss Sharon Bewry, Res. Mgr. Residence for Developmentally Disabled Adults.

En El, Inc., 75 Greene Ave., 11238.

Good Shepherd Volunteers, Saint Germaines Services, 235 Prospect Park W., 11215. Tel: 718-768-8452. Sr. Maureen McGowan, R.G.S., Dir.

Jornada Movement, 118 Congress St., 11201. Tel: 718-624-5670. Rev. Balduino Martinez, C.M. (Spain), Dir.

Latvian Roman Catholic Mission. (Our Lady of Aglona Center), 361 Highland Blvd., 11207. Rev. Msgr. Leons Varna, S.T.D., Dir.

Manhattan Career Development Center, 1386 Ralph Ave., 11236. Bro. John Linhardt, F.S.C., Ph.D., Dir.; Sr. Sally Ann Dowd, O.P., Assoc. Dir.

**MCIF Center, Inc.*, 138 Bleeker St., 11221.

Mercy Montessori School, 1397 Brooklyn Ave., 11203. Tel: 718-469-2834. Sr. Mary Harvey, R.S.M., Dir.

Neighbors Together, 160 Thomas S. Boyland St., P.O. Box 330-562, 11233. Tel: 718-498-7256. Anne Kohler, Exec. Dir. Services for the Poor. Soup Kitchen and Social Services Advocacy.

New Horizons Adult Education Program, Inc., St. John's Center, 75 Lewis Ave., 11206. Tel: 718-455-1166; 455-1033; Fax: 718-452-3047. Sr. Ann Spencer, D.C., Exec. Dir.

Pro Sanctity Movement, 730 E. 87th St., 11236. Tel: 718-649-0324; Fax: 718-272-5012. Ms. Gloria Florez, Co-Dir.; Mrs. Liz Shellman, Co-Dir.; Rev. John J. Costello, Spiritual Advisor.

The Roman Catholic Pontifical Lay Association Memores Domini, 181 Senator St., 11220. Tel: 718-833-3992; Fax: 718-833-7374.

Men's House, 181 Senator St., 11220. Tel: 718-833-3992. Angelo Sala, Head of the House.

Women's House, 1122 71 St., 11228. Tel: 718-745-3649. Lorna Beretta, Head of the House.

St. James Cathedral Foundation, Inc., 250 Cathedral Pl., 11201. Tel: 718-852-4002. Rev. John C. Tosi, Sec.

St. John's Bread & Life Program, Inc. (Soup Kitchen, Employment Counseling, HIV/AIDS Support Group/ Food Pantry, Counseling, Referrals and Advocacy), 75 Lewis Ave., 11206. Tel: 718-574-0058. Mr. Hossein Saadat, M.S.A., Exec. Dir.; Sr. Bernadette Szyhczak, D.C., Soup Kitchen Coord.

**The Maura Clarke-Ita Ford Center*, 138 Bleeker St., 11221. Tel: 718-452-0167; Fax: 718-452-5173. Sr. Mary Burns, S.C., Co-Dir.; Sr. Mary Dowd, O.S.U., Co-Dir.

ASTORIA. *Flowers With Care Youth Services, Diocese of Brooklyn, Inc.*, 23-40 Astoria Blvd., 11102. Tel: 718-726-9790. Paula Beltrone, Exec. Dir.

BRENTWOOD. *Congregation of the Sisters of St. Joseph*, Charitable Trust, Brentwood Rd., 11717. Sr. Joan Larkin, Treas.

CAMBRIA HEIGHTS. *National Center of the Haitian Apostolate*. 455 E. 29th St., Brooklyn, 11226. Tel: 718-856-3323. Rev. Guy Sansariq, Exec. Dir.

DOUGLASTON. *Brooklyn-Queens Environmental Management Corporation*, Immaculate Conception Center, 7200 Douglaston Pkwy., 11362. Tel: 718-229-8001. James A. O'Brien. Legal Title: *Brooklyn-Queens Environmental Management Corporation of the Roman Catholic Diocese of Brooklyn.*

Society of the Immaculate Conception of Brooklyn. (Missionary Society), 7200 Douglaston Pkwy., 11362. Tel: 718-229-8001, Ext. 743. Rev. John J. Brogan, Exec. Dir.

JAMAICA. *Mary Immaculate, Inc.*, 88-25 153rd St., 11432. Tel: 718-558-6900.

Vincentian Service Corps.-East Inc., Saint John's University - SVH 102, 11439. Tel: 718-990-6266; Fax: 718-990-8939. A program for laywomen and men willing to commit to one year of service to the poor. Rev. Paul K. Cavanaugh, C.M., Dir.

QUEENS. *Focolare Movement*. Queens Office, 6359 83rd St., Middle Village, 11379. Tel: 718-898-2611.

ROCKVILLE CENTRE.

**Women Helping Women*, 255 Merrick Rd., 11570.

RELIGIOUS INSTITUTES OF MEN REPRESENTED IN THE DIOCESE

For further details refer to the corresponding bracketed number in the Religious Institutes of Men or Women section.

[0140]—*The Augustinians*.—O.S.A.

[1350]—*Brothers of St. Francis Xavier*. (Sacred Heart Prov.).—C.F.X.

[0330]—*Brothers of the Christian Schools*.—F.S.C.

[0600]—*Brothers of the Congregation of Holy Cross*.—C.S.C.

[1100]—*Brothers of the Sacred Heart*.—S.C.

[0470]—*The Capuchin Friars*. (Prov. of St. Mary).—O.F.M.Cap.

[0270]—*Carmelite Fathers & Brothers*. (St. Elias Prov.).—O.Carm.

[1330]—*Congregation of the Mission*. (Eastern, New England, Spanish Provs.).—C.M.

[1210]—*Congregation of the Missionaries of St. Charles*.—C.S.

[1000]—*Congregation of the Passion*. (Prov. of St. Paul of the Cross).—C.P.

[0480]—*Conventual Franciscans.* (Polish Prov.).—O.F.M.Conv.
[0490]—*Franciscan Brothers of Brooklyn.*—O.S.F.
[0520]—*Franciscan Friars.* (Immaculate Conception Prov.; Lithuanian Vicariate).—O.F.M.
[0650]—*Holy Ghost Fathers.*—C.S.Sp.
[0690]—*Jesuit Fathers and Brothers.* (New York Prov.).—S.J.
[0770]—*The Marist Brothers.*—F.M.S.
[0780]—*The Marist Fathers.*—S.M.
[0870]—*Montfort Missionaries.*—S.M.M.
[0950]—*Oratorians.* (Brooklyn).—C.O.
[0610]—*Priests of the Congregation of Holy Cross.* (Eastern Prov.).—C.S.C.
[1070]—*The Redemptorists.*—C.SS.R.
[0760]—*Society of Mary (Marianists).* (New York Prov.).—S.M.
[0370]—*Society of St. Columban.*—S.S.C.
[0990]—*Society of the Catholic Apostolate.*—S.A.C.
[1200]—*Society of the Divine Savior.*—S.D.S.

RELIGIOUS INSTITUTES OF WOMEN REPRESENTED IN THE DIOCESE

[]—*Altagracia Sisters.* (Dominican Republic).
[0340]—*Carmelite Sisters of Charity.*—C.Ch.
[0330]—*Carmelite Sisters of the Aged and Infirm.*—O.Carm.
[2980]—*Congregation of Notre Dame.*—C.N.D.
[2950]—*Congregation of Notre Dame de Sion.*—N.D.S.
[]—*Congregation of Olivetan Benedictine Sisters.* (Korea).
[3110]—*Congregation of Our Lady of the Retreat in the Cenacle.*—R.C.
[2230]—*Congregation of the Infant Jesus.*—C.I.J.
[0760]—*Daughters of Charity of St. Vincent de Paul.*—D.C.
[0960]—*Daughters of Wisdom.*—D.W.
[0420]—*Discalced Carmelite Nuns.*—O.C.D.
[1070-01]—*Dominican Sisters.*—O.P.
[1070-02]—*Dominican Sisters.*—O.P.
[1070-05]—*Dominican Sisters.*—O.P.
[1070-06]—*Dominican Sisters.*—O.P.
[1070-11]—*Dominican Sisters.*—O.P.
[1400]—*Franciscan Missionary Sisters of the Sacred Heart.*—F.M.S.C.
[1180]—*Franciscan Sisters of Allegany, NY.*—O.S.F.
[1425]—*Franciscan Sisters of Peace.*—F.S.P.
[1420]—*Franciscan Sisters of Ringwood.*—F.S.R.
[1470]—*Franciscan Sisters of St. Joseph.*—F.S.S.J.
[1190]—*Franciscan Sisters of the Atonement.*—S.A.
[]—*Franciscan Sisters of the Immaculate (Honduras).*—H.F.I.
[1440]—*Franciscan Sisters of the Poor.*—S.F.P.
[1840]—*Grey Nuns of the Sacred Heart.*—G.N.S.H.
[]—*Little Sisters of the Gospel.* (France).—L.S.G.
[2340]—*Little Sisters of the Poor.*—L.S.P.
[2420]—*Marist Missionary Sisters (Missionary Sisters of the Society of Mary) Inc..*—S.M.S.M.
[2470]—*Marknoll Sisters of St Dominic.*—M.M.
[2710]—*Missionaries of Charity.*—M.C.
[2860]—*Missionaries of the Sacred Heart.*—M.S.C.
[1360]—*Missionary Franciscan Sisters of the Immaculate Conception.*—O.S.F.
[2790]—*Missionary Servants of the Most Blessed Trinity.*—M.S.B.T.
[3160]—*Parish Visitors of Mary Immaculate.*—P.V.M.I.
[2070]—*Religious of the Holy Union of the Sacred Hearts.*—S.U.S.C.
[3465]—*Religious of the Sacred Heart of Mary.*—R.S.H.M.
[3430]—*Religious Teachers Filippini.*—M.P.F.
[2970]—*School Sisters of Notre Dame.* (Wilton, CT; Baltimore, MD).—S.S.N.D.
[0110]—*Sisters Adorers of the Precious Blood.*—A.P.B.
[0650]—*Sisters of Charity of St. Vincent de Paul of New York.*—S.C.
[0640]—*Sisters of Charity of St. Vincent de Paul, Halifax.*—S.C.
[0430]—*Sisters of Charity of the Blessed Virgin Mary.*—B.V.M.
[1000]—*Sisters of Divine Providence of Kentucky.*—C.D.P.
[2575]—*Sisters of Mercy of the Americas.* (Brooklyn, NY; Dallas, TX).—R.S.M.
[3000]—*Sisters of Notre Dame de Namur.*—S.N.D.deN.
[2670]—*Sisters of Our Lady of Mercy.*—S.O.L.M.
[3820]—*Sisters of St. John the Baptist.*—C.S.J.B.
[3830-05]—*Sisters of St. Joseph.*—C.S.J.
[3140]—*Sisters of the Catholic Apostolate-Pallottine.*—C.S.A.C.
[3180]—*Sisters of the Cross and Passion.*—C.P.
[1830]—*Sisters of the Good Shepherd.*—R.G.S.
[1970]—*Sisters of the Holy Family of Nazareth.* (Immaculate Heart of Mary Prov.).—C.S.F.N.
[3320]—*Sisters of the Presentation of the B.V.M..* (Newburgh).—P.B.V.M.
[2160]—*Sisters, Servants of the Immaculate Heart of Mary.*—I.H.M.
[2460]—*Society of Mary Reparatrix.*—S.M.R.
[4070] *Society of the Sacred Heart.*—R.S.C.J.
[4130]—*Ursuline Sisters of the Congregation of Tildonk, Belgium.*—O.S.U.
[4190]—*Visitation Nuns.*—V.H.M.

DIOCESAN CEMETERIES

BROOKLYN. *Holy Cross,* Brooklyn & Tilden Ave., 11203. Rev. Msgr. Anthony J. Barretta, Chap.

FARMINGDALE. *Resurrection,* Conklin St., 11735. Tel: 516-249-8700.

St. Charles, Conklin St., 11735. Tel: 516-249-8700. Rev. Msgr. August C. Bednartz, Chap.

FLUSHING. *Mount St. Mary,* 172-00 Booth Memorial Ave., 11365. Tel: 718-353-1560. Rev. Romano Zanon, Chap.

MIDDLE VILLAGE. *St. John's.* Administration Offices for the Diocesan Cemeteries. 80-01 Metropolitan Ave., 11379. Tel: 718-894-4888. Rev. Ralph Guarracino, Chap.

PARISH CEMETERIES

AMITYVILLE. *Most Holy Trinity.* Most Holy Trinity Parish, Brooklyn.

Trinity. Most Holy Trinity Parish, Brooklyn.

ROCKAWAY. *St. Mary Star of the Sea,* Rockaway Blvd., 11691. Tel: 718-894-4888.

NECROLOGY

† Bartley, William J, Brooklyn, NY Holy Name. —Died Aug. 18, 1996.
† Benincasa, Albert E, Brooklyn, NY St. Mary Mother of Jesus. —Died May 28, 1996.
† Brown, Rev. Msgr. Douglas L, Brooklyn, NY St. Ephrem's Church. —Died Dec. 10, 1996.
† Brown, Stewart R, Glendale, NY St. Pancras. —Died Feb. 26, 1996.
† Burke, Rev. Msgr. Edward T, Brooklyn, NY Monastery of the Sisters Adorers of the Precious Blood. —Died Dec. 25, 1996.
† Dougherty, Rev. Msgr. T. David, Brooklyn, NY St. Athanasius Church. —Died Dec. 12, 1996.
† Ferris, Rev. Msgr. Richard W, Rockaway Point, NY St. Genevieve. —Died April 21, 1996.
† Gallagher, Michael, (Retired). —Died June 24, 1996.
† Gately, Thomas A, Brooklyn, NY St. Francis of Assisi-St. Blaise Church. —Died Sept. 4, 1996.
† Ghirlando, Roland J, Brooklyn, NY Assumption of the Blessed Virgin Mary Church. —Died Dec. 27, 1996.
† Kakizaki, John T, Rockaway Beach, NY St. Camillus. —Died May 15, 1996.
† Kammer, Arthur C., (Retired). —Died Feb. 1, 1996.
† Lawrie, Edward A., (Retired). —Died Aug. 8, 1996.
† Mahoney, Rev. Msgr. John T., (Retired). —Died Oct. 14, 1996.
† Matters, William F, Elmhurst, NY Ascension. —Died April 23, 1996.
† Mihouich, George R., (Retired). —Died Dec. 8, 1996.
† Murphy, Rev. Msgr. Francis J, Brooklyn, NY St. Anselm. —Died Jan. 24, 1996.
† O'Grady, James B., (Retired). —Died Dec. 12, 1996.
† Ryan, Rev. Msgr. William G, Bayside, NY Queen of Peace Residence. —Died June 21, 1996.
† Savage, John H, Brooklyn, NY St. Saviour. —Died Aug. 15, 1996.
† Schmidt, Rev. Msgr. John J, Brooklyn, NY St. Mary's. —Died Jan. 31, 1996.
† Schmidt, John J, Brooklyn, NY St. Mark's Church. —Died Jan. 31, 1996.
† Sclafani, Rev. Msgr. Dominic A, Brooklyn, NY Our Lady of Grace. —Died May 4, 1996.
† Sherman, John T, Douglaston, NY Bishop Mugavero Residence. —Died Oct. 1, 1996.
† Sickler, James G, Brooklyn, NY St. Finbar. —Died Oct. 14, 1996.
† Tessier, Victor J, Far Rockaway, NY St. Gertrude. —Died June 26, 1996.
† Varriale, Rev. Msgr. Alfred A, Brooklyn, NY Our Lady of Guadalupe. —Died Jan. 18, 1996.

Diocese of Brownsville

(Dioecesis Brownsvillensis)

Most Reverend

RAYMUNDO J. PENA, D.D.

Bishop of Brownsville; ordained May 25, 1957; appointed Titular Bishop of Trisipa and Auxiliary of San Antonio October 16, 1976; consecrated December 13, 1976; appointed Bishop of El Paso April 29, 1980; installed June 18, 1980; appointed Bishop of Brownsville May 23, 1995; installed August 6, 1995. *Mailing Address: P.O. Box 2279, Brownsville, TX, 78522-2279.*

Most Reverend

JOHN J. FITZPATRICK, D.D.

Retired Bishop of Brownsville; ordained December 13, 1942; appointed Auxiliary of Miami June 24, 1968; consecrated August 28, 1968; appointed Bishop of Brownsville April 27, 1971; installed May 27, 1971; retired November 30, 1991. *Mailing Address: P.O. Box 2279, Brownsville, TX, 78522-2279.*

ESTABLISHED JULY 10, 1965.

Square Miles 4,226.

Comprises the four Counties of Cameron, Hidalgo, Starr and Willacy in the State of Texas.

For legal titles of parishes and diocesan institutions, consult the Catholic Pastoral Center.

Catholic Pastoral Center: 1910 E. Elizabeth St., P.O. Box 2279, Brownsville, TX, 78522-2279. Tel.: 210-542-2501; Fax: 210-542-6751.

STATISTICAL OVERVIEW

Personnel	
Bishop	1
Retired Bishops	1
Priests: Diocesan Active in Diocese	39
Priests: Active Outside Diocese	4
Priests: Retired, Sick or Absent	14
Number of Diocesan Priests	57
Religious Priests in Diocese	51
Extern Priests in Diocese	8
Ordinations:	
Diocesan Priests	1
Religious Priests	2
Permanent Deacons in Diocese	82
Total Brothers	18
Total Sisters	139
Parishes	
Parishes	63
With Resident Pastor:	
Resident Diocesan Priests	29
Resident Religious Priests	25
Without Resident Pastor:	
Administered by Priests	9
Missions	45
Pastoral Centers	1
New Parishes Created	2
Professional Ministry Personnel:	
Brothers	1
Sisters	22
Lay Ministers	52
Welfare	
Health Care Centers	2
Total Assisted	177
Homes for the Aged	2
Total Assisted	13,292
Day Care and Extended Day Care Centers	1
Total Assisted	53
Specialized Homes	1
Total Assisted	700
Special Centers for Social Services	4
Total Assisted	107,608
Other Institutions	2
Total Assisted	1,229
Educational	
Diocesan Students in Other Seminaries	9
Total Seminarians	9
High Schools, Private	1
Total Students	673
Elementary Schools, Diocesan and Parish	6
Total Students	2,090
Elementary Schools, Private	2
Total Students	523
Catechesis/Religious Education:	
High School Students	7,065
Elementary Students	26,163
Total Students Under Catholic Instruction	36,523
Teachers in the Diocese:	
Brothers	6
Sisters	15
Lay Teachers	211
Vital Statistics	
Receptions into the Church:	
Infant Baptism Totals	9,280
Adult Baptism Totals	674
Received into Full Communion	448
First Communions	6,879
Confirmations	2,709
Marriages:	
Catholic	1,470
Interfaith	98
Total Marriages	1,568
Deaths	2,314
Total Catholic Population	717,056
Total Population	888,112

Former Prelates—Rt. Rev. DOMINIC MANUCY, Titular Bishop of Delma and Vicar Apostolic of Brownsville; cons. Dec. 8, 1874; transferred to Mobile, March 9, 1884 reappointed to Vicariate Apostolic of Brownsville, Feb. 1, 1885; died Dec. 4, 1885.—Rt. Rev. PETER VERDAGUER, Titular Bishop of Aulon and Vicar Apostolic of Brownsville; cons. Nov. 9, 1890; died Oct. 26, 1911.—Rt. Rev. CLAUDE JAILLET, O.P., Administrator of Vicariate Apostolic of Brownsville, 1911-1913.

Former Bishops—Most Rev. ADOLPH MARX, D.D., J.C.D., First Bishop of Brownsville; ord. May 2, 1940; appt. Titular Bishop of Citrus and Auxiliary Bishop of Corpus Christi, July 6, 1956; cons. Oct. 9, 1956; appt. first Bishop of Brownsville, July 19, 1965; installed Sept. 2, 1965; died in Cologne, Germany Nov. 1, 1965.—His Eminence HUMBERTO CARDINAL MEDEIROS, D.D., second Bishop of Brownsville; appt. April 14, 1966; cons. June 9, 1966; installed Bishop of Brownsville, June 29, 1966; appt. Archbishop of Boston, Sept. 8, 1970; installed Archbishop of Boston, Oct. 7, 1970; created Cardinal, March 5, 1973; died Sept. 17, 1983.—Most Rev. JOHN J. FITZPATRICK, third Bishop of Brownsville; ord. Dec 13, 1942; appt. Auxiliary Bishop of Miami, June 24, 1968; cons. Aug. 28, 1968; appt. Bishop of Brownsville, April 27, 1971; installed May 27, 1971; retired Nov. 30, 1991.—Most Rev. ENRIQUE SAN PEDRO, S.J., S.T.D., S.S.L., fourth Bishop of Brownsville; ord. March 18, 1957; appt. Auxiliary Bishop of Galveston-Houston April 1, 1986; cons. June 29, 1986; appt. Coadjutor of Brownsville, August 13, 1991; installed Sept. 26, 1991; succeeded to the See, Nov. 30, 1991; died July 17, 1994.

Catholic Pastoral Center—P.O. Box 2279, Brownsville, 78522-2279. Tel: 210-542-2501; Fax: 210-542-6751.

Vicar General—Rev. Msgr. PATRICK J. DOHERTY, V.G.

Vicar Episcopal for Evangelization—Rev. JUAN NICOLAU.

Moderators of the Curia—Lower Valley: Rev. IVAN M. ROVIRA; Upper Valley: Rev. ARMANDO ESCOBEDO.

Bishop's Administrative Assistant—Rev. EDUARDO ORTEGA.

Vice-Chancellor—CLARA M. MARTINEZ.

Presbyteral Council—Rev. Msgr. PATRICK J. DOHERTY, V.G., Commissioner for Parish Needs; Revs. CRAIG CAROLAN, Commissioner for Justice and Peace; F. ROBERT DAVOLA, Commissioner for Vocations/ Seminarians; HERMAN J. DEFLER, M.S.F., Commissioner for Administration; EDWARD T. DE LEON, O.M.I., Commissioner for Worship and Liturgy; ARMANDO ESCOBEDO, Commissioner for Permanent Deacons and Lay Ministry; GERALD W. FRANK, Commissioner for Marriage and Family Life; JUAN VICTOR HEREDIA, Commissioner for Social Services; MICHAEL MONTOYA, C.I.C.M., Commissioner for Evangelization; JUAN NICOLAU, Commissioner for Priestly Life and Ministry; IVAN M. ROVIRA, Commissioner for Education and Formation; PATRICK K. SEITZ, Commissioner for the Diocesan Shrine; EDUARDO ORTEGA, Sec. & Notary, Commissioner for Youth and Young Adult Ministry.

Diocesan College of Consultors—Rev. Msgr. PATRICK J. DOHERTY; Revs. F. ROBERT DAVOLA; EDWARD T. DE LEON, O.M.I.; ARMANDO ESCOBEDO; JUAN VICTOR

HEREDIA; IVAN M. ROVIRA.

Deans—Brownsville Deanery: Rev. GUSTAVO BARRERA; Harlingen Deanery: Rev. JAIME CABANAS; Weslaco Deanery: Rev. FRANCISCO CASTILLO; McAllen Deanery: Rev. AGOSTINHO S. PACHECO; Mission Deanery: Rev. ROBERT E. MAHER; Rio Grande City Deanery: Vacant.

Parish Priests' Consultors & Priests' Personnel Board—Revs. F. ROBERT DAVOLA; RUBEN M. DELGADO; GEORGE E. HARRIS; GREGORY M. KUCZMANSKI.

Diocesan Liturgist/Bishop's Master of Ceremonies—Rev. EDWARD T. DE LEON, O.M.I.

Assistant Master of Ceremonies—Rev. EDUARDO ORTEGA.

Diocesan Tribunal—*P.O. Box 2279, Brownsville, 78522-2279.* Tel: 210-550-1512; Fax: 210-542-6751.

Judicial Vicar—Rev. GILBERT M. PIETTE, J.C.L.

Adjutant Judicial Vicar—Rev. ADRIAN R. CORREA.

Promoter of Justice—Rev. GUSTAVO BARRERA.

Director of the Tribunal/Notary—SYLVIA W. GARCIA.

Defenders of the Bond—Revs. GUSTAVO BARRERA; F. ROBERT DAVOLA.

Judges—Most. Rev. JOHN J. FITZPATRICK; Revs. MICHAEL ANNUNZIATO, SS.CC.; ADRIAN R. CORREA; HERMAN J. DEFLER, M.S.F.; THOMAS G. KULLECK.

Procurator/Advocate—Sr. MARY DOLORES DOYLE, C.C.V.I.

Comptroller—ANITA A. RODRIGUEZ, *P.O. Box 2279, Brownsville, 78522-2279.* Tel: 210-550-1534; Fax: 210-542-6751.

Accountant—Mrs. SOCORRO PADILLA.

Parish Accounting Services—MARY GUAJARDO.

Insurance and Pension Plans—JUDY PLATA.

Diocesan Finance Council—NOBLE ALLEN; ALONSO CANTU; CHARLES ELLERD; MATT GORGES; JOSE A. HINOJOSA; MICHAEL POWERS.

Diocesan Offices and Directors

Human Resources Office—BENJAMIN SANDOVAL, *P.O. Box 2279, Brownsville, 78522-2279.* Tel: 210-550-1541; Fax: 210-542-6751.

Ministry Resource Center—Sr. MAUREEN CROSBY, S.S.D., Audio/Visual; Sr. SUSAN KLEIN, O.P., Library Resource, *P.O. Box 547, Alamo, 78516-0547.* Tel: 210-787-8571; Fax: 210-787-5778.

Vicar for Religious—Rev. F. ROBERT DAVOLA, *1119 Francisco Ave., Mission, 78572.* Tel: 210-585-2701; Fax: 210-581-4801.

Office of Youth Ministry—FELIPE C. SALINAS, Coord., *P.O. Box 547, Alamo, 78516-0547.* Tel: 210-787-8571; Fax: 210-787-5778.

Building & Property Manager—JAIME ENRIQUEZ, *P.O. Box 2279, Brownsville, 78522-2279.* Tel: 210-787-0033; Fax: 210-787-2908.

Director of Seminarians—Rev. IVAN M. ROVIRA, *P.O. Box 2279, Brownsville, 78522-2279.* Tel: 210-550-1547; Fax: 210-542-6751.

Director of Communications—Rev. PEDRO BRISENO, *KMBH-TV60, P.O. Box 2147, Harlingen, 78551.* Tel: 210-421-4111; Fax: 210-421-4150.

Superintendent of Catholic Schools—Sr. MARCELLA EWERS, D.C., *P.O. Box 547, Alamo, 78516-0547.* Tel: 210-787-8571; Fax: 210-787-5778.

Office of Permanent Deacons—Deacon ALFRED V. CRIXELL, *P.O. Box 547, Alamo, 78516-0547.* Tel: 210-787-8571; Fax: 210-787-5778.

Young Adult Ministry—Sr. GLORIA ANN FIEDLER, C.D.P., *1850 Ridgely Rd., Brownsville, 78520.* Tel: 210-542-3942. See Campus Ministry for more listings.

Encuentro Matrimonial—Rev. ALFONSO M. GUEVARA, *2255 Southmost Rd., Brownsville, 78521.* Tel: 210-546-1982.

Engaged Encounter—GEORGE GANDARA; ANA GANDARA, *1524 S. 14th St., Edinburg, 78539.* Tel: 210-318-1035.

Girl Scouts—Sr. ARMIDA RANGEL, M.J., Moderator, *1055 Military Hwy., Brownsville, 78520.* Tel: 210-541-8341.

Boy Scouts—Rev. CRAIG CAROLAN, Chap., *P.O. Box 216, Progreso, 78579.* Tel: 210-565-6856.

Marriage Encounter—English: JAVIER ROCHA; ESTHER ROCHA, *Rte. 1, Box 8, Magnum Rd., Mission, 78572.* Tel: 210-580-9010. Spanish: ALFONSO GONZALEZ; MINERVA GONZALEZ, *R.R. 3, Box 6095, Harlingen, 78550.* Tel: 210-428-0433.

Movimiento Familiar Cristiano—VICTOR CASTILLO; ESTELLA CASTILLO, *Rte. 3, Box 171, Los Fresnos.* Tel: 210-233-6438. RICARDO CABALLERO; ORALIA CABALLERO, *100 N. Pleasant View, Weslaco, 78596.* Tel: 210-968-7843.

Catholic Foundation of the Diocese of Brownsville—Most Rev. RAYMUNDO J. PENA; Rev. Msgr. PATRICK J. DOHERTY, V.G.; Ms. GRACIELA GUTIERREZ, *P.O. Box 2279, Brownsville, 78522-2279.* Tel: 210-542-2501; Fax: 210-542-6751.

Catholic Social Services Office—TELMA LONGORIA, *P.O. Box 128, San Juan, 78589.* Tel: 210-702-4088. (See separate listing for branch offices and extended services).

Campaign for Human Development—HERNAN GONZALEZ, *P.O. Box 747, San Juan, 78589.* Tel: 210-787-0033; Fax: 210-787-2908.

Office of Evangelization—Rev. JUAN NICOLAU, V.E., Dir., *P.O. Box 2279, Brownsville, 78522-2279.* Tel: 210-550-1528; Fax: 210-542-6751.

Office of Family Life—Mrs. GLENDA GUERRA, *P.O. Box 547, Alamo, 78516.* Tel: 210-787-8571; Fax: 210-787-5778.

Virgen de San Juan del Valle Shrine—

Board of Directors—Most Rev. RAYMUNDO J. PENA; Revs. EDWARD T. DE LEON, O.M.I.; PATRICK K. SEITZ; RICHARD ALANIZ; FERNANDO MANCIAS, *P.O. Box 2279, Brownsville, 78522-2279.* Tel: 210-550-1510; Fax: 210-542-6751.

Housing Board—HERNAN GONZALEZ; SANTIAGO FERNANDEZ; ANITA A. RODRIGUEZ; ANA ZAMARRIPA, Mgr., *El Rosario Homes, P.O. Box 971, Mission, 78572.* Tel: 210-585-5051., *La Merced Homes, P.O. Box 806, Mercedes, 78570.* Tel: 210-565-2622.

Jail Ministry—Cameron County Jail and Bayview Detention Center, Sr. JULIANA GARCIA, M.J., *1850 Ridgely Rd., Brownsville, 78520.* Tel: 210-541-0220. Hidalgo County Jail, Deacon JOSE SOLIS, *315 E. Peter St., Edinburg, 78539.* Tel: 210-383-4324. Starr County Jail, Deacon R. C. SALINAS, *304 North East St., Rio Grande City, 78582.* Tel: 210-487-3112.

Office of Catechesis—LYDIA PESINA, *P.O. Box 547, Alamo, 78516.* Tel: 210-787-8571; Fax: 210-787-5778.

Diocesan Offices—

Archives—CLARA M. MARTINEZ, *P.O. Box 2279, Brownsville, 78522-2279.* Tel: 210-550-1531; Fax: 210-542-6751.

Attorney—DAVID C. GARZA, *P.O. Box 2025, Brownsville, 78520.* Tel: 210-541-4914; Fax: 210-542-7403.

Catholic Lawyers Guild—Mr. FIDENCIO GUERRA, JR., *P.O. Box 4227, McAllen, 78501.* Tel: 210-682-1465.

Holy Childhood Association—Sr. MARY DOLORES DOYLE, C.C.V.I., *P.O. Box 2279, Brownsville, 78522-2279.* Tel: 210-542-2501; Fax: 210-542-6751.

Legion of Mary—Rev. JOHN A. O'MALLEY, Spiritual Moderator, *901 N. Texas Blvd., Weslaco, 78596.* Tel: 210-968-2691; Fax: 210-968-1473.

Natural Family Planning—Mrs. WILLY KOPECKY, *1012 W. Third, Weslaco, 78596.* Tel: 210-969-3079.

Propagation of the Faith—Rev. Msgr. PATRICK J. DOHERTY, V.G., *P.O. Box 2279, Brownsville, 78522-2279.* Tel: 210-550-1526.

Serra Club International—Brownsville: ROLANDO RAMIREZ, *1905 W. Madison, Brownsville, 78520.* Tel: 210-541-1453. Rev. GUSTAVO BARRERA, Chap., *1914 Barnard Rd., Brownsville, 78520.* Tel: 210-546-3800. McAllen: LEONEL BARRERA, JR., *117 W. Camellia, McAllen, 78501.* Tel: 210-687-4922. Rev. IVAN M. ROVIRA, Chap., *P.O. Box 2279, Brownsville, 78522-2279.* Tel: 210-550-1547. Rio Grande City: BENITO SAENZ, Pres., *Rte. 2, Box 102X, Rio Grande City, 78582.* Tel: 210-487-3416. Rev. EDUARDO VILLA, Chap., *P.O. Box 1, Rio Grande City, 78582.* Tel: 210-487-2317.

Office of Public & Governmental Relations—PAMELA DOWNING, *P.O. Box 2279, Brownsville, 78522-2279.* Tel: 210-550-1541; Fax: 210-542-6751.

Office of Vocations—Rev. IVAN M. ROVIRA; Sr. NINFA GARZA, M.J., *P.O. Box 2279, Brownsville, 78522-2279.* Tel: 210-550-1547; Fax: 210-542-6751.

Office of Planning & Resource Development—JESUS SALINAS, *P.O. Box 2279, Brownsville, 78522-2279.* Tel: 210-550-1543; Fax: 210-542-6751.

Pro-Life Activities—Rev. JOHN A. O'MALLEY, *901 N. Texas Blvd., Weslaco, 78596.* Tel: 210-968-2691; Fax: 210-968-1473.

R.C.I.A.—Rev. LAWRENCE J. KLEIN, *920 Anacuitas, Mission, 78570.* Tel: 210-565-0271.

Knights of Columbus—Rev. Msgr. PATRICK J. DOHERTY, V.G., *P.O. Box 2279, Brownsville, 78522-2279.* Tel: 210-550-1526; Fax: 210-542-6751.

CLERGY, PARISHES, MISSIONS AND PAROCHIAL SCHOOLS

CITY OF BROWNSVILLE
(Cameron County)

1—IMMACULATE CONCEPTION CATHEDRAL (1849), Revs. Pasquale Lanese, O.M.I.; Charles Moran, O.M.I.; Deacons John Kinch; Arturo Rodriguez.
Res., 1218 E. Jefferson St., P.O. Box 311, 78522. Tel: 210-546-3178; Fax: 210-546-1284.
Missions—Brownsville, Cameron Co., St. Thomas, 155 E. Jefferson St., 78520.; Brownsville, Cameron Co., Sacred Heart, 602 E. Elizabeth St., 78520.
Chapel—La Muralla, D St., 78520.

2—CHRIST THE KING (1953), Revs. Alfonso M. Guevara; James P. Fischler, C.I.C.M.; Deacons Alfred L. Webre, Jr.; Felipe Trevino.
2255 Southmost Rd., 78521. Tel: 210-546-1982; Fax: 210-546-7120.
Chapel—Kopernik Shores, St. Michael Archangel.

3—CHURCH OF THE GOOD SHEPHERD (1968), Rev. Horacio Chavarria; Deacon Paul McArdle.
Res., 2645 Tulipan, 78521. Tel: 210-542-5142; Fax: 210-542-5278.

4—HOLY FAMILY (1966), Revs. Ivan M. Rovira; Eduardo Ortega; Deacon Alejandro Flores.
Res., 2308 E. Tyler, 78520. Tel: 210-546-6975; Fax: 210-546-4883.

5—OUR LADY OF GOOD COUNSEL (1966), Rev. Ruben Delgado; Deacons Enrique Saldana; Alvino C. Olvera.
Res., 1055 Military Hwy., 78520. Tel: 210-541-8341; Fax: 210-548-0229.
Mission—San Pedro, San Pedro.

6—OUR LADY OF GUADALUPE (1928), Rev. Msgr. Patrick J. Doherty, V.G.; Deacons Jose Guerra; Ramon Leal.
Res., 1200 E. Lincoln St., 78521. Tel: 210-542-4823; Fax: 210-542-5944.

7—ST. EUGENE DE MAZENOD (1996), Rev. Harry Schuckenbrock, O.M.I.; Deacon Bruno Cedillo.
Res., 5409 Austin Rd., 78251. Tel: 210-831-9923.

8—ST. JOSEPH (1953), Revs. John G. Castro, O.M.I.; Jan Rademaker, O.M.I.; Deacon Frank Galvan.
Res., 555 W. St. Francis St., 78520. Tel: 210-542-2709; Fax: 210-546-5162.

9—ST. LUKE (1974), Revs. Juan Nicolau; Pedro Briseno; Deacons Francisco Garza; Juan Pablo Navarro.
Res., 2800 Rockwell Dr., 78521. Tel: 210-541-1480; 541-4973; Fax: 210-542-8043.
School—2850 Price Rd., 78521. Tel: 210-544-7982; Fax: 210-544-4874. Sr. Helen Rottier, C.S.J., Prin.
Religious 2; Lay Teachers 30; Students 304.

10—SAINT MARY, MOTHER OF THE CHURCH (1967), Revs. Gustavo Barrera; Lionel Lopez; Deacons Gilbert Borja; Roberto Cano; Heriberto Solis; Heriberto Trevino. In res., Most Rev. John J. Fitzpatrick, (Retired).
Res., 1914 Barnard Rd., 78520. Tel: 210-546-3800; Fax: 210-546-1589.
School—1300 Los Ebanos Blvd., 78520. Tel: 210-546-1805; Fax: 210-546-0787. Mr. Juan Barrera, Prin.
Religious 3; Lay Teachers 28; Students 565.

11—SAN FELIPE DE JESUS (1996), Rev. Michael Seifert, S.M.; Bro. Albert Phillipp, F.M.S., Pastoral Assoc.
Mailing Address: P.O. Box 8956, 78526-8956.
Res., 2215 Avenida Rancho Viejo, 78521. Tel: 210-982-2007.

OUTSIDE THE CITY OF BROWNSVILLE

Alamo, Hidalgo Co., Resurrection (1926). (Formerly St. Joseph/Our Lady of Fatima). Revs. Patrick McDonnell; Plutarco A. Belanggoy, C.I.C.M.; Deacon Jesus P. Galvan.
Res., 834 E. Citrus St., P.O. Box 1159, 78516. Tel: 210-787-2963; Fax: 210-787-6788.

Alton, Hidalgo Co., San Martin de Porres (1967), Rev. Anselme Malonda, C.I.C.M.; Deacon Israel Sagredo.
Res., Five Miles N. Conway W., P.O. Box 9023, Mission, 78572. Tel: 210-585-8001; Fax: 210-585-0715.

Donna, Hidalgo Co., St. Joseph (1928), Revs. Philip Sosa, M.S.F.; Herman J. Defler, M.S.F. In res., Bro. Berthold Papkalla, M.S.F.
Res., 306 S. D Salinas Blvd., 78537. Tel: 210-464-3331; Fax: 210-464-6808.
Missions—Colonia Nueva, Christ the King; Donna, Hidalgo Co., Holy Cross Center, 400 Scobey, 78537.

Edcouch, Hidalgo Co., St. Theresa of the Infant Jesus (1948), Rev. Gregory M. Kuczmanski; Deacon Alvin H. Gerbermann.
Res., 600 P. Salazar, P.O. Box 307, 78538. Tel: 210-262-1347.
Mission—La Villa, Our Lady of Guadalupe.

Edinburg, Hidalgo Co., Holy Family (1967), Rev. Esteban Hernandez, M.S.F.; Deacons Inocencio Diaz; Ruben Lopez.
Res., 1302 E. Champion, 78539-4864. Tel: 210-383-5472; 383-4593; Fax: 210-383-5034.

Sacred Heart (1927), Revs. Michael Annunziato, SS.CC.; Richard Czerwien, SS.CC.; Deacons Jose Solis; Oscar Cuevas; Gilberto Lopez.
Res., 215 N. 16th Ave., 78539. Tel: 210-383-3253.
Mission—Lull, Capilla de San Jose.

St. Joseph (1948), Rev. Robert E. Maher; Deacons Silvestre Garcia; Irineo Gonzalez, Jr.
Res., 122 W. Fay St., 78539. Tel: 210-383-3728; Fax: 210-383-8630.

School—119 W. Fay St., 78539. Tel: 210-383-3957; Fax: 210-383-8630. Mr. Edward Lopresto, Prin. Religious 3; Lay Teachers 22; Students 204.

Elsa, Hidalgo Co., Sacred Heart (1948), Rev. Emmanuel Bialoncik, O.F.M.; Deacon Hugo de la Cruz.
Res., 1100 N. Broadway, P.O. Box 6, 78543. Tel: 210-262-1406; Fax: 210-262-4265.
Mission—Monte Alto, Hidalgo Co., Christ the King, Holy Cross Catechetical Center, Mile 15, Monte Alto, 78538.

Escobares, Starr Co., Sacred Heart (1967), Rev. Juan Victor Heredia.
Res., P.O. Box 1180, Roma, 78584. Tel: 210-849-1741; Fax: 210-849-4589.
Missions—Rosita, Santa Rosa de Lima; El Sauz, Our Lady of Guadalupe.

Grulla, Starr Co., Holy Family (1967), Rev. Lee DaCosta; Deacon Benito Saenz, Jr.
Res., P.O. Box 67, 78548. Tel: 210-487-3365.
Mission—Cristo Rey, La Victoria.

Harlingen, Cameron Co.,

1—Our Lady of the Assumption, (1958), Rev. R. Jaime Cabanas; Deacon Ignacio Gonzales.
Res., 1313 W. Buchanan St., 78550. Tel: 210-423-4670; Fax: 210-423-5970.
Mission—San Felipe, Austin Co., Rangerville Rd., San Felipe, 77473.

2—Immaculate Heart of Mary, (1927), Rev. Terence L. Fowler; Deacon Abel Castillo.
Res., 412 S. C St., 78550. Tel: 210-423-0855; Fax: 210-421-1071.

3—Queen of Peace, (1967), Revs. Matthias Shanley, SS.CC.; Emilio Vega, SS.CC.; Deacon Juan Valenzuela.
Res., 1509 New Combes Hwy., 78550. Tel: 210-423-6341; Fax: 210-423-2864.

4—St. Anthony, (1940), Revs. Gilbert M. Piette; Hernan Quintero Diaz; Deacon Julio Flores, Jr.
Res., 209 S. 10th, 78550. Tel: 210-428-6111; Fax: 210-428-4276.
School—1015 E. Harrison St., 78550. Tel: 210-423-2486. Ms. Johna Hays, Prin.
Lay Teachers 27; Students 222.
Mission—Le Moyne Chapel.

Hidalgo, Hidalgo Co., Sacred Heart (1967), Rev. Joseph Bukase, C.I.C.M.
Res., 308 E. Camelia St., P.O. Box 742, 78557. Tel: 210-843-2463.

La Feria, Cameron Co., St. Francis Xavier (1930), Rev. Thomas Pincelli.
Res., 500 S. Canal St., P.O. Box 116, 78559. Tel: 210-797-2666; Fax: 210-797-3387.

La Joya, Hidalgo Co., Our Lady, Queen of Angels (1960), Revs. Michael Montoya, C.I.C.M.; Romero "Butch" Olivares, C.I.C.M.; Deacons Alberto Chapa; Lucio Flores.
Res., P.O. Drawer D, 78560. Tel: 210-585-5223; Fax: 210-585-4878.
Missions—Abram, St. Mary Magdalene; Penitas, St. Anthony; Los Ebanos, St. Michael; Sullivan City, St. William.

Los Fresnos, Cameron Co., St. Cecilia (1964), Rev. George E. Harris; Deacons Augusto Chapa, Jr.; Andres Munoz.
Res., 606 W. Ocean Blvd., P.O. Box 39, 78566. Tel: 210-233-5619.
Mission—Olmito, Our Heavenly Father.

Lyford, Willacy Co., Prince of Peace (1967), Revs. Richard J. MacDonald, S.C.J.; David Jackson, S.C.J.
Res., 1100 Park Ave., P.O. Box 460, 78569. Tel: 210-347-3580; Fax: 210-347-3649.
Missions—Santa Monica, Santa Monica; Sebastian, Willacy Co., St. Martin, Box 247, Sebastian, 78594.

McAllen, Hidalgo Co.,

1—Our Lady of Perpetual Help, (1967), Rev. Francisco Acosta; Deacon Rene Villalon, Sr., S.F.O.
Res., 2209 Kendlewood Ave., 78501. Tel: 210-682-4238.

2—Our Lady of Sorrows, (1941), Rev. Agostinho S. Pacheco; Deacon John Schwarz.
Res., 1108 Hackberry St., 78501-4304. Tel: 210-686-0251; Fax: 210-686-0322.
School—1100 Gumwood, 78501. Tel: 210-686-3651; Fax: 210-686-0324. Mrs. Jeanne L. Bruton, Prin. & Dir. of Day Care.
Lay Teachers 29; Students 587.
Day Care—.

3—Sacred Heart, (1917), Rev. James Pfeifer, O.M.I.; Deacon Eduardo Reyna.
Res., 306 S. 15th St., P.O. Box 370, 78505-0370. Tel: 210-686-7711.

4—St. Joseph the Worker, (1967), Revs. Bart A. Flaat, C.I.C.M.; Albert Lelo-Luemba, C.I.C.M.; Deacons Alejandro Gamboa; Salvador Rojas.
Res., 2315 Ithaca St., 78501. Tel: 210-682-1351; Fax: 210-971-9480.

5—Holy Spirit, (1981), Revs. Gerald W. Frank; John Taosan, C.I.C.M.; Deacons Lorenzo Contreras, Jr.; Carlos S. Trevino.
Res., 2201 Martin Ave., 78504. Tel: 210-631-5295; Fax: 210-631-5460.
Preschool & Day Care Center—Tel: 210-682-6562. Mrs. Toni F. Espinosa, Dir.

McCook, Hidalgo Co., Immaculate Conception (1950), Rev. Thomas Kulleck.
Rte. 3, Box 188-E, Edinburg, 78539. Tel: 210-842-3663.

Mercedes, Hidalgo Co., Our Lady of Mercy (1909), Rev. Armando Escobedo; Deacon Juan Trevino.
Res., 322 S. Vermont Ave., P.O. Box 805, 78570. Tel: 210-565-1141.
Sacred Heart Church (1969), Rev. Lawrence J. Klein; Deacon Roberto Cantu.
Res., 920 Anacuitas, 78570. Tel: 210-565-0271.

Mission, Hidalgo Co.,

1—Our Lady of Guadalupe, (1899), Revs. Roy Lee Snipes, O.M.I.; Norman Racette, O.M.I.; Bro. Timothy Paulsen, O.M.I.; Deacon Ricardo Ayala, Jr.
Res., 620 Dunlap St., P.O. Box 1047, 78572-1047. Tel: 210-585-2623. [CEM]

2—Our Lady of the Holy Rosary, (1968), Rev. Vicente Azcoiti.
Res., 923 Matamoros St., P.O. Box 1439, 78572. Tel: 210-581-2193.
Missions—Madero, Our Lady of Lourdes; Granjeno, Our Lady of Fatima.

3—Our Lady of St. John of the Fields, (1967), Revs. Ricardo Garcia; Anton Hestasusilo, C.I.C.M.; Deacons Daniel Zamora; Peter Requenez.
Res., 1052 Washington St., 78572. Tel: 210-585-2325; Fax: 210-585-8179.

4—St. Paul, (1915), Rev. F. Robert DaVola; Deacons Ismael Garcia; Robert Ledesma. In res., Rev. Thomas Kulleck.
Res., 1119 Francisco Ave., 78572. Tel: 210-585-2701; Fax: 210-581-4801.

Pharr, Hidalgo Co., St. Anne, Mother of Mary (1973), Rev. Gerry Shanley, SS.CC.; Deacon Jose R. Castro.
Res., 710 E. Lucas, 78577. Tel: 210-787-8122.
St. Jude Thaddeus (1951), Very Rev. Leo Francis Daniels, C.O.; Rev. Jose Encarnacion Losoya, C.O.; Bro. Mario Alberto Aviles, C.O.
Res., 505 S. Ironwood, P.O. Drawer J, 78577-1210. Tel: 210-781-2489; Fax: 210-783-4614.
School—Oratory Academy, P.O. Drawer ii, 78577. Tel: 210-781-3056; Fax: 210-702-3047. Mrs. G. Yvonne Perez, Dir.
Priests 1; Lay Teachers 21; Students 295.
Mission—Las Milpas, Nuestro Senor del Sagrado Corazon, Tel: 210-787-3554.
St. Margaret Mary (1927), Rev. James Brown; Deacon Pedro F. Sanchez.
Res., 122 W. Hawk Ave., 78577. Tel: 210-787-8563.

Port Isabel, Cameron Co., Our Lady Star of the Sea (1927), Revs. Joseph J. O'Brien, O.M.I.; Jack Franko, O.M.I.
Res., 705 S. Longoria St., Box 6504, 78578. Tel: 210-943-1297; Fax: 210-943-1907.

Progreso, Hidalgo Co., Holy Spirit (1969), Rev. Craig G. Carolan.
Res., P.O. Box 216, 78579. Tel: 210-565-6856; 565-1231.
Missions—Santa Maria, St. Margaret Ann; Bluetown, Cristo Rey.

Ranchito, Cameron Co., St. Ignatius (1967), Rev. Ignacio Luna; Deacon Salvador G. Saldivar.
Res., Rte. 10, Box 159, San Benito, 78586. Tel: 210-399-2022.
Missions—La Paloma, Our Lady of Lourdes; Las Rucias, Sacred Heart.

Raymondville, Willacy Co., Our Lady of Guadalupe (1927), Revs. Richard J. MacDonald, S.C.J.; Steve Pujdak, S.C.J.; Gregory M. Speck, S.C.J.; Deacon Juan Francisco Gonzalez.
Res., 693 N. Third St., 78580. Tel: 210-689-2408; Fax: 210-689-3583.
Missions—La Sara, St. Patrick; Hargill, St. Frances Xavier Cabrini.
St. Anthony (1907), Rev. Edward E. Day.
Res., 464 S. First St., 78580. Tel: 210-689-3380.
Mission—San Perlita, Sacred Heart.

Rio Grande City, Starr Co., Immaculate Conception (1880), Revs. Eduardo Villa; Lee DaCosta; Deacon R.C. Salinas.
Res., P.O. Box 1, 101 E. Third St., 78582. Tel: 210-487-2317; Fax: 210-487-8246. [CEM]
School—305 N. Britton Ave., 78582. Tel: 210-487-2558; Fax: 210-487-1033. Sr. Christine Garcia, S.S.N.D., Prin.
School Sisters of Notre Dame 1; Lay Teachers 13; Students 208.
Missions—La Puerta, St. Paul; Los Garcias Ranch, Sacred Heart.

Rio Hondo, Cameron Co., St. Helen (1943), Rev. Terrence Gorski, O.F.M.; Deacons Albert C. Lopez; Genaro Ibarra.
Res., 228 Huisache, P.O. Box 451, 78583. Tel: 210-748-2327.
Mission—Lozano, St. Vincent de Paul.

Roma, Starr Co., Our Lady of Refuge (1853), Rev. Hugo Van den Bussche, O.M.I.
Res., P.O. Box 156, 78584. Tel: 210-849-1455; Fax: 210-849-2257.
Missions—Falcon Heights, Holy Trinity; Salineno, St. Joseph; Los Saenz, Holy Family; Fronton, Lamb of God.

San Benito, Cameron Co., Our Lady, Queen of the Universe (1960), Revs. Norbert J. Deddens (L); Jorge A. Gonzalez.
Res., 121 Garrison Dr., 78586. Tel: 210-399-2865; Fax: 210-399-2045.
Mission—San Benito, St. Joseph, 1001 W. Hwy. 77, 78586.
St. Benedict (1912), Rev. Richard Guerra, O.M.I.; Deacons Manuel Sanchez; Margarito Briones.
Res., 351 S. Bowie, P.O. Box 950, 78586. Tel: 210-399-2353.
St. Theresa (1954), Rev. Patrick K. Seitz; Deacon Benito Flores.
Res., 1300 Combes St., P.O. Box 1830, 78586. Tel: 210-399-3247; Fax: 210-399-3247.

San Carlos, Hidalgo Co., St. Joseph the Worker (1970), Rev. Samuel Arizpe; Deacon Hector Perez.
Res., Rte. 1, Box 202-E, Edinburg, 78539-9801. Tel: 210-383-5880.
Missions—San Manuel, St. Anne; Faysville, St. Theresa.

San Isidro, Starr Co., St. Isidore (1964), Rev. Jose M. Villalon, Jr.
Res., Rte. 1, Box 2, 78588. Tel: 210-481-3392.

San Juan, Hidalgo Co., Virgen de San Juan del Valle Shrine, Revs. Edward T. de Leon, O.M.I., Rector; Leo Gauvin, O.M.I.; Bernard Doyon, O.M.I.; Henri Janssen, O.M.I.; Francis Schoutteten, O.M.I.
Res., P.O. Box 747, 78589. Tel: 210-787-0033.
St. John the Baptist (1949), Rev. Richard J. Sheehan, O.M.I.; Deacons Agapito L. Cantu; Julio Castilleja.
Res., 216 W. First St., P.O. Box 1196, 78589. Tel: 210-783-1196.
Mission—Lopezville, Immaculate Conception.

Santa Rosa, Cameron Co., St. Mary (1967), Rev. Alfredo Garcia, SS.CC.
Res., 101 San Antonio Ave., P.O. Box 365, 78593. Tel: 210-636-1211.

Weslaco, Hidalgo Co., St. Joan of Arc (1929), Rev. Francisco Castillo; Deacons Jesus Aguayo; Francisco Cabellero.
Res., 109 S. Illinois Ave., 78596. Tel: 210-968-3670.
San Martin de Porres (1967), Revs. John A. O'Malley; Carlos Garza; Deacons Abraham Cardosa; Juan Delgado; Jose G. Garza.
Res., 901 N. Texas Blvd., 78596. Tel: 210-968-2691; Fax: 210-968-1473.
Missions—Weslaco, St. Jude Chapel; Expressway Heights, Nuestra Senora de Guadalupe.
St. Pius X (1955), Rev. William Zapalac, O.M.I.; Deacon Jose Oscar Perez.
Res., 600 S. Oklahoma Ave., 78596. Tel: 210-968-7471; Fax: 210-969-3040.

Chaplains of Public Institutions

Brownsville. *Brownsville Medical Center,* 1040 W. Jefferson St., 78520. Tel: 210-544-1426, Ext. 26. Dr. Ethel Winchester-Didsbury, Chap.; Deacon Frank Galvan, Chap. Asst.
Cameron County Jail. Sr. Juliana Garcia, M.J., Chap. Mailing Address: 1850 Ridgely Rd., 78521. Tel: 210-541-0220.
HCA Valley Regional Medical Center, One Ted Hunt Blvd., 78521. Tel: 210-831-9611. Dr. Ethel Winchester-Didsbury, Chap.; Deacon Frank Galvan, Chap. Asst.

Edinburg. *Edinburg Hospital,* 333 W. Freddy Gonzalez Dr., 78539. Tel: 210-383-6211; 585-0019. Sr. Gloria Morales, M.J. Mailing Address: 1501 W. Adams St., Brownsville, 78520. Tel: 210-542-2180.
Hidalgo County Jail. Deacon Jose Solis, Chap. Mailing Address: 315 E. Peter St., 78539. Tel: 210-383-4324.

Harlingen. *Valley Baptist Medical Center,* 2101 Pease St., 78550. Tel: 210-421-1100. Rev. Frank Clancy, S.C.J., Chap.; Sr. Therese Rodriguez, O.P., Chap.

Los Fresnos. *Bayview Detention Center,* Buena Vista Rd., 78577. Tel: 210-541-0220. Sr. Juliana Garcia, M.J., Chap.

McAllen. *McAllen Medical Center,* 701 S. Main St., 78501. Tel: 210-632-4000; 686-3912. Rev. Willy Verboomen, C.I.C.M., Chap.
Rio Grande Regional Hospital, 101 E. Ridge Rd., 78501. Tel: 210-632-6616. Sr. Helen Roper, S.S.N.D., Chap.

Mission. *Mission Hospital.* Sr. Gloria Morales, M.J.,

Chap. Mailing Address: 1501 W. Adams St., Brownsville, 78520. Tel: 210-542-2180. Deacon Arturo Villarreal.

RIO GRANDE CITY. *Starr County Jail.* Deacon R. C. Salinas, Chap. Mailing Address: 304 N. East, 78582. Tel: 210-487-3112.

WESLACO. *Knapp Memorial Medical Center,* P.O. Box 1895, 78596. Tel: 210-969-5258; 973-1968. Sr. Dominga Mosqueda, S.F.C.C., Chap.

Graduate Studies:
Reverend Fathers—
Correa, Adrian R., 906 N. Iverson St., #203, Alexandria, VA 22304. Tel: 703-823-5698

On Assignment Outside the Diocese:
Reverend Fathers—
Brum, Louis, St. Elizabeth Church, 577 Wood St., Bristol, RI 02809-2395
Garza, Amador, St. Meinrad Seminary, St. Meinrad, IN 47577-1030
Mestas, Leonard J., St. Joseph the Worker Church, 10816 Mount View Ave., Loma Linda, CA 92354

On Leave:
Reverend Fathers—
Ayala, Richardo, III

Absent:
Reverend Fathers—
Acosta, Humberto J.
Anderson, Ronald C.
Ellerbrock, Timothy
Farias, Jorge
Mireles, Richard
Zuber, Marti G.

Retired:
Reverend Fathers—
Diaz, Robert, P.O. Box 2279, Brownsville, TX 78520-2279
Gomez, Frank, 6803 N. Navarro, Apt. 4, Victoria, TX 77904. Tel: 512-578-2376
Lambert, John C., 2212 Betty Blvd., Edinburg, TX 78539. Tel: 210-383-4037
Mateos, Tomas, R.R. 15, Box 7747, Mission, TX 78572
Ortiz, Benedicto, 2735 E. 31st St., Brownsville, TX 78521. Tel: 210-546-6790
Smith, Peter J., P.O. Box 570, Rhineback, NY 12572
Sweeney, Robert L., 709 Toronto, Apt. E-2, McAllen, TX 78503. Tel: 210-631-1880

Permanent Deacons:
Aguayo, Jesus, St. Joan of Arc, Weslaco
Aiken, Bruce, Reired
Ayala, Ricardo, Jr., Our Lady of Guadalupe, Mission
Barrera, Ernesto, On Leave
Borja, Gilberto, St. Mary, Mother of the Church, Brownsville
Briones, Margarito, St. Benedict, San Benito
Caballero, Francisco, St. Joan of Arc, Weslaco
Cano, Roberto, St. Mary, Mother of the Church, Brownsville
Cantu, Agapito L., St. John the Baptist, San Juan
Cantu, Roberto, Sacred Heart, Mercedes
Cardosa, Abraham, San Martin de Porres, Weslaco
Casas, Noe, Inactive
Castilleja, Julio, St. John the Baptist, San Juan
Castillo, Abel, Immaculate Heart of Mary, Harlingen
Castro, Jose R., St. Anne, Mother of Mary, Pharr
Cedillo, Bruno, St. Eugene de Mazenod, Brownsville
Chapa, Alberto X., Our Lady, Queen of Angels, La Joya
Chapa, Augusto, Jr., St. Cecilia, Los Fresnos
Contreras, Lorenzo, Jr., Holy Spirit, McAllen
Crixell, Alfred V., Coord., Office of Family Life
Cuevas, Oscar, Sacred Heart, Edinburg
de la Cruz, Hugo, Sacred Heart, Elsa
Delgado, Juan, San Martin de Porres, Weslaco
Diaz, Inocencio, Holy Family, Edinburg
Eklund, Bruce, Albuquerque, NM
Flores, Alejandro, Holy Family, Brownsville
Flores, Benito, St. Theresa, San Benito
Flores, Julio, Jr., St. Anthony, Harlingen
Flores, Lucio, Our Lady, Queen of Angels, La Joya
Galvan, Frank, St. Joseph, Brownsville
Galvan, Jesus P., Resurrection, Alamo
Gamboa, Alejandro, St. Joseph the Worker, McAllen
Garcia, Ismael, St. Paul, Mission
Garcia, Silvestre, St. Joseph, Edinburg
Garza, Francisco, St. Luke, Brownsville
Garza, Jose G., San Martin de Porres, Weslaco
Gerbermann, Alvin H., St. Theresa of the Infant Jesus, Edcouch
Gonzales, Ignacio R., Our Lady of Assumption, Harlingen
Gonzalez, Irineo, Jr., St. Joseph, Edinburg
Gonzalez, Juan F., Our Lady of Guadalupe, Raymondville
Gonzalez, Leopoldo, Inactive
Grimaldo, Jose N., Inactive
Guerra, Jose, Our Lady of Guadalupe, Brownsville
Ibarra, Genaro, St. Helen, Rio Hondo
Jurado, Mariano, St. Theresa Mission, Faysville
Kinch, John, Immaculate Conception Cathedral, Brownsville
Leal, Ramon G., Our Lady of Guadalupe, Brownsville
Ledesma, Robert, St. Paul, Mission
Lopez, Albert C., St. Helen, Rio Hondo
Lopez, Gilberto, Sacred Heart, Edinburg
Lopez, Ruben, Holy Family, Edinburg
McArdle, Paul, Good Shepherd, Brownsville
Munoz, Andres, Our Heavenly Father Mission, Olmito
Navarro, Juan Pablo, St. Luke, Brownsville
Oden, Luis, Inactive
Olvera, Alvino C., Our Lady of Good Counsel, Brownsville
Ovalle, Eduardo, Sr., St. Joseph, Donna
Perez, Hector, St. Joseph the Worker, San Carlos
Perez, Jose Oscar, St. Pius X, Weslaco
Requenez, Peter, Our Lady of St. John of the Fields, Mission
Reyna, Eduardo, Sacred Heart, McAllen
Rodriguez, Arturo, Immaculate Conception Cathedral, Brownsville
Rojas, Salvador, St. Joseph the Worker, McAllen
Rousset, Louis, Inactive
Saenz, Benito, Jr., Holy Family, Grulla
Sagredo, Israel, San Martin de Porres, Alton
Saldana, Enrique, Our Lady of Good Counsel, Brownsville
Saldivar, Salvador G., St. Ignatius, Ranchito
Salinas, Rodolfo C., Immaculate Conception, Rio Grande City
Sanchez, Manuel, St. Benedict, San Benito
Sanchez, Pedro F., St. Margaret Mary, Pharr
Schwarz, John, Our Lady of Sorrows, McAllen
Solis, Heriberto, St. Mary, Mother of the Church, Brownsville
Solis, Jose, Sacred Heart, Edinburg
Trevino, Carlos S., Holy Spirit, McAllen
Trevino, Felipe, Christ the King, Brownsville
Trevino, Heriberto, St. Mary, Mother of the Church, Brownsville
Trevino, Juan, Our Lady of Mercy, Mercedes
Valenzuela, Juan, Queen of Peace, Harlingen
Villalon, Rene, Sr., S.F.O., Our Lady of Perpetual Help, McAllen
Villarreal, Arturo, Retired
Webre, Alfred L., Jr., Retired
Zamora, Daniel, Our Lady of St. John of the Fields, Mission

INSTITUTIONS LOCATED IN THE DIOCESE

[A] HIGH SCHOOLS, PRIVATE

BROWNSVILLE. *St. Joseph Academy.* (Grades 7-12), 101 St. Joseph Dr., 78520. Tel: 210-542-3581. Bro. John Venturella, F.M.S., Prin. Marist Brothers, Esopus Province. Religious 8; Lay Teachers 39; Students 673.

[B] ELEMENTARY SCHOOLS, PRIVATE

BROWNSVILLE. *Incarnate Word Academy Elementary and Middle School.* (Convent Academy of the Incarnate Word), 244 Resaca Blvd., 78520. Tel: 210-546-4486. Sisters of the Incarnate Word and Blessed Sacrament. Miss Christina Moreno, Prin. Religious 5; Lay Teachers 20; Students 228.

PHARR. *Oratory Academy,* P.O. Drawer ii, 78577. Tel: 210-781-3056. Mrs. Yvonne D. Perez, Dir. Religious 1; Lay Teachers 2; Students 295.

[C] CATHOLIC SOCIAL SERVICES

BROWNSVILLE. *Bayview Detention Center Ministry,* 1850 Ridgely Rd., 78520. Tel: 210-541-0220. Sr. Juliana Garcia, S.J., Chap.

Catholic Charities, P.O. Box 2279, 78522. Tel: 210-542-2501. Legal Title: *Catholic Charities of the Diocese of Brownsville, a Texas Non-Profit Corporation.* Most Rev. Raymundo J. Pena, Chm.; Mr. Hernan Gonzalez, Exec. Dir.

Catholic Social Services Branch Office, 1850 Ridgely Rd., 78520. Tel: 210-541-0220. Sr. Norma Pimentel, M.J., Family Counselor; Telma Longoria. Tel: 210-702-4088; Fax: 210-702-4042.

SAN JUAN. *Catholic Social Services Office,* 400 N. Nebraska, P.O. Box 128, 78589. Tel: 210-702-4088; Fax: 210-702-4042. Telma Longoria, Coord.; Deacon Ricardo Ayala, Jr., Family Counseling.

[D] HOMES FOR THE AGED

BROWNSVILLE. *Mother of Perpetual Help Home,* 519 E. Madison St., 78520. Tel: 210-546-6745; 546-0711. *For a complete listing, refer to the Special Care Facilities section.*

SAN JUAN. *San Juan Home Health and Hospice,* 400 N. Nebraska, P.O. Box 2359, 78589. Tel: 210-782-0333; Fax: 210-782-0335. *For a complete listing, refer to the Special Care Facilities section.*

San Juan Nursing Home, 300 N. Nebraska, P.O. Box 1238, 78589. Tel: 210-787-1771; Fax: 210-787-8091. *For a complete listing, refer to the Special Care Facilities section.*

[E] RESIDENCES FOR PRIESTS AND BROTHERS

BROWNSVILLE. *El Rancho Grande Apartments,* 1225 Central Blvd., #903, 78520. Tel: 210-542-4744. Rev. Edward W. Wichmann (PBL).

Marist Brothers of the Schools, Champagnat Hall, 105 St. Joseph Dr., 78520. Tel: 210-546-3038. Brothers 2.

Marist Brothers, St. Joseph Academy, 101 St. Joseph Dr., 78520. Tel: 210-546-2608. Brothers 7.

HARLINGEN. *Priests of the Sacred Heart,* 144 W. Spencer Ct., 78550. Tel: 210-428-8344. Rev. Frank Clancy, S.C.J.

PHARR. *Oratory of St. Philip Neri, of Pontifical Right,* P.O. Box ii, 78577-1235. Tel: 210-843-8217; Fax: 210-843-2946. Very Rev. Leo Francis Daniels, C.O., Provost; Revs. Jose Encarnacion Losoya, C.O., Sec. & Treas.; David Garcia, C.O.; Bro. Mario Alberto Aviles, C.O.

RAYMONDVILLE. *Sacred Heart Fathers,* Rte. 2, Box 788, 78580. Tel: 210-689-6428. Priests 4; Brothers 1.

SAN BENITO. *Our Lady of Tenderness Hermitage.* (El Ranchito), Rte. 1, Box 159, 78586. Tel: 210-399-2552. In res., Bro. David Lopez.

[F] CONVENTS AND RESIDENCES FOR SISTERS

BROWNSVILLE. *Dominican Sisters of Charity of the Presentation,* 934 W. St. Charles St., 78520. Tel: 210-542-7225. Sisters 3.

Incarnate Word Convent, 700 W. Jefferson St., 78520. Sisters 14; Sisters of Christian Charity 1; Sisters of the Holy Spirit 1; Sisters of the Incarnate Word and Blessed Sacrament 12.

Missionaries of Jesus, 1501 W. Adams, 78520. Tel: 210-542-2180. Sisters 7; Novices 1.

Mother of Perpetual Help Nursing Home, 519 E. Madison, 78520. Tel: 210-546-0711. Sisters of the Holy Spirit and Mary Immaculate 3.

School Sisters of Notre Dame, 600 Lakeside Blvd., Apt. 6AA, 78520. Tel: 210-548-0056. Sisters 2.

Sisters of Charity of the Incarnate Word. (San Antonio Prov.), 1218 E. Jefferson St., 78522. Tel: 210-504-3343. Mailing Address: P.O. Box 1973, 78522.

Sisters of Charity of the Incarnate Word (San Antonio), 600 Lakeside Blvd., Apt. 5E, 78520. Tel: 210-548-1963. Mailing Address: P.O. Box 2279, 78522.

Sisters of St. Joseph of Carondelet, 1955 W. Monroe, 78520. Tel: 210-541-4038.

Sisters of the Incarnate Word and Blessed Sacrament, Casa de Vida, Rte. 8, Box 684-F, 78520. Tel: 210-504-2131.

Sisters of the Incarnate Word and Blessed Sacrament, 535 W. St. Charles St., 78520. Tel: 210-544-2542; 546-8298. Sisters 3.

ALAMO. *Missionary Sisters of the Immaculate Heart of Mary,* Rte. 2, Box 133A, 78516. Tel: 210-702-0524. Sisters 2.

EDINBURG. *Sisters of St. Joseph of Carondelet,* 502 E. Kuhn St., 78539. Tel: 210-383-6870.

HARLINGEN. *Franciscan Sisters of Mary,* 3401 Business 83, #85, 78552-3517. Tel: 210-423-9447.

Sisters of Charity of the Incarnate Word (Houston), 502 E. Polk St., 78550. Tel: 210-428-3567. Sisters 2.

LA FERIA. *Congregation of Notre Dame of Montreal,* 208 W. Cypress St., P.O. Box 1476, 78559-1116. Tel: 210-797-2774.

Missionary Sisters of the Immaculate Heart of Mary, 317 S. West St., Box 5803, 78559. Tel: 210-797-3973. Sisters 3.

MCALLEN. *Maryknoll Sisters of St. Dominic, Inc.,* 700 Jackson Ave., #161, 78501. Tel: 210-682-3112. Sisters 2.

Missionary Sisters of the Immaculate Heart of Mary, 816 S. 27th St., 78501-7750. Tel: 210-631-0208. Sisters 2.

School Sisters of Notre Dame, Casa de Paz, 700 W. Jackson Ave., #151, 78501. Tel: 210-682-2482. Sisters 2.

Sisters of Mercy of the Americas. (St. Louis), 1400 N. 16th St., Apt. 111, 78501-4460. Tel: 210-687-2620.

Sisters of Mercy of the Americas. (St. Louis), Rte. 2, Box 1680, 78504. Tel: 210-686-6047. Sisters 2.

MISSION. *Misioneras Catequistas de los Pobres*, 615 Dunlap, 78572. Tel: 210-585-1376. Sisters 2.

Misioneras Eucaristicas Franciscanas, 2207 Washington St., 78572. Tel: 210-581-3741. Sisters 3.

Sisters of Charity of Leavenworth, P.O. Box 9023, 78572. Tel: 210-585-8139.

Sisters of St. Joseph of Carondelet, 1711 W. Gastel Cir., 78572-3037. Tel: 210-585-4870. Sisters 2.

PHARR. *Congregation of Divine Providence*, Rte. 2, Box 228-A, 78577. Tel: 210-682-3990.

Missionary Catechists of Divine Providence, 1501 W. Kelly, #367, 78577. Tel: 210-702-0453. Sisters 3.

Sisters of Mercy of the Americas. (St. Louis), La Casa de ARISE, 6900 Mars Ln., 78577. Tel: 210-781-5208.

PORT ISABEL. *Sisters of St. Francis*, 705 Manautau St., P.O. Box 6504, 78578. Tel: 210-943-2136.

PROGRESO. *Sisters of St. Dorothy*, P.O. Box 536, Holy Spirit Convent, 78579. Tel: 210-565-9430. Sisters 4.

RAYMONDVILLE. *Sisters of Mercy of the Americas.* (St. Louis), 693 N. Third St., 78580. Tel: 210-689-3151.

Sisters of the Holy Cross, Casa de la Luz, 317 S. King St., 78580-2307. Tel: 210-689-3059. Sisters 3.

RIO GRANDE CITY. *Benedictine Sisters of Crookston, MN*, 612 E. Mira Soles St., 78582. Tel: 210-487-7927. Sisters 3.

Benedictine Sisters of the Good Shepherd, Rte. 1, Box 3401, 78582. Tel: 210-486-2680. Sisters 3.

SAN BENITO. *Missionary Sisters of the Immaculate Heart of Mary*, 1221 Combes St., 78586. Tel: 210-399-8122. Sisters 3.

Sisters of St. Francis of Penance and Charity, R.R. 1, Box 65C, 78586. Tel: 210-399-4394.

SAN JUAN. *Sisters of the Sacred Heart of Jesus*, P.O. Box 464, 78589. Tel: 210-702-1967. Sisters 3.

WESLACO. *Sisters of St. Francis*, Siesta Village, Box 332, 78596. Tel: 210-968-0471. Sisters 2.

[G] RETREAT HOUSES

BROWNSVILLE. *Sisters of the Incarnate Word Casa de Vida*, P.O. Box 684-F, 78520. Tel: 210-504-2131. Sr. Jude Janecek, I.W.B.S.

SAN JUAN. *San Juan Diocesan Retreat Center*, P.O. Box 747, 78589. Tel: 210-787-0033.

[H] CAMPUS MINISTRY

BROWNSVILLE. *Young Adult Ministry / University of Texas at Brownsville-Texas Southmost College*, 1850 Ridgely Rd., 78520. Tel: 210-542-3942. Sr. Gloria Ann Fiedler, C.D.P.; Hilda Escandon.

EDINBURG. *University of Texas Pan American Campus at Edinburg*, 1615 W. Kuhn St., 78539. Tel: 210-383-0133. Sr. Gloria Ann Fiedler, C.D.P.; Marilyn Hagerty.

[I] MISCELLANEOUS

BROWNSVILLE. *Society of St. Vincent De Paul District Council*, 1158 E. Jefferson St., 78520. Tel: 210-541-1755; Fax: 210-541-2374. Joan Cortinas, District Pres.

Villa Maria Language Institute, 224 Resaca Blvd., 78520. Tel: 210-546-7196. Sr. Mary Lelia Aguilar, I.W.B.S., Dir.

EDINBURG. *Cursillos*, 900 S. Second, 78539. Tel: 210-383-5137. Mr. Ruben Alfaro, Contact Person; Deacon Salvador Rojas, Spiritual Dir.

HARLINGEN. *KMBH-TV 60 / KHID-FM 88.1 / KMBH-FM 88.9*, P.O. Box 2147, 78551. Tel: 210-421-4111; Fax: 210-421-4150. Rev. Pedro Briseno, Admin. Supvr.

MCALLEN. *Secular Franciscan Order, Fraternity of Our Lady of Guadalupe*, 3600 N. 23rd, Ste. 205, 78501. Tel: 210-687-6816. Rev. Tomas Mateos, S.F.O., Spiritual Dir.; Paula Cortez, Min. Prefect; Maria Celia Solis, Vice Min. Prefect; Rafael Solis, Sec. & Treas.; Sr. Teresita L. MacLang, S.F.O., Formator.

MERCEDES. *La Merced Charitable Trust*, 413 S. Virginia, P.O. Box 806, 78570. Tel: 210-565-2622.
Housing Board: Mr. Santiago (Jimmy) Fernandez; Mr. Hernan Gonzalez; Mrs. Anita A. Rodriguez; Mrs. Ana Zamarripa, Res. Mgr.

MISSION. *El Rosario Charitable Trust*, 119 Retama, P.O. Box 971, 78572. Tel: 210-585-5051.
Housing Board: Mr. Santiago (Jimmy) Fernandez; Mr. Hernan Gonzalez.

SAN JUAN. *Virgen de San Juan del Valle Shrine*, P.O. Box 747, 78589. Tel: 210-787-0033; Fax: 210-787-2908. Rev. Edward T. DeLeon, O.M.I., Rector. Associates: Revs. Leo Gauvin, O.M.I.; Bernard Doyon, O.M.I.; Henri Janssen, O.M.I.; Francis Schoutteten, O.M.I.; Hernan Gonzalez, General Mgr.

San Juan Retreat Center. Tel: 210-787-0033.

San Juan Pilgrim House / Hotel. Tel: 210-787-0033, Ext. 249.

Religious Gift & Book Store. Tel: 210-787-0033, Ext. 332.

San Juan Print Shop. Tel: 210-787-0033, Ext. 350.

WESLACO. *Holy Family Services-Birth Center*, Rte. 1, Box 257, 78596-9705. Tel: 210-969-2538. Sr. Angela Murdaugh, F.S.M.

RELIGIOUS INSTITUTES OF MEN REPRESENTED IN THE DIOCESE

For further details refer to the corresponding bracketed number in the Religious Institutes of Men or Women section.

[0630]—*Congregation of the Missionaries of the Holy Family.*—M.S.F.

[1130]—*Congregation of the Priests of the Sacred Heart.*—S.C.J.

[1140]—*Fathers of the Sacred Hearts.*—SS.CC.

[0410]—*Franciscans-Assumption BVM Province.*—O.F.M.

[0770]—*The Marist Brothers.*—F.M.S.

[0780]—*Marist Fathers.*—S.M.

[0860]—*Missionhurst Congregation of the Immaculate Heart of Mary.*—C.I.C.M.

[0910]—*Oblates of Mary Immaculate.*—O.M.I.

[0950]—*Oratorians of St. Philip Neri.*—C.O.

RELIGIOUS INSTITUTES OF WOMEN REPRESENTED IN THE DIOCESE

[]—*Adorers of the Blood of Christ.*

[]—*Benedictine Sisters of Crookston, Minnesota.*—O.S.B.

[]—*Benedictine Sisters of the Good Shepherd (Monastery).*—O.S.B.

[]—*Congregation of Divine Providence (Helotes).*—C.D.P.

[]—*Congregation of Notre Dame.*

[0470]—*Congregation of the Sisters of Charity of the Incarnate Word, Houston, Texas.*—C.C.V.I.

[1920]—*Congregation of the Sisters of the Holy Cross.*—C.S.C.

[0760]—*Daughters of Charity of St. Vincent de Paul.*—D.C.

[]—*Dominican Sisters.*

[]—*Dominican Sisters of Grand Rapids, Michigan.*—O.P.

[]—*Dominican Sisters of St. Catherine of Kentucky.*

[1070-09]—*Dominican Sisters of St. Dominic.* (Racine, WI).—O.P.

[]—*Dominican Sisters of the Congregation of Our Lady of the Sacred Heart.*

[1070-05]—*Dominican Sisters of the Presentation.*—O.P.

[1200]—*Franciscan Sisters of Baltimore.*—O.S.F.

[1415]—*Franciscan Sisters of Mary.*—F.S.M.

[]—*Franiscan Sisters of Little Falls, Minnesota.*—O.S.F.

[2470]—*Maryknoll Sisters of St. Dominic, Inc.*.—M.M.

[1150]—*Misioneras Eucaristicas Franciscanas.*—M.E.F.

[2690]—*Missionary Catechists of Divine Providence.*—M.C.D.P.

[]—*Missionary Eucharistic Franciscan Sisters.*

[]—*Missionary Sisters of Jesus.*—M.J.

[2750]—*Missionary Sisters of the Immaculate Heart of Mary.*—I.C.M.

[]—*Missioneras Catequistas de los Pobres.*—M.C.P.

[]—*Racine Dominicans of Racine, Wisconsin.*

[2970]—*School Sisters of Notre Dame.* (Prov. of Dallas).—S.S.N.D.

[]—*School Sisters of Notre Dame.* (Mankato Prov.).—S.S.N.D.

[]—*Sinsinawa Dominican Sisters.*—O.P.

[0440]—*Sisters of Charity of Cincinnati, Ohio.*—S.C.

[0480]—*Sisters of Charity of Leavenworth, Kansas.*—S.C.L.

[0460]—*Sisters of Charity of the Incarnate Word.* (San Antonio, TX).—C.C.V.I. []—Sisters for a Christian Community.—S.F.C.C.

[]—*Sisters of Christian Charity.*—S.C.C.

[]—*Sisters of Divine Providence.* (Pennsylvania).—C.D.P.

[1010]—*Sisters of Divine Providence of St. Louis.*—C.D.P.

[2575]—*Sisters of Mercy of the Americas.* (St. Louis, MO; Cincinnati, OH).—R.S.M.

[3790]—*Sisters of St. Dorothy.*—S.S.D.

[1720]—*Sisters of St. Francis of Our Lady of Lourdes.*—O.S.F.

[1760]—*Sisters of St. Francis of Penance and Charity.*—O.S.F.

[3840]—*Sisters of St. Joseph of Carondelet.* (St. Paul & St. Louis Provs.).—C.S.J.

[2980]—*Sisters of the Congregation of Notre Dame of Montreal.*—C.N.D.

[2050]—*Sisters of the Holy Spirit and Mary Immaculate.*—S.H.Sp.

[2200]—*Sisters of the Incarnate Word and Blessed Sacrament.*—I.W.B.S.

[]—*Sisters of the Living Word.*—S.L.W.

[3320]—*Sisters of the Presentation of the Blessed Virgin Mary.*—P.B.V.M.

[3670]—*Sisters of the Sacred Heart of Jesus of Saint Jacut.*—S.S.C.J.

NECROLOGY

† Yanez-Moreno, Eduardo, Brownsville, TX, Saint Mary, Mother of the Church. —Died Feb. 18, 1996.

Diocese of Buffalo

(Dioecesis Buffalensis)

Most Reverend

EDWARD D. HEAD, D.D.

Bishop Emeritus of Buffalo; ordained January 27, 1945; appointed Titular Bishop of Ardstratha and Auxiliary of New York January 27, 1970; consecrated March 19, 1970; appointed to Buffalo January 17, 1973; installed March 19, 1973; retired June 12, 1995. *Res., 795 Main St., Buffalo, NY, 14203-1250.*

Most Reverend

BERNARD J. McLAUGHLIN, D.D., V.G.

Retired Auxiliary Bishop of Buffalo; Titular Bishop of Mottola; ordained December 21, 1935; appointed December 28, 1968; consecrated January 6, 1969; retired January 15, 1988. *Res., 204 Knoche Rd., Tonawanda, NY, 14150.*

Most Reverend

HENRY J. MANZELL, D.D.

Bishop of Buffalo; ordained December 19, 1962; appointed Titular Bishop of Marazane and Auxiliary of New York November 24, 1992; ordained January 6, 1993; appointed to Buffalo April 18, 1995; installed June 12, 1995. *Res., 77 Oakland Pl., Buffalo, NY, 14222.*

Chancery Office: 795 Main St., Buffalo, NY, 14203. Tel.: 716-847-5500; Fax: 716-847-5557.

Web site address: http://www.buffalodiocese.org

E-mail address: dob@servtech.com

Most Reverend

EDWARD M. GROSZ, D.D.

Auxiliary Bishop of Buffalo; Titular Bishop of Morosbisdo; ordained May 29, 1971; appointed November 22, 1989; consecrated February 2, 1990. *Res., St. Stanislaus Kostka Rectory, 2437 Niagara St., Niagara Falls, NY, 14303-1925.*

ESTABLISHED APRIL 23, 1847.

Incorporated under the laws of the State of New York October 30th, 1897. Re-incorporated by special act passed April 5, 1951, Chapter 568 of the laws of 1951. Corporate Title: *The Diocese of Buffalo, N.Y.*

Square Miles 6,357.

Comprises the Counties of Erie, Niagara, Genesee, Orleans, Chautauqua, Wyoming, Cattaraugus and Allegany in the State of New York.

For legal titles of parishes and diocesan institutions, consult the Chancery Office.

STATISTICAL OVERVIEW

Personnel	
Bishop	1
Auxiliary Bishops	1
Retired Bishops	2
Priests: Diocesan Active in Diocese	334
Priests: Active Outside Diocese	13
Priests: Diocesan in Foreign Missions	1
Priests: Retired, Sick or Absent	102
Number of Diocesan Priests	450
Religious Priests in Diocese	194
Extern Priests in Diocese	2
Ordinations:	
Diocesan Priests	4
Transitional Deacons	6
Permanent Deacons	5
Permanent Deacons in Diocese	85
Total Brothers	47
Total Sisters	1,489
Parishes	
Parishes	266
With Resident Pastor:	
Resident Diocesan Priests	215
Resident Religious Priests	15
Without Resident Pastor:	
Administered by Priests	35
Administered by Women Religious	1
Missions	10
Welfare	
Catholic Hospitals	7
Total Assisted	908,267
Homes for the Aged	16
Total Assisted	1,653
Day Care and Extended Day Care Centers	2
Total Assisted	192
Specialized Homes	3
Total Assisted	302
Special Centers for Social Services	4
Total Assisted	2,893
Educational	
Seminaries, Diocesan	2
Students from This Diocese	15
Students from Other Diocese	15
Diocesan Students in Other Seminaries	6
Total Seminarians	21
Colleges and Universities	7
Total Students	13,298
High Schools, Private	17
Total Students	6,029
Elementary Schools, Diocesan and Parish	88
Total Students	22,896
Elementary Schools, Private	6
Total Students	1,763
Catechesis/Religious Education:	
High School Students	12,433
Elementary Students	42,328
Total Students Under Catholic Instruction	98,768
Teachers in the Diocese:	
Priests	18
Brothers	6
Sisters	127
Lay Teachers	1,812
Vital Statistics	
Receptions into the Church:	
Infant Baptism Totals	8,094
Adult Baptism Totals	501
Received into Full Communion	447
First Communions	8,588
Confirmations	5,964
Marriages:	
Catholic	2,367
Interfaith	946
Total Marriages	3,313
Deaths	7,268
Total Catholic Population	753,117
Total Population	1,613,258

Former Bishops—Rt. Rev. JOHN TIMON, D.D., C.M., cons. Oct. 17, 1847; died April 16, 1867.—Rt. Rev. STEPHEN V. RYAN, D.D., C.M., cons. Nov. 8, 1868; died April 10, 1896.—Rt. Rev. JAMES EDWARD QUIGLEY, D.D., cons. Bishop of Buffalo, Feb. 24, 1897; promoted to the Archdiocese of Chicago, Feb. 19, 1903; died July 10, 1915.—Rt. Rev. CHARLES HENRY COLTON, D.D., cons. Aug. 24, 1903; died May 9, 1915.—His Eminence DENIS CARDINAL DOUGHERTY, D.D., cons. Bishop of Nueva Segovia, June 14, 1903; transferred to the Diocese of Jaro, April 19, 1908; transferred to the Diocese of Buffalo, Dec. 6, 1915; promoted to Archdiocese of Philadelphia, May 1, 1918; created Cardinal, March 7, 1921; died May 31, 1951.—Most Rev. WILLIAM TURNER, D.D., cons. March 30, 1919; died July 10, 1936.—Most Rev. JOHN A. DUFFY, D.D., cons. Bishop of Syracuse, June 29, 1933; transferred to the Diocese of Buffalo, April 14, 1937; died Sept. 27, 1944.—His Eminence JOHN CARDINAL O'HARA, C.S.C., ord. Sept. 9, 1916; appt. Military Delegate of the Armed Forces and Titular Bishop of Mylasa, Dec. 11, 1939; cons. Jan. 15, 1940; transferred to Buffalo, March 10, 1945; installed May 8, 1945; promoted to the Archdiocese of Philadelphia, Nov. 23, 1951; created Cardinal, Dec. 15, 1958; died Aug. 28, 1960.—Most Rev. JOSEPH A. BURKE, D.D., cons. Titular Bishop of Vita and Auxiliary, June 29, 1943; promoted to the See, Feb. 9, 1952; died Oct. 16, 1962.—Most Rev. JAMES A. MCNULTY, D.D., cons. Oct. 7, 1947; Titular Bishop of Methone and Auxiliary Bishop of Newark, NJ; appt. Bishop of Paterson, NJ April 9, 1953; transferred to Buffalo, Feb. 12, 1963; died Sept. 4, 1972.—Most Rev. EDWARD D. HEAD, D.D., ord. Jan. 27, 1945; appt. Titular Bishop of Ardstratha and Auxiliary of New York, Jan. 27, 1970; cons. March 19, 1970; appt. Bishop of Buffalo, Jan. 17, 1973; installed March 19, 1973; retired June 12, 1995.

Vicars General—Most Rev. EDWARD M. GROSZ, D.D.; Rev. Msgr. ROBERT J. CUNNINGHAM, P.A., J.C.L.

Chancery Office—795 Main St., Buffalo, 14203. Tel: 716-847-5500; Fax: 716-847-5557. Office Hours: Mon.-Fri. 9-4:30.

Chancellor—Rev. Msgr. ROBERT J. CUNNINGHAM, P.A., J.C.L., V.G.

Vice Chancellor—Rev. PAUL A. LITWIN, J.C.L.

Secretary to Ordinary and Assistant Chancellor—Rev. Msgr. PETER J. POPADICK.

Diocesan Tribunal—795 Main St., Buffalo, 14203. Tel: 716-847-8769; Fax: 716-847-8772. Send all rogatory commissions to the Tribunal.

Judicial Vicar—Rev. SALVATORE MANGANELLO, S.T.L., J.C.L.

Adjunct Judicial Vicars—Revs. PAUL P. SABO; PAUL A. LITWIN, J.C.L.

Defenders of the Bond—Revs. FRANCIS T. NOWAK; EDWARD R. CZARNECKI; FRANCIS X. MAZUR; GREGORY M. FAULHAUBER; DENNIS A. FRONCZAK; DONALD E. LEVAN, J.C.L.; ROBERT E. ZAPFEL, S.T.D.; DAVID A. ZWIFKA, J.C.L.

Advocates—Deacons DANIEL E. BRICK; MICHAEL P. MCKEATING; Revs. RICHARD DIGIULIO; ROBERT W. VOGT.

Auditor—Sr. MARY HARTLEY, S.S.M.N.; Sr. JOLENE JASINSKI, C.S.S.F.
Promotor of Justice—Rev. Msgr. JEROME W. SULLIVAN, J.C.D.
Judges—Rev. Msgr. ANTHONY J. CALIGIURI; Rev. Msgr. ROBERT J. CUNNINGHAM, J.C.L., V.G.; Rev. Msgr. JOHN W. MADSEN; Rev. Msgr. GEORGE B. YIENGST; Rev. Msgr. WILLIAM J. GALLAGHER; Revs. CHESTER S. FRYSIAK; JAMES M. AUGUSTYN; HENRY A. ORSZULAK; WALLACE T. BORUCKI; VINCENT J. BECKER; SALVATORE MANGANELLO, J.C.L.; DONALD E. LEVAN, J.C.L.; PAUL R. BOSSI; JOHN R. GAGLIONE; FRED D. INGALLS; BERNARD OLSZEWSKI, O.F.M.Conv., J.C.D.; DAVID A. ZWIFKA, J.C.L.; JEROME E. KOPEC, J.C.L.; Sr. SANDRA MAKOWSKI, J.C.L.; Revs. PAUL A. LITWIN, J.C.L.; PAUL SABO; Rev. Msgr. DAVID S. SLUBECKY, S.T.L., J.C.L.
Notaries—Sr. AGNITA BROWN; LUCILLE BUCZEK; ROBIN COLVIN.
Consultors, College of—Most Rev. EDWARD M. GROSZ, D.D.; Rev. Msgr. ROBERT J. CUNNINGHAM, P.A., J.C.L., V.G.; Rev. RODERICK M. BROWN, O.P.; Rev. Msgr. RICHARD M. CAHILL; Rev. Msgr. GERALD L. GREEN; Rev. JEROME E. KOPEC; Rev. Msgr. JOHN W. MADSEN; Rev. LOUIS P. TROTTA, C.M.
Council of Priests—Most Rev. HENRY J. MANSELL, D.D., Pres.; Most Rev. EDWARD M. GROSZ, D.D.; Rev. Msgr. ROBERT J. CUNNINGHAM, P.A., J.C.L., V.G.; Rev. JOSEPH BAYNE, O.F.M.Conv.; Rev. Msgr. VINCENT J. BECKER; Rev Msgr. LEONARD E. BINISZKIEWICZ; Rev. RODERICK M. BROWN, O.P.; Rev. Msgr. RICHARD M. CAHILL; Rev. Msgr. JOHN J. CONNIFF; Revs. RICHARD C. COVENY; GREGORY J. DOBSON; JOSEPH G. FIFAGROWICZ; Rev. Msgr. DAVID A. GERNATT; Rev. Msgr. GERARD L. GREEN; Rev. Msgr. HENRY J. GUGINO; Revs. JEROME E. KOPEC; JOHN J. LEISING; BARTHOLOMEW W. LIPIEC; DAVID G. LIPUMA; Rev. Msgr. JOHN W. MADSEN; Revs. ROBERT A. MARTIN; JOHN J. MITKA; Rev. Msgr. ROBERT E. MURPHY; Revs. SEBASTIAN C. PIERRO; JOSEPH F. POWER, O.S.F.; RICHARD A. REINA; Rev. Msgr. EDWARD J. SCANLAN; Revs. JEROME J. STELMACH; PAUL F. STENGEL; WALTER J. SZCZESNY; LOUIS P. TROTTA, C.M.; MICHAEL G. UEBLER; EUGENE P. ULRICH; ROBERT W. VOGT; Rev. Msgr. JAMES E. WALL; Revs. DANIEL P. WALSH; MARK J. WOLSKI; Rev. Msgr. RUPERT A. WRIGHT; Rev. RICHARD E. ZAJAC.
Vicariates—
Vicars—Northwest Buffalo: Rev. PAUL R. BOSSI; Central Buffalo: Rev. RODERICK M. BROWN, O.P.; Southeast Buffalo: Rev. Msgr. MATTHEW S. KOPACZ; Northern Erie: Rev. Msgr. RUPERT A. WRIGHT; Eastern Erie: Rev. Msgr. DAVID S. SLUBECKY; Western Erie: Rev. Msgr. ROBERT C. WURTZ; Allegany: Rev. DENNIS G. WOLF; Northern Cattaraugus: Rev. LAWRENCE M. MILBY; Southern Cattaraugus: Rev. GREGORY J. DOBSON; Northern Chautauqua: Rev. PATRICK H. ELLIS; Southern Chautauqua: Rev. Msgr. ANTOINE P. ATTEA; Genesee: Rev. Msgr. LEO F. MCCARTHY; Eastern Niagara: Rev. Msgr. DONALD R. WANGLER; Western Niagara: Most Rev. EDWARD M. GROSZ; Orleans: Rev. RICHARD A. CSIZMAR; Wyoming: Rev. RICHARD W. BLAZEJEWSKI.
The Diocese of Buffalo, N.Y.—A corporation under the laws of the State of New York. Most Revs. HENRY J. MANSELL, D.D., Pres. EDWARD M. GROSZ, D.D., Vice Pres.; Rev. Msgr. ROBERT J. CUNNINGHAM, J.C.L., Sec.

Diocesan Offices and Directors

All offices are located at: *795 Main St., Buffalo, 14203.* Tel: 716-847-8700; Fax: 716-847-5557. (Unless otherwise noted)
Apostleship of Prayer—Rev. Msgr. WALTER O. KERN, Dir., *5337 Genesee St., Bowmansville, 14026.*
Apostleship of the Sea—Rev. Msgr. JOHN I. DUCETTE, Dir., *Res., 565 E. Park Dr., Tonawanda, 14150.*
Archives—Rev. Msgr. WALTER O. KERN, Dir. Tel: 716-847-5500.
Bishop's Committee for Christian Home and Family—Rev. Msgr. FRED R. VOORHES, Moderator. Tel: 716-847-2210.
Boy Scouts—Rev. Msgr. FRANCIS G. WELDGEN, Chap. Tel: 716-847-8789. VINCENT J. HARMON, Lay Dir., *99 Clark St., Tonawanda, 15150.* Tel: 716-693-7558.
Buildings and Properties—JOHNSTONE N. REID, JR. Tel: 716-847-8750.
Camping—Rev. GARY J. BAGLEY. Tel: 716-847-8789.
Catholic Alumni Club—ROBERT A. LIPOME, Pres.; Rev. RICHARD W. BLAZEJEWSKI, Chap., *P.O. Box 87, Kenmore, 14223.*
Catholic Charities—Rev. Msgr. HENRY J. GUGINO, Dir., *525 Washington St., Buffalo, 14203.* Rev. JOSEPH J. SICARI, Assoc. Dir. Tel: 716-856-4494; Fax: 716-856-2005.
Catholic Charities Appeal—Rev. Msgr. HENRY J. GUGINO, Dir., Office: *525 Washington St., Buffalo, 14203.* Tel: 716-856-4494.
Catholic Relief Services—Rev. Msgr. HENRY J. GUGINO, Dir., *525 Washington St., Buffalo, 14203.* Tel: 716-856-4494.
Church Ministry, Office of—Mrs. KATHLEEN B. HEFFERN, Coord. Tel: 716-847-5531.
Council of Catholic Men—Rev. Msgr. WILLIAM A. SCHWINGER, Moderator, *50 Franklin St., Buffalo, 14202.* Tel: 716-852-6040.
Council of Catholic Women—Rev. Msgr. JAMES E. WALL, Moderator, *6892 Lake Shore, P.O. Box 816, Derby, 14047.*
Cemeteries—CARMEN COLAO, Dir., *Mt. Olivet Cemetery, 4000 Elmwood Ave., Kenmore.* Tel: 716-873-6500.
Censors—Board of Diocesan Censors of Books and Vigilance for the Faith—Rev. Msgr. SAMUEL J. FAIOLA, S.T.D.; Rev. Msgr. THOMAS E. CRANE, S.S.L.
Charismatic Renewal Program—Vacant, *795 Main St., Buffalo, 14203.* Tel: 716-847-8700.
Christian Life Communities (Sodalities)—Rev. JOHN D. GARVEY, S.J., Diocesan Dir., *2001 Main St., Buffalo, 14208.* Tel: 716-883-7000.
Central City Apostolate—Rev. RODERICK BROWN, O.P., Vicar, *795 Main St., Buffalo, 14203.* Tel: 716-847-8391.
Clergy Personnel Board—Rev. JEROME E. KOPEC, Coord. Tel: 716-847-5537. Rev. Msgr. WILLIAM G. STANTON; Rev. Msgr. RICHARD M. CAHILL; Rev. Msgr. FRANCIS G. WELDGEN; Revs. EUGENE P. ULRICH; CHARLES E. SLIZ; JAY W. MCGINNIS.
Commission on Women in Church and Society—ESTHER RAE, Chm., *215 Lamarck Dr., Snyder, 14226.* Tel: 716-839-0797.
Communication—Rev. Msgr. DAVID M. LEE, Dir. Tel: 716-847-8719.
Diocesan Directory—Mrs. ROMANA REGER.
Public Relations, Assistant Director of Communications—MICHELLE KACZMAREK.
Assistant Director of Communications for Radio—GREGG PRINCE.
Telecommunications—LYDIA S. SZYJKA.
Computer Services (Diocesan)—JAMES C. KAVANAGH, Dir. Tel: 716-847-5500.
Continuing Education for Clergy—Co-Directors: Rev. Msgr. JAMES E. WALL; Rev. RICHARD W. SIEPKA, *Christ the King Seminary, P.O. Box 607, East Aurora, 14052.* Tel: 716-652-8900.
Cursillo Movement—ROBERT HELLER, Lay Coord.
Deaf—Rev. CONRAD P. STACHOWIAK, Chap., *4125 Union Rd., Cheektowaga, 14225.* Tel: 716-634-3420.
Due Process—Rev. SALVATORE MANGANELLO, J.C.L., Chm., Catholic Center. Tel: 716-847-8769.
Ecumenism—(Ecumenical Liaison Committee); Revs. RICHARD E. ZAJAC; THOMAS D. DOYLE; A. MARK ILLIG; JACOB C. LEDWON; BRENDA EASLEY-WEBB; Sr. MARITA LANNEN, O.S.F.; Rev. FRANCIS X. MAZUR, Ecumenical Officer.
Education (Office of Catholic Education)—Tel: 716-847-5501; Fax: 716-847-5593. ROBERT R. BIMONTE, F.S.C., Supt. of Catholic Education; Sr. M. CHRISTELLE SAWICKI, C.S.S.F., Assoc. Dir. Schools; DENISE MCKENZIE, Diocesan Dir. Religious Education; MARY LOUISE SCHULZ, Assoc. Dir. Religious Education; VIRGINIA M. SCHULTZ, Coord. Religious Education for Persons with Disabilities & Adult Christian Formation; Sr. JULIE UHRICH, O.S.F., Reg. Dir. Religious Education (Allegany & Southern Cattaraugus Counties); DAVID J. SAMPSON, Coord. Devel. THOMAS E. PETERS, Dir. Govt. Programs; Sr. MARIE PARES, O.S.F., Dir. Athletics & Physical Education; BRUCE EVERT, Dir. School Finances; SUE HILL, Senior Accountant for Diocesan Education; Sr. M. CYNTHIA KILIAN, C.S.S.F., Reg. Dir. Religious Education (Chautauqua, Genesee and Northern Cattaraugus Counties); Sr. M. EVARISTA GOLEN, F.S.S.J., School Psychologist; SALLY DAVIS, Dir. Food Serv.
Evangelization Commission—Rev. DANIEL J. PALYS, Chm., *5271 Clinton St., Elma, 14059.* Tel: 716-668-4017.
Family Life—Rev. Msgr. FRED R. VOORHES, Dir. Tel: 716-847-2210.
Finance Office—JOHN R. O'BRIEN. Tel: 716-847-5500.
Guild for the Blind, Inc.—Rev. Msgr. HENRY J. GUGINO, Chap., Office: *525 Washington St., Buffalo.* Tel: 716-856-4494.
Health Care Apostolate—Rev. Msgr. HENRY J. GUGINO, Bishop's Rep., *525 Washington St., Buffalo, 14203.* Tel: 716-856-4494.
Holy Childhood (Pontifical) Association—Rev. Msgr. HAROLD WAGNER, Dir. Tel: 716-847-8773.
Holy Name Society—Rev. Msgr. FRANCIS B. JUCHNOWSKI, Moderator. Tel: 716-847-2202.
Hospital Chaplains—Rev. RICHARD H. AUGUSTYN, Dir. Hospital Ministry, *100 High St., Buffalo, 14203.* Tel: 716-859-5600.
Human Resources—PAUL C. EBERHARDT, Dir. Tel: 716-847-8376.
Legion of Mary—Rev. DAVID W. BIALKOWSKI, Moderator. Tel: 716-847-5545.
Liturgical Commission—Revs. DAVID G. LIPUMA, Dir. Office of Worship & Catechumenate. Tel: 716-847-5545. KAREN PODD, Pres. MARK DIGIAMPAOLO, Vice Pres.
Newman Club Chaplains—Rev. PAUL W. STELLER, *Vicar Campus Ministry and Newman Club Centers, 6325 Main St., Williamsville, 14221.* Tel: 716-632-8898.
Newspaper—*"The Western New York Catholic Visitor";* Rev. Msgr. DAVID M. LEE, Editor-in-Chief. Tel: 716-847-8719. Sr. M. FRANCIS GANGLOFF, O.S.F., Managing Editor. Tel: 716-849-8719.
Pamphlet Society (Catholic) of Buffalo, Inc.—Rev. Msgr. WALTER O. KERN, Dir., *120 Old Maryvale Dr., Cheektowaga, 14225.* Tel: 716-833-6617.
Pastoral Council—Rev. Msgr. WILLIAM J. MCDONNELL, Pres., *885 Sweet Home Rd., Buffalo, 14226.* Tel: 716-835-8905.
Peace and Justice (Diocesan Commission)—Rev. Msgr. JAMES G. KELLY.
Permanent Diaconate—Vacant. Tel: 716-847-5543.
Priests, Vicar for—Rev. Msgr. JAMES E. WALL.
Pro-Life Activities—JUDITH A. GORMAN, Coord. Tel: 716-847-2205.
Propagation of the Faith—Rev. Msgr. HAROLD WAGNER. Tel: 716-847-8711.
Purchasing (Diocesan)—Mr. PETER M. MCKEE. Tel: 716-847-8700.
Research and Planning—Sr. REGINA MURPHY, S.S.M.N. Tel: 716-847-5539.
St. Peter Claver Youth Program, Inc.—HOSIE ARNOLD, Exec. Dir., *185 Lang Ave., Buffalo, 14215.* Tel: 716-893-4651.
St. Vincent de Paul Society—Rev. Msgr. HENRY J. GUGINO, Spiritual Moderator, *1298 Main St., Buffalo, 14209.* Tel: 716-882-3360; Fax: 716-882-3556.
Spanish Speaking Apostolate—AMADOR LOPEZ, Dir.
Television-Daybreak TV Productions, Inc.—Rev. Msgr. DAVID M. LEE; CLAIRE RUNG. Tel: 716-847-8719.
Worship, Office of—Rev. DAVID G. LIPUMA, Dir.
Vicar for Religious—Sr. MARY DOLORES COOK, O.S.F.; Rev. JAMES J. RUDDICK, S.J., Assoc. Dir. Tel: 718-847-5529.
Vocations—Rev. ROBERT A. WOZNIAK, Dir. Tel: 716-847-5535.
Diocesan Youth Council—Rev. GARY J. BAGLEY, Dir. Tel: 716-847-8789.
Young Adult Ministry—PATRICIA BUBAR. Tel: 716-847-8788.
Dunkirk-Fredonia Youth Ministry—GAIL HASSETT, Dir., *145 E. Main St., Fredonia, 14063.* Tel: 716-679-7172.

CLERGY, PARISHES, MISSIONS AND PAROCHIAL SCHOOLS

CITY OF BUFFALO
(Erie County)

1—ST. JOSEPH'S CATHEDRAL (1851), Rev. Msgr. William J. Gallagher, Rector. In res., Rev. Msgr. William A. Schwinger; Rev. Jerome E. Kopec.
Res., 50 Franklin St., 14202. Tel: 716-854-5855; Fax: 716-854-5861.
School—Catholic Academy of West Buffalo Regional School. See separate listing under Regional and Consolidated Elementary Schools in the Institutions located in the Diocese.

2—ST. ADALBERT'S BASILICA (1886) (Polish), Rev. Thaddeus Nicholas Bocianowski.
Res., 212 Stanislaus St., 14212. Tel: 716-895-8091. [CEM]

3—ST. AGATHA (1921), Rev. James W. Fliss.
Res., 54 Alamo Pl., 14220. Tel: 716-822-2668.
School—Tel: 716-824-4510. Ms. Dolores Oakes, Prin.
Lay Teachers 13; Students 190.

4—ST. AGNES (1883), Rev. Guy F. Siracuse.
Res., 194 Ludington St., 14206. Tel: 716-893-0509.
School—Tel: 716-892-1441. Sr. Ann Helene Koenig, O.S.F., Prin.
Lay Teachers 14; Students 275.
Catechesis/Religious Programs—Sr. Monica Piyac, O.S.F., D.R.E.
Students 105.
Parish Catholic Charities—Tel: 716-893-6418. Sr. Rose Therese Di Gregorio, O.S.F., Outreach Coord.

5—ALL SAINTS (1911), Rev. Msgr. Albert W. Clody; Rev. Dennis J. Mancuso; Sr. Patrice Yarborough, S.S.M.N., Pastoral Assoc.
Res., 127 Chadduck Ave., 14207-1531. Tel: 716-875-8183; Fax: 716-875-6597.
School—Tel: 716-875-4174. Mrs. Cynthia Jacobs, Prin.

Sisters 2; Lay Teachers 20; Students 335.
Catechesis/Religious Programs—Nancy Schorb, D.R.E.
Students 150.

6—ST. AMBROSE (1930), Rev. Msgr. William G. Stanton; Rev. R.B. Michael Oliver.
Res., 65 Ridgewood Rd., 14220. Tel: 716-822-5962; Fax: 716-822-0966.
School—Tel: 716-824-6360. June F. Neuner, Prin.
Sisters 3; Lay Teachers 21; Students 436.
Catechesis/Religious Programs—Tel: 716-826-4125. Sr. Pauline Petruzzella, R.S.M., D.R.E.
Students 352.

7—ST. ANN (1858), Rev. William Frankhauser, S.J.; Sr. Marie Davis, O.S.F., Pastoral Assoc.; Bro. Eugene H. Aste, S.J.
Office: 491 Emslie St., 14212. Tel: 716-852-3316.
Res., 501 Emslie St., 14212. Tel: 716-854-3742; Fax: 716-854-4131.
School—Catholic Central Regional School. See separate listing under Regional and Consolidated Elementary Schools in the Institutions located in the Diocese.

8—ANNUNCIATION (1885), Rev. James G. Judge. In res., Rev. James M. Monaco, Weekend Asst.
Res., 18 Greenwood Pl., 14213. Tel: 716-885-2469.
Church—Lafayette Ave. & Grant St., 14213.
School—Catholic Academy of West Buffalo Regional School. See separate listing under Regional and Consolidated Elementary Schools in the Institutions located in the Diocese. Tel: 716-886-5384.
Catechesis/Religious Programs—Tel: 716-885-3714.
Students 146.
Convent—257 Lafayette Ave., 14213. Tel: 716-885-6252. Sisters of St. Mary of Namur

9—ST. ANTHONY OF PADUA (1891) (Italian), Rev. Secondo Casarotto, C.S.
Res., 160 Court St., 14202. Tel: 716-854-2563.
School—Catholic Academy of West Buffalo Regional School. See separate listing under Regional and Consolidated Elementary Schools in the Institutions located in the Diocese.

10—ASSUMPTION (1888) (Polish), Rev. Msgr. Daniel J. Myszka.
Res., 435 Amherst St., 14207. Tel: 716-875-7626.
School—Our Lady of Black Rock Consolidated, 16 Germain St., 14207. Tel: 716-873-7497.
Felician Sisters 3; Students 183.

11—ST. BARTHOLOMEW. Closed 1993. Merged with Blessed Trinity Church. Records at the Catholic Center, 795 Main St., Buffalo, 14203.

12—ST. BENEDICT THE MOOR. Closed. For inquiries for parish records contact the Chancery.

13—ST. BERNARD (1906), Rev. Msgr. Francis B. Juchnowski; Revs. Francis J. Chmielewski; Donald J. Lutz.
Res., 414 S. Ogden, 14206. Tel: 716-822-8856.
School—Tel: 716-822-8057.
Congregation of Sisters of St. Felix 4; Lay Teachers 16; Students 335.

14—BLESSED SACRAMENT (1887), Rev. Paul R. Bossi. In res., Revs. Franklin J. Tuchols; Salvatore Manganello.
Res., 330 Linwood Ave., 14209-1689. Tel: 716-884-0053; Fax: 716-884-2279.
School—Catholic Academy of West Buffalo Regional School. See separate listing under Regional and Consolidated Elementary Schools in the Institutions located in the Diocese. Tel: 716-885-6111.
Catechesis/Religious Programs—James J. Kennedy, D.R.E.
Students 80.

15—BLESSED TRINITY (1906), Rev. George L. Reger.
Res., 317 Leroy Ave., 14214. Tel: 716-833-0301; Fax: 716-834-4711.
School—Catholic Central Regional School. See separate listing under Regional and Consolidated Elementary Schools in the Institutions located in the Diocese.

16—ST. BONIFACE. Closed. For inquiries for parish records contact the Chancery.

17—ST. BRIGID. Merged with St. Columba. For inquiries for parish records contact SS. Columba & Brigid.

18—ST. CASIMIR (Polish), Rev. Msgr. Matthew S. Kopacz; Rev. James T. Bartnik. In res., Rev. Msgr. Eugene V. Marcinkiewicz.
Res., 160 Cable St., 14206. Tel: 716-824-9589.

19—SS. COLUMBA & BRIGID, Rev. Roderick M. Brown, O.P., Admin.
Res., 418 N. Division St., 14204. Tel: 716-852-3331.
School—Catholic Central Regional School. See separate listing under Regional and Consolidated Elementary Schools in the Institutions located in the Diocese.

20—CORONATION OF THE BLESSED VIRGIN MARY (1950), Rev. Msgr. Eugene M. Radon.
Res., 348 Dewitt St., 14213. Tel: 716-882-2650.
School—Our Lady of Black Rock School. See separate listing under Regional and Consolidated Elementary Schools in the Institutions located in the Diocese.
Catechesis/Religious Programs—Tel: 716-882-6360. Frank Antonucci, D.R.E.
Students 89.

21—CORPUS CHRISTI (Polish). (St. Anthony's Convent). Revs. Karl Kolodziejski, O.F.M.Conv.; Anthony M. Konieczny, O.F.M.Conv., Pastor Emeritus; Gregory Kwapisz, O.F.M.Conv.; Joseph Trawinski, O.F.M.Conv.; Bruno Pysz, O.F.M.Conv.; Roman Siola, O.F.M.Conv. In res., Revs. Benvenute Gorczyca, O.F.M.Conv.; Valentine Rajter, O.F.M.Conv.
Res., 199 Clark St., 14212. Tel: 716-896-1050.

22—ST. ELIZABETH OF HUNGARY (1906) (Hungarian), Rev. John Skrapits.
Res., 986 Grant St., 14207. Tel: 716-875-6586.
Convent—89 Military Rd., 14207. Tel: 716-876-2168.
Sisters of the Divine Redeemer 3.

23—ST. FLORIAN (1917), Rev. Msgr. Edward F. Synowiak; Rev. Jan Pasiewala, S.A.C.
Res., 567 Hertel Ave., 14207. Tel: 716-875-3246.
School—Our Lady of Black Rock Consolidated School. See separate listing under Regional and Consolidated Elementary Schools in the Institutions located in the Diocese.

24—ST. FRANCIS OF ASSISI, Rev. Msgr. Michael E. DelVecchio; Sr. Grace Cascia, S.S.J., Pastoral Assoc.
Res., 118 Schiller St., 14206. Tel: 716-895-6813.

25—ST. FRANCIS XAVIER (1849) (German). Attended by St. John the Baptist, Buffalo. Rev. George J. Stephan; Sr. Leandra Kosmoski, S.S.J., Pastoral Assoc.
Res., 157 East St., 14207. Tel: 716-873-1911. [CEM]
School—Our Lady of Black Rock Consolidated School. See separate listing under Regional and Consolidated Elementary Schools in the Institutions located in the Diocese. Tel: 716-873-7497.
Catechesis/Religious Programs—Students 38.

26—ST. GERARD (1902) (German), Rev. Joseph P. Badding, Admin.
Res., 1190 E. Delavan Ave., 14215. Tel: 716-895-5761; Fax: 716-895-6311.
Catechesis/Religious Programs—Tel: 716-895-3751. Debra Stafford, D.R.E.
Students 51.

27—HOLY ANGELS (1852), Revs. Anthony Rigoli, O.M.I.; Martin J. McMahon, O.M.I.; Louis Longen, O.M.I.; Sr. Mary Courts, G.N.S.H., Pastoral Assoc. In res., Revs. Brendan Hunt, O.M.I.; Eugene Tremblay, O.M.I.; Stephen Vasek, O.M.I.; George Kirwin, O.M.I.; Daniel F. O'Leary, O.M.I., Dean of Studies, Niagara Univ.; Bro. Richard Schultz, O.M.I.
Res., 348 Porter Ave., 14201. Tel: 716-885-3767.
School—Catholic Academy of West Buffalo Regional School. See separate listing under Regional and Consolidated Elementary Schools in the Institutions located in the Diocese.
Catechesis/Religious Programs—Sr. Mary Courts, G.N.S.H.
Students 140.

28—HOLY APOSTLES SS. PETER AND PAUL (1909) (Polish), Rev. Ronald A. Bagienski.
Res., 660 Smith St., 14210. Tel: 716-854-8971.
Catechesis/Religious Programs—Tel: 716-856-5790.
Students 180.

29—HOLY CROSS (1914), Revs. Dennis W. Mende; Ivan Torres; Deacons Reinaldo Santana; Carlos Ramos.
Res., 345 Seventh St., 14201. Tel: 716-847-6930; Fax: 716-847-6934.
School—Catholic Academy of West Buffalo Regional School. See separate listing under Regional and Consolidated Elementary Schools in the Institutions located in the Diocese. Tel: 716-885-6111; Fax: 716-885-6452.
Catechesis/Religious Programs—D.R.E.: Marangely Gonzalez; Ann Moquin.
Students 109.

30—HOLY FAMILY (1902) (Irish), Rev. William R. Bigelow.
Res., 1885 S. Park Ave., 14220. Tel: 716-822-0308.
School—Sisters of Mercy 3; Lay Teachers 15; Students 260.

31—HOLY NAME OF JESUS (1887), Rev. Robert J. Hora, Admin.
Res., 1947 Bailey Ave., 14211. Tel: 716-892-8056.

32—HOLY SPIRIT (1910), Rev. Msgr. Charles T. Griffin; Rev. Paul D. Seil.
Res., 91 Dakota Ave., 14216. Tel: 716-875-8102.
School—85 Dakota Ave., 14216. Tel: 716-875-9478. Miss Karen Adamski, Prin.
Lay Teachers 10; Students 149.

33—IMMACULATE CONCEPTION (1849), Rev. Antonio L. Rodriguez.
Res., 144 Edward St., 14201. Tel: 716-886-5627.
School—Catholic Academy of West Buffalo Regional School. See separate listing under Regional and Consolidated Elementary Schools in the Institutions located in the Diocese. Tel: 716-885-6111.
Catechesis/Religious Programs—Sr. Olivia Ortiz, D.R.E.
Students 106.

34—IMMACULATE HEART OF MARY (1946), Rev. Msgr. Raymond J. Kozlowski, Admin. In res., Rev. Richard H. Augustyn.
Res., 381 Edison St., 14215. Tel: 716-894-6953.

35—ST. JAMES (1916), Revs. Robert L. Gebhard, Admin.; Peter Nami, O.M.I.; Sr. Patricia Kerin, F.M.D.C., Pastoral Assoc.
Res., 10 Hastings Ave., 14215. Tel: 716-834-5601.
Convent—36 Davidson St., 14215. Tel: 716-836-7835.

36—ST. JOACHIM. Closed. For inquiries for parish records contact the Chancery.

37—ST. JOHN THE BAPTIST (1867). Attended by St. Francis Xavier, Buffalo. Rev. George J. Stephan.
Res., 60 Hertel Ave., 14207-2595. Tel: 716-875-4390.
Parish Center—410 East St., 14207. Tel: 716-873-8660.
School—Our Lady of Black Rock Consolidated. See separate listing under Regional and Consolidated Elementary Schools in the Institutions located in the Diocese.

38—ST. JOHN THE EVANGELIST (1906), Revs. Mark J. Wolski; Ronald P. Sajdak; Sr. Catherine McGady, G.N.S.H., Pastoral Assoc.
Res., 2315 Seneca St., 14210. Tel: 716-822-2315.

39—ST. JOHN KANTY (Polish), Rev. Anthony Lutostanski. In res., Rev. Msgr. Joseph P. Waclawski.
Res., 101 Swinburne St., 14212. Tel: 716-893-0412; Fax: 716-893-9864.

40—ST. JOSEPH (1850), Rev. Jacob C. Ledwon; Sr. Jeremy Midura, Pastoral Assoc.; Deacon Thaddeus V. Pijacki.
Res., 3269 Main St., 14214. Tel: 716-833-0298; Fax: 716-833-7339.
School—3275 Main St., 14214. Tel: 716-835-7395.
Sisters of St. Joseph 1; Lay Teachers 18; Students 264.

41—ST. LAWRENCE (1929), Rev. Richard A. Reina; Sr. Jolene Ellis, O.S.F., Pastoral Assoc.; Deacon Paul Weisenburger. In res., Rev. Norbert F. Orsolits.
Res., 1520 E. Delavan Ave., 14215. Tel: 716-892-2471; Fax: 716-892-2478.
School—Kolbe Catholic Regional School. See St. John Gualbert, Cheektowaga for details. Tel: 716-895-3127.
Catechesis/Religious Programs—Tel: 716-896-0047. Sr. Joanne Fogarty, O.S.F., D.R.E.
Students 120.

42—ST. LOUIS (1829), Rev. Msgr. Robert A. Mack.
Res., 35 Edward St., 14202. Tel: 716-852-6040.
School—Catholic Academy of West Buffalo Regional School. See separate listing under Regional and Consolidated Elementary Schools in the Institutions located in the Diocese.

43—ST. LUKE (Polish). Closed. For inquiries for parish records contact the Chancery.

44—ST. MARGARET (1916), Rev. Msgr. James G. Kelly; Rev. Joseph F. Moreno; Deacon Alex Molnar.
Res., 1395 Hertel Ave., 14216. Tel: 716-876-5318; Fax: 716-876-5519.
School—Tel: 716-876-8885; Fax: 716-875-9068.
Sisters of St. Joseph 1; Lay Teachers 15; Students 207.
Catechesis/Religious Programs—Tel: 716-876-6122.
Students 195.

45—ST. MARK (1908), Rev. Msgr. Francis Braun.
Res., 401 Woodward Ave., 14214. Tel: 716-836-1600.
School—Tel: 716-836-1191.
Sisters of St. Joseph 2; Lay Teachers 15; Students 300.
Convent—223 Summit Ave., 14214. Tel: 716-837-9055.

46—ST. MARTIN (1926), Revs. Vincent J. Becker; Samuel J. Venne. In res., Rev. Thomas N. Shepherd.
Res., 1140 Abbott Rd., 14220. Tel: 716-823-7077; Fax: 716-823-4197.
School—Tel: 716-824-0727; 824-0726. Sr. M. Roberta, R.S.M., Prin.
Lay Teachers 20; Students 386.
Catechesis/Religious Programs—D.R.E.: Christine Penner; Libbyanne Cowan.
Students 130.

47—ST. MARY OF SORROWS (1872), Sr. Mary Augusta Kaiser, S.S.J., Parish Life Coord.; Sr. Jean Marie Zirnheld, S.S.J., Pastoral Assoc.; Deacon Jimmie L. Boyd, Sr.
Church & Offices—333 Guilford St., 14211. Tel:

716-892-4115.
School—Catholic Central Regional School. See separate listing under Regional and Consolidated Elementary Schools in the Institutions located in the Diocese.
Convent—20 Rich St., 14211. Tel: 716-892-4116; Fax: 716-896-5332. Sisters of St. Joseph. Sisters of St. Francis of Penance & Christian Charity.

48—St. Matthew. Closed. For inquiries for parish records contact St. Martin de Porres.

49—St. Martin de Porres (1993) (African American), Rev. Roderick M. Brown, O.P.; Deacon Ronald Walker; Sr. Philip Marie.
Office: 80 Durham Ave., 14215. Tel: 716-892-0528.
Res., 26 Wyoming Ave., 14215. Tel: 716-893-6079.
School—Catholic Central Regional School. See Regional and Consolidated Elementary Schools under Institutions Located in the Diocese.

50—St. Michael (1851), Revs. Patrick T. Sullivan, S.J.; Robert J. Boyle, S.J.; Edward L. Guth, S.J.; Thomas D. McMahon, S.J.; John G. Sturm, S.J.; Joseph R. Spellerberg, S.J.; H. James Roleke, S.J. In res., Rev. Richard J. Zanoni, S.J.
Res., 651 Washington St., 14203. Tel: 716-854-6726; Fax: 716-854-4616.
School—Catholic Academy of West Buffalo Regional School. See separate listing under Regional and Consolidated Elementary Schools in the Institutions located in the Diocese. Tel: 716-885-6111; 886-5384.

51—St. Monica. Closed. For inquiries for parish records contact the Chancery.

52—The Nativity of the Blessed Virgin (1898), Rev. Angelo M. Chimera; Deacon Caesar Zymanek.
Res., 20 Herkimer St., 14213. Tel: 716-885-1344; Fax: 716-885-2385.
School—Catholic Academy of West Buffalo Regional School. See separate listing under Regional and Consolidated Elementary Schools in the Institutions located in the Diocese. Tel: 716-885-6111.
Catechesis/Religious Programs—Tel: 716-885-4017. Mr. Len Rizzo, D.R.E.
Students 92.

53—Our Lady of Loretto, Rev. Ronald A. Lord; Deacon Roberto Miranda.
Res., 172 15th St., 14213. Tel: 716-885-7573.
School—Catholic Academy of West Buffalo Regional School. See separate listing under Regional and Consolidated Elementary Schools in the Institutions located in the Diocese.
Catechesis/Religious Programs—Cathy Pritchard, D.R.E.
Students 75.

54—Our Lady of Lourdes. Closed. For inquiries for parish records contact the Chancery.

55—Our Lady of Perpetual Help, Rev. Dennis G. Riter.
Res., 115 O'Connell Ave., 14204. Tel: 716-852-2671.

56—Precious Blood (1899) (Polish), Rev. Msgr. Ronald P. Sciera.
Res., 140 Lewis St., 14206. Tel: 716-854-4623.

57—Queen of the Most Holy Rosary (Polish). Closed. For inquiries for parish records contact the Chancery.

58—Queen of Peace (1920) (Polish), Rev. Msgr. Chester S. Frysiak, Admin.
Res., 1955 Genesee St., 14211. Tel: 716-892-5646.

59—SS. Rita & Patrick (1854), Revs. Ronald Pecci, O.F.M.; Paul Osborne, O.F.M. Pastoral Assocs: Bro. Maurice V. Swartout, O.F.M.; Mary A. Masters. In res., Rev. Robert Struzynski, O.F.M.; Bros. Timothy S. Dauenhauser, O.F.M.; Michael Oberst, O.F.M.
Res., St. Patrick Friary, 102 Seymour St., 14210. Tel: 716-856-5790; Fax: 716-856-4019.

60—St. Rose of Lima (1926), Rev. Msgr. Francis V. Engler; Rev. Francis J. Zmozynski. In res., Rev. David G. LiPuma.
Res., 500 Parker Ave., 14216. Tel: 716-834-6688.
School—201 Winston Rd., 14216. Tel: 716-833-4100.
Grey Nuns of the Sacred Heart 2; Lay Teachers 15; Students 234.
Catechesis/Religious Programs—Tel: 716-833-4130. Sr. Caesaria Keslo, F.S.S.J., D.R.E.
Students 203.

61—St. Stanislaus (1873) (Polish), Rev. Msgr. John R. Gabalski, P.A.
Res., 123 Townsend St., 14212. Tel: 716-854-5511. [CEM]
School—Tel: 716-854-1803.
Felician Sisters 5; Lay Teachers 9; Students 117.

62—St. Stephen (1875). (Formerly Shrine of St. Jude). Rev. Robert A. Stolinski.
Res., 193 Elk St., 14210-1499.

63—St. Teresa (1897), Rev. Msgr. S. Theodore Berg. In res., Rev. Msgr. Richard C. Crumlish.
Res., 1974 Seneca St., 14210. Tel: 716-822-0608.
School—Tel: 716-822-4546.
Sisters 1; Lay Teachers 12; Students 340.
Catechesis/Religious Programs—Students 170.

64—St. Thomas Aquinas (1920), Revs. Arthur J. Smith; Raymond R. Russell. In res., Rev. Msgr. Eugene E. O'Loughlin.
Res., 450 Abbott Rd., 14220-1796. Tel: 716-822-1250; Fax: 716-824-2594.
School—20 Athol St., 14220-1796. Tel: 716-824-5046; Fax: 716-824-2539.
Sisters 1; Lay Teachers 23; Students 441.

65—Transfiguration (Polish). Closed. For inquiries for parish records contact the Chancery.

66—St. Valentine, Rev. Dennis G. Riter.
Res., 522 S. Park Ave., 14204. Tel: 716-854-7193.

67—St. Vincent de Paul. Closed. For inquiries for parish records contact the Chancery.

68—The Visitation of the B.V.M. (1898), Rev. Paul P. Sabo.
Res., 1040 Lovejoy St., 14206. Tel: 716-892-2289.

OUTSIDE THE CITY OF BUFFALO

Akron, Erie Co., St. Teresa of Avila (1859), Rev. Msgr. Robert J. Williamson.
Res., 5771 Buell St., 14001. Tel: 716-542-9103. [CEM]
Catechesis/Religious Programs—Tel: 716-542-9717. Sr. Mary Ruth Warejko, C.S.S.F., D.R.E.
Students 187.

Albion, Orleans Co., St. Mary Assumption (1891) (Polish), Rev. Richard A. Csizmar; Deacon James L. Collichio.
Res., 47 Brown St., 14411. Tel: 716-589-4243; 589-5162.
St. Joseph (1852), Rev. Richard A. Csizmar; Deacon James L. Collichio.
Res., 106 S. Main St., 14411. Tel: 716-589-4243.
Catechesis/Religious Programs—Tel: 716-589-4492. D.R.E.: Sally Rytlewski; Carla Nellist.
Students 350.

Alden, Erie Co., St. John the Baptist (1850), Revs. Fred D. Ingalls; Ivan Skenderovic; Deacon Richard J. Mahaney.
Res., 2021 Sandridge Rd., 14004. Tel: 716-937-6959. [CEM]
School—Tel: 716-937-9483; Fax: 716-937-9483. Mary Jane Liszewski, Prin.
Lay Teachers 15; Students 218.
Catechesis/Religious Programs—Tel: 716-937-3448. Mary Weisenburger, D.R.E.
Students 510.

Allegany, Cattaraugus Co., St. Bonaventure (1854), Revs. Bernardine Kessing, O.F.M.; Aquinas Reding, O.F.M.
Res., 95 E. Main St., 14706. Tel: 716-373-1330; Fax: 716-373-4220.
School—Southern Tier Catholic Regional School. See separate listing under Regional and Consolidated Elementary Schools in the Institutions located in the Diocese. Tel: 716-372-2891.
Catechesis/Religious Programs—Tel: 716-373-0430. Mrs. Margaret Duch, D.R.E.
Students 273.
Mission—Vandalia, Cattaraugus Co., St. John the Baptist.

Almond, Allegany Co., SS. Brendan and Jude (1992), Rev. Eugene P. Ulrich. Pastoral Assocs.: Susan Fowler; Robert Donius.
Res., 14804. Tel: 607-276-5304; Fax: 607-587-9411.
Church—11 S. Main St., Box G, 14804.

Amherst, Erie Co., St. Leo (1953), Rev. Msgr. William J. McDonnell; Revs. Karl E. Loeb; Robert A. Wozniak.
Res., 885 Sweet Home Rd., Buffalo, 14226. Tel: 716-835-8905; Fax: 716-835-8997.
School—Tel: 716-832-6340. Mr. George J. Drescher, Prin.
Sisters of Third Order of St. Francis 1; Lay Teachers 10; Students 185; Preschool Students 76.
Catechesis/Religious Programs—Tel: 716-833-8359. Sr. Judith Beiswanger, O.S.F., D.R.E.
Students 374.

Andover, Allegany Co., Blessed Sacrament (1855), Rev. Fred G. Fingerle.
Res., One Church St., Box 761, 14806-0761. Tel: 607-478-8885. [CEM]

Angelica, Allegany Co., Sacred Heart (1848), Rev. John E. Kelly.
Res., 5 Milton St., Belmont, 14813-1119. Tel: 716-268-7272; Fax: 716-268-7272.
Church—Park Cir., 14709.

Angola, Erie Co., Most Precious Blood, Rev. Msgr. J. Grant Higgins. In res., Rev. Msgr. Gerald J. Kreuzer.
Res., 22 Prospect St., 14006. Tel: 716-549-0420. [CEM]
School—17 Prospect St., 14006. Tel: 716-549-1818.
Franciscan Sisters of St. Joseph 3; Lay Teachers 7; Students 200.

Arcade, Wyoming Co., SS. Peter and Paul, Rev. Msgr. Patrick J. Woods, Temp. Admin.; Rev. Michael G. Uebler.
Res., 417 Main St., 14009-1195. Tel: 716-492-5330. [CEM]

Athol Springs, Erie Co., St. Francis of Assisi (1929), Revs. David M. Stopyra, O.F.M.Conv.; Michael Englert, O.F.M.Conv.
Res., 14010. Tel: 716-627-2710; Fax: 716-627-5263.
School—Tel: 716-627-2841. Sr. Mary Anne Siwak, F.S.S.J., Prin.
Franciscan Sisters of St. Joseph 1; Lay Teachers 6; Students 71.
Catechesis/Religious Programs—Tel: 716-627-3357. Annette Breen, D.R.E.
Students 450.

Attica, Wyoming Co., St. Vincent de Paul (1857), Rev. Stanley R. Chwalinski.
Res., 50 East Ave., 14011. Tel: 716-591-1228; Fax: 716-591-1614. [CEM]
School—Genesee-Wyoming Catholic Central Consolidated School. See separate listing under Regional and Consolidated Elementary Schools in the Institutions located in the Diocese. Tel: 716-591-2515; Fax: 716-741-9762.
Catechesis/Religious Programs—Students 236.

Barker, Niagara Co., St. Patrick (1856), Rev. James F. Hassett.
Res., 14012. Tel: 716-795-3331; Fax: 716-795-3919.
Catechesis/Religious Programs—Students 207.

Batavia, Genesee Co.,

1—St. Anthony, (1908) (Italian), Rev. Msgr. Paschal L. Acquavia.
Res., 122 Liberty St., 14020. Tel: 716-343-0914.
School—Tel: 716-343-5561.
Sisters of Mercy 2; Lay Teachers 13; Students 147.
Catechesis/Religious Programs—Students 245.

2—St. Joseph, (1849), Rev. Msgr. Leo F. McCarthy; Deacon John Stone. In res., Rev. Robert A. Martin.
Res., 303 E. Main St., 14020. Tel: 716-343-5800; Fax: 716-345-9525. [CEM]
School—Tel: 716-343-6154. Samuel Zalacca, Prin.
Lay Teachers 15; Students 269; Preschool Students 50.
Catechesis/Religious Programs—Samuel Zalacca, D.R.E.
Students 283.
Mission—South Byron, Genesee Co., St. Michael, (1892). Rev. Msgr. Leo F. McCarthy.

3—St. Mary, (1906), Revs. Donald W. Becker; Ivan R. Trujillo.
Res., 18 Ellicott St., 14020. Tel: 716-343-5400; Fax: 716-344-0213.
School—Tel: 716-343-6866.
Felician Sisters 1; Lay Teachers 8; Students 153.
Catechesis/Religious Programs—St. Mary's School, 40 Woodrow Rd., 14020. Tel: 716-343-6866.
Students 160.
Mission—Batavia, Genesee Co., St. Pius X, 18 1/2 Ellicott St., 14020. Tel: 716-343-2134.

4—Sacred Heart, (1904) (Polish), Rev. Eugene S. Slomba.
Res., 15 Sumner St., 14020. Tel: 716-343-1796; Fax: 716-344-3752.

Belfast, Allegany Co., St. Patrick (1859), Rev. Francis J. Jann.
Res., 31 E. Hughes St., 14711. Tel: 716-365-2115. [CEM]

Belmont, Allegany Co., St. Mary (1861), Rev. John E. Kelly.
Res., 5 Milton St., 14813. Tel: 716-268-7272.
Mission—Scio, Allegany Co., St. Joseph. [CEM]

Bemus Point, Chautauqua Co., Our Lady of Lourdes (1948), Rev. Ralph P. Federico.
Res., 42 Main St., P.O. Box 500, 14712. Tel: 716-386-2400; Fax: 716-386-2400.

Bennington Center, Wyoming Co., Sacred Heart of Jesus (1872) (Polish), Rev. Joseph A. Fiore.
Res., 1230 Clinton St., Attica, 14011. Tel: 716-591-0176. [CEM]
School—Genesee-Wyoming Catholic Central Consolidated School. See separate listing under Regional and Consolidated Elementary Schools in the Institutions located in the Diocese. Tel: 716-591-2515.
Catechesis/Religious Programs—Tel: 716-591-0205. Ms. Tammy Acquard, D.R.E.
Students 106.

Bergen, Genesee Co., St. Brigid (1861), Rev. Richard J. Keppeler.
Res., P.O. Box 219, 14416. Tel: 716-494-1110. [CEM]
Catechesis/Religious Programs—Students 160.

Blasdell, Erie Co., Our Mother of Good Counsel (1905), Revs. Lawrence E. Burns; Edward R. Czarnecki.
Res., 3688 S. Park Ave., 14219. Tel: 716-822-2630.
School—15 Oakwood Ave., 14219. Tel: 716-823-6286. Sr. Ellen McCarthy, S.S.J., Prin.
Sisters of St. Joseph 3; Lay Teachers 13; Students 200.

Catechesis/Religious Programs—Cheryl McNerney.
Students 350.

Bliss, Wyoming Co., St. Joseph, Rev. Edward E. Muerder.
Res., St. Nicholas Rectory, Rte. 98, North Java, 14113. Tel: 716-535-7457.
Church—P.O. Box 80, 14024. Tel: 716-322-8866.

Blossom, Erie Co., St. Gabriel (1925), Revs. Daniel J. Palys; Perry A. Ciambella; Arthur Mattulke; Ann Bauman, Pastoral Assoc.
Res., 5271 Clinton St., P.O. Elma, 14059-7617. Tel: 716-668-4017; Fax: 716-656-0616.
Catechesis/Religious Programs—Tel: 716-668-2070. Rose Andrews, D.R.E.
Students 1,029.

Bolivar, Allegany Co., St. Mary, Rev. Richard M. Poblocki.
Res., Sacred Heart, 43 Maple Ave., Portville, 14770. Tel: 716-933-6394. [CEM]
Church—111 Wellsville St., 14715. Tel: 716-928-1024.

Boston, Erie Co., St. John the Baptist (1869), Rev. Msgr. Paul F. Stengel.
Res., 14025. Tel: 716-941-3549. [CEM]
Catechesis/Religious Programs—Tel: 716-941-6363.
Students 246.

Bowmansville, Erie Co., Sacred Heart (1920), Rev. Msgr. Walter O. Kern; Rev. Msgr. Arnold J. Schneider.
Res., 5337 Genesee St., 14026-1098. Tel: 716-683-2375. [CEM]
School—SS. Peter & Paul Consolidated School. See separate listing under Regional and Consolidated Elementary Schools in the Institutions located in the Diocese. Tel: 716-683-8049.

Brant, Erie Co., Our Lady of Mt. Carmel (1906), Rev. James E. Fitzgerald.
Res., 10708 Brant-Angola Rd., P.O. Box 225, 14027-0225. Tel: 716-549-2418. [CEM]

Brocton, Chautauqua Co., St. Patrick (1922), Rev. Robert G. Beiter.
Res., 12 Central Ave., P.O. Box P, 14716-0675. Tel: 716-792-4125.
School—Northern Chautauqua Catholic Regional School. See separate listing under Regional and Consolidated Elementary Schools in the Institutions located in the Diocese.
Catechesis/Religious Programs—Diana Giambra, D.R.E.
Students 120.

Canaseraga, Allegany Co., St. Mary (1855), Rev. Robert M. Mock.
Res., 7 North St., Box 234, 14822. Tel: 607-545-8943. [CEM]

Cassadaga, Chautauqua Co., Immaculate Conception, Rev. Patrick H. Elis.
Res., 14718. Tel: 716-595-3141.

Cattaraugus, Cattaraugus Co., St. Mary's (1863), Rev. Wallace T. Borucki.
Res., 36 Washington St., 14719. Tel: 716-257-9351.
Convent—65 South St., 14719. Tel: 716-257-9781. Missionary Sisters of the Divine Child.

Cheektowaga, Erie Co.,

1—St. Aloysius Gonzaga, (1940), Rev. Richard S. DiGiulio; Deacons Donald Shultz; Melvin Carroll.
Res., 157 Cleveland Dr., Buffalo, 14215. Tel: 716-833-1715.
School—Tel: 716-836-4549. Sr. Paul Marie Baczkowski, C.S.S.F., Prin.
Sisters of St. Felix of Cantalice 5; Lay Teachers 27; Students 311.

2—Infant of Prague, (1946), Rev. Msgr. Angelo M. Caligiuri; Rev. Richard A. Massar; Deacon Alan A. Meister. In res., Rev. Patrick Zengierski.
Res., 921 Cleveland Dr., 14225. Tel: 716-634-3660; Fax: 716-634-3661.
School—Tel: 716-632-5482; 632-5539.
Sisters 1; Lay Teachers 21; Students 348.
Catechesis/Religious Programs—Sr. M. Antonita Sikorski, C.S.S.F., D.R.E.
Students 348.

3—St. John Gualbert, (1917) (Polish), Revs. Daniel A. Pokornowski; David W. Bialkowski. In res., Rev. Eugene S. Slomba; Deacon Franklyn C. Steffen.
Res., 83 Gualbert Ave., 14211. Tel: 716-892-5746.
School—Kolbe Catholic, Tel: 716-895-3127. Sr. Loriette Tokasz, Prin.
Felician Sisters 1; Lay Teachers 16; Students 236.
Catechesis/Religious Programs—Tel: 716-897-2619. Mrs. Karen Pszczolkowski, D.R.E.
Students 125.

4—St. Josaphat, (1906) (Polish), Rev. Charles E. Slisz; Sr. Joseph Marie Marczak, C.S.S.F., Pastoral Assoc. In res., Revs. Bernard T. Sokolowski; Robert A. Wozniak.
Res., 20 Peoria Ave., 14206. Tel: 716-893-1086; Fax: 716-893-1099.
School—Tel: 716-893-6448. Sr. Mary Thomas Frys, C.S.S.F., Prin.
Felician Sisters 2; Lay Teachers 14; Students 208.
Catechesis/Religious Programs—Tel: 716-896-5007. Maryanne Mann, D.R.E.
Students 218.

5—Most Holy Redeemer, Rev. F. Norman Sullivan. In res., Rev. Francis D. Sullivan, O.F.M.
Res., 25 Avery Pl., 14225. Tel: 716-895-7589.
School—Kolbe Catholic. See St. John Gualbert, Cheektowaga.
Catechesis/Religious Programs—Mr. Dennis Hughes, D.R.E.
Students 55.

6—Mother of Divine Grace, (1946), Rev. Msgr. S. Paul Ayoub.
Res., 120 Old Maryvale Dr., 14225. Tel: 716-834-8488; Fax: 716-834-8489.
Catechesis/Religious Programs—Tel: 716-834-8533.
Students 160.

7—Our Lady Help of Christians, (1890). National Historic Society. Rev. Msgr. Paul R. Letourneau; Revs. Martin L. Pavlock; Conrad P. Stachowiak.
Res., 4125 Union Rd., 14225. Tel: 716-634-3420; 634-3428. [CEM]
School—Tel: 716-632-4199.
Lay Teachers 15; Students 123; Preschool 78.
Catechesis/Religious Programs—Tel: 716-632-3532. Nancy Roscoe, D.R.E.
Students 372.

8—Our Lady of Czestochowa, (1922) (Polish American), Rev. Harry F. Szczesniak. In res., Rev. James H. Kasprzyk.
Res., 23 Willowlawn Pkwy., Buffalo, 14206. Tel: 716-822-5590.
School—Tel: 716-824-2225.
Lay Teachers 13; Students 129.

9—St. Philip the Apostle, (1967), Revs. Joseph H. Penkaus; James B. Cunningham; Deacon Dennis W. Kapsiak. In res., Rev. Msgr. Anthony J. Jasinski, Pastor Emeritus.
Res., 950 Losson Rd., 14227. Tel: 716-668-8370; Fax: 716-668-3824.
Catechesis/Religious Programs—Tel: 716-668-3344. Madeline Fuller, D.R.E.
Students 972.

10—Queen of Martyrs, (1946), Rev. Msgr. Max M. Kozminski; Rev. Walter Grabowski. In res., Rev. John J. Sardina.
Res., 180 George Urban Blvd., Buffalo, 14225-3095. Tel: 716-892-1746.
School—Tel: 716-895-6280. Sr. M. Marcia, C.S.S.F., Prin.
Felician Sisters 3; Lay Teachers 10; Students 140.
Catechesis/Religious Programs—Tel: 716-895-2162. Kathy Seibold, D.R.E.
Students 252.

11—Resurrection, (1944), Rev. Walter L. Matuszak; Rev. Msgr. George E. Maj, S.A.C.
Res., 130 Como Park Blvd., 14227. Tel: 716-683-3712; Fax: 716-683-3712.
School—Tel: 716-683-8785; Fax: 716-683-8785. Sr. M. Christinnete Lojewski, Prin.
Sisters 1; Lay Teachers 10; Students 112.
Catechesis/Religious Programs—Tel: 716-683-3422.
Students 205.

Cherry Creek, Chautauqua Co., St. Elizabeth. Closed. For inquiries for parish records contact the Chancery.

Clarence, Erie Co., Our Lady of Peace (1922), Rev. Msgr. Richard L. Wetter. In res., Rev. Abraham Pulikoottil.
Res., 10950 Main St., 14031. Tel: 716-759-8554; Fax: 716-759-8537.

Clarence Center, Erie Co., St. Augustine (1949), Rev. Edward H. Schroeder; Deacon Norman Foster.
Res., 8700 Goodrich Rd., 14032. Tel: 716-741-2258.
Catechesis/Religious Programs—Rosey Frost, D.R.E.
Students 262.

Colden, Erie Co., Our Lady of the Sacred Heart (1912), Rev. Richard C. Coveny.
Res., 8428 Heath Rd., 14033. Tel: 716-941-5817.

Collins Center, Erie Co., St. Frances Cabrini (1955), Rev. Lawrence P. Damian.
Res., 13940 Sisson Hwy., P.O. 332, 14035. Tel: 716-532-9431.

Corfu, Genesee Co., St. Francis of Assisi, Rev. Robert E. Waters.
Res., 14036. Tel: 716-599-4933.
Mission—Crittenden, St. Patrick.

Cuba, Allegany Co., Our Lady of Angels (1850), Rev. Jerome M. Dissek.
Res., 50 South St., 14727. Tel: 716-968-2885; Fax: 716-968-0123. [CEM]
School—Southern Tier Catholic Regional School. See separate listing under Regional and Consolidated Elementary Schools in the Institutions located in the Diocese.
Catechesis/Religious Programs—Students 192.

Darien Center, Genesee Co., Our Lady of Good Counsel, Rev. Joseph A. Fiore. In res., Rev. Roy T. Herberger.
Res., 14040. Tel: 716-547-3547. [CEM]
School—Genesee-Wyoming Catholic Central Consolidated School. See separate listing under Regional and Consolidated Elementary Schools in the Institutions located in the Diocese. Attica.

Dayton, Cattaraugus Co., St. Paul of the Cross. Closed. For inquiries for parish records contact St. John Fisher, South Dayton.

Delevan, Cattaraugus Co., Blessed Sacrament (1947), Rev. Raymond F. Uschold.
Res., 10 N. Main St., P.O. Box 188, 14042. Tel: 716-492-2383.
Catechesis/Religious Programs—Kathleen Morris, D.R.E.
Students 131.

Depew, Erie Co.,

1—St. Augustine, (1909) (Polish), Rev. Msgr. Henry J. Stachewicz.
Res., 425 Penora St., 14043. Tel: 716-683-3038. [CEM]

2—St. Barnabas, (1960), Rev. Msgr. John W. Madsen; Rev. Joseph E. Vatter. In res., Revs. Donald L. Measer; Robert J. Schober; Deacon Thaddeus P. May.
Res., 2049 George Urban Blvd., 14043. Tel: 716-685-2350; Fax: 716-685-8679.
School—Tel: 716-684-1444. Sr. M. Rosa Mystica, O.S.F., Prin.
Sisters 1; Lay Teachers 15; Students 193.
Catechesis/Religious Programs—2099 George Urban Blvd., 14043. Tel: 716-685-2000. Sharon Lowery, D.R.E.
Students 400.

3—St. James, (1897), Rev. David J. Borowiak. In res., Rev. Henry M. Borowiak.
Res., 496 Terrace Blvd., 14043. Tel: 716-683-2746; Fax: 716-683-3121.
School—500 Terrace Blvd., 14043. Tel: 716-683-0050. Sr. Mary Georgette, Prin.
Sisters 2; Lay Teachers 17; Students 154.
Catechesis/Religious Programs—Kermy Herazko, D.R.E.
Students 240.
Convent—55 Westfield Ave., 14043. Tel: 716-683-6653. Felician Nuns

4—SS. Peter and Paul, (1896) (Polish), Rev. Stanley F. Nowak.
Res., 86 Burlington Ave., 14043. Tel: 716-683-1645.
School—SS. Peter & Paul Consolidated School. See separate listing under Regional and Consolidated Elementary Schools in the Institutions located in the Diocese. Tel: 716-683-8049.
Catechesis/Religious Programs—Barbara Schmitt, D.R.E.
Students 170.

5—Our Lady of the Blessed Sacrament, (1965), Rev. Louis S. Dolinic. In res., Rev. Msgr. Dino J. Lorenzetti.
Res., 10 French Rd., 14043. Tel: 716-684-6342; Fax: 716-684-1853.
School—20 French Rd., 14043. Tel: 716-685-2544; Fax: 716-685-9103.
Felician Sisters 1; Lay Teachers 12; Students 256.
Catechesis/Religious Programs—Tel: 716-684-2546.
Students 647.

Dunkirk, Chautauqua Co.,

1—St. Hedwig, (Polish), Rev. Joseph J. Janaczek.
Res., 324 Townsend St., 14048. Tel: 716-366-1615. [CEM]
School—Northern Chautauqua Catholic Regional School. See separate listing under Regional and Consolidated Elementary Schools in the Institutions located in the Diocese.

2—Holy Trinity, (1908), Rev. Sebastian C. Pierro.
Res., 1032 Central Ave., 14048. Tel: 716-366-2306; Fax: 716-366-2309. [CEM]
School—Northern Chautauqua Catholic Regional School. See separate listing under Regional and Consolidated Elementary Schools in the Institutions located in the Diocese. Tel: 716-366-0630.
Catechesis/Religious Programs—Tel: 716-366-0499. Ruth Wilson, D.R.E.
Students 230.

3—St. Hyacinth, (1875) (Polish American), Rev. Richard A. Jedrzejewski; Deacon Daniel Mackowiak.
Res., 295 Lakeshore Dr., E., 14048. Tel: 716-366-7266; Fax: 716-363-0031. [CEM]
School—Tel: 716-366-1950.
Felician Sisters 4; Lay Teachers 7; Students 138.

4—St. Elizabeth Ann Seton, (1975), Rev. Thomas J.

Wopperer; Deacons Thomas Nadeau; Moises N. Cruz.
Res., 328 Washington Ave., 14048. Tel: 716-366-1750; Fax: 716-366-4398. [CEM]
School—Northern Chautauqua Catholic Regional School. See separate listing under Regional and Consolidated Elementary Schools in the Institutions located in the Diocese. Tel: 716-366-0630.
Catechesis/Religious Programs—Tel: 716-366-2827. Samuel Mancuso, D.R.E.
Students 350.

East Arcade, Wyoming Co., St. Mary's (1846), Rev. Michael G. Uebler.
Rectory: 6785 E. Arcade Rd., Arcade, 14009. Tel: 716-492-2282.
Res., 417 Main St., Arcade, 14009. Tel: 716-492-5330.

East Aurora, Erie Co., Immaculate Conception (1901), Rev. Msgr. Kevin T. O'Neill; Rev. Joseph D. Wolf.
Res., 520 Oakwood Ave., 14052. Tel: 716-652-6400; Fax: 716-652-7168. [CEM]
School—510 Oakwood Ave., 14052. Tel: 716-652-5855. Susan K. Gregg, Prin.
Lay Teachers 16; Students 220.
Catechesis/Religious Programs—Tel: 716-655-0067. Rosemary A. Sacilowski, D.R.E.
Students 642.

East Bethany, Genesee Co., Immaculate Conception, Rev. Thomas L. Kemp.
Res., 5865 Ellicott St., 14054. Tel: 716-343-4537.
Catechesis/Religious Programs—Students 125.

East Eden, Erie Co., St. Mary (1835) (German-Polish), Rev. James A. Grimmer.
Res., 8175 E. Eden Rd., 14057. Tel: 716-992-4237. [CEM]
Catechesis/Religious Programs—Tel: 716-992-3123. Dorothy Zydel, D.R.E.
Students 173.

East Otto, Cattaraugus Co., St. Isidore (1957), Rev. Wallace T. Borucki.
Res., 36 Washington St., Cattaraugus, 14719.
Church—E. Otto Rd., 14729. Tel: 716-257-3377.

East Pembroke, Genesee Co., Holy Name of Mary, Rev. David J. Scheider, Admin.
Res., P.O. Box 219, 14056. Tel: 716-762-9006.

Eden, Erie Co., Immaculate Conception (1908), Rev. David J. Peter; Deacon Richard H. Kelsey; Sr. Phyllis Fuest, O.S.F., Pastoral Assoc.
Res., 8791 S. Main St., 14057. Tel: 716-992-3933.
School—8783 S. Main St., 14057. Tel: 716-992-3508. Elaine Poleto, Prin.
Lay Teachers 16; Students 130.
Catechesis/Religious Programs—Sharon Reed, D.R.E.
Students 344.

St. Mary of Immaculate Conception (1858), Rev. Lawrence P. Damian.
Res., (New Oregon) 5107 Langford Rd., 14057. Tel: 716-337-2291. [CEM]

Eggertsville, Erie Co., St. Benedict (1920), Rev. Msgr. John M. Ryan; Rev. A. Mark Illig.
Res., 1317 Eggert Rd., 14226. Tel: 716-834-1041; Fax: 716-835-5949.
School—Tel: 716-835-2518. Sr. Aline Henderson, Prin.
Sisters of St. Francis of Penance and Christian Charity 4; Lay Teachers 21; Students 373.
Catechesis/Religious Programs—Tel: 716-836-6444. Sr. Virginia Judge, O.S.P., D.R.E.
Students 402.

Elba, Genesee Co., Our Lady of Fatima, Rev. William G. Ward.
Res., P.O. Box 185, 14058-0185. Tel: 716-757-6891.

Ellicottville, Cattaraugus Co., Holy Name of Mary (1850), Rev. Ronald B. Mierzwa.
Res., P.O. Box 543, 14731. Tel: 716-699-2592. [CEM]

Elma, Erie Co., Annunciation of the Blessed Virgin Mary (1906), Revs. Emil P. Swiatek; Robert W. Wood; Deacon Joseph Mercurio.
Res., 7580 Clinton St., 14059. Tel: 716-683-5254; Fax: 716-685-2401. [CEM]
School—Tel: 716-681-1327.
Sisters 2; Lay Teachers 19; Students 198; Preschool Students 59.
Catechesis/Religious Programs—Tel: 716-683-5515.
Students 675.

Falconer, Chautauqua Co., Our Lady of Loreto (1912) (Italian), Rev. Carlton J. Westfield.
Res., 309 W. Everett St., 14733. Tel: 716-665-4253.
Catechesis/Religious Programs—Tel: 716-665-3764. Beverly Smeragliuolo, D.R.E.
Students 130.

Farnham, Erie Co., St. Anthony's (1904), Rev. James E. Staebell.
Res., 417 Commercial St., 14061. Tel: 716-549-1159; Fax: 716-549-7722. [CEM]
Catechesis/Religious Programs—Kathleen Brachmann, D.R.E.
Students 227.

Fillmore, Alleghany Co., St. Patrick (1881), Rev. Francis P. Kowalewski.
Res., 14735. Tel: 716-567-2282. [CEM]

Forestville, Chautauqua Co., St. Rose of Lima (1850), Rev. Gerald P. Sheehan.
Res., 2773 Main Rd., Sheridan, 14135. Tel: 716-679-4951.

Franklinville, Cattaraugus Co., St. Philomena (1906), Rev. Michael D. O'Hara.
Res., 26 N. Plymouth Ave., 14737. Tel: 716-676-3629.
Catechesis/Religious Programs—Tel: 716-676-2123. Kathy Berry, D.R.E.
Students 68.

Fredonia, Chautauqua Co., St. Anthony (1905) (Italian), Rev. Daniel P. Walsh; Deacon Moises Cruz.
Res., 42 Orchard St., 14063. Tel: 716-679-4050; 674-4046 (Office).
School—Northern Chautauqua Catholic Regional School. See separate listing under Regional and Consolidated Elementary Schools in the Institutions located in the Diocese. Tel: 716-366-0630.
Catechesis/Religious Programs—Tel: 716-674-1268. Mrs. Barbara O'Connell, D.R.E.
Students 300.

St. Joseph (1899), Rev. James C. O'Connor; Deacon Matthew A. Podniesinski.
Res., 145 E. Main St., 14063. Tel: 716-679-4116; Fax: 716-679-1352 (1-5 P.M.).
School—Northern Chautauqua Catholic Regional School. See separate listing under Regional and Consolidated Elementary Schools in the Institutions located in the Diocese. Tel: 716-366-0630.
Catechesis/Religious Programs—Tel: 716-672-2647.
Students 200.

French Creek, Chautauqua Co., St. Matthias, Rev. Bernard C. Staszak.
Res., 1762 French Creek Mina Rd., 14724-0660. Tel: 716-355-8891. [CEM]
Mission—Panama, Our Lady of the Snows.

Frewsburg, Chautauqua Co., Our Lady of Victory (1950), Rev. Carlton J. Westfield.
Res., 14738. Tel: 716-569-4725.
Catechesis/Religious Programs—Ellen Weber, D.R.E.
Students 73.

Friendship, Allegany Co., Sacred Heart (1912), Rev. Jerome M. Dissek.
Res., 81 W. Main St., 14739. Tel: 716-973-2871. [CEM]

Gasport, Niagara Co., St. Mary (1968), Rev. Msgr. James E. Streng; Deacon Victor P. Crimi.
Res., 8110 West Ave., 14067. Tel: 716-772-7803.
Catechesis/Religious Programs—Joan Kaczmarczyk, D.R.E.
Students 142.

Getzville, Erie Co., St. Pius X (1958), Rev. Msgr. George B. Yiengst. In res., Rev. John J. Fox.
Res., 1700 N. French Rd., P.O. Box 162, 14068-0162. Tel: 716-688-9143; Fax: 716-688-5417.
Catechesis/Religious Programs—Tel: 716-688-5417.
Students 669.

Gowanda, Erie Co., St. Joseph (1900), Rev. Lawrence M. Milby; Deacon Louis A. Pais.
Res., 26 Erie Ave., 14070. Tel: 716-532-5100; 337-0120. [CEM]
School—Tel: 716-532-2520. Sr. Frances Clare Perry, O.S.F., Prin.
Sisters of St. Francis of Penance and Christian Charity 1; Lay Teachers 8; Students 101.

Grand Island, Erie Co., St. Stephen (1862), Rev. Msgr. Richard M. Cahill; Revs. Dennis A. Fronczak; Francis X. Mazur; Deacon John A. Polizzi.
Res., 2100 Baseline Rd., 14072. Tel: 716-773-7647; Fax: 716-773-5792. [CEM]
School—2080 Baseline Rd., 14072. Tel: 716-773-4347. Sr. Christina Marie Luczynski, C.S.S.F., Prin.
Felician Sisters 2; Lay Teachers 19; Students 274.
Catechesis/Religious Programs—Tel: 716-773-2002. D.R.E.: Angela Diebold; Donna Wilson.
Students 804.

Hamburg, Erie Co., SS. Peter and Paul (1844), Rev. Msgr. Gerard L. Green; Rev. Msgr. Stanley A. Ropelski; Rev. Walter J. Szczesny; Deacon Lawrence D. Eschbach.
Res., 66 E. Main St., 14075. Tel: 716-649-2765; Fax: 716-649-5218. [CEM]
School—68 E. Main St., 14075. Tel: 716-649-7030. Judith MacDonald, Prin.
Lay Teachers 23; Students 286.
Catechesis/Religious Programs—Tel: 716-649-0231. D.R.E.: Mary Ann Senchyne; Sr. Eileen Steen, R.S.M.; Margery Helinski.
Students 1,085.

St. Mary of the Lake (1948), Rev. Msgr. W. Jerome Sullivan.
Res., S-4737 Lake Shore Rd., 14075. Tel: 716-627-3123; Fax: 716-627-7062.
School—Tel: 716-627-7700. Mr. Daniel Mackowiak, Prin.
Franciscan Sisters of St. Joseph 3; Lay Teachers 14; Students 208.
Catechesis/Religious Programs—Tel: 716-627-7150. Ms. Mary Margaret Joyce, D.R.E.
Students 389.

Harris Hill, Erie Co., Nativity of the Blessed Virgin Mary (1954), Rev. Msgr. Raymond F. Paa; Rev. Daniel A. Young; Deacon Frank R. Krahling; Rev. Msgr. Daniel J. Fawls.
Res., 4375 Harris Hill Rd., Wiliamsville, 14221. Tel: 716-632-8838; Fax: 716-632-7898.
School—Tel: 716-633-7441. Mrs. Cherie M. Ansuini, Prin.
Lay Teachers 15; Students 190.
Catechesis/Religious Programs—Tel: 716-634-3130. Mrs. Mary Ann Hoag, D.R.E.
Students 830.

Hinsdale, Cattaraugus Co., St. Helen (1947), Rev. Barry J. Allaire, Admin.
Res., 10 N. Main St., 14743. Tel: 716-557-8841.
School—Southern Tier Catholic Regional School. See separate listing under Regional and Consolidated Elementary Schools in the Institutions located in the Diocese.

Holland, Erie Co., St. Joseph (1890), Rev. Msgr. Mecislaus S. Wendzikowski.
Res., 46 N. Main St., 14080-0006. Tel: 716-537-9434. [CEM 2]
Catechesis/Religious Programs—Tel: 716-537-9336. D.R.E.: Mrs. Theresa Leach Tel: 716-537-9868; Mrs. Joyce Faust.
Students 304.

Holley, Orleans Co., St. Mary (1866), Rev. Joseph F. Kozlowski.
Res., 11 S. Main St., 14470-1107. Tel: 716-638-6718; Fax: 716-638-3210. [CEM]
Catechesis/Religious Programs—Tel: 716-638-6027. Jean M. Mullins, D.R.E.
Students 172.
Mission—Hulberton, Orleans Co., St. Rocco, 115 Main St., 14470.

Humphrey, Cattaraugus Co., St. Pacificus, Mission of St. Bonaventure University Friary (1855), Rev. J. Gregory Brennan, O.F.M.
Res., St. Bonaventure University, St. Bonaventure, 14778. Tel: 716-375-2000; Fax: 716-375-2424. [CEM]

Jamestown, Chautauqua Co., St. James (1915) (Italian), Rev. Msgr. Antoine Attea. In res., Rev. John L. Kuhlmann.
Res., 27 Allen St., 14701. Tel: 716-487-0125. [CEM]
Catechesis/Religious Programs—Tel: 716-664-4237. Anne Gordon, D.R.E.
Students 54.

St. John (1939), Rev. Donald S. Fafinski.
Res., 270 Newton Ave., 14701. Tel: 716-664-4556.
Parish Center: Tel: 716-484-1875.
Catechesis/Religious Programs—Tel: 716-484-1875.
Students 82.

St. Peter and Paul (1854), Rev. John J. Mitka.
Res., 508 Cherry St., 14701. Tel: 716-664-5703; Fax: 716-661-3660. [CEM]
School—1135 N. Main St., 14701. Tel: 716-483-3245; Fax: 716-484-8492.
Sisters 1; Lay Teachers 19; Students 284.
Catechesis/Religious Programs—Tel: 716-484-8958.
Students 300.

Java Center, Wyoming Co., St. Patrick, Rev. Edward E. Muerder.
Res., 14082. Tel: 716-457-9532.
School—Genesee-Wyoming Catholic Central Consolidated School. See separate listing under Regional and Consolidated Elementary Schools in the Institutions located in the Diocese.
Catechesis/Religious Programs—Mary Gentner, D.R.E.
Students 118.

Kendall, Orleans Co., St. Mark (1984), Rev. Joseph F. Kozlowski. In res., Rev. Elmer A. McNamara (ROC).
Res., 11 S. Main St., Holley, 14470-1107. Tel: 716-638-6718; Fax: 716-638-3210.
Catechesis/Religious Programs—Tel: 716-659-8631. Sr. Mary Anne Rapp, O.S.F., D.R.E.
Students 150.

Kenmore, Erie Co.,

1—St. Andrew, (1944), Rev. Msgr. Richard A. Graeber; Rev. Jeffrey M. Sturmer; Deacon Thomas J. Hart. In res., Rev. Vincent J. Ferraro, Chap.
Res., 1525 Sheridan Dr., 14217. Tel: 716-873-6716; Fax: 716-873-2214.

School—Tel: 716-877-0422.
Felician Sisters 2; Lay Teachers 40; Students 643.
Catechesis/Religious Programs—Students 444.

2—BLESSED SACRAMENT, Rev. Msgr. Robert K. Golombek; Rev. Adolph M. Kowalozyk.
Res., 263 Claremont Ave., 14223. Tel: 716-834-4282.
School—Felician Sisters 3; Lay Teachers 13; Students 208.

3—ST. JOHN THE BAPTIST, (1836), Rev. Msgr. Kenneth M. Menge; Revs. Thomas J. McCarthy; Michael H. Burzynski; Deacon Bernard M. Thomann. In res., Rev. Edward C. Metzger, O.F.M.
Res., 1085 Englewood Ave., 14223. Tel: 716-873-1122; Fax: 716-873-3305. [CEM]
School—Englewood & Belmont, 14223. Tel: 716-877-6401; Fax: 716-877-9139. Marilynn Camp, Prin.
Sisters 1; Lay Teachers 45; Students 637.
Catechesis/Religious Programs—Tel: 716-877-0474. Catherine Salzman, D.R.E.
Students 433.

4—ST. PAUL, (1897), Revs. Paul M. Nogaro; Richard E. Sowinski; William J. Quinlivan.
Res., 33 Victoria Blvd., 14217. Tel: 716-875-2730; Fax: 716-877-3475.
School—Tel: 716-877-6308; Fax: 716-877-3874. Louise Lopardi, Prin.
Lay Teachers 28; Students 470.
Catechesis/Religious Programs—Tel: 716-873-9429.
Students 700.

Knapp Creek, Cattaraugus Co., Sacred Heart, Mission of Allegany. Closed. For sacramental records contact St. Mary of the Angels.

Lackawanna, Erie Co.,

1—BASILICA OF OUR LADY OF VICTORY, (1854). (National Shrine). Rev. Msgr. Robert C. Wurtz, P.A.; Rev. Msgr. Robert E. Murphy; Revs. Joseph Klos; Matthew J. Zirnheld; Deacon Thomas M. Forcucci.
Res., 767 Ridge Rd., 14218. Tel: 716-828-9444; Fax: 716-828-9429.
School—Tel: 716-828-9434. Sr. Ellen O'Keefe, Prin.
Sisters 5; Lay Teachers 20; Students 406.
Catechesis/Religious Programs—Tel: 716-828-9437. Sheila Flynn, D.R.E.
Students 125.

2—ST. ANTHONY, (1917) (Italian), Rev. Frank E. Barone.
Res., 306 Ingham Ave., 14218. Tel: 716-823-0782.

3—ASSUMPTION, (1918) (Hungarian), Rev. Kalman Miskolczy, Sch.P., Admin.
Church—80 Steelawanna Ave., 14218. Tel: 716-822-9828.

4—ST. BARBARA, (1903) (Polish), Rev. Lawrence F. Cobel.
Res., 551 Ridge Rd., 14218. Tel: 716-822-3470.

5—ST. HYACINTH, (1911) (Polish), Rev. Henry A. Orszulak, Admin.
Res., 253 Ridge Rd., 14218. Tel: 716-823-0845.

6—ST. MICHAEL THE ARCHANGEL, (1921) (Polish), Rev. James M. Augustyn.
Res., 144 Warsaw St., 14218. Tel: 716-826-0880.
Catechesis/Religious Programs—Tel: 716-822-8526. Sr. Mary Alisette Skotnicki, C.S.S.F., D.R.E.
Students 137.

7—OUR LADY OF BISTRICA, (1917) (Croatian), Revs. Christopher Coric, O.F.M.Conv. (Croatia); Zarco Mula, O.F.M.Conv. (Croatia). In res., Rev. Msgr. Stephen F. Lackovic (Croatia).
Res., 1619 Abbott Rd., 14218. Tel: 716-822-0818.
Coordinator for Croatian Conventual Franciscans—

8—QUEEN OF ALL SAINTS, (1949), Rev. Thomas P. Taton, Admin.
Res., 206 Ridge Rd., 14218. Tel: 716-824-8797.
Catechesis/Religious Programs—Cynthia Lopez, D.R.E.
Students 135.

Lake View, Erie Co., Our Lady of Perpetual Help (1922), Rev. Msgr. John W. Zeitler; Sr. Sharon Erickson, R.S.M.
Res., 2052 Lake View Ave., 14085. Tel: 716-627-2910; Fax: 716-627-7972.
School—Southtowns Catholic Consolidated School. See separate listing under Regional and Consolidated Elementary Schools in the Institutions located in the Diocese. Tel: 716-627-5011.
Catechesis/Religious Programs—Tel: 716-627-9397. Sr. Catherine Taberski, S.S.M.N., D.R.E.
Students 415.

Lakewood, Chautauqua Co., Sacred Heart (1912), Rev. Msgr. Joseph M. Dowdell.
Res., 380 E. Fairmount Ave., 14750-2197. Tel: 716-763-2815.
Catechesis/Religious Programs—Marilyn Wozneak, Pastoral Assoc. & D.R.E.
Students 291.

Lancaster, Erie Co., St. Mary of the Assumption (1850), Rev. Msgr. Frederick D. Leising; Revs. Berard Pulikoottil; David R. Glassmire.
Res., 14086-2033. Tel: 716-683-6445; Fax: 716-684-8446. [CEM]
School—Tel: 716-683-2112. Sr. Barbara Jean Wajda, O.S.F., Prin.
Sisters of Third Order of St. Francis 3; Lay Teachers 21; Students 371.
Catechesis/Religious Programs—Tel: 716-683-8564. Mrs. Elaine Driscoll, D.R.E.
Students 900.

Our Lady of Pompeii (1909), Rev. Jay W. McGinnis; Deacon John Klein. In res., Rev. John P. Mack.
Res., 158 Laverack Ave., 14086. Tel: 716-683-6522; Fax: 716-685-8066.
School—(Grades PreK-8). Tel: 716-684-4664. Mrs. Christine M. Schierer, Prin.
Sisters 4; Lay Teachers 14; Students 275.
Catechesis/Religious Programs—D.R.E.: Antoinette Duran, (Elementary); Joseph Blatz, (High School).
Students 545.

Langford, Erie Co., St. Martin (1851), Rev. Lawrence P. Damian.
Res., 10893 Sisson Hwy. (Langford), North Collins, 14111. Tel: 716-337-2686. [CEM]

Le Roy, Genesee Co., St. Joseph (Italian), Rev. Msgr. Emil P. Zupa.
Res., 27 Lake St., 14482. Tel: 716-768-6600.
Catechesis/Religious Programs—Students 100.

St. Peter (1849), Rev. Robert W. Wardenski.
Res., 44 Lake St., Leroy, 14482. Tel: 716-768-6543. [CEM]
School—Tel: 716-768-7390. Mrs. Barbara McVean, Prin.
Lay Teachers 7; Students 143.
Catechesis/Religious Programs—Students 175.
Mission—Lime Rock, Genesee Co., St. Anthony.

Lewiston, Niagara Co., Holy Family (1953) (Tuscarora Indian Nation), Rev. Ubaldo M. Fior, C.R.S.P.
Res., 1023 Swan Rd., Youngstown, 14174-9797. Tel: 716-754-7489. [JC]

St. Peter, Rev. Msgr. Anthony J. Caligiuri, P.A. In res., Rev. Slawomir Siok, S.A.C.
Res., 620 Center St., 14092. Tel: 716-754-4118.
School—Mary Donald, Prin. Franciscan Sisters of St. Joseph 3; Lay Teachers 7; Students 225.
Catechesis/Religious Programs—Students 470.
Convent—421 Plain St., 14092.

Limestone, Cattaraugus Co., St. Patrick (1875), Rev. Jerome J. Stelmach.
Res., 16 Church St., 14753. Tel: 716-925-8596. [CEM]

Little Valley, Cattaraugus Co., St. Mary (1874), Revs. Wallace T. Borucki; Joseph K. Lowry, Jr., Pastor Emeritus.
Mailing Address: 36 Washington St., Cattaraugus, 14719. Tel: 716-257-9351.
Res., 425 Erie St., 14755.

Lockport, Niagara Co.,

1—ST. ANTHONY, (1928), Rev. Louis F. Della Neve.
Res., 9 Bristol Ave., 14094. Tel: 716-434-5025.
School—Lockport Catholic Consolidated School. See separate listing under Regional and Consolidated Elementary Schools in the Institutions located in the Diocese.
Catechesis/Religious Programs—D.R.E.: Patricia Riexenger; Kathleen D'Agostino.
Students 140.

2—ST. JOHN THE BAPTIST, (1834), Rev. Msgr. Donald L. Wangler; Rev. Joseph C. Dumphrey, O.S.F.S.
Res., 168 Chestnut St., 14094. Tel: 716-433-8118.
School—Lockport Catholic Consolidated School. See separate listing under Regional and Consolidated Elementary Schools in the Institutions located in the Diocese. Tel: 716-433-6422.
Catechesis/Religious Programs—Tel: 716-434-2492. Sr. Mary Helen, F.M.D.C., D.R.E.
Students 900.
Convent—159 Chestnut St., 14094. Tel: 716-434-8303.

3—ST. JOSEPH, (1912) (Italian), Rev. Nicholas A. Rossello.
Res., 391 Market St., 14094. Tel: 716-433-5792.
School—Lockport Catholic Consolidated School. See separate listing under Regional and Consolidated Elementary Schools in the Institutions located in the Diocese. Tel: 716-433-6422.
Catechesis/Religious Programs—Tel: 716-433-3194. Mrs. Marea Eggert, D.R.E.
Students 149.

4—ST. MARY, (1859) (German), Rev. Msgr. Michael J. Yunk.
Res., 5 Saxton St., 14094. Tel: 716-434-6316.
School—DeSales Catholic School. See separate listing under Regional and Consolidated Elementary Schools in the Institutions located in the Diocese. Tel: 716-433-6222.
Catechesis/Religious Programs—Tel: 716-433-0340.
Students 160.

5—ST. PATRICK, (1864) (Irish), Rev. Francis Schimscheiner, O.S.F.S. In res., Revs. Gerald Bartko, O.S.F.S.; Joseph Dumphrey, O.S.F.S.
Res., 76 Church St., 14094. Tel: 716-433-3707. [CEM]
School—See separate listing for DeSales Catholic School, Lockport, under Regional and Consolidated Elementary Schools in the Institutions located in the Diocese.
Catechesis/Religious Programs—Tel: 716-433-6672. Sr. Rene Ruberto, S.S.M.N., D.R.E.
Students 190.
Convent—138 N. Transit St., 14094. Tel: 716-433-9193.

Lyndonville, Orleans Co., St. Joseph (1962), Revs. Joseph G. Fifagrowicz; Albert J. Bosack.
Res., 38 Lake Ave., P.O. Box 308, 14098. Tel: 716-765-9722.

Machias, Cattaraugus Co., Holy Family (1948), Rev. Raymond F. Uschold.
Res., 10 N. Main St., P.O. Box 188, Delevan, 14042. Tel: 716-492-2383.

Mayville, Chautauqua Co., St. Mary, Rev. Raymond A.J. Donohue.
Res., 18 E. Chautauqua St., Box 148, 14757. Tel: 716-753-2332.

Medina, Orleans Co., St. Mary (1840), Rev. Msgr. Paul J. Whitney; Deacon Nelson Darroch.
Res., 211 Eagle St., 14103. Tel: 716-798-0112. [CEM]
Catechesis/Religious Programs—Tel: 716-798-5399. Marguerite J. Moriarty, D.R.E.
Students 237.

Sacred Heart (1910), Rev. Joseph G. Fifagrowicz.
Res., 208 Ann St., 14103. Tel: 716-798-0356. [CEM]

Middleport, Niagara Co., St. Stephen (1854), Rev. Msgr. James E. Streng.
Res., 19 Vernon St., 14105-1321. Tel: 716-735-9433. [CEM]
Catechesis/Religious Programs—Tel: 716-735-7008.
Students 183.

Newfane, Niagara Co., St. Bridget (1859), Rev. John J. Leising.
Res., 3455 Ewings Rd., Box 87, 14108-0087. Tel: 716-778-9822. [CEM]
Catechesis/Religious Programs—Carol Piech, D.R.E.
Students 260.

Niagara Falls, Niagara Co.,

1—ST. CHARLES, (1970), Rev. Joseph C. Carlo.
Res., 5604 Lindbergh Ave., 14304. Tel: 716-283-7602. [CEM]

2—ST. GEORGE, (1915) (Lithuanian), Rev. Seweryn J. Koszyk, S.A.C.
Res., 1910 Falls St., 14303. Tel: 716-282-4587.

3—HOLY TRINITY, (1902) (Polish), Most Rev. Edward M. Grosz, D.D., V.G.; Deacon Walter Fudala.
Res., 1419 Falls St., 14303. Tel: 716-284-6628. [CEM]

4—ST. JOHN DE LA SALLE, (1907), Rev. Msgr. Robert J. Hogan; Rev. Norman P. McTigue; Deacon David P. Slish.
Res., 8469 Buffalo Ave., 14304. Tel: 716-283-2238.
School—Tel: 716-283-3031.
Lay Teachers 9; Students 196.

5—ST. JOSEPH, (1903) (Italian), Rev. Msgr. Richard S. Amico; Sr. Francis Marie Vallone, F.M.D.C., Pastoral Assoc.
Res., 1413 Pine Ave., 14301. Tel: 716-282-1379; Fax: 716-282-6005. [CEM]
School—625 Tronolone Pl., 14301. Tel: 716-282-8144.
Franciscan Sisters of Allegany 1; Lay Teachers 21; Students 246.
Catechesis/Religious Programs—Students 154.

6—ST. LEO, (1957), Rev. David G. Griffin.
Res., 2748 Military Rd., 14304. Tel: 716-297-3690.
Catechesis/Religious Programs—Tel: 716-297-5010.
Students 310.

7—ST. MARY OF THE CATARACT, Rev. Msgr. William J. Stillwell. In res., Revs. John P. Duggan, Pastor Emeritus; Mark M. Friel, Chap., Memorial Medical Center; Francis Gross, O.S.F.S.; Bro. Francis Murray, O.S.F.S.
Res., 259 Fourth St., 14303. Tel: 716-282-0059.

8—OUR LADY OF LEBANON, (1914), Rev. William E. McKeon, C.M., Admin.
Res., 1120 Niagara St., 14303. Tel: 716-282-0729.

9—OUR LADY OF MOUNT CARMEL, (1949), Rev. Msgr. Edward J. Scanlan. In res., Rev. Robert S. Hughson.
Res., 2486 Grand Ave., 14301. Tel: 716-282-5546; Fax: 716-282-6395.
School—2499 Independence Ave., 14301. Tel: 716-282-0645.

Lay Teachers 12; Students 279.
Catechesis/Religious Programs—Students 200.

10—Our Lady of the Rosary, (1906), Rev. John R. Gaglione.
Res., 339 22nd St., 14303. Tel: 716-282-0264.

11—Prince of Peace, (1943), Revs. William C. McGarry; Stewart M. Lindsay, O.S.F.S. In res., Rev. Salvatore J. Cusimano.
Res., 1040 Cayuga Dr., 14304. Tel: 716-283-2715.
School—(Grades PreK-6). Tel: 716-283-1455. Sr. Mary Asarese, S.S.M.N., Prin.
Sisters 1; Students 258.
Catechesis/Religious Programs—Tel: 716-283-0569.
Students 342.

12—Sacred Heart, (1854), Revs. James J. Kasinski, Admin.; Richard Strassberger, Senior Assoc. In res.,
Res., 1917 11th St., 14305. Tel: 716-282-1749.
School—Tel: 716-282-8484. Sr. Mary Walz, S.S.J., Prin.
Sisters of St. Joseph 1; Lay Teachers 10; Students 130.
Catechesis/Religious Programs—Patricia McCarthy, D.R.E.
Students 87.

13—St. Stanislaus Kostka, (1917), Revs. Richard A. Jesionowski; Edward M. Grosz, D.D., V.G.; Deacon Walter Fudala.
Res., 2437 Niagara St., 14303. Tel: 716-285-3604. [JC]

14—St. Teresa of the Infant Jesus, (1930), Rev. Msgr. Leonard E. Biniszkiewicz.
Res., 3840 Macklem Ave., 14305. Tel: 716-282-5583; Fax: 716-282-0453.
Catechesis/Religious Programs—Tel: 716-282-0795. Catherine Halliday, D.R.E.
Students 189.

North Collins, Erie Co., Holy Spirit (1958), Rev. Msgr. Daniel J. Szostak.
Res., 2017 Halley Rd., 14111. Tel: 716-337-2544. [CEM]
Catechesis/Religious Programs—Tel: 716-337-3803. Sr. Julia Witkowski, D.R.E.
Students 165.

North Evans, Erie Co., St. Vincent (1914), Revs. William R. Tuyn; Brian M. Hatrick.
Res., 2050 S. Creek Rd., 14112. Tel: 716-627-3382. [CEM]
School—Southtowns Catholic Consolidated School. See separate listing under Regional and Consolidated Elementary Schools in the Institutions located in the Diocese. Tel: 716-627-5011.
Catechesis/Religious Programs—Tel: 716-627-7673. Ann Kirkpatrick, D.R.E.
Students 455.

North Java, Wyoming Co., St. Nicholas, Rev. Edward E. Muerder.
Res., 14113. Tel: 716-535-7457. [CEM]
School—Genesee-Wyoming Catholic Central Consolidated School. See separate listing under Regional and Consolidated Elementary Schools in the Institutions located in the Diocese.

North Tonawanda, Niagara Co.,

1—Ascension, (1887), Rev. Gary Szczepankiewicz.
Res., 168 Robinson St., 14120. Tel: 716-693-1211; Fax: 716-693-1263.
School—North Tonawanda Consolidated Catholic School. See separate listing under Regional and Consolidated Elementary Schools in the Institutions located in the Diocese. Tel: 716-693-2828; Fax: 716-693-0169.
Catechesis/Religious Programs—Tel: 716-694-3754. Mr. Gary Szezepankiewitz; Mrs. Jeanne Wantz.
Students 430.

2—St. Albert the Great, Rev. Msgr. Edward T. Fisher; Deacon Daniel E. Brick. In res., Rev. Duane G. Fimbel.
Res., 1520 Kingston Ave., 14120. Tel: 716-694-0540.

3—St. Joseph, (1947) (Polish), Rev. Msgr. Thomas E. Crane.
Res., 1451 Payne Ave., 14120. Tel: 716-693-2791; Fax: 716-743-1405.
School—North Tonawanda Catholic Consolidated School. See separate listing under Regional and Consolidated Elementary Schools in the Institutions located in the Diocese. Tel: 716-693-4769.
Catechesis/Religious Programs—Tel: 716-693-0421. Mrs. Lorraine Schintzius, D.R.E.
Students 400.

4—Our Lady of Czestochowa, (1903) (Polish), Revs. Dennis F. Fronckowiak; Michael R. Kopczynski.
Res., 64 Center Ave., 14120. Tel: 716-693-3822; Fax: 716-693-3882.
School—North Tonawanda Catholic Consolidated School. See separate listing under Regional and Consolidated Elementary Schools in the Institutions located in the Diocese. Tel: 716-694-3644.
Catechesis/Religious Programs—Students 150.
Convent—Tel: 716-692-0276.

Oakfield, Genesee Co., St. Cecilia (1907), Rev. Thomas D. Doyle.
Res., 56 Maple Ave., 14125. Tel: 716-948-5344. [CEM]
Mission—Wheatville, Genesee Co., St. Patrick.

Olcott, Niagara Co., St. Charles Borromeo (1912), Rev. James F. Hassett. In res., Rev. Eugene L. Wagner, Pastor Emeritus.
Res., 5969 Washington St., 14126. Tel: 716-778-7592; 795-3331 (Church).

Olean, Cattaraugus Co., St. John (1896) (Irish-Italian), Rev. Msgr. William O. Wangler.
Res., 931 N. Union St., 14760. Tel: 716-372-5313.
School—Southern Tier Catholic Regional School. See separate listing under Regional and Consolidated Elementary Schools in the Institutions located in the Diocese. Tel: 716-372-2891.
Catechesis/Religious Programs—Tel: 716-372-6633.
Students 205.

St. Mary of the Angels (1876), Rev. Thomas J. Quinlivan.
Res., 202 S. Union St., 14760. Tel: 716-372-4841; Fax: 716-372-5905.
School—Southern Tier Catholic Regional School. See separate listing under Regional and Consolidated Elementary Schools in the Institutions located in the Diocese.

Transfiguration (1912) (Polish), Rev. Jerome J. Stelmach.
Res., 1102 Walnut St., 14760. Tel: 716-372-5430; Fax: 716-373-4719.
School—Southern Tier Catholic Regional School. See separate listing under Regional and Consolidated Elementary Schools in the Institutions located in the Diocese.

Orchard Park, Erie Co.,

1—Nativity, (1908), Rev. Msgr. Thomas J. Beasley; Revs. Joseph A. Gullo; Joseph D. Porpigilia. In res., Rev. Msgr. H. Gil Weil.
Res., 26 Thorn Ave., 14127. Tel: 716-662-9339; Fax: 716-662-2195. [CEM]
School—Tel: 716-662-7572. Ruth Frost, Prin.
Sisters of St. Francis of Penance and Christian Charity 1; Lay Teachers 27; Students 350.
Catechesis/Religious Programs—Tel: 716-662-2169. Mary Ann Pietrzak, D.R.E.
Students 770.

2—St. Bernadette, (1957), Rev. Msgr. Richard T. Nugent; Rev. Raymond McNicholas, S.S.C.
Res., 5930 S. Abbott Rd., 14127-4516. Tel: 716-649-3090; Fax: 716-649-0211.
School—Tel: 716-649-3369. Sr. Diane Swanson, Prin.
Lay Teachers 17; Students 220.
Catechesis/Religious Programs—Tel: 716-648-1720. Joan Ersing, D.R.E.
Students 876.

3—Our Lady of the Sacred Heart, (1920), Rev. Msgr. Paul J.E. Burkard; Revs. Gregory Dobson; Mieczyslaw F. Nycz.
Res., S-3148 Abbot Rd., 14127. Tel: 716-824-2935; Fax: 716-827-7643.
School—3144 Abbott Rd., 14127. Tel: 716-824-8208. Sr. Monica Riordan, R.S.M., Prin.
Sisters of Mercy 4; Lay Teachers 34; Students 661.
Catechesis/Religious Programs—Tel: 716-824-8209. Paula White, D.R.E.
Students 676.

4—St. John Vianney, (1958), Rev. Theodore C. Rog.
Res., 2950 Southwestern Blvd., 14127. Tel: 716-674-9133; Fax: 716-674-9134.
School—Tel: 716-674-9232.
Lay Teachers 14; Students 145.
Catechesis/Religious Programs—Tel: 716-674-9145. Sharon Kirsch, D.R.E.
Students 600.

Pavilion, Genesee Co., St. Mary (1870), Rev. Robert P. Conlin.
Res., 14525. Tel: 716-584-3280. [CEM]
Catechesis/Religious Programs—Students 173. D.R.E.: Carol Kistner Tel: 716-343-7823; Mary Shaughnessy Tel: 716-584-3827.

Pendleton, Niagara Co., Good Shepherd (1847), Rev. Msgr. Paul J. Belzer.
Res., 5442 Tonawanda Creek Rd., North Tonawanda, 14120-9699. Tel: 716-625-8594. [CEM]
Catechesis/Religious Programs—Tel: 716-625-8817. Elizabeth McDermott, D.R.E.
Students 240.

Perry, Wyoming Co., St. Joseph (1879) (Italian), Rev. Richard W. Blazejewski.
Res., 8 Park St., 14530. Tel: 716-237-2625. [CEM]

St. Stanislaus Kostka (1910) (Polish), Rev. Richard J. Blazejewski.
Res., 8 Park St., 14530. Tel: 716-237-3869. [CEM]

Perrysburg, Cattaraugus Co., St. Joan of Arc (1950), Rev. John S. Kwiecien.
Office St. John Fisher Church:South Dayton, 14138. Tel: 716-988-5568.
Res., All records are kept at St. John Fisher. P.O. Box 222, 14129-0222. Tel: 716-532-4556.

Portageville, Wyoming Co., Assumption B.V.M. (1849), Rev. Robert M. Mock.
Res., P.O. Box 404, 14536. Tel: 716-468-2643. [CEM]

Portville, Cattaraugus Co., Sacred Heart, Rev. Richard M. Poblocki.
Res., 14770. Tel: 716-933-6394.
School—Southern Tier Catholic Regional School. See separate listing under Regional and Consolidated Elementary Schools in the Institutions located in the Diocese.

Randolph, Cattaraugus Co., St. Patrick (1853), Rev. Msgr. Leon M. Neu.
Res., 189 Main St., 14772. Tel: 716-358-2991. [CEM]
Catechesis/Religious Programs—Students 110.

Ransomville, Niagara Co., Immaculate Conception (1891), Revs. Herold M. Nuwer; Salvatore J. Piazza, (Retired).
Res., 4671 Townline Rd., Rte. 429, 14131-9799. Tel: 716-731-4822.
Catechesis/Religious Programs—Mrs. Judith A. Kirkpatrick, D.R.E.
Students 448.

Rushford, Allegany Co., St. Mark (1948), Rev. Francis J. Jann, Admin.
Res., 14777. Tel: 716-437-5332.

Salamanca, Cattaraugus Co., Holy Cross (1893) (Polish), Rev. Constantine Kwiatkowski.
Res., 284 Broad St., 14779. Tel: 716-945-4966. [JC]

St. Patrick (1868), Rev. Michael P. Juran.
Res., 101 River St., 14779. Tel: 716-945-5522. [CEM]

Sardinia, Erie Co., St. Jude (1953), Rev. Bonifice D. Ferens, Admin.
Res., 12820 Genesee Rd., 14134-0267. Tel: 716-496-7535.

Sheldon, Wyoming Co., St. Cecilia (1848), Rev. Donald C. Weber; Deacon Daniel Molik.
Res., Strykersville, 14145. Tel: 716-457-9437. [CEM]
School—Genesee-Wyoming Catholic Central Consolidated School. See separate listing under Regional and Consolidated Elementary Schools in the Institutions located in the Diocese.

Sheridan, Chautauqua Co., St. John Bosco (1949), Rev. Gerald P. Sheehan.
Res., Box 3, 14135. Tel: 716-679-4951.

Sherman, Chautauqua Co., St. Isaac Jogues, Rev. Raymond A.J. Donohue.
Res., 18 E. Chautanqua St., Box 148, Mayville, 14757. Tel: 716-753-2332.

Silver Creek, Chautauqua Co., Our Lady of Mt. Carmel (1882), Rev. Msgr. Richard J. Gill.
Res., 165 Central Ave., 14136. Tel: 716-934-2233. [CEM]
School—Northern Chautauqua Catholic Regional School. See separate listing under Regional and Consolidated Elementary Schools in the Institutions located in the Diocese. Tel: 716-366-0630.
Catechesis/Religious Programs—Tel: 716-934-4891.
Students 207.

Silver Springs, Wyoming Co., St. Mary, Rev. Edward J. Sheedy; Deacon John Kelly.
Res., 23 Church St., Box 305, 14550. Tel: 716-493-5265. [CEM]

Sinclairville, Chautauqua Co., St. John the Evangelist, Rev. Patrick H. Elis.
Res., 14782. Tel: 716-962-3781.

Sloan, Erie Co., St. Andrew (1915) (Polish), Rev. Robert D. Moss.
Res., 34 Francis St., 14212. Tel: 716-892-0425.
School—14212.
Felician Sisters 2; Lay Teachers 15; Students 153.

Snyder, Erie Co., Christ the King (1926), Rev. Msgr. James J. Lichtenthal; Rev. David A. Bellittiere.
Res., 30 Lamarck Dr., 14226. Tel: 716-839-1430; 839-1433.
School—Tel: 716-839-0473.
Franciscan Sisters of Allegany 1; Lay Teachers 18; Students 246.

South Dayton, Cattaraugus Co., St. John Fisher (1946), Rev. John S. Kwiecien.
Office: P.O. Box 242, 14138. Tel: 716-988-5568.
Res., Perrysburg, 14129. Tel: 716-532-4556.

Springbrook, Erie Co., St. Vincent (1850), Revs. James A. Walter; Edward F. Jost.
Res., 14140. Tel: 716-652-3972. [CEM]
School—Tel: 716-652-8697. Ms. Julia Gorman, Prin.
Sisters of the Third Order of St. Francis 2; Lay Teachers 9; Students 170.

Catechesis/Religious Programs—Tel: 716-652-7242. Marjory Moretta, D.R.E.
Students 280.

Springville, Erie Co., St. Aloysius (1853), Rev. Charles J. Zadora.
Res., 190 Franklin St., 14141-1199. Tel: 716-592-2701; Fax: 716-592-4347. [CEM]
School—Tel: 716-592-7002. Sr. Marie McTarnaghan, Prin.
Sisters of Third Order of St. Francis 3; Lay Teachers 13; Students 217.
Catechesis/Religious Programs—Tel: 716-592-4869. Ms. Sharon Stachowiak, D.R.E.
Students 348.

Strykersville, Wyoming Co., St. Mary, Queen of the Rosary (1885), Rev. Michael P. McNicholl.
Res., 3854 Main St., 14145. Tel: 716-457-3021; 457-3222; Fax: 716-457-3021. [CEM]
Catechesis/Religious Programs—Sr. Mary Jane Reisdorf, O.S.F., D.R.E.
Students 175.

Swormville, Erie Co., St. Mary (1849), Revs. Robert M. Yetter; Patrick T. O'Keefe; Deacon Howard J. Edbauer, Jr.
Res., 6919 Transit Rd., Box 460, 14146. Tel: 716-688-9380; Fax: 716-688-6173. [CEM]
School—Tel: 716-689-8424.
Sisters of the Third Order of St. Francis 2; Lay Teachers 15; Students 192.
Catechesis/Religious Programs—Tel: 716-688-0599.
Students 775.

Tonawanda, Erie Co.,

1—St. Amelia, (1953), Rev. Msgr. Thomas F. Maloney; Revs. Leon J. Biernat; Michael J. Parker; Sr. Rita Claire, S.S.M.N., Pastoral Assoc.; Deacon Richard W. Parker. In res., Rev. Msgr. John L. McHugh, Pastor Emeritus.
Res., 210 St. Amelia Dr., 14150. Tel: 716-836-0011; Fax: 716-832-5439.
School—Tel: 716-836-2230. James Mule, Prin.
Lay Teachers 25; Students 375.
Catechesis/Religious Programs—Tel: 716-833-8647. Elaine Dankowski, D.R.E.
Students 758.

2—St. Christopher, (1928), Rev. Msgr. Francis G. Weldgen.
Res., 2660 Niagara Falls Blvd., 14150. Tel: 716-692-2660; Fax: 716-693-5639.
School—Tel: 716-693-5604; Fax: 716-693-5639.
Lay Teachers 27; Students 484.
Catechesis/Religious Programs—Tel: 716-694-4310.
Students 800.

3—St. Edmund, (1965), Rev. Msgr. Onofrio R. Smiroldo; Deacon Robert Bauer.
Res., 530 Ellicott Creek Rd., 14150. Tel: 716-694-5656.
School—Tel: 716-694-5900.
Felician Sisters 1; Lay Teachers 9; Students 122.
Catechesis/Religious Programs—Students 250.

4—St. Francis of Assisi, (1858), Rev. Robert W. Vogt. In res., Rev. Merrick J. Bednar.
Res., 73 Adam St., 14150. Tel: 716-693-1150; Fax: 716-693-2025. [CEM]
School—Tel: 716-694-5342; Fax: 716-692-7886.
Lay Teachers 17; Students 204.
Catechesis/Religious Programs—Tel: 716-694-5342.
Students 482.

5—St. Timothy, (1960), Rev. Msgr. John I. Ducette; Deacon Gordon J. Steinagle. In res., Rev. Msgr. John Kempczynski; Rev. Paul Keppner, S.S.C.
Res., 565 E. Park Dr., 14150. Tel: 716-875-9430.
Catechesis/Religious Programs—Students 165.

Vandalia, Cattaraugus Co., St. John the Baptist, Rev. Bernadine Kessing, O.F.M.
Res., St. Bonaventure, 14778. Tel: 716-375-2531.
School—Southern Tier Catholic Regional School. See separate listing under Regional and Consolidated Elementary Schools in the Institutions located in the Diocese.

Varysburg, Wyoming Co., St. Joseph (1910) (German), Rev. Msgr. Joseph A. Boruszewski.
Res., 14167. Tel: 716-535-7342. [CEM]
School—Genesee-Wyoming Catholic Central Consolidated School. See separate listing under Regional and Consolidated Elementary Schools in the Institutions located in the Diocese.

Warsaw, Wyoming Co., St. Michael (1858), Rev. Bart Lipiec; Deacon John J. Kelly.
Res., 171 N. Main St., 14569. Tel: 716-786-2400. [CEM]
School—(Grades PreK-6) 16 North St., 14569. Tel: 716-786-8561. Don Felix, Prin.
Lay Teachers 6; Students 75.
Catechesis/Religious Programs—Students 70.

Wellsville, Allegany Co., Immaculate Conception (1850) (Irish-German), Rev. Dennis G. Wolf.
Res., 6 Maple Ave., 14895. Tel: 716-593-4834; Fax: 716-593-7167. [CEM]
School—(Grades PreK-8) 24 Maple Ave., 14895. Tel: 716-593-5840. Sr. Alice Roach, Prin.
Sisters of Mercy 2; Lay Teachers 13; Students 176.
Catechesis/Religious Programs—Tel: 716-593-1862. D.R.E.: Mrs. Carol Gardner, (Grades 9-11); Sr. Margaret M. Gleason, (Grades PreK-8).

West Falls, Erie Co., St. George (Jewettville) (1912), Rev. Albert M. Hansen.
Res., 74 Old Glenwood Rd., 14170. Tel: 716-652-3153.
Catechesis/Religious Programs—Tel: 716-652-0126.
Students 155.

Westfield, Chautauqua Co., St. James (1860), Rev. Daniel A. Lapinski.
Res., 15 Union St., 14787-1494. Tel: 716-326-2816; Fax: 716-326-4863. [CEM]
Catechesis/Religious Programs—Tel: 716-326-2338; Fax: 716-326-2732. D.R.E.: Mrs. Cecilia Filipkowski; Mr. Robert Ducato.
Students 114.
Mission—Ripley, Chautauqua Co., St. Thomas More, 66 E. Main St., Ripley, 14775. Tel: 716-736-5200.

West Seneca, Erie Co.,

1—St. Bonaventure, (1918), Revs. Benoit J. Drapeau, C.J.M.; Ronald M. Bagley, C.J.M., Dir.; Robert J. Perelli, C.J.M., Aids Family Services; J. Gregory Sampson, C.J.M., Supr.; Louis Levesque, C.J.M.
Total in Residence 5; Total Staff 5.
Res., 36 Flohr Ave., 14224. Tel: 716-823-1090.
School—2784 Seneca St., 14224. Tel: 716-822-7260.
Lay Teachers 13; Students 160.
Catechesis/Religious Programs—Tel: 716-825-5053. Mrs. Lynn Lipczynski, D.R.E.
Students 318.

2—St. Catherine of Siena, (1967), Rev. Pascal D. Ipolito; Deacon Joseph M. Barr.
Res., 4928 Seneca St., 14224. Tel: 716-675-0531; Fax: 716-675-1530.
Catechesis/Religious Programs—Students 317.

3—Fourteen Holy Helpers, (1864) (German-Polish), Rev. Msgr. David S. Slubecky; Revs. Duane R. Klizek; Theodore Caffarelli, S.S.C.
Res., 1345 Indian Church Rd., Buffalo, 14224. Tel: 716-674-2374. [CEM]
School—Tel: 716-674-1670. Ms. Susan Jagosh, Prin.
Lay Teachers 20; Students 364.
Catechesis/Religious Programs—Tel: 716-674-2180.
Students 380.

4—St. William, (1926), Rev. James L. Breitnauer; Joan Morreal, Pastoral Assoc. & D.R.E.
Res., Arcade St., 14224. Tel: 716-822-5449.
School—Affiliated with St. Bonaventure. Tel: 716-822-7260.
Catechesis/Religious Programs—Tel: 716-822-1531.
Students 196.

5—Queen of Heaven, (1955), Rev. Msgr. James F. Campbell; Rev. Peter J. Cronin, S.S.C.
Res., 4220 Seneca St., 14224. Tel: 716-674-3468; Fax: 716-674-3475.
School—839 Mill Rd., 14224. Tel: 716-674-5206. Mrs. Judith Talbot, Prin.
Lay Teachers 24; Students 335.
Catechesis/Religious Programs—Tel: 716-675-3714. D.R.E.: Elizabeth Vitko; Dorothy Flynn.
Students 676.

West Valley, Cattaraugus Co., St. John the Baptist (1904), Rev. Carl L. Kuehmeier.
Res., 5381 Depot St., P.O. Box 315, 14171-0315. Tel: 716-942-3259. [CEM]
Catechesis/Religious Programs—Janet Vant, D.R.E.
Students 105.

Whitesville, Allegany Co., St. John of the Cross (1949), Rev. Fred G. Fingerle.
Res., One Church St., Box 761, Andover, 14806. Tel: 607-478-8885.
Church—540 Main St., Box 137, 14897.

Williamsville, Erie Co., St. Gregory the Great (1958), Rev. Msgr. Rupert A. Wright; Revs. James R. Bastien; Joseph S. Rogliano; James Ciupek.
Res., 100 St. Gregory Ct., 14221. Tel: 716-688-5678; 5679; Fax: 716-688-2315.
School—250 St. Gregory Ct., 14221. Tel: 716-688-5323; Fax: 716-688-6629. Mrs. Patricia Boyd, Prin.
Sisters 1; Lay Teachers 37; Students 628.
Catechesis/Religious Programs—Tel: 716-688-5760. Mrs. Joan Rischmiller, D.R.E.
Students 1,957.

SS. Peter and Paul (1836), Rev. Msgr. David M. Gallivan; Revs. Alfons M. Osiander; Robert J. Schober; Mrs. Linda Downey, Pastoral Assoc.
Res., 5480 Main St., 14221. Tel: 716-632-2559; Fax: 716-626-0971. [CEM 2]
School—Tel: 716-632-6146. Sr. Joan Hupp, O.S.F., Prin.
Lay Teachers 16; Students 260.
Catechesis/Religious Programs—Tel: 716-632-2678. Ms. Susan Golebiewski, D.R.E.
Students 520.

Wilson, Niagara Co., Our Lady of the Rosary (1920), Rev. John J. Leising.
Res., 359 Lake St., Box 116, 14172-0116. Tel: 716-751-6459.
Catechesis/Religious Programs—Mrs. Barbara Mosher, D.R.E.
Students 124.

Woodlawn, Erie Co., Our Lady of Grace (1940), Rev. John F. Kasprzak.
Res., S. 3319 Lake Shore Rd., 14219. Tel: 716-822-0607.
Catechesis/Religious Programs—BettyLou Regueira, D.R.E.
Students 140.

Youngstown, Niagara Co., St. Bernard's (1946), Rev. Msgr. J. Thomas Moran.
Res., 218 Hinman St., 14174. Tel: 716-745-7460. [CEM]
Catechesis/Religious Programs—Blanche Sylvester, D.R.E.
Students 275.

Chaplains of Public Institutions

Buffalo. *Buffalo General Hospital*. Revs. Douglas F. Faraci; Norbert F. Orsolits; Richard H. Augustyn.
Buffalo Psychiatric Center. 400 Forest Ave., 14213. Rev. John J. O'Connor.
Children's Hospital. Vacant.
Columbus Hospital. Attended by Oblates from Holy Angeles.
Erie County Medical Center. Rev. Robert A. Stolinski.
Millard Fillmore Hospital. Rev. Robert J. Schober.
Roswell Park Memorial Institute. Rev. Douglas F. Faraci.
Sheehan Memorial Emergency Hospital. Vacant.
Veterans Hospital. Sr. Denise McKenzie, G.N.S.H.

Albion. *Albion Correctional Facility*. Vacant.

Alden. *Erie County Correctional Facility*. Rev. Francis T. Nowak.

Amherst. *Millard Fillmore Suburban Hospital*. Rev. Joseph W. Bertha.

Attica. *Attica Correctional Facility*. Rev. John Kilian.

Batavia. *Veterans Hospital*. Rev. John P. Bernard.

Dunkirk. *Brooks Memorial Hospital*. Deacon Matthew A. Podnieskinski, Chap.

Helmuth. *Collins Correctional Facility*. Vacant.

Jamestown. *Jamestown Women's Christian Association Hospital*. 27 Allen St., 14701. Tel: 716-487-0125. Rev. John L. Kuhlmann, Chap.

Niagara Falls. *Niagara Falls Memorial Medical Centers*. Rev. Mark M. Friel.

North Tonawanda. *DeGraff Memorial Hospital*. 1520 Kingston Ave., 14120. Tel: 716-694-4500. Rev. Duane G. Fimbel.
Orleans Correction Facility. Vacant.

Perrysburg. *J. N. Adam Memorial Hospital*. St. Aloysius Chapel. Deacon Robert A. Bauer.
Wende Correctional Facility. Rev. Frank Barone.

West Seneca. *Development Center*. Carol Ann Corey.
Wyoming Correctional Facility. Rev. Roy T. Herberger.

On Duty Outside the Diocese:
Reverend Monsignors—
Kraus, Theodore W., 521 Boden Way, Oakland, CA 94610-3609
Reverend Fathers—
Blesnuk, Donald J., Casilla 313, Linares, Chile
Conoscenti, Frederick M., 605 Grove St., D4, Clifton, NJ 07013
Enright, James C., Auburn Correctional Facility, 135 State St., Auburn, NY 13021
Krysa, Czeslaw M., SS. Cyril & Methodius Seminary, Orchard Lake, MI 48033
Nielsen, Kenneth M., SS. Peter & Paul Church, 55 W. Broadway, Boston, MA 02127
Sheedy, Edward J., Wadhams Hall Seminary, Ogdensburg, NY 13669
Wild, Robert A., Madonna House, Combermere, Ontario, Canada
Zapfel, Robert E., S.T.D., Congregation for Catholic Education, 00120 Vatican City State

---

Military Chaplains:
Reverend Fathers—
Koester, Timothy J., HQ BTN, HQ USMC, Henderson Hall, Arlington, VA 22214-5001
Nowak, Bernard U., 2/8 2nd Marine Division, PSC Box 20103, Camp Lejeune, NC 28542-0103
Rappl, Joseph P., U.S. Army Chaplaincy Svcs. Support Group, 2750 Army Pentagon, Washington, DC 20310-2750

Spatorico, Joseph S., Comdr. Chap. U.S.N., Office of Wing Chap., 2D MAW, Cherry Point, NC 28533
Zuffoletto, Michael P., U.S. Navy, 3747 Bengal Rd., Gulf Breeze, FL 32561

Absent on Leave:
Reverend Fathers—
Biesinger, Robert J.
Gresock, Thomas G.
Maryanski, Fabian J.
Ronald, Roy K.
Swartz, Michael R.
Tuchols, Franklin J.

Retired:
Reverend Monsignors—
Brennan, George J., 4 Lockwood Ln., Orchard Parl, NY 14127
Bugman, John H., Our Lady of Victory, 767 Ridge Rd., Lackawanna, NY 14218
Caine, Martin J., 4000 Ridgeline Dr., Austin, TX 78731
Connelly, James N., O'Hara Residence, 69 O'Hara Rd., Tonawanda, NY 14150
Conniff, John J., 1088 Delaware Ave., Buffalo, NY 14209
Coughlin, Joseph F., Queen of Heaven Rectory, 4220 Seneca St., West Seneca, NY 14224
Cronin, Paul T., Sheehan Residence, 330 Linwood Ave., Buffalo, NY 14209
Crumlish, Richard C., 1974 Seneca St., Buffalo, NY 14210
Dawidziak, Stanley J., 6796 Woodland Dr., Hamburg, NY 14075
Duggan, John M., 127 Keil St., N. Tonawanda, NY 14120
Englehardt, Herbert G., 43 Circle End Dr., West Seneca, NY 14224
Faiola, Samuel J., 72B Lexington Ct., Lockport, NY 14094
Gernatt, David A., 11742 Markham Rd., Gowanda, NY 14070
Hammerl, Leo E., O'Hara Residence, 69 O'Hara Rd., Tonawanda, NY 14783-0224
Hanna, Francis J., Brothers of Mercy, 10570 Bergtold Rd., Clarence, NY 14031-2198
Jasinski, Anthony J., 950 Losson Rd., South Cheektowaga, NY 14227
Joseph, Joseph D., 10537 Oldro Hill Rd., Steamburg, NY 14783-0224
Juenker, Paul R., O'Hara Residence, 69 O'Hara Rd., Tonawanda, NY 14150
Kazmierczak, Edward L., 32 Gregory Dr., West Seneca, NY 14224
Kempczynski, John, St. Timothy Rectory, 565 East Park Dr., Tonawanda, NY 14150
Klein, Stanley H., Chap. Col., 11 Philip Dr., Buffalo, NY 14227
Krajewski, Walter M., Brookview Condominiums, 1108-22 Indian Church Rd., W., Seneca, NY 14224
Kreuzer, Gerald J., Most Precious Blood Rectory, 22 Prospect St., Angola, NY 14006
Krupa, Francis A., 5829 Shoreham Dr., Lakeview, NY 14085
Lackovic, Stephen F., Our Lady of Bistrica, 1619 Abbott Rd., Lackawanna, NY 14218
LaRusch, Alton J., 132 E. Main St., Hamburg, NY 14075
Lombardo, Samuel L., 129 Laverack Ave., Lancaster, NY 14086
Lorenzetti, Dino J., 10 French Rd., Depew, NY 14043
Marcinkiewicz, Eugene V., St. Casimir Rectory, 160 Cable St., Buffalo, NY 14206
McHugh, John L., St. Amelia Rectory, 210 St. Amelia Dr., Tonawanda, NY 14150
Meloch, Chester A., 12 Christian Dr., Cheektowaga, NY 14225
Murphy, Robert E., Our Lady of Victory Basilica, 767 Ridge Rd., Lackawanna, NY 14218
O'Loughlin, Eugene E., St. Thomas Aquinas Rectory, 450 Abbott Rd., Buffalo, NY 14220-1796
Ormsby, Basil A., P.O. Box 4, Buffalo, NY 14240
Schwab, Robert C., 2160 N.E. 36th St., Apt. 49, Lighthouse Point, FL 33064
Schwinger, William A., 50 Franklin St., Buffalo, NY 14202
Setlock, William A., S. 4647, Southwestern Blvd., Apt. 206, Hamburg, NY 14075
Skupien, Francis M., 46 Mill St., Middleport, NY 14105-1018
Skupien, Joseph F., P.O. Box 287, N. Boston, NY 14110
Sobierajski, Edward J., O'Hara Residence, 69 O'Hara Rd., Tonawanda, NY 14150
Sorci, Francis P., 34 Loch Lee, Williamsville, NY 14221
Sutherland, William J., P.O. Box 106, Cassadaga, NY 14718
Swiatkowski, Francis M., O'Hara Residence, 69 O'Hara Rd., Tonawanda, NY 14150
Szabo, Julius J., O'Hara Residence, 69 O'Hara Rd., Tonawanda, NY 14150
Waclawski, Joseph P., 101 Swinburne St., Buffalo, NY 14212-9864
Walker, Edward J., 31 Stevenson St., Buffalo, NY 14220
Woods, Patrick J., c/o Harold O'Connor, 49 Landings Dr., Amherst, NY 14228-1479
Zak, Casimir A., O'Hara Residence, 69 O'Hara Rd., Tonawanda, NY 14150
Reverend Fathers—
Bilotta, Anthony J., 851 Washington Ave., Dunkirk, NY 14048
Bohn, Raymond G., Sheehan Residence, 330 Linwood Ave., Buffalo, NY 14209
Borowiak, Henry M., St. James Rectory, 496 Terrace Blvd., Depew, NY 14043
Bosack, Albert J., St. Joseph Rectory, 38 Lake Ave., Box 308, Lydonville, NY 14098
Coppola, Paul R., Rte. 3, Box 221 P, Interlachen, FL 32148
Cusimano, Salvatore J., Prince of Peace Rectory, 1040 Cayuga Rd., Niagara Falls, NY 14304
Czechowicz, Bernard J., Oceans Clover Leaf North, Four Oceans West Blvd., 206-C, Daytona Beach, FL 32118
Daley, James M., Quaker Towne Apartments, 150 Countryside Ln., Orchard Park, NY 14127
Fitzgerald, Donald J., Box 3100, Bonita Springs, FL 33959
Flynn, James P., Trocaire Place, 427 E. Main St., Batavia, NY 14020
Fox, John J., P.O. Box 852, Amherst, NY 14226
Gagliardo, Anthony F., P.O. Box 7184, Colorado Springs, CO 80933-7184
Gimbrone, Richard J., 157 Pennsylvania Ave., Buffalo, NY 14201
Gonter, Louis J., 9980 S.E. 161st Pl., Summerfield, FL 34491
Hall, Francis J., Sheehan Residence for Priests, 330 Linwood Ave., Buffalo, NY 14209
Haran, James E., 81 South St., Cattaraugus, NY 14719
Hennessey, John P., 1955 Eleventh St., S.W., Largo, FL 33778-1118
Hogan, Francis T., 2792 N. Breeze Rd., Melbourne, FL 32935
Hughes, Donald R., McAuley Residence, 2950 Elmwood Ave., Kenmore, NY 14217
Kasprzyk, James H., Our Lady of Czestochowa, 23 Willowlawn Pkwy., Buffalo, NY 14206
Kaukus, Edwin J., 245 Richmond Ave., Buffalo, NY 14222
Klos, Walter, Albertine Home, 1501 Hoffman St., Hammond, IN 46327
Kuntz, Aloysius G., Sheehan Residence, 330 Linwood Ave., Buffalo, NY 14209
Kwolek, Joseph, 580 Doat St., Buffalo, NY 14211
Lex, Henry V., Sheehan Residence, 330 Linwood Ave., Buffalo, NY 14209
Lowry, Joseph K., Jr., 124 Division St., Salamanca, NY 14779
Martlock, Loville N., Our Lady of Good Counsel Rectory, 10675 Allegany Rd., Darien Center, NY 14040
McCarthy, John P., 197 Southgate Rd., Buffalo, NY 14215
McGrath, James R., Ellicot Sta., P.O. Box 1292, Buffalo, NY 14205
Measer, Donald L., 2049 George Urban Blvd., Depew, NY 14043
Meegan, William H., 62 Eagan Dr., Lackawanna, NY 14218
Miller, Francis N., Our Lady of Victory Hospital, 55 Melroy St., Lackawanna, NY 14218
Naber, John T., P.O. Box 868, Buffalo, NY 14205-0868
O'Shea, John T., 3178 Merchant Rd., Warsaw, NY 14565
Paa, Joseph F., 21 Foxwood Row, Depew, NY 14043
Piazza, Salvatore J., 3743 Ridge Rd., Lockport, NY 14094
Priester, Robert E., Father Baker Manor, 6400 Powers Rd., Orchard Park, NY 14301
Pulikoottil, Abroham, 297 Collins Ave., West Seneca, NY 14224
Roche, Christopher J., Sheehan Residence, 330 Linwood Ave., Buffalo, NY 14209
Roche, David V., 1525 Sheridan Dr., Kenmore, NY 14217
Selzler, Norbert E., 5020 Carpenter Rd., Hamburg, NY 14075
Shepherd, Thomas N., 1140 Abbot Rd., Buffalo, NY 14220
Snyder, Clatus E., 101 Century Rd., Buffalo, NY 14215
Sokolowski, Bernard T., St. Josaphat Rectory, 20 Peoria Ave., Cheektowaga, NY 14206
Strassberger, H. Richard, 1917 11th St., Niagara Falls, NY 14305
Sweeney, Robert S., 302 Littletown Quarter, Williamsburg, VA 23185
Tomiak, Walter L., St. Elizabeth Home, 5539 Broadway, Lancaster, NY 14086
Vallone, Louis A., 7931 Villa Nova Dr., Boca Raton, FL 33433
Wagner, Eugene L., St. Charles Borromeo, 5969 Washington St., Olcott, NY 14126
Werth, Charles M., 108 Wellington Ct., Buffalo, NY 14221-6750
Wright, Vincent L., 10848 Bowen Rd., Attica, NY 14011
Zancan, Robert D., St. Michael's Community, 13270 Maple Dr., St. Louis, MO 63127

Permanent Deacons:
Barr, Joseph M.
Bauer, Robert A.
Boyd, Jimmie L., Sr.
Brick, Daniel E.
Bringenberg, Thomas B.
Bryant, Stanley W.
Burke, John H.
Burns, Robert E.
Burns, William R.
Calby, Edward T.
Carroll, Melvin W.
Collichio, James L.
Crimi, Victor
Cruz, Moises C.
Dains, Ronald
Darroch, Nelson
Edbauer, Howard J., Jr.
Eschbach, Lawrence D.
Farstad, Dan K.
Forcucci, Thomas M.
Fortuna, Chester J., M.D.
Foster, Norman E.
Fox, Albert F.
Friedman, Heinz H.
Fudala, Walter N.
Gainey, John C.
Gill, Joseph J.
Griesbaum, Charles J., Jr.
Hart, Thomas J.
Jerome, David R.
Kane, Joseph P.
Kapsiak, Dennis W.
Karnes, John R.
Kelly, John J.
Kelsey, Richard H.
Klein, George L.
Klein, John P.
Kopczynski, Michael R.
Krahling, Francis R.
Lankes, George A.
Lewandowski, Stephen J.
Mackowiak, Daniel H.
Mahaney, Richard J.
Maloney, Timothy
Marino, Benjamin
Markowski, Lawrence
May, Thaddeus P.
McKeating, Michael P.
Meister, Alan A.
Menke, Richard A.
Mercurio, Joseph P.
Miranda, Roberto G.
Molik, Daniel J.
Molnar, Alexander
Moses, Robert J.
O'Connell, Edward G.
Parker, Richard W.
Penksa, Daniel M.
Pijacki, Thaddeus V.
Podniesnski, Matthew A.
Polizzi, Frank S.
Polizzi, John A.
Prince, James A.
Radlinski, Donald
Ramos, Carlos W.
Santana, Reinaldo
Sarikey, Augustine
Schultz, Thomas E.
Shaunhnessey, Frank J.
Shultz, Donald W., Sr.
Slish, David P.
Stahl, Raymond H.
Steffen, Franklyn C.
Steinagle, Gordon J.
Stone, John G.
Suffoletto, Albert D.
Thomann, Bernard M.
Walders, Peter J.
Walek, Edward S.
Walker, Ronald
Walkowiak, Brian C.

Weisenburger, Paul F.
Wetter, Donald A.
Wick, John G.
Willis, William W.
Zwack, Francis A.
Zymanek, Caesar F.

INSTITUTIONS LOCATED IN THE DIOCESE

[A] SEMINARIES

BUFFALO. *Pope John II Residence*, 217 Winston Rd., 14216. Tel: 716-836-5526. Rev. Joseph C. Gatto, Acting Dir. Students 7; Priests 1; Total Staff 1.

EAST AURORA. *Christ the King Seminary*. Graduate School of Theology, 711 Knox Rd., P.O. Box 607, 14052. Tel: 716-652-8900. Interdiocesan Theologate. Owned and operated by the Diocese of Buffalo. Seminarians are assigned by the Bishop of any diocese for preparation for ordination to Priesthood. Administration and Faculty: Revs. Richard W. Siepka, M.A., S.T.L., Pres.-Rector; Joseph C. Gatto, S.T.D., Vice-Rector; Alfons M. Osiander, Th.D., Academic Dean; Mrs. Nancy Ehlers, Treas.; Mr. Joseph Roos, Dir. of Institutional Advancement; Rev. Bonaventure F. Hayes, O.F.M., M.A., S.T.L, M.L.S., Dir. Library; Sr. Jean Thompson, O.S.F., M.S. Counselor Ed., M.A., Registrar; Coordinator of Graduate Students. Faculty: Revs. Charles R. Amico, Ph.D., S.T.D.; Richard Cassidy, Ph.D.; Charles O'Connor, O.F.M., S.T.D.; Gabriel Scarfia, O.F.M., S.T.D.; Gregory Faulhaber, S.T.D.; Roger M. Haas, O.F.M. Conv., Ph.D.; Sr. Charlene Nowak, C.S.S.F., M.A.; Rev. Thomas Sheehan, O.F.M.; Sr. M. Tiburtia, Gorecki, F.S.S.J., M.L.S., Librarian; Rev. Peter Drilling, Th.D.; Dr. Susan Roll, Ph.D.; Rev. David Zwifka, M.A., J.C.D. Formation Faculty: Revs. Joseph Gatto; Gregory Faulhaber, S.T.D. Priests 13; Sisters 3; Lay Staff 17; Students 147; Total Staff 34.

[B] SEMINARIES, RELIGIOUS

YOUNGSTOWN. *St. Anthony Zaccaria Seminary*, Provincial Headquarters, 1023 Swann Rd., 14174. Tel: 716-754-7489; Fax: 716-754-9130. Revs. Paul M. Keeling, C.R.S.P.; Julio M. Ciavaglia, C.R.S.P., Shrine Dir., Prov. Supr, & Comm. Supr.; Ubaldo M. Fior, C.R.S.P.; Joseph M. Gariolo, C.R.S.P.; Luciano M. Visconti, C.R.S.P. The Barnabite Fathers staff the Shrine of Our Lady of Fatima. Priests 5; Students 2; Total Staff 28.

[C] COLLEGES AND UNIVERSITIES

BUFFALO. *Canisius College*, 2001 Main St., 14208-1098. Tel: 716-883-7000; Fax: 716-888-2525.
For a complete listing, refer to the Colleges and Universities section.

**D'Youville College*, 320 Porter Ave., 14201. Tel: 716-881-3200; Fax: 716-881-7780.
For a complete listing, refer to the Colleges and Universities section.

Trocaire College, 110 Red Jacket Pkwy., 14220. Tel: 716-826-1200.
For a complete listing, refer to the Colleges and Universities section.

Villa Maria College of Buffalo, 240 Pine Ridge Rd., 14225-3999. Tel: 716-896-0700; Fax: 716-896-0705.
For a complete listing, refer to the Colleges and Universities section.

HAMBURG. *Hilbert College*, 5200 S. Park Ave., 14075. Tel: 716-649-7900.
For a complete listing, refer to the Colleges and Universities section.

NIAGARA UNIVERSITY. *Niagara University*, Lewiston Rd., 14109-2016. Tel: 716-285-1212; Fax: 716-286-8355.
For a complete listing, refer to the Colleges and Universities section.

ST. BONAVENTURE. *St. Bonaventure University*, 14778. Tel: 716-375-2000; Fax: 716-375-2055.
For a complete listing, refer to the Colleges and Universities section.

[D] HIGH SCHOOLS, PRIVATE

BUFFALO. *Bishop Timon-St. Jude High School*, 601 McKinley Pkwy., 14220. Tel: 716-826-3610. Owned and operated by Bishop Timon Board of Trustees. Mr. Thomas J. Sullivan, Prin. Franciscans 2; Lay Teachers 31; Students 373.

Canisius High School, 1180 Delaware Ave., 14209. Tel: 716-882-0466; Fax: 716-883-1870. Society of Jesus. Revs. Charles F. Kelley, S.J., Pres.; David S. Ciancimino, S.J., Prin.; Louis T. Garaventa, S.J.; Joseph J. Kamiensky, S.J.; James R. Van Dyke, S.J.; Ronald W. Sams, S.J.; Richard J. Zanoni, S.J.; Eugene A. Zimpfer, S.J.; Bro. James T. Dennehy, S.J.; Mr. David McCallum, S.J. Priests 8; Brothers 1; Scholastic 1; Lay Teachers 44; Students 650; Total Staff 72.

Holy Angels' Academy, 24 Shoshone Dr., 14214-1097. Tel: 716-834-7120. Jo Anne Grippi, Prin. Priests 1; Grey Nuns of the Sacred Heart 7; Lay Teachers 25; Religious 2; Students 240; Total Staff 28.

Mt. Mercy Academy, 88 Red Jacket Pkwy., 14220. Tel: 716-825-8796. Sisters of Mercy. Mrs. Barbara E. Ochterski, Prin. Students 493; Total Staff 68.

Nardin Academy High School, 135 Cleveland Ave., 14222. Tel: 716-881-6262; Fax: 716-881-4190. Miss Barbara Rapier, D.H.M., Pres.; Rev. Jeffrey Sturmer, Chap. Lay Teachers 48; Girls 403.

St. Joseph's Collegiate Institute, 845 Kenmore Ave., 14223. Tel: 716-874-4024; Fax: 716-874-4956. Brothers of the Christian Schools. (De La Salle Christian Brothers). Rev. James Croglio, Chap. of School and Brothers' Community; Bros. Thomas Lackey, F.S.C., Prin.; Edward Martin, F.S.C., Community Dir. Priests 1; Brothers 5; Lay Teachers 49; Students 801; Total Staff 55.

Turner Carroll High School, 185 Lang Ave., 14215. Tel: 716-896-4911; Fax: 716-896-4947. Owned and operated by Turner/Carroll Board of Trustees. Sisters 1; Lay Teachers 17; Students 175.

Villa Maria Academy, 600 Doat St., 14211. Tel: 716-894-0398; Fax: 716-892-4177. Felician Sisters. Sr. Mary Kevin Szeluga, Prin.; Rev. Gregory J. Dobson, Chap. Sisters 16; Lay Teachers 20; Students 203; Total Staff 36.

ATHOL SPRINGS. *St. Francis High School*, 4129 Lake Shore Rd., 14010-0185. Tel: 716-627-1200; Fax: 716-627-4610. St. Anthony Province of the Order of Friars Minor Conventual. Revs. Robert Augustine Twele, OFM Conv., Prin.; Brad Heckathorne, OFM Conv., Asst. Prin.; Joseph Benicewicz, OFM Conv., Asst. Prin.; Aurelian Brzezniak, OFM Conv.; Charles Jagodzinski, OFM Conv.; Mark David Skura, OFM Conv.; Mark Thomas Booth, OFM Conv.; Felix Bracikowski, OFM Conv.; Bernard Olszewski, OFM Conv.; Roger Haas, OFM Conv.; Adrian Gallagher, OFM Conv.; Bro. Lawrence LaFlame, OFM Conv. Priests 9; Brothers 1; Sisters 3; Lay Teachers 37; Total Staff 49; Students 575.

BATAVIA. *Notre Dame High School of Batavia*, 73 Union St., 14020. Tel: 716-343-2783. Owned and operated by Notre Dame Board of Trustees. Mr. Frank C. Ferrando, Pres./Prin.; Mr. Lance Bennett, Asst. Prin.; Rev. Robert A. Martin. Priests 1; Lay Teachers 19; Students 174; Total Staff 20.

EGGERTSVILLE. *Buffalo Academy of the Sacred Heart*, 3860 Main St., 14226-3398. Tel: 716-834-2101. Sisters of St. Francis of Penance and Christian Charity. Sr. Edith Wyss, O.S.F., Prin. Sisters 12; Lay Teachers 29; Students 385.

HAMBURG. *Immaculata Academy*, 5138 S. Park Ave., 14075. Tel: 716-649-6161. Franciscan Sisters of St. Joseph. Sr. M. Paulette Tirone, Prin. Sisters 4; Lay Teachers 19; Students 156.

KENMORE. *Mt. St. Mary Academy*, 3756 Delaware Ave., 14217. Tel: 716-877-1358. Sisters of St. Mary of Namur. Mrs. Joan M. Spencer, Prin. Sisters 1; Lay Teachers 27; Girls 225; Day Care Center 130.

LANCASTER. *St. Mary's High School*, 142 Laverack Ave., 14086. Tel: 716-683-4824; Fax: 716-683-4996. Owned and operated by St. Mary's Board of Trustees. Miss Mary Sue Sciandra, Prin.; Mr. Lewiston Manuel, Assoc. Prin.; Mrs. Catherine Oldenburg, Asst. Prin.; Revs. Michael G. Uebler; John Mack. Priests 2; Sisters 1; Lay Teachers 31; Students 385; Total Staff 34.

NIAGARA FALLS. *Niagara Catholic Junior-Senior School*, 520-66th St., 14304. Tel: 716-774-8000. Owned and operated by Niagara Catholic Board of Trustees. Ronald K. Buggs, Prin.; Sr. M. Jacqueline Benbenek, C.S.S.F., Assoc. Prin. for Student Affairs; Ms. Antonia Pellegrino, Assoc. Prin. for Academic Affairs; Rev. Robert S. Hughson. Priests 2; Sisters 1; Lay Teachers 32; Students 393.

OLEAN. *Archbishop Walsh High School*, 208 N. 24th St., 14760. Tel: 716-372-8122. Owned and operated by Archbishop Walsh Board of Trustees. Ms. Mary Jane Telford, Prin.; Rev. Barry J. Allaire. Priests 1; Lay Teachers 15; Students 103.

TONAWANDA. *Cardinal O'Hara High School*, 39 O'Hara Rd., 14150. Tel: 716-695-2600. Owned and operated by Cardinal O'Hara Board of Trustees.

Cardinal O'Hara Residence, Faculty Residence, 69 O'Hara Rd., 14150. Rev. Merrick J. Bednar, Chap.; Mr. James E. Walline, Prin. Priests 1; Sisters 4; Lay Teachers 31; Students 342. Convent, 9 O'Hara Rd., 14150. Tel: 716-694-2370. Felician Sisters. Franciscan Missionary Sr. of the Divine Child.

[E] ELEMENTARY SCHOOLS, PRIVATE

BUFFALO. *Mount St. Joseph Academy*. Elementary Division: 2064 Main St., 14208. Tel: 716-883-1515. Mr. Theodore A. Callisto, Prin. Sisters 4; Lay Teachers 28; Students 320.

Nardin Academy, 135 Cleveland Ave., 14222. Tel: 716-881-6262. (Montessori-Grade 12).

LEWISTON. *Sacred Heart Villa School*. (Grades PreK-6), 5269 Lewiston Rd., 14092. Tel: 716-284-8273; Fax: 716-284-8273. Sr. Elizabeth Domin, S.S.H.J., Prin. Sisters 9; Lay Teachers 1; Students 105.

STELLA NIAGARA. *Stella Niagara Education Park*, 4421 Lower River Rd., 14144. Sisters of St. Francis of Penance and Christian Charity. Sr. Nicholas Macoretta, O.S.F. Sisters 9; Lay Teachers 18; Students 265.

[F] ELEMENTARY SCHOOLS, SPECIAL

BUFFALO. *Cantalician Center for Learning, Inc.*, 3233 Main St., 14214. Tel: 716-833-5353. Program for the disabled: Infant, Toddler and Preschool; Elementary and Secondary. Workshop for adult individuals with disabilities, day treatment-like program, & day habilitation for retired, disabled adults. Group homes/I.R.A. for adult individuals with disabilities. Sr. Patricia Tomasik, C.S.S.F., Exec. Dir.; Rev. Msgr. Harold Wagner, Chap. Priests 1; Brothers 1; Sisters 4; Laystaff 257; Students 474; Total Staff 263.

[G] REGIONAL AND CONSOLIDATED ELEMENTARY SCHOOLS

BUFFALO. *Catholic Academy of West Buffalo*. Delaware Campus: (Grades 3-8), 1069 Delaware Ave., 14209. Tel: 716-885-6111. Lafayette Campus: (Grades PreK-2), 279 Lafayette Ave., 14213. Tel: 716-886-5384. Miss Louise M. Myszka, Supervising Prin.; Sr. Gail Glenn, S.S.J., Bldg. Prin. (Delaware Campus); Mrs. Geraldine Kizielewicz, Bldg. Prin., (Lafayette Campus), Loretto Campus: Child Care Center, 301 14th St., 14213. Tel: 716-882-3071.
Sponsoring parishes: Annunciation, St. Anthony, Blessed Sacrament, Holy Angels, Holy Cross, Immaculate Conception, St. Joseph's Cathedral, St. Louis, St. Michael, Nativity, Our Lady of Loretto. Sisters 2; Lay Teachers 24; Students 429; Total Staff 26.

Catholic Central School. (Grades K-8), 476 Emslie St., 14212. Sr. Roberta Fulton, S.M.N.N., Prin.
Sponsoring parishes: St. Ann, Blessed Trinity, SS. Columba & Brigid, St. James, St. Mary of Sorrows, & St. Martin de Porres. Sisters 7; Lay Teachers 18; Students 335; Total Staff 25.

Our Lady of Black Rock, 16 Germain St., 14207. Tel: 716-873-7497. Sr. Mary Francianne Zielezinski, C.S.S.F., Prin.
Sponsoring parishes: Assumption, St. Florian, St. Francis Xavier, Coronation, St. Elizabeth, St. John the Baptist. Sisters 1; Lay Teachers 9; Students 183.

ATTICA. *Genesee-Wyoming Catholic Central Consolidated School*, 72 East Ave., 14011. Tel: 716-591-2515. Sr. M. Anthonille Tyczkowski, C.S.S.F., Prin.
Sponsoring parishes: Attica, St. Vincent; Bennington Center, Sacred Heart; Darien Center, Our Lady of Good Counsel; Java Center, St. Patrick; North Java, St. Nicholas; Sheldon, St. Cecelia; Varysburg, St. Joseph; Warsaw, St. Michael. Sisters 2; Lay Teachers 15; Students 141.

CHEEKTOWAGA. *Kolbe Catholic Regional School*, 120 Alexander Ave., 14211. Sr. M. Loriette, C.S.S.F., Prin.
Sponsoring parishes: St. Lawrence, Holy Name, St. Gerard, St. John Kanty, St. John Gualbert, Most Holy Redeemer. Lay Teachers 16; Students 236; Total Staff 17.

DEPEW. *SS. Peter & Paul Catholic School*, 52 Burlington Ave., 14043. Tel: 716-683-8049.
Sponsoring parishes: SS. Peter & Paul, Depew; Sacred Heart, Bowmansville. Sisters 1; Lay Teachers 14; Students 218; Total Staff 15.

DUNKIRK. *Northern Chautauqua Catholic*, 336 Washington Ave., 14048. Tel: 716-366-0630. Mary E. Margerum, Prin.
Sponsoring parishes: Brocton, St. Patrick; Dunkirk: St. Elizabeth Ann Seton, St. Hedwig, Holy Trinity; Fredonia: St. Anthony, St. Joseph Newman Center; Silver Creek: Our Lady of Mt. Carmel. Lay Teachers 15; Students 194.

LAKE VIEW. *Southtowns Catholic*, 2052 Lakeview Rd., Box 86, 14085. Tel: 716-627-5011. Sr. M. Diane Miller, C.S.S.F., Prin.
Sponsoring Parishes: St. Vincent de Paul, North Evans; Our Lady of Perpetual Help, Lake View. Sisters 2; Lay Teachers 23; Students 258; Total Staff 25.

LOCKPORT. *DeSales Catholic School*, 6914 Chestnut School, 14094. Tel: 716-433-6422. Sr. Roberta Thoen, S.S.M.N. Sisters 2; Lay Teachers 33; Students 623; Total Staff 35.

NORTH TONAWANDA. *North Tonawanda Catholic*. Ascension Campus: (Grades 6-8), 75 Keil St., 14120. Tel: 716-693-2828. Sr. Rosemarie Kutsko, C.S.S.F., Supervising Prin., OLC Campus: (Grades PreK-2), 57 Center Ave., 14120. Tel: 716-694-3644. St. Joseph Campus: (Grades 3-5), 1469 Payne Ave., 14120. Tel: 716-693-4769. Mrs. Diane Vigrass, Bldg. Prin.
Sponsoring parishes: Ascension, Our Lady of Czestochowa, St. Albert the Great and St. Joseph.

Sisters 3; Lay Teachers 22; Students 286; Total Staff 25.

OLEAN. *Southern Tier Catholic*, 205 W. Henley St., 14760. Tel: 716-372-2891. Mr. Lawrence D. Ford, Sr., Prin.
Sponsoring parishes: Allegany, St. Bonaventure; Cuba, Our Lady of the Angels; Hinsdale, St. Helen; Portville, Sacred Heart; Olean, St. Mary of the Angels, St. John, Transfiguration; Vandalia, St. John the Baptist. Lay Teachers 17; Students 214; Total Staff 21.

[H] CATHOLIC CHARITIES

BUFFALO. *The Catholic Charities of the Diocese of Buffalo*, 525 Washington St., 14203. Tel: 716-856-4494. Rev. Msgr. Henry J. Gugino, Diocesan Dir.
Central Office: All Offices, Directors, and Supervisors are located at 525 Washington St., Buffalo, NY 14203, unless otherwise indicated.
Finance Dept. Theodore S. Lesinski, Comptroller. Tel: 716-856-4494; Mrs. Margaret Connors, Admin. Asst.
Catholic Charities Manpower Services. Rev. Msgr. Henry J. Gugino, Exec. Dir. Tel: 716-856-4494.
Department of Metropolitan Services. Mr. Michael V. Avanzato, Dir. Tel: 716-856-4494 Ext. 3045.
Central Intake. Mrs. Kathryn Heavey, Supvr.
Parish Social Work Program, 188 Oakmont Ave., 14215. Tel: 716-835-6894. Jesselyn Garcia, Supvr.
Black Rock/Riverside Office, 819 Tonawanda St., 14207. Tel: 716-877-4716.
West Side Family Counseling Center, 412 Niagara St., 14201. Tel: 716-854-3622.
Lackawanna Family Counseling Center, 33-37 Wilkesbarre Ave., Lackawanna, 14218. Tel: 716-822-6877.
Preventative Services & Batterer's Intervention Program, 1581 Bailey Ave., 14212. Tel: 716-896-6390. Diane Greenaway, Coord. Legal Title: *Preventative Services and Batterer's Intervention Program, and Therapeutic Supervised Visitation Program.*
School Intervention Service, 3370 Delaware Ave., Kenmore, 14217. Tel: 716-877-8822. Adele Wawrzynek, Supvr., 9 E. Union, P.O. Box 94, Hamburg, 14075. Tel: 716-648-6515. Linda Dinger, Supvr., 3719 Union Rd., Ste. 214, Cheektowaga, 14225. Tel: 716-681-7394. Sara Murphy, Supvr., 4498 Main St., Amherst, 14226. Tel: 716-839-4066. Maria Picone, Supvr.
Department of Manpower & Educational Services, 33 Main St., P.O. Box 33, Bowmansville, 14026. Tel: 716-685-3400. Michael Talluto, Dir.
Day Care Services. Tel: 716-856-4494.
Diocesan Resettlement Division, 73 Edward St., 14203. Tel: 716-842-6816. Ann Brittain, Supvr.
Youth Careers Program, 33 Main St., P.O. Box 33, Bowmansville, 14026. Tel: 716-685-3400.
Department of Parish Based Social Services. Tel: 716-856-4494. Sr. Mary Anne Weldon, R.S.M., Dir.
Parish Outreach Program.
Office of Pastoral Ministry With Handicapped Persons. Tel: 716-856-4494. Sr. Rose Mary Cauley, G.N.S.H., Supvr.
South Chautauqua Elderly Project, 116 Aldren Ave., Jamestown, 14701. Tel: 716-665-4374. Claire Trubits, Supvr.
Department of District Services. Tel: 716-856-4494. Mr. Leonard J. Haefner, Dir.
Adoptions, Child Care Division, and Young Parents Program. Miss Mary M. Horrigan, Supvr.
Batavia, 113-119 Main St., Batavia, 14020. Tel: 716-343-0614. Mrs. Margaret Meyer, Supvr.
Dunkirk, 173 Lakeshore Dr. E., Dunkirk, 14048. Tel: 716-366-3533. Randy Hulbert, Supvr. Dunkirk & Jamestown.
Jamestown, 413 N. Main St., Jamestown, 14701. Tel: 716-484-9188.
Niagra Falls, 345 Third St., Ste. 515, Niagra Falls, 14303. Tel: 716-282-2351. Kathleen Hall, Supvr.
Olean, 520 W. State St., P.O. Box 554, Olean, 14140. Tel: 716-372-0101. Mrs. Kim Moricca, Supvr.
Women, Infants & Children (W.I.C) of Niagra County, 237 Fourth St., Niagra Falls, 14303. Tel: 716-285-0975. Mrs. Claudia Weber, Coord.
Catholic Charities Satellite Offices: Blackrock-Riverside: 819 Tonawanda St., 14207. Tel: 716-877-4716. East Side: 1581 Bailey Ave., 14212. Tel: 716-896-6390. Grider St.: 359 Grider St., 14215. Tel: 716-895-7715. Oakmont Ave.: 188 Oakmont Ave., 14215. Tel: 716-835-6894. Perry St.: 488 Perry St., 14204. Tel: 716-856-4456. South Buffalo: 2315 Seneca St., 14210. Tel: 716-821-1929. Albion: 243 S. Main St., Albion, 14411. Tel: 716-589-7477. Amherst: 4498 Main St., Amherst, 14226. Tel: 716-839-4066. Cheektowaga: 3719 Union Rd., Cheektowaga, 14225. Tel: 716-681-7394. Hamburg: 9 E. Union St., 14075. Tel: 716-648-6515. Kenmore: 3370 Delaware Ave., Kenmore, 14217. Tel: 716-877-8822. Lockport: 39 East Ave., Lockport, 14094. Tel: 716-433-0246. North Tonawanda: 74 Webster St., North Tonawanda, 14120. Tel: 716-692-1440. Southtowns Office: 34 Barnstead Dr., Springville, 14141. Tel: 716-592-3420. Warsaw: 2-10 W. Buffalo St., Warsaw, 14569. Tel: 716-786-3440. Wellsville: 25 E. Pearl St., Wellsville, 14895. Tel: 716-595-2015. West Seneca: 4105 Seneca St., West Seneca, 14224. Tel: 716-675-3785.
Catholic Charities Appeal, 525 Washington St., 14203. Tel: 716-856-4494. Rev. Msgr. Henry J. Gugino, Diocesan Dir.; Rev. Joseph J. Sicari, Assoc. Dir.
Department of Clinical Services. Christopher J. Pino, Ph.D., Dir.
Marriage Counseling Center, 525 Washington St., 14203. Tel: 716-856-4494. David Catalano, Supvr.
St. Joseph's Day Training Center, 930 Fillmore Ave., 14211. Tel: 716-896-6038. Marsha Sladeski, Ph.D., Supvr.
Developmental Disabilities/Family Support Program, 359 Grider St., 14215. Tel: 716-895-7715. Maryruth Morris, R.N.
Diocesan Counseling Service for Clergy and Religious, 16 Columbus St., Cheektowaga, 14227. Tel: 716-894-2743. Sr. Anne Marie Jablonicky, C.S.S.F., Dir.
Chemical Dependency Program, Substance Abuse Prevention & Counseling Program. Tel: 716-835-9745. Judith Vogtli, Ph.D., Dir.
Geriatrics Outreach Treatment Team, 359 Grider St., 14215. Tel: 716-895-7715. Suzanna Mattingly, Supvr.
Department of Services to the Aging. Tel: 716-856-4494. Ms. Mary Jo Giambelluca, Dir.
Home Care Services. Deborah Alberth, R.N., Supvr.
Family Focus Program, 30 Rich St., 14211. Tel: 716-896-8262. Kathleen Pharris, Supvr.
Senior Day Center, 30 Rich St., 14211. Tel: 716-896-6388. Mrs. Kathleen Pharris, Dir.
Housing and Supportive Services. Tel: 716-856-4494. Mrs. Marie Bakowski, Supvr.; Deborah Alberth, R.N., Supvr.
Foster Grandparents Program, 525 Washington St., 14203. Tel: 716-856-4494. Dorothy Turchiarelli, Supvr.
Friendly Phones, 525 Washington St., 14203. Tel: 718-856-4494. Dorothy Turchiarelli, Supvr.
Department of Institutional Services to Aging, 525 Washington St., 14203. Tel: 716-856-4494. Carol Kennedy, R.N., Dir.
Volunteer Agencies:
Catholic Guild for the Blind. Tel: 716-856-4494. Sr. Rosemary Cauley, Prog. Dir.
Guild of St. Apollonia. Tel: 716-856-4494. Rev. Msgr. Henry J. Gugino, Spiritual Dir.
Ladies of Charity, 1122 Broadway, 14212. Tel: 716-895-4001. Rev. Msgr. Henry J. Gugino; Mrs. Eileen Nowak, Prog. Dir.
Society of St. Vincent de Paul, 72 E. Huron St., 14203. Tel: 716-852-7415. Rev. Msgr. Henry J. Gugino, Spiritual Dir.; Mr. Mark S. Zirnheld, Dir.
Delta Development Low Income Housing Development & Management, 525 Washington St., 14203. Tel: 716-856-4494. Janet Meiselman, Supvr. Total Assisted 418; Total Staff 35.

[I] ORPHANAGES AND INFANT HOMES

BUFFALO. *German Roman Catholic Orphan Home*, 795 Main St., 14203.
For a complete listing, refer to the Special Care Facilities section.

[J] PROTECTIVE INSTITUTES

BUFFALO. *The Franciscan Center, Inc.*, 1910 Seneca St., 14210-1842. Tel: 716-822-8017.
For a complete listing, refer to the Special Care Facilities section.

LACKAWANNA. *Baker Victory Services*, 780 Ridge Rd., 14218. Tel: 716-828-9500.
For a complete listing, refer to the Special Care Facilities section.
Our Lady of Victory Infant Home, 790 Ridge Rd., 14218. Tel: 716-828-9500.
For a complete listing, refer to the Special Care Facilities section.

[K] GENERAL HOSPITALS

BUFFALO. *McAuley Mercy Corporation*, 515 Abbott Rd., 14220. Tel: 716-828-2750.
For a complete listing, refer to the Hospitals section.
Mercy Health System of Western New York. Marian Professional Center, 515 Abbott Rd., Ste. 508, 14220. Tel: 716-828-2750.
For a complete listing, refer to the Hospitals section.
Mercy Hospital, 565 Abbott Rd., 14220. Tel: 716-826-7000.
For a complete listing, refer to the Hospitals section.
Sisters Hospital Foundation, Inc., 2130 Main St., 14214. Tel: 716-862-2533.
For a complete listing, refer to the Hospitals section.
Sisters of Charity Hospital of Buffalo, NY, 2157 Main St., 14214. Tel: 716-862-1000; Fax: 716-862-1899.
For a complete listing, refer to the Hospitals section.

BATAVIA. *St. Jerome Hospital*, 16 Bank St., 14020. Tel: 716-343-3131.
For a complete listing, refer to the Hospitals section.

CHEEKTOWAGA. *McAuley-Seton Home Care*, 14 Apple Tree Business Park, 14227. Tel: 716-685-4870.
For a complete listing, refer to the Hospitals section.
St. Joseph Hospital, 2605 Harlem Rd., 14225-4097. Tel: 716-891-2400; Fax: 716-891-2616.
For a complete listing, refer to the Hospitals section.

KENMORE. *Kenmore Mercy Foundation Inc.*, 2950 Elmwood Ave., 14217. Tel: 716-879-6204.
For a complete listing, refer to the Hospitals section.
Kenmore Mercy Hospital, 2950 Elmwood Ave., 14217. Tel: 716-447-6100; Fax: 716-447-6090.
For a complete listing, refer to the Hospitals section.

LACKAWANNA. *Our Lady of Victory Hospital*, 55 Melroy at Ridge Rd., 14218. Tel: 716-825-8000; Fax: 716-825-4681.
For a complete listing, refer to the Hospitals section.
Our Lady of Victory Hospital Auxiliary, 55 Melroy Ave., 14218. Tel: 716-825-8000.
For a complete listing, refer to the Hospitals section.

LEWISTON. *Mount St. Mary's Hospital of Niagara Falls*, 5300 Military Rd., 14092-1997. Tel: 716-297-4800.
For a complete listing, refer to the Hospitals section.

LOCKPORT. *Niagara Homemaker Services, dba Mercy Home Care of Western New York*, 111 Main St., 14094. Tel: 716-434-2388.
For a complete listing, refer to the Hospitals section.

[L] HEALTH CARE FACILITIES

BUFFALO. *St. Francis Geriatric & Healthcare Services, Inc.*, 2787 Main St., 14214. Tel: 716-837-4200; Fax: 716-837-2924.
For a complete listing, refer to the Special Care Facilities section.

[M] HOMES FOR AGED

BUFFALO. *Nazareth Nursing Home*, 291 North St., 14201. Tel: 716-881-2323.
For a complete listing, refer to the Special Care Facilities section.

BATAVIA. *St. Luke Manor*, 17 Wiard St., 14020. Tel: 716-343-8806.
For a complete listing, refer to the Special Care Facilities section.

CLARENCE. *Brothers of Mercy Housing Co., Inc.*, 10500 Bergtold Rd., 14031. Tel: 716-795-2122.
For a complete listing, refer to the Special Care Facilities section.
Brothers of Mercy Nursing & Rehabilitation Center, 10570 Bergtold Rd., 14031. Tel: 716-759-6985.
For a complete listing, refer to the Special Care Facilities section.
Brothers of Mercy Sacred Heart Home, Inc., 4520 Ransom Rd., 14031. Tel: 716-759-2644.
For a complete listing, refer to the Special Care Facilities section.

DUNKIRK. *St. Vincent's Home for the Aged*, 319 Washington Ave., 14048. Tel: 716-366-2066; Fax: 716-366-0545.
For a complete listing, refer to the Special Care Facilities section.

KENMORE. *KMH Homes, Inc.*. Administrative Offices, 2950 Elmwood Ave., 14217.
For a complete listing, refer to the Special Care Facilities section.

LANCASTER. *St. Elizabeth's Home*, 5539 Broadway, 14086. Tel: 716-683-5150; Fax: 716-683-4049.
For a complete listing, refer to the Special Care Facilities section.

LOCKPORT. *St. Clare Manor*, 543 Locust St., 14094 Fax: 716-434-5900.
For a complete listing, refer to the Special Care Facilities section.

NIAGARA FALLS. *Mount St. Mary's LTC Facility, Inc.*, 2600 Main St., 14305.
For a complete listing, refer to the Special Care Facilities section.
St. Mary's Manor, 515 Sixth St., 14301.
For a complete listing, refer to the Special Care Facilities section.

OLEAN. *St. Joseph Manor*, 2211 W. State St., 14760 Fax: 716-373-4375.
For a complete listing, refer to the Special Care Facilities section.

ORCHARD PARK. *W.N.Y. Catholic LongTerm Care, Inc. dba Father Baker Manor*, 6400 Powers Rd., 14127. Tel: 716-667-0001.
For a complete listing, refer to the Special Care Facilities section.

SILVER CREEK. *St. Columbans on the Lake, Home for the Aged*, 2546 Lake Rd., 14136. Tel: 716-934-4515.
For a complete listing, refer to the Special Care Facilities section.

WILLIAMSVILLE. *Holy Family Home*, 410 Mill St., 14221. Tel: 716-634-5400.
For a complete listing, refer to the Special Care Facilities section.
St. Francis Home of Williamsville, 147 Reist St., 14221. Tel: 716-633-5400; Fax: 716-663-6404.

For a complete listing, refer to the Special Care Facilities section.

[N] DAY CARE CENTERS

BUFFALO. *Guardian Angel Day Care Center*, 1193 Delaware Ave., 14209. Dana M. Cassiano, Admin. Lay Staff 16; Children 72; Total Staff 17.

Holy Innocents Day Care Center, 30 Rich St., 14211. Tel: 716-896-6386. Mrs. Ann Marie Zaccarine, Dir. Day care for children age 6 weeks to 12 yrs. Total Staff 19.

[O] MONASTERIES AND RESIDENCES OF PRIESTS AND BROTHERS

BUFFALO. *Bishop's Residence*, 77 Oakland Pl., 14222. Most Rev. Henry J. Mansell, D.D.; Rev. Msgr. Robert J. Cunningham; Rev. Msgr. Peter J. Popadick; Rev. Paul A. Litwin.

Canisius Jesuit Community, 2001 Main St., 14208. Tel: 716-883-7000. Legal Title: *The Jesuits of Canisius College, Inc.* Revs. James J. Ruddick, S.J.; Richard J. Hoar, S.J., Min.; William C. Carroll, S.J.; Bro. Thomas J. Casey, S.J.; Revs. David S. Ciancimino, S.J.; J. Peter Conroy, S.J.; Vincent M. Cooke, S.J.; Bro. James T. Dennehy, S.J.; Revs. James L. Dugan, S.J.; Paul J. Dugan, S.J.; Edward T. Dunn, S.J.; Benjamin Fiore, S.J.; Thomas E. Fleming, S.J.; Richard H. Galligan, S.J.; Louis T. Garaventa, S.J.; John J. Garvey, S.J.; Robert A. Haus, S.J.; James P. Higgins, S.J.; Daniel P. Jamros, S.J.; Ladislaus F. Juhasz, S.J. (Hungary); Joseph J. Kamiensky, S.J.; Charles F. Kelley, S.J.; Mark G. Kriz, S.J.; Daniel P. Liderbach, S.J.; Patrick J. Lynch, S.J.; Paul J. McCarthy, S.J.; Martin X. Moleski, S.J.; Paul W. Nochelski, S.J.; Thomas A. O'Connor, S.J.; Michael H. Pastizzo, S.J.; Frederick J. Reisert, S.J.; Ronald W. Sams, S.J.; Brendan T. Scott, S.J.; Edward P. Sullivan, S.J.; Michael F. Tunney, S.J.; James R. Van Dyke, S.J.; Eugene Zimpfer, S.J.; Daniel J. Lusch, S.J., Elmwood 4, 4845 Transit Rd., 14043. Rev. Harry A. Reese, S.J., U.S. Dept. of Housing & Urban Devel., 16 Spindrift Ct., #4, 14221. Total in Residence 40; Total Staff 15.

Maryknoll House, 71 Jewett Pkwy., 14214-2396. Tel: 716-834-6065. Revs. Douglas May, M.M., Dir.; Richard S. Kardian, M.M. Total in Residence 2; Total Staff 2.

Sheehan Residence for Priests, 330 Linwood Ave., 14209-1689. Tel: 716-884-0053. Residence for retired priests. Revs. Robert J. Biesinger; Raymond G. Bohn; Rev. Msgr. Paul T. Cronin; Revs. Francis J. Hall; Aloysius G. Kuntz; Henry V. Lex; Christopher J. Roche.

ATHOL SPRINGS. *Father Justin Rosary Hour Radio Apostolate*, St. Anthony of Padua Friary, 4190 St. Francis Dr., 14010. Tel: 716-627-3861; Fax: 716-627-4059. Revs. Marion M. Tolczyk, O.F.M.Conv., Guardian & Dir.; Lucian Krolikowski, O.F.M.Conv.; Eligius Kozak, O.F.M.Conv. (Poland); Walter Mezyk, O.F.M.Conv. (Poland). Staff to the Rosary Apostolate: Sr. Mary Angelica Bielski, C.S.S.F., Executive Secretary; Sr. Mary Rosette Kubisty, C.S.S.F.

St. Francis of Assisi Friary, 4129 Lake Shore Rd., 14010-0185. Tel: 716-627-5762; Fax: 716-627-4610. Faculty Residence for St. Francis High School. Revs. Robert Augustine Twele, O.F.M.Conv., Guardian & Prin.; Aurelian W. Brzezniak, O.F.M.Conv.; Bernard Olszewski, O.F.M.Conv.; Charles Jagodzinski, O.F.M.Conv.; Felix Bracikowski, O.F.M.Conv.; Mark David Skura, O.F.M.Conv., Vicar; Joseph Benicewicz, O.F.M.Conv.; Roger Haas, O.F.M.Conv.; Brad Heckathorne, O.F.M.Conv.; Mark Thomas Booth, O.F.M.Conv.; Adrian Gallagher, O.F.M.Conv.; Bros. Lawrence LaFlame, O.F.M.Conv.; Paschal Kolodziej, O.F.M.Conv. Priests 11; Brothers 2; Total in Residence 13.

CLARENCE. *Provincial Motherhouse of Brothers of Mercy*, 4520 Ransom Rd., 14031. Tel: 716-759-8341. Legal Title: *Brothers of Mercy, Inc.* Bro. Jude Holzfoerster, F.M.M., Prov.; Rev. John J. Sardina, Chap. Brothers 14; In Formation 4.

DERBY. *Piarist Fathers*, 6472 Lake Shore Rd., Box 786, 14047. Tel: 716-947-4412. Revs. Alphonse Vercek, Sch.P.; Kalman Miskolczy, Sch.P., Supr.; Nicholas Vitez Fodor, Sch.P. Total in Residence 3; Total Staff 2.

Society of St. Paul Provincial Residence, 6746 Lake Shore Rd., Box 757, 14047. Tel: 716-947-5407; Fax: 716-947-5407. Very Rev. Jeffrey Mickler, S.S.P., Prov. Supr.; Revs. Anthony C. Warren, S.S.P., Vice Prov.; Francis J. Parella, S.S.P., Prov. Sec. Priests 2; Brothers 1.

LEROY. *Order of the BVM of Mercy/Mercedarian Friars*, Mercygrove, 7758 E. Main Rd., 14482-9701. Tel: 716-768-7110; Fax: 716-768-4803. United States headquarters for the community. Pre-novitiate and Novitiate formation community. Very Rev. Marino Frascati, O.de.M., Vicar Prov. & Local Supr.; Revs. Jerome Laubacker, O.de.M., Dir. of Retreats; Michael Rock, O.de.M., Postulant Master; James Mayer, O.de.M., Novice Master. Total in Community: Professed Religious 4; Novices 5; Postulants 9.

St. Raymond Nonnatus Novitiate. Order of the BVM of Mercy. Mercygrove, 7758 E. Main Rd., 14482-9701. Tel: 716-768-7110. Rev. James Mayer, O.de.M., Novice Master. Novices 5.

NIAGARA FALLS. *Catholic Worker Center*, 931 Niagara Ave., 14305. Tel: 716-282-8683. Jim Serafin, Exec. Dir.

NIAGARA UNIVERSITY. *Vincentian Community at Niagara University*, Meade Hall, 14109-2209. Tel: 716-286-8110; Fax: 716-286-8766.
E-Mail: meade@niagara.edu
Revs. John A. Kettleberger, C.M., Supr.; Joseph G. Hubbert, C.M., Asst.; Bro. Augustine D. Towey, C.M., Sub-Asst.; Revs. Patrick S.L. Flanagan, C.M., Procurator; John C. Bowes, C.M.; Edward J. Burke, C.M.; Kevin G. Creagh, C.M.; Peter A. Fitzgerald, C.M.; Paul L. Golden, C.M.; William L. Green, C.M.; Thomas P. Mallaghan, C.M.; Thomas P. McGourty, C.M.; Daniel F. O'Leary, O.M.I.; Vincent J. O'Malley, C.M.; Martin J. Sleasman, C.M.; John J. Trainor, C.M.; Louis P. Trotta, C.M.; Michael J. Tumulty, C.M.; Hugo M. Vascones, C.M.; Bros. Stephen J. Kennedy, C.M.; Martin J. Schneider, C.M.

NORTH TONAWANDA. *Society of the Catholic Apostolate.* Infant Jesus Delegature, 3452 Niagara Falls Blvd., P.O. Box 563, 14120-0563. Tel: 716-694-4313. Revs. Anthony Zemula, S.A.C., Supr. & Prov. Delegate; Francis A. Cegielka, S.A.C., Shrine Dir.; Jan B. Posiewala, S.A.C.; Andrzej Kurowski, S.A.C.; Seweryn J. Koszyk, S.A.C.; Benedict Barszcz, S.A.C.; Slavomir Siok, S.A.C.; George Poltorak, S.A.C. Chaplains, VA Hospital: Revs. Ignatius Curzydlo, S.A.C.; George Maj, S.A.C.

ST. BONAVENTURE. *St. Bonaventure Friary*, 14778. Tel: 716-375-2000; Fax: 716-375-2424. Bro. Anthony J. LoGalbo, O.F.M., Vicar; Revs. Jack Zibert, O.F.M., Guardian; Michael Blastic, O.F.M.Conv.; David D. Blake, O.F.M.; Thomas Blow, O.F.M.Conv.; J. Gregory Brennan, O.F.M.; Joel A. Campbell, O.F.M.; Anthony M. Carrozzo, O.F.M.; Mathias F. Doyle; Regis A. Duffy, O.F.M.; Richard C. Flaherty, O.F.M.; Gedeon Gal, O.F.M.; Romuald Green, O.F.M. (Australia); Cyprian J. Lynch, O.F.M.; Francis Storms, O.F.M., Treas.; Peter Schneible, O.F.M.; Robert Stewart, O.F.M.; Alphonsus A. Trabold, O.F.M.; Allen Weber, O.F.M.; Gervase White, O.F.M.; Robert H. White, O.F.M.; Bros. Thomas Cole, O.F.M.; David Haack, O.F.M.; Michael W. Montgomery, O.F.M.; Adrian A. Riester, O.F.M.; Julian Riester, O.F.M.; Basil J. Valente, O.F.M. Fathers 21; Brothers 7.

TONAWANDA. *O'Hara Residence*, 69 O'Hara Rd., 14150. Tel: 716-743-0037. Rev. Msgr. James N. Connelly; Rev. Msgr. Leo E. Hammerl; Rev. Msgr. Paul R. Juenker, P.A.; Rev. Msgr. Edward J. Sobierojski; Rev. Msgr. Francis M. Swiatkowski; Rev. Msgr. Julius J. Szabo; Rev. Msgr. Casimir A. Zak. Total in Residence 6; Total Staff 3.

WEST SENECA. *St. Bonaventure*, 36 Flahr Ave., 14224-1818. Tel: 716-823-1090. Revs. Benoit Drapeau, C.J.M., Pastor; Ronald M. Bagley, C.J.M., Dir. St. John Eudes Center; Robert J. Perelli, C.J.M., AIDS Family Services; J. Gregory Sampson, C.J.M., Supr.; Louis Levesque, C.J.M. Total in Residence 5; Total Staff 5.

[P] CONVENTS AND RESIDENCES FOR SISTERS

BUFFALO. *Congregation of the Sisters of St. Joseph Generalate.* Total in Residence 79; Total Staff 39. Administrative Offices, 23 Agassiz Cir., 14214. Tel: 716-838-4400. Professed Sisters 158.

Discalced Carmelite Monastery of St. Teresa of the Child Jesus (1920), 75 Carmel Rd., 14214. Tel: 716-837-6499. Mother Marie Therese of the Child Jesus, O.C.D., Prioress. Cloistered Professed Sisters 16; Extern Professed Sisters 3; Novices 2.

Immaculate Heart of Mary Provincial House and Convent. Villa Maria, 600 Doat St., 14211. Tel: 716-892-4141. Sr. Mary Raymond Kasprzak, C.S.S.F., Prov. Min.; Revs. Donald E. Levan, Provincial House Chap.; Joseph Kwolek, Infirmary Chap. Felician Sisters 317.

Monastery of Our Lady of the Rosary. Dominican Nuns of the Perpetual Rosary, 335 Doat St., 14211-2199. Tel: 716-892-0066. Contemplative Dominican Nuns of the Perpetual Rosary. Mother Rose of St. Mary, O.P., Prioress; Rev. Jacob Restrick, O.P., Chap. Dominican Nuns of the Perpetual Rosary 30; Total in Residence 30.

Mount Mercy Convent, 625 Abbott Rd., 14220. Tel: 716-826-6192. Total in Residence 26.

St. Mary's Convent, 138 Wesley St., 14214. Tel: 716-837-5816. Sisters of St. Mary of Namur. Professed Sisters 3.

Sisters of Social Service District Residence, 440 Linwood Ave., 14209. Tel: 716-883-0112. Sr. Angela Homoki-Szabo, S.S.S., District Moderator. Sisters 9.
Other Convents: Generalate Res. and Novitiate, 296 Summit Ave., 14214. Tel: 716-834-0197. Sr. Anne Lehner, S.S.S., Gen. Moderator. Sisters 5. Scholastica House, 210 Winston Rd., 14216. Tel: 716-833-7412. Sisters 2; Sisters Living Alone 2; Sisters in Other Religious Retirement Homes 1.

Sisters of St. Mary, 250 Bryant St., 14222. Tel: 716-884-8221; Fax: 716-884-2950. Provincial House of the Sisters of St. Mary of Namur. Sr. Maureen Quinn, S.S.M.N., Prov. Supr.; Sr. Barbara Riter, S.S.M.N., Prov. Councillor. Professed Sisters 110.

ALLEGANY. *St. Elizabeth's Motherhouse*, 14706. Tel: 716-373-0200; Fax: 716-372-5774. Motherhouse of the Franciscan Sisters of Allegany. Sr. Margaret Mary Kimmins, O.S.F., Gen. Min.; Sr. Marigene Kennedy, O.S.F., Local Min.; Sr. Patricia Perry, O.S.F., Local Min. Sisters 95; Total Staff 15.

BELMONT. *Immaculate Conception Convent*, R.F.D. 1, Box 19, 14813. Franciscan Missionary Sisters of the Divine Child. Conducts catechetical centers in 7 villages. Sr. Rosemary Benson, Supr. Sisters 2.

CLARENCE. *Sisters of St. Joseph.* Clarence Residence, 4975 Strickler Rd., 14031. Tel: 716-759-6893. Coordinators: Sr. Marian Schwenk, S.S.J.; Sr. Marie Denise Heineman, S.S.J. Total in Residence 48; Total Staff 35.

DELEVAN. *Franciscan Sisters of Allegany, New York-Blessed Sacrament Mission Center*, 8 N. Main St., 14042. Tel: 716-492-2266. Conducted by Franciscan Sisters of Allegany. Services Region 21. Sr. Mary Richard Burke, O.S.F., Chaplaincy Svc.; Sr. Veronica Mary Louis, Field Mgr. Mission Society; Sr. Ellen Michael Schafer, O.S.F., Dir. Oleon Southern Tier Catechetical Office.

DERBY. *Sisters of St. Mary of Namur*, 7110 Lake Shore Rd., 14047. Tel: 716-947-4061. Sr. Kathleen Kane; Sr. Catherine Taberski. Sisters 2.

HAMBURG. *Immaculate Conception Convent*, 5286 S. Park Ave., 14075; Fax: 716-649-5958. Motherhouse of the Franciscan Sisters of St. Joseph. Sr. M. Andrea Ciszewski, F.S.S.J., Gen. Min.; Rev. Ronald Sermak, O.F.M.Conv., Chap. Sisters 120.

North American Union of the Sisters of Our Lady of Charity, 3800 Howard Rd., 14075. Tel: 716-648-4988. Legal Title: *Sisters of Our Lady of Charity of the Refuge, Inc.* Sr. Rosemary Toth, Local Supr. Sisters 24.

LACKAWANNA. *Sisters of Charity of St. Vincent de Paul of Zagreb, Croatia*, 211 W. Elmview Ave., 14218. Tel: 716-825-1461. Sr. Stella, Supr. Sisters 2.

LEWISTON. *Sisters of the Sacred Heart of Jesus (S.S.H.J.)*, Sacred Heart School & Convent, 5269 Lewiston Rd., 14092. Tel: 716-284-8273. Sr. M. Terenzia Giudice, S.S.H.J., Supr. Sisters 9.

LOCKPORT. *St. Joseph's Convent - Sisters of St. Mary of Namur*, 104 Garden St., 10494. Tel: 716-433-3966. Sisters of St. Mary of Namur. Professed Sisters 3; Total in Residence 3.

ORCHARD PARK. *Sisters of Mercy of the Buffalo Diocese Retirement Corp.*, 5245 Murphy Rd., 14127. Tel: 716-662-9836; 662-5120; Fax: 716-662-9766. Sr. Peggy Gorman, R.S.M., Pres.

Sisters of Mercy-Regional Community Offices, 5245 Murphy Rd., 14127. Tel: 716-662-9836; 662-5120; Fax: 716-662-9766. Sisters of Mercy. Sr. Peggy Gorman, R.S.M., Pres.; Rev. Msgr. Cyril I. Trevett, Chap. Sisters Professed 205; Candidates 5.

SILVER CREEK. *Missionary Sisters of St. Columbans, St. Columban's on the Lake*, 14136. Rev. John C. Healy, S.S.C., Chap. Professed Sisters 12.

STELLA NIAGARA. *Stella Niagara Education Park*, 4421 Lower River Rd., 14144. Tel: 716-754-4312; Fax: 716-754-7657. Provincial Offices of the Sisters of St. Francis of Penance and Christian Charity. Sr. Claudia Steger, O.S.F., Prov. Min.; Rev. Joseph Power, O.S.F.S., Chap. Sisters in the Providence 251; Professed Sisters in Residence 78.

WEST SENECA. *Sisters of Charity of St. Vincent de Paul of Zagreb, Croatia*, 171 Knox Ave., 14224. Tel: 716-825-5859; 822-6841. Sr. Mary Adelina Cizmesija, Supr. Professed Sisters 26. Legal Title: *Sisters of Charity of St. Vincent de Paul of Zagreb, Croatia - U.S.A. Delegacy Headquarters.*

WILLIAMSVILLE. *Franciscan Missionary Sisters of the Divine Child, Inc.*, 6380 Main St., 14221. Tel: 716-632-3144. Sr. Marie Dorothy Clitheroe, Min. Gen.; Sr. Bernadine Salazar, Asst. Supr.; Sr. Margaret C. Krantz, Min. Gen.; Sr. Marianne Ferguson, Asst. Supr. Sisters 33.

Formation Center, 6380 Main St., 14221. Tel: 716-631-5147.

Private Kindergarten, 6380 Main St., 14221. Sr. Renee Kopacz, F.M.D.C., Prin.; Rev. Gary J. Bagley, Community Chap.

Sisters of St. Francis of the Third Order Regular, St. Mary of the Angels, 400 Mill St., P.O. Box 275, 14231-0275. Tel: 716-632-2155. Motherhouse of the Sisters of St. Francis of the Third Order Regular. Sr. Patricia Burkard, Gen. Min.; Rev. Msgr. Fred R. Voorhes, Chap. Sisters 143.

[Q] RETREAT HOUSES

DERBY. *St. Columban's Center*, 6892 Lake Shore Rd., P.O. Box 816, 14047-0816. Tel: 716-947-4708; Fax: 716-947-5759. Rev. Msgr. James E. Wall, Dir.; Sr. Mary Leah Krauth, O.S.F., Assoc. Dir.; Sr. Mary Catherine Cummins, O.S.U., Assoc. Dir. Total in Residence 3; Total Staff 14.

LEROY. *St. Peter Nolasco Spiritual Center*, Mercygrove, 7770 E. Main Rd., 14482-9701. Tel: 716-768-7110; 768-6408. Offering directed or private retreats. Facility available for overnight programs. Rev. Jerome Laubacker, O.de.M., Dir.

STELLA NIAGARA. *Stella Niagara Center of Renewal*, 4421 Lower River Rd., 14144. Tel: 716-754-7376. Directors: Revs. John J. Mergenhagen; Joseph Power, O.S.F.S.; Sr. Karen Allen, O.S.F. Total in Residence 1; Total Staff 6.

WEST CLARKSVILLE. *Mount Irenaeus, Franciscan Mountain Retreat & Holy Peace Friary*, P.O. Box 100, 14786. Tel: 716-973-2470. Order of Friars Minor Holy Name Province. Revs. Daniel Riley, O.F.M., Pres. & Guardian; Daniel Hurley, O.F.M.; Bro. Joseph Kotula, O.F.M.; Rev. Louis McCormick, O.F.M. Total in Residence 4.

[R] CAMPUS MINISTRY AND NEWMAN CENTERS

WILLIAMSVILLE. *Newman Club Chaplains*, 6325 Main St., 14221. Tel: 716-632-8898. Rev. Paul W. Steller, Episcopal, Vicar of Campus Ministry.

Canisius College. Campus Ministry Office, 2001 Main St., Buffalo, 14208. Tel: 716-888-2420. Sr. Marlene Butler, G.N.S.H., Dir. Assoc. Campus Ministers: Revs. Richard R. Galligan, S.J.; Thomas A. O'Connor, S.J.; Mark Kriz, S.J.; Sr. Patricia Brady, S.S.M.N.; Mr. J. Joseph Volkenburg.

Daemen College. Campus Ministry Office, 4380 Main St., Buffalo, 14226. Tel: 716-839-3600. Ms. Joanne Stiller, Dir.; Rev. A. Mark Illig.

D'Youville College. 320 Porter Ave., Buffalo, 14201. Tel: 716-881-3200. Bro. James Sarach, T.O.R., Dir.; Rev. Anthony Rigoli, O.M.I.

Erie Community College. City Campus, 121 Ellicott St., Buffalo, 14203. Tel: 716-842-2770. Sr. Ruth Marie Penksa, G.N.S.H., Dir. Campus Ministry, North Campus, Newman Center, 6325 Main St., 14221. Tel: 716-632-8898. Rev. Msgr. Paul W. Steller, Dir.; Carol Kwadrans, Sec., South Campus, Newman Center, 4196 Abbott Rd., Orchard Park, 14127. Tel: 716-648-5400; 649-6186. Rev. Msgr. David M. Lee, Dir.

Medaille College. Campus Ministry, 18 Agassiz Cir., Buffalo, 14214.

Niagra University, Lewiston Rd., Buffalo, 14109. Tel: 716-285-1212. Revs. Patrick Flanagan, C.M.; Kevin Creagh, C.M.; Ms. Mary Beth Coates, Dir.; Mr. Thomas Hughes.

State University College at Buffalo. Newman Center, 1219 Elmwood Ave., Buffalo, 14222. Tel: 716-882-1080. Rev. John C. Weimer, Dir. Assoc. Directors: Sr. Charlene Fontana, S.S.J.; Susan Spadinger; Dorothy Gardiner, Sec.

State University of New York at Buffalo (Main St. South Campus), Newman Center, Buffalo, 14214. Tel: 716-833-0298. Rev. Jacob C. Ledwon, Dir.; Mr. Matthew Smith.

Trocaire College, 110 Red Jacket Pkwy., Buffalo, 14220. Tel: 716-826-1200. Ms. Nicole Lusmann, Dir.

Villa Maria College, 240 Pine Ridge Rd., Buffalo, 14225. Tel: 716-896-0700. Sr. Barbara Juszkiewicz, C.S.S.F.

St. Jude's Chapel at Alfred University & Alfred State College, Box 1154, Elm St., Alfred, 14802. Tel: 607-587-9411. Rev. Eugene P. Ulrich, Dir.; Robert Donius; Sue Fowler.

State University of New York at Buffalo (North Campus) Newman Center, UB Commons, Amherst, 14228. Rev. J. Patrick Keleher, Dir.; Anne Tupper.

Genesee Community, One College Rd., Batavia, 14020.

State University College at Fredonia, 222 Temple St., Fredonia, 14063. Tel: 716-679-4686. Rev. James Vacco, O.F.M., Dir.; Karen M. Cave, Sec.

Hilbert College. Campus Ministry Office, 5200 S. Park Ave., Hamburg, 14075. Tel: 716-649-7900. Rev. Bernard Olszewski, O.F.M.Conv., Dir.; Ms. Sheila Dunphy.

St. Bonaventure University, St. Bonaventure, 14778. Tel: 716-375-2000. Revs. David Blake, O.F.M.; Daniel Hurley, O.F.M.; David Blake, O.F.M.; Mr. Jason Free; Bro. Thomas Cole, O.F.M., Dir.; Janet Fusco, Sec.

[S] CAMPS AND COMMUNITY CENTERS

ALLEGANY STATE PARK. *Camp Turner*. Office, 795 Main St., 14203. (Coed). Rev. Gary J. Bagley.

ANGOLA. *St. Vincent de Paul Camp*. Office, 72 E. Huron St., Buffalo, 14203. (Camp for needy boys and girls). Rev. Msgr. John J. Conniff, Spiritual Dir.

[T] MISCELLANEOUS

BUFFALO. *Catholic Charities of Buffalo, NY, Foundation, Inc.*, 525 Washington St., 14203.

Catholic Union Store, 795 Main St., 14203. Tel: 716-847-8715; Fax: 716-847-8702. Peter M. McKee, Dir.

Federation of Catholic School Parents, Diocese of Buffalo, NY, 795 Main St., 14203. Tel: 716-847-5501. Barbara B. Ashcroft, Pres.

The Foundation of the Roman Catholic Diocese of Buffalo, NY, Inc., 795 Main St., 14203-1250.

Good Counsel Apartments, 525 Washington St., 14203. Housing for handicapped & elderly of low income. Rev. Msgr. John J. Conniff, Pres.; Rev. Msgr. Robert J. Cunningham; Rev. Msgr. Henry J. Gugino, Sec. & Treas. Total in Residence 39; Total Staff 4.

Hope of Buffalo, Inc., 335 Grider St., 14215. Tel: 716-892-8224. Rev. Roy T. Herberger, Pres.; Sr. Karen Klimczak, Dir.

Kolping Catholic Young Men's Association of Buffalo, NY dba Kolping Society of Buffalo, 29 Delphi Dr., 14227. Tel: 716-668-0120. Ludwig Haberle, Jr., Pres.; Rev. Msgr. Paul R. Letourneau, Mod.

La Casa Del Tainos Housing Development Fund Company, Inc., 525 Washington St., 14203. Rev. Msgr. Henry J. Gugino, Dir.

Mercy Health System of Western New York. Marian Professional Center, 515 Abbott Rd., Ste. 508, 14220.

Monsignor Adamski Village Housing Development Fund Company, Inc., 123 Townsend St., 14212. Rev. Msgr. Robert J. Cunningham, Pres.

Monsignor Adamski Village, Inc., 123 Townsend St., 14212. Rev. Msgr. John R. Gabalski. Facility for elderly and handicapped persons of low income.

Monsignor Carr Institute, 76 W. Humboldt Pkwy., 14214. Tel: 716-835-9745. Field Agency of Catholic Charities for Psychiatric and Psychological Services. Christopher J. Pino, Ph.D., Dir. Total Assisted 19,984; Total Staff 37.

Monsignor Kirby Apartments Housing Development Fund Company, Inc., 525 Washington St., 14203. Tel: 716-853-4424, Ext. 3095. Rev. Msgr. Henry J. Gugino, Contact Person. Total in Residence 39; Total Staff 2.

Mother of Divine Grace Housing Development Fund Company, Inc., 3233 Main St., 14214. Tel: 716-833-5353. Purpose: To provide housing for persons of low income, particularly handicapped mentally retarded and developmentally disabled adults. Sr. Mary Patricia Tomasik, Exec. Dir. Total in Residence 10; Total Staff 10.

Nativity Housing Development Fund Company, Inc., 3233 Main St., 14214. Tel: 716-833-5353. Purpose: To provide housing for persons of low income, particularly handicapped mentally retarded and developmentally disabled adults. Sr. Mary Patricia Tomasik, Exec. Dir. Total in Residence 11; Total Staff 10.

St. Francis Respite Program, Inc.

St. Timothy's Park Villa Housing Development Fund Company, Inc., 525 Washington St., 14203. Tel: 716-853-4424, Ext. 3095. Rev. Msgr. Henry J. Gugino, Contact Person. Total in Residence 49; Total Staff 3.

Santa Maria Towers, Office, 525 Washington St., 14203. Housing for handicapped and elderly of low income.

Monsignor Gambino Tower, Ltd. Most Rev. Edward D. Head, Pres.

Timon Towers Housing Development Fund Company, Inc., 525 Washington St., 14203. Rev. Msgr. John J. Conniff, Pres. Low income housing for the handicapped and elderly. Total Staff 6.

AMHERST. *St. Andrew Kim Roman Catholic Church Society of Amherst, NY, Diocese of Buffalo*. 795 Main St., 14203-1250. Tel: 716-847-5529. Rev. James J. Ruddick, S.J.

BOWMANSVILLE. *International Institute of the Heart of Jesus*. North American Office (IIHJ-NAO), 5337 Genesee St., 14026. Tel: 716-683-2375. Rev. Msgr. Walter O. Kern.

LACKAWANNA. *Our Lady of Victory Homes of Charity*, 780 Ridge Rd., 14218. Tel: 716-828-9648. Rev. Msgr. Robert C. Wurtz, Exec. Vice Pres. & Treas. (Formerly Association of Our Lady of Victory). Legal Titles: *Our Lady of Victory Homes of Charity; Society for the Protection of Destitute Roman Catholic Children at Buffalo, NY; Father Baker's*. Includes the following Institutions: Baker Victory Services 716-828-9500 or 716-888-9500 (Formerly Baker Hall, St. Joseph Orphanage and Our Lady of Victory Infant Home) and Our Lady of Victory Hospital. Total Assisted 2,500; Total Staff 800.

Western New York Catholic Healthcare Corporation, Our Lady of Victory Hospital, 55 Melroy Ave., 14218.

NIAGARA UNIVERSITY. *Our Lady of Angels Association*. Marian House, 14109-1918. Tel: 716-286-8150; Fax: 716-286-8155. Rev. William J. O'Brien, C.M., Dir. Development Office for the Congregation of the Mission, Eastern Province. Total Staff 11.

NORTH TONAWANDA. *Shrine of the Infant Jesus*. Administered by the Pallottine Fathers. 3452 Niagara Falls Blvd., P.O. Box 563, 14120-0563.

WEST SENECA. *Victorious Missionaries*, 791 Seneca Creek Rd., 14224. Tel: 716-675-5891. Deacon William W. Willis, Spiritual Dir. A spiritual and social movement for the handicapped and chronically ill.

RELIGIOUS INSTITUTES OF MEN REPRESENTED IN THE DIOCESE

For further details refer to the corresponding bracketed number in the Religious Institutes of Men or Women section.

[0810]—*Brothers of Mercy*.—F.M.M.
[0330]—*Brothers of the Christian Schools*. (New York Prov.).—F.S.C.
[0160]—*Clerics Regular of St. Paul*.—C.R.S.P.
[0450]—*Congregation of Jesus and Mary*.—C.J.M.
[1330]—*Congregation of the Mission*. (Eastern Prov.).—C.M.
[0390]—*Consolata Missionaries*.—I.M.C.
[0480]—*Conventual Franciscans*. (St. Anthony of Padua).—O.F.M.Conv.
[0520]—*Franciscan Friars*. (Holy Name Prov.).—O.F.M.
[0690]—*Jesuit Fathers and Brothers*. (New York Prov.).—S.J.
[0800]—*Maryknoll*. (Buffalo).—M.M.
[1210]—*Missionaries of St. Charles-Scalabrinians*.—C.S.
[0910]—*Oblates of Mary Immaculate*. (Eastern Prov.).—O.M.I.
[0920]—*Oblates of St. Francis De Sales*.—O.S.F.S.
[0970]—*Order of Our Lady of Mercy*. (Le Roy).—O.deM.
[0430]—*Order of Preachers-Dominicans*. (Provs. of St. Joseph; St. Albert the Great).—O.P.
[1020]—*Pauline Fathers and Brothers*. (Derby).—S.S.P.
[1040]—*Piarist Fathers*.—Sch.P.
[0370]—*Society of St. Columban*.—S.S.C.
[0990]—*Society of the Catholic Apostolate*. (Christ the King Prov.).—S.A.C.

RELIGIOUS INSTITUTES OF WOMEN REPRESENTED IN THE DIOCESE

[0760]—*Daughters of Charity of St. Vincent de Paul*.—D.C.
[0810]—*Daughters of the Heart of Mary*.—D.H.M.
[0420]—*Discalced Carmelite Nuns*.—O.C.D.
[1060]—*Dominican Contemplative Sisters*.—O.P.
[1170]—*Felician Sisters*.—C.S.S.F.
[1340]—*Franciscan Missionary Sisters of the Divine Child*.—F.M.D.C.
[1180]—*Franciscan Sisters of Allegany, New York*.—O.S.F.
[1470]—*Franciscan Sisters of St. Joseph*.—F.S.S.J.
[1280]—*Franciscan Sisters of the Immaculate Conception*.—O.S.F.
[1840]—*Grey Nuns of the Sacred Heart*.—G.N.S.H.
[2575]—*Institute of the Sisters of Mercy of the Americas*.—R.S.M.
[2830]—*Missionary Sisters of Our Lady of Mercy*.—M.O.M.
[2880]—*Missionary Sisters of St. Columban*.—S.S.C.
[3040]—*Oblate Sisters of Providence*.—O.S.P.
[0630]—*Sisters of Charity of St. Vincent de Paul*.—S.V.Z.
[]—*Sisters of Christ the King*.—S.C.K.
[3070]—*Sisters of Our Lady of Charity*.—N.A.U.-O.L.C.
[3950]—*Sisters of Saint Mary of Namur*.—S.S.M.N.
[4090]—*Sisters of Social Service*.—S.S.S.
[1630]—*Sisters of St. Francis of Penance and Christian Charity*.—O.S.F.
[1800]—*Sisters of St. Francis of the Third Order Regular*. (Williamsville, NY).—O.S.F.
[3830]—*Sisters of St. Joseph*.—C.S.J.
[1020]—*Sisters of the Divine Redeemer*.—S.D.R.
[]—*Sisters of the Sacred Heart of Jesus*.—S.S.H.J.
[1720]—*Sisters of the Third Order Regular of St. Francis of the Congregation of Our Lady of Lourdes*.—O.S.F.

DIOCESAN CEMETERIES

CHEEKTOWAGA. *Holy Sepulchre*.

GRAND ISLAND. *Assumption*.

KENMORE. *Mount Olivet*, 4000 Elmwood Ave., 14217. Tel: 716-873-6500.

LACKAWANNA. *Holy Cross*.

LOCKPORT. *Queen of Heaven*.

NIAGARA FALLS. *Gate of Heaven*.

NECROLOGY

† Bialek, Rev. Msgr. Joseph L., Buffalo, NY, St. Adalbert Basilica. —Died March 3, 1996.

† Conlin, Rev. Msgr. Norman R., (Retired). —Died March 26, 1996.

† Coveney, Edwin J., (Retired). —Died Jan. 21, 1996.
† Duggan, John P., (Retired). —Died Dec. 29, 1996.
† Hanna, Rev. Msgr. Francis J., (Retired). —Died March 28, 1996.
† Kozlowski, Rev. Msgr. Raymond J., Buffalo, NY, Immaculate Heart of Mary. —Died June 22, 1996.
† Schieder, Rev. Msgr. Joseph E., (Retired). —Died June 12, 1996.
† Selbert, Rev. Msgr. Eugene H., (Retired). —Died July 16, 1996.
† Smith, Gregory L., Clarence, NY, Clarence Residence. —Died Jan. 2, 1996.
† Swick, Robert J., (Retired). —Died June 23, 1996.
† Trapp, Donald G., (Retired). —Died March 24, 1996.
† Weiss, Bernard A., (Retired). —Died March 3, 1996.
† Zenns, Rev. Msgr. William C., (Retired). —Died Aug. 7, 1996.

Diocese of Burlington

(Dioecesis Burlingtonensis)

Most Reverend

KENNETH A. ANGELL, D.D.

Bishop of Burlington; ordained May 26, 1956; appointed Auxiliary Bishop of Providence August 9, 1974; consecrated October 7, 1974; transferred to Bishop of Burlington October 6, 1992; installed November 9, 1992. *Mailing Address: 351 North Ave., Burlington, VT, 05401-2999; Fax: 802-658-0436.*

ESTABLISHED JULY 29, 1853.

Square Miles 9,135.

Comprises the State of Vermont.

For legal titles of parishes and diocesan institutions, consult the Chancery Office.

Chancery Office: 351 North Ave., Burlington, VT, 05401. Tel.: 802-658-6110; Fax: 802-658-0436.

STATISTICAL OVERVIEW

Personnel	
Bishop	1
Priests: Diocesan Active in Diocese	92
Priests: Active Outside Diocese	6
Priests: Retired, Sick or Absent	41
Number of Diocesan Priests	139
Religious Priests in Diocese	48
Extern Priests in Diocese	1
Ordinations:	
Diocesan Priests	1
Religious Priests	1
Permanent Deacons in Diocese	40
Total Brothers	21
Total Sisters	263
Parishes	
Parishes	93
With Resident Pastor:	
Resident Diocesan Priests	79
Resident Religious Priests	14
Without Resident Pastor:	
Administered by Priests	6
Missions	39
Pastoral Centers	1
Professional Ministry Personnel:	
Sisters	15
Lay Ministers	39
Welfare	
Catholic Hospitals	1
Total Assisted	32,691
Homes for the Aged	4
Total Assisted	143
Residential Care of Children	1
Total Assisted	14
Other Institutions	1
Total Assisted	7,628
Educational	
Diocesan Students in Other Seminaries	11
Total Seminarians	11
Colleges and Universities	3
Total Students	4,029
High Schools, Diocesan and Parish	2
Total Students	695
Elementary Schools, Diocesan and Parish	9
Total Students	1,780
Elementary Schools, Private	2
Total Students	653
Catechesis/Religious Education:	
High School Students	1,118
Elementary Students	5,846
Total Students Under Catholic Instruction	14,132
Teachers in the Diocese:	
Priests	2
Brothers	2
Sisters	22
Lay Teachers	228
Vital Statistics	
Receptions into the Church:	
Infant Baptism Totals	2,012
Adult Baptism Totals	130
Received into Full Communion	157
First Communions	1,934
Confirmations	1,194
Marriages:	
Catholic	522
Interfaith	531
Total Marriages	753
Deaths	1,531
Total Catholic Population	147,190
Total Population	584,771

Former Bishops—Rt. Rev. LOUIS DE GOESBRIAND, D.D., cons. Oct. 30, 1853; died Nov. 3, 1899.—Rt. Rev. JOHN S. MICHAUD, D.D., cons. June 29, 1892; died Dec. 22, 1908.—Most Rev. JOSEPH J. RICE, D.D., cons. April 14, 1910; died April 1, 1938.—Most Rev. MATTHEW F. BRADY, D.D., cons. Oct. 26, 1938; transferred to Manchester, NH, Nov. 11, 1944; died Sept. 20, 1959.—Most Rev. EDWARD F. RYAN, D.D., cons. Jan. 3, 1945; died Nov. 3, 1956.—Most Rev. ROBERT F. JOYCE, D.D., cons. Auxiliary Bishop Oct. 28, 1954; installed Diocesan Bishop Feb. 26, 1957; retired Jan. 25, 1972; died Sept. 2, 1990.—Most Rev. JOHN ALOYSIUS MARSHALL, D.D.,elected Bishop of Burlington November 30, 1971; ord. and installed January 25, 1972; transferred to Springfield, MA, Dec. 27, 1991; died July 3, 1994.

Vicar General and Moderator of the Curia—Rev. Msgr. JOHN R. MCSWEENEY, V.G., J.C.L.

Vicar General—Rev. WENDALL H. SEARLES, V.G.

Chancery Office—351 North Ave., Burlington, 05401. Tel: 802-658-6110; Fax: 802-658-0436. Office Hours: Mon.-Fri. 9-12 & 1-5.

Finance Officer—Mr. KEVIN J. HEFFERNAN, C.P.A.

Episcopal Vicar for Administration—Rev. JAY C. HASKIN, M.Ch.A.

Episcopal Vicar for Lay Apostolates—Rev. Msgr. W. JOHN FRADET.

Episcopal Vicar for Clergy and Youth—Vacant.

Chancellor—Rev. JAY C. HASKIN, M.Ch.A.

Secretary to the Most Reverend Bishop and Vice Chancellor—Rev. WALTER D. MILLER, J.C.D., *351 North Ave., Burlington, 05401.* Tel: 802-658-6110.

Diocesan Tribunal—351 North Ave., Burlington, 05401. Tel: 802-658-6110; Fax: 802-658-4118.

Judicial Vicar—Rev. WALTER D. MILLER, M.Div., J.C.D.

Adjutant Judicial Vicar—Rev. GERALD W. BOMBARDIER, M.A., J.C.L.

Judges—Rev. Msgr. JOHN R. MCSWEENEY, V.G., J.C.L.; Revs. THOMAS V. MATTISON, M.Div., J.C.L., M.C.L.; WILLIAM D. CORCORAN, J.C.L.

Promoter of Justice—Rev. BERNARD F. DEPEAUX, J.C.L.

Defenders of the Bond—Revs. ROGER L. CHARBONNEAU; MICHEL J. ST.-PIERRE; ROBERT B. WHALEN.

Advocates—Revs. JOHN G. FELTZ; RAYMOND A. GIROUX; PETER A. ROUTHIER.

Notaries—Mrs. SHIRLEY J. MEACHAM; Mrs. JANE B. KELLNER; Mrs. ELSA M. WHEEL.

Diocesan Administrative Board—Most Rev. KENNETH A. ANGELL, D.D., Chm.; Rev. Msgr. JOHN R. MCSWEENEY, V.G., J.C.L.; Rev. WENDELL H. SEARLES, V.G.; Rev. Msgr. W. JOHN FRADET; Sr. MARY BOISELLE, R.S.M.; Rev. JAY C. HASKIN, Sec.

Diocesan Consultors—Rev. Msgr. JOHN R. MCSWEENEY, V.G., J.C.L.; Rev. Msgr. PAUL M. BRESNEHAN; Revs. JAY C. HASKIN; WENDELL H. SEARLES, V.G.; REID C. MAYO; MICHAEL W. DEFORGE; JOHN W. HAMILTON.

Deans—Revs. ROBERT CAMPBELL, M.S.; RICHARD A. FOWLER; JOHN W. HAMILTON; JULIEN J. LAFLAMME; PIERRE A. LAVALLEE; RICHARD G. LAVALLEY; JOSEPH A. LIVELY; JAMES J. MCSHANE; BERNARD MESSIER; MAURICE J. ROY; RICHARD W. TINNEY; DONAL WARD.

Diocesan Offices and Directors

Alcohol Advisory Committee—Rev. RAYMOND A. GIROUX, Chm., *St. John Vianney Rectory, 160 Hinesburg Rd., South Burlington, 05403.* Tel: 802-864-4166.

Apostolate for the Deaf—Rev. PETER Y. WILLIAMS, *351 North Ave., Burlington, 05401.* Tel: 802-658-6110.

Apostolate for the Handicapped—LINDA PREVITI, Coord., *Office of Catholic Formation, Special Needs Ministry, 351 North Ave., Burlington, 05401.* Tel: 802-658-6110.

Bishop's Commission on Women—Ms. DIANE FOSTER, Chm., *351 North Ave., Burlington, 05401.* Tel: 802-658-6110.

Boy Scouts—Rev. YVON J. ROYER, *St. Joseph Rectory, 85 Elmwood Ave., Burlington, 05401.* Tel: 802-863-2388.

Building Commission—Rev. PETER A. ROUTHIER, Chm., *Chancery Office, 351 North Ave., Burlington, 05401.* Tel: 802-658-6110.

Vermont Catholic Charities—Rev. ROLAND J. RIVARD, Dir., *Central Office, 351 North Ave., Burlington, 05401.* Tel: 802-658-6110; Fax: 802-860-0451. Mrs. MARY M. MCNAMARA, A.C.S.W., Supvr. Professional Svcs., *351 North Ave., Burlington, 05401.* Tel: 802-658-6110., Rutland Office: *24 1/2 Center St., Rutland, 05701.* Tel: 802-773-3379.

Campaign for Human Development—Rev. ROLAND J. RIVARD, Dir., *351 North Ave., Burlington, 05401.* Tel: 802-658-6110.

Catholic Daughters of The Americas—Rev. PATRICK J. FORMAN, *St. Michael Rectory, 20 Walnut St., Brattleboro, 05301.* Tel: 802-257-5101.

Catholic Relief Services—Rev. ROLAND J. RIVARD, *351 North Ave., Burlington, 05401.* Tel: 802-658-6110.

Catholic Women, Vermont Council of—Rev. GEORGE H. DUPUIS, Diocesan Moderator, *St. Margaret Mary Rectory, Main St., Arlington, 05250.* Tel: 802-375-2849. Mrs. THERESA BIASUZZI, Pres.

Censor Librorum—Rev. MICHEL J. ST-PIERRE, *351 North Ave., Burlington, 05401.* Tel: 802-658-6110.

Charismatic Renewal—Rev. FORREST W. ROUELLE, *St. Mary Star of the Sea Rectory, 5 Clermont Ter., Newport, 05855.* Tel: 802-334-5066.

Chief Administrator for Catholic Formation—Sr. MARIANNE READ, R.S.M., M.Ed., C.A.E.S.

Continuing Education for Clergy—Rev. WILLIAM R. BEAUDIN, Dir., *North American Martyrs Rectory, P.O. Box 221, Marshfield, 05658-0221.* Tel: 802-426-3233; Fax: 802-426-3525.

Diocesan Archives—WILLIAM GOSS, *351 North Ave., Burlington, 05401.* Tel: 802-658-6110.

Diocesan Development Office—LORRAINE CLARKE, Dir., *351 North Ave., Burlington, 05401.* Tel: 802-658-6110.

Director of Communications—GLORIA J. GIBSON, *351 North Ave., Burlington, 05401.* Tel: 802-658-6110.

Daughters of Isabella—Rev. BERNARD H. MESSIER, Chap., *St. Monica Rectory, 79 Summer St., Barre, 05641.* Tel: 802-479-3253.

Diocesan Cemeteries—ROBERT DELARICHELIERE, Chm.; DONALD MCKENZIE, Supvr., *Resurrection Park, South Burlington, 05403.* Tel: 802-862-1530., *St. Joseph's Cemetery, Burlington, 05401.*

Diocesan Finance Council—Ex-Officio Members: Most Rev. KENNETH A. ANGELL; Rev. WENDELL H. SEARLES, V.G.; KEVIN J. HEFFERMAN, Finance Officer & Chm. Board Members: Sr. MARY I. GRANT, R.S.M.; JAMES STROUSE; CAROL MARKEY; JOHN KELLY.

Diocesan Pastoral Planning—Rev. WENDELL H. SEARLES, V.G., Dir., *351 North Ave., Burlington, 05401.* Tel: 802-658-6110.

Ecumenical Commission—JAMES G. CASE, *St Michael's College, Winooski Park, Colchester, 05439.* Tel: 802-654-2464.

Education, Board of—Ms. MADELEINE ROY, *P.O. Box 338, Barton, 05822.*

Evangelization—Vacant.

Liturgical Commission—Rev. PETER A. ROUTHIER, Chm., *St. Stephen Rectory, 115 Barlow St., Winooski, 05404.* Tel: 802-655-0318.

Director of Liturgical Formation—Rev. PETER A. ROUTHIER, Dir., *St. Stephen Rectory, 115 Barlow St., Winooski, 05404.* Tel: 802-655-0318.

Family Life—RUTH CHARLESWORTH, Dir., *351 North Ave., Burlington, 05401.* Tel: 802-658-6110.

Diocesan Coordinator for Health Affairs—Rev. LEOPOLD J. BILODEAU, *Fletcher Allen Health Care, 111 Colchester Ave., Burlington, 05401.*

Holy Childhood Association—Rev. ROBERT C. RICHARDSON, Dir., *351 North Ave., Burlington, 05401.* Tel: 802-658-6110.

House of Discernment—Revs. MICHAEL W. DEFORGE, Dir.; PETER Y. WILLIAMS, *The Catholic Center at UVM, 390 South Prospect St., Burlington, 05401.* Tel: 802-862-8403; Fax: 802-865-9480.

Knights of Columbus—Rev. JOHN C. LEDOUX, *State Chaplain, 16 Clover Dr. 9-C, Essex Junction, 05452.* Tel: 802-879-0623.

Leap—Rev. MICHAEL P. CRONOGUE, S.S.E., *St. Michael's College, Winooski Park, Colchester, 05439.* Tel: 802-654-2386.

Marriage Encounter, Vermont—DAVID ERKSON; JENNIE ERKSON, *R.R. 1, Box 462, Jericho Rd., Richmond, 05477.* Tel: 802-434-4218.

Diocesan Master of Ceremonies—Rev. WALTER D. MILLER, J.C.D., *St. Jude Rectory, Box 69, Hinesburg.* Tel: 802-482-2290; Fax: 802-482-3952.

Office of Ministerial Formation—Rev. WILLIAM R. BEAUDIN, Dir., *P.O. Box 221, Marshfield, 05658.* Tel: 802-426-3233; Fax: 802-426-3525.

National Catholic Conference for Interracial Justice—Rev. WALTER D. MILLER, J.C.D., Diocesan Coord., *St. Jude Rectory, Box 69, Hinesburg.* Tel: 802-482-2290; Fax: 802-482-3952.

National Shrine of the Immaculate Conception, Washington—Rev. ROGER L. CHARBONNEAU, *Holy Cross Rectory, 47 Church Rd., Colchester, 05446.* Tel: 802-863-3002.

Office of Catholic Formation—Deacon IVAN HAWK, Dir. Coordinators: FLORA HAND; TERESA MIELE.

Permanent Diaconate—Rev. WILLIAM BEAUDIN, Dir., *P.O. Box 221, Marshfield, 05658.* Tel: 802-426-3233; Fax: 802-426-3525.

Diocesan Presbyteral Council—Members Ex-Officio: Most Rev. KENNETH A. ANGELL; Rev. Msgr. JOHN R. MCSWEENEY, V.G., J.C.L.; Revs. WENDELL H. SEARLES, V.G.; JAY C. HASKIN; MICHAEL W. DEFORGE; WILLIAM R. BEAUDIN. Elected Members: Revs. PIERRE A. LAVALLEE; ALBERT G. BALTZ; GEORGE H. DUPUIS; DENIS R. BRETON; MAURICE J. ROY; REID C. MAYO; JOHN W. HAMILTON; JAMES J. MCSHANE; WILLIAM P. GIROUX; STEPHEN J. NICHOLS; ROLAND J. RIVARD; LEOPOLD J. BILODEAU; FRANCIS M. HOLLAND; ROBERT CAMPBELL, M.S.

Press, (Diocesan)—Diocesan Media Board: HENRY DELBIANCO, Chm. Newspaper: "The Vermont Catholic Tribune"; Most Rev. KENNETH A. ANGELL, Publisher; Rev. RAYMOND A. GIROUX, Assoc. to the Publisher; PAT GORE, Editor, Editorial and Business Office: *351 North Ave., Burlington, 05401.* Tel: 802-658-6110; Fax: 802-658-0436.

Priests' Benefit Fund—Rev. ROBERT B. WHALEN, Chm., *351 North Ave., Burlington, 05401.* Tel: 802-658-6110.

Prison Ministry—Deacon STEPHEN RATTE, *351 North Ave., Burlington, 05401.* Tel: 802-658-6110.

Pro-Life—RUTH CHARLESWORTH, Dir., *351 North Ave., Burlington, 05401.* Tel: 802-658-6110; Fax: 802-860-0451.

Propagation of the Faith—Rev. ROBERT C. RICHARDSON, Dir., *351 North Ave., Burlington, 05401.* Tel: 802-658-6110.

Rural Life—Deacon JEAN LOUIS RAINVILLE, *Box 122G, R.F.D., Gore Rd., Highgate Center, 05459.*

Schools—Sr. MARIANNE READ, R.S.M., M.Ed., C.A.E.S., Supt. of Schools, *351 North Ave., Burlington, 05401.* Tel: 802-658-6110.

Secular Franciscans—Rev. RICHARD A. FOWLER, *St. James Rectory, P.O. Box 407, Island Pond, 05846.* Tel: 802-723-4312.

Senate of Sisters—Sr. MARY POLWORTH, S.S.J., *Sisters of St. Joseph Convent, 131 Convent Ave., Rutland, 05701.* Tel: 802-775-5133.

Liaison for Religious—Sr. FRANCES AGNES BLAKE, C.S.J., *The Catholic Center at UVM, 390 S. Prospect St., Burlington, 05401.* Tel: 802-862-8403; Fax: 802-865-9480.

Vermont Cursillo Secretariat—HELENE LOUX, Pres., *P.O. Box 48, North Troy, 05859.* Tel: 802-988-2983.

Vocations and Seminarians—Rev. MICHAEL W. DEFORGE, Dir., *The Catholic Center at UVM, 390 South Prospect St., Burlington, 05401.* Tel: 802-862-8403; Fax: 802-865-9480.

CLERGY, PARISHES, MISSIONS AND PAROCHIAL SCHOOLS

CITY OF BURLINGTON (Chittenden County)

1—CATHEDRAL OF THE IMMACULATE CONCEPTION (1830), Rev. Thomas J. Ball.
Res., 20 Pine St., 05401. Tel: 802-658-4333. [CEM]

2—ST. ANTHONY'S (1903), Rev. Msgr. W. John Fradet, Admin.; Deacon Louis Meunier. In res., Revs. Michel J. St-Pierre; Roland J. Rivard.
Res., 305 Flynn Ave., 05401. Tel: 802-864-0478.

3—CHRIST THE KING (1940), Rev. Msgr. W. John Fradet.
Res., 305 Flynn Ave., 05401-4834. Tel: 802-862-5784.
School—36 Locust St., 05401. Tel: 802-862-6696. Sisters of Mercy 3; Lay Teachers 20; Students 242.

4—ST. JOSEPH'S (1850), Revs. Pierre A. Lavallee; Yvon J. Royer.
Res., 85 Elmwood Ave., 05401. Tel: 802-863-2388. [CEM]
School—Sisters 1; Lay Teachers 15; Students 168.

5—ST. MARK'S (1940), Rev. Msgr. John R. McSweeney, V.G., J.C.L.; Rev. Paul C. Houde.
Res., 1251 North Ave., 05401. Tel: 802-864-7686; Fax: 802-651-9391.

OUTSIDE THE CITY OF BURLINGTON

Alburg, Grand Isle Co., St. Amadeus (1886), Rev. Maurice U. Boucher, S.S.E.
Res., 05440. Tel: 802-796-3481; Fax: 802-928-3305. [CEM]
Mission—Isle LaMotte, Grand Isle Co., St. Joseph, P.O. Box 65, Isle LaMotte, 05463. [CEM]
Chapel—Isle La Motte, St. Anne's Shrine, Tel: 802-928-3362; Fax: 802-928-3305.

Arlington, Bennington Co., St. Margaret Mary (1946), Rev. George H. Dupuis; Deacon Peter Putis.
Res., Main St., Box 36, 05250-0036. Tel: 802-375-2849. [CEM]

Barre, Washington Co., St. Monica (1892), Revs. Bernard H. Messier; Bernard W. Bourgeois; William D. Corcoran; Deacons Fernand Rivard; David Bisson.
Res., 79 Summer St., 05641. Tel: 802-479-3253.
School—Tel: 802-476-5015.
Lay Teachers 18; Students 180.
Convent—73 Summer St., 05641. Tel: 802-476-6514.

Barton, Orleans Co., Conversion of St. Paul (1893), Rev. James H. Mattison.
Res., Eastern Ave., 05822. Tel: 802-525-3711. [CEM]
School—Tel: 802-525-6178.
Sisters 1; Lay Teachers 7; Students 73.
Mission—East Albany, Orleans Co., St. John of the Cross. [CEM]

Bellows Falls, Windham Co., St. Charles (1871), Rev. James J. McShane.
Res., 31 Cherry Hill, 05101. Tel: 802-463-3128. [CEM]
Sacred Heart (1909), Rev. Felix J. Reczek, O.F.M., Admin.; Deacon John Blicharz.
Res., 39 Green St., 05101. Tel: 802-463-4110. [CEM]

Bennington, Bennington Co., Sacred Heart-St. Francis de Sales (1995), Revs. Laurence M. Olszewski, C.S.C.; William H. Kelley, C.S.C.; Deacon Eugene M. Krawczyk Tel: 802-442-7979.
Parish Office: 238 W. Main St., 05201. Tel: 802-442-3141; Fax: 802-442-3142.
School—Sacred Heart School, 307 School St., 05201. Tel: 802-442-2446; Fax: 802-442-3584. Mr. David B. Estes, Prin.
Lay Teachers 11; Students 166.
Mission—North Pownal, Our Lady of Lourdes.
Station—Vermont Veterans Home, Tel: 802-442-6353.

Bethel, Windsor Co., St. Anthony (1950), Rev. John J. Arnott, Admin.
Res., P.O. Box 63, Church St., 05032. Tel: 802-234-9916.
Missions—Pittsfield, Rutland Co., St. Denis; Rochester, Windsor Co., St. Elizabeth; South Royalton, Windsor Co., St. Matthew.

Bradford, Orange Co., Our Lady of Perpetual Help (1945), Rev. Philip R. Lamothe; Deacon Kelly Fitzpatrick.
Res., Box 314, 05033. Tel: 802-222-5268.
Missions—Norwich, Windsor Co., St. Francis of Assisi; Wells River, Orange Co., St. Eugene; South Strafford, Orange Co., Our Lady of Light.

Brandon, Rutland Co., St. Mary's (1867), Rev. Douglas W. Hawkins, C.S.C.
Res., 38 Carver St., 05733. Tel: 802-247-6351. [CEM]
Mission—Leicester, Addison Co., St. Agnes.

Brattleboro, Windham Co., St. Michael (1855), Revs. J.H. Normand Nadeau; Patrick J. Forman.
Res., 20 Walnut St., 05301. Tel: 802-257-5101. [CEM]
School—Mr. Frank J. Vara, Prin. Lay Teachers 8; Students 163.
Convent—27 Grove St., 05301. Tel: 802-254-9431.

Bristol, Addison Co., St. Ambrose (1893), Rev. Albert G. Baltz.
Res., 11 School St., 05443. Tel: 802-453-2488. [CEM]

Cambridge, Lamoille Co., St. Mary (1964), Rev. Robert C. Richardson.
Res., P.O. Box 129, 05444. Tel: 802-644-5073; Fax: 802-644-2546.
Mission—Johnson, Lamoille Co., St. John the Apostle.

Canaan, Essex Co., Assumption of the Blessed Virgin Mary (1950), Rev. John B. Loughnane, Jr (MAN).
Res., P.O. Box 176, Beecher Falls, 05902. Tel: 802-246-8829. [CEM]

Castleton, Rutland Co., St. John the Baptist (1899), Rev. Robert B. Whalen.
Res., P.O. Box 128, 05735. Tel: 802-468-5706.

Charlotte, Chittenden Co., Our Lady of Mount Carmel (1858), Rev. Gerald Ragis, O.S.B.
Res., P.O. Box 158, Spear St., 05445. Tel: 802-425-2637. [CEM]

Chester, Windsor Co., St. Joseph (1946), Rev. William P. Giroux; Deacon Eugene Allen, Jr.
Res., P.O. Box 40, 05143. Tel: 802-875-2610.
Mission—Proctorsville, Windsor Co., Holy Name of Mary.
Station—Londonderry, St. Joseph.

Chittenden, Rutland Co., St. Robert, Rev. Adam J. Krempa.
Res., c/o Rev. Adam J. Krempa, Immaculate Heart of Mary, 18 Lincoln Ave., Rutland, 05701. Tel: 802-747-7088.

Colchester, Chittenden Co., Holy Cross (1950), Rev. Roger L. Charbonneau.
Res., 47 Church Rd., 05446. Tel: 802-863-3002. [CEM]
Our Lady of Grace (1966), Rev. Brian E. Mead; Deacon William Glinka.
Res., 76 Main St., 05446. Tel: 802-878-5987.

Derby Line, Orleans Co., St. Edward (1946), Rev. Ernest Passero, S.J.; Deacon John P.E. Gratton.
Res., 24 Main St., 05830. Tel: 802-873-3522. [CEM]
Mission—West Charleston, Orleans Co., St. Benedict Labre.

East Dorset, Bennington Co., St. Jerome (1868), Rev. Michael A. Demasi, Admin.
Res., 05253. Tel: 802-362-2320. [CEM]
Mission—Danby, Rutland Co., Holy Trinity.

Enosburg Falls, Franklin Co., St. John the Baptist (1874), Rev. Gerard P. Leclere.
Res., P.O. Box 563, 05450. Tel: 802-933-4464; Fax: 802-933-8940. [CEM]

Essex Center, Chittenden Co., St. Pius X (1957), Rev.

Edward F. Moore.
Res., 20 Jericho Rd., Essex Junction, 05452-2707. Tel: 802-878-5997.

Essex Junction, Chittenden Co., Holy Family (1893), Rev. Charles P. Davignon.
Res., 4 Prospect St., 05452. Tel: 802-878-5331. [CEM]

St. Lawrence, Martyr (1966), Rev. Paul F. St. James.
Res., 158 West St., 05452. Tel: 802-878-8271.

Fairfax, Franklin Co., St. Luke (1943), Rev. John G. Feltz; Deacon Stephen Ratte.
Res., 17 Huntsville Rd., P.O. Box 7, 05454. Tel: 802-849-6205. [CEM]
Mission—Georgia, Franklin Co., Ascension.

Fairfield, Franklin Co., St. Patrick (1858), Rev. Thomas V. Mattison, Admin.; Deacon James Rock.
Res., 05455. Tel: 802-827-3203. [CEM]
Mission—East Fairfield, Franklin Co., St. Anthony-St. George.

Fair Haven, Rutland Co., Our Lady of Seven Dolors (1866), Rev. Raymond G. Maloney.
Res., 10 Washington St., 05743. Tel: 802-265-3135. [CEM]
Mission—West Castleton, Rutland Co., St. Matthew of Avalon.

Gilman, Essex Co., St. Theresa (1939), Revs. Joseph A. Lively; Lance Harlow; Deacon William J. Brown, III.
Res., Commercial Ave., Box 119, 05904. Tel: 802-892-5380.
Mission—Lunenburg, Essex Co., St. Leo.

Graniteville, Washington Co., St. Sylvester (1899), Rev. William S. Chant.
Res., Rte. 1, Box 1, 05654. Tel: 802-476-3913. [CEM]
Mission—Williamstown, Orange Co., St. Edward.

Greensboro Bend, Orleans Co., St. Michael (1954), Rev. Michael E. Augustinowitz.
Mailing Address: c/o St. Norbert Parish, P.O. Box 496, Hardwick, 05843. [CEM]
Res., 05842. Tel: 802-533-2377. [CEM]
Mission—Craftsbury, Orleans Co., Our Lady of Fatima.

Hardwick, Caledonia Co., St. Norbert (1911), Rev. Michael E. Augustinowitz.
Mailing Address: P.O. Box 496, 05843.
Res., 15 S. Main St., 05843. Tel: 802-472-5544. [CEM]

Highgate Center, Franklin Co., St. Louis (1886), Rev. Charles H. Ranges, S.S.E.; Deacon Jean-Louis Rainville.
Mailing Address: P.O. Box 78, 05459.
Res., 65 Canada St., Swanton, 05488. Tel: 802-862-4502. [CEM 2]

Hinesburg, Chittenden Co., St. Jude the Apostle (1946), Rev. Walter D. Miller, J.C.D.
Res., P.O. Box 69, 05461-0069. Tel: 802-482-2290; Fax: 802-482-3952.

Hyde Park, Lamoille Co., St. Teresa (1888), Rev. Denis R. Breton; Deacon Thomas Cooney.
Res., c/o Holy Cross Rectory, P.O. Box 339, Morrisville, 05661.
Church—05655. Tel: 802-888-3318.
Mission—Eden, Lamoille Co., St. Gabriel.

Island Pond, Essex Co., St. James the Greater (1871), Rev. Richard A. Fowler.
Res., P.O. Box 407, 05846. Tel: 802-723-4312. [CEM]
Mission—Norton, Essex Co., St. Bernard.

Ludlow, Windsor Co., Annunciation (1885), Rev. James A. Lawrence.
Res., 7 Depot St., 05149. Tel: 802-228-3451.

Lyndonville, Caledonia Co., St. Elizabeth (1891), Rev. Thomas Mosher (DEN); Deacon Alfred Toborg.
Res., 7 East St., P.O. Box 141, 05851-0141. Tel: 802-626-5267. [CEM]

Manchester Center, Bennington Co., Conversion of St. Paul (1896), Rev. Julien J. LaFlamme.
Res., Bonnet St., R.R. 2, Box 2830, 05255. Tel: 802-362-1380.

Marshfield, Washington Co., North American Martyrs (1963), Rev. William R. Beaudin.
Res., Box 221, 05658. Tel: 802-426-3233; Fax: 802-426-3525.
Mission—Danville, Calendonia Co., Our Lady Queen of Peace, P.O. Box 51, 05828. Tel: 802-684-3944.

Middlebury, Addison Co., Assumption of the Blessed Virgin Mary (1855), Rev. John J. McDermott.
Res., 19 College St., 05753. Tel: 802-388-2943. [CEM]
Mission—Bridport, Addison Co., St. Bernadette.

Middletown Springs, Rutland Co., St. Anne (1963), Rev. Paul E. Sackevich; Deacon Richard Perkins.
Res., 05757. Tel: 802-235-2156.
Missions—West Pawlet, Rutland Co., St. Frances Cabrini; Wells, Rutland Co., St. Paul.

Milton, Chittenden Co., St. Ann (1866), Rev. Donald J. Roy; Deacon Roger Lauziere.
Res., P.O. Box 1, 05468. Tel: 802-893-2487. [CEM]

Montgomery Center, Franklin Co., St. Isidore (1890). Attended by All Saints, Richford.
152 Main St., Richford, 05476. Tel: 802-848-7741. [CEM]

Montpelier, Washington Co., St. Augustine (1850), Revs. Bernard E. Gaudreau; Charles R. Danielson; Deacons Regis Cummings; Daniel Pudvah.
Res., 16 Barre St., 05602. Tel: 802-223-5285. [CEM]
School—St. Michael School, 46 Barre St., 05602. Tel: 802-223-6430.
Sisters 2; Lay Teachers 8; Students 123.

Morrisville, Lamoille Co., Holy Cross (1946), Rev. Denis R. Breton; Deacon Thomas Cooney.
Res., Brooklyn St., P.O. Box 339, 05661. Tel: 803-888-3318.

Newport, Orleans Co., St. Mary Star of the Sea (1873), Revs. Forrest W. Rouelle; Anthony Ventura (HRT).
Res., 5 Clermont Ter., 05855. Tel: 802-334-5066. [CEM]

North Bennington, Bennington Co., St. John the Baptist (1885), Rev. Robert J. Baffa.
Res., 05257. Tel: 802-447-7504. [CEM]

Northfield, Washington Co., St. John the Evangelist (1865), Rev. Kevin E. Rooney.
Res., 23 Vine St., 05663. Tel: 802-485-8313. [CEM]

North Troy, Orleans Co., St. Vincent de Paul (1939), Rev. George A. Paulin.
Res., Pleasant St., 05859. Tel: 802-988-2608. [CEM]

Orleans, Orleans Co., St. Theresa of Child Jesus (1942), Rev. Thomas A. Bransfield, Admin.
Res., 5 Willoughby Ave., 05860. Tel: 802-754-6049. [CEM]
Mission—Irasburg, Orleans Co., St. John Vianney. [CEM]

Orwell, Addison Co., St. Paul (1886), Rev. Robert J. McKnight.
Res., P.O. Box 41, 05760. Tel: 802-948-2951. [CEM]
Mission—Shoreham, Addison Co., St. Geneviere.

Pittsford, Rutland Co., St. Alphonsus Liguori (1893), Rev. Joseph E. Romano.
Res., R.R. 2, Box 2114, 05763. Tel: 802-483-2301; Fax: 802-483-2136. [CEM]

Poultney, Rutland Co., St. Raphael (1894), Rev. Joseph M. Vignoe.
Res., Main St., 05764. Tel: 802-287-5703. [CEM]

Proctor, Rutland Co., St. Dominic (1888), Rev. Msgr. Paul M. Bresnehan.
Res., 45 South St., 05765. Tel: 802-459-2221. [CEM]

Putney, Windham Co., Our Lady of Mercy (1931), Revs. John T. Scully, S.S.E.; Frederick E. McLachlan, S.S.E.; Deacon Robert Degnon.
Res., Old Depot Rd., 05346. Tel: 802-387-5861.
Missions—Saxtons River, Windham Co., St. Edmund of Canterbury; Stratton Mountain, Windham Co., Chapel of the Snows; Townshend, Windham Co., Our Lady of the Valley; Wardsboro, Windham Co., Our Lady of Hope.

Randolph, Orange Co., SS. Donatian and Rogatian (1903), Rev. John M. Milanese, Admin.; Deacon Paul Lissandrello.
Res., 25 S. Pleasant St., 05060. Tel: 802-728-3227. [CEM]

Readsboro, Bennington Co., St. Joachim (1895), Rev. James E. Beauregard.
Res., 36 Tunnel St., 05350-9738. Tel: 802-423-5267.
Mission—Stamford, Bennington Co., St. John Bosco.

Richford, Franklin Co., All Saints (1899), Rev. Francis C. Eksterowicz; Deacons Clifford Chagnon; Jon Ramey.
Res., 152 Main St., 05476. Tel: 802-848-7741. [CEM]
Mission—East Berkshire, Franklin Co., Our Lady of Lourdes.

Richmond, Chittenden Co., Our Lady of the Holy Rosary (1857), Rev. Ronald H. Benoit.
Res., P.O. Box 243, 05477. Tel: 802-434-2521. [CEM 2]

Rutland, Rutland Co., Christ the King (1907), Revs. Reid C. Mayo; J. Charles Durham.
Res., 66 S. Main St., 05701. Tel: 802-773-6820; Fax: 802-773-6820, Ext. 136.
School—Sisters 2; Lay Teachers 24; Students 418.

Immaculate Heart of Mary (1869), Rev. Richard W. Tinney. In res., Rev. Adam J. Krempa.
Res., 18 Lincoln Ave., 05701. Tel: 802-775-0846. [CEM]

St. Peter (1855), Revs. Wilfred Andre Houle; John J. Herbert. In res., Rev. John A. Guischard, (Retired).
Res., 134 Convent Ave., 05701. Tel: 802-775-1994; Fax: 802-775-0178. [CEM]

St. Albans, Franklin Co., Holy Angels (1872), Rev. Maurice J. Roy.
Res., 246 Lake St., 05478. Tel: 802-524-2585. [CEM]

Immaculate Conception (1847), Rev. Leonidas B. Laroche; Deacon John Rixon.
Res., 45 Fairfield St., 05478. Tel: 802-527-7775. [CEM]

St. Albans Bay, Franklin Co., Our Lady of the Lake (1904). Closed. For inquiries for parish records contact the Chancery.

St. Johnsbury, Caledonia Co., St. John the Evangelist (1896), Revs. Joseph A. Lively; Lance Harlow; Robert Lapan; Deacons Bruce Burk; Raymond Desilets; Bernier Mayo.
Res., 2 Winter St., 05819. Tel: 802-748-8129. [CEM]

Shelburne, Chittenden Co., St. Catherine of Siena (1906), Rev. John W. Hamilton.
Res., Church St., P.O. Box 70, 05482. Tel: 802-985-2373. [CEM]

Sheldon Springs, Franklin Co., St. Anthony (1906), Rev. Bernard J. Bechard, S.S.E.
Res., Mill St., P.O. Box 97, 05485-0097. Tel: 802-933-8921; Fax: 802-933-8921. [CEM]
Mission—Franklin, Franklin Co., St. Mary.

Sherburne, Rutland Co., Our Lady of the Mountains, Rev. Adam J. Krempa.
Res., c/o Rev. Adam J. Krempa, Immaculate Heart of Mary, 18 Lincoln Ave., Rutland, 05701. Tel: 802-747-7088.

South Burlington, Chittenden Co., St. John Vianney (1940), Rev. Raymond A. Giroux; Deacons Joseph Lane; Anthony Previti.
Res., 160 Hinesburg Rd., 05403. Tel: 802-864-4166; Fax: 802-863-6065.

South Hero, Grand Isle Co., St. Rose of Lima (1895), Rev. Philip J. Branon.
Res., 501 Rte. 2, 05486. Tel: 802-372-4092; Fax: 802-372-4770.
Missions—Grand Isle, Grand Isle Co., St. Joseph, 185 Rte. 2, 05458. Tel: 802-372-5627; North Hero, Grand Isle Co., St. Benedict Joseph Labre.

Springfield, Windsor Co., Maternity of the Blessed Virgin Mary (1901), Rev. James M. Shea.
Res., 40 Summer St., 05156. Tel: 802-885-3400; 885-2250. [CEM]

Stowe, Lamoille Co., Blessed Sacrament (1954), Rev. John B. Kenney.
Res., Mountain Rd., P.O. Box 27, 05672. Tel: 802-253-7536.

Swanton, Franklin Co., Nativity of the Blessed Virgin Mary (1854), Rev. Charles H. Ranges, S.S.E., Admin.
Res., 65 Canada St., 05488. Tel: 802-868-4517; Fax: 802-868-4262. [CEM]

Troy, Orleans Co., Sacred Heart of Jesus (1931), Rev. Stephen J. Nichols.
Res., 05868. Tel: 802-744-2239. [CEM]
Mission—Lowell, Orleans Co., St. Ignatius Loyola.

Underhill Center, Chittenden Co., St. Thomas (1856), Rev. Francis R. Prive.
Res., P.O. Box 3, 05490-0003. Tel: 802-899-4632; Fax: 802-899-4770. [CEM 3]

Vergennes, Addison Co., St. Peter (1881), Rev. Donal Ward.
Res., 85 S. Maple St., P.O. Box 324, 05491. Tel: 802-877-2367; Fax: 802-877-1063. [CEM]

Waitsfield, Washington Co., Our Lady of the Snows (1964), Rev. Donald E. Ritchie.
Mailing Address: c/o 109 S. Main St., Waterbury, 05676. Tel: 802-244-7734.
Mission—Moretown, Washington Co., St. Patrick.

Wallingford, Rutland Co., St. Patrick (1910), Rev. Joseph M. Quinn, C.S.C.
Res., 30 N. Main St., 05773. Tel: 802-446-2161. [CEM]
Mission—Mount Holly, Rutland Co., St. Mary.

Washington, Orange Co., St. Cecilia (1961), Rev. William P. Morgan.
Res., P.O. Drawer 4, 05675. Tel: 802-883-2285.
Mission—East Barre, Orange Co., Mother Cabrini.

Waterbury, Washington Co., St. Andrew (1869), Rev. Donald E. Ritchie.
Res., 109 S. Main St., 05676. Tel: 802-244-7734. [CEM]

West Rutland, Rutland Co., St. Bridget (1857), Rev. Raymond D. Walsh.
Res., One Church St., 05777-0087. Tel: 802-438-2490. [CEM 2]

St. Stanislaus Kostka (1904), Rev. Frank S. Warzocha.
Res., 9 Barnes St., 05777. Tel: 802-438-5671. [CEM]

White River Junction, Windsor Co., St. Anthony (1869), Revs. Ronald Saunders, S.M.; Adrien O. Pelletier, S.M.; Deacon John P. Guarino.
Res., One Church St., 05001. Tel: 802-295-2225;

Fax: 802-296-6008. [CEM]
Convent—7 Church St., 05001. Tel: 802-295-7176.
Station—White River Junction, Veterans Administration Hospital, Tel: 802-295-9363.

Williston, Chittenden Co., Immaculate Heart of Mary (1951), Rev. Donald J. Ravey.
Res., P.O. Box 1047, 05495. Tel: 802-878-4513.

Wilmington, Windham Co., Our Lady of Fatima (1959), Rev. Joseph H. Tate, C.S.C.; Deacon Paul Mello.
Res., P.O. Box 188, 05363. Tel: 802-464-7329.

Windsor, Windsor Co., St. Francis of Assisi (1886), Rev. Robert J. Campbell, M.S.
Res., 30 Union St., P.O. Box 46, 05089. Tel: 802-674-2157; 674-2156. [CEM]

Winooski, Chittenden Co., St. Francis Xavier (1868), Rev. Richard G. LaValley; Deacons Norman Langlois; John F. Place. In res., Rev. Gerald W. Bombardier.
Res., St. Peter St., 05404. Tel: 802-655-2290; Fax: 802-655-3036. [CEM]
School—Tel: 802-655-2600.
Brothers 1; Sisters 3; Lay Teachers 6; Students 260.
Convent—Tel: 802-655-2395; Fax: 802-655-3888.
St. Vincent de Paul Center—Tel: 802-655-3006.
Daycare—Tel: 802-655-4660.
St. Stephen (1882), Rev. Peter A. Routhier. In res., Rev. Jay C. Haskin.
Res., 115 Barlow St., 05404. Tel: 802-655-0318; Fax: 802-655-1615. [CEM]

Woodstock, Windsor Co., Our Lady of the Snows (1894), Rev. William P. Gallagher.
Res., 7 South St., 05091. Tel: 802-457-2322; Fax: 802-457-5805.

Chaplains of Public Institutions

BURLINGTON. *Fletcher Allen Health Care,* 05401. Tel: 802-656-2770. Revs. Leopold J. Bilodeau; Francis E. Connors; Sr. Monica Rock, R.H.S.J., Pastoral Assoc.

WATERBURY. *State Hospital*. Rev. Louis R. Logue.

WHITE RIVER JUNCTION. *Veterans Administration Hospital*. Rev. Adrien O. Pelletier, S.M.

On Duty Outside the Diocese:
Reverend Fathers—
Courcy, Leo J., Mt. Saviour Monastery, Mt. Savior Rd., Pine City, NY 14871
Daley, Daniel P., St. Mary, 307 N. Church St., Bloomfield, NM 87413
Dowd, Barry G., Mary Queen of the Universe Shrine, 8300 Vineland Ave., Orlando, FL 32821

Military Chaplains:
Reverend Fathers—
Soutiere, Ronald, USN

Unassigned:
Reverend Fathers—
Bean, Donald

Other Residence:
Reverend Fathers—
Bruder, John W., O.C.S.O., R.R. 1, Box 143, West Danville, VT 05873-9801

Retired:
Reverend Monsignors—
Adams, Raymond A., 9 Cascadnac Ave., Essex Junction, VT 05452
Buckley, Edwin T., 22 Wellesley Grove, 630 Hinesburg Rd., South Burlington, VT 05403
Flanagan, Francis B., 59 Meadow St., Rutland, VT 05701
Foster, Edward C., The Waterford, 3333 University Blvd., Kensington, MD 20895
Gelineau, Edward J., St. Joseph's Home, 243 N. Prospect St., Burlington, VT 05401
Powers, Robert J., St. Albert Rectory, 1130 Washington St., Weymouth, MA 02189
Reverend Fathers—
Beary, Thomas J., St. Joseph's Home, 243 N. Prospect St., Burlington, VT 05401
Brackett, Anthony H., 9854 Wildginger Dr., S.W., Fort Myers, FL 33919
Brochu, Gerard H., P.O. Box 7223, Statesville, NC 28687
Couture, Bernard G., Box 202, East Barre, VT 05639
Demasi, Michael A., St. Jerome, East Dorset, VT 05253
Dennigan, Patrick J., P.O. Box 931, North Adams, MA 01247
Depeaux, Bernard F., P.O. Box 4000, Shelburne, VT 05482
Dufault, Omer L., St. Joseph's Home, 243 N. Prospect St., Burlington, VT 05401
Duquette, Lucien G., 6 Roland Ct., Winooski, VT 05404
Falvella, Richard J., Crystal Haven Rd., Bomoseen, VT 05732
Foley, James F., Burlington Health & Rehab Center, 300 Pearl St., Burlington, VT 05401
Gagnon, John, Loretto Home, 59 Meadow St., Rutland, VT 05701
Guischard, John A., St. Peter Rectory, 134 Convent Ave., Rutland, VT 05701
Hackett, John P., 59 Upper Welden St., Apt. 15, St. Albans, VT 05478
Hart, Edward J., St. Joseph's Home, 243 N. Prospect St., Burlington, VT 05401
Holland, Francis M., 8 Cedar Glen N., South Burlington, VT 05403
Kennedy, David G., 4580 N. Kolb Rd., Tucson, AZ 85715-6103
Lagor, Joseph J., Box 28, Sharon, VT 05065
Laliberte, William F., 113 Robbins St., Rutland, VT 05701
Laplante, Jean-Paul, 64 N. Elm St., St. Albans, VT 05478
Lawlor, Brendan W., 695 Americana Dr., Apt. 17, Annapolis, MD 21403
Ledoux, John C., 16 Clover Dr., 9-C, Essex Junction, VT 05452
McCarthy, Joseph, 130 Curtis Ave., Burlington, VT 05401
Mulligan, William R., 20 N. 28th Ave., Longport, NJ 08403
Murtagh, George O., 2640 N.E. 52nd Ct., #42, Silver Springs, FL 34488-9402
Pagliuca, Joseph P., Villaggio S. Berardo, No. 16, Pescina, Province L'Aguila, 67057 Italy
Pray, Joseph N, P.O. Box 85, Castleton, VT 05735
Provost, Raymond C., Birchwood Terrace Healthcare, 43 Starr Farm Rd., Burlington, VT 05401
Rousseau, Peter A., D10, Stonehedge Dr., South Burlington, VT 05403
Von Fauer, Stephen C., Mary Theotokos Center, P.O. Box 88, West Burke, VT 05871

Permanent Deacons:
Allen, Eugene, Jr., St. Joseph, Chester
Bisson, David A., St. Monica, Barre
Blicharz, John F., Sacred Heart, Bellow Falls
Brown, William, III, St. Theresa, Gilman
Burk, Bruce, St. John, St. Johnsbury
Chagnon, Clifford, All Saints, Richford
Cooney, Thomas, Holy Cross, Morrisville
Cummings, Regis E., St. Augustine, Montpelier
Degnon, Robert F, Our Lady of Hope, West Wardsboro
Desilets, Raymond J., St. John, St. Johnsbury
Fitzpatrick, Kelly, Our Lady of Perpetual Help, Bradford
Glinka, William, Our Lady of Grace, Colchester
Gratton, John, St. Benedict, West Charleston
Guarino, John P., St. Anthony, White River Junction
Hawk, Ivan, Holy Cross, Colchester
Herrick, Eugene, St. Mark, Burlington
Krawczyk, Eugene, Sacred Heart-St. Francis de Sales, Bennington
Lane, Joseph W., Sr., St. John Vianney, South Burlington
Langlois, Norman S., St. Francis Xavier, Winooski
Lauziere, Roger J., St. Ann, Milton
Lissandrello, Paul, Sts. Donatian and Rogatian, Randolph
Mayo, Bernier L., St. John, St. Johnsbury
Mello, Paul, Our Lady of Fatima, Wilmington
Meunier, Louis A., St. Anthony, Burlington
Nadeau, Thomas, On Duty Outside the Diocese
Perkins, Richard, St. Francis Cabrini, West Pawlet
Place, John F., St. Francis Xavier, Winooski
Previti, Anthony, St. John Vianney, South Burlington
Pudvah, Daniel, St. Augustine, Montpelier
Putis, Peter, St. Margaret Mary, Arlington
Rainville, John L., St. Louis, Highgate Center
Ramey, Jon, St. Isidore, Montgomery Center
Ratte, Stephen J., St. Luke, Fairfax
Rivard, Fernand R., St. Monica, Barre
Rixon, John, St. Mary, St. Albans
Rock, James E., St. Patrick, Fairfield
Toborg, Alfred, St. Elizabeth, Lyndonville
Vincelette, Alan, St. Amadeus, Alburg

INSTITUTIONS LOCATED IN THE DIOCESE

[A] COLLEGES AND UNIVERSITIES

BURLINGTON. *Trinity College of Vermont*, President's Office, 208 Colchester Ave., 05401. Tel: 802-658-0337.
For a complete listing, refer to the Colleges and Universities section.

COLCHESTER. *St. Michael's College*, Winooski Park, 05439. Tel: 802-654-2211; Fax: 802-655-4079.
For a complete listing, refer to the Colleges and Universities section.

RUTLAND. *College of St. Joseph in Vermont*, 71 Clement Rd., 05701-3899. Tel: 802-773-5900.
For a complete listing, refer to the Colleges and Universities section.

[B] CENTRAL HIGH SCHOOLS, DIOCESAN AND PAROCHIAL

RUTLAND. *Mt. St. Joseph Academy*, 127 Convent Ave., 05701. Tel: 802-775-0151. Sisters of St. Joseph. Sr. Shirley A. Davis, S.S.J., Prin.; Richard Horn, Guidance Dir.; Gregory Schillinger, Vice Prin. Priests 2; Sisters 2; Lay Teachers 23; Students 205.

SOUTH BURLINGTON. *Rice Memorial High School*, 99 Proctor Ave., 05403. Tel: 802-862-6521. Bro. Roger Lemoyne, S.C., Prin.; Thomas Walsh, Guidance Dir. Sisters 3; Brothers 2; Lay Teachers 35; Students 490.

[C] ELEMENTARY SCHOOLS, PAROCHIAL

BURLINGTON. *Christ The King*. (Grades PreK-8), 136 Locust St., 05401. Tel: 802-862-6696. Mr. James Provost, Prin. Sisters 3; Lay Teachers 20; Students 242.
Mater Christi School, 50 Mansfield Ave., 05401. Tel: 802-658-3992. Sr. Laura Della Santa, R.S.M., Prin. Sisters 4; Lay Teachers 35; Students 443.
St. Joseph. (Grades PreK-8), 20 Allen St., 05401. Tel: 802-864-5623. Keith Cieplicki, Prin. Sisters 1; Lay Teachers 15; Students 168.

BARRE. *St. Monica's*. (Grades PreK-8), 73 Summer St., 05641. Tel: 802-476-5015. Mrs. Betty Foley, Prin. Lay Teachers 18; Students 180.

BARTON. *St. Paul's*. (Grades K-8), Eastern Ave., 05822. Tel: 802-525-6578. Mrs. Jane Williams, Prin. Sisters 1; Lay Teachers 6; Students 73.

BENNINGTON. *Sacred Heart*. (Grades K-6), 307 School St., 05201. Tel: 802-442-2446; Fax: 802-442-3584. Mr. David Estes, Prin. Lay Teachers 11; Students 166.

BRATTLEBORO. *St. Michael's*. (Grades PreK-6), 23 Walnut St., 05301. Tel: 802-254-5666. Mr. Frank J. Vara, Prin. Lay Teachers 9; Students 190.

MONTPELIER. *St. Michael's School*. (Grades K-6), 46 Barre St., 05602. Tel: 802-223-6430. Sr. Nancy Mencel, S.N.D., Prin. Sisters 2; Lay Teachers 8; Students 123.

NEWPORT. *Sacred Heart Schools, Inc*. (Grades PreK-8), P.O. Box 930, 05855. Tel: 802-334-8185; 334-7803 (Bus. Office). Mrs. Nancy Croteau, Prin. Sisters 1; Lay Teachers 13; Students 215.

RUTLAND. *Christ the King*. (Grades PreK-8), 60 S. Main St., 05701. Tel: 802-773-6820, Ext. 17. Mr. Jeffrey G. Johnson, Prin. Sisters 2; Lay Teachers 24; Students 418.

WINOOSKI. *St. Francis Xavier*. (Grades PreK-8), St. Peter St., 05404. Tel: 802-655-2600. Mr. Roderick Marcotte, Prin. Sisters 3; Brothers 1; Lay Teachers 6; Students 260.

[D] CHILD CARE INSTITUTIONS

BURLINGTON. *St. Joseph's Group Home*, c/o Vermont Catholic Charities, Inc., 351 North Ave., 05401. Tel: 802-862-2623.
For a complete listing, refer to the Special Care Facilities section.

[E] GENERAL HOSPITALS

COLCHESTER. *Fanny Allen Hospital*, 101 College Pkwy., 05446. Tel: 802-655-1234; Fax: 802-654-1109.
For a complete listing, refer to the Hospitals section.

[F] HOMES FOR AGED

BURLINGTON. *St. Joseph's Home for Aged*, 243 N. Prospect St., 05401. Tel: 802-864-0264.
For a complete listing, refer to the Special Care Facilities section.

DERBY LINE. *Michaud Memorial Manor*, 05830. Tel: 802-873-3152.
For a complete listing, refer to the Special Care Facilities section.

RUTLAND. *Loretto Home for Aged*, 05701. Tel: 802-773-8840.
For a complete listing, refer to the Special Care Facilities section.
St. Joseph Assisted Living Residence/Kervick Home, 131 Convent Ave., 05701. Tel: 802-775-5133.
For a complete listing, refer to the Special Care Facilities section.

[G] MONASTERIES AND RESIDENCES OF PRIESTS AND BROTHERS

BURLINGTON. *Brothers of the Sacred Heart*. 190 White St., South Burlington, 05403. Tel: 802-658-6624. Bros. Damian Goudreau, S.C., Dir.; Roger

Lemoyne, S.C.; Roger Fountain, S.C.; Richard Labbe, S.C. Brothers 4.

ARLINGTON. *Carthusian Foundation, Charterhouse of the Transfiguration*, R.R. 2, Box 2411, 05250. Revs. Francois Rheault, O.Cart. (Canada); Lorenzo Maria Tolentino de la Rosa, Jr., O.Cart. (Philippines), Rector, Novice Master of Brothers; Mary Joseph Kim, O.Cart (Korea), Novice Master of Cloister Monks; Mary Paul Chapeau, O.Cart. (France), Antiquior; Marianus Marck, O.Cart. (Germany); Mary Bernard Thompson, O.Cart. (U.S.A.); Mary Michael Tobias, O.Cart. (Czechoslovakia).
Carthusian Foundation, Association Fraternelle Romande. Choir Monks: Solemn Professed 7; Temporary Professed 3; Postulants 2; Converse Brothers: Solemn Professed 4; Temporary Professed 2; Perpetual Donates 2.

COLCHESTER. *Society of St. Edmund*. (Edmundite Generalate), 270 Winooski Park, 05439. Tel: 802-654-3400.
Central Offices, Society of Saint Edmund. Revs. Joseph L. Hart, S.S.E., Supr. Gen.; James R. Coombs, S.S.E.; Eymard Galligan, S.S.E.; Edward J. Dubriske, S.S.E. (Venezuela); Howard J. Muehlberger, S.S.E. (Venezuela); Philippe Simonnet, S.S.E. (France).
Society of St. Edmund. (Edmundite Community at St. Michael's College), 05439. Tel: 802-654-2000. Revs. Marcel Rainville, S.S.E., Supr.; Richard N. Berube, S.S.E.; Paul E. Couture, S.S.E.; Michael P. Cronogue, S.S.E.; Brian J. Cummings, S.S.E.; Lorenzo D'Agostino, S.S.E.; Raymond J. Doherty, S.S.E.; Joseph M. McLaughlin, S.S.E.; Robert J. Sheehey, S.S.E.; John A. Stankiewicz, S.S.E.; Romeo A. Trahan, S.S.E.; Richard L. VanderWeel, S.S.E.; Bros. Anthony Krutch, S.S.E.; Daniel H. Manzano, S.S.E.

WESTON. *Priory of Benedictine Monks*, 58 Priory Hill Rd., 05161. Tel: 802-824-5409. Very Rev. John Hammond, O.S.B., Prior; Revs. Richard Iaquinto, O.S.B., Asst. Prior; Peter Claude Anctil, O.S.B.; Robert J. Kiernan, O.S.B.; Mark Ronald Nicolosi, O.S.B. Priests 5; Brothers 9.

[H] CONVENTS AND RESIDENCES OF SISTERS

BURLINGTON. *Mount St. Mary Convent*, 100 Mansfield Ave., 05401. Tel: 802-863-6835. Motherhouse and Novitiate of Sisters of Mercy. Sr. Jeannine Mercure, R.S.M., Pres. In res., Rev. Wendell H. Searles, Chap.
Institute for Spiritual Development, 208 Colchester Ave., 05401. Tel: 802-658-0339, Ext. 410. Sisters 92.

BARRE. *Discalced Carmelite Monastery*, Beckley Hill, R.R. 2, Box 4784, 05641-8922. Tel: 802-476-8362. Sr. Jeanne M. Gonyon, Prioress. Professed Nuns 10.

COLCHESTER. *Religious Hospitallers of St. Joseph*, 101 College Pkwy., 05446. Tel: 802-655-1160. Sr. Rita Vallee, R.H.S.J., Supr. Sisters 16.

NEWPORT. *Sacred Heart Convent*, P.O. Box 375, 05855. Tel: 802-334-7058. Sr. Solange Poutre, F.C.S.C.J., Supr. Sisters 13.

RUTLAND. *Sisters of St. Joseph Society, Inc.*, 131 Convent Ave., 05701. Tel: 802-775-5133. Administrative Offices, 129 Convent Ave., 05701. Tel: 802-775-0665.
Other Residences: St. Francis Residence, 11 Clement Rd., 05701.
Guest Houses: Avila Hall, 7 Clement Rd., 05701. Marion Hall, 9 Clement Rd., 05701. St. Joseph, 333 Elm St., Bennington, 05201. Fontbonne Hall, 13 Clement Rd., 05701. Sisters 53.

WESTFIELD. *Monastery of the Immaculate Heart of Mary*, H.C.R. #13, Box 11, 05874. Tel: 802-744-6525. Benedictine Cloistered Nuns, Congregation of Solesmes. Rev. Mother Marguerite Derome, O.S.B., Prioress; Rev. Dom Guy-Marie Oury, O.S.B., Res. Chap., Monk of Solesmes, France. Professed Nuns 14.

WINOOSKI. *Missionary Sisters of Our Lady of Africa (M.S.O.L.A.)*, 47 W. Spring St., 05404. Tel: 802-655-4003. Sr. Lucille Pilotte, District Supr. Sisters 15.
Our Lady of Providence Convent, 47 W. Spring St., 05404. Tel: 802-655-2395. Sr. Theresa Dufresne, S.P., Supr. Sisters 27.

[I] SUMMER CAMPS

BURLINGTON. *Camp Holy Cross, Inc.*, 351 North Ave., 05401. Summer Camp for Boys. Day Camp for Boys and Girls. Diocesan institution under direction of Board of Trustees. Capacity 100.
Camp Tara, Catholic Charities Central Office, 351 North Ave., 05401. Tel: 802-658-6110. Summer camp for underprivileged Vermont children. Diocesan institution under direction of Vermont Catholic Charities. Capacity 222.

MARLBORO. *Camp Neringa*. R.F.D. No. 4, Box 155, West Brattleboro, 05301. Sr. Igne Marijosius, Dir. Coed under direction of the Sisters of the Immaculate Conception of the Blessed Virgin Mary, Putnam, CT. Capacity 120.

[J] NEWMAN CENTERS

BURLINGTON. *University of Vermont-The Catholic Center at UVM*, 390 S. Prospect St., 05401. Tel: 802-862-8403; Fax: 802-865-9480. Chaplains: Revs. Michael W. DeForge; Peter Y. Williams.
Castleton State College, St. John Rectory, P.O. Box 128, Castleton, 05735. Rev. Robert B. Whalen, Chap.
Goddard College, Plainfield, 05667. Rev. William R. Beaudin, Chap., North American Martyrs, Box 221, Marshfield, 05658-0221.
Green Mountain College, St. Raphael Rectory, Main St., Poultney, 05764. Rev. Joseph M. Vignoe, Chap.
Johnson State College (Johnson). Attended by St. Mary, Cambridge. P.O. Box 129, Cambridge, 05444. Rev. Robert C. Richardson, Chap.
Lyndon State College, Lyndon Center, 05850. Rev. Thomas Mosher, Chap., St. Elizabeth Church, P.O. Box 141, Lyndonville, 05851.
Middlebury College, St. Mary Rectory, 19 College St., Middlebury, 05753. Rev. John McDermott, Chap.
Norwich Newman Apostolate, Norwich University, Northfield, 05663. Chaplains: Rev. Michael W. DeForge, The Catholic Center at UVM, 390 S. Prospect St., 05401. Rev. Richard G. LaValley, St. Francis Xavier Rectory, St. Peter St., Winooski, 05404.
Vermont Technical College, Sts. Donatian and Rogatian Rectory, 25 S. Pleasant St., Randolph, 05060. Rev. John M. Milanese, Chap.

[K] MISCELLANEOUS

BURLINGTON. *Institute for Spiritual Development*, 208 Colchester Ave., 05401. Tel: 802-658-0337, Ext. 410.

BENSON. *Lumen Christi Retreat House*, 05731. Tel: 802-537-4531. Reservations for retreat call Tel: 802-658-0337, Ext. 410.

ISLE LA MOTTE. *St. Anne's Shrine*, 05463. Tel: 802-928-3362; Fax: 802-928-3305. Conducted by Fathers of Society of St. Edmund. Rev. Maurice U. Boucher, S.S.E.
Open May 15-Oct. 15.

RANDOLPH. *Opus Dei*, Wynnview Center, R.D. 1, 05060. Tel: 802-728-5414; Fax: 802-728-3334.
Legal Names: Opus Dei; The Work of God.

RELIGIOUS INSTITUTES OF MEN REPRESENTED IN THE DIOCESE

For further details refer to the corresponding bracketed number in the Religious Institutes of Men or Women section.

[0200]—*Benedictine Monks.*—O.S.B.
[1100]—*Brothers of the Sacred Heart.* (New England Prov.).—S.C.
[0300]—*Cistercian Order of the Strict Observance (Trappists).*—O.C.S.O.
[0520]—*Franciscan Friars.*—O.F.M.
[0690]—*Jesuit Fathers and Brothers.*—S.J.
[0780]—*Marist Fathers.*—S.M.
[0720]—*The Missionaries of Our Lady of La Salette.* (Prov. of the Immaculate Heart of Mary).—M.S.
[0280]—*Order of Carthusians.*—O.Cart.
[0610]—*Priests of the Congregation of Holy Cross.* (Eastern Prov.).—C.S.C.
[0440]—*Society of Saint Edmund.*—S.S.E.

RELIGIOUS INSTITUTES OF WOMEN REPRESENTED IN THE DIOCESE

[0170]—*Benedictine Cloistered Nuns of the Congregation of Solesmes.*—O.S.B.
[0750]—*Daughters of the Charity of the Sacred Heart of Jesus.*—F.C.S.C.J.
[0820]—*Daughters of the Holy Spirit.*—D.H.S.
[0960]—*Daughters of Wisdom.*—D.W.
[0420]—*Discalced Carmelite Nuns.*—O.C.D.
[1070]—*Dominican Sisters.*—O.P.
[1190]—*Franciscan Sisters of the Atonement.*—S.A.
[]—*Missionary Sisters of Our Lady of Africa.*—M.S.O.L.A.
[3440]—*Religious Hospitallers of Saint Joseph.*—R.H.S.J.
[1930]—*Sisters of Holy Cross.*—C.S.C.
[2550]—*Sisters of Mercy.*—R.S.M.
[3000]—*Sisters of Notre Dame de Namur.*—S.N.D.deN.
[3340]—*Sisters of Providence.*—S.P.
[3830-01]—*Sisters of St. Joseph (Boston, MA).*—C.S.J.
[3830-07]—*Sisters of St. Joseph (Burlington, VT).*—S.S.J.
[4130]—*Ursuline Sisters of the Congregation of Tildonk, Belgium.*—O.S.U.

DIOCESAN CEMETERIES

BURLINGTON. *St. Joseph's Cemetery*, 05401.
SOUTH BURLINGTON. *Resurrection Park Cemetery*, 05403.

NECROLOGY

† Fitzsimons, Rev. Msgr. Edward J., (Retired). —Died Aug. 6, 1996.

Diocese of Camden

(Dioecesis Camdensis)

Most Reverend

JAMES T. McHUGH, S.T.D.

Bishop of Camden; ordained May 25, 1957; appointed Titular Bishop of Morosbisdo and Auxiliary Bishop of Newark November 20, 1987; consecrated January 25, 1988; appointed Bishop of Camden May 13, 1989; installed June 20, 1989. *Res., Marywood, P.O. Box 577, 1600 Peter Cheeseman Rd., Blackwood, NJ, 08012. Office: Camden Diocesan Center, P.O. Box 709, Camden, NJ, 08101-0709.*

Most Reverend

JAMES L. SCHAD, D.D.

Retired Auxiliary Bishop of Camden; appointed Titular Bishop of Panatoria October 18, 1966; consecrated December 8, 1966; retired January 26, 1993. *Res., Neumann House, St. Mary's Home, Ste. 102, 1730 Kresson Rd., Cherry Hill, NJ, 08003.*

Legal Corporate Title: "The Diocese of Camden, New Jersey."

ESTABLISHED DECEMBER 9, 1937.

Square Miles 2,691.

Comprises six Counties in the State of New Jersey—viz., Atlantic, Camden, Cape May, Cumberland, Gloucester and Salem.

For legal titles of parishes and diocesan institutions, consult the Chancery Office.

The Chancery: Camden Diocesan Center, 1845 Haddon Ave., P.O. Box 709, Camden, NJ, 08101-0709. Tel.: 609-756-7900; Fax: 609-963-2655.

STATISTICAL OVERVIEW

Personnel	
Bishop	1
Retired Bishops	1
Priests: Diocesan Active in Diocese	293
Priests: Active Outside Diocese	36
Priests: Diocesan in Foreign Missions	2
Number of Diocesan Priests	331
Religious Priests in Diocese	42
Extern Priests in Diocese	16
Ordinations:	
Transitional Deacons	2
Permanent Deacons in Diocese	96
Total Brothers	14
Total Sisters	372
Parishes	
Parishes	126
With Resident Pastor:	
Resident Diocesan Priests	119
Resident Religious Priests	7
Without Resident Pastor:	
Pastoral Centers	31
Welfare	
Catholic Hospitals	1
Total Assisted	243,221
Health Care Centers	2
Total Assisted	9,320
Homes for the Aged	5
Total Assisted	1,020
Residential Care of Children	2
Total Assisted	11
Day Care and Extended Day Care Centers	1
Total Assisted	60
Special Centers for Social Services	12
Total Assisted	7,833
Educational	
Diocesan Students in Other Seminaries	21
Total Seminarians	21
High Schools, Diocesan and Parish	8
Total Students	4,766
High Schools, Private	3
Total Students	1,071
Elementary Schools, Diocesan and Parish	61
Total Students	15,662
Catechesis/Religious Education:	
High School Students	543
Elementary Students	31,774
Total Students Under Catholic Instruction	53,837
Teachers in the Diocese:	
Priests	17
Brothers	3
Sisters	90
Lay Teachers	959
Vital Statistics	
Receptions into the Church:	
Infant Baptism Totals	7,305
Adult Baptism Totals	642
Received into Full Communion	540
First Communions	6,813
Confirmations	4,917
Marriages:	
Catholic	1,506
Interfaith	622
Total Marriages	2,128
Total Catholic Population	406,383
Total Population	1,286,240

Former Bishops—Most Rev. BARTHOLOMEW J. EUSTACE, S.T.D., First Bishop of Camden; cons. March 25, 1938; died Dec. 11, 1956.—Most Rev. JUSTIN J. MCCARTHY, S.T.D., LL.D., Second Bishop of Camden; cons. June 17, 1954; appt. to Camden, Jan. 27, 1957; died Dec. 26, 1959.—Most Rev. CELESTINE J. DAMIANO, D.D., Third Bishop of Camden; cons. Feb. 11, 1953; transferred to Camden, Jan. 24, 1960, with the personal title of Archbishop; died Oct. 2, 1967.—Most Rev. GEORGE H. GUILFOYLE, D.D., J.D., ord. March 25, 1944; appt. Titular Bishop of Marazanae and Auxiliary Bishop of New York, Oct. 17, 1964; cons. Fourth Bishop of Camden, Nov. 30, 1964; appt. Jan. 2, 1968; installed March 4, 1968; retired May 22, 1989; died June 11, 1991.

Chancery:

Camden Diocesan Center—1845 Haddon Ave., P.O. Box 709, Camden, 08101-0709. Tel: 609-756-7900; Fax: 609-963-2655. Address all official business to this office.

The Diocese of Camden—A corporation under the laws of the State of New Jersey.

Officers—Most Rev. JAMES T. MCHUGH, S.T.D., Pres.; Rev. Msgr. DAVID F. BUDNEY, V.G., Vice Pres.; Rev. Msgr. JOSEPH W. POKUSA, J.C.D., Sec.

Diocesan Bishop—Most Rev. JAMES T. MCHUGH, S.T.D. Tel: 609-756-7913.

Retired Auxiliary Bishop—Most Rev. JAMES L. SCHAD, D.D.

Vicar General—Rev. Msgr. DAVID F. BUDNEY, V.G. Tel: 609-756-7906.

Judicial Vicar—Rev. Msgr. LEONARD G. SCOTT, J.C.D. Tel: 609-756-7972.

Chancellor—Rev. Msgr. JOSEPH W. POKUSA, J.C.D. Tel: 609-756-7916.

Secretariat—Rev. GEORGE C. SEITER, Sec. to Bishop McHugh and Vice Chancellor. Tel: 609-756-7907.

Episcopal Vicars:

City of Camden—Rev. Msgr. ROBERT T. MCDERMOTT, V.E., *St. Joseph Pro-Cathedral, 2907 Federal St., Camden, 08105.* Tel: 609-964-2776.

Clergy—Rev. Msgr. JAMES P. MCINTYRE, V.E. Tel: 609-756-7915.

Communications and Community Relations—Rev. Msgr. CHARLES J. GIGLIO, V.E., Ph.D. Tel: 609-756-7926.

Pastoral Services—Rev. Msgr. THOMAS J. MCINTYRE, V.E. Tel: 609-756-7908.

Vicars:

For Religious—Rev. Msgr. EDWARD F. MULLEN, *St. Augustine, 1310 Ocean Ave., Ocean City, 08226-3295.* Tel: 609-399-0648.

For Clergy—Rev. Msgr. JAMES P. WELSH, *St. Pius X, 344 Kresson Rd., Cherry Hill, 08034.* Tel: 609-429-1330.

Deaneries and Vicars Forane—

Atlantic Deanery—Rev. Msgr. MICHAEL J. COYNE, V.F., *St. Elizabeth Ann Seton, 591 New Jersey Ave., Absecon, 08201-2424.* Tel: 609-641-1480.

Cape May Deanery—Rev. Msgr. WILLIAM QUINN, V.F., *St. Ann, 2900 Pacific Ave., Wildwood, 08260-4943.* Tel: 609-522-5583.

Camden City Deanery—Rev. Msgr. ROBERT T. MCDERMOTT, V.E., *St. Joseph Pro-Cathedral, 2907 Federal St., Camden, 08105-2229.* Tel: 609-964-2776.

Camden North Deanery—Rev. Msgr. JAMES R. TRACY, Ph.D., V.F., *St. Peter Celestine, 402 Kings Hwy. N., Cherry Hill, 08034-1091.* Tel: 609-667-2440.

Camden South Deanery—Rev. Msgr. EDWARD J. KORDA, V.F., *St. Gregory, 340 Evesham Ave., Magnolia, 08049-1098.* Tel: 609-784-4090.

Camden West Deanery—Rev. Msgr. JOSEPH C. DOWNING, V.F., *St. Stephen, 6306 Browning Rd., Pennsauken, 08109-1549.* Tel: 609-662-9338.

Central Deanery—Rev. JOHN F. BOURKE, V.F., *Our Lady of Mount Carmel, 178 W. White Horse Pike, Berlin, 08009-2023.* Tel: 609-767-2563.

Cumberland Deanery—Rev. Msgr. JOSEPH G. STOERLEIN, P.A., V.F., *Sacred Heart, 1010 E. Landis Ave., Vineland, 08360-4096.* Tel: 609-691-0420.

Gloucester Deanery—Rev. JAMES P. CURRAN, V.F., *Our Lady of Lourdes, 500 Greentree Rd., Glassboro, 08028-1427.* Tel: 609-881-0909.

Southwest Deanery—Rev. Msgr. ROCCO A. CONTINILLO, V.F., *Corpus Christi, 369 Georgetown Rd., Carneys Point, 08069-2598.* Tel: 609-299-3833.

Diocesan Tribunal:

Judicial Vicar—Rev. Msgr. LEONARD G. SCOTT, J.C.D. Tel: 609-756-7972.

Adjutant Judicial Vicars—Rev. Msgr. PATRICK J. MADDEN; Rev. Msgr. JAMES J. ZEGERS, P.A.; Rev. EDWARD J. LIPINSKI.

Judges—Rev. Msgr. EDWARD D. ALLEYNE; Rev. Msgr. BERNARD P. HEWITT, V.F.; Rev. Msgr. JOHN R. LUBICKY; Rev. Msgr. EDWARD F. MULLEN; Rev. Msgr. THOMAS F. SHARKEY, J.C.D.

Notaries—ROSE MCFADDEN; ROSEMARY MANZO; DEBORAH MORAN; ALICE PEDERSEN; JOAN WHITELOCK.

Promoter of Justice—Rev. Msgr. EUGENE J. FITZSIMMONS, J.C.D., *St. Michael, 313 Memorial Ave., Gibbstown, 08027.* Tel: 609-423-0007.

Presbyteral Council—Most Rev. JAMES T. MCHUGH, S.T.D., Chm. Officers: Revs. DANIEL M. SHERMAN, Pres.; CADMUS D. MAZZARELLA, Vice Pres.; ROBERT E. HUGHES, Sec. Representatives by Age: Revs. CHARLES P. BARTH; PATRICK S. CHIARILLI; JOHN J. VIGNONE. Representatives by Geography: Revs. RONALD S. FALOTICO; THOMAS B. FITZSIMMONS; WILLIAM P. GRAHAM; ROBERT E. HUGHES; MICHAEL J. MATVEENKO. Representatives by Ministry: Revs. FRANCIS X. HUDSON; HARRY J. JORDON; STEPHEN LAROSA, O.S.A.; ROBERT C. PALSEY; DANIEL A. SHERMAN. Members by Appointment: Rev. Msgr. EDWARD D. ALLEYNE; Rev. Msgr. RICHARD J. CALLAHAN; Rev. Msgr. ROCCO A. CONTINILLO, V.F.; Rev. Msgr. MICHAEL J. COYNE, V.F.; Rev. Msgr. JOSEPH C. DOWNING, V.F.; Rev. Msgr. J. GERALD GALLAGHER; Rev. Msgr. JOSEPH P. HERRON, V.E.; Rev. Msgr. EDWARD L. KORDA, V.F.; Rev. Msgr. ROBERT T. MCDERMOTT, V.E.; Rev. Msgr. VICTOR S. MURO; Rev. Msgr. CIARAN P. O'MEARAIN; Rev. Msgr. WILLIAM QUINN, V.F.; Rev. Msgr. JOSEPH G. STOERLEIN, P.A., V.F.; Rev. Msgr. PATRICK M. TIERNEY; Rev. Msgr. JAMES R. TRACY; Revs. JOHN F. BOURKE, V.F.; JAMES P. CURRAN, V.F.; JOHN T. FREY; CADMUS D. MAZZARELLA; RUSSELL L. ROCK. Ex-Officio Members: Most Rev. JAMES L. SCHAD, D.D.; Rev. Msgr. DAVID F. BUDNEY, V.G.; Rev. Msgr. JOSEPH W. POKUSA, J.C.D. Permanent Observers: Rev. Msgr. CHARLES J. GIGLIO, V.E.; Rev. Msgr. JAMES P. MCINTYRE, V.E.; Rev. Msgr. THOMAS J. MCINTYRE, V.E.; Rev. Msgr. LEONARD G. SCOTT.

College of Consultors—Most Rev. JAMES L. SCHAD, D.D.; Rev. Msgr. DAVID F. BUDNEY, V.G.; Rev. Msgr. RICHARD J. CALLAHAN; Rev. Msgr. ROCCO A. CONTINILLO, V.F.; Rev. Msgr. MICHAEL J. COYNE, V.F.; Rev. Msgr. J. GERALD GALLAGHER; Rev. Msgr. JOSEPH P. HERRON, V.E.; Rev. Msgr. THOMAS J. MCINTYRE, V.E.; Rev. Msgr. CIARAN P. O'MEARAIN; Rev. Msgr. WILLIAM QUINN, V.F.; Rev. Msgr. PATRICK M. TIERNEY; Rev. RUSSELL L. ROCK.

Diocesan Pastoral Council—Most Rev. JAMES T. MCHUGH, S.T.D., Chm.; Rev. Msgr. THOMAS J. MCINTYRE, Ph.D., Vice Chm.; EDWARD G. BARRY, Pres., *198 Briar Hill Ln., Woodbury, 08096.* Tel: 609-848-6870. VINCENT PREMONE, Vice Pres., *410 S. Breaker Dr., Galloway Twp., 08201.* Tel: 609-748-1168.

Sisters' Council—Sr. MARIANNE MCCANN, M.P.F., Pres., *Paul VI Convent, Hopkins Rd., Haddon Twp., 08033.* Tel: 609-854-3678.

Diocesan Finance Council—Most Rev. JAMES L. SCHAD, D.D.; Rev. Msgr. DAVID F. BUDNEY, V.G.; Rev. Msgr. CHARLES J. BARTH; Rev. Msgr. J. GERALD GALLAGHER; Rev. Msgr. JOSEPH P. HERRON; Rev. Msgr. JOSEPH W. POKUSA; Rev. Msgr. WILLIAM QUINN, V.F.; Rev. Msgr. PATRICK M. TIERNEY, V.F.; WILLIAM J. MURRAY; WILLIAM CONWAY.

Finance Council Committee Chairmen—Rev. Msgr. JOSEPH P. HERRON, Audit; Rev. Msgr. J. GERALD GALLAGHER, Finance; Rev. Msgr. CHARLES J. BARTH, Buildings & Property; Rev. Msgr. DAVID F. BUDNEY, V.G., Investment; Rev. Msgr. PATRICK M. TIERNEY, Insurance; Rev. Msgr. JOSEPH W. POKUSA, Employee Benefits & Compensation.

Diocesan Offices and Directors

The following offices and directors are located at the Camden Diocesan Center unless otherwise indicated.

Camden Diocesan Center—1845 Haddon Ave., P.O. Box 709, Camden, 08101-0709. Tel: 609-756-7900.

Office of the Vicar General

Vicar General—Rev. Msgr. DAVID F. BUDNEY, V.G. Tel: 609-756-7906.

Agencies Reporting to the Vicar General:

Special Committees—Interparochial Cooperation Board; Deposit and Loan Fund; Parish Finance Councils; New Parish Development Committee.

House of Charity—Rev. Msgr. THOMAS A. GUENTHER, Dir. Tel: 609-756-7939.

Stewardship Program—Rev. Msgr. J. GERALD GALLAGHER, *St. Patrick, 64 Cooper St., Woodbury, 08096.* Tel: 609-845-0123.

Secretariat for Diocesan & Parish Finances:

Secretary—WILLIAM J. MURRAY. Tel: 609-756-7934.

Accounting Services—Mrs. LISA M. CILIBERTO, C.P.A., Dir. Tel: 609-756-7980.

Department of Finance—STEPHEN M. TALAROWSKI, Dir. Tel: 609-756-7912.

Department of Insurance—JAMES SMITH, Consultant. Tel: 609-756-7953; 756-7928.

Department of Lay Personnel and Insurance Programs—PAUL F. ZAKULEC, Dir. Tel: 609-756-7928.

Secretariat for Diocesan & Parish Operations:

Secretary—ROBERT SPEAKMAN. Tel: 609-756-7935.

Special Projects Coordinator—THOMAS BECHARD. Tel: 609-756-7989.

Department of Buildings—ARTHUR BASCIANO, A.I.A., Diocesan Architect & Dir. JOSEPH COSTANZO, Assoc. Dir. Tel: 609-756-7979.

Department of Cemeteries—ARTHUR HEINTZ, Dir., Mailing Address: *1845 Haddon Ave., P.O. Box 709, Camden, 08101-0709.* Tel: 609-424-8728 (Cherry Hill).

Department of Real Estate—KENNETH MCILVANE, Assoc. Dir. Tel: 609-756-7937.

Vicariate for Clergy Personnel

Vicar—Rev. Msgr. JAMES P. MCINTYRE.

Office of Priest Personnel—Rev. Msgr. JAMES P. MCINTYRE, Dir. Tel: 609-756-7915.

Priests Personnel Board—Rev. THOMAS J. MORGAN, Chm., *Christ the King, 200 Windsor Ave., Haddonfield, 08033-1499.* Tel: 609-429-1600. Members: Rev. Msgr. JAMES A. CARR; Rev. Msgr. JOSEPH F. O'CONNELL; Revs. LEWIS A. BATTISTI; JAMES P. CURRAN, V.F.; NEAL F. DANTE; RONALD S. FALOTICO; JOSEPH R. FERRARA; WILLIAM H. HART; ROBERT E. HUGHES; PETER M. JOYCE; EDWARD J. LIPINSKI; DANIEL M. SHERMAN; ERNEST R. SOPRANO. Non-Voting Members: Most Rev. JAMES T. MCHUGH; Rev. Msgr. DAVID F. BUDNEY, V.G.; Rev. Msgr. JAMES P. MCINTYRE, V.E.; Rev. Msgr. JOSEPH W. POKUSA; Rev. THOMAS J. MORGAN.

Permanent Diaconate—Rev. FREDERICK G. LINK, Dir. Tel: 609-756-7950.

Vocations Apostolate—Rev. LOUIS A. MARUCCI, Dir.; Sr. DOROTHY ALOYSIO, Assoc. Dir.; Rev. JOSEPH T. SZOLACK, Liaison, St. Charles Borromeo Seminary. Tel: 609-756-7966.

Vocation Advisory Board—Rev. Msgr. LAWRENCE P. BOYLE, V.F.; Rev. Msgr. RICHARD J. CALLAHAN; Rev. Msgr. MARTIN J. MANNION; Rev. Msgr. ROBERT T. MCDERMOTT; Rev. Msgr. JAMES P. MCINTYRE; Rev. Msgr. JAMES R. TRACY, Ph.D.; Revs. WILLIAM A. HODGE; LOUIS A. MARUCCI; CADMUS D. MAZZARELLA; Sr. DOROTHY ALOYSIO.

Friends of the Sacred Heart—Rev. Msgr. CHARLES P. BARTH, J.C.D., Chap., *St. Peter, 43 W. Maple Ave., Merchantville, 08109-5141.* Tel: 609-663-1373.

Serra Clubs International—District 15: THOMAS HALPIN, Governor; Atlantic City East: JOHN PARIS, Pres.; Rev. BRENDAN V. SULLIVAN, Chap.; Cape May County: RICHARD MILLER, Pres.; Rev. MARK CAVAGNARO, Chap.; Cumberland County: PHILLIP BORGESE, Pres.; Rev. RAYMOND GORMLEY, Chap.

Continuing Education and Spiritual Formation of Priests—Rev. KENNETH JOHNSTON, Dir. Tel: 609-756-7908.

Liaison with Retired Priests—Rev. HARRY J. JORDAN.

Clergy Health Panel—Rev. Msgr. JAMES P. MCINTYRE, Chm.; Rev. Msgr. JAMES A. CARR; Rev. Msgr. JOSEPH P. HERRON; Rev. Msgr. ROBERT T. MCDERMOTT; Revs. LEWIS A. BATTISTI; JOHN T. FREY; WILLIAM H. HART; Dr. JOSEPH W. SOKOLOWSKI.

Vicariate for Communications and Community Relations

Vicar—Rev. Msgr. CHARLES J. GIGLIO, Ph.D. Tel: 609-756-7926.

Secretariat for Communications:

Newspaper—"The Catholic Star Herald," (Official organ of the Diocese of Camden). A corporation under the laws of NJ.

Trustees and Officers—Most Rev. JAMES T. MCHUGH, S.T.D., Pres. & Treas.; Rev. Msgr. DAVID F. BUDNEY, V.G., Vice Pres.; Rev. Msgr. JOSEPH W. POKUSA, J.C.D., Sec.; Rev. Msgr. JOSEPH P. HERRON; Rev. Msgr. THOMAS H. SHARKEY, J.C.D.; Rev. Msgr. PATRICK M. TIERNEY, V.F.; Sr. MARIANNE MCCANN, M.P.F.

Executive Editor—Rev. Msgr. CHARLES J. GIGLIO, Ph.D. Tel: 609-756-7910.

Managing Editor—CARL D. PETERS. Tel: 609-756-7910.

Editorial and Business Office—1845 Haddon Ave., Camden, 08101. Tel: 609-756-7910.

Office of Public Relations and Telecommunications—Rev. Msgr. CHARLES J. GIGLIO, Ph.D., Dir.; Rev. GEORGE C. SEITER, Asst. Dir. Tel: 609-756-7907.

Censor Librorum—Rev. Msgr. THOMAS H. SHARKEY, J.C.D., *Our Lady of Good Counsel, 3948 Central Ave., Ocean City, 08226.* Tel: 609-399-2085.

Diocesan Historian—Rev. Msgr. CHARLES J. GIGLIO, Ph.D. Tel: 609-756-7910.

Secretariat for Community Relations:

Propagation of the Faith; Society of the Holy Childhood; Brazilian Missions—Rev. Msgr. THOMAS A. GUENTHER, Dir. Tel: 609-756-7924.

Ecumenical and Interreligious Affairs—Rev. JOSEPH D. WALLACE, Coord. Tel: 609-756-7982.

Commission on Ecumenical and Interreligious Affairs—Rev. Msgr. EUGENE J. FITZSIMMONS, J.C.D., Chm., *St. Michael's, 313 Memorial Ave., Gibbstown, 08027.* Tel: 609-423-0007.

Pro-Life Office—JOYCE LIVELY, Coord. Tel: 609-756-7992.

Prison Ministry—Vacant.

Hospital Ministry—Vacant.

Community Affairs—Rev. EDWARD J. WALSH, Coord.

Campaign for Human Development—Rev. EDWARD J. WALSH, Dir., *Immaculate Heart of Mary, 201 Cooper St., Woodlynne, 08107.* Tel: 609-962-8610.

Special Collections—Rev. GEORGE C. SEITER, Coord. Tel: 609-756-7907.

Catholic Relief Services—Vacant.

Operation Rice Bowl—Vacant.

Jubilate Deo Chorale and Orchestra—Rev. LOUIS A. MARUCCI, Exec. Dir.; Rev. Msgr. CARL J. MARUCCI, Conductor. Tel: 609-756-7966.

Secretariat for Social Services:

Catholic Social Services—"Catholic Social Services of the Diocese of Camden, NJ"—A Corporation under the laws of the State of New Jersey.

Trustees and Officers—Most Rev. JAMES T. MCHUGH, S.T.D., Pres.; Rev. Msgr. DAVID F. BUDNEY, V.G., Vice Pres.; Rev. Msgr. JOSEPH W. POKUSA, J.C.D., Sec.; Rev. Msgr. CHARLES P. BARTH; Rev. Msgr. ROCCO A. CONTINILLO, V.F.; Rev. Msgr. CHARLES J. GIGLIO; Rev. Msgr. THOMAS J. MCINTYRE; Rev. Msgr. JOSEPH G. STOERLEIN; Rev. Msgr. THOMAS A. GUENTHER; CHARLES DUNN; WILLIAM J. MURRAY; NORA HUGHES.

Executive Director—PATRICIA D. LANGAN, M.A., M.Ed. Tel: 609-663-9800.

Counseling Services—Rev. EDWARD A. IGLE, A.C.S.W., Clinical Dir., *Catholic Social Services, P.O. Box 737, Newfield, 08344-0737.* Tel: 609-697-0744.

Pregnancy and Adoption Services—ANN GALLAGHER, A.C.S.W., Supvr., *Catholic Social Services, 810 Montrose Ave., Vineland, 08360.* Tel: 609-691-1841.

Project Rachel—(Post-Abortion Counseling and Support)—SYLVIA LOUMEAU, M.S.W., Coord., *P.O. Box 737, Newfield, 08344-0737.* Tel: 609-756-7954. Rev. ANDREW J. BOLCAR, Moderator. Tel: 609-456-4136.

Aids Ministry—Sr. RUTH HARKINS, I.H.M., M.A., *2830 Marlton Pike, Pennsauken, 08105.* Tel: 609-663-0085.

Immigration and Refugee Services—THOMAS B. HENKEL, P.D., *6981 N. Park Dr., Ste. 104W, Pennsauken, 08109.* Tel: 609-317-0202.

Legal Assistance to the Poor—Rev. DAVID C. BROOKS, S.J., J.D., *511 State St., Camden, 08102.* Tel: 609-966-8896.

Ladies of Charity—Rev. JAMES J. DURKIN, Spiritual Dir., *Our Lady of Pompeii, 4680 Dante Ave., Vineland, 08360-6810.* Tel: 609-691-7526. Sr. MARY VINCENT SHARP, M.S.B.T., A.C.S.W., Moderator, *Parish Ministry, 3107 Alabama Rd., Camden, 08104.* Tel: 609-962-9725. Mrs. KATALINA UYEHARA, *167 N. Mansfield Blvd., Cherry Hill, 08034.* Tel: 609-795-4340.

St. Vincent De Paul Society—Rev. Msgr. THOMAS H. SHARKEY, J.C.D., Spiritual Dir., *Our Lady of Good Counsel, 3948 Central Ave., Ocean City, 08226.* Tel: 609-399-2085.

Vicariate for Pastoral Services

Vicar—Rev. Msgr. THOMAS J. MCINTYRE. Tel: 609-756-7908.

Assistant to Vicar—Rev. MICHAEL P. ORSI, Ed.D. Tel: 609-756-7908.

Agencies Reporting to the Vicar:

Office for Pastoral Statistics and Data—Rev. DOUGLAS R. TOBIN, Coord. Tel: 609-756-7932.

Office of Black Ministry—Mr. LARRY CHATHAM. Tel: 609-756-7908.

Ministry with the Deaf—Rev. BRIAN E. O'NEILL, *St. Mary, 426 Monmouth St., Gloucester, 08030.* Tel: 609-456-0052.

Apostolate to Hispanics—Rev. Msgr. VICTOR S. MURO, Dir., *Spanish Catholic Center, 410 S. 8th St., Vineland, 08360.* Tel: 609-692-8992.

Office of Pastoral Planning and Research—Vacant.

Institute for Religious Studies—Rev. ROBERT J. GREGORIO, Dir., *St. Edward, 500 Erial Rd., Pine Hill, 08021.* Tel: 609-784-2272.

Secretariat for Education and Religious Formation:

Department of Schools—DAVID T. COGHLAN, Ph.D., Supt. Schools; Sr. STELLA LOTZ, S.S.J., Asst. Supt. Lay Personnel & Govt. Programs; Sr. ANTOINE THERESE LAWLOR, I.H.M., Asst. Supt. Relig. Education; Sr. ST. EUGENE FIORINO, O.S.F., Asst. Supt. Educational Svcs.; Sr. ROSE DIFLURI, I.H.M., Asst. Supt. Educational Programs. Tel: 609-756-7988.

Board of Education—Most Rev. JAMES T. MCHUGH, S.T.D., Chm. CHARLES DICIANO, Pres.

Special Education—Miss KATHLEEN FLYNN, Dir. Tel: 609-756-7993.

Office of Religious Education—MICHAEL E. STEIER, D.Min., Dir. THERESA H. GERLACH, Asst. Dir. Elementary Religious Education. Tel: 609-756-7987.

Media Resource Center—CONNIE TEESDALE, *St. Pius X Retreat House, P.O. Box 216, Blackwood, 08012.* Tel: 609-228-6881.

Parent-Teacher Association—Rev. JAMES P. CURRAN, Moderator, *Our Lady of Lourdes, 500 Greentree Road, Glassboro, 08028.* Tel: 609-881-0909. Sr. ST. EUGENE FIORINO, O.S.F., Honorary Pres. Tel: 609-756-7988. MAUREEN MCLOONE, Pres., *17 E. Chestnut Ave., Merchantville, 08109.* Tel: 609-665-6271. Mrs. RAE O'NEILL, Vice Pres., *702 N. New St., Clayton, 08312.* Tel: 609-881-7185. Mrs. CAROL BASARA, Sec., *4 Dorset Dr., Cherry Hill, 08003.* Tel: 609-424-3976. Mr. GARY BATTISTINI, Treas., *4 Northfield Plaza, Northfield, 08225.* Tel: 609-646-4880.

Secretariat for Family Life:

Family Life Bureau—Rev. MICHAEL P. ORSI, Ed.D., Dir. Tel: 609-756-7957.

Resource Development—TERRY WARNICK, Assoc. Dir. Tel: 609-756-7964. Parish Family Ministry; Parents of Gays/Lesbians; Collaborative Ministry; Leadership Training; Elizabeth Ministry.

Singles / Single Again; Bereavement Ministry—Sr. KATHLEEN DUFFY, R.S.M., Coord. Tel: 609-756-7942. Grief Mgmt. Support Groups (death, separation, divorce); Affiliate Groups; Enrichment retreats and workshops, Bereavement Ministry Training, Rainbows Program - Rainbows- Elementary Schools, Spectrum - High School, Prism - Parents.

Marriage Preparation—Rev. PAUL D. HARTE, Coord. Tel: 609-756-7965. Pre-Cana, Engaged Encounter, Second Marriages.

Marriage Enrichment—STEVEN BOZZA, Coord. Tel: 609-756-7921. Covenant Love, Infertility Support, Diocesan Wedding Anniversary, World Marriage Day, Retrouvaille.

Natural Family Planning—MARY ANN CHEZIK, Ph.D., Coord. Tel: 609-756-7965. Natural Family Planning, Human Sexuality Education, Diocesan Devel. Program for NFP, Chastity Education.

Parenting Programs—BOB LENTO, Consultant. Tel: 609-756-7957. Positive Parenting; The Emerging Adolescent; Self Esteem; Getting Ready for Kindergarten; Sibling Rivalry.

Office of Youth and Young Adult Ministry—JEFFREY CORDNER, Dir. Tel: 609-756-7919. Rev. CADMUS D. MAZZARELLA, Moderator.

Life Teen—TOM HOFACKER, Consultant. Tel: 609-783-2045.

Scouting—Rev. ALBERT E. HARSHAW, Chaplain; EDMUND A. DOMANSKI, Chm. Tel: 609-784-3153.

Young Adult Ministry—LARA HILL, Coord. Tel: 609-939-6357.

Campus Ministry—Rev. CADMUS P. MAZZARELLA. Tel: 609-881-5642.

C.Y.O. Youth and Family Fitness Center—Mr. JOHN MILLER, Dir., *P.O. Box 250, Blackwood, 08012.* Tel: 609-227-1359.

Secretariat for Parish Life:

Secretary—Vacant. Tel: 609-756-7908.

Parish Spiritual Development—Vacant.

St. Pius X Spiritual Life Center—Rev. DAVID E. BEEBE, Dir., *P.O. Box 216, Blackwood, 08012.* Tel: 609-227-1436.

RCIA Implementation—Rev. MICHAEL J. FIELD, Dir. Tel: 609-756-7947.

RCIA Commission—Rev. Msgr. JAMES R. TRACY, Chm. Members: Rev. Msgr. JOSEPH P. JOYNES; Revs. JOSEPH ADAMSON; JOHN H. BURTON; WAYNE PATRICK LAVIN; STANLEY L. WITCOSKIE; Sr. ALICE GALLAGHER, S.S.J.; Ms. CHRIS FITZPATRICK; Mr. BERNARD GARBOWSKI; Ms. PATRICIA MAJER; Ms. JOAN MULLIN; Ms. ALICE POLOCZ; Mrs. KAREN KUDLISS; Mrs. TERRY WARNICK, *St. Celestine, 402 Kings Hwy. N., Cherry Hill, 08034.* Tel: 609-667-2440.

Office of Worship—Rev. JOHN H. BURTON, Dir. Tel: 609-756-7900.

Diocesan Music Office—JON RANIA, Dir. Tel: 609-756-7948, Ext. 355.

Liturgical Commission—Rev. JOHN BURTON, Chm.; Rev. Msgr. JOSEPH W. POKUSA, J.C.D.; Revs. THOMAS B. FITZSIMMONS; DAVID A. GROVER; ROBERT E. HUGHES; MICHAEL J. MATVEENKO; THOMAS A. NEWTON; GEORGE C. SEITER; Sr. EMILY MCMULLEN, S.S.J.; Sr. MARIA G. PINO, S.S.J.; Mrs. CARL INNOCENZO; Mrs. JAMES KEOUGH; Mrs. KATHLEEN RANDO; Deacon THOMAS O'BRIEN; JON RANIA.

Office of Evangelization—Vacant.

Office of Lay Ministry Development—Vacant.

Office of Parish Council Development—Vacant.

Office of Social Justice—Vacant.

Marian Commission—Rev. WILLIAM A. HODGE, Chm., *St. James, 114 State St., Penns Grove, 08069.* Tel: 609-299-0399.

Legion of Mary—Rev. WILLIAM A. HODGE, Spiritual Dir. Tel: 609-229-0399.

Holy Name Society—Rev. JEROME C. ROMANOWSKI, Dir., *St. Lucy, 250 S. Rte. 73, Blue Anchor, 08037.* Tel: 609-561-6116.

Charismatic Movement—Rev. Msgr. JAMES P. MCINTYRE, Moderator For information contact FRANK IULA, M.D., P.D. Tel: 609-547-4875.

Cursillo—Rev. LEONARD CARRIERI, M.SS.CC., Spiritual Dir. Spanish Cursillo, *Villa Pieta, 2249 Shore Rd., Linwood, 08221.* Tel: 609-927-5600.

CLERGY, PARISHES, MISSIONS AND PAROCHIAL SCHOOLS

CITY OF CAMDEN
(Camden County)

1—IMMACULATE CONCEPTION CATHEDRAL (1864), Rev. Msgr. Charles J. Giglio; Rev. Thomas A. Harkins; Deacons William P. Iannuzzi; William L. Watts. In res., Rev. David J. Klein.
Res., 642 Market St., 08102. Tel: 609-964-1580; Fax: 609-757-0438. [CEM]

2—ST. ANTHONY OF PADUA (1945), Revs. Ramon Gomez Vazquez, O.F.M.; Christopher Posch, O.F.M.; Bro. Christoper Coccia, O.F.M., Admin.
Res., 2818 River Ave., 08105. Tel: 609-963-5884; Fax: 609-635-1286.
School—Tel: 609-966-6791; 966-1616. Mrs. Linda Meehan, Prin.
Sisters of the Third Franciscan Order, Minor Conventuals (Syracuse, NY) 3; Lay Teachers 8; Students 220.

3—ST. BARTHOLOMEW'S (1940), Rev. Wayne Patrick Lavin.
Res., 751 Kaighns Ave., 08103. Tel: 609-365-0573; Fax: 609-963-3146.
School—St. Bartholomew Parkside School, 1725 Park Blvd., Tel: 609-963-3133; Fax: 609-963-3146. Joan Ciccone, Ph.D., Prin.
Sisters 3; Lay Teachers 7; Students 150.
Convent—Tel: 609-964-0603; Fax: 609-963-3146. Sr. Anna Cox, S.B.S.; Sr. Bernadette Stack, S.B.S.

4—HOLY NAME (1913), Revs. Frank T. Kaminski, S.J.; Donald Ward, S.J.; Sr. Linda Stilling, S.S.N.D., Pastoral Assoc. In res., Revs. Mark C. Aita, S.J., M.D.; David R. Brooks, S.J., Esq.; Richard G. Malloy, S.J.; Mr. Daniel Joyce, S.J.
Res., 522 State St., 08102-1919. Tel: 609-963-1621; Fax: 609-338-0793.
School—Tel: 609-365-7930; Fax: 609-365-8041. Mrs. Patricia Munyan, Prin.
Sisters 4; Lay Teachers 7; Students 217.
Convent—517 State St., Tel: 609-964-1233. Sisters of St. Joseph (Chestnut Hill) School Sisters of Notre Dame (Baltimore). Sr. Dorothy Crowley, S.S.J., Coord.

5—ST. JOAN OF ARC (1920), Rev. James P. Rush.
Res., 3107 Alabama Rd., 08104. Tel: 609-962-8642; Fax: 609-962-7123.
School—Tel: 609-962-7226. Miss Mary Beth Holahan, Prin.
Lay Teachers 10; Students 140.

6—ST. JOSEPH'S (1892) (Polish), Rev. Msgr. Edward H. Bucia; Rev. Jacek Stefanski. In res., Rev. Charles J. Becker, S.S.
Res., 1010 Liberty St., 08104. Tel: 609-963-1285. [CEM]

7—ST. JOSEPH'S PRO-CATHEDRAL (1893), Rev. Msgr. Robert T. McDermott; Revs. Kenneth P. Hallahan; Joseph An Nguyen; Sr. Margaret Mary Schmiher, O.S.F., Pastoral Min.; Deacon Bienvenido Negron. In res., Rev. Andrew Martin.
Res., 2907 Federal St., 08105. Tel: 609-964-2776; Fax: 609-964-0044.
School—Tel: 609-964-4336. Mrs. Kathleen Shiflet, Prin.
Lay Teachers 10; Students 260.
Nursery School—17 Church St., 08105. Tel: 609-963-0452. Franciscan Sisters of the Infant Jesus. Sr. Maria DeRosia, F.M.I.J., Supr.
Sisters 2; Children 46.

8—OUR LADY OF FATIMA AND MOUNT CARMEL (1953), Revs. Salvatore A. Scuderi, M.SS.CC.; Bruce Bumbarger, M.SS.CC.; Deacon Miguel Rivera; Bro. David Graber, M.SS.CC.
Res., 832 S. 4th St., 08103. Tel: 609-541-7618; Fax: 609-541-2835.

9—SACRED HEART (1885), Revs. Michael Doyle; Charles G. Gonzalez, S.J. In res., Rev. Arthur T. Anderson.
Res., 1739 Ferry Ave., 08104. Tel: 609-966-6700; Fax: 609-756-0102.
School—Fourth St. & Jaspers St., 08104. Tel: 609-963-1341. Mrs. Janet Williams, Prin.
Sisters 1; Lay Teachers 11; Students 253. Records for St. George kept at Sacred Heart, Camden. Records for Sts. Peter and Paul kept at the Cathedral of the Immaculate Conception, Camden. Records for St. John the Baptist kept at St. Joseph Pro-Cathedral, Camden.

OUTSIDE THE CITY OF CAMDEN

Absecon, Atlantic Co., St. Elizabeth Ann Seton (1975), Rev. Msgr. Michael J. Coyne; Rev. Thomas S. Donio; Deacon Joseph Becker.
Res., 591 New Jersey Ave., 08201. Tel: 609-641-1480; Fax: 609-641-7396.
School—Assumption Regional School, Pomona. See separate listing.

Atco, Camden Co., Assumption (1947), Revs. Howard E. Muhlbaier; Michael Coffey; Deacon Charles McAleer.
Res., 2116 Atco Ave., 08004. Tel: 609-767-0719; Fax: 609-753-7917.
School—Tel: 609-767-3414; Fax: 609-753-7917. Mrs. Paula Angiletta, Prin., Tel: 609-767-0569.
Lay Teachers 8; Students 225.

Atlantic City, Atlantic Co.,

1—HOLY SPIRIT, (1908), Revs. Eldridge T. Evans; Felipe Moyano; Deacon Angel Vega.
Res., 626 Oriental Ave., 08401. Tel: 609-344-6533.

2—ST. MICHAEL'S, (1904) (Italian), Rev. Msgr. Francis A. Sprecace; Rev. John L. O'Connor; Deacon Raymond Ferrario.
Res., 10 N. Mississippi Ave., 08401. Tel: 609-344-8536.

3—ST. MONICA'S, (1925), Rev. J. Overton Jones.
Res., 108 N. Pennsylvania Ave., 08401. Tel: 609-345-1786.

4—ST. NICHOLAS OF TOLENTINE, Revs. Joseph X. O'Connor, O.S.A.; Bernard J. O'Dowd, O.S.A.; Terence J. O'Rourke, O.S.A.
Res., 1409 Pacific Ave., 08401. Tel: 609-344-1040; Fax: 609-344-2471.

5—OUR LADY STAR OF THE SEA, (1894), Revs. Patrick J. Brady; Paul C. Wise; Joseph An Nguyen; Deacons Agatino Garufi; James Tully.
Res., 2651 Atlantic Ave., 08401. Tel: 609-345-1878; Fax: 609-348-0248.
School—Tel: 609-345-0648. Sr. Mary Shamus, R.S.M., Prin. & Supr.
Sisters 7; Lay Teachers 9; Students 325.
Convent—15 N. California Ave., Tel: 609-347-0434. Sisters of Mercy

Audubon, Camden Co., Church of the Holy Maternity (1957), Revs. Michael J. McGilley; Edward J. Lipinski.
Res., 431 W. Nicholson Rd., 08106. Tel: 609-547-0444; Fax: 609-547-0045.
School—Sacred Heart Regional School, Mount Ephraim. See separate listing.

Avalon, Cape May Co., Maris Stella (1961), Rev. Msgr. Patrick M. Tierney.
Res., 5012 Dune Dr., 08202. Tel: 609-967-3746.
School—St. Joseph Regional School, Sea Isle City. See separate listing. Tel: 609-263-4296.

Barrington, Camden Co., St. Francis de Sales (1955), Rev. Francis J. McLaughlin; Deacon Michael Harkins. In res., Rev. Msgr. William F. Poyatt; Rev. Robert E. Hughes.
Res., 199 Willmont Ave., 08007. Tel: 609-547-2313; Fax: 609-547-8225.
School—St. Francis de Sales Regional School. See separate listing.
Convent—424 Browning Rd., Bellmawr, 08031. Tel: 609-931-8973.

Bellmawr, Camden Co., Annunciation (1951), Rev.

William F. Ryan.
Res., 601 W. Browning Rd., 08031. Tel: 609-931-6307; Fax: 609-931-0155.
School—Tel: 609-931-0122; Fax: 609-931-4390. Sr. Marie St. James, I.H.M., Prin.
Sisters 3; Lay Teachers 9; Students 194.
Convent—603 W. Browning Rd., Tel: 609-931-7192. Sisters Servants of Immaculate Heart of Mary

Mary, Mother of the Church (1965), Rev. Francis P. Gaffney. In res., Rev. John J. Byrnes; Deacon Ron Olesienicz.
Res., 20 Braisington Ave., 08031. Tel: 609-931-0204.
School—St. Francis de Sales Regional, Barrington. See separate listing.

Berlin, Camden Co., Our Lady of Mt. Carmel (1903), Revs. John F. Bourke; Edward M. Friel; Henry J. McBride; Deacons Joseph Beebe; Richard F. McCarthy.
Res., 178 W. White Horse Pike, 08009. Tel: 609-767-2563. [CEM]
School—Our Lady of Mt. Carmel Regional School. See separate listing. Tel: 609-767-1537; Fax: 609-767-1293.

Blackwood, Camden Co., St. Agnes (1946), Rev. Msgr. Joseph V. DiMauro; Revs. John E. Bruni; Cornelius F. Lambert; Deacons Henry S. Custodio; Phillip Giordano. In res., Rev. Msgr. John R. Lubicky, (Retired).
Res., 701 Little Gloucester Rd., 08012. Tel: 609-228-4331; Fax: 609-227-0743.
School—St. Agnes Regional School, Blackwood. See separate listing.

St. Jude's (1961), Rev. Msgr. Thomas J. McIntyre; Rev. Carmel F. Polidano; Deacons William J. Drum; Michael McDonaugh.
Res., 402 S. Black Horse Pike, 08012. Tel: 609-227-0572; Fax: 609-227-1276.
School—St. Jude Regional School, Blackwood. See separate listing.

Blue Anchor, Camden Co., St. Lucy's (1925), Rev. Thomas S. Tracey. In res., Rev. Albert E. Harshaw.
Res., 250 S. Rte. 73, 08037. Tel: 609-561-6116; Fax: 609-561-9305.
School—St. Joseph Regional School, Hammonton. See separate listing.
Mission—Cedar Brook, Sacred Heart, (1904).

Bridgeton, Cumberland Co., Immaculate Conception (1874), Rev. Msgr. Ciaran P. O'Mearain; Rev. Thomas J. Barcellona; Deacons C. J. Achee; Carmen Bischer. In res., Rev. John P. Connor.
Res., 312 N. Pearl St., 08302. Tel: 609-451-0254. [CEM]
School—Immaculate Conception Regional School, Bridgeton. See separate listing.

St. Teresa of Avila, Cumberland, (1961), Rev. Stanley E. Kloskowski. In res., Rev. Daniel A. DiNardo.
Res., 46 Central Ave., 08302. Tel: 609-455-2323; Fax: 609-455-7291.
School—Immaculate Conception Regional School, Bridgeton. See separate listing.

Brigantine, Atlantic Co., St. Thomas (1958), Rev. Msgr. Lawrence P. Boyle; Rev. Bernard J. Gannon. In res., Rev. Joseph A. Perreault.
Res., 331 8th St., S., 08203. Tel: 609-266-2123; Fax: 609-266-6416.
School—Tel: 609-266-3154. Sr. M. Annunziata, D.M., Prin.
Sisters 1; Lay Teachers 9; Students 156.
Convent—42nd and Brigantine Ave., Tel: 609-266-3507. St. Philip the Apostle Daughters of Our Lady of Mercy

Brooklawn, Camden Co., St. Maurice's (1955), Rev. Thomas E. Ploude.
Res., 401 Community Rd., 08030. Tel: 609-456-9039.

Cape May, Cape May Co., Our Lady Star of the Sea (1878), Rev. Msgr. Timothy A. Ryan; Rev. Edward W. Garay.
Res., 525 Washington St., 08204. Tel: 609-884-5311; Fax: 609-884-0162. [CEM]
School—Our Lady Star of the Sea Regional School, Cape May. See separate listing.
Chapel—Cape May Point, St. Agnes.

Cape May Court House, Cape May Co., Our Lady of the Angels (1956), Rev. Msgr. Donald D. Velozo. In res., Rev. Max S. Fasciglione.
Res., 106 Mechanic St., P.O. Box 324, 08210. Tel: 609-465-5245.
School—Our Lady Star of the Sea Regional School, Cape May. See separate listing.

Carneys Point, Salem Co., Corpus Christi (1966), Rev. Msgr. Rocco A. Continillo, V.F.
Res., 369 Georgetown Rd., 08069. Tel: 609-299-3833.
School—St. James Regional School, Penns Grove. See separate listing.

Cedarville, Cumberland Co., St. Michael's (1942), Rev. Sean A. McArdle. In res., Rev. Robert P. Weber.
Res., 367 Main St., 08311. Tel: 609-447-3480.
School—Immaculate Conception Regional School, Bridgeton. See separate listing.
Mission—Port Norris, St. Anthony.
Stations—NJ State Medium Security Prison, Bayside Prison; Laurel Lake, Our Lady of the Lake Chapel; Delmont, Southern State Correctional Facility.

Cherry Hill, Camden Co.,

1—St. Mary's, (1961), Revs. John C. Killeen; David A. Grover.
Res., 2001 Springdale Rd., 08003. Tel: 609-424-1454; Fax: 609-424-8270.
School—Holy Rosary Regional School, Cherry Hill. See separate listing.

2—Holy Rosary, Revs. Michael M. Signiski; Robert Fritz; Deacon Raymond Radziak. In res., Rev. Msgr. Leonard G. Scott.
Res., 99 Burnt Mill Rd., 08003. Tel: 609-428-2212 (Res.); 609-428-9456 (Office); Fax: 609-428-9152.
School—Tel: 609-428-4855. Mrs. Patricia Connell, Prin.
Lay Teachers 9; Students 180.
Catechesis/Religious Programs—Sr. Alice Gallagher, S.S.J., D.R.E.
Students 175.
Convent—Tel: 609-429-1364. Sisters of Saint Joseph

3—St. Peter Celestine, (1961), Rev. Msgr. James R. Tracy; Revs. Michael J. Field; Donald F. Trinkle; William Iannuzzi; Deacons W. Leo McBlain; William Watts.
Res., 402 N. Kings Hwy., 08034. Tel: 609-667-2440; Fax: 609-482-0332.
School—Tel: 609-667-3034; Fax: 609-667-9160. Mrs. Camille Forrest, Prin.
Sisters of St. Joseph (Chestnut Hill, PA) 2; Lay Teachers 19; Students 359; Special Educ. Students 17.

4—St. Pius X, (1961), Revs. William P. Brennan; William B. Cannon; Timothy E. Byerley.
Res., 344 Kresson Rd., 08034. Tel: 609-429-1330; Fax: 609-429-8679.
School—Christ the King Regional School, Haddonfield. See separate listing.

5—St. Thomas More, (1968), Rev. Msgr. David F. Budney; Rev. Patsy C. Amabile. In res., Rev. William C. Hart.
Res., 1439 Springdale Rd., 08003. Tel: 609-424-3212; Fax: 609-424-2411, Ext. 51.
School—Holy Rosary Regional School, Cherry Hill. See separate listing.

6—Queen of Heaven, (1955), Rev. Msgr. Edward D. Alleyne; Rev. Carlton C. Stoegbauer; Deacons Charles C. Reiss; James H. Rocks. In res., Rev. Thomas H. Jarka.
Res., 700 W. Marlton Pike, 08002. Tel: 609-429-3334.
School—Tel: 609-428-2890. Sr. Marita Regina, I.H.M., Prin.
Sisters 4; Lay Teachers 8; Students 247.
Convent—Queen of Heaven Convent, 10 Massachusetts Ave., 08002. Tel: 609-428-8818.

Clayton, Gloucester Co., St. Catherine's (1943), Rev. James F. Barry; Deacon Matthew J. Hanrahan. In res., Rev. Cadmus Mazzarella.
Res., 49 W. North St., 08312. Tel: 609-881-9155; Fax: 609-881-9166.
School—51 W. North St., 08312. Tel: 609-881-0067. Miss Janice Bruni, Prin.
Lay Teachers 9; Students 220.

Collings Lakes, Atlantic Co., Our Lady of the Lakes (1976), Rev. Marjan L. Bober; Deacon Edward Freed.
Res., 19 Malaga Rd., 08094. Tel: 609-561-8313.
School—Notre Dame Regional School, Landisville. See separate listing.

Collingswood, Camden Co., St. John's (1903), Rev. Msgr. Martin J. Mannion; Rev. Michael P. Hegarty; Deacon Frank P. Gargin. In res., Rev. Robert C. Pasley.
Res., 809 Park Ave., 08108. Tel: 609-858-0298.
School—Tel: 609-858-1562. Miss Joan Simpson, Prin.
Lay Teachers 15; Students 236.

Delair, Camden Co., St. Veronica's (1961), Rev. James T. McCall.
Res., 8329 Holman Ave., 08110. Tel: 609-662-8050.

Deptford, Gloucester Co., St. John Vianney, Rev. Msgr. James J. Rynne. In res., Rev. Kenneth Johnston.
Res., 2901 Good Intent Rd., 08096. Tel: 609-227-2623; Fax: 609-228-1823.
School—St. Agnes Regional School, Blackwood. See separate listing.

Egg Harbor City, Atlantic Co., St. Nicholas (1864), Revs. Calogero N. LaVerde; Ivan Callone, I.M.C.; Deacon Michael H. Guerrieri.
Res., 525 St. Louis Ave., 08215-2224. Tel: 609-965-0350.
School—526 Chicago Ave., Tel: 609-965-2398. Sr. Kathleen Kelly, O.S.F., Prin.
Sisters 2; Lay Teachers 9; Students 150.
Convent—526 St. Louis Ave., 08215. Tel: 609-965-0890.

Elmer, Salem Co., St. Ann's (1961), Rev. Anthony L. Minniti; Deacon Edward J. Harkins.
Res., 115 Broad St., 08318. Tel: 609-358-3106.
School—St. Rose Regional School, Newfield. See separate listing.

Franklinville, Gloucester Co., Nativity (1961), Rev. William F. Collins.
Res., P.O. Box 296, 08322. Tel: 609-694-2349.
School—St. Rose Regional School, Newfield. See separate listing.

Gibbsboro, Camden Co., St. Andrew the Apostle (1963), Rev. Msgr. Glendon E. Robertson; Rev. Gerald C. Marable; Deacon Thomas B. Henkel.
Res., 120 United States Ave., 08026. Tel: 609-784-3878; Fax: 609-435-7508.
School—Our Lady of Mt. Carmel Regional School, Berlin. See separate listing.

Gibbstown, Gloucester Co., St. Michael's, Rev. Msgr. Eugene J. Fitzsimmons; Rev. Victor J. Jurkowski, O.F.M.Cap.; Deacon James Kiley.
Res., 313 Memorial Ave., 08027. Tel: 609-423-0007; Fax: 609-423-1445.

Glassboro, Gloucester Co., St. Bridget's (1887), Revs. Robert V. Smith; Vincent G. Carpinelli.
Res., 125 Church St., 08028. Tel: 609-881-2753; Fax: 609-881-9697. [CEM]
School—St. Bridget's Regional School, Glassboro. See separate listing.

Our Lady of Lourdes (1966), Revs. James P. Curran; John D. Bohrer. In res., Rev. Msgr. James J. Gaffney, (Retired).
Res., 500 Greentree Rd., 08028. Tel: 609-881-0909; Fax: 609-881-5457.
School—St. Bridget Regional School, Glassboro. See separate listing.

Gloucester, Camden Co., St. Mary's (1848), Revs. Harry J. Jordan; Walter N. Smith; Teofilo Useche. In res., Rev. Brian E. O'Neill.
Res., 426 Monmouth St., 08030. Tel: 609-456-0052; Fax: 609-456-1837. [CEM]
School—Tel: 609-456-0913; Fax: 609-456-7382. Sr. Nora Foley, O.P., Prin.
Dominican Sisters of Hope 2; Lay Teachers 11; Students 355.

Haddonfield, Camden Co., Christ the King Regional School (1927), Rev. Msgr. Thomas J. Morgan; Rev. Daniel Rocco; Deacon Thomas Hafner. In res., Rev. Paul D. Harte.
Res., 200 Windsor Ave., 08033. Tel: 609-429-1600; Fax: 609-429-2734.
School—Christ the King Regional School, Haddonfield. See separate listing.
Convent—168 Hopkins Ave., 08033. Tel: 609-429-3988. Sr. Mary Therese Maher, O.S.F., Local Min.

Haddon Heights, Camden Co., St. Rose's (1896), Rev. Msgr. Richard J. Callahan; Revs. Krzysztof Wtorek; Joseph D. Wallace; Deacon Frank A. Iula, M.D. In res., Rev. Msgr. Michael A. Argullo; Rev. Alfred J. Hewett.
Res., 300 Kings Hwy, 08035. Tel: 609-547-0564; Fax: 609-547-7311.
School—Tel: 609-546-6166. Mrs. Kathryn Lange, Prin.
Sisters of St. Dominic (Newburgh, NY) 1; Lay Teachers 17; Students 376.

Haddon Township, Camden Co., St. Vincent Pallotti (1963), Rev. Msgr. Salvatore J. Adamo; Rev. Msgr. John H. Casey. In res., Rev. Russell L. Rock.
Res., 901 Hopkins Rd., Haddonfield, 08033. Tel: 609-858-1313; 1314; Fax: 609-869-9010.

Hammonton, Atlantic Co., St. Anthony of Padua (1965), Rev. Joseph H. Burns; Deacon Rocco A. Mangino. In res., Rev. John M. Fleming.
Res., P.O. Box 1087, 285 Rte. 206, 08037. Tel: 609-561-3313; Fax: 609-567-7764.
School—St. Joseph Regional School, Hammonton. See separate listing.

St. Joseph's (1886), Revs. Joseph Mungari, S.A.C.; Nicholas Rinaldi, S.A.C.; Michael Parente, S.A.C.; Deacon Ismael Perez Tavarez.
Res., 226 French St., 08037. Tel: 609-561-0180. [CEM]
School—St. Joseph Regional School, Hammonton. See separate listing.

St. Martin de Porres (1962), Rev. John A. DelDuca. In res., Rev. Msgr. Pasquale DiBuono.
Res., 129 Park Ave., 08037. Tel: 609-561-4322.
School—St. Joseph Regional School, Hammonton. See separate listing.

Landisville, Atlantic Co., Our Lady of Victories (1952), Revs. Ernest R. Soprano; Ireneo Lopez-Tovar.
Res., 202 North Blvd., 08326. Tel: 609-697-1450.
School—Notre Dame Regional School, Landisville. See separate listing.

Lindenwold, Camden Co., St. Lawrence's (1896), Revs. Patrick A. McCabe; Paul A. Olszewski. In res., Rev. Zbigniew J. Jezierski.
Res., 100 South Ave., 08021. Tel: 609-627-2222; 627-7522.
School—Tel: 609-783-0710. Sr. Joan Boyle, O.P., Supr. & Prin.
Sisters of St. Dominic 3; Lay Teachers 10; Students 229.

Linwood, Atlantic Co., Our Lady of Sorrows (1965), Revs. Malcolm C. McLeod, M.SS.CC.; John Perdue, M.SS.CC.
Res., 200 Wilson Ave., 08221. Tel: 609-927-1154.

Longport, Atlantic Co., Epiphany (1954), Rev. Stanley J. Barr.
Res., 2801 Ventnor Ave., 08403. Tel: 609-822-8940.
School—Blessed Sacrament Regional School, Margate. See separate listing.

Magnolia, Camden Co., St. Gregory's (1955), Rev. Msgr. Edward L. Korda; Rev. A. Robert Cairone; Deacon Leonard P. Carlucci.
Res., Evesham Ave., 08049. Tel: 609-784-4090; Fax: 609-784-6371.
School—Our Lady of Grace Regional School, Somerdale. See separate listing.
Convent—230 E. Evesham Ave., 08049. Tel: 609-784-1576. Sr. Victoria Masterpaul, O.S.F., Local Min.

Malaga, Gloucester Co., St. Mary's (1961), Rev. Abbott J. Hope.
Res., Dutch Mill Rd., P.O. Box M, 08328. Tel: 609-694-2576.
School—Notre Dame Regional School, Newfield. See separate listing.

Mantua, Gloucester Co., Incarnation (1956), Rev. Thomas A. Newton; Deacon Thomas F. O'Brien.
Res., 234 Shadow Pl., P.O. Box 295, 08051. Tel: 609-468-1314; Fax: 609-468-4886.
School—School St. Margaret Regional School, Woodbury Heights. See separate listing.

Margate, Atlantic Co., Blessed Sacrament (1945), Revs. Lewis A. Battisti; Robert F. Walker.
Res., 11 N. Kenyon Ave., 08402. Tel: 609-822-7105; Fax: 609-822-3817.
School—Blessed Sacrament Regional School, Margate. See separate listing.
Convent—14 N. Jerome Ave., 08402. Tel: 609-822-5543. Sr. Kathryn Rush, O.S.F., Local Supr.

Marmora, Cape May Co., The Church of the Resurrection (1975), Revs. Mark R. Cavagnaro; Joseph M. Reilly.
Res., 200 W. Tuckahoe Rd., 08223. Tel: 609-390-0664; Fax: 609-390-7700.
School—St. Augustine Regional School, Ocean City. See separate listing.

Mays Landing, Atlantic Co., St. Vincent de Paul (1906), Revs. John F. Sugrue; Edward J. Maher; Deacon Richard Wigglesworth.
Res., 114 Rte. 50, 08330. Tel: 609-625-2124. [CEM]
School—Tel: 609-625-1565. Miss Linda Pirolli, Prin.
Sisters 1; Lay Teachers 8; Students 241.
Convent—5807 Main St., 08330. Tel: 609-625-1566. Sisters of St. Joseph of Chestnut Hill Sr. Marie Fenton, S.S.J., Local Coord.
Mission—Dorothy, St. Bernard. [CEM]

Merchantville, Camden Co., St. Peter's (1903), Rev. Msgr. Charles P. Barth; Revs. Glenn R. Hartman; Pawel Kryszkiewicz; Deacons Peter J. Gilmartin; Ray Ellis. In res., Rev. Joseph T. Szolack.
Res., 43 W. Maple Ave., 08109. Tel: 609-663-1373; Fax: 609-488-0647.
School—Tel: 609-665-5789; Fax: 609-665-4943. Sr. Louise Lauretti, M.P.F., Prin.
Lay Teachers 18; Students 528.

Millville, Cumberland Co., St. Mary Magdalen's (1864), Revs. Anthony J. Manuppella; David V. Minniti.
Res., 621 Dock St., 08332. Tel: 609-825-0021; Fax: 609-825-0073. [CEM]
School—7 W. Powell St., 08332. Tel: 609-825-3600. Armida of the Holy Eucharist M.D.P.V.M., Prin.
Sisters 8; Lay Teachers 9; Students 330.
Convent—3 W. Powell St., 08332. Tel: 609-327-2235. Missionary Daughters of the Holy Eucharist Mother Armida of the Holy Eucharist M.D.P.V.M., Supr.

St. John Bosco (1966), Rev. William Graham. In res., Rev. Francis X. Hudson.
Res., 2 Hillcrest Ave., 08332. Tel: 609-825-1513; Fax: 609-327-7752.

Minotola, Atlantic Co., St. Michael's (1902), Rev. Donald C. Chiavello.
Res., P.O. Box 587, West Ave., 08341. Tel: 609-697-0942.
School—Notre Dame Regional School, Newfield. See separate listing.

Mount Ephraim, Camden Co., Sacred Heart (1939), Revs. Robert J. Dunphy; James O. Dabrowski; Deacon William Norquist.
Res., 11 N. Black Horse Pike, 08059. Tel: 609-931-1441; Fax: 609-931-9433.
School—Sacred Heart Regional School, Mount Ephraim. See separate listing.

Mullica Hill, Gloucester Co., Holy Name of Jesus (1901), Rev. Michael P. Rush; Deacon Sam Nastasi. In res., Rev. William J. Bleiler, Area Spanish Apostolate.
Res., 17 Earlington Ave., 08062. Tel: 609-478-2294. [CEM]

National Park, Gloucester Co., St. Matthew's (1915), Revs. Edward F. Sobolewski; William C. Pierce; Deacon William J. Rumaker.
Res., 214 Columbia Blvd., 08063. Tel: 609-845-2523; Fax: 609-251-0822.
School—St. Matthew Regional School, National Park. See separate listing.
Convent—Hessian Ave., Verga, 08093. Tel: 609-845-7204.

Newfield, Gloucester Co., St. Rose of Lima (1922), Rev. John Joseph Tumosa. In res., Rev. Edward A. Igle.
Res., 104 Catawba Ave., 08344. Tel: 609-697-3232; Fax: 609-697-1455.
School—Notre Dame Regional School, Newfield. See separate listing.

North Cape May, Cape May Co., St. John of God (1966), Revs. Andrew Duignan; Jaromir Michalak.
Res., 680 Town Bank Rd., 08204. Tel: 609-884-1656.
School—St. Raymond Regional School, Villas. See separate listing.

Northfield, Atlantic Co., St. Bernadette (1966), Rev. Msgr. Donald D. Velozo; Rev. Perry A. Cherubini.
Res., 1421 New Rd., 08225. Tel: 609-646-3499; 646-5611; Fax: 609-484-8345.
School—Blessed Sacrament Regional School, Margate. See separate listing.

Oaklyn, Camden Co., St. Aloysius (1935), Revs. Thomas M. Flynn; Robert M. Gomes. In res., Rev. Douglas R. Tobin.
Res., 37 W. Haddon Ave., 08107. Tel: 609-858-2848; 854-2352.
School—St. John Regional School, Collingswood. See separate listing.

Ocean City, Cape May Co., St. Augustine's (1894), Rev. Msgr. Edward F. Mullen; Rev. William S. Vandegrift. In res., Rev. Edward D. Lyons.
Res., 1310 Ocean Ave., 08226. Tel: 609-399-0648; Fax: 609-399-0063.
School—St. Augustine Regional School, Ocean City. See separate listing.

St. Frances Cabrini (1966), Rev. Msgr. Joseph P. Herron; Rev. Michael H. D'Amico.
Res., 114 Atlantic Ave., 08226. Tel: 609-399-4776; Fax: 609-391-9412.
School—St. Augustine Regional School, Ocean City. See separate listing.

Our Lady of Good Counsel (1961), Rev. Msgr. Thomas H. Sharkey; Deacon James J. Teeney.
Res., 3948 Central Ave., 08226. Tel: 609-399-2085; 398-3654 (Office).
School—St. Augustine Regional School, Ocean City. See separate listing.

Paulsboro, Gloucester Co., St. John's, Revs. William J. Fallon; Alfred S. Aversa.
Res., 647 Beacon Ave., 08066. Tel: 609-423-0086; Fax: 609-423-0123.
School—712 Mantua Ave., 08066. Tel: 609-423-0099.
Lay Teachers 9; Students 143.
Convent—700 Seventh St., 08066. Tel: 609-423-0723. Sr. Ann Byrnes, R.S.M., Supr.

Pennsauken, Camden Co., St. Cecilia's (1939), Revs. Fred Voltaggio; Anthony DiBardino; Deacon D. Eugene Burns. In res., Rev. James R. Ryan.
Res., 4824 Camden Ave., 08110. Tel: 609-662-2721; Fax: 609-486-2089.
School—Tel: 609-662-0149. Miss Patricia Flannery, Prin.
Lay Teachers 9; Students 201.

St. Stephen (1961), Rev. Msgr. Joseph C. Downing; Rev. Antoine F. St. Germain.
Res., 6306 Browning Rd., 08109. Tel: 609-662-9338.
School—Tel: 609-662-5935. Sr. Kathleen M. Boyle, S.S.J., Prin.
Sisters of St. Joseph 1; Lay Teachers 12; Students 182.

Penns Grove, Salem Co., St. James (1901), Rev. William A. Hodge; Deacon Joseph A. Ganci.
Res., 114 State St., 08069. Tel: 609-299-0399; Fax: 609-299-3728.
School—St. James Regional School, Penns Grove. See separate listing.

Pennsville, Salem Co., Queen of the Apostles (1955), Rev. William F. Moore; Deacon Jack Cromer. In res., Rev. Peter J. Osinski.
Res., 391 S. Broadway, 08070. Tel: 609-678-5400; Fax: 609-627-9373.
School—St. Mary Regional School, Salem. See separate listing. Tel: 609-784-4853.

Pine Hill, Camden Co., St. Edward's (1953), Revs. John P. Ward; Dennis W. Bajkowski. In res., Rev. Robert J. Gregorio.
Res., 500 Erial Rd., 08021. Tel: 609-783-2670; Fax: 609-627-9373.
School—Sr. Bridget Gedji, S.O.L.M., Prin. & Supr.
Sisters of Mercy (Rome) 4; Lay Teachers 5; Students 151.

Pitman, Gloucester Co., Our Lady Queen of Peace (1949), Rev. Msgr. John F. Cooke.
Res., 161 Pitman Ave., 08071. Tel: 609-589-5673; Fax: 609-589-0102.
School—St. Bridget Regional School, Glassboro. See separate listing.

Pleasantville, Atlantic Co., St. Peter's (1896), Revs. Ronald S. Falotico; Michael Kim; Laserian I. Nwoga. In res., Rev. C. Jeffries Burton, S.J.
Res., 25 W. Verona Ave., 08232. Tel: 609-641-0285; Fax: 609-641-0385.
School—Tel: 609-646-3057. Miss Patricia Ellis, Prin.
Lay Teachers 9; Students 170.

Pomona, Atlantic Co., Assumption (1938), Revs. Joseph P. Rush; Daniel M. Sherman. In res., Rev. Peter F. Finnerty.
Res., 276 W. White Horse Pike, 08240. Tel: 609-965-4021; Fax: 609-965-4149.
School—Assumption Regional School, Pomona. See separate listing.

Rosenhayn, Cumberland Co., St. Mary's, Rev. Joseph A. Salerno. In res., Rev. Sebastian V. Annino.
Res., Morton Ave., P.O. Box 376, 08352-0376. Tel: 609-451-8763. [CEM]
School—Immaculate Conception Regional School, Bridgeton. See separate listing.

Runnemede, Camden Co., St. Maria Goretti (1965), Rev. Msgr. James P. McIntyre; Rev. Joseph J. Adamson.
Res., 321 Orchard Ave., 08078. Tel: 609-933-0037; Fax: 609-933-0036.
School—St. Teresa Regional School, Runnemede. See separate listing.

St. Teresa of the Infant Jesus, Rev. Msgr. Joseph W. Pokusa, J.C.D.; Rev. John J. Vignone; Deacon A. Kenneth Bandiera.
Res., 13 E. Evesham Rd., 08078. Tel: 609-939-1681.
School—St. Teresa Regional School, Runnemede. See separate listing.

Salem, Salem Co., St. Mary's (1864), Revs. Richard J. Hadyka; Joseph F. Ganiel.
Res., 25 Oak St., 08079. Tel: 609-935-0288. [CEM]
School—St. Mary Regional School, Salem. See separate listing.

Sea Isle City, Cape May Co., St. Joseph's (1884), Revs. Stephen Carey; John A. Cavagnaro.
Res., 4308 Landis Ave., 08243. Tel: 609-263-8696.
School—St. Joseph Regional School, Sea Isle City. See separate listing.

Sicklerville, Camden Co., St. John Neumann (1977), Revs. Edward B. Rosinski; Brendan J. Meaney; Deacons Frank J. Engel; Anthony Kijonka.
Res., 234 Sicklerville Rd., Box G, 08081-0438. Tel: 609-728-1060.

Somerdale, Camden Co., Our Lady of Grace (1954), Rev. Msgr. Dominic J. Bottino; Rev. Richard L. Forbes; Deacon Frank Pepe. In res., Rev. Timothy Hubbs; Rev. Msgr. J. Francis Flaherty, P.A.
Res., 35 N. White Horse Pike, 08083. Tel: 609-783-2256; Fax: 609-435-1722.
School—Our Lady of Grace Regional School, Somerdale. See separate listing.

Somers Point, Atlantic Co., St. Joseph's (1946), Rev. Msgr. Josef A. Wagenhoffer; Rev. Vicente Moreno Martin; Deacons Jerome Wilson; John L. Glasser. In res., Rev. Robert T. Matysik.
Res., 606 Shore Rd., 08244. Tel: 609-927-3568.
School—St. Joseph Regional School. Regionalized with Our Lady of Sorrows Parish, Linwood. Sr. Gloria Schaab, Prin.
Sisters 3; Lay Teachers 11; Students 261.
Convent—580 Shore Rd., 08244. Tel: 609-927-2228. Sisters of St. Joseph

Stone Harbor, Cape May Co., St. Paul's (1911), Rev. Eugene J. Kernan.
Res., 9910 Third Ave., 08247. Tel: 609-368-3091.
School—St. Joseph Regional School, Sea Isle City. See separate listing.

Stratford, Camden Co., St. Luke's (1961), Revs. Thomas B. Fitzsimmons; Peter M. Joyce; Deacon James D'Angelillio.
Res., 55 Warwick Rd., 08084. Tel: 609-783-5555; Fax: 609-782-8336.
School—Tel: 609-783-3088. Mrs. Cathleen Sheridan, Prin.
Lay Teachers 12; Students 300.
Special Education— Lay Teachers 2; Students 15.

Swedesboro, Gloucester Co., St. Joseph's (1854), Revs. John F. Bloh; Paul Hao Trinh; Deacon Robert W. Hardy.
Res., 140 N. Broad St., 08085. Tel: 609-467-0037;

Fax: 609-467-0038. [CEM]
School—225 Kings Hwy., 08085. Tel: 609-467-1154. Mr. Dennis Reitano, Prin.
Lay Teachers 9; Students 161.

Ventnor, Atlantic Co., St. James (1922), Revs. Brendan V. Sullivan; Herman N. Burger; Deacon James Clair.
Res., 6415 Atlantic Ave., 08406. Tel: 609-822-2176; Fax: 609-487-8137.
School—Tel: 609-822-2234. Sr. Kathleen Hayes, O.P., Prin.
Sisters 2; Lay Teachers 8; Students 262.
Convent—Portland & Atlantic Ave., 08406. Tel: 609-487-8110. Dominican Sisters (Sinsinawa, WI)

Villas, Cape May Co., St. Raymond (1937), Revs. John H. Burton; Peter Saporito.
Res., 25 E. Hudson Ave., 08251. Tel: 609-886-5366; Fax: 609-886-9415.
School—St. Raymond Regional School, Villas. See separate listing.

Vineland, Cumberland Co.,

1—OUR LADY OF POMPEII, (1909), Rev. James J. Durkin.
Res., 4680 Dante Ave., 08360. Tel: 609-691-7526; Fax: 609-692-2686.
School—St. Mary Regional School, Vineland. See separate listing.

2—SACRED HEART, (1874), Rev. Msgr. Joseph G. Stoerlein, V.F.; Revs. Salvatore L. DeIelse; Raymond P. Gormley; Deacon Robert Andreacchio. In res., Rev. Msgr. Joseph A. von Hartleben.
Res., 1010 Landis Ave., 08360. Tel: 609-691-0420; Fax: 609-691-1516. [CEM]
School—Sacred Heart Regional School, Vineland. See separate listing.

3—ST. FRANCIS OF ASSISI, (1961), Rev. Msgr. Patrick S. Chiarilli; Rev. Hugh J. Bradley. In res., Rev. Msgr. Victor S. Muro.
Res., 23 W. Chestnut Ave., 08360. Tel: 609-691-9181; Fax: 609-794-9029.
School—Tel: 609-691-9184. Mrs. Anita Meale, Prin.
Sisters 4; Lay Teachers 15; Students 325.
Convent—W. Chestnut Ave., 08360. Tel: 609-691-8129. Daughters of Mercy

4—ST. ISIDORE, (1962), Rev. John T. Frey. In res., Revs. Edward P. Sommers; Alvaro Diaz, O.F.M.
Res., 1655 Magnolia Ave., 08360. Tel: 609-691-9077; Fax: 609-692-3305.
School—Sacred Heart Regional School, Vineland. See separate listing.

5—ST. MARY'S, (1887), Revs. Paul P. Onufer; Julian K. Karczewski; Edward F. Namiotka.
Res., 9 S. Union Rd., 08360. Tel: 609-691-9721; Fax: 609-692-5034. [CEM]
School—St. Mary Regional School. See separate listing.
Mission—Richland, St. Joseph.

Washington Township, Gloucester Co., St. Charles Borromeo (1965), Rev. Msgr. Joseph F. O'Connell; Rev. John O'Leary; Deacon John R. Gallimore.
Res., 176 Stagecoach Rd., Sicklerville, 08081. Tel: 609-629-0411.
School—St. Jude Regional School, Blackwood. See separate listing.

SS. Peter and Paul (1973), Revs. John A. Clarke; Joseph A. Newell, S.J.; Deacons Edward X. Guidotti; Liberato F. Tumulo. In res., Rev. Michael J. Bourke.
Res., Ganttown Rd., P.O. Box 1022, Turnersville, 08012. Tel: 609-589-3366.
School—St. Jude Regional School, Blackwood. See separate listing.

Holy Family (1974), Rev. Msgr. Joseph P. Joynes; Rev. Marcel Tabone; Deacons Vincent Fausto; George M. Ferland.
Res., 226 Hurffville Rd., Sewell, 08080. Tel: 609-228-1616; Fax: 609-228-6332.
School—St. Jude Regional School, Blackwood. See separate listing.

Waterford, Camden Co., St. Anthony (1966), Revs. Ambrose S. Bryce; Charles E. Kuhl.
Res., 436 Pennington Ave., 08089. Tel: 609-767-7535.
School—St. Joseph Regional School, Hammonton. See separate listing.

West Collingswood, Camden Co., Transfiguration (1950), Revs. Richard J. Lodge; Nathan I. DeMarco; Deacon William C. Robinson. In res., Rev. Msgr. Thomas A. Guenther.
Res., 445 White Horse Pike, 08107. Tel: 609-854-0364.
School—PreSchool Cares Program, Tel: 609-858-2200; Fax: 609-858-7013. Miss Diane Mary Felke, Dir.

Westmont, Camden Co., Holy Saviour (1928), Revs. Terry M. Odien; Edward F. Heintzelman. In res., Rev. Michael P. Orsi.
Res., 50 Emerald Ave., 08108. Tel: 609-854-0022; Fax: 609-854-5741.
School—30 Emerald Ave., 08108. Tel: 609-858-1966. Sr. Janice Novak, Prin.; Sr. Bernadra Ribeiro, Supr.
Sisters, Franciscan Missionaries of the Immaculate Heart of Mary 4; Lay Teachers 7; Students 239.

Westville, Gloucester Co., St. Anne's (1921), Rev. Andrew J. Bolcar; Deacon Anthony C. Como. In res., Rev. Frederick G. Link.
Res., 213 Woodbine Ave., 08093. Tel: 609-456-4136; Fax: 609-742-0619.
School—St. Matthew Regional School, National Park. See separate listing.

Westville Grove, Gloucester Co., Most Holy Redeemer (1958), Revs. Neil F. Dante; Piotr Szamocki.
Res., Rte. 1, Box 595, Delsea Dr., 08093. Tel: 609-848-6779; Fax: 609-848-6208.
School—Mrs. Donna DiPasquale, Prin.; Sr. Hugh Marie Layton, S.S.J., Supr. Sisters of St. Joseph (Chestnut Hill) 2; Lay Teachers 7; Students 245.

Wildwood, Cape May Co., St. Ann's (1895), Rev. Msgr. William Quinn, V.F.; Rev. Stanley Witcoskie; Deacon Alfred W. Lewis. In res., Revs. Paul J. Maguire, (Retired); Charles Conaty.
Res., 2900 Pacific Ave., 08260. Tel: 609-522-5583; Fax: 609-522-9375.
School—St. Ann Regional School Regionalized with Assumption Parish, Wildwood Crest, 2901 New Jersey Ave., 08260. Tel: 609-522-2704; Fax: 609-522-5721. Sr. Sheila Murphy, S.S.J., Prin.
Sisters of St. Joseph 3; Lay Teachers 8; Students 290.
Convent—119 E. Glenwood Ave., 08260. Sr. Marie Scherr, S.S.J., Supr.

Wildwood Crest, Cape May Co., Assumption B.V.M., Revs. Francis J. Gramigna; James R. Plummer; Deacon Joseph A. Costello. In res., Rev. Msgr. John J. Kelly, (Retired).
Res., 7110 Seaview Ave., 08260. Tel: 609-522-4114; 522-6071.
School—St. Ann Regional School, Wildwood. See separate listing under St. Ann's Parish.

Williamstown, Gloucester Co., St. Mary's (1906), Revs. Carmen A. Carlone; John Muscat; Conleth Eleanya; Deacon John J. Leyden.
Res., 32 Carrol Ave., 08094. Tel: 609-629-6142; Fax: 609-875-2097.
School—Tel: 609-629-6190; Fax: 609-728-1437. Miss Judith McBride, C.S.S.F., Prin.
Sisters 3; Lay Teachers 24; Students 570.
Convent—640 S. Main St., 08094. Tel: 609-262-1358. St. Joseph Sisters

Woodbine, Cape May Co., St. Casimir's (1939), Rev. Robert Yori.
Res., 304 Clay St., P.O.Box 533, 08270. Tel: 609-861-3771; Fax: 609-861-7112. [CEM]
School—St. Joseph Regional School, Sea Isle City. See separate listing.
Mission—Goshen, St. Elizabeth. [CEM]

Woodbury, Gloucester Co., St. Patrick's (1877), Revs. J. Gerald Gallagher; E. Joseph Byerley; Deacon Robert Lorenzo.
Res., 64 Cooper St., 08096. Tel: 609-845-0123; Fax: 609-845-7409.
School—Mrs. Dorice Palumbo, Prin. Lay Teachers 11; Students 250.

Woodbury Heights, Gloucester Co., St. Margaret's (1961), Rev. Msgr. Felix M. O'Neill; Rev. Michael J. Matveenko; Deacon Robert M. Kenney.
Res., P.O. Box 186, 334 Beech Ave., 08097. Tel: 609-848-0047; Fax: 609-384-8123.
School—St. Margaret Regional School, Woodbury Heights. See separate listing.

Woodlynne, Camden Co., Immaculate Heart of Mary (1949), Rev. Edward J. Walsh.
Res., 201 Cooper Ave., 08107. Tel: 609-962-8610.

Woodstown, Salem Co., St. Joseph's (1895), Rev. Stephen F. Cervoni; Deacon Kenneth H. Demarest. In res., Rev. Joseph R. Ferrara.
Res., 51 Broad St., 08098. Tel: 609-769-0004. [CEM]

Chaplains of Public Institutions

ANCORA. *New Jersey State Mental Hospital*. Rev. Albert E. Harshaw, St. Lucy's Church, 250 S. Rte. 73, Blue Anchor, 08037.

DELMONT. *Southern State Correctional Facility*. Tel: 609-785-1300. Rev. Robert P. Weber.

LAKELAND. *Camden County Hospital at Lakeland*. Sr. Mary de Sales Vesey, S.S.J., St. Jude's Church, 402 S. Black Horse Pike, Blackwood, 08012. Tel: 609-227-0572.

St. Joseph's Chapel. Vacant. Camden County Hospital, Blackwood Post Office, 08012.

LEESBURG. *New Jersey State Medium Security Prison*, 08327. Revs. Sean P. McArdle; Robert P. Weber.

VINELAND. *Vineland State School*. Attended by Sacred Heart Church, Vineland. Tel: 609-691-0420.

WOODBINE. *State Colony*. Rev. Robert Yori, St. Casimir's Church, Tel: 609-861-3771.

On Duty Outside the Diocese:

Reverend Monsignors—
Daiber, Sean J., Brazilian Missions, Central Mailing Address, Paroguia de Sao Jose Rua 107, Setor Sul, Caiza Postal 716, 74,000 Goiania Goias, Brazil S.A.
Marucci, Carl J., The Permanent Observer., Mission of the Holy See to the U.N., 25 E. 39th St., New York, NY 20016-0903. Tel: 212-370-7885
O'Leary, Cornelius, 25098 Jaclyn Ave., Moreno Valley, CA 92387

Reverend Fathers—
Checchio, James F., North American College, Rome, Italy
Chirico, Peter F., S.S., St. James Cathedral, 804 Ninth Ave., Seattle, WA 98104
Davis, Charles J., RRI, Box 20-1, Woodsville, NH 03785
Kocik, Franc W., St. Patrick, Pincourt, Ile Perrot, Province of Quebec, Canada
Kunzman, Richard T., P.O. Box 61, Big Flats, NY 14814
Mannion, Michael, Office of Catholic Ministry, Catholic University of America., 620 Michigan Ave., N.E., Washington, DC 20064-1567
McGrath, Roger E., St. Mary Seminary and University, 5400 Roland Ave., Baltimore, MD 21210. Tel: 410-323-3200
Norton, Daniel J., Brazilian Missions
Reese, Donald B., Lake Dr., Lake Hauto, Box 40c, RD 1, Nesquehoning, PA 18240
Selleck, John P., St. of Francis of Assisi, 334 Gaskin St., Blountstown, FL 32424-2127
Stout, O. Hugh, Holy Ghost, 2015 Louisiana Ave., New Orleans, LA 70015
Wade, Edward C., Our Lady of Perpetual Help, 15 Lebreton St., Ottawa, ON K1R-7H1 Canada. Tel: 613-232-6960; Fax: 613-234-4568

Military Chaplains:
Reverend Fathers—
Betz, James, U.S. Army
McLaughlin, Peter A., U.S. Navy
Newton, John G., U.S. Navy

On Sick Leave:
Reverend Fathers—
Bean, Charles S.
Gerbino, A. Richard
Hardin, Roy
O'Sullivan, James
Pisik, Timothy E.
Shannon, Joseph E.

On Leave of Absence:
Reverend Fathers—
Weaver, Patrick

Retired:
Reverend Monsignors—
Adamo, Salvatore J.
Argullo, Michael A., St. Rose of Lima Church, 3 Green St., Haddon Heights, NJ 08035
Beausang, Charles C., 13595 Clara Ln., Port Charlotte, FL 33981
Cannon, Thomas, St. Peter, 359 W. New York Ave., P.O. Box 3700, Deland, FL 32723
Carr, James A., 918 Society Hill, Cherry Hill, NJ 08003
Chmielewski, Joseph, 5 S. Suffolk Ave., Ventnor, NJ 08406
Clark, John J., 644 Pleasure Ave., Ocean City, NJ 08226
Conlon, Joseph E., St. Mary Nursing Home, 1730 Kresson Rd., Cherry Hill, NJ 08003
DiBuono, Pasquale M., St. Martin de Porres, 129 Park Ave., Hammonton, NJ 08037
Flaherty, J. Francis, Our Lady of Grace, 35 N. White Horse Pike, Somerdale, NJ 08083-1796
Gaffney, James J., J.C.D., Our Lady of Lourdes, 500 Green Tree Rd., Glassboro, NJ 08028-1427
Giammarino, Vincent J., St. Mary Nursing Home, 1730 Kresson Rd., Cherry Hill, NJ 08003
Hewitt, Bernard P., Garden Lakes Trailer Park, Lot 144, Eighth Ave., Court House, Cape May, NJ 08210
Hudzik, Leo A., 705 Pilgrim Plaza, North Cape May, NJ 08204
Kelly, John J., Assumption, 710 Seaview Ave., Wildwood Crest, NJ 08260-3826
Kennedy, Edward J., 4901 Harbor Beach Blvd., Apt. P-12, Brigantine, NJ 08203. Tel: 609-266-6244
Leary, Joseph W., 130 N. Railroad, Frockville, PA 17931
Lubicky, John R., St. Agnes, 701 Little Gloucester Rd., Blackwood, NJ 08012-7309
Madden, Patrick J., 401 Washington Mall, Cape May, NJ 08204
McCaffrey, John, 201 N. Flagler Dr. Room 501, West Palm Beach, FL 33401

McDaid, Edward J., Sacred Heart Priests Residence, 200 St. Mary's Dr., Cherry Hill, NJ 08003-2517
O'Connor, Edward J., 46 Asbury Rd., Ocean City, NJ 08226
O'Connor, Paul, 23 N. Wissahickan Ave, Ventnor, NJ 08406
Rigney, Philip, 139 Fairview W., Tequesta, FL 33458
Seidenburg, Augustine J., 150 W. Cedar Ave., Somers Point, NJ 08244
Wieckowski, John F., Grand View Apts., 428-C, Crafton Ave., Pitman, NJ 08071
Zegers, James J., P.A., 21 Red Clover Dr., Marmora, NJ 08223

Reverend Fathers—
Becker, Charles J., S.S., St. Joseph's, 1010 Liberty St., Camden, NJ 08104
Bernard, John P., 4327 Lockport Rd., Elba, NY 14058
Burns, Thomas E., 6713A Monmouth Ave., Ventor, NJ 08406-2128. Tel: 609-822-7102
Campuzano, J. Eduardo, Puerto del Carmen 4-A, Maspalomas 35100 (Las Palmas), Spain
Carta, Umberto, 23 Pine Ave., Elmtown E, Hammonton, NJ 08037
Darby, Bernard M., 6548 165th St., Flushing, NY 11365
Eckert, William F., 9 Lori Ct., Pittsfield, MA 01201-7145
Hayden, Joseph M., 4747 N. Road 33, Lot 354, Lakeland, FL 33805
Hewett, Alfred, St. Rose of Lima, 300 Kings Hwy., Haddon Heights, NJ 08035-1397
Kolton, Stanislaus J., P.O. Box 72, Spring Lake, NJ 07762
Maguire, Paul J., St. Ann, 2900 Pacific Ave., Wildwood, NJ 08260-4943
McCormick, George, Dow Rd., RR1 Box 32, Deer Isle, ME 04629
McDonnell, Cyril, 1920 S. Ocean Dr., Apt. 201, Fort Lauderdale, FL 33316
McGarvey, Joseph F., 32 Central Ave., Audubon, NJ 08106-1904
Melvin, James M., Sacred Heart Priests Residence, 200 St. Mary's Dr., Cherry Hill, NJ 08003-2517
Mroczkowski, Leonard A., 1981 Washington Ave., Seaside Heights, NJ 08751
Orsini, Joseph E., 42 W. 50th St., Bayonne, NJ 07002
Weber, George A., Box 272114, Tampa, FL 33688-2114

Permanent Deacons:
Achee, C. J.
Andreaccho, Robert A.
Bandiera, A. Kenneth
Beebe, Joseph
Bischer, Carmen
Bradley, Patrick
Bucher, Joseph L.
Burns, D. Eugene
Carlucci, Leonard P.
Cassidy, Joseph P.
Clair, John
Como, Anthony C.
Costello, Joseph A.
Cromer, John
Custodio, Henry S.
D'Angelillio, James J.
Demarest, Kenneth H.
Donohue, J. Frank
Drum, William J.
Ellis, Raymond V.
Engel, Frank J.
Fausto, Vincent
Ferland, George M.
Ferrario, Raymond C.
Freed, Edward E.
Gallimore, John R.
Ganci, Joseph A.
Gargin, Frank P.
Garufi, Agatino
Gilmartin, Peter J.
Giordano, Philip
Glasser, John L.
Gonzalez, Carmelo
Guerrieri, Michael H.
Guidotti, Edward
Hafner, Thomas J.
Hagan, William T.
Hanrahan, Matthew J.
Hardy, Robert W.
Harkins, Edward J.
Harkins, Michael J.
Harris, Philip
Henkel, Thomas B.
Hynes, John C.
Iannuzzi, William P.
Iula, Dr. Frank A.
Johnson, Paul F.
Kearney, J. Brian
Kenney, Robert M.
Kijonka, Anthony
Kiley, James
Kulesa, Stanley
Leone, John
Lewis, Alfred W.
Leyden, John J.
Lorenzo, Robert
Lytle, George V.
Majewski, Walter, Jr.
Mangino, Rocco A.
McAleer, Charles
McBlain, Leo
McCarthy, Richard F.
McDonaugh, Michael
McLeer, Eugene L.
Mija, Theodore
Nastasi, Santo
Norquist, William V.
O'Brien, Thomas F.
Olesiewicz, Ronald J.
Pepe, Frank, Jr.
Porowicz, Alfred T.
Quiles, Bernardino
Radziak, Raymond
Raftovich, Robert V.
Ralbusky, Emil A.
Reiss, Dr. Charles C.
Rios, Jose R.
Rivera, Miguel A.
Robinson, William C.
Rocks, James H.
Rumaker, William J.
Seppanen, Henry R.
Tavarez, Ismael Perez
Teeney, James J.
Traxler, Harold G., Jr.
Tully, James
Tumulo, Liberato F.
Valle, Wilfredo
Vargo, Frank T.
Vega, Angel Ramos
Verycken, Edward J.
Watts, William L.
Wigglesworth, Richard
Wilson, Jerome I.

INSTITUTIONS LOCATED IN THE DIOCESE

[A] HIGH SCHOOLS, DIOCESAN

ABSECON. *Holy Spirit High School*, New Rd., 08201. Tel: 609-646-3000; Fax: 609-646-1770. Revs. Joseph A. Perreault, Prin.; Edward D. Lyons. Sisters of Mercy 5; Priests 2; Lay Teachers 35; Students 904.

CARNEYS POINT. *St. James High School*, 350 Georgetown Rd., 08069. Tel: 609-299-0400. Revs. Peter J. Osinski, Prin.; Joseph R. Ferrara. Priests 2; Lay Teachers 16; Students 250.

CHERRY HILL. *Camden Catholic High School*, Rte. 38 and Cuthbert Rd., 08002. Tel: 609-663-2247. Rev. Andrew E. Martin, Prin.; Joan Urello, Vice Prin.; Revs. William C. Hart; Robert Pasley. Priests 4; Sisters of Mercy 4; Lay Teachers 38; Students 876.

HADDONFIELD. *Paul VI High School*, 901 Hopkins Rd., Ste. B, 08033. Tel: 609-858-4900. Rev. Russell L. Rock, Prin.; Sr. Marianne McCann, M.P.F., Asst. Prin.; Revs. John J. Byrnes; Timothy Hubbs; Robert E. Hughes. Priests 4; Religious Teachers Filippini 3; Lay Teachers 43; Students 1,050.

HAMMONTON. *St. Joseph*, 133 N. 3rd St., 08037. Tel: 609-561-0689. Mr. James J. Cavalieri, Prin.; Rev. Edward F. Namiotka. Religious Sisters Filippini 2; Lay Teachers 20; Students 343.

[B] HIGH SCHOOLS, PAROCHIAL

GLOUCESTER. *Gloucester Catholic High School*, 333 Ridgeway St., 08030. Tel: 609-456-4400. Rev. Kenneth J. Johnston, Prin. Priests 1; Deacons 1; Dominican Sisters 1; Lay Teachers 36; Students 748.

VINELAND. *Sacred Heart High School*, N. East Ave., 08360. Tel: 609-691-4491. Sr. Clare de Chantal, S.S.J., Prin. Sisters of St. Joseph 2; Lay Teachers 16; Students 260.

WILDWOOD. *Wildwood Catholic High School*, 1500 Central Ave., 08260. Tel: 609-522-7257. Sr. Mary Ellen Ford, S.S.J., Prin.; Richard Turco, Asst. Prin.; Rev. Charles Conaty. Priests 1; Brothers 1; Sisters of St. Joseph 3; Lay Teachers 19; Students 330.

[C] HIGH SCHOOLS, PRIVATE

NEWFIELD. *Our Lady of Mercy Academy*, 1001 Main Rd., 08344. Tel: 609-697-2008. Daughters of Our Lady of Mercy. Sr. Grace Marie, D.M., Prin. Sisters 2; Lay Teachers 9; Students 140.

PENNSAUKEN. *Bishop Eustace Prep School*, 5552 Rte. 70, 08109-4798. Tel: 609-662-2160; 662-0865 (Res.). Society of the Catholic Apostolate, Province of the Immaculate Conception. Revs. Ralph Firneno, S.A.C., Rector & Prin.; Alex Dryden, S.A.C.; Joseph Capella, S.A.C.; Frank Donio, S.A.C.; Robert J. Nolan, S.A.C.; Bro. James Beamesderfer, S.A.C. Priests 4; Brothers 1; Lay Teachers 52; Students 750.

RICHLAND. *St. Augustine Preparatory School*. (Boys), N. Cedar Ave., 08350. Tel: 609-697-2600. Order of St. Augustine, Province of St. Thomas of Villanova. Revs. Paul W. Galetto, O.S.A.; Stephen J. La Rosa, O.S.A., Pres.; Cherubin Kerr, O.S.A.; Bros. Frank Cucinotta, O.S.A.; David Graber, M.SS.CC. Priests 3; Brothers 2; Lay Teachers 13; Students 211.

[D] REGIONAL SCHOOLS, ELEMENTARY

BARRINGTON. *St. Francis de Sales*, 199 Wilmont Ave., 08007. Tel: 609-547-2313; Fax: 609-399-7586. Sr. Catherine Mulcahy, F.D.N.S.C., Supr. & Prin. Daughters of Our Lady of the Sacred Heart 6; Lay Teachers 9; Students 287. Serving St. Francis de Sales, Barrington and Mary, Mother of the Church, Bellmawr.

BERLIN. *Our Lady of Mt. Carmel*, One Maple Ave., 08009. Tel: 609-767-2115. Sr. M. Agnes, R.S.M., Prin.; Sr. Annette, Supr. Sisters of Mercy (American Province) 6; Lay Teachers 12; Students 290. Serving Our Lady of Mt. Carmel, Berlin and St. Andrew, Gibbsboro.

BLACKWOOD. *St. Agnes*, 117 W. Church St., 08012. Tel: 609-228-7076. Mr. John T. Cafagna, Prin. Lay Teachers 10; Students 266. Serving St. Agnes, Blackwood; St. John Vianney, Deptford.

St. Jude, 400 S. Black Horse Pike, 08012. Tel: 609-227-4442. Sr. Paula Marie Randow, O.S.F., Prin.; Sr. Janice Novak, F.M.I.H.M., Supr. Franciscan Sisters 3; Lay Teachers 23; Students 464. Serving St. Jude, Blackwood; SS. Peter & Paul, St. Charles Borromeo, & Holy Family, Washington Township.

BRIDGETON. *Immaculate Conception Regional School*, 398 N. Pearl St., 08302. Tel: 609-451-2134. Mrs. Kathleen Bischer, Prin. Lay Teachers 10; Students 172. Serving Immaculate Conception, St. Teresa of Avila, Bridgeton; St. Michael, Cedarville; St. Mary, Rosenhayn.

CAPE MAY. *Our Lady, Star of the Sea*, 520 Lafayette St., 08204. Tel: 609-884-4437. Sr. Jeannette M. Daily, S.S.J., Prin. Sisters of St. Joseph 3; Lay Teachers 11; Students 206. Serving Our Lady, Star of the Sea, Cape May; Our Lady of the Angels, Cape May Court House.

COLLINGSWOOD. *St. John*, 100 Lees Ave., 08108. Tel: 609-858-1562. Miss Joan Simpson, Prin. Lay Teachers 10; Students 217. Serving St. John, Collingswood; St. Aloysius, Oaklyn.

GLASSBORO. *St. Bridget Regional School*, W. High St., 08028. Tel: 609-881-2578. Sr. Lisa Marie, C.S.S.F., Prin. Felician Sisters 2; Lay Teachers 14; Students 299. Serving St. Bridget, Our Lady of Lourdes, Glassboro; Our Lady, Queen of Peace, Pitman.

HADDONFIELD. *Christ the King Regional School*, 168 Hopkins Ave., 08033. Tel: 609-429-2084. Miss Jane M. McErlane, Prin. Franciscan Sisters of Allegany 1; Lay Teachers 15; Students 275. Serving Christ the King, Haddonfield; St. Vincent Pallotti, Haddon Township; St. Pius X, Cherry Hill.

HAMMONTON. *St. Joseph*, 133 N. 3rd St., 08037. Tel: 609-561-5980. Sr. Barbara Ranere, M.P.F., Prin. Religious Teachers Filippini 5; Lay Teachers 12; Students 307. Serving St. Joseph, St. Martin de Porres, St. Anthony of Padua, Hammonton; St. Anthony, Waterford; St. Lucy, Blue Anchor; Sacred Heart Mission, Cedar Brook.

MARGATE. *Blessed Sacrament*, 14 N. Jerome St., 08402. Tel: 609-822-9243. Sr. Rosaline Walters, O.S.F., Prin. Sisters of St. Francis of Syracuse, NY. Lay Teachers 9; Students 203. Serving Blessed Sacrament, Margate; St. Bernadette, Northfield; Epiphany, Longport.

MOUNT EPHRAIM. *Sacred Heart School*, W. Buckingham Ave., 08059. Tel: 609-931-5498. Ms. Rosemarie DelCorio, Prin. Lay Teachers 10; Students 175. Serving Sacred Heart, Mt. Ephraim; Holy Maternity, Audubon.

NATIONAL PARK. *St. Matthew*, Hessian Ave., 08063. Tel: 609-845-7203. Sr. Maria Liber, Prin. Little Servant Sisters of the Immaculate Conception 4; Lay Teachers 8; Students 290. Serving St. Matthew, National Park; St. Anne, Westville.

NEWFIELD. *Notre Dame Regional School*, 108 Church St., 08344. Tel: 609-697-0155, (Newfield) (Grades 1-4); 609-697-3456, (Grades 5-8); (Landisville). Miss Kathleen Brown, Prin. Daughters of Mercy 2; Lay Teachers 16; Students 320. Serving Our Lady of Victories, Landisville; St. Michael, Minotola; Our

Lady of the Lakes, Collings Lakes; St. Rose, Newfield; St. Mary, Malaga; Nativity, Franklinville; St. Ann, Elmer.

OCEAN CITY. *St. Augustine*, 1337 Asbury Ave., 08226. Tel: 609-399-1435. Sr. M. Marjorie Smith, R.S.M., Prin.; Sr. Joanne Tarpey, R.S.M., Supr. Sisters of Mercy (NJ) 3; Lay Teachers 8; Students 251. Serving St. Augustine, St. Frances Cabrini, Our Lady of Good Counsel, Ocean City; Resurrection, Marmora.

PENNS GROVE. *St. James*, Beach Ave., 08069. Tel: 609-299-0397. Mrs. Claire Whittaker. Lay Teachers 11; Students 150. Serving St. James, Penns Grove; Corpus Christi, Carneys Point; St. Joseph, Woodstown.

POMONA. *Assumption*, White Horse Pike, 08240. Tel: 609-652-7134. Mr. Joseph S. Mancuso, Prin. Lay Teachers 10; Students 205. Serving Assumption, Pomona; St. Elizabeth Ann Seton, Absecon.

RUNNEMEDE. *St. Teresa*, 18 Ardmore Rd., 08078. Tel: 609-939-0333. Sr. Margaret M. Langer, I.H.M., Supr. & Prin. Sisters Servants of the Immaculate Heart of Mary 8; Lay Teachers 8; Students 299. Serving St. Teresa, St. Maria Goretti, Runnemede.

SALEM. *St. Mary*, 31 Oak St., 08079. Tel: 609-935-0660. Sr. Marian, C.S.J.P., Prin. Sisters of St. Joseph of Peace 2; Lay Teachers 8; Students 136. Serving St. Mary, Salem; Queen of Apostles, Pennsville.

SEA ISLE CITY. *St. Joseph*, 132 44th St., 08243. Tel: 609-263-4296. Sr. Rosalie Pronsati, R.S.M., Prin.; Sr. Patricia Tomlin, S.S.J., D.R.E. Sisters of Mercy (Merion, PA) 1; Lay Teachers 12; Students 279. Serving St. Joseph, Sea Isle City; Maris Stella, Avalon; St. Casimir, Woodbine; St. Paul, Stone Harbor.

SOMERDALE. *Our Lady of Grace School*, 105 N. White Horse Pike, 08083. Tel: 609-784-0372. Sr. Patricia O'Donnell, I.H.M., Prin.; Sr. Helen Marie Gates, I.H.M., Supr. Sisters Servants of Immaculate Heart of Mary 3; Lay Teachers 17; Students 385. Serving Our Lady of Grace, Somerdale; St. Gregory, Magnolia.

VILLAS. *St. Raymond*, 25 E. Ocean Ave., 08251. Tel: 609-886-2893. Sr. M. Margaret Ann Quinn, Supr. & Prin. Servants of the Immaculate Heart of Mary 8; Lay Teachers 9; Students 212. Serving St. Raymond, Villas; St. John of God, North Cape May.

VINELAND. *Sacred Heart*, 922 E. Landis Ave., 08360. Tel: 609-691-4490. Sr. Bernadette Mary Leahy, S.S.J., Prin.; Sr. Inez Patricia, S.S.J., Supr. Sisters of St. Joseph 3; Lay Teachers 16; Students 462. Serving Sacred Heart, St. Isidore, Spanish Catholic Center, Vineland.

St. Mary, 8 S. Union Rd., 08360. Tel: 609-692-8537. Sr. M. Bernardine, D.M., Prin. Daughters of Our Lady of Mercy 2; Lay Teachers 9; Students 314. Serving St. Mary; St. Joseph Mission, Richland; Our Lady of Pompeii, East Vineland; St. Mary Mission, Milmay.

WOODBURY HEIGHTS. *St. Margaret*, 3rd & Beech St., 08097. Tel: 609-845-5200. Sr. Lorraine Klein, F.M.I.J., Prin.; Sr. Rosaria Sillitti, F.M.I.J., Supr. Sisters 4; Lay Teachers 6; Students 372. Serving St. Margaret, Woodbury Heights; Incarnation, Mantua.

[E] SCHOOLS FOR SPECIAL CHILDREN

WESTVILLE GROVE. *Archbishop Damiano School*. St. John of God Community Svcs., 1145 Delsea Dr., Box 1979, 08093. Tel: 609-848-4700. Ms. Muncie Buckalew, Exec. Dir. Brothers 4; Lay Teachers 33; Students 440.

[F] CATHOLIC FOUNDATIONS

CAMDEN. *The Frank J. and Rosina W. Suttill Catholic Foundation*, 1845 Haddon Ave., P.O. Box 709, 08101. Rev. Msgr. Joseph P. Herron, Sec.

The Tuition Assistance Fund, Inc., 1845 Haddon Ave., P.O. Box 709, 08100. Rev. Msgr. Thomas J. McIntyre, Sec.

OCEAN CITY. *The Sharkey Family Charitable Trust*. Our Lady of Good Counsel, 3948 Central Ave., 08226. Rev. Msgr. Thomas H. Sharkey, Trustee.

[G] GENERAL HOSPITALS

CAMDEN. *Our Lady of Lourdes Medical Center, Inc.*. 1600 Haddon Ave., 08103. Tel: 609-757-3500.
For a complete listing, refer to the Hospitals section.

[H] NURSING HOMES

CHERRY HILL. *St. Mary's Nursing Home*, 1730 Kresson Rd., 08003. Tel: 609-424-9521.
For a complete listing, refer to the Special Care Facilities section.

NEWFIELD. *Mater Dei Nursing Home*, 176 Rte. 40, 08344. Tel: 609-358-2061.
For a complete listing, refer to the Special Care Facilities section.

PLEASANTVILLE. *Our Lady's Residence*, 1100 Clematis Ave., 08232.
For a complete listing, refer to the Special Care Facilities section.

VINELAND. *Bishop McCarthy Residence*, 1045 E. Chestnut Ave., 08360.
For a complete listing, refer to the Special Care Facilities section.

[I] VISITING NURSES

CAPE MAY. *Holy Redeemer Rehabilitation Center*, 1261 Rte. 9 S., Ste. 1, Cape May Court House, 08210. Tel: 609-465-3866. Carol Frankenfield, P.T., Chief Therapist.

MAYS LANDING. *Atlantic Co. Office*, 701 Rte. 50, 08330. Tel: 609-625-220; 800-788-3029. Jennifer Savon, R.N., Admin.

SWAINTON. *Holy Redeemer Visiting Nurse Agency, Inc.* Subsidiary of Holy Redeemer Health System, Inc. 1801 Rte. 9 N., 08210. Tel: 609-465-2082; 800-745-4693; Fax: 609-463-0196. Sponsored by Sisters of the Holy Redeemer, C.S.R. Mr. Jerold S. Cohen, R.N., Pres.

[J] HOUSING FOR AGED

CAPE MAY. *Victorian Towers Associates*, 608 Washington St., 08204. Tel: 609-884-5883.
For a complete listing, refer to the Special Care Facilities section.

CHERRY HILL. *The Manor at St. Mary's*, 1743 Kresson Rd., 08003.
For a complete listing, refer to the Special Care Facilities section.

Marian Residence, 1000 Cropwell Rd., 08003. Tel: 609-424-1131.
For a complete listing, refer to the Special Care Facilities section.

Village Apartments of Cherry Hill, NJ, Inc., 212 Lourdes Ct., 08003. Tel: 609-424-7913.
For a complete listing, refer to the Special Care Facilities section.

[K] CHILD CARE CENTERS

CAMDEN. *St. Joseph's Nursery School*, 17 Church St., P.O. Box 1443, 08105. Tel: 609-963-0452; 365-4653 (Convent); Fax: 609-963-0103. Sr. Maria DiRosa, Prin.; Sr. Angela D'Alessandro, Supr. Franciscan Missionary Sisters of the Infant Jesus 2.

[L] MONASTERIES AND RESIDENCES OF PRIESTS AND BROTHERS

CAMDEN. *Dominican Sisters of the Perpetual Rosary Chaplain's Residence*, 1500 Haddon Ave., 08103. Tel: 609-365-4427. Rev. Raymond M. McCabe. Trustees: Very Rev. Peter T. Sticco, S.A.C.; Rev. Francis Gaetano, S.A.C.

BLACKWOOD. *Bishop's Residence*. Marywood, 1600 Peter Cheeseman Rd., P.O. Box 577, 08012. In res., Most Rev. James T. McHugh, S.T.D.; Rev. George C. Serter.

CHERRY HILL. *Neumann House, Village of St. Mary*, 1730 Kresson Rd., 08003.

Vianney Villa, 1730 Kresson Rd., 08003. Tel: 609-424-2035. Rev. William D. Titmas, Dir. In res., Rev. Msgr. Joseph W. Devlin; Revs. Charles S. Bean; A. Richard Gerbino; James O'Sullivan.

LINWOOD. *Villa Pieta*. Missionaries of the Sacred Hearts of Jesus & Mary. 2249 Shore Rd., 08221. Tel: 609-927-5600. Revs. Roque Longo, M.SS.CC.; Anthony Patrizio, M.SS.CC., Rector & Delegate; Leonard Carrieri, M.SS.CC.; Bros. Carlos Lopez, M.SS.CC.; Sigfried Troche, M.SS.CC.

MARGATE. *Franciscan Friars' Vacation Home*. Holy Name Province. 118 S. Mansfield Ave., 08402. Tel: 609-822-9552. Rev. Joel Munzing, O.F.M., Curator.

OCEAN CITY. *Augustinian Friars Summer Home*. St. Rita of Cascia Cottage, 823 5th St., 08226. Tel: 609-398-1299.

Ocean Rest Summer School and Retreat House, 31st and Central Ave., 08226. Brothers of Christian Schools Summer Home and Retreat House. Bro. James F. Rieck, F.S.C., Dir. Tel: 609-399-6480, Mailing Address: LaSalle College High School, 8605 Cheltenham Ave., Wyndmoor, PA, 19038. Tel: 215-233-2911.

PITTSGROVE. *Villa St. Joseph*, 9 Harding Hwy., 08318. Tel: 609-358-2841. Oblates of St. Francis de Sales. Revs. John P. Connolly, O.S.F.S., Supr.; James E. Cassidy, O.S.F.S.; Joseph A. Connolly, O.S.F.S.; Nicholas C. DiIenno, O.S.F.S.; Stuart Dooling, O.S.F.S.; Edward J. Friel, O.S.F.S.; Thomas W. Kelly, O.S.F.S.; John M. McDevitt, O.S.F.S.; Edmund F. O'Rourke, O.S.F.S.; Joseph P. Schaefer, O.S.F.S.; Joseph A. Travers, O.S.F.S.; Bro. Eugene J. Rehrman, O.S.F.S.

WESTVILLE GROVE. *Hospitaller Order of St. John of God*, 532 Delsea Dr., 08093. Tel: 609-848-4700. Bros. Bernard Farrell, O.H., Supr.; Derek O'Connell, O.H., Dir. Vocations. Brothers 4.

[M] CONVENTS AND RESIDENCES FOR SISTERS

CAMDEN. *Monastery of the Dominican Nuns of the Perpetual Rosary*, 1500 Haddon Ave., 08103. Mother Mary of the Immaculate Heart, O.P., Prioress; Rev. Raymond M. McCabe, O.P., Chap. Sisters 8.

ATLANTIC CITY. *St. John's Retreat House and Rest Home*, 128 S. Dover Ave., 08401. Little Servant Sisters of the Immaculate Conception. Sr. Xavier Czachor, L.S.I.C., Supvr. Sisters 4.

CHERRY HILL. *Franciscan Missionary Sisters of the Infant Jesus*. U.S. Province and Novitiate, 1215 Kresson Rd., 08003. Tel: 609-428-7930; Fax: 609-428-7930. Sr. Chiara Lilia Ferrario, F.M.I.J., Delegate Supr. Sisters 4.

Little Servant Sisters of the Immaculate Conception. Provincialate and Novitiate. 1000 Cropwell Rd., 08003. Tel: 609-424-1962. Mother M. Leonarda, L.S.I.C., Prov. Professed Sisters 17; Novices 1.

Queen of Heaven Convent, 10 Massachusetts Ave., 08002. Tel: 609-428-8818. Sr. Barbara Ann Colligon, Supr. Sisters Servants of the Immaculate Heart of Mary 4.

HADDONFIELD. *St. Mary of the Angels Convent*, 134 Kings Hwy. W., 08033. Tel: 609-428-0824. Franciscan Sisters of Allegany. Sr. Poverello Wells, O.S.F., Local Min. & Admin. Sisters 9.

MAPLE SHADE. *Emmaus Community*, Ryan's Run East Apts. #2312, 1330 E. Kings Hwy., 08052. Tel: 609-365-4642. School Sisters of Notre Dame 2.

NEWFIELD. *Villa Rossello*. Provincial House and Novitiate of Daughters of Our Lady of Mercy. 1009 Main Rd., 08344. Tel: 609-697-2983. Sr. Grace Marie, D.M., Prov. Sisters 26.

PLEASANTVILLE. *Hospitaler Sisters of Mercy Novitiate*, 915 S. Main St., 08232. Sr. Teresa Thadathil, Supr.

SEA ISLE CITY. *The Sisters of St. Francis of Philadelphia*, 55th & Landis Ave., 08243. Mailing Address: Our Lady of Angels Convent 19014, 609 S. Convent Rd., Aston, PA.

STONE HARBOR. *Villa Maria by the Sea*. Retreat House, 08247. Sisters, Servants of the Immaculate Heart of Mary (Immaculata, PA).

SWAINTON. *Sisters of the Holy Redeemer, C.S.R.* Our Lady of Peace Convent, 8 Brooks Ave., 08210. Tel: 609-465-3549.

VENTNOR. *The Benedictine Sisters of Elizabeth, NJ*, 114 S. Troy Ave., 08406.

Convent of Mary the Ocean Star, 112 S. Dorset Ave., 08406. Tel: 609-823-3977. Sisters of Charity of St. Vincent De Paul (Mt. St. Vincent, NY).

Holy Family, Seaside Convent, 110 S. Dorset Ave., 08406. Sisters of St. Dominic (Blauvelt, NY). Sr. Jane McDermott, O.P.

McAuley House, 102 S. Derby Pl., 08406. Sisters of Mercy (Baltimore Regl. Community).

Mercy By-the-Sea, 114 S. Portland Ave., 08406. Sisters of Mercy (Plainfield - Watchung).

Mercy Villa, 104 S. Derby Pl., 08406. Sisters of Mercy (Prov. of New York).

St. Joseph House by the Sea, 107 S. Derby Ave., 08406. Tel: 609-823-1159. Franciscan Sisters of Peace. 317 Charleston E., Wildwood Crest, 08260. Tel: 609-523-1167.

VINELAND. *Bishop McCarthy Residence Convent*, 1045 E. Chestnut Ave., 08360. Sr. Eletta Felli, Supr. Hospitaler Sisters of Mercy 5.

[N] RETREAT HOUSES

BLACKWOOD. *St. Pius X Spiritual Life Center*. St. Pius X Retreat House, Peter Cheeseman Rd., Box 216, 08012. Tel: 609-227-1436; Fax: 609-227-2907. Rev. David E. Beebe, Dir.; Sr. Ann Newell, I.H.M.; Bro. Nicholas Crosby, S.D.S. In res., Revs. Joseph M. Messina; Louis A. Marucci.

[O] APOSTOLIC CENTERS

CAPE MAY POINT. *Marianist Family Retreat Center*, 415 Yale Ave., Box 502, 08212-0456. Tel: 609-884-3829. Rev. Richard V. Kuhn, S.M.; Bros. Albert Koch, S.M., Local Community Dir.; Raymond McQuade, S.M., Dir.; Walter Oberster, S.M.; Edward Underdorfer, S.M.

VINELAND. *Spanish Catholic Center*, 410 S. 8th St., 08360. Tel: 609-692-8992. Rev. Victor S. Muro, Dir., 23 W. Chestnut Ave., 08360. Rev. Alvaro Diaz, St. Isidore, 1655 Magnolia Rd., 08360.

[P] LOCAL OFFICES OF CATHOLIC SOCIAL SERVICES

CAMDEN. *Catholic Social Services*, 1035 Mechanic St., 08104. Tel: 609-964-2133. Ms. Cereida Medina, Dir.

St. John the Baptist Pre-Natal Clinic, 6th St. & Erie St., 08102. Tel: 609-757-9540. Patricia A. Chico, L.P.N., B.A., Admin.

ATLANTIC CITY. *Catholic Social Services*, 9 N. Georgia Ave., 08401. Tel: 609-345-3448. Sr. Grace Nolan, R.S.M., Coord.

CAPE MAY. *Catholic Social Services Senior Center*. Victorian Towers, 608 Washington St., 08204. Tel: 609-884-5624. Sr. Terese Elizabeth Cunningham, S.S.J., Dir.

GIBBSTOWN. *Catholic Social Services, Camden/ Gloucester Regional Counseling Center*, 320 Memorial Ave., 08027. Tel: 609-224-0945. Ms. Mary Nicoletto, Dir.

NEWFIELD. *Catholic Social Services Regional Counseling Center*, P.O. Box 737, 08344. Tel: 609-697-0744. Rev. Frank X. Hudson, L.C.S.W., C.A.D.C., Dir.

PENNSAUKEN. *Catholic Social Services Central Office*, 2830 Marlton Pike, 08105. Tel: 609-663-9800; Fax: 609-663-0253. Miss Patricia Langan, M.A., M.Ed., Exec. Dir.

PLEASANTVILLE. *Catholic Social Services*. Cape Atlantic Counseling Center, 21 W. Verona Ave., 08232. Tel: 609-383-0909. Mr. Michael Murphy, L.C.S.W., Dir.

RIO GRANDE. *Catholic Social Services*. Cape May County Office: 3808 Rte. 9, Box 482, 08242. Tel: 609-886-2662. Eileen Henderson, Coord.

SALEM. *Catholic Social Services*. Salem County Office: 21 W. Main St., Penns Grove, 08069. Tel: 609-299-1296. An Emergency Services Agency.

VINELAND. *Catholic Social Services of Vineland*, 810 Montrose St., 08360. Tel: 609-691-1841. Mr. John Desparrois, Coord.

WOODBURY. *Catholic Social Services, Gloucester County Office*, 8 Green Ave., 08096. Tel: 609-845-9200. Mr. Robert S. Skrzot, Coord.

[Q] NEWMAN CENTERS

CAMDEN. *Camden Diocesan Center*, 1845 Haddon Ave., 08101. Tel: 609-756-7900.

Rutgers College of South Jersey, 406 Penn St., 08102. Rev. Thomas A. Newton.

GLASSBORO. *Rowan College of New Jersey*. Rev. Cadmus D. Mazzarella, Rte. 322 & Bowe Blvd., 08028.

MAYS LANDING. *Atlantic Community College*, 08330. Rev. C. Jeffries Burton, S.J., St. Peter, 25 W. Verona Ave., Pleasantville, 08232. Tel: 609-641-0285.

POMONA. *Richard Stockton College of New Jersey*, Jim Leeds Rd., 08240. Rev. C. Jeffries Burton, S.J.

[R] MEDICAL CLINICS

CAMDEN. *Saint Luke's Catholic Medical Services, Inc.*, 511 State St., 08102. Tel: 609-365-4642.

For a complete listing, refer to the Hospitals section.

[S] LEGAL SERVICES

CAMDEN. *Camden Center for Law and Social Justice, Inc.*, 509 State St., 08102. Tel: 609-966-8896; Fax: 609-541-8826. Rev. David R. Brooks, S.J., J.D.

[T] FOOD CENTERS

CAMDEN. *The Cathedral Soup Kitchen, Inc.*, 642 Market St., 08102. Tel: 609-964-1580.

[U] MISCELLANEOUS

CAMDEN. *Guadalupe Family Services*, 511 State St., 08102.

NORTH CAPE MAY. *The National Christ Child Society, Inc.* (Cape May County Chapter), P.O. Box 882, 08204.

RELIGIOUS INSTITUTES OF MEN REPRESENTED IN THE DIOCESE

For further details refer to the corresponding bracketed number in the Religious Institutes of Men or Women section.

[0140]—*The Augustinians*. (Vice Prov. of Our Lady of Good Counsel, Villanova, PA).—O.S.A.

[0330]—*Brothers of the Christian Schools*.—F.S.C.

[0480]—*Conventual Franciscans*. (Syracuse, NY).—O.F.M.Conv.

[0520]—*Franciscan Friars*. (Prov. of the Most Holy Name of Jesus).—O.F.M.

[0670]—*Hospitaller Brothers of St. John of God*.—O.H.

[0690]—*Jesuit Fathers and Brothers*.—S.J.

[1120]—*Missionaries of the Sacred Hearts of Jesus and Mary*.—M.SS.CC.

[0920]—*Oblates of St. Francis De Sales*. (Wilmington-Philadelphia).—O.S.F.S.

[0430]—*Order of Preachers-Dominicans*. (St. Joseph Prov., New York).—O.P.

[0760]—*Society of Mary*.—S.M.

[0990]—*Society of the Catholic Apostolate*.—S.A.C.

[1200]—*Society of the Divine Savior*.—S.D.S.

[0560]—*Third Order Regular of Saint Francis*.—T.O.R.

RELIGIOUS INSTITUTES OF WOMEN REPRESENTED IN THE DIOCESE

[0230]—*Benedictine Sisters of Pontifical Jurisdiction*. (Newark, NJ).—O.S.B.

[2410]—*Congregation of the Marianites of Holy Cross*.—M.S.C.

[0850]—*Daughters of Mary Help of Christians*. (Paterson).—F.M.A.

[0900]—*Daughters of Our Lady of the Sacred Heart*.—F.D.N.S.C.

[1050]—*Dominican Contemplative Nuns*.—O.P.

[1070-03]—*Dominican Sisters*.—O.P.

[1070-06]—*Dominican Sisters*.—O.P.

[1070-13]—*Dominican Sisters*.—O.P.

[1070-15]—*Dominican Sisters*.—O.P.

[1170]—*Felician Sisters*. (Immaculate Conception Prov., Lodi, NJ).—C.S.S.F.

[1400]—*Franciscan Missionary Sisters of the Sacred Heart*.—F.M.S.C.

[1180]—*Franciscan Sisters of Allegany, New York*.—O.S.F.

[1190]—*Franciscan Sisters of the Atonement*.—S.A.

[2575]—*Institute of the Sisters of Mercy of the Americas*. (Merion, PA; Baltimore, MD).—R.S.M.

[2300]—*Little Servant Sisters of the Immaculate Conception*.—L.S.I.C.

[]—*Missionary Daughters of the Most Pure Virgin Mary*.—M.D.P.V.M.

[2790]—*Missionary Servants of the Most Blessed Trinity*.—M.S.B.T.

[3430]—*Religious Teachers Filippini*. (Morristown, NJ).—M.P.F.

[2970]—*School Sisters of Notre Dame*. (Baltimore Prov.).—S.S.N.D.

[0650]—*Sisters of Charity of St. Vincent de Paul, of New York*.—S.C.

[2517]—*Sisters of Mercy*.

[2670]—*Sisters of Our Lady of Mercy*.—S.O.L.M.

[3893]—*Sisters of Saint Joseph of Chestnut Hill, Philadelphia*.—S.S.J.

[1650]—*Sisters of St. Francis of Philadelphia*.—O.S.F.

[3890]—*Sisters of St. Joseph of Peace*.—C.S.J.P.

[0260]—*Sisters of the Blessed Sacrament for Indians and Colored People*.—S.B.S.

[2000]—*Sisters of the Holy Redeemer*.—C.S.R.

[1490]—*Sisters of the Third Franciscan Order*.—O.S.F.

[2170]—*Sisters, Servants of the Immaculate Heart of Mary*.—I.H.M.

NECROLOGY

† Conlon, Rev. Msgr. Joseph E., (Retired). —Died Dec. 11, 1996.

† Follett, John E., Runnemede, NJ, St. Maria Goretti. —Died Feb. 4, 1996.

† Giammarino, Rev. Msgr. Vincent J., (Retired). —Died Feb. 14, 1996.

† Keis, Rev. Msgr. Gottfried, (Retired). —Died March 4, 1996.

† Leonard, Francis J., Audubon, NJ, Holy Maternity. —Died Oct. 3, 1996.

† Reynolds, Rev. Msgr. William J., Raymond, NJ, St. Villas. —Died April 22, 1996.

† Taxter, John F., Waterford, NJ, St. Anthony. —Died May 16, 1996.

† Zemrowski, Rev. Msgr. Anthony, (Retired). —Died Feb. 14, 1996.

Diocese of Charleston

(Dioecesis Carolopolitana)

Most Reverend

DAVID B. THOMPSON, D.D., J.C.L.

Bishop of Charleston; ordained May 27, 1950; appointed Coadjutor Bishop of Charleston April 22, 1989; ordained May 24, 1989; succeeded to Bishop of Charleston February 22, 1990. *Res., 114 Broad St., Charleston, SC, 29401. Office: 119 Broad St., Charleston, SC, 29401. Mailing Address: P.O. Box 818, Charleston, SC, 29402.* Tel.: 803-723-3488; Fax: 803-724-6387.

Chancery Office: 119 Broad St., P.O. Box 818, Charleston, SC, 29402. Tel.: 803-723-3488; Fax: 803-724-6387.

ESTABLISHED JULY 11, 1820.

Square Miles 31,055.

Comprises the State of South Carolina.

For legal titles of parishes and diocesan institutions, consult the Chancery Office.

STATISTICAL OVERVIEW

Personnel	
Bishop	1
Abbots	1
Retired Abbots	1
Priests: Diocesan Active in Diocese	67
Priests: Active Outside Diocese	4
Priests: Diocesan in Foreign Missions	1
Priests: Retired, Sick or Absent	23
Number of Diocesan Priests	95
Religious Priests in Diocese	33
Extern Priests in Diocese	6
Ordinations:	
Diocesan Priests	2
Transitional Deacons	4
Permanent Deacons in Diocese	62
Total Brothers	26
Total Sisters	164
Parishes	
Parishes	86
With Resident Pastor:	
Resident Diocesan Priests	57
Resident Religious Priests	14
Without Resident Pastor:	
Administered by Priests	4
Administered by Permanent Deacons	3
Administered by Women Religious	7
Administered by Pastoral Teams, etc.	1
Missions	27
Pastoral Centers	10
Professional Ministry Personnel:	
Brothers	2
Sisters	38
Lay Ministers	54
Welfare	
Catholic Hospitals	3
Total Assisted	302,548
Health Care Centers	1
Total Assisted	325
Homes for the Aged	1
Total Assisted	20
Special Centers for Social Services	8
Total Assisted	199,500
Educational	
Diocesan Students in Other Seminaries	13
Total Seminarians	13
High Schools, Diocesan and Parish	3
Total Students	1,416
Elementary Schools, Diocesan and Parish	25
Total Students	6,449
Catechesis/Religious Education:	
High School Students	1,942
Elementary Students	9,311
Total Students Under Catholic Instruction	19,131
Teachers in the Diocese:	
Priests	1
Sisters	12
Lay Teachers	538
Vital Statistics	
Receptions into the Church:	
Infant Baptism Totals	2,122
Adult Baptism Totals	239
Received into Full Communion	467
First Communions	2,405
Confirmations	3,881
Marriages:	
Catholic	319
Interfaith	435
Total Marriages	754
Deaths	904
Total Catholic Population	109,629
Total Population	3,673,000

Former Bishops—Rt. Rev. JOHN ENGLAND, D.D., first Bishop; cons. Sept. 21, 1820; died April 11, 1842.—Rt. Rev. WILLIAM CLANCY, D.D., cons. Dec. 21, 1834, Coadjutor made Vicar-Apostolic of British Guiana, April 12, 1837; died June 19, 1847.—Rt. Rev. IGNATIUS A. REYNOLDS, D.D., second Bishop; cons. March 19, 1844; died March 6, 1855.—Rt. Rev. PATRICK N. LYNCH, D.D., third Bishop; cons. March 14, 1858; died Feb. 26, 1882.—Rt. Rev. HENRY P. NORTHROP, D.D., fourth Bishop; cons. Titular-Bishop of Rosalia and Vicar-Apostolic of North Carolina, Jan. 8, 1882; transferred to Charleston, S. C., by brief dated Jan. 27, 1883; died June 7, 1916.—Rt. Rev. WILLIAM T. RUSSELL, D.D., fifth Bishop; cons. March 15, 1917; died March 18, 1927.—Most Rev. EMMET M. WALSH D.D., cons. Sept. 8, 1927; transferred to Youngstown, Ohio, as Coadjutor Bishop, Sept. 8, 1949.—Most Rev. JOHN J. RUSSELL, D.D., cons. March 14, 1950; transferred to Bishop of Richmond, July 10, 1958.—Most Rev. PAUL J. HALLINAN, D.D., cons. Oct. 28, 1958; transferred to Archbishop of Atlanta, Feb. 21, 1962.—Most Rev. FRANCIS F. REH, S.T.L., J.C.D., cons. June 29, 1962; appt. Titular Bishop of Macriana in Mauretania and Rector of North American College, Rome, Italy, Sept. 5, 1964; transferred to Saginaw, Dec. 18, 1968; installed Feb. 26, 1969; retired April 29, 1980.—Most Rev. ERNEST L. UNTERKOEFLER, D.D., J.C.D., S.T.L., Bishop of Charleston; ord. May 18, 1944; appt. Titular Bishop of Latopolis and Auxiliary Bishop of Richmond, Dec. 13, 1961; cons. Feb. 22, 1962; appt. Bishop of Charleston, Dec. 12, 1964; resigned Feb. 22, 1990; died Jan. 4, 1993.

Vicar General—Rev. Msgr. SAM R. MIGLARESE, V.G.

Chancery Office—119 Broad St., P.O. Box 818, Charleston, 29402. Tel: 803-723-3488; Fax: 803-724-6387.

Chancellor for Administration—CLEO E. CANTEY.

Archivist—SUSAN L. KING. Tel: 803-724-8372.

Office of Finance—DENNIS F. ATWOOD, Chief Financial Officer; BERNADETTE M. WORSHAM, Controller, *1662 Ingram Rd., Charleston, 29407.* Tel: 803-769-4480; Fax: 803-769-2179.

Diocesan Curia—Rev. Msgr. SAM R. MIGLARESE, V.G., Moderator; Rev. Msgr. JAMES A. CARTER, Vicar for Clergy; Rev. Msgr. LEIGH A. LEHOCKY, V.F., Vicar for Ecumenical Affairs & Pastoral Organizations; Rev. Msgr. CHARLES H. ROWLAND, Vicar for Judicial Affairs; Sr. SUSAN SCHORSTEN, H.M., Dir., Catholic Charities & Diocesan Social Ministry; Dr. THOMAS W. MAHAN, Dir., Synod Implementation; Dr. GAY G. ROWZIE, Dir., Christian Formation/Education; DENNIS F. ATWOOD, Chief Financial Officer; SANDY FERENCZ, Dir., Stewardship & Devel. MARY M. JEFFCOAT, Dir., Office of Communications & Information; MICHAEL R. MYERS, Assoc. Dir., Synod Implementation.

Diocesan Tribunal—114 Rear Broad St., P.O. Box 818, Charleston, 29402. Tel: 803-724-8363; Fax: 803-724-6366.

Vicar Judicial—Rev. Msgr. CHARLES H. ROWLAND, J.C.L.

Adjutant Vicar Judicial—Rev. THOMAS X. HOFMANN, J.C.L.

Director of the Tribunal—MARY M. SMIRCIC.

Judges—Rev. Msgr. CHARLES H. ROWLAND, J.C.L.; Rev. Msgr. ROBERT J. KELLY; Rev. Msgr. LAWRENCE B. MCINERNY, J.C.L.; Rev. Msgr. SAM R. MIGLARESE, V.G.; Rev. Msgr. JOSEPH R. ROTH; Revs. THOMAS X. HOFMANN, J.C.L.; JOSEPH J. MAHER; H. GREGORY WEST, J.C.L.

Defenders of the Bond—Rev. Msgr. THOMAS R. DUFFY; Rev. Msgr. EDWARD D. LOFTON; Revs. J. SCOTT NEWMAN, J.C.L.

Promotor of Justice—Rev. DENNIS B. WILLEY.

Advocates—Sr. AGNES ASSISI, O.S.F.; MARY M. SMIRCIC.

Notaries—ELIZABETH S. BECKER; CLEO E. CANTEY; JOANNE M. COMAR.

College of Consultors—Rev. Msgr. SAM R. MIGLARESE, V.G.; Rev. Msgr. JAMES A. CARTER; Rev. Msgr. THOMAS R. DUFFY, V.F.; Rev. Msgr. ROBERT J. KELLY; Rev. Msgr. E. CHRISTOPHER LATHEM, V.F.; Rev. Msgr. LEIGH A. LEHOCKY, V.F.; Rev. Msgr. CHARLES H. ROWLAND; Rev. MICHAEL F. MCCAFFERTY; Very Rev. JOSEPH A. WAHL C.O.; Revs. PETER CLARKE; THOMAS A. EVATT; PAUL M. WILLIAMS, O.F.M.

Deans—Rev. Msgr. E. CHRISTOPHER LATHEM, V.F., Coastal Deanery; Rev. Msgr. LEIGH A. LEHOCKY, V.F., Midlands Deanery; Rev. Msgr. THOMAS R. DUFFY, V.F., Pee Dee Deanery; Very Rev. CHESTER M. MOCZYDLOWSKI, V.F., Piedmont Deanery.

Diocesan Finance Committee—Rev. Msgr. SAM R. MIGLARESE, V.G., Chm., *P.O. Box 818, Charleston, 29402.* Tel: 803-723-3488.

Presbyteral Council—Most Rev. DAVID B. THOMPSON; Rev. Msgr. SAM R. MIGLARESE, V.G., Facilitator; Rev. Msgr. JAMES A. CARTER; Rev. Msgr. THOMAS R. DUFFY, V.F.; Rev. Msgr. ROBERT J. KELLY; Rev. Msgr. E. CHRISTOPHER LATHEM, V.F.; Rev. Msgr. LEIGH A. LEHOCKY, V.F.; Rev. Msgr. LAWRENCE B. MCINERNY; Rev. Msgr. CHARLES H. ROWLAND; Very Revs. CHESTER M. MOCZYDLOWSKI, V.F.; JOSEPH A. WAHL, C.O.; Revs. PETER CLARKE; THOMAS A. EVATT; RICHARD D. HARRIS; TIMOTHY M. LIJEWSKI; JEROME F. SCHWAB;

PAUL M. WILLIAMS, O.F.M.; Sr. BRIDGET SULLIVAN, O.L.M., Sec.

Bishop's Missionary Support Committee—Rev. Msgr. ROBERT J. KELLY, *P.O. Box 1257, Folly Beach, 29439.* Tel: 803-588-2336.

Building Committee—Rev. Msgr. JAMES A. CARTER, Chm., *P.O. Box 724, Mt. Pleasant, 29465.* Tel: 803-884-5587.

Catholic Charities—Sr. SUSAN SCHORSTEN, H.M., Dir., *1662 Ingram Rd., Charleston, 29407.* Tel: 803-769-4466.

Catholic Women, Council of—Rev. WILLIAM F. PENTIS, C.O., Moderator, *P.O. Box 11586, Rock Hill, 29731.* Tel: 803-327-2097.

Cemeteries—DENNIS F. ATWOOD, Dir., *1662 Ingram Rd., Charleston, 29407.* Tel: 803-769-4480.

Charismatic Renewals and Prayer Groups—JOSEPH BALAZS, Diocesan Liaison, *114 Horseshoe Cove, Sumter, 29150.* Tel: 803-773-1160.

Commission for Divine Worship and Sacraments—WILLIAM N. SCHLITT, Chm., *120 Broad St., Charleston, 29401.* Tel: 803-724-8395.

Ministry with Persons with Disabilities—CHARLES M. LUCE, Dir., *P.O. Box 4711, Columbia, 29240.* Tel: 803-782-2706.

Christian Formation / Education—Dr. GAY G. ROWZIE, Dir., Christian Formation & Supt. of Schools; LAWRENCE OLEKSIAK, M.S., Asst. Supt. of Schools; DIANE LAMPITT, M.Ed., Dir., Catechesis/ Evangelization; Rev. MICHAEL F. MCCAFFERTY, Dir., Campus Ministry, *1610 Greene St., Columbia, 29201.* Tel: 803-799-5870., *1662 Ingram Rd., Charleston, 29407.* Tel: 803-769-2160.

Holy Childhood Association—Rev. Msgr. ROBERT J. KELLY, Dir., *P.O. Box 1257, Folly Beach, 49439.* Tel: 803-588-2336.

Marian Programs—Rev. D. ANTHONY DROZE, Moderator, *111 Hampton Ave., Greenville, 29601.* Tel: 864-271-8422.

Master of Episcopal Ceremonies—Diocesan- Rev. H. GREGORY WEST, J.C.L., *P.O. Box 487, Hardeeville, 29927.* Tel: 803-784-2943. Episcopal- Rev. DENNIS B. WILLEY, *120 Broad St., Charleston, 29401.* Tel: 803-724-8395.

Office of Prayer & Worship—Rt. Rev. FRANCIS KLINE, O.C.S.O., *P.O. Box 818, Charleston, 29402.* Tel: 803-724-6364.

Newspaper—"The New Catholic Miscellany," P.O. Box 818, Charleston, 29402. Tel: 803-724-8375; Fax: 803-724-8368.

Propagation of the Faith—Rev. Msgr. ROBERT J. KELLY, Dir., *P.O. Box 1257, Folly Beach, 29439.* Tel: 803-588-2336.

Office of Communications & Information—MARY M. JEFFCOAT, Dir., *P.O. Box 818, Charleston, 29402.* Tel: 803-724-8375; Fax: 803-724-8368.

Vocations—Rev. HENRY T. BARRON, *1662 Ingram Rd., Charleston, 29407.* Tel: 803-769-2184; 795-3821.

Bishop's Missionary League—P.O. Box 818, Charleston, 29402. Tel: 803-723-3488.

Cursillo Movement—Rev. CHARLES J. SNOPEK, Spiritual Dir., *Waverly-Shell Rd., Rte. 3, Box 455, Pawley's Island, 29585.* Tel: 803-237-3428.

Permanent Diaconate—Rev. Msgr. JOSEPH R. ROTH, Dir., *503 37th Ave. N., Myrtle Beach, 29577.* Tel: 803-448-5930.

Campaign for Human Development—Sr. SUSAN SCHORSTEN, H.M., Chm., *1662 Ingram Rd., Charleston, 29407.* Tel: 803-769-4466.

Office of Stewardship & Development—SANDY FERENCZ, Dir., *P.O. Box 818, Charleston, 29402.* Tel: 803-724-6369.

Migration & Refugee Services—PEGGY SOOKIKIAN, Coord., *P.O. Box 7245, Columbia, 29202-7245.* Tel: 803-254-9776; Fax: 803-252-7605.

Office of Family Life—KATHLEEN J. MACARON, Coord., *1662 Ingram Rd., Charleston, 29407.* Tel: 803-769-4466.

Personnel Committee—Rev. Msgr. JAMES A. CARTER, Chm.; Rev. Msgr. THOMAS R. DUFFY, V.F.; Rev. Msgr. E. CHRISTOPHER LATHEM, V.F.; Rev. Msgr. LEIGH A. LEHOCKY, V.F.; Rev. Msgr. JOSEPH R. ROTH; Very Rev. CHESTER M. MOCZYDLOWSKI, V.F.; Rev. HENRY T. BARRON; Sr. BERNADINE JAX, O.S.F.; Mr. JOHN CARROLL.

Priests' Retirement—Rev. Msgr. SAM R. MIGLARESE, V.G., Dir., *P.O. Box 818, Charleston, 29402.* Tel: 803-723-3488.

Scouting Programs—SAM E. HANVEY, *P.O. Box 639, Charleston, 29402.* Tel: 803-577-2600.

Office of the Synod Implementation—THOMAS W. MAHAN, Ph.D., Dir. MICHAEL R. MYERS, Assoc. Dir., *P.O. Box 818, Charleston, 29402.* Tel: 803-724-8366; 724-6384.

Vietnamese Ministry—Rev. VINCENT THE' QUANG NGUYEN, *111 Hampton Ave., Greenville, 29601.* Tel: 803-271-8422.

Vicar for African American Catholics—Rev. PAUL M. WILLIAMS, O.F.M., *307 Gower St., Greenville, 29611.* Tel: 803-233-7717.

Vicar for Ecumenism—Rev. Msgr. LEIGH A. LEHOCKY, V.F., *P.O. Box 1896, Columbia, 29202.* Tel: 803-779-0036.

Office for Hispanics—Sr. SUSAN SCHORSTEN, H.M., *1662 Ingram Rd., Charleston, 29407.* Tel: 803-769-4466.

Society of St. Vincent de Paul—MICHAEL S. DUM, Pres., *1054 Anna Knapp Blvd., #2B, Mt. Pleasant, 29464.* Tel: 803-881-1364.

CLERGY, PARISHES, MISSIONS AND PAROCHIAL SCHOOLS

GREATER CHARLESTON
(Charleston County)

1—CATHEDRAL OF ST. JOHN THE BAPTIST, Rev. Msgr. Sam R. Miglarese, V.G.; Rev. Dennis B. Willey.
Mailing Address: Cathedral Center, 120 Broad St., 29401. Tel: 803-724-8395; Fax: 803-724-6386.
Res., 105 Queen St., 29401.
School—Charleston Catholic School. See Sacred Heart for details.

2—ST. MARY'S, Rev. Msgr. John A. Simonin.
Res., 89 Hasell St., 29401. Tel: 803-722-7696; Fax: 803-577-5036. [CEM]

3—ST. PATRICK'S, Rev. Richard D. Harris.
Res., 125 St. Philip St., P.O. Box 20726, 29413. Tel: 803-723-6066; Fax: 803-853-8114. [CEM]
School—Charleston Catholic School. See Sacred Heart for details.

4—SACRED HEART, Rev. Michael J. Davino.
Res., 888 King St., 29403-4139. Tel: 803-722-7018; Fax: 803-577-4055.
School—Charleston Catholic School, Tel: 803-577-4495. Sr. Carol Ann Kleindinst, S.S.M.N., Prin.
Lay Teachers 20; Students 220.

5—OUR LADY OF MERCY, Rev. Richard D. Harris; Sr. Maigread Conway, O.S.F., Pastoral Admin.
Res., 77 America St., 29403. Tel: 803-723-5129.

6—ST. JOHN'S,
Res., 3921 St. John's Ave., North Charleston, 29405-7158. Tel: 803-744-6201.
School—Tel: 803-744-3901; Fax: 803-744-3689. Mrs. Harriet M. Condon, Prin.
Lay Teachers 13; Students 120.

7—BLESSED SACRAMENT, Rev. Joseph F. Hanley.
Res., 5 St. Teresa Dr., 29407. Tel: 803-556-0801; Fax: 803-556-2851.
School—7 St. Teresa Dr., 27407. Tel: 803-766-2128. Sr. Linda Marie Bolinski, SS.C.M., Prin.
Sisters of SS. Cyril and Methodius 2; Lay Teachers 31; Students 464.
Convent—O Moore Dr., 29407. Tel: 803-766-5120.

8—ST. PETER'S. Closed. For inquiries for parish records contact St. Patrick, P.O. Box 20726, Charleston, SC 29413.

9—DIVINE REDEEMER, Berkeley Co., Rev. J. Scott Newman, J.C.L.
Office: 1106 Fort Dr., Hanahan, 29406. Tel: 803-553-0340; Fax: 803-553-0346.
Res., 1022 Recess Rd., Hanahan, 29406. Tel: 803-572-3532.
School—1104 Fort Dr., Hanahan, 29406. Tel: 803-553-1521. Mrs. Jean Steinhoff, Prin.
Lay Teachers 17; Students 288.

10—STELLA MARIS, Rev. Msgr. Lawrence B. McInerny.
Res., 1204 Middle St., P.O. Box 280, Sullivan's Island, 29482. Tel: 803-883-3108 (Office); 883-9158 (Rectory); Fax: 803-883-3160.

11—CHURCH OF THE NATIVITY, Revs. Henry T. Barron; William Gladstone Kinney, Jr. In res., Rev. Joseph G. Maher.
Office & Mailing Address: 1061 Folly Rd., 29412. Tel: 803-795-3821; Fax: 803-795-2714.
Res., 1129 Pittsford Cir., 29412. Tel: 803-795-5525; Fax: 803-795-2714.
School—Tel: 803-795-3975. Mrs. Margaret Neises, Prin.
Sisters of SS. Cyril and Methodius 1; Lay Teachers 21; Students 320.
Mission—Folly Beach, Charleston Co., Our Lady of Good Counsel, 56 Center St., P.O. Box 1257, Folly Beach, 29439. Tel: 803-588-6384. Rev. Msgr. Robert J. Kelly.

12—ST. JOSEPH, Rev. Gabriel J. Smith.
Office & Mailing Address: 1695 Wallenberg Blvd., 29407. Tel: 803-556-4611; Fax: 803-556-4612.
Res., 1549 Montclair St., 29407.

13—ST. JOSEPH'S. Closed. For inquiries for parish records contact St. Joseph, 1695 Wallenberg Blvd., Charleston, SC 29407.

14—ST. THOMAS THE APOSTLE, Rev. Msgr. Edward D. Lofton.
Res., 6650 Dorchester Rd., Charleston Heights, 29418. Tel: 803-552-9045; 552-2223; Fax: 803-552-2223.

15—CHURCH OF THE HOLY SPIRIT, Rev. James Parker.
Res., 2545 Bohicket Rd., Johns Island, 29455. Tel: 803-559-0353. [CEM]

16—CHRIST THE DIVINE TEACHER, Rev. Michael J. Davino.
Mailing Address: MSC 58, The Citadel, 171 Moultrie St., 29409. Tel: 803-953-7692; 722-7018 (Res.).

17—CHRIST OUR KING, Rev. Msgr. James A. Carter; Rev. James Leo LeBlanc.
Res., 1122 Russell Dr., P.O. Box 724, Mount Pleasant, 29465. Tel: 803-884-5587; Fax: 803-884-7086.
School—Christ Our King-Stella Maris School, 1183 Russell Dr., Mount Pleasant, 29464. Tel: 803-884-4721. Sr. Stella Maris Craven, O.L.M., Prin.
Sisters 1; Lay Teachers 27; Students 634.

OUTSIDE OF THE CITY OF CHARLESTON

Abbeville, Abbeville Co., Sacred Heart, Sr. Joan Kobe, D.W., Pastoral Admin.
Res., N. Main St. at Pinckney St., P.O. Box 812, 29620. Tel: 864-459-5150.
Mission—McCormick, McCormick Co., Good Shepherd, P.O. Box 1468, McCormick, 29835. Sr. Joan Kobe, D.W., Pastoral Admin.
Station—Abbeville, McCormick Correction Institution.

Aiken, Aiken Co., St. Mary, Help of Christians, Revs. Thomas A. Evatt; Edward W. Fitzgerald.
Res., 219 York St. S.E., P.O. Box 438, 29802. Tel: 803-649-4777; Fax: 803-642-6421. [CEM]
School—Tel: 803-649-2171; Fax: 803-643-0092. Sr. Rosemary Boyd, O.L.M., Prin.
Sisters of Charity of Our Lady of Mercy 1; Lay Teachers 29; Students 321.

St. Gerard's, Rev. Thomas M. Gillin, S.J.
Res., 640 Edrie St. N.E., 29801. Tel: 803-649-3030.
School—Merged with St. Mary's School.

Anderson, Anderson Co., St. Joseph's, Rev. Thomas D. Timlin.
Office: Windsor Place Shopping Center, 29622. Tel: 864-225-5341; Fax: 864-224-0538.
Res., 1107 McLees Rd., P.O. Box 1013, 29622. Tel: 864-224-4415.
Church—1200 Cornelia Rd., 29621.
School—1200 Cornelia Rd., 29621. Mrs. Marilyn Butterfoss, Prin.
Lay Teachers 11; Students 163.

St. Mary of the Angels, Rev. David L. Hyman, O.F.M.
In res., Rev. Thomas F. Vigliotta, O.F.M.
Res., 1821 White St., P.O. Box 3, 29622. Tel: 864-226-8621.

Batesburg, Lexington Co., St. John of the Cross, Rev. Filemon Juya (Garagoa) Admin.
Res., 320 W. Columbia Ave., P.O. Box 438, 29006. Tel: 803-532-1208.

Beaufort, Beaufort Co., St. Peter's, Rev. Ronald R. Cellini (PIT).
Res., 70 Lady's Island Dr., 29902. Tel: 803-522-9555; Fax: 803-522-0667. [CEM]
School—Tel: 803-522-2163. Mr. William Gabrielson, Prin.
Lay Teachers 10; Students 193.
Mission—Saint Helena Island, Beaufort Co., Holy Cross.

Bluffton, Beaufort Co., St. Andrew's, Rev. H. Gregory West.
Res., 220 Pinckney Colony Rd., 29910. Tel: 803-757-2986.
Office & Mailing: 19 E. Main St., P.O. Box 487, Hardeeville, 29927. Tel: 803-784-2943; Fax: 803-784-5612. [CEM]
Mission—Hardeeville, Jasper Co., St. Anthony's.

Camden, Kershaw Co., Our Lady of Perpetual Help, Rev. John P. Coffey.
Res., 1709 Lyttleton St., 29020. Tel: 803-432-6131.

Chapin, Lexington Co., Our Lady of the Lake, Rev. Andrew J. Vollkommer.
Mailing Address: 195 Amicks Ferry Rd., P.O. Box 631, 29036. Tel: 803-345-3962; Fax: 803-345-8933.
Res., 2 Oakstand Ct., Irmo, 29063. Tel: 803-781-8767.

Cheraw, Chesterfield Co., St. Peter's, Rev. Patrick E. Cooper.
Res., 602 Market St., P.O. Box 905, 29520. Tel: 803-537-7351.
Missions—Bennettsville, Marlboro Co., St. Denis; Pageland, Chesterfield Co., St. Ernest.

Chester, Chester Co., St. Joseph's, Rev. Thomas F. Morrison; Deacon Jon E. Dwyer, Pastoral Admin.
Res., 110 West End, P.O. Box 869, 29706. Tel: 803-377-4695.

Clemson, Pickens Co., St. Andrew, Revs. Johns J. Kenny, C.S.P.; Gerard J. Aylward, C.S.P.; Thomas

D. Allain, C.S.P.; James M. Brucz, C.S.P.
Res., 123 Folger St., P.O. Box 112, 29633. Tel: 864-654-2711; 654-1757; Fax: 864-654-2950.
Missions—Seneca, Oconee Co., St. Paul the Apostle; Walhalla, Oconee Co., St. Francis of Assisi.
Station—Clemson, Clemson University.

Columbia, Richland Co.,

1—St. Peter's, Rev. Msgr. Leigh A. Lehocky.
Mailing Address: P.O. Box 1896, 29202.
Res., 2125 Raven Tr., West Columbia, 29169.
Church—1529 Assembly St., 29201. Tel: 803-779-0036; Fax: 803-799-2438. [CEM]
School—Tel: 803-252-8285. Mrs. Madeline McMillion, Prin.
Lay Teachers 17; Students 192.
Station—Columbia, South Carolina State Hospital.

2—St. Joseph, Rev. Msgr. Charles H. Rowland; Rev. Gary S. Linsky.
Office: 3512 Devine St., 29205. Tel: 803-254-7646; Fax: 803-799-7607.
Res., 3451 Blossom St., 29205. Tel: 803-540-1910.
Church—3600 Devine St., 29205.
School—3700 Devine St., 29205. Tel: 803-254-6736; Fax: 803-540-1903. Sr. Christina Murphy, S.N.D., Prin.
Ursuline Nuns of the Congregation of Paris 3; Lay Teachers 20; Students 263.
Mission—Winnsboro, Fairfield Co., St. Theresa. Rev. Michael F. McCafferty.
Res., 1610 Greene St., 29201. Tel: 803-799-5870.

3—Saint Martin de Porres, Sr. Mary Laura Lesniak, S.S.M.N., Pastoral Admin. In res., Rev. John E. Keefer, O.P.
Res., 2229 Hampton St., P.O. Box 4187, 29240. Tel: 803-254-6862; Fax: 803-779-4720.
School—Tel: 803-254-6862. Sr. Carol Bongaarts, O.P., Coord. of Education Programs.
Lay Teachers 9; Students 190.
Station—Columbia, Correctional Institutions in the Greater Columbia Area.

4—Our Lady of the Hills, Rev. Robert H. Fix.
Mailing Address: & Religious Education Center: 2700 Ashland Rd., 29210. Tel: 803-772-7400; Fax: 803-798-8030.
Res., 120 Marydale Ln., 29210. Tel: 803-772-6692.

5—St. John Neumann, Rev. Frederick F. Masad.
Res., 2816 Bancroff Rd., P.O. Box 23689, 29224. Tel: 803-788-1274; 788-0811 (Office); Fax: 803-788-1501 (Office).
Church—100 Polo Rd., 29223. Tel: 803-788-1478.
School—721 Polo Rd., 29223. Tel: 803-788-1367; Fax: 803-788-7330. Dr. Margaret Adams, Prin.
Sisters 1; Lay Teachers 24; Students 343.

6—Good Shepherd, Rev. William D. Ladkau.
Mailing Address: P.O. Box 1298, 29202.
Res., 1625 Granby Rd., Cayce, 29033. Tel: 803-791-4596; 765-1334 (Office).

Conway, Horry Co., St. James, Rev. Frederick LaBrecque.
Church & Office: 1071 Academy Dr., 29526. Tel: 803-347-5168; Fax: 803-347-1212.
Res., 181 Long Ave., 29526. Tel: 803-248-7148.
Mission—Loris, Horry Co., Church of the Resurrection, 1929 Business Hwy. 9E, Loris, 29569. Tel: 803-756-6168.

Dillon, Dillon Co., St. Louis, Sr. Bernadine Jax, O.S.F., Pastoral Admin.
Res., 607 N. Fourth Ave., 29536. Tel: 803-744-9401.
Mission—Marion, Marion Co., Infant Jesus.

Edgefield, Edgefield Co., St. Mary's, Rev. Robert W. Ninedorf.
Res., 302 Jeter St., P.O. Box 386, 29824. Tel: 803-637-6248. [CEM]
Church—305 Buncombe St., 29824.

Florence, Florence Co., St. Anthony's All Souls Memorial, Rev. Msgr. Thomas R. Duffy.
Res., 2536 W. Hoffmeyer Rd., P.O. Box 5327, 29502. Tel: 803-665-5853; 662-5674; Fax: 803-662-5673.
School—Tel: 803-662-1910; Fax: 803-662-5674. Mr. Frank J. Cottone, Prin.
Lay Teachers 24; Students 257.

St. Ann, Rev. Michael T. Corrigan (GAL).
Res., 113 S. Kemp St., 29501. Tel: 803-662-1736.
Convent—Tel: 803-662-6360.
Sisters of St. Mary of Namur 3.

Gaffney, Cherokee Co., Sacred Heart, Rev. Donald F. Grady, S.J.
Res., 407 Grace St., 29340. Tel: 864-489-9453.

Garden City, Horry Co., St. Michael, Rev. William C. Bleiler.
Mailing Address: P.O. Box 14357, Surfside Beach, 29587.
Res., 574 Cypress Ave., 29576. Tel: 803-651-3737; Fax: 803-651-6316.

Georgetown, Georgetown Co., St. Mary's. (Our Lady of Ransom). Rev. Steven L. Brovey.
Office: 317 Broad St., P.O. Box 766, 29442. Tel: 803-546-7416.
Res., 810 Highmark St., 29442.
Missions—Andrews, Georgetown Co., St. Leo the Great; McClellanville, Charleston Co., McClellanville Mission.

St. Cyprian, Rev. Steven L. Brovey; Sr. Kathleen Driscoll, D.C., Pastoral Admin.
Center & Mailing Address: 1905 Front St., P.O. Box 2037, 29442. Tel: 803-546-1470.

Gloverville, Aiken Co., Our Lady of the Valley, Rev. John L. Lawlor, C.M.; Deacon Robert J. Waters, Pastoral Admin.
Mailing Address: P.O. Box 419, 29828. Tel: 803-593-2241.
Res., 2429 Augusta Rd., 29828. Tel: 803-593-2241.
Parish Community Center—Tel: 803-593-2241.
Convent—Horsecreek Valley Convent, P.O. Box 358, 29828. Tel: 803-593-9862.
Daughters of Charity 5.

Goose Creek, Berkeley Co., Immaculate Conception, Rev. Frank Palmieri, C.R.M.
Res., 510 St. James Ave., 29445. Tel: 803-553-1386; 572-1270.

Greenville, Greenville Co., St. Mary's, Rev. Msgr. Charles J. Baum, Pastor Emeritus; Revs. D. Anthony Droze; Charles J. McPadden, M.M. In res., Rev. Vincent The' Quang Nguyen.
Mailing Address: 111 Hampton Ave., 29601. Tel: 864-271-8422; Fax: 864-370-9880.
Res., 338 W. Washington St., 29601. Fax: 864-235-2868.
School—101 Hampton Ave., 29601. Tel: 864-271-3870. Sr. Veronica Janas, O.L.M., Prin.
Sisters of Charity of Our Lady of Mercy 1; Lay Teachers 14; Students 300.

Our Lady of the Rosary, Rev. Charles J. Day.
Res., 3710 Augusta Rd., P.O. Box 8396, 29604. Tel: 864-277-5971.
School—Tel: 864-277-5350; Fax: 864-277-7745. Mr. D. Keith Darr, Prin.
Lay Teachers 13; Students 184.

St. Anthony of Padua, Rev. Paul M. Williams, O.F.M. In res., Rev. Francis A. Gorman, O.F.M., (Retired).
Res., 307 Gower St., 29611. Tel: 864-233-7717; Fax: 864-233-2852.
School—309 Gower St., 29611. Tel: 864-271-0167; Fax: 864-271-2936. Sr. Catherine Noecker, O.S.F., Prin.
Sisters of St. Francis of Williamsville 4; Lay Teachers 9; Students 111.

Greenwood, Greenwood Co., Our Lady of Lourdes, Rev. Hayden J. Vaverek.
Office: 110 E. Laurel Ave., 29649. Tel: 864-223-8410; Fax: 864-223-4039.
Res., 120 Colonial Dr., 29649. Tel: 864-223-3003.

Greer, Greenville Co., Blessed Trinity, Rev. Nicholas R. Bayard.
Res., 111 Becky Don Dr., Apt. 9, 29651. Tel: 864-879-3812.
Church—901 River Rd., P.O. Box 1371, 29652. Tel: 864-879-4225.

Hartsville, Darlington Co., St. Mary the Virgin Mother, Rev. Gerald J. Ryfinski.
Res., 115 Church St., P.O. Box 1378, 29551. Tel: 803-332-6664; 332-3136.
Mission—Darlington, Darlington Co., St. Joseph the Worker.

St. Joseph's. Closed. For inquiries for parish records contact St. Mary's, P.O. Box 1378, Hartsville, SC 29550.

Hilton Head Island, Beaufort Co., Holy Family, Rev. Edmund M. McCaffrey.
Res., 24 Pope Ave., P.O. Box 5397, 29938. Tel: 803-785-2895; 785-2876; Fax: 803-842-7494.

St. Francis By the Sea, Rev. Martin T. Laughlin (DUB).
Res., 45 Beach City Rd., P.O. Box 22239, 29925. Tel: 803-681-6350; Fax: 803-689-5502.
School—P.O. Box 1482, 29925. Tel: 803-681-6501. Dr. Kathleen Sutcliffe, Prin.
Students 40.

Joanna, Laurens Co., St. Boniface, Rev. James M. Crowley, O.M.I.
Res., 403 Main St., P.O. Box 188, 29351. Tel: 864-697-6745.
Station—Joanna, Whitten Center.

Kingstree, Williamsburg Co., St. Ann's, Rev. Arturo O. Dalupang.
Res., 300 Ashton Ave., 29556. Tel: 803-354-7798.
Center—906 Thorne Ave., 29556. Tel: 803-354-9415.
Convent—908 Thorne Ave., 29556. Tel: 803-354-9415.
Felician Sisters 2.

Lake City, Florence Co., St. Philip's, Rev. Arturo O. Dalupang; Sr. Diane V. Tomkinson, O.S.F., Admin.
Res., 146 Anderson St., P.O. Box 399, 29560. Tel: 803-394-8343.
Mission—Johnsonville, Florence Co., St. Patrick.

Lancaster, Lancaster Co., St. Catherine's, Rev. Thomas F. Morrison.
Res., 720 W. Meeting St., P.O. Box 814, 29720. Tel: 803-283-3362; Fax: 803-283-3363.
Mission—Great Falls, Chester Co., St. Michael.

Lexington, Lexington Co., Corpus Christi, Rev. Jerome F. Schwab.
Res., 2350 Augusta Hwy., 29072. Tel: 803-359-4391; Fax: 803-359-8885.

Mauldin, Greenville Co., St. Elizabeth Ann Seton, Rev. Howard L. Coughlin.
Mailing Address: & Office: P.O. Box 672, 29662-0672. Tel: 864-963-3959; 963-8428; Fax: 864-967-9726.
Res., 115 Ivy Dr., Simpsonville, 29680-6124. Tel: 864-967-3125.

Moncks Corner, Berkeley Co., St. Philip Benizi, Rev. Thomas X. Hofmann.
Res., 1404 Old Hwy. 52 S., 29461. Tel: 803-761-3777.
Mission—Bonneau, Berkeley Co., Our Lady of Peace, 224 Murry Ferry Rd., 29461.

Murphy Village, Edgefield Co., St. Edward, Rev. Peter Clarke.
Res., 1370 Edgefield Rd., P.O. Box 6340, North Augusta, 29861. Tel: 803-279-1837.

Myrtle Beach, Horry Co., St. Andrew's, Rev. Msgr. Joseph R. Roth; Rev. Paul A. McDuffie.
Res., 503 37th Ave. N., 29577. Tel: 803-448-5930; Fax: 803-448-3947.
School—3601 N. Kings Hwy., 29577. Tel: 803-448-6062. Mrs. Molly Halasz, Prin.
Lay Teachers 13; Students 264.
Parish Center—512 36th Ave. N., 29577. Tel: 803-448-5930; Fax: 803-448-3947.

Newberry, Newberry Co., St. Mark, Rev. James M. Crowley, O.M.I.
Res., 928 Boundary St., 29108. Tel: 803-276-6446; Fax: 803-276-0856.

North Augusta, Alken Co., Our Lady of Peace, Revs. C. Alexander McDonald; Luis Augusto Soler (Tunja).
Res., 856 Old Edgefield Rd., P.O. Box 6605, 29861-6605. Tel: 803-279-0315; Fax: 803-279-5247.
School—Tel: 803-279-8396. Mrs. Kathleen Morton, Prin.
Lay Teachers 15; Students 204.

North Myrtle Beach, Horry Co., Our Lady Star of the Sea, Rev. George F. Moynihan.
Office: 1000 Eighth Ave. N., 29582. Tel: 803-249-2356; Fax: 803-249-8514.
Res., 1105 Golf View Dr., 29582. Tel: 803-249-8049.

Orangeburg, Orangeburg Co., Holy Trinity, Rev. Michael J. Polewczak (ALB).
Res., 2161 Griffith Dr., N.W. P.O. Box 1207, 29116. Tel: 803-534-8177; Fax: 803-535-0012.
School—2202 Riverbank Dr. N.W., 29118. Tel: 803-534-0461. Mrs. Josephine Evan, Prin.
Lay Teachers 8; Students 76.
Brothers Residence—1710 Amelia St., N.E., 29116. Tel: 803-534-2302.
Xaverian Brothers (St. Joseph Prov.) 4.
Missions—Allendale, Barnwell Co., St. Mary; Barnwell, Barnwell Co., St. Andrew the Apostle, c/o Rev. Louis J.P. Kennedy, P.O. Box 604, 29812. Tel: 803-259-7593; Blackville, Barnwell Co., Sacred Heart; Springfield, Orangeburg Co., St. Theresa.
Station—Orangeburg, Santee.

Christ the King. Closed. For inquiries for parish records contact Holy Trinity, 351 Amelia St. N.E., P.O. Box 1207, Orangeburg, SC 29115. Tel: 803-534-8177.

Pawleys Island, Georgetown Co., Precious Blood of Christ, Rev. Charles J. Snopek.
Res., 489 Brace Dr., 29585.
Office: 1633 Waverly Rd., 29585. Tel: 803-237-3428.

Pickens, Pickens Co., Holy Cross, Rev. Francis J. Travis.
Res., 416 John St., P.O. Box 855, 29671. Tel: 864-878-0574.
Church—558-560 Hampton St., 29671. Tel: 864-878-3820; Fax: 864-878-0028.
Mission—Easley, Anderson Co., St. Luke, Tel: 803-269-6891.

Ridgeland, Jasper Co., St. Anthony's, Rev. Michael J. Hussey, O.M.I.
Res., U.S. Hwy. 17, P.O. Box 548, 29936. Tel: 803-726-3606; 943-4019.
Mission—Hampton, Hampton Co., St. Mary.

Rock Hill, York Co., St. Anne's, Rev. William F. Pentis, C.O.
Office & Mailing Address: 1694 Bird St., P.O. Box 3000, 29732. Tel: 803-329-2662; Fax: 803-329-2190.
Res., 434 Charlotte Ave., 29731. Tel: 803-327-3236.
School—Tel: 803-324-4814; Fax: 803-324-4281. Mr. Frederick McKay, Prin.
Lay Teachers 30; Students 335.
Mission—Fort Mill, York Co., St. Philip Neri, P.O. Box 3413, Fort Mill, 29715. Tel: 803-328-2620. Rev. John P. Giuliani, C.O., Admin.
St. Mary's, Bro. David Boone, C.O., Pastoral Admin.; Sr. Francis K. Saring, M.S.B.T., Pastoral Admin.
Office—Bannon Hall, 902 Crawford Rd., P.O. Box 11982, 29731. Tel: 803-329-1008.
Convent—Missionary Servants of the Most Blessed Trinity. 915 Crawford Rd., 29730. Tel: 803-327-7450. St. Mary's Missionary Cenacle
Saint Martin de Porres Recreation Center—911 Crawford Rd., 29730.

Simpsonville, Greenville Co., St. Mary Magdalene, Rev. Herbert K. Conner, S.J.
Res., 107 Wickersham Dr., 29681. Tel: 864-234-5323.
Church & Office: 2252 Woodruff Rd., 29681. Tel: 864-288-4884; Fax: 864-297-5804.

Spartanburg, Spartanburg Co., St. Paul the Apostle, Rev. Michael R. DeAntonio.
Res., 161 N. Dean St., 29302. Tel: 864-582-0674; Fax: 864-582-0716.
School—Tel: 864-582-6645; Fax: 864-582-0716. Mrs. Ann Marie Sullivan, Prin.
Lay Teachers 22; Students 243.
St. Joseph's, Rev. Michael R. DeAntonio.
Office: 450 Duncan St., P.O. Box 5091, 29304. Tel: 864-582-1870.
Res., 161 N. Dean St., 29302. Tel: 864-582-0674.
Jesus Our Risen Savior, Rev. Eugene A. Leonard.
Res., 2565 Reidville Rd., P.O. Box 17059, 29301. Tel: 864-576-1164; 576-0726.

Summerton, Clarendon Co., St. Mary's, Rev. Raymond E. DuMouchel; Deacon Charles M. Walsh, Pastoral Admin.
Res., 10 N. Cantey St., P.O. Box 960, 29148. Tel: 803-485-2925.
Mission—Holly Hill, Orangeburg Co., St. Ann, 8309 Old State Rd., Holly Hill, 29059. Tel: 803-485-2925. Rev. Raymond E. DuMouchel.

Summerville, Dorchester Co., St. John the Beloved, Rev. Msgr. E. Christopher Lathem; Rev. Duane T. Riplog.
Res., 28 Sumter Ave., 29483. Tel: 803-873-0631; Fax: 803-873-9327.
School—Summerville Regional Catholic School, (Grades K-8) 226 Black Oak Blvd., 29483. Tel: 803-873-9310; Fax: 803-873-5709. Ms. Carole Anne White, Prin.
Lay Teachers 26; Students 436.
St. Theresa the Little Flower, Rev. David J. Schiller.
Res., 11001 Dorchester Rd., 29485. Tel: 803-875-5002; 875-3609; Fax: 803-875-4884.
Station—Summerville, MacDougall Correction Center.

Sumter, Sumter Co., St. Anne's, Rev. David J. Sharrock, C.SS.R.
Res., 216 E. Liberty St., 29150. Tel: 803-773-3524; Fax: 803-778-1644. [CEM]
School—Tel: 803-775-3692. Mr. John Fer, Prin.
Lay Teachers 17; Students 193.
St. Jude, Rev. Michael Varady, C.SS.R.
Res., 611 W. Oakland Ave., P.O. Box 1589, 29150. Tel: 803-773-9244.
Preschool & Tutorial Program—114 S. Purdy St., 29150. Tel: 803-775-4895.
Convent—609 W. Oakland Ave., P.O. Box 1197, 29150. Tel: 803-775-3721.
Sisters of St. Mary of Namur 4.

Taylors, Greenville Co., Prince of Peace, Very Rev. Chester M. Moczydlowski.
Mailing Address: 1209 Brushy Creek Rd., 29687. Tel: 864-268-4352; Fax: 864-322-2239.
Res., 1201 Brushy Creek Rd., 29687. Tel: 864-244-7799.

Union, Union Co., St. Augustine's, Rev. Timothy M. Lijewski.
Res., 103 E. South St., P.O. Box 507, 29379. Tel: 864-427-7240.
Mission—Laurens, Laurens Co., Holy Spirit.

Walterboro, Colleton Co., St. Anthony's, Rev. Paul F.X. Seitz.
Res., 925 S. Jefferies Blvd., P.O. Box 933, 29488. Tel: 803-549-5230.
Mission—Ritter, Colleton Co., St. James. [CEM]
St. Joseph's. Closed. For inquiries for parish records contact St. Anthony's, P.O. Box 933, Walterboro, SC 29488.

Ward, Saluda Co., St. William's, Rev. Robert W. Ninedorf; Deacon John P. Klein, Pastoral Admin.
Res., Saluda Hwy. No. 39, 29166. Tel: 864-445-7215. [CEM]
Convent—Tel: 864-445-3302. Daughters of Wisdom

Yonges Island, Charleston Co., St. Mary, Rev. Basil P. Congro.
Res., 4255 State Hwy. 165, 29449. Tel: 803-889-8549.
Mission—Edisto Island, Charleston Co., SS. Frederick & Stephen.

York, York Co., Divine Saviour, Rev. Edward P. McDevitt, C.O.
Res., 232 Herndon Ave., P.O. Box 341, 29745. Tel: 803-684-3431; 327-2097.
Mission—Lake Wylie, York Co., All Saints.

Chaplains of Public Institutions

LEXINGTON. *Correctional Institutions in the Greater Columbia Area,* 4214 Grand St., 29203. Tel: 803-786-7177. Mr. Roland L. Thomas.

Special Assignment:
Rev.—
Kennedy, Ernest E., 105 Driftwood, Bonneau, SC 29431

On Duty Outside the Diocese:
Reverend Fathers—
Abbott, Donald S., St. Dorothy's Church, 11 Harnden St., Wilmington, MA 01887-3519
Gorski, J. Donald, Casa Parroquial, Corritos-Tumbes, Peru
White, Leland J., Theology Dept., St. John's Univ., Grand Central Pkwy. & Utopia Pkwy., Jamaica, NY 11439
Zaratti, Filiberto, Via Di Morena 45, Ciampino, Roma, 00043 Italy

Military Chaplains:
Reverend Fathers—
Keating, Pius F., S.A., (Retired), Commander, CHC, U.S. Navy, P.O. Box 1498, Tryon, NC 28782-1498. Tel: 704-859-2054
Mintegui, Marc A., U.S. Army
Torm, Agustin, U.S. Army

Absent On Leave:
Reverend Fathers—
Bench, John F.
Condon, Eugene L.
Dilley, Gary D.
Sorce, John J.

Retired:
Reverend Monsignors—
Aiken, Roy F., P.O. Box 1728, Columbia, SC 29202
Baum, Charles J., 7 S. Memminger St., P.O. Box 2406, Greenville, SC 29602
Hamburger, Donald C., P.O. Box 1051, Columbia, SC 29202
Hopwood, Frederick J.
McManus, J. Fleming, 1809 Mepkin Dr., Charleston, SC 29407
Sterker, Louis F., P.A., P.O. Box 1728, Columbia, SC 29202
Reverend Fathers—
Berberich, Peter K., 147 Honey Bee Rd., Moncks Corner, SC 29461
Burke, Henry J., 720 Garden Lake St., Murrells Inlet, SC 29576
Burn, William C., 2107 Westchase Dr., Charleston, SC 29407-8829
Chmely, Edward V., White Oak Manor of York, P.O. Box 629, York, SC 29745
Cilwick, Theodore T., 2225 Ashley River Rd., Apt. 182, Charleston, SC 29414
Faase, Albert A., P.O. Box 1195, Beaufort, SC 29901
Mullen, Edward F., 8155 Tydor Dr., Jonesboro, GA 30236
Murphy, Joseph J., 203 Center St., Mount Pleasant, SC 29464
Owens-Howard, Robert J.
Patat, St. John E., 2 Riverdale Dr., Charleston, SC 29407
Powers, Jerome C., 1405 Sarsfield Ave., Camden, SC 29020
Suggs, Fred H., Brian Center, 3514 Sidney Rd., Columbia, SC 29210

Permanent Deacons:
Anonie, Joseph A., Immaculate Conception Church, Goose Creek
Barth, Kenneth J. (BUF), St. Michael's Church, Garden City
Biviano, Joseph P., Our Lady of the Lake Church, Chapin
Brown, John H., St. Joseph's Church, Charleston
Cahill, Joseph F., Christ Our King Church, Mount Pleasant
Carmody, Joseph E., St. Mary Help of Christians Church, Aiken
Cassandra, Anthony J., Our Lady of the Rosary Church, Greenville
Cole, Stephen D., St. Peter's Church, Columbia
Conick, John E., On Duty Outside the Diocese
Crocker, Dr. Jack L., Our Lady of the Hills Church, Columbia
Cuomo, Nicholas G., Sacred Heart Church, Charleston
Dashnaw, Donald R. (OG), Divine Redeemer Church, Hanahan
Davis, Thomas E., St. Thomas the Apostle Church, Charleston
DeBlasio, Anthony A. (MET), St. Andrew's Church, Myrtle Beach
Delmonte, Richard (HRT), St. John the Beloved Church, Summerville
Dillard, Henry, St. Anthony's Church, Greenville
DiRusso, Charles R., Our Lady of the Hills Church, Columbia
Dwyer, John E., St. Joseph, Chester
Easterling, Charles M., St. Peter's Church, Columbia
Ellis, Billy, Maj. Gen. (Retired), St. Jude's Church, Sumter
Farina, Frank J., St. Mary's Church, Greenville
Gorman, Chester E., St. Andrew's Church, Myrtle Beach
Grismore, Gerald, Prince of Peace Church, Taylors
Hanvey, Samuel E., Cathedral of St. John the Baptist, Charleston
High, Raymond, Corpus Christi Church, Lexington
Hoffmann, Frederick G., Corpus Christi Church, Lexington
Hyland, James P., St. Anne's Church, Rock Hill
Johnson, James H., St. Ann's Church, Florence
Jones, Dennis N.
Jones, Robert L., On Duty Outside the Diocese
Karandisevsky, John F., St. Mary's Church, Greenville
Kemper, Joseph C., (Retired)
Kiely, John D. (TR), St. James Church, Conway
Klein, John P. (NY), St. William's Church, Ward
Langford, Walter H., Jr., On leave
Lenny, William P. (DET), St. Elizabeth Ann Seton Church, Mauldin
Lorenzo, Anthony J. (RVC), St. Andrew's Church, Myrtle Beach
Mahaffey, Robert L., Jr., St. Paul the Apostle Church, Spartanburg
McCabe, Farrell W., Sr., Blessed Sacrament Church, Charleston
McDonald, Thomas F., Divine Redeemer Church, Hanahan
Meyer, John P. (PAT), Unassigned
Meyer, Philip M., Stella Maris Church, Sullivan Island
Mirande, August J., Our Lady Star of the Sea Church, North Myrtle Beach
Murtaugh, Richard J., Jr., St. Mary's Church, Greenville
Nazzaro, Joseph J. (NEW), St. Francis by the Sea Church, Hilton Head
O'Connor, Joseph P., St. Andrew's Church, Myrtle Beach
O'Donnell, John D., St. Anthony's Church, Florence
Osbourne, R. Michael, Stella Maris Church, Sullivan's Island
Pecko, Harry C., Unassigned
Petrusak, Frank T., St. Thomas the Apostle Church, Charleston
Pezanowski, Walter S., Stella Maris Church, Sullivan's Island
Poole, Charles P., Jr., St. Joseph's Church, Columbia
Richardson, David W. (NEW), Holy Spirit Church, Johns Island
Rock, Paul J., On Duty Outside the Diocese
Rush, James J. (NY), Unassigned
Sharkey, Donald F., St. John the Beloved Church, Summerville
Shook, Paul F., St. Joseph Church, Anderson
Sturm, Robert M., Our Risen Savior Church, Spartanburg
Thomas, Roland L., St. Martin de Porres Church, Columbia
Tierney, George, St. Mary's Magdalene Church, Simpsonville
Traxler, Harold Gr. Jr. (CAM), St. Andrew's Church, Clemson
Walsh, Charles Michael (CHI), St. Mary's Church, Summerton
Waters, Robert J., St. Mary Help of Christians Church, Aiken
West, James L., Holy Cross Church, Pickens
Williams, Thomas P., St. Patrick's Church, Charleston
Wright, Winston C., St. Anthony's Church, Greenville
Young, James R., St. Mary's Church, Georgetown

INSTITUTIONS LOCATED IN THE DIOCESE

[A] HIGH SCHOOLS, DIOCESAN

CHARLESTON. *Bishop England High School,* 203 Calhoun St., 29401-3522. Tel: 803-723-3637. Rev. Msgr. Lawrence B. McInerny, Rector; Mr. Nicholas J. Theos, Prin. Priests 1; Sisters 1; Lay Teachers 44; Students 835.

COLUMBIA. *Cardinal Newman High School.* (Grades 7-12), 4701 Forest Dr., 29206. Tel: 803-782-2814. Mr. Harold J. Bayerl, Prin. Sisters 2; Lay Teachers 30; Students 426.

SUMTER. *Sumter Catholic High School.* (Grades 7-12), 21 Council St., P.O. Box 1589, 29151. Tel: 803-775-0119. Mrs. Susan Anderson, Interim Prin. Lay Teachers 18; Students 163.

[B] GENERAL HOSPITALS

CHARLESTON. *Bon Secours-St. Francis Xavier Hospital,* 2095 Henry Tecklenburg Dr., 29414. Tel: 803-402-1000.
For a complete listing, refer to the Hospitals section.

DILLON. *Saint Eugene Community Hospital,* 301 E. Jackson St., 29536. Tel: 803-774-4111; Fax: 803-774-1563.
For a complete listing, refer to the Hospitals section.

*GREENVILLE. *Franciscan Health System of South Carolina, Inc.,* One St. Francis Dr., 29601. Tel: 803-255-1000.
For a complete listing, refer to the Hospitals section.

[C] HOSPICE

MYRTLE BEACH. *Mercy Hospice of Horry County,* P.O. Box 1409, 29578. Tel: 803-236-2282.
For a complete listing, refer to the Special Care Facilities section.

[D] HOMES FOR AGED

CHARLESTON. *Carter-May Home,* 1660 Ingram Rd., 29407. Tel: 803-556-8314.
For a complete listing, refer to the Special Care Facilities section.

[E] MONASTERIES AND RESIDENCES OF PRIESTS AND BROTHERS

MONCKS CORNER. *Mepkin Abbey.* (Trappist Monks), 1098 Mepkin Abbey Rd., 29461. Tel: 803-761-8509; Fax: 803-761-6719. Rt. Revs. Francis Kline, O.C.S.O.; Christian Aidan Carr, O.C.S.O., (Retired); Revs. Benjamin Clark, O.C.S.O.; Leonard A. Cunningham, O.C.S.O.; Aelred Hagan, O.C.S.O., Novice Dir.; Guerric Frederick A. Heckel (RIC); Richard G. McGuire, O.C.S.O.; Malachy Wall, O.C.S.O.; Feliciano Manalili (Philippines); Bro. Stan Gumula, O.S.C.O., Bus. Mgr. Professed Monks 25; Priests 9; Novices 3; Postulants 1; Number in Community 29.

ROCK HILL. *Oratory of St. Philip Neri, Congregation of the Oratory of Pontifical Rite,* 434 Charlotte Ave., Box 11586, 29730. Tel: 803-327-2097. Very Rev. Joseph A. Wahl, C.O., S.T.D., Provost; Revs. William F. Pentis, C.O., First Deputy & Vicar; David D. Valtierra, C.O., Deputy; Bros. David Boone, C.O., Treas.; Joseph Guyon, C.O., Sec.; Revs. Robert S. Dell, C.O.; John P. Giuliani, C.O.; Edward P. McDevitt, C.O.; James Moran, C.O.; Paul C. Proodian, C.O.; Halbert Weidner, C.O., Ph.D.; Clarence Edward Jones, C.O. Fathers 10; Brothers 4; Scholastics 2.

[F] CONVENTS AND RESIDENCES FOR SISTERS

CHARLESTON. *Convent of the Franciscan Sister,* 5 Riverside Dr., 29403. Tel: 803-722-2335. Sr. M. Maigread, Coord. Sisters of the Third Order Regular of St. Francis of the Congregation of Our Lady of Lourdes 2.

Daughters of St. Paul Convent, 243 King St., 29401. Tel: 803-577-0175; Fax: 803-577-9833. Sr. Christine Virginia Orfeo, F.S.P., Local Supr. Sisters 4.

May Forest, Generaltae and Motherhouse of the Sisters of Charity of Our Lady of Mercy, 424 Ft. Johnson Rd., P.O. Box 12410, 29422. Tel: 803-795-2866; Fax: 803-795-6083. Sr. Anne Francis Campbell, O.L.M., Gen. Supr. & Coord. of the Motherhouse, Maria Hall: Tel: 803-795-3351. St. Joseph & Barry Halls: Tel: 803-795-6851. Professed Sisters in Community 33.

St. Katharine Convent, 34 Wentworth St., 29401. Tel: 803-723-0053. Sr. Elsa Maria Lopez, O.S.P., Coord. Oblate Sisters of Providence 3.

Sisters of Bon Secours Convent, 878 Friendly Cir., 29407. Tel: 803-763-2336. Sisters 2.

Sisters of St. Mary Convent, 60 Pitt St., 29401. Tel: 803-722-4198. Sisters 3.

COLUMBIA. *Dominican House,* 3605 Hanson Ave., 29204. Tel: 803-738-0890. Sisters 2.

Ursuline Convent, 1607 Edgehill Rd., 29204. Tel: 803-782-3121. Sr. Maria Lovett., O.S.U., Local Supr. Ursline Nuns of the Congregation of Paris (Louisville, KY) 2.

CONWAY. *St. Joseph's Convent,* 1210 Main St., 29526. Tel: 803-248-3564.

DILLON. *Emmaus Community,* 803 N. 6th Ave., 29536. Tel: 803-774-7008. Franciscan Sisters of Mary 2.

GREENVILLE. *Monastery of St. Clare,* 1916 N. Pleasantburg Dr., 29609-4080. Tel: 864-244-4514. Franciscan Poor Clare Nuns. Sr. Maryalice Pierce, O.S.C., Abbess. Cloistered Nuns in Solemn Vows 16; Postulants 1; Extern in Perpetual Vows 1.

RIDGEVILLE. *Sisters of St. Dominic.* (Givhans), 2151 Hwy. 61, 29472. Tel: 803-875-4817. Sisters of St. Dominic (Adrian, MI) 2.

ST. HELENA ISLAND. *Franciscan Center,* Mattis Rd., U.S. Hwy. 21, P.O. Box 682, 29920. Tel: 803-838-3924. Sisters of St. Francis of Philadelphia, Glen Riddle-Aston, PA 2.

[G] CATHOLIC CHARITIES

CHARLESTON. *Catholic Charities of the Diocese of Charleston,* 1662 Ingram Rd., 29407. Tel: 803-769-4466. Sr. Susan Schorsten, H.M., Dir., Midlands Regional Office, 1012 Taylor St., P.O. Box 7245, Columbia, 29202-7245. Tel: 803-254-9776. Mrs. Peggy Sookikian, Regl. Coord., Pee Dee Regional Office, 1071 Academy Dr., Conway, 29526. Tel: 803-347-5157. Mrs. Diane Bullard, Regl. Coord., Piedmont Regional Office, 123 Sumner St., Greenville, 29601. Tel: 864-370-9446. Mrs. Leigh Allen Guth, Regl. Coord.

Echo House-Inner City Apostolate, 1911 Hackemann Ave., 29405. Tel: 803-554-7319. Sr. Maigread Conway, O.S.F., Dir. Sisters of the Third Order Regular of St. Francis of the Congregation of Our Lady of Lourdes 2.

Neighborhood House-Inner City Apostolate, 77 America St., 29403. Tel: 803-723-5129. Center for Social Service. Sr. Maigread Conway, O.S.F., Dir. Sisters of the Third Order of St. Francis of the Congregation of Our Lady of Lourdes 2.

[H] NEWMAN CENTERS

CHARLESTON. *The Citadel,* MSC 58, The Citadel, 171 Moultrie St., 29409. Tel: 803-953-7692; 722-7018; Fax: 803-953-7692. Rev. Michael J. Davino.

The College of Charleston Newman Center, Medical University of South Carolina, c/o 120 Broad St., 29401. Tel: 803-724-8395; 724-6368; 588-2336. Rev. Msgr. Sam R. Miglarese; Rev. Dennis B. Willey; Mrs. Jane Myers.

AIKEN. *University of South Carolina, Aiken Extension Newman Center,* P.O. Box 438, 29802. Tel: 803-649-4777. Rev. Thomas A. Evatt.

ANDERSON. *Anderson College Newman Center,* P.O. Box 1013, 29622. Tel: 864-225-5341. Rev. Thomas D. Timlin.

BEAUFORT. *University of South Carolina, Beaufort Extension Newman Center,* 70 Lady's Island Dr., 29902. Tel: 803-522-9555. Rev. Ronald R. Cellini (PIT).

CLEMSON. *Clemson University,* 209 Sloan St., P.O. Box 112, 29633. Tel: 864-654-7804; 654-1757; 654-9670. Rev. James M. Brucz, C.S.P. Legal Title: *Clemson University - Catholic Campus Ministry at St. Andrew's Church and the Catholic Student Association.*

CLINTON. *Presbyterian College Newman Center.* c/o 928 Boundry St., Newberry, 29108. Tel: 803-276-6446. Rev. James M. Crowley.

COLUMBIA. *Allen University, Benedict College Newman Center,* c/o St. Martin de Porres Church, 2229 Hampton St., P.O. Box 4187, 29240. Tel: 803-254-6862.

University of South Carolina, Columbia College, Thomas More Center, 1610 Greene St., 29201. Tel: 803-799-5870; Fax: 803-765-0800. Rev. Michael F. McCafferty.

DUE WEST. *Erskine College Newman Center.* P.O. Box 812, Abbeville, 29620. Tel: 864-459-5150. Sr. Joan Kobe, D.W.

FLORENCE. *Francis Marion University Newman Center,* 113 S. Kemp St., 29501. Tel: 803-662-1736. Rev. Michael T. Corrigan (GAL).

GAFFNEY. *Limestone College Newman Center,* 407 Grace St., 29340. Tel: 864-489-9453. Rev. Donald F. Grady, S.J.

GREENVILLE. *Furman University Newman Center,* 338 W. Washington St., 29601. Tel: 864-233-7717; Fax: 864-233-2852. Rev. Paul M. Williams.

GREENWOOD. *Lander College Newman Center,* Office, 110 E. Laurel Ave., 29649. Tel: 864-223-8410. Rev. Hayden J. Vaverek.

HARTSVILLE. *Coker College Newman Center,* 115 Church St., P.O. Box 1378, 29550. Tel: 803-332-6664; 332-3136. Rev. Gerald J. Ryfinski.

NEWBERRY. *Newberry College Newman Center,* 928 Boundry St., 29108. Tel: 803-276-6446. Rev. James M. Crowley.

ORANGEBURG. *South Carolina State University Newman Center & Claflin College,* 1710 Amelia St., N.E., 29115. Tel: 803-534-2302. Bro. Jim Connolly, C.F.X., Campus Minister.

ROCK HILL. *Winthrop University, York Co. Tech Center Newman Center,* 434 Charlotte Ave., Box 11586, 29731. Tel: 803-327-2097. Rev. David D. Valtierra, C.O.

SPARTANBURG. *Converse College, Wofford College, Spartanburg Methodist College Newman Center,* 161 N. Dean St., 29302. Tel: 864-582-0674. Rev. Michael R. DeAntonio.

[I] RETREAT CENTERS

EDISTO BEACH. *Sea of Peace House of Prayer,* 802 Jungle Rd., 29438. Tel: 803-869-0513.

KINGSTREE. *Springbank Christian Center-Dominican Retreat House,* Rte. 2, Box 180, 29556. Tel: 803-382-3426.

[J] MISCELLANEOUS

CHARLESTON. *Ladies of Charity of Sacred Heart Church,* 888 King St., 29403-4138. Tel: 803-722-7018.

Pauline Books & Media, 243 King St., 29401. Tel: 803-577-0175; Fax: 803-577-9833. Daughters of St. Paul.

The Sisters of Charity of Our Lady of Mercy Charitable Trust, 424 Ft. Johnson Rd., P.O. Box 12410, 29422. Tel: 803-795-2866; Fax: 803-795-6083.

COLUMBIA. *CSA Providence Ministries,* 2601 Laurel St., Ste. 150, 29204. Tel: 216-696-5560; Fax: 216-696-2204.

Sisters of Charity Foundation of South Carolina, 2601 Laurel St., Ste. 150, 29204. Tel: 803-254-1230; Fax: 803-749-0444.

JOHNS ISLAND. *Our Lady of Mercy Community Outreach Services, Inc.,* 1684 Brownswood Rd., 29455. Tel: 803-559-4109. P.O. Box 607, 29457.
Sponsored by Sisters of Charity of Our Lady of Mercy.

RELIGIOUS INSTITUTES OF MEN REPRESENTED IN THE DIOCESE

For further details refer to the corresponding bracketed number in the Religious Institutes of Men or Women section.

[0100]—*Adorno Fathers.*—C.R.M.
[1350]—*Brothers of St. Francis Xavier.* (St. Joseph Prov.).—C.F.X.
[0350]—*Cistercians Order of the Strict Observance-Trappist.*—O.C.S.O.
[1330]—*Congregation of the Mission.* (Eastern Prov.).—C.M.
[0520]—*Franciscan Friars.* (Prov. of the Most Holy Name).—O.F.M.
[0690]—*Jesuit Fathers and Brothers.* (New Orleans; New England Provs.).—S.J.
[0800]—*Maryknoll.*—M.M.
[0910]—*Oblates of Mary Immaculate.* (Eastern American Prov.).—O.M.I.
[0950]—*Oratorians.*—C.O.
[1030]—*Paulist Fathers.*—C.S.P.
[1070]—*Redemptorist Fathers.* (Richmond Vice Prov.).—C.SS.R.

RELIGIOUS INSTITUTES OF WOMEN REPRESENTED IN THE DIOCESE

[0270]—*Congregation of Bon Secours.*—C.B.S.
[1010]—*Congregation of Divine Providence.* (Texas).—C.D.P.
[1000]—*Congregation of Divine Providence.* (KY).—C.D.P.
[1730]—*Congregation of the Sisters of the Third Order of St. Francis.* (Oldenburg, IN).—O.S.F.
[0760]—*Daughters of Charity of St. Vincent de Paul.*—D.C.
[0960]—*Daughters of Wisdom.* (American Prov.).—D.W.
[1070-03]—*Dominican Sisters.* (Sinsinawa, WI).—O.P.
[1070-09]—*Dominican Sisters.* (Racine, WI).—O.P.
[1070-13]—*Dominican Sisters.* (Adrian, MI).—O.P.
[1070-04]—*Dominican Sisters.* (San Rafael, CA).—O.P.
[1170]—*Felician Sisters.*—C.S.S.F.
[1310]—*Franciscan Sisters of Little Fall.* (Minnesota).—O.S.F.
[1415]—*Franciscan Sisters of Mary.*—F.S.M.
[1440]—*Franciscan Sisters of the Poor.*—S.F.P.
[2790]—*Missionary Servants of the Most Blessed Trinity.*—M.S.B.T.
[3040]—*Oblate Sisters of Providence.*—O.S.P.
[3760]—*Order of St. Clare.*—O.S.C.
[0950]—*Pious Daughters of St. Paul.*—F.S.P.
[2970]—*School Sisters of Notre Dame.*—S.S.N.D.

[1680]—*School Sisters of St. Francis.* (Milwaukee).—O.S.F.
[0500]—*Sisters of Charity of Nazareth.*—S.C.N.
[0510]—*Sisters of Charity of Our Lady of Mercy.*—O.L.M.
[0580]—*Sisters of Charity of St. Augustine.*—C.S.A.
[2575]—*Sisters of Mercy of the Americas.* (Belmont, NC; Dallas, PA;).—R.S.M.
[3000]—*Sisters of Notre Dame de Namur.* (Baltimore; Boston).—S.N.D.deN.
[3950]—*Sisters of Saint Mary of Namur.*—S.S.M.N.
[3780]—*Sisters of Saints Cyril and Methodius.*—SS.C.M.
[1540]—*Sisters of St. Francis.* (Clinton, IA).—O.S.F.
[1650]—*Sisters of St. Francis of Philadelphia.*—O.S.F.
[1800]—*Sisters of St. Francis of the Third Order Regular.* (Williamsville, New York).—O.S.F.
[3840]—*Sisters of St. Joseph of Carondelet.* (Prov. of St. Louis).—C.S.J.
[2110]—*Sisters of the Humility of Mary.*—H.M.
[1720]—*Sisters of the Third Order of St. Francis of the Congregation of Our Lady of Lourdes.* (Rochester).—O.S.F.
[1890]—*Society of Helpers.*—H.H.S.
[4120-03]—*Ursuline Nuns, of the Congregation of Paris.*—O.S.U.

DIOCESAN CEMETERIES

CHARLESTON. *St. Lawrence and Holy Cross,* 1662 Ingram Rd., 29407. Tel: 803-769-4480. Mr. Dennis F. Atwood, Dir.

NECROLOGY

† Chassagne, Rt. Rev. M. Anthony, (Retired). —Died Oct. 9, 1996.

† Degan, David Arthur, (Retired). —Died Feb. 5, 1996.

† Goodwin, Justin Leo, (Retired). —Died Dec. 25, 1995.

Diocese of Charlotte

(Dioecesis Carolinana)

Most Reverend

WILLIAM G. CURLIN, D.D.

Bishop of Charlotte; ordained May 25, 1957; appointed Auxiliary Bishop of Washington November 2, 1988; consecrated December 20, 1988; appointed Bishop of Charlotte February 22, 1994; installed April 13, 1994. *Res., 1521 Dilworth Rd., Charlotte, NC, 28203.* Tel.: 704-376-4337; Fax: 704-375-7359.

Most Reverend

MICHAEL J. BEGLEY, D.D.

Retired Bishop of Charlotte; ordained May 26, 1934; appointed November 30, 1971; consecrated First Bishop of Charlotte January 12, 1972; resigned 1984. *Mailing Address: 3104 Stone Orchard Pl., Charlotte, NC, 28209.*

Chancery: P.O. Box 36776, Charlotte, NC, 28236. Tel.: 704-377-6871; 331-1702; Fax: 704-358-1208.

ESTABLISHED JANUARY 12, 1972.

Square Miles 20,470.

Comprises the Counties of Alexander, Alleghany, Anson, Ashe, Avery, Buncombe, Burke, Cabarrus, Caldwell, Catawba, Cherokee, Clay, Cleveland, Davidson, Davie, Forsyth, Gaston, Graham, Guilford, Haywood, Henderson, Iredell, Jackson, Lincoln, Macon, Madison, McDowell, Mecklenberg, Mitchell, Montgomery, Polk, Randolph, Richmond, Rockingham, Rowan, Rutherford, Stanley, Stokes, Surry, Swain, Transylvania, Union, Watauga, Wilkes, Yadkin and Yancey in the State of North Carolina.

For legal titles of parishes and diocesan institutions, consult the Chancery.

STATISTICAL OVERVIEW

Personnel	
Bishop	1
Retired Bishops	1
Abbots	1
Retired Abbots	1
Priests: Diocesan Active in Diocese	52
Priests: Active Outside Diocese	10
Priests: Retired, Sick or Absent	20
Number of Diocesan Priests	82
Religious Priests in Diocese	62
Extern Priests in Diocese	6
Ordinations:	
Diocesan Priests	2
Transitional Deacons	2
Permanent Deacons in Diocese	60
Total Brothers	5
Total Sisters	192
Parishes	
Parishes	66
With Resident Pastor:	
Resident Diocesan Priests	42
Resident Religious Priests	22
Without Resident Pastor:	
Administered by Women Religious	2
Missions	24
Pastoral Centers	4
Professional Ministry Personnel:	
Brothers	2
Sisters	23
Lay Ministers	63
Welfare	
Catholic Hospitals	1
Total Assisted	82,452
Health Care Centers	8
Total Assisted	149,235
Homes for the Aged	1
Total Assisted	115
Day Care and Extended Day Care Centers	4
Total Assisted	346
Specialized Homes	2
Total Assisted	85
Special Centers for Social Services	1
Total Assisted	75
Residential Care of Disabled	1
Total Assisted	65
Other Institutions	2
Total Assisted	28,175
Educational	
Diocesan Students in Other Seminaries	22
Total Seminarians	22
Colleges and Universities	2
Total Students	902
High Schools, Diocesan and Parish	2
Total Students	1,084
Elementary Schools, Diocesan and Parish	15
Total Students	5,462
Catechesis/Religious Education:	
High School Students	3,888
Elementary Students	10,639
Total Students Under Catholic Instruction	21,997
Teachers in the Diocese:	
Priests	3
Brothers	1
Sisters	16
Lay Teachers	380
Vital Statistics	
Receptions into the Church:	
Infant Baptism Totals	2,484
Adult Baptism Totals	574
Received into Full Communion	465
First Communions	2,402
Confirmations	1,219
Marriages:	
Catholic	309
Interfaith	424
Total Marriages	733
Deaths	631
Total Catholic Population	110,302
Total Population	3,715,535

Former Bishops—Most Rev. MICHAEL J. BEGLEY, ord. May 26, 1934; appt. Nov. 30, 1971; cons. first Bishop of Charlotte Jan. 12, 1972; resigned 1984.—Most Rev. JOHN F. DONOGHUE, ord. June 4, 1955; appt. Nov. 6, 1984; cons. Dec. 18, 1984; appt. Archbishop of Atlanta June 22, 1993; cons. Aug. 19, 1993.

Vicar General In Curia—Very Rev. MAURICIO W. WEST, *P.O. Box 36776, Charlotte, 28236.* Tel: 704-377-6871.

Chancery—*P.O. Box 36776, Charlotte, 28236.* Tel: 704-377-6871; 331-1702; Fax: 704-358-1208.

Chancellor—Very Rev. MAURICIO W. WEST, *P.O. Box 36776, Charlotte, 28236.* Tel: 704-377-6871.

Vice Chancellor—Deacon CURTISS P. TODD, *P.O. Box 36776, Charlotte, 28236.* Tel: 704-331-1727.

Secretary to the Bishop—Rev. ANTHONY J. MARCACCIO.

Fiscal Manager—WILLIAM G. WELDON, C.P.A., *P.O. Box 36776, Charlotte, 28236.* Tel: 704-331-1726.

Controller—TRACY CLARK, *P.O. Box 36776, Charlotte, 28236.* Tel: 704-331-1707.

Diocesan Properties—Deacon GUY A. PICHE, Dir., *P.O. Box 36776, Charlotte, 28236.* Tel: 704-331-1704.

Employee Benefits—TERRI WILHELM, Coord., *P.O. Box 36776, Charlotte, 28236.* Tel: 704-331-1724.

Diocesan Tribunal—*1524 E. Morehead St., Charlotte, 28207.* Tel: 704-331-1708.

Judicial Vicar—Rev. PETER J. JUGIS, J.C.D.; MARY L. HILDRETH, Dir., *1524 E. Morehead St., Charlotte, 28207.*

Diocesan Consultors—Very. Rev. MAURICIO W. WEST, V.G.; Rev. Msgr. JOSEPH S. SHOWFETY; Rev. Msgr. RICHARD ALLEN; Revs. JAMES DEVEREUX; PETER J. JUGIS; M. JOSEPH KELLEHER.

Vicars—Asheville: Very Rev. JOHN SCHNEIDER, V.F., Boone: Very Rev. ROLAND HAUTZ, Glmy., Charlotte: Very Rev. EDWARD J. SHERIDAN, V.F., Gastonia: Very Rev. PETER J. JUGIS, V.F., Greensboro: Very Rev. JAMES P. O'NEILL, O.S.F.S., V.F., Hickory: Very Rev. WILBUR N. THOMAS, V.F., Albemarle: Very Rev. THOMAS P. CLEMENTS, V.F., Smoky Mountains: Very Rev. JAMES P. CAHILL, V.F., Winston-Salem: Very Rev. JOSEPH M. KELLEHER, V.F.

Vicar for Priests—Vacant.

Diocesan Offices and Directors

Apostleship of Prayer—Rev. EUGENE MCCREESH, S.J., *St. Peter Church, 507 S. Tryon St., Charlotte, 28202.* Tel: 704-332-2901.

Archives—JOHANNA MIMS, Dir., *1524 E. Morehead St., Charlotte, 28207.* Tel: 704-377-6871; Fax: 704-358-1208.

Boy Scouts—Deacon JAMES R. JOHNSON, *St. Charles Borromeo Church, 714 W. Union St., Morganton, 28655.* Tel: 704-437-3221; 437-3461.

Campus Ministry—Rev. JAMES HAWKER, Interim Dir., *3104 Park Rd., Charlotte, 28209.* Tel: 704-523-2157; Fax: 704-523-3413.

Communications—JOANN KEANE, Dir., *1524 E. Morehead St., Charlotte, 28207.* Tel: 704-331-1731; Fax: 704-377-0842.

Office of Faith Formation—Dr. CRIS VILLAPANDO, Dir., *3104 Park Rd., Charlotte, 28207.* Tel: 704-523-2118;

Fax: 704-523-3413.
Campaign for Human Development—Vacant; Coord.
Justice and Peace—JOANNE FRAZIER, Coord., *1524 E. Morehead St., Charlotte, 28207.* Tel: 704-331-1736; Fax: 704-358-1208.
Youth Ministry—PAUL KOTLOWSKI.

Charismatic Renewal Services—Vacant, *1524 E. Morehead St., Charlotte, 28207.* Tel: 704-377-6871.

Cursillo—Rev. Msgr. ANTHONY KOVACIC, Dir.

Development—JAMES K. KELLEY, Dir. BARBARA ROHRMAN, Assoc. Dir., *1524 E. Morehead St., Charlotte, 28207.* Tel: 704-331-1709; 1710; Fax: 704-358-1208.

Evangelization—Rev. EDWARD VILKAUSKAS, C.S.Sp., Dir., *1621 Dilworth Rd. E., Charlotte, 28203.* Tel: 704-334-1805; 334-2283.

Foundation of the Roman Catholic Diocese of Charlotte, Inc., The—JAMES KELLEY, Exec. Dir., *1524 E. Morehead St., Charlotte, 28207.* Tel: 704-331-1709.

Hispanic Ministry—Rev. VINCENT H. FINNERTY, C.M., Diocesan Dir., *Centro Catolico Hispano, 2117 Shenandoah Ave., Charlotte, 28205-6021.* Tel: 704-335-1281; 527-6745.

Holy Childhood Association—Rev. Msgr. ANTHONY KOVACIC, Dir., *1524 E. Morehead St., Charlotte, 28207.* Tel: 704-377-6871; Fax: 704-358-1208.

Home Missions—Rev. ANTHONY KOVACIC, *1524 E. Morehead St., Charlotte, 28207.* Tel: 704-377-6871; Fax: 704-358-1208.

Human Resources—CURTISS P. TODD, Dir. TERRI WILHELM, Assoc., *1524 E. Morehead St., Charlotte, 28207.* Tel: 704-331-1727; 331-1724; Fax: 704-358-1208.

Korean Catholic Cultural Center—Rev. JAE YEONG (CHOI), Dir., *7101 Robinson Church Rd., Charlotte, 28215.* Tel: 704-531-8417.

Lay Ministry—Sr. M. TIMOTHY WARREN, R.S.M., Dir., *1621 Dilworth Rd., E., Charlotte, 28203.* Tel: 704-334-1805; 334-2283.

African-American Ministry—Deacon CURTISS P. TODD, Coord., *1524 E. Morehead St., Charlotte, 28236.* Tel: 704-377-6871.

Media Resource Center & Telecommunications—GAIL HUNT VIOLETTE, Dir., *1524 E. Morehead, Charlotte, 28207.* Tel: 704-331-1717.

Cathedral Publishing Corporation—Mailing Address: P.O. Box 37267, Charlotte, 28237. Tel: 704-377-6871. *1524 E. Morehead, Charlotte, 28207.* Tel: 704-331-1717.

Newspaper: "Catholic News & Herald"—MICHAEL KROKOS, Editor, *P.O. Box 37267, Charlotte, 28237.* Tel: 704-331-1713; Fax: 704-377-0842.

Permanent Diaconate—Very Rev. MAURICIO W. WEST, V.G., *P.O. Box 36776, Charlotte, 28236.* Tel: 704-377-6871; Fax: 704-358-1208.

Planning—GEORGE COBB, Dir., *1524 E. Morehead St., Charlotte, 28207.* Tel: 704-331-1721; Fax: 704-258-1208.

Propagation of the Faith—Rev. Msgr. ANTHONY KOVACIC, *1524 E. Morehead St., Charlotte, 28207.* Tel: 704-377-6871; Fax: 704-358-1208.

St. Vincent de Paul—ELIZABETH THURBEE, A.C.S.W., *1524 E. Morehead St., Charlotte, 28207.*

School—MICHAEL F. SKUBE, Ed.D., Supt. of Schools, *3104 Park Rd., Charlotte, 28209.* Tel: 704-523-2157; Fax: 704-523-3413.

Mecklenburg Area Catholic Schools—Dr. CHARLES LEBLANC, Reg. Supt., *1524 E. Morehead St., Charlotte, 28207.* Tel: 704-335-1334; Fax: 704-335-1580.

Presbyteral Council—Most Rev. WILLIAM G. CURLIN, D.D.; Very Rev. MAURICIO W. WEST, V.G.; Rev. Msgr. RICHARD ALLEN; Rev. Msgr. JOSEPH S. SHOWFETY; Revs. RICHARD BELLOW, O.F.M.Conv.; FRANCIS T. CANCRO; JAMES DEVEREUX, S.J.; PAUL Q. GARY; PETER J. JUGIS; JOSEPH KELLEHER; DENNIS R. KUHN; BERNARD A. MANLEY; ANTHONY MARCACCIO; KIERAN NIELSON, O.S.B.; FRANCIS J. O'ROURKE; JAMES W. O'NEILL, O.S.F.S.; JOHN W. SCHNEIDER; WILBUR N. THOMAS; EDWARD VILKAUSKAS, C.S.Sp., *1524 E. Morehead St., Charlotte, 28207.*

Social Services—ELIZABETH THURBEE, A.C.S.W., Diocesan Dir., *1524 E. Morehead St., Charlotte, 28207.* Tel: 704-331-1720.

Vietnamese Apostolate—*c/o St. Ann Church, 3635 Park Rd., Charlotte, 28209.* Tel: 704-529-0553. Rev. TAN VAN LE, Chap.

Vocations—Rev. FRANCIS J. O'ROURKE, Dir., *P.O. Box 130, Clemmons, 27012.* Tel: 910-766-1882; Fax: 910-766-1882.

Worship—Rev. KENNETH WHITTINGTON, *714 W. Union St., Morganton, 28655.* Tel: 704-437-3108.

CLERGY, PARISHES, MISSIONS AND PAROCHIAL SCHOOLS

CITY OF CHARLOTTE
(Mecklenburg County)

1—ST. PATRICK CATHEDRAL. (Phelan Memorial). Revs. Paul Q. Gary; Thomas Williamson; Deacon Nicholas Fadero.
Res., 1621 Dilworth Rd., E., 28203. Tel: 704-334-2283; Fax: 704-377-6403.
Catechesis/Religious Programs—Students 137.

2—OUR LADY OF THE ASSUMPTION, Rev. Francis J. Gillespie, S.J.; Deacons Stephen J. Horai; Peter Duca.
Res., 4207 Shamrock Dr., 28215. Tel: 704-535-9965; 535-9970; Fax: 704-535-3621.
Catechesis/Religious Programs—Michael S. Hjellming, C.R.E., Tel: 704-535-3310.
Students 275.

3—OUR LADY OF CONSOLATION, Rev. Cecil W. Tice; Deacon Curtiss P. Todd. In res., Rev. Damion J. Lynch.
Res., 2301 Statesville Ave., 28206-2491. Tel: 704-375-4339; Fax: 704-375-8039.
Catechesis/Religious Programs—Tel: 704-344-0821.
Students 109.

4—ST. ANN, Rev. Msgr. Richard F. Allen; Revs. John D. Hanic; Tan Van Le.
Church—3635 Park Rd., 28209. Tel: 704-523-4641.
Res., 632 Hillside Ave., 28209.
Catechesis/Religious Programs—Tel: 704-523-0122.
Students 165.
Convent—3452 Willow Oak Rd., 28209. Tel: 704-523-0331.

5—ST. GABRIEL, Very Rev. Edward J. Sheridan; Revs. Leigh Fuller, S.J.; Dennis R. Kuhn; Deacons Bernard Wenning; Fred Dobens; Robert Gettlefinger.
Res., 3016 Providence Rd., 28211. Tel: 704-364-5431; Fax: 704-362-5049.
Catechesis/Religious Programs—Susan Krasniewski, D.R.E., Tel: 704-366-2738.
Students 936.

6—ST. JOHN NEUMANN, Revs. Richard M. Bellow, O.F.M.Conv.; Carmelo V. Malacari, O.F.M.Conv.; Deacons Neil Chirico; Joseph Mack.
Res., 8451 Idlewild Rd., 28227. Tel: 704-536-6520; Fax: 704-536-3147.
Catechesis/Religious Programs—Tel: 704-535-4197.
Students 734.

7—ST LUKE, Rev. Joseph V. Mulligan.
Res., 13700 Lawyers Rd., 28227. Tel: 704-545-1224; Fax: 704-545-7288.
Catechesis/Religious Programs—Tel: 704-545-0065.
Students 231.

8—ST. MATTHEW, Revs. Edmund Walker, O.F.M. Cap.; Stephen Hoyt, O.F.M. Cap.; Bro. Jesu "Jay" Perez, O.F.M. Cap., Pastoral Assoc.; Sr. Jeanne Marie Kienast, R.S.M., Pastoral Assoc.; Deacons James Hamrlik; Keith Kolodzies.
Office: 8015 Ballantyne Commons Pkwy., 28277. Tel: 704-543-7677; Fax: 704-542-7244.
Res., 5725 Providence Rd., W., 28277. Tel: 704-846-6311.
Catechesis/Religious Programs—Tel: 704-541-8362; Fax: 704-542-7244.
Students 1184.

9—ST. PETER, Revs. James A. Devereux, S.J.; Eugene P. McCreesh, S.J. In res., Rev. Robert J. Paquet, S.J.
Res., 507 S. Tryon St., 28202. Tel: 704-372-6808; Fax: 704-358-0050.
Catechesis/Religious Programs—Tel: 704-332-2901; Fax: 704-358-0050.
Students 90.

10—ST. THOMAS AQUINAS, Revs. Ignatius Zampino, O.F.M.Cap.; Thomas Crangle, O.F.M.Cap.; Miriam Ficconi, Pastoral Assoc.
Res., 1400 Suther Rd., 28213. Tel: 704-549-1607; Fax: 704-549-1614.
Catechesis/Religious Programs—Sr. Carol L. Bennett, O.S.F., D.R.E.
Students 1082.

11—ST. VINCENT DE PAUL, Rev. Msgr. William N. Pharr; Rev. Richard N. Hanson; Deacons Kurt Fohn; Gerald P. Hickey. In res., Rev. Gordon Pillon.
Res., 6828 Old Reid Rd., 28210. Tel: 704-554-7088; Fax: 704-554-0490.
Catechesis/Religious Programs—Tel: 704-554-1622; Fax: 704-554-0490. Joan Mahony, D.R.E.
Students 135.

OUTSIDE THE CITY OF CHARLOTTE

Albemarle, Stanly Co., Our Lady of the Annunciation, Rev. Joseph Ayathupadam.
Res., 416 N. Second St., 28001. Tel: 704-982-2910.
Catechesis/Religious Programs—Barbara Newkirk, D.R.E.
Students 108.
Mission—Biscoe, Montgomery Co., Our Lady of the Americas, 105 Hyde St., P.O. Box 1187, Biscoe, 27209. Tel: 910-428-3051. Rev. Gerardo R. Clarke, O.S.F.S., Admin.

Andrews, Cherokee Co., Holy Redeemer, Rev. James J. Wilmes.
Res., 32 Aquone Rd., P.O. Box 698, 28901. Tel: 704-321-4463.
Mission—Robbinsville, Graham Co., Prince of Peace.
Catechesis/Religious Programs—Students 10.

Arden, Buncombe Co., St. Barnabas, Very Rev. John W. Schneider; Deacon Arthur J. Kingsley.
Mailing Address: P.O. Box 38, 28704. Tel: 704-684-6098; Fax: 704-684-6152.
Res., 4 Pointview Ct., 28704. Tel: 704-684-5343.
Catechesis/Religious Programs—Miss Sheryl Peyton, D.R.E.
Students 290.

Asheboro, Randolph Co., St. Joseph, Rev. Joseph W. Mack.
Res., 326 S. Park St., 27203. Tel: 910-629-0221.

Asheville, Buncombe Co., Basilica of St. Lawrence, Rev. Msgr. John J. McSweeney.
Res., 97 Haywood St., 28801. Tel: 704-252-6042; Fax: 704-254-0414.
Catechesis/Religious Programs—Mrs. Karen Ascik, D.R.E.
Students 124.

St. Eugene, Rev. Francis T. Cancro; Deacons Joseph Vandermeer, Pastoral Assoc.; Lou Rinkus, Prison Ministry.
Mailing Address: P.O. Box 8160, 28814. Tel: 704-254-5193; Fax: 704-254-5797.
Office: One Culvern St., 28814.
Catechesis/Religious Programs—Ms. Vicki Fedor, D.R.E.
Students 345.

St. Joan of Arc, Rev. C. Morris Boyd.
Res., 919 Haywood Rd., 28806. Tel: 704-252-3151.
Catechesis/Religious Programs—Mary Ann Poli, D.R.E.
Students 120.

Belmont, Gaston Co., Queen of the Apostles, Very Rev. Peter J. Jugis, J.C.D.; Deacon Guy Piche.
Res., 503 N. Main St., 28012. Tel: 704-825-5277.
Catechesis/Religious Programs—Students 241.
Mission—Spencer Mountain, St. Helen.

Boone, Watauga Co., St. Elizabeth, Rev. Conrad Hoover.
Office: 259 Pilgrim's Way, 28607. Tel: 704-264-8338; 264-6347; Fax: 704-262-3721.
Res., 199 Highland Ave., Apt. 1, 28607. Tel: 704-264-4503.
Catechesis/Religious Programs—Carol Brown, D.R.E.
Students 110.
Mission—Blowing Rock, Epiphany.

Brevard, Transylvania Co., Sacred Heart, Rev. Carl Del Giudice.
Res., 4 Fortune Cove, 28712. Tel: 704-883-9572.
Catechesis/Religious Programs—Students 108.
Mission—Sapphire Valley, Transylvania Co., St. Jude, P.O. Box 543, Highlands, 28741. Tel: 704-526-2418.

Bryson City, Swain Co., St. Joseph, Rev. Thomas E. Field, Glmy.
Res., P.O. Box 727, 28713. Tel: 704-488-6766.
Catechesis/Religious Programs—Students 30.
Mission—Cherokee, Our Lady of Guadalupe.

Clemmons, Forsyth Co., Holy Family, Revs. Francis J. O'Rourke; Fidel Melo; Deacons Gerard Schumacher; Michael Langsdorf.
Res., 2890 Knobb Hill Dr., P.O. Box 130, 27012. Tel: 910-766-1882; Fax: 910-766-8133.
Catechesis/Religious Programs—Tel: 910-766-8189. Marcy Boyer, D.F.F.; Mary Langsdorf, Coord., Youth Ministry.
Students 566.
Mission—Yadkinville, Yadkin Co., Cristo Rey Catholic Hispanic Center of Yadkin Valley, U.S. Hwy. 601 & Hoot Rd., P.O. Box 788, Yadkinville, 27055. Tel: 910-463-5533. Sr. Andrea Inkrott, O.S.F., Coord.

Concord, Cabarrus Co., St. James, Revs. Daniel J. Carboy, C.SS.R.; Francis Sands, C.SS.R.; Karl Aschmann, C.SS.R.; Deacon J. Daniel Carl.
Mailing Address: P.O. Box 123, 28026. Tel: 704-786-9131; Fax: 704-786-5412.
Res., 251 Union St., N., 28025.
Catechesis/Religious Programs—Cecelia Rouse, D.R.E.
Students 400.
Mission—Kannapolis, St. Joseph, Tel: 704-932-4607.

Eden, Rockingham Co., St. Joseph of the Hills, Sr. Bernadette McNamara, R.S.M., Parochial Admin.; Deacon Gerald W. Potkay.
Res., 316 Boone Rd., 27288. Tel: 910-623-2661.
Catechesis/Religious Programs—Students 52.

Forest City, Rutherford Co., Immaculate Conception, Rev. Gabriel Meehan; Deacon Andrew Cilone.
Res., 940 W. Main St., 28043. Tel: 704-245-4017.
Catechesis/Religious Programs—Students 85.

Franklin, Macon Co., St. Francis of Assisi, Revs. Richard T. McCue; James M. Collins.
Res., 150 Maple St., 28734. Tel: 704-524-2289.
Catechesis/Religious Programs—Tel: 704-369-8131. D.R.E.: Sharon Edwards; Ron Brahmer.
Students 95.
Mission—Highlands, Macon Co., Our Lady of the Mountains, P.O. Box 543, Highlands, 28741. Tel: 704-526-2418.

Gastonia, Gaston County, St. Michael, Rev. George M. Kloster.
Res., 708 St. Michael's Ln., 28052. Tel: 704-853-8808.
Church—Tel: 704-867-6212; Fax: 704-867-6379.
School—Tel: 704-865-4382.
Lay Teachers 14; Students 241.
Catechesis/Religious Programs—Students 325.

Greensboro, Guilford Co.,

1—OUR LADY OF GRACE. (Ethel Clay Price Memorial). Revs. Mark Lamprich, M.I.C.; David Lord, M.I.C.; Waldek Ziolkowski, M.I.C. (Poland); Deacons Timothy Rohan; Paul Teich.
Res., 2205 W. Market St., 27403. Tel: 910-274-6520; 275-5376; Fax: 910-274-7326.
School—Tel: 910-275-1522. Roberta Hutchcraft, Prin.
Lay Teachers 26; Students 455.
Catechesis/Religious Programs—James D. McCullough, D.R.E.
Students 307.

2—ST. BENEDICT, Rev. Msgr. Joseph S. Showfety; Deacon Philip Killian.
Res., 109 W. Smith St., 27401. Tel: 910-272-0303.
Catechesis/Religious Programs—Students 18.

3—ST. MARY, Revs. Robert J. Prior, C.M.; Manh H. Nguyen, C.M.; Deacon Vincent Shaw. In res., Rev. Vincent H. Finnerty, C.M.
Mailing Address: P.O. Box 21012, 27420.
Res., 812 Duke St., 27401. Tel: 910-272-8650; Fax: 910-274-5396.
Social Ministry Office—Tel: 910-275-8377.
St. Vincent de Paul Office—Tel: 910-272-0336.
Catechesis/Religious Programs—Students 130.

4—ST. PAUL THE APOSTLE, Very Rev. James W. O'Neill, O.S.F.S.; Revs. Bob Bazzoli, O.S.F.S.; John Gilvey, O.S.F.S.; Deacons Gordon L. Forester; William Shaw.
Res., 2715 Horsepen Creek Rd., 27410. Tel: 910-294-6160; 294-4696 (Office); Fax: 910-294-6149.
Catechesis/Religious Programs—Students 864.

5—ST. PIUS X, Rev. Francis T. Connolly; Sr. Phyllis Tierney, S.S.J., M.S.W., Pastoral Assoc. In res., Rev. Louis Canino, O.F.M.
Office: 2210 N. Elm St., 27408. Tel: 910-272-4681; 272-8598; Fax: 910-274-8112.
School—Tel: 910-273-9865; Fax: 910-273-0199. Mrs. Sue Geraghty, Prin.
Lay Teachers 20; Students 374.
Catechesis/Religious Programs—Students 180.
Convent—19-A Fountain Manor Dr., 27405. Tel: 910-275-5915; Fax: 910-275-5915.
Daughters of Charity 3.
Franciscan Center—233 N. Greene St., 27401. Tel: 910-273-2554.
Catholic Campus Connection (Thea House)—1009 Bluford St., 27401. Tel: 910-272-5868.

Hamlet, Richmond Co., St. James, Rev. Robert Spangenberg, C.S.Sp.
Mailing Address: P.O. Box 1208, 28345. Tel: 910-582-0207; 582-8776 (Rectory).
Catechesis/Religious Programs—Ann Peters, D.R.E.
Students 44.
Mission—Wadesboro, Anson Co., Sacred Heart, P.O. Box 1123, Wadesboro, 28170. Tel: 704-694-5183.

Hendersonville, Henderson Co., Immaculate Conception, Revs. John C. Aurilia, O.F.M.Cap.; Alfonso Pagliara, O.F.M.Cap.
Parish Office: 229 Sixth Ave., W., 28739-4305. Tel: 704-693-6901; Fax: 704-697-1656.
Res., 717 Buncombe St., 28791-3609. Tel: 704-692-0550.
School—Immaculata, 711 Buncombe St., 28739. Tel: 704-693-3277. Sr. Judith McKenna, Prin.
Sisters of the Holy Cross 2; Lay Teachers 17; Students 200.
Catechesis/Religious Programs—Lauretta Franz, D.R.E.
Students 175.
Convent—2 Springside Dr., 28792. Tel: 704-692-1399.

Hickory, Catawba Co., St. Aloysius, Rev. William H. Tanguay; Deacons Joseph E. Garavaglia; Hugo L. May; Thomas A. Rasmussen. In res., Very Rev. Wilbur N. Thomas, V.F.; Rev. William H. Tanguay (RI).
Res., 902 Second St., N.E., 28601. Tel: 704-327-2341; Fax: 704-327-3376.
Catechesis/Religious Programs—Sr. Mary Norman Woodend, C.L.H.C., D.R.E.
Students 511.

High Point, Guilford Co., Immaculate Heart of Mary, Revs. Joseph C. Zuschmidt, O.S.F.S.; Thomas P. Norris, O.S.F.S.; Deacons Thomas Kak; Joseph T. Smith.
Res., 512 Montlieu Ave., 27262. Tel: 910-884-5212; Fax: 910-884-1849.
School—Tel: 910-887-2613; Fax: 910-884-1849. Frank McGrail, Prin.
Sisters 1; Lay Teachers 15; Students 260.
Catechesis/Religious Programs—Tel: 910-885-5210. Sr. Mary Sheehan, S.M.G., D.R.E.
Students 279.
Christ the King, Rev. Philip Kollithanath.
Res., 1505 Kivett Dr., 27260. Tel: 910-884-0244; Fax: 910-887-1200.

Jefferson, Ashe Co., St. Francis of Assisi, Very Rev. Roland Hautz, Glmy.
Mailing Address: P.O. Box 1, 28640. Tel: 910-246-9151.
Res., Tel: 910-246-5925.
Catechesis/Religious Programs—Students 76.
Mission—Sparta, Alleghany Co., St. Frances of Rome, P.O. Box 935, Sparta, 28675. Tel: 910-372-2119; 372-8846. Bro. Ken Woods, Glmy.

Kernersville, Forsyth Co., Holy Cross, Rev. Thomas J. Fitzpatrick, O.S.F.S.
Res., 616 S. Cherry St., 27284. Tel: 910-996-5109; Fax: 910-996-5115.
Child Developmental Center—Tel: 910-996-5144; Fax: 910-996-5115. Maria Rosato, Dir.
Catechesis/Religious Programs—Tel: 910-996-5109; Fax: 910-996-5115. Louise Hiatt, D.R.E.
Students 163.

Lenoir, Caldwell Co., St. Francis of Assisi, Rev. Michael Buttner; Deacon Ronald Caplette.
Res., 1025 College Ave., S.W., 28645-5433. Tel: 704-754-5281; Fax: 704-754-5281.
Catechesis/Religious Programs—Students 76.
Mission—Taylorsville, Alexander Co., Holy Trinity, Hwy. 90 W., 655 W. Main Ave., Taylorsville, 28681. Tel: 704-632-8009. In res., Rev. Joseph Waters.

Lexington, Davidson Co., Our Lady of the Rosary, Very Rev. M. Joseph Kelleher; Deacon Edward Morovich.
Res., 619 S. Main St., 27292. Tel: 910-246-2463.
Catechesis/Religious Programs—Students 85.

Lincolnton, Lincoln Co., St. Dorothy, Rev. Richard B. Farwell.
Res., 148 St. Dorothy Ln., 28092. Tel: 704-735-5575.
Catechesis/Religious Programs—Students 100.

Maggie Valley, Haywood Co., St. Margaret, Rev. Eric Houseknecht, Admin.; Deacon Robert Dotson. In res., Rev. James M. Byer.
Mailing Address: P.O. Box 1359, 28751. Tel: 704-926-0106.
Res., 1422 Soco Rd., 28751. Tel: 704-926-0025.

Mars Hill, Madison Co., St. Andrew the Apostle, Rev. Edward M. Ifkovits, S.J.; Sr. Margaret Verstege, R.S.M., Pastoral Assoc.
Mailing Address: P.O. Box 947, 28754. Tel: 704-689-3719; 649-2781.
Res. & Church—100 W. Brook St., 28754.
Missions—Burnsville, Yancey Co., Sacred Heart; Hot Springs, Madison Co., Chapel of the Redeemer. Jesuit House of Prayer. P.O. Box 7, Hot Springs, 28743. Tel: 704-622-7366. Revs. Vincent Alagia, S.J.; Joseph McGovern, S.J.
Catechesis/Religious Programs—Students 31.

Mocksville, Davie Co., St. Francis of Assisi, Sr. M. Anita Sherin, R.S.M., Parochial Admin.
Mailing Address: P.O. Box 642, 27028. Tel: 704-634-2973.
Church—862 Yadkinville Rd., 27028.
Catechesis/Religious Programs—Students 57.

Monroe, Union Co., Our Lady of Lourdes, Revs. Edward J. Vilkauskas, C.S.Sp.; Vincent J. Donovan, C.S.Sp.
Res., 725 Deese St., 28112. Tel: 704-289-2773; Fax: 704-283-7210.
Catechesis/Religious Programs—Tel: 704-289-2773; Fax: 704-283-7210.
Students 178.

Mooresville, Iredell Co., St. Therese, Revs. Robert D. Wiesenbaugh, S.J.; James V. Keogh, S.J.; William J. Lynch, S.J.
Res., 217 Brawley School Rd., 28115-1364. Tel: 704-664-3992.
Mission—Denver, Lincoln Co., Holy Spirit, 537 N. Hwy. 16, Denver, 28037-9235. Tel: 704-483-6638. Rev. Conrad L. Kimbrough, Admin.
Catechesis/Religious Programs—Students 455.

Morganton, Burke Co., St. Charles Borromeo, Revs. Kenneth L. Whittington; John J. Murray, Pastor Emeritus; Deacons James R. Johnson; John J. Gallen.
Res., 714 W. Union St., 28655. Tel: 704-437-3108;704-437-6262.
Catechesis/Religious Programs—Terri Martino, D.R.E.
Students 188.
Mission—Marion, McDowell Co, Our Lady of the Angels. Rev. Jerome Aung Shwe (Burma).

Mt. Airy, Surry Co., Holy Angels, Rev. Thomas D. Stott.
Res., 1208 N. Main St., 27030. Tel: 910-786-8147; Fax: 910-786-1968.
Mission—Dobson, Sacred Heart.
Catechesis/Religious Programs—Mrs. Gloria Bunn, D.R.E.
Students 67.

Murphy, Cherokee Co., St. William, Rev. Edmund D. Kirsch.
Res., 109 Andrews Rd., P.O. Box 546, 28906. Tel: 704-837-2000.
Mission—Hayesville, Clay Co., Immaculate Heart of Mary.
Catechesis/Religious Programs—Students 34.

Newton, Catawba Co., St. Joseph, Rev. Richard P. Hokanson (WOR) Admin.; Deacon Harold Markle.
Church—720 W. 13th St., 28658-3899. Tel: 704-464-9207.
Holy Family Parish Center—Tel: 704-465-2878.
Catechesis/Religious Programs—Tel: 704-465-2878.
Students 135.

North Wilkesboro, Wilkes Co., St. John Baptist de LaSalle, Rev. Francis M. Cintula; Deacon Frank Aversa.
Res., 275 C.C. Wright School Rd., 28659. Tel: 910-838-5562.
Catechesis/Religious Programs—Students 112.
Mission—Elkin, Surry Co., St. Stephen, 101 Hawthorne, Elkin, 28621. Tel: 910-835-3007.

Reidsville, Rockingham Co., Holy Infant, Rev. Joseph R. Valentine, Admin.
Res., 1042 Freeway Dr., P.O. Box 1197, 27323. Tel: 910-342-1448.
Catechesis/Religious Programs—Students 100.

Salisbury, Rowan Co., Sacred Heart, Very Rev. Thomas P. Clements; Rev. Samuel W. Orlando; Deacon Patrick Vallandingham.
Res., 128 N. Fulton St., 28144. Tel: 704-633-0591; Fax: 704-647-0126.
School—Tel: 704-633-2841. Sr. Mary John Madden, Prin.
Sisters of Mercy 2; Lay Teachers 24; Students 270.
Convent—425 W. Council St., 28144. Tel: 704-636-4070; Fax: 704-636-2564. Sisters of Mercy
Catechesis/Religious Programs—Tel: 704-638-0172.
Students 160.

Shelby, Cleveland Co., St. Mary's, Rev. Msgr. Carl E. Kaltreider.
Res., 818 McGowan Rd., 28150. Tel: 704-484-3241.
Mission—Kings Mountain, Cleveland Co., Christ the King, 714 Stone St., Kings Mountain, 28086. Tel: 704-739-3214.
Catechesis/Religious Programs—D.R.E.: Ron Maskarinec; Helen Turpish; Ann Marie Bridges.
Students 145.

Spruce Pine, Mitchell Co., St. Lucien, Rev. Aloysius J. D'Silva.
Res., 503 Summit St., P.O. Box 688, 28777. Tel: 704-765-2224.
Mission—Linville, Avery Co., St. Bernadette, P.O. Box 1252, Linville, 28646. Tel: 704-898-6900.
Catechesis/Religious Programs—Students 40.

Statesville, Iredell Co., St. Philip the Apostle, Rev. Paul L. Fitzgibbons; Deacon Charles Brantley.
Mailing Address: P.O. Box 882, 28687-0882. Tel: 704-873-8641.
Office: Tel: 704-872-2579; Fax: 704-872-2579.
Res., 525 Camden Dr., 28677.
Catechesis/Religious Programs—Tel: 704-872-2579; Fax: 704-872-2579.
Students 204.

Swannanoa, Buncombe Co., St. Margaret Mary, Rev. Andrew J. Latsko.
Res., 102 Andrews Pl., Box 98, 28778. Tel: 704-686-3243.

Sylva, Jackson Co., St. Mary, Very Rev. James P. Cahill.
Res., 22 Bartlett St., 28779. Tel: 704-586-9496.
Catechesis/Religious Programs—Tel: 704-586-9496.
Students 86.

Thomasville, Davidson Co., Our Lady of the Highways, Rev. John B. Murphy, O.S.F.S.
Res., 943 Ball Park Rd., 27360. Tel: 910-475-2732;

Fax: 910-476-3337.
Catechesis/Religious Programs—Tel: 910-475-2732; Fax: 910-476-3337.
Students 75.

Tryon, Polk Co., St. John the Baptist, Rev. Lawrence W. Heiney (HBG); Deacon Bruce H. Haslett.
Mailing Address: P.O. Box 1597, 28782.
Res., 600 Laurel Ave., 28782. Tel: 704-859-9574; Fax: 704-859-5932.
Catechesis/Religious Programs—Students 41.

Waynesville, Haywood Co., St. John the Evangelist, Rev. Raymond B. Hourihan.
Res., 409 Church St., 28786. Tel: 704-456-6707.
Catechesis/Religious Programs—Students 60.
Mission—Canton, Haywood Co., Immaculate Conception.

Winston-Salem, Forsyth Co., Our Lady of Mercy, Rev. Conall McHugh, O.F.M.Conv. In res., Revs. Michael McCaffrey, O.F.M.Conv.; Edgar Holden, O.F.M.Conv.; George Sullivan, O.F.M.Conv.; Deacons Joseph Schumacher; Pedro Herran.
Res., 1910 S. Main St., 27127. Tel: 910-724-6806; Fax: 910-768-8292.
School—Tel: 910-722-7204; Fax: 910-725-2294. Sandra McMonagle, Prin.
Sisters of St. Joseph 2; Lay Teachers 17; Students 276.
Convent—1922 S. Main St., 27127. Tel: 910-727-0925.
Mission—Winston-Salem, Forsyth Co., Our Lady of Fatima, 211 W. 3rd St., Winston-Salem, 27101. Tel: 910-723-8238.
Catechesis/Religious Programs—Students 178.

St. Benedict the Moor, Rev. Lawrence J. Hunt, S.J.
Res., 1625 E. Twelfth St., 27101. Tel: 910-725-9200; Fax: 910-777-1062.
Mission—King, Stokes Co., Good Shepherd, P.O. Box 1149, King, 27021. Tel: 910-725-9200; Fax: 910-777-1062.
Catechesis/Religious Programs—Students 117.

St. Leo's, Revs. James K. Solari; Mark Lawlor; Deacons Dennis O'Madigan; Robert DeSautels; Rev. Thomas O'Connell.
Res., 406 Springdale Ave., 27104. Tel: 910-724-5314.
Church—335 Springdale Ave., 27104. Tel: 910-724-0561; Fax: 910-724-7036.
School—333 Springdale Ave., 27104. Tel: 910-748-8252; Fax: 910-748-9005.
Sisters of St. Joseph 2; Lay Teachers 18; Students 296.
Catechesis/Religious Programs—Students 290.
Convent—1975 Georgia Ave., 27104. Tel: 910-723-3639.

Special Assignment:
Reverend Fathers—
Hoover, John P.
Marcaccio, Anthony J., Sec. to Bishop
West, Mauricio W., Vicar Gen. & Chancellor

On Duty Outside the Diocese:
Reverend Fathers—
Farrell, William, Diocese of Ogdensburg, NY
Marecki, Ronald A., Diocese of Rochester, NY
Pagel, John M., Diocese of San Antonio, TX
Tarasi, Carlo D., Diocese of Trenton, NJ
Wilderotter, Paul C., Diocese of Charleston, SC

Graduate Studies:
Reverend Fathers—
Putnam, John T., Jr., Catholic University, Washington

Military Chaplains:
Reverend Fathers—
Fitzgibbons, Peter L., U.S. Army
Klepacki, Michael S., U.S. Navy

Sabbatical:
Reverend Monsignors—
Kerin, Joseph A.

Absent On Leave:
Reverend Fathers—
Baker, Donald P.
Bradley, John Paul
Choquet, Robert M.
Evans, William M.

Retired:
Reverend Monsignors—
Burke, Thomas P., 207 Eagle St., Belmont, NC 28012
Duncan, Arthur L., Maryfield Nursing Home, 1315 Greensboro Rd., High Point, NC 27260
Kelaher, Felix R., 7401 Ashfield Ct., Charlotte, NC 28226
Roueche, John F., St. Joseph of the Pines Hospital, 590 Central Ave., Southern Pines, NC 28387
Wellein, William G., Little Flower Assisted Living, 8700 Lawyers Rd., Charlotte, NC 28227
Reverend Fathers—
Berg, Ramon A., 2500 Morgan Mill Rd., Brevard, NC 28712
Erb, Vincent I., 1001 Easton Rd., Apt. 615, Willow Grove, PA 19090
Gavigan, P. Patrick, 2945 Reynolda Rd., Room 217, Winston-Salem, NC 27106
Lash, Joseph J., 3078 W. 136th St., Cleveland, OH 44111. Tel: 216-476-9610
Manley, Bernard A., 420 Lakeshore Dr., Asheville, NC 28804
McCarthy, Joseph L., Sardis Nursing Home, 5151 Sardis Rd., Charlotte, NC 28270
Morse, Guy E., Teresian House, 200 Washington Ave. Ext., Albany, NY 12203-5394
O'Doherty, Edward, Tubbercurry, Co. Sligo, Ireland
Reese, Charles T., 800 Bay Dr., No. 25, Niceville, FL 32578
Sullivan, D. Edward
Walsh, Thomas R., 12 N. 6th St., Allegany, NY 14706

Permanent Deacons:
Adams, Wayne, Our Lady of the Highways, Thomasville
Aversa, Frank, St. John, N. Wilkesboro
Brantley, Charles, St. Philip the Apostle, Statesville
Burke, John, Sacred Heart, Brevard
Caplette, Ronald, St. Francis of Assisi, Lenoir
Carl, Daniel, St. James, Concord
Chirico, Neil, St. John Neumann, Charlotte
Cilone, Andrew, Immaculate Conception, Forest City
DeSauntels, Charles, St. Leo, Winston-Salem
Dobens, Frederick, St. Gabriel, Charlotte
Dotson, Robert, St. Margaret, Maggie Valley
Duca, Peter, Our Lady of the Assumption, Charlotte
Fadero, Nick, St. Patrick, Charlotte
Fohn, Kurt, St. Vincent De Paul, Charlotte
Forester, Gordon L., St. Paul the Apostle, Greensboro
Garavaglia, Joseph E., St. Aloysius, Hickory
Gettlefinger, Robert, St. Gabriel, Charlotte
Hamrlik, James, St. Matthew, Charlotte
Haslett, Bruce, St. John the Baptizer, Tryon
Herbers, Jerome, St. Mary, Sylva
Herran, Pedro, Our Lady of Mercy, Winston-Salem
Hickey, Gerald P., St. Vincent, Charlotte
Horai, Stephen J., Our Lady of the Assumption, Charlotte
Johnson, James R., St. Charles, Morganton
Kak, Thomas, Immaculate Heart of Mary, High Point
Killian, Philip, Jr., St. Benedict, Greensboro
Kingsley, Arthur, St. Barnabas, Arden
Kolodziej, Keith, St. Matthew, Charlotte
Langsdorf, Michael, Holy Family, Clemmons
Mack, Joseph H., Jr., St. John Neumann, Charlotte
Manning, Franklin L., Sr., Christ the King, High Point
Marini, Anthony, St. William, Murphy
Markle, Harold, St. Joseph, Newton
May, Hugo L., (Retired)
Medina, Carlos, Hispanic Center, Charlotte
Morovich, Edward, (Retired)
O'Connell, Thomas, St. Leo, Winston-Salem
O'Madigan, Dennis T., St. Leo, Winston-Salem
Piche, Guy, Queen of Apostles, Belmont
Pivarnik, William, Immaculate Conception, Hendersonville
Potkay, Gerald, St. Joseph of the Hills, Eden
Rasmussen, Thomas, St. Aloysius, Hickory
Renuart, Albert, Immaculate Conception, Hendersonville
Rinkus, Louis, (Retired)
Rodriguez, Edwin, Hispanic Center, Charlotte
Rohan, Timothy, Our Lady of Grace, Greensboro
Schumacher, Gerard, Holy Family, Clemmons
Schumacher, Joseph N., Our Lady of Mercy, Winston-Salem
Shaw, Vincent, Jr., St. Mary, Greensboro
Shaw, William, St. Paul the Apostle, Greensboro
Sims, John, St. Therese, Mooresville
Smith, Joseph T., Immaculate Heart of Mary, High Point
Steinkamp, Ronald, Our Lady of the Highways, Thomasville
Szalony, George, St. Luke, Charlotte
Teich, Paul, Our Lady of Grace, Greensboro
Todd, Curtiss, Our Lady of Consolation, Charlotte
Torres, Rafael, Hispanic Center, Charlotte
Vallandingham, Patrick, Sacred Heart, Salisbury
Vandermeer, Jos A., St. Eugene, Asheville
Weisenhorn, John, St. Michael, Gastonia
Wenning, Bernard, St. Gabriel, Charlotte

INSTITUTIONS LOCATED IN THE DIOCESE

[A] COLLEGES AND UNIVERSITIES

*BELMONT. *Belmont Abbey College*, 100 Belmont-Mount Holly Rd., 28012-2795. Tel: 704-825-6700; Fax: 704-825-6670.
For a complete listing, refer to the Colleges and Universities section.
Sacred Heart College, 28012. Tel: 704-829-5100; Fax: 704-829-5137.
For a complete listing, refer to the Colleges and Universities section.

[B] HIGH SCHOOLS, INTER-PAROCHIAL

WINSTON-SALEM. *Bishop McGuinness High School*, 1730 Link Rd., 27103. Tel: 910-725-4247; Fax: 910-725-6669. George L. Repass, M.Ed., Prin. Sisters of St. Joseph 4; Brothers 1; Lay Teachers 25; Students 355.

[C] ELEMENTARY SCHOOLS, INTER-PAROCHIAL

ASHEVILLE. *Asheville Catholic School*, 12 Culvern St., 28804. Tel: 704-252-7896. Judith E. Cavallo, Prin. Lay Teachers 18; Students 216.

[D] REGIONAL SCHOOLS

CHARLOTTE. *Mecklenburg Area Catholic Schools (M.A.C.S.)*, 1524 E. Morehead St., 28207. Dr. Charles LeBlanc, Reg. Supt.
Charlotte Catholic High School (Bishop Hafey Memorial), 7702 Matthews-Mint Hill Rd., 28226. Tel: 704-543-1127; Fax: 704-543-1217. Sr. Paulette Williams, R.S.M., Prin.; Rev. Stephen Hoyt, O.F.M. Cap., Chap. Priests 2; Sisters 1; Lay Teachers 56; Students 731.
Charlotte Catholic High School Athletic Association.
Charlotte Catholic High School Alumni Association.
Charlotte Catholic High School Home School Association.
Holy Trinity Middle School, 3100 Park Rd., 28209. Tel: 704-527-7822; Fax: 704-525-7288. Gerald A. Healy, Prin. Lay Teachers 48; Students 840.
All Saints Catholic School, 7100 Endhaven Ln., 28277. Tel: 704-544-2070. Mrs. Betsy Denoyer, Prin. Lay Teachers 37; Students 558.
Our Lady of the Assumption School, 4225 Shamrock Dr., 28215. Tel: 704-531-0067. Mrs. Patricia Murphy, Prin. Lay Teachers 20; Students 238.
St. Ann School, 600 Hillside Ave., 28209. Tel: 704-525-4938. Sr. Helene Nagle, S.S.J., Prin. Lay Teachers 22; Students 315.
St. Gabriel School, 3028 Providence Rd., 28211. Tel: 704-366-2409. Deacon Fred Dobens, Prin. Lay Teachers 30; Students 549.
St. Patrick School, 1125 Buchanan St., 28203. Tel: 704-333-3174. Mr. Joseph Puceta, Prin. Lay Teachers 21; Students 316.

[E] GENERAL HOSPITALS

CHARLOTTE. *Selwyn Life Center at Mercy*, 1921 Vail Ave., 28207. Tel: 704-379-5005.
For a complete listing, refer to the Hospitals section.
ASHEVILLE. *St. Joseph's Health Services Corporation*, 345 Biltmore Ave., 28801.
For a complete listing, refer to the Hospitals section.
St. Joseph's Hospital, 428 Biltmore Ave., 28801. Tel: 704-255-3100.
For a complete listing, refer to the Hospitals section.
St. Joseph's Urgent Care, Inc., 345 Biltmore Ave., 28801. Tel: 704-258-6569.
For a complete listing, refer to the Hospitals section.

[F] SPECIAL CARE FACILITIES

*BELMONT. *Holy Angels, Inc.*, P.O. Box 710, 28012. Tel: 704-825-4161; Fax: 704-825-0553.
For a complete listing, refer to the Special Care Facilities section.

[G] CATHOLIC SOCIAL SERVICES

CHARLOTTE. *Catholic Social Services of the Diocese of Charlotte, Inc.*
The Catholic Center, 1524 E. Morehead St., 28207. Tel: 704-331-1720. Elizabeth K. Thurbee, A.C.S.W., Diocesan Dir.
Area Offices:
Asheville-Smoky Mountain Vicariates, 35 Orange St., Asheville, 28801. Tel: 704-255-0146. Sr. Marie Frechette, M.S.B.T., A.C.S.W., Dir.
Albemarle-Charlotte-Gastonia Vicariates, 116 E. First St., 28202. Tel: 704-343-9954. Geri King, M.S.W., Dir.
Boone-Greensboro-Hickory-Winston-Salem Vicariates. P.O. Box 10962, Winston-Salem, 27108. 621 W. Second St., Winston-Salem, 27101. Tel: 910-727-0705. David W. Harold, A.C.S.W., Dir.

Catholic Social Services Refugee Office, 2217 Eastway Dr., 28205. Tel: 704-568-8806. Cira Ponce, Dir.
Special Ministries:
Adoption. Contact the Domestic Adoption Unit at CSS offices. 704-255-0146, Asheville; 910-727-0505, Winston-Salem. Tel: 704-343-9954, Charlotte.
Adoption International, Asheville. Tel: 704-255-0146. Carol Meyerriecks, M.S.W.
CRISM. Catholic Retirees Invited to Special Ministries, Contact Diocesan Office. Suzanne Bach, Contact Person. Tel: 704-331-1720.
Disaster. Contact the Office of Special Ministries. Tel: 910-922-3628. Gerard Carter, Contact Person.
Engaged Encounter. Contact Diocesan Office. Tel: 704-331-1720. Marlow Wallace, Contact Person; Carl & Mary Shultz, Chm.
Family Life. Contact the Office of Special Ministries. Gerard Carter, Dir. Tel: 910-922-3628.
Hand to Hand. Contact Winston-Salem Office. Tel: 910-727-0705. Connie McVey, Contact Person.
Hispanic/Migrant Outreach. Contact Asheville or Winston-Salem Offices. Tel: 704-255-0146 (Asheville); 910-727-0705 (Winston-Salem).
Host Homes. Contact Winston-Salem Office. Tel: 910-727-0705. Mable Stevenson, Contact Person.
Natural Family Planning. Contact the Diocesan Office. Tel: 704-331-1720. Jay Hamilton, Contact Person.
Prison Ministry. Contact Diocesan Office. Tel: 704-331-1720. Mr. Bill Matevie, Contact Person.
Problem Pregnancy. Contact the pregnancy support worker at any of the CSS offices. Tel: 704-343-9954 (Charlotte); 255-0146 (Asheville); 910-727-0705 (Winston-Salem).
Respect Life. Contact the Diocesan Office. Tel: 704-331-1720. Maggi Nadol, Contact Person.
Retrouvaille. Contact Diocesan Office. Tel: 704-331-1720. Karen Ridino, Contact Person.
Widowed-Separated-Divorced. Contact the Diocesan Office. Tel: 704-331-1720. Suzanne Bach, Contact Person.

HAMPTONVILLE. *Well of Mercy*, 181 Mercy Ln., 27020. Tel: 704-539-5449. Co-Directors: Sr. Brigid McCarthy, R.S.M.; Sr. Donna Marie Vaillancourt, R.S.M. Counseling and psycho-spiritual development retreat programs.

[H] HOME HEALTH CARE

HAYESVILLE. *Good Shepherd Home Health & Hospice Agency, Inc.*, P.O. Box 465, 28904. Tel: 704-389-6311; Fax: 704-389-9584.
For a complete listing, refer to the Special Care Facilities section.

*ROSMAN. *Frances Warde Health Service*, Star Rte. 1, Box 581, 28772. Tel: 704-884-7990; Fax: 704-966-9609.
For a complete listing, refer to the Special Care Facilities section.

[I] NURSING HOMES

HIGH POINT. *Maryfield Nursing Home*, 1315 Greensboro Rd., 27260. Tel: 910-886-2444; Fax: 910-886-4036.
For a complete listing, refer to the Special Care Facilities section.

[J] MONASTERIES AND RESIDENCES OF PRIESTS AND BROTHERS

CHARLOTTE. *Jesuit Community*, 507 S. Tryon St., 28202. Tel: 704-372-6808. Legal Title: *Jesuit Community in Western North Carolina*. Revs. James A. Devereux, S.J., Supr.; Vincent P. Alagia, S.J.; Leigh Fuller, S.J.; Francis J. Gillespie, S.J.; Lawrence J. Hunt, S.J.; Edward M. Ifkovits, S.J.; James P. Keogh, S.J.; William J. Lynch, S.J.; Eugene P. McCreesh, S.J.; Joseph J. McGovern, S.J.; Robert J. Paquet, S.J.; Peter S. Rogers, S.J.; Robert D. Weisenbaugh, S.J.

BELMONT. *Belmont Abbey*, 100 Belmont-Mount Holly Rd., 28012-2795. Tel: 704-825-6675. Legal Title: *Southern Benedictine Society of North Carolina, Inc.* Rt. Revs. Oscar C. Burnett, O.S.B.; Walter A. Coggin, O.S.B., Ph.D., D.D., (Retired), Abbot-Nullius; Very Rev. Kenneth A. Geyer, O.S.B., Prior; Bro. Paul J. Shanley, O.S.B., Sub-Prior; Revs. Bernard L. Rosswog, O.S.B.; Anselm G. Biggs, O.S.B., Ph.D.; Raymond J. Geyer, O.S.B.; Matthew T. McSorley, O.S.B.; John A. Oetgen, O.S.B.; Raphael G. Bridge, O.S.B.; Kenneth A. Geyer, O.S.B.; David R. Kessinger, O.S.B.; Kieran A. Neilson, O.S.B.; Francis P. Forster, O.S.B.; Arthur J. Pendleton, O.S.B.; Lawrence R. Willis, O.S.B.; W. Frederick George, O.S.B.; David G. Brown, O.S.B.; Paschal M. Baumstein, O.S.B., Archivist; Placid D. Solari, O.S.B.; Christopher A. Kirchgessner, O.S.B. Abbots 2; Monk Priests of Abbey 17; Priests in Residence 16; Brothers 2.

[K] CONVENTS AND RESIDENCES FOR SISTERS

CHARLOTTE. *Blessed Trinity Missionary Cenacle*, 801 Bromley Rd., 28207. Tel: 704-377-3254. Social work. Sisters 2.
Coolock House, 2328 Red Barn Ln., 28210. Tel: 704-554-1967. Parish and health care. Sisters of Mercy of the Americas 2.
Missionaries of Charity, 236 S. Torrence St., 28204. Tel: 704-334-8685. Ministry for poor. Sisters 4.
Sisters of St. Francis Convent, 4516 Randolph Rd., Apt. 87, 28211. Tel: 704-364-1361. Sisters 2.
Sisters' Residence, Carmel House, 3035 Carmel Rd., 28226. Tel: 704-552-2899; Fax: 704-552-2899. Teaching, administration, vocation ministry, liturgical & musical ministry. Sisters 4.

ASHEVILLE. *St. Genevieve of the Pines*, 103 Victoria Rd., 28801. Tel: 704-252-2811. Sr. Patricia Dolan, R.C.E., Local Supr. Religious of Christian Education at St. Genevieve 5. Residence for teaching and health care ministry and retired and semi-retired sisters.
St. Joseph Hospital Convent, 428 Biltmore Ave., 28801. Tel: 704-253-1243; 255-3100 (Hospital). Sisters 6; Health Care 4.

BELMONT. *Sisters of Mercy of North Carolina on Guam - Sacred Heart Convent*, 100 Mercy Dr., 28012-2738. Tel: 704-829-5103; Fax: 704-829-5137. Motherhouse and Novitiate of Sisters of Mercy of the Americas, Regional Community of North Carolina. Sr. Rosalind M. Picot, R.S.M., Pres.; Sr. Mary Andrew Ray, R.S.M., Motherhouse Coord. Sisters in Motherhouse 46; Professed Sisters in Community 135. Connected with the Motherhouse are Holy Angels, Inc., the McAuley Center, House of Mercy, Inc., and Catherine's House, Inc.

CHEROKEE. *Our Lady of Guadalupe Convent*, P.O. Box 202, 28719. Tel: 704-497-2029. Sisters of St. Francis (Tiffin, OH) 2. Pastoral work.

MAGGIE VALLEY. *Living Waters Convent*, 1420 Soco Rd., 28751. Tel: 704-926-9393. Sisters 3. Retreat work.

ROSMAN. *Sisters Residence*, Star Rte. 1, Box 581, 28772. Tel: 704-884-7990; 884-9528; 883-2789; Fax: 704-966-9609. Sisters 4. Health service.

VALE. *Maryvale Motherhouse*, 2522 June Bug Rd., 28168. Tel: 704-276-2626. Mother Mary Louis, Foundress and Supr. Congregation of Our Lady Help of the Clergy, (Maryvale Sisters). Sisters 5. Parish ministry, day-care center, spiritual/retreat center, religious education and pastoral ministry.

[L] CAMPUS MINISTRY CENTERS

CHARLOTTE. *Diocesan Office of Campus Ministry*. Rev. James Hawker, Interim Dir., Res., 3104 Park Rd., 28209. Tel: 704-523-2157; Fax: 704-523-3413.
University of North Carolina-Charlotte, ORA, 9201 University City Blvd., UNC-Charlotte, 28223-0001. Tel: 704-547-4069; 394-8308. Barbara L. Neff-Hutchinson, Catholic Campus Min.
Belmont Abbey College, Belmont, 28012. Tel: 704-829-7196; 825-6697. Rev. Frederick George, O.S.B., Dir. Campus Ministry.
Appalachian State University, 232 Faculty St., Boone, 28607. Tel: 704-264-7067; Fax: 704-262-3721.
Catholic Campus Ministry: Rev. Ed Alton; Mr. Julian Fitzgerald.
Brevard College, 5 Atsadi Ct., Brevard, 28712. Tel: 704-883-3242; 885-2001. Tony Asalone; Helen Asalone.
Western Carolina University, Catholic Student Center, P.O. Box 364, Cullowhee, 28723-0364. Tel: 704-293-9374; 586-8068. Gloria Schweizer, Catholic Campus Min.
Davidson College. (Davidson), 217 Brawley School Rd., P.O. Box 1364, Mooresville, 28115-1364. Tel: 704-664-3992. Rev. Robert Weisenbaugh, S.J., Catholic Campus Min.
NC Agricultural and Technical State University & Bennett College, 1009 Bluford St., Greensboro, 27401. Tel: 910-272-5868; 545-1468. Alberta Hairston.
University of North Carolina-Greensboro, Greensboro College & Guilford College, 1331 W. Friendly Ave., Greensboro, 27403. Tel: 910-334-5548; 691-0592. Rev. John A. Gilvey, O.S.F.S.; Anita Rose. Tel: 910-691-1229.
Wake Forest University, NC School of the Arts, Salem College and Winston-Salem State University, P.O. Box 7204, Reynolda Station, 27109. Tel: 910-759-5018; 727-7590. Shawn Adams, Catholic Campus Min. Tel: 910-759-5962; Rev. Michael McCaffrey, O.F.M.Conv.

[M] RETREAT CENTERS

HOT SPRINGS.
**Jesuit House of Prayer*, P.O. Box 7, 28743. Tel: 704-622-7366. Revs. Vincent P. Alagia, S.J., Dir.; Joseph J. McGovern, S.J. Directed, private individual retreats and small group retreats for men and women, as well as ecumenical. Overnight hostel for Appalachian hikers.

[N] REFLECTION CENTERS

BELMONT. *The McAuley Center*, Center for Adult Religious Education Sacred Heart Convent, 28012. Tel: 704-829-5113. Sr. Mary Hugh Mauldin, Dir.

MAGGIE VALLEY. *Living Waters Catholic Reflection Center*, 1420 Soco Rd., 28751. Tel: 704-926-3833. Sr. Jane Schmenk, O.S.F., Dir.; Sr. Jean Linder, O.S.F.; Sr. Francine Sartor, O.S.F. Retreats, days of recollection, and continuing education.

[O] HISPANIC MINISTRY

CHARLOTTE. *Centro Catolico Hispano*, 2117 Shenandoah Ave., 28205-6021. Tel: 704-335-1281. Rev. Vincent H. Finnerty, C.M., Diocesan Dir. of Hispanic Ministry.

[P] CONFERENCE CENTERS

HICKORY. *Catholic Conference Center*, 1551 Trinity Lane, 28602-9247. Tel: 704-327-7441; Fax: 704-327-0872. Deacon Guy A. Piche, Dir.

[Q] MISCELLANEOUS

CHARLOTTE.
**Room at the Inn, Inc.*, 3737 Weona Ave., 28209. Mailing Address: P.O. Box 30544, 28230-0544. Tel: 704-525-4673. Rev. Conrad L. Kimbrough, Pres.; Albert Hodges, Exec. Dir. A long-term residence for single pregnant women, with or without previous children.
Sisters of Mercy of North Carolina Foundation, Inc., 2115 Rexford Rd., Suite 401, 28211. Tel: 704-366-0087. Sr. Mary Jerome Spradley, R.S.M., Pres.

ASHEVILLE. *St. Joseph Addictions Recovery Program*, 129 Biltmore Ave., 28801. Tel: 704-254-2700.

BELMONT.
**Catherine's House*, 402 Mercy Dr., P.O. Box 1633, 28012. Tel: 704-825-9599; Fax: 704-829-5137. Sr. Mary Barbara Sullivan, R.S.M., CEO. Transitional housing for women and women with children, who are homeless.
House of Mercy, Inc., 701 Mercy Dr., 28012. Tel: 704-825-4711; Fax: 704-825-9976. Mailing Address: P.O. Box 808, 28012. Provides a home for persons living with AIDS in the advanced stages who have no other housing alternative in an 11 county region, and Case Management services for persons living with HIV/AIDS in Gaston, Lincoln, and Cleveland counties. Sr. Margaret J. Straney, R.S.M., Pres. & CEO. Beds 6.
Sisters of Mercy of North Carolina on Guam - Mercy Administration Center, 101 Mercy Dr., 28012. Tel: 704-829-5103. Sr. M. Rosalind Picot, R.S.M., Pres.

RELIGIOUS INSTITUTES OF MEN REPRESENTED IN THE DIOCESE

For further details refer to the corresponding bracketed number in the Religious Institutes of Men or Women section.

[0200]—*Benedictine Monks*. (Belmont, NC).—O.S.B.
[0470]—*The Capuchin Friars Province of the Stigmata*.—O.F.M.Cap.
[]—*Carmelites of Mary Immaculate*. (India).—C.M.I.
[0740]—*Congregation of Marians of the Immaculate Conception*.—M.I.C.
[1330]—*Congregation of the Mission*. (Eastern Prov.).—C.M.
[0480]—*Conventual Franciscans*. (Union City, NJ).—O.F.M.Conv.
[0520]—*Franciscan Friars*. (New York, NY).—O.F.M.
[0530]—*Franciscan Friars of the Atonement*.—S.A.
[0570]—*Glenmary Home Missioners*.—Glmy.
[0650]—*Holy Ghost Fathers*. (Bethel Park, PA).—C.S.Sp.
[0690]—*Jesuit Fathers and Brother*. (Maryland Prov.; Milwaukee, WI).—S.J.
[0920]—*Oblates of St. Francis De Sales*. (Wilmington-Philadelphia).—O.S.F.S.
[1070]—*Redemptorist Fathers*. (Baltimore Prov.).—C.SS.R.

RELIGIOUS INSTITUTES OF WOMEN REPRESENTED IN THE DIOCESE

[0230]—*Benedictine Sisters of Pontifical Jurisdiction*.—O.S.B.
[3080]—*Congregation of Our Lady, Help of the Clergy*.—C.L.H.C.
[1920]—*Congregation of the Sisters of the Holy Cross*.—C.S.C.
[0760]—*Daughters of Charity of St. Vincent de Paul*.—D.C.
[1070-13]—*Dominican Sisters*.—O.P.
[2710]—*Missionaries of Charity*.—M.C.
[2790]—*Missionary Servants of the Most Blessed Trinity*.—M.S.B.T.
[3640]—*Poor Servants of the Mother of God*.—S.M.G.
[3410]—*Religious of Christian Education*. (Asheville).—R.C.E.

[0590]—*Sisters of Charity of Saint Elizabeth, Convent Station.*—S.C.

[0650]—*Sisters of Charity of St. Vincent de Paul, of New York.*—S.C.

[0990]—*Sisters of Divine Providence.* (Allison Park, PA).—C.D.P.

[2570]—*Sisters of Mercy.* (Belmont, NC; Watchung, NJ).—R.S.M.

[2580]—*Sisters of Mercy of the Union in the United States of America.* (Dallas, TX; Detroit, MI; Cincinnati, OH).—R.S.M.

[3000]—*Sisters of Notre Dame de Namur.*—S.N.D.deN.

[3893]—*Sisters of Saint Joseph of Chestnut Hill, Philadelphia.*—S.S.J.

[1570]—*Sisters of St. Francis of the Holy Family.*—O.S.F.

[1760]—*Sisters of the Third Order of St. Francis of Penance and Charity.*—O.S.F.

[4060]—*Society of the Holy Child Jesus.* (Drexel Hill).—S.H.C.J.

NECROLOGY

† Hoban, Michael J., (Retired). —Died Dec. 29, 1995.

Diocese of Cheyenne

(Dioecesis Cheyennensis)

Most Reverend

JOSEPH HART, D.D.

Bishop of Cheyenne; ordained May 1, 1956; appointed July 1, 1976; appointed Titular Bishop of Timida Regia; episcopal ordination August 31, 1976; installed June 12, 1978. *Res., Box 468, Cheyenne, WY, 82003.*

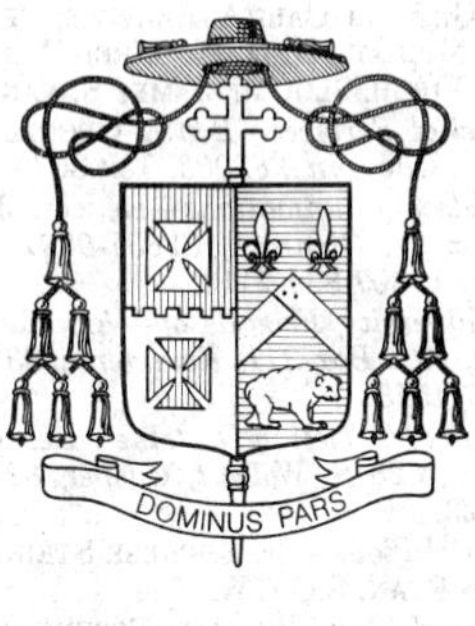

Chancery Office: 2121 Capitol Ave., Box 426, Cheyenne, WY, 82003-0426. Tel.: 307-638-1530; Fax: 307-637-7936.

ESTABLISHED AUGUST 2, 1887.

Square Miles 97,548.

Comprises the State of Wyoming and Yellowstone National Park.

For legal titles of parishes and diocesan institutions, consult the Chancery Office.

STATISTICAL OVERVIEW

Personnel	
Bishop	1
Priests: Diocesan Active in Diocese	41
Priests: Active Outside Diocese	1
Priests: Retired, Sick or Absent	10
Number of Diocesan Priests	52
Religious Priests in Diocese	11
Extern Priests in Diocese	1
Ordinations:	
Diocesan Priests	1
Permanent Deacons	4
Permanent Deacons in Diocese	7
Total Brothers	1
Total Sisters	34
Parishes	
Parishes	36
With Resident Pastor:	
Resident Diocesan Priests	30
Resident Religious Priests	4
Without Resident Pastor:	
Administered by Priests	1
Administered by Permanent Deacons	1
Missions	42
Closed Parishes	1
Professional Ministry Personnel:	
Sisters	15
Lay Ministers	36
Welfare	
Homes for the Aged	2
Total Assisted	94
Day Care and Extended Day Care Centers	5
Total Assisted	200
Specialized Homes	1
Total Assisted	107
Special Centers for Social Services	9
Total Assisted	12,137
Educational	
Diocesan Students in Other Seminaries	1
Total Seminarians	1
Elementary Schools, Diocesan and Parish	7
Total Students	1,322
Catechesis/Religious Education:	
High School Students	1,684
Elementary Students	5,753
Total Students Under Catholic Instruction	8,760
Teachers in the Diocese:	
Priests	2
Sisters	2
Lay Teachers	94
Vital Statistics	
Receptions into the Church:	
Infant Baptism Totals	1,071
Adult Baptism Totals	218
Received into Full Communion	265
First Communions	1,070
Confirmations	775
Marriages:	
Catholic	131
Interfaith	166
Total Marriages	297
Deaths	606
Total Catholic Population	48,427
Total Population	480,184

Former Bishops—Rt. Rev. MAURICE F. BURKE, D.D., cons. Oct. 28, 1887; transferred to the See of St. Joseph, MO, June 19, 1893; died March 17, 1923.—Rt. Rev. THOMAS M. LENIHAN, D.D., cons. Feb. 24, 1897; died Dec. 15, 1901.—Most Rev. JAMES J. KEANE, D.D., cons. Bishop of Cheyenne Oct. 28, 1902 raised to the archiepiscopal dignity and transferred to Archdiocese of Dubuque, Aug. 11, 1911; died Aug. 2, 1929.—Most Rev. PATRICK A. McGOVERN, D.D., LL.D., ord. Aug. 18, 1895 assistant at the Pontifical Throne; appt. Jan. 19, 1912; cons. April 11, 1912; died Nov. 8, 1951.—Most Rev. HUBERT M. NEWELL, D.D., LL.D., ord. June 15, 1930; appt. Coadjutor Aug. 2, 1947; cons. Sept. 24, 1947; succeeded to the See Nov. 8, 1951; retired Jan. 3, 1978; died Sept. 8, 1987.

Chancery Office—2121 Capitol Ave., P.O. Box 426, Cheyenne, 82003-0426. Tel: 307-638-1530; Fax: 307-637-7936.

Catholic Ministries Office—623 S. Wolcott, Casper, 82601. Tel: 307-237-2723; Fax: 307-235-9157.

Vicar-General/Moderator of the Curia—Very Rev. EUGENE SULLIVAN, V.G., *P.O. Box 2024, Sheridan, 82801.* Tel: 307-674-7441; 672-2848; Fax: 307-674-9187.

Chancellor—CAROL DELOIS, *P.O. Box 426, Cheyenne, 82003-0426.* Tel: 307-638-1530; Fax: 307-637-7936.

Vice-Chancellors—Revs. CARL A. BEAVERS; VERNON CLARK, M.C.L., J.C.L.; Very Revs. MICHAEL CARR; CHARLES F. TAYLOR, J.C.D.

College of Consultors—Very Rev. EUGENE SULLIVAN, V.G.; Revs. THOMAS E. CRONKLETON, JR., J.C.L.; AUGUST KOEUNE; GARY RUZICKA; JOHN SAVIO; GERALD A. SULLIVAN.

Council of Priests—Most Rev. JOSEPH HART, D.D.; Very Rev. EUGENE SULLIVAN, V.G., Ex-Officio; Revs. AUGUST KOEUNE, Chm. CARL GALLINGER, Vice-Chm. THOMAS E. CRONKLETON, JR., J.C.L.; ANDREW DUNCAN; WILLIAM ESPENSHADE; Rev. Msgr. LAWRENCE ETCHINGHAM; Revs. GARY RUZICKA; JOHN SAVIO; GERALD A. SULLIVAN; Very Rev. CHARLES TAYLOR; Rev. CHARLES VELASQUEZ.

Episcopal Vicar for Priestly Life and Ministry—Rev. GARY RUZICKA, *P.O. Box 50397, Casper, 82605-0397.* Tel: 307-235-5535; Fax: 307-237-7244.

Vicars Forane—Casper Deanery: Very Rev. JOHN MURRAY; Cheyenne Deanery: Very Rev. MICHAEL CARR; Rock Springs Deanery: Very Rev. CHARLES F. TAYLOR; Sheridan Deanery: Very Rev. EUGENE SULLIVAN, V.G.; Thermopolis Deanery: Very Rev. RONALD STOLCIS.

Director of Diocesan Programs—FINN MCCARTHY, *623 S. Wolcott, Casper, 82601.* Tel: 307-235-9157; Fax: 307-235-9157.

Finance Officer—JAMES S. VANCE, *P.O. Box 426, Cheyenne, 82003-0426.* Tel: 307-638-1530; Fax: 307-637-7936.

Finance Council—Most Rev. JOSEPH HART, D.D. Ex-Officios, Voting: Very Rev. EUGENE SULLIVAN, V.G.; Rev. CARL A. BEAVERS; TONY HASKEY; EDWARD F. MURRAY. Ex-Officios, Non-Voting: Revs. THOMAS E. CRONKLETON, JR.; THOMAS OGG; JAMES S. VANCE; FINN MCCARTHY; ROBERT MAYOR. Appointed: HOWARD BAKER, Chm. PATTI BURRIS; RODNEY KINSKEY; ORION LORENZI; JOHN OSTLUND; FRANK ROTELLINI; Rev. JOHN SAVIO; JANE SCHNAUBER; CY WALLACE.

Tribunal Office—All marriage correspondence is to be directed to: *The Tribunal Office: P.O. Box 426, Cheyenne, 82003-0426.* Tel: 307-638-1530; 800-788-4606; Fax: 307-637-7936.

Judicial Vicar—Rev. THOMAS E. CRONKLETON, JR., J.C.L., J.C.D. (Cand.).

Director of the Tribunal—DARLENE FLYNN.

Auditors—DARLENE FLYNN; CONNIE KASSAHN.

Administrative Assistant/Ecclesiastical Notary—CONNIE KASSAHN.

Bookkeeper/Clerk/Ecclesiastical Notary—LESLIE CONNAGHAN.

Promoter of Justice—Very Rev. CHARLES F. TAYLOR, J.C.D.

Judges—Very. Rev. MICHAEL CARR; Revs. GERALD F. CHLEBORAD, J.C.L.; THOMAS E. CRONKLETON, JR., J.C.L.; DAVID ALAN ZWIFKA, J.C.L.

Defenders of the Bond—Revs. VERNON F. CLARK, M.C.L., J.C.L.; WILLIAM T. ESPENSHADE; ANGEL ORNELAS; THOMAS G. OGG; SAMUEL HAYES; GERALD A. SULLIVAN; RICHARD R. RYAN, J.C.D.; Very Rev. CHARLES F. TAYLOR, J.C.D.; Deacon LEE PICO.

Advocates—SUSAN SIMON; BONNIE BAUMBERGER.

Diocesan Administrative Offices and Boards

Catholic Social Services of Wyoming, Inc.—BETSY GROOM, M.S.W., Dir., *P.O. Box 1026, Cheyenne, 82003-1026.* Tel: 307-638-1530; Fax: 307-637-7936. Board of Directors: Most Rev. JOSEPH HART, D.D.; Very Rev. EUGENE SULLIVAN, V.G.; PAUL NOVAK, Chm. Board of Trustees: Rev. GERALD A. SULLIVAN; MARY SHARP, Vice-Chm. ELIZABETH GROOM, M.S.W., Dir. HELEN CHADEY; HENRY CHADEY; JAN COBB; DICK DESOMBER; JO DESOMBER; JIM ZANCANELLA; LILLIAN ZANCANELLA.

Education Office—Deacon ED MCCARTHY, Dir.; Sr. MARY ST. LUKE BELUS, Media Consultant, *623 S. Wolcott, Casper, 82601.* Tel: 307-237-2723; Fax: 307-235-9157.

Education Office Board—Most Rev. JOSEPH HART,

D.D.; Deacon ED MCCARTHY, Supt. Education; Revs. ANDREW DUNCAN; ROBERT G. LYNCH, S.J.; RAY RODRIGUEZ; Sr. MARY ST. LUKE BELUS, Media Consultant; Sr. RUTH ELLERT, O.L.V.M.; Sr. MARY SCHAEFER, C.S.J.; Sr. ELIZABETH SKALICKY, S.C.L.; ANDREA CHOJNACKY, (Glenrock): APRIL CRAMER, (Lander): MARY ANN CUMMINS, (Buffalo): DONNA DUNCAN, (Torrington): PAM EVANOFF, (Rock Springs): JANE JOHNSON, (Gillette): SUSIE PALMER, (Jackson): SUE SANDEEN, (Laramie): MARY SUTTON, (Casper): PAT MCCARTHY, Family Life Dir. JIM ZIERDEN, Youth Dir.

Family Services Office—PAT MCCARTHY, Dir., *623 S. Wolcott, Casper, 82601.* Tel: 307-237-2723; Fax: 307-235-9157.

Family Services Board—Most Rev. JOSEPH HART, D.D.; Very Rev. EUGENE SULLIVAN, V.G.; Rev. RAY ROGRIGUEZ; MARY ANN DURAN; RUTHIE HALVORSEN; LINDA HURLESS; CHARLIE LUX; FRANK MCGINTY; DICK MILLS; PAT MILLS; RALPH SPECHT; CAROL SPECHT; BETSY VIGNERI; BRAD ZETTL; JENNIFER ZETTL; BYRON ZUEHLSDORFF; TRACY ZUEHLSDORFF.

Lay Ministry Office—Sr. ESTELLE SCULLY, S.P., Dir., *623 S. Wolcott, Casper, 82601.* Tel: 307-237-2723; Fax: 307-235-9157.

Lay Ministry Formation Board—Most Rev. JOSEPH HART, D.D.; Sr. ESTELLE SCULLY, S.P., Dir.; Rev. Msgr. JAMES O'NEILL; Revs. AUGUST KOEUNE; THOMAS OGG; Dr. MARY BURKE; Dr. TOM BURKE; ALISON MCNULTY; DAVID MCNULTY; THERESA WYBURN.

Newspaper "Wyoming Catholic Register"—published by the Catholic Press Society of Wyoming. SCOTT FARRIS, Editor, *P.O. Box 1308, Cheyenne, 82003-1308.* Street Address: *2121 Capitol Ave., Cheyenne, 82003-1308.* Tel: 307-638-1530; Fax: 307-637-7936.

Newspaper, Wyoming Catholic Register Board—Most Rev. JOSEPH HART, D.D.; SCOTT FARRIS, Editor; Rev. Msgr. JAMES O'NEILL; Rev. WILLIAM ESPENSHADE; Sr. ESTELLE SCULLY, S.P.; JOAN BARRON; GLORIA CARLSON; HELEN FITCH; SALVADOR MANZANARES.

Planned Giving Office—FINN MCCARTHY, Dir., *623 S. Wolcott, Casper, 82601.* Tel: 307-237-2723; Fax: 307-235-9157.

Vocation Office—Rev. CARL GALLINGER, Dir., *1800 E. Grand Ave., Laramie, 82070.* Tel: 307-745-5461; Fax: 307-742-0521.

Youth Office—JIM ZIERDEN, Dir. ELIZABETH LOVELETT, Asst. Dir., *623 S. Wolcott, Casper, 82601.* Tel: 307-237-2723; Fax: 307-235-9257.

Youth Ministry Board—Rev. CARL GALLINGER; SANDY BECKSTEAD; BEN CAROTTA; JOHN CHICK; ANDREA EICKE; MONICA ELSINGER; NICOLE LECLERE; LIZ LOVELETT; PHILANN LUX; PAUL NEEL; JILL RAMAKER; JIM SCALIA; SARA STRIKE; CHRIS TRUJILLO; JIM ZIERDEN.

Other Diocesan Boards, Councils and Programs

Diocesan Trustees, Board of Directors—Most Rev. JOSEPH HART, D.D.; Very Rev. EUGENE SULLIVAN, V.G.; Rev. CARL A. BEAVERS; ANTHONY HASKEY; EDWARD F. MURRAY, JR.

Apostolate for Evangelization—Rev. RAY MOSS, *617 S. 4th St., Laramie, 82070.* Tel: 307-745-3115.

Bishop's Annual Campaign, "Bishop's Appeal"—JAMES S. VANCE, *P.O. Box 426, Cheyenne, 82003.* Tel: 307-638-1530; Fax: 307-637-7936. FINN MCCARTHY, *623 S. Wolcott, Casper, 82601.* Tel: 307-237-2723; Fax: 307-235-9157.

Boy and Girl Scouts—Rev. THOMAS KADERA, *St. Ann's Church, P.O. Box 667, Saratoga, 82331-0667.* Tel: 307-326-5461.

Building Commission—Most Rev. JOSEPH HART, D.D.; ROGER BAALMAN, Chm.; Very Rev. EUGENE SULLIVAN, V.G.; Revs. CARL A. BEAVERS; GERALD F. CHLEBORAD; MICHAEL HELLMAN; FRED WENDEL; CLINTON BLACK; VIRGIL SLOUGH; JAMES S. VANCE, Sec.

Catholic Relief Services—BETSY GROOM, M.S.W., *P.O. Box 426, Cheyenne, 82003.* Tel: 307-638-1530.

Catholic Telecommunications—Deacon JOHN ALOISIO, *P.O. Box 27, Glenrock, 82637-0027.* Tel: 307-436-9529; Fax: 307-864-2110.

Catholic University, Friends of—Very Rev. CHARLES F. TAYLOR, *P.O. Box 311, Kemmerer, 83101-0311.* Tel: 307-877-4573.

Confraternity of Christian Doctrine—Deacon ED MCCARTHY, Dir., *623 S. Wolcott, Casper, 82601.* Tel: 307-237-2723.

Council of Religious—Sr. THERESE STEINER, S.C.L.; Sr. BRIDGID RYAN, S.O.L.W.

Cursillo Board—Rev. WILLIAM ESPENSHADE; DAVE ZELENKA, Pres. VIRGINIA SPINDLER; MARY BONOGOFSKY.

Diaconate Program, Permanent—Rev. GARY RUZICKA, *P.O. Box 50397, Casper, 82605-0397.* Tel: 307-235-5535; Fax: 307-237-7244.

Diaconate Board—Most Rev. JOSEPH HART, D.D.; Revs. CARL GALLINGER, Bishop's Delegate; GARY RUZICKA, Dir. Deacons; THOMAS OGG; RONALD STOLCIS; Deacons JOHN ALOISIO; JOSEPH KRISTUFEK.

Ecumenism Commission—Revs. JOSEPH DALEY, Chm. GERALD F. CHLEBORAD.

Endowment Funds and Trusts—

Catholic Schools Endowment Fund, Seminarian Education Endowment—JAMES S. VANCE, *P.O. Box 426, Cheyenne, 82003.* Tel: 307-638-1530.

Knights of Columbus Charitable Trust for Seminarian Education and Priests' Retirement—FINN MCCARTHY, *623 S. Wolcott, Casper, 82601.* Tel: 307-237-2723.

St. Mary's School Foundation—Rev. CARL A. BEAVERS, *P.O. Box 1268, Cheyenne, 82003.* Tel: 307-635-9261.

Family Services Divisions—PAT MCCARTHY, Dir.

Beginning Experience for Divorced or Widowed—VIKKI EPPERSON; JESS THIEL, *P.O. Box 9953, Casper, 82609.* Tel: 307-234-2551; 237-6013.

Divorced / Separated / Widowed Ministry—LINDA HURLESS. Tel: 307-254-3509.

Engaged Encounter—JAN MARTIN; STEVE MARTIN, *1340 Nottingham Dr., Casper, 82609.* Tel: 307-577-3009.

Marriage Encounter—DEBBIE ROBBINS; STEVE ROBBINS, *1103 Overdale, Gillette, 82718.* Tel: 307-686-7471.

Marriage Preparation—PAT MCCARTHY.

Natural Family Planning—PAT MCCARTHY.

Rainbows for All God's Children—AMY ROJO, *121 S. Connor, Sheridan, 82801.* Tel: 307-674-7301.

Respect Life Catholic Pro-Life Ministry—PAT MCCARTHY.

Retrouvaille, Ministry for Hurting Marriages—PAT MCCARTHY.

Holy Child Pontifical Association—Deacon ED MCCARTHY, Dir., *623 S. Wolcott, Casper, 82601.* Tel: 307-237-2723.

Housing—Rev. CARL A. BEAVERS, *P.O. Box 1268, Cheyenne, 82003-1268.* Tel: 307-635-9261., *St. Anthony Manor, 211 E. Sixth, Casper, 82601.* Tel: 307-237-0843., *Holy Trinity Manor, 2516 E. 18th St., Cheyenne, 82001.* Tel: 307-778-8850.

Information Office—SCOTT FARRIS, *P.O. Box 1308, Cheyenne, 82003-1308.* Tel: 307-638-1530; Fax: 307-637-7936.

Liturgical Commission—Most Rev. JOSEPH HART, D.D.; Revs. GARY RUZICKA, Exec. Sec. GERALD F. CHLEBORAD; THOMAS CRONKLETON, JR.; MICHAEL HELLMAN; FRED WENDEL; BETTY MCCARTHY; BRENDA WILKING.

Pastoral Council—Most Rev. JOSEPH HART, D.D., Chm. CYNTHIA JOHNSON, Vice-Chm.; Very Rev. EUGENE SULLIVAN, V.G., Ex-Officio; CAROL DELOIS, Chancellor; FINN MCCARTHY, Dir. Diocesan Programs; JAMES S. VANCE, Finance Officer; Sr. ESTELLE SCULLY, S.P., Exec. Sec., *623 S. Wolcott, Casper, 82601.* Tel: 307-237-2723. Casper Deanery: Very Rev. JOHN MURRAY; WILLIAM COUGHLIN; DOLLY MEEHAN; CATHY STRONG. Cheyenne Deanery: Rev. RAY RODRIGUEZ; SANDY GADDIS; CHARLES GARCIA; JOSEPH NIES. Rock Springs Deanery: Rev. AUGUST KOEUNE; JAN HOTCHKIN; PHILANN LUX; DOTTIE PASENELLI. Sheridan Deanery: Rev. RICHARD MACLELLAN; SHIRLEY GENEREAUX; BLASE GILTNER; RAY O'LEARY. Thermopolis Deanery:; Vacant; Clergy Rep. JIM HEISER; CYNTHIA JOHNSON; APRIL PENDLETON. Religious: Sr. RITA DOWNEY, O.S.B.; Sr. RUTH ANN HEHN, S.C.L., Recording Sec.; Sr. LETITIA LENHERR, S.C.L. Hispanic Rep.:; Vacant. Native American Rep.: MARY ANN WHITEMAN.

Priests' Eucharistic League—Very Rev. EUGENE SULLIVAN, V.G., *P.O. Box 2024, Sheridan, 82801-2024.*

Priests' Personnel Board—Most Rev. JOSEPH HART, D.D., Chm.; Very Revs. MICHAEL CARR; CHARLES F. TAYLOR, J.C.D.; Revs. WILLIAM ESPENSHADE; SAMUEL HAYES.

Propagation of the Faith—Deacon JOHN ALOISIO, *P.O. Box 27, Glenrock, 82637.* Tel: 307-436-9529; Fax: 307-864-2110.

Rural Life Conference—Rev. SAM HAYES, *P.O. Box 992, Jackson, 83001.* Tel: 307-733-2516.

St. Joseph's Society for Sick and Retired Priests (Clergy Mutual Benefit Society)—Most Rev. JOSEPH HART, D.D.; Rev. THOMAS OGG, Pres.; Rev. Msgr. LAWRENCE ETCHINGHAM; Very Revs. RONALD STOLCIS; CHARLES F. TAYLOR, J.C.D.; Revs. DANIEL COLIBRARO; THOMAS E. CRONKLETON, JR., J.C.L.; KEVIN KOCH; GERALD A. SULLIVAN.

Spanish-Speaking Apostolate Board—Most Rev. JOSEPH HART, D.D.; Rev. CHARLES VELAZQUEZ, Chap., *1009 9th St., Wheatland, 82201.* Tel: 307-322-2070.

CLERGY, PARISHES, MISSIONS AND PAROCHIAL SCHOOLS

CITY OF CHEYENNE
(Laramie County)

1—ST. MARY'S CATHEDRAL (1868), Revs. Carl A. Beavers; Rory Schiffbauer; Roy Rodriguez; Deacon Lee Pico. In res., Rev. Joseph Moroney.
Mailing Address: P.O. Box 1268, 82003-1268. Tel: 307-635-9261; Fax: 307-637-7936. [CEM]
School—Tel: 307-638-9268; Fax: 307-635-2347. Dr. James Schumacher, Supt./Prin.
Lay Teachers 20; Students 349.
Catechesis / Religious Programs—Tel: 307-637-4009; 635-9261; Fax: 307-637-7936. D.R.E.: Charlene Jonart, (Grades PreK-8); Cathy Mohatt, (Grades 9-12).
Students 632.
Convent—716 E. 21st St., 82001. Tel: 307-638-6005. Sisters 2.

2—HOLY TRINITY (1957), Rev. Gerald A. Sullivan. In res., Rev. Msgr. William Delaney, (Retired); Rev. Msgr. Lawrence Etchingham, (Retired); Rev. James Doudican, (Retired).
Res., 1836 Hot Springs Ave., P.O. Box 5720, 82003-5720. Tel: 307-632-5872; 637-7150; Fax: 307-637-7150. [CEM]
Catechesis / Religious Programs—Tel: 307-632-4482. D.R.E.: Martha Thein; Terri Mercer.
Sisters of Charity of Leavenworth 1; Students 271.

3—ST. JOSEPH'S (1929) (Hispanic), Rev. Michael Carr. In res., Rev. Gerald Chleborad.
Mailing Address: P.O. Box 1141, 82003-1141. Tel: 307-634-4625; Fax: 307-635-4700.
Office: 314 E. Sixth St., 82007.
Res., 515 House, 82007. Tel: 307-634-4625; Fax: 307-635-4700. [CEM]
Church—300 E. 6th St., 82007.
Catechesis / Religious Programs—Students 292.

OUTSIDE CITY OF CHEYENNE

Buffalo, Johnson Co., St. John the Baptist (1885) (Basque), Rev. Vernon F. Clark.
Res., 532 N. Lobban, 82834. Tel: 307-684-7268; Fax: 307-684-5490.
Catechesis / Religious Programs—Tel: 307-684-7217. Mary Ann Cummins, D.R.E.
Students 211.
Missions—Clearmont, Johnson Co., St. Mary, 82834; Kaycee, Johnson Co., St. Hubert, 82834.

Casper, Natrona Co., St. Anthony of Padua (1903), Rev. Msgr. James O'Neill; Rev. Clifford Jacobson; Deacon Don Stewart.
Office: 604 S. Center, 82601. Tel: 307-266-2666; Fax: 307-266-4127.
School—218 E. Seventh, 82601. Tel: 307-234-2873; Fax: 307-235-4946. Mrs. Mary Kozola, Prin.
Sisters 1; Lay Teachers 18; Students 267.
Catechesis / Religious Programs—Ruthie Halvorsen, D.R.E.
Students 391.
Convent—604 S. Durbin St., 82601. Tel: 307-237-7691.
Mission—Midwest, Natrona Co., St. Francis Mission, Midwest, WY 82643.

Our Lady of Fatima (1954), Revs. Daniel Colibraro, Co-Pastor; Philip Colibraro, Co-Pastor; Deacon Ed McCarthy.
Res., 1401 CY Ave., 82604. Tel: 307-237-9837; Fax: 307-266-2958.
Catechesis / Religious Programs—Tel: 307-234-3971; Fax: 307-266-2958. D.R.E.: Teresa Sears; Donna Macklin.
Students 107.

Saint Patrick's (1963), Rev. Gary J. Ruzicka; Deacon Russ Humphreys.
Res., 425 S. Illinois, Box 50397, 82605-0397. Tel: 307-235-5535; 266-2495; Fax: 307-237-7244.
Catechesis / Religious Programs—Tel: 307-265-4881. D.R.E.: Marilyn Crull; Ellen Klym; Mary Lou Stoecklin.
Students 605.

Cody, Park Co., St. Anthony (1942), Rev. Joseph A. Daley.
Res., 1333 Monument Dr., 82414-3406. Tel: 307-587-3388; Fax: 307-587-3383.
Catechesis / Religious Programs—Tel: 307-587-2567. Audrey Du Montier, D.R.E.
Students 262.
Missions—Yellowstone National Park, Park Co. Sunday Masses at Old Faithful, Lake Lodge, Canyon Lodge, and Grant Village in summer only. 82414; Meeteetsee, Park Co., St. Theresa, 82414.

Douglas, Converse Co., St. James (1907), Very Rev. John E. Murray.
Res., 243 S. Fifth St., P.O. Box 1500, 82633-1500. Tel: 307-358-2338.
Catechesis / Religious Programs—Tel: 307-358-5540. Kathi Cox, D.R.E.
Students 160.

Mission—Glendo, Platte Co., Our Lady of Lourdes, 423 A St., Glendo, 82213. Tel: 307-358-2338.

Evanston, Uinta Co., St. Mary Magdalen (1878), Rev. August Koeune.
Mailing Address: Box 163, 82931-0163. Tel: 307-789-2189; Fax: 307-789-9480.
Catechesis/Religious Programs—Tel: 307-789-9046; Fax: 307-789-9480. Peggy Ducharme, D.R.E. Students 200.
Mission—Fort Bridger, Uinta Co., St. Helen, P.O. Box 183, Fort Bridger, 82933. Tel: 307-782-6190.
Catechesis/Religious Programs—Tel: 307-787-6590. Bonnie La Fond, D.R.E. Students 70.

Gillette, Campbell Co., St. Matthew's (1926), Revs. Thomas Ogg; Andrew Duncan.
Res., 900 Butler Spaeth Rd., 82716. Tel: 307-682-3319; Fax: 307-682-6386.
Catechesis/Religious Programs—Tel: 307-682-5321. Jane Johnson, D.R.E. Students 840.
Missions—Wright, Campbell Co., Blessed Sacrament, 624 Wright Blvd., Wright, 82732. Tel: 307-464-0809; Moorcroft, Crook Co., St. Patrick, 216 N. Belle Fourche, Moorcroft, 82721. Tel: 307-756-9478.

Glenrock, Converse Co., St. Louis (1920), Deacon John Aloisio.
Mailing Address: P.O. Box 27, 82637-0027. Tel: 307-436-9529.
Catechesis/Religious Programs—Tel: 307-436-5769. Andrea Chojnacky, D.R.E. Students 60.

Green River, Sweetwater Co., Immaculate Conception (1884), Rev. Michael P. Hellman.
Mailing Address: P.O. Box 70, 82935-0128. Tel: 307-875-2441.
Catechesis/Religious Programs—Tel: 307-875-2184. Peggy Hyslope, D.R.E. Students 262.

Greybull, Big Horn Co., Sacred Heart (1919), Rev. Peter Johnson.
Mailing Address: P.O. Box 231, 82426-0231. Tel: 307-765-2438.
Catechesis/Religious Programs—Esther Lindsey, D.R.E. Students 42.
Mission—Basin, Big Horn Co., St. Philip.

Guernsey, Platte Co., St. Anthony's (1969), Rev. Robert H. Cousineau, S.J.
Res., P.O. Box 430, 82214-0430. Tel: 307-836-2586.
Catechesis/Religious Programs—Tel: 307-836-2051. Kari Gerhold, D.R.E. Students 45.

Jackson, Teton Co., Our Lady of the Mountains (1955), Rev. Sam Hayes.
Mailing Address: P.O. Box 992, 83001-0992. Tel: 307-733-2516; Fax: 307-733-2516.
Catechesis/Religious Programs—Tel: 307-733-6391. Susie Palmer, D.R.E. Students 131.
Mission—Afton, Lincoln Co., Holy Family.
Chapel—Moran, Sacred Heart.

Kemmerer, Lincoln Co., St. Patrick's (1901), Rev. Charles F. Taylor.
Mailing Address: Box 311, 83101-0311. Tel: 307-877-4573; Fax: 307-877-4079.
Catechesis/Religious Programs—Students 98.
Missions—Cokeville, Lincoln Co., St. Dominic; La Barge, Lincoln Co., La Barge Catholic Community.

Lander, Fremont Co., Holy Rosary (1882), Revs. John Savio; Robert K.C. Siu (HON).
Res., 163 Leedy Rd., P.O. Box 1047, 82520-0503. Tel: 307-332-4952; Fax: 307-332-9332.
Catechesis/Religious Programs—Tel: 307-332-4803. Sr. Ruth Ellert, D.R.E. Students 172.
Missions—Hudson, Ascension; Jeffrey City, St. Brendan.

Laramie, Albany Co., St. Laurence O'Toole (1872), Revs. Angel Ornelas, Jr.; Ray Moss.
Mailing Address: 617 S. Fourth St., 82070-1045. Tel: 307-745-3115; Fax: 307-745-3131.
School—(Grades PreK-6). Tel: 307-742-6363; Fax: 307-745-3131.
Sisters 1; Lay Teachers 8; Students 118.
Catechesis/Religious Programs—Students 123. D.R.E.: Sr. Elizabeth Skalicky, (Grades PreK-6); Alicen Krahling, (Grades 7-12).
Convent—420 Kearney St., 82070. Tel: 307-745-9278.
Station—Rock River.

St. Paul's Newman Center (1957), Revs. Roger W. Schmit, O.S.B.; Carl J. Gallinger; Sr. Mary Frost, S.D.S., Pastoral Assoc.; Joseph A. Zenk, Campus Min.
Office & Mailing Address: 1800 E. Grand Ave., 82070-4316. Tel: 307-745-5461; Fax: 307-745-0521.
Res., 1819 E. Garfield, 82070-4338. Tel: 307-745-7783.

Catechesis/Religious Programs—Students 78.

Lovell, Big Horn Co., St. Joseph's (1979), Rev. Peter Johnson.
Res., 100 Wyoming St., P.O. Box 185, 82431-0185. Tel: 307-548-2282.
Church—1141 Shoshone Ave., 82431.
Catechesis/Religious Programs—Rochelle Haupster, D.R.E. Students 78.

Lusk, Niobrara Co., St. Leo's (1911), Rev. Evan P. Shea.
Res., 900 W. Fifth St., Box 959, 82225-0959. Tel: 307-334-2702; Fax: 307-334-3161.
Catechesis/Religious Programs—Tel: 307-334-3096. Connie Sampers, D.R.E. Students 55.

Newcastle, Weston Co., Corpus Christi (1890), Rev. Richard H. MacLellan; Sr. Frances Schaf, O.S.U., Ministries Coord.
Res., 19 W. Winthrop, 82701. Tel: 307-746-4219.
Catechesis/Religious Programs—Students 183.
Missions—Sundance, Crook Co., St. Paul, P.O. Box 28, Sundance, 82729. Tel: 307-283-2382; Upton, Weston Co., St. Anthony, P.O. Box 177, Upton, 82730. Tel: 307-468-2236; Hulett, Crook Co., St. Matthew's, 26 Hunter, Hulett, 82720.

Pine Bluffs, Laramie Co., St. Paul's (1913), Rev. Thomas E. Cronkleton, Jr.
Res., P.O. Box 97, 82082-0097. Tel: 307-245-3761.
Catechesis/Religious Programs—Tel: 307-246-3255. Carleen Graves, D.R.E. Students 76.
Missions—Albin, Laramie Co., St. Joseph; Carpenter, Laramie Co., St. Peter.

Pinedale, Sublette Co., Our Lady of Peace (1940), Rev. Robert G. Lynch, S.J.
Mailing Address: P.O. Box 70, 82941-0070. Tel: 307-367-2359.
Catechesis/Religious Programs—Tel: 307-367-2802. Bernie Majhanovich, D.R.E. Students 70.
Missions—Big Piney, Sublette Co., St. Anne, Box 742, Big Piney, 83113. Tel: 307-276-3227; Eden, Sweetwater Co., St. Christopher, Eden, 82926.

Powell, Park Co., St. Barbara (1910), Rev. John A. Wright.
Res., 115 E. Third, P.O. Box 818, 82435-0818. Tel: 307-754-2480.
Catechesis/Religious Programs—Tel: 307-754-3361. Blanche Roehr, D.R.E. Students 131.
Mission—Clark, Park Co., Our Lady of the Valley, P.O. Box 818, 82435. Tel: 307-754-2480.

Rawlins, Carbon Co., St. Joseph's (1867), Rev. Malcolm Reid.
Mailing Address: P.O. Box 68, 82301-0068. Tel: 307-324-4631.
Catechesis/Religious Programs—Tel: 307-324-4033. Catherine Faber, D.R.E. Students 252.
Mission—Baggs, Carbon Co., Our Lady of the Sage, P.O. Box 26, Baggs, 82321. Tel: 307-383-2695.

Riverton, Fremont Co., St. Margaret's (1908), Revs. William T. Espenshade; Jan J. Santich, O.S.B., Pastoral Assoc.; Frits J. Braakhuis, C.M.
Res., 622 E. Park, P.O. Box 888, 82501-0888. Tel: 307-856-3757; Fax: 307-856-8533.
School—(Grades PreK-5). Tel: 307-856-5922; Fax: 307-857-5892. Jane Rainwater, Prin.
Lay Teachers 15; Students 131.
Catechesis/Religious Programs—Tel: 307-856-3757; Fax: 307-856-8533. Patricia Newlin, D.R.E. Students 178.
Missions—Shoshoni, Fremont Co., St. Joseph, 211 Wyoming St., Shoshoni, 82649. Tel: 307-876-2760; Dubois, Fremont Co., Our Lady of the Woods, 4 S. Riverton St., P.O. Box 1134, Dubois, 82513. Tel: 307-455-2533; Kinnear, Fremont Co., St. Edward, Kinnear Rectory, 11350 US Hwy. 26, P.O. Box 34, Kinnear, 82516. Tel: 307-856-5502.

Rock Springs, Sweetwater Co., Our Lady of Sorrows (1887). Consolidated with Sts. Cyril & Methodius Church, Rock Springs. Revs. Fred Wendel; Bruce Clapham.
Res., 633 Bridger Ave., P.O. Box 6038, 82901. Tel: 307-362-2611.
School—Rock Springs Catholic School. (Bi-parish). Tel: 307-362-6077. Mr. Gene McConnell, Prin.
Lay Teachers 10; Students 168.
Catechesis/Religious Programs—Tel: 307-382-4911. Pam Evanoff, D.R.E. Students 426.
Missions—Superior, Sweetwater Co., St. Vivian; Table Rock, Sweetwater Co., Catholic Community.

SS. Cyril and Methodius (1911). Consolidated with Our Lady of Sorrows Church, Rock Springs. Revs. Fred Wendel; Bruce Clapham.
Res., 633 Bridger Ave., P.O. Box 6038, 82901. Tel: 307-362-2611.
Catechesis/Religious Programs—Tel: 307-382-4911. Pam Evanoff, D.R.E. Students 325.

Our Lady of Sorrows/Sts. Cyril & Methodius Church. Our Lady of Sorrows and Sts. Cyril & Methodius Church consolidated to form Our Lady of Sorrows/Sts. Cyril & Methodius Church. Revs. Fred Wendel; Bruce Clapham.
Res., P.O. Box 6038, 82901. Tel: 307-362-2611; Fax: 307-362-2611.

Saratoga, Carbon Co., St. Ann's (1960), Rev. Thomas Kadera.
Mailing Address: P.O. Box 667, 82331-0667. Tel: 307-326-5461; Fax: 307-326-5461.
Catechesis/Religious Programs—Tel: 307-327-5722. D.R.E.: Cathy Lynch; Ginger Miller. Students 50.
Missions—Hanna, Carbon Co., St. Joseph, P.O. Box 782, Hanna, 82327; Medicine Bow, Carbon Co., St. Malachy, P.O. Box 223, Medicine Bow, 82329.

St. Stephens, Fremont Co., St. Stephen's (1884) (Native American). Indian Mission for the Shoshone and Arapahoe Indians. St. Stephen's Indian Mission, Inc. Revs. Eugene Zimmerman, S.J.; Daniel J. Gannon, S.J.; John A. Apel, S.J.
Catechesis/Religious Programs—Students 130.
Mailing Address: Box 250, 82524-0250. Tel: 307-856-5937; Fax: 307-856-6797.
Missions—Ethete, Fremont Co., St. Joseph, Box 8358, Ethete, 82520. Tel: 307-332-4415; Fort Washakie, Fremont Co., Blessed Sacrament, Box 307, Fort Washakie, 82514-0307. Tel: 307-332-2252.

Sheridan, Sheridan Co., Holy Name (1885), Very Rev. Eugene P. Sullivan; Rev. James A. Schumacher; Deacon Joe Kristufek.
Mailing Address: Box 2024, 82801-2024. Tel: 307-674-7441; Fax: 307-674-9187.
School—121 S. Connor, 82801. Tel: 307-672-2021; Fax: 307-672-2021. Mr. Gilbert Sanchez, Prin.
Sisters of Charity (Leavenworth) 1; Lay Teachers 13; Students 196.
Catechesis/Religious Programs—Tel: 307-672-7455. Cel Hope, D.R.E. Students 285.
Missions—Story, Sheridan Co., Our Lady of the Pines, P.O. Box 2024, 82801. Tel: 307-674-7441; Ranchester, Sheridan Co., St. Edmund, P.O. Box 197, Ranchester, 82839. Tel: 307-655-2357.

Thermopolis, Hot Springs Co., St. Francis (1906), Rev. William A. Caspers.
Mailing Address: P.O. Box 272, 82443-0272. Tel: 307-864-2674.
Catechesis/Religious Programs—Tel: 307-864-2674. Madonna McIntosh, D.R.E. Students 93.

Torrington, Goshen Co., St. Rose (1906), Rev. Kevin A. Koch.
Res., 605 E. 22nd Ave., 82240. Tel: 307-532-5556; Fax: 307-534-2329.
Catechesis/Religious Programs—Tel: 307-532-5880. D.R.E.: Cindy Haught; Donna Duncan. Students 235.

Wheatland, Platte Co., St. Patrick's (1891), Rev. Charles J. Velasquez.
Res., 1009 Ninth St., 82201. Tel: 307-322-2070; Fax: 307-322-2386.
Catechesis/Religious Programs—Tel: 307-322-4213. Students 82.
Mission—Chugwater, Platte Co., St. Theresa, 1009 9th St., 82201. Tel: 307-322-2070.

Worland, Washakie Co., St. Mary Magdalen (1949), Very Rev. Ronald A. Stolcis; Sr. Dorothy Henscheid, S.C.L., Pastoral Assoc.
Mailing Address: Box 901, 82401-0901. Tel: 307-347-2820; Fax: 307-347-2450.
Shipping Address: 1099 Charles Ave., 82401.
Catechesis/Religious Programs—Tel: 307-347-6441. Students 156.

Chaplains of Public Institutions

CHEYENNE. *U.S. Veterans Administration Hospital 1,* 90 MW/HC, F.E. Warren AFB, 82005. Revs. Dennis Hanley Tel: 307-775-2451; 772-3434; Carl A. Beavers, Chap., Tel: 800-788-4606; 638-1530.

EVANSTON. *Wyoming State Hospital.* Vacant.

RAWLINS. *Wyoming State Penitentiary.* Mailing Address: P.O. Box 468, 82301-0068. Tel: 307-324-4631. Rev. Malcolm Reid.

SHERIDAN. *U.S. Veterans Administration Hospital.* Mailing Address: Box 4013, 82801-4013. Tel: 307-672-3473, Ext. 263. Rev. John Norton, O.P.

On Leave of Absence:
Reverend Fathers—
Robinson, John, O.S.B.

In Residence:
Reverend Fathers—
Siu, Robert, Holy Rosary Church, P.O. Box 1047, Lander, WY 82520-1047

On Duty Outside the Diocese:
Reverend Fathers—
Jablonowski, Anthony, C.M.M.I., St. Theresa Parish, P.O. Box 435, Patagonia, AZ 85624

Retired:
Reverend Monsignors—
Carroll, Daniel, 639 Ave. H, #157, Powell, WY 82435. Tel: 307-754-9746
Delaney, William, P.O. Box 5720, Cheyenne, WY 82003-5720
Etchingham, Lawrence, P.O. Box 5720, Cheyenne, WY 82003
Godley, James, Ballyheige, Kerry Ireland
Reverend Fathers—
Doudican, James, P.O. Box 5720, Cheyenne, WY 82003
Fahey, Thomas, O.F.M., Chap., Victory Noll Sisters, 1900 W. Park Dr., Box 109, Huntington, IN 46750
Fraher, Joseph P., Church of St. Mary Magdalen, 2771 Zenobia St., Denver, CO 80212
Gianola, William, 3954 Quail Ln. N., Chattanooga, TN 37415
Moroney, Joseph E., 100 W. 21st St., Cheyenne, WY 82001
Prado, Cletus, 802 N. 29th St., Phoenix, AZ 85008

Permanent Deacons:
Aloisio, John, St. Francis, Thermopolis
Humphreys, Russ, St. Patrick's Church, Casper
Kristufek, Joseph, Holy Name Church, Sheridan
McCarthy, Ed, Our Lady of Fatima, Casper
Piasecki, Stanley, St. Matthew, Gillette
Pico, Lee, St. Mary's Cathedral, Cheyenne
Stewart, Don, St. Anthony's Church, Casper

INSTITUTIONS LOCATED IN THE DIOCESE

[A] PROTECTIVE INSTITUTIONS

TORRINGTON. *St. Joseph's Children's Home*, Box 1117, 82240-1117. Tel: 307-532-4197; Fax: 307-532-8405.
For a complete listing, refer to the Special Care Facilities section.

[B] HOUSING FOR THE ELDERLY (LOW INCOME)

CHEYENNE. *Holy Trinity Manor*, 2516 E. 18th St., 82001. Tel: 307-778-8850.
For a complete listing, refer to the Special Care Facilities section.

CASPER. *St. Anthony Manor*, 211 E. Sixth St., 82601. Tel: 307-237-0844.
For a complete listing, refer to the Special Care Facilities section.

[C] MONASTERIES AND RESIDENCES FOR PRIESTS AND BROTHERS

ST. STEPHENS. *St. Stephens Mission - Jesuit Community*, Box 250, 82524. Tel: 307-865-5937. Revs. Eugene Zimmerman, S.J.; Daniel J. Gannon, S.J.; John A. Apel, S.J.

[D] CONVENTS AND RESIDENCES FOR SISTERS

DAYTON. *Benedictine Sisters of Perpetual Adoration*, San Benito Monastery, P.O. Box 520, 82836-0520. Tel: 307-655-9013. Sr. M. Benita Luetkemeyer, O.S.B., Supr. Sisters 5.

[E] CAMPUS MINISTRY

CASPER. *Casper Community College*, St. Francis Newman Center, 1732 S. Elm St., 82601. Tel: 307-577-1421. Total Staff 3.
Attended by St. Anthony of Padua, Casper.

LARAMIE. *University of Wyoming*, St. Paul's Newman Center, University Catholic Parish, 1800 E. Grand Ave., 82070-4316. Tel: 307-745-5461. Rev. Roger W. Schmit, O.S.B., Admin. Total Staff 7.

POWELL. *NorthWest College*, John Henry Newman Center, 674 N. Absaroka, 82435. Tel: 307-745-5316. Rev. John Wright, Chap. & Dir.; Jennifer Martinez, Asst. Dir.
Attended by St. Barbara, Powell.

[F] MISCELLANEOUS LISTINGS

CHEYENNE. *St. Mary's Goods Bookstore*, 2417 Central Ave., 82001. Tel: 307-635-4228. Zula Samuelson, Mgr.

CASPER.
**Holy Cross Food Center, Inc.*, 1030 N. Lincoln, 82601. Tel: 307-577-1041. Operated by Holy Cross Brothers. Bro. Francis Kjeldgaard, C.S.C., Dir. Total Staff 18; Total Assisted 11,160.
**Mother Seton Housing, Inc.*, 906 N. Beach St., 82601. Tel: 307-577-8026. Emergency/Transitional Housing for Homeless Women and Children/Homeless Men and Children. Debra Starks, Exec. Dir., Shelter, 324 E. H St., 82601. Tel: 307-234-1119. Total Assisted 60-65 families per year; Individuals 417.

ROCK SPRINGS. *Rock Springs Catholic School Foundation*, P.O. Box 6038, 82901-0038. Rev. Fred Wendel.

ST. STEPHENS. *St. Stephens Indian Mission Foundation* (1974), P.O. Box 278, 82524-0278. Tel: 307-856-6797. Rev. Eugene Zimmerman, S.J., Dir.

RELIGIOUS INSTITUTES OF MEN REPRESENTED IN THE DIOCESE

For further details refer to the corresponding bracketed number in the Religious Institutes of Men or Women section.

[0200]—*Benedictine Monks.*—O.S.B.
[0600]—*Brothers of the Congregation of Holy Cross.* (South-West Prov.).—C.S.C.
[0275]—*Carmelites of Mary Immaculate.*—C.M.I.
[1330]—*Congregation of the Mission.*—C.M.
[0690]—*Jesuit Fathers and Brothers Jesus.*—S.J.
[0430]—*Order of Preachers (Dominicans).*—O.P.

RELIGIOUS INSTITUTES OF WOMEN REPRESENTED IN THE DIOCESE

[0230]—*Benedictine Sisters of Pontifical Jurisdiction.*—O.S.B.
[1070-03]—*Dominican Sisters.*—O.P.
[3130]—*Our Lady of Victory Missionary Sisters.*—O.L.V.M.
[]—*Religious Sisters of Mercy.*—R.S.M.
[1680]—*School Sisters of St. Francis.* (Milwaukee, WI).—O.S.F.
[0480]—*Sisters of Charity of Leavenworth, Kansas.*—S.C.L.
[0430]—*Sisters of Charity of the Blessed Virgin Mary.*—B.V.M.
[2360]—*Sisters of Loretto At the Foot of the Cross.*—S.L.
[3360]—*Sisters of Providence of Saint Mary-of-the-Woods, IN.*—S.P.
[1650]—*Sisters of St. Francis of Philadelphia.*—O.S.F.
[3830]—*Sisters of St. Joseph.*—C.S.J.
[4120]—*Ursuline Nuns, of the Congregation of Paris.*—O.S.U.

DIOCESAN CEMETERIES

CHEYENNE. *Olivet Cemetery.*

NECROLOGY

† Bauer, Vincent Louis, (Retired). —Died Sept. 27, 1996.
† Bianco, Bernard, (Retired). —Died July 21, 1996.
† Kimmett, Rev. Msgr. Frederick J., (Retired). —Died April 2, 1996.

Archdiocese of Chicago

(Archidioecesis Chicagiensis)

(Vacant See)

The Pastoral Center: P.O. Box 1979, Chicago, IL, 60690. Tel.: 312-751-7999 ext. 8200.

Web site address: http://www.archdiocese-chgo.org

Most Reverend

ALFRED L. ABRAMOWICZ

Retired Auxiliary Bishop of Chicago; ordained May 1, 1943; appointed Auxiliary Bishop of Chicago and Titular Bishop of Paestum on May 8, 1968; consecrated June 13, 1968; retired January 24, 1995. *Res., 6101 S. 75th Ave., Summit-Argo, IL, 60501.*

Most Reverend

TIMOTHY J. LYNE

Retired Auxiliary Bishop of Chicago; ordained May 1, 1943; appointed Auxiliary Bishop of Chicago and Titular Bishop of Vamalla October 31, 1983; consecrated December 13, 1983; retired January 24, 1995. *Res., 730 N. Wabash, Chicago, IL, 60611.*

Most Reverend

THAD J. JAKUBOWSKI

Auxiliary Bishop of Chicago; ordained May 3, 1950; appointed Auxiliary Bishop of Chicago and Titular Bishop of Plestia February 16, 1988; consecrated April 11, 1988. *Res., 6002 W. Berteau Ave., Chicago, IL, 60634-1630.* Tel.: 312-202-7720.

Most Reverend

JOHN R. GORMAN

Auxiliary Bishop of Chicago and Titular Bishop of Catula; ordained May 1, 1952; appointed February 16, 1988; consecrated April 11, 1988. *Res., 2330 W. 118th St., Chicago, IL, 60643.*

Most Reverend

RAYMOND E. GOEDERT

Auxiliary Bishop of Chicago; ordained May 1, 1952; appointed Auxiliary Bishop of Chicago and Titular Bishop of Tamazeni July 8, 1991; consecrated August 29, 1991; Diocesan Administrator. *Res., 1555 N. State Pkwy., Chicago, IL, 60611.*

Most Reverend

EDWIN M. CONWAY

Auxiliary Bishop of Chicago; ordained May 3, 1960; appointed Auxiliary Bishop of Chicago and Titular Bishop of Auguro January 24, 1995; consecrated and installed March 20, 1995. *Res., 126 N. Desplaines, Chicago, IL, 60661.*

Most Reverend

GERALD F. KICANAS

Auxiliary Bishop of Chicago; ordained April 27, 1967; appointed Auxiliary Bishop of Chicago and Titular Bishop of Bela January 24, 1995; consecrated and installed March 20, 1995. *Res., 200 N. Milwaukee Ave., Libertyville, IL, 60048.*

Most Reverend

GEORGE V. MURRY, S.J.

Auxiliary Bishop of Chicago; ordained 1979; appointed Auxiliary Bishop of Chicago and Titular Bishop of Fuerteventura January 24, 1995; consecrated and installed March 20, 1995. *Mailing Address: P.O. Box 733, South Holland, IL, 60473-0733.*

Most Reverend

JOHN R. MANZ

Auxiliary Bishop of Chicago; ordained May 12, 1971; appointed Auxiliary Bishop of Chicago and Titular Bishop of Mulia January 23, 1996; installed March 5, 1996. *Mailing Address: 1820 S. Leavitt St., Chicago, IL, 60608.*

ESTABLISHED NOVEMBER 28, 1843.; CREATED 1880.

Square Miles 1,411.

Comprises the Counties of Cook and Lake in the State of Illinois.

Legal Title: The Catholic Bishop of Chicago, a Corporation Sole.

For legal titles of institutions, consult The Pastoral Center.

STATISTICAL OVERVIEW

Personnel	
Auxiliary Bishops	7
Retired Bishops	2
Priests: Diocesan Active in Diocese	621
Priests: Active Outside Diocese	29
Priests: Diocesan in Foreign Missions	5
Priests: Retired, Sick or Absent	303
Number of Diocesan Priests	958
Religious Priests in Diocese	859
Extern Priests in Diocese	78
Ordinations:	
Diocesan Priests	6
Religious Priests	10
Transitional Deacons	7
Permanent Deacons	30
Permanent Deacons in Diocese	595
Total Brothers	444
Total Sisters	3,434
Parishes	
Parishes	378
With Resident Pastor:	
Resident Diocesan Priests	314
Resident Religious Priests	51
Without Resident Pastor:	
Administered by Priests	12
Administered by Women Religious	1
Missions	11
Pastoral Centers	8
New Parishes Created	2
Closed Parishes	1
Professional Ministry Personnel:	
Brothers	11
Sisters	192
Lay Ministers	464
Welfare	
Catholic Hospitals	19
Total Assisted	2,680,658
Health Care Centers	1
Total Assisted	4,500
Homes for the Aged	28
Total Assisted	5,200
Day Care and Extended Day Care Centers	11
Total Assisted	2,100
Specialized Homes	20
Total Assisted	11,000
Special Centers for Social Services	45
Total Assisted	93,000
Residential Care of Disabled	9
Total Assisted	1,300
Other Institutions	45
Total Assisted	330,000
Educational	
Seminaries, Diocesan	3
Students from This Diocese	328
Students from Other Diocese	143
Diocesan Students in Other Seminaries	4
Seminaries, Religious	1
Students Religious	93
Total Seminarians	425
Colleges and Universities	6
Total Students	40,599
High Schools, Diocesan and Parish	9
Total Students	2,727
High Schools, Private	39
Total Students	30,698
Elementary Schools, Diocesan and Parish	274
Total Students	100,842
Elementary Schools, Private	2
Total Students	1,182
Non-residential Schools for the Disabled	7
Total Students	600
Catechesis/Religious Education:	
High School Students	10,797
Elementary Students	93,812
Total Students Under Catholic Instruction	281,682
Teachers in the Diocese:	
Priests	55
Brothers	67
Sisters	357
Lay Teachers	5,710
Vital Statistics	
Receptions into the Church:	
Infant Baptism Totals	39,989
Adult Baptism Totals	1,804
Received into Full Communion	1,544
First Communions	29,219
Confirmations	19,827
Marriages:	
Catholic	9,038
Interfaith	2,277
Total Marriages	11,315
Deaths	18,948
Total Catholic Population	2,342,000
Total Population	5,712,000

Former Bishops—Rt. Rev. WILLIAM QUARTER, D.D., cons. March 10, 1844; died April 10, 1848.—Rt. Rev. JAMES O. VAN DE VELDE, D.D., cons. Feb. 11, 1849; transferred to Natchez, July 29, 1853; died Nov. 13, 1855.—Rt. Rev. ANTHONY O'REGAN, D.D., cons. July 25, 1854; resigned 1858; died Nov., 1866.—Rt. Rev. JAMES DUGGAN, D.D., cons. Bishop of Antigone, and Coadjutor to the Archbishop of St. Louis, May 1, 1857; transferred to Chicago, Jan. 21, 1859; hospitalized, 1869; died March 27, 1899.—Rt. Rev. THOMAS FOLEY, D.D., Coadjutor-Bishop and Administrator of the diocese; cons. Bishop of Pergamus, Feb. 27, 1870; died Feb. 19, 1879.—Most Rev. PATRICK A. FEEHAN, D.D., First Archbishop of Chicago; cons. Bishop of Nashville, Nov. 1, 1865; promoted to Chicago, Sept. 10, 1880; died July 12, 1902.—Most Rev. JAMES EDWARD QUIGLEY, D.D., Archbishop of Chicago; ord. April 12, 1879; cons. Bishop of Buffalo, Feb. 24, 1897; promoted to Archbishop of Chicago, Jan. 8, 1903; died July 10, 1915.—His Eminence GEORGE CARDINAL MUNDELEIN, Archbishop of Chicago; ord. June 8, 1895; cons. Titular Bishop of Loryma and Auxiliary Bishop of Brooklyn, Sept. 21, 1909; promoted to the See of Chicago, Dec. 9, 1915; created Cardinal Priest, March 24, 1924; died Oct. 2, 1939.—His Eminence SAMUEL CARDINAL STRITCH, Archbishop of Chicago; ord. May 21, 1910; appt. Bishop of Toledo, Aug. 10, 1921; promoted to Archbishop of Milwaukee, Aug. 26, 1930; transferred to Archbishop of Chicago, Dec. 27, 1939; created Cardinal Priest Feb. 18, 1946; elevated to the Roman Curia, Sacred Congregation for the Propagation of the Faith, March 1, 1958; died in Rome, May 27, 1958.—His Eminence ALBERT CARDINAL MEYER, Archbishop of Chicago; ord. July 11, 1926; appt. Bishop of Superior, Feb. 18, 1946; promoted to Archbishop of Milwaukee, July 21, 1953; transferred to Archbishop of Chicago, Sept. 19, 1958; created Cardinal Priest, Dec. 14, 1959; died April 9, 1965.—His Eminence JOHN CARDINAL CODY, Archbishop of Chicago; ord. Dec. 8, 1931; appt. Auxiliary Bishop of St. Louis, May 14, 1947; cons. July 2, 1947; promoted to Coadjutor of St. Joseph, Jan. 27, 1954; transferred to Kansas City-St. Joseph, Aug. 29, 1956; promoted to Coadjutor Archbishop of New Orleans, Aug. 14, 1961; acceded the See of New Orleans, Nov. 8, 1964; transferred to the Archdiocese of Chicago, June 16, 1965; created Cardinal Priest in the Consistory, June 26, 1967; died April 25, 1982.—His Eminence JOSEPH CARDINAL BERNADIN, Archbishop of Chicago; ord. April 26, 1952; appt. Auxiliary Bishop of Atlanta, March 9, 1966; cons. April 26, 1966; appt. Archbishop of Cincinnati, Nov. 21, 1972; appt. Archbishop of Chicago, July 10, 1982; installed Aug. 25, 1982; created Cardinal Priest, Feb. 2, 1983; died Nov. 14, 1996.

Diocesan Administrator—Most Rev. RAYMOND E. GOEDERT.

Vicar General/Vicar for Regional Services—Most Rev. RAYMOND E. GOEDERT.

Episcopal Vicars—Most Rev. GERALD KICANAS, Vicariate I (Deaneries A, B); Most Rev. EDWIN M. CONWAY, Vicariate II (Deaneries A, B, C, D, E, F); Most Rev. JOHN R. MANZ, Vicariate III (Deaneries A, B, C, D, E); Most Rev. THAD J. JAKUBOWSKI, Vicariate IV (Deaneries A, B, C); Most Rev. JOHN L. GORMAN, Vicariate V (Deaneries A, B, C, D, E); Most Rev. GEORGE V. MURRY, S.J., Vicariate VI (Deaneries A, B, C, D).

Deans—Revs. FARRELL KANE, Deanery I-A; JOHN J. HURLEY, Deanery I-B; EDWARD HOOVER, Deanery II-A; LAWRENCE F. MADDOCK, Deanery II-B; ROBERT J. HEIDENREICH, Deanery II-C; JOHN R. HOFFMAN, Deanery II-D; RONALD N. KALAS, Deanery II-E; MICHAEL A. WULSCH, Deanery II-F; THOMAS A. TIVY, Deanery III-A; MICHAEL DANEK, C.R., Deanery III-B; ANTHONY M. TALARICO, Deanery III-C; LAWRENCE M. CHOATE, O.S.M., Deanery III-D; JAMES T. KACZOROWSKI, Deanery III-E; DANIEL G. MAYALL, Deanery IV-A; FRANCIS C. JENKS, Deanery IV-B; JOHN C. ROSEMEYER, Deanery IV-C; JOSEPH R. BENNETT, Deanery V-A; JEROME S. SIWEK, Deanery V-B; PATRICK M. LYONS, Deanery V-C; PAUL C. BURAK, Deanery V-D; EDWARD F. UPTON, Deanery V-E; JAMES J. MARTIN, Deanery VI-A; LAWRENCE M. DURIS, Deanery VI-B; THOMAS FRANZMAN, Deanery VI-C; THOMAS E. CIMA, Deanery VI-D.

College of Consultors—Revs. GINO DALPIAZ; THOMAS M. DORE; LAWRENCE F. HANLEY; JOHN L. HARVEY; FRANCIS C. JENKS; JAMES T. KACZOROWSKI; J. CLETUS KILEY; JOHN KUZINSKAS; PATRICK J. POLLARD; DONALD SENIOR, O.P.; MICHAEL A. WULSCH; THOMAS J. PAPROCKI, Sec.

Presbyteral Council—Revs. JEREMIAH M. BOLAND, Chm. JOHN M. COLLINS, Vice Chm. RONALD J. MASS, Sec. CURTIS A. LAMBERT, Treas.

Finance Council—Vice Chairmen: Rev. R. PETER BOWMAN; Mr. FRANK W. CONSIDINE; Mr. JAMES M. DENNY; Rev. KEVIN J. SPIESS. Members: Miss EILEEN T. CORCORAN; Mr. JOHN W. CROGHAN; Most Rev. RAYMOND E. GOEDERT; Mr. WILLIAM M. GOODYEAR; Mr. DONALD GOSS; Sr. LOIS GRAVER, R.S.M.; Rev. RICHARD M. HOMA; Mr. MITCHELL KOBELINSKI; Hon. GEORGE N. LEIGHTON; Mr. WILLIAM A. MCINTOSH; Mr. ANDREW J. MCKENNA, SR.; Mr. HENRY MENDOZA; Mr. R. MICHAEL MURRAY, JR.; Mr. OLIVER NICKLIN; Mr. THOMAS H. QUINN; Mr. PHILIP P. ROONEY; Rev. GEORGE L. SCHOPP; Mr. EDMUND A. STEPHAN; Mr. JEROME VAN GORKOM; Mr. FIDELIS N. UMEH; Mr. ARTHUR R. VELASQUEZ; Rev. THOMAS F. VENTURA; Mrs. PATRICIA A. WEIR.

Pastoral Council—DAVID SHERMAN, Chm. ANNA CANNON, Vice Chm. ANN SUPPLITT, Exec. Sec. Tel: 312-751-5357.

Consejo Pastoral Hispano Arquidiocesano—Co-Chm.: GRACIELA CONTRERAS. Tel: 708-286-0078. TERESA HERNANDEZ. Tel: 312-641-4838. Sr. DOMINGA ZAPATA, S.W., Exec. Dir. Tel: 312-751-8343.

Provincial Offices

The Catholic Conference Of Illinois—Mr. DOUGLAS DELANEY, Exec. Dir., *500 N. Clark St., Chicago, 60610-4202.* Tel: 312-467-4375.

Interdiocesan Appellate Tribunal—Revs. ROBERT L. KEALY, S.T.L., J.D., J.C.D., Judicial Vicar; JOHN P. LUCAS, Adjutant Judicial Vicar; Ms. JANE HALPIN, Chief Notary, *20 N. Wacker Dr., Ste. 3420, Chicago, 60606.* Tel: 312-553-4080; 800-572-7835 (In Illinois); Fax: 312-553-4085.

Archdiocesan Offices

All Archdiocesan Departments can be contacted through *The Pastoral Center, 155 E. Superior St., Chicago, IL 60611.* (Street & Package Delivery Address). Address all mail to: *P.O. Box 1979, Chicago, IL 60690.* Tel: 312-751-7999, Ext. 8200 unless otherwise indicated.

Office of the Archbishop—Bro. DENNIS DUNNE, F.M.S., Exec. Asst. to the Cardinal. Tel: 312-751-7999, Ext. 8219. Sr. MARY BRIAN COSTELLO, R.S.M., Chief of Staff. Tel: 312-751-7999, Ext. 8236. Rev. ALPHONSE P. SPILLY, C.PP.S., Spec. Asst. to the Cardinal. Tel: 312-751-7999, Ext. 8299. MARIE KNOLL, Communications Assoc. Tel: 312-751-7999, Ext. 8238.

The Chancery See Office of the Chancellor.

The Metropolitan Tribunal—See Office of the Chancellor.

Research Theologian for the Curia & Consul for Policy Development—Rev. MICHAEL D. PLACE, S.T.D. Tel: 312-751-7999, Ext. 8354.

Senior Administrators Serving the Archbishop

Vicar for Regional Services/Vicar General—Most Rev. RAYMOND E. GOEDERT. Tel: 312-751-7999, Ext. 8271.

Vicar for Administration/Moderator of the Curia—Rev. R. PETER BOWMAN. Tel: 312-751-7999, Ext. 5250.

Chief of Staff—Sr. MARY BRIAN COSTELLO, R.S.M. Tel: 312-751-7999, Ext. 8236.

Executive Assistant to the Cardinal—Bro. DENNIS DUNNE, F.M.S. Tel: 312-751-7999, Ext. 8219.

Vicar for Regional Services/Vicar General

Vicar for Regional Services/Vicar General—Most Rev. RAYMOND E. GOEDERT. Tel: 312-751-7999, Ext. 8271.

Office of Research & Planning—Rev. DAVID E. BALDWIN. Tel: 312-751-7999, Ext. 8345.

Office of Ethnic Ministries—Rev. JOHN P. BOIVIN. Tel: 312-751-7999, Ext. 8308.

Vicar for Administration/Moderator of the Curia

Vicar for Administration/Moderator of the Curia—Rev. R. PETER BOWMAN. Tel: 312-751-7999, Ext. 5250.

Department Directors—JOHN F. BENWARE, Financial Svcs.; Most Rev. EDWIN M. CONWAY, Human Svcs.; Rev. DONALD J. NEVINS, Ministry Formation; Dr. CAROL FOWLER, Personnel Svcs.

Legal Services—JOHN C. O'MALLEY, Dir. Tel: 312-751-7999, Ext. 5379.

Research & Planning—Rev. DAVID E. BALDWIN, Dir. Tel: 312-751-7999, Ext. 8345. Assoc. Dirs. of Planning: Mr. TONY M. FIDANZO. Tel: 312-751-7999, Ext. 5283. Mr. CHARLES A. HOLLAND, JR. Tel: 312-751-7999, Ext. 5370. Ms. CONSTANCE O'BRIEN. Tel: 312-751-7999, Ext. 5371. DAVID F. SCHWARTZ, Assoc. Dir., Research. Tel: 312-751-7999, Ext. 8344. Rev. ROBERT L. EBROM, Research Asst. Tel: 312-751-7999, Ext. 5338.

Office of the Chancellor

The Chancery—Fax: 312-751-5381.

Chancellor—Rev. THOMAS J. PAPROCKI, S.T.L., J.D., J.C.D. Tel: 312-751-7999, Ext. 8220.

Vice-Chancellors—Revs. RICHARD B. SAUDIS; EMMETT J. GAVIN, O.Carm. Tel: 312-751-7999, Ext. 8207.

Associate Chancellor—Rev. ROBERT GEISINGER, S.J., J.C.D. Tel: 312-751-7999, Ext. 8211.

Assistant to the Chancellor—Rev. JEFFREY S. GROB. Tel: 312-751-7999, Ext. 8213.

Assistant Chancellor for Archives and Records—JOHN J. TREANOR, *711 W. Monroe St., Chicago, 60606.* Tel: 312-831-0711.

Metropolitan Tribunal—

Judicial Vicar—Rev. MICHAEL A. HACK, J.C.D. Tel: 312-751-7999, Ext. 8250.

Adjutant Judicial Vicar—Rev. PATRICK R. LAGGES, J.C.D.

Applications Coordinator—GLENDA MCFADDEN. Tel: 312-751-7999, Ext. 8523.

Promoter of Justice—Rev. MICHAEL A. KURZ, J.C.D.

Judges—Rev. MICHAEL A. HACK, J.C.D.; Sr. JOYCE HOBEN, S.N.D.; Revs. STANLEY DREWRIAK; ROBERT GEISINGER, S.J., J.C.D.; MICHAEL KURZ, J.C.L.; PATRICK R. LAGGES, J.C.D.; DAVID J. MULVIHILL, J.C.D.; DANIEL SMILANIC, J.C.D.; Sr. CARMEN GONZALEZ, C.D.P., J.C.L.

Defenders of the Bond—Rev. JOHN A. ROLEK, B.A.

Delegate of the Archbishop for Privilege Cases—Rev. JOHN A. ROLEK, B.A.

Advocates—Revs. JOHN GRIFFITHS; MICHAEL BRADLEY; JOSEPH MOL; Deacon STEFAN STANCZAK.

Office of Conciliation—RALPH BONACCORSI, Exec. Dir. Tel: 312-751-8291.

Office of Professional Fitness Review—Ms. BERNADETTE CONNOLLY, Admin., *One E. Superior St., Ste. 504, Chicago, 60611.* Tel: 312-751-5205; 800-994-6200.

Office of Professional Responsibility—RALPH BONACCORSI, Dir. MYRA FLORES, Admin. Asst., *676 N. St. Clair, Ste. 2240, Chicago, 60611.* Tel: 312-751-8256.

Department of Communications and Development

Department of Communications and Development—Vacant. Tel: 312-751-7999, Ext. 8200.

Communications, Office of—Mr. ROBERT A. QUAKENBUSH, Chief Communications Officer; Ms. MARY MCDONOUGH, Communications Mgr.; Ms. NANCY WILSON, Asst. Communications Mgr. Tel: 312-751-7999, Ext. 8227.

Catholic Information Service—BECKY SUTTON, Dir. Tel: 312-751-7999, Ext. 8204.

Office of Radio & TV—JOE LOUGHLIN, Dir. Tel: 312-751-7999, Ext. 8277.

Consultant—THOMAS DEMINT. Tel: 312-751-8264.

New World Publications—MARY CLAIRE GART, Editor Pro Tem, *1144 W. Jackson, Chicago, 60607.* Tel: 312-243-1300.

Media Chaplain—Rev. JOHN J. WALL, Dir., *718 W. Adams, Chicago, 60606.* Tel: 312-243-1300.

Director of Archdiocesan Development—RAYMOND P. COUGHLIN, Dir., *225 S. Aberdeen Ave., Chicago, 60607.* Tel: 312-563-5737.

Cardinal's Appeal—JOAN B. PATTERSON-TURK, Internal Coord. Tel: 312-563-5735. ANNE R. DEMKE, External Coord. Tel: 312-563-5715.

Planned Giving/Annuities—Mr. RICHARD GOODE. Tel: 312-563-5711.

Parish Development—DAN CHORNEY, Dir. Tel: 312-563-5738.

Stewardship—MICHAEL GLEASON. Tel: 312-563-5740.

Seminary Development-Archbishop Quigley Preparatory Seminary—Mr. THOMAS LECLAIR. Tel: 312-787-9343., *St. Joseph Seminary,* MARIE COMPOSTO. Tel: 773-631-1017., *St. Mary of the Lake, Mundelein;* Mr. BRUCE HOLMES. Tel: 708-566-6401.

Donor Research—PATRICIA MCNICHOLAS. Tel: 312-563-5736.

Big Shoulders Fund—WALTER HANSEN. Tel: 312-751-8337.

Department of Financial Services

Director—JOHN F. BENWARE. Tel: 312-751-8218.

Facilities Services and Construction—C. GREGORY VEITH, Mgr. Tel: 312-751-8342.

Controller's Operations—JAMES C. ROJEK, Mgr. Tel: 312-751-5277.

Accounting—MARK COSENTINO, Mgr. Tel: 312-751-5266.

Office Services—PHIL WAGNER, Mgr. Tel: 312-751-8246.

Management Information Services (MIS)—Mr. GANG CHEN, Mgr. Tel: 312-751-5349.

Property and Insurance—MICHAEL J. DOLAN, Mgr. Tel: 312-751-8221.

Vicariate Administrative Consultants (VACS)—

Vicariate I—MARY P. HALL. Tel: 312-751-5322. Vicariate Office: Tel: 847-549-0165.

Vicariate II—GENE MYERS. Tel: 312-751-5321. Vicariate Office: Tel: 773-763-1661.

Vicariate III—KENT BEAUSOLEIL. Tel: 312-751-5323. Vicariate Office: Tel: 312-243-1135.

Vicariate IV—TAFFIE NEVILLE. Tel: 312-751-5312. Vicariate Office: Tel: 773-202-7722.

Vicariate V—ALEX BECKER. Tel: 312-751-5318. Vicariate Office: Tel: 773-779-9165.

Vicariate VI—JASON BERTRAND. Tel: 708-333-6132. Vicariate Office: Tel: 312-493-2993.

Catholic Cemeteries—Rev. PATRICK J. POLLARD, Dir. DONALD MASSARO, Exec. Dir.; Rev. Msgr. FRANCIS

J. McElligott, Consultant, *1400 S. Wolf Rd., Hillside, 60162.* Tel: 708-449-6100; Fax: 708-449-3419.

Department of Evangelization and Christian Life

Director—Rev. Raymond Baumhart S.J., Dir. Tel: 312-751-8346.

Archdiocesan Council of Catholic Women (ACCW)—Clarice Brown, Pres. Tel: 312-751-8325.

Catholic Charismatic Renewal Center of Chicago (CCRCC)—Revs. Patrick J. Henry, Cardinal's Liaison; Richard T. Simon, Liaison for Hispanics, *12905 S. Division St., Blue Island, 60406.* Tel: 708-371-2727.

Catholic Missions Office—

Propagation of the Faith—Co-Dirs.: Rev. John J. Grace; Sr. Ann Carol Kaufenberg, S.S.N.D., *225 S. Aberdeen Ave., Chicago, 60607.* Tel: 312-563-5750.

Holy Childhood Association—Co-Dirs.: Rev. John J. Grace; Sr. Ann Carol Kaufenberg, S.S.N.D., *225 S. Aberdeen Ave., Chicago, 60607.* Tel: 312-563-5750.

Partnership in Mission Archdiocese of Chicago/Diocese of Chilpancingo-Chilapa-Catholic Missions Office—225 S. Aberdeen Ave., Chicago, 60607. Tel: 312-563-5750.

Catholic Youth Office—Revs. John P. Smyth, Dir. David Ryan, Asst. Exec. Dir., *1658 W. Grand Ave., Chicago, 60622.* Tel: 312-733-7405.

Chaplaincies—

The Catholic Ministry at Chicago O'Hare International Airport—Rev. John A. Jamnicky, Chap.; Deacon James O'Malley, Assoc. Chap., *P.O. Box 66353, Chicago, 60666-0353.* Tel: 773-686-2636.

Airport, Midway—Rev. George P. McKenna, Chap. Tel: 773-767-0500.

Firefighters/Paramedics—Rev. Thomas A. Mulcrone, Chap., *1140 W. Jackson Blvd., Chicago, 60607.* Tel: 312-738-9246.

Police—Rev. Thomas R. Nangle, Chap., *1140 W. Jackson Blvd., Chicago, 60607.* Tel: 312-738-7588.

Seafarers—Rev. James P. Keating, Chap., *10201 S. Ewing, Chicago, 60617.* Tel: 773-734-1383.

Cursillo Movement, Chicago Catholic Office of—Vacant, *2226 N. Hoyne Ave., Chicago, 60647.* Tel: 773-486-5101; Fax: 773-486-5111.

Ecumenism and Interreligious Affairs, Office for—Revs. Thomas Baima, Dir. Tel: 312-751-7999, Ext. 5325. Daniel Montalbano, Assoc Dir. Tel: 773-478-9705. Sr. Mary Ellen Coombe, N.D.S., Assoc Dir. Tel: 312-751-5325. Dr. Jon Nilson, Asst. Dir. Tel: 773-508-2347. Adjunct Staff: Rev. Leonard Dubi; Deacon Edmund Gronkiewicz; Revs. Henry Kricek; Andrew Luczak; Mr. J. Michael Thompson; Rev. Raymond Webb.

Ethnic Ministries, Office for—Rev. John P. Boivin, Dir.; Mrs. Sheila Adams, African-American Consultant; Mrs. Teresita L. Nuval, Asian-American Consultant; Mrs. Krystyna Zambrzycki, European-American Consultant; Sr. Dominga Zapata, S.H., Hispanic-American Consultant. Tel: 312-751-8301; Fax: 312-751-5313. Rev. Joseph Glab, C.R., Polish Liaison.

Vicariate Hispanic Coordinators—

Vicariate I—Graciela Contreras, O.S.A., *200 N. Milwaukee Ave., Ste. 212, Libertyville, 60048.* Tel: 847-549-0164.

Vicariate II—Vacant, *4419 N. Kedzie, Chicago, 60625.* Tel: 773-463-5339.

Vicariate III—Roberto Rivas, *1840 S. Leavitt, Chicago, 60608.* Tel: 312-432-9804; 432-9805.

Vicariate IV—Ms. Modesta Martinez, *912 Dolores Dr., Bensenville, 60106.* Tel: 630-238-1593.

Vicariate V—Ms. Olga Torres, *2330 W. 118th St., Chicago, 60643.* Tel: 773-779-9324.

Vicariate VI—Mr. Mario Delgado, *16160 Seton Rd., South Holland, 60473.* Tel: 708-339-1779.

Ministry Missions or Centers—

American Indian Apostolate—Sr. Antoinette Harris, Dir., *Anawin Center, 4545 N. Broadway, Ste. 258, Chicago, 60640.* Tel: 773-561-6155.

Angel Guardian Croatian Catholic Mission—Rev. Nicholas Dugandzic, O.P., Dir., *6346 N. Ridge Ave., Chicago, 60660.* Tel: 773-262-0535.

Chinese Catholic Mission (St. Therese Chinese Mission)—Rev. Christopher Wong, *218 W. Alexander, Chicago, 60616.* Tel: 312-842-6777.

Haitian Catholic Center—Vacant, *Our Lady of Peace, 7851 S. Jeffrey, Chicago, 60649.* Tel: 773-768-0105.

Holy Trinity Polish Mission—Rev. Wladyslaw Gowin, S.Ch., Dir., *1118 N. Noble, Chicago, 60622.* Tel: 773-489-4140.

Indochinese Catholic Center—Rev. Peter Hung, Dir., *4827 N. Kenmore, Chicago, 60640.* Tel: 773-784-1932.

Italian Catholic Apostolate—Rev. Ermete Nazzani, C.S., Dir., *1621 N. 39th Ave., Stone Park, 60165.* Tel: 708-345-3842.

Knanya Catholic Mission—Rev. Simon Edadthiparambil, Dir., *3834 N. Spaulding, Chicago, 60618.* Tel: 773-509-9147.

Korean Catholic Mission of Chicago—Rev. John Smith, S.S.C., Dir., *4115 N. Kedvale, Chicago, 60641.* Tel: 773-283-3979.

Blessed George Matulaitis Lithuanian Catholic Mission—Rev. Algirdas Paliokas, S.J., Dir., *14915 127th St., Unit 101, Lemont, 60439.* Tel: 630-257-5613.

St. Paul Chong Hasang Korean Catholic Mission—Rev. Thomas Kim, Dir., *675 Dursey Ln., Des Plaines, 60016.* Tel: 847-699-6334; Fax: 847-966-1029.

Sacred Heart Mission House—Rev. Leszek Balczewski, S.J., Supr., *4105 N. Avers Ave., Chicago, 60618.* Tel: 773-588-7476.

Slovenian Catholic Mission—Rev. David Srumpf, Dir., *14246 Main St., P.O. Box 608, Lemont, 60439.* Tel: 630-257-2068.

Slovak Catholic Mission—Rev. Edward Slosarcik, Dir., *5900 W. 147th St., Oak Forest, 60452.* Tel: 708-535-1090.

Syro-Malabar Catholic Mission—Rev. Jos Kandathikudy, Dir., *Mar Thoma Shleeha Center, 5000 St. Charles Rd., Bellwood, 60104.* Tel: 708-544-7250.

Syro-Malankara Catholic Center—Rev. Zacharias Nanthiyattu, O.I.C., Dir., *1634 W. Gregory St., Chicago, 60640., 1208 Ashland Ave., Evanston, 60202.* Tel: 773-907-2092.

Family Ministries—Mr. Francis P. Hannigan, Dir. Tel: 312-751-8351. Assoc. Dirs.: Eunice Joan Dohra. Tel: 312-751-8353. Alicia Rivera. Tel: 312-751-8240.

Cana Conference—Mr. Francis P. Hannigan, Contact. Tel: 312-751-8340.

Hispanic Family Ministries—Alicia Rivera, Contact. Tel: 312-751-8240.

Natural Family Planning—Sharon Dausman, Contact. Tel: 312-751-8351.

Phoenix Ministry—For Separated, Divorced and Remarried. Beginning Experience, Single Parenting. Eunice Joan Dohra, Contact. Tel: 312-751-8353.

Widowed, Ministry to the—Rita Anton, Coord. Tel: 312-751-8351.

Food Service Professionals, Archdiocese—Mr. Ron Hunter, Dir., *5150 Northwest Hwy., Chicago, 60638.* Tel: 773-286-7038.

Ministry in Higher Education—Jan Slattery, Dir., *700 S. Morgan, Chicago, 60607.* Tel: 312-829-0670.

Office of Catholic Education—Elaine M. Schuster, Ph.D., Supt. Tel: 312-751-5200.

Divine Worship, Office for—Mrs. Sheila McLaughlin, Dir.; Sr. Marilyn Barnett, C.S.J., Assoc. Dir.; Ms. Mary Beth Kunde-Anderson, Dir. Liturgical Music; Ms. Kathleen Sullivan-Stewart, Prog. Coord. & L.I.C. Dir.; Mr. Jose Castillo, Coord. Hispanic Programs; Ms. Denise LaGiglia, Asst. Prog. Dir.; Mr. David Phillippart, Acting Admin., Environment & Art Liturgy Training Publications (LTP): Mr. Gabe Huck, Dir., *1800 N. Hermitage Ave., Chicago, 60622.* Tel: 773-486-5153 (ODW); 486-8970 (LTP); Fax: 773-486-7094.

Office of Religious Education—Dr. Carol Eipers, Dir. Asst. Directors: Mr. Christopher Anderson; Jacquelynne Pokorny, *1025 W. Fry St., Chicago, 60622.* Tel: 312-243-3700; Fax: 312-243-3801.

Parish Pastoral Councils—Ms. Rita Kattner, Dir. Tel: 312-751-8364.

Christ Renews His Parish—Ms. Rita Kattner, Dir. Tel: 312-751-8364.

Office for the Ministry of Peace & Justice—Mr. James Lund, Dir. Tel: 312-751-7999, Ext. 8390, 8367, 4333, 5383.

Catholic Relief Services/International Affairs—Mr. James Lund, Dir. Tel: 312-751-5383.

Campaign for Human Development—Dr. Mary Heidkamp, Dir. Tel: 312-751-5333.

Parish Sharing Program—Mr. James Lund, Dir. Tel: 312-751-7999, Ext. 8390.

Prison Ministry/Kolbe House—Rev. Lawrence J. Craig, Dir., *2434 S. California, Chicago, 60608.* Tel: 773-247-0700.

Respect Life/Pro-Life Activities—Ms. Mary A. Hallan, Dir. Tel: 312-751-5355; Fax: 312-787-1554.

Project Rachel—155 E. Superior St., Chicago, 60611. Tel: 312-337-1962.

Special Religious Education (SPRED)—Rev. James H. McCarthy, Dir., *2956 S. Lowe, Chicago, 60616.* Tel: 312-842-1039; Fax: 312-842-4449. Sr. Mary Therese Harrington, S.H.; Sr. Susanne Gallagher, S.P.

Young Adult Ministry/Singles—Rev. John C. Cusick, Dir.; Ms. Katherine F. DeVries, Assoc. Dir., *122 S. Desplaines, Chicago, 60661-3519.* Tel: 312-263-0267.

Lay Groups and Organizations—

Archdiocesan Council of Catholic Men—Rev. John C. Cusick, *122 S. Desplaines, Chicago, 60606.* Tel: 312-782-6171.

Christian Family Movement—Rev. R. Peter Bowman, Chap., *155 E. Superior St., Chicago, 60611.* Chicago Federation Chaircouple: Mary Lou Gorman; Phil Gorman, *900 E. Wilmette Rd., #122, Palatine, 60067.* Tel: 847-202-1032. Area Chaircouple: Jim Quinlan; Bonnie Quinlan, *20 Sarah's Grove, Schaumburg, 60193.* Tel: 630-529-2575.

Knights of Columbus—Tel: 312-751-7999, Ext. 5377.

Legion of Mary—Rev. Charles Lenaghan, S.J., Spiritual Dir., *St. Philomena Parish.* Tel: 773-489-1100.

Marriage Encounter—Rev. Edmund J. Schreiber, Spiritual Dir. Tel: 708-445-0971.

Naim (Widowers & Widows)—Rev. George A. Slominski, Chap., *721 N. LaSalle, Chicago, 60610.* Tel: 312-944-1286.

Department of Human Services

Director—Most Rev. Edwin M. Conway, D.D., *126 N. Desplaines St., Chicago, 60661.* Tel: 312-655-7031.

Catholic Charities of Chicago—Rev. Michael M. Boland, Admin.; Mr. Donald W. Kent, Exec. Dir.; Mr. Jimmy M. Lago, Assoc. Exec. Dir.; Rev. Charles T. Rubey, Dir., Programs. Assoc. Admins.: Revs. Richard E. Bulwith; Francis A. Cimarrusti; Roger J. Coughlin; Daniel M. Holihan; Daniel C. Jankowski; James M. Ray; Rev. Msgr. Vincent W. Cooke, Consultant, *126 N. Desplaines St., Chicago, 60661-2357.* Tel: 312-655-7000. (Refer to Catholic Charities section under the Institutions located in the Archdiocese for further listings.).

Catholic Office of the Deaf—Rev. Joseph A. Mulcrone, Dir.; Ms. Nancy Huber, Religious Education Dir., *721 N. LaSalle, Chicago, 60610.* Tel: 312-655-7899.

Apostolate of the Handicapped—Rev. Charles F. Kelly, Moderator, *5330 S. Nashville, Chicago, 60638.* Tel: 312-586-1223.

Health/Hospital Affairs—Tel: 312-655-7040.

Mercy Home for Boys and Girls—Rev. James J. Close, Pres.; Rev. Scott Donahue, Assoc. Pres., *1140 W. Jackson, Chicago, 60607.* Tel: 312-738-7560; Fax: 312-738-0484.

Office for Persons with Disabilities—Rev. Michael Solazzo, *6300 N. Ridge, Chicago, 60660.* Tel: 773-973-6300.

Department of Ministry Formations

Director—Rev. Donald J. Nevins, *Mundelein Seminary of the University of St. Mary of the Lake.* Tel: 847-566-6401.

University of St. Mary of the Lake—

Mundelein Seminary—Revs. John F. Canary, Rector; Martin A. Zielinski, Academic Dean; Bartholomew S. Winters, Dean of Formation, *Mundelein, 60060.* Tel: 847-566-6401.

Center for Development in Ministry (CDM)—Sr. Judy Connolly, S.S.N.D., Assoc. Dir.; Dr. Juan Lorenzo Hinojosa, Dir., Hillenbrand Institute. Educational Associates: Sr. Joye Gros, O.P.; Rose Henebry-Keane; Revs. William J. Stenzel; George Schopp, *University of St. Mary of the Lake, Mundelein, 60060.* Tel: 847-566-8290; Fax: 847-566-7971.

St. Joseph Seminary at Loyola University—Rev. James Presta, Rector, *6551 N. Sheridan Rd., Chicago, 60626.* Tel: 773-973-9700.

Archbishop Quigley Preparatory Seminary—Revs. John G. Klein, Pres. Michael G. Foley, Rector, *103 E. Chestnut, Chicago, 60611.* Tel: 312-787-9343.

Vocation Office—Rev. John G. Klein, Dir.; Sr. Judith Anne Haase, O.P., Coord. Tel: 312-787-9343.

Amate House/Young Adult Volunteer Program—Mrs. Christina R. Zaker, Dir., *2601 N. Zayre Ave., Chicago, 60635.* Tel: 773-745-0002; 800-383-2038.

Cardinal Stritch Retreat House—Rev. Edmund J. Siedlecki, Dir., *P.O. Box 455, Mundelein, 60060.* Tel: 847-566-6060; Fax: 847-566-6082.

Casa Jesus—Rev. Michael T. Herman, Dir., *1335 W. Harrison St., Chicago, 60607.* Tel: 773-243-7400.

Lay Ministry Programs—Kathryn Jo Cunningham, Assoc. Dir., *1025 Columbian, Oak Park, 60302-1327.* Tel: 708-383-3727; Fax: 708-383-4509.

Diaconate Permanent—1025 Columbia Ave., Oak Park, 60302. Tel: 708-383-9200. Rev. Edward P. Salmon, Vicar/Diaconate Community; Thomas McGorey, Assoc. Dir., Personnel; Charles O'Donnell, Assoc. Dir., Formation.

Instituto De Liderazgo Pastoral (Hispanic Programs for Lay Ministry and Permanent Diaconate).—Mr. Enrique Alonso, Dir. Assoc. Directors: Mrs. Ana M. Rivas; Mrs. Rebecca Vilanueva, *1025 Columbian Ave., Oak Park, 60302.* Tel: 708-383-7948; Fax: 708-383-4509.

Department of Personnel Services

Director—Dr. CAROL FOWLER. Tel: 312-751-8349.

Employee Services—FRED VAN DEN HENDE, Mgr. Tel: 312-751-5352.

Lay Pastoral Ministry, Office for—Mrs. LUCILLE M. MERLIHAN, Dir. HEIDI WEBB, Coord. Placement. Tel: 312-751-5262; 751-5284 (Job Hotline); Fax: 312-751-5281.

Vicar for Priests—Revs. DANIEL P. COUGHLIN; LAWRENCE P. MCBRADY, Vicar for Priests, *645 N. Michigan Ave., Ste. 543, Chicago, 60611.* Tel: 312-642-1837. Rev. ANDREW J. MCDONAGH, Asst. to Vicar for Priests, *6939 N. Hiawatha, Chicago, 60646.* Tel: 312-631-2428.

Vicar for Senior Priests—Most Rev. TIMOTHY J. LYNE, Vicar; Rev. Msgr. FRANCIS MCELLIGOTT, Asst. Vicar. Tel: 312-787-8040.

Religious, Office for—Sr. JOAN MCGLINCHEY, M.S.C., Dir.; Sr. MARGARET COLEMAN, Retirement Collection. Tel: 312-751-8333.

Vicar for Diaconate Community—Rev. EDWARD P. SALMON, *1025 Columbian Ave., Oak Park, 60302.* Tel: 708-383-9200.

Priests' Retirement and Mutual Aid Association (PRMAA)—Rev. DONALD J. AHEARN, Chm., *7142 N. Osceola, Chicago, 60631.* Tel: 773-631-4127.

Priests' Placement Board—Rev. JEREMIAH BOLAND, Exec. Dir. Tel: 312-751-5270; Fax: 312-751-5281.

Commission on the Mission and Life of the Diocesan Priest—Rev. DANIEL P. COUGHLIN, Chm., *645 N. Michigan Ave., Ste. 543, Chicago, 60611.* Tel: 312-642-1837.

Parish Staffing Team—Most Rev. RAYMOND E. GOEDERT, Chm. Tel: 312-751-8271.

Office of Ministeral Evaluation—MARY YUNGER, Dir. Tel: 312-751-5265; Fax: 312-751-5281.

Miscellaneous Archdiocesan Agencies

Apostleship of Prayer—Rev. Msgr. JAMES C. HARDIMAN, Dir., *4126 W. 99th St., Oak Lawn, 60453.* Tel: 708-425-8732.

Pilgrimage and Shrine Apostolate—Rev. DAVID J. BYRNE, Dir., *P.O.Box 557816, Chicago, 60655.* Tel: 708-499-3283; Fax: 708-422-8699.

CLERGY, PARISHES, MISSIONS AND PAROCHIAL SCHOOLS

CITY OF CHICAGO (Cook County)

1—CATHEDRAL OF THE HOLY NAME, Revs. Robert E. McLaughlin, Rector and Pastor of Parish; William J. Sheridan; John Boivin. Pastoral Ministers: Ms. Cathleen Mika; Mrs. Ann Klocke; Deacon Michael McCloskey; Sr. Roberta Popara, O.P., Minister of Care; Mr. Matthew Walsh, Dir. Music; Mrs. Jean Surma, Business Mgr.; Mrs. Elaine Kern, Parish Sec.; Sr. Michaeleen Gibbons, B.V.M., Financial Admin. In res., Most Rev. Timothy J. Lyne, Pastor Emeritus (Retired); Rev. Msgr. John J. Egan; Revs. John J. McDonnell; William J. Moriarity; James P. Roache; Thomas J. Paprocki; Eugene F. Durkin, (Retired).
Rectory: 730 N. Wabash Ave., 60611. Tel: 312-787-8040; Fax: 312-787-9113.
Domestic Dept., Little Sisters of the Holy Family 7.
Cardinal's Residence—1555 N. State Pkwy., 60610. Most Rev. Raymond E. Goedert, Auxiliary Bishop & Vicar General; Bro. Dennis Dunne, F.M.S., Exec. Asst. to the Cardinal.
School—Frances Xavier Warde School, 751 N. State St., 60611. Tel: 312-466-0700. Sr. Mary Ellen Caron, R.S.M., Prin.
Religious 1; Lay Teachers 34; Students 475.
Convents—750 N. Wabash Ave., 60611. Tel: 312-664-1462. Sisters of Charity of the Blessed Virgin Mary; 740 N. Wabash Ave., 60611. Tel: 312-787-8040; Fax: 312-787-9113. Little Sisters of the Holy Family

2—ST. ADALBERT, Rev. James Kaczorowski.
Res., 1650 W. 17th St., 60608. Tel: 312-226-0340.

3—ST. ADRIAN, Rev. Theodore L. Ostrowski.
Res., 7000 S. Fairfield Ave., 60629. Tel: 773-434-3223.
Church—70th and S. Washtenaw Ave., 60619.
School—Sisters of the Institute of the Blessed Virgin Mary (Ladies of Loretto) 4; Lay Teachers 9; Students 260.
Convent—7020 S. Washtenaw Ave., 60629.

4—ST. AGATHA, Revs. Michael T. Ivers; Matthew S. Eyerman; Sr. Jo Mary Davis, S.N.D., Pastoral Assoc.; Deacon Roy Warren.
Res., 3147 W. Douglas Blvd., 60623. Tel: 773-522-3050; Fax: 773-522-3842.
School—Campus No. One—Our Lady of the Westside Catholic School. Serving the following parishes: St. Agatha, Precious Blood and Presentation. Totals represent all three campuses. Tel: 773-762-1809.
Sisters 6; Lay Teachers 23; Students 609.
Convent—3143 W. Douglas Blvd., 60623. Tel: 773-762-7969.

5—ST. AGNES OF BOHEMIA, Revs. J. Cletus Kiley; Francis T. Pribyl, Pastor Emeritus; Mark Bartosic; Alejandro Garrido. Pastoral Assocs.: Sr. Sandra Luz Dominguez; Sr. Maria del Carmen Valenzuela; Sr. Yolanda Gil; Deacons Gregorio Bustos; Jesus Medina.
Res., 2651 S. Central Park Ave., 60623. Tel: 773-522-0142.
School—2643 S. Central Park Ave., 60623. Tel: 773-522-0143.
Sisters 1; Lay Teachers 19; Students 630.
Convents—2658 S. Drake, 60623. Franciscan Sisters; 2658 S. Central Park Ave., 60623. Misioneras de San Pio X

6—ST. AILBE, Revs. John S. Breslin; Daniel J. McCormack; Deacon Bruce T. McElrath; Mrs. Marie C. Davis, Pastoral Assoc.
Res., 9015 S. Harper Ave., 60619. Tel: 773-374-2345; Fax: 773-374-7096.
School—9137 S. Harper Ave., 60619. Tel: 773-734-1386. Sr. Kathryn Hartnett, Prin.
Sisters of St. Dominic (Adrian, MI) 1; Lay Teachers 15; Students 320.

7—ALL SAINTS-ST. ANTHONY, Rev. Raymond P. Devereux; Deacons Peter Liberti; Martin Mackert; Duke Vemich. In res., Rev. Robert Ebrom.
Res., 518 W. 28th Pl., 60616. Tel: 312-842-2744; Fax: 312-842-2791.
School—Participant in Bridgeport Catholic Academy. See separate listing for Consolidated Elementary Schools.

8—ST. ALOYSIUS, Revs. Michael S. Michelini; Moises M. Marin; Deacons Santiago Rodriguez; Jose Gonzalez; Adolph Lopez; Dennis Ramos. In res., Rev. Sebastian Ugochukwu.
Res., 2300 W. Le Moyne St., 60622. Tel: 773-278-4808; Fax: 773-278-4898.

9—ST. ALPHONSUS (German), Revs. Joseph Morin, C.Ss.R.; John Schmidt, C.Ss.R.; Deacons William Kostock; Joseph Riffner; Raul Mendieta. In res., Revs. Manuel Borg, C.Ss.R.; Americo Dalbelo, C.Ss.R.; John Dowd, C.Ss.R.; Edward Castaldo, C.Ss.R.; Walter George, C.Ss.R.; James Gleason, C.Ss.R.; Bernard Guenther, C.Ss.R.; Stephen Rehauer, C.Ss.R.; Peter Schavitz, C.Ss.R.
Res., 1429 W. Wellington Ave., 60657. Tel: 773-525-0709.
Co-Redemptorist Association Office—Tel: 773-472-8509. Rev. John Andree, C.Ss.R.
School—School Sisters of Notre Dame 2; Lay Teachers 12; Students 280.
Convent—1456 Oakdale Ave., 60657.

10—ST. AMBROSE, Rev. David A. Jones.
Res., 1012 E. 47th St., 60653. Tel: 773-624-3695; Fax: 773-624-3697.
School—1014 E. 47th St., 60653-3698. Tel: 773-373-7311.
Lay Teachers 10; Students 250.

11—ST. ANDREW, Rev. John W. Parker; Rev. Msgr. John S. Quinn, Pastor Emeritus; Rev. Thai Van Nguyen. In res., Rev. Philip X. Guerin, (Retired).
Res., 3546 N. Paulina St., 60657. Tel: 773-525-3016; Fax: 773-248-2709.
School—1710 W. Addison, 60613. Tel: 312-248-2500.
Lay Teachers 14; Students 311.

12—ST. ANGELA, Rev. Dennis S. Riley; Rev. Msgr. Edward M. Pellicore, Pastor Emeritus; Rev. Aloysius M. Funtilla, C.I.C.M.; Deacon Jose Uroza.
Res., 5758 W. Potomac Ave., 60651. Tel: 773-379-7700.
School—Sisters 5; Lay Teachers 16; Students 543.
Convent—1325 N. Menard Ave., 60651.

13—ANGEL GUARDIAN CROATIAN CATHOLIC MISSION. (Independent Mission). In res., Rev. Harvey Blaschko, O.P.
Res., 6346 N. Ridge, 60660. Tel: 773-262-0535; Fax: 773-262-4603.

14—ST. ANN, Rev. John J. Keehan; Deacons Rodrigo Silva; Bricio Lopez. In res., Rev. Louis J. Zake.
Res., 1840 S. Leavitt St., 60608. Tel: 312-733-7486.
School—2211 W. 18th Pl., 60608. Sr. Michael Marie Franzak, Prin.
Lay Teachers 7; Students 324.

15—ANNUNCIATA, Revs. Christopher L. Krymski, O.S.M.; Mark Dennehy, O.S.M., Assoc.; Bro. Brian Fitzpatrick, O.S.M., Pastoral Assoc. In res., Rev. Conrad Borntrager, O.S.M.; Sr. Judene Studer, S.S.N.D., D.R.E.
Res., 11128 S. Avenue G, 60617. Tel: 773-221-1040; Fax: 773-221-1556.
School—Lay Teachers 13; Students 340.

16—ST. ANSELM, Rev. William Hegarty; Bro. Jim Fisher, S.V.D., Pastoral Assoc. In res., Rev. Hector Maldonado, S.V.D.
Res., 6045 S. Michigan Ave., 60637. Tel: 773-493-5959; Fax: 773-363-1887.

17—ST. ANTHONY (Italian), Revs. Charles LaVerde, C.S.; Peter Corbellini, C.S.; Deacon Edward Ryan.
Res., 11530 S. Prairie Ave., 60628. Tel: 773-468-1200; Fax: 773-468-3570.
School—Lay Teachers 11; Students 155.

18—ASSUMPTION OF THE BLESSED VIRGIN MARY, Revs. Augustine M. Kulbis, O.S.M.; Paul M. Cullen, O.S.M. In res., Revs. Anthony M. O'Connell, O.S.M.; John Pawlikowski, O.S.M.
Res., 323 W. Illinois St., 60610. Tel: 312-644-0036; Fax: 312-644-1838.

19—ASSUMPTION OF THE B.V.M./ST. CATHERINE OF GENOA, Rev. Robert C. Behnke; Deacon Tommy West.
Res., 640 W. 118th St., 60628. Tel: 773-785-6600.
School—11756 S. Lowe, 60628. William P. Donegan, Prin.
Lay Teachers 10; Students 320.

20—ASSUMPTION, Revs. Lawrence J. Craig; David A. Kelly, C.PP.S.
Res., 2434 S. California Ave., 60608. Tel: 773-247-6644; Fax: 773-247-0569.
Convent—2831 W. 24th St. Blvd., 60623. Tel: 773-247-3560.
Kolbe House—Catholic Prison Ministry. Tel: 773-247-0070. Rev. Lawrence J. Craig, Dir.

21—ST. BARBARA, Revs. Michael T. Yakaitis; Edward D. Skupien, Pastor Emeritus; Deacon Andrew Brongiel.
Res., 2859 S. Throop St., 60608. Tel: 312-842-7979; Fax: 312-842-7978.
School—2867 S. Throop St., 60608. Tel: 312-326-6243.
Sisters of St. Joseph of the Third Order of St. Francis (Chicago, IL) 1; Lay Teachers 11; Students 257.
High School—Tel: 312-842-0042.
Sisters of St. Joseph of the Third Order of St. Francis (Chicago, IL) 2; Lay Teachers 12; Students 170.

22—ST. BARNABAS, Revs. Raymond J. Tillrock; Martin T. Marren; Coletta Hogan, Pastoral Assoc.; Deacons James Temple; William Sullivan; James L. Conway.
Res., 10134 S. Longwood Dr., 60643. Tel: 773-779-1166; Fax: 773-445-9671.
School—10121 S. Longwood Dr., 60643. Tel: 773-445-7711.
Dominican Sisters (Sinsinawa, WI) 1; Lay Teachers 27; Students 624.

23—ST. BARTHOLOMEW, Revs. George F. Cerny; Casimir J. Kozien, (Retired); J. Edward Duggan, (Retired); Deacon Robert Jablonski; Mr. Robert Puhala, Lay Min.
Res., 4949 W. Patterson Ave., 60641. Tel: 773-286-7871; Fax: 773-286-4808.
School—4941 W. Patterson Ave., 60641. Tel: 773-282-9373.
Sisters 1; Lay Teachers 24; Students 483.
Convent—Tel: 773-545-2119; Fax: 773-282-4757.

24—ST. BASIL/VISITATION, Rev. Brian G. Walker, O.P.; Deacon Roosevelt Jones. In res., Revs. Thomas Jackson, O.P.; Jesse Cox, O.P.; Robert Mutlow, O.P.; Gerald Koreger, O.P.; Kevin Niehoff, O.P.
Res., 843 W. Garfield Blvd., 60621. Tel: 773-846-3570; Fax: 773-925-7091.
Schools—St. Basil School, 1824 W. Garfield Blvd., 60609. Tel: 773-778-4448; Fax: 773-925-7091.
Sisters 1; Lay Teachers 10; Students 147; Visitation School, 900 W. Garfield Blvd., 60609.
Dominican Sisters (Sinsinawa, WI) 3; Lay Teachers 15; Students 353.

25—ST. BEDE THE VENERABLE, Revs. Jeremiah C. Duggan; Francis G. Scanlan; Thomas R. Koys; Deacons Donald Kotwas; James F. Delaney.
Res., 8200 S. Kostner Ave., 60652. Tel: 773-582-9100; Fax: 773-582-0026.
School—4420 W. 83rd St., 60652. Tel: 773-582-8800.
Lay Teachers 44; Students 1,100.

26—ST. BENEDICT, Revs. Robert A. Heidenreich; Phien Nguyen; Dennis B. O'Neill; Deacon Robert Jacob.
Res., 2215 W. Irving Park Rd., 60618. Tel: 773-588-6484; Fax: 773-588-4927.
School—3920 N. Leavitt St., 60618. Tel: 773-463-6797.
Lay Teachers 22; Students 471.
High School—Priests 1; Sisters 10; Lay Teachers 31; Students 561.

27—ST. BENEDICT THE AFRICAN (WEST), Revs. James J. Martin; John L. Harvey; Deacon Louis Constanopolis; Sr. Joann Sambs, Pastoral Assoc.
Worship Site—7033 S. Honore, 60636.
Office—6012 S. Laflin St., 60636. Tel: 773-476-4831; Fax: 773-925-1010.

School—Academy of St. Benedict the African.
Total Students for 3 Sites 840.
Honore Site—7033 S. Honore St., 60636. Tel: 773-476-2258.
Laflin Site—6020 S. Laflin St., 60636. Tel: 773-776-3316.
Stewart Site—6547 S. Stewart St., 60636. Tel: 773-994-6100.

28—St. Benedict the African (East), Rev. David E. Baldwin; Sr. Mary Pokorny, Pastoral Assoc.
340 W. 66th St., 60621. Tel: 773-873-4464; Fax: 773-925-1010.
School—Academy of St. Benedict the African.
Total Students for 3 Sites 800.
Stewart Site—6547 S. Stewart, 60621. Tel: 773-944-6100.

29—Blessed Sacrament, Rev. Richard A. Boever, C.Ss.R.; Bros. Eugene Patin, C.Ss.R.; Paul Jorns, C.Ss.R.; Deacon Juan Sierra. In res., Rev. John Phelps, C.Ss.R.
Res., 2153 S. Millard Ave., 60623. Tel: 773-521-5595; Fax: 773-521-6076.
School—2130 S. Central Park Ave., 60623.
Lay Teachers 11; Students 265.
Convents—2128 S. Central Park Ave., 60623. Dominican Sisters (Sinsinawa, WI); 2135 S. Central Park Ave., 60623. Sisters of Charity of the Blessed Virgin

30—St. Bonaventure, Rev. James P. Heneghan; Deacons Emiliano Rodriguez; Tito Roman; Jose Alvarez. In res., Revs. Richard Bulwith; Joseph Moffat, C.S.B.
Res., 1641 W. Diversey Pkwy., 60614. Tel: 773-281-6588; Fax: 773-281-1051.

31—St. Bride, Revs. Robert J. Kyfes; Robert E. Burns, Pastor Emeritus.
Res., 7811 S. Coles Ave., 60649. Tel: 773-731-8822.
School—7760 South Shore Dr., 60649. Tel: 773-721-5459.
Sisters of Institute of the B.V.M. 4; Lay Teachers 9; Students 270.

32—St. Bronislava, Revs. Michael J. Bonner, S.V.D., Admin.; Frank Drzaic, S.V.D., Pastoral Assoc.
Res., 8708 S. Colfax Ave., 60617. Tel: 773-734-0776; Fax: 773-734-0776.

33—St. Bruno, Revs. Joseph P. Grembla; Ernest Ciemiega; Edmund S. Szlanga, Pastor Emeritus; Idzi Stacherczak; Deacon Sal Villa.
Res., 4751 S. Harding Ave., 60632. Tel: 773-523-3467; Fax: 773-523-4253.
School—Tel: 773-847-0697.
Lay Teachers 14; Students 301.

34—St. Cajetan, Revs. William Maloney; Thomas J. Hurley, Sr.; Sr. Annette Kelley, O.P., Pastoral Assoc.; Deacon Don Newhall.
Res., 11234 S. Artesian Ave., 60655. Tel: 773-238-4100.
School—2447 W. 112th St., 60655. Tel: 773-233-8844.
Lay Teachers 27; Students 619.

35—St. Callistus (Italian). Closed. Merged with Notre Dame. For inquiries for parish records contact Notre Dame.

36—St. Camillus, Rev. Norman M. Czajka. In res., Rev. Stanley Drewniak.
Res., 5426 S. Lockwood Ave., 60638. Tel: 773-767-8183; Fax: 773-284-3812.
School—5432 S. Lockwood Ave., 60638.
Sisters of the Holy Family of Nazareth 6; Lay Teachers 8; Students 250.

37—Christ the King, Revs. Joseph W. Seitz; Edward F. Myers, Pastor Emeritus; Thomas J. Raftery, (Retired); Deacons Larry Antonsen; William Hurley; Terry Childers. In res., Rev. William T. Corcoran.
Res., 9235 S. Hamilton Ave., 60620. Tel: 773-238-4877; Fax: 773-238-4963.
School—9240 S. Hoyne Ave., 60620. Tel: 773-779-3329.
Lay Teachers 23; Students 336.

38—Christ the Redeemer Byzantine Bielarusian, Rev. John McDonnell, Admin.
Res., 3107 W. Fullerton Ave., 60647. Tel: 773-342-7373.

39—St. Christina, Revs. Martin E. O'Donovan; Patrick J. Henry; Christopher E. Gustafson; Deacon Thomas Ryan.
Res., 11005 S. Homan Ave., 60655. Tel: 773-779-7181; Fax: 773-238-2942.
School—Tel: 773-445-2969; Fax: 773-445-0444.
Dominican Sisters (Springfield, IL) 2; Lay Teachers 27; Students 638.
Convent—11033 S. Christiana, 60655.

40—St. Clare of Montefalco, Revs. Anthony B. Pizzo, O.S.A.; John Flynn, O.S.A. In res., Rev. Daniel Hartigan, O.S.A.
Res., 5443 S. Washtenaw Ave., 60632. Tel: 773-436-4422; Fax: 773-476-1888.
School—5450 S. Talman Ave., 60632. Tel: 773-434-2427. Iris Foley, Prin.
Religious 3; Lay Teachers 10; Students 230.

41—St. Clement, Revs. Thomas E. Hickey; John W. McGivern, Assoc.; Sr. Diane Boutet, O.P., Pastoral Assoc. In res., Rev. Daniel P. Coughlin.
Res., 642 W. Deming Pl., 60614. Tel: 773-281-0371; Fax: 773-281-2509.
School—2524 N. Orchard St., 60614. Tel: 773-348-8212; Fax: 773-348-4712.
Lay Teachers 17; Students 301.

42—St. Clotilde, Rev. Michael G. Meany.
Res., 8430 Calumet Ave., 60619. Tel: 773-874-1022; Fax: 773-874-1736.
School—321 E. 84th St., 60619. Tel: 773-488-4214. Mr. Joseph Cailles, Prin.
Lay Teachers 8; Students 210.
Convent—8414 S. Prairie Ave., 60619.

43—St. Columba, Revs. Kilian J. Knittel; Henry A. Olejniczak, Pastor Emeritus.
Res., 13323 S. Green Bay Ave., 60633. Tel: 773-646-2660; Fax: 773-646-6821.
School—Tel: 773-646-0751.
School Sisters of Notre Dame 1; Lay Teachers 7; Students 180.

44—St. Columbanus, Revs. Philip E. Cyscon; David R. Straub; Deacons William McKinnis; George Borka.
Res., 331 E. 71st St., 60619. Tel: 773-224-1022.
School—7120 S. Calumet, 60619.
Lay Teachers 16; Students 350.

45—St. Constance, Revs. Thomas R. Rzepiela; Martin R. Borowczyk, Pastor Emeritus; Andrew Izyk; Philip J. Grib; Sr. Marie Ellen Sullivan, Pastoral Assoc.; Deacons Ted Lisowski; James Schlitz; George Gniech; Edward Lukaszewski.
Res., 5843 W. Strong St., 60630. Tel: 773-545-8581; Fax: 773-545-0227.
School—5841 W. Strong St., 60630. Tel: 773-283-2311.
Lay Teachers 17; Students 260.

46—St. Cornelius, Revs. Edwin D. Pacocha; Erwin J. Friedl; Marion A. Matlak, Pastor Emeritus; Deacon Carl D. Olson. In res., Rev. Robert S. Brodfuehrer, (Retired).
Res., 5205 N. Lieb Ave., 60630. Tel: 773-283-5222.
School—Tel: 373-283-2192; Fax: 373-283-1377.
Lay Teachers 19; Students 373.

47—Corpus Christi, Revs. Christian Reuter, O.F.M.; Michael Perry, O.F.M.; Howard A. Tuite. In res., Rev. Edward Shea, O.F.M.
Res., Corpus Christi Friary, 4920 King Dr., 60615. Tel: 773-285-7720.

48—St. Daniel the Prophet, Revs. Lawrence J. Malcolm; John M. Cassidy; Peter Gacki; Charles F. Kelly, Pastor Emeritus; Sr. Eileen Tierney, C.N.D., Pastoral Assoc.; Deacons Albert Malec; Chester Golab.
Res., 5330 S. Nashville Ave., 60638. Tel: 773-586-1223; Fax: 773-586-1238.
School—5337 S. Natoma Ave., 60638.
Lay Teachers 26; Students 615.

49—St. David. Closed. For inquiries for parish records contact the Chancery.

50—St. Denis, Revs. Lawrence R. Dowling; Patrick J. Pollard; Sr. Norine Burns, O.P., Pastoral Assoc.; Deacons Thomas Ewers; Thomas Solon; Sr. Mary Anne Yanz, O.P., D.R.E.
Res., 8301 S. St. Louis Ave., 60652. Tel: 773-434-3313; Fax: 773-776-3922.
School—8332 S. St. Louis Ave., 60652. Sr. Elizabeth Lynch, O.P., Prin.
Sisters 2; Lay Teachers 27; Students 567.

51—St. Dorothy, Revs. Kenneth J. Fischer; Joseph Odama.
Res., 450 E. 78th St., 60619. Tel: 773-651-7000; Fax: 773-651-0969.
School—7740 S. Eberhart Ave., 60619.
Sisters of the Presentation of the Blessed Virgin Mary 2; Lay Teachers 16; Students 511.

52—St. Edward, Revs. John M. Murphy; John J. Donohue, Pastor Emeritus; Joseph C. Taylor, Assoc.; Edward A. Carlson, Assoc. In res., Revs. Louis J. Cameli; Joseph A. Kelly, (Retired).
Res., 4350 W. Sunnyside Ave., 60630-4147. Tel: 773-545-6496; Fax: 773-545-1136.
School—4343 W. Sunnyside Ave., 60630-4147. Tel: 773-736-9133; Fax: 773-736-9280.
Dominican Sisters (Springfield, IL) 5; Lay Teachers 23; Students 576.

53—St. Elizabeth, Rev. Donald J. Ehr, S.V.D.; Bros. Thomas Joseph, S.V.D.; Gary Burr, S.V.D.
Res., 50 E. 41st St., 60653. Tel: 773-268-1518; Fax: 773-373-8640.
School—4052 S. Wabash, 60653. Tel: 773-548-4100; Fax: 773-548-8641.
Sisters 5; Lay Teachers 17; Students 435.

54—Epiphany, Rev. Kevin W. Hays; Rev. Msgr. John M. Hayes, Pastor Emeritus.
Res., 2524 S. Keeler Ave., 60623. Tel: 773-521-1112.
School—4225 W. 25th St., 60623. Sr. Leona Bruck, O.P., Prin.; Sr. Berta Lopez, M.H.S.P.X., D.R.E.
Sisters 3; Lay Teachers 13; Students 245.

55—St. Ethelreda, Rev. James F. Nallen.
Res., 8754 S. Paulina St., 60620. Tel: 773-238-6118; Fax: 773-238-6059.
School—8734 S. Paulina St., 60620. Tel: 773-238-1757.
Lay Teachers 14; Students 328.

56—St. Eugene, Revs. James J. O'Brien; Francis W. Shaunessy, Pastor Emeritus; Frank L. Schouten; Fred W. Tomzik; Deacons Gerard Kwasegroch; Charles Tipperreiter; Edward O'Leary. In res., Rev. George J. Helfrich, (Retired).
Res., 7958 W. Foster Ave., 60656-1698. Tel: 773-775-6659; Fax: 773-775-2832.
School—7930 W. Foster Ave., 60656.
Sisters of Charity B.V.M. 1; Lay Teachers 28; Students 575.

57—St. Felicitas, Revs. John T. Boyle; Thomas S. Boyle, Pastor Emeritus; Deacons James Hubbard; Ralph Shaw. In res., Rev. Damain Adugu.
Res., 1526 E. 84th St., 60619. Tel: 773-734-2300; Fax: 773-731-5381.
School—1521 E. 83rd Pl., 60652. Tel: 773-721-0858.
Lay Teachers 10; Students 250.

58—St. Ferdinand, Revs. David J. Cortesi; Philip M. Danaher, S.V.D.; Maxim Lasrado, O.C.D.; Tadeucz Dzieszko; Deacons Carmen Cesario; Irwin Hotcaveg. In res., Rev. Joseph Kromenaker.
Res., 5900 W. Barry Ave., 60634. Tel: 773-622-5900; Fax: 773-622-5903.
School—3131 N. Mason Ave., 60634. Tel: 773-622-3022. Mrs. Marilyn Hilberg, Prin.
Lay Teachers 34; Students 638.

59—St. Fidelis, Sr. Leonette Kaluzny, S.Sp.S., Pastoral Coord.; Rev. Francis A. Cimmarrusti, Sacramental Min.
Res., 1406 N. Washtenaw Ave., 60622. Tel: 773-486-8700; Fax: 773-486-8944.

60—Five Holy Martyrs, Rev. Andrew P. Wypych; Most Rev. Alfred L. Abramowicz, D.D., Pastor Emeritus; Revs. John Latka (Poland); Leonard M. Kruzel; Deacon Richard Wieczorek.
Res., 2905 W. Pope John Paul II Dr., 60632. Tel: 773-254-3636; Fax: 773-254-7541.
Bishop's Residence—6101 S. 75th Ave., Argo, 60501.
School—4325 S. Richmond St., 60632. Tel: 773-523-6161.
Franciscan Sisters of Chicago 2; Lay Teachers 18; Students 343.

61—St. Florian, Revs. Casimir M. Szatkowski, Admin.; Joe Pachorek, Pastor Emeritus.
Res., 13145 S. Houston Ave., 60633. Tel: 773-646-4877; Fax: 773-646-5965.
School—Lay Teachers 12; Students 241.

62—St. Francis of Assisi (Spanish Speaking Parish), Rev. Donald J. Nevins; Deacons Zeferino Ochoa; Manuel Rodriguez; Arturo Velasco. In res., Rev. Arturo J. Perez.
Res., 813 W. Roosevelt Rd., 60608. Tel: 312-226-7575.

63—St. Francis of Assisi/Our Lady of the Angels, Revs. Nicholas R. Desmond; Wojiech Kwiecen; Sr. Anita Franz, O.S.F., Pastoral Assoc.
Res., 3808 W. Iowa St., 60651. Tel: 773-235-3132; Fax: 773-486-7726.
School—3814 W. Iowa St., 60651.
Sisters 3; Lay Teachers 6; Students 245.

64—St. Francis Borgia, Revs. Daniel G. Mayall; Robert S. Brodfuehrer, Pastor Emeritus; Joseph A. Mulcrone; Joseph T. Noonan; Martin R. Borowczyk.
Res., 8033 W. Addison St., 60634. Tel: 773-625-1118; Fax: 773-625-1110.
School—Tel: 773-589-1000.
Sisters 2; Lay Teachers 20; Students 545.
Convent—3521 N. Panama St., 60634.

65—St. Francis de Sales, Rev. James P. Keating; Deacon Joseph Pastirik. In res., Rev. Ildephonse Skorup, O.F.M.
Res., 10201 S. Ewing Ave., 60617. Tel: 773-734-1383; Fax: 773-734-3022.

66—St. Gabriel, Revs. William J. Hastings; John M. Michet, Assoc.
Res., 4522 S. Wallace St., 60609. Tel: 773-268-9595; Fax: 773-268-9586.
Church—45th St. and Lowe Ave., 60609.
School—4500 S. Wallace St., 60609. Tel: 773-268-6636; Fax: 773-268-2501.
Lay Teachers 14; Students 285.

67—St. Gall, Revs. David P. Dowdle; William Wilkosz; Deacons Bernie Kut; Michael Slajchert.
Res., 5511 S. Sawyer Ave., 60629. Tel: 773-737-3113; Fax: 773-737-0272.
School—5515 S. Sawyer Ave., 60629.
Sisters Servants of the Holy Heart of Mary 2; Lay Teachers 12; Students 316.

68—St. Gelasius, Rev. Peter McGarry, O.Carm.; Bro.

Damien Chong, O.Carm., Pastoral Assoc.; Deacon James Morgan. In res., Rev. Martin Curtis, O.Carm.
Res., 6415 S. Woodlawn Ave., 60637. Tel: 773-363-6500; Fax: 773-363-3279.
School—Lay Teachers 10; Students 287.

69—ST. GENEVIEVE, Revs. Eugene W. Gratkowski; Thomas F. Maher, Pastor Emeritus; Rev. Msgr. Thomas J. Mohan, Pastor Emeritus; Rev. Sergio Romo; Sr. Jean Michael Rafferty, S.P., Pastoral Assoc.; Deacon Benito Centeno.
Res., 4835 W. Altgeld St., 60639. Tel: 773-237-3011; Fax: 773-237-3043.
School—4854 W. Montana St., 60639. Tel: 773-237-7131; Fax: 773-237-7265.
Sisters of Providence of St. Mary-of-the-Woods, IN 1; Lay Teachers 18; Students 286.

70—ST. GEORGE (Slovenian), Rev. Raphael A. Sesek, O.F.M.
Res., 9546 S. Ewing Ave., 60617. Tel: 773-734-0554.

71—ST. GERTRUDE, Rev. William G. Kenneally; Mr. Peter Buttitta, Pastoral Assoc.
Res., 1420 W. Granville Ave., 60660. Tel: 773-764-3621; Fax: 773-761-4164.
School—Northside Catholic Academy, 6216 N. Glenwood Ave., 60660.
Sisters 1; Lay Teachers 17; Students 333.

72—GOOD SHEPHERD, Rev. Donald J. Lund.
Res., 2719 S. Kolin Ave., 60623. Tel: 773-762-2322.
School—2733 S. Kolin Ave., 60623.
Lay Teachers 11; Students 254.

73—ST. GREGORY, Revs. John W. Clemens; Edward H. Baseheart, Pastor Emeritus; Mark J. Krylowicz; Sr. Barbara Quinn, S.N.D.deN., Pastoral Assoc. In res., Rev. Zacharias Nanthiyattu, O.I.C.
Res., 1634 W. Gregory St., 60640. Tel: 773-561-3546.
School—Northside Catholic Academy, Tel: 773-907-2094.
Lay Teachers 17; Students 300.
High School—1677 W. Bryn Mawr Ave., 60660. Tel: 773-907-2100.
Lay Teachers 30; Students 350.

74—ST. HEDWIG, Revs. Michael E. Danek, C.R.; Casimir V. Polinski, C.R.; Gary Hogan, C.R. In res., Revs. Walter Wilczek, C.R.; Eugene Szarek, C.R.; Bro. Ed Howe, C.R.; Deacons Gilberto Cintron; Salomon Villegas.
Res., 2226 N. Hoyne Ave., 60647. Tel: 773-486-1660.

75—ST. HELEN, Rev. Bronislaus Chmiel.
Res., 2315 W. Augusta Blvd., 60622. Tel: 773-235-3575; Fax: 773-235-3576.
School—2347 W. Augusta Blvd., 60622.
Lay Teachers 15; Students 263.

76—ST. HELENA, Rev. Steven W. Patte; Sr. Mary Leroy Rowland, S.S.N.D., Pastoral Assoc.
Res., 10121 S. Parnell Ave., 60628. Tel: 773-779-2243; Fax: 773-779-2749.
School—10115 S. Parnell Ave., 60628.
Sisters 1; Lay Teachers 9; Students 242.

77—ST. HENRY, Rev. Edward A. Harasim, Admin.; Deacon Frank G. Duffy.
Res., 6335 N. Hoyne Ave., 60659. Tel: 773-764-7413; Fax: 773-761-9770.
School—Northside Catholic Academy, 6325 N. Hoyne, 60659. Tel: 773-274-5227; Fax: 773-274-2157.
Convent—1956 W. Devon, 60660.

78—ST. HILARY, Revs. Robert G. Darow; Matt A. Bednarz, Pastor Emeritus; Deacons Edmund Tryba; Donald Wehling.
Res., 5600 N. Fairfield Ave., 60659. Tel: 773-561-3474; Fax: 773-561-6409.
School—5614 N. Fairfield Ave., 60659. Tel: 773-561-5885.
Lay Teachers 17; Students 355.

79—HOLY ANGELS, Rev. John W. Calicott; Deacons Robert Miller; Willie Foggie; Jasper Roy; Dexter Watson. In res., Revs. James L. Mollohan; Paul B. Smith.
Res., 607 E. Oakwood Blvd., 60653. Tel: 773-624-5375.
School—545 E. Oakwood Blvd., 60653.
Priests 1; Sisters 18; Lay Teachers 30; Students 1,300.

80—HOLY CROSS/IMMACULATE HEART OF MARY, Revs. Peter Rodriguez, C.M.F.; Tom Joyce, C.M.F.; Miguel Estrada, C.M.F.; John Cirone, C.M.F.; Tom Enneking, O.S.C.
Res., 4557 S. Wood St., 60609. Tel: 773-376-3900; Fax: 773-376-8929.

81—HOLY FAMILY, Rev. Donald J Nevins.
Res., 1019 S. May St., 60607. Tel: 312-226-7575; Fax: 312-226-6283.

82—HOLY INNOCENTS, Revs. Richard J. Klajbor; Richard Milek (Poland); Marco Antonio Alvarado (Guatemala).
Res., 743 N. Armour St., 60622. Tel: 312-666-3675; Fax: 312-666-0714.
School—1444-56 W. Superior St., 60622.
Felician Sisters (Chicago, IL) 8; Lay Teachers 11; Students 280.

83—HOLY NAME OF MARY, Revs. Anthony J. Vader; James E. Flynn.
Res., 11159 S. Loomis St., 60643. Tel: 773-238-6800.
School—1421 W. 112th St., 60643. Tel: 773-445-3277.
Oblate Sisters of Providence 3; Lay Teachers 8; Students 180.
Mission—Chicago, Cook Co., Sacred Heart, 11652 S. Church St., 60643.

84—HOLY ROSARY, Rev. Richard C. Creagh.
Res., 351 E. 113th St., 60628. Tel: 773-568-4455; Fax: 773-568-4456.

85—HOLY ROSARY, Rev. Anthony M. Talarico; Deacons Jose Colon, (Retired); Martin Hare, (Retired); Jorge Rozo. In res., Rev. Joseph Kavunkal.
Res., 612 N. Western Ave., 60612. Tel: 773-278-4820; Fax: 773-278-3770.

86—HOLY TRINITY (Croatian), Rev. Charles W. Dahm, O.P., Admin.
Res., 1850 S. Throop St., 60608. Tel: 312-226-2736.
Catechesis/Religious Programs—1840 S. Throop St., 60608.
Priests 1; Sisters of St. Francis of Christ the King 3.

87—HOLY TRINITY MISSION (Polish), Revs. Wladyslaw Gowin, S.Chr.; Jacek Walkiewicz, S.Chr.
Res., 1118 N. Noble St., 60622. Tel: 773-489-4140; Fax: 773-489-5918.

88—ST. HYACINTH, Revs. Michael Osuch, C.R.; Francis Rog, C.R.; Andrzej Lewandowski, C.R.; Jerzy Zieba, C.R.; Wieslaw Janowski, C.R.; Deacons Fred Girjatowicz; Edward Rozanski; Stefan Stanczak. In res., Rev. Joseph Wise, C.R.
Res., 3636 W. Wolfram St., 60618. Tel: 773-342-3636; Fax: 773-342-3638.
School—3640 W. Wolfram St., 60618.
Sisters of the Holy Family of Nazareth (Des Plaines) 3; Lay Teachers 21; Students 365.

89—ST. IGNATIUS, Revs. Richard J. Baumann, S.J.; Richard J. Murphy, S.J. In res., Revs. Robert Geisinger, S.J.; David Smolira, S.J.; Bro. Anthony McCaffrey, S.J.
Res., 6559 N. Glenwood Ave., 60626. Tel: 773-764-5936; Fax: 773-764-4360.

90—IMMACULATE CONCEPTION OF THE BLESSED VIRGIN MARY, Rev. Patrick J. Lee.
Res., 1431 N. North Park Ave., 60610. Tel: 773-944-1230; Fax: 773-944-0673.

91—IMMACULATE CONCEPTION, Revs. Michael J. Hoolahan, C.P.; Eric Meyer, C.P.; Alan Phillip, C.P.
Res., 7211 W. Talcott Ave., 60631. Tel: 773-775-3833.
School—7263 W. Talcott Ave., 60631.
Sisters of Providence of Saint Mary-of-the-Woods, IN 1; Lay Teachers 37; Students 663.

92—IMMACULATE CONCEPTION (Lithuanian), Rev. Anthony C. Puchenski; Rev. Msgr. Damasus A. Mozeris, Pastor Emeritus; Revs. Edward J. Maxa; Fabian V. Kireilis.
Res., 2745 W. 44th St., 60632-1999. Tel: 773-523-1402.
School—4426 S. Fairfield Ave., 60632.
Sisters of St. Casimir 3; Lay Teachers 8; Students 248.

93—IMMACULATE CONCEPTION OF THE BLESSED VIRGIN MARY, Rev. Michael P. Enright. In res., Rev. Edward J. McKenna.
Parish Office and Rectory: 2944 E. 88th St., 60627. Tel: 773-768-2100; Fax: 773-221-9121.
Church—88th & Commercial Ave., 60617.

94—IMMACULATE HEART OF MARY, Revs. James F. Blazek; John P. McNalis; Norbert J. Zawistanowicz, Pastor Emeritus; Deacon John Kearney. In res., Rev. Simon Edathiparampil.
Res., 3834 N. Spaulding Ave., 60618. Tel: 773-478-1157; Fax: 773-478-6044.
School—3820 N. Spaulding Ave., 60618.
Sisters of the Holy Family of Nazareth (Des Plaines, IL) 2; Lay Teachers 24; Students 466.
Convent—3817 N. Christiana Ave., 60618.

95—IMMACULATE HEART OF MARY VICARIATE. See Holy Cross, Wood St.

96—SAINT ITA, Revs. Laurence F. Maddock; Robert G. Casey; Vinh Ha; Deacon Frank Gaughan.
Res., 1220 West Catalpa Ave., 60640. Tel: 773-561-5343; Fax: 773-561-5609.
School—Northside Catholic Academy, 5525 N. Magnolia Ave., 60640.
Sisters 2; Lay Teachers 11; Students 230.

97—ST. JAMES, Rev. Thomas M. Frayne.
Res., 2942 S. Wabash Ave., 60616. Tel: 312-842-1919; Fax: 312-842-3612.
School—2920 S. Wabash Ave., 60616.
Sisters 2; Lay Teachers 12; Students 270.

98—ST. JAMES, Revs. Joseph R. Szabelski; John L. Wodniak, Pastor Emeritus; Joseph Weligala. In res., Rev. Joseph Lee.
Res., 5730 W. Fullerton Ave., 60639. Tel: 773-237-1474.
School—2456 N. Mango Ave., 60639. Tel: 773-237-0549.
Felician Sisters (Chicago, IL) 4; Lay Teachers 7; Students 290.

99—ST. JANE DE CHANTAL, Rev. Paul B. Marszalek; Sr. Jan Brynda, O.P., Pastoral Assoc.; Deacon Ron Morowczynski. In res., Rev. Edmund S. Szlanga.
Res., 5252 S. Austin Ave., 60638. Tel: 773-767-2411; Fax: 773-767-2769.
School—5201 S. McVicker Ave., 60638.
Lay Teachers 13; Students 276.

100—ST. JEROME, Revs. Harold A. Bonin; Juan Sanchez; Sr. Marie Paryse, S.S.S.F., Pastoral Assoc.; Deacons Fritz Jean-Pierre; Sigifredo Hernandez; Victor LaCoursiere; Robert Murphy; Raymond Ward. In res., Rev. William P. Grogan.
Res., 1709 W. Lunt Ave., 60626. Tel: 773-262-3170; Fax: 773-262-2834.

101—ST. JEROME (Croatian), Revs. Zvonimir Kutlesa, O.F.M.; Mark Kozina, O.F.M.
Res., 2823 S. Princeton Ave., 60616. Tel: 312-842-1871; Fax: 312-842-6427.
School—2813 S. Princeton Ave., 60616.
Sisters Adorers of the Blood of Christ 3; Lay Teachers 8; Students 169.

102—ST. JOACHIM, Rev. Frank M. Sasso.
Res., 700 E. 91st St., 60619. Tel: 773-488-4488; Fax: 773-994-8945.
School—9035 S. Langley Ave., 60619. Tel: 773-488-4491.
Lay Teachers 9; Students 175.

103—ST. JOHN THE BAPTIST (Slovak). Closed. For inquiries for parish records contact the Chancery.

104—ST. JOHN DE LA SALLE, Rev. Oliver Jennings.
Res., 10205 King Dr., 60628. Tel: 773-785-2022.
School—Tel: 773-785-2331. Sharon Dale, Prin.
Lay Teachers 10; Students 256.

105—ST. JOHN BERCHMANS, Revs. William B. Gubbins; Michael G. Foley; Deacons Virgilio Bonifazi; Jorge Cabrera; Guillermo Mendizabal; Marcial Herrera.
Res., 2517 W. Logan Blvd., 60647. Tel: 773-486-4300.
School—2509 W. Logan Blvd., 60647. Tel: 773-486-1334; Fax: 773-486-1782.
Dominican Sisters (St. Catherine, KY) 1; Lay Teachers 24; Students 435.

106—ST. JOHN BOSCO, Revs. John Edward Mulvihill; Salvatore J. Ognibene, Pastor Emeritus; Deacons Wilfredo Perez; Pedro Soto; Ronald Swiatek.
Res., 2250 N. McVicker Ave., 60639. Tel: 773-622-4620; Fax: 773-622-5040.

107—ST. JOHN CANTIUS (Polish), Revs. C. Frank Phillips, C.R.; Edwin Karlowicz, C.R.
Res., 825 N. Carpenter St., 60622. Tel: 312-243-7373; Fax: 312-666-4653.

108—ST. JOHN FISHER, Rev. Thomas J. Purtell; Rev. Msgr. Francis J. McElligott, Pastor Emeritus; Revs. Thomas P. May; Thomas J. Kaminski; Deacons Sidney Mench; Raymond Reilly; Clayton Kort; John Rohan, (Retired).
Res., 10234 S. Washtenaw Ave., 60655. Tel: 773-445-6565; Fax: 773-445-1644.
School—10200 S. Washtenaw Ave., 60642. Tel: 773-445-4737.
Sisters of St. Joseph (LaGrange, IL) 2; Lay Teachers 44; Students 765.

109—ST. JOSAPHAT, Revs. Dominic J. Grassi; Daniel R. Whiteside; Deacon Bienvenido Nieves.
Res., 2311 N. Southport Ave., 60614. Tel: 773-327-8955; Fax: 773-327-2047.
School—2245 N. Southport Ave., 60614.
Lay Teachers 16; Students 296.

110—ST. JOSEPH, Rev. Sebastian C. Lewis, O.S.B. In res., Rev. Julius Ogolla (Tanzania).
Res., 1107 N. Orleans St., 60610. Tel: 312-787-7174; Fax: 312-787-9825.
School—Sisters 1; Lay Teachers 10; Students 261.

111—ST. JOSEPH, Revs. Anthony Cirignani, O.F.M.; Paschal Grigus, O.F.M.; Bro. Mark Zapczynski, O.F.M.
Res., 4821 S. Hermitage Ave., 60609. Tel: 773-254-2366.
School—4800 S. Paulina St., 60609.
Sisters 5; Lay Teachers 15; Students 365.
High School—4831 S. Hermitage Ave., 60609.
Felician Sisters 2; Lay Teachers 20; Students 215.
Convent—4818 S. Paulina St., 60609.

112—ST. JULIANA, Revs. Philip J. Dressler; Donald J. Ahearn, Pastor Emeritus; Deacons Michael Finnegan; Robert Ryan; Edward Dolan. In res., Rev. L. Scott Donahue; Pam Francisco, Pastoral Assoc.
Res., 7142 N. Osceola Ave., 60631. Tel: 773-631-4127; Fax: 773-631-4150.
School—7400 W. Touhy, 60648.

Lay Teachers 34; Religious 2; Students 719.

113—St. Kevin, Revs. Alfred Gundrum, O.F.M.Cap.; W. Bernard Scheid, Pastor Emeritus.
Res., 10509 S. Torrence Ave., 60617. Tel: 773-721-2563.

114—St. Kilian, Revs. William E. Vanecko; Daniel J. Murtaugh; Hugh V. O'Brien, Pastor Emeritus; John W. Shirey, (Retired).
Res., 8725 S. May St., 60620. Tel: 773-651-4000.

115—St. Ladislaus, Revs. Stephen F. Kanonik; William J. Lisowski, Pastor Emeritus; Walter J. Zmija, Pastor Emeritus; Walter Takuski.
Res., 5345 W. Roscoe St., 60641. Tel: 773-725-2300.
School—3330 N. Lockwood Ave., 60641. Tel: 773-545-5600.
Sisters of the Holy Family of Nazareth (Des Plaines, IL) 4; Lay Teachers 16; Students 420.

116—St. Laurence, Rev. Gerald K. O'Reilly; Deacons Willie Cooper; Roy Lilly.
Res., 7140 S. Dorchester Ave., 60619. Tel: 773-493-1118.

117—St. Leo The Great, Rev. Michael J. Furlan; Deacons Dorsey Chappell; Mervin O. Johnson.
Res., 7747 S. Emerald Ave., 60620. Tel: 773-846-6146.
School—7746 S. Emerald Ave., 60620. Tel: 773-483-2335.
Lay Teachers 11; Students 250.

118—Santa Lucia-Santa Maria Incoronata, Rev. Nicholas A. Marro, C.S.
Res., 3022 S. Wells St., 60616. Tel: 312-842-6115.
School—3017 S. Wells St., 60616. Geraldine Maratea, Prin.
Lay Teachers 11; Students 236.

119—St. Malachy, Rev. Ralph E. Starus.
Res., 2248 W. Washington Blvd., 60612. Tel: 312-733-1068.
School—2252 W. Washington Blvd., 60612.
Sisters 6; Brothers 2; Lay Teachers 10; Students 250.

120—St. Margaret of Scotland, Revs. Daniel J. Mallette; Robert A. Sheridan. In res., Rev. Claude Souffrant, S.J. (Haiti).
Res., 9837 S. Throop St., 60643. Tel: 773-779-5151; Fax: 773-779-6198.
School—9833 S. Throop St., 60643. Tel: 773-238-1088; Fax: 773-238-1033.
School Sisters of Notre Dame 3; Lay Teachers 15; Students 320.
Convent—1209 W. 98th St., 60643. Tel: 773-233-3470.

121—St. Margaret Mary, Revs. Mark B. Sorvillo; John J. O'Shea, (Retired); Deacon Thomas Stanton. In res., Rev. Oliver Nwachukwu.
Res., 2324 W. Chase Ave., 60645. Tel: 773-764-0615; Fax: 773-764-0641.
School—Tel: 773-764-0641.
Lay Teachers 21; Students 455.

122—Santa Maria Addolorata, Revs. Louis Gandolfi, C.S.; Alex Peloso, C.S., Pastor Emeritus; Miguel Alvarez, C.S.; Deacon Arthur DeLuna.
Res., 528 N. Ada St., 60622. Tel: 312-421-3122.
School—1337 W. Ohio St., 60622. Tel: 312-421-5482.
School Sisters of St. Francis 1; Lay Teachers 9; Students 211.

123—St. Mark, Revs. Domingo Hurtado-Badillo, Admin.; Peter B. McQuinn, Admin.; Deacons Jorg Gutierrez; Abraham Rosa; Andrew Matuga; Ignacio Ortega; Antonio Villalobos; Mel Maldonado.
Res., 1048 N. Campbell Ave., 60622. Tel: 773-342-1516; Fax: 773-342-1372.
School—2510 W. Cortez St., 60622. Tel: 773-486-0430.
Sisters of Providence 3; Religious 1; Lay Teachers 9; Students 270.

124—St. Martin De Porres, Revs. Austin Mac Adam, M.Afr.; Abdon Gamulani, M.Afr. (Malawi, Central Africa).
Res., 5112 W. Washington Blvd., 60644. Tel: 773-287-0206.
Schools—Resurrection, 5072 W. Jackson Blvd., 60661.
Sisters 4; Lay Teachers 17; Students 530; St. Thomas Aquinas, 116 N. LeClaire, 60644.
Lay Teachers 11; Students 310.

125—Old St. Mary, Revs. James W. Donovan, C.S.P.; Charles Brunick, C.S.P.; Richard C. Sparks, C.S.P. In res., Rev. James O'Gara, C.S.P.; Deacon Timothy Donovan.
Res., 21 E. Van Buren St., 60605. Tel: 312-922-3444; Fax: 312-922-3447.

126—St. Mary, Rev. Joseph T. Cook; Mr. Joseph Paprocki, Pastoral Assoc.; Deacons John Amberg; Thomas Duffner.
Res., 310 E. 137th St., 60627. Tel: 773-568-1611; Fax: 773-568-6268.
School—Our Lady of the Gardens, 13300 S. Langley Ave., 60627. Tel: 773-568-4099.
Sisters 4; Lay Teachers 9.
Daughters of Charity.

127—St. Mary of the Angels, Revs. Hilary F. Mahaney; John P. Debicki. In res., Rev. Charles M. Ferrer.
Res., 1850 N. Hermitage Ave., 60622. Tel: 773-278-2644; Fax: 773-278-8904.
School—1810 N. Hermitage Ave., 60622.
Sisters of the Resurrection (Chicago, IL) 1; Lay Teachers 13; Students 230.

128—St. Mary of the Lake, Revs. Robert G. Mair; Eduardo Pinzon, S.J.; Deacon Paul Spalla, Pastoral Assoc. In res., Revs. Daniel J. Collins; Patrick J. O'Malley.
Res., 4200 N. Sheridan Rd., 60613. Tel: 773-472-3711.
School—1026 W. Buena Ave., 60613. Tel: 773-281-0018.
Lay Teachers 12; Students 225.

129—St. Mary Magdalene, Revs. Philip Howard, C.S.Sp.; Egbert J. Figaro, C.S.Sp.
Res., 8426 S. Marquette Ave., 60617. Tel: 773-768-1700; Fax: 773-734-8518.

130—St. Mary of Perpetual Help, Rev. Donald J. Mulsoff.
Res., 1039 W. 32nd St., 60608. Tel: 773-927-6646.
School—Participant in Bridgeport Catholic Academy. See separate listing under Consolidated Elementary Schools in the Institutions section.

131—St. Mary, Star of the Sea, Revs. Michael J. Adams; Ralph H. Zwirn; Robert Kilbridge, O.P.; Deacons Jesse Navarro; Gregory Serratore.
Res., 6435 S. Kilbourn Ave., 60629. Tel: 773-767-1246.
School—6424 S. Kenneth Ave., 60629.
Lay Teachers 32; Students 902.

132—St. Mary of the Woods, Revs. Leo Mahon; Andrew J. McDonagh, Pastor Emeritus; Gregory Sakwoicz; Deacon William Mages. In res., Rev. Thomas F. Maher.
Res., 7033 N. Moselle Ave., 60646. Tel: 773-763-0206; Fax: 773-763-4968.
School—Religious 1; Lay Teachers 26; Students 498.

133—Maternity of the Blessed Virgin Mary, Rev. Thomas Pelton, Admin.; Deacons Jose R. Vazquez; Benito Velasco; Milton Rodriguez.
Res., 3647 W. North Ave., 60647. Tel: 773-772-9401.
School—1537 N. Lawndale Ave., 60651.
Sisters of Providence of Saint Mary-of-the-Woods, IN 2; Lay Teachers 15; Students 432.

134—St. Matthias, Revs. Miguel B. Alcantara; Thomas J. McHugh, Pastor Emeritus. In res., Rev. Francis A. Cimarrusti.
Res., 2310 W. Ainslie St., 60625. Tel: 773-561-6020.
School—4910 N. Claremont Ave., 60625.
Sisters 7; Lay Teachers 15; Students 387.

135—St. Maurice, Rev. John W. Dearhammer.
Res., 3615 S. Hoyne Ave., 60609. Tel: 773-847-3357.
School—3625 S. Hoyne Ave., 60609.
School Sisters of St. Francis 1; Lay Teachers 9; Students 210.

136—St. Michael, Very Revs. James Keena, C.SS.R.; Edward Wilhelm, C.SS.R.; Kenneth Sedlak, C.SS.R. In res., Revs. Milton Girse, C.SS.R.; Albert Castellino, C.SS.R.; Francis Novak, C.SS.R.; John Andree, C.SS.R.; John Schmidt, C.SS.R.
Res., 1633 N. Cleveland Ave., 60614. Tel: 312-642-2498; Fax: 312-642-9283.
Perpetual Help Confraternity Office—Tel: 312-642-9399. Bro. Patrick Considine, C.SS.R.

137—St. Michael Archangel (Italian), Rev. Daniel Lapolla, C.S.
Res., 2325 W. 24th Pl., 60608. Tel: 773-847-2727; Fax: 773-847-7618.
School—2315 W. 24th Pl., 60608. Tel: 773-847-9070; Fax: 773-847-7618.
Missionary Sisters of St. Charles 4; Lay Teachers 6; Students 206.

138—St. Michael, Revs. Thomas R. Franzman; Joseph G. Nowak, Pastor Emeritus; Deacon Albin J. Wegner, Jr.
Res., 8237 South Shore Dr., 60617. Tel: 773-734-4921; Fax: 773-734-8723.
School—8231 South Shore Dr., 60617. Tel: 773-221-0212. Sr. Judine Hilbing, O.P., Prin.
Poor Handmaids of Jesus Christ 2; Lay Teachers 12; Students 311.

139—St. Michael the Archangel (Slovak), Revs. John E. Tilford; Alfredo Del Toro, M.C.C.J.
Res., 4821 S. Damen Ave., 60609. Tel: 773-523-1248.

140—St. Monica, Revs. Michael A. Wulsch; Edward B. Panek; John T. Beyenka, Pastor Emeritus; Sr. Kathleen Maloney, O.S.B., Pastoral Assoc. In res., Rev. Michaelsami Arockiam.
Office—5136 N. Nottingham Ave., 60656. Tel: 773-763-1661; Fax: 773-763-4917.
Res., 5135 N. Mont Clare Ave., 60656.
School—Tel: 773-631-7880; Fax: 773-631-3266.
Sisters 1; Lay Teachers 19; Students 428.

141—Nativity of the Blessed Virgin Mary, Revs. John A. Kuzinskas; Anthony J. Zakarauskas, Pastor Emeritus; Vaclovas Zakarauskas, (Retired); Vito E. Mikolaitis, (Retired); Francis J. Kelpsas, (Retired).
Res., 6812 S. Washtenaw Ave., 60629. Tel: 773-776-4600; Fax: 773-776-0677.
School—6820 S. Washtenaw Ave., 60629. Tel: 773-476-0571.
Sisters of St. Casimir 3; Lay Teachers 8; Students 248.
Convent—6804 S. Washentaw Ave., 60629.

142—Nativity of Our Lord, Revs. James P. Kehoe; Edward P. O'Brien, Pastor Emeritus; Michael Flynn, O.Carm., Resident; Deacon Francis Henry.
Res., 653 W. 37th St., 60609. Tel: 773-927-6263.
School—Participant in Bridgeport Catholic Academy. See separate listing under Consolidated Elementary Schools in the Institutions section.

143—St. Nicholas of Tolentine, Revs. Stanley G. Rataj; Edward J. Brzozowski, Pastor Emeritus; Francis P. Cassidy; William Zimmer; Deacon Chester Brzoski.
Res., 3721 W. 62nd St., 60629. Tel: 773-735-1121; Fax: 773-735-1135.
School—3743 W. 62nd St., 60629.
Lay Teachers 25; Students 550.

144—Notre Dame, Revs. Steven M. Lanza, Admin.; Michael T. Herman. In res., Most Rev. John R. Manz, Auxiliary Bishop of Chicago; Rev. Thomas Mulcrone, Chap. Chicago Fire Dept.; Deacons Candelario Rodriguez; Joseph Siranovic.
Res., 1335 W. Harrison St., 60607-3318. Tel: 312-243-7400; Fax: 312-243-7614.

145—Our Lady of Fatima, Revs. Joseph R. Bennett; Pierre J. Barr, Pastor Emeritus; Raymond J. Gerrity, Pastor Emeritus; Richard Vogt, S.J.; Deacon Candido Torres.
Res., 2751 W. 38th Pl., 60632. Tel: 773-927-2421.
School—2744 W. Pershing Rd., 60632.
Lay Teachers 12; Students 325.

146—Our Lady Gate of Heaven, Rev. John Celichowski, O.F.M.Cap. In res., Revs. Brian Braun, O.F.M.Cap.; Alfredo Gundrum, O.F.M.Cap.
Res., 2338 E. 99th St., 60617. Tel: 773-375-3059; Fax: 773-375-3091.

147—Our Lady of Good Counsel, Revs. James M. Hyland; Richard J. O'Donnell, Pastor Emeritus.
Res., 3528 S. Hermitage Ave., 60609. Tel: 773-523-3917.
School—McKinley Park Catholic. (Merged with St. Maurice & SS. Peter & Paul). 3540 S. Hermitage Ave., 60609.
Lay Teachers 9; Students 170.

148—Our Lady of Grace, Revs. Thomas A. Tivy; Stanley J. Rokicinski, Pastor Emeritus; Esequiel Sanchez; Michael Rochford; Sr. Florence Norton, S.P., Pastoral Assoc.; Deacons Russell Drinan; Enrique Alonso; James Kwasigroch; Gaston Fernandez; Gregorio Lugo; Carlos Nazario. In res., Rev. Lawrence E. Gorski.
Res., 2455 N. Hamlin Ave., 60647. Tel: 773-772-5900.
School—2446 N. Ridgeway Ave., 60647.
Dominican Sisters (Springfield, IL) 6; Lay Teachers 12; Students 286.

149—Our Lady of Guadalupe, Revs. Michael Fernandez, C.M.F.; Mark Brummel, C.M.F.; John-Marie Lemrise, C.M.F.; George Morgan, C.M.F.; Deacons Salvador Cornejo; Margarito Alvarez; Raul Nunez; Juan Valdivia.
Res., 3200 E. 91st, 60617. Tel: 773-768-0793.
School—Lay Teachers 10; Students 297.
Shrine—National Shrine of St. Jude. (Claretian Missionaries).

150—Our Lady Help of Christians, Rev. Kenneth M. Brigham.
Res., 832 N. Leclaire Ave., 60651. Tel: 773-287-0244.
School—847 N. Leamington, 60651. Tel: 773-626-5700.
Lay Teachers 10; Students 189.

151—Our Lady of Lourdes, Revs. Curtis Lambert; Daniel Cassidy; Deacons Roy Henry; John Klemanovic; Moises Ramos. In res., Revs. Carlos Liagas, S.J.; Urban Osuji, C.M.
Res., 4640 N. Ashland Ave., 60640. Tel: 773-561-2141; Fax: 773-561-9853.
School—4641 N. Ashland Ave., 60640. Mrs. Anne Balzanto, Prin.
Lay Teachers 14; Students 250.

152—Our Lady of Lourdes, Rev. Ramon Dompke, C.SS.R.; Sr. Caritas Wehrman, S.S.N.D., Pastoral Assoc.
Res., 1444 S. Keeler Ave., 60623. Tel: 773-521-5217;

Fax: 773-762-5960.
School—Blessed Sacrament/Our Lady of Lourdes, Central Park and Cermak, 60623.
Students 250.

153—OUR LADY OF MERCY, Revs. Donald J. Headley; Leonicia S. Santiago; Patrick R. Lagges, Resident.
Res., 4432 N. Troy St., 60625. Tel: 773-588-2620.
School—4416 N. Troy, 60625. Dr. Patricia Colfer, Prin.
Sisters 1; Lay Teachers 19; Students 578.

154—OUR LADY, MOTHER OF THE CHURCH, Revs. Daniel R. Fallon; Joseph F. Ognibene; Peter F. Hayes, Pastor Emeritus.
Res., 8747 W. Lawrence Ave., 60656. Tel: 773-625-3369; Fax: 773-625-0226.

155—OUR LADY OF MOUNT CARMEL, Revs. Thomas I. Healy; Thomas E. Srenn; Deacon Edmund Gronkiewicz. In res., Rev. Peter Snieg.
Res., 690 W. Belmont Ave., 60657. Tel: 773-525-0453; Fax: 773-525-9438.
School—708 W. Belmont Ave., 60657.
Lay Teachers 19; Students 323.

156—OUR LADY OF PEACE, Rev. Lawrence M. Duris, Admin.; Deacon John Hill.
Res., 7851 S. Jeffrey Ave., 60649. Tel: 773-768-0105.
School—Lay Teachers 11; Students 217.

157—OUR LADY OF POMPEII. Closed. For inquiries for parish records contact the Chancery.

158—OUR LADY OF THE SNOWS, Rev. James A. Mezydlo. In res., Rev. Dennis Ziomek.
Res., 4858 S. Leamington Ave., 60638. Tel: 773-582-2266.
School—4810 S. Leamington Ave., 60638. Tel: 773-735-4810.
Lay Teachers 12; Students 240.

159—OUR LADY OF SORROWS, BASILICA OF, Revs. David Brown, O.S.M., Admin.; Lawrence M. Choate, O.S.M.; Deacons Roosevelt Davis, Jr.; Joseph Lewis.
Res., 3121 W. Jackson Blvd., 60612. Tel: 773-638-5800; Fax: 773-638-3036.
School—3141 W. Jackson Blvd., 60612. Tel: 773-638-5010.
Lay Teachers 9; Students 290.

160—OUR LADY OF TEPEYAC, Revs. James W. Miller; William P. Malone; Sr. Carol Ann Berte, O.S.F., Pastoral Assoc.; Deacons Ramon Echeverria; Vincente Limon.
Res., 2226 S. Whipple St., 60623. Tel: 773-521-8400; Fax: 773-927-1610.
School—2235 S. Albany, 60623.
Lay Teachers 9; Students 165.
High School—2228 S. Whipple St., 60623.
Sisters of the Resurrection (Chicago) 1; Lay Teachers 9; Students 165.

161—OUR LADY OF VICTORY, Revs. Daniel P. McCarthy; Gary J. Lewanski; Deacons Thomas Handrigan; Robert Leck; Rudolph Schoewe; Dennis Ranke. In res., Revs. Norbert J. Zawistanowicz, (Retired); Edward M. Mikolajczyk; Denis Carneiro.
Res., 5212 W. Agatite Ave., 60630. Tel: 773-286-2950; Fax: 773-286-8579.
School—4434 N. Laramie, 60630. Tel: 773-283-2229.
School Sisters of St. Francis 1; Lay Teachers 30; Students 540.
Convent—5240 W. Agatite Ave., 60630.
School Sisters of St. Francis 5.

162—OUR LADY OF AGLONA (Latvian), (Independent Mission), Revs. Boleslaus Baginskis, M.I.C.; Victor Civzelis, M.I.C.
Res., 2541 W. Wabansia, 60647. Tel: 773-276-9566.

163—ST. PANCRATIUS, Revs. Andrew P. Wypych; Walter Stefanski, Pastor Emeritus; Richard Bartlett, C.M.F.
Res., 4025 S. Sacramento Ave., 60632. Tel: 773-523-5666; Fax: 773-523-5666.
School—2940 W. 40th Pl., 60632.
Franciscan Sisters of Chicago 3; Lay Teachers 8; Students 190.

164—ST. PASCAL, Revs. Gary M. Miller; Tirso S. Villaverde; Edmund J. Fitzpatrick, Weekend Assistance; Deacons Eugene Dorgan; Thomas Stubstad; Ms. Catherine Crino, Pastoral Assoc.
Res., 3935 N. Melvina Ave., 60634. Tel: 773-725-7641; Fax: 773-725-9368.
School—6143 W. Irving Park Rd., 60634. Tel: 773-736-8806.
Lay Teachers 27; Students 595.
Convent-Senior Center—3954 N. Meade Ave., 60634. Tel: 773-545-9453.

165—ST. PATRICK, Revs. John J. Wall; John C. Cusick; Gene F. Smith; Anthony Aravindassery (India).
Res., 700 W. Adams St., 60606. Tel: 312-782-6171.

166—ST. PAUL, Revs. George Ruffolo, C.M.F.; Marco Cardenas, C.M.F.
Res., 2127 W. 22nd Pl., 60608. Tel: 773-847-7622; Fax: 773-847-8687.
School—2124 W. 22nd Pl., 60608.
Sisters 3; Lay Teachers 8; Students 295.

167—ST. PETER'S, Revs. Thomas Aldworth; Thomas Fratus, O.F.M.; Bill Rooney, O.F.M.
Res., St. Peter's Friary, 110 W. Madison St., 60602. Tel: 312-372-5111; Fax: 312-853-2361.
Priests 22; Brothers 11. (For complete listing see Section [N] Residences of Priests and Brothers.).

168—ST. PETER CANISIUS, Rev. Robert E. Bridge; Deacon Jose Gonzalez. In res., Rev. John T. Hillenbrand.
Res., 5057 W. North Ave., 60639-4565. Tel: 773-637-2075; Fax: 773-889-3929.

169—SS. PETER AND PAUL, Revs. Robert C. Behnke, Admin.; Bruno B. Grinis, Pastor Emeritus.
Res., 12433 S. Halsted St., 60628. Tel: 773-785-1200.

170—SS. PETER AND PAUL, Revs. Robert J. Roll; Joseph F. Mytch, Pastor Emeritus; Michael V. Kalck; Steven Bauer, O.S.C.
Res., 3745 S. Paulina St., 60609. Tel: 773-523-3410; Fax: 773-523-0540.
Convent—1640 W. 38th St., 60608. Tel: 773-523-0916.
Felician Sisters 2; Poor Handmaids of Jesus Christ 3.

171—ST. PHILIP NERI, Revs. Lawrence M. Duris; William H. Sheridan; Deacons Aaron Pressie; Wilmer Hatch.
Res., 2132 E. 72nd St., 60649. Tel: 773-363-1700.
School—2110 E. 72nd St., 60649.
Lay Teachers 13; Students 345.

172—ST. PHILOMENA, Revs. Robert P. Coleman; Charles G. Lenaghan, S.J.; Stephen F. Lesniewski; Deacons Francisco Ramos; Pedro Soto; Israel Valentin; Edwin Martinez; Benjamin Diaz.
Res., 1921 N. Kedvale Ave., 60639. Tel: 773-489-1100.
School—4131 W. Cortland Ave., 60639.
Lay Teachers 10; Students 250.

173—ST. PIUS V, Revs. Charles W. Dahm, O.P.; Matthias R. Mueller, O.P.; Antonio Romero, O.P. In res., Rev. Martin Aitesbaomo, O.P.
Res., 1914 S. Ashland Ave., 60608. Tel: 312-829-1931.
School—1919 S. Ashland Ave., 60608. Mrs. Nancy Nasko, Prin.
Dominican Sisters 1; Lay Teachers 9; Students 268.
Shrine—Shrine of St. Jude Thaddeus.

174—PRECIOUS BLOOD, Revs. William Mason, O.M.I.; Mark Stroba, O.M.I. Pastoral Assocs.: Latessa Harper; Mr. Sabino Gaytan, (Hispanic Community); Deacons Curba Merrill; Mario Avila. In res., Revs. Gregory Cholewa, O.M.I.; Joseph Pitts, O.M.I.
Res., 2411 W. Congress Pkwy., 60612. Tel: 312-733-5331.
School—Campus No. Two—Our Lady of the Westside School. See St. Agatha Parish listing for further details.

175—PRESENTATION, Rev. Thomas P. Walsh; Sr. Marylyn Welter, S.S.S.F., Pastoral Assoc.
Res., 734 S. Springfield Ave., 60624. Tel: 773-533-2820; Fax: 773-638-2316.
School—Campus No. Three—Our Lady of the Westside School. See St. Agatha Parish listing for further details.

176—ST. PRISCILLA, Revs. John J. Cunningham; Darrio L. Boscutti; Albert Tanahal; Deacons Robert Odegard; Fred Spitzerri. In res., Rev. Albert Judy, O.P.
Res., 6949 W. Addison St., 60634. Tel: 773-545-8840; Fax: 773-545-8919.
School—7011 W. Addison St., 60634. Tel: 773-685-3581.
Lay Teachers 24; Students 510.

177—ST. PROCOPIUS, Revs. James G. Gartland, S.J.; Thomas D. Hoffman, S.J.; Charles W. Niehaus, S.P. In res., Rev. John P. Foley, S.J.
Res., 1641 S. Allport St., 60608. Tel: 312-226-7887.
School—Lay Teachers 10; Students 220.

178—PROVIDENCE OF GOD, Rev. Robert R. Perez; Deacon Max Carrizales.
Res., 717 W. 18th St., 60616. Tel: 312-226-2929.

179—QUEEN OF ALL SAINTS BASILICA, Revs. Wayne F. Prist; H. Robert Clark, Pastor Emeritus; Thomas J. Bradley; Mrs. Charlene Keane, Pastoral Assoc.; Deacons Michael Monnelly; Raymond Ward. In res., Revs. Wayne F. Watts; George Velloorattil.
Res., 6280 N. Sauganash Ave., 60646. Tel: 773-736-6060; Fax: 773-736-6099.
School—Sisters 3; Lay Teachers 28; Students 759.
Convent—6275 N. Ionia Ave., 60646.

180—QUEEN OF ANGELS, Revs. Thomas E. Lamping; Terence M. Keehan; Deacons Roberto Figueroa; Donald O'Grady.
Res., 2330 W. Sunnyside Ave., 60625. Tel: 773-561-5118; Fax: 312-561-2510.
School—4520 N. Western Ave., 60625.
Lay Teachers 23; Students 442.

181—QUEEN OF THE UNIVERSE, Revs. Lawrence R. McNally; Richard L. Skriba; Michael G. McGovern; Deacon Everett W. Helmer.
Res., 7114 S. Hamlin Ave., 60629. Tel: 773-582-4662; Fax: 773-581-3313.
School—7130 S. Hamlin Ave., 60629.
Lay Teachers 20; Students 404.

182—ST. RENE GOUPIL, Revs. Peter P. Paurazas; Edward M. Flannery, Pastor Emeritus; Deacon Owen Boehm. In res., Rev. James Sweeney, M.H.M.
Res., 6949 W. 63rd Pl., 60638. Tel: 773-229-8523.
School—6340 S. New England Ave., 60638. Valerio Bellucci, Prin.
Sisters 1; Lay Teachers 13; Students 330.

183—RESURRECTION, Revs. Daniel F. Montalbano; Phillip C. Kiley; Deacons Efrain Ayala; Paul Bovyn; Feliciano Crespo; George Fuller, (Retired); Camilo Vera.
Business Office: 3043 N. Francisco Ave., 60618. Tel: 773-478-9705; Fax: 773-478-1387.
Res., 2840 W. Nelson St., 60618. Tel: 773-478-1441.
School—2845 W. Barry, 60618. Tel: 773-478-9191.
Lay Teachers 12; Students 280.

184—ST. RICHARD, Revs. Jerome S. Siwek; Peter Galek; Andrew S. Grzela; Deacon Albert Schroetlin.
Res., 5032 S. Kostner Ave., 60632. Tel: 773-585-1221; Fax: 773-585-4959.
School—5025 S. Kenneth Ave., 60632.
Lay Teachers 15; Students 320.

185—ST. RITA OF CASCIA, Revs. William E. Lego, O.S.A.; Edward J. Kersten, O.S.A.; Bros. John Patrick Currier, O.S.A.; William Wiegel, O.S.A.; Deacons John Flanagan; Juan Rodriguez; George Steinhable.
Res., 6243 S. Fairfield Ave., 60629. Tel: 773-434-9600; Fax: 773-434-9668.

186—ST. ROBERT BELLARMINE, Revs. Michael A. Goergan; Kevin J. Sheahan; Deacon Edward Swiech.
Res., 4646 N. Austin Ave., 60630. Tel: 773-777-2666; Fax: 773-777-2770.
School—6036 W. Eastwood Ave., 60630.
Sisters 6; Lay Teachers 20; Students 402.

187—ST. ROMAN, Revs. Juan J. Huitrado; John G. Klein; Deacons Jose Marrero; Vicente Estrada; Sr. Irma Fuentes, Pastoral Assoc. & D.R.E. In res., Rev. Arturo J. Perez.
Res., 2311 S. Washtenaw Ave., 60608. Tel: 773-247-6645; Fax: 773-927-1610.

188—ST. SABINA, Rev. Michael L. Pfleger.
Res., 1210 W. 78th Pl., 60620. Tel: 773-483-4300.
School—7801 S. Throop St., 60620.
Dominican Sisters (Sinsinawa, WI) 4; Lay Teachers 21; Students 503.

189—SACRED HEART (Croatian), Revs. Paul Maslach, O.F.M.; Jago Soce, O.F.M.
Res., 2864 E. 96th St., 60617. Tel: 773-768-1423; Fax: 773-768-3750.
School—2906 E. 96th St., 60617.
School Sisters of St. Francis 3; Lay Teachers 8; Students 220.

190—SACRED HEART MISSION OF HOLY NAME OF MARY, Rev. Anthony J. Vader.
Res., 11652 S. Church St., 60643. Tel: 773-238-6800; 233-3955.

191—ST. SIMON THE APOSTLE, Rev. Francis Q. Kub; Laura L. Zbella, Pastoral Assoc.; Deacon Angelo Cordoba. In res., Rev. Charles J. Kouba, (Retired).
Res., 5157 S. California Ave., 60632. Tel: 773-436-1045; Fax: 773-436-4684.
School—5135 S. California Ave., 60632. Tel: 773-434-5036.
Sisters of SS. Cyril & Methodius 3; Lay Teachers 8; Students 254.

192—ST. STANISLAUS, BISHOP AND MARTYR, Revs. Anthony Dziorek, C.R.; Francis Grzechowiak, C.R.; Marion Wroblewski, C.R.; Edmund Jastrzebski, C.R.; Deacons Zygfryd Oborski; Mitchell Szady.
Res., 5352 W. Belden Ave., 60639. Tel: 773-237-5800; Fax: 773-237-7029.
School—2342 N. Lorel Ave., 60639. Tel: 773-622-3342; Fax: 773-622-9160.
Franciscan Sisters of Chicago 2; Lay Teachers 20; Students 400.

193—ST. STANISLAUS KOSTKA (Polish, Spanish, English), Revs. Anthony Bus, C.R.; Emil Stec, C.R.; Jacek Praski; Deacons Nicolas Flores; Miguel Garcia; Juan Ibarra.
Res., 1351 W. Evergreen Ave., 60622. Tel: 773-278-2470; Fax: 773-278-2471.
School—1255 N. Noble St., 60622.
Sisters 3; Lay Teachers 9; Students 220.

194—ST. STEPHEN, Revs. Blase Chemazar, O.F.M.; Callistus F. Langerholz, O.F.M.; Deacon John Vidmar.
Res., 1852 W. 22nd Pl., 60608. Tel: 773-376-4334.

195—ST. STEPHEN, KING OF HUNGARY, Rev. Joseph Somos (STL).
Res., 2015 W. Augusta Blvd., 60622. Tel: 773-486-1896.

196—ST. SYLVESTER, Revs. Kevin J. Feeney; Joseph

Tito; Deacons Confessor DeJesus; Sigifredo Ortiz; Santos Soto; Francisco Roman; Bienvenido Nieves. Res., 2157 N. Humboldt Blvd., 60647. Tel: 773-235-3646; Fax: 773-489-0974.
School—Sisters 3; Lay Teachers 15; Students 351.

197—ST. SYMPHOROSA AND SEVEN SONS, Revs. Marcel J. Pasciak; Francis Maniola, Pastor Emeritus; Thomas A. Bernas.
Res., 6135 S. Austin Ave., 60638. Tel: 773-767-1523.
School—6125 S. Austin Ave., 60638.
Benedictine Sisters of Pontifical Jurisdiction 3; Lay Teachers 28; Students 609.

198—ST. TARCISSUS, Revs. John J. Grace; Leonard J. Felczak, Pastor Emeritus; Edward X. Detloff; Thomas F. Baldonieri; Sleeva R. Policetta; Deacon Gregory M. Bzdon. In res., Revs. William T. Hock; Bruno Switalski.
Res., 6020 W. Ardmore Ave., 60646. Tel: 773-763-8228.
School—6040 W. Ardmore Ave., 60646.
Lay Teachers 30; Students 712.

199—ST. TERESA, Rev. John R. Hoffman; Deacon Roberto Figueroa. In res., Revs. Frank Latzko; R. Peter Bowman.
Res., 1037 W. Armitage Ave., 60614. Tel: 773-528-6650; Fax: 773-871-6766.
School—1930 N. Kenmore Ave., 60614.
Sisters of Christian Charity (Wilmette, IL) 1; Lay Teachers 10; Students 134.

200—ST. THADDEUS, Rev. John M. Collins; Deacon Jimmie Flewellen.
Res., 9540 S. Harvard Ave., 60628. Tel: 773-568-7077; Fax: 773-928-5447.
School—Lay Teachers 10; Students 265.

201—ST. THECLA, Revs. Gerard E. Rogala; Matt A. Bednarz, Pastor Emeritus; Leon J. Rezula; Deacon Eugene Bates. In res., Rev. Wojtech Zieba.
Res., 6725 W. Devon Ave., 60631. Tel: 773-792-3077; Fax: 773-792-3820.
School—6323 N. Newcastle Ave., 60631.
Lay Teachers 17; Students 335.

202—ST. THERESE OF THE INFANT JESUS. Closed. For inquiries for parish records contact the Chancery. (The Little Flower).

203—ST. THERESE CATHOLIC CHINESE CHURCH, Rev. Christopher Wong.
Res., 218 W. Alexander St., 60616. Tel: 312-842-6777.
School—247 W. 23rd St., 60616.
Sisters 1; Lay Teachers 14; Students 240.

204—ST. THOMAS APOSTLE, Revs. John A. Farry; Thomas J. Fitzgerald, Pastor Emeritus; Thomas R. Seitz, (Retired); Deacon Robert Monica.
Res., 5472 S. Kimbark Ave., 60615. Tel: 773-324-2626; Fax: 773-753-7415.
School—5485 S. Woodlawn Ave., 60615.
Dominican Sisters (Sinsinawa, WI) 4; Lay Teachers 27; Students 453.

205—ST. THOMAS OF CANTERBURY, Revs. Richard T. Simon; Trinh Peter Hung (SCL) (Vietnamese Apostolate); Deacons Richard Leigh; Orlando Perez.
Res., 4827 N. Kenmore Ave., 60640. Tel: 773-878-5507.
School—Lay Teachers 10; Students 271.

206—ST. THOMAS MORE, Revs. Anthony J. Brankin; Theodore McNulty; John J. Sullivan; John Frawley, (Retired); Thomas J. Curley, (Retired).
Res., 2825 W. 81st St., 60652. Tel: 773-436-4444.
School—8130 S. California Ave., 60652.
Dominican Sisters (Sinsinawa, WI) 3; Lay Teachers 17; Students 357.

207—ST. TIMOTHY, Revs. Harold B. Murphy; Gilbert A. Carroll, Pastor Emeritus. In res., Rev. M. Arul Raj.
Res., 6326 N. Washtenaw Ave., 60659. Tel: 773-262-6600; Fax: 773-262-9214.

208—TRANSFIGURATION OF OUR LORD, Rev. John J. Rudnik. In res., Rev. Kevin Ugomadi.
Res., 2609 W. Carmen Ave., 60625. Tel: 773-561-7953.
School—5044 N. Rockwell, 60625.
Lay Teachers 12; Students 235.

209—ST. TURIBIUS, Revs. Raymond M. Barlog; Michael Bowler; Rev. Msgr. Joseph Mroczkowski, Pastor Emeritus. In res., Rev. Stanley J. Rokicinski.
Res., 5646 S. Karlov Ave., 60629. Tel: 773-581-2730.
School—4120 W. 57th St., 60629.
Felician Sisters 7; Lay Teachers 17; Students 465.

210—ST. VIATOR, Revs. William L. Carpenter, C.S.V.; Robert T. Bolser, C.S.V.; C. Gregory Jones, C.S.V.; Donald Wehnert, C.S.V.
Res., 4170 W. Addison St., 60641. Tel: 773-286-4040; Fax: 773-286-4058.
School—4140 W. Addison St., 60641.
Sisters of St. Joseph of Carondelet (St. Louis, MO) 5; Lay Teachers 25; Students 550.

211—ST. VINCENT DE PAUL, Rev. Donald Ours, C.M.
Res., 1010 W. Webster Ave., 60614. Tel: 773-327-1113; Fax: 773-327-2326.

212—ST. WALTER, Revs. John M. Sevick; Joseph D. Ryan, (Retired); Sr. Christine Kub, O.P., Pastoral Assoc.; Deacons Thomas O'Connell; Daniel Carroll; Donald Niersbach.
Res., 11722 S. Oakley Ave., 60643. Tel: 773-779-1515; Fax: 773-779-0381.
School—11741 S. Western Ave., 60643. Tel: 773-445-8850.
Lay Teachers 10; Students 207.

213—ST. WENCESLAUS, Rev. Eugene R. Winkowski.
Res., 3400 N. Monticello Ave., 60618. Tel: 773-588-1135.

214—ST. WILLIAM, Revs. Robert C. Rizzo; Henry J. Michalek, Pastor Emeritus; Michael G. Zaniolo; Thomas Hoffman; Deacons Christopher Virruso; Dennis Colgan.
Res., 2600 N. Sayre Ave., 60635. Tel: 773-637-6565; Fax: 773-745-4200.
School—2559 N. Sayre Ave., 60635.
Lay Teachers 25; Students 320.

OUTSIDE THE CITY OF CHICAGO

Alsip, Cook Co., St. Terrence, Revs. William J. Lyons; Patrick J. O'Neill.
Res., 4300 W. 119th Pl., 60658. Tel: 708-597-0970.

Antioch, Lake Co., St. Peter, Revs. Lawrence F. Hanley; William J. Costello; Deacons Robert A. Gagnon; Frank M. Colette, (Retired); Paul M. Newrauter; Jeffrey Barton.
Res., 557 W. Lake St., 60002. Tel: 847-395-0274; Fax: 847-395-4553.
School—Lay Teachers 16; Students 275.

Argo, Cook Co., St. Blase, Rev. Norbert J. Waszak; Deacon Antonio Ponce. In res., Most Rev. Alfred L. Abramowicz, D.D.; Rev. Joseph Mytych.
Res., 6101 S. 75th Ave., 60501. Tel: 708-458-0007.

Arlington Heights, Cook Co., St. Edna, Revs. John J. Hurley; Daniel F. Sullivan; Deacons Raymond Graffia, Jr.; Robert Manthie; Vern Valenziano. In res., Rev. Eugene J. Faucher.
Res., 2525 N. Arlington Heights Rd., 60004. Tel: 847-398-3362; Fax: 847-394-5226.

St. James, Revs. William J. Zavaski; Hugh V. O'Brien, Pastor Emeritus; Lawrence R. Dowling; Timothy J. Fairman; Sr. Kathleen A. Donohoe, O.S.F., Pastoral Assoc.; Deacons Richard Dinneen; Robert Plantz; Joseph Phillippi; Louis Lekan; John Lyons; Armand Ferrani; Matt Hennessy.
Office: 820 N. Arlington Heights Rd., 60004. Tel: 847-253-6305; Fax: 847-253-0269.
School—821 Arlington Heights Rd., 60004.
School Sisters of St. Francis 2; Lay Teachers 33; Students 909.

Our Lady of the Wayside, Revs. Vincent F. Costello; Ronald C. Lewandowski; John J. Mackin, Pastor Emeritus; Harold T. O'Hara, Pastor Emeritus; Deacons Robert Duffy; Donald Grossnickle; Brendan Foley; Denise Niziolek, Pastoral Assoc.
Res., 432 W. Park St., 60005. Tel: 847-253-5353; Fax: 847-253-7175.
School—Lay Teachers 42; Students 631.

Barrington, Lake Co., St. Anne, Revs. John W. Dewes; Arthur J. Dillon, Pastor Emeritus; Dennis J. Stafford; Deacons Richard Baum; Robert C. Brauch; James Condill; Richard Seveska.
Res., 120 N. Ela St., 60010. Tel: 847-382-5300; Fax: 847-382-5363.
School—312 E. Chestnut St., 60010.
School Sisters of St. Francis 6; Lay Teachers 30; Students 625.

Bartlett, Cook Co., St. Peter Damian, Revs. William L. Lupo; Jerome G. Klug, Pastor Emeritus; Deacons David Sattler; Robert Newton.
Res., 109 S. Crest Ave., 60103. Tel: 630-837-5411; Fax: 630-837-9424.

Bellwood, Cook Co., St. Simeon, Revs. John J. McCarville; Mariano L. Vita, Pastor Emeritus. In res., Rev. Joseph Ekpo.
Res., 430 Bohland Ave., 60104. Tel: 708-547-6868.
School—501 Bellwood Ave., 60104. Tel: 708-547-7350.
Lay Teachers 13; Students 200.

Berwyn, Cook Co., St. Leonard, Rev. William J. Curran; Rev. Msgr. John J. Farrell, Pastor Emeritus; Revs. Kenneth S. Laske; Edward G. Corcoran; Deacon Joel Chrastka.
Res., 3318 S. Clarence Ave., 60402. Tel: 708-484-0015; Fax: 708-484-6982.
School—3322 S. Clarence Ave., 60402. Tel: 708-749-3666.
Lay Teachers 18; Students 424.
Convent—6634 W. 34th St., 60402. Sisters of St. Joseph (La Grange, IL)

St. Mary of Celle, Revs. Richard J. Prendergast; Thang T. Le; Deacon Larry Spohr.
Res., 1428 Wesley Ave., 60402. Tel: 708-788-0876; Fax: 708-788-0242.
School—1448 S. Wesley Ave., 60402. Tel: 708-749-1989.
Lay Teachers 15; Students 217.

St. Odilo, Rev. Peter J. Cyscon. In res., Revs. Richard B. Saudis; David J. Mulvihill; Thomas J. Kaveney, (Retired); William P. Fegan.
Res., 2244 S. East Ave., 60402. Tel: 708-484-2161.
School—2301 S. Clarence Ave., 60402. Tel: 708-484-0755. William Donegan, Prin.
Sisters of Charity B.V.M. 2; Lay Teachers 14; Students 303.
National Shrine—Poor Souls.

Blue Island, Cook Co., St. Benedict, Revs. George L. Schopp; Edward P. Connors, Pastor Emeritus; Roger J. Caplis; John Bola Atoyebi (Nigeria); Deacons Thomas Grotto; Juan Limon; Ellery Shandro; Jose Zapata.
Res., 2339 York St., 60406. Tel: 708-385-8510; Fax: 708-371-2631.
School—2324 New St., 60406.
School Sisters of Notre Dame 1; Adrian Dominicans 3; Lay Teachers 7; Students 299.
Mission—Robbins, Cook Co., St. Peter Claver, 14125 Claire Blvd., Robbins, 60472. Tel: 708-389-2434.

St. Donatus, Revs. Robert Kleiner, M.C.C.J.; Patrick Burns, M.C.C.J.; Hugo Riva, M.C.C.J.
Res., 1939 Union St., 60406. Tel: 708-385-2890; Fax: 708-385-4708.

St. Isidore, Revs. Gregory A. Rom; Sylvester W. Dudzinski, Pastor Emeritus.
Res., 1811 W. Burr Oak Ave., 60406. Tel: 708-388-0807.
School—12731 S. Wood St., 60406.
Sisters 2; Lay Teachers 9; Students 154.

Bridgeview, Cook Co., St. Fabian, Revs. Walter J. Turlo; Walter A. Strus; Deacons Kenneth Schoenfeld; Kenneth Zawadzki.
Res., 8300 S. Thomas Ave., 60455. Tel: 708-599-1110; Fax: 708-599-0673.

Brookfield, Cook Co., St. Barbara, Revs. Maurice J. Kissane; Norman J. Trela; Sr. Margaret Halligan, C.S.J., Pastoral Assoc.; Deacons John Debnar; Robert Motycka; Gerald Fox. In res., Rev. John Birk (SPK).
Res., 4008 Prairie Ave., 60513. Tel: 708-485-0589.
School—8900 Windemere Ave., 60513.
Sisters 1; Lay Teachers 15; Students 255.

Buffalo Grove, Lake Co., St. Mary, Revs. Kenneth G. Kiepura; Donald J. Duffy, Pastor Emeritus; Thomas A. Bishop; John S. Plotkowski; Deacons I. James Young, M.D.; Dennis Brown; Robert LaCosse; Eugene Kukla; Bruce Peters; Kevin Kanter.
Res., 75 N. Buffalo Grove Rd., 60089. Tel: 847-541-1450; Fax: 847-541-2443. [CEM]
School—50 N. Buffalo Grove Rd., 60089.
Lay Teachers 45; Students 736.

Burbank, Cook Co., St. Albert the Great, Revs. Edward M. Mackowiak; Joseph P. Lynch, Pastor Emeritus; Frank J. Burek; Bruno Janik; Deacon Irvin Bryce.
Res., 5555 W. State Rd., 60459. Tel: 708-423-0321.
School—5535 W. State Rd., 60459. Tel: 708-424-7757.
Dominican Sisters (Adrian, MI) 4; Lay Teachers 22; Students 400.

Burnham, Cook Co., Mother of God, Rev. Edmund F. Guz.
Res., 14207 S. Green Bay Ave., 60633. Tel: 708-862-8777; Fax: 708-891-1349.

Calumet City, Cook Co., St. Andrew the Apostle, Revs. Martin E. Michniewicz; Michael G. Zaniolo; Deacon Robert Banet.
Res., 768 Lincoln Ave., 60409. Tel: 708-862-4165.
School—331-155th Pl., 60409.
Sisters of the Holy Family of Nazareth (Des Plaines, IL) 2; Lay Teachers 17; Students 267.

Our Lady of Knock, Revs. Donald J. Fenske; Michael L. Zoufal; Sr. Alban Hermes, O.P., Pastoral Assoc.; Deacon Albert Lundy.
Res., 501 163rd St., 60409. Tel: 708-862-3011; Fax: 708-862-9618.
School—497 163rd St., 60409.
Lay Teachers 11; Students 245.

St. Victor, Revs. Thomas E. Cima; Victor Miranda; Sr. Clara Chandler, H.M., D.R.E.; Deacons Eugene Kilinski; Romeo Munoz; Daniel Ragonese; Ronald Schultz. In res., Rev. Michael Kurz.
Res., 553 Hirsch Ave., 60409. Tel: 708-891-8920; Fax: 708-891-8943.
School—Lay Teachers 15; Students 412.

Calumet Park, Cook Co., Seven Holy Founders, Revs. Robert Kleiner, M.C.C.J.; Hugo Riva, M.C.C.J.
Res., 12400 S. Ada St., 60643. Tel: 708-385-8459.

Chicago Heights, Cook Co., St. Agnes, Rev. John S. Siemanowski; Deacon Thomas Nowack.
Res., 1501 Chicago Rd., 60411. Tel: 708-709-2694; Fax: 708-709-2693.
School—1501 Chicago Rd., 60411.
Sisters of St. Francis of the Perpetual Adoration 2; Lay Teachers 16; Students 290.

St. Kieran, Revs. William A. Eddy; Daniel A. Flens; Deacons Eugene La Belle; William Jablonski;

Bernard Halper.
Res., 724 W. 195th St., 60411. Tel: 708-755-0074.
School—700 W. 195th St., 60411.
Lay Teachers 12; Students 267.

St. Paul, Revs. William T. O'Connor; Bernard G. Guirsch, Pastor Emeritus; Deacon Juan Garza.
Res., 206 E. 25th St., 60411. Tel: 708-754-3120; Fax: 708-754-0076.

Chicago Ridge, Cook Co., Our Lady of the Ridge, Rev. Paul Burak; Rev. Msgr. M. Edward Roche, Pastor Emeritus; Rev. Robert J. Keener; Sr. Dominic Krivich, O.S.F., Pastoral Assoc.; Deacon Michael Krapez.
Res., 10811 S. Ridgeland Ave., 60415. Tel: 708-425-3800; Fax: 708-425-2792.
School—10859 S. Ridgeland Ave., 60415. Tel: 708-424-4409.
Franciscan Sisters of Our Lady of Perpetual Help 2; Lay Teachers 11; Students 287.

Cicero, Cook Co.,

1—St. Anthony, Rev. James J. Kastigar; Deacons Alfonso Salgado; Gilberto Mercado; Claude Hensley. In res., Rev. Michael J. Bradley.
Res., 1515 S. 50th Ave., 60650. Tel: 708-652-0231; Fax: 708-652-0228.
St. Anthony Center—1506 S. 49th Ct., 60650. Tel: 708-652-0081; 656-7260.

2—St. Frances of Rome, Revs. Mark P. Canavan; Daniel P. Buck.
Res., 1428 S. 59th Ct., 60650. Tel: 708-652-2140.
School—1400 S. Austin Blvd., 60650. Tel: 708-652-2277.
School Sisters of Charity of the Incarnate Word (St. Louis, MO) 3; Lay Teachers 19; Students 470.

3—St. Mary of Czestochowa, (Polish), Revs. Thaddeus J. Makuch; Waldemar Dynak.
Res., 3010 S. 48th Ct., 60650. Tel: 708-652-0948.
School—3009 S. 49th Ave., 60650.
Sisters of St. Joseph of the Third Order of St. Francis 3; Lay Teachers 10; Students 221.

4—Mary, Queen of Heaven, Revs. John R. Price; Francis J. Spellman, Pastor Emeritus; Deacon Julio Rosado. In res., Rev. Edward N. Coffey.
Res., 5300 W. 24th St., 60650. Tel: 708-863-6608.
School—5314 W. 24th Pl., 60650. Tel: 708-652-6312.
Lay Teachers 10; Students 287.

5—Our Lady of Charity, Revs. Charles E. Ezerskis; Medard P. Laz, Admin. In res., Rev. John A. Rolek.
Res., 3600 57th Ct., 60650. Tel: 708-863-1207.
School—3620 57th Ct., 60650. Tel: 708-652-0262.
Lay Teachers 12; Students 217.
Convent—School Sisters of St. Francis 8.

6—Our Lady of the Mount, Revs. Joseph T. LeVoy; James T. O'Connor, (Retired); Deacons Robert E. Devereux; Bill Ciston; Antonio Llano.
Res., 2414 S. 61st Ave., 60804. Tel: 708-652-2791; Fax: 708-863-6014.
School—2400 S. 61st Ave., 60804.
Lay Teachers 10; Students 305.

Country Club Hills, Cook Co., St. Emeric, Revs. Paul G. Seaman; John J. Rochford, Pastor Emeritus; Deacons James Detloff; Thomas O'Brien, (Retired).
Res., 4330 W. 180th St., 60478. Tel: 708-798-0757.
School—4300 W. 180th St., 60478.
Lay Teachers 10; Students 142.

Deerfield, Lake Co., Holy Cross, Rev. John M. Thinnes. Pastoral Assocs.: Sr. Dee Peppard, B.V.M.; Anne Schank; Deacons Thomas Bresler; Jerome Kasimatis; Anthony Sabato; Robert Smith. In res., Rev. Jeremiah M. Boland.
Res., 724 Elder Ln., 60015. Tel: 847-945-0430; Fax: 847-945-7651.
School—720 Elder Ln., 60015. Ms. Lorraine Gawlik, Prin.; Mrs. Marilyn Peters Krawczyk, D.R.E.
Lay Teachers 28; Students 418.

Des Plaines, Cook Co.,

1—St. Mary, Revs. Eugene J. Dyer; Paul F. Rosemeyer, Pastor Emeritus; Flavio Gonzalez; Edward J. Barrett; Deacon Fred Kruse.
Res., 794 Pearson St., 60016. Tel: 847-824-8144; Fax: 847-824-3906.
School—Our Lady of Destiny (North Campus), 795 Center St., 60016.
Lay Teachers 7; Students 138.

2—St. Paul Chong Hasang, Cook, Rev. Thomas Kim.
Res., 675 Dursey Ln., 60016. Tel: 847-699-6334; Fax: 847-966-1029.

3—St. Stephen Protomartyr, Revs. Michael A. Olivero; Leonard T. Mezydlo, Pastor Emeritus; Deacon Donald J. Telposky.
1267 Everett Ave., 60018-2398. Tel: 847-824-2026; Fax: 847-824-3842.
School—Our Lady of Destiny (South Campus), 1880 Ash St., 60018-2343. Tel: 847-827-2900.
Lay Teachers 6; Students 130.

4—St. Zachary, Revs. Joseph P. McGinnity; Thomas P. Conley, (Retired); Lawrence F. Springer; Deacons Peter Lagges; Robert W. Blue, (Retired).
Res., 567 W. Algonquin Rd., 60016. Tel: 847-956-7020; Fax: 847-956-7313.
School—Sisters 3; Lay Teachers 13; Students 261.

Elk Grove Village, Cook Co., St. Julian Eymard Church, Rev. John F. Dedek.
Res., 601 Biesterfield Rd., 60007. Tel: 847-956-0130; Fax: 847-956-0189.

Queen of the Rosary, Revs. Arthur J. Fagan; Francis J. Cerniglia; John A. Robinson; Deacon Ted Czarnecki.
Res., 750 Elk Grove Blvd., 60007. Tel: 847-437-0403; Fax: 847-981-7192.
School—690 Elk Grove Blvd., 60007.
Lay Teachers 20; Students 370.

Elmwood Park, Cook Co., St. Celestine, Revs. Walter G. DeRoeck; Lawrence J. Sullivan. Pastoral Assocs.: Sr. Jean Schulte, R.S.M.; Deacons John Nolan; James Devine; Michael DeLarco; Gregory Stevens. In res., Rev. Bernard C. White.
Res., 3020 N. 76th Ct., 60707. Tel: 708-453-2555; Fax: 708-462-0560.
School—Lay Teachers 22; Students 598.

Evanston, Cook Co., St. Athanasius, Rev. William D. Mannion; Deacon Richard S. Jay.
Res., 1615 Lincoln St., 60201. Tel: 847-328-1430; Fax: 847-328-1809.
School—2510 Ashland, 60201. Tel: 847-864-2650.
Lay Teachers 25; Students 335.

St. Mary, Revs. Edward F. Hoover; Jackson Colomb; Deacon John Arndt; Christopher M. Murphy, Pastoral Assoc. In res., Rev. Valerian Laini (Africa).
Res., 1421 Oak Ave., 60201. Tel: 847-864-0333.
Parish Center—1012 Lake St., 60201. Fax: 847-864-0354.
School—Consolidated with St. Nicholas Parish to form Pope John XXIII School. See St. Nicholas for further details.

St. Nicholas, Rev. Robert H. Oldershaw. In res., Rev. James Halstead, O.S.A.
Res., 806 Ridge Ave., 60202. Tel: 847-864-1185; Fax: 847-864-7810.
School—Consolidated with St. Mary Parish to form Pope John XXIII School. 1120 Washington, 60202. Tel: 847-475-5678. Mrs. Nancy Schultz, Prin.
Lay Teachers 21; Students 344.

Evergreen Park, Cook Co., St. Bernadette, Rev. David J. Byrne. In res., Revs. Alfredo J. Salera; Bernard Blasich.
Res., 9343 Francisco Ave., 60642. Tel: 708-422-8995; Fax: 708-422-8699.
School—9311 S. Francisco Ave., 60642.
Dominican Sisters (Springfield, IL) 3; Lay Teachers 16; Students 422.

Most Holy Redeemer, Revs. Richard J. Dempsey; Brian A. Lisowski; Anthony L. Markus. In res., Rev. Albert R. Adamich, (Retired).
Res., 9525 S. Lawndale Ave., 60642. Tel: 708-425-5354.
School—3650 W. 96th St., 60642.
Sisters of the Holy Cross (South Bend, IN) 2; Lay Teachers 17; Students 492.

Queen of Martyrs, Revs. Patrick M. Lyons; William P. Murphy, Pastor Emeritus; Rev. Msgr. John J. Doyle; Rev. Daniel R. Steiner; Sr. Mary Lou Henerson, S.S.N.D., Pastoral Assoc.
Res., 10233 S. Central Park, 60805-3799. Tel: 708-423-8110; Fax: 708-423-7372.
School—3550 W. 103rd St., 60805.
Sisters of Mercy 1; Lay Teachers 28; Students 750.

Flossmoor, Cook Co., Infant Jesus of Prague, Revs. Michael A. Hack; William J. Flaherty, Pastor Emeritus; Joseph D. Ryan, Pastor Emeritus; Richard L. Hills, Pastor Emeritus; Thomas Winnikates; Deacon George Brooks. In res., Rev. Matthias Hoffman.
Res., 1131 Douglas Ave., 60422. Tel: 708-799-5400.
School—1101 Douglas Ave., 60422.
Lay Teachers 22; Students 514.

Forest Park, Cook Co., St. Bernardine, Revs. Patrick M. Tucker; John F. Fearon, Pastor Emeritus; Phillip F. Cioffi; William J. Quinlan, Pastor Emeritus; Deacons Timothy Rehor; John Walters. In res., Rev. Francis J. Grady, S.S.C.
Res., 7246 Harrison St., 60130. Tel: 708-366-0839.
School—815 Elgin Ave., 60130.
Lay Teachers 12; Students 232.
Convent—816 Marengo Ave., 60130.

Franklin Park, Cook Co., St. Gertrude, Revs. Alfred P. Corbo; Ramon Perez; Deacons Robert Murphy; Sebastian Rivera; Roman Flores; Lorenzo Chaidez. In res., Revs. Edmund J. Schreiber; William T. Hock, Pastor Emeritus.
Res., 9613 Schiller Blvd., 60131. Tel: 847-455-1100; Fax: 847-455-1209.
School—9617 Schiller Blvd., 60131. Tel: 847-455-5810.
Lay Teachers 9; Students 140.

Glenview, Cook Co., St. Catherine Laboure, Rev. James P. Murphy; Deacons Ray Gavin; Michael Bretz; Frank Beil.
Res., 3535 Thornwood Ln., 60025. Tel: 847-729-1414.
School—3425 Thornwood Ln., 60025.
Sisters 1; Lay Teachers 16; Students 212.

Our Lady of Perpetual Help, Revs. John E. Flavin; Marc W. Reszel; Richard J. Jakubik; Deacons James Revord; Alan Sedivy. In res., Rev. Jerome J. Hartmann, (Retired).
Res., 1775 Grove St., 60025. Tel: 847-729-1525; Fax: 847-724-7025.
School—1123 Church St., 60025.
School Sisters of St. Francis 4; Lay Teachers 66; Students 1010.

Glenwood, Cook Co., St. John, Revs. John R. Kauzlarich; Stanley C. Limanowski, Pastor Emeritus; Paul E. Schwartz.
Res., 301 S. Cottage Grove Ave., 60425. Tel: 708-758-5098.

Grayslake, Lake Co., St. Gilbert, Revs. Robert W. Beaven; Thomas Refermat; Deacons Chester Kozuchowski; Henry Iwan; Jeffrey Newman. In res.,
Res., 301 E. Belvidere Rd., 60030. Tel: 847-223-4731.
School—251 E. Belvidere Rd., 60030. Tel: 847-223-8600.
Sisters of the Holy Family of Nazareth 3; Lay Teachers 18; Students 527.

Gurnee, Lake Co., St. Paul the Apostle, Revs. Farrell J. Kane, O.Carm.; Philip Nessinger, O.Carm.; Deacon Michael Penich.
Res., 6401 Gages Lake Rd., 60031. Tel: 847-918-0600; Fax: 847-918-0640.

Hanover Park, Cook Co., St. Ansgar, Revs. John W. Tapper; Jerome F. Riordan, Pastor Emeritus; Deacons Louis Barone; Nick Tereza; Robert Ziomek; Clem Petricca; Oscar Monterosa.
Res., 2041 Poplar Ave., 60103. Tel: 630-837-5553; Fax: 630-837-9847.

Harvey, Cook Co., Ascension-St. Susanna, Rev. Joseph W. Altman; Deacons Thomas R. Carvlin; Henry Burke, Jr.
Res., 15234 Myrtle Ave., 60426. Tel: 708-333-0931; Fax: 708-333-3281.
School—Mary of Nazareth, 15727 S. Emerald Ave., 60426.
Sisters of the Holy Family of Nazareth 4; Lay Teachers 5; Students 201.

St. John the Baptist (Polish), Revs. Edward Romanski (Poland) Admin.; Clarence J. Juchcinski, Pastor Emeritus; Michael Wasiel, (Retired).
Res., 15746 Union Ave., 60426. Tel: 708-333-0184.
School—15727 Emerald Ave., 60426.
Sisters of the Holy Family of Nazareth (Des Plaines, IL) 3; Lay Teachers 8; Students 163.

Harwood Heights, Norridge, Cook Co., St. Rosalie, Revs. John C. Cain; Richard J. Ehrens; Deacon Joseph E. Bishop, Pastoral Assoc.
Res., 4401 N. Oak Park Ave., Harwood Heights-Norridge, 60656. Tel: 708-867-8817.

Hazel Crest, Cook Co., St. Anne, Rev. Leonard A. Dubi; Sr. Joan Klega, S.P., Pastoral Assoc.; Deacons John Leonas, (Retired); Theodore Perez; Herman Benthey; Steven Moore.
Res., 16802 S. Lincoln St., 60429. Tel: 708-335-3221; Fax: 708-335-1953.
School—16801 Dixie Hwy., 60429. Tel: 708-335-2288.
Lay Teachers 10; Students 263.
Early Learning Center—16777 Dixie Hwy., 60429. Tel: 708-335-4831.

Hickory Hills, Cook Co., St. Patricia, Revs. Gerald F. Mulcahy; Norbert A. Chapell, Pastor Emeritus; Michael E. Flynn; Joseph C. Mol; Deacons Charles Keegan; Norbert Weitendorf.
Res., 9050 S. 86th Ave., 60457. Tel: 708-598-5222; Fax: 708-598-5280.
School—9000 S. 86th Ave., 60457.
Sisters of the Holy Family of Nazareth (Des Plaines, IL) 4; Lay Teachers 17; Students 500.

Highland Park, Lake Co., Immaculate Conception, Revs. Robert L. Kealy; John E. O'Brien, Pastor Emeritus; Alec J. Wolff; Deacons Robert T. Fitzsimon (Retired); William L. Moorman.
Res., 770 W. Deerfield Rd., 60035. Tel: 847-433-0130; Fax: 847-433-0669.

Highwood, Lake Co., St. James, Revs. Ronald E. Scarlata; James O'Malley; Deacons Bruno Pagliai; Ellsworth Cordesman; James Gallagher.
Res., 134 North Ave., 60040. Tel: 847-433-1494.
School—140 North Ave., 60040.
Lay Teachers 11; Students 211.

Hillside, Cook Co., St. Domitilla, Revs. Donald Gantley, O.S.M.; Frank M. Falco, O.S.M.; Deacons Angelo Marotto; Kenneth Bell. In res., Rev. Micahel M. Guimon, O.S.M.
Res., 4940 Washington St., 60162. Tel: 708-449-8430; Fax: 708-449-2009.

School—601 Hillside Ave., 60162.
Sisters 4; Lay Teachers 10; Students 298.

Hoffman Estates, Cook Co., St. Hubert, Rev. Eugene J. Nowak; Deacon James Knippen.
Res., 729 Grand Canyon St., 60194. Tel: 847-885-7700; Fax: 847-885-4631.
School—Lay Teachers 42; Students 822.

Hometown, Cook Co., Our Lady of Loretto, Revs. Ronald J. Mass; John J. Mackin, (Retired); Sr. Kathryn McDonald, B.V.M., Pastoral Assoc.; Deacon Thomas Meehan.
Res., 8925 S. Kostner Ave., 60456. Tel: 708-424-7471.
School—Lay Teachers 13; Students 242.

Homewood, Cook Co., St. Joseph, Revs. James M. Sayers; Robert A. Stepek; Deacons Jack O'Leary; George Maddock. In res., Rev. John W. Curran.
Res., 17951 Dixie Hwy., 60430. Tel: 708-798-0622; Fax: 708-798-6137.
School—17949 Dixie Hwy., 60430.
Dominican Sisters (Adrian, MI) 1; Lay Teachers 17; Students 239.

Ingleside, Lake Co., St. Bede, Revs. John F. Krebs; Richard M. Zborowski; Deacons John McMahon; Edward Quakenbush. Pastor Emeriti: Revs. Robert J. Fitzpatrick; Laverne J. Cure.
Res., 36455 N. Wilson Rd., 60041. Tel: 847-587-2251.
School—36399 N. Wilson Rd., 60041.
Lay Teachers 11; Students 208.

Inverness, Cook Co., Holy Family, Rev. Patrick J. Brennan; Deacons Andrew Repak; Robert Anstiss.
Res., 2515 W. Palatine Rd., 60067. Tel: 847-359-0042; Fax: 847-359-0639.

La Grange, Cook Co., St. Cletus, Revs. Raymond F. Klees; Edward Fialkowski; Charles Gallagher, Pastor Emeritus; Deacon Walter Klimke, (Retired).
Res., 600 W. 55th St., 60525. Tel: 708-352-6209; Fax: 708-352-0707.
School—700 W. 55th St., 60525. Tel: 708-352-4820.
Lay Teachers 25; Students 417.

St. Francis Xavier, Revs. William J. Stenzel; Pierce J. Joyce, Pastor Emeritus; Michael J. Shanahan; Lawrence M. Lisowski.
Res., 124 N. Spring Ave., 60525. Tel: 708-352-0168; Fax: 708-352-4904.
School—145 N. Waiola Ave., 60525. Tel: 708-352-2175.
Lay Teachers 24; Students 453.

La Grange Park, Cook Co., St. Louise de Marillac, Revs. John C. Hergenrother; Cletus J. Lynch, Pastor Emeritus; Michael J. Wanda; Deacons Michael McLynn; Dennis Huslig; James Grevenites.
Res., 1144 Harrison Ave., 60526. Tel: 708-352-7388; Fax: 708-352-0714.
School—Lay Teachers 20; Students 250.
Youth Ministry—1125 Harrison Ave., 60526.

Lake Forest, Lake Co., St. Mary, Revs. George J. Rassas; Michael F. McMahon; James D. Brett, Pastor Emeritus; Deacons James L. Kenney; Joseph G. Krakora. Pastoral Assocs.: Joan O'Keefe; Patricia Moran.
Res., 175 E. Illinois Rd., 60045. Tel: 847-234-0205; Fax: 847-234-9860.
School—185 E. Illinois Rd., 60045. Tel: 847-234-0371; Fax: 847-234-9593.
Lay Teachers 31; Students 598.

St. Patrick, Rev. William J. McNulty.
Res., 991 S. Waukegan Rd., 60045. Tel: 847-234-1401; Fax: 847-615-2749.

Lake Villa, Lake Co., Prince of Peace, Revs. Richard W. Fassbinder; James F. Ouletta; Deacons Timothy Leonard; Leonard Milender.
Res., P.O. Box 265, 60046. Tel: 847-356-7915.
School—Lay Teachers 12; Students 213.

Lake Zurich, Lake Co., St. Francis de Sales, Revs. Ronald J. Gollatz; Richard M. Yanos; Deacon Frank Bertagnoli.
Res., 277 E. Main St., 60047. Tel: 847-438-6622; Fax: 847-438-6638.
School—11 S. Buesching Rd., 60047.
Lay Teachers 25; Students 540.

Lansing, Cook Co., St. Ann, Revs. Michael A. Gabriel; Joseph P. Allen; William A. Burke; Deacons Richard Mauch, (Retired); Erwin Chojnacki, (Retired); John Rowe; Joseph Winblad; D. Todd Williamson, Pastoral Assoc.
Res., 3010 Ridge Rd., 60438. Tel: 708-895-6700; Fax: 708-895-6877.
School—3014 Ridge Rd., 60438. Tel: 708-895-1661.
Lay Teachers 21; Students 464.

Lemont, Cook Co.,

1—St. Alphonsus, Revs. Kevin J. Speiss; Julian G. Grinis, Pastor Emeritus.
Res., 215 E. Logan, 60439. Tel: 630-257-2414; Fax: 630-257-2476.
School—St. Alphonsus-St. Patrick Consolidated, (Grades K-8) Admin. Office: 205 Cass St., 60439. Tel: 708-257-2380.
Sisters 4; Lay Teachers 9; Students 260.

2—Blessed Jurgis Matulaitis, Rev. Algirdas Paliokas, S.J.
Res., Lithuanian Catholic Mission, 14915 - 127th St., Unit 101, 60439. Tel: 708-257-5613.

3—SS. Cyril and Methodius, Revs. Victor J. Sivore; Richard M. Jozwiak, Pastor Emeritus; Peter Nowacki, O.P.; Deacons Norbert Lesnieski; Gilbert Ende.
Res., 608 Sobieski St., 60439. Tel: 630-257-2776; Fax: 630-257-9372.
School—607 Sobieski St., 60439. Tel: 630-257-6488; Fax: 630-257-6465.
Lay Teachers 13; Students 419.

4—St. James at Sag Bridge, Revs. Edwin V. Bohula; George F. Aschenbrenner, Pastor Emeritus; James P. Davitt, Pastor Emeritus.
Res., 106th Archer Rd., 60439. Tel: 708-257-7000; Fax: 708-257-7912. [CEM]

5—St. Patrick, Rev. Richard J. Shannon; Rev. John J. McCaig, Pastor Emeritus; Deacon Edward C. Perini.
Res., 200 Illinois St., 60439. Tel: 708-257-6134.
School—St. Alphonsus-St. Patrick Consolidated, (Grades 4-8) Admin. Office: 205 Cass St., 60439. Tel: 708-257-2380.
Lay Teachers 9; Students 325.

Libertyville, Lake Co., St. Joseph, Revs. Ronald H. Anglim; Ronald H. Folger; James E. Schmaus; Deacons Dennis I. Mudd; Dennis J. Dunn; Robert E. Matthews. In res., Rev. Victor J. Ivers.
Res., 121 E. Maple Ave., 60048. Tel: 847-362-2073; Fax: 847-362-6821.
School—221 Park Pl., 60048. Tel: 847-362-0730.
Lay Teachers 28; Students 530.

Lyons, Cook Co., St. Hugh, Revs. Thomas A. Moran; James W. Keating, Pastor Emeritus; James F. Galivan.
Res., 7939 W. 43rd St., 60534. Tel: 708-447-3108; Fax: 708-447-9870.
School—4315 Joliet Ave., 60534.
Lay Teachers 13; Students 159.
Catechesis/Religious Programs—Tel: 708-447-5711.
Students 93.

Markham, Cook Co., St. Gerard Majella, Revs. Michael J. Wallen, Admin.; John J. Heffernan, Pastor Emeritus.
Res., 3536 W. 161st St., 60426. Tel: 708-331-8400.

Matteson, Cook Co., St. Lawrence O'Toole, Revs. James P. Finno; Danilo C. Soriano; Deacons Timothy Keating; Wayne Morton; Gerald Savercool; Ronald Zanardo.
Res., 4101 St. Lawrence Ave., 60443. Tel: 708-748-6090; Fax: 708-748-4055.
School—Lay Teachers 24; Students 519.

Maywood, Cook Co., St. Eulalia, Rev. James V. Quinlan; Rev. Msgr. William J. Quinn, Pastor Emeritus; Deacons Ben Bacchi; Giulio Camerini; George Lambert. In res., Rev. Robert A. Bacchi.
Res., 1851 S. 9th Ave., 60153. Tel: 708-343-6120.
School—815 Lexington St., 60153.
Sisters 4; Lay Teachers 10; Students 340.

St. James, Rev. Herbert J. Meyr; Sr. Jane McCarthy, O.S.F., Pastoral Assoc.; Deacons Antonio Maney; Roman Revering; Norberto Ojeda.
Res., 305 S. 6th Ave., 60153. Tel: 708-343-5210; Fax: 708-343-9317.

Melrose Park, Cook Co., St. Charles Borromeo, Rev. Claire Antonio Orso, C.S.; Deacon Dominic Marella.
Res., 1637 N. 37th Ave., 60160. Tel: 708-343-7646; Fax: 708-343-3527.

Our Lady of Mount Carmel (Italian), Revs. Vincent J. Gennardo, C.S.; Vincent Cutrara, C.S.; Peter Sordi, C.S.; Deacon Rafael Donates.
Res., 1101 N. 23rd Ave., 60160. Tel: 708-344-4140.
School—1102 N. 22nd Ave., 60160. Tel: 708-343-7030. Bro. Charles Muscat, C.S., D.R.E.
Lay Teachers 10; Students 280.

Sacred Heart, Revs. Cosmo F. Militello; Edward J. Kniewel, Pastor Emeritus; Richard J. Kozak; Deacons Raymond Behrendt; Victor Colucci; John Hendricks.
Res., 819 N. 16th Ave., 60160. Tel: 708-344-0757; Fax: 708-344-5906.
School—1503 W. Rice St., 60160.
Sisters of the Third Order of St. Francis of the Holy Family 1; Lay Teachers 20; Students 301.

Midlothian, Cook Co., St. Christopher, Revs. William E. Killeen; Terrence M. Johnson; William M. Henkel, Resident, (Retired); Deacons Joseph Brady; Charles Yucuis; James Giancarlo.
Res., 14641 S. Keeler Ave., 60445. Tel: 708-388-8190; Fax: 708-388-0072.
School—14611 S. Keeler Ave., 60445. Tel: 708-385-8776.
Sisters 2; Lay Teachers 22; Students 511.

Morton Grove, Cook Co., St. Martha, Rev. Robert J. Burnell; Deacon Peter Meehan.
Res., 8523 Georgiana Ave., 60053. Tel: 847-965-0262.
School—Lay Teachers 14; Students 190.
Catechesis/Religious Programs—Tel: 847-965-8062. Mrs. Barbara Koop, D.R.E.
Students 250.
Convent—8519 Georgiana Ave., 60053.

Mt. Prospect, Cook Co.,

1—St. Cecilia, Revs. Daniel J. Brady; Raymond A. Pavis, Pastor Emeritus; Elzear Gehlen, S.V.D.
Res., 700 S. Meier Rd., 60056. Tel: 847-437-6208; Fax: 847-437-6209.

2—St. Emily, Revs. Robert L. Tuzik; John McLoraine, Pastor Emeritus; Denis Condon; Deacons James Sanford; Bill DiCanio.
Res., 101 N. Horner Ln., 60056. Tel: 847-824-5049; Fax: 847-297-0358.
School—1400 E. Central Rd., 60056. Tel: 847-296-3490.
Sisters of the Holy Family of Nazareth 4; Lay Teachers 30; Students 635.

3—St. Raymond de Penafort, Revs. Bernard J. Pietrzak; William J. Buhrfeind, Pastor Emeritus; Steven Dombrowski; Deacons Chester Cheki; Thomas Corcoran; Thomas Lambert; William Reinert; John Lorbach.
Res., 311 S. Ioka St., Box 509, 60056. Tel: 847-253-2444; Fax: 847-253-0023.
School—300 S. Elmhurst Rd., 60056.
Lay Teachers 33; Students 611.

4—St. Thomas a Becket, Revs. John W. Roller; Ralph R. Mollan, Pastor Emeritus; Catherine Weiland, Pastoral Assoc.
Res., 1321 Burning Bush Ln., 60056. Tel: 847-827-9220; Fax: 847-827-0370.

Mundelein, Lake Co., Santa Maria Del Popolo, Revs. James W. Kinn; William J. Shields, (Retired); Edward J. Maloney; Deacons John Simmons; Bill Dunn; Dave Auld; William Sands.
Res., 116 N. Lake St., 60060. Tel: 847-949-8300.
School—126 N. Lake St., 60060. Tel: 847-949-2335.
Lay Teachers 18; Students 411.
Convent—133 N. Lincoln Ave., 60060.

St. Mary (Fremont Center), Revs. Ronald J. Lewinski; James E. Morrissey, Pastor Emeritus; Deacon Robert A. Poletto.
Res., 22333 W. Erhart Rd., 60060. Tel: 847-223-0010; Fax: 847-223-5960.
School—Franciscan Sisters of the Sacred Heart 3; Lay Teachers 8; Students 210.

Niles, Cook Co., St. Isaac Jogues, Revs. John E. Hennessey; George Koeune; Deacons Frederick W. Ray; Robert C. O'Keefe.
Res., 8149 Golf Rd., 60714. Tel: 847-967-1060; Fax: 847-967-1070.

St. John Brebeuf, Revs. Robert S. Banzin; Andrew A. Barzyk; David F. Mannelli; Deacons John Perkowitz; Lawrence Skaja; John Dulen.
Res., 8307 N. Harlem Ave., 60648. Tel: 847-966-8145.
School—8301 Harlem Ave., 60648.
Sisters 4; Lay Teachers 26; Students 554.

Our Lady of Ransom, Revs. John R. Hall; James J. Donovan; Deacons Russell Benko; Robert Crandall; Daniel Collins; Charles O'Donnell.
Ministry Center: 8624 W. Normal, 60714. Tel: 847-823-2550; Fax: 847-823-4291.
School—8350 N. Greenwood, 60714.
Felician Sisters 3; Lay Teachers 22; Students 527.

Norridge, Cook Co., Divine Savior, Revs. Stephen J. Tebes; William A. Schackmuth, Pastor Emeritus; Ronald R. Turcich, O.S.A (PEO); Deacons Gus Jeffery; William Lehman.
Res., 7740 W. Montrose, 60634. Tel: 708-456-9000.
School—7750 W. Montrose, 60634-1098.
Sisters 4; Lay Teachers 9; Students 234.

Northbrook, Cook Co., St. Norbert, Revs. Richard J. Mueller; Robert J. Lutz, Pastor Emeritus; Richard J. Valker; Mr. Daniel P. Costigan, Pastoral Assoc.
Res., 1809 Walters Ave., 60062. Tel: 847-272-7090; Fax: 847-272-7771.
School—1817 Elm St., 60062. Tel: 847-272-0051. Sr. Ann Busch, S.S.S.F., Prin.
Sisters of St. Casimir 2; Lay Teachers 22; Students 315.

Our Lady of the Brook, Revs. Richard E. Sztorc; Robert G. Herne, Pastor Emeritus; Kenneth F. Tabor.
Res., 3700 W. Dundee Rd., 60062. Tel: 847-272-5686; Fax: 847-498-0899.

North Chicago, Lake Co., Queen of Peace, Rev. James E. Merold; Deacons Michael Boucha; Gary Munda; Dean Hermann; Julio Negron.
Res., 910 14th St., 60064. Tel: 847-473-4079.

Northfield, Cook Co., St. Philip the Apostle, Rev. Laurence J. Dunn. In res., Rev. Timothy R. Fiala.
Res., 1962 Old Willow Rd., 60093. Tel: 847-446-8383; Fax: 847-446-8338.
School—1980 Old Willow Rd., 60093.

Lay Teachers 15; Students 120.

Northlake, Cook Co., St. John Baptist Vianney, Cure of Ars, Revs. Charles V. Fanelli; Raymond J. Morrison, Pastor Emeritus; Joseph S. Thomas; Deacons William Ruppert; Robert Hjelmgren; John Zurawski. In res., Rev. Salvador Simoni.
Res., 46 N. Wolf Rd., 60164. Tel: 708-562-0500; Fax: 708-562-1824.
School—Lay Teachers 18; Students 240.

North Riverside, Cook Co., Mater Christi, Rev. M. Cyril Nemecek; Deacon Richard Gordus.
Res., 2431 S. 10th Ave., 60546. Tel: 708-442-5611.
School—2400 S. 10th Ave., 60546.
Lay Teachers 9; Students 162.

Oak Forest, Cook Co., St. Damian, Rev. James L. Cullinen; Rev. Msgr. Martin J. O'Day, Pastor Emeritus; Revs. Michael P. Knotek; Francis Kaucky; Deacons Michael Kush; Patrick O'Donnell, (Retired); Len Steinbeigle; Thomas Hipelius; William Stearns.
Res., 5220 W. 155th St., 60452. Tel: 708-687-1370; Fax: 708-687-1377.
School—5300 W. 155th St., 60452. Barbara Wesolowski, Prin.
Lay Teachers 29; Students 732.

Oak Lawn, Cook Co.,

1—St. Catherine of Alexandria, Revs. William J. Lion; John R. Dolehide, O.P.; Daniel F. Jarosewic; George P. McKenna, Pastor Emeritus; Deacons James Hughes; James Crane.
Res., 4100 W. 107th St., 60453. Tel: 708-425-2850; Fax: 708-425-2313.
School—10621 S. Kedvale Ave., 60453.
Lay Teachers 19; Students 549.

2—St. Gerald, Revs. Richard J. LoBianco; William J. White, Pastor Emeritus; Rev. Msgr. William J. McNichols, Pastor Emeritus; Rev. John E. Heffernan. In res., Revs. Edward P. O'Brien; William J. Buhrfeind.
Res., 9349 S. Central Ave., 60453. Tel: 708-422-0234.
School—9320 S. 55th Ct., 60453.
Sisters of St. Francis (Clinton, IA) 5; Lay Teachers 24; Students 565.

3—St. Germaine, Revs. William E. Malloy; Edward S. Stockus; William O. Goedert, Pastor Emeritus; Deacons John Flanagan; Donald Daum; John L. Malone. In res., Rev. William O. Goedert, (Retired).
Res., 4240 W. 98th St., 60453. Tel: 708-636-5060; Fax: 708-636-8007.
School—9735 S. Kolin, 60453.
Sisters of the Presentation of the B.V.M. 1; Lay Teachers 18; Students 390.

4—St. Linus, Rev. Joseph E. Auer; Rev. Msgr. John I. Cardiff, Pastor Emeritus; Rev. Charles Balaskus; Deacons Richard Feltes; Edward Gadomski; James Reinhart.
Res., 10300 S. Lawler Ave., 60453. Tel: 708-422-2400; Fax: 708-422-2707.
School—10331 Linus Ln., 60453.
Felician Sisters 5; Lay Teachers 25; Students 550.

5—St. Louis De Montfort, Revs. William J. Quinn; Marion A. Soprych; Deacons Michael Karnoski; Michael Sharwarko; William Sullivan.
Res., 8808 S. Ridgeland, 60453. Tel: 708-599-5300; Fax: 708-599-2678.
School—Lay Teachers 10; Students 283.

Oak Park, Cook Co.,

1—Ascension, Revs. Francis C. Jenks; John Moulder. In res., Rev. Harold B. Stanger.
Res., 815 S. East Ave., 60304. Tel: 708-848-2703.
School—601 Van Buren, 60304.
Lay Teachers 24; Students 461.

2—St. Catherine of Siena-St. Lucy, Revs. John R. Lynch; John J. Carolan; Deacon Bruce Bradford.
Res., 38 N. Austin Blvd., 60302. Tel: 708-386-8077; Fax: 708-386-7755.
School—27 Washington Blvd., 60302. Tel: 708-386-5286; Fax: 708-386-7328.
Sisters of Mercy 2; Lay Teachers 12; Students 400.

3—St. Edmund, Rev. Joseph B. Ruiz; Deacon Edward P. DeLorenzo. In res., Revs. John P. Lucas; Edward C. Dufficy. Pastoral Assocs.: Deacon Edward P. DeLorenzo; Sr. Madeleva Deegan, R.S.M.
Res., 188 S. Oak Park Ave., 60302. Tel: 708-848-4417; Fax: 708-848-0049.
School—200 S. Oak Park Ave., 60302.
Lay Teachers 17; Students 220.

4—St. Giles, Revs. Thomas M. Dore; Thomas J. Campana; Leroy Wickowski; Dan Ostdiek, O.P.; Deacons Loretto J. Madonia; Gerald Zych. In res., Rev. Edward M. Salmon.
Res., 1045 Columbian Ave., 60302. Tel: 708-383-3430; Fax: 708-383-8644.
School—1030 Columbian Ave., 60302.
Lay Teachers 26; Students 450.

Orland Hills, Cook Co., St. Elizabeth Seton, Revs. William T. O'Mara; Ronald A. Hicks; Brian Ardagh.
Res., 9300 W. 167th St., 60477. Tel: 708-403-0101; Fax: 708-403-0105.

Orland Park, Cook Co., St. Francis of Assisi, Revs. Edward F. Upton; Michael J. Weidman.
Res., 15050 S. Wolf Rd., 60462. Tel: 708-460-0042; Fax: 708-460-0136.

St. Michael, Revs. Edward J. McLaughlin; Michael A. Nacius; Louis J. Tylka; Sr. Marietta Umlor, C.S.C., Pastoral Assoc.; Deacons Michael McDonough; Thomas Bartholomew; Tony Cocco. In res., Rev. Reynaldo B. Treyes.
Res., 14327 Highland Ave., 60462. Tel: 708-349-0903; Fax: 708-349-6015. [CEM]
School—14355 Highland Ave., 60462.
Sisters 1; Lay Teachers 29; Students 849.

Our Lady of the Woods, Revs. William J. Finnegan; Thomas Libera; Deacons John Benware; Daniel Welter.
Res., 10731 W. 131st St., 60462. Tel: 708-361-4754; Fax: 708-361-5965.

Palatine, Cook Co., St. Theresa, Revs. John P. McNamara; Charles M. Schlax; Deacons Stephen Norys; John Conick; Frank Gildea; Richard Pizzato; Lou Riccio.
Res., 467 N. Benton, 60067. Tel: 847-358-7760.
Church—465 N. Benton, 60067.
Ministry Center: 455 N. Benton, 60067. Tel: 847-359-2846.
School—445 N. Benton, 60067. Tel: 847-359-1820.
Lay Teachers 40; Students 780.

Santa Teresita Vicariate, Revs. John P. Enright; Raphael Orozco, Pastor Emeritus.
Res., 35 W. Wood St., 60067. Tel: 847-358-6337.

St. Thomas of Villanova, Revs. Raymond A. Yadron; James J. Rowley, Pastor Emeritus; Joseph M. Jackson; Deacons Terry Dineen; Edward Kaczmarek; Kevin Leo; Thomas Maloney; Ray Braski, (Retired); Thomas Dunne; James Zdeb.
Office: 1152 E. Anderson Dr., 60067. Tel: 847-358-6999.
School—1141 E. Anderson Dr., 60067.
Lay Teachers 18; Students 280.

Palos Heights, Cook Co., Incarnation, Revs. Robert E. Dovick; William B. Lynch, Pastor Emeritus; Richard J. Martin; Deacons John Seitz; James Langwell.
Res., 5757 W. 127th St., 60463. Tel: 708-597-3180.
School—Felician Sisters 4; Lay Teachers 13; Students 345.

St. Alexander, Revs. John M. Crosby; Thomas M. McKiernan; Stanley R. Rudcki; Mr. Harry Leddy, Pastoral Assoc.
Res., 7025 W. 126th St., 60463. Tel: 708-448-4861; Fax: 708-448-0039.
School—126th St. at 71st Ave., 60463.
Sisters of Providence of Saint Mary-of-the-Woods, IN 2; Lay Teachers 20; Students 401.

Palos Hills, Cook Co., Sacred Heart, Revs. Robert F. McGinnity; Michael J. Walsh; Deacon William Barker. In res., Rev. Robert G. Herne.
Res., 8245 W. 111th St., 60465. Tel: 708-974-3336; Fax: 708-974-3556.

Park Forest, Cook Co., St. Irenaeus, Revs. Daniel J. O'Sullivan; Francis A. Garrity, Pastor Emeritus.
Res., 78 Cherry St., 60466. Tel: 708-748-6891.

Park Ridge, Cook Co., Mary, Seat of Wisdom, Revs. Ronald N. Kalas; Michael F. Conroy, S.P.S.; Theodore Stone; Deacon Michael Ruffner.
Res., 920 Granville Ave., 60068. Tel: 847-825-3153; Fax: 847-825-3184.
School—1352 S. Cumberland, 60068.
Sisters 1; Lay Teachers 23; Students 594.

St. Paul of the Cross, Revs. Carl Morello; Joseph J. Kinane, Pastor Emeritus; Kenneth A. Budzikowski; Deacon Aloysius J. Memmel. In res., Rev. Daniel A. Smilanic.
Res., 320 S. Washington St., 60068. Tel: 847-825-7605.
School—Sisters 1; Lay Teachers 24; Students 498.

Posen, Cook Co., St. Stanislaus Bishop and Martyr, Rev. David B. Krolczyk; Deacon Joseph Wilczynski.
Res., 14414 McKinley Ave., 60469. Tel: 708-597-4910.
School—14418 McKinley Ave., 60469.
Lay Teachers 10; Students 250.

Prospect Heights, Cook Co., St. Alphonsus Liguori, Revs. Robert P. Heinz; Richard J. Maginot, Pastor Emeritus; Raymond A. Dunne, S.J.; Deacons Norbert Ciesil; James Dahn.
Res., 411 N. Wheeling Rd., 60070. Tel: 847-255-7452; Fax: 847-255-7520.
School—Sisters 1; Lay Teachers 15; Students 300.

Riverdale, Cook Co., Queen of Apostles, Revs. Daniel M. Tomich; John F. Gorman, Pastor Emeritus; Sr. Dorothy Wolsiffer, S.P., Pastoral Assoc.; Deacon Gerald Hahn.
Res., 207 W. 145th St., 60627. Tel: 708-849-4901.
School—14419 S. Atlantic, 60627.
Lay Teachers 10; Students 295.

River Forest, Cook Co., St. Luke, Revs. A. Paul Reicher; Gery W. Stefanski; Deacons Terry Norton; John O'Neill; Robert Zima; Thomas Coffey; Paul Faherty. In res., Rev. Michael M. Boland.
Res., 528 Lathrop Ave., 60305. Tel: 708-771-8250; Fax: 708-771-8809.
School—519 Ashland Ave., 60305.
Lay Teachers 26; Students 330.

St. Vincent Ferrer Priory, Revs. John G. McGreevy, O.P.; Thomas Saucier, O.P.; Robert J. Botthof, O.P. In res., Revs. James B. Kelly, O.P.; Vincent I. Zarlenga, O.P.; John J. O'Malley, O.P.; Martin F. McCormick, O.P.; Steven F. Kuhlmann, O.P.; Giles Klapperich, O.P.; Bro. John Patrick Mulkeen, O.P.
Res., 1530 Jackson Ave., 60305. Tel: 708-366-7090; Fax: 708-366-7092.
Church—Lathrop and North Aves., 60305.
School—1515 Lathrop Ave., 60305.
Dominican Sisters 2; Lay Teachers 21; Students 366.

River Grove, Cook Co., St. Cyprian, Revs. Ronald E. Navoy; Thomas M. Powers, Pastor Emeritus; Waldemar Kilian, O.S.J.; Deacon James Platt.
Res., 2601 Clinton St., 60171. Tel: 708-453-4800; Fax: 708-453-6141.
School—2565 Clinton St., 60171.
Religious 4; Lay Teachers 9; Students 192.

Riverside, Cook Co., St. Mary, Revs. Gerald T. Gunderson; Leon R. Wagner, Pastor Emeritus; Thomas R. Kasputis; Sr. Margaret Sannasardo, B.V.M., Pastoral Assoc.
Res., 126 Herrick Rd., 60546. Tel: 708-447-1020; Fax: 708-447-3309.
School—97 Herrick Rd., 60546.
Sisters 5; Lay Teachers 19; Students 378.

Rolling Meadows, Cook Co., St. Colette, Rev. Michael P. Ahlstrom; Deacons John Connor; John Gallagher. In res., Rev. Joseph F. Ognibene, (Retired).
Res., 3900 S. Meadow Dr., 60008. Tel: 847-394-8100; Fax: 847-394-8102.
School—Lay Teachers 16; Students 288.

Rosemont-Des Plaines, Cook Co., Our Lady of Hope, Rev. Thomas E. Schwab.
Res., 9711 W. Devon Ave., Rosemont, 60018. Tel: 847-825-HOPE (4673).

Round Lake, Lake Co., St. Joseph, Rev. Raymond F. Skriba; Deacons John Brooks; Theodore Kuntz. In res., Rev. Robert J. Fitzpatrick, (Retired).
Res., 114 N. Lincoln Ave., 60073. Tel: 847-546-3449.
School—Lay Teachers 16; Students 403.

Sauk Village, Cook Co., St. James, Rev. Thomas P. Conde; Deacons Thomas McCarthy; Thomas Schroeder.
Res., 22244 S. Torrence Ave., 60411-5144. Tel: 708-757-2170; Fax: 708-757-2176.
School—22410 S. Torrence Ave., 60411-5144. Tel: 708-757-2175.
Dominican Sisters (Springfield, IL) 3; Lay Teachers 8; Students 208.
Convent—22412 S. Torrence Ave., 60411-5144. Tel: 708-757-2179.

Schaumburg, Cook Co., St. Marcelline, Revs. Warren J. McCarthy; Peter M. Yangas; Deacons Edward Boggio; Joe Garcia; Phil Ontiveros; John Zeller.
Res., 822 Springinsguth, 60193. Tel: 847-529-4429; Fax: 847-529-4597.

Church of the Holy Spirit, Revs. William Tkachuk; George J. Kane, Pastor Emeritus; Deacons Raymond Doud; Lowell Taylor; Timothy Kryszak, Sr.; Luis Trevino.
Res., 1451 W. Bode Rd., 60194. Tel: 847-882-7580; Fax: 847-882-1845.

St. Matthew, Revs. Joseph M. Wilk; Edward J. Hughes, Pastor Emeritus; Kenneth R. Bratko, C.R.; Deacons Thomas Halt; William Reisen; Thomas Duszynski; Stanley Kozloski.
Res., 1001 E. Schaumburg Rd., 60194. Tel: 847-893-1220; Fax: 847-893-2575.

Schiller Park, Cook Co., St. Beatrice, Rev. John J. Bresnahan.
Res., 4157 Atlantic Ave., 60176. Tel: 847-678-0138; Fax: 847-678-3974.
School—Religious 2; Lay Teachers 9; Students 241.

St. Maria Goretti, Rev. Thomas C. McNeff. In res., Rev. Anthony K. Chen.
Res., 3929 N. Wehrman Ave., 60176. Tel: 847-678-3988.
School—Lay Teachers 10; Students 203.

Skokie, Cook Co., St. Joan of Arc, Revs. James L. Barrett; James F. Moriarty, Pastor Emeritus; John J. McMahon, Pastor Emeritus. In res., Rev. Matthew D. McDonald.
Res., 9248 N. Lawndale Ave., Evanston, 60203. Tel: 847-673-0409; Fax: 847-673-9626.
School—Lay Teachers 18; Students 220.

St. Lambert, Revs. Andrew E. Luczak; James J. Murtaugh, Pastor Emeritus; William P. Welsh.
Res., 8148 Karlov Ave., 60076. Tel: 847-673-5090; Fax: 847-677-5135.
School—Sisters 1; Lay Teachers 15; Students 180.

St. Peter, Revs. Edward D. Grace; Kenneth P. Klose,

Pastor Emeritus; Leo F. Carton, (Retired); Henry C. Kricek; James D. Beath; Deacons James Wills; William D. Miller. In res., Rev. Thomas A. Baima.
Res., 8116 Niles Center Rd., 60077. Tel: 847-673-1492; Fax: 847-673-6979.
School—8140 Niles Center Rd., 60077. Tel: 847-673-0918.
School Sisters of St. Francis 1; Lay Teachers 19; Students 305.

South Holland, Cook Co., St. Jude the Apostle, Revs. Thomas S. Cabala; John J. Powers, Pastor Emeritus; Deacons Herbert Drazba; Arthur Nylen.
Res., 880 E. 154th St., 60473. Tel: 708-333-3550; Fax: 708-339-3336.
School—900 E. 154th St., 60473.
Sisters 2; Lay Teachers 22; Students 486.
Holy Ghost, Rev. Richard J. Feller.
Res., 700 E. 170th St., 60473. Tel: 708-333-7011; Fax: 708-333-7020.
School—Lay Teachers 12; Students 286.

Stickney, Cook Co., St. Pius X, Revs. Thomas E. Unz; Thomas P. Conley, Pastor Emeritus; Deacon Marvin Kocar. In res., Rev. James F. Moriarty.
Res., 4314 S. Oak Park Ave., 60402. Tel: 708-484-7951; Fax: 708-749-8515.

Streamwood, Cook Co., St. John the Evangelist, Revs. Robert F. Tonelli; Fred C. Pesek; John M. Kyle, Pastor Emeritus; Deacons Michael Braddock; Earl Dahl; Lawrence Kancler; Ronald Lino; Charles Moran; Michael Nugent.
Res., 427 Cedarcrest Dr., 60107. Tel: 603-837-6500; Fax: 603-483-3153.
School—Lay Teachers 9; Students 267.

Summit, Cook Co., St. Joseph, Revs. Thaddeus J. Bojczuk; Henry Pozdol, Pastor Emeritus; Gerald Kroeger, O.P.; Deacons Ben Michalowski; Peter Manning.
Res., 7240 W. 57th St., 60501. Tel: 708-458-0501.
School—5641 S. 73rd Ave., 60501. Tel: 708-458-2927.
Sisters 1; Lay Teachers 9; Students 252.

Tinley Park, Cook Co., St. George, Revs. Donald C. Cahill; Gerald Walsh; Marek Grzela; Deacons Richard Kristinat; Paul Gilbert; Dominick Dattoli; Joseph Stalcup; John Ficker; Joseph Chausse.
Res., 6707 W. 175th St., 60477. Tel: 708-532-2243; Fax: 708-532-2055.
School—6700 W. 176th St., 60477.
Mantellate Sisters 1; Lay Teachers 23; Students 465.
Saint Julie Billiart, Revs. Richard M. Homa; Robert M. Duffy, (Retired); James Curry; Deacons Joseph Callahan; Richard Miska.
Res., 7399 W. 159th St., 60477. Tel: 708-429-6767; Fax: 708-429-6788.

Vernon Hills, Lake Co., St. Mary of Vernon, Revs. John P. Finnegan; Dennis J. Stafford; Deacons Mark R. Zwolski; Dante D. Virgilio; James Wogan.
Res., 236A U.S. Hwy. 45, Indian Creek, 60061. Tel: 847-362-1005; Fax: 847-362-6375.

Volo, Lake Co., St. Peter, Rev. James P. Doyle.
Res., 27551 W. Hwy. 120, 60073. Tel: 815-385-5496.

Wadsworth, Lake Co., St. Patrick, Revs. Patrick G. Cecil; George J. Dyer, Pastor Emeritus; Paul B. McDermott (PEO); Deacons John Richardson; Louis Abboud; Phillip Fragassi; Edward Tomkowiak; David Egan.
Res., 15000 Wadsworth Rd., 60083. Tel: 847-244-4161; Fax: 847-336-0630.
School—Marcella Bosnak, Prin. Lay Teachers 18; Students 528.

Wauconda, Lake Co., Transfiguration, Revs. Thomas M. Enright; Robert G. Aguirre; Byron G. Maher, Pastor Emeritus; Thomas J. Curley, Pastor Emeritus; Deacons Stephen Cenek; Marion Omiatek; John Zimmerman. Pastoral Assocs.: Marilyn Omiatek; Dee Zimmerman.
Res., 318 Bangs St., 60084. Tel: 847-526-2400; Fax: 847-526-2961.
School—Lay Teachers 16; Students 323.

Waukegan, Lake Co.,

1—St. Anastasia, Revs. Terrence A. McCarthy; Edward S. Maraczewski, Pastor Emeritus.
Res., 624 Douglas Ave., 60085. Tel: 847-623-2875; Fax: 847-623-4882.
School—Lay Teachers 18; Students 439.

2—St. Bartholomew. Merged with St. Joseph. See Holy Family for details.

3—St. Dismas, Revs. John M. Ryan; Paul J. Cull, Pastor Emeritus; Deacons Anthony Sacramento; Paul Telle. In res., Revs. Regis Kleene, S.D.S.; Edward E. Lisowski.
Res., 2600 Sunset Ave., 60087. Tel: 847-623-5050.

4—Holy Family, Revs. Gary M. Graf; William O'Connell, Pastor Emeritus; Gerardo Garcia, O.S.A.; Michael J. Boehm. Pastoral Assocs.: Sr. Loretta Tiernan, S.H.C.J.; Julie O'Reilly; Deacons Edward Scarbalis; Ralph Bufano. In res., Rev. Thomas W. McQuaid.
Res., 501 S. Utica St., P.O. Box 440, 60085. Tel: 847-623-2655.
School—Participant in Lake Shore Catholic Academy. 515 S. Utica St., 60085.

5—St. Joseph. Merged with St. Bartholomew. See Holy Family listing for details.

6—Immaculate Conception B.V.M., Rev. Frank W. Plotka.
Res., 508 Grand Ave., 60085. Tel: 847-336-3684; Fax: 847-336-9040.
School—Lay Teachers 12; Students 256.

Westchester, Cook Co., Divine Infant, Revs. Gerald P. Joyce; William M. Henkel, Pastor Emeritus; Dean F. Semner; Deacon John Harrington.
Res., 1601 Newcastle Ave., 60154. Tel: 708-865-8071.
School—Lay Teachers 18; Students 356.
Convent—Institute of the Blessed Virgin Mary (I.B.V.M.)
Divine Providence, Revs. John C. Rosemeyer; Joseph J. Wojcik; Deacons Frank DeVita; William Casey.
Res., 2550 S. Mayfair Ave., 60154. Tel: 708-562-3364; Fax: 708-562-3134.
School—2500 S. Mayfair Ave., 60154. Tel: 708-562-2258.
Sisters of Divine Providence (Normandy, MO) 2; Lay Teachers 14; Students 232.

Western Springs, Cook Co., St. John of the Cross, Revs. Richard P. Hynes; Joseph F. McDonnell, Pastor Emeritus; William J. Martin; Edward J. Fealey; Sr. Jeanne Bonneau, C.N.D., Pastoral Assoc.; Deacons William Engler; Thomas McGorey; Joseph Pepitone.
Res., 4920 Caroline Ave., 60558. Tel: 708-246-4404; Fax: 708-246-4566.
School—705 51st St., 60558. Tel: 708-246-4454; Fax: 708-246-9010.
Sisters 1; Lay Teachers 38; Students 800.
Convent—5103 Caroline Ave., 60558. Tel: 708-246-0014.

Wheeling, Cook Co., St. Joseph the Worker, Rev. Frederick L. Brandstrader; Deacon Perry Duderstadt. In res., Rev. John C. Massion.
Res., 181 W. Dundee Rd., 60090. Tel: 847-537-2740; Fax: 847-537-7914.

Wilmette, Cook Co., St. Francis Xavier, Revs. Edward F. Harnett; George W. Klein. Pastoral Assocs.: Patty Jane Pelton; Sr. Joyce Shanabarger, O.S.F.; Deacon Michael Cavanaugh. In res., Rev. Michael D. Place.
Office: 524 Ninth St., 60091. Tel: 847-256-4250; Fax: 847-256-4254.
Res., 912 Linden Ave., 60091.
School—808 Linden Ave., 60091. Tel: 847-256-0644. Sr. Mary K. O'Brien, B.V.M., Prin.
Sisters 1; Lay Teachers 23; Students 374.
St. Joseph, Rev. Francis J. Kane; Rev. Msgr. Charles N. Meter, Pastor Emeritus; Rev. John Szmyd; Ms. Dana McKenna, Pastoral Assoc.
Res., 1747 Lake Ave., 60091. Tel: 847-251-0771; Fax: 847-251-5715.

Winnetka, Cook Co., SS. Faith, Hope and Charity, Rev. Thomas F. Ventura; Rev. Msgr. Eugene F. Lyons, Pastor Emeritus; Rev. Jeffrey Grob; Deacons Terrence Levins; Roger Mullaney. In res., Rev. William Flaherty.
Res., 191 Linden St., 60093. Tel: 847-446-7646; Fax: 847-446-7630.
School—180 Ridge Ave., 60093. Tel: 847-446-0031.
Sisters 1; Lay Teachers 24; Students 359.
Sacred Heart, Revs. Robert E. Ferrigan; Thomas J. Raftery, Pastor Emeritus; Mark Simpson; Deacons D. J. Shinkle; Michael McNulty; John Fay.
Res., 905 Burr Ave., 60093. Tel: 847-446-0856; Fax: 847-501-5311.
School—1095 Gage St., 60093.
Lay Teachers 17; Students 189.
Parish Center—1077 Tower Rd., 60093. Tel: 847-446-0856.

Zion-Beach Park, Lake Co., Our Lady of Humility, Revs. Joseph C. Curtis; John E. Hayes, Pastor Emeritus; Sr. Mary O'Connell, S.H.C.J., Pastoral Assoc.; Deacons Philip Horne; Max Jinkens; Michael Mercure.
Res., 10655 Wadsworth Rd., 60099. Tel: 847-872-8778; Fax: 847-872-8780.
School—10601 Wadsworth Rd., 60099. Sr. Jane Roach, S.H.C.J., Prin.
Lay Teachers 12; Students 275.

Syro-Malabar Rite

Chicago, Cook Co., Knanite Syro-Malabar Catholic Mission of the Archdiocese of Chicago, Rev. Simon Edathiparampil, Dir.
Res., Immaculate Heart of Mary, 3834 N. Spaulding, 60618. Tel: 312-478-1157.

Northlake, Cook Co., Syro-Malabar Catholic Mission of the Archdiocese of Chicago, Rev. Joseph Kandathiduky, Dir.
Center Mar Thoma Shleeha Church: 5000 St. Charles Rd., Bellwood, 60104. Tel: 708-544-7250; Fax: 708-544-5890.

Malankara Rite

Chicago, Cook Co., Syro-Malankara Catholic Mission of the Archdiocese of Chicago,
Divine Liturgy at: 1208 Ashland St., Evanston, 60202. Tel: 708-475-4093. Rev. Zacharias Nanthiyattu, O.I.C., Dir.

Chaplains of Public Institutions

Chicago. *Chicago O'Hare International Airport,* P.O. Box 66353, 60666. Rev. John A. Jamnicky.
Cook County Hospital. Revs. George Wallenhorst, S.J.; William O. Madden, S.J.; Deacon James Davis; Sr. Marie Louise Julk, S.Sp.S.
Hines V.A. Hospital. Revs. John G. Birk (SPK); Bruno H. Kowalkowski, O.P.
V.A. Lakeside Medical Center. Rev. Robert J. Borre (MAD).
West Side V.A. Hospital. Rev. John D. Carroll.
Oak Forest. *Oak Forest Hospital.* Revs. Melchior Toczek, O.F.M.; Victorian Haladus, O.F.M.; Michael Windolf, O.F.M.; Bro. Innocent Gill, O.F.M.

On Duty Outside the Archdiocese:
Reverend Monsignors—
Sarauskas, R. George, Office to Aid Central/Eastern Europe Catholic Church, 3211 4th St. N.E., Washington, DC 20017-1194
Trisco, Robert F., Curley Hall, Catholic University of America, Washington, DC 20064
Reverend Fathers—
Barnum, Martin, Sacred Heart School of Theology, 7335 S. Hwy. 100, P.O. Box 429, Hales Corners, WI 53130-0429
Brankin, Patrick M., St. Theresa Church, P.O. Box 297, Collinsville, OK 74021-0297
Broccolo, Gerard T., 256 Jacaranda Dr., Battle Creek, MI 49015-8662
Clements, George H., 1146 29th St., N.W., Suite 250, Washington, DC 20036
Dempsey, Robert J., Editor, L'Osservatore Romano, Villa Stritch, Via della Nocetta, 63, 00164 Rome, Italy
Filipetto, Silvano, Via Roma #224, 0038 Spina (VE), Italy
Garza, Jesus, Campus Ministry, Edgewood High School, 2219 Monroe St., Madison, WI 53711
Hotchkin, John F., Bishops' Commission for Ecumenical Affairs, 3211 Fourth St. N.E., Washington, DC 20017-1194
Lorenz, Matthais E., 5531 E. Lake Dr., Lisle, IL 60532
Martinek, John B., Our Lady of the Snows Parish, P.O. Box 89, Nulato, AK 99765
Pollard, John E., Office of the Catechism, National Conference for Catholic Bishops, 3211 4th St. N.E., Washington, DC 20017
Rugen, Patrick J., St. Mary University, Campus Box 1431, 700 Terrace Heights, Winona, MI 55987-1399

Military Chaplains:
Reverend Monsignors—
Dobes, George E., 3370 S. Second St., Arlington, VA 22204-1709
Reverend Fathers—
Baldwin, John F., CAPT, CHC, USN, Office of the Chap., Naval Postgraduate School, University Cir., Rm. 126, Monterey, CA 93943-5009
Ball, David, USN, 109 Northport Pl., Northport, MI 46970
Bykowski, Norbert H., Office of the Chap., Bldg. 3714, Redstone Arsenal, AL 35898
Falkenthal, Thomas W., Group Chaplain's Office, 2nd FSSG, PSC Box 20002, Camp Lejeune, NC 28542-0002
Grace, James N., CMR 438, Box 1095, APO, AE 09111
Joslyn, James W., 72 White Oak, Fox Lake, IL 60020
Kastigar, John J., Military Chap., U.S.A.F., 1774 Lexington Dr., Sierra Vista, AZ 85635
Kloak, David G., Office of the Chap., Naval Air Station, Alameda, CA 94501
Murray, John W., Chaplain, V.A. Medical Center (125), 1201 N.W. 16th St., Miami, FL 33125
Simpson, Brian C., 6B Kamakami Pl., Honolulu, HI 96818
Stake, Ronald P., CHC USNR, 1st Tank Battalion, MCAGCC, Twentynine Palms, CA 92289

Graduate Studies:
Reverend Fathers—
Ford, David R., 1709 Shattuck Ave., 118, Berkeley, CA 94709
Griffiths, John M., Casa Santa Maria, Via dell' Umilta 30, 00187 Rome, Italy

O'Connell, Michael W., Casa Santa Maria, Via dell' Umilta 30, 00187 Rome, Italy

Missionary Work:
Reverend Fathers—
Cleary, Philip C., Nuestros Pequenos Hermanos, Apartado Postal, 333, 62000 Cuernavaca, Morelos, Mexico
Colleran, James A., Archdiocesan Mission Team, St. James the Apostle, Diocese of Chilpancingo-Chilapa, Santiago Apostol, Quachultanango, 39250
Cowell, Raymond, Parroquia Nuestra Senoria de Fatima, El Pari Casilla 919, Santa Cruz, Bolivia
Foley, Matthew, Mission of St. James the Apostle, Santiago Apostal, Quechultenango Guerrero, Mexico
Rochford, E. Michael, Society of St. James, 2455 N. Hamlin Ave., Chicago, IL 60647

Other Assignments:
Reverend Fathers—
Becker, Charles P., 24955 N. Hwy. 12, Lake Zurich, IL 60047
Carroll, Clement D., 960 Wexford Leas Blvd., Palm Harbor, FL 34683
Durkin, Charles T., 163 Vandera, Robertsville, MO 63072
Egan, Gerard P., Loyola University, 820 N. Michigan, Chicago, IL 60611
Fleck, Kenneth J., 7851 S. Jeffrey, Chicago, IL 60649
Gilligan, Michael J., American Catholic Press, 16160 S. Seton Dr., South Holland, IL 60473
Gleeson, Edward D., P.O. Box 653, Oak Lawn, IL 60454
Greeley, Andrew M., N.O.R.C., 1155 E. 60th St., Chicago, IL 60637
Hannigan, John T., 611 E. Clark, Litchfield, IL 62056
Hoder, James A., P.O. Box 455, Mundelein, Il 60060
Hurley, John W., 1315 S. 50th Ct., 1st Rear, Cicero, IL 60650
Keeley, Thomas R., 645 N. Michigan Ave., Suite #543, Chicago, IL 60622
LaChance, Charles P., 810 W. Montrose Ave., Chicago, IL 60613
Leja, Casimir, 646 N. Michigan Ave., Ste. 543, Chicago, IL 60611
Maday, Norbert J., P.O. Box 455, Mundelein, IL 60060
McCarthy, James H., Special Religious Ed. Div., 2953 S. Lowe, Chicago, IL 60616
McGlinn, Robert J., Cristo Rey Parish, 800 Wisconsin Ave., Racine, WI 53403
Motycka, Robert R., 14327 Highland Ave., Orland Park, IL 60462
Mysliwiec, Haldane R., 116 N. Lake St., Mundelein, IL 60060
Nangle, Thomas R., Police Chaplaincy, 1140 W. Jackson, Chicago, IL 60607
Nicola, John J., P.O. Box 1505, Pinehurst, NC 28374
O'Brien, Joseph J., 605 Burr Ave., Winnetka, IL 60093
O'Keefe, Millard, 2525 59th St., Wood Ridge, IL 60517-1114
Perkins, Robert S., 13428 Maxella Ave., #104, Marina del Ray, CA 90292
Pokladowski, Gregory S., 1430 Hale St., Vallejo, CA 94591-4134
Ray, James M., P.O. Box 455, Mundelein, IL 60060
Ruge, Kenneth C., P.O. Box 455, Mundelein, IL 60060
Shea, John J., 718 W. Adams St., Chicago, IL 60661
Shields, James P., 116 N. Lake St., Mundelein, IL 60060
Solazzo, Michael J., Misericordia-North, 6300 N. Ridge Ave., Chicago, IL 60660
Strand, Ralph S., P.O. Box 455, Mundelein, IL 60060
Swade, Thomas J., P.O. Box 455, Mundelein, IL 60060
Vitro, Thomas J., P.O. Box 932, Lake Geneva, WI 53147
Wurst, Wayne H., 1000 E. Maple Rd., P.O. Box 455, Mundelein, IL 60060

Retired:
Reverend Monsignors—
Bergin, Clifford E., 1245 W. Norwood, Chicago, IL 60660
Brackin, Francis A., 30571 Magician Terr., Dowagiac, MI 49047
Cardiff, John I., St. Linus, 10300 S. Lawler Ave., Oak Lawn, IL 60453
Carroll, Donald M., 7260 W. Peterson, Chicago, IL 60631
Chess, Edwin R., 11812 Song Dr., San Antonio, TX 78216
Cooke, Vincent W., c/o Catholic Charities, 126 N. DesPlaines St., Chicago, IL 60661
Egan, John J., 730 N. Wabash, Chicago, IL 60611
Farrell, John J., St. Andrew Home, 7000 N. Newark, Niles, IL 60714
Hardiman, James C., 4126 W. 99th St., Oak Lawn, IL 60453
Hayes, John M., 2524 S. Keeler, Chicago, IL 60623
Higgins, George C., Curley Hall 220, Catholic University of America, Washington, DC 20064
Koenig, Harry C., Addolorata Villa, 555 McHenry Rd., Wheeling, IL 60090
Lyons, Eugene F., Addolorata Villa, 555 McHenry Rd., Wheeling, IL 60090
McDermott, Ignatius D., The McDermott Foundation, 932 W. Washington St., Chicago, IL 60607
McElligott, Francis J., St. John Fisher, 10234 S. Washtenaw, Chicago, IL 60642
McNichols, William J., Holy Family Villa, 123rd & Will Cook Rd., Lemont, IL 60439
Meter, Charles N., 1747 Lake Ave., Wilmette, IL 60091
Mohan, Thomas J., Addolorata Villa, 559 McHenry Rd., Wheeling, IL 60090
Mozeris, Damasus A., Immaculate Conception, 2745 W. 44th St., Chicago, IL 60632
Mroczkowski, Joseph J., 1501 Hoffman St., Hammond, IN 46327
O'Day, Martin J., 13240 W. Circle Dr., No. 305, Crestwood, IL 60445
Pellicore, Edward M., 1801 35th St., Apt. 1421, Oak Brook, IL 60521
Quinn, John S., St. Andrew, 3546 N. Paulina St., Chicago, IL 60657
Quinn, William J., St. Eulalia, 1851 S. 9th Ave., Maywood, IL 60153
Roche, M. Edward, 10811 S. Ridgeland, Chicago Ridge, IL 60415
Stanek, Wenceslaus, St. Benedict's Home, 6930 W. Touhy Ave., Niles, IL 60714
Reverend Fathers—
Ackerman, Raymond J., Little Sisters of the Poor, 2325 N. Lakewood Ave., #1412, Chicago, IL 60614
Adamich, Albert R., Most Holy Redeemer, 9525 S. Lawndale Ave., Evergreen Park, IL 60042
Ahearn, Donald J., St. Juliana, 7142 N. Osceola, Chicago, IL 60631
Ahern, John J., 765 Busse Hwy., Apt. #1C, Park Ridge, IL 60068-2455
Ahern, John J., 6804 Joliet Rd., Indian Head Park, IL 60525
Aschenbrenner, George F., 1598 Main St., Lemont, IL 60439
Ballweber, Eugene L., 2302 Julie S.W., Albuquerque, NM 87105
Barr, Pierre J., 3825 S. California Ave., Chicago, IL 60633
Barron, Edward M., 1515 E. 154th St., #130, Dolton, IL 60419
Baseheart, Edward H., 1598 Main St., Lemont, IL 60439
Bednarz, Matt A., 5600 N. Fairfield, Chicago, IL 60659-4817
Beyenka, John T., Addolorata Villa, 555 McHenry Rd., Wheeling, IL 60090
Boreczky, John V., 35 Rosada Dr., Bravard, NC 28712
Borowczyk, Martin R., St. Francis Borgia, 8033 W. Addison, Chicago, IL 60634
Boyle, Thomas S., One Cambridge Ct., Michigan City, IN 46360
Braun, David F., P.O. Box 745, Sublette, IL 61637
Brett, James D., P.O. Box 268, Delevan, WI 53115
Brodfuehrer, Robert S., 5205 N. Lieb, Chicago, IL 60630-1433
Brzozowski, Edward J., 13356 Buffalo Ave., Chicago, IL 60633
Buhrfeind, William J., St. Gerald, 9349 S. Central, Oak Lawn, IL 60453
Bull, Albert D., 13047 W. Ballad Dr., Sun City West, AZ 85375-1812
Burns, Eugene P., 797 Waverly Rd., LaPorte, IN 46350
Burns, Robert E., St. Bride, 7811 S. Coles, Chicago, IL 60649
Carolan, John J., St. Juliana, 7142 N. Osceola Ave., Chicago, IL 60631
Carroll, Gilbert A., St. Timothy, 6326 N. Washtenaw, Chicago, IL 60659
Carton, Leo F., 8116 Niles Center Rd., Skokie, IL 60077
Cerniglia, Francis J., Queen of the Rosary, 750 Elk Grove Blvd., Elk Grove, IL 60007-4298
Chapell, Norbert A., 7737 Golf View Dr., Palos Heights, IL 60463
Chen, Anthony K., 3929 Wehrman, Schiller Park, IL 60176
Chisek, Anthony S., 1 Thornwood Mall, Apt. 1002, University Park, IL 60466
Clark, H. Robert, Queen of All Saints Basilica, 6280 N. Sauganash Ave., Chicago, IL 60646
Coffey, Edward N., 5300 W. 24th St., Cicero, IL 60650
Coneglio, Andrew, P.O. Box 34956, Las Vegas, NV 89133-4956
Conley, Thomas P., St. Zachary, 567 N. Algonquin Rd., Des Plaines, IL 60016
Connors, Edward P., 2339 York St., Blue Island, IL 60406
Coughlin, Roger J., 721 N. LaSalle St., Chicago, IL 60610
Cross, Robert A., c/o James and Mary Catherine Meeks, 700 Ashland, River Forest, IL 60305
Cull, Paul J., 920 Vost Dr., Apt. #212, Gurnee, IL 60031
Cullen, George H., St. Benedict Home for the Aged, 6930 W. Touhy, Niles, IL 60714
Curley, Thomas J., 2825 W. 81st St., Chicago, IL 60652
Davitt, James P., St. James, 106 Archer Rd., Lemont, IL 60439
Devine, William J., P.O. Box 53, Worth, IL 60482
Diemer, Charles J., 35801 W. Cook Ave., Antioch, IL 60002
Dilla, Francis E., P.O. Box 88, New Carlisle, IN 46552
Dillon, Arthur J., P.O. Box 125, Powers Lake, WI 53159
Dolciamore, John V., Mundelein Seminary of the University of St. Mary of the Lake, Mundelein, IL 60060
Donohue, John J., 2400 Archbury Ln., Park Ridge, IL 60068
Downes, Thomas J., 2630 Sierra Dr., Colorado Springs, CO 80917
Dudzinski, Sylvester W., Mother Theresa Home, 1270 Franciscan Dr., #114, Lemont, IL 60437
Dufficy, Edward C., St. Edmund, 188 S. Oak Park Ave., Oak Park, IL 60302
Duffy, Donald J., 75 N. Buffalo Grove Rd., Buffalo Grove, IL 60089
Duffy, Robert M., 7399 W. 159th St., Tinley Park, IL 60477
Duggan, J. Edward, St. Bartholomew, 4949 W. Patterson Ave., Chicago, IL 60641
Durkin, Eugene F., Holy Name Cathedral, 730 N. Wabash Ave., Chicago, IL 60611
Dyer, George J., St. Patrick, 15000 Wadsworth Rd., Wadsworth, IL 60083
Faucher, Eugene J., St. Edna, 2525 N. Arlington Hts. Rd., Arlington Heights, IL 60004
Fearon, John F., St. Bernardine, 7246 W. Harrison, Forest Park, IL 60130
Felczak, Leonard J., 4325 S. Spaulding, Chicago, IL 60632
Festle, Robert H., 5046 N. Ashland Ave., Chicago, IL 60640
Fisher, Frederick J., Little Company of Mary, Health Facility, 7520 S. 421, San Pierre, IN 46374
Fitzgerald, Edward P., Mercy Hospital and Medical Center, Stevenson Expwy. at King Dr., Chicago, IL 60616
Fitzgerald, Thomas J., 5472 S. Kimbark, Chicago, IL 60615
Fitzpatrick, Edmund J., St. Pascal, 3935 N. Melvina Ave., Chicago, IL 60634
Fitzpatrick, Robert J., St. Joseph, 114 N. Lincoln Ave., Round Lake, IL 60073
Flaherty, William J., 191 Linden St., Winnetka, IL 60093-3832
Flannery, Edward M., 21 Spinning Wheel Dr., Hinsdale, IL 60521
Fraser, Gerald D., 900 Center St., #2F, Des Plaines, IL 60016-6562
Frawley, John P., 2825 W. 81st St., Chicago, IL 60652-2722
Gallagher, Charles G., St. Cletus, 600 W. 55th St., La Grange, IL 60525
Garrity, Francis A., 78 Cherry St., Park Forest, IL 60466
Gerrity, Raymond J., 917 S. 8th Ave., #2, LaGrange, IL 60525
Giese, Vincent J., P.O. Box 772, Rensselaer, IN 47978
Goedert, William O., St. Germaine, 2330 W. 118th St., Chicago, IL 60643-4710
Gorman, John F., Resurrection Nursing Pavilion, 1001 N. Greenwood, Park Ridge, IL 60068
Gorman, Lawrence J., c/o Mr. & Mrs. Henry Lenz, 7706 Sequoia Dr., Palos Heights, IL 60463
Graff, J. Austin, 1141 Iroquois, Apt. 215, Naperville, IL 60540
Grinis, Bruno B., 12433 S. Halsted St., Chicago, IL 60628
Grinis, Julian G., Box 108, Oak Lawn, IL 60453
Gruchot, Stanley J., 7000 Newark, Chicago, IL 60643
Guerin, Philip X., 3546 N. Paulina St., Chicago, IL 60657
Guirsch, Bernard G., 206 E. 25th St., Chicago Heights, IL 60411
Gunia, Edward S., 850 Front St., Lisle, IL 60532

Hanlon, Thomas C., 8536 W. Berwyn, Chicago, IL 60656
Hayes, John E., Rte. 1, Box 4E, Dakota, MN 55925
Hayes, Peter F., 4623 N. Chester, No. 207-W, Chicago, IL 60656
Heffernan, John J., 9724 S. Karlov, Oak Lawn, IL 60453
Helfrich, George J., 7958 W. Foster Ave., Chicago, IL 60656
Henkel, William M., 1601 Newcastle Ave., Westchester, IL 60154
Herne, Robert G., Sacred Heart Parish, 8245 W. 111th St., Palos Hills, IL 60465
Hills, Richard L., St. Benedict Home, 6930 W. Touhy Ave., Niles, IL 60714
Hock, William T., St. Tarcissus Parish, 6020 W. Ardmore, Chicago, IL 60646
Hoffman, Matthias H., 1131 Douglas Ave., Flossmoor, IL 60422
Hosty, Edward, Little Company of Mary Health Facility, San Pierre, IN 46374
Hosty, Thomas J., 8419 Bailey Rd., Darien, IL 60561
Huske, Leonard G., 14619 S. Keystone, Midlothian, IL 60445
Ivers, Victor J., St. Joseph, 121 E. Maple Ave., Libertyville, IL 60048-2283
Janiak, Anthony J., St. Benedict Home, 6930 W. Touhy Ave., Niles, IL 60714
Jarzynski, Edward A., 1009 S. Cook St., Barrington, IL 60010
Jasinski, Raymond J., 1813 6th Ave, Kearney, NE 68847
Joyce, Pierce J., 124 N. Spring Ave., La Grange, IL 60525
Jozwiak, Richard M., 385 N. Edinburgh, Frankfort, IL 60423
Juchcinski, Clarence J., 16001 Lowe Ave., Harvey, IL 60426
Kane, George J., 1700 Cambourne, Schaumburg, IL 60194
Kash, Robert J., 21 S. Spring Ave., Unit A, LeGrange, IL 50525-2272
Kaveney, Thomas J., St. Odilo, 2244 S. East Ave., Berwyn, IL 60402
Keating, James W., 7939 W. 43rd St., Lyons, IL 60534
Kelly, Charles F., St. Daniel the Prophet, 5330 S. Nashville Ave., Chicago, IL 60638
Kelly, Joseph A., St. Edward, 4350 W. Sunnyside, Chicago, IL 60630
Kelly, William J., c/o Jones, 3332 S. 59th Ave., Cicero, IL 60650
Kelpsas, Francis J., Nativity B.V.M., 6812 S. Washtenaw St., Chicago, IL 60629
Kinane, Joseph J., St. Paul of the Cross, 320 S. Washington St., Park Ridge, IL 60068
Kireilis, Fabian P., Immaculate Conception, 2745 W. 44th St., Chicago, IL 60632
Kirkilas, Michael, 6666 20th Ave., N.E., St. Petersburg, FL 33710
Kleiber, Kenneth R., 15202 N. 40th St., #223-2, Phoenix, AZ 85032-4652
Klose, Kenneth P., 8116 Niles Center Rd., Skokie, IL 60077
Klug, Jerome G., 26166 W. Mattalina Ct., Ingleside, IL 60041
Kniewel, Edward J., 2600 N. Nordica, Chicago, IL 60635
Kouba, Charles J., 5157 S. California, Chicago, IL 60632
Kozien, Casimir J., 4949 W. Patterson Ave., Chicago, IL 60641
Kupinski, Raymond P., P.O. Box 357, Williams Bay, WI 53191
Kyle, John M., 7000 N. Newark, No. 516, Niles, IL 60648
Lambert, Rollins E., 10112 Menaul N.E. #L-23, Albuquerque, NM 87112
Limanowski, Stanley C., 100 Mutiny Ln., Apt. #104, Merritt Island, FL 32952-2521
Lisowski, William J., 15714 Old Orchard Ct., Orland Park, IL 60462
Lutz, Robert J., St. Norbert, 1809 Walters Ave., Northbrook, IL 60062
Lynch, Cletus J., 1010 American Eagle Blvd., #609, Sun City Center, FL 33573
Lynch, Joseph P., 14130 Green Valley Dr., Orland Park, IL 60462
Lynch, William B., 5727 W. 127th St., Palos Heights, IL 60463
Lyons, James W., 520 Donovan St., Woodstock, IL 60098
Lyons, Leo J., 14226 - 84th Ave., Orland Park, IL 60462
Mackin, John J., 8925 S. Kostner, Hometown, IL 60456
Maginot, Richard J., St. Alphonsus Liguori, 411 N. Wheeling Rd., Prospect Heights, IL 60070
Maher, Byron G., 416 E. Jefferson, Burlington, WI 53105
Maher, Thomas F., St. Mary-of-the-Woods, 7033 N. Moselle Ave., Chicago, IL 60646
Makaras, Joseph V., c/o Ms. Irene Tumas, 817 S. Theodore St., Appleton, WI 54915
Maniola, Francis N., 6135 S. Austin, Chicago, IL 60638
Maraczewski, Edward S., 1516 E. Lowden, Mt. Prospect, IL 60056
Matlak, Marion A., 7264 W. Peterson Ave., C-218, Chicago, IL 60631-3624
McCaig, John J., St. Patrick, 200 Illinois St., Lemont, IL 60439
McDonagh, Andrew J., 6939 N. Hiawatha, Chicago, IL 60646
McDonald, Matthew D., 9248 N. Lawndale, P.O., Evanston, IL 60203
McDonnell, Joseph F., 17 W. 706 Butterfield Rd., Oakbrook Terrace, IL 60181
McGrath, John F., 10726 S. Sacramento, Chicago, IL 60655
McHugh, Thomas J., St. Matthias Parish, 2310 W. Ainslie, Chicago, IL 60625
McKenna, George P., Bayport Apartments, 9820 S. Pulaski Rd., Oak Lawn, IL 60453
McLaughlin, Charles J., Box 2308 R.F.D., Long Grove, IL 60047
McLoraine, John A., 790 McCormick Dr., Lake Forest, IL 60045
McMahon, John J., 2535 Lake Ave., Wilmette, IL 60092
Meyer, Charles R., Mundelein Seminary, University of St. Mary-of-the-Lake, Mundelein, IL 60060
Mezydlo, Leonard T., St. Stephen Protomartyr Parish, 1267 Everett St., Des Plaines, IL 60018
Michalek, Henry J., 7264 W. Peterson Ave., C-605, Chicago, IL 60631
Mikolaitis, Vito E., 6812 S. Washtenaw, Chicago, IL 60629
Millea, Thomas V., 4342 N Lieb, Chicago, IL 60630
Mollan, Ralph R., 1321 Burning Bush Ln., Mt. Prospect, IL 60056
Mollohan, James L., 1451 W. Bode Rd., Schaumburg, IL 60194
Morgan, Edward J., 119 Evergreen Dr., Frankfort, IL 60423
Moriarty, James F., St. Pius X, 4314 S. Oak Park, Stickney, IL 60402
Morris, John J., 2214 S.W. 29th Ter. No. 33, Topeka, KS 66611-1956
Morrison, Raymond J., St. Andrew Home for the Aged, 7000 N. Newark, Niles, IL 60714
Morrissey, James E., Maryhaven West, 1700 E. Lake St., Glenview, IL 60025
Murphy, William P., Queen of Martyrs, 10233 S. Central Pk., Evergreen Park, IL 60642
Murtaugh, Daniel J., St. Kilian, 8725 S. May St., Chicago, IL 60620
Murtaugh, James J., 400 E. Randolph, #3107, Chicago, IL 60602
Myers, Edward F., 9343 S. Francisco, Evergreen Park, IL 60642
Mytych, Joseph F., 6101 S. 75th Ave., Argo, IL 60501
Nikliborc, Francis U., Box 162, Cary, IL 60013
Norkett, Edward J., 26 S. Central, Highwood, IL 60040
Novak, Robert J., 2960 N. Lake Shore Dr., Apt. 1209, Chicago, IL 60657
Nowak, Joseph G., 8237 S. Shore Dr., Chicago, IL 60617
O'Brien, Edward P., Bethlehem Woods #1147, 1571 W. Ogden Ave., LaGrange Park, IL 60525
O'Brien, Hugh V., 841 N. Arlington Heights Rd., Arlington Heights, IL 60004
O'Brien, John E., 12329 First Ct., Kenosha, WI 53140
O'Connell, William M., 2310 Greentree Ct., Lindenhurst, IL 60046
O'Connor, James T., Our Lady of the Mount, 2414 S. 61st Ave., Cicero, IL 60804-2698
O'Donnell, Richard J., 3528 S. Hermitage, Chicago, IL 60609
O'Hara, Harold T., 170 N.W. 27th St., Pompano Beach, FL 33064
O'Shea, John J., 2324 W. Chase Ave., Chicago, IL 60645
Ognibene, Joseph F., St. Colette, 3900 S. Meadow Dr., Rolling Meadows, IL 60008
Ognibene, Salvatore J., St. Mary of Providence Home, 4200 N. Austin, Chicago, IL 60634
Olejniczak, Henry A., 15704 Lake Hills Ct., Orland Park, IL 60462
Orozco, Raphael R., P.O. Box 1006, Palatine, IL 60068
Pachorek, Joseph J., Albertine Home, 1505 Hoffman St., Hammond, IN 46327
Pastick, Joseph A., 4939 Floramar Terr., #608, New Port Richey, FL 34652-3310
Pavis, Raymond A., P.O. Box 12, Powers Lake, WI 53159
Peng, John B., 3420 N. Kolmar, Chicago, IL 60641
Powers, John J., St. Jude the Apostle, 880 E. 154th St., South Holland, IL 60473
Powers, Thomas M., St. Cyprian Parish, 2601 Clinton St., River Grove, 60171
Pozdol, Henry, 7240 W. 57th St., Summit, IL 60501
Pribyl, Francis T., 2651 S. Central Park, Chicago, IL 60623
Quinlan, William J., June- November, Our Lady of the Wayside, 432 W. Park St., Arlington Heights, IL 60005
Raftery, Thomas J., Christ the King, 9235 S. Hamilton, Chicago, IL 60620
Riordan, Jerome F., 7114 Hawthorne Ln., Hanover Park, IL 60102
Rochford, John J., 18102 S. 66th Ct., #401, Tinley Park, IL 60477
Rodell, Jeremiah J., 6015 Lakeside Pl., #201, Tinley Park, IL 60477
Rokicinski, Stanley J., 5646 S. Karlov, Chicago, IL 60629
Rooney, William J., Curley Hall, Catholic University of America, Washington, DC 20064
Rosemeyer, Paul F., St. Theresa, 467 Benton, Palatine, IL 60067
Rowley, James J., 1138 E. Anderson Dr., Palatine, IL 60067
Ryan, Joseph D., 11722 S. Oakley, Chicago, IL 60643
Schackmuth, William A., 4041 W. 97th St., Oak Lawn, IL 60453
Scheid, W. Bernard, 5659 N. Rockwell, Chicago, IL 60659
Schreiber, Edmund J., 9613 Schiller Blvd., Franklin Park, IL 60131
Schroeder, Richard F., 7216 Oxford Cir., Fox Lake, IL 60020
Seitz, Thomas R., St. Thomas the Apostle, 5472 S. Kimbark, Chicago, IL 60615
Shannon, Robert J., Mercy Hospital, Stevenson Expy. at King Dr., Chicago, IL 60616
Shaunessy, Francis W., P.O. Box 528, Powers Lake, WI 53159
Sheridan, Robert A., St. Margaret of Scotland, 9837 S. Throop St., Chicago, IL 60643
Shirey, John W., 8725 S. May, Chicago, IL 60620
Skach, Charles J., P.O. Box 509, Mt. Prospect, IL 60056
Skriba, Richard L., 1130 S. Michigan Ave., #3209, Chicago, IL 60605
Skupien, Edward D., St. Andrew Home for the Aged, 7000 N. Newark, Niles, IL 60714
Slominski, George A., 6727 S. California, Chicago, IL 60629
Slosarcik, Edward A., 13950 Main St., Lemont, IL 60439
Somerville, Walter F., 7574 E. Camine de Querabi, Tuscon, AZ 85715
Spellman, Francis J., St. Benedict's Home for the Aged, 6930 W. Touhy, Niles, IL 60714
Stankevicius, John P., 16294 Avenida Nobleza, San Diego, CA 92128
Stefanski, Walter, 29 E. McEldowney St., Chicago Heights, IL 60411
Stoga, Stanley C., 8200 S. Kostner, Chicago, IL 60652
Sullivan, C. Otis, St. Benedict Home, 6930 W. Touhy Ave., Niles, IL 60714
Sullivan, Daniel J., 3217 W. 184th St., Homewood, IL 60430
Szatkowski, Casimir M., 8030 S. Pulaski, Chicago, IL 60652
Szlanga, Edmund S., St. Jane de Chantal, 5252 S. Austin Ave., Chicago, IL 60638
Tessmer, Richard A., 800 W. Biesterfield Rd., Elk Grove Village, IL 60007
Tlapa, Richard J., 6350 S. Taft Ave., Merrillville, IN 46410
Troy, Henry A., c/o Mr. Edward L. Troy, 9727 Lindgren Ave., Sun City, AZ 85373
Ubowski, Chester, Resurrection Hospital, 7435 W. Talcott, Chicago, IL 60631
Ulatowski, Donald F., 2839 County Z, Adams, WI 53910
Velutis, John, 11129 S. Homan, Chicago, IL 60655
Vita, Mariano, 1809 E. 31st St., La Grange Park, IL 60525
Wagner, Leon R., 2435 Seabrook Island Rd., John Island, SC 29455
Wasiel, Michael J., 546 E. 155th St., Harvey, IL 60426
Weber, Gerard P., 4316 Lanai Rd., Encino, CA 91436
White, Bernard C., St. Henry, 6335 North Hoyne, Chicago, IL 60659
Windle, John J., 459 Homestead, La Grange Park, IL 60525
Wodniak, John L., 5730 W. Fullerton, Chicago, IL 60639
Wojcik, Richard J., Mundelein Seminary of the University of St. Mary-of-the-Lake, Mundelein, 60060

Wozny, William J., 1318 S. 61st Ave., Cicero, IL 60650
Zakarauskas, Anthony J., 6812 S. Washtenaw, Chicago, IL 60629
Zakarauskas, Vaclovas, 6812 S. Washtenaw, Chicago, IL 60629
Zawistanowicz, Norbert J, Our Lady of Victory Parish, 5212 W. Agatite Ave., Chicago, IL 60630
Zmiga, Walter J., 5345 W. Roscoe, Chicago, IL 60641
Zukowski, John A., c/o Maruska, 7080 Loba Ct., La Mesa, CA 92041

Permanent Deacons:
Abboud, Louis, St. Patrick, Wadsworth
Allen, Leslie, Jr., St. Sabina, Chicago
Allen, Warren, (Retired), St. Gelasius, Chicago
Alonso, Enrique, Our Lady of Grace, Chicago
Alvarez, Jose, St. Bonaventure, Chicago
Alvarez, Margarito, Our Lady of Guadalupe, Chicago
Amberg, John, St. Mary of the Assumption, Chicago
Antiss, Robert S., Holy Family, Inverness
Antonsen, Larry, Christ the King, Chicago
Arndt, John, St. Mary, Evanston
Auld, David D., Santa Maria del Popolo, Mundelein
Avila, Mario, Precious Blood, Chicago
Ayala, Efrain, Resurrection, Chicago
Bacchi, Benedict, St. Eulalia, Maywood
Banet, Robert, St. Andrew the Apostle, Calumet City
Barker, William, Sacred Heart, Palos Hills
Barone, Louis, St. Ansgar, Hanover Park
Bartholomew, Thomas, St. Michael, Orland Park
Barton, Jeffrey, St. Peter, Antioch
Bates, Eugene, St. Thecla, Chicago
Baum, Richard, St. Anne, Barrington
Behrendt, Raymond J., Sacred Heart, Melrose Park
Beil, Frank, St. Catherine Laboure, Glenview
Belanger, James, (Retired)
Bell, Kenneth, St. Domitilla, Hillside
Benthey, Herman, St. Anne, Hazel Crest
Benware, John, Our Lady of the Woods, Orland Park
Bergquist, Bernard, St. Tarcissus, Chicago
Bertagnoli, Frank, St. Francis de Sales, Lake Zurich
Bishop, Joseph, St. Rosalie, Harwood Heights
Blais, Emile, St. Mary of the Angels
Blue, Robert, St. Zachary, Des Plaines
Boehm, Owen, St. Rene, Chicago
Boggio, Edward, St. Marcelline, Schaumburg
Bohannon, Morris E., St. Clotilde, Chicago
Boivin, Edward, Catholic Charities
Bonifazi, Virgilio, St. John Berchmans, Chicago
Borha, George, St. Columbanus, Chicago
Boucha, Michael, Queen of Peace, North Chicago
Bovyn, Paul, Resurrection, Chicago
Braddock, J. Michael, St. John the Evangelist, Streamwood
Bradford, Bruce, St. Catherine of Siena/St. Lucy, Oak Park
Brady, Joseph, St. Christopher, Midlothian
Braski, Ray, St. Thomas of Villanova, Palatine
Brauch, Robert, St. Anne, Barrington
Bresler, Thomas, Holy Cross, Deerfield
Bretz, Michael, St. Catherine Laboure, Glenview
Bretzlauf, John, St. Anastasia, Waukegan
Brongiel, Andrew, St. Barbara, Chicago
Brooks, George, Infant Jesus of Prague, Flossmoor
Brooks, John, St. Joseph, Round Lake
Brown, Dennis G., St. Mary, Buffalo Grove
Bryce, Irvin, St. Albert the Great, Burbank
Brzoski, Chester, St. Nicholas of Tolentine, Chicago
Burke, Henry, Ascension/St. Susanna, Harvey
Burns, James, St. Donatus, Blue Island
Bustos, Gregorio, St. Clare of Montefalco, Chicago
Bzdon, Gregory M., St. Tarcissus, Chicago
Cabrera, Jorge, St. John Berchmans, Chicago
Callahan, Joseph, St. Julie Billiart, Tinley Park
Camerini, Guilio, St. Eulalia, Maywood
Carrizales, Maximiliano, Providence of God, Chicago
Carroll, Daniel, St. Walter, Chicago
Carvlin, Thomas, Ascension/St. Susanna, Harvey
Cascino, Joseph, Jr., St. Mary-of-the-Woods
Casey, William, Divine Providence, Westchester
Castanon, Toribio, Holy Cross-Immaculate Heart of Mary, Chicago
Cavanaugh, Michael, St. Francis Xavier, Wilmette
Cenek, Stephen, Transfiguration, Wauconda
Centeno, Benito, St. Genevieve, Chicago
Cesario, Carmen, Our Lady, Mother of the Church
Chaldez, Lorenzo, St. Gertrude, Franklin Park
Chappel, Dorsey, St. Leo the Great, Chicago
Chausse, Joseph, St. George, Tinley Park
Chavez, Abraham, Immaculate Conception, Chicago
Checki, Chester, St. Raymond de Penafort, Mt. Prospect
Childers, Terry D., Christ the King, Chicago
Chrastka, Joel, St. Leonard, Berwyn
Churilla, William L.
Ciesil, Norbert, St. Alphonsus, Prospect Heights
Cintron, Gilberto, St. Hedwig, Chicago
Ciston, William, Our Lady of the Mount, Cicero
Cnota, Robert F., St. Francis Borgia, Chicago
Cocco, Anthony, St. Michael, Orland Park
Coffey, Thomas W., St. Luke, River Forest
Colgan, Dennis L., St. William, Chicago
Collins, Dan, Our Lady of Ransom, Niles
Colon, Jose, (Retired)
Colucci, Victor, Sacred Heart, Melrose Park
Condill, James, St. Anne, Barrington
Conick, John, St. Theresa, Palatine
Connor, John, St. Colette, Rolling Meadows
Constanopolis, Louis, St. Benedict the African (West), Chicago
Conway, James, St. Barnabas, Chicago
Cooper, Willie, St. Laurence, Chicago
Corcoran, Thomas, St. Raymond de Penafort, Mount Prospect
Cordesman, Ellsworth, St. James, Highwood
Cordoba, Angelo, St. Simon the Apostle, Chicago
Cornejo, Salvador, Our Lady of Guadalupe, Chicago
Crandall, Robert, Our Lady of Ransom, Niles
Crane, Walter James, St. Catherine of Alexandria, Oak Lawn
Crespo, Feliciano, Resurrection, Chicago
Cruz, Esteban
Czarnecki, Thaddeus, Queen of the Rosary, Elk Grove Village
Dahl, Earl, St. John the Evangelist, Streamwood
Dahn, James, St. Alphonsus Ligouri, Prospect Heights
Dattoli, Dominick, St. George, Tinley Park
Daum, Donald, St. Germaine, Oak Lawn
Davis, James, St. Martin de Porres, Chicago
Deabel, Raymond
Debnar, John, St. Barbara, Brookfield
DeFiore, Robert, St. John the Evangelist, Streamwood
DeJesus, Confesor, St. Sylvester, Chicago
Del Llano, Manuel, Our Lady of Mercy, Chicago
Delaney, James, St. Bede the Venerable, Chicago
DeLarco, Michael, St. Celestine, Elmwood Park
DeLorenzo, Edward, St. Edmund, Oak Park
DeLuna, Arthur, Sta. Maria Addolorata, Chicago
DeRose, Ronald, Kolbe House, Chicago
Detloff, James, St. Emeric, Country Club Hills
Devereux, Robert, Our Lady of the Mount, Cicero
Devine, James, St. Celestine, Elmwood Park
DeVita, Frank, Divine Providence, Westchester
Diaz, Benjamin, St. Philomena, Chicago
DiCanio, Vito W., St. Emily, Mt. Prospect
Dienberg, Clifford, St. Vincent Ferrer, River Forest
Dineen, Terry, St. Thomas of Villanova, Palatine
Dinneen, Richard, St. James, Arlington Heights
Disparte, Philip, Alexian Brothers Hospital, Elk Grove Village
DiVirgilio, Dante, St. Mary of Vernon, Indian Creek
Dolan, Edward, St. Juliana, Chicago
Donates, Rafael, Our Lady of Mt. Carmel, Melrose Park
Donovan, Timothy, Old St. Mary's, Chicago
Dorgan, Eugene J., St. Pascal, Chicago
Doud, Raymond, Church of the Holy Spirit, Schaumburg
Downs, Sylvester, St. Joachim, Chicago
Drazba, Herbert, St. Jude the Apostle, South Holland
Drinan, Russell, Our Lady of Grace, Chicago
Duderstadt, Peery, St. Joseph the Worker, Wheeling
Duffner, Thomas, St. Mary of the Assumption, Chicago
Duffy, Frank, St. Henry, Chicago
Duffy, Robert, Our Lady of the Wayside, Arlington Heights
Dulen, John, St. John Brebeuf, Niles
Dunn, Dennis, St. Joseph, Libertyville
Dunn, William F., Jr., Santa Maria del Popolo, Mundelein
Dunne, Thomas, St. Thomas of Villanova, Palatine
Duszynski, Thomas, St. Matthew, Schaumburg
Dwyer, James T., Church of the Holy Spirit, Schaumburg
Echevarria, Ramon, Our Lady of Tepeyac, Chicago
Egan, David, Immaculate Conception, Waukegan
Ende, Gilbert, SS. Cyril & Methodius, Lemont
Engler, William, St. John of the Cross, Western Springs
Ernst, James, Our Lady of Hope, Rosemont
Estrada, Vincente, St. Roman, Chicago
Ewers, Thomas, St. Denis, Chicago
Faherty, Paul, St. Luke, River Forest
Favila, Angel, St. Agnes of Bohemia, Chicago
Fay, John, Sacred Heart, Winnetka
Feltes, Richard, St. Linus, Oak Lawn
Fernandez, Dismas, St. Maurice, Chicago
Ferrini, Armand, St. James, Arlington Heights
Ficker, John, St. George, Tinley Park
Figueroa, Roberto, Queen of Angels, Chicago
Finnegan, Michael, St. Juliana, Chicago
Fitzsimon, Robert, Immaculate Conception, Highland Park
Flam, Richard, St. Marcelline, Schaumburg
Flanagan, John, St. Germaine, Oak Lawn
Flewellen, James, St. Thaddeus, Chicago
Flores, Nicolas, St. Stanislaus Kostka, Chicago
Flores, Roman, St. Gertrude, Franklin Park
Foley, Brendan, Our Lady of the Wayside, Arlington Heights
Fox, Gerald, St. Barbara, Brookfield
Fragassi, Phillip, St. Patrick, Wadsworth
Fronczek, Casimir, St. Francis Borgia Deaf Center, Chicago
Fuller, George, Resurrection, Chicago
Gadomski, Edward, St. Linus, Oak Lawn
Gagnon, Robert, St. Peter, Antioch
Gallagher, James, St. James, Highwood
Gallagher, John, St. Colette, Rolling Meadows
Garcia, Jose, St. Marcelline, Schaumburg
Garcia, Miguel, St. Stanislaus Kostka, Chicago
Garstki, Edwin, Office of the Vicar for the Diaconate
Garza, Juan L., St. Paul, Chicago Heights
Gaughan, Francis, St. Ita, Chicago
Gavin, Raymond, St. Catherine Laboure, Glenview
Gembara, Emil, St. Mary Star of the Sea, Chicago
Giancarlo, James, St. Christopher, Midlothian
Gilbert, Paul, St. George, Tinley Park
Gildea, Francis, St. Theresa, Palatine
Gniech, George, St. Constance, Chicago
Golab, Chester J., St. Daniel the Prophet, Chicago
Gonzalez, Jose, St. Aloysius, Chicago
Gonzalez, Jose M., St. Peter Canisius, Chicago
Gordus, Richard, Mater Christi, North Riverside
Graffia, Raymond, St. Edna, Arlington Heights
Green, Richard, St. Turibius, Chicago
Grevenites, James, St. Louise de Marillace, LaGrange Park
Gronek, Ronald, Divine Savior, Norridge
Gronkiewicz, Edmund, Our Lady of Mount Carmel, Chicago
Grossnickle, Donald R., Our Lady of the Wayside, Arlington Heights
Grotto, Thomas, St. Benedict, Blue Island
Gutierrez, Jorge, St. Mark, Chicago
Hahn, Gerald E., Queen of Apostles, Riverdale
Halper, Bernard, St. Kieran, Chicago Heights
Halt, Thomas, St. Matthew, Schaumburg
Handrigan, Thomas, Our Lady of Victory, Chicago
Hare, Martin, Holy Rosary, Chicago
Harrington, John, Kolbe House
Harris, Wallace, St. Dorothy, Chicago
Hart, Vernon, Seven Holy Founders, Calumet Park
Hatch, Wilmer, St. Philip Neri, Chicago
Helmer, Everett, Queen of the Universe, Chicago
Hempen, Harold, St. Irenaeus, Park Forest
Hennessy, Matthew, St. James, Arlington Heights
Henricks, John, Sacred Heart, Melrose Park
Henry, Francis, Nativity of Our Lord, Chicago
Henry, Roy, Our Lady of Lourdes, Chicago
Hensley, Claude, St. Anthony, Cicero
Hermann, Dean, Queen of Peace, North Chicago
Hernandez, Armando, St. Michael, Chicago
Hernandez, Sigifredo, St. Jerome, Chicago
Herrera, Armando, Mary Queen of Heaven, Chicago
Herrera, Marcial, St. John Berchmans, Chicago
Hill, John, Our Lady of Peace, Chicago
Hinch, Ralph, St. Francis Borgia Deaf Center, Chicago
Hipelius, Thomas, St. Damian, Oak Forest
Hjelmgren, Bob, St. John Vianney, Northlake
Hogan, Ralph, St. Mary of Vernon, Mundelein
Horne, Philip G., Our Lady of Humility, Zion
Hotcaveg, Irwin E., St. Ferdinand, Chicago
Hubbard, James, St. Felicitas, Chicago
Huber, Charles, St. Francis Borgia, Chicago
Hughes, James, St. Catherine of Alexandria, Oak Lawn
Hurley, William, Christ the King, Chicago
Huslig, Dennis, St. Louise de Marillac, La Grange Park
Ibarra, Juan, St. Stanislaus Kostka, Chicago
Iwan, Henry, St. Gilbert, Grayslake
Jablonski, Robert, St. Bartholomew, Chicago
Jablonski, William, St. Kiernan, Chicago Heights
Jacob, Robert, St. Benedict, Chicago
Jay, Richard, St. Athanasius, Evanston
Jean-Pierre, Fritz, St. Jerome, Chicago
Jeffrey, August, Divine Savior, Norridge
Jenney, Kenneth, Jr., Immaculate Heart of Mary, Chicago
Jinkens, Max R., Our Lady of Humility, Zion
Johnson, Mervin, St. Leo the Great, Chicago
Jones, Roosevelt, St. Basil-Visitation, Chicago
Kaczmarek, Edward, St. Thomas of Villanova, Palatine

Kalivoda, Bill, Addolorata Villa, Wheeling
Kancler, Lawrence, St. John the Evangelist, Streamwood
Kanter, Kevin, St. Mary, Buffalo Grove
Karnoski, Michael, St. Louis de Montfort, Oak Lawn
Kasimatis, Jerome, Holy Cross, Deerfield
Kearney, John, Immaculate Heart of Mary, Chicago
Keating, Timothy, St. Lawrence O'Toole, Matteson
Keegan, Charles, St. Patricia, Hickory Hills
Kenney, James, St. Mary, Lake Forest
Klemanovic, John, Our Lady of Lourdes, Chicago
Klimcke, Walter, St. Cletus, LaGrange
Knippen, James, St. Hubert, Hoffman Estates
Kocar, Marvin, St. Pius X, Stickney
Kort, Clayton, St. John Fisher, Chicago
Kotleba, Rudolf, Holy Family/St. Francis Assisi, Chicago
Kotwas, Donald, St. Bede the Venerable, Chicago
Kozloski, Stanley, St. Matthew, Schaumburg
Kozuchowski, Chester, St. Gilbert, Grayslake
Krakora, Joseph, St. Mary, Lake Forest
Krapez, Michael, Our Lady of the Ridge, Chicago Ridge
Kristinat, Richard L., St. George, Tinley Park
Kryszak, Timothy, Holy Spirit, Schaumburg
Kukla, Eugene, St. Mary, Buffalo Grove
Kush, Michael, St. Damian, Oak Forest
Kut, Bernard, St. Gall, Chicago
Kwasegroch, Gerald, St. Eugene, Chicago
Kwasigroch, James, Our Lady of Grace, Chicago
La Belle, Eugene, St. Kieran, Chicago Heights
LaCosse, Robert, St. Mary, Buffalo Grove
LaCoursiere, Victor, St. Jerome, Chicago
Lagges, Peter, St. Zachary, Des Plaines
Lambert, George, St. Eulalia, Maywood
Lambert, Thomas, St. Raymond, Mt. Prospect
Langwell, James E., Incarnation, Palos Heights
Leck, Robert, Our Lady of Victory, Chicago
Lehman, William B., Divine Savior, Norridge
Lekan, Louis, St. James, Arlington Heights
Leo, Kevin, St. Thomas of Villanova, Palatine
Leonard, Timothy, Prince of Peace, Lake Villa
Leonas, John, St. Anne, Hazel Crest
Lesnieski, Norbert, SS. Cyril & Methodius, Lemont
Levins, Terrence, SS. Faith, Hope & Charity, Winnetka
Lewis, Joseph, Our Lady of Sorrows, Chicago
Liberti, Peter, All Saints-St. Anthony, Chicago
Lilly, Leroy, St. Laurence, Chicago
Limon, Juan, St. Benedict, Blue Island
Limon, Vincente, Our Lady of Tepeyac, Chicago
Lino, Ronald, St. John the Evangelist, Streamwood
Lisowski, Thaddeus, St. Constance, Chicago
Llano, Antonio, Our Lady of the Mount, Cicero
Llorens, Anthony, St. Martin de Porres, Chicago
Lopez, Adolf, St. Aloysius, Chicago
Lopez, Bricio
Lorbach, John, St. Raymond de Penafort, Mt. Prospect
Lugo, Gregorio, Our Lady of Grace, Chicago
Lukaszewski, Edward, St. Constance, Chicago
Lundy, Albert, Our Lady of Knock, Calumet City
Lyons, John, St. James, Arlington Heights
Mackert, Martin, All Saints-St. Anthony, Chicago
Maddock, George, St. Joseph, Homewood
Madonia, Loretto, St. Giles, Oak Park
Mages, William, St. Mary of the Woods, Chicago
Maldonado, Meliquides, St. Mark
Malec, Albert, St. Daniel the Prophet, Chicago
Mally, Joseph, St. Adalbert, Chicago
Malone, Jack, St. Germaine, Oak Lawn
Maloney, Thomas J., St. Thomas of Villanova, Palatine
Maney, Antonio, St. James, Maywood
Manning, Peter, St. Joseph, Summit
Manthie, Robert, St. Edna, Arlington Heights
Marella, Dominic, St. Charles Borromeo, Melrose Park
Marotto, Angelo, St. Domitilla, Hillside
Marquez, J. Frank, (Retired)
Marrero, Jose, St. Roman, Chicago
Martinez, Francisco, St. Philomena, Chicago
Mason, Frederick, Catholic Youth Organization
Matthews, Robert, St. Joseph, Libertyville
Mauch, Richard, St. Ann, Lansing
Maune, William, St. Irenaeus, Park Forest
Maurer, William, Infant Jesus of Prague, Flossmoor
McCarthy, Thomas, St. James, Sauk Village
McCloskey, Michael, Holy Name Cathedral, Chicago
McDonough, Michael, St. Michael, Orland Park
McElrath, Bruce, St. Ailbe, Chicago
McGorey, Thomas, St. John of the Cross, Western Springs
McKinnis, William, St. Columbanus, Chicago
McLynn, Michael, St. Louis de Marillac, La Grange Park
McMahon, John, St. Bede, Ingleside
McNulty, Michael, Sacred Heart, Winnetka
Meehan, Peter, St. Martha, Morton Grove
Meehan, Thomas, Our Lady of Loretto, Hometown
Mele, John, Special Ministry
Melkovitz, Emil, St. Francis Borgia, Chicago
Memmel, Aloysius, St. Paul of the Cross, Park Ridge
Mench, Sidney, St. John Fisher, Chicago
Mendieta, Raul, St. Alphonsus, Chicago
Mendizabal, Guillermo, St. John Berchmans, Chicago
Mendoza, Jose Luis, St. Agnes of Bohemia, Chicago
Mercure, Michael, Our Lady of Humility, Zion-Beach Park
Metallo, Arthur, St. Francis Hospital, Evanston
Michalowski, Benedict, St. Joseph, Summit
Milender, Leonard, Prince of Peace, Lake Villa
Miller, William, St. Peter, Skokie
Miska, Richard, St. Julie Billiart, Tinley Park
Mongan, Martin, St. Bernadette, Evergreen Park
Monica, Robert, St. Thomas the Apostle, Chicago
Monnelly, Michael, Queen of All Saints, Chicago
Monterroso, Oscar, St. Ansgar, Hanover Park
Moore, Steven, St. Anne, Hazel Crest
Moorman, William, Immaculate Conception, Highland Park
Morales, Juan, St. John the Baptist, Harvey
Moran, Charles, St. John the Evangelist, Streamwood
Morgan, James, St. Gelasius, Chicago
Morowczynski, Romuald, St. Jane de Chantal, Chicago
Morton, Wayne, St. Lawrence O'Toole, Matteson
Motycka, Robert, St. Barbara, Brookfield
Mudd, Dennis, Sr., St. Joseph, Libertyville
Mujica, Ines, St. Mary, Riverside
Mullaney, Roger, SS. Faith, Hope & Charity, Winnetka
Munda, Gary, Sr., Queen of Peace, North Chicago
Munoz, Romeo, St. Victor, Calumet City
Murphy, Robert, St. Gertrude, Franklin Park
Murphy, Robert, St. Jerome, Chicago
Murray, Michael, Our Lady of the Brook, Northbrook
Navarro, Anthonio, St. Mark, Chicago
Navarro, Jesse, St. Mary, Star of the Sea, Chicago
Nazario, Carlos, Our Lady of Grace, Chicago
Negron, Julio A., Queen of Peace, North Chicago
Neurauter, Paul, St. Peter, Antioch
Newhall, Redondo, St. Cajetan, Chicago
Newman, Jeffrey, St. Gilbert, Grayslake
Newton, Robert, St. Peter Damian, Bartlett
Nguyen, Duc Van, St. Thomas of Canterbury, Chicago
Niersbach, Donald, St. Walter, Chicago
Nieves, Bienvenido, St. Josaphat, Chicago
Nimietz, James, St. John the Evangelist, Streamwood
Nolan, John, St. Celestine, Elmwood Park
Norton, Terrence, St. Luke, River Forest
Norys, Stephen, St. Theresa, Palatine
Nowak, Thomas, St. Agnes, Chicago Heights
Nugent, J Michael, St. John the Evangelist, Streamwood
Nunez, Raul, Our Lady of Guadalupe, Chicago
Nylen, Arthur A., St. Jude the Apostle, South Holland
O'Brien, Thomas, St. Emeric, Country Club Hills
O'Connell, Thomas, St. Walter, Chicago
O'Donnell, Charles, Our Lady of Ransom, Niles
O'Donnell, Patrick, St. Damian, Oak Forest
O'Grady, Donald A., Queen of Angels, Chicago
O'Keefe, Robert C., St. Isaac Jogues, Niles
O'Leary, Edward, St. Eugene, Chicago
O'Leary, John A., St. Joseph, Homewood
O'Malley, James, O'Hare Airport Chapel, Chicago
O'Neill, John, St. Luke, River Forest
Oborski, Zygfryd, St. Stanislaus Bishop & Martyr, Chicago
Ochoa, Zeferino, Holy Family/St. Francis of Assisi, Chicago
Odegard, Robert, St. Priscilla, Chicago
Ojeda, Norberto, St. James, Maywood
Olson, Carl, St. Cornelius, Chicago
Omiatek, Marion, Transfiguration, Wauconda
Ontiveros, Philip, St. Marcelline, Schaumburg
Ortego, Ignacio, St. Mark, Chicago
Ortiz, Sigifredo, St. Sylvester, Chicago
Pagliai, Bruno, St. James, Highwood
Panek, Joseph, Office of the Vicar for Diaconate
Pastirik, Joseph, St. Francis de Sales, Chicago
Pecson, Andres, St. Mathias, Chicago
Penich, Michael, Jr., St. Paul the Apostle, Gurnee
Pepitone, Joe, St. John of the Cross, Western Springs
Perez, Alphonse M., Assumption, Chicago
Perez, Carlos, St. Joseph, Chicago
Perez, Luis, Santa Maria Addolorata, Chicago
Perez, Miguel, St. Pius V., Chicago
Perez, Orlando, St. Thomas of Canterbury, Chicago
Perez, Teodoro, St. Anne, Hazel Crest
Perez, Wilfredo, St. John Bosco, Chicago
Perkowitz, John, St. John Brebeuf, Niles
Peters, Bruce, St. Mary, Buffalo Grove
Peterson, George A., (Retired)
Petricca, Clemente, St. Ansgar, Hanover Park
Phillippi, Joseph, St. James, Arlington Heights
Pincich, Samuel, St. Isaac Jogues, Niles
Pineda, Javier, St. Adrian, Chicago
Pineiro, Ismael, St. Simeon, Bellwood
Pizzato, Richard, St. Theresa, Palatine
Plantz, Robert, St. James, Arlington Heights
Platt, James, St. Cyprian, River Grove
Poletto, Robert, St. Mary, Fremont Center, Mundelein
Ponce, Antonio, St. Blase, Summit
Quackenbush, Edward, St. Bede, Ingleside
Quinn, Eugene, Holy Ghost, South Holland
Ragonese, Dan, St. Victor, Calumet City
Ramirez, Jorge V., Our Lady of Good Counsel, Chicago
Ramos, Dennis, St. Aloysius, Chicago
Ramos, Francisco, St. Philomena, Chicago
Ranke, Dennis, Our Lady of Victory, Chicago
Ray, Frederick W., St. Isaac Jogues, Niles
Rehor, Timothy, St. Bernardine, Forest Park
Reilly, Raymond, St. John Fisher, Chicago
Reinert, William, St. Raymond de Penafort, Mount Prospect
Reinhart, James, St. Linus, Oak Lawn
Reisen, William, St. Matthew, Schaumburg
Renk, Dennis, St. Joseph, Chicago
Revering, Roman, St. James, Maywood
Revord, James, Our Lady of Perpetual Help, Glenview
Riccio, Louis, Charismatic Renewal, St. Theresa
Richardson, John, St. Patrick, Wadsworth
Richardson, Leonard M., St. Sabina, Chicago
Riffner, Joseph, St. Alphonsus, Chicago
Riner, Edwin
Rios, Jamie, St. Fidelis, Chicago
Rivas, Roberto, Our Lady of Mercy, Chicago
Rivera, Hector, St. Teresa of Avila, Chicago
Rivera, Sebastian, St. Gertrude, Franklin Park
Rodriguez, Candelario, Notre Dame, Chicago
Rodriguez, Emiliano, St. Bonaventure, Chicago
Rodriguez, Juan, St. Rita of Cascia, Chicago
Rodriguez, Manuel, St. Francis of Assisi, Chicago
Rodriguez, Milton, Maternity of B.V.M., Chicago
Rodriguez, Santiago, St. Aloysius, Chicago
Rodriguez, Uriol, Resurrection, Chicago
Roman, Francisco, St. Sylvester, Chicago
Roman, Tito, St. Bonaventure, Chicago
Romano, Michael, Columbus Hospital, Chicago
Rosa, Abraham, St. Mark, Chicago
Rosado, Julio, Mary, Queen of Heaven, Cicero
Rowe, John, St. Ann, Lansing
Roy, Jasper, Holy Angels, Chicago
Rozo, Jorge, Holy Rosary, Chicago
Ruffner, R. Michael, Mary, Seat of Wisdom, Park Ridge
Ruppert, William, St. John Vianney, Northlake
Ryan, Edward, St. Anthony, Chicago
Ryan, Robert E., Sr., St. Juliana, Chicago
Ryan, Thomas, St. Christina, Chicago
Sabato, Anthony, Holy Cross, Deerfield
Sacramento, Anthony, St. Dismas, Waukegan
Salgado, Alfonso, St. Anthony, Cicero
Sanchez, Salvador, St. Francis of Assisi/Our Lady of the Angels, Chicago
Sands, William, Sta. Maria Del Popolo, Mundelein
Sanford, James, St. Emily, Mount Prospect
Sanzone, Michael J., Immaculate Conception, Waukegan
Sassetti, Robert C., St. Vincent Ferrer, River Forest
Sassone, Michael, Blue Island
Sattler, David, St. Peter Damien, Bartlett
Savercool, Gerald, St. Lawrence O'Toole, Matteson
Scarbalis, Edward, SS. Joseph & Bartholomew, Waukegan
Schiltz, James, St. Constance, Chicago
Schoenfeld, Kenneth, St. Fabian, Bridgeview
Schoewe, Rudolph, Our Lady of Victory, Chicago
Schroeder, Thomas, St. James, Sauk Village
Schroetlin, Albert, St. Richard, Chicago
Schultz, Ronald, St. Victor, Calumet City
Sedivy, Alan, Our Lady of Perpetual Help, Glenview
Seitz, John, Incarnation, Palos Heights
Serratore, Gregory, St. Mary Star of Sea, Chicago
Seveska, Richard, St. Anne, Barrington
Shandro, Ellery, St. Benedict, Blue Island
Sharwarko, Michael, St. Louis de Monfort, Oak Lawn
Shaw, Ralph, St. Felicitas, Chicago
Shinkle, Derald, Sacred Heart, Winnetka
Sierra, Juan, Blessed Sacrament, Chicago
Silva, Rodrigo, St. Ann, Chicago
Simmons, John, Santa Maria del Popolo, Mundelein
Siranovic, Joseph, Notre Dame de Chicago, Chicago
Skaja, Lawrence, St. John Brebeuf, Niles

Slajchert, Michael, St. Gall, Chicago
Smith, Robert S., Jr., Holy Cross, Deerfield
Solon, Thomas, St. Denis, Chicago
Soto, Pedro, St. Philomena, Chicago
Soto, Santos, St. Sylvester, Chicago
Spalla, Paul, St. Mary-of-the-Lake, Chicago
Spitizzeri, Fred, St. Priscilla, Chicago
Spohr, Lawrence, St. Mary of Celle, Berwyn
Stalcup, Joseph, Sr., St. George, Tinley Park
Stanczak, Stefan, St. Hyacinth, Chicago
Stearns, William, St. Damian, Oak Forest
Steinbeigle, Francis, St. Damian, Oak Forest
Stevens, Gregory, St. Celestine, Elmwood Park
Stubstad, Thomas, St. Pascal, Chicago
Sullivan, William, St. Barnabas, Chicago
Sullivan, William, St. Louis de Montfort, Oak Lawn
Sutton, Daniel, St. Helena of the Cross, Chicago
Swiatek, Ronald, St. John Bosco, Chicago
Swiech, Edward, St. Robert Bellarmine, Chicago
Szady, Mitchell, St. Stanislaus B & M, Chicago
Taylor, Lowell, Church of the Holy Spirit, Schaumburg
Telle, Paul, St. Dismas, Waukegan
Telposky, Donald, St. Stephen, Des Plaines
Temple, James, St. Barnabas, Chicago
Tereza, Nick, St. Ansgar, Hanover Park
Tipperreiter, Charles, St. Eugene, Chicago
Tomkowiak, Edward, St. Patrick, Wadsworth
Torres, Candido, Our Lady of Fatima, Chicago
Trakszelis, Jerome, St. Vincent Ferror, River Forest
Trevino, Luis, Church of the Holy Spirit, Schaumburg
Troy, Daniel J., Holy Ghost, South Holland
Tryba, Edmund, St. Hilary, Chicago
Tryjefaczka, Richard, St. Turibius, Chicago
Uroza, Jose, St. Angela, Chicago
Valdivia, Juan, Our Lady of Guadalupe, Chicago
Valentin, Israel, St. Philomena, Chicago
Valenziano, Vern, St. Edna, Arlington Heights
Valle, Miguel Angel, Our Lady of Lourdes, Chicago
Van Dyke, Neil, Riverside
Vazquez, Jose, Maternity B.V.M., Chicago
Velasco, Arturo, St. Francis of Assisi, Chicago
Velasco, Benito, Maternity B.V.M., Chicago
Velazquez, Angel, SS. Joseph & Bartholomew, Waukegan
Vemich, Duke, All Saints-St. Anthony, Chicago
Vera, Camilo, Resurrection, Chicago
Vidmar, John, St. Stephen, Chicago
Villa, Salvatore, St. Bruno, Chicago
Villalobos, Antonio, St. Mark, Chicago
Villegas, Salomon, St. Hedwig, Chicago
Virruso, Christopher, Our Lady, Mother of the Church, Chicago
Walters, John, St. Bernardine, Forest Park
Ward, Raymond, Queen of All Saints, Chicago
Ward, Raymond E., St. Jerome, Chicago
Warfield, Richard, Chap. Police Dept., Chicago
Warren, Roy, St. Agatha, Chicago
Watson, Dexter, Holy Angels, Chicago
Wegner, Albin J., Jr., St. Michael, Chicago
Wehling, Donald, St. Hilary, Chicago
Weiner, Ronald, St. John Bosco, Chicago
Weitendorf, Norbert, St. Patricia, Hickory Hills
Welter, Daniel, Our Lady of the Woods, Orland Park
West, Tommy, Assumption/St. Catherine of Genoa, Chicago
White, Philip, Mercy Mission, Chicago
Wieczorek, Richard, Five Holy Martyrs, Chicago
Wilczynski, Joseph, St. Stanislaus B & M, Posen
Williams, Rufus, St. Benedict the African, Chicago
Wills, James, St. Peter, Skokie
Winblad, Joseph, St. Ann, Lansing
Wogan, James, St. Mary of Vernon, Indian Creek
Young, Irving, St. Mary, Buffalo Grove
Yucuis, Charles, St. Christopher, Midlothian
Zadruzny, Wieslaw, St. Fidelis, Chicago
Zanardo, Ronald, St. Lawrence O'Toole, Matteson
Zapata, Jose, St. Benedict, Blue Island
Zawadzki, Kenneth, St. Fabian, Bridgeview
Zdeb, James, St. Thomas of Villanova, Palatine
Zeller, John, St. Marcelline, Schaumburg
Zima, Robert, Office for Peace and Justice
Zimmerman, Edward
Zimmermann, John, Transfiguration, Wauconda
Ziomek, Robert, St. Ansgar, Hanover Park
Zurawski, John, St. John Vianney, Northlake
Zwolski, Mark, St. Mary of Vernon, Mundelein
Zych, Gerald, St. Giles, Oak Park

INSTITUTIONS LOCATED IN THE ARCHDIOCESE

[A] SEMINARIES, ARCHDIOCESAN

CHICAGO. *Archbishop Quigley Preparatory Seminary*, 103 E. Chestnut St., 60611. Tel: 312-787-9343. Revs. John G. Klein, Pres.; Michael G. Foley, Rector; Wayne Watts; Peter Snieg; Frank Latzko; Edward M. Mikolajczyk, Dean of Students; Louis J. Zake; Dennis A. Ziomek; William T. Corcoran, Dean of Formation. Priests 9; Lay Teachers 19; Students 223.

Institute of Vocation Awareness, 103 E. Chestnut St., 60611. Tel: 312-787-9343. Revs. John G. Klein, Pres.; Harold B. Stanger.

A Vocation Out-Reach Program for the Archdiocese of Chicago.

St. Joseph Seminary, The Seminary College at Loyola University, 6551 N. Sheridan Rd., 60626. Tel: 773-973-9700; Fax: 773-973-9718. Administration: Revs. James Presta, M. Div., S.T.L., Rector-Pres.; John J. Clair, M.Div., Vice Pres.; Anthony A. Englert, M.Div., Vice Rector & History Instructor; Dennis J. Lyle, M.Div., S.T.L., Academic Dean & Theology Instructor; Mr. Dennis M. Composto, M.P.A., M.Ed., Comptroller & Dir. Financial Aid, Political Science Lecturer; Mr. Michael D. Martino, M.A., Dir. of Pre-College Prog.; Mr. Patrick McCarthy, B.S., Assoc. Dir. of Recruitment; Mrs. Marie Composto, Dir. Seminary Devel.; Ms. Yuvanka Juarez, B.A., Financial Aid Admin.; Mr. Paul Harrington, B.A., Dir. Alumni Rels.; Ms. Theresa Rooney, Dir. of Community Relations. Faculty: Mr. Michael Martino, M.A., English Instructor; Rev. James Presta, M. Div., S.T.L., Theology Instructor.

MUNDELEIN. *University of St. Mary of the Lake-Mundelein Seminary*, 60060. Tel: 847-566-6401; Fax: 847-566-7330. Resident Faculty: Very Rev. John F. Canary, Rector, Pres.; Revs. Bartholomew S. Winters, M. Div., M.A.S., S.T.D.; Martin A. Zielinski, Ph.D., Academic Dean; Leo D. Lefebure, Ph.D., Dean of Canonically Recognized Faculty; Sr. Linda Sevcik, S.M., S.T.L., Dir. Field Ed.; Revs. Raymond J. Webb, Ph.D., Dir. Newly Ordained Program; John H. Barkemeyer, Dir. Vocations; August J. Belauskas, Ph.D. (Cand.), Admissions Dir.; Kurt D. Boras; Patrick J. Boyle, S.J., Ph.D.; Sr. Sara Butler, M.S.B.T., Ph.D.; Sr. Dorothy Folliard, O.P., Ph.D., M.A.R.S.; Sr. Veronica Mendez, R.C.D., M.T.S.; Revs. Louis J. Cameli, S.T.D.; Edward J. Cronin, M.A.S.; Robert E. Barron, S.T.D. (Cand.); John V. Dolciamore, J.C.L., Canonical Recorder; Brian J. Fischer, S.L.D. (Cand.); Lawrence R. Hennessey, Ph.D.; Leo D. Lefebure, Ph.D.; Jerome E. Listecki, J.C.D., J.D., S.T.D.; John G. Lodge, S.S.L., D.Min., S.T.D.; Charles R. Meyer, S.T.D., Prof. Emeritus; John J. McDonnell, S.T.D.; James P. McIlhone, Ph.D.; Arlene Michna, Mus. B., Mus. M.; Rev. B. James Murphy, M.Div. (JOL); David P. Pavlik, B.A., M. Div.; Revs. Robert L. Schoenstene, S.S.L. (JOL); Daniel S. Siwek, S.T.L.; Paul H. Wachdorf, M.C.Sp.; Richard J. Wojcik, M.C.G., Prof. Emeritus; Dennis M. Zalecki; Bro. Henry Baldwin, F.S.C., M.Ed., Librarian; Rev. Anthony M. O'Connell, O.S.M., Psy.D., Non-Resident. Sisters 4; Brothers 1; Lay Teachers 1; Students 191.

Convent. Sr. Consuelo Vazquez, Supr. Oblate Sisters of Jesus the Priest 9.

[B] SEMINARIES, RELIGIOUS OR SCHOLASTICATES

CHICAGO. *The Catholic Theological Union at Chicago*, 5401 S. Cornell Ave., 60615. Tel: 773-324-8000. Major Seminary. Serving the following: Franciscans, Servites, Passionists, Augustinians, Norbertines, Society of the Divine Word, Missionaries of the Precious Blood, Claretians, Crosier Fathers, Holy Ghost Fathers, Sacred Heart Missionaries, Viatorians, Comboni Missionaries, Franciscans Capuchins, Sacred Heart Fathers and Brothers, Ukrainian Catholic Diocese, Congregation of the Blessed Sacrament, Columban Missionaries, Redemptorist Fathers, Oblates of Mary Immaculate, Xaverian Missionaries, Maryknoll Missionaries, Conventual Franciscans, Oratorians, Scalabrinians, Discalced Carmelites, Vincentians. Revs. Norman Bevan, C.S.Sp., S.T.D., Pres.; Gary Riebe-Estrella, S.V.D., S.T.D., Vice Pres. & Academic Dean; Ms. Virginia A. Piecuch, M.Div., Dean of Students & C.T.U. Community Svcs.; Mr. Cyrin Maus, S.T.D., Dir. Institutional Advancement; JoAnn McCaffrey, D. Min. Cand., Registrar; Rev. Kenneth O'Malley, C.P., Ph.D., Dir. Library; Ms. Priscilla Sporrong, M.B.A., Dir., Public Rels.; Rev. Kevin Madigan, P.H.D., Dir. M.A. Prog.; Mrs. Keiren M. O'Kelly, M.Div., Dir. Admissions & Recruiting; Sr. Eleanor Holland, I.B.V.M., M.A., Dir. Continuing Educ. Prog.; Revs. Genska DePaul, O.F.M., M.T.S., Admin.; Gerald Persha, M.M., Ph.D., S.T.D., Dir. M.Div. Prog. Faculty: Dr. Herbert Anderson, Ph.D.; Dr. Claude-Marie Barbour, S.T.D.; Sr. Dianne Bergant, C.S.A., Ph.D., Dir. M. Div. Prog.; Revs. Stephen B. Bevans, S.V.D., Ph.D.; Timothy Lenchak, S.V.D.; Sr. Barbara Bowe, R.S.C.J., Th.D.; Sr. Jeanette Lucinio, S.P., D.Min., Prog. & Dir. Field Education; Sr. Eleanor Doidge, L.O.B., D.Min.; Dr. Kevin Madigan, Ph.D.; Revs. Edward Foley, O.F.M.Cap., Ph.D., M.Mus., Dir. D.Min. Prog.; Archimedes Fornasari, M.C.C.J., Ph.D.; Richard Fragomeni, Ph.D.; Mark Francis, C.S.V., S.L.D.; Dr. Mary Frolich, Ph.D.; Sr. Marianne Race, C.S.J., M.A., Dir. Israel Study Programs; Revs. Anthony Gittins, C.S.Sp., Ph.D.; Zachary Hayes, O.F.M., Dr.Th.; Leslie J. Hoppe, O.F.M., Ph.D.; John M. Kaserow, M.M., Ph.D.; John Linnan, C.S.V., S.T.D.; Eugene A. LaVerdiere, S.S.S., Ph.D.; Thomas Nairn, O.F.M., Ph.D.; James C. Okoye, C.S.Sp.; Sr. Carolyn Osiek, R.S.C.J., Th.D.; Rev. John Pawlikowski, O.S.M., Ph.D.; Rabbi Hayim Goren Perelmuter, D.H.L.; Rev. Gerald Persha, M.M., Ph.D., S.T.D.; Sr. Jamie Phelps, O.P., Ph.D.; Sr. Ana Maria Pineda, R.S.M., S.T.D.; Sr. Barbara Reid, O.P., Ph.D.; Revs. Gary Riebe-Estrella, S.V.D., Ph.D., S.T.D.; Robert Schreiter, C.PP.S., Th.D.; Roger P. Schroeder, S.V.D., D.Miss.; Donald Senior, C.P., S.T.D.; Paul Wadell, C.P., Ph.D.; Mr. Bruce Lescher, Ph.D. Priests 23; Sisters 10; Lay Teachers 3; Non-Catholic Clergy 3; Students 353.

TECHNY. *Divine Word Residence*. (Formerly Divine Word Seminary-St. Mary's Mission House), P.O. Box 6000, 60082-6000. Tel: 847-272-2700; Fax: 847-272-2873. Legal Title: *Divine Word Techny Community Corporation*. Revs. Kazimerz Garbacz, S.V.D., Rector; James Bergin, S.V.D.; William Blake, S.V.D.; Michael Bonner, S.V.D.; Edward Borkowski, S.V.D.; James Braband, S.V.D.; Walter Bracken, S.V.D.; Thomas Commons, S.V.D.; Joseph Connors, S.V.D.; Paul Connors, S.V.D.; Philip Danaher, S.V.D.; Emmanuel DeLeon, S.V.D.; John Donaghey, S.V.D.; Daniel Driscoll, S.V.D.; Leo Dusheck, S.V.D.; Alphonse Elsbernd, S.V.D.; Lawrence Freidel, S.V.D.; Gerald Garry, S.V.D.; Gilbert Gawlick, S.V.D.; Elzear Gehlen, S.V.D.; Thomas Griffith; Walter Hafner, S.V.D.; Joseph Henkels, S.V.D.; Gerard Hofstee, S.V.D.; Leo Hotze, S.V.D.; Francis Hughes, S.V.D.; Henry Jungbluth, S.V.D.; Francis Kamp, S.V.D.; John Koster, S.V.D.; Francis Kowalski, S.V.D.; Anthony Krajci, S.V.D.; Thomas Krosnicki, S.V.D.; Joseph LeBeau, S.V.D.; Paschal LoBianco, S.V.D.; Louis Luzbetak, S.V.D.; Andrew Masters, S.V.D.; Wilbert Morman, S.V.D.; Robert Myers, S.V.D.; Edward Norton, S.V.D.; Chester Nowicki, S.V.D.; Edward Peklo, S.V.D.; Lawrence Poetz, S.V.D.; Raymond Quetchenbach, S.V.D.; Claire Risse, S.V.D.; Charles Roesslein, S.V.D.; Frederick Rudolph, S.V.D.; Charles Schoderbek, S.V.D.; Eugene Stoll; Robert Studeny, S.V.D.; John Swift, S.V.D.; Lawrence Thornton, S.V.D.; Stanley Uroda, S.V.D.; John Vogelgesang, S.V.D.; Bros. John Carlucci, S.V.D.; Douglas Edmonds, S.V.D.; Rene Gawlik, S.V.D.; George Haegele, S.V.D.; Rudolph Heckel, S.V.D.; Jude Heeks, S.V.D.; James Hunt, S.V.D.; Clement Meyer, S.V.D.; David Noonan, S.V.D.; Joachim Oros, S.V.D.; Stephen Pardy, S.V.D.; George Pashia, S.V.D.; Pius Resch, S.V.D.; James Ryan, S.V.D.; Conrad Schmid, S.V.D.; Cyril Schroeder, S.V.D.; Richard Sullivan, S.V.D.; Alois Terendy, S.V.D.; Joseph Urban, S.V.D.; Kenneth Valois, S.V.D.; Edwin Wirth, S.V.D.; Matthew Zemel, S.V.D.

Divine Word Theologate. Major Seminary of the Chicago Province. 5342 S. University Ave., Chicago, 60615. Tel: 773-288-2777; Fax: 773-288-6307. Rev. Mark Weber, S.V.D., Rector. Staff: Revs. Roger Arnold, S.V.D.; Stephen Bevens, S.V.D.; Phelim Jordan, S.V.D.; Timothy Lenchak, S.V.D.; Gary Riebe-Estrella, S.V.D.; Roger Schroeder, S.V.D.; Derek Simons, S.V.D.; Higinio Yescas, S.V.D.

[C] COLLEGES AND UNIVERSITIES

CHICAGO. *De Paul University*, One E. Jackson Blvd., 60604.

For a complete listing, refer to the Colleges and Universities section.

Jesuit Community at Loyola University of Chicago, Jesuit Residence, 6525 N. Sheridan Rd., 60626. Tel: 773-508-8800; Fax: 773-508-2098.

For a complete listing, refer to the Colleges and Universities section.

Loyola University-Chicago, 6525 N. Sheridan Rd., 60626. Tel: 312-274-3000.

For a complete listing, refer to the Colleges and Universities section.

Saint Xavier University, 3700 West 103rd St., 60655. Tel: 773-298-3000.

For a complete listing, refer to the Colleges and Universities section.

Vincentian Community at DePaul University, 2233 N. Kenmore Ave., 60614. Tel: 312-880-2968.

For a complete listing, refer to the Colleges and Universities section.

LAKE FOREST. *Barat College*, 700 Westleigh Rd., 60045. Tel: 708-234-3000.

For a complete listing, refer to the Colleges and Universities section.

RIVER FOREST. *Dominican University (Formerly Rosary*

College), 7900 W. Division St., 60305. Tel: 708-366-2490.
For a complete listing, refer to the Colleges and Universities section.

[D] HIGH SCHOOLS, PRIVATE

CHICAGO. *Academy of Our Lady,* 1309 W. 95th St., 60643. Tel: 312-445-2300. Legal Title: *Academy of Our Lady.* A Day School (Girls). School Sisters of Notre Dame. Mrs. Trudy L. Hunter, Prin. Sisters 1; Lay Teachers 18; Students 308.

Brother Rice High School, 10001 S. Pulaski Rd., 60655-3356. Tel: 773-779-3410. Congregation of Christian Brothers. Bro. Daniel J. Casey, C.F.C., Prin. Brothers 15; Lay Teachers 67; Students 1,425.

Cristo Rey Jesuit High School, Inc., 1852 W. Cermak Rd., 60608. Tel: 312-523-6800. Rev. John P. Foley, S.J., Pres.; Sr. Judith Murphy, O.S.B., Prin. Priests 1; Sisters 1; Brothers 1; Lay Teachers 8; Students 150.

Cristo Rey Work/Study Program, Inc., 1852 W. Cermak Rd., 60608. Tel: 312-523-6800. Preston Kendall, Dir.

De La Salle High School, 3455 S. Wabash Ave., 60616. Tel: 312-842-7355. Legal Title: *De La Salle Institute.* Brothers of the Christian Schools. Bro. Michael Quirk, F.S.C., Pres.; Dr. James M. Gay, Prin. Brothers 6; Sisters 1; Lay Teachers 55; Students 975.

Good Counsel High School, Inc., 3900 Peterson Ave., 60659. Tel: 773-478-3655. Legal Title: *Good Counsel High School, Inc.* Day School. Sr. Beatrice Knipple, C.S.S.F., Prin. Sisters 14; Lay Teachers 54; Students 679.

Gordon Technical High School, 3633 N. California Ave., 60618. Tel: 773-539-3600. Bro. William Hallas, C.R., Pres.; Mr. Casimir Kozlik, Prin.; Revs. Marion Gienko, C.R.; Joseph J. Glab, C.R.; Edward J. Jaskula, C.R.; Stephen Juda, C.R.; Thomas Kubik, C.R.; Joseph Malczyk, C.R.; Chester Norkiewicz, C.R.; Aloysius M. Orzechowski, C.R.; Paul Sims, C.R., Supr.; John Stephen, C.R.; Donald Zinn, C.R. Priests 10; Brothers 2; Lay Teachers 49; Students 850.

**Hales Franciscan High School, Inc.,* 4930 Cottage Grove Ave., 60615. Tel: 773-285-8400. Mr. Timothy King, Pres.; Mr. Thomas Calhoun, V.P. of Academic Affairs; Revs. John Paul Cafiero, O.F.M., Head of Counseling Dept.; Phil D. Hogan, O.F.M., Campus Minister; David Rodriguez, O.F.M., Guardian. Priests 5; Brothers 3; Lay Teachers 20; Students 350.

Holy Spirit Friary. Revs. Charles E. Payne, O.F.M., Ph.D.; Thomas Nairn, O.F.M.; Salvador Valdez, O.F.M.

Holy Trinity High School, 1443 W. Division St., 60622. Tel: 312-278-4212. Brothers of Holy Cross. Bro. Philip R. Smith, C.S.C. Priests 1; Brothers 5; Sisters 6; Lay Teachers 40; Students 470.

Josephinum High School, 1501 N. Oakley Blvd., 60622. Tel: 773-276-1261. Legal Title: *Josephinum High School, Inc.* Fully accredited high school. Lay Teachers 21; Girls 253.

Leo High School, 7901 S. Sangamon, 60620. Tel: 312-224-9600. Mr. Robert W. Foster, Prin. Boys 200.

Lourdes High School, 4034 W. 56th St., 60629. Tel: 773-581-2555; Fax: 773-581-9358. Sisters of St. Joseph, Third Order of St. Francis. Ms. Mary Iannucilli, Prin. Sisters 7; Lay Teachers 35; Students 542.

Madonna High School, 4055 W. Belmont, 60641. Tel: 312-282-2552. Franciscan Sisters of Chicago. Sr. Carol Marie Schommer, O.S.F., Prin. Priests 1; Sisters 6; Lay Teachers 22; Students 350.

Maria High School. (Formerly St. Casimir Academy), 6727 S. California Ave., 60629. Tel: 312-925-8686; Fax: 312-925-8885. Sisters of St. Casimir. Local Coordinators: Sr. M. Georgine; Sr. Helene Chernesky; Sr. M. Reginald; Sr. Zalot Margaret, Pres.; Mrs. Barbara McKee, Prin.; Rev. George A. Slominski, Chap. Sisters 14; Lay Teachers 59; Students 820.

Marist High School, 4200 W. 115th St., 60655-4397. Tel: 773-881-6360. Marist Brothers. Tel: 773-881-5300. Bro. Hank Hammer, F.M.S. Brothers 14; Sisters 4; Priests 1; Lay Teachers 69; Students 1,435.

Mother McAuley Liberal Arts High School, 3737 W. 99th St., 60642. Tel: 773-881-6500. Sisters of Mercy. Sr. Corinne Raven, R.S.M. Sisters 11; Lay Teachers 108; Students 1,995.

Mt. Carmel High School, 6410 S. Dante Ave., 60637. Tel: 773-324-1020; Fax: 773-324-9235. Res., 6401 S. Harper Ave., 60638. Carmelite Fathers. Revs. Carl J. Markelz, O.Carm., Prin.; John Knoernschild, O.Carm.; Daniel Carroll, O.Carm.; Glen Snow, O.Carm.; Leander Troy, O.Carm.; George L. O'Keefe, O.Carm.; Bro. Timothy Sklopan, O.Carm., Prior. Priests 8; Brothers 1; Lay Teachers 40; Students 770.

Notre Dame High School, 3000 N. Mango Ave., 60634. Tel: 773-622-9494. Sisters of Notre Dame de Namur. Sr. Mary Bridget Murphy, Pres.; Mrs. Judy Schutter, Prin. Sisters 4; Lay Teachers 47; Girls 675.

Resurrection High School, 7500 W. Talcott Ave., 60631. Tel: 773-775-6616; Fax: 773-775-0611. Sisters of the Resurrection. Ms. Therese M. Fenney, Prin. Sisters 4; Lay Teachers 51; Girls 910.

St. Francis de Sales High School, 10155 S. Ewing Ave., 60617. Tel: 312-773-7272. Mr. Walter Schultz, Prin. Sisters 1; Priests 1; Lay Teachers 30; Students 500.

St. Ignatius College Prep, 1076 W. Roosevelt Rd., 60608-1594. Tel: 312-421-5900; Fax: 312-829-5846. Rev. Donald F. Rowe, S.J., Pres.; Dr. James Lalley, Prin.; Revs. Joseph T. Brennan, S.J.; George R. Menke, S.J.; Robert C. Thul, S.J.; Gerald Walling, S.J. Priests 5; Sisters 2; Lay Teachers 93; Students 1,269.

St. Ignatius Jesuit Community, 1025 W. Taylor, 60607. Tel: 312-829-2297; Fax: 312-829-9552. Revs. Joseph T. Brennan, S.J., Rector; Louis E. Busemeyer, S.J.; M. Joseph Casey, S.J.; James C.L. Arimond, S.J.; Michael D. Class, S.J.; John P. Coakley, S.J.; James J. Creighton, S.J.; Francis J. Daly, S.J.; John M. Dennis, S.J.; Matthew T. Gamber, S.J.; Phillip J. Grib, S.J.; John H. Lane, S.J.; William O. Madden, S.J.; George R. Menke, S.J.; Bradley M. Schaeffer, S.J.; Robert C. Thul, S.J.; Richard J. Vogt, S.J.; James F. Vorwoldt, S.J.; George A. Wallenhorst, S.J.; Bro. Anthony R. Kreutzjans, S.J.

St. Martin de Porres Academy, 250 E. 111th St., 60628. Tel: 312-995-3700. Sr. Ann M. Welch, R.S.M. Sisters 3; Lay Teachers 19; Students 355.

St. Patrick High School, 5900 W. Belmont Ave., 60634. Tel: 773-282-8844; Fax: 773-282-2361. Legal Title: *St. Patrick High School.* Brothers of the Christian Schools. Bro. Konrad Diebold, F.S.C., Pres.; Dr. Joseph Schmidt, Prin.; Mr. Charles Schmidt, Asst. Prin. Brothers 4; Lay Teachers 56; Students 904.

St. Rita High School. (See separate listing for residence information), 7740 S. Western Ave., 60620. Tel: 773-925-6600. Rev. Michael J. O'Connor, O.S.A., Pres.; Mr. Joseph F. Bamberger, Prin.; Rev. Edward Andrews, O.S.A., Prior; Mr. James F. Segredo, Vice Pres. Priests 7; Sisters 1; Brothers 1; Lay Teachers 39; Students 698.

St. Scholastica Academy, 7416 N. Ridge Blvd., 60645. Tel: 773-764-5715. Sr. Judith Zonsius, O.S.B., Prin. Sisters 8; Lay Teachers 27; Students 291.

Convent, 7430 N. Ridge Blvd., 60645.

Weber High School, 5252 W. Palmer St., 60639. Tel: 312-637-7500. Faculty Res., 2250 N. Latrobe Ave., 60639. Tel: 312-622-0477. Conducted by the Fathers and Brothers of the Congregation of the Resurrection. Very Rev. Richard P. Balazs, C.R., Prov. Supr.; Revs. Fred Ciesla, C.R.; Jerome Andracki, C.R.; Steve Bartczyszyn, C.R.; John Nowak, C.R., Supr.; Henry Blaski, C.R.; Joseph Przysucha, C.R.; Adolph Istok, C.R.; Bro. Edward Jaszkowski, C.R.; Revs. Leonard Krzywda; Joseph Korabik, C.R.; Mitchell Pawelko, C.R.; Frank Majewicz, C.R.; Charles Mrowinski, C.R.; Francis Rog, C.R.; Jerome Twarog, C.R.; Gary Young, C.R. Priests 8; Brothers 1; Lay Teachers 42; Students 565.

ARLINGTON HEIGHTS. *St. Viator High School,* 1213 E. Oakton St., 60004. Tel: 708-392-4050; Fax: 708-392-4101. Clerics of St. Viator. Revs. Charles G. Bolser, C.S.V., Pres.; George G. Harris, C.S.V.; Arnold E. Perham, C.S.V.; John E. VanWiel, C.S.V.; Bros. Robert Ruhl, C.S.V.; Brian Cooper, C.S.V.; Michael Rice, C.S.V. Priests 4; Brothers 3; Lay Teachers 53; Students 813.

BURBANK. *Queen of Peace High School.* (Girls). 7659 S. Linder Ave., 60459. Tel: 708-458-7600. Ms. Patricia Nolan Fitzgerald, Prin. Sisters 5; Lay Teachers 89; Students 1,556.

St. Laurence High School, Inc., 5556 W. 77th St., 60459. Tel: 708-458-6900. Congregation of Christian Brothers. Mr. Thomas J. Ondrla, Prin. Priests 1; Brothers 9; Lay Teachers 48; Students 975.

CHICAGO HEIGHTS. *Marian Catholic High School,* 700 Ashland Ave., 60411. Tel: 708-755-7565; Fax: 708-755-0042. Dominican Sisters (Springfield, IL). Sr. M. Paul McCaughey, O.P., Prin. Sisters 17; Lay Teachers 70; Students 1,536.

LAKE FOREST. *Woodlands Academy of the Sacred Heart,* 760 E. Westleigh Rd., 60045-3298. Tel: 708-234-4300. Religious of Sacred Heart. Sr. Claude Demoustier, R.S.C.J., Prin. Sisters 1; Lay Teachers 27; Students 191.

LEMONT. *Mt. Assisi Academy for Girls,* 13860 Main St., 60439. Tel: 708-257-7844; Fax: 708-257-6362. Sisters of St. Francis of Christ the King. Sr. Paula Nasanbneny, O.S.F., Prin. Sisters 12; Lay Teachers 38; Students 365.

MUNDELEIN. *Carmel High School,* One Carmel Pkwy., 60060. Tel: 708-566-3000; Fax: 708-566-8465. Revs. William J. Harry, O.Carm., Pres.; Robert Carroll, O.Carm., Prin. Priests 3; Sisters 4; Brothers 1; Lay Teachers 68; Students 1,280.

NILES. *Notre Dame High School.* (Boys), 7655 Dempster St., 60648. Tel: 708-965-2900; Fax: 708-965-2975. Revs. Kenneth Molinaro, C.S.C., Prin.; Jerome Esper, C.S.C.; Mr. John Ziebell, Dir. Devel.; Mr. Steven Zeier, Asst. Prin. Academics; Mr. Michael Hennessey, Asst. Prin. Student Life; Mr. James Boylan, Dean of Men; Bro. Patrick Lynch, C.S.C., Finance Officer; Mrs. Donna Cassidy, Dir. Guidance; Mr. Michael Hennessey, Dir. Athletics; Revs. William Brinker, C.S.C., (Retired); Jerome Esper, C.S.C.; Christopher A. Kuhn, C.S.C.; Norbert Hess, C.S.C., (Retired); Randall Rentner, C.S.C.; Bro. Patrick Lynch, C.S.C. Priests 5; Retired Priests 2; Brothers 1; Sisters 2; Lay Teachers 40; Students 666.

OAK PARK. *Fenwick High School,* 505 Washington Blvd., 60302. Tel: 708-386-0127. Dominican Order. Revs. Daniel C. Davis, O.P., Pres.; William J. Bernacki, O.P.; Malachy R. Dooley, O.P.; Joseph Ekpo; John M. Gambro, O.P.; Clinton P. Honkomp, O.P.; Joseph I. Hren, O.P.; Kevin Niehoff, O.P.; Bro. Gabriel J. Dault, O.P.; Sr. Mary Nugent, O.P.; Sr. Louise J. Brogacz, O.P. Priests 7; Brothers 1; Sisters 2; Lay Teachers 66; Students 1,106.

RIVER FOREST. *Trinity High School,* 7574 W. Division St., 60305. Tel: 708-771-8383. Dominican Sisters (Sinsinawa, WI). Sr. Michelle Germanson, O.P., Pres.; Sr. Jeanne Bessette, O.S.F., Prin. Sisters 5; Lay Teachers 40; Students 491.

RIVER GROVE. *Holy Cross High School,* 3000-80th, 60171. Tel: 708-456-5110. Brothers of Holy Cross. Bros. Robert L. Brown, Pres.; Donald Fleischhacker, C.S.C., Dir. Brothers 10; Lay Teachers 32; Students 500.

Mother Theodore Guerin High School, 8001 Belmont Ave., 60171. Tel: 312-625-3278; Fax: 708-453-6296. Sisters of Providence. Sr. Cathy Campbell, S.P., Pres.; Sr. Jeanette Hagelskamp, S.P., Prin. Sisters 18; Lay Teachers 53; Students 810.

SOUTH HOLLAND. *Seton Academy,* 16100 Seton Rd., 60473-1899. Tel: 708-333-6300. Sisters 1; Lay Teachers 24; Students 400.

WESTCHESTER. *Immaculate Heart of Mary High School,* 10900 W. Cermak Rd., 60154. Tel: 708-562-3115. Sisters, Servants of the Immaculate Heart of Mary. Catherine A. Karl, Ph.D., Prin. Sisters 3; Lay Teachers 36; Students 600.

St. Joseph High School, 1840 Mayfair, 60154-4299. Tel: 708-562-4433. Brothers of the Christian Schools. Mr. Charles J. Lynch, Jr., Pres.; Mr. David L. Hotek, Prin.; Mr. Thomas Reif, Asst. Prin. Brothers 3; Lay Teachers 45; Students 530.

WILMETTE. *Loyola Academy,* 1100 N. Laramie Ave., 60091. Tel: 708-256-1100; Fax: 708-251-4031. Revs. Raymond J. Callahan, S.J., Pres.; Norman E. Harland, S.J., Rector; Dr. Bernard L. Bouillette, Headmaster; Mr. William A. Graf, Athletic Dir.; Mr. John E. Hoerster, Dir. Admissions; Dr. Lorraine Ozar, Academic Dean; Mr. Kenneth Maziarka, Dean of Students; Mr. Karl J. Costello, Asst. Dean of Students; Mr. John P. Brady, Business Mgr.; Revs. Mark W. Andrews, S.J.; John V. Moorman, S.J.; Robert G. Humbert, S.J.; Raymond A. Dunne, S.J.; Bros. James W. Small, S.J.; David L. Henderson, S.J.; Robert J. Schneider, S.J.; Rev. Robert A. Ytsen, S.J. Priests 7; Sisters 5; Brothers 3; Lay Teachers 131; Students 1,925.

Regina Dominican High School, 701 Locust Rd., 60091. Tel: 847-256-7660; Fax: 847-256-3726. Sisters of St. Dominic (Adrian, MI). Sr. Carol Fleming, O.P., Pres.; Sr. Marilee Ewing, O.P., Prin. Sisters 14; Lay Teachers 33; Students 468. Sisters 14; Lay Teachers 33; Students 468.

[E] ELEMENTARY SCHOOLS, PRIVATE

CHICAGO. *Sacred Heart Schools (Academy of the Sacred Heart for Girls, Hardey Prep. for Boys).* (Grades K-8), 6250 N. Sheridan Rd., 60660. Tel: 312-262-4446. Religious of the Sacred Heart. Sr. Carol Campbell, R.S.C.J., Dir. of Schools; Mrs. Janet Underwood, Head of Schools. Sisters 2; Lay Teachers 45; Students 354.

[F] CONSOLIDATED ELEMENTARY SCHOOLS

CHICAGO. *Bridgeport Catholic Academy,* Admin. Office, 1040 W. 32nd Pl., 60608. Tel: 312-376-0142. Nona Barrientos, Prin.
Serving the following parishes: All Saints-St. Anthony (518 W. 28th Pl.); St. Mary of Perpetual Help (1039 W. 32nd St.); Nativity of Our Lord (653 W. 37th St.). Lay Teachers 24; Students 400.

[G] CATHOLIC CHARITIES

CHICAGO. *Catholic Charities of the Archdiocese of Chicago-Archdiocesan Offices,* 126 N. Desplaines St., 60661. Tel: 312-655-7000. Administers charitable activities of the Archdiocese. Rev. Michael M. Boland, Admin.; Mr. Jimmy M. Lago, Assoc. Exec. Dir.; Rev. Charles T. Rubey, Dir.-Programs. Assoc. Admins.: Revs. Roger J. Coughlin; Richard E. Bulwith; Daniel C. Jankowski; Daniel M. Holihan;

James M. Ray; Francis A. Cimarrusti; Most Rev. Edwin M. Conway, Consultant; Rev. Msgr. Vincent W. Cooke, Consultant.
Office of Annual and Deferred Giving. Tel: 312-655-7003. Ms. Christine Kenny-Sheputis, Dept. Dir.
Dept. of Communications. Tel: 312-655-7024. Mr. William J. Sullivan, Jr., Dir.
Office of Board Relations and Major Events. Tel: 312-655-7768. Mr. Brian Wileym, Dir.
Office of Major Gifts. Tel: 312-655-7394. Mr. John O'Connell, Dir.
Financial Services, 721 N. LaSalle, 60610. Ms. Cynthia Smetana, Dir. of Finance.
Division of Family and Parish Support Services. Tel: 312-655-7136. Ms. Ellen E. Gorney, Div. Mgr.
Central Information and Referral Services. Tel: 312-655-7700. Ms. Kathleen Donahue, Dept. Dir.
Emergency Assistance Program, 121 W. Superior St., 60610. Tel: 312-665-7500. Ms. Christene Dykes, Program Dir.
Southeast Chicago Information and Referral Services, 10160 Avenue J, 60617. Tel: 773-768-2850.
Northwest Suburban Family Shelter, c/o 1911 Rohlwing Rd., Ste. E, Rolling Meadows, 60008. Tel: 708-870-0560.
Dept. of Family and Aging Services. Tel: 312-655-7153. Ms. Veronica Glodowski, Dept. Dir.
Archdiocesan AIDS Ministry Office. Tel: 312-655-7294. Mrs. Marianne Zelewsky, Dir.
Specialized Mental Health Services Network. Tel: 312-655-7298. Dr. Angela Chemazar, Assoc. Div. Mgr.
Holbrook Center for Counseling and Psychotherapy, 721 N. LaSalle, 60610. Tel: 312-655-7550. Ms. Dorothy Auw, Dept. Dir.
Community Family Service Center, 2189 W. Bowler, 60612. Tel: 312-733-5661. Ms. Sigrid Brooks, Prog. Dir.
Immigration & Naturalization Services and Refuge Resettlement Program, 126 N. Desplaines St., 60661. Tel: 312-655-7359. Mr. J. Zeferino Ochoa, Dept. Dir.
LOSS (Loving Outreach to Survivors of Suicide). Tel: 312-655-7283. Ms. Laina Lurito, Prog. Dir.
Parish Social Ministry Consultation Services, 721 N. La Salle, 60610. Tel: 312-655-7403. Ms. Betty Siuba, Dept. Dir.
Transitional Shelter Program for Families and Individuals, 126 N. Desplaines St., 60661. Tel: 312-655-7268. Ms. Mildred Lincoln, Dept. Dir.
Assumption B.V.M. Family Shelter, 12242 S. Parnell, 60628.
St. Francis de Paula Hospitality House, 7811 S. Ellis, 60619.
St. Sylvester Family Shelter, 2915 W. Palmer St., 60647.
St. Susanna Family Shelter, 14926 S. Honore, Harvey, 60426.
Sousa Transitional Shelter & Sousa Support Center.
Sousa Overnight Shelter, 7000 S. Aberdeen, 60621. Tel: 773-874-4161. Mr. Samuel Porter, Supr. Tel: 312-874-4400.
Cooke's Manor Transitional Housing For Men, 124 N. Sangamon, 60607. Tel: 312-997-2756. Rev. Richard E. Bulwith, Dept. Dir.
Pioneer House, 3909 N. Bell, 60618.
Forever Free-Women's Wholistic Recovery Home, 4539 S. Wells St., 60609. Tel: 773-548-9500. Ms. Josephine Abi-Rached, Prog. Dir.
Forever Free Phase II-Transitional Housing For Women, 7021 S. May St., 60621. Tel: 312-224-3232. Ms. Josephine Abi-Rached, Prog. Dir.
Society of St. Vincent De Paul of Chicago, 645 W. Randolph St., 60661. Tel: 312-655-7181. Mrs. Claudia Pieske, Pres.; Rev. Thomas A. Grace, C.M., Exec. Dir.; Mr. William Dolan, Budget Dir.; Revs. Michael M. Boland, Spiritual Advisor; Michael Zoufal, Asst. Spiritual Advisor; Mr. Patrick Gaughen, Pres. District Council I; Mr. Donald Walsh, Pres. District Council III; Mr. John Winter, Pres. District Council IV; Mr. Ben Gallardo, Pres. District Council VII; Mr. John Hovorka, Pres. District Council VIII; Mr. Richard Kress, Pres. District Council IX; Mrs. John Rosenthal, Pres. District Council X; Ms. Rose Reynaud, Pres. District Council XI; Mrs. Bernice O'Leske, Pres. District Council XII; Mr. Richard Kress, Regional Coord.; Ms. Janet Deckenbach, Regional Coord.; Mrs. Kathy Keith, Youth Coord.; Mr. Thomas Van Wazer, Disaster Chm. & Coord.; Mrs. Mary Van Wazer, Advocate and Elder Care Coord.; Mr. Edward Bara, Sr., Ozanam Cause Coord.; Deacon John Perkowitz, Funding & Twinning Coord.-Asst. to Pres.; Mr. Karl Gawlas, Treas.; Mrs. Barbara Collins, ADC Sec.; Mrs. Marge Walsh, Gen. Mgr.
Stores & Warehouse Operation.
St. Stanislaus Kostka Soup Kitchen, 1351 W. Evergreen, 60622. Tel: 773-278-2470. Sr. Ann Schaffer, Dir.
Pathways (Employee Assistance Program), 721 N. La Salle, 60610. Tel: 312-266-7550. Ms. Dorothy Auw, Dept. Dir.
Cara Program (Supportive Housing Services). Tel: 312-655-7003. Ms. Anne Marie Crowe, Prog. Dir.
Lake County Services, 1 N. Genessee St., Ste. 203, Waukegan, 60085. Tel: 847-249-3500. Ms. Mary Clare Jakes, Assoc. Div. Mgr., Community Casework Services, 1 N. Genessee St., Ste. 203, Waukegan, 60085. Tel: 847-249-3500. Ms. Maureen Murphy, Prog. Dir.
Samaritan House, 601 Tenth St., North Chicago, 60064. Tel: 847-689-1414. Ms. Patricia Lynch, Supr.
Consumer Credit Counseling Services, 1 N. Genesee St., Ste. 205, Waukegan, 60085. Tel: 847-249-3500. Ms. Charlene Foster, Supr.
Regional Services Dept., 1911 Rohlwing Rd., Ste. E, Rolling Meadows, 60008. Tel: 847-870-0560. Mr. Stephen O'Brien-Combs, Assoc. Div. Mgr., Cicero: West Suburban Services, 1400 S. Austin Blvd., Cicero, 60804. Tel: 708-222-1491. Calumet Park: South Suburban Services, 12420 S. Ada, Calumet Park, 60643. Tel: 708-388-0743. Chicago Southside Services Regional Office, 7020 S. Aberdeen St., 60621. Tel: 773-488-8028. Southwest Suburban Services, 10661 Roberts Rd., Palos Hills, 60465. Tel: 708-430-0428. North Suburban Services, 1700 E. Lake St., Room 207, Glenview, 60025. Tel: 847-657-0946. Physician Referral Service, 1911 Rohlwing Rd., Ste. E, Rolling Meadows, 60008. Tel: 847-870-0202. Ms. Karen Kordisch, Prog. Dir.
Division of Non-Residential Services for Children and Youth for Cook and Lake Counties, 641 W. Lake St., Ste. 306, 60661. Tel: 312-655-7097. Mr. Everett T. Petlicki, Div. Mgr.; Mr. Jadonal Ford, Sr. Assoc. Div. Mgr. Tel: 312-655-7100.
Child Protective Services, 901 W. Jackson, 60607. Tel: 312-382-2521. One N. Genesee St., Waukegan, 60085. Tel: 847-249-3500. Linda Gee, Dept. Dir.
Family Based Services, 916 N. Western Ave., 60622. Tel: 312-655-7601. Patricia Green, Dept. Dir.
Maternity/Adoption Services, 651 W. Lake St., 60661. Tel: 312-655-7076. Miss Ann Abrams, Dept. Dir.
Madonna/Saint Joseph Center, 1114 W. Grace St., 60613. Tel: 773-472-3343. Ms. Sally Heyneman, Prog. Admin.
Roseland Adolescent Parent Program, 10809 S. State St., 60628. Tel: 773-995-1737. Velma Brown-Walker, Dept. Dir.
Children & Adolescent Parent Program, 721 N. La Salle, 60610. Tel: 312-655-7848. Sandra Braine, Dept. Dir.
Teen Parent Initative Program, 3040 W. Walnut St., 60612. Tel: 773-826-0506. Ms. Catarina Williamson, Supvr.; Ms. Sandra Braine, Program Dir.
Arts of Living-Core Program, 721 N. La Salle, 60610. Tel: 312-655-7388. Ms. Patricia Canessa, Dept. Dir.
Relative Family Care Services, 901 W. Jackson, 60607. Tel: 312-655-7646. Ms. Sylvia Flory, Assoc. Div. Mgr.
Traditional and Specialized Foster Care Services, 651 W. Lake St., 60661. Tel: 312-655-7250. Mr. George Thibeault, Assoc. Div. Mgr.
Div. of Residential Child-Adult Care Services. Tel: 312-655-7289. Ms. Michelle A. Arnold, Div. Mgr.
Division of Community Development Services, 721 N. La Salle, 60610. Tel: 312-655-7474. Mr. Walter H. Ousley, Div. Mgr.; Ms. Michele Bianchi, Assoc. Div. Mgr. Tel: 312-655-7538; Mr. Dennis McSwain, Assoc. Div. Mgr. Tel: 312-655-7482; Mr. Richard Klemundt, Assoc. Div. Mgr. Tel: 312-655-7568.
Addiction Consultation and Educational Services, 721 N. La Salle, 60610. Tel: 312-655-7450. Ms. Mary Ellen Flynn, Prog. Dir.
Central States Institute for Addiction, 120 W. Huron St., 60610. Tel: 312-655-7540. Mr. Anthony Rizzato, Dept. Dir.
Disruptive Behavior Intervention. Tel: 312-655-7474. Bro. William Tomes, Consultant.
El Centro Drop-In Center, 1545 W. 18th St., 60608. Tel: 312-733-7006. Mr. Richard Martinez, Program Dir.
Respond Now, 1439 Emerald Ave., P.O. Box 215, 60411. Tel: 708-755-4357. Mr. Dennis Condon, Prog. Dir.
Keen Ager News, 721 N. La Salle, 60610. Tel: 312-655-7425. Ms. Yolanda Roman, Editor.
Mother and Child Food and Nurtition Program, 721 N. La Salle, 60610. Tel: 312-655-7484. Mr. Aldo Pedrosa, Dir. Legal Title: *Mother and Child Food Nutrition Program & Temporary Emergency Food Assistance Program and Commodity Supplemental Food Program.*
Roseland Center, 11013 S. Indiana Ave., 60628.
Westside Center, 1017 N. Cicero Ave., 60651.
WIC Food Centers Program, 721 N. La Salle St., 60610. Tel: 312-655-7480. Mr. Phil Parson, Dir.
WIC Food Centers: 907 N. Larrabee, Chicago, IL 60610; 2907 S. Wabash Ave., Chicago, IL 60616; 416 E. 43rd St., Chicago, IL 60653; 5060 S. State St., Chicago, IL 60609; 6202 S. Halsted St., Chicago, IL 60621; 2310 W. Roosevelt Rd., Chicago, IL 60608; 5332 S. Western, Chicago, IL 60609; 3110 W. Armitage, Chicago, IL 60647; WIC Warehouse: 4500 W. Chicago Ave., Chicago, IL 60651; 5125 W. Chicago Ave., Chicago, Il 60651; 1643 W. Cermak Rd., Chicago, IL 60608; 1734 W. Chicago Ave., Chicago, IL 60622; 3932 W. Madison St., Chicago, IL 60624.
Garfield Alternative High School, 220 W. 45th Pl., 60609. Tel: 773-924-0543. Mr. Oyemola Kale, Prog. Dir.
Employment Services, 5332 S. Western, 60609. Tel: 773-778-2412. Ms. Christine L. Tamani, Prog. Dir.
Day Care Services. Tel: 312-655-7875. Ms. Ethel Barnes, Dept. Dir.
Head Start Services. Tel: 312-655-7896. Mr. Neil Myrie, Dept. Dir.
Day Care Services, 2822 W. Jackson Blvd., 60612. Tel: 312-722-7440. Sr. Yvonne Thranow, D.C., Consultant.
Division of Senior Social Services, 721 N. La Salle Dr., 60610. Tel: 312-655-7572. Wendy S. Thomas, Div. Mgr.
Northeast/Northwest Chicago Case Management Services, 5801 N. Pulaski, Bldg. A, 60646. Tel: 773-583-9224. Sarah Cohen, Dept. Dir.
South Suburban Senior Services and Senior Activity Center, 15300 S. Lexington, Harvey, 60426. Tel: 708-596-2222. Gwen Westley, Dept. Dir.
Lake County Senior Case Management Services, 116 N. Lincoln, Round Lake, 60073. Tel: 847-546-5733. Jan Ahlgrin, Dept. Dir.
Congregate Senior Housing, Maplehurst, 2312 Elisha, Zion, 60099. Tel: 847-872-7527. Frank Phillps, Dept. Dir.
Lake County Senior Community Services & Nutrition Program Site, 414 S. Lewis Ave., Waukegan, 60085. Tel: 847-662-0085. Frank Phillips, Dept. Dir., Antioch Area Center, 817 Holbeck St., Antioch, 60002. Tel: 847-395-7120. Mr. Paul Howard, Ctr. Dir., Ela Township Area Center, 95 E. Main St., Lake Zurich, 60047. Tel: 847-438-0303. Mr. Rusty Miller, Ctr. Dir., Libertyville Civic Center, 135 W. Church St., Libertyville, 60048. Tel: 847-367-8210. Ms. Lois Pacente, Ctr. Dir.
Lake County Nutrition Programs for Seniors. Round Lake Senior Center, 814 Hart Rd., Round Lake, 60073. Tel: 847-546-0056. Fox Lake Community Senior Center, 79 E. Keystone, Fox Lake, 60020. Tel: 847-587-3335.
Northwest Suburban Senior Services, 306 W. Park St., Arlington Heights, 60005. Tel: 847-253-5500. Ms. Cindy Gunderson, Prog. Dir.
Cook County Senior Community Services, 6414 S. Halsted, 60621. Tel: 773-994-8923. Ms. Barbara Carlo, Dept. Dir.
De Sales Senior Center, 10160 Ave. J, 60617. Tel: 773-768-2850. Ms. Carole Kozak, Prog. Dir.
Ada S. Niles Senior Center and Adult Day Care Services, 6412-14 S. Halsted St., 60621. Tel: 773-874-2400. Ms. Denise King, Senior Ctr. Dir.; Ms. Norma Nalls, Day Care Senior Center Supvr.
Senior Aides Employment Program. Tel: 773-874-2400. Mr. Victor Dodd, Supr.
St. Joseph Center, 7240 W. 57th St., Summit, 60501. Tel: 708-458-0501. Mr. Henry Lambke, Ctr. Dir.
Catholic Home Care, Inc., 721 N. La Salle St., 60610. Tel: 312-655-7415. Ms. Anne Demke, R.N., Dept. Dir.
Division of Senior Residential Services, 721 N. LaSalle, 60610. Tel: 312-655-7492. Mr. William D'Arcy, Div. Mgr.
Bethlehem Woods Retirement Living Center, 1571 W. Ogden Ave., LaGrange Park, 60525.
Casa San Carlo, 420 N. Wolf Rd., Northlake, 60164.
Cortland Manor, 1900 N. Karlov, 60639.
Hayes Manor, 1211 W. Marquette Rd., 60636.
Matthew Manor, 271 N. Albany Ave., 60612.
Roseland Manor, 11717 S. State St., 60628.
St. Brendan Apartments, 6715 S. Elizabeth, 60636.
St. Theodore Apartments, 6209 S. Paulina, 60636.
Tolton Manor, 6345 S. Stewart, 60621.
Catholic Charities Housing Development Corp., 721 N. LaSalle St., 60610. Tel: 312-655-7975. Mr. Lawrence Prozek, Assoc. Div. Mgr.
Under Development: Frances Manor, Lawrence Manor, Casimir Apartments Bernardin Manor and St. Ailbe Manor.
Human Resources. Tel: 312-655-7115. Ms. Violet Sabo, Dir.
Facilities Operations. Tel: 312-655-7104. Mr. Richard Whalen, Dept. Dir.
Governmental Relations, 721 N. La Salle, 60610. Tel: 312-655-7314. Ms. Laurie Barretto, Dept. Dir.
Research and Planning Services, 721 N. La Salle, 60610. Tel: 312-655-7492. Ms. Jean Welter, Dept. Dir.
Mission of the Holy Cross, 126 N. Deplaines St., 60606. Tel: 312-655-7460. Rev. Michael M. Boland.

Catholic Charities Activity Center, 6250 N. Winchester, 60659. Tel: 312-508-7203. Mr. Ed Collins, Prog. Dir.

[H] RESIDENTIAL CHILD-YOUTH CARE

CHICAGO. *Mission of Our Lady of Mercy-Mercy Home for Boys and Girls*, 1140 W. Jackson Blvd., 60607. Tel: 312-738-7560. Revs. James J. Close, Pres.; L. Scott Donahue, Assoc. Pres.; Maureen Meter, Chief Admin. Officer; Theresa Gossman, Exec. Vice Pres. Youth Prog.; Mark Mroz, Exec. Vice Pres. Communications; Mark Teresi, Exec. Vice Pres. Devel.; Sr. Mary Hrovat, O.P., Asst. to Pres.; Rob Gaskill, The Mission Press. Staff 63; Full Time Religious 7; Youths 221.

DES PLAINES. *Maryville Academy*, 1150 N. River Rd., 60016. Tel: 708-824-6126. Legal Title: *Maryville Academy*. Rev. John P. Smyth, Exec. Dir. Students 273.

[I] DAY NURSERIES, SETTLEMENTS AND SOCIAL CENTERS

CHICAGO. *Cordi-Marian Center*, 1100 S. May St., 60607. Tel: 312-666-3787. Cordi-Marian Missionary Sisters. Sr. M. Theresa Alonso, M.C.M., Supr. Sisters 5; People under care 1,061; Day Care capacity 358.

Marillac Social Center, 2822 W. Jackson Blvd., 60612. Tel: 773-722-7440. Sr. Yvonne Thranow, D.C., Exec. Dir. Day care for children ages 2 1/2 to 12 years; Recreation programs for ages 6 to 25 years; emergency assistance food and clothing for poor families; day shelter for the homeless; child abuse and neglect treatment; counselling services; programs for pregnant & parenting teens and their babies; home bound elderly; services for teenage mothers. Day Care capacity 422.

Resurrection Day Care Center, 1849 N. Hermitage Ave., 60622. Tel: 773-384-7142. Sisters of the Resurrection. Sr. M. Paulette Pieta, C.R., Supr. and Admin. Sisters 4; Daily Attendance 30 Children.

St. Rose Center, 4911 S. Hoyne, 60609. Tel: 773-436-1433. Sr. Marcellina Erne, D.S.M.P., Admin. Day school and workshop for mentally handicapped children. Sisters 2; Lay Teachers 3; Classroom Aides 6; Therapists 3; Capacity 60.

St. Vincent de Paul Center, 2145 N. Halsted St., 60614. Tel: 312-943-6776. Sr. Cathrine Mary Norris, D.C., Admin. Day care for children 4 mos. to 11 yrs.; family social services; therapeutic program for child abuse referred families. Daughters of Charity 5; Capacity 451. Provides youth and adult recreational and athletic programs for ages 9 years through adult. Individual registration 468. Provides recreational and supportive programming for senior citizens. Individual registration 349.

**San Miguel Center, Inc.* Operated by DeLaSalle Christian Brothers and Secular Franciscans. Free Catholic Middle School for at risk youth; Adult education (ESL, GED & Job Training); after school and evening youth programs, ages 11-21; emergency assistance with food, clothing and housing. 1949 W. 48th St., 60609. Tel: 773-890-0233. Officers: Gene Downs, Officer; Sandra Downs; Bros. Gordon Hannon, F.S.C.; Ed Siderewicz, F.S.C. Total Staff 12; Total Assisted 500.

**The Port*. A Franciscan outreach of the Assumption of the Blessed Virgin Mary Province, Pulaski, WI. Soup Kitchen, food pantry, overnight shelters (men, women & family), GED, ESL, family services. 5013 S. Hermitage Ave., 60609. Tel: 773-778-5955. Rev. Augustin Milon, O.F.M., Founder & Pres. Total Staff 10; Total Assisted 3,000.

[J] HOSPITALS

CHICAGO. *Columbus Hospital*, 2520 N. Lakeview Ave., 60614.
For a complete listing, refer to the Hospitals section.

Holy Cross Hospital, 2701 W. 68th St., 60629. Tel: 312-471-8000.
For a complete listing, refer to the Hospitals section.

Mercy Hospital and Medical Center, 2525 S. Michigan Ave. Stevenson Expwy. at King Dr., 60616. Tel: 312-567-2100; Fax: 312-567-6575.
For a complete listing, refer to the Hospitals section.

**Our Lady of the Resurrection Medical Center*, 5645 W. Addison, 60634. Tel: 312-282-7000.
For a complete listing, refer to the Hospitals section.

Resurrection Medical Center, 7435 Talcott Ave., 60631. Tel: 773-774-8000.
For a complete listing, refer to the Hospitals section.

St. Anthony Hospital, 2875 W. 19th St., 60623. Tel: 773-521-1710.
For a complete listing, refer to the Hospitals section.

St. Bernard Hospital, 326 W. 64th St., 60621. Tel: 773-962-3900.
For a complete listing, refer to the Hospitals section.

St. Elizabeth's Hospital, 1431 N. Claremont Ave., 60622. Tel: 773-278-2000.
For a complete listing, refer to the Hospitals section.

St. Joseph Hospital, 2900 N. Lake Shore Dr., 60657. Tel: 773-665-3000.
For a complete listing, refer to the Hospitals section.

St. Mary of Nazareth Hospital Center, 2233 W. Division, 60622. Tel: 312-770-2000.
For a complete listing, refer to the Hospitals section.

BLUE ISLAND. *St. Francis Hospital and Health Center*, 12935 S. Gregory St., 60406. Tel: 708-597-2000.
For a complete listing, refer to the Hospitals section.

CHICAGO HEIGHTS. *Alverno Lakeside Corporation*, 1423 Chicago Rd., 60411.
For a complete listing, refer to the Hospitals section.

St. James Hospital and Health Centers, 1423 Chicago Rd., 60411. Tel: 708-756-1000.
For a complete listing, refer to the Hospitals section.

CRESTWOOD. *St. Francis Family Health Center*, 13755 Cicero Ave., 60445.
For a complete listing, refer to the Hospitals section.

DES PLAINES. *Holy Family Medical Center*, 100 N. River Rd., 60016. Tel: 847-297-1800; Fax: 847-297-1863.
For a complete listing, refer to the Hospitals section.

DOLTON. *St. Francis Family Health Center*, 13826 S. Lincoln Ave., 60419.
For a complete listing, refer to the Hospitals section.

ELK GROVE VILLAGE. *Alexian Brothers Medical Center, Inc.*, 800 Biesterfield Rd., 60007-3397. Tel: 708-437-5500.
For a complete listing, refer to the Hospitals section.

EVANSTON. *Saint Francis Hospital of Evanston*, 355 Ridge Ave., 60202. Tel: 708-316-4000.
For a complete listing, refer to the Hospitals section.

EVERGREEN PARK. *Little Company of Mary Hospital and Health Care Centers*, 2800 W. 95th St., 60642. Tel: 708-422-6200; Fax: 708-425-9369.
For a complete listing, refer to the Hospitals section.

MAYWOOD. *Foster G. McGaw Hospital of Loyola University of Chicago*, 2160 S. First Ave., 60153. Tel: 708-216-9056.
For a complete listing, refer to the Hospitals section.

OAK PARK. *Oak Park Hospital*, 520 S. Maple Ave., 60304. Tel: 708-383-9300.
For a complete listing, refer to the Hospitals section.

TINLEY PARK. *St. Francis Family Health Center*, 17148 S. Harlem Ave., 60477.
For a complete listing, refer to the Hospitals section.

WAUKEGAN. *Saint Therese Medical Center*, 2615 Washington St., 60085. Tel: 708-249-3900.
For a complete listing, refer to the Hospitals section.

WORTH. *St. Francis Family Health Center*, 11415 S. Harlem Ave., 60482.
For a complete listing, refer to the Hospitals section.

[K] HEALTH CARE CENTERS

CHICAGO. *St. Basil Health Service - Free People's Clinic*, 1850 W. Garfield, 60609. Tel: 773-436-6496.
For a complete listing, refer to the Hospitals section.

[L] PROTECTIVE INSTITUTIONS

CHICAGO. *Big Sisters*, 203 N. Wabash Ave., 60601. Tel: 312-346-0075.
For a complete listing, refer to the Special Care Facilities section.

House of the Good Shepherd, 1114 W. Grace St., 60613. Tel: 773-935-3434; Fax: 773-935-3523.
For a complete listing, refer to the Special Care Facilities section.

Misericordia Home South, 2916 W. 47th St., 60632. Tel: 773-254-9595.
For a complete listing, refer to the Special Care Facilities section.

Misericordia/Heart of Mercy Center, 6300 N. Ridge, 60660. Tel: 773-973-6300.
For a complete listing, refer to the Special Care Facilities section.

St. Joseph's Carondelet Child Center, 739 E. 35th St., 60616. Tel: 773-624-7443; Fax: 773-624-7676.
For a complete listing, refer to the Special Care Facilities section.

St. Mary of Providence, 4200 N. Austin Ave., 60634. Tel: 773-545-8300; Fax: 773-545-8035.
For a complete listing, refer to the Special Care Facilities section.

BARTLETT. *Bartlett Learning Center*, 801 W. Bartlett Rd., 60103. Tel: 630-289-4221.
For a complete listing, refer to the Special Care Facilities section.

LAKE ZURICH. *Mt. St. Joseph Home*, 24955 North Hwy. 12, 60047. Tel: 847-438-5050; Fax: 847-438-1561.
For a complete listing, refer to the Special Care Facilities section.

OAK PARK. *Ephpheta Center and Hearing Conservation Service*, 119 S. Harvey Ave., 60302.
For a complete listing, refer to the Special Care Facilities section.

PALOS PARK. *St. Coletta's of Illinois*, 123rd and Wolf Rd., 60464. Tel: 708-448-6520.
For a complete listing, refer to the Special Care Facilities section.

[M] SENIOR CARE INSTITUTIONS

CHICAGO. *Cortland Manor Retirement Home*, 1900 N. Karlov, 60639. Tel: 773-235-3670.
For a complete listing, refer to the Special Care Facilities section.

Jugan Terrace, 2300 N. Racine, 60614. Tel: 773-935-9600; Fax: 773-935-4291.
For a complete listing, refer to the Special Care Facilities section.

Little Sisters of the Poor Center for the Aging, 2325 N. Lakewood Ave., 60614. Tel: 773-935-9600; Fax: 773-935-9614.
For a complete listing, refer to the Special Care Facilities section.

Resurrection Retirement Community, 7262 W. Peterson Ave., 60631. Tel: 773-792-7930.
For a complete listing, refer to the Special Care Facilities section.

St. Joseph Home of Chicago, Inc., 2650 N. Ridgeway Ave., 60647. Tel: 773-235-8600; Fax: 773-235-2933.
For a complete listing, refer to the Special Care Facilities section.

DES PLAINES. *Holy Family Health Center*, 2380 Dempster, 60016. Tel: 708-296-3335.
For a complete listing, refer to the Special Care Facilities section.

Nazarethville, 300 N. River Rd., 60016. Tel: 708-297-5900.
For a complete listing, refer to the Special Care Facilities section.

GLENVIEW. *Maryhaven Inc.*, 1700 East Lake Ave., 60025. Tel: 708-729-1300; Fax: 708-729-9202.
For a complete listing, refer to the Special Care Facilities section.

HOMEWOOD. *Mercy Health Care and Rehabilitation Center*, 19000 S. Halsted St., 60430. Tel: 708-957-9200; Fax: 708-799-4787.
For a complete listing, refer to the Special Care Facilities section.

JUSTICE. *Rosary Hill Home*, 9000 W. 81st St., 60458. Tel: 708-458-3040.
For a complete listing, refer to the Special Care Facilities section.

LEMONT. *Alvernia Manor*, 13950 Main St., 60439. Tel: 708-257-7721.
For a complete listing, refer to the Special Care Facilities section.

Holy Family Villa, 12375 McCarthy Rd., 60439.
For a complete listing, refer to the Special Care Facilities section.

Mother Theresa Home, 1270 Franciscan Dr., 60439. Tel: 708-257-5801; Fax: 708-257-1328.
For a complete listing, refer to the Special Care Facilities section.

NILES. *St. Andrew Home for the Aged*, 7000 N. Newark Ave., 60714-4497. Tel: 847-647-8332.
For a complete listing, refer to the Special Care Facilities section.

St. Benedict Home for the Aged, 6930 W. Touhy Ave., 60714. Tel: 847-647-0003.
For a complete listing, refer to the Special Care Facilities section.

NORTHLAKE. *Villa Scalabrini Home for the Aged*, 480 N. Wolf Rd., 60164-1667. Tel: 708-562-0040.
For a complete listing, refer to the Special Care Facilities section.

OLYMPIA FIELDS. *Mercy Residence at Tolentine Center*, 20300 Governors Hwy., 60461. Tel: 708-748-9500; Fax: 708-481-2090.
For a complete listing, refer to the Special Care Facilities section.

PALATINE. *St. Joseph's Home for the Elderly*, 80 W. Northwest Hwy., 60067. Tel: 847-358-5700; Fax: 847-358-5763.
For a complete listing, refer to the Special Care Facilities section.

PARK RIDGE. *Resurrection Nursing and Rehabilitation Center*, 1001 N. Greenwood, 60068. Tel: 708-692-5600; Fax: 708-692-2305.
For a complete listing, refer to the Special Care Facilities section.

WHEELING. *Addolorata Villa, Inc.*, 555 McHenry Rd., 60090. Tel: 708-537-2900; Fax: 708-215-5805.
For a complete listing, refer to the Special Care Facilities section.

[N] MONASTERIES AND RESIDENCES OF PRIESTS AND BROTHERS

CHICAGO. *Brandsma House*, 1036 W. Loyola Ave., #3, 60626-5233. Tel: 773-761-5139. Revs. Eamon R. Carroll, O.Carm.; Leopold G. Gluekert, O.Carm.

Carmelite Fathers Residence, 4747 S. Dorchester Ave., 60615. Tel: 773-268-9745. Very Rev. Quinn R. Conners, O.Carm., Prior Prov.; Revs. Emmett Gavin, O.Carm.; Daniel O'Neill, O.Carm.

Carmelite Priory of St. Cyril, 6401 S. Harper Ave., 60637. Tel: 312-684-0112; Fax: 312-684-0113. Bro. Timothy Sklopan, O.Carm., Prior & Prin.; Revs. Jerry Williams, O.Carm.; Leander Troy, O.Carm., (Retired); Daniel Carroll, O.Carm.; George L. O'Keefe, O.Carm., (Retired); Glenn Snow, O.Carm. Residing here are all the priests who teach at Mt. Carmel High School. Revs. Carl Markelz, O.Carm.,

Prin.; John Knoerschild, O.Carm.

Chicago Province of the Society of Jesus-Provincial Office, 2050 N. Clark St., 60614. Tel: 773-975-6363; Fax: 773-975-0230. Very Rev. Bradley M. Schaeffer, S.J., Prov.; Revs. Francis J. Daly, S.J., Exec. Asst. & Asst. for Formation; Gerald P. Grace, S.J., Asst. for Intl. Apostolates & Jesuit Intl. Missions; James A. Stoeger, S.J., Asst. for Secondary Education; James P. Gschwend, S.J., Asst. for Continuing Ed. & Asst. for Jesuits in Diaspora; Richard H. McGurn, S.J., Asst. for Pastoral & Social Ministries; John F. Costello, S.J., Asst. for Devel. & Communications; Paul V. Robb, S.J., Asst. Treas.; Daniel L. Flaherty, S.J., Asst. for Business & Finance; Joseph F. Small, S.J., Asst. for Records & Res.; Brian G. Paulson, S.J., Asst. for Vocation Promotion.

Jesuits Serving Abroad: Rev. Kevin E. Gallagher, S.J., Interprovince Liaison, Apdo 10226, Lima 1, Peru. Revs. Robert E. Beckman, S.J.; Fred F. Bergewisch, S.J.; Kevin H. Flaherty, S.J.; Daniel F. Hartnett, S.J.; Jeffrey L. Klaiber, S.J.; Lewis C. Murtaugh, S.J.; John R. Sima, S.J. (Peru); Henry T. Chamberlain, S.J. (Rome); James M. O'Leary, S.J. (Peru); John D. Baggerly, S.J. (Rome); Paul V. Mankowski, S.J. (Rome); John P. Murphy, S.J. (Rome).

Residing elsewhere in the U.S.: Revs. Richard J. Bautch, S.J., Notre Dame, IN; Francis P. O'Donnell, S.J., Albuquerque, NM.

Clark Street Jesuit Residence, 2050 N. Clark St., 60614. Tel: 773-975-6900. Bro. Donald J. Butler, S.J.; Revs. James F. Bresnahan, S.J.; John F. Costello, S.J.; Gerald P. Grace, S.J.; James P. Gschwend, S.J.; George A. Lane, S.J.; James M. Dixon, S.J.; John F. Pennington, S.J.; Edward W. Schmidt, S.J.; Richard H. McGurn, S.J. Priests 9; Brothers 1.

Woodlawn Jesuit Community, 5554 S. Woodlawn Ave., 60637. Tel: 773-667-1395. Revs. Philip J. Chmielewski, S.J., Supr.; Robert E. Finn, S.J.; Thomas W. Florek, S.J.; Paul R. Mueller, S.J.; Robert S. Flack, S.J.; Joseph M. Fung, S.J.; Pablo Mora Mendoza, S.J.; Thomas C. Widner, S.J.; Paul V. Robb, S.J.

Claretian Missionaries, St. Jude League, Inc., 205 W. Monroe, 60606. Tel: 312-236-7782; Fax: 312-236-7230.

Editorial Offices: "U.S. Catholic", "Salt", and other Claretian newsletters; U.S. Catholic Bookstore. Directors: Revs. Mark J. Brummel, C.M.F.; Theodore Cirone, C.M.F.; Robert Fath, C.M.F., Asst. Dir.

Columban Fathers Mission Center, 6449 N. Magnolia Ave., 60626. Tel: 773-274-9111. Revs. Thomas P. Reynolds, S.S.C.; Thomas G. Glennon, S.S.C.; Sean Conneely, S.S.C.

Columban Fathers Theologate, 5722 S. Drexel, 60637. Tel: 312-955-5044. Rev. Mark Mengel, S.S.C., Rector. Priests 1; Lay Missionaries in formation 7.

Comboni Missionaries Theologate (M.C.C.J.), Verona Fathers, 5512 Hyde Park Blvd., 60637. Tel: 312-667-8920. Revs. Guido Oliana, M.C.C.J. (Italy); Mengheesteab Tesfamarian, M.C.C.J. (Ethiopia). Theology students 19.

Congregation of Alexian Brothers-Alexian Brothers Novitiate, 6007 N. Kenmore Ave., 60660. Tel: 773-275-9300. Bro. John Howard, C.F.A., Dir. Novices. Professed Brothers 2; Novices 7.

Congregation of Christian Brothers, Brother Rice Community, 10001 S. Pulaski Rd., 60642. Tel: 312-445-5048. Bros. Eugene O. Carty, C.F.C., Supr.; Michael S. Segvich, C.F.C., Prin.; Thomas J. Collins, C.F.C.; Edmund V. Corrigan, C.F.C.; Austin D. Devane, C.F.C.; Charles E. Joyce, C.F.C.; James A. Houlihan, C.F.C.; Peter J. Martin, C.F.C.; John B. Moore, C.F.C.; Patrick B. Martin, C.F.C.; John Toole, C.F.C.; James B. Sloan, C.F.C.; Ross E. Willatz, C.F.C.; Patrick T. Varilla, C.F.C.; Frank S. Verre, C.F.C.; John S. O'Keefe, C.F.C.; Francis R. Finch, C.F.C.; William F. Kramer, C.F.C. Brothers 18.

Congregation of Marian Fathers of the Immaculate Conception, 6336 S. Kilbourn Ave., 60629. Tel: 773-582-1666; 767-1687 (Religious House); Fax: 773-582-8961(Provincial Office). Very Rev. Donald Petraitus, M.I.C., Prov.; Revs. Victor Rimselis, M.I.C., Councillor I; Timothy Roth, M.I.C., Councillor II; Boniface Vaisnoras, M.I.C., Councillor III; Bro. Donald Schaefer, M.I.C., Councillor IV & Prov. Treas.; Rev. Vytautas Bagdanavicius, M.I.C., Moderator.

Lithuanian Book Club. Revs. Jonas Duoba, M.I.C., Sec.; John Jancius, M.I.C.; Anthony Miciunas, M.I.C.; Bros. Matthew Pulauskas, M.I.C.; Vincent Zvingilas, M.I.C. Priests 4; Brothers 3. Priests 4; Brothers 3.

Conventual Franciscans of St. Bonaventure Province, 6107 N. Kenmore Ave., 60660. Tel: 773-274-7681; Fax: 773-274-9751. Very Revs. Anthony Labedis, O.F.M.Conv., Prov.; Justin Kusibab, O.F.M.Conv., Vicar Prov.; Bro. Thomas Surmann, O.F.M.Conv., Treas.

The Conventual Franciscans of Saint Bonaventure Province Corporation. Legal Title: *The Conventual Franciscans of Saint Bonaventure Province Charitable Continuing Care Trust Fund.*

Franciscan Friars Educational Corporation.

St. Hedwig Cemetery and Mausoleum Corporation. Legal Title: *Franciscan Friars Retirement Corporation.*

Croatian Dominican Fathers, 6346 N. Ridge, 60660. Tel: 773-262-0535. Revs. Nicholas Dugandzic, O.P., Chap., Croatian Catholic Mission; Harvey Blaschko, O.P., Asst. Chap.

Croatian Franciscan Custody of the Holy Family, 4848 S. Ellis Ave., 60615. Tel: 773-373-3463. Revs. Slavko Soldo, Custos; Jerome Kucan, O.F.M.; Mark Kozina, O.F.M.; Ljubo Krasic, O.F.M.; Timothy Majic, O.F.M.; Dionizije Lasic, O.F.M.; Vjekoslav Bambir, O.F.M.; Doiminik Coric; Miron Lasic; Kvirin Vasilj, O.F.M.

Crosier Community of Chicago, 5401 S. Cornell Ave., 60615. Tel: 773-684-6975. Revs. Stephan Bauer, O.S.C.; Thomas Enneking, O.S.C.; Bros. Michael McNiel, O.S.C.; David Donnay, O.S.C.; William Deziel, O.S.C.

Daneo Hall. (Passionist Retirement Wing), 7233 W. Talcott Ave., 60631. Tel: 312-631-5179. Revs. Finan Storey, C.P.; Ralph Briski, C.P.; Kyron O'Connor, C.P.; Andrew Lane, C.P., Dir. Priests 4.

Divine Word Theologate, 5342 S. University, 60615. Tel: 312-288-2777; Fax: 312-288-6307. Very Rev. Roger P. Schroeder, S.V.D.; Revs. Mark E. Weber, S.V.D., Rector; Timothy A. Lenchak, S.V.D., Vice-Rector; Roger S. Arnold, S.V.D., Dir. Formation; Gary L. Riebe-Estrella, S.V.D.; Stephen B. Bevans, S.V.D.; Thomas Kovattiyil, S.V.D.; Derek Simons, S.V.D.; Phelim Jordan, S.V.D.; Higinio M. Yescas, S.V.D. Priests 10; Students 27.

Dominican Community, 1914 S. Ashland Ave., 60608. Tel: 312-829-0074. Revs. Charles W. Dahm, O.P.; Matthias Mueller, O.P.

Dominicans (Provincial Office), St. Pius V. Priory, 1909 S. Ashland Ave., 60608. Tel: 312-226-0075. Provincial Office. Tel: 312-666-3244; Fax: 312-829-8471. Legal Title: *Dominicans, Province of St. Albert the Great, U.S.A. (Central Dominican Province).* Provincial Staff: Very Revs. Edward M. Ruane, O.P., Prior Prov.; David F. Wright, O.P., Socius & Vicar Prov.; Gerald L. Stookey, O.P., Vicar Prov.; Revs. David L. Delich, O.P., Dir. Devel.; Dennis R. Zusy, O.P., Dir. of Soc. for Vocational Support & Regent of Studies; Michael A. Winkels, O.P., Economic Admin.; Very Revs. David F. Wright, O.P., Prov. Archivist; Jesse deP. Cox, O.P., Dir. Vocations; Revs. Bede R. Jagoe, O.P., Dir. St. Dominic Mission; Jerome M. Walsh, Dir. Shrine of St. Jude Thaddeus; Michael A. Winkels, O.P., Dir. Dominican Conference Center; Charles W. Dahm, O.P., Promoter of Social Justice; Steven F. Kuhlmann, O.P., Dir. Dominican Social Action Fund; Regis R. Hovald, O.P., Prov. Rep. to Dominican Laity; Vincent I. Zarlenga, O.P., Dir., Fra Angelico Art Foundation.

St. Pius V Priory. Very Revs. Edward M. Ruane, O.P., Prior Prov.; David F. Wright, O.P., Socius & Vicar Prov.; Gerald L. Stookey, O.P., Vicar, Prov.; Jerome M. Walsh, O.P., Prior; Revs. Patrick M.J. Clancy, O.P.; Daniel C. Davis, O.P.; David L. Delich, O.P.; Richard de Ranitz, O.P.; Kevin R. Fane, O.P.; Michael A. Garcia, O.P.; Robert A. Goedert, O.P.; Bruno H. Kowalkowski, O.P.; James V. Marchionda, O.P.; Robert J. Miller, O.P.; Thomas A. Morrison, O.P.; Anthony E. Romero, O.P.; David J. Staszak, O.P.; Deacon J. Reid Perkins-Buzo, O.P.; Bros. Paul T. Leahy, O.P.; Gerald Pidcock, O.P.

Assigned but Serving Elsewhere: Revs. Raymond N. Ashenbrenner, O.P.; Roderick M. Brown, O.P.; Vincent W. Bryce, O.P.; Paul H. Colloton, O.P.; Francis R. Crowe, O.P.; John R. Dolehide, O.P.; Thomas C. Donlan, O.P.; Francis X. Dyer, O.P.; John C. Fabian, O.P.; Rapael A. Fabish, O.P.; James M. Karepin, O.P.; Thomas L. Kearney, O.P.; John J. McDonald, O.P.; Gerald C. Kroeger, O.P.; James V. Marchionda, O.P.; Daniel W. Morrissey, O.P.; Frank M. Nouza, O.P.; Robert F. Pieper, O.P.; Matthew D. Powell, O.P. (PRO); Ceslaus R. Prazan, O.P.; Richard V. Weber, O.P.; Richard J. Woods, O.P.; Bros. Benedict G. Baer, O.P.; Michael F. McGreal, O.P.; Joachim M. Thiel, O.P.

Priests of the Province Serving Abroad: Revs. James Q. Barnett, O.P., Honduras; Gerard B. Cleator, O.P. (Mexico); Eric deWasseige, O.P., Bolivia; David M. Hynous, O.P. (Rome); Thomas P. Lynch, O.P., Bolivia; Joseph P. Kenny, O.P., Nigeria; John J. Meany, O.P. (Jerusalem); Thomas K. McDermott, O.P., Nigeria; Peter Otillio, O.P., Nigeria; Justus M. Pokrzewinski, O.P., Nigeria; Edward H. Riley, O.P., Nigeria; Lewis M. Shea, O.P., Kenya; James A. Spahn, O.P., Bolivia; Benedict T. Viviano, O.P., Switzerland; Ambrose P. Windbacher, O.P., Nigeria; Bros. Kevin Carroll, O.P., Honduras; Carlos Griego, O.P. (Mexico); Stephen D. Lucas, O.P., Nigeria. Legal Titles: *Spirituality Today Journal, Inc.*; *Shrine of St. Jude Thaddeus*; *Society for Vocational Support, Inc.*; *St. Dominic Mission Society*; *Dominican Social Action Fund*; *Dominican Laity*; *Fra Angelico Art Foundation.*

Edith Stein House of Studies, 5401 S. Cornell Ave., 60615. Tel: 312-572-6943; 324-8000 Ext. 384 (Office); Fax: 312-572-6594. Legal Title: *Edith Stein House of Studies of the Order of Discalced Carmelite Friars.* Revs. Bonaventure Lussier, O.C.D., Rector; Marc Foley, O.C.D., Sub-Rector; Kevin Culligan, O.C.D. Friars: Alan Meyer, O.C.D.; Steven Schmirler, O.C.D.; Mark DeVelis, O.C.D.; Joseph Girouard, O.C.D.; Donald Brick, O.C.D. Priests 3; Students 5.

Franciscan House of Studies, 6107 N. Kenmore Ave., 60660. Tel: 312-764-8811. A Formation House of Conventual Franciscan Friars. Revs. Ferdinand Kintop, O.F.M.Conv., (Retired); Thomas A. Blow, O.F.M.Conv., Guardian & Dir. Vocations; Patrick W. Greerough, O.F.M.Conv., Vicar & Dir. Formation. Priests 3; Professed Students 1; Candidates 9.

The Holy Evangelists Friary. Order of Friars Minor. 4513 N. Ashland Ave., 60625. Revs. Laurence Jagdfeld; Robert Powell; Eulogio Roselada. Priests 3.

Holy Name Friary-Franciscan House of Formation, Assumption BVM Province, 5103 S. Ellis Ave., 60615. Tel: 312-947-9147.

Franciscan Vocation Office. Tel: 312-667-9113. Revs. John E. Wojtowicz, O.F.M., Local Supr./Dir.-Vocations; Colman Majchrzak, O.F.M., Asst. Dir.-Candidates & Temp. Professed; Leslie J. Hoppe, O.F.M., Academic Advisor/Prof. Catholic Theological Union; Joseph Mika, O.F.M.; Stanley Janowski, O.F.M.

Immaculate Conception Monastery, 5700 N. Harlem Ave., 60631. Tel: 773-631-1686; Fax: 773-631-8059. Revs. James Thoman, C.P., Supr.; Myron Gohmann, C.P.; Luke Connolly, Dir., Passionist Missions Appeals; Finan Storey, C.P.; Christopher Gibson, C.P.; Frederick Sucher, C.P.; John Cyril Jablonovsky, C.P.; Andrew Lane, C.P., Dir. of Daneo Hall; Louis Doherty, C.P.; Michael Hoolahan, C.P., Pastor, Immaculate Conception Parish; Alan Phillip, C.P.; Lawrence Browning, C.P.; Paul I. Bechtold, C.P.; Roger Mercurio, C.P., Prov. Archivist; Rian Clancy, C.P.; John T. Render, C.P., Dir. Passionist Resource Center; Leon Grantz, C.P., Chap., Our Lady of the Resurrection Hospital; Francis X. Keenan, C.P., Chap., Lutheran General Hospital; Brian Mahedy, C.P.; John F. Kobler, C.P.; Ralph Brisk, C.P.; Eric Meyer, C.P.; Bros. William Baalman, C.P., Asst. Supr., Immaculate Conception Community; Peter Fitzpatrick, C.F.X.; Raymond Sanchez, C.P., Chap. Cook Co. Jail; Joseph Stadtfeld, C.P. Priests 22; Brothers 4. Legal Title: *Congregation of the Passion: Immaculate Conception Community.*

Institute for Spiritual Leadership, 4906 S. Greenwood Ave., 60615. Tel: 312-373-7953; Fax: 312-373-5794. Legal Title: *Institute for Spiritual Leadership.* ISL offers personal formation and professional training in spiritual direction. Rev. Martin J. Dean, M.S.C. (Australia); Patricia M. Bombard, B.V.M., Exec. Dir.; Ann McElhatton, R.S.C.J., Pres.

Korean Catholic Center, 4115 N. Kedvale, 60641. Tel: 773-283-3979. Rev. John Smith, S.S.C., Dir.

Lithuanian American Jesuits. (Della Strada Residence and Lithuanian Youth Center), 2345 W. 56th St., 60636. Tel: 773-737-8400; Fax: 773-737-0486. Legal Title: *Jesuit Fathers of Della Strada.* Revs. Antanas V. Saulaitis, S.J., Supr.; Jonas Kidykas, S.J., Minister; Kazimieras Raudeliunas, S.J., Treas. Members of the Community: Revs. Vaclovas Gutauskas, S.J.; Bruno Markaitis, S.J.; Juozas Vaisnys, S.J., Editor of, Letters to Lithuanians; Algirdas Paliokas, S.J., Chap. Dir.

Blessed Jurgis Matulaitis Mission, 14911 E. 127th St., Lemont, 60439. Tel: 630-257-5613. Bros. Jurgis Janeliunas, S.J.; Petras Kleinotas, S.J. Priests 7; Brothers 2.

Lithuanian Youth Center, 5620 S. Claremont Ave., 60636. Tel: 773-778-7500.

Marist Brothers, Monastery Community, 4200 W. 115th St., 60655. Tel: 773-881-6380. Bros. Patrick Magee, Dir.; M. Oswald Ouellette; Clement Legare; Philip McEnaney; Brice Byzynski; Julian Roy; Thomas Kelly; Richard Sharpe; Paul Forgues; Nicholas Caffrey; Gerard Brown; Richard Grenier; Martin Doherty, O.S.M.

Marist Brothers, St. Ann Residence, 10114 S. Leavitt, 60643. Tel: 773-239-4116. Bros. Timothy Brady, Dir.; Vito Aresto, Dir.; Louis Richard; Hugh Turley; Henry Hammer.

Maryknoll Fathers & Brothers, 3600 S. Seeley Ave., 60609. Tel: 773-927-9257. Legal Title: *The Catholic Foreign Mission Society of America.* Revs. Benedict A. Zweber, M.M., Dir.; Edward O. Custer, M.M.; John R. Heisse, M.M.; James J. Madden, M.M.; Bro. Anthony Lopez, M.M.

Missionaries of Africa, St. Martin de Porres, 5112 W.

Washington, 60644. Tel: 312-287-0206. Revs. Austin MacAdam, M.Afr. (Canada); Abdon Gamulani, M.Afr. (Malawi, Central Africa). Priests 2.

Monastery of the Holy Cross, 3111 S. Aberdeen St., 60608-6503. Tel: 773-927-7424; Fax: 773-927-5734. Benedictine Monks. Revs. Thomas Baxter, O.S.B., Prior; Patrick D. Creeden, O.S.B.; Edward J. Glanzmann, O.S.B.

The Oblate House of Theology, 5535 S. Kenwood Ave., 60637. Tel: 773-493-3590; Fax: 773-493-6239. Revs. James Allen, O.M.I., Supr.; Francis Demers, O.M.I., Assoc. Scholastics 5.

Passionist Community-CTU, 5401 S. Cornell Ave., 60615. Tel: 773-324-2704. Revs. Kenneth O'Malley, C.P., Supr.; Alfred Pooler, C.P., Dir.-Students; James Barry, C.P.; Robert Carbonneau, C.P.; Owen Dougherty, C.P.; Leo O'Boyle, C.P.; Kevin O'Malley, C.P.; Paul Fatt Lean Saw, F.M.S.; Donald Senior, C.P.; Paul Wadell, C.P.; Kurt Wernert, C.P. Priests 7; Scholastics 3; Brothers 2. Legal Title: *Congregation of the Passion: St. Vincent Strambi Community.*

Passionist Provincial Office, 5700 N. Harlem Ave., 60631. Tel: 773-631-6336. Very Rev. Michael Joseph Stengel, C.P., Prov.; Revs. Michael Higgins, C.P., Asst. Prov.; Blaise Czaja, C.P., Consultor; Clemente Barron, C.P., Consultor; James Thoman, C.P., Consultor.

Special Assignment: Most Rev. Paul M. Boyle, C.P., Apostolic Vicar of Mandeville, P.O. Box 8, Mandeville, Jamaica, West Indies. Rev. Paul Placek, C.P., Passionist Novitiate, P.O. Box 61 Lagao - 9500 S. Cotabato, General Santos City, Philippines. Rev. Jerome Stowell, C.P., 50 Cedar Bluff Dr., #8, Lake St. Louis, MO, 63367. Rev. Richard Johnson, C.P., 2412 Linda Ave., Key West, FL, 33040-5100. Rev. John Gabriel R. Mulnix, C.P., 3001 N. Texas St., #128, Fairfield, CA, 94533. Rev. Robert Coward, C.P., Curia Generalizia Dei Passionist, Piazza SS. Giovanni e Paolo 13, Rome, Italy, 00184. Rev. Arhtur Carrillo, C.P., Curia Generalizia Dei Passionisti, Piazza SS. Giovanni e Paolo 13, Rome, Italy, 00184. Rev. Joseph Vanleeuwen, C.P., Ashram J.X.P., Pallichal Rd. - Palluruthy, Cochin 682-006, India. Rev. John Patrick Day, C.P., St. Catherine Laboure, 913 Rome Ln., Cahokia, 62206. Rev. Thomas M. Newbold, C.P., Sisters of Mercy Motherhouse, 535 Sacramento St., Auburn, CA, 95603. Bro. John Monzyk, C.P., Prof., St. Francis Xavier Rectory, 303 S. Poplar St., Carbondale, 62901. Rev. Robert Weiss, C.P., 1226 Danville Dr., St. Louis, MO, 63137. Rev. Joseph Moons, C.P., Regl. Vicar, Passionist Community, Carmelaramn P.O., Bangalore, India, 560-035. Rev. Warren Womack, C.P., Katolska Forsamlingen, Parkgatan 14, Box 413, Gothenburg, Sweden, 401 26.

Stauros U.S.A. Sr. Ardis Cloutier, O.S.F., Exec. Dir., Catholic Theological Union at Chicago, 5401 S. Cornell Ave., 60615. Tel: 773-752-5732.

Passionist Missions of India, 5700 N. Harlem Ave., 60631. Tel: 773-631-6336. Rev. Walter Kaelin, C.P., Procurator.

Congregation of the Passion. Mother of Good Counsel Community, 5700 N. Harlem Ave., 60634. Tel: 773-631-1686.

Passionist Missions, Inc., 5700 N. Harlem Ave., 60636. Tel: 773-631-1686. Mr. Edward Scholl, Dir.; Rev. Luke Connolly, C.P., Mission Appeals.

Passionist Lay Missioners, 5700 N. Harlem Ave., 60636. Tel: 773-631-6336. Anne Avellone, Dir. Legal Title: *Congregation of the Passion (Holy Cross Province).*

Premonstratensian Fathers and Brothers (Norbertines), 4841 S. Woodlawn Ave., 60615. Tel: 773-548-8020. Holy Spirit House of Studies. Revs. Alan D. Scheible, O.Praem., Supr.; Dane Radecki, O.Praem.; Paul Therly, O.Praem.; Bro. Terrence Lauerman, O.Praem.; Revs. Jay Fostner, O.Praem.; Brian Prunty, O.Praem.; James Stein, O.Praem.; Jeremy Tobin, O.Praem. Priests 1; Norbertine seminarians attending Catholic Theological Union 2.

Priests of the Sacred Heart. (House of Studies), 4840 S. Woodlawn Ave., 60615-1920. Tel: 773-373-2739. Revs. Michael Burke, S.C.J., Dir.; Stephen Huffstetter, S.C.J.; Robert W. Bossie, S.C.J., 4946 N. Sheridan, Apt. 222, 60640. Tel: 773-275-9516. Rev. Michael McMillen, S.C.J., 6227 N. Magnolia, #2, 60660. Tel: 773-743-7247. Priests 4; Scholastics 3.

Provincial Office of the Congregation of the Resurrection, 2250 N. Latrobe Ave., 60639. Tel: 773-637-0999. Very Rev. Richard P. Balazs, C.R., Prov.; Rev. John H. Nowak, C.R., Vocation Dir. Tel: 773-622-0477.

Priests serving abroad: Very Rev. Norbert W. Raszeja, C.R., Via San Sebastianello 11 00187, 00187 Rome, Italy. Tel: 011-39-6-679-5908. Revs. James Gibson, C.R.; Casimir Tadla, C.R.; Gerald Watt, C.R., Our Lady of Guadalupe House Mission, APDO 1512, 68000 Oaxaca, Oaxaca, Mexico. Tel: 011-52-951-507-56. Stella Maria Catholic Church, P.O. Box G378, St. George's, Bermuda GE BX. Tel: 441-297-0512. Rev. Glen Baptiste, C.R.

Redemptorist Theology Residence, 1027 E. Hyde Park Blvd., 60615-2807. Tel: 773-363-2094. Revs. Harry A. Grile, C.SS.R., Supr. & Formation Dir.; Gilbert A. Enderle, C.SS.R., Formation Dir.; Bros. Joseph The Pham, C.SS.R.; Tuan Anh Pham, C.SS.R.; Eugene Harrison, C.SS.R.; Scott Katzenberger, C.SS.R.; Lamar Partin, C.SS.R.; Martin Pham, C.SS.R. Priests 2; Students 6.

Sacred Heart Mission House, 4105 N. Avers Ave., 60618. Tel: 773-588-7476; Fax: 773-588-6517. Legal Title: *The Polish Messenger of The Sacred Heart, Inc.* Revs. Leslaw Balczewski, S.J., Supr.; Stefan Filipowicz, S.J., Editor, The Messenger of The Sacred Heart in Polish language; Stanislaw Gron, S.J.; August Smyda, S.J.; Jerzy Sermak, S.J.; Bros. Wladyslaw Hadam, S.J.; Edward Jawor, S.J. Priests 5; Brothers 2.

Jan Beyzym Society, Inc. (Polish Jesuit Foreign Missions), 4105 N. Avers Ave., 60618. Tel: 773-588-7476. Rev. Leslaw Balczewski, S.J.

St. Clare Friary, 3407 S. Archer Ave., 60608-6817. Tel: 773-890-1238; Fax: 773-890-0484. Rev. Mark J. Costello, O.F.M.Cap., Local Min.; Friars Leonard Gibeault, O.F.M.Cap.; Raymond Stadmeyer, O.F.M.Cap.; Robert Torn, O.F.M.Cap.; Jon Stuttgen, O.F.M.Cap.; Jozef Timmers, O.F.M.Cap.; David Heffron, O.F.M.Cap.; Mark Carrico, O.F.M.Cap.; Thomas Belanger, O.F.M.Cap.; Robert Roemer, O.F.M.Cap.

St. John Stone Friary, 1165 E. 54th Pl., 60615. Tel: 773-684-6510. Revs. Wes Benak, O.S.A., Prior; James Thompson, O.S.A., Dir. Formation; Michael Slattery, O.S.A., Treas.; R. William Sullivan, O.S.A.

St. Joseph Friary. (A Franciscan House of the Sacred Heart) Province, 5495 S. Hyde Park Blvd., 60615. Tel: 773-363-0072; Fax: 773-363-0076. Revs. Tod Laverty, O.F.M., Formation Staff; Gino Correa, O.F.M., Guardian & Formation Staff; Arthur Anderson, O.F.M., Formation Staff; Zachary Hayes, O.F.M.; Gil Ostdiek, O.F.M. Professed 16.

St. Mary Magdalene Friary, 8425 S. Saginaw Ave., 60617. Tel: 312-374-1590. Franciscan House of Formation (St. John the Baptist Province, Cincinnati, OH). Bro. Tim Sucher, O.F.M., Local Guardian & Formation Dir.; Rev. Tod Laverty, O.F.M.; Bros. Edward Gura, O.F.M.; Francis Williams, O.F.M.; Brian Maloney, O.F.M. Priests 1; Brothers 4; Temporary Professed Clerics 2; Temporary Professed Brothers 1.

St. Patrick's Missionary Society, 1347 W. Granville Ave., 60660. Tel: 773-973-3737. Revs. Karl Langsdorf, Supr.; Sean Cullen.

St. Peter's Friary, 110 W. Madison St., 60602-4196. Tel: 312-372-5111. Order of Friars Minor. Revs. Thomas Aldworth; Elric Sampson; Boniface Baum; Jerome Baum; Bro. John Bush; Revs. Vincent Callahan; Wenceslaus Church; Bro. Berchmans Cifra; Rev. Michael Clarahan; Bro. Sammy Danna; Revs. Barnabas DieKemper; Kenan Dulzer; Thomas Ess; Charles Faso; Bro. James Finn; Revs. Tarsicius Fischer; Thomas Fratus; Francis Jerome Gray; Bro. Patrick Hanrahan; Revs. Robert Hutmacher; Robert Kamis; Bros. Clarence Klingert; Thomas Krull; Rev. Paul Lachance; Bro. William Lanning; Revs. Clement Leahy; George Musial; Fred Radtke; Bill Rooney; Bros. Terrence Santiapillai, O.F.M.; Raymond Shuhert; Rev. Joseph Windolph.

St. Rita Monastery, 7740 S. Western Ave., 60620-5867. Tel: 773-476-3879. (For information concerning school, see separate listing). Revs. Michael J. O'Connor, O.S.A.; Thomas McCarthy, O.S.A.; John A. Kret; Gerald VanOverbeek, O.S.A.; Edward Andrews, O.S.A., Prior.

Scalabrini House of Theology, 5121 S. University Ave., 60615. Tel: 773-684-5230; 684-4340; Fax: 773-684-5240. Revs. Raniero Alessandrini, C.S., Rector; Edison Osorio, C.S., Animator; Angelo Moscato, C.S., Spiritual Dir. Priests 3; Students 13.

Servite Friars - Eastern Province, Provincial Center, 3121 W. Jackson Blvd., 60612-2729. Tel: 773-533-0360; Fax: 773-533-8307. Very Rev. Michael M. Guimon, O.S.M., Prior Prov.; Revs. Joseph M. Chamblain, O.S.M., Asst. Prov.; James M. Dore, O.S.M., Prov. Councilor; Paul M. Cullen, O.S.M., Prov. Councilor; Paul M. Novak, O.S.M., Prov. Councilor; Bros. Edmund Baran, O.S.M., Prov. Treas.; Michael M. Callary, O.S.M., Prov./Corp. Sec.; Revs. Conrad M. Borntrager, O.S.M., Prov. Archivist & Historian; Donald M. Siple, O.S.M., Natl. Vocation Dir.; Robert M. Warsey, O.S.M.

Monastery of Our Lady of Sorrows, 3121 W. Jackson Blvd., 60612-2729. Tel: 773-638-5800. Bros. Edmund M. Baran, O.S.M.; Robert M. Fandel, O.S.M.; Kevin O'Byrne, O.S.M.; Revs. Charles M. Brennan, O.S.M.; Walter M. Brennan, O.S.M.; David O. Brown, O.S.M.; Joseph M. Chamblain, O.S.M.; Lawrence M. Choate, O.S.M.; Jerome M. Hurley, O.S.M.; Donald M. Sipe, O.S.M.; Robert M. Warsey, O.S.M.

Annunciata Regional Priory, 11128 S. Avenue G, 60617. Tel: 773-221-1043; Fax: 773-221-1556. Bros. Michael M. Callary, O.S.M.; Martin M. Doherty, O.S.M.; Brian M. Fitzpatrick, O.S.M.; Revs. Conrad M. Borntrager, O.S.M.; Mark M. Dennehy, O.S.M.; Christopher M. Krymski, O.S.M.

Assumption Priory, 323 W. Illinois St., 60610. Tel: 312-644-0392; Fax: 312-644-1838. Revs. Paul M. Cullen, O.S.M.; Augustine M. Kulbis, O.S.M.; Anthony M. O'Connell, O.S.M.; John M. Pawlikowski, O.S.M.

St. Bonfilius Priory, 3401 S. Home Ave., Berwyn, 60402-3399. Tel: 708-484-2595; Fax: 708-484-0064. Bro. Joel A. Lechner, O.S.M.; Revs. Bernard M. Barnes, O.S.M.; Thomas M. Heskin, O.S.M.; Paul M. Novak, O.S.M.; Peter M. Rookey, O.S.M.

Servite Development Office, 1439 S. Harlem Ave., Berwyn, 60402. Tel: 708-795-8885; Fax: 708-795-8892.

St. Domitilla Priory, 4940 Washington, Hillside, 60162-1297. Tel: 708-449-8430; Fax: 708-449-2009. Revs. Frank M. Falco, O.S.M.; Donald M. Gantley, O.S.M.; Very Rev. Michael M. Guimon, O.S.M.; Rev. Philip M. McGlynn, O.S.M.

Members of the Province Located Elsewhere in the Archdiocese of Chicago and Other Locations in the U.S.: Revs. Frank M. Calkins, O.S.M., Addolorata Villa, Wheeling IL; Lawrence (Leroy) M. Calkins, O.S.M., U.S. Veterans Admin. Hospital, Roseburg, OR; Damian M. Charbonneau, O.S.M., Our Lady of Grace Priory, Palm Bay, FL.; Louis M. Cortney, O.S.M., Addolorata Villa, Wheeling, IL; Thomas M. Crotty, O.S.M., St. Catherine of Siena Mission, Kissimmee, FL.; James M. Dore, O.S.M., Our Lady of Grace Priory, Palm Bay, FL; Lawrence Michael Doyle, O.S.M., United States Air Force, Denver, CO; Thomas M. Duff, O.S.M., St. Joseph Husband of Mary Parish, Las Vegas, NV.; Edward M. Edwards, O.S.M., St. Mary Academy, North Plainfield, NJ; Carl M. Feil, O.S.M., Our Lady of Belen Priory, Belen, NM.; John M. Fontana, O.S.M., Seven Holy Founders Priory, Affton, MO; Albert M. Gallegos, O.S.M., Our Lady of Belen Priory, Belen, NM.; David M. Gallegos, O.S.M., Our Lady of Belen Priory, Anaheim, CA; Anthony M. Gaydos, O.S.M., St. Marie du Lac Parish, Ironton, MO; Paul M. Gins, O.S.M., Seven Holy Founders Priory, Anaheim, CA.; Thomas M. Greaney, O.S.M., Our Lady of Belen Priory, Belen, NM.; Damian M. Kobus, O.S.M., St. John Neumann, Yuma, AZ; David M. Kondik, O.S.M., St. Juliana Falconieri Priory, Fullerton, CA; Timothy M. Kremen, O.S.M., Seven Holy Founders Priory, Affton, MO; Thomas M. LoCascio, O.S.M., Addolorata Villa, Wheeling, IL; Francis M. Martin, O.S.M., Seven Holy Founders Priory, Affton, MO; John J. Martin, O.S.M., Our Lady of Grace Priory, Palm Bay, FL.; Vidal Martinez, O.S.M., St. Catherine of Siena Mission, Kissimmee, FL; George M. O'Connell, O.S.M., Little Sisters of the Poor, Chicago, IL; Vincent M. O'Shea, O.S.M., St. John, St. Petersburg Beach, FL; Michael M. Scanlon, O.S.M., Addolorata Villa, Wheeling, IL; Philip M. Scherer, O.S.M., Mother of Sorrows Convent, Blue Island, IL; Luke M. Stano, O.S.M., St. John Berchmans-St. Juliana, Detroit, MI; John M. Topper, O.S.M., The Sanctuary of Our Sorrowful Mother, Portland, OR; Bros. Bonifilius M. McGovern, O.S.M., Seven Holy Founders Priory, Anaheim, CA; Christopher Moran, O.S.M., Our Lady of Belen Priory, Belen, NM.

Members of the Province Serving Abroad: Revs. Matthew M. Ford, O.S.M., Benburb, Northern Ireland; John M. Huels, O.S.M., Zululand, South Africa; John M. LeMay, O.S.M., Zululand, South Africa; Edwin M. Kinch, O.S.B., Manilla, Philippines; Robert M. Kucera, O.S.M., Zululand, South Africa; Frederick Reiman, O.S.M., Zululand, South Africa; Amideus M. Wickers, O.S.M., Dusseldorf-Nord, Germany; Bro. Andrew M. Motsko, O.S.M., Zululand, South Africa. Priests 56; Brothers 9; Novices 1.

Viatorian Residence, 1201 W. Belden, 60614. Revs. Thomas F. McMahon, C.S.V.; John E. Linnan, C.S.V.; Mark R. Francis, C.S.V.; Bros. Michael T. Gosch, C.S.V.; Donald P. Houde, C.S.V.; Leo V. Ryan, C.S.V. Priests 3; Brothers 3.

Vincentian Community, Congregation of the Mission, Midwest Province, 2210-12 N. Racine Ave., 60614. Tel: 773-880-2968. Revs. Thomas Croak, C.M., Supr.; Joseph C. Geders, C.M., Treas.; Ronald Hoye, C.M.; Robert Lucas, C.M.; Edward Udovic, C.M.; Thomas A. Grace, C.M.; J. Patrick Murphy, C.M.; David Nygren, C.M.; Daniel Theiss, C.M.; Anthony J. Dosen; Paul A. Sisul; Bro. Mark Elder, C.M.

Xaverian Missionaries (S.X.), 1347 E. Hyde Park Blvd., 60615. Tel: 312-643-5745. Revs. Ivan J. Marchesin, S.X., Rector; Lino Sgarbossa, S.X.; Vittorio Falsina, S.X.

ARLINGTON HEIGHTS. *Clerics of St. Viator-Provincial Residence*, 1212 E. Euclid St., 60004. Tel: 708-398-1354; Fax: 708-394-4507. Revs. Robert M. Egan, C.S.V., Prov.; Richard A. Rinn, C.S.V., Asst. Prov.; Donald J. Fitzsimmons, C.S.V.; James F. Fanale,

C.S.V.; Robert E. Erickson, C.S.V.; Bro. Michael A. Rice, C.S.V. Priests 5; Brothers 1.

Viatorian Mission House, 1212 E. Euclid St., 60004. Tel: 708-255-9292. Clerics of St. Viator. Rev. Richard A. Rinn, C.S.V., Mission Procurator, Dir. of Viatorian Seminary Aid Assn. & Dir. of Pious A.

Viatorian Province Center-Clerics of St. Viator, 1212 E. Euclid St., 60004. Tel: 847-398-1350. Revs. George Auger, C.S.V.; Philip M. Clifford, C.S.V.; Thomas G. O'Brien, C.S.V.; Michael J. Ranahan, C.S.V.; Thomas L. Sullivan, C.S.V.; William C. Meyer, C.S.V.; Charles L. Maranto, C.S.V.; Thomas P. McCarthy, C.S.V.; Casimir C. Kicmal, C.S.V.; James F. Fanale, C.S.V.; Michael J. O'Brien, C.S.V.; John C. Puisis, C.S.V.; Joseph M. Lofy, C.S.V.; Robert E. Erickson, C.S.V.; Christopher J. Glancy, C.S.V.; Richard A. Rinn, C.S.V.; John A. Toolan, C.S.V.

Priests of the Province Serving Abroad: Revs. Pedro E. Herrera, C.S.V.; Luis E. Lopez, C.S.V.; John A. Pisors, C.S.V.; Albeyro Vanagas, C.S.V., Colegio San Viator, Kilmetro 14, Autopista del Norte, Bogota 2, D.E., Columbia, 54-11-62. Mailing Address: Apartado Aereo 102413, Bogota 10, D.E., Columbia. Bros. Alejandro Adame, C.S.V.; Fredy Santos, C.S.V.; Fernando Nunez, C.S.V.; Carlos Luis Claro, C.S.V.; Carlos Florez, C.S.V.; Carlos Chaves, C.S.V.; Rev. Roger C. Drolet, C.S.V., 38 Takan-Tsuen, Pali Hsiang, Taipei, Hsien (249), Taiwan, R.O.C. Military Chaplains: Rev. Daniel Hall, C.S.V., 107 Grant St., Sneads Ferry, NC, 28460.

Priests Serving Elsewhere In U.S.A.: Rev. Victor E. Bertrand, Gulfort, MS. Rev. Joseph B. Tremonti, 240 S. Curtis St., Kankakee, 60901. Tel: 815-932-3001. Revs. Donald W. Huntimer, C.S.V., Tucson, AZ; Thomas G. Kass, C.S.V., Manchester, NH; Alan M. Syslo, C.S.V., Highland Park, NJ; Robert H. Carey, C.S.V., San Jose, CA.

ASLIP. *Marist Brothers*, 3623 W. 120th St., #1N, 60658. Tel: 708-489-1238. Bros. Brendan Brennan, Dir.; John Murray.

BANGKOK, THAILAND, 123/19 Ruam Rudi Ln., 10330. Most Rev. Alfred Novak, C.Ss.R., Rua Consulheiro Sinimbu, 83200 Paranagua, Panama, Brazil. Rev. William Bueche, C.Ss.R., Rua Conselheiro Sinimbu, 83200 Paranagua, Parana, Brazil. Revs. Anthony Smith, C.Ss.R.; Joseph W. Tobin, C.Ss.R., Casa Sant' Alfonso, C.P. 2458, Rome, Italy, 00100. Redemptorists: Revs. William Cleary, C.Ss.R.; William Peterson, C.Ss.R.; Robert Wirth, C.Ss.R.; John Willett, C.Ss.R.; Bro. Daniel Hall, C.Ss.R., P.O. Box 29585 Secretariat, Bodija, Ibadan, Oyo State, Nigeria. Rev. William Fitzgerald, C.Ss.R., C.P. 400, Juazerio, Babia, Brazil, 48900. Rev. Harold Thiel, C.Ss.R., T. Chang Phuek A. Muang, 88 Chotana Rd., Chaing Mai, 50300.

Serving Elsewhere, Not Listed: Rev. John McPhee, C.Ss.R., 61847 Glenview Terrace, Washington, MI, 49084. Rev. Thomas Franciscus, C.Ss.R., The Tribunal, 1550 N. Fresno St., Fresno, CA, 93703-3788. Rev. T. William Coyle, C.Ss.R., 608 Broadway, Fargo, ND, 58102. Rev. Pascal Dreici, C.Ss.R., 1035 E. Walthen, Fresno, CA, 93710. Rev. Ricardo Elford, C.Ss.R., P.O. Box 574, Cortaro, AZ, 85652. Rev. Joseph Nuttmann, C.Ss.R., P.O. Box 235, Carlin, NV, 89822. Rev. Richard Strass, C.Ss.R., P.O. Box 207, Seward, Alphonsus, 99664.

BLUE ISLAND. *Marist Brothers*, 12212 Irving Ave., 60406. Tel: 708-385-1488. Bros. Dennis Dunne, Dir.; Sumner Herrick; Michael Marsan; Luke Pearson.

COUNTRYSIDE. *St. Gratian Friary, Franciscan Friars*, 5536 S. Edgewood Ave., 60525. Tel: 708-482-4546. Revs. James Walton, O.F.M.; Dennis Koopman, O.F.M.; James Hoffman, O.F.M.; Albert Merz, O.F.M.; Ildephonse Skorup, O.F.M.; Kieran Kemner, O.F.M.; Bros. Leon Beranek, O.F.M.; Herbert Rempe, O.F.M. Fathers 6; Brothers 2.

ELK GROVE VILLAGE. *Congregation of Alexian Brothers Immaculate Conception Province, Inc.*, 600 Alexian Way, 60007. Tel: 708-640-7550; Fax: 708-981-5561. Affiliate: Brothers of St. Alexius Health and Welfare Fund, Inc. Bro. Edward Walsh, C.F.A., Prov. Supr. Provincial Councilors: Bros. Philip Kennedy, C.F.A.; Thomas Keusenkothen, C.F.A.; Lawrence Krueger, C.F.A.; Andrew Thome, C.F.A., Dir.-Vocations/ Community. Brothers 12. Res., 801 Gloucester Dr., 60007. Tel: 708-439-5845.

EVANSTON. *Canisius House*. (Loyola Press Jesuit Authors Residence), 201 Dempster St., 60201-4704. Tel: 847-475-1825; Fax: 847-475-1869. Revs. Joseph F. Downey, S.J., Supr.; Daniel L. Flaherty, S.J.; Thomas L. Kenealy, S.J.; Donald J. McGuire, S.J.

GLENVIEW. *The Redemptorists of Glenview, Illinois*. Villa Redeemer: North American Redemptorist Novitiate and Retreat Center, 1111 N. Milwaukee Ave., P.O. Box 6, 60025. Tel: 847-724-0425; Fax: 847-724-8953. Revs. Gary Heinecke, C.Ss.R., Local Supr. & Asst. Retreat Dir.; Joseph J. Hurley, C.Ss.R., Novice Dir., Vicar, & 1st Consultor; Henry Novak, C.Ss.R., 2nd Consultor; Kevin Fraher, C.Ss.R., Retreat Dir. & Asst. Novice Dir.; Bro. Thomas Sanhuber, C.Ss.R.

Redemptorist Denver Province Foreign Mission Office. Rev. Wilfred Lowery, C.Ss.R., Dir., Redemptorist Theology Residence, 1027 E. Hyde Park Blvd., Chicago, 60615.

LA GRANGE PARK. *Comboni Mission Center*, 1615 E. 31st St., 60526. Tel: 708-354-1999; Fax: 708-354-2006. Revs. Angelo Biancalana, M.C.C.J., Dir., C. Lay Miss. Prog.; Tom Vermiglio, M.C.C.J., Mission Dir.; Valentino Saoncella, M.C.C.J., Supr.; Sixtus Agostino, M.C.C.J., Lay Miss. Prog. Priests 4.

LEMONT. *The Slovene Franciscan Fathers, Order of Friars Minor, Commissariat of the Holy Cross*, 14246 Main St., P.O. Box 608, 60439. Tel: 708-257-2494; Fax: 708-257-8559. Revs. Blase Chemazar, O.F.M., Pres.; Vendelin Spendov, O.F.M., Guardian; Leonard Bogolin, O.F.M.; Benno Korbic, O.F.M.; Bernardin Susnik, O.F.M.; Fortunat Zorman, O.F.M.; Martin Stepanich, O.F.M.; Athanasius Lovrencic, O.F.M.; David Srumpf, O.F.M.; Bro. Robert Hochevar, O.F.M. Priests 9; Brothers 1.

LIBERTYVILLE. *Marytown, Our Lady of Fatima Friary*, 1600 W. Park Ave., 60048. Tel: 847-367-7800. Community of Conventual Franciscan Friars administering the U.S. National Center of the Militia of the Immaculata Movement (M.I.). Bro. Juniper Kriss, O.F.M.Conv., Vicar; Rev. Patrick Greenough, O.F.M.Conv., Guardian & Prov. Asst., J.I. Editorial Office for Immaculata Magazine & Prow Books.

Conventual Franciscan Friars of Marytown.

Shrine of St. Maximilian Kolbe.

MUNDELEIN. *Carmelite Monastery*, 999 E. McKinley Ave., 60060. Tel: 847-566-4070. Bro. Dominic Saganich, O.Carm., Prior; Revs. John-Benedict Weber, O.Carm.; William J. Harry, O.Carm.; John J. Comerford, O.Carm.; Robert Carroll, O.Carm.; Cletus Sullivan, O.Carm.; Bro. John Sprissler, O.Carm.

OAK FOREST. *St. Roch Friary-Franciscan Fathers*, 4700 W. 159th St., 60452. Tel: 708-687-2035. Chaplains: Revs. Melchior Toczek, O.F.M., Supr.; Victorian Haladus, O.F.M., Vicar; Conrad Schneider, O.F.M. In res., Rev. Michael Windolph, O.F.M. Priests 4.

OAK PARK. *Claretian Fathers Headquarters of U.S.A. Eastern Province*, 400 N. Euclid, 60302. Tel: 708-848-2076; Fax: 708-848-2069. Very Rev. Theodore Salvatore Cirone, C.M.F., Prov.; Revs. Robert Fath, C.M.F., Supr.; Richard Bartlett, C.M.F.; Thomas Paramo, C.M.F.; Ronald Luka, C.M.F.; James Maloney, C.M.F.; Raymond O'Connor, C.M.F.; Milton Alvarez, C.M.F.; Jesse Carrero, C.M.F.; James Curran, C.M.F.; Bros. Richard Wilga; James Santmiguel Oriols.

Priests serving outside Province: Rev. Richard J. Todd, C.M.F., Via Sacro Cuore di Maria, 5, Rome, Italy, 00197. Rev. Donald Lavelle, C.M.F., Dominguez Retreat Renewal Center, 18127 S. Alameda St., Rancho Dominguez, CA, 90220. Revs. Walter Mischke, C.M.F.; Edmundo Andres, C.M.F.; Daniel Vogt, C.M.F., Parroquia San Pedro, El Estor, Izabal, Guatemala, C.A. Revs. Daniel Drinan, C.M.F.; Thomas Moran, C.M.F., Parroquia Nuestra Senora del Rosario, Livingston, Izabal, Guatemala, C.A. Rev. Thomas Brummel, C.M.F., Claretian Theologate, Attakwu P.O. Box 80, Enugu, Enugu State, Nigeria. Priests 43; Scholastics 1; Brothers 4.

Claretian Missionaries Community Support Trust, 400 N. Euclid Ave., 60302. Tel: 708-848-2076. Rev. Theodore Salvatore Cirone, C.M.F., Pres. Vice Presidents: Revs. Mark J. Brummel, C.M.F.; Gregory Kenny, C.M.F.; Ronald Stua; David Liners, C.M.F., Sec.

Dominican Community of St. Martin de Porres, 204 S. Humphrey, 60302. Bros. Joseph Kilikevice, O.P.; Gabriel Dault, O.P.

Missionaries of Saint Charles, Provincial Residence, 546 N. East Ave., 60302. Tel: 708-386-4430; Fax: 708-386-4457. Legal Title: *Fathers of St. Charles*. Rev. Livio Stella, C.S., Prov., Scalabrini Development Office, 3800 W. Division, Stone Park, 60165. Tel: 708-345-2626.

Scalabrinians Community Support Corporation, Oak Park.

Scalabrinians Community Formation Corporation, Oak Park.

Italian Cultural Center, 1621 N. 39th Ave., Stone Park, 60165. Tel: 708-345-3842.

OLYMPIA FIELDS. *The Augustinian Provincialate Tolentine Center*, 20300 Governors Hwy., 60461. Tel: 708-748-9500; 468-6700. Very Rev. David L. Brecht, O.S.A., Prior Prov.; Bros. Kenneth D. Mehn, O.S.A., Prov. Sec.; Bruce A. Jendraszak, O.S.A., Prov. Treas. & Dir. Tolentine Ctr.; Mr. Michael Kiley, Acting Dir. Devel.; Revs. G. Jerome Kneis, O.S.A., Personnel Dir. & Asst. Prov.; W. Timothy Cuny, O.S.A., Vocation Dir.; John W. Beretta, O.S.A.; James V. Corrigan, O.S.A.; Robert J. Dodaro, O.S.A.; Edward G. Grace, O.S.A.; Bernard R. Danber, O.S.A.; Bro. Mark D. Emken, O.S.A.; Rev. Thomas F. Martin, O.S.A.; Bro. Jerome A. Sysko, O.S.A.; Revs. Karl A. Gersbach, O.S.A.; Donald W. Harkabus, O.S.A.; Richard M. Jacobs, O.S.A.; Martin S. Laird, O.S.A.; John R. Mabarak, O.S.A.

Foreign Missionaries assigned to the Provincialate: Revs. Alfred M. Burke, O.S.A.; Charles J. Bodden, O.S.A.; David R. Klotz, O.S.A.; Most Rev. John J. McNabb, O.S.A.; Revs. Richard D. Palmer, O.S.A.; Robert F. Prevost, O.S.A.; Bro. David A. Sharp, O.S.A.; Revs. John P. Tasto, O.S.A.; Daniel T. Turley, O.S.A.; John A. Tyma, O.S.A.

Austin Friary, 20300 Governors Hwy., 60461-1081. Tel: 708-748-9500. Revs. G. Jerome Kines, O.S.A., Prior; Donald J. Bates, O.S.A.; Terry A. Deffenbaugh, O.S.A. Priests 3; Brothers 2.

Tolentine Monastery at Tolentine Center, 20300 Governors Hwy., 60461. Tel: 708-748-9500; Fax: 708-481-2090; 748-0018. Very Rev. David L. Brecht, O.S.A., Prior Prov.; Rev. James Friedel, O.S.A., Prior; Bro. Martin Shaw, O.S.A., Sub-Prior; Revs. W. Timothy Cuny, O.S.A., Treas.; John Mabarak, O.S.A.; John J. Flaherty, O.S.A.; Edwin R. Kuczynski, O.S.A.; Thomas A. McGowan, O.S.A.; Bros. Anthony Schander, O.S.A.; John Stobba, O.S.A., Sacristan; Angelo Sturn, O.S.A.

Viatorian Residence, 20300 Governors Hwy., Apt. 23, 60461. Rev. John E. Durkee, C.S.V., Chap., Marian Catholic H.S.

PARANA, BRAZIL. *Rua Consulheiro Sinimbu*, 83200 Paranagua. Revs. Anthony Smith, C.Ss.R.; Joseph W. Tobin, C.Ss.R., Casa Sant Alfonso, C.P. 2458, Rome, Italy, 00100. Revs. William Cleary, C.Ss.R.; William Peterson, C.Ss.R.; Robert Wirth, C.Ss.R.; John Willett, C.Ss.R.; Bro. Daniel Hall, C.Ss.R., P.O. Box 29585 Secretariat, Bodija, Ibadan, Oyo State, Nigeria. Rev. William Fitzgerald, C.Ss.R., C.P. 400, Juazeiro, Babia, 48900. Rev. Harold Thiel, C.Ss.R., 88 Chotana Rd. T. Chang Phuek A. Muang, Chaing Mai, Thailand, 50300. 61847 Glenview Ter., Washington, MI, 49084. Rev. Thomas Fransiscus, C.Ss.R., The Tribunal, 1550 N. Fresno St., Fresno, CA, 93703-3788. Rev. T. William Coyle, C.Ss.R., 608 Broadway, Fargo, ND, 58102. Rev. Pascal Dreici, C.Ss.R., 1035 E. Walthen, Fresno, CA, 93710. Rev. Ricardo Elford, C.Ss.R., P.O. Box 574, Cortaro, AZ, 85652. Rev. Joseph Nuttmann, C.Ss.R.

RIVER FOREST. *St. Thomas Aquinas Priory*, 7200 Division St., 60305. Tel: 708-771-3030. Very Revs. Peter J. Herely, O.P., Prior; William J. Bernacki, O.P., Subprior; Revs. Richard R. Farmer, O.P., Business Mgr.; Jordan Aumann, O.P.; Robert L. Barry, O.P.; Robert I. Campbell, O.P.; Edward L. Cleary, O.P.; Joseph C. Della Penta, O.P.; Malachy R. Dooley, O.P.; James M. Erwin, O.P.; Hilary J. Freeman, O.P.; John M. Gambro, O.P.; Gilbert J. Graham, O.P.; Clinton P. Honkomp, O.P.; Joseph I. Hren, O.P.; Albert Judy, O.P.; Robert A. Kilbridge, O.P.; Victor S. LaMotte, O.P.; Richard C. LaPata, O.P.; Robert J. Miller, O.P.; Quentin E. Moriarty, O.P.; Walter T. O'Connell, O.P.; Jerome A. O'Leary, O.P.; Thomas Aquinas F. O'Meara, O.P.; Robert F. O'Riley, O.P.; David J. Santoro, O.P.; James Regan, O.P.; Very Rev. Timothy H. Sparks, O.P.; Rev. Michael A. Winkels, O.P., Vicar; Bros. Terence G. Bullock, O.P.; Regis R. Hovald, O.P.; Reginald Neu, O.P.; Michael McGovern, O.P. Priests 29; Brothers 4.

Legal subsidiaries and holdings: The Priory Press, Theology texts for high schools; "Listening", journal of Religion and Culture; Vestments and Vessels; Dominican Conference Center; Carpentier Art Collection.

STONE PARK. *Scalabrini Mission Center*. (Formerly Sacred Heart Seminary- Scalabrini Renewal Center), 3800 W. Division St., 60165. Tel: 708-345-8270. Revs. Gino Dalpiaz, C.S., Dir.; Aldo Vendramin, C.S., Dir. Scalabrini Devel. Office; Gina Corradin, C.S., Asst., Mission Center. Priests 2; Brothers 1; Missionary Sisters of St. Charles Borromeo 2.

TECHNY. *Society of the Divine Word, Provincial Headquarter-Chicago Prov.* (Province of Blessed Joseph Freinademetz, S.V.D.), 1985 Waukegan Rd., P.O. Box 6038, 60082-6038. Tel: 708-272-2700; Fax: 708-272-2517. Very Rev. Stanley Uroda, S.V.D., Prov., 1985 Waukegan Rd., P.O. Box 6038, 60082-6038. Tel: 708-272-2700; Fax: 708-272-2517. Bro. Douglas Edmonds, S.V.D., Vice Prov.; Revs. Thomas Griffith, S.V.D., Treas.; Chester Nowicki, S.V.D., Asst. Treas. Legal Title: *Divine Word Missionaries, Inc.; Divine Word Funds, Inc.; Catholic Universities, Inc.; Blessed Arnold Charitable Trust*. Revs. Thomas A. Krosnicki, S.V.D., Pres.; Francis Kamp, S.V.D., Mission Treas.; Walter Bracken, S.V.D., Delegated Supr. For Missionaries on Leave; John Donaghey, S.V.D., Prov. Admin.; James Braband, S.V.D., Sec. of Education/Formation/Recruitment; Bro. Dennis Newton, S.V.D., Vocation Dir.

Blessed Arnold Charitable Trust. Rev. Thomas Griffith, S.V.D., Pres.

S.V.D. Funds, Inc. Revs. Stanley Uroda, S.V.D., Pres.; Thomas Griffith, S.V.D., Treas.; Chester Nowicki, S.V.D., Asst. Treas.; Raymond Quetchenbach, S.V.D., Dir., Charitable Gift Annuities.

Divine Word International, 2001 Waukegan Rd., P.O. Box 176, 60082-0176. Tel: 847-272-1100; Fax:

847-272-9363. Bro. David Noonan, S.V.D., Dir.; Revs. Paul Connors, S.V.D.; Gilbert Gawlik, S.V.D.; Bro. Richard Sullivan, S.V.D.

House of Religious Men: Divine Word Theologate, 5342 University Ave., Chicago, 60615. Tel: 312-288-2777. Revs. Mark Weber, S.V.D., Rector; Roger Arnold, S.V.D.; Phelim Jordan, S.V.D.; Timothy Lenchak, S.V.D.; Roger P. Schroeder, S.V.D., Rector; Derek Simons, S.V.D.; Higinlo Yescas, S.V.D.

Edward McGuinn House of Studies, 5487 S. Hyde Park, #1N, Chicago, 60615. Tel: 773-643-1518. Revs. Stephan Bevans, S.V.D.; Gary Riebe-Estrella, S.V.D.

Divine Word Novitiate, 1940 Waukegan Rd., 60082-6000. Tel: 847-272-0299. Rev. Edward Peklo, S.V.D., Novice Dir.

Divine Word Residence, 1901 Waukegan Rd., P.O. Box 6000, 60082-6000. Tel: 847-272-2700; Fax: 847-272-2873. Rev. Kazimerz Garbacz, S.V.D., Rector.

Slovak Department, 1985 Waukegan Rd., P.O. Box 6068, 60082-6068. Tel: 847-272-2700. Rev. Emil Cernaj, S.V.D.

Werbisci, 1985 Waukegan Rd., P.O. Box 6024, 60082-6024. Rev. Kazimerz Garbacz, S.V.D.

Catholic Chinese Cultural Center, 856 W. Fullerton Ave., Chicago, 60614. Tel: 312-348-6856. Rev. John Fu, S.V.D. Fathers 62; Brothers 22.

WILLOW SPRINGS. *Cistercian Fathers*, Our Lady Mother of the Church, 8121 Archer Rd., 60480. Tel: 708-839-6808. Mailing Address: Box 334, Argo, 60501. Rt. Rev. Hubert Kostrzanski, S.O.Cist., Abbot of Szczyrzyc (Poland); Revs. Michael Blicharski, S.O-.Cist.; Gregory Szydlowski, S.O.Cist.; Alberic Lipinski, S.O.Cist.; John Muc, S.O.Cist.
Cistercian Priory dependant monastery of the Abbey in Szczyrzyc, Poland (Polish Congregation) est. 1982. Legal Title: *Cistercian Monasteries Auxiliary*. Priests 4.

[O] CONVENTS AND RESIDENCES FOR SISTERS

CHICAGO. *Administrative Center of the Sisters of Mercy of the Americas*, Regional Community of Chicago, 10024 S. Central Park, 60655-3132. Tel: 773-779-6011. Sr. Lucille McKillop, R.S.M., Pres. Sisters 14.

Sisters of Mercy of the Americas, Regional Community of Chicago Charitable Trust.

Comboni Missionary Sisters, 1125 E. 50th St., 60615. Tel: 773-624-1122. Sisters 4.

Daughters of St. Mary of Providence, Provincialate: 4200 N. Austin Ave., 60634. Tel: 773-545-8300. Sr. Bernardine Kauffmann, Prov.

Daughters of St. Paul, 172 N. Michigan, 60601. Tel: 312-346-4228; 346-3240. Sr. Frances Aurelia Obrovac, F.S.P., Supr. Sisters 4.

Little Sisters of Jesus, 1551 S. Sawyer St., 60623. Sisters 3.

Little Sisters of the Poor, The, 2325 N. Lakewood Ave., 60614; Fax: 773-935-9614. Sr. Maria Christine, L.S.P., Supr. Legal Title: *Little Sisters of the Poor of Chicago, Inc.* Sisters 15.

Medical Missionaries of Mary, 3410 W. 60th Pl., 60629. Tel: 773-737-3458; Fax: 773-737-4582. Sisters 4.

Missionaries of Charity, 2234 W. Washington Blvd., 60612. Tel: 312-421-0038. Sr. M. Marilyn, M.C.

Missionary Sisters of Christ the King, 1118 N. Noble St., 60622. Tel: 773-489-0714. Irena Gertruda Szymanska, Supr., 5936 W. Barry Ave., 60634-5130. Tel: 773-889-7979. Sr. Weronika E. Ilnicka, Supr. Sisters 9.

Missionary Sisters of the Sacred Heart of Jesus. Cabrini Hall, 428 St. James Pl., 60614.
Other Addresses: 422 W. Deming Pl., 60614. 420 W. Deming Pl., 60614. 9430 Golf Rd., Des Plaines, 60016. 2826 W. Cermak Rd., 60623. Sisters 26.

Mother of Good Counsel Convent, 3800 Peterson Ave., 60659. Tel: 773-463-3020. Provincialate of the Felician Sisters, Good Counsel High School, Novitiate, Our Lady of the Angels. Sr. Mary Barbara Ann Bosch, C.S.S.F., Prov. Min.; Revs. Michael Suszynski, O.F.M.Conv., Chap. of Provincialate; Philip Wozniak, O.F.M.Conv., Chap. of Infirmary. Professed Sisters 289. Our Lady of the Angels, 3800 W. Peterson, 60659.

Queen of the Resurrection House of Prayer, 7430 W. Talcott Ave., 60631. Sr. Mary Julianne, C.R., Supr. Sisters 30.

St. Scholastica Priory and Academy, Benedictine Sisters of Chicago. (Motherhouse), 7430 N. Ridge Blvd., 60645. Sr. Karen Bland, O.S.B., Prioress. Sisters 96.

Sisters of St. Casimir, Motherhouse and Novitiate, 2601 W. Marquette Rd., 60629-1817. Tel: 773-776-1324. Sr. Marilyn Kuzmickus, S.S.C., Gen. Supr. Sisters 209.

Sisters of the Holy Cross, 7422 N. Harlem, 60631-4409. Tel: 773-774-5449. Sr. Karen Anne Jackson, C.S.C.
Other Residences: 1040 W. Granville, 60660. 3650 W. 96th St., Evergreen Park, 60805. 15119 Catalina Dr., Orland Park, 60462. 6918 W. 112th Pl., Worth, 60482. Sisters of the Holy Cross 8.

Sisters of the Resurrection Provincial House and Novitiate, 7432 Talcott Ave., 60631. Sr. Virginia Ann Wanzek, C.R., Prov. Supr. Sisters 34. Congregation of the Sisters of the Resurrection, Chicago Province. Legal Title: *Sisters of the Resurrection*. Attended by Passionist Fathers.

Society of Helpers, 303 W. Barry, 60657. Tel: 312-486-5359; 384-7707. Provincial Office, 2956 S. Lowe., 60616. Tel: 312-842-1039. Sr. Mary Therese Harrington, Prov. Professed Sisters 30.
Other residences: 1536 W. Wellington, 60657. 2043 N. Humboldt Blvd., 60647. 2039 N. Humboldt Ave., 60647. 2933 N. Sheridan Rd., 60657. 4546 S. Wood, 60609. 515 W. Barry, #458, 60657. 1930 N. Kenmore, 60614. 1850 S. Throop St., 60608. 3130 N. Lake Shore Dr., 60657.

Wright Hall-Sisters of Charity B.V.M., 6364 Sheridan Rd., 60660. Tel: 773-761-7550. Professed Sisters B.V.M. 96.

ALSIP. *Hospital Sisters of the Third Order of St. Francis*, 11923 S. Ridgeway, #10, 60658.

ARLINGTON HEIGHTS. *Missionaries of the Sacred Heart of Jesus and Our Lady of Guadalupe M.S.C.Gpe.*, 1212 E. Euclid Ave., 60004. Tel: 847-255-5616.

Sisters of the Living Word, 800 N. Fernandez Ave. B, 60004-5316. Tel: 708-577-5972; Fax: 708-577-5980. Sr. Mary Ann Zrust, S.L.W., Supr. Gen. & Coord. of Spiritual Life. Sisters 80.

BARTLETT. *Immaculata Congretional Home*, 801 W. Bartlett Rd., 60103-4061. Tel: 708-837-3502; Fax: 708-837-0052. Congregational Home of the Sisters of St. Joseph, T.O.S.F. Management Team: Sr. Lydia Bilecki, S.S.J.-T.O.S.F.; Sr. Elaine Haiduk, S.S.J.-T.O.S.F.; Sr. Patricia Schafke, S.S.J.-T.O.S.F. Sisters in Residence 58.

BERWYN. *Poor Handmaids of Jesus Christ*, 1916 S. Clarence Ave., 60402. Tel: 708-749-0125. Sisters 3.

School Sisters of Notre Dame. (Chicago Province), 1431 Euclid Ave., 60402. Tel: 708-749-1380; 749-1381. Sr. Catherine Sarther, S.S.N.D., Prov. Leader. Professed Sisters 162.

BLUE ISLAND. *Franciscan Sisters of Mary*, 12101 Artesian Ave., 60406-1047. Tel: 708-597-2720. Sisters 3.

Mother of Sorrows Convent, 13811 S. Western Ave., 60406. Tel: 708-385-2103. Legal Title: *Mantellate Sisters Servants of Mary*.
Motherhouse of the Servants of Mary. Sr. M. Gabriel Cossa, O.S.M., Prov. Sisters 23.

DES PLAINES. *Monastery of Discalced Carmelities*, River Rd. and Central, 60016. Tel: 708-298-4241. Mother Catherine of the Mother of God, Prioress.
Attended by Holy Cross Fathers.

Provincial House of the Sisters of the Holy Family of Nazareth, 310 N. River Rd., 60016-1211. Tel: 847-298-6760; Fax: 847-803-1941. Sr. M. Lucille Madura, C.S.F.N., Prov. Supr. Professed Sisters 45.

EVERGREEN PARK. *American Province of Little Company of Mary Sisters*. (Little Company of Mary Sisters), 9350 S. California, 60805. Tel: 708-422-0130; Fax: 708-422-2212. Sr. Carol Pacini, Prov. Leader. Total in Community 32.
Charitable Trust: American Province of Little Company of Mary Sisters Charitable Trust.

HIGHWOOD. *Daughters of Divine Love Congregation*, 140 North Ave., St. James Convent, 60040. Tel: 847-432-9003. Sr. Mary Paul Asoeqwu, D.D.L., Supr.

HOFFMAN ESTATES. *Poor Handmaids of Jesus Christ, Annunciation Convent*, 1480 Ashley Rd., 60195. Tel: 847-519-1384.

HOMETOWN. *Adrian Dominican Sisters, Upper Midwest Mission Chapter*, 8925 S. Kostner Ave., 60456-1006. Tel: 708-636-8178; Fax: 708-636-0031. Sr. Patricia Brady, O.P., Chapter Prioress.

Adrian Dominican Sisters, Midwest Dominican Mission Chapter, 8925 S. Kostner Ave., 60456-1006. Tel: 708-636-7566; Fax: 708-636-0031. Sr. Joella Miller, O.P., Chapter Prioress.

JUSTICE. *Immaculate Conception Prov. House and Novitiate of the Dominican Sisters*, 9000 W. 81st St., 60458. Sr. Natalie, O.P., Prov. Sisters 17.

LA GRANGE PARK. *Sisters of St. Joseph of La Grange*. Sponsored ministries include retirement care cosponsored with Catholic charities, secondary education and School on Wheels, and adult literacy program. 1515 W. Ogden Ave., 60525. Tel: 708-354-9200; Fax: 708-354-9573. Legal Title: *Bethlehem Woods Retirement Living Center, Nazareth Academy, Sisters of St. Joseph Charitable Trust*. Sr. Carol J. Crepeau, C.S.J., Pres. Total in Community 114.

LAKE VILLA. *Handmaids of the Precious Blood-Priory of the Heart of Mary*, 24140 W. Petite Lake Rd., 60046. Tel: 847-356-7729. Sr. Mel Pierre, H.P.B., Prioress. Sisters 3.

LAKE ZURICH. *Daughters of St. Mary of Providence*, Novitiate: 24955 N. Hwy. 12, 60047. Tel: 847-438-5050. Sr. Caryn Haas, Formation Dir.

LEMONT. *Mount Assisi Convent, Sisters of St. Francis of Christ the King*, 13900 Main St., 60439-9736. Sr. M. Ann Barbara Plavac, O.S.F., Prov. Supr. Sisters 80.

Our Lady of Victory Convent, 14700 Main St., 60439. Tel: 630-257-7776; Fax: 630-257-7887. General Motherhouse and Novitiate of the Franciscan Sisters of Chicago. Legal Title: *Franciscan Sisters of Chicago*. Sr. M. Francis Clare Radke, Gen. Supr. Professed Sisters 78.

MELROSE PARK. *Sisters of St. Charles Borromeo*. Missionary Sisters of St. Charles Borromeo (Scalabrinians), 1414 N. 37th Ave., 60160. Tel: 708-343-2162. Sr. Marciana Zambiasi, M.S.S.C., Prov. Supr. Sisters 63; Residents 13.

Charitable Trust: Sisters of St. Charles Borromeo, Province of Our Lady of Fatima Charitable Trust.

OAK FOREST. *Our Lady of Sorrows Priory, Benedictine Sisters of Pontifical Jurisdiction*, 5900 W. 147th St., 60452. Tel: 708-687-2877. Sr. Irene Sebo, O.S.B., Prioress. In res., Rev. Martin N. Winters. Professed 6.

TECHNY. *Provincial Motherhouse of the Missionary Sisters Servants of the Holy Spirit*, 2600 Waukegan Rd., P.O. Box 6026, 60082-6026. Tel: 847-272-5930. Sr. Priscilla Burke, Prov. Supr.; Sr. Dolores Marie Kuhl. Professed Sisters 105.

Arnold Janssen Foundation.

WAUKEGAN. *Franciscan Missionaries of Mary*, 726 S. Lincoln St., 60085. Tel: 847-662-8439. Sr. Noreen Murray, F.M.M., Coord. Sisters 4.

WILMETTE. *Maria Immaculata Convent*, 1041 Ridge Rd., 60091-1560. Tel: 847-853-3400; Fax: 847-251-0482. Motherhouse and Novitiate of the Sisters of Christian Charity. Sr. M. Judith Moran, S.C.C., Prov. Supr. Sisters 28.

Sacred Heart Convent, 2221 Elmwood Ave., 60091-1435. Tel: 847-251-3770. A home for aged and infirm Sisters of Christian Charity. Motherhouse in Wilmette, Illinois. Sr. Anna Domeier, S.C.C., Supr. Retired Sisters 45; Sisters 25.

[P] SECULAR INSTITUTES

RIVER FOREST. *Caritas Christi*, P.O. Box 5162, 60305. Legal Title: *Cultural Crossroads, Inc.* An International Secular Institute of Pontifical Rite, which forms and gives to the Church laywomen who according to their callings, talents, and professional skills seek to respond to the love of Christ in their providential environment by following the demands of the Gospel.

[Q] PIOUS UNIONS AND OTHER SOCIETIES

CHICAGO. *Teresian Institute*, 3926 N. Kildare, 60641. Tel: 773-545-2979. C. Fernandez-Aguinaco, Contact Person.
An international association of the faithful of pontifical right, founded in Spain in 1911. Aim: To promote the integration of Christian faith and culture, through the professional activity of its members. They live out their Christian call from within existing temporal structures, seeking to order and illumine them according to the plan of God, in the manner of leaven.

LIBERTYVILLE. *Marytown, U.S. National Center of the Militia of the Immaculata Movement*, Shrine of St. Maximilian Kolbe, 1600 W. Park Ave., 60048-2593. Tel: 847-367-7800.
International Latin name: Militia Immaculatae (M.I.). An association of clergy, religious and laity dedicated to Catholic evangelization, founded 1917 in Rome by St. Maximilian Kolbe. Revs. Bernard M. Geiger, O.F.M.Conv., Natl. Asst. for Adult M.I. Focus Groups; Patrick Greenough, O.F.M.Conv., Prov. Asst. for M.I.; Bros. Martin Schmitz, O.F.M.Conv., Dir. Volunteers; Francis M. Kalvelage, O.F.M.Conv., Natl. Asst. for Youth Mission of the Immaculata (YMI). Conventual Franciscan Friars 15; Volunteers 6.

[R] VISITING AND NURSING OF THE SICK IN THEIR HOMES

CHICAGO. *Catholic Home Care*, 721 N. LaSalle St., 60610. Tel: 312-655-7415.
For a complete listing, refer to the Special Care Facilities section.

Catholic Home Care Home Services, 721 N. LaSalle St., 60610. Tel: 312-655-7573.
For a complete listing, refer to the Special Care Facilities section.

[S] SOCIETIES, CLUBS AND RESIDENCES

CHICAGO. *Catholic Chinese Cultural Center*. (Formerly: Chinese Friendship House), 856 W. Fullerton Ave., 60614. Tel: 312-348-6856. Rev. John Fu, S.V.D., Dir.

Equestrian Order of the Holy Sepulchre of Jerusalem. (North Central Lieutenancy), 1454 N. Dearborn Pkwy., 60610. Tel: 312-944-5595; Fax: 312-280-2568. Sir Matthew J. Lamb, K.G.C.H.S., Lieutenant; Sir Thomas J. McCabe, K.C.H.S., Sec.

Kolping Center, 5826 N. Elston, 60646. Tel: 773-792-2190. Rev. Richard J. Ehrens.

The Catholic Kolping Society of Chicago.

[T] RETREAT HOUSES

CHICAGO. *Congregation of Our Lady of the Retreat in the Cenacle*, 513 Fullerton Pkwy., 60614. Tel: 312-528-6300. Sr. Marguerite Gautreau, Prov.; Sr. Elizabeth Galbrath, Supr. Professed Sisters 37.

Focolare Movement-Mariapolis Center, 5001 S. Greenwood Ave., 60615. Tel: 773-285-2746. Daytime Capacity 60; Overnight Capacity 30.

BARRINGTON. *Bellarmine Hall*, Box 268, 60011. Tel: 847-381-1261. Jesuit retreat house for laity, priests, and religious. Revs. Donald J. Hayes, S.J.; Bernard J. Mulhern, S.J.; Bros. William R. Haas, S.J.; George A. Prickril, S.J.

The Jesuit Retreat League of Chicago. Tel: 847-381-1261. Revs. George W. Steenken, S.J.; Robert J. Lab, S.J.; J. Michael Sparough, S.J.; Michael E. Dorrler, S.J.

DES PLAINES. *Cabrini Retreat Center*. (Formerly St. Frances Cabrini Retreat House), 9430 Golf Rd., 60016. Tel: 847-297-6530. Sr. Ilaria Povero, M.S.C., Dir. Sisters 3. Retreats for priests, religious, laity & youth. Staffed by Missionary Sisters of the Sacred Heart of Jesus.

GLENVIEW. *Villa Redeemer*, 1111 N. Milwaukee Ave., Box 6, 60025. Tel: 847-724-7804; Fax: 847-724-7816. Retreats for men, women, married and engaged couples and special groups. Conducted by the Redemptorists. Rev. Kevin Fraher, Dir. Legal Title: *The Redemptorists of Glenview, IL*.

LEMONT. *St. Mary's Retreat House*, 14230 Main St., P.O. Box 608, 60439. Tel: 630-257-5102. Bro. Robert Hochevar, O.F.M., Acting Dir.

MUNDELEIN. *Cardinal Stritch Retreat House*, 60060. Tel: 847-566-6060; Fax: 847-566-6082. Rev. Edmund J. Siedlicki, Admin.
Serves the clergy of Chicago and Region VII. Retreatants during year 1,600.

[U] NATIONAL INSTITUTIONS

CHICAGO. *The Catholic Church Extension Society*, Headquarters, 35 E. Wacker Dr., 60601-2105. Tel: 312-236-7240; Fax: 312-236-5276. Legal Title: *The Catholic Church Extension Society of the United States of America*. Most Rev. Oscar H. Libscomb, Vice Chancellor; Rev. Msgr. Kenneth J. Velo, Pres.; Mr. Richard A. Ritter, Vice Pres./Treas.; Paul E. Flaherty, Gen. Sec.

Catholic Kolping Society of America-National Endowment Fund. 1804 Aspen Dr., Mount Prospect, 60056. Tel: 847-824-8768. William B. Mahrenholz, Treas.

Catholic League for Religious Assistance to Poland, Headquarters, 1200 N. Ashland Ave., 60622. Tel: 773-276-2334. Legal Title: *Catholic League*. Most Rev. Thad J. Jakubowski, D.D., Exec. Dir.; Rev. Matt A. Bednarz, Asst. Dir.

Jan Beyzym Society, Inc., 4105 N. Avers Ave., 60618. Tel: 773-588-7476; Fax: 773-588-6517. Polish Jesuits Foreign Missions.

National Association of Diaconate Directors (NADD), 1337 W. Ohio, 60622. Tel: 312-226-4033; Fax: 312-829-8915. Rev. Msgr. Joseph Roth, Pres.; Deacon Maury Reed, Pres. Elect.

National Coalition for Church Vocations, 1603 S. Michigan Ave. #400, 60616. Tel: 312-663-5453; Fax: 312-663-5030. Sr. Diane Poplawski, O.P., Exec. Dir.

National Organization for Continuing Education of Roman Catholic Clergy, Inc., 1337 W. Ohio, 60622. Tel: 312-226-1890; Fax: 312-829-8915. Rev. Francis S. Tebbe, O.F.M., Pres.; Bro. Paul J. Murray, C.F.X., Exec. Dir. Description: A professional organization of those involved in the continuing education-formation of clergy in the Catholic Church. Dioceses and religious communities in the U.S. are full members. Institutions and organizations which are concerned with continuing education-formation of clergy are associate members. Dioceses and provinces outside the U.S. may also be associate members. NOCERCC was founded in 1973 through the efforts of the National Federation of Priests Councils. It is governed by a Board of Directors which involves a president selected by the membership, elected representatives from the 13 NCCB Regions and 2 elected religious representatives. Its services include bi-monthly NewsNotes, Resource publications, an Annual Convention, training for new and experienced directors, regional meetings, consultations and service to regional and interdiocesan programs.

National Religious Vocation Conference, 1603 S. Michigan Ave. #400, 60616. Tel: 312-663-5454; Fax: 312-663-5030. Sr. Catherine Bertrand, S.S.N.D., Exec. Dir.

**The Catholic Guild for the Blind*. Provides devotional services including large print Mass, free tapelending library, spiritual magazine available in Braille, large print and on audio cassette and programs for Catholic schools. 180 N. Michigan Ave., STE. 1700, 60601-7463. Tel: 312-236-8569; Fax: 312-236-8128. Mr. David M. McGowan, CFRE, Exec. Dir.

**Trinity House*. Treatment Center for Clergy and Religious. 3230 S. Lituanica Ave., 60608. Tel: 312-247-7707; Fax: 312-247-1588. Rev. John Keenan, S.S.S., Psy.D., Ph.D., Dir.

**Zambian Rehabilitation Institute*. Organized to raise funds and recruit volunteers in the U.S. to assist in the establishment of an addictions treatmment center for clergy, religious and laity. Initial location of center in Zambia will also serve Eastern and South Africa. 5414 N. Luna Ave., 60630-1310. Tel: 773-792-2380; Fax: 773-792-9093. Mr. Thomas F. Healy, Contact Person.

RIVER FOREST.

**American Friends of the Ecole Biblique*, 7200 W. Division St., 60305-1294. Tel: 708-771-3030; Fax: 708-771-4510. Rev. Peter J. Hereley, O.P., Pres.; Judy Valentine Gerth, Managing Dir. Tel: 847-475-4114. Organized to raise funds in the U.S. to support the work of the Ecole Biblique et Archeologique Francaise de Jerusalem and promote the dissemination of biblical scholarship and archeological research is provided through newsletters, receptions, and seminars with biblical scholars.

Dominican Leadership Conference, 7200 W. Division St., 60305. Tel: 708-771-0909; Fax: 708-771-4510. Sr. Elizabeth Schaefer, O.P., Exec. Dir. Legal Title: *Dominican Leadership Conference of Dominican Men and Women Religious in the United States of America*.
Conferences:
Parable Conference for Dominican Life and Mission.
Opus: A History of the Order of Preachers in the United States.

TECHNY. *Divine Word Missionaries, Inc., Divine Word Funds, Inc.*, 1835 Waukegan Rd., Box 6099, 60082-6099. Tel: 847-272-7600; Fax: 847-272-8572. Revs. Thomas A. Krosnicki, S.V.D., Pres.; Francis J. Kamp, S.V.D., Treas.

S.V.D., Catholic Universities, Inc., 1835 Waukegan Rd., Box 6099, 60082-6099. Tel: 847-272-7600; Fax: 847-272-8572. Revs. Thomas A. Krosnicki, S.V.D., Pres.; Francis J. Kamp, S.V.D., Treas.

[V] MINISTRY IN HIGHER EDUCATION

CHICAGO. *Ministry in Higher Education*, 700 S. Morgan St., 60607. Tel: 312-829-0670. Ms. Jan Slattery, Dir.
Non-Catholic Institutions:
Chicago State University, 95th & Martin Luther King Dr., 60628. Tel: 312-995-3869. Ms. Corrine Grant.
College of Lake County, 19351 W. Washington, Grayslake, 60030. Tel: 847-2236-6601, Ext. 290.
Moraine Valley Community College, P.O. Box 311, Worth, 60482. Tel: 708-974-4300, Ext. 4263. Mr. William Droel.
Northeastern Illinois University/North Park College, c/o Precious Blood, 2411 W. Congress Pkwy., 60612. Tel: 312-733-5331. Rev. Joseph A. Pitts, O.M.I.
Northwestern University/Kendall College, Sheil Center, 2110 N. Sheridan Rd., Evanston, 60201. Tel: 847-328-4648. Rev. Kenneth C. Simpson, B.S., M.Div., D.Min., Dir.
University of Chicago Calvert House, 5735 S. University Ave., 60637. Tel: 312-288-2311; 2312. Rev. Willard F. Jabusch, Ph.D., Dir.
University of Illinois at Chicago - John Paul II Newman Center, 700 S. Morgan St., 60607-3429. Tel: 312-226-1880. Rev. Patrick Marshall.
University of Illinois at the Medical Center, 916 S. Wolcott Ave., 60612. Tel: 312-733-6370. Rev. Patrick M. Marshall.
Triton Community College, Triton Campus Ministry, 3005 N. 76th Ct., Elmwood Park, 60635. Tel: 708-456-0300; 456-5225, Ext. 752. Sr. Christine Myskow, O.S.F.
Illinois Institute of Technology, c/o St. James, 2942 S. Wabash Ave., 60616. Tel: 312-842-1919. Mr. Eric Schwister.
Truman City College, c/o 4827 N. Kenmore Ave., 60640. Tel: 312-784-1932. Rev. Trinh Peter Hung.
Wilbur Wright College, c/o 3005 W. 76th Ct., Elmwood Park, 60707. Tel: 312-481-8874. Sr. Judith Flinn, C.S.J.
Columbia College/Roosevelt University/Art Institute/John Marshall Law School, c/o Old St. Mary's, 21 E. Van Buren St., 60605. Tel: 312-922-3444.
Lake Forest College, c/o St. Mary, 175 E. Illinois St., 60045. Tel: 708-234-0205.
Catholic Institutions:
Barat College, 700 E. Westleigh Rd., Lake Forest, 60045. Tel: 708-234-3000, Ext. 341. Ms. Karen Rushen; Sr. Patricia Reiss, R.S.C.J.
De Paul University, Campus Ministry-Stewart Center, 2311 N. Seminary Ave., 60614. Tel: 312-362-8515. Ms. Cathy Flaherty, Admin. Asst.
De Paul University, Campus Ministry Department, 25 E. Jackson Blvd., 60604. Tel: 312-362-6910. Dr. Robert Ludwig, Dir.
Loyola University of Chicago, Univeristy Ministry Dept., 6525 N. Sheridan Rd., 60626. Tel: 312-508-2200. Mr. Lucien Roy, Dir.; Rev. Lawrence Reuter, S.J., Vice Pres. of University Ministry. Tel: 773-508-2089.
Loyola University of Chicago, 800 N. Michigan Ave., 60611. Tel: 312-915-600. Mr. Lucien Roy, Dir.
Loyola University Medical Center, 2160 S. First Ave., Maywood, 60153. Tel: 708-216-3561. Ms. Maureen Fuechtmann, Dir.
Rosary College, 7900 W. Division St., River Forest, 60305. Tel: 708-524-6685. Ms. Mary Mertzlufft.
St. Xavier University, 3700 W. 103rd St., 60655. Tel: 773-298-3140; 298-3126. Ms. Eileen Doherty.

[W] PERSONAL PRELATURE

CHICAGO. *Midtown Center*, 1825 N. Wood St., 60622. Tel: 773-292-5450; 292-0660. Revs. Charles Ferrer; James Socias.

Northview University Center, 7225 N. Greenview Ave., 60626. Tel: 773-465-3468. Revs. Fred Piegl; Claudio Urbano.

Opus Dei. (Prelature of the Holy Cross and Opus Dei), Delegate Vicariate, 5800 N. Keating Ave., 60646. Tel: 773-283-5800. Very Rev. William H. Stetson, Delegate Vicar; Revs. Peter V. Armenio; John R. Meyer.

OAK PARK. *Oak Park Study Center*, 831 S. Euclid Ave., 60304. Tel: 708-383-0928. Revs. Richard L. Schendt; Barry Cole. Legal Title: *The Work of God, Inc.*

[X] MISCELLANEOUS LISTINGS

CHICAGO. Conducted by Inter-Cultural Association. Janet E. MacLean, Dir.

**Aid for Women*. Dedicated to upholding the principles of Human Vitae and Evangelium Vitae, the organization maintains a crisis center where any pregnant woman will find help and encouragement to choose life for her unborn child through pregnancy testing, confidential counseling and referral to community resources. 8 S. Michigan Ave., 60603. Tel: 312-621-1100; Fax: 312-621-1972. Ms. Megan Lynch, Dir.

Angel Guardian German Catholic Orphan Society of Chicago, 126 N. Des Plaines St., 60661. Tel: 312-655-7040.

Apostolate of the Handicapped, 721 N. LaSalle, 60610. Tel: 312-655-7188. James Grady, Pres.; Rev. Charles F. Kelly, St. Daniel the Prophet, 5330 S. Nashville, 60638. Active membership 750.

The Aquin Guild, 1025 W. Fry St., 60622. Tel: 312-280-9199. Rev. John W. Clemens, Dir. Provides spiritual direction to Catholics engaged in public and parochial education.

Bonaventure House, Inc., P.O. Box 148187, 60614-8187. Tel: 773-327-9921; Fax: 773-327-9113. Mr. Timothy McCormick, CEO. Congregation of Alexian Brothers, Immaculate Conception Province. Residence for persons with AIDS.

Catholic Chaplaincy at O'Hare. Mailing Address: Chicago O'Hare International Airport, P.O. Box 66353, 60666. Tel: 773-686-2636; Fax: 773-686-0130. Rev. John A. Jamnicky, Chap.; Deacon James O'Malley, Assoc. Chap.

Catholic Conference of Illinois, 500 N. Clark, 60610. Tel: 312-467-4375. 200 Broadway, Springfield, 62701. Tel: 217-528-9200. Mr. Doug Delaney, Exec. Dir. Assoc. Directors: Ms. Jura S. Scharf; Ms. Joan McKinney.

Catholic Health Alliance for Metropolitan Chicago, 203 N. Wabash Ave., Suite 1404, 60601. Tel: 312-606-0266; Fax: 312-606-0357. Sr. Tommasina Lanski, M.S.C.

Catholic Health Partners Services. Sponsored by the Daughters of Charity National Health System-East Central, Inc. and the Missionary Sisters of the Sacred Heart of Jesus to operate St. Anthony, Columbus and St. Joseph hospitals. 2913 N. Commonwealth Ave., 60657. Tel: 312-665-3170.

Catholic Office of the Deaf, 721 N. LaSalle, 60610. Tel: 312-655-7899 (Voice); 751-8368 (TDD). Rev. Joseph Mulcrone, Dir.

Catholic Youth, Archdiocese of Chicago, 1658 W. Grand Ave., 60622. Tel: 312-733-7405. Revs. John Smyth, Dir.; David Ryan, Dir., Oper. Mgmt.; Joanne Walczynski, Youth Ministry Coord. of Vicariate I; Patrick Pacer, Youth Ministry Coord. of Vicariate II; Jesse Estrade, Youth Ministry Coord. of Vicariate III; Michael Molitor, Youth Ministry Coord. of Vicariate IV; Maria Perez Eraci, Youth Ministry Coord. of Vicariate V; Deacon Frederick Mason, Youth Ministry Coord. of Vicariate VI; Ms. Kimberly Williams, Coord. Athletics; Irene Friend, Coord. of Training & Faith Formation; Arlene Nash, Sec. & Admin. Asst. to TEC, Day of the Spirit, Boy Scouts, Girl Scouts, Campfire; James Eraci, Dir., Archdiocesan Camping Prog. Office Mgr., Special Events, Newsletter (Shout).

**Central American Martyrs Center (Su Casa Catholic Worker Community)*, 5045 S. Laflin, 60609. Tel: 773-376-9263. Sr. Mary Davis, I.H.M.; Monica Sandschafer, Cabrini Vol.; Bros. Denis Murphy, F.S.C.; James Krause, F.S.C.; Alan Partham, F.S.C.

The Chicago Center for Peace Studies, P.O. Box 909706,

60690. Tel: 312-701-7262. James A. Serritella, Contact Person.
The Chicago Marian Center, 7262 W. Foster Ave., 60656. Tel: 773-774-7700. Kathleen Long, Contact Person.
Claret Center, 5540 S. Everett, 60637. Tel: 312-643-6259. Resources for Counseling and Spiritual Direction. Anne M. Luther, Exec. Dir.
Claretian Associates, Inc. Organization to provide affordable housing and encourage neighborhood improvement in South Chicago. 9108 S. Brandon Ave., 60617. Tel: 773-734-9181. Ms. Donna Drinan, Contact Person.
Claretian Volunteers and Lay Missionaries, 205 W. Monroe St., 60606. Tel: 312-236-7846; Fax: 312-236-7230. Directors: Ms. Becky Morrill; Ms. Michelle Scheidt.
Court of Appeals-Province of Chicago, 20 N. Wacker Dr., Ste. 3420, 60606. Tel: 312-553-4080. The Court of Second Instance in matrimonial cases for the Tribunals of the Province of Chicago. Revs. Robert L. Kealy, S.T.L., J.D., J.C.D., Judicial Vicar; John P. Lucas, S.T.L., J.C.L., Adjutant Judicial Vicar; Ms. Jane McCarthy, Chief Notary.
Focolare Movement, P.O. Box 53426, 60653. Tel: 773-285-2746. Women, 5017 S. Greenwood Ave., 60615. Tel: 773-536-7873; Fax: 773-536-5054. Ms. Paola Santostefano, Contact Person, Men, 1112 S. Oak Park Ave., Oak Park, 60304. Tel: 708-848-6576; Fax: 708-848-6950. Mr. William Neu, Contact Person.
Work of Mary founded in Trent, Italy in 1943. International headquarters are in Rome, Italy; national formation center in New York.
Foundation for Adult Catechetical Teaching Aids, 6007 N. Sheridan Rd., Suite 22A, 60660. Tel: 818-990-4694; Fax: 773-334-6774. Rev. Msgr. Gerard P. Weber, Pres.; Mr. Buckley, Contact Person.
Franciscan Friars Retirement Corporation, 6107 Kenmore Ave., 60660.
Franciscan Outreach Assoc., 1645 W. LeMoyne St., 60622. Tel: 773-278-6724. Bro. Herb Rempe, O.F.M., Exec. Dir.
Owns & operates: Marquard Center and House of Mary & Joseph in Chicago, and St. Anthony Pilgrim House in Harvey.
Friends of the Metropolitan Andrew Sheptysky Hospital, 126 N. DesPlaines, 60661. Most Rev. Edwin Conway, Pres.
Holy Family Church Inc., 2050 N. Clark St., 60614.
Institute for Spiritual Leadership, 4906 S. Greenwood Ave., 60615. Tel: 773-373-7953; Fax: 773-373-5794. Education Center for Spiritual Direction and Renewal. Sr. Patricia M. Bombard, B.V.M., Exec. Dir.
Intercommunity Housing Corporation, 2900 N. Lakeshore Dr., 60657. Tel: 773-665-3129. Janet Bilandic, Exec. Dir.
Jesuit International Missions, Inc., 2050 N. Clark St., 60614. Tel: 312-975-6363. Rev. Gerald P. Grace, S.J.
Kolbe House, 2434 S. California Ave., 60608. Tel: 312-773-0070. Catholic prison ministry. Revs. Lawrence J. Craig, Exec. Dir.; David A. Kelly, C.PP.S.; Deacon George Brooks; Sr. Miriam Wilson, O.S.B.; Deacons James Morgan; Ronald DeRose.
Loyola Press, 3441 N. Ashland Ave., 60657. Tel: 773-281-1818. Rev. George A. Lane, S.J., Dir.
Marist Volunteer Program, 4200 W. 115th St., 60655. Tel: 773-881-5300.
Martin de Porres House, 3322 Washington Blvd., 60624. Tel: 773-826-9336. Margaret Brooks, Pres.; Cathryn Peters, Vice Pres.; Claire Cummings, Sec.
Mercy Housing Corporation, 10024 S. Central Park, 60655-3132. Tel: 773-779-6011. Sisters of Mercy of the Americas, Regional Community of Chicago. Sr. Lucille McKillop, R.S.M., Contact Person.
The Midwest Patrons of the Arts in the Vatican Museums, 1454 N. Dearborn Pkwy., 60610. Tel: 312-280-8385. Mr. Matthew J. Lamb, Pres.
Mother Cabrini League, 434 W. Deming Pl., 60614. Tel: 773-883-7329. The purpose of the League is to spread devotion to St. Frances Xavier Cabrini. Sr. Philippa Provenzano, M.S.C.; Sr. Melba Russo, M.S.C; Joan Conrath; Anna Grenvich.
The New World, 1144 W. Jackson Blvd., 60607. Tel: 312-243-1300. Publishers of The New World; Chicago Catolico; and the Archdiocesan Directory. Mary Claire Gart, Editor Pro Tem.
Nowe Zycie Association, 5026 W. Diversey Ave., 60693. Tel: 773-283-4700. Mr. Roman Harmata, Contact Person.
Polish Manual Training School for Boys, 126 N. Des Plaines St., 60661. Tel: 312-655-7040.
S.F.V., Inc., 1645 W. LeMoyne St., 60622. Tel: 773-278-6724. Sponsor corporation of St. Francis Village (a retirement village) in Crowley, TX. Rev. J. Michael Ewert, O.F.M., Pres.
St. Anthony Pucci Charitable Trust, 3121 W. Jackson Blvd., 60612. Tel: 773-533-0360.
St. Hedwig's Industrial School for Girls, 126 N. Des Plaines St., 60661. Tel: 312-655-7040.
St. Joseph Bohemian Orphanage, 126 N. Des Plaines St., 60661. Tel: 312-655-7040.
St. Thomas Aquinas Foundation. (STAF) (St. Albert the Great Prov.), 1909 S. Ashland Ave., 60608-2994. Very Rev. Edward H. Ruane, O.P., Sec. & Treas.
Serra International. U.S./Canada Council, 65 E. Wacker Pl., Ste. 1210, 60601-7203. Tel: 312-782-2163; Fax: 312-782-2358. Mr. Robert Raccuglia, Exec. Dir., Sierra International; Mr. E. V. Verbeke, Exec. Admin., U.S./Canada Council.
Servite Friars-Eastern Province Retirement Trust, 3121 W. Jackson Blvd., 60612. Tel: 773-533-0360.
Servite Friars-Eastern Province, Inc., 3121 W. Jackson Blvd., 60612. Tel: 773-533-0360.
Shelters for the Homeless, Inc., 126 N. Desplaines St., 60606. Tel: 312-236-5172.
**The Institute on Religious Life*, 3051 N. Christiana, 60618. Tel: 773-267-1195; Fax: 773-267-2044. Mailing Address: P.O. Box 41007, 60641. Rev. L. Dudley Day, O.S.A., Assoc. Exec. Dir.
United Stand Family Center, 3731 W. 62nd St., 60629. Tel: 773-585-4499. Dr. Kim Mis, C.S.S.F., Exec. Dir. Staff 34. Education, Prevention, Problem Identification, Consultation, and Intervention with Children and Families.
Villa Guadalupe Senior Services Corporation, 9108 S. Brandon Ave., 60617. Tel: 773-734-9181. Organization to provide affordable housing and related services for Senior Citizens in South Chicago. Marta C. Bukata, Chair.; Carmen Mendoza, Treas.
The Warde Corporation, 10024 S. Central Park, 60655-3132. Tel: 773-779-6011. Sisters of Mercy of the Americas, Regional Community of Chicago. Sr. Lucille McKillop, R.S.M., Contact Person.

BERWYN. *Servants of Mary, Inc.*, 1439 S. Harlem Ave., 60402. Tel: 708-795-8885.

BLUE ISLAND. *St. Francis Health Care Foundation*, 12935 S. Gregory St., 60406. Tel: 708-597-2000. A Member of the SSM Health Care System.

ELK GROVE VILLAGE. *Alexian Brothers Health Management, Inc., (ABHM)*, 600 Alexian Way, 60007; Fax: 708-981-5561. Congregation of Alexian Brothers, Immaculate Conception Province.
Alexian Brothers Health System Inc., 600 Alexian Way, 60007; Fax: 708-981-5561. Congregation of Alexian Brothers, Immaculate Conception Province.
Alexian Brothers of America, Inc., 600 Alexian Way, 60007; Fax: 708-981-5561. Congregation of Alexian Brothers, Immaculate Conception Province.
**Chicago Catholic Healthcare System, Inc.*, 600 Alexian Way, 60007; Fax: 708-981-5561. Congregation of Alexian Brothers, Immaculate Conception Province.

EVERGREEN PARK. *American Province of Little Company of Mary Sisters Charitable Trust*, 9350 S. California, 60805. Tel: 708-422-0130; Fax: 708-422-2212.
Little Company of Mary Hospital and Health Care Centers, 2800 W. 95th St., 60642.

LAGRANGE PARK. *Nazareth Academy*, 1209 W. Ogden Ave., 60525.
Sisters of St. Joseph of LaGrange Charitable Trust, 1515 W. Ogden Ave., 60525. Tel: 708-354-9200; Fax: 708-354-9573.

MUNDELEIN. *Civitas Dei Foundation*, 232 W. Park St., Box 665, 60060. Tel: 847-566-1462. The Journal is named Chicago Studies. Rev. George J. Dyer.

NORTHLAKE. *Italian Catholic Federation*, 46 N. Wolf Rd., 60164. Tel: 708-562-0500. Rev. Charles V. Fanelli, Chap.
Scalabrini Village, 444 N. Wolf Rd., 60164. Tel: 708-562-4402.

SCHAUMBURG. *Rainbows for All God's Children, Inc.*, 1111 Tower Rd., 60173-4305. Tel: 847-310-1880; Fax: 847-310-0120. Mrs. Suzy Yehl Marta, Founder & Pres.

TECHNY. *Blessed Arnold Religious Charitable Trust*, 1985 Waukegan Rd., 60082. Tel: 847-205-1565. Society of the Divine Word. Rev. Thomas Griffith, S.V.D., Contact Person.

WAUKEGAN. *Lake Shore Catholic Academy*, 510 Tenth St., 60085. Tel: 847-623-4070. Sr. Miriam Patrick Cummings, S.S.N.D., Admin.

WESTCHESTER. *Christian Brothers Counseling Center, Inc.*, 1840 Mayfair Ave., 60154. Tel: 708-562-1260. Sr. M. Jean Keeley, O.P., Ph.D., Dir. Staff Psychologists & Counselors: James Zullo, F.S.C., Ph.D.; Sr. Joan Scanlon, O.P., Ph.D.; Sr. M. Jean Keeley, O.P., Ph.D.; Patricia Campion, Psy.D.; Denise Simmons Giblin, M.S.W., L.C.S.W.; Barbara DeCoursey Roy, M.A.; Joseph Fortunato, Psy.D. (Cand.).

WILMETTE. *Musica Pacis*, Office of the Treasurer, P.O. Box 969, 60091. Tel: 847-624-2559. Revs. Willard F. Jabusch, Pres.; Robert H. Festle, Sec.; Alec J. Wolff, Treas.

[Y] CLOSED INSTITUTIONS

CHICAGO. *Chicago Archdiocesan Archives and Records Center*, 711 West Monroe St., 60606. Tel: 312-831-0711; Fax: 312-831-0610. The following parish, school or institution records may be found at the above address unless otherwise indicated. Notations to sacramental records of closed parishes held by the Archives and Records Center should be directed to the Archives and Records Center and should specify the name of the parish. The location of records periodically changes. Inquiries for records of parishes, schools or institutions not on this list should be directed to the above address.
Academy of St. Benedict the African (May St.).
St. Adalbert School, St. Adalbert Parish, 1650 W. 17th St., 60608. Tel: 312-226-0340.
St. Agatha School.
Blessed Agnes Commercial High School, St. Agnes of Bohemia School, 2643 S. Central Park, 60623. Tel: 312-522-0143.
St. Agnes (39th & Washtenaw).
St. Agnes School (39th & Washtenaw).
Alexine Center School (La Grange).
All Saints (State St.).
All Saints School (State St.).
All Saints (Wallace St.).
Sacramental Records: All Saints/St. Anthony Parish, 518 W. 28th Pl., 60616. Tel: 312-842-2744.
School Records:
St. Aloysius School & Commercial High School.
St. Alphonsus School (Lemont), St. Alphonsus/St. Patrick, 205 Cass St., Lemont, 60439. Tel: 708-257-2380.
St. Alphonsus Commercial High School.
Alvernia High School.
St. Andrew Misson (Wadsworth), St. Patrick Parish, 15000 Wadsworth Rd., Wadsworth, 60083. Tel: 708-244-4161.
Angel Guardian Orphanage.
St. Ann (Chicago Heights).
St. Ann School (Chicago Heights).
St. Ann High School (Leavitt), St. Ann, 2211 W. 18th Pl., 60608. Tel: 312-829-4153.
St. Anne (Garfield Blvd.).
St. Anne School (Garfield Blvd.).
St. Anne (Waukegan), Immaculate Conception, 508 Grand Ave., Waukegan, 60085. Tel: 708-336-3684.
St. Anne Mission Chapel (Richton), St. Liborius, 71 W. 35th St., Steger, 60475. Tel: 708-754-1363.
Annunciation (Wabansia).
Annunciation School (Wabansia).
St. Anthony of Padua (24th Pl.), All Saints-St. Anthony, 518 W. 28th Pl., 60616. Tel: 312-842-2744.
St. Anthony School & Commercial High School (24th Pl.).
Aquinas Catholic High School.
Aquinas Dominican High School.
Ascension (Harvey), Ascension-St. Susanna, 15234 Myrtle, Harvey, 60426-3194. Tel: 708-333-0931.
Ascension of Our Lord (Evanston).
Ascension of Our Lord School (Evanston).
Assumption School (24th St.).
Assumption (Marshfield Ave.).
Assumption School (Marshfield Ave.).
Assumption BVM (123rd St.).
Assumption BVM School (123rd St.).
St. Attracta (Cicero).
St. Attracta School (Cicero).
St. Attracta-St. Valentine.
St. Attracta-St. Valentine School (Cicero).
St. Augustine (S. Laflin).
St. Augustine School & High School.
St. Bartholomew (Waukegan), Sts. Joseph & Bartholomew, 501 S. Utica, Waukegan, 60079-0440. Tel: 708-623-2655.
St. Bartholomew School (Waukegan), St. Bartholomew, 730 S. Lincoln, Waukegan, 60085. Tel: 708-623-0468.
St. Basil, St. Basil/Visitation 5443 S. Honore, 60609.
Bellarmine School of Theology-Loyola University of Chicago, Dean of Students of Arts and Sciences, 820 N. Michigan Ave., 60611.
St. Bernard (65th St.).
St. Bernard School.
Bishop Quarter Boarding School for Motherless Boys.
Bishop Quarter Junior Military School.
St. Blase School, St. Joseph School, 5641 S. 73rd St., Summit, 60501. Tel: 708-458-2927.
St. Bonaventure School (Diversey).
St. Boniface (N. Noble).
St. Boniface School (N. Noble).
St. Brendan (Racine).
St. Brendan School (Racine).
St. Bridget.
St. Bridget School & High School.
St. Bronislava School.
Cabrini Green Alternate High School. Catholic Charities, Division of Services for Children and Youth, 126 N. Des Plaines, 60606. Tel: 312-236-5172, Ext. 429.
Cardinal Stritch High School.
Carmel High School. (Boys and Girls), Carmel High

School, One Carmel Pkwy., Mundelein, 60060-2499. Tel: 708-566-3000.
St. Carthage (73rd St.).
St. Carthage School.
St. Casimir (Chicago Heights).
St. Casimir School (Chicago Heights).
St. Casimir (Whipple St.), Our Lady of Tepeyac, 2226 S. Whipple St., 60623. Tel: 773-521-8400.
St. Casimir School (Whipple St.).
St. Catherine Academy.
St. Catherine High School. see Siena High School.
St. Catherine of Genoa.
St. Catherine of Genoa School.
St. Catherine of Siena (Oak Park).
Sacramental Records: St. Catherine/St. Lucy Parish, 38 N. Austin Blvd., Oak Park, 60302. Tel: 708-386-8077.
School Records: St. Catherine/St. Lucy School, 27 W. Washington Blvd., Oak Park, 60302. Tel: 708-386-5286.
St. Cecelia (Wells St.).
St. Cecelia School (Wells St.).
St. Charles Borromeo (Hoyne).
St. Charles Borromeo School (Chicago).
St. Charles Borromeo School (Melrose Park).
St. Charles Lwanga (W. Garfield).
St. Charles Lwanga School (W. Garfield).
St. Clara (Woodlawn).
St. Clara School (Woodlawn), St. Gelasius School, 6358 S. Blackstone, 60637. Tel: 312-324-8430.
St. Clara-St. Cyril (S. Woodlawn).
St. Clara-St. Cyril School (Woodlawn), St. Gelasius School, 6358 S. Blackstone, 60637. Tel: 312-324-8430.
St. Clement High School.
St. Columbkille (Paulina).
St. Columbkille School (Paulina).
St. Columbkille High School, Mother Guerin High School, 8001 Belmont Ave., River Grove, 60171. Tel: 708-453-6233.
St. Constance High School.
Corpus Christi High School, Hales Franciscan High School, 4930 S. Cottage Grove, 60615. Tel: 312-285-8400.
St. Cyril (Blackstone).
St. Cyril School (Blackstone), St. Gelasius School, 6358 S. Blackstone, 60637. Tel: 312-324-8430.
Ss. Cyril & Methodius Church & School (Hermitage Ave.).
Ss. Cyril & Methodius Church & School (Walton St.).
St. David School.
St. David Church, All Saints-St. Anthony, 518 W. 28th Pl., 60616. Tel: 312-842-2744.
De Lourdes College (Des Plaines), Holy Family College, Registrar's Office, Grant Ave. & Frankford Ave., Philadelphia, PA, 19114. Tel: 215-637-4851.
DePaul Academy, DePaul University, Registrar's Office, 243 S. Wabash, 60604. Tel: 312-341-8610.
St. Dionysius (Cicero).
St. Dionysius School (Cicero).
St. Dominic (Locust).
St. Dominic School & High School.
St. Donatus School.
St. Elizabeth High School.
Englewood Catholic Academy.
Englewood Catholic Academy (Laflin St.), Academy of St. Benedict the African, 6020 S. Laflin, 60636. Tel: 312-776-3316.
Englewood Catholic Academy (May St.).
Englewood Catholic Academy.
St. Fidelis School (N. Washtenaw).
St. Finbarr (14th St.).
St. Finbarr High School.
St. Florian Mission (52nd & Archer), St. Camillus, 5426 S. Lockwood Ave., 60638. Tel: 312-767-8183.
Ford City Catholic Center.
Fornier Institute, DePaul University, Registrar's Office, 243 S. Wabash, 60604. Tel: 312-341-8610.
St. Frances Xavier Cabrini (Lexinton St.).
St. Frances Xavier Cabrini School (Lexinton St.).
St. Francis de Paula.
St. Frances de Paula School (S. Ellis).
St. Francis of Assisi Church (Kostner Ave.), St. Francis of Assisi/Our Lady of the Angels, 3808 W. Iowa St., 60651. Tel: 773-235-3132.
St. Francis of Assisi School (Kostner Ave.).
St. Francis Xavier (Nelson), Resurrection, 2840 W. Nelson, 60618-7012. Tel: 312-478-9705.
St. Francis Xavier School (Nelson).
St. Gabriel Commercial High School.
St. Gabriel School, 4500 S. Wallace St., 60609. Tel: 312-268-6636.
St. George (Lituanica Ave.).
St. George School & Commercial High School (Lituanica Ave.).
St. George School (Ewing Ave.).
St. George (Wentworth Ave.).
St. George School (Wentworth Ave.).
St. George High School (Evanston), Christian Brothers Center, 200 De La Salle Dr., Romeoville, 60441. Tel: 312-242-1240.
St. Gerard Majella School (Markham).
Good Shepherd Chapel. (Illinois Technical School for Colored Girls).
Heart of Mary High School.
St. Hedwig Mission, St. John Berchmans, 2517 W. Logan Blvd., 60647. Tel: 312-486-4300.
St. Hedwig Orphanage (Niles).
Holy Child High School (Waukegan), St. Anastasia School, 629 Glen Flora, Waukegan, 60685. Tel: 708-623-8320.
Holy Cross (65th St.).
Holy Cross School (65th St.).
Holy Cross School.
Holy Family (North Chicago).
Holy Family School (North Chicago).
Holy Family Academy (Division St.).
Holy Family Extension High School (Des Plaines), Sisters of Holy Family of Nazareth, Provincial Archives, 353 N. River Rd., Des Plaines, 60016. Tel: 708-298-6760.
Holy Ghost Church & School.
Holy Guardian Angel (Arthington/Cabrini).
Holy Guardian Angel School.
Holy Rosary Slovak (108th St.).
Holy Rosary Slovak School (108th St.).
Holy Rosary School (113th & King Dr.).
Holy Rosary (North Chicago).
Holy Rosary School (North Chicago).
Holy Rosary School (Western Ave.).
Holy Trinity School (Noble St.).
Holy Trinity (Wolcott Ave.).
Holy Trinity School (Wolcott Ave.).
St. Hyacinth Mission (Spaulding), St. Hyacinth Parish, 3636 N. Wolfram, 60618. Tel: 312-342-3636.
Immaculata High School.
Immaculate Conception School (Aberdeen St.).
Immaculate Conception Commercial High School (Aberdeen St.).
Immaculate Conception-St. Bridget School.
Immaculate Conception (Aberdeen St.).
Immaculate Conception School (Exchange St.).
Immaculate Conception School (Highland Park).
Immaculate Conception School (North Park).
Immaculate Heart of Mary Vicariate (Ashland Ave.), Holy Cross-Immaculate Heart of Mary Parish, 4541 S. Wood St., 60609. Tel: 312-376-3900.
St. Irenaeus School (Park Forest).
St. James (Fremont Center), St. Mary, 22333 W. Erhart Rd., Mundelein, 60060. Tel: 708-223-0010.
St. Jarlath (Jackson).
St. Jarlath School (Jackson).
St. Jean Baptiste (33rd Pl. & Wood St.).
Jesuit School of Theology. Loyola University of Chicago, Office of the Dean of Graduate School, 820 N. Michigan Ave, 60611.
Old St. John (18th St.).
St. John Cantius School.
St. John Chrysostom (Bellwood).
St. John Chrysostom School (Bellwood).
St. John Nepmucene Church & School.
St. John of God Church & School (S. Throop).
St. John the Baptist (50th Pl.).
St. John the Baptist School (50th Pl.).
St. John the Baptist School (Harvey), Mary of Nazareth School, 15727 S. Emerald, Harvey, 60426. Tel: 708-331-5076.
St. Joseph (Saginaw St.).
St. Joseph School (Saginaw St.).
St. Joseph (Chicago Heights).
St. Joseph School (Chicago Heights).
St. Joseph (Saginaw).
St. Joseph School (Saginaw).
St. Joseph (Waukegan), Sts. Joseph & Bartholomew, 501 S. Utica, Waukegan, 60079-0440. Tel: 708-623-2655.
St. Joseph School (Waukegan).
St. Joseph School (Wilmette), St. Joseph Parish, 1747 Lake Ave., Wilmette, 60091. Tel: 708-251-0771.
St. Joseph & St. Anne, Our Lady of Fatima, 2751 W. 38th Pl., 60632-1686. Tel: 312-927-2421.
St. Joseph & St. Anne Commercial High School, Our Lady of Fatima, 2751 W. 38th Pl., 60632-1686. Tel: 312-927-2421.
St. Joseph Academy (La Grange).
St. Joseph Mission (13th St.).
St. Joseph Mission (13th St.).
St. Joseph Servite Seminary (Elgin-St. Charles), Provincial Archives, Servite Provincial Center, 3121 W. Jackson Blvd., 60612. Tel: 312-533-0360.
St. Josaphat Commercial High School.
St. Justin Martyr (71st St.).
St. Justin Martyr School.
St. Kevin School.
St. Leonard Commercial High School (Berwyn), St. Leonard School, 3322 S. Clarence, Berwyn, 60402. Tel: 708-749-1989.
Lewis Memorial Maternity Hospital.
Little Flower High School.
Loretto Academy (Woodlawn).
Loretto Academy & High School (Englewood).
St. Louis de France (117th St.).
St. Louis de France School (117th St.).
St. Louis (Polk St.).
St. Louis Academy (117th Ave.), St. Jude the Apostle Convent, 890 E. 154th St., South Holland, 60473. Tel: 708-333-7595.
St. Lucy. Sacramental Records: St. Catherine-St. Lucy, 38 N. Austin Blvd., Oak Park, 60302. Tel: 708-386-8077.
School Records:
St. Lucy. St. Ludimilla, Our Lady of Tepeyac, 2226 S. Whipple St., 60623. Tel: 773-521-8400.
St. Ludmilla School.
St. Malachy High School, St. Malachy School, 2252 W. Washington, 60612. Tel: 312-733-2252.
Marian School. Catholic Charities, Division of Services for Children & Youth, 126 N. Des Plaines, 60606. Tel: 312-236-5172, Ext. 429.
St. Mark the Evangelist School.
Marquette Institute (Clark St.).
St. Martin (Princeton).
St. Martin School & Commerical High School (Princeton).
St. Mary School (DesPlaines).
St. Mary School (Evanston).
St. Mary (Lemont), St Patrick, 200 Illinois St., Lemont, 60439. Tel: 708-257-6134.
St. Mary (Waukegan), Immaculate Conception, 508 Grand Ave., Waukegan, 60085. Tel: 708-336-3684.
St. Mary Alternative High School. (to 1976), Collections University of Illinois at Chicago, University Library, Special Collections, Dawson Technical School and University of Chicago Library, P.O. 8198, 60680. Tel: 312-996-2742.
St. Mary Alternative High School (Grenshaw). (1976-1979; some to Dawson Technical School), Chicago City-Wide College-Admissions and Records, 226 W. Jackson Blvd., 60606. Tel: 312-368-7159; 312-641-2595, Ext. 2539.
St. Mary Magdalen School.
St. Mary of Mt. Carmel (Hermitage).
St. Mary of Mt. Carmel School (Hermitage).
St. Mary of Perpetual Help School, Bridgeport Catholic Academy West Campus, 1040 W. 32nd Pl., 60608. Tel: 312-927-1041.
St. Mary of Perpetual Help High School.
St. Mary Training School, Maryville Academy, 1150 N. River Rd., Des Plaines, 60016. Tel: 708-824-6126.
St. Mary School of Nursing (Des Plaines), Holy Family College, Registrar's Office, Grant Ave. & Frankford Ave., Philadelphia, PA, 19114. Tel: 215-637-4851.
Marywood High School (Evanston), Mother Guerin High School, 8001 Belmont Ave., River Grove, 60171. Tel: 312-625-3278.
Mater Dolorosa Seminary (Hillside). See Servite Seminary.
St. Matthew (Walnut St.).
St. Matthew School (Walnut St.).
St. Mel & St. Mel-Holy Ghost.
St. Mel & St. Mel-Holy Ghost School.
St. Mel High School. (up to 1969), Christian Brothers Center, 200 De La Salle Dr., Romeoville, 60441. Tel: 312-242-1240.
Mendel High School.
Mercy High School.
Mercy Mission High School.
St. Michael School (Hudson).
St. Michael Central High School.
St. Michael (Waubansia St.).
St. Michael School (Waubansia St.).
St. Michael Commercial High School (South Shore Dr.).
Misericordia Hospital. Sacramental Records: Our Lady of Fatima, 2751 W. 38th Pl., 60632-1686. Tel: 312-927-2421. Client Records & Adoption Placements: Catholic Charities, 126 N. Des Plaines, 60606. Tel: 312-876-2288; 236-5172, Ext. 330.
Mission of the Holy Ghost (Techny), St. Norbert, 1809 Walters Ave., Northbrook, 60062. Tel: 312-272-7090.
St. Monica (36th St.).
Monastery of Mt. St. Phillip Servite Novitiate. (Granville, WI), Provincial Archives, Servite Provincial Center, 3121 W. Jackson Blvd., 60612. Tel: 312-533-0360.
Mother of God (Waukegan).
Mother of God School (Waukegan).
Mother of Sorrows Grade and High School (Blue Island).
Mount Carmel School (Chicago Heights).
Mundelein High School.
Municipal Tuberculosis Sanitarium. (Sacred Heart Chapel).
Nativity of Our Lord School & Commercial High School, Bridgeport Catholic Academy South Campus, 3700 S. Lowe, 60609. Tel: 312-376-6223.
St. Nicholas School (Evanston).

St. Nicholas (State St.).
St. Nicholas School (State St.).
Notre Dame de Chicago School.
Our Lady of Bethlehem Academy.
Our Lady of Fatima Mission, St. Hyacinth Parish, 3636 N. Wolfram, 60618. Tel: 312-342-3636.
Our Lady of Good Counsel (Western Ave.).
Our Lady of Good Counsel School (Western Ave.).
Our Lady of Guadalupe Chapel, Holy Cross-Immaculate Heart of Mary, 4541 S. Wood St., 60609. Tel: 312-376-3900.
Our Lady of Hope School (Des Plaines).
Our Lady of Hungary (93rd St.).
Our Lady of Hungary School (93rd St.).
Our Lady of Perpetual Help Vicariate (13th St.).
Our Lady of Perpetual Help Vicariate School (13th St.).
Our Lady of Providence Academy. See Providence Academy.
Our Lady of Solace (Sangamon).
Our Lady of Solace School (Sangamon).
Our Lady of the Angels, St. Francis of Assisi/Our Lady of the Angels, 3808 W. Iowa St., 60651. Tel: 773-235-3132.
Our Lady of Angels (Iowa).
Our Lady of the Cross Mission Chapel, St. Margaret Mary, 2324 W. Chase, 60645. Tel: 312-764-0615.
Our Lady of Vilna (23rd St.).
Our Lady of Vilna School (23rd St.), St. Paul School, 2114 W. 22nd Pl., 60608. Tel: 312-847-6078.
St. Patrick Academy (Chicago), McAulay High School, 3737 W. 99th St., 60642. Tel: 312-881-6522.
St. Patrick School (Lemont), St. Alphonsus-St. Patrick School, 205 Cass St., Lemont, 60439. Tel: 708-257-2380.
St. Patrick (Commercial Ave.).
St. Patrick School (Commercial Ave.).
St. Patrick Academy (Des Plaines), McAulay High School, 3737 W. 99th St., 60642. Tel: 312-881-6522.
St. Patrick High School. (Boys), 5900 W. Belmont, 60634. Tel: 312-282-8844.
St. Patrick High School. (Girls),
St. Paul High School, Christian Brother Center, 200 De La Salle Dr., Romeoville, 60441. Tel: 312-242-1240.
St. Peter School (Volo), St. Peter, 27551 W. Hwy. 120, Round Lake, 60073. Tel: 708-385-5496.
St. Peter Canisius School.
SS. Peter and Paul (Exchange St.).
SS. Peter and Paul School (Exchange St.).
St. Peter & Paul School (S. Halsted).
Ss. Peter & Paul School (Paulina St.).
SS. Peter & Paul (Libertyville), St. Joseph, 121 E. Maple, Libertyville, 60048. Tel: 708-362-2073.
SS. Peter & Paul High School, St. Francis de Sales High School, 10155 S. Ewing, 60617. Tel: 312-731-7272.
St. Philip Benizi (Maypole St.).
St. Philip Benizi (Oak St.).
St. Philip Benizi School (Oak St.).
St. Philip High School.
St. Philomena Commercial High School, St. Philomena School, 4131 W. Cortland, 60639. Tel: 312-235-0120.
St. Pius V Commercial High School, St. Pius V School, 1919 S. Ashland, 60608. Tel: 312-226-1590.
Precious Blood School.
Presentation School.
Presentation-Precious Blood Unit School. Our Lady of the West Side Catholic, Precious Blood Campus, 2401 W. Congress, 60612. Tel: 312-421-6157.
St. Procopius High School.
Providence Academy & High School, Mother Guerin High School, 8001 Belmont Ave., River Grove, 60171. Tel: 312-625-3278.
Providence-St. Mel High School, 119 S. Central Park Blvd., 60624. Tel: 312-722-4600.
Quigley Preparatory Seminary North & South, Archbishop Quigley Preparatory Seminary, 103 E. Chesnut St., 60611. Tel: 321-787-9343.
St. Raphael.
St. Raphael (60th St.).
St. Raphael School (60th St.).
Resurrection (Jackson Blvd.).
St. Rocco (Chicago Heights). School Records: see Mt. Carmel School.
St. Roman School.
St. Rosalie School (Harwood Heights).
St. Rose of Lima (W. 48th St.).
St. Rose of Lima School.
Sacred Heart (19th St.).
Sacred Heart School & High School (70th St.).
Sacred Heart (Oakley Blvd.).
Sacred Heart School & High School (May St.).
Sacred Heart (N. Oakley).
Sacred Heart School (N. Oakley).
Sacred Heart (Church St.), Sacred Heart Mission, 11652 S. Church St., 60643. Tel: 312-233-3955.
Sacred Heart of Jesus (Honore St.).
Sacred Heart of Jesus School (Honore St.).
Sacred Heart of Jesus High School (Honore St.).
Sacred Heart of Mary High School (Arlington Heights), St. Viator High School, 1213 E. Oakton St., Arlington Heights, 60004. Tel: 708-392-4050.
St. Salomea (S. Indiana).
St. Salomea School (S. Indiana).
San Callisto Mission.
San Marcello Mission (Evergreen), Immaculate Conception, 1415 N. North Park, 60610. Tel: 312-944-1230.
Santa Lucia Mission. Sacramental Records: Santa Lucia-Santa Maria Incoranata, 3022 S. Wells, 60616. Tel: 312-842-6115. School Records: Santa Lucia School, 3017 S. Wells, 60616. Tel: 312-326-1839.
Santa Maria Incoranata. Sacramental Records: Santa Lucia-Santa Maria Incoranata, 3022 S. Wells, 60616. Tel: 312-842-6115. School Records: Santa Lucia School, 3017 S. Wells, 60616. Tel: 312-326-1839.
St. Sebastian (W. Wellington).
St. Sebastian School & High School.
Servite Seminary (Hillside), Provincial Archives, Servite Provincial Center, 3121 W. Jackson Blvd., 60612. Tel: 312-533-0360.
Seven Holy Founders School (Calumet Park).
Sheil Institute.
Siena High School, McAulay High School, 3737 W. 99th St., 60642. Tel: 312-881-6522.
St. Stanislaus College, Weber High School, 5252 W. Palmer, 60639. Tel: 312-637-7500.
St. Stanislaus Kostka High School, St. Stanislaus Kostka Elementary, 1255 N. Noble, 60622. Tel: 312-278-4560.
Old St. Stephen (Ohio St.).
Old St. Stephen School.
St. Susanna (Harvey), Ascension-St. Susanna, 15234 Myrtle, Harvey, 60426-3194. Tel: 708-333-0931.
St. Susanna School (Harvey).
St. Sylvester High School, St. Sylvester School, 3027 W. Palmer, 60647. Tel: 312-772-5222.
St. Theodore (S. Paulina).
St. Theodore School.
St. Thomas Aquinas (Washington).
St. Thomas Mission (River Forest), St. Luke, 528 Lathrop, River Forest, 60305. Tel: 708-771-8250.
St. Thomas the Apostle High School, St. Thomas the Apostle School, 5467 S. Woodlawn, 60615. Tel: 312-667-1142.
Unity High School.
St. Valentine (Cicero).
St. Valentine School (Cicero).
St. Veronica, Resurrection, 2840 W. Nelson, 60618. Tel: 312-478-9705.
St. Veronica School (Whipple St.).
Villa Nazareth High School (Whipple St.).
St. Vincent de Paul School.
St. Vincent Academy. (Girls)(Depaul High School & St. Vincent Academy, location of records unknown).
St. Vincent Orphanage. Client & School Records: Catholic Charities, Division of Services for Children and Youth, 126 N. Des Plaines, 60606. Tel: 312-876-2288; 236-5172, Ext. 330. Sacramental Records: Holy Name Cathedral, 730 N. Wabash, 60611. Tel: 312-787-8040.
St. Vincent Infant Hospital School of Child Care, St. Vincent de Paul Center, 2145 N. Halsted, 60614. Tel: 312-943-6776.
Visitation.
Visitation Academy (Evanston). see Marywood High School.
Visitation High School.
St. Vitus (S. Paulina).
St. Vitus School.
St. Wenceslaus (DeKoven St.).
St. Willibrord (114th St.).
St. Willibrord School (114th St.).
Willibrord Catholic High School.
St. Willibrord High School.

RELIGIOUS INSTITUTES OF MEN REPRESENTED IN THE ARCHDIOCESE

For further details refer to the corresponding bracketed number in the Religious Institutes of Men or Women section.

[0120]—*Alexian Brothers.*—C.F.A.
[0140]—*The Augustinians (Mother of Good Counsel).* Chicago.—O.S.A.
[0200]—*Benedictine Monks.*—O.S.B.
[0330]—*Brothers of the Christian Schools.*—F.S.C.
[0600]—*Brothers of the Congregation of Holy Cross.*—C.S.C.
[0900]—*Canons Regular of Premontre.* (U.S. Circary).—O.Praem.
[0400]—*Canons Regular of the Order of the Holy Cross.* (Prov. of St. Odilia, Minneapolis, MN).—O.S.C.
[0470]—*The Capuchin Friars.*—O.F.M.Cap.
[0270]—*Carmelite Fathers & Brothers.* (Most Pure Heart of Mary).—O.Carm.
[0360]—*Claretian Missionaries.*—C.M.F.
[1320]—*Clerics of St. Viator.* (Chicago, IL).—C.S.V.
[0380]—*Comboni Missionaries of the Heart of Jesus-Verona.*—M.C.C.J.
[0310]—*Congregation of Christian Brothers.*—C.F.C.
[0750]—*Congregation of Marianhill Missionaries.*—C.M.M.
[0220]—*Congregation of the Blessed Sacrament.* (Rome, Italy).—S.S.S.
[1330]—*Congregation of the Mission.* (Western Prov.).—C.M.
[1210]—*Congregation of the Missionaries of St. Charles.* (Western Prov.).—C.S.
[1000]—*Congregation of the Passion.* (Western Prov.).—C.P.
[1130]—*Congregation of the Priests of the Sacred Heart.*—S.C.J.
[1080]—*Congregation of the Resurrection.* (Chicago Prov.).—C.R.
[0480]—*Conventual Franciscans.* (St. Bonaventure, Our Lady of Consolation Provs.).—O.F.M.Conv.
[0260]—*Discalced Carmelite Friars.*—O.C.D.
[0520]—*Franciscan Friars.* (Sacred Heart, Assumption of B.V.M. Provs.; Commissariats of the Holy Cross, Holy Family).—O.F.M.
[0650]—*Holy Ghost Fathers.* (Eastern Prov.).—C.SS.P.
[0690]—*Jesuit Fathers and Brothers.* (Chicago, Polish, Lithuanian Provs.).—S.J.
[0740]—*Marian Fathers.*—M.I.C.
[0770]—*The Marist Brothers.*—F.M.S.
[0780]—*Marist Fathers.*—S.M.
[0800]—*Maryknoll.*—M.M.
[0830]—*Mill Hill Missionaries.*—M.H.M.
[0860]—*Missionhurst Congregation of the Immaculate Heart of Mary.*—C.I.C.M.
[0910]—*Oblates of Mary Immaculate.*—O.M.I.
[0430]—*Order of Preachers-Dominicans.*—O.P.
[1030]—*Paulist Fathers.* (New York Prov.).—C.S.P.
[0610]—*Priests of the Congregation of Holy Cross.* (Notre Dame, IN).—C.S.C.
[1070]—*Redemptorist Fathers.* (Denver).—C.SS.R.
[1170]—*St. Patrick Missionary Society.*—S.P.S.
[1220]—*Servants of Charity.*—S.C.
[1240]—*Servites.* (Chicago, IL).—O.S.M.
[1260]—*Society of Christ.*—S.Ch.
[0760]—*Society of Mary.*—S.M.
[0850]—*Society of Missionaries of Africa.*—M.Afr.
[0370]—*Society of St. Columban.*—S.S.C.
[1200]—*Society of the Divine Savior.*—S.D.S.
[0420]—*Society of the Divine Word.*—S.V.D.
[1060]—*Society of the Precious Blood.* (Kansas City Prov.).—C.PP.S.
[1360]—*Xaverian Missionary Fathers.*—S.X.

RELIGIOUS INSTITUTES OF WOMEN REPRESENTED IN THE ARCHDIOCESE

[0100]—*Adorers of the Blood of Christ.*—A.S.C.
[0230]—*Benedictine Sisters of Pontifical Jurisdiction.* (Chicago, IL; Duluth, MN).—O.S.B.
[0690]—*Comboni Missionary Sisters.*—C.M.S.
[3110]—*Congregation of Our Lady of the Retreat in the Cenacle.*—R.C.
[1860]—*Congregation of the Handmaids of the Precious Blood.*—H.P.B.
[2100]—*Congregation of the Humility of Mary.*—C.H.M.
[0460]—*Congregation of the Sisters of Charity of the Incarnate Word.*—C.C.V.I.
[3710]—*Congregation of the Sisters of Saint Agnes.*—C.S.A.
[1920]—*Congregation of the Sisters of the Holy Cross.*—C.S.C.
[1780]—*Congregation of the Sisters of the Third Order of St. Francis of Perpetual Adoration.*—F.S.P.A.
[1710]—*Congregation of the Third Order of St. Francis of Mary Immaculate, Joliet, IL.*—O.S.F.
[1730]—*Congregation of the Third Order of St. Francis, Oldenburg, IN.*—O.S.F.
[0760]—*Daughters of Charity of St. Vincent de Paul.*—D.C.
[0793]—*Daughters of Divine Love.*—D.D.L.
[0940]—*Daughters of St. Mary of Providence.*—D.S.M.P.
[0810]—*Daughters of the Heart of Mary.*—D.H.M.
[0420]—*Discalced Carmelite Nuns.*—O.C.D.
[1070-01]—*Dominican Sisters.*—O.P.
[1070-03]—*Dominican Sisters.*—O.P.
[1070-10]—*Dominican Sisters.*—O.P.
[1070-13]—*Dominican Sisters.*—O.P.
[1070-27]—*Dominican Sisters.*—O.P.
[1170]—*Felician Sisters.*—C.S.S.F.
[1370]—*Franciscan Missionaries of Mary.*—F.M.M.
[1210]—*Franciscan Sisters of Chicago.*—O.S.F.
[1230]—*Franciscan Sisters of Christian Charity.*—O.S.F.

[1310]—*Franciscan Sisters of Little Falls, Minnesota.*—O.S.F.
[1415]—*Franciscan Sisters of Mary.*—F.S.M.
[1430]—*Franciscan Sisters of Our Lady of Perpetual Help.*—O.S.F.
[1450]—*Franciscan Sisters of the Sacred Heart.*—O.S.F.
[1240]—*Franciscan Sisters, Daughters of the Sacred Hearts of Jesus and Mary.*—O.S.F.
[1820]—*Hospital Sisters of the Third Order of St. Francis.*—O.S.F.
[2370]—*Institute of the Blessed Virgin Mary (Loretto Sisters).*—I.B.V.M.
[2330]—*Little Sisters of Jesus.*—L.S.J.
[2320]—*Little Sisters of the Holy Family.*—P.S.S.F.
[2340]—*Little Sisters of the Poor.*—L.S.P.
[3570]—*Mantellate Sisters, Servants of Mary of Blue Island.*—O.S.M.
[2420]—*Marist Missionary Sisters.*—S.M.S.M.
[2430]—*Marist Sisters Congregation of Mary.*—S.M.
[2470]—*Maryknoll Sisters of St. Dominic.*—M.M.
[2480]—*Medical Missionaries of Mary.*—M.M.M.
[2680]—*Misericordia Sisters.*—S.M.
[2710]—*Missionaries of Charity.*—M.C.
[2865]—*Missionaries of the Sacred Heart of Jesus and Our Lady of Guadalupe.*—M.S.C.Gpe.
[2790]—*Missionary Servants of the Most Blessed Trinity.*—M.S.B.T.
[2715]—*Missionary Sisters of Christ the King for Polonia.*—M.S.C.K.
[2900]—*Missionary Sisters of St. Charles Borromeo.*—M.S.S.C.B.
[3990]—*Missionary Sisters of St. Peter Claver.*—S.S.P.C.
[2860]—*Missionary Sisters of the Sacred Heart.*—M.S.C.
[3530]—*Missionary Sisters Servants of the Holy Spirit.*—S.Sp.S.
[3040]—*Oblate Sisters of Providence.*—O.S.P.
[3130]—*Our Lady of Victory Missionary Sisters.*—O.L.V.M.
[0950]—*Pious Society Daughters of St. Paul.*—F.S.P.
[3230]—*Poor Handmaids of Jesus Christ.*—P.H.J.C.
[3440]—*Religious Hospitallers of Saint Joseph.*—R.H.S.J.
[2970]—*School Sisters of Notre Dame.*—S.S.N.D.
[1680]—*School Sisters of St. Francis.*—O.S.F.
[3590]—*Servants of Mary (Servite Sisters).*—O.S.M.
[3520]—*Servants of the Holy Heart of Mary.*—S.S.C.M.
[0440]—*Sisters of Charity of Cincinnati, Ohio.*—S.C.
[0570]—*Sisters of Charity of Seton Hill, Greensburg, Pennsylvania.*—S.C.
[0630]—*Sisters of Charity of St. Vincent de Paul.*—S.V.Z.
[0430]—*Sisters of Charity of the Blessed Virgin Mary.*—B.V.M.
[0660]—*Sisters of Christian Charity.*—S.C.C.
[0990]—*Sisters of Divine Providence.*—C.D.P.
[2360]—*Sisters of Loretto at the Foot of the Cross.*—S.L.
[2575]—*Sisters of Mercy of the Americas.* (Chicago, IL).—R.S.M.
[3000]—*Sisters of Notre Dame de Namur.*—S.N.D.deN.
[3080]—*Sisters of Our Lady Christian Doctrine.*—R.C.D.
[3350]—*Sisters of Providence.*—S.P.
[3360]—*Sisters of Providence of Saint Mary-of-the-Woods, IN.*—S.P.
[1620]—*Sisters of Saint Francis of Millvale, Pennsylvania.*—O.S.F.
[1540]—*Sisters of Saint Francis, Clinton, Iowa.*—O.S.F.
[3780]—*Sisters of Saints Cyril and Methodius.*—SS.C.M.
[3740]—*Sisters of St. Casimir.*—S.S.C.
[1520]—*Sisters of St. Francis of Christ the King.*—O.S.F.
[1640]—*Sisters of St. Francis of Perpetual Adoration.*—O.S.F.
[1570]—*Sisters of St. Francis of the Holy Family.*—O.S.F.
[1800]—*Sisters of St. Francis of the Third Order Regular (Williamsville, New York).*—O.S.F.
[3830-02]—*Sisters of St. Joseph.*—C.S.J.
[3830-15]—*Sisters of St. Joseph.*—C.S.J.
[3840]—*Sisters of St. Joseph of Carondelet.*—C.S.J.
[3930]—*Sisters of St. Joseph of the Third Order of St. Francis.*—S.S.J.-T.O.S.F.
[0260]—*Sisters of the Blessed Sacrament for Indians and Colored People.*—S.B.S.
[2980]—*Sisters of the Congregation de Notre Dame.*—C.N.D.
[1030]—*Sisters of the Divine Savior.*—S.D.S.
[1830]—*Sisters of the Good Shepherd.*—R.G.S.
[1970]—*Sisters of the Holy Family of Nazareth.*—C.S.F.N.
[2110]—*Sisters of the Humility of Mary.*—H.M.
[2140]—*Sisters of the Immaculate Conception of the Blessed Virgin Mary.* (Lithuanian).
[2270]—*Sisters of the Little Company of Mary.*—L.C.M.
[2350]—*Sisters of the Living Word.*—S.L.W.
[3320]—*Sisters of the Presentation of the B.V.M.*—P.B.V.M.
[3480]—*Sisters of the Resurrection.*—C.R.
[1705]—*Sisters of the Third Order of St. Francis of Assisi.*—O.S.F.
[1720]—*Sisters of the Third Order of St. Francis of the Congregation of Our Lady of Loudes.*—O.S.F.
[2150]—*Sisters, Servants of the Immaculate Heart of Mary.*—I.H.M.
[1890]—*Society of Helpers.*—H.H.S.
[4060]—*Society of the Holy Child Jesus.*—S.H.C.J.
[4070]—*Society of the Sacred Heart.*—R.S.C.J.

ARCHDIOCESAN CEMETERIES

CHICAGO. *Central Office.* Catholic Cemeteries, 1400 S. Wolf Rd., Hillside, 60162-2197. Tel: 708-449-6100; Fax: 708-449-3419. Rev. Patrick J. Pollard, Archdiocesan Dir.; Mr. Donald A. Massaro, Exec. Dir.
Mt. Olivet.
St. Boniface.
St. Casimir.
St. Henry.
CALUMET CITY. *Holy Cross.*
CRESTWOOD. *St. Benedict.*
DES PLAINES. *All Saints.*
EVANSTON. *Calvary.*
EVERGREEN PARK. *St. Mary.*
FOX LAKE. *St. Bede.*
FREMONT CENTER. *St. Mary.*
GLENWOOD. *Assumption.*
HIGHLAND PARK. *St. Mary.*
HILLSIDE. *Mt. Carmel.*
Our Lady of Sorrows.
Queen of Heaven.
JUSTICE. *Resurrection.*
LAKE FOREST. *St. Mary.*
LEMONT. *St. Alphonsus.*
St. James, Sag Bridge.
St. Patrick.
SS. Cyril & Methodius.
LIBERTYVILLE. *Ascension.*
NILES. *Maryhill.*
St. Adalbert.
NORTHBROOK. *Sacred Heart.*
OAK FOREST. *St. Gabriel.*
ORLAND PARK. *St. Michael.*
PALATINE. *St. Michael the Archangel.*
PARK FOREST. *St. Anne.*
RIVER FOREST. *St. Joseph.*
ROSENCRANS. *St. Patrick.*
ROUND LAKE. *St. Joseph.*
SAUK VILLAGE. *St. James.*
SKOKIE. *St. Peter.*
STEGER. *Calvary.*
VOLO. *St. Peter.*
WAUCONDA. *Transfiguration.*
WAUKEGAN. *St. Mary.*
WEST LAKE FOREST. *St. Patrick.*
WILMETTE. *St. Joseph.*
WORTH. *Holy Sepulchre.*

NECROLOGY

✠ Bernardin, His Eminence Joseph. —Died Nov. 14, 1996.
† Banahan, John S., (Retired). —Died Jan. 5, 1996.
† Buckley, Albert J., (Retired). —Died Oct. 3, 1996.
† Cantwell, Rev. Msgr. Daniel M., (Retired). —Died Jan. 2, 1996.
† Cronin, Charles E., Chicago, IL, Queen of All Saints. —Died Jan. 9, 1996.
† Cunningham, John P., (Retired). —Died Nov. 13, 1996.
† Cure, Laverne J., (Retired). —Died Oct. 2, 1996.
† Cusack, Donald E., Chicago, IL, St. Therese Medical Center. —Died Nov. 17, 1996.
† Daley, John M., Chicago, IL, Archbishop Quigley Seminary. —Died March 14, 1996.
† Duda, Thaddeus Z., Chicago, IL, St. Constance. —Died April 25, 1996.
† Dudek, Anthony A., (Retired). —Died March 1, 1996.
† Finn, Daniel E., (Retired). —Died June 21, 1996.
† Grimmel, Richard R., Oak Forest, IL, St. Damian. —Died Dec. 30, 1995.
† Gryzik, Charles P., (Retired). —Died July 28, 1996.
† Halpin, Rev. Msgr. George C., (Retired). —Died April 28, 1996.
† Hartmann, Jerome J., (Retired). —Died Nov. 12, 1996.
† Karpowicz, Boleslaus P., (Retired). —Died June 21, 1996.
† Kelly, Laurence D., (Retired). —Died May 23, 1996.
† Klug, Elmer C., (Retired). —Died Jan. 7, 1996.
† Loftus, Robert J., Chicago, IL, St. Raymond de Penafort. —Died April 27, 1996.
† Macholz, Ignatius M., (Retired). —Died March 15, 1996.
† Rogers, William J., (Retired). —Died April 30, 1996.
† Ryzner, Stanley L., (Retired). —Died Dec. 24, 1995.
† Smaza, Rev. Msgr. Edward J., (Retired). —Died Nov. 28, 1995.
† Urbanek, Sylvester M., (Retired). —Died Feb. 8, 1996.
† Wild, Philip T., (Retired). —Died Feb. 3, 1996.
† Wisniewski, Robert E., Tinley Park, IL, St. George. —Died April 19, 1996.

Archdiocese of Cincinnati

(Archidioecesis Cincinnatensis)

Most Reverend

DANIEL E. PILARCZYK, S.T.D., PH.D.

Archbishop of Cincinnati; ordained December 20, 1959; appointed Titular Bishop of Hodelm and Auxiliary Bishop of Cincinnati November 12, 1974; consecrated December 20, 1974; appointed Archbishop of Cincinnati November 2, 1982; installed December 20, 1982. *Res., 100 E. Eighth St., Cincinnati, OH, 45202.*

Most Reverend

CARL K. MOEDDEL, M.A., M.DIV., D.D.

Auxiliary Bishop of Cincinnati; ordained August 15, 1962; appointed Titular Bishop of Bistue and Auxiliary Bishop of Cincinnati August 24, 1993. *Res., 100 E. Eighth St., Cincinnati, OH, 45202.*

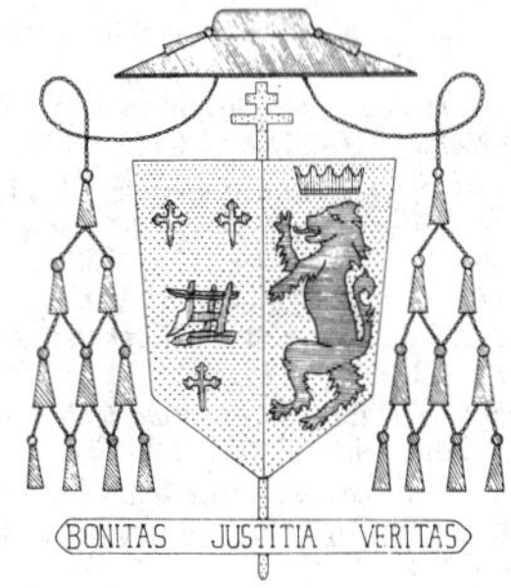

ERECTED DIOCESE JUNE 19, 1821; ARCHDIOCESE JULY 19, 1850.

Square Miles 8,543.

Comprises that part of the State of Ohio lying south of 40 degrees, 41 minutes, being the 19 Counties south of the northern line of Mercer, Auglaize, and Logan, all west of the eastern line of Logan, Champaign, Clark, Greene, Clinton, Highland and Adams Counties.

For legal titles of parishes and archdiocesan institutions, consult the Chancery Office.

Archdiocesan Offices: 100 E. Eighth St., Cincinnati, OH, 45202. Tel.: 513-421-3131; Fax: 513-421-6225.

STATISTICAL OVERVIEW

Personnel	
Archbishop	1
Auxiliary Bishops	1
Priests: Diocesan Active in Diocese	242
Priests: Active Outside Diocese	12
Priests: Diocesan in Foreign Missions	2
Priests: Retired, Sick or Absent	102
Number of Diocesan Priests	358
Religious Priests in Diocese	281
Extern Priests in Diocese	7
Ordinations:	
Diocesan Priests	1
Permanent Deacons	5
Permanent Deacons in Diocese	128
Total Brothers	179
Total Sisters	1,471
Parishes	
Parishes	236
With Resident Pastor:	
Resident Diocesan Priests	166
Resident Religious Priests	32
Without Resident Pastor:	
Administered by Priests	38
Pastoral Centers	1
Closed Parishes	1
Professional Ministry Personnel:	
Brothers	7
Sisters	85
Lay Ministers	295
Welfare	
Catholic Hospitals	11
Total Assisted	1,572,000
Health Care Centers	1
Total Assisted	265
Homes for the Aged	11
Total Assisted	1,629
Residential Care of Children	4
Total Assisted	740
Day Care and Extended Day Care Centers	2
Total Assisted	201
Specialized Homes	3
Total Assisted	205
Special Centers for Social Services	6
Total Assisted	97,200
Residential Care of Disabled	1
Total Assisted	18
Other Institutions	4
Total Assisted	960
Educational	
Seminaries, Diocesan	1
Students from This Diocese	22
Students from Other Diocese	5
Diocesan Students in Other Seminaries	4
Total Seminarians	26
Colleges and Universities	4
Total Students	18,805
High Schools, Diocesan and Parish	18
Total Students	12,568
High Schools, Private	4
Total Students	2,816
Elementary Schools, Diocesan and Parish	111
Total Students	39,512
Elementary Schools, Private	2
Total Students	1,009
Catechesis/Religious Education:	
High School Students	5,880
Elementary Students	34,464
Total Students Under Catholic Instruction	115,080
Teachers in the Diocese:	
Priests	13
Brothers	28
Sisters	132
Lay Teachers	3,159
Vital Statistics	
Receptions into the Church:	
Infant Baptism Totals	8,476
Adult Baptism Totals	1,206
Received into Full Communion	865
First Communions	9,030
Confirmations	8,144
Marriages:	
Catholic	1,944
Interfaith	1,389
Total Marriages	3,333
Deaths	4,702
Total Catholic Population	546,100
Total Population	2,892,000

Former Bishops—Rt. Rev. EDWARD FENWICK, O.P., D.D., cons. Jan. 13, 1822; died Sept. 26, 1832.—Most Rev. JOHN BAPTIST PURCELL, D.D., cons. Oct. 13, 1833; appt. Archbishop, July 19, 1850; died July 4, 1883.—Most Rev. WILLIAM HENRY ELDER, D.D., cons. Bishop of Natchez May 3, 1857; appt. Titular Bishop of Avar, and Coadjutor to the Archbishop of Cincinnati *cum jure successionis,* Jan. 30, 1880; succeeded to the See of Cincinnati, July 4, 1883; died Oct. 31, 1904.—Most Rev. HENRY MOELLER, D.D., cons. Bishop of Columbus, Aug. 25, 1900; promoted to Archiepiscopal See of Areopolis and made Coadjutor to the Most Rev. WILLIAM HENRY ELDER *cum jure successionis,* April 27, 1903; appt. Archbishop of Cincinnati, Oct. 31, 1904; died Jan. 5, 1925.—Most Rev. JOHN T. MCNICHOLAS, O.P., S.T.M., cons. Bishop of Duluth, MN Sept. 8, 1918; promoted to Archiepiscopal See of Cincinnati, July 8, 1925; appt. Assistant at the Pontifical Throne, Feb. 18, 1923; died April 22, 1950.—Most Rev. KARL J. ALTER, D.D., cons. Bishop of Toledo, June 17, 1931; appt. Assistant to the Pontifical Throne, May 30, 1950; elevated to Archbishop of Cincinnati, June 21, 1950; retired July 23, 1969; died Aug. 23, 1977.—Most Rev. PAUL F. LEIBOLD, D.D., J.C.D., appt. Titular Bishop of Trebenna and Auxiliary of Cincinnati, April 10, 1958; cons. June 17, 1958; installed as Bishop of Evansville, June 15, 1966; transferred to Archdiocese of Cincinnati, July 23, 1969; installed Oct. 2, 1969; died June 1, 1972.—His Eminence JOSEPH CARDINAL BERNARDIN, D.D., appt. Titular Bishop of Lugura and Auxiliary Bishop of Atlanta, March 9, 1966; cons. April 26, 1966; appt. Archbishop of Cincinnati, Nov. 21, 1972; installed Dec. 19, 1972; appt. Archbishop of Chicago, July 5, 1982; installed Aug. 25, 1982; created Cardinal Priest, Feb. 2, 1983.

Vicar General—Most Rev. CARL K. MOEDDEL.

Archdiocesan Department Directors—ROBERT DAVIS, Dir., Community Svcs.; Sr. KATHRYN ANN CONNELLY, S.C., Dir., Educational Svcs.; Revs. CHRISTOPHER R. ARMSTRONG, Dir., Exec. Svcs. HOWARD P. PECQUET, Dir., Financial Svcs.; Most Rev. CARL K. MOEDDEL, Dir., Pastoral Svcs. VINCENT FRASHER, Dir., Personnel Svcs.

Presbyteral Council—Ex-Officio Members: Most Rev. DANIEL E. PILARCZYK; Most Rev. CARL K. MOEDDEL. Priest Councilors: Revs. TIM BUNCH; THOMAS DIEHL, S.J.; PATRICK DUFFY; GERARD A. EVERS; ROBERT FARRELL; ANTHONY J. GERACI; EDWARD A. HASKAMP; TED KOSSE; FRANCIS G. LAMMEIER; JAMES J. MANNING; JIM MEADE; ROBERT J. MONNIN; RICHARD RIEDEL, C.PP.S.; JOSEPH RIGALI.

Vicarri Foranei (Deans)—Cathedral Deanery: Rev. JAMES

A. BRAMLAGE; St. Andrew Deanery: Rev. MICHAEL PUCKE; St. Francis de Sales Deanery: Rev. GERALD R. HAEMMERLE; St. Lawrence Deanery: Rev. JAMES R. COLLINS; St. Margaret Mary Deanery: Rev. RAYMOND E. LARGER; Hamilton Deanery: Rev. JEFFREY P. SILVER; St. Martin Deanery: Rev. JOHN P. FISHER; Dayton Deanery: Rev. Msgr. LAWRENCE K. BRESLIN; Springfield Deanery: Rev. JOHN D. MACQUARRIE; Sidney Deanery: Rev. EUGENE F. VONDERHAAR; St. Mary's Deanery: Rev. RONALD H. WILKER.

Consultors—Most Rev. CARL K. MOEDDEL, Aux. Bishop; Revs. ERWIN J. BERTKE; TIMOTHY S. BUNCH; WILLIAM H. CROSS; ANTHONY J. GERACI; JEFFREY M. KEMPER; TED KOSSE; DONALD G. MCCARTHY; JAMES J. MANNING; JAMES MEADE; ROBERT J. MONNIN; JOHN E. WESSLING.

Archdiocesan Offices

All Archdiocesan Offices and Directors are located at 100 E. Eighth St., Cincinnati, OH 45202. Tel: 513-421-3131; Fax: 513-421-6225, unless otherwise indicated.

Office of the Archbishop—Rev. MALCOLM S. GRAD, Admin. Asst. LINDA CHOUTEAU, Exec. Sec. to the Archbishop; JOAN RANZ, Sec.

Office of Mediation—JOSEPH B. CROWE, Admin. Tel: 513-421-3131, Ext. 408.

Department Of Executive Services

Rev. CHRISTOPHER R. ARMSTRONG, Dir.

Chancery—

Chancellor—Rev. CHRISTOPHER R. ARMSTRONG.

Vice Chancellor—Rev. MALCOLM S. GRAD.

Archivist—DON H. BUSKE,(Special Address & Phone No. for Historical Archives Only), *6616 Beechmont Ave., Cincinnati, 45230.* Tel: 513-231-0810.

Censors—Revs. ROBERT J. BUSCHMILLER; EDWARD J. GRATSCH; RALPH J. LAWRENCE; ROBERT L. HAGEDORN; CHRISTOPHER R. ARMSTRONG, J.C.L.

Communications Office—Deacon RAYMOND W. GEORGE, Dir.

Newspaper—"The Catholic Telegraph"—Most Rev. DANIEL E. PILARCZYK, Publisher.

Planning and Research—JEFFRY W. REXHAUSEN, Dir.

Tribunal-Archdiocese of Cincinnati—Tel: 513-421-3145; Fax: 513-723-1035.

Director—Sr. VICTORIA VONDENBERGER, R.S.M., J.C.L.

Judicial Vicar—Rev. EDWIN F. GEARHART, J.C.L.

Adjutant Judicial Vicars—Revs. DENNIS J. CAYLOR, J.C.L.; RAYMOND C. KELLERMAN, J.C.L.

Judges—Deacon MICHAEL A. ASCOLESE; Rev. Msgr. LAWRENCE K. BRESLIN; Revs. CHRISTOPHER R. ARMSTRONG, J.C.L.; MICHAEL D. BEATTY; JAMES A. BRAMLAGE; JOHN L. CAVANAUGH, J.C.D.; R. DANIEL CONLON, J.C.D.; J. RAYMOND FAVRET; DAVID E. FAY; JOHN P. FISCHER; MICHAEL T. FLAHERTY; GERALD R. HAEMMERLE; TIMOTHY S. KALLAHER; RICHARD L. KLUG; EMIL J. LABBE, J.C.D.; FRANCIS G. LAMMEIER; NORMAN W. LANGENBRUNNER; RALPH J. LAWRENCE; WALTER J. MACPHERSON; ROBERT J. MOONEY; THOMAS C. NOLKER; ROBERT A. OBERMEYER; EDWARD L. RUDEMILLER; JEROME A. SCHAEPER; MICHAEL A. SEGER; OSCAR H. SEGER; R. MARC SHERLOCK; TERRENCE W. SMITH; PAUL L. STOLZ; EDWARD B. STOLZE; LAWRENCE R. STRITTMATTER; RICHARD J. SWEENEY; LARRY P. THARP; JAMES J. WALSH; JOHN R. WHITE; BARRY M. WINDHOLTZ, J.C.L.; WILLIAM H. WYSONG.

Defenders of the Bond—Revs. HERMAN H. KENNING; THOMAS A. SNODGRASS, J.C.L.; Sr. VICTORIA VONDENBERGER, R.S.M., J.C.L.

Promoter of Justice—Sr. VICTORIA VONDENBERGER, R.S.M., J.C.L.

Auditors—ELVA BRUNNER; SUSAN E. JINKENS; BETTY MEDER; KELLY M. TERRY; MARY G. WILKIE.

Secretary—JULIANN BUCHER.

Department Of Community Services

Robert Davis, Dir.

Archdiocesan Office of Catholic Charities—RAYMOND F. EGAN, Dir.

Association of Ladies of Charity—LENDRA WRIGHT, Pres. Tel: 513-421-3131.

Catholic Federation for the Mentally Retarded—DONALD MINK, Pres. Tel: 513-741-9689.

Catholic Social Services of Hamilton—MAUREEN KRAH, Exec. Dir., *140 N. Fifth St., Hamilton, 45011.* Tel: 513-863-6129.

Catholic Social Services of Miami Valley—RONALD A. ECKERLE, Exec. Dir., *922 W. Riverview Dr., Dayton, 45407.* Tel: 513-223-7217.

Catholic Social Services of Southwest Ohio—RAYMOND F. EGAN, Exec. Dir. Tel: 513-241-7745.

Catholic Social Services of Springfield—VINCENT CHASE, Exec. Dir., *641 High St., Springfield, 45505.* Tel: 513-325-8715.

Cemeteries—ROBERT DAVIS, Dir. IRVIN BENKIN, Asst. Dir., *11000 Montgomery Rd., Cincinnati, 45242.* Tel: 513-489-0300.

Ecumenical and Interfaith Relations—LOUISE BARNES, Program Coord.

St. Vincent de Paul Society—MARK CASELLA, Pres.; Rev. HERMAN KENNING, Spiritual Dir.; (See Special Listing: St. Vincent de Paul Society).

Health Affairs—ROBERT DAVIS. Tel: 513-241-7745.

Rural Life Conference—BRIAN HENTIES, *266 Bainbridge St., Dayton, 45402.* Tel: 513-224-3026.

Social Action and World Peace—THOMAS CHOQUETTE, Exec. Dir. *Dayton Office,* BRIAN HENTIES, Assoc. Dir., *266 Bainbridge St., Dayton, 45402.* Tel: 513-224-3026.

Department Of Educational Services

Sr. KATHRYN ANN CONNELLY, S.C., Dir.

School Office—Sr. KATHRYN ANN CONNELLY, S.C., Supt., Schools, Dayton North; MICHAEL T. MCCORMICK, Area Supt., *266 Bainbridge St., Dayton, 45402.* Tel: 513-223-5151.

Religious Education Office—KENNETH GLEASON, Archdiocesan Dir. DAVID RILEY, Regional Dir., *226 Bainbridge St., Dayton, 45402.* Tel: 513-223-4075. *Sidney,* JANE PIERRON, Regl. Dir., *401-A S. Main St., Sidney, 45365.* Tel: 513-498-1192.

Department Of Financial Services

HOWARD P. PECQUET, Treas./Dir.

Office of Property Management-Central Services—GARY RAFFEL, Dir.

Office for Financial Development—JOAN SCHROEDER, Dir.

Department Of Pastoral Services

Most Rev. CARL K. MOEDDEL, Dir.

Evangelization/Parish Renewal—JANE M. BENSMAN, Coord., *266 Bainbridge St., Dayton, 45402.* Tel: 513-222-0227.

Campus Ministry—Dr. JANE STEINHAUSER, Dir., *444 W. Third St., Dayton, 45402.* (See Special Listing: Campus Ministry).

African American Catholic Ministries—GEORGE C. FINDLEY, Dir.

Family Life—MARGARET BLACK, Dir. *Dayton:* MARILYN PORCINO, Assoc. Dir., *266 Bainbridge St., Dayton, 45402.* Tel: 513-222-0227. *Northern Area:* VELMA JEAN BORGERT, *401-A S. Main St., Sidney, 45365.* Tel: 513-492-4449.

Missions—

Pontifical Mission Aid Societies—Most Rev. CARL K. MOEDDEL.

Missions Office—ARCHIE BRUUN, Dir., *100 E. Eighth St., Cincinnati, 45202.*

Pastoral Council Secretariat—Rev. MALCOLM S. GRAD, Exec. Sec.

Hispanic Catholic Ministry, Dayton—Ms. PURISSIMA MIRA, Moderator, *266 Bainbridge St., Dayton, 45402.* Tel: 513-222-1340.

Hispanic Catholic Ministry, Cincinnati—Rev. JOSEPH NELSON, O.F.M., Moderator-Chap., *100 E. Eighth St., Cincinnati, 45202.* Tel: 513-421-3131.

Worship—Rev. LAWRENCE R. TENSI, Dir.

Youth—Mr. SEAN REYNOLDS, Dir., *100 East Eighth St., Cincinnati, 45202.* Tel: 513-421-3131. TIMOTHY E. COLBERT, Reg. Dir.; *Dayton & Northern Area: 266 Bainbridge St., Dayton, 45402.* Tel: 513-223-1001.

Department of Personnel Services

VINCENT FRASHER, Dir.

Office of Religious—Sr. MARY GARKE, C.PP.S., Dir.

Permanent Diaconate Office—Vacant.

Personnel Office for Archdiocesan Administrative Offices—VINCE FRASHER, Dir.

Priestly Formation—Rev. THOMAS P. DI FOLCO, Dir.

Priests' Personnel Director—Most Rev. CARL K. MOEDDEL, Dir.

Vocations Office—Rev. MARK T. WATKINS, Dir.

CLERGY, PARISHES, MISSIONS AND PAROCHIAL SCHOOLS

GREATER CINCINNATI (HAMILTON COUNTY)

1—ST. PETER IN CHAINS CATHEDRAL, Revs. James A. Bramlage; James M. Willig. In res., Revs. Carl J. Geers; Louis F. Funk.
Res., 325 W. Eighth St., 45202. Tel: 513-421-5354; Fax: 513-241-9517.
Church—Eighth & Plum St., 45202.

2—ST. AGNES (Bond Hill), Rev. George P. Jaquemine; Sr. M. Jerome Buchert, O.S.U., Pastoral Admin.
Res., 1619 California Ave., 45237. Tel: 513-242-4747; Fax: 513-641-3983.

3—ALL SAINTS (Kenwood), Rev. J. Dennis Jaspers; Mrs. Jennifer Cmar, Pastoral Assoc. In res., Rev. Mark Schmieder.
Res., 8939 Montgomery Rd., 45236. Tel: 513-791-6351; Fax: 513-792-4730.
School—Tel: 513-792-4732; Fax: 513-792-4730. Mrs. Mary E. Stratford, Prin.
Lay Teachers 25; Students 491.
Catechesis/Religious Programs—Tel: 513-791-6351, Ext. 103; Fax: 513-792-4730. Mrs. Tanya Monsour Stager, D.R.E.
Students 330.

4—ST. ALOYSIUS GONZAGA (Bridgetown), Revs. Paul Rehling; Paul L. Friedrichs; Sr. Josetta Boeing, S.C., Pastoral Assoc.
Res., 4366 Bridgetown Rd., 45211. Tel: 513-574-4840; Fax: 513-574-4402.
School—4390 Bridgetown Rd., 45211. Tel: 513-574-4035. Bernadine Stone, Prin.
Lay Teachers 14; Students 357.
Catechesis/Religious Programs—Tel: 513-574-4840; Fax: 513-574-4402. Kevin Hibner, D.R.E.
Students 257.

5—ST. ALOYSIUS-ON-THE-OHIO, Rev. Donald R. Rettig.
Res., 134 Whipple St., 45233. Tel: 513-941-3445.
School—6207 Portage, 45233. Tel: 513-941-7831. Sr. Daria Mitchell, O.F.M., Prin.
Lay Teachers 12; Students 220.
Catechesis/Religious Programs—Tel: 513-941-2797; Fax: 513-941-7831.
Students 45.

6—ST. ALOYSIUS (Elmwood Pl.), Rev. Thomas A. Snodgrass.
Res., 115 W. Seymour Ave., 45216. Tel: 513-821-2971.
Church—314 Township Ave., 45216. Tel: 513-242-5496.

7—ST. ANDREW, Rev. Terence A. Meehan.
Res., 3401 Reading, P.O. Box 29064, 45229. Tel: 513-281-7504.
Church—609 Maple Ave., 45229.

8—ST. ANN (Groesbeck), Revs. William M. Kennedy; Charles Mentrup.
Res., 2900 Galbraith Rd., 45239. Tel: 513-521-8440; Fax: 513-521-8447.
School—2940 W. Galbraith Rd., 45239. Tel: 513-931-3070. Mary E. Henninger, Prin.
Sisters 1; Lay Teachers 20; Students 383.
Catechesis/Religious Programs—Tel: 513-729-2180. Diane C. Ferrier, D.R.E.
Students 185.

9—ANNUNCIATION OF THE BLESSED VIRGIN MARY, Rev. Richard L. Klug.
Res., 3547 Clifton Ave., 45220. Tel: 513-861-1295.
School—3545 Clifton Ave., 45220. Tel: 513-221-1230; Fax: 513-221-0219. Mrs. Lynn Sundermann, Prin.
Lay Teachers 11; Students 220.
Catechesis/Religious Programs—Tel: 513-861-1295.
Students 22.

10—ST. ANTHONY (Madisonville), Rev. George P. Jacquemin.
Res., 6104 Desmond St., 45227. Tel: 513-271-0920; Fax: 513-271-6630. [CEM]
School—See St. John Vianney Cure of Ars. Tel: 513-271-5510.
Catechesis/Religious Programs—Tel: 513-271-0920. D.R.E.: Tim Cronin, (Youth); Nancy Tunat, (Adults).
Students 153.

11—ST. ANTONINUS, Revs. Donald G. McCarthy; James Brichetto, S.J.; Deacon William Petrie.
Res., 1500 Linneman Rd., 45238. Tel: 513-922-5400; Fax: 513-451-5871.
School—5425 Julmar Dr., 45238. Tel: 513-922-2500. Mr. James Leisring, Prin.
Lay Teachers 24; Students 582.
Catechesis/Religious Programs—Tel: 513-922-4759. Mr. Robert Schroeder, D.R.E.
Students 63.

12—ASSUMPTION OF THE BLESSED VIRGIN MARY (Walnut Hills), Rev. Thomas Bokenkotter.
Res., 2622 Gilbert Ave., 45206. Tel: 513-961-3242.

13—ASSUMPTION (Mount Healthy), Revs. Francis G. Lammeier; John Robert Jack; Deacon Thomas J. Austing.
Res., 7711 Joseph St., 45231. Tel: 513-521-7274.
School—1500 McMakin Ave., Mt. Healthy, 45231. Tel: 513-522-0071. William J. Walborn, Prin.
Lay Teachers 18; Students 410.
Catechesis/Religious Programs—Tel: 513-728-4953. Sr. Marietta Sharkey, O.S.F., D.R.E.
Students 90.

14—ST. BARTHOLOMEW, Revs. William F. Krumpe; Robert W. Hasselhoff; Raymond C. Kellerman.
Res., 9375 Winton Rd., 45231. Tel: 513-522-3680; Fax: 513-728-3141.

School—St. Bartholomew Consolidated School. See separate listing.
Catechesis/Religious Programs—Jenny Luchsinger, D.R.E.
Students 129.

15—St. Bernard, Revs. James Shappelle; Michael Paraniuk.
Res., 740 Circle Ave., 45232. Tel: 513-541-3732.
Catechesis/Religious Programs—Students 24.

16—St. Bernard (Taylor's Creek), Rev. Robert J. Mick; Mr. Charles Karst, Pastoral Assoc.
Res., 7130 Harrison Rd., 45247. Tel: 513-353-4207; Fax: 513-353-4156.
School—Tel: 513-353-4224.
Sisters of Notre Dame of Covington, KY 2; Lay Teachers 13; Students 257.

17—St. Bonaventure, Rev. David Reilly; Sr. Joseph Marion Shappelle, S.C., Pastoral Assoc.
Res., 1798 Queen City Ave., 45214. Tel: 513-921-2547; Fax: 513-921-2548.
Chapel—Cincinnati, San Antonio di Padova. (Italian). Tel: 513-921-6411.

18—St. Boniface, Rev. Joseph A. Robinson; Deacon Ted Schmidt.
Res., 1750 Chase Ave., 45223. Tel: 513-541-1563.
School—St. Boniface Consolidated. See separate listing.

19—St. Catharine, Rev. Robert E. Schmitz; Deacon Thomas Gargan; Therese Bower, Pastoral Min.
Res., 2848 Fischer Pl., P.O. Box 111115, 45211. Tel: 513-661-0651; Fax: 513-661-0652.
School—3324 Wunder Ave., 45211. Tel: 513-481-7683; Fax: 513-661-0652. William Schlater, Prin.
Lay Teachers 20; Students 463.
Catechesis/Religious Programs—Tel: 513-481-7977; Fax: 513-661-0652.
Students 54.

20—St. Cecilia (Oakley), Rev. Elmer W. Smith; Deacon John Slattery. In res., Rev. Robert J. Buschmiller, (Retired).
Res., 3105 Madison Rd., 45209. Tel: 513-871-5757.
School—4115 Taylor Ave., 45209. Tel: 513-533-6060; Fax: 513-533-6068. Sr. Mary Ellen Matts, R.S.M., Prin.
Sisters 2; Lay Teachers 12; Students 255.
Catechesis/Religious Programs—Barbara Browarsky, D.R.E.
Students 71.
Parish Center—4030 Gilmore Ave., 45209. Tel: 513-553-6067.

21—St. Charles Borromeo (Carthage), Rev. Thomas A. Snodgrass.
Res., 115 W. Seymour Ave., 45216. Tel: 513-821-2971.

22—St. Clare (College Hill), Rev. Dale Peterka; Sr. Mary Luke Prickel, O.S.F., Pastoral Assoc. In res., Rev. Robert J. Hater.
Res., 1443 Cedar Ave., 45224. Tel: 513-541-2100.
School—5800 Salvia Ave., 45224. Tel: 513-541-5751. Mrs. Carol Graler, Prin.
Catechesis/Religious Programs—Students 214.

23—St. Clement (St. Bernard), Revs. Al D. Hudepohl, O.F.M.; Donnul Suttmann, O.F.M.; Bro. Joel Soldenski, O.F.M.
Res., St. Clement Friary, 4536 Vine St., 45217. Tel: 513-641-3176; 641-2257 (Friary).
School—4534 Vine St., 45217. Tel: 513-641-2137. Mr. Gerard K. Myers, Prin.
Sisters 2; Lay Teachers 15; Students 397.
Catechesis/Religious Programs—Colleen Gerke, D.R.E.
Students 92.

24—Corpus Christi, Revs. Don Holtgrewe, O.F.M.; Fridolin Voegele, O.F.M.; Deacon John Gingras. In res., Revs. Jeremy Harrington, O.F.M.; Thomas Speier, O.F.M.; Connie Leyendecker, Business Mgr.
Res., 2014 Springdale Rd., 45231. Tel: 513-825-0618; Fax: 513-825-0674.
School—St. Bartholomew Consolidated. See separate listing.
Catechesis/Religious Programs—Tel: 513-825-0182. Barbara Conway, D.R.E.
Students 180.

25—St. Dominic (Delhi Hills), Revs. James R. Collins; Joseph R. Binzer.
Res., 4551 Delhi Pike, 45238. Tel: 513-471-7741; Fax: 513-471-0363.
School—371 Pedretti Ave., 45238. Tel: 513-251-1276. Sr. Patrick Ann O'Connor, S.C., Prin.
Sisters 4; Lay Teachers 30; Students 751.
Catechesis/Religious Programs—Students 231.

26—St. Francis Seraph, Revs. E. John Stein, O.F.M.; Paul Desch, O.F.M.; Bro. Josef Anderlohr, O.F.M.
Res., St. Francis Friary, 1615 Vine St., 45210. Tel: 513-721-4700; Fax: 513-421-9672.
School—14 E. Liberty St., 45210. Tel: 513-721-7778. Sr. Janet Linz, O.S.F., Prin.
Brothers 1; Sisters 3; Lay Teachers 10; Students 150.

27—St. Francis de Sales, Rev. Edward M. Jach, S.M.; Bro. Giancarlo Bonutti, S.M., Pastoral Assoc.
Res., 1600 Madison Rd., 45206. Tel: 513-961-1945; Fax: 513-221-4907.
School—Tel: 513-961-1953; Fax: 513-221-4907. Sr. Carol Ann Wenning, R.S.M., Prin.
Brothers 1; Sisters 1; Lay Teachers 10; Students 225.

28—St. Francis Xavier, Revs. Thomas J. Diehl, S.J.; Paul A. Huber, S.J.; Donald O. Nastold, S.J.; Frederic G. Middendorf, S.J. In res., Revs. Carl J. Moell, S.J.; Robert J. Thesing, S.J.
Res., 607 Sycamore St., 45202. Tel: 513-721-4045; Fax: 513-723-0451.

29—St. Gabriel (Glendale), Rev. David E. Fay; Sr. Mary Doeker, Pastoral Assoc.; Deacon Herman H. Bryant.
Res., 48 W. Sharon Ave., 45246. Tel: 513-771-4700.
School—St. Gabriel Consolidated School. See separate listing. Tel: 513-771-5220.
Catechesis/Religious Programs—Sr. Charlotte Foppe, R.S.M., D.R.E.
Students 118.

30—St. Gertrude (Madeira), Revs. Clement Burns, O.P.; Joseph Ambrose Eckinger, O.P., Novice Master & Subprior; George Schommer, Assoc.; William A. Holt, O.P., Assoc. & Prior. In res., Revs. Thomas F. Carroll, O.P., Pastoral Assoc.; Harvey B. Schaller, O.P.; James M. Sullivan, O.P.; Bro. Ignatius Perkins, O.P.
Res., 7630 Shawnee Run Rd., 45243. Tel: 513-561-5954; Fax: 513-561-6740.
School—6551 Miami Ave., 45243. Tel: 513-561-8020; Fax: 513-561-7184. Sr. Mary Michael, O.P., Prin.
Dominican Sisters (Nashville, TN) 3; Lay Teachers 15; Students 470.
Catechesis/Religious Programs—Tel: 513-561-8369. Mr. Dan Faloon, D.R.E.
Students 575.

31—Good Shepherd (1973), Rev. Thomas R. Axe. Pastoral Assocs.: Donald S. Kruse; Stephen P. Lindner; Sr. Jeannine Selzer, S.C.; Elmer H. Fischesser; Scott Mussari; Patricia Blomer.
Res., 8815 East Kemper Rd., 45249. Tel: 513-489-8815; Fax: 513-489-8521.
Catechesis/Religious Programs—Students 1,400.

32—Guardian Angels (Mt. Washington), Revs. Thomas C. Nolker; William Schroeder, (Retired); Carl J. Wollering; Carol Niemeier, Pastoral Assoc.; Deacons Rick Novick; Bill Wakefield.
Res., 6531 Beechmont Ave., 45230. Tel: 513-231-7440; Fax: 513-624-3145.
School—6539 Beechmont Ave., 45230. Tel: 513-624-3141; Fax: 513-624-3145. Mr. David A. Reker, Prin.
Lay Teachers 40; Students 862.
Catechesis/Religious Programs—Tel: 513-624-3146; Fax: 513-624-3145.
Students 459.

33—Holy Angels, Rev. Msgr. Robert A. Amann; Deacon Philip Wersching.
Res., 2130 Grandin Rd., 45208. Tel: 513-321-3880.

34—Holy Cross-Immaculata (Mount Adams), Rev. Stanley H. Neiheisel. In res., Rev. Terence A. Meehan.
Res., 30 Guido St., 45202. Tel: 513-721-6544; Fax: 513-721-6177.

35—Holy Family (Price Hill). Includes the consolidation of Our Lady of Grace and Our Lady of Perpetual Help Parishes. Rev. Mark J. Burger; Deacon Dave Childers.
Res., 814 Hawthorne Ave., 45205. Tel: 513-921-7527; Fax: 513-921-6033.
School—(Grades K-8) 3001 Price Ave., 45205. Tel: 513-921-8483. Sr. Kathleen Ann Murray, S.C., Prin.
Sisters 10; Lay Teachers 2; Students 176.

36—Holy Name, Rev. Terence Meehan; Sr. Elizabeth Bowyer, S.N.D.deN., Pastoral Admin.
Res., 2448 Auburn Ave., 45219. Tel: 513-721-5608.

37—Holy Trinity Church (Norwood) (1994), Revs. Michael L. Bidwell; Edward F. Haskamp.
Res., 2420 Drex Ave., 45212. Tel: 513-366-4400; Fax: 513-366-4400.
School—Holy Trinity School, Tel: 513-366-4406; Fax: 513-366-4420.
Lay Teachers 17; Students 312.
Catechesis/Religious Programs—Tel: 513-366-4400; Fax: 513-366-4404.
Students 30.

38—St. Ignatius Loyola (Monfort Heights), Revs. Thomas L. Bolte; John J. Mattscheck; Deacon Luis Riva; Barb Campbell, Business Mgr.; Drago Bubalo, Music Dir. In res., Rev. J. Paul Gruber.
Res., 5222 N. Bend Rd., 45247. Tel: 513-661-6565; Fax: 513-389-3241.
School—Tel: 513-389-3242. Timothy Reilly, Prin.
Sisters of Mercy (Oakwood) 1; Lay Teachers 24; Students 697.
Catechesis/Religious Programs—Kris Schoettmer, D.R.E.
Students 179.

39—Immaculate Heart of Mary (Forestville), Rev. Jan Kevin Schmidt; Deacons Jim Sonnenberg; Gene Miller.
Res., 7820 Beechmont Ave., 45255. Tel: 513-474-5570; Fax: 513-388-4097.
School—Tel: 513-388-4086; Fax: 513-388-4097. Bro. Edward Kesler, Prin.
Brothers 1; Lay Teachers 29; Students 565.
Catechesis/Religious Programs—Tel: 513-388-4093; Fax: 513-388-4097. D.R.E.: Sr. Marie Re, S.C., (Adult); Leisa Anslinger; Rita Balcom, (Youth); Patrick Lesher, (Youth).
Students 775.

40—St. James the Greater (White Oak), Revs. Raymond E. Larger; Bernard J. Weldishofer; Sr. Joan Roach, O.S.U., Pastoral Assoc.; Deacon Paul J. Kluener.
Res., 3565 Hubble Rd., 45247. Tel: 513-741-5300; Fax: 513-741-5302. [CEM]
School—6111 Cheviot Rd., 45247. Tel: 513-741-5333; Fax: 513-741-5312. John Merritt, Prin.
Lay Teachers 40; Students 1,092.
Catechesis/Religious Programs—Tel: 513-741-5335; Fax: 513-741-5302.
Students 115.

41—St. James (Wyoming), Rev. Robert B. Buening; Deacons John Cooper; Louis Rekers. In res., Revs. Thomas Fitzsimmons; James E. Ulrich.
Res., 411 Springfield Pk., 45215. Tel: 513-948-1218; Fax: 513-948-1225.
School—Tel: 513-821-9054; Fax: 513-821-9556. Lisa Schaffer, Prin.
Lay Teachers 12; Students 197.
Catechesis/Religious Programs—Tel: 513-948-1212; Fax: 513-948-1225. Mrs. Jeanne Hunt, D.R.E.
Students 261.
Convent—35 Linden Dr., 45215. Tel: 513-761-3511. Sisters of Notre Dame de Namur.

42—St. Jerome, Rev. Carl J. Wollering.
Church—5858 Kellogg Ave., 45228.
Res., 6531 Beechmont Ave., 45230. Tel: 513-231-7042.

43—St. John the Baptist (Dry Ridge), Rev. Charles Bowes.
Res., 5361 Dry Ridge Rd., 45252. Tel: 513-385-8010.
School—5375 Dry Ridge Rd., 45252. Tel: 513-385-7970; Fax: 513-385-5554. Mrs. Sandi Buschmann, Prin.
Sisters 2; Lay Teachers 18; Students 458.
Catechesis/Religious Programs—Tel: 513-385-6239.
Students 125.

44—St. John the Baptist (Harrison), Revs. Edward J. Shine; Robert A. Marine.
Res., 110 N. Hill St., Harrison, 45030. Tel: 513-367-9086. [CEM]
School—Tel: 513-367-6826; Fax: 513-367-6864.
Sisters 4; Lay Teachers 25; Students 501.
Catechesis/Religious Programs—Tel: 513-367-9878.
Students 481.

45—St. John the Evangelist, Rev. Lawrence J. Mick.
Res., 7121 Plainfield Rd., 45236. Tel: 513-791-3238.
School—7131 Plainfield Rd., 45236. Tel: 513-791-6283; Fax: 513-791-6345.
Lay Teachers 17; Students 230.
Catechesis/Religious Programs—Students 65.

46—St. John Fisher (Newtown), Rev. Giles H. Pater.
Office: 3227 Church St., 45244. Tel: 513-561-9431; Fax: 513-561-7513.
Res., 3211 Church St., 45244.
Catechesis/Religious Programs—Tel: 513-561-9431.
Students 52.

47—St. John Vianney (Madison Pl.), Revs. Paul J. Edrich; William H. Cross.
Res., 4448 Berwick, 45227. Tel: 513-271-5490.
School—Cure of Ars, Tel: 513-271-5510; Fax: 513-271-0205.
Lay Teachers 9; Students 145.
Catechesis/Religious Programs—Tel: 513-272-6347.
Students 25.

48—St. John Neumann (Springfield Township), Rev. Robert C. Waller. Pastoral Assocs.: Sr. Adria Connors, C.S.C.; Mary Striebich; Deacons Thomas M. Kiley; John R. Gobbi.
Res., 12191 Mill Rd., 45240. Tel: 513-742-0953; Fax: 513-742-5875.
School—St. Bartholomew Consolidated. See separate listing.
Catechesis/Religious Programs—Tel: 513-742-0953. Mary Lou Tansey, D.R.E.
Students 319.

49—St. Joseph, Rev. Michael A. Noonan; Deacon Raphael Simmons.
Res., 745 Ezzard Charles Dr., 45203. Tel: 513-381-4526.

School—Tel: 513-381-2126. Mr. Wilbur Sanford, Prin.
Lay Teachers 13; Students 221.
Catechesis/Religious Programs—Bro. Rey Taylor, C.F.P., D.R.E.
Students 30.

50—ST. JOSEPH (North Bend), Rev. Harry J. Gerdes; Sr. Helen Groeber, S.C.
Res., 25 E. Harrison Ave., 45052. Tel: 513-941-3661.
Catechesis/Religious Programs—Tel: 513-941-0733. Susan K. Rensing, D.R.E.
Students 155.

51—ST. JUDE THE APOSTLE, Revs. Richard E. Dressman; Gerard Hiland; G. R. Keith Albrecht; Deacon James Sunderman.
Res., 5924 Bridgetown Rd., 45248. Tel: 513-574-1230.
School—5940 Bridgetown Rd., 45248. Tel: 513-598-2100; Fax: 513-598-2118. Joan Axt, Prin.
Lay Teachers 22; Students 457.
Catechesis/Religious Programs—Tel: 513-598-2101.
Students 221.

52—ST. LAWRENCE (Price Hill), Rev. Ralph A. Westerhoff. Pastoral Assocs.: Sr. Helen Julia Hahn. In res., Rev. Erwin J. Bertke.
Res., 3680 Warsaw Ave., 45205. Tel: 513-921-0328.
School—1020 Carson Ave., 45205. Tel: 513-921-4996. Mrs. Mary DeBrunner, Prin.
Sisters 4; Lay Teachers 16; Students 378.
Catechesis/Religious Programs—Students 55.

53—ST. LEO THE GREAT, Rev. Edwin F. Gearhart.
Res., 2573 St. Leo Pl., 45225. Tel: 513-921-0025.
School—St. Boniface Consolidated. See separate listing.
Catechesis/Religious Programs—Students 19.

54—ST. LOUIS, Revs. Edward B. Stolze; Barry M. Windholtz, Res. Assoc.; Sr. Mary William Luxford, O.S.U., Pastoral Assoc. In res., Revs. Edwin F. Gearhart; Arokiyam Amirtharaj, S.D.B. (India).
Res., 29 E. Eighth St., 45202-2086. Tel: 513-421-3157; Fax: 513-333-0579.

55—ST. MARGARET OF CORTONA (Madisonville), Rev. Michael T. Flaherty; Deacon William Aufderheide.
Res., 4100 Watterson St., 45227. Tel: 513-271-0856; Fax: 513-271-1513.
School—4100 Simpson Ave., 45227. Tel: 513-271-8288; Fax: 513-272-1740. Sr. Sharon Ann Wiedmar, R.S.M., Prin.
Sisters 1; Lay Teachers 10; Students 170.
Convent—Tel: 513-271-1956. Sisters of Mercy.

56—ST. MARGARET MARY (North College Hill), Rev. John E. Wall; Deacon Raymond S. Burger. In res., Rev. Anthony G. Andres.
Res., 1830 W. Galbraith Rd., 45239. Tel: 513-521-7387; Fax: 513-521-7388.
School—1820 W. Galbraith Rd., 45239. Tel: 513-521-8619; Fax: 513-521-8620. Ann Heilman, Prin.
Lay Teachers 19; Students 340.
Catechesis/Religious Programs—Tel: 513-729-1551. Al Cuchetti, D.R.E.
Students 3.

57—ST. MARK, Rev. Raymond J. Zarate, C.PP.S.
Res., 3500 Montgomery Rd., 45207. Tel: 513-961-0472.
School—1712 Duck Creek Rd., 45207. Tel: 513-751-3257. Mr. Robert A. Veite, Prin.
Lay Teachers 21; Students 220.

58—ST. MARTIN OF TOURS (Cheviot), Revs. George C. Kunkel; Gregory J. Konerman; Deacon Howard R. Wiehe.
Res., 3720 St. Martin Pl., 45211. Tel: 513-661-2000; Fax: 513-661-8102.
School—3729 Harding Ave., 45211. Tel: 513-661-7609; Fax: 513-661-8102. Sr. Mary Reinette Kroeger, S.N.D., Prin.
Sisters 2; Lay Teachers 23; Students 562.
Catechesis/Religious Programs—Tel: 513-661-2000; Fax: 513-661-8102.
Students 48.

59—ST. MARTIN DE PORRES (Lincoln Heights), Rev. Thomas P. DiFolco.
Res., 9927 Wayne Ave., 45215. Tel: 513-554-4010.
School—St. Gabriel School. See separate listing.

60—OLD ST. MARY, Rev. Francis W. Voellmecke.
Res., 123 E. 13th St., 45210. Tel: 513-721-2988.

61—ST. MARY (Hyde Park), Rev. David C. Robisch; Mrs. Judy Wickert, Pastoral Assoc.; Deacon John Thamann.
Res., 2853 Erie Ave., 45208. Tel: 513-321-1207; Fax: 513-533-5518.
School—2845 Erie Ave., 45208. Tel: 513-321-0703; Fax: 513-533-5518. Jane Welling, Prin.
Lay Teachers 20; Students 530.
Catechesis/Religious Programs—Tel: 513-321-0703; Fax: 513-533-5518.
Students 70.

62—ST. MATTHIAS (Forest Park), Revs. William A. Drain; Gerard A. Evers; Deacons Raymond George; Michael Metz.
Res., 1050 W. Kemper Rd., 45240. Tel: 513-851-1930; Fax: 513-589-3850.
Catechesis/Religious Programs—Tel: 513-589-3845; Fax: 513-589-3850.
Students 85.

63—ST. MICHAEL, Rev. Mark Burger.
Res., 2110 St. Michael St., 45204. Tel: 513-921-0766.

64—ST. MICHAEL (Sharonville), Rev. Michael U. Pucke; William J. Frantz, Admin. Assoc.; Michael Gable, Pastoral Assoc.; Brian Bisig, Dir. Music.
11144 Spinner Ave., 45241. Tel: 513-563-6377; Fax: 513-554-3543.
School—Tel: 513-554-3555; Fax: 513-554-3543. Jody Farrell, Prin.
Lay Teachers 20; Students 507.
Catechesis/Religious Programs—Tel: 513-554-3547; Fax: 513-554-3543. Sr. Carol Gaeke, O.P., D.R.E.
Students 277.

65—ST. MONICA-ST. GEORGE PARISH NEWMAN CENTER, Revs. Jeff Scheeler, O.F.M.; Leonard J. Fecko; Al Hirt; Sr. Lucy Zientek, C.D.P., Pastoral Assoc.
Res., 328 W. McMillan St., 45219. Tel: 513-381-6400.
Church—Tel: 513-381-6400.

66—MOTHER OF CHRIST, Rev. James Shappelle; Sr. Mary Macke, O.S.U., Pastoral Admin.
Church—5301 Winneste Ave., 45232. Tel: 513-242-0164; 242-7588.
Res., 740 Circle Ave., 45232. Tel: 513-541-3732.
Catechesis/Religious Programs—Students 10.

67—NATIVITY OF OUR LORD (Pleasant Ridge), Rev. Robert J. Farrell.
Res., 5935 Pandora Ave., 45213. Tel: 513-531-3164; Fax: 513-531-6368.
School—5936 Ridge Ave., 45213. Tel: 513-531-5138; Fax: 513-531-6368. Robert C. Herring, Prin.
Lay Teachers 21; Students 457.
Catechesis/Religious Programs—Students 60.

68—OUR LADY OF LOURDES (Westwood), Revs. Edward L. Rudemiller; Christopher Lack; Deacon Thomas E. Westerfield; Sr. Ann Mary Lay, Pastoral Min. In res., Revs. Robert R. Wolfer; Paul J. Wolfer.
Res., 2832 Rosebud Dr., 45238. Tel: 513-922-0715; 347-2641 (Res.); Fax: 513-347-2644.
School—5835 Glenway Ave., 45238. Tel: 513-347-2660; Fax: 513-347-2663. Sr. Madonna Ratermann, C.PP.S., Prin.
Sisters 3; Lay Teachers 26; Students 644.

69—OUR LADY OF THE ROSARY (Greenhills), Rev. Paul A. Bader; Deacon Harry S. Walker.
Res., 17 Farragut Rd., 45218. Tel: 513-825-8626; Fax: 513-825-2783.
School—Tel: 513-825-2336; Fax: 513-825-2783. Mrs. Judy Grubb, Prin.
Lay Teachers 17; Students 271.
Catechesis/Religious Programs—19 Farragut Rd., 45218. Tel: 513-825-2338; Fax: 513-825-2783. Sr. Mary Laura Miceli, S.C., D.R.E.
Students 240.

70—OUR LADY OF THE SACRED HEART (Reading), Rev. Jack W. Wehman; Deacons James Geraci; Robert Glassmeyer.
Res., 162 Siebenthaler Ave., 45215. Tel: 513-733-4950.
School—Tel: 513-733-5225. Ms. Barbara Adelmann, Prin.
Lay Teachers 18; Students 320.
Catechesis/Religious Programs—Tel: 513-733-4950.
Students 50.

71—OUR LADY OF VICTORY (Delhi Hills), Revs. Patrick P. Duffy; Peter Thomas St. George; Deacons Charles Jenkins; Joseph Schultheis; Ms. Donna Watts, Pastoral Min.
Res., 810 Neeb Rd., 45233. Tel: 513-922-4460; Fax: 513-922-5476.
School—808 Neeb Rd., 45233. Tel: 513-347-2072; Fax: 513-922-5476. Mr. Melschlomer, Prin.
Lay Teachers 28; Students 680.
Catechesis/Religious Programs—Tel: 513-347-2071; Fax: 513-922-5476. Mary Jo Wolfram, D.R.E.
Students 226.

72—OUR LADY OF VISITATION (Mack), Revs. John E. Wessling; W. Michael Hay; Deacon William A. Dehmer; Sr. Gertrude Ann Knipper, C.D.P., Pastoral Assoc.
Res., 3172 South Rd., 45248. Tel: 513-922-2056; Fax: 513-347-2238.
School—3180 South Rd., 45248. Tel: 513-347-2222; Fax: 513-347-2225. Mr. Terry P. Chapman, Prin.
Sisters 1; Lay Teachers 33; Students 836.
Catechesis/Religious Programs—Tel: 513-347-2228; Fax: 513-347-2225. Sr. Mary Tewes, O.S.B., D.R.E.
Students 164.

73—OUR LORD, CHRIST THE KING (Mt. Lookout), Revs. Gerald R. Haemmerle; Anthony Muller.
Res., 3223 Linwood Rd., 45226. Tel: 513-321-4121; Fax: 513-871-3978.
School—Cardinal Pacelli, 927 Ellison, 45226. Tel: 513-321-1048; Fax: 513-871-3978. Fran Moore, Prin.
Lay Teachers 20; Students 458.
Catechesis/Religious Programs—Students 45.

74—OUR MOTHER OF SORROWS (Roselawn), Rev. Steven P. Walter; Deacon Michael A. Ascolese.
Res., 7243 Eastlawn Dr., 45237. Tel: 513-731-6480; Fax: 513-731-4640.
School—Tel: 513-731-8838; Fax: 513-731-4640. Paul F. McLaughlin, Prin.
Lay Teachers 13; Students 180.
Catechesis/Religious Programs—Students 170.

75—STS. PETER AND PAUL (Reading), Rev. Paul L. Stolz. In res., Rev. Mark T. Watkins.
Res., 417 W. Vine St., Reading, 45215. Tel: 513-554-1010; Fax: 513-554-0190.
School—Tel: 513-554-1311; Fax: 513-554-4667. Mr. Paul D. Mertzman, Prin.
Sisters 2; Lay Teachers 6; Students 144.
Catechesis/Religious Programs—Tel: 513-821-7448. Sr. Judith Wessels, S.N.D.de N., D.R.E.
Students 70.

76—ST. PIUS, Rev. Michael Noonan. In res., Rev. Martin Smith.
Res., 1814 Dreman Ave., 45223. Tel: 513-541-0211.

77—RESURRECTION OF OUR LORD, Rev. Robert E. Keller.
Res., 1744 Iliff Ave., 45205. Tel: 513-471-2700.
School—1740 Iliff Ave., 45205. Tel: 513-471-6600. Thomas F. Miller, Prin.
Sisters 2; Lay Teachers 10; Students 190.
Catechesis/Religious Programs—Students 2.

78—ST. ROBERT BELLARMINE, Rev. Richard W. Bollman, S.J.; Lauren McDonough Renneker, Dir. Pastoral Min., Tel: 513-745-3008; Guy M. Vanasse, Dir. Music Min., Tel: 513-745-3270; Michael W. Jarrold-Grapes, Dir. Youth Min., Tel: 513-745-4224.
Res., Xavier University, 3844 Victory Pkwy., 45207. Tel: 513-745-3398; Fax: 513-745-2031.
Catechesis/Religious Programs—Tel: 513-745-3317; Fax: 513-745-2031. Rosemary G. Conrad, D.R.E.
Students 123.

79—ST. ROSE OF LIMA, Lawrence R. Krusling.
Res., 2501 Eastern Ave., 45202. Tel: 513-871-1162.

80—SACRED HEART, Rev. Mario Rauzi, C.S. In res., Rev. Angelo Cugnidoro, C.S.
Res., 2733 Massachusetts Ave., 45225. Tel: 513-541-4654; Fax: 513-541-4662.
School—Corryville Catholic Elementary School. See separate listing.

81—ST. SAVIOUR (Rossmoyne), Rev. Robert W. Goebel; Deacon Jerry Cain.
Res., 4136 Myrtle Ave., 45236. Tel: 513-791-9004; Fax: 513-791-6530.
School—4122 Myrtle Ave., 45236. Tel: 513-791-2734; Fax: 513-791-6530. Donna Beebe, Prin.
Lay Teachers 12; Students 183.
Catechesis/Religious Programs—Students 76.

82—ST. SIMON THE APOSTLE, Rev. Michael D. Beatty.
Res., 825 Pontius Rd., 45233. Tel: 513-941-3656; Fax: 513-941-2329.
Catechesis/Religious Programs—Tel: 513-941-6173; Fax: 513-941-3656. Carolyn Meyers, D.R.E.
Students 255.

83—ST. STEPHEN, Rev. Ronald J. Averbeck.
Res., 320 Donham Ave., 45226. Tel: 513-871-3373.

84—ST. TERESA, Revs. Larry R. Tharp; John L. Cavanaugh; Deacon Michael Davenport.
Res., 1175 Overlook Ave., 45238. Tel: 513-921-9200; Fax: 513-921-4446.
School—1194 Rulison Ave., 45238. Tel: 513-471-4530. Barbara A. Cooke, Prin.
Sisters 1; Lay Teachers 18; Students 451.
Catechesis/Religious Programs—Tel: 513-471-4530. David L. Donovan, D.R.E.
Students 90.

85—ST. THERESE, THE LITTLE FLOWER (Mt. Airy), Revs. Thomas M. King; Robert A. Stricker.
Res., 5560 Kirby Ave., 45239. Tel: 513-541-5560; Fax: 513-681-2631.
School—5555 Little Flower Ave., 45239. Tel: 513-542-6787. Mrs. Patricia Kennedy, Prin.
Lay Teachers 23; Students 519.
Catechesis/Religious Programs—Mr. James Dunn, D.R.E.
Students 70.

86—ST. VINCENT FERRER (Kenwood), Rev. Terence J. Hamilton. In res., Rev. Joseph Heskamp, (Retired).
Res., 7754 Montgomery Rd., 45236. Tel: 513-791-9030; Fax: 513-791-7405.
School—Tel: 513-791-6320; Fax: 513-791-7405.
Lay Teachers 15; Students 260.
Catechesis/Religious Programs—Tel: 513-791-6321; Fax: 513-791-7405. Sr. Kaye Lednik, C.S.J., D.R.E.

Students 141.

87—ST. VINCENT DE PAUL, Rev. Gary J. Witsken.
Res., 4026 River Rd., 45204. Tel: 513-451-5714.
School—4044 River Rd., 45204. Tel: 513-451-5656. Sr. Miriam Clare Glandorf, S.C., Prin.
Sisters 1; Lay Teachers 5; Students 80.

88—ST. VIVIAN, Rev. John E. Filippine; Mr. Greg Hogg, Pastoral Assoc.; Deacons William R. Michael; Gerald Coomes.
Res., 7600 Winton Rd., 45224. Tel: 513-728-4331; Fax: 513-728-4335.
School—885 Denier Pl., 45224. Tel: 513-522-6858; Fax: 513-728-4335.
Lay Teachers 18; Students 370.
Catechesis/Religious Programs—Tel: 513-728-4333; Fax: 513-728-4335. Christine Siciliano, D.R.E. Students 91.

89—ST. WILLIAM, Rev. Philip O. Seher; Deacon C. Edward Brockman; Sr. Claire Foken, S.C., Pastoral Min. In res., Rev. Msgr. Francis Kennedy; Rev. Christopher R. Armstrong.
Res., 4108 W. Eighth St., 45205. Tel: 513-921-0247; Fax: 513-921-2810.
School—4125 St. William Ave., 45205. Tel: 513-471-2989; Fax: 513-471-8226. Elaine Haas, Prin.
Sisters 1; Lay Teachers 25; Students 457.

OUTSIDE THE CITY OF CINCINNATI

Amelia, Clermont Co., St. Bernadette's, Rev. Hans H. Gruenbauer.
Res., 1479 Locust Lake Rd., 45102. Tel: 513-753-5566; Fax: 513-753-5566.
School—1453 Locust Lake Rd., 45102. Tel: 513-753-4744. Mr. Dan Teller, Prin.
Lay Teachers 13; Students 200.
Catechesis/Religious Programs—Tel: 513-753-5566. Kelly Lafferty, D.R.E.
Students 110.

Arnheim, Brown Co., St. Mary, Rev. Dohrman W. Byers.
Res., 6647 Van Buren St., Georgetown, 45121. Tel: 513-446-2555.
Catechesis/Religious Programs—Tel: 937-446-2555.
Students 83.

Batavia, Clermont Co., Holy Trinity, Rev. William R. Stockelman; Deacon James Hennessey.
Res., 140 N. 6th St., 45103. Tel: 513-732-2024.
Catechesis/Religious Programs—Tel: 513-732-2024. Patricia Bruce, D.R.E.
Students 117.

Beavercreek, Greene Co., St. Luke, Rev. William J. Kramer.
Res., 1440 N. Fairfield Rd., 45432. Tel: 937-426-1733; Fax: 937-426-3965.
School—(Grades K-8) 1442 N. Fairfield Rd., 45432. Tel: 937-426-8551; Fax: 937-426-6435. Ms. Constance Wildenhaus, Prin.
Lay Teachers 21; Students 507.
Catechesis/Religious Programs—1444 N. Fairfield Rd., 45432. Tel: 937-426-5656.
Students 400.

Bellefontaine, Logan Co., St. Patrick's, Rev. Henry F. Albietz; Deacon Harold Dipple.
Res., 328 E. Patterson Ave., 43311. Tel: 937-592-1656.
Catechesis/Religious Programs—320 E. Patterson Rd., 43311. Tel: 937-592-6621. Sr. Vincent Marie Willman, S.C., D.R.E.
Students 244.

Bethel, Clermont Co., St. Mary, Rev. Patrick H. Crone.
Res., 3398 S.R. 125, 45106. Tel: 513-734-4041.
Catechesis/Religious Programs—Tel: 513-734-3676. Joan St. Clair, D.R.E.
Students 209.

Blanchester, Clinton Co., Holy Name, Rev. Michael A. Savino.
Res. & Church: 746 S. S.R. 133, 45107. Tel: 937-783-3956.
Catechesis/Religious Programs—Kathy Baxter, D.R.E.
Students 76.

Botkins, Shelby Co., Immaculate Conception, Rev. James J. O'Connor.
Res., 116 N. Mill St., P.O. Box 519, 45306. Tel: 937-693-2561.
Catechesis/Religious Programs—Students 311.

Bradford, Miami Co., Immaculate Conception, Rev. James S. Duell.
Res., 5874 N. Buckneck Rd., R.R. 2, 45308. Tel: 937-448-6220.
Catechesis/Religious Programs—Students 58.

Burkettsville, Mercer Co., St. Bernard, Rev. Albert A. Reed, C.PP.S.
Res., 71 W. Main St., P.O. Box 146, 45310. Tel: 419-375-2333.
St. Henry Catechetical Center—See St. Henry, St. Henry for details.

Camden, Preble Co., St. Mary's, Rev. Francis R. Monnig.
Res., 5304 Jacksonburg Rd., Trenton, 45067. Tel: 937-726-6294.
Church—7721 N. Main St., 45311. Tel: 937-452-3352.

Carthagena, Mercer Co., St. Aloysius, Rev. David A. Hoying, C.PP.S.
Res., 1509 Cranberry Rd., St. Henry, 45883. Tel: 419-925-4776.
Church—State Rte. 274, Celina, 45822.
St. Henry Catechetical Center—For details call Tel: 419-678-3811.

Cassella, Mercer Co., Nativity of the Blessed Virgin Mary, Rev. Frederick Ryder, C.PP.S.
Res., 6524 State Rte. 119, Maria Stein, 45860. Tel: 419-925-4630. [CEM]
Catechesis/Religious Programs—Carolyn Stucke, D.R.E.
Students 127.

Celina, Mercer Co., Immaculate Conception of the Blessed Virgin Mary, Revs. James C. Seibert, C.PP.S.; Richard R. Riedel, C.PP.S. In res., Deacon Thomas Huff.
Res., 229 W. Anthony St., 45822. Tel: 419-586-6648; Fax: 419-586-6649. [CEM]
School—Tel: 419-586-2379; Fax: 419-586-6649. Ms. Kathryn Mescher, Prin.
Sisters of the Precious Blood 1; Lay Teachers 15; Students 254.
Catechesis/Religious Programs—Wayne & Walnut Sts., Tel: 419-586-2370; Fax: 419-586-6649.
Students 575.

Centerville, Montgomery Co., Incarnation, Revs. Thomas A. Kuhn; Kenneth E. Schartz; Daniel J. Meyer. Pastoral Assocs.: Mary Fogler; Tim Niesel; Deacon Robert Zinck.
Res., 55 Williamsburg Ln., 45459. Tel: 937-433-1188; Fax: 937-433-3263.
School—45 Williamsburg Ln., 45459. Tel: 937-433-1051; Fax: 937-433-9796. Cheryl Reichel, Prin.
Lay Teachers 27; Students 642.
Catechesis/Religious Programs—Tel: 937-433-3377; Fax: 937-433-3263. Mrs. Ann Osgood, D.R.E. Students 532.

St. Francis of Assisi (1969), Revs. John B. Turnbull, O.F.M.; Knute Kinross, O.F.M.; Sharon Wilson, Parish Sec.; Francis Obringer, Sec. of Rel. Ed.
Res., 6245 Wilmington Pike, 45459. Tel: 937-433-1013; Fax: 937-433-1699.
Catechesis/Religious Programs—Tel: 937-433-0128; Fax: 937-433-1699. D.R.E.: Mary Ellen Singer; Mary Ann Monseur.
Students 624.

Chickasaw, Mercer Co., Most Precious Blood, Rev. John L. Bensman.
Res., Box 26, 35 S. Maple St., 45826-0026. Tel: 419-925-4391.
Catechesis/Religious Programs—Margie Ronnebaum, D.R.E.
Students 192.

Coldwater, Mercer Co., Holy Trinity, Revs. Ronald H. Wilker; Frank Amberger.
Res., 116 E. Main St., 45828. Tel: 419-678-4802; Fax: 419-678-4803.
Catechesis/Religious Programs—110 N. Second St., 45828. Tel: 419-678-3328. D.R.E.: Helen Vagedes; Catherine Wenning.
Students 1,113.

Covington, Miami Co., St. Teresa, Rev. James S. Duell.
Res., 6925 W. U.S. 36, 45318. Tel: 937-473-2970. [JC]
Catechesis/Religious Programs—Tel: 937-473-2970. Donald Kuether, D.R.E.
Students 69.

Cranberry Prairie, Mercer Co., St. Francis, Rev. David A. Hoying, C.PP.S.
Res., 1509 Cranberry Rd., St. Henry, 45883. Tel: 419-925-4776. [CEM]
St. Henry Catechetical Center—See St. Henry, St. Henry for details. Tel: 419-678-3811.

Dayton, Montgomery Co.,

1—ST. ADALBERT'S, (Polish), Rev. Michael J. Holloran; Deacon Robert Kozlowski. Office 1511 Valley St., 45404. Tel: 937-228-8782.
Catechesis/Religious Programs—1509 Valley St., 45404. Tel: 937-228-8604. Doreen Matulavitch, D.R.E.
Students 40.

2—ST. AGNES, Rev. James R. Schutte; Nympha Clark, Pastoral Admin.
Res., 811 N. Paul L. Dunbar St., 45407. Tel: 937-274-2212; Fax: 937-274-0976.
School—Dayton Catholic Elementary Consolidated. See separate listing. Tel: 937-275-8114.

3—ST. ALBERT THE GREAT, Revs. James J. Manning; Lawrence R. Strittmatter; Sr. Patrice Vales, S.C., Pastoral Assoc.; Deacons Ray Blum; Steve Bermick. In res., Rev. Benedict O'Cinnsealaigh.
Res., 3033 Far Hills Ave., 45429. Tel: 937-293-1191; Fax: 937-293-1848.
School—Tel: 937-293-9452; Fax: 937-293-1848. Mrs. Leslie Kearney, Prin.
Lay Teachers 26; Students 547.
Catechesis/Religious Programs—104 Dorothy Ln., Kettering, 45429. Tel: 937-298-2402; Fax: 937-293-1848.
Students 370.

4—ST. ANTHONY OF PADUA, Rev. Thomas M. Shearer. In res., Revs. Thomas Ballman; Christian A. Rohmiller.
Res., 820 Bowen St., 45410. Tel: 937-253-9132; Fax: 937-253-6658.
School—Tel: 937-253-6251; Fax: 937-253-1541.
Lay Teachers 19; Students 457.

5—ASCENSION, Revs. David E. Brinkmoeller; James Wedig. In res., Rev. Ronald Nuzzi. Pastoral Assocs.: Sr. Florence Seifert, C.PP.S.; Sr. Marie Langhals, C.PP.S.
Res., 2025 Woodman Dr., Kettering, 45420. Tel: 937-253-5171.
School—Tel: 937-245-5411; Fax: 937-254-1105. Sr. Maureen Heavey, R.S.M., Prin.
Sisters 1; Lay Teachers 17; Students 380.
Catechesis/Religious Programs—Tel: 937-254-0622. Mary Ellen Fargey, D.R.E.
Students 375.
Convent—2005 Woodman Dr., Kettering, 45420. Tel: 937-254-1751.

6—ASSUMPTION, Rev. John E. Krumm; Sr. Mary M. Garascia, Pastoral Admin.
Parish Address: 3805 Kings Hwy., 45406. Tel: 937-275-9042.
School—Dayton Catholic Elementary Consolidated. See separate listing. Tel: 937-275-8144; Fax: 937-275-5737.

7—ST. CHARLES BORROMEO, Rev. Msgr. Lawrence K. Breslin; Rev. George Schmitz; Deacon Leonard Baltes. In res., Rev. Isacc Ebeicbe (Nigeria).
Res., 4500 Ackerman Rd., 45429. Tel: 937-434-6081; Fax: 937-434-6251.
School—Tel: 937-434-4933. Miss Judy Ellerbrock, Prin.
Sisters 3; Lay Teachers 29; Students 661.
Catechesis/Religious Programs—Students 405.

8—CORPUS CHRISTI, Rev. James R. Schutte; Deacon Milton Royer.
Res., 224 Squirrel Rd., 45405. Tel: 937-228-6672.
School—200 Homewood Ave., 45405. Tel: 937-228-3091; Fax: 937-461-0611.
Lay Teachers 13; Students 184.

9—EMMANUEL, Revs. Lee Sciarrotta, S.M.; Francis J. Kenney, S.M.
Res., 149 Franklin St., 45402. Tel: 937-228-2013.
Catechesis/Religious Programs—Tel: 937-228-5354.
Students 141.

10—ST. HELEN, Rev. Paul F. DeLuca; Deacons John J. Jachimowicz; Susano Mascorro; Roy Deardorff.
Res., 605 Granville Pl., 45431. Tel: 937-254-6233; Fax: 937-256-6117.
School—Tel: 937-256-1761. Sr. Annette Paveglio, S.C., Prin.
Sisters 6; Lay Teachers 15; Students 445.
Catechesis/Religious Programs—Tel: 937-256-8815. Joan Torres, D.R.E.
Students 155.
Convent—5098 Burkhardt Rd., 45431. Tel: 937-252-7972. Sisters of Notre Dame

11—ST. HENRY, Revs. Lawrence E. Mierenfeld; Steven L. Shoup; Sr. Joanne Termini, S.C., Pastoral Assoc.; Deacon Alan W. Arber.
Res., 6666 Springboro Rd., 45449. Tel: 937-434-9231; Fax: 937-434-6798.
School—Bishop Leibold Consolidated. See separate listing. Tel: 937-434-9343.
Catechesis/Religious Programs—Students 420.

12—HOLY ANGELS, Rev. Thomas E. Meyer; Sr. Rose Marie Burns, S.C., Pastoral Assoc.; Deacon Eldon M. Cotterman.
Parish Office: 218 K St., 45409. Tel: 937-222-7807; Fax: 937-222-8167.
Church—Brown & L Sts., 45409.
School—Tel: 937-222-0365. Louise P. Moore, Prin.
Lay Teachers 17; Students 265.
Catechesis/Religious Programs—Tel: 937-222-2641. Karen D. Davis, D.R.E.
Students 256.

13—HOLY CROSS, (Lithuanian), Rev. Michael J. Holloran, Admin.
Res., 1924 Leo St., 45404-1997. Tel: 937-228-8902.

14—HOLY FAMILY, Rev. Thomas M. Gaeke; Deacon William Stevenson, Jr. In res., Revs. Edward Haggerty; Ernesto Caro (Mexico).
Res., 140 S. Findlay St., 45403. Tel: 937-253-1109; Fax: 937-253-2172.
School—121 S. Monmouth St., 45403. Tel: 937-253-4859. G. Janell Postawski, Prin.

Sisters 2; Lay Teachers 8; Students 220.
Convent—141 S. Monmouth St., 45403. Tel: 937-252-0101. Sisters of Notre Dame de Namur.
Catechesis/Religious Programs—St. Mary Church, 310 Allen St., 45410. Tel: 937-256-5633; Fax: 937-256-7138.

15—HOLY TRINITY, Rev. Walter J. MacPherson; Deacon George Zvonar; Sr. Helen McDermott, S.N.D., Pastoral Asst.; Mary C. Wlodarski, Christian Formation Min.
Res., 272 Bainbridge St., 45402. Tel: 937-228-1223; Fax: 937-445-0232.

16—ST. JAMES, Revs. Freddy Washington, C.S.Sp.; George Crocenzi, C.S.Sp., Assoc.
Res., 719 Edgemont Ave., 45408. Tel: 937-228-7023.
Church—Heck & Cincinnati St., 45408.
School—Dayton Catholic Elementary. See separate listing.
Catechesis/Religious Programs—Anna Burns, D.R.E.
Students 30.

17—ST. JOSEPH, Rev. Louis Osterhage, C.PP.S.
Res., 411 E. Second St., 45402. Tel: 937-228-9272; 228-9522.

18—ST. MARY'S, Rev. Thomas M. Gaeke; Deacon William Saluke.
Res., 310 Allen St., 45410. Tel: 937-256-5633; Fax: 937-256-7138.
Catechesis/Religious Programs—Tel: 937-256-5633; Fax: 937-256-7138. Dr. Robert Obach, D.R.E.
Students 39.

19—OUR LADY OF THE IMMACULATE CONCEPTION, Rev. Timothy S. Kallaher. Pastoral Assocs.: Pauline Everman; Deacons Dan Kraus; Vince Orlando; Art Kronenberger.
Res., 2300 S. Smithville Rd., 45420. Tel: 937-252-9919; Fax: 937-252-0890.
School—Tel: 937-253-8831; Fax: 937-252-8832. Rachelle Cordonnier, Prin.
Sisters 2; Lay Teachers 20; Students 460.
Catechesis/Religious Programs—Students 60.
Convent—2272 Smithville Rd., 45420. Sisters of Notre Dame de Namur.

20—OUR LADY OF MERCY, Rev. John E. Krumm. Pastoral Assocs.: Carolyn Mackenzie; Bill Painter; Kathy Shirley; Deacon Thomas Platfoot.
Res., 220 W. Siebenthaler Ave., 45405. Tel: 937-274-2107; Fax: 937-274-4363.
School—Tel: 937-278-5483. Sr. M. Karen Sammons, S.C., Prin.
Lay Teachers 16; Students 275.
Catechesis/Religious Programs—Students 30.

21—OUR LADY OF THE ROSARY, Rev. Anthony M. Dattilo; Deacon Henry B. Beck.
Res., 22 Notre Dame Ave., 45404. Tel: 937-228-8802.
School—40 Notre Dame Ave., 45404. Tel: 937-222-7231; Fax: 937-222-7393. Genevieve S. Ritzel, Prin.
Lay Teachers 11; Students 210.

22—ST. PETER, (Huber Heights), Revs. Earl Francis Simone; Francis B. Pilliod; Michael T. Mahoney; Deacons Allen K. Miller; Robert Borgerding.
Res., 6161 Chambersburg Rd., 45424. Tel: 937-233-1503; Fax: 937-237-3523.
School—Tel: 937-233-8710; Fax: 937-237-3974. Feliza Poling, Prin.
Lay Teachers 43; Students 936.
Catechesis/Religious Programs—Tel: 937-237-3516; Fax: 937-233-5717. Mrs. Janet Lewis, D.R.E.
Students 516.

23—PRECIOUS BLOOD, Rev. Mark Hoying, C.PP.S.; Deacon Richard Janowiecki. In res., Rev. Angelo Anthony, C.PP.S.; Bro. Bernard Barga, C.PP.S.
Res., 4961 Salem Ave., 45416. Tel: 937-276-5954; Fax: 937-276-5955.
School—4870 Denlinger Rd., 45426. Tel: 937-277-2291. Sr. Anne Schulz, C.PP.S., Prin.
Lay Teachers 19; Students 416.
Catechesis/Religious Programs—Tel: 937-277-2454.
Students 129.

24—QUEEN OF APOSTLES, Greene Co., Rev. James Bartlett, S.M., Priest Coord.
Church—4400 Shakertown Rd., 45430-1095. Tel: 937-429-0510; Fax: 937-429-0881.
Res., Trinity Community, 1903 Trinity Ave., 45409-2445. Tel: 513-293-9744.
Catechesis/Religious Programs—Tel: 937-426-0881; Fax: 937-429-0881. Marilyn McCrate, D.R.E.
Students 104.

25—QUEEN OF MARTYRS, (Northridge), Rev. Thomas R. Hopp; Sr. Ann Merkle, C.PP.S., Pastoral Assoc.
Res., 4144 Cedar Ridge Rd., 45414. Tel: 937-277-2092.
School—Tel: 937-274-5592. Lucianne Lilienthal, Prin.
Sisters 2; Lay Teachers 7; Students 200.
Catechesis/Religious Programs—Tel: 937-277-2092. Sr. Ann Merkle, C.PP.S., D.R.E.
Students 44.

26—RESURRECTION OF OUR LORD, Rev. Freddy Washington; Deacon Jacob Jernigan.
Res., 130 Gramont Ave., 45417. Tel: 937-268-6697.
School—Tel: 937-268-6391; Fax: 937-268-9775.
Lay Teachers 9; Students 156.

27—ST. RITA, Rev. Kenneth R. Baker.
Res., 5401 N. Main St., 45415. Tel: 937-278-5815; Fax: 937-275-3302.
School—Tel: 937-277-8978. Mary Ann Eismann, Prin.
Lay Teachers 16; Students 332.
Catechesis/Religious Programs—Karen Sipos, D.R.E.
Students 98.

28—ST. STEPHEN, (North Dayton), Rev. Anthony M. Dattilo.
Res., 1114 Troy St., 45404. Tel: 937-223-8306.

Eaton, Preble Co., Visitation of the Blessed Virgin Mary, Rev. Ralph J. Lawrence; Deacon Joseph James.
Res., 407 E. Main St., 45320. Tel: 937-456-3380.
Catechesis/Religious Programs—Tel: 937-456-3395. Sharon Stump, D.R.E.
Students 160.

Egypt, Auglaize Co., St. Joseph, Rev. Thomas Brenberger, C.PP.S. In res., Rev. Oscar H. Seger.
Res., 02441 SR 364, 45865. Tel: 419-628-2614; Fax: 419-628-2958.
Catechesis/Religious Programs—Students 32.

Englewood, Montgomery Co., St. Paul's, Rev. Todd Grogan; Deacon Joseph Subler.
Res., 1000 W. Wenger Rd., 45322. Tel: 937-836-7535.
Catechesis/Religious Programs—Tel: 937-836-2337. Dr. Sandra Chakeres, D.R.E.
Students 585.

Fairborn, Greene Co., Mary Help of Christians, Revs. Joseph R. Raudabaugh; John R. Kummer; Anne Rusen, Pastoral Assoc.; Deacon Max Roadruck.
Res., 954 N. Maple Ave., 45324-5498. Tel: 937-878-8353; Fax: 937-879-8800.
School—934 N. Maple Ave., 45324-5499. Tel: 937-878-9152. Joseph L. Pizza, Prin.
Lay Teachers 16; Students 350.
Catechesis/Religious Programs—1030 N. Maple Ave., 45324. Tel: 937-878-7325. Gloria L. Leigh, D.R.E.
Students 159.

Fairfield, Butler Co., Sacred Heart of Jesus, Revs. Norman Langenbrunner; Jerome Gardner.
Church—400 Nilles Rd., 45014. Tel: 513-829-4383; Fax: 513-829-4387.
Res., 5202 Mississippi Dr., 45014. Tel: 513-863-5318; Fax: 513-863-5318.
School—Tel: 513-829-6501; Fax: 513-829-0268. Joseph Nagle, Prin.
Lay Teachers 19; Students 470.
Catechesis/Religious Programs—Tel: 513-829-6493.
Students 266.

Fayetteville, Brown Co., St. Patrick's, Rev. Donald T. Noll.
Res., P.O. Box 279, 45118. Tel: 937-875-2082.
Catechesis/Religious Programs—Tel: 937-875-2161. Debbie Rosselot, D.R.E.
Students 100.

Felicity, Clermont Co., Our Mother of Good Counsel, Rev. Patrick H. Crone.
Res., 3398 S.R. 125, Bethel, 45106. Tel: 513-734-4041.
Catechesis/Religious Programs—Tel: 513-734-3676. Joan St. Clair, D.R.E.
Students 31.

Fort Loramie, Shelby Co., St. Michael's, Revs. Timothy S. Bunch; Aloysius B. Boeke; Deacon Werner Bensman.
Res., 33 Elm St., P.O. Box 7, 45845. Tel: 937-295-2891; Fax: 937-295-3349.
Catechesis/Religious Programs—Tel: 937-295-2179; Fax: 937-295-3349. D.R.E.: Marge Rethman; Frank Turner.
Students 560.

Fort Recovery, Mercer Co., Mary Help of Christians, Revs. Paul W. Wohlwend, C.PP.S.; Norbert Loshe, C.PP.S.; Deacon John Parker.
Res., 403 Sharpsburg Rd., 45846. Tel: 419-375-4153.
Catechesis/Religious Programs—Tel: 419-375-4153.
Students 372.
St. Peter, Rev. George Kuzara, C.PP.S.
Res., 1477 Philothea Rd., St. Peter, 45846. Tel: 419-375-4344.
Catechesis/Religious Programs—Tel: 419-375-4344. Ginny Fortkamp, D.R.E.
Students 176.

Franklin, Warren Co., St. Mary's, Rev. Joseph B. Bruening.
Res., 115 S. Main St., 45005. Tel: 513-746-5404; Fax: 513-746-1404.
Catechesis/Religious Programs—Tel: 513-746-1404; Fax: 513-746-1404.
Students 204.

Frenchtown, Darke Co., Holy Family, Rev. Leo A. Hoying.
Res., 14 E. Wood St., Versailles, 45380. Tel: 937-526-4945.
Catechesis/Religious Programs—Students 100.

Fryburg, Auglaize Co., St. John, Rev. Charles F. Lang.
Res., 11319 Van Buren St., Wapokoneta, 45895-8467. Tel: 419-738-6043.
Catechesis/Religious Programs—Tel: 419-738-6043. Richard Westbay, D.R.E.
Students 84.

Georgetown, Brown Co., St. George, Rev. Earl O. Metz.
Res., 109 Elm St., 45121. Tel: 937-378-6829.
Church—507 E. State St.
Catechesis/Religious Programs—Mary Gaskin, D.R.E.
Students 66.

Germantown, Montgomery Co., St. Augustine, Rev. Paul F. Hurst.
Res., 6891 Weaver Rd., 45327. Tel: 937-855-2289.
Catechesis/Religious Programs—Tel: 937-855-2289.
Students 76.

Glynwood, St. Patrick, Rev. Charles F. Lang.
Res., 06959 Glynwood Rd., St. Marys, 45885. Tel: 419-738-6308.
Catechesis/Religious Programs—Tel: 419-394-8458. Irene Heilers, D.R.E.
Students 62.

Greenfield, Highland Co., St. Benignus, Rev. Ronald C. Cooper.
Res., 218 S. Second St., 45123. Tel: 937-981-2785.
Catechesis/Religious Programs—Jessie Spangler, D.R.E.
Students 65.

Greenville, Darke Co., St. Mary, Rev. Harold W. Kist.
Res., 233 W. 3rd St., 45331. Tel: 937-548-1616.
School—238 W. Third St., 45331. Tel: 937-548-2345; Fax: 937-548-0878.
Lay Teachers 10; Students 138.
Catechesis/Religious Programs—Tel: 937-548-1616. Sr. Elaine Beimesche, C.S.J., D.R.E.
Students 228.

Hamilton, Butler Co.,

1—ST. ANN'S, Rev. Dennis Dettenwanger; Deacon Mark E. Brunner.
Res., 646 Clinton Ave., 45015. Tel: 513-863-4963.
School—3064 Pleasant Ave., 45015. Tel: 513-863-0604; Fax: 513-863-2073. Mrs. Donna L. Weber, Prin.
Sisters 1; Lay Teachers 10; Students 234.
Catechesis/Religious Programs—Tel: 513-863-4963.
Students 38.
Convent—(Oldenburg, IN) 646 Clinton Ave., 45015. Tel: 513-863-1701. Sisters of the Third Order Regular of St. Francis.

2—ST. JOSEPH'S, Rev. Dennis Dettenwanger; Sr. Mary Ann Klohr, C.S.J., Pastoral Admin.
Res., 171 Washington St., 45011. Tel: 513-863-1424.
School—Tel: 513-863-8758; Fax: 513-863-5253. Gail Kist Kline, Ph.D., Ed., Prin.
Lay Teachers 12; Students 175.

3—ST. JULIE BILLIART, (1989). (This parish is the successor in interest to St. Mary, St. Stephen and St. Veronica parishes, formerly located in Hamilton, Ohio.). Rev. Jeffrey P. Silver; Deacons James S. McCormick; William B. Renneker.
Church—224 Dayton St., 45011. Tel: 513-863-1040; Fax: 513-863-1132.
School—(Grades K-8) 1206 Shuler Ave., 45011. Tel: 513-867-8477. Mrs. Margaret Hunsberger, Prin.
Lay Teachers 12; Students 225.

4—ST. PETER IN CHAINS, Rev. William H. Schwartz.
Res., 382 Liberty Ave., 45013. Tel: 513-863-3938; Fax: 513-863-3344.
School—451 Ridgelawn Ave., 45013. Tel: 513-863-0685.
Lay Teachers 20; Students 447.
Catechesis/Religious Programs—Tel: 513-863-3344.
Students 90.

Hillsboro, Highland Co., St. Mary's, Rev. Stanley E. Luehrmann; Miss Carole J. Grady, Pastoral Assoc. & D.R.E.
Res., 212 S. High St., 45133-1445. Tel: 937-393-1742.
Catechesis/Religious Programs—Tel: 937-393-4017.
Students 119.

Jamestown, Greene Co., St. Augustine, Rev. William V. Thomas.
Res., 31 S. Chillicothe St., P.O. Box F, South

Charleston, 45368-0806. Tel: 937-462-8971.
Catechesis/Religious Programs—D.R.E.: Rita Canty Tel: 937-675-3219; Carmen Montgomery Tel: 937-675-3707.
Students 60.

Lebanon, Warren Co., St. Francis de Sales, Rev. Lou Hohlmayer; Deacons Herschel Steward; John Taylor; Ned Ostendorf.
Res., 15 DeSales Ave., 45036. Tel: 513-932-2601.
School—20 DeSales Ave., 45036. Tel: 513-932-6501; Fax: 513-932-9919. Jo Anne Fischesser, Prin.
Sisters 1; Lay Teachers 8; Students 194.
Catechesis/Religious Programs—Tel: 513-438-3381.
Students 211.

Loveland, Clermont Co., St. Columban, Rev. Terrance W. Smith; Deacons Joseph Coll; James Miller.
Office: 894 Oakland Rd., 45140. Tel: 513-683-7903; Fax: 513-683-1389.
Res., 855 Oakland Rd., 45140. Tel: 513-677-8084; Fax: 513-683-7904.
School—896 Oakland Rd., 45140. Tel: 513-683-7903. Sr. Mary Suzanne Rose, S.N.D., Prin.
Sisters 2; Lay Teachers 19; Students 510.
Catechesis/Religious Programs—Students 240.
Convent—(Covington, KY) 896 Oakland Rd., 45140. Tel: 513-683-0255. Sisters of Notre Dame.

Manchester, Adams Co., St. Mary. (Vicariate). Rev. David Glockner, Glmy.
Res., 612 E. Mulberry St., West Union, 45693. Tel: 937-544-2757.

Maria Stein, Mercer Co., St. John the Baptist, Rev. Emil J. Labbe, C.PP.S.; Deacons Carl Franzer; Omer Bertke.
Res., 8533 State Rte. 119, 45860. Tel: 419-925-4522.
Catechesis/Religious Programs—Tel: 419-925-4442.
Students 278.

Mason, Warren Co., St. Susanna, Rev. Harry J. Meyer; Karen Gottschall, Pastoral Assoc. for Youth; Deacons James A. Merritt; Daniel L. Rader; Gerald L. Barney; Ralph W. Popp, Bus. Mgr.
Res., 305 Fourth Ave., 45040. Tel: 513-398-3821; Fax: 513-398-2254.
School—500 Reading Rd., 45040. Tel: 513-398-5826. Kenneth L. Beiser, Prin.
Lay Teachers 14; Students 375.
Catechesis/Religious Programs—Tel: 513-398-1234.
Students 890.

McCartyville, Shelby Co., Sacred Heart of Jesus, Rev. Gerald E. Bensman.
Res., 9333 State Rte. 119, Anna, 45302. Tel: 937-394-3823; 419-628-2502.
Catechesis/Religious Programs—Tel: 937-394-3823. Barbara Riethman, D.R.E.
Students 384.

Mechanicsburg, Champaign Co., St. Michael's, Rev. Clarence G Heis.
Res., 40 Walnut St., 43044. Tel: 513-834-2413.

Miamisburg, Montgomery Co., Our Lady of Good Hope, Rev. Bernard H. Bruening; Deacon Joseph J. Sprinkle.
Res., 6 S. Third St., 45342. Tel: 937-866-1432.
School—Bishop Leibold Consolidated, Dayton. See separate listing.

Middletown, Butler Co., Holy Family. (This parish is the successor in interest to Holy Trinity, St. John the Baptist and St. Mary parishes, formerly located in Middletown, OH). Rev. John R. Civille; Sr. Jean Sora, O.S.F., Pastoral Assoc. In res., Revs. Charles L. Moore, (Retired); Paul L. Gebhardt; Deacons Thomas Coyle; William Krumm.
Office: 201 Clark St., 45042. Tel: 513-422-0602; Fax: 513-424-7416.
School—John XXIII Consolidated, Middletown. See separate listing. Tel: 513-424-0838; Fax: 513-420-8475.
Catechesis/Religious Programs—Tel: 513-422-0602; Fax: 513-424-7416.
Students 180.

Milford, Clermont Co., St. Andrew, Rev. William C. Wagner.
Res., 552 Main St., 45150. Tel: 513-831-3353; Fax: 513-831-6597.
School—St. Andrew-St. Elizabeth Seton, (Grades K-8). Consolidated. 555 Main St., 45150. Tel: 513-831-5277. Mr. James Renner, Prin.
Lay Teachers 20; Students 503.
Catechesis/Religious Programs—Tel: 513-831-3812; Fax: 513-831-6597. Barbara Aluotto, D.R.E.
Students 205.

Millville, Butler Co., Queen of Peace, Rev. Kenneth J. Schoettmer; Deacon Bill Brunsman.
Res., 2550 Millville Rd., Hamilton, 45013. Tel: 513-863-4344; Fax: 513-863-4364.
School—Tel: 513-863-8705; Fax: 513-863-4310. Kathleen Daulton, Prin.
Lay Teachers 14; Students 276.
Catechesis/Religious Programs—Students 115.

Minster, Auglaize Co., St. Augustine's, Rev. Thomas Brenberger, C.PP.S.; Deacons Cliff Perryman; John J. Schmiesing; Bro. Tim Cahill, C.PP.S., Pastoral Assoc.
Res., 48 N. Hanover St., P.O. Box 93, 45865. Tel: 419-628-2614; Fax: 419-628-1078.
Catechesis/Religious Programs—47 N. Lincoln St., P.O. Box 93, 45865. Tel: 419-628-3434. D.R.E.: Jane Boeke; Kathy Sommer.
Students 690.

Monroe, Butler Co., Our Lady of Sorrows, Rev. John Kroeger.
Res., 416 Lebanon St., 45050. Tel: 513-539-8383.
Catechesis/Religious Programs—330 Lebanon St., 45050. Tel: 513-539-8061. Sr. Bridget Cottle, S.C.N., D.R.E.
Students 118.

Montezuma, Mercer Co., Our Lady of Guadalupe, Rev. Carl A. Wise, C.PP.S., Admin.
Res., P.O. Box 69, 45866. Tel: 419-268-2312.
Catechesis/Religious Programs—Tel: 419-268-2312. Carol Niekamp, D.R.E.
Students 195.

Morrow, Warren Co., St. Philip the Apostle, Rev. Joseph C. Allison.
Res., 944 East U.S. 22-3, 45152. Tel: 513-899-3601; Fax: 513-899-3601.
Catechesis/Religious Programs—Tel: 513-899-3785; Fax: 513-899-2079. Sr. Jane Roberts, S.N.D.deN., D.R.E.
Students 170.

Mount Carmel, Clermont Co., St. Veronica, Rev. Dennis J. Caylor; Sr. Therese Beringer, C.S.J., Pastoral Assoc.
Res., 4473 Mt. Carmel-Tobasco Rd., Cincinnati, 45244. Tel: 513-528-1622; Fax: 513-528-1622.
School—Tel: 513-528-0442. Ms. Kay Hohner Stefanics, Prin.
Sisters 3; Lay Teachers 17; Students 475.
Catechesis/Religious Programs—Tel: 513-528-1622.
Students 172.

Mount Orab, Brown Co., St. Michael, Rev. Earl O. Metz.
Res., St. George Church, 109 Elm St., Georgetown, 45121. Tel: 937-378-6829.
Church—220 S. High St., 45154.
Catechesis/Religious Programs—Connie Carroll, D.R.E.
Students 54.

Mount Repose, Clermont Co., St. Elizabeth Ann Seton, Rev. Thomas J. Dennemann.
Res., 5890 Buckwheat Rd., Milford, 45150. Tel: 513-575-0119.
School—5900 Buckwheat Rd., Milford, 45150. Tel: 513-375-0093; Fax: 513-575-1078. Mr. James Renner, Prin.
Lay Teachers 25; Students 550.
Preschool—Tel: 513-575-0093. Mrs. Terri Imming, Dir.
Lay Teachers 8; Students 130.
Catechesis/Religious Programs—Students 290.

New Bremen, Auglaize Co., Holy Redeemer, Rev. R. Daniel Conlon.
Res., 120 S. Eastmoor Dr., 45869. Tel: 419-629-2543.
Catechesis/Religious Programs—Tel: 513-629-2343.
Students 492.

New Carlisle, Clark Co., Sacred Heart, Rev. John MacQuarrie.
Res., 476 N. Scott St., 45344. Tel: 937-845-3121; Fax: 937-846-1223.
Catechesis/Religious Programs—Tel: 937-845-1373; Fax: 937-846-1223.
Students 265.

New Paris, Preble Co., St. John, Rev. Ralph J. Lawrence, Admin.
Res., Visitation, 407 E. Main St., Eaton, 45320. Tel: 937-456-3380.
Catechesis/Religious Programs—Students 40.

Newport, Shelby Co., SS. Peter and Paul, Rev. Donald E. Shelander.
Res., 6788 State Rte. 66, Ft. Loramie, 45845. Tel: 937-295-3001.
Catechesis/Religious Programs—Tel: 937-295-2536. Susan Francis, D.R.E.
Students 180.

New Richmond, Clermont Co., St. Peter, Rev. Theodore C. Kosse.
Res., 1192 Bethel-New Richmond Rd., 45157. Tel: 513-553-3267; Fax: 513-553-4321.
Catechesis/Religious Programs—Sr. Patricia Corbett, C.S.J., D.R.E.
Students 157.

New Vienna, Clinton Co., St. Michael, Rev. Ronald C. Cooper.
Res., St. Benignus, 218 S. Second St., Greenfield, 45123. Tel: 937-981-2785.

North Lewisburg, Champaign Co., Immaculate Conception, Rev. Clarence G. Heis.
Res., 40 Walnut St., Mechanicsburg, 43044. Tel: 937-834-2413.

North Star, Darke Co., St. Louis, Rev. James M. Schmitmeyer.
Parish Office: P.O. Box 9, Osgood, 45351. Tel: 419-582-2531; Fax: 419-582-2531. [CEM]
Catechesis/Religious Programs—Linda Wehrkamp, D.R.E.
Students 206.

Osgood, Darke Co., St. Nicholas, Rev. James M. Schmitmeyer.
Office: 128 Church St., P.O. Box 9, 45351. Tel: 419-582-2531; Fax: 419-582-2531.
Catechesis/Religious Programs—Donna Grieshop, D.R.E.
Students 169.

Owensville, Clermont Co., St. Louis, Rev. John R. Wolbert.
Res., 210 N. Broadway, 45160. Tel: 513-732-2218.
School—250 N. Broadway, 45160. Tel: 513-732-0636; Fax: 513-732-1748. Sr. Mary Lottinville, Prin.
Ursuline Sisters 2; Lay Teachers 12; Students 201.
Catechesis/Religious Programs—Tel: 513-732-2580.
Students 52.

Oxford, Butler Co., St. Mary Church and Catholic Campus Ministry (Miami U.), Rev. Terrance L. Schneider; Sr. Ann Hunt, S.C., Pastoral Assoc.; Jeffrey J. Piccirilli, Dir. Campus Min.
Res., 111 E. High St., 45056. Tel: 513-523-2153.

Peebles, Adams Co., St. Mary Queen of Heaven. (Vicariate). Rev. David Glockner, Glmy.
Res., Holy Trinity, 612 E. Mulberry St., West Union, 45693. Tel: 513-544-2757.
Catechesis/Religious Programs—Students 38.

Philothea, Mercer Co., St. Mary's, Rev. Louis J. Barga, C.PP.S.
Res., 3821 Philothea Rd., Coldwater, 45828. Tel: 419-678-2795.
Catechesis/Religious Programs—Esther Homan, D.R.E.
Students 98.

Piqua, Miami Co., St. Boniface, Rev. Rick Unwin.
Res., 310 S. Downing St., 45356. Tel: 937-773-1656; Fax: 937-773-2665. Rev. Angelo C. Caserta Tel: 513-778-9526.
School—Piqua Catholic School, Piqua. (Consolidated) See separate listing. Tel: 937-773-3876.
Catechesis/Religious Programs—Tel: 937-773-0710.
Students 479.

St. Mary, Rev. Francis J. Keferl; Joan Dunn, Pastoral Assoc. In res., Rev. Anselm F. Boeke, (Retired).
Res., 528 Broadway, 45356. Tel: 937-773-1327; Fax: 937-773-2313.
School—Piqua Catholic School, Piqua. See separate listing. Tel: 937-773-1564.
Catechesis/Religious Programs—Tel: 937-778-8770. Helen Metzger, D.R.E.
Students 55.

Princeton, Butler Co., St. Maximilian Kolbe (1989), Rev. John Porter; Rev. Msgr. Earl L. Whalen; Deacon R. Daniel Murphy. Pastoral Assocs.: Joan Stoltz; Carol Heuser.
Res., 7168 St. Albans Way, Hamilton, 45011. Tel: 513-777-4322; Fax: 513-777-7264.
Church—5720 Hamilton-Mason Rd., Liberty Township, 45011.
School—St. Gabriel Consolidated School. See separate listing.
Catechesis/Religious Programs—Tel: 513-779-3433. Beth Moyer, D.R.E.
Students 997.

Rhine, Shelby Co., St. Lawrence, Rev. James J. O'Connor.
Res., 16053 Botkins Rd., P.O. Box 519, Botkins, 45306. Tel: 937-693-2561.
Catechesis/Religious Programs—Students 112.

Ripley, Brown Co., St. Michael, Rev. Thomas F. Feldhaus.
Res., 16 N. Fourth St., 45167. Tel: 937-392-1116.
School—Tel: 937-392-4202. Sr. Sharon Blank, O.S.F., Prin.
Sisters 1; Lay Teachers 4; Students 65.
Catechesis/Religious Programs—Tel: 937-392-1335. Joseph P. Shadle, D.R.E.
Students 50.

Rockford, Mercer Co., St. Teresa, Rev. Clement B. Alt, C.PP.S.
Res., 213 S. Franklin St., P.O. Box 445, 45882. Tel: 419-363-2633.
Catechesis/Religious Programs—Tel: 419-363-2327. Alice Provci, D.R.E.
Students 78.

Russells Point, Logan Co., St. Mary of the Woods, Rev. Anthony J. Geraci.

Res., P.O. Box 278, 43348. Tel: 937-843-3127; Fax: 937-843-4792.
Catechesis/Religious Programs—Madison Ave., 43348. Tel: 937-843-4227; Fax: 937-843-4792.
Students 156.

Russia, Shelby Co., St. Remy, Rev. Eugene F. Vonderhaar.
Res., 108 E. Main St., P.O. Box 275, 45363. Tel: 937-526-3437; Fax: 937-526-5326.
Catechesis/Religious Programs—Tel: 937-526-3437. Nancy Luthman, D.R.E.
Students 330.

St. Anthony, Mercer Co., St. Anthony, Rev. Bernard Meiring, C.PP.S.; Deacon Cletus H. Homan.
Res., 471 St. Anthony Rd., Fort Recovery, 45846. Tel: 419-942-1795. [CEM]
Catechesis/Religious Programs—Tel: 419-942-1795.
Students 104.

St. Henry, Mercer Co., St. Henry, Rev. Larry Wyen, C.PP.S.
Res., Box 301, 272 E. Main St., 45883. Tel: 419-678-4118; Fax: 419-678-8285.
Inter-parish Center—162 S. Walnut, 45883. Tel: 419-678-3811.
Catechesis/Religious Programs—Bro. Thomas Bohman, C.PP.S., D.R.E.
Students 715.

St. Joseph, Mercer Co., St. Joseph 1839 (German), Rev. George Kuzara, C.PP.S.
Res., 1477 Philothera Rd., St. Peter, 45846. Tel: 419-375-4344. [CEM]
Church—1689 St. Joe Rd., Fort Recovery, 45846.

Saint Martin, Brown Co., Saint Martin, Rev. Michael A. Savino, Admin.
Res., 6616 Beechmont Ave., Cincinnati, 45230. Tel: 513-875-2790. [CEM]
Church—20864 State Rte. 251 N., St. Martin, 45118.
Catechesis/Religious Programs—Terry Brinkman, D.R.E.
Students 95.

St. Marys, Auglaize Co., Holy Rosary, Rev. David A. Heinl. In res., Rev. James O. Byrne.
Res., 511 E. Spring St., 45885. Tel: 419-394-5050.
School—Tel: 419-394-5291. Bruce Ludwig, Prin.
Lay Teachers 16; Students 245.
Catechesis/Religious Programs—Tel: 419-394-5291. Connie Bargdill, D.R.E.
Students 230.

St. Paris, Champaign Co., Sacred Heart, Rev. Thomas R. Espelage.
Res., 231 Washington Ave., Urbana, 43078-1728. Tel: 937-653-1375.
Catechesis/Religious Programs—Students 52.

St. Rose, Mercer Co., St. Rose, Rev. Frederick Ryder.
Res., 7428 State Rte. 119, Maria Stein, 45860. Tel: 419-925-4775. [CEM]
Catechesis/Religious Programs—Students 91.

St. Sebastian, Mercer Co., St. Sebastian, Rev. John L. Bensman.
Res., Precious Blood Church, 35 S. Maple St., Box 26, Chickasaw, 45826-0026. Tel: 419-925-4391.
Catechesis/Religious Programs—Nancy Broering, D.R.E.
Students 79.

St. Wendelin, Mercer Co., St. Wendelin, Rev. Milton A. Ballor, C.PP.S.
Res., 517 Meiring Rd., Fort Recovery, 45846. Tel: 419-375-2603.
Catechesis/Religious Programs—Students 77.

Sardinia, Brown Co., St. Elizabeth Parish, Rev. Dohrman W. Byers.
Res., 6647 Van Buren St., Georgetown, 45121. Tel: 937-446-2555.
Church—122 N. Main St., 45171. Tel: 937-446-2555.
Catechesis/Religious Programs—Students 50.

Shandon, Butler Co., St. Aloysius, Rev. William J. Dorrmann; Deacon Lawrence A. Maag.
Res., P.O. Box 95, 45063. Tel: 513-738-1014; Fax: 513-738-2084.
Catechesis/Religious Programs—Tel: 513-738-4641. Joan Mills, D.R.E.
Students 270.

Sharpsburg, Mercer Co., St. Paul, Rev. Milton A. Ballor, C.PP.S.
Res., 517 Meiring Rd., Fort Recovery, 45846. Tel: 419-375-2603.
Catechesis/Religious Programs—Cleopha Link, D.R.E.
Students 246.

Sidney, Shelby Co., Holy Angels, Revs. Glen W. Perin; David L. Zink; Deacon Philip Myers.
Res., 324 S. Ohio Ave., 45365. Tel: 937-498-2307.
School—Tel: 937-492-9293; Fax: 937-492-8578. Regina Seubert, Prin.
Lay Teachers 18; Students 476.
Catechesis/Religious Programs—Tel: 937-498-0433. Marianne Dunson, D.R.E.
Students 371.

South Charleston, Clark Co., St. Charles Borromeo, Rev. William V. Thomas.
Res., 31 S. Chillicothe St., P.O. Box F, 45368-0806. Tel: 513-462-8971.
Catechesis/Religious Programs—Denise Federle, D.R.E.
Students 44.

Springfield, Clark Co.,

1—St. Bernard, Rev. Donald C. Huebner.
Res., 910 Lagonda Ave., 45503. Tel: 937-322-5243; Fax: 937-322-3788.
School—800 Lagonda Ave, 45503. Tel: 937-324-4551; Fax: 937-322-3788.
Sisters of Charity (Cincinnati, OH) 2; Lay Teachers 12; Students 247.
Catechesis/Religious Programs—Tel: 937-324-2870; Fax: 937-322-3788. Sr. Teresa Noser, O.S.F., D.R.E.
Students 117.

2—St. Joseph, Rev. J. Frederick McGuire.
Res., 802 Kenton St., 45505. Tel: 937-323-8483; Fax: 937-323-8471.
School—Holy Trinity Catholic School, Springfield. See separate listing.
Catechesis/Religious Programs—Tel: 937-327-4057. Sr. Angela Jarboe, D.R.E.
Students 85.

3—St. Mary, Rev. David P. Vincent.
Res., 1027 W. High St., 45506-1398. Tel: 513-322-7272; Fax: 937-322-7272.
School—Holy Trinity Catholic School, Springfield. See separate listing.
Catechesis/Religious Programs—Tel: 937-322-7272. Denis Forsting, D.R.E.
Students 45.

4—St. Raphael, Rev. M. Edmund Hussey; Deacon Norman G. Horstmann.
Res., 225 E. High St., 45505. Tel: 937-323-7523.
School—Holy Trinity Catholic School, Springfield. See separate listing.
Catechesis/Religious Programs—Tel: 937-323-7523.
Students 185.

5—St. Teresa of the Child Jesus, Rev. Richard W. Walling.
Res., 137 Floral Ave., 45504. Tel: 937-399-4339; Fax: 937-399-5451.
School—Tel: 937-399-5451. Mrs. Martha Szczesny, Prin.
Lay Teachers 11; Students 245.
Catechesis/Religious Programs—Tel: 937-399-5451.
Students 65.

Stonelick, Clermont Co., St. Philomena, Rev. John R. Wolbert.
Res., 210 N. Broadway, Box 85, Owensville, 45160. Tel: 513-732-2218; Fax: 513-732-1748.

Tipp City, Miami Co., St. John the Baptist, Rev. Thomas A. Dorenbusch.
Res., 218 S. Third St., 45371. Tel: 937-667-3419; Fax: 937-667-9267.
Catechesis/Religious Programs—Tel: 937-667-6092. Nelda Schwab, D.R.E.
Students 363.

Trenton, Butler Co., Holy Name, Rev. George W. Klein; Deacon William Martin.
Res., 222 Hamilton Ave., 45067. Tel: 513-988-6335.
Catechesis/Religious Programs—Tel: 513-988-9348.
Students 90.

Troy, Miami Co., St. Patrick, Revs. Thomas J. Brunner; Charles B. Rohrkemper.
Res., 409 E. Main St., 45373. Tel: 937-335-2833; Fax: 937-335-1453.
School—Tel: 937-339-3705. James O'Leary, Prin.
Lay Teachers 9; Students 189.
Catechesis/Religious Programs—409 E. Main St., 45373. Tel: 937-339-5517.
Students 325.

Twenty Mile Stand, Warren Co., St. Margaret of York, Rev. Thomas W. Kreidler; Deacon Raymond Kroger.
Res., 9483 Columbia Rd., Loveland, 45140. Tel: 513-683-7100; Fax: 513-683-7101.
School—Tel: 513-683-9793. Co-Principals: Sr. Mary Ann Trotta, R.S.M.; Sr. Ann Gorman, R.S.M.
Lay Teachers 24; Students 580.
Catechesis/Religious Programs—Tel: 513-583-0536. Mark Spanyer, D.R.E.
Students 401.

Urbana, Champaign Co., St. Mary, Rev. Thomas R. Espelage.
Res., 231 Washington Ave., 43078. Tel: 937-653-1375.
School—Tel: 937-653-1370. Sr. Mary Annice Quinter, Prin.
Sisters 1; Lay Teachers 9; Students 147.
Catechesis/Religious Programs—Tel: 937-788-2251.
Students 104.

Vandalia, Montgomery Co., St. Christopher, Rev. Robert J. Monnin.
Res., 435 E. National Rd., 45377. Tel: 937-898-3542; Fax: 937-898-1017.
School—(Grades K-8). Tel: 937-898-5104.
Lay Teachers 13; Students 289.
Catechesis/Religious Programs—Tel: 937-788-2251; Fax: 937-898-1017.
Students 332.

Versailles, Darke Co., St. Denis, Rev. Leo A. Hoying.
Res., 14 E. Wood St., 45380. Tel: 937-526-4945.
Catechesis/Religious Programs—D.R.E.: Arlene Niekamp; Judy Pierron.
Students 600.

Wapakoneta, Auglaize Co., St. Joseph, Rev. William O'Donnell, C.PP.S.
Res., 309 S. Perry St., 45895. Tel: 419-738-2115; Fax: 419-738-4525. [CEM]
School—1101 Lincoln Hwy., 45895. Tel: 419-738-3311; Fax: 419-738-7706.
Lay Teachers 13; Students 235.
Catechesis/Religious Programs—Tel: 419-738-2115; Fax: 419-738-4525.
Students 370.

Waynesville, Warren Co., St. Augustine, Rev. Raymond Kammerer.
Res., 5715 Lytle Rd., 45068. Tel: 513-897-2821.
Catechesis/Religious Programs—Tel: 513-932-8275. Christine Burroughs, D.R.E.
Students 164.

West Chester, Butler Co., St. John, Rev. James W. Meade. In res., Rev. J. Raymond Favret.
Res., 9080 Cincinnati-Dayton Rd., 45069. Tel: 513-777-6433.

West Milton, Miami Co., Transfiguration, Rev. Thomas J. Grilliot; Deacon Robert Huffman.
Res., 972 S. Miami St., 45383. Tel: 937-698-4520.
Catechesis/Religious Programs—Students 220.

West Union, Adams Co., Holy Trinity, Rev. David Glockner, Glmy. In res., Rev. Robert Berson, Glmy.
Res., 612 E. Mulberry St., 45693. Tel: 937-544-2757.
Catechesis/Religious Programs—Students 55.

Williamsburg, Clermont Co., St. Ann, Rev. William R. Stockelman.
Res., 140 N. Sixth St., Batavia, 45103. Tel: 513-732-2024.
Catechesis/Religious Programs—Tel: 513-732-2024. Patricia Bruce, D.R.E.
Students 25.

Wilmington, Clinton Co., St. Columbkille, Rev. R. Marc Sherlock; Deacons Robert G. Baker; Robert E. Meyer.
Res., 73 N. Mulberry St., 45177-2277. Tel: 937-382-2236.
Catechesis/Religious Programs—Tel: 937-382-1596. Daniel L. Thomas, D.R.E.
Students 277.

Withamsville, Clermont Co., St. Thomas More, Rev. John P. Fischer; Deacon Michael E. Metz. Pastoral Assocs.: Sr. Kay Garnett; Mr. Michael Thomas. In res., Rev. Francis E. Fritz, (Retired).
Res., 800 Ohio Pike, Cincinnati, 45245. Tel: 513-753-2578; 752-2080 (Office); Fax: 513-753-2542.
School—788 Ohio Pike, Cincinnati, 45245. Tel: 513-753-2540; Fax: 513-753-2542. Mr. Michael Kirry, Prin. & D.R.E.
Lay Teachers 14; Students 236.
Catechesis/Religious Programs—Tel: 513-753-2548; Fax: 513-753-2542.
Students 182.

Xenia, Greene Co., St. Brigid, Rev. Stanley D. Doerger.
Res., 258 Purcell Ave., 45385. Tel: 937-372-3193; Fax: 937-374-3622. [CEM]
School—Tel: 937-372-3222. Sr. Lois Jean Goettke, Prin.
Sisters 1; Lay Teachers 10; Students 233.
Convent—216 Purcell Ave., 45385. Tel: 937-372-0994. Sisters of Charity of Cincinnati, OH
Catechesis/Religious Programs—Tel: 937-372-3222.
Students 125.

Yellow Springs, Greene Co., St. Paul, Rev. Joseph W. Goetz; Deacon Paul E. Richardson.
Res., 308 Phillips St., 45387. Tel: 937-767-7450.
Catechesis/Religious Programs—Students 110.

Closed and Merged Parishes

Greater Cincinnati

1— Community of Hope. Consolidated with Holy Family Parish.

2—St. Elizabeth Church (Norwood). Merged with Holy Trinity Church (Norwood).

3—St. George Parish & Newman Center. Closed. For

inquiries for parish records contact St. Monica-St. George Newman Center.
4—St. Matthew Church (Norwood). Merged with Holy Trinity Church (Norwood).
5—Our Lady of Grace (Price Hill). Consolidated with Holy Family Parish.
6—Our Lady of Loretto. Merged with St. Margaret of Cortona.
7—Our Lady of Perpetual Help (Sedamsville). Consolidated with Holy Family Parish.
8—Our Lady of Presentation. Closed. For inquiries for parish records contact St. Leo the Great, Cincinnati.
9—St. Patrick (Northside). Merged with St. Boniface, Cincinnati. See listing for details.
10—Sts. Peter and Paul Church (Norwood). Merged with Holy Trinity Church (Norwood).
11—St. Richard of Chichester (College Hill). Merged with St. Therese, the Little Flower, Cincinnati. See listing for details.
12—St. Thomas Aquinas. Closed. For inquiries for parish records contact the Chancery.
13—San Antonio di Padova (Italian). Refer to St. Bonaventure for details.

Blue Creek, Adams Co., St. Joseph. Closed. For inquiries for parish records contact the Chancery.
Dayton, Sacred Heart. Closed. For inquiries for parish records contact Emmanuel, Dayton. Hamilton, St. Mary. Merged. Now known as St. Julie Billiart.
St. Stephen. Merged. Now known as St. Julie Billiart.
St. Veronica. Merged. Now known as St. Julie Billiart.
Middletown, Holy Trinity. Merged. Now known as Holy Family.
St. John the Baptist. Merged. Now known as Holy Family.
St. Mary. Merged. Now known as Holy Family.
New Miami, St. Lawrence. Merged. Now known as St. Julie Billiart, Hamilton.
St. Patrick, Shelby Co., St. Patrick. Closed. For inquiries for parish records contact St. Michael, Fort Loramie.
Vera Cruz, Brown Co., Holy Ghost (Vicariate). Closed. For inquiries for parish records contact St. Patrick, Fayetteville. [CEM]

Chaplains of Public Institutions

On Special and Diocesan Assignment:
Reverend Fathers—
DeVore, David G., 520 E. Epworth Ave., Cincinnati, OH 45232
Friedrichs, Paul, 2702 Jefferson Ave., Cincinnati, OH 45219
Grad, Malcolm, Admin. Asst., Archbishop's Office, 100 E. 8th St., Cincinnati, OH 15202
Guntzelman, Louis J., 10709 Adventure Lane, Cincinnati, OH 45242
Lauer, Albert E., 123 E. 13th St., Cincinnati, OH 45210
Mick, Lawrence E., 3103 Observation Trail, Dayton, OH 45449
Nguyen, Huan Tien, 5440 Moeller Ave., Cincinnati, OH 45212
Rivers, Clarence J., 17 Erkenbrecher Ave., Cincinnati, OH 45220
Seger, Oscar H., 782 Osterloh, Minster, OH 45865
Tensi, Lawrence R., Dir. Worship Office, 100 E. Eighth St., Cincinnati, OH 45202

On Duty Outside the Archdiocese:
Reverend Fathers—
Conlon, Edward F., St. Andrew R.C. Church, Grenada, West Indies
Kelly, William T., 4015 Yupon St., Houston, TX 47006-4840
Lemkuhl, David A., Maryknoll Assoc. Program, Maryknoll, NY 10545
Pater, Daniel R., Secretariat of State, Nunciature Apostolic Au Carrie, Vatican City, 00120 Italy
Smith, Edward P., North American College, Vatican City State, 00120 Italy
Umberg, Andrew J., Pontifical College Josephinum, College of Liberal Arts, 7625 N. High St., Columbus, OH 43235-1498
Walsh, James J., NCEA, Seminary Dept., 1077 30th St. N.W., Washington, DC 20007-3852
Wenke, Leonard C., 1001 Spring St. #306, Silver Springs, MD 20910

Military Chaplains:
Reverend Fathers—
Breaker, Donald J., CH MAJ, Office of Post Chaplain, Fort Leonard Wood, MO 65473
Janning, Timothy J., CHC USNR, 3800 Parkview Ln. #26C, Irvine, CA 92715
Kaising, John J., CH COL, 3709 S. George Mason Dr. #608E, Falls Church, VA 22041
Leurck, Raymond J., CH LTC, Chief of Chap., HQ USA F/HCS, 172 Luke Ave., Bolling AFB, DC 20332-5113
Niemeier, Dennis, CH MAJ, 6th ADA BDE Chap., Fort Bliss, TX 79916
Whalen, Frank J., CH COL, Installation Staff Chap., 3100 Indiana Ave., Fort Campbell, KY 42223-6202

Leave of Absence:
Reverend Fathers—
Albrecht, G.R. Keith
Cooley, George J.

Retired:
Reverend Monsignors—
Evans, Ferdinand A., 850 Ohio Ave., Englewood, FL 34223. Tel: 813-474-2178
Franer, William J., 4124 Settle Rd., Apt. A, Cincinnati, OH 45227. Tel: 513-271-9401
Kennedy, Francis B., 4108 W. 8th St., Cincinnati, OH 45205. Tel: 513-921-0247
Klocker, Henry J., 5440 Moeller Ave., Cincinnati, OH 45212. Tel: 513-631-2913
Krusling, James L., Priests' Personnel Office, c/o 100 E. 8th St., Cincinnati, OH 45202
Vogelpohl, Henry J., 977 Bayley Place Dr., Cincinnati, OH 45233. Tel: 513-347-5566
Whalen, Earl L., 872 Bayley Place Dr., Cinncinnati, OH 45233. Tel: 513-347-5638
Reverend Fathers—
Andres, Joseph P., P.O. Box 54458, Cincinnati, OH 45254. Tel: 513-231-0508
Ballman, Thomas J., 820 Bowen St., Dayton, OH 45410. Tel: 513-253-9132
Bastian, Robert J., 1585 N.W. Washington Blvd., Hamilton, OH 45013. Tel: 513-894-7425
Beckman, Joseph F., 6616 Beechmont Ave., Cincinnati, OH 45230. Tel: 513-624-0554
Behler, Donald, 4551 Delhi Pike, Cincinnati, OH 45238. Tel: 513-471-8962
Berning, Cornelius C., St. Margaret Hall, 1960 Madison Rd., Cincinnati, OH 45206
Berning, John B., P.O. Box 4023, St. Petersburg, FL 23731
Bertke, Erwin J., 3680 Warsaw Ave., Cincinnati, OH 45205. Tel: 513-921-1995
Birarelli, Carl A., Queen of Martyrs, 833 Magellan Dr., Sarasota, FL 34243. Tel: 813-377-6654
Boeke, Aloysius B., 33 Elm St., Fort Loramie, OH 45845. Tel: 513-295-2891
Boeke, Anselm F., 528 Broadway, Piqua, OH 45356. Tel: 513-773-1327
Bramlage, Vincent J., 148 Thomas Blvd., Hamilton, OH 45013. Tel: 513-894-7426
Braun, Norbert L., 7303 Estate Ct., Cincinnati, OH 45224. Tel: 513-522-4662
Brennan, Elmer F., 7283 Kingswood Dr., West Chester, OH 45069. Tel: 513-777-7372
Brinkman, Norbert C., 100 Compton Rd., Cincinnati, OH 45215
Broering, Victor F., 9568 Dry Fork Rd., Harrison, OH 45030. Tel: 513-367-0091
Bruemmer, Joseph A., St. Andrew, 552 Main St., Milford, OH 45150. Tel: 513-248-4995
Buerger, Francis J., Schroder Manor Retirement Community, 1302 Millville Ave., Hamilton, OH 45103. Tel: 513-844-6486
Burns, John T., 8843 Carrousel Park Cir. #19, Cincinnati, OH 45251. Tel: 513-385-1032
Buschmiller, Robert J., 3105 Madison Rd., Cincinnati, OH 45209. Tel: 513-871-5757
Byrne, James O., 511 Spring St., St. Marys, OH 45885. Tel: 513-394-5050
Calme, Stephen J., 3630 W. Liberty St., Cincinnati, OH 45205. Tel: 513-471-2464
Caserta, Angelo C., P.O. Box 1656, Piqua, OH 45356. Tel: 513-778-9526
Caserta, Charles W., 133 Douglas, Lewisburg, OH 45338. Tel: 513-962-2500
Cavanaugh, John L., 1175 Overlook Ave., Cincinnati, OH 45238. Tel: 513-921-9200
Coghlan, John C., 8414 Donna Ln., #8, Cincinnati, OH 45236. Tel: 513-891-4261
DeFrancesco, Albert J., 6059 State Rte. 221, Georgetown, OH 45121. Tel: 513-375-4281
Diegelman, Clarence L., St. Charles Seminary, Carthagena, OH 45822. Tel: 513-925-4516
Drapp, Alfred E., 29 E. 8th St., Cincinnati, OH 45202
Evers, Gerard A., 1044 W. Kemper Rd., Cincinnati, OH 45240. Tel: 513-851-1930
Felix, Bernard J., 100 Compton Rd., Cincinnati, OH 45215. Tel: 513-948-1945
Francis, A. Edwin, Dorothy Love Retirement Home, 2500 N. Kuther Rd. #110, Sidney, OH 45365. Tel: 513-497-7271
Fritz, Francis E., 800 Ohio Pike, Cincinnati, OH 45245. Tel: 513-753-2545
Frommeyer, James F., Mallard Core, 1410 Mallard Cove Dr., Sharonville, OH 452466
Funk, Louis F., 325 W. Eighth St., Cincinnati, OH 45208. Tel: 513-421-5354
Geers, Carl J., 325 W. 8th St., Cincinnati, OH 45202. Tel: 513-421-5354
Gratsch, Edward J., 6616 Beechmont Ave., Cincinnati, OH 45230. Tel: 513-232-0631
Griese, Roger E., Oak Creek Terrace, 2316 Springmill Rd., Kettering, OH 45440. Tel: 513-439-9509
Gruber, J. Paul, 5403 Bluesky Dr., #6, Cincinnati, OH 45247. Tel: 513-598-1424
Gude, George W., West Park Retirement Community, 2950 West Park Dr., Cincinnati, OH 45238
Hagedorn, Robert L., 808 Schiff Ave. #1, Cincinnati, OH 45205. Tel: 513-921-0379
Haskamp, Edward F., 11080 Montgomery, Cincinnati, OH 45249
Henz, Kenneth W., 1805 John Glenn Rd., Dayton, OH 45420. Tel: 513-253-2829
Heskamp, Joseph C., 7754 Montgomery Rd., Cincinnati, OH 45236. Tel: 513-791-9030
Jacquemin, John M., 6700 Beechmont Ave., Cincinnati, OH 45230. Tel: 513-231-6433
Jaekle, Lawrence E., 24 Catalpa, Versailles, OH 45380. Tel: 513-526-5862
Jennings, John P., 1227 Ebenezer Rd., Cincinnati, OH 45238. Tel: 513-941-0932
Keller, Neil J., 1085 Parkridge Ct. #4, Cincinnati, OH 45240. Tel: 513-742-8592
Kenning, Herman H., 60 Compton Rd., Cincinnati, OH 45215. Tel: 513-821-1886
Kesting, Philip A., 2497 Eastern Ave., Cincinnati, OH 45202. Tel: 513-221-7011
Kneipp, August J., Leibold Home, 476 Riddle Rd., Cincinnati, OH 45220. Tel: 513-281-2648
Koegel, Victor C., Parkwood Estates, Lot 150, 2900 Gulf to Bay Blvd., Clearwater, FL 34619
Kylius, Ferdinand W., 100 Compton Rd., Cincinnati, OH 45215. Tel: 513-761-2623
Lutmer, Joseph H., 4688 Largo Dr., Cincinnati, OH 45236. Tel: 513-793-9937
Massarella, Francis A., 235 W. Orchard Springs Dr., Dayton, OH 45415. Tel: 513-275-4377
Mauntel, Robert J., 19 Mohave Dr., Sardinia, OH 45171. Tel: 513-446-3491
McNicholas, Timothy J., Nativity B.V.M. Rectory, 30 E. Franklin St., Media, PA 19603. Tel: 215-566-0185
McWilliam, James J., 6616 Beechmont Ave., Cincinnati, OH 45230. Tel: 513-232-5080
Miller, Francis J., 4988 Lord Alfred Ct., Cincinnati, OH 45241-2196. Tel: 513-247-0966
Minic, John F., 968 Sharewood Ct., Kettering, OH 45429. Tel: 513-299-2747
Moore, Charles L., 3917 Central Ave., Middletown, OH 45042. Tel: 513-423-9692
Mueller, Eugene J., 3525 Burke St., Cincinnati, OH 45241. Tel: 513-563-2640
Niehaus, Francis H., P.O. Box 727, Florence, KY 40142
Pater, Thomas G., Catholic University of America, Curley Hall, Washington, DC 20064
Peaker, James N., 5858 Kellogg Ave., Cincinnati, OH 45228. Tel: 513-232-6006
Perryman, John E., 138 Heritage Dr., Urbana, OH 43078. Tel: 937-663-5749
Pilliod, Francis B., 6161 Chambersburg Rd., Dayton, OH 45424. Tel: 513-233-1503
Plagge, Robert J., 6210 Cleves-Warsaw Pike, Cincinnati, OH 45233. Tel: 513-467-2751
Powers, Alfred J., 2344 N. Limestone #1, Springfield, OH 45503
Poynter, Gail A., 6509 Azure Way, West Carrollton, OH 45449. Tel: 513-438-9001
Putnick, Robert J., West Park Community, 2950 West Park Dr., Cincinnati, OH 45238. Tel: 513-922-2836
Ries, Victor F., 6161 Chambersburg Rd., Dayton, OH 45424
Rohrkemper, Charles B., 109 Freedom Ct., Sidney, OH 45365. Tel: 513-492-3010
Sahlfeld, Francis J., 8 Muirfield Ln., Cincinnati, OH 45241-3257. Tel: 513-891-6852
Schetter, Albert E., Otterbein-St. Mary's Retirement Community, 11329 Bobwhite Ln., St. Mary's, OH 45885. Tel: 419-394-8672
Schroeder, William L., 7432 Tower View, Cincinnati, OH 45255. Tel: 513-232-3074
Schutte, Robert W., 2783 Losantiridge Ave., Cincinnati, OH 45213. Tel: 513-351-0971
Steinbicker, Carl R., 3636 Semloh Ave., Cincinnati, OH 45247. Tel: 513-923-3816
Stricker, Robert A., 5560 Kirby Rd., Cincinnati, OH 45239. Tel: 513-541-5560
Suver, Robert J., 8100 Clyo Rd., Centerville, OH 45458. Tel: 513-434-1312
Tenoever, Donald A., 2532 Meyerhill Dr., Cincinnati, OH 45211
Thorsen, Robert J., 5002 Lord Alfred Ct., Cincinnati, OH 45241. Tel: 513-469-0921
Urbain, Joseph V., 2692 Enterprise Rd., E. #1303,

Clearwater, FL 34619. Tel: 813-799-2546
Volker, Edward H., 100 Compton Rd., Cincinnati, OH 45215
Wiemeyer, Raymond G., 5367 Julmar Dr., Cincinnati, OH 45238. Tel: 513-922-2791
Will, Carl G., 8731 Washington Colony Dr., Centerville, OH 45459. Tel: 513-438-9583
Williams, Edward T., 6210 Cleves-Warsaw Ave. #424, Cincinnati, OH 45233. Tel: 513-467-2785
Wintermeyer, William P., 1080-A Wittshire Ln., Cincinnati, OH 45255
Wolfer, Paul J., 2832 Rosebud Dr., Cincinnati, OH 45238. Tel: 513-922-0715
Wolfer, Robert, 2832 Rosebud Dr., Cincinnati, OH 45238. Tel: 513-922-0715
Zugelter, Alvin T., 1550 N. Astor, Chicago, IL 60610. Tel: 312-337-5952

Permanent Deacons:
Arber, Alan W., St. Henry, Dayton
Ascolese, Michael A., Our Mother of Sorrows, Cincinnati
Aufderheide, William, St. Margaret of Cortona, Cincinnati
Austing, Thomas J., Assumption, Mount Healthy
Baker, Robert, St. Columbkille, Wilmington
Baltes, Leonard W., St. Charles, Kettering
Barney, Gerald L., St. Susanna, Mason
Beck, Henry B., Our Lady of the Rosary, Dayton
Bensman, Werner, SS. Peter & Paul, Newport; St. Michael, Ft. Laramie
Bermick, Stephen C., III, St. Albert the Great, Kettering
Bertke, Omer H., St. John the Baptist, Maria Stein
Blum, Raymond, St. Albert the Great, Dayton
Borgerding, Robert H., St. Peter, Dayton
Brockmann, C. Edward, St. William, Cincinnati
Brunner, Mark E., St. Ann, Hamilton
Brunsman, Willard, Queen of Peace, Millville
Bryant, Herman, St. Gabriel, Cincinnati
Burger, Raymond S., St. Margaret Mary, Cincinnati
Cain, Jerome J., St. Saviour, Cincinnati
Camele, David G., (Retired)
Cecere, Gregory, Unassigned
Childers, David E., Holy Family, Cincinnati
Coll, Joseph J., St. Columban, Loveland
Coomes, Gerald L., St. Vivian, Cincinnati
Cooper, John H., St. James, Wyoming
Cotterman, Eldon, Holy Angels, Dayton
Couzins, Jerome, Unassigned
Coyle, Thomas J., Holy Family, Middletown
Davenport, Michael D., St. Teresa of Avila, Cincinnati
Dawson, David A., Holy Trinity, West Union
Deardorff, Roy L., St. Helen, Dayton
Dehmer, William A., Our Lady of Visitation, Cincinnati
Dipple, Harold I., St. Patrick, Bellefontaine
Fischesser, Elmer, New Jerusalem Community, Cincinnati
Franzer, Carl C., St. John the Baptist, Maria Stein
Gargan, Thomas, St. Catharine, Cincinnati
George, Raymond W., St. Matthias, Cincinnati
Geraci, James L., Our Lady of the Sacred Heart, Reading
Gingras, John J., Corpus Christi, New Burlington
Glassmeyer, Robert A., Our Lady of the Sacred Heart, Reading
Gobbi, John R., St. John Neumann, Cincinnati
Haas, Frederick J., Unassigned
Hennessey, James F., Holy Trinity, Batavia
Homan, Cletus H., St. Anthony, Ft. Recovery
Horstman, Norman G., St. Raphael, Springfield
Huff, Thomas, Immaculate Conception, Celina
Huffman, Robert J., Transfiguration, West Milton
Jachimowicz, John J., St. Helen, Dayton
James, Joseph, Visitation, Eaton
Janowiecki, Richard J., Precious Blood, Dayton
Jenkins, Charles J., Our Lady of Victory, Cincinnati
Jernigan, Jacob, Resurrection, Dayton
Keller, David R., St. Clement, Cincinnati
Kelly, George J., (Retired)
Kiley, Thomas M., St. John Neumann, Cincinnati
Kluener, Paul J., St. James, White Oak
Kowalski, James, Unassigned
Kozlowski, Robert R., St. Adalbert, Dayton
Kraus, Daniel E., Immaculate Conception, Dayton
Kroger, Raymond, St. Margaret of York, Twenty Mile Stand
Kronenberger, Arthur, Immaculate Conception, Dayton
Krumm, William T., Holy Family, Middletown
Maag, Lawrence A., St. Aloysius, Shanoon
Martin, William, Holy Name, Trenton
Mascorro, Susano, St. Helen, Dayton
McCormick, James S., St. Julie Billiart, Hamilton
Metz, Michael, St. Thomas More, Withamsville
Meyer, Robert E., St. Columbkille, Wilmington
Michael, William R., St. Vivian, Cincinnati
Miller, Allen K., St. Peter, Dayton
Miller, Eugene M., Immaculate Heart of Mary, Cincinnati
Miller, James A., St. Columban, Loveland
Montgomery, Michael, O.F.M., St. Francis of Assisi, Centerville
Murphy, Robert D., St. Maximilian Kolbe, Hamilton
Myers, Philip B., Holy Angels, Sidney
Novick, Rick, Guardian Angels, Cincinnati
Orlando, Vincent, Immaculate Conception, Dayton.
Ostendorf, Edward B., St. Francis de Sales, Lebanon
Parker, John G., Mary, Help of Christians, Fort Recovery
Perry, Robert, Our Lady, Queen of Peace, Wright Patterson Air Force Base
Perryman, Clifton, St. Augustine, Minster
Petrie, William J., St. Antoninus, Cincinnati
Platfoot, Thomas F., Our Lady of Mercy, Dayton
Rader, Daniel L., St. Susanna, Mason
Reeves, Paul S., Unassigned
Rekers, Louis J., St. James, Wyoming
Renneker, William B., St. Julie Billiart, Hamilton
Richardson, Paul E., St. Paul, Yellow Springs
Riva-Saleta, Luis O., St. Ignatius, Cincinnati
Roadruck, Max, Mary Help of Christians, Fairborn
Royer, Milton W., Corpus Christi, Dayton
Runnels, Arthur, St. Charles Borromeo, Carthage; St. Aloysius, Elmwood Place
Saluke, William M., St. Mary, Dayton
Schmidt, Joseph Ted, St. Boniface, Cincinnati
Schmiesing, John J., St. Augustine, Minster
Schneider, Jerry R., Unassigned
Schroeder, Robert J., St. Antoninus, Cincinnati
Schultheis, Joseph R., Our Lady of Victory, Cincinnati
Simmons, Raphael, St. Joseph, Cincinnati
Slattery, John M., St. Cecilia, Cincinnati
Smith, James E., Unassisgned
Sonnenberg, James J., Immaculate Heart of Mary, Cincinnati
Sprinkle, Joseph, Our Lady of Good Hope, Miamisburg
Stevenson, William, Holy Family, Dayton
Steward, Herschel R., St. Francis De Sales, Lebanon
Subler, Joseph, St. Paul, Englewood
Sunderman, James P., St. Jude the Apostle, Cincinnati
Taylor, John, St. Francis de Sales, Lebanon
Thamann, John D., St. Mary, Cincinnati
Vilaboy, Manuel D., Spanish Community, Cincinnati
Wakefield, W. Bill, Guardian Angels, Cincinnati
Waldbillig, Urban J., Unassigned
Walker, Harry S., Our Lady of the Rosary, Cincinnati
Weitzel, Paul J., St. Teresa, Springfield
Wersching, J. Phillip, Holy Angels, Cincinnati
Westerfield, Thomas E., Our Lady of Lourdes, Cincinnati
Zinck, Robert C., Jr., Incarnation, Centerville
Zvonar, George J., St. Christopher, Vandalia

INSTITUTIONS LOCATED IN THE ARCHDIOCESE

[A] THE ATHENAEUM OF OHIO

CINCINNATI. *The Athenaeum of Ohio*, Mt. St. Mary's Seminary, 6616 Beechmont Ave., 45230. Tel: 513-231-2223. Most Rev. Daniel E. Pilarczyk, D.D., Archbishop of Cincinnati, Chancellor, Chm. of Bd. of Trustees; Rev. Robert J. Mooney, M.A., Pres.; Dr. Terrance D. Callan, Ph.D., Dean, Athenaeum of Ohio; Mr. Dennis K. Eagan, B.B.A., Bus. Mgr. It was incorporated March 24, 1928 by the State of Ohio and presently has three divisions: Mt. St. Mary's Seminary of the West; the Lay Pastoral Ministry Program and the Special Studies Division.

Lay Pastoral Ministry Program, 6616 Beechmont Ave., 45230. Tel: 513-231-1200. Ms. Mary Sue O'Donnell, M.A.R., Dir.; Ms. Judith Ebbeler, M.A., Assoc. Dir.; Sr. Nancy McMullen, C.PP.S., Program Coord.; Sr. Susan Keferl, S.N.D.deN., M.A., Assoc. Dir.

The St. Gregory Seminary Trust, 100 E. Eighth St., 45202.

[B] SEMINARIES

CINCINNATI. *Mt. St. Mary's Seminary of the West*. (Diocesan), 6616 Beechmont Ave., 45230. Tel: 513-231-2223; Fax: 513-231-3254. Major seminary for students in Theology. Rev. Robert J. Mooney, M.A., Rector; Dr. Terrance D. Callan, Ph.D., Athenaeum Academic Dean; Revs. Richard A. Marzheuser, S.T.D., Seminary Dean; Raymond P. Aichele, M.R.E., Dir. Formation; Sr. Barbara Ann Hoying, C.PP.S., M.A.R.Ed., Dir. Field Education Prog.; Rev. Michael A. Savino, M.Div., Dean of Students and Assoc. Dir., Field Ed. & Dir. of Pastoral Internship; Mr. Michael E. Sweeney, M.A., M.A.T., Registrar; Dennis K. Eagan, Business Mgr.; John Gutting, Ph.D., Dir. Pastoral Counseling Degree. In res., Most Rev. Carl K. Moeddel; Revs. Raymond P. Aichele, M.R.E.; James M. Daprile, M.A.; Jeffrey M. Kemper, Ph.D.; Richard A. Marzheuser, S.T.D.; Robert J. Mooney, M.A.; Michael A. Savino, M.Div.; Timothy P. Schehr, Ph.D.; Michael Seger, S.T.L.; P. Del Staigers, M.A. Non-Resident Faculty: Mr. Terrance Callan, Ph.D.; Mr. Anthony Dicello, M.M.; Sr. Barbara Fiand, Ph.D.; John Gutting, Ph.D.; Sr. Deborah Harmeling, M.S.L.; Sr. Betty Jane Lillie, Ph.D. In res., Revs. Joseph Beckman; Edward Gratsch; John M. Jacquemin; James J. McWilliam.

CARTHAGENA. *St. Charles*, Society of the Precious Blood, 45822. Tel: 419-925-4516. Revs. William Eilerman, C.PP.S., Dir.; Joseph Anthamatten, C.PP.S.; Casper Bonifas, C.PP.S.; John Bosch, C.PP.S.; Robert Conway, C.PP.S.; Leonard Fullenkamp, C.PP.S.; Robert Gaertner, C.PP.S.; Benedict D'Angelo, C.PP.S.; Clarence Diegelman; Harold Diller, C.PP.S.; William Donohoe, C.PP.S.; Mark Dorenkemper, C.PP.S.; William Dougherty, C.PP.S.; Kilian Dreiling, C.PP.S.; Urban Dumminger, C.PP.S.; Richard Elo, C.PP.S.; Cornelius Fenton, C.PP.S.; Aloys Friedrich, C.PP.S.; Anthony Gamble, C.PP.S.; Leo Gaulrapp, C.PP.S.; Raymond Grevencamp, C.PP.S.; Joseph Hajduch, C.PP.S.; Augustine Hanchak, C.PP.S.; Florian Hartke, C.PP.S.; Ambrose Heimann, C.PP.S.; Leo Herber, C.PP.S.; James Hinton, C.PP.S.; John Jadgchew, C.PP.S.; Alphonse Jungwirth, C.PP.S.; Edgar Jutte, C.PP.S.; James Kelley, C.PP.S.; Gerold Koller, C.PP.S.; Henry Langhals, C.PP.S.; Robert Lechner, C.PP.S.; John Lefko, C.PP.S.; Ambrose Lengerich, C.PP.S.; Joseph Lima, C.PP.S.; Carl Longanback, C.PP.S.; Robert Lux, C.PP.S.; Arnold Meiring, C.PP.S.; Charles Meyer, C.PP.S.; James Miller, C.PP.S.; Othmar Missler, C.PP.S.; Alfred Naseman, C.PP.S.; Andrew Pollack, C.PP.S.; Daniel Raible, C.PP.S.; Ambrose Ruschau, C.PP.S.; Bernard Schmitt, C.PP.S.; Vincent Schuster, C.PP.S.; Raymond Seifert, C.PP.S.; Robert Siebeneck, C.PP.S.; Joseph Smolar, C.PP.S.; John Spatt, C.PP.S.; Leonard Sudhoff, C.PP.S.; Anthony Traser, C.PP.S.; Hugh Ulrich, C.PP.S.; Bro. Jude Brown, C.PP.S., Treas. Priests 56; Brothers 18; Sisters 4.

[C] NOVITIATES AND HOUSES OF STUDY

CINCINNATI. *Dominican Novitiate*, 7630 Shawnee Run Rd., 45243. Tel: 513-527-3972; Fax: 513-527-3973. Rev. Joseph Ambrose Eckinger, O.P., Novice Master. Novices 4.

St. Anthony Shrine, Francisan Candidacy, St. John the Baptist Province, 5000 Colerain Ave., 45223. Tel: 513-541-2146. Revs. Clyde Young, O.F.M., Vicar; Dennis Bosse, O.F.M., Instructor; Varian Slacke, O.F.M., (Retired); Kenan Freson, O.F.M., Prov. Treas.; Frank Geers, O.F.M., Dir. of Candidates; Bros. Vincent Delorenzo, O.F.M., Guardian; Scott Obrecht, O.F.M.; Donald Rewers, O.F.M. Priests 5; Brothers 3; Candidates 6.

DAYTON. *Marianist Novitiate*, 4435 E. Patterson Rd., 45430-1095. Tel: 937-426-5721. Rev. Theodore K. Cassidy, S.M., Dir. Novices; Bro. Steven P. O'Neil, S.M., Asst. Dir. Novices. Priests 2; Brothers 9.

[D] COLLEGES AND UNIVERSITIES

CINCINNATI. *College of Mount St. Joseph*, 5701 Delhi Rd., 45233-1670. Tel: 513-244-4200.
For a complete listing, refer to the Colleges and Universities section.

Xavier University, 3800 Victory Pkwy. at Dana Ave., 45207. Tel: 513-745-3000.
For a complete listing, refer to the Colleges and Universities section.

DAYTON. *The University of Dayton*, (1850) 300 College Park Ave., 45469-1624. Tel: 937-229-1000.
For a complete listing, refer to the Colleges and Universities section.

SAINT MARTIN. *Chatfield College*, Brown County Ursulines, 20918 State Rte. 251, 45118. Tel: 937-875-3344; Fax: 937-875-3912.
For a complete listing, refer to the Colleges and Universities section.

[E] HIGH SCHOOLS, INTER-PAROCHIAL

CINCINNATI. *Elder High School*, 3900 Vincent Ave., 45205. Tel: 513-921-3744. Revs. Jerome A. Schaeper, Prin.; James G. Kiffmeyer; Donald R. Rettig. Priests 3; Lay Teachers 57; Students 1023.

LaSalle High School, 3091 N. Bend Rd., 45239-7696. Tel: 513-741-3000; Fax: 513-741-2666. Mr. John M. Strathern, Prin. Diocesan Priests 1; Lay Teachers 50; Students 940.

McAuley High School, 6000 Oakwood Ave., 45224. Tel: 513-681-1800. Mrs. Cheryl A. Sucher, Prin.; Mrs. Connie Kampschmidt, Asst. Prin.; Rev. Chuck

Mentrup. Sisters of Mercy 2; Lay Teachers 64; Girls 942. Convents, 1768 Cedar Ave. 5925 Oakwood Ave. 5764 Belmont Ave., 45224.

McNicholas High School, 6536 Beechmont Ave., 45230. Tel: 513-231-3500. Sisters of St. Joseph of Medaille (Cincinnati Prov.). Mr. Jerome P. Couzins, Prin. Priests 1; Sisters 1; Lay Teachers 51; Students 783.

Moeller High School, 9001 Montgomery Rd., 45242. Tel: 513-791-1680. Mr. Daniel J. Ledford, Prin.; Rev. Michael F. Leshney. Sisters of Mercy 1; Diocesan Priest 1; Brothers 7; Lay Teachers 45; Students 880.

Mother of Mercy High School, 3036 Werk Rd., 45211. Tel: 513-661-2740. Sr. Nancy Merkle, R.S.M., Prin. Priests 1; Sisters of Mercy 2; Lay Teachers 54; Girls 638.

Mt. Notre Dame High School, 711 E. Columbia Ave., 45215. Tel: 513-821-3044; Fax: 513-821-6068. Mrs. Maureen Baldock, Prin. Sisters 4; Lay Teachers 56; Girls 707.

Purcell Marian High School. (Walnut Hills), 2935 Hackberry St., 45206. Tel: 513-751-1230. Janis M. Rich, Prin.; Brenda Pfeiffer, Business Mgr.; Mr. Miguel Lopez-Madrazo, Dir. Ministry. Priests 1; Brothers 3; Sisters 1; Lay Teachers 50; Students 732.

Roger Bacon High School, 4320 Vine St., 45217. Tel: 513-641-1300; Fax: 513-641-0498. Franciscan Friars of the Cincinnati Province of St. John the Baptist. Revs. Roger Bosse, O.F.M., Prin.; Patrick McCloskey, O.F.M., Chap., Teacher; Dennis Bosse, O.F.M., Student Activity Dir., Teacher; Bros. Christopher Cahill, O.F.M., Computer Network Coordinator; Conrad Rebmann, O.F.M., Community Svcs. Coord. Priests 3; Brothers 2; Sisters 3; Lay Teachers 53; Students 880.

Seton High School. (Price Hill), 3901 Glenway Ave., 45205. Tel: 513-471-2600; Fax: 513-471-0529. Sr. Brenda Busch, S.C., Prin.; Miss Susan M. Gibbons, Assoc. Prin.; Mr. Thomas E. McKiernan, Assoc. Prin.-Treas. Priests 1; Sisters of Charity of Cincinnati 7; Lay Teachers 35; Students 685.

DAYTON. *Archbishop Alter High School*, 940 E. David Rd., 45429. Tel: 937-434-4434. Mr. Walter J. Klimaski, Prin. Sisters 2; Lay Teachers 49; Students 755.

Carroll High School, 4524 Linden Ave., 45432. Tel: 513-253-8188. Mr. Joseph R. Sens, Prin. Sisters 2; Lay Teachers 58; Students 1,092.

Chaminade-Julienne High School, 505 S. Ludlow St., 45402. Tel: 937-461-3740. Conducted by the Society of Mary (Marianists) and Sisters of Notre Dame de Namur. Mr. Lorcan Barnes, Pres.; Bro. Edward Brink, S.M., Prin.; Mr. Antonio F. Ferraro, Dir. Student Svcs.; Mrs. Shirley Kuchta, Dir. of Faculty & Staff Devel.; Mrs. Debra M. Schenk, Dir. Admin. Svcs.; Ms. Karen Seitz, Dir. Pastoral Svcs.; Sr. Damienne Grismer, S.N.D.deN. Priests 2; Brothers 3; Sisters 5; Lay Teachers 70; Students 958.

HAMILTON. *Stephen T. Badin High School*, 571 New London Rd., 45013. Tel: 513-863-3993. Ms. Margaret R. Winkeljohn, Prin. Lay Teachers 50; Students 774.

MIDDLETOWN. *Fenwick High School*, 3800 Manchester Rd., 45042. Tel: 513-423-0723; Fax: 513-420-8690. Ms. Katherine A. Beimesche, Prin.; Rev. Paul L. Gebhardt. Priests 1; Lay Teachers 26; Students 356.

SIDNEY. *Lehman High School*, 2400 St. Mary's Ave., 45365. Tel: 937-498-1161; Fax: 937-492-3911. Mr. Michael Barhorst, Prin. Sisters 1; Lay Teachers 25; Students 345.

SPRINGFIELD. *Catholic Central High School*, 1200 E. High St., 45505-1124. Tel: 937-325-9204. Sr. Teresa Marie Laengle, S.C., Prin. Sisters 2; Lay Teachers 19; Students 340.

[F] HIGH SCHOOLS, PRIVATE

CINCINNATI. *St. Ursula Academy High School*, 1339 E. McMillan St., 45206. Tel: 513-961-3410; Fax: 513-961-3856. Francis Romweber, Prin. Sisters 5; Lay Teachers 45; Girls 524.

St. Xavier High School, 600 N. Bend Rd., 45224. Tel: 513-761-7600. Mr. David B. Mueller, Prin.; Rev. William L. Verbryke, S.J., Pres.; Mr. William Sandquist, Jr., Asst. Prin.; Revs. John J. Beckman, S.J.; J. Paul O'Brien, S.J.; Edward L. Pigott, S.J., Rector. Priests 4; Sisters 1; Scholastics 1; Lay Teachers 83; Students 1,408.

Summit Country Day Upper School, 2161 Grandin Rd., 45208. Tel: 513-871-4700; Fax: 513-533-5373. Mr. Edward C. Tyrrell, Headmaster and Pres.; Mr. Thomas G. Monaco, Prin. Lay Teachers 37; Students 293.

Ursuline Academy of Cincinnati. Senior High School. 5535 Pfeiffer Rd., 45242. Tel: 513-791-5791. Ursuline Sisters of Brown Co. Saint Martin, OH. Rev. John E. Wessling; Mrs. Shirley G. Speaks, Exec. Dir. Priests 1; Sisters 5; Lay Teachers 65; Girls 615.

[G] CONSOLIDATED ELEMENTARY SCHOOLS

CINCINNATI. *Corryville Catholic Elementary School*, 108 Calhoun St., 45219. Tel: 513-281-4856. Sr. Marie Smith, S.N.D., Prin. Sisters 5; Lay Teachers 7; Students 153.
Consolidated school serving the parishes of St. George, St. Monica, Holy Name, St. Andrew, Assumption and Sacred Heart.

St. Bartholomew. (Grades K-8), 9375 Winton Rd., 45231. Tel: 513-521-0860. Mrs. Anne Crowe, Prin.; Mrs. Sally Hicks, Asst. Prin. Sisters of St. Francis 1; Lay Teachers 29; Students 750.
Consolidated school serving the parishes of St. Bartholomew, Corpus Christi and St. John Neumann, Cincinnati.

St. Boniface School, 4305 Pitts Ave., 45223. Tel: 513-541-5122. Sr. Joanne Geis, S.C., Prin. Sisters 4; Lay Teachers 5; Students 200.
Serving the parishes of St. Boniface and St. Leo, Cincinnati.

St. Gabriel. (Grades K-8), 18 W. Sharon Ave., 45246. Tel: 513-771-5220. Florence Edelmann, Prin. Sisters 1; Lay Teachers 15; Students 360.
Consolidated school serving the parishes of St. Gabriel, Glendale; St. John, West Chester; St. Martin de Porres, Lincoln Heights; St. Matthias, Forest Park; St. Maximilian Kolbe, West Chester.

DAYTON. *Bishop Leibold School*. West Campus: (Grades K-3), 24 S. Third St., 45342. Tel: 937-866-3021. East Campus: (Grades K, 4-8), 6666 Springboro Rd., 45449. Tel: 937-434-9343. Mr. Charles Lanasa, Prin. Lay Teachers 24; Students 495.
Serving the Parishes of St. Henry, Dayton and Our Lady of Good Hope, Miamisburg.

Dayton Catholic Elementary School. (Grades K-8), 3805 King's Hwy., 45406. Tel: 937-275-8114. Mrs. Karyn J. Hecker, Prin. Lay Teachers 12; Students 258.
Serving the parishes of St. Agnes, Assumption and St. James, Dayton.

HAMILTON. *St. Joseph Consolidated School*. (Grades K-8), 925 S. Second St., 45011. Tel: 513-863-8758; Fax: 513-863-5253. Dr. Gail Kist-Kline, Prin. Lay Teachers 11; Students 174.
Serving the parishes of St. Aloysius, Shandon and St. Joseph, Hamilton.

MIDDLETOWN. *John XXIII Elementary School*. (Grades K-5). East Campus: 3907 Central Ave., 45044. Tel: 513-424-0838. North Campus: (Grades 6-8), 3806 Manchester Rd., 45042. Tel: 513-424-1196. Sr. Nancy Krista, S.N.D., Prin. Sisters 3; Lay Teachers 25; Students 468.
Serving the parishes of Holy Family, Middletown and St. Mary, Franklin.

PIQUA. *Piqua Catholic School*. North St. Campus: (Grades 4-8), 503 W. North St., 45356. Tel: 937-773-1564. Downing St. Campus: (Grades K-3), 218 S. Downing St., 45356. Tel: 937-773-3876. Mr. David Skelton, Prin. Lay Teachers 23; Students 480.
Serving the parishes of St. Boniface and St. Mary.

SPRINGFIELD. *Holy Trinity Catholic School*. (Grades K-8), 1035 W. High St., 45506. Tel: 937-322-8781. Mrs. Kathy A. Grott, Prin. Lay Teachers 11; Students 230.
Serving the parishes of St. Joseph, St. Mary and St. Raphael.

[H] ELEMENTARY SCHOOLS, PRIVATE

CINCINNATI. *St. Ursula Villa*. (Grades PreK-8), 3660 Vineyard Pl., 45226. Tel: 513-871-7218. Mr. Paul Loechle. Sisters 2; Lay Teachers 34; Students 500.

Summit Country Day School PreK-8, 2161 Grandin Rd., 45208. Tel: 513-871-4700; Fax: 513-533-5373. Edward C. Tyrrell, Headmaster and Pres. Lay Teachers 80; Students 711.

[I] CHILD CARE INSTITUTIONS

CINCINNATI. *St. Aloysius Orphanage*, 4721 Reading Rd., 45237. Tel: 513-242-7600; Fax: 513-242-2845.
For a complete listing, refer to the Special Care Facilities section.

St. Joseph Infant and Maternity Home dba St. Joseph Home, 10722 Wyscarver Rd., 45241. Tel: 513-563-2520.
For a complete listing, refer to the Special Care Facilities section.

St. Joseph Orphanage, 5400 Edalbert, 45239.
For a complete listing, refer to the Special Care Facilities section.

[J] SPECIAL SCHOOLS

CINCINNATI. *St. Rita School for the Deaf*, 1720 Glendale-Milford Rd., 45215. Tel: 513-771-7600. Mr. Gregroy R. Ernst, Supt.; Ms. Mary Ann Stansfield, Prin.; Mr. Peter Keller, Dir. of Student Life; Rev. William H. Wysong. Sisters of Charity 3; Lay Teachers 35; High School Students 48; Elementary Students 85; Pre-School 35. Residential and day school for deaf and hard of hearing children.

[K] GENERAL HOSPITALS

CINCINNATI. *Franciscan Hospital, Mt. Airy Campus*, 2446 Kipling Ave., 45239. Tel: 513-853-5000.
For a complete listing, refer to the Hospitals section.

Franciscan Hospital, Western Hills Campus, 3131 Queen City Ave., 45238. Tel: 513-389-5000.
For a complete listing, refer to the Hospitals section.

Good Samaritan Hospital, 375 Dixmyth Ave., 45220. Tel: 513-872-1400; Fax: 513-872-3435.
For a complete listing, refer to the Hospitals section.

Mercy Hospital Anderson, 7500 State Rd., 45255. Tel: 513-624-4500.
For a complete listing, refer to the Hospitals section.

BATAVIA. *Clermont Mercy Hospital*, 3000 Hospital Dr., 45103. Tel: 513-732-8200.
For a complete listing, refer to the Hospitals section.

DAYTON. *Good Samaritan Hospital*, 2222 Philadelphia Dr., 45406. Tel: 937-278-2612.
For a complete listing, refer to the Hospitals section.

St. Elizabeth Medical Center, Inc., 601 Edwin C. Moses Blvd., 45408. Tel: 513-229-6000.
For a complete listing, refer to the Hospitals section.

FAIRFIELD. *Mercy Health Plaza*, 2990 Mack Rd., 45014. Tel: 513-874-6440.
For a complete listing, refer to the Hospitals section.

HAMILTON. *Mercy Hospital of Hamilton-Fairfield*, 100 Riverfront Plaza, P.O. Box 418, 45011. Tel: 513-867-6400; Fax: 513-867-9043.
For a complete listing, refer to the Hospitals section.

SPRINGFIELD. *Mercy Medical Center*, 1343 N. Fountain Blvd., 45501-1380. Tel: 937-390-5000; Fax: 937-328-8003.
For a complete listing, refer to the Hospitals section.

URBANA. *Mercy Memorial Hospital*, 904 Scioto St., 43078. Tel: 937-653-5231.
For a complete listing, refer to the Hospitals section.

[L] SENIOR RESIDENCES

CINCINNATI. *Archbishop Leibold Home for the Aged*, 476 Riddle Rd., 45220-2493. Tel: 513-281-8001.
For a complete listing, refer to the Special Care Facilities section.

The Franciscan at St. Clare, 100 Compton Rd., 45215. Tel: 513-761-9036.
For a complete listing, refer to the Special Care Facilities section.

The Franciscan at West Park, 2950 West Park Dr., 45238. Tel: 937-451-8900.
For a complete listing, refer to the Special Care Facilities section.

Mercy St. Theresa Center, 7010 Rowan Hill Dr., Ste. 200, 45227. Tel: 513-271-7010; Fax: 513-527-0181.
For a complete listing, refer to the Special Care Facilities section.

St. Margaret Hall, 1960 Madison Rd., 45206-1896. Tel: 513-751-5880; Fax: 513-751-9813.
For a complete listing, refer to the Special Care Facilities section.

Sisters of Charity Senior Care Corp., dba Bayley Place, 990 Bayley Place Dr., 45233. Tel: 513-347-5500; Fax: 513-347-5553.
For a complete listing, refer to the Special Care Facilities section.

CENTERVILLE. *The Franciscan at St. Leonard*, 8100 Clyo Rd., 45458. Tel: 937-433-0480.
For a complete listing, refer to the Special Care Facilities section.

DAYTON. *The Maria Joseph Living Care Center*, 4830 Salem Ave., 45416. Tel: 937-278-2692; Fax: 937-278-9016.
For a complete listing, refer to the Special Care Facilities section.

Mercy Siena Woods, 235 W. Orchard Springs Dr., 45415. Tel: 937-278-8211; Fax: 937-278-8046.
For a complete listing, refer to the Special Care Facilities section.

Siena Springs, 6215 N. Main St., 45415. Tel: 937-274-4790.
For a complete listing, refer to the Special Care Facilities section.

HAMILTON. *The Franciscan at Schroder*, 1302 Millville Ave., 45013. Tel: 513-867-1300; Fax: 513-867-1415.
For a complete listing, refer to the Special Care Facilities section.

SPRINGFIELD. *Oakwood Village Retirement Community*, 1500 Villa Rd., 45503. Tel: 937-390-9000; Fax: 937-390-9333.
For a complete listing, refer to the Special Care Facilities section.

URBANA. *Mercy McAuley Center-Mercy Health Systems*, 906 Scioto St., 43078. Tel: 937-653-5432; Fax: 937-652-2072.
For a complete listing, refer to the Special Care Facilities section.

[M] MONASTERIES AND RESIDENCES OF PRIESTS AND BROTHERS

CINCINNATI. *The Catholic Foreign Mission Society of America, Inc.*, 104 Elm Ave., Wyoming, 45215. Tel:

513-761-5888. Maryknoll Fathers. Revs. Robert W. Greene, M.M.; Leslie F. Blowers, M.M., Dir.

Comboni Missionaries (Verona Fathers)-Comboni Mission Center. Houses Comboni Missionaries of the Heart of Jesus, Inc., The Offices of the Province of North America, including the Office of the Provincial. 8108 Beechmont Ave., 45255-3194. Tel: 513-474-4997; Fax: 513-474-0382.

E-mail: comboni@igc.apc.org. Revs. John Converset, M.C.C.J., Prov. Tel: 513-474-3818; Joseph Bragotti, M.C.C.J., Vice Prov.; Sergio Contran, M.C.C.J., Prov. Treas.; Sr. Rosanne White, O.S.U., Finance Dir.; Rev. Mario Ongaro, M.C.C.J., Personnel Dir.; Patricia Meder, Editor Comboni Missions Newsletter & Comboni Press Feature Service; Cindy Browne, Mgr. Justice & Peace Center, Resource Center & Editor, CPN Newsletter; Tim McDowell, Development Dir.; Rev. Kenneth Gerth, M.C.C.J., Chap., St. Joseph's Hospital, 3001 W. Dr. Martin Luther King, Jr. Blvd., Tampa, FL, 33607-6387. 8417 N. Armenia Ave. #606, Tampa, FL, 33604-2627. Tel: 813-915-9800. Rev. Charles Walter, M.C.C.J. Priests 4.

Faber Jesuit Community, 790 Clinton Springs Ave., 45229. Tel: 513-961-7700. Revs. Joseph M. Becker, S.J.; Edward W. Burke, S.J.; J Peter Carey, S.J.; Edward W. Carter, S.J.; Richard T. Deters, S.J.; Robert Dressman, S.J.; Daniel Foley, S.J.; John N. Felten, S.J.; John M. Ferone, S.J.; Robert J. Hagee, S.J.; John P. Heim, S.J., Supr.; Herbert J Raterman, S.J.; Harold Sommer, S.J.; William G. Topmoeller, S.J.; John J. Beckman, S.J.

4105 Hoffman Ave., 45236. Rev. James M. Brichetto, S.J.

St. Antoninus, 1500 Linneman Rd., 45238. Rev. Robert J. Ross, S.J.

2028 Mackoy Ave., 41014. Bros. Donald H. Bengert, S.J.; Robert G. Cardosi, S.J.; John P. Martin, S.J. Priests 17; Brothers 3.

Jesuit Community at St. Xavier High School, Jesuit Community, 7361 View Pl., 45224. Tel: 513-761-5522; Fax: 513-761-0514. Revs. Edward L. Pigott, S.J., Rector; Lester A. Linz, S.J.; Eugene J. Nevins, S.J.; J. Paul O'Brien, S.J.; William L. Verbryke, S.J.

Jesuit Community at Xavier Unversity, Jesuit Community Residence, 3844 Victory Pkwy., 45207. Tel: 513-745-3591. Members of the Jesuit Community (Society of Jesus, S.J.). Revs. Joseph A. Bracken, S.J., Rector; Robert C. Baumiller, S.J.; Richard W. Bollman, S.J.; Louis A. Bonacci, S.J.; Eugene J. Carmichael, S.J.; Michael J. Graham, S.J.; James E. Hoff, S.J.; Francis D. Johnson, S.J.; Thomas P. Kennealy, S.J.; William F. King, S.J.; J. Leo Klein, S.J.; John J. LaRocca, S.J.; Edward T. O'Donnell, S.J.; Robert W. Schmidt, S.J.; Theodore C. Thepe, S.J.; Benjamin J. Urmston, S.J.; George B. Wilson, S.J.; Bro. Jerome J. Pryor, S.J. Priests 18; Brothers 1.

Marianist Community, 2708 Johnstone Pl., 45206-1822. Tel: 513-961-6244. Revs. John S. Putka, S.M., Dir.; Louis Wiesner, S.M. Priests 2; Brothers 6.

Marianist Community, 1600 Madison Rd., 45206-1815. Tel: 513-961-1945. Bros. Giancarlo Bonutti, S.M., Dir.; Lawrence Corbin, S.M.; Revs. Edward M. Jach, S.M.; Daniel Winters, S.M. Priests 2; Brothers 2.

Marianist Community, 9025 Montgomery Rd., 45242-7711. Tel: 513-793-4777. Bro. Robert M. Flaherty, S.M., Dir.; Rev. Joseph L. Kerr, S.M. Priests 1; Brothers 9.

Marianist Community, 118 Findlay St., Apt. #1, 45210-2402. Tel: 513-369-0388; Fax: 513-369-0408. Rev. Michael L. Lisbeth, S.M.; Bros. J. Mitchell Schweickart, S.M., Dir.; Robert P. Donovan, S.M.; Paul Hoffman, S.M. Brothers 3; Priests 1.

Pleasant Street Friary, 1723 Pleasant St., 45210. Tel: 513-621-0599. Friars Daniel J. Anderson, O.F.M.; Jovian C. Weigel, O.F.M.; Jack R. Wintz, O.F.M.; Murray L. Bodo, O.F.M.

St. Ann Friary, 2936 W. Galbraith Rd., 45239. Tel: 513-522-7420. Revs. Nicholas Lohkamp, O.F.M.; Conan Taylor, O.F.M.; Joseph Rayes, O.F.M.; Joseph Ricchini, O.F.M.; Dominic Wachtel, O.F.M.; Carl Langenderfer, O.F.M.; Bro. John Schreck, O.F.M.

St. Clare Friary, 5831 Saranac Ave., 45224. Tel: 513-541-5742. Revs. Patrick McCloskey, O.F.M.; James Bok, O.F.M.; Bros. Gene Mayer, O.F.M.; Francisco Meyer, O.F.M.

St. Clement Friary. St. John the Baptist Province. Residence for Faculty of Roger Bacon High School, Pastors of St. Clement Parish and other Friars. 4536 Vine St., 45217. Tel: 513-641-2257. Revs. Joachim N. Lux, O.F.M., Guardian; Al D. Hudepohl, O.F.M., Pastor; Stanley Bir, O.F.M., Prov. Personnel Advisor; Christopher Schneider, O.F.M.; Vincent A. Dieckman, O.F.M.; Frank D. Frey, O.F.M.; Warren Zeisler, O.F.M.; Cyril Hermann, O.F.M.; Otto Krische, O.F.M.; Roger T. Bosse, O.F.M.; Donnul Suttmann, O.F.M.; William Reichel, O.F.M.; Valens Waldschmidt; Bros. Conrad F. Rebmann, O.F.M., Vicar; Louis Lamping, O.F.M., Treas.; Louis Zant, O.F.M.; Bernard Jennings, O.F.M.; Kenneth Beetz, O.F.M.; Joel Soldenski, O.F.M.; Jude Sukup, O.F.M.; Didacus Casanave, O.F.M.; Jerry Jackson, O.F.M.; Joseph Haley, O.F.M.; Francis Williams, O.F.M. Priests 13; Brothers 11.

St. Francis Center, 10290 Mill Rd., 45231. Tel: 513-825-4465. Vocation Office. Tel: 513-825-1082. St. John the Baptist Province. Revs. Ed Slater, Dir. Renewal Center; Noel William, O.F.M., Guardian; Celsus Griese, O.F.M., Chap. Bob Hope House; Ernest Porsch; Bruno Kremp, O.F.M., Vocation Dir.; Aloys Held, O.F.M.; Marcan Hetteberg, O.F.M., Franciscan Archives; Melvin Holtel, O.F.M.; Adrian Schneider, O.F.M.; Germain Krizmanich, O.F.M., Drake Hospital; Bros. Linus Border, O.F.M.; Bill Ollendick, O.F.M.; Kevin Duckson, O.F.M., Vicar.

St. Francis Seraph Friary. Provincial Headquarters of the Province of St. John the Baptist of the Order of Friars Minor. 1615 Vine St., 45210. Tel: 513-721-4700; Fax: 513-421-9672. Revs. Paul Desch, O.F.M., Pastor; John Stein, O.F.M., Assoc.; John Bok, O.F.M., Prov. Min.; Alan Hirt, O.F.M., Vicar Prov.; Kenan Freson, O.F.M., Prov. Treas.; James Bok, O.F.M., Dir. Devel.; John R. Boehman, O.F.M., Office for Senior Friars; Francis S. Tebbe, O.F.M., Dir. Ongoing Formation; Rock Travnikar, O.F.M., Vocation Dir.; Bruno Kremp, O.F.M., Vocation Dir.; Toni Cashnelli, Dir. Communications; Henry Beck, O.F.M., Office of Justice, Peace and Integrity of Creation; Bert Heise, O.F.M., Guardian; Theobald Hattrup, O.F.M., (Retired); Paschal Varnskuhler, O.F.M., (Retired); Peter Paul James, O.F.M., (Retired); Bros. Scott Obrecht, O.F.M., Dir. Franciscan Mission Office & Missionary Union; Gene Mayer, O.F.M., Prov. Sec.; Josef Anderlohr, O.F.M.; Christopher Cahill, O.F.M.; John Carey, O.F.M.; Dominic Lococo, O.F.M.; Robert Lucero, O.F.M.; Kevin Schroeder, O.F.M.; Bill Spond, O.F.M. Priests 9; Brothers 8.

Priests of the Province Serving Abroad: Rev. James Fehrenbach, O.F.M., Ainmillerstr, 5 Whg. 608, Munchen, Germany, 80801. Rev. Max Langenderfer, O.F.M., Franciscans, P.O. Box 14355. Rev. John Quigley, O.F.M., Curia Generale, Via. S. Maria Mediatrice, 25, 00165. Rev. Daniel Kroger, O.F.M., Our Lady of the Angels Seminary, P.O. Box 191.

St. Gertrude Priory, 7630 Shawnee Run Rd., 45243. Tel: 513-561-5954. Revs. William A. Holt, O.P., Prior & Assoc.; Joseph Ambrose Eckinger, O.P., Novice Master & Subprior; Clement Burns, O.P., Pastor; Thomas F. Carroll, O.P., Assoc.; George Schommer, O.P., Assoc.; James M. Sullivan, O.P., Assoc. In res., Rev. Harvey B. Schaller, O.P.; Bro. Ignatius Perkins, O.P.

DAYTON. *Marianist Provincialate*. Cincinnati Province of the Society of Mary (Brothers of Mary, Marianists), 4435 E. Patterson Rd., 45430-1095. Tel: 937-513-429-0794; Fax: 937-513-429-3195. Very Rev. James F. Fitz, S.M., Prov.; Rev. Bertrand A. Buby, S.M., Councilor; Bros. Joseph H. Kamis, S.M., Asst. Provincial & Asst. for Education; Ronald L. Overman, S.M., Asst. for Temporalities & Prov. Treas.; Thomas J. Pieper, S.M., Asst. Relgious Life; Robert J. Metzger, S.M., Asst. Treas.; Ms. Phyllis J. Lipker, Sec.

Priests of the Province on Special Assignment: Rev. Robert E. Hogan, S.M., St. Joseph Marianist Community, 520 Fordham Ln., San Antonio, TX, 78228-4800. Rev. Thomas J. Stanley, S.M., Marianist Community, 5000 Monroe St., Hollywood, FL, 33021-7270. Rev. Dennis J. Gatto, S.M., The Madeline House, 1614 S. Carrollton Ave., New Orleans, LA, 70118-2826. Rev. James A. Russell, S.M., 500 Chaminade Dr. East, Hollywood, FL, 33021-5853. Rev. Joseph H. Lackner, S.M., Marianist Seminary, 175 Phelan Ave., San Francisco, CA, 94112-1897. Rev. John L. Bakle, S.M., St. Agatha Rectory, 1860 Northam Rd., Columbus, 43221-3299. Rev. Norbert C. Brockman, S.M., St. Mary's University, Casa Maria, One Camino Santa Maria, San Antonio, TX, 78228-8518. Rev. Robert J. Bouffier, S.M., 21 Easton St., Allston, MA, 02134. Rev. Raymond J. Kacirk, S.M., 25149 Hanover St., Dearborn, MI, 48125-1831. Rev. Edmund L. Rhodes, S.M., 5000 Monroe St., Hollywood, FL, 33021-7270. Rev. Kenneth J. Sommer, S.M., 5541 Bosworth Pl., Cincinnati, 45212. Rev. James F. Kunes, S.M., 4649 D Country Ln., St. Louis, MO, 63074. Rev. Anthony E. Victoria, S.M., St. Joseph Church, 172 Leslie St., Toronto, Canada, M4M 3C7.

Priests of the Province Serving Overseas: Rev. Michael R. Reaume, S.M., St. Columba, Ballybrack, Ireland.

Priests of the Province Serving in the Missions: Rev. William R. Behringer, S.M., Brother Vincent House, P.O. Box 25156, Nairobi, Kenya. Rev. Robert W. Hertweck, S.M., Marianist Novitiate, P.O. Box 210, Limuru, Kenya. Rev. Martin A. Solma, S.M., Reg. Supr. & Reg. Admin., P.O. Box 50504, Nairobi, Kenya. Rev. Charles J. Stander, S.M., Marianist Novitiate, P.O. Box 210, Limuru, Kenya. Rev. Richard A. Loehrlein, S.M., Chaminade Marianist Community, P.O. Box 100, Karonga, Malawi.

Marianist Community, 100 Chambers St., 45409-2817. Tel: 937-223-7150. Revs. Eugene J. Contadino, S.M.; Bertrand A. Buby, S.M; Bro. Thomas E. Oldenski, S.M, Dir. Priests 2; Brothers 4.

Marianist Community, 149 Franklin St., 45402-2598. Tel: 937-228-2013. Revs. Lee Sciarrotta, S.M., Dir.; Francis J. Kenney, S.M. Priests 2; Brothers 2.

Marianist Community, Meyer Hall, 4435 East Patterson Rd., 45430-1095. Tel: 937-426-7852. Revs. Richard K. Knuge, S.M.; John D. Mulligan, S.M. (NY); Bro. Thomas A. Payne, S.M., Dir. Priests 2; Brothers 7.

Marianist Community, Novitiate, 4435 E. Patterson Rd., 45430-1095. Tel: 937-426-5721. Rev. Theodore K. Cassidy, S.M. (NY), Dir. Priests 2; Brothers 8.

Marianist Community, 141 Washington St., 45402-2530. Tel: 937-224-9978. Bro. Robert N. Wiethorn, S.M., Dir.; Revs. James F. Fitz, S.M.; John A. McGrath, S.M. (NY); Thomas A. Schroer, S.M.; Christopher T. Wittmann, S.M. Priests 4; Brothers 7.

Marianist Community, 62 Indiana Ave, 45410-2308. Tel: 937-258-3212. Bro. John J. Jansen, S.M., Dir.; Revs. Charles T. Bergedick, S.M.; Norbert C. Burns, S.M.; Cyril Middendorf, S.M. Tel: 513-258-3250. Priests 3; Brothers 3.

Marianist Community, 340 Stonemill Rd., 45409-2543. Tel: 937-285-8611; 285-8612. Revs. Gerald T. Chinchar, S.M., Dir.; Christopher W. Conlon, S.M. (NY). Priests 2; Brothers 2.

Marianist Community, 121 Sawmill Rd., 45409-2524. Tel: 937-222-4928. Revs. Matthew F. Kohmescher, S.M., Dir.; Thomas A. Schoen, S.M. Priests 2; Brothers 3.

Marianist Community, 1903 Trinity Ave., 45409-2445. Tel: 937-293-9744. Bro. Bernard J. Ploeger, S.M., Dir.; Revs. H. James Bartlett, S.M.; James L. Heft, S.M. Priests 2; Brothers 4.

The Marianist Mission, Mount St. John, 45481-0001. Tel: 513-222-4641. Rev. John D. Mulligan, S.M., Dir., Marianist Community, Alumni Hall, University of Dayton, 45469-0300. Tel: 937-229-2721. Revs. Paul F. Vieson, S.M., Dir.; John J. Kelley, S.M.; Theodore A. Koehler, S.M. (France); Joseph F. Kozar, S.M.; Johann B.G. Roten, S.M. (Suisse); Thomas A. Thompson, S.M.; Adolf M. Windisch, S.M. (STL). Priests 7; Brothers 22.

The Franciscan at St. Leonard, Assisted Living & Nursing Assistance, 8100 Clyo Rd., 45458. Tel: 937-433-0480. Bro. John J. Schneider, S.M., Dir.; Revs. Joseph S. McDonald, S.M.; Bernard C. Stueve, S.M. Priests 3; Brothers 15.

Marianist Community, 1234 Duckview Ct., 45458. Tel: 937-439-5941. Bro. John J. Schneider, Dir.; Rev. Philip C. Hoelle, S.M. Brothers 3; Priests 1.

Marianist Community, 57 Woodland Ave., 45409-2853. Tel: 937-285-8091. Bro. Philip T. Aaron, S.M., Dir. Brothers 3.

Marianist Press. Religious 2; Total Staff 5.

Marianist Network for the Arts. Religious 3; Total Staff 3.

North American Center for Marianist Studies. Religious 3; Total Staff 4.

Marianist Mission. Religious 5; Total Staff 63.

Marianist Voluntary Service Communities. Religious 2; Total Staff 4.

Marianist Environmental Education Center. Religious 2; Total Staff 2.

Provincial House of the Cincinnati Province of the Society of the Precious Blood, 431 East Second St., 45402. Tel: 937-228-9263; Fax: 937-228-6878. Very Rev. Kenneth F. Pleiman, C.PP.S., Prov. Dir.; Bro. Joseph J. Fisher, C.PP.S., Treas.; Rev. James F. McCabe, C.PP.S., Sec. Members of the Executive Committee: Rev. James F. McCabe, C.PP.S., Vice Prov., 431 E. Second St., 45402. Rev. Clarence E. Williams, C.PP.S., 1st Councilor, 11430 Morang Dr., Detroit, MI, 48224. Rev. William A. O'Donnell, C.PP.S., 2nd Councilor, 309 S. Perry St., Wapakoneta, 45895. Rev. Jame Seibert, C.PP.S., 3rd Councilor, 229 W. Anthony St., Celina, 45822. Bro. Joseph J. Fisher, C.PP.S., 4th Councilor, 431 E. Second St., 45402. Bro. Benjamin Basile, C.PP.S., 5th Councilor, 2400 New York Ave., Whiting, IN, 46394. Vocation Office, 431 E. 2nd St., 45402-1764. Tel: 937-228-6224; Fax: 937-228-6878. Rev. Angelo Anthony, C.PP.S., Vocation Dir.

Military: Rev. Louis L. Schmit, C.PP.S., HQ USAR EUR & 7A, CMR 420, Box 2977, APO, AE, 09063. Rev. Eugene H. Schnipke, C.PP.S., 4204-H West Muledeer Dr., USAF Academy, CO, 80840-1137. Rev. Kenneth J. Schroeder, C.PP.S., United States Army Garrison, Post Chapel, Bldg. #4419, Fort George, G. Meade, MD, 20755-5065. Rev. John S. Srode, C.PP.S., 2 Heritage Rd., Hanscom AFB, MA, 01731-2632.

Priests of the Province Serving Abroad: Rev. Frederick T. Licciardi, C.PP.S., Hirschengraben 72,8001, Zurich, Switzerland.

Foreign Mission: Rev. Richard L. Beischel, C.PP.S., Casilla 619, Valdivia, Chile. Rev. William J. Beuth, C.PP.S., Apartado 2483, 01901. Rev. Paul A. Buehler, C.PP.S., Apartado 1983, Lima 100, Peru. Rev. Joseph F. Deardorff, C.PP.S., Apartado 2348, Lima, 100, Peru. Rev. Gerald G. Dreiling, C.PP.S., Apartado 07-0148, Lima 07, Peru. Rev. John F. Falter, C.PP.S., Casilla 619, Valdivia, Chile. Rev. Barry J. Fischer, C.PP.S., Moderator General, Viale Di Porta Ardeatina 66, Rome, Italy, I-00154. Rev. James E. Gaynor, C.PP.S., Apartado 36, La Oroya, Peru. Rev. James W. Bender, C.PP.S., Apartado 36, LaOroya, Peru. Rev. Daniel J. Mangen, C.PP.S., Casilla 194, Purranque, Chile. Rev. Bernard J. Mores, C.PP.S., Casilla 163 Correo 55, Santiago 55, Chile. Rev. Ernest W. Ranly, C.PP.S., Apartado 1983, Lima, 100, Peru. Rev. Donald J. Thieman, C.PP.S., Casilla 176-2, Santiago, Chile.

Returned to U.S.A.: Revs. William A. Volk, C.PP.S.; Thomas W. Hemm, C.PP.S.; Ambrose R. Lengerich, C.PP.S.; Patrick E. Patterson, C.PP.S.

In Residences Not Listed Elsewhere: 6451 Cypress Rd., Plantation, FL, 33317. Revs. Benjamin J. Berinti, C.PP.S.; John E. Bolan, C.PP.S., 16359 Emerald Point Dr., Middleburg Hts., 44130. Rev. James K. Grothjan, C.PP.S., 1135 Bayshore Dr., Valparaiso, FL, 32580. Rev. Robert W. Hunt, C.PP.S., P.O. Box 389, Bellevue, 44811. Rev. Howard J. Lesch, C.PP.S., 1115 Coral Dr., Niceville, FL, 32578. Rev. Edward A. Maziarz, C.PP.S., 1033 W. Loyola Ave., #1007, Chicago, IL, 60626-5225. Rev. Francis W. McCarthy, C.PP.S., 52411 C.R. 425, Fresno, 43824. 2497 Eastern Ave., Cincinnati, 45202. Rev. William A. Nordenbrock, C.PP.S., 5401 S. Cornell Ave., Chicago, IL, 60615. Rev. Paul F. Schaaf, C.PP.S., 100 Bluff View Dr., 106C, Belleair Bluffs, FL, 34640. Rev. Emil A. Schuwey, C.PP.S., 1108 Fenley Ave., Louisville, KY, 40222. Rev. Alphonse P. Spilly, C.PP.S., P.O. Box 1979, Chicago, IL, 60690. Rev. David J. Van Horn, C.PP.S., 1247 E. Siena Heights Dr., Adrian, MI, 49221.

FAIRFIELD. *Headquarters of Glenmary Home Missioners*, P.O. Box 465618, 45246-5618. 4119 Glenmary Trace, 45014. Tel: 513-874-8900; Fax: 513-874-1690. The Home Missioners of America. Revs. Jerry Dorn, Glmy., Pres.; Will Steinbacher, Glmy., 1st Vice Pres. & Dir. of Education Dept.; Bro. Jack Henn, Glmy., 2nd Vice Pres. & Dir. of Vocation Dept. Senior Members: Revs. Edward Haggerty, Glmy.; Del Holmes, Glmy.; Charles Hughes, Glmy.; Patrick O'Donnell, Glmy.; John Otterbacher, Glmy.; Raymond Orlett, Glmy.; George Mathis, Glmy.; John McNearney, Glmy.; Joseph Dean, Glmy.; Robert Healy, Glmy.; William Smith, Glmy.; Joseph Gartner, Glmy.; James Kelly, Glmy.; Francisco Schenk, Glmy.; Bob Berson, Glmy.; John Garvey, Glmu.; Bros. Arthur Miller; Vincent Wilmes; George Sauer; Paul Wilhelm; Bernie Stern; Revs. Pete Richardson, Glmy., Editor of the Glenmary Challenge; August Guppenberger, Glmy., Mission Office; Dominic Duggins, Glmy., Mission Office & Cincinnati House Dir.; Richard Kreimer, Glmy., Mission OFC; Bros. Mike Springer, Glmy., Senior Member Coordinator; Bob Hoffman, Vocation Counselor.

On Special Assignment: Revs. Thomas Meehan, AIDS Ministry, Atlanta, GA; John Rausch, Human Economics Ministry, Berea, KY; Donald Levernier, Glmy., On Loan to Lithuania.

HAMILTON. *St. Francis Friary*, 723 Main St., 45013-2548. Tel: 513-896-5326. Brothers of the Poor of St. Francis. Bros. Eric Lauer, C.F.P.; Howard Parent, C.F.P.

HUNTSVILLE. *St. George Chapel of Marianist Community*, 9636 Lakeshore Dr., E., 43324-9633. Tel: 513-842-4902. Bros. Donald L. Smith, S.M., Dir.; Robert V. Kelly, S.M.; Revs. John F. Mueller, S.M.; Robert J. Hoeper, S.M. Priests 2; Brothers 2.

[N] CONVENTS AND RESIDENCES FOR SISTERS

CINCINNATI. *Central Office of Sisters of St. Joseph of Medaille*, 1821 Summit Rd., Ste. 210, 45237-2819. Tel: 513-761-2888; Fax: 513-761-9957. Sr. Lucy Silvio, C.S.J., Pres.; Sr. Maria Hill, C.S.J., Vice Pres. General Councilors: Sr. Joan Hartlaub, C.S.J.; Sr. Janice Miller, C.S.J. Sisters in Archdiocese 26; Total Congregation 198.

Cincinnati Regional Community, Institute of the Sisters of Mercy of the Americas, 2335 Grandview Ave., 45206. Tel: 513-221-1800. Sr. Marie Hartmann, R.S.M., Pres. Reg. Community; Sr. Wanda Smith, R.S.M., Vocation Dir.; Sr. Mary Carol Temming, R.S.M., Formation Dir. Professed Sisters 400; Candidates 1.

Convent of St. Dominic, 916 York St., 45214. Tel: 513-621-5899. Dominican Sisters of Hope 5; Sisters of Saint Francis of Oldenburg, IN 1.

Director of Higher Education, 1768 Cedar Ave., 45224. Tel: 513-681-5328. Sr. Mary Virginia Sullivan, R.S.M., Dir.

Dominican Sisters, 3840 Applegate, Apt. 604, 45211. Tel: 513-481-6691. Sr. Clarita Elder, O.P.; Sr. Laurene Hagman, O.P.; Sr. Vivian Kessler, O.P. Dominican Sisters 3.

Franciscan Monastery of St. Clare (Poor Clares), 868 Finney Trail, 45224-1319. Tel: 513-522-4795. Contemplative Sisters 3; Candidates 1; Novices 1.

McAuley Convent, 1768 Cedar Ave., 45224. Tel: 513-681-2100. Sr. Joanne Mary Braeunig, R.S.M., Local Coord. Sisters of Mercy 50.

Mercy Center, 2335 Grandview Ave., 45206. Tel: 513-221-1800. Mr. John Payne, Building Mgr.; Sr. Bernice O'Neil, R.S.M., Local Coord. Professed Sisters 9.

Mercy Hall, 2317 Grandview Ave., 45206. Tel: 513-475-6726. Professed Sisters 6.

Provincial House, Health Center of Sisters of Notre Dame de Namur, 701 E. Columbia Ave., 45215. Tel: 513-821-7448. Sr. Claire Foley, S.N.D.deN., Prov. Supr.; Sr. Anne Flanagan, S.N.D.deN., Local Coord.; Sr. Phyllis Angerer, S.N.D.deN., Admin. Sisters 117.

St. Clare Convent, Franciscan Sisters of the Poor, 60 Compton Rd., 45215. Tel: 513-761-9036. Sr. Rosalita Losonsky, S.F.P., Local Minister; Rev. Herman Kenning, Res. Chap. Sisters 25.

St. Joseph Center, 6532 Beechmont Ave., 45230. Tel: 513-232-5230. Sr. Marlene Favre, House Admin. Sisters of St. Joseph of Medaille. Sisters 8.

St. Rose Convent, 3952 W. Eighth St., 45205.

Sisters of Charity of Cincinnati, Ohio, 5900 Delhi Rd., 45051. Tel: 513-347-5201; Fax: 513-347-5228. Sr. Mary Ellen Murphy, S.C., Pres. Sisters in Congregation 686; Sisters in Archdiocese 506. Franciscan Fathers, St. John the Baptist Province. Tel: 513-721-4700.

Sisters of Mercy, Corner Residence, 3107 Epworth Ave., 45211. Tel: 513-662-3018. Institute of the Sisters of Mercy of the Americas 3.

Sisters of the Good Shepherd. (Cincinnati Province), 2849 Fischer Pl., 45211-5915. Tel: 513-661-1833; Fax: 513-661-1216. Sr. Dolores Kalina, Prov.; Sr. Marilyn Atwell, Sec. Sisters 2.

Sisters of the Good Shepherd, 2108 Hatmaker St., 45204-1906. Tel: 513-921-5923. Sisters 4.

Ursulines of Cincinnati, 1339 E. McMillan St., 45206. Tel: 513-961-3410; Fax: 513-961-0129. Ursuline Sisters. Sr. Mary Cabrini Durkin, Supr. Sisters 31. Sisters of this community own and teach in one high school, sponsor one elementary school, serve in pastoral ministry, counseling, chaplaincy, secondary education administration, adult education and state university.

BATAVIA. *Sisters of Mercy*, Clermont, 4315 Elizabeth Dr., 45103. Tel: 513-732-6335.

DAYTON. *Sisters of the Precious Blood Generalate*, 4000 Denlinger Rd., 45426. Tel: 937-837-3302. Sr. Joyce Langhals, C.PP.S., Pres.; Sr. Nancy Raley, C.PP.S., Vice Pres. & Councilor; Sr. Judy Kroeger, C.PP.S., Councilor & Sec.; Sr. Joyce Lehman, C.PP.S., Councilor; Sr. Benita Volk, C.PP.S., Councilor; Sr. Barbara Brown, C.PP.S., Treas.

Sisters of the Precious Blood, Salem Heights Convent, 4960 Salem Ave., 45416. Tel: 937-278-0871. Sr. Corinne Staub, O.P., Admin.; Sr. Mary Ellen Andrisin, C.PP.S., Dir. Resident Life; Rev. Joseph Pax, C.PP.S., Chap. Sisters 110.

HAMILTON. *Franciscan at St. Raphael, Inc.*, 233 Dayton St., 45011. Tel: 513-893-1370. Mr. Robert Moore, Exec. Dir. Assist Social Service.

SAINT MARTIN. *Ursuline Convent of the Immaculate Heart of Mary*. (Also known as Ursulines of Brown County), Ursuline Center, 20860 State Rte. 251, 45118-9705. Tel: 937-875-2020. Ursuline Order, Congregation of Paris. Sr. Anne Maureen Maher, O.S.U., Supr. Sisters 43.

[O] RESIDENCES FOR ADULTS AND YOUTHS

CINCINNATI. *Catholic Residential Services with People with Mental Retardation*, 100 E. Eighth St., 45202. Tel: 513-241-7745; Fax: 513-241-4333. Ms. Christine Hoekzema. Legal Title: *Catholic Residential Services of Archdiocese of Cincinnati with People with Mental Retardation*.

Connelly Homes, 5591 Colerain Ave., 45239. Tel: 513-741-0035. Ms. Roxanne Hall, Mgr.

Villa Maria, 923 Bank St., 45214. Tel: 513-369-0870. Ms. Ann Williams, Mgr.

Friars Club, 65 W. McMillan St., 45219. Tel: 513-381-5432. Beth Bowsky, Exec. Dir.; Rev. James M. Bok, O.F.M., Pres., Bd. of Trustees. Residential programs for male teens, residency for men, transitional living for mentally ill, counseling, education for teen school dropouts, youth sports, and community outreach for high risk youth, family resource center, housing & support for homeless families.

[P] RETREAT HOUSES, CONFERENCE AND RENEWAL CENTERS

CINCINNATI. *Friarhurst Retreat Center*, 8136 Wooster Pike, 45227. Tel: 513-561-2270. Revs. Hilarion H. Kistner, O.F.M.; Lambert R. Dannenfelser, O.F.M.; Bro. Stephen Richter, O.F.M.

DAYTON. *Bergamo*, 4400 Shakertown Rd., 45430-1075. Tel: 937-426-2363; Fax: 937-426-1090. Mr. Thomas A. Cox, Exec. Dir.; Bro. Joseph Markel, S.M., Dir. of Operations; Sr. Madeline Columbro, S.N.D., Dir. of Adult Development; Barbara Kozlowski, Dir. of Youth Development; Patricia O'Grady, Dir. of Reservations; Robert Broderick, Dir. of Food Services.

LOVELAND. *Grailville*, 932 O'Bannonville Rd., 45140. Tel: 513-683-2340; Fax: 513-683-4752. National Center of International Grail Movement. Audrey Sorrento, Program Dir.; Frances McLaughlin, Sec.

MARIA STEIN. *Maria Stein Center*, Retreat House, 2365 St. Johns Rd., Box 128, 45860. Tel: 419-925-4538; Fax: 419-925-5413. Shrine of the Holy Relics, 2291 St. Johns Rd., 45860. Tel: 419-925-4532. Suzanne Budde, Reservations; Sr. Patricia Gist, C.PP.S., Admin. Retreat Staff: Rev. Richard Nieberding, C.PP.S., Youth Dir.; Sr. Marguerite Holz, H.M., Prog. Dir.; Sr. Mary Catherine Kunk, C.PP.S.; Sr. Mary Lou Schmersal, C.PP.S.; Sr. Elizabeth Kammerer, C.PP.S. Sisters 8; Lay Staff 20.

Chapel Hill Preschool, 2291 St. Johns Rd., 45860. Tel: 419-925-5411. Maria Rethman, Dir.

MILFORD. *Milford Spiritual Center*, 5361 S. Milford Rd., 45150-9746. Tel: 513-248-3500; Fax: 513-248-3503. Revs. Joseph E. Peschel, S.J., Supr.; R. Michael Brophy, S.J.; Frank M. Oppenheim, S.J.; George W. Traub, S.J.; Thomas J. Diehl, S.J.; Kenneth Overberg, S.J.; Bro. Paul F. Mattingly, S.J.; Daniel O. Roche, Exec. Dir. Officers: Sr. Janice Bachman, O.P., Chm.; Rev. William Verbryke, S.J., Vice Chm.; William Michael, Sec.

[Q] CAMPUS MINISTRY AND NEWMAN CENTERS

CINCINNATI. *College of Mt. St. Joseph Campus Ministry*, 5701 Delhi Rd., 45233-1670. Tel: 513-244-4245. Sr. Marge Kloos, S.C., Campus Ministry. Tel: 513-244-4245.

University of Cincinnati Newman Center, 328 W. McMillan St., 45219-1224. Tel: 513-381-6400. Revs. Jeffrey Scheeler, O.F.M.; Leonard Fecko; Al Hirt, O.F.M.; Sr. Lucy Zientek, C.D.P.; Ms. Peggy Hilvers; Ms. Jill Hack.

Xavier University Campus Ministry, 3800 Victory Pkwy., 45207-2411. Tel: 513-745-3567. Ms. Chris Potter, Dir.; Mr. Tom Sheilbley, Retreat Coord.; Rev. Louis Bonacci, S.J., Coord. Pastoral Ministry in Residence Halls; Mr. Guy Vanasse, Coord. Liturgical Music; Marci Kerscher, Campus Ministry Intern; Debbie Brawn, Campus Ministry Intern.

DAYTON. *Sinclair Community College Campus Ministry*, 444 W. Third St., 45402. Tel: 513-226-2768. Dr. V. Jane Steinhauser, Archdiocesan Dir. of Campus Ministry.

E-mail: jsteinha@sinclair.edu.

University of Dayton Campus Ministry, 45469; Fax: 937-229-2035. Revs. Gerald T. Chinchar, S.M. Tel: 937-229-2725; Christopher W. Conlon, S.M., Dir. Tel: 937-229-3339; Sr. Eileen J. Cehyra, F.M.I. Tel: 937-229-3339; Sr. Nancy Bramlage, S.C. Tel: 937-229-2576; Sr. Mary Louise Foley, F.M.I. Tel: 937-229-2093; Sr. Jody O'Neil, S.P. Tel: 937-229-2574; Sr. Kathleen Rossman, O.S.F. Tel: 937-229-3310; Sr. Monica Gundler, S.C. Tel: 937-229-2010; Bro. Philip Aaron, S.M. Tel: 937-229-2575.

FAIRBORN. *Wright State Campus Ministry Center*, 3640 Colonel Glenn Hwy., 45324. Tel: 937-426-1836. Rev. Christian A. Rohmiller, Campus Min.; Mrs. Constance Newman, Sec.

OXFORD. *Miami University Catholic Campus Ministry*, 111 E. High St., 45056. Tel: 513-523-2153. Rev. Terrance L. Schneider; Sr. Ann Hunt, S.C., Pastoral Assoc.; Jeffrey J. Piccirilli, Dir. Campus Ministry; Christina M. Flum, D.R.E.

SPRINGFIELD. *Mercy Medical Center, Wittenberg University Campus Ministry*, 1343 N. Fountain Blvd., 45501. Tel: 513-390-5000. Rev. Marvin R. Hackman, Dir. Pastoral Care.

URBANA. *Urbana University Campus Ministry*, 231 Washington Ave., 43078. Tel: 937-653-1375. Rev. Thomas R. Espelage.

Pastoral care available through St. Mary Parish.

WILBERFORCE. *Central State and Wilberforce Universities Campus Ministry*., Box 386, 45384. Tel: 937-376-8033.

WILMINGTON. *Wilmington College Campus Ministry*, 73 N. Mulberry St., 45177. Tel: 937-382-2236. Rev. R. Marc Sherlock.

Pastoral care available through St. Columbkille Parish.

YELLOW SPRINGS. *Antioch College Campus Ministry*, 308 Phillips St., 45387. Tel: 937-767-7450. Rev. Joseph W. Goetz.

Pastoral care available through St. Paul Parish.

[R] COMMUNITY CENTERS

CINCINNATI. *The Franciscan at St. John*, P.O. Box 14368,

45250. A member of the Franciscan Health System of the Ohio Valley, Inc. 121 E. 13th St., 45210. Tel: 513-241-2186. Ms. Marylyn Middendorf, Exec. Dir.; R. Christopher West, Pres.
Provides a full-range of emergency and educational services, encourages self-determination and self-improvement to over 25,000 clients annually.
Program for the Medically Underserved of Cincinnati, 3131 Queen City Ave., 45238. Tel: 513-389-5295. Sr. Kathleen Brogle, R.S.M., M.S.W., Exec. Dir. Annual Participants 2,750.

HAMILTON. *The Franciscan at St. Raphael, Inc.* A member of the Franciscan Health System of the Ohio Valley, Inc. 233 Dayton St., 45011. Tel: 513-893-1370. R. Christopher West, Pres. of FHSOV, Inc.; Robert Moore, Exec. Dir.; Sr. Bonnieen Steinlage, Pearly Gates Program.
Provides food and other emergency services and self sufficiency programs to over 10,000 clients annually.

SPRINGFIELD. *Mercy-St. John's Center*, 100 W. McCreight Ave., 45504. Tel: 937-399-9910. Marianne S. Wildermuth, Pres.
Day care center for adults, skilled & intermediate long term care facility for all ages, Alzheimer's unit, ventilator unit.

[S] ST. VINCENT DE PAUL SOCIETY

CINCINNATI. *Archdiocesan Central Council of Cincinnati*, 1125 Bank St., 45214. Tel: 513-562-8841; 8842. Rev. Louis R. Hohlmayer, Spiritual Advisor.
Central Council: Mr. Richard J. Powell, Pres.; Mr. Carl Rayles, Vice Pres.; Mr. Richard Niklas, Sec.; Mr. Marvin E. Doane, Treas.
District Council of Cincinnati and Subordinate Parish Conferences. 1125 Bank St., 45214. Mr. Mark A. Casella, Pres.; Rev. Herman Kenning, Spiritual Advisor.
District Council of Dayton and Subordinate Parish Conferences. 695 Fulmer Dr., Dayton, 45403. Tel: 937-254-0115. Deacon Robert Zink, Spiritual Advisor; Mr. Jack L. Vandegrift, Pres. & Contact; Philip A. Parmley, Treas.
District Council of Hamilton and Subordinate Parish Conferences, 401 N. Washington Blvd., Hamilton, 45013. Tel: 513-863-5091. Mr. Howard Hetterich, Pres.; Mr. James Meyer, Sec.; Mr. Donald Arent, Treas.; Rev. Charles E. Moore, Spiritual Advisor.
District Council of Springfield and Subordinate Parish Conferences, 2425 E. High St., Springfield, 45505. Deacon Norman G. Horstman, Spiritual Advisor; Mr. Melvin Buck, Pres.; Ms. Audrey Farland, Vice Pres.; Mrs. Janice Drake, Sec.; Mr. Richard Hale, Treas.
District Council of Saint Martin and Subordinate Parish Conferences, 5969 Pinto Pl., Milford, 45150. Tel: 513-575-1246. Mr. Marvin E. Hudson, Pres.; Rev. James N. Peaker, Spiritual Advisor. Tel: 513-232-6006.
St. Vincent de Paul Stores, Inc., 1125 Bank St., 45214. J. Timothy Heile, Dir.
St. Vincent de Paul Stores of Dayton, Ohio, Inc. Tel: 937-222-5555. 945 S. Edwin C. Moses Blvd., Dayton, 45408. Tel: 513-222-5555. Mr. Tony Staub, Dir.
St. Vincent Hotel, Inc., 212 W. Fifth St., Dayton, 45402. Tel: 937-461-7837. James H. Butler, Dir.
De Paul Industries, 15 S. Sinclair St., Dayton, 45402. Tel: 937-461-7837. Mr. James H. Butler, Dir.
Ozanam Center, 5829 Vine St., Elmwood Place, 45215. Tel: 513-562-8841; 8842. Mark A. Casella, Pres.

[T] HEALTH CARE SYSTEMS

CINCINNATI. *Franciscan Health System of the Ohio Valley*, 2446 Kipling Ave., 45239. Tel: 513-853-5000. James Strieby, C.E.O.; R. Christopher West, Pres.; Sr. Arlene McGowan, Vice Pres. Mission and Support Svcs.; Don Rohling, Dir. of Mission. Sisters 3. Includes Franciscan Hospital-Mt. Airy Campus, Franciscan Hospital- Western Hills Campus; the Franciscan at St. Clare; the Franciscan at West Park; Franciscan at St. John; Franciscan Home Development; Franciscan at St. Raphael; Franciscan Home Health Services; Franciscan Diabetes Centers; Franciscan Center for Sight; Franciscan Medicenter-Harrison Campus; Franciscan/University of Cincinnati Family Practice Center; Franciscan Rehabilitation Centers; Franciscan Sports Medicine Centers; Franciscan Holistic Health Center; Franciscan Workplace Health; Franciscan Senior Network; Franciscan Medical Management Services.
Franciscan Health System of the Ohio Valley (FHSOV). A member of the Franciscan Health System of Cincinnati, Inc. 2446 Kipling Ave., 45239. Tel: 513-853-5000. James Strieby, C.E.O.; R. Christopher West, Pres.; Sr. Arlene McGowan, Vice Pres., Mission and Support Svcs.; Don Rohling, Dir. of Mission. Sisters 1.
Mercy Health System, 2335 Grandview Ave., 45206. Tel: 513-221-2736; Fax: 513-559-3835. Michael Connelly, Pres. & CEO. 18 acute care hospitals, 8 long-term care facilities, 1 congregate care residence, 4 elderly housing projects. Mercy Health System is co-sponsored by the Sisters of Mercy, Cincinnati Regional Community; Sisters of Mercy, Dallas (PA) Regional Community; the Sisters of Charity of Montreal, St. Joseph Province. Patients assisted annually 2.3 Million; Residence for Senior Citizens: 325.
Mercy Health System, Greater Cincinnati Regional, 4340 Glendale-Milford Rd., Ste. 100, 45242. Julia Hanser, Pres. & CEO.
Mercy Home Care, 7010 Rowan Hill Dr., 45227. Tel: 513-271-6700.
Sisters of Charity Health Care Systems, Inc., 345 Neeb Rd., 45233. Tel: 513-347-1000. An affiliate of Catholic Health Initiatives.

DAYTON. *Franciscan Health System of the Ohio Valley operations in Dayton, OH*, One Franciscan Way, 45408. Tel: 937-229-6000. Sr. Karen Hartman, S.F.P., Vice Pres.; Allen Weimer, Dir. of Pastoral Care. Includes Franciscan Medical Center-Dayton; the Franciscan at Schroder; the Franciscan at St. Leonard; Franciscan Medicenters; Franciscan Family Practice Center; St. Elizabeth Hopeland Health Center; St. Elizabeth Family Practice Residency Program; Franciscan Home Health Services; Franciscan Rehabilitation Centers; Franciscan Sports Medicine Centers; Franciscan Senior Network; Franciscan Workplace Health; Franciscan Medical Management Services.
Samaritan Health Partners, 2222 Philadelphia Dr., 45406. Tel: 937-278-2612. Affiliate of Catholic Health Initiative.

SPRINGFIELD. *Mercy Health System - Western Ohio, Sisters of Mercy*, 1 S. Limestone St., P.O. Box 688, 45501-0688. Tel: 513-328-7013. Jerrold A. Maki, Pres. & C.E.O.; Roy T. Santarella, Exec. Vice Pres. & C.O.O.

[U] FOUNDATIONS AND ENDOWMENTS

CINCINNATI. *Community Support Charitable Trust*, 1615 Vine St., 45210. Tel: 513-721-4700; Fax: 513-421-9672. Trustees: Revs. Kenan Freson, O.F.M.; Roger Bosse, O.F.M.; Bart Pax, O.F.M. Legal Title: *Community Support Charitable Trust for the Province of St. John the Baptist of the Order of Friars Minor.*
The Congregation of Our Lady of Charity of the Good Shepherd, Community Support Trust, 2849 Fischer Pl., 45211-5915. Tel: 513-661-1833; Fax: 513-661-1216. Sr. Dolores Kalina, Prov.
Eldercare Foundation, Inc. c/o CHI Services, 345 Neeb Rd., 45233. Tel: 513-347-1054. Sr. Celestia Koebel, S.C., Pres.; Mitch H. Milfi, Esq., Sec.
Good Samaritan Hospital Foundation of Cincinnati, Inc., 375 Dixmyth Ave., 45220-2489. Tel: 513-872-3786.
Mercy Hospital Anderson Foundation, 7500 State Rd., 45255. Tel: 513-624-4910; Fax: 513-624-3299. Helen B. Balush, Vice Pres. A Subsidiary of Mercy Hospital Anderson.
Roger Bacon High School Endowment, 4320 Vine St., 45217. Tel: 513-641-1300. Rev. Roger Bosse, O.F.M.
Seton High School Foundation, 3901 Glenway Ave., 45205. Tel: 513-471-2600; Fax: 513-471-0529. Mr. Thomas E. McKiernan, Chm.; Sr. Brenda Busch, S.C., Pres.
Sisters of Charity Foundation, Inc., 345 Neeb Rd., 45233. Tel: 513-347-1000. Sr. Mary Ellen Murphy, S.C., Pres.
Sisters of Charity of Cincinnati-Charitable Trust, 5900 Delhi Rd., 45051. Tel: 513-347-5201. A designated trust fund to primarily support older and infirmed members of the congregation. Sr. Mary Ellen Murphy, S.C., Pres.
Sisters of Notre Dame De Namur, Ohio Province, Charitable Trust, 701 E. Columbia Ave., 45215. Tel: 513-761-7636. Sr. Clare Foley, Prov.
The Summit Country Day School Foundation, 2161 Grandin Rd., 45208. Tel: 513-579-6560. Edward C. Tyrrell, Pres.; Thomas Grote, Jr., Chm.; Richard Alder, Sec. & Treas.
Ursulines of Cincinnati, Ohio Charitable Trust, 1339 E. McMillan St., 45206. Tel: 513-961-3410. Sr. Mary Cabrini Durkin, O.S.U.

DAYTON. *Community Support Charitable Trust*, 431 E. Second St., 45402. Tel: 937-228-9263. Trustees: Revs. Albert A. Reed, C.PP.S.; Thomas R. Brenberger, C.PP.S.; Angelo P. Anthony, C.PP.S.; Scott T. Kramer, C.PP.S.; Thomas J. Beischel, C.PP.S.; Bros. Joseph J. Fisher, C.PP.S.; Thomas R. Bohman, C.PP.S.
**Samaritan Health Foundation*, 2222 Philadelphia Dr., 45406. Tel: 513-278-5770; Fax: 513-874-5140. J. Kay Timmons, Pres. Affiliate of Catholic Health Initiatives.

FAIRFIELD. *Glenmary Home Missioners Charitable Trust*, 4119 Glenmary Trace, 45014. Tel: 513-874-8900. Rev. Robert C. Berson, Trustee.

[V] MISCELLANEOUS LISTINGS

CINCINNATI. *Apostleship of Prayer*, 607 Sycamore St., 45202. Rev. Paul Huber, S.J.
Apostolate to Aid the Dying, 80 Compton Rd., 45215. Tel: 513-821-6332. Sr. M. Cornelia Evans, S.F.P.
Catholic Alumni Club (Cincinnati Chapter), 100 E. 8th St., 45202. Tel: 513-421-3131.
Catholic Charismatic Renewal Liaison, 5924 Bridgetown Rd., 45248. Tel: 513-574-1230. Rev. Richard Dressman.
Catholic Cursillo of Cincinnati, 10290 Mill Rd., 45231. Tel: 513-851-9399. Mary Pat Golden, Dir.; Rev. Allan Schmitz, O.F.M., Spiritual Advisor.
Cincinnati Catholic Women's Association, 958 Marion Ave., 45229. Tel: 513-961-3566. Mary K. Mairose, Pres.
The Comboni Lay Missionaries Association, 8108 Beechmont Ave., 45255-3194. Tel: 513-474-4997. Rev. Angelo Biancalana, M.C.C.J., Pres.; Ms. Sue Howard, Vice Pres.; Sr. Jeanne Oursler, C.S.J., Sec./Treas.
The Comboni Missionaries Auxiliary, Inc., 8108 Beechmont Ave., 45255. Tel: 513-474-4997. Evelyn Huber, Pres.; Catherine Ewers, Vice Pres.; Terry Kunke, Treas.; Janet Tate, Sec.; Mario Ongaro, M.C.C.J., Spiritual Advisor.
Franciscan Brothers Work Crew, St. Clement Friary, 4536 Vine St., 45217. Tel: 513-641-2257. Bro. Louis P. Zant, O.F.M., Mgr.
Franciscan Central Purchasing, St. Clement Friary, 4536 Vine St., 45217. Tel: 513-641-2257. Bro. Louis Zant, O.F.M., Dir.
Franciscan Home Development, Inc. A member of the Franciscan Health System of the Ohio Valley, 1300 Main St., 45210. Tel: 513-651-6457. R. Christopher West, Pres.; Ms. Stephanie Sweeney, Ex. Dir.
Provides housing to over 200 persons in over 171 residential units.
Franciscan Missionary Union, 1615 Vine St., 45210-1297. Tel: 513-721-4700, Ext. 3222. Bro. Scott Obrecht, O.F.M., Exec. Dir.
HIV/AIDS Ministry Team, Archdiocese of Cincinnati, 100 E. Eighth St., 45202. Tel: 513-357-6187. Ms. Kathy Cox, Coord.
Jesuit Development Office, 2245 Gilbert Ave., 45206. Tel: 513-751-6688. Mark J. McLaughlin, Dir.
Legion of Mary, 3105 Madison Rd., 45209. Rev. Elmer W. Smith, Dir.
Living Monuments of Reparation, P.O. Box 29372, 45229. Tel: 513-569-4587. Rev. Herbert J. Raterman, S.J., Dir.
Marian Center of Cincinnati, P.O. Box 388061, 45238. Tel: 513-922-1250. Mr. Robert E. Hater, Lay Dir.; Rev. Robert J. Plagge, Spiritual Dir.
Ministers of Service, 745 Ezzard Charles, 45203. Tel: 513-381-0630. Mr. Jack D. McWilliams, Dir.
New Jerusalem Community, 745 Derby Ave., 45232. Tel: 513-541-4748; Fax: 513-541-4811. Leadership Council: Gerry Becker; Debbie Metz; Jerry Carrico; Charlie Stenken; Kate Ploucha, Coord. Community Life; William A. Zins, Admin.
North American Ursuline Education Services, 1339 E. McMillan St., 45206. Tel: 513-961-3410. Sr. Bernadette Hannaway, O.S.U., Pres.; Sr. Lois Castillion, O.S.U., Exec. Dir.
Priests Eucharistic League, 5222 N. Bend Rd., 45247. Rev. John J. Mattscheck, Dir.
St. Andrew Kim Korean Catholic Society, 3171 Struble Rd., 45251. Tel: 513-851-3065. Revs. John E. Porter; Leslie F. Blowers, M.M.; Mr. Benedict U. Lee, Council Pres.
St. Anthony Messenger, St. Anthony Messenger Press and Franciscan Communications, 1615 Republic St., 45210. Tel: 513-241-5615.
Operated by the St. John the Baptist Province of the Franciscan Friars.
St. Dymphna Chapel, The Lewis Center, State Mental Hospital, P.O. Box 16061, 45216. Tel: 513-821-1608. Rev. Valens J. Waldschmidt, O.F.M.
St. Francis Bookshop. Conducted by the St. John the Baptist Province of the Franciscan Friars. 1618 Vine St., 45210. Tel: 513-241-7304.
Secular Franciscan Order. Holy Trinity Regional Fraternity, Inc. Founded by St. Francis of Assisi before A.D. 1215. Information concerning the Secular Franciscan Order can be obtained from SFO Office, St. Francis Center, 10290 Mill Rd. St. Francis Center, 10290 Mill Rd., 45231. Roo Potts, Minister, (Beaver Creek, OH); Bette Dries, V-Min., (Louisville, KY); Don Lipps, Sec., (Cincinnati, OH); Ralph Bidelman, Treas., (Cincinnati, OH); Ralph Schluetter, Formation Dir., (Cincinnati, OH).
Stimuli, Inc., 17 Erkenbrecher Ave., 45220-2202. Tel: 513-221-3889; 221-5538. Consultants in worship & cultural adaptation and in revitalizing traditional worship. Rev. Clarence R.J. Rivers, Ph.D., Pres.
**The Couple to Couple League International*, 4290 Delhi Pk., 45238. Tel: 513-471-2000; Fax: 513-557-2449. Mailing Address: P.O. Box 111184, 45211. John F. Kippley, Pres.
Vietnamese-Catholic Community, 5440 Moeller Ave.,

45212. Tel: 513-531-3307. Rev. Huan Tien Nguyen.

CENTERVILLE. *Catholic Alumni Club (Dayton Chapter)*, 55 Williamsburg Ln., 45459. Tel: 937-433-1188. Rev. Daniel J. Meyer, Chap.

St. Leonard Faith Community, 8100 Clyo Rd., 45458. Tel: 937-435-3626; 433-7224 (Friary). Rev. Msgr. Anthony J. Giannamore, Moderator/Chap.

DAYTON. *Marianist Voluntary Service Communities, MVSC*, P.O. Box 9224, Wright Bros. Branch, 45409. Tel: 937-229-4630; 229-3287. Michelle Cano, Assoc. Dir.; Ms. Laura Libertore, Dir.

MARIA STEIN. *Maria Stein Shrine of the Holy Relics*, 2291 St. John Rd., 45860. Tel: 419-925-4532; Fax: 513-925-5413. Sr. Patricia Gist, C.PP.S., Admin.

RELIGIOUS INSTITUTES OF MEN REPRESENTED IN THE ARCHDIOCESE

For further details refer to the corresponding bracketed number in the Religious Institutes of Men or Women section.

[]—*Brothers of the Christian Service*.—B.C.S.
[0460]—*Brothers of the Poor of St. Francis*.—C.F.P.
[0380]—*Comboni Missionaries of the Heart of Jesus (Verona)*.—M.C.C.J.
[0520]—*Franciscan Friars*.—O.F.M.
[0570]—*Glenmary Home Missioners*.—Glmy.
[0650]—*Holy Ghost Fathers*. (Eastern Province).—C.S.Sp.
[0690]—*Jesuit Fathers and Brothers*. (Chicago Province).—S.J.
[0800]—*Maryknoll*.—M.M.
[1210]—*Missionaries of St. Charles (Scalabrinians)*.—C.S.
[0430]—*Order of Preachers (Dominicans)*. (St. Joseph Province).—O.P.
[0760]—*Society of Mary (Marianists)*. (Cincinnati Province).—S.M.
[1060]—*Society of the Precious Blood*. (Cincinnati Province).—C.PP.S.
[1310]—*Trinitarians-St. (Servants/Most Holy Trinity)*.—O.SS.T.

RELIGIOUS INSTITUTES OF WOMEN REPRESENTED IN THE ARCHDIOCESE

[0230]—*Benedictine Sisters of Pontifical Jurisdiction*. (Crookston, MN; Covington, KY).—O.S.B.
[0330]—*Carmelite Sisters for the Aged and Infirm*.—O.Carm.
[0870]—*Congregation of the Daughters of Mary Immaculate (Marianist Sisters)*.—F.M.I.
[3710]—*Congregation of the Sisters of Saint Agnes*.—C.S.A.
[1920]—*Congregation of the Sisters of the Holy Cross*.—C.S.C.
[1730]—*Congregation of the Sisters of the Third Order of St. Francis, Oldenburg, IN*.—O.S.F.
[1710]—*Congregation of the Third Order of St. Francis of Mary Immaculate, Joliet, IL*.—O.S.F.
[1070-02]—*Dominican Sisters*. (Blamvelt, NY).—O.P.
[1070-07]—*Dominican Sisters*. (Adrian, MI).—O.P.
[1070-13]—*Dominican Sisters*. (St. Mary of the Springs, Columbus, OH).—O.P.
[1070-15]—*Dominican Sisters*. (Sick Poor).—O.P.
[1070-16]—*Dominican Sisters*. (Nashville, TN).—O.P.
[1440]—*Franciscan Sisters of the Poor*.—S.F.P.
[2340]—*Little Sisters of the Poor*.—L.S.P.
[2470]—*Maryknoll Sisters of St. Dominic*.—M.M.
[2490]—*Medical Mission Sisters*.—M.M.S.
[3760]—*Order of St. Clare-Poor Clares*.—O.S.C.
[3130]—*Our Lady of Victory Missionary Sisters*.—O.L.V.M.
[3230]—*Poor Handmaids of Jesus Christ*.—P.H.J.C.
[0440]—*Sisters of Charity of Cincinnati, Ohio*.—S.C.
[0500]—*Sisters of Charity of Nazareth*.—S.C.N.
[0570]—*Sisters of Charity of Seton Hill, Greensburg, Pennsylvania*.—S.C.
[1000]—*The Sisters of Divine Providence of Kentucky*.—C.D.P.
[2360]—*Sisters of Loretto at the Foot of the Cross*.—S.L.
[2630]—*Sisters of Mercy of the Holy Cross*.—S.C.S.C.
[2580]—*Sisters of Mercy of the Union of the United States of America*.—R.S.M.
[2990]—*Sisters of Notre Dame*. (Covington Prov.).—S.N.D.
[3000]—*Sisters of Notre Dame de Namur*.—S.N.D.deN.
[3360]—*Sisters of Providence of Saint Mary-of-the-Woods, Indiana*.—S.P.
[1630]—*Sisters of St. Francis of Penance and Christian Charity, Stella Niagara, NY*.—O.S.F.
[1530]—*Sisters of St. Francis of the Congregation of Our Lady of Lourdes, Sylvania, Ohio*.—O.S.F.
[3880]—*Sisters of St. Joseph of Medaille*. (Cincinnati Prov.).—C.S.J.
[3840]—*Sisters of St. Joseph of Medaille of Carondelet*. (Latham, NY and St. Louis, MO).—C.S.J.
[1830]—*The Sisters of the Good Shepherd*.—R.G.S.
[2110]—*Sisters of the Humility of Mary*.—H.M.
[3260]—*Sisters of the Precious Blood (Dayton, Ohio)*.—C.PP.S.
[1760]—*Sisters of the Third Order of St. Francis of Penance and Charity*.—O.S.F.
[2150]—*Sisters, Servants of the Immaculate Heart of Mary*.—I.H.M.
[4110]—*Ursuline Nuns (Roman Union)*.—O.S.U.
[4120]—*Ursuline Nuns of the Congregation of Paris*. (Saint Martin).—O.S.U.
[4120-01]—*Ursuline Nuns of the Congregation of Paris (Cincinnati, OH)*.—O.S.U.

CEMETERIES

CINCINNATI. *Calvary*, 1721 Duck Creek Rd., 45207. Tel: 513-961-2179.

Gate of Heaven, 11000 Montgomery Rd., 45242. Tel: 513-489-0300.

St. John, 701 Ross Ave., 45217. Tel: 513-242-4191.

St. Joseph, Eighth St. & Seton Ave., 45205. Tel: 513-921-3050.

St. Joseph New, 4500 Foley Ave., 45238. Tel: 513-251-3110.

St. Mary, 701 Ross Ave., 45217. Tel: 513-242-4191.

DAYTON. *Calvary*, Calvary & Dixie Ave., 45409. Tel: 513-293-1221.

SPRINGFIELD. *Calvary*, 3155 E. Possum Rd., 45502. Tel: 513-513-7474.

NECROLOGY

† Andres, Anthony G., (Retired). —Died Sept. 29, 1996.
† Aufderheide, Edwin J., (Retired). —Died Jan. 16, 1996.
† Molloy, William J., (Retired). —Died Nov. 14, 1996.
† Sauter, John D., (Retired). —Died Sept. 28, 1996.
† Sherman, Rev. Msgr. James E., (Retired). —Died July 20, 1996.
† Williams, Brian J, St. Martin, OH St. Martin Church. —Died Aug. 1, 1996.

Diocese of Cleveland

(Dioecesis Clevelandensis)

Most Reverend

ANTHONY M. PILLA, D.D., M.A.

Bishop of Cleveland; ordained May 23, 1959; appointed Auxiliary and Titular Bishop of Scardona June 30, 1979; consecrated August 1, 1979; named Apostolic Administrator of Cleveland July 29, 1980; appointed Bishop of Cleveland November 18, 1980; installed January 6, 1981. *Office: 1027 Superior Ave., Cleveland, OH, 44114.* Tel.: 216-696-6525; 800-869-6525 (Ohio only); Fax: 216-696-6547.

Most Reverend

A. EDWARD PEVEC, PH.D.

Auxiliary Bishop of Cleveland; ordained April 29, 1950; appointed Auxiliary and Titular Bishop of Mercia April 13, 1982; consecrated July 2, 1982. *Office: Center for Pastoral Leadership, 28700 Euclid Ave., Wickliffe, OH, 44092.* Tel.: 216-944-1400; Fax: 216-943-7577.

Most Reverend

A. JAMES QUINN, J.C.D., J.D.

Auxiliary Bishop of Cleveland; ordained May 24, 1958; appointed Auxiliary and Titular Bishop of Socia October 14, 1983; consecrated December 5, 1983. *Office: 2500 Elyria Ave., Lorain, OH, 44055.* Tel.: 216-244-2120; 579-0326 (Cleveland Line); Fax: 216-899-1122.

ESTABLISHED APRIL 23, 1847.

Square Miles 3,414.

Comprises since July 22, 1943, eight Counties in the north-central part of the State of Ohio, namely Ashland, Cuyahoga, Geauga, Lake, Lorain, Medina, Summit and Wayne Counties.

For legal titles of parishes and diocesan institutions, consult the Chancery Office.

Chancery Building: 1027 Superior Ave., Cleveland, OH, 44114. Tel.: 216-696-6525; 800-869-6525 (Ohio only); Fax: 216-621-7332.

STATISTICAL OVERVIEW

Personnel	
Bishop	1
Auxiliary Bishops	2
Abbots	1
Priests: Diocesan Active in Diocese	375
Priests: Active Outside Diocese	17
Priests: Diocesan in Foreign Missions	5
Priests: Retired, Sick or Absent	105
Number of Diocesan Priests	502
Religious Priests in Diocese	147
Extern Priests in Diocese	26
Ordinations:	
Diocesan Priests	2
Transitional Deacons	3
Permanent Deacons	11
Permanent Deacons in Diocese	155
Total Brothers	74
Total Sisters	1,628
Parishes	
Parishes	236
With Resident Pastor:	
Resident Diocesan Priests	214
Resident Religious Priests	18
Without Resident Pastor:	
Administered by Priests	2
Administered by Permanent Deacons	1
Administered by Women Religious	1
Missions	1
Pastoral Centers	3
Closed Parishes	1
Professional Ministry Personnel:	
Brothers	5
Sisters	115
Lay Ministers	205
Welfare	
Catholic Hospitals	2
Total Assisted	134,514
Homes for the Aged	24
Total Assisted	3,117
Residential Care of Children	1
Total Assisted	248
Day Care and Extended Day Care Centers	6
Total Assisted	1,204
Specialized Homes	5
Total Assisted	1,173
Special Centers for Social Services	21
Total Assisted	532,748
Residential Care of Disabled	1
Total Assisted	188
Other Institutions	3
Total Assisted	68,221
Educational	
Seminaries, Diocesan	2
Students from This Diocese	49
Students from Other Diocese	2
Diocesan Students in Other Seminaries	1
Students Religious	7
Total Seminarians	57
Colleges and Universities	3
Total Students	6,190
High Schools, Diocesan and Parish	7
Total Students	4,360
High Schools, Private	16
Total Students	10,087
Elementary Schools, Diocesan and Parish	134
Total Students	49,471
Elementary Schools, Private	7
Total Students	2,479
Non-residential Schools for the Disabled	1
Total Students	76
Catechesis/Religious Education:	
High School Students	7,108
Elementary Students	44,943
Total Students Under Catholic Instruction	124,771
Teachers in the Diocese:	
Priests	28
Brothers	29
Sisters	252
Lay Teachers	3,146
Vital Statistics	
Receptions into the Church:	
Infant Baptism Totals	11,294
Adult Baptism Totals	1,053
Received into Full Communion	930
First Communions	12,220
Confirmations	9,324
Marriages:	
Catholic	3,096
Interfaith	1,825
Total Marriages	4,921
Deaths	8,610
Total Catholic Population	830,130
Total Population	2,811,515

Former Bishops—Rt. Rev. AMADEUS RAPPE, D.D., cons. Oct. 10, 1847; resigned Aug. 22, 1870; died Sept 8, 1877.—Rt. Rev. RICHARD GILMOUR, D.D., cons. April 14, 1872; died April 13, 1891.—Rt. Rev. IGNATIUS F. HORSTMANN, D.D., cons. Feb. 25, 1892; died May 13, 1908.—Rt. Rev. JOHN P. FARRELLY, D.D., cons. May 1, 1909; died Feb. 12, 1921.—Most Rev. JOSEPH SCHREMBS, S.T.D., Archbishop-Bishop of Cleveland; cons. Feb. 22, 1911; transferred to the See of Cleveland, June 16, 1921; installed Sept. 8, 1921; appt. Archbishop, March 25, 1939; died November 2, 1945.—Most Rev. EDWARD F. HOBAN, S.T.D., Ph.D., L.L.D., Archbishop-Bishop of Cleveland; cons. Dec. 21, 1921; transferred to Cleveland as Coadjutor Bishop "cum jure successionis" Nov. 14, 1942; succeeded to See of Cleveland, Nov. 2, 1945; appt. Archbishop, July 23, 1951; died Sept. 22, 1966.—Most Rev. CLARENCE G. ISSENMANN, S.T.D., cons. May 25, 1954; transferred to Cleveland as Coadjutor Bishop "cum jure successionis" and Titular Bishop of Filaca. Ap-Adm. Oct. 7, 1964; succeeded to See of Cleveland, Sept. 22, 1966; retired June 5, 1974; died July 27, 1982.—Most Rev. JAMES A. HICKEY, S.T.D., J.C.D., cons. April 14, 1967; appt. Bishop of Cleveland, June 5, 1974; installed July 16, 1974; appt. Archbishop of Washington, DC June 18, 1980; created Cardinal by Pope John Paul II in the consistory on June 28, 1988.

Vicars General—Most Rev. A. EDWARD PEVEC, Ph.D., *Center For Pastoral Leadership, 28700 Euclid Ave., Wickliffe, 44092.* Tel: 216-944-1400. Most Rev. A. JAMES QUINN, J.C.D., J.D., *2500 Elyria Ave., Lorain, 44055.* Tel: 216-244-2120; 579-0326 Cleveland Line. Rev. RALPH E. WIATROWSKI, Chancellor, *1027 Superior Ave., Cleveland, 44114.* Tel: 216-696-6525.

College of Consultors—Rt. Rev. ROGER GRIES, O.S.B.; Rev. Msgr. ROBERT BACHER; Revs. RAY BARTNIKOWSKI; JOHN CREGAN; MARK HOLLIS; JOSEPH H.

KRAKER; THOMAS MCGOVERN; JOHN OLSAVSKY; PAUL ROSING; ROBERT SANSON; ANTHONY ZEPP; RALPH E. WIATROWSKI, Sec.

Presbyteral Council—Revs. MARK L. HOLLIS, Moderator; RICHARD C. ANTALL; ROBERT E. BACHER; LEONARD BACIK; RALPH L. COLETTA; EDWARD T. ESTOK; THOMAS A. MCGOVERN; STEPHEN RADECKY; LAWRENCE JURCAK; Rt. Rev. ROGER GRIES, O.S.B.; Revs. DANIEL F. SCHLEGEL; DAVID R. TRASK; ANTHONY W. ZEPP,Presbyteral Conveners: Revs. NELSON CALLAHAN; THOMAS A. HAREN; DENNIS J. KLEINWEBER; JOHN R. OLSAVSKY; WILLIAM B. PADAVICK; PAUL J. ROSING; JOHN J. CREGAN; MARK A. DINARDO; MARK L. HOLLIS; DAVE R. IRELAND; DANIEL L. BEGIN; DOUGLAS MAKOWSKI; ROBERT C. WOLFF.

Finance Council—Most Rev. ANTHONY M. PILLA, Pres.; Sr. MARY NATHAN, S.N.D.; ANTHONY LANG; JOHN P. MCGINTY; CASIMIR J. RUTT; KEVIN O'DONNELL; NORMAN T. PATTON; WILLIAM J. REIDY.

Diocesan Pastoral Council—Most Rev. ANTHONY M. PILLA, Pres.; DONALD R. BECK, Vice Pres.; MARY CHRISTINE JACKMAN; RICHARD KRIVANKA, Exec. Sec.

Conference of Religious Leadership—Sr. MARGARET TAYLOR, S.I.W., Chm., *6618 Pearl Rd., Parma Heights, 44130*. Tel: 216-886-6440. Sr. ROCHELLE GUERTAL, O.SS.T., Sec./Treas., *1355 W. 70th St., Cleveland, 44102*. Tel: 216-281-7146.

Diocese of Cleveland—

Chancery Building—1027 Superior Ave., Cleveland, 44114.

Catholic Center—1031 Superior Ave., Cleveland, 44114.

All Diocesan Offices in the Chancery Building or in the Catholic Center may be reached at Tel: 216-696-6525 or 800-869-6525 (Ohio only); Fax: 216-781-8243.

Address dispensations and all business communication to the Chancery Office.

Chancellor—Rev. RALPH E. WIATROWSKI, J.C.D. S.T.L., Office: *Chancery Building*. Fax: 216-621-7332.

Vice-Chancellor—Rev. DAVID J. WALKOWIAK, J.C.D., Office: *Chancery Building*.

Assistant Chancellors—Revs. THEODORE MARSZAL, Office: *Catholic Center,* JOSEPH E. LEHANE, Office: *40 University Ave., Akron, 44308*. Tel: 330-434-4114. Sr. LAURA BOUHALL, O.S.U., Office: *Chancery Building*.

Secretary to Bishop Pilla—Rev. THEODORE MARSZAL, Office: *Catholic Center.*

Judicial Offices—

Office of Mediation—Sr. DONNA MIKULA, O.S.U., *Chancery Building*. Tel: 216-696-6525; 800-869-6525.

Tribunal—Office: *1027 Superior Ave., Ste. 500, Cleveland, 44114*. Tel: 216-696-6525 Ext. 400; 800-869-6525 (Ohio only); 800-676-4431; Fax: 216-696-3226.

Judicial Vicar—Rev. MARK Q. FEDOR, J.C.D.

Adjutant Vicars—Revs. DONALD P. BRICKMAN, J.C.L.; LAWRENCE JURCAK, J.C.L.; THOMAS A. MORAN, J.C.D.; GARY D. YANUS, J.C.D.

Judges—Deacon LOUIS G. PECEK, Ph.D.; Sr. JEAN C. IFFARTH, O.S.U., J.C.L.

Defenders of the Bond—Revs. JOSEPH A. BACEVICE, M.Div.; WILLIAM M. JERSE, J.C.L.; Sr. CHRISTINE MARIE RODY, V.S.C., J.C.L.; Revs. MICHAEL J. TROHA, M.A., M.Div.; PETER D. WASLO, J.C.L.

Associate Judicial Vicars—Revs. MIRKO HLADNI, J.C.L.; EDWARD J. LUCA, J.C.D.; JOHN R. OLSAVSKY, J.C.L.; WILLIAM P. O'NEILL, J.C.L.; ROBERT F. PFEIFFER, J.C.L.; ROBERT J. SANSON, J.C.D.; DAVID J. WALKOWIAK, J.C.D.; EDWARD F. WEIST, J.C.D.; RALPH E. WIATROWSKI, J.C.D.

Associate Judges—Deacon JAMES L. AGRIPPE; Rev. MARTIN J. AMOS; Sr. MARY ANN ANDREWS, C.S.A., J.C.L.; Revs. NELSON J. CALLAHAN, M.Div.; GARY D. CHMURA, M.Div.; CHARLES T. DIEDRICK, M.A.; JEROME J. DUKE; JOHN R. HENGLE; ALAN R. LAUBENTHAL, S.T.D.; JOHN E. MANNING, M.Div.; LAWRENCE N. MARTELLO, M.Div.; THOMAS W. MCCANN; JOHN J. MUELLER; CORNELIUS J. MURRAY, M.S.E.; PAUL J. ROSING, M.Div.; THOMAS R. SMITH, M.Div.; ARTHUR SNEDEKER, M.Div.; DONALD E. SNYDER, M.Div.; CHARLES J. STOLLENWERK, M.Div.; ALBERT J. TESEK; ROBERT M. WENDELKEN, M.Div.; ANTHONY W. ZEPP, M.Div.

Assessor—Mr. WILLIAM P. GILMORE, L.I.S.W.

Auditor/Assessor—Revs. ALLEN F. CORRIGAN, M.Div.; DONALD P. OLEKSIAK, M.Div.

Procurators—Revs. JOSEPH HILINSKI, M.Div.; ROBERT J. KROPAC, S.T.B.; THEODORE MARSZAL, S.T.D.; DAVID R. TRASK, M.Div.; DAVID J. WEBER, M.Div.

Promoter of Justice—Sr. CHRISTINE C. RODY, V.S.C., J.C.L.

Notaries—Ms. MARY M. BRYAN. Notary Public: Miss CYNTHIA M. QUINLAN; Miss DENISE C. RABATIN.

Translators—Mr. RIAD BAHUR; Revs. RICHARD R. BOBER, Ph.D.; EDWARD ESTOK, M.A., M.Div.; BEDE KOTLINSKI, O.S.B.; AUGUSTINE PHAM VAN LAN, Ph.D.; JOHN F. WESSEL.

Administrator of Buildings—MICHAEL E. SUHY, *Chancery Building*.

Archivist—Rev. RALPH E. WIATROWSKI; CHRISTINE L. KROSEL, Dir., *Chancery Building*.

Catholic Cemeteries Association—Rev. JAMES J. GRANDILLO, Dir. THOMAS J. KELLEY, Admin., *10000 Miles Ave., Box 05310, Cleveland, 44105*. Tel: 216-641-7575.

Callistian Guild—P.O. Box 605044, Cleveland, 44105. Tel: 216-641-7575.

Central Purchasing—EDWARD J. ZAMISKA, Dir., *3020 Superior Ave., Cleveland, 44114*. Tel: 216-696-4811; 800-362-9016.

Communications Department—Rev. MICHAEL G. DIMENGO, Dir., *Chancery Building*. Tel: 216-696-6525, Ext. 454.

Office for Public Relations—ROBERT A. POLOMSKY, Assoc. Dir., *Chancery Building*.

Radio and Television Productions—MARY FLYNN, Assoc. Dir.

Audio Communications Center, Inc.—Rev. MICHAEL G. DIMENGO, Dir., Office: *Chancery Building*.

"Catholic Universe Bulletin"—Most Rev. ANTHONY M. PILLA, Publisher; Rev. MICHAEL G. DIMENGO, Assoc. Publisher; JOSEPH M. POLITO, Gen. Mgr., Office: *Chancery Building*. Tel: 216-696-6525, Ext. 587; 696-6525, Ext. 277 (after 5 p.m.).

Catholic Universe Bulletin Publishing Company, Inc.—Chancery Building.

Diocesan Pastoral Planning Office—RICHARD S. KRIVANKA, Dir. MARIE HIRSCH, Coord., Special Projects; Sr. MARY PATRICIA RICKARD, S.N.D., Consultant, Parish Pastoral Council Svcs. JEAN S. CLEARY, Office Coord., Office: *Chancery Building*.

Mission Office, Society for the Propagation of the Faith—Rev. DENIS L. ST. MARIE, Dir., Office: *The Catholic Center*, Ext. 424.

Pontifical Programs—Society for the Propagation of the Faith; Society of St. Peter the Apostle; Missionary Union of the Clergy; Holy Childhood Assoc.

National Programs—Latin-American Program; Lay Mission Volunteers.

Diocesan Programs—Missionary Cooperation Plan; St. Francis Xavier Mission Assoc.; Cleveland Diocesan Mission, C.A.

National Shrine of Immaculate Conception—Washington, DC. Rev. RALPH E. WIATROWSKI, Chancellor, *Chancery Building*.

Financial & Legal

Financial—Rev. JOHN J. WRIGHT, J.D., Financial/Legal Sec. JOSEPH H. SMITH, Treasurer, *Chancery Building*.

Legal—SANTIAGO FELICIANO, *Chancery Building*.

Catholic Lawyers' Guild of Cleveland—Chancery Building.

Catholic Lawyers' Guild of Cleveland Endowment Trust—Chancery Building.

Diocesan Budget Committee—RICHARD MARRAPESSE, Chm., *Chancery Building*.

Diocesan Building Commission—Rev. JOHN J. WRIGHT, J.D., Coord.

Department of Diocesan Fund Development—AUGUST A. NAPOLI, Jr., Coord.

Diocesan Insurance Service Committee—(DISC). Members: J. THOMAS HANNON; THOMAS MCGOWAN, III; DENNIS P. TOP.

Diocesan Financial Advisory Committee—JACK P. MCGINTY, Chm.

Health Benefits—PALMIRA JUREVICIUS, *Catholic Center.*

Group Life and Pension Plans—JORDAN J. USSAI, *Catholic Center.*

Workers' Compensation Office—JORDAN J. USSAI, Admin., *Catholic Center.*

Informational Services Office—MICHAEL NOVICKY, Office: *Chancery Building*.

Secretariat for Education

Secretary—Sr. CAROL ANNE SMITH, H.M., *The Catholic Center.* Tel: 216-696-6525, Ext. 328; Fax: 216-696-8646.

Departments—

Administrative Services/School Food Services/Summer Food Service Program—RENE WEBER, Dir., *Catholic Center.*

Buildings and Grounds—DANIEL BRODNIK, Dir., *Catholic Center.*

Department of Fund Development—Mrs. KENDRA GEVRY, Dir., *Catholic Center.*

Catholic Education Endowment Trust—Catholic Center—

Inner-City School Fund—Catholic Center—

Office of Catechetical Services—DORIS KOSKO, Office Mgr., *Catholic Center.* Fax: 216-696-6206.

Newman Campus Ministry—WILLIAM FICHTER, Assoc. Dir., *Catholic Center.*

Ministers—EMILY HOLTEL, *Akron University*. Tel: 330-376-3585. MARIE DE LABRUERE, *Case Western Reserve University, Hallinan Center.* Tel: 216-421-1522. MATTHEW MARUGGI, *Lakeland Community College*. Tel: 216-953-4803. Rev. EDWIN A. DOWLING, *Ashland University*. Tel: 419-994-4396. MAUREEN MASTERSON, *College of Wooster.* Tel: 216-263-2096. WILLIAM A. FICHTER, *Baldwin-Wallace College*. Tel: 216-243-4955. Rev. EDWARD KORDAS, *Oberlin College*. Tel: 216-775-8103. MAUREEN MASTERSON, *Cuyahoga Community College-West*. Tel: 216-886-1327. MATTHEW MARUGGI, *Case Western Reserve University, Hallinan Center.* Tel: 216-421-1522. WILLIAM FICHTER, *Cuyahoga Community College-Metro*. Tel: 216-987-4239. EMILY HOLTEL, *Lorain County Community College*. Tel: 216-365-5222, ext. 7661; 800-995-5222.

Religious Education Office—DENISE SMITHBERGER, Assoc. Dir., *Catholic Center.*

Area Religious Education Consultants—Vacant, *Western Area Office, 2500 Elyria Ave., Lorain, 44055*. Tel: 216-233-1612, 216-871-5246 (Cleveland line). DENISE SMITHBERGER; WILLIAM B. MILLER, *Southern Area, 1025 Clay St., Akron, 44301*. Tel: 330-773-7621. MARY LOU NECKEL, *Eastern Area Office, Hallinan Center, 11303 Euclid Ave., Cleveland, 44106*. Tel: 216-421-1522. MICHAEL YOUNGBLOOD, *Central Area Office, Catholic Center, 1031 Superior Ave., Cleveland, 44114*. Tel: 216-696-6525, Ext. 320.

Media Library—Sr. JOAN PETERSEN, O.S.U., *Catholic Center,* KATHLEEN RHAMY, *Catholic Center.*

Office of Catholic Education—Sr. CAROL ANNE SMITH, H.M., Sec. for Education/Supt.; Sr. KATHLEEN SKUTA C.S.F.N., Sec. Asst., *Catholic Center.* Tel: 216-696-6525, Ext. 328.

Curriculum—Sr. MARY THERESE BERRY, H.M., Dir. Catholic Ctr.

Field Directors—Sr. BARBARA BROMEIER, H.M., *Eastern Area Office, Hallinan Center, 11303 Euclid Ave., Cleveland, 44106*. Tel: 216-421-1522. Sr. LUCIA BUCHOLTZ, S.S.J.-T.O.S.F., *Western Area Office, 2500 Elyria Ave., Lorain, 44055*. Tel: 216-244-1612; 871-5246 (Cleveland line). Sr. PATRICIA KIDDER, I.H.M., *Southern Area Office, 1025 Clay St., Akron, 44301*. Tel: 330-773-7621.

School Planning Process—Sr. ANNE GLASER, S.N.D., Dir., *Catholic Center.*

Registrar—CASEY SCAFIDI, *Catholic Center.*

Catholic Parent Teacher League—CHARLOTTE TARICSKA, Pres., *1031 E. 68th St., Cleveland, 44103*. Tel: 216-431-6690. MARIANNE SOMMERFELT, Corresponding Sec., *3825 Independence Rd., Cleveland, 44105*. Tel: 216-883-6855.

Finance, Policy and Planning—LISA A.B. RACHUL, Business Mgr., *Catholic Center.*

Secondary Education—MARGARET LYONS, Dir., *Catholic Center.*

Government Programs—MICHAEL VOINOVICH, Dir., *Catholic Center.*

Mandated Services—Consultants: CHERYL FASCIANO; RAY PUDELSKI; MICHELE WINTER, *Catholic Center.*

Secretariat for Parish Life and Development

Secretary—Sr. RITA MARY HARWOOD, S.N.D., *Catholic Center*, Ext. 350.

Blue Army of Our Lady of Fatima—Marian Center, 6626 Pearl Rd., Parma Heights, 44130-3808. Tel: 216-888-8553.

Catholic Renewal Ministries—Rev. ROBERT FRANCO, *16271 Pearl Rd., Strongsville, 44136*. Tel: 216-238-1770., *Bishop's Delegate, Presentation House, 28706 Euclid Ave., Wickliffe, 44092*. Tel: 216-944-9445.

Central City Ministry with Poor—Rev. JAMES P. O'DONNELL, *2186 E. 35th St., Cleveland, 44115*. Tel: 216-566-0531.

Cleveland Diocesan Council, NCCW—MARYALICE O'BRIEN, Pres., *Catholic Center;* Rev. RALPH HUDAK, Moderator, *4427 Rocky River Dr., Cleveland, 44135*. Tel: 216-251-8286.

Diocesan Interfaith Commission—Rev. JOSEPH J. HILINSKI, Delegate, *Catholic Center,* Ext. 511.

Enthronement of the Sacred Heart—Diocesan Center, St. John Cathedral Rectory, 1007 Superior Ave., Cleveland, 44114. Tel: 216-267-4713. MARGARET OLLE, Sec.

Ethnic Ministries—

Diocesan Hispanic Office—Sr. JOAQUINA CARRION, M.S.B.T., Dir., *Catholic Center,* Ext. 430.

Korean Catholic Apostolate—Rev. PETER YOUNG-KEU SIN, *St. Andrew Kim (Korean Pastoral Center), 2310 West 14th St., Cleveland, 44113*. Tel: 216-861-4630.

Native American Ministry—Sr. JOAN LANG, C.S.J., Dir., *Catholic Center,* Ext. 350.

Office of Ministry to African American Catholics—VANESSA GRIFFIN CAMPBELL, Dir., *Catholic Center,* Ext. 302.

Philippine-American Ministry—Rev. GREGORIO BANGA, Dir., *12021 Mayfield Rd., Cleveland, 44106*. Tel: 216-421-2995.

Vietnamese-American Apostolate—Rev. AUGUSTINE PHAM VAN LAN, Dir., *3545 W. 54th St., Cleveland,*

44102. Tel: 216-961-2713.
Office of Evangelization—Sr. VIRGINIA STASIUM, S.S.N.D., Dir., *Catholic Center,* Ext. 254.
Holy Name Societies, Cleveland Diocesan Union—Rev. THOMAS HAREN, Spiritual Dir., *15000 Lake Shore Blvd., Cleveland, 44110-1298.* Tel: 216-481-8200.
Pastoral Ministry Office—KATHLEEN HAASE-FALBO, Dir., *Center for Pastoral Leadership, 28700 Euclid Ave., Wickliffe, 44092.* Tel: 216-943-7670.
Legion of Mary—Rev. HERMAN B. PETERS, Spiritual Dir., Office: *1007 Superior Ave., Cleveland, 44114.*
Office for Pastoral Liturgy—Rev. J-GLENN MURRAY, Dir., *Catholic Center,* Ext. 412.
Office for Women in Church and Society—DEBRA MARSEY, Acting Dir., *Catholic Center,* Ext. 307.
St. Joseph Christian Life Center—Rev. WALTER J. HYCLAK, Exec. Dir., *18485 Lake Shore Blvd., Cleveland, 44119.* Tel: 216-531-7370.

Secretariat for Clergy and Religious

Secretary—Rev. JOHN F. MURPHY, Ph.D., Vicar for Clergy and Religious, *The Catholic Center.*
Borromeo Seminary—See Seminaries.
Clergy Personnel Board—Rev. LAWRENCE JURCAK, J.C.L., M.Div., Dir., *The Catholic Center.*
Continuing Education and Formation of Ministers—Rev. DONALD E. SNYDER, M.Div., Dir., *The Center for Pastoral Leadership, 28700 Euclid Ave., Wickliffe, 44092.*
Office for Religious—Sr. CHRISTINE RODY, V.S.C., Delegate, *The Catholic Center.*
Permanent Diaconate—Deacon KENNETH PIECHOWSKI, Dir., *The Center for Pastoral Leadership, 28700 Euclid Ave., Wickliffe, 44092.*
Retirement Board—Revs. JAMES CONRY, Chm., *Sacred Heart Parish, 272 Broad St., Wadsworth, 44281.* Tel: 216-336-3049. Rev. THOMAS L. WEBER, Sec., *Holy Family, 7367 York Rd., Parma, 44130.* Tel: 216-842-5533.
St. Mary Seminary—See Seminaries.
Senior Priests—Rev. JOSEPH MCMAHON, Delegate, *St. Vincent Charity Hosp., 2351 E. 22nd St., Cleveland, 44115.* Tel: 216-861-6200.
Vocations Office—Co-Dirs.: Rev. ROBERT STEC; Sr. MARY ROSE KOCAB, S.I.W., *The Catholic Center.*
Avilas of the Diocese of Cleveland—RUTH MERRIMAN, Pres., *The Catholic Center.*
Parents of Priests—DONALD TRASK, Pres., *The Catholic Center.*

Secretariat for Social Concerns

Secretary—J. THOMAS MULLEN, M.S.W., C.S.W., *The Catholic Center, 1111 Superior Ave., Cleveland, 44114.* Tel: 216-696-6525, Ext. 416; Fax: 216-344-9962.
Catholic Charities Parish Services—TERRENCE FLANAGAN, Senior Dir., *1031 Superior Ave., Cleveland, 44114.* Tel: 216-696-6525, Ext. 503; Fax: 216-344-9962.
Office of Ministry for Persons with Disabilities—Rev. JOSEPH MCNULTY, M.Div., M.Th., Exec. Dir., *St. Augustine Church, 2486 W. 14th St., Cleveland, 44113.* Tel: 216-781-5530; Fax: 216-781-1124.
Marriage and Family Office—Rev. STEPHEN J. DOHNER, Dir., *1031 Superior Ave., Cleveland, 44114.* Tel: 216-696-6525, Ext. 357.
Catholic Information and Referral Service (CIRS)—JANE HORRIGAN, Dir., *1031 Superior Ave., Cleveland, 44114.* Tel: 216-696-HELP (4357); 800-869-6525, Ext. 243; 439; Fax: 216-344-9962.
Youth and Young Adult Ministry and CYO Office—GREG MOSER, Dir., *1031 Superior Ave., Cleveland, 44114.* Tel: 216-696-6525.
Migration and Refugee Services—DIANE SHERBAN, Dir., *1736 Superior Ave., Cleveland, 44114.* Tel: 216-566-9500; Fax: 216-566-9161.
Pro Life Office—COLLEEN GALLAGHER, Dir., *1031 Superior Ave., Cleveland, 44114.* Tel: 216-696-6525 (Ext. 360); 800-869-6525 (Central Office of Diocese); Fax: 216-781-8243., Satellite Office:: *795 Russell, Akron, 44037.* Tel: 330-535-5767.
Catholic Charities Services Corporation—J. THOMAS MULLEN, Pres. & CEO; JOHN P. KLEE, Exec. Vice Pres. and COO, *1111 Superior Ave., Cleveland, 44114.* Tel: 216-696-6525, Ext. 416; Fax: 216-344-9962.
Children and Family Services—THOMAS WOLL, Senior Dir., , Ext. 802.
Disabilities Services—DENNIS MCNULTY, Senior Dir., , Ext. 249.
Emergency and Transitional Assistance Program—CHIP JOSEPH, Senior Dir., , Ext. 352.
Other Adult Services—JEAN THERRIEN, Senior Dir., , Ext. 393.
Catholic Charities Facilities Corp.—LAWRENCE E. MURTAGH, Pres. & CEO, *1111 Superior Ave., Cleveland, 44114.* Tel: 216-696-6525, Ext. 554; Fax: 216-344-9962.
Catholic Charities Corporation—AUGUST A. NAPOLI, JR., Pres. & CEO, *1111 Superior Ave., Cleveland, 44114.* Tel: 216-696-6525, Ext. 604; Fax: 216-348-0740.
Diocesan Social Action Office—THOMAS J. ALLIO, Dir., *1031 Superior Ave., Cleveland, 44114.* Tel: 216-696-6525, Ext. 374; Fax: 216-781-8243.
Catholic Action Commission of Lorain County—SHARON KLEPPEL, Dir., *2500 Elyria Ave., Lorain, 44055.* Tel: 216-244-6037; Fax: 216-899-1122.
Catholic Commission of Lake and Geauga Counties—Sr. MADELINE SHEMO, H.M., Dir., *Schrembs Hall, 28706 Euclid Ave., Wickliffe, 44092.* Tel: 216-585-7745; Fax: 216-585-7747.
Catholic Commission (Summit County)—THOMAS J. ALLIO, Dir., *729 Russell Ave., Akron, 44307.* Tel: 330-535-2787; Fax: 330-535-9040.
Catholic Commission of Wayne, Ashland and Medina Counties—PATRICK O'BRIEN, Exec. Dir., *521 Beall Ave., P.O. Box 15, Wooster, 44691.* Tel: 330-263-6176; Fax: 330-262-4633., Satellite Office: *72 Public Square, Ste. 2, Medina, 44256.* Tel: 330-722-1851.
Campaign for Human Development—ROCKY ORTIZ, Coord., *1031 Superior Ave., Cleveland, 44114.* Tel: 216-696-6525, Ext. 228; Fax: 216-781-8243.

CLERGY, PARISHES, MISSIONS AND PAROCHIAL SCHOOLS

CITY OF CLEVELAND
(Cuyahoga County)

1—CATHEDRAL OF ST. JOHN THE EVANGELIST (1848), Revs. David C. Weber, Rector; James J. Grandillo; Deacon Kenneth J. Piechowski. In res., Revs. Theodore Marszal; Lawrence Jurcak; John F. Murphy; Michael G. Dimengo; Donald P. Brickman.
Res., 1007 Superior Ave., N.E., 44114-2582. Tel: 216-771-6666; Fax: 216-781-5646.
Church—E. 9th St. & Superior Ave. N.E., 44114.
Catechesis/Religious Programs—Students 150.

2—ST. ADALBERT (1883), Rev. Jerome Steinbrunner, C.PP.S.; Lemuel J. Walcott, Pastoral Assoc.
Res., 2347 E. 83rd St., 44104. Tel: 216-881-7647.
School—2345 E. 83rd St., 44104. Tel: 216-881-6250; Fax: 216-881-9030. Mrs. Lydia M. Harris, Prin.
Lay Teachers 16; Students 400.

3—ST. AGNES - OUR LADY OF FATIMA (1980), Rev. Michael K. Barth, S.T.
Res., 6805 Quimby Ave., 44103. Tel: 216-391-3947; 391-1655 (Office); Fax: 216-391-7919.
Church—6800 Lexington Ave., 44103. Tel: 216-391-1655.

4—ST. ALOYSIUS - ST. AGATHA (1975), Revs. Paul M. Marshall, S.M.; Eldon Reichert, S.M.; Bro. Michael O'Grady, Pastoral Assoc.
Res., 10932 St. Clair Ave., 44108-1939. Tel: 216-451-3262; 3263; Fax: 216-268-3830.
Schools—640 Lakeview Rd., N.E., 44108. Tel: 216-451-2050; Fax: 216-541-1601. Sr. Sandra Lea Sabo, S.S.J.-T.O.S.F., Prin.
Sisters 2; Lay Teachers 8; Students 258; St. Joseph School, Tel: 216-451-2143; Fax: 216-451-8832.
Lay Teachers 8; Students 258.
Convent—653 E. 109th St., 44108-1939. Tel: 216-791-9530.

5—ST. ANDREW (1906) (Slovak), Rev. Raphael Zbin, O.S.B.
Res., 5135 Superior Ave., 44103. Tel: 216-431-2057.

6—ST. ANDREW KIM (1988) (Korean), Rev. Peter Young Keu Sin; Sr. Benedicta Young Hee Ha, Admin.
Res., 2310 West 14th St., 44113. Tel: 216-861-4630; Fax: 216-241-6366.
Convent—2496 W. 14th St., 44113. Tel: 216-861-4408.

7—ANNUNCIATION (1924), Rev. Russell J. Banner. Pastoral Assocs.: Sr. Janet Bednar, C.S.J.; Sr. Marilyn Nickol, C.S.J.
Res., 4697 W. 130th St., 44135-3798. Tel: 216-671-2015; Fax: 216-941-1014.

8—ASCENSION (1946), Rev. Joseph J. Fortuna. Pastoral Assocs.: Ms. Laurel A. Jurecki; Ms. Lori Ashyk; Deacon John Koch.
Res., 14040 Puritas Ave., 44135. Tel: 216-671-5890; 5891; Fax: 216-671-2320.
School—4400 W. 140th St., 44135. Tel: 216-941-3715. Sr. Laura Bregar, O.S.U., Prin.
Lay Teachers 21; Students 467.
Convent—4370 W. 140th St., 44135.

9—ST. AUGUSTINE (1860), Rev. Joseph D. McNulty. Pastoral Assocs.: Sr. Corita Ambro, C.S.J.; Mary Ellen Czelusniak; Sr. Audrey Koch, C.S.J.; Deacons John M. Rivera; Edmund J. Karecki; Louis Woyton.
Res., 2486 W. 14th St., 44113. Tel: 216-781-5530.
School—Metro Catholic Parish School. See Separate Listing under Elementary Schools, Parochial and Diocesan.
Catechesis/Religious Programs—Mrs. Sheila Gelzinis, D.R.E.
Students 435.
Convent—2432 W. 14th St., 44113. Tel: 216-579-1306.

10—ST. BARBARA (1905) (Polish), Rev. Chester C. Cudnik.
Res., 1505 Denison Ave., 44109. Tel: 216-741-2067.
Convent—3855 W. 16th St., 44109. Tel: 216-661-0547.

11—ST. BENEDICT. Closed. For inquiries for parish records contact the Chancery.

12—BLESSED SACRAMENT (1903), Rev. Matthew A. Ischay; Deacon William E. Schill.
Res., 3381 Fulton Rd., 44109. Tel: 216-741-8338.
School—3389 Fulton Rd., 44109. Tel: 216-741-0172; Fax: 216-741-0172. Nancy Brewer, Prin.
Lay Teachers 10; Students 172.

13—ST. BONIFACE (1903), Rev. Alex E. Brazynetz; Sr. Dianne Skubby, C.PP.S., Pastoral Assoc. In res., Revs. Mark Q. Fedor; Augustine Pham Van Lan.
Res., 3545 W. 54th St., 44102. Tel: 216-961-2713; 961-2714; Fax: 216-634-2844.
Convent—3588 W. 52nd St., 44102. Tel: 961-0669.

14—ST. CASIMIR (1891) (Polish), Rev. Msgr. Leo Telesz.
Res., 8223 Sowinski Ave., 44103. Tel: 216-361-4322.
Convent—1116 East 82nd St., 44103. Tel: 216-361-5008.

15—ST. CATHERINE (1898), Rev. Walter H. Jenne, Admin. Pastoral Assocs.: Sr. Mary Jane Vonk, S.N.D.; Sr. Mary Janeta Stamper, S.N.D.
Res., 9412 Heath Ave., 44104-5512. Tel: 216-341-3353; 341-5542.
Church—E. 93rd & Catherine Ave., 44104.
School—3443 E. 93rd St., 44104. Tel: 216-341-7212; Fax: 216-641-8184. Mr. Nash Thompson, Prin.
Sisters 2; Lay Teachers 8; Students 217.

16—ST. CECILIA (1915), Revs. Daniel L. Begin; Herman B. Peters, Pastor Emeritus; Sr. Rosella Holloman, C.S.A., Pastoral Assoc.
Res., 3476 E. 152nd St., 44120. Tel: 216-921-3310; 921-3311.
Church—Kinsman Rd. & E. 152nd St., 44120.
School—Mount Pleasant Catholic Elementary Education Center. See separate listing under Institutions Located in the Diocese.

17—ST. COLMAN (1880), Administrators: Sr. Carol English, C.S.J.; Sr. Lucy Dragonette, C.S.J. In res., Rev. Robert T. Begin.
Res., 2027 W. 65th St., 44102. Tel: 216-651-0550; Fax: 216-651-1663.
Convent—2007 W. 65th St., 44102. Tel: 216-961-1550.

18—CONVERSION OF ST. PAUL (1931), Revs. Senan Glass, O.F.M.Cap.; Andrew Hohman, O.F.M.Cap. In res., Pastoral Assocs.: Bros. James Allman; Mike Letosak.
Res., Connected with the monastery of the Poor Clares of Perpetual Adoration. 4120 Euclid Ave., 44103-3728. Tel: 216-431-8854; Fax: 216-361-1951.
Convent—4108 Euclid Ave., 44103-3728.

19—CORPUS CHRISTI (1935), Rev. Ronald J. Szudarek; Deacons David J. Lundeen; Charles Zawadzki.
Res., 5204 Northcliff Ave., 44144-4065. Tel: 216-351-8738; 8739; Fax: 216-741-5620.
School—5007 Archmere Ave., 44144. Tel: 216-351-2974; Fax: 216-661-9188. Sr. M. Maureen Ryba, S.S.J.-T.O.S.F., Prin.
Sisters of St. Joseph III Order of St. Francis 1; Lay Teachers 9; Students 196.
Convent—Tel: 216-741-5001.

20—CRISTO REY, CAPILLA DE (1983) (Hispanic), Pastoral Team: Rev. James H. McCreight; Deacon Frederick F. Simon; Mrs. Millie Simon.
Res., 3402 Clark Ave., 44109-1136. Tel: 216-631-6817; Fax: 216-636-9351.
School—Metro Catholic Parish School. See Separate Listing under Elementary Schools, Parochial and Diocesan.

21—ST. ELIZABETH (1892) (Magyar), Rev. Andras Antal (Hungary) Admin.
Mailing Address: P.O. Box 20175, 44120-0175.
Church—9016 Buckeye Rd., 44104. Tel: 216-231-0325; Fax: 216-231-0325.

22—ST. EMERIC (1904 & Territorial 1964) (Magyar), Rev. Sandor Siklodi (Hungary) Admin.; Deacon Geza J. Balassy.
Res., 1860 W. 22nd St., 44113. Tel: 216-861-1937.

23—EPIPHANY (1944), Rev. Daniel L. Begin; Mrs. Mary James, Admin.; Deacon Troy F. Stokes.
Res., 11901 Oakfield Ave., 44105. Tel: 216-561-3975.
School—See Mount Pleasant Catholic Elementary Education Center, 3845 E. 131st St., 44105. Tel: 216-991-1615.

24—ST. FRANCIS (1887), Rev. Thomas F. Martin; Deacon Frank Lozada.
Office: 7206 Myron Ave., 44103. Tel: 216-361-4133; Fax: 216-361-1673.
School—Tel: 216-361-4858. Sr. Karen Somerville, S.N.D., Prin.
Sisters of Notre Dame 4; Lay Teachers 7; Students 267.
Convent—7119 Superior Ave., 44103. Tel: 216-361-5094.

25—ST. GEORGE (1901) (Lithuanian), Revs. Joseph A. Bacevice; Balys C. Ivanauskas, Pastor Emeritus.
Res., 6527 Superior Ave., 44103-2698. Tel: 216-431-5794; Fax: 216-391-8233.
Hunger Center—Tel: 216-391-9160.

26—ST. HENRY (1946), Rev. Robert J. Kropac. Pastoral Assocs.: Gerry Kynkor; Ms. Barbara Price; Ms. Patricia Polk. In res., Revs. J. Glenn Murray, S.J.; Dennis J. Kristancic; Simon Engler, T.O.R.
Res., 18200 Harvard Ave., 44128. Tel: 216-921-0725; 921-0726; 921-7030; Fax: 216-991-9470.
School—Archbishop James P. Lyke Elementary School. See Elementary Schools, Parochial and Diocesan under Institutions Located in the Diocese.

27—HOLY FAMILY (1911). Closed. For inquiries for parish records contact the Chancery.

28—HOLY NAME (1854), Revs. Vincent J. Moraghan; John C. Dalton, Pastor Emeritus, Senior Assoc.; Deacon Martin J. Wendzicki.
Res., 8328 Broadway Ave. S.E., 44105-3931. Tel: 216-271-4242; 4243.
School—Tel: 216-341-0084; Fax: 216-341-1122. Sr. Marie Patrice Joyce, S.C., Prin.
Sisters 3; Lay Teachers 7; Students 219.
Catechesis/Religious Programs—Students 163.

29—HOLY REDEEMER (1924) (Italian), Revs. Martin F. Polito; James J. Grandillo, Pastor Emeritus.
Res., 15712 Kipling Ave., 44110. Tel: 216-531-3313; Fax: 216-531-4717.
School—15720 Kipling Ave., 44110. Tel: 216-486-0935. Sr. Maureen Spillane, S.N.D., Prin.
Sisters of Notre Dame 1; Lay Teachers 7; Students 157.
Convent—924 Ruple Rd., 44110. Tel: 216-481-2740.

30—HOLY ROSARY (1892) (Italian), Rev. Philip G. Racco; Sr. Mary Johnica D'Amico, S.N.D., Pastoral Assoc. In res., Revs. Francis X. Klamet; Gregg Banaga, C.M.
Res., 12021 Mayfield Rd., 44106. Tel: 216-421-2995; 2996.

31—HOLY TRINITY - ST. EDWARD (1975), Revs. Senan Glass, O.F.M.Cap.; Peter J. Woll, Pastor Emeritus.
Res., 7211 Woodland Ave., 44104. Tel: 216-431-1134; 431-8854.

32—ST. HYACINTH (1906) (Polish), Rev. John S. Deka.
Res., 6114 Francis Ave., 44127. Tel: 216-641-3944.
Convent—2971 E. 61st St., 44127. Tel: 216-641-1508.

33—ST. IGNATIUS (1902), Rev. James R. McGonegal; Rev. Msgr. James P. McIntyre, Pastor Emeritus; Rev. Timothy M. Daw; Sr. Dianne Piunno, S.N.D., Pastoral Assoc.; Deacons Daniel J. Hancock; Billy Malcolm. In res., Rev. Gary D. Yanus.
Res., 10205 Lorain Ave., 44111-5470. Tel: 216-251-0300; 0301; 0302; Fax: 216-251-0302.
School—Tel: 216-671-0535. Sr. Theresine Cregan, C.S.J., Prin.
Lay Teachers 19; Students 432.
Convent—10212 Bernard Ave., 44111. Tel: 216-251-3446.

34—IMMACULATE CONCEPTION (1865), Revs. Michael J. Troha; Albert J. Mackert, Pastor Emeritus; Sr. Eileen Quinn, O.S.U., Pastoral Assoc. In res., Revs. John J. Hayes; David A. Novak.
Res., 4129 Superior Ave., 44103-1179. Tel: 216-431-5900; Fax: 216-881-4274.
School—Tel: 216-361-1883. Dr. Marlene M. Matis, Prin.
Ursuline Nuns of Cleveland 2; Lay Teachers 8; Students 209.
Convent—Tel: 216-541-3050.

35—IMMACULATE HEART OF MARY (1894) (Polish), Revs. Stanley Klasinski; Marian Bendyk.
Res., 6700 Lansing Ave., 44105. Tel: 216-341-2734. [CEM]
School—Jesus and Mary Consolidated, (Grades 4-8). (See Sacred Heart of Jesus listing). 6804 Lansing Ave., 44105-3797. Tel: 216-441-0886; Fax: 216-441-1515. Mr. Frank W. Przybojewski, Prin.
Sisters 1; Lay Teachers 10; Students 254.
Convent—Tel: 216-641-7121.

36—ST. JEROME (1919), Revs. Thomas A. Haren; Anthony Cassese; Deacon Peter Travalik.
Res., 15000 Lake Shore Blvd., 44110-1298. Tel: 216-481-8200; Fax: 216-481-8201.
School—15100 Lake Shore Blvd., 44110. Tel: 216-486-3587; Fax: 216-486-4288. Mr. Nicholas DiBartolemeo, Prin.
Ursuline Nuns of Cleveland 1; Lay Teachers 11; Students 296.
Convent—15025 Ridpath Ave., 44110. Tel: 216-531-6118.

37—ST. JOHN CANTIUS (1898) (Polish), Rev. Ralph A. Bodziony. In res., Rev. Msgr. Casimir S. Ciolek.
Res., 906 College Ave., S.W., 44113. Tel: 216-781-9095; Fax: 216-696-6065.
School—2357 Tremont Ave., 44113. Tel: 216-861-0118. Miss Rosemary DiPetro, Prin.
Sisters 1; Lay Teachers 5; Students 88.
Convent—2265 W. 10th St., 44113. Tel: 216-861-1349.

38—ST. JOHN NEPOMUCENE (1902) (Bohemian), Revs. William F. Tezie; Joseph R. Spolny.
Res., 3785 Independence Rd., 44105-3357. Tel: 216-641-8444; 8445; Fax: 216-341-4466.
Church—Fleet Ave. & E. 50th St., 44105.
School—3777 Independence Rd., 44105. Tel: 216-341-1347; Fax: 216-341-4466. Mrs. Roswitha Wunker, Prin.
Lay Teachers 11; Students 245.
Convent—Tel: 216-341-6393.

39—ST. JOSAPHAT (1908), Rev. David A. Novak, Admin.; Rev. Msgr. Alexander I. Goldikovskis, Pastor Emeritus.
Res., 1411 E. 33rd St., 44114-4032. Tel: 216-579-0173.

40—ST. JOSEPH (Woodland). Closed. For inquiries for parish records contact the Chancery.

41—ST. JOSEPH (Collinwood) (1877). Closed. For inquiries for parish records contact St. Aloysius, Cleveland.

42—ST. LAWRENCE (1901) (Slovenian), Rev. Anthony Rebol. In res., Rev. Frank G. Godic.
Res., 3547 E. 80th St., 44105. Tel: 216-341-0496.
Church—3532 E. 81st St., 44105.
Convent—23531 E. 80th St., 44105. Tel: 216-341-1235.

43—ST. LEO THE GREAT (1948), Revs. Edward F. Weist; William D. Eylar, Pastor Emeritus; John A. Ocilka; Kevin C. Shemuga; Sr. Joyce Joecken, C.S.J., Pastoral Assoc.; Deacon Thomas J. Waken. In res., Rev. Msgr. Kenneth W. Saunders.
Res., 4940 Broadview Rd., 44109. Tel: 216-661-1006; 1007; 1008; Fax: 216-661-7125.
School—4900 Broadview Rd., 44109. Tel: 216-661-2120. Michael Fasciano, Prin.
Lay Teachers 22; Students 646.
Catechesis/Religious Programs—Students 139.

44—COMMUNITY OF ST. MALACHI (1975). (Personal Parish). Revs. Paul J. Hritz, Pastor Emeritus; Anthony J. Schuerger.
Res., 2459 Washington Ave., 44113-2380. Tel: 216-781-3110; Fax: 216-861-5340.
Church—W. 25th & Detroit Ave., 44113.

45—ST. MALACHI (1865), Revs. Paul J. Hritz, Pastor Emeritus; Anthony J. Schuerger. Pastoral Assocs.: Donna K. Rego; Sr. M. Francis Borgia Allwine, O.S.U.
Res., 2459 Washington Ave., 44113-2380. Tel: 216-861-5343; 5344; Fax: 216-861-5340.
School—Urban Community School. (Intermediate Level) (See St. Wendelin listing for Primary Level) 2401 Washington Ave., 44113. Tel: 216-771-8014; Fax: 216-771-7888. Sr. Maureen Doyle, O.S.U., Prin.
Sisters 4; Lay Teachers 20; Students 408.
Convent—2456 Vermont Ave., 44113. Tel: 216-781-3481.

46—ST. MARK (1945), Revs. Douglas H. Koesel, Admin.; Anthony J. Muzic; Joseph F. Wagner, Pastor Emeritus.
Res., 15800 Montrose Ave., 44111. Tel: 216-226-7577; 7578.
School—15724 Montrose Ave., 44111. Tel: 216-521-4115; Fax: 216-221-8664. Dr. Marilyn Kurnath, Prin.
Sisters of Immaculate Heart of Mary 2; Lay Teachers 20; Students 517.
Convent—15604 Fisher Rd., 44111. Tel: 216-221-2117.

47—ST. MARY (1905) (Slovenian), Revs. John M. Kumse; Victor N. Tomc, Pastor Emeritus; Sr. Nina Vitale, O.S.U., Pastoral Assoc. In res., Rev. Joze Cerne.
Res., 15519 Holmes Ave., 44110. Tel: 216-761-7740; 761-1837; 761-5524 (Ministry House); Fax: 216-451-7911.
School—716 E. 156th St., 44110. Tel: 216-451-1717. Sr. Mary Ellen Brinovec, O.S.U., Prin.
Religious 2; Lay Teachers 5; Students 122.
Convent—717 E. 155th St., 44110. Tel: 216-851-3234.
Catechesis/Religious Programs—Students 109.

48—ST. MARY OF CZESTOCHOWA (1913) (Polish). Closed. For inquiries for parish records contact the Chancery.

49—ST. MEL (1945), Revs. Edwin J. Schenkelberg; Ray J. Horley; Donna Winbiscus, Pastoral Assoc.
Res., 14436 Triskett Rd., 44111. Tel: 216-941-4313; 4314.
School—14440 Triskett Rd., 44111. Tel: 216-941-6879. Patricia Kelly, Prin.
Lay Teachers 18; Students 379.
Catechesis/Religious Programs—Students 374.
Convent—14538 Grapeland Ave., 44111. Tel: 216-941-6589.

50—ST. MICHAEL (1882), Revs. Dennis R. O'Grady; James H. McCreight; Sr. Mary Reean Coyne, S.N.D., Pastoral Assoc.; Deacon Miquel Figueroa. In res., Rev. Thomas V. O'Donnell.
Res., 3114 Scranton Rd., 44109. Tel: 216-861-6297; 6298; 621-3847 (Spanish).
Convent—2202 Prame Ave., 44109. Tel: 216-351-0855.

51—NATIVITY OF THE BLESSED VIRGIN MARY. Closed. For inquiries for parish records contact the Chancery.

52—OUR LADY OF ANGELS (1922), Rev. John J. Cregan. Pastoral Assocs.: Sr. Rita Henley, H.M.; Ann Steinbrunner. In res., Rev. Stephen J. Walick.
Res., 3644 Rocky River Dr., 44111. Tel: 216-252-2332; Fax: 216-252-2383.
School—Tel: 216-251-6841; Fax: 216-251-7831. Miss Kathleen A. Lynch, Prin.
Lay Teachers 23; Students 586.
Convent—3550 Rocky River Dr., 44111.

53—OUR LADY OF GOOD COUNSEL (1873), Revs. Leroy Moreeuw, C.PP.S.; George J. Albers, C.PP.S.; John Zivjak, C.PP.S.; Bro. Thomas R. Bohman, C.PP.S., Pastoral Assoc.; Deacon Patrick F. Berigan.
Res., 4423 Pearl Rd., S.W., 44109. Tel: 216-749-2323; 2324; Fax: 216-741-7183.
School—4419 Pearl Rd., 44109. Tel: 216-741-3685. Mr. Paul Deitrick, Prin.
Lay Teachers 19; Students 433.

54—OUR LADY OF LOURDES (1883) (Bohemian), Rev. James J. Masek. In res., Rev. Stephen F. Radecky.
Res., 3395 E. 53rd St., 44127-1692. Tel: 216-641-2829; 2830.
Convent—3401 E. 53rd St., 44127.

55—OUR LADY OF MERCY (1922) (Slovak), Revs. Joseph T. Hilinski; Andrew P. Laheta, Pastor Emeritus.
Res., 2425 W. 11th St., 44113. Tel: 216-781-8277.

56—OUR LADY OF MOUNT CARMEL (East) (1936) (Italian). Officially closed as a parish on July 29, 1990, however, still in existence as an Oratory. Mrs. Rose Marie Criniti, Admin.
Res., 2615 Martin Luther King Blvd., 44104-2553. Tel: 216-421-0140.
Oratory—Cleveland, 11501 Mount Carmel Rd., 44104.

57—OUR LADY OF MOUNT CARMEL (West) (1926) (Italian), Revs. Richard Rasch, O.de.M.; Anthony M. Fortunato, O.de.M.; Eugene Costa, O.de.M.; Deacon Clarence A. Chrosniak. In res., Rev. Vincent Caruso, O.de.M.
Res., 6928 Detroit Ave., 44102-3093. Tel: 216-651-5043; 651-2547; 651-1611; Fax: 216-651-6641.
School—1355 W. 70th St., 44102. Tel: 216-281-7146; Fax: 216-281-6651. Sr. M. Rochelle Guertal, O.SS.T., Prin.
Sisters of Most Holy Trinity 2; Lay Teachers 8; Students 254.
Convent—1355 W. 70th St., 44102.

58—OUR LADY OF PEACE (1919), Rev. Gary D. Chmura; Deacon William E. Dirk; Mrs. Nancy McIntosh, Pastoral Assoc. In res., Rev. Thomas A. Moran.
Res., 12503 Buckingham Ave., 44120-1498. Tel: 216-421-4211; 4212; Fax: 216-421-0988.
Church—Shaker Blvd. & E. 126th St., 44120.
School—12406 Buckingham Ave., 44120-1419. Tel: 216-795-7161; Fax: 216-795-7161. Mrs. Sheila Bolek, Prin.
Lay Teachers 10; Students 229.

59—OUR LADY OF PERPETUAL HELP (1929) (Lithuanian), Rev. Gediminas Kijauskas, S.J. Pastoral Assocs.: Nijole Kersnauskas; Stasys Ignatavicius.
Res., 18022 Neff Rd., 44119-2644. Tel: 216-531-4263; Fax: 216-531-8441.
Convent—18021 Marcella Rd., 44119.

60—ST. PATRICK (1853), Rev. Mark A. DiNardo; Mary Jane Treichel, Pastoral Assoc.
Res., 3602 Bridge Ave., 44113-3314. Tel: 216-631-6872; 6873; 6874; Fax: 216-281-8459.
School—Urban Community School. See St. Malachi listing. Tel: 216-771-8014.

61—ST. PATRICK (West Park) (1848), Revs. Thomas J. Hagedorn; Ralph G. Hudak; Deacons Richard C. Beercheck; John Koch. In res., Rev. Joseph C. Pednekar, M.S.F.S.
Res., 4427 Rocky River Dr., 44135-2551. Tel: 216-251-8286; 8287; Fax: 216-251-8555. [CEM]
School—17720 Puritas Ave., 44135. Tel: 216-671-4314. Joyce Needham, Prin.
Ursuline Nuns of Cleveland 2; Lay Teachers 24; Students 645.
Convent—17712 Puritas Ave., 44135. Tel: 216-941-1088.

62—ST. PAUL (1902) (Croatian), Revs. Mirko Hladni; Stephen A. Mrakuzic, Pastor Emeritus.
Res., 1369 E. 40th St., 44103-1194. Tel: 216-431-1895; Fax: 216-431-1128.

63—ST. PETER (1853), Rev. Robert J. Marrone.
Res., 1533 E. 17th St., 44114. Tel: 216-861-1798; 861-1799.

64—SS. PHILIP AND JAMES (1950), Revs. J. Brendan McNulty; Robert F. Brennan, Pastor Emeritus, (Retired). In res., Rev. John F. McMahon.
Res., 10812 Adeline Rd., 44111-4806. Tel: 216-941-6808; 6809.
Church—3727 Bosworth Rd., 44111.
School—Tel: 216-941-7070. Miss Joan Woost, Prin.
Lay Teachers 9; Students 164.
Convent—10909 Oliver Rd., 44111. Tel: 216-941-7387.

65—ST. PHILIP NERI (1914), Rev. Gary Stakem, O.F.M.Cap.; Sr. Wilma Apack, C.S.J., Pastoral Assoc.
Res., 8215 St. Clair Ave., 44103. Tel: 216-431-2583.
School—St. Thomas Aquinas-St. Philip Neri, 9101 Superior Ave., 44106. Tel: 216-421-4668; Fax: 216-721-8444. Mrs. Berkely Dixon, Prin.
Religious 1; Lay Teachers 15; Students 364.
Convent—799 E. 82nd St., 44103. Tel: 216-431-0224.

66—ST. PROCOP (1872) (Bohemian), Rev. Mark J. Peyton.
Res., 3181 W. 41st St., 44109-1275. Tel: 216-631-0365; 631-0367.
School—Metro Catholic Parish School. See Separate Listing under Elementary Schools, Parochial and Diocesan.

67—ST. ROCCO (1922) (Italian), Revs. Michael Contardi, O.de.M.; Paschal Rosca, O.de.M.; Kenneth Breen, O.de.M.
Res., 3205 Fulton Rd., 44109-1495. Tel: 216-961-8331; 961-7384; Fax: 216-961-1845.
School—Tel: 216-961-8557; Fax: 216-961-1112. Sr. Judith Wulk, O.SS.T., Prin.
Sisters of Most Holy Trinity 2; Lay Teachers 8; Students 217.
Convent—Tel: 216-961-2378.

68—ST. ROSE (1899), Rev. James A. Viall; Sr. Ruth Donnelly, O.S.U., Pastoral Assoc. In res., Rev. Albert Veigas.
Res., 11411 Detroit Ave., 44102. Tel: 216-521-0133; Fax: 216-521-1306.
Church—Detroit Ave. & W. 114th St., 44102.
School—1441 W. 116th St., 44102. Tel: 216-226-4525; Fax: 216-226-0413. Sr. Maria Olga Palma, O.C.D., Prin.
Sisters 2; Lay Teachers 10; Students 161.
Convent—1418 W. 114th St., 44102. Tel: 216-521-5605.

69—SACRED HEART OF JESUS (1888) (Polish), Rev. Francis M. Bednar.
Res., 6916 Krakow Ave., 44105. Tel: 216-341-2828; Fax: 216-271-1889.
Church—E. 71st & Kazimier Ave., 44105.
School—Jesus and Mary Consolidated, (Grades K-3). See Immaculate Heart of Mary listing. 6804 Lansing Ave., 44105.
Convent—Tel: 216-641-2797.

70—SAN JUAN BAUTISTA (1975) (Spanish-Non Territorial), Rev. David F. Fallon. Pastoral Assocs.: Sr. Florence Cremering, S.C.; Sr. Ann Dorenbusch, S.C.; Deacons Ceferino Medina; Epifanio Torres; Victor Colon; Ignacio Miranda.
Res., 1946 W. 32 St., 44113. Tel: 216-631-2888; Fax: 216-631-2999.
School—Metro Catholic Parish School. See Separate Listing under Elementary Schools, Parochial and Diocesan.
Convent—3215 Carroll Ave., 44113. Tel: 216-281-7215.

71—ST. STANISLAUS (1873) (Polish), Revs. William Gulas, O.F.M.; Alcuin L. Mikulanis, O.F.M.
Res., 3649 E. 65th St., 44105-1293. Tel: 216-341-9091; 9092; Fax: 216-341-2688.
Church—Forman Ave. & E. 65th St., 44105.
School—6615 Forman Ave., 44105. Tel: 216-883-3307; Fax: 216-883-0514. Mrs. Alice Torrence, Prin.
Sisters 4; Lay Teachers 13; Students 384.
Convent—Tel: 216-341-0934.

72—ST. STEPHEN (1869) (German), Rev. S. Michael Franz; Sr. Carol Marie McHenry, S.N.D., Pastoral Assoc.
Res., 1930 W. 54th St., 44102. Tel: 216-631-5633; Fax: 216-631-5634.
School—Metro Catholic Parish School. See Separate Listing under Elementary Schools, Parochial and Diocesan.
Convent—1891 W. 57th St., 44102. Tel: 216-631-0754.

73—ST. THOMAS AQUINAS. Closed. For inquiries for parish records contact the Chancery.

74—TRANSFIGURATION (1943). Closed. For inquiries for parish records contact the Chancery.

75—ST. VINCENT DE PAUL (1922), Revs. John E. Manning; Urban A. Reichlin, Pastor Emeritus; Daniel P. Redmond; Deacon Kenneth J. Hill.
Res., 13400 Lorain Ave., 44111. Tel: 216-252-2626; Fax: 216-251-0455.
Church—Lorain Ave. & Berea Rd., 44111.
School—13442 Lorain Ave., 44111. Tel: 216-251-3932. Sr. Caroline Kocur, O.S.U., Prin.
Sisters 2; Lay Teachers 18; Students 423.
Convent—3483 W. 135th St., 44111. Tel: 216-252-1080.

76—ST. VITUS (1893) (Slovenian), Revs. Joseph P. Boznar; Richard D. Evans; Sr. Mary Avsec, S.N.D., Pastoral Assoc.
Res., 6019 Glass Ave., 44103. Tel: 216-361-1444; 1445; Fax: 216-361-1445.
School—6111 Glass Ave., 44103. Tel: 216-881-1689. Mrs. Jeanette Polomsky, Prin.
Sisters of Notre Dame 1; Lay Teachers 10; Students 212.
Catechesis/Religious Programs—Students 179.
Convent—6104 Glass Ave., 44103. Tel: 216-361-7330.

77—ST. WENDELIN (1903) (Slovak), Rev. Jerome M. Lajack.
Res., 2281 Columbus Rd., 44113. Tel: 216-861-1141.
School—Urban Community School. (Primary and Junior High) (See St. Malachi listing for Intermediate Level) 2281 Columbus Rd., 44113. Tel: 216-861-4706; Fax: 216-781-0034.
Convent—2259 Columbus Rd., 44113. Tel: 216-241-1773.

OUTSIDE THE CITY OF CLEVELAND

Akron, Summit Co.,

1—ANNUNCIATION, (1907), Rev. Paul J. Rosing. Pastoral Ministers: Jean J. Jordan; Diana Herhold. In res., Revs. James J. Berardi; Augustine Ukwuoma.
Res., 87 Broad St., 44305. Tel: 330-535-4141; Fax: 330-762-8456.
Church—Broad St. & Kent St., 44305.
School—Annunciation-St. John the Baptist, 88 Kent St., 44305. Tel: 330-253-5311; Fax: 330-762-8456. Barbara Mesko, Prin.
Lay Teachers 12; Students 282.

2—ST. ANTHONY OF PADUA, (1933) (Italian), Revs. James V. Ragnoni; Robert Labella.
Res., 83 Mosser Pl., 44310. Tel: 330-762-7277.
School—80 E. York St., 44310. Tel: 330-253-6918. Sr. Elizabeth Szilvasi, M.P.F., Prin.
Religious Teachers Filippini 2; Lay Teachers 7; Students 215.
Convent—93 Mosser Pl., 44310. Tel: 216-376-1735.

3—ST. BERNARD, (1861), Rev. Paul E. Schindler; Deacon Daniel J. Matusicky. In res., Revs. Jude Onwana; Albert Reymann, M.M.
Res., 44 University Ave., 44308-1609. Tel: 330-253-5161; 5162; 253-5265; 253-5364; Fax: 330-253-6949. [CEM]

4—CHRIST THE KING, (1935), Revs. Francis J. Basa; Victor J. Cimperman, Pastor Emeritus.
Res., 1584 Creighton Ave., 44310-2699. Tel: 330-633-8418.
School—1558 Creighton Ave., 44310. Tel: 330-633-1383; Fax: 330-633-4512. Sr. Paula Krizancic, Prin.
Daughters of Divine Charity 3; Lay Teachers 6; Students 137.
Convent—Tel: 330-633-8217.

5—ST. FRANCIS DE SALES, (1948), Revs. James R. Schleicher; Robert E. Stein. In res., Rev. Charles L. Byrider.
Res., 4019 Manchester Rd., 44319. Tel: 330-644-2225.
School—4009 Manchester Rd., 44319. Tel: 330-644-0638. Carol Trifonoff, Prin.
Sisters Servants of Immaculate Heart of Mary 1; Lay Teachers 18; Students 456.
Catechesis/Religious Programs—Students 344.

6—ST. HEDWIG, (1912) (Polish), Rev. Thaddeus M. Swirski.
Res., 215 E. Glenwood Ave., 44310-3837. Tel: 330-376-6979.
Convent—211 E. Glenwood Ave., 44310.

7—ST. HILARY, (1958), Revs. Gordon A. Yahner; John P. Miceli; Deacon Lee F. Hindersheid. Pastoral Assocs.: Sr. Marlene LoGrasso; Mrs. Mary Lou Grossman; Ms. Christina Kitts; Mrs. Patricia Schnee.
Mailing Address: 2750 W. Market St., Fairlawn, 44333.
Res., 615 Moorfield Rd., Fairlawn, 44333. Tel: 330-867-1055; 1056; Fax: 330-869-2312.
Church—2750 W. Market St., Fairlawn, 44333.
School—645 Moorfield Rd., Fairlawn, 44333. Tel: 330-867-8720; Fax: 330-867-5081. Miss Patricia Nugent, Prin.
Lay Teachers 29; Students 577.
Catechesis/Religious Programs—Students 497.

8—IMMACULATE CONCEPTION, (1923), Rev. Arthur A. Snedeker; Melissa Keegan, Pastoral Assoc.; Deacon Dennis L. Smith. In res., Rev. Samuel R. Ciccolini.
Res., 2101 17th St. S.W., 44314-2315. Tel: 330-753-8429; Fax: 330-753-7440.
Church—2100 16th St. S.W., 44314.
School—2128 16th St. S.W., 44314. Tel: 330-745-3544; Fax: 330-745-2051. Mrs. Rosemary Capotosto, Prin.
Lay Teachers 10; Students 198.

9—ST. JOHN THE BAPTIST, (1907) (Slovak), Rev. Ralph V. Coletta.
Res., 1034 Brown St., 44301. Tel: 330-773-9114.
School—Annunciation-St. John the Baptist School, 88 Kent St., 44305. Tel: 330-253-5311. Barbara Mesko, Prin.
Lay Teachers 12; Students 282.

10—ST. MARTHA, (1919), Revs. Norman K. Douglas; Peter Colletti. Pastoral Assocs.: Sr. Mary Jane Simmons, H.M.; Sr. Eileen Keating, C.S.A.
Res., 300 E. Tallmadge Ave., 44310-2399. Tel: 330-376-5144; 5145; 376-5858; Fax: 330-376-5311.
School—Tel: 330-535-8817. Mrs. Mary Dean, Prin.
Lay Teachers 11; Students 277.
Catechesis/Religious Programs—Students 179.

11—ST. MARY, (1887), Revs. John J. Hilkert; Raymond J. Smith.
Res., 750 S. Main St., 44311-1094. Tel: 330-762-9247.
School—Tel: 330-253-1233. Miss Joan Krill, Prin.
Lay Teachers 11; Students 223.
Convent—743 Dunbar Dr., 44311. Tel: 330-762-9496.

12—ST. MATTHEW, (1943), Rev. Thomas A. McGovern. In res., Rev. William P. Lyons.
Res., 2603 Benton St., 44312-1694. Tel: 330-733-9944; Fax: 330-733-9424.
Church—Berne & Woolf St., 44312.
School—2580 Benton St., 44312. Tel: 330-784-1711. Mr. Thomas S. Maroon, Prin.
Dominican Sisters 1; Lay Teachers 18; Students 360.
Catechesis/Religious Programs—Students 200.
Convent—2578 Benton St., 44312. Tel: 330-733-1001.

13—NATIVITY OF THE LORD JESUS, (1977), Rev. David J. Halaiko; Sr. Susanne Gill, H.M., Pastoral Assoc.
Res., 2425 Myersville Rd., 44312. Tel: 330-699-5086.
Catechesis/Religious Programs—Students 247.

14—ST. PAUL, (1919), Revs. John M. Jenkins; Steven K. Brunovsky; Therese Nesline, Pastoral Assoc.; Deacon Francis R. Lonteen.
Res., 433 Mission Dr., 44301-2798. Tel: 330-724-1263; Fax: 330-724-7680.
Church—1580 Brown St., 44301.
School—Tel: 330-724-1253. Mrs. Teresa A. Bica, Prin.
Lay Teachers 24; Students 452.

15—ST. PETER, (1917). Closed. For inquiries for parish records contact St. Mary Parish, Akron.

16—SACRED HEART OF JESUS, (1915) (Hungarian), Rev. Robert E. Clancy, Admin.; Deacon Geza Balassy.
Res., 212 E. Voris St., 44311. Tel: 330-434-4348.
Church—734 Grant St., 44311.

17—ST. SEBASTIAN, (1928), Revs. William D. Karg; John T. McDonough, Pastor Emeritus; Charles L. Byrider, Pastor Emeritus; Neil G. Walters; Deacon Terry W. Peacock.
Res., 476 Mull Ave., 44320-1299. Tel: 330-836-2233; 2234; 2235.
School—500 Mull Ave., 44320. Tel: 330-836-9107; Fax: 330-836-7690. Sr. Mary Patricia Leopold, H.M., Prin.
Sisters of the Humility of Mary 1; Lay Teachers 19; Students 495.
Catechesis/Religious Programs—Students 112.
Convent—352 Elmdale Ave., 44320. Tel: 330-864-2902.

18—ST. VINCENT, (1837), Revs. Joseph H. Kraker; Edward N. Schwet.
Res., 164 W. Market St., 44303-2395. Tel: 330-535-3135; Fax: 330-535-4160. [CEM]
Church—W. Market St. & Maple St., 44303.
School—17 S. Maple St., 44303. Tel: 216-762-5912. William D. Hackman, Prin.
Lay Teachers 14; Students 251.

Amherst, Lorain Co., St. Joseph (1864), Revs. Lawrence N. Martello; Anthony L. Kreps, Pastor Emeritus; James P. Schmitz; Sr. Mary Ann Burke, S.N.D., Pastoral Assoc.
Res., 200 St. Joseph Dr., 44001-1663. Tel: 216-988-2848; 2849; 871-4415 (Cleveland); Fax: 216-984-2301. [CEM]
School—175 St. Joseph Dr., 44001. Tel: 216-988-4244. Sr. Mary Jo Ludwig, S.N.D., Prin.
Sisters of Notre Dame 1; Lay Teachers 14; Students 323.
Catechesis/Religious Programs—Students 531.
Convent—151 St. Joseph Dr., 44001. Tel: 216-988-2621.

Ashland, Ashland Co., St. Edward (1853), Rev. James M. Cassidy; Deacon James A. Kaniecki.
Res., 501 Cottage St., 44805-2167. Tel: 419-289-7224; Fax: 419-289-0515.
Administration Center—149 Pleasant St., 44805.
School—433 Cottage St., 44805. Tel: 419-289-7456. Douglas J. Mark, Prin.
Lay Teachers 9; Students 201.
Catechesis/Religious Programs—Students 172.
Convent—Tel: 419-289-8333.

Avon, Lorain Co., Holy Trinity (1833), Revs. John J. Gorski; Michael J. Ondik, Pastor Emeritus.
Res., 33601 Detroit Rd., 44011-1999. Tel: 216-937-5363. [CEM]
School—2610 Nagel Rd., 44011. Tel: 216-937-6420. Sr. Patricia Vovk, S.N.D., Prin.
Notre Dame Sisters 2; Lay Teachers 8; Students 231.
Catechesis/Religious Programs—Students 59.
Convent—2620 Nagel Rd., 44011. Tel: 216-937-5005.

St. Mary of the Immaculate Conception (1841), Revs. Arthur B. Egan; John F. Wessel.
Res., 2640 Stoney Ridge Rd., 44011. Tel: 216-934-4212; Fax: 216-934-6246. [CEM]
School—2680 Stoney Ridge Rd., 44011. Tel: 216-934-6246. Miss Linda A. Kenzik, Prin.
Sisters of Notre Dame 2; Lay Teachers 8; Students 173.
Convent—Tel: 216-934-5173.

Avon Lake, Lorain Co., Holy Spirit (1965), Revs. James H. Beatty; James J. Mosovsky, Pastor Emeritus; Sr. Mary Popoczy, S.N.D., Pastoral Assoc.; Deacon Harold R. Dietrich.
Res., 410 Lear Rd., 44012-2004. Tel: 216-933-3777; 933-3789; 871-8157; Fax: 216-871-8157.
Catechesis/Religious Programs—Students 394.

St. Joseph's (1949), Rev. Timothy J. O'Connor; Sr. Thomasine Antenucci, S.S.J.-T.O.S.F., Pastoral Assoc.; Deacon James R. Stewart.
Res., 32929 Lake Rd., 44012. Tel: 216-933-3152; 871-0616 (Cleveland); Fax: 216-933-8919.
School—Tel: 216-933-6233; Fax: 216-933-2463. Mrs. Patricia Vaccaro, Prin.
Religious 1; Lay Teachers 9; Students 278.
Catechesis/Religious Programs—Students 301.
Convent—32911 Lake Rd., 44012. Tel: 216-933-5769.

Bainbridge Township, Geauga Co., Holy Angels (1977), Rev. Joseph P. Labbe.
Res., 8390 Stoneybrook Dr., Cleveland, 44023-4851. Tel: 216-543-7227; 543-2636; Fax: 216-543-4876.
Church—18046 Chillicothe Rd., Chagrin Falls, 44023-4851.
Catechesis/Religious Programs—Students 417.

Barberton, Summit Co.,

1—St. Augustine, (1898), Revs. Richard Burchell; Stephen Spisak; Paul J. Clines, Pastor Emeritus; Deacon Robin Adair.
Res., 204 Sixth St., N.W., 44203. Tel: 330-745-0011; 0012; Fax: 330-745-0012.
Church—Sixth St. & Lake St., 44203.
School—195 Seventh St., N.W., 44203. Tel: 330-753-6435. Sr. Marie Damicone, O.P., Prin.
Lay Teachers 19; Students 432.
Catechesis/Religious Programs—Students 297.
Convent—633 W. Paige Ave., 44203. Tel: 330-745-5735.

2—SS. Cyril and Methodius, (1906), Revs. Edward F. Lajack; James A. Yavorsky, Pastor Emeritus.
Res., 189 15th St. N.W., 44203-2329. Tel: 330-825-7089.
Church—183 15 St. N.W., 44203-2329.

3—Holy Trinity, (1911) (Hungarian), Rev. Carl A. Ciprian.
Res., 398 Van St., 44203-2329. Tel: 330-745-4735.
Church—380 Wooster Rd. N., 44203-2329.

4—St. Mary's, (1912), Revs. Richard Arko, Admin.; Claude J. Gaebelein, Pastor Emeritus.
Res., 122 21st St. N.W., 44203. Tel: 330-825-6231.

5—Sacred Heart, (1916) (Slovenian), Revs. Albert A. Kunkel; Joseph J. Ozimek, Pastor Emeritus.
Res., 1263 Shannon Ave., N.W., 44203-6792. Tel: 330-825-9543.

Bay Village, Cuyahoga Co., St. Raphael (1946), Revs. Nelson J. Callahan; C. Thomas Cleaton; Sr. Ardath Blake, H.M., Pastoral Assoc.
Res., 525 Dover Center Rd., 44140-2366. Tel: 216-871-1100; Fax: 216-871-1358.
School—Tel: 216-871-6760. Beverly Nemec, Prin.
Lay Teachers 30; Students 778.
Catechesis/Religious Programs—Students 549.

Bedford, Cuyahoga Co., St. Mary (1910), Rev. Thomas J. Winkel; Rev. Msgr. Francis E. Gasbarre, Pastor Emeritus; Rev. Edward A. Burba.
Res., 300 Union St., 44146-4594. Tel: 216-232-9393; 9394; Fax: 216-232-2303.
Church—340 Union St., 44146.
School—270 Union St., 44146. Tel: 216-232-2303. Michelle Nowakowski, Prin.
Vincentian Sisters of Charity 2; Lay Teachers 9; Students 272.
Convent—36 Paul St., 44146. Tel: 216-439-1667.

St. Pius X (1952), Revs. Desmund Hunt, S.M.; John Jazwiecki, S.M.; Deacons Willard C. Payne; Robert Rapp.
Res., 400 Center Rd., 44146-2296. Tel: 216-232-8166; 8167.
School—370 Center Rd., 44146-2297. Tel: 216-232-1531. Mrs. Mary Ann Murnyack, Prin.
Vincentian Sisters of Charity 1; Lay Teachers 9; Students 244.
Convent—Tel: 216-232-0571.

Bedford Heights, Cuyahoga Co., Holy Trinity (1965), Rev. Ernest C. Hepner. Pastoral Assocs.: Josephine Jendrisak; Joan McGinty; Leonard Duritsky.
Res., 24821 Columbus Rd., 44146-2599. Tel: 216-232-2044; 2045; Fax: 216-232-3720.

Berea, Cuyahoga Co., St. Adalbert (1873) (Polish), Revs. Gerald J. Keller; Joseph Batkiewicz; Deacon Donald P. Butkovic; Sr. Thelma Gerhart, C.S.J., Pastoral Assoc.
Res., 66 Adelbert St., 44017-1799. Tel: 216-234-6830; Fax: 216-234-2588. [CEM]
School—56 Adelbert St., 44017. Tel: 216-234-5529. Mrs. Stephanie West, Prin.
Lay Teachers 10; Students 218.
Catechesis/Religious Programs—Students 152.
Convent—Tel: 216-234-1096.

St. Mary's (1852), Rev. John M. Garrity.
Res., 250 Kraft St., 44017-1449. Tel: 216-243-3877; 243-3878; Fax: 216-891-9417. [CEM]
School—265 Baker St., 44017-1515. Tel: 216-243-4555; Fax: 216-243-6214. Mrs. Nancy C. Kaesgen, Prin.
Lay Teachers 10; Students 338.
Catechesis/Religious Programs—Students 697.

Brecksville, Cuyahoga Co., St. Basil the Great (1960), Revs. Walter H. Jenne; Edward J. Camille, Pastor Emeritus; Robert F. Wenz. Pastoral Assocs.: Sr. Maureen Grady, O.S.U.; Mrs. Carol Gaby.
Res., 8700 Brecksville Rd., 44141. Tel: 216-526-1686; 1687; Fax: 216-526-2373.
Catechesis/Religious Programs—Tel: 216-526-3520; 526-3587.
Students 905.
Convent—6901 Mill Rd., 44141. Tel: 216-526-2850; 2851.

Broadview Heights, Cuyahoga Co., Assumption (1857), Revs. Christopher Schwartz, O.S.B.; William T. Matyas, O.S.B.; Ronald Mahnke, O.S.B.; Deacon Robert C. Bubnick, Sr.
Res., 9183 Broadview Rd., 44147. Tel: 216-526-1177; 1178.
School—Tel: 216-526-4877; Fax: 216-526-0683. Sr. Carol Tobler, S.I.W., Prin.
Sisters of Incarnate Word 2; Lay Teachers 9; Students 265.
Catechesis/Religious Programs—Students 403.
Convent—9139 Broadview Rd., 44147. Tel: 216-526-4069.

Brooklyn, Cuyahoga Co., St. Thomas More (1946), Revs. James J. Vesely; John S. Juhas; Gregory F. Schaut; Sr. Elaine Theresa Burrows, S.I.W., Pastoral Assoc.; Deacons Rudolph Jarosh, Jr.; Martin A. Thiel. In res., Rev. Andrew F. O'Boyle.
Res., 4170 N. Amber Dr., 44144-1399. Tel: 216-749-0414; Fax: 216-749-1001.
School—4180 N. Amber Dr., 44144. Tel: 216-749-1660; Fax: 216-398-4265. Nancy D. Brewer, Prin.
Lay Teachers 20; Students 486.
Catechesis/Religious Programs—Students 270.

Brook Park, Cuyahoga Co., Assumption of Mary (1860), Revs. Thomas A. Boone; Dennis M. McNeil; Anthony J. Dodd. In res., Mrs. Joan Mahon, Pastoral Assoc.; Deacon Francis B. Wilson.
Res., 5445 Smith Rd., 44142-2077. Tel: 216-267-0630; Fax: 216-267-0632. [CEM]
Church—5555 Smith Rd., 44142.

St. Peter the Apostle (1968), Rev. George W. Balaun; Deacon Robert G. Sabol. In res., Rev. Dismas Boeff, O.S.B.
Res., 6455 Engle Rd., 44142-3503. Tel: 216-433-1440; 1441.
Catechesis/Religious Programs—Students 441.

Brunswick, Medina Co., St. Ambrose (1957), Revs. Robert C. Hilkert; Robert H. Jackson; Joseph L. Labak; Deacons Clement J. Belter; John Miklosovic; Thomas J. Sheridan.
Res., 929 Pearl Rd., 44212. Tel: 330-225-3116; Fax: 330-225-5425.
School—923 Pearl Rd., 44212. Tel: 330-225-2116. Sr. Mary Ann Senia, H.M., Prin.
Sisters of Humility of Mary 2; Lay Teachers 16; Students 462.
Catechesis/Religious Programs—Students 1,364.

St. Colette (1977), Rev. Thomas G. Montavon; Deacon Howard Masony. In res., Rev. Joseph F. Wagner.
Res., 330 W. 130th St., 44212. Tel: 330-273-5500; Fax: 330-273-1355.
Catechesis/Religious Programs—Students 270.

Chagrin Falls, Holy Angels (1995). Unassigned.
Res., 8390 Stoney Brook Dr., 44023-4851.

St. Joan of Arc, Cuyahoga Co., (1948), Revs. John R. Olsavsky; John J. Kinkopf, Pastor Emeritus; John W. Wolf, Pastor Emeritus; James F. Mazanec; Sr. Joanne Laurienzo, S.N.D., Pastoral Min.; Deacon Louis J. Capek.
Res., 496 E. Washington St., 44022-2999. Tel: 216-247-7183; 7184; Fax: 216-247-2327.
School—498 E. Washington St., 44022-2998. Tel: 216-247-6530; Fax: 216-247-2045. Mrs. Jean Takacs, Prin.
Sisters of Notre Dame 1; Lay Teachers 10; Students 223.
Catechesis/Religious Programs—Students 544.
Convent—456 E. Washington St., 44022. Tel: 216-247-4419.

Chardon, Geauga Co., St. Mary (1909), Revs. Thomas C. Gilles; David R. Durkee; Deacon Edward J. McCarthy, Jr.
Res., 400 North St., 44024. Tel: 216-285-7051.
School—401 North St., 44024. Tel: 216-286-3590; Fax: 216-285-2818. Sr. Mary Sandra Nativio, S.N.D., Prin.
Sisters of Notre Dame 2; Lay Teachers 17; Students 355.
Catechesis/Religious Programs—Students 471.
Convent—315 North St., 44024. Tel: 216-286-5641.

Chesterland, Geauga Co., St. Anselm (1961), Revs. Thomas M. Sweany; John F. Anderson, Pastor Emeritus; Eric B. Leissa; Deacons Dale A. Bacik; Donald E. Sill.
Res., 12969 Chillicothe Rd., 44026-3199. Tel: 216-729-9575; Fax: 216-729-9103.
Church—13013 Chillicothe Rd., 44026.
School—Tel: 216-729-7806; Fax: 216-729-3524. Sr. Mary Donna Galetovich, S.N.D., Prin.
Sisters of Notre Dame 2; Lay Teachers 20; Students 400.
Catechesis/Religious Programs—Students 529.
Convent—13055 Chillicothe Rd., 44026. Tel: 216-729-0292.

Chippewa Lake, Medina Co., Jesus Divine Redeemer (1976). Attended by Our Lady Help of Christians, Litchfield.

Cleveland Heights, Cuyahoga Co., St. Ann (1915), Revs. James E. Singler; Robert J. Glepko; Sr. Donna Mikula, O.S.U., Pastoral Assoc. In res., Rev. Donald B. Cozzens.
Res., 2175 Coventry Rd., 44118-2898. Tel: 216-321-0024; 321-0025; 321-0048; 321-4599.
School—2160 Stillman Rd., 44118. Tel: 216-932-4177; Fax: 216-932-7439. Sr. Dorothy Ann Krolikowski, S.S.J.-T.O.S.F., Prin.
Sisters 4; Lay Teachers 18; Students 355.
Convent—12764 Cedar Rd., 44118-2899. Tel: 216-932-1438.

St. Louis (1947), Rev. Leonard J. Zamborsky; Deacon Richard E. Woods; Sr. Marie Manning, S.N.D., Pastoral Assoc. In res., Rev. Stephen J. Dohner.
Res., 2475 N. Taylor Rd., 44118-1397. Tel: 216-382-0440; Fax: 216-382-1605.
Church—2463 N. Taylor Rd., 44118.
School—Tel: 216-382-0033; Fax: 216-382-5933. Sr. Maurene Gilmore, S.N.D., Prin.
Sisters of Notre Dame 1; Lay Teachers 9; Students 175.
Convent—2425 N. Taylor Rd., 44118. Tel: 216-381-3034.

Clinton, Summit Co., St. George (1908), Rev. Msgr. Robert E. Bacher; Deacon Ronald J. Volek.
Res., 7615 Second Ave. N., 44216. Tel: 330-882-3353.
Church—7609 Second Ave. N., 44216.

Columbia Station, Lorain Co., St. Elizabeth Ann Seton (1976), Rev. Charles J. Ryba.
Mailing Address: P.O. Box 968, 44028-0968.
Res., 25777 Royalton Rd., 44028-0968. Tel: 216-236-8595.
Church—25801 Royalton Rd., 44028. Tel: 216-236-5095.
Catechesis/Religious Programs—Tel: 216-236-3711.
Students 200.

Concord Twp., Lake Co., St. Gabriel (1966), Revs. Frederick F. Pausche; Eric S. Orzech; Michael J. Guggenbiller; Deacon Norman H. Davis. In res., Rev. David G. Woost.
Res., 9925 Johnnycake Ridge Rd., 44060-6294. Tel: 216-352-8282; 953-3867 (Cleveland); Fax: 216-354-7558.
School—9935 Johnnycake Ridge Rd., 44060. Tel: 216-352-6169; Fax: 216-939-0143. Sr. Josephmarie Bunosky, S.N.D., Prin.
Sisters of Notre Dame 2; Lay Teachers 19; Students 517.
Catechesis/Religious Programs—Students 949.
Convent—9918 Johnnycake Ridge Rd., 44060. Tel:

216-354-7553.

Copley, Summit Co., Guardian Angels (1964), Rev. J. Norman Riley; Rev. Msgr. Robert C. Wolff, Pastor Emeritus.
Res., 1676 Cleveland-Massillon Rd., 44321-1976. Tel: 330-666-1373.
Church—1686 Cleveland-Massillon Rd., 44321-1976.
Catechesis/Religious Programs—Students 211.

Cuyahoga Falls, Summit Co., Immaculate Heart of Mary (1952), Revs. Thomas W. McCann; John R. Rathfon, Pastor Emeritus; Michael B. Smith; Deacon J. David Seal.
Res., 1905 Portage Trail, 44223. Tel: 330-929-8361; Fax: 330-929-8496.
School—2859 Lillis Dr., 44223. Tel: 330-923-1220; Fax: 330-929-4373. Mr. John Mark, Prin.
Lay Teachers 22; Students 586.
Catechesis/Religious Programs—Students 224.

St. Eugene (1963), Rev. B. Thomas Zeisig.
Res., 1821 Munroe Falls Ave., 44221-3699. Tel: 330-923-5244; Fax: 330-923-8436.
Catechesis/Religious Programs—Students 224.

St. Joseph (1831), Revs. James J. Marsick; Raymond G. Hamlin; Mr. Robert Kochanski, Pastoral Assoc.
Res., 215 Falls Ave., 44221. Tel: 330-928-2173; Fax: 330-928-2173.
Church—1761 Second St., 44221.
School—1909 Third St., 44221-3894. Tel: 330-928-2151; Fax: 330-928-2151. Robert Kochanski, Prin.
Lay Teachers 14; Students 330.
Catechesis/Religious Programs—Students 209.

Doylestown, Wayne Co., SS. Peter and Paul (1827), Rev. David J. McCarthy.
Res., 161 W. Clinton St., 44230-1297. Tel: 330-658-2145; Fax: 330-658-2287. [CEM][JC]
School—169 W. Clinton St., 44230. Tel: 330-658-2804. Marian Gillen, Prin.
Lay Teachers 10; Students 205.
Catechesis/Religious Programs—Students 159.

East Cleveland, Cuyahoga Co., Christ the King (1928), Rev. Louis M. Papes; Deacon Raymond Daull.
Res., 1862 Noble Rd., 44112-1636. Tel: 216-851-4388; 4389; Fax: 216-851-4040.
School—Noble & Terrace Rd., 44112. Tel: 216-451-4756; Fax: 216-451-0831. Mr. Kevin James, Prin.
Lay Teachers 10; Students 200.
Convent—16005 Terrace Rd., 44112.

St. Philomena (1902), Rev. Dennis J. Kleinweber; Delores Breckenridge, Pastoral Assoc. In res., Rev. John R. McCarthy (STU).
Res., 13824 Euclid Ave., 44112. Tel: 216-541-3540; Fax: 216-541-3545.

Eastlake, Lake Co., St. Justin Martyr (1962), Revs. Kevin M. Liebhardt; Daniel A. Lonteen; Joanne E. Novak, Pastoral Assoc.
Mailing Address: 35781 Stevens Blvd., 44095.
Administration Center—Tel: 216-946-1177; Fax: 216-946-2074.
Res., 35701 Stevens Blvd., 44095.
School—35741 Stevens Blvd., 44095. Tel: 216-946-5414; Fax: 216-946-2074. Sr. Mary Quinlan, Prin.
Sisters of Notre Dame 4; Lay Teachers 8; Students 319.
Catechesis/Religious Programs—Students 484.
Convent—35711 Stevens Blvd., 44095. Tel: 216-946-1013.

Elyria, Lorain Co.,

1—St. Agnes, (1914), Rev. Michael D. Ausperk.
Res., 611 Lake Ave., 44035-3541. Tel: 216-322-5622; 236-8276 (Cleveland); Fax: 216-322-0231.
Church—611 Lake Ave., 44035.

2—Holy Cross, (1922) (Polish), Rev. James D. Schorr, Admin.
Res., 417 West Ave., 44035. Tel: 216-323-1022; Fax: 216-323-8277.
Church—1417 West Ave., 44035.

3—St. Jude, (1943), Revs. Frank P. Kosem; Patrick J. O'Connor; Deacon Patrick J. Humphrey. Pastoral Assocs.: Sr. Marie Gillich, C.S.J.; Sr. Angela Nihill.
Res., 590 Poplar St., 44035. Tel: 216-366-5711; 366-6052; Fax: 216-366-1916.
School—594 Poplar St., 44035. Tel: 216-366-1681. Sr. Mary Berigan, S.N.D., Prin.
Sisters of Notre Dame 2; Lay Teachers 17; Students 543.
Catechesis/Religious Programs—Students 421.
Convent—628 Poplar St., 44035. Tel: 216-366-1551.

4—St. Mary, (1845), Revs. Joseph C. Weigand; Gary J. Malin; Deacon Frank A. Humphrey, III.
Res., 320 Middle Ave., 44035. Tel: 216-323-5530; 323-5539; 777-7380 (Cleveland); Fax: 216-322-2329. [CEM]
School—237 Fourth St., 44035. Tel: 216-322-2808; Fax: 216-323-0886. Sr. Geraldine M. Tengler, S.N.D., Prin.
Sisters of Notre Dame 1; Lay Teachers 12; Students 386.
Catechesis/Religious Programs—Tel: 216-322-3054.
Students 320.
Convent—Tel: 216-322-1423.

5—Sacred Heart of Jesus, (1922) (Magyar), Rev. George M. Guschwan.
Res., P.O. Box 417, 44036-0417. Tel: 216-323-3382.
Church—162 Irondale St., 44036.

Elyria Township, Lorain Co., St. Vincent de Paul (1949), Revs. James R. Ols; Liam J. Kitt, Pastor Emeritus.
Res., 41295 N. Ridge Rd., 44035. Tel: 216-324-4212; 277-5285; Fax: 216-324-2892.
School—41315 N. Ridge Rd., 44035. Tel: 216-277-6208. Mrs. Margaret Malenich, Prin.
Lay Teachers 10; Students 264.
Catechesis/Religious Programs—Students 215.

Euclid, Cuyahoga Co.,

1—St. Christine, (1925), Revs. Francis R. Sterk; Francis M. Paik, Pastor Emeritus; Keith M. Alberts.
Res., 840 E. 222nd St., 44123-3317. Tel: 216-261-1410; 261-6210; 261-6144; 261-6383; Fax: 216-261-6003.
School—860 E. 222nd St., 44123. Tel: 216-731-6244. Mrs. Mary Benns, Prin.
Lay Teachers 12; Students 266.

2—St. Felicitas, (1950), Pastoral Team: Revs. Richard J. Bober, Coord.; John J. Kraker; Miss Marybeth Muehle.
Res., 140 Richmond Rd., 44143. Tel: 216-289-0770.
School—Tel: 216-261-1240; Fax: 216-261-5843.
Lay Teachers 22; Students 531.
Catechesis/Religious Programs—Students 292.

3—Holy Cross, (1924), Revs. John P. McNulty; Daniel F. Schlegel. Pastoral Assocs.: Sr. Kathleen Flannery, O.S.U.; Sr. Marcia Carlile, O.S.U.; Deacons Jerome B. Vrabel; Robert Payne.
Res., 19951 Lake Shore Blvd., 44119. Tel: 216-486-0850; Fax: 216-486-0851.
Church—Lake Shore Blvd. & E. 200th St., 44119.
School—Tel: 216-481-6824; Fax: 216-481-9841. Mrs. Sharon Stupica, Prin.
Ursuline Nuns of Cleveland 2; Lay Teachers 17; Students 454.
Catechesis/Religious Programs—Students 224.
Convent—19951 Lake Shore Blvd., 44119. Tel: 216-486-0088.

4—St. Paul, (1860), Rev. Francis C. Mulvanity; Deacon Louis G. Pecek. In res., Rev. William M. Jerse.
Res., 1231 Chardon Rd., 44117-1192. Tel: 216-531-0900; 0901; Fax: 216-481-0919. [CEM]
School—1200 E. 200th St., 44117. Tel: 216-481-6060. Sr. Margaret O'Brien, O.S.U., Prin.
Ursuline Nuns of Cleveland 3; Lay Teachers 7; Students 205.
Convent—1050 E. 200th St., 44117. Tel: 216-531-9178.

5—St. Robert Bellarmine, (1950), Rev. John T. Burkley. In res., Rev. Peter J. Woll.
Res., 23802 Lake Shore Blvd., 44123-1200. Tel: 216-731-2606; 2607.
School—Tel: 216-731-2108; Fax: 216-731-2109. Mary A. Pittinger, Prin.
Lay Teachers 11; Students 237.
Convent—23805 Elmwood Dr., 44123. Tel: 216-731-3020.

6—St. William, (1946), Revs. David G. Baugh; Edward T. Estok. In res., Rev. John E. Lesniak, (Retired); Sr. Jeanette Kearns, O.S.U., Pastoral Assoc.
Res., 367 E. 260th St., 44132-1495. Tel: 216-731-1515.
School—351 E. 260th St., 44132. Tel: 216-731-3060. Mary Heramb, Prin.
Lay Teachers 19; Students 427.
Catechesis/Religious Programs—Students 189.
Convent—584 Lloyd Rd., 44132. Tel: 216-261-1895.

Fairport Harbor, Lake Co., St. Anthony of Padua (1887), Revs. Peter M. Mihalec; William J. Englert, Pastor Emeritus; Deacon Clemens J. Urbanski.
Res., 316 Fifth St., 44077. Tel: 216-354-4525.

Fairview Park, Cuyahoga Co., St. Angela Merici (1923), Revs. Richard E. Hudak; Timothy W. Gareau; Douglas M. Proehl; Anthony Iezzi, Ph.D., Pastoral Assoc.; Deacon James L. Agrippe.
Res., 20970 Lorain Rd., 44126-2096. Tel: 216-333-2133; Fax: 216-333-8061.
School—20830 Lorain Rd., 44126. Tel: 216-333-2126; Fax: 216-333-8480. Mrs. Harriet Davis, Prin.
Lay Teachers 31; Students 626.
Catechesis/Religious Programs—Tel: 216-333-8061.
Students 417.
Convent—4317 W. 210th St., 44126. Tel: 216-331-1948.

Garfield Heights, Cuyahoga Co.,

1—St. Monica, (1952), Rev. John P. Seabold, Coord. of Pastoral Team. Pastoral Team: Rev. Donald P. Oleksiak; Sr. Helen Weis, S.J.S.M.; Deacon Ralph W. Netzband; Ms. Maureen Dowd.
Res., 13623 Rockside Rd., 44125-5197. Tel: 216-662-8685; 8686; 8687; 662-8625; Fax: 216-662-1245.
School—13633 Rockside Rd., 44125. Tel: 216-662-9380; Fax: 216-662-3137. Sr. Helen Weis, S.J.S.M., Prin.
Sisters of St. Joseph Third Order of St. Francis 2; Lay Teachers 19; Students 485.
Catechesis/Religious Programs—Students 263.

2—SS. Peter and Paul, (1927) (Polish), Rev. Anthony W. Zepp; Rev. Msgr. Casimir S. Ciolek, Pastor Emeritus; Rev. Lucjan Stokowski.
Res., 4750 Turney Rd., 44125. Tel: 216-429-1515; 1516; Fax: 216-429-1889.
School—4740 Turney Rd., 44125. Tel: 216-271-6564; Fax: 216-271-0504. Sr. M. Theresine Swigonski, S.S.J.-T.O.S.F., Prin.
Lay Teachers 17; Students 458.
Convent—Tel: 216-429-2666.

3—St. Therese, (1927), Revs. Norman A. Gajdzinski; Mark R. Blinn, Pastor Emeritus; Stephen J. Kaminski; Deacon Lawrence Cermak.
Res., 5276 E. 105th St., 44125. Tel: 216-581-2852; 2853.
School—10608 Penfield Ave., 44125. Tel: 216-581-3080; Fax: 216-581-3031. Sr. M. Anne Cecile Muldoon, O.S.U., Prin.
Ursuline Nuns of Cleveland 1; Lay Teachers 18; Students 410.
Catechesis/Religious Programs—Students 185.
Convent—10430 Granger Rd., 44125. Tel: 216-581-2864.

4—St. Timothy, (1923), Rev. Michael A. Matusz; Deacon Joseph H. Newman.
Res., 4341 E. 131st St., 44105. Tel: 216-581-0981; 0982; Fax: 216-581-8222.
School—Archbishop James P. Lyke Elementary School. See Elementary Schools, Parochial and Diocesan under Institutions Located in the Diocese. Tel: 216-991-9644.

Gates Mills, Cuyahoga Co., St. Francis of Assisi (1943), Revs. James L. Caddy; Thomas J. Pajk; Jean Vitak, Pastoral Assoc.
Res., 6850 Mayfield Rd., P.O. Box 8003, 44040-8003. Tel: 216-461-0066; Fax: 216-461-9053.
School—Tel: 216-442-7450; Fax: 216-446-1132. Sr. Mary Patricia Griesmar, S.N.D., Prin.
Sisters of Notre Dame 2; Lay Teachers 12; Students 287.
Catechesis/Religious Programs—Students 335.
Convent—Tel: 216-449-1352.

Grafton, Lorain Co., Assumption (1894) (Polish), Rev. John M. Tezie.
Res., 1033 Elm St., 44044. Tel: 216-926-2364.

Immaculate Conception (1835), Rev. Robert R. Vieweg.
Res., 708 Erie St., 44044. Tel: 216-926-2268. [CEM]
Catechesis/Religious Programs—Students 232.

Green, Summit Co., Queen of Heaven (1964), Revs. Robert E. Pahler; Robert J. Teknipp, Pastor Emeritus; Deacons Francis R. Lonteen; James A. White.
Res., P.O. Box 296, 44232. Tel: 330-896-2345; Fax: 330-896-3332.
Church—1800 Steese Rd., 44232.
Catechesis/Religious Programs—Students 345.

Highland Heights, Cuyahoga Co., St. Paschal Baylon (1953), Revs. Mario Marzocchi, S.S.S.; Frederico J. Ablog, S.S.S.; William Young, S.S.S.; Deacon Robert J. Bowers.
Res., 5384 Wilson Mills Rd., 44143. Tel: 216-442-3410; 449-7532; 449-7758; Fax: 216-446-9037.
School—5360 Wilson Mills Rd., 44143. Tel: 216-442-6766. Mr. John V. Bednar, Prin.
Sisters of Notre Dame 2; Lay Teachers 24; Students 541.
Catechesis/Religious Programs—Students 444.
Convent—Tel: 216-442-2380.

Hinckley, Medina Co., Our Lady of Grace (1965), Rev. William P. O'Neill. In res., Rev. John T. McDonough.
Res., 1088 Ridge Rd., 44233-9602. Tel: 216-278-2834; 278-4121; Fax: 216-278-2834.
Catechesis/Religious Programs—Students 298.

Hudson, Summit Co., St. Mary (1860), Revs. Joseph J. Costello; Vincent P. O'Dea, Pastor Emeritus; William R. Dickinson; Kathee Sterbenz, Pastoral Assoc.
Res., P.O. Box 657, 44236. Tel: 216-653-8118; 656-2558 (Cleveland); 650-0722 (Akron); Fax: 216-463-5759. [CEM]
Church—340 N. Main St., 44236.
Catechesis/Religious Programs—Students 1,694.

Independence, Cuyahoga Co., St. Michael (1851), Revs. Carl L. D'Agostino; Denis L. St. Marie; Adelbert J. Gassert, Pastor Emeritus; Deacon Robert Weniger. In res., Rev. William F. Gibbons.
Res., 6912 Chestnut Rd., 44131-3399. Tel: 216-524-1394; 1395; Fax: 216-524-7538. [CEM]
Church—Brecksville Rd., 44131.
School—6906 Chestnut Rd., 44131. Tel: 216-524-6405. Sr. Carol Marek, S.N.D., Prin.
Sisters of Notre Dame 2; Lay Teachers 13; Students 369.

Parish Annex—6800 Chestnut Rd., 44131. Tel: 216-524-4212.
Catechesis/Religious Programs—Students 359.
Convent—Tel: 216-447-4406.

Kirtland, Lake Co., Divine Word (1977), Rev. Norman N. Smith; Deacon Carl M. Varga, Pastoral Assoc. In res., Rev. John J. Kinkopf.
Res., 8100 Eagle Rd., 44094. Tel: 216-256-1412; 1413; Fax: 216-256-4929.
Catechesis/Religious Programs—Students 213.

Lakewood, Cuyahoga Co.,

1—ST. CLEMENT, (1922), Revs. Alfred H. Winters; Robert J. Jasany; Sr. Mary Jame Masterson, C.S.J., Pastoral Assoc.
Res., 2022 Lincoln Ave., 44107-6099. Tel: 216-226-5116; Fax: 216-226-9459.
Church—Madison & Lincoln Aves., 44107.
School—14505 Madison Ave., 44107. Tel: 216-226-1942. Mrs. Arlene Polen, Prin.
Lay Teachers 12; Students 219.
Catechesis/Religious Programs—Students 262.
Convent—14505 Madison Ave., 44107.

2—SS. CYRIL AND METHODIUS, (1902) (Slovak), Revs. Richard J. Ondreyka, M.S.; Jerome J. Duke.
Res., 12608 Madison Ave., 44107-4997. Tel: 216-521-7288; 521-9091; Fax: 216-221-8516.
Church—Madison Ave. & Lakewood Ave., 44107.
School—1639 Alameda Ave., 44107. Tel: 216-221-9409. Mrs. June Seman, Prin.
Lay Teachers 10; Students 196.
Convent—1635 Alameda Ave., 44107. Tel: 216-221-3164.

3—ST. HEDWIG, (1905) (Polish), Rev. John J. Bryk.
Res., 12903 Madison Ave., 44107. Tel: 216-521-5086; 521-4463.
Church—12905 Madison Ave., 44107.

4—ST. JAMES, (1908), Revs. John J. Weigand; William L. Andrews, Pastor Emeritus; Mark R. Riley; Miss Kathryn Haag, C.PP.S., Pastoral Assoc. In res., Rev. Thomas P. Kowatch.
Res., 17514 Detroit Ave., 44107. Tel: 216-221-0233.
Church—Detroit & Granger Ave., 44107.
School—17415 Northwood Ave., 44107. Tel: 216-221-1225; Fax: 216-529-7950. Miss Sheila Mannix, Prin.
Sisters of Humility of Mary 2; Lay Teachers 18; Students 359.
Catechesis/Religious Programs—Students 325.
Convent—17400 Northwood Ave., 44107. Tel: 216-521-4125.

5—ST. LUKE, (1922), Revs. Francis P. Walsh; Kenneth J. Jakubowski; Sr. Miriam Erb, C.S.A., Pastoral Assoc.; Deacon David A. Streeter. In res., Rev. Ralph E. Wiatrowski.
Res., 1212 Bunts Rd., 44107-2699. Tel: 216-521-0184; 0185; 0186.
School—13889 Clifton Blvd., 44107. Tel: 216-521-7033; Fax: 216-521-9124. Sr. Marilynn Kozak, O.S.U., Prin.
Ursuline Nuns of Cleveland 2; Lay Teachers 15; Students 332.
Catechesis/Religious Programs—Students 181.
Convent—1221 Chase Ave., 44107.

Litchfield, Medina Co., Our Lady Help of Christians Parish (1976), Rev. Robert A. Burge, Coord. Pastoral Team. Pastoral Team: Revs. Ronald J. Bryda; Michael A. Wittman; Deacon John M. Buda; Sr. Monica Niemira, C.S.J.; Sr. Mary Lou Misciasci, C.S.J.; Sandra J. Lynn.
Administration Center—9608 Norwalk Rd., 44253-9598. Tel: 330-722-1180; 273-1500 (Cleveland).
Catechesis/Religious Programs—Students 464.
Convent—9608 Norwalk Rd., 44253.

Lodi, Medina Co., Jesus Our Teacher (1976). Closed.

Lorain, Lorain Co.,

1—ST. ANTHONY OF PADUA, (1923), Revs. Christian Moore, O.F.M.Conv.; Conrad Sutter, O.F.M.Conv. In res., Bros. Stephen Pfiher, O.F.M.Cap.; Campion Erdei, O.F.M.Cap.
Res., 1305 E. Erie Ave., 44052. Tel: 216-288-0106; Fax: 216-288-9550.
School—1339 E. Erie Ave., 44052. Tel: 216-288-2155. Mrs. Barbara Goebl, Prin.
Lay Teachers 11; Students 332.
Catechesis/Religious Programs—Students 131.

2—SS. CYRIL AND METHODIUS, (1905) (Slovenian), Rev. Paul Krajnik.
Res., 1709 E. 31st St., 44055. Tel: 216-277-8286.
Church—1705 E. 31st St., 44055.

3—HOLY TRINITY, (1906) (Slovak), Rev. Leonard M. Bacik.
Res., 2428 Elyria Ave., 44055-1392. Tel: 216-244-1253; 244-2418.

4—SACRED HEART CHAPEL, (1952) (Hispanic), Rev. Robert J. Reidy; Sr. Suzanne Susany, Pastoral Assoc.; Deacons Tomas Badillo; Jose A. Flores; Carlos Rivera; Prudo Vicens; Jose A. DeGracia; Juan Diaz, Sr.; Jose Luis Piniero.
Res., 3921 Seneca Ave., 44055. Tel: 216-277-7231; 7232; 277-7379 (Rectory); Fax: 216-277-7232.
Church—4301 Pearl Ave., 44055.
Catechesis/Religious Programs—Students 383.

5—ST. JOHN, (1900), Revs. Thomas V. Rath, Pastor Emeritus; Thomas R. Smith.
Res., 2143 Homewood Dr., 44055-2799. Tel: 216-277-7266.
School—2140 E. 36th St., 44055-2798. Tel: 216-277-6285. Mrs. Vera Darmafall, Prin.
Lay Teachers 11; Students 207.

6—ST. JOSEPH, (1896) (German), Revs. Robert J. Reidy; Williams Gibbons, Pastor Emeritus; Deacon Luis Maldonado, Admin.
Res., 317 W. 15th St., 44052-3488. Tel: 216-244-2179.
Church—Reid Ave. & 15th St., 44052.

7—ST. LADISLAUS, (1890) (Hungarian), Revs. Patrick J. Shields, Admin. Pro Tem; Alex D. Demetzky, Pastor Emeritus.
Res., 1412 E. 29th St., 44055. Tel: 216-277-8187; 277-6607 (School).

8—ST. MARY, (1873), Revs. Daniel O. Divis; John J. Kline, Pastor Emeritus; Mrs. Patricia Shullick, Pastoral Assoc.
Res., 310 Eighth St., 44052-1879. Tel: 216-245-5283.
School—307 Seventh St., 44052. Tel: 216-244-1697. Mr. Richard Dargo, Prin.
Lay Teachers 13; Students 190.
Administration Center—309 Seventh St., 44052.

9—NATIVITY OF THE BLESSED VIRGIN MARY, (1898) (Polish), Rev. Robert M. Bielek; Deacon Robert J. Dybo.
Res., 418 W. 15th St., 44052. Tel: 216-244-9090; 621-6445 (Cleveland).
Church—1454 Lexington Ave., 44052.
Catechesis/Religious Programs—Students 65.

10—ST. PETER, (1909), Revs. Kenneth J. Wolnowski; Patrick Henry; Deacon Ralph Krupp. In res., Rev. Jonathan Zingales.
Res., 3501 Oberlin Ave., 44053-2759. Tel: 216-282-9103; 9104; 282-8104; 892-8641 (Cleveland); Fax: 216-892-1693.
School—3601 Oberlin Ave., 44053. Tel: 216-282-9909. Sr. Annamae Murphy, S.N.D., Prin.
Sisters of Notre Dame 2; Lay Teachers 29; Students 620.
Catechesis/Religious Programs—Students 374.
Convent—3651 Oberlin Ave., 44053. Tel: 216-282-2378.

11—ST. STANISLAUS, (1908) (Polish), Rev. Dennis J. Kristancic.
Res., 2702 Elyria Ave., 44055. Tel: 216-244-4185.

12—ST. VITUS, (1922) (Croatian), Rev. Simon J. Nekic.
Res., 1785 E. 32nd St., 44055. Tel: 216-277-8210.

Loudonville, Ashland Co., St. Peter (1870), Rev. Edwin A. Dowling.
Res., 132 N. Wood St., 44842. Tel: 419-994-4396. [CEM]
Catechesis/Religious Programs—Tel: 419-994-3329.
Students 136.

Lyndhurst, Cuyahoga Co., St. Clare (1944), Revs. Stanley J. Klasinski; Louis A. Pizmoht; Joseph Cappelletti; Deacons Ross C. DeJohn, Sr.; Bill Elwood; Leo F. McNulty; Robert J. Matoney, Jr.
Res., 5659 Mayfield Rd., 44124. Tel: 216-449-4242; 4243; 4244; Fax: 216-646-9648.
School—5655 Mayfield Rd., 44124. Tel: 216-449-1554; Fax: 216-449-1497. Miss Ruth Downey, Prin.
Ursuline Nuns of Cleveland 2; Lay Teachers 24; Students 513.
Catechesis/Religious Programs—Students 443.
Convent—5687 Mayfield Rd., 44124. Tel: 216-382-7409.

Macedonia, Summit Co., Our Lady of Guadalupe (1967), Revs. Joseph E. Lehane; Lloyd J. Boymer, Pastor Emeritus; Deacon Mario Vinciguerra; Mrs. Nancy Freibatt, Pastoral Assoc.
Res., 9080 Shepard Rd., 44056-1450. Tel: 216-468-2194; Fax: 216-468-2196.
Catechesis/Religious Programs—Students 351.

Madison, Lake Co., Immaculate Conception (1863), Revs. Luigi C. Miola; Harry J. Fagan, Pastor Emeritus; Deacons Thomas G. Hupertz; Richard F. Kuhlman.
Res., 2846 Hubbard Rd., 44057-2998. Tel: 216-428-5164; 5165; 975-0729 (Cleveland); Fax: 216-428-3075.
Catechesis/Religious Programs—Students 519.

Maple Heights, Cuyahoga Co., St. Martin of Tours (1960), Revs. John G. Vrana; John J. Gerrity, Pastor Emeritus; Allen F. Corrigan; Deacon John R. Bender.
Res., 14600 Turney Rd., 44137-4788. Tel: 216-475-4300; 4301; Fax: 216-475-8242.
School—Tel: 216-475-3633; Fax: 216-475-2484. Rozann Swanson, Prin.
Lay Teachers 11; Students 252.
Catechesis/Religious Programs—Students 239.

St. Wenceslas (1923), Rev. Raymond B. Bartnikowski; Deacon Daniel C. Terrion. In res., Rev. Msgr. Joseph C. Heruday, Pastor Emeritus.
Res., 17825 Libby Rd., 44137-1598. Tel: 216-475-2477; 2478; 475-3304; Fax: 216-662-8101.
Church—Libby Rd. & Cato St., 44137.
School—5254 Arch St., 44137. Tel: 216-662-0180. Sr. Mary Ellen Ryan, S.I.W., Prin.
Sisters 4; Lay Teachers 7; Students 279.

Medina, Medina Co., St. Francis Xavier (1860), Revs. Mark L. Hollis; Ronald J. Wearsch; Sue Kirkham, Pastoral Assoc.; Deacons Joseph E. Loutzenhiser; Leonard A. Sloan; James T. Schlund.
Res., 606 E. Washington St., 44256. Tel: 330-725-4968; 225-3940 (Cleveland); Fax: 330-725-5886. [CEM]
Church—600 E. Washington St., 44256.
School—612 E. Washington St., 44256. Tel: 330-725-3345. Sr. Sandra Bevec, C.S.S.F., Prin.
St. Felix of Cantalice 1; Lay Teachers 24; Students 554.
Catechesis/Religious Programs—Students 812.

Holy Martyrs (1980), Rev. Robert F. Pfeiffer. Pastoral Assocs.: Mary Frances Ehlinger; Suzanne Kozub.
Res., 3100 S. Weymouth Rd., 44256. Tel: 330-722-6633; 722-8951; 216-273-1188 (Cleveland); Fax: 216-273-1188.
Catechesis/Religious Programs—Students 480.

Mentor, Lake Co., St. Bede the Venerable (1964), Rev. John J. Sullivan. Pastoral Assocs.: Mrs. Judith A. Cox; Mrs. Lottie A. Sroczynski; Mrs. Karen J. Roman; Deacons Robert P. Ulman; John Burke, Jr.; Kenneth Knight.
Res., 9114 Lake Shore Blvd., 44060-1697. Tel: 216-257-5544; 5545; Fax: 216-257-2318.
Catechesis/Religious Programs—Tel: 216-257-6988.
Students 643.

St. John Vianney (1969), Revs. Robert W. Kline; Thomas W. Johns; Donald A. Rooney; Deacons James J. Duffy; Wayne W. Snyder.
Administration Office—7575 Bellflower Rd., 44060-3997. Tel: 216-943-3445 (Cleveland); 255-0600 (Cleveland Res.); Fax: 216-255-8832.
School—All Saints of St. John Vianney, Wickliffe. See separate listing under Institutions Located in the Diocese.
Catechesis/Religious Programs—Students 1,255.

St. Mary of the Assumption (1857), Revs. Wilfred T. Smith; Ronald J. Turek; Deacons Raymond C. Beebe; James T. Martin.
Res., 8560 Mentor Ave., 44060-5853. Tel: 216-255-3404; 3405; 942-1774 (Cleveland); Fax: 216-974-8107.
School—8540 Mentor Ave., 44060. Tel: 216-946-7087. Mrs. Judy A. Tucci, Prin.
Ursuline Nuns of Cleveland 3; Lay Teachers 16; Students 420.
Catechesis/Religious Programs—Students 314.
Convent—Tel: 216-942-1656.

Middleburg Heights, Cuyahoga Co., St. Bartholomew (1956), Rev. John A. Leahy; Rev. Msgr. Kenneth W. Saunders, Pastor Emeritus; Rev. Thomas G. Elsasser; Deacon Russell Glorioso; Ms. Joan Skalak, Pastoral Assoc.
Res., 14865 E. Bagley Rd., 44130. Tel: 216-842-5400; Fax: 216-842-2691.
School—Academy of St. Bartholomew, 14875 E. Bagley Rd., 44130. Tel: 216-845-6660; Fax: 216-845-6672. Mr. Frank E. Dobos, Prin.
Sisters 2; Lay Teachers 13; Students 430.
Catechesis/Religious Programs—Students 322.

Middlefield, Geauga Co., St. Lucy (1958), Rev. Harry S. Winca.
Mailing Address: P.O. Box 178, 44062-0178. Tel: 216-632-5824; 548-8091.
Church—16280 Kinsman Rd., 44062.

Newbury, Geauga Co., St. Helen (1949), Revs. James G. McPhillips; Andrew F. O'Boyle, Pastor Emeritus; Deacon Frederick F. Giel. In res., Rev. William J. Johnson.
Res., 12060 Kinsman Rd., 44065. Tel: 216-564-5805; 338-3358 (Cleveland); Fax: 216-338-1734.
School—Tel: 216-564-7125. Sr. Jean Marie Dick, S.N.D., Prin.
Sisters of Notre Dame 2; Lay Teachers 7; Students 212.
Catechesis/Religious Programs—Students 338.

Northfield, Summit Co., St. Barnabas (1956), Revs. Charles T. Diedrick; R. Stephen Vellenga; Sr. Regina Kusnir, V.S.C., Pastoral Assoc.; Deacon Gerald Butler.
Res., 9451 Brandywine Rd., 44067. Tel: 216-467-7959; 467-7941; 467-6424; 650-0240 (Akron); Fax: 216-467-6424.
School—9200 Olde Eight Rd., 44067. Tel: 216-467-7921; Fax: 216-468-1926. Miss Beverly Tabacco, Prin.
Vincentian Sisters of Charity 1; Lay Teachers 21;

Students 612.
Catechesis/Religious Programs—Students 626.

North Olmsted, Cuyahoga Co., St. Brendan (1964), Revs. Cornelius J. Murray; Stephen P. Moran; Sr. Mary Ann Phillip, O.P., Pastoral Assoc. In res., Rev. Albert J. Myers.
Res., 3920 Brendan Ln., No. 615H, 44070-2999. Tel: 216-777-7222; 7223.
Church—4242 Brendan Ln., 44070.
School—Tel: 216-772-8433. Mary Mackin, Prin.
Lay Teachers 14; Students 318.
Catechesis/Religious Programs—Students 348.

St. Clarence (1978), Rev. Thomas A. Flynn; Sr. Sonna M. Bradesca, O.S.U., D.Min., Pastoral Assoc.; Deacons Wayne A. Bosau; Homer L. Sherman.
Res., 30106 Lorain Rd., 44070-3986. Tel: 216-734-2414; Fax: 216-734-4255.
Catechesis/Religious Programs—Students 618.
Convent—30337 Lorain Rd., 44070. Tel: 216-779-0704.

St. Richard (1950), Revs. Charles J. Stollenwerk; George A. Vrabel; Sr. M. Jerome Fitzgerald, S.I.W., Pastoral Assoc.; Sr. Laurie Divoky, S.N.D. In res., Rev. Elmer E. Marquard.
Res., 26855 Lorain Rd., 44070. Tel: 216-777-5050; 5051; 5052; Fax: 216-777-3577.
School—Tel: 216-777-2922; Fax: 216-777-7374. Sr. Julie Demchak, H.M., Prin.
Sisters 4; Lay Teachers 19; Students 563.
Catechesis/Religious Programs—Students 374.
Convent—5053 Whitethorn Ave., 44070. Tel: 216-777-2168.

North Ridgeville, Lorain Co., St. Julie Billiart (1978), Rev. Richard A. Gonser; Deacon John M. Rivera.
Res., 5545 Opal Dr., 44039-2025. Tel: 216-327-1978; 1979; Fax: 216-327-1994.
Church—5500 Lear Nagle Rd., 44039.
Catechesis/Religious Programs—Students 122.

St. Peter (1875), Revs. Thomas J. Hyland; David R. Trask.
Res., 35777 Center Ridge Rd., 44039. Tel: 216-327-2201; 327-2204 (Cleveland). [CEM]
School—35749 Center Ridge Rd., 44039. Tel: 216-327-3212; Fax: 216-327-6843. Sr. Marcia Wilkomm, S.N.D., Prin.
Sisters of Notre Dame 3; Lay Teachers 16; Students 444.
Catechesis/Religious Programs—Students 417.
Convent—Tel: 216-327-8713.

North Royalton, Cuyahoga Co., St. Albert the Great (1959), Revs. John L. Viall; Albert J. Tesek; Robert W. Wisniewski.
Res., 6667 Wallings Rd., 44133. Tel: 216-237-6760; 6761; Fax: 216-237-5945.
School—Tel: 216-237-1032; Fax: 216-237-3308. Mr. John J. Krupinski, Prin.
Lay Teachers 25; Students 671.
Catechesis/Religious Programs—Students 945.

Norton, Summit Co., St. Andrew the Apostle (1951), Revs. James G. Maloney; John A. Wittreich, Pastor Emeritus.
Res., 4022 Johnson Rd., 44203. Tel: 216-825-2617; Fax: 216-825-5309.
Church—Johnson & Hametown Rd., 44203.
Catechesis/Religious Programs—Students 253.

Oberlin, Lorain Co., Sacred Heart (1880). Closed. Parish listings are included under Our Lady Help of Christians, Litchfield. Revs. William B. Padavick; Robert A. Bonnell, Pastor Emeritus.
Res., 410 W. Lorain St., 44074. Tel: 216-774-6791; Fax: 216-774-1337.

Olmsted Falls, Cuyahoga Co., St. Mary of the Falls (1854), Revs. Robert J. Cole; Daniel R. Fickes; Ralph W. Thomas.
Res., 25615 Bagley Rd., 44138-1915. Tel: 216-235-2222; 2223; Fax: 216-235-2937. [CEM]
School—8262 Columbia Rd., 44138. Tel: 216-235-4580. Mrs. Priscilla Shields, Prin.
Lay Teachers 10; Students 245.
Catechesis/Religious Programs—Tel: 216-235-2808.
Students 659.

Orange Village, Cuyahoga Co., St. Margaret of Hungary (1921) (Hungarian), Rev. Ladislaus Rosko.
Res., 4680 Lander Rd., 44022. Tel: 216-248-2618; 248-8148.

Orrville, Wayne Co., St. Agnes (1879), Rev. Paul J. Wysocki.
Res., 541 Spring St., 44667. Tel: 216-682-3606; 682-2611.
Church—E. Oak St. & Lake St., 44667.
Catechesis/Religious Programs—Students 240.

Painesville, Lake Co., St. Mary (1848), Revs. Michael Sdyrcz; Joseph S. Mecir; Richard C. Antall.
Res., 242 N. State St., 44077-4095. Tel: 216-354-4381; 4382; Fax: 216-352-8712. [CEM]
School—268 N. State St., 44077. Tel: 216-352-9414; Fax: 216-352-8712. Sr. Mary Ann Raycher, V.S.C., Prin.
Vincentian Sisters of Charity 3; Lay Teachers 17; Students 321.
Catechesis/Religious Programs—Students 451.
Convent—339 Erie St., 44077-4095. Tel: 216-354-3762.

Parkman, Geauga Co., St. Edward (1928), Rev. Harry S. Winca.
Res., P.O. Box 709, 44080-0709. Tel: 216-548-8091.
Church—16150 Center St., 44080.

Parma, Cuyahoga Co.,

1—St. Anthony of Padua, (1959), Revs. Dale W. Staysniak; John C. Chlebo; William G. Bouhall; Deacons Thomas J. Senn; Robert J. Jasany.
Res., 6750 State Rd., 44134-4518. Tel: 216-842-2666; 2667; 2668; Fax: 216-845-9549.
School—6800 State Rd., 44134. Tel: 216-845-3444; Fax: 216-884-4548. Mr. Frank M. Kuhar, Prin.
Lay Teachers 19; Students 558.
Catechesis/Religious Programs—Students 286.

2—St. Bridget, (1956), Revs. Lawrence J. Bayer; Jerome A. Lukachinsky. In res., Rev. William R. Krizner.
Res., 5620 Hauserman Rd., 44130. Tel: 216-886-4434; 4435; Fax: 216-886-5121.
School—Tel: 216-886-1468. Sr. Alice Rooney, C.S.J., Prin.
Sisters of St. Joseph 2; Lay Teachers 11; Students 331.
Convent—Tel: 216-886-2555.

3—St. Charles Borromeo, (1923), Revs. John T. Carlin; Russell P. Lowe; Richard A. Evans, M.Div.; Sr. Denise Marie Vlna, O.S.U., Pastoral Assoc.; Deacon John A. Talerico. In res., Rev. Dwayne A. Bednar.
Res., 5891 Ridge Rd., 44129-3642. Tel: 216-884-3030; 3031; 884-3232; Fax: 216-884-5326.
School—7107 Wilber Ave., 44129. Tel: 216-886-5546; Fax: 216-886-1163. Sr. Maryann Murphy, O.S.U., Prin.
Ursuline Nuns of Cleveland 3; Lay Teachers 27; Students 847.
Catechesis/Religious Programs—Students 468.
Convent—6902 Charles Ave., 44129. Tel: 216-886-0390.

4—St. Columbkille, (1956), Revs. Neil D. O'Connor; Stephen F. Radecky, Pastor Emeritus; Donald A. Rooney; John A. Misenko; Deacon Edward A. Telepak.
Res., 6740 Broadview Rd., 44134. Tel: 216-524-1987; 1988; 524-1516; Fax: 216-524-9146.
School—Tel: 216-524-4816. Miss Rita Klement, Prin.
Lay Teachers 23; Students 619.
Catechesis/Religious Programs—Students 413.
Convent—Tel: 216-524-1738.

5—St. Francis de Sales, (1931), Revs. Russell G. Rauscher; Donald J. Balogh, Pastor Emeritus; Robert L. Hoban; Neil P. Kookoothe; Deacon Robert J. Piskach.
Res., 3434 George Ave., 44134-2904. Tel: 216-884-2319; 2320; 2321; Fax: 216-884-1661.
Church—State & Snow Rd., 44134.
School—3421 Snow Rd., 44134-2596. Tel: 216-884-2340; Fax: 216-884-8211. Anne Sweeney, Prin.
Ursuline Nuns of Cleveland 1; Lay Teachers 19; Students 395.
Catechesis/Religious Programs—Students 318.
Convent—3425 Snow Rd., 44134. Tel: 216-884-7242.

6—Holy Family, (1872), Revs. James P. Costello; Thomas Sheehan; James McManamon, O.F.M.; Edwin M. Leonard; Thomas L. Weber; Sr. Mary Petronella, V.S.C., Pastoral Assoc.; Deacons Russell J. Glorioso; Joseph P. Litke.
Res., 7367 York Rd., 44130-5162. Tel: 216-842-5533; Fax: 216-842-6658. [CEM]
School—Tel: 216-842-7785; Fax: 216-842-3634. Kathleen Hrutkay, Prin.
Lay Teachers 32; Students 647.
Catechesis/Religious Programs—Students 438.
Convent—Tel: 216-843-9145.

7—St. Matthias, (1980), Rev. Raymond A. Sutter.
Res., 1200 W. Sprague Rd., 44134-6801. Tel: 216-888-8220; 8221; Fax: 216-888-8146.
Catechesis/Religious Programs—Students 248.

Parma Heights, Cuyahoga Co., St. John Bosco (1963), Revs. David D. Liberatore; Edward M. Tulley, Pastor Emeritus; Sean J. Donnelly; Stephen L. Shields; Sr. Therese Horan, O.S.U., Pastoral Assoc.; Deacon Roger Polefko.
Res., 6480 Pearl Rd., 44130. Tel: 216-886-3500; 3501; 3502; Fax: 216-886-0966.
School—6460 Pearl Rd., 44130. Tel: 216-886-0061; Fax: 216-884-4115. Sr. Jane Morgan, O.S.U., Prin.
Ursuline Nuns of Cleveland 2; Lay Teachers 19; Students 523.
Catechesis/Religious Programs—Students 441.
Convent—6485 Beverly Dr., 44130. Tel: 216-888-5229.

Peninsula, Summit Co., Mother of Sorrows (1882), Revs. John D. Terzano; Robert W. Donohoe, Pastor Emeritus; Rev. Msgr. Thomas J. Kelly, Pastor Emeritus.
Res., 6034 S. Locust St., 44264. Tel: 216-657-2631; 657-2075; 467-5549(Cleveland Line); Fax: 216-657-2631.
Catechesis/Religious Programs—Students 159.

Perry, Lake Co., St. Cyprian (1968), Revs. James J. Patton; Anthony F. Alexander, Pastor Emeritus; Deacon Andrew Novak.
Res., 4223 Middle Ridge Rd., 44081. Tel: 216-259-2344; Fax: 216-259-2344.
Catechesis/Religious Programs—Students 327.

Richfield, Summit Co., St. Victor (1964), Rev. Arthur A. Bacher; Deacon Frank O'Connell.
Res., P.O. Box 461, 44286-0461. Tel: 216-659-6591; 659-6321; Fax: 216-659-3618.
Church—3435 Everett Rd, 44286.
Catechesis/Religious Programs—Students 243.

Rittman, Wayne Co., St. Anne (1855), Revs. Phillip P. Pritt; Frank J. Kuta, Pastor Emeritus.
Res., 139 S. First St., 44270-1492. Tel: 216-927-2941. [CEM]
Church—E. Ohio & S. First St., 44270.

Rocky River, Cuyahoga Co., St. Christopher (1922), Revs. Edward F. Prendergast; Thomas G. Fanta. Pastoral Assocs.: Sr. Elizabeth Pierik, C.S.A.; Ms. Gayle Cilimburg. In res., Rev. Msgr. James P. McIntyre.
Res., 20141 Detroit Rd., 44116-2420. Tel: 216-331-4255; 4256; Fax: 216-331-0674.
School—1610 Lakeview Ave., 44116-2409. Tel: 216-331-3075. Sr. Patricia Twohig, Prin.
Sisters of Humility of Mary 1; Lay Teachers 23; Students 457.
Catechesis/Religious Programs—Tel: 216-331-6226.
Students 445.

Seville-Creston, Medina-Wooster Counties, Jesus Emmanuel (1976). Closed.

Shaker Heights, Cuyahoga Co., St. Dominic (1945), Rev. Martin J. Amos; Deacon Bruce R. Cowell. In res., Rev. Herman B. Peters.
Res., 3450 Norwood Rd., 44122-4967. Tel: 216-991-1444; 991-1445; Fax: 216-561-1573.
Church—19000 Van Aken Blvd., 44122.
School—3455 Norwood Rd., 44122-4901. Tel: 216-561-4400. Sr. Mary Ann Mozser, C.PP.S., Prin.
Sisters of the Precious Blood 2; Lay Teachers 9; Students 228.
Catechesis/Religious Programs—Students 294.

Sheffield, Lorain Co., St. Teresa (1845), Revs. Edward J. Luca; Raymond J. Grismer, Pastor Emeritus; John H. Walker, Pastor Emeritus; Sr. Mary Floranne, S.N.D., Pastoral Assoc.
Church—1878 Abbe Rd., 44054-2322. Tel: 216-934-4227. [CEM]

Sheffield Lake, Lorain Co., St. Thomas the Apostle (1962), Rev. John J. McCaffrey.
Res., 521 Harris Rd., 44054. Tel: 216-949-7744.
School—715 Harris Rd., 44054. Tel: 216-949-6275; Fax: 216-949-6275. Sr. Helene F. Minut, S.N.D., Prin.
Sisters of Notre Dame; Sisters 1; Lay Teachers 9; Students 198.
Catechesis/Religious Programs—Students 186.
Convent—4855 E. Lake Rd., 44054. Tel: 216-949-6232.

Solon, Cuyahoga Co., St. Rita (1929), Revs. Robert M. Wendelken; Robert A. Lorkowski; Clyde K. Foster; Mr. Albert E. Leko, Pastoral Assoc.; Deacons William Donlin; Gerard Ziemkiewicz.
Res., 32820 Baldwin Rd., 44139-4098. Tel: 216-248-1350; Fax: 216-248-2094.
School—33200 Baldwin Rd., 44139. Fax: 216-248-9442. Mrs. Phyllis Nemetz, Prin.
Lay Teachers 21; Students 553.
Catechesis/Religious Programs—Students 762.

Resurrection of Our Lord (1971), Rev. J. Mark Hobson, Coord., Pastoral Team. Pastoral Team: Rev. Theodore Lucas; Ms. Elizabeth Frey; Sr. Patricia Adams, C.S.J.
Res., 31600 Farm Dr., 44139. Tel: 216-248-0980; 0981; Fax: 216-248-0992.
Church—32001 Cannon Rd., 44139.
Catechesis/Religious Programs—Students 394.
Convent—5710 Janet Blvd., 44139. Tel: 216-248-4364.

South Amherst, Lorain Co., Nativity of Blessed Virgin Mary (1933), Revs. Edward J. Kordas; Wallace F. Roth, Pastor Emeritus.
Res., 333 S. Lake St., 44001. Tel: 216-986-7011.

South Euclid, Cuyahoga Co., St. Gregory the Great (1922), Rev. Msgr. William N. Novicky; Revs. Stephen A. Towell, Pastor Emeritus; Francis G. Van Bergen; John G. Crawford. Pastoral Assocs.: Sr. Monica Schmitt, S.N.D.; Sr. Mary Callista Antolik, S.N.D.; Sr. Lucille Myers, S.I.W.; Mrs. Mary Ann Trask; Deacon John P. Sferry.

Res., 1545 S. Green Rd., 44121-4085. Tel: 216-382-7601; Fax: 216-382-4992.
School—4478 Rushton Rd., 44121-4084. Tel: 216-381-0363; Fax: 216-691-0435. Miss Lucy Iemmolo, Prin.
Sisters of Notre Dame 1; Lay Teachers 32; Students 789.
Catechesis/Religious Programs—Students 339.
St. Margaret Mary (1948), Revs. Thomas J. Lusoski; Neal J. Buckon; Deacon John T. Wenzel.
Res., 4217 Bluestone Rd., 44121-3427. Tel: 216-382-4114; 4115.
School—4205 Bluestone Rd., 44121. Tel: 216-382-4272; Fax: 216-382-4559. Sr. Mary Barbara Morscher, S.N.D., Prin.
Sisters of Notre Dame 2; Lay Teachers 8; Students 196.
Catechesis/Religious Programs—Students 103.
Convent—4215 Bluestone Rd., 44121. Tel: 216-381-8787.

Spencer, Medina Co., Jesus Our Savior (1976). Closed.

Stow, Summit Co., Holy Family (1946), Revs. Edward J. Szabo; Joseph J. Lieberth; James F. Flood; Sr. Noel Marra, O.S.U., Pastoral Assoc.; Deacon Philip P. Kamlowsky.
Res., 3450 Sycamore Dr., 44224-3999. Tel: 330-688-6411; 6412; 6413; Fax: 330-688-3474.
Church—3179 Kent Rd., 44224.
School—3163 Kent Rd., 44224. Tel: 330-688-3816. Miss Susan Jelenic, Prin.
Lay Teachers 32; Students 699.
Catechesis/Religious Programs—Students 679.

Strongsville, Cuyahoga Co., St. John Neumann (1977), Revs. Robert J. Kraig; F. Christopher Esmurdoc; Robert J. Franco; Sr. Patricia Sylvester, S.N.D., Pastoral Assoc.; Deacon Thomas Grasson.
Res., 16271 Pearl Rd., 44136. Tel: 216-238-1770; 1771; Fax: 216-238-2030.
School—SS. Joseph & John Interparochial. See St. Joseph, Strongsville. Tel: 216-238-4877.
Catechesis/Religious Programs—Students 1,039.
St. Joseph (1946), Revs. Robert J. Sanson; Charles F. Strebler; Douglas Makowski; Sr. Betty Gulick, S.S.J.-T.O.S.F., Pastoral Assoc.; Deacons Alfred J. Koch; Howard Masony.
Res., 12700 Pearl Rd., 44136-3484. Tel: 216-238-5555; 5556; 238-1038; Fax: 216-238-1059.
School—SS. Joseph and John Interparochial, 12580 Pearl Rd., 44136. Tel: 216-238-4877; Fax: 216-238-8745. Mrs. Darlene Thomas, Prin.
Sisters of St. Joseph 1; Lay Teachers 30; Students 840.
Catechesis/Religious Programs—Tel: 216-238-5231.
Students 608.
Convent—12600 Pearl Rd., 44136. Tel: 216-238-6352.

Tallmadge, Summit Co., Our Lady of Victory (1944), Rev. John R. Hengle; Sr. Dolores Bourquin, H.M., Pastoral Assoc. & D.R.E.
Administration Center—73 North Ave., 44278-1996. Tel: 330-633-3637; 633-3672; Fax: 330-633-6978.
Church—105 North Ave., 44278.
Catechesis/Religious Programs—Students 550.

Thompson, Geauga Co., St. Patrick (1854), Rev. Paul F. Smith; Deacon Andrew J. Novak.
Res., 16550 Rock Creek Rd., Rte. 166, 44086-8753. Tel: 216-298-1327; Fax: 216-298-1846. [CEM]

Twinsburg, Summit Co., SS. Cosmas and Damian (1963), Rev. Robert E. Friedel; Deacon Vincent L. Belsito, Prin. In res., Rev. Joseph A. Goebel.
Res., 10419 Ravenna Rd., 44087-1726. Tel: 216-425-8141; 8142; Fax: 216-963-6597.
Church—10439 Ravenna Rd., 44087-1726. Tel: 216-425-8141.
School—Tel: 216-425-4279.
Lay Teachers 5; Students 61.
Catechesis/Religious Programs—Students 508.

University Heights, Cuyahoga Co., Gesu (1926), Revs. John V. White, S.J.; Edward M. Nemeth, S.J.; Deacon James K. O'Donnell.
Res., 2470 Miramar Blvd., 44118. Tel: 216-932-0617; 0618; Fax: 216-932-0731.
Church—2490 Miramar Blvd., 44118.
School—2450 Miramar Blvd., 44118. Tel: 216-932-0620; Fax: 216-932-8326. Sr. Mary Reiling, S.N.D., Prin.
Sisters of Notre Dame 2; Lay Teachers 40; Students 763.
Catechesis/Religious Programs—Students 330.
Convent—2440 Miramar Blvd., 44118. Tel: 216-932-1660.

Valley City, Medina Co., St. Martin of Tours (1840), Rev. Thomas R. Dunphy; Deacon James E. Petrus.
Res., 1824 Station Rd., 44280. Tel: 330-483-3808; Fax: 330-483-3848. [CEM]
Catechesis/Religious Programs—Students 370.

Wadsworth, Medina Co., Sacred Heart (1866), Revs. James A. Conry; Neil A. Crosby.
Res., 272 Broad St., 44281. Tel: 330-336-3049.
School—110 Humbolt Ave., 44281. Tel: 330-334-6272; Fax: 330-334-3236. Mrs. Joan Thompson, Prin.
Vincentian Sisters of Charity 2; Lay Teachers 12; Students 341.
Catechesis/Religious Programs—Students 457.
Convent—268 Broad St., 44281. Tel: 330-334-5063.

Warrensville Heights, Cuyahoga Co., St. Jude (1945), Rev. Thomas Carolan, O.F.M.; Susan Horvath, Pastoral Assoc. In res., Rev. Emmanuel Beunen, O.F.M.; Bro. Joseph DiSanto.
Res., 4760 Richmond Rd., 44128-5986. Tel: 216-292-6600; 6601; 6602.

Wellington, Lorain Co., St. Patrick (1851), Rev. James J. Reymann.
Res., 512 N. Main St., 44090-1198. Tel: 216-647-4375.
Catechesis/Religious Programs—Students 262.

Westlake, Cuyahoga, Co., St. Bernadette (1950), Revs. James F. Kramer; John W. Krasen; James T. Klein. Pastoral Assocs.: Mrs. Catherine Vaughan; Sr. Theresa Sullivan, C.S.J.; Mrs. Diane Portorreal; Deacon Stanley J. Fulton. In res., Rev. James A. O'Neill, Pastor Emeritus.
Res., 2256 Clague Rd., 44145-4328. Tel: 216-734-1300; Fax: 216-734-1584.
School—2300 Clague Rd., 44145. Tel: 216-734-7717; Fax: 216-734-9198. Mrs. Denise King, Prin.
Lay Teachers 18; Students 564.
Catechesis/Religious Programs—Students 489.
St. Ladislas (1973), Rev. Thomas F. Cullen. Pastoral Assocs.: Sr. Mary Joan Grisez, O.S.U.; Robert C. Hertl; Deacons David L. Kinzel; William Gorman. In res., Most Rev. A. James Quinn.
Res., 2335 Bassett Rd., 44145-2999. Tel: 216-835-2300; 2301; 2302; Fax: 216-835-2300.
Church—2345 Bassett Rd., 44145.
Catechesis/Religious Programs—Students 361.

West Salem, Wayne Co., St. Stephen (1952), Revs. Carl A. Uhler; Paul W. Hackman, Pastor Emeritus; Deacon Joseph W. Johnson.
Res., 44 Britton St., 44287. Tel: 419-853-4946.
Catechesis/Religious Programs—Students 124.

Wickliffe, Lake Co., Our Lady of Mount Carmel (1921), Revs. David L. McCafferty; Dave R. Ireland; Nestor Almazan; Sr. Rosemary Diba, V.S.C., Pastoral Assoc.; Deacon John W. Strmac.
Res., 1730 Mount Carmel Dr., 44092-1835. Tel: 216-585-0700; Fax: 216-585-0870.
Church—29850 Euclid Ave., 44092.
School—29840 Euclid Ave., 44092. Tel: 216-585-0800. Mrs. Ellen Samuels, Prin.
Lay Teachers 14; Students 338.
Catechesis/Religious Programs—Students 307.

Willoughby, Lake Co., Immaculate Conception (1866), Revs. Francis D. Curran; Jeffrey M. Weaver.
Res., 37935 Wright St., 44094-5899. Tel: 216-942-4500.
School—37940 Euclid Ave., 44094. Tel: 216-942-2121; Fax: 216-942-6766. Mrs. Rosalie A. Lewis, Prin.
Ursuline Nuns of Cleveland 1; Lay Teachers 20; Students 409.
Catechesis/Religious Programs—Students 313.

Willoughby Hills, Lake Co., St. Noel (1980), Rev. George Smiga. Pastoral Assocs.: Miss Alice Hinkel; Anthony Camino; Deacons Lawrence Somrack; Robert C. Anderson; Edward Feldkamp. In res., Rev. Thomas M. Dragga.
Res., 35200 Chardon Rd., Tel: 216-946-0887; Fax: 216-946-4331.
Catechesis/Religious Programs—Students 310.

Willowick, Lake Co., St. Mary Magdalene (1949), Pastoral Team: Revs. John P. Singler, Coord. Pastoral Team; David L. Enzman; Sr. Nancy Hendershot, C.S.A.; Sr. Mercia Madigan, O.S.U.
Res., 460 East 321 St., 44095-3663. Tel: 216-943-2133; Fax: 216-943-4450.
Church—32114 Vine St., 44095.
School—Tel: 216-944-7222; Fax: 216-944-8416. Ms. Judy Novey, Prin.
Ursuline Nuns of Cleveland 1; Lay Teachers 13; Students 297.
Catechesis/Religious Programs—Tel: 216-944-2523.
Students 508.
Convent—32301 Willowick Dr., 44095. Tel: 216-944-1134.

Wooster, Wayne Co., St. Mary of the Immaculate Conception (1846), Revs. John J. Mueller; Kevin M. Conroy; Deacon Bernard E. Hosfeld. Pastoral Assocs.: Mrs. Jacquelynn Lee; Sr. Maria Kurrie, S.S.J.-T.O.S.F.
Res., P.O. Box 109, 44691. Tel: 330-264-8824; 264-8822; Fax: 330-262-4633. [CEM]
Church—527 Beall Ave., 44691.
School—535 E. Bowman St., P.O. Box 85, 44691. Tel: 330-262-8671. Cathleen Mark, Prin.
Lay Teachers 9; Students 250.
Catechesis/Religious Programs—Students 322.
Convent—546 E. Bowman St., 44691. Tel: 330-264-5569.

Cleveland Diocesan Mission

EL SALVADOR, C.A. *The Catholic Center*. Rev. Denis St. Marie, Dir. Society for the Propagation of the Faith; Sr. Lisa Marie Belz, O.S.U.
Parroquial de Nuestra Senora de Guadalupe. Chirilagua Depto San Miguel, El Salvador. Revs. Joseph H. Callahan; John D. King; Sr. Catherine Walsh, C.S.A.
Parroquial Immaculada Concepcion. Puerto de La Libertad, El Salvador. Revs. Albert Krupp; William A. Thaden; Sr. Catherine McConnell, H.M.; Sr. Roberta Goebel, O.S.U.
Senora del Pilar, Villa de Zaragoza. Rev. G. Michael Williamson.

Chaplains of Public Institutions

CLEVELAND. *Airport, Cleveland Hopkins International*. Vacant.
Bedford Municipal Hospital. Attended from St. Pius X. Tel: 216-232-8166.
Children's Receiving Home. Attended from the Metzenbaum Center.
Cleveland Clinic Hospital. Rev. Dwayne Bednar. Tel: 216-884-3030; Joseph P. Owens, S.J. Tel: 216-397-4689.
Cleveland House of Correction. Rev. Emmanuel Beunen, O.F.M. Tel: 216-292-6602.
Cleveland Psychiatric. (CPI). Rev. Thomas Gallagher. Tel: 216-361-1444.
Cuyahoga County Detention Home. Rev. James P. O'Donnell, on call, Tel: 216-566-9953.
Cuyahoga County Jail. Rev. Kenneth Breen, O.de.M. Tel: 216-651-5043.
Cuyahoga County Nursing Home. Rev. John F. McMahon. Tel: 216-292-6602.
Cuyahoga Hills Boys School. Rev. Emmanuel Beunen, O.F.M. Tel: 216-292-6602.
Deaconess Hospital. Rev. Raymond Schultheis, C.PP.S. Tel: 216-749-2323.
Dept. of Youth Services. Rev. Emmanuel Beunen, O.F.M. Tel: 216-292-6602.
Fairview General Hospital. Rev. Steven Walick. Tel: 216-252-2332.
Grace Hospital. Attended from St. Augustine. Tel: 216-781-5530.
Health Hill Hospital for Children. Vacant.
Kaiser Foundation Hospital. Attended from St. Ann, Fairhall. Tel: 216-321-0024.
Kaiser Foundation Hospital. Attended from St. Bridget. Snow Rd., 44129. Tel: 216-886-4434.
Lakewood Hospital. Tel: 216-226-5116. Rev. Thomas P. Kowatch. Tel: 216-221-0233.
Lutheran Medical Center. Rev. Eugene A. Costa, O. de M., Tel: 216-651-5043.
Meridia Euclid General Hospital. Vacant.
Meridia Hillcrest Hospital. Attended from St. Francis of Assisi. Tel: 216-461-0066.
Meridia Huron Road Hospital. Attended from St. Philomena. Tel: 216-541-3540.
Meridia South Pointe Hospital. Rev. Michael Matusz. Tel: 216-581-0982.
Metro Health Center for Rehabilitation. Deacon Charles O. Johnson, Chap., Tel: 216-459-4663.
Metro Health Medical Center. (Hospital). Rev. Thomas V. O'Donnell Tel: 216-861-6297; Deacon Charles O. Johnson, Chap., Tel: 216-671-9472.
Metzenbaum Children's Center. Attended from St. Augustine. Tel: 216-781-5330.
Mount Sinai Hospital. Catholic Chaplain Service. Tel: 216-486-8253. Deacon William Dirk, Chap.
Northeast Pre Release Center. Rev. James O'Donnell. Tel: 216-566-9953.
Parma Community Hospital. Rev. James R. Semonin. Tel: 216-843-8781.
Rainbow Hospital. (See University Hospitals).
Richmond Heights General Hospital. Attended from St. Felicitas. Tel: 216-289-0770.
St. Luke Hospital. Attended from Our Lady of Peace. Tel: 216-421-4211.
SouthWest General Hospital. Rev. Dismas Boeff. Tel: 216-433-0696.
Sunny Acres Skilled Nursing Facility. Rev. Emmanuel Beunen, O.F.M. Tel: 216-292-6602.
University Hospitals. Rev. John J. Hayes. Tel: 216-431-5900.
Veterans Administration Hospitals, Brecksville V.A 1000 Brecksville Rd., 44141. Tel: 216-526-3030. Chaplains: Revs. Thomas Gallagher; John E. Bolan, C.PP.S., Cleveland V.A., 10701 East Blvd., 44106. Tel: 216-791-3800, Ext. 305.

AKRON. *Akron City Hospital*. Rev. James J. Berardi. Tel: 216-535-4141.
Akron General Hospital. Rev. Robert E. Clancy. Tel: 216-434-4348.
Edwin C. Shaw Hospital. Attended from Nativity of the Lord Jesus. Tel: 216-699-5086.

AMHERST. *Amherst Hospital*. Attended from St. Joseph. Tel: 216-988-2848.

APPLE CREEK. *Apple Creek State Institute*. Vacant. Tel: 216-696-6525.
ASHLAND. *Samaritan Hospital*. Attended from St. Edward. Tel: 419-289-0491.
AVON. *Our Lady of the Wayside*. 38125 Colorado Ave., 44011. Tel: 216-934-4327. Rev. Robert T. Begin.
BARBERTON. *Barberton Citizens Hospitals*. Attended from St. Augustine. Tel: 216-745-0011.
Juvenile Court Center. Vacant. 122 21 St., N.W., 44203. Tel: 216-825-6231.
CHAGRIN FALLS. *Windsor Hospital*. Attended from St. Joan of Arc. Tel: 216-247-7183.
CHARDON. *Geauga Community Hospital*. Attended from St. Helen, Newbury. Tel: 216-564-5805; 338-3358 (Cleveland).
CUYAHOGA FALLS. *Fallsview Mental Health Center*. Attended from St. Eugene. Tel: 216-923-5244.
General Hospital. Attended from St. Joseph. Tel: 216-928-2173.
ELYRIA. *Elyria Memorial Hospital*. St. Mary, Elyria. Tel: 216-323-5539; 777-7380 (Cleveland). Sr. Joan Tomchey, O.S.U., Chap., Pastoral Care, Tel: 216-933-5769.
GRAFTON. *Grafton Correctional Institution*. Tel: 216-781-1161. Deacons Edward Dillon, Chap., Tel: 216-323-7331; James Petrus, Chap., Tel: 216-723-6100.
HUDSON. *Youth Development Center*. Attended from St. Andrew Abbey. Tel: 216-721-5300.
LODI. *Lodi Hospital, Our Lady Help of Christians, Litchfield*. Tel: 216-722-1180; 273-1500 (Cleveland).
LORAIN. *Lorain Community / St. Joseph Regional Health Care Center*. Tel: 216-967-3997; 282-9121. Deacon Thomas Waken, Chap., Tel: 216-888-7799.
LOUDONVILLE. *Kettering Hospital*. Attended from St. Peter. Tel: 419-994-4396.
MEDINA. *Medina Community Hospital*. Attended from St. Francis Xavier. Tel: 216-725-4968.
NORTHFIELD. *Western Reserve Psychiatric Habilitation Center*. P.O. Box 305, 44067. Tel: 216-467-7131. Rev. Adelbert Gassert.
OBERLIN. *Allen Memorial Hospital*. Attended from Sacred Heart. Tel: 216-774-6791.
ORRVILLE. *Dunlap Memorial Hospital*. Attended from St. Agnes. Tel: 216-682-3606.
PAINESVILLE. *Lake County Memorial Hospital-East*. Attended from St. Mary. Tel: 216-354-4381.
SMITHVILLE. *Boys Village of Ohio*. Attended from St. Mary, Wooster. Tel: 216-264-8824.
WADSWORTH. *Wadsworth Health Care Center*. Attended from Sacred Heart of Jesus. Tel: 216-336-3049.
Wadsworth-Rittman Hospital. Attended from Sacred Heart of Jesus. Tel: 216-336-3049.
WILLOUGHBY. *Lake County Memorial Hospital-West*. Attended from Immaculate Conception. Tel: 216-942-4500.
WOOSTER. *Wooster Community Hospital*. Attended from St. Mary. Tel: 216-264-8824.

Released from Diocesan Assignment:
Reverend Monsignors—
Broglio, Timothy, Secretariat of State, Vatican City State, 00120
Reverend Fathers—
Berthiaume, Gary D., Cenacle Retreat House, P.O. Box 340, Warrenville, IL 60555
Cooper, R. John, 4379 Plumwood Dr., North Olmsted, OH 44070
Klamet, Francis X., Holy Rosary, 12021 Mayfield Rd., Cleveland, OH 44106
Lang, Joseph J., Church of the Resurrection, 9504 100th Ave., Fort St. John, BC V1J 1X7 Canada
Lynch, James M., Casilla 53303, Santiago, Chile
McShane, Patrick E., Veterans Administration Medical Center, 940 Belmont St., Brockton, MA 02401
Myers, Kenneth C., Missionaries of Pastoral Charity Society, 1135 Mission Rd., San Antonio, TX 78210-4598
Obloy, Leonard G., Faculty & Vice Rector, St. Mary Seminary, Emmitsburgh, MD 21727
Patrick, William J., St. Jude Hospital & Rehabilitation Center, 101 E. Valencia Mesa Dr., Fullerton, CA 92634
Petcavage, Leonard, Order of Benedict, O.S.B., 10510 Buckeye Rd., Cleveland, OH 44104
Piskura, Joseph H., P.O. Box 316, Fort Belvoir, VA 22060
Valley, John, 37825 Lake Shore Blvd., Eastlake, OH 44095

Military Chaplains:
Reverend Fathers—
Czech, Edward M.
McCausland, Joseph E.
Sheil, James

Graduate Studies:
Reverend Fathers—
Woost, Michael G.

Absent on Leave:
Reverend Fathers—
Baranek, Raymond
Brodnick, Joseph
Burg, Thomas R.
Chojnacki, David
Richards, John M.
Severt, William H.

Retired:
Reverend Monsignors—
Ciolek, Casimir S., 906 College Ave., Cleveland, OH 44113
Gasbarre, Francis E., Holy Trinity, 24821 Columbus Rd., Bedford Heights, OH 44146
Goldikovskis, Alexander I., 21362 Milan Ave., Cleveland, OH 44119
Heruday, Joseph C., St. Wenceslas, 17825 Libby Rd., Maple Heights, OH 44137
Kelly, Thomas J., Issenmann Place, 4185 Brookway Ln., Brooklyn, OH 44144
McIntyre, James P., 20141 Detroit Rd., Rocky River, OH 44116
Moriarty, Joseph T., 6620 Pearl Rd., Parma Heights, OH 44130. Tel: 216-885-0320
Spitzig, Joseph, 1264 Tupelo Ln., West Salem, OH 44287
Wolff, Robert C., 4516 Rex Lake Dr., Akron, OH 44319
Reverend Fathers—
Alexander, Anthony, 344 Sanford St., Painesville, OH 44077
Anderson, John F., 12969 Chillicothe Rd., Chesterland, OH 44026
Andrews, William L., 35990 Westminster Ave., North Ridgeville, OH 44039
Balogh, Donald J., 785 W. Perimeter Rd., Frewsburg, NY 14738
Becherer, James R., 4963 E. Lake Rd., Sheffield Lake, OH 44054
Blinn, Mark R., West Bay Manor, 27601 Westchester Pkwy., Westlake, OH 44145
Bonnell, Robert A., 143 E. College St., Apt. 313, Oberlin, OH 44074
Boymer, Lloyd J., St. Barnabas, 1105 Canyonview, #304, Sagamore, OH 44067
Brennan, Robert, 1076 Sylvan Ave., Lakewood, OH 44107
Bruening, Allen
Byrider, Charles L., St. Francis De Sales Parish, 4019 Manchester Rd., Akron, OH 44319
Camille, Edward J., St. Basil, 8700 Brecksville Rd., Brecksville, OH 44141
Cauley, Robert W., Eliza Jennings, 10603 Detroit Ave., Lakewood, OH 44107
Cimperman, Victor J., 1240 E. 61st St., Cleveland, OH 44103
Clines, Paul J., St. Augustine Parish, 965 Norton Ave., Barberton, OH 44203
Conway, Neil, 4045 Wetmore Rd., Cuyahoga Falls, OH 44223
Cook, William R., Parkway S., #165, Phoenix, AZ 85032
Cullen, Thomas F., 2335 Bassett Rd., Westlake, OH 44145
Dalton, John, Holy Name, 8328 Broadway, Cleveland, OH 44105
Demetzky, Alex D., 7611 Eve Ave., Cleveland, OH 44102
Dodd, Anthony J., Assumption, 5445 Smith Rd., Brook Park, OH 44142
Donohue, Robert W., St. Jude, 590 Poplar St., Elyria, OH 44035
Englert, William J., 534 W. Bullard Ave., Fresno, CA 93704
Eylar, William D., 6163 E. Akron St., Mesa, AZ 85205
Fagan, Harry J., 7600 South Ridge Rd., Madison, OH 44057
Gaebelein, Claude J., 4291 Richmond Rd., Warrenville Heights, OH 44122
Gassert, Adelbert, 925 Canyon View Dr., #205, Akron, OH 44067
Gerrity, John J., 4291 Richmond Rd., Warrensville Heights, OH 44122
Gibbons, William, 6912 Chestnut Rd., Independence, OH 44131
Goebel, Joseph, 10419 Ravenna Rd., Twinsburg, OH 44087-1726
Grandillo, James, 1007 Superior Ave., Cleveland, OH 44144
Grismer, Raymond J., Issenmann Place, 4185 Brookway Ln., Brooklyn, OH 44144
Hackman, Paul W., 5232 Broadview Rd., Richfield, OH 44286
Hanzo, Robert, 5406 Pebble Creek Ln., Painesville, OH 44077
Hritz, Paul, 28700 Euclid Ave., Wickliffe, OH 44092
Ivanauskas, Balys C., 200 S. Silvery Ln., Dearborn, MI 48124-1225
Jezeski, Henry, 7551 Pleasant Run Rd., Seven Hills, OH 44131-5906
Johnson, William J., 12060 Kinsman Rd., Newbury, OH 44065
Kilcoyne, John, Issenmann Place, 4185 Brookway Ln., Brooklyn, OH 44144
Kinkopf, John J., Divine Word, 8100 Eagle Rd., Kirtland, OH 44094
Kitt, William J., Castleblakeney, Ballinasloe, Co. Galway, Ireland
Kline, John J., 33803 Electric Blvd., #E-6, Avon Lake, OH 44012
Kreps, Anthony L., 2920 Hamlin Rd., Medina, OH 44256
Kuta, Frank, 8795 N. Kane Rd., Warrensville, OH 44281
Laheta, Andrew P., 5232 Broadview Rd., Richfield, OH 44286
Lesniak, John, 367 E. 260th St., Euclid, OH 44132
Lyons, William P., 2603 Benton St., Akron, OH 44312
Mackert, Albert J., 13719 Tartan Dr., Sun City West, AZ 85375
McDonough, John T., 1088 Ridge Rd., Hinckley, OH 44233
McMahon, John F., 10812 Adeline Rd., Cleveland, OH 44111
Michalski, Thaddeus C., Issenmann Place, 4185 Brookway Ln., Brooklyn, OH 44144
Minnoggio, Ferrando, North American College, Vatican City State, 00120
Mosovsky, James J., 7801 Detroit Ave., Cleveland, OH 44102
Mrakuzic, Stephen A., Mailing Address: 4849 Grace Rd., North Olmsted, OH 44070
Mulica, James, 255 N. El Cielo Rd., No. 366, Palm Springs, CA 92262
Myers, Albert, 3920 Brendan Ln., North Olmstead, OH 44070
O'Boyle, Andrew F., 4170 N. Amber Dr., Brooklyn, OH 44144
O'Dea, Vincent P., Issenmann Place, 4185 Brookway Ln., Brooklyn, OH 44144
O'Neill, James A., St. Bernadette Parish, 2225 Clague Rd., Westlake, OH 44145
Ondik, Michael J., 1045 S. 70th St., Mesa, AZ 85208
Paik, Francis M., 12340 Bass Lake Rd., #B27, Chardon, OH 44024
Patragnoni, Ettore, Viale Principe di Piemonte No. 18, Stresa, (Novara) 28049 Italy
Peters, Herman B., St. Dominic Parish, 3450 Norwood Rd., Shaker Heights, OH 44122
Plafcan, Paul, 5232 Broadview Rd., Richfield, OH 44286
Radecky, Stephen, 3395 E. 53rd St., Cleveland, OH 44127
Rath, Thomas V., 200 St. Joseph Dr., Amherst, OH 44001
Rathfon, John R., 263 Woodpecker Rd., Naples, FL 33961
Reichlin, Urban A., 76 Westshore Dr., Avon Lake, OH 44012
Roth, Wallace F., Issenmann Place, 4185 Brookway Lane, Brooklyn, OH 44144
Schneid, Michael, 6765 State St., Cleveland, OH 44134
Silva, David E., 2788 E. Ridgewood Dr., Seven Hills, OH 44131
Smith, James A., 5163 Broadway, Cleveland, OH 44127
Storey, John R., 5232 Broadview Rd., Richfield, OH 44286
Sullivan, Thomas F., 39 N. Portage Path, Akron, OH 44303
Teknipp, Robert J., 45 Lethbridge Ln., Akron, OH 44321-1369
Tomc, Victor N., 20654 Centuryway Rd., Maple Heights, OH 44137
Tomicky, Ronald, 6164 Westminster Dr., Parma, OH 44129-4924
Towell, Stephen A., 4483 Ardendale Rd., South Euclid, OH 44121
Trapp, Raymond A., 6360 Elmdale Ave., Brook Park, OH 44142
Trivison, Louis J., 283 Union St., Bedford, OH 44146
Valentini, Francis M., 2749 Orchid Oaks Dr., #302-A, Sarasota, FL 34239
Wagner, Joseph F., St. Colette, 330 W. 130th St., Brunswick, OH 44212
Walker, John H., 5550 Harvest Hill Rd., #T-280, Dallas, TX 75230
Wilson, John F., St. Edward Home, 3131 Smith Rd., Akron, OH 44313
Wittreich, John A., 18592 Edward Rd., Lot 143 Butternut, Doylestown, OH 44230
Wolf, John W., 5232 Broadview Rd., Richfield, OH 44286
Woll, Peter J., St. Robert Parish, 23802 Lake Shore Blvd., Euclid, OH 44123

Yavorsky, James A., 4722 Bali Dr., Akron, OH 44319

Permanent Deacons:
Adair, Robin, St.Augustine, Barberton
Agrippe, James L., St. Angela Merici, Fairview Park
Anderson, Robert C., St. Noel, Willoughby Hills
Bacik, Dale A., St. Anselm, Chesterland
Badillo, Tomas, Sacred Heart Chapel, Lorain
Balassy, Geza J., St. Emeric, Cleveland; St. Albert the Great, North Royalton
Bals, Jerry J., On Leave, St. Justin Martyr, Eastlake
Beebe, Raymond C., St. Mary, Mentor
Beercheck, Richard C., St. Patrick, (Rocky River), Cleveland
Belsito, Vincent L., Sts. Cosmas and Damian, Twinsburg
Belter, Clement J., St. Ambrose, Brunswick
Bender, John R., St. Martin of Tours, Maple Heights
Berigan, Patrick F., Our Lady of Good Counsel, Cleveland
Bosau, Wayne A., St. Clarence, North Olmsted
Bowers, Robert J., St. Paschal Baylon, Highland Heights
Broering, J. Harry, Jr., NC
Bubnick, Robert C., Sr., Apostolate for the Mentally Retarded, Assumption, Broadview Heights
Buda, John M., Our Lady Help of Christians, Litchfield
Burke, John Jr., St. Bede the Venerable, Mentor
Butkovic, Donald P., St. Adalbert, Berea; St. Thomas Hospital, Akron
Capek, Louis J., Rep. Diocesan Vocation Council, St. Joan of Arc, Chagrin Falls
Cermak, Lawrence, St. Therese, Garfield Heights
Chrosniak, Clarence A., Our Lady of Mount Carmel (West), Cleveland
Coleman, Gerald T., (Retired)
Colon, Victor R., San Juan Bautista, Cleveland
Corrigan, William H., St. Colman, Cleveland
Cowell, Bruce R., St. Dominic, Shaker Heights
Damukaitis, Joseph B., On Leave
Daull, Raymond L., Christ the King, Cleveland
Davis, Norman H., St. Gabriel, Mentor
Davison, John H., On Leave
DeGracia, Jose A., Diaconate Staff, Sacred Heart Chapel, Lorain
DeHaas, Thomas B., Jr., St. Felicitas, Euclid
DeJohn, Ross C., Sr., St. Clare, Lyndhurst
Diaz, Juan A., Sacred Heart, Lorain
Dietrich, Harold R., Holy Spirit, Avon Lake
Dillon, Edward R., Sacred Heart of Jesus & Grafton Prison, Elyria
Dirk, William E., Our Lady of Peace, Cleveland; Mount Sinai Hospital; St. Luke Hospital
Donlin, William A., St. Rita, Solon
Duffy, James J., DPC Representative, St. John Vianney, Mentor
Dybo, Robert J., Nativity of the Blessed Virgin Mary, Lorain
Elwood, William T., St. Clare, Lyndhurst; Youth & Family Ministry, Eastern Region
Feldkamp, Edward J., St. Noel, Willoughby Hills
Figueroa, Miguel A., St. Michael, Cleveland
Flores, Jose A., Sacred Heart Chapel, Lorain
Friend, Shelby M., St. Henry, Cleveland
Fulton, Stanley J., St. Bernadette, Westlake
Giel, Frederick F., St. Helen, Newbury
Girard, Charles C., Tuscon, AZ
Glorioso, Russell J., Holy Family, Parma; St. Bartholomew, Middleburg Heights
Grasson, Thomas J., St. John Neumann, Strongsville
Hancock, Daniel J., Region VI Rep., St. Ignatius, Cleveland
Hill, Kenneth J., St. Vincent de Paul, Cleveland
Hinderscheid, Lee F., St. Hilary, Fairlawn
Hosfeld, Bernard E., St. Mary of the Immaculate Conception, Wooster
Humphrey, Frank A., III, St. Mary, Elyria
Humphrey, Patrick J., St. Jude, Elyria
Hupertz, Thomas G., Immaculate Conception, Madison
Jarosh, Rudolph, Jr., D.P.C. Rep., St. Thomas More, Brooklyn
Jasany, Robert J., St. Anthony of Padua, Parma
Johnson, Charles O., Metropolitan General Hospital; St. Aloysius-St. Agatha, Cleveland
Johnson, Joseph W., St. Stephen, West Salem
Kamlowsky, Philip P., Holy Family, Stow
Kaniecki, James A., St. Edward, Ashland
Karecki, Edmund J., St. Augustine, Cleveland
Kinzel, David L., St. Ladislas, Westlake
Knight, Kenneth, St. Bede the Venerable, Mentor
Koch, Alfred J., St. Joseph, Strongsville
Koch, John A., Ascension, Cleveland
Krupp, Ralph J., St. Peter, Lorain
Kuhlman, Richard F., Immaculate Conception, Madison
Litke, Joseph P., Holy Family, Parma
Lobdell, Donald W., Nadeau, MI
LoCascio, Phillip A., Phoenix, AZ
Lonteen, Francis R., St. Paul, Akron; Queen of Heaven, Greensburg
Loutzenhiser, Joseph E., St. Francis Xavier, Medina
Love, Wm. Ansley, (Retired)
Lozada, Frank, St. Francis, Cleveland
Lundeen, David J., Corpus Christi, Cleveland
Malcolm, Billy J., St. Ignatius of Antioch, Cleveland
Maldonado, Louis, St. Joseph Lorain
Martin, James T., St. Mary of the Assumption, Mentor
Masony, Howard J., Diaconate Staff, St. Jospeh the Worker, Strongsville
Matoney, Robert, Jr., St. Clare, Lyndhurst
Matusicky, Daniel J., St. Bernard, Akron
McCarthy, Edward J., Jr., Diaconate Staff, St. Mary, Chardon
McNulty, Leo F., St. Clare, Lyndhurst; St. Joseph Christian Life Center
Medina, Ceferino, San Juan Bautista, Cleveland
Miklosovic, John, St. Ambrose, Brunswick
Miranda, Ignacio, San Juan Bautista, Cleveland
Netzband, Ralph W., St. Monica, Garfield Heights
Newman, Joseph H., Asst. Chap. Port of Cleveland, St. Timothy, Garfield Heights
Novak, Andrew J., St. Cyprian, Perry; St. Patrick, Thompson
O'Donnell, James K., Interfaith Commission, Diaconate Staff, Gesu, University Heights
Paroff, John A., Grand Rapids, MI
Payne, Robert H., Holy Cross, Euclid
Payne, Willard C., St. Pius X, Bedford
Peacock, Terry W., St. Sebastian, Akron
Pecek, Louis G., Diocesan Tribunal, St. Paul, Euclid
Petrus, James E., St. Martin of Tours, Valley City
Piechowski, Kenneth J., Dir., Permanent Diaconate Program & Cathedral of St. John
Pineiro, Jose L., Sacred Heart Chapel, Lorain
Piskach, Robert J., St. Francis de Sales, Parma
Polefko, Roger F., St. John Bosco, Parma Heights
Quiles, Rafael, St. Petersburg, FL
Rapp, Robert, Garrettsville, Ohio
Reiland, George J., Jr., (Retired)
Rivera, Carlos, Sacred Heart Chapel, Lorain
Rivera, John M., Diaconate Staff, St. Augustine, Cleveland; St. Julie Billiart, North Ridgeville
Rodriguez, Alfonso, Palm Bay, FL
Sabol, Robert G., St. Peter the Apostle, Brook Park
Savage, Joseph J., Plymouth, MI
Schad, Kenneth E., On Leave
Schill, William E., Blessed Sacrament, Cleveland
Seal, J. David, Immaculate Heart of Mary, Cuyahoga Falls
Senn, Thomas J., St. Anthony of Padua, Parma; Cuyahoga County Jail
Sferry, John P., St. Gregory, South Euclid
Sherman, Homer L., St. Clarence, North Olmsted
Sill, Donald E., St. Anselm, Chesterland
Simon, Frederick F., Capilla de Cristo Rey, Cleveland
Skrha, Joseph W., M.D., Dir., Pastoral Care Dept., St. Alexis Hospital, Cleveland
Sloan, Leonard A., St. Francis Xavier, Medina; University Hospitals
Smith, Dennis L., Immaculate Conception, Akron
Snyder, Wayne W., St. John Vianney, Mentor
Somrack, Lawrence A., St. Augustine Hunger Center, Cleveland; St. Noel, Willoughy Hills
Stewart, James R., St. Joseph, Avon Lake
Stokes, Troy F., Epiphany, Cleveland
Streeter, David A., St. Luke, Lakewood
Strmac, John W., Diaconate Staff, Our Lady of Mount Carmel, Wickliffe
Talerico, John A., St. Charles Borromeo, Parma
Telepak, Edward A., Diaconate Staff, St. Columbkille, Parma
Terrion, Daniel C., St. Wenceslas, Maple Heights
Thiel, Martin A., St. Thomas More, Brooklyn
Torres, Epifanio, San Juan Bautista, Cleveland
Travalik, Peter M., St. Jerome, Cleveland
Ulman, Robert P., St. Bede the Venerable, Mentor
Urbanski, Clemens J., St. Anthony of Padua, Fairport Harbor
Varga, Carl M., Divine Word, Kirtland
Vicens, Prudo, Sacred Heart Chapel, Lorain
Vincent, James C., St. Peter the Apostle, Brook Park
Vinciguerra, Mario J., Our Lady of Guadelupe, Macedonia
Volek, Ronald J., Guardian Angels
Vrabel, Jerome B., Holy Cross, Euclid
Waken, Thomas J., Pastoral Care Coord., St. Joseph Hospital; St. Leo, Cleveland
Walsh, John J. (Y), Pittsburgh, Pennsylvania
Weglicki, Frank L., Jr., St. Ambrose, Brunswick
Wendzicki, Martin J., Holy Name, Cleveland
Weniger, Robert L., St. Michael, Independence
Wenzel, John T., St. Margaret Mary, South Euclid
Wilson, Francis B., Assumption of Mary, Brook Park
Woods, Richard E., St. Louis, Cleveland Heights
Woyton, Louis M., St. Augustine, Cleveland
Zawadzki, Charles W., Corpus Christi, Cleveland
Zdolshek, John R., St. Richard, N. Olmstead
Ziemkiewicz, Gerard J., NADO Rep., St. Rita, Solon

INSTITUTIONS LOCATED IN THE DIOCESE

[A] SEMINARIES, DIOCESAN

WICKLIFFE. *Borromeo Seminary*, 28700 Euclid Ave., 44092-2585. Tel: 216-943-7600. Very Rev. Thomas M. Dragga, D.Min., Rector; Rev. Robert Stec, M.A., M.Div., Recruiter; Kathryn C. Simmons, Registrar; Revs. Donald Lippert, O.F.M.Cap., M.A.; John Loya, M.Div., Spiritual Dir.; Lee Monroe, M.A., Ph.D., Academic Advisor; Michael Greb, O.F.M.Cap., M.A.; Mr. Brian F. Houlahan, Treas.; Rev. Timothy Plavac, M.Div. Priests 6; Lay Teachers 3; Seminarians 34.

St. Mary Seminary. (Our Lady of the Lake), 28700 Euclid Ave., 44092-2585. Tel: 216-943-7600. Revs. Donald B. Cozzens, Ph.D., Pres. & Rector; Thomas W. Tifft, Ph.D., Vice Rector & Academic Dean; Peter M. Mihalic, S.T.D.; John F. Loya, M.A., M.Div., Spiritual Dir.; Ms. Kathryn C. Simmons, Registrar; Sr. Donna Marie Bradesca, O.S.U., D.Min.; Revs. Gerald J. Bednar, Ph.D.; Donald Dunson, Ph.D.; Thomas Dragga, D.Min.; Mark Latcovich, Ph.D., Dean of Students; Thomas H. Weber, S.T.L., S.S.L.; Lorenzo Tosco, C.S.J., S.S.L.; Paul Hritz, Ph.D.; Mr. Edward J. Kaczuk, M.M.; Rev. David Walkowiak, J.C.D.; Mr. Alan K. Rome, M.L.S., Librarian; Mr. Brian F. Houlahan, Treas. Priests 12; Sisters 1; Adjunct Faculty 9; Students for Priesthood, Diocesan 28; Permanent Diaconate 25; Other 58.

[B] SEMINARIES, RELIGIOUS OR SCHOLASTICATES

CLEVELAND. *Blessed Sacrament Seminary, Congregation of the Blessed Sacrament*, 5384 Wilson Mills Rd., 44143. Tel: 216-442-6311. Very Rev. Anthony Schueller, S.S.S., Provincial; Revs. Eugene LaVerdiere, S.S.S.; John Thomas Lane, S.S.S., Dir. of Vocations; Jack Dowling, Dir. of Scholasticates.

[C] COLLEGES AND UNIVERSITIES

CLEVELAND. *John Carroll Jesuit Community*. John Carroll University, University Heights, 44118. Tel: 216-397-1886; Fax: 216-397-4228.

For a complete listing, refer to the Colleges and Universities section.

John Carroll University, North Park & Miramar Blvd., 44118. Tel: 216-397-1886.

For a complete listing, refer to the Colleges and Universities section.

Notre Dame College of Ohio. 4545 College Rd. South Euclid, 44121. Tel: 216-381-1680; Fax: 216-381-3802.

For a complete listing, refer to the Colleges and Universities section.

Ursuline College. 2550 Lander Rd. Pepper Pike, 44124. Tel: 216-449-4200; Fax: 216-646-8102.

For a complete listing, refer to the Colleges and Universities section.

[D] HIGH SCHOOLS, DIOCESAN

CLEVELAND. *Cleveland Central Catholic High School*, Administration: Forman Campus, 6550 Baxter Ave., 44105. Tel: 216-441-4700. Scranton Campus, 3146 Scranton Rd., 44109. Janice T. Roccosalva, Prin. Sisters 2; Lay Teachers 33; Students 528.

Holy Name High School. (Coed). 6000 Queens Hwy., Parma Heights, 44130. Tel: 216-886-0300. Raymond R. Ramicone, Prin.; Rev. William R. Krinzner, Chap. Priests 1; Sisters 6; Lay Teachers 61; Students 1,192.

Villa Angela-St. Joseph High School, 18491 Lake Shore Blvd., 44119. Tel: 216-481-8414; Fax: 216-486-1035. Sr. Maria Berlec, O.S.U., Prin. Marianists 2; Ursuline Nuns 4; Lay Teachers 34; Students 571.

BEDFORD. *St. Peter Chanel High School*, 480 Northfield Rd., 44146. Tel: 216-232-5900; Fax: 216-232-9283. Mr. Roger R. Abood, Prin. Sisters of Notre Dame 2; Lay Teachers 26; Students 380.

ELYRIA. *Elyria Catholic High School*. (Coed), 725 Gulf Rd., 44035. Tel: 216-365-1821; Fax: 216-365-7536. Mr. Wayne Uehlein, M.A., Prin.
Serving Elyria, Avon, Sheffield, North Ridgeville, Grafton, Oberlin, and Amherst. Sisters of Notre Dame 2; Lay Teachers 35; Students 550.

LORAIN. *Lorain Catholic High School*. (Grades 7-12), 760 Tower Blvd., 44052. Tel: 216-282-8216. Rev. A.

Jonathan Zingales, M.Ed., J.C.L.; Mr. Kenneth E. Fisher, J.D., Asst. Prin. for Student Affairs; Revs. Leo Dechant, C.S.J., M.Ed., M.A., Asst. Prin. for Academic Affairs; Giampetro Gasparin, C.S.J., M.Div., Chap. Priests 3; Sisters of Notre Dame 1; Lay Teachers 25; Students 350.

MENTOR. *Lake Catholic High*, 6733 Reynolds Rd., 44060. Tel: 216-951-0077; Fax: 216-974-9087. Sr. St. Ann Waldron, O.S.U., Prin.; Rev. David Woost, Chap. Priests 1; Ursuline Nuns of Cleveland (O.S.U.) 3; Lay Teachers 48; Students 860.

[E] HIGH SCHOOLS, PRIVATE

CLEVELAND. *Beaumont School*. 3301 N. Park Blvd., Cleveland Heights, 44118. Beaumont Convent, 3240 Fairmount Blvd., 44118. Tel: 216-321-2157. Ursuline Sisters. Sr. Margaret Ann Kelley, O.S.U., Pres.; Sr. Susan Mary Rathbun, O.S.U., Prin. Sisters 14; Lay Teachers 38; Students 437.

Benedictine High School, 2900 Martin Luther King Dr., 44104-4898. Tel: 216-421-2080; Fax: 216-421-1100. Rt. Rev. Roger W. Gries, O.S.B., Pres.; Mr. Dennis Sutcliffe, Chm., Board of Governors; Mr. Charles Reynolds, Prin.; Rev. Gerard Gonda, O.S.B., Vice Prin. Academic Affairs; Mr. Anthony Russ, Dean Student Affairs; Mr. David A. Smith, Business Mgr.; Revs. Albert Marflak, O.S.B.; Michael Brunovsky, O.S.B.; Timothy Buyansky, O.S.B.; Gary Hoover, O.S.B.; Bede Kotlinski, O.S.B.; Joachim Pastirik, O.S.B., School Chap.; Benedict Sellers, O.S.B.; Clement Zeleznik, O.S.B.; Anselm Zupka, O.S.B.; Dominic Mondzelewski; Bros. Peter Ancel, O.S.B.; Theodore Girard, O.S.B.; Ignatius Isaac, O.S.B. Priests 11; Brothers 3; Lay Teachers 20; Students 350.

Magnificat High School. (Girls), 20770 Hilliard Rd., 44116. Tel: 216-331-1572; Fax: 216-331-7257. Sr. Carolyn Marshall, H.M., Prin. Sisters 4; Lay Teachers 63; Students 826.

Padua Franciscan High School, 6740 State Rd., 44134. Tel: 216-845-2444. Rev. Walter Dolan, O.F.M., Pres.; Gerald R. Jindra, Vice Pres. for Development & Public Information; Timothy Giulivo, Prin.; Rev. Dan Senger, O.F.M. Campus Ministry: Rev. Tony Posadas, O.F.M.; Bro. Tom Carroll, O.F.M., Academic Dean. Priests 3; Sisters 1; Brothers 1; Lay Teachers 61; Students 1,035.

Regina High School. (Girls), 1857 S. Green Rd., 44121. Tel: 216-382-2110; Fax: 216-382-3555. Sisters of Notre Dame. Sr. Maureen Burke, S.N.D., Prin. Sisters 10; Lay Teachers 20; Students 250.

St. Augustine Academy, 14808 Lake Ave., 44107. Tel: 216-221-4227. Sr. Patricia Lenard, C.S.F.N., Dir. Sisters of the Holy Family of Nazareth 5; Lay Teachers 29; Girls 318.

St. Edward High School. (Boys). 13500 Detroit Ave., Lakewood, 44107. Tel: 216-221-3776; Fax: 216-221-4609. Bro. James Spooner, C.S.C., Pres. Brothers 8; Lay Teachers 51; Students 870.

St. Ignatius High School, 1911 W. 30th St., 44113. Tel: 216-651-0222; Fax: 216-651-6313. Revs. Robert J. Welsh, S.J., Pres.; Lawrence M. Ober, S.J., Rector; Richard F. Clark, Prin.; Revs. Stephen J. Agostino, S.J.; Thomas J. Bain, S.J.; Henry F. Birkenhauer, S.J.; James Farrell, S.J.; John H. Kleinhenz, S.J.; James V. Lewis, S.J.; Bernard J. Streicher, S.J.; Glenn F. Williams, S.J.; Carl Bonk, S.J.; Dennis Dillon, S.J.; Martin Connell, S.J.; Michael Vincent, S.J. Priests 14; Lay Teachers 80; Students 1,343.

St. Joseph Academy, 3430 Rocky River Dr., 44111. Tel: 216-251-6788; Fax: 216-251-5809. Jacqualine Kasprowski, Prin. Sisters 13; Lay Teachers 49; Students 580.

Trinity High School, 12425 Granger, 44125. Tel: 216-581-1644; 662-3290 (Res.). Sisters of St. Joseph of the Third Order of St. Francis. Sr. Catherine Britton, S.S.J., Pres.; Patrick J. Riley, D.Min., Asst. to Pres.; Thomas M. Maher, Ph.D., Prin.; Mr. Daniel J. Thomeier, Business Mgr.; Mr. Joseph A. Waler, M.A., Assoc. Admissions. Sisters of St. Joseph 7; Lay Teachers 46; Students 720.

AKRON. *Archbishop Hoban High School*. (Coed), 400 Elbon Ave., 44306. Tel: 330-773-6658; Fax: 330-773-9100. Brothers of Holy Cross. Bro. Kenneth Haders, C.S.C., Pres.; Mrs. Mary Anne Beiting, Prin. Brothers 7; Lay Teachers 40; Students 645.

Our Lady of the Elms High School, 1375 W. Exchange St., 44313. Tel: 216-867-0880; Fax: 216-864-6488. Sisters of St. Dominic. Mrs. Connie Hardy, Prin. Sisters 3; Lay Teachers 31; Girls 326.

St. Vincent-St. Mary High School, 15 North Maple St., 44303. Tel: 216-253-9113; Fax: 216-996-0020. Margaret T. Lynch, Prin. Priests 1; Lay Teachers 36; Students 605.

CHARDON. *Notre Dame-Cathedral Latin School*, 13000 Auburn Rd., 44024. Tel: 216-946-3314; 286-6226; Fax: 216-286-7199. Sisters of Notre Dame. Sr. Judith Lynne Mucheck, S.N.D., Prin. Sisters 8; Lay Teachers 51; Students 810.

CUYAHOGA FALLS. *Walsh Jesuit High School*, 4550 Wyoga Lake Rd., 44224. Tel: 216-929-4205; 800-686-4694 (Cleveland). Revs. Donald J. Petkash, S.J., Pres.; Emmett P. Holmes, S.J., Religious Supr.; Richard M. Rosenfelder, S.J.; Thomas M. Ryan, S.J.; James J. King, S.J.; Daniel D. Dunnigan, S.J.; Bro. Bernard L. Polinak, S.J.; Priests 6; Lay Teachers 60; Students 840.

GATES MILLS. *Gilmour Academy*. (Grades PreK-12). Private. 34001 Cedar Rd., 44040. Tel: 216-442-1104; Fax: 216-473-8010. Day and Resident College Preparatory School. Congregation of Holy Cross. Mr. Murlan J. Murphy, Jr., Chm., Board of Trustees; Bro. Robert Lavelle, C.S.C., Headmaster; Dr. Elizabeth Fesler, Ph.D., Dir. of Upper School; Ms. Monica Veto, M.S., M.A., Dir. of Lower School; Rev. John Blazek, C.S.C., Campus Minister. Priests 1; Sisters 2; Brothers 9; Students 629; Residents 33; Lay Teachers 63.

[F] ELEMENTARY SCHOOLS

CLEVELAND. *Incarnate Word Academy*, 6618 Pearl Rd., 44130. Tel: 216-842-6818; Fax: 216-888-1377. Sr. Eileen Fitzgerald, S.I.W., Prin.; Rev. Msgr. Joseph T. Moriarty, Chap. Sisters 8; Lay Teachers 21; Students 624.

AKRON. *Our Lady of Elms Elementary School*, 1290 W. Market St., 44313. Tel: 330-864-7210. Sr. Rosemary Quinn, O.P., Prin. Sisters 5; Lay Teachers 18; Students 184.

CHARDON. *Notre Dame Elementary School*, 13000 Auburn Rd., 44024. Sr. Margaret Hartman, S.N.D., Prin. Sisters of Notre Dame 12; Lay Teachers 18; Students 447.

Notre Dame Montessori School, 13000 Auburn Rd., 44024. Tel: 216-286-7101, Ext. 592. Sr. Carol Urmetz, S.N.D., Prin. Sisters of Notre Dame 1; Lay Teachers 3; Students 48.

[G] ELEMENTARY SCHOOLS, PAROCHIAL AND DIOCESAN

CLEVELAND. *Archbishop James P. Lyke Elementary School*. St. Henry and St. Timothy Schools consolidated to form Archbishop James P. Lyke Elementary School. 18230 Harvard Ave., 44128. Sr. Brigetta Waldron, O.S.U., Co-Prin.; Mrs. Margarete Smith, Co-Prin. Lay Teachers 14; Students 340.

Mount Pleasant Catholic Elementary Education Center. Serving St. Cecilia, Epiphany. Holy Family Parish Building, 3845 E. 131st St., 44120. Tel: 216-991-1615. Lay Teachers 9; Religious 2; Students 199.

Urban Community School, 2401 Washington Ave., 44113. Tel: 216-771-8014; Fax: 216-771-7888. Sr. Maureen Doyle, O.S.U., Dir. Ursuline Nuns 4; Lay Teachers 21; Students 408.

WICKLIFFE. *All Saints of St. John Vianney School*. (Grades PreK-8), 28702 Euclid Ave., 44092. Tel: 216-943-1395. Mrs. Rosemary Wilson, Prin. Sisters 1; Lay Teachers 17; Students 381.

[H] SPECIAL SCHOOLS AND CENTERS

For Exceptional Children

CLEVELAND. *Julie Billiart*. 4982 Clubside Rd., Lyndhurst, 44124-2596. Tel: 216-381-1191. Non-graded school for children having learning problems. Sr. Agnesmarie, S.N.D., Prin. Sisters of Notre Dame of Chardon 10; Lay Staff 4; Students 114.

OLA-St. Joseph Center, 2346 W. 14th St., 44113. Tel: 216-621-3451; Fax: 216-621-6104. Non-graded school for developmentally handicapped children, ages 6-16. Mrs. Pamela Delly, Prin. Lay Teachers 10; Students 80.

[I] PRESCHOOL AND DAY CARE CENTERS

CLEVELAND. *Head Start Catholic Center*, 1031 Superior Ave., 44114. Tel: 216-696-6525, Ext. 287. Lois Reed, Dir. Lay Teachers 38; Children 1,294.

Villa Montessori Center, 5620 Broadway Ave., 44127. Tel: 216-641-4770. Sr. Marie Veres, H.M., Dir./Prin.

AKRON. *Our Lady of Elms Pre-School*, 1295 W. Exchange St., 44313. Tel: 330-864-6817. Miss Suzanne M. Scarpitti, Dir. Lay Teachers 12; Students 90.

GARFIELD HEIGHTS. *Marymount Child Care Center*, 12215 Granger Rd., 44125. Tel: 216-581-3540; Fax: 216-518-1435. Sr. Felicia Mann, S.S.J.-T.O.S.F., Dir. Total Assisted 200; Total Staff 18.

TWINSBURG. *Preschool Activity and Learning Sessions, Inc.*, 9550 Ravenna Rd., 44087. Florence Bonacci, Dir. Children 100; Total Staff 5.

[J] GENERAL HOSPITALS

(For information on other Catholic related hospitals please contact the Chancery Office.)

CLEVELAND. *Marymount Hospital, Inc.*, 12300 McCracken Rd., 44125. Tel: 216-581-0500.
For a complete listing, refer to the Hospitals section.

St. John Hospital, 2351 E. 22nd St., 44115. Tel: 216-696-5560.
For a complete listing, refer to the Hospitals section.

[K] TRAINING SCHOOLS FOR NURSES

CLEVELAND. *Marymount School of Practical Nursing*. 12300 McCracken Rd., Garfield Heights, 44125. Tel: 216-587-8160. Louise M. Evans, R.N., B.S.N., M.S., Dir. Students 29.

[L] SPECIAL HOSPITALS

CLEVELAND. *Holy Family Home*, 6707 State Rd., 44134. Tel: 216-885-3100; Fax: 216-885-0644.
For a complete listing, refer to the Special Care Facilities section.

Rose Mary, The Johanna Grasselli Rehabilitation and Education Center, 19350 Euclid Ave., 44117. Tel: 216-481-4823.
For a complete listing, refer to the Special Care Facilities section.

[M] PROTECTIVE INSTITUTIONS

CLEVELAND. *Christ Child - DePaul Day Care Center*, 2320 E. 24th St., 44115. Tel: 216-687-0006; Fax: 216-687-0403.
For a complete listing, refer to the Special Care Facilities section.

INDEPENDENCE. *Marycrest*, 7800 Brookside Rd., 44131. Tel: 216-524-5280; Fax: 216-524-2127.
For a complete listing, refer to the Special Care Facilities section.

PARMA. *Parmadale*, 6753 State Rd., 44134. Tel: 216-845-7700; Fax: 216-845-5910.
For a complete listing, refer to the Special Care Facilities section.

[N] HOMES FOR AGED

CLEVELAND. *Jennings Hall Inc.*, 10204 Granger Rd., 44125. Tel: 216-581-2900; Fax: 216-581-1517.
For a complete listing, refer to the Special Care Facilities section.

Mount Alverna Home, Inc. & Mount Alverna Home Annex, Inc.. 6765 State Rd. Parma, 44134. Tel: 216-843-7800; Fax: 216-843-7107.
For a complete listing, refer to the Special Care Facilities section.

Mount St. Joseph, 21800 Chardon Rd., 44117. Tel: 216-531-7426; Fax: 216-531-4033.
For a complete listing, refer to the Special Care Facilities section.

St. Augustine Manor, 7801 Detroit Ave., 44102. Tel: 216-634-7400; Fax: 216-634-7483.
For a complete listing, refer to the Special Care Facilities section.

Sts. Mary and Joseph Home for the Aged, 4291 Richmond Rd., 44122-6199. Tel: 216-464-1222.
For a complete listing, refer to the Special Care Facilities section.

AKRON. *Francesca Residence*, 39 N. Portage Path, 44303. Tel: 330-867-6334.
For a complete listing, refer to the Special Care Facilities section.

BEACHWOOD. *Villa Sancta Anna Home for the Aged, Inc.*, 25000 Chagrin Blvd., 44122-5665. Tel: 216-464-9250.
For a complete listing, refer to the Special Care Facilities section.

BEDFORD. *Light of Hearts Villa, Inc.*, 283 Union St., 44146. Tel: 216-232-1991.
For a complete listing, refer to the Special Care Facilities section.

FAIRLAWN. *St. Edward Home dba The Village at Saint Edward Nursing Care and Assisted Living*, 3131 Smith Rd., 44333. Tel: 330-666-1183.
For a complete listing, refer to the Special Care Facilities section.

RICHFIELD. *Regina Health Center*, 5232 Broadview Rd., 44286-9608. Tel: 216-659-4161; Fax: 216-659-3899.
For a complete listing, refer to the Special Care Facilities section.

[O] RESIDENCE FOR RETIRED PRIESTS

BROOKLYN. *Issenmann Place*, 4185 Brookway Ln., 44144. Tel: 216-661-1470. Thomas Willson, Asst. Admin. Total in Residence 8; Total Staff 3.

[P] MONASTERIES AND RESIDENCES OF PRIESTS AND BROTHERS

CLEVELAND. *Benedictine Order of Cleveland*, St. Andrew Abbey, 10510 Buckeye Rd., 44104. Tel: 216-721-5300. Rt. Rev. Roger W. Gries, O.S.B.; Very Rev. Joachim Pastirik, O.S.B., Prior; Revs. Clement Zeleznik, O.S.B., Novice Master; Timothy Buyansky, O.S.B.; Dominic Mondzelewski, O.S.B.; Placid Pientek, O.S.B.; Dismas Boeff, O.S.B., Chap., Southwest General Hospital, St. Peter, 6455 Engle Rd., 44142. Revs. Matthew Bonk, O.S.B.; Gerard Gonda, O.S.B.; Armand E. Gress, O.S.B.; Gary Hoover, O.S.B.; Kenneth Katricak, O.S.B., Chap., Villa Santa Anna, 25000 Chagrin Blvd., 44122. Revs. Albert

Marflak, O.S.B., Vocation Dir. & Abbey Procurator; Gregory Oravec, O.S.B.; Andrew Pier, O.S.B., Little Sisters of the Poor, 4291 Richmond Rd., Warrensville Heights, 44122. Revs. Benedict Sellers, O.S.B.; Lawrence Sevcik, O.S.B.; Bernard Slimak, O.S.B.; Robert Wilkes, O.S.B.; Anselm Zupka, O.S.B. Priests 27; Brothers 14.

Other Assignments: Rev. Bede Kotlinski, O.S.B., Incarnate Word, 6618 Pearl Rd., Parma Heights, 44130. Revs. William T. Matyas, O.S.B.; Ronald Mahnke, O.S.B., Assumption, 9183 Broadview Rd., Broadview Heights, 44147. Rev. Anthony Ozimek, O.S.B., St. Vincent Hospital, Billings, MT, 59107-5200. Rev. Christopher Schwartz, O.S.B., Assumption Church, 9183 Broadview Rd., 44147. Rev. Raphael Zbin, O.S.B., St. Andrew, 5135 Superior Ave., 44103. Rev. Michael Brunovsky.

Blessed Sacrament Community, 5384 Wilson Mills Rd., 44143. Tel: 216-442-6311. Revs. Anthony L. Schueller, Prov. Supr.; Patrick J. Fenton, S.S.S., Supr.; Thomas E. Waldie; John Thomas Lane, Vocation Dir.; Mario T. Marzocchi; Raymond J. Dubois, S.S.S.; Edward J. Stapleton, S.S.S., Prov. Treas.; William F. Fickel, S.S.S.; William T. Young, S.S.S.; Frederico J. Ablog, S.S.S.; Frederick Roberge, S.S.S.; Bros. Edmund Hardy, S.S.S.; Thomas F. Flanagan, S.S.S.; Gary L. Laverdiere, S.S.S.; Michael J. O'Leary, S.S.S.; Ignatius J. Montgomery, S.S.S. Priests 11; Brothers 5. Regina Health Center, 5232 Broadview Rd., Richfield, 44286-9608. Revs. George Evans, S.S.S.; John Gartner, S.S.S.; Bros. Fernand Duquette, S.S.S.; Raymond Lussier, S.S.S.; Mark Proulx, S.S.S. Priests 2; Brothers 3.

Congregation of the Blessed Sacrament Provincial House. 5384 Wilson Mills Rd., Highland Heights, 44143. Tel: 216-442-6311; Fax: 216-449-3862.

Province of St. Ann. Very Rev. Anthony Schueller, S.S.S., Prov. Supr.; Rev. Edward J. Stapleton, S.S.S., Prov. Treas.

Priests Serving Outside Country: Very Rev. Norman Pelletier, S.S.S., General Supr.; Revs. Thomas Wiese, S.S.S., General Sec.; Rafko Ropret, S.S.S., Dir. of International Scholasticate; G. B. de Rossi, (Italy).

Priests attached to Provincialate: Rev. Andrew Beaudoin, S.S.S., 11487 Kerridale Ave., Spring Hill, FL, 34608. Rev. Rene A. Belanger, S.S.S., 58 Dudley St., New Bedford, MA, 02744. Rev. Peter Cops, S.S.S., Retreat House, Rte. 1, Box 110, Waverly, NE, 68462. Rev. Edward Roberts, S.S.S., 34 Soley St., Apt. 2, Charleston, MA, 02129-3311. Rev. John Keenan, S.S.S., 320 W. Illinois, #1609, Chicago, IL, 60610. Rev. Robert S. Pittman, S.S.S., P.O. Box 410, Waldorf, MD, 20604. Rev. Joachim Viet-Chau, S.S.S., Vietnamese Apostolate, P.O. Box 1429, Gretna, LA, 70053. Bro. Eugene Blee, S.S.S., Regina Health Center, 5232 Broadview Rd., Richfield, 44286-9608. Revs. John Gartner, S.S.S.; George Evans, S.S.S.; Bros. Fernand Duquette, S.S.S.; Raymond Lussier, S.S.S.; Mark Proulx, S.S.S.

Marianist Community, 18340 Marcella Rd., 44119-2622. Tel: 216-481-1007. Priests 2; Brothers 4.

Maryknoll Fathers, 10309 Edgewater Dr., 44102. Tel: 216-651-2121. Rev. Robert L. Depinet, M.M., Dir., P.O. Box 80938, Davao City, Philippines, 8000. Revs. George H. Ratermann, M.M.; James H. Huvane, M.M.; Richard S. Kardian, M.M. Total in Residence 3; Total Staff 2.

Mercedarians, 6928 Detroit Ave., 44102. Tel: 216-651-5043. Order of Our Lady of Mercy. Rev. Richard Rasch, O.de.M., Supr. In res., Revs. Vincent Caruso, O.de.M., (Retired); Anthony M. Fortunato, O.de.M.; Eugene Costa, O.de.M. Priests 4.

Missionary Servants of the Most Holy Trinity. St. Agnes-Our Lady of Fatima, 6800 Lexington Ave., 44103. Tel: 216-391-1655. Revs. Michael Barth, S.T.; John Ford, S.T.

Padua Franciscan Friary. 7022 State Rd., Parma, 44134. Tel: 216-888-7742. Revs. Cecil Koop, O.F.M.; Eugene Katoski, O.F.M.; Walter Dolan, O.F.M.; Daniel Senger, O.F.M.; Jose Antonio Posadas, O.F.M.; Bro. Thomas Carroll, O.F.M. Priests 6; Brothers 1.

St. Jude Friary, 4760 Richmond Rd., 44128. Tel: 216-292-6602. Revs. Emmanuel Beunen, O.F.M.; Thomas Carolan, O.F.M., Supr.; Bro. Joseph Di Santo, O.F.M. Priests 2; Brothers 1; Total Assisted 60.

St. Paul Friary, 4120 Euclid Ave., 44103. Tel: 216-431-8854. Revs. Senan Glass, O.F.M.Cap.; Gary Stakem, O.F.M.Cap.; Andrew Hohman, O.F.M.Cap.; Bro. James Allman, O.F.M.Cap. Priests 3; Brothers 1.

St. Stanislaus Friary, 3649 E. 65th St., 44105-1293. Tel: 216-341-9091; Fax: 216-341-2688. Revs. Alcuin L. Mikulanis, O.F.M.; William E. Gulas, O.F.M.; George Jaskulski, O.F.M. (Pulaski, WI), Chap., Marymount Convent, Garfield Heights. Rev. Lazarus Macior, O.F.M. (Pulaski, WI), Prof., University of Akron, Akron. The Franciscan Friars, Province of the Assumption of the Blessed Virgin. Priests 3.

AVON. *Congregation of St. Joseph*, 4076 Case Rd., 44011. Tel: 216-934-6270. Revs. Lawrence Tosco, C.S.J.; Leo Dechant, C.S.J.; Libero Ballestrazzi, C.S.J.; Gaetano Menegatto, C.S.J.; Giampietro Gasparin, C.S.J. Priests 5.

[Q] CONVENTS AND RESIDENCES FOR SISTERS

CLEVELAND. *Carmel of the Holy Family*, 3176 Fairmount Blvd., 44118-4199. Tel: 216-321-6568. Discalced Carmelite Nuns. Sr. Patricia O'Brien, O.C.D., Prioress. Professed Nuns 16; Vowed Religious Transfer Sisters in Formation 2.

Marymount Congregational Home. 12215 Granger Rd., Garfield Heights, 44125. Tel: 216-581-3535. Residence of the Sisters of St. Joseph, Third Order of St. Francis. Contact Persons: Sr. Esther Romalke; Sr. Dominica Fick; Rev. George Jaskulski, O.F.M., Chap. Sisters 83.

Monastery of the Poor Clares, 3501 Rocky River Dr., 44111-2998. Tel: 216-941-2820. Poor Clare Nuns (Colettine).

Observing the Primitive Rule of St. Clare (strictly cloistered solemn vows). Perpetual exposition of the Blessed Sacrament. Rev. Eugene Katoski, O.F.M., Chap. Cloistered Nuns 23; Extern Sisters 3.

Motherhouse and Novitiate of the Sisters of the Holy Spirit, 10102 Granger Rd., 44125. Tel: 216-581-2941. Sr. Assumpta Zabas, C.S.Sp., Supr. Gen.; Rev. John J. Wright, Chap. Professed Sisters 9.

Motherhouse and Novitiate of the Ursuline Nuns, 2600 Lander Rd., 44124. Tel: 216-449-1200. Sr. Virginia DeVinne, O.S.U., Gen. Supr. Legal Title: *The Ursuline Academy of Cleveland*. Professed Nuns 287.

Motherhouse of the Sisters of St. Joseph, 3430 Rocky River Dr., 44111. Tel: 216-252-0440; Fax: 216-941-3430. Exec. Team: Sr. Barbara Green; Sr. Donna Hawk; Sr. Marietta Starrie. Sisters 168.

Poor Clares of Perpetual Adoration, 4108 Euclid Ave., 44103. Tel: 216-361-0783. Mother Mary Angela, P.C.P.A., Supr. Cloistered Sisters 23; Novice 1.

Monastery adjoins Conversion of St. Paul Church, where they maintain Perpetual Adoration.

Provincialhouse of Sisters of the Most Holy Trinity, 21281 Chardon Rd., 44117. Tel: 216-481-8232; Fax: 216-481-6577. Sr. M. Valentine, O.SS.T., Reg. Delegate.

Attended from Borromeo Seminary. Sisters 29; Total in Residence 14.

Sisters of St. Joseph of St. Mark. General Motherhouse and Novitiate of Sisters of St. Joseph of St. Mark-Generalate, Diocese of Cleveland. 21800 Chardon Rd., 44117. Tel: 216-531-7426; Fax: 216-531-4033. Mother M. Therese Trunk, Gen. Supr. Sisters 20.

Sisters of the Incarnate Word and Blessed Sacrament, 6618 Pearl Rd., 44130. Tel: 216-886-6440; Fax: 216-888-1377. Sr. Margaret Taylor, Congregational Leader. Legal Title: *Motherhouse and Novitiate of the Sisters of the Incarnate Word and and Blessed Sacrament*. Final Professed Sisters 43. In res., Rev. Msgr. Joseph T. Moriarty, 6620 Pearl Road, Parma Heights, 44130. Tel: 216-885-0320. Rev. Bede Kotlinski, O.S.B., 6634 Pearl Rd., Parma Heights, 44130. Tel: 216-886-6996.

AKRON. *Motherhouse of the Sisters of St. Dominic of the Immaculate Heart of Mary*, Our Lady of the Elms Convent, 1230 W. Market St., 44313-7185. Tel: 330-836-4908. Sisters 111.

Provincial Motherhouse and Novitiate of the Daughters of Divine Charity, 39 N. Portage Path, 44303-1183. Tel: 330-867-4960. Sr. Maria Bakich, F.D.C., Prov. Supr.; Rev. Thomas F. Sullivan, Chap. Tel: 330-864-6700. Sisters 23.

BEDFORD. *Motherhouse and Novitiate of the Vincentian Sisters of Charity*, Villa San Bernardo, 1160 Broadway, 44146-4523. Tel: 216-232-4755. Sr. Margaret Mach, Gen. Supr.; Sr. Dorothy Ann Blatnica, Formation Dir.; Sr. Ruthann Rody, Vocation-Contact Person. Sisters 77; Novices 1.

CHARDON. *Provincial House of the Sisters of Notre Dame, Juniorate, Novitiate*, Notre Dame Educational Center, 13000 Auburn Rd., 44024. Tel: 216-286-7101. Rev. Paul J. Sciarrotta, Chap. Sisters 472; Novices 1.

INDEPENDENCE. *Contemplative Sisters of the Good Shepherd*. (Infirmary), 7800 Brookside Rd., 44131. Tel: 216-524-8692. Sr. Mary Josephine Fritz, C.G.S., Supr. Sisters 27.

Sisters of the Good Shepherd, Marycrest, 7800 Brookside Rd., 44131. Tel: 216-524-4578; Fax: 216-524-6669. Sr. Rose Catherine Wuensch, R.G.S., Supr., Marycrest Euphrasia Center, 2320 E. 24th St., Cleveland, 44115. Tel: 216-687-0313. Sisters 4; Total in Residence 70; Total Staff 130.

RICHFIELD. *Mount Augustine, Motherhouse of the Sisters of Charity of St. Augustine*, 5232 Broadview Rd., 44286-9608. Tel: 216-659-5100; Fax: 216-659-3899. Sr. Judith Ann Karam, C.S.A., Major Supr.; Sr. Nancy Hendershot, C.S.A., Dir. of Formation. Finally Professed Sisters 103.

[R] SECULAR INSTITUTES

CLEVELAND HEIGHTS. *Society of Our Lady of the Way*, c/o Mary Ann Tady, 1064 Oxford Rd., 44121. Tel: 216-381-5502. Secular Institute for Single Women.

[S] HOMES FOR WOMEN

AKRON. *Leonora Hall*, 39 N. Portage Path, 44303. Tel: 216-867-1752.

For a complete listing, refer to the Special Care Facilities section.

[T] LAY ASSOCIATIONS

CLEVELAND. *Community of Little Brothers and Sisters of the Eucharist, Inc.*, 2186 East 35th St., 44115-3039. Tel: 216-566-0531; Fax: 216-566-9370. Sr. Maggie Conrad, Dir.

[U] RETREAT HOUSES

CLEVELAND. *Jesuit Retreat House*, 5629 State Rd., 44134. Tel: 216-884-9300; Fax: 216-885-1055. Rev. James Riley, S.J. Spirituality Team: Revs. James Farrell, S.J.; Joseph Scharf, S.J.; Dennis Dillon, S.J.; Carl Bonk, S.J.; Henry F. Birkenhauer, S.J.

St. Joseph Christian Life Center, 18485 Lake Shore Blvd., 44119-1299. Tel: 216-531-7370; Fax: 216-531-0629. Rev. Walter J. Hyclak, Exec. Dir.; Jackie Cherep, Oper. Mgr. & Finance Coord.; Deacon Leo McNulty. In res., Rev. Donald Snyder, Diocesan Judge & Dir., Continuing Education & Formation of Priests. Tel: 216-486-8391. Total Staff 34.

AKRON. *Loyola of the Lakes Jesuit Retreat House*. 700 Killinger Rd., Clinton, 44216. Tel: 216-896-2315; 800-827-1416; Fax: 216-896-0858. Mrs. Elizabeth R. Flynt, Exec. Dir. In res., Rev. Vincent A. Hagarman, S.J.

BEDFORD. *Poustinia*, 1160 Broadway, 44146. Tel: 216-232-4755. Vincentian Sisters of Charity.

Tabor Center, 1160 Broadway, 44146. Tel: 216-232-4755. Vincentian Sisters of Charity. Sr. Irene Mraz, V.S.C., Contact Person. Maximum Capacity 5.

[V] SOCIAL SERVICE AGENCIES AND INSTITUTIONS

For information call Catholic Information and Referral Services (CIRS) Tel: 216-696-HELP (4357).

CLEVELAND. *Bishop William M. Cosgrove Center*, 1736 Superior Ave., 44114. Tel: 216-781-8262. Total Assisted 110,000; Total Staff 7.

Catholic Charities Services Corporation, Eaton Center, 1111 Superior Ave., 44114. Tel: 216-696-6525; Fax: 216-344-9962. Provides management services and direction to Catholic Charities agencies and institutions to enhance the effectiveness and efficiency of human services within the Diocese. J. Thomas Mullen, M.S.W., Pres. & CEO; John Klee, Exec. Vice Pres. & COO; Patrick Ertle, Gen. Counsel; Jean Hutzler, M.S.W., Exec. Asst. to Pres.; Wayne Peel, CFO; Claire Gavin, Vice Pres. Human Resources; Margaret Wojcik Stefanov, Dir., MIS; Thomas Woll, Senior Dir., Children & Family Services; Jean Therrien, Senior Dir., Older Adult Services; Dennis McNulty, Senior Dir., Disability Services; Charles Joseph, III, Senior Dir., Emergency & Transitional Services; Patsy Holian, Dir. System Development.

Catholic Charities Services Corporation.

Bishop William M. Cosgrove Center, 1736 Superior Ave., 44114. Tel: 216-781-8262. Pat Wehner, Exec. Dir.

Catholic Social Services of Ashland, Medina, and Wayne Counties, 246 Northland Dr., Medina, 44256. Tel: 330-723-9615 (Medina); 419-289-1903 (Ashland); 330-262-7386 (Wooster). Timothy Putka, Dir.

Catholic Social Services of Cuyahoga County, 7800 Detroit Ave., 44102. Tel: 216-631-3499. Service Directors: Maureen Dee, Dir. Behavioral Health Services; David Modarski, Dir. Community Services.

Catholic Services of Geauga County, 1077 Mayfield Rd., 44024. Tel: 800-242-9755. Anthony J. Marjenin, Dir.

Catholic Social Services of Lake County, 8 N. State St., Suite 455, Painesville, 44077. Tel: 216-946-7264; 352-6191. James R. Clements, Dir.

Catholic Social Services of Lorain County, 2136 N. Ridge Rd., Elyria, 44035. Tel: 216-324-2614; 277-7228. Bernadette Washington, Dir.

Fatima Community Center, 6707 Quimby Ave., 44103. Tel: 216-391-0505. LaJean Ray, Dir.

Hispanic Senior Center, 7800 Detroit Ave., 44102. Tel: 216-631-3599. Virginia Gomez, Acting Dir.

Matt Talbot Inn, 2270 Professor Ave., 44113. Tel: 216-781-0288. Ruby Black, Dir.

OLA/St. Joseph Center, 2346 W. 14th St., 44113-3697. Tel: 216-621-3451. Pamela Delly, Prin.

St. Martin de Porres Center, 1264 E. 123rd St., 44108. Tel: 216-268-3909. Marsha Banks, Dir.

Special Ministry to the Aged, 6804 Lansing Ave., 44105. Tel: 216-441-5402. Sr. Anna Kaszuba, Dir.

CATHOLIC CHARITIES PARISH SERVICES: Camps:

Camp Corde, 2901 Ridgewood Ave., Parma, 44134. Tel: 216-884-3950.
Camp Christopher, Ira & Hametown Rd., Bath, 44210. Tel: 800-CYO-CAMP.
AFFILIATED CORPORATIONS WITHIN THE SECRETARY FOR SOCIAL CONCERNS (Under membership structure of Bishop, Secretary for Social Concerns & Chairperson of Board of Trustees):
Catholic Social Services of Summit County.
CYO & Community Services of Summit County.
Jennings Hall, Inc.
The LeBlond Housing Corporation.
Parmadale.
Rose-Mary, The Johanna Grasselli Rehabilitation and Education Center.
St. Augustine Corporation.
The Village at St. Edward.
The Society of St. Vincent de Paul (not under membership structure).
Catholic Social Services of Ashland, Medina, and Wayne Counties. 246 Northland Dr., Medina, 44256-1598. Medina. Tel: 330-723-9615. Ashland. Tel: 419-289-1903. Brunswick-Cleveland. Tel: 330-225-7100. Wadsworth-Akron. Tel: 330-336-6657. Wooster. Tel: 330-262-7836. Timothy J. Putka, M.S., Exec. Dir. Provides counseling, casework, and family life education in Ashland, Wayne, and Medina Counties.
Catholic Social Services of Cuyahoga County, St. Augustine Towers, 7800 Detroit Ave., 44102-2895. Tel: 216-631-3499. Maureen Dee, L.I.S.W., C.C.D.C. III, Dir. Behavioral Health Services; David J. Modarski, A.C.S.W., L.I.S.W., Dir. Community Services; Sanford Waldman, M.D., Medical Dir. A multi-function social service agency which offers social service programs. Individual, family, and group counseling; marital counseling, psychiatric consultations; and outpatient psychiatric services for children, youth, and adults. Chemical dependency assessments and outpatient counseling for youth and families having alcohol and other drug-related problems. Bilingual services for Hispanic youth and families. Child day care; school for pregnant teens; pregnancy counseling and planning; adoption; big brothers/sisters; older adult programs, senior citizens counseling and respite care; employment services.
Satellite Offices: Midtown Center, 3135 Euclid Ave., Ste. 202, 44115-2507. 1414 S. Green Rd., Rm. 310, South Euclid, 44121. 5510 Pearl Rd., Rm. 305, Parma, 44129. 2012 W. 25th St., Rm. 517, 44113. 3510 Chatham Ave., 44113. St. Vincent School, 2320 E. 24th St., 44115. Total Assisted 3,500; Total Staff 94.
Catholic Social Services of Geauga County. 10771 Mayfield Rd., Chardon, 44024-9323. Tel: 216-285-3537; 800-242-9755 (Ohio); Fax: 216-285-4909. Anthony J. Marjenin, M.S.S.A., L.I.S.W., Exec. Dir. Outpatient counseling for families and individuals. Substance abuse counseling. Parenting programs. Services for the elderly. Services to strengthen and enrich the valued relationships of families and individuals for effective and healthy living.
Catholic Social Services of Lake County. 8 N. State St., No. 455, Painesville, 44077-3954. Tel: 216-352-6191; 946-7264. James Clements, L.P.C.C., L.S.W., Exec. Dir.
Satellite Offices: 28706 Euclid Ave., Wickliffe, 44092. 2041 Hubbard Rd., Madison, 44057. Total Assisted 6,232; Total Staff 25.
The LeBlond Housing Corporation, 431 The Catholic Center, 1031 Superior Ave., 44114. Tel: 216-696-6525, Ext. 449; Fax: 216-781-8243. Brian Gillen, M.S.S.A., L.I.S.W., Pres.
Malachi House, Inc., 2810 Clinton Ave., 44113. Tel: 216-621-8831. Total assisted annually 60; Total Staff 15.
St. Malachi Center, Inc., 2459 Washington Ave., 44113. Tel: 216-771-3036. Total Assisted 65 per day (Neighborhood Center); 30 per Monday (Health Services); Total Staff 11.
Society of St. Vincent de Paul, Diocesan Central Council, Chancery Bldg., 1027 Superior Ave., 44114. Tel: 216-696-6525, Ext. 358. Rev. Msgr. Casimir S. Ciolek, A.C.S.W., Spiritual Dir.; Frank J. Fearon, Diocesan Pres.; Lawrence Lauter, A.C.S.W., L.I.S.W., Exec. Dir.; Rev. James R. Schleicher, Spiritual Dir.; Frank Fearon, Pres.
Akron District Council, 388 W. Bath Rd., Cuyahoga Falls, 44223. Tel: 216-929-4478.
Cleveland District Council, Chancery Building, 1027 Superior Ave., 44114. Chancery Building, 1027 Superior Ave., 44114. Lawrence Lauter, Exec. Dir.
Lorain District Council, 221 Columbia, Elyria, 44035. Tel: 216-322-6250. Donald Smith, Pres.
St. Vincent de Paul Thrift Stores, 875 E. 70th, 44103. Tel: 216-391-9655. 4726 Superior Ave., 44103. Tel: 216-391-1337. 3074 W. 25th St., 44113. Tel: 216-694-2060. 16730 Lorain Ave., 44111. Tel: 216-252-8764. 5462 Broadway Ave., 44127. Tel: 216-341-3445. 10322 Lorain Ave., 44111. Tel: 216-941-7780. 4125 Lee Rd., 44128. Tel: 216-921-5550. 700 E. 185th St., 44119. Tel: 216-486-9122.
AKRON. *Catholic Social Services of Summit County, Inc.*, 640 N. Main St., 44310-3098. Tel: 216-762-7481. Susan E. Milne, M.S.W., Exec. Dir. Service sites throughout Summit County. Total Assisted 15,000; Total Staff 30.
CYO & Community Services, 812 Biruta St., 44307. Tel: 216-762-2961.
CYO Adult Day Care Services, 812 Biruta St., 44307. Tel: 216-762-2000. Donald P. Finn, Exec. Dir. Total Assisted 145; Total Staff 8.
Recreation (camping and athletics): Total Assisted 14,998; Total Staff 27.
Interval Brotherhood Home Alcohol-Drug Rehabilitation Center, 3445 S. Main St., 44319. Tel: 330-644-4095. Rev. Samuel R. Ciccolini, Dir. Total Assisted 385; Total Staff 72.
Leonora Hall. (Refer to Homes for Women).
ELYRIA. *Catholic Social Services of Lorain County*, 2136 N. Ridge Rd., 44035-1241. Tel: 216-324-2614; 277-7228 (Lorain); Fax: 216-324-2985. Bernadette Washington, Exec. Dir.
Senior Achievement Center, 3114 Pearl Ave., Lorain, 44055. Tel: 216-277-4860. Barbara A. Alflen, Prog. Dir.
Catholic Community Services, 203 Eighth St., Lorain, 44052. Tel: 216-244-9915.
GARFIELD HEIGHTS. *Brendan Manor, Inc.*, 13401 Cranwood Dr., 44105. Tel: 216-475-5230. Diane Kalchert, Admin. Licensed nonprofit, nondenominational shared living home for low to moderate income older adults. Total in Residence 16; Total Staff 6.
NORTHFIELD. *St. Barnabas Villa, Inc.*, 9234 Olde Eight Rd., 44067. Tel: 216-467-3758; 467-4044. A shared living facility for nine people over 60 years of age. Sr. M. Germaine Maximovich, V.S.C., Mgr.; Mrs. Jo Ann Smith, Asst. Mgr. Total in Residence 9; Total Staff 4.

[W] SHRINES

CLEVELAND. *Our Lady of Lourdes.* Euclid, (U.S. Rtes. 20 & 6). Administered by the Sisters of the Most Holy Trinity. 21281 Chardon Rd., 44117. Tel: 216-481-8232; Fax: 216-481-6577. Sr. M. Valentine, O.SS.T., Contact Person. Total in Residence 14.
BEDFORD. *Our Lady of Levocha.* (Ohio Rte. 14). Administered by the Vincentian Sisters of Charity (V.S.C.). 1160 Broadway, 44146. Tel: 216-232-4755. Sr. M. Gertrude, V.S.C., Contact Person.
GARFIELD HEIGHTS. *Our Lady of Czestochowa Shrine.* (Ohio Rte. 17). Administered by the Sisters of St. Joseph Third Order of St. Francis (S.S.J. -T.O.S.F.), 12215 Granger Rd., 44125. Tel: 216-581-3535. Sr. Dominica, Shrine Contact.
PARMA. *Our Lady, Queen of the Holy Rosary.* (U.S. Rte. 42). Administered by the Sisters of the Incarnate Word and Blessed Sacrament (S.I.W.). 6618 Pearl Rd., 44130. Tel: 216-886-6440; Fax: 216-888-1377.

[X] MINISTRY TO THE SPANISH SPEAKING

CLEVELAND. *Diocesan Hispanic Office*, 1031 Superior Ave., 44114-2519. Tel: 216-696-6525, Ext. 253. Sr. Joaquina Carrion, M.S.B.T., Dir.
Hispanic Parishes: San Juan Bautista Parish, 1946 W. 32nd St., 44113. Tel: 216-631-2888. Rev. David F. Fallon.
Sacred Heart Chapel, 4301 Pear Ave., Lorain, 44055. Tel: 216-277-7231; 277-7379. Rev. Robert J. Reidy.
Cristo Rey Mission, 3402 Clark Ave., 44109. Tel: 216-631-6817. Pastoral Team: Rev. Jim McCreight, Admin.; Deacon Frederick F. Simon; Millie Simon.
Parishes with Ministry to Spanish Speaking: St. Bernard, 47 University Ave., Akron, 44308. Tel: 216-253-5161. Rev. Paul E. Schindler.
St. Francis, 7119 Superior Ave., 44103. Tel: 216-361-4133. Rev. Thomas F. Martin; Deacon Frank Lozada.
St. Josaphat, 1411 E. 33rd St., 44114. Tel: 216-579-0173.
St. Michael, 3114 Scranton Rd., 44109. Tel: 216-861-6297. Rev. Dennis R. O'Grady.
St. Mary's - Painesville, 242 N. State St., Painesville, 44077. Tel: 216-354-4381. Rev. Richard C. Antall.

[Y] NEWMAN CENTERS

CLEVELAND. *Office of Newman Campus Ministry*, The Catholic Center, 1031 Superior Ave., 44114. Mr. William A. Fichter, Assoc. Diocesan Dir.
Newman Foundation Corp. Catholic Center, Case-Western Reserve University, 1031 Superior Ave., 44114. Tel: 216-696-6525, Ext. 325; Fax: 216-696-6206.
Hallinan Center, 11303 Euclid Ave., 44106. Tel: 216-421-1522; Fax: 216-421-2925. Ms. Marie deLaBruere, Campus Min.
Case-Western Reserve Hallinan Chair of Catholic Studies, 2501 Kemper, Shaker Heights, 44106. Tel: 216-368-2210. Rev. James W. Flanagan (DUB).
Cleveland State University Newman Ministry, Hallinan Center, 11303 Euclid Ave., 44106. Tel: 216-421-1522; Fax: 216-696-2925. Mr. Matthew Maruggi, Campus Min.
Cuyahoga Community College, Metro Campus, 2900 Community College Dr., 44115. Tel: 216-987-4239. Mr. William A. Fichter, Assoc. Diocesan Dir.
Western Campus, 11000 Pleasant Valley, Parma, 44130. Tel: 216-886-1327. Maureen Masterson, Campus Min.
Lakeland Community College, Mentor, 44060. Tel: 216-953-4803. Mr. Matthew Maruggi, Campus Min.
University of Akron. (Akron), Newman Center, 44 University Ave., Akron, 44308. Tel: 216-376-3585. Ms. Emily Holtel, Campus Min.
Ashland College. (Ashland), c/o St. Peter Church, 132 N. Wood St., Loudonville, 44842. Rev. Edwin A. Dowling, Campus Min.
Baldwin-Wallace College Newman Center. (Berea), 170 E. Center St., Berea, 44017. Tel: 216-243-4955; Fax: 216-243-0354. Mr. William A. Fichter, Assoc. Diocesan Dir.
Oberlin College. (Oberlin), Office of Chaplains, 217 Wilder Hall, Oberlin, 44074. Tel: 216-775-8103. Rev. Edward J. Kordas, D.Min.
The College of Wooster. (Wooster), Box C-3135, Wooster, 44691. Tel: 216-263-2096. Ms. Maureen Masterson, Campus Min.
Lorain County Community College, 1005 N. Abbey Rd., Elyria, 44035. Tel: 216-365-5222, Ext. 7661; 800-995-5222. Emily Holtel, Campus Min. Total Staff for 12 Newman Centers 8.

[Z] ENDOWMENT TRUSTS

CLEVELAND. *Good Shepherd-Marycrest Endowment Fund*, 7800 Brookside Rd., 44131. Tel: 216-524-5280; Fax: 216-524-6669.
St. John Cathedral Endowment Trust, 1007 Superior Ave., 44114.
Sisters of St. Joseph Community Support Charitable Trust, 3430 Rocky River Dr., 44111. Tel: 216-252-0440; Fax: 216-941-3430. Sr. Marrieta Starrie, C.S.J., Contact Person.
Villa Angela - St. Joseph High School Education Endowment Foundation, 18491 Lake Shore Blvd., 44119.
AKRON. *The Daughters of Divine Charity, St. Mary Province, Charitable Trust*, 39 N. Portage Path, 44303-1188. Tel: 330-867-4960.
Our Lady of the Elms / Our Lady of the Elms Foundation, 1230 W. Market St., 44313; Fax: 330-836-5913.
St. Vincent-St. Mary High School Endowment Fund, 15 N. Maple St., 44303. Tel: 216-253-9116; Fax: 216-996-0020.
**St. Hilary Parish Foundation*, 657 Moorfield Rd., 44313. Tel: 330-666-2403. Mr. Edward F. Carter, Pres.
CHARDON. *The Sisters of Notre Dame Charitable Trust*, 13000 Auburn Rd., 44024. Tel: 216-942-6716. Sr. Mary Frances Murray, S.N.D., Chm.
MENTOR. *St. Mary of the Assumption Parish Endowment Trust*, 8560 Mentor Ave., 44060-5853.
PARMA HEIGHTS. *Incarnate Word Endowment Trust*, 6618 Pearl Rd., 44130. Tel: 216-886-6440; Fax: 216-888-1377. Sr. Margaret Taylor, Chm.
WELLINGTON. *St. Patrick Church Endowment Trust*, 512 N. Main St., 44090.
WOOSTER. *St. Mary Elementary Day School Endowment Trust*, 527 Beall Ave., P.O. Box 109, 44691.

[AA] MISCELLANEOUS

CLEVELAND. *Catholic Tours of Ohio, Inc.*, 17825 Libby Rd., 44137. Tel: 330-475-2478. Rev. Msgr. Joseph C. Heruday, Pres. & Sec.; Stanley Streiner, Treas. Nonprofit organization.
Christa Center, 18515 Underwood Ave., 44119. Tel: 216-481-1015. Sr. Barbara Walter, H.M., Co-Dir.
Holistic Spirituality and Wellness Center. Total Assisted 1,220; Total Staff 2.
COAR Peace Mission, Inc., 4395 Rocky River Dr., 44135-2569. Sr. Ann Mary Brangan, C.C.V.I., Exec. Dir.; Margaret M. McBride, Office Mgr.
COAR Children's Village. (Zaragoza, El Salvador, C.A.). Sr. M. Audrey Walsh, C.C.V.I., Dir.; Rev. Kenneth C. Myers, Founder. COAR Children's Village is an orphanage in Zaragoza, El Salvador, serving 125 children whose parents have died in the violence or have been abandoned in refugee centers. 650 children attend the COAR school. This includes children from the surrounding area. The COAR Clinic serves the medical and dental needs of the resident orphaned children and assists 193 people on a weekly basis. COAR was begun in August 1980 by Rev. Kenneth C. Myers.
CSA St. John Ministries fka St. John West Shore Hospital, 2351 E. 22nd St., 44115. Tel: 216-696-5560; Fax: 216-696-2204. Sr. Mary Ann Andrews, CSA Pres. & CEO.
CSA St. Vincent Charity Ministries fka St. Vincent

Charity Hospital, 2351 E. 22nd St., 44115. Tel: 216-696-5560; Fax: 216-696-2204. Sr. Mary Ann Andrews, CSA Pres. & CEO.

The Greater Cleveland/Akron Corporation United for Education, 1027 Superior Ave., 44114. Tel: 216-696-6525, Ext. 436; Fax: 216-696-8084. Rev. John J. Wright, Exec. Dir.; Andrej N. Lah, Attorney; Joseph Smith, Treas.

H.M. Center for Women and Children, 2100 Broadway Ave., 44052. Tel: 216-356-5707. Sr. Cathleen Walsh, H.M., Chm., Board of Trustees; Kathryn Csank, Dir.

Heartbeats, 2259 Columbus Rd., 44113. Tel: 216-241-1504; 1-800-808-1991. Sr. Margaret Cessna, H.M., Dir.

L'Arche, Cleveland, 2634 E. 127 St., P.O. Box 20540, 44120. Tel: 216-721-5719. An ecumenical community providing homes for adults with mental retardation and developmental disabilities. Residents 9.

National Catholic Ministry to the Bereaved, Inc., 9412 Heath Ave., 44104. Tel: 216-441-2125.

Sisters of Charity of St. Augustine Health Network, 2351 East 22nd St., 44115. Tel: 216-659-5560; Fax: 216-696-2204. Sr. Mary Ann Andrews, C.S.A., Pres. & CEO. Serves as the general partner to the joint venture ownership of Catholic healthcare providers.

Sisters of Charity of St. Augustine Health System, 2351 E. 22nd St., 44115. Tel: 216-696-5560; Fax: 216-696-2204. Sr. Mary Ann Andrews, C.S.A., Pres. & CEO.
Serves as the Member of foundations and human service corporations sponsored by the Sisters of Charity of St. Augustine, Richfield, OH.

**St. Augustine Development Corporation*, 7801 Detroit Ave., 44102-2895. Tel: 216-634-7400, Ext. 2345; Fax: 216-634-7483. Joan M. Steidl, Pres.

**St. Augustine Services Corporation*, 7801 Detroit Ave., 44102. Tel: 216-634-7400; Fax: 216-634-7483. Provides administrative and support services to St. Augustine Manor and St. Augustine Development Corp. - both 509(a)(2) organizations. Raymond S. Lesniak, Jr., Pres. Total Staff 55.

AKRON. *H.M. Life Opportunity Services*, Box 8174, 44320. Central Office, 1220 W. Market St., 44313. Tel: 330-869-5600; Fax: 330-869-8168. Sr. Loretta Rafter, H.M., Pres. & CEO.

Humility of Mary Housing, Inc., P.O. Box 22250, 44302-0250. Tel: 216-836-8660. Sr. Denise Maher, H.M., Pres. & CEO. Affordable housing and housing related services for low and moderate income individuals. Total Assisted 2,500; Total Staff 2.

BEDFORD. *Emmaus Conference Center*, Vincentian Sisters of Broadway, 1160 Broadway, 44146. Tel: 216-232-4755.

BROADVIEW HEIGHTS. *Alliance for Access dba Medical Center South*, 2001 E. Royalton Rd., 44147. Tel: 216-526-3333; Fax: 216-526-1369. A corporation operating an urgent and ambulatory acute care sponsored by Marymount Hospital and St. Vincent Charity Hospital health facility. Edgar Maloney, Admin.

CHARDON. *Christ Child Society-Geauga Chapter*, 12010 Burlington Glen, 44024. Linda L. Toth, Pres.

EUCLID. *Faith and Light U.S.A., Inc.*, 26351 Drakefield Ave., 44132. Pearl Cahoon; Posie O'Connor.

St. Robert's Holy Name Society Boosters, 23802 Lakeshore Blvd., 44123. Tel: 216-731-2606. Rev. John T. Burkley, Pastor.

GARFIELD HEIGHTS. *Marymount Health Care Systems*. Provides comprehensive health and human services in response to the needs of the local community by owning, leasing, and operating health care facilities and services, including Marymount Place, a 104-unit Senior Living Community for the Well-elderly/Assisted Living, within the philosophy and objectives of the Sisters of St. Joseph of the Third Order of St. Francis and is the special Member of Marymount Hospital, Inc. 12200 McCracken Rd., 44125.

HUDSON.
**Laurel Lake Retirement Community, Inc.*, 200 Laurel Lake Rd., 44236. Tel: 216-656-3651. Paul Younger, Pres. & CEO. Independent Living Residents 363; Assisted Living Residents 18; Skilled Nursing Residents 75; Total Staff 270.

LORAIN. *St. Joseph Health Care Foundation, Inc.*, 205 W. 20th St., 44052. Tel: 216-233-1099.

MIDDLEBURG HEIGHTS. *Humility of Mary Health Care Corporation*, Plaza One South, 7251 Engle Rd., Ste. 410, 44130-3496. Tel: 800-884-9374; 216-234-0059. Sr. Frances Flanigan, H.M., Pres. & CEO.

St. Elizabeth Health Center, Youngstown. Medical Staff 507; Employees 2,465; Inpatient 18,305; Outpatient 239,860; Beds 550; Bassinets 60.

H.M. Health Services. Consolidated with St. Joseph Health Center., Warren. Medical Staff 461; Employees 695; Inpatient 5,665; Outpatient 43,254; Bed Capacity 165.

Lorrain Community/St. Joseph Regional Health Center, Lorain. Medical Staff 320; Employers 2,135; Inpatient 14,512; Outpatient 182,317; Bed Capacity 359.

Laurel Lake Retirement Community, Hudson.

OBERLIN. *Common Ground Center for Community Renewal, Inc.*, P.O. Box 613, 44074. Tel: 216-965-5551. Sr. Rose Bator, H.M., Dir.

PARMA. *Society of St. Joseph the Worker*, 7033 State Rd., 44134-4952. Tel: 216-888-4872. Lawrence R. Verbiar, Dir.

PEPPER PIKE. *The O'Neill Brothers Foundation*, 3550 Lander Rd. #140, 44124. Tel: 216-464-2121; Fax: 216-464-1517. Mr. Robert K. Healey, Pres.

**Ursuline Sophia Center*, 2600 Lander Rd., 44124. Tel: 216-442-4160. Sr. Carolyn Clines, O.S.U., Dir.

ROCKY RIVER. *The Center for Learning*, 21590 Center Ridge Rd., 44116. Tel: 216-331-1404; Fax: 216-331-5414. Sr. Rose Schaffer, H.M., M.A., Pres. & CEO; Sr. Bernadette Vetter, H.M., M.A., Vice Pres. Educational Development Center and Publisher of values-based instructional materials: Religion for Catholic schools and parishes; English/Language Arts, Social Studies, Novel/Drama, and Elementary Curriculum Units for all schools. Owned and operated by the Sisters of the Humility of Mary. Directed by an ecumenical lay board. Administrative-Editorial Office in Rocky River. Shipping-Business Office, Evergreen Rd., P.O. Box 910, Villa Maria, PA, 16155. Tel: 800-767-9090; 412-964-8083; Fax: 888-767-8080.

SAN ANTONIO, TX, 1135 Mission Rd., 78210-4598. Rev. Kenneth C. Myers, Dir.

WICKLIFFE. *Center for Pastoral Leadership Services, Inc.*, 28700 Euclid Ave., 44092-2585. Tel: 216-943-7600. Revs. Donald B. Cozzens, Pres.; Brian F. Howlahan, Chief Operating Officer.

RELIGIOUS INSTITUTES OF MEN REPRESENTED IN THE DIOCESE

For further details refer to the corresponding bracketed number in the Religious Institutes of Men or Women section.

[0200]—*Benedictine Monks*. (St. Andrew Abbey).—O.S.B.
[0600]—*Brothers of the Congregation of Holy Cross*. (Midwest Prov.).—C.S.C.
[0470]—*The Capuchin Friars*.—O.F.M.Cap.
[1150]—*Congregation of St. Joseph*.—C.S.J.
[0220]—*Congregation of the Blessed Sacrament*.—S.S.S.
[0520]—*Franciscan Friars*. (Provs. of Sacred Heart & Assumption).—O.F.M.
[0480]—*Franciscan Friars (Conv.)*.—OFM.Conv.
[0690]—*Jesuit Fathers and Brothers*. (Maryland Prov.).
[0690]—*Jesuit Fathers and Brothers*. (Detroit Prov.).
[0780]—*Marist Fathers*. (Washington Prov.).—S.M.
[0800]—*Maryknoll*.—M.M.
[]—*Missionaries of St. Francis de Sales*.—M.S.F.S.
[0840]—*Missionary Servants of the Most Holy Trinity*.—S.T.
[0910]—*Oblates of Mary Immaculate*.—O.M.I.
[0970]—*Order of Our Lady of Mercy*.—O.de.M.
[0610]—*Priests of the Congregation of the Holy Cross*. (Indiana Prov.).—C.S.C.
[0760]—*Society of Mary-Marianists*. (Dayton, OH).—S.M.
[1060]—*Society of the Precious Blood*. (Cincinnati Prov.).—C.PP.S.

RELIGIOUS INSTITUTES OF WOMEN REPRESENTED IN THE DIOCESE

[0230]—*Benedictine Sisters of Pontifical Jurisdiction*. (Erie, PA).—O.S.B.
[]—*Byzantine Nuns of St. Clare*.—B.N.S.C.
[0370]—*Carmelite Sisters of the Most Sacred Heart of Los Angeles*.—O.C.D.
[0470]—*Congregation of the Sisters of Charity of the Incarnate Word*. (Houston).—C.C.V.I.
[1730]—*Congregation of the Sisters of the Third Order of St. Francis*. (Oldenburg).—O.S.F.
[1710]—*Congregation of the Third Order of St. Francis of Mary Immaculate, Joliet, IL*.—O.S.F.
[1830]—*Contemplative Sisters of the Good Shepherd*.—C.G.S.
[0790]—*Daughters of Divine Charity*.—F.D.C.
[0820]—*Daughters of the Holy Spirit*.—D.H.S.
[0420]—*Discalced Carmelite Nuns*.—O.C.D.
[1070-13]—*Dominican Sisters*.—O.P.
[1070-14]—Dominican Sisters.—O.P.
[1070-23]—*Dominican Sisters*.—O.P.
[1070-28]—*Dominican Sisters*.—O.P.
[1170]—*Felician Sisters*.—C.S.S.F.
[1210]—*Franciscan Sisters of Chicago*.—O.S.F.
[1840]—*Grey Nuns of Sacred Heart*.—G.N.S.H.
[2340]—*Little Sisters of the Poor*.—L.S.P.
[2490]—*Medical Mission Sisters*.—M.M.S.
[2790]—*Missionary Servants of the Most Blessed Trinity*.—M.S.B.T.
[3760]—*Order of St. Clare-Poor Clare Colettine Nuns*.—P.C.C.
[3130]—*Our Lady of Victory Missionary Sisters*.—O.L.V.M.
[0950]—*Pious Society Daughters of St. Paul*.—F.S.P.
[3210]—*Poor Clares of Perpetual Adoration*.—P.C.P.A.
[1020]—*Religious of the Divine Redeemer*.—S.D.R.
[1830]—*Religious of the Good Shepherd*.—R.G.S.
[3430]—*Religious Teachers Filippini*.—M.P.F.
[2970]—*School Sisters of Notre Dame*.—S.S.N.D.
[0440]—*Sisters of Charity of Cincinnati, Ohio*.—S.C.
[0580]—*Sisters of Charity of St. Augustine*.—C.S.A.
[0990]—*Sisters of Divine Providence*.—C.D.P.
[2580]—*Sisters of Mercy of the Union of the United States of America*.—R.S.M. (Provs. of Cincinnati & Detroit).
[2990]—*Sisters of Notre Dame*.—S.N.D.
[1620]—*Sisters of St. Francis of Millvale*. (PA).—O.S.F.
[1640]—*Sisters of St. Francis of Perpetual Adoration*.—O.S.F.
[3830-08]—*Sisters of St. Joseph*.—C.S.J.
[3910]—*Sisters of St. Joseph of St. Mark*.—S.J.S.M.
[3930]—*Sisters of St. Joseph of the Third Order of St. Francis*.—S.S.J.-T.O.S.F.
[1970]—*Sisters of the Holy Family of Nazareth*.—C.S.F.N.
[2030]—*Sisters of the Holy Spirit*.—C.S.Sp.
[2110]—*Sisters of the Humility of Mary*.—H.M.
[2210]—*Sisters of the Incarnate Word and Blessed Sacrament*.—S.I.W.
[2350]—*Sisters of the Living Word*.—S.L.W.
[2060]—*Sisters of the Most Holy Trinity*.—O.SS.T.
[3730]—*Sisters of the Order of St. Basil the Great*.—O.S.B.M.
[3260]—*Sisters of the Precious Blood*. (Dayton, Ohio).—C.PP.S.
[1490]—*Sisters of the Third Franciscan Order*.—O.S.F.
[3620]—*Sisters, Servants of Mary Immaculate*.—S.S.M.I.
[2150]—*Sisters, Servants of the Immaculate Heart of Mary*.—I.H.M.
[4120-04]—*Ursuline Nuns of the Congregation of Paris*.—O.S.U.
[4120-07]—*Ursuline Nuns of the Congregation of Paris*.—O.S.U.
[]—*Sisters of Divine Providence*. Korea.
[4170]—*Vincentian Sisters of Charity*. (Bedford, OH).—V.S.C.

DIOCESAN CEMETERIES

CLEVELAND. *Assumption of Mary*.
Calvary.
St. John.
St. Joseph.
St. Mary.
St. Mary of the Falls.
AKRON. *Holy Cross*.
AVON. *Holy Trinity*, Detroit Rd.
Holy Trinity, Jaycox Rd.
BROOK PARK. *Holy Cross*.
CHARDON. *All Souls*.
CUYAHOGA HEIGHTS. *St. Mary*.
ELYRIA. *St. Mary*.
LORAIN. *Calvary*.
NORTHFIELD. *All Saints*.
VALLEY CITY. *Resurrection*.

NECROLOGY

† Angelaitis, Joseph F., Cleveland, OH, Our Lady of Perpetual Help. —Died Oct. 6, 1996.
† Bartnikowski, Francis G., Grafton, OH, Assumption. —Died Jan. 6, 1996.
† Blair, Rev. Msgr. Robert C., Cleveland, OH, Cathedral of St. John the Evangelist. —Died June 5, 1996.
† Cartmell, J. Richard, (Retired). —Died May 29, 1996.
† DeAngelis, Nazareno, Cleveland, OH, Our Lady of Mount Carmel (East). —Died July 1, 1996.
† Kane, Eugene C., (Retired). —Died Jan. 3, 1996.
† Knuff, Robert C., Euclid, OH, St. Robert Bellarmine. —Died May 17, 1996.
† Minnich, John C., Bedford Heights, OH, Holy Trinity. —Died July 9, 1996.
† Monroe, Lee J., Wickliffe, OH, Borromeo Seminary. —Died Nov. 2, 1996.
† Murphy, Edward J., (Retired). —Died Nov. 10, 1996.
† Ozimec, Joseph J., Barberton, OH, Sacred Heart. —Died Nov. 10, 1996.
† Saunders, Rev. Msgr. Kenneth W., Middleburg Heights, OH, St. Bartholomew. —Died Oct. 19, 1996.
† Sodja, Max F., (Retired). —Died Feb. 16, 1996.
† Trapp, Raymond A., Brook Park, OH, Assumption of Mary. —Died April 11, 1996.
† Zahorsky, Julius, Cleveland, OH, St. Elizabeth. —Died Dec. 4, 1995.

Diocese of Colorado Springs

Most Reverend

RICHARD C. HANIFEN, D.D., J.C.L.

Bishop of Colorado Springs; ordained June 6, 1959; appointed Titular Bishop of Abercorn and Auxiliary of Denver July 6, 1974; consecrated September 20, 1974; appointed First Bishop of Colorado Springs November 10, 1983; installed January 30, 1984. *Office: 29 West Kiowa, Colorado Springs, CO, 80903-1498.* Tel.: 719-636-2345; Fax: 719-636-1216.

Diocesan Offices: 29 West Kiowa, Colorado Springs, CO, 80903-1498. Tel.: 719-636-2345; Fax: 719-636-1216.

Legal Title: Diocese of Colorado Springs.

ESTABLISHED AND CREATED A DIOCESE, JANUARY 30, 1984.

Square Miles Approximately 15,500.

Comprising the Counties of Chaffee, Cheyenne, Douglas, Elbert, El Paso, Kit Carson, Lake, Lincoln, Park and Teller.

For legal title of parishes and diocesan institutions, consult the Diocesan Offices.

STATISTICAL OVERVIEW

Personnel	
Bishop	1
Priests: Diocesan Active in Diocese	22
Priests: Active Outside Diocese	1
Priests: Retired, Sick or Absent	8
Number of Diocesan Priests	31
Religious Priests in Diocese	18
Extern Priests in Diocese	9
Ordinations:	
Transitional Deacons	4
Permanent Deacons in Diocese	21
Total Brothers	3
Total Sisters	145
Parishes	
Parishes	30
With Resident Pastor:	
Resident Diocesan Priests	15
Resident Religious Priests	8
Without Resident Pastor:	
Administered by Priests	3
Administered by Permanent Deacons	2
Administered by Lay People	2
Missions	9
Professional Ministry Personnel:	
Sisters	3
Lay Ministers	75
Welfare	
Catholic Hospitals	3
Total Assisted	265,000
Health Care Centers	2
Total Assisted	113
Homes for the Aged	2
Total Assisted	103
Educational	
Diocesan Students in Other Seminaries	7
Total Seminarians	7
Elementary Schools, Diocesan and Parish	4
Total Students	1,212
Catechesis/Religious Education:	
High School Students	1,785
Elementary Students	4,936
Total Students Under Catholic Instruction	7,940
Teachers in the Diocese:	
Lay Teachers	74
Vital Statistics	
Receptions into the Church:	
Infant Baptism Totals	1,312
Adult Baptism Totals	140
Received into Full Communion	269
First Communions	1,406
Confirmations	618
Marriages:	
Catholic	178
Interfaith	153
Total Marriages	331
Deaths	370
Total Catholic Population	86,462
Total Population	593,175

Diocesan Offices—29 W. Kiowa St., Colorado Springs, 80903-1498. Tel: 719-636-2345; Fax: 719-636-1216. Office Hours: Mon.-Fri. 8:30-4:30.

Vicar General and Moderator of the Curia—Very Rev. DONALD F. DUNN.

Chancellor—Rev. GEORGE V. FAGAN, J.C.L., *29 W. Kiowa St., Colorado Springs, 80903.* Tel: 719-636-2345.

Diocesan Consultors—Revs. DONALD BROWNSTEIN; RICHARD BUHLER, S.J.; ROBERT JAEGER; WILLIAM C. VOLLMER; WILLIAM WACK, C.S.C.; AUGUST STEWART.

Finance Officer—ROBERT G. DOERFLER, JR.

Archivist—Sr. JOSEPH MARIE JACOBSEN, O.S.B.

Judicial Vicar—Rev. GEORGE V. FAGAN, J.C.L.

Associate Judges—Revs. JAMES I. DONLON, J.C.D.; JOSEPH KOURY, S.J., J.C.D.

Defender of the Bond—Rev. MARK PLEWKA, J.C.L.

Procurator-Advocates—Revs. KARL USELDINGER; ERNEST W. BOND; Sr. JOSEPH MARIE JACOBSEN, O.S.B.; Deacon GEORGE D. LINEHAN, JR.

Auditors—Sr. JOSEPH MARIE JACOBSEN, O.S.B.

Ecclesiastical Notaries—Rev. GEORGE V. FAGAN, J.C.L.; Sr. JOSEPH MARIE JACOBSEN, O.S.B.; SHIRLEY WELLS.

Catholic Community Services, The Diocese of Colorado Springs, Inc.—GAIL DUSING, Exec. Dir.

Diocesan Resource Center—KAREN BAKER, Resource Ctr. Mgr.

Office of Pastoral Administration—ROBERT G. DOERFLER, JR., Dir.

Office of Stewardship and Development—HERMAN GUENTHER, Dir.

Office of the Superintendent of Schools—Sr. JUDITH CAULEY, C.S.J., Supt.

Propagation of the Faith—Very Rev. DONALD F. DUNN, Diocesan Dir.

Vocations Office—Rev. GEORGE V. FAGAN, JR., Dir.

Regionalization—Very Rev. DONALD F. DUNN, Vicar General; Douglas/Elbert Cos. Region: Rev. DENNIS DWYER, Vicar; Metro-Central Region (Colorado Springs): Rev. MICHAEL BUTLER, Vicar; Metro-North Region (Colorado Springs): Rev. PAUL WICKER, Vicar; Metro-South Region (Colorado Springs): Rev. DONALD F. DUNN, Vicar (Acting); Mountain Region: Rt. Rev. WARREN HEIDGEN, O.S.B., Vicar; Plains Region: Rev. R. WILLIAM RHINEHART, C.M., Vicar.

CLERGY, PARISHES, MISSIONS AND PAROCHIAL SCHOOLS

CITY OF COLORADO SPRINGS
(County of El Paso)

1—ST. MARY'S CATHEDRAL, Very Revs. John F. Slattery, Rector; Theodore A. Haas, Rector Emeritus; Deacon John Baumbach. In res., Rev. Matthew T. Minh.
Res., 15 West View Pl., 80903.
Office: 22 W. Kiowa St., 80903. Tel: 719-473-4633.
Catechesis/Religious Programs—Kerry Susser, D.R.E.
Students 103.

2—CORPUS CHRISTI, Rev. Lawrence W. Carmody; Deacon Benedict Cruise.
Res., 2318 N. Cascade Ave., 80907. Tel: 719-633-1457; Fax: 719-473-7567.
School—2410 N. Cascade Ave., 80907. Tel: 719-632-5092. Martha Frauenheim, Prin.
Lay Teachers 14; Students 333.
Catechesis/Religious Programs—Tel: 719-473-8363. Barb Maloney, D.R.E.
Students 142.

3—DIVINE REDEEMER, Revs. Michael C. Butler; William Jarema; Deacon David Van Matre.
Res., 1520 E. Yampa St., 80909. Tel: 719-633-5559; Fax: 719-575-9180. [JC]
School—901 N. Logan, 80909. Tel: 719-471-7771; Fax: 719-575-9180. Patricia Beckert, Prin.
Lay Teachers 25; Students 422.
Catechesis/Religious Programs—Bernadette Tittle, D.R.E.
Students 190.

4—HOLY APOSTLES, Revs. Paul F. Wicker; Martin Hunckler.
Res., 4925 N. Carefree Cir., 80917. Tel: 719-597-4249; Fax: 719-591-1816.
Preschool—4925 N. Carefree, 80917. Tel: 719-591-1566; Fax: 719-591-1816. Mary Parsons, Dir.
Lay Teachers 12; Students 145.
Catechesis/Religious Programs—Mary Margaret Melanson, D.R.E.
Students 685.

5—HOLY TRINITY, Deacon James Whittle; Ms. CoCo Soper, Parish Dir.
Office: 3122 Poinsetta Dr., 80907. Tel: 719-633-2132; Fax: 719-633-0975.
Res., 1522 Hollyhock, 80907.
School—3115 Larkspur Dr., 80907.
Lay Teachers 12; Students 217.

6—KOREAN CATHOLIC COMMUNITY, Rev. Adrian Jae Cheol Lee (Korea). Office 2126 Mount Vernon Pl., 80906. Tel: 719-635-8970; Fax: 719-635-5688.

7—OUR LADY OF GUADALUPE, Rev. Donald F. Dunn, V.G.; Deacon Emilio S. Reyes, Parish Dir.
Res., 2715 E. Pikes Peak, 80909. Tel: 719-633-7204.
Catechesis/Religious Programs—Students 369.

8—OUR LADY OF THE PINES-BLACK FOREST, Revs. Gerard J. Borer, S.J.; Curtis Van Del, S.J.; Deacons Gene Eastham; Lynn Sherman.
Res., 11020 Teachout Rd., 80908. Tel: 719-495-2351.
Catechesis/Religious Programs—D.R.E.: Mrs. Susan Ames; Mrs. Karen Weber.
Students 150.

9—SACRED HEART, Revs. James A. Bracke, C.S.C.; William Wack, C.S.C.; James W. Thornton, C.S.C.; Sr. Kathleen Elliott, C.S.J., Pastoral Assoc.
Office: 2021 W. Pikes Peak Ave., 80904. Tel:

719-633-8711; Fax: 719-633-1859.
Catechesis/Religious Programs—Kathleen Moriarty, D.R.E.
Students 280.
Missions—Manitou Springs, El Paso Co., Our Lady of Perpetual Help, 218 Ruxton Ave., 80829; Cascade, El Paso Co., Holy Rosary, 4435 Holiday Trail, 80809.

10—ST. FRANCIS OF ASSISI, Deacon Charles W. Specht, Parish Dir.; Revs. Edward L. Maginnis, S.J.; Owen J. McHugh; Deacon Michael Ciletti.
Office: 2650 Parish View, 80919. Tel: 719-599-5031.
Catechesis/Religious Programs—Tel: 719-548-0374; Fax: 719-599-3360. Kathy Kredo, D.R.E.
Students 550.

11—ST. JOSEPH'S (Southgate), Mr. David Kenney, Parish Dir.; Rev. Patrick McLoughlin; Deacon Albert E. Kimminau, Pastoral Assoc.
Res., 1830 S. Corona Ave., 80906. Tel: 719-632-9903; Fax: 719-632-9170.
Catechesis/Religious Programs—Tel: 719-635-3166. Randall Brungardt, D.R.E.
Students 223.

12—ST. PATRICK'S, Revs. Donald Brownstein; William Thro, S.J.
Office: 1925 Dominion Way, 80918. Tel: 719-598-3595; Fax: 719-599-5741.
Res., 6602 Snowbird Dr., 80918.
Catechesis/Religious Programs—Angelita M. Dykes, D.R.E.
Students 1037.

13—SAINT PAUL, Revs. John Auer; August Stewart; Deacon Patrick Bidon.
Res., 9 El Pomar Rd., 80906. Tel: 719-471-9700; Fax: 719-471-3009.
School—Pauline Memorial Catholic School, Tel: 719-632-1846.
Lay Teachers 16; Students 238.
Catechesis/Religious Programs—D.R.E.: Joanne Pittz; Francis Pittz.
Students 421.

14—THE VIETNAMESE HOLY MARTYRS QUASI-PARISH, Rev. Matthew T. Minh Thanh Tran.
Res. & Mailing Address: 15 West View Pl., 80903. Tel: 719-634-6172.
Parish Center—29 W. Kiowa, 80903. Tel: 719-633-2274.

OUTSIDE THE CITY OF COLORADO SPRINGS

Bailey, Park Co., St. Mary's of the Rockies, Rev. Ernest W. Bond.
Res., P.O. Box 319, 80421-8319. Tel: 303-838-2375.

Buena Vista, Chaffee Co., St. Rose of Lima, Rt. Rev. Warren J. Heidgen, O.S.B.; Deacon Richard Willburn.
Res., 114 S. Gunnison, P.O. Box 458, 81211. Tel: 719-395-8424.
Catechesis/Religious Programs—Students 72.
Mission—Fairplay, Park Co., St. Joseph. (Send all correspondence to Buena Vista address.)

Burlington, Kit Carson Co., St. Catherine of Siena, Rev. Jay Gibson, C.M.
Res., P.O. Box 57, Stratton, 80836. Tel: 719-346-7156; Fax: 719-348-5336.
Church—P.O. Box 38, 80836. Tel: 719-348-5336; Fax: 719-348-5336.
Catechesis/Religious Programs—Students 155.

Calhan, El Paso Co., St. Michael's, Rev. James F. Halloran, Admin.
Res., Box 199, 80808. Tel: 719-347-2290.
Catechesis/Religious Programs—Students 55.

Castle Rock, Douglas Co., St. Francis of Assisi, Rev. William C. Vollmer; Deacon Robert Hunter.
Res., 2746 E Hwy. 86, 80104. Tel: 303-688-3025; 688-3057; Fax: 303-688-4016.
Catechesis/Religious Programs—Tel: 303-688-9522. Lynne K. Lane, D.R.E.
Students 435.

Cheyenne Wells, Cheyenne Co., Sacred Heart, Rev. Thomas Kloppenborg, C.M.
Res., P.O. Box 819, 80810. Tel: 719-767-5272.
Mission—Kit Carson, Cheyenne Co., St. Augustine, P.O. Box 82, Kit Carson, 80825. Tel: 719-962-3552.
Catechesis/Religious Programs—D.R.E.: Dianne Smith; Sharon Baker; Eleanor Dechant.
Students 73.

Fountain, El Paso Co., St. Joseph, Deacon Roger K. Eberwein, Parish Dir.
Res., Box 277, 80817. Tel: 719-382-7086.
Catechesis/Religious Programs—Students 72.

Highlands Ranch, Douglas Co., Pax Christi Catholic Church, Mr. Jeff Kelling Parish Dir.
Office: 9777 S. Yosemite, Ste. 210, Littleton, 80124. Tel: 303-799-1036; Fax: 303-799-1072.
Catechesis/Religious Programs—Chris Holmes, D.R.E.
Students 500.

Leadville, Lake Co., Catholic Community of Leadville, Annunciation & St. Joseph, Rev. Thomas Killeen, O.M.I., Admin.
Res., 609 Poplar St., 80461. Tel: 719-486-1382. [CEM]
Catechesis/Religious Programs—Students 115.

Limon, Lincoln Co., Our Lady of Victory, Rev. R. William Rhinehart, C.M.
Res., 489 H Ave., P.O. Box 790, 80828. Tel: 719-775-2118.
Catechesis/Religious Programs—Limon & Missions.
Students 95.
Missions—Hugo, Lincoln Co., St. Anthony of Padua. (Send all correspondence to Limon address.) 133 Fifth St., P.O. Box 275, Hugo, 80821. Tel: 719-743-2373. [CEM]
Flagler, Kit Carson Co., St. Mary. (Send all correspondence to Limon address.) Flagler, 80815.

Monument, El Paso Co., St. Peter, Rev. Robert E. Jaeger.
Res., 55 N. Jefferson, Box 827, 80132. Tel: 719-481-2554; Fax: 719-481-9606.
Catechesis/Religious Programs—Kathy Campbell, D.R.E.
Students 470.

Parker, Douglas Co., Ave Maria, Revs. Dennis E. Dwyer; Khanh San Hoang; Donald Sutton; Sr. Monica Marie Ehnie, S.C., Pastoral Assoc.; Deacon George D. Linehan, Jr.
Res., 9056 E. Parker Rd., P.O. Box 189, 80134. Tel: 303-841-3750; Fax: 303-841-2412.
Catechesis/Religious Programs—Wavelyn Dreher, D.R.E.
Students 1,089.

Salida, Chaffee Co., St. Joseph, Rev. Kenneth Przybyla. In res., Rev. Anthony C. Uhl, Chap. Colorado Dept. of Corrections.
Res., P.O. Box 847, 81201. Tel: 719-539-6419.
Catechesis/Religious Programs—Students 135.

Security, El Paso Co., Holy Family, Rev. Patrick W. Battiato.
Res., 331 Main St., 80911. Tel: 719-392-7653; Fax: 719-392-1651.
Catechesis/Religious Programs—Cathy Jane King, D.R.E.
Students 595.

Stratton, Kit Carson Co., St. Charles Borromeo, Rev. Jay L. Gibson, C.M.
Res., P.O. Box 57, 80836. Tel: 719-348-5336; Fax: 719-348-5336.
Catechesis/Religious Programs—Students 128.

Woodland Park, Teller Co., Our Lady of the Woods, Rev. Karl J. Useldinger; Deacon Allen Breaux.
Res., P.O. Box 416, 80866. Tel: 719-687-9345.
Catechesis/Religious Programs—Students 165.
Missions—Cripple Creek, Teller Co., St. Peter's. (Send all correspondence to Woodland Park address.); Victor, Teller Co., St. Victor's. (Send all correspondence to Woodland Park address.)

On Duty Outside Diocese:
Reverend Fathers—
Grabrian, Dennis, P.O. Box 1418, Millville, NJ 08332

On Administrative Leave:
Reverend Fathers—
Kelleher, Jerome

Retired:
Reverend Fathers—
Bruggeman, Gerald H., Chap., Penrose Hospital, 2215 N. Cascade Ave., Colorado Springs, CO 80907
Dresen, Arthur G., 4559 Sunnyhill Dr., Colorado Springs, CO 80916
Halloran, Joseph H., Fountain Terrace Apartments, 3211 E. Fountains Blvd., #103, Colorado Springs, CO 80910
Kekeisen, Robert E., 4895-B El Camino Dr., Colorado Springs, CO 80918
Leonard, Edward, 15 Hewlett Ave., New Castle, DE 19720
Myers, Rawley, St. Mary's Cathedral, 22 W. Kiowa, Colorado Springs, CO 80903

Permanent Deacons:
Baumbach, John, St. Mary's, Colorado Springs
Bidon, Patrick, St. Paul's, Colorado Springs
Breaux, Allen, Our Lady of the Woods, Woodland Park
Ciletti, Michael, Service to mentally and physically challenged communities, St. Francis of Assisi, Colorado Springs
Cruise, Ben, Corpus Christi & Fort Carson, Colorado Springs
Eastham, Eugene S., Our Lady of the Pines, Colorado Springs
Eberwein, Roger, Parish Dir., St. Joseph, Fountain
Huber, Robert A., Douglas/Elbert Counties Prison Ministry; Northern Region Ministry
Hunter, Robert, St. Francis of Assisi, Castle Rock
Kimminau, Albert E., St. Joseph's, Southgate, Colorado Springs
Leverington, Michael, St. Peter's, Monument
Linehan, George D., Jr., Ave Maria, Parker
McLean, Arthur, (Retired)
Parrish, Thomas E., Jail Ministry
Reyes, Emilio, Our Lady of Guadalupe, Colorado Springs
Sherman, Lynn, Our Lady of the Pines, Colorado Springs
Sherpa, Lee, (Retired)
Specht, Charles W., Dir., Office of Permanent Diaconate & Parish Dir., St. Francis of Assisi, Colorado Springs
Van Matre, Dave, Divine Redeemer, Colorado Springs
Whittle, James B., Holy Trinity, Colorado Springs
Willburn, Richard, St. Rose of Lima, Buena Vista

INSTITUTIONS LOCATED IN THE DIOCESE

[A] EDUCATIONAL INSTITUTIONS

COLORADO SPRINGS.
**The Center at Benet Hill Monastery*, 2577 N. Chelton Rd., 80909. Tel: 719-473-6184. Sr. Marilyn Carpenter, O.S.B., Contact person. Sisters 5; Lay Staff 2.

[B] GENERAL HOSPITALS

COLORADO SPRINGS. *The Penrose Foundation*, 7606 N. Union Blvd., Ste. D, 80920. Tel: 719-528-5883.
For a complete listing, refer to the Hospitals section.
Penrose-St. Francis Health Services.
For a complete listing, refer to the Hospitals section.

[C] NURSING HOMES

*COLORADO SPRINGS. *St. Francis Nursing Center*, 7550 Assisi Heights, 80920. Tel: 719-598-1336.
For a complete listing, refer to the Special Care Facilities section.

[D] SPECIAL CARE FACILITIES

COLORADO SPRINGS. *Medalion (East)*, 1719 E. Bijou St., 80909. Tel: 719-471-4800; Fax: 719-471-4807.
For a complete listing, refer to the Special Care Facilities section.
Medalion West, 417 E. Kiowa St., 80903. Tel: 719-471-2578; Fax: 719-471-4807.
For a complete listing, refer to the Special Care Facilities section.
Namaste Alzheimer Center, 2 Penrose Blvd., 80906. Tel: 719-560-2000.
For a complete listing, refer to the Special Care Facilities section.

[E] RESIDENCES FOR MEN RELIGIOUS

CASCADE. *Holy Cross Novitiate*, Box 749, 80809. Tel: 719-684-9277. Congregation of Holy Cross (Indiana Prov., Marigreen Pines). Rev. William Dorwart, C.S.C., Dir. Novices & Supr. Staff: Rev. Thomas A. Stella, C.S.C.; Bro. Thomas Moser, C.S.C. Priests 2; Brothers 1; Novices 13.

SEDALIA. *Sacred Heart Retreat House - Jesuit Community*, Box 185, 80135. Tel: 303-688-5196. Revs. Richard O. Buhler, S.J., Supr.; Vincent E. Hovley, S.J.; Robert F. Houlihan, S.J.; James J. Costello, S.J.; William W. Williams, S.J.; Bros. Richard P. May, S.J.; David L. Ward, S.J.

[F] RESIDENCES FOR WOMEN RELIGIOUS

COLORADO SPRINGS.
**Benet Hill Monastery*, 2555 N. Chelton Rd., 80909. Tel: 719-633-0655. Motherhouse of the Sisters of St. Benedict (1963). Sr. Anne Stedman, O.S.B., Prioress; Sr. Diane Liston, O.S.B., Community Archivist. Professed Sisters 47.
Properties owned: The Center at Benet Hill Monastery and Benet Pines.
Mount St. Francis, 7665 Assisi Hts., 80919. Tel: 719-598-5486. Provincial and Formation House. Sisters of St. Francis of Perpetual Adoration, Province of St. Joseph (The Sisters of St. Francis of Colorado Springs). Sr. Clarice Gentrup, O.S.F., Prov.; Rev. George V. Fagan, Jr., Chap. Professed Sisters 118.

[G] RETREAT CENTERS

COLORADO SPRINGS.
**Benet Pines*, 15780 Hwy. 83, 80921. Tel: 719-495-2574. Sr. Jan Ginzkey, O.S.B.; Sr. Clare Carr, O.S.B.; Dick Pfalmer; Francie Pfalmer; Ed Summers; Karen Summers.
Franciscan Center, 7665 Assisi Hts., 80919-3836. Tel: 719-598-5486. Sr. Christine Hayes, O.S.F., Dir.

SEDALIA. *Sacred Heart Jesuit Retreat House*, Box 185, 80135. Tel: 303-688-4198. Revs. Richard O. Buhler, S.J., Dir.; Vincent E. Hovley, S.J.; Robert F. Houlihan, S.J.; James J. Costello, S.J.; William W. Williams, S.J.; Bros. David L. Ward, S.J.; Richard P. May, S.J.; Sr. Eleanor Sheehan, C.S.J.

[H] MISCELLANEOUS LISTINGS

COLORADO SPRINGS. *Catholic Charismatic Renewal Services*. (CCRS), 926 Farragut Ave., 80909. Tel: 719-633-2302. Rev. William Jarema, Liaison to Bishop Hanifen for Charismatic Renewal.

The Catholic Foundation of the Diocese of Colorado Springs, Inc., 29 W. Kiowa, 80903-1498. Herman H. Guenther, Pres./Exec. Dir.

Colorado Springs Council of Black Catholics, 29 W. Kiowa St., 80909.

Colorado Springs Diocesan Council of Catholic Women, 720 Orion Dr., 80906. Tel: 719-635-7398. Phyllis E. Hinsey, Pres.

The Diocese of Colorado Springs - Lay Retirement Plan, 29 W. Kiowa St., 80903-1498. Robert G. Doerfler, Jr., Plan Admin.

The Diocese of Colorado Springs - Priests' Retirement Plan, 29 Kiowa St., 80903-1498. Robert G. Doerfler, Jr., Plan Admin.

Franciscan Family Wellness Program, Inc., 7665 Assisi Hts., 80919. Sr. Judith Ann Schaeffer, Ph.D., Exec. Dir.

The Franciscan Foundation of Colorado Springs, 7665 Assisi Hts., 80919-3836. Sr. Clarice Gentrup, O.S.F., Contact Person.

Jail Ministries, c/o Diocese of Colorado Springs, 29 W. Kiowa St., 80903. Tel: 719-635-5881. Deacon Thomas E. Parrish, Coord.

S.E.T. of Colorado Springs, 2413 N. Cascade, 80907. Barbara Counts, Contact Person.

Theresians of the United States aka Theresians World Ministry, 2577 N. Chelton Rd., Ste. 207, 80909. Tel: 719-636-3643. Sr. Rose Ann Barmann, Exec. Dir.

**Villa San Jose, Inc.*, 1810 S. Corona, 80906. Tel: 719-632-7444. Karla Ross, Acting Admin. & Res. Svcs. Coord.

**Villa Santa Maria, Inc.*, 405 E. St. Elmo Ave., 80906. Tel: 719-520-9344. Karla Ross, Acting Dir. & Res. Svcs. Coord.

NECROLOGY

† Shimalonis, Albert L., (Retired). —Died Nov. 30, 1996.

Diocese of Columbus

(Dioecesis Columbensis)

Most Reverend

JAMES A. GRIFFIN, J.D., J.C.L.

Bishop of Columbus; ordained May 28, 1960; consecrated Titular Bishop of Holar and Auxiliary to the Bishop of Cleveland August 1, 1979; appointed Tenth Bishop of Columbus February 7, 1983; installed April 25, 1983. *Res., 198 E. Broad St., Columbus, OH, 43215.* Tel.: 614-224-2251.

Most Reverend

EDWARD G. HETTINGER, D.D.

Retired Auxiliary Bishop and Titular Bishop of Teos; ordained June 2, 1928; appointed December 6, 1941; consecrated February 24, 1942; retired October 14, 1977. *Res., Convalarium at Indian Run, 6430 Post Rd., Dublin, OH, 43017.* Tel.: 614-761-1188.

Most Reverend

EDWARD J. HERRMANN, D.D.

Retired Bishop of Columbus; ordained June 12, 1947; appointed Auxiliary Bishop of Washington and Titular Bishop of Lamzella March 4, 1966; consecrated April 26, 1966; appointed Ninth Bishop of Columbus June 26, 1973; installed August 21, 1973; retired September 18, 1982; Apostolic Administrator September 1982 to April 1983. *Res., St. Raphael Home, 1550 Roxbury Rd., Columbus, OH, 43212.* Tel.: 614-224-2251.

Chancery Office: 198 E. Broad St., Columbus, OH, 43215. Tel.: 614-224-2251; 224-8718 (Sat.-Sun. and other times); Fax: 614-224-6306.

ESTABLISHED 1868.

Square Miles 11,310.

Comprises the following 23 Counties in the State of Ohio: Hardin, Marion, Morrow, Knox, Holmes, Tuscarawas, Union, Delaware, Licking, Coshocton, Madison, Franklin, Muskingum, Fayette, Pickaway, Fairfield, Perry, Ross, Hocking, Pike, Jackson, Vinton and Scioto.

For legal titles of parishes and diocesan institutions, consult the Chancery Office.

STATISTICAL OVERVIEW

Personnel	
Bishop	1
Retired Bishops	2
Priests: Diocesan Active in Diocese	143
Priests: Active Outside Diocese	11
Priests: Retired, Sick or Absent	49
Number of Diocesan Priests	203
Religious Priests in Diocese	45
Extern Priests in Diocese	11
Ordinations:	
Diocesan Priests	3
Permanent Deacons in Diocese	48
Total Brothers	8
Total Sisters	411
Parishes	
Parishes	108
With Resident Pastor:	
Resident Diocesan Priests	95
Resident Religious Priests	8
Without Resident Pastor:	
Administered by Priests	4
Administered by Women Religious	1
Missions	8
Professional Ministry Personnel:	
Brothers	1
Sisters	31
Lay Ministers	54
Welfare	
Catholic Hospitals	4
Total Assisted	906,461
Homes for the Aged	16
Total Assisted	1,021
Day Care and Extended Day Care Centers	4
Total Assisted	1,612
Specialized Homes	3
Total Assisted	1,623
Special Centers for Social Services	13
Total Assisted	375,723
Educational	
Seminaries, Diocesan	1
Students from This Diocese	8
Students from Other Diocese	95
Diocesan Students in Other Seminaries	2
Students Religious	7
Total Seminarians	17
Colleges and Universities	1
Total Students	1,883
High Schools, Diocesan and Parish	11
Total Students	4,819
Elementary Schools, Diocesan and Parish	45
Total Students	15,161
Elementary Schools, Private	2
Total Students	232
Catechesis/Religious Education:	
High School Students	1,548
Elementary Students	14,832
Total Students Under Catholic Instruction	38,492
Teachers in the Diocese:	
Priests	3
Sisters	23
Lay Teachers	844
Vital Statistics	
Receptions into the Church:	
Infant Baptism Totals	3,787
Adult Baptism Totals	448
Received into Full Communion	702
First Communions	3,857
Confirmations	3,063
Marriages:	
Catholic	1,013
Interfaith	912
Total Marriages	1,925
Deaths	1,562
Total Catholic Population	216,676
Total Population	2,170,007

Former Bishops—Rt. Rev. SYLVESTER HORTON ROSECRANS, D.D., cons. Titular Bishop of Pompeiopolis and Auxiliary to the Bishop of Cincinnati, March 25, 1862; transferred to Columbus, March 3, 1868; died Oct. 21, 1878.—Rt. Rev. JOHN AMBROSE WATTERSON, cons. Aug. 8, 1880; died April 17, 1899.—Most Rev. HENRY MOELLER, D.D., cons. Bishop of Columbus, Aug. 25, 1900; promoted to the Archiepiscopal See of Areopolis and made Coadjutor to the Archbishop of Cincinnati, with the right of succession, April 27, 1903; succeeded to the See of Cincinnati, Oct. 31, 1904; died Jan. 5, 1925.—Most Rev. JAMES JOSEPH HARTLEY, D.D., cons. Feb. 25, 1904; died Jan. 12, 1944.—Most Rev. MICHAEL JOSEPH READY, D.D., cons. Dec. 14, 1944; died May 2, 1957.—Most Rev. CLARENCE GEORGE ISSENMANN, S.T.D., cons. Titular Bishop of Phytea and Auxiliary Bishop of Cincinnati May 25, 1954; appt. Bishop of Columbus Dec. 5, 1957; transferred to Cleveland as Apostolic Administrator. "cum jure successionis," Oct. 7, 1964; died July 27, 1982.—His Eminence JOHN CARDINAL CARBERRY, D.D., appt. Titular Bishop of Elis and Coadjutor of Lafayette in Indiana "cum jure successionis," May 3, 1956; cons. July 25, 1956; succeeded to See Nov. 20, 1957; transferred to Columbus Jan. 20, 1965; transferred to the Archdiocese of St. Louis, March 24, 1968; created Cardinal April 28, 1969.—Most Rev. CLARENCE E. ELWELL, D.D., cons. Dec. 21, 1962; appt. to Columbus May 29, 1968; died Feb. 16, 1973.

Vicar General / Chancellor—Rev. Msgr. JOSEPH M. HENDRICKS, S.T.B., M.A.

Episcopal Vicar for Charities and Social Concerns—Rev. STANLEY BENECKI, Ph.D.

Episcopal Vicar for Education—Rev. PAUL A. NOBLE.

Episcopal Vicar for Church Ministry—Sr. JOAN M. HARPER, C.D.P.

Episcopal Vicar for Communications—Rev. THOMAS KESSLER, S.T.D.

Episcopal Vicar for Spiritual Life—Rev. Msgr. STEPHAN J. MOLONEY, M.A., M.Div., J.C.L.

Chancery Office—198 E. Broad St., Columbus, 43215. Office Hours: Mon.-Fri. 8-4:30. Tel: 614-224-2251 (Sat.-Sun.). Tel: 614-224-8718 (other times); Fax: 614-224-6306.

Chancellor—Rev. Msgr. JOSEPH M. HENDRICKS, S.T.B., M.A.

Vice Chancellor—Rev. Msgr. STEPHAN J. MOLONEY, M.A., M.Div., J.C.L.

Diocesan Consultors—Most Rev. JAMES A. GRIFFIN, J.D., J.C.L.; Rev. Msgr. FRANK P. LANE; Rev. Msgr. JOSEPH M. HENDRICKS; Rev.Msgr. STEPHAN J. MOLONEY; Revs. RODNEY DAMICO; WILLIAM DUNN; JAMES GEIGER; MARK GHILONI; STEPHEN KRILE.

Parochial Examiners—Revs. CARL P. CLAGETT; CHARLES E. COTTON; Rev. Msgr. FRANK J. MEAGHER.

Vicars Forane—Vicariate 1: Center City: Vacant. Vicariate 2: Northwest: Rev. MARK J. HAMMOND, *St. Andrew Church, 1899 McCoy Rd., Columbus, 43220.* Vicariate 3: North High: Rev. Msgr. MARIO A. SERRAGLIO, *St. John the Baptist Church, 720 Hamlet St., Columbus, 43215.* Vicariate 4: Northland: Rev. RODRIC J. DIPIETRO, *St. Elizabeth Church, 1682 Lynnhurst Rd., Columbus, 43229.* Vicariate 5: West:

Rev. JOHN L. BAKLE, S.M., *St. Agatha Church, 1860 Northam Rd., Columbus, 43221.* Vicariate 6: South: Rev. MICHAEL B. WATSON, *St. Mary Church, 684 S. 3rd St., Columbus, 43206.* Vicariate 7: East: Rev. DANIEL L. OCHS, *St. Pius X Church, 1051 Waggoner Rd., Reynoldsburg, 43068.* Vicariate 8: Marion: Rev. WILLIAM J. FAUSTNER, *Immaculate Comception Church, 215 E. North St., Kenton, 43326.* Vicariate 9: Zanesville: Rev. DWAYNE A. MCNEW, *St. Nicholas Church, 925 E. Main St., Zanesville, 43701.* Vicariate 10: Knox-Licking: Rev. G. MICHAEL GRIBBLE, *St. Edward Church, 785 Newark Rd., Granville, 43023.* Vicariate 11: Tusc.-Holmes: Rev. Msgr. GEORGE J. SCHLEGEL, *Sacred Heart Church, 139 3rd St., N.E., New Philadelphia, 44663.* Vicariate 12: Lancaster: Rev. JEFFREY J. RIMELSPACH, *St. Mary Church, 602 Marietta St., Bremen, 43107.* Vicariate 13: Chillicothe: Rev. DONALD E. FRANKS, *St. Mary Church, 61 S. Paint St., Chillicothe, 45601.* Vicariate 14: Scioto County: Rev. MARK V. GHILONI, *Holy Redeemer Church, 1325 Gallia St., Portsmouth, 45662.* Vicariate 15: Perry County: Rev. Msgr. RICHARD F. DODD, *St. Patrick Church, 1170 State Rt. 668 South, Junction City, 43748.*

Priests' Senate—Rev. Msgr. JAMES L. RUEF, Chm.; Revs. WILLIAM D. HUBER, Vice Chm. & Treas. JAMES A. WALTER, Sec. THOMAS G. PETRY; THOMAS SHONEBARGER; CHARLES E. COTTON; DAVID E. GETREU; DANIEL J. MILLISOR; FRANK P. MILLER; DEAN MATHEWSON; MARTIN J. RALKO; RICHARD J. PENDOLPHI; JAMES L. COLOPY; PETER GIDEON. Ex Officio Members: Rev. Msgr. JOSEPH M. HENDRICKS; Rev. Msgr. STEPHAN J. MOLONEY.

Diocesan Pastoral Council—JOSEPH STEIGER, Chm.; Sr. PHYLLIS DUGAN, S.N.D.deN., Exec. Sec., *197 E. Gay St., Columbus, 43215.* Tel: 614-228-1646.

Tribunal—*197 E. Gay St., Ste. 500, Columbus, 43215-3290.* Tel: 614-241-2500. Commissions should be addressed to the Diocese of Columbus, Tribunal.

Judicial Vicar—Rev. MARK J. HAMMOND, S.T.L., J.C.L.

Court of First Instance—

Adjutant Vicar Judicial—Rev. Msgr. JOHN G. JOHNSON, J.C.D.

Diocesan Judges—Rev. Msgr. JOHN K. CODY, M.Div.; Rev. Msgr. F. THOMAS GALLEN, C.G.M.; Rev. Msgr. FRANK P. LANE, Ph.D.; Revs. LEO CONNOLLY, M.Div.; JOHN DITTOE, S.T.L.; WM. THOMAS KESSLER, S.T.D.; CHARLES F. KLINGER, M.Div., Ph.D.; WILLIAM A. METZGER, B.A.; JEFFREY J. RIMELSPACH, M.A., M.Div.; CHARLES T. THOMAS, M.A., M.Div.; EILEEN C. JARAMILLO, M.A., M.Div., J.C.L.

Defenders of the Bond—Rev. DENNIS STEVENSON, M.Div., J.C.L.; Sr. WANDA SCHERER, O.S.F., M.A.

Auditors/Notaries—Sr. MARY LINDA LORENZ, O.P., M.A.; HELEN THOMAS; JANET BAIRD, A.L.A.; SAUNDRA BURNS.

Notaries—Sr. RAYMUNDA BROOKS, O.P., M.A.; ANGELA NESMITH.

Promoter of Justice—Rev. EDWARD F. TRENOR, J.C.L.

Court of Second Instance—

Presiding Judge—Rev. Msgr. JAMES L.T. RUEF, M.A., J.D., J.C.L.

Appellate Judges—Rev. Msgr. ANTHONY BORRELLI, J.C.L.; Rev. Msgr. JOHN J. DREESE, S.S.L., J.C.L.; Rev. Msgr. DAVID V. SOROHAN, M.A., S.T.L., Ph.D.; Rev. Msgr. EDWARD F. TRENOR, J.C.L.; Rev. Msgr. JOHN V. WOLF, S.T.D.; Revs. THOMAS J. CADDEN, M.A.; JAMES A. GEIGER, A.B., Ph.D.

Defender of the Bond—EILEEN C. JARAMILLO, M.A., M.Div., J.C.L.

Apostleship of Prayer—Rev. Msgr. RICHARD DODD, Dir., *St. Patrick, Junction City, 43478.* Tel: 614-987-2691.

Bishop's Delegate for Priests—Rev. THOMAS BENDER, *St. Joan of Arc Church, 10700 Liberty Rd. S., Powell, 43065-9303.* Tel: 614-761-0905.

Building Commission—Rev. Msgr. EDWARD F. TRENOR, Chm. & Contact Person, *Christ the King, 2770 Dover Rd., Columbus, 43209.*

Catholic Center—Diocesan Office Building, 197 E. Gay St., Columbus, 43215. Tel: 614-228-2453.

Catholic Charities and Social Concerns—Rev. STANLEY BENECKI, Vicar, *197 E. Gay St., Columbus, 43215.* Tel: 614-241-2540; Fax: 614-268-8130.

Catholic Conference of Ohio—TIMOTHY V. LUCKHAUPT, Dir., *Nitsche Building, 35 E. Gay St., Ste. 502, Columbus, 43215.* Tel: 614-224-7147.

Catholic Record Society—DONALD SCHLEGEL, Sec., *197 E. Gay St., Columbus, 43215.* Tel: 614-241-2571.

Catholic Relief Services—MARK HUDDY, Diocesan Admin., *Dept. of Social Concerns, 197 E. Gay St., Columbus, 43215.* Tel: 614-241-2540.

Catholic Social Services—SARA K. MURPHY, Pres., *197 E. Gay St., Columbus, 43215.* Tel: 614-221-5891.

Cemeteries—RICHARD FINN, Dir., *6440 S. High St., Lockbourne, 43137.* Tel: 614-491-2751.

Censors of Books—Rev. Msgr. JOHN V. WOLF, S.T.D.; Rev. THOMAS KESSLER, S.T.D.

Central Purchasing Service, Inc.—STEPHEN DEEDRICK, Dir., *1567 Loretta Ave., Ste. 212, Columbus, 43211.* Tel: 1-800-842-8319; 614-262-0010.

Charismatic Renewal—Rev. JUSTIN REIS, Bishop's Liaison, *St. Bernadette, 1343 Wheeling Rd., Lancaster, 43130-8701.* Tel: 614-654-1893. MAXINE POWERS, Dir., *Catholic Charismatic Center, P.O. Box 32296, Columbus, 43232-0296.* Tel: 614-575-1971.

Columbus Family and Child Guidance Centers—WILLIAM J. HAMBOR, Pres. & C.E.O., *1490 E. Main St., Columbus, 43205.* Tel: 614-252-0731.

St. Vincent Campus—1490 E. Main St., Columbus, 43205. Tel: 614-252-0731.

Franklinton Office—840 W. State St., Columbus, 43222. Tel: 614-221-7855.

Wayne Avenue Center—880 S. Wayne Ave., Columbus, 43204. Tel: 614-272-0018.

Communication Office—MARK MORETTI, Media Rels., *197 E. Gay St., Columbus, 43215.* Tel: 614-241-2555.

Council of Religious—Sr. WANDA SCHERER, O.S.F., Pres., *5070 Zimmer Dr., Columbus, 43232-6048.* Tel: 614-833-6760.

Deaf Apostolate—Rev. STANLEY BENECKI, *Sts. Augustine and Gabriel, 1567 Loretta Ave., Ste. 111, Columbus, 43211.* Tel: 614-261-0339 (TDD); 268-3123 (Voice).

Department of Education—Rev. PAUL NOBLE, Vicar-Supt., *197 E. Gay St., Columbus, 43215.* Tel: 614-221-5829.

Diocesan Council of Catholic Women—MARGUERITE KRAUSE, Pres., *197 E. Gay St., Columbus, 43215.* Tel: 614-228-8601.

Development Office—HELMUT NAUNHEIMER, Dir., *197 E. Gay St., Columbus, 43215.* Tel: 614-241-2550.

Diocesan Finance Committee—FRANK BETTENDORF, Chm.; Most Rev. JAMES A. GRIFFIN; Rev. Msgr. STEPHAN J. MOLONEY; Rev. Msgr. JOSEPH M. HENDRICKS; Rev. Msgr. EDWARD F. TRENOR; Rev. PAUL NOBLE; ANN O'ROURKE; DONALD BORROR; HUGH DORRIAN; WILLIAM HEROLD; THOMAS MCAULIFFE; JAMES J. NOLL; W. MATTHEW BROWN, *198 E. Broad St., Columbus, 43215.* Tel: 614-224-1221.

Diocesan Finance Council—Most Rev. JAMES A. GRIFFIN; Rev. Msgr. JOSEPH M. HENDRICKS; Rev. Msgr. STEPHAN J. MOLONEY; JAMES J. NOLL, *198 E. Broad St., Columbus, 43215.* Tel: 614-224-1221.

Priests Personnel Board—Rev. CRAIG R. EILERMAN, Chm., *132 S. High St., Lancaster, 43130.* Tel: 614-653-0997.

Diocesan Retirement Plans for Priests, Lay Employees and Lay Teachers—PAUL D. RITTER, JR., Chm. Admin. Board for Plans. Tel: 614-462-5442.

Family Life Office—STEPHANIE JENEMANN, Dir., *197 E. Gay St., Columbus, 43215.* Tel: 614-241-2560.

Finance Office—JAMES J. NOLL, Dir., *198 E. Broad St., Columbus, 43215.* Tel: 614-224-1221; 224-1235.

Foundation of the Catholic Diocese of Columbus—KATHLEEN SPENCER, Exec. Dir., *197 E. Gay St., Columbus, 43215.* Tel: 614-241-2566.

Health Affairs Department (Hospitals)—Rev. Msgr. ANTHONY BORRELLI, Coord., *197 E. Gay St., Columbus, 43215.* Tel: 614-279-1690.

Holy Childhood, Pontifical Association—Sr. M. PAULETTE BOLL, O.P., Dir., *197 E. Gay St., Columbus, 43215.* Tel: 614-228-8603.

House of Retreats—MARY MURPHY, Dir., *St. Therese Retreat Center, 5277 E. Broad St., Columbus, 43213.* Tel: 614-866-1611.

Insurance—Diocesan Finance Office, 198 E. Broad St., Columbus, 43215. Tel: 614-224-1221.

J.O.I.N. (Joint Organization for Inner-City Needs)—Mrs. RUTH BECKMAN, Dir., *197 E. Gay St., Columbus, 43215.* Tel: 614-241-2530.

Legion of Mary—Rev. Msgr. CHARLES FOELLER, Dir., *Sacred Hearts Church, 4680 U.S. Rt. 42, Cardington, 43315.* Tel: 419-946-3611.

Liturgical Commission—Rev. JAMES P. BLACK, Chm., *212 E. Broad St., Columbus, 43215.* Tel: 614-224-1295.

Liturgy Office—Rev. LARRY J. HEMMELGARN, C.PP.S., Dir., *197 E. Gay St., Columbus, 43215.* Tel: 614-221-4640.

Ministry Formation Office—LESLIE J. YOUNG, Ph.D., Dir. JAMES HATFIELD, Coord., *197 E. Gay St., Columbus, 43215.* Tel: 614-241-2544.

Newspaper—"The Catholic Times"; Rev. THOMAS KESSLER, S.T.D., Editor, *P.O. Box 636, Columbus, 43216.* Tel: 614-224-5195.

Missions Office—Sr. M. PAULETTE BOLL, O.P., Dir., *197 E. Gay St., Columbus, 43215.* Tel: 614-228-8603.

Pastoral Services, Office of—Sr. PHYLLIS DUGAN, S.N.D-.deN., Dir., *197 E. Gay St., 4th Floor, Columbus, 43215.* Tel: 614-228-1646.

Permanent Diaconate Program—Deacons FRANK IANNARINO, Dir. THOMAS JOHNSTON, Assoc. Dir. Formation, Office: *197 E. Gay St., Columbus, 43215.* Tel: 614-241-2545., School: *Pontifical College Josephinum, 7625 N. High St., Columbus, 43085.* Tel: 614-885-5585.

Personnel Services—JOAN PALKUTI, Sec., *197 E. Gay St., Columbus, 43215.* Tel: 614-241-2590.

Priests Continuing Education—Rev. Msgr. FRANK LANE, *St. Andrew Church, 1899 McCoy Rd., Columbus, 43220.* Tel: 419-451-4290.

Propagation of the Faith and Opus Sancti Petri—Sr. PAULETTE BOLL, O.P., Dir., *197 E. Gay St., Columbus, 43215.* Tel: 614-228-8603.

Printing Services—NANCY EYERMAN, Mgr., *197 E. Gay St., Columbus, 43215.* Tel: 614-224-0261.

Real Estate—DONALD A. BORROR, Consultant, *5501 Frantz Rd., P.O. Box 7166, Dublin, 43017.* Tel: 614-761-6000.

Religious Education Office—Co-Directors: KATHLEEN KING; Sr. JANE MCCAFFREY, O.P., *197 E. Gay St., Columbus, 43215.* Tel: 614-221-4633.

Retreats—MARY MURPHY, Dir., *St. Therese Retreat Center, 5227 E. Broad St., Columbus, 43213.* Tel: 614-866-1611.

Rural Life Apostolate—Deacon RALPH PARSONS, Assoc. Dir., *P.O. Box 28, West Jefferson, 43162-0028.*

St. Stephen's Community House—JUDITH STATTMILLER, Dir., *1500 E. 17th Ave., Columbus, 43219.* Tel: 614-294-6347.

St. Vincent de Paul Society—BILL WISSE, Pres., *197 E. Gay St., Columbus, 43215.* Tel: 614-221-3554.

St. Vincent de Paul Shop—424 E. Locust St., Lancaster, 43130. Tel: 614-653-6037.

Scout Chaplain—Deacon PETER LABITA, Dir., *Christ the King Church, 2770 Dover Rd., Columbus, 43209.*

Department of Social Concerns—MARK HUDDY, Dir., *197 E. Gay St., Columbus, 43215.* Tel: 614-241-2540.

Spanish Speaking Apostolate—Vacant, *St. Patrick Church, 376 E. Naghten St., Columbus, 43215.*

Vocations Office—Rev. THEODORE K. SILL, Dir., *197 E. Gay St., Columbus, 43215.* Tel: 614-221-5565.

Youth Ministry Office—PATRICIA M. CLANCY, Dir., *197 E. Gay St., Columbus.* Tel: 614-241-2565.

CLERGY, PARISHES, MISSIONS AND PAROCHIAL SCHOOLS

CITY OF COLUMBUS
(Franklin County)

1—ST. JOSEPH CATHEDRAL (1878), Rev. Msgr. Joseph N. Fete, Rector; Rev. James P. Black; Deacon Thomas Johnston. In res., Rev. Paul A. Noble.
Res., 212 E. Broad St., 43215. Tel: 614-224-1295; Fax: 614-224-1176.
Church—E. Broad St. & N. Fifth St., 43215.

2—ST. AGATHA (Upper Arlington) (1940), Rev. Msgr. David R. Funk; Rev. Patrick J. Naughton; Sr. Mary Catherine Kaeppner, Pastoral Min. In res., Revs. Robert J. Schuer; John L. Bakle, S.M.
Res., 1860 Northam Rd., 43221. Tel: 614-488-6149; Fax: 614-488-6596.
School—2767 Andover Rd., 43221. Tel: 614-488-9000; Fax: 614-488-5783. Mrs. Joan Mastell, Prin. Lay Teachers 22; Students 392.
Catechesis/Religious Programs—Tel: 614-488-4975. Mrs. Jeanne Altiero, D.R.E. Students 368.

3—ST. AGNES (1954), Rev. William A. Metzger.
Res., 2364 W. Mound St., 43204-2997. Tel: 614-276-5413; Fax: 614-276-5608.
Catechesis/Religious Programs—Students 21.

4—ST. ALOYSIUS (1906), Rev. Dennis E. Stevenson, J.C.L., Admin. In res., Rev. Msgr. Donald C. Schulz.
Res., 32 Clarendon Ave., 43223. Tel: 614-276-6587.
Catechesis/Religious Programs—2350 W. Mound St., 43204. Fax: 614-276-5608.
Students 21.

5—ST. ANDREW (1955), Rev. Msgr. Frank Lane; Rev. Thomas Buffer. In res., Rev. Mark Hammond.
Res., 1899 McCoy Rd., 43220. Tel: 614-451-4290; Fax: 614-451-8300.
School—McCoy Rd. & Reed Rd., 43220. Tel: 614-451-1626. Raenita Kownacki, Prin.
Lay Teachers 26; Students 540.
Catechesis/Religious Programs—Tel: 614-451-2855. Ann Brown, D.R.E.
Students 330.

6—SAINT ANTHONY (1963), Rev. John L. Swickard; Mrs. Eileen Funk, Pastoral Min.
Res., 4913 Atwater Dr., 43229. Tel: 614-885-4857.
School—1300 Urban Dr., 43229. Tel: 614-888-4268; Fax: 614-888-4435. Richard Shisler, Prin.

Lay Teachers 13; Students 265.
Catechesis/Religious Programs—Tel: 614-888-8190. Judy McElwee, D.R.E.
Students 91.

7—STS. AUGUSTINE AND GABRIEL (1984), Rev. Stanley Benecki; Deacon Roger Pry.
Office: 1567 Loretta Ave., Ste. 111, 43211-1507. Tel: 614-268-3123; Fax: 614-268-8130.
Church—1550 E. Hudson St., 43211.
Catechesis/Religious Programs—Students 39.

8—ST. CATHARINE (1931), Rev. Msgr. David V. Sorohan; Rev. Joseph John Trapp, II; Sr. Christella Ritchey, O.S.F., Pastoral Assoc.; Donald Kegelmeyer, Chap., Pastoral Care, Tel: 614-235-7495. In res., Rev. Robert E. Willmann.
Res., 500 S. Gould Rd., 43209. Tel: 614-231-4509; Fax: 614-231-8366.
School—2865 Fair Ave., 43209. Tel: 614-235-1396. Mrs. Margaret Crabtree, Prin.
Lay Teachers 14; Students 266.
Catechesis/Religious Programs—Tel: 614-231-4500. Sr. Christella Ritchey, O.S.F., D.R.E.
Students 217.

9—ST. CECILIA (1882), Rev. Raymond Larussa.
Res., 434 Norton Rd., 43228. Tel: 614-878-5353; Fax: 614-878-0459.
School—440 Norton Rd., 43228. Tel: 614-878-3555. Sr. Regina Snyder, O.S.F., Prin.
Lay Teachers 16; Students 281.
Catechesis/Religious Programs—Tel: 614-878-0133. Richard Keyes, D.R.E.
Students 330.

10—CHRIST THE KING (1946), Rev. Msgr. Edward F. Trenor; Rev. R. Michael Ellifritz; Deacon Peter Labita. In res., Revs. Clement Faistl; Thomas Kessler.
Res., 2770 Dover Rd., 43209. Tel: 614-237-0401; Fax: 614-237-4689.
School—2855 E. Livingston Ave., 43209. Tel: 614-231-3391. Ms. Chris Iaconis, Prin.
Sisters of St. Dominic 2; Lay Teachers 23; Students 424.
Catechesis/Religious Programs—Tel: 614-231-8374. Karen Laihr, D.R.E.
Students 77.

11—ST. CHRISTOPHER (1947), Revs. Michael J. Reis; Arthur W. Wiles. In res., Rev. Jerome Stluka.
Res., 1420 Grandview Ave., 43212. Tel: 614-486-0457; Fax: 614-486-0433.
School—Trinity, 1381 Ida Ave., 43212. Tel: 614-488-7650. Mrs. Diane Hayhurst, Prin.
Sisters 1; Lay Teachers 12; Students 256.
Catechesis/Religious Programs—Susan Bellotti, D.R.E.
Students 143.

12—CORPUS CHRISTI (1925), Rev. Samuel E. Ritchey; Deacon J. Jerry Butts.
Res., 1111 E. Stewart Ave., 43206. Tel: 614-444-9871.

13—SANTA CRUZ (1993) (Spanish). Unassigned.
Res., St. Patrick Church, 376 E. Naghten St., 43215. Tel: 614-224-9522.
Church—256 E. Rich St., 43215. Tel: 614-469-9178.

14—ST. DOMINIC (1889) (African American), Rev. Thomas G. Petry; Deacon Robert Neely.
Mailing Address: P.O. Box 83572, 43203.
Res., 453 N. 20th St., 43203. Tel: 614-252-4913.

15—ST. FRANCIS OF ASSISI (1892), Rev. Msgr. John K. Cody.
Res., 386 Buttles Ave., 43215. Tel: 614-299-5781; Fax: 614-299-2933.

16—ST. ELIZABETH (1967), Rev. Rodric J. DiPietro; Deacon Frank X. Ball.
Res., 1682 Lynnhurst Rd., 43229. Tel: 614-882-1782; Fax: 614-882-1782.
Church—6077 Sharon Woods Blvd., 43229. Tel: 614-891-0150; Fax: 614-891-3243.
Catechesis/Religious Programs—Tel: 614-891-0151.
Students 131.

17—ST. GABRIEL. Merged with St. Augustine. See separate listing.

18—HOLY CROSS (1833) (German), Rev. Msgr. James Berendt. In res., Rev. Msgr. Lawrence J. Corcoran, P.A.
Res., 204 S. Fifth St., 43215. Tel: 614-224-3416.

19—HOLY FAMILY (1877), Rev. Msgr. Francis X. Schweitzer. In res., Rev. Jan C.P. Sullivan.
Res., 43 S. Skidmore St., 43215-2724. Tel: 614-221-4323.

20—HOLY NAME (1905), Rev. Msgr. James L.T. Ruef.
Res., 154 E. Patterson Ave., 43202. Tel: 614-262-0390.

21—HOLY SPIRIT (Whitehall) (1947), Rev. J. Colby Grimes.
Res., 4383 E. Broad St., 43213. Tel: 614-861-1521; Fax: 614-861-3746.
School—4382 Duchene Ln., 43213. Tel: 614-861-0475. Sr. Shawn Fitzpatrick, O.P., Prin.
Lay Teachers 10; Students 294.
Catechesis/Religious Programs—Tel: 614-861-4559. Paul E. Saelzler, D.R.E.
Students 40.

22—IMMACULATE CONCEPTION (1957), Rev. Anthony N. Missimi; Rev. Msgr. Thomas Bennett.
Res., 414 E. North Broadway, 43214. Tel: 614-267-9241.
School—366 E. North Broadway, 43214. Tel: 614-267-6579. Suzanne Wehinger, Prin.
Lay Teachers 13; Students 480.
Catechesis/Religious Programs—440 E. North Broadway, 43214. Tel: 614-267-0279. Patricia Sharkey, D.R.E.
Students 73.

23—ST. JAMES THE LESS (1947), Revs. James H. Dugal, C.PP.S.; Scott T. Kramer, C.PP.S.; Deacon Joseph Checca. In res., Rev. Leon J. Flaherty, C.PP.S.
Res., 1652 Oakland Park Ave., 43224. Tel: 614-262-1179; 1170; Fax: 614-262-6798.
School—1628 Oakland Park Ave., 43224. Tel: 614-268-3311. Kathleen O'Reilly, Prin.
Lay Teachers 20; Students 463.
Catechesis/Religious Programs—Mary Souder, D.R.E.
Students 80.

24—ST. JOHN THE BAPTIST (1896) (Italian), Rev. Mario Serraglio.
Res., 720 Hamlet St., 43215. Tel: 614-294-5319.

25—COMMUNITY OF HOLY ROSARY AND ST. JOHN (1979), Revs. Robert J. Scullin, S.J.; James Hasse, S.J.; John E. Beez, S.J.; Bro. James F. Gates; Deacon James Davis.
Res., 648 S. Ohio Ave., 43205. Tel: 614-252-5926; Fax: 614-252-5933.
Catechesis/Religious Programs—Sr. Diane Kozlowski, O.P., D.R.E.
Students 70.

26—ST. LADISLAS (1908) (Hungarian), Rev. William D. Huber; Sr. Andrew Marie, S.C.N., Pastoral Assoc.; Deacon Frank McDevitt. In res., Rev. David M. Schilder.
Res., 260 Reeb Ave., 43207. Tel: 614-444-5009.

27—ST. LEO (1903) (German), Rev. Bernard J. McClory.
Res., 221 Hanford St., 43206. Tel: 614-443-7685.
School—Bruck St. & Frebis Ave., 43206. Tel: 614-444-6683. Suzanne Emsweller, Prin.
Lay Teachers 10; Students 156.
Catechesis/Religious Programs—Students 247.

28—ST. MARGARET OF CORTONA (1921), Rev. Msgr. Anthony Borrelli.
Res., 1600 Hague Ave., 43204-1606. Tel: 614-279-1690; Fax: 614-279-2386.
Catechesis/Religious Programs—Sharon Curtin, D.R.E.
Students 152.

29—ST. MARY (1865) (German), Rev. Michael B. Watson; Mary Koors, Pastoral Assoc. In res., Rev. Arthur Dimond.
Res., 684 S. Third St., 43206. Tel: 614-445-9668; Fax: 614-445-9669.
School—700 S. Third St., 43206. Tel: 614-444-8994; Fax: 614-444-8145. Kathleen McClernon, Interim Prin.
Lay Teachers 9; Students 252.

30—ST. MARY MAGDALENE (1928), Revs. Charles Cotton; Carmen Arcuri. In res., Rev. Theodore Sill.
Res., 473 S. Roys Ave., 43204. Tel: 614-274-1121; Fax: 614-274-1122.
School—2940 Parkside Rd., 43204. Tel: 614-279-9935. Mary Ann Piela, Prin.
Lay Teachers 25; Students 435.
Catechesis/Religious Programs—Tel: 614-875-0346.
Students 52.

31—ST. MATTHIAS (1956), Rev. James T. Smith; Sr. Marie Shields, S.N.D.deN., Pastoral Assoc. In res., Rev. Richard Huelsman, S.J.
Res., 1582 Ferris Rd., 43224. Tel: 614-267-3406.
School—1566 Ferris Rd., 43224. Tel: 614-268-3030. Mr. Daniel Kinley, Prin.
Sisters 1; Lay Teachers 10; Students 290.
Catechesis/Religious Programs—Nancy Mead, D.R.E.
Students 85.

32—ST. MICHAEL (1946), Revs. William A. Dunn; Michael F. Nimocks; Willis E. Everett; Deacons John Crerand; John Vellani; Sr. Barbara Sir, C.S.J., Pastoral Min.
Res., 5750 N. High St., Worthington, 43085. Tel: 614-885-7814; Fax: 614-885-3446.
School—64 E. Selby Blvd., Worthington, 43085-3986. Tel: 614-885-3149; Fax: 614-885-1249. Miss Christine Armbrust, Prin.
Religious 2; Lay Teachers 22; Students 605.
Catechesis/Religious Programs—Tel: 614-888-5384. Mrs. Carol O'Connor, D.R.E.
Students 235.

33—OUR LADY OF THE MIRACULOUS MEDAL (1967), Rev. Carl P. Clagett; Deacon Joseph D. Poland. Pastoral Assocs.: Mrs. Anita Remy; Deacon Steve Venturini.
Res., 5225 Refugee Rd., 43232. Tel: 614-861-1242.
Catechesis/Religious Programs—Tel: 614-868-1414. Mrs. Sandy Venturini, D.R.E.
Students 107.

34—OUR LADY OF PEACE (1946), Rev. Msgr. Kenneth F. Grimes; Rev. Francis M. Stanton; Deacon Jack Rankin; Sr. Mary Agnes Jones, O.P., Pastoral Min.
Res., 20 E. Dominion Blvd., 43214. Tel: 614-263-8824; Fax: 614-263-3383.
School—40 Dominion Blvd., 43214. Tel: 614-267-4535. Carol Folian, Prin.
Lay Teachers 15; Students 270.
Catechesis/Religious Programs—Andrea McAuliffe, D.R.E.
Students 35.

35—OUR LADY OF VICTORY (1922), Rev. Thomas J. Cadden; Deacon Richard Baumann. In res., Revs. Christlin Rajendram, S.J.; Wayne Miller.
Res., 1559 Roxbury Rd., 43212. Tel: 614-488-2428; Fax: 614-488-0507.
School—Trinity. See St. Christopher, Columbus for details. Tel: 614-486-7650.
Catechesis/Religious Programs—Tel: 614-486-7678. Jane Leach, D.R.E.
Students 163.

36—ST. PATRICK (1852) (Irish), Revs. Kenneth A. France-Kelly, O.P.; Stephen D. Hayes, O.P.; James Vincent Watson, O.P. In res., Rev. Kenneth Sicard, O.P.
Res., 376 E. Naghten St., 43215. Tel: 614-224-9522; Fax: 614-240-5928.
Catechesis/Religious Programs—Tel: 614-240-5925.
Students 198.

37—ST. PETER (1970), Rev. Msgr. John G. Johnson; Rev. David E. Young; Deacons Joe Schermer; Phil Paulucci.
Res., 6899 Smoky Row Rd., 43235-1998. Tel: 614-889-2221; Fax: 614-889-6612.
Catechesis/Religious Programs—Tel: 614-889-1407; Fax: 614-889-0543.
Students 873.

38—ST. PHILIP THE APOSTLE (1956), Rev. Leo L. Connolly; Sr. Mary Caryl Perkinson, O.S.F., Pastoral Assoc.; Deacon Joseph Farry. In res., Rev. Patrick W. Rogers.
Res., 1573 Elaine Rd., 43227. Tel: 614-237-1671; Fax: 614-231-8416.
School—1555 Elaine Rd., 43227. Tel: 614-237-5278. Janet J. Nungesser, Prin.
Sisters of St. Francis 1; Lay Teachers 11; Students 225.
Catechesis/Religious Programs—Tel: 614-237-6500. Brad Walters, D.R.E.
Students 60.

39—SAINT STEPHEN THE MARTYR (1963), Rev. John L. Bakle, S.M.; Rev. Msgr. Stephan Moloney; Sr. Anne McCarrick, S.N.D.deN., Pastoral Admin.
Res., 4031 Clime Rd., 43228. Tel: 614-272-5200.
Catechesis/Religious Programs—Students 84.

40—ST. TIMOTHY (1961), Rev. Thomas Shonebarger. In res., Rev. Msgr. Michael A. Nugent; Rev. Msgr. James Nugent, (Retired).
Res., 1088 Thomas Ln., 43220. Tel: 614-451-2671.
School—1070 Thomas Ln., 43220. Tel: 614-451-0739; Fax: 614-451-3108. Norma A. Horan, Prin.
Lay Teachers 10; Students 220.
Catechesis/Religious Programs—Tel: 614-451-3867. Margaret Gercke, D.R.E.
Students 93.

41—SACRED HEART (1875), Rev. William H. DeVille. In res., Rev. James W. Jones.
Res., 893 Hamlet St., 43201. Tel: 614-299-4191; 4192.

42—SHRINE OF BLESSED MARGARET OF CASTELLO (1957), Rev. Kenneth A. France-Kelly, O.P., Dir.
262 N. Grant Ave., 43215-2623. Tel: 614-240-5915; 240-5917; Fax: 614-240-5928.

43—ST. THOMAS THE APOSTLE (1900), Rev. Ronald J. Atwood.
Res., 2692 E. Fifth Ave., 43219. Tel: 614-252-0976; Fax: 614-252-0977.
School—767 N. Cassady Ave., 43219. Tel: 614-252-7136. Sr. Petra Flavin, Prin.
Lay Teachers 9; Students 250.

44—KOREAN CATHOLIC COMMUNITY, Rev. Msgr. John K. Cody; Rev. Jin Hum Na.
St. Francis of Assisi Parish: 386 Buttles Ave., 43215. Tel: 614-457-4736.

OUTSIDE THE CITY OF COLUMBUS

Ada, Hardin Co., Our Lady of Lourdes (1874), Rev. Daniel J. Millisor.
Res., 222 E. Highland Ave., 45810. Tel: 419-634-2626.
Catechesis/Religious Programs—Students 99.

Bremen, Fairfield Co., St. Mary (1917), Rev. Jeffrey J. Rimelspach.
Res., 602 Marietta St., 43107. Tel: 614-569-4272. [CEM]
Catechesis/Religious Programs—Tel: 614-569-7724. Patricia Davis, D.R.E.
Students 80.

Bolivar, Tuscarawas Co., Holy Trinity. Unassigned. Rev. Michael F. Nimocks.
Res., 141 Water St. S.W., 44612. Tel: 330-874-4716.

Buckeye Lake, Licking Co., Our Lady of Mt. Carmel (1929), Rev. Msgr. Frank J. Meagher. Pastoral Assocs.: Barbara Diewald; Betty Friend; Deacon Joe Farmer.
Res., P.O. Box 45, 5133 Walnut Rd. S.E., 43008. Tel: 614-928-3266.
Catechesis/Religious Programs—Tel: 614-928-3264. Silvia Zaborowski, D.R.E.
Students 118.

Cardington, Morrow Co., Sacred Hearts (1868), Rev. Msgr. Charles J. Foeller.
Res., 4680 U.S. Rte. 42, 43315. Tel: 419-946-3611.
Catechesis/Religious Programs—D.R.E.: Gene McCurdy; Molly McCurdy.
Students 69.

Chillicothe, Ross Co., St. Mary (1837), Rev. Donald E. Franks; Deacon George Lovensheimer.
Res., 61 S. Paint St., 45601. Tel: 614-772-2061; Fax: 614-772-2061. [CEM][JC]
School—James Condron, Prin. Sisters 1; Lay Teachers 22.
Catechesis/Religious Programs—570 Parsons Ave., 45601.
Students 101.

St. Peter (1845) (German), Rev. Msgr. A. Anthony Frecker; Deacon Richard T. Krick. In res., Rev. Charles R. Griffin.
Res., 122 Church St., 45601. Tel: 614-773-4391. [CEM][JC]
School—Bishop Flaget Consolidated, (Grades PreK-8) 570 Parsons Ave., 45601. Tel: 614-774-2970; Fax: 614-774-2889. Mr. James Condron, Prin.
Lay Teachers 19; Students 323.
Catechesis/Religious Programs—Tel: 614-773-3455.
Students 136.

Circleville, Pickaway Co., St. Joseph's (1840), Rev. Robert Reilly. Pastoral Assocs.: Mary Kay Wood; Nancy Plescia; Deacon William Whalen.
Res., 134 W. Mound St., P.O. Box 659, 43113. Tel: 614-477-2549. [CEM]
Catechesis/Religious Programs—Theresa Jenkins, D.R.E.
Students 275.

Corning, Perry Co., St. Bernard (1882), Rev. John L. Metzger; Sr. Mary Ann Creely, O.S.F., Pastoral Min.; Sr. Assunta Ghiloni, O.S.F., D.R.E.
Res., 425 Adams St., 43730. Tel: 614-347-4700.

Coshocton, Coshocton Co., Sacred Heart (1897), Rev. Msgr. Robert E. Schneider; Sr. Mary Emma Muckensturm, Pastoral Assoc.; Deacon Andy Duda.
Res., 805 Main St., 43812. Tel: 614-622-8817.
School—39 Burt Ave., 43812. Tel: 614-622-3728; Fax: 614-622-9151. Sr. Johanna Eberly, O.P., Prin.
Sisters of St. Dominic 2; Lay Teachers 8; Students 155.
Catechesis/Religious Programs—(Grades PreK-6) 128 Burt Ave., 43812. Tel: 614-623-0882. Deacon Andy Duda, D.R.E.
Students 125.
Mission—Wills Creek, Coshocton Co., Our Lady of Lourdes, 805 Main St., 43812.

Crooksville, Perry Co., Church of the Atonement (1896), Rev. John M. Fulcher.
Res., 320 Winter St., 43731. Tel: 614-982-3816. [CEM]
Catechesis/Religious Programs—Patricia Musick, D.R.E.
Students 119.

Danville, Knox Co., St. Luke (1820), Rev. F. Richard Snoke.
Res., 307 S. Market St., P.O. Box P, 43014. Tel: 614-599-6362. [CEM]
Catechesis/Religious Programs—St. Luke Community Center, 7 W. Rambo, P.O. Box P, 43014-0616. Tel: 614-599-7367. Thomas Harrmann, D.R.E.
Students 162.

Delaware, Delaware Co., St. Mary (1835), Rev. Kevin J. Kavanagh; Sr. Cecilia Taphorn, C.PP.S., Pastoral Assoc.; Deacon Felix Azzola.
Res., 82 E. William St., 43015. Tel: 614-363-4641; 548-6050; Fax: 614-363-9915. [CEM]
School—66 E. William St., 43015. Tel: 614-362-8961; Fax: 614-363-9915. Eleanor Wagner, Prin. (Grades PreK-8).
Lay Teachers 16; Students 329.
Catechesis/Religious Programs—Tel: 614-369-8228. Sandra Murray, D.R.E. (Grades K-8).
Students 280.

Dennison, Tuscarawas Co., Immaculate Conception (1871), Rev. Martin J. Ralko. In res., Rev. Kenneth F. Wise.
Res., 206 N. First St., 44621. Tel: 614-922-3533. [CEM]
School—100 Sherman St., 44621. Tel: 614-922-3539; Fax: 614-922-2486. John Zucal, Prin.
Lay Teachers 9; Students 170.
Catechesis/Religious Programs—Brenda McCloud, D.R.E.
Students 29.

Dover, Tuscarawas Co., St. Joseph (1849), Rev. William L. Arnold; Deacon Ronald Fondriest.
Res., 613 N. Tuscarawas Ave., 44622. Tel: 330-364-6661. [CEM 2]
School—600 N. Tuscarawas Ave., 44622. Tel: 330-343-9134; Fax: 330-343-3704. Thomas Topolewski, Prin.
Lay Teachers 14; Students 251.
Catechesis/Religious Programs—Tel: 330-364-8257. Mrs. Linda Allison, D.R.E.
Students 226.

Dresden, Muskingum Co., St. Ann's (1889), Rev. Frank P. Miller.
Res., 405 Chestnut St., Box 107, 43821. Tel: 614-754-2221.
Catechesis/Religious Programs—Tel: 614-754-3018.
Students 70.
Mission—Mattingly Settlement, Muskingum Co., St. Mary, 6280 St. Mary's Rd., Nashport, 43830.

Dublin, Franklin Co., St. Brigid of Kildare (1987), Rev. Msgr. Paul P. Enke; Rev. David W. Sizemore; Deacon Frank A. Iannarino; Jean Bonk, Dir. Liturgy. In res., Rev. Msgr. Joseph Hendricks.
Res., 7179 Avery Rd., P.O. Box 3130, 43016-0062. Tel: 614-761-3734; Fax: 614-889-6638.
School—7175 Avery Rd., 43017. Tel: 614-718-5825. Mr. Kevan Hartman, Prin.
Lay Teachers 17; Students 259.
Catechesis/Religious Programs—Tel: 614-761-1176. Mary Fran Cassidy, D.R.E.
Students 1,023.

Gahanna, Franklin Co., St. Matthew (1959), Rev. Msgr. Edward J. McFarland; Rev. David E. Getreu. In res., Rev. Msgr. Stephan J. Moloney.
Res., 807 Havens Corners Rd., 43230. Tel: 614-471-0212; Fax: 614-471-0247.
School—795 Havens Corners Rd., 43230. Tel: 614-471-4930. Carole G. Marsh, Prin.
Lay Teachers 23; Students 550.
Catechesis/Religious Programs—Tel: 614-471-2067. Julie Zarichny, D.R.E.
Students 666.

Granville, Licking Co., St. Edward the Confessor (1946), Rev. G. Michael Gribble; Deacon Paul Belhorn.
Res., 785 Newark Rd., 43023. Tel: 614-587-3254; Fax: 614-587-0149.
Catechesis/Religious Programs—Linda Baus, D.R.E.
Students 325.

Grove City, Franklin Co., Our Lady of Perpetual Help (1954), Rev. Msgr. Romano Ciotola.
Res., 3710 Broadway, 43123. Tel: 614-875-3322; Fax: 614-875-3329.
School—3752 N. Broadway, 43123. Tel: 614-875-6779. Mr. William R. Groce, Prin.
Sisters 1; Lay Teachers 16; Students 369.
Catechesis/Religious Programs—Tel: 614-875-9345. Mrs. Martha J. Hurd, D.R.E.
Students 410.

Groveport, Franklin Co., St. Mary's (1871), Rev. J. Lawrence Reichert; Deacon Fred Schmitt.
Res., 5684 Groveport Rd., 43125. Tel: 614-497-1324; Fax: 614-497-2706.
Catechesis/Religious Programs—Tel: 614-497-1437. Rosemarie Watters, D.R.E.
Students 264.

Heath, Licking Co., St. Leonard (1962), Rev. Harold E. Schneider; Deacon Albert E. Cain.
Res., 57 Dorsey Mill Rd., 43056. Tel: 614-522-5270.
Catechesis/Religious Programs—Betty Witalec, D.R.E.
Students 40.

Hilliard, St. Brendan (1957), Rev. Msgr. William J. Maroon; Rev. Thomas J. Brosmer; Deacon Patrick Wiggins.
Res., 4475 Dublin Rd., 43026. Tel: 614-876-1272; Fax: 614-876-1482.
School—(Grades 1-8). Tel: 614-876-6132. Mary Lang, Prin.
Lay Teachers 17; Students 325.
Catechesis/Religious Programs—Tel: 614-876-9533. Mrs. Patricia Davidson, D.R.E.
Students 1,090.

Jackson, Jackson Co., Holy Trinity (1875), Rev. Msgr. Robert E. Metzger.
Res., 215 Columbia St., 45640. Tel: 614-286-1428. [CEM]
Catechesis/Religious Programs—Karen Ochsenbein, D.R.E.
Students 65.

Johnstown, Licking Co., Church of the Ascension (1912), Rev. Richard L. Metzger.
Res., 276 S. Main St., 43031. Tel: 614-967-7871. [CEM]
Catechesis/Religious Programs—Tel: 614-967-1203. Kathy Wahlenmaier, D.R.E.
Students 100.

Junction City, Perry Co., St. Patrick's (1820), Rev. Msgr. Richard F. Dodd; Mr. Al Kunkler, Pastoral Assoc.
Res., 1170 S. SR668, 43748. Tel: 614-987-2691.
Catechesis/Religious Programs—Mary Sawtelle, D.R.E.
Students 95.

Kenton, Hardin Co., Immaculate Conception (1836), Rev. William J. Faustner.
Res., 215 E. North St., 43326. Tel: 419-675-1162. [CEM]
Parish Center—220 E. North St., 44326. Tel: 419-675-9461.
Catechesis/Religious Programs—Tel: 419-675-1162. Jean M. Bruner, D.R.E.
Students 84.

Lancaster, Fairfield Co., St. Bernadette (1963), Rev. Justin J. Reis.
Res., 1343 Wheeling Rd., 43130-8701. Tel: 614-654-1893.
School—1325 Wheeling Rd., 43130. Tel: 614-654-3137. Pam Eltringham, Prin.
Lay Teachers 7; Students 173.
Catechesis/Religious Programs—Tel: 614-468-2268. Mary Good, D.R.E.
Students 100.

St. Mark (1960), Rev. Ronald Arter; Sr. Rita Walker, O.P., Pastoral Min.
Res., 324 Gay St., 43130. Tel: 614-654-2874.
Catechesis/Religious Programs—331 Gay St., 43130. Tel: 614-653-1229. Cheryl Oelker, D.R.E.
Students 145.

St. Mary (1818), Revs. Martin V. Weithman; Jack Maynard, S.F.O.; Craig R. Eilerman; Sr. Mary Cecil Grandpre, O.P., Pastoral Assoc.; Deacon Eugene Dawson.
Res., 132 S. High St., 43130. Tel: 614-653-0997; Fax: 614-653-0337. [CEM]
School—309 E. Chestnut St., 43130. Tel: 614-654-1632. Carlton B. Rider, Prin.
Sisters of St. Dominic 1; Lay Teachers 20; Students 460.
Catechesis/Religious Programs—Tel: 614-653-5054. Sr. Louis Mary Passeri, O.P., D.R.E.
Students 163.

La Rue, Marion Co., St. Joseph's (1864), Rev. Joseph Losh.
Res., 285 N. High St., P.O. Box 347, 43332-0347. Tel: 614-499-3614.

Logan, Hocking Co., St. John (1841), Rev. Richard J. Pendolphi; Deacon Frank Paniccia.
Res., 351 N. Market St., 43138. Tel: 614-385-2549; Fax: 614-380-2837. [CEM]
School—321 N. Market St., 43138. Tel: 614-385-2767. Tonya C. Stump, Prin.
Lay Teachers 4; Students 80.
Catechesis/Religious Programs—Lisa Lanning, D.R.E.
Students 60.
Mission—Murray City, Hocking/Athens, St. Philip Neri.

London, Madison Co., St. Patrick's (1865) (German-Irish), Rev. Donald Maroon.
Res., 61 S. Union St., 43140. Tel: 614-852-0942. [CEM]
School—(Grades K-8) 226 Elm St., 43140. Tel: 614-852-0161. James Moeller, Prin.
Lay Teachers 9; Students 146.
Catechesis/Religious Programs—Students 235.

Marion, Marion Co., St. Mary (1864), Revs. James A. Klima; Rodney M. Damico. In res., Rev. Frederick Furey, SS.CC.
Res., 251 N. Main St., 43302. Tel: 614-382-2118; Fax: 614-382-2110. [CEM]
School—274 North Prospect St., 44302. Tel: 614-382-1607. Robert Dendinger, Prin.
Lay Teachers 15; Students 262.
High School—(Grades 7-12).
Lay Teachers 15; Students 106.

Marysville, Union Co., Our Lady of Lourdes (1869), Rev. John Bentz; Deacon Gordon T. Kunkler.
Res., 1033 W. Fifth St., 43040. Tel: 513-644-6020; Fax: 513-644-6020.
Catechesis/Religious Programs—Tel: 513-644-6030. Maryanne Feeney, D.R.E.
Students 269.

Millersburg, Holmes Co., St. Peter (1877), Rev. Ronald J. Aubry.
Res., 379 S. Crawford St., 44654-1463. Tel: 330-674-1671. [CEM][JC]

Catechesis/Religious Programs—Tel: 330-674-0333. Patricia A. Huebner, D.R.E.
Students 101.
Mission—Glenmont, Holmes Co., SS. Peter and Paul, SR 520, Glenmont, 44628.

Mineral City, Tuscarawas Co., Saint Patrick. Closed. For sacramental records contact Holy Trinity, Bolivar.

Mt. Vernon, Knox Co., St. Vincent de Paul (1842), Rev. Charles Theodore Thomas; Sr. Jean Welling, S.C., Pastoral Assoc.
Res., 303 E. High St., P.O. Box 587, 43050. Tel: 614-392-4711. [CEM]
School—206 E. Chestnut St., 43050. Tel: 614-393-3611. Deborah Leibold, Prin.
Lay Teachers 11; Students 172.
Catechesis/Religious Programs—Tel: 614-393-0826. Shirley Lower, D.R.E.
Students 146.

New Albany, Franklin Co., Church of the Resurrection (1983), Revs. Jerome P. Rodenfels; Matthew N. Hoover; Sr. Sarah Gass, S.C., Pastoral Assoc.
Res., 6300 E. Dublin-Granville Rd., 43054. Tel: 614-855-1400; Fax: 614-855-0779.
Catechesis/Religious Programs—(Grades K-6). Mrs. Diana Leister, D.R.E.
Students 275.

Newark, Licking Co., St. Francis de Sales (1842), Revs. Dean Mathewson; Richard Weyls; Patrick Toner; Sr. Barbara Catalano, O.P., Pastoral Assoc.
Res., 66 Granville St., 43055. Tel: 614-345-9874. [CEM 2]
School—38 Granville St., 43055. Tel: 614-345-4049. Kathleen Mullooly-Erhard, Prin.
Sisters of St. Dominic 2; Lay Teachers 19; Students 520.
Catechesis/Religious Programs—Tel: 614-349-7978. Richard LaBrake, D.R.E.
Students 286.

Church of the Blessed Sacrament (1904), Rev. Timothy M. Hayes; Deacons Charles Stevens, (Retired); Jack Elam; Robert Ghiloni.
Res., 378 E. Main St., 43055. Tel: 614-345-4290. [JC]
School—15 Penny Ave., 43055. Tel: 614-345-4125; Fax: 614-345-6168. Joseph A. Rogers, Prin.
Lay Teachers 10; Students 215.
Catechesis/Religious Programs—Tel: 614-763-4304. Debbie Wills, D.R.E.
Students 60.

New Boston, Scioto Co., St. Monica (1915), Revs. Peter M. Gideon; William Patterson; Sr. Theresa Kehres, Pastoral Assoc.
Res., 4252 Pine St., 45662. Tel: 614-456-5154.

Newcomerstown, Tuscarawas Co., St. Francis de Sales (1918), Rev. Edward L. Keck.
Res., 440 River St., 43832. Tel: 614-498-7368.
Catechesis/Religious Programs—Cindy Branch, D.R.E.
Students 115.

New Lexington, Perry Co., St. Rose of Lima (1867), Rev. Msgr. John J. Dreese; Sr. Mary Ann Creely, O.S.F., Pastoral Min.
Res., 309 N. Main St., 43764. Tel: 614-342-1348.
School—119 W. Water St., 43764. Tel: 614-342-3043; Fax: 614-342-3206. J. Steven Holekamp, Prin.
Lay Teachers 8; Students 141.
Catechesis/Religious Programs—Tel: 614-347-4700. Sr. Assunta Ghiloni, O.S.F., D.R.E.
Students 63.

New Philadelphia, Tuscarawas Co., Sacred Heart (1895), Rev. Msgr. George J. Schlegel. In res., Rev. Robert T. Manning.
Res., 139 3rd St., N.E., 44663-3900. Tel: 330-343-6976. [CEM 2]
School—320 Fair Ave., N.E., 44663-3914. Tel: 330-343-1721; Fax: 330-364-4334. Scott Power, Prin.
Lay Teachers 11; Students 202.
Catechesis/Religious Programs—Tel: 330-364-2527.
Students 105.

Otway, Scioto Co., Our Lady of Lourdes (1917), Rev. John E. Stattmiller.
Res., 2215 Galena Pike, West Portsmouth, 45663. Tel: 614-858-4600. [CEM]
Otway Community Service Center—P.O. Box 8, 45657. Tel: 614-372-2202. Tom Loar, Mgr.

Pickerington, Fairfield Co., Seton Parish (1978), Revs. Stephen B. Hawkins; Dennis S. Kigozi; David A. Poliafico.
Res., 600 Hill Rd., 43147. Tel: 614-833-0482; Fax: 614-833-4154.
Catechesis/Religious Programs—Tel: 614-833-0485. Mrs. Mary Houze, D.R.E.
Students 805.

Plain City, Madison Co., St. Joseph (1864), Rev. Kevin Lutz.
Res., 6604 Perry Pk., 43064. Tel: 614-873-8850; Fax: 614-873-8850.
Catechesis/Religious Programs—Heidi Kellett, D.R.E.
Students 85.
Mission—Milford Center, Union Co., Sacred Heart, P.O. Box 166, 43064.

Portsmouth, Scioto Co., St. Mary (1841) (German), Rev. John J. Marquis; Sr. Gavin Hagan, Pastoral Assoc.; Deacon George Horsley.
Res., 524 Sixth St., 45662. Tel: 614-354-4551; Fax: 614-354-4552. [CEM]
Catechesis/Religious Programs—Students 176.

Holy Redeemer (1852), Rev. Mark Ghiloni. In res., Rev. William C. Patterson.
Res., 1325 Gallia St., 45662. Tel: 614-354-2716. [CEM]
School—Notre Dame Elementary, (Grades PreK-6). Serving all 7 parishes in Scioto County. 1401 Gallia St., 45662. Tel: 614-353-8610; Fax: 614-353-6769. Kay Kern, Prin.
Sisters 1; Lay Teachers 20; Students 448.

Powell, Delaware Co., St. Joan of Arc (1987), Rev. Msgr. Thomas G. Bender; Revs. Raymond E. Lavelle; Frederick A. Loyd; Deacon Thomas M. Berg.
Res., 10700 Liberty Rd. S., 43065-9303. Tel: 614-761-0905; Fax: 614-761-0850.
Catechesis/Religious Programs—Tel: 614-761-0903. Natalie Hutchison, D.R.E.
Students 1090.

Reynoldsburg, Franklin Co., St. Pius X (1958), Revs. Daniel L. Ochs; Joseph A. Ehwald; David Gwinner. Pastoral Assocs.: Sr. Catherine Sullivan, O.P.; Ms. Regina Courey.
Res., 1051 Waggoner Rd., 43068. Tel: 614-866-2859; Fax: 614-866-1499.
School—1061 Waggoner Rd., 43068. Tel: 614-866-6050. Catherine Fields, Prin.
Lay Teachers 25; Students 638.
Catechesis/Religious Programs—Tel: 614-864-3505. Anne Grossman, D.R.E.
Students 450.

Roswell, Tuscarawas Co., St. Elizabeth. Closed. For sacramental records contact Sacred Heart Parish, New Philadelphia.

Shawnee, Perry Co., St. Mary & St. Augustine. Closed. For sacramental records contact St. Rose of Lima Parish, New Lexington.

Somerset, Perry Co., St. Joseph's (1818), Rev. Adrian L. Dionne, O.P.
Res., 5757 State Rte. 383 N.E., P.O. Box 190, 43783. Tel: 614-743-1317. [CEM]

Holy Trinity (1827), Rev. Adrian L. Dionne, O.P.
Res., 5757 State Rte. 383 N.E., P.O. Box 190, 43783. Tel: 614-743-1317. [CEM]
School—S. Columbus St., 43783. Tel: 614-743-1324. Sr. Valerie Shaul, O.P., Prin.
Sisters of St. Dominic 3; Lay Teachers 6; Students 150.
Catechesis/Religious Programs—Tel: 614-246-5719.
Students 46.

Strasburg, Tuscarawas Co., St. Aloysius (1911). Closed. For sacramental records contact Holy Trinity, Bolivar.

Sugar Grove, Fairfield Co., St. Joseph (1892), Rev. James A. Geiger.
Res., 306 Elm St., 43155. Tel: 614-746-8302. [CEM] [JC]
Catechesis/Religious Programs—Tel: 614-746-8302. Kathy Krile, D.R.E.
Students 63.

Sunbury, Delaware Co., St. John Neumann (1981), Rev. James A. Walter; Mrs. Linda K. Haas, Pastoral Assoc.
Res., 36 Domigan Rd., 43074.
Church—9633 E. State Rte. 37, 43074-9593. Tel: 614-965-1358; Fax: 614-965-1358.
Catechesis/Religious Programs—Tel: 614-965-4877. Robert J. Steinbauer, D.R.E.
Students 258.

Utica, Licking Co., Church of the Nativity (1909), Rev. Stephen A. Metzger, Admin.
Res., 271 Jefferson St., P.O. Box 506, 43080. Tel: 614-892-2321.
Catechesis/Religious Programs—Rose Gorius, D.R.E.
Students 58.

Wainwright, Tuscarawas Co., Parish Community of St. Therese and St. Paul. Closed. For St. Therese's sacramental records contact Immaculate Conception, Dennison. For St. Paul's sacramental records contact Sacred Heart, New Philadelphia.

Washington Court House, Fayette Co., St. Colman (1885), Rev. Jerome K. Raiser; Deacon William Whalen.
Office: 219 S. North St., 43160. Tel: 614-335-5000.
Res., 223 E. East St., 43160. [CEM]
Catechesis/Religious Programs—Tel: 614-335-5005. D.R.E.: Kathy Henry, (Grades PreK-5); Rita Wheaton, (Grades 6-12).
Students 133.

Waverly, Pike Co., St. Mary, Queen of the Missions (1878), Rev. William J. Metzger.
Res., 407 S. Market St., 45690. Tel: 614-947-2436. [JC]
Catechesis/Religious Programs—Students 17.

Wellston, Jackson Co., SS. Peter and Paul (1881), Rev. Stephen Krile.
Res., 227 S. New York Ave., 45692. Tel: 614-384-2359. [CEM]
School—229 S. New York Ave., 45692. Tel: 614-384-6354. Sr. Theresa Feldkamp, Prin.
Franciscan Sisters of Christian Charity 4; Lay Teachers 4; Students 127.
Catechesis/Religious Programs—Students 128.

Westerville, Delaware Co., St. Paul the Apostle (1913), Rev. Msgr. Edward J. Fairchild; Revs. Homer Blubaugh; Theodore Machnik; Deacon Thomas Barford. In res., Rev. Joseph Jerabeck.
Res., 313 N. State St., 43082. Tel: 614-882-2109.
School—61 Moss Rd., 43082. Tel: 614-882-2710; Fax: 614-882-5998. Walter Miller, Prin.
Lay Teachers 26; Students 744.
Catechesis/Religious Programs—Tel: 614-882-5045. Janet Brewer, D.R.E.
Students 795.

West Jefferson, Madison Co., SS. Simon and Jude (1866) (German-Irish), Rev. Michael J. Devaney, O.M.I.; Deacon Ralph Parsons.
Res., 95 W. Main St., 43162-1295. Tel: 614-879-8562. [CEM]
Catechesis/Religious Programs—Students 120.

West Portsmouth, Scioto Co., Our Lady of Sorrows (1944), Rev. John Stattmiller.
Res., 2215 Galena Pike, 45663. Tel: 614-858-4600.
New To You Service Center—Mary Horn, Dir.
Catechesis/Religious Programs—P.O. Box 31, Otway, 45657. Tel: 614-372-7115.
Students 77.
Mission—Pond Creek, Scioto Co., Holy Trinity, 2215 Galena Pike, 45663.

Wheelersburg, Scioto Co., St. Peter (1855), Revs. Peter M. Gideon; William C. Patterson.
Res., 2167 Lick Run Lyra Rd., 45694. Tel: 614-574-5486. [CEM]
Catechesis/Religious Programs—Barbara Schwabklaco, D.R.E.
Students 151.

Zaleski, Vinton Co., St. Sylvester (1862), Rev. James L. Colopy.
Res., 22 N. Second St., 45698. Tel: 614-596-5474. [CEM]

Zanesville, Muskingum Co., St. Nicholas (1842) (German), Revs. Charles F. Klinger; Dwayne A. McNew. Pastoral Assocs.: Sr. Anne Marie Selinsky, O.S.F.; Sr. Nadine Overbeck, O.S.F.; Deacons B. N. Peterson, Jr.; Jeffrey Coning.
Res., 925 E. Main St., 43701. Tel: 614-453-0597; Fax: 614-453-0590. [CEM]
School—1030 E. Main St., 43701. Tel: 614-453-2637. Sr. Leonette Kochan, O.S.F., Prin.
Franciscan Sisters of Christian Charity 4; Lay Teachers 12; Students 321.
Catechesis/Religious Programs—Tel: 614-453-3931. Judy Schiele, D.R.E.
Students 127.

St. Thomas Aquinas (1820), Revs. Thomas J. Ertle, O.P.; Paul J.D. Scanlon, O.P.; William P. Garrott, O.P.; Thomas V. DiFede, O.P. Pastoral Assocs.: Sr. Teresa Sommer, O.P.; Sr. Edwina Devlin, O.P.
Res., 130 N. Fifth St., 43701. Tel: 614-453-3301; Fax: 614-453-0333. [CEM]
School—139 N. Fifth St., 43701. Tel: 614-454-9731; Fax: 614-454-9732. M. Patricia Russi, Prin.
Lay Teachers 9; Students 280.
Catechesis/Religious Programs—Melanie Von Gunten, D.R.E.
Students 155.
Mission—Philo, Muskingum Co., St. Ann, 79 Main St., Philo, 43771. Tel: 614-674-6448.

Chaplains of Public Institutions

COLUMBUS. *Children's Hospital*. Rev. Jan C.P. Sullivan. *Regency Manor*. Rev. Samuel E. Ritchey.

CHILLICOTHE. *Chillicothe Correctional Institution*. Rev. Charles R. Griffin. Mailing Address: P.O. Box 5500, 45601. Tel: 614-773-2616, Ext. 248. Res., 122 Church St., 45601. Tel: 614-773-4391.
Ross Correctional Institution and Honor Camp. Rev. Charles R. Griffin. Mailing Address: P.O. Box 7010, 45601. Tel: 614-774-4182, Ext. 2519. Res., 122 Church St., 45601. Tel: 614-773-4391.
Veteran's Administration Medical Center. Tel: 614-773-1141. Rev. Richard F. Engle.

LANCASTER. *Southeastern Correctional Institution*. Tel: 614-653-4324. Rev. Edward L. Kessler, Chap., Res., P.O. Box 264, Sugar Grove, 43155. Tel: 614-746-8007.

LONDON. *London Correctional Institution.*
LUCASVILLE. *Southern Ohio Correctional Facility* Tel: 614-259-5544.
MARION. *Marion Correctional Institution.* Rev. Frederick Furey, SS.CC. Tel: 614-382-5781 Ext. 346.
MARYSVILLE. *Ohio Reformatory for Women.* Rev. John Bentz Tel: 513-642-1065; Deacon Gregory Eiden, 305 Acton Rd., Columbus, 43214. Tel: 614-267-7500.
MOUNT VERNON. *Mount Vernon State Institute* St. Vincent de Paul Parish, 303 E. High St., 43050. Tel: 614-392-4711. Rev. Wayne Meyer Tel: 614-397-5094.
ORIENT. *Orient Correctional Institution.* Rev. David M. Schilder Tel: 614-877-4367.

Special Assignment:
Reverend Fathers—
Ascencio, Joseph A.
Sprenger, Alan M., Exec. Dir., Syntaxis, Inc., 5300 N. Hamilton Rd., Gahanna, OH 43230. Tel: 614-855-1224; 855-1333

On Duty Outside the Diocese:
Reverend Monsignors—
Spiers, Edward F., Chap., St. Joseph Hospital, 590 Central Dr., Southern Pines, NC 28387
Reverend Fathers—
Byrne, J. Patrick, Chap., V.A. Medical Center, 1202 N.W. 16th St., Miami, FL 33125. Tel: 305-324-4455, Ext. 3258
Jacobs, Philip
Martin, Thomas
Pickett, James

Military Chaplains:
Reverend Fathers—
Bernans, Arvids
Hummer, Lawrence L.

Graduate Studies:
Reverend Fathers—
Bay, Joseph N.
Klein, Terrance W.
Willmann, Robert

Leave of Absence:
Reverend Fathers—
Drake, Carl
Virginia, Stephen

Absent on Sick Leave:
Reverend Fathers—
Hanrahan, Michael
Thomas, Raymond

Retired:
Reverend Monsignors—
Applegate, P.A Bennett, 793 W. State St., Columbus, OH 43222
Carroll, James, 12915 Galaxy Dr., Sun City W., AZ
Corcoran, Lawrence J., Holy Cross, 204 S. 5th St., Columbus, OH 43215
Dittoe, John T., 3547 Chowning Ct., Columbus, OH 43220
Faistl, Clement, Christ the King Church, 2770 Dover Rd., Columbus, OH 43209
Griffin, Patrick, 3881 Montorey Dr., Grove City, OH 43123
Hanley, James P., 2492 Timberside Dr., Columbus, OH 43235
Healey, Edward, 5415-B5 Yorkshire Terrace Dr., Columbus, OH 43232
Huntzinger, Ralph, 8797 State Rte. 273 W., Belle Center, OH 43310-9580
Klinec, Julius G., P.A., St. Raphael Home, 1550 Roxbury Rd., Columbus, OH 43212-2799
Noon, Robert L., St. Mark Church, 132 Gay St., Lancaster, OH 43130
Nugent, Michael A., St. Timothy Church, 1088 Thomas Ln., Columbus, OH 43220
Schmidt, Robert R., 2647 Schaaf Dr., Columbus, OH 43209
Schulz, Donald, St. Aloysius Church, 32 Clarendon Ave., Columbus, OH 43223
Schwendeman, Francis J., R.R. #4, Box 343, Marietta, OH 45750
Winel, Roland T., P.A., Nazareth Towers, 300 E. Rich St., Apt. 1306, Columbus, OH 43215
Wolf, John V., 104 N. Mulberry St., Fredericktown, OH 43019-1051. Tel: 614-694-2502
Reverend Fathers—
Buzek, Joseph L., 1858 Maywood Rd., Winter Park, FL 32792
Carter, Raymond, 5325-301 Portland St., Columbus, OH 43235
Connor, William J., 10248 Snead Cir. N., Sun City, AZ 85351
Dermody, Ralph, 2 Lake View Dr., Mt. Vernon, OH 43050
Dimond, Arthur, St. Mary, 684 S. 3rd St., Columbus, OH 43206
Durbin, Clement B., Sharon Brook Inn, 920 Sharon Vally Rd., Newark, OH 43055
Engle, Richard F., 192 Grand Ave., Chillicothe, OH 45601
Essman, Charles P., Thurber Towers, 645 Neil Ave. #409, Columbus, OH 43215
Gamba, John J., P.O. Box 184, Doylestown, OH 44230
Gately, Robert E., P.O. Box 40232, St. Petersburg, FL 33743
Graf, John H., 155 Primrose Ln., McDermott, OH 45652
Haluska, Charles A., 37950 TR 344, Rte. 3, Warsaw, OH 43844
Jerabeck, Joseph, St. Paul Church, 313 N. State St., Westerville, OH 43082
Jones, Bernard, 17423 N. Appaloosa Dr., Sun City, AZ 85373
Kessler, Edward L., 107 W. 4th St., P.O. Box 264, Sugar Grove, OH 43155
Klee, Robert, St. Charles Preparatory School, 2010 E. Broad St., Columbus, OH 43209
Laurinaitis, Saulius P., 1185 Studer Ave., Columbus, OH 43206
Manning, Robert, Sacred Heart, 139 3rd St. N.E., New Philadelphia, OH 44663
Marzluf, George J., 7807 Rockville Rd.S.W., Navarre, OH 44662
McNulty, Edwin J., St. Rita Home, 880 Greenlawn Ave., Columbus, OH 43223
Meyer, Paul Wayne, 406 E. High St., Mount Vernon, OH 43050
Schaefer, Francis R., 11438 E. Huffman Rd. #4, Cleveland, OH 44130
Schuer, Robert J., St. Agatha, 1860 Northam Rd., Columbus, OH 43221
Stanton, Joseph, St. Leo Church, 221 Hanford St., Columbus, OH 43206
Tabit, Michael J., Our Lady of the Rosary, 9500 S.W. 184th St., P.O. Box 570247, Perrine, FL 33157
Totten, Raymond F., 329 Carnegie, Pittsburgh, PA 15208
Wise, Kenneth, Immaculate Conception Church, 206 N. First St., Dennison, OH 44621

Permanent Deacons:
Azzola, Feliz, St. Mary, Delaware
Ball, Frank X., St. Elizabeth, Columbus
Barford, Thomas M., St. Paul, Westerville
Baumann, Richard L., Our Lady of Victory, Columbus
Belhorn, Paul, St. Edward, Granville
Berg, Thomas, St. Joan of Arc, Powell
Butts, Jerome J., Corpus Christi, Columbus
Cain, Al, St. Leonard, Heath
Checca, Joseph, St. James the Less, Columbus
Crerand, John R., St. Michael, Worthington
Davis, James R., Holy Rosary-St. John Community, Columbus
Dawson, Gene, St. Mary, Lancaster
Duda, Frank, Sacred Heart, Coshocton
DuPrey, John L., Leave of Absence
Eiden, Gregory L., Chap., Ohio Reformatory for Women
Elam, Jack W., Blessed Sacrament, Newark
Farmer, Joseph, Our Lady of Mt. Carmel, Buckeye Lake
Farry, Joseph W., St. Philip, Columbus
Fondriest, Ronald H., St. Joseph, Dover
Gorman, William J., Leave of Absence
Horsley, George E., St. Mary, Portsmouth
Iannarino, Frank, St. Brigid of Kildare, Dublin
Johnston, Thomas V., St. Joseph Cathedral, Columbus
Koebel, Lawrence, Chap., Pickaway Correctional Institute
Krick, Richard T., St. Peter, Chillicothe
Kunkler, Gordon, Our Lady of Lourdes, Marysville
Labita, Peter C., Christ the King, Columbus
Lampe, Elmer, Leave of Absence
Larcomb, Dwight, Leave of Absence
Lovensheimer, George, St. Mary, Chillicothe
McCurry, William, County Sheriff's Office, Marion
McDevitt, Frank, St. Ladislas, Columbus
Neely, Robert, St. Dominic, Columbus
Paniccia, Frank A., St. John, Logan
Parsons, Ralph J., Jr., Sts. Simon & Jude, West Jefferson
Paulucci, Philip, St. Peter, Columbus
Peterson, Burdette, St. Nicholas, Zanesville
Poland, Joseph D., Our Lady of the Miraculous Medal, Columbus
Pry, Roger, St. Augustine, Columbus
Rankin, John, Our Lady of Peace, Columbus
Schermer, Joseph E., St. Peter, Columbus
Schmitt, Frederick J., St. Mary, Groveport
Spina, Philip, Jr., Leave of Absence
Stevens, Charles F., Blessed Sacrament, Newark
Vellani, Albert J., St. Michael, Worthington
Venturini, Stephen A., Our Lady of the Miraculous Medal, Columbus
Whalen, William T., St. Joseph, Circleville; St. Colman, Washington Court House
Wiggins, Patrick J., St. Brendan, Hilliard

INSTITUTIONS LOCATED IN THE DIOCESE

[A] SEMINARIES, DIOCESAN

COLUMBUS. *Pontifical College Josephinum*, 7625 N. High St., 43235-1498. Tel: 614-885-5585; Fax: 614-885-2307.
General Administrative Offices: Most Revs. Agostino Cacciavillan, Pro-Nuncio, Chancellor; James A. Griffin, J.D., J.C.L., Bishop of Columbus & Vice Chancellor; Rev. Msgr. Blase J. Cupich, S.T.D. (OM), Pres. & Rector; Rev. Msgr. Thomas J. Olmsted, J.C.D., Pres./Rector-Elect & Dean of Personal Formation; Mr. Patrick J. O'Reilly, Treas.; Dr. Byron W. Thorsen, Registrar; Mr. Peter Veracka, Dir. of the Library.
Theology Administrative Offices: Rev. Brian R. Moore, Ph.D. (DOD), Academic Dean; Mary Patricia Mulligan, M.A., Dir. Field Education School Theology & Dir. M.Div. Program; Revs. Richard J. Tomasek, S.J., S.T.L., Dir. Spiritual Formation; Roger P. Cooney, M.A. (COV), Vice Rector Theology & Dean of Men. Priests on Theology Teaching Staff: Revs. Robert J. Bauer, S.D.B., S.S.L.; John D. Corbett, O.P.; Jiri Kasny, S.D.B.; William D. Lynn, S.J., S.T.D.; William Dettling, O.P., S.T.D. Theology Teaching Staff: Sr. Carolyn Thomas, S.C.N., Ph.D.; James Keating, Ph.D.; Jaime Vidal, Ph.D.; James A. Yeager, D.M.A.
College Administrative Offices: Steven Snyder, Ph.D., Academic Dean; Revs. Andrew J. Umberg, Dean of Students & Dir. of Pastoral Works; Robert A. Gonzales, Ph.D. (TUC); Thomas L. Gwozdz, S.D.B., Dir. Spiritual Formation; Charles A. Jackson, S.T.L., Coord. Personal Formation. College Teaching Staff: Alma Amell, Ph.D.; David J. DeLeonardis, Ph.D.; Linda G. Schoen, Ph.D.; Michael J. Tori, Ph.D.; Judith B. Reuning, M.Ed. In res., Rev. Msgr. Anthony A. Kleinschmidt, B.L.S. (SCL); Rev. Msgr. Gerald F. Durst (SUP); Rev. Msgr. Clarence M. DeRuntz, M.A., M.Div. (KCK). Total Staff 31; Total Enrollment 136.

[B] COLLEGES AND UNIVERSITIES

COLUMBUS. *Ohio Dominican College*, 1216 Sunbury Rd., 43219. Tel: 614-253-2741; Fax: 614-252-0776.
For a complete listing, refer to the Colleges and Universities section.

[C] HIGH SCHOOLS, DIOCESAN OR INTERPAROCHIAL

COLUMBUS. *Bishop Hartley High School*, 1285 Zettler Rd., 43227. Tel: 614-237-5421. Jim Silcott, Prin.; Don Burger, Dean of Students; Erskine Braggs, Athletic Dir. Religious 1; Lay Teachers 37; Students 500.
Bishop Ready High School, 707 Salisbury Rd., 43204. Tel: 614-276-5263; Fax: 614-276-5116. Celene A. Seamen, Prin. Lay Teachers 32; Students 494.
Bishop Watterson High School, 99 E. Cooke Rd., 43214. Tel: 614-268-8671. Mr. John J. Durant, Prin. Deacons 1; Sisters 1; Lay Teachers 60; Students 1,082. Convent, 100 Indian Springs Dr., 43214.
St. Charles Preparatory School, 2010 E. Broad St., 43209. Tel: 614-252-6714. Dominic J. Cavello, Prin.; Scott M. Pharion, Asst. Prin.; James Lower, Asst. Prin.; Rev. Msgr. Thomas M. Bennett; Rev. Msgr. F. Thomas Gallen; Sr. Margaret Hoffman. Lay Teachers 35; Students 487.
St. Francis de Sales High School, 4212 Karl Rd., 43224. Tel: 614-267-7808. Mr. Patrick D. Rossetti, Prin.; Mr. Dan Garrick, Asst. Prin.; Ms. Molly Feesler, Asst. Prin. Convent, 4212 Karl Rd., 43224. Lay Teachers 47; Students 890.
LANCASTER. *William V. Fisher Catholic High School*, 1803 Granville Pike, 43130. Tel: 614-654-1231. Sr. Gail Morgan, O.P., Prin. Sisters 2; Lay Teachers 20; Students 296.
MARION. *Marion Catholic High School*, 1001 Mt. Vernon Ave., 43302; Fax: 614-389-5243. Beth Hill, Prin. Lay Teachers 14; Students 153.
NEW PHILADELPHIA. *Central Catholic High School*, 777 Third St., N.E., 44663. Tel: 216-343-3302. Joe Martin, Prin. Lay Teachers 10; Students 180.
NEWARK. *Newark Catholic High School*, 1 Green Wave

Dr., 43055. Tel: 614-344-3594. Susie Gribble, Campus Min. Lay Teachers 24; Students 288.

PORTSMOUTH. *Notre Dame High School.* (Grades 7-12), 2220 Sunrise Ave., 45662. Tel: 614-353-0719. Kathleen Milligan, Prin. Sisters 1; Lay Teachers 17; Students 220.

ZANESVILLE. *Bishop Rosecrans High School,* 1040 E. Main St., 43701. Tel: 614-452-7504. Joseph Brannon, Ph.D., Prin.; Rev. Dwayne A. McNew. Priests 1; Lay Teachers 16; Students 252.

[D] MONTESSORI SCHOOLS

COLUMBUS. *St. Joseph Montessori School,* 933 Hamlet St., 43201. Tel: 614-291-8601. Donna Barton, Admin. Lay Teachers 21; Students 268.

St. Mary of the Springs Montessori School, 2320 Airport Dr., 43219. Tel: 614-258-0024. Sr. Sheila Marie McIntyre, O.P., Sec. Sisters 1; Lay Teachers 3; Students 75.

[E] GENERAL HOSPITALS

COLUMBUS. *Holy Cross Care Services, Inc. dba Northland Terrace Medical Center,* 5700 Karl Rd., 43229. Tel: 614-846-5420; Fax: 614-438-5873.
For a complete listing, refer to the Hospitals section.

Mohun Health Care Center, 2320 Airport Dr., 43219. Tel: 614-253-8517.
For a complete listing, refer to the Hospitals section.

Mount Carmel Health System, 793 W. State St., 43222. Tel: 614-234-5423; Fax: 614-234-5985.
For a complete listing, refer to the Hospitals section.

ZANESVILLE. *Good Samaritan Medical Center and Rehabilitation Center,* 800 Forest Ave., 43701. Tel: 614-454-5000.
For a complete listing, refer to the Hospitals section.

[F] PROTECTIVE INSTITUTIONS

COLUMBUS. *Rosemont Center,* 2440 Dawnlight Ave., 43211. Tel: 614-471-2626.
For a complete listing, refer to the Special Care Facilities section.

[G] HOMES FOR AGED AND HOUSING FOR ELDERLY

COLUMBUS. *Nazareth Towers,* 300 E. Rich St., 43215. Tel: 614-464-4780; Fax: 614-464-1733.
For a complete listing, refer to the Special Care Facilities section.

St. Raphael Home for the Aged, Inc., 1550 Roxbury Rd., 43212. Tel: 614-486-0436; Fax: 614-486-1640.
For a complete listing, refer to the Special Care Facilities section.

St. Rita Home, 880 Greenlawn Ave., 43223. Tel: 614-443-9433; Fax: 614-443-1196.
For a complete listing, refer to the Special Care Facilities section.

Seton London, Inc.. 350 Cambridge Dr. London, 43140. Tel: 614-852-4233.
For a complete listing, refer to the Special Care Facilities section.

Seton South Columbus, Inc., 155 Highview Blvd., 43207. Tel: 614-492-9944.
For a complete listing, refer to the Special Care Facilities section.

Seton Square North, 1776 Drew Ave., 43235. Tel: 614-451-1995.
For a complete listing, refer to the Special Care Facilities section.

Seton Washington Court House, Inc.. 400 N. Glenn Ave. Washington Court House, 43160. Tel: 614-335-2292.
For a complete listing, refer to the Special Care Facilities section.

COSHOCTON. *Seton Coshocton, Inc.,* 377 Clow Ln., 43812. Tel: 614-451-1995.
For a complete listing, refer to the Special Care Facilities section.

DOVER. *Seton Square Dover, I, Inc.,* 501 James St., 44622. Tel: 330-343-3611.
For a complete listing, refer to the Special Care Facilities section.

Seton Square Dover, II, Inc., 139 Fillmore St., 44622. Tel: 330-343-3611.
For a complete listing, refer to the Special Care Facilities section.

KENTON. *Seton Kenton, Inc.,* 699 Morningside Dr., 43326. Tel: 419-673-7202.
For a complete listing, refer to the Special Care Facilities section.

LANCASTER. *Seton Lancaster, Inc.,* 232 Gay St., 43130. Tel: 614-681-1403.
For a complete listing, refer to the Special Care Facilities section.

MARION. *Seton Square Marion, Inc.,* 255 Richland Rd., 43302. Tel: 614-389-4746.
For a complete listing, refer to the Special Care Facilities section.

REYNOLDSBURG. *Seton Square East, Inc.,* 1235 Briarcliff Rd., 43068. Tel: 614-861-4860.
For a complete listing, refer to the Special Care Facilities section.

WELLSTON. *Seton Square Wellston, Inc.,* 570 W. First St., 45692. Tel: 614-384-6174.
For a complete listing, refer to the Special Care Facilities section.

ZANESVILLE. *Seton Housing, Inc.,* 516 Sheridan St., 43701. Tel: 614-453-4422.
For a complete listing, refer to the Special Care Facilities section.

[H] MONASTERIES AND RESIDENCES OF PRIESTS AND BROTHERS

COLUMBUS. *Salesian Center,* 80 S. 6th St., 43215. Tel: 614-464-4047. Revs. Steven Shafran, S.D.B., Dir.; Robert Bauer, S.D.B.; James Hurley, S.D.B., Exec. Dir. Boys & Girls Club; William Bucciferro, S.D.B., Youth Min. & Vice Dir.; Richard Alejunas, S.D.B., Financial Admin.; Jiri Kasny, S.D.B.; Thomas Gwozdz. Students of Theology 7; Brothers 1; Total Staff 40; Total Assisted 15.

NEWARK. *P.I.M.E. Mission & Prayer Center,* 2734 Seminary Rd. S.E., 43056-9339. Tel: 614-928-4246; Fax: 614-928-1512. Revs. Dino S. Vanin, P.I.M.E., Rector; James Coleman, P.I.M.E.; Ronnie Boccali, P.I.M.E. In res., Revs. Casto Marrapese, P.I.M.E.; Charles Sala, P.I.M.E. Franciscan Sisters of St. Joseph (Mexico City) 4; Total Staff 2; Total in Residence 5.

SOMERSET. *St. Joseph's Rectory,* 5757 State Rte. 383 N.E., P.O. Box 190, 43783. Tel: 614-743-1317. Rev. Adrian L. Dionne, O.P. Total Staff 2; Total in Residence 1.

WEST JEFFERSON. *SS. Simon and Jude,* 95 W. Main St., 43162-1225. Tel: 614-879-8562. Rev. Michael J. Devaney, O.M.I.; Deacon Ralph Parsons.

[I] CONVENTS AND RESIDENCES FOR SISTERS

COLUMBUS. *House of the Good Shepherd of Columbus.* (aka Rosemont Center), 2440 Dawnlight Ave., 43211. Tel: 614-471-2626. Sr. Monica Nowak, Exec. Dir. Sisters of Our Lady of Charity of the Good Shepherd 10; Total Staff 125.

Our Lady of Bethlehem Convent, 4567 Olentangy River Rd., 43214. Tel: 614-451-3900. American Region of the Sisters of the Poor Child Jesus. Sr. Frances Teresa Holzberger, P.C.J., Reg. Supr. Sisters 5.

Our Lady of Bethlehem Early Child Education Center. Sisters 1; Lay Teachers 13; Children 230.

St. Mary of the Springs, 2320 Airport Dr., 43219-2098. Tel: 614-252-2137. Leadership Team: Sr. Mary Faith Geelan, O.P., Prioress; Sr. Anne Kilbride, O.P., Vicaress; Sr. Sheila Marie McIntyre, O.P., Councilor, Secretary-General; Sr. Ellen Dunn, O.P., Councilor; Sr. Arleen Kisiel, O.P., Councilor. Sisters' Residence: Sr. Francis de Sales Heffernan, O.P., Superior.

Mohun Health Care Center. Sr. Jacqueline Baum, O.P., Admin.; Sr. Virginia King, O.P., Dir. of Resident Life; Rev. Benedict Joseph, O.P., Chap.

St. Mary of the Springs Montessori School. (Pre-Primary and Kindergarten). Sr. Marietta Miller, O.P., Dir. Sisters 120; Novices 2; Candidates 1; Total in Congregation 340.

Sisters of Notre Dame de Namur, 85 S. Roys Ave., 43204. Tel: 614-276-9521.

Sisters of the Holy Cross, Our Lady of Mount Carmel Convent, 266 McNaughton Rd., 43213. Tel: 614-866-9397. 1750 Lane Rd., 43220. Tel: 614-459-0727. 1381A Bluff Ave., 43221. Legal Title: *Sisters of the Holy Cross, Inc.* Sisters 9. Sisters 4.

NEWARK. *Franciscan Sisters of St. Joseph (Mexico City),* P.I.M.E. Mission Convent, 2734 Seminary Rd. S.E., 43056-9339. Tel: 614-928-4246. Sr. Angelina Landa, H.F.deS.J., Supr. Sisters 4.

PORTSMOUTH. Oratory. *St. Joseph Adoration Monastery, Poor Clares of Perpetual Adoration,* 2311 Stockham Ln., 45662. Tel: 614-353-4713. Mother Mary Agnes, Abbess. Professed Cloistered Nuns 6; Extern Sisters 1; Postulants 1.

[J] NEWMAN CENTERS

COLUMBUS. *Campus Ministry.* P.O. Box 587, Mt. Vernon, 43050. Ohio State University, 64 W. Lane Ave., Columbux, 43201. Revs. David O'Brien, C.S.P., Dir.; Vincent McKiernan, C.S.P.; Donald Andrie, C.S.P.; C. Theodore Thomas, Diocesan Dir. Campus Min., P.O. Box 587, Mt. Vernon, 43050.

[K] FOUNDATIONS

COLUMBUS.

**The Foundation of the Catholic Diocese of Columbus,* 197 E. Gay St., 43215. Tel: 614-241-2566. Kathy Spencer, Exec. Dir.

Legacy of Catholic Learning Endowment Program, 198 E. Broad St., 43215. Tel: 614-224-1221. Ann Ball, Coord.

LANCASTER.

**William V. Fisher Catholic High School Endowment Fund,* 1803 Granville Pike, 43130.

MARION. *Marion Catholic High School Endowment Fund,* 1001 Mount Vernon Ave., 43302.

NEW PHILADELPHIA. *Tuscarawas Central Catholic High School Endowment Fund,* 777 Third St. N.E., 44663.

NEWARK.

**Newark Catholic High School Endowment Fund,* One Green Wave Dr., 43055.

ZANESVILLE. *Bishop Rosecrans High School Foundation,* 1040 E. Main St., 43701. Tel: 614-452-7504.

[L] MISCELLANEOUS

COLUMBUS. *Blessed Margaret Guild, Inc.,* 262 N. Grant Ave., 43215. Tel: 614-240-5915;240-5917; Fax: 614-240-5928. Rev. Kenneth A. France-Kelly, O.P., Exec. Dir. Total Staff 51; Total Assisted 35,483.

Catholic Alumni Club, P.O. Box 695, 43216. Peggy Schano, Contact Person. Tel: 614-263-7686; Dan Doell, Contact Person. Tel: 614-846-7489.

The Christ Child Society of Columbus, Inc., P.O. Box 340091, 43234. Mrs. Catherine Hayes, Pres.

Diocesan Retirement Community Corp., 198 E. Broad St., 43215-3766. Mrs. Carol Oravec, Project Coord.

St. Stephen's Community House, 1500 E. 17th Ave., 43219. Tel: 614-294-6347; Fax: 614-294-0258. Ms. Judith Stattmiller, Exec. Dir. Total Assisted 110; Total Staff 15.

ZANESVILLE. *St. Nicholas Foundation,* 925 E. Main St., 43701. Tel: 614-453-0597; Fax: 614-453-0590.

RELIGIOUS INSTITUTES OF MEN REPRESENTED IN THE DIOCESE

For further details refer to the corresponding bracketed number in the Religious Institutes of Men or Women section.

[0350]—*Cistercians Order of the Strict Observance-Trappists.*—O.C.S.O.

[1140]—*Fathers of the Sacred Hearts.*—SS.CC.

[0520]—*Franciscan Friars.* (Prov. of St. John the Baptist).—O.F.M.

[0690]—*Jesuit Fathers and Brothers.* (Detroit, Maryland, and Sri Lanka Provs.).—S.J.

[0910]—*Oblates of Mary Immaculate.*—O.M.I.

[0430]—*Order of Preachers-Dominicans.* (Prov. of St. Joseph).—O.P.

[1030]—*Paulist Fathers.*—C.S.P.

[1050]—*Pontifical Institute for Foreign Missions.*—P.I.M.E.

[1190]—*Salesians of St. John Bosco.*—S.D.B.

[0760]—*Society of Mary.*—S.M.

[1060]—*Society of the Precious Blood.* (Cincinnati Prov.).—C.PP.S.

RELIGIOUS INSTITUTES OF WOMEN REPRESENTED IN THE DIOCESE

[0330]—*Carmelite Sisters for the Aged and Infirm.*—O.Carm.

[1920]—*Congregation of the Sisters of the Holy Cross.*—C.S.C.

[1730]—*Congregation of the Sisters of the Third Order of St. Francis, Oldenburg, IN.*—O.S.F.

[1710]—*Congregation of the Third Order of St. Francis of Mary Immaculate, Joliet, IL.*—O.S.F.

[1070-02]—*Dominican Sisters.*—O.P.

[1070-13]—*Dominican Sisters.*—O.P.

[1070-25]—*Dominican Sisters.*—O.P.

[1230]—*Franciscan Sisters of Christian Charity.*—O.S.F.

[1480]—*Franciscan Sisters of St. Joseph.* (Mexico City).—H.F.deS.J.

[1440]—*Franciscan Sisters of the Poor.*—S.F.P.

[3790]—*Institute of the Sisters of St. Dorothy.*—S.S.D.

[3210]—*Poor Clares of Perpetual Adoration.*—P.C.P.A.

[1070-03]—*Sinsinawa Dominican Congregation of the Most Holy Rosary.*—O.P.

[0440]—*Sisters of Charity of Cincinnati, Ohio.*—S.C.

[0500]—*Sisters of Charity of Nazareth, Kentucky.*—S.C.N.

[0990]—*Sisters of Divine Providence.*—C.D.P.

[2575]—*Sisters of Mercy of the Americas.* (Detroit & St. Louis Provs.).—R.S.M.

[3000]—*Sisters of Notre Dame de Namur.*—S.N.D.deN.

[1630]—*Sisters of St. Francis of Penance and Christian Charity.* (Stella Niagara, NY).—O.S.F.

[1530]—*Sisters of St. Francis of the Congregation of Our Lady of Lourdes, Sylvania, OH.*—O.S.F.

[3830-05]—*Sisters of St. Joseph.*—C.S.J.

[3830-08]—*Sisters of St. Joseph.*—C.S.J.

[3830-13]—*Sisters of St. Joseph.*—C.S.J.

[1830]—*Sisters of the Good Sheperd.*—R.G.S.

[3220]—*Sisters of the Poor Child Jesus.*—P.C.J.

[3260]—*Sisters of the Precious Blood.* (Dayton, Ohio).—C.PP.S.

[3320]—*Sisters of the Presentation of the B.V.M.*—P.B.V.M.

[1760]—*Sisters of the Third Order of St. Francis of Penance and of Charity.*—O.S.F.

[1720]—*Sisters of the Third Order Regular of St. Francis of the Congregation of Our Lady of Lourdes.*—O.S.F.

[4120-04]—*The Ursuline Nuns of Cleveland.*—O.S.U.

DIOCESAN CEMETERIES

COLUMBUS. *Mount Calvary*, 581 Mt. Calvary Ave., 43223-2217. Tel: 614-491-2751. Rich Finn, Dir. & Gen. Mgr.

LEWIS CENTER. *Resurrection*, 9571 N. High St., 43035-9413. Tel: 614-888-1805. Rich Finn, Dir. & Gen. Mgr.

LOCKBOURNE. *St. Joseph*, 6440 S. High St., 43137-9208. Tel: 614-491-2751. Rich Finn, Dir. & Gen. Mgr.

PATASKALA. *Holy Cross*, 11539 National Rd. S.W., 43062-8304. Tel: 614-927-4442. Rich Finn, Dir. & Gen. Mgr.

NECROLOGY

† Dermody, Ralph R., (Retired). —Died Jan. 31, 1996.

† Graf, John H., (Retired). —Died Dec. 16, 1996.

† Klinec, Rev. Msgr. Julius G., (Retired). —Died Dec. 20, 1996.

† McGinnis, Daniel P., Columbus, OH, Holy Trinity Church. —Died Oct. 21, 1996.

Diocese of Corpus Christi

(Dioecesis Corporis Christi)

Most Reverend

RENE H. GRACIDA, D.D.

Bishop of Corpus Christi; ordained May 23, 1959; appointed Titular Bishop of Masuccaba and Auxiliary of Miami December 6, 1971; consecrated January 25, 1972; appointed Bishop of Pensacola-Tallahassee October 1, 1975; transferred to Corpus Christi May 19, 1983; installed July 11, 1983. *Res., 4126 Ocean Dr., Corpus Christi, TX, 78411-1224. Office: 620 Lipan St., P.O. Box 2620, Corpus Christi, TX, 78403-2620.* Tel.: 512-882-6191.

Most Reverend

ROBERTO O. GONZALEZ, O.F.M.

Coadjutor Bishop of Corpus Christi; ordained May 1977; appointed Titular Bishop of Ursona and Auxiliary Bishop of Boston July 19, 1988; ordained Bishop October 3, 1988; appointed Coadjutor Bishop of Corpus Christi May 16, 1995; transferred to Corpus Christi June 26, 1995. *Res., 4109 Ocean Dr., Corpus Christi, TX, 78411. Office: 620 Lipan St., P.O. Box 2620, Corpus Christi, TX, 78403-2620.* Tel.: 512-882-6191.

ERECTED A VICARIATE APOSTOLIC IN 1874.

ELEVATED TO A DIOCESE MARCH 23, 1912.

Square Miles 17,294.

The territory embraced by the Diocese of Corpus Christi comprises the Counties of Aransas, Bee, Brooks, Duval, Jim Hogg, Jim Wells, Kleberg, Kenedy, Live Oak, Nueces, Refugio, San Patricio, Webb, Zapata, and parts of LaSalle and McMullen in the State of Texas.

For legal titles of parishes and diocesan institutions, consult the Chancery Office.

The Chancery Office: 620 Lipan St., P.O. Box 2620, Corpus Christi, TX, 78403-2620. Tel.: 512-882-6191; Fax: 512-882-1018; 883-8850.

STATISTICAL OVERVIEW

Personnel	
Bishop	1
Abbots	1
Retired Abbots	1
Priests: Diocesan Active in Diocese	76
Priests: Active Outside Diocese	7
Priests: Diocesan in Foreign Missions	2
Priests: Retired, Sick or Absent	23
Number of Diocesan Priests	108
Religious Priests in Diocese	62
Extern Priests in Diocese	4
Ordinations:	
Diocesan Priests	3
Religious Priests	2
Transitional Deacons	3
Permanent Deacons	3
Permanent Deacons in Diocese	66
Total Brothers	22
Total Sisters	565
Parishes	
Parishes	84
With Resident Pastor:	
Resident Diocesan Priests	53
Resident Religious Priests	20
Without Resident Pastor:	
Administered by Priests	10
Administered by Permanent Deacons	1
Missions	59
Pastoral Centers	11
Professional Ministry Personnel:	
Brothers	8
Sisters	22
Lay Ministers	29
Welfare	
Catholic Hospitals	5
Total Assisted	384,228
Homes for the Aged	2
Total Assisted	160
Residential Care of Children	1
Total Assisted	64
Day Care and Extended Day Care Centers	3
Total Assisted	210
Specialized Homes	2
Total Assisted	1,107
Special Centers for Social Services	8
Total Assisted	33,926
Residential Care of Disabled	1
Total Assisted	4
Other Institutions	2
Total Assisted	250
Educational	
Seminaries, Diocesan	1
Students from This Diocese	9
Diocesan Students in Other Seminaries	16
Seminaries, Religious	1
Students Religious	1
Total Seminarians	26
High Schools, Diocesan and Parish	2
Total Students	722
High Schools, Private	1
Total Students	315
Elementary Schools, Diocesan and Parish	23
Total Students	3,751
Elementary Schools, Private	5
Total Students	1,347
Catechesis/Religious Education:	
High School Students	4,276
Elementary Students	15,947
Total Students Under Catholic Instruction	26,384
Teachers in the Diocese:	
Priests	7
Sisters	70
Lay Teachers	409
Vital Statistics	
Receptions into the Church:	
Infant Baptism Totals	5,989
Adult Baptism Totals	240
Received into Full Communion	504
First Communions	5,500
Confirmations	6,145
Marriages:	
Catholic	1,080
Interfaith	172
Total Marriages	1,252
Deaths	2,291
Total Catholic Population	361,500
Total Population	792,300

Former Bishops—Rt. Rev. DOMINIC MANUCY, cons. Dec. 8, 1874; transferred to Mobile March 9, 1884 reappointed to Vicariate Apostolic of Brownsville Feb. 1, 1885; died Dec. 4, 1885, before taking possession.—Rt. Rev. PETER VERDAGUER, cons. Nov. 9, 1890; died Oct. 26, 1911.—Rt. Rev. PAUL JOSEPH NUSSBAUM, C.P., D.D., cons. May 20, 1913; resigned March 26, 1920; Bishop of Marquette; appt. Nov. 14, 1922; died June 24, 1935.—Most Rev. EMMANUEL B. LEDVINA, D.D., LL.D., appt. April 30, 1921; cons. June 14, 1921; Assistant at Pontifical Throne May 30, 1931; resigned March 15, 1949; died Dec. 15, 1952.—Most Rev. MARIANO S. GARRIGA, D.D., LL.D., Coadjutor *cum jure successionis,* appt. June 20, 1936; cons. Sept. 21, 1936; succeeded to See March 15, 1949; assistant at Pontifical Throne April 14, 1951; died Feb. 21, 1965.—Most Rev. THOMAS J. DRURY, D.D., Fourth Bishop of Corpus Christi; Bishop of San Angelo; appt. Oct. 16, 1961; cons. Jan. 24, 1962; fourth Bishop of Corpus Christi; appt. July 19, 1965; installed Sept. 1, 1965; retired Bishop of Corpus Christi; appt. May 19, 1983; died July 22, 1992.

Diocesan Curia and Administrative Council—620 Lipan St., P.O. Box 2620, Corpus Christi, 78403-2620. Most Rev. RENE H. GRACIDA, Chm., Bishop of Corpus Christi; Most Rev. ROBERTO O. GONZALEZ, O.F.M., Coadjutor Bishop & Vicar General; Rev. Msgr. ROBERT E. FREEMAN, P.A., Episcopal Vicar for Social Services and Communications; Rev. Msgr. LEONARD D. PIVONKA, J.C.D., V.J., Judicial Vicar and Secretary for Canonical Affairs; Rev. Msgr. JAMES HARRIS, V.E., Episcopal Vicar for the Western Vicariate of the Diocese of Corpus Christi; Rev. Msgr. THOMAS L. MEANY, V.E., Episcopal Vicar for Religious and Admin. of the Diocesan Tribunal; Rev. Msgr. THOMAS P. MCGETTRICK, V.E., Episcopal Vicar for Priests; Rev. Msgr. MICHAEL HERAS, V.E., Episcopal Vicar for Evangelization and Parish Renewal; Rev. Msgr. DANIEL E. FLORES, V.E., Episcopal Vicar for Priestly Formation and Education; Deacons ROY M. GRASSEDONIO, Chancellor; STANLEY MILLSAP, Vicar for the Permanent Diaconate; Dr. FRANK LUCIDO, Ed.D., Dir. of Education; GREGOR A. SEAGRAVE, Fiscal Officer; MARTY WIND, Exec.

Vice Pres. & Gen. Mgr. Diocesan Telecommunications. Members: ROBIN PERRONE; MARY WHITMIRE.

Consultative Bodies—620 Lipan St., P.O. Box 2620, Corpus Christi, 78403-2620.

College of Consultors—Rev. Msgr. WILLIAM T. THOMPSON, P.A.; Rev. Msgr. ROBERT E. FREEMAN, P.A.; Rev. Msgr. LEONARD D. PIVONKA, J.C.D., V.J.; Rev. Msgr. THOMAS L. MEANY, V.E.; Rev. Msgr. LOUIS KIHNEMAN, V.E.; Rev. Msgr. LAWRENCE WHITE; Rev. Msgr. THOMAS P. MCGETTRICK, V.E.; Rev. Msgr. MICHAEL HERAS, V.E.; Rev. Msgr. DANIEL E. FLORES, V.E.

Council of Deacons—Deacons LUPE VASQUEZ, Chm. ANASTACIO BERNAL, Vice Chm. RONALD DEBUQUE, Sec. ALAN BORSE, Treas. STANLEY MILLSAP, Vicar.

Council Of Religious—Very Rev. THOMAS L. MEANY, V.E., Episcopal Vicar for Religious; Sr. AGNES MARIE TENGLER, I.W.B.S., Pres., *2930 S. Alameda, Corpus Christi, 78404.* Tel: 512-882-5413.

Deans—Alice, Rev. Msgr. STANLEY SLIWIAK; *Beeville,* Rev. THOMAS FEENEY; *Corpus Christi Central,* Rev. Msgr. LEONARD PIVONKA, J.C.D.; *Corpus Christi Five Points,* Rev. Msgr. THOMAS MEANY, V.E.; *Corpus Christi Southside,* Rev. Msgr. WILLIAM T. THOMPSON, P.A.; *Corpus Christi Westside,* Rev. Msgr. LAWRENCE E. WHITE; *Kingsville,* Rev. Msgr. STANLEY SLIWIAK; *Portland,* Rev. Msgr. LOUIS KINHEMAN; *Sinton,* Rev. Msgr. JOHN P. KILLEEN; *Collegiate Parishes,* Rev. Msgr. DANIEL E. FLORES, V.E.

Finance Council—Most Rev. RENE H. GRACIDA. Consultants: JOE MOKRY; R. C. ALLEN; DANIEL J. DAVIS; GREGOR A. SEAGRAVE; JOHN BUCKLEY; DONALD KINGSBURY.

Diaconal Screening Committee—Deacons JAMES CARLISLE, Chm. RICARDO COSTLEY, Vice Chm. LEONEL SAN MIGUEL, Sec. Western Vicariate; STANLEY MILLSAP, Vicar.

Personnel Board - Priests—Rev. Msgr. THOMAS P. MCGETTRICK, V.E., Chm.; Rev. Msgr. RICHARD SHIRLEY; Revs. MATTHEW LYNG; MARK CHAMBERLIN; PAUL HESSE; Rev. Msgr. DANIEL E. FLORES, V.E.; Rev. Msgr. JAMES HARRIS, V.E.

Presbyteral Council—Rev. Msgr. STANLEY SLIWIAK, Chm.; Rev. Msgr. MICHAEL HERAS, V.E., Sec.; Rev. Msgr. JOHN P. KILLEEN, Vice Chm.

Telecommunications Corporation—Rev. Msgr. ROBERT E. FREEMAN, P.A., V.G., Pres.; MARTY WIND, Exec. Vice Pres. & Gen. Mgr.

Tribunal—Rev. Msgr. LEONARD PIVONKA, J.C.D., V.J., Judicial Vicar; Rev. Msgr. THOMAS L. MEANY, V.E., Admin.

Judges—Rev. Msgr. THOMAS MEANY, V.E.; Revs. THOMAS P. FEENEY; JAMES HAMILTON; DONALD DOWNEY, J.C.L.; Deacon BRUCE AYCOCK.

Advocates—Rev. Msgr. JAMES HARRIS, V.E.; Revs. EDWARD KIRCHER; MORGAN ROWSOME; Sr. PATRICK BRUEN, O.L.C.; Sr. SARA CARTER; Sr. ESPERANZA MANAS, O.P.; Sr. MARGARET MANION, C.C.V.I.; Sr. MARY WALDEN, O.S.U.; Sr. MARIE ELISE VAN DIJK, C.D.P.; Deacons ANTONIO CASTILLO; ANTONIO LARA; GERARD MORALES; RAUL ROSALES; CRISPIN O. SOTO; JOHN SUTHERLAND; ANASTACIO BERNAL; LEONAL SAN MIGUEL; M. M. HORSEMAN; EMMA GONZALEZ; MARIO ALAMEIDA; MARY ALICE AMAYA; STELLA ARAIZA; BARBARA BASSETT; MARY C. CHRISTMAS; FRANCES COLLING; GARLAND FRAZIER; YOLANDA GUARJARDO; EVELYN MANSHEIM; RAMONA MORENO; ROBERT MOYA, JR.; BETTY PARKOS; BERNICE QUINTANILLA; CY RICHARDS; GRACIE SOSA; TED STRASSER, JR.; ELLEN STRASSER; ROMIE VARGAS.

Defenders of the Bond—Rev. Msgr. MICHAEL HERAS, V.E.; Rev. ROGER SMITH.

Notaries-Secretaries—SARA VARGAS; BELINDA HARRIS.

Villa Maria, Inc., Board—Rev. Msgr. ROBERT E. FREEMAN, P.A., Pres.; Sr. PATRICK BRUEN, O.L.C.; BRIAN CHAMBERLIN.

Administrative Offices

The Chancery Office—620 Lipan St., P.O. Box 2620, Corpus Christi, 78403-2620. Tel: 512-882-6191; Fax: 512-882-1018 (Admin.); 883-8850 (Fiscal Office). Office Hours: Mon.-Fri., 8:30-5. Closed holidays.

Office of the Bishop—Most Rev. RENE H. GRACIDA, D.D.

Office of the Coadjutor Bishop—Most Rev. ROBERTO O. GONZALEZ, O.F.M., Coadjutor Bishop.

Secretary for Canonical Affairs—Rev. Msgr. LEONARD D. PIVONKA, J.C.D., V.J.

Secretary to the Bishop and Master Of Ceremonies—Rev. JAMES STEMBLER; RENE H. GRACIDA.

Master of Ceremonies to Bishop Roberto O. Gonzalez, O.F.M.—Rev. FRANCISCO LOPEZ.

Administrative Assistant to Bishop—RENE H. GRACIDA; LALI WATSON.

Secretary to Bishops for Appointments—ANNA DE LEON.

Secretary to Coadjutor Bishop for Correspondence—LUCIA CARRERA.

Vicar General—Most Rev. ROBERTO O. GONZALEZ, O.F.M., V.G.

Judicial Vicar—Rev. Msgr. LEONARD D. PIVONKA, J.C.D., V.J.

Episcopal Vicar for Evangelization and Parish Renewal—Rev. Msgr. MICHAEL HERAS, V.E.

Episcopal Vicar for Religious and Admin. of the Diocesan Tribunal—Rev. Msgr. THOMAS L. MEANY, V.E.

Episcopal Vicar for Permanent Diaconate—Deacon STANLEY MILLSAP.

Episcopal Vicar for Priests—Rev. Msgr. THOMAS P. MCGETTRICK, V.E.

Chancellor—Deacon ROY M. GRASSEDONIO.

Administrative Assistant to the Chancellor—SUSAN D. CAMPBELL.

Family Life Office—BILL LARA, Dir.

Fiscal Officer—GREGOR SEAGRAVE.

C.P.A.—PAUL A. DAMEROW.

Catholic Sharing Appeal—GREGOR SEAGRAVE.

Data Processing Office—PAUL DAMEROW, Supvr.

Human Life Office—REX MOSES, Dir.

Office of Priests—Rev. Msgr. THOMAS P. MCGETTRICK, V.E., Dir.

Office of Worship—NELDA CRUG MUNGUIA, Dir.

Personnel Office—Deacon STANLEY MILLSAP.

Permanent Diaconate Office—Deacons STANLEY MILLSAP, Vicar; MICHAEL MANTZ, Admin. Asst.

Propagation of the Faith Office—Deacon ROY GRASSEDONIO.

Vocation Office—Rev. Msgr. DANIEL FLORES, V.E., Episcopal Vicar for Priestly Formation and Education, *Corpus Christi Academy Complex, 3036 Saratoga Blvd., Corpus Christi, 78415.* Tel: 512-851-0908. Rev. ALEJANDRO SALAZAR, Assoc. Dir.-Laredo; Rev. FRANK X. MARTINEZ, Assoc. Dir. Corpus Christi.

The Corpus Christi Pastoral Center—1200 Lantana St., Corpus Christi, 78407. Tel: 512-289-6501; Fax: 512-289-1867. Office Hours: Mon.-Fri., 8:30-5. Closed holidays.

Archives—Mr. CY RICHARDS, III, Archivist Mon.-Thurs. 9-2.

Catholic Schools Office—Dr. FRANK LUCIDO, Supt., *Corpus Christi Academy Complex, 3036 Saratoga, Corpus Christi, 78415.* Tel: 512-814-0444.

Catholic Cemeteries—Deacon ROLAND OUELLETTE, Dir. Tel: 512-289-1528.

Construction Office—Deacon H.H. (PETE) HORSEMAN, JR., Mgr. Tel: 512-289-1937.

Diocesan Telecommunications Corporation—Tel: 512-289-6437. Rev. Msgr. ROBERT E. FREEMAN, P.A.; MARTY WIND, Exec. Vice Pres. & Gen. Mgr.

Education—Dr. FRANK LUCIDO, Supt., *Corpus Christi Academy Complex, 3036 Saratoga, Corpus Christi, 78415.* Tel: 512-814-0475.

Natural Family Planning - Understanding Sexuality—4639 Corona, Ste. 13B, Corpus Christi, 78411. Tel: 512-852-0222; 852-2067. MARGE HARRIGAN, R.N., Dir.

Maintenance Office—BILL TRBULA, Mgr. Tel: 512-289-9317.

Newspaper "The South Texas Catholic"—Most Rev. RENE H. GRACIDA, Publisher; PAULA ESPITIA, Interim Editor. Tel: 512-289-1752.

Pastoral Institute For Ministry and Christian Service—Rev. BRADLEY A. BARBER, Dir., *Corpus Christi Academy Complex, 3036 Saratoga, Corpus Christi, 78415.* Tel: 512-814-5030.

Office for Persons with Disabilities—Rev. DAVID WALSH, C.Ss.R., Dir., *Corpus Christi Academy Complex, 3036 Saratoga, Corpus Christi, 78415.* Tel: 512-814-2181.

Real Property Office—WILLIAM TAGLIABUE, Mgr. Tel: 512-289-1528.

Religious Education—Dr. FRANK LUCIDO, Diocesan Coord., *Corpus Christi Academy Complex, 3036 Saratoga, Corpus Christi, 78415.* Tel: 512-814-5689.

Office of Youth And Young Adult Ministry—TONI CHAPA, Dir., *Corpus Christi Academy Complex, 3036 Saratoga, Corpus Christi, 78415.* Tel: 512-814-3806.

Episcopal Vicar for Western Vicariate for the Diocese of Corpus Christi—Rev. Msgr. JAMES HARRIS, V.E., Episcopal Vicar, *214 San Bernardo Ave., Laredo, 78040.* Tel: 210-722-1382; Fax: 210-722-5599.

Religious Education Office—Sr. MARIA GUADALUPE HERRERA, R.S.M., Laredo Area Coord., *1512 Logan St., Laredo, 78040.* Tel: 210-722-0950; Fax: 210-722-2238.

Other Offices and Organizations

Adoption Services—ROXANNA GUERRA, Admin., *1901 Corpus Christi St., Laredo, 78044.* Tel: 210-722-2443.

Alhambra—ROBERT BATTERSON, Grand Commander, *13829 Sea Horse, Corpus Christi, 78418.* Tel: 512-949-8337. Dr. MARY MCCASKEY, Grand Sultana, *250 Cape Henry, Corpus Christi, 78412.* Tel: 512-991-6200.

Apostleship of The Sea—Rev. VINCENT PATRIZI, Dir., *Our Lady Star of the Sea, P.O. Box 1899, Corpus Christi, 78403.* Tel: 512-883-4507.

Birthright Counseling—ROXANNA GUERRA, Admin., *1901 Corpus Christi St., Laredo, 78044.* Tel: 210-722-2443. DONNA CISNEROS, Pres., *1422 Baldwin, Corpus Christi.* Tel: 512-884-2662.

Blue Army (World Apostolate of Fatima)—Mrs. AGNES BOCKHOLTZ, Pres., *Rte. 2, Box 885, Corpus Christi, 78410.* Tel: 512-265-9156. Rev. Msgr. LEONARD PIVONKA, J.C.D., V.J., Spiritual Leader, *505 N. Upper Broadway, Corpus Christi, 78401.*

Boy Scouts—Deacon CESAR M. PONCE, *P.O. Box 91, Tuleta, 78162.* Tel: 512-358-5390.

Campus Ministries—Texas A&M University-Kingsville, Collegiate Parish of St. Thomas Aquinas, Rev. ROGER SMITH, *P.O. Box 2193, Kingsville, 78363.* Tel: 512-592-5781. *Del Mar College, Collegiate Parish of St. Thomas More,* Rev. HANH VAN PHAM, *2045 18th St., Corpus Christi, 78404.* Tel: 512-883-9308. *The Cardinal John Henry Newman Catholic Student Center, at Texas A&M University-Corpus Christi,* Rev. Msgr. RICHARD SHIRLEY, *6300 Ocean Dr., Corpus Christi, 78412.* Tel: 512-993-5898. *Bee County College,* Rev. JAMES KELLEHER, *4000 N. St. Mary's St., Beeville, 78102.* Tel: 512-358-4968. *Laredo State University and Junior College,* Bro. ROBERT WARREN, F.M.S., Campus Min., *P3, Fort McIntosh, Laredo, 78040.* Tel: 210-722-2324.

Catholic Daughters of the Americas—Rev. Msgr. LEONARD PIVONKA, J.C.D., V.J., *Corpus Christi Cathedral, 505 N. Upper Broadway, Corpus Christi, 78401.* Tel: 512-883-4213. Ms. JUANITA AGUILAR, *District 15, 1201 Chihuahua, Laredo, 78040.* Tel: 210-723-3037. VICTORIA GONZALES, Dist. 16: *4442 Carlton, Corpus Christi, 78415.* Tel: 512-855-9646. ALICIA SALINAS, Dist. 23: *Rte. 3, Box 22, Alice, 78332.* Tel: 512-664-6932. DELPHA R. GONZALES, Dist. 36: *330 Cheyenne St., Corpus Christi, 78406.* Tel: 512-884-6970. TERRY SKORUPPA, Dist. 41: *4021 Pernitas Creek, Corpus Christi, 78410.* Tel: 512-242-2892.

Catholic Social Services of Corpus Christi, Inc.—Rev. Msgr. ROBERT E. FREEMAN, P.A.; Sr. MILAGROS TORMO, M.J.M.J., Admin., *1322 Comanche, Corpus Christi, 78401.* Tel: 512-884-0651; Fax: 512-884-3956.

Catholic Social Services of Laredo, Inc.—Rev. Msgr. ROBERT E. FREEMAN, P.A.; ROXANNA GUERRA, Admin., *1901 Corpus Christi St., Laredo, 78044.* Tel: 210-722-2443; Fax: 210-725-2238.

Cemeteries—(Laredo); Deacon ROLAND OUELLETTE, Diocesan Dir. Tel: 210-723-6811.

Center For Spiritual Direction—Sr. JOAN MICHELE RAKE, C.D.P., Spiritual Dir., *4103 Ocean Dr., Corpus Christi, 78411.* Tel: 512-853-0171.

Charismatic Movement—Deacon ANTONIO LARA, Diocesan Dir.; Corpus Christi Area: *624 W. Fulton, Mathis, 78368.* Tel: 512-547-5819.

Cursillo Movement—Rev. Msgr. VLADIMIRO MANETE, O.M.I., Spiritual Dir., *Diocesan Secretariat & Center, P.O. Box 1175, Laredo, 78042.* Tel: 210-723-3850. Deacon NOEL BRELAND, Spiritual Dir. (English), *Rte. 1, Box 109R-5, Sandia, 78383.* Tel: 512-547-9263. Deacon RAUL HINOJOSA, Spiritual Dir. (Spanish), *P.O. Box 101, Premont, 78375.* Tel: 512-348-3847. Bro. JOE HERRERA, Spiritual Dir., Youth Cursillo (English), *611 E. Cherry Hill, Laredo, 78041.* Tel: 210-724-2651.

Diocesan Council Of Catholic Women—LORRAINE LUNCHEON, *P.O. Box 22, Beeville, 78102.* Rev. JAMES STEMBLER, Spiritual Moderator. Tel: 512-882-6191, Ext. 669.

Disaster Relief—Rev. Msgr. ROBERT E. FREEMAN, P.A., Dir., *1322 Comanche St., Corpus Christi, 78401.* Tel: 512-884-0651.

Ecumenical And Interreligious Affairs—Rev. JOHN WOJTASCZYK, Dir., *St. Joseph Church, 609 E. Gramman, Beeville, 512-358-3239.*

Emergency Aid—Sr. MILAGROS TORMO, M.J.M.J., Admin., *1322 Comanche, Corpus Christi, 78401.* Tel: 512-884-0651.

Family Counseling—Laredo Catholic Social Services; ROXANNA GUERRA, Admin., *1901 Corpus Christi, Laredo, 78044.* Tel: 210-722-2443. CSS-Corpus Christi Catholic Social Services: Sr. MILAGROS TORMO, M.J.M.J., Admin., *1322 Comanche St., Corpus Christi, 78401.* Tel: 512-884-0651.

Catholic Engaged Encounter—Rev. Msgr. MICHAEL HERAS, V.E., Dir., *P.O. Box 2620, Corpus Christi, 78403.* Tel: 512-882-6191, Ext. 356.

Holy Childhood, Pontifical Association of the—FRANK LUCIDO, Dir., *Corpus Christi Academy Complex, 3036 Saratoga, Corpus Christi, 78415.* Tel: 512-814-5689.

Immigration Services—Sr. MILAGROS TORMO, M.J.M.J., Admin., *1322 Comanche, Corpus Christi, 78401.* Tel: 512-884-0651. ROXANNA GUERRA, Admin., *Servicios Para Inmigrantes, 1901 Corpus Christi St., Laredo, 78044.* Tel: 210-722-2443.

Jail Ministries—Bee County: Deacon MANUEL CARRANCO, Chap. Brooks County: Deacon GONZALO RIVERA, Chap. Kleberg County: Deacon TONY BARBOUR

Webb County: Deacon JOSE RODRIGUEZ; SALVADOR MADRIGAL. Nueces County: Rev. Msgr. MICHAEL HERAS, V.E., Spiritual Dir.; Deacon ARMANDO CAVADA, McConnell Unit, Beeville.

La Frontera Halfway House—ROXANNA GUERRA, Admin., *1616 Callaghan, Laredo, 78040.* Tel: 210-722-7271.

Lay Maryans—MANUEL GARCIA, Dir., *5310 Hitching Post Ln., Corpus Christi, 78415.* Tel: 512-855-9288.

Legion of Mary—BUNNIE HERMAN, Pres., *610 Wilshire, Corpus Christi, 78411.* Tel: 512-855-8321. Rev. Msgr. LEONARD PIVONKA, J.C.D., J.V., Spirit. Dir., *Corpus Christi*, JUAN VILLARREAL, Pres., *4415 Santa Maria, Laredo, 78041.* Tel: 210-723-9348. Deacon JOSE RODRIQUEZ, Spirit. Dir., *Laredo.*

Marriage Encounter—Rt. Rev. LUKE BUERGLER, O.S.B., Spiritual Dir., *Corpus Christi Abbey, HCR 2, Box 6300, Sandia, 78383.* Tel: 512-547-3257.

Pre-Release Prisoner Program—ROXANNA B. GUERRA, Admin., *1616 Callaghan, Laredo, 78040.* Tel: 210-722-7271.

Radio Stations - KLUX FM—RUSSEL WAYNE MARTIN, Dir. Broadcast Operations, *1200 Lantana St., Corpus Christi, 78407.* Tel: 512-289-2487.

KHOY FM—BENNETTE MCBRIDE, Mgr., *1901 Corpus Christi St., Laredo, 78040.* Tel: 210-722-4167.

Religious Education—Corpus Christi Area: Dr. FRANK LUCIDO, D.R.E., *Corpus Christi Academy Complex, 3036 Saratoga, Corpus Christi, 78415.* Tel: 512-289-5689. Laredo Area: Sr. M. GUADALUPE HERRERA, R.S.M., Coord., *1512 Logan St., Laredo, 78040.* Tel: 210-722-0959; Fax: 210-725-2238.

Serra International—Rev. Msgr. DANIEL E. FLORES, V.E., Chap., *3036 Saratoga Blvd., Corpus Christi, 78415.* Tel: 512-851-0908. JAMES RIDLEY, Pres. Tel: 512-852-8367.

Theresians—Rev. Msgr. DANIEL E. FLORES, V.E., Spiritual Dir., *3036 Saratoga Blvd., Corpus Christi, 78415.* Tel: 512-851-0908. ELLA NICHOLAS, Pres., *629 Moray, Corpus Christi, 78411.* Tel: 512-855-8656.

Villa Maria, Inc.—Deacon GARLAND FRAZIER, Dir., *Box 4, 3146 Saratoga Blvd., Corpus Christi, 78415.* Tel: 512-857-6171.

CLERGY, PARISHES, MISSIONS AND PAROCHIAL SCHOOLS

CITY OF CORPUS CHRISTI
(Nueces County)

1—CORPUS CHRISTI CATHEDRAL (1912), Rev. Msgr. Leonard Pivonka, J.C.D., Rector; Rev. John C. Ouellette; Deacons Michael Mantz; Bruce Aycock.
Res., 505 N. Upper Broadway, 78401. Tel: 512-883-4213; Fax: 512-883-1918. [CEM]
Catechesis/Religious Programs—Tel: 512-883-4213; Fax: 512-883-1918.
Students 150.
Chapels—Emmanuel; Blessed Sacrament; Perpetual Eucharistic Adoration.

2—CHRIST THE KING (1946) (Mexican), Rev. Bernard Mlapah, O.SS.T.; Deacon Antonio Castillo.
Res., 3423 Rojo, 78415. Tel: 512-883-2821; Fax: 512-883-3448.
Catechesis/Religious Programs—Tel: 512-883-1404. Carol A. Enloe, D.R.E.
Students 250.
Convent—1625 Arlington, 78415. Tel: 512-883-0212.

3—HOLY CROSS (1914) (African American), Rev. Msgr. Patrick Higgins.
Res., 1109 N. Staples St., 78401. Tel: 512-888-4012; Fax: 512-888-5338.

4—HOLY FAMILY (1946), Revs. James Janecek, Pastor; Jesus Francisco Lopez; Deacon Alex Carrizales.
Res., 2509 Nogales St., 78416. Tel: 512-882-3245; Fax: 512-882-4968.
Catechesis/Religious Programs—512-882-3245. Tel: 512-882-4968.
Students 250.
Convent—1723 Frio St., 78417. Tel: 512-884-9142.
Sisters of Mercy of the Blessed Sacrament 5.
Mission—Corpus Christi, Nueces, Mary, Mother of the Church, 1755 Frio St., 78417.

5—MOST PRECIOUS BLOOD (1966), Rev. Msgr. William Thompson; Rev. Bradley A. M. Barber.
Res., 3502 Saratoga Blvd., 78415. Tel: 512-854-3800; Fax: 512-854-9253.
Catechesis/Religious Programs—Tel: 512-854-9219. Sr. Margaret Hesse, D.R.E.
Students 484.

6—OUR LADY OF GUADALUPE (1969) (Hispanic), Rev. Eduardo H. Garcia; Deacon Armando Botello.
Res., 540 Hiawatha, 78405. Tel: 512-882-1951; Fax: 521-888-5813.
Catechesis/Religious Programs—Estela Almeida, D.R.E.
Students 245.
Convent—541 Virginia St., 78405.

7—OUR LADY OF THE ROSARY (1967) (Hispanic), Deacon Homer T. Martinez, Jr., Admin.
Res., 1123 Main Dr., 78409. Tel: 512-241-2004; Fax: 512-242-1099.
Catechesis/Religious Programs—Students 110.
Missions—Petronila, Nueces Co., St. Vivian, FM 665, Petronila, 78415; Corpus Christi, Nueces Co., Our Lady of Mount Carmel, 1080 S. Clarkwood, 78406. Tel: 512-265-9109.

8—OUR LADY OF PERPETUAL HELP (1954), Rev. Msgr. Michael Heras, Pastor. In res., Rev. David Walsh.
Res., 5830 Williams Dr., 78412-4415. Tel: 512-991-7891; Fax: 512-993-1211.
Catechesis/Religious Programs—Tel: 512-991-3261.
Students 430.

9—OUR LADY OF THE PILLAR (1964), Rev. Marcos Martinez; Deacon Armando Bolanos.
Res., 1101 Bloomington St., 78416. Tel: 512-852-6327; Fax: 512-852-2614.
Catechesis/Religious Programs—Tel: 512-852-6843.
Students 500.

10—OUR LADY STAR OF THE SEA (1950), Rev. Vincent M. Patrizi.
Res., 3110 E. Causeway Blvd., P.O. Box 1899, 78403. Tel: 512-883-4507; Fax: 512-888-6411.
Catechesis/Religious Programs—Students 60.

11—SACRED HEART (1936) (Hispanic), Rev. Jose M. Gutierrez.
Res., 422 N. Alameda, 78401. Tel: 512-883-6082; Fax: 512-883-6248. [CEM]
Catechesis/Religious Programs—Students 49.
Stations—Nueces County Jail; Navarro Place.

12—SAINT ANDREW BY THE SEA PARISH (1986), Rev. Richard Filice.
Res., 14238 Encantada Ave., Padre Island, 78418-6432. Tel: 512-949-7193; Fax: 512-949-0717.

13—ST. ANSELM ANGLICAN USE COMMUNITY (1992), Rev. W.T. St. John Brown, Chap.
Res., 3036 Saratoga Blvd., 78415-5715. Tel: 512-854-3688; Fax: 512-852-8965.

14—SS. CYRIL AND METHODIUS (1947), Revs. Lawrence E. White; Robert DeCock, I.S.S.S.; Deacon Ron Dubuque.
Res., 3210 S. Padre Island Dr., 78415. Tel: 512-853-7371; Fax: 512-851-1438.
Catechesis/Religious Programs—Tel: 512-852-1651. Mona Lucido, D.R.E.
Students 600.

15—ST. JOSEPH (1952), Revs. David Tonary, M.S.F.; Joseph Lawless, M.S.F.; Deacon Pedro Ybarra; Bro. Rolland Kapsner, M.S.F.
Res., 710 S. 19th St., P.O. Box 5196, 78465-5196. Tel: 512-882-7912; Fax: 512-882-6853.
Catechesis/Religious Programs—Elizabeth Contreras, D.R.E.
Students 130.
Convent—2100 Morris St., 78405. Tel: 512-884-4027.
Sisters 2.

16—ST. MICHAEL THE ARCHANGEL LATIN MASS COMMUNITY (1995),
Res., 2233 Waldron Rd, 78418-4699. Tel: 512-937-3864; Fax: 512-939-7774. Rev. Carlos S. Casavantes, F.S.P.

17—ST. PATRICK (1944), Rev. Msgr. Robert E. Freeman; Revs. Glen Mullan; Manuel Hernandez, Jr.; Deacon W. Oliver.
Res., 3350 S. Alameda St., 78411. Tel: 512-855-7391; Fax: 512-855-7552.
Catechesis/Religious Programs—Tel: 512-855-7567.
Students 265.

18—ST. PAUL THE APOSTLE (1967), Rev. Bruno Mikolajczyk. In res., Rev. Carlos Casavantes, F.S.P.
Res., 2233 Waldron Rd., 78418. Tel: 512-937-3864; Fax: 512-939-7774.
Catechesis/Religious Programs—Tel: 512-937-6908. Sr. M. Purificion Palis, O.P., D.R.E.
Students 300.

19—ST. PETER PRINCE OF APOSTLES (1967), Rev. Morgan Rowsome.
Res. & Mailing Address—3901 Violet Rd., 78410. Tel: 512-241-3249; Fax: 512-241-0533.
Catechesis/Religious Programs—Tel: 512-241-3372; Fax: 512-241-0533. Marian Tajchman, D.R.E.
Students 559.
Mission—Corpus Christi, Nueces Co., St. Mary, 4849 Cynthia, 78410. Tel: 512-241-3432.

20—ST. PHILIP THE APOSTLE (1982), Rev. Msgr. Thomas P. McGettrick; Deacons Roy Grassedonio; Garland Frazier; Stacy Millsap.
Res., 6333 N. Washam St., 78414. Tel: 512-993-9474.
Church—3513 Cimarron Rd., 78414. Tel: 512-991-5146; Fax: 512-991-9135.
Catechesis/Religious Programs—Tel: 512-993-1710.
Students 371.

21—ST. PIUS X (1963), Rev. Msgr. Richard Shirley; Rev. Jerome Zurovetz; Deacon Michael DeShetler.
Res., 5620 Gollihar Rd., 78412. Tel: 512-993-4053; Fax: 512-992-0352.
Catechesis/Religious Programs—Tel: 512-993-9024.
Students 235.

22—ST. THERESA (1947), Rev. Mark Chamberlin. In res., Rev. Msgr. Raymond F. Rau (BRK).
Res., 1302 Lantana St., 78407. Tel: 512-289-2759.
Catechesis/Religious Programs—Tel: 512-289-2238. Mrs. Josie Martinez, D.R.E.
Students 150.
Convent—1253 Lantana St., 78407. Tel: 512-289-5534.

23—COLLEGIATE PARISH OF ST. THOMAS MORE (1990), Rev. Hanh Van Pham.
Church—2045 18th St., 78404-3862. Tel: 512-888-9308; Fax: 512-888-6119.

OUTSIDE THE CITY OF CORPUS CHRISTI

Agua Dulce, Nueces Co., St. Frances of Rome (1934), Rev. James A. Hayes, M.S.C.
Mailing Address: P.O. Box 598, 78330. Tel: 512-998-2216.
Catechesis/Religious Programs—Mrs. Doretta McDonough, D.R.E.
Students 135.
Mission—Banquete, Nueces Co., St. Michael, Banquete, 78339. Tel: 512-998-2216.
Catechesis/Religious Programs—Otelia Pena, D.R.E.
Students 195.

Alice, Jim Wells Co., Our Lady of Guadalupe (1969), Rev. Thomas L. Goodwin.
Res., 1318 Guerra St., P.O. Box 411, 78332. Tel: 512-664-2953; Fax: 512-664-4001.
Catechesis/Religious Programs—Tel: 512-664-2957. D.R.E.: Rosaura Garcia; Delicia Rodriguez; Dora Rosales.
Students 327.
Convent—Tel: 512-664-0437. Carmelite Sisters
Mission—Alice, Jim Wells Co., Santo Nino De Atocha, Rte. 3 Box 273, 78332. Tel: 512-664-2953.

St. Elizabeth (1918), Rev. Stanley A. Sliwiak, Ph.D.; Deacons James A. Carlisle; Alan K. Borse.
Res., 518 N. Almond St., P.O. Box 1009, 78333. Tel: 512-664-6481; Fax: 512-664-7243.
Catechesis/Religious Programs—Tel: 512-664-7719.
Students 244.
Convent—603 E. 5th St., 78332.
Mission—Ben Bolt, St. Peter's Church, P.O. Box 1009, 78333.

St. Joseph (1911) (Hispanic), Revs. Francisco X. Martinez; James E. Janecek; Deacons Jose A. Vitela; Mario Rivera.
Res., 801 S. Reynolds St., P.O. Box 2026, 78333. Tel: 512-664-7551; Fax: 512-664-2388.
Catechesis/Religious Programs—Tel: 512-664-5625.
Students 630.
Convent—311 Dewey St., P.O. Box 157, 78332. Tel: 512-664-6283.
Sisters 5.
Mission—Alice, Jim Wells Co., Sacred Heart, 110 S. Texas, 78332. Tel: 512-664-6225.
Chapel—Perpetual Eucharistic Adoration.

Aransas Pass, San Patricio Co., St. Mary, Star of the Sea (1948), Rev. Charles Doherty. In res., Rev. James Hamilton.
Res., 342 S. Rife St., 78336. Tel: 512-758-2662.
Catechesis/Religious Programs—Ginny Vega, D.R.E.
Students 278.

Beeville, Bee Co.,

1—OUR LADY OF VICTORY, (1908), Revs. Joseph R. Audet, M.S.F.; Simon Brzozowski, M.S.F. In res., Rev. Edward Zaborowski.
Res., 403 W. Carter St., 78102. Tel: 512-358-3761; Fax: 512-358-2028. [CEM 2][JC]
Catechesis/Religious Programs—Tel: 512-358-3518. Sr. Encarnacion D.R.E.
Students 80.
Convent—707 N. Avenue E, 78102. Tel: 512-358-3518.
Sisters 5.

2—SACRED HEART MISSION, (1966) (Hispanic). (Independent). Rev. Simmon P. Brzozowski, M.S.F.
403 W. Carter St., 78102. Tel: 512-375-2973; 375-2512 (Church); Fax: 512-358-2028.
Catechesis/Religious Programs—Guadalupe Aguirre, D.R.E.
Students 3.

3—ST. JAMES, (Alta Vista) (1966) (Hispanic), Revs.

Eugene T. Ronan, M.S.F., Pastor; Edward Zaborowski, M.S.F.; Deacon Juan Vasquez.
Res., 605 Alta Vista, 78102. Tel: 512-358-4825; Fax: 512-358-5150.
Catechesis/Religious Programs—Miss Mary Elizabeth Garcia, D.R.E.
Students 170.

4—St. Joseph, (Alta Vista) (1891), Rev. Michael A. DeLeon, O.S.B.
Res., 609 E. Gramman St., 78102. Tel: 512-358-3239; Fax: 512-358-4270. [CEM]
Catechesis/Religious Programs—Robin Pate, D.R.E.
Students 150.
Convent—610 E. Gramman St., 78102. Tel: 512-358-5089; 358-9405.
Sisters 6.

Benavides, Duval Co., St. Rose of Lima (1941) (Hispanic), Rev. Epifanio Rodriguez, O.P.
Res., Hackberry St., P.O. Drawer W, 78341. Tel: 512-256-3427.
Catechesis/Religious Programs—Tel: 512-256-3319. Gracie Garcia, D.R.E.
Students 177.
Mission—San Jose Ranch, Duval Co., St. Joseph, P.O. Box W, 78341.

Bishop, Nueces Co., St. James (1938), Rev. Patrick O'Connor, M.S.C.
Res., 601 W. 3rd St., P.O. Box 843, 78343. Tel: 512-584-3250. [CEM]
Catechesis/Religious Programs—Students 228.
Mission—Driscoll, Nueces Co., St. James.

Encinal, La Salle Co., Immaculate Heart of Mary, Rev. Alejandro Salazar.
Mailing Address: P.O. Box 275, 400 Santa Fe St., 78019. Tel: 210-948-5328. [JC]
Catechesis/Religious Programs—Students 55.

Falfurrias, Brooks Co., Sacred Heart (1914), Rev. Matthew J. Stephan.
Res., 304 S. Caldwell St., 78355. Tel: 512-325-3455; Fax: 512-325-2486.
Catechesis/Religious Programs—Tel: 512-325-5067.
Students 640.
Mission—Encino, Brooks Co., St. Ann. c/o Sacred Heart Parish 78355.

Freer, Duval Co., St. Mary (1968), Rev. Gregory A. Boensch.
Res., 1500 Duval St., Box B, 78357. Tel: 512-394-6832.
Catechesis/Religious Programs—Tel: 512-394-7188. D.R.E.: Mrs. A. Bitoni; Mr. Teeka Mendiola.
Students 251.

George West, Live Oak Co., St. George (1924), Rev. John P. Killeen.
Oratory—George West, Live Oak Co., Crockett St., P.O. Box 580, 78022. Tel: 512-449-1893; Fax: 512-449-1886. [CEM][JC]
Catechesis/Religious Programs—Tel: 512-449-2137. D.R.E.: Rev. John P. Killeen; Debbie Brown; Noreen Brown.
Students 250.
Mission—Gussetville, St. Joseph, Tel: 512-449-1893. [CEM][JC]

Gregory, San Patricio Co., Immaculate Conception (1926) (Hispanic), Rev. Robert Dunn.
Res., 107 Church St., P.O. Box 108, 78359-0108. Tel: 512-643-4505; Fax: 512-643-1509.
Catechesis/Religious Programs—Sr. Therese Cunnigham, S.H.Sp., D.R.E.
Students 372.

Hebbronville, Jim Hogg Co., Our Lady of Guadalupe (1926) (Hispanic), Revs. Adalberto Rameriz, O.F.M.; Eduardo Jayme, O.F.M.; Bro. Armando Martinez, O.F.M.
Res., 504 E. Santa Clara St., 78361. Tel: 512-527-3865; Fax: 512-527-5548. [CEM 2]
School—502 E. North St., 78361. Tel: 512-527-3611.
Little Flower Day Care Center—Tel: 512-527-3515. Mrs. Mary Garza, Prin.
Lay Teachers 3; Students 35.
Catechesis/Religious Programs—Chala Garcia, D.R.E., Tel: 512-527-4281.
Students 230.
Missions—Hebbronville, Jim Hogg Co., Immaculate Conception; Mirando City, Webb Co., St. Agnes; Oilton, Webb Co., St. Bridget; Bruni, Webb Co., Sacred Heart; Realitos, Duval Co., Sacred Heart.

Ingleside, San Patricio Co., Our Lady of the Assumption (1970), Rev. Thomas Wellar.
Res., 2414 Main, 78362. Tel: 512-776-2644; Fax: 512-776-2446.
Catechesis/Religious Programs—Faith Repka, D.R.E.
Students 160.
Our Lady of the Assumption Early Learning Center—Tel: 512-776-3643.

Kingsville, Kleberg Co.,

1—Our Lady of Good Counsel, (1967) (Mexican), Rev. Michael Lenihan.
Res., 1102 E. Kleberg, 78363. Tel: 512-592-3489.
Catechesis/Religious Programs—Tel: 512-592-9546. Amparo Quintanilla, D.R.E.
Students 103.

2—St. Gertrude, (1908), Rev. Roger Smith.
Res., 1120 S. 8th St., 78363. Tel: 512-592-7351; Fax: 512-592-0028.
School—(Grades K4-6). Tel: 512-592-6522; Fax: 512-592-6591.
Students 210.
Catechesis/Religious Programs—Tel: 512-595-0974. D.R.E.: Sr. Emma Marie Stillman, I.W.B.S.; Sr. Therese Ann Ridge, I.W.B.S.
Students 394.
Convent—400 E. Caesar Ave., 78363. Tel: 512-592-2443.
Sisters 2.
Missions—Ricardo, Kleberg Co., Sacred Heart, W. County Rd. 2160, Ricardo, 78363; Kingsville, Kleberg Co., Christ the King, King Ranch, 78363.

3—St. Joseph, (1973), Rev. Richard Philion, O.M.I.
Res., 1400 Brookshire, P.O. Box 1602, 78364-1602. Tel: 512-592-5689.
Catechesis/Religious Programs—Tel: 512-592-5689. Rosalinda Vidal, D.R.E.
Students 200.

4—St. Martin, (1914), Rev. James Foelker, O.M.I.; Deacons Tiburcio Garcia; Raul G. Rosales.
Res., 715 N. Eighth St., 78363. Tel: 512-592-4602; Fax: 512-592-4602.
Catechesis/Religious Programs—Tel: 512-592-0881. Gloria DeLeon, D.R.E.
Students 142.
Convent—919 N. Ninth St., 78363. Tel: 512-595-1087.
Sisters 7.

5—Collegiate Parish of St. Thomas Aquinas, (1990), Rev. Roger Smith.
Mailing Address: 1120 S. 8th, 78363. Tel: 512-592-5781.
Res., 614 Retama St., 78363. Fax: 512-592-8617. [CEM]
Church—1119 W. Santa Gertrudis, 78363. Tel: 512-592-7351.

Laredo, Webb Co.,

1—Blessed Sacrament, (1950), Rev. Pedro Nolasco Hinojosa, Jr., Pastoral Assoc.
Res., 2219 Galveston St., 78043. Tel: 210-722-1295; 722-1231; Fax: 210-722-2823.
Catechesis/Religious Programs—Tel: 512-725-7045. Eva Escamilla, D.R.E.
Students 220.

2—Christ the King, (1954), Rev. James Harris; Deacon Guillermo De La Garza.
Res., 1105 Tilden Ave., 78040. Tel: 210-723-4267; Fax: 210-791-8034. [JC]
School—Tel: 210-722-7821. Mrs. Mary Martinez, Prin.
Lay Teachers 4.
Catechesis/Religious Programs—Mr. Ricardo A. Ramon, Jr., D.R.E.
Students 223.

3—Holy Family, (1984) (Hispanic), Rev. Alejandro Salazar.
Res., 2705 McPherson, P.O. Box 1603, 78044. Tel: 210-724-6881.
Catechesis/Religious Programs—Students 128.

4—Holy Redeemer, (1940) (Hispanic), Revs. Jose Romero, O.S.A.; Ruben Zamudio, O.S.A.
Res., 1602 Garcia St., P.O. Box 1087, 78042. Tel: 210-723-7171; Fax: 210-723-7194. [CEM][JC]
Catechesis/Religious Programs—D.R.E.: Sonia Rendon; Josefina Garza.
Students 194.
Mission—Laredo, Webb Co., Santa Cruz, 2002 Lee Ave., 78040.

5—Our Lady of Guadalupe, (1910), Revs. Edward Ward, O.M.I.; Edward Vrazel.
Res., 1718 San Jorge Ave., P.O. Box 671, 78042. Tel: 210-723-6954; Fax: 210-723-6047.
Catechesis/Religious Programs—Olga Juarez, D.R.E.
Students 241.

6—San Augustine, (1879) (Mexican), Revs. Thomas Davis; Silvestre Rodriguez, O.F.M.
Res., 214 San Bernardo Ave., 78040. Tel: 210-722-1382; Fax: 210-722-5599. [JC]
Catechesis/Religious Programs—Maria Elena Requejo, D.R.E.
Students 122.
Missions—Musquiz, Coahuila Co., Desert Apostolate Mission. (Mexico) 214 San Bernardo Ave., 78040; Laredo, Webb Co., Santo Nino Mission, 2720 Ireland, 78043. Tel: 210-724-6638. Rev. Vladimiro Manente, O.M.I.; Laredo, Webb Co., San Francisco Javier, 2502 Zargoza St., P.O. Box 1175, 78040. Tel: 210-723-3850.

7—San Luis Rey, (1958), Revs. Joseph A. Farias, S.D.B.; Thomas Juarez, S.D.B.
Res., 3502 Sanders Ave., P.O. Box 2294, 78041. Tel: 210-723-6587; Fax: 210-723-6825.
Catechesis/Religious Programs—Tel: 210-722-3323. Mary Ann Gamez, D.R.E.
Students 507.

8—Santa Margarita De Escocia Independent Mission, Rev. Francis Stodola, Admin.; Deacon Leonel San Miguel.
Res., 320 Segovia Dr., 78046. Tel: 210-724-9669.

9—San Martin De Porres, (1979), Revs. Domingo de Llano; Angel Vizcarra, O.P.
Res., 1704 Sandman, P.O. Box 2666, 78044-2666. Tel: 210-723-5215; Fax: 210-723-9443.
Catechesis/Religious Programs—Tel: 210-725-2440. Laura Leyendecker, D.R.E.
Students 525.

10—Santa Rita De Casia Independent Mission, Rev. Mariano Martinez.
Res., 1001 Espejo Molina, 78043. Tel: 210-725-7215.

11—St. Frances Cabrini, (1958), Rev. Alessandro DiTaddeo.
Res., 3018 Davis Ave., 78040. Tel: 210-722-2919; Fax: 210-791-5453.
Catechesis/Religious Programs—Tel: 210-722-8315. Agustina Bustos, D.R.E.
Students 259.

12—St. John Neumann, (1979), Rev. Randy Cain.
Res., 5408 Gallagher, 78041. Tel: 210-726-9488; Fax: 210-726-0540.
Catechesis/Religious Programs—Cynthia Barreda, D.R.E.
Students 245.

13—St. Joseph, (1953), Rev. Jesus M. Madariaga, O.P., Admin.; Deacons Salvador Madrigal; Crispin O. Soto.
Res., 109 N. Meadow St., 78040. Tel: 210-723-4172.
Catechesis/Religious Programs—Mrs. Yolanda Molina, D.R.E.
Students 232.

14—St. Jude, Rev. Santiago Domingo.
Res., 2031 Lowry Rd., 78045. Tel: 210-722-2280; Fax: 210-726-8017.
Rectory—101 Biscayne Loop, 78045. Tel: 210-726-6318.
Catechesis/Religious Programs—Students 304.

15—St. Patrick, (1970) (Irish), Rev. Thomas A. Davis.
Res., 555 E. Del Mar Blvd., 78041. Tel: 210-722-6215; Fax: 210-722-6266. [CEM]
Catechesis/Religious Programs—Tel: 210-722-8451; Fax: 210-722-6266.
Students 500.

16—St. Peter the Apostle, (1897), Rev. Donald E. Critchlow.
Res., 1510 Matamoros St., P.O. Box 26, 78042. Tel: 210-723-6301; Fax: 210-723-6301.
Catechesis/Religious Programs—Students 210.

17—St. Vincent de Paul, (1969) (Hispanic), Revs. Roberto Vargas, O.S.A. (Mexico); Alberto Palmeno, O.S.A. (Mexico).
Res., 1119 S. Louisiana St., 78043. Tel: 210-722-3034; Fax: 210-722-4829.
Catechesis/Religious Programs—Tel: 210-726-4134. Graciela Ramirez, D.R.E.
Students 450.

Mathis, San Patricio Co., Sacred Heart (1942), Rev. Jose Angel Salazar.
Res., 114 S. Aransas, P.O. Box 608, 78368-0608. Tel: 512-547-9181; Fax: 512-547-6111. [JC]
Catechesis/Religious Programs—Rosie Aguilar, D.R.E.
Students 220.
Mission—San Patricio, San Patricio Co., St. Patrick, Tel: 512-547-5748.

Odem, San Patricio Co., Sacred Heart (1919), Rev. Paul A Hesse, Admin.
Res., 401 Willis St., P.O. Box 276, 78370. Tel: 512-368-9156; Fax: 512-368-2247.
Catechesis/Religious Programs—Tel: 512-368-2746. D.R.E.: Sr. Arellano R. Soledad, C.M.S.T.; Juan Orta, (Elementary); Manuela Cantu; Robert Mancias, (High School); Marina Rodriguez, (Junior High).
Students 296.
Convent—402 Borden, 78370. Tel: 512-368-2560.
Sisters 4.
Mission—Edroy, San Patricio Co., Our Lady of Guadalupe, P4D W. 5th, #N1, Edroy, 78352. Tel: 512-368-9156.

Orange Grove, Jim Wells Co., St. John of the Cross (1925), Rev. Brendan Ashe (Ireland).
Mailing Address: P.O. Box 329, 78372. Tel: 512-384-2795; Fax: 512-384-2795. [CEM]
Catechesis/Religious Programs—Tel: 512-384-2246.
Students 255.
Mission—Orange Grove, Jim Wells, St. Pius X, P.O. Box 329, 78372. Tel: 512-384-2795.

Port Aransas, Nueces Co., St. Joseph (1860), Rev. Gregory S. Deane.
Mailing Address: 412 Lantana St., 78373. Tel: 512-749-5825; Fax: 512-749-5509.

Portland, San Patricio Co., Our Lady of Mount Carmel (1961), Rev. John Vega; Deacon John W. Sutherland.
Res., 1008 Austin St., 78374. Tel: 512-643-7533; Fax: 512-643-5544.
Catechesis/Religious Programs—Tel: 512-643-3548. Sr. Lourdes Untalan, O.P., D.R.E.
Students 450.

Premont, Jim Wells Co., St. Theresa of the Infant Jesus (1958), Rev. Jose A. Almazan, C.M. (Spain); Deacon Raul Hinojosa.
Res., 235 S.W. 4th St., P.O. Box 569, 78375. Tel: 512-348-2202; Fax: 512-348-2137.
Catechesis/Religious Programs—Tel: 512-348-3955. Laura Howell, D.R.E.
Students 298.
Missions—Concepcion, Duval Co., Immaculate Conception, 78375; Rios, Duval Co., St. Francis of Assisi, 78375; Ramirez, Duval Co., Our Lady of Guadalupe, 78375.

Refugio, Refugio Co., Our Lady of Refuge (1795), Rev. Thomas Feeney.
Res., 1008 S. Alamo St., 78377. Tel: 512-526-2083; Fax: 512-526-5653. [CEM][JC]
Catechesis/Religious Programs—106 W. Roca, 78377. Tel: 512-526-2053.
Students 233.
Mission—Blanconia, Bee Co., St. Catherine, 1008 S. Alamo, 78377.

St. James the Apostle (1886) (Hispanic), Rev. Thomas P. Feeney.
Res., 205 E. Santiago St., P.O. Box 326, 78377-0326. Tel: 512-526-2252; Fax: 512-526-5379. [CEM][JC]
Catechesis/Religious Programs—Tel: 512-526-2714.
Students 127.

Robstown, Nueces Co., St. Anthony (1914), Revs. Vincent Albano, S.O.L.T.; James Flanagan, S.O.L.T.; Robert Rank, S.O.L.T.; Isidore Usit Nyein, S.O.L.T.; Anthony Anderson, S.O.L.T.; Robert Copsey, S.O.L.T.; Paul Grala, S.O.L.T.; Alfredo Gaytan, S.O.L.T.
Res., 204 Dunne St., P.O. Box 792, 78380. Tel: 512-387-2774; Fax: 512-387-5114. [CEM]
Catechesis/Religious Programs—Tel: 512-387-9874. Eva Hernandez, D.R.E.
Students 395.
Convent—612 Indiana, 78380. Tel: 512-387-3810.

St. John Nepomucene, Rev. Joseph O'Connell, S.O.L.T.
Res., 603 N. First St., 78380. Tel: 512-387-3705; Fax: 512-387-3681.
Catechesis/Religious Programs—Joann Charba, D.R.E.
Students 127.

St. Thomas the Apostle (1980), Rev. Matthew Lyng.
Office: Rte. 1, Box 67-S, 78380. Tel: 512-387-1312; Fax: 512-387-9311.
Catechesis/Religious Programs—Shirley Syamken, D.R.E.
Students 230.

Rockport, Aransas Co., Sacred Heart (1838), Rev. Msgr. Louis F. Kihneman; Deacons Ciprian Martinez; Jerre Ledbetter; George Wiest.
Res., 704 Cornwall St., 78382. Tel: 512-729-2174; Fax: 512-729-1989.
Catechesis/Religious Programs—Tel: 512-729-8283.
Students 225.
Convent—114 N. Church St., 78382. Tel: 512-729-5311.
Sisters 2.

St. Peter Indo-Chinese Parish (1989) (Vietnamese), Rev. Peter Phan Van Nguyen, C.S.S.R. In res., Rev. Quang Dang Nguyen, (Retired).
Mailing Address: P.O. Box 1060, 78382. Tel: 512-729-3008.

San Diego, Duval Co., St. Francis de Paula (1866) (Mexican), Revs. Benito Retortillo, O.P.; Juan Suarez, O.P.
Res., Victoria & St. Peter St., P.O. Box 279, 78384. Tel: 512-279-3596; Fax: 512-279-8288.
Catechesis/Religious Programs—411 S. Victoria St., 78384. Tel: 512-279-3586.
Students 540.
Missions—La Rosita, Duval Co., Holy Cross; Palito Blanco, Jim Wells Co., St. Joseph.

Sarita, Kenedy Co., Our Lady of Guadalupe (1935), Rev. Angel Villalba, O.M.I.
Mailing Address: P.O. Box 6, 78385. Tel: 512-294-5350; Fax: 512-294-5350.
Mission—Norias Ranch, Santa Elena.

Sinton, San Patricio Co., Our Lady of Guadalupe (1954) (Hispanic), Rev. David Taurasi, Pastor.
Res., 725 Sodville Ave., 78387. Tel: 512-364-2210; Fax: 512-364-5818. [JC]
Catechesis/Religious Programs—Tel: 512-364-4542.
Students 378.

Sacred Heart (1918), Rev. Seamus J. McGowan.
Res., 906 E. Sinton St., P.O. Box 266, 78387. Tel: 512-364-1768; Fax: 512-364-5325. [JC 3]
Catechesis/Religious Programs—Tel: 512-364-1772. D.R.E.: Mary Connors; Marilyn Knox.
Students 163.
Mission—St. Paul, St. Paul, 78387.

Skidmore, Bee Co., Immaculate Conception (1915), Rev. James R. Kelleher, S.O.L.T.
Res., 600 First St., P.O. Box 189, 78389. Tel: 512-287-3256.
Catechesis/Religious Programs—Students 115.
Convent—Tel: 512-287-3830.
Sisters 4.
Mission—Tynan, Bee Co., St. Francis Xavier, 78384.

Taft, San Patricio Co., Holy Family (1957), Rev. Patrick K. Donohoe.
Mailing Address: P.O. Box 868, 78390-0868.
Res., 646 McIntyre, 78390-2904. Tel: 512-528-3132; Fax: 512-528-3907.
Catechesis/Religious Programs—Students 67.

Immaculate Conception (1928), Rev. Patrick K. Donohoe; Deacon Alonzo T. Rodriguez.
Mailing Address: P.O. Box 868, 78390. Tel: 512-528-2626; Fax: 512-528-3907.
Res., 120 E. Escobedo St., 78390. Tel: 512-528-2626; Fax: 512-528-3907.
Catechesis/Religious Programs—Tel: 512-528-5300.
Students 532.

Three Rivers, Live Oak Co., Sacred Heart (1948), Rev. Zanon Konowalek.
300 Alexander, P.O. Box 729, 78071-0729. Tel: 512-786-3398.
Mission—Pawnee, Bee Co., Our Lady of Guadalupe, P.O. Box 729, 78071. Tel: 512-786-3398.

Tivoli, Refugio Co., Our Lady of Guadalupe (1936), Rev. John J. Feminelli.
Mailing Address: P.O. Box I, 77990. Tel: 512-286-3349; Fax: 512-286-3665.
Catechesis/Religious Programs—Joyce Lenhart, D.R.E.
Students 85.
Missions—Austwell, Refugio Co., St. Anthony of Padua, Drawer 1, 77990-0250; O'Connor Ranch, Refugio Co., St. Dennis, 77990-0250.

Vattman, Kleberg Co., Our Lady of Consolation (1914), Rev. Wojciech Kosowicz.
Res., Rte. 1, Box 21, 78379. Tel: 512-297-5255; Fax: 512-297-5578. [CEM]
Catechesis/Religious Programs—Students 52.
Mission—Riviera, Kleberg Co., Our Lady of Guadalupe, 78379.

Violet, Nueces Co., St. Anthony (1910), Rev. Aidan J. Leddy.
Res., Rte. 3, P.O. Box 134, Robstown, 78380. Tel: 512-387-4434; Fax: 512-387-4434. [CEM]
Catechesis/Religious Programs—Students 36.

Woodsboro, Refugio Co., St. Therese, The Little Flower (1915), Rev. Celestine Murray.
Res., 315 Pugh St., Drawer 1076, 78393-1140. Tel: 512-543-4166; Fax: 512-543-5922. [CEM]
Catechesis/Religious Programs—Students 125.
Mission—Bayside, Refugio Co., St. Mary, 78393.

Zapata, Zapata Co., Our Lady of Lourdes (1940) (Mexican), Rev. Peter J. McNamara.
Res., Hidalgo & 17th Ave., P.O. Box 3213, 78076. Tel: 210-765-4216; Fax: 210-765-6188. [JC 2]
Catechesis/Religious Programs—Tel: 210-765-6711.
Students 710.
Missions—San Ignacio, Zapata Co., St. Ignatius, 78076; Lopeno, Zapata Co., San Pedro, 78076; Falcon, Zapata Co., Santa Ana, 78076.

On Special Assignment:
Reverend Monsignors—
Flores, Daniel, Episcopal Vicar for Priestly Vocations & Education, 3036 Saratoga, Corpus Christi, TX 78415. Tel: 512-851-0908
Meany, Thomas, Chancery Office, 620 Lipan, P.O. Box 2620, Corpus Christi, TX 78403-2620
Reverend Fathers—
Feminelli, John, Our Lady of Guadalupe Parish, P.O. Drawer 1, Tivoli, TX 77990
Gutierrez, Jose, Chap., Spohn Hospital
Hamilton, James, St. Mary Star of the Sea, 342 S. Rife, Aransas Pass, TX 78336
Kenna, John Thomas, Mount Carmel Home, 4130 S. Alameda, Corpus Christi, TX 78411
Nguyen, Liep Van Joseph, Chap., Shoenstatt Retreat House, HCO, Box 101, Rockport, TX 78382
O'Donovan, Thomas, Mercy Hospital, P.O. Drawer 2068, Laredo, TX 78041
Ramirez, Hernando, S.J., Mercy Regional Hospital, 1515 Logan, Laredo, TX 78041
Rodriguez, Antonio, I.S.S.S., 4343 Gains, Corpus Christi, TX 78412
Stembler, James, Sec. to the Bishop
Vega, Hector, I.S.S.S., 4343 Gaines, Corpus Christi, TX 78412
Vizcarra, Angel, O.P., Broadcast Ministry Catholic Radio Network
Walsh, David, C.SS.R., Dir., Office of Persons with Disabilities

---

On Duty Outside the Diocese:
Reverend Fathers—
Bauta, Krzysztof T.
Bergin, Pascal
Howell, Michael, St. Mary's Seminary, 9845 Memorial Dr., Houston, TX 77024
Martinez, Benjamin
Masin, Richard H., Russia
Masterson, Clyde
McGerity, Francis X., 26 Fairbanks St., Brighton, MA 02135
Mercer, Timmothy
Walsh, Arthur
Wojtaszczyk, John

Military Chaplains:
Reverend Fathers—
Chilen, Michael D., LTC, P.O. Box 4173, Fort Polk, LA 71459
Kinast, Timothy, Cpt., Guantanamo Bay, Cuba
Shuley, Keith
Williams, Gary, Lt., Corpus Christi Naval Air Station, Bldg. 5, Corpus Christi, TX 78419

Retired:
Reverend Monsignors—
Adams, Michael, Mount Carmel Home, 4130 S. Alameda, Corpus Christi, TX 78411
Brasley, Lucian R., 9140 Timber Path, No. 2303, San Antonio, TX 78250
Clark, Robert, Villa Maria Apartments, 3146 Saratoga Blvd., Box 18, Corpus Christi, TX 78415
Clarke, Hugh, Coneyburro Rd., Lifford, Co. Donegal, Ireland
Kinlough, William C., St. Mary, P.O. Box 866, Lampasas, TX 76550
Tengler, Alvin, 1011 7th St., Corpus Christi, TX 78404
Reverend Fathers—
Arguelles, Antonio G., 3404 South Texas Ave., Laredo, TX 78043
Berger, Joseph, S.L.T., Trinity Towers, 101 N. Upper Broadway, Apt. 408, Corpus Christi, TX 78401
Bradley, Robert, Villa Maria Apartments, 3146 Saratoga Blvd., Box 45, Corpus Christi, TX 78415. Tel: 512-855-3767
Burke, Michael, St. Francis of Assisi, P.O. Box 878, Mount Kisco, NY 10549. Tel: 914-666-5986
DeAngelis, William, O.S.B., Villa Maria Apartments, 3146 Saratoga Blvd., Box 20, Corpus Christi, TX 78415
Fidalgo, Federico, 8326 N. Vandiver, #508, San Antonio, TX 78209
Iglesias, Luis Fernando, Mieres-Urbies (33613), Asturias, Spain
Joseph, Louis, 4334 Ocean Dr., Corpus Christi, TX 78412. Tel: 512-814-3007
Kircher, Edward, 310 East Ward St., Refugio, TX 78377
Nguyen, Quang Dang, P.O. Box 916, Fulton, TX 78358
Noone, Sean, Villa Maria Apartments, 3146 Saratoga Blvd., Box 12, Corpus Christi, TX 78415. Tel: 512-853-4814
Vidiella, Felix, 5702 Santa Clara, Santa Clara Estates, Robstown, TX 78380
Zagari, Joseph

Permanent Deacons:
Aycock, J. Bruce, Corpus Christi Cathedral, Corpus Christi
Barbour, Tony R., St. Thomas Aquinas Collegiate Parish, Kingsville
Bernal, Anastacio, Our Lady of Guadalupe, Laredo
Bolanos, Armando M., Our Lady of Pillar, Corpus Christi
Borse, Alan T., St. Elizabeth, Alice
Botello, Armando, Our Lady of Guadalupe, Corpus Christi
Breland, Walter N., Spiritual Dir., Cursillo Movement, St. John of the Cross, Orange Grove
Carlisle, James A., Dir., Diaconate Formation, St. Elizabeth, Alice
Carranco, Manuel G., Chap., Our Lady of Victory; Bee County Jail, Beeville.
Carrizales, Alejandro, Admin., Holy Family, Corpus Christi
Castillo, Antonio M., Christ the King, Corpus Christi
Cavada, Armando, Chap., McConnell Unit, Beeville
Cavazos, Jesus Z., Our Lady of Lourdes, Zapata

Cleavelin, William, St. Thomas the Apostle, Robstown
Costley, Ricardo E., Assoc. Dir. of Formation, Sacred Heart, Falfurrias
de Anda, Candido, St. Francis of Rome, Agua Dulce
De la Garza, Guillermo, Mercy Regional Medical Center; Christ the King, Laredo
DeShelter, Michael, Liturgical Commission, St. Pius X, Corpus Christi
Dubuque, Roland, SS. Cyril & Methodius Parish, Corpus Christi
Flores, Arturo, St. Gertrude, Kingsville
Frazier, Garland, Exec. Dir. Villa Maria Apartments, St. Philip the Apostle, Corpus Christi
Garcia, Tiburcio, St. Martin, Kingsville
Garza, Jorge J., St. Francisco Javier Mission, Laredo
Gomez, Juan, Immaculate Conception, Taft
Grassedonio, Roy M., Diocesan Chancellor & Admin. Council, St. Philip the Apostle, Corpus Christi
Hinojosa, Raul, Spiritual Dir. Cursillo Movement, Mission of St. Theresa of the Infant Jesus, Premont
Horseman, M. M. (Pete), Construction Mgr., Most Precious Blood, Corpus Christi
Kaizen, Joseph, Our Lady of Guadalupe Chapel, N.A.S., Corpus Christi
Lara, Antonio S., Diocesan Dir. Charismatic Renewal, Immaculate Conception, Skidmore
Ledbetter, Jerre H., Sacred Heart, Rockport
Lickteig, Wayne, S.O.L.T., Dir., Lay Council of Society
Madrigal, Salvador, Assoc. Dir. Jail & Refugee Ministry, St. Joseph, Laredo
Mantz, Michael, Youth & Drug Abuse Prog. & Admin. Asst. to Vicar for Permanent Diaconate, Corpus Christi Cathedral, Corpus Christi
Martinez, Ciprian, Sacred Heart, Rockport
Martinez, Homer, Jr., Our Lady of the Rosary, Corpus Christi
Millsap, Stacy, St. Phillip the Apostle, Corpus Christi
Millsap, Stanley, Diocesan Human Resources Dir. & Vicar for Deacons
Morales, Gerardo, Assoc. Dir. of Formation of Western Vicariate, St. John Neumann, Laredo; St. Theresa, San Carlos, Sacred Heart, Catholic Community
Nartowicz, Edward, Catholic Social Services, Assoc. Spiritual Dir. Cursillo Movement, St. Paul the Apostle, Our Lady of Guadalupe Chapel, N.A.S., Corpus Christi
Nowicki, Edward, (Retired)
Oliver, Willard F., St. Patrick, Corpus Christi
Ouellette, Roland, Outreach Coord. for Catholic Social Services & Dir. of Diocesan Cemeteries
Panas, George, Our Lady Star of the Sea, Corpus Christi
Ponce, Cesar, Chap. for Catholic Scouting, St. Joseph, Beeville
Rivera, Gonzalo, Chap., Sacred Heart, Rockport; Brooks County Jail, Falfurrias
Rivera, Mario, Area Coord. Cursillo Movement, St. Joseph, Alice
Rodriguez, Alonzo, Immaculate Conception, Taft
Rodriguez, Fernando G., Most Precious Blood, Corpus Christi
Rodriguez, Jose, Jr., Outreach Coord. for La Frontera Halfway House & San Luis Rey, Laredo; Dir. Ministry to Jails & Refugees
Rodriguez, Reynaldo, Jr., Diocesan Chap., St. Therese, Woodsboro
Rosales, Raul G., Consultant for Mission 2000 Regional Dept. of Schools, St. Martin, Kingsville
Salazar, Rolando R., St. Joseph, Beeville
San Miguel, Leonel, Sr., Assoc. Vicar for Deacons, Western Vicariate Facilitator, Santa Margarita De Escocia Independent Mission, Laredo
Sandlin, Larry, (Retired)
Smith, George F., Our Lady Star of the Sea, Corpus Christi
Soto, Crispin O., St. Joseph, Laredo
Sutherland, John W., Our Lady of Mount Carmel, Portland
Trevino, Luis, St. Joseph, Beeville; Our Lady of Good Counsel, Kingsville
Vallarata, David, San Augustin, Laredo; Asst. at Colonia San Carlos Mission
Vargas, David, Blessed Sacrament, Laredo; Asst. at Colonia San Carlos Mission
Vasquez, Juan, St. James, Beeville
Vasquez, Guadalupe C., Mary, Mother of the Church Mission, Corpus Christi
Vitela, Jose Angel, St. Joseph, Alice
Wiest, George Joe, Outreach Coord. for St. Vincent de Paul Society & Chap., Shoreline Treatment Facility, Taft, Sacred Heart, Rockport
Ybarra, Pedro M., St. Joseph, Corpus Christi

INSTITUTIONS LOCATED IN THE DIOCESE

[A] HIGH SCHOOLS

CORPUS CHRISTI. *Corpus Christi Academy*. (Diocesan), 3036 Saratoga Blvd., 78415. Tel: 512-853-6227. Rev. Carlos Casavantes; Rev. Msgr. Daniel Flores; Rev. James G. Stembler; Judith Herrera, Prin.; Deacon Ron Dubuque. Religious 2; Lay Teachers 14; Students 162.

Incarnate Word Academy High School. (Private), 2910 S. Alameda, 78404. Tel: 512-883-0857; Fax: 512-883-2185. Sr. Martha O'Gara, Prin. Sisters 8; Lay Teachers 27; Students 310.

LAREDO. *St. Augustine High School*. (Diocesan), 1300 Galveston St., 78040. Tel: 210-724-8131; Fax: 210-724-8131. Sr. Antoninette Billeaud, C.D.P., Prin. Lay Teachers 35; Students 567.

[B] JUNIOR HIGH AND ELEMENTARY SCHOOLS

CORPUS CHRISTI. *Bishop Garriga Middle School*. (Diocesan), 3114 Saratoga Blvd., 78415. Tel: 512-851-0853. Mrs. Margaret McGettrick, Prin.; Rev. James G. Stembler, Chap. Lay Teachers 9; Students 135.

Central Catholic School. (Parochial), 1218 Comanche St., 78401. Tel: 512-883-3873. Sr. Denise Cassidy, I.W.B.S., Prin. Sisters 2; Lay Teachers 7; Students 155.

Christ the King School. (Parochial), 1625 Arlington Dr., 78415. Tel: 512-883-5391. Sr. Colette Brehony, I.W.B.S., Prin. Sisters 1; Lay Teachers 8; Students 158.

Corpus Christi Academy Middle School. (Diocesan), 3036 Saratoga Blvd., 78415. Tel: 512-882-1601. Mrs. Esmeralda Perez-Gonzalez, Prin.; Rev. David Tonary, M.S.F., Chap. Sisters 1; Lay Teachers 8; Students 85.

Holy Family School. (Parochial), 2526 Soledad St., 78416. Tel: 512-884-9142. Sr. Rosario Vega, H.M.S.S., Prin. Sisters 5; Lay Teachers 14; Students 240.

Incarnate Word Elementary. (Private), 450 Chamberlain, 78404. Tel: 512-883-0857; Fax: 512-883-2185. Sisters 3; Lay Teachers 9; Students 239.

Incarnate Word Middle School. (Private), 2917 Austin St., 78404. Tel: 512-883-0857. Sr. Barbara Netek, I.W.B.S., Prin. Sisters 2; Lay Teachers 20; Students 267.

Most Precious Blood School. (Parochial), 3502 Saratoga Blvd., 78415. Tel: 512-852-4800; Fax: 512-855-8707. Mrs. Anna Galvan, Prin. Religious Teachers 1; Lay Teachers 14; Students 262.

Our Lady of Perpetual Help School. (Parochial), 5814 Williams Dr., 78412. Tel: 512-991-3305. Ms. Linda Cantu, Prin. Lay Teachers 13; Students 190.

St. Patrick School. (Parochial), 3350 S. Alameda, 78411. Tel: 512-852-1211. Dr. Maria M. Barrera, Prin. Sisters 1; Lay Teachers 21; Students 323.

St. Pius X School. (Parochial), 747 St. Pius Dr., 78412. Tel: 512-992-1343. Mrs. Patricia Stegall, Prin. Lay Teachers 13; Students 229.

SS. Cyril and Methodius School. (Parochial), 5002 Kostoryz Rd., 78415. Tel: 512-853-9392. Mrs. Nannette Hatch, Prin. Lay Teachers 18; Students 250.

ALICE. *St. Elizabeth School*. (Parochial), 615 E. Fifth, 78332. Tel: 512-664-6271. Ms. Julia Strubhart, Prin. Lay Teachers 12; Students 127.

St. Joseph School. (Parochial), P.O. Box 157, 78332. Tel: 512-664-4642. Mrs. Margarita Longoria, Prin. Sisters 3; Lay Teachers 8; Students 90.

BEEVILLE. *St. Mary's Academy Elementary School*. (Parochial), 707 North Ave. E., 78102. Tel: 512-358-1913; Fax: 512-592-6591. Sr. Maria Paz Aribon, O.P., Prin. Sisters 4; Lay Teachers 8; Students 84.

St. Mary's Academy Middle School. (Parochial), 410 N. Tyler, 78102. Tel: 512-358-5089; Fax: 512-358-4270. Sr. Esperanza Manas, O.P., Prin. Sisters 5; Lay Teachers 7; Students 86.

KINGSVILLE. *St. Gertrude School*. (Parochial), 400 E. Caesar St., 78363. Tel: 512-592-6522. Mrs. Jean Claire Turcotte, Prin. Lay Teachers 9; Students 156.

St. Martin Catholic School. (Parochial), 903 N. Ninth St., 78363. Tel: 512-592-5011. Sisters 1; Lay Teachers 5; Students 110.

LAREDO. *Blessed Sacrament School*, 1501 N. Bartlett St., 78043. Tel: 210-722-1222. Mrs. Viola Moore, Prin. Lay Teachers 8; Students 125.

Mary Help of Christians School. (Private), 10 E. Del Mar Blvd., 78045. Tel: 210-722-3966. Sr. Barbara Campbell, F.M.A., Prin. Sisters 1; Lay Teachers 55; Students 724.

Our Lady of Guadalupe School. (Parochial), 400 Callaghan St., 78040-3834. Tel: 210-722-3915. Sr. Julia Hickey, O.S.U., Prin. Sisters 3; Lay Teachers 7; Students 170.

St. Augustine Elementary School. (Diocesan), 1300 Galveston, 78040. Tel: 210-724-1176; Fax: 210-725-9891. Sr. Marie Elise van Dijk, Prin. Sisters 1; Lay Teachers 11; Students 223.

St. Peter's Memorial School. (Diocesan), 1519 Houston St., P.O. Box 430211, 78043-0211. Tel: 210-723-6302. Ms. Alicia C. Valdez, Prin. Sisters 2; Lay Teachers 19; Students 145.

ROBSTOWN. *St. Anthony School*. (Parochial), 203 Dunne St., 78380. Tel: 512-387-3814. Rev. Robert Rank, Prin. Sisters 1; Lay Teachers 15; Students 140.

ROCKPORT. *Sacred Heart School*. (Parochial), 111 N. Church St., 78382. Tel: 512-729-2672; Fax: 512-729-1989. Mary E. Sierra-Lopez, Prin. Sisters 1; Lay Teachers 7; Students 153.

[C] DAY NURSERY, PRE-KINDER, KINDER

CORPUS CHRISTI. *Carmelite Learning Center of Corpus Christi*. (Private), 4015 MacArthur St., 78416-1907. Tel: 512-853-6970; Fax: 512-853-6670. Sr. M. Michelle, Carmel.D.C.J., Dir. Day Care and Kindergarten. Carmelite Sisters of the Divine Heart of Jesus 4; Lay Teachers 14; Students 75.

Our Lady of the Rosary Learning Center, 2237 Waldron Rd., 78418. Tel: 512-939-9847. Sr. Assumpta Guevara, O.P., Dir. Students 50.

LAREDO. *Christ the King Learning Center*, 1100 Hendricks, 78040. Tel: 210-722-7821. Mrs. Mary Martinez, Prin. Lay Teachers 3; Students 85.

[D] ORPHANAGES AND INFANT HOMES

LAREDO. *Sacred Heart Children's Home*, 3310 S. Zapata Hwy., 78046. Tel: 210-723-3343.

For a complete listing, refer to the Special Care Facilities section.

[E] GENERAL HOSPITALS

CORPUS CHRISTI. *Spohn Hospital*, 600 Elizabeth St., 78404. Tel: 512-881-3000; Fax: 512-881-3149.

For a complete listing, refer to the Hospitals section.

Spohn Hospital South, 5950 Saratoga Blvd., 78414. Tel: 512-985-5000; Fax: 512-985-5109.

For a complete listing, refer to the Hospitals section.

Spohn Memorial Hospital. Mailing Address: P.O. Box 5280, 78465-5280.

For a complete listing, refer to the Hospitals section.

KINGSVILLE. *Spohn-Kleberg Memorial Hospital*, 1300 General Cavazos Blvd., 78363. Tel: 512-595-1661; Fax: 512-595-9888.

For a complete listing, refer to the Hospitals section.

LAREDO. *Mercy Regional Medical Center*, 1515 Logan, P.O. Box 2068, 78044. Tel: 210-718-6222; Fax: 210-718-6904.

For a complete listing, refer to the Hospitals section.

[F] HOMES FOR THE AGED

CORPUS CHRISTI. *Mount Carmel Home*, 4130 S. Alameda St., 78411. Tel: 512-855-6243.

For a complete listing, refer to the Special Care Facilities section.

Villa Maria, Inc., 3146 Saratoga Blvd., 78415. Tel: 512-857-6171; Fax: 512-857-6173.

For a complete listing, refer to the Special Care Facilities section.

[G] RETREAT HOUSE

CORPUS CHRISTI. *Bishop Rene H. Gracida Retreat House*, 3036 Saratoga Blvd., 78415. Tel: 512-814-3806. Deacon Homer Martinez, Dir.

Bishop Thomas J. Drury Retreat Center, 1200 Lantana St., 78407. Tel: 512-289-6501. Mr. William Tribula, Mgr.

LAREDO. *Holy Spirit Retreat and Conference Center*, 501 S. Century Dr., 78043. Tel: 210-726-4352. Rev. Marie Tarcisius Lemarie, F.J. (France), Spiritual Dir.; Deacon Jose Rodriguez, Mgr. Total Staff 3; Total in Residence 1.

SANDIA. *Benedictine Retreat Center*, HC 2, Box 6300, 78383-9989. Tel: 512-547-3257; Fax: 512-547-5184. Very Rev. Bartholomew Leon, O.S.B., Prior.

SARITA. *Lebh Shomea House of Prayer*, La Parra Ranch, 78385-1580. Tel: 512-294-5369; Fax: 512-294-5791. Rev. Francis Kelly Nemeck, O.M.I.

[H] MONASTERIES AND RESIDENCES OF PRIESTS AND BROTHERS

HEBBRONVILLE. *Catholic Solitudes*, Rancho Maria, P.O. Box 748, 78361. Tel: 512-527-4636; Fax: 512-527-4482. Rev. M. Brendan Meaney, F.J., Dir.; Jean-Baptiste LePichone, Dir. Special Apostolate: A fraternal community stressing neremitical contemplative prayer, welcoming eremitcal vocations and spiritual formational retreats for young people under directives of Diocesan Bishop. Total Staff 1; Total in Residence 6.

Franciscan Friars - O.F.M., 504 E. Santa Clara St., 78361. Tel: 512-527-3865; Fax: 512-527-5548. Rev. Adalberto Ramirez, O.F.M., Pastor. Total Staff 3; Total Assisted 35.

LAREDO. *Marist Brothers*, 1511 E. Cherry Hill Dr., 78041. Tel: 210-724-2651; Fax: 210-724-1963. Bros. Philip R. Degagne, F.M.S., Dir.; Joseph E. Herrera,

F.M.S.; Robert W. Warren, F.M.S.; Thomas W. Coyne, F.M.S.; John A. Allen, F.M.S.; Gregory Avina, F.M.S. Marist Brothers 6.

St. John's Priory, (F.J.), 505 Century Dr. S., 78046. Tel: 210-722-3399. Congregation of St. John. Revs. Marie-Tarcisius LeMarie (France), Prior; Juan de Dios Saavedra (Spain); Didier-Marie Dugas Viallis (France); Deacon Jean Marie Bernard (France). Priests 3; Brothers in Formation (Postulants) 3; Total in Residence 5.

ROBSTOWN. *Society of Our Lady of the Most Holy Trinity*, P.O. Box 152, 78380-0792. Tel: 512-387-2774; Fax: 512-387-5114. Deacon Roy M. Grassedonio, Chancellor; Revs. Vincent Albano, S.O.L.T.; Anthony Anderson, S.O.L.T., Voc. Dir.; Peter J. Auer, S.O.L.T. (GF); James H.T. Brady, S.O.L.T. (WH); Alberto A. Brancaccio, S.O.L.T. (ALB); George Carlin, S.O.L.T.; Phillip Chavez, S.O.L.T.; Robert Copsey, S.O.L.T.; John Corapi, S.O.L.T. (SAC); Robert Cronin, S.O.L.T. (GLP); Jacques Dolbec, S.O.L.T. (FAR); James Flanagan, S.O.L.T.; Peter Fremont-Smith, S.O.L.T.; Alfredo Gaytan, S.O.L.T.; Thomas P. Gier, S.O.L.T.; Paul Grala, S.O.L.T.; Joseph Hadgkiss, S.O.L.T.; Gene Hart, S.O.L.T.; Edward Horan, S.O.L.T.; Jeffrey Johnson, S.O.L.T. (BO); Michael Jordan, S.O.L.T.; Eckley Macklin, S.O.L.T. (KC); John McHugh, S.O.L.T.; Glenn Meaux, S.O.L.T.; Christopher Myers, S.O.L.T.; Thien Chi Nguyen, S.O.L.T.; Vincent A. Nicosia, S.O.L.T. (SFE); Joseph O'Connell, S.O.L.T.; Frank Papa, S.O.L.T. (HRT); Tan Pham, S.O.L.T.; Santan Pinto, S.O.L.T. (SFE); John Purtell, S.O.L.T. (BO); William Sharkey, S.O.L.T.; Gerald Sheehan, S.O.L.T.; Maurice Shepherd, S.O.L.T.; James Tamborino, S.O.L.T. (MIL); Deacon Wayne Lickteig, S.O.L.T. In res., Rev. Robert Rank, S.O.L.T.; Deacon Francis Hohenadel, S.O.L.T.

SAN DIEGO. *Vicariate of Holy Rosary*, St. Francis de Paul Church, P.O. Box 279, 78384. Tel: 512-279-3596. Order of Preachers, U.S. Foundation of the Province of Spain. Revs. Benito Retortillo, O.P., Local Supr.; Epifanio Rodriguez, O.P.; Juan Suarez, O.P.

SANDIA. *Corpus Christi Abbey*. (Benedictine Monastery), HC2, Box 6300, 78383. Tel: 512-547-3257. Order Saint Benedict-Swiss-American Congregation. Very Rev. Bartholomew Leon, O.S.B.; Rt. Revs. Bonaventure Knaebel, O.S.B., Admin.; Luke Buergler, O.S.B., (Retired); Revs. William DeAngelis, O.S.B.; Michael DeLeon, O.S.B.; Louis-Marie Hacker, O.S.B.; Augustine Linbeck, O.S.B.; John Harold McKenzie, O.S.B.; Sylvester Schad, O.S.B.; Gregory Yockey, O.S.B.; Maryon Jordan, O.S.B.; Deacon Dominic Mazoch, O.S.B. Brothers 13; Priests 11; Novices 3; Postulants 3.

[I] CONVENTS AND RESIDENCES FOR SISTERS

CORPUS CHRISTI. *Bethany Convent*, 2962 Austin St., 78404. Tel: 512-888-7537. Sisters of the Incarnate Word and Blessed Sacrament 2.

Blessed Sacrament Chapel, 4105 Ocean Dr., 78411-1223. Tel: 512-852-6212. Sr. Mary Lourdes Cervino, S.Sp.S. de A.P., Supr. Sister-Servants of the Holy Spirit of Perpetual Adoration (Motherhouse, Steyl, Holland) 10.

Congregation of the Sisters of the Holy Cross, Holy Cross Convent, 1109 N. Staples, 78401-1836. Tel: 512-888-7753; 888-4012.

Corpus Christi Academy Convent, 3036 Saratoga Blvd., 78415. Tel: 512-853-5772. Sisters of St. Ann. Sr. Emiliana Mampallil, S.S.A., Supr.

Incarnate Word Convent, 2930 S. Alameda, 78404. Tel: 512-882-5413. Sisters of the Incarnate Word and Blessed Sacrament. Legal Title: *Convent Academy of the Incarnate Word*. Sr. Michelle Marie Kuntscher, I.W.B.S., Supr. Tel: 512-882-5413; Rev. Robert McGrath, O.M.I. Sisters 33; Total Staff 17; Total in Residence 33.

Mount Carmel Home Convent, 4130 S. Alameda St., 78411. Tel: 512-855-6243. Carmelite Sisters of the Divine Heart of Jesus 9.

Mount Tabor Convent, 12940 Up-River Rd., 78410. Tel: 512-241-1955. Novitiate and Central Regional House of the Missionary Sisters of Jesus, Mary, and Joseph. Sr. Avelina Sosa, M.J.M.J., Delegation Supr.; Sr. Angeles Berrozpe, M.J.M.J., Supr. Sisters 5; Total Staff 5; Total Assisted 5.

Pax Christi Residence, 4601 Calallen Dr., 78410. Tel: 512-241-2833.

Pax Christi Institute. Mother Teresa Santoyo, P.C.I., Supr.; Rev. Msgr. Thomas Meany, Chap. Tel: 512-241-6329. Sisters 12; Total Staff 8; Total Assisted 3,640.

Religious Missionaries of St. Dominic, Inc. (Congregacion de Religiosas Misioneras de Santo Domingo), 2237 Waldron Rd., 78418. Tel: 512-939-8102.

Our Lady of the Rosary Learning Center. Sr. Mary Purificacion Palis, O.P., Contact Person; Sr. Assumpta Guevara; Sr. Isabel Montemayor; Sr. Soledad Oliva; Sr. Lourdes Untalan; Sr. Antonina Ferrer; Sr. Paula Elesterio; Sr. Visitacion Ponce; Sr. Antonia Egar; Sr. Angela Lavador; Sr. Susan de Guzman. Sisters 33; Sisters Staffing the Learning Center 9; Total Staff 9; Total Assisted 50.

St. Joseph School, Alice. Sr. Evelina Enerva, Supr.; Sr. Rosario Empainado; Sr. Rogelia Perez; Sr. Margarita Lacandola; Sr. Joaquina Perez; Sr. Rosario Reyes; Sr. Julien Valdevieso.

St. Joseph School, Beeville. Sr. Esperanza Manas; Sr. Fatima Cabuguas; Sr. Helen Cannu; Sr. Julia Macaraeg; Sr. Julien Valdevieso.

Our Lady of Victory School, Beeville. Sr. Encarnacion de los Santos, Supr.; Sr. Paz Aribon; Sr. Flaviana Macasling; Sr. Amor Vigare; Sr. Guadalupe de Vela.

Dominican Convent, Oxnard, CA. Sr. Imelda Alcober, Supr.; Sr. Rebecca Ortega; Sr. Corazon Gamotin.

Nuestra Senora de Guadalupe Convent, Santa Paula, CA. Sr. Araceli Diaz, Supr.; Sr. Germaine Marie Quinones; Sr. Filomena Villacruzada.

St. Joseph Home Convent, 4015 MacArthur St., 78416-1907. Tel: 512-853-6970; Fax: 512-853-6670. Carmelite Sisters of the Divine Heart of Jesus. Sr. M. Michelle Miranda Carmel, D.C.J., Supr. Total Staff 14; Sisters 4; Total Assisted 75.

Sisters of Our Lady of Charity Convent, 1201 Lantana St., 78407. Tel: 512-289-2611. Sisters of Our Lady of Charity. Sisters 2.

Spohn Hospital Convent, 1725 2nd St., 78404. Tel: 512-881-3000; 884-0702; Fax: 512-881-3634. Congregation of Sisters of Charity of the Incarnate Word - San Antonio. Sisters 3.

Stella Maris Convent, 1739 Second St., 78404. Tel: 512-887-7920. Congregation of Sisters of Charity of the Incarnate Word - San Antonio. Sisters 2.

KINGSVILLE. *Missionary Daughters of the Most Pure Virgin Mary*, 919 N. Ninth St., 78363. Sr. Consuelo Ramirez, M.D.P.V.M., Supr. Sisters 11.

LAREDO. *Mary, Help of Christians Convent*, 10 E. Del Mar Blvd., 78041. Tel: 512-722-3966. Daughters of Mary Help of Christians Salesian Sisters. Sr. Teresita Delgado, F.M.A., Supr.; Sr. Barbara Campbell, F.M.A., Prin.; Sr. Refugio Gallardo, F.M.A.; Sr. Rosalba Garcia, F.M.A.; Sr. Maria Guadalupe Medina, F.M.A.; Sr. Teresa Nguyen Xuan Thi, F.M.A.; Sr. Socorro Ortega, F.M.A.; Sr. Trinidad Reyes, F.M.A.; Sr. Assunta Sanchez, F.M.A.; Sr. Josephine Sanchez, F.M.A.; Sr. Mary Ann Villagomez, F.M.A. Sisters 11; Total Staff 55.

Sacred Heart Children's Home Convent, 3310 S. Zapata Hwy., 78046. Tel: 210-723-3343. Servants of the Sacred Heart of Jesus and of the Poor. Sr. Maria Yolanda Fernandez, S.S.H.J.P., Supr. Sisters 15.

St. Augustine's Convent, 1707 Galveston, 78043. Tel: 210-722-3245. Sisters of Divine Providence. Sr. Maria Elise van Dijk, C.D.P.; Sr. Miriam Fidelis Mellein, C.D.P. Sisters 2.

Sisters of Mercy of the St. Louis Regional Community, Inc., 1414 Hendricks Ave., 78040. Tel: 210-723-1364. Religious Sisters of Mercy. Sr. Amelia Zepeda, R.S.M., Local Coord. Sisters 16; Total Staff 14.

Mercy Hospital Convent, Sisters' Retirement Center. Su Casa, 3906 Monterrey, 78043-6648. Tel: 210-718-8762.

Sisters of St. John, 504 Century Dr. S., 78046. Tel: 210-727-1028. Sr. Maria Immakulata Dziegielewska, Local Supr. Total in Residence 6.

Ursuline Convent, 2302 Corpus Christi St., 78043. Tel: 210-723-9185. 1415 Jarvis St., 78043. Tel: 210-723-8968. Roman Union Central Province of the U.S. Sr. Mary Walden, O.S.U., Prioress. Sisters 12.

ROCKPORT. *Schoenstatt Sisters of Mary*, 130 Front St., Lamar, HC 04, Box 100, 78382-9606. Tel: 512-729-1868; Fax: 512-729-1685. Secular Institute of the Schoenstatt Sisters of Mary. Sr. M. Antoinette Buffler, I.S.S.M., Prov. Supr. Sisters 26; Total in Residence 15.

SARITA. *Lebh Shomea, House of Prayer*, La Parra Ranch, 78385-1580. Tel: 512-294-5369. Total Staff 7; Total in Residence 4.

SKIDMORE. *Our Lady of the Most Holy Trinity Convent*, General Motherhouse, P.O. Box 189, 78389. Tel: 512-287-3256; 287-3830. Sr. Mary of the Redemption, Gen. Sister Severant; Sr. Mary Carmen Sandoval, S.O.L.T., Regional Sister Servant. Sisters 9.

[J] MISCELLANEOUS

CORPUS CHRISTI. *The Catholic Campaign of America, Inc.*, P.O. Box 2620, 78403-2620; Fax: 512-882-1018.

Center for Spiritual Direction, 4103 Ocean Dr., 78411. Tel: 512-853-0170. Sr. Joan Michele Rake, C.D.P., Spiritual Dir.

The Counseling Center, 1322 Commache, 78401. Tel: 512-883-7611; Fax: 512-884-7175. Ms. Gloria Garcia, Lead Counselor. Total Staff 7; Patients assisted annually 768.

Hope, Faith & Love, Inc., 658 Robinson, 78404. Total Staff 2; Total Assisted 49.

Incarnate Word Academy Foundation, 2930 S. Alameda, 78404. Tel: 512-882-5413. Sr. Michelle Marie Kuntscher, I.W.B.S., Pres.

Pope John Paul, II Library, Corpus Christi Academy, 3036 Saratoga Blvd., 78415.

LAREDO. *St. Augustine School Endowment Fund, Inc.*, 1300 Galveston, 78040. Tel: 210-724-5119. Sr. Antoinette Billeaud, Contact Person.

San Augustin Historical Preservation & Restoration Society, Inc., 214 San Bernardo, 78040. Tel: 210-722-1382. Rev. Thomas A. Davis, Contact Person.

SARITA. *Food Co-op of Sarita, Inc.*, P.O. Box 6, 78385. Tel: 512-294-5350. Rev. Angel Villalba, O.M.I., Contact Person. Total Assisted 300.

RELIGIOUS INSTITUTES OF MEN REPRESENTED IN THE DIOCESE

For further details refer to the corresponding bracketed number in the Religious Institutes of Men or Women section.

[0140]—*The Augustinians.*—O.S.A.
[0200]—*Benedictine Monks.*—O.S.B.
[]—*Congregation of St. John.* (Priorato de San Juan).—F.J.
[]—*Congregation of the Missionaries of the Holy Family.*—M.S.F.
[0520]—*Franciscan Friars.*—O.F.M.
[0770]—*The Marist Brothers.*—F.M.S.
[0910]—*Oblates of Mary Immaculate.* (Southwest Prov.).—O.M.I.
[1310]—*Order of the Holy Trinity.* (Province of Baltimore).—O.SS.T.
[1070]—*Redemptorists.*—C.Ss.R.
[1190]—*Salesians of St. John Bosco.*—S.D.B.
[]—*Society of Our Lady of the Most Holy Trinity.*—S.O.L.T.

RELIGIOUS INSTITUTES OF WOMEN REPRESENTED IN THE DIOCESE

[0360]—*Carmelite Sisters of the Divine Heart of Jesus.*—Carmel.D.C.J.
[0460]—*Congregation of Sisters of Charity of the Incarnate Word.*—C.C.V.I.
[]—*Congregation of Sisters of St. John.*
[1920]—*Congregation of the Sisters of the Holy Cross.*—C.S.C.
[0850]—*Daughters of Mary Help of Christians.*—F.M.A.
[]—*Dominican Sisters.*—O.P.
[]—*Eucharistic Missionary Society.*—E.M.S.
[]—*Misioneras del Perpetua Socorro.*—M.P.S.
[0390]—*Missionary Carmelites of St. Teresa.*—C.M.S.T.
[]—*Missionary Daughters of the Most Pure Virgin Mary.* (U.S. Foundation-Mexico).—M.D.P.V.M.
[2770]—*Missionary Sisters of Jesus, Mary, and Joseph.*—M.J.M.J.
[3070]—*North American Unions of Sisters of Our Lady of Charity.*—O.L.C.
[]—*Pax Christi Institute.*—P.C.I.
[]—*Religious Missionaries of St. Dominic.* (Spanish Prov.).—O.P.
[2519]—*Religious Sisters of Mercy.*—R.S.M.
[]—*Schoenstatt Sisters of Mary Secular Institute.*—I.S.S.M.
[3660]—*Servants of the Sacred Heart of Jesus and of the Poor.*—S.S.H.J.P.
[1010]—*Sisters of Divine Providence of San Antonio, Texas.*—C.D.P.
[2590]—*Sisters of Mercy of the Blessed Sacrament.*—H.M.S.S.
[]—*Sisters of Our Lady of the Rosary of Fatima, Zapata.*—H.M.R.F.
[3360]—*Sisters of Providence of Saint Mary-of-the-Woods, IN.*—S.P.
[3718]—*Sisters of St. Anne.*—S.S.A.
[1930]—*Sisters of the Holy Cross.*—C.S.C.
[2040]—*Sisters of the Holy Spirit.*—S.H.Sp.
[2205]—*Sisters of the Incarnate Word and Blessed Sacrament.*—I.W.B.S.
[]—*Sisters of the Society of Our Lady of the Most Holy Trinity.*—S.O.L.T.
[3540]—*Sisters-Servants of the Holy Spirit of Perpetual Adoration.*—S.Sp.S.deA.P.
[4110]—*Ursuline Nuns (Roman Union).*—O.S.U.

NECROLOGY

† Dunne, Rev. Msgr. Kevin, (Retired). —Died April 8, 1996.
† Hayes, Damien J., (Retired). —Died Oct. 4, 1996.
† Herrero, Bernardino, (Retired). —Died Aug. 3, 1996.
† McNaboe, Charles, Laredo, TX, St. Patrick Church. —Died Jan. 26, 1996.
† Powell, Thomas, Corpus Christi, TX, Most Precious Blood Church. —Died June 7, 1996.

Diocese of Covington

(Dioecesis Covingtonensis)

Most Reverend

ROBERT W. MUENCH, D.D.

Bishop of Covington; ordained May 18, 1968; appointed Titular Bishop of Mactaris and Auxiliary of New Orleans May 8, 1990; consecrated June 29, 1990; appointed January 5, 1996; installed March 19, 1996. *Mailing Address: P.O. Box 18548, Erlanger, KY, 41018-0548.* Tel.: 606-283-6215.

Most Reverend

WILLIAM A. HUGHES, D.D.

Retired Bishop of Covington; ordained April 6, 1946; appointed Titular Bishop of Inis Cathaig and Auxiliary of Youngstown July 23, 1974; consecrated September 12, 1974; appointed Bishop of Covington April 13, 1979; transferred to Covington May 8, 1979; retired July 4, 1995. *Res., Cathedral Basilica of the Assumption, 1140 Madison Ave., Covington, KY, 41011-3116.*

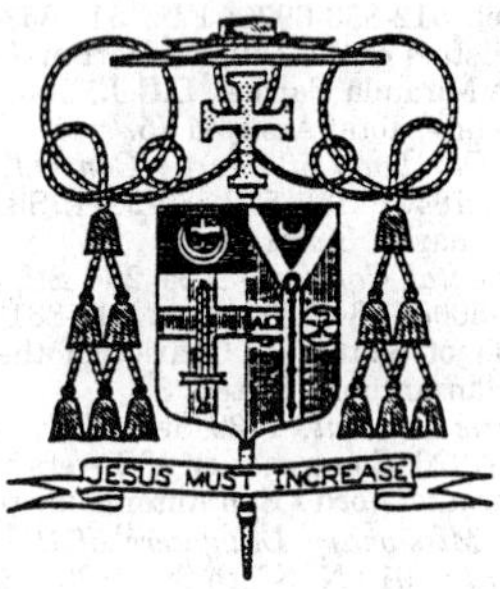

The Catholic Center: P.O. Box 18548, Erlanger, KY, 41018-0548. Tel.: 606-283-6200; Fax: 606-283-6334.

ESTABLISHED JULY 29, 1853.

Square Miles 3,359.

Comprises 14 Counties of the Commonwealth of Kentucky in the north and east of the Commonwealth, including Bracken, Boone, Campbell, Carroll, Fleming, Gallatin, Grant, Harrison, Kenton, Lewis, Mason, Owen, Pendleton and Robertson Counties.

For legal titles of parishes and diocesan institutions, consult the Chancery Office.

STATISTICAL OVERVIEW

Personnel	
Bishop	1
Retired Bishops	1
Priests: Diocesan Active in Diocese	69
Priests: Active Outside Diocese	4
Priests: Retired, Sick or Absent	46
Number of Diocesan Priests	119
Religious Priests in Diocese	1
Ordinations:	
Diocesan Priests	3
Transitional Deacons	1
Permanent Deacons	16
Permanent Deacons in Diocese	17
Total Brothers	7
Total Sisters	464
Parishes	
Parishes	51
With Resident Pastor:	
Resident Diocesan Priests	45
Without Resident Pastor:	
Administered by Priests	3
Administered by Women Religious	3
Missions	5
Professional Ministry Personnel:	
Sisters	15
Lay Ministers	29
Welfare	
Catholic Hospitals	3
Total Assisted	220,722
Homes for the Aged	4
Total Assisted	579
Residential Care of Children	2
Total Assisted	78
Day Care and Extended Day Care Centers	1
Total Assisted	81
Special Centers for Social Services	4
Total Assisted	24,383
Other Institutions	1
Total Assisted	5,512
Educational	
Diocesan Students in Other Seminaries	4
Total Seminarians	4
Colleges and Universities	1
Total Students	1,426
High Schools, Diocesan and Parish	7
Total Students	2,391
High Schools, Private	2
Total Students	773
Elementary Schools, Diocesan and Parish	30
Total Students	7,972
Elementary Schools, Private	2
Total Students	492
Catechesis/Religious Education:	
High School Students	416
Elementary Students	4,207
Total Students Under Catholic Instruction	17,681
Teachers in the Diocese:	
Priests	1
Brothers	1
Sisters	57
Lay Teachers	584
Vital Statistics	
Receptions into the Church:	
Infant Baptism Totals	1,603
Adult Baptism Totals	174
Received into Full Communion	153
First Communions	1,473
Confirmations	1,375
Marriages:	
Catholic	375
Interfaith	234
Total Marriages	609
Deaths	703
Total Catholic Population	82,341
Total Population	401,127

Former Bishops—Rt. Rev. GEORGE ALOYSIUS CARRELL, S.J., D.D., cons. Nov. 1, 1853; died Sept. 25, 1868.—Rt. Rev. AUGUSTUS MARIA TOEBBE, D.D., cons. Jan. 9, 1870; died May 2, 1884.—Rt. Rev. CAMILLUS PAUL MAES, D.D., cons. Jan. 25, 1885; died May 11, 1915.—Rt. Rev. FERDINAND BROSSART, D.D., cons. Jan. 25, 1916; resigned March 14, 1923; died Aug. 6, 1930.—Most Rev. FRANCIS W. HOWARD, D.D., cons. July 15, 1923; died Jan. 18, 1944.—Most Rev. WILLIAM T. MULLOY, D.D., LL.D., cons. Jan. 10, 1945; died June 1, 1959.—Most Rev. RICHARD H. ACKERMAN, C.S.Sp., D.D., cons. May 26, 1956; transferred to Covington April 6, 1960; retired Nov. 28, 1978; died Nov. 18, 1992.—Most Rev. WILLIAM A. HUGHES, D.D., cons. Sept. 12, 1974; appt. April 13, 1979; retired July 4, 1995.

Vicar General and Chancellor—Very Rev. ROGER L. KRIEGE, S.T.B., V.G.

Assistant to Bishop and Assistant Chancellor—Rev. THOMAS B. SACKSTEDER.

Diocesan Tribunal—Very Rev. JOHN R. SCHULTE, J.C.L., Judicial Vicar; JOHN M. MEECE, Notary & Cast Promoter. Defenders of the Bond: Revs. GREGORY E. OSBURG, M.A., J.C.L.; GERALD E. TWADELL, Ph.D.; PAUL BERSCHIED; JOSEPH GALLENSTEIN.

Diocesan Consultors—Very Rev. ROGER L. KRIEGE, V.G.; Rev. Msgr. JOHN F. MURPHY; Rev. Msgr. DONALD F. HELLMANN; Revs. WILLIAM F. CLEVES; GEORGE E. SCHNEIDER; ROBERT C. WEHAGE.

Deans—Covington: Rev. RAYMOND C. HOLTZ; Northern Kenton County: Rev. Msgr. DONALD F. HELLMANN; Southwest: Rev. EDWARD J. BRODNICK; Newport, Bellevue, Dayton: Rev. JOHN H. KROGER; Campbell County: Rev. JOSEPH C. BRINK; Southeast: Rev. DANIEL J. SANER.

Diocesan Pastoral Council—Deacon THOMAS NOLAN, Chm.; Sr. JO ANN MCMASTER, O.P., Exec. Sec.

Presbyteral Council—Rev. Msgr. DONALD F. HELLMANN, Chm.; Revs. RAYMOND S. HOLTZ, Vice-Chm.; EDWARD J. BRODNICK, Sec.; G. MICHAEL GREER, Treas.

Due Process Board of Administrative Review—MICHAEL HAMMONS, J.D., Chm.; STEPHEN KOPLYAY, Sec.

Diocesan Offices and Directors

The Catholic Center—947 Donaldson Hwy., P.O. Box 18548, Erlanger, 41018-0548. Tel: 606-283-6200; Fax: 606-283-6334. Office Hours: Mon.-Fri. 8:30-4:30.

Archives—DAVID E. SCHROEDER.

Board of Total Catholic Education—LAWRENCE W. BOWMAN, Ph.D.; SCOTT GROSSER, Chm.

Building Committee—JOSEPH SCHWAB, Chm.

Campus Ministry-Newman Centers—AL CUCCHETTI, Pastoral Admin., *Northern Kentucky Univ., 512 Johns Hill Rd., P.O. Box 76174, Highland Heights, 41076-1449.* Tel: 606-781-3775.

Cathedral Foundation, Inc.—CAROL SROCZYNSKI, Exec. Dir., *1140 Madison Ave., Covington, 41011-3116.* Tel: 606-431-2060; Fax: 606-431-2060.

Catholic Charities—Sr. JOAN MARIE BOBERG, C.D.P., Dir., *3629 Church St., Covington, 41015-1499.* Tel: 606-581-8974; Fax: 606-581-9595.

Catholic Scouting—Rev. JEROME BRITT, Chap.; PEG HERINGER, Chm.

Cemeteries—JOHN NIENABER, Dir.

Censor Librorum—Rev. JAMES E. QUILL, S.T.D.

Charismatic Renewal—HARRY HUMPERT, Contact Person.

Communication—Rev. THOMAS B. SACKSTEDER, Dir.

Continuing Education of Priests—Rev. RONALD KETTELER, Dir.

Corpus Central Purchasing—SANDRA NARE, Gen. Mgr. MIKE FREUDENBERG, Buyer, *845 Isabella St., Newport, 41071.* Tel: 606-491-8100; 800-955-2541; Fax: 606-491-6587.

Cursillo Movement—Rev. GERALD L. REINERSMAN, Spiritual Dir. RON KIRKWOOD, Lay Dir.

Development and Missions—SUE GRETHEL, Dir. Includes Pontifical Aid Societies, Campaign for Human Development, Catholic Relief Fund, Holy Childhood Assoc., Inner City Missions.

Disabilities Commission—TOM FRICKE, Chm.

Ecumenism—Rev. RONALD KETTELER, *Thomas More College, 333 Thomas More Pkwy., Crestview Hills, 41017-3428.* Tel: 606-344-3393.

Evangelization and Initiation Commission—MADONNA KLING, C.D.P., Chm.

Family Ministry—SUSAN VOGT, Dir.

Finance—ANTHONY G. DEPENBROCK, Dir.

Justice and Peace Center—Sr. RUTH KETTMAN, C.S.J., Dir.

Lay Retreat Movement—Deacon EDWARD STIERITZ, Dir., *945 Donaldson Hwy., Erlanger, 41018-1093.*

Legion of Mary—Rev. JOSEPH RUETER, Spiritual Dir.

Liaison for Retired Priests—Rev. ROBERT L. VATER.

Ministry Development Program—GINGER HOLSTEIN, Dir.; Sr. MARY GALLAGHER, S.C., Assoc. Dir.

Mission Services, Pontifical Mission Aid Societies, Campaign for Human Development, Catholic Relief Fund, Holy Childhood Assoc., Inner City Missions—See Development and Missions.

Missions Among Black and Native Americans—Sr. JANET BUCHER, C.D.P.

Mustard Seed Community—HARRY HUMPERT, Contact Person.

Newspaper "Messenger"—GERALD H. ENDERLE, Editor-in-Chief.

Pastoral Ministry Formation—Rev. GERALD L. REINERSMAN, Dir.

Pastoral Office for the Deaf—Sr. ROBIN CONNELL, C.S.J.

Pastoral Planning and Research—Sr. JO ANN MCMASTER, O.P., Acting Dir., Consultant Parish Svcs.

Permanent Diaconate Formation—Rev. GERALD L. REINERSMAN, Dir.

Priest Personnel—Rev. ROBERT C. ROSING, Dir.

Priests' Eucharistic League—Rev. LOUIS B. BRINKER, Dir.

Priests' Retirement Board—Very Rev. ROGER L. KRIEGE, V.G., Chm.

Religious—Sr. M. JOAN DOHMEN, Dir.

Serra Club of Diocese of Covington—Rev. GERALD L. REINERSMAN, Chap.

St. Vincent de Paul Society—Rev. ROBERT J. REINKE, Spiritual Dir.

Total Catholic Education—LAWRENCE M. BOWMAN, Ph.D., Dir. Catholic Education & Supt. EUGENE A. KUEHNE, Dir. Business Svcs.; Sr. STELLA MARIE GOUGH, O.S.B., Dir. Catechetical Svcs.

Vocation Council—Rev. GERALD L. REINERSMAN, Dir.

Worship Commission—MADONNA MARIE KLING, C.D.P., Chm.

Office of Worship, Evangelization & Initiation—MADONNA MARIE KLING, C.D.P.

Office of Youth Ministry—BETH WORLAND, Dir.

CLERGY, PARISHES, MISSIONS AND PAROCHIAL SCHOOLS

CITY OF COVINGTON
(Kenton County)

1—CATHEDRAL, BASILICA OF THE ASSUMPTION (1837), Very Rev. John W. Cahill; Deacon John Dunning.
Res., 1140 Madison Ave., 41011-3116. Tel: 606-431-2060; Fax: 606-431-8444.

2—ST. AGNES (1930), Rev. Msgr. Donald F. Hellmann; Revs. John J. Sterling; James E. Quill, (Retired); Deacons Joseph Cleves; David Flynn.
Res., 1680 Dixie Hwy., Fort Wright, 41011-2779. Tel: 606-431-1802.
School—Tel: 606-261-0543; Fax: 606-261-9778.
Sisters of Notre Dame 1; Lay Teachers 35; Students 515.
Catechesis/Religious Programs—Students 85.

3—ST. ANN (1860), Rev. Mark Steidle.
Res., 1274 Parkway, 41011-1060. Tel: 606-261-9548.

4—ST. AUGUSTINE (1870), Rev. Leo C. Schmidt.
Res., 1839 Euclid Ave., 41014-1162. Tel: 606-431-3943.
School—Tel: 606-261-5564; Fax: 606-261-5402.
Sisters of Notre Dame 3; Lay Teachers 7; Students 151.

5—ST. BENEDICT (1885), Rev. Mark A. Keene. In res., Rev. Donald A. Enzweiler.
Res., 338 E. 17th St., 41014-1315. Tel: 606-431-5607.
Catechesis/Religious Programs—Students 160.

6—HOLY CROSS (1890), Rev. Thomas C. Barnes; Ms. Marg Wilburs, Pastoral Assoc. In res., Revs. Charles J. Garvey, (Retired); Charles Hoffer, (Retired); Deacon Ralph Colatrella.
Res., 3612 Church St., 41015-1431. Tel: 606-431-0636; Fax: 606-431-6917.
School—Tel: 606-581-6599.
Lay Teachers 12; Students 233.
Catechesis/Religious Programs—Students 70.

7—ST. JOHN (1854), Rev. David B. Gamm.
Res., 627 Pike St., 41011-1926. Tel: 606-431-5314.

8—MOTHER OF GOD (1841), Rev. Raymond C. Holtz; Deacon Thomas Runge.
Res., 119 W. 6th St., 41011-1409. Tel: 606-291-2288; Fax: 606-291-2065.

9—CHURCH OF OUR SAVIOR (1943), Sr. Janet Marie Bucher, C.D.P., Admin.; Rev. Donald A. Enweiler.
Res., 246 E. 10th St., 41011-3026. Tel: 606-491-5872.
Catechesis/Religious Programs—Students 169.

OUTSIDE THE CITY OF COVINGTON

Alexandria, Campbell Co., St. Mary of the Assumption (1860), Very Rev. Joseph C. Brink; Rev. Michael D. Barth.
Res., 5 S. Jefferson St., 41001-1315. Tel: 606-635-4188; Fax: 606-635-4189. [CEM]
School—9 S. Jefferson St., 41001-1398. Tel: 606-635-9539; Fax: 606-635-4189.
Sisters of Notre Dame 2; Lay Teachers 25; Students 482.
Catechesis/Religious Programs—Students 315.

Augusta, Bracken Co., St. Augustine (1860), Very Rev. Daniel J. Saner; Deacon Frank Estill.
Res., 215 E. Fourth St., 41002-1117. Tel: 606-756-2377. [JC]
School—Tel: 606-756-3229; Fax: 606-756-2377.
Sisters of Notre Dame 3; Lay Teachers 5; Students 72.

Bellevue, Campbell Co., Sacred Heart (1874), Rev. Lawrence R. Robotnik. In res., Rev. Lawrence W. Keller, (Retired).
Res., 318 Division St., 41073-1104. Tel: 606-261-6172.

St. Anthony (1889), Rev. John H. Kroger.
Res., 320 Poplar St., 41073-1196. Tel: 606-431-7143; Fax: 606-491-4735.
Catechesis/Religious Programs—Students 20.

Brooksville, Bracken Co., St. James (1868), Rev. James L. McHugh.
Res., P.O. Box 27, 41004-0027. Tel: 606-735-2271. [CEM]
Catechesis/Religious Programs—Students 56.
Mission—Minerva, Mason Co., St. James.

California, Campbell Co., Sts. Peter and Paul (1854), Rev. Joseph N. Boschert.
Res., Rte. 2, Box 134, 41007-9713. Tel: 606-635-2924. [CEM 2]
School—Tel: 606-635-4382; Fax: 606-635-9841.
Lay Teachers 7; Students 117.
Mission—Stepstone, Pendleton Co., Immaculate Conception.

Camp Springs, Campbell Co., St. Joseph (1845), Rev. Paul F. Tenhundfeld.
Res., Box 225, 41059-9746. Tel: 606-635-2491. [CEM]
School—Tel: 606-635-5652.
Religious 1; Lay Teachers 3; Students 55.
Catechesis/Religious Programs—Students 13.

Carrollton, Carroll Co., St. John the Evangelist (1853), Rev. William B. Neuhaus.
Res., 507 Fifth St., 41008-1203. Tel: 502-732-5776. [CEM]
Catechesis/Religious Programs—Students 85.
Mission—Perry Park, Owen Co., Transfiguration.

Cold Spring, Campbell Co., St. Joseph (1870), Revs. Robert J. Henderson; James B. Egbers. In res., Rev. Joseph J. Rueter, (Retired).
Res., 4011 Alexandria Pk., 41076-1817. Tel: 606-441-1604; Fax: 606-441-7681. [CEM]
School—Tel: 606-441-2025; Fax: 606-441-7681.
Sisters of Notre Dame 4; Lay Teachers 37; Students 647.
Catechesis/Religious Programs—Students 81.

Crescent Springs, Kenton Co., St. Joseph (1916), Revs. Raymond S. Hartman; Douglas J. Lauer; Deacons Marvin Holstein; Joseph Baker. In res., Rev. Ronald M. Ketteler.
Res., 2470 Lorraine Ct., 41017-1406. Tel: 606-341-6609; Fax: 606-578-2741.
School—Tel: 606-578-2742; Fax: 606-578-2754.
Lay Teachers 30; Students 570.
Catechesis/Religious Programs—Students 175.

Cynthiana, Harrison Co., St. Edward (1872), Rev. Louis B. Brinker.
Res., 123 N. Walnut St., 41031-1225. Tel: 606-234-5444; Fax: 606-234-9823. [CEM]
School—Tel: 606-234-2731.
Sisters of Notre Dame 1; Lay Teachers 3; Students 81.

Dayton, Campbell Co., St. Bernard (1853), Revs. Michael E. Comer; Paul Brinker, (Retired); Deacon Charles Dietz.
Res., Fifth & Berry Sts., 41074. Tel: 606-261-8506.
School—Tel: 606-581-6759.
Sisters of Divine Providence of Kentucky 4; Lay Teachers 3; Students 93.

Edgewood, Kenton Co., St. Pius X (1958), Revs. Douglas F. Fortner; Jeffrey D. Von Lehmen; Deacon Robert J. Hermann.
Res., 340 Dudley Rd., 41017-2609. Tel: 606-341-4888; Fax: 606-341-0508.
School—Tel: 606-341-3435.
Priests 2; Sisters 1; Lay Teachers 33; Students 627.
Catechesis/Religious Programs—Students 246.

Erlanger, Kenton Co., St. Barbara (1967), Rev. G. Michael Greer; Deacon Bernard J. Kaiser.
Res., 4042 Turkeyfoot Rd., 41018-2921. Tel: 606-371-3100; Fax: 606-371-3101.
Catechesis/Religious Programs—Students 209.

St. Henry (1890), Revs. Robert C. Wehage; Ralph C. Hartman; Anthony H. Deye, (Retired).
Res., 3813 Dixie Hwy., 41018-1809. Tel: 606-342-2540; 727-2035; Fax: 606-342-2542.
School—Tel: 606-342-2551; Fax: 606-342-2554.
Religious 1; Lay Teachers 25; Students 523.
Catechesis/Religious Programs—Students 178.

Mary, Queen of Heaven, Boone Co., (1955), Rev. John J. McGuire. In res., Rev. James P. Gerrety, (Retired).
Res., 1150 Donaldson Hwy., 41018-1048. Tel: 606-525-6909.
School—Tel: 606-371-8100.
Sisters 1; Lay Teachers 8; Students 235.

Falmouth, Pendleton Co., St. Francis Xavier (1880), Rev. Louis H. Dickmann.
Res., 202 Second St., 41040-1118. Tel: 606-654-8241. [CEM]
Catechesis/Religious Programs—Students 81.

Flemingsburg, Fleming Co., St. Charles (1859), Rev. Verne F. Hogan.
Res., 211 Mt. Carmel Ave., 41041-1315. Tel: 606-845-4601.

Florence, Boone Co., St. Paul (1874), Revs. George E. Schneider; Joseph Gallenstein.
Res., 7301 Dixie Hwy., 41042-2126. Tel: 606-371-8051; Fax: 606-647-4061.
School—Tel: 606-647-4070.
Lay Teachers 23; Students 531.
Catechesis/Religious Programs—Students 360.

Fort Mitchell, Kenton Co., Blessed Sacrament (1920), Revs. Albert E. Ruschman; Mark G. Witte; Sr. Ann Middendorf, O.S.B., Pastoral Assoc.
Res., 2415 Dixie Hwy., 41017. Tel: 606-331-4302; Fax: 606-578-4752.
School—Tel: 606-331-3062; Fax: 606-344-7323.
Lay Teachers 33; Students 565.
Catechesis/Religious Programs—Students 230.

Fort Thomas, Campbell Co., St. Catherine of Siena (1930), Rev. Daniel J. Vogelpohl; Deacon Edward Stieritz. In res., Rev. Robert L. Vater, (Retired).
Mailing Address: 1803 N. Ft. Thomas Ave., 41075-1170. Tel: 606-441-1352; Fax: 606-572-2685.
School—Lay Teachers 15; Students 221.
Catechesis/Religious Programs—Students 195.

St. Thomas (1902), Revs. John J. Riesenberg; Richard W. Frazier; Deacon James Sweigart.
Res., 26 E. Villa Pl., 41075-2218. Tel: 606-441-1282; Fax: 606-572-4640.
School—Tel: 606-572-4641.
Sisters of Divine Providence of Kentucky 3; Lay Teachers 21; Students 275.
Catechesis/Religious Programs—Students 126.

Burlington, Boone Co., Immaculate Heart of Mary (1954), Rev. Jerome C. Britt.
Church—5876 Veterans Way, 41005-8824. Tel: 606-689-4488; Fax: 606-689-5636.
School—Tel: 606-689-4303.
Sisters of Divine Providence of Kentucky 3; Lay Teachers 18; Students 355.
Catechesis/Religious Programs—Students 373.

Independence, Kenton Co., St. Cecilia (1880), Rev. Paul L. Berschied.
Res., 5313 Madison Pk., 41051-8611. Tel: 606-356-3251. [CEM]
School—Tel: 606-356-6119; Fax: 606-356-5492.
Lay Teachers 8; Students 194.
Catechesis/Religious Programs—Students 194.

Kenton, Kenton Co., St. Matthew (1909), Rev. Gregory E. Osburg.

Res., 13816 Decoursey Pk., P.O. Box 82, 41053-0082. Tel: 606-356-6530. [CEM]
Catechesis/Religious Programs—Students 68.
Mission—Morning View, Kenton Co., Assumption of the Blessed Virgin, 3711 St. Mary Rd., Morning View, 41063.

Ludlow, Kenton Co., Sts. Boniface and James (1872), Rev. Allan W. Bradley.
Res., 304 Oak St., 41016-1417. Tel: 606-261-5340.

May's Lick, Mason Co., St. Rose of Lima (1864), Rev. Verne F. Hogan.
Church—P.O. Box 100, 41055. Tel: 606-763-6304.

Maysville, Mason Co., St. Patrick (1874), Rev. William H. Hinds; Deacon Ernest B. Hillenmeyer.
Res., 110 E. Third St., P.O. Box 248, 41056-0248. Tel: 606-564-9015. [CEM]
School—Tel: 606-564-5949; Fax: 606-564-8795. Lay Teachers 13; Students 220.
High School—Lay Teachers 14; Students 100.
Catechesis/Religious Programs—Students 45.

Melbourne, Campbell Co., St. Philip (1908), Rev. James M. Ryan.
Res., R.R. #1, Box 1, 41059-9701. Tel: 606-441-8949; Fax: 606-441-2611.
School—Tel: 606-441-3423.
Sisters of Divine Providence of Kentucky 3; Lay Teachers 4; Students 111.

Newport, Campbell Co.,

1—CORPUS CHRISTI, (1884), Rev. Richard Bolte.
Res., 841 Isabella St., 41071-1338. Tel: 606-261-2541; Fax: 606-491-6587.

2—ST. STEPHEN, (1854), Rev. Eugene E. Wolfzorn.
Res., 825 Washington Ave., 41071-1943. Tel: 606-431-2533.
Catechesis/Religious Programs—Students 62.

3—ST. FRANCIS DE SALES, (1911), Rev. Eugene Wolfzorn.
10 Chesapeake Ave., 41071-1945. Tel: 606-292-0452; Fax: 606-292-0452.
Res., 825 Washington Ave., 41071-1943.
Catechesis/Religious Programs—Students 62.

4—ST. VINCENT DE PAUL, (1916), Rev. Robert J. Reinke.
Res., 119 Main St., 41071-2353. Tel: 606-261-4391. [JC]

Southgate, Campbell Co., St. Therese of the Infant Jesus (1927), Revs. Clarence J. Heitzman; Robert L. Gruber. In res., Rev. Msgr. Elmer Grosser, (Retired).
Res., 11 Temple Pl., 41071-3133. Tel: 606-441-1654.
School—Tel: 606-441-0449; Fax: 606-441-7988.
Sisters of Notre Dame 2; Lay Teachers 9; Students 251.
Catechesis/Religious Programs—Students 65.

Taylor Mill, Kenton Co., St. Anthony (1878), Rev. Thomas P. Robbins.
Res., Grand & Howard Ave., P.O. Box 15219, Covington, 41015-0219. Tel: 606-431-1773.
School—Tel: 606-431-5987.
Lay Teachers 10; Students 185.
Catechesis/Religious Programs—Students 60.

St. Patrick (1968), Rev. B. Gerald Witzemann.
Res., 3285 Mills Rd., Covington, 41015-2480. Tel: 606-356-2171.
Catechesis/Religious Programs—Students 185.

Union, Boone Co., St. Timothy (1989), Rev. Edward J. Brodnick; Deacon Thomas Nolan.
Res., 10272 Hwy. 42, P.O. Box 120, 41091-0120. Tel: 606-384-1100; Fax: 606-384-1709.
Catechesis/Religious Programs—Students 317.

Vanceburg, Lewis Co., Holy Redeemer (1965), Sr. Joseph Fillenwarth, S.P., Admin.; Rev. Bruce Brylinski, Pastoral Supvr.
Res., P.O. Box 8, 41179-0008. Tel: 606-796-3052.

Walton, Boone Co., All Saints (1951), Rev. Edwin B. Heile.
Res., 46 Needmore St., 41094-1029. Tel: 606-485-4476. [CEM 2]
Catechesis/Religious Programs—Students 151.

Warsaw, Gallatin Co., St. Joseph (1864), Rev. George J. Schuhmacher.
Mailing Address: P.O. Box 495, 41095-0495.
Res., 602 Sparta Pike, 41095-0495. Tel: 606-567-2425. [CEM]
Mission—Owenton, Owen Co., St. Edward, 1335 Hwy. 22 E., R.R. 4, Box 35B, Owenton, 40359-9003. Tel: 606-567-2425.

Wilder, Campbell Co., St. John (1847), Rev. Richard H. McGrath.
Res., 641 Licking Pike, 41076-9076. Tel: 606-781-2117. [CEM]

Williamstown, Grant Co., St. William (1912), Sr. Carol Leveque, S.C., Pastoral Admin.; Rev. Roger L. Kriege.
Res., 6 Church Dr., 41097. Tel: 606-824-5381. [CEM 2]
Catechesis/Religious Programs—Students 63.
Mission—Dividing Ridge, Pendleton Co., St. John's, (1956).

Chaplains of Public Institutions

COVINGTON. *Children's Psychiatric Hospital of Northern Kentucky*. Rev. Charles E. Weber.
St. John's Nursing Home. Attended by St. Augustine Church, Covington.

COLD SPRING. *Lakeside Place*. Attended by St. Joseph Parish, Cold Spring.

FLORENCE. *St. Luke West*. Rev. Charles E. Weber.

FORT THOMAS. *St. Luke Hospital East*. Rev. John A. Seiler.
Veterans Hospital. Attended by the Franciscan Fathers (O.F.M.), Cincinnati, Ohio.

On Duty Outside the Diocese:
Reverend Fathers—
Callahan, Leonard F., 3725 Blackburn, Dallas, TX 75219-0507
Cooney, Roger P., Pontifical College Josephinum, 7625 N. High St., Columbus, OH 43235-1499
Rutz, Gilbert J., 1224 E. Northern Ave., Phoenix, AZ 85020-4274

Leave of Absence:
Reverend Fathers—
Goeke, John W.
Schott, Fred
Wilcoxson, Thomas J.

Military Chaplains:
Reverend Fathers—
Leslie, Larry B., MCMWTC, Chaplain's Office, Bridgeport, CA 93517-5001

Retired:
Reverend Monsignors—
Finn, Thomas B., Regina Cleri Home, 100 Carmel Manor Rd., Fort Thomas, KY 41075-2300
Fleming, W. Stanley, Regina Cleri Home, 100 Carmel Manor Rd., Fort Thomas, KY 41075-2300
Grosser, Elmer J., St. Therese Rectory, 11 Temple Pl., Southgate, KY 41071-3133
Hegenauer, John V., Regina Cleri Home, 100 Carmel Manor Rd., Fort Thomas, KY 41075-2300
Hickey, Edward T., Highland Crossing, #112, 400 Farrell Dr., Covington, KY 41011-3286
Meier, Allen J., Notre Dame Academy, 1699 Hilton Dr., Covington, KY 41011-2705
Murphy, John F., 2727 Leatherwood Ct., Crestview Hills, KY 41017-2274
Welp, Harry J., 726 Meadowood, Apt. 1, Villa Hills, KY 41017-4607

Reverend Fathers—
Bierman, Earl C., The Catholic Center, P.O. Box 18548, Erlanger, KY 41018-0548
Brinker, Paul J., P.O. Box 17321, Dayton, KY 41017-0321
Broering, Raymond L., 2 Cypress Run, SMW-B21, Homosassa, FL 34446-4211
Deye, Anthony H., St. Henry Rectory, 3813 Dixie Hwy., Erlanger, KY 41018-1809
Garvey, Charles J., Holy Cross Rectory, 3612 Church St., Covington, KY 41015-1431
Gerrety, James P., Mary, Queen of Heaven Rectory, 1150 Donaldson Hwy., Erlanger, KY 41018-1048
Hoffer, Charles, Holy Cross Rectory, 3612 Church St., Covington, KY 41015-1431
Holtz, Louis J., Newman Rd., R.R. 4, Box 195A, Falmouth, KY 41040-9417
Jasper, Louis H., 1400 Sleepy Hollow, Apt. 4, Covington, KY 41011-2757
Kamlage, Herman, Hathaway Court, #416, 1200 Highway Ave., Covington, KY 41011-1095
Keller, Lawrence W., Sacred Heart Rectory, 318 Division St., Bellevue, KY 41073-1104
Kelly, Francis J., 32 Widrig St., Newport, KY 41071-2746
Klein, Robert P., 3516 Misty Creek Dr., Erlanger, KY 41018-2627
Krebs, Paul F., 14 Orchard St., Southgate, KY 41071-3126
Mertes, William H., 228 Covington Ave., Covington, KY 41011-1414
Mulhern, Raymond F., 6537 W. 173rd Pl., Tinley Park, IL 60477-3554
Nieman, Raymond L., 705 Gripshover Ln., Crittenden, KY 41030-8257
Quill, James E., St. Agnes Rectory, 1680 Dixie Hwy., Covington, KY 41011
Reifsnyder, John A., Sacred Heart Rectory, 310 Shady Ave., Pittsburgh, PA 15206-4306
Rooks, Charles W., 1601 Dixie Hwy., Covington, KY 41011-2798
Rueter, Joseph J., St. Joseph Rectory, 4011 Alexandria Pike, Cold Spring, KY 41076-1817
Schmidt, Vincent F., Carmel Manor, 100 Carmel Manor Rd., Fort Thomas, KY 41075-2300
Schutzman, John S., Carmel Manor, 100 Carmel Manor Rd., Fort Thomas, KY 41075-2300
Shockey, David P., St. Joseph Convent, 13 Mulberry St., Walton, KY 41094-1036
Smith, R. Leroy, 5440 Moeller Ave., Norwood, OH 45212-1211
Steinhauser, Raymond W., 705 Gripshover Ln., Crittenden, KY 41030-8257
Toner, Edward R., 5614 Long Commons Cir., Sarasota, FL 34235-2401
Trimbur, Edwin H., P.O. Box 452, El Paso, TX 79943-0452
Urlage, Robert J., P.O. Box 75254, Fort Thomas, KY 41075
Vater, Robert L., St. Catherine of Siena Rectory, 10 Wesley Hills Dr., Fort Thomas, KY 41075-1213
Werner, John P., 104 Highland Dr., Apt. 1, Fort Mitchell, KY 41017-2920
Witt, Robert G., P.O. Box 2844, Capistrano Beach, CA 92624-0844

Permanent Deacons:
Baker, Joseph, St. Joseph, Crescent Springs
Cleves, Joe, St. Agnes, Covington
Colatrella, Ralph, Holy Cross, Latonia
Dietz, Charles, St. Bernard, Dayton
Dunning, John, Cathedral, Covington
Estill, Andrew (Frank), St. Augustine, Augusta
Flynn, David, St. Agnes, Covington
Hermann, Robert J., St. Pius, Edgewood
Hillenmeyer, Ernest, St. Patrick, Maysville
Holstein, Marvin, St. Joseph, Crescent Springs
Kaiser, Bernard, St. Barbara, Erlanger
Lehmkuhl, Dennis, St. Mary, Alexandria
Nolan, Thomas, St. Timothy, Union
Norris, Eugene, (Retired)
O'Donnell, Richard, (Retired)
Runge, Thomas, Mother of God, Covington
Stieritz, Edward, St. Catherine, Fort Thomas
Sweigart, Jim, St. Thomas, Fort Thomas

PILGRIMAGE SHRINES

COVINGTON. *Shrine of St. Ann*. Attached to St. Ann Church.

SOUTHGATE. *Shrine of the Little Flower*. Attached to St. Therese Church.

INSTITUTIONS LOCATED IN THE DIOCESE

[A] COLLEGES AND UNIVERSITIES

COVINGTON. *Thomas More College*, Crestview Hills, 41017-3428. Tel: 606-341-5800.
For a complete listing, refer to the Colleges and Universities section.
Thomas More College, Student Dormitory, 333 Thomas More Pkwy., 41017.
For a complete listing, refer to the Colleges and Universities section.

[B] HIGH SCHOOLS, DIOCESAN

COVINGTON. *Covington Catholic High School*, 1600 Dixie Hwy., 41011-2797. Tel: 606-431-5351. Mr. Jack Kennevan, Prin.; Rev. John Sterling, Chap. Lay Teachers 30; Boys 509.
Covington Latin School, 21-23 E. 11th St., 41011-3196. Tel: 606-291-7044. Mr. Richard Stewart, Dean; Mr. Robert R. Larcher, Headmaster; Rev. Mark Steidle, Chap. Lay Teachers 16; Boys 120; Girls 70.
Holy Cross High School, 3617 Church St., 41015-1498. Tel: 606-431-1335. Mr. William Goller, Prin.; Rev. Thomas P. Robbins, Chap. Religious 3; Lay Teachers 28; Students 344.

ALEXANDRIA. *Bishop Brossart High School*, 41001-1295. Tel: 606-635-2108. Mr. Thomas H. Seither, Prin.; Rev. Michael Barth, Chap. Sisters of Notre Dame 2; Sisters of Divine Providence 1; Lay Teachers 25; Students 421.

ERLANGER. *St. Henry District High School*, 3837 Dixie Hwy., 41018-1864. Tel: 606-342-2544. Mr. David M. Otte, Prin.; Rev. Donald A. Enzweiler, Chap. Lay Teachers 34; Religious 1; Priests 1; Students 435.

MAYSVILLE. *St. Patrick High School*, 318 Limestone St., 41056-1248. Mrs. Sarah C. Kalb, Prin.; Rev. William Hinds, Chap. Lay Teachers 14; Students 100.

NEWPORT. *Newport Central Catholic High School*, 13 Carothers Rd., 41071-2497. Tel: 606-292-0001. Mr. Carl Foster, Prin.; Rev. Richard Bolte, Chap. Administrative Team: Mr. Greg Burwinkel; Mr. Robert Schneider. Lay Teachers 25; Students 392.

[C] HIGH SCHOOLS, PRIVATE

COVINGTON. *Academy of Notre Dame*, 1699 Hilton Dr., 41011-2705. Tel: 606-261-4300. Sisters of Notre Dame. Sr. Mary Rita, S.N.D., Prin. Chaplains: Rev. Msgr. Allen J. Meier; Rev. Mark Witte. Sisters 17;

Lay Teachers 35; Girls 638.

Villa Madonna High School. 2500 Amsterdam Rd., Villa Hills, 41017-3798. Tel: 606-331-6333. Sr. Victoria Eisenman, O.S.B., Dir.; Ms. Pamela McQueen, Prin.; Rev. Douglas J. Lauer, Chap. Sisters 4; Lay Teachers 12; Students 135.

[D] ELEMENTARY SCHOOLS, INTERPAROCHIAL

COVINGTON. *Holy Family Catholic School*, 338 E. 16th St., 41014-1304. Tel: 606-581-0290. Lay Teachers 10; Students 162.

Prince of Peace School, 625 Pike St., 41011-2798. Tel: 606-431-5153. Sr. Mary Sharron Goller, S.N.D., Prin. Sisters of Notre Dame 3; Lay Teachers 6; Students 128.

BELLEVUE. *St. Michael School*, 235 Division St., 41073-1101. Tel: 606-291-6937. Sr. M. Patrycia Sweeney, S.N.D., Prin. Sisters of Notre Dame 3; Lay Teachers 8; Students 149.

NEWPORT. *Holy Spirit Elementary School*, 840 Washington Ave., 41071-2485. Tel: 606-431-8745. Sr. Juanita Nadicksbernd, C.D.P., Prin. Sisters 2; Lay Teachers 5; Students 118.

Holy Spirit Junior High School, Chesapeake Ave. & Grand Ave., 41071-2485. Tel: 606-292-0487. Sr. Juanita Nadicksbernd, C.D.P., Prin. Sisters of Divine Providence 2; Lay Teachers 3; Students 72.

[E] ELEMENTARY SCHOOLS, DIOCESAN

FORT MITCHELL. *Guardian Angel*, P.O. Box 17007, Orphanage Rd., 41017-0007. Tel: 606-331-2040. Sr. Pamela Mae Geiger, S.N.D., Prin. Sisters 1; Lay Teachers 3; Students 19.

[F] ELEMENTARY SCHOOLS, PRIVATE

COVINGTON. *Villa Madonna Elementary School*. 2500 Amsterdam Rd., Villa Hills, 41017-3798. Tel: 606-331-6333. Sr. Victoria Eisenman, O.S.B., Dir.; Mrs. Becky Moeller, Prin. Sisters 3; Lay Teachers 22; Students 261.

WALTON. *St. Joseph Academy*, 48 Needmore St., 41094. Tel: 606-485-6444. Sisters of St. Joseph the Worker. Sr. Patricia Jean, S.J.W., Prin. Sisters 6; Lay Teachers 7; Students 227.

Attended from All Saints, Walton; St. William, Williamstown; St. Joseph, Warsaw; and St. Timothy, Union.

[G] MONTESSORI SCHOOLS (PRESCHOOL)

VILLA HILLS. *Villa Madonna Montessori*, 2402 Amsterdam Rd., 41017-5316. Tel: 606-341-5145. Sr. Mary Peter, O.S.B., Prin. & Admin. Sisters of St. Benedict 3; Lay Teachers 4; Students 50.

[H] GENERAL HOSPITALS

COVINGTON. *St. Elizabeth Medical Center, North*, 401 E. 20th St., 41014-1585. Tel: 606-292-4000; Fax: 606-292-4487.

For a complete listing, refer to the Hospitals section.

EDGEWOOD. *St. Elizabeth Medical Center, South*, One Medical Village Dr., 41017-3441. Tel: 606-344-2000.

For a complete listing, refer to the Hospitals section.

WILLIAMSTOWN. *St. Elizabeth Medical Center, Grant County*, 238 Barnes Rd., 41097-9482. Tel: 606-291-6738.

For a complete listing, refer to the Hospitals section.

[I] NURSING HOMES

COVINGTON. *Madonna Manor, Inc.* 2344 Amsterdam Rd. Villa Hills, 41017-3712. Tel: 606-341-3981.

For a complete listing, refer to the Special Care Facilities section.

St. Charles Care Center, Inc., 500 Farrell Dr., 41011-3798. Tel: 606-331-3224.

For a complete listing, refer to the Special Care Facilities section.

[J] PROTECTIVE INSTITUTIONS

COVINGTON. *Diocesan Catholic Children's Home*. Orphanage Rd., P.O. Box 17007 Fort Mitchell, 41017-2730.

For a complete listing, refer to the Special Care Facilities section.

COLD SPRING. *Campbell Lodge Boys Home*, 150 Skyline Dr., 41076-2099. Tel: 606-781-1214.

For a complete listing, refer to the Special Care Facilities section.

[K] HOMES FOR AGED

FORT THOMAS. *Carmel Manor*, 100 Carmel Manor Rd., 41075-2395. Tel: 606-781-5111.

For a complete listing, refer to the Special Care Facilities section.

Regina Cleri Home for Retired Priests, 100 Carmel Manor Rd., 41075-2395. Tel: 606-781-5111.

For a complete listing, refer to the Special Care Facilities section.

[L] MONASTERIES AND RESIDENCES OF PRIESTS AND BROTHERS

COVINGTON. *Brothers of the Poor of St. Francis*, 716 Bakewell St., 41011. Tel: 606-431-3202; Fax: 606-431-7667. International Office. Bro. James Phelan, C.F.P., Res. Minister Gen. In res., Bros. James Phelan, C.F.P.; John Walsh, C.F.P.; Rock Larson.

[M] CONVENTS AND RESIDENCES FOR SISTERS

COVINGTON. *St. Joseph Heights Provincialate and Novitiate of the Sisters of Notre Dame*, 1601 Dixie Hwy., 41011-2798. Tel: 606-291-2040. Sr. Mary Shauna Bankemper, S.N.D., Prov. Supr.; Rev. Charles W. Rooks, Chap. Sisters in Community 187; Sisters in Prov. House 73.

St. Walburg Monastery, 2500 Amsterdam Rd., 41017-3798. Tel: 606-331-6324; Fax: 606-331-2136. Sisters of St. Benedict. Sr. Mary Catherine Wenstrup, O.S.B., Prioress; Rev. Gerald L. Reinersman, Chap. Professed Sisters 110.

ERLANGER. *Monastery of the Sacred Passion*, 1151 Donaldson Hwy., 41018-1000. Tel: 606-371-8568. Passionists Nuns. Sr. Margaret Mary, C.P., Supr.; Rev. John R. Schulte, Chap. Professed 9.

FORT THOMAS. *Sisters of the Good Shepherd*, Pelletier Hall, 930 Highland Ave., 41075. Tel: 606-441-5531. Rev. Richard H. McGrath, Chap. Sisters of the Good Shepherd 22.

KENTON HILLS. *St. Vincent's Convent*, 630 Jerol Ave., 41011. Tel: 606-431-5388. Intercongregational Residence. Sisters 4.

MELBOURNE. *Holy Family Home*, Rte. 8, 2000 St. Anne Dr., 41059-9604. Tel: 606-781-0712. Rev. John Modica, Chap. Sisters in Residence 65.

St. Anne Convent, 1000 St. Anne Dr., 41059-9603. Tel: 606-441-0679. Provincial House and Novitiate of the Sisters of Divine Providence of Kentucky. Sr. Lynn Stenken, C.D.P., Prov. Supr. Sisters in Community 201; Sisters in Provincial House 33; Sisters in Residence 56.

WALTON. *St. William Convent*, One St. Joseph Ln., 41094-1036. Tel: 606-485-4914; 485-4256; Fax: 606-485-9302. Sisters of St. Joseph the Worker. Mother Ellen Curran, S.J.W., Supr.; Rev. David P. Shockey, Chap., Res., 13 Mulberry St., 41094-1036. Sisters in Community 21; Sisters in Motherhouse 10.

[N] SECULAR INSTITUTES

COVINGTON. *Society of St. Vincent de Paul*, 2655 Crescent Springs Rd., 41017-1504. Tel: 606-341-3219. William H. Schneider, Pres. District Council of Northern Kentucky. Executive Offices and Thrift Stores. 30 Parish Conferences in Northern Kentucky Thrift Stores, including Dayton, Newport, Crescent Springs, Latonia, Ludlow, Covington, and Walton. Total stores 7. A Catholic lay organization of over 875,000 members worldwide whose members meet in parish and district groups in order to help in a personal way those in need.

[O] SOCIAL SERVICES

COVINGTON. *Catholic Social Services*, 3629 Church St., 41015-1499. Tel: 606-581-8974; Fax: 606-581-9595. Sr. Joan Marie Boberg, C.D.P., Dir. Total Assisted 8,383.

Parish Kitchen, Pike St. & Russell St., 41011. Tel: 606-581-7745. Ms. Molly Navin, Dir. Total Assisted 60,000.

Welcome House of Northern Kentucky, Inc., 141 Pike St., 41011-2521. Tel: 606-431-8717; Fax: 606-431-6297. 203-205 Pike St., 41011. Shelter for homeless women and their children, 24 hours a day. Emergency Assistance Center and Representative Payee Program.

VANCEBURG. *Appalachian Apostolate, Inc.*, Rte. 1, Box 6A, 41179-0008. Tel: 606-796-3289. Sr. Conall O'Connell, Dir. Persons assisted annually 1,200.

[P] DIOCESAN RETREAT HOUSES

ERLANGER. *Marydale Retreat Center*, 945 Donaldson Hwy., 41018-1093. Tel: 606-371-4224. Edward Stieritz, Dir.

[Q] NEWMAN CENTERS

HIGHLAND HEIGHTS. *Catholic Newman Center - Northern Kentucky University*, 512 Johns Hill Rd., P.O. Box 76174, 41076-1449. Tel: 606-781-3775. Mr. Al Cucchetti, Pastoral Admin.

[R] INTERFAITH CENTERS

COVINGTON. *Interfaith Commission of Northern Kentucky*. P.O. Box 72296, Newport, 41072-0296. Tel: 606-581-2237. Rev. William C. Neuroth, Exec. Dir. Purpose: A religious organization committed to understanding the various faith traditions of our member bodies, while working together in response to the spiritual and human needs of all people of the Northern Kentucky area.

[S] MISCELLANEOUS

DAYTON. *Connective Ministries*, 416 10th Ave., 41074. Tel: 606-261-9040. Co-Chairmen: Sr. Mary Priniski, O.P.; Mrs. Sarah Price. Purpose: Seeks to encourage grassroots empowerment efforts by developing linkages between local organizing groups, providing opportunities for shared reflection among church workers, and connecting unorganized poor people with resource groups.

ERLANGER. *Women of Providence in Collaboration*, National Office, The Catholic Center, 947 Donaldson Rd., P.O. Box 18548, 41018-0548. Tel: 606-283-6303; Fax: 606-283-6334. Sr. Mary Catherine Hunt, C.D.P., Dir. Purpose: To investigate and develop intercongregationally a contemporary theology and spirituality of Providence and to undertake collaborative projects which communicate these understandings through our mission of witnessing Providence to the world.

FORT THOMAS. *Mission Share*, P.O. Box 242, 41075. Tel: 606-525-6909. Rev. John J. McGuire, Pres. Purpose: A mission society whose principal activity is to carry out and advance the function, practices, and liturgy of the Catholic Church in Cali, Colombia, and for medical and dental programs, educational programs, the construction of parish and archdiocesan buildings, and the advancement of the Catholic faith and various other civic and social programs.

RELIGIOUS INSTITUTES OF MEN REPRESENTED IN THE DIOCESE

For further details refer to the corresponding bracketed number in the Religious Institutes of Men or Women section.

[0460]—*Brothers of the Poor of St. Francis*. (Aachen, Germany).—C.F.P.

[0570]—*Glenmary Home Missioners*.—Glmy.

[0690]—*Jesuit Fathers and Brothers*. (Chicago Prov.).—S.J.

RELIGIOUS INSTITUTES OF WOMEN REPRESENTED IN THE DIOCESE

[0230]—*Benedictine Sisters of Pontifical Jurisdiction*.—O.S.B.

[0330]—*Carmelite Sisters for the Aged and Infirm*. (Germantown, NY).—O.Carm.

[1070-01]—*Congregation of St. Catharine of Siena*. (Louisville, KY).—O.P.

[3180]—*Congregation of the Passion of Jesus Christ*.—C.P.

[1920]—*Congregation of the Sisters of the Holy Cross*. (Notre Dame, IN).—C.S.C.

[1070-21]—*Dominican Sisters of Edmonds*.—O.P.

[0440]—*Sisters of Charity of Cincinnati, Ohio*.—S.C.

[0500]—*Sisters of Charity of Nazareth*.—S.C.N.

[1000]—*Sisters of Divine Providence of Kentucky*.—C.D.P.

[2990]—*Sisters of Notre Dame*.—S.N.D.

[3000]—*Sisters of Notre Dame de Namur*. (Cincinnati, OH).—S.N.D.deN.

[3360]—*Sisters of Providence of Saint Mary-of-the-Woods, IN*.—S.P.

[3880]—*Sisters of St. Joseph of Medaille*. (Cincinnati, OH).—C.S.J.

[3920]—*Sisters of St. Joseph the Worker*.—S.J.W.

[1830]—*Sisters of the Good Shepherd*.—R.G.S.

[3260]—*Sisters of the Precious Blood*. (Dayton, Ohio).—C.PP.S.

[1730]—*Sisters of the Third Order of St. Francis*. (Oldenburg, IN).—O.S.F.

[1720]—*Sisters of the Third Order Regular of St. Francis of the Congregation of Our Lady of Lourdes*. (Rochester, MN).—O.S.F.

[4120]—*Ursuline Nuns, of the Congregation of Paris*. (Brown County, OH).—O.S.U.

DIOCESAN CEMETERIES

COLD SPRING. *St. Joseph*.

FORT MITCHELL. *St. John*.

St. Mary.

FORT THOMAS. *St. Stephen*.

WILDER. *St. Joseph*.

NECROLOGY

† Elsaesser, John Severin, (Retired). —Died Aug. 17, 1996.

Diocese of Crookston

(Dioecesis Crookstoniensis)

Most Reverend

VICTOR H. BALKE, D.D., PH.D.

Bishop of Crookston; ordained May 24, 1958; appointed July 7, 1976; Episcopal ordination September 2, 1976. *Res., 1200 Memorial Dr., Crookston, MN, 56716.* Tel.: 218-281-4533.

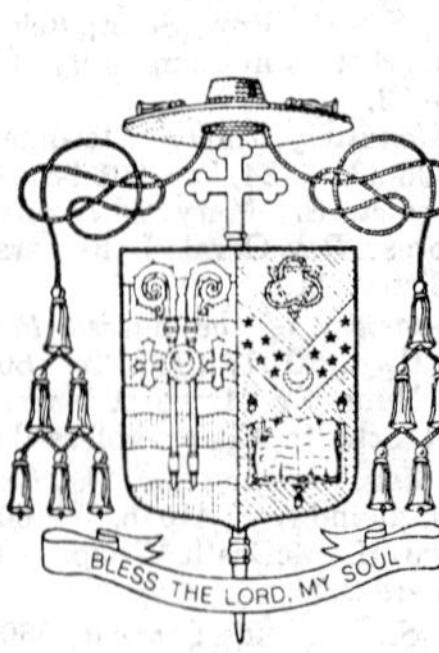

Chancery Office: 1200 Memorial Dr., P.O. Box 610, Crookston, MN, 56716. Tel.: 218-281-4533; Fax: 218-281-3328.

ESTABLISHED BY HIS HOLINESS PIUS X, DECEMBER 31, 1909.

Square Miles 17,210.

Comprises the Counties of Becker, Beltrami, Clay, Clearwater, Hubbard, Kittson, Lake of the Woods, Marshall, Mahnomen, Norman, Pennington, Polk, Red Lake and Roseau in the State of Minnesota.

PATRONESS OF THE DIOCESE: The Immaculate Conception.

Legal Title: Diocese of Crookston.

For legal titles of parishes and diocesan institutions, consult the Chancery Office.

STATISTICAL OVERVIEW

Personnel	
Bishop	1
Priests: Diocesan Active in Diocese	31
Priests: Active Outside Diocese	3
Priests: Diocesan in Foreign Missions	1
Priests: Retired, Sick or Absent	14
Number of Diocesan Priests	49
Religious Priests in Diocese	5
Extern Priests in Diocese	3
Ordinations:	
Diocesan Priests	2
Permanent Deacons	3
Permanent Deacons in Diocese	8
Total Brothers	2
Total Sisters	214
Parishes	
Parishes	76
With Resident Pastor:	
Resident Diocesan Priests	24
Resident Religious Priests	5
Without Resident Pastor:	
Administered by Priests	38
Administered by Permanent Deacons	1
Administered by Women Religious	6
Administered by Lay People	2
Pastoral Centers	1
Professional Ministry Personnel:	
Brothers	2
Sisters	12
Lay Ministers	19
Welfare	
Catholic Hospitals	3
Total Assisted	48,118
Homes for the Aged	3
Total Assisted	473
Day Care and Extended Day Care Centers	1
Total Assisted	53
Educational	
Diocesan Students in Other Seminaries	4
Total Seminarians	4
High Schools, Diocesan and Parish	1
Total Students	150
Elementary Schools, Diocesan and Parish	8
Total Students	1,165
Elementary Schools, Private	1
Total Students	85
Catechesis/Religious Education:	
High School Students	2,726
Elementary Students	3,614
Total Students Under Catholic Instruction	7,744
Teachers in the Diocese:	
Sisters	6
Lay Teachers	95
Vital Statistics	
Receptions into the Church:	
Infant Baptism Totals	776
Adult Baptism Totals	15
Received into Full Communion	93
First Communions	696
Confirmations	756
Marriages:	
Catholic	148
Interfaith	161
Total Marriages	309
Deaths	440
Total Catholic Population	42,934
Total Population	236,100

Former Bishops—Most Rev. TIMOTHY CORBETT, D.D., ord. June 12, 1886; cons. May 19, 1910; resigned See Aug. 6, 1938; appt. Titular Bishop of Vita; died July 20, 1939.—Most Rev. JOHN H. PESCHGES, D.D., ord. April 15, 1905; cons. Nov. 9, 1938; died Oct. 30, 1944.—Most Rev. FRANCIS J. SCHENK, D.D., ord. June 13, 1926; cons. May 24, 1945; transferred to Duluth Jan. 27, 1960; died Oct. 28, 1969.—Most Rev. LAURENCE A. GLENN, D.D., ord. June 11, 1927; cons. Sept. 12, 1956; retired July 28, 1970; died Jan. 26, 1985.—Most Rev. KENNETH J. POVISH, D.D., ord. June 3, 1950; appt. Bishop of Crookston July 28, 1970; cons. Sept. 29, 1970; transferred to Lansing Oct. 21, 1975.

Vicar General—Rev. Msgr. ROGER L. GRUNDHAUS, J.C.L., *Cathedral of the Immaculate Conception, 702 Summit Ave., Crookston, 56716.*

Chancery Office—1200 Memorial Dr., P.O. Box 610, Crookston, 56716. Tel: 218-281-4533; Fax: 218-281-3328.

Chancellor—Rev. MICHAEL H. FOLTZ, J.C.L.

Moderator of the Curia—Rev. MICHAEL H. FOLTZ, J.C.L.

Episcopal Vicar for Canonical Affairs—Rev. MICHAEL H. FOLTZ, J.C.L.

Information Officer—Rev. MICHAEL H. FOLTZ, J.C.L.

Pastoral Office of Administration—GEORGE NOEL.

Finance Manager—GEORGE NOEL.

Diocesan Tribunal—1200 Memorial Dr., P.O. Box 610, Crookston. Tel: 218-281-4533.

Officialis—Rev. MICHAEL SULLIVAN, J.C.L.

Defenders of the Bond—Revs. RICHARD BOYD; RICHARD LAMBERT.

Advocate—JOANNE TOLLEFSON.

Notary—ROSE MARIE WISE.

Psychological Consultant—ELIZABETH BARAGA SUPER, Ph.D.

Diocesan Offices And Directors

Diocesan Consultors—Rev. Msgr. ROGER L. GRUNDHAUS, J.C.L.; Revs. GARY LAMOINE; RAYMOND PALCISKO; JOHN KLEINWACHTER; MICHAEL SULLIVAN; AUGUST GOTHMAN.

Finance Council—Most Rev. VICTOR H. BALKE, D.D.; Rev. Msgr. ROGER L. GRUNDHAUS, V.G.; Rev. MICHAEL H. FOLTZ, J.C.L.; Rev. Msgr. MICHAEL PATNODE; Revs. DAVID SUPER; AL HENGER, O.M.I.; Sr. MARY DANIEL NEUMANN, O.S.B.; IRENE CAMPBELL; ELAINE WHITE; RICHARD TAYLOR; DEAN MITZEL.

Advocacy, Adoption Referral—ROSE MARIE WISE, *P.O. Box 610, Crookston, 56716.* Tel: 218-281-4533.

Beginning Experience—JAY NORBY, Pres. BERNADETTE DUNN, Bishop's Liaison, *P.O. Box 610, Crookston, 56716.* Tel: 218-281-4533.

Boy Scouts—DON VOTAVA, *Rte. 2, Box 172A, Warren, 56762.* Tel: 218-745-5423. Rev. MICHAEL SULLIVAN, Chap.

Campaign for Human Development—BERNADETTE DUNN, *P.O. Box 610, Crookston, 56716.* Tel: 218-281-4533.

Catholic Relief Services—Rev. MICHAEL H. FOLTZ, J.C.L., Dir., *P.O. Box 610, Crookston, 56716.* Tel: 218-281-4533.

Clergy Relief Society—Legal Title: *St. Joseph's Priest Fund Inc.* Rev. TIMOTHY MCGEE, Sec. & Treas.

Commission on Building and Planning—Rev. RICHARD LAMBERT; Sr. MARGUERITE STREIFEL, O.S.B.; Sr. BRIAN WILD, O.S.B.; RICHARD RUDE; JIM SHULIND; CATHY BELMONT.

Commission on Catholic-Lutheran Rural Life—MILO MATHISON, Chm., *Rte. 1, Box 244, Mentor, 56736.* Tel: 218-637-6456.

Commission on Ecumenism—KEVIN ERPELDING, Chm. JANICE SEMANKO; SUZANNE NELSON; ROY DUFAULT; MILDRED OVERGAARD; CHERYL YARNOTT; STEPHEN TAYLOR; AL OVERGAARD; Sr. PAT MURPHY, C.S.J., Bishop's Liaison, *P.O. Box 610, Crookston, 56716.* Tel: 218-281-4533.

Commission on Liturgy, Sacred Music and Art—JIM DOTTENWHY, Chm.; Sr. MARGUERITE STREIFEL, O.S.B., Dir.; Sr. MARDELLE MOHS, O.S.B.; Sr. PATRICE EBLEN, O.S.B.; JULIE MAREK; MAGGIE FRAHER; JANEL KRESL; Rev. AUGIE GOTHMAN.

Commission on Respect Life—BERNADETTE DUNN, *P.O. Box 610, Crookston, 56716.* Tel: 218-281-4533.

Commission on Social Justice—Rev. DUANE PRIBULA, *P.O. Box 610, Crookston, 56742.* Tel: 218-796-5844.

Commission on Women—JOYCE STOLTMAN, *3807 Simonview Ct., Grand Forks, ND, 58201.* Tel: 701-746-0729.

Crookston Council of Women Religious—Sr. MAUREEN SUPRENANT, C.S.J., Pres.; Sr. MARY JEAN GUST, O.S.B., Sec.

Cursillo—OSCAR ELSHAUG, Chm. of the Secretariat, *602 S. Ash St., Crookston, 56716.*

Deans—Rev. MICHAEL SULLIVAN, Northwest: Rev. RAYMOND PALCISKO, Northeast: Rev. GERALD NOESEN, Western: Rev. RICHARD LAMBERT, Eastern: Rev. DAVID SUPER, Southwest: Rev. JERRY ROGERS, Southeast:

Diaconate Office—Rev. ROBERT SCHREINER, Dir., *Rte.2, Box 9, Middle River, 56737.* Tel: 218-222-3392.

Diocesan Board of Conciliation and Arbitration—Rev. Msgr. WILLIAM MEHRKENS, *Red Lake, 56671.* Sr. ELAINE DUFRESNE, C.S.J., *Crookston, 56716.* Judge MICHAEL KRAKER, *Mahnomen, 56557.*

School Board, Diocesan—MICHAEL STOLTMAN, Chm. SUE WOYTASSEK, Vice Chm. Ex Officio Members: Most Rev. VICTOR H. BALKE, D.D.; Sr. PAT MURPHY, C.S.J.,Members: Dr. JOHN HALCROW; JUDY SCHOENEBERGER; GREG KAISER; DAVID VIPOND; MICHELLE VOELLER; VICTORIA GRAVES; DAN OLSON; Rev. Msgr. MICHAEL PATNODE; Rev. DENNIS WIELAND.

Hispanic Ministry—Sr. TERESA ANN WOLF, O.S.B., Co-ord., *P.O. Box 610, Crookston, 56716.* Tel: 218-281-4533.

Holy Childhood Association—Rev. WILLIAM J. KEEFE, Dir., *516 Walsh St., Crookston, 56716.*

Native American Task Force—Rev. Msgr. WILLIAM MEHRKENS, Chm., *St. Mary's Mission Church, P.O. Box 189, Red Lake, 56671.* Tel: 218-679-3614.

Natural Family Planning—MARK WHELAN; JANE WHELAN, *RR 4, Box 78D, Detroit Lakes, 56501.* Tel: 218-847-6521.

Newspaper, "Our Northland Diocese"—CAROL EVENSON, Editor & Business Mgr., *Diocese of Crookston, 1200 Memorial Dr., P.O. Box 610, Crookston, 56716-0610.* Tel: 218-281-4533.

Pastoral Council—Most Rev. VICTOR H. BALKE, D.D.; Revs. JOE KIESELBACH; DENNIS WIELAND; Sr. MARY JEAN GUST, O.S.B.; Sr. ELAINE DUFRESNE, C.S.J.; TOM ROGUS; GIL DIAZ; TONY GUST; ELVERN VANYO; JAN DELAGE; ANDREW NISTLER; KERMIT ERICKSON; STEPHANIE WALTER; ANDY VANYO; GINNY MCDOUGALL; JOANN KERSTING; WALLY LAMB, *P.O. Box 610, Crookston, 56716.* Tel: 218-281-4533.

Pastoral Office of Christian Service—BERNADETTE DUNN, Dir. ROSE MARIE WISE, Sec., *1200 Memorial Dr., P.O. Box 610, Crookston, 56716.* Tel: 218-281-4533.

Pastoral Office of the Word—Sr. PAT MURPHY, C.S.J., Dir., *1200 Memorial Dr., P.O. Box 610, Crookston, 56716.* Tel: 218-281-4533.

Pastoral Office of Worship—Sr. MARGUERITE STREIFEL, O.S.B., Dir., *1200 Memorial Dr., P.O. Box 610, Crookston, 56716.* Tel: 218-281-4533.

Priests' Personnel Board—Rev. Msgr. ROGER L. GRUNDHAUS, V.G. Ex Officio Members: Rev. Msgr. MICHAEL PATNODE; Revs. GERALD NOESEN; DONALD BRAUKMANN.

Propagation of the Faith—Rev. MICHAEL H. FOLTZ, Dir., *P.O. Box 610, Crookston, 56716.*

Religious Education & Youth Ministry Office—RAY LAGASSE, Dir., *P.O. Box 610, Crookston, 56716.* Tel: 218-281-4533.

Schools & Adult Faith Formation—Sr. PAT MURPHY, C.S.J., Dir. Office of the Word, *1200 Memorial Dr., P.O. Box 610, Crookston, 56716.* Tel: 218-281-4533.

TEC (Teens Encounter Christ)—NANCY BOUCHER, Mgr., *P.O. Box 610, Crookston, 56716.* Tel: 218-281-4533.

Vocations—Revs. MICHAEL H. FOLTZ, J.C.L., Dir. LARRY DELANEY, Assoc. Dir., *P.O. Box 610, Crookston, 56716.* Tel: 218-281-4533.

CLERGY, PARISHES, MISSIONS AND PAROCHIAL SCHOOLS

CITY OF CROOKSTON
(Polk County)

1—CATHEDRAL OF THE IMMACULATE CONCEPTION, Rev. Msgr. Roger L. Grundhaus; Revs. Timothy F. Bushy; David Baumgartner; Sr. Mary Jean Gust, O.S.B., Pastoral Assoc.; Deacon Dennis Bivens.
Parish Office—702 Summit Ave., 56716. Tel: 218-281-1735; Fax: 218-281-1747.
Res., 319 S. Ash St., 56716. Tel: 218-281-2638. [JC]
School—The Cathedral School, (Grades K-6). Tel: 218-281-1835. Rev. Timothy F. Bushy, Prin.
Lay Teachers 8; Students 120.
Missions—Euclid, Polk Co., St. Mary; Gentilly, Polk Co., St. Peter; Ada, Norman Co.; Halstad, Norman Co.; Twin Valley, Norman Co.

OUTSIDE THE CITY OF CROOKSTON

Ada, Norman Co., St. Joseph's. Served by Cathedral of the Immaculate Conception, Crookston. Tel: 218-281-1735. Sr. Patrice Eblen, O.S.B., Pastoral Admin.
Res., 405 E. Thorpe Ave., 56510. Tel: 218-784-4131. [CEM]
Missions—Halstad, Norman Co., Holy Family; Twin Valley, Norman Co., St.William.

Akeley, Hubbard Co., St. John's, Rev. Edward Nistler.
Res., 56433. Tel: 218-652-2785.
Missions—Nevis, Hubbard Co., Immaculate Conception; Laporte, Hubbard Co., St. Theodore.

Alma, Marshall Co., St. John the Baptist. Served by St. Rose, Argyle. Tel: 218-437-6341.

Argyle, Marshall Co., St. Rose, Rev. Michael H. Foltz.
Res., P.O. Box 277, 56713. Tel: 218-437-6341. [CEM]
Mission—Alma.

Badger, Roseau Co., St. Mary's. Served by Sacred Heart, Roseau. Tel: 218-463-2441.

Bagley, Clearwater Co., St. Joseph, Sr. Joanne Johnson, C.S.J., Pastoral Admin.
Res., P.O. Box 67, 56621. Tel: 218-694-6416.
Mission—Shevlin, Clearwater Co., Our Lady of Victory. [CEM]

Barnesville, Clay Co., Assumption, Rev. Msgr. Stanley C. Bourassa; Sr. Mardelle Mohs, O.S.B., Pastoral Min.
Res., 307 Front St. N., P.O. Box 339, 56514. Tel: 218-354-7320. [CEM]
Mission—Sabin, Clay Co., St. Cecilia.

Baudette, Lake of the Woods Co., Sacred Heart, Rev. Cyril Foppe, O.M.I.; Deacon James Lukenbill.
Res., P.O. Box 738, 56623. Tel: 218-634-2689.
Mission—Williams, Lake of the Woods Co., St. Joseph. [CEM]

Beaulieu, Mahnomen Co., St. Joseph. Served by St. Michael, Mahnomen. Tel: 218-935-2503.

Bejou, Mahnomen Co., Immaculate Conception. Served by Rev. Gerald Noesen, Rte. 1, Box 561, Mentor, MN 56736. Tel: 218-574-2424.

Bemidji, Beltrami Co., St. Philip's, Rev. Msgr. Michael Patnode; Rev. James H. Lyons; Deacon John Schuiling. In res., Rev. William F. Lemen.
Res., 710 Beltrami Ave., 56601. Tel: 218-751-4262; Fax: 218-751-4262. [CEM]
School—Mrs. Carol Rettinger, Prin. Lay Teachers 13; Students 276.
Missions—Wilton, Beltrami Co., Sacred Heart; Lake Itasca, Clearwater Co., St. Catherine; Bemidji, Beltrami Co., Newman Center.

Benwood, Roseau Co., St. Joseph, The Worker. Served by Sacred Heart, Roseau. Tel: 218-463-2441.

Big Elbow Lake, Becker Co., St. Francis Cabrini. Served by St. Ann, Waubun. Tel: 218-473-2101.

Blackduck, Beltrami Co., St. Ann's, Rev. Alcuin J. Henger, O.M.I.
Res., P.O. Box G, 56630. Tel: 218-835-6673; Fax: 218-835-6675.
Missions—Kelliher, Beltrami Co., St. Patrick; Northome, Koochiching Co., St. Michael.

Brooks, Red Lake Co., St. Joseph. Served by St. Francis, Oklee. Tel: 218-796-5844.

Callaway, Becker Co., Assumption. Served by St. Mary of the Lakes, Lake Eunice Township. Tel: 218-532-2513. Deacon Randy Bauer, Pastoral Admin.
Res., P.O. Box 67, 56521. Tel: 218-375-3571; Fax: 218-847-6367.
Mission—Lake Itasca, Clearwater Co., St. Catherine.

Detroit Lakes, Becker Co., Holy Rosary, Rev. Jerry Rogers; Deacons Randall J. Bauer; James Thomas.
Res., 1016 Washington Ave., 56501. Tel: 218-847-1393; Fax: 218-847-6367. [CEM]
School—Tel: 218-847-5306. Mitchell J. Vogt, Prin.
Sisters of St. Benedict 2; Lay Teachers 9; Students 133.

Dilworth, Clay Co., St. Elizabeth, Rev. Joseph Kieselbach.
Res., P.O. Box 307, 56529. Tel: 218-287-2705.
Mission—Georgetown, Clay Co., St. John.

Dorothy, Red Lake Co., St. Dorothy. Served by St. Joseph's, Red Lake Falls. Tel: 218-253-2685.

East Grand Forks, Polk Co., Sacred Heart, Revs. Timothy H. McGee; Larry Delaney.
Res., 202 Third St. N.W., 56721. Tel: 218-773-0877; Fax: 218-773-8312. [CEM]
School—Tel: 218-773-1579. Mr. David Andrys, Prin.
Lay Teachers 13; Students 159.
High School—Tel: 218-773-0230. Mr. Phillip E. Meyer, Prin.
Sisters 1; Lay Teachers 15; Students 150.
Convent—Sr. Marguerite Streifel, O.S.B., Coord.

Euclid, Polk Co., St. Mary. Served by the Cathedral of the Immaculate Conception, Crookston. Tel: 218-281-1735.

Falun, Roseau Co., St. Philip. Served by St. Mary's, Warroad. Tel: 218-386-1178.

Fertile, Polk Co., St. Joseph, Rev. Gerald L. Noesen.
Mailing Address: 201 S.E. Elm St., 56540. Tel: 218-945-6649.
Res., Rte. 1, Box 561, Mentor, 56736. Tel: 218-574-2424. [CEM]
Mission—Bejou, Mahnomen Co., Immaculate Conception.

Fisher, Polk Co., St. Francis. Served by Sacred Heart, East Grand Forks. Tel: 218-773-0877. Ms. Bernadette Dunn, Pastoral Admin.
Res., 304 Park Ave., 56723. Tel: 218-891-2406. [CEM]

Florian, Marshall Co., Assumption. Served by Blessed Sacrament, Greenbush. Tel: 218-782-2467. Rev. Donald Braukman.
Mailing Address: Rte. 2, Box 110, Strandquist, 56758. Tel: 218-478-3578.
Res., P.O. Box A, Greenbush, 56726. Tel: 218-782-2467.

Fosston, Polk Co., St. Mary's, Rev. Richard D. Lambert.
Res., Rte. 3, Box 19A, 56542. Tel: 218-435-6484. [CEM]

Frazee, Becker Co., Sacred Heart, Rev. Joseph DeCrans.
Res., P.O. Box 357, 56544. Tel: 218-334-4221. [CEM]

Gentilly, Polk Co., St. Peter's. Served by Cathedral of the Immaculate Conception, Crookston. Tel: 218-281-1735.
Mailing Address: Rte. 2, Box 80, Crookston, 56716. Tel: 218-281-1688. [CEM]

Georgetown, Clay Co., St. John. Served by St. Elizabeth's, Dilworth. Tel: 218-287-2705.

Goodridge, Pennington Co., St. Anne. Served by St. Bernard's, Thief River Falls. Tel: 218-681-3571.

Greenbush, Roseau Co., Blessed Sacrament, Rev. Donald Braukmann.
Res., P.O. Box A, 56726. Tel: 218-782-2467. [CEM]
Missions—Leo, Roseau Co., St. Aloysius. [CEM] Florian.

Grygla, Marshall Co., St. Clement. Served by St. Bernard's, Thief River Falls. Tel: 218-681-3571.

Hallock, Kittson Co., St. Patrick's, Rev. Timothy T. Noah.
Res., P.O. Box 519, 56728. Tel: 218-843-2323.
Mission—Lancaster, Kittson Co., Holy Rosary.

Halstad, Norman Co., Holy Family. Served by Cathedral of the Immaculate Conception, Crookston. Tel: 218-281-1735. Sr. Patrice Eblen, O.S.B., Pastoral Admin.
Res., 405 E. Thorpe Ave., Ada, 56510. Tel: 218-784-4131.

Hawley, Clay Co., St. Andrew. Served by St. Francis Xavier, Lake Park. Tel: 218-238-6639; Fax: 218-238-6619.
Mailing Address: P.O. Box 688, 56549.

Kelliher, Beltrami Co., St. Patrick. Served by St. Ann's, Blackduck. Tel: 218-835-6673.

Lake Eunice Township, Becker Co., St. Mary of the Lakes, Rev. Eugene L. Wesely.
Mailing Address: R.R. 5, Box 364D, Detroit Lakes, 56501. Tel: 218-532-2513.
Mission—Callaway.

Lake Itasca, Clearwater Co., St. Catherine. Served by St. Philip's, Bemidji. Tel: 218-751-4262.

Lake Park, Becker Co., St. Francis Xavier's, Rev. Bernard Friedl, O.S.B.
Res., 2066 Second St., 56554-4402. Tel: 218-238-6639; Fax: 218-238-6619. [CEM]
Mission—Hawley, Clay Co., St. Andrew.

Lancaster, Kittson Co., Holy Rosary. Served by St. Patrick, Hallock. Tel: 218-843-2323.

Laporte, Hubbard Co., St. Theodore. Served by St. John's, Akeley. Tel: 218-652-2785.

Leo, Roseau Co., St. Aloysius. Served by Blessed Sacrament, Greenbush. Tel: 218-782-2467.

Mahnomen, Mahnomen Co., St. Michael's, Rev. John Kleinwachter. In res., Rev. Frank Reid.
Res., Rte. 1, Box 22, 56557. Tel: 218-935-2503. [CEM]
School—Sisters of St. Benedict 2; Lay Teachers 6; Students 74.
Catechesis/Religious Programs—Sr. Yvonne Schafer, D.R.E.
Students 190.
Mission—Beaulieu, Mahnomen Co., St. Joseph. [CEM]

Mentor, Polk Co., St. Lawrence, Rev. Gerald L. Noesen; Deacon John A. Bruggeman.
Mailing Address: Box 51, 56736. Tel: 218-637-8178.
Res., Rte. 1, Box 561, 56736. Tel: 218-574-2424.

Middle River, Marshall Co., St. Joseph, Husband of Mary, Rev. Robert C. Schreiner, S.T.L.
Res., Rte. 2, Box 9, 56737. Tel: 218-222-3392.
Mission—Strandquist, Marshall Co., St. Edward, The Confessor. [CEM]

Moorhead, Clay Co., St. Francis de Sales, Rev. David J. Super.
Res., 804 N. 13th St., 56560. Tel: 218-236-1505. [JC]
Church—601 15th Ave. N., 56560. Tel: 218-233-4780.
St. Joseph's, Rev. Msgr. Donald H. Krebs; Rev. August Gothman.
Office: 218 10th St. S., 56560. Tel: 218-236-5066; 236-9503 (Res.); Fax: 218-236-1624.
School—Tel: 218-233-0553. Sr. Mary Ann Welsch, Prin.
Sisters 2; Lay Teachers 17; Students 216.

Catechesis/Religious Programs—Tel: 218-236-1979. Barbara Schmidt, D.R.E.
Students 524.
Mission—Moorhead, Clay Co., St. Thomas Newman Center, 707-11th St. S., Tel: 218-236-9596.

Naytahwaush, Mahnomen Co., St. Anne. Served by St. Ann's, Waubun. Tel: 218-473-2101.
Mailing Address: P.O. Box 70, 56566. Tel: 218-935-5676.

Nebish, Beltrami Co., St. John. Served by St. Mary's Mission, Red Lake. Tel: 218-679-3614.

Nevis, Hubbard Co., Immaculate Conception. Served by St. John's, Akeley. Tel: 218-652-2785.

Ogema, Becker Co., Most Holy Redeemer. Served by St. Benedict's, White Earth. Tel: 218-983-3519. Rev. Martin F. Machovec, O.M.I.
Mailing Address: P.O. Box 57, 56569. Tel: 218-983-3261. [CEM]

Oklee, Red Lake Co., St. Francis Xavier's, Rev. Duane J. Pribula.
Res., P.O. Box 160, 56742. Tel: 218-796-5844; Fax: 218-796-5844. [CEM]
Missions—Brooks, Red Lake Co., St. Joseph. [CEM]
Plummer, Red Lake Co., St. Vincent de Paul. [CEM]

Oslo, Marshall Co., St. Joseph. Served by SS. Peter and Paul, Warren. Tel: 218-745-4511. Sr. Lucille Adelman, O.S.B., Pastoral Admin.
Res., P.O. Box 97, 56744. Tel: 218-695-2641.

Park Rapids, Hubbard Co., St. Peter's, Rev. Richard Boyd.
Res., P.O. Box 353, 56470. Tel: 218-732-5142 (Office); 732-8852 (Res.); Fax: 218-732-5142. [CEM]
Mission—Two Inlets.

Pennington, Beltrami Co., St. Charles. (Under the jurisdiction of the Diocese of Crookston; administered by the Diocese of Duluth.). Rev. Bogumil Kosciesza.
P.O. Box 368, Cass Lake, 56633. Tel: 218-335-2359.

Plummer, Red Lake Co., St. Vincent de Paul. Served by St. Francis Xavier's, Oklee. Tel: 218-796-5844.

Ponsford, Becker Co., St. Theodore. Served by St. Benedict's, White Earth. Tel: 218-983-3519.

Red Lake, Beltrami Co., St. Mary's Mission Church, Rev. Msgr. William Mehrkens.
Res., P.O. Box 189, 56671. Tel: 218-679-3614. [CEM]
School—Sr. Philip Zimmer, Prin. Sisters 1; Lay Teachers 6; Students 85.
Mission—Nebish, Beltrami Co., St. John.

Red Lake Falls, Red Lake Co., St. Joseph's, Rev. Gary W. LaMoine; Sr. Lucille Schafer, O.S.B., Pastoral Assoc.
Res., P.O. Box 400, 56750. Tel: 218-253-2004. [CEM]
School—112 Edward Ave. N.W., Box 215, 56750. Tel: 218-253-2188; Fax: 218-253-2188. Val Gagnon, Prin.
Lay Teachers 7; Students 78.
Missions—Dorothy, Red Lake Co., St. Dorothy. [CEM]
Terrebonne, Red Lake Co., St. Anthony. [CEM]

Roseau, Roseau Co., Sacred Heart, Rev. Raymond Palcisko.
Res., P.O. Box 118, 403 Main Ave. N., 56751. Tel: 218-463-2441. [CEM]
Missions—Badger, Roseau Co., St. Mary's. [CEM]
Benwood, Roseau Co., St. Joseph, The Worker. [CEM]

Sabin, Clay Co., St. Cecilia. Served by Assumption, Barnesville. Tel: 218-354-7320.

Shevlin, Clearwater Co., Our Lady of Victory. Served by St. Mary's, Fosston. Tel: 218-435-6484. Sr. Joanne Johnson, Pastoral Admin.
Res., P.O. Box 67, Bagley, 56621. Tel: 218-694-6416. [CEM]

Stephen, Marshall Co., St. Stephen's, Rev. Robert C. Schreiner, S.T.L.
Res., 515 Fifth St., P.O. Box 507, 56757. Tel: 218-478-2231. [CEM]

Strandquist, Marshall Co., St. Edward, The Confessor. Served by St. Joseph's, Middle River. Tel: 218-222-3392.

Tabor, Polk Co., Holy Trinity Catholic. Served by SS. Peter and Paul, Warren. Tel: 218-745-4511.

Terrebonne, Red Lake Co., St. Anthony. Served by St. Joseph's, Red Lake Falls. Tel: 218-253-2004.

Thief River Falls, Pennington Co., St. Bernards, Revs. Dennis J. Wieland; Robert J. LaPlante; Deacon John Eisbrenner.
Res., 105 Knight Ave. N., 56701. Tel: 218-681-3571. [CEM]
School—Tel: 218-681-1539. Sr. Kathy Kuchar, O.S.B., Prin.
Lay Teachers 7; Students 109.
Missions—Goodridge, Pennington Co., St. Ann; Grygla, Marshall Co., St. Clement.

Twin Valley, Norman Co., St. William. Served by Cathedral of the Immaculate Conception, Crookston. Tel: 218-281-1735. Sr. Patrice Eblen, O.S.B., Pastoral Admin.
Res., 405 E. Thorpe Ave., Ada, 56510. Tel: 218-784-4131.

Two Inlets, Becker Co., St. Mary's. Served by St. Peter's, Park Rapids. Tel: 218-732-5142. Rev. Rick Boyd, O.M.I.; Ms. Mary Ellen Kenney, Pastoral Admin.
Mailing Address: P.O. Box 287, Park Rapids, 56470. Tel: 218-732-4046.

Warren, Marshall Co., SS. Peter and Paul, Rev. Michael Sullivan.
Res., 208 N. Seventh St., 56762. Tel: 218-745-4511. [CEM]
Missions—Oslo, Marshall Co., St. Joseph, P.O. Box 97, 56744. Tel: 218-695-2641. Sr. Lucille Adelman, O.S.B., Admin.; Tabor, Polk Co., Holy Trinity Catholic.

Warroad, Roseau Co., St. Mary's, Rev. Patrick Sullivan; Deacon Robert Marvel.
Res., P.O. Box 33, 56763. Tel: 218-386-1178. [CEM]
Mission—Falun, Roseau Co., St. Philip.

Waubun, Mahnomen Co., St. Ann, Rev. Ronald J. Meyer, O.M.I.
Res., Rte. 2, Box 6, 56589. Tel: 218-473-2101.
Missions—Naytahwaush, Mahnomen Co., St. Anne; Big Elbow Lake, Becker Co., St. Francis Cabrini.

White Earth, Becker Co., St. Benedict, Rev. Martin F. Machovec, O.M.I.; Bro. Craig Bonham, O.M.I., Pastoral Assoc.
Res., P.O. Box 417, 56591-0417. Tel: 218-983-3519. [CEM]
Missions—Ogema, Becker Co., Most Holy Redeemer; Ponsford, Becker Co., St. Theodore.

Williams, Lake of the Woods Co., St. Joseph. Served by Sacred Heart, Baudette. Tel: 218-634-2689.

Wilton, Beltrami Co., Sacred Heart. Served by St. Philip's, Bemidji. Tel: 218-751-4262.

Special Assignment:
Reverend Fathers—
Foley, Gerald K.

On Duty Outside the Diocese:
Reverend Fathers—
Bester, Robert
Skoczylas, Walter
Wieseler, Lawrence A.

Leave of Absence:
Reverend Fathers—
Richards, Joseph D.
Troska, Llewelyn J.

Retired:
Reverend Monsignors—
Stearns, John D., 5320 12th St. S., #227, Fargo, ND 58104
Reverend Fathers—
Archer, W. Donald, 1444 N. Recker Rd., #144, Mesa, AZ 85205
Bernauer, James, P.O.Box 7, Dent, MN 56528
Carriere, Henry G., 506 E. Esther St. #101, Badger, MN 56714
Felion, Jerome, 1514 Bamboo Cir., Harlingen, TX 78552
Keefe, William, Villa St. Vincent, 516 Walsh St. #212, Crookston, MN 56716. Tel: 218-281-5303
Kulhawik, Frank, St. William's, P.O. Box 306, Twin Valley, MN 56584. Tel: 218-584-5200
Lemen, William F., 710 Beltrami Ave., Bemidji, MN 56601. Tel: 218-751-4262
Merth, John P., 1405 7th St. S. #210, Moorhead, MN 56560-3497
Noah, Daniel, Rte. 2, Box 291, Crookston, MN 56716
Pryor, G. Robert, U.S.A.F, 286 Grantwood Dr., Henderson, NV 89014
Reid, Francis R., Rte. 1, Box 22, Mahnomen, MN 56557

Permanent Deacons:
Bauer, Randall, Holy Rosary, Detroit Lakes
Bivens, Dennis, Cathedral of the Immaculate Conception, Crookston
Bruggeman, John, St. Lawrence, Mentor
Eisbrener, John, St. Bernard, Thief River Falls
Lukenbill, James, Sacred Heart, Baudette
Marvel, Robert, St. Mary's, Warroad
Schuiling, John, St. Philip, Bemidji
Thomas, James, Holy Rosary, Detroit Lakes

INSTITUTIONS LOCATED IN THE DIOCESE

[A] ELEMENTARY SCHOOLS, PRIVATE

RED LAKE. *St. Mary's Mission School*, 56671. Benedictine Sisters (St. Joseph, MN). Sr. Philip Zimmer, O.S.B., Prin.; Rev. William Mehrkens. Sisters 1; Lay Teachers 6; Students 85.

[B] CONFRATERNITY OF CHRISTIAN DOCTRINE

CROOKSTON. *Cathedral - Religious Education/Faith Formation*, 702 Summit Ave., 56716. Tel: 218-281-1735; Fax: 218-281-1747. Rev. Timothy F. Bushy, Dir.; Sr. Mary Jean Gust, Prog. Asst.; Michael Gerads, Junior High Coord.; Nancy Boucher, Senior High Coord. Students (Grades K-8) 275; High School Students (Grades 9-11) 138.

ADA. *St. Joseph Parish, R.E. Program*, 56510. Tel: 218-784-4131. Students 150.

ARGYLE. *St. Rose Parish, R.E. Program*, Box 277, 56713. Tel: 218-437-8336. Judy Adolphson, Dir. Students 146.

BEMIDJI. *St. Philips Parish, R. Formation Program*, 620 Beltrami Ave., 56601. Tel: 751-5849. D.R.E.: Kathy Burwell, (Grades PreK-5); Kris Jensen, (Grades 6-8); Mary Hoody, (Grades 9-12). Students (Grades PreK-5) 210; Students (Grades 6-12) 300.

DETROIT LAKES. *Holy Rosary Parish, R.E. Program*, 1032 Washington Ave., 56501. Tel: 218-847-8970. JoAnne Knuttila, Coord. Students 340.

EAST GRAND FORKS. *Sacred Heart Parish, R.E. Program*, 131 N.W. Fourth, 56721. Tel: 218-773-0531. D.R.E.: Ginny Osowski, (Grades PreK-6); Sheryl Guzek, (Grades 7-12). Students 503.

GREENBUSH. *Religious Education Program*, P.O. Box A, 56726. Tel: 218-782-2263. Coordinators: Gerry Nubson. Students 124.

THIEF RIVER FALLS. *Religious Education Program*, 105 Knight Ave. N., 56701. Tel: 218-681-6268; 6269. Jan Halling, Coord. Students 224; High School Students 171.

[C] GENERAL HOSPITALS

BAUDETTE. *LakeWood Health Center*, 600 South Main Ave., Box 2120, 56623. Tel: 218-634-2120; Fax: 218-634-1307.
For a complete listing, refer to the Hospitals section.

*DETROIT LAKES. *St. Mary's Regional Health Center*, 1027 Washington Ave., 56501. Tel: 218-847-5611; Fax: 218-847-7674.
For a complete listing, refer to the Hospitals section.

PARK RAPIDS. *St. Joseph's Area Health Services*, 600 Pleasant Ave., 56470. Tel: 218-732-3311.
For a complete listing, refer to the Hospitals section.

[D] HOMES FOR THE AGED

CROOKSTON. *Villa St. Vincent*, 516 Walsh St., 56716.
For a complete listing, refer to the Special Care Facilities section.

DETROIT LAKES. *St. Mary's Nursing Center*, 56501.
For a complete listing, refer to the Special Care Facilities section.

[E] CONVENTS AND RESIDENCES FOR SISTERS

CROOKSTON. *Marywood Residential Community*. (Retirement Residence). Community, R.R. 2, Box 16, 56716-9603. Tel: 218-281-3093. Congregation of the Sisters of St. Joseph of Medaille (Pontifical Jurisdiction). Mr. Willie Larson, Admin.; Sr. Elaine DuFresne, Dir. of Pastoral Care; Rev. Msgr. Roger Grundhaus, Chap. Marywood Residential Community 22; Crookston Regional Community 36.
Mount St. Benedict Monastery, 620 Summit Ave. E., 56716-2799. Tel: 218-281-3441; Fax: 218-281-3441, Ext. 26. Motherhouse of the Order of the Sisters of St. Benedict of Pontifical Jurisdiction-The Federation of St. Gertrude. Sr. Michelle McGurran, O.S.B., Prioress; Sr. Lenore Paschke, Subprioress. Sisters in Community 156.
Sisters of St. Benedict Initial Formation. Sr. Lois Spors, O.S.B.

[F] NEWMAN CENTERS

CROOKSTON. *University of Minnesota Cooperative Campus Ministry*, 56716. Collette M. Conati, Dir. Coop. Campus Ministry.

BEMIDJI. *Holy Spirit Newman Center*, 1701 Birch Ln. N.E., 56601-2607. Tel: 218-751-3724. Rev. Msgr. Michael Patnode; Rev. James H.C. Lyons; Lois Jenkins, Pastoral Assoc.

MOORHEAD. *St. Thomas Newman Center*, 707 11th St. S., 56560. Tel: 218-236-9596. Rev. August Gothman, Dir.; Shirley Wallace, Coord.

[G] MISCELLANEOUS

CROOKSTON.

**Mount Saint Benedict Foundation*, 620 Summit Ave., 56716.

**The Diocese of Crookston Catholic Community Foundation*, 1200 Memorial Dr., 56716.

RELIGIOUS INSTITUTES OF MEN REPRESENTED IN THE DIOCESE

For further details refer to the corresponding bracketed number in the Religious Institutes of Men or Women section.

[0200]—*Benedictine Monks*.—O.S.B.

[0910]—*Oblates of Mary Immaculate*.—O.M.I.

RELIGIOUS INSTITUTES OF WOMEN REPRESENTED IN THE DIOCESE

[0230]—*Benedictine Sisters of Pontifical Jurisdiction*. (Congregation of St. Gertrude).—O.S.B.

[]—*Benedictine Sisters of Pontifical Jurisdiction (Federation of St. Benedict)*.—O.S.B.

[1070-03]—*Dominican Sisters (Sinsinawa, WI)*. (Western Prov.).—O.P.

[1310]—*Franciscan Sisters of Little Falls, Minnesota*.—O.S.F.

[3880]—*Sisters of St. Joseph of Medaille*.—C.S.J.

NECROLOGY

† Patnode, Keough, (Retired). —Died Dec. 14, 1995.

† Pickla, John, (Retired). —Died Aug. 23, 1996.

† Seitz, Aloys, (Retired). —Died May 29,1996.

† Sullivan, Jeremiah, (Retired). —Died June 24, 1996.

Diocese of Dallas

(Dioecesis Dallasensis)

Most Reverend

CHARLES V. GRAHMANN, D.D.

Bishop of Dallas; ordained March 17, 1956; appointed Titular Bishop of Equilio and Auxiliary of San Antonio June 30, 1981; consecrated August 29, 1981; appointed First Bishop of Victoria April 14, 1982; installed May 29, 1982; appointed Coadjutor of Dallas December 18, 1989; Reception as Coadjutor of Dallas February 21, 1990; appointed Bishop of Dallas July 14, 1990.

Most Reverend

THOMAS TSCHOEPE

Retired Bishop of Dallas; ordained May 30, 1943; appointed Bishop of San Angelo January 12, 1966; consecrated March 9, 1966; transferred to Dallas August 27, 1969; resigned July 14, 1990. *Res., St. Joseph, P.O. Box 190, Waxahachie, TX, 75165.*

ESTABLISHED DIOCESE OF DALLAS ON JULY 15, 1890.

REDESIGNATED DIOCESE OF DALLAS-FORT WORTH ON OCTOBER 20, 1953.

REDESIGNATED DIOCESE OF DALLAS ON AUGUST 27, 1969.

Square Miles 7,523.

Comprises the following nine Counties in the State of Texas: Collin, Dallas, Ellis, Fannin, Grayson, Hunt, Kaufman, Navarro and Rockwall.

For legal titles of parishes and diocesan institutions, consult the Chancery Office.

Chancery Office: 3725 Blackburn, P.O. Box 190507, Dallas, TX, 75219. Tel.: 214-528-2240; Fax: 214-526-1743.

Web site address: http://www.diocese-of-dallas.org/

E-mail address: catholic@flash.net

STATISTICAL OVERVIEW

Personnel	
Bishop	1
Retired Bishops	1
Abbots	1
Priests: Diocesan Active in Diocese	80
Priests: Active Outside Diocese	8
Priests: Retired, Sick or Absent	16
Number of Diocesan Priests	104
Religious Priests in Diocese	84
Extern Priests in Diocese	19
Ordinations:	
Diocesan Priests	6
Transitional Deacons	4
Permanent Deacons in Diocese	145
Total Brothers	4
Total Sisters	161
Parishes	
Parishes	64
With Resident Pastor:	
Resident Diocesan Priests	54
Resident Religious Priests	10
Without Resident Pastor:	
Missions	7
New Parishes Created	1
Professional Ministry Personnel:	
Brothers	1
Sisters	28
Lay Ministers	121
Welfare	
Catholic Hospitals	1
Total Assisted	33,400
Homes for the Aged	1
Total Assisted	45
Day Care and Extended Day Care Centers	7
Total Assisted	695
Special Centers for Social Services	17
Total Assisted	61,350
Educational	
Seminaries, Diocesan	1
Students from This Diocese	10
Diocesan Students in Other Seminaries	18
Total Seminarians	28
Colleges and Universities	1
Total Students	2,740
High Schools, Diocesan and Parish	3
Total Students	1,269
High Schools, Private	4
Total Students	1,794
Elementary Schools, Diocesan and Parish	29
Total Students	10,082
Elementary Schools, Private	3
Total Students	700
Non-residential Schools for the Disabled	1
Total Students	101
Catechesis/Religious Education:	
High School Students	4,802
Elementary Students	29,014
Total Students Under Catholic Instruction	50,530
Teachers in the Diocese:	
Priests	15
Scholastics	2
Brothers	2
Sisters	24
Lay Teachers	859
Vital Statistics	
Receptions into the Church:	
Infant Baptism Totals	10,266
Adult Baptism Totals	769
Received into Full Communion	637
First Communions	6,609
Confirmations	4,231
Marriages:	
Catholic	1,386
Interfaith	618
Total Marriages	2,004
Deaths	1,301
Total Catholic Population	324,820
Total Population	2,733,974

Former Bishops—Rt. Rev. THOMAS F. BRENNAN, D.D., cons. April 5, 1891; resigned Nov. 17, 1892; died March 21, 1916.—Rt. Rev. EDWARD JOSEPH DUNNE, D.D., cons. Nov. 30. 1893; died Aug. 5, 1910.—Most Rev. JOSEPH PATRICK LYNCH, D.D., LL.D., appt. June 8, 1911; cons. July 12, 1911 Assistant at Pontifical Throne, May 13, 1936; died Aug. 19, 1954.—Most Rev. THOMAS K. GORMAN, D.D., D.Sc.Hist., ord. June 23, 1917; Bishop of Reno; appt. April 24, 1931; cons. July 22, 1931 Assistant at the Pontifical Throne, May 4, 1942; appt. Titular Bishop of Rhasus and Coadjutor to the Bishop of Dallas, Feb. 8, 1952; succeeded to Aug. 19, 1954; resigned and appointed Titular Bishop of Pinhel, Aug. 27, 1969. (Title rescinded); died Aug. 16, 1980.

Vicar General—Rev. Msgr. GLENN D. GARDNER, J.C.D.

Chancery Office—3725 Blackburn, P.O. Box 190507, Dallas, 75219. Tel: 214-528-2240; Fax: 214-526-1743. Office Hours: 9-5.

Chancellor—Rev. Msgr. JOHN P. BELL, J.C.L.

Diocesan Tribunal—P.O. Box 190507, Dallas, 75219. Tel: 214-528-9970.

Judicial Vicar—Rev. Msgr. JOHN P. BELL, J.C.L.

Assistant Judicial Vicar—Rev. JACK HOPKA, S.F.O., J.C.L.

Director of the Tribunal—WILLIAM HARE, III, J.C.L.

Secretary to the Tribunal—MARGARET GILLETT.

Defensores Vinculi—JOHN P. GARGAN, J.C.D.; Revs. JOSEPH MITCHELL, J.C.L.; MICHAEL DUCA, J.C.L.

Diocesan Judges—Rev. Msgr. GLENN D. GARDNER, J.C.D.; Rev. DAVID L. COLELLA, O.SS.T, J.C.D.

Notaries—MARGARET GILLETT; JANE HOFMEISTER.

Procurator-Advocates—Rev. RAMON ALVAREZ; SUSAN O'CONNOR BURKE; BEBE CANTU; ANN CARMODY; JUDY CLARK; Deacon DON FORBRICH; JEANNE MARIE GIRSCH; AGNES A. GLADBACH; MARY CATHERINE HARE; WILLIAM E. HEBEKEUSER; VIRGINIA G. HEMMI; MARY HOEFER; Deacon JUAN IBARRA; MARY L. IZAK; Rev. GREG KELLY; Deacon JOHN PAUL KELLY; LINDA MOSES; MARY A. RASINS; Deacon MICHAEL RASINS; PAUL W. REITTINGER; Deacon ROBERT RICARD; MARY KAY RITCHIE; Deacons ROBERT SANCHEZ; WILLIAM J. SCHUSTER; Rev. MARK SEITZ; ELAINE STIEBER; Deacon LEE J. STIEBER; FRANCIS XAVIER VUONG ANH THUONG; Deacon GARY M. VOGEL; MARGE WICK; DANNY WILCOX.

Consultors of Pastors—Rev. Msgr. RICHARD JOHNSON; Rev. Msgr. JOHN MYERS; Revs. HENRY PETTER; TIM GOLLOB.

Diocesan Consultors—Rev. RAMON ALVAREZ; Rev. Msgr. JOHN BELL; Rev. TOM CLOHERTY; Rev. Msgr. DONALD FISCHER; Rev. Msgr. G. DUFFY GARDNER; Rev. HENRY PETTER; Rev. Msgr. DON ZIMMERMAN.

Presbyteral Council—Rev. Msgr. GLENN D. GARDNER, V.G., Ex-Offico; Revs. RAMON ALVAREZ; JAMES BALINT; Rev. Msgr. JOHN BELL; Revs. STEPHEN BIERSCHENK; IGNACIO CIZUR, O.F.M.Cap.; TOM CLOHERTY; MIKE DUCA; Rev. Msgr. DONALD FISCHER; Revs. TIM GOLLOB; ANDREW KOLZOW, O.P.; Rev. Msgr. JOHN MEYERS; Revs. ROBERT O'ROURKE, S.S.C.; HENRY PETTER; KENNETH A. BUDDENDORF, S.J.; Rev. Msgr. DONALD ZIMMERMAN.

Censor Librorum—Rev. Msgr. GLENN D. GARDNER; Rev. ROBERT M. COERVER.

Diocesan Offices and Directors

Finance Committee—WILLIAM COX; EUGENE VILFORDI; LOUIS G. MUNIN; J. OLIVER MCGONIGLE; MICHAEL T. WEIS.

Building Commission—Rev. Msgr. JEROME P. DUESMAN; Rev. Msgr. LAWRENCE PICHARD; AL SALEM; DAVID FURLOW; MICHAEL T. WEIS. Tel: 214-528-2240.

Teaching Division

I. Total Catholic Education—

Division Head—Rev. LEONARD CALLAHAN, *P.O. Box 190507, Dallas, 75219.* Tel: 214-528-2360.

Associates—DOUGLAS J. HAMILTON; TONI UNDERWOOD.

Resource Center—Tel: 214-528-2360.

II. Media—

Sub-Division Head—Rev. Msgr. JOHN BELL, *P.O. Box 190507, Dallas, 75219.* Tel: 214-528-2240.

Newspaper—*"The Texas Catholic"*, Official Catholic Newspaper for the Diocese of Dallas; Most Rev. CHARLES V. GRAHMANN, D.D., Publisher; BRONSON HAVARD, Exec. Editor; ANTONIO RAMIREZ, JR., Business Mgr. Tel: 241-528-8792; Fax: 241-528-3411.

"El Catolico de Texas"—Spanish Language Paper.

Communications Office—Dir.: MICHAEL MCGEE. Tel: 214-528-2240.

Sanctifying Division

Division Head—PATRICIA LENOIR, *P.O. Box 190507, Dallas, 75219.* Tel: 214-528-2360.

Worship Office—Dir.: PATRICIA LENOIR. Tel: 214-528-2360.

Spiritual Director—Rev. ROBERT COERVER. Tel: 214-582-2360.

Sacred Places—

Cemeteries—JAMES FOUCH, Exec. Dir., *3235 Lombardy Ln., 75220.* Tel: 214-357-5754.

Cathedral Santuario de Guadalupe—Rev. Msgr. LARRY PICHARD, Rector. Tel: 214-871-1362.

Catholic Conference and Formation Center—BARBARA LANDREGAN, Dir., *901 S. Madison Ave., Dallas, 75208. Mailing Address: P.O. Box 190507, Dallas, 75219.* Tel: 214-943-6585; Fax: 214-943-6587.

Sacramental Life Office—PATRICIA LENOIR, Dir. Tel: 214-582-2360.

Sacraments of Initiation—BILL HEBEKEUSER, *Holy Spirit, 1111 W. Danieldale Rd., Duncanville, 75137.* Tel: 972-298-4971.

Sacraments of Healing—PATRICIA LENOIR. Tel: 214-582-2360.

Sacrements of Orders—

Seminary—Very Rev. MICHAEL DUCA, *Holy Trinity Seminary, P.O. Box 140309.* Tel: 972-438-2212.

Seminarian Relations—Rev. JOHN LIBONE. Tel: 972-596-5505.

Vocations—Rev. GREG KELLY. Tel: 972-562-0638.

Diaconal Ministry—STEVE LANDREGAN, *901 S. Madison Ave., Dallas, 75208. Mailing Address: P.O. Box 190507, Dallas, 75219.* Tel: 214-943-6585.

Sacrament of Marriage—DIANE DANIELS. Tel: 214-528-2360.

Governing Division

Division Head—MICHAEL T. WEIS, *P.O. Box 190507, Dallas, 75219.* Tel: 214-528-2240.

Business Office—Dir.: MICHAEL T. WEIS. Tel: 214-528-2240.

Catholic Community Appeal—Dir.: R. MICHAEL GEORGE. Tel: 214-528-2240.

Pastoral Planning and Research—Dir.: MARY EDLUND. Tel: 214-528-2240.

Tribunal—Dir.: Rev. Msgr. JOHN P. BELL. Tel: 214-528-2240.

Archives—Archivist: ESTELLE METZGER. Tel: 214-528-2240.

Mission Division

Division Head—Rev. Msgr. KILIAN BRODERICK, *P.O. Box 190507, Dallas, 75219.* Tel: 214-520-6590.

Catholic Charities—Dir.: Rev. Msgr. KILIAN BRODERICK. Tel: 214-520-6590.

Mission Awareness / Justice and Peace—Vacant. Tel: 214-528-2240.

CHD Coordinator—Vacant. Tel: 214-528-2240.

Propagation of Faith and Holy Childhood—Dir.: Sr. AGNES CHRISTINE MULLEN, C.PP.S. Tel: 214-528-2240.

Pastoral Care Ministries—

Addictions Ministry—PHIL PASCHKE. Tel: 972-960-2166.

Ministries to People with Disabilities—Rev. AUSTIN GREEN, O.P. Tel: 214-528-2240.

Hospital Ministry—Rev. Msgr. DUFFY GARDNER. Tel: 214-528-2240.

Prison Ministry—Rev. PAUL GRAY, *All Saints Parish, 5231 Meadowcreek, 75248.* Tel: 972-661-9282.

Networks

MARY EDLUND, Chm., *P.O. Box 190507, Dallas, 75219.* Tel: 214-528-2240

Family Life Network—SUE PARKER, Chm. Tel: 214-526-2772, Ext. 192.

Asian Network—VIVIEN RIVERA, Chm. Tel: 214-920-8384.

Black Network—Co-Chairs: LARI NEWMAN-WILLIAMS. Tel: 214-375-3715. PETER GRANGER. Tel: 972-227-4631.

Hispanic Network—RAUL OJEDA, Chm. Tel: 972-262-1744.

CLERGY, PARISHES, MISSIONS AND PAROCHIAL SCHOOLS

CITY OF DALLAS
(Dallas County)

1—CATHEDRAL-SANTUARIO DE GUADALUPE (1869), Rev. Msgr. Lawrence Pichard; Rev. Anibal Adorno; Deacons Juan Ibarra; Charles Stump.
Res., 2215 Ross Ave., 75201. Tel: 214-871-1362; Fax: 214-954-1557.
Catechesis / Religious Programs—Sr. Esther Guerrero, M.C.D.P., D.R.E.
Students 1,183.

2—ALL SAINTS (1976), Rev. Msgr. Robert C. Rehkemper; Revs. Lonnie Honea; Paul Gray; Deacons Denis Simon; Vincent Bathea; William Friedman.
Res., 5231 Meadowcreek, 75248. Tel: 972-661-9282; Fax: 972-233-5401.
Catechesis / Religious Programs—Rosemary Quagliana, D.R.E.
Students 475.

3—BLESSED SACRAMENT (1901), Rev. Paul L. Weinberger; Deacons Joe Vollmer-Konig; Jose R. Robles. In res., Rev. Msgr. William A. Botik, (Retired).
Res., 231 N. Marsalis Ave., 75203. Tel: 214-948-6535; Fax: 214-948-1660.
Catechesis / Religious Programs—D.R.E.: Mr. Francisco Manzo; Mrs. Rosie Delgado, Coord./CCD Volunteers.
Students 1,386.

4—CHRIST THE KING, Rev. Msgr. Donald F. Zimmerman; Deacons Sam Franklin; Ben Stabile.
Res., 8017 Preston Rd., 75225. Tel: 214-365-1200; Fax: 214-365-1205.
School—4100 Colgate St., 75225. Tel: 214-365-1264; Fax: 214-365-1236.
Lay Teachers 27; Students 377.
Catechesis / Religious Programs—Students 255.

5—HOLY CROSS (1956), Rev. Timothy A. Gollob; Deacons Antonio Trevino; Henry Vault. In res., Rev. James George McKenna.
Res., 2926 E. Ledbetter Dr., 75216. Tel: 214-374-7952.
Catechesis / Religious Programs—Students 225.

6—HOLY TRINITY (1907), Revs. Paul W. Sauerbier, C.M.; Warren F. Dicharry, C.M.; George J. Weber, C.M.; Deacons Paul Husting; Don Forbrich.
Mailing Address: 3826 Gilbert Ave., 75219.
Res., 3811 Oak Lawn Ave., 75219. Tel: 214-526-8555; Fax: 214-526-3477.
School—3815 Oak Lawn Ave., 75219.
Lay Teachers 21; Students 215.
Catechesis / Religious Programs—Students 470.

7—MARY IMMACULATE (1956), Rev. Msgr. Albert A. Cuschieri; Revs. Joseph Son Van Nguyen; Luis Gongora; Deacons Don Van-Scoy; Gerard L. Bauwens; Robert G. Hoch; Robert J. Dalton; Patrick Hayes.
Res., 14032 Dennis Ln., 75234. Tel: 972-243-7104; Fax: 972-406-1254.
School—Tel: 972-243-7105.
Lay Teachers 24; Students 579.
Catechesis / Religious Programs—Judy Grimmett, D.R.E.
Students 1,021.

8—OUR LADY OF LOURDES (1954), Revs. Jesse Torre, O.F.M.Cap. (Spain); Roberto Garcia, O.F.M.Cap. (Spain); Alfonso Casteig, O.F.M.Cap. (Spain).
Res., 5605 Bernal Dr., 75212. Tel: 214-637-6673.
Catechesis / Religious Programs—D.R.E.: Pete Rodriguez; Amy Rodriguez.
Students 925.

9—OUR LADY OF PERPETUAL HELP (1942), Revs. Ignacio Cizur, O.F.M.Cap. (Spain); Sabino Erro, O.F.M. (Spain); Deacons Albert Montes; Adolph Orozco, Jr.; Jesse J. Rojas. In res., Rev. Juan Cruz Gaston, O.F.M.Cap.
Res., 7617 Cortland Ave., 75235. Tel: 214-352-6012; Fax: 214-352-6012.
School—7625 Cortland Ave., 75235. Tel: 214-351-3396; Fax: 214-352-5635.
School Sisters of Notre Dame 2; Lay Teachers 10; Students 167.
Catechesis / Religious Programs—Olivia Vallenzuela, D.R.E.
Students 803.

10—OUR LADY OF SAN JUAN DE LOS LAGOS AND ST. THERESA (1928), Rev. Juan Cruz Gaston, O.F.M.Cap.
Res., 2601 Singleton Blvd., 75212. Tel: 214-631-9627; Fax: 214-631-6267.
Catechesis / Religious Programs—Tel: 214-688-0942.
Students 220.

11—ST. ANDREW KIM (1977), Rev. John Hogan, S.S.C.
Res., 2712 Swiss Ave., 75204. Tel: 214-651-9150; Fax: 214-826-9099.
Catechesis / Religious Programs—Moses Chung, D.R.E.
Students 155.

12—ST. ANTHONY (1938), Rev. Anthony Nwaogu.
Res., 2711 Romine St., 75215. Tel: 214-428-6926.
School—3732 Myrtle St., 75215. Tel: 214-421-3645.
Lay Teachers 18; Students 215.

13—ST. AUGUSTINE (1937), Revs. Ernesto Torres; A. Oscar Diez; Deacons Jesus Cerrato; Ismael Guerra.
Res., 1047 N. St. Augustine Dr., 75217. Tel: 214-398-1583; Fax: 214-398-2580.
School—1064 N. St. Augustine Dr., 75217.
Sisters 2; Lay Teachers 10; Students 225.
Catechesis / Religious Programs—Sr. Catherine Killoran, D.R.E.
Students 1,060.

14—ST. BERNARD OF CLAIRVAUX (1947), Rev. August A. Melito; Deacons Robert Garcia; John Kelly.
Res., 1404 Old Gate Ln., 75218. Tel: 214-321-0454; Fax: 214-320-0119.
School—1420 Old Gate Ln., 75218. Tel: 214-321-2897; Fax: 214-321-4060.
Lay Teachers 25; Students 355.
Catechesis / Religious Programs—Juanita Mitchell, D.R.E.
Students 375.

15—ST. CECILIA (1933), Revs. Edmundo Paredes; Jesus Hernandez (Mexico); H. Fred Caldwell; Santos Mendoza (Philippines); Deacon Gonzalo Gonzales.
Res., 1809 W. Davis St., 75208. Tel: 214-941-5821; Fax: 214-946-4466.
School—635 Marycliff Rd., 75208. Tel: 214-948-8628.
Sisters of St. Mary of Namur 1; Lay Teachers 10; Students 210.
Catechesis / Religious Programs—Students 1,175.

16—ST. EDWARD (1903), Revs. Ramon Alvarez; Luis Serna; Deacons Juan G. Gonzalez; Guadalupe Carreon; Paul Johansen.
Res., 4007 Elm St., 75226. Tel: 214-823-1291; Fax: 214-823-2911.
Catechesis / Religious Programs—Sylvia Orozco-Joseph, D.R.E.
Students 1,200.

17—ST. ELIZABETH (1956), Revs. T. Michael Dugan; Danielo Ramos; Deacons Joseph Vollmer-Konig; Denis Simon; Sr. Denise Thompson, Pastoral Assoc.
Res., 4015 S. Hampton Rd., 75224. Tel: 214-331-4328; Fax: 214-331-2464.
School—4019 S. Hampton Rd., 75224. Tel: 214-331-5139; Fax: 214-467-4346.
Lay Teachers 24; Students 401.
Catechesis / Religious Programs—Mr. Bebe Cantu, D.R.E.
Students 108.

18—ST. JAMES (1934), Rev. Efren Ortega, Admin.; Deacon Vincent F. Jimenez.
Mailing Address: P.O. Box 763338, 75376.
Res., 1002 E. Saner Ave., 75216. Tel: 214-371-9209; Fax: 214-371-0226.
Catechesis / Religious Programs—Fax: 214-371-9672.
Students 407.

19—ST. JUDE CHAPEL AND INFORMATION CENTER (Downtown Dallas) (1968), Rev. Gilbert J. Graham, O.P., Admin.
Res., 1521 Main St., 75201. Tel: 214-742-2508; Fax: 214-748-5282.

20—ST. MARY OF CARMEL (1944), Rev. Jesus Sancho, O.C.D.
Res., 2900 Vilbig Rd., 75212. Tel: 214-747-1433; Fax: 214-748-7481.
School—1716 Singleton Blvd., 75212. Tel: 214-748-2934; Fax: 214-760-9052.
Sisters of the Holy Spirit 3; Lay Teachers 10; Students 206.
Catechesis / Religious Programs—Students 501.

21—ST. MONICA (1954), Revs. John F. Meyers; Brindley Mills; Joseph Mehan; Deacons John M. Votruba; Larry Lucido; Bob Marrinan.
Res., 9933 Midway Rd., 75220. Tel: 214-358-1453; Fax: 214-351-1887.
School—4140 Walnut Hill Ln., 75229. Tel: 214-351-5688; Fax: 214-352-2608.
Lay Teachers 53; Students 779.
Catechesis / Religious Programs—Ms. Patricia Foley, D.R.E.
Students 330.

22—ST. PATRICK (1963), Rev. Msgr. Richard E. Johnson; Rev. James S. Orosco; Deacons Clifford H. Kopinski; John C. Nordick.
Res., 9643 Ferndale Rd., 75238. Tel: 214-348-7380; Fax: 214-340-5956.
School—9635 Ferndale Rd., 75238. Tel: 214-348-8070; Fax: 214-340-5956.
Sisters of the Incarnate Word and Blessed Sacrament 2; Lay Teachers 27; Students 475.
Catechesis / Religious Programs—Mrs. Martha Noel, D.R.E.
Students 646.

23—ST. PETER (1905), Rev. Stanislaw Michalek, S.Ch.; Deacon Fred Delin.
Res., 2907 Woodall Rodgers Fwy., 75204. Tel: 214-855-1384; Fax: 214-855-1309.
Catechesis / Religious Programs—Mercy Hamilton. Students 77.

24—ST. PHILIP (1954), Rev. David J. Flori.
Res., 8131 Military Pkwy., 75227. Tel: 214-388-5464.
School—8151 Military Pkwy., 75227. Tel: 214-381-4973.
Sisters of the Holy Spirit 3; Lay Teachers 16; Students 234.
Catechesis / Religious Programs—D.R.E.: Susan Laurence; Pat Kountz.
Students 204.

25—ST. PIUS X (1954), Rev. Msgr. Thomas W. Weinzapfel; Revs. Jacob Angadiath (India); Joseph Lien Thien Tong (Vietnam); Denis O'Brien, M.M.; Deacons David Leerssen; Michael Shaw; George Zacek; John Schell.
Res., 3030 Gus Thomasson Rd., 75228. Tel: 972-279-6155; Fax: 972-686-7510.
School—Lay Teachers 30; Students 618.
Catechesis / Religious Programs—Virginia Hemmi, D.R.E.
Students 714.

26—ST. RITA (1961), Revs. Gerald Hughes, S.J.; George F. Wiltz, S.J.; Edward Coles, S.J.; Deacons William Schuster; Charles Sylvester.
Office: 12521 Inwood Rd., 75244. Tel: 972-934-8388; Fax: 972-934-8965.
Res., 12626 Planters Glen, 75244. Tel: 972-239-5205.
School—12525 Inwood Rd., 75244. Tel: 972-239-3203; Fax: 972-934-3657.
Lay Teachers 35; Students 619.
Catechesis / Religious Programs—Deacon William Schuster, D.R.E.
Students 545.

27—ST. THOMAS AQUINAS (1952), Revs. Stephen W. Bierschenk; James R. Sharp. In res., Rev. Msgr. John T. Gulczynski.
Res., 6306 Kenwood Ave., 75214. Tel: 214-821-3360; Fax: 214-821-5395.
School—3741 Abrams Rd., 75214.
Lay Teachers 45; Students 563.
Catechesis / Religious Programs—Mrs. Mary Xuereb, D.R.E.
Students 193.

28—SANTA CLARA (1993), Revs. David L. Colella, O.SS.T.; Antonio Liberman Ormaza, S.C.S. (Ecuador); Deacons Roberto Sanchez; Alberto Villarreal.
Res., 321 Calumet St., 75211. Tel: 214-337-3936; Fax: 214-333-9148.
School—St. Clare of Assisi Catholic School, Tel: 214-333-9423; Fax: 214-467-1158. Frank Romero, Prin.
Catechesis / Religious Programs—Rosalinda Rodriguez, D.R.E.
Students 500.

OUTSIDE THE CITY OF DALLAS

Allen, Collin Co., St. Jude (1981), Revs. Bruce A. Bradley; Loyd Morris; Deacon Ronald Fejeran.
Mailing Address: P.O. Box 869, 75013.
Res., 1515 N. Greenville, 75002. Tel: 214-727-1177; Fax: 214-727-1401.
Catechesis / Religious Programs—Carole Anne Horstman, D.R.E.
Students 1,075.

Bonham, Fannin Co., St. Elizabeth, Rev. Jose Saldana; Deacon Joe Culling.
Res., 409 W. 10th St., 75418. Tel: 903-583-7359.

Commerce, Hunt Co., St. Joseph, Rev. D. Stanley Corcoran.
Res., 2904 Melmar Pk., 75428. Tel: 903-886-7135.
Catechesis / Religious Programs—Students 68.

Coppell, Dallas Co., St. Ann (1985), Rev. Msgr. Kilian J. Broderick; Rev. Tim Church, Assoc.; Deacon Ed Scarbrough.
Church—180 Samuel Blvd., 75019. Tel: 972-393-5544; Fax: 972-462-1617.
Res., 129 Lansdowne Cir., 75019. Tel: 972-393-7951.
Catechesis / Religious Programs—Sr. Ruth Ellen Dean, D.R.E.
Students 1,568.

Corsicana, Navarro Co., Immaculate Conception (1871), Rev. Robert Williams; Deacon Lewis Palos.
Res., 3000 Hwy. 22 W., P.O. Box 798, 75151. Tel: 903-874-4473; Fax: 903-874-2619.
School—James L. Collins Catholic School.
Sisters of St. Francis of Sylvania, OH 2; Lay Teachers 13; Students 191.
Catechesis / Religious Programs—Mrs. Therese Miller, D.R.E.
Students 162.

Denison, Grayson Co., St. Patrick (1872), Rev. George P. Monaghan; Deacon Gary Vogel.
Res., 314 N. Rusk Ave., 75020. Tel: 903-463-3275; Fax: 903-463-3278.
Catechesis / Religious Programs—Marge Orrick, D.R.E.
Students 150.

Duncanville, Dallas Co., Holy Spirit (1974), Rev. Michael J. Barone; Deacons Eugene Schlebach; Les Alt; Edward Armstead.
Res., 1111 W. Danieldale Rd., 75137-3719. Tel: 972-298-4971; Fax: 972-709-1443.
Catechesis / Religious Programs—William Hebekeuser, D.R.E.
Students 950.

Ennis, Ellis Co., St. John Nepomucene (1902), Revs. Fred Sidler; John Dick; Deacons Dean Darnall; Don Griffith; Ralph Gordon.
Res., 401 E. Lampasas St., 75119. Tel: 972-878-2834; Fax: 972-875-2452. [CEM]
School—701 S. Paris St., 75119. Tel: 972-878-5411.
Sisters of Divine Providence 3; Lay Teachers 12; Students 193.
High School—Lay Teachers 15; Students 173.
Catechesis / Religious Programs—Students 445.
Mission—Ferris, Ellis Co., Corpus Christi, 117 N. Wood, Ferris, 75125. Tel: 972-842-2288. Rev. Eduardo Gonzalez.
Catechesis / Religious Programs—Students 213.

Forney, Kaufman Co., St. Martin (1891), Rev. Arthur D. Mallinson; Deacons James Burkel; Hector Pena. In res., Rev. Thomas Speiser.
Res., 806 N. Washington St., P.O. Box 619, Kaufman, 75142. Tel: 972-962-3247; Fax: 972-962-3247.

Garland, Dallas Co.,

1—GOOD SHEPHERD, (1944), Revs. Robert R. Crisp; Ernesto Villarroya (Philippines); Deacons Kenneth R. Badough; Walter R. Gove. In res., Revs. Abraham Samuel; Jose Moreno.
Res., 201 S. 13th St., 75040. Tel: 972-276-8587; Fax: 972-494-3653.
School—214 S. Garland Ave., 75040. Tel: 214-272-6533.
Brothers 1; Lay Teachers 27; Students 354.
Catechesis / Religious Programs—Students 1,073.

2—MOTHER OF PERPETUAL HELP, (Vietnamese), Revs. Augustine Nguyen; Hai Dinh, C.SS.R.; Thong Nguyen, C.SS.R.
Res., 2121 Apollo Rd., P.O. Box 451568, 75044. Tel: 972-414-7073.
Catechesis / Religious Programs—Bro. Hoa, D.R.E.
Students 300.

3—ST. MARY MALANKARA, (1996), Rev. Abraham Samuel Kadamala.
116 E. Ave. D, 75040. Tel: 972-494-5356.
Res., c/o Good Shepherd Church, 201 S. 13th St., 75040. Tel: 972-272-4641.

4—ST. MICHAEL THE ARCHANGEL, (1980), Rev. Msgr. Leon Duesman; Deacons Richard L. Sykora; Joe Perez.
Res., 950 Trails Pkwy., 75043. Tel: 972-279-6581; 681-8026 (Rectory); Fax: 972-279-6647.
Catechesis / Religious Programs—Adela Miller, D.R.E.
Students 1,051.

5—ST. THOMAS THE APOSTLE, (1992), Rev. Jacob Angadiath.
Res., 4922 Rose Hill Rd., 75043. Tel: 972-270-4939.
Catechesis / Religious Programs—Students 106.

Grand Prairie, Dallas Co., Immaculate Conception, Revs. Dennis O'Mara, S.S.C.; Bernard Toal, S.S.C.; Robert O'Rourke, S.S.C.; Deacons Fernando L. Argumaniz; Manuel Veyna; Michael S. Rasins.
Res., 610 N.E. 17th St., 75050. Tel: 972-262-5137.
School—400 N.E. 17th St., 75050. Tel: 972-264-8777.
Sisters of the Holy Family of Nazareth 3; Lay Teachers 13; Students 227.
Catechesis / Religious Programs—Diane Gutierrez, D.R.E.
Students 725.

St. Joseph Vietnamese Catholic Community (1993), Rev. Peter Phong Nguyen; Bro. Hong Phuc Le.
Res., 1902 S.E. 8th St., 75051. Tel: 972-642-6747; Fax: 972-264-9441.

St. Michael the Archangel (1985), Rev. Richard F. Tullius; Deacon Robert Ricard.
2910 Corn Valley, 75052.
Res., 2925 Lake Park Dr., 75051. Tel: 972-262-0552; Fax: 972-642-5429.
Catechesis / Religious Programs—Tel: 972-262-6590. Aggie Gladback, D.R.E.
Students 447.

Greenville, Hunt Co., St. William (1892), Rev. Robert M. Cox; Deacon Lee Davis.
Res., 4300 Stuart St., 75401. Tel: 903-450-1177; Fax: 903-455-7134.
Catechesis / Religious Programs—Tel: 903-455-8201; Fax: 903-455-8201. Carolyn Dorman, D.R.E.
Students 171.
Mission—Quinlan, Hunt Co., Our Lady of Fatima.

Irving, Dallas Co., Chapel of the Incarnation (1973), Rev. Tom Cloherty, Chap., Admin.; Ms. Christine G. Edmonds, Asst. Chap.
Res., University of Dallas, 75062. Tel: 972-721-5375; Fax: 972-721-5351.

Holy Family of Nazareth (1964), Rev. Msgr. Jerome P. Duesman; Deacons Lee Stieber; Kenneth Hale.
Res., 2330 Cheyenne St., 75062. Tel: 972-252-5521; Fax: 972-252-5523.
School—2323 Cheyenne St., 75062. Tel: 972-255-0205.
Sisters of the Holy Family of Nazareth 3; Lay Teachers 25; Students 403.
Catechesis / Religious Programs—Monica Duyka, D.R.E.
Students 247.

St. Luke (1902), Revs. J. Douglas Deshotel; John W. Fowler; Deacons Louis F. Adelmann; Marvin M. Barron; Jose Lincon.
Res., 1015 Schulze Dr., 75060. Tel: 972-259-3222; Fax: 972-259-3339.
School—1023 Schulze Dr., 75060.
Sisters of the Holy Family of Nazareth 1; Lay Teachers 20; Students 356.
Catechesis / Religious Programs—Jo Ann Dreyer, D.R.E.
Students 722.

Kaufman, Kaufman Co., St. Ann (1935), Rev. Arthur Mallinson; Deacons James Burkel; Hector Pena. In res., Rev. Thomas Speiser.
Res., 806 N. Washington St., P.O. Box 619, 75142. Tel: 972-962-3247.
Catechesis / Religious Programs—Nick Guigneaux, D.R.E.
Students 202.

Lancaster, Dallas Co., St. Francis of Assisi (1973), Rev. Stephen J. Mocio; Deacon Jose F. Hernandez.
Res., 1001 Alicia, 75134. Tel: 972-227-4124.
Catechesis / Religious Programs—Tel: 972-227-0770. Jeannine McClellan, D.R.E.
Students 300.

McKinney, St. Gabriel the Archangel,
2214 Forest Creek, 75070. Tel: 972-562-0638. Rev. Gregory Kelly.

St. Michael, Collin Co., (1892), Rev. J. Carl Vogel.
Res., 411 Paula Rd., 75069. Tel: 972-562-4444.
Catechesis / Religious Programs—Barbara Woodroof, D.R.E.
Students 301.
Missions—Van Alstyne, Grayson Co., Holy Family; Frisco, Collin Co., St. Francis of Assisi, 8760 Third St., Frisco, 75034. Tel: 972-335-3448. Rev. Joseph Mitchell (Mexico); Deacon Stanley Storozuk.

Plano, Collin Co., Prince of Peace (1991), Revs. R. James Balint; Lawrence A. Beyer; Deacons Robert Staib; Bernard Schroedle.
Res., 5100 W. Plano Pkwy., 75093. Tel: 972-380-2100; Fax: 972-380-5162.
School—Tel: 972-380-5505; Fax: 972-380-5162.
Lay Teachers 34; Students 340.
Catechesis / Religious Programs—Students 530.

St. Elizabeth Ann Seton (1976), Revs. John Libone; Timothy Heines; Robert Shortall (DAV); Deacons Ted Perez; Thomas Roche; Bill Flynn; Harry Pusateri.
Res., 2701 Piedra Ln., 75023. Tel: 972-596-5505;

Fax: 972-985-7573.
Catechesis/Religious Programs—Tel: 972-596-1923. Mary Frazier, D.R.E.
Students 2,054.

St. Mark the Evangelist, Rev. Msgr. Claude Smyth; Rev. Luis Buitrago; Deacons Bob Scoggins; Michael A. Carrell; Ed Putonti; Arnold Picon.
Res., 1201 Alma Dr., 75075. Tel: 972-423-5609; Fax: 972-423-5024.
School—Tel: 972-578-0610; Fax: 972-423-3299.
Lay Teachers 29; Students 550.
Catechesis/Religious Programs—Deacon Mike Carrell, D.R.E.
Students 1,399.

Richardson, Dallas Co., Mission of the Sacred Heart of Jesus (Chinese), Rev. John Chen.
Res., 14277 Preston Rd. #1027, Dallas, 75240. Tel: 972-716-0077; Fax: 972-980-8211.

St. Joseph (1976), Rev. Msgr. Don L. Fischer; Rev. Clifford G. Smith; Deacon Jim Daniels.
Res., 600 S. Jupiter Rd., 75081. Tel: 972-231-2951; Fax: 972-231-2875.
Catechesis/Religious Programs—Tel: 972-690-5588.
Students 764.

St. Paul the Apostle (1956), Revs. Henry V. Petter; Paul W. Barrus; Deacon Carl Thelin.
Res., 709 James Dr., 75080. Tel: 972-235-6105; Fax: 972-480-8528.
School—720 S. Floyd Rd., 75080. Tel: 972-235-3263.
Lay Teachers 25; Students 478.
Catechesis/Religious Programs—Tel: 972-235-2598; Fax: 972-664-9993. Jeremy (Jerri) Brandenburg, D.R.E.
Students 512.

Rockwall, Rockwall Co., Our Lady of the Lake (1974), Rev. William Richard; Deacons John Catsoris; Jesus Cerrato.
Res., P.O. Box 191, 75087. Tel: 972-771-6671 (Office); Fax: 972-722-9310.
Catechesis/Religious Programs—Tel: 214-771-4253. Aline Kindle, D.R.E.
Students 378.

Rowlett, Dallas Co., Sacred Heart (1899), Rev. Daniel J. Clayton; Deacons Frank Dunlop, Sr.; James Welsh.
Res., 3905 Hickox Rd., 75088. Tel: 972-475-4405; Fax: 972-475-6658.
Catechesis/Religious Programs—Sandy Guancial, D.R.E.
Students 432.

Sherman, Grayson Co., St. Mary (1872), Revs. Jeremy Myers; Juan R. Lira; Deacon John Le Blanc.
Res., 727 S. Travis, 75090. Tel: 903-893-5148; Fax: 903-813-5489.
School—713 Travis St., 75090. Tel: 903-893-2127.
Lay Teachers 15; Students 165.
Catechesis/Religious Programs—Annie Kremers, D.R.E.
Students 335.
Mission—Whitesboro, Grayson Co., St. Francis of Assisi.

Terrell, Kaufman Co., St. John (1876), Rev. Raymond J. Scott.
Res., 701 N. Frances St., 75160. Tel: 972-563-3643.
Catechesis/Religious Programs—Susan Warner, D.R.E.
Students 203.

Waxahachie, Ellis Co., St. Joseph (1875), Rev. Mark Joseph Seitz; Most Rev. Thomas Tschoepe; Deacons Denver Crawley; Hugo Monsanto; Larry Hatch.
Res., 504 E. Marvin St., P.O. Box 190, 75165. Tel: 972-938-1953.
School—St. Joseph Catholic School, 506 E. Marvin St., 75165. Tel: 972-938-2652. Edith Kosydar, Prin.
Lay Teachers 20; Students 150.
Catechesis/Religious Programs—Denis Corbin, D.R.E.
Students 590.
Mission—Italy, Ellis Co., Epiphany, 434 S. Ward, Italy 76651.

Wylie, Collin Co., St. Anthony (1900), Rev. Anthony W. Pondant; Deacons Peter Martinez; Warner Washington.
Res., 404 N. Ballard, 75098. Tel: 972-442-2765. [CEM]
Catechesis/Religious Programs—Anthony Pondant, D.R.E.
Students 400.

Chaplains of Public Institutions

DALLAS. *Veterans Administration Hospital* 2926 E. Ledbetter Dr., 75216. Tel: 214-374-7952. Rev. Timothy A. Gollob.

BONHAM. *Veterans Administration Hospital* 404 W. 10th St., 75418. Tel: 903-583-4942. Rev. Jose Saldana.

GRAND PRAIRIE. *Hensley Field Naval Base*. Vacant.

SEAGOVILLE. *Federal Correctional Institution*. Rev. Raymond Dowling.

TERRELL. *State Hospital* 702 N. Frances St., 75160. Tel: 972-563-3643. Rev. Raymond J. Scott.

Special Assignment:
Reverend Fathers—
Eades, B. G., 1503 Cedar Hills Ave., Dallas, TX 75205
Lucio, Justin, 5904 Ross Ave., Dallas, TX 75206

On Duty Outside the Diocese:
Reverend Fathers—
Drozd, Henry J., P.O. Box 42063, Savannah, GA 31409-0001
Martin, Sean C., St. Mary's Seminary, Houston, TX
McKenna, James G., P.O. Box 190507, Dallas, TX 75219
Phan, Cho Dink Peter, Catholic University
Roberts, Kenneth J., 611 Rosetta, Florissant, MO 63031

Absent on Leave:
Reverend Fathers—
Brown, Richard

Retired:
Reverend Monsignors—
Hughes, Gerald
Johnson, Edwin, 213 Goodford Rd., Philadelphia, PA 19154
McCallum, John V., 3406 Tipps Dr., Greenville, TX 75401
O'Rourke, John G.
Reverend Fathers—
Fernandez, Edward P., 5392 Bramble Ln., Las Vegas, NV 89120
Haberman, Lawrence R., 1518 E. Mulberry, Sherman, TX 75090
White, Gale, P.O. Box 699, Mineola, TX 75773

Permanent Deacons:
Adelman, Louis
Alt, Les
Argumaniz, Fernando L.
Armstead, Edward
Arredondo, Pastor G., (Retired)
Avila, Tomas
Badough, Kenneth
Barron, Marvin
Bathea, Val Vincent
Bauwens, Gerald
Burkel, James
Carrell, Michael A.
Carreon, Guadalupe A.
Catsoris, John A.
Cerrato, Jesus, Jr.
Coffey, Thomas, On Duty Outside the Diocese
Crawley, Denver
Culling, Joseph
Dalton, Robert J.
Daniels, James
Darnall, Dean
Davis, Lee B.
Delin, Fred O.
Dorsey, Timothy, On Duty Outside the Diocese
Dunlop, Frank W., Sr.
Elsberg, Alick, On Duty Outside the Diocese
Eschbach, Frank
Fejeran, Ronald
Flynn, Bill
Forbrich, Donald
Franklin, Sam
Friedman, William L.
Garcia, Robert
Gonzales, Gonzalo
Gonzales, Juan G.
Gonzalez, Ronald, On Duty Outside the Diocese
Gordon, Ralph R.
Gove, Walter
Griffith, Don
Guerra, Ismael A.
Guerrero, Joseph D., Leave of Absence
Hale, Kenneth
Hancock, John, On Duty Outside the Diocese
Hayes, Pat
Henvey, Thomas
Hernandez, Jose F.
Hoch, Robert G., (Retired)
Husting, Paul
Ibarra, Juan
Jimenez, Roberto, On Duty Outside the Diocese
Jimenez, Vincent
Johansen, Paul
Jorgensen, John, (Retired)
Kelly, John Paul
Kopinski, Clifford H.
LeBlanc, John D.
Leerssen, David
Leicht, Robert R., Jr., On Duty Outside the Diocese
Lincon, Jose
Lucido, Larry
Macero, Carl, On Duty Outside the Diocese
Marrinan, Robert, Sr.
Martinez, Pete A., (Retired)
McAlister, Craig
Miller, Carl V., On Duty Outside the Diocese
Milliken, Frank M.
Monsanto, Hugo
Montes, Alberto
Nordick, John C.
Noriega, Ramon, On Duty Outside the Diocese
Orozco, Adolph, Jr.
Palos, Lewis J.
Pena, Hector B.
Perez, Joe R.
Perez, Ted, Jr.
Picon, Arnold
Pilger, Rex, Jr., On Duty Outside the Diocese
Pusateri, Harry
Putonti, Edward
Rasins, Michael
Reisor, Kenneth
Reyna, Frank
Ricard, Robert A.
Robles, Jose R.
Roche, Thomas
Rojas, Jessie
Ross, Donald, Leave of Absence
Salerno, John, On Duty Outside the Diocese
Salvo, Joseph
Sanchez, Robert
Scarbrough, Ed
Schell, John A.
Schlebach, Eugene M.
Schnurr, Don
Schroedle, Bernard E.
Schuster, William J.
Scoggins, Robert C., Jr.
Shaw, Michael, Jr.
Sifuentez, Stephen Q., Leave of Absence
Simon, Denis
Slovacek, Emil
Stabile, Benjamin, (Retired)
Staib, Bob
Stieber, Lee, (Retired)
Storozuk, Stanley
Stump, Charles, Jr.
Sykora, Richard
Sylvester, Charles T.
Thelin, Carl
Trevino, Antonio D.
Valdes, Alfonso, (Retired)
Van Scoy, Donald G.
Vara, Rudolph R., (Retired)
Vault, Henry, Jr.
Veyna, Manuel
Villarreal, Albert
Vogel, Gary M.
Vollmer-Konig, Josef
Votruba, John M., (Retired)
Washington, Warner
Webb, Philip E., On Duty Outside the Diocese
Weithman, James C., (Retired)
Welsh, James L.
Wong, Peter
Zacek, George E.
Zoeller, William C., On Duty Outside the Diocese

INSTITUTIONS LOCATED IN THE DIOCESE

[A] SEMINARIES, DIOCESAN

IRVING. *Holy Trinity Seminary*, P.O. Box 140309, 75014-0309. Tel: 972-438-2212; Fax: 972-438-6530. Diocesan College and Pre-Theology Seminary. Very Rev. Michael Duca, Rector; Rev. John Collet, Spiritual Dir. & Coord. Liturgy; Mr. Larry LeNoir, L.M.S.W., Dir. Field Education & Counseling Svcs.; Ms. Gail Tillman, M.Mus., Dir. Music & Tutoring. Priests 2; Seminarians 31.

[B] COLLEGES AND UNIVERSITIES

IRVING. *University of Dallas*, President's Office, 1845 E. Northgate, 75062. Tel: 214-721-5000; Fax: 214-721-5017.
For a complete listing, refer to the Colleges and Universities section.

[C] HIGH SCHOOLS, DIOCESAN

DALLAS. *Bishop Dunne High School*. (Grades 8-12). (Coed), 3900 Rugged Dr., 75224. Tel: 214-339-6561; Fax: 214-339-1438. Kate C. Collins, Prin. Sisters 1; Lay Teachers 29; Students 354.

Bishop Lynch High School, 9750 Ferguson Rd., 75228. Tel: 214-324-3607; Fax: 214-324-3600. Mr. Edward E. Leyden, Pres.; Dale Kennedy, Prin.; Rev. Richard

Weaver. Lay Teachers 58; Students 815.

[D] HIGH SCHOOLS, PRIVATE

DALLAS. *Jesuit College Preparatory School.* (Boys), 12345 Inwood Rd., 75244. Tel: 214-387-8700; Fax: 214-661-9349. Society of Jesus. Revs. Kenneth A. Buddendorff, S.J., Rector; Philip S. Postell, S.J., Pres.; John F. Deeves, S.J.; Paul Deutsch, S.J., Prin.; Michael D. Dooley, S.J.; Charles A. Leininger, S.J.; James A. Marshall, S.J.; John G. Stack, S.J.; Mark Thibodeaux, S.J.; Mitchell Pacwa, S.J. Priests 8; Lay Teachers 66; Students 815; Scholastics 2.

Ursuline Academy. (Girls), 4900 Walnut Hill Ln., 75229. Tel: 214-363-6551; Fax: 214-363-5524. Mrs. Shaun Underhill, Principal; Sr. Margaret Ann Moser, O.S.U., Pres. Faculty 71; Students 755.

IRVING. *Cistercian Preparatory School.* (Boys), One Cistercian Rd., 75039-4599. Tel: 972-438-4956; Fax: 972-554-0736. Cistercian Fathers of Our Lady of Dallas Abbey. Rev. Peter Verhalen, O.Cist., Headmaster. Priests 10; Lay Teachers 23; Students 145.

Highland School, 1451 E. Northgate Dr., 75062. Tel: 972-554-1980. Rev. Steven Reilly, L.C., Pres.; Dr. Michael Dennell, Prin.

[E] SCHOOLS, PAROCHIAL

DALLAS. *Prince of Peace - Dallas*, 4500 W. Davis St., 75211. Tel: 214-337-0244. Mr. Christopher Cavnar, Prin.

[F] ELEMENTARY SCHOOLS, INTERPAROCHIAL

DALLAS. *John XXIII Regional School*, 4910 Bonnie View Rd., 75241. Tel: 214-371-8522. Dr. Armando Murillo, Prin. Lay Teachers 14; Students 191.

[G] ELEMENTARY SCHOOLS, PRIVATE

IRVING. *Cistercian Preparatory School.* (Boys), One Cistercian Rd., 75039. Tel: 214-438-4956; Fax: 214-554-0736. Cistercian Fathers of Our Lady of Dallas Abbey. Rev. Peter Verhalen, O.Cist., Headmaster. Priests 10; Lay Teachers 23; Students 181.

Highland School, 1451 E. Northgate Drive, 75062. Tel: 972-554-1980. Rev. Steven Reilly, L.C., Pres.; Mark Salisbury, Prin.

[H] SPECIAL SCHOOLS, PRIVATE

DALLAS. *Notre Dame of Dallas Schools, Inc.*, 2018 Allen St., 75204. Tel: 214-720-3911; Fax: 214-720-3913. Day School: Provides instructional education for mentally retarded children, ages 3-15. Ms. Theresa Francis, Prin. Students 110. Vocational Center: Provides vocational training for young adults, ages 15-21. Lay Staff 28.

[I] GENERAL HOSPITALS

DALLAS. *Parkland Hospital*, 5201 Harry Hines Blvd., 75235. Tel: 214-590-8512.

For a complete listing, refer to the Hospitals section.

St. Paul Medical Center, 5909 Harry Hines Blvd., 75235. Tel: 214-879-1000.

For a complete listing, refer to the Hospitals section.

St. Paul Medical Center, 5909 Harry Hines Blvd., 75235.

For a complete listing, refer to the Hospitals section.

St. Paul Medical Center Foundation Inc., 2777 Stemmons Fwy., #957, 75207.

For a complete listing, refer to the Hospitals section.

[J] CATHOLIC CHARITIES

DALLAS. *Catholic Charities*, 3725 Blackburn St., P.O. Box 190507, 75219. Tel: 214-520-6590; Fax: 214-520-6595. Rev. Kilian J. Broderick, Exec. Dir.

Catholic Counseling Services, 3725 Blackburn St., P.O. Box 190507, 75219. Tel: 214-526-2772.

Immigration Counseling Services, 325 W. 12th St., 75208. Tel: 214-946-4889. Ms. Vanna Slaughter, M.S.W., Admin.

Marillac Social Center, 2827 Lapsley, 75212. Tel: 214-638-4997. Sr. Rose Ann Aguilar, D.C., Admin. Sisters 2; Lay Staff 58.

Migration Refugee Services; Refugee Resettlement; Refugee Job Placement, 3915 Lemmon Ave., 75219. Tel: 214-520-9845; 520-9849. English as a second language. Mr. Art Granzeier, Admin.

Monsignor John P. Brady Center, 4009 Elm St., 75226. Tel: 214-826-8330. Sr. Mary N. Brown, S.S.N.D., Admin. Conducted by Catholic Charities. Lay Staff 23.

St. Joseph Adolescent & Family Counseling Center, 325 W. 12th St., 75208. Tel: 214-946-4896. Dr. Grant C. Hellyer, Admin. Treatment Center for adolescent boys and girls ages 13-17. Lay Staff 4; Capacity 20.

St. Joseph Residence, 330 W. Pembroke, 75208. Tel: 214-948-3597; Fax: 214-948-1209. Sr. Adelaide Bocanegra, Bethl., Admin. For elderly ladies, gentlemen, and couples. Conducted by Daughters of the Sacred Heart of Jesus (Bethlemitas). Sisters 6; Residents 45.

St. Jude, Inc., 3725 Blackburn St., P.O. Box 190507, 75219. Tel: 214-520-6590; Fax: 214-520-6595.

Purpose: To obtain housing for the elderly and needy in Dallas.

St. Martin Family Service Center, Inc., 325 W. 12th St., 75208. Tel: 214-520-6590; Fax: 214-520-6595.

Purpose: To provide social services to assist the poor and indigent families of Oak Cliff to become self-reliant.

St. Stephen, Inc., 3725 Blackburn St., 75219. Tel: 214-520-6590; Fax: 214-520-6595. Rev. Msgr. Kilian J. Broderick, Pres.; David D.W. Bain, Vice Pres.; Joseph W. Dingman, Sec. & Treas.; Peter Larson, Vice Pres.; Karl Locker, Vice Pres.; Alice Murray, Vice Pres.

Purpose: To provide affordable housing for very low-income families and individuals in South Oak Cliff area of Dallas.

Villa Santa Maria, Inc., 3725 Blackburn St., P.O. Box 190507, 75219. Tel: 214-520-6590; Fax: 214-520-6595.

Purpose: To obtain housing for the elderly and needy in Dallas.

COPPELL. *St. Martin de Porres, Inc.*, 180 Samuel Blvd., 75019. Tel: 214-393-5544.

Purpose: To obtain housing for low-income families.

[K] EDUCATION CENTERS

DALLAS. *Mount Carmel Center*, 4600 W. Davis St., 75211-3498. Tel: 214-331-6224. Discalced Carmelite Fathers of the Southwestern Province. Revs. M. Philip Wurth, O.C.D., Dir.; Sam Anthony Morello, O.C.D.; John Michael Payne, O.C.D., Asst. Dir. In res., Rev. Joseph Neilson, O.C.D.

Mount St. Michael Spiritual Life Center, 4500 W. Davis St., 75211. Tel: 214-331-1754; Fax: 214-339-6322. Sr. Margaret McCaffrey, Supr. Sisters of Our Lady of Charity of Refuge 16.

[L] PERSONAL PRELATURES

DALLAS. *Marian Servants of the Holy Spirit*, 3930 Rugged Dr., 75224. Tel: 214-330-0410. Revs. Michael McDonagh, M.S.H.S., Supr./Dir.; Matthew Riemer, M.S.H.S., Vocation Dir. Total in Residence 6.

IRVING. *Opus Dei.* (Prelature of the Holy Cross and Opus Dei), 3610 Wingren, 75062. Tel: 972-650-0064. Rev. Jack Solarski.

[M] MONASTERIES AND RESIDENCES OF PRIESTS

DALLAS. *Capuchin Franciscan Friars, Vice Province of Texas*, 2601 Singleton Blvd., 75212. Tel: 214-630-7933. Rev. Juan Cruz Gaston, O.F.M.Cap. Priests 16; Brothers 2.

Congregation of the Mission, Southern Province, 3826 Gilbert Ave., 75219. Tel: 214-526-2421; Fax: 214-526-3477. Rev. George J. Weber, C.M. Priests 34; Brothers 1.

IRVING. *Cistercian Abbey of Our Lady of Dallas*, One Cistercian Rd., 75039. Tel: 214-438-2044. Rt. Rev. Denis M. Farkasfalvy, O.Cist., S.S.L., M.S., S.T.D., Abbot, Vicar of the Abbot Pres. of Zirc; Revs. Peter Verhalen, O.Cist., M.A., Prior; Henry Marton, O.Cist., Subprior; Christopher Rabay, O.Cist., S.T.L.; Damian Szodenyi, O.Cist., Ph.D.; Placid Csizmazia, O.Cist., Ph.D.; George Ferenczy, O.Cist., Ph.D.; Benedict Monostori, O.Cist., Ph.D.; Balthasar Szarka, O.Cist.; Bede Lackner, O.Cist., Ph.D.; Pascal Kis-Horvath, O.Cist.; Aloysius Kimecz, O.Cist.; David Balas, O.Cist., Ph.D., S.T.D.; Matthew Kovacs, O.Cist.; Melchior Chladek, O.Cist.; Rochus Kereszty, O.Cist., S.T.D.; Julius Leloczky, O.Cist., S.T.D.; Bernard Marton, O.Cist., S.T.D.; James Lehrberger, O.Cist.; Robert Maguire, O.Cist., Ph.D.; Gregory Schweers, O.Cist.; Timothy Coble, O.Cist.; Mark Ripperger, O.Cist.; Bros. Paul McCormick, O.Cist.; William Wheat, O.Cist.; Andrew Farr, O.Cist. Priests 24; Scholastics 3.

Priests of the Abbey Serving Abroad: Rev. Ralph March, O.Cist., Ph.D., Germany.

Dominican Priory of St. Albert the Great, Prior of Dominican Community, University of Dallas, 1845 E. Northgate Dr., 75062-4799. Tel: 214-438-1626. Very Rev. Andrew K. Kolzow, O.P., Prior; Revs. Paul G. Hinnebusch, O.P., Subprior; Thomas M. Cain, O.P.; Edward M. Robinson, O.P.; Daniel P. Brady, O.P.; Austin E. Green, O.P.; John B. Balsam, O.P.; Daniel A. Shanahan, O.P.

Assigned to this Priory but residing elsewhere due to Ministry: Revs. Thomas M. Cumiskey, O.P., Holy Trinity Seminary, Irving; Eduardo Gabriel, O.P.

Legionaries of Christ, 1451 E. Northgate Dr., 75062. Tel: 972-438-2556. Revs. Steven Reilly, L.C., Supr.; Martin Pollock, L.C.; Bro. Jason Wallace, L.C.

[N] CONVENTS AND RESIDENCES FOR SISTERS

DALLAS. *Bethany House*, 3017 Mallory, 75216. Tel: 214-371-4867. Sisters of St. Mary of Namur. Sr. Patricia Ann Ridgley, S.S.M., Contact Person.

The Institute of Divine Mercy Convent, 8351 San Fernando Way, 75218. Tel: 214-969-7500. Sr. Maria Faustina; Sr. Mary Francis; Sr. Maria Barterte.

Marillac Social Center Residence, 2911 Lapsley St., 75212. Tel: 214-631-6757. Sr. Noreen Crean, D.C., Supr. Daughters of Charity of St. Vincent de Paul 7.

Missionaries of Charity, 2704 Harlandale, 75216. Tel: 214-374-3351. Sr. M. Bernice, M.C. Sisters 4.

Missionary Catechist of the Poor, 950 N. Montclair Ave., 75208. Tel: 214-942-6243. Sr. Norma Edith Munoz, M.C.P., Supr. Sisters 8.

Monastery of Discalced Carmelites, 600 Flowers Ave., 75211. Mother Celine, O.C.D., Prioress. Professed Sisters 9.

School Sisters of Notre Dame, P.O. Box 227275, 75222. Tel: 214-330-9152; Fax: 214-330-9197. Sr. Juliette Daigle, S.S.N.D.

Provincial House of the Dallas Province, 4500 W. Davis, 75211. Sr. Elizabeth Newman, S.S.N.D. Prov. Sisters 203.

Other Convents: 2930 Storey Ln., Apts. 202 & 101, 75220. 2810 Storey Ln., Apt. 101, 75220. 7625 Cortland, 75235. 4401 Highview, 75211. 1406 Glenwick, Irving, 75060. 2826 Storey Ln., Apts. 100 & 101, 75220. 2910 Storey Ln., Apt. 104, 75220.

Ursuline Convent, 9905 Inwood Rd., 75220. Tel: 214-369-8159; Fax: 214-369-4004. Academy, 4900 Walnut Hill Ln., 75229. Tel: 214-363-6551; Fax: 214-369-4034. Sr. Catherine Chandler, O.S.U., Prioress; Sr. Margaret Ann Moser, O.S.U., Pres. Nuns 19.

GRAND PRAIRIE. *Sisters of the Holy Family of Nazareth.* (Blessed Frances Siedliska Provincialate), 1814 Egyptian Way, P.O. Box 530959, 75053. Tel: 972-641-4496. Sr. M. Ancilla, C.S.F.N., Prov. Supr. Sisters 48.

[O] CAMPUS MINISTRY

IRVING. *Diocese of Dallas Campus Ministry*, University of Dallas, 75062. Tel: 972-721-5375. Rev. Thomas Cloherty, Diocesan Dir.; Christine Edmonds, Campus Minister.

Southern Methodist University, P.O. Box 282, Dallas, 75275. Tel: 214-692-4504. Rev. Jeremiah J. Cullinane; Judy Henneberger, Campus Minister.

East Texas State University, St. Joseph Church, 2904 Melmar Pk., Commerce, 75428. Tel: 903-886-7135. Rev. D. Stanley Corcoran.

[P] MISCELLANEOUS LISTINGS

DALLAS. *Cathedral Preservation Fund, Inc.*, 6517 Hillcrest Ave., Ste. 402, 75205. Tel: 214-361-8941. W. David Holliday, Contact.

Catholic Alumni Club, 6322 Azalea Ln., 75230. Ann Weaver.

Catholic Community Appeal, Inc., 3725 Blackburn St., P.O. Box 190507, 75219. Tel: 214-528-2240. Michael T. Weis, Treas.

Christian Community of God's Delight, 4500 W. Davis-Keating Hall, P.O. Box 225008, 75211. Tel: 214-333-2337; Fax: 214-333-2595.

Collin County Catholic High School Campaign, Inc., 3725 Blackburn St., P.O. Box 190507, 75219. Tel: 214-528-2240. Michael T. Weis, Treas.

Commission on Ecumenism, P.O. Box 190507, 75219. Tel: 214-528-2240. Rev. Robert Crisp, Chm.

Diocesan Charitable Trust, 3725 Blackburn, P.O. Box 190507, 75219. Tel: 214-528-2240. Sponsor of Rent Subsidizing Housing, Colonia Tepeyeac Apartments.

The Institute of Divine Mercy, Inc., 8351 San Fernando Way, 75218. Nonprofit corporation formed under the supervision of the diocese of Dallas for the purpose of starting a new order of cloistered nuns.

International Catholic Network, 419 Cockrell Hill Rd., 75211.

Ladies of Charity of Dallas, P.O. Box 595666, 75359-0666. Tel: 214-821-5713.

The National Cursillo Center and Office of the National Secretariat, 4500 W. Davis, 75211. Mailing Address: P.O. Box 210226, 75211. Tel: 214-339-6321. Thomas E. Sarg, Exec. Dir.; Joachim Thong Le, Vietnamese Coord., 9362 Asbery Cir., Westminster, CA, 92683. Tel: 714-891-6216. Juan Ruiz, Hispanic Coord., 15839 Hillgate Dr., Whittier, CA, 90604. Tel: 310-947-7824. Ken Sittenauer, English Coord., 3312 W. 50th Ter., Shawnee Mission, KS, 66205. Tel: 913-831-2936.

Patrons of the Arts in the Vatican Museum. (Vacant).

School Sisters of Notre Dame of Dallas Charitable Trust, 4500 W. Davis, 75211. Tel: 214-330-9152; Fax: 214-330-9197. Mailing Address: P.O. Box 227275, 75222-7275.

Scouting - Camp Fire, 3616 Bon Park Ct., 75228. Deacon Mike Shaw, Chap.

Society of St. Vincent de Paul, 3826 Gilbert St., 75219. Tel: 214-528-7837. Central Office for all society activities in the Diocese of Dallas. Mr. Philip Young, Pres.; Mr. Robert J. Little, Exec. Dir.

Southwestern Lieutenancy, Equestrian Order of the

Holy Sepulchre of Jerusalem, 9716 Trailhill Dr., 75238. Tel: 214-341-4457; 349-6196; Fax: 214-341-6262. Albin J. Brezna, Lieutenant.

White Rose Women's Center, 4300 N. Central Expwy., Ste. 110, 75206. Tel: 214-821-6292. John Everett, Dir.; Rev. Robert M. Cox, Chap.
Purpose: Catholic crisis pregnancy center offering free pregnancy tests, complete information on pregnancy and abortion, and concrete, practical assistance with awkward pregnancy situations.

CARROLLTON. *Council of Catholic Women, DDCCW*. (Dallas Diocesan Council of Catholic Women), 1846 Rosemeade Pkwy #160, 75007. Tel: 972-492-7698.

COMMERCE. *Apostleship of Prayer*, St. Joseph, 2904 Melmar Pk., 75428. Rev. Msgr. Robert Johnson, Dir.

FERRIS. *Holy Name Society*, Corpus Christi Mission, 117 N. Wood St., 75125. Rev. Eduardo Gonzalez, S.D.B.

IRVING. *Diocesan Historian*, Campus Ministry Office - University of Dallas, 1845 E. Northgate Dr., 75067. Tel: 972-721-5375. Rev. Thomas P. Cloherty, K.C.H.S.

RELIGIOUS INSTITUTES OF MEN REPRESENTED IN THE DIOCESE

For further details refer to the corresponding bracketed number in the Religious Institutes of Men or Women section.

[0470]—*The Capuchin Friars*.—O.F.M.Cap.
[0340]—*Cistercian Fathers*.—O.Cist.
[0260]—*Discalced Carmelite Friars*. (Oklahoma Prov.).—O.C.D.
[0690]—*Jesuit Fathers and Brothers*. (New Orleans Prov.).—S.J.
[0730]—*Legionaries of Christ*.—L.C.
[]—*Marian Servants of the Holy Spirit*.—M.S.H.S.
[1110]—*Missionaries of Sacred Heart*.—M.S.C.
[0430]—*Order of Preachers (Dominicans)*. (Southern Dominican Prov.).—O.P.
[1260]—*Society of Christ*.—S.Ch.
[0370]—*Society of St. Columba*.—S.S.C.
[1330]—*Vincentian Fathers*. (Southern Prov.).—C.M.

RELIGIOUS INSTITUTES OF WOMEN REPRESENTED IN THE DIOCESE

[1810]—*Bernardine Sisters of the Third Order of St. Francis*.—O.S.F.
[1920]—*Congregation of the Sisters of the Holy Cross*.—C.S.C.
[0760]—*Daughters of Charity of St. Vincent de Paul*. (St. Louis Prov.).—D.C.
[]—*Daughters of the Sacred Heart of Jesus*.—S.C.I.F.
[0420]—*Discalced Carmelite Nuns*.—O.C.D.
[1070-03]—*Dominican Sisters*.—O.P.
[2710]—*Missionaries of Charity*.—M.C.
[]—*Missionary Catechists of the Poor*. (Mexico).
[3070]—*North American Union Sisters of Our Lady of Charity*.—N.A.U.-O.L.C.
[2970]—*School Sisters of Notre Dame*.—S.S.N.D.
[1010]—*Sisters of Divine Providence of San Antonio, Texas*.—C.D.P.
[3950]—*Sisters of Saint Mary of Namur*. (Western Prov.).—S.S.M.N.
[1970]—*Sisters of the Holy Family of Nazareth*. (Sacred Heart Vice Prov.).—C.S.F.N.
[2050]—*Sisters of the Holy Spirit and Mary Immaculate*.—S.H.Sp.
[4110]—*Ursuline Nuns (Roman Union)*. (Central Prov.).—O.S.U.

DIOCESAN CEMETERIES

DALLAS. *Calvary Hill Cemetery & Mausoleum*.
DESOTO. *Holy Redeemer Cemetery & Mausoleum*.
ROWLETT. *Sacred Heart Cemetery & Mausoleum*.
WYLIE. *St. Paul*.

NECROLOGY

† Forliti, Rev. Msgr. Robert Q., (Retired). —Died May 10, 1996.
† McGill, Rev. Msgr. Henry, (Retired). —Died Dec. 29, 1996.
† Weinzapel, Joseph J., (Retired). —Died May 1, 1996.

Diocese of Davenport

(Dioecesis Davenportensis)

Most Reverend

WILLIAM E. FRANKLIN, D.D.

Bishop of Davenport; ordained February 4, 1956; appointed Titular Bishop of Surista and Auxiliary Bishop of Dubuque January 29, 1987; ordained Bishop April 1, 1987; transferred to Davenport November 12, 1993; installed January 20, 1994. *Res., 2761 Scott St., Davenport, IA, 52803.* Tel.: 319-324-4774. *Office: St. Vincent Center, 2706 N. Gaines St., Davenport, IA, 52804-1998.* Tel.: 319-324-1911.

Most Reverend

GERALD FRANCIS O'KEEFE, D.D.

Retired Bishop of Davenport; ordained January 29, 1944; appointed Auxiliary Bishop of St. Paul and Titular Bishop of Candyba May 5, 1961; consecrated July 2, 1961; transferred to Davenport October 20, 1966; installed January 4, 1967; retired November 12, 1993. *Res., 2706 N. Gaines St., Davenport, IA, 52804.*

ERECTED MAY 8, 1881.

Square Miles 11,438.

Comprises that part of the State of Iowa bounded on the east by the Mississippi River; on the west by the western boundaries of the counties of Jasper, Marion, Monroe and Appanoose; on the south by the State of Missouri; on the north by the northern boundaries of the Counties of Jasper, Poweshiek, Iowa, Johnson, Cedar and Clinton.

For legal titles of parishes and diocesan institutions, consult the Chancery.

Chancery: St. Vincent Center, 2706 N. Gaines St., Davenport, IA, 52804-1998. Tel.: 319-324-1911; Fax: 319-324-5842.

STATISTICAL OVERVIEW

Personnel	
Bishop	1
Retired Bishops	1
Priests: Diocesan Active in Diocese	94
Priests: Active Outside Diocese	11
Priests: Diocesan in Foreign Missions	1
Priests: Retired, Sick or Absent	40
Number of Diocesan Priests	146
Religious Priests in Diocese	7
Extern Priests in Diocese	4
Ordinations:	
Diocesan Priests	1
Transitional Deacons	3
Permanent Deacons in Diocese	50
Total Brothers	2
Total Sisters	214
Parishes	
Parishes	93
With Resident Pastor:	
Resident Diocesan Priests	59
Resident Religious Priests	4
Without Resident Pastor:	
Administered by Priests	28
Administered by Lay People	2
Pastoral Centers	1
New Parishes Created	1
Closed Parishes	11
Professional Ministry Personnel:	
Brothers	1
Sisters	20
Lay Ministers	4
Welfare	
Catholic Hospitals	3
Total Assisted	275,966
Homes for the Aged	3
Total Assisted	441
Educational	
Seminaries, Diocesan	1
Students from This Diocese	4
Students from Other Diocese	1
Diocesan Students in Other Seminaries	7
Total Seminarians	11
Colleges and Universities	2
Total Students	3,119
High Schools, Diocesan and Parish	7
Total Students	1,278
Elementary Schools, Diocesan and Parish	45
Total Students	4,627
Catechesis/Religious Education:	
High School Students	3,200
Elementary Students	9,600
Total Students Under Catholic Instruction	21,835
Teachers in the Diocese:	
Priests	29
Sisters	18
Lay Teachers	538
Vital Statistics	
Receptions into the Church:	
Infant Baptism Totals	1,543
Adult Baptism Totals	236
Received into Full Communion	221
First Communions	2,110
Confirmations	1,928
Marriages:	
Catholic	346
Interfaith	384
Total Marriages	730
Deaths	1,117
Total Catholic Population	106,460
Total Population	707,123

Former Bishops—Rt. Rev. JOHN MCMULLEN, D.D., cons. July 25, 1881; died July 4, 1883.—Rt. Rev. HENRY COSGROVE, D.D., cons. Sept. 14, 1884; died Dec. 22, 1906.—Rt. Rev. JAMES DAVIS, D.D., cons. Nov. 30, 1904; died Dec. 2, 1926.—Most Rev. HENRY P. ROHLMAN, D.D., cons. July 25, 1927; appt. Coadjutor-Archbishop of Dubuque and Titular Archbishop of Macra in Rhodope, June 15, 1944; Archbishop of Dubuque, Nov. 18, 1946; appt. Titular Archbishop of Cotrada, Dec. 2, 1954; died Sept. 13, 1957.—Most Rev. RALPH LEO HAYES, D.D., ord. Sept. 19, 1909; appt. Bishop of Helena June 23, 1933; cons. Sept. 21, 1933; appt. Rector of North American College in Rome in Sept. 1935; transferred to Titular See of Hierapolis Oct. 26, 1935; transferred to Davenport Nov. 16, 1944; appt. Assistant at the Pontifical Throne April 30, 1958; transferred to Titular See of Naraggara; retired Oct. 20, 1966; died July 4, 1970.—Most Rev. GERALD FRANCIS O'KEEFE, D.D., ord. Jan. 29, 1944; appt. Auxiliary Bishop of St. Paul and Titular Bishop of Candyba May 5, 1961; cons. July 2, 1961; transferred to Davenport Oct. 20, 1966; installed Jan 4, 1967; retired Nov. 12, 1993.

Chancery—St. Vincent Center, 2706 N. Gaines St., Davenport, 52804-1998. Tel: 319-324-1911; Fax: 319-324-5842.

Vicar General—Rev. Msgr. MICHAEL J. MORRISSEY, J.C.L.

Chancellor—Rev. Msgr. LEO J. FEENEY.

Vice-Chancellor—Rev. Msgr. JAMES F. PARIZEK, J.C.L.

Diocesan Tribunal—St. Vincent Center, 2706 N. Gaines St., Davenport, 52804-1998. Tel: 319-324-1911.

Judicial Vicar—Rev. Msgr. JAMES F. PARIZEK, J.C.L.

Adjutant Judicial Vicar—Rev. Msgr. MICHAEL J. MORRISSEY, J.C.L.

Assistant to the Judicial Vicar—HELEN HART.

Promoter of Justice—Rev. FRANCIS C. HENRICKSEN.

Defenders of the Bond—Rev. Msgr. LEO J. FEENEY; Revs. JOHN P. GALLAGHER, J.C.L.; WILLIAM E. REYNOLDS, J.C.L.

Notaries—JOANN KAKERT; HELEN HART; BARBARA MORRISSEY.

Pro-Synodal Judges—Rev. Msgr. JAMES F. PARIZEK; Rev. Msgr. MICHAEL J. MORRISSEY; Rev. Msgr. LEO J. FEENEY; Revs. JOHN P. BOYLE; ROBERT J. BUSHER; JOSEPH B. DENNING; EDWARD J. FITZPATRICK; JOHN P. GALLAGHER; RUDOLPH T. JUAREZ; ROBERT T. MCALEER; GEORGE W. MCDANIEL; WILLIAM E. REYNOLDS.

Diocesan Consultors—Rev. Msgr. MICHAEL J. MORRISSEY, V.G.; Very Revs. JOHN M. HYLAND; MARVIN A. MOTTET; Revs. JOSEPH B. DENNING; FRANCIS C. HENRICKSEN; JOSEPH R. SPARKS.

Deans—Davenport: Very Rev. MARVIN A. MOTTET, Clinton: Very Rev. H. ROBERT HARNESS, Iowa City: Very Rev. EDWARD J. FITZPATRICK, Keokuk: Very Rev. JOHN M. HYLAND, Ottumwa: Very Rev. ANTHONY J. HEROLD, Grinnell: Very Rev. ERNEST E. BRAIDA.

Diocesan Administrative Council—Rev. Msgr. MICHAEL J. MORRISSEY; Rev. Msgr. LEO J. FEENEY; ROBERT VAN VOOREN; KATHY BUSH. Tel: 319-324-1911.

Finance Council—Most Rev. WILLIAM E. FRANKLIN; Rev. Msgr. MICHAEL J. MORRISSEY; JAMES MURPHY;

MICHAEL BAUER; ROBERT VAN VOOREN; DON BLOUGH; KATHY BUSH.

Episcopal Vicar for Priests—Rev. Msgr. W. ROBERT SCHMIDT, E.V., *St. Vincent Center, 2706 N. Gaines St., Davenport, 52804-1998.* Tel: 319-324-1911.

Episcopal Vicar of Iowa City—Very Rev. HARRY H. LINNENBRINK, *St. Wenceslaus Rectory, 618 E. Davenport, Iowa City, 52245.*

Missionary Vicar—Rev. RUDOLPH T. JUAREZ, *516 Fillmore St., Davenport, 52802.*

Diocesan Offices and Directors

Operations—*St. Vincent Center, 2706 N. Gaines St., Davenport, 52804-1998.* Tel: 319-324-1911.

Director of Finances and Operations—STEPHEN J. SCHMALL.

Human Resource Coordinator—DAN CRUSE.

Stewardship and Development Coordinator—JENNIFER MAAS.

Director of Communications—DAVID MONTGOMERY.

Database/Publications Coordinator—CAROLINE BARTLING.

Technology Coordinator—MICHELE TRAVER.

Archivist—Sr. MADELEINE MARIE SCHMIDT, C.H.M.

Departments—*St. Vincent Center, 2706 N. Gaines St., Davenport, 52804-1998.* Tel: 319-324-1911.

Parish Services Department—

Director of Parish Services and Director of Ministry Formation—Vacant.

Coordinating Director of Social Action—DAN EBENER.

Ethnic Ministry Coordinator—MARTHA YERINGTON.

Immigration Program Coordinator—LAURA TORRES.

Coordinating Director of Education—Vacant.

Superintendent of Schools—Rev. Msgr. W. ROBERT SCHMIDT.

Family Formation Coordinator—MARIE HOWARD.

Youth Formation Coordinator—ROB BUTTERWORTH.

Adult Formation Coordinator—Sr. ANGELA IRELAND, S.S.S.F.

Religion Formation Coordinator—Vacant.

Media Resource Coordinator—SHARON HELM.

School Curriculum Coordinator—Vacant.

Coordinating Director of Worship and Liturgy—Rev. JAMES J. VRBA.

Other Offices and Directors—

Boy Scouts—Deacon RICHARD J. RASMUSSEN, *3236 Somerset Dr., Bettendorf, 52722.* Tel: 319-332-7558.

Catholic Relief Services—Rev. Msgr. MICHAEL J. MORRISSEY, Dir., *St. Vincent Center, 2706 N. Gaines St., Davenport, 52804-1998.* Tel: 319-324-1911.

Catholic Woman's League—Rev. CHARLES E. GANNON, Chap., *St. Vincent Center, 2706 N. Gaines St., Davenport, 52804-1998.* Tel: 319-322-7837.

Cemetery Committee—JOHN MCCABE, Sec., *614 Main St., Davenport, 52801.* Tel: 319-322-4438.

Campaign for Human Development—DAN R. EBENER, *St. Vincent Center, 2706 N. Gaines St., Davenport, 52804-1998.* Tel: 319-324-1911.

Continuing Education of the Clergy—Rev. Msgr. MICHAEL J. MORRISSEY, *St. Vincent Center, 2706 N. Gaines St., Davenport, 52804-1998.* Tel: 319-324-1911.

Commission on Women in the Church—*St. Vincent Center, 2706 N. Gaines St., Davenport, 52804-1998.* Tel: 319-324-1911.

Commission on Worship and Prayer—Rev. JAMES J. VRBA, *St. Patrick Rectory, 228 E. Court St., Iowa City, 52240-4998.* Tel: 319-337-2856.

Department of Communications—Rev. FRANCIS C. HENRICKSEN, Dir., *P.O. Box 460, 103 E. Second St., Davenport, 52805.* Tel: 319-323-9959.

D.C.C.W.—Rev. TIMOTHY J. REGAN, Dir., *109 N. Lincoln St., Keota, 52248-9757.* Tel: 515-636-3883.

Holy Childhood, Pontifical Association—Rev. Msgr. W. ROBERT SCHMIDT, Dir., *St. Vincent Center, 2706 N. Gaines St., Davenport, 52804-1998.* Tel: 319-324-1911.

Hospital Association—Rev. JAMES P. CONROY, Bishop's Rep., *St. Vincent Center, 2706 N. Gaines St., Davenport, 52804-1998.* Tel: 319-324-1911.

Legion of Mary—Chaplaincy Vacant. Contact Chancery.

Marriage Encounter—*St. Vincent Center, 2706 N. Gaines St., Davenport, 52804-1998.* Tel: 319-324-1911.

Newspaper—*"The Catholic Messenger"*; Rev. FRANCIS C. HENRICKSEN, Mng. Editor, *P.O. Box 460, Davenport, 52805.*

Pastoral Council—Most Rev. WILLIAM E. FRANKLIN, D.D., Chm., *St. Vincent Center, 2706 N. Gaines St., Davenport, 52804-1998.* Tel: 319-324-1911.

Permanent Diaconate—*St. Vincent Center, 2706 N. Gaines St., Davenport, 52804-1998.* Tel: 319-324-1911.

Personnel Board—*St. Vincent Center, 2706 N. Gaines St., Davenport, 52804-1998.* Tel: 319-324-1911.

Presbyteral Council—Rev. ROBERT T. MCALEER, *St. Mary Rectory, 1013 Ave. E, Fort Madison, 52627-2816.* Tel: 319-372-3139.

Priests' Aid Society—Very Rev. ERNEST E. BRAIDA, *Sacred Heart Rectory, P.O. Box 1478, Newton, 50208-1478.* Tel: 319-792-2050.

Priests Eucharistic League—Rev. MICHAEL T. PHILLIPS, Dir., *Holy Family Rectory, 1923 N. Fillmore St., Davenport, 52804.* Tel: 319-322-0901.

Propagation of the Faith—Rev. Msgr. LEO J. FEENEY, Dir., *St. Vincent Center, 2706 N. Gaines St., Davenport, 52804-1998.* Tel: 319-324-1911.

Research and Development—Rev. Msgr. MICHAEL J. MORRISSEY, Dir., *St. Vincent Center, 2706 N. Gaines St., Davenport, 52804-1998.* Tel: 319-324-1911.

Refugee Resettlement Office—NORA DVORAK, Dir., *St. Vincent Center, 2706 N. Gaines St., Davenport, 52804-1998.* Tel: 319-324-1911.

Respect Life—DAN R. EBENER, *St. Vincent Center, 2706 N. Gaines St., Davenport, 52804-1998.* Tel: 319-324-1911.

Rural Life—DAN R. EBENER, Dir., *St. Vincent Center, 2706 N. Gaines St., Davenport, 52804-1998.* Tel: 319-324-1911.

Serra Club—BILL BARRETT, *2901 Marquette St., Davenport, 52803.* Tel: 319-391-0510.

Sisters' Council—Sr. REBECCA DOBBELS, C.H.M., *608 5th St. #9, Coralville, 52241.* Tel: 319-339-0118.

Substance Abuse Council—Rev. DANIEL C. MANNHARDT, Chm., *4105 N. Division, Davenport, 52806.* Tel: 319-391-4245.

Vicar for Indo-Chinese—Rev. JOSEPH KAHN V. NGUYEN, *St. Vincent Center, 2706 N. Gaines St., Davenport, 52804-1998.* Tel: 319-324-3134.

Vicar for Religious—Rev. FRANCIS C. HENRICKSEN, *4097 18th St., Bettendorf, 52722.* Tel: 319-332-7910; 323-9959.

Vocations—Rev. CHARLES ADAM, Dir., *St. Vincent Center, 2706 N. Gaines St., Davenport, 52804-1998.* Tel: 319-333-6151.

CLERGY, PARISHES, MISSIONS AND PAROCHIAL SCHOOLS

CITY OF DAVENPORT (Scott County)

1—SACRED HEART CATHEDRAL (1856), Very Rev. Marvin A. Mottet; Sr. Charla Bulko, S.S.S.F., Pastoral Assoc. In res., Rev. Thomas Stratman.
Res., 422 E. 10th St., 52803-5499. Tel: 319-324-3257; Fax: 319-326-6014. [JC]
School—Tel: 319-326-6278. Dr. Joan Kuvaitis, Prin. Sisters 1; Lay Teachers 13; Students 203.
Catechesis/Religious Programs—Sr. Mary Schmidt, O.S.B., D.R.E.
Students 160.

2—OUR LADY OF VICTORY (1962), Revs. E. William Kaska; Martin G. Goetz; Deacons Paul Hittner; Marcel Mosse. In res., Rev. Daniel C. Mannhardt.
Res., 4105 N. Division St., 52806. Tel: 319-391-4245. [JC]
School—John F. Kennedy Catholic, Tel: 319-391-3030. Judith C. Calcari, Prin.
Lay Teachers 21; Students 458.
Catechesis/Religious Programs—Tel: 319-391-8384. Kay Carruthers, D.R.E.
Students 345.

3—HOLY FAMILY (1897), Revs. Michael T. Phillips; Patrick Lumsden; Deacons Gerald Timmerman; Joseph Rosenthal; Richard Rasmussen.
Res., 1923 Fillmore St., 52804. Tel: 319-322-0902 (Rectory); 322-0901; 326-3836 (Office); Fax: 319-322-1637.
School—1926 Marquette St., 52804. Tel: 319-324-3205; Fax: 319-324-9331. Mr. William R. Fox, Prin. Lay Teachers 24; Students 465.
Catechesis/Religious Programs—Carol Kovach, D.R.E.
Students 190.

4—ST. ALPHONSUS, Revs. Theodore Lawson, C.SS.R., Rector; John Morton, C.SS.R.; Gerald Heim, C.SS.R., (Retired).
Res., 2618 Boies Ave., 52802. Tel: 319-322-0987; Fax: 319-323-1458.
School—Mrs. C. J. Albertson, Prin. Franciscan Sisters of Christ the Divine Teacher 2; Lay Teachers 9; Students 173.
Catechesis/Religious Programs—Mary Ann Hagemann, D.R.E.
Students 81.

5—ST. ANTHONY'S (1837), Rev. James P. Conroy.
Res., 417 N. Main St., 52801. Tel: 319-322-3303.

6—ST. JOSEPH'S (1855), Rev. E. James Wilson.
Res., 615 Marquette St., 52802. Tel: 319-322-3473; Fax: 319-323-7278.
School—Tel: 319-322-3723. William Meehan, Prin. Sisters 2; Lay Teachers 8; Students 128.
Catechesis/Religious Programs—516 Fillmore St., 52802. Tel: 319-322-3383.

7—ST. MARY'S (1867) (Irish), Very Rev. Rudolph T. Juarez; Deacons George D. Strader; Julian Gutierrez.
Res., 516 Fillmore St., 52802. Tel: 319-322-3383.
Catechesis/Religious Programs—Students 95.

8—ST. PAUL THE APOSTLE (1909), Revs. Joseph B. Denning; Robert D. Gruss; Deacons William Jones; Robert McCoy.
Res., 916 E. Rusholme St., 52803. Tel: 319-322-7994.
School—Tel: 319-322-2923. William Schneden, Prin. Sisters of Charity of the Blessed Virgin Mary 1; Lay Teachers 21; Students 508.
Catechesis/Religious Programs—Tel: 319-322-3768. Terri Doran, D.R.E.
Students 514.

OUTSIDE THE CITY OF DAVENPORT

Albia, Monroe Co., St. Mary's (1874), Rev. Thomas R. Doyle.
Res., P.O. Box 365, 52531. Tel: 515-932-5130. [CEM]
Catechesis/Religious Programs—Tel: 515-932-5589. Jackie Maddy, D.R.E.
Students 248.

Ardon, Muscatine Co., St. Malachy. Closed. For sacramental records, inquiries should be addressed to St. Joseph Parish, 815 2nd St., Columbus Junction, IA, 52738.

Augusta, Des Moines Co., St. Mary's (1881). Closed. For inquiries for parish records contact the Chancery.

Bauer, Marion Co., St. Joseph. Closed. For inquiries for parish records contact the Chancery.

Bettendorf, Scott Co., Our Lady of Lourdes (1903), Revs. Thomas J. Spiegel; Gary L. Beckman; Sr. Rita Lenaghan, C.H.M., Pastoral Assoc.; Deacons Dennis Duff; Warren Jensen; Tom Nolan; Terry Starns.
Res., 1506 Brown St., 52722. Tel: 319-359-0345.
School—Tel: 319-359-3466. Mrs. Barbara Herter, Prin.
Sisters of the Humility of Mary 1; Lay Teachers 23; Students 418.
Catechesis/Religious Programs—Tel: 319-359-1869. Ms. Ada Davis, D.R.E.
Students 525.

St. John Vianney (1967), Revs. Francis C. Henricksen; Richard J. Poster; Deacons William Donnelly; Thomas Sink.
Res., 4097 18th St., 52722. Tel: 319-332-7910; Fax: 319-332-8407. [JC]
Catechesis/Religious Programs—Tel: 319-332-7564. Barbara Hesenius, D.R.E. (Elementary).
Students 594.

Bloomfield, Davis Co., St. Mary Magdalen (1953), Rev. L. H. Goettemoeller, C.PP.S.
Res., 52537. Tel: 515-664-2553. [CEM]

Blue Grass, Scott Co., St. Andrew (1976), Rev. Rudolph C. Berndt.
Res., 534 N. Moselle St., 52726. Tel: 319-381-2865.
Catechesis/Religious Programs—Tel: 319-263-7301. D.R.E.: Dorothy Spiess; Deacons Allen Haut; Donald Frericks; James Becker; Dan & Judy Freeman.
Students 144.

Brooklyn, Poweshiek Co., St. Patrick, Rev. Joseph Rogers.
Res., 215 Jackson St., 52211-0512. Tel: 515-522-7714. [CEM]

Bryant, Clinton Co., St. Mary. Consolidated with St. Joseph, Sugar Creek to form Sts. Mary and Joseph, Sugar Creek.

Buffalo, Scott Co., St. Peter's. Attended by St. Andrew, Blue Grass. Rev. Rudolph C. Berndt; Deacon Larry Dankert.
Mailing Address: 406 Fourth St., P.O. Box 488, 52728. Tel: 319-381-2265; 381-2865. [CEM]

Burlington, Des Moines Co., St. John's (1855), Very Rev. John M. Hyland, V.F.; Deacon Robert R. Gengenbacher.
Res., 700 Division St., 52601. Tel: 319-752-6733; Fax: 319-753-5211. [CEM]
Catechesis/Religious Programs—Students 550.

St. Patrick's (1870), Revs. Gerald E. Stouvenel; John K. Sterling; Deacon Richard Hammer.
Res., 420 W. Mt. Pleasant St., P.O. Box 415, West Burlington, 52655. Tel: 319-752-4035. [JC]
Catechesis/Religious Programs—Tel: 319-753-0277. Sr. Mary Jean Assell, S.S.J., D.R.E.
Students 510.

St. Paul's (1840), Very Rev. John M. Hyland.
Res., 700 Division St., 52601-5415. Tel: 319-752-6933; Fax: 319-753-5211. [JC]
Catechesis/Religious Programs—Tel: 319-752-8771. Sr. Mary Assell, D.R.E.
Students 565.

Camanche, Clinton Co., Church of the Visitation

(1966), Rev. John J. Stack; Deacon John H. Schmitt. 1032 Middle Rd., 52730-1032. Tel: 319-259-1188.
Catechesis/Religious Programs—Tel: 319-522-2720. Mrs. Sue Schmitt, D.R.E.
Students 200.

Centerville, Appanoose Co., St. Mary's, Rev. Joseph Miller, C.PP.S.; Bro. Daryl Charron, C.PP.S.
Res., 828 S. 18th St., 52544. Tel: 515-437-1984.
School—Tel: 515-437-1984. Robert Wells, Prin.
Sisters 1; Lay Teachers 6; Students 64.
Catechesis/Religious Programs—Students 150.

Charlotte, Clinton Co., Assumption of the Blessed Mary. Consolidated with St. Patrick's, Villa Nova to form Assumption and St. Patrick's, Charlotte.
Assumption and St. Patrick's, Rev. David G. Steinle.
Res., 52731. Tel: 319-677-2758. [CEM]

Clear Creek, Keokuk Co., SS. Peter & Paul. See Holy Trinity, Keota.

Clinton, Clinton Co., Jesus Christ, Prince of Peace, Revs. Ronald E. Young; Joseph M. Wolf; Deacons Arthur Donart; Ramon Hilgendorf; Patrick Lennon; Aloysius Mueller.
Parish Office—(Maintained for all five churches in Clinton.) 505 Ninth Ave., S., 52732. Tel: 319-242-3311; Fax: 319-242-3323.
Churches—St. Mary's, 520 Ninth Ave., S., 52732; Sacred Heart, 316 S. Fourth Ave., 52732; St. Boniface, 2500 N. Pershing Blvd., 52732; St. Irenaeus, 2811 N. Second St., 52732; St. Patrick's, 240 Fourth Ave., N., 52732.

Colfax, Jasper Co., Immaculate Conception (1898). Attended by Sacred Heart, Newton.
Mailing Address: P.O. Box 1478, Newton, 50208-1478. Tel: 515-792-2050.

Columbus Junction, Louisa Co., St. Joseph, Rev. Bernard E. Weir.
Res., 815 Second St., 52738. Tel: 319-728-8210.

Cosgrove, Johnson Co., St. Peter's. Unassigned.
4022 Cosgrove Rd. S.W., Oxford, 52322. Tel: 319-645-2077.

Delmar, Clinton Co., St. Patrick's, Rev. Edward A. Botkin.
Res., 52037. Tel: 319-674-4240. [CEM]

DeWitt, Clinton Co., St. Joseph's (1880), Very Rev. H. Robert Harness, V.F.; Rev. David Brownfield; Sr. Theresa Ann Spitz, R.S.M., Pastoral Assoc.; Deacon Mike Sheil.
Res., 417 Sixth Ave., 52742. Tel: 319-659-3514; Fax: 319-659-2599. [CEM]
School—Tel: 319-659-3812. Gerald Streit, Prin.
Sisters of Mercy 1; Lay Teachers 12; Students 234.
Catechesis/Religious Programs—Kathy McGarry, D.R.E.
Students 210.

Dodgeville, Des Moines Co., St. Mary's (1850), Revs. Gerald E. Stouvenel; John K. Sterling; Deacon Clifford Beckman.
Res., 13204 Dodgeville Rd., Sperry, 52650-9875. Tel: 319-985-2122. [CEM]
Catechesis/Religious Programs—Tel: 319-865-7451. Frieda Vantiger, D.R.E.
Students 98.

East Pleasant Plain, Jefferson Co., St. Joseph's (1902). Attended by St. Francis Xavier Cabrini, Richland. Rev. Paul E. Connolly.
Mailing Address: P.O. Box 130, Richland, 52585. Tel: 319-456-3161; Fax: 319-456-6408. [CEM]
Catechesis/Religious Programs—Students 30.

Eddyville, Mahaska Co., St. Mary's. Attended by Sacred Heart, Ottumwa. Rev. James E. Grubb.
Mailing Address: Box 446, 52553.

Eldon, Wapello Co., St. Aloysius. Attended by St. Mary Magdalen, Bloomfield. Rev. L. H. Goettemoeller, C.PP.S.
Church—52554. Tel: 515-664-2553.

Fairfield, Jefferson Co., St. Mary's (1864), Rev. Stephen C. Page; Deacon Art Anderson.
Res., 402 N. Third, P.O. Box 903, 52556-0903. Tel: 515-472-3179.
Catechesis/Religious Programs—Tel: 515-472-5991. Therese Cummiskey, D.R.E.
Students 268.

Farmington, Van Buren Co., St. Boniface (1862), Rev. David F. Wilkening.
Res., 609 Washington St., 52626. Tel: 319-878-3736. [CEM]
Catechesis/Religious Programs—Students 129.

Fort Madison, Lee Co.,

1—St. Joseph's. Consolidated with St. Mary's to form SS.Mary & Joseph Parish.

2—St. Mary's. Consolidated with St. Joseph's to form SS. Mary & Joseph Parish.

3—SS. Mary & Joseph, Rev. Robert T. McAleer; Sr. Mary Helen Hotze, S.S.N.D., Pastoral Assoc.
Res., 1013 Ave. E, 52627. Tel: 319-372-3139.

4—Sacred Heart, (1893), Rev. Timothy J. Sheedy; Deacons John Clough; Ronald Stein.
Res., 2204 Ave. I, 52627. Tel: 319-372-3179; Fax: 319-372-3321.
Catechesis/Religious Programs—Tel: 319-372-6428; 372-2486.
Students 377.

Georgetown, Monroe Co., St. Patrick's (1851) (Irish). Attended by St. Patrick, Melrose. Rev. Mark W. Swanson.
Mailing Address: P.O. Box 183, Albia, 52531. Tel: 515-726-3529. [CEM]

Grand Mound, Clinton Co., Church of St. Philip and James (1876), Rev. David L. Brownfield.
Res., 606 Fulton St., P.O. Box 287, 52751-0287. Tel: 319-847-2271. [CEM]
Catechesis/Religious Programs—Students 110.

Grinnell, Poweshiek Co., St. Mary's, Rev. Anthony G. Farrell; Deacons Stephen J. Witt; William D. Olson.
Res., 1018 Broad St., P.O. Box 623, 50112. Tel: 515-236-5289. [CEM]

Harper, Keokuk Co., St. Elizabeth's. See Holy Trinity, Keota.

Hills, Johnson Co., St. Joseph's (1902), Rev. Louis J. Leonhardt.
Res., 52235. Tel: 319-679-2271.
Catechesis/Religious Programs—Students 72.

Holbrook, Iowa Co., St. Michael. Closed. For inquiries for parish records contact the Chancery.

Houghton, Lee Co., St. John's (1895), Rev. John D. Spiegel.
Res., Box 100, 52631. Tel: 319-469-2001. [CEM]
School—(Grades PreK-6). Tel: 319-837-6544. Sr. Pat Siepker, Prin.
Lay Teachers 11; Students 219.
High School—Tel: 319-837-6282. Mr. Dan Kieler, Prin.
Religious 2; Lay Teachers 13; Students 164.
Catechesis/Religious Programs—Tel: 319-469-2000.
Students 381.

Iowa City, Johnson Co.,

1—St. Mary of the Assumption, (1856) (German), Revs. Kenneth E. Kuntz; Brian J. Shepley; Sr. Mary Agnes Giblin, B.V.M., Pastoral Assoc.
Res., 220 E. Jefferson St., 52245. Tel: 319-337-4314. [CEM 2][JC]
Catechesis/Religious Programs—Tel: 319-351-7638.
Students 802.

2—St. Patrick's, (1872) (Irish), Rev. James J. Vrba. In res., Rev. Paul A. Deyo.
Res., 228 E. Court St., 52240. Tel: 319-337-2856; Fax: 319-354-5590. [JC]

3—St. Thomas More, Rev. David F. Hitch; Sr. Margaret Kruse, O.S.F., Pastoral Assoc.
Res., 108 McLean St., 52246. Tel: 319-337-2173. [JC]
Catechesis/Religious Programs—Mary Lu Gallahan, D.R.E.
Students 533.

4—St. Wenceslaus, (1893) (Bohemian), Very Rev. Harry H. Linnenbrink, E.V.
Res., 618 E. Davenport St., 52245. Tel: 319-337-4957. [JC]

Keokuk, Lee Co., All Saints (1982), Revs. Michael J. Spiekermeier; Dennis L. Hoffman; Deacon William Cosgrove.
Res., 310 S. Ninth St., 52632. Tel: 319-524-8334.
Catechesis/Religious Programs—Students 75.

Keota, Keokuk Co., Holy Trinity (1992), Rev. Timothy J. Regan.
Res., 109 N. Lincoln St., 52248-9757. Tel: 515-636-3883. [CEM 3]
Churches—St. Mary's, 109 N. Lincoln St., 52248-9757.; St. Elizabeth's, 20486 285th Ave., Harper, 52231. Tel: 515-635-2662; SS. Peter & Paul, 30832 242nd St., Harper, 52231. Tel: 515-635-2028.
Catechesis/Religious Programs—Tel: 515-636-3731.
Students 182.
St. Mary's. See Holy Trinity, Keota.

Keswick, Keokuk Co., Our Lady of Lourdes. Attended by St. Mary's, Sigourney. Rev. Philip R. Ryan.
Mailing Address: 415 E. Pleasant Valley St., Sigourney, 52591-1730. [CEM]
Church—50136.

Kinross, Keokuk Co., Sacred Heart. Closed. For inquiries for parish records contact the Chancery.

Knoxville, Marion Co., St. Anthony's (1870), Revs. Thomas L. Parlette; Charles Fladung.
Res., 1202 Woodland St., 50138. Tel: 515-828-7050; Fax: 515-828-7915. [CEM]
Catechesis/Religious Programs—Tel: 515-842-6249. Sr. Rachel Beeson, C.H.M., D.R.E.
Students 202.

Le Claire-Princeton, Scott Co., Our Lady of the River, Rev. John F. Hynes.
Res., 28225 226th St., LeClaire, 52753. Tel: 319-289-5736.
Catechesis/Religious Programs—Cheryl O'Klock, D.R.E.
Students 209.

Lone Tree, Johnson Co., St. Mary's. Unassigned.
Res., Box 187, Hills, 52235. Tel: 319-679-2271.

Long Grove, Scott Co., St. Ann's (1853), Rev. Stephen P. Ebel.
Res., 16550 290th St., 52756. Tel: 319-285-4596. [CEM]
Catechesis/Religious Programs—Tel: 319-285-4020. D.R.E.: Janice Uitenbroek; Fiona Wilson; Margaret Liske; Chris Behnke; Tammy Zimmer; Betty Zimmer.
Students 538.

Lost Nation, Clinton Co., Sacred Heart, Rev. William E. Reynolds.
Res., P.O. Box 127, 52254. Tel: 319-678-2200. [CEM]

Lovilia, Monroe Co., St. Peter's, Rev. Sylvester Conrad.
Res., 50150. Tel: 319-946-4621. [CEM]

Marengo, Iowa Co., St. Patrick's (1878), Rev. Joseph F. Roost.
Mailing Address: P.O. Box 183, 52301. Tel: 319-642-5438; Fax: 319-642-5648. [CEM]
Catechesis/Religious Programs—609 E. Randolph, 52301. Tel: 319-642-3825. Peggy Walton, D.R.E.
Students 100.

Mechanicsville, Cedar Co., St. Mary's (1872), Rev. William O. Meyer.
Res., 52306-0457. Tel: 319-432-6236.
Catechesis/Religious Programs—Shirley Jarzombek, D.R.E.
Students 84.

Melcher, Marion Co., Sacred Heart (1912), Revs. Thomas L. Parlette; Charles Fladung.
315 S. Main, Box 277, 50163. Tel: 515-947-3261. [CEM]
Catechesis/Religious Programs—Tel: 515-947-2902. Jean Bishop, D.R.E.
Students 110.

Melrose, Monroe Co., St. Patrick's, Rev. Mark W. Swanson.
Res., P.O. Box 154, 52569. Tel: 515-726-3457.

Montrose, Lee Co., St. Joseph's, Rev. Gerald A. Hoenig.
Res., Box 206, 52639. Tel: 319-463-5443.

Mount Pleasant, Henry Co., St. Alphonsus (1862) (Irish), Rev. Nicholas Adam; Sr. Marilyn Schierbrock, C.H.M., Pastoral Min.; Deacon Joe Demeter.
Res., 607 S. Jackson St., 52641. Tel: 319-385-8410; Fax: 319-385-0545. [CEM]
Catechesis/Religious Programs—Tel: 319-385-4937. D.R.E.: Mary Hassenfritz, (Grades PreK-5); Janine Lukaszonas, (Grades 6-10); Mark Porth, (Grades 11-12).
Students 309.

Muscatine, Muscatine Co., St. Mary's (1876), Rev. Walter B. Helms; Sr. Irma Ries, P.B.V.M., Pastoral Assoc.; Deacon Anton Tometich.
Res., 417 Green St., 52761. Tel: 319-263-7788. [JC]
Catechesis/Religious Programs—Tel: 319-263-3848. Gayle Sayles, D.R.E.
Students 280.
St. Mathias, Rev. George B. Hoenig.
Res., 215 W. Eighth St., 52761. Tel: 319-263-1878.
Our Lady of Guadalupe Catholic Mission, Deacons Juan Leza; Juan Cadena.
Res., 501 E. Sixth St., P.O. Box 243, 52761. Tel: 319-263-0296.

Mystic, Appanoose Co., St. Francis. Closed. For inquiries for parish records contact the Chancery.

Newport, Johnson Co., St. Mary. Closed. For inquiries for parish records contact the Chancery.

Newton, Jasper Co., Sacred Heart (1867), Revs. Ernest E. Braida; Philip A. Cardenzana; Betty Hummel, Pastoral Assoc.; Ila Mae Hanisch, Pastoral Min.; Deacon William Schroeder.
Mailing Address: P.O. Box 1478, 50208-1478. Tel: 515-792-4625. [CEM]
McCann Center—(Parish Office and Religious Education Center) 1115 S. Eighth Ave. E., P.O. Box 1478, 50208. Tel: 515-792-2050; Fax: 515-792-5963.
Catechesis/Religious Programs—D.R.E.: Cathi Fouts, (Grades K-6); Marybeth Wagner, (Grades 7-12).
Students 360.

Nichols, Muscatine Co., St. Mary's. Unassigned.
Box 187, Hills, 52235. Tel: 319-679-2271. [CEM]

Nolan Settlement, Johnson Co., St. Bridget's. Closed. For inquiries for parish records contact the Chancery.

North English, Iowa Co., St. Joseph's (1963), Rev. John J. Whalen.
Res., 52316. Tel: 319-664-3325; Fax: 319-668-2582. [JC]
Catechesis/Religious Programs—Students 63.

Oskaloosa, Mahaska Co., St. Mary's (1871), Rev. Robert J. Busher; Deacon William Wiegand.
Res., 311 First Ave. E., 52577. Tel: 515-673-6680. [CEM]
Catechesis/Religious Programs—Mrs. Madonna Bowie, D.R.E.
Students 200.

Ottumwa, Wapello Co., St. Mary of the Visitation, Rev. Robert M. Striegel.
Res., 216 N. Court St., 52501-2586. Tel: 515-682-4559.
Sacred Heart, Rev. James E. Grubb.
Res., 1101 E. Second St., 52501. Tel: 515-682-5587.
St. Patrick's (1880), Rev. Anthony J. Herold; Gail Bates, Pastoral Assoc.
Res., 222 N. Ward St., 52501. Tel: 515-682-4212.
Catechesis/Religious Programs—Tel: 515-682-0320. Vickie Renfrew, D.R.E.
Students 243.

Oxford, Johnson Co., St. Mary's. Unassigned.
Box 80, 52322. Tel: 319-628-4180.

Parnell, Iowa Co., St. Joseph's. Attended by St. Joseph, North English. Rev. John J. Whalen.
52325. Tel: 319-668-2366. [CEM]

Pella, Marion Co., St. Mary's (1869), Revs. Thomas L. Parlette; Charles Fladung; Sr. Carol Grawe, S.S.N.D., Parish Admin.
Res., 1104 Peace St., Box 144, 50219. Tel: 515-628-3078; Fax: 515-628-3165. [CEM]
Catechesis/Religious Programs—Students 199.

Petersville, Clinton Co., Immaculate Conception (1853), Rev. Edward A. Botkin.
Church—2885 145th St., Charlotte, 52731-9646. Tel: 319-674-4240. [CEM]

Rathbun, Appanoose Co., St. Anthony (1895). Closed. For inquiries for parish records contact the Chancery.

Richland, Keokuk Co., St. Frances Xavier Cabrini (1946), Rev. Paul E. Connolly.
Res., 309 Main St., P.O. Box 130, 52585-0130. Tel: 319-456-3161; Fax: 319-456-6408.
Catechesis/Religious Programs—Students 54.

Richmond, Washington Co., Holy Trinity, Rev. Scott G. Lemaster.
Res., 580 Howard St., Kalona, 52247-9558. Tel: 319-656-2802. [CEM]
Catechesis/Religious Programs—Students 120.

Riverside, Washington Co., St. Mary of the Assumption, Rev. John P. Gallagher.
Res., 52327. Tel: 319-648-2331; Fax: 319-648-5024. [CEM]

St. Paul, Lee Co., St. James (1838). Attended by St. John, Houghton. Rev. John D. Spiegel. [CEM]
Catechesis/Religious Programs—1249 Hwy. 218, West Point, 52656. Tel: 319-469-2000. Rose Jennings, D.R.E.
Students 381.

Sigourney, Keokuk Co., St. Mary's, Rev. Philip V. Ryan; Deacon James Striegel.
Res., 415 E. Pleasant Valley St., 52591. Tel: 515-622-3426 (Rectory); 622-2316 (Business). [CEM][JC]
Catechesis/Religious Programs—Sr. Angela Keil, O.S.F., D.R.E.
Students 125.

Solon, Johnson Co., St. Mary's, Rev. Joseph R. Sparks.
Res., Box 64, 52333. Tel: 319-644-2228. [CEM]
SS. Peter & Paul. Closed. For inquiries for parish records contact the Chancery.

String Prairie, Lee Co., St. Mary. Closed. For inquiries for parish records contact the Chancery.

Sugar Creek, Clinton Co., St. Joseph's. Consolidated with St. Mary, Bryant, to form Sts. Mary and Joseph, Sugar Creek.
Sts. Mary and Joseph (1993), Rev. Vincent J. Fabula, O.C.S.O., Admin.
Res., 3218 110th St., Preston, 52069. Tel: 319-689-4355. [CEM 2]
Catechesis/Religious Programs—Tel: 319-689-6122. Barbara Skoff, D.R.E.
Students 102.

Tipton, Cedar Co., St. Mary's (1856), Rev. M. Eugene Benda; Deacons Adrian Panther; Robert Snavely.
Res., 52772. Tel: 319-886-2506. [CEM]
Catechesis/Religious Programs—Tel: 319-886-2506. Mary Wethington, D.R.E.
Students 245.

Toronto, Clinton Co., St. James. Attended by Sacred Heart, Lost Nation. Rev. William E. Reynolds.
Mailing Address: P.O. Box 127, Lost Nation, 52254. Tel: 319-678-2200. [CEM]
Catechesis/Religious Programs—Mary Stevenson, D.R.E.
Students 62.

Valeria, Jasper Co., Sacred Heart (1892). Closed. For inquiries for parish records contact the Chancery.

Victor, Iowa Co., St. Bridget's, Rev. Richard U.O. Okumu.
Res., 104 Third St., P.O. Box 266, 52347. Tel: 319-647-2220; Fax: 319-647-2294. [CEM]

Villa Nova, Clinton Co., St. Patrick. Consolidated with Assumption of the Blessed Virgin Mary, Charlotte, to form Assumption and St. Patrick's, Charlotte.

Wapello, Louisa Co., St. Mary's (1867). Attended by St. Joseph, Columbus Junction. Rev. Bernard E. Weir.
Mailing Address: 815 Second St., Columbus Junction, 52738. Tel: 319-728-8210.

Washington, Washington Co., St. James (1860), Rev. Dennis C. Martin.
Res., 602 W. Second St., 52353-1994. Tel: 319-653-4504. [JC]
School—Tel: 319-653-3631; Fax: 319-653-3631. Ms. BethAnn McBride, Prin.
Lay Teachers 10; Students 148.
Catechesis/Religious Programs—Tel: 319-653-6213. Sr. Therese Demers, D.R.E.
Students 282.

Wellman, Washington Co., St. Joseph, Rev. Scott G. Lemaster; Deacon David Reha.
Mailing Address: 580 Howard St., Kalona, 52247-9558. Tel: 319-656-2802.
Catechesis/Religious Programs—Tel: 319-646-2807. D.R.E.: Donna Johnson; Barry Johnson.
Students 64.

Weller, Monroe Co., St. Mary. Closed. For inquiries for parish records contact the Chancery.

Welton, Clinton Co., St. Anne (1910). Attended by St. Patrick, Delmar. Rev. Edward A. Botkin.
Mailing Address:Delmar, 52037. Tel: 319-674-4240.
Catechesis/Religious Programs—Students 87.

West Branch, Cedar Co., St. Bernadette (1960). Attended by St. Joseph, West Liberty. Rev. Edward A. O'Melia.
Church—307 E. Orange St., P.O. Box 103, 52358-0103.
Mailing Address: 107 W. Sixth St., West Liberty, 52776-1246. Tel: 319-627-2229.
Catechesis/Religious Programs—Marilyn Hanson, D.R.E.
Students 115.

West Burlington, Des Moines Co., St. Mary's (1886), Revs. Gerald E. Stouvenel; John K. Sterling.
Res., 420 W. Mt. Pleasant St., P.O. Box 415, 52655. Tel: 319-752-4035. [CEM]
Catechesis/Religious Programs—520 W Mt. Pleasant St., 52655. Tel: 319-753-0277. Sr. Mary Jean Assell, S.S.J., D.R.E.
Students 510.

West Liberty, Muscatine Co., St. Joseph's, Rev. Edward A. O'Melia.
Res., 107 W. Sixth St., 52776-1246. Tel: 319-627-2229. [CEM]

West Point, Lee Co., Assumption of the Blessed Virgin Mary, Rev. David F. Wilkening.
Res., 52656. Tel: 319-837-6808. [CEM]

What Cheer, Keokuk Co., St. Joseph's. Closed. For inquiries for parish records contact the Chancery.

Williamsburg, Iowa Co., St. Mary's (1891), Rev. Joseph F. Roost.
Res., 52361. Tel: 319-668-1397. [CEM]
Catechesis/Religious Programs—Tel: 319-668-2757.
Students 216.

Wilton, Muscatine Co., St. Mary's. Attended by St. Alphonsus, Davenport.
Res., 52778. Tel: 319-732-2271. [CEM]

Chaplains of Public Institutions

FORT MADISON. *Iowa State Penitentiary*. Rev. Gerald A. Hoenig.

IOWA CITY. *Oakdale Sanitorium*. Attended from St. Thomas More, Iowa City.
State University of Iowa Hospital. Revs. Vitolds Valainis; Jerry D. Lasley.
Veteran's Administration Hospital. Attended from Mercy Hospital, Iowa City. Revs. Andrew E. Kelly; Francis E. Bass; Louis J. Leonhardt.

KNOXVILLE. *Veteran's Administration Hospital*. Revs. Sylvester A. Conrad; Mark W. Swanson.

MOUNT PLEASANT. *Mental Health Institute, St. Dymphna Chapel*. Rev. Barnabas Barker, T.O.R.

Special Assignment:
Rev.—
Martinez, Frank, 2706 N. Gaines St., Davenport, IA 52804
Mulligan, Louis J., 1140 E. 37th St., #114, Davenport, IA 52807

On Duty Outside the Diocese:
Reverend Fathers—
Bevenour, Richard F., 622 W. Escalon, Fresno, CA 93704
Beyer, Richard J., 1401 Chapelwood Dr., Waco, TX 76712
Cassidy, Dominic J., St. Joseph Hospital, 77 N. Airlite St., Elgin, IL 60120
Colonnese, Louis M., Apartado 109, Sonsonate, Depto. Sonsonate, El Salvador
Otto, John A., 215 11th Ave., Apt. 5, Cold Springs, MN 56320
Shortall, Robert, 916 E. University, No. 147, Dallas, TX 75206
Steckel, Gregory A., 2351 McKinley Ave., Davenport, IA 52802-1769
Weibler, William F., 750 Burlington Ave., Apt. 3F, St. Petersburg Beach, FL 33701

Military Chaplains:
Reverend Fathers—
Borger, Theodore R., U.S. Navy, 3265 Landis Ave., San Diego, CA 92104
Burnett, James E., U.S. Air Force, The Sovereign, Penthouse South, 1040 W. Granville Ave., Chicago, IL 60660-2119
Spiegel, Robert H., U.S. Army, Command Chaplain's Office, USFK 7 EUSA-FKCH, Unix 15237, APO, AP 96205-0010
Spring, Mark P., U.S. Air Force, 222 BSB CMR 405, Box 1370, APO AE 09034

Absent on Leave:
Reverend Fathers—
Bernemann, Timothy C.
Leu, James E.
Mohr, Thomas H.

Retired:
Reverend Monsignors—
Burke, Ambrose J., B-6 Condo, 1014 Hickory Hill Ct., Clinton, IA 52732
Madsen, Cletus P., St. Vincent Center, 2706 N. Gaines St., Davenport, IA 52804
Menke, S. G.
Walter, Robert J., 3406 Spring St., #3, Davenport, IA 52807-2117
Reverend Fathers—
Albers, Paul C., 611 Bel Aire Dr., West Point, IA 52656
Bass, Francis E., 109 N. Dodge St., Iowa City, IA 52245
Bergthold, LeRoy J., St. Vincent Center, 2706 N. Gaines St., Davenport, IA 52804
Brothersen, Maynard J., St. Vincent Center, 2706 N. Gaines St., Davenport, IA 52804
Brownfield, Robert L., O'Keefe Hall, 104 E. Jefferson St., Iowa City, IA 52245
Collins, Edward F., P.O. Box 1180, Fair Oaks, CA 95628
Conrad, Anthony J., St. Vincent Center, 2706 N. Gaines St., Davenport, IA 52804
Cross, Peter, 2220 10th St., Coralville, IA 52241
Dinh, Dominic, 602 B Gemini Ct., Arlington, TX 76011
Donahue, Paul H., St. Vincent Center, 2706 N. Gaines St., Davenport, IA 52804
Durkin, John R., 8927 Willmon Way, San Antonio, TX 78239
Egert, Clifford A., St. Vincent Center, 2706 N. Gaines St., Davenport, IA 52804
Ferrara, Pasquale L., Kahl Home, 1101 W. Ninth St., Davenport, IA 52804
Gannon, Charles E., St. Vincent Center, 2706 N. Gaines St., Davenport, IA 52804
Graham, John E., The Graham House, Belle Plaine, IA 52208
Hratz, Joseph A., Kahl Home, 1101 W. Ninth St., Davenport, IA 52804
Janssen, James M., St. Vincent Center, 2706 N. Gaines St., Davenport, IA 52804
Kelleher, James P., A201, Canterbury Village, 1323 Derbyshire Ct., Naples, FL 33999
Kelly, Daniel J., 5645 Westwind Ln., Sarasota, FL 34231
Lenoch, Francis J., P.O. Box 69, Solon, IA 52333-0069
Leveling, Carlos F., St. Vincent Center, 2706 N. Gaines St., Davenport, IA 52804
Manning, Martin B., St. Vincent Center, 2706 N. Gaines St., Davenport, IA 52804
McMahan, Frederick J., 518 W. Locust St., Davenport, IA 52803
Morrissey, John J., St. Vincent Center, 2706 N. Gaines St., Davenport, IA 52804
Shepler, Charles C., 518 W. Locust St., Davenport, IA 52803
Stratman, Thomas F., 422 E. 10th St., Davenport, IA 52803
Stratman, William J., 518 W. Locust St., Davenport, IA 52803
Strub, Herman A., Kahl Home, 1101 W. Ninth St., Davenport, IA 52804

Waldschmidt, Donald L., St. Vincent Center, 2706 N. Gaines St., Davenport, IA 52804
Weeg, Edmund J., 364 22nd Pl., Clinton, IA 52732-6104

Permanent Deacons:
Anderson, Arthur, Batavia
Barry, James T., Kansas City, MO
Becker, James L., Muscatine
Beckman, Clifford C., Sperry
Cadena, Juan J., Muscatine
Carl, Robert L., Muscatine
Clough, John R., West Point
Cord, Michael H., Des Moines
Cosgrove, William T., Keokuk
Dankert, Larry F., Davenport
Demeter, M. Joseph W., Mount Pleasant
Donart, Arthur C., Thomson, IL
Donnelly, William G., Bettendorf
Duff, Dennis L., Bettendorf
Frericks, Donald E., Blue Grass
Gengenbacher, Robert, Burlington
Gutierrez, Julian, Davenport
Hammer, Richard D., Burlington
Haut, Allen A., Bettendorf
Hilgendorf, Paul F., Davenport
Hittner, Paul F., Davenport
Jensen, Warren F., Davenport
Jones, William, Bettendorf
Lennon, Patrick, Clinton
Leonard, Timothy, Lake Villa, IL
Lester, Jary, Sioux City
Leza, Juan B., Muscatine
McCoy, Robert C., Davenport
Mosse, Marcel G., Davenport
Mueller, Aloysius P., Clinton
Nolan, Thomas, Bettendorf
O'Connor, Arthur, Olatha, KS
Olson, William D., Grinnell
Pacha, Richard F., Washington
Panther, Adrian B., Tipton
Rasmussen, Richard J., Bettendorf
Reha, David, Wellman
Rosenthal, Joseph I., Davenport
Schmitt, John H., Low Moor
Schroeder, William E., Newton
Sheil, Michael D., DeWitt
Sink, Thomas, Bettendorf
Snavely, Robert E., Tipton
Starns, Terry L., Bettendorf
Stein, Ronald K., Donnellson
Strader, George D., Davenport
Striegel, James L., Delta
Timmerman, Gerald L., Davenport
Tometich, Anton I., Muscatine
Wiegand, William R., Oskaloosa
Witt, Stephen J., Grinnell

INSTITUTIONS LOCATED IN THE DIOCESE

[A] SEMINARIES, DIOCESAN

DAVENPORT. *St. Ambrose University Seminary*, 52803. Tel: 319-333-6151. Revs. Charles A. Adam, Rector; Edmond J. Dunn, Spiritual Dir. Students 5.

[B] COLLEGES AND UNIVERSITIES

DAVENPORT. *St. Ambrose University*, 52803-2898. Tel: 319-333-6300; Fax: 319-333-6243.
For a complete listing, refer to the Colleges and Universities section.

CLINTON. *Mt. St. Clare College*, Bluff Blvd. & Springdale Dr., 52732. Tel: 319-242-4023.
For a complete listing, refer to the Colleges and Universities section.

[C] SECULAR CAMPUSES

IOWA CITY. *Catholic Chair of Religion*, School of Religion, 314 Gilmore Hall, University of Iowa, 52242-1376. Tel: 319-335-2164. Rev. John P. Boyle, Ph.D, Res., 2413 Walden Ct., 52246-4118. Tel: 319-338-8634.

[D] ADULT RELIGIOUS EDUCATION

DAVENPORT. *New Horizons of Faith, Inc.*, 820 W. Central Park Ave., 52804. Tel: 319-323-8533. Sr. Joann K. Kuebrich, C.H.M.

[E] HIGH SCHOOLS, INTERPAROCHIAL

DAVENPORT. *Assumption High School*, 1020 W. Central Park Ave., 52804. Tel: 319-326-5313. Dr. Thomas Sunderbruch, Prin.; Rev. Paul E. Connolly. Sisters 1; Lay Teachers 43; Students 584.

BURLINGTON. *Notre Dame High School*, 702 S. Roosevelt Ave., 52601. Tel: 319-754-8431. Sr. Mary McGreevy, S.S.N.D., Prin. Lay Teachers 20; Students 207.

CLINTON. *Mater Dei High School*, 525 Eighth Ave. S., 52732. Tel: 319-242-1663. Mr. James Anderson, Prin. Sisters of Charity B.V.M. 1; Lay Teachers 9; Students 89.

FORT MADISON. *Aquinas Junior-Senior High School*, 2600 Ave. A., 52627. Tel: 319-372-2486. Mr. Thomas Walljasper, Prin. Lay Teachers 17; Students 194.

WEST POINT. *Marquette School, Inc.* (Marquette School System). See separate listing under Elementary Schools in the Institution section. Tel: 319-837-6131.

[F] EDUCATION CENTERS

CLINTON. *Trinity Early Learning Center.* (Grades PreK-K), 2520 Pershing Blvd., 52732. Tel: 319-242-9258. Mr. James M. Anderson, Admin. Teachers 3; Students 80.
Trinity Elementary. (Grades 1-6), 312 S. Fourth St., 52732. Tel: 319-242-8929. Mr. James M. Anderson, Admin. Teachers 7; Students 158.

IOWA CITY. *The Regina Catholic Education Center*, 2140 Rochester Ave., 52245. Tel: 319-337-2580.
Regina Junior Senior High School, 2150 Rochester Ave., 52245. Tel: 319-338-5436. Ms. Joy Kelly, Prin.; Rev. Paul A. Deyo. Sisters 2; Lay Teachers 25; Students 300.
Regina Elementary School, 2120 Rochester Ave. Tel: 319-337-5739. Mr. Raymond Pechous, Prin. Lay Teachers 31; Students 502.
Regina Religious Education, 2140 Rochester Ave., 52245. Tel: 319-351-7638. Sr. Mary Frances Michalec.
Regina Development Office. Tel: 319-354-5688.

KEOKUK. *Keokuk Catholic Schools, Inc.*, 2981 Plank Rd., 52632-2399. Tel: 319-524-2399. Jack Turner, Chief Admin.
St. Vincent's Elementary School. (Grades K-6). (Keokuk Catholic Schools, Inc.).
St. Vincent's Extended Day Care Program, 610 Timea St., 52632-5452. Tel: 319-524-6375. Paul Gaylord, Prin. Lay Teachers 9; Students 125.
Cardinal Stritch Junior Senior High School. (Grades 7-12). (Keokuk Catholic School, Inc.), 2981 Plank Rd., 52632-5452. Tel: 319-524-6375. Jack Turner, Prin. Lay Teachers 10; Students 120.

[G] ELEMENTARY SCHOOLS, INTERPAROCHIAL

DAVENPORT. *Holy Trinity Catholic Mission School*, 615 Marquette St., 52802. Tel: 319-322-3723. Sisters 2; Lay Teachers 8; Students 129.

BURLINGTON. *Burlington Catholic School System: St. Paul Center.* (Grades K-3), 520 N. Fourth St., 52601. Tel: 319-754-4417. Ms. Corinne Trautner, Prin. Lay Teachers 9; Students 161.
St. John Center. (Grades PreK, 4-6). (Intermediate), 712 Division St., 52601. Tel: 319-752-3776. Lay Teachers 12; Students 189.

FORT MADISON. *Aquinas East and West.* (Grades PreK-3). (Primary), Aquinas East, 509 Avenue F, 52627. Tel: 319-372-5013. Mr. Robert Clifton, Prin. East and West. Lay Teachers 8; Students 169.
Aquinas West. (Grades 4-6). (Intermediate), 2213 Avenue J, 52627. Tel: 319-372-6428. Sisters 1; Lay Teachers 5; Students 86.

MUSCATINE. *Hayes Elementary School*, 2407 Cedar St., 52761. Tel: 319-263-3264. Sr. Rachel Beeson, C.H.M., Prin. Sisters 1; Lay Teachers 10; Students 218.

OTTUMWA. *Seton Catholic School*, 117 E. Fourth St., 52501. Tel: 515-682-8826. Lay Teachers 7; Students 138.

WEST POINT. *Marquette School, Inc.* (Marquette School System), 52656.
Marquette School System: Marquette Primary. (K-3 at Houghton Center), P.O. Box 134, Houghton, 52631. Tel: 319-469-3581. Sr. Pat Siepker, Prin.
Marquette School System: Marquette Intermediate. (PreK, 4-6 at St. Paul Center), Box 71, St. Paul, 52657. Tel: 319-469-3881. Sr. Pat Siepker, Prin.
Marquette School System: Marquette Jr./Sr. High. (7-12, West Point), 413 Avenue C, 52656. Tel: 319-837-6131. Mr. Daniel J. Kieler, Prin. Religious 2; Lay Teachers 27; Students 392.

[H] CATHOLIC STUDENT CENTERS

IOWA CITY. *Newman Catholic Student Center*, 104 E. Jefferson St., 52245. Tel: 319-337-3106. Revs. Edward J. Fitzpatrick, Dir.; John E. Stecher.

[I] RESIDENTIAL ADOLESCENT CARE CENTERS

*BURLINGTON. *Young House Family Services, Inc.*, Central Office, 724 N. 3rd St., P.O. Box 845, 52601. Tel: 319-752-4000; Fax: 319-752-6933.
For a complete listing, refer to the Special Care Facilities section.

CLINTON. *Arch Office*, Box 278, 52733-0278. Tel: 319-243-9035.
For a complete listing, refer to the Special Care Facilities section.

[J] GENERAL HOSPITALS

CENTERVILLE. *St. Joseph's Mercy Hospital*, One St. Joseph's Dr., 52544. Tel: 515-437-4111.
For a complete listing, refer to the Hospitals section.

CLINTON. *Samaritan Health System, Inc.*, 1410 N. Fourth St., 52732. Tel: 319-244-5555.
For a complete listing, refer to the Hospitals section.

IOWA CITY. *Mercy Hospital*, 52240. Tel: 319-339-0300; Fax: 319-339-3788.
For a complete listing, refer to the Hospitals section.

[K] SOCIAL ACTION DEPARTMENTS

DAVENPORT. *Central Fiscal Services, Inc.*, St. Vincent Center, 2706 N. Gaines St., 52804-1998. Tel: 319-324-1911.
John Lewis Coffee Shop/Miriam House, 904 W. Sixth St., P.O. Box 3245, 52808-3245. Tel: 319-322-0518. Kate Ridge, Agent.
Project Renewal of Davenport, Inc., Nazarath House, 906 W. Fifth St., 52802. Tel: 319-324-0800. Ann Schwickerath.
Refugee Resettlement Office, St. Vincent Center, 2706 N. Gaines St., 52804-1998. Tel: 319-324-1911; Fax: 319-324-5811. Nora Dvorak, Dir.
St. Vincent Center, 2706 N. Gaines St., 52804-1998. Tel: 319-324-1911. Mr. Dan R. Ebener.
Thomas Merton House, Inc., c/o 422 E. 10th St., 52803. Tel: 319-324-3257. Rev. Marvin A. Mottet.

[L] HOMES FOR AGED

DAVENPORT. *Kahl Home for the Aged and Infirm*, 1101 W. Ninth St., 52804. Tel: 319-324-1621.
For a complete listing, refer to the Special Care Facilities section.

BURLINGTON. *St. Francis Continuation Care and Nursing Home*, 52601. Tel: 319-752-4564.
For a complete listing, refer to the Special Care Facilities section.

CLINTON. *The Alverno Health Care Facility*, 52732. Tel: 319-242-1521; Fax: 319-243-3016.
For a complete listing, refer to the Special Care Facilities section.

[M] MONASTERIES AND RESIDENCES FOR PRIESTS AND BROTHERS

DAVENPORT. *St. Vincent Center*, 2706 N. Gaines St., 52804. Most Rev. Gerald O'Keefe; Rev. Msgr. Leo J. Feeney; Rev. Msgr. Cletus P. Madsen; Rev. Msgr. Sebastian J. Menke; Rev. Msgr. Michael J. Morrissey; Rev. Msgr. James F. Parizek; Rev. Msgr. W. Robert Schmidt; Revs. LeRoy J. Bergthold; Maynard J. Brothersen; Anthony J. Conrad; Paul H. Donahue; Clifford A. Egert; Charles E. Gannon; James M. Janssen; James T. Lawrence; Carlos F. Leveling; Martin B. Manning; Frank R. Martinez; John J. Morrissey; Joseph Kahn V. Nguyen; Donald Waldschmidt.

IOWA CITY. *O'Keefe Hall*, #104 E. Jefferson St., 52245. Rev. Edward J. Fitzpatrick. In res., Revs. John E. Stecher; Robert L. Brownfield.

[N] CONVENTS AND RESIDENCES FOR SISTERS

DAVENPORT. *Franciscan Sisters of Christ the Divine Teacher*, 2605 Boies Ave., 52802. Tel: 319-323-1502. Sisters 5. 4130 Nobis Dr., 52802. Tel: 319-323-7038. Sr. Bernadette Counihan, O.S.F., Superior. Sisters 3.
Humility Convent, 1310 W. Pleasant St., 52804. Tel: 319-326-3257.
Humility of Mary Center-Motherhouse of the Congregation of the Humility of Mary, 820 W. Central Park Ave., 52804. Tel: 319-323-9466; Fax: 319-323-5209. Sr. Jude Fitzpatrick, Pres. Total in Residence 31; Total Staff 9.
Humility of Mary Novitiate, 820 W. Central Park Ave., 52804. Tel: 319-323-8533; Fax: 319-323-5209.

CLINTON. *Mount St. Clare Convent*, 400 N. Bluff Blvd., 52732. Tel: 319-242-1827; Fax: 319-243-0007. Motherhouse and Novitiate of the Sisters of St. Francis, Clinton. Sr. Marilyn Huegerich, O.S.F., Pres.; Rev. John Stack, Chap.

ELDRIDGE. *Carmel of the Queen of Heaven Discalced Carmelite Nuns*, 17937 250th St., 52748. Tel: 319-285-8387. Sr. Mary Joan Loebig, O.C.D., Prioress. Professed Sisters 12; Novices 2.

IOWA CITY. *Dominican Sisters*, Provincial Office: 304 Oberlin St., 52245. Tel: 319-339-0993. Sr. Marguerite Gregoire, O.P., Prioress; Sr. Jacqueline Provencher, O.P., Prov. Prioress.

[O] RETREAT PROGRAMS-CENTERS

BURLINGTON. *Beacon House, House of Prayer*, 915 N. Third, 52601. Tel: 319-752-2121. Sr. Mary Francis Houin, P.H.J.C.

IOWA CITY. *Emmanuel House of Prayer Country Retreat and Solitude Center.* Mailing Address: 4427 Kotts Ln. N.E., 52240. Tel: 319-351-5839. Betsy Coester, Dir.

WHEATLAND. *Our Lady of the Prairie Retreat*, 2774 145th Ave., 52777. Tel: 319-374-1092. Rev. Vincent J. Fabula, O.C.S.O., Dir.

[P] MISCELLANEOUS

DAVENPORT. *Assumption High School Foundation*, 1020 W. Central Park Ave., 52804. Tel: 319-326-5313. Dr. Thomas A. Sunderbruch.

Catholic Service Board, St. Vincent Center, 2706 N. Gaines St., 52804. Tel: 319-324-1911.

Commitment, St. Vincent Center, 2706 N. Gaines St., 52804. Tel: 319-324-1911. Rev. L. Michael Colonnese, Dir.; Sandy Carlson, Assoc. Dir.

Congregation of the Humility of Mary Charitable Trust, 820 W. Central Park Ave., 52804; Fax: 319-323-5209. Sr. Jude Fitzpatrick, C.H.M., Contact Person. Humility of Mary Shelter, Inc., 820 W. Central Park Ave., 52804. Tel: 319-323-9466; Fax: 319-323-5209. Sr. Jude Fitzpatrick, C.H.M., Contact Person. Total Assisted 160; Total Staff 9; Total in Residence 15.

Interfaith Housing, Ltd., 422 E. 10th St., 52803-5499. Tel: 319-324-3257. Rev. Marvin A. Mottet, Contact Person.

Kingdom Co., 2706 N. Gaines St., 52804-1998; Fax: 319-324-5842. Rev. Msgr. Michael J. Morrissey, Contact Person.

Quad Cities Catholic Deaf Ministry, 2706 N. Gaines St., 52804-1998. Rev. Msgr. James F. Parizek, Contact Person.

St. Vincent Home Corporation, 2706 N. Gaines St., 52804. Tel: 319-324-1911. Mr. Dan R. Ebener, Contact Person.

Spirit, Inc., 2219 E. Central Park, 52803. Tel: 319-324-9233. Mr. Harold Meier.

BROOKLYN. *St. Patrick Parish Foundation*, 215 Jackson St., 52211-0512. Tel: 515-522-7714. Rev. Joseph Rogers, Dir.

BURLINGTON. *Burlington Notre Dame Foundation*, 702 S. Roosevelt Ave., 52601. Tel: 319-752-8690. Debbie Trine.

St. Vincent De Paul Society, St. John the Baptist Church Conference, 712 Division St., 52601. Tel: 319-752-9332.

R.E.B.A. (Religious Education Burlington Area) Trust Fund, 702 S. Roosevelt Ave., 52601. Tel: 319-754-8431.

CENTERVILLE. *St. Mary School Foundation*, 838 S. 18th St., 52544.

CLINTON. *Amicare Home Health Services*, 562 Second Ave. S., 52732. Tel: 319-243-7261. Karen Roode, Dir.; Gary Baum, Chm.

Mount St. Clare Speech & Hearing Center, 400 N. Bluff Blvd., 52732. Tel: 319-242-7609; 242-4070. Sisters of St. Francis. Sr. Marcella Marie Narlock, Dir.

Sisters of St. Francis, Clinton, Iowa, Charitable Trust, 400 N. Bluff Blvd., 52732-3998. Tel: 319-242-5631; 242-7609; Fax: 319-243-0007. Sr. Marilyn Huegerich, O.S.F., Pres.

IOWA CITY. *Mercy Hospital Foundation*, 500 E. Market St., 52245. Tel: 319-339-3540; Fax: 319-339-3788.

Mercy Hospital Guild of Iowa City, Iowa.

Mercy Outreach Iowa City, Inc.

Mercy Hospital, Iowa City, Iowa.

The Regina Foundation, 2140 Rochester Ave., 52245; Fax: 319-337-4109.

WEST POINT. *Marquette Foundation*. Mailing Address: Box AA, 52656. Tel: 319-837-6749. Mr. Gene Winnike.

RELIGIOUS INSTITUTES OF MEN REPRESENTED IN THE DIOCESE

For further details refer to the corresponding bracketed number in the Religious Institutes of Men or Women section.

[0460]—*Brothers of the Poor of St. Francis.*—C.F.P.

[0350]—*Cistercian Order of the Strict Observance (Trappists).*—O.C.S.O.

[1070]—*Redemptorist Fathers.*—C.SS.R.

[1060]—*Society of the Precious Blood.*—C.PP.S.

[0560]—*Third Order Regular of Saint Francis.*—T.O.R.

RELIGIOUS INSTITUTES OF WOMEN REPRESENTED IN THE DIOCESE

[0230]—*Benedictine Sisters of Pontifical Jurisdiction.*—O.S.B.

[0330]—*Carmelite Sisters for the Aged and Infirm.*—O.Carm.

[2100]—*Congregation of the Humility of Mary.*—C.H.M.

[1780]—*Congregation of the Sisters of the Third Order of St. Francis of Perpetual Adoration.*—F.S.P.A.

[1710]—*Congregation of the Third Order of St. Francis of Mary Immaculate, Joliet, IL.*—O.S.F.

[0420]—*Discalced Carmelite Nuns.*—O.C.D.

[1070-03]—*Dominican Sisters.*—O.P.

[1120]—*Dominican Sisters of the Roman Congregation.*—O.P.

[]—*Franciscan Sisters of Christ the Divine Teacher.*—O.S.F.

[2575]—*Institute of the Sisters of Mercy of the Americas.* (Chicago).—R.S.M.

[2420]—*Marist Missionary Sisters.*—S.M.S.M.

[3230]—*Poor Handmaids of Jesus Christ.*—P.H.J.C.

[2970]—*School Sisters of Notre Dame.*—S.S.N.D.

[1680]—*School Sisters of St. Francis.*—O.S.F.

[0430]—*Sisters of Charity of the Blessed Virgin Mary.*—B.V.M.

[1540]—*Sisters of Saint Francis, Clinton, Iowa.*—O.S.F.

[1570]—*Sisters of St. Francis of the Holy Family.*—O.S.F.

[3830]—*Sisters of St. Joseph.*—C.S.J.

[3320]—*Sisters of the Presentation of the B.V.M.*—P.B.V.M.

[1770]—*Sisters of the Third Order of St. Francis.* (Peoria, Illinois).—O.S.F.

[1705]—*Sisters of the Third Order of St. Francis of Assisi.*—O.S.F.

[1760]—*Sisters of the Third Order of St. Francis of Penance and of Charity.* (Tiffin, Ohio).—O.S.F.

NECROLOGY

† Boeckmann, Walter F., (Retired). —Died July 19, 1996.

† Greene, James E., (Retired). —Died June 21, 1996.

† Mackey, Daniel P., Davenport, IA, St. Vincent Center. —Died Feb. 20, 1996.

† McGivern, Carroll A., (Retired). —Died April 2, 1996.

† Snell, George E., (Retired). —Died Jan. 1, 1996.

† Sullivan, William J., Fairfield, IA, St. Mary Church. —Died May 28, 1996.

Archdiocese of Denver

Archidioecesis Denveriensis

Most Reverend

CHARLES J. CHAPUT, O.F.M.Cap., D.D.

Archbishop of Denver; ordained August 29, 1970; Episcopal ordination July 26, 1988; appointed Bishop of Rapid City April 11, 1988; appointed Archbishop of Denver February 18, 1997.

Pastoral Center: 200 Josephine St., Denver, CO, 80206. Tel.: 303-388-4411; Fax: 303-388-0517.

ESTABLISHED A VICARIATE-APOSTOLIC IN 1868.

ERECTED A DIOCESE AUGUST 16, 1887.

CREATED AN ARCHDIOCESE NOVEMBER 15, 1941.

Square Miles 40,154.

Comprises the northern part of the State of Colorado, including the 24 Counties of Adams, Arapahoe, Boulder, Clear Creek, Denver, Eagle, Garfield, Gilpin, Grand, Jackson, Jefferson, Larimer, Logan, Moffat, Morgan, Phillips, Pitkin, Rio Blanco, Routt, Sedgwick, Summit, Washington, Weld and Yuma.

For legal titles of parishes and archdiocesan institutions, consult the Chancery.

STATISTICAL OVERVIEW

Personnel	
Archbishop	1
Retired Archbishops	1
Abbots	1
Priests: Diocesan Active in Diocese	119
Priests: Active Outside Diocese	6
Priests: Diocesan in Foreign Missions	1
Priests: Retired, Sick or Absent	26
Number of Diocesan Priests	151
Religious Priests in Diocese	133
Extern Priests in Diocese	12
Ordinations:	
Diocesan Priests	1
Transitional Deacons	15
Permanent Deacons	9
Permanent Deacons in Diocese	117
Total Brothers	19
Total Sisters	433
Parishes	
Parishes	112
With Resident Pastor:	
Resident Diocesan Priests	83
Resident Religious Priests	18
Without Resident Pastor:	
Administered by Priests	8
Administered by Permanent Deacons	1
Administered by Lay People	1
Administered by Pastoral Teams, etc.	1
Missions	39
Professional Ministry Personnel:	
Brothers	4
Sisters	49
Lay Ministers	185
Welfare	
Catholic Hospitals	3
Total Assisted	412,832
Health Care Centers	2
Total Assisted	31,950
Homes for the Aged	7
Total Assisted	1,050
Residential Care of Children	1
Total Assisted	40
Day Care and Extended Day Care Centers	28
Total Assisted	1,950
Specialized Homes	2
Total Assisted	75
Special Centers for Social Services	4
Total Assisted	7,550
Residential Care of Disabled	1
Total Assisted	65
Other Institutions	2
Total Assisted	1,419
Educational	
Diocesan Students in Other Seminaries	25
Seminaries, Religious	2
Students Religious	13
Total Seminarians	38
Colleges and Universities	1
Total Students	9,648
High Schools, Diocesan and Parish	2
Total Students	569
High Schools, Private	3
Total Students	1,714
Elementary Schools, Diocesan and Parish	36
Total Students	10,959
Elementary Schools, Private	1
Total Students	469
Non-residential Schools for the Disabled	2
Total Students	465
Catechesis/Religious Education:	
High School Students	5,716
Elementary Students	22,171
Total Students Under Catholic Instruction	51,749
Teachers in the Diocese:	
Priests	3
Brothers	3
Sisters	31
Lay Teachers	726
Vital Statistics	
Receptions into the Church:	
Infant Baptism Totals	9,389
Adult Baptism Totals	735
Received into Full Communion	968
First Communions	6,686
Confirmations	4,187
Marriages:	
Catholic	1,454
Interfaith	800
Total Marriages	2,254
Deaths	2,661
Total Catholic Population	358,600
Total Population	2,628,800

Former Bishops—Most Rev. JOSEPH PROJECTUS MACHEBEUF, D.D., cons. Titular Bishop of Epiphania and Vicar Apostolic of Colorado and Utah, Aug. 16, 1868; first Bishop of Denver in 1887; died July 10, 1889.—Most Rev. NICHOLAS CHRYSOSTOM MATZ, D.D., cons. Titular Bishop of Telmessa and Coadjutor of Denver *cum jure successionis,* Oct. 28, 1887; succeeded to the See of Denver, July 10, 1889; died Aug. 9, 1917.—Most Rev. J. HENRY TIHEN, D.D., ord. April 26, 1886; cons. Bishop of Lincoln, July 6, 1911; transferred to the See of Denver, Sept. 21, 1917; resigned Jan. 6, 1931; Apostolic Admin. until July 16, 1931; died Jan. 14, 1940.—Most Rev. URBAN J. VEHR, D.D., ord. May 29, 1915; Bishop of Denver; appt. April 17, 1931; cons. June 10, 1931; installed July 16, 1931; elevated to Archiepiscopal dignity, Nov. 15, 1941; installed as Archbishop of Denver; appt. Jan. 6, 1942; resigned Feb. 22, 1967; died Sept. 19, 1973.—Most Rev. JAMES V. CASEY, D.D., ord. Dec. 8, 1939; Titular Bishop of Citium and Auxiliary of Lincoln; appt. April 5, 1957; cons. April 24, 1957; promoted to Archbishop of Denver, Feb. 22, 1967; died March 14, 1986.—Most Rev. J. FRANCIS STAFFORD, D.D., ord. Dec. 15, 1957; cons. Auxiliary Bishop of Baltimore, Feb. 29, 1976; installed Bishop of Memphis; appt. Nov. 16, 1982; installed Archbishop of Denver; appt. June 3, 1986; appt. President of the Pontifical Council for the Laity in Rome, Aug. 1996.

The Pastoral Center—200 Josephine St., Denver, 80206. Tel: 303-388-4411; Fax: 303-388-0517.

Vicars General—Rev. Msgr. RAYMOND N. JONES; Rev. Msgr. R. WALKER NICKLESS.

Moderator of the Curia—Rev. Msgr. RAYMOND N. JONES.

Chancellor—Sr. MARY HUGHES, C.S.J.

Vice Chancellor—Rev. TIMOTHY J. MCCARTHY, J.C.L.

Executive Assistant to the Archdiocesan Administrator—PATRICIA J. MCDONALD.

Secretary for Permanent Deacons—Rev. MARCIAN T. O'MEARA.

Secretary of Finance and Administration—Vacant.

Secretary for Priests and Seminarians—Rev. Msgr. R. WALKER NICKLESS.

Assistant Secretary for Priests—Rev. THOMAS S. FRYAR.

Secretary for Religious—Rev. MARCIAN T. O'MEARA.

Secretary for Social Concerns—Vacant.

Secretary for Catholic Education—Rev. SAMUEL J. AQUILA.

Secretary for Hispanics—Vacant.

Archdiocesan Ecumenical Officer—Vacant.

Archdiocesan Master of Ceremonies—Rev. MICHAEL GLENN.

Presbyteral Council—Vacant.

Priest Personnel Board—Rev. Msgr. MICHAEL CHAMBERLAIN; Revs. THOMAS S. FRYAR; MICHAEL W. GASS; KENNETH KOEHLER; DONALD WILLETTE; Rev. Msgr. R. WALKER NICKLESS; Rev. REINHOLD WEISSBECK.

Priests' Continuing Education Committee—Rev. Msgr. R. WALKER NICKLESS; Revs. SAMUEL AQUILA; JAMES E. FOX; DORINO DELAZZER; ROGER LASCELLE; ANDREW KEMBERLING, O.S.B.; SEAN MCGRATH; GARY MUELLER, C.M.

Consultors—Rev. ROBERT L. AMUNDSON; Rev. Msgr. EDWARD M. HOFFMANN, V.F.; Rev. Msgr. RAYMOND N. JONES; Rev. Msgr. EDWARD T. MADDEN, V.F.; Rev. Msgr. R. WALKER NICKLESS; Rev. EDWARD J. POEHLMANN.

Finance Council—RICHARD O. CAMPBELL; Dr. DORIS M. DRURY; DENNIS D. RUSSELL; CAROL A. MCCOLL; THOMAS E. RODRIGUEZ; Rev. Msgr. RAYMOND N. JONES; Rev. Msgr. R. WALKER NICKLESS.

Council for Religious—Rev. GEORGE FITZGERALD, C.S.P.; Sr. SHARON FORD, R.S.M., Sec.; Sr. CHRISTINE HOCK, R.G.S.; Sr. MACRINA SCOTT, O.S.F.; Bro. CHARLES MILLER, F.S.C.; Rev. LAWRENCE CHRISTENSEN C.M.; Sr. MARY DEL RAY EKLER, R.S.M.; Sr. LAVONNE GUIDONI, S.C.L.; Rev. CHARLIE MARTINEZ, O.F.M.; Sr. ANN MARTIN KLEE, S.C.; Sr. MARGARET THOMAS, O.P.

Chairman of Deans—Rev. Msgr. R. WALKER NICKLESS, Sec. for Priests & Seminarians, *200 Josephine St., Denver, 80206.* Tel: 303-388-4411.

Deaneries—East Denver: Very Rev. DARRELL SCHAFFER, V.F., North Denver: Very Rev. MARTIN LALLY, V.F., West Denver: Very Rev. MELVIN THOMPSON, V.F., Southeast Denver: Rev. Msgr. EDWARD HOFFMANN S.T.D., J.C.L., Southwest Denver: Very Rev. JOSEPH E. MONAHAN, V.F., Aurora: Very Rev. DAVID P. CROAK, V.F., Boulder: Rev. Msgr. EDWARD MADDEN, V.F., Fort Collins: Very Rev. ELBERT V. CHILSON, V.F., Eastern Plains: Very Rev. ROBERT WHIPKEY, V.F., Greeley: Very Rev. ROBERT FISHER, V.F., Western Slope: Rev. Msgr. THOMAS F. DENTICI, V.F.

Metropolitan Tribunal

Judicial Vicar—Very Rev. JAMES S. MORENO, J.C.D.

Executive Director—TIMOTHY J. MCCARTHY, J.C.L.

Clerk of Due Process—TIMOTHY J. MCCARTHY, J.C.L., Pro Tem.

Promoters of Justice—Rev. Msgr. JOHN HARLEY SCHMITT, J.C.D.; Rev. Msgr. EDWARD L. BUELT, J.C.L.

Judges—Very Rev. JAMES S. MORENO, J.C.D.; Rev. RONALD F. WALTERS, O.F.M., J.C.L.; Rev. Msgr. MICHAEL J. CHAMBERLAIN, J.C.L.; Revs. GEORGE P. MILLER, J.C.L.; ROBERT P. HUNDT, J.C.L.; TIMOTHY J. MCCARTHY, J.C.L.

Defender of the Bond—Rev. Msgr. EDWARD L. BUELT, J.C.L.

Judicial Assessor—CATHERINE A. DAVISIO.

Canonical Advisors—Revs. MARK PLEWKA, J.C.L.; J. ANTHONY MC DAID, J.C.D.

Advocates—Mr. KENNETH DOBBINS, Ex Officio Additional advocates appointed individually for particular cases.

Ecclesiastical Notary—RONDA WHITEHURST.

Coordinator of Second Instance—ELIZABETH O'MALLEY.

The Metropolitan Tribunal—Handles all marriage permissions and dispensations by delegation.

Archdiocesan Offices and Directors

The Archdiocese of Denver, a corporation sole—Rev. Msgr. RAYMOND N. JONES, Admin., *200 Josephine St., Denver, 80206.* Tel: 303-388-4411.

Archdiocesan Archives—Sr. MARY HUGHES, C.S.J., *200 Josephine St., Denver, 80206.* Tel: 303-388-4411.

Archdiocesan Campaign for Human Development—DAN MONDRAGON, Dir., *200 Josephine St., Denver, 80206.* Tel: 303-388-4411, Ext. 156.

Archdiocesan Liaison for Health Care—Vacant. Tel: 303-388-4491, Ext. 151.

Chief Financial Officer—DENNIS D. RUSSELL, *200 Josephine St., Denver, 80206.* Tel: 388-4411.

Director of Construction and Engineering—WALTER E. WOSTENBERG, *200 Josephine St., Denver, 80206.*

Director of Property & Real Estate—DONNA BARR.

A.C.C.W.—VIC THORGREN, Spiritual Moderator, *3716 S. Forest Way, Denver, 80277.* Tel: 303-757-3722.

AIDS Task Force Members—DENNIS KELLY, Chm.

Archdiocesan Housing Committee, Inc.—ANNA STROBEL, Exec. Dir., *1580 Logan, Ste. #700, Denver, 80203.* Tel: 303-830-0215.

Boy and Girl Scouts—JAY ZOLITAR, *2071 S. Gray Dr., Denver, 80227.* Tel: 303-987-2306.

Building Committee—Rev. SAMUEL J. AQUILA; RAYMOND L. CRITES; RICHARD G. DUCEY; PETER J. FURSTENBERG; ALAN D. GILLAN; JAMES M. KLINK; JOHN F. MCGUIRE; GERHARD R. MUELLER; Rev. Msgr. JAMES W. RASBY; MICHAEL D. VANEK; WALTER E. WOSTENBERG.

Catholic Education Secretariat—Rev. SAMUEL J. AQUILA, Sec. Catholic Education; WILLIAM BECKMAN, Dir., Office of Catechetics & Mile Hi Congress; Sr. MACRINA SCOTT, O.S.F., Coord., Catholic Biblical School, *200 Josephine St., Denver, 80206.* Tel: 303-388-4411. Rev. LAWRENCE M. FREEMAN, Dir. Special Religious Education & Pastoral Care, *3101 W. Hillside Pl., Denver, 80219.* Tel: 303-934-1999. DAVID WARNER, Dir. of Catechetical School/Biblical School; Deacon RICHARD BAKER, Dir. Archdiocesan Charismatic Ministries.

Mt. Olivet Cemetery Association—MICHAEL WRIGHT, Dir., *12801 W. 44th Ave., 80033.* Tel: 303-424-7785.

Catholic Charities and Community Services of the Archdiocese of Denver, Inc.—JAMES H. MAUCK, Pres., *200 Josephine St., Denver, 80206.* Tel: 303-388-4435., *460 Linden Center Dr., Ft. Collins, 80524.* Tel: 303-484-5010. (For further details see Catholic Community Services-Northern, Inc. under Institutions located in the Archdiocese.).

Catholic Relief Services—DENISE MADDEN, Dir., *Pastoral Center, 200 Josephine St., Denver, 80206.* Tel: 303-388-4491, Ext. 154.

Colorado Catholic Conference 501(c)(4)—JIM TATTEN, *200 Josephine St., Denver, 80206.* Tel: 303-388-4411.

Secretary for Communications—FRANCIS X. MAIER, *200 Josephine St., Denver, 80206.* Tel: 303-388-4411.

Office of Development—MOLLY MOORE, Dir. Devel. & Dir. Corp. & Foundation Rels., *200 Josephine St., Denver, 80206.* Tel: 303-388-4411.

Holy Childhood Assn.—DENISE MADDEN, Dir., *200 Josephine St., Denver, 80201.* Tel: 303-388-4491, Ext. 154.

Archdiocesan Housing Committee, Inc.—(For further details see the listing under Institutions.).

John Paul II Center for the New Evangelization—Vacant, *1300 S. Steele St., Denver, 80210.* Tel: 303-722-4687; Fax: 303-722-7422.

Justice and Peace Office—MIKE SHEEHAN, Dir., *200 Josephine St., Denver, 80206.* Tel: 303-388-4491, Ext. 155.

Legion of Mary—Rev. JOSEPH CAMPBELL, C.SS.R., Chap., *605 W. 6th Ave., Denver, 80204.* Tel: 303-534-4408.

Migrant Ministry Archdiocesan Hispanic Center—*3600 Zuni, Denver, 80211.* Tel: 303-433-9013; 433-9028.

Archdiocesan Hispanic Center—Sr. IRENE MUNOZ, C.H.M., *3600 Zuni, Denver, 80211.* Tel: 303-433-9013; 433-9028.

Office of Liturgy—Revs. CYPRIAN CONSTANTINE, O.S.B., Dir. MICHAEL PAVLAKOVICH, Chm., Commission on the Sacred Liturgy, *200 Josephine St., Denver, 80206.* Tel: 303-388-4411, Ext. 285.

Permanent Diaconate Program—Rev. MARCIAN T. O'MEARA, Sec. Associate Secretaries: Deacons JOHN PONTILLO; L. KENNETH DREILING; GEORGE FORTUNATO; WARREN LYBARGER, *200 Josephine St., Denver, 80206.* Tel: 303-388-4411.

Priests' Eucharistic League—Rev. Msgr. JOHN V. ANDERSON, Dir., *1530 Logan St., Denver, 80202.* Tel: 303-831-7010.

Propagation of the Faith and Missions Office—DENISE M. MADDEN, Dir., *200 Josephine St., Denver, 80206.* Tel: 303-388-4491, Ext. 154. ANDREW PASINI, Coord. for Monteria Mission. Tel: 303-388-4411, Ext. 110.

Religious—Sr. SHARON FORD, R.S.M., Sec., *200 Josephine St., Denver, 80206.* Tel: 303-388-4411, Ext. 299; Fax: 303-388-0517.

Rural Life Conference—RITA MAILANDER, *3990 S. Syracuse Way, Denver, 80237.* Tel: 303-741-2133.

Vocation Office—Rev. MICHAEL GLENN, Dir.; Sr. SHARON FORD, R.S.M., Assoc. Dir., *200 Josephine St., Denver, 80206.* Tel: 303-388-4411.

CLERGY, PARISHES, MISSIONS AND PAROCHIAL SCHOOLS

CITY OF DENVER
(County of Denver)

1—CATHEDRAL OF THE IMMACULATE CONCEPTION, Rev. Msgr. John V. Anderson, Rector; Revs. James K. Goggins; Charles Martinez; Deacons Dominic Deprofio; Michael Dunn. In res., Rev. Msgr. Raymond N. Jones, V.G.; Rev. Samuel Aquila.
Res., 1530 Logan St., 80203. Tel: 303-831-7010; Fax: 303-831-9514.
Catechesis/Religious Programs—Students 102.

2—ALL SAINTS (1950), Rev. James R. Purfield.
Res., 2559 S. Federal Blvd., 80219. Tel: 303-922-3758; Fax: 303-922-3750.
Parish Center—2560 S. Grove St., 80219.
Catechesis/Religious Programs—Students 281.

3—ANNUNCIATION (1883), Rev. Gene J. Emrisek, O.F.M.Cap. In res., Revs. Matthew Gross, O.F.M.Cap.; John Cousins, O.F.M.Cap.; Edward Judy, O.F.M.Cap.; Cyrus Gallagher, O.F.M.Cap.; Gregory Beyer, O.F.M.Cap.; Jeffrey Ernst, O.F.M.Cap.
Res., 3621 Humboldt St., 80205. Tel: 303-296-1024; Fax: 303-296-1026.
School—1408 E. 36th Ave., 80205. Tel: 303-296-8132.
Sisters of Charity of Leavenworth 5; Lay Teachers 10; Students 181.
Catechesis/Religious Programs—Students 181.
Mission—Denver, Denver Co., St. Patrick, 3401 Pecos St., 80211. Tel: 303-433-6328.

4—ASSUMPTION (1912), Revs. Gabriel M. Ramacciotti, O.S.M.; Hugh Guentner, O.S.M.
Res., 2361 E. 78th Ave., 80229. Tel: 303-288-2442; Fax: 303-289-2713.
School—2341 E. 78th Ave., 80229. Tel: 303-288-2159. Jane E. Schissel, Prin.
Lay Teachers 10; Students 119.
Catechesis/Religious Programs—Tel: 303-289-2713.
Students 125.

5—BLESSED SACRAMENT (1912), Revs. Roland Freeman; Lawrence Freeman; Deacon Nathan Coursey.
Res., 4930 Montview Blvd., 80207. Tel: 303-355-7361; Fax: 303-355-0894.
School—1973 Elm St., 80220. Tel: 303-377-8835.
Lay Teachers 14; Students 192.
Catechesis/Religious Programs—Students 192.

6—CHRIST THE KING (1947), Rev. J. Darrell Schaffer; Deacon Harold Del Real.
Res., 845 Fairfax St., 80220. Tel: 303-388-1643; Fax: 303-355-0141.
School—860 Elm St., 80220. Tel: 303-321-2123.
Lay Teachers 18; Students 246.
Catechesis/Religious Programs—Students 337.

7—CURE D'ARS (1952), Rev. John P. Cousins, O.F.M.Cap.; Deacon Clarence G. McDavid.
Office: 3050 Dahlia St., 80207. Tel: 303-322-1119; Fax: 303-322-9335.
Church—3201 Dahlia St., 80207. Tel: 303-322-7709.

8—CHURCH OF THE GOOD SHEPHERD (1981). (Formerly St. John the Evangelist & St. Philomena). Revs. Marcian T. O'Meara; Terrence T. Kissel; Hermanagild Jayachandra; Deacon Stephen M. Blake.
Church and Res.—2626 E. Seventh Ave. Pkwy., 80206-3809. Tel: 303-322-7706; Fax: 303-399-1382.
Business and D.R.E. Offices—2626 E. Seventh Ave. Pkwy., 80206.
School—940 Fillmore St., 80206. Tel: 303-377-8018; Fax: 303-377-4034.
Middle School—Tel: 303-321-6231.
Lay Teachers 24; Students 360.

9—GUARDIAN ANGELS (1954), Rev. Robert J. Reycraft.
Res., 1843 W. 52nd Ave., 80221. Tel: 303-433-8361; Fax: 303-477-2066.
School—Tel: 303-480-9005.
Lay Teachers 13; Students 231.
Catechesis/Religious Programs—Students 107.

10—HOLY CROSS (Thornton) (1957), Rev. Thomas Coyte; Deacons Tim Ritchey; Russell Halpine.
Res., 9371 Wigham St., 80229. Tel: 303-289-2258; 287-5204 (TDD); Fax: 303-289-2259.
Catechesis/Religious Programs—Students 387.

11—HOLY FAMILY (1889), Rev. Robert J. Greenslade; Deacon Leonard E. Polak.
Res., 4377 Utica St., 80212. Tel: 303-455-1664; Fax: 303-455-7732.
Church—W. 44th Ave. & Utica St., 80212.
School—(Grades PreK-8) 4380 Utica St., 80212. Tel: 303-477-4023.
Lay Teachers 12; Students 176.
Catechesis/Religious Programs—4377 Utica St., 80212. Tel: 303-433-9781.
Students 90.

12—HOLY GHOST (1905), Revs. Henry W. Grodecki, C.M.; Robert A. Schwane, C.M.; Charles E. Prost, C.M.; Gary A. Mueller, C.M.; Mark Pranaitis, C.M.; Deacon Vernon L. Rompot.
Res., 1900 California St., 80202. Tel: 303-292-1556; Fax: 303-292-5378.
Convent—2161 Tremont, 80202. Tel: 303-296-1740.
Missionary Sisters of Our Lady of Victory 2.
Mission—Denver, Denver Co., St. Elizabeth of Hungary, 1060 St. Francis Way, 80204. Tel: 303-534-4014; Fax: 303-534-4140.

13—HOLY ROSARY (1918), Rev. Joseph A. Meznar.
Mailing Address: P.O. Box 8685, 80201-8685.
Res., 4695 Pearl St., 80216. Tel: 303-296-3283.
Catechesis/Religious Programs—Students 185.

14—MONTBELLO CATHOLIC PARISH-CHURCH OF THE ASCENSION (1972), Rev. Thomas M. Dona; Deacon Luis A. Usera.
Res., 14050 Maxwell Pl., 80239. Tel: 303-371-0786; 303-373-4950 (Church); Fax: 303-373-4954.

15—MOST PRECIOUS BLOOD (1952), Rev. Kenneth Koehler; Deacons George Hendricks; Lewis Barbato, (Retired).
Res., 2250 S. Harrison, 80210. Tel: 303-756-3083; Fax: 303-756-5628.
School—3959 E. Iliff, 80210. Tel: 303-757-1279.
Lay Teachers 18; Students 487.
Catechesis/Religious Programs—Students 112.

16—MOTHER OF GOD (1949), Rev. Msgr. Michael J. Chamberlain; Rev. Jude Geilenkirchen.
Res., 475 Logan St., 80203. Tel: 303-744-1715; Fax: 303-744-1716.

17—NOTRE DAME (1957), Revs. Leo R. Horrigan; Walter Huber, S.M.B.; Peter Quang Nguyen.
Mailing Address: 5100 W. Evans Ave., 80219.
Church—2190 S. Sheridan Blvd., 80227.
Parish Center—Tel: 303-935-3900; Fax: 303-937-6699.
School—2165 S. Zenobia St., 80219. Tel: 303-935-3549; Fax: 303-937-4868.
Students 588.
Catechesis/Religious Programs—2160 S. Zenobia St., 80219. Tel: 303-922-9875; Fax: 303-937-6699.
Students 425.

18—OUR LADY OF GRACE, Rev. Patrick Kennedy.
Res., 2645 E. 48th Ave., 80216. Tel: 303-297-3440; Fax: 303-297-3430.

19—OUR LADY OF GUADALUPE (1936) (Hispanic), Rev. Marshall Gourley, C.R.; Deacon Alfonso M. Sandoval.

Res., 1209 W. 36th Ave., 80211. Tel: 303-477-1402; 477-8113; Fax: 303-477-4013.

20—OUR LADY OF LOURDES (1947), Rev. David S. Blue Jacket.
Res., 2200 S. Logan St., 80210. Tel: 303-722-6861; Fax: 303-722-4810.
School—2256 S. Logan St., 80210. Tel: 303-722-7525.
Sisters 1; Lay Teachers 12; Students 200.
Catechesis / Religious Programs—Students 124.

21—OUR LADY OF MT. CARMEL (1894) (Italian), Revs. Justin M. Pisciotta, O.S.M.; Joseph M. Carbone, O.S.M.; Benedict M. Rori, O.S.M., (Retired). In res., Rev. Michael L. Doyle, O.S.M.
Res., 3549 Navajo St., 80211. Tel: 303-455-0447; Fax: 303-455-5487.

22—PRESENTATION OF OUR LADY, Rev. David A. Stahl. In res., Rev. James O. Abosike (Nigeria).
Res., 665 Irving St., 80204. Tel: 303-534-4882; Fax: 303-893-5056.
School—660 Julian St., 80204. Tel: 303-629-6562.
Lay Teachers 12; Students 248.

23—CHURCH OF THE RISEN CHRIST (1967), Very Rev. Edward M. Hoffmann, S.T.D., V.F.; Rev. Sean J. McGrath.
Church—3060 S. Monaco Pkwy., 80222. Tel: 303-758-8826; Fax: 303-782-9667.
Catechesis / Religious Programs—Students 531.

24—SACRED HEART (1879) (Mexican), Rev. Marcus Medrano; Deacons Henry Sandoval; Edward Lujan.
Res., 2760 Larimer St., 80205. Tel: 303-294-9830; Fax: 303-296-0171.

25—ST. ANTHONY OF PADUA (1947), Rev. Joseph C. Sullivan; Deacon A. Paul Garcia, (Retired).
Res., 3801 W. Ohio Ave., 80219. Tel: 303-935-2431; Fax: 303-935-8969.
Parish Center—775 S. Newton St., 80219.
Catechesis / Religious Programs—Tel: 303-936-5386; Fax: 303-935-8969.
Students 86.

26—ST. CAJETAN'S (Spanish), Revs. James Prohens, C.R.; Tomas Fraile, C.R.; Deacon Filemon F. Gonzales, (Retired).
Res., 299 S. Stuart, 80219. Tel: 303-922-6306; Fax: 303-936-8285.
Church—299 S. Raleigh, 80219.
Catechesis / Religious Programs—4325 W. Alameda, 80219.
Students 334.

27—ST. CATHERINE OF SIENA (1912), Revs. Robert P. Meznar; Steven V. Padilla.
Res., 4200 Federal Blvd., 80211. Tel: 303-455-9090; Fax: 303-455-6651.
School—4280 Federal Blvd., 80211. Tel: 303-477-8035.
Lay Teachers 12; Students 216.
Catechesis / Religious Programs—Students 144.

28—ST. DOMINIC'S (1889), Revs. Jose M. Santiago, O.P.; John C. Risley, O.P. In res., Revs. Louis S. Morrone, O.P.; John J. Markey, O.P.; Thomas V. Flynn, O.P.; Michael G. Kyte, O.P.; Ronald G. Kruel, O.P.; Bros. Anthony D. Kalinowski, O.P.; Henry A. Denier, O.P.
Res., 3005 W. 29th Ave., 80211. Tel: 303-455-3613; Fax: 303-455-3087.
Catechesis / Religious Programs—Students 188.

29—ST. FRANCIS DE SALES (1892), Rev. Msgr. Frank G. Morfeld.
Res., 301 S. Sherman St., 80209. Tel: 303-744-7211; Fax: 303-744-7211.
School—235 S. Sherman St., 80209. Tel: 303-744-7231.
Sisters of St. Joseph 4; Lay Teachers 9; Students 227.

30—ST. IGNATIUS LOYOLA (1924), Revs. Stephen T. Yavorsky, S.J.; John F. Brady, S.J.; Deacon Guffie Menogan. In res., Rev. J. Patrick Walsh, S.J.
Res., 2305 Gaylord St., 80205. Tel: 303-322-8042; Fax: 303-322-2927.
School—2350 Gaylord, 80205.
Sisters of Charity of Cincinnati 4; Lay Teachers 7; Students 140.
Catechesis / Religious Programs—Students 137.

31—ST. JAMES (1909), Revs. Brian S. Morrow; David Sobieszczyk.
Res., 1314 Newport St., 80220. Tel: 303-322-7449; Fax: 303-399-2850.
School—Tel: 303-333-8275.
Lay Teachers 14; Students 227.
Catechesis / Religious Programs—Tel: 303-333-5189.
Students 69.

32—ST. JOSEPH'S, Revs. Anthony Judge, C.SS.R.; Joseph Campbell, C.SS.R.; John P. Fahey, C.SS.R.; Deacon Alfredo Sanchez. In res., Rev. Michael McAndrew, C.SS.R.
Res., 605 W. 6th Ave., 80204. Tel: 303-534-4408; Fax: 303-534-4412.
Catechesis / Religious Programs—Students 230.

33—ST. JOSEPH'S (1902) (Polish), Rev. Jan Mucha.
Res., 517 E. 46th Ave., 80216. Tel: 303-296-3217.

34—ST. MARY MAGDALENE'S (1907), Rev. Robert Greenslade; Deacon Richard Vieira. In res., Revs. Joseph Fraber (CHY); John Gibbons; Robert Staes, O.P.; Thomas Noeson, O.P.
Res., 2771 Zenobia St., 80212. Tel: 303-455-1968; Fax: 303-477-2049.

35—ST. ROSE OF LIMA (1924), Rev. James Brennan; Deacon Sidney Atencio.
Res., 1320 W. Nevada Pl., 80223. Tel: 303-778-7673; Fax: 303-778-6601.
School—1345 W. Dakota Ave., 80223. Tel: 303-733-5806.
Lay Teachers 8; Students 142.
Catechesis / Religious Programs—Students 84.

36—ST. VINCENT DE PAUL, Rev. R. Christopher Hellstrom; Deacons Marvin A. Hegarty; Joseph Babish.
Res., 2375 E. Arizona Ave., 80210. Tel: 303-744-6119; Fax: 303-744-6124.
School—1164 S. Josephine St., 80210. Tel: 303-777-3812.
Sisters 4; Lay Teachers 26; Students 550.

SUBURBAN PARISHES OF DENVER

Arvada, Jefferson Co., Shrine of St. Anne (1920), Rev. John D. McCormick; Deacons Kenneth Hawkins; Michael Ritz, (Retired); Richard Bowles; Rodger Creel; Hugh Downey. In res., Rev. Kenneth J. Liuzzi.
Res., 7555 Grant Pl., 80002. Tel: 303-420-1280; Fax: 303-420-1341. [CEM]
School—Tel: 303-422-1800; Fax: 303-420-1341.
Lay Teachers 22; Students 505.
Catechesis / Religious Programs—Loretta Flom, D.R.E.
Students 480.

St. Joan of Arc (1967), Revs. James E. Kleiner; Walter Watson, S.J.; Deacons Gordon Hudec; John Smith.
Res., 12735 W. 58th Ave., 80002. Tel: 303-420-1232; Fax: 303-420-0126.
Catechesis / Religious Programs—Students 306.

Spirit of Christ Parish (1974), Revs. Robert J. Kinkel; James Baird; James J. Cuneo; Deacons Michael Howard; Richard Baker.
Res., 7400 W. 80th Ave., 80003. Tel: 303-422-9173; Fax: 303-422-8251.
Catechesis / Religious Programs—Students 761.

Aurora, Arapahoe Co.,

1—QUEEN OF PEACE, (1968), Revs. William E. Breslin; Donald G. Romero; Malachy R. McBride, O.F.M. Cap.; Deacons William Sorber; Martin A. Wilhelm. In res., Rev. Msgr. Robert F. Hoffman, (Retired).
Res., 13120 E. Kentucky Ave., 80012. Tel: 303-364-1056; Fax: 303-364-3944.
Catechesis / Religious Programs—Students 910.

2—ST. MICHAEL THE ARCHANGEL, (1978), Revs. Dorino De Lazzer; David W. Allen; Robert Syrianey, (Retired); Deacon Robert Austin.
Res., 3320 S. Cathay St., 80013.
Parish Center and Office: 19099 E. Floyd Ave., 80013. Tel: 303-690-6797; Fax: 303-690-6932.
Catechesis / Religious Programs—Tel: 303-690-7697.
Students 872.

3—ST. PIUS X, (1956), Rev. Angelo Ossino; Deacons Gregory Martin; John Thunblom.
Res., 13670 E. 13th Pl., 80011. Tel: 303-364-7435; Fax: 303-364-7525.
School—13680 E. 14th Pl., 80011. Tel: 303-364-6515; Fax: 303-364-7525. Sr. Helen Weber, C.P.P.S., Prin.
Lay Teachers 25; Students 404.

4—ST. THERESE, (1926), Rev. David P. Croak; Deacon Richard Brady.
Res., 1243 Kingston St., 80010. Tel: 303-344-0132; Fax: 303-344-0133.
School—Tel: 303-364-7494.
Sisters 2; Lay Teachers 22; Students 335.
Catechesis / Religious Programs—Students 170.

5—ST. LAWRENCE KOREAN CATHOLIC COMMUNITY, Rev. Andrew Myeong Rae Cho.
Res., 4310 S. Pitkin St., 80015-1974. Tel: 303-617-7555; Fax: 303-617-8265.

Broomfield, Boulder, Nativity of Our Lord (1958), Rev. Dennis K. Ryan; Deacon Richard Medenwaldt.
Res., 900 W. Midway Blvd., 80020. Tel: 303-469-5171; Fax: 303-469-5172.
Parish Center Office—580 W. 3rd Ave. Dr., P.O. Box 302, 80020.
School—Tel: 303-466-4177.
Lay Teachers 18; Students 360.

Commerce City, Adams Co., Our Lady Mother of the Church (1946), Rev. Thomas McCormick; Deacon Samuel R. Trujillo. In res., Rev. Peter Urban, (Retired).
Res., 6690 E. 72nd Ave., 80022. Tel: 303-289-6489; Fax: 303-289-6480.
Catechesis / Religious Programs—Students 399.

Englewood, Arapahoe Co.,

1—ALL SOULS, (1955), Rev. Thomas S. Fryar. In res., Rev. Msgr. Thomas P. Barry; Deacon Gordon Milhone.
Res., 4950 S. Logan, 80110. Tel: 303-789-0007; Fax: 303-789-0491.
School—4951 S. Pennsylvania, 80110. Tel: 303-789-2155; Fax: 303-789-0491.
Brothers 1; Lay Teachers 30; Students 585.
Catechesis / Religious Programs—Students 222.

2—HOLY NAME, (1894), Rev. William P. Murphy; Deacon Jack Sutton.
Res., 3290 W. Milan, 80110. Tel: 303-781-6093; Fax: 303-781-6398.
Catechesis / Religious Programs—Students 145.

3—ST. LOUIS, (1911), Revs. Roger W. Mollison; Gaston Muyombo (Zaire); Deacons Dennis Kelly; Frank Bocovich; Marty Wager. In res., Rev. Simon Kalonga (Zaire).
Res., 3310 S. Sherman St., 80110. Tel: 303-761-3940; Fax: 303-781-7931.
School—3301 S. Sherman St., 80110. Tel: 303-762-8307.
Lay Teachers 11; Students 171.
Catechesis / Religious Programs—Students 85.

4—ST. THOMAS MORE, (1972), Revs. Michael Walsh; John J. McGinn; Patrick Dolan; Deacons Gary Rogge; Henry Becker (SAN); Mark Salvato. In res., Rev. Martin Whealen, S.J.
Res., 8035 S. Quebec St., 80112. Tel: 303-770-1155; Fax: 303-220-3399.
School—7071 E. Otero Ave., 80112. Tel: 303-770-0441.
Catechesis / Religious Programs—Students 1746.

Golden, Jefferson Co., St. Joseph (1867), Rev. John F. Wind.
Res., 969 Ulysses St., 80401. Tel: 303-279-4464; Fax: 303-273-9811.
Catechesis / Religious Programs—Students 331.

Lakewood, Jefferson Co.,

1—ST. BERNADETTE, (1947), Rev. Frank Deml; Deacon Gene Vitello.
Res., 7240 W. 12th Ave., 80215. Tel: 303-233-1523; Fax: 303-233-7285.
Church—W. 12th Ave. & Teller St., 80215.
School—1100 Upham St., 80215. Tel: 303-237-0401.
Sisters 1; Lay Teachers 10; Students 194.
Catechesis / Religious Programs—Deacon Ken Dreiling D.R.E.
Students 80.

2—CHRIST ON THE MOUNTAIN PARISH, (1975), Rev. John F.X. Burton, S.J.
Church—13922 W. Utah Ave., 80228-4110. Tel: 303-988-2222; Fax: 303-986-6956.
Catechesis / Religious Programs—Students 223.

3—OUR LADY OF FATIMA, Revs. Melvin F. Thompson; Tim Evans; Deacon Joseph W. Hawley. In res., Very Rev. R. Walker Nickless, V.G.
Res., 1985 Miller St., 80215. Tel: 303-233-6236; Fax: 303-237-6097.
School—Tel: 303-233-2500. Sr. Patricia Dunphy, C.S.J., Prin.
Lay Teachers 27; Students 491.

4—ST. JUDE, (1967), Rev. Michael W. Gass; Deacons Joel J. Paulson; Tom Quinlan.
Office: 9405 W. Florida Ave., 80232. Tel: 303-988-6435; Fax: 303-988-6735.
Res., 1666 S. Jellison St., 80226.
Catechesis / Religious Programs—Students 540.

Littleton, Jefferson Co., St. Frances Cabrini Parish (1972), Rev. Kenneth Leone; Deacons Ronald Claussen; Craig Fucci; Paul Grimm.
Res., 6673 W. Chatfield Ave., 80123. Tel: 303-979-7688; Fax: 303-972-8566.
Catechesis / Religious Programs—Students 932.

Light of the World Parish (1979), Revs. Patrick Tierney; Gregorio Mirto; Deacons Charles Lamar; Eugene Mooneyham, (leave of absence); Chester Ubowski; Dick Kramb, (Retired).
Res., 5903 S. Kline St., 80127. Tel: 303-973-3969; Fax: 303-973-2122.
Catechesis / Religious Programs—Georgia Glover, D.R.E.
Students 1,042.

St. Mary, Arapahoe Co., (1901), Very Rev. Joseph E. Monahan, V.F.; Rev. Vincent Phung; Deacons Edward Clements; William H. Ward.
Res., 6853 S. Prince, 80120. Tel: 303-798-8506; Fax: 303-347-2270. [JC]
School—(Grades K-8). Tel: 303-794-4757 (Grades K-3); 798-2375 (Grades 4-8).
Lay Teachers 44; Students 640.

Northglenn, Adams Co., Immaculate Heart of Mary (1967), Very Rev. Martin Lally, V.F.; Rev. Gregg Beyer, O.F.M.Cap.; Deacons Leo Oehrle; Lynn Waring.
Offices & Mailing Address: 11385 Grant Dr., 80233. Tel: 303-452-2041; Fax: 303-452-7546.

Res., 335 E. 112th Dr., 80233. Tel: 303-452-9104.
Catechesis/Religious Programs—Students 1,100.

Westminster, Adams Co., Holy Trinity (1956), Revs. George M. Luznicky, O.S.M.; Mark Franceschini, O.S.M.; Deacon Lloyd Quintana. In res., Rev. Nicholas M. Norusis, O.S.M.
Res., 7595 N. Federal, 80030. Tel: 303-428-3594; Fax: 303-427-4125.
School—Tel: 303-427-5632; Fax: 303-427-4125.
Sisters 2; Lay Teachers 16; Students 298.
Friary—3100 W. 76th Ave., 80030. Tel: 303-428-1693.
Mission—Westminster, Adams Co., Our Lady of Visitation.
Catechesis/Religious Programs—Students 278.

St. Mark (1973), Rev. James R. Fox; Deacons John Pontillo; Darryl Dunn.
Res., 3141 W. 96th Ave., 80030. Tel: 303-466-8720; Fax: 303-466-0998.

Wheat Ridge, Jefferson Co., Queen of Vietnamese Martyrs (1976) (Asian), Revs. Bartholomew Do Thai Hoa, C.M.C.; Louis M. Ha Pham, C.M.C.; Deacon Joseph Le Van Tam.
Res., 4655 Harlan St., 80033. Tel: 303-431-0382; Fax: 303-431-1876.

SS. Peter and Paul (1949), Rev. John Hilton; Deacons Gary E. Miller; Jim Wall.
Res., 3900 Pierce St., 80033. Tel: 303-424-3706; Fax: 303-424-0819.
School—Tel: 303-420-0402.
Lay Teachers 17; Students 346.
Catechesis/Religious Programs—Students 381.

OUTSIDE THE CITY OF DENVER

Akron, Washington Co., St. Joseph (1917), Rev. Thomas Clement.
Res., 551 W. 6th St., 80720. Tel: 970-345-6996; Fax: 970-345-6504. [CEM]
Catechesis/Religious Programs—Students 118.

Aspen, Pitkin Co., St. Mary (1892), Rev. Lawrence T. Solan.
Res., 104 S. Galena St., 81611. Tel: 970-925-7339; Fax: 970-925-1889.
Catechesis/Religious Programs—Students 82.
Mission—Aspen, Snowmass in Snowmass Village.

Ault, Weld Co., St. Mary. See Our Lady of Peace, Greeley.

Basalt, Eagle Co., St. Vincent (1970), Rev. Frank Maroney.
Res., P.O. 518, 81621. Tel: 970-927-3934; Fax: 970-927-3934.
Catechesis/Religious Programs—Students 50.
Mission—Carbondale, Garfield Co., St. Mary of the Crown, P.O. Box 64, 81623. Tel: 970-963-1270.

Boulder, Boulder Co.,

1—Sacred Heart of Jesus, (1875), Very Rev. Edward T. Madden; Rev. Jerome M. Rohr; Deacon Robert J. Howard. In res., Rev. George L. Weibel.
Res., 2312 14th St., 80302. Tel: 303-442-6158; Fax: 303-442-7905. [JC]
School—(Grades PreK-8). Tel: 303-447-2362; Fax: 303-443-2466.
Lay Teachers 23; Students 423.
Catechesis/Religious Programs—Students 270.
Mission—Nederland, Boulder Co., St. Rita, P.O. Box 901, Nederland, 80466. Tel: 303-642-7348; Fax: 303-642-7348. Deacon Joseph Young, Admin.

2—Sacred Heart of Mary, (1874), Rev. Andrew Kemberling, O.S.B.
Res., 6739 S. Boulder Rd., 80303. Tel: 303-494-7572; Fax: 303-494-7581. [CEM]
Rectory: Tel: 303-494-1266; Fax: 303-494-7581.
Catechesis/Religious Programs—Students 264.

3—St. Martin de Porres, (1968), Rev. Manuel Gabel; Deacons Karl T. Matz; Francis A. Boselli.
Res., 3700 Armer Dr., 80303. Tel: 303-499-7744; Fax: 303-494-8754.
Catechesis/Religious Programs—Students 109.

4—St. Thomas Aquinas University Parish, (1950). (Campus Ministry), University of Colorado. Revs. George R. Fitzgerald, C.S.P.; Joseph A. Ciccone, C.S.P.
Pastoral Center: 904 14th St., 80302. Tel: 303-443-8383; Fax: 303-443-8399.
Catechesis/Religious Programs—Students 85.

Breckenridge, Summit Co., St. Mary (1875), Rev. Vincent Leo Smith.
Mailing Address: No. 2 W. Miner's Cr. Rd., P.O. Box 2670, Frisco, 80443. Tel: 970-668-3141; Fax: 970-668-3213.
Catechesis/Religious Programs—Students 180.
Mission—Dillon Valley, Summit Co., Our Lady of Peace.

Brighton, Adams Co., St. Augustine (1887), Rev. Reinhold B. Weissbeck; Deacon Gilbert Rael.
Res., 675 E. Egbert St., 80601. Tel: 303-659-1410; Fax: 303-659-6449.
Catechesis/Religious Programs—Students 271.

Brush, Morgan Co., St. Mary (1911), Rev. Michael G. Pavlakovich.
Res., 340 Stanford St., 80723. Tel: 970-842-2216; Fax: 970-842-4461.
Catechesis/Religious Programs—Students 125.
Mission—Stoneham, Morgan Co., St. John, 340 Stanford, Brush 80723.

Byers, Arapahoe Co., Our Lady of the Plains (1978), Rev. Thomas M. Dona; Deacon William M. Sorber.
Res., 186 N. McDonnell, Box 519, 80103. Tel: 303-822-5880; Fax: 303-822-5780.
Catechesis/Religious Programs—Students 105.

Conifer, Our Lady of The Pines (1979), Rev. Reuben Payo; Deacon Wally Kullman.
Mailing Address: 9444 Eagle Cliff Rd., 80433. Tel: 303-838-0338; Fax: 303-697-5335.
Catechesis/Religious Programs—Students 216.
Mission—Buffalo Creek, Jefferson Co., St. Elizabeth, 9444 Eagle Cliff, 80433.

Craig, Moffat Co., St. Michael (1920), Rev. Cathal Longwill.
Res., 678 School St., 81625. Tel: 970-824-4822; Fax: 970-824-9724.
Catechesis/Religious Programs—Students 110.

Eagle, Eagle Co., St. Mary. See St. Patrick, Minturn.

Edwards, St. Clare of Assisi (1993), Rev. Edward J. Poehlmann.
Mailing Address: P.O. Box 1900, Eagle, 81631. Tel: 970-926-2821; Fax: 970-926-5350.
Res., 53 Old County Ln., 81631. Tel: 970-328-6396.
Catechesis/Religious Programs—Students 110.
Missions—Eagle, Eagle Co., St. Mary, 215 Capitol, Eagle, 81631.; Beaver Creek, Eagle Co., Beaver Creek Chapel. Not a mailing address. 33 Elktrack Rd., Tel: 970-845-9449.

Erie, Weld Co., St. Scholastica (1946). Unassigned. See St. Theresa, Frederick.
Office: 436 Fifth St., Box 418, Frederick, 80530. Tel: 303-833-2966; 654-1106.
Church—615 Main St., 80516.

Estes Park, Larimer Co., Our Lady of the Mountains (1947), Rev. James G. Simko; Deacon Jason Dorwart.
Res., P.O. Box 1706, 80517. Tel: 970-586-8111; Fax: 970-586-8112.
Catechesis/Religious Programs—Barry Emmett, D.R.E.
Students 70.

Evergreen, Jefferson Co., Christ the King (1932), Rev. John J. Murphy; Deacons George Fitterer (CHI); Norman Beabout (JOL).
Res., 4291 Evergreen Pkwy., 80439-7723. Tel: 303-674-3155; Fax: 303-674-3285.
Catechesis/Religious Programs—Tel: 303-674-5282.
Students 272.

Fort Collins, Larimer Co.,

1—St. Joseph, (1879), Revs. Philip S. Meredith; Michael V. Delaney, S.J.; Deacon John Mckeown.
Res., 308 W. Mountain Ave., P.O. Box 502, 80522. Tel: 970-482-4148; Fax: 970-221-0635.
School—Tel: 303-484-1171; Fax: 970-221-0635.
Lay Teachers 16; Students 253.
Catechesis/Religious Programs—Students 400.
Mission—Red Feather Lakes, Larimer Co., Our Lady of the Lakes, P.O. Box 502, 80522.

2—Holy Family, (1924) (Hispanic), Rev. Joseph Romero, C.R.
Res., 326 N. Whitcomb St., 80521. Tel: 970-482-6599.
Catechesis/Religious Programs—Students 90.

3—John XXIII University Parish, (1967), Rev. Robert L. Amundsen.
Res., 1220 University Ave., 80521. Tel: 970-484-3356; Fax: 970-484-3434.
Catechesis/Religious Programs—Students 346.

4—St. Elizabeth Ann Seton, (1981), Very Rev. Elbert V. Chilson, V.F.; Deacons William Trewartha; Howard Frisinger.
Res., 5450 S. Lemay Ave., 80525. Tel: 970-226-1303; Fax: 970-226-5780.
Catechesis/Religious Programs—Students 634.

Fort Lupton, Weld Co., St. William (1909), Rev. Gary Ziuraitis, C.SS.R. In res., Rev. James Shea, C.SS.R.
Res., 1025 Fulton Ave., 80621. Tel: 303-857-6642; 659-3519; 785-6400; Fax: 303-857-6643.
Catechesis/Religious Programs—Students 412.
Mission—Platteville, Weld Co., St. Nicholas. See Wattenberg, Our Lady of Grace. 514 Marion, 80621. Tel: 970-785-2143; Fax: 970-857-6643.

Fort Morgan, Morgan Co., St. Helena (1910), Revs. Lawrence B. Kaiser; Adalberto DeGante (GLP).
Res., 917 W. 7th Ave., 80701. Tel: 970-867-2885.
Catechesis/Religious Programs—923 Pawnee, Ft. Morgan, 80701. Tel: 970-867-5768.
Students 250.
Mission—Weldona, Morgan Co., St. Francis of Assisi, 80701.

Frederick, Weld Co., St. Theresa (1923), Rev. G. Timothy Gaines.
Res., 436 Fifth St., P.O. Box 418, 80530. Tel: 970-833-2966; 303-654-1106 (Metro).
Catechesis/Religious Programs—Students 100.
Mission—Mead, Weld Co., Guardian Angels, 80530.

Glenwood Springs, Garfield Co., St. Stephen (1885), Rev. Cliff J. McMillan; Deacons Victor Kimminau; Charles Sprick.
Res., 1010 Grand Ave., 81601. Tel: 970-945-6673; Fax: 970-945-2089.
School—414 S. Hyland Park Dr., 81601. Tel: 970-945-7746.
Sisters 1; Lay Teachers 9; Students 102.
Catechesis/Religious Programs—Tel: 970-945-2580.
Students 323.

Grand Lake, Grand Co., St. Anne (1957), Rev. Francis J. Gerber, Jr.
Res., 219 Hancock St., P.O. Box 510, 80447. Tel: 970-627-3450; Fax: 970-627-3064.
Missions—Granby, Grand Co., Our Lady of the Snow, P.O. Box 510, 80447.; Winter Park, Grand Co., St. Bernard, P.O. Box 510, 80447.

Greeley, Weld Co., St. Mary (1965), Rev. Robert D. Fisher; Deacon Joseph H. Meilinger.
Res., 2222 23rd Ave., 80631. Tel: 970-352-1724; Fax: 970-352-1729.

St. Peter (1903), Rev. Gregory Ames; Deacon Frederick Torrez. In res., Rev. Isaac Raney, M.Ss.A.
Office: 915 12th St., 80631. Tel: 970-352-1060; Fax: 970-352-1062.
Catechesis/Religious Programs—Students 460.

Our Lady of Peace (1945), Revs. Kyle Fisher, C.SS.R.; Matthew Kessler, C.SS.R. In res., Rev. Eugene Oates, C.SS.R.
Res., 1311 3rd St., 80631. Tel: 970-353-1747; Fax: 970-353-4830.
Catechesis/Religious Programs—1303 13th St., 80631. Tel: 970-351-6473; Fax: 970-353-4830.
Students 425.
Missions—Ault, Weld Co., St. Mary, 267 E. 4th St., 80610. Tel: 970-834-1609; Gilcrest, Weld Co., Sacred Heart, 4th St. & Starbird Rd., Gilcrest 80623.; Eaton, Weld Co., St. Michael.

Holyoke, Phillips Co., St. Patrick (1893), Rev. Neal A. Pfister.
Res., 535 S. Interocean, 80734. Tel: 970-854-2762; 859-2866 (Hall); Fax: 970-854-2781. [CEM]
Missions—Haxtun, Phillips Co., Christ the King, 306 N. Iris, Haxtun 80731. Tel: 974-774-7640; Fax: 974-854-2781; Fleming, Logan Co., St. Peter the Apostle, 40027 CR 18, Rt. 1, Fleming 80728. Tel: 970-265-2792. [CEM]

Idaho Springs, Clear Creek Co., St. Paul's (1881), Rev. Michael F. Kerrigan.
Res., P.O. Box 848, 1632 Colorado Blvd., 80452. Tel: 303-567-4662; Fax: 303-567-4662.
Catechesis/Religious Programs—Tel: 303-567-4138; Fax: 303-567-4662.
Students 51.
Missions—Central City, Gilpin Co., St. Mary of the Assumption, P.O. Box 848, 80452.; Georgetown, Clear Creek Co., Our Lady of Lourdes, P.O. Box 848, Idaho Springs 80452. [CEM]

Iliff, Logan Co., St. Catherine of Siena (1927), Very Rev. Robert G. Whipkey, V.F.; Rev. Adalberto DeGante (GLP).
Res., 111 S. Fifth St., P.O. Box 221, 80736. Tel: 970-522-8040; Fax: 970-334-2227.

Johnstown, Weld Co., St. John the Baptist (1937), Rev. Stephen E. Adams.
Res., 809 Charlotte St., 80534. Tel: 970-587-2879.
Catechesis/Religious Programs—Students 132.
Mission—Windsor, Weld Co., Our Lady of the Valley, P.O. Box 1018, 80534. Tel: 970-686-5084.

Julesburg, Sedgwick Co., St. Anthony (1907), Rev. Christopher A. Renner.
Res., 606 W. 3rd St., 80737. Tel: 970-474-2655.
Catechesis/Religious Programs—Students 55.
Mission—Crook, Logan Co., St. Peters, 612 E. 3rd, Crook 80726.

Kremmling, Grand Co., St. Peter (1944), Rev. John Kauffman.
Church and Office: 106 S. 5th St., P.O. Box 428, 80459. Tel: 970-724-3428.
Mission—Walden, Grand Co., St. Ignatius, 80459.

Lafayette, Boulder Co., Immaculate Conception (1906), Rev. Joseph A. Hartmann; Deacon Merle Runck.
Res., 110 W. Simpson, 80026. Tel: 303-665-5103; Fax: 303-604-9077.
Catechesis/Religious Programs—Tel: 303-665-9334.
Students 157.

Longmont, Boulder Co., St. John the Baptist (1882), Revs. James E. Fox; Lawrence P. Christensen, C.M.; Deacons William Lee; Nehemias Ruiz.
Parish Center: 336 Emery St., 80501. Tel: 303-776-0737; 449-7745 (Metro); Fax: 303-772-5636. [JC]

School—350 Emory St., 80501. Tel: 303-449-7745. Dr. Paul Czaja, Prin.
Lay Teachers 20; Students 299.
Catechesis/Religious Programs—Tel: 303-772-5637; Fax: 303-772-5636.
Students 362.

Spirit of Peace Parish (1982), Revs. Daniel J. Flaherty; John Markey, O.P. Pastoral Team: Mary Franch; Sr. Dorothy Feehan, B.V.M.; Julie Lupien; Waldemar Perez; John Rejeske; Tom Shugrue.
Church and Office: 1500 Hover Rd., 80501. Tel: 303-772-6322; Fax: 303-772-9415. [JC]

Louisville, Boulder Co., St. Louis (1884), Rev. Donald Willette; Deacon Richard F. Pelis.
Res., 902 Grant Ave., 80027. Tel: 303-666-6401; Fax: 303-666-0826.
School—925 Grant Ave., 80027. Tel: 303-666-6220. Lay Teachers 13; Students 230.
Preschool—901 Grant Ave., 80027. Tel: 303-665-0606.
Catechesis/Religious Programs—841 Grant Ave., 80027. Tel: 303-604-6055.
Students 450.

Loveland, Larimer Co., St. John the Evangelist (1902), Rev. John J. Grabrian; Deacons Richard Johnson; Warren Lybarger; Robert Haigh.
Office: 1515 Hilltop Dr., 80537. Tel: 970-669-2720; Fax: 970-669-5743.
Res., 1523 Hilltop Dr., 80537. Tel: 970-663-3457.
School—1730 W. 12th St., Tel: 970-667-6846.
Sisters 1; Lay Teachers 10; Students 228.
Catechesis/Religious Programs—Students 445.

Meeker, Rio Blanco Co., Holy Family (1905), Rev. Roger L. Lascelle.
Res., 889 Park, Box 866, 81641. Tel: 970-878-3300; Fax: 970-878-3300.
Mission—Rangely, Rio Blanco Co., St. Ignatius, 109 S. Stanolind Ave., Rangely, 81648. Tel: 970-675-8935; Fax: 970-675-8935.

Minturn, Eagle Co., St. Patrick's (1913), Very Rev. Msgr. Thomas Dentici, V.F.
Res., 476 Pine St., P.O. Box 219, 81645. Tel: 970-827-5784; Fax: 970-827-9454.
Catechesis/Religious Programs—Students 140.
Missions—Red Cliff, Eagle Co., Our Lady of Mt. Carmel, P.O. Box 219, 81645.; Vail, Eagle Co., The Interfaith Chapel, P.O. Box 219, 81645.

Oak Creek, Routt Co., St. Martin. See Holy Name, Steamboat Springs.

Peetz, Logan Co., Sacred Heart, Very Rev. Robert G. Whipkey, V.F.; Rev. Adalberto DeGante (GLP).
Res., 621 Logan, P.O. Box D, 80747. Tel: 970-334-2227; Fax: 970-334-2227. [CEM]

Platteville, Weld Co., St. Nicholas. See St. William, Fort Lupton.

Rangely, St. Ignatius (1931), Rev. Roger L. Lascelle; Deacon George Fortunato.
Res., 109 S. Stanolind Ave., 81648. Tel: 970-675-8935; Fax: 970-675-8935.
Catechesis/Religious Programs—Students 63.

Red Feathers Lakes, Larimer Co., Our Lady of the Lakes. See St. Joseph, Fort Collins.

Rifle, Garfield Co., St. Mary's (1910), Rev. Robert E. Hehn.
Res., 323 1/2 E. Fifth St., P.O. Box 191, 81650. Tel: 970-625-2547. [JC]
Catechesis/Religious Programs—341 E. 5th St., 81650. Tel: 970-625-3914.
Students 173.
Missions—Silt, Garfield Co., Sacred Heart, P.O. Box 191, 81650.; Parachute, Garfield Co., St. Brendan, P.O. Box 191, 81650.

Roggen, Weld Co., Sacred Heart (1924), Rev. Joseph J. Blanco.
Res., 38044 Weld County Rd. 16, 80652. Tel: 303-849-5313; Fax: 303-849-5674.
Catechesis/Religious Programs—Students 110.
Missions—Keenesburg, Weld Co., Holy Family, 38044 Weld County Rd. 16, 80652.; Wiggins, Morgan Co., Our Lady of Lourdes, 38044 Weld County Rd. 16, 80652.

Steamboat Springs, Routt Co., Holy Name (1907), Rev. George Schroeder; Deacon Rex H. Pilger, Jr.
Res., 504 Oak St., P.O. Box 774198, 80477-4198. Tel: 970-879-0671; Fax: 970-879-7406.
Catechesis/Religious Programs—Tel: 970-879-1225.
Students 253.
Mission—Oak Creek, Routt Co., St. Martin Church.

Sterling, Logan Co., St. Anthony (1888), Revs. Adalberto DeGante; Robert G. Whipkey, Jr., V.F.
Res., 327 S. 3rd St., 80751. Tel: 970-522-6422; Fax: 970-522-6442.
School—Tel: 970-522-7567; Fax: 970-522-6442.
Sisters of the Third Order of St. Francis of Assisi 1; Lay Teachers 10; Students 114.
Catechesis/Religious Programs—326 S. 3rd St., 80751. Tel: 970-522-7568; Fax: 970-522-6442.
Students 305.

Stoneham, Weld Co., St. John. See St. Mary, Brush.

Vail, Eagle Co., The Interfaith Chapel. See St. Patrick's, Minturn.

Walden, Jackson Co., St. Ignatius. See St. Peter, Kremmling.

Wattenberg, Fort Lupton Co., Our Lady of Grace. See St. William, Fort Lupton.

Weldona, Morgan Co., St. Francis of Assisi. See St. Helena, Fort Morgan.

Wiggins, Morgan Co., Our Lady of Lourdes. See Sacred Heart, Roggen.

Winter Park, Grand Co., St. Bernard of Montjoux. See St. Anne, Grand Lake.

Windsor, Weld Co., Our Lady of the Valley, Very Rev. Stephen E. Adams, V.F.; Deacon Harold Kimble.
Office: P.O. Box 1018, 80550. Tel: 970-686-5084; Fax: 970-587-2879.
Res., 809 Charlotte St., Johnstown, 80534. Tel: 303-587-2879.

Wray, Yuma Co., St. Andrew (1891), Rev. Gerald A. Young (LA).
Res., 412 Dexter St., 80758. Tel: 970-332-5858; Fax: 970-332-4604.
Catechesis/Religious Programs—Students 107.

Yuma, Yuma Co., St. John (1888), Rev. Gerald A. Young, Admin.
Res., 508 S. Ash St., 80759. Tel: 970-848-5973; Fax: 970-332-4604.
Catechesis/Religious Programs—Students 125.

Chaplains of Public Institutions

DENVER. *Veterans Hospital*. Rev. Thomas J. Woerth.
AURORA. *Fitzsimons Army Medical Center*. Rev. Edward Kucera, O.S.B.

On Duty Outside the Archdiocese:
Reverend Fathers—
Denig, Philip, Chap. (Capt.), HHC 1 SB Unit, 31520, APO AE, 09832
Kelly, Thomas D., 15 ABW / HC, Hickam AFB, HI 96853-5112
McDaid, J. Anthony, Villa Stritch, Via Della Nocetta 63, Rome, 00164 Italy
Owlrich, Robert E., Casa Santa Maria, Via Dell' Umilta 30, Rome, 00187 Italy
Revello, James K.I., Chap. (Lt. Col.), USAF, 2703 San Juan Loop, Holloman, NM 88330
Schmitz, Bernard A., Monteria Mission, A.A. 1393, Monteria, Colombia

---

Absent on Leave:
Reverend Fathers—
Bradtke, Thomas A.
Dold, John F.
Fuller, Roger J.
McInerney, Maurice
Scezney, Leonard J.
Schlut, Michael
St. Peter, Lawrence
White, Robert H.

Retired:
Reverend Monsignors—
Barry, Thomas P., 4950 S. Logan St., Englewood, CO 80110-6921
Foxhoven, Omer V., 3342 Marshall St., Wheat Ridge, CO 80033
Hoffman, Robert F., 13120 E. Kentucky Ave., Aurora, CO 80012
Jones, William H., 7125 E. 11th Ave., Denver, CO 80220
Rasby, James W., 1011 S. Valencia, Villa 3, Denver, CO 80231
Schmitt, J. Harley, Chap., Mullen Home, 3629 W. 29th Ave., Denver, CO 80211
Reverend Fathers—
Alimena, Leonard S.
Banigan, Herbert, 5817 S. Mount Vernon, Spokane, WA 99223
Breunig, Robert L., Villa Madeline, 2771 Zenobia St., Denver, CO 80212
Canjar, John A.
Durrie, Robert L., 1580 S. Dahlia, Denver, CO 80222
Gibbons, Charles
Jones, Charles, 1129 Fillmore, Denver, CO 80206. Tel: 303-322-0624
Kearney, George W., 3373 W. 36th Ave., Denver, CO 80211
McCallin, Frederick D., Mullen Home, 3629 W. 29th Ave., Denver, CO 80211
Mihelich, Leopold, 6305 W. 5th Pl., Lakewood, CO 80226
Nevans, Robert V., Villa Madeleine, 2771 Zenobia St., Denver, CO 80212
O'Malley, Joseph M., 1542 E. Nicholas Dr., Littleton, CO 80161
Puhl, Albert E., 800 Pennsylvania St., Denver, CO 80203
Salmon, Charles P., 2835 W. 32nd, Denver, CO 80211
Sanger, Charles P., 10450 Oakmont Dr., Sun City, AZ 85351
Scannell, John W., 6333 Rancho Mission Rd., San Diego, CA 92108
Sullivan, Patrick, Box 274, 8962 E. Hampden Ave., Denver, CO 80231-4996
Syrianey, Robert, 13902 E. Marina Ave., Apt. 207, Aurora, CO 80014
Weibel, George L., 2312 14th St., Boulder, CO 80304

Permanent Deacons:
Ansay, Ronald J., (Retired)
Atencio, Sidney, St. Rose of Lima, Denver
Austin, Robert, St. Michael the Archangel, Aurora
Babish, Joseph T., St. Vincent de Paul, Denver
Baker, Richard L., Spirit of Christ, Arvada
Barbato, Lewis, M.D., (Retired)
Beabout, Norman, Christ the King, Evergreen
Becker, Henry Jr. (SAN), St. Thomas More, Englewood
Benzel, Leonard, John XXIII University, Fort Collins
Blake, Stephen M., Church of the Good Shepherd, Denver
Bocovich, Frank J., St. Louis, Englewood
Boselli, Francis A., St. Martin de Porres, Boulder
Bowles, Richard J., Jr., Shrine of St. Anne, Arvada
Bradley, Patrick (CAM), St. Catherine of Siena, Denver
Brady, Richard A., St. Therese, Aurora
Burgess, Lou A., On Duty in the Diocese of Phoenix
Clausson, Ronald L., St. Francis Cabrini, Littleton
Clements, Edward R., St. Mary, Littleton
Coker, Richard, Military Service
Combs, Richard E., On Duty in the Archdiocese of Seattle
Coursey, Nathan D., Contemplative Outreach Ministry, Blessed Sacrament Parish, Denver
Creel, Rodger L., Shrine of St. Anne, Arvada
Decker, Myles M., On Duty in the Diocese of Palm Beach
Del Real, Harold, Sabbatical
DeProfio, Dominic, St. Louis, Englewood
Dolan, L. Stephen, St. Thomas Aquinas, Boulder
Dorwart, Jason, Our Lady of the Mountains, Estes Park
Downey, Hugh, Spirit of Christ Community, Arvada
Dreiling, L. Kenneth, Handicapped Ministry, St. Joseph, Golden
Dunn, Michael A., On Duty in the Diocese of San Jose
Fitterer, George (JOL), Christ the King, Evergreen
Fortunato, George R., St. Ignatius Parish, Rangely
Frisinger, Howard, (Retired)
Fucci, Craig (LA), St. Francis Cabrini, Littleton
Gamache, Robert K., On Duty in the Archdiocese of St. Louis
Garcia, A. Paul, (Retired)
Gonzales, Filemon F., (Retired)
Grimm, R. Paul, St. Francis Cabrini, Fort Logan Medical Center, Littleton
Haigh, Robert, St. John the Evangelist, Loveland
Halpine, Russell, Holy Cross, Thorton
Hamersky, Alfons, St. Bernadette Parish, Lakewood
Harrington, Philip, Notre Dame Parish, Denver
Hawkins, Kenneth I., Jr., Archdiocesan Family Center, Airport Ministry
Hawley, Joseph W., Our Lady of Fatima, Lakewood
Hegarty, Marvin A., St. Vincent de Paul, Denver
Heissenbuttel, Thomas, St. Paul, Idaho Springs
Hendricks, George, St. Catherine of Siena, Denver
Hillyer, Granby, On Duty in the Diocese of San Francisco
Howard, Michael J., Spirit of Christ, Arvada
Howard, Robert J., Sacred Heart of Jesus, Boulder
Hronek, Dennis R., Unassigned
Hudec, Gordon D., St. Joan of Arc, Arvada
Johnson, Richard, St. John the Evangelist, Loveland
Kelly, Dennis M., St. Louis, Englewood
Kerby, Brian J., Mt. Evans Hospice (Evergreen), St. Elizabeth, Buffalo Creek
Kimble, Harold, Our Lady of the Valley, Windsor
Kimminau, Victor H., St. Stephen, Glenwood Springs
Koch, Kenneth, (Retired)
Kramb, Richard F., (Retired)
Kulinski, Jerome N., (Retired)
Kullman, Frank W., Our Lady of the Pines Parish, Conifer
Lamar, Charles (CHI), Light of the World Parish, Littleton
Lee, William S., St. John the Baptist, Longmont
Linton, William J., (Retired)
Lujan, Edward, Sacred Heart, Denver
Lybarger, Warren G., St. Joseph, Fort Collins
Martin, Gregory, St. Pius X, Aurora
Matz, Karl T., (Retired)

McDavid, Clarence G., Cure D'Ars, Denver
McKeown, John, St. John the Evangelist, Loveland
Medenwaldt, Richard A., Nativity of Our Lord, Broomfield
Meilinger, Joseph H., St. Mary, Greeley
Menogan, Guffie E., St. Ignatius Loyola, Denver
Mich, Lawrence E., (Retired)
Milhone, Gordon G., Holy Name, Englewood
Miller, Gary E., Sts. Peter and Paul Parish, Wheat Ridge
Mooneyham, E. Gene, Light of the World, Littleton
Oehrle, Leo A., Immaculate Heart of Mary, Northglenn
Padilla, Carlos L., (Retired)
Paulson, Joel J., St. Jude, Lakewood
Pelis, Richard F., St. Louis Parish, Louisville
Pilger, Rex H., Jr., Holy Name Parish, Steamboat Springs
Polak, Leonard E., Holy Family, Denver
Pontillo, John E., St. Mark, Westminster
Power, Winfield S., (Retired)
Quinlan, Thomas, St. Jude, Lakewood
Quintana, Lloyd, Holy Trinity, Westminster
Rael, Gilbert E., Adams County Jail, St. Augustine, Brighton
Reynolds, Philip J., Arapahoe County Jail, St. Mary, Littleton
Ritchey, Ronald T., Denver County Jail, Holy Cross, Thornton
Ritz, Michael P., Jr., (Retired)
Rogge, Gary, St. Thomas More, Englewood
Rompot, Vernon L., Holy Ghost Church, Denver
Ruiz, Nehemias (SEA), St. John the Baptist, Longmont
Runck, Merle, D.D.S., Immaculate Conception, Lafayette
Salvato, Mark, St. Thomas More, Englewood, Airport Ministry
Sanchez, Alfredo (SFE), St. Mark Parish, Westminister
Sanchez, Maclovio, (Retired)
Sanchez, Wilfred G., St. Elizabeth, Denver
Sandoval, Alfonso M., Our Lady of Guadalupe, Denver
Sandoval, Henry, (Retired)
Scholz, Franz, On Duty in the Diocese of San Diego
Slinkard, Alan, Our Lady of the Pines, Estes Park
Smith, John L., St. Joan of Arc, Arvada
Sorber, William M., Queen of Peace Parish, Aurora
Sprick, Charles B., (Retired)
Stephenson, Billy C., (Retired)
Sutton, Jack, Cathedral of Immaculate Conception, Denver
Thunblom, John, St. Pius X Parish, Aurora
Tirgrath, Howard L., On Duty in the Diocese of Reno-Las Vegas
Torrez, Frederick L., St. Peter, Greeley
Trewartha, William D.P.M., St. Elizabeth Ann Seton, Fort Collins
Trujillo, Samuel R., Our Lady Mother of the, Commerce City
Ubowski, Chester W., Light of the World Parish, Littleton
Usera, Luis A., Sr., Ascension, Denver
Van Tam Le, Joseph, (Retired)
Vieria, Richard, Jefferson County Jail, St. Mary Magdalene Parish, Denver
Vigil, Arthur A., All Saints Parish, Denver
Vitello, Eugene, St. Catherine of Siena, Denver
Wager, Martin A., St. Louis, Englewood, Handicapped Ministry
Wall, James R., Sts. Peter and Paul, Wheat Ridge
Ward, William (SLC), St. Mary, Littleton
Waring, Lynn E., Immaculate Heart of Mary, Northglenn
Webster, Earl, Leave of Absence
Wilhelm, Martin A., St. Michael the Archangel, Aurora
Young, John Joseph, All Souls, Englewood

INSTITUTIONS LOCATED IN THE ARCHDIOCESE

[A] SEMINARIES, RELIGIOUS OR SCHOLASTICATES

DENVER. *Provincial House at St. Andrew, Seminary (C.R.)*, 1050 S. Birch St., 80220. Tel: 303-756-5522. Preparatory students in residence. Theatine Fathers. Very Rev. Patrick Valdez, C.R., Prov. Supr.; Revs. Bart Nadal, C.R., Rector; Mark Matson, C.R. In res., Rev. Angelo Urdiain, C.R.

Redemptoris Mater House of Formation, 3434 E. Arizona Ave., 80210. Tel: 303-733-2220; Fax: 303-733-2223. Rev. Angel Molina, Vice Rector. Priests 2.

St. Dominic Priory, 3005 W. 29th Ave., 80211. Tel: 303-455-3613. Province of St. Albert the Great. Rev. Michael G. Kyte, O.P.

[B] COLLEGES AND UNIVERSITIES

DENVER. *Regis University*, 3333 Regis Blvd., 80221-1099. Tel: 303-458-4100.
For a complete listing, refer to the Colleges and Universities section.

[C] INTER-PAROCHIAL HIGH SCHOOLS

DENVER. *Holy Family High School*, 4343 Utica St., 80212. Tel: 303-458-8822. Sr. Mary Rose Lieb, O.S.F., Prin. Priests 1; Sisters 3; Lay Teachers 29; Students 315.

Machebeuf Catholic High School, 1958 Elm St., 80220. Tel: 303-322-1810. Bill Giddings, Prin. Sisters 1; Lay Teachers 18; Students 279.

[D] HIGH SCHOOLS, PRIVATE

DENVER. *J.K. Mullen High School, Corp.*, 3601 S. Lowell Blvd., 80236. Tel: 303-761-1764. Legal Title: *The Christian Brothers of J.K. Mullen High School*. Coed Day School. Brothers of the Christian Schools. Vincent J. Greco, Jr., Prin. Brothers 1; Sisters 3; Lay Teachers 50; Students 865.

St. Mary's Academy High School, 4545 S. University Blvd., 80110. Tel: 303-762-8300; Fax: 303-783-6201. Sisters of Loretto at the Foot of the Cross. Jennifer Fox, Prin. Lay Teachers 27; Girls 256.

AURORA. *Regis Jesuit High School*, 16300 E. Weaver Pl., 80016. Tel: 303-699-1598. Day School for Boys. Revs. Walter Sidney, S.J., Pres.; Chris Pramuk, Head of Theology; Philip Steele, S.J., Rector; Mr. Rick Sullivan, Prin.; Bro. Joe Gockel, S.J. Priests 3; Brothers 1; Lay Teachers 54; Students 794.

[E] ELEMENTARY SCHOOLS, PRIVATE

DENVER. *St. Mary's Academy Lower School.* (Grades PreK-5), 4545 S. University Blvd., 80110. Tel: 303-762-8300; Fax: 303-761-4146. Sisters of Loretto at the Foot of the Cross. Sr. Susan Swain, S.L., Prin. Sisters 1; Lay Teachers 38; Students 302.

ENGLEWOOD. *St. Mary's Academy, Middle School.* (Grades 6-8), 4545 S. University Blvd., 80110. Tel: 303-762-8300. Mike Radigan, Prin. Lay Teachers 20; Students 167.

[F] SPECIAL EDUCATION

DENVER. *Mt. St. Vincent's Home*, 4159 Lowell Blvd., 80211. Tel: 303-458-7220. Sr. Vickie Perkins, Exec. Dir. Sisters of Charity of Leavenworth 8; Students 70.

[G] MINISTRY TO THE HANDICAPPED

DENVER. *The Carron Center*, 1050 S. Birch St., 80222. Tel: 303-759-5150. Mrs. Cary Carron, Supvr.

Religious Education-Pastoral Care of Developmentally Disabled Persons, 3101 W. Hillside Pl., 80219. Tel: 303-934-1999. Rev. Lawrence M. Freeman, Dir.; Sr. Mary Catherine Widger, S.L., Assoc. Dir.; Sr. Sue Rogers, S.L., Dir. Bridge Community Group Home. Religious education of approximately 400 mentally retarded children and adults; One 8 bed group home.

[H] GENERAL HOSPITALS

*DENVER. *Centura Health*, 1601 Lowell Blvd., 80204.
For a complete listing, refer to the Hospitals section.

St. Joseph Hospital, 1835 Franklin St., 80218. Tel: 303-837-7111.
For a complete listing, refer to the Hospitals section.

[I] HOMES FOR AGED

DENVER. *Francis Heights, Inc.*, 3805 W. 26th Ave., 80211. Tel: 303-433-6268.
For a complete listing, refer to the Special Care Facilities section.

**Gardens at St. Elizabeth*, 2835 W. 32nd Ave., 80211. Tel: 303-477-4442.
For a complete listing, refer to the Special Care Facilities section.

Mullen Home, 3629 W. 29th Ave., 80211. Tel: 303-433-7221.
For a complete listing, refer to the Special Care Facilities section.

[J] HOMES AND SERVICES FOR AGED AND INFIRM

DENVER. *Hospice of Peace*, 1601A Lowell Blvd., 80204-1545. Tel: 303-575-8393; 575-8350.
For a complete listing, refer to the Special Care Facilities section.

[K] HOUSING FOR THE ELDERLY AND FOR FAMILIES (LOW INCOME)

DENVER. *Archdiocesan Housing Committee*, 1544 Pearl St., 80203. Tel: 303-830-0215; Fax: 303-830-2885.
For a complete listing, refer to the Special Care Facilities section.

Damen House, 2851 W. 52nd Ave., P.O. Box 11580, 80211. Tel: 303-433-4280.
For a complete listing, refer to the Special Care Facilities section.

Dayspring Villa, Inc., 3777 W. 26th Ave., 80211. Tel: 303-455-5066 (local).
For a complete listing, refer to the Special Care Facilities section.

Francis Heights, 3805 W. 26th Ave., 80212. Tel: 303-433-6268.
For a complete listing, refer to the Special Care Facilities section.

Franciscan Ministries, Inc., 3805 W. 26th Ave., 80212. Tel: 303-433-6268; Fax: 708-462-4977.
For a complete listing, refer to the Special Care Facilities section.

WESTMINSTER. *Villa Maria, Inc.*, 2451 W. 82nd Pl., 80030-4065. Tel: 303-433-6268 (local); 303-427-4406.
For a complete listing, refer to the Special Care Facilities section.

[L] CATHOLIC CHARITIES & COMMUNITY SERVICES

DENVER. *Catholic Charities and Community Services of the Archdiocese of Denver, Inc.*, 200 Josephine St., 80206. Tel: 303-388-4435. James H. Mauck, Pres., Admin.

Samaritan House, 2301 Lawrence St., 80205. Tel: 303-294-0241. Samaritan House Resource Center, 360 Acoma St., 80223. Tel: 303-715-9525.

Shelter for Homeless.

Transitional Housing, Courtyard Commons, 1122 Pearl St., 80203. Tel: 303-860-9098.

The Carron Center, 1050 S. Birch St., 80222. Tel: 303-759-5150.

Aurora Family Assistance Center, 1468 Iola St., Aurora, 80010. Tel: 303-363-9543.

North Area Cares Emergency Assistance, 7301 Federal Blvd. #20, Westminister, 80030. Tel: 303-427-6256.

Northeast E.A. Center, 6621 E. 72nd Ave., Commerce City, 80022. Tel: 303-287-1127.

Central Emergency Assistance Center, 1440 Poplar St., 80220. Tel: 303-399-1558.

Southwest Emergency Assistance Center, 902 S. Sheridan Blvd., 80226. Tel: 303-922-5205.

Brighton Emergency Assistance Center, 178 S. Sixth St., Brighton, 80601. Tel: 303-654-1040.

Catholic Charities and Community Services East Office, 1445 Emporia St., Aurora, 80010. Tel: 303-360-9686. Counseling and Case Management.

The Family Center, 1020 Upham St., Lakewood, 80215. Tel: 303-238-0521.

Camp Santa Maria. Tel: 303-238-0521. Counseling Services, Family and Children Services, Family Life and Marriage Ministry, Senior Services and Youth Ministry.

Immigration and Resettlement, 3417 W. 38th Ave., 80211. Tel: 303-458-0222.

Mulroy Neighborhood Center, 3550 W. 13th Ave., 80204. Tel: 303-892-1540.

SHARE Colorado, 9360 Federal Blvd., Federal Heights, 80221. Tel: 303-428-0400.

Catholic Charities and Community Services Northern, Hostel of Hospitality/The Mission, 460 Linden Center Dr., Fort Collins, 80524. Tel: 970-484-5010. Emergency Services, Hope Job Bank, Hospitality Kitchen, Hostel of Hospitality, Homeless Shelter, Pregnancy Counseling and Adoption, SHARE Colorado and Volunteer Program. 1311 11th St., Greeley, 80631. Tel: 970-353-6433. Elderly Outreach, Caregiver Empowerment Project, Guadalupe Shelter, Migrant Program, Senior Companions and Spanish Elderly Outreach.

CCS North-Loveland, 574 E. 23rd St., Loveland, 80538. Tel: 970-663-1880.

Catholic Charities & Community Services Farm Labor Housing Corp., 200 Josephine St., 80206. Tel: 303-388-4435.

[M] MONASTERIES AND RESIDENCES OF PRIESTS AND BROTHERS

DENVER. *Annunciation Friary*, 3621 Humboldt St., 80205. Tel: 303-296-1024. Capuchin Friars. In res., Revs. Gene Emrisek, O.F.M.Cap., Guardian; Edward Judy, O.F.M.Cap., Vicar; Matthew Gross, O.F.M.Cap.; John Cousins, O.F.M.Cap.; Gregory Beyer, O.F.M.Cap.; Cyrus Gallagher, O.F.M.Cap.

Christian Brothers (F.S.C.)- St. Joseph Community, 115 Galapago, 80223. Tel: 303-295-2515. Bro. Mariano Lopez, Contact.

Congregation of the Mission Midwest Province: De Paul House, 2340 S. University Blvd., 80210. Tel: 303-698-1618; Fax: 303-777-0468. Revs. John H. Karssen, C.M., Supr.; Richard R. Ryan, C.M.; E. Hartrick Sullivan, C.M.; Thomas J. Nelson, C.M.; John Q. O'Connell, C.M.

Holy Trinity Friary, 2924 W. 43rd Ave., 80211. Tel: 303-561-1474. Rev. Chas. Martinez, O.F.M., Guardian. Priests 4; Brothers 2; Students 2.

Loyola Parish - Jesuit Community, 2305 Gaylord St.,

80205-5627. Tel: 303-322-8042; Fax: 303-322-2927. Revs. Stephen T. Yavorsky, S.J., Supr.; John F. Brady, S.J.; J. Patrick Walsh, S.J.; James C. Sunderland, S.J.

Maryknoll Fathers, Catholic Foreign Mission Society of America (Legal Title), 4460 Federal Blvd., 80211. Tel: 303-455-5669; Fax: 303-455-5753. Rev. Francis B. Higdon, M.M.

The Redemptorists / Denver Province, Provincial Residence, Box 300399, 80203-0399. Tel: 303-370-0035; Fax: 303-370-0036. Res., 2130 E. Fourteenth Ave., 80206. Very Rev. Richard Thibodeau, C.Ss.R., Prov. Supr.; Revs. J. Robert Fenili, C.Ss.R., Prov. Vicar; Stephen Meyer, C.Ss.R., Prov. Consultor; John Steingraeber, C.Ss.R., Co-Dir., Financial Svcs.; Bro. Thomas Wright, C.Ss.R., Co-Dir., Financial Svcs. Priests 21; Brothers 2.

Serving abroad: Most Rev. Clarence Duhart, C.Ss.R., 123/19 Ruam Rudi Ln., Bangkok, Thailand, 10330. Rev. Alfred Novak, C.Ss.R., Rua Consulheiro Sinimbu, 83200 Paranagua, Parana, Brazil. Revs. Anthony Smith, C.Ss.R.; Joseph W. Tobin, C.Ss.R., Casa Sant'Alfonso, C.P. 2458, 00100 Rome, Italy. Revs. William Cleary, C.Ss.R.; William Peterson, C.Ss.R.; Robert Wirth, C.Ss.R.; John Willett, C.Ss.R.; Bro. Daniel Hall, C.Ss.R., P.O. Box 29585 Secretariat, Bodija, Ibadan, Oyo State, Nigeria. Rev. William Fitzgerald, C.Ss.R., C.P. 400, 48900 Juazeiro, Bahia, Brazil. Rev. Harold Thiel, C.Ss.R., 88 Chotana Rd., T. Chang Phuek A. Muang, Chaing Mai 50300, Thailand.

Serving elsewhere, not listed: Rev. John McPhee, C.Ss.R., 61847 Glenview Ter., Washington, MI, 49084. Rev. Thomas Fransiscus, C.Ss.R., The Tribunal, 1550 N. Fresno St., Fresno, CA, 93703-3788. Rev. T. William Coyle, C.Ss.R., 608 Broadway, Fargo, ND, 58102. Rev. Pascal Dreici, C.Ss.R., 1035 E. Walthen, Fresno, CA, 93710. Rev. Ricardo Elford, C.Ss.R., P.O. Box 574, Cortaro, AZ, 85652. Rev. Joseph Nuttmann, C.Ss.R., P.O. Box 235, Carlin, NV, 89822. Rev. Richard Strass, C.Ss.R., P.O. Box 207, Seward, Alphonsus, 99664.

Regis Jesuit Community (The Jesuits at Regis University), Jesuit House M12, 3333 Regis Blvd., 80221-1099. Tel: 303-458-4100; Fax: 303-964-5525. Revs. John J. Callahan, S.J., Rector; David M. Clarke, S.J.; Thomas W. Cummings, S.J.; James B. Guyer, S.J.; Edward L. Maginnis, S.J.; Edward T. Oakes, S.J.; Patrick H. O'Liddy, S.J.; James S. Richard, S.J.; John K. Ridgway, S.J.; James G. Sampson, S.J.; Michael J. Sheeran, S.J.; Charles M. Shelton, S.J.; Thomas J. Steele, S.J.

St. Francis of Assisi Friary, 3553 Wyandot St., 80211-2948. Tel: 303-477-5542; Fax: 303-477-6925. In res., Rev. Harvey P. Dinkel, O.F.M.Cap., Vicar, Exec. Sec./Treas.; Very Rev. David Gottschalk, O.F.M.Cap., Prov. Min., Guardian; Revs. Thomas More Janeck, O.F.M.Cap., Chap. Poor Clares; John Lager, O.F.M.Cap., Dir. Devel.; Eric Lindbloom, O.F.M.; Malachy McBride, O.F.M. Cap.; Regis Scanlon, O.F.M.Cap., Preaching Ministry; Michael Suchnicki, O.F.M.Cap., Assoc. Dir. Samaritan House.

Xavier Jesuit Center, 3450 W. 53rd, 80221-6568. Tel: 303-480-3900; Fax: 303-433-6235. Revs. John P. Teeling, S.J., Supr.; Richard F. Bocklage, S.J.; Joseph F. Bona, S.J.; John J. Campbell, S.J.; Frederick T. Daly, S.J.; Robert R. DeRouen, S.J.; Edward F. Flaherty, S.J.; John C. Futrell, S.J.; Harry E. Hoewischer, S.J.; Carl G. Kloster, S.J.; Timothy J. Lawless, S.J.; William T. Miller, S.J.; Anthony J. Short, S.J.; James C. Sunderland, S.J.; Edward A. Thro, S.J.; William S. Udick, S.J.; Bros. Herbert A. Bussen, S.J.; A. Albert Knoll, S.J.

AURORA. *Regis Jesuit High School - Jesuit Community*, 16810 E. Caley Ave., 80016. Tel: 303-699-1598; 690-4782. Revs. Philip G. Steele, S.J., Supvr.; Walter T. Sidney, S.J.; David A. Wayne, S.J.; Bro. Joseph L. Gockel, S.J.

SNOWMASS. *St. Benedict's Monastery*, 1012 Monastery Rd., 81654. Tel: 970-927-3311; Fax: 970-927-3399. The Order of Cistercians of the Strict Observance (Trappists). Rt. Rev. Joseph Boyle, O.C.S.O.; Revs. Thomas Keating, O.C.S.O.; Theophane Boyd, O.C.S.O.; Daniel Kelliher, O.C.S.O.; William Meninger, O.C.S.O. Professed Monks 12; Novices 1.

[N] CONVENTS AND RESIDENCES FOR SISTERS

DENVER. *Dominican Sisters of Hope*, 2501 Gaylord St., 80205. Tel: 303-322-1413; Fax: 303-322-1608. Sr. Anne Frances Goedert, O.P., Contact. Dominican Sisters home health agency served 105 patients. Sisters 3.

Marycrest Convent Franciscan Sisters, 2851 W. 52nd Ave., 80221. Tel: 303-433-2276; 458-6270; Fax: 303-433-5865. Sr. Gloria Shuffer, O.S.F., Provincial Min. Provincial Motherhouse of Sisters of St. Francis of Penance and Christian Charity, Province of the Sacred Heart #1630. Sr. Helena Hager, Min. Sisters 28.

Missionaries of Charity, 1840 Grant St., 80203. Tel: 303-860-8040. Sr. M. Shanti Prabha, M.C., Contact.

Monastery of Our Lady of Light (Capuchin Poor Clares). (Strict Enclosure), 3325 Pecos, 80211. Tel: 303-458-6339. Legal Title: *Capuchin Poor Clares of Denver, Inc.* Mother Maria de Cristo Palafox, O.S-.C.Cap., Abbess; Rev. Thomas More Janeck, O.F.M.Cap., Chap. Sisters 9.

Queen of Peace Convent, 5360 Columbine Rd., 80221. Tel: 303-477-9139. Sisters of St. Francis of Penance and Christian Charity. Sisters 8.

Sisters of the New Covenant, 10620 Livingston Dr., 80234. Tel: 303-451-8677; Fax: 303-438-9556. Pious Union. Sr. Angeline Bukowiecki, S.N.C. Sisters 3.

BOULDER. *Abbey of St. Walburga*, 6717 S. Boulder Rd., 80303. Tel: 303-494-5733; Fax: 303-494-4357. Mother Maria-Thomas Beil, O.S.B., Abbess; Rev. Cyprian Constantine, O.S.B., Chap. Confessors: Revs. Andrew Kemberling, O.S.B.; Walter Watson, S.J. Benedictine Nuns 20; Novices 2; Postulants 1.

GOLDEN. *Mother Cabrini Shrine*, 20189 Cabrini Blvd., 80401. Tel: 303-526-0758; Fax: 303-526-9795. Sr. Bernadette Casciano, M.S.C., Contact; Thomas M. James, Registered Agent. Missionary Sisters of the Sacred Heart of Jesus(M.S.C.) 4.

LAKEWOOD. *Benedictine Sisters of Denver, Inc.*, Spirit of Life Monastery, 10760 W. Glennon Dr., 80226. Tel: 303-986-9234. Sr. Charlotte Redpath, O.S.B., Prioress. Sisters 2.

LITTLETON. *Carmel of Holy Spirit*, 6138 S. Gallup St., 80120-2702. Tel: 303-798-4176. Discalced Carmelites (O.C.D.). Mother Judith of the Immaculate Heart, D.C., Prioress; Rev. Gaston Muyombo (Zaire), Chap. Sisters 9.

Loretto Center, 4000 S. Wadsworth, 80123-1309. Tel: 303-986-1541; Fax: 303-986-8453. Sr. Ann Lucille Ryan, S.L., Coord. Sisters 34.

Sisters of Benedict of Colorado, Inc., 4264 W. Ponds View Dr., 80123. Tel: 303-795-2378. Sr. Judith Elms, O.S.B., Supr.

[O] RETREAT CENTERS

ALLENSPARK. *St. Malo Conference, Retreat Center*, 10758 Hwy. 7, 80510. Tel: 303-747-2892; 970-586-6061 (Estes Park); 303-444-5177 (Denver); Fax: 303-747-2892. Blake Fischer, Dir.

[P] CAMPUS MINISTRY

DENVER. *Auraria Campus.*

Community College of Denver.

Metropolitan State College.

University of Colorado at Denver. Rev. Gary Mueller.

Vincentian Fathers.

St. Elizabeth Parish.

St. Francis Center, 1030 St. Francis Center, 80204. Tel: 303-534-4014; 556-3864.

Director of Campus Ministry, 200 Josephine St., 80206. Tel: 303-388-4411, Ext. 280; Fax: 303-388-7638. Mr. Thomas McCabe.

Regis University (Denver), 3333 Regis Blvd., Ste. 200, 80221. Tel: 303-458-4153; Fax: 303-964-5530. Rev. Louis S. Morrone, O.P.; Kathy Schaefer, Dir.; Mr. Ken Phillips, Asst. Dir.

University of Denver, Catholic Campus Ministry House, 1795 S. Williams St., 80210. Tel: 303-778-7657. Sr. Maria Regis, S.C.J.

BOULDER. *University of Colorado (Boulder)*, St. Thomas Aquinas Parish, 904 Fourteenth St., 80302. Tel: 303-443-8383; Fax: 303-443-8399. Revs. George Fitzgerald, C.S.P.; Joseph A. Ciccone, C.S.P.; Ms. Sandy Swegel; Ms. Kathleen Ahl.

FORT COLLINS. *Colorado State University (Fort Collins)*, John XXIII University Center, 1220 University Ave., 80521. Tel: 303-484-3356; Fax: 303-484-3434. Rev. Robert L. Amundsen; Ms. Kathy Kautzky.

GOLDEN. *Colorado School of Mines (Golden)*, 15755 W. 3rd Ave., 80401. Tel: 303-273-3460. Mr. Edward Mantz.

GREELEY. *University of Northern Colorado (Greeley)*, St. Peter's Parish, 915 12th St., 80631. Tel: 970-352-1060; Fax: 970-352-1062. Rev. Gregory K. Ames.

LITTLETON. *Arapahoe Community College*, c/o Al Rodriguez, 2500 W. College Ave., P.O. Box 9002, 80160-9002. Tel: 303-797-5910; Fax: 303-797-5935.

RANGELY. *Colorado Northwestern Community College (Rangely)*, 109 S. Stanolind Ave., P.O. Box 370, 81648. Tel: 303-675-8935; Fax: 303-878-5736 (Meeker). Rev. Roger Lascelle; Deacon George G. Fortunato.

STEAMBOAT SPRINGS. *Colorado Mountain College*, c/o Holy Name Catholic Church, P.O. Box 774198, 80477-7406. Tel: 970-870-4444; Fax: 970-879-7406. Rev. George M. Schroeder.

STERLING. *Northeastern Junior College (Sterling)*, St. Anthony Church, 327 S. Third St., 80751. Tel: 303-525-6422. Very Rev. Robert G. Whipkey, V.F.; Michael Wolsbauer.

WESTMINSTER. *Front Range Community College*, c/o Mr. Frank Sullivan, 3645 W. 112 St., 80030. Tel: 303-466-8811; Fax: 303-466-1623.

[Q] MISCELLANEOUS LISTINGS

DENVER. *Catholic Alumni Club of Denver, Inc.* P.O. Box 6111, Cherry Creek Station, 80206. Tel: 303-756-7659.

**Colorado Vincentian Volunteers*, 1732 Pearl St., 80203. Tel: 303-863-8141. Bill Jaster, Exec. Dir.

Denver Catholic Register, Archdiocesan Religious Newspaper, 200 Josephine St., 80206. Tel: 303-388-4411. Francis X. Maier, General Mgr.

Elementary Education Fund, 200 Josephine St., 80206. Tel: 303-388-4411.

Francis of Assisi Foundation of Colorado, Inc., 2626 Osceola St., 80211. Tel: 303-433-6268. Franciscan Sisters, Daughters of the Sacred Hearts of Jesus and Mary, (Wheaton, IL).

Hmong Catholic Community, All Saints Parish, 2559 S. Federal Blvd., 80219. Tel: 303-922-3758; 429-6427.

Kateri Catholic Indian Community of Colorado, 2340 S. University Blvd #32, 80210. Tel: 303-778-5966. Rev. John Q. O'Connell, C.M.

Marycrest Health System, 2861 W. 52nd Ave., 80221. Tel: 303-458-8611; Fax: 303-477-4105.

Mercy Housing, Inc., 601 E. 18th Ave., Ste. 150, 80203. Tel: 303-830-3300; Fax: 303-830-3301. Sr. Lillian Murphy, Pres.

Mercy Services Corp., 601 E. 18th Ave., Ste. 150, 80203. Tel: 303-830-3300. Geraldine M. Hoyler, C.S.C., Pres.

Decatur Place, 601 E. 18th Ave., Ste. 150, 80203. Tel: 303-830-3300. Mary Helen Sandoval, Pres.

Homes Again Program, 601 E. 18th Ave., Ste. 150, 80203. Tel: 303-830-3300. Mary Helen Sandoval, Pres.

Mercy Housing Colorado, 601 E. 18th Ave., Ste. 150, 80203. Tel: 303-830-3300. Mary Helen Sandoval, Pres.

Mercy Properties, Inc., 601 E. 18th Ave., Ste. 150, 80203. Tel: 303-830-3397. Mary Helen Sandoval, Contact Person.

Willow Street Apartments, 601 E. 18th Ave., Ste. 150, 80203. Tel: 303-830-3397. Mary Helen Sandoval, Contact Person.

Mercy Holly Park East, 601 E. 18th Ave., Ste. 150, 80203. Tel: 303-830-3397. Mary Helen Sandoval, Contact Person.

Mercy Holly Park West, 601 E. 18th Ave., Ste. 150, 80203. Tel: 303-830-3397. Mary Helen Sandoval, Contact Person.

Mercy Green Mountain Manor, 601 E. 18th Ave., Ste. 150, 80203. Tel: 303-830-3397. Mary Helen Sandoval, Contact Person.

S.E.T. of Colorado, Inc., dba Health S.E.T., Raleigh Bldg., 4200 N. Conejos #436, 80204. Tel: 303-534-8002. Jim Elfeine, Exec. Dir.

Sacred Heart House of Denver, 2844 Lawrence, 80205. Tel: 303-296-6686. Sr. Maureen Kottenstette, C.S.J., Exec. Dir.

Saint Joseph Hospital Foundation, 1835 Franklin St., 80218. Tel: 303-837-7043; Fax: 303-837-7115. Roger A. Goodwin, Exec. Dir.

St. Vincent DePaul Society Denver-Metro Council, 1300 S. Steele St., 80210. Tel: 303-777-8367. Leonard J. Langenderfer, Pres.; Robert S. Huff, Exec. Sec.

**Sisters of St. Francis Foundation*, 2861 W. 52nd Ave., 80221. Tel: 303-458-5084; Fax: 303-477-4105. Sisters of St. Francis. Sr. Cecelia Linenbrink, O.S.F., Contact.

ARVADA.

**Buena Vista, Inc.*, P.O. Box 745475, 80006-5475. Tel: 303-426-6622; 941-947-8545; Fax: 303-657-9428. Peg Bisgrove, Pres.

ENGLEWOOD. *Queen of the Apostles Mission Association, Inc.*, 8035 S. Quebec St., 80112-3118. Tel: 303-770-3240; Fax: 303-770-0415. Rachel Bresnahan, Pres.

ESTES PARK.

**Our Lady of Tenderness, Poustinia*, Box 4311, 80517. Tel: 970-586-9433; 586-0656. Lucille Dupuis, Dir.

GLENDALE.

**Havican Insurance Co.*, 4100 E. Mississippi Ave., Ste. 1500, 80222. Sisters of the Holy Cross.

LITTLETON. *Auxiliary of Mother Cabrini Shrine*, 7295 S. Steele Cir., 80122. Tel: 303-771-4386. Zoraide Scordo, Founder.

RELIGIOUS INSTITUTES OF MEN REPRESENTED IN THE ARCHDIOCESE

For further details refer to the corresponding bracketed number in the Religious Institutes of Men or Women section.

[0200]—*Benedictine Monks.* (Canon City, CO).—O.S.B.

[]—*Bethlehem Fathers.*—S.M.B.

[0330]—*Brothers of the Christian Schools.*—F.S.C.

[0460]—*Brothers of the Poor of St. Francis.*—C.F.P.

[0470]—*The Capuchin Friars.* (Denver, CO).—O.F.M.Cap.

[0350]—*Cistercians of the Strict Observance-Trappists.* (St. Benedict Abbey).—O.C.S.O.

[]—*Congregation of Mother Coredemptrix.* (Carthage, MO).—C.M.C.

[1330]—*Congregation of the Mission.* (Western Prov.).—C.M.

[0520]—*Franciscan Friars*. (Provs. of the Most Holy Name of Jesus & Our Lady of Guadalupe).—O.F.M.
[0690]—*Jesuit Fathers and Brothers*. (Missouri, Milwaukee, Oregon, Maryland Provs.).—S.J.
[0800]—*Maryknoll*. (Denver).—M.M.
[0430]—*Order of Preachers-Dominicans*. (Prov. of St. Albert the Great).—O.P.
[1030]—*Paulist Fathers*.—C.S.P.
[1070]—*Redemptorist Fathers*. (St. Louis Prov.).—C.SS.R.
[1240]—*Servites*. (Western Prov.).—O.S.M.
[1300]—*Theatine Fathers*. (Rome, Italy).—C.R.

RELIGIOUS INSTITUTES OF WOMEN REPRESENTED IN THE ARCHDIOCESE

[0190]—*Benedictine Nuns*.—O.S.B.
[0230]—*Benedictine Sisters of Pontifical Jurisdiction*. (Colorado Springs, CO; Boulder, CO; Denver, CO; Oklahoma City, OK).—O.S.B.
[]—*Capuchin Poor Clares*.—O.S.C.Cap.
[3110]—*Congregation of Our Lady of the Retreat in the Cenacle*.—R.C.
[2100]—*Congregation of the Humility of Mary*. (Davenport, IA).—C.H.M.
[1780]—*Congregation of the Sisters of the Third Order of St. Francis of Perpetual Adoration*. (La Crosse, WI).—F.S.P.A.
[0760]—*Daughters of Charity of St. Vincent de Paul*.—D.C.
[0960]—*Daughters of Wisdom*.—D.W.
[0420]—*Discalced Carmelite Nuns*.—O.C.D.
[1070-14]—*Dominican Sisters*.—O.P.
[1070-16]—*Dominican Sisters*.—O.P.
[1070-18]—*Dominican Sisters*.—O.P.
[1070-24]—*Dominican Sisters*.—O.P.
[1070-28]—*Dominican Sisters*.—O.P.
[1070-03]—*Dominican Sisters*. Sinsinawa.—O.P.
[]—*Dominican Sisters of the Congregation of St. Cecilia*. (Nashville).
[1240]—*Franciscan Sisters, Daughters of the Sacred Hearts of Jesus and Mary*. (Wheaton, IL).—O.S.F.
[2575]—*Institute of the Sisters of Mercy of the Americas*.—R.S.M.
[2340]—*Little Sisters of the Poor*.—L.S.P.
[2710]—*Missionaries of Charity*.—M.C.
[]—*Missionaries of Charity of Mary Immaculate*.—M.C.M.I.
[2860]—*Missionary Sisters of the Sacred Heart*.—M.S.C.
[3130]—*Our Lady of Victory Missionary Sisters*.—O.L.V.M.
[1680]—*School Sisters of St. Francis*. (Milwaukee, WI).—O.S.F.
[0440]—*Sisters of Charity of Cincinnati, Ohio*.—S.C.
[0480]—*Sisters of Charity of Leavenworth, Kansas*.—S.C.L.
[0430]—*Sisters of Charity of the Blessed Virgin Mary*.—B.V.M.
[2360]—*Sisters of Loretto at the Foot of the Cross*. (Nerinx, KY).—S.L.
[2990]—*Sisters of Notre Dame*.—S.N.D.
[1705]—*Sisters of St. Francis of Assisi*. (Milwaukee, WI).—O.S.F.
[1630]—*Sisters of St. Francis of Penance and Christian Charity*.—O.S.F.
[1640]—*Sisters of St. Francis of Perpetual Adoration*. (Colorado Springs, CO).—O.S.F.
[3830-05]—*Sisters of St. Joseph*.—C.S.J.
[3830-15]—*Sisters of St. Joseph*.—C.S.J.
[3840]—*Sisters of St. Joseph of Carondelet*.—C.S.J.
[3930]—*Sisters of St. Joseph of the Third Order of St. Francis*. (Immaculate Conception Prov.).—S.S.J.-T.O.S.F.
[1830]—*Sisters of the Good Shepherd*.—R.G.S.
[]—*Sisters of the New Covenant*.—S.N.C.
[3260]—*Sisters of the Precious Blood (Dayton, OH)*.—C.PP.S.
[1720]—*Sisters of the Third Order Regular of St. Francis of the Congregation of Our Lady of Lourdes*. (Rochester, MN).—O.S.F.

ARCHDIOCESAN CEMETERIES

WHEAT RIDGE. *Archdiocese of Denver Mortuary at Mt. Olivet, Inc.*, 12801 W. 44th Ave., 80033. Tel: 303-425-9511.

Mount Olivet Cemetery, 12801 W. 44th Ave., 80033. Tel: 303-424-7785.

NECROLOGY

† Gottschalk, Andrew E., (Retired). —Died April 1, 1996.
† Lievens, Joseph J., (Retired). —Died Nov. 3, 1995.
† McMahon, Donald A., (Retired). —Died Nov. 18, 1995.

Diocese of Des Moines

(Dioecesis Desmoinensis)

Most Reverend

JOSEPH L. CHARRON, C.PP.S., S.T.D.

Bishop of Des Moines; ordained June 3, 1967; appointed Titular Bishop of Bencenna and Auxiliary Bishop of Saint Paul and Minneapolis; appointed November 6, 1989; consecrated January 25, 1990; appointed Bishop of Des Moines; appointed November 12, 1993.

Chancery: 601 Grand Ave., P.O. Box 1816, Des Moines, IA, 50306. Tel.: 515-243-7653; Fax: 515-237-5070.

Web site address: http://members.aol.com/cathdiodm

E-mail address: cathdiodm@aol.com

ERECTED BY POPE S. PIUS X, AUGUST 12, 1911.

Square Miles 12,446.

Legal Title: "The Roman Catholic Diocese of Des Moines."

Comprises that part of the State of Iowa which is bounded on the east by the eastern boundaries of the Counties of Polk, Warren, Lucas and Wayne; on the south by the State of Missouri; on the west by the Missouri River; and on the north by the northern boundaries of the Counties of Harrison, Shelby, Audubon, Guthrie, Dallas and Polk.

PATRONS OF THE DIOCESE: I. BLESSED VIRGIN MARY QUEEN; II. POPE SAINT PIUS X. Diocese solemnly consecrated to the Immaculate Heart of Mary on May 16, 1948.

For legal titles of parishes and diocesan institutions, consult the Chancery Office.

STATISTICAL OVERVIEW

Personnel	
Bishop	1
Priests: Diocesan Active in Diocese	85
Priests: Active Outside Diocese	5
Priests: Diocesan in Foreign Missions	1
Priests: Retired, Sick or Absent	24
Number of Diocesan Priests	115
Religious Priests in Diocese	7
Extern Priests in Diocese	3
Ordinations:	
Diocesan Priests	4
Transitional Deacons	1
Permanent Deacons in Diocese	53
Total Brothers	4
Total Sisters	128
Parishes	
Parishes	87
With Resident Pastor:	
Resident Diocesan Priests	60
Resident Religious Priests	1
Without Resident Pastor:	
Administered by Priests	25
Administered by Permanent Deacons	1
Missions	1
Welfare	
Catholic Hospitals	3
Total Assisted	583,890
Health Care Centers	1
Total Assisted	5,389
Homes for the Aged	1
Total Assisted	237
Specialized Homes	1
Total Assisted	205
Special Centers for Social Services	4
Total Assisted	31,970
Educational	
Diocesan Students in Other Seminaries	8
Total Seminarians	8
High Schools, Diocesan and Parish	2
Total Students	1,380
Elementary Schools, Diocesan and Parish	15
Total Students	4,673
Catechesis/Religious Education:	
High School Students	2,064
Elementary Students	9,232
Total Students Under Catholic Instruction	17,357
Teachers in the Diocese:	
Priests	1
Brothers	1
Sisters	11
Lay Teachers	305
Vital Statistics	
Receptions into the Church:	
Infant Baptism Totals	1,801
Adult Baptism Totals	238
Received into Full Communion	544
First Communions	1,852
Confirmations	1,628
Marriages:	
Catholic	319
Interfaith	335
Total Marriages	654
Deaths	709
Total Catholic Population	97,105
Total Population	671,091

Former Bishops—Most Rev. AUSTIN DOWLING, D.D., first Bishop of Des Moines; ord. June 24, 1891; appt. Bishop Jan. 31, 1912; cons. April 25, 1912; promoted to the See of St. Paul, Jan., 1919.—Most Rev. THOMAS W. DRUMM, D.D., Bishop of Des Moines; ord. Dec. 21, 1901; cons. May 21, 1919; died Oct. 24, 1933.—Most Rev. GERALD T. BERGAN, D.D., ord. Oct. 28, 1915; appt. Mar. 24, 1934; cons. June 13, 1934; enthroned June 21, 1934; elevated to Archiepiscopal dignity and promoted to Omaha Feb. 9, 1948.—Most Rev. EDWARD C. DALY, O.P., S.T.M., Bishop of Des Moines; ord. June 12, 1921; appt. March 13, 1948; cons. May 13, 1948; named Asst. at Papal Throne, May 23, 1958; died Nov. 23, 1964.—Most Rev. GEORGE J. BISKUP, D.D., ord. March 19, 1937; appt. Auxiliary Bishop of Dubuque, March 9, 1957; cons. April 24, 1957; appt. Bishop of Des Moines, Feb. 3, 1965; appt. Coadjutor Archbishop of Indianapolis, July 26, 1967; succeeded to See Jan. 14, 1970.—Most Rev. MAURICE J. DINGMAN, D.D., Retired Bishop of Des Moines; ord. Dec. 8, 1939; appt. Bishop of Des Moines April 2, 1968; cons. June 19, 1968; installed July 7, 1968; retired Oct. 14, 1986; died Feb. 1, 1992.—Most Rev. WILLIAM H. BULLOCK, ord. June 7, 1952; appt. Auxiliary Bishop of St. Paul and Minneapolis and Titular Bishop of Natchez June 3, 1980; cons. Aug. 12, 1980; appt. Bishop of Des Moines Feb. 10, 1987; installed April 2, 1987; appt. to Diocese of Madison April 13, 1993.

Vicar General and Moderator of the Curia—Rev. Msgr. LAWRENCE BEESON, *P.O. Box 1816, Des Moines, 50306.* Tel: 515-237-5044; 246-5983 (Residence).

Chancery—601 Grand Ave., P.O. Box 1816, Des Moines, 50306. Tel: 515-243-7653; Fax: 515-237-5070. Office Hours: Mon.-Fri. 8:30-4:30.

Chancellor—LAWRENCE BREHENY,All Matrimonial Correspondence to Tribunal.

Secretary to the Bishop—PATRICIA ROSS, *P.O. Box 1816, Des Moines, 50306.* Tel: 515-237-5039; Fax: 515-237-5071.

Finance Officer—MARY LOU HERRING, *P.O. Box 1816, Des Moines, 50306.* Tel: 515-237-5012.

Vicar for Finance—Rev. Msgr. EDWARD HURLEY.

Diocesan Tribunal—601 Grand Ave., P.O. Box 1816, Des Moines, 50306. Tel: 515-237-5030.

Judicial Vicar—Rev. Msgr. LAWRENCE BEESON, J.C.D.

Director of Tribunal—Sr. CAMILLA HUBER, O.S.M.

Defenders of the Bond—Revs. MICHAEL AMADEO, J.C.L.; LAWRENCE R. HOFFMANN; DANIEL F. KRETTEK, J.C.L.; DAVID J. POLICH; Deacons ROBERT L. BRAY, J.D.; ROBERT L. HOWE.

Judges—Rev. Msgr. LAWRENCE A. BEESON, J.C.D.; Revs. DANIEL L. CLARKE; GARRY A. CULVER, J.C.L.; Rev. Msgr. STEPHEN L. ORR; Rev. SAMUEL I. PALMER, J.C.L.; Rev. Msgr. EDWARD B. PFEFFER, J.C.L.; Rev. THOMAS J. PFEFFER, J.C.L.

Notary—DORIS KLANG.

Advocates—JOAN BERNER; RICHARD E. GUBBELS; Sr. CAMILLA HUBER, O.S.M.; Revs. EUGENE R. KOCH; JOHN P. LUDWIG; VINCE G. ROSONKE.

Diocesan Consultors—Rev. Msgr. LAWRENCE BEESON; Rev. Msgr. FRANK BOGNANNO; Rev. Msgr. GERALD STESSMAN; Rev. Msgr. JOHN MCILHON; Revs. JOHN ACREA; PAUL BIANCHI; GORDON GITTINS.

Diocesan Corporation Board—Most Rev. JOSEPH L. CHARRON; Rev. Msgr. LAWRENCE A. BEESON; CYNTHIA EISENHAUER; MICHAEL RILEY; MARY LOU HERRING; LAWRENCE BREHENY.

Diocesan Offices and Directors

Catholic Charities—LAWRENCE BREHENY, Exec. Dir.; Rev. DUANE WEILAND, Assoc. Dir., *601 Grand Ave., P.O. Box 723, Des Moines, 50303.* Tel: 515-237-5058.

Social Service Division—Des Moines Office, 601 Grand Ave., P.O. Box 723, Des Moines, 50303. Tel: 515-237-5026.

Council Bluffs Office—411 E. Broadway, Council Bluffs, 51503. Tel: 712-328-3086; Fax: 712-322-1388.

Charismatic Renewal Liaison—Rev. Msgr. FRANK E. BOGNANNO, *St. Augustin, 545 42nd, Des Moines, 50312.* Tel: 515-255-1175.

Communications, Office of—THOMAS CHAPMAN, Dir., *P.O. Box 1816, Des Moines, 50306.* Tel: 515-237-5041; Fax: 515-237-5071.

Continuing Education for Clergy—Rev. GORDON GITTINS, Dir., *St. Michael's Church, 1912 18th St., Harlan, 51537.* Tel: 712-755-5244.

Deaf-Handicapped, Office of—Sr. HELEN SEIVERT, O.S.F., Dir., *315 W. Pierce St., Council Bluffs, 51501.* Tel: 712-328-3086.

Advancement Office—JACK JONES, Exec. Dir., *P.O. Box 1816, Des Moines, 50306.* Tel: 515-237-5007.

Diocesan Council of Catholic Women—LOIS SCHMID, Pres., *Rte. 3 Box. 217, Red Oak, 51566.* Tel: 712-623-4075. Rev. GORDON GITTINS, *St. Michael's Church, 1912 18th St., Harlan, 51537.* Tel: 712-755-5244.

Diaconate (Permanent)—Deacon GENE JAGER, Dir.

Evangelization, Office of—JIM BOND, Dir., *P.O. Box 1816, Des Moines, 50306.* Tel: 515-237-5046.

Hispanic Ministry, Office of—Rev. KEVIN CAMERON, *Visitation, 1271 E. 9th St., Des Moines, 50316.* Tel: 515-266-6695.

Holy Childhood, Pontifical Association—Dr. LUVERN GUBBELS, *P.O. Box 1816, Des Moines, 50306.* Tel: 515-237-5013.

Legislative Activities, Office of—Vacant, *601 Grand Ave., P.O. Box 723, Des Moines, 50303.* Tel: 515-237-5021.

Newspaper—"The Catholic Mirror", TOM CHAPMAN, Editor, *601 Grand Ave., P.O. Box 10372, Des Moines, 50306.* Tel: 515-237-5060.

Priests' Pension Fund Society—Most Rev. JOSEPH L. CHARRON; Rev. ED KELLY; Rev. Msgr. EDWARD HURLEY; Rev. ROBERT SCHOEMANN; Rev. Msgr. RAYMOND CONLEY.

Propagation of the Faith—Rev. PAUL BIANCHI, Dir., *Box 1816, Des Moines, 50306-1816.* Tel: 515-237-5058.

Religious Education Office—NANCY THOMPSON, Dir., *P.O. Box 1816, Des Moines, 50306.* Tel: 515-237-5052.

St. Vincent de Paul Society—Rev. JOHN LUDWIG, Chap., *Drake Newman Center, 1342 30th St., Des Moines, 50311.* Tel: 515-274-3473.

Schools—Dr. LUVERN GUBBELS, Supt./Dir. Educ. Elementary School Coords.: Sr. JUDITH SHEAHAN, B.V.M.; MARJ CANAN, *P.O. Box 1816, Des Moines, 50306.* Tel: 515-237-5013.

Office of Social Justice—Vacant, *P.O. Box 723, Des Moines, 50303.*

Vocations—Rev. DAVID FLEMING, Dir.; Sr. EILEEN MALLOY, C.S.C., Assoc. Dir., *P.O. Box 1816, Des Moines, 50306.* Tel: 515-237-5014.

Office of Worship (Liturgy, Music, Art and Architecture)—JIM BOND, Dir., *601 Grand Ave., P.O. Box 1816, Des Moines, 50306.* Tel: 515-237-5043.

Youth Ministry, Office of—Rev. JAMES WILWERDING, *St. Thomas More Center, 6177 Panorama Rd., Panora, 50216.* Tel: 515-755-3164.

CLERGY, PARISHES, MISSIONS AND PAROCHIAL SCHOOLS

CITY OF DES MOINES
(Polk County)

1—ST. AMBROSE CATHEDRAL (1856), Revs. James W. Kiernan, Rector; Felix Onuora, C.S.Sp.; Sr. Patricia Scherer, Pastoral Min.; Sr. Virginia Jennings, O.S.F., D.R.E.; Deacons Lee Pao Yang; Robert Bray; Dave Garza; Joseph Huynh; Michael McCarthy.
Res., 607 High St., 50309. Tel: 515-288-7411. [JC]

2—ALL SAINTS (1914), Rev. Anthony Aiello.
650 N.E. 52nd Ave., 50313.
Res., 3509 3rd St., 50313. Tel: 515-288-7539. [JC]
Parish Center: 3411 3rd St., 50313. Tel: 515-243-5987.

3—CHRIST THE KING (1939), Rev. David J. Polich. Pastoral Ministers: Sr. Barbara L. Marshall, S.F.C.C.; Sr. Susan D. Widdel, R.S.M.
Res., 5711 S.W. 9th St., 50315. Tel: 515-285-2888.
School—701 Wall St., 50315. Tel: 515-285-3349; Fax: 515-285-0381.
Lay Teachers 15; Students 209.
Catechesis/Religious Programs—Students 260.

4—DRAKE NEWMAN PARISH (1969). (Non-Territorial University Parish). Rev. John Ludwig.
Church—1342 30th St., 50311. Tel: 515-274-3473; Fax: 515-274-3474.

5—HOLY TRINITY (1920), Rev. Msgr. Gerald J. Stessman; Rev. Mike McLaughlin; Deacons Robert Howe; Jeff Boehlert.
Res., 2926 Beaver Ave., 50310. Tel: 515-255-3162; Fax: 515-255-1381.
School—Lay Teachers 30; Students 552.
Catechesis/Religious Programs—Students 145.

6—ST. ANTHONY'S (1905), Revs. Lawrence R. Hoffmann; Raymond Higgins.
Res., 15 Indianola Rd., 50315. Tel: 515-244-4709.
School—16 Columbus Ave., 50315. Tel: 515-243-1874.
Sisters 2; Lay Teachers 23; Students 377.
Catechesis/Religious Programs—Tel: 515-244-1119.
Students 255.

7—ST. AUGUSTIN'S (1923), Rev. Msgr. Frank E. Bognanno; Rev. John Lorenz; Deacon Dennis Luft.
Res., 545 42nd St., 50312. Tel: 515-255-1175; Fax: 515-255-7969.
School—4320 Grand Ave., 50312. Tel: 515-279-5947; Fax: 515-279-8049.
Lay Teachers 16; Students 290.

8—BASILICA OF SAINT JOHN (1905), Rev. Msgr. Frank Chiodo; Rev. Richard Wagner; Deacons John Jarvis; George Catanzano.
Res., 1915 University Ave., 50314. Tel: 515-244-3101; Fax: 515-244-3165.
School—Holy Family School, (Grades PreK-3). (Consolidated) 1913 University Ave., 50314. Tel: 515-288-6455.
Lay Teachers 19; Students 202.

9—ST. JOSEPH'S (1924), Rev. Msgr. Robert J. Chamberlain; Rev. Remigius Okere; Deacon Marvin Brewer.
Res., 3300 Easton Blvd., 50317. Tel: 515-266-2226.
School—Tel: 515-266-3433.
Lay Teachers 14; Students 196.
Catechesis/Religious Programs—Students 150.

10—ST. MARY OF NAZARETH (1964), Revs. Gerald E. Ryan; David Santoro, O.P.
Res., 4605 N.W. 47th Ct., P.O. Box 13170, 50310. Tel: 515-276-4042; Fax: 515-252-1995.
Catechesis/Religious Programs—Tel: 515-276-7589.
Students 387.

11—ST. PETER'S (1915), Rev. John Dorton; Deacon Eugene Jager.
Res., 607 E. 18th St., 50316. Tel: 515-266-4265.

12—ST. THERESA OF THE CHILD JESUS (1951), Revs. Robert A. Hoefler; Tan Van Tran; James Kirby.
Res., 1230 Merle Hay Rd., 50311. Tel: 515-279-4654; Fax: 515-277-0838. [JC]
School—5810 Carpenter, 50311. Tel: 515-277-0178; Fax: 515-277-0838.
Lay Teachers 20; Students 386.
Catechesis/Religious Programs—Students 150.

13—VISITATION (1882), Revs. Thomas Pfeffer; Kevin Cameron, Hispanic Ministry.
Res., 1271 E. 9th St., 50316. Tel: 515-266-6695.
School—Holy Family, (Grades 4-8). (Consolidated). Tel: 515-262-8025.
Lay Teachers 6; Students 204.
Catechesis/Religious Programs—Tel: 515-266-1027.
Students 180.
Mission—Des Moines, Polk Co., Our Lady of Guadalupe, 601 S.E. 8th St., 50316. Tel: 515-243-9585.

OUTSIDE THE CITY OF DES MOINES

Adair, Adair Co., St. John (1879). Attended by St. Mary, Anita. Rev. Albert G. Sherbo.
Res., P.O. Box 277, Anita, 50020. Tel: 712-762-3484; 762-3773 (Office).

Adel, Dallas Co., St. John (1917), Rev. Martin G. Chevalier; Sr. Christine F. Ramirez, Pastoral Min.
Mailing Address: P.O. Box 151, 50003-0151. Tel: 515-993-4482.
Catechesis/Religious Programs—Students 128.

Afton, Union Co., St. Edward (1878). Attended by Paul VI Pastoral Ministry from Creston.
Mailing Address: 406 W. Clark, Creston, 50801. Tel: 515-782-5278; Fax: 515-782-5924.
Church—104 W. Union, 50830. Tel: 515-347-8452.

Altoona, Polk Co., SS. John and Paul (1983), Rev. Vince G. Rosonke.
Res., 114 13th St., S.E., 50009. Tel: 515-967-3796; Fax: 515-967-7197.
Catechesis/Religious Programs—Students 340.

Anita, Cass Co., St. Mary (1924), Rev. Albert Sherbo.
Church—P.O. Box 277, 50020. Tel: 712-762-3484; 762-3773 (Office).

Ankeny, Polk Co., Our Lady's Immaculate Heart (1961), Revs. Gregory Leach; Randy Richman; Deacons Dan McGuire; Richard Ziller.
Res., 510 E. First St., 50021. Tel: 515-964-3038; Fax: 515-964-5997.
Catechesis/Religious Programs—Tel: 515-964-3545.
Students 1,071.

Atlantic, Cass Co., SS. Peter and Paul (1871), Rev. Richard Gubbels, Admin.; Deacon Fred Cornwell, Pastoral Assoc.
Res., 106 W. 6th St., 50022. Tel: 712-243-4721.
Catechesis/Religious Programs—Tel: 712-243-2144.
Students 305.

Audubon, Audubon Co., St. Patrick (1918), Rev. John C. Maier.
Res., 116 E. Division St., 50025. Tel: 712-563-2283. [CEM]
Catechesis/Religious Programs—Students 200.

Avoca, Pottawattamie Co., St. Mary, Mediatrix of All Graces (1882), Rev. Fred P. Reischl; Deacon Clarence Christensen.
Res., 326 N. Maple St., P.O. Box 38, 51521. Tel: 712-343-6948.
Catechesis/Religious Programs—Students 94.

Bayard, Guthrie Co., St. Patrick (1882), Rev. Tan Van Tran.
Res., 214 Prairie St., P.O. Box 274, 50029. Tel: 712-651-2676.

Bedford, Taylor Co., Sacred Heart. Attended by St. Clare, Clarinda.
Mailing Address: 300 E. Lincoln Blvd., Clarinda, 51632.

Carlisle, Warren Co., St. Elizabeth Seton (1979), Rev. Nelo A. Leto.
Mailing Address: P.O. Box 35, 50047. Tel: 515-989-0659.

Carter Lake, Pottawattamie Co., Our Lady of Carter Lake (1970). Attended by Our Lady, Queen of Apostles, Council Bluffs. Rev. Dennis Trausch.
Church—3501 N. 9th St., 51510. Tel: 712-347-6631; Fax: 712-325-2411.

Casey, Guthrie Co., St. Joseph (1898). Attended by St. Mary, Anita. Rev. Albert Sherbo.
Mailing Address: P.O. Box 277, Anita, 50020. Tel: 712-762-3484.

Chariton, Lucas Co., Sacred Heart (1869), Rev. Allan Stetz. Pastoral Ministers: Sr. Mary Lenz, O.S.F.; Sr. Marie Hodapp, S.S.S.F. Tel: 515-774-5486.
Res., 407 N. Main, 50049. Tel: 515-774-5486 or 515-766-6786.

Churchville, Warren Co., Assumption of the Blessed Virgin Mary (1855), Rev. John O. Bertogli.
Res., P.O. Box 88, St. Mary's, 50241. Tel: 515-297-2267.

Clarinda, Page Co., St. Clare (1942), Rev. Tom Coenen.
Res., 300 E. Lincoln Blvd., 51632. Tel: 712-542-2030.
Catechesis/Religious Programs—Students 58.

Corning, Adams Co., St. Patrick's, Rev. Daniel E. Siepker.
Res., 504 Grove Ave., 50841. Tel: 515-322-3363. [CEM]

Corydon, Wayne Co., St. Francis (1969). Attended by Chariton of the South Central Catholic Ministry Team.
Mailing Address: 213 W. Jackson, 50060. Tel: 515-774-4978.

Council Bluffs, Pottawattamie Co.,

1—HOLY FAMILY, (1908), Rev. Kenneth A. Gross; Deacon Joseph Scurlock.
Res., 2217 Ave. B, 51501. Tel: 712-328-3869.

2—OUR LADY, QUEEN OF APOSTLES, (1957), Revs. Phillip Kruse; Dan Kirby; Deacon Monty Montagne.
Res., 3304 4th Ave., 51501. Tel: 712-323-2916; Fax: 712-328-0228.
Catechesis/Religious Programs—Students 164.

3—ST. PATRICK, (1924), Rev. Msgr. Edward Kelly; Rev. Raphael Masabakhwa; Deacons Charles Hannan; Larry Knotek.
Res., 223 Harmony St., 51503. Tel: 712-323-1484.
Catechesis/Religious Programs—Students 268.

4—ST. PETER, (1887) (German), Rev. Charles Kottas; Deacon Stephen Rallis, Pastoral Min.
Res., One Bluff St., 51503. Tel: 712-322-8889; Fax: 712-323-1442.
St. Francis Worship Center—238 6th St., 51501. Tel: 712-328-7272.

Creston, Union Co., Holy Spirit (1975), Revs. Leonard A. Kenkel, Pastor; John W. Acrea, Assoc. Pastor.
Res., 406 W. Clark, 50801. Tel: 515-782-5278.
Church—Also serving the parish of St. Edward, Afton. 107 W. Howard St., Afton, 50801. Tel: 515-782-2716.
School—St. Malachy, Tel: 515-782-7125; Fax: 515-782-5924.
Lay Teachers 11; Students 103.

Cumberland, Cass Co., St. Timothy (Reno) (1883), Rev. Daniel Krettek.
Mailing Address: P.O. Box 605, Griswold, 51535-0605. Tel: 712-778-4540.

Cumming, Warren Co., St. John (1892), Rev. Robert J. Aubrey; Deacon David O'Brien.
Res., P.O. Box 5, 50061. Tel: 515-981-4855.
Catechesis/Religious Programs—Students 225.

Defiance, Shelby Co., St. Peter (1882), Rev. Thomas G. Crowley.
Res., P.O. Box 127, 51527. Tel: 712-748-3501.

Dunlap, Harrison Co., St. Patrick, Rev. Howard Fitzgerald.
Res., 509 S. 3rd St., 51529. Tel: 712-643-5808.
Catechesis/Religious Programs—Students 164.

Earling, Shelby Co., St. Joseph (1882) (German), Rev. Michael Berner.
Res., P.O. Box 225, 51530. Tel: 712-747-2091.
School—See Shelby County Board of Catholic Education under Education Centers in the Institution section. Tel: 712-747-3081.

Elkhart, Polk Co., St. Mary/Holy Cross (1914), Rev. Randy Richman, Admin.
Res., 214 Washington, P.O. Box 110, 50073. Tel: 515-367-2685.

Exira, Audubon Co., Holy Trinity. Attended by St. Patrick.
116 E. Division St., Audubon, 50025.

Glenwood, Mills Co., Our Lady of the Holy Rosary

(1955), Rev. Paul Monahan; Deacons Joseph Blankenship; Ronald Kohn; Richard Maiers; James Parr.
Res., 24116 Marian Ave., 51534-5291. Tel: 712-527-5211.
Catechesis/Religious Programs—Students 201.

Grand River, Decatur Co., St. Patrick, Rev. John M. Frost.
Res., 222 E. Pearl, Osceola, 50213. Tel: 515-342-2850.

Granger, Dallas Co., Assumption of the Blessed Virgin Mary (1871), Rev. Eugene R. Koch.
Res., 1906 Sycamore, P.O. Box 177, 50109. Tel: 515-999-2239.
School—Tel: 515-999-2211.
Lay Teachers 7; Students 85.
Mission—Woodward, Dallas Co., St. Ann.

Greenfield, Adair Co., St. John (1907), Rev. Dean Nimerichter.
Res., 303 N.E. Elm St., 50849. Tel: 515-743-2641.
Catechesis/Religious Programs—Students 129.

Griswold, Cass Co., Our Lady Of Grace (1911), Rev. Daniel Krettek.
Mailing Address: P.O. Box 605, 51535-0605. Tel: 712-778-4540.

Guthrie Center, Guthrie Co., St. Mary (1906), Rev. Benedict J. Kenkel.
Res., 603 Main St., 50115. Tel: 515-747-2569.

Hamburg, Fremont Co., St. Mary (1874). Attended by St. Mary, Shenandoah. Rev. Donald Bruck.
Res., 1306 Washington St., 51640. Tel: 712-382-2871.

Harlan, Shelby Co., St. Michael (1888), Rev. Gordon Gittins; Deacons Patrick Davitt; Donald Jacobi; John Stessman.
Res., 1912-18th St., 51537. Tel: 712-755-5244; Fax: 712-755-3332.
School—See Shelby County Board of Catholic Education under Education Centers in the Institution section.
Catechesis/Religious Programs—Tel: 712-755-5366; Fax: 712-755-3332.
Students 309.

Imogene, Fremont Co., St. Patrick (1880), Rev. John W. Clarke.
Res., P.O. Box 205, 51645. Tel: 712-386-2123.
Catechesis/Religious Programs—Students 105.

Indianola, Warren Co., St. Thomas Aquinas (1958), Rev. Frank Palmer.
Res., 1202 W. Iowa Ave., 50125. Tel: 515-961-3026.
Catechesis/Religious Programs—Tel: 515-961-0447.
Students 300.

Irish Settlement, Madison Co., St. Patrick (1852), Rev. John O. Bertogli.
Res., P.O. Box 88, St. Marys, 50241. Tel: 515-297-2267.

Jamaica, Guthrie Co., St. Joseph (1903). Attended by St. Patrick, Bayard.
214 Prairie, P.O. Box 274, Bayard, 50029. Tel: 712-651-2676.

Lacona, Warren Co., Holy Trinity Church of Southeast Warren County (1978), Rev. Frank Cordaro.
Res., P.O. Box 145, 50139. Tel: 515-534-4691.
Worship Centers—St. Mary of the Assumption Church, Lacona; St. Augustine Church, Milo; St. Mary of Perpetual Help Church, Rosemont.

Lenox, Taylor Co., St. Patrick (1875). Attended by St. Patrick, Corning.
Church—600 W. Michigan, 50851. Tel: 515-336-2893.

Leon, Decatur Co., St. Brendan (1865) (Irish), Rev. Thomas V. Dooley.
Res., 1001 N.W. Church St., 50144. Tel: 515-446-4789.

Logan, Harrison Co., St. Anne, Rev. John Harmon.
Res., 112 W. 3rd St., P.O. Box 142, 51546. Tel: 712-644-2535.

Maloy, Ringgold Co., Immaculate Conception (1874), Rev. Thomas V. Dooley.
Res., 1001 N.W. Church St., Leon, 50144. Tel: 515-446-4789. [CEM]

Massena, Cass Co., St. Patrick (1888), Deacon Fred Cornwell.
Res., P.O. Box 180, 50853. Tel: 712-779-3397.

Missouri Valley, Harrison Co., St. Patrick (1877), Rev. James F. Kleffman.
Res., 215 N. Seventh St., 51555. Tel: 712-642-3124; Fax: 712-642-2518.
School—219 N. Seventh St., 51555. Tel: 712-642-3155.
Lay Teachers 5; Students 70.

Mondamin, Harrison Co., Holy Family. Attended by St. Anne.
112 W. 3rd St., P.O. Box 142, Logan, 51546.

Mt. Ayr, Ringgold Co., St. Joseph (1913). Attended by St. Brendan.
Church—100 N. Polk, 50854. Tel: 515-446-4789.

Neola, Pottawattamie Co., St. Patrick (1882), Rev. Wayne Gubbels; Deacon Mark Stageman.
Res., P.O. Box 127, 51559. Tel: 712-485-2124.

Orient, Adair Co., St. Mark. Attended by St. John, Greenfield. Rev. Dean Nimerichter.
Res., 303 N.E. Elm, Greenfield, 50849. Tel: 515-743-2641.

Osceola, Clarke Co., St. Bernard (1885), Rev. John M. Frost.
Res., 222 E. Pearl, 50213. Tel: 342-2850.

Panama, Shelby Co., St. Mary of the Assumption (1899) (German), Rev. Michael G. Peters.
Res., Box 130, 51562. Tel: 712-489-2030.
School—See Shelby County Board of Catholic Education under Education Centers in the Institution section.

Panora, Guthrie Co., St. Cecilia (1907). Attended by St. Mary, Guthrie Center.
Church—220 N. First St., 50216. Tel: 515-755-2658.

Perry, Dallas Co., St. Patrick (1881), Rev. Daniel J. Clarke.
Res., 1312 3rd St., 50220. Tel: 515-465-4387.
School—1324 5th St., 50220. Tel: 515-465-4186.
Lay Teachers 10; Students 132.

Portsmouth, Shelby Co., St. Mary (1885), Rev. Paul Bianchi.
Res., P.O. Box 98, 51565. Tel: 712-743-2625; Fax: 712-743-2010.
Catechesis/Religious Programs—Students 124.

Red Oak, Montgomery Co., St. Mary (1902), Rev. Jon Kautzky.
Res., 1510 Highland Ave., 51566. Tel: 712-623-2744.
Catechesis/Religious Programs—Students 158.

St. Marys, Warren Co., Immaculate Conception (1871), Rev. John O. Bertogli.
Res., P.O. Box 88, 50241. Tel: 515-297-2267.

Shenandoah, Page Co., St. Mary, Rev. Donald Bruck.
Res., 512 W. Thomas Ave., 51601. Tel: 712-246-1718.
Catechesis/Religious Programs—Students 185.

Stuart, Guthrie Co., All Saints (1876), Rev. Richard L. Bergman.
Res., P.O. Box 605, 50250. Tel: 515-523-1497.
Catechesis/Religious Programs—Students 111.

Urbandale, Polk Co., St. Pius X (1955), Rev. Msgr. Edward Hurley; Rev. Samuel Palmer. Pastoral Ministers: Mary Sue Lone; Barbara Mease; June Wilwert.
Res., 3663 66th St., Des Moines, 50322. Tel: 515-276-2059; Fax: 515-276-8351.
School—3601 66th St., Des Moines, 50322. Tel: 515-276-1061. Roberta Harvey, Prin.
Sisters 1; Lay Teachers 26; Students 400.
Catechesis/Religious Programs—Tel: 515-278-5684. D.R.E.: Mary Heinrich; Mary Green.
Students 630.

Villisca, Montgomery Co., St. Joseph (1947). Attended by St. Clare, Clarinda.
304 E. Lincoln St., Clarinda, 51632. Tel: 712-826-8841.

Walnut, Pottawattamie Co., St. Patrick (1882). Attended by St. Mary, Mediatrix of All Graces, Avoca. Rev. Fred P. Reischl.
Mailing Address: 326 N. Maple St., P.O. Box 38, Avoca, 51521. Tel: 712-343-6948.
Catechesis/Religious Programs—Students 86.

Waukee, Dallas Co., St. Boniface (1880), Rev. Robert L. Schoemann; Sr. Theresa Engel, S.S.S.F., Pastoral Min.
Res., 250 4th St., 50263-9623. Tel: 515-987-4597; Fax: 515-987-5272.
Catechesis/Religious Programs—Students 225.

West Des Moines, Polk Co., Sacred Heart (1892), Rev. Msgr. Joseph J. McDonnell; Rev. Christopher Hartshorn; Deacon Chris Rohwer; Sr. Mary Margaret O'Toole, Pastoral Assoc.
Res., 1627 Grand Ave., 50265. Tel: 515-225-6414.
School—1601 Grand Ave., 50265. Tel: 515-223-1284; Fax: 515-223-9413.
Sisters 2; Lay Teachers 26; Students 517.
Catechesis/Religious Programs—Tel: 515-225-7030; Fax: 515-225-0286.
Students 383.

St. Francis of Assisi, Dallas Co., (1991), Rev. Msgr. Stephen Orr.
7075 Ashworth Rd., 50266. Tel: 515-223-4577; Fax: 515-223-4768.
Catechesis/Religious Programs—Students 505.

Weston, Pottawattamie Co., St. Columbanus (1883). Attended by St. Patrick. Rev. Wayne Gubbels.
Res., St. Patrick's Church, P.O. Box 127, Neola, 51559. Tel: 712-485-2124.

Westphalia, Shelby Co., St. Boniface (1873), Rev. Thomas G. Crowley.
Church—207 Duren Strasse, P.O. Box 86, 51578. Tel: 712-627-4255.

Winterset, Madison Co., St. Joseph (1911), Rev. Msgr. Edward B. Pfeffer.
Res., 607 W. Green St., 50273. Tel: 515-462-1083.
Catechesis/Religious Programs—Students 127.

Woodbine, Harrison Co., Sacred Heart. Attended by St. Patrick's, Dunlap. Rev. Howard Fitzgerald.
33 Seventh St., 51579.

Woodward, Dallas Co., St. Ann (1934). Attended by Assumption of the Blessed Virgin Mary.
1906 Sycamore St., P.O. Box 177, Granger, 50109. Tel: 515-999-2239.

Chaplains of Public Institutions

DES MOINES. *City Chaplaincy Program,* 1610 60th St., 50322. Rev. Arthur McCann.
United States Veterans Hospital, 3019 Pleasant, 50310. Rev. Paul Holt.

CLARINDA. *State Hospital.* Served from St. Clare Church, Clarinda.

COUNCIL BLUFFS. *Iowa School for the Deaf,* 411 E. Broadway, 51503. Tel: 712-322-2449. Sr. Helen Seivert, Chap. & D.R.E.

GLENWOOD. *Glenwood State School.* Vacant.

MITCHELLVILLE. *Iowa Correctional Institution for Women.* Deacon Jim Doyle, Chap. & Coord., Svcs. to Catholic Residents.

On Special Assignment:
Reverend Monsignors—
Beeson, Lawrence A., Vicar Gen.
Reverend Fathers—
Amadeo, Michael, Diocesan Tribunal Office
Culver, Garry, Pastoral Assistance
Fleming, David, Diocesan Dir. Vocations
Weiland, Duane J., Clinical Therapist, Catholic Charities

On Duty Outside the Diocese:
Reverend Fathers—
Fitzgerald, P. Timothy, Notre Dame Center for Pastoral Liturgy, P.O. Box 81, Notre Dame, IN 46556
Freeman, James, Holy Trinity Church, 1300 N. Greasewood, Tucson, AZ 85745
Grant, Robert, St. Ambrose University, Davenport, IA 52803
Koch, Paul M., Casilla 919, Santa Cruz, Bolivia
Polich, James, Conception Seminary College, Conception, MO 64433
Richter, John, 2001 Westfield Ct., Apt. C, St. Louis, MO 63143

Retired:
Reverend Monsignors—
Conley, Raymond J., 1390 Buffalo Rd., West Des Moines, IA 50265
Connelly, Paul J., 615 Park St., #1501, Des Moines, IA 50309
Deere, Gerald, 128 Baughn St., Council Bluffs, IA 51503
Devine, W. J., Sagamore Towers No. 2, 95 Squantum St., Apt. 609, Quincy, MA 02169
Gorman, John, 1390 Buffalo Rd., West Des Moines, IA 50265
Kane, Bartholomew, 600 Locust St., Atlantic, IA 50022
Kovacs, John F., 1390 Buffalo Rd., West Des Moines, IA 50265
McIlhon, John J., 1390 Buffalo Rd., West Des Moines, IA 50265
Ring, Arthur R., 4317 Ovid Ave., Des Moines, IA 50310
Ryan, Joseph P., 1390 Buffalo Rd., West Des Moines, IA 50265
Schulte, Joseph M., 1390 Buffalo Rd., West Des Moines, IA 50265
Schwarte, Michael W., P.O. Box 43, Portsmouth, IA 51565
Wadsworth, James, 600 Locust, Atlantic, IA 50022
Reverend Fathers—
Cunningham, John E., 1390 Buffalo Rd., West Des Moines, IA 50265
Daleke, Don, 9125 Meadow Run Way, San Diego, CA 92100
Elias, Woodrow, 100 W. Moore Rd., No. 414, Pharr, TX 78577
Fenelon, David, 934 Lincoln St., Waterloo, IA 50703
Gaul, Cornelius, P.O. Box 59, R.R., Earling, IA 51530
Klein, Eugene J., R.R. 1, Box 83, Earling, IA 51530
Peterson, Cyril, Longview Home, Inc., Rm. 20, 1010 Longview Dr., Missouri Valley, IA 51555
Reece, Frederick W., 2929-35th St., Des Moines, IA 50310
Reisz, Adam, R.R. 2, Dunlap, IA 51529
Ryan, John R., 1173 20th Pl., West Des Moines, IA 50265

Permanent Deacons:
Blankenship, Joseph
Boehlert, Jeffrey
Bray, Robert
Brewer, Marvin
Catanzano, George
Christensen, Clarence
Coan, Joseph
Cord, Michael
Cornwell, Fred
Critelli, Anthony
Davitt, Patrick
Doyle, James
Erickson, Gregg
Garza, David
Gaul, Leo
Hannan, Charles
Heitkotter, Jerome
Herman, James
Howe, Robert
Huynh, Joseph
Jacobi, Donald
Jager, Gene
Jarvis, John
Kirlin, Dennis
Klein, Marvin
Knotek, Lawrence
Kohn, Ronald
Leininger, Jerry
Lovell, David
Lovell, Dennis
Luft, Dennis
Maiers, Richard
McCarthy, Michael
McGuire, Dan
Miller, Edward
Montagne, Monty
O'Brien, David
Parr, James
Rallis, El
Richardson, Alan
Rohwer, Chris
Scurlock, Joseph
Stageman, Mark
Starbuck, Tom
Stessman, Gail
Stessman, John
Sullivan, Robert
Von Behren, Lyle
Webering, James
Wolford, Charles
Yang, LyPao
Ziller, Richard

INSTITUTIONS LOCATED IN THE DIOCESE

[A] EDUCATION CENTERS

COUNCIL BLUFFS. *Council Bluffs Area Catholic Education Systems, Inc.*, 400 Gleason Ave., 51503. Tel: 712-328-9567. John F. Cronin, Ph.D., President.

St. Albert Junior High School. (Grades 7-8), 400 Gleason Ave., 51503. Tel: 712-328-2316. Rev. Phillip Hobt. Lay Teachers 8; Students 172.

St. Albert Intermediate School. (Grades 4-6), 3330 Fourth Ave., 51501. Tel: 713-322-7004. Lay Teachers 7; Students 177.

St. Albert Primary School. (Grades PreK-3), 2912 9th Ave., 51501. Tel: 712-323-3703. Lay Teachers 15; Students 362.

Religious Education Center, 424 Gleason Ave., 51503. Tel: 712-322-4339. Mary B. Fisher, Dir.

PANAMA. *Shelby County Board of Catholic Education*, 208 St. Mary's Ave., 51562-0183.

Elementary Schools: Shelby County Catholic Schools. Attendance Centers:

St. Mary's Center. (Grades PreK-3), 208 St. Mary's Ave., 51562-0183. Tel: 712-489-2727. Lay Teachers 5; Students 113.

St. Joseph's Center. (Grades 4-8), 208 Main St., Earling, 51530-0227. Tel: 712-747-3081. Lay Teachers 5; Students 103.

St. Michael's Center. (Grades K-6), 205 College Blvd., Harlan, 51537. Tel: 712-755-5634. Lay Teachers 7; Students 114.

WEST DES MOINES. *St. Joseph Educational Center*, 1400 Buffalo Rd., 50265. Tel: 515-225-3000. Rev. Msgr. Michael N. Hess, Pres.; Rev. James M. Laurenzo.

Religious Education. Sr. Nancy Brousseau, O.P., Dir. Adult and Youth Ministries.

[B] HIGH SCHOOLS, INTERPAROCHIAL

COUNCIL BLUFFS. *Saint Albert Catholic Schools*, 400 Gleason Ave., 51503. Tel: 712-328-2316. John F. Cronin, Ph.D., Pres., Saint Albert High School (Grades 9-12).
Serving all parishes in Council Bluffs; St. Patrick, Missouri Valley; St. Patrick, Neola; Holy Rosary, Glenwood; St. Columbanus, Weston. Priests 1; Lay Instructors 37; Students 297.

WEST DES MOINES. *Dowling High School*, 1400 Buffalo Rd., 50265. Tel: 515-225-3000; Fax: 515-222-1056. Rev. Msgr. Michael N. Hess, Pres.; James Dowdle, Prin.; Mary Bustin, Registrar; Rev. Lyle Peters.
Serving all parishes in Des Moines; Sacred Heart, West Des Moines; St. Francis of Assisi, West Des Moines; St. Boniface, Waukee; Assumption, Granger; St. John, Cumming; St. Mary, Elkhart; Holy Cross, Elkhart; SS. John and Paul, Atoona; Immaculate Heart, Ankeny. Priests 3; Sisters 3; Lay Teachers 61; Students 1,070.

[C] GENERAL HOSPITALS

DES MOINES. *Mercy Hospital Medical Center*, 6th & University Ave., 50314. Tel: 515-247-3121.
For a complete listing, refer to the Hospitals section.

CORNING. *Mercy Midlands: Mercy Hospital*, Rosary Dr., P.O. Box 368, 50841. Tel: 515-322-3121; Fax: 515-322-4872.
For a complete listing, refer to the Hospitals section.

COUNCIL BLUFFS. *Bergan Mercy Health System: Mercy Hospital*, 800 Mercy Dr., 51502. Tel: 712-328-5000; Fax: 712-328-5202.
For a complete listing, refer to the Hospitals section.

[D] HOMES FOR AGED

JOHNSTON. *Bishop Drumm Retirement Center*, 5837 Winwood Dr., 50131. Tel: 515-270-1100; Fax: 515-276-1714.
For a complete listing, refer to the Special Care Facilities section.

[E] SPECIAL CARE FACILITIES

DES MOINES. *House of Mercy*, 1409 Clark St., 50314-1964. Tel: 515-243-2424; Fax: 515-243-0318.
For a complete listing, refer to the Special Care Facilities section.

[F] SECULAR INSTITUTES

DES MOINES. *Institute of the Heart of Jesus*, P.O. Box 4634, 50306. Secular Priests and Lay People. Rev. John F. Lorenz.

[G] SPIRITUAL MINISTRY TO THE DIOCESE

DES MOINES. *Emmaus House*, 1521 Center St., 50314. Tel: 515-282-4839. Co-Directors: Sr. Mary Dingman, S.S.S.F.

[H] NEWMAN CENTERS

DES MOINES. *Drake Newman Center*, 1342-30th St., 50311. Tel: 515-274-3473.
E-mail: newman@acad.drake.edn
Rev. John Ludwig. Students 750; Non-Students 250.

[I] MISCELLANEOUS LISTINGS

DES MOINES. *American-International-Agrimissio*, 1900 Hub Tower, 50309.

Bishop's Endowment Fund Foundation, 601 Grand Ave., 50309.

City Hospital Chaplaincy Service, 1610 60th St., 50322-6106. Tel: 515-255-1846. Rev. Arthur McCann.
Serving all non-Catholic hospitals in Des Moines.

Dowling-St. Joseph Alumni Foundation, 1400 Buffalo Rd., 50265. Tel: 515-225-3000. James Swift, Pres.; Rev. Msgr. Michael N. Hess, Sec.; Bob Ligouri, Vice Pres. Devel.

Life in the Spirit Community, Inc., 4601 Ovid Ave., 50310. Tel: 515-255-7534. Michael Freilinger, Coord.

Mercy Child Development Center, 6th & University, 50314. Tel: 515-247-4200. Diane Kraemer, Mgr.

Mercy Foundation of Des Moines, 921 Sixth Ave., Ste. A, 50314-1200. Tel: 515-247-3248. William G. Bolin, Pres.

National Catholic Rural Life Conference, 4625 Beaver Ave., 50310. Tel: 515-270-2634; Fax: 515-270-9447.
E-mail: ncrlc@aol.com
Most Rev. William Skylstad, S.J., Pres., (Bishop of Spokane); Bro. David G. Andrews, C.S.C., Exec. Dir.

Roman Catholic Pastoral Center Foundation, 601 Grand Ave., 50309.

Roman Catholic Priests' Medical Fund Foundation, 601 Grand Ave., 50309.

Roman Catholic Seminary Fund Foundation, 601 Grand Ave., 50309.

St. Joseph Emergency Shelter, 1535 - 11th St., 50314.

St. Mary Family Center, 1248 E. 12th, 50316.

Society of Saint Vincent de Paul, 1426 6th Ave., 50314. Tel: 515-282-8327. Virginia Klemm, District Pres.; Larry Schmitz, Vice Pres.

Society of St. John (Brothers of Saint Benedict), 1915 University Ave., 50314. Tel: 515-244-3101. Rev. Frank E. Chiodo, Supr. Brothers 4; Oblates 1.

COUNCIL BLUFFS. *Mercy Hospital Foundation, Council Bluffs*, 800 Mercy Dr., P.O. Box 1C, 51502. Tel: 712-328-5585. Richard A. Hachten, II, Pres.

St. Albert Educational Foundation, 400 Gleason Ave., 51503. Tel: 712-328-9567.

St. Joseph Catholic Cemetery Association, Box 32, R.R. 3, 51501. Tel: 712-322-7963. John E. O'Connor, Mgr.

GRISWOLD. *Wakonda Prayer House*, Box 370, 51535. Tel: 712-778-4325. Rev. La Vern Wingert.

HARLAN. *Shelby County Catholic Education Foundation*, 711 Court St., 51537.

JOHNSTON. *Bishop Drumm Foundation*, 5837 Winwood Dr., 50131. Tel: 515-270-1100.

PANORA. *St. Thomas More Center*, 6177 Panorama Rd., 50216. Tel: 515-755-3164. Rev. James Wilwerding.

RELIGIOUS INSTITUTES OF MEN REPRESENTED IN THE DIOCESE

For further details refer to the corresponding bracketed number in the Religious Institutes of Men or Women section.

[0600]—*Brothers of the Congregation of the Holy Cross.*—C.S.C.

[0690]—*Jesuit Fathers and Brothers.* (Wisconsin Prov.).—S.J.

[0430]—*Order of Preachers-Dominicans.*—O.P.

[0200]—*Order of St. Benedict.* (Conception, MO).—O.S.B.

RELIGIOUS INSTITUTES OF WOMEN REPRESENTED IN THE DIOCESE

[0230]—*Benedictine Sisters of Pontifical Jurisdiction.*—O.S.B.

[2100]—*Congregation of the Holy Humility of Mary.*—C.H.M.

[1920]—*Congregation of the Sisters of the Holy Cross.*—C.S.C.

[1070-14]—*Dominican Sisters.*—O.P.

[1070-03]—*Dominican Sisters.*—O.P.

[1070-13]—*Dominican Sisters.*—O.P.

[1120]—*Dominican Sisters of the Roman Congregation.*—O.P.

[2575]—*Institute of the Sisters of Mercy of the Americas.* (Cedar Rapids, IA; Omaha, NE; Chicago, IL).—R.S.M.

[1680]—*School Sisters of St. Francis.*—O.S.F.

[3580]—*Servants of Mary.*—O.S.M.

[0480]—*Sisters of Charity of Leavenworth, Kansas.*—S.C.L.

[0430]—*Sisters of Charity of the Blessed Virgin Mary.*—B.V.M.

[2630]—*Sisters of Mercy of the Holy Cross.*—S.C.S.C.

[3000]—*Sisters of Notre Dame de Namur.*—S.N.D.de.N.

[3320]—*Sisters of Presentation of the Blessed Virgin Mary.*—P.B.V.M.

[1540]—*Sisters of Saint Francis, Clinton, Iowa.*—O.S.F.

[1705]—*The Sisters of St. Francis of Assisi.*—O.S.F.

[2960]—*Notre Dame Sisters.* Omaha, NE.—N.D.

[1570]—*Sisters of St. Francis of the Holy Family.*—O.S.F.

NECROLOGY

† Devlin, Rev. Msgr. Joseph A., (Retired). —Died July 22, 1996.

† Lawler, Phillip, Cumming, IA, St. John's Church. —Died Dec. 16, 1995.

† Varna, Rev. Msgr. Leons, (Retired). —Died Feb. 15, 1996.

Archdiocese of Detroit

(Archidioecesis Detroitensis)

Most Reverend

ARTHUR H. KRAWCZAK, D.D.

Retired Auxiliary Bishop of Detroit and Titular Bishop of Subbar; ordained May 18, 1940; appointed February 8, 1973; consecrated April 3, 1973; resigned August 17, 1982. *Res., 14453-D Levan Rd., Livonia, MI, 48154-5022.*

Most Reverend

THOMAS J. GUMBLETON, D.D.

Auxiliary Bishop of Detroit, Titular Bishop of Ululi; ordained June 2, 1956; appointed March 8, 1968; consecrated May 1, 1968. *Office: 1234 Washington Blvd., Detroit, MI, 48226.*

Most Reverend

WALTER J. SCHOENHERR, D.D.

Retired Auxiliary Bishop of Detroit, Titular Bishop of Timidana; ordained October 27, 1945; appointment March 8, 1968; consecrated May 1, 1968; retired March 7, 1995. *Office: 1234 Washington Blvd., Detroit, MI, 48226.*

Most Reverend

MOSES B. ANDERSON, S.S.E., D.D.

Auxiliary Bishop of Detroit, Titular Bishop of Vatarba; ordained May 30, 1958; appointed December 3, 1982; consecrated January 27, 1983. *Office: 1234 Washington Blvd., Detroit, MI, 48226.*

Most Reverend

KEVIN M. BRITT, D.D.

Auxiliary Bishop of Detroit, Titular Bishop of Esco; ordained June 28, 1970; appointed November 23, 1993; consecrated January 6, 1994. *Office: 1234 Washington Blvd., Detroit, MI, 48226.*

His Eminence

ADAM CARDINAL MAIDA, J.C.L., J.D., S.T.L.

Archbishop of Detroit; ordained May 26, 1956; appointed to Green Bay November 8, 1983; consecrated January 25, 1984; installed as Archbishop of Detroit June 12, 1990; created Cardinal on November 26, 1994.

Cardinal's Office: 1234 Washington Blvd., Detroit, MI, 48226; Fax: 313-237-4642.

Most Reverend

BERNARD J. HARRINGTON, D.D.

Auxiliary Bishop of Detroit, Titular Bishop of Uzali; ordained June 6, 1959; appointed November 23, 1993; consecrated January 6, 1994. *Office: 1234 Washington Blvd., Detroit, MI, 48226.*

Most Reverend

ALLEN J. VIGNERON, D.D.

Auxiliary Bishop of Detroit, Titular Bishop of Sault Ste. Marie; ordained July 27, 1975; appointed June 12, 1996; consecrated July 9, 1996. *Office: 1234 Washington Blvd., Detroit, MI, 48226.*

Most Reverend

JOHN C. NIENSTEDT

Auxiliary Bishop of Detroit, Titular Bishop of Alton; ordained July 27, 1974; appointed June 12, 1996; consecrated July 9, 1996. *Office: 1234 Washington Blvd., Detroit, MI, 48226.*

ESTABLISHED MARCH 8, 1833.; CREATED AN ARCHBISHOPRIC AUGUST 3, 1937.

Square Miles 3,901.

Comprises the Counties of Lapeer, Macomb, Monroe, Oakland, St. Clair and Wayne.

For legal titles of parishes and archdiocesan institutions, consult the Cardinal's Office.

STATISTICAL OVERVIEW

Personnel	
Cardinal	1
Auxiliary Bishops	6
Retired Bishops	2
Priests: Diocesan Active in Diocese	336
Priests: Active Outside Diocese	17
Priests: Retired, Sick or Absent	136
Number of Diocesan Priests	489
Religious Priests in Diocese	230
Extern Priests in Diocese	37
Ordinations:	
Diocesan Priests	7
Transitional Deacons	8
Permanent Deacons in Diocese	151
Total Brothers	71
Total Sisters	1,687
Parishes	
Parishes	306
With Resident Pastor:	
Resident Diocesan Priests	274
Resident Religious Priests	32
Without Resident Pastor:	
Missions	5
Pastoral Centers	6
New Parishes Created	1
Professional Ministry Personnel:	
Brothers	5
Sisters	147
Lay Ministers	436
Welfare	
Catholic Hospitals	11
Total Assisted	1,520,112
Health Care Centers	8
Total Assisted	9,391
Homes for the Aged	13
Total Assisted	1,921
Residential Care of Children	8
Total Assisted	1,477
Day Care and Extended Day Care Centers	2
Total Assisted	499
Specialized Homes	8
Total Assisted	1,855
Special Centers for Social Services	11
Total Assisted	16,397
Residential Care of Disabled	1
Total Assisted	118
Educational	
Seminaries, Diocesan	2
Students from This Diocese	41
Students from Other Diocese	78
Diocesan Students in Other Seminaries	6
Seminaries, Religious	2
Students Religious	11
Total Seminarians	58
Colleges and Universities	4
Total Students	16,122
High Schools, Diocesan and Parish	18
Total Students	6,123
High Schools, Private	17
Total Students	8,009
Elementary Schools, Diocesan and Parish	134
Total Students	40,103
Elementary Schools, Private	6
Total Students	1,075
Catechesis/Religious Education:	
High School Students	7,469
Elementary Students	72,267
Total Students Under Catholic Instruction	151,226
Teachers in the Diocese:	
Priests	32
Brothers	25
Sisters	180
Lay Teachers	2,579
Vital Statistics	
Receptions into the Church:	
Infant Baptism Totals	17,215
Adult Baptism Totals	1,285
Received into Full Communion	1,642
First Communions	14,962
Confirmations	11,861
Marriages:	
Catholic	4,488
Interfaith	1,799
Total Marriages	6,287
Deaths	10,126
Total Catholic Population	1,424,616
Total Population	4,266,654

Former Bishops—Rt. Rev. FREDERIC RESE, D.D., cons. Oct. 6, 1833; resigned Aug. 19, 1840; died Dec. 30, 1871.—Rt. Rev. PETER PAUL LEFEVERE, D.D., cons. Nov. 22, 1841; Bishop of Zela, coadjutor and admin. of Detroit; died March 4, 1869.—Rt. Rev. CASPAR HENRY BORGESS, D.D., cons. April 24, 1870; Bishop of Calydon, coadjutor and admin. of Detroit became Bishop of Detroit Dec. 30, 1871; resigned April 16, 1887; died May 3, 1890.—Rt. Rev. JOHN SAMUEL FOLEY, D.D., cons. Nov. 4, 1888; died Jan. 5, 1918.—Most Rev. MICHAEL JAMES GALLAGHER, D.D., cons. Sept. 8, 1915; Bishop of Tipasa, coadjutor of Grand

Rapids became Bishop of Grand Rapids Dec. 26, 1916; transferred to Detroit July 18, 1918; died Jan. 20, 1937.—His Eminence EDWARD CARDINAL MOONEY, D.D., appt. Apostolic Delegate in India Jan. 8, 1926; appt. Titular Archbishop of Irenopolis Jan. 18, 1926; cons. Jan. 31, 1926; appt. Apostolic Delegate in Japan Feb. 25, 1931; transferred to the Diocese of Rochester, Aug. 28, 1933; transferred to the Archdiocese of Detroit, Aug. 3, 1937; created Cardinal Priest of the title of S. Susanna, Feb. 18, 1946; died October 25, 1958.—His Eminence JOHN CARDINAL DEARDEN, D.D., ord. Dec. 8, 1932; cons. Titular Bishop of Sarepta and coadjutor Bishop of Pittsburgh Dec. 22, 1950; installed Archbishop of Detroit Jan. 29, 1959; created Cardinal April 28, 1969; resigned as Archbishop July 15, 1980; died Aug. 1, 1988.—His Eminence EDMUND CARDINAL SZOKA, J.C.L., D.D., Archbishop Emeritus of Detroit; ord. June 5, 1954; appt. Bishop of Gaylord June 15, 1971; cons. July 20, 1971 and; installed July 20, 1971; promoted to See of Detroit March 28, 1981; installed May 17, 1981 created Cardinal June 28, 1988. appt. Pres., Prefacture for Economic Affairs of the Holy See June 25, 1990.

Archdiocesan Departments and Divisions

Information and Reference—Tel: 313-237-5800.

Cardinal's Office—1234 Washington Blvd., Detroit, 48226; Fax: 313-237-4642. All official mail should be directed to this office. Rev. G. MICHAEL BUGARIN, Cardinal's Appointments Sec. Tel: 313-237-5816. Rev. Msgr. JOHN P. ZENZ, Moderator of the Curia. Tel: 313-237-5783. Sr. BARBARA CELESKEY, S.J., Chancellor. Tel: 313-237-5847; Fax: 313-237-4643.

Auxiliary Bishops—Most Rev. BERNARD J. HARRINGTON, D.D., Region 2. Tel: 313-237-5859. Most Rev. KEVIN M. BRITT, D.D., Region 3. Tel: 313-237-5848. Most Rev. MOSES B. ANDERSON, D.D., Region 1. Tel: 313-237-5843.

College of Consultors—Revs. JEROME A. BRZEZINSKI; FRANCIS X. DIETZ; DONALD HANCHON; Rev. Msgr. DENNIS HARRITY; Rev. KEVIN O'BRIEN; Rev. Msgr. JAMES P. ROBINSON, S.S.E.

Presbyteral Council—Revs. LOUIS E. GRANDPRE; DAVID BUERSMEYER; LAWRENCE DELONNAY; BRADLEY FORINTOS; Rev. Msgr. JOHN P. ZENZ; Sr. BARBARA CELESKEY, S.J.; Rev. Msgr. EDWARD J. BALDWIN; Revs. BOHDAN W. KOSICKI; WILLIAM J. MCGOLDRICK; MICHAEL HIGGINS, C.P.; RONALD JOZWIAK; Rev. Msgr. JAMES MOLONEY; Revs. RAYMOND SAYERS; THOMAS SUTHERLAND; Revs. DONALD ARCHAMBAULT; FRANCIS BURNS; PATRICK HALFPENNY; MICHAEL HRYDZIUSZKO; Rev. Msgr. F. GERALD MARTIN; Revs. MICHAEL MOLNAR; JOHN LEO PHALEN; DAVID PRUESS, O.F.M.Cap.; JAMES SCHEICK; TIMOTHY SZOTT; Rev. Msgr. ANTHONY TOCCO; Revs. STANLEY ULMAN; RONALD WILLIAMS.

Archdiocesan Vicars—East Region: Revs. JAMES E. COMMYN, Belle River; RICHARD MEVISSEN, The Hub; DUANE NOVELLY, Detroit/Grosse Pointe; GARY T. SMETANKA, East Macomb; VALENTINE GATTARI, East Side; DAVID E. WEISNER, Gratiot; GARY MICHALIK, North Central; WILLIAM J. PROMESSO, North Macomb; RENE L. DESMARAIS, Port Huron; JAMES L. BJORUM, Serf; ARTHUR H. JACOBI, Warren-Center Line *South Region:* LAWRENCE KAISER, Dearborn; Revs. JAMES F. WIEGING, Downriver; GERALD A. MCENHILL, Farmington/Southfield; WILLIAM FISHER, O.S.F.S., Monroe; THOMAS F. SLOWINSKI, Northwest Wayne; NEIL EMON, O.S.C., Southland; GERARD BECHARD, Western Wayne *West Region:* Revs. DANIEL J. MURPHY, Birmingham/Bloomfield/Troy; Revs. RONALD DEHONDT, Grand River; TIMOTHY F. BABCOCK, Pontiac; LAWRENCE ZURAWSKI, Southeast Oakland; KENNETH CHASE, Southwest; Rev. Msgr. ROBERT S. HUMITZ, Vicariate of the Lakes; MARK BRAUER, West Detroit; Rev. Msgr. JAMES ROBINSON, S.S.E., West Side Inner City; DOUGLAS J. TERRIEN, Thumb.

Archdiocesan Pastoral Council—Sr. BARBARA CELESKEY, S.J.

The Metropolitan Tribunal—305 Michigan Ave., Detroit, 48226. Tel: 313-237-5865; Fax: 313-237-5872. Office Hours: Mon.-Fri. 8:30-4:30.

Judicial Vicar—Very Rev. NORMAN D. NAWROCKI, J.C.L.

Adjutant Judicial Vicars—Revs. GEORGE P. MILLER, J.C.L.; RONALD J. JOZWIAK, J.C.L.

Diocesan Judges—Revs. WILLIAM CARNAGO, J.C.L.; JEROME SLOWINSKI, J.C.L.; Rev. Msgr. JOHN WEIER, J.C.L.; Revs. TIMOTHY BABCOCK; JAMES BJORUM, J.C.L.; ROBERT BURKE, J.C.L.; JOHN GAGALA, J.C.L.; KENNETH KAUCHECK, J.C.D.; MICHAEL A. MOLNAR, J.C.L.; GARY TIERNEY, J.C.L.; ROBERT H. WILLIAMS, J.C.L.

Office Manager—SALLY BAIRD.

Notaries—GLORIA ANFIELD; SALLY BAIRD; ALICE LILEY; ANDREA PINTO; CAROL SAMULSKI; MARJORIE SEERY; DARNELL MCQUEEN.

Defenders of Bond—Revs. RICHARD CAVELLIER, J.C.L.; FRANCIS REISS, J.C.L.; Rev. Msgr. RICARDO BASS, J.C.L.; FRANCIS SYLVESTER; Rev. Msgr. WALTER A. HURLEY, J.C.L.; Sr. DIANE MASSON, C.S.S.F., J.C.L.

Auditors—Rev. MAREK STOCHMAL; ROBERT CADOTTE.

Court Expert—Sr. JUDITH MCMANUS, O.P., A.C.S.W., C.S.W.

Department of Christian Service—DANIEL PIEPSZOWSKI, Dir., *305 Michigan Ave., Detroit, 48226.* Tel: 313-237-5900; Fax: 313-237-5866.

Office of Human Services and Pastoral Care—KRISTA BAJOKA. Tel: 313-237-5962.

Office of Institutions and Agencies—PHIL WELLS. Tel: 313-237-5903.

Office of Social Ministries—Sr. JUDE VAN BAALEN. Tel: 313-237-5958.

Department of Communications—NED MCGRATH, Dir., *305 Michigan Ave., Detroit, 48226.* Tel: 313-237-5943; Fax: 313-237-4644.

Office of Information Technology—CLIFF TRUDEAU. Tel: 313-237-5797; Fax: 313-237-5979.

Office of Public Relations—NED MCGRATH. Tel: 313-237-5943; Fax: 313-237-4644.

Office of Printing and Mailing—DENNIS MILLIGAN. Tel: 313-237-5967; Fax: 313-965-8471.

Office of Television—KEN KOLB. Tel: 313-237-5943; Fax: 313-237-5928.

Department of Education—Rev. Msgr. JOHN M. QUINN, Dir., *305 Michigan Ave., Detroit, 48226.* Tel: 313-237-4675; Fax: 313-237-5867.

Catholic Schools—Sr. FRANCES NADOLNY, O.P., Ph.D., Supt. Tel: 313-237-5775.

Office of Catechetics / Religious Education—Sr. ELIZABETH FLAHERTY, O.P. Tel: 313-237-4670.

Office of Family Life / Youth Ministry—FRANCIS OZAR. Tel: 313-237-5892.

St. John Center for Family and Youth—Rev. JOHN WEST, Rector. Tel: 313-237-4668; Fax: 313-414-1154.

Department of Development—MICHAEL E. MURPHY, Dir., *1234 Washington Blvd., Detroit, 48226.* Tel: 313-883-8657; Fax: 313-883-8681.

Office of Catholic Services Appeal—Tel: 313-883-8656.

Department of Finance and Administrative Services—Sr. MARY V. KORB, R.S.M., Dir., *1234 Washington Blvd., Detroit, 48226.* Tel: 313-237-5834; Fax: 313-237-5868.

Archdiocesan Buildings—DONALD J. SCHEIBLE. Tel: 313-237-5845. JEMAR HARVILLE, Asst. Dir. Bldgs. Tel: 313-237-5806.

Archdiocesan Properties—GERALD T. CHUHRAN. Tel: 313-237-5820.

Financial Services—ABELARDO B. BUSQUE. Tel: 313-237-5828.

Human Resources—CAROL MEYERS. Tel: 313-237-5947.

Sacred Heart Building Administration—JOHN DUNCAN. Tel: 313-883-8599.

Archdiocese of Detroit Endowment Foundation—1234 Washington Blvd., Detroit, 48226.

Administration—Sr. MARY V. KORB, R.S.M., Dir. Tel: 313-237-5834; Fax: 313-237-5868.

Development—MICHAEL E. MURPHY, Dir. Tel: 313-883-8657; Fax: 313-883-8681.

Department of Parish Life—CATHERINE WAGNER, Dir. LORY MCGLINNEN, Assoc. Dir.; Rev. DANIEL HAVRON, O.F.M., Coord. Evangelization. Tel: 313-237-4686., *305 Michigan Ave., Detroit, 48226.* Tel: 313-237-5934; Fax: 313-237-5869.

Office of Christian Worship—MICHAEL MCCALLION. Tel: 313-237-5932.

Council of Catholic Women—MARY LABUDIE, Pres. Tel: 313-237-5896.

Director of Hispanic Catholic Ministries—RAUL FELICIANO. Tel: 313-237-5761.

Director of African-American Catholic Ministries—Rev. CLARENCE WILLIAMS, C.P.P.S. Tel: 313-237-5934.

Office of Leadership Formation—JAMES R. KIEFER. Tel: 313-237-5887.

Office of Pastoral Ministers and Deacons Office—Deacon JOHN BALL. Tel: 313-237-5778.

Delegate for Religious—Sr. MARGARET STECHSHULTE, O.P. Tel: 313-237-4682.

"The Michigan Catholic" Newspaper—KAREN M. PITTON, Editor, *305 Michigan Ave., Detroit, 48226.* Tel: 313-224-8000.

Archivist—ROMAN P. GODZAK, *1234 Washington Blvd., Detroit, 48226.* Tel: 313-237-5846; Fax: 313-237-4643.

Propagation of the Faith (Missions)—Rev. Msgr. JAMES A. MOLONEY, *17650 W. Outer Dr., Dearborn Heights, 48127.*

Holy Childhood Association—1230 Washington Blvd., Detroit, 48226. Tel: 313-237-5807.

Catholic Youth Organization—Detroit: *Gabriel Richard Bldg., 305 Michigan Ave., Detroit, 48226.* Tel: 313-963-7172. Branch office, RAYMOND HILLEN, Dir., *22235 Fenkell, Detroit.* Tel: 313-534-4620. Neighborhood Development, Brightmoor Community.

Archdiocesan Theological Commission—Rev. Msgr. JOHN P. ZENZ. Tel: 313-237-5783.

Vocation Office—Rev. ROBERT J. FISHER, Dir. Tel: 313-237-5875. Sr. ANGELA CERNA-PLATA, I.H.M., Asst. Dir., . Fax: 313-237-6070.

Office of Pastoral Services for Clergy—Most Rev. KEVIN M. BRITT, Dir.; Deacon EUGENE KRZEMINSKI, Exec. Asst., *1234 Washington Blvd., Detroit, 48226.* Tel: 313-237-5848; Fax: 313-237-5844.

Office of Parish Support Services—Rev. DONALD MCLEOD, C.S.B. Tel: 313-237-6059; Fax: 313-237-4643.

CLERGY, PARISHES, MISSIONS AND PAROCHIAL SCHOOLS

CITY OF DETROIT
(Wayne County)

1—CATHEDRAL, CHURCH OF THE MOST BLESSED SACRAMENT, Rev. Msgr. James P. Robinson, S.S.E., Rector.
Res., 9844 Woodward Ave., 48202. Tel: 313-865-6300; Fax: 313-867-4613.

2—ALL SAINTS, Rev. Edward F. Zaorski.
Res., 7824 W. Fort St., 48209. Tel: 313-841-1428; Fax: 313-841-3009.

3—ST. ALOYSIUS, Revs. Mark Soehner, O.F.M.; Mel P. Brady, O.F.M.; Bro. James Ebaugh, O.F.M., Pastoral Assoc. In res., Rev. Charles Smiech, O.F.M.
Res., Chancery Bldg., 1234 Washington Blvd., 48226. Tel: 313-237-5810; Fax: 313-963-9076.

4—ST. ANDREW (Polish), Rev. Julian Chmura.
Res., 7060 McGraw Ave., 48210. Tel: 313-361-1717; Fax: 313-361-9816.

5—SS. ANDREW AND BENEDICT (Slovak), Rev. Edward F. Zaorski.
Res., 2430 S. Beatrice St., 48217. Tel: 313-381-1184.

6—ST. ANDREW KIM KOREAN CATHOLIC CHURCH, Rev. Blose Lee.
Res., 20131 Berg Rd., 48219. Tel: 313-535-3130; Fax: 313-535-3314.

7—STE. ANNE, Rev. Robert J. Duggan, C.S.B.; Sr. Mary Clare Yates, R.S.M.
Res., 1000 Ste. Anne St., 48216. Tel: 313-496-1701; Fax: 313-496-0429.

8—ANNUNCIATION, Rev. Valentine A. Gattari; Deacon Peter Schlesser.
Res., 1265 Parkview Ave., 48214. Tel: 313-822-1262; Fax: 313-824-1908.
Stapleton Center—9341 Agnes, 48214. Tel: 313-822-0397.

9—ST. ANTHONY, Rev. Robert Kotlarz; Deacon Elgia L. McCoy, Exec. Admin.
Office: 5247 Sheridan Ave., 48213. Tel: 313-921-0263; Fax: 313-924-4040.

10—ST. ANTHONY (Lithuanian), Rev. Alphonse Babonas.
Res., 1750 25th St., 48216. Tel: 313-554-1284.

11—ASSUMPTION GROTTO, Rev. Eduard Perrone. In res., Rev. Boleslaus Lipczewski; Bro. Matthew Hincks, O.R.C.
Res., 13770 Gratiot Ave., 48205. Tel: 313-372-0762; Fax: 313-372-2064. [CEM]

12—ST. AUGUSTINE AND ST. MONICA, Rev. Daniel J. Trapp, Admin.
Res., 4151 Seminole St., 48214. Tel: 313-921-4107; Fax: 313-921-1115.

13—ST. BARTHOLOMEW, Rev. Boleslaus Krol. In res., Rev. Edward Kaszak.
Res., 2291 E. Outer Dr., 48234. Tel: 313-892-1446; Fax: 313-892-1149.
School—Sr. Albina Prin. Lay Teachers 8; Students 158.
Convent—2251 E. Outer Dr., 48234. Tel: 313-366-0525.
Sisters 4.

14—ST. BRENDAN, Rev. Victor Roman.
Res., 11433 Beaconsfield, 48224. Tel: 313-372-1644; Fax: 313-372-7195.
School—Tel: 313-839-0434. Ann H. O'Grady, Prin. Lay Teachers 6; Students 134.
Convent—11430 Morang, 48224.

15—ST. CECILIA, Rev. Msgr. Thomas J. Finnigan.
Res., Box 04209, 10400 Stoepel Ave., 48204. Tel: 313-933-6788; Fax: 313-933-1439.
Church—Livernois at Stearns, 48204.
School—Tel: 313-933-2400. Sr. Margaret Sweeney, I.H.M., Prin.
Sisters-Servants of the Immaculate Heart of Mary 2; Lay Teachers 16; Students 400.
High School—Sunbeam Hughes, Prin. Priests 1; Sisters 3; Lay Teachers 24.
Convent—6336 Burlingame Ave., 48204.

16—ST. CHARLES BORROMEO, Revs. David Preuss, O.F.M.Cap.; Augustine Cops; Sr. Francis W. Schnell,

O.P., Pastoral Assoc. In res., Rev. Ben Markwell, O.F.M.Cap.
Res., 1491 Baldwin Ave., 48214. Tel: 313-331-0253; Fax: 313-331-4834.

17—ST. CHRISTINE, Rev. Mark S. Brauer.
Office: 22303 Fenkell St., 48223. Tel: 313-535-7272; Fax: 313-535-3439.
Res., 23450 W. Davison, 48223.
School—13550 Virgil, 48223. Tel: 313-535-9342; Fax: 313-455-7355. Sr. M. Josephine Lechowicz, C.S.S.F., Prin.
Felician Sisters 2; Lay Teachers 11; Students 246.

18—CHRIST THE KING, Rev. Victor Clore. Pastoral Assocs.: Sr. Fiorentina D'Amore; Mrs. Katherine Paul.
Res., 16805 Pierson, 48219. Tel: 313-532-1211; Fax: 313-532-1216.
Church—20800 Grand River & Burt Rd., 48219. Tel: 313-532-1213.
School—Mrs. Margaret Pic-Kell, D.R.E. Lay Teachers 18; Students 267.

19—ST. CHRISTOPHER, Rev. Richard A. Hartmann; Deacons John Marku; Norbert Motowski; Sr. Celeste Hupert.
Res., 7800 Woodmont Ave., 48228. Tel: 313-584-7460; Fax: 313-584-6361.
School—Tel: 313-846-1430. Ronald Mysliwiec, Prin. Sisters of the Holy Family of Nazareth 1; Lay Teachers 7; Students 217.
Convent—7800 Woodmont Ave., 48228.

20—ST. CUNEGUNDA, Rev. Mitchell Szarek.
Res., 5900 St. Lawrence Ave., 48210. Tel: 313-841-4000.
School—Tel: 313-843-0004. Sr. Mary Alexander, C.S.S.F., Prin.
Lay Teachers 8; Religious 3; Students 159.

21—ST. DOMINIC, Revs. Malcolm S. Willoughby, O.P.; James Murray, O.P.; Charles D. Farrell, O.P. In res., Revs. Daniel Casey, O.P.; Francis Maguire, O.P.
Res., 4844 Trumbull Ave., 48208. Tel: 313-831-8790; Fax: 313-831-2965.
Shrine—Rosary Shrine of St. Jude, Tel: 313-831-7566; Fax: 313-831-2965.
Convent—4835 Lincoln Ave., 48208. Tel: 313-831-1028. Missionaries of Charity
Sisters 4.

22—ST. ELIZABETH, Rev. John W. Markham.
Res., 3138 E. Canfield Ave., 48207. Tel: 313-921-9225; Fax: 313-921-9475.

23—ST. FRANCIS D'ASSISI, Rev. Robert J. Wojciechowski.
Res., 4500 Wesson St., 48210. Tel: 313-897-7229; Fax: 313-897-7485.
School—Tel: 313-897-8720. Ms. Susan Perna, Prin. Lay Teachers 8; Lay Librarian 1; Students 187.

24—ST. FRANCIS DE SALES, Rev. James E. O'Reilly, S.J.; Deacon Benjamin Prince.
Res., 10600 Fenkell Ave., 48238. Tel: 313-861-4020; Fax: 313-861-4718.

25—ST. GABRIEL, Rev. Donald F. Hanchon. In res., Rev. Anthony F. Bologna.
Res., 8118 W. Vernor Hwy., 48209-1524. Tel: 313-841-0753; Fax: 313-841-0916.
Catechesis/Religious Programs—Students 140.

26—ST. GEMMA GALGANI, Rev. Mark S. Brauer.
Res., 23450 W. Davison, 48223. Tel: 313-255-3666; Fax: 313-537-0598.
School—13550 Virgil, 48223. Tel: 313-535-9342.
Lay Teachers 11; Students (Grades K-8) 195.

27—ST. GERARD, Rev. Donald Archambault; Deacon Alfons Hogrebe.
Res., 19800 Pembroke, 48219. Tel: 313-537-5770.
School—19900 Evergreen Rd., 48219. Tel: 313-533-4353.
Sisters 3; Lay Teachers 10; Students 216.
Catechesis/Religious Programs—Tel: 313-533-0197. Sr. Laura Kendrick, H.V.M., D.R.E.
Students 258.
Convent—19900 Evergreen Rd., 48219.

28—GESU, Rev. James F. Lotze, S.J.; Deacon Ronald McIntyre. In res., Revs. John A. Kardon, S.J.; Kenneth J. Noetzel, S.J.; Bro. Richard C. Conroy, S.J.
Res., 17204 Oak Dr., 48221. Tel: 313-862-4400; Fax: 313-862-1083.
School—Sr. Stella Rabaut, I.H.M., Prin., Tel: 313-863-4677. Sisters-Servants of the Immaculate Heart of Mary 1; Lay Teachers 27; Students 528.
Convent—17180 Oak Dr., 48221. Tel: 313-861-8877.

29—ST. GREGORY, Rev. Ronald J. DeHondt; Deacon Benjamin Prince.
Res., 15031 Dexter, 48238. Tel: 313-861-0363; Fax: 313-862-6805.

30—GUARDIAN ANGELS, Rev. Sidney J. Eckert.
Res., 12545 Kelly Rd., 48224. Tel: 313-526-0735; Fax: 313-526-7382.

31—ST. HEDWIG, Rev. Kenneth M. Chase.
Res., 3245 Junction Ave., 48210. Tel: 313-894-5409; Fax: 313-894-4730.

32—HOLY CROSS (Hungarian), Revs. Barnabas G. Kiss, O.F.M.; Angelus Ligeti, O.F.M.
Res., 8423 South St., 48209. Tel: 313-842-1133; Fax: 313-842-2773.

33—HOLY FAMILY (Italian), Rev. Noel Patacconi, O.S.B.
Res., 641 Walter P. Chrysler Expwy., 48226. Tel: 313-963-2046; Fax: 313-961-0065.

34—HOLY REDEEMER, Revs. Robert Halter, C.SS.R.; Larry Sanders, C.SS.R.; Richard Mevissen, C.SS.R.; Gregory Moy, C.SS.R.; Robert Hirsch, C.SS.R. In res., Revs. James Sullivan, C.SS.R.; Robert P. McCarthy, C.SS.R.; George Jolly, C.SS.R.; John E. Bellon, C.SS.R.; Bros. Gerard Patin, C.SS.R.; Robert Ruffing, C.SS.R.
Res., 1721 Junction Ave., 48209. Tel: 313-842-3450; Fax: 313-849-0539.
School—Tel: 313-841-5230. Sr. Elizabeth Fleckenstein, I.H.M., Prin.
Sisters Servants of the Immaculate Heart of Mary 4; Lay Teachers 16; Students 408.
High School—Tel: 313-841-4433. Miriam Snyder, Prin.
Sisters 4; Lay Teachers 14; Students 227.
Convent—5678 Eldred Ave., 48209. Tel: 313-841-8420.

35—ST. HYACINTH (Polish), Rev. Francis S. Skalski.
Res., 3151 Farnsworth Ave., 48211. Tel: 313-922-1507; Fax: 313-922-2459.

36—IMMACULATE HEART OF MARY, Rev. William J. Carnago; Mary Caroline Jonah, Pastoral Assoc.
Res., 16000 Pembroke Ave., 48235. Tel: 313-272-0990; Fax: 313-272-9772.
School—19940 Mansfield, 48235. Tel: 313-835-0258. Sr. Stephanie Holub, R.S.M., Prin.
Sisters of Mercy of the Union 1; Lay Teachers 10; Students 129.
Convent—19960 Mansfield Ave., 48235. Tel: 313-272-6810; Fax: 313-272-6811.

37—ST. JEROME. Closed. For inquiries for parish records contact the Chancery.

38—ST. JOHN BERCHMANS-ST. JULIANA, Rev. Luke Stano, O.S.M.; Sr. Barbara Dakoske, H.V.M., Pastoral Assoc.
Res., 9801 Chalmers, 48213. Tel: 313-526-7254; Fax: 313-526-7553.
School—St. Juliana, 9755 Chalmers, 48213. Tel: 313-526-0062.
Servite Sisters 1; Lay Teachers 10; Students 236.

39—ST. JOHN CANTIUS (Polish), Rev. Edwin A. Szczygiel.
Res., 844 Harbaugh Ave., 48209. Tel: 313-842-2276; Fax: 313-842-2268.

40—ST. JOSAPHAT (Polish), Rev. Ronald J. Jozwiak.
Res., 691 E. Canfield Ave., 48201. Tel: 313-831-1072.

41—ST. JOSEPH, Rev. Msgr. John F. Schweder.
Res., 1828 Jay St., 48207. Tel: 313-393-8212; Fax: 313-393-8294.

42—ST. JUDE, Revs. Raymond J. Sayers; Christopher Maus; Sr. Judy Lieder, O.P., Pastoral Assoc.
Res., 15889 E. Seven Mile Rd., 48205. Tel: 313-527-0380; Fax: 313-527-3511.
School—15865 E. Seven Mile, 48205.
Sisters of St. Dominic 2; Lay Teachers 22; Students 417.
Catechesis/Religious Programs—Mrs. Joyce Francois, D.R.E.
Students 167.

43—ST. LEO, Most Rev. Thomas J. Gumbleton. Pastoral Assocs.: William Morrow; Daniel Maxwell.
Church & Res.: 4860 15th St., 48208. Tel: 313-894-0357; Fax: 313-896-2804.
School—4851 14th St., 48208. Mary Lou Van Antwerp, Prin., Tel: 313-896-6078.
Sisters 2; Lay Teachers 7; Students 200.

44—ST. LOUIS THE KING, Revs. Boleslaus Krol; Ron Borg, C.S.B.
Res., 18891 St. Louis Ave., 48234. Tel: 313-891-1766; Fax: 313-891-7959.

45—ST. LUKE, Rev. Msgr. John M. Quinn; Sr. Judith Mouch, R.S.M., Parish Nurse Ministry; Sr. Marie Roy, S.S.J., Pastoral Assoc.
Res., 8017 Ohio Ave., 48204. Tel: 313-935-6161; Fax: 313-935-0788.
School—St. Luke & St. Brigid Elementary School, St. Brigid Montessori Preschool, 8091 Ohio, 48204. Tel: 313-933-9611. Clima Fields, Prin.
Lay Teachers 9; Students 200.

46—MADONNA, Rev. William T. Cunningham; Sr. Ellen Ann Gardner, S.C.
Res., 1125 Oakman Blvd., 48238. Tel: 313-868-4308; Fax: 313-868-9771.

47—MARTYRS OF UGANDA, Rev. Tyrone Robinson; Deacons Douglas Jackson; Allen McNeeley.
Res., 7601 Rosa Parks Blvd., 48206. Tel: 313-896-2335; Fax: 313-896-0925.
School—Martyrs of Uganda Catholic Academy, 4317 Blaine, 48204. Tel: 313-361-1065.
Lay Teachers 17; Students 320.
Catechesis/Religious Programs—Mrs. Mary Brown, D.R.E.
Students 310.

48—ST. MARY, Revs. Norman G. Hannahs, C.S.Sp.; Martin J. Conroy, C.S.Sp.
Res., 646 Monroe Ave., 48226. Tel: 313-961-8711; Fax: 313-961-4994.

49—ST. MARY'S OF REDFORD, Rev. Ronald R. Williams.
Mailing Address: 14750 St. Mary's, 48227. Tel: 313-273-1100; Fax: 313-273-2002.
School—St. Mary of Redford Grade School, 14751 Mansfield, 48227. Tel: 313-835-6834. Sr. Joan McGrath, I.H.M., Prin.
Religious 2; Lay Teachers 18; Students 430.
Convent—14601 Mansfield, 48227. Tel: 313-272-2727.
Sisters 3.

50—ST. MATTHEW, Rev. Duane R. Novelly; Sr. Karen Eklund, I.H.M., Pastoral Min.; Deacon William H. Johr.
Res., 6021 Whittier Ave., 48224. Tel: 313-884-4470; Fax: 313-884-4276.
School—John Walker, Prin. Lay Teachers 10; Students 114.

51—MOST HOLY TRINITY, Revs. Russell E. Kohler; Grace Agius.
Res., 1050 Porter St., 48226. Tel: 313-965-4450; Fax: 313-965-4453.
School—Tel: 313-961-8855. Sr. Irene Therese Gumbleton, Prin.
Sisters-Servants of the Immaculate Heart of Mary 2; Lay Teachers 5; Students 160.
St. Vincent Middle School—(Grades 5-8) 2020 14th St., 48216. Tel: 313-961-6773. Ms. Kathleen McBride, Prin.
Lay Teachers 4; Students 92.
Convent—1234 Porter St., 48226. Tel: 313-961-6683.

52—NATIVITY OF OUR LORD, Rev. Jerome C. Singer.
Res., 5900 McClellan Ave., 48213. Tel: 313-922-0033; Fax: 313-922-0033.

53—OUR LADY GATE OF HEAVEN, Rev. Dennis D. Duggan, Admin.; Sr. Rosemarie Kieffer, O.P., Pastoral Assoc.; Deacon William Krauskoff.
Church—9555 St. Mary's, 48227. Tel: 313-270-5350; Fax: 313-838-3207.

54—OUR LADY OF GOOD COUNSEL, Revs. David E. Weisner; Emiliano Ahurwendeire; Deacon Donald Sandstrom, Pastoral Assoc.; Sr. Betty Zeestraten, O.S.F., Pastoral Assoc.; Patricia Gillis, Pastoral Assoc.
Res., 17142 Rowe Ave., 48205. Tel: 313-372-1698; Fax: 313-372-1211.

55—OUR LADY HELP OF CHRISTIANS (Polish), Rev. George A. Rutkowski.
Res., 12635 McDougall Ave., 48212. Tel: 313-892-6116.
School—Tel: 313-893-5666. Sr. M. Maristella-Nowakowski, Prin.
Felician Sisters 4; Lay Teachers 5; Students 87.
Convent—12541 McDougall Ave., 48212. Tel: 313-891-5280.

56—OUR LADY OF MT. CARMEL, Rev. Bartolomeo Santino Ferrero. Pastoral Associates: Ms. Mary Jane Jarczak; Tom Di Giacomo; Rosalie DeLoye; Cyndy Guerra.
Res., 555 Oakwood Blvd., 48217. Tel: 313-841-8478.

57—OUR LADY OF THE ROSARY, Rev. Robert Morand.
Res., 5930 Woodward Ave., 48202. Tel: 313-875-6011; Fax: 313-872-0758.

58—OUR LADY OF SORROWS, Revs. David Preuss, O.F.M.Cap.; Augustine Cops, O.F.M.Cap.
Mailing Address: 2965 Meldrum, 48207. Tel: 313-471-4643 (parish).
Res., 1491 Baldwin, 48214. Tel: 313-331-0253; Fax: 313-331-4834.

59—OUR LADY QUEEN OF ANGELS, Rev. Michael Rozewicz, O.F.M.Conv. In res., Rev. Ferdinand Kintop, O.F.M. Conv.
Res., 4200 Martin Ave., 48210. Tel: 313-897-8160; Fax: 313-897-8126.
School—Tel: 313-894-6266. Mr. Carl E. Weiss, Prin. Franciscan Sisters of St. Joseph 2; Lay Teachers 7; Students 233.
Convent—4108 Martin Ave., 48210. Tel: 313-894-3462.

60—OUR LADY QUEEN OF HEAVEN, Rev. Donald A. Sopiak; Sr. Anne Bockhorst, S.C., Pastoral Assoc.
Res., 8200 Rolyat Ave., 48234. Tel: 313-891-4553; Fax: 313-891-5782.

61—ST. PATRICK, Rev. Thomas J. Duffey; Floria Ellison, Pastoral Assoc.
Church—58 Parsons, 48201. Tel: 313-833-0857; Fax: 313-833-0128.
St. Patrick Senior Center, Inc.—Tel: 313-833-7080. Sr. Mary Watson, O.P., Pres.

62—SS. PETER AND PAUL JESUIT, Rev. Robert R. Hartigan, S.J. In res., Revs. Arthur E. Loveley, S.J.; Francis X. Budovic, S.J.; George R. Follen, S.J.
Res., 438 St. Antoine St., 48226. Tel: 313-961-8077; Fax: 313-961-5134.

63—SS. PETER AND PAUL (West Side), Revs. Francis R. Reiss; Jozef Mitek; John Kubik.
Res., 7685 Grandville Ave., 48228. Tel: 313-846-2222; Fax: 313-584-1484.
School—Tel: 313-336-3600. Patricia Gajewski, Prin.
Sisters of St. Francis (Sylvania) 1; Lay Teachers 9; Students 214.

64—ST. PHILOMENA, Rev. Peter S. Lentine.
Res., 4281 Marseilles Ave., 48224. Tel: 313-882-4300; Fax: 313-882-1661.
Catechesis/Religious Programs—Kathleen McKenzie, D.R.E., Tel: 313-884-2422.
Students 190.

65—PRECIOUS BLOOD, Most Rev. Moses B. Anderson, S.S.E.
Res., 13305 Grove Ave., 48235. Tel: 313-342-5292; Fax: 313-342-3513.

66—PRESENTATION-OUR LADY OF VICTORY, Rev. Kenneth C. Stewart, O.F.M.Cap.
Res., 19760 Meyers Rd., 48235. Tel: 313-342-1333; Fax: 313-342-4182.
School—Tel: 313-864-0595; Fax: 313-864-2271.
Lay Teachers 11; Students 138.

67—ST. RAYMOND, Rev. David E. Weisner.
Res., 20103 Joann Ave., 48205. Tel: 313-527-0525; Fax: 313-527-9776.
Community House—20055 Joann Ave., 48205. Tel: 313-521-4615.

68—ST. RITA, Rev. Timothy Kane.
Res., 1000 E. State Fair, 48203. Tel: 313-366-2340; Fax: 313-891-0677.

69—SACRED HEART-CHALDEAN PARISH, Rev. Jacob O. Yasso.
Res., 310 W. Seven Mile Rd., 48203. Tel: 313-368-6214; Fax: 313-891-0132.

70—SACRED HEART OF JESUS, Rev. Norman P. Thomas.
Res., 1000 Eliot St., 48207. Tel: 313-831-1356; Fax: 313-831-8603.
Catechesis/Religious Programs—Barbara Hunt, D.R.E.
Students 266.

71—ST. SCHOLASTICA, Rev. Livius Paoli, O.S.B.
Res., 17320 Rosemont Rd., 48219. Tel: 313-531-0140; Fax: 313-531-0739.
Church—Southfield Rd. & West Outer Dr., 48219.
School—Tel: 313-532-1916. Eric Westley, Elementary Prin.
Sisters of St. Dominic (Adrian) 1; Lay Teachers 25; Students 425.
High School—Benedictine High School, Tel: 313-532-1274; Fax: 313-532-5767. Sam Walker, High School Prin.
Sisters 1; Lay Teachers 19; Students 312.
Catechesis/Religious Programs—Students 737.
Convent—17305 Ashton, 48219. Tel: 313-531-3694.

72—ST. STEPHEN-MARY MOTHER OF THE CHURCH, Revs. Mark Gawronski; Rafael Jimenez.
Res., 4311 Central Ave., 48210. Tel: 313-841-0783.
School—Tel: 313-841-2739. Sr. Mary Laurene Smolinski, C.S.S.F., Prin.
Religious 4; Lay Teachers 7; Students 227.
Convent—4329 Central Ave., 48210. Tel: 313-843-9080.

73—ST. SUZANNE, Rev. Dennis D. Duggan; Sr. Lucy Abbey, I.H.M., Pastoral Assoc.
Res., 9357 Westwood Ave., 48228. Tel: 313-838-6780; Fax: 313-838-1063.
School—Joan Cullinan, Prin., Tel: 313-836-7030.
Lay Teachers 9; Students 180.

74—SWEETEST HEART OF MARY (Polish), Rev. Bernard Backiel, M.I.C.
Res., 4440 Russell St., 48207. Tel: 313-831-6659; Fax: 313-831-8522. [CEM]

75—ST. THOMAS AQUINAS, Rev. Leo F. Sabourin. Pastoral Assocs.: Bros. Michael Graf, O.F.M.; Micheleen Troutman.
Res. & Parish Center: 5780 Evergreen Rd., 48228. Tel: 313-271-3266; Fax: 313-271-8773.
School—Tel: 313-271-4170. Sr. Jan Stocking, R.S.M., Prin.
Sisters of Mercy 2; Lay Teachers 12; Students 237.
Catechesis/Religious Programs—Tel: 313-271-0813. Clare Cooper, D.R.E.
Students 152.
Convent—5890 Evergreen Rd, 48228. Tel: 313-336-4559.

76—TRANSFIGURATION, Rev. Andrew Wesley; Deacon Don Sobolewski.
Res., 5830 Simon K. St., 48212. Tel: 313-892-1310.
School—Sr. Angelica Zajkowski, Prin. Sisters of the Holy Family of Nazareth 2; Lay Teachers 10; Students 250.
Convent—5821 Rupert, 48212. Tel: 313-891-9273.

OUTSIDE THE CITY OF DETROIT

Algonac, St. Clair Co., St. Catherine, Rev. Leo P. Broderick; Deacon Kenneth A. Nowicki.
Res., 1103 Washington, 48001. Tel: 810-794-3301; Fax: 810-794-1849. [CEM]
School—1106 St. Clair Blvd., 48001. Marie Dewitte, Prin., Tel: 810-794-4966.
Sisters 2; Lay Teachers 6; Students 122.
Catechesis/Religious Programs—Tel: 810-794-3843. Anna Mae Lines, D.R.E.
Students 220.

Allen Park, Wayne Co., St. Frances Cabrini, Revs. Gary Bueche; Gerald J. LeBoeuf; P. Larry Siroskey. In res., Rev. Michael Gormley, S.A.C.
Res., 9000 Laurence Ave., 48101. Tel: 313-381-5601; Fax: 313-381-7837.
School—Tel: 313-928-6610; Fax: 313-381-7837. Bernadette Sugrue, Prin.
Lay Teachers 24; Students 479.
High School—Tel: 313-388-0110. R. Edward Smith, Prin.
Lay Teachers 21; Students 360.
Catechesis/Religious Programs—Jerome Green, D.R.E.
Students 501.

Allenton, St. Clair Co., St. John the Evangelist, Rev. Salvino Briffa; Deacon James Gennette.
Res., 872 Capac Rd., 48002. Tel: 810-395-7074; Fax: 810-395-7718.
Catechesis/Religious Programs—Tel: 810-395-2305.
Students 237.

Anchorville, St. Clair Co., Immaculate Conception, Rev. Sigismund Kowalczyk.
Mailing Address: P.O. Box 106, 48004. Tel: 810-725-3051; 725-1121; Fax: 810-725-2474. [CEM]
School—7403 Church Rd., 48004. Tel: 810-725-0078; Fax: 810-725-2474. Irene Heidtke, Prin.
Lay Teachers 12; Students 305.
Catechesis/Religious Programs—Jane Petitpren, D.R.E, Tel: 810-725-1762.
Students 231.

Armada, Macomb Co., St. Mary Mystical Rose, Rev. Paul Xuereb.
Res., 24040 Armada Ridge, 48005. Tel: 810-784-5966; Fax: 810-784-9330.
Catechesis/Religious Programs—Students 252.

Auburn Hills, Oakland Co., Sacred Heart, Rev. Daniel Rebain; Sr. Sharon Simon, O.P., Pastoral Assoc.
Res., 3400 Adams Rd., 48326. Tel: 810-852-4170; Fax: 810-852-5745.
Catechesis/Religious Programs—Tel: 810-852-3620.
Students 334.

St. John Fisher Chapel University Parish, Rev. Jerome A. Brzezinski. Pastoral Assocs.: Sr. Mary Bodde; Sr. Mary Van Gilder; Sr. Mary Ann Dixon; Ms. Linda Coleman; Mr. Eugene Mahon; Mrs. Susan Burrato.
Res., 3665 Walton Blvd., 48326. Tel: 810-373-6457; Fax: 810-373-5479.
Catechesis/Religious Programs—Tel: 810-373-3130. Sr. Mary Ann Dixon, O.P., D.R.E.
Students 470.

Belleville, Wayne Co., St. Anthony, Rev. Thomas H. Cusick; Terrence D. Taylor, Pastoral Assoc.; Deacon Peter Cornell.
Res., 409 W. Columbia Ave., 48111. Tel: 313-697-1211; Fax: 313-697-6217.
School—Tel: 313-699-4313; Fax: 313-699-0824. Sr. Denise Seymour, Prin.
Sisters of St. Joseph of the Third Order of St. Francis 2; Lay Teachers 10; Students 259.
Convent—371 W. Columbia Ave., 48111.

Berkley, Oakland Co., Our Lady of La Salette, Rev. Lawrence Zurawski; Deacon Daniel Darga.
Res., 2600 Harvard Rd., 48072. Tel: 810-541-3762; Fax: 810-541-4250.
School—Tel: 810-542-3757. Sr. Barbara Beerkle, O.P., Prin.
Sisters 2; Lay Teachers 9; Students 268.
Catechesis/Religious Programs—Tel: 810-547-1150.
Students 215.

Beverly Hills, Franklin Co., Our Lady of Albanians, Rev. Primus P. Ndrevashay.
Res., 20855 W. Thirteen Mile Rd., 48025. Tel: 810-642-0816; Fax: 810-642-0251.

Birmingham, Oakland Co.,

1—ST. COLUMBAN, Very Rev. Msgr. John A. Trese; Patricia Costigan, Pastoral Assoc.; Deacon Robert Ovies.
Res., 2200 Dunstable, 48009. Tel: 810-642-1148; Fax: 810-642-4636.
Church—1775 Melton, 48009. Tel: 810-646-5224.
Catechesis/Religious Programs—Tel: 810-646-5225. Nancy Sullivan, D.R.E.
Students 205.

2—HOLY NAME, Rev. Robert E. Burke. Pastoral Assocs.: Donna M. Hansen; Mary A. Pineau; Sr. Shirlee Hoski, S.S.J.-T.O.S.F.; Deacon Michael J. McKale.
Parish Office—630 Harmon St., 48009.
Res., 645 Woodland Ave., 48009. Tel: 810-646-2244; Fax: 810-646-2286.
School—Tel: 810-644-2722. Sr. Annice Mordenski, O.P., Prin.
Sisters 2; Lay Teachers 16; Students 321.
Catechesis/Religious Programs—Mary Marian, D.R.E.
Students 380.

3—OUR LADY QUEEN OF MARTYRS, Rev. Richard F. Wyzgoski. In res., Rev. Michael J. Heppen, C.S.C.
Res., 32340 Pierce Ave., Beverly Hills, 48025. Tel: 810-644-8620; Fax: 810-644-8623.
School—32460 Pierce Ave., Beverly Hills, 48025. Tel: 810-642-2616. Peter J. Ferguson, Prin.
Lay Teachers 15; Students 330.
Catechesis/Religious Programs—Marie Therese Walbridge, D.R.E.
Students 235.

4—ST. REGIS, Revs. Daniel J. Murphy; Patrick J. Connell; Deacon Brian Carroll. In res., Rev. Duane Doherty, O.F.M.Conv.
Res., 3695 Lincoln, 48301. Tel: 810-646-2686; Fax: 810-646-4643.
School—Tel: 810-644-4466. Barbara S. Stork, Prin.
Lay Teachers 18; Students 342.
Catechesis/Religious Programs—Robert Metz, D.R.E.
Students 158.

Bloomfield Hills, Oakland Co., St. Hugo of the Hills, Rev. Msgr. Anthony M. Tocco; Rev. James Bilot; Sr. Barbara Rund, O.P., Pastoral Assoc.; Deacon Michael T. Smith.
Res., 2215 Opdyke Rd., 48304. Tel: 810-644-5460; Fax: 810-644-1758.
School—380 E. Hickory Grove, 48304. Tel: 810-642-6131; Fax: 810-642-4457. Sr. Margaret Van Velzen, I.H.M., Prin.
Sisters, Servants of the Immaculate Heart of Mary 5; Lay Teachers 35; Students 870.
Catechesis/Religious Programs—Tel: 810-642-6062.
Students 359.

St. Owen, Rev. Msgr. Edward J. Baldwin. Pastoral Ministers: Sr. Carolyn Nelson; Sr. Anne McGinn; Mrs. Kathryn Michalik. In res., Rev. Msgr. William Sherzer, (Retired).
Res., 6869 Franklin Rd., 48301. Tel: 810-626-0840; Fax: 810-626-0345.
Catechesis/Religious Programs—Tel: 810-626-2300. Mrs. Kathryn Michalik, D.R.E.
Students 400.

Canton, Wayne Co., Saint John Neumann, Rev. George Charnley; Eugene Kijek, Pastoral Min. In res., Rev. Robert Cislo.
Res., 44800 Warren Rd., 48187. Tel: 313-455-5910; Fax: 313-455-6779.
Catechesis/Religious Programs—Ms. Fran Dawson, D.R.E.
Students 1,324.

Resurrection, Rev. Richard A. Perfetto.
48755 Warren Rd., 48187-1216. Tel: 313-451-0444; Fax: 313-451-0454.
Catechesis/Religious Programs—Students 200.

St. Thomas a Becket, Rev. C. Richard Kelly.
Res., 555 S. Lilley Rd., 48188. Tel: 313-981-1333; Fax: 313-981-1481.
Catechesis/Religious Programs—Tel: 313-981-6680.
Students 930.

Capac, St. Clair Co., St. Nicholas, Rev. Bogdan Milosz.
Res., 15096 W. Park, 48014.
Church—4331 Capac Rd., Tel: 810-395-7572; Fax: 810-395-7572.

Carleton, Monroe Co., St. Patrick, Rev. Robert A. Bauer.
Res., 2996 Labo Rd., 48117. Tel: 313-654-2500; Fax: 313-654-6594. [CEM]
School—Tel: 313-654-2522. Sr. Jeanne Twomey, S.S.J., Prin.
Sisters 1; Lay Teachers 11; Students 205.
Catechesis/Religious Programs—Tel: 313-654-6444. Diane Janssens, D.R.E.
Students 250.
Convent—2970 Labo Rd., 48117. Tel: 313-654-2904.

Centerline, Macomb Co., St. Clement, Revs. Arthur H. Jacobi, Jr.; James A. Mayworm; Carl J. Yagley; Sr. Emeline Bash, O.P., Pastoral Assoc.
Res., 8075 Ritter Ave., 48015-1499. Tel: 810-757-3306; Fax: 810-757-5390. [CEM]
School—Tel: 810-757-7500; Fax: 810-757-4724. Patricia A. Downey, Prin.
Lay Teachers 25; Students 420.
High School—Tel: 810-757-1739; Fax: 810-757-1797. Deborah A. Michon, Prin.
Lay Teachers 22; Students 207.
Catechesis/Religious Programs—Tel: 810-757-3306; Fax: 810-757-5390. Thomas P. Oppat, D.R.E.

Students 300.

Clarkston, Oakland Co., St. Daniel, Rev. Msgr. Robert S. Humitz; Deacon Alexander Jablonowski.
Res., 7010 Valley Park Dr., 48346. Tel: 810-625-4580; Fax: 810-620-9839.
Catechesis/Religious Programs—Tel: 810-625-1750. Frieda Arpoika, D.R.E.
Students 850.

Clawson, Oakland Co., Guardian Angels, Revs. Gary M. Tierney; David G. Burgard; Deacon Eugene Tombler. In res., Revs. Vincent Nguyen An Ninh (Vietnamese); Bernard Schroll; John Blaska.
Res., 581 E. 14 Mile Rd., 48017. Tel: 810-588-1222; Fax: 810-588-8767.
School—Tel: 810-588-5545. Mr. Frank Spencer, Prin.
Dominican Sisters (Adrian) 1; Lay Teachers 23; Students 462.
Catechesis/Religious Programs—Eilleen Burke, D.R.E.
Students 411.

Clinton Twp., Macomb Co.,

1—St. Claude, Rev. Edward J. Wilk.
Res., 33826 Beaconsfield, 48035. Tel: 810-791-6630; Fax: 810-791-0017.
Catechesis/Religious Programs—Donna Hartner, D.R.E.
Students 133.

2—St. Louis, Rev. Pasquale LoGrasso; Sr. Rose Arnold, S.C., Pastoral Assoc.; Deacon Donald C. Junak. In res., Rev. Thomas Physician.
Res., 24415 Crocker Blvd., 48036. Tel: 810-468-8734; Fax: 810-468-9647.
Catechesis/Religious Programs—Tel: 810-468-4332. Joyce Appelt, D.R.E.
Students 400.
Convent—39173 Ormsby St., 48036. Tel: 810-468-4574.

3—St. Paul of Tarsus, Rev. Louis E. Grandpre; Rev. Msgr. Eugene Edyk; Rev. Clifford Ruskowski; Deacon Edward Wilson.
Res., 41300 Romeo Plank Rd., 48038. Tel: 810-228-1210; Fax: 810-228-8935.
Catechesis/Religious Programs—Tel: 810-228-0047. Audrey Wentz, D.R.E.
Students 1,067.

4—St. Ronald, Rev. Lawrence T. Fares.
Res., 17701 15 Mile Rd., 48035-2401. Tel: 810-792-1190; Fax: 810-792-0765.
Catechesis/Religious Programs—Tel: 810-792-1276.
Students 130.

5—St. Thecla, Revs. Gary T. Smetanka; Michael Hrydziuszko; Sr. M. Francesca, C.S.S.F., Pastoral Assoc.
Res., 20740 Nunneley Rd., 48035-1628. Tel: 810-791-3930; Fax: 810-791-3890.
School—Tel: 810-791-2170.
Felician Sisters 3; Lay Teachers 18; Students 508.
Catechesis/Religious Programs—Tel: 810-792-0550.
Students 531.

6—St. Valerie of Ravenna, Rev. Richard Cavellier.
Res., 23300 King Dr., 48035. Tel: 810-791-5450; Fax: 810-791-6876.

7—San Francesco Community, Rev. Giulio Schiavi, P.I.M.E.
Res., 22870 S. Nunneley Rd., 48035. Tel: 810-792-5346; Fax: 810-792-5119.
Catechesis/Religious Programs—Students 155.

Columbus, St. Clair Co., St. Philip Neri, Rev. Francis A. Zielinski.
Res., 9735 Dolan Rd., 48063. Tel: 810-727-7263. [CEM]
Mission—Smiths Creek, St. Clair Co., Holy Rosary.

Dearborn, Wayne Co.,

1—St. Alphonsus, Rev. Michael W. Quaine.
Res., 7455 Calhoun Ave., 48126. Tel: 313-581-5218; Fax: 313-584-9560.
School—Tel: 313-581-1886. John Rashid, Grade & High School Prin.
Lay Teachers 13; Students 270.
High School—Tel: 313-582-4266; Fax: 313-584-9589.
Adrian Dominican Sisters 1; Lay Teachers 20; Students 305.
Catechesis/Religious Programs—Tel: 313-581-5218. Judith Bedard, D.R.E.
Students 100.
Convent—13541 Gould Ave., 48126. Tel: 313-584-4350.

2—St. Barbara, Rev. Zbigniew W. Grankowski; Deacon Richard B. Hulan, Pastoral Assoc.
Res., 13534 Colson Ave., 48126. Tel: 313-582-8383; Fax: 313-582-1581.

3—St. Bernadette, Rev. Robert Cini, M.S.S.P. (Malta).
Res., 2600 Saulino Court, 48120. Tel: 313-841-0400; Fax: 313-841-2140.

4—St. Clement, Rev. Arnold V. Dachille; Sr. Ann Dineen, S.M., Pastoral Assoc.
Res., 5275 Kenilworth Ave., 48126. Tel: 313-581-7495; Fax: 313-581-4233.
Catechesis/Religious Programs—Tel: 313-846-2443. Tim Pilon, D.R.E.
Students 90.

5—Divine Child, Rev. Msgr. Herman W. Kucyk. In res., Revs. Matthew Ellis; John C. Riccardo.
Res., 25001 Hollander, 48128. Tel: 313-277-3110; Fax: 313-277-3211.
School—Tel: 313-562-1090; Fax: 313-562-2045. Sr. Cecilia Bondy, Elementary Prin.
Bernardine Sisters 9; Lay Teachers 25; Students 842.
High School—Tel: 313-562-1990. Sr. Elena Sabalausky, High School Prin.
Bernardine Sisters 7; Lay Teachers 56; Students 912.
Catechesis/Religious Programs—Sr. Helen Therese Bodziak, D.R.E.
Students 264.
Convent—1045 N. Silvery Ln., 48128. Tel: 313-561-5455.

6—St. Joseph, Rev. Adolph Redwick.
Res., 16101 Rotunda Dr., 48120. Tel: 313-336-3227; Fax: 313-441-6769.

7—St. Martha, Rev. John F. Child.
Res., 18200 Oakwood Blvd., 48124. Tel: 313-336-4090; Fax: 313-336-3318.

8—Sacred Heart, Revs. James P. Kenneally; Jack H. Baker; Fran Helner, Pastoral Assoc.
Res., 22430 W. Michigan Ave., 48124. Tel: 313-278-4654; Fax: 313-278-8582. [CEM]
School—22513 Garrison, 48124. Tel: 313-561-9192; Fax: 313-561-1598. Keiren Stoller, Prin.
Sisters 2; Lay Teachers 17; Students 397.
Catechesis/Religious Programs—Denise Daniel, D.R.E.
Students 335.

Dearborn Heights, Wayne Co.,

1—St. Albert the Great, Rev. Lawrence Kaiser; Sr. Mary Downey, I.H.M., Pastoral Assoc.; Deacon Robert Rowland.
Res., 4855 Parker, 48125. Tel: 313-292-0430; Fax: 313-292-8565.
School—Tel: 313-292-1144.
Sisters, Servants of the Immaculate Heart of Mary 1; Lay Teachers 9; Students 231.
Catechesis/Religious Programs—Tel: 313-292-9370. Mrs. Barbara Brown, D.R.E.
Students 215.
Convent—4864 Parker, 48127. Tel: 313-292-0493.

2—St. Anselm, Rev. Msgr. James A. Moloney, Pastor and Dir., Society for The Propagation; Sr. Mary Ann Thue, R.S.M., Pastoral Assoc. & Prin.
Res., 17650 W. Outer Dr., 48127. Tel: 313-565-4808; Fax: 313-565-7514.
School—Tel: 313-563-3430.
Sisters 4; Lay Teachers 6; Students 270.
Catechesis/Religious Programs—Tel: 313-561-0512. Sr. Mary Ann Thue, R.S.M., D.R.E.
Students 155.
Convent—20495 Brooklawn, 48127. Tel: 313-271-2287.

3—St. John the Baptist, Rev. Edwin W. Balazy.
Res., 26123 McDonald Ave., 48125. Tel: 313-292-9693; Fax: 313-292-1755.

4—St. Linus, Rev. Randall R. Phillips; Deacon George Cochrane. In res., Rev. George Miller.
Parish Office: 6466 Evangeline, 48127-2086.
Res., 6465 N. Gulley Rd., 48127-2086. Tel: 313-274-4500; Fax: 313-562-2821.
School—Tel: 313-274-5320. Thomas Judd, Prin.
Lay Teachers 11; Students 303.
Catechesis/Religious Programs—Tel: 313-274-5778.
Students 295.
Convent—25450 Hass, 48127.

5—St. Mel, Rev. William G. Petron; Sr. Carmen Dominguez, O.P., Pastoral Assoc.
Church—7506 Inkster Rd., 48127. Tel: 313-274-0684; Fax: 313-274-9080.
School—Tel: 313-274-6270. Ann-Marie Hergott, Prin.
Lay Teachers 9; Students 147.
Catechesis/Religious Programs—Tel: 313-274-3977. Nancy Liebau, D.R.E.
Students 225.

6—Our Lady of Grace, Rev. Ronald Cyprys; Deacon Robert DeWitt. In res., Rev. Charles O'Neill.
Res., 8679 Riverview, 48127. Tel: 313-561-6373; Fax: 313-359-2727.
Church—23700 Joy Rd., 48127.
School—Tel: 313-562-6524.
Lay Teachers 10; Students 185.
Convent—8664 Appleton Ave., 48127. Tel: 313-562-7476. Shalom Spiritual Life Center

7—St. Sabina, Rev. Joseph L. Romano.
Res., 25605 Ann Arbor Tr., 48127. Tel: 313-561-1977; Fax: 313-561-7898.
School—Tel: 313-274-5628.
Sisters 2; Lay Teachers 8; Students 231.
Catechesis/Religious Programs—Tel: 313-274-5635.
Students 80.

8—St. Sebastian, Revs. William B. Brennan; John Cusmano; Rita Oleksiak, Pastoral Min.
Res., 3850 Merrick Ave., Dearborn, 48124. Tel: 313-562-5356; Fax: 313-562-0058.
School—Tel: 313-563-6640.
Franciscan Sisters of St. Joseph 4; Lay Teachers 16; Students 443.
Catechesis/Religious Programs—Tel: 313-563-0960. Judy Valiguette, D.R.E.
Students 445.
Convent—20700 Colgate Ave., 48125. Tel: 313-562-7733.

Dryden, Lapeer Co., St. Cornelius, Rev. Wayne G. Ureel.
Res., 3834 Mill St., P.O. Box 208, 48428. Tel: 810-796-2926; Fax: 810-796-9713.

Dundee, Monroe Co., St. Irene, Rev. Ronald J. Alder.
Res., 576 Main St., 48131. Tel: 313-529-2160; Fax: 313-529-2160.

Eastpointe, Macomb Co., St. Barnabas, Rev. William J. Keveney; Deacon Thomas M. Thomas.
Res., 24800 Phlox Ave., 48021. Tel: 810-775-2284; Fax: 810-775-6933.
Catechesis/Religious Programs—Geraldine Combetta, D.R.E.
Students 180.

St. Basil, Rev. James H. Profota; Deacon Rocco Mauiri.
Parish Center—22851 Lexington Ave., 48021. Tel: 810-777-5610; Fax: 810-779-3341.
Catechesis/Religious Programs—Tel: 810-772-5434.
Students 282.

St. Veronica, Revs. Stanley L. Pachla, Jr.; Daniel Zaleski; Januscz Iwan; Kulan Daisamy Arokiasamy.
Res., 21440 Universal Dr., 48021. Tel: 810-777-0331; Fax: 810-777-0615.
School—Tel: 810-775-8333. Sr. Gloria Jean Zieske, Prin.
Sisters of St. Joseph 4; Adrian Dominican 1; Lay Teachers 14; Students 418.
Catechesis/Religious Programs—D.R.E.: Sr. Mary Ann Ankoviak, S.S.J.; Sr. Geraldine Arnold, S.S.J.
Students 285.
Convent—21357 Redmond, 48021. Tel: 810-777-0321.

Ecorse, Wayne Co., St. Francis Xavier, Rev. Jeffrey Anifer.
Res., 4250 W. Jefferson Ave., 48229. Tel: 313-383-8514; Fax: 313-383-7508. [CEM]
Catechesis/Religious Programs—Cathy Borsch, D.R.E.
Students 174.

Emmett, St. Clair Co., Our Lady of Mount Carmel, Rev. Jasper Sirianni.
Res., 10828 Brandon Rd., 48022. Tel: 810-384-1338; Fax: 810-384-1338.
Catechesis/Religious Programs—Tel: 810-384-6925.
Students 214.
Convent—10832 Brandon Rd., 48022. Tel: 313-384-6925.

Erie, Monroe Co., St. Joseph, Rev. Joseph Plawecki.
Res., 2214 Manhattan Ave., 48133. Tel: 313-848-6125; Fax: 313-848-2784. [CEM]
School—Tel: 313-848-6985.
Sisters 2; Lay Teachers 12; Students 240.
Convent—2238 Manhattan Ave., 48133. Tel: 313-848-8754.

Farmington, Oakland Co., St. Colman, Rev. Norbert V. Kendzierski; Mrs. Kathleen O. Dardy, Pastoral Assoc.
Res., 32500 Middlebelt Rd., Farmington Hills, 48334. Tel: 810-626-0285; Fax: 810-626-5420.
Catechesis/Religious Programs—Tel: 810-626-0287.
Students 61.

St. Gerald, Rev. Gerald A. McEnhill.
Res., 21300 Farmington Rd., 48336. Tel: 810-477-7470; Fax: 810-477-3878.
Catechesis/Religious Programs—Tel: 810-476-7677. Mary Taylor, D.R.E.
Students 410.

Our Lady of Sorrows, Rev. Msgr. Walter A. Hurley; Revs. Douglas J. Bignall; Loren F. O'Dea; Sr. Christine Mihelcic, S.J., Dir. In res., Rev. Arthur W. Fauser.
Res., 23815 Power Rd., 48336. Tel: 810-474-5720; Fax: 810-474-1340.
School—(Grades K-8). Tel: 810-476-0977 (Elem.); 810-615-5574 (Middle). Roberta Clemak, Prin. (Grades K-8).
Lay Teachers 40; Students 785.

Catechesis/Religious Programs—Tel: 810-474-6480. Bette Jannott, D.R.E.
Students 527.

Farmington Hills, Oakland Co., St. Alexander, Rev. James B. Wright.
Res., 27835 Shiawassee, 48336. Tel: 810-474-5748; Fax: 810-474-5776.
Catechesis/Religious Programs—Tel: 810-474-8126; Fax: 810-474-8231.
Students 243.

St. Clare of Assisi, Rev. Frederick J. Klettner.
Res., 29200 W. Ten Mile, 48336. Tel: 810-477-9870; Fax: 810-477-4785.

St. Fabian, Rev. Brian J. Chabala.
Church—32200 W. 12 Mile Rd., 48334. Tel: 810-553-4610; Fax: 810-553-6296.
Res., 32265 Red Clover Rd., 48334.
School—Tel: 810-553-2750. Sr. M. Loretelle, O.S.F., Prin.
Bernardine Sisters 3; Lay Teachers 13; Students 330.
Catechesis/Religious Programs—Gina Karl, D.R.E.
Students 651.
Convent—32170 Twelve Mile Rd., 48334. Tel: 313-553-4186.

Ferndale, Oakland Co., St. James, Rev. Robert L. Wurm; Sr. Eveleen Forkin, Pastoral Min.; W. Michael O'Neill, Pastoral Assoc.
Res., 241 W. Pearson Ave., 48220. Tel: 810-542-8835; Fax: 810-542-0267.
Catechesis/Religious Programs—W. Michael O'Neill, D.R.E.
Students 390.

Flat Rock, Wayne Co., St. Roch, Rev. Frederick Misiolek; Deacon Harold Goodhue.
Res., 25022 Gibraltar Rd., 48134. Tel: 313-782-4471; Fax: 313-782-5450.

Fraser, Macomb Co., Our Lady Queen of All Saints, Rev. Ronald J. Babich; Sr. Nancy Zajac, O.P., Pastoral Assoc.
Res., 31740 Cyril Dr., 48026. Tel: 810-293-4050; Fax: 810-293-1041.
Catechesis/Religious Programs—Tel: 810-294-6180; Fax: 810-293-1041.
Students 421.

Garden City, Wayne Co., St. Dunstan, Rev. Donald Demmer; Deacon Michael Markulike.
Res., 1646 Belton Ave., 48135. Tel: 313-425-6720; Fax: 313-425-8511.
School—1615 Belton Ave., 48135. Tel: 313-425-4380. Sr. Mariella Chrusciel, Prin.
Sisters 1; Lay Teachers 10; Students 244.
Catechesis/Religious Programs—Tel: 313-425-4396. Sr. Mary Martin, D.R.E.
Students 206.

St. Raphael the Archangel, Rev. Edward Prus; Sr. Ritamary Pyzick, Pastoral Min.
Parish Center—31530 Beechwood, 48135. Tel: 313-427-1533; Fax: 313-427-8594.
Parish Hall—5875 Merriman, 48135. Tel: 313-422-9617.
School—Tel: 313-425-9771. Judith McBride, Prin.
Lay Teachers 20; Students 440.
Catechesis/Religious Programs—Tel: 313-425-5550. Sr. Patricia Donnelly, D.R.E.
Students 336.

Gibraltar, Wayne Co., St. Victor, Rev. Roger A. Knapp.
Res., 14100 Navarre, 48173. Tel: 313-675-0100; Fax: 313-675-6952.

Grosse Ile, Wayne Co., Sacred Heart, Rev. Thomas P. Flynn; Sr. Mary Ann Kasper, S.J., Pastoral Assoc.; Deacon Robert Tremmel.
Res., 21526 E. River Rd., 48138. Tel: 313-671-3043. [CEM]
Parish Center—21599 Parke Ln., 48138. Tel: 313-676-1378; Fax: 313-676-3623.
Catechesis/Religious Programs—Tel: 313-676-1378.
Students 697.
Convent—21537 Parke Ln., 48138. Tel: 313-671-3056.

Grosse Pointe, Wayne Co., Our Lady Star of the Sea, Rev. Msgr. Dennis Harrity; Rev. John J. Mech.
Church—467 Fairford, 48236. Tel: 313-884-5554; Fax: 313-885-5591.
School—Tel: 313-884-1070. Dr. Lois Masouris, Prin.
Lay Teachers 26; Students 419.
Catechesis/Religious Programs—Tel: 313-884-7407. Helen L. Goettl, D.R.E.
Students 401.
Convent—19950 Morningside Dr., 48236. Tel: 313-884-4074.

Grosse Pointe Farms, Wayne Co., St. Paul Catholic Church, Rev. Msgr. F. Gerald Martin; Rev. George W. Williams. Pastoral Assocs.: Deacon Richard Shubick; Sr. Ruthanne Reed, O.P. In res., Rev. Michael O'Leary.
Res., 157 Lake Shore Rd., 48236. Tel: 313-885-8855; Fax: 313-886-6467. [CEM]
School—170 Grosse Pointe Blvd., 48236. Tel: 313-885-3430; Fax: 313-885-9357. Elizabeth A. Burns, Prin.
Sisters 3; Lay Teachers 24; Students 495.
Catechesis/Religious Programs—Sr. Janet Schaeffler, O.P., D.R.E.
Students 514.

Grosse Pointe Park, Wayne Co., St. Ambrose, Rev. Timothy R. Pelc. Pastoral Assocs.: Sr. Irene Kerich, O.P.; Deacons John Schaible, Emeritus; William Jamieson.
Res., 15020 Hampton, 48230. Tel: 313-822-2814; Fax: 313-822-9838.
School—Tel: 313-823-0177. Sr. Marie Cyril DeLisi, I.H.M., Prin.
Religious 4; Lay Teachers 9; Students 200.
Catechesis/Religious Programs—Julie Telang, D.R.E.
Students 210.

St. Clare of Montefalco, Rev. Joseph E. McCormick, O.S.A. In res., Revs. John J. Burkhart, O.S.A.; Joseph F. Hartman, O.S.A.; Francis R. McDonnell, O.S.A.; Robert Gardella, O.S.A.
Res., 1401 Whittier Rd., 48230. Tel: 313-885-4960; Fax: 313-885-8533.
School—16231 Charlevoix, 48230. Tel: 313-886-1440; Fax: 313-886-1437.
Catechesis/Religious Programs—Tel: 313-884-2110. Paula Miller, D.R.E.
Students 490.

Hamtramck, Wayne Co., St. Florian, Revs. Wojciech Baryski, S.Ch.; Darrell Roman, S.Ch.
Res., 2626 Poland Ave., 48212. Tel: 313-871-2778; Fax: 313-871-5947.
Church—Florian and Latham Aves., 48212.
School—Tel: 313-875-3040.
Felician Sisters 2; Lay Teachers 8; Students 261.
High School—Tel: 313-875-6347. Sr. Mary Estelle, C.S.S.F., Prin.
Felician Sisters 2; Lay Teachers 12; Students 148.
Convent—2622 Florian Ave., 48212. Tel: 313-872-5775.

St. Ladislaus (Polish), Rev. Stanley A. Ulman. In res., Rev. Stanislaus Czapiewski, S.J.
Res., 2730 Caniff Ave., 48212. Tel: 313-872-0709; Fax: 313-872-5906.
Convent—2697 Caniff Ave., 48212. Tel: 313-365-6610. Sisters of St. Francis (Sylvania, OH)

Our Lady Queen of Apostles (Polish), Revs. Gary M. Michalik; Wojciech Wojcicki.
Res., 3851 Prescott Ave., 48212-3115. Tel: 313-891-1520; 1521; Fax: 313-891-3552.
School—11420 Conant, 48212. Tel: 313-892-8130. Sr. Florence M. Owczarzak, C.S.S.F., Prin.
Sisters 4; Lay Teachers 8; Students 190.
Convent—3891 Prescott Ave., 48212-3115. Tel: 313-891-7121.

Harper Woods, Wayne Co., Our Lady Queen of Peace, Rev. Daniel C. Complo. In res., Revs. John M. Fee, SS.CC.; Eugene Fedewa; John T. Gordon.
Res., 20955 Bournemouth Ave., 48225. Tel: 313-881-5212; Fax: 313-881-7813.
School—Tel: 313-881-3629. Richard Flaherty, Prin. & D.R.E.
Lay Teachers 11; Students 203.
Catechesis/Religious Programs—Tel: 313-884-8744.
Students 160.

St. Peter the Apostle, Rev. Robert J. Keller.
Res., 19851 Anita St., 48225. Tel: 313-886-1771; Fax: 313-886-1489.
School—Tel: 313-885-8062. Sr. Kathleen DeSmedt, I.H.M., Prin.
Sisters 3; Lay Teachers 16; Students 254.

Harrison Twp., Macomb Co., St. Hubert, Rev. James J. O'Leary; Sr. Susan Ouwerkerk, O.P., Pastoral Assoc.
Res., 38775 Prentiss, 48045. Tel: 810-463-5877; 463-7796; Fax: 810-463-1734.
Catechesis/Religious Programs—Tel: 810-463-5875. Mr. Allan Ranusch, D.R.E.
Students 476.

Harsens Island, St. Clair Co., St. Mark, Rev. Erwin J. Bauer, Admin.
Res., Church and Rectory, 4190 Green Dr., Harsen's Island, 48028. Tel: 810-748-3828; Fax: 810-748-9148.

Hazel Park, Oakland Co., St. Justin, Rev. Robert Hayes Williams.
Res., 1631 E. Elza St., 48030. Tel: 810-542-2129.

St. Mary Magdalen, Revs. Michael Bertram, O.F.M.Cap.; Malcolm Maloney, O.F.M.Cap.
Res., 50 E. Annabelle, 48030. Tel: 810-542-8060; Fax: 810-542-4563.
School—Tel: 810-547-3363. Suzanne Kisseberth, Prin.
Sisters 2; Lay Teachers 9; Students 210.
Catechesis/Religious Programs—Tel: 810-547-0323. Anne Fox-McGrath, D.R.E.
Students 223.

Highland, Oakland Co., Church of the Holy Spirit, Rev. Leo T. Lulko.
Church—3700 Harvey Lake Rd., 48356.
Res., 1673 Apollo Dr., 48356. Tel: 810-887-9029; Fax: 810-889-1374.
Catechesis/Religious Programs—Tel: 810-887-9029. Joann Dalton, D.R.E.
Students 666.

Highland Park, Wayne Co., St. Benedict, Rev. Robert B. McGrath; Deacon Richard Conlin.
Res., 60 Church Ave., 48203. Tel: 313-868-3876; Fax: 313-868-0110.
School—53 Candler, 48203. Tel: 313-868-7502. Kathleen Freeman, Prin.
Sisters 3; Lay Teachers 10; Students 260.

Holly, Oakland Co., St. Rita, Rev. Joseph P. Killeen.
Res., 309 E. Maple, 48442. Tel: 810-634-4841; Fax: 810-634-4858.
Catechesis/Religious Programs—Tel: 810-634-1658. Dawn M. Sliwa, D.R.E.
Students 209.

Ida, Monroe Co., St. Joseph, Rev. John P. LaCasse, Admin.
Res., 8295 Van Akin St., 48140. Tel: 313-269-3895. [CEM]
Catechesis/Religious Programs—Tel: 313-269-3414. Sr. Mary Johnson D.R.E.
Students 274.

Imlay City, Lapeer Co., Sacred Heart, Rev. Ezequiel Mondragon.
Res., 700 Maple Vista, 48444. Tel: 810-724-1135; Fax: 810-724-0870. [CEM]
Catechesis/Religious Programs—Tel: 810-724-1145.
Students 185.

Inkster, Wayne Co., Holy Family Parish, Revs. John Lehner, O.S.F.S.; Festus Ejimadu.
Res., 27800 Annapolis Rd., 48141. Tel: 313-563-8242.

St. Kevin and St. Norbert, Revs. John Lehner, O.S.F.S.; Festus Ejimadu.
Office: 27355 Woodsfield, 48141.
Res., 604 Sherbourne Dr., 48141. Tel: 313-563-0993; Fax: 313-563-3148.
Catechesis/Religious Programs—Tel: 313-278-4924; Fax: 313-563-3148.
Students 160.

Lake Orion, Oakland Co., St. Joseph, Revs. John L. Phalen; Bernard J. Mullen. Pastoral Assocs.: Sr. Barbara Jean Pelak, O.P.; William Chamberlin; Deacon Thomas Yezak. In res., Rev. Daniel Thottakara, C.M.I.
Res., 715 N. Lapeer Rd., 48362. Tel: 810-693-0440; Fax: 810-693-3724.
School—Tel: 810-693-6215; Fax: 810-693-0958. Sr. Theresa Darga, O.S.F., Prin.
Lay Teachers 13; Students 288.
Catechesis/Religious Programs—Regina Moskal, D.R.E.
Students 693.

Lakeport, St. Clair Co., St. Edward's on the Lake, Rev. Leonard P. Wallace.
Res., 6945 Lakeshore Rd., 48059. Tel: 810-385-4340; Fax: 810-364-3472.
School—(Grades K-5). For grades 6-8 please refer to McCormick Consolidated Academy, Port Huron, under Elementary Schools, Inter-Parochial in the Institutions Located in the Archdiocese section. Tel: 810-385-4461.
Students 95.
Convent—6975 Lakeshore Rd., 48059. Tel: 810-385-9531.

Lapeer, Lapeer Co., Immaculate Conception of the Blessed Virgin Mary, Revs. Douglas J. Terrien; David Lesniak; Deacon Gerald Deshaw.
Res., 814 Nepessing, 48446. Tel: 810-664-8594; Fax: 810-664-4564. [CEM]
School—Bishop Kelley School, Tel: 810-664-5011. Miss Barbara Davis, Prin.
Lay Teachers 9; Students 190.
Catechesis/Religious Programs—Tel: 810-664-0868.
Students 540.

Lincoln Park, Wayne Co., Christ the Good Shepherd, Revs. David A. Buersmeyer; Marek Stochmal; Sr. Marge Zacharias, Pastoral Assoc.
Res., 1531 Riverbank Ave., 48146. Tel: 313-928-1324; Fax: 313-928-1326.
School—Tel: 313-386-0633. Thomas Caruso, Prin.
Lay Teachers 24; Students 485.
Catechesis/Religious Programs—Sr. Diann Cousino, D.R.E.
Students 310.

St. Henry, Rev. Gerald J. Cupple.
Res., 1358 Council Ave., 48146. Tel: 313-381-0711; 0712; Fax: 313-381-6746.
Catechesis/Religious Programs—Anne Martus, D.R.E.
Students 150.

Livonia, Wayne Co.,
1—ST. AIDAN, Rev. Gerald K. Flannery; Dr. Jerard E.

Delaney, II, Pastoral Assoc. & D.R.E.; Deacon Ray Gabel.
Res., 17500 Farmington Rd., 48152. Tel: 313-425-5950; Fax: 313-425-3687.
Catechesis/Religious Programs—Tel: 313-425-9333. Mary Ellen Skene, Assoc. D.R.E.
Students 600.

2—St. Colette, Revs. Henry W. Roodbeen; Robert McCabe; Deacons Al Morad; Leo D'Argis.
Res., 17600 Newburgh, 48152-2699. Tel: 313-464-4433; Fax: 313-464-1694.
Catechesis/Religious Programs—Tel: 313-464-4435; Fax: 313-464-7817. Linda Tuss, D.R.E.
Students 892.

3—St. Edith, Revs. James C. Scheick; John Castelot; Deacons John Kenny; Ric Misiak.
Res., 15089 Newburgh, 48154. Tel: 313-464-1222; Fax: 313-464-7582.
School—Tel: 313-464-1250. Sr. Margaret Kijek, C.S.S.F., Prin.
Felician Sisters 1; Lay Teachers 8; Students 300.
Catechesis/Religious Programs—Tel: 313-464-2020. Elizabeth Nowak, D.R.E.
Students 500.

4—St. Genevieve, Rev. Kean D. Cronin; Deacon R. P. Piro, Pastoral Assoc.
Res., 29015 Jamison, 48154. Tel: 313-427-5220; Fax: 313-422-1763.
School—Tel: 313-425-4420. Sr. M. Juanita Szymanski, C.S.S.F., Prin.
Sisters 3; Lay Teachers 7; Students 315.
Catechesis/Religious Programs—Tel: 313-261-5920. D.R.E.: Gail Shymanski; Georgene Wojciechowski.
Students 331.

5—St. Maurice, Rev. John P. Maierle; Darlene Bellmore, Pastoral Assoc.
Res., 32765 Lyndon Ave., 48154. Tel: 313-522-1616; Fax: 313-522-5092.
Catechesis/Religious Programs—Tel: 313-421-5240. Lezlie Allison, D.R.E.
Students 149.

6—St. Michael, Rev. Alberto P. Bondy; Deacon Robert C. Fitzgerald.
Res., 11441 Hubbard Ave., 48150. Tel: 313-261-1455; Fax: 313-522-1123.
School—Tel: 313-421-7360. Sr. M. Carolyn Ratkowski, C.S.S.F., Prin.
Felician Sisters 6; Lay Teachers 25; Students 764.
Religious Education—Tel: 313-261-1790.
Students 277.
Catechesis/Religious Programs—Students 277.
Convent—11400 Fairfield, Tel: 313-421-7522.

7—St. Priscilla, Rev. Kevin P. O'Brien; Deacon Ray Kunik.
Res., 19120 Purling Brook Rd., 48152. Tel: 810-442-9419; Fax: 810-476-7831.
Catechesis/Religious Programs—Tel: 810-476-4702.
Students 490.

Macomb, Macomb Co., St. Isidore, Revs. Frank J. Berge; Kevin Thomas, M.M.; Karl DeLisle, Pastoral Assoc.
Res., 18201 Twenty-three Mile Rd., 48042. Tel: 810-286-1700; Fax: 810-286-8753.
Catechesis/Religious Programs—Tel: 810-286-4433. Betty Frei, D.R.E.
Students 1,251.

Madison Heights, Oakland Co., St. Vincent Ferrer, Rev. Steven C. Koehler; Deacon Ralph Hardwick; Sr. Mary Jo Seig, O.P., Pastoral Assoc.
Res., 1087 E. Gardenia Ave., 48071. Tel: 810-542-8720; Fax: 810-542-8721.
School—1075 E. Gardenia, 48071. Tel: 810-398-4190. Mrs. Suzanne Pientak, Prin.
Lay Teachers 14; Students 140.
Catechesis/Religious Programs—Sandra Wishart, D.R.E.
Students 221.

Marine City, St. Clair Co., Holy Cross, Rev. James R. Wysocki; Deacon Gary Krueger.
Res., 610 S. Water St., 48039. Tel: 810-765-3568; Fax: 810-765-2974. [CEM]
School—Holy Cross Elementary, Tel: 810-765-3591. Mrs. Dianne Lovette, Prin.
Dominican Sisters 1; Lay Teachers 8; Students 171.
High School—Cardinal Mooney Catholic, Tel: 810-765-3591; Fax: 810-765-8825. Dr. Elsie L. Ogden, Prin.
Priests 1; Sisters 4; Lay Teachers 16; Students 197.
Catechesis/Religious Programs—Tel: 810-765-8300. Kathleen Mulso, O.S.F., D.R.E.
Students 250.

Marysville, St. Clair Co., St. Christopher, Rev. Arthur R. Baranowski; Sr. Doris Wood, S.S.J., Pastoral Min.; Sr. Geraldine Nowak, O.S.F., Pastoral Assoc.
Res., 1000 Michigan Ave., 48040. Tel: 810-364-4100; Fax: 810-364-5947.
Catechesis/Religious Programs—Tel: 810-364-7080. Patricia Radacsy, D.R.E.
Students 484.

Maybee, Monroe Co., St. Joseph, Rev. Casimir Wiercioch.
Res., 9207 Joseph St., Box 125, 48159. Tel: 313-587-8835; Fax: 313-587-3490. [CEM]
Convent—9147 Joseph St., Box 126, 48159. Tel: 313-587-8785.

Melvindale, Wayne Co., St. Conrad, Rev. Joseph A. Gagnon.
Res., 3320 Melwood, 48122. Tel: 313-383-0303; Fax: 313-383-5704.

St. Mary Magdalen, Revs. James E. Curtin; John Melepuram (India).
Res., 19624 Wood St., 48122. Tel: 313-381-8566; Fax: 313-381-1319.
School—Tel: 313-382-6060. James A. Bouvy, Prin.
Lay Teachers 12; Students 320.
Catechesis/Religious Programs—Tel: 313-382-1099. Mrs. Patricia Dincau, D.R.E.
Students 100.
Mission—Melvindale, St. Thomas Indian Catholic Mission, Tel: 313-381-1773.

Memphis, Macomb Co., All Saints, Rev. Dennis Nowinski.
Church—79780 Main St., 48041. Tel: 810-392-2056; 392-3232; Fax: 810-392-3043.
Catechesis/Religious Programs—Tel: 810-392-2056. Toni Zweng, D.R.E.
Students 225.

Milford, Oakland Co., St. Mary, Our Lady of the Snows, Rev. Ronald Anderson; Sr. Lucille Janowiak, O.P., Pastoral Assoc.; Deacon Archie Noon.
Res., 1851 E. Commerce, 48381. Tel: 810-685-1482; Fax: 810-684-5642. [CEM]
Catechesis/Religious Programs—Tel: 810-685-2702. Michael Maras, D.R.E.
Students 883.

Monroe, Monroe Co.,

1—St. Anne, Rev. Thomas R. Byrne; Deacon Patrick Belleman, D.R.E.
Res., 2420 N. Dixie Hwy., 48161. Tel: 313-289-2910; Fax: 313-289-1098.
Catechesis/Religious Programs—Students 233.

2—St. John, Rev. Terrence D. Kerner.
Res., 511 S. Monroe St., S., 48161. Tel: 313-241-8910; Fax: 313-241-1943.
School—Tel: 313-241-1670. Rita Linnenkugel, Prin.
Lay Teachers 10; Students 224.
Catechesis/Religious Programs—D.R.E.: Sharon DuVall; Karon Kinsey.
Students 251.

3—St. Joseph's, Rev. William F. Fisher, O.S.F.S.; Sr. Harriet Fitzmaurice, I.H.M., Pastoral Assoc.
Res., 924 E. Second St., 48161. Tel: 313-241-9590; Fax: 313-241-5296. [JC]
Catechesis/Religious Programs—Mrs. Judy Collins, D.R.E.
Students 160.

4—St. Mary's, Rev. Anthony F. Sulkowski; Sr. Geraldine Nowak, O.S.F., Pastoral Assoc.
Res., 127 N. Monroe St., 48161. Tel: 313-241-1644; Fax: 313-241-3077. [JC]
School—Mary Ann Lapinski, Prin. Lay Teachers 14; Students 329.
Catechesis/Religious Programs—Deacon Daniel Fraser, D.R.E.
Students 287.

5—St. Michael, Rev. Stephen Rooney; Deacons Michael M. Ingels; Alfred H. Hoffman.
Res., 502 W. Front St., 48161. Tel: 313-241-8645; Fax: 313-241-6132. [JC]
School—Tel: 313-241-3923. Karen Pilon, Prin.
Lay Teachers 12; Students 256.
Catechesis/Religious Programs—Susan Pacitti, D.R.E.
Students 175.

Mount Clemens, Macomb Co., St. Peter, Rev. Michael N. Cooney; Sheila Roy, Pastoral Min.; Doris Kalleck, Admin.
Admin. Bldg.—98 New St., 48043. Tel: 810-468-4578; Fax: 810-468-3199.
Res., 100 New St., 48043. [CEM]
School—St. Mary, Tel: 810-468-4570. Elizabeth McMillan, Prin.
Lay Teachers 20; Students 513.
Catechesis/Religious Programs—Judy Coll, D.R.E.
Students 380.

New Baltimore, Macomb Co., St. Mary, Revs. Nicholas Zukowski; Bradley Forintos; Mary Frances Van Hollenbeck, Parish Nurse Coord.; Deacon Anthony Lewandoski.
Res., 51041 Maria St., 48047. Tel: 810-725-2441; Fax: 810-725-3647. [CEM]
Catechesis/Religious Programs—Carolyn Bissett, D.R.E.
Students 883.

New Boston, Wayne Co., St. Stephen, Revs. Alexander J. Wytrwal; Joseph Szewczyk.
Res., 18800 Huron River Dr., 48164-9599. Tel: 313-753-4305; Fax: 313-753-5828. [CEM]
School—Tel: 313-753-4175. Sr. M. Virginia Gola, C.S.S.F., Prin.
Felician Sisters 2; Lay Teachers 9; Students 205.
Catechesis/Religious Programs—Tel: 313-753-4722. Sr. Mary Patricia Pyszynski, C.S.S.F., D.R.E.
Students 102.
Convent—Tel: 313-753-9937.

New Haven, Macomb Co., St. Francis of Assisi, Rev. Daniel O'Sullivan.
Res., 57775 Main St., P.O. Box 308, 48048. Tel: 810-749-9584; Fax: 810-749-6021.

Newport, Monroe Co., St. Charles Borromeo, Rev. William H. Tindall.
Res., 8109 Swan Creek Rd., 48166. Tel: 313-586-2531; Fax: 313-586-3900. [CEM]
School—Tel: 313-586-2171. Krista Seibert, Prin.
Lay Teachers 10; Students 224.
Catechesis/Religious Programs—Tel: 313-586-3304. Mrs. Marshia Valleau, D.R.E.
Students 220.

North Branch, Lapeer Co., St. Mary's Burnside, Rev. Richard M. Schmidberger.
Res., 5622 Summers Rd., 48461. Tel: 313-688-3648. [CEM]
Mission—Brown City, Sanilac Co., Sacred Heart. [CEM]

SS. Peter and Paul, Rev. Jude T. Ellinghausen.
Res., Box 208, 6645 Washington, 48461. Tel: 810-688-3797. [CEM]
Catechesis/Religious Programs—Tel: 810-688-9019. Charlotte Kalbfleisch, D.R.E.
Students 273.
Mission—Clifford, St. Patrick's. [CEM]

Northville, Wayne Co., Our Lady of Victory, Revs. Ernest M. Porcari; Todd J. Lajiness; Patricia Ernst, Pastoral Assoc.
Res., 770 Thayer, 48167. Tel: 810-349-2621; Fax: 810-349-7329.
School—Tel: 810-349-6610.
Lay Teachers 11; Students 363.
Catechesis/Religious Programs—D.R.E.: Ms. Eileen Moss; Sr. Gail Singel, O.P.
Students 620.
Convent—103 Orchard Dr., 48167. Tel: 810-349-6698.

Novi, Oakland Co., Holy Family, Rev. John G. Budde; Deacon William Waldmann.
Res., 39654 Squire Dr., 48375. Tel: 810-478-4676; Fax: 810-349-3711.
Catechesis/Religious Programs—Tel: 810-349-8837. Dorothy Morse, D.R.E.
Students 1,038.

St. James, Rev. James F. Cronk.
46325 Ten Mile Road, 48374-3007.
Res., 24491 Riverview Ln., 48374-3052. Tel: 810-347-7778; Fax: 810-347-9625.
Catechesis/Religious Programs—Wendy Duvall-Angelocci, D.R.E.
Students 842.

Oak Park, Oakland Co., Our Lady of Fatima, Rev. Paul F. Chateau; Sr. Jane Zoltek, S.S.J., Pastoral Assoc.
In res., Rev. Nicholas H. Amico (Ecuador).
Res., 13500 Oak Park Blvd., 48237. Tel: 810-545-2310; Fax: 810-545-2312.

Orchard Lake, Oakland Co., Our Lady of Refuge, Rev. William J. Murphy; Deacon Robert Goetz.
Res., 3663 Erie Dr., P.O. Box 240485, 48324. Tel: 810-682-0920; Fax: 810-682-3794.
School—Tel: 810-682-3422; Fax: 810-682-0479. Sr. Mary Ruth Koralewski, C.S.S.F., Prin.
Sisters 3; Lay Teachers 22; Students 488.
Catechesis/Religious Programs—Patricia Allsteadt, D.R.E.
Students 345.
Convent—3725 Erie Dr., 48324. Tel: 810-682-1876.

Orion Township, Oakland Co., Christ the Redeemer, Rev. Joseph E. Dailey.
Res., 4005 Baldwin, Orion, 48359. Tel: 810-391-1621; Fax: 810-391-3412.
Catechesis/Religious Programs—Tel: 810-391-4074. Marilyn Lynes, D.R.E.
Students 492.

Ortonville, Oakland Co., St. Anne, Rev. A. Frank Pollie; Deacon Bernard Braun.
Res., 825 Ortonville Rd., 48462. Tel: 810-627-3965; Fax: 810-627-3965.
Catechesis/Religious Programs—Tel: 810-627-3753. Diana Frechette, D.R.E.
Students 339.

Plymouth, Wayne Co., Our Lady of Good Counsel, Revs. John J. Sullivan; James G. Livingston; Deacon Don Leach. In res., Rev. Robert Fisher.
Res., 1062 Church St., 48170. Tel: 313-453-0326; Fax: 313-416-9257.
School—Tel: 313-453-3053. Theodore Behn, Prin.
Lay Teachers 21; Students 567.
Catechesis/Religious Programs—Tel: 313-455-0242. D.R.E.: Diane M. Michaelson; Marilyn Olszewski.

Students 587.
St. Kenneth, Rev. William J. Pettit; Deacon Eugene Krzeminski.
Res., 14951 Haggerty Rd., 48170. Tel: 313-420-0288; Fax: 313-420-2921.
Catechesis/Religious Programs—Tel: 313-420-3031. Mrs. Laurel McGrane, D.R.E.
Students 393.

Pontiac, Oakland Co., St. Joseph, Revs. Patrick F. Halfpenny, Admin.; Fabian B. Slominski, Liturgical Presider; Deacon John M. Fleming; Sr. M. Patricia Malone, R.S.M., Pastoral Assoc.
400 S. Blvd. W., 48341-2465.
Res., 150 E. Wide Track, 48342. Tel: 810-332-0283; Fax: 810-334-0528.

St. Michael, Rev. John P. Wynnycky; Deacons Edward Strye; Richard Vestuto, Pastoral Assoc.
Res., 120 Lewis, 48342. Tel: 810-332-9167; Fax: 810-332-3901.

St. Vincent de Paul, Rev. John P. Wynnycky, Admin. Pastoral Assocs.: Sr. Carmen Coccimiglio, S.L.W.; Maria Jimenez; Willie McCray, Minister of Service; Deacons Fernando Valdez; Rafael Rivera; Jesus Vasquez; Brigido Rodriguez; Norman LaLone.
Res., 150 E. Wide Track Dr., 48342. Tel: 810-332-0283; Fax: 810-332-7041.

Port Huron, St. Clair Co., St. Joseph, Rev. Rene Desmarais; Mary Fran Canza, Pastoral Assoc.
Res., 1317 7th St., 48060. Tel: 810-985-9616; Fax: 810-985-9807. [JC]
School—Tel: 810-982-3701.
Sisters 1; Lay Teachers 7; Students 77.
Catechesis/Religious Programs—Tel: 810-982-2343. Mrs. Fran Warsalla, D.R.E.
Students 112.

St. Mary, Rev. Stanley Wyczawski.
Res., 1505 Ballentine St., 48060. Tel: 810-982-7906; Fax: 810-987-3441.
School—Tel: 810-982-1091. Mrs. Karen Pawlak.
Lay Teachers 8; Students 189.

St. Stephen, Revs. Frederick A. Bodde; C. Paul Hidgon.
Res., 325 32nd St., 48060. Tel: 810-984-2689; 984-3220; Fax: 810-984-8559.
Parish Center—2865 Henry, 48060. Tel: 810-985-9069.
Catechesis/Religious Programs—Amy Miles, D.R.E.
Students 294.

Redford, Wayne Co.,

1—St. Agatha, Rev. Thomas F. Slowinski.
Parish Office—19750 Beech Daly Rd., 48240.
Res., 19650 Beech Daly Rd., 48240. Tel: 313-531-0371; Fax: 313-531-1805.
School—Tel: 313-532-6940. Lorelei Darga, Prin.
Sisters 1; Lay Teachers 13; Students 311.
High School—Sisters 1; Lay Teachers 11; Students 202.
Catechesis/Religious Programs—Students 155.

2—St. John Bosco, Rev. Richard A. Osebold.
Res., 12100 Beech-Daly Rd., 48239. Tel: 313-937-9690; Fax: 313-937-2927.
School—Tel: 313-937-3856. Sr. Rita Sieg, O.P., Prin.
Lay Teachers 8; Students 133.

3—Our Lady of Loretto, Rev. Joseph M. Esper; Sr. Marcella Clancy, S.S.J., Pastoral Assoc.; Deacon Gary Pardo.
Res., 17116 Olympia Ave., 48240. Tel: 313-534-9000; Fax: 313-534-6744.
School—Tel: 313-532-4764.
Lay Teachers 14; Students 260.
Catechesis/Religious Programs—Tel: 313-532-3707. Patricia M. Metz, D.R.E.
Students 220.

4—St. Valentine, Rev. Thomas A. Belczak. In res., Rev. Norman Nawrocki.
Res., 25881 Dow, 48239. Tel: 313-532-4394; Fax: 313-532-2237.
School—25800 Dow St., 48239. Tel: 313-533-7149. Carol Budchuk, Prin.
Lay Teachers 21; Students 320.
Catechesis/Religious Programs—Tel: 313-538-9161. Sharon Larkin, D.R.E.
Students 400.
Convent—25900 Dow St., 48239. Tel: 313-533-7828.

Redford Township, Wayne Co., St. Robert Bellarmine, Revs. John B. Zwers; Donald L. Walker.
Res., 27101 W. Chicago, 48239. Tel: 313-937-1500; Fax: 313-937-1185.
School—Tel: 313-937-1655. Lynn Matlenga, Prin.
Lay Teachers 19; Students 330.
Catechesis/Religious Programs—Tel: 313-937-1531. Jan Lopata, D.R.E.
Students 256.

St. Hilary, Rev. John T. Nowlan; Sr. Marie Miller, I.H.M.
Res., 23901 Elmira, 48239. Tel: 313-533-1560; Fax: 313-533-1735.

Richmond, Macomb Co., St. Augustine, Rev. James E. Commyn.
Res., 68035 Main St., 48062. Tel: 810-727-5215; Fax: 810-727-3760. [CEM]
School—Tel: 810-727-9365.
Sisters 1; Lay Teachers 13; Students 259.
Catechesis/Religious Programs—Tel: 810-727-9290.
Students 298.
Convent—67900 Howard St., 48062. Tel: 810-727-1517.

River Rouge, Wayne Co., Our Lady of Lourdes, Rev. James F. Wieging; Dr. Paul D. Bodrie, Pastoral Assoc.; Deacon Edward E. Quirouette.
Res., 1440 Coolidge Highway, 48218. Tel: 313-842-3320; 3321; Fax: 313-842-4507.

Riverview, Wayne Co., St. Cyprian, Revs. Jude Verley, O.S.C.; Richard Leliaert, O.S.C.; Sr. Kathleen Horvat, Pastoral Assoc. In res., Revs. Neil Emon, O.S.C.; Dale Redwanski, O.S.C.
Res., 13249 Pennsylvania, 48192. Tel: 313-283-1366; Fax: 313-283-2809.
School—Tel: 313-283-9442. Ann Roush, Prin.
Lay Teachers 14; Students 191.
Catechesis/Religious Programs—Mrs. Kathleen Duford, D.R.E.
Students 409.

Rochester, Oakland Co., St. Andrew, Revs. Timothy F. Babcock; Dennis C. Laesch; Sr. Carmela Whitton, O.S.F., Pastoral Assoc.; Deacon Charles G. Skubick.
Res., 1400 Inglewood, 48307. Tel: 810-651-7486; Fax: 810-651-3950.
Catechesis/Religious Programs—Tel: 810-651-6401. Judith Petterson, D.R.E.
Students 1,275.

St. Irenaeus, Rev. Edward J. Mitchell; Patricia Egan-Myers, Pastoral Assoc. & D.R.E.
Res., 771 Old Perch Rd., Rochester Hills, 48309. Tel: 810-651-9595; Fax: 810-651-1504.
Catechesis/Religious Programs—Tel: 810-651-2443.
Students 702.

Rochester Hills, St. Mary's of the Hills, Rev. Eugene Strain.
Res., 2675 John R, 48307. Tel: 810-853-5390; Fax: 810-853-7989.
Catechesis/Religious Programs—Tel: 810-853-5390. Nancy A. Mason, D.R.E.
Students 576.

Rockwood, Wayne Co., St. Mary, Rev. Thomas M. Sauter; Deacon Thomas C. Murphy.
Res., P.O. Box 249, 48173. Tel: 313-379-9248; Fax: 313-379-6548. [CEM]
School—Tel: 313-379-9285. Michelle E. Seward, Prin.
Lay Teachers 11; Students 190.
Catechesis/Religious Programs—Tel: 313-379-9406. Ms. Theresa Borawski, D.R.E.
Students 199.
Convent—32477 Church St., 48173.

Romeo, Macomb Co., St. Clement of Rome, Rev. Stephen C. Reckker.
Res., 343 S. Main St., 48065. Tel: 810-752-9611; Fax: 810-752-7795.
Catechesis/Religious Programs—Ellen Licavoli, D.R.E.
Students 790.

Romulus, Wayne Co., St. Aloysius, Rev. Michael D. Malawy.
Res., 11280 Ozga Rd., 48174. Tel: 313-941-5056; Fax: 313-941-6018.
School—Tel: 313-941-3340. Gladys Bosel, Prin.
Lay Teachers 7; Students 108.

Roseville, Macomb Co.,

1—St. Angela, Revs. George T. Browne; Lambert Smits, C.I.C.M.; Peter Mubiru (Uganda).
Res., 25001 Chippendale, 48066. Tel: 810-445-6360; Fax: 810-445-6366.
Church—Ten Mile Rd. and Chippendale, 48066.
School—Tel: 810-445-6375; Fax: 810-445-6382. Sr. M. LaVerne, C.S.B., Prin.
Sisters 8; Lay Teachers 12; Students 335.
Catechesis/Religious Programs—Tel: 810-445-6377. Diane McDonald, D.R.E.
Students 302.
Convent—25165 Chippendale, 48066. Tel: 810-445-6370.

2—St. Athanasius, Rev. Gerard Hadad; Deacon Ron Channell.
Res., 18720 Thirteen Mile Rd., 48066. Tel: 810-772-1170; Fax: 810-776-2945.
Catechesis/Religious Programs—Sr. Theresa Bray, O.P., D.R.E.
Students 356.

3—St. Donald, Rev. Michael A. Donovan.
Res., 16330 Twelve Mile Rd., 48066. Tel: 313-773-3440; Fax: 810-773-1235.

4—Holy Innocents, Rev. Richard C. Welsh; Lena Kocis, Pastoral Assoc.; Deacon James Pallarito.
Res., 26100 Ridgemont Rd., 48066. Tel: 810-777-7543; Fax: 810-777-1536.
School—Tel: 810-777-5286.
Lay Teachers 12; Students 268.
Catechesis/Religious Programs—Robert Dugas, D.R.E.
Students 184.

5—Sacred Heart, Rev. William Bonnici; Sr. Frances Chirco, Pastoral Assoc.
Res., 18430 Utica Rd., 48066. Tel: 810-777-9116; Fax: 810-777-7958.
Catechesis/Religious Programs—Tel: 810-777-8150. Patricia DeBruce, D.R.E.
Students 198.

Royal Oak, Oakland Co., St. Dennis, Revs. John Christ, O.S.C.; Gerald Thaar, O.S.C.; Sr. Connie Parran, I.H.M., Pastoral Assoc.
Res., 2200 E. 12 Mile Rd., 48067-1504. Tel: 810-544-2181; Fax: 810-544-9443.
School—1415 N. Stephenson, 48067-1504. Tel: 810-398-6555; Fax: 810-398-2878. Cheryl Hermann, Prin.
Sisters 2; Lay Teachers 18; Students 443.
Catechesis/Religious Programs—Tel: 810-545-1926. Mrs. B. Gutowski, D.R.E.
Students 325.

St. Mary, Rev. Michael A. Woroniewicz; Rev. Msgr. Thomas H. Villerot; Deacon James A. Cron; Sr. Therese Allgeyer, O.P. In res., Rev. Richard Yost, O.S.F.S.
Res., 730 Lafayette Ave., S., 48067. Tel: 810-547-1818; Fax: 810-547-4577. [CEM]
School—628 Lafayette Ave., S., 48067. Tel: 810-545-2140. William R. Farrand, Prin.
Lay Teachers 8; Students 102.
Catechesis/Religious Programs—Tel: 810-547-1810. Ms. Bridget Gasior, D.R.E.
Students 107.

Shrine of the Little Flower, Rev. Msgr. William M. Easton; Revs. Reginald Brady; Ralph L. Quane; Dr. Ronald E. Rohlman.
Res., 2123 Roseland Ave., 48073. Tel: 810-541-4122 (Office); Fax: 810-541-2838.
Church—2123 Roseland, 48067.
School—Tel: 810-541-4622. Patricia Crowe, Prin.
Lay Teachers 22; Students 601.
Academy—Tel: 810-549-2928. Timothy Kelly, Dir.
Lay Teachers 12; Students 168.
High School—3500 W. Thirteen Mile Rd., 48073. Tel: 810-549-2925; Fax: 810-549-2953. Thomas Kirkwood, Prin.
Lay Teachers 21; Students 277.
Catechesis/Religious Programs—Judy Dantzer, D.R.E.
Students 460.

St. Clair, St. Clair Co., St. Mary, Rev. Edward W. Ritter; Sr. Eileen Meyers, O.P., Pastoral Assoc.
Res., 415 N. 6th St., 48079. Tel: 810-329-2255; Fax: 810-329-5997. [CEM]
School—Tel: 810-329-4150. Mrs. Marilynn Pavlov, Prin.
Lay Teachers 12; Students 330.
Catechesis/Religious Programs—Tel: 810-329-7801. Sr. Janice Marie Peer, O.S.F., D.R.E.
Students 537.
Convent—811 Orchard St., 48079. Tel: 810-329-2400.

St. Clair Shores, Macomb Co.,

1—St. Germaine, Rev. James L. Bjorum; Deacon Terrance Downey, Pastoral Assoc.
Office: 28301 Little Mack, 48081. Tel: 810-771-1750; Fax: 810-771-7634.
School—Tel: 810-771-0890. Mrs. Kay O'Leary, Prin.
Sisters 2; Lay Teachers 18; Students 450.
Catechesis/Religious Programs—Sr. Helen Williams, I.H.M., D.R.E.
Students 154.

2—St. Gertrude, Revs. Thomas J. Johnston, O.P.; Gerald B. Morahan, O.P.; Michael B. Ruthenberg, O.P. In res., Rev. Michael Monshau, O.P.
Res., 28839 Jefferson Ave., 48081. Tel: 810-777-9120; Fax: 810-777-8390. [CEM]
Catechesis/Religious Programs—Tel: 810-775-5820. Paul Lippard, D.R.E.
Students 200.

3—St. Isaac Jogues, Revs. Ronald J. Victor; Francisco Restrepo Diaz (Mexico); Ms. Alice Murphy, Pastoral Assoc.
Parish Center—21120 Benjamin Dr., 48081. Tel: 810-778-5100; Fax: 810-778-4458.
School—Tel: 810-771-3525.
Lay Teachers 22; Students 405.
Catechesis/Religious Programs—Tel: 810-778-5100. Mrs. Claudia Givinsky, D.R.E.
Students 450.

4—St. Joan of Arc, Rev. Msgr. Ricardo E. Bass; Revs. Roman Pasieczny (Poland); Michael J. Byrnes; Sr. Margaret Moran, O.P., Pastoral Assoc.; Deacons Eugene E. DiCresce; Robert F. Busch.
Parish Center—22412 Overlake, 48080. Tel: 810-777-3670; Fax: 810-774-5528.
School—22415 Overlake, 48080. Tel: 810-777-8370;

Fax: 810-447-3574. Mr. Don Ancypa, Prin.
Sisters of St. Joseph (Nazareth) 1; Lay Teachers 30; Students 766.
Catechesis/Religious Programs—Tel: 810-772-1282. Sr. Marie Houle, O.P., D.R.E.
Students 651.

5—St. Lucy, Rev. Bohdan W. Kosicki; Deacon Robert Herta.
Res., 23401 Jefferson, 48080. Tel: 810-771-8300; Fax: 810-447-4220.
Catechesis/Religious Programs—Sr. Kathy Payne, O.S.M., D.R.E.
Students 424.

6—St. Margaret, Rev. Ronald W. Kurzawa; Deacon Kenneth Braman. In res., Rev. Mark A. Borkowski.
Res., 21201 Thirteen Mile Rd., 48082. Tel: 810-293-2240; Fax: 810-293-0116.
Catechesis/Religious Programs—Tel: 810-293-3280. Mary Paonessa, D.R.E.
Students 725.

Shelby Twp., St. John Vianney Church, Rev. Jerome J. Machlik.
Res., 54045 Schoenherr Rd., 48315. Tel: 810-781-6525; Fax: 810-781-6527.
Catechesis/Religious Programs—Tel: 810-781-2627. D.R.E.: Fritzi Bohlman; Mary Lundgaard; Ida Johns.
Students 903.

St. Kieran, Rev. H. Thomas Johnson; Deacon Ronald W. Cook, Pastoral Assoc.
Res., 53600 Mound Rd., 48316. Tel: 810-781-4901; Fax: 810-781-6516.
Catechesis/Religious Programs—Nancy Clancy, D.R.E.
Students 750.

St. Therese of Lisieux, Rev. Thomas J. Sutherland.
Res., 49230 Arlington Ct., 48315-3903. Tel: 810-247-5428.
Church—48115 Schoenherr Rd., 48315-4225. Tel: 810-254-4433; Fax: 810-254-5463.
Catechesis/Religious Programs—Students 515.

Southfield, Oakland Co.,

1—St. Beatrice, Rev. John Gagala.
Res., 17235 Mt. Vernon, 48075. Tel: 810-557-3342; Fax: 810-557-3427.

2—St. Bede, Rev. Lawrence A. Pettke; Joyce Fry, Pastoral Assoc. In res., Rev. Toma A. Behman.
Res., 18290 Twelve Mile Rd. W, 48076. Tel: 810-559-0577; Fax: 810-559-0752.
Church—Twelve Mile and Southfield Rds., 48076.
School—Tel: 810-559-0572. Mona Cioffi, Prin.
Lay Teachers 13; Students 183.
Catechesis/Religious Programs—Pat Metz, D.R.E.
Students 65.

3—Divine Providence, Rev. Valdas Valdemaras.
Res., 25335 W. 9 Mile Rd., 48034. Tel: 810-354-3429; Fax: 810-354-1773.

4—St. Ives, Rev. William D. Sinatra; Deacon Brian J. Black; Linda Simonelli, Pastoral Assoc.
Res., 29350 Lahser, 48034. Tel: 810-353-3410; Fax: 810-353-5412.
Catechesis/Religious Programs—Students 157.

5—St. Michael, Revs. Lawrence W. Zurek, O.F.M.; John C. Market, O.F.M., (Retired); Theophane Dattilo, O.F.M., (Retired); Roch Farland, O.F.M., (Retired); Bro. Michael Schebeci, O.F.M., Pastoral Asoc.
Res., 25225 Code Rd., 48034. Tel: 810-356-8787; Fax: 810-356-1240.
School—Tel: 810-356-6113. Sr. M. Presentine, Prin.
Sisters 1; Lay Teachers 11; Students 273.
Convent—22750 10 Mile Rd., 48034. Tel: 810-356-8785.

Southgate, Wayne Co., St. Pius X, Rev. Peter Petroske.
Office: 14101 Superior Ave., 48195. Tel: 313-285-1100; Fax: 313-285-5310.
Res., 14160 Longtin Ave., 48195.
School—Tel: 313-285-1100. Clara Seeley, Elementary Prin.
Lay Teachers 18; Students 400.
High School—Sue Kodyk, High School Prin.(interim). Religious 2; Lay Teachers 18; Students 254.
Catechesis/Religious Programs—Jerry Sabatowich, D.R.E.
Students 345.

St. Hugh, Eugene E. Wojtewicz.
Res., 11300 Reeck Rd., 48195. Tel: 313-287-6990; Fax: 313-287-8109.

South Lyon, Oakland Co., St. Joseph, Rev. Howard L. Vogan. Pastoral Assocs.: Sr. Colleen Morris, S.M.; Deacon William Otto.
Res., 810 S. Lafayette, 48178. Tel: 810-437-1121; Fax: 810-437-3784.
Catechesis/Religious Programs—Mary Ann Sikorski, D.R.E.
Students 654.

Sterling Heights, Macomb Co.,

1—St. Blase, Rev. Msgr. Michael C. LeFevre; Rev. Thomas P. Kirwan; Sr. Megan McElroy, O.P., Pastoral Assoc.; Deacon Donald Cox.
Res., 12151 E. 15 Mile Rd., 48312-5120. Tel: 810-268-2244; Fax: 810-268-1174.
Catechesis/Religious Programs—Students 802.

2—SS. Cyril and Methodius, Rev. Elemir Joseph Mikus.
Res., 41233 Ryan Rd., 48314. Tel: 810-726-6911; Fax: 810-726-5913.

3—St. Ephrem, Revs. Timothy P. Mazur; Ronald Milligan.
Res., 38900 Dodge Rd., 48312. Tel: 810-264-1230; Fax: 810-264-2757.
Catechesis/Religious Programs—Tel: 810-264-2777.
Students 395.

4—St. Jane Frances de Chantal, Revs. Leon J. Page; John Vargas.
Res., 38750 Ryan Rd., 48310. Tel: 810-977-8080; Fax: 810-977-9305.

5—St. Malachy, Revs. Joseph J. Gembala; William P. Siebert. Pastoral Assocs.: Sr. Alys Currier, I.H.M.; Sr. Pat McCarthy, S.F.C.C.
Res., 14115 14 Mile Rd., 48312-6506. Tel: 810-264-1220; Fax: 810-264-1656.
Catechesis/Religious Programs—Tel: 810-268-4430. Ms. Patricia Whelan, D.R.E.
Students 410.

6—St. Matthias, Revs. Richard E. Cyr; Thomas J. Moloney, S.A.C.
Res., 12509 Nineteen Mile Rd., 48313. Tel: 810-731-1300; Fax: 810-731-2576.
Catechesis/Religious Programs—Tel: 810-731-0650. Mary A. Lang, D.R.E.
Students 784.

7—St. Michael, Rev. Lawrence J. Jackson; Sr. Monica Stuhlreyer, I.H.M., Pastoral Assoc.; Deacon Lawrence Healy. In res., Rev. Stanislaw Tokarski.
Church—40501 Hayes Rd., 48313. Tel: 810-247-0020; Fax: 810-247-4081.
Res., 39443 Heatherheath, Clinton Twp., 48038. Tel: 810-286-3322.
Catechesis/Religious Programs—Tel: 810-247-0098. D.R.E.: Emily Gordon; Catherine McInerney.
Students 1,070.

8—Our Lady of Czestochowa, Revs. Jan Rudzewicz, S.Ch.; Jacek Nowak, S.Ch.; Konrad Urbanowski, S.Ch.
Res., 3100 18 Mile Rd., 48314-3810. Tel: 810-977-7267; Fax: 810-977-2074.
Catechesis/Religious Programs—Sr. Elizabeth Lepiarczyk, D.R.E.
Students 376.

9—St. Rene Goupil, Revs. Frederick J. Schweihofer; William J. Promesso; Sr. Mary Schmidlin, O.S.F., Pastoral Assoc.; Deacon John Santeramo.
Res., 35955 Ryan Rd., 48310. Tel: 810-939-7500; Fax: 810-939-7839.
Catechesis/Religious Programs—Tel: 810-939-7688. Mary Gagnon, D.R.E.
Students 657.

Taylor, Wayne Co.,

1—St. Alfred, Revs. C. Michael Verschaeve; Neil Emon, O.S.C.
Res., 9500 Banner, 48180. Tel: 313-291-6464; Fax: 313-291-2733.
School—Tel: 313-291-0247; 291-4600. A. Francis Bontumasi, Prin.
Sisters 1; Lay Teachers 21; Students 415.
Catechesis/Religious Programs—Tel: 313-291-3210. Beth A. Oley, D.R.E.
Students 271.

2—St. Constance, Rev. John D. Canavan; Deacon Joseph Mouro.
Res., 21555 Kinyon Rd., 48180. Tel: 313-291-4050; Fax: 313-291-5655.

3—St. Cyril of Jerusalem, Rev. Gary Morelli; Deacons Daniel J. Hurley; William A. Thome. Pastoral Assocs.: Sr. Marion Therese Mackey, O.P.; Joan Forrest; Patricia Mueller.
Res., 6442 Pelham Rd., 48180. Tel: 313-381-3000; Fax: 313-381-5528.
School—Tel: 313-383-8585. John Champion, Prin.
Lay Teachers 10; Students 214.
Catechesis/Religious Programs—Tel: 313-383-5663. Stacie Battaglia, D.R.E.
Students 142.
Convent—20170 Pinecrest, 48180. Tel: 313-389-1678.

4—St. Paschal, Rev. Richard Macey.
Res., 22210 Champaign St., 48180. Tel: 313-291-4880; Fax: 313-291-7514.
School—Tel: 313-291-6650. Marcia Guerra, Prin.
Lay Teachers 10; Students 156.

Temperance, Monroe Co., St. Anthony, Rev. Gregory J. Deters; Deacon Robert J. Snyder.
Res., 4605 St. Anthony Rd., 48182. Tel: 313-854-1143; Fax: 313-854-4622. [CEM]
School—Tel: 313-854-1160. Sr. M. Joan Furlong, S.N.D., Prin.
Sisters of Notre Dame 2; Dominican Sisters 1; Lay Teachers 13; Students 127.
Catechesis/Religious Programs—Students 173.
Convent—4607 St. Anthony Rd., 48182. Tel: 313-854-2779.

Our Lady of Mt. Carmel, Rev. Alfred J. Miller; Sr. Pam Nosbusch; Hazel Destatte, Pastoral Assoc.
Res., 810 Donna Dr., 48182. Tel: 313-847-2805; Fax: 313-847-8970.
Catechesis/Religious Programs—Tel: 313-847-1725.
Students 467.

Trenton, Wayne Co., St. Joseph, Rev. James A. Vedro, O.S.C.; Sr. Ellen Baker, I.H.M., Pastoral Assoc.
Res., 2623 3rd St., 48183. Tel: 313-676-9082; Fax: 313-676-6255. [JC]
School—Tel: 313-676-2565; Fax: 313-676-9744. Wanda Rovenskie, Prin.
Lay Teachers 8; Students 221.
Catechesis/Religious Programs—Tel: 313-676-7115. Jacqueline Pangborn, D.R.E.
Students 314.
Convent—250 Elm St., 48183. Tel: 313-676-3082.

St. Timothy, Rev. Charles S. Fontana.
Parish Office: 2901 Manning Dr., 48183. Tel: 313-676-5115; Fax: 313-676-6863.
Catechesis/Religious Programs—D.R.E.: Fritzi Bohlmann; Geraldine Mooney.
Students 304.

Troy, Oakland Co.,

1—St. Thomas More, Rev. Edward A. Belczak; Deacon John Ball.
Res., 4580 Adams Rd., 48098. Tel: 810-647-2222; Fax: 810-647-8192.
Catechesis/Religious Programs—Tel: 810-647-4680.
Students 1,142.

2—St. Alan, Revs. Thaddeus J. Blaszczyk; Edward F. Konopka, Pastor Emeritus; Sr. Mary Choiniere, S.S.J., Pastoral Assoc.
Church—3077 Glouchester, 48084.
Res., 2345 Coolidge Rd., 48084. Tel: 810-649-5510; Fax: 810-649-6729.

3—St. Anastasia, Rev. Kenneth R. Kaucheck. Pastoral Assocs.: Sr. Kay Allberry, O.P.; Deacon Mark Springer. In res., Rev. William B. Davidson.
Res., 4571 John R. Rd., 48098. Tel: 810-689-8380; Fax: 810-689-7489.
Catechesis/Religious Programs—Tel: 810-689-1431. Elizabeth Murray, D.R.E.
Students 1,008.

4—St. Elizabeth Ann Seton, Rev. Ronald J. Essman. Pastoral Assocs.: Mary Persinger; Judy Manturuk; Donna Mylenek.
Res., 280 E. Square Lake Rd., 48098. Tel: 810-879-1310; Fax: 810-879-2886.
Catechesis/Religious Programs—Tel: 810-879-1314.
Students 235.

5—St. Lucy, Rev. Joseph Galic, O.F.M.
Res., 200 E. Wattles, 48098. Tel: 810-619-9910; Fax: 810-619-9912.

Utica, Macomb Co., St. Lawrence, Revs. Timothy J. Szott; Robert C. Schuster; Sr. Janet Sullivan, I.H.M., Pastoral Assoc.
Res., 44633 Utica Rd., 48317. Tel: 810-731-5347; Fax: 810-731-5393.
School—Tel: 810-731-0135. Paul Gielow, Prin.
Lay Teachers 22; Students 587.
Catechesis/Religious Programs—Tel: 810-731-5072. Linda Sheets, D.R.E.
Students 662.

Walled Lake, Oakland Co., St. William, Rev. Michael G. Savickas; Deacon Richard Smith. In res., Rev. Christopher Chukwu.
Res., 531 Common St., 48390. Tel: 810-624-1421; Fax: 810-624-5273.
School—135 O'Flaherty, 48390. Tel: 810-669-4440; Fax: 810-669-2245. Alexandra Leidlein, Prin.
Lay Teachers 11; Students 243.
Catechesis/Religious Programs—Tel: 810-624-1371. Alexandra Leidlein, D.R.E.
Students 530.

Warren, Macomb Co.,

1—St. Anne's, Revs. Michael Kazer; Jerome Slowinski; Sr. Alice Miller, I.H.M., Pastoral Assoc.; Deacon Marvin Strzyzewski.
Res., 32000 Mound Rd., 48092. Tel: 810-268-3434; Fax: 810-268-4142.
School—Tel: 810-264-2911. Dr. Thomas Engel, Prin.
Intercommunity Sisters 1; Lay Teachers 30; Students 875.
Catechesis/Religious Programs—Patricia Berry, D.R.E.
Students 490.

2—Ascension, Rev. Norbert Maciejewski.
Res., 21050 Ascension St., 48089. Tel: 810-754-4000; Fax: 810-757-2342.

Catechesis/Religious Programs—Tel: 810-754-6741.
Students 128.

3—ST. CLETUS, Rev. Philip Briffa.
Office: 26256 Ryan Rd., 48091. Tel: 810-755-1313.
Res., 26262 Ryan Rd., 48091.
Catechesis/Religious Programs—Tel: 810-755-1350. Virginia Filar, D.R.E.
Students 230.

4—ST. DOROTHY, Revs. Francis A. Weingartz; Thomas Puzio; Sr. Carlotta Lammers, Pastoral Assoc.
Res., 12255 Frazho, 48089. Tel: 810-754-3232; Fax: 810-754-3152.
Catechesis/Religious Programs—Tel: 810-759-1040.
Students 290.

5—ST. EDMUND, Revs. Robert J. Witkowski; Eugene T. Katcher; Deacon Val Buyle.
Res., 14025 Twelve Mile Rd., 48093. Tel: 810-772-2720; Fax: 810-772-5576.
Catechesis/Religious Programs—Tel: 810-773-9220.
Students 530.

6—ST. LEONARD OF PORT MAURICE, Rev. Andrew J. Tomasko; Sr. Patricia Eeckhout, Pastoral Assoc.; Deacon Edward Swartz.
Res., 14057 E. Nine Mile, 48089. Tel: 810-777-1350; Fax: 810-777-1247.

7—ST. LOUISE, Rev. Thomas G. Rice; Sr. Kathleen Israel, Pastoral Assoc.; Deacons Wilhelm Kessler; Anthony Morici.
Res., 2500 Twelve Mile Rd., 48092. Tel: 810-751-3340; Fax: 810-751-0603.
Catechesis/Religious Programs—Tel: 810-751-3486. Mrs. Irmgard Kovacs, D.R.E.
Students 240.

8—ST. MARK, Rev. Robert A. Ruedisueli; Deacon George R. Posavetz.
Res., 4257 Bart, 48091. Tel: 810-759-3020; Fax: 810-759-3024.
Catechesis/Religious Programs—Tel: 810-759-3022. Suzanne Cornelius, D.R.E.
Students 415.

9—ST. MARTIN DE PORRES, Revs. Timothy J. Murray; Joseph Mallia. Pastoral Assocs.: Sr. Dorothy Krupp, O.S.F.; Sr. Joan Popovits, O.P.
Res., 31555 Hoover Rd., 48093. Tel: 810-264-7515; Fax: 810-264-4013.
Catechesis/Religious Programs—Tel: 810-264-7970. Mrs. Diane Bucko, D.R.E.
Students 345.
Convent—31014 Shaw, 48093. Tel: 810-264-4894.
Sisters 2.

10—ST. PAUL ALBANIAN CATHOLIC COMMUNITY, Rev. Anton Kcira, Admin.
Office: 3411 Twelve Mile Rd., 48092. Tel: 810-573-8110; Fax: 810-573-4107.
Res., 3239 E. Twelve Mile Rd., 48092. Tel: 810-573-8799.

11—ST. SYLVESTER, Revs. Gary Schulte; Stanislaw J. Obloj; Deacons John L. Skladanowski, Pastoral Min.; Daniel Darga, D.R.E.
Res., 11200 Twelve Mile Rd., 48093. Tel: 810-751-3636; Fax: 810-751-1766.
Catechesis/Religious Programs—Tel: 810-751-3510.
Students 496.

Washington, Macomb Co., SS. John and Paul, Rev. Terence F. Treppa.
Res., 7777 W. 28 Mile Rd., 48094. Tel: 810-781-9010; Fax: 810-781-7061.
Catechesis/Religious Programs—Tel: 810-781-9488. Deborah Knoblock, D.R.E.
Students 341.

Waterford, Oakland Co., Our Lady of the Lakes, Revs. Lawrence Delonnay; Jacek Brewczynski; Deacon Charles F. Johnson.
Res., 5481 Dixie Hwy., 48329. Tel: 810-623-0274; Fax: 810-623-2723.
School—Tel: 810-623-0250. Carol Hanrahan, Elementary Prin.
Lay Teachers 15; Students 481.
High School—Tel: 810-623-0340. Carl Uberti, High School Prin.
Sisters 1; Lay Teachers 19; Students 300.
Catechesis/Religious Programs—Tamzien Tallenger, D.R.E.
Students 396.

St. Benedict, Rev. James P. O'Hagan; Maria Geryk, Pastoral Assoc.
Parish Office—80 S. Lynn, 48328. Tel: 810-681-1534; Fax: 810-681-4501.
Res., 1160 Myrtle St., 48328.
School—Tel: 810-682-5580. Dr. Eugene Mignacca, Prin.
Lay Teachers 13; Students 255.
Catechesis/Religious Programs—Tel: 810-681-1536. Patricia Tola, D.R.E.
Students 206.

St. Perpetua, Rev. Richard S. Rakoczy.
Res., 134 Airport Rd., 48327. Tel: 810-682-6431; Fax: 810-682-7088.
Catechesis/Religious Programs—Joseph Leddy, D.R.E.
Students 428.

Wayne, Wayne Co., St. Mary, Rev. Raymond H. Bucon. Pastoral Assocs.: Sr. Eleanor Sekol, I.H.M.; Sr. Patricia Hergenroether, S.S.J.; Deacon William Meahan.
34530 Michigan Ave., 48184. Tel: 313-721-8745; Fax: 313-467-7381.
School—34516 Michigan Ave., 48184. Tel: 313-721-1240. Ms. Catherine Myszka, Prin.
Lay Teachers 10; Students 295.
Catechesis/Religious Programs—Tel: 313-326-8180.
Students 331.

West Bloomfield, Oakland Co., Prince of Peace, Rev. Arnold J. Kosco.
Res., 4300 Walnut Lake Rd., 48323. Tel: 810-681-9424; Fax: 810-681-5543.
Catechesis/Religious Programs—Tel: 810-681-5070. Irma Macy, D.R.E.
Students 420.

Westland, Wayne Co.,

1—ST. BERNARDINE, Rev. Ronald Sayes.
Res., 31463 Ann Arbor Trail, 48185. Tel: 313-427-5150; Fax: 313-427-3319.
Catechesis/Religious Programs—Tel: 313-261-3050. Mary Jane Ayotte, D.R.E.
Students 220.

2—ST. DAMIAN, Rev. John Hall, Admin.
Res., 29825 Joy Rd., 48185. Tel: 313-421-6130; Fax: 313-513-4916.
School—Tel: 313-427-1680. Sr. M. Pauline, C.S.S.F., Prin.
Felician Sisters 2; Lay Teachers 9; Students 238.
Catechesis/Religious Programs—Elaine O'Neill, D.R.E.
Students 159.
Convent—30055 Joy Rd., 48185. Tel: 313-427-0031.

3—CHURCH OF THE DIVINE SAVIOR, Rev. Alexander A. Kuras; Deacon Paul F. Pelchat.
Church—39375 Joy Rd., 48185. Tel: 313-455-3620; Fax: 313-455-7998.
Res., 9249 Caprice, Plymouth, 48170. Tel: 313-455-6964.
Catechesis/Religious Programs—Mary Ann Newton, D.R.E.
Students 227.

4—ST. RICHARD, Rev. John F. Hall.
Res., 35637 Cherry Hill, 48185. Tel: 313-729-2240; Fax: 313-729-3132.
Church—Church & C.C.D. Office, 35851 Cherry Hill Rd., 48185. Tel: 313-729-4411; Fax: 313-729-3132.
Catechesis/Religious Programs—Jeanne Martin, D.R.E.
Students 286.

5—SS. SIMON AND JUDE, Rev. Gerard V. Bechard.
Office: 32500 Palmer Rd., 48186. Tel: 313-722-1343; Fax: 313-326-5466.
Res., 1700 Hubbard Ave., 48186.
Catechesis/Religious Programs—D.R.E.: Mary Ann Kocsis; Phoebe Jankowski.
Students 220.

6—ST. THEODORE OF CANTERBURY, Revs. Michael A. Molnar; H. Thomas Kuehnemund; Deacon Anthony Kendzierski.
Res., 8200 Wayne Rd., 48185. Tel: 313-425-4421; Fax: 313-425-0650.
Catechesis/Religious Programs—Tel: 313-425-7310.
Students 394.

White Lake, Oakland Co., St. Patrick, Rev. Thomas L. Meagher.
Res., 9086 Hutchins Rd., 48386. Tel: 810-698-3100; Fax: 810-698-2350.
School—9040 Hutchins Rd., 48386. Tel: 810-698-2340. Mrs. Linda Meese, Prin.
Lay Teachers 10; Students 301.
Catechesis/Religious Programs—Students 857.

Woodhaven, Wayne Co., Our Lady of the Woods, Rev. Richard J. Bartoszek; Deacon Dennis Scanland.
Res., 21892 Gudith Rd., 48183. Tel: 313-671-5102; Fax: 313-671-2901.
Catechesis/Religious Programs—Tel: 313-671-0525. Patricia Butler, D.R.E.
Students 925.

Wyandotte, Wayne Co.,

1—ST. ELIZABETH, Rev. Charles M. Morris.
Res., 138 Goodell St., 48192. Tel: 313-284-7727; Fax: 313-284-7891.

2—ST. HELENA, Rev. George Kowalski.
Res., 753 Forest St., 48192. Tel: 313-284-4988.

3—ST. JOSEPH, Rev. Gerard Frawley, S.A.C.
Res., 353 Elm St., 48192. Tel: 313-285-9840; Fax: 313-285-9745.
School—Tel: 313-285-2030; Fax: 313-285-0327. Mary Swinkey, Prin.
Lay Teachers 10; Students 175.
Catechesis/Religious Programs—Doreen Calvin, D.R.E.
Students 229.

4—OUR LADY OF MT. CARMEL, (Polish), Rev. Walter J. Ptak.
Res., 976 Superior Blvd., 48192. Tel: 313-284-9135; Fax: 313-284-1367. [CEM]
School—2609 Tenth St., 48192. Tel: 313-285-5520. Sr. Mary Anita Niemiec, C.S.S.F., Elementary Prin.
Felician Sisters 3; Lay Teachers 15; Students 318.
High School—Tel: 313-284-7311; Fax: 313-284-6235. Sr. Mary Cordelia, C.S.S.F., High School Prin.
Felician Sisters 2; Lay Teachers 12; Students 140.
Catechesis/Religious Programs—Tel: 313-284-6145. Sr. Mary Adonia, C.S.S.F., D.R.E.
Lay Teachers 14; Students 180.
Convent—2609 Tenth St., 48192. Tel: 313-284-7253.

5—ST. PATRICK, Rev. Raymond H. Lewandowski.
Office: 135 Superior Blvd., 48192.
Res., 105 Superior Blvd., 48192. Tel: 313-285-9472; Fax: 313-285-1623. [JC]
School—Wyandotte Catholic Consolidated School, Tel: 313-285-2030. Mary Swinkey, Elementary Prin.
Lay Teachers 9; Students 176.
High School—Gabriel Richard H.S., Tel: 313-284-1875. John Bres, High School Prin.
Students 520.

6—ST. STANISLAUS KOSTKA, (Polish), Rev. John P. Hedges.
Res., 266 Antoine St., 48192. Tel: 313-285-9509.
School—240 Antoine St., 48192. Tel: 313-282-3105.
Sisters 1; Lay Teachers 8; Students 153.

Yale, St. Clair Co., Sacred Heart, Rev. Lawrence E. Dunn.
Res., 310 N. Main St., 48097. Tel: 810-387-2998. [CEM]
Catechesis/Religious Programs—Tel: 810-387-3361. Marian Boike, D.R.E.
Students 106.

Chaplains of Public Institutions

DETROIT. *Alexander Blaine Memorial*. Attended from St. Peter and Paul. Tel: 313-961-8077.
Annapolis. Rev. Bernard Pilarski.
Art Centre Hospital. Attended from Lady of the Rosary. Tel: 313-875-6011.
Beaumont Hospital. Revs. Christopher Welch; Lloyd Thiel, O.F.M. Cap.
Bi-County Osteopathic. Rev. Theo Meyer.
Bon Secours. Rev. Donald J. Kresmer; Sr. Therese Tighe, O.P., Chap.; Rita McEachen Neal, Chap.
Children's Hospital. Tel: 313-745-5917. Sr. Janet Ryan, I.H.M., Dir.; Sr. Beverly Hindson, I.H.M., Chap.
Clinton Valley Center. Tel: 810-338-7241, Ext. 425. Rev. Daniel Thottakara, C.M.I.
Cottage Hospital. Attended from St. Paul's. Tel: 810-785-8855.
Crittendon Hospital. Rev. Walter Lezochowski.
Detroit General Hospital, 48226. Tel: 313-224-0541. Sr. Adelaide Eiden, Chap.
Detroit Osteopathic Hospital. Attended from Cathedral of the Most Blessed Sacrament. 48226. Tel: 313-865-6300.
Detroit Psychiatric Institute, 48226. Tel: 313-427-1533. Rev. Daniel O'Sullivan.
Detroit Receiving Hospital, 48226. Rev. Bernard Backiel, M.I.C.; Sr. Janet Hudspeth, Chap.
Detroit Riverview Hospital. Attended from St. Charles.
Doctor's Hospital. Vacant. St. Peter and Paul, 48226. Tel: 313-961-8077.
Garden City Osteopathic Hospital. Rev. Bernard Pilarski.
Glen Eden Hospital. Attended from the Capuchin Community.
Grace Hospital-Northwest University. Deacon Dan Sweeney, Chap.; Mary Bartnik, Chap.
Harper Hospital and Rehabilitation Center. Rev. Gabriel Cohelo, O.F.M.Cap.
Henry Ford Hospital. Rev. Charles Hart, O.F.M.; Sr. Kathleen Miotke, O.P., Chap.; Mrs. Marie Handley, Chap.
Heritage Hospital. Tel: 810-295-6700. Rev. Richard Bartoszek.
Hutzel Hospital. Tel: 313-831-3139. Rev. James L. Meyer.
Kirkwood Hospital. Attended from St. Gregory. Tel: 313-861-0363.
Lapeer Regional. Attended from Immaculate Conception. Tel: 810-664-8594.
Lincoln Hospital. Attended from Holy Redeemer. Tel: 313-842-3450.
Macomb Hospital Center. Mrs. Katherine Breslin, Chap.
Martin Place East Hospital. Attended from St.

Vincent Ferrer. Tel: 810-542-8720.
McNamara Hospital. Attended from the Capuchin Community. Tel: 810-751-0410.
Mercy Hospital Detroit, 48226. Sr. Rose Petrozzo, O.P., Chap.
Michigan Health Care Corporation. Rev. Bernard Backiel, M.I.C.
North Woodward Hospital. Attended from Blessed Sacrament Cathedral. Tel: 313-865-6300.
Northville State Hospital. Tel: 810-349-1800. Rev. Stanislaus C. Kukulski.
Oakland General Osteopathic. Sr. Stephanie Thompson, Chap.
Oakwood Hospital. Revs. Michael Gormley, S.A.C.; Richard Lileart; Sr. Ann Foley, Chap.
Palmer Osteopathic Hospital. Attended from St. Benedict. Tel: 313-868-3876.
Palmer Osteopathic Hospital-East. Attended from St. Matthew. Tel: 313-881-4049.
Pontiac Correction Camp. Attended from St. Patrick, Union Lake. Tel: 810-363-2441.
Pontiac General Hospital. Diane Guappone, Chap.
Pontiac Osteopathic Hospital. Diane Guappone, Chap.
Redford Community Hospital. Attended from St. Agatha. Tel: 313-531-0371.
Rehabilitation Institute. Sr. Therese LeBlanc, Dir.; Sr. Leslie Hartway, Chap.
Riverside Osteopathic Hospital. Attended from St. Joseph. Tel: 313-676-9082. Sr. Fran Pokrifka, I.H.M., Chap.
Saratoga General Hospital. Rev. Louis Resma.
Sinai Hospital. Vacant.
Southwest Detroit Hospital, 48226. Tel: 313-963-4539. Rev. Thomas Lumpkin.
Veterans Administration Hospital. Vacant.
Warren Memorial Hospital. Vacant.
Wayne and Monroe County-Adults, 305 Michigan Ave., 48226. Tel: 313-237-4684. John Humphrey, Chap.
Wayne Co., 305 Michigan Ave., 48226. Tel: 313-237-4684. Don Portwood, Chap.
Wayne County Juvenile Justice, c/o Team for Justice, 1035 St. Antoine, 48226. Tel: 313-965-3242. Bill Kresse, Chap.
Wayne County Youth Home. Tel: 313-831-1356. Rufus Knighton, Chap.
Wyandotte General Hospital. Attended from St. Helena. Tel: 313-284-4988. Rev. George Kowalski.
Yale Community Hospital. Attended from Sacred Heart. Tel: 810-387-2998.
Zieger Osteopathic Hospital. Attended from Our Lady Queen of Angels. Tel: 313-825-4696.

CLINTON TOWNSHIP. *Macomb Regional,* 23823 15 Mile Rd., 48035. Tel: 810-792-6740. Deacon John Barbera, Chap.
State Prisons, 24415 Crocker Blvd., 48036. Tel: 810-755-9359. Rev. Tom Physician.

FARMINGTON. *Botsford General Hospital,* St. Alexander's, 810-474-5748. Rev. Louis Resma.

MOUNT CLEMENS. *Macomb County Adults,* c/o Macomb County Jail, 43565 Elizabeth Rd., 48043. Tel: 810-307-9326. Jo Kudela, Chap.
Macomb County Jail, 43565 Elizabeth, 48043. Tel: 810-307-9326. Don Portwood, Chap.
Macomb County Jail and Macomb County Youth Home. Attended from St. Peter's, Mount Clemens. Tel: 313-237-5962.
Mount Clemens General Hospital. Ms. Connie Walker, Dir.

PONTIAC. *Oakland and Lapeer County-Adults,* 14 Judson St., 3rd Floor, P.O. Box 431366, 48343-1366. Tel: 810-338-9310. Peggy Devaney, Chap.
Oakland, Lapeer, and St. Clair County, 14 Judson St., 3rd Floor, P.O. Box 431366, 48343-1366. Tel: 810-338-9310. Harry Lawrence, Chap.
Oakland, Lapeer, Macomb, and St. Clair Counties-Juveniles, 14 Judson St., 3rd Floor, P.O. Box 431366, 48343-1366. Tel: 810-338-9310. Carleen Ward, Chap.

PORT HURON. *Mercy Hospital Port Huron,* 48060. Sr. Margaret Weber, R.S.M., Chap.; Sr. M. Frances Villerot, R.S.M., Chap.
Port Huron Hospital. Attended from St. Joseph. 48060. Tel: 810-985-7750.

Special Assignment:
Reverend Monsignors—
Gordon, John, Archdiocesan Cemeteries
Quinn, John M., Dept. of Education
Sable, Robert M., Prelate Auditor of the Roman Rota, Vatican
Zenz, John P., Moderator of the Curia
Reverend Fathers—
Bugarin, Michael, Sec. Cardinal
Byrne, Thomas R., Monroe Vicariate
Carnago, William, Tribunal & Pastor, Immaculate Heart of Mary, Detroit
Fisher, Robert J., Vocations Office
Havron, Daniel, O.F.M., Office of Evangelization
Heppen, Michael, C.S.C., Special Projects
Jozwiak, Ronald J., Tribunal & Admin., St. Josaphat, Detroit
Kosnik, Anthony, Marygrove College
McLeod, Donald, C.S.B., Parish Support Svcs.
Miller, George, Tribunal
Nawrocki, Norman, Tribunal
Slowinski, Jerome, Tribunal
Taube, Sylvester, Family Life Office
West, John H., Rector, St. John's Center for Youth & Families
Williams, Clarence, C.PP.S., African American Catholic Ministries Office
Williams, Robert H., Tribunal & Pastor, St. Justin, Hazel Park

---

On Duty Outside the Archdiocese:
Reverend Fathers—
Bartos, Kris A., Archdiocese of Miami
Cassidy, Richard, East Aurora, NY
Singelyn, Robert K., Recife, Brazil
Trent, James F., Chaplaincy Admin., Federal Bureau of Prisons-Western Region, 7950 Dublin Blvd., Dublin, CA 94568. Tel: 510-803-4776
Walsh, Jerome, Jackson Heights, NY

Military Chaplains:
Reverend Fathers—
Bjorklund, Brian, U.S. Navy
Borycz, Edmund S., U.S. Army
Goodrow, Robert, U.S. Navy
Hogan, Timothy D., U.S. Navy
Jagielski, James, U.S. Army
Kaul, John, U.S. Naval Reserves

Graduate Studies:
Reverend Fathers—
Browne, Ronald, Pontifical University of St. Thomas Aquinas, Rome
Kasza, John, Pontifical Intl. Inst. of San Anselmo
Monforton, Jeffrey, Pontifical Gregorian Univ.
Spezia, Robert, North American College

Absent on Leave:
Reverend Fathers—
Crepeau, John J.
Hogan, Richard
Koss, David F.
Kramer, Thomas
Loyson, Michael
McLaughlin, Andrew
Sam, James
Shirilla, Gerald

Absent on Sick Leave:
Reverend Fathers—
DuCharme, Lawrence M.
Lipczewski, Boleslaus
MacLennan, Donald
Morgan, Colum

Retired:
Reverend Monsignors—
Canfield, Francis X., St. Paul Parish, 157 Lakeshore Rd., Grosse Pointe Farms, MI 48236
DeCneudt, Ferdinand, Father Tallieu Senior Citizen Residence, Apt. B104, 18740 Thirteen Mile Rd., Roseville, MI 48066
Flanigan, Gerald A., 14469-B Levan Rd., Livonia, MI 48154
Horkan, Vincent J., 36800 Schoolcraft, Livonia, MI 48150
Lorenz, Victor O., 6504 Marina Dr., Algonac, MI 48001
Sawher, Clifford F., 716 Clinton Ave., St. Clair, MI 48079
Sherzer, William J., St. Owen Parish, 6869 Franklin Rd., Bloomfied Hills, MI 48301
Villerot, Thomas H., 14453-A Levan Rd., Livonia, MI 48154-5022
Weier, John A., Maryhaven, 11350 Reeck Rd., Rm. 73, Southgate, MI 48195
Reverend Fathers—
Bartone, Donald E., 1715 N. River Rd., Apt. 21, St. Clair, MI 48079
Bauer, Erwin J., 75 S. Channel, Harsens Island, MI 48028
Bell, Arthur J., 15131 Newburg, Apt. 47, Livonia, MI 48154
Berg, Paul, Sacred Heart Major Seminary, 2701 Chicago Blvd., Detroit, MI 48206
Blaska, John A., 541 E. 14 Mile Rd., Clawson, MI 48017
Bologna, Anthony F., St. Gabriel Parish, 8118 W. Vernor, Detroit, MI 48209
Borowski, Ladislaus, DeSerrano Res., C-226, 17255 Common Rd., Roseville, MI 48066
Bresnahan, Thomas, 14453-B Levan Rd., Livonia, MI 48154
Britz, Gerald F., 8781 Lakeshore, Lexington, MI 48450
Burke, Walter E., HC48 Box 101, Paradise, MI 49768
Burkholder, Robert, 84 - 770 Kili Dr., Apt. 632, Waianae, HI 96792
Burns, Francis H., 810 North Shore, St. Clair Shores, MI 48080
Butkus, Casimir, 6467 Warwick, Detroit, MI 48228
Castelot, John, 42555 Plymouth Hollow, Plymouth, MI 48170
Ciesniewski, Richard P., St. Elizabeth Seton Parish, 9728 Palmeras Ln., Sun City, AZ 85373
Dacey, Donald, Fairlane Meadows, 5148 Heather Dr., #116, Dearborn, MI 48126
David, Basilio, 64 Kennedy, San Juan, Metro-Manila, Philippines
Davidson, William, St. Anastasia Parish, 4571 John Rd., Troy, MI 48098
Decker, Maurice C., Rapalo North Condominiums, 306, 1701 S. Flagler, West Palm Beach, FL 33401
Dietz, Francis, 14453-C Levan Rd., Livonia, MI 48154
Dorr, Richard J., 38110 John P. Rd., Clinton Twp., MI 48036-1218
Dowell, William J., 14467-A Levan Rd., Livonia, MI 48154-5022
Drogowski, Joseph, P.O. Box 372, Cohoctah, MI 48816-0372
Dunn, John, Casa Maria, 670 Maple Vista, Imlay City, MI 48444
Edwards, Lawrence A., 8181 Wayne Rd., Apt. K-1093, Westland, MI 48185
Esper, Thomas, 164 Shoreline Rd., East Port Sanilac, MI 48469-9769
Fauser, Arthur W., Our Lady of Sorrows Parish, 23815 Powers, Farmington, MI 48336
Fedewa, Eugene F., Our Lady Queen of Peace Parish, 20955 Bournemouth, Harper Wds., MI 48225
Femminineo, Joseph P.
Ferens, Joseph F., 1870 Lakesview Blvd., Oxford, MI 48371
Foley, John L., Marybrook Manor, 36975 Five Mile Rd., Livonia, MI 48154
Forish, Andrew, 19450 Mayfield, Apt. 104, Livonia, MI 48152
Fortuna, George B., 14467-C Levan Rd., Livonia, MI 48154-5022
Fraser, Thomas, 9375 Meskill Rd., Columbus, MI 48063
Gierut, Joseph A., 9106 Del Prado Dr., Palos Hills, IL 60525-0807
Goentges, Charles J., 14468-A Levan Rd., Livonia, MI 48154-5022
Haener, Robert W., 14467-B Levan Rd., Livonia, MI 48154
Haney, Richard M., Maryhaven Apt. 25, 11350 Reeck Rd., Southgate, MI 48195
Hardy, John J., P.O. Box 488, Ortonville, MI 48462
Hayes, James L., Villa Maria, Apt. 1, 15131 Newburg Rd., Livonia, MI 48154
Heidelberger, Ronald, 1431 Washington Blvd., Apt. 1402, Detroit, MI 48226
Hennes, Paul R., 102 Wild Cherry Cove, Leesburg, FL 34748-8621
Herman, Jerome A., 1604 E. 9th St., Stuart, FL 34996
Higdon, C. Paul, 325 32nd St., Port Huron, MI 48060
Hillebrand, Albert J., 1116 Shore Club Dr., St. Clair Shores, MI 48080
Hoffmaster, Harry, 2500 River Rd. #41, Marysville, MI 48040
Hubble, Karl D., 1593 N. River Rd., Apt. 1-D, St. Clair, MI 48079
Immel, William A., 7300 Orchard St., P.O. Box 236, Port Sanilac, MI 48469
Janiga, Joseph, 7039 Sarena, Detroit, MI 48210
Jones, Raymond, 779 Hawk Ave. N.W., Lake Placid, FL 33852
Kaznowski, Valentine J., 7758 Colony Dr., Algonac, MI 48001
Kenna, John A., Maryhaven, 11350 Reeck Rd., Apt. 74, Southgate, MI 48195
Koenig, Robert B., Chalet Apts., 33373 Utica Rd., Apt. 2, Fraser, MI 48026
Koltuniak, Michael P., 14454-C Levan Rd., Livonia, MI 48154-5022
Konopka, Edward F., 2345 Coolidge Hwy., Troy, MI 48084
Kowalski, Ralph E., 14467-D Levan Rd., Livonia, MI 48154-5022
Kreft, Henry S., 3621 Port Austin Rd., Port Austin, MI 48467
Kresmer, Donald J., Maryhaven #26, 11350 Reeck Rd., Southgate, MI 48195-2285
Kress, Joseph J., 203 S. Huron St., Ypsilanti, MI 48197-5452
Krieg, Jerome L., 2300 Watkins Lake Rd., Waterford, MI 48328
Krisciunevicius, Victor, 12942 Brixham, Warren, MI 48093

Kubik, John M., St. Peter & Paul Parish, 7685 Grandville, Detroit, MI 48228
Kundrat, Michael J., 81393 Belle River Rd. #15, Memphis, MI 48041
Kuntz, Donald B., 9245 North River Rd., Algonac, MI 48001
Lederman, Paul, 14455-C Levan Rd., Livonia, MI 48154
Lombardi, Albert U., 14465-B Levan Rd., Livonia, MI 48154-5022
Machak, James A., 27216 Lorraine, Warren, MI 48093
Malaric, Stephen L., 5325 Pointe Dr., E. China, MI 48054-4161
Maliszewski, Francis S., 986 Wexford Way, Rochester Hills, MI 48309
Maloney, Richard E., 390 Mt. Vernon, Grosse Pointe Farms, MI 48236
Marshall, Raymond, 19650 Eastland Village Dr., Apt.#1, Harper Woods, MI 48225
Matheson, Paul V., 14469-D Levan Rd., Livonia, MI 48154-5022
Matlenga, Joseph, Sacred Heart Home for the Aged, 4900 Navarre, Oregon, OH 43616
McGoldrick, William J., Fernhill Village Apts., 38271 Fairway Ct., #99A, Clinton Township, MI 48038
Muir, Edmund D., 443 Cerromar Ln., Apt. 300, Venice, FL 34293
Neffy, Arthur, 17825 15 Mile Rd. #25, Clinton Twp., MI 48035
O'Callaghan, John F., 5617 Tequesta Dr., West Bloomfield, MI 48323
O'Hara, Michael J., 22612 St. Joan, St. Clair Shores, MI 48080-3866
O'Leary, Michael G., St. Paul Parish, 157 Lake Shore Dr., Grosse Pointe Farms, MI 48236
O'Neill, Charles F., Our Lady of Grace Parish, 8679 Riverview, Dearborn Heights, MI 48127
Partensky, Leonard J., 6747 N. Wayne Rd., 440A-3, Westland, MI 48185
Perkowski, Joseph, 16113 Inla Ln., Ocqueoc, MI 49759
Reckinger, Robert A., 3300 Jeffries Fwy., Detroit, MI 48208
Redwick, Stanislaus J., Marywood Nursing Center, 36975 W. Five Mile Rd., Livonia, MI 48154
Rybinski, Marvin, Maryhaven #1, 11350 Reeck Rd., Southgate, MI 48195
Ryder, Joseph F., 3015 Moonlake Dr., W. Bloomfield, MI 48323
Sadler, Alfred H., 5571 Pointe Dr., E. China, MI 48054
Samonie, Jacob, 34644 Spring Valley, Westland, MI 48185
Scheuerman, Edward L., 14453-D Levan Rd., Livonia, MI 48154
Schmitt, Thomas G., 53880 Sunderlund Dr., Shelby Township, MI 48316
Schroll, Bernard A., Guardian Angels Parish, 581 E. 14 Mile, Clawson, MI 48017
Schweihofer, Walter J., 49310 Bay Shore Dr., New Baltimore, MI 48047
Sierocki, Paul E., 1723 N. Lafayette, Dearborn, MI 48128
Sirianni, Jasper F., Our Lady of Mt. Carmel Parish, 10828 Brandon Rd., Emmett, MI 48022
Sito, Joseph, 14455-B Levan Rd., Livonia, MI 48154-5022
Slominski, Fabian B., 5405 Christi Dr., Warren, MI 48091
Stanievich, J. Walter, 22295 Green Hill, Apts. 29, Farmington Hills, MI 48335
Stine, Jerome E., 20198 Omira, Detroit, MI 48203
Tucci, Italo, Fr. Taillieu Sr. Citizens #107, 18700 13 Mile Rd., Roseville, MI 48066
Ugolik, Richard, 57088 Copper Creek Dr., Washington Township, MI 48094-2822
Van Der Linden, Peter J., 1370 Aspen Dr., Apt. 4, Marysville, MI 48040
Villerot, Henry E., De Serrano Residence, 17255 Common Rd. B-200, Roseville, MI 48066
Welch, William F., 14455-A Levan Rd., Livonia, MI 48154-5022
Wittstock, John J., 3603 Villa Knolls Dr., Las Vegas, NV 89120
Wolber, Ferdinand A., Woodlore Condominiums, 33399 Fargo, Livonia, MI 48152
Zdrodowski, Francis, 2397 20th St., Wyandotte, MI 48192
Zeeb, Charles, 18569 Manorwood West, Clinton Township, MI 48039
Zielinski, Thomas J., Madonna Villa, 17825 15 Mile Rd., Apt. 28, Clinton Twp., MI 48035
Ziemba, Walter, SS. Cyril & Methodius Seminary, 3535 Indian Trail, Orchard Lake, MI 48324

Permanent Deacons:
Abler, Donald, VA Medical Center, Allen Park
Ball, John H., St. Thomas More, Troy
Barbera, John
Belleman, Patrick
Black, Brian J., St. Ives, Southfield
Braman, Kenneth, St. Elizabeth Ann Seton, Troy
Braun, Bernard, St. Anne, Ortonville
Bruen, Patrick T., St. Stanislaus Kostka, Wyandotte
Busch, Robert F., St. Joan of Arc, St. Clair Shores
Buyle, Valere, St. Edmund, Warren
Carroll, Brian, St. Regis, Birmingham
Channell, Ronald, St. Athanasius, Roseville
Cochrane, George, St. Linus, Dearborn Heights
Cominotto, Anthony, St. Augustine, Richmond
Conlin, Richard R., St. Benedict, Highland Park
Connors, John J., St. Stephen, Port Huron
Cook, Ronald W., St. Kieran, Utica
Cornell, Peter, St. Anthony, Belleville
Cousino, Wesley, St. Joseph, Utica
Cox, Donald J., St. Blase, Sterling Heights
Cron, James A., St. Mary, Royal Oak
Daratony, Joseph J., Resurrection, Canton
Darga, Daniel J., Our Lady of La Salette, Berkley
Delbeke, Robert G., St. Rita, Detroit
Deshaw, Gerald, Immaculate Conception, Lapeer
Desjarlais, Eugene B., Madonna University, Livonia
Desmedt, Frank, St. Lawrence, Utica
DeWitt, Robert N., Our Lady of Grace, Dearborn Heights
DiCresce, Eugene, St. Joan of Arc, St. Clair Shores
Downey, Terrance E., St. Germaine, St. Clair Shores
Dullinger, Aloysius, Senior Status
Emery, Harry R., Senior Status
Fitzgerald, Robert C., St. Michael, Livonia
Fleming, John Michael, St. Joseph, Pontiac
Fraser, Daniel, St. Mary, Monroe
Gabel, Raymond, St. Aidan, Livonia
Gennette, James, St. John, Allenton
Girard, Lawrence, St. Sebastian, Dearborn Heights
Goetz, Robert, Our Lady of Refuge, Orchard Lake
Gonzalez, Norman, Senior Status
Goodhue, Harold, St. Roch, Flat Rock
Hardwick, Ralph, St. Vincent Ferrer, Madison Heights
Healey, Lawrence, St. Michael, Sterling Heights
Hensel, James L., Senior Status
Herta, Robert, St. Lucy, St. Clair Shores
Hoffman, Alfred H., St. Michael, Monroe
Hulan, Richard, St. Barbara, Dearborn
Hurley, Daniel, St. Cyril, Taylor
Igoe, James, St. Richard, Westland
Ingles, Michael M., St. Michael, Monroe
Iskra, Joseph, All Saints, Holy Cross, SS. Andrew & Benedict, Detroit
Jablonowski, Alexander, St. Daniel, Clarkston
Jackson, Douglas, Jr., Martyrs of Uganda, Detroit
Jamieson, William E., St. Ambrose, Grosse Point Park
Jimenez, Rafael, St. Stephen, Mary Mother of the Church
Johnson, Charles, Our Lake of the Lakes, Waterford
Johr, William H., St. Matthew, Detroit
Jones, Wyatt, St. Cecelia, Detroit
Junak, Donald C., St. Louis, Mount Clemens
Kendzierski, Anthony, St. Theodore, Westland
Kenny, John, St. Edith, Livonia
Kessler, Wilhelm, St. Louise, Warren
Krauskoff, William, Our Lady Gate of Heaven, Detroit
Krueger, Gary R., Holy Cross, Marine City
Krzeminski, Eugene, St. Kenneth, Plymouth
Kunik, Raymond L., St. Priscilla, Livonia
LaLone, Norman C., Senior Status
Leach, Donald, Our Lady of Good Counsel, Plymouth
Lennon, Joseph, St. Stanislaus Kostka, Wyandotte
Lewandoski, Anthony, St. Mary Church, New Baltimore
Lubien, Raymond J., St. Bartholomew, Detroit
Machus, Paul H., St. William, Walled Lake
Maiuri, Rocco, St. Basil, Eastpointe
Marku, John, St. Christopher, Detroit
Markulike, Michael J., St. Dunstan, Garden City
Marquis, Joseph, St. Paul of the Cross Retreat Center, Detroit
Martin, John, Senior Status
McCoy, Elgia, St. Anthony, Detroit
McIntyre, Ronald L., Gesu, Detroit
McKale, Michael, Holy Name, Birmingham
McLeod, Robert E., St. Mary, St. Clair
McNeeley, Allen J., Martyrs of Uganda, Detroit
Meahan, William, St. Mary, Wayne
Misiak, Richard, St. Edith, Livonia
Modes, Robert, St. John Bosco, Redford
Morad, Alfred J., Senior Status
Morello, Steven, St. Agatha, Redford
Morici, Anthony, St. Jane Frances de Chantal, Sterling Heights
Motowski, Norbert, St. Christopher, Detroit
Mouro, Joseph, St. Constance Parish, Taylor
Murphy, Thomas, St. Mary, Rockwood
Noon, Archie J., St. Mary, Milford
Nowicki, Kenneth, St. Catherine, Algonac
Otto, William, St. Joseph, South Lyon
Ovies, Robert, St. Columban, Birmingham
Pallarito, James R., Holy Innocents, Roseville
Pardo, Gary, Our Lady of Loretto, Redford
Pelchat, Paul, Divine Savior, Westland
Piro, Rudolph P., St. Genevieve, Livonia
Posavetz, George, St. Mark, Warren
Prince, Benjamin, St. Frances DeSales, Detroit
Quirouette, Edward E., Our Lady of Lourdes Parish, River Rouge
Riopelle, Ernest, St. Conrad, Melvindale
Rivera, Rafael, St. Vincent de Paul, Pontiac
Rivier, Robert, St. Elizabeth, Wyandotte
Rodriguez, Brigido, St. Vincent de Paul, Pontiac
Rohlman, Ronald, Shrine of the Little Flower, Royal Oak
Rowland, Robert, St. Albert the Great, Dearborn
Sandstrom, Donald, Our Lady of Good Counsel, Detroit
Santeramo, John, St. Rene Goupil, Sterling Heights
Scanland, Dennis, Our Lady of the Woods, Woodhaven
Schaible, John, Senior Status
Schlesser, Peter, Annunciation, Detroit
Shubik, Richard, St. Paul, Grosse Pointe Farms
Skladanowski, John L., St. Sylvester, Warren
Skubick, Charles G., St. Andrew, Rochester
Smith, Michael T., Our Lady Gate of Heaven, Detroit
Smith, Richard, St. Hugo of the Hills, Bloomfield Hills
Snyder, Robert J., St. Anthony, Temperance
Sobolewski, Don F., Transfiguration, Detroit
Solomon, James, Redemption, Melkite, Warren
Springer, Mark, St. Anastasia, Troy
Stankiewicz, Clement, St. Christine/St. Gemma, Detroit
Stimpson, Bill, Jr., Precious Blood, Detroit
Strye, Edward, St. Michael, Pontiac
Strzyzewski, Marvin, St. Anne, Warren
Sullivan, Lawrence
Swartz, Edward, St. Leonard, Warren
Thomas, Thomas M., St. Martin, Warren
Thome, William A., St. Cyril of Jerusalem, Taylor
Tombler, Eugene, Guardian Angels, Clawson
Tremmel, Robert, Sacred Heart, Grosse Ile
Valdez, Ferando, St. Vincent de Paul, Pontiac
Van Brook, Arthur, Holy Spirit, Highland
Vanneste, Johnny M., St. Jane Frances DeChantal, Sterling Heights
Vasquez, Jesus, St. Vincent de Paul, Pontiac
Vestuto, Richard, St. Benedict, Waterford
Waldmann, William L., Holy Family, Novi
Wilson, Edward C., Jr., St. Paul of Tarsus, Clinton Township
Yezak, Thomas, St. Joseph, Lake Orion

INSTITUTIONS LOCATED IN THE ARCHDIOCESE

[A] SEMINARIES, ARCHDIOCESAN

DETROIT. *Sacred Heart Major Seminary, Inc.*, 2701 Chicago Blvd., 48206. Tel: 313-883-8500. Allen H. Vigneron, Rector & Pres.; Revs. Patrick Halfpenny, Vice Rector & Dean of Seminarians; Earl Boyea, Dean of Studies; Sr. Mary Ward, O.P., Registrar.

The College of Liberal Arts. Revs. Charles Kosanke, Dir. Undergraduate Seminarians; John Esper, Spiritual Dir.; Sr. Mary Finn, H.V.M., Dir. The Apostolic Experience Program; Mrs. Karen Meheffey, Dir. of Libraries; Mr. John Goyette.

The School of Theology. Revs. Paul Kreimes, Dir. Graduate Seminarians; Daniel Trapp, Spiritual Dir.; Clifford Ruskowski; Ronald De Hondt; James Jorgenson, (Orthodox Church in America); Dr. Patricia Cooney-Hathaway; Mr. Mark Latkovic; Sr. Mary Lou Putrow, O.P.; Dr. William Riordan.

The Institute for Pastoral Ministry. Mrs. Patricia A. Rennie, Dean of The Institute for Ministry; Ms. Suzanne Schreiber, Asst. Dean of The Institute for Recruitment & Retention.

Seminary Total: Priests 10; Sisters 4; Lay Faculty 8; Students 242.

ORCHARD LAKE. *SS. Cyril and Methodius Seminary*, 3535 Indian Trail, 48324. Tel: 810-683-0311; 313-963-8075. Rev. Msgr. Stanley E. Milewski, D.H.L., Chancellor; Rev. Msgr. Francis B. Koper, D.Min. (WIL), Rector, Vice Chancellor; Rev. John C. Kemper, S.S., D.Min. (HBG), Vice Rector & Dir. Formation; Mr. Edward Chaczyk, Comptroller; Rev. Albin J. Grous, S.T.D. (PH), Academic Dean; Mrs. Mary Jo

Wagener, Registrar; Rev. Msgr. Jan Jagodzinski, M.A. (Poland); Revs. Stanislaw Flis, S.T.D. (Poland), Dir. Admissions and Recruitment; James K. Mazurek, M.Div. (PIT), Devel. Exec. Sec., Natl. Alumni Assoc.; Roman Nir (Poland), Archivist; Kathleen Castillo, M.A., Dir. Field Ed.; David Troiano, Dir. Liturgical Music; Nancy Ward, M.S.L.S., Librarian. Full Time Resident Faculty: Rev. Msgr. Jerome S. Smalarz, J.C.L., Emeritus; Rev. Msgr. Zdzislaw Peszkowski, Ph.D. (Poland), Emeritus; Revs. Gregory Banazak, S.T.D.; Czeslaw M. Krysa, S.T.L. (BUF); Janusz Kukulka, M.A. (Poland); Michael Monshau, O.P., Ph.D.; David West, S.T.B.; Joseph Szewczyk, S.T.D. (Poland); Walter J. Ziemba, Ph.D., Emeritus. Students 105.

[B] SEMINARIES, RELIGIOUS OR SCHOLASTICATES

DETROIT. *Duns Scotus.* (Corporate Title: Duns Scotus), St. Aloysius Friary, 1234 Washington Blvd., 48226. Tel: 313-237-5811. Order of Friars Minor, St. John Baptist Province (Cincinnati). Revs. Maynard Tetreault, O.F.M., Pres.; Daniel Havron, O.F.M., Sec. Priests 2; Brothers 1.

BERKLEY. *Loyola House.* (Novitiate of the Chicago-Detroit Provinces of the Society of Jesus), 2599 Harvard Rd., 48072. Tel: 810-399-8132. Revs. Joseph H. Boel, S.J., Supr.; Timothy J. Shepard, S.J., Dir. Formation & Novices; Mark J. Andrews, S.J., Asst. Dir. Novices; Norman J. Dickson, Dir. Vocations; Sr. Melaine Svoboda, S.N.D., Spirituality & Min.; Bro. Henry C. Kuhn, S.J., Socius. Priests 5; Brothers 1; Sisters 1; Scholastics 7.

OXFORD. *St. Benedict Monastery*, 2711 E. Drahner Rd., 48370. Tel: 810-628-2249. Headquarters Novitiate House of Sylvestrine Benedictine Monks in the United States. Revs. Daniel J. Homan, O.S.B., Conventual Prior & Retreat Dir.; Michael R. Green, O.S.B., Subprior. Priests 2; Brothers 7; Chapels 2.

[C] COLLEGES AND UNIVERSITIES

DETROIT. *Marygrove College*, 8425 W. McNichols Rd., 48221. Tel: 313-862-8000.
For a complete listing, refer to the Colleges and Universities section.

University of Detroit Mercy, McNichols Campus, 4001 W. McNichols Rd. at Livernois, 48219-0900. Tel: 313-993-1000.
For a complete listing, refer to the Colleges and Universities section.

LIVONIA. *Madonna University*, 36600 Schoolcraft Rd., 48150. Tel: 313-432-5300; Fax: 313-432-5393.
For a complete listing, refer to the Colleges and Universities section.

ORCHARD LAKE. *Saint Mary's College*, 3535 Indian Trail, 48324. Tel: 810-682-1885.
For a complete listing, refer to the Colleges and Universities section.

[D] HIGH SCHOOLS, INTER-PAROCHIAL

DETROIT. *Bishop Borgess High School*, 11685 Appleton, 48239. Tel: 313-255-1100; Fax: 313-255-1102. Sr. Joan Charnley, I.H.M., Prin.; Ms. Patrice Evans, Youth Minister. Priests 1; Sisters 2; Lay Teachers 18; Lay Admin. & Personnel 4; Students 297.

East Catholic High School, 7320 St. Anthony Pl., 48213. Tel: 313-921-9650. R. Munson-Griffin, S.L.W., Prin. Sisters 1; Lay Teachers 11; Students 169.

St. Martin de Porres High, 13436 Grove, 48235. Tel: 313-864-3330. Ms. Sunbeam Hughes, Prin. Priests 1; Sisters 2; Lay Teachers 24; Students 354.

St. Vincent Middle School, 2020 14th St., 48216. Tel: 313-961-6773. Ms. Kathleen McBride, Prin. Lay Teachers 4; Students 100.

HARPER WOODS. *Bishop Gallagher High School*, 19360 Harper, 48225. Tel: 313-886-0855. Francis Turk, Prin. Sisters 2; Lay Teachers 14; Students 275.

MADISON HEIGHTS. *Bishop Foley High School*, 32000 Campbell Rd., 48071. Tel: 810-585-1210; Fax: 810-585-3667. Alex M. Gajewski, Prin. Priests 1; Sisters 12; Lay Teachers 46; Students 633.

Bishop Foley Venture Fund, 32000 Campbell Rd., 48071. Tel: 810-585-1210. Paul Manzec, Pres.

MARINE CITY. *Cardinal Mooney Catholic College Preparatory School*, 660 S. Water St., 48039. Tel: 810-765-8825. Dr. Elsie L. Ogden, Prin. Priests 1; Sisters 4; Lay Teachers 16; Students 197.

MONROE. *St. Mary Catholic Central High School.* (Coed), 108 W. Elm Ave., 48161. Tel: 313-241-0663. Bro. Robert Livernois, C.S.C., Prin. Brothers 1; Sisters 4; Lay Teachers 28; Students 452.

PONTIAC. *Notre Dame Preparatory High School and Marist Academy*, 1300 Giddings Rd., 48340-2108. Tel: 810-373-5300. Revs. Leon M. Olszamowski, S.M., Prin.; James G. Strasz, S.M. Priests 3; Brothers 1; Lay Teachers 34; Students 586.

RIVERVIEW. *Gabriel Richard High School*, 15325 Pennsylvania Rd., 48192. Tel: 313-284-1875. John A. Bres., Prin. Brothers 2; Sisters 4; Lay Teachers 33; Students 506.

ROYAL OAK. *Shrine High School*, 3500 W. 13 Mile Rd., 48073. Tel: 810-549-2925; Fax: 810-549-2953. Mr. Thomas P. Kirkwood, Prin. Lay Teachers 23; Students 297.

SOUTHGATE. *Aquinas High School*, 15601 North Line Rd., 48195. Tel: 313-283-3190. Rev. James F. Bradley, O.S.F.S.; Susan M. Kotyk, Prin. Priests 1; Brothers 1; Lay Teachers 18; Students 255.

[E] HIGH SCHOOLS, PRIVATE

DETROIT. *Dominican High School and Academy*, 9740 McKinney Ave., 48224. Tel: 313-882-8500 (High School & Academy). Adrian Dominican Sisters. Admin. Team: Sr. Joan Weitz, O.P., Prin.; Sr. Patricia Sporer, O.P., Asst. Prin. Sisters 12; Lay Teachers 12; Students 290.

Loyola High School, 15325 Pinehurst, 48238-1633. Tel: 313-861-2407; Fax: 313-861-4718. Rev. Michael A. Evans, S.J.

University of Detroit Jesuit High School and Academy, 8400 S. Cambridge, 48221. Tel: 313-862-5400. Revs. Timothy T. Shannon, S.J., Pres.; Kenneth A. Styles, S.J., Rector; J. Daniel Daly, S.J.; R. James Kurtz, S.J.; John Libens, S.J.; Patrick F. Peppard, S.J.; Patrick J. Rice, S.J.; Keith Esenther, S.J.; Bro. James J. Boynton, S.J. Priests 9; Scholastics 1; Lay Teachers 38; Students 656; Chapels 2.

BLOOMFIELD HILLS. *Academy of the Sacred Heart*, 1250 Kensington Rd., 48304. Tel: 810-646-8900; Fax: 810-646-4143. Religious of the Sacred Heart. Sr. Margaret Mary Canty, R.S.C.J., Headmistress. Sisters 5; Lay Teachers 51; Students 398.

Brother Rice Endowment Fund. (The "Foundation"), 7101 Lahser Rd., 48301-4045. Tel: 810-647-2526. Bro. William A. Dogan, C.F.C.; Mr. Thomas Sklut, Contact Person.

Brother Rice High School, 7101 Lahser Rd., 48301-4045. Tel: 810-647-2526. Congregation of Christian Brothers. Bro. William A. Dogan, C.F.C., Prin. Brothers 9; Sisters 2; Lay Teachers 42; Students 712.

Marian High School for Young Women, 7225 Lahser Rd., 48301. Tel: 810-644-1750. Sr. Lenore Pochelski, I.H.M., Prin. Sisters 2; Lay Teachers 32; Students 460.

FARMINGTON HILLS. *Mercy High School for Girls*, 29300 Eleven Mile Rd., 48336. Tel: 810-476-8020. Sisters of Mercy. Sr. Regina Marie Doelker, R.S.M., Prin. Faculty 63; Students 875.

HARPER WOODS. *Notre Dame High School*, 20254 Kelly Rd., 48225-1287. Tel: 313-371-8965. Marist Fathers. Mr. Richard Kuhn, Prin.; Revs. John Bryson, S.M.; Raymond Ouellette, S.M.; John Kiselica, S.M.; Normand Martin, S.M. Priests 4; Sisters 3; Lay Teachers 27; Students 455.

Regina High School for Girls, 20200 Kelly Rd., 48225-1284. Tel: 313-526-0220; Fax: 313-526-5850. Sr. Mary Leanne, Prin. Sisters of St. Joseph of the Third Order of St. Francis 11; Lay Teachers 43; Students 775.

LIVONIA. *Ladywood High School*, 14680 Newburgh Rd., 48154. Tel: 313-591-1544. (Private School for Girls). Sr. Mary Ann Smith, C.S.S.F., Prin.

ORCHARD LAKE. *St. Mary's Preparatory*, 3535 Indian Trail, 48324. Tel: 810-683-0531. Rev. Msgr. Stanley E. Milewski, Chancellor; Larry Reeside, Prin.; Mr. Richard Rychcik, Dean of Residence. Priests 1; Lay Teachers 23; Students 230.

REDFORD. *The Catholic Central Endowment Trust* 48239-2999, 14200 Breakfast Dr. Tel: 313-534-0660. Gregory Grabowski, Dir.

Catholic Central High School, 14200 Breakfast Dr., 48239. Tel: 313-534-0660; 261-3387 (Res). Basilian Fathers. Revs. Harold B. Gardner, C.S.B., Prin.; Richard J. Elmer, C.S.B., Supr.; John J. Ward, C.S.B.; Frank H. Bredeweg, C.S.B.; Edward Doneher, C.S.B.; Kenneth B. McKernan, C.S.B.; John H. Menner, C.S.B.; Raymond Paramo, C.S.B.; Charles C. Smith, C.S.B. Priests 9; Lay Teachers 60; Students 991.

WARREN. *De La Salle Collegiate for Boys*, 14600 Common Rd., 48093-3397. Tel: 810-778-2207. High School Brothers of the Christian Schools. Bros. Joseph Jozwiak, F.S.C., Prin.; Kevin Gilhooly, F.S.C., Supr. Brothers 6; Sisters 1; Lay Teachers 40; Students 800.

La Salle Warren, Inc., 14600 Common Rd., 48093. Tel: 908-842-7420. Bro. Kevin Gilhooly, F.S.C., Contact Person.

[F] ELEMENTARY SCHOOLS, INTER-PAROCHIAL

DETROIT. *Genesis Catholic Elementary School*, 20045 Joann, 48205. Tel: 313-839-2330. (Combined Parish Schools from Our Lady of Good Counsel and St. Raymond). Mr. Richard Enright, Prin. Lay Teachers 10; Total Enrollment 205.

CANTON. *All Saints Regional School*, 48735 Warren Rd., 48187-1233. Tel: 313-459-2490; Fax: 313-459-0981. Mrs. Mary Rita Allen, Prin.

PORT HURON. *McCormick Catholic Academy.* (Grades 6-8), 2865 Henry, 48060. Tel: 810-985-9599. Mrs. Deborah A. Krueger, Prin. Lay Teachers 11; Students 90. A consolidation of the following three parish schools in Port Huron: St. Edward (Lakeport), St. Joseph and St. Mary.

ROCHESTER. *Holy Family Regional School*, 1240 Inglewood, 48307. Tel: 810-656-1234. (Regional). Sr. Karen Hawver, S.C., Prin. Students 553.

[G] ELEMENTARY, PRIVATE

BLOOMFIELD HILLS. *Academy of the Sacred Heart*, 1250 Kensington Rd., 48304. Tel: 810-646-8900. Religious of the Sacred Heart. Sr. Margaret Mary Canty, R.S.C.J., Headmistress. Sisters 4; Lay Teachers 53; Students 373.

[H] GENERAL HOSPITALS

DETROIT. *Holy Cross Hospital*, 4777 E. Outer Dr., 48234. Tel: 313-369-9100.
For a complete listing, refer to the Hospitals section.

Mercy Family Care Program Unit, 5555 Conner Ave., 48213. Tel: 313-579-4300.
For a complete listing, refer to the Hospitals section.

Mercy Hospital, 5555 Conner Ave., 48213. Tel: 313-579-4000.
For a complete listing, refer to the Hospitals section.

St. John Hospital and Medical Center, 22101 Moross Rd., 48236. Tel: 313-343-4000.
For a complete listing, refer to the Hospitals section.

CLINTON TOWNSHIP. *Mercy Mount Clemens Corporation*, 15855 Nineteen Mile Rd., 48038. Tel: 810-263-2707.
For a complete listing, refer to the Hospitals section.

GROSSE POINTE. *Bon Secours Hospital*, 468 Cadieux Rd., 48230. Tel: 313-343-1000.
For a complete listing, refer to the Hospitals section.

LIVONIA. *Marian Village Corporation*, 36475 Five Mile Rd., 48154. Tel: 313-464-4800, Ext. 2300.
For a complete listing, refer to the Hospitals section.

St. Mary Hospital, 36475 W. Five Mile Rd., 48154. Tel: 313-655-4800.
For a complete listing, refer to the Hospitals section.

PONTIAC. *St. Joseph Mercy - Oakland*, 900 Woodward Ave., 48341-2985. Tel: 810-858-3000.
For a complete listing, refer to the Hospitals section.

PORT HURON. *Mercy Hospital of Port Huron*, 2601 Electric, 48060-6518. Tel: 810-985-1500.
For a complete listing, refer to the Hospitals section.

SOUTHFIELD. *Providence Hospital*, 16001 W. Nine Mile Rd., P.O. Box 2043, 48037. Tel: 810-424-3000.
For a complete listing, refer to the Hospitals section.

[I] SPECIAL HOSPITALS AND SANATORIA FOR INVALIDS

LAKE ORION. *Guest House for Women Religious*, 1840 W. Scripps Rd., Box 68, 48360. Tel: 248-391-3100.
For a complete listing, refer to the Special Care Facilities section.

LIVONIA. *Marycrest Manor*, 15475 Middlebelt Rd., 48154. Tel: 313-427-9175.
For a complete listing, refer to the Special Care Facilities section.

Marywood Nursing Care Center, 36975 W. Five Mile Rd., 48154. Tel: 313-464-0600.
For a complete listing, refer to the Special Care Facilities section.

MOUNT CLEMENS. *St. Joseph Mercy Living Care Center*, 37700 Harper, 48043. Tel: 810-468-0827.
For a complete listing, refer to the Special Care Facilities section.

ST. CLAIR SHORES. *Sisters of Bon Secours Nursing Care Center*, 26001 E. Jefferson, 48081. Tel: 810-779-7000.
For a complete listing, refer to the Special Care Facilities section.

WATERFORD. *Lourdes Nursing Home*, 2300 Watkins Lake Rd., 48328. Tel: 810-674-2241.
For a complete listing, refer to the Special Care Facilities section.

[J] HOUSING AND/OR COMMUNITY FACILITIES FOR THE AGING

DETROIT. *St. Catherine's House*, 1641 Webb Ave., 48206. Tel: 313-868-4505.
For a complete listing, refer to the Special Care Facilities section.

St. Joseph's Home, 4800 Cadieux Rd., 48224. Tel: 313-882-3800; Fax: 313-882-6944.
For a complete listing, refer to the Special Care Facilities section.

ALLEN PARK. *Little Sisters of the Poor*, P.O. Box 610, 48101.
For a complete listing, refer to the Special Care Facilities section.

BLOOMFIELD HILLS. *St. Elizabeth's Briarbank*, 1315 N. Woodward Ave., 48304. Tel: 810-644-1011.
For a complete listing, refer to the Special Care Facilities section.

Villa Francesca, 565 W. Long Lake Rd., 48302. Tel: 810-644-5390.

For a complete listing, refer to the Special Care Facilities section.

FARMINGTON HILLS. *Mercy Services for Aging*, 34605 Twelve Mile Rd., 48331-3221. Tel: 810-305-7920.
For a complete listing, refer to the Special Care Facilities section.

LIVONIA. *Marybrook Manor*, 36975 W. Five Mile Rd., 48154. Tel: 313-464-9667.
For a complete listing, refer to the Special Care Facilities section.

Ryan Senior Residences of the Archdiocese of Detroit. Inc., Central Office, 14469-C Levan Rd., 48154. Tel: 313-953-5873.
For a complete listing, refer to the Special Care Facilities section.

ST. CLAIR SHORES. *Sisters of Bon Secours Nursing Care Center*, 26001 E. Jefferson, 48081. Tel: 810-779-7000.
For a complete listing, refer to the Special Care Facilities section.

SOUTHFIELD. *Sheltering Arms*, 18310 W. 12 Mile, 48076. Tel: 810-557-7373.
For a complete listing, refer to the Special Care Facilities section.

WARREN. *A Friends House Adult Day Care Center*, 28111 Imperial Dr., 48093. Tel: 810-751-6260.
For a complete listing, refer to the Special Care Facilities section.

WATERFORD. *Fox Manor, Inc.*, 2350 Watkins Lake Rd., 48238. Tel: 810-674-9590.
For a complete listing, refer to the Special Care Facilities section.

St. Jude Home, Inc., 2270 Marwood, 48328. Tel: 810-673-5179.
For a complete listing, refer to the Special Care Facilities section.

[K] MONASTERIES AND RESIDENCES OF PRIESTS AND BROTHERS

DETROIT. *Jesuit Community at the University of Detroit*, Lansing-Reilly Hall, 4001 W. McNichols Rd., 48221. Tel: 313-993-1000.
(Corporate Title: The Jesuit Community Corporation at the University of Detroit Mercy). Mailing Address: P.O. Box 19900, 48219. Revs. Arthur F. McGovern, S.J., Rector; John C. Kehres, S.J.; Gregory Chisholm, S.J.; Malcolm Carron, S.J.; Gerald F. Cavanagh, S.J.; Paul F. Conen, S.J.; Terrence M. Curry, S.J.; Paulinus F. Forsthoefel, S.J.; George F. Lundy, S.J.; Brian P. O'Donnell, S.J.; Oswald A. Mascarenhas, S.J. (India); Frank C. McGough, S.J.; Norman G. McKendrick, S.J.; Herman J. Muller, S.J.; John D. O'Neill, S.J.; Sushil Sah India; John A. Saliba, S.J. (Malta); D. Clayton Schario, S.J.; Raphael Shen, S.J. (China); John M. Staudenmaier, S.J.; R. Gerard Albright, S.J.; Joseph P. Daoust, S.J.; John E. Dister, S.J.; Eugene L. Donahue, S.J.; Benjamin B. Hawley, S.J.

Jesuit Provincial Office-Detroit Province of the Society of Jesus, 7303 W. Seven Mile, 48221-2198. Tel: 313-861-7500. Very Rev. John F. Libens, S.J., Prov.; Revs. Keith J. Esenther, S.J., Exec. Asst. & Asst. for Higher Education; Norman J. Dickson, S.J., Asst. Intl. Missions & Vocations; John E. Dister, S.J., Asst. for Pastoral & Social Ministries; Walter L. Farrell, S.J., Treas.; Timothy J. Shepard, S.J., Asst. for Formation; James E. Von Tobel, S.J., Asst. for Health Care. Priests 168; Brothers 25; Scholastics 16. Priests assigned outside the U.S.: Rev. Richard M. Mackowski, S.J., Piazza S. Maria Maggiore 7, Rome, Italy, 00187. Tel: 39-6-6701-7140; Fax: 3964465576. Rev. Thomas H. Radloff, S.J., Spiritual Dir. at North American College, 000120 Vatican City State. Tel: 3966869441; Fax: 3966867561. Rev. W. Jared Wicks, S.J., Piazza della Pilotta 4, Rome, Italy, 00187. Tel: 39667015454; Fax: 39667015413. Rev. Mark G. Henninger, S.J., Arrupe College, P.O. M.P 320 Mount Pleasant, Harare, Zimbabwe. Tel: 0112634745411. Rev. Kenneth M. Kunert, S.J., Xavier House, P.O. Box 7300, Kampala, Uganda, 25641267614. Bro. Joseph A. Shubitowski, S.J., c/o CARITAS, P.O. Box 103, Bugene, Tanzania. Rev. Richard H. Tuohig, S.J., P.O. Box 9533, Dar es Salaam, Tanzania; Fax: 25505175579. Rev. Michael J. Vjecha, S.J., American Refugee Committee, P.O. Box 39694, Nairobi, Kenya. Rev. Theodore W. Walters, S.J., Nyegezi Social Training Institute, P.O. Box 307, Mwanza, Tanzania. Tel: 2556850560. Rev. Martin L. Chase, S.J., Campion House, 99 Studley Park Rd., Kew, Victoria, Australia, 3101. Tel: 011038538329.
E-mail: nsksj@inet.unic.dk
Rev. Kevin L. Flannery, S.J., Campion House, 99 Studley Park Rd., Kew, Victoria, Australia, 3101. Tel: 011038538329.
E-mail: flannery@mvgre.unigre.urbe.it
Rev. Joseph E. Mulligan, S.J., Colegio Centroamericano, Apdo. 2419, Managua, Nicaragua. Tel: 5052786965; Fax: 5052783359.
E-mail: guvols@nicarao.apc.org
Rev. Joseph G. Mueller, S.J., 9, Rue Raynouard, Paris, France, 75016. Tel: 33144146620; 33144146626 (private); Fax: 33144146622. Rev. John A. Lucal, S.J., Via Massimi, 114A, Rome, Italy, 00136. Tel: 011396355881; Fax: 01139635588352. Members in the U.S. residing outside the Province: Revs. Thomas S. Acker, S.J.; David C. Bayne, S.J.; Peter J. Bernardi, S.J.; Martin J. Calkins, S.J.; Joseph F. Downey, S.J.; Edward A. Flint, S.J.; Thomas W. Gedeon, S.J., Exec. Dir., Retreats International; Thomas W. Gensler, S.J.; Francis T. Gignac, S.J.; Howard J. Gray, S.J.; Fred M. Henley, S.J.; Francis J. Houdek, S.J.; Joseph B. Kappes, S.J.; John L. Kieffer, S.J.; William F. King, S.J.; Stephen T. Krupa, S.J.; Robert J. Lab, S.J.; John P. Langan, S.J.; Daniel P. Liderbach, S.J.; Mark S. Massa, S.J.; Edward J. Mattimoe, S.J.; George C. Maynard, S.J.; J. Thomas McClain, S.J.; Richard A. McCormick, S.J.; John M. McManamon, S.J.; Timothy J. Meier, S.J.; George B. Murray, S.J.; Jerome K. Odbert, S.J., Treas. Jesuit Refugee Services, Eastern Africa; John W. O'Malley, S.J.; Philip C. Rule, S.J.; Donald M. Serva, S.J.; Michael F. Steltenkamp, S.J.; Earl A. Weis, S.J.; Eric A. Zimmer, S.J.; Bro. Jerome J. Pryor, S.J.

Maryknoll Fathers and Brothers, 12709 Pembroke, 48235. Tel: 313-342-0330. Rev. Paul Brien, M.M., Dir.

P.I.M.E. College Community, 17330 Quincy Ave., 48221. Tel: 313-861-2866; Fax: 313-342-6816. Rev. Giorgio Paleari, P.I.M.E., Formation. Seminarians 5. P.I.M.E. Missionaries. (Pontifical Institute for Foreign Missions). P.I.M.E. Mission Center, 17330 Quincy Ave., 48221. Tel: 313-342-4066; Fax: 313-342-6816. Revs. Bruno Piccolo, P.I.M.E., Mission Office Dir.; Claudio Corti, P.I.M.E., Vocation Dir. Vocations Office; Foster Parents Mission Club; Leprosy Relief Society; Printing Press; P.I.M.E. World Magazine; Public Relations Office.

P.I.M.E. Missionaries of SS. Peter and Paul. (Pontifical Institute for Foreign Missions). P.I.M.E. Motherhouse in Detroit, 17330 Quincy, 48221. Tel: 313-342-4066; Fax: 313-342-6816. Revs. Bruno Piccolo, P.I.M.E., Prov. Supr.; Steven Baumbusch, P.I.M.E., Procurator; Angelo Villa, P.I.M.E., Asst. Rector; John B. Boracco, P.I.M.E., House Rector; Luciano Ghezzi, P.I.M.E.; Giorgio Paleari, P.I.M.E.; Luigi Maggioni, P.I.M.E.; Edward Miley, P.I.M.E. Brothers 1; Franciscan Sisters of St. Joseph (Mexico City) 4.

St. Bonaventure Friary, 1740 Mt. Elliott Ave., 48207-3496. Tel: 313-579-2100; Fax: 313-579-2275. Legal Title: *Province of St. Joseph of the Capuchin Order, Inc.* Provincialate: Revs. Daniel Fox, O.F.M.Cap., Prov. Min.; Perry McDonald, O.F.M.Cap., Prov. Vicar; Bros. Mark McDonough, Sec. & Treas.; David Swab, O.F.M.Cap., Sec. Religious Affairs; Larry LaCross, O.F.M.Cap., Public Rels. & Devel.; Revs. Loran Miller, O.F.M.Cap., Mission Secretariat; James Wolf, O.F.M.Cap., Archivist.
Priests of the Province Assigned Outside the U.S.: Rev. Charles Bantle, O.F.M.Cap., Diocese of Naha - Chancery, 3 chome 7-2 Asato (Naha), Okinawa, Japan, 902; Fax: 011-098-863-8474. Rev. Carmel Flora, O.F.M.Cap., St. Lawrence Community, 545 Tingal Rd., Wynnum North, Qld. 4178, Australia; Fax: 011-61-7-893-2905. Rev. Patrick McSherry, O.F.M.Cap., Capuchin General Curia, Via Piemonte, 70, Rome, Italy, 00187; Fax: 011-39-6-482-8267. Rev. John Myers, O.F.M.Cap., St. Lawrence Community, 392 Albert St., Balcatta, Perth, West Australia, 6021. In Residence in the Archdiocese of Detroit (excluding parishes): Rev. Blase Gitzen, O.F.M.Cap., 4030 W. 13 Mile Rd., Apt. J-3, Royal Oak, 48073-6638. Bro. Sam Ciraulo, O.F.M.Cap, Canterbury Woods, 700 Tobin Dr., Apt. 15, Inkster, 48141. Bro. Michael Graf, O.F.M.Cap., Canterbury Woods, 700 Tobin Dr., Apt. 15, Inkster, 48141. Assigned to St. Bonaventure Friary: Rev. James Hast, O.F.M.Cap., Local Min.; Bro. Richard Merling, O.F.M.Cap., Vicar; Revs. Gabriel Prashant Coelho, O.F.M.Cap.; Daniel Fox, O.F.M.Cap.; Charles Hart, O.F.M.; James Leary, O.F.M.Cap.; Joseph Maloney, O.F.M.Cap.; Perry McDonald, O.F.M.Cap.; Philip Naessens, O.F.M.Cap.; Albert Sandor, O.F.M.Cap.; Lloyd Thiel, O.F.M.Cap.; Donald Wiest, O.F.M.Cap.; James Wolf, O.F.M.Cap.; Bros. Gabriel Badalamenti, O.F.M.Cap.; Michael Drobnicki, O.F.M.Cap.; Paul Hanisko, O.F.M.Cap.; Joseph Howe, O.F.M.Cap.; Thomas Kroll, O.F.M.Cap.; Ignatius Milne, O.F.M.Cap.; Joseph Monachino, O.F.M.Cap.; John Raniszewski, O.F.M.Cap.; Daniel Vena, O.F.M.Cap.; Leo Wollenweber, O.F.M.Cap.

St. Mary's Friary, 121 E. Boston Blvd., 48202. Tel: 313-867-5200. Revs. Michael Gaffney, O.F.M.Cap., Local Min.; Anthony Scannell, O.F.M.Cap., Prov. Min.; James Zelinski, O.F.M.Cap., Prov. Asst.; Rick Samyn, O.F.M.Cap.; Paul Detaege, O.F.M.Cap.; Mark Freedman, O.F.M.Cap.; Patrick McSherry, O.F.M.Cap.; Larry Groescher, O.F.M.Cap.; Daniel Kabat, O.F.M.Cap.

St. Paul of the Cross Community, Congregation of the Passion, 23300 W. Davison Ave., 48223. Tel: 313-531-0562; Fax: 313-531-6911. A center for the Passionist Fathers & Brothers in mid-western & north central United States. Members of this community conduct parish missions, renewals & retreats for laity, clergy & religious, Forty Hours, Devotion & other ministries. Revs. Sebastian McDonald, C.P., Supr.; Rene Champagne, C.P.; Ronald Corl, C.P.; John Devany, C.P.; Michael Higgins, C.P., Dir., Retreat Center; Randal Joyce, C.P.; John A. Parenza, C.P., St. Mary's Hospital, Livonia; John Baptist Pechulis, C.P.; Philip Schaefer, C.P.; Emil Womack, C.P.; Bros. John Gebauer, C.P.; Patrick Keeney, C.P.; Jerome Milazzo, C.P. Priests 11; Brothers 3.

St. Sylvester Monastery, 17320 Rosemont Rd., 48219. Tel: 313-532-6064. Revs. Livius Paoli, O.S.B., Prior; Bartholomew Kraemer, O.S.B.; John Stopponi, O.S.B.; Leo Cornelli, O.S.B.; John Colautti, O.S.B.; Noel Patacconi, O.S.B.; Dom Bernard Schinn, O.S.B., Holy Family Church, 641 Chrysler Express Way.

Society of St. Paul, 7050 Pinehurst, 48126. Tel: 313-582-2033. Revs. Joseph Chircop, S.S.P., Supr.; Joseph A. Triano, S.S.P.; Ernesto Tigreros; Bros. Gerard T. Roche, S.S.P.; John Naranjo, S.S.P.; Emmanuel Canas. Priests 3; Brothers 3.

BLOOMFIELD HILLS. *Congregation of Christian Brothers, Brother Rice Community*, Caroll Hall, 3575 Lincoln Dr., 48301. Tel: 810-647-1547. Bros. Patrick L. O'Hare, C.F.C., Supr.; G. Gerard Gremley, C.F.C., Prin. In res., Bros. Robert E. Beckstrom, C.F.C.; William Alexander Dogan, C.F.C.; Norbert B. Hueller, C.F.C.; E. Vincent Kelly, C.F.C.; David A. McIntyre, C.F.C.; Donald F. McGovern, C.F.C.; W. Rudolph Younghans, C.F.C.; Arthur M. Arndt, C.F.C. Brothers 10.

DEARBORN HEIGHTS. *Our Lady of Grace Monastery*, Mariannhill Mission Society, 23715 Ann Arbor Trail, 48127. Tel: 313-561-7140; 561-8888; Fax: 313-561-9486. Vocation Office: Tel: 313-274-2893. Revs. Francis Claerr, C.M.M.; Egbert Heinlein, C.M.M., (Retired); Anthony Kirschner, C.M.M.; Anthony Gathen, C.M.M., Supr.; Raymond Lucasinsky, C.M.M., Mission Procurator; Timothy Mock, C.M.M., Prov. Treas.; Thomas Szura, C.M.M., Asst. Prov. Treas.; Aloysius Blonigen, C.M.M., Prov., Retreat Dir.; Reinhold Schmitt, C.M.M.; Thomas Heier, C.M.M., Editor of LEAVES; Vergil Heier, C.M.M. In res., Bros. Otto Waldmueller, C.M.M.; Jamie Miller, C.M.M.; Kenneth Shatz, C.M.M.; Gregory Jones, C.M.M.; Kenneth Lansing, C.M.M.; William Simon, C.M.M. Priests 11; Brothers 4.

RIVERVIEW. *Crosier Community of Riverview*, 13249 Pennsylvania Rd., 48192. Tel: 313-283-0112; Fax: 313-283-2809. Revs. Jude Verley, O.S.C.; John P. Christ, O.S.C.; Bruce C. Maxwell, O.S.C., U.S. Navy; Neil J. Emon, O.S.C.; Gordon Van Hoof, O.S.C.; Very Rev. Richard M. Leliaert, O.S.C., Supr.; Revs. Dale H. Redwanski, O.S.C.; James Vedro, O.S.C.; Steven Henrich, O.S.C.; Gerald Thaar, O.S.C.; Richard Thompson, O.S.C. Priests 11.

STERLING HEIGHTS. *Society of Christ Provincial Home*, Provincial Home, 3000 18 Mile Rd., 48314. Tel: 810-939-5022. Revs. Andrzej Maslejak, S.Ch., Prov.; Stanislaw Kuczaik, S.Ch., Asst. Prov.; Gerald Grupczynski, S.Ch., Treas.

WYANDOTTE. *Pallottine Fathers*, 3352 Fourth St., 48192. Tel: 313-285-2966. Rev. Stephen Keogh, S.A.C., Rector & Mission Promotions Dir.; Bro. Faustino Paez, S.A.C.

[L] CONVENTS AND RESIDENCES FOR SISTERS

DETROIT. *Adrian Dominican Sisters - Great Lakes Mission Chapter*, 9400 Courville, 48224-2517. Tel: 313-882-8484; Fax: 313-882-0436. Sr. Rosemary Asaro, O.P., Chapter Prioress.

Franciscan Sisters of St. Joseph (Mexico City), 17330 Quincy Ave., 48221. Tel: 313-342-0825; Fax: 313-342-6816. Sr. Magdalena Santiago Chenete, F.S.S.J., Supr. Sisters 4.

Missionaries of Charity, 4835 Lincoln St., 48208. Tel: 313-831-1028. Sr. M. Christophine, M.C., Supr.

Sisters, Home Visitors of Mary Convent, 356 Arden Park, 48202. Tel: 313-875-1123. Sr. Elizabeth Harris, H.V.M., Admin.

BLOOMFIELD HILLS. *Daughters of Divine Charity - Holy Trinity Province* (1972), Holy Trinity Provincialate, 1315 N. Woodward Ave., 48304. Tel: 810-644-1011; Fax: 810-644-1596. Sr. M. Paschal Grand, F.D.C., Prov. Supr. Sisters in Community 30.

CLARKSTON. *Servants of Jesus*, 9075 Big Lake Rd., Box 128, 48347. Tel: 810-625-8483. Leadership Team: Sr. Barbara Celeskey, S.J., Pres.; Sr. Roberta Kolasa, S.J.; Sr. Ann Ozog, S.J.

S.J. Charitable Trust (Retired & Infirm Sisters), Servants of Jesus Community Support Trust, 9075 Big Lake Rd., Box 128, 48347.

CLINTON TWP. *Monastery of St. Therese of the Child Jesus*, 35750 Moravian Dr., 48035-2138. Tel: 810-790-7255. Discalced Carmelite Nuns. Mother Mary of the Eucharist, O.C.D., Prioress. Professed Nuns 8; Extern Sisters 2; Extern Novice 1.

DEARBORN HEIGHTS. *Adrian Dominican Sisters, Nokomis Mission Chapter*, 7506 N. Inkster Rd., 48127-1668. Tel: 313-274-3543. Sr. Nancyann Turner, O.P., Chapter Prioress.

FARMINGTON HILLS. *Adrian Dominican Sisters, Southeast Adrian Mission Chapter*, 28650 Eleven Mile Rd., 48336-1502. Tel: 810-426-9185; Fax: 810-426-9186. Sr. Lorraine Mordenski, O.P., Chapter Prioress.

Bernardine Franciscan Sisters, 27405 W. 10 Mile Rd., 48336. Tel: 810-476-4111. Our Lady of the Rosary Convent Sisters of the Third Order of St. Francis. Sr. Maria Christine Keller, O.S.F., Province Min. Sisters in Area 55.

Mercy Center, 28650 Eleven Mile Rd., 48336.

Monastery of the Blessed Sacrament, 29575 Middlebelt Rd., 48334-2311. Tel: 810-626-8253; Fax: 810-626-8724. Dominican Nuns of Perpetual Adoration (Strictly Cloistered). Sr. Mary Thomas, O.P., Prioress; Rev. Thomas Poulsen, O.P., Chap. Cloistered Sisters 37; Extern Sister 3.

Sisters of Mercy-Regional Community of Detroit, Inc., 29000 Eleven Mile Rd., 48336. Tel: 810-476-8000; Fax: 810-476-4222. Sr. Gretchen Elliott, R.S.M., Pres. Sisters 304; U.S.Professed 270; Novices 1; In Argentine-Professed 32; Candidates 1.

Sisters of Mercy of the Americas. Regional Community of Detroit, Charitable Trusts 1 & 2.

IDA. *St. Joseph's Convent*, 2882 Southwick, Box 187, 48140. Tel: 313-269-2505. Missionary Sisters of Our Lady of Victory 2.

LIVONIA. *Provincial House and Novitiate of the Sisters of St. Felix*, 36800 Schoolcraft Rd., 48150. Tel: 313-591-1730. Sr. Mary Dennis Glonek, C.S.S.F., Prov. Min.; Rev. Michael Daly, Res. Chap.; Rev. Msgr. Vincent Horkan, Infirmary Chap. Legal Title: *Provincial House and Novitiate of the Congregation of the Sisters of St. Felix, C.S.S.F., Felician Sisters*. Professed Sisters 271; Novices 3.

MONROE. *Sisters, Servants of the Immaculate Heart of Mary, Leadership Council*, 610 W. Elm Ave., 48162-9909. Tel: 313-241-0092; Fax: 313-241-9114. Sr. Mary M. McCann, I.H.M., Pres.; Sr. Nancy Sylvester, I.H.M., Vice Pres.; Sr. Frances Mlocek, I.H.M., Chief Financial Officer; Sr. Paula Cathcart, I.H.M., Leadership Council; Sr. Anne Crimmins, I.H.M., Leadership Council; Sr. Mary Ann Markel, I.H.M., Leadership Council; Sr. Kathleen O'Brien, I.H.M., Leadership Council; Sr. Mary Agnes Ryan, I.H.M., Leadership Council.

SSIHM Charitable Trust (Retired and Infirm Sisters), 610 W. Elm Ave., 48162-7907. Tel: 313-241-0092. Sr. Frances Miocek, I.H.M., Chief Financial Officer.

ORTONVILLE. *Our Lady of Mt. Thabor Monastery*, 1295 Bald Eagle Lake Rd., 48462. Tel: 810-627-4355. Dominican Sisters of Mt. Thabor. Sr. Mary Martin, Prioress.

OXFORD. *Dominican Sisters, Congregation of St. Rose of Lima, St. Joseph Convent*, 775 W. Drahner Rd., Box 167, 48371. Tel: 810-628-2872. Sr. Frances Mary Kernasovich, O.P., Pres.; Sr. Mary Ann Fedor, O.P., First Vice Pres.; Sr. Virginia Berak, O.P., Second Vice Pres. Professed Sisters 46. General Mother House and Novitiate of the Dominican Sisters; St. Mary Retreat House; Dominican Center; St. Raphael's.

PORT HURON. *Sisters of Mary Reparatrix*, 2532 South Blvd., 48060. Tel: 810-364-3326. Sisters 2.

Full Circle House of Prayer.

[M] HOMES FOR MEN AND WOMEN

DETROIT. *St. Mary's Residence*, 2120 Orleans St., 48207. Tel: 313-259-6874; 259-0459.

For a complete listing, refer to the Special Care Facilities section.

[N] CATHOLIC SOCIAL SERVICE AGENCIES

DETROIT. *Catholic Social Services of Wayne County*, 9851 Hamilton Ave., 48202. Tel: 313-883-2100; Fax: 313-883-3957. Patrick J. Heron, Pres. Family service, marriage counseling, adoption services, services to unwed mothers, planned respite care, substance abuse counseling, foster family care & services to youth & older persons including Foster Grandparent, Senior Companion & Retired Senior Volunteer Program.

Branches: 24331 Van Born Rd., Taylor, 48180. Tel: 313-292-5690. 17332 Farmington Rd., Livonia, 48152. Tel: 313-421-3730. 19653 Mack Ave., Grosse Pte. Woods, 48236. Tel: 313-881-6645. 1035 St. Antoine, 48226. Tel: 313-965-3242.

LAPEER. *Christian Family Services of Lapeer County, Inc.*, 441 Clay St., 48446. Tel: 810-664-4557.

MONROE. *Catholic Social Services of Monroe County*, 16 E. Fifth St., 48161. Tel: 313-242-3800; Fax: 313-242-6203. Mark T. Robinson, M.S.W., A.C.S.W., Pres./CEO, South County Office: 8330 Lewis Ave., Temperance, 48182. Tel: 313-847-1523.

MOUNT CLEMENS. *Catholic Services of Macomb*, 235 S. Gratiot, 48043. Tel: 810-468-2616. Mr. Thomas Reed, Pres. & C.E.O.

Branch Offices: 12434 Twelve Mile Rd., Ste. 202, Warren, 48093. Tel: 810-558-7551. 18720 Thirteen Mile Rd., Roseville, 48066. Tel: 810-558-7551. 45100 Sterrit, Suite 103, Utica, 48087. Tel: 810-254-2900.

Friend's House Adult Day Care for the Elderly, 16931 Nineteen Mile Rd., Ste. 140, Clinton Township, 48038. Tel: 810-412-8494.

PONTIAC. *Catholic Social Services of Oakland County*, 50 Wayne St., 3rd Floor, 48342. Tel: 810-333-3700. Margaret A. Huggard, M.S.W., Pres.

Branches: 53 Franklin Blvd., 48341. Tel: 810-334-3595. 6637 Highland Rd., Waterford, 48327. Tel: 810-666-8870. 26105 Orchard Lake Rd., Suite 303, Farmington, 48334. Tel: 810-471-4140. 1424 E. Eleven Mile Rd., Royal Oak, 48067. Tel: 810-548-4044.

Sheltering Arms Adult Day Care, 18310 W. 12 Mile Rd., Southfield, 48076. Tel: 810-557-7373.

PORT HURON. *Catholic Social Services of St. Clair County, Inc.*, 2601 Thirteenth St., 48060. Tel: 810-987-9100. Patrick L. Cogley, M.A., Pres.

[O] SPECIALIZED CHILD CARE FACILITIES AND SCHOOLS

DETROIT. *Christ Child House*, 15751 Joy Rd., 48228. Tel: 313-584-6077; Fax: 313-584-1148.

For a complete listing, refer to the Special Care Facilities section.

Don Bosco Hall, Inc., 10001 Petosky, 48204. Tel: 313-834-8677.

For a complete listing, refer to the Special Care Facilities section.

DEARBORN HEIGHTS. *Vista Maria*, 20651 W. Warren Ave., 48127. Tel: 313-271-3050.

For a complete listing, refer to the Special Care Facilities section.

FARMINGTON HILLS. *Marillac Programs*. 22255 Greenfield, Ste. 330 Southfield, 48334. Tel: 810-559-2272; Fax: 810-559-2226.

For a complete listing, refer to the Special Care Facilities section.

St. Vincent and Sarah Fisher Center, 27400 W. Twelve Mile Rd., 48334. Tel: 313-538-6000; 810-626-7527.

For a complete listing, refer to the Special Care Facilities section.

Seton Nursery School and Infant-Toddler Child Care Center, 29475 Inkster Rd., 48018. Tel: 810-626-6990.

For a complete listing, refer to the Special Care Facilities section.

NORTHVILLE. *Our Lady of Providence Center*, 16115 Beck Rd., 48167. Tel: 313-453-1300.

For a complete listing, refer to the Special Care Facilities section.

SOUTHFIELD. *Boysville of Michigan, Inc.*, Community Resource Office, 17117 W. Nine Mile Rd., Ste. 445, 48075. Tel: 810-569-6630; Fax: 810-569-8171.

For a complete listing, refer to the Special Care Facilities section.

St. Francis Family Services, 17500 W. Eight Mile Rd., 48075. Tel: 810-552-0750.

For a complete listing, refer to the Special Care Facilities section.

[P] RETREAT HOUSES

DETROIT. *St. Paul of the Cross Retreat Center*. Conducted by the Passionist Community. 23333 Schoolcraft, 48223-2499. Tel: 313-535-9563; Fax: 313-535-9207. Rev. Michael Higgins, C.P., Retreat Dir. Team Members: Revs. Rene Champagne, C.P.; Ronald Corl, C.P., Asst. Retreat Dir.; Bro. John Gebauer, C.P.

BLOOMFIELD HILLS. *Manresa Jesuit Retreat House*, 1390 Quarton Rd., 48304-3554. Tel: 313-564-6455; 810-644-4933; Fax: 810-644-8291. Revs. James K. Serrick, S.J., Dir. Supr.; Jules J. Toner, S.J., Writer; John A. McGrail, S.J., Retreat Dir.; Bernard J. Owens, S.J., Retreat Dir.; John T. Schuett, S.J., Retreat Dir.; Benno G. Kornely, S.J., Retreat Dir.; Eugene P. Simon, S.J. Priests 7.

CLARKSTON. *Colombiere Center*, 9075 Big Lake Rd., Box 139, 48347. Tel: 810-625-5611; Fax: 810-625-3526. Spirituality Conference Center and Jesuit Health Care Community for the Detroit Province and Chicago Province. Revs. James E. Von Tobel, S.J., Dir. & Supr.; Paul L. Allen, S.J.; Thomas F. Ankenbrandt, S.J.; Leo J. Belanger, S.J.; Thomas C. Biecker, S.J.; Francis A. Bittenz, S.J.; John L. Blanchard, S.J.; Robert C. Broome, S.J.; Edward E. Cincoski, S.J.; Jerome A. Clifford, S.J.; Thomas P. Conry, S.J.; George A. Curran, S.J.; Stanislaus Czapiewski, S.J., St. Ladislaus, 2730 Caniff, Hamtramck, 48212. Tel: 313-872-0709. Revs. J. Richard Dempsey, S.J.; Lester J. Evett, S.J.; Edward L. Fergus, S.J.; Henry C. Gelin, S.J.; Francis X. Grollig, S.J.; Cletus F. Hartmann, S.J.; Luis Iscla Rovira, S.J.; Lawrence E. Isenecker, S.J.; Howard L. Kerner, S.J.; J. Robert Koch, S.J.; Joseph V. Loftus, S.J.; Edward M. Loveley, S.J.; John E. Mahoney, S.J.; Joseph T. Mangan, S.J.; Oswald J. Marshall, S.J.; David F. McCarthy, S.J.; Stephen A. Meder, S.J.; David E. Meier, S.J.; Harold R. Meirose, S.J., Pastoral Care, Asst. Dir.; Edmund J. Montville, S.J.; Charles A. Mooney, S.J.; Francis M. Moore, S.J.; Edwin A. Mousbrugger, S.J.; Donald J. O'Shaughnessy, S.J., Asst. Supr.; Joseph C. Osuch, S.J.; Joseph J. Peters, S.J.; Robert A. Pollauf, S.J.; Francis D. Rabaut, S.J.; Robert D. Rosenfelder, S.J.; LeRoy F. Ryan, S.J.; Joseph D. Scallon, S.J., St. James, P.O. Box 145, Beaver Island, 49782. Tel: 616-448-2230. Revs. William F. Schmoldt, S.J.; Gerald A. Streeter, S.J.; George T. Tolbert, S.J.; Jerome F. Treacy; Bernard J. Wuellner, S.J.; Bros. Philip J. Anton, S.J.; William J. Balconi, S.J.; Tomasz Dziemba, S.J.; Herman F. Elsaesser, S.J.; John E. Foy, S.J.; Frederick A. Frowerk, S.J.; Charles W. Hocter, S.J.; Bruno W. Karpinski, S.J.; Valerian F. Luterick, S.J.; Daniel J. McCullough, S.J.; Clayton P. Morell, S.J.; John J. Petrus, S.J.; Bernard L. Polinak, S.J.; Frederick F. Readence, S.J.; Edward B. Richert, S.J.; Clarence M. Riedlinger, S.J.; Albert J. Savoie, S.J.; Erwin L. Schloff, S.J. Priests 49; Brothers 13.

MONROE. *Visitation*, 529 Stewart Rd., 48161. Tel: 313-242-5520. Sponsorship of I.H.M. Congregation. Sisters 6.

WASHINGTON. *Capuchin Retreat*, 62460 Mt. Vernon Rd., P.O. Box 188, 48094. Tel: 810-651-4826. Revs. Simon Hesse, O.F.M.Cap.; James R. Andres, O.F.M.Cap.; Gerald Kessel, O.F.M.Cap.; Gerald Pehler, O.F.M.Cap.; Bro. Raymond Meier, O.F.M.Cap.

[Q] SPECIAL SERVICES

DETROIT. *Capuchin Soup Kitchen*, 1760 Mt. Elliott, 48207. Tel: 313-579-2100. Rev. James Leary, O.F.M.Cap., Dir.; Mr. Lewis Hickson, Exec. Dir.

Jefferson House, 8311 E. Jefferson, 48214. Tel: 313-331-8900. Transitional alcohol-drug residence. Mr. James Fleming, Site Dir.

Catholic Community Services of the Archdiocese of Detroit, Inc., 1234 Washington Blvd., 48226. Tel: 313-237-5885; Fax: 313-237-4642. His Eminence Adam J. Maida, Pres.; Rev. Msgr. John P. Zenz, Sec.; Sr. Mary V. Korb, R.S.M., Treas.

Community Food Depots, Society of St. Vincent de Paul, 2929 E. Grand Blvd., 48202. Tel: 313-972-3100. Ellen Kennedy, Dir.

Manna Community Meal. (Soup Kitchen), 1950 Trumbull, 48226. Tel: 313-963-8708.

Pope John XXIII Hospitality House, 3977 2nd Ave., 48201. Tel: 313-832-HELP. Cancer outpatient-residents, Transportation for Area Pediatric Cancer Patients. Rev. Russell E. Kohler.

Sacred Heart Rehabilitation Center, Inc., 2203 St. Antoine, 48201. Tel: 313-961-0612; 962-7472 (Admissions). John Sass, Jr., Pres. Treatment for alcoholism and drug dependency to adult men and women. 400 Stoddard Rd., Memphis, 48041. Beds 80. Detox and Residential services. Admission & Outpatient Services, 2203 St. Antoine, 48201. Outpatient and family service. 214 E. Elm St. #107, Monroe, 48161. Outpatient and aftercare service.

St. Mary's Residence, 2120 Orleans, 48207. Tel: 313-259-6874; 259-0459. Sr. M. Fidelis, F.D.C., Admin. Conducted by the Daughters of Divine Charity. A licensed adult foster care home for mentally or physically handicapped women, ages 30-65. Staff 6; Residents 60.

St. Patrick's Senior Center, Inc., 58 Parsons, 48201. Tel: 313-833-7080. Sr. Mary Watson, O.P., Pres.; Rev. Thomas J. Duffey, Vice Pres. Lay Staff 10; Patients assisted annually 1,400.

St. Vincent de Paul Society, Archdiocesan Council, 2929 E. Grand Blvd., 48202. Tel: 313-972-3100; Fax: 313-972-3147. James Dumont, Pres.; Rev. Msgr. F. Gerald Martin, Spiritual Dir.; Patrick Adamcik, Exec. Sec.; James Carron, Exec. Dir.

ONSTED. *St. Patrick's Retreat*, 11528 Killarney Hwy., 49265. Tel: 517-467-7492. Rev. Russell E. Kohler, Dir. Tel: 313-832-4357. Retreats for Family with cancer outpatient; small groups of handicapped-developmentally disabled; small parish team meetings; hospice & chaplain's meetings.

TROY. *Gabriel Richard Institute*, 2820 W. Maple #101, 48084. Tel: 810-643-4039; 800-382-8609; Fax: 810-643-4045. Adult and youth Christopher Leadership training for Catholic laymen, women, clergy & religious. Rev. Thomas J. Bresnahan, Dir.; Dolores Ammar, Natl. Mgr.

WARREN. *St. John's Deaf Center*, 8245 Fisher, 48089. Tel: 810-758-0710 (TDD); 758-0714 (Voice). Revs. Richard J. Yost, O.S.F.S., Dir.; Kenneth N. McKenna, O.S.F.S., Assoc.

WATERFORD. *Lourdes Alzheimers Special Care Center*, 2300 Watkins Lake Rd., 48328. Tel: 810-674-2241. Sr. Sue McMahon, O.P., Contact.

[R] CAMPS AND COMMUNITY CENTERS

DETROIT. *C.Y.O. Boys Camp*, CYO Camps, Catholic Youth Organization, 305 Michigan Ave., 48226. Tel: 313-963-7172. Brian Cokonougher, Camp Dept. Dir.

C.Y.O. Girls Camp, CYO Camps, Catholic Youth Organization, 305 Michigan Ave., 48226. Tel: 313-963-7172. Brian Cokonougher, Camp Svcs. Dir.

Camp Ozanam, Central Office-St. Vincent de Paul Society, 2929 E. Grand Blvd., 48202-0518. Tel: 313-972-3100. A free week long christian camping experience for boys 8-12. Recruitment through Parish Conferences of the Society of St. Vincent de Paul.

Camp Stapleton, Central Office, 2929 E. Grand Blvd., 48202. Tel: 313-972-3100. A free week long christian camping experience for girls 8-12. Recruitment through Parish Conferences of the Society of St. Vincent de Paul.

[S] NEWMAN CENTERS

DETROIT. *Marygrove College Campus Ministry*, 8425 West McNichols Rd., 48221. Tel: 313-862-8000, Ext. 275. Sr. Marie Sweeney, I.H.M., Campus Ministry.

University of Detroit Mercy Campus Ministry, 4001 W. McNichols, 48221. Tel: 313-993-1560. Sr. Beth Ann Finster, S.S.J., Acting Dir.

University of Detroit-Mercy Campus Ministry, 8200 W. Outer Dr., P.O. Box 19900, 48219. Tel: 313-993-6216.

Wayne State University, Newman Center, 761 Student Center, 48202. Tel: 313-577-3462. Sr. Martha M. Curry, R.S.C.J., Dir.

AUBURN HILLS. *St. John Fisher Chapel University Parish*, 3665 Walton Blvd., 48326. Tel: 810-373-6457. Campus Ministry for Oakland University. Rev. Jerome A. Brzezinski; Sr. Mary Bodde, S.C.; Mrs. Susan Burrato; Sr. Mary Dixon, O.P.; Sr. Mary Van Gilder, I.H.M.; Mr. Eugene Mahon.

DEARBORN. *Univ. of Michigan, Dearborn, Henry Ford Community College Newman Center*. Gabriel Richard Campus Ministry Center, 5001 Evergreen Rd., 48128. Tel: 313-271-6000. Thomas Salas, M.A., Campus Ministry Dir.; Shannon Dyer, B.A., Campus Min.

LIVONIA. *Madonna University Newman Center*, 36600 Schoolcraft, 48150. Tel: 313-591-5000. Deacon Eugene Desjarlais, Dir. Campus Min.

Schoolcraft College, Newman House. (Campus Ministry), 17300 Haggerty Rd., 48152. Tel: 313-464-2160. Rev. J. Robert Schaden; Ms. Bert Kelly.

PORT HURON. *John Courtney Murray Newman Center*, 505 Huron Ave., 48060. Tel: 810-948-5195. Rev. Rene L. Desmarais.

WARREN. *Macomb Community College Campus Ministry*, 14500 Twelve Mile Rd., 48093. Tel: 810-445-7378. Sr. Joyce Campbell, I.H.M.; Kathy Eubanks; Michael Lauchlan.

[T] MISCELLANEOUS LISTINGS

DETROIT. *The Black Catholic Televangelization Network*, 11430 Morang, 48224. Tel: 313-521-7777. Rev. Clarence Williams, C.PP.S., Pres. Search, This Far by Faith (Radio), Black and Catholic (TV) and the Catholic African World Network.

Cardinal Club, 1234 Washington, 48226. An organization of Catholic laymen in business and professional fields.

Christ Child Society, 15751 Joy Rd., 48228; Fax: 313-584-1148. Rev. Msgr. John P. Zenz, Spiritual Dir.; Susan Manion, Pres.

Clergy Health Plan, Chancery Building, 1234 Washington Blvd., 48226. Rev. Jack Fabian, Dir.

Council of Catholic Women, 305 Michigan Ave., 48226. Tel: 313-237-5896. Patricia A. Kendro, Pres.

Detroit Federation of Christian Life Communities, 1234 Washington Blvd., 48226. Mrs. Shirley Boots, Pres.

Dominican Literacy Center, 9400 Courville, 48224. Tel: 313-882-4853. Sr. Marie Schdenlein, O.P., Dir.

Foster Parents Mission Club, 17330 Quincy Ave., 48221. Tel: 313-342-4066; Fax: 313-342-6816. Rev. Bruno Piccolo, P.I.M.E., Dir.; Alice Marino, Exec. Sec. An agency of the P.I.M.E. Missionaries.

Guest House Alumni Assn., 1601 Joslyn Rd., Box 420, 48361. Tel: 248-391-4445. Daniel Webster, Dir. Communications; William C. Morgan, Dir. Rochester Treatment Facility; Sr. Mae Kierans, C.S.J., Clinical Svcs. Coord.; Rev. Andrew J. Tomasko, Pres. Alumni Assoc.; William C. Morgan, Dir. Rochester Treatment Facility.

Jesuit Seminary Association, 7303 W. Seven Mile Rd., 48221. Tel: 313-861-4438. Rachel M. Brennan, Dir. of Development; Rev. Eugene P. Simon, S.J., Dir., Jesuit Seminary Assoc.

Jesuit International Missions. Rev. Norman J. Dickson.

Jesuit Volunteer Corps. Midwest, Inc., 438 St. Antoine, 48226-4318. Tel: 313-963-4112; Fax: 313-963-9620. Timothy McCabe, Exec. Dir.

Latino Catholic Pastoral Center, 5680 Konkel, 48210. Tel: 313-897-5277. Sr. Juanita Flores, O.P., Dir.

Leprosy Relief Society, 17330 Quincy Ave., 48221. Tel: 313-342-4066; Fax: 313-342-6816. Barbara J. Rubaie, Dir. An agency of the P.I.M.E. Missionaries.

Pope John Paul II Cultural Foundation, Inc., 2701 Chicago Blvd., 48206. Tel: 313-883-8518. His Eminence Adam J. Maida, Episcopal Moderator; Rev. Michael R. Dylag, Admin. Asst.

St. John Health System. Holding Company Sponsored by Sisters of St. Joseph which operates: St. John Hospital & Medical Center; St. John Ambulatory Corp.; The Oxford Institute; The St. John Dialysis Center Corporation; St. John Hospital-Macomb Center; Affiliated Health Services; St. John-Bon Secours Senior Community; Eastwood Community Clinics; Holy Cross Hospital; Oakland General Hospital; Saratoga Community Hospital. 22101 Moross Rd., 48236. Tel: 313-343-4000. Rev. James Krasman, O.F.M., Chap.; Dr. Anthony R. Tersigni, Ed.D., Pres. & CEO.

St. John Newco, 22101 Moross, 48236. Tel: 313-343-7880. Arthur F. deVaux, Contact Person.

St. Mary Magdalen Catholic Community, Ryan Correctional Facility, 305 Michigan Ave., 48226. Tel: 313-237-4688. Rev. Thomas R. Physician, Chaplaincy Coord.

SS. Peter & Paul Jesuit Church Historical Fund, 438 St. Antoine, 48226. Tel: 313-961-8077. Rev. Robert Hartigan, S.J., Contact Person.

BLOOMFIELD HILLS. *Amicare Home Health Care - Metro Detroit*, 281 Enterprise Dr., Ste. 200, 48302. Tel: 810-858-7735. Gary Baum, Pres.

Ladies of Charity of St. Vincent de Paul Oakland County Associaton, 1466 Glengarry, 48301. Patricia Hurlbert, Contact Person.

The Legion of Christ, Inc., 2460 Opdyke Rd., 48013. Tel: 810-644-2954. Rev. Lorenzo Gomez, Contact.

Logos, Inc. (Michigan), 2460 Opdyke Rd., 48103. Tel: 203-281-4798. Rev. Lorenzo Gomez, L.C., Contact.

Opdyke, Inc., 2460 Opdyke Rd., 48103. Tel: 810-644-2954. Rev. Lorenzo Gomez, Contact.

DEARBORN. *Leo XIII Society*, 1734 N. Waverly, 48128. Tel: 313-561-2155. Ernie Scarano, Contact Person.

DEARBORN HEIGHTS. *Dominican Center for Religious Development*, 7430 N. Inkster Rd., 48127. Tel: 313-730-8759. Sr. Charlotte Hoefer, O.P.

EASTPOINTE. *Detroit Catholic Charismatic Renewal*, Coordinating Center, 22851 Lexington, 810-777-7780. Rev. John Esper, Assoc. Liason. Diocesan Service Committee: Arlene Apone; Al Schindler; John Sherry.

FARMINGTON HILLS.

**Amicare Home Health Services, Inc.*, P.O. Box 9185, 48333-9185; Fax: 810-305-7632. Gary Baum, Pres.

**Amicare Hospice Services, Inc.*, 34605 Twelve Mile Rd., 48331; Fax: 810-489-6204. Gary Baum, Pres.

Mercy Health Foundation, 34605 Twelve Mile Rd., 48331-3292. Tel: 810-489-6084. Nancy Van Zandt, M.S.Ed., V.P. Devel. Svcs.

Mercy Health Services (Formerly Sisters of Mercy Health Corporation), 34605 Twelve Mile Rd., 48331. Tel: 810-489-6000. Judith Pelham, Pres. Organization owns & operates 14 hospital divisions in Michigan & Iowa. Owns & operates 13 nursing home facilities, manages senior housing facilities, alternative health financing activities, home care services, hospice services, rehabilitation services and foundation activities.

Mercy Information Systems, 34605 Twelve Mile Rd., 48331. Tel: 810-489-6500.

Mercy International Health Services, 34605 Twelve Mile Rd., 48331. Tel: 810-489-6100. David Vellinga, Pres.

Mercy Services for Aging. Wholly-owned subsidiary of Mercy Health Services, 34605 Twelve Mile Rd., 48331. Tel: 810-305-7920. Gerald Bruen, Pres.

Mercy Services for Aging, Non-profit Housing Corporation. Wholly owned subsidiary of Mercy Services for Aging, 34605 Twelve Mile Rd., 48331. Tel: 810-305-7920. Gerald Bruen, Pres.

GROSSE POINTE. *John Paul II Foundation of Michigan, Inc.*, 35 Warner Rd., 48236. Tel: 313-882-2140. Mrs. Frank A. Germack, Jr., Pres. Conducts religious, cultural, educational, humanitarian and fund raising activities in Michigan in liaison with the John Paul Foundation in Rome. Regular, supporting and life memberships.

GROSSE POINTE FARMS. *American Friends of the Vatican Library*, 157 Lakeshore Rd., 48236. Tel: 313-884-8761. Rev. Msgr. Francis X. Canfield, Contact.

LIVONIA.

**Angela Hospice Home Care, Inc.*, 14100 Newburgh Rd., 48154-1871. Tel: 313-464-7810.

MARYSVILLE. *National Alliance of Parishes Restructuring into Communities*, 1000 Michigan Ave., 48040-1466. Tel: 810-364-3500; Fax: 810-364-3555. Rev. Art Baranowski, Pres.; Sr. Geraldine Nowak, O.S.F., Nat'l Coord.; Larry & Judy Berch, Editors; Joseph Piro, Treas. The N.A.P.R.C. networks and supports American & intl. parishes developing small church communities as the primary restructuring of the parish.

NEWPORT. *Companions of Christ the Lamb*, P.O. Box 115, 48166. Tel: 810-486-5051. Rev. Jack Fabian, Dir.

NOVI.

**Mission Health Corporation*, 47601 Grand River Ave., 48374. Tel: 810-380-4850; Fax: 810-380-4859. Brian Connolly, Pres.

REDFORD. *Siena Literacy Center*, 11685 Appleton, 48239. Tel: 313-532-8404. Sr. Mary Hemmen, O.P., Dir.

ROSEVILLE. *Cursillos in Christianity Movement of the Archdiocese of Detroit*, 18430 Utica Rd., 48066. Tel: 810-776-4533. Rev. Charles M. Morris, Spiritual Advisor; Mr. William Pfannes, Lay Dir. Tel: 810-524-1951.

ST. CLAIR SHORES. *Catholic Kolping Society of America, Detroit Branch, Inc.*, 24409 Jefferson, 48080. Tel: 810-775-9159. Mary Margaret Hubert, Pres. Tel: 810-689-7975; Thekla Abels, Contact Person. Tel: 313-885-1189; Revs. James Leary, O.F.M.Cap., Praeses; Bohdan W. Kosicki.

**Celebrate Life Ministries*, 28111 Jefferson, A6, 48081. Tel: 810-778-4446. Mrs. Patricia Haas, Coord.

Dominican Consultation Center, 22811 Greater Mack, Ste. L-11, 48080. Tel: 810-775-5620. 24225 W.Nine Mile Rd., Ste. 114A, Southfield, 48034-3990. Tel: 810-353-9080. Sr. Diane Burgermeister, O.P.

SOUTHFIELD. *Seton Health Corporation of Southeast Michigan*, 16001 W. Nine Mile Rd., 48037. Tel: 810-424-3011. Brian Connolly, Pres.

WARREN. *Catholic Campus Ministers Association*, Macomb County Community College, 14500 Twelve Mile Rd., K-320, 48093. Tel: 810-445-7378. Bonnie Krauskoff, Chm.; Sr. Margaret Dowd, Chm. & Treas.; Sally McCuen, Sec.; Rev. Jerome Brzezinski.

WATERFORD. *Voluntas Dei Institute*, 4557 Fairway Ct., 48328. Tel: 810-380-4850; Fax: 810-380-4859. Rev. George F. Hazler, Contact Person.

[U] CLOSED INSTITUTIONS

DETROIT. *Archdiocesan Archives*. The following institutional sacramental records can be found at the following address unless otherwise indicated: 1234 Washington Blvd., 48226. Tel: 313-237-5846; Fax: 313-237-4643.

St. Agnes.
St. Albertus.
Anawim Community.
Assumption of the Blessed Virgin Mary.
St. Augustine.
St. Benedict the Moor.
St. Bernadette Chapel.
St. Bernard.
St. Boniface.
St. Brigid.
St. Camillus.
Cardinal Leger Community.
St. Catherine.
St. Casimir.
Corpus Christi.
St. David.
St. Edward.
Emmaus Community.
Epiphany.
St. Eugene.
St. Francis Hospital.
Holy Ghost.
Holy Name of Jesus.
St. Ignatius of Antioch.
Immaculate Conception.
St. Joachim.
St. John the Evangelist.
St. John Nepomucene.
St. John Vianney.
St. Lawrence.
St. Margaret Mary.
St. Martin.
St. Mary Hospital - Detroit Memorial Hospital.
St. Monica.
Mother of Consolation.
Mother of Our Savior.
Mount Carmel Mercy Hospital.
Our Lady of Guadalupe.
Our Lady of Help.
Our Lady of the Hills.
Our Lady Queen of Hope.
St. Paul Maltese.
Patronage of St. Joseph.
St. Peter (Lithuanian).
St. Philip Neri.
Resurrection.
St. Rose of Lima.
St. Stanislaus Bishop and Martyr.
St. Theresa.
St. Thomas the Apostle.
St. Vincent de Paul.
Santa Maria.
Vida Nueva Community.
Visitation.
St. Wenceslaus.

RELIGIOUS INSTITUTES OF MEN REPRESENTED IN THE ARCHDIOCESE

For further details refer to the corresponding bracketed number in the Religious Institutes of Men or Women section.

[0140]—*The Augustinians.* (Chicago).—O.S.A.
[0170]—*Basilian Fathers.* (Toronto, Ont.).—C.S.B.
[0200]—*Benedictine Monks.* (Detroit Prov.).—O.S.B.
[0330]—*Brothers of the Christian Schools.* (New York Prov., Chicago, IL).—F.S.C.
[0600]—*Brothers of the Congregation of Holy Cross.* (Midwest Prov.).—C.S.C.
[0460]—*Brothers of the Poor of St. Francis.*—C.F.P.
[0400]—*Canons Regular of the Order of the Holy Cross.* (Prov. of St. Odilia).—O.S.C.
[0470]—*The Capuchin Friars.* (St. Joseph Prov.).—O.F.M.Cap.
[0275]—*Carmelites of Mary Immaculate.*—C.M.I.
[0310]—*Congregation of Christian Brothers.* (American Prov.).—C.F.C.
[0750]—*Congregation of Marianhill Missionaries.*—C.M.M.
[0740]—*Congregation of Marians of the Immaculate Conception.* (St. Stanislaus Kostka Prov.).—M.I.C.
[1000]—*Congregation of the Passion.* (Western Prov.).—C.P.
[1140]—*Congregation of the Sacred Hearts of Jesus and Mary.*—SS.CC.
[0480]—*Conventual Franciscans.*—O.F.M.Conv.
[0520]—*Franciscan Friars (Custody of St. John Capristran; Prov. of St. Stephen, King; Custody of the Holy Family / Croatian).*—O.F.M.
[0650]—*Holy Ghost Fathers.* (Eastern Prov.).—C.S.Sp.
[0690]—*Jesuit Fathers and Brothers.* (Detroit Prov.).—S.J.
[0730]—*Legionaries of Christ.*—L.C.
[]—*Little Brothers of Jesus.*
[0780]—*Marist Fathers.* (Northeastern Prov.).—S.M.
[0800]—*Maryknoll.*—M.M.
[0720]—*The Missionaries of Our Lady of La Salette.*—M.S.
[0860]—*Missionhurst Congregation of the Immaculate Heart of Mary.*—C.I.C.M.
[0920]—*Oblates of St. Francis De Sales.*—O.S.F.S.
[0430]—*Order of Preachers-Dominicans.* (Provs. of St. Joseph & St. Albert the Great).—O.P.
[1020]—*Pauline Fathers and Brother.*—S.S.P.
[1050]—*Pontifical Institute for Foreign Missions.*—P.I.M.E.
[1070]—*Redemptorist Fathers.* (St. Louis Prov.).—C.SS.R.
[1260]—*Society of Christ.* (American-Canadian Prov.).—S.Ch.
[0440]—*Society of Saint Edmund.*—S.S.E.
[0990]—*Society of the Catholic Apostolate.*—S.A.C.
[1060]—*Society of the Precious Blood.* (Cincinnati Prov.).—C.PP.S.

RELIGIOUS INSTITUTES OF WOMEN REPRESENTED IN THE ARCHDIOCESE

[1810]—*Bernardine Sisters of the Third Order of St. Francis.*—O.S.F.
[0360]—*Carmelite Sisters of the Divine Heart of Jesus Carmel.*—D.C.J.
[3810]—*Catholic Mission Sistersof St. Francis Xavier.*—X.S.
[0270]—*Congregation of Bon Secours.*—C.B.S.
[2410]—*Congregation of the Marianites of Holy Cross.*—M.S.C.
[1730]—*Congregation of the Sisters of the Third Order of St. Francis Oldenburg, IN.*—O.S.F.
[1710]—*Congregation of the Third Order of St. Francis of Mary Immaculate, Joliet, IL.*—O.S.F.
[1830]—*Contemplative Sisters of the Good Shepherd.*—C.G.S.
[0760]—*Daughters of Charity of St. Vincent de Paul.*—D.C.
[0790]—*Daughters of Divine Charity.*—F.D.C.
[]—*Daughters of Mary Immaculate (Chaldean).*—D.M.I.
[0940]—*Daughters of St. Mary of Providence.*—D.S.M.P.
[0810]—*Daughters of the Heart of Mary.*—D.H.M.
[0420]—*Discalced Carmelite Nuns.*—O.C.D.
[1050]—*Dominican Contemplative Nuns.*—O.P.
[1070-13]—*Dominican Sisters (Adrian, MI).*—O.P.
[1070-02]—*Dominican Sisters (Columbus,OH).*—O.P.
[1070-17]—*Dominican Sisters (Elkin Park).*—O.P.
[1070-14]—*Dominican Sisters (Grand Rapids, MI).*—O.P.
[1070-16]—*Dominican Sisters (Hope).*—O.P.
[1070-26]—*Dominican Sisters (Oxford, MI).*—O.P.
[1070-09]—*Dominican Sisters (Racine, WI).*—O.P.
[]—*Dominican Sisters of Mt. Thabor.*—O.P.
[1170]—*Felician Sisters.*—C.S.S.F.
[1470]—*Franciscan Sisters of St. Joseph.*—F.S.S.J.
[1480]—*Franciscan Sisters of St. Joseph.* (Mexico).
[1440]—*Franciscan Sisters of the Poor.*—S.F.P.
[2430]—*Marist Sisters Congregation of Mary.*—S.M.
[2470]—*Maryknoll Sisters of St. Dominic.*—M.M.
[2720]—*Mission Helpers of the Sacred Heart.*—M.H.S.H.
[2710]—*Missionaries of Charity.*—M.C.
[]—*Missionaries of the Kingship of Christ.*—S.I.M.
[]—*Missionary Sisters of Christ the King for Polonia.*—M.S.K.C.P.
[3130]—*Our Lady of Victory Missionary Sisters.*—O.L.V.M.
[2970]—*School Sisters of Notre Dame.*—S.S.N.D.
[3560]—*Servants of Jesus.*—S.J.
[3590]—*Servants of Mary (Servite Sisters).*—O.S.M.
[0440]—*Sisters of Charity of Cincinnati, Ohio.*—S.C.
[0520]—*Sisters of Charity of Our Lady, Mother of Mercy.*—S.C.M.M.
[0990]—*Sisters of Divine Providence.*—C.D.P.
[2360]—*Sisters of Loretto.*—S.L.
[2575]—*Sisters of Mercy of the Americas.*—R.S.M.
[2990]—*Sisters of Notre Dame.*—S.N.D.
[1530]—*Sisters of St. Francis of the Congregation of Our Lady of Lourdes, Sylvania, Ohio.*—O.S.F.
[1570]—*Sisters of St. Francis of the Holy Family.*—O.S.F.
[1600]—*Sisters of St. Francis of the Martyr St. George.*—O.S.F.
[3830-11]—*Sisters of St. Joseph.*—S.S.J.
[3930]—*Sisters of St. Joseph of the Third Order of St. Francis.*—S.S.J.-T.O.S.F.
[1830]—*Sisters of the Good Shepherd.*—R.G.S.
[1970]—*Sisters of the Holy Family of Nazareth.*—C.S.F.N.
[1990]—*Sisters of the Holy Names of Jesus and Mary.*—S.N.J.M.
[2350]—*Sisters of the Living Word.*—S.L.W.
[3730]—*Sisters of the Order of St. Basil the Great.*—O.S.B.M.
[3260]—*Sisters of the Precious Blood (Dayton, Ohio).*—C.PP.S.
[2090]—*Sisters, Home Visitors of Mary.*—H.V.M.
[3610]—*Sisters, Servants of Mary Immaculate.*—S.S.M.I.
[2150]—*Sisters, Servants of the Immaculate Heart of Mary.*—I.H.M.
[2460]—*Society of Mary Reparatrix.*—S.M.R.
[4070]—*Society of the Sacred Heart.*—R.S.C.J.
[4120-06]—*Ursuline Nuns of the Congregation of Paris.*—O.S.U.
[]—*Vestiarski Sisters of Jesus.*—V.S.

ARCHDIOCESAN CEMETERIES

DETROIT. *Owned and Operated by the Archdiocese of Detroit.*
Holy Cross.
Holy Sepulchre, Southfield.
Our Lady of Hope, Southgate.
Owned and Operated by the Mt. Elliott Cemetery Association.
Mt. Elliott.
Mt. Olivet.
Resurrection, Clinton Township.
All Saints, Waterford.
Owned and Operated by the Conventual Franciscan Friars.
St. Hedwig, Dearborn Heights.

NECROLOGY

† Bogus, Daniel, (Retired). —Died Oct. 4, 1996.
† Borkowicz, Rev. Msgr. Vincent P., (Retired). —Died July 27, 1996.
† Canaan, Joseph A., (Retired). —Died Feb. 8, 1996.
† Fedewa, Rev. Msgr. Stanley, (Retired). —Died Sept. 7, 1996.
† Griffith, J. William, (Retired). —Died Feb. 12, 1996.
† Lis, Edward, (Retired). —Died June 11, 1996.
† Murphy, James, (Retired). —Died June 17, 1996.
† Nardone, Michael, Sterling Heights, MI, St. Malachy Parish. —Died May 2, 1996.
† Paul, Harry, (Retired). —Died March 20, 1996.
† Pouget, Richard A., Allenton, MI, St. John the Evangelist Parish. —Died Feb. 14, 1996.
† Radziecki, Sylvester L., (Retired). —Died April 16, 1996.
† Rokicki, Stanley C., (Retired). —Died July 16, 1996.
† Walling, Edward, (Retired). —Died Sept. 14, 1996.
† Wallis, Anthony I., (Retired). —Died Sept. 4, 1996.
† Werenski, Robert J., Oakland, CO, Hospice of Southeastern Michigan. —Died Dec. 10, 1996.

Diocese of Dodge City

(Dioecesis Dodgepolis)

Most Reverend

STANLEY G. SCHLARMAN, D.D.

Bishop of Dodge City; ordained July 13, 1958; appointed to the Titular See of Capri and Auxiliary Bishop of Belleville, March 13, 1979; consecrated May 14, 1979; appointed Bishop of Dodge City March 1, 1983; installed May 4, 1983. *Office: 910 Central Ave., Box 137, Dodge City, KS, 67801.*

Most Reverend

MARION F. FORST, D.D.

Retired Bishop of Dodge City; ordained June 10, 1934; consecrated Bishop of Dodge City March 24, 1960; installed April 5, 1960; resigned from Dodge City; appointed Auxiliary Bishop of Kansas City in Kansas October 16, 1976; retired as Auxiliary Bishop December 23, 1986. *Res., St. Joseph Care Center, 759 Vermont Ave., Kansas City, KS, 66601.*

ESTABLISHED MAY 19, 1951.

Square Miles 23,000.

Comprises the following Counties in the State of Kansas: Barton, Stafford, Pratt, Barber, Rush, Ness, Lane, Scott, Wichita, Greeley, Hamilton, Kearny, Finney, Hodgeman, Pawnee, Edwards, Ford, Gray, Haskell, Grant, Stanton, Morton, Stevens, Seward, Meade, Clark, Kiowa and Comanche.

Principal Patron: Our Lady of Guadalupe.

Secondary Patron: St. John the Baptist.

For legal titles of parishes and diocesan institutions, consult the Chancery Office.

Catholic Church Offices: 910 Central Ave., P.O. Box 137, Dodge City, KS, 67801-0137. Tel.: 316-227-1500; Fax: 316-227-1570.

STATISTICAL OVERVIEW

Personnel	
Bishop	1
Retired Bishops	1
Priests: Diocesan Active in Diocese	30
Priests: Active Outside Diocese	3
Priests: Retired, Sick or Absent	18
Number of Diocesan Priests	51
Religious Priests in Diocese	3
Ordinations:	
Permanent Deacons in Diocese	6
Total Sisters	122
Parishes	
Parishes	57
With Resident Pastor:	
Resident Diocesan Priests	26
Resident Religious Priests	2
Without Resident Pastor:	
Administered by Priests	26
Administered by Professed Men Religious	2
Administered by Women Religious	1
Professional Ministry Personnel:	
Sisters	5
Lay Ministers	5
Welfare	
Catholic Hospitals	3
Total Assisted	97,722
Special Centers for Social Services	4
Total Assisted	62,737
Educational	
Diocesan Students in Other Seminaries	3
Total Seminarians	3
Elementary Schools, Diocesan and Parish	10
Total Students	1,378
Catechesis/Religious Education:	
High School Students	2,453
Elementary Students	4,311
Total Students Under Catholic Instruction	8,145
Teachers in the Diocese:	
Sisters	4
Lay Teachers	120
Vital Statistics	
Receptions into the Church:	
Infant Baptism Totals	944
Adult Baptism Totals	219
Received into Full Communion	264
First Communions	1,060
Confirmations	658
Marriages:	
Catholic	171
Interfaith	130
Total Marriages	301
Deaths	303
Total Catholic Population	44,504
Total Population	212,147

Former Bishops—Most Rev. JOHN BAPTIST FRANZ, D.D., cons. Aug. 29, 1951; transferred to the See of Peoria Aug. 8, 1959.—Most Rev. MARION F. FORST, D.D., cons. March 24, 1960; transferred to See of Kansas City, KS as Auxiliary Oct. 16, 1976; retired as Auxiliary Bishop Dec. 23, 1986.—Most Rev. EUGENE J. GERBER, D.D., cons. Dec. 14, 1976; transferred See of Wichita, KS Nov. 23, 1982.

Vicar General—Rev. JOHN J. MAES.

Chancellor & Moderator of the Curia—Rev. WARREN L. STECKLEIN.

Vice Chancellor—Sr. LORETTA GEGEN, A.S.C., Ph.D.

Catholic Church Offices—910 Central Ave., P.O. Box 137, Dodge City, 67801-0137. Tel: 316-227-1500; Fax: 316-227-1570. Office Hours: Mon.-Fri. 9-4:30 All rogatonial commissions should be sent to the Catholic Church Offices.

Finance Director—Mr. DANIEL M. STREMEL, C.P.A., *Catholic Church Offices, 910 Central Ave., P.O. Box 137, Dodge City, 67801-0137.* Tel: 316-227-1500.

Presbyteral Council & Diocesan Board of Consultors—Most Rev. STANLEY G. SCHLARMAN; Revs. DENNIS REED, Chm. TED SKALSKY, Vice Chm. JAMES E. BAKER, J.C.L., Sec. & Treas. BRIAN D. HIPP; GERALD A. HAMMEKE; MICHAEL L. HELMS; GILBERT HERRMAN; HENRY HILDEBRANDT; PASCAL L. KLEIN; JOHN J. MAES, V.G.; FRANCIS KHOI NGUYEN; WARREN L. STECKLEIN.

Deans—Dodge City: Rev. JAMES E. BAKER, V.F.; Garden City: Rev. JOHN P. KOWAL, V.F.; Great Bend: Rev. JOSEPH E. BAHR, V.F.

Council of Administration—Sr. LORETTA GEGEN, A.S.C., Ph.D.; Rev. JOHN J. MAES, V.G.; Mr. DANIEL M. STREMEL, C.P.A.; Rev. WARREN L. STECKLEIN.

Matrimonial Tribunal—910 Central Ave., P.O. Box 137, Dodge City, 67801-0137.

Judicial Vicar—Rev. JAMES E. BAKER, J.C.L.

Synodal Judge—Rev. JAMES E. BAKER, J.C.L.

Promotor of Justice—Rev. GERALD A. HAMMEKE, *100 Main St., P.O. Box 187, Spearville, 67876.* Tel: 316-385-2212.

Defender of the Bond—Rev. DAVID H. KRAUS, J.C.L., *723 S. Baca, P.O. Box 570, Elkhart, 67950-0570.* Tel: 316-697-4622.

Advocates—All priests in active ministry in the diocese.

Notary—LORRAINE KINCAID.

Diocesan Offices and Directors

Catholic Education Office and Superintendent of Schools - Elementary School Religious Education—Sr. ROSEMARY HENRICHS, A.S.C., *P.O. Box 137, Dodge City, 67801-0137.* Tel: 316-227-1500.

Catholic Social Service Offices—Rev. TED A. SKALSKY, Exec. Dir., *332 N. Oak, Pratt.* Tel: 316-672-6352. DEBBIE SNAPP, Program Dir., *P.O. Box 137, Dodge City, 67801-0137.* Tel: 316-227-1500.

Commission for Continuing Education for Priests—Revs. JAMES E.BAKER, J.C.L.; JOHN P. KOWAL.

Commission for Ministry to Priests—Revs. EUGENE P. KENNY; JOHN J. MAES, V.G.; WARREN L. STECKLEIN.

Council of Catholic Women—Sr. LORETTA GEGEN, A.S.C., Moderator.

Development Office—JACK SCHRAMM, *P.O. Box 137, Dodge City, 67801-0137.* Tel: 316-227-1500.

Diocesan Attorney—Frigon Chartd., *208 W. Wyatt Earp Blvd., P.O. Box 1695, Dodge City, 67801.* Tel: 316-225-0600.

Diocesan Commission for the Promotion of Christian Unity—Vacant.

Diocesan Finance Council—ED MICHEL, C.P.A., Chm.; Rev. GERALD A. HAMMEKE, Vice Chm.; Mr. DANIEL M. STREMEL, C.P.A., Ex-Officio, Treas.; EUGENE BERNING; CLARINE HEIMAN; EUGENE HEIMAN; CARL HELFRICH, C.P.A.; JACK SCHRAMM; SID SHRIWISE; Rev. WARREN STECKLEIN; ANN STEGMAN; RON VRATIL, C.P.A.

Due Process—Vacant.

Diocesan Fitness Review Board—DAVID H. SNAPP, Admin. Tel: 316-225-5051 (Office); 316-225-2412 Iome).

Diocesan Pastoral Council—Sr. LORETTA GEGEN, A.S.C., Coord.; Rev. JOSEPH E. BAHR, V.F.; Sr. JOEL CHRISTOPH, O.P.; DEBBIE HELFRICH; JEANETTE SIEMENS; Rev. JAMES E. BAKER, V.F.; CAROLYN GLEASON; BECKY

HESSMAN; Mrs. PAT KRIER; Rev. JOHN P. KOWAL, V.F., Dean; VICTOR GRAFF; GENE JUNO; Deacon ERASMO RODRIGUEZ.

Diocesan Priests' Trust Fund—Revs. ROBERT A. SCHREMMER, Chm.; JOHN R. STRASSER, Vice Chm.; JAMES P. DIEKER, Sec.; Rev. Msgr. A. F. PREISNER, Treas.; Revs. EUGENE P. KENNY; GEORGE E. MUELLER; MARVIN W. REIF.

Diocesan School Council—Sr. ROSEMARY HENRICHS, A.S.C., Supt. of Schools; Revs. JOSEPH BAHR; PASCAL KLEIN; ROBERT A. SCHREMMER; DERMOT F. TIGHE; BILL VOGEL; CHRIS HIMMELWRIGHT; BRUCE REICHMUTH; ALLEN SCHULER; JANICE SCOTT; JOHN STROBEL.

Health Affairs Office—Sr. BETTY WERNER, O.P., Dir., *3600 Broadway, Great Bend, 67530.*

Lay Employees' Retirement Plan—Mr. DANIEL M. STREMEL, C.P.A.

League of the Apostleship of Prayer—Vacant.

Newspaper Office—"The Southwest Kansas Register", Diocesan Weekly, TIM WENZL, Editor, *P.O. Box 137, Dodge City, 67801-0137.* Tel: 316-227-1500.

Office of Family Ministries—Co-Directors: Sr. ROSE MARY STEIN, O.P.; STEVEN POLLEY, *P.O. Box 137, Dodge City, 67801-0137.* Tel: 316-227-1500.

Office of Leadership Formation and Planning—Sr. LORETTA GEGEN, A.S.C., Dir., *P.O. Box 137, Dodge City, 67801-0137.* Tel: 316-227-1500.

Office of Liturgy and Worship (R.C.I.A.)—Rev. DAVID A. FLAGOR, Dir.; JANE STEIN, Coord., *523 W. 6th, Ashland, 67831.* Tel: 316-635-2284.

Ministry to Parents and the Aging—Sr. ROSE MARY STEIN, O.P., *910 Central, P.O. Box 137, Dodge City, 67801-0137.* Tel: 316-227-1500.

Catholic Agency - Migration and Refugee Services—LEVITA ROHLMAN, Exec. Dir., *1510 Taylor Plaza E., Garden City, 67846.* Tel: 316-276-7610; Fax: 316-276-9228.

Permanent Diaconate Office—Rev. BRIAN D. HIPP, Dir., *P.O. Box 137, Dodge City, 67801-0137.* Tel: 316-227-1500.

Propagation of the Faith and Pontifical Association of the Holy Childhood—Sr. KAREN ACKERMAN, A.S.C., *P.O. Box 137, Dodge City, 67801-0137.* Tel: 316-227-1500.

High School Religious Education, Youth Ministry, Confirmation Retreats—STEVEN D. POLLEY, Dir., *P.O. Box 137, Dodge City, 67801-0137.* Tel: 316-227-1500.

Scouting—Rev. JAMES E. BAKER, *P.O. Box 278, Jetmore, 67854-0278.* Tel: 316-357-8791.

Vigilance for the Faith—The Rev. Deans.

Vocation Director—Rev. BRIAN HIPP, *P.O. Box 137, Dodge City, 67801-0137.* Tel: 316-227-1500.

CLERGY, PARISHES, MISSIONS AND PAROCHIAL SCHOOLS

CITY OF DODGE CITY
(Ford County)

1—CATHEDRAL OF THE SACRED HEART (1882), Revs. John R. Strasser; Gregory S. LeBlanc; Sr. Rose Hacker, S.S.S.F., Pastoral Min.
Office: 903 Central Ave., 67801. Tel: 316-225-4802.
Res., 903 Central, 67801. Tel: 316-227-3772.
School—905 Central Ave., 67801. Tel: 316-227-6532. Mrs. Phyllis Johnson, Prin.
Religious 1; Lay Teachers 20; Students 404.
Catechesis/Religious Programs—Sr. Greta Fitzgerald, D.R.E.
Students 253.

2—OUR LADY OF GUADALUPE (1915), Sr. Patricia Schlarman, A.S.C., Pastoral Admin.
Res., 805 Ave. J, 67801. Tel: 316-227-3442 (Office).
Catechesis/Religious Programs—Elaine Campbell, D.R.E.
Students 350.

OUTSIDE THE CITY OF DODGE CITY

Ashland, Comanche Co., Holy Spirit (1984). Attended by St. Joseph, Ashland. Rev. David A. Flagor.
Mailing Address: c/o St. Joseph Church, 514 Main St., Box 577, 67831. Tel: 316-635-2338; Fax: 316-635-4066.

St. Joseph, Clark Co., (1886), Rev. David A. Flagor.
Res., 514 Main St., P.O. Box 577, 67831-0577. Tel: 316-635-2338; Fax: 316-635-4066.
Catechesis/Religious Programs—Jan Fast, D.R.E.
Students 60.

Beaver, Barton Co., St. Joseph. Closed. For inquiries for parish records contact the Chancery.

Belpre, Edwards Co., St. Bernard (1921), Rev. Robert A. Schremmer; Deacon Richard Rondeau.
Res., 203 Hudson St., P.O. Box 188, 67519-0188. Tel: 316-995-4305.
Catechesis/Religious Programs—Eileen Loomis, D.R.E.
Students 69.

Bucklin, Ford Co., St. George (1943). Attended by Our Lady of Guadalupe, Dodge City. Sr. Patricia Schlarman, A.S.C., Pastoral Admin.
Church—321 S. Dodge Ave., P.O. Box 611, 67834. Tel: 316-826-3335.

Burdett, Pawnee Co., Holy Rosary (1951). Attended by St. Lawrence, Jetmore. Rev. James E. Baker.
Mailing Address: c/o St. Lawrence Church, P.O. Box 278, Jetmore, 67854. Tel: 316-357-8791. [JC]

Claflin, Barton Co., Immaculate Conception (1904), Rev. Joseph E. Bahr; Sr. Catherine Therese Paulie, C.S.J., Pastoral Min.
Mailing Address: P.O. Box 197, 67525. Tel: 316-587-3628.
Catechesis/Religious Programs—Tammi Miller, D.R.E.
Students 128.

Deerfield, Kearney Co., Christ the King (1937), Revs. Pascal L. Klein; John J. Waters, S.J.
Mailing Address: P.O. Box 455, 67838. Tel: 316-275-4204.
Catechesis/Religious Programs—Marilyn Danler, D.R.E.
Students 81.

Dighton, Lane Co., St. Theresa (1927). Attended by St. Joseph, Scott City. Rev. Francis X. Khoi Nguyen.
Res., 322 S. First St., P.O. Box 787, 67839. Tel: 316-397-5357. [JC]
Catechesis/Religious Programs—Annette Wilson, D.R.E.
Students 58.

Dubuque, Barton Co., St. Catherine (1902), Rev. John J. Maes, V.G.
Mailing Address: c/o St. John the Evangelist Parish, 122 E. 5th St., Hoisington, 67544. Tel: 316-792-1396. [CEM]

Elkhart, Morton Co., St. Joan of Arc (1921), Rev. David H. Kraus, J.C.L.
Res., 723 S. Baca, P.O. Box 570, 67950-0570. Tel: 316-697-4622.
Catechesis/Religious Programs—Tel: 316-697-4587. Sarita Blakeley, D.R.E.
Students 60.

Ellinwood, Barton Co., St. Joseph (1876), Rev. Joseph E. Bahr.
Res., 214 N. Main St., 67526. Tel: 316-564-2534. [CEM]
School—111 W. Third, 67526. Tel: 316-564-2721. Sr. Noella Blick, A.S.C., Prin.
Adorers of the Blood of Christ 2; Lay Teachers 6; Students 88.
Catechesis/Religious Programs—D.R.E.: Tammy Sturn; Mary Tudor.
Students 171.

Fowler, Meade Co., St. Anthony (1910). Attended by St. John the Baptist, Meade. Rev. George E. Mueller; Deacon Dwaine Lampe.
Res., 310 Fourth St., P.O. Box 80, Meade, 67844. Tel: 316-646-5297; Fax: 316-646-5207. [JC]
Catechesis/Religious Programs—Pat Dierking, D.R.E.
Students 113.

Garden City, Finney Co., St. Dominic (1965), Revs. Dennis L. Reed; Louis Trung Hoang.
Office: 615 J. C. St., 67846. Tel: 316-276-2024; Fax: 316-276-2086.
School—617 J. C. St., 67846. Tel: 316-276-8981. Mrs. Sue Glodt, Prin.
Lay Teachers 9; Students 154.
Catechesis/Religious Programs—Tel: 316-276-3500. Michael Dorsey, D.R.E.
Students 315.

St. Mary (1898), Revs. Pascal L. Klein; John J. Waters, S.J.
Res., 509 St. John St., 67846. Tel: 316-275-4204; Fax: 316-272-9971.
School—503 W. St. John St., 67846. Tel: 316-276-2241. Trina Delgado, Prin.
Lay Teachers 9; Students 137.
Catechesis/Religious Programs—Tel: 316-276-2716. Patricia Nieman, D.R.E.
Students 535.
Mission—Deerfield, Kearny Co., Christ the King, 812 Main St., Deerfield, 67838. Tel: 316-426-6996.

Great Bend, Barton Co., St. Patrick (1960), Revs. Dermot F. Tighe; Patrick M. Downey.
Res., 4100 Broadway, 67530. Tel: 316-792-1396; Fax: 316-792-1397. [JC]
School—4200 Broadway, 67530. Tel: 316-793-3265. Mr. Fred Meyers, Prin.
Lay Teachers 10; Students 156.
Catechesis/Religious Programs—Kathy Pike, D.R.E.
Students 497.

St. Rose of Lima (1878), Revs. Charles J. Mazouch; Vincent Bork.
Res., 1423 Holland St., P.O. Box 1007, 67530. Tel: 316-792-3641. [JC]
School—1400 Baker Ave., 67530. Tel: 316-793-5662. Mr. Fred Meyers, Prin.
Lay Teachers 7; Students 118.
Catechesis/Religious Programs—Students 230.

Greensburg, Kiowa Co., St. Joseph (1952). Attended by St. Joseph, Ashland. Rev. David A. Flagor.
Res., 514 Main St., P.O. Box 577, Ashland, 67831-0577. Tel: 316-635-2338; Fax: 316-635-4066.

Hanston, Hodgeman Co., St. Anthony (1908). Attended by St. Lawrence, Jetmore. Rev. James E. Baker.
Mailing Address: c/o St. Lawrence Church, P.O. Box 278, Jetmore, 67854. Tel: 316-357-8791. [CEM]

Hoisington, Barton Co., St. John the Evangelist (1892), Rev. John J. Maes, V.G.; Sr. Alvina Miller, O.P., Pastoral Min.; Sr. Marie Zoglman, A.S.C., Pastoral Min.
Office: 122 E. 5th St., 67544. Tel: 316-653-2963.;
Rectory: 108 E. 5th St., 67544. Tel: 316-653-2695. [CEM]
Catechesis/Religious Programs—Ms. Judy Linsner, D.R.E.
Students 211.

Hugoton, Stevens Co., St. Helen (1948), Rev. Emil Dinkel, C.PP.S.
Parish Office: 1011 S. Jefferson St., 67951-2823. Tel: 316-544-2551.
Catechesis/Religious Programs—Tel: 316-544-4644. Phyllis Ackerman, D.R.E.
Students 115.

Ingalls, Gray Co., St. Stanislaus (1909), Revs. Dennis L. Reed; Louis Trung Hoang.
Mailing Address: P.O. Box 175, 67853.
Catechesis/Religious Programs—Kathy Hornung, D.R.E.
Students 142.

Jetmore, Hodgeman Co., St. Lawrence (1923), Rev. James E. Baker.
Mailing Address: P.O. Box 278, 67854. Tel: 316-357-8791. [JC]
Catechesis/Religious Programs—Marge Jacobs, D.R.E.
Students 60.

Johnson, Stanton Co., St. Bernadette (1949) (Hispanic). Attended by Mary Queen of Peace, Ulysses. Rev. John P. Kowal.
Mailing Address: c/o Mary, Queen of Peace Church, 804 Colorado, Ulysses, 67880. Tel: 316-356-1532; Fax: 316-424-1065.
Catechesis/Religious Programs—Tel: 316-495-2471. Judy Cullen, D.R.E.
Students 65.

Kinsley, Edwards Co., St. Nicholas (1883), Rev. William Vogel.
Res., 706 E. Sixth St., 67547. Tel: 316-659-2692. [CEM]
School—720 E. Sixth St., 67547. Tel: 316-659-2521. Mrs. Rebecca Burcher, Prin.
Lay Teachers 5; Students 64.

Kiowa, Barber Co., St. John the Apostle (1885). Attended by Holy Rosary, Medicine Lodge and St. Boniface, Sharon. Rev. Anthony J. Suellentrop.
Res., 920 E. Main St., 67070. Tel: 316-825-4361.
Catechesis/Religious Programs—Julie Sterling, D.R.E.
Students 54.

LaCrosse, Rush Co., St. Michael (1911), Rev. James P. Deiker, Admin.
Res., 918 Lincoln St., P.O. Box 309, 67548. Tel: 913-222-2561. [JC]
Catechesis/Religious Programs—Ardis Viegra, D.R.E.
Students 127.

Lakin, Kearny Co., St. Anthony (1909), Rev. Gilbert P. Herrman.
Res., 600 Soderberg St., P.O. Box 983, 67860. Tel: 316-355-6405. [JC]
Catechesis/Religious Programs—Delia Stahlecker, D.R.E.
Students 135.

Larned, Pawnee Co., Sacred Heart (1912), Rev. Robert A. Schremmer.
Res., 1111 State St., 67550. Tel: 316-285-2035.
School—527 W. 12th St., 67550. Tel: 316-285-3025. Diane Dodez, Prin.
Lay Teachers 6; Students 79.
Catechesis/Religious Programs—Jeane Debes, D.R.E.
Students 121.

Leoti, Wichita Co., St. Anthony of Padua (1887), Rev. Michael Helms.
Res., 600 S. Fourth St., R.R. 2, Box 114, 67861. Tel: 316-375-2292. [CEM]
Catechesis/Religious Programs—Tel: 316-375-4996. Diana Long, D.R.E.
Students 95.

Liberal, Seward Co., St. Anthony (1916), Rev. Henry F. Hildebrandt; Deacon Erasmo Rodriguez.

Res., 419 W. First St., 67901. Tel: 316-624-4135; Fax: 316-624-3553.
Catechesis/Religious Programs—Kathy Berry, D.R.E.
Students 681.

Liebenthal, Rush Co., St. Joseph (1905). Attended by St. Michael, LaCrosse. Rev. James P. Dieker, Admin.
Mailing Address: P.O. Box 98, 67553. Tel: 913-222-3160. [CEM]

Marienthal, Wichita Co., St. Mary (1886), Rev. Michael Helms.
Mailing Address: P.O. Box 7, 67863. Tel: 316-379-4431. [CEM]
Catechesis/Religious Programs—Tel: 316-379-4658. Jenni Winter, D.R.E.
Students 90.

McCracken, Rush Co., St. Mary (1905), Rev. Eugene P. Kenny.
Mailing Address: P.O. Box 157, 67556. Tel: 913-394-2251. [CEM]

Meade, Meade Co., St. John the Baptist (1889), Rev. George E. Mueller; Deacon Dwaine Lampe.
Res., 412 W. Carthage St., P.O. Box 706, 67864. Tel: 316-873-2003. [JC]

Medicine Lodge, Barber Co., Holy Rosary, Rev. Anthony J. Suellentrop.
Mailing Address: 808 N. Cedar, 67104. Tel: 316-886-3596.
Catechesis/Religious Programs—Diane Seiler, D.R.E.
Students 48.

Ness City, Ness Co., Sacred Heart (1912), Rev. Marvin Reif.
Res., 606 S. School St., P.O. Box 310, 67560. Tel: 913-798-3195. [CEM]
School—520 S. School St., 67560. Tel: 913-798-3530. Ann Depperschmidt, Prin.
Adorers of the Blood of Christ 2; Lay Teachers 6; Students 67.
Catechesis/Religious Programs—Joby Henning, D.R.E.
Students 97.

North Kinsley, Edwards Co., SS. Peter and Paul. Closed. For inquiries for sacramental records contact the Chancery.

Odin, Barton Co., Holy Family (1879), Rev. John J. Maes, V.G.
Mailing Address: c/o St. John the Evangelist Parish, 122 E. 5th St., Hoisington, 67544. [CEM]
Catechesis/Religious Programs—Teresa Hickel, D.R.E.
Students 62.

Offerle, Edwards Co., St. Joseph (1876), Rev. William Vogel.
Mailing Address: P.O. Box 7, 67563. Tel: 316-659-2692. [CEM 2]

Olmitz, Barton Co., St. Ann (1889), Rev. Ultan P. Murphy.
Res., 115 Cleveland St., P.O. Box 8, 67564. Tel: 316-586-3306. [CEM]
Catechesis/Religious Programs—Tel: 316-586-3282. Terese Frieb, D.R.E.
Students 107.

Plains, Meade Co., St. Patrick (1916). Attended by St. John the Baptist, Meade. Rev. George E. Mueller; Deacon Dwaine Lampe.
Res., St. John the Baptist, 412 W. Carthage, P.O. Box 706, Meade, 67864.
Church—601 Superior, P.O. Box 247, 67869. Tel: 316-563-7663. [CEM]
Catechesis/Religious Programs—Ann Amerin, D.R.E.
Students 66.

Pratt, Pratt Co., Sacred Heart (1887), Rev. Ted A. Skalsky.
Res., 332 N. Oak St., 67124. Tel: 316-672-6352.
School—(Grades PreK-5) 330 N. Oak St., 67124. Tel: 316-672-3687. Mr. Dallas Woolf, Prin.
Lay Teachers 6; Students 58.
Catechesis/Religious Programs—Tel: 316-672-6352. Rita Hitt, D.R.E.
Students 171.

Ransom, Ness Co., St. Aloysius (1903). Attended by Sacred Heart, Ness City. Rev. Marvin W. Reif.
Mailing Address: P.O. Box 96, 67572. Tel: 913-731-2497. [CEM]
Catechesis/Religious Programs—Loretta Flax, D.R.E.
Students 89.

St. John, Stafford Co., St. John the Apostle (1947). Attended by St. Francis Xavier, Steward. Rev. Rene Guesnier, O.S.B.
Res., 609 E. Fourth St., Rte. 2, Box 100, 67576. Tel: 316-549-3538.
Catechesis/Religious Programs—Johnna Stanford, D.R.E.
Students 63.

St. Mary, Hodgeman Co., St. Mary (1904) (Irish), Rev. Gerald A. Hammeke.
Mailing Address: c/o P.O. Box 187, Spearville, 67876-0187. [CEM]

Satanta, Haskell Co., St. Alphonsus (1946), Rev. Emil Dinkel, C.PP.S.
Res., 603 Tecumseh, Box 65, 67870. Tel: 316-649-2692.
Church—601 Tecumseh, 67870.
Catechesis/Religious Programs—Students 97.

Scott City, Scott Co., St. Joseph (1911), Rev. Francis Khoi Nguyen.
Res., 1004 Main St., P.O. Box 248, 67871. Tel: 316-872-3644. [JC]
Catechesis/Religious Programs—Marilee Cramer, D.R.E.
Students 196.

Seward, Stafford Co., St. Francis Xavier (1886), Rev. Rene Guesnier, O.S.B.
Mailing Address: 504 Main St., 67576. Tel: 316-458-5691.

Sharon, Barber Co., St. Boniface (1904). Attended by Holy Rosary, Medicine Lodge and St. John the Apostle, Kiowa. Rev. Anthony J. Suellentrop.
Res., 410 N. Main St., P.O. Box 118, 67138. Tel: 316-294-5526. [CEM]
Catechesis/Religious Programs—Marge Rankin, D.R.E.
Students 75.

Spearville, Ford Co., St. John the Baptist (1904), Rev. Gerald A. Hammeke.
Res., 100 Main St., P.O. Box 187, 67876. Tel: 316-385-2212. [CEM]
Catechesis/Religious Programs—Carol Durler, D.R.E.
Students 190.

Syracuse, Hamilton Co., St. Raphael (1906), Rev. Gilbert P. Herrman.
Mailing Address: P.O. Box 731, 67878. Tel: 316-384-7357. [CEM]

Timken, Rush Co., Holy Trinity (1904) (Czech). Attended by St. Ann, Olmitz. Rev. Ultan Murphy.
Mailing Address: c/o St. Ann Church, P.O. Box 8, Olmitz, 67564. Tel: 316-586-3306. [CEM][JC]
Catechesis/Religious Programs—Tel: 913-387-2552. Marie Stremel, D.R.E.
Students 50.

Tribune, Greeley Co., St. Joseph (1950). Attended by St. Mary's, Marienthal. Rev. Michael Helms.
Mailing Address: c/o St. Mary's, 801 Broadway, Marienthal, 67879. Tel: 316-376-2292.
Catechesis/Religious Programs—Brian Reuber, D.R.E.
Students 59.

Ulysses, Grant Co., Mary Queen of Peace (1948) (Hispanic), Rev. John P. Kowal.
Res., 804 N. Colorado, 67880. Tel: 316-356-1532; Fax: 316-424-1065.
Catechesis/Religious Programs—Tel: 316-356-4911.
Students 254.

Windthorst, Ford Co., Immaculate Heart of Mary (1878). Attended by St. John the Baptist, Spearville. Rev. Gerald A. Hammeke.
Res., c/o Box 187, Spearville, 67876. [CEM]
Mission—Spearville, Ford Co., St. John the Baptist.

Wright, Ford Co., St. Andrew (1909), Rev. Warren L. Stecklein.
Mailing Address: 10893 St. Andrew Rd., P.O. Box 125, 67882. Tel: 316-227-3363. [CEM]
Parish Center—11792 Jewel Rd., 67882. Tel: 316-225-7345.
Catechesis/Religious Programs—Diane Lix, D.R.E.
Students 69.

Shrines

ELLINWOOD. *Sts. Peter & Paul,* R.R. 1, 67526. Leona Klein.

LORETTO. *St. Mary Help of Christians.* Box 98, Liebenthal, 67553. Rev. Eugene P. Kenny.

On Duty Outside the Diocese:
Reverend Fathers—
Fiedler, Donald J.
Joyce, Thomas J.
Moore, Brian R.

Retired:
Reverend Monsignors—
Leahy, Patrick J., 6900 E. 45th St. N., Wichita, KS 67226
Preisner, A. F., 105 Kent, Dodge City, KS 67801
Stewart, George N., 304 W. Williamson, P.O. Box 191, Claflin, KS 67525
Weller, Arnold J., P.O. Box 411, Spearville, KS 67876
Reverend Fathers—
Birzer, W. L., 308 E. Third St., P.O. Box 37, Ellinwood, KS 67526
Dreher, Jacob J., 3706 Meadowlark, Great Bend, KS 67530
Haberthier, John A., 3440 Cottonwood C-9, San Jacinto, CA 92582
Kelly, James, 6900 E. 45th St. N., Apt. D-4, Wichita, KS 67226
Klenke, Elmer A., 205 N. Lakin St., P.O. Box 1213, Lakin, KS 67860-1213
Lavrih, John, 6900 E. 45th St. N., Apt. D-2, Wichita, KS 67226
O'Neill, Rory, 6900 E. 45th St. N., Wichita, KS 67226
Pottorff, Lisle J., Rte. 2, Box 247, Douglass, KS 67039
Tuzicka, Fred M., 2611 27th St., Apt. 3-38, Great Bend, KS 67530
van Sloun, Eugene G., Rijksweg C.10, 6161EE, Geleen, Netherlands
Wylie, Stephen, 6900 E. 45th St. N., Apt. D-3, Wichita, KS 67226

Permanent Deacons:
Crowley, Norman
Lampe, Dwaine, St. Anthony, Fowler
Rodriguez, Erasmo, St. Anthony, Liberal
Rondeau, Richard, St. Bernard, Belpre
Stickney, Harold

INSTITUTIONS LOCATED IN THE DIOCESE

[A] GENERAL HOSPITALS

GARDEN CITY. *St. Catherine Hospital,* 410 E. Walnut, 67846-5672. Tel: 316-272-2222; Fax: 316-272-2566.
For a complete listing, refer to the Hospitals section.

GREAT BEND. *Central Kansas Medical Center,* 3515 Broadway, 67530. Tel: 316-792-2511.
For a complete listing, refer to the Hospitals section.

LARNED. *Central Kansas Medical Center, St. Joseph Campus,* 923 Carroll St., 67550. Tel: 316-285-3161.
For a complete listing, refer to the Hospitals section.

[B] RETREAT CENTERS

GREAT BEND. *Heartland Center for Spirituality,* 3600 Broadway, 67530-3692. Tel: 316-792-1232; Fax: 316-792-1746. Retreat Center. Sr. Louise Hageman, O.P., Dir.; Sr. Geraldine Eakes. Total Staff 6.

[C] EDUCATIONAL ENDOWMENT FUNDS

DODGE CITY. *The Sacred Heart School Endowment,* 903 Central, 67801.

ELLINWOOD. *St. Joseph School Education Endowment Fund,* 214 N. Main St., 67526.

GARDEN CITY. *St. Dominic Grade School Endowment Fund,* 615 J.C. St., 67846.
The St. Mary Catholic Education Endowment Fund, 509 St. John St., 67846.

GREAT BEND. *Catholic Social Services Endowment Fund,* 2546 20th St., 67530.
The St. Patrick Grade School Education Endowment Fund, 4100 Broadway, 67530.
The St. Rose of Lima Grade School Education Endowment Fund, 1423 Holland St., Box 1007, 67530.

LARNED. *The Sacred Heart Grade School of Larned Education Endowment Fund,* 527 W. 12th St., 67550.

PRATT. *The Sacred Heart School Education Endowment, Inc.,* 332 N. Oak St., 67124.

[D] CONVENTS AND RESIDENCES FOR SISTERS

GREAT BEND. *Immaculate Conception Convent,* 3600 Broadway, 67530-3692. Tel: 316-792-1232; Fax: 316-792-1746. Dominican Sisters of Great Bend. Legal Title: *Immaculate Conception Convent, Motherhouse and Novitiate of the Nuns of the Third Order of St. Dominic.* Sr. Betty Werner, O.P., Prioress; Sr. Peggy Ann Martin, Asst. Prioress. Council Members: Sr. LeAnn Probst, O.P.; Sr. Rita Brizer, O.P.; Sr. Terence Wasinger, O.P. Final Professed Sisters 134; Novices 1; Lay Associates 58.
Great Bend Dominican Sisters Office of Mission and Ministry, 3600 Broadway, 67530-3692. Tel: 316-792-8661. Total in Residence 49. Retreat Center.

[E] SERVICES FOR THE ELDERLY

GREAT BEND. *Cedar Park Place, Inc.,* 3910 Cedar Park Pl., 67530-3692. Tel: 316-793-8115; Fax: 316-792-1746. Low and Middle Income Housing for Elderly and Handicapped.

[F] MISCELLANEOUS

DODGE CITY. *Manna House*, 1012 First, 67801. Tel: 316-227-7606; 227-6707. Margaret Witsken, Exec. Dir. Short-term housing and food distribution for those in need. Total Staff 3; Total Assisted 2,328.

GARDEN CITY. *Catholic Agency-Migration & Refugee Service*, 1510 Taylor Plaza E., 67846. Tel: 316-276-7610; Fax: 316-276-9228. Ms. Levita Rohlman, Exec. Dir. Total Staff 1; Assisted 1500.

Emmaus House, 802 N. Fifth St., 67846-5638. Tel: 316-275-2008. Special Center for Social Services & Assistance. Mrs. Marjorie R. Williams, Dir. Total Staff 2; Total Assisted 59,271.

GREAT BEND. *Family Crisis Center*, 1300 Kansas, 67530. Tel: 316-793-1965; 1966; 792-1885 (Crisis Line). Patty Linsner, Contact Person. Total Staff 6; Total Assisted 633.

Sommerset Place, 5803 16th Terrace, 67530. 60 Unit Apartment Complex.

RELIGIOUS INSTITUTES OF MEN REPRESENTED IN THE DIOCESE

For further details refer to the corresponding bracketed number in the Religious Institutes of Men or Women section.

[0200]—*Benedictine Monks.*—O.S.B.

[]—*Dominican Fathers.*—O.P.

[0690]—*Jesuit Fathers and Brothers.*—S.J.

[1060]—*Society of the Precious Blood.* (Kansas City Prov.).—C.PP.S.

RELIGIOUS INSTITUTIONS OF WOMEN REPRESENTED IN THE DIOCESE

[0100]—*Adorers of the Blood of Christ.*—A.S.C.

[2100]—*Congregation of the Humility of Mary.*—C.H.M.

[1070-24]—*Nuns of the Third Order of St. Dominic.*—O.P.

[1680]—*School Sisters of St. Francis.*—S.S.S.F.

[]—*Sisters of St. Francis.*—O.S.F.

[3830-18]—*Sisters of St. Joseph.*—C.S.J.

[]—*Sisters of the Presentation of the Blessed Virgin Mary.*—B.V.M.

NECROLOGY

† Dziemian, Rev. Msgr. Anthony Bernard, (Retired). —Died April 24, 1996.

† Simms, Russell J., (Retired). —Died Sept. 25, 1996.

† Stremel, Rev. Msgr. Joseph A., (Retired). —Died Feb. 28, 1996.

† Temaat, Norbert C., Garden City, KS, St. Mary Parish. —Died Feb. 16, 1996.

Archdiocese of Dubuque

(Archidioecesis Dubuquensis)

Most Reverend

JEROME HANUS, O.S.B., D.D.

Archbishop of Dubuque; ordained July 30, 1966; appointed Bishop of St. Cloud July 6, 1987; ordained and installed August 24, 1987; appointed Coadjutor Archbishop of Dubuque August 23, 1994; welcomed October 27, 1994; succeeded to the See October 16, 1995. *Office: Box 479, Dubuque, IA, 52004-0479.*

Most Reverend

DANIEL W. KUCERA, O.S.B., PH.D., D.D.

Retired Archbishop of Dubuque; ordained May 26, 1949; appointed Titular Bishop of Natchez and Auxiliary Bishop of Joliet June 6, 1977; ordained Bishop July 21, 1977; appointed Bishop of Salina March 11, 1980; installed May 7, 1980; appointed Archbishop of Dubuque December 20, 1983; installed February 23, 1984; retired October 16, 1995. *13952 E. Marina Dr., #612:, Aurora, CO, 80014.*

Chancery-Archdiocesan Center: P.O. Box 479, Dubuque, IA, 52004-0479. Tel.: 319-556-2580; Fax: 319-556-5464.

ESTABLISHED JULY 28, 1837.

CREATED AN ARCHDIOCESE JUNE 15, 1893.

Square Miles 17,403.

PATRONS OF THE ARCHDIOCESE: Primary: St. Raphael, the Archangel; Secondary: St. John Mary Vianney, Cure of Ars.

Corporate Title: "The Archdiocese of Dubuque."

Comprises 30 Counties, that part of the State of Iowa north of the Counties of Polk, Jasper, Poweshiek, Iowa, Johnson, Cedar and Clinton and east of the Counties of Kossuth, Humboldt, Webster and Boone.

For legal titles of parishes and archdiocesan institutions, consult the Chancery.

STATISTICAL OVERVIEW

Personnel	
Archbishop	1
Retired Archbishops	1
Abbots	1
Retired Abbots	4
Priests: Diocesan Active in Diocese	168
Priests: Active Outside Diocese	7
Priests: Diocesan in Foreign Missions	2
Priests: Retired, Sick or Absent	91
Number of Diocesan Priests	268
Religious Priests in Diocese	32
Extern Priests in Diocese	1
Ordinations:	
Diocesan Priests	1
Transitional Deacons	4
Permanent Deacons in Diocese	63
Total Brothers	28
Total Sisters	1,054
Parishes	
Parishes	213
With Resident Pastor:	
Resident Diocesan Priests	130
Resident Religious Priests	1
Without Resident Pastor:	
Administered by Priests	75
Administered by Permanent Deacons	3
Administered by Women Religious	4
Missions	2
Pastoral Centers	1
Professional Ministry Personnel:	
Brothers	1
Sisters	62
Lay Ministers	436
Welfare	
Catholic Hospitals	6
Total Assisted	781,597
Health Care Centers	3
Total Assisted	391
Homes for the Aged	5
Total Assisted	399
Day Care and Extended Day Care Centers	1
Total Assisted	61
Educational	
Seminaries, Diocesan	1
Students from This Diocese	9
Students from Other Diocese	3
Diocesan Students in Other Seminaries	13
Seminaries, Religious	1
Students Religious	115
Total Seminarians	137
Colleges and Universities	3
Total Students	4,198
High Schools, Diocesan and Parish	8
Total Students	3,189
Elementary Schools, Diocesan and Parish	54
Total Students	12,447
Catechesis/Religious Education:	
High School Students	7,058
Elementary Students	16,726
Total Students Under Catholic Instruction	43,755
Teachers in the Diocese:	
Priests	10
Brothers	1
Sisters	44
Lay Teachers	1,015
Vital Statistics	
Receptions into the Church:	
Infant Baptism Totals	3,564
Adult Baptism Totals	158
Received into Full Communion	405
First Communions	3,639
Confirmations	3,127
Marriages:	
Catholic	1,065
Interfaith	705
Total Marriages	1,770
Deaths	2,151
Total Catholic Population	206,199
Total Population	923,000

Former Bishops—Most Rev. MATHIAS LORAS, D.D., cons. Dec. 10, 1837; died Feb. 19, 1858.—Most Rev. CLEMENT SMYTH, O.C.S.O., D.D., cons. May 3, 1857; died Sept. 22, 1865.—Most Rev. JOHN HENNESSY, D.D.,First Archbishop, cons. Sept. 30, 1866 raised to the Archiepiscopal Dignity, June 15, 1893; died March 4, 1900.—Most Rev. JOHN J. KEANE, D.D., cons. Bishop of Richmond, Aug. 25, 1878; transferred to the Titular See of Jasso, Aug. 12, 1888; elevated to the Archiepiscopal Dignity with the title of Archbishop of Damascus, Jan. 9, 1897; transferred to the See of Dubuque, July 24, 1900; resigned April 3, 1911; appt. Titular Archbishop of Cios, April 28, 1911; died June 22, 1918.—Most Rev. JAMES JOHN KEANE, D.D., ord. Dec. 23, 1882; cons. Bishop of Cheyenne, Oct. 28, 1902; elevated to the Archiepiscopal Dignity and transferred to Dubuque, Aug. 1, 1911; died Aug. 2, 1929.—Most Rev. FRANCIS J. L. BECKMAN, S.T.D., Titular Archbishop of Phulli; ord. June 20, 1902; appt. Bishop of Lincoln, Dec. 23, 1923; cons. Bishop of Lincoln, May 1, 1924 Apostolic Administrator of Omaha, June 1, 1926 to July 4, 1928; elevated to Archiepiscopal Dignity and transferred to Dubuque, Jan. 17, 1930; appt. Assistant at the Pontifical Throne, April 21, 1928; resigned Nov. 11, 1946; died Oct. 17, 1948.—Most Rev. HENRY P. ROHLMAN, D.D., appt. Bishop of Davenport, May 20, 1927; cons. July 25, 1927; appt. Coadjutor Archbishop of Dubuque "cum jure successionis" and Apostolic Administrator, June 15, 1944; installed Sept. 12, 1944; succeeded to Nov. 11, 1946; named Assistant at Pontifical Throne, Sept. 2, 1950; resigned and named Titular Archbishop of Cotrada, Dec. 2, 1954; died Sept. 13, 1957.—Most Rev. LEO BINZ, D.D., ord. March 15, 1924; appt. Titular Bishop of Pinara, Coadjutor Bishop and Apostolic Administrator of Winona, Nov. 21, 1942; cons. Dec. 21, 1942; named Titular Archbishop of Silyum and Coadjutor to the Archbishop of Dubuque "cum jure successionis," Oct. 15, 1949; named Assistant at the Pontifical Throne, June 11, 1954 Archbishop of Dubuque, Dec. 2, 1954; Pallium conferred, June 12, 1958; appt. Archbishop of St. Paul, Dec. 16, 1961; retired July, 1975; died Oct. 9, 1979.—Most Rev. JAMES J. BYRNE, S.T.D., appt. Titular Bishop of Etenna and Auxiliary Bishop of St. Paul, May 10, 1947; ord. Bishop, July 2, 1947; transferred Boise, ID, June 16, 1956; appt. Archbishop of Dubuque, March 19, 1962; retired Aug. 23, 1983; named Apostolic Administrator; died Aug. 2, 1996.—Most Rev. DANIEL KUCERA, O.S.B., Ph.D., D.D., ord. March 26, 1949; appt. Titular Bishop of Natchez and Auxiliary Bishop of Joliet, June 6, 1977; ord. Bishop, July 21, 1977; appt. Bishop of Salina, KS, March 11, 1980; installed May 7, 1980; named Archbishop of Dubuque, Dec. 20, 1983; installed Feb. 23, 1984; retired Oct. 16, 1995.

Archbishop—Most Rev. JEROME HANUS, O.S.B., *Archdiocesan Center, 1229 Mt. Loretta Ave., P.O. Box 479, Dubuque, 52004-0479.* Tel: 319-556-2580.

Vicar General and Episcopal Vicar for Dubuque Region—Rev. Msgr. DAVID A. WHEELER, J.C.D., *Archdiocesan*

Center, 1229 Mt. Loretta Ave., P.O. Box 479, Dubuque, 52004-0479. Tel: 319-556-2580.

Episcopal Vicar for Cedar Rapids Region—Rev. Msgr. JAMES O. BARTA, Ph.D., *P.O. Box 8293, Cedar Rapids, 52408-8293.* Tel: 319-366-1647.

Episcopal Vicar for Waterloo Region—Rev. Msgr. W. DEAN WALZ, J.C.L., *320 Mulberry St., Waterloo, 50703.* Tel: 319-235-5566.

Judicial Vicar—Rev. JOSEPH L. HAUER, J.C.L., *Archdiocesan Center, 1229 Mt. Loretta Ave., P.O. Box 479, Dubuque, 52004-0479.* Tel: 319-556-2580.

Chancellor—Rev. JOSEPH L. HAUER, J.C.L., *Archdiocesan Center, 1229 Mt. Loretta Ave., P.O. Box 479, Dubuque, 52004-0479.* Tel: 319-556-2580.

Finance Officer—RICHARD L. RUNDE, *Archdiocesan Center, 1229 Mt. Loretta Ave., P.O. Box 479, Dubuque, 52004-0479.* Tel: 319-556-2580.

College of Consultors—Most Rev. JEROME HANUS, O.S.B.; Rev. Msgr. W. DEAN WALZ; Rev. Msgr. DAVID A. WHEELER; Rev. Msgr. JAMES O. BARTA; Rev. Msgr. JOSEPH J. SLEPICKA; Rev. DONALD L. KLEIN; Rev. Msgr. WALTER L. BRUNKAN.

Deans—Bellevue: Very Rev. DENNIS R. CAIN; Cedar Rapids: Very Rev. CHARLES E. LANG; Charles City: Rev. Msgr. STANLEY J. HAYEK; Decorah: Very Rev. GARY F. KRAPFL; Dubuque: Very Rev. DANIEL A. KRAPFL; Dyersville: Rev. Msgr. NEIL W. TOBIN; Elkader: Very Rev. FREDERICK C. FANGMANN; Independence: Very Rev. RALPH P. SIMINGTON; Marshalltown: Very Rev. EVERETT HEMANN; Mason City: Rev. Msgr. JOSEPH J. SLEPICKA; New Hampton: Very Rev. CARL L. SCHMITT; Waterloo: Very Rev. DONALD J. HAWES; Webster City: Very Rev. GERALD A. CONDON; Loras College: Rev. Msgr. ROBERT R. VOGL.

Archdiocesan Central Offices

Archdiocesan Pastoral Center—Mailing Address: P.O. Box 479, Dubuque, 52004-0479. 1229 Mt. Loretta Ave., Dubuque, 52003-7800. Tel: 319-556-2580; Fax: 319-556-5464. Office Hours: Mon.-Fri. 8:30-4:30; Most Rev. JEROME HANUS, O.S.B.; BETTY SCHUELLER, Sec.; Rev. Msgr. DAVID A. WHEELER, Vicar Gen. LU LECONTE, Sec.; Rev. JOSEPH L. HAUER, Chancellor; BEV RECH, Sec.; Rev. THOMAS E. TOALE, Moderator of the Curia; PHYLLIS BERTHEL, Sec.

Adult Catechesis/Evangelization—Archdiocesan Center, 1229 Mt. Loretta Ave, P.O. Box 479, Dubuque, 52004-0479. Tel: 319-556-2580. Sr. MARY DIDIER, O.S.F., Dir. GINNY NEUWOHNER, Sec.

Archives—Rev. LORAS OTTING, Dir.; Rev. Msgr. EDGAR J. KURT, Archivist Emeritus; LINDA MATHEWSON, Sec.

Archdiocesan Educational System—

Office of Educational Services—Rev. THOMAS E. TOALE, Ph.D., Dir., *Archdiocesan Center, 1229 Mt. Loretta Ave., Dubuque, 52003-7800.* Tel: 319-556-2580.

Superintendent of Schools—Rev. THOMAS E. TOALE, Ph.D.

Office Secretary—PHYLLIS BERTHEL.

Administrative Assistant—Sr. NONA MEYERHOFER, O.S.F., M.Ed.

Curriculum Coordinator—JOAN MANTERNACH.

Director of Educational Planning and Technology—JAMES OSTERBERGER, M.A.

Secondary Coordinator—CHERYL CASEY, M.A.

Regional Directors of Educational Services—Sr. JEAN MARIE BRADY, B.V.M., M.Ed.; LORETTA RYAN, M.A.

Director of Catechetical Services—Sr. JOAN MEYER, O.S.F.

Office Secretary—Sr. MILDRED STREIF, R.S.M.

Associate Director—THERESA HARVEY.

Regional Consultants—THERESA HARVEY, Dubuque Region; JULIE JOHNSON, Cedar Rapids Region; PAM JOHNSTON, Waterloo Region; Sr. MARGARET ANNE KRAMER P.B.V.M., Northeast Region.

Associate Director of Catechetical Services/Coordinator of Special Services—Sr. MARCI BLUM, O.S.F.

Dubuque Metropolitan System of Catholic Education—CHERYL CASEY, M.A., Assoc. Dir., *2005 Kane St., Dubuque, 52001.* Tel: 319-582-5456.

Cedar Rapids Metropolitan System of Catholic Education—Sr. JEAN MARIE BRADY, B.V.M., Assoc. Dir., *516 A Ave., N.W., P.O. Box 8293, Cedar Rapids, 52408.* Tel: 319-366-2517.

Cedar Valley Catholic Education System—LORETTA RYAN, Assoc. Dir., *123 E. Parker St., Waterloo, 50703.* Tel: 319-232-1422.

Boy Scouts—Rev. LYLE L. WILGENBUSCH, Archdiocesan Chap. & Spiritual Dir., *St. Joseph the Worker, 60 S. Algona St., Dubuque, 52001.* Tel: 319-588-1433.

Campaign for Human Development—JAMES L. YEAST, Dir., *1229 Mt. Loretta Ave., P.O. Box 1309, Dubuque, 52004-1309.* Tel: 319-556-2580; 588-0558. KEN RAHE, Admin. Asst.

Campus Ministry—Rev. JOHN S. HAUGEN, Dir., *St. Stephen the Witness Catholic Student Center, 1019 W. 23rd St., Cedar Falls, 50613.* Tel: 319-266-9863; Fax: 319-266-3706.

Catholic Cemeteries of the Archdiocese of Dubuque—RICHARD L. RUNDE, Dir., Finance Office: *1229 Mt. Loretta Ave., Dubuque, 52003-7800.* Tel: 319-556-2580.

Catholic Charities—

Administrative Offices—JAMES L. YEAST, A.C.S.W., Dir. JUDE PANSINI, Housing Admin. JOE FEATHERSTON, M.A., Dir., Professional Svcs. KEN RAHE, Admin. Asst. Office Secs.: MARTHA DEVEAUX; SUE HIRD; CAROL CALLAHAN, Business Office: *1229 Mt. Loretta Ave., P.O. Box 1309, Dubuque, 52004-1309.* Tel: 319-556-2580.

Branch Offices—

Dubuque—JOSEPH FEATHERSTON, Supvr. JOYCE CONNORS; TOM SHEA; ANGELLA LINK, *P.O. Box 1309, Dubuque, 52004-1309.* Tel: 319-556-2580.

Decorah—DONALD KLAUKE, *P.O. Box 1309, Dubuque, 52004-1309.* Tel: 800-772-2758.

Cedar Rapids—GARY STEJSKAL, Supvr. KIM MARTENSEN; LYN PIOTROWSKI, Sec., *1430 Second Ave. S.E., Cedar Rapids, 52403.* Tel: 319-364-7121.

Ames—JULIA PETERS, *208 Fifth St., Ames, 50010.* Tel: 515-232-7421.

Waterloo—THOMAS FLAHERTY, Supvr. ORLYN WATHIER; Rev. KENNETH STECHER; MICHELLE SPRIO, Sec., *Kimball Ridge Center, 2101 Kimball Ave., Ste. LL-11, Waterloo, 50702.* Tel: 319-292-2453.

Mason City—THOMAS FLAHERTY, *Will F. Muse Center, 600 First St. N.W., Mason City, 50401.* Tel: 515-424-9683.

Special Programs—

Adoption—NANCY KINLEY, Dubuque Office.

Family Ministry—CHARLOTTE MCCOY, Coord. Tel: 319-556-2580.

Refugee Resettlement—JOE FEATHERSTON, Dubuque Office.

Social Concerns/Parish-Based Social Service—JAMES L. YEAST, Dubuque Office *Catholic Charities may be telephoned toll-free from anyplace in Iowa: 1-800-772-2758.*

Communications Coordinator—Sr. CAROL HOVERMAN, O.S.F., *Archdiocesan Center, 1229 Mt. Loretta Ave., Dubuque, 52003-7800.* Tel: 319-556-2580. PEG HENNAGIR, Sec.

Continuing Formation of Clergy and Young Priests Program—Rev. JOSEPH L. HAUER, Dir., *Archdiocesan Center, 1229 Mt. Loretta Ave., Dubuque, 52003-7800.* Tel: 319-556-2580. BEV RECH, Sec.

Council of Catholic Women—Rev. Msgr. W. DEAN WALZ, Moderator; MARY ANN SPITLER, Exec. Pres., *2698 143rd St., Belmond, 50421.* Tel: 515-444-3174., Office: *Archdiocesan Center, 1229 Mt. Loretta Ave., Dubuque, 52003.* Tel: 319-556-2580. Bellevue Deanery: HELEN ZEIMET, Springbrook. Tel: 319-689-4466. Cedar Rapids Deanery: HELEN HANSON, Cedar Rapids. Tel: 319-393-8105. Charles City Deanery: PHYLLIS LEAVENS, Charles City. Tel: 515-435-2353. Decorah Deanery: HELEN PINTER, Fort Atkinson. Tel: 319-534-7489. Dubuque Deanery: RITA WHALEN, Dubuque. Tel: 319-582-0203. Dyersville Deanery: JANAAN KRAUS, Monticello. Tel: 319-465-4699. Elkader Deanery: NEVA FISCHER, Strawberry Point. Tel: 319-933-4957. Independence Deanery: MARY ANN JAEGER, Manchester. Tel: 319-927-4049. Marshalltown Deanery: MARY ANN HUSAK, Toledo. Tel: 515-484-2159. Mason City Deanery: PHYLLIS PEDERSON, Lake Mills. Tel: 515-592-5182. New Hampton Deanery: BETTY HUMPAL, Sumner. Tel: 319-578-5357. Waterloo Deanery: KAREN ROTTINGHAUS, LaPorte City. Tel: 319-342-2694. Webster City Deanery: CHRISTINA BALDUS, Jewell. Tel: 515-827-5376.

Education Resource Center—MARY MESCHER, Dir., *1229 Mt. Loretta Ave., Dubuque, 52003-7800.* Tel: 319-556-2580; 800-876-3546. Media Clerks: JUDY MCCARTHY; CONNIE MCDERMOTT.

Educational Development Office—PAUL FROMMELT, Dir., *P.O. Box 479, Dubuque, 52004-0479.* Tel: 319-556-2580. NANCY TRUMM, Sec.

Family Life Office—Rev. MELVIN D. HEMANN, Dir. GINNY NEUWOHNER, Office Sec., *Archdiocesan Center, 1229 Mt. Loretta Ave., Dubuque, 52003-7800.* Tel: 319-556-2580.

Engaged Encounter—Coords.: JUDY BECK; PAUL BECK, *2485 Maryville Dr., Dubuque, 52001.* Tel: 319-556-1438. BARB LUDESCHER; JACK LUDESCHER, *2780 Andrew Ct., Dubuque, 52001.* Tel: 319-583-7039. Rev. PHIL SCHMITT, Spiritual Advisor, *St. Mark, 415 Main St., Iowa Falls.* Tel: 515-648-9547.

For Registration—Family Life Office, 1229 Mt. Loretta Ave., Dubuque, 52003-7800. Tel: 319-556-2580.

Marriage Encounter—Family Life Office, 1229 Mt. Loretta Ave., Dubuque, 52003-7800. Tel: 319-556-2580.

Marriage Retorno—Dirs.: Deacon MICHAEL OATES; MAUREEN OATES, *127 Kaspend Pl., Cedar Falls, 50613.* Tel: 319-268-0202.

Natural Family Planning—COREY WESTHOFF; MICHELLE WESTHOFF, *R.R. 2, Box 63, Dyersville, 52040.* Tel: 319-875-8363.

NEET Experience—GINNY WEBER, *3477 Kingswood Pl., Waterloo, 50701.* Tel: 319-235-1247.

Pre-Cana—Family Life Office, 1229 Mt. Loretta Ave., Dubuque, 52003-7800. Tel: 319-556-2580. AREA I: Dubuque Deanery, JOHN MAUSS; MARYLOU MAUSS, *1515 Auburn St., Dubuque, 52001.* Tel: 319-588-2143. AREA II: Dyersville Deanery, Dirs.: JERRY BECKER; CATHY BECKER, *P.O. Box 91, Earlville, 52041.* Tel: 319-875-8656. AREA III: Elkader, New Hampton, Decorah Deaneries, KRIS CROATT, Dir., *306 E. Main St., Ossian, 52161.* Tel: 319-532-9618. AREA IV: Independence & Waterloo Deaneries, Dirs.: MIKE BLAD; JANET BLAD, *205 Toneff Dr., Elk Run Hts., 50707.* Tel: 319-234-2748. AREA V: Cedar Rapids Deanery, Dirs.: PAT MURPHY; SANDY MURPHY, *1130 33rd St. S.E., Cedar Rapids, 52403.* Tel: 319-365-9839. AREA VI: Ames & Marshalltown Deaneries, Co-Dirs.: JAMES AMFAHR; JUDITH AMFAHR, *623 Agg Ave., Ames, 50014.* Tel: 515-292-4433. AREA VII: Charles City & Mason City Deaneries, Dirs.: CHUCK COOPER; JENNY COOPER, *710 N. Adams, Mason City, 50401.* Tel: 515-424-6251.

Retrouvaille—Contacts: STEVE LAWSON; MARY LAWSON, *424 Ardmore, Waterloo, 50701.* Tel: 319-232-8475. DICK SMITH; JOYCE SMITH, *420 10th Ave., S.E., Dyersville, 52040.* Tel: 319-875-8791.

Sponsor Couple—Family Life Office, 1229 Mt. Loretta Ave., Dubuque, 52003-7800. Tel: 319-556-2580.

To Trust Again—DAVID STER; ELIZABETH STER, *2509 Falbrook Dr. N.W., Cedar Rapids, 52402.* Tel: 319-393-9432.

Finance Office—RICHARD L. RUNDE, Finance Officer; JULIE KNIPPER, Controller; EDWARD HABERKORN, Financial Svcs. Clerk; JANICE TUEGEL, Accounting Clerk; MARY FLECKENSTEIN, Bookkeeper/Sec., *P.O. Box 479, Dubuque, 52004-0479.* Tel: 319-556-2580.

Health Care—JANINE MARIE IDZIAK, Ph.D., Consultant, *P.O. Box 479, Dubuque, 52004-0479.* Tel: 319-556-2580. MARTHA DEVEAUX, Sec.

Hispanic Ministry—Marshalltown: Rev. LLOYD PAUL OUDERKIRK; Sr. ANNE MARIE MANTERNACH, O.S.F., *12 W. Linn, Marshalltown, 50158.* Tel: 515-753-7815. Waterloo: Sr. KATHLEEN GRACE, O.S.F., *329 Mulberry St., Waterloo, 50703.* Tel: 319-234-6744. Sacramental Services provided by Rev. Mark McGovern, 319-635-2211.

Holy Childhood, Pontifical Association—ROBERT L. FERRING, Dir., *Archdiocesan Center, 1229 Mt. Loretta Ave., Dubuque, 52003-7800.* Tel: 319-556-2580. NANCY EISBACH, Sec.

Insurance: Property and Liability (Dubuque Archdiocesan Protection Program)—DAVID ROTH, Field Rep., *Archdiocesan Center, 1229 Mt. Loretta Ave., Dubuque, 52003-7800.* Tel: 319-556-2580. PATSY BURKEN, Sec.

Lay Ministry Formation & Young Adult—Sr. CARLA POPES, P.B.V.M., Dir. CAROL RAUSCH, Sec., *Archdiocesan Center, 1229 Mt. Loretta Ave., P.O. Box 479, Dubuque, 52004-0479.* Tel: 319-556-2580.

Legion of Mary—Rev. JOHN HUSSMANN, *P.O. Box 479, Dubuque, 52004-0479.* Tel: 319-556-2580.

Metropolitan Tribunal—P.O. Box 479, Dubuque, 52004-0479. Tel: 319-556-2580. (Please send all dispensation requests to the Tribunal.).

Judicial Vicar—Rev. JOSEPH L. HAUER, J.C.L.

Director of the Metropolitan Tribunal—Sr. FRANCINE QUILLIN, P.B.V.M., J.C.L.; CHARLOTTE NEISES, Asst. to the Dir. and Notary.

Defenders of the Bond—Rev. DONALD J. PLAMONDON, J.C.L.; Rev. Msgr. DAVID A. WHEELER, J.C.D.

Auditors—Deacons GERALD JORGENSEN, Ph.D.; TIMOTHY LOBIANCO.

Judges—Revs. JOSEPH HAUER, J.C.L.; MARK R. NEMMERS; Rev. Msgr. ROBERT L. SPAIGHT, J.C.D.; Rev. Msgr. RICHARD P. FUNKE, J.C.L.; Rev. Msgr. W. DEAN WALZ, J.C.L.; Sr. FRANCINE QUILLEN, P.B.V.M., J.C.L.

Ecclesiastical Attorneys—Rev. Msgr. W. DEAN WALZ, J.C.L.; Rev. Msgr. RICHARD P. FUNKE, J.C.L.; Rev. MARK R. NEMMERS.

Promoter of Justice—Rev. Msgr. DAVID A. WHEELER, J.C.D.

Notary and Office Secretary—THERESA HOUSELOG.

Management Information Services—LOIS THILMANY, Co-ord. PATSY BURKEN, Sec.

Newspaper "The Witness"—Rev. Msgr. THOMAS J. RALPH, Editor, *Archdiocesan Center, 1229 Mt. Loretta Ave., P.O. Box 917, Dubuque, 52004-0917.* Tel: 319-588-0556. Sr. M. DONALDA KEHOE, O.S.F., Sec. Staff: JUDY BANDY; BRET FEAR; STEVE MCMAHON; BETTY BERRIE, Circulation.

Pastoral Planning Office—Sr. MARY MONTGOMERY, O.P., Dir. LUANN LECONTE, Sec., *P.O. Box 479, Dubuque, 52004-0479.* Tel: 319-556-2580.

Permanent Diaconate Program—Deacon LEN FROYEN, Dir. REGENA HUFFMAN, Sec., *St. Stephen the Witness Student Center, 1019 W. 23rd St., Cedar Falls, 50613.* Tel: 319-266-9863. Asst. Directors: Deacons GERALD JORGENSEN; MICHAEL OATES.

Print Shop—ROBERT GOLDTHORPE, Mgr., *P.O. Box 479, Dubuque, 52004-0479.* Tel: 319-556-2580.

Propagation of the Faith—Rev. Msgr. ROBERT L. FERRING; NANCY EISBACH, Sec., *Archdiocesan Center, 1229 Mt. Loretta Ave., Dubuque, 52003-7800.* Tel: 319-556-2580.

Respect Life Coordinator—JAMES L. YEAST, Dir., Catholic Charities; KEN RAHE, Admin. Asst., *P.O. Box 1309, Dubuque, 52004-1309.* Tel: 319-556-2580; 800-772-2758.

Rural Life Conference—DONALD KLAUKE, Archdiocesan Dir. MARY KLAUKE, Sec., *1229 Mt. Loretta Ave., P.O. Box 479, Dubuque, 52004-0479.* Tel: 319-556-2580.

St. Mary's Home, Inc.—JAMES L. YEAST, A.C.S.W., Dir. JAMES GIESEN, Admin., *1229 Mt. Loretta Ave., P.O. Box 1309, Dubuque, 52003-7800.* Tel: 319-556-2580.

Saint Raphael Priest Fund Society—Most Rev. JEROME HANUS, O.S.B., Pres.; Rev. Msgr. DAVID A. WHEELER, Vice Pres.; Rev. Msgr. JAMES O. BARTA, Sec. & Treas., *P.O. Box 8293, Cedar Rapids, 52408-8293.* Dirs.: Rev. Msgr. RICHARD P. FUNKE; Rev. Msgr. STANLEY J. HAYEK; Rev. Msgr. JOSEPH P. HERARD; Rev. Msgr. NEIL W. TOBIN; Revs. FREDERICK C. FANGMANN; JERRY KOPACEK; KARL L. GLOVIK; CHARLES W. WHALEN; THOMAS R. ZINKULA.

Seminarians—Rev. JOSEPH L. HAUER, Dir. BEV RECH, Sec., *1229 Mt. Loretta Ave., Dubuque, 52003-7800.* Tel: 319-556-2580.

Stewardship/Sacrificial Giving—Rev. Msgr. ROBERT G. HOGAN, Dir., *2310 First Ave. N.E., Cedar Rapids, 52402.* Tel: 319-363-8269.

Vocations—Rev. JOSEPH L. HAUER, Dir., Seminarians; Sr. JENNIFER RAUSCH, P.B.V.M., Dir.; Rev. DOUGLAS J. LOECKE, Assoc. Dir., Waterloo Region; Rev. JON SEDA, Assoc. Dir., Cedar Rapids Region, *Archdiocesan Center, 1229 Mt. Loretta Ave., Dubuque, 52003-7800.* Tel: 319-556-2580.

Worship Office—Rev. NEIL J. MANTERNACH, Dir., *1229 Mt. Loretta Ave., P.O. Box 479, Dubuque, 52004-0479.* Tel: 319-556-2580. HELEN ENGELKEN, Sec.

Youth Formation—JUDY ARLEN, Sec., *Archdiocesan Center, 1229 Mt. Loretta Ave., Dubuque, 52003.* Tel: 319-556-2580.

Archdiocesan Boards

Archdiocesan Administrative Board—Most Rev. JEROME HANUS, O.S.B.; Rev. Msgr. DAVID A. WHEELER; Rev. JOSEPH L. HAUER; Sr. MARY MONTGOMERY, O.P.; RICHARD L. RUNDE.

Archdiocesan Board of Education—BRIAN KANE, Pres., Dubuque Deanery; DON BERGAN, Vice Chm.; Sr. HELEN NELSON, O.S.F., Appointed Sec. Bellevue Deanery: JULIE BYBEE,Cedar Rapids Deanery: CAROL VOLK,Charles City Deanery: PAM POPELKA,Decorah Deanery: MARY HOLTHAUS,Dyersville Deanery: GLENDA NICKOL,Elkader Deanery: DIANNE FETTE,Independence Deanery: WILMA BILLHORN-,Marshalltown Deanery: MARGARET BOWMAN,Mason City Deanery: MARY KOPACEK,New Hampton Deanery: STEVEN LAURES,Waterloo Deanery: DEB BARSCHOW,Webster City Deanery: CLEONE MENAGE. Appointed by the Archbishop: MATT BRANDES; ROSA MARIA DE FINDLEY; MARTHA NASH. Priest Representative: Rev. MAURICE J. LYNCH,Priest Council Representative: Rev. DONALD P. SCHMITT. Sister Representatives: Sr. THERESE BECK, B.V.M.; Sr. HELEN NELSON, O.S.F.; Sr. FRANCESCA OLDHAM, R.S.M. Ex-Officio Members: Most Rev. JEROME HANUS, O.S.B.; Rev. Msgr. DAVID A. WHEELER; Rev. Msgr. JAMES O. BARTA; Rev. Msgr. W. DEAN WALZ; Rev. THOMAS E. TOALE; Sr. JOAN MEYER, O.S.F.; Sr. NONA MEYERHOFER, O.S.F.

Archdiocesan Building Commission—Rev. Msgr. JAMES O. BARTA, Exec. Sec. RICHARD L. RUNDE; Rev. Msgr. STANLEY HAYEK; Rev. Msgr. ROBERT G. HOGAN; Rev. Msgr. NEIL TOBIN; Rev. JOHN R. GALLAGHER; JAMES HYNES; JOHN D. KILBY; Rev. NEIL J. MANTERNACH; WAYNE SNYDER; LEO THEISEN; JAMES YOUNGBLUT.

Archdiocesan Campaign for Human Development Board of Directors—JAMES YEAST, Chm. JOANN MILLER; Rev. WILLIAM JOENSEN; HELEN SORENSEN; TOM HOMAN; RANDALL KREIG; ANN MICHALSKI; STEVE HINDMAN; Rev. Msgr. RICHARD FUNKE; COLLEEN MACFARLAND.

Archdiocesan Chemical Dependency Board—Rev. Msgr. ROBERT L. SPAIGHT, Chm.; Revs. DENNIS J. COLTER; PAUL C. MCMANUS; STEVEN J. ROSONKE; CARL L. SCHMITT.

Archdiocesan Church Design/Renovation Commission—Rev. NEIL J. MANTERNACH, Exec. Sec. PAM JOHNSTON; Rev. DENNIS D. JUHL; Rev. LYLE L. WILGENBUSCH.

Archdiocesan Continuing Formation of Clergy—Rev. JOSEPH L. HAUER, Chm.; Rev. Msgr. RUSSELL M. BLEICH; Rev. Msgr. JOSEPH P. HERARD; Revs. JAMES A. DUSTER; CARL A. RIES; GARY KRAPFL; JAMES SECORA; THOMAS E. TOALE, Ex-Officio; DAVID H. O'CONNOR, Liaison to Priests' Council.

Archdiocesan Diaconal Council—Most Rev. JEROME HANUS, O.S.B., Pres.; Deacons TIM LOBIANCO, Chm. LEN FROYEN, Ph.D., Exec. Sec.

Ames Region—Deacons JOHN MCCULLY; IRV VASKE.

Cedar Rapids Region—Deacons J. C. OTTO; ED PANTALONI.

Dubuque Region—Deacons TIM LOBIANCO; BILL BIVER.

Elkader Region—Deacon PAUL CARROLL.

Mason City Region—Deacons MATT BERRY; LEO STATTELMAN.

Waterloo Region—Deacons JOHN BAKER; JOHN HERMAN.

Appointed—Deacons DARYL FORTIN; MICHAEL OATES; MICHAEL BLOUIN, APC Liaison.

Archdiocesan Due Process Board—MIKE BLOUIN; Rev. JOHN FRIEDERICK; Sr. KATHLEEN GRACE, O.S.F.; Rev. JERRY KOPACEK; Bro. BRIAN MCLAUCHLIN, S.V.D.; JOYCE MERRITT; Sr. ELIZABETH PRESSLER, P.B.V.M.; REX REYNOLDS; LEO ROLING; JOHN WHALEN.

Archdiocesan Finance Commission—Most Rev. JEROME HANUS, O.S.B., Chm. RICHARD L. RUNDE, Exec. Sec.; Rev. THOMAS E. TOALE, Recording Sec. PAUL J. FROMMELT; Rev. Msgr. RICHARD P. FUNKE; Rev. Msgr. ROBERT G. HOGAN; ARTHUR NIXA; ANN OSTERHAUS; ROBERT VERHILLE; STEVE WEIDNER; DAN WELU.

Archdiocesan Lay Ministry Advisory Board—JOANNE DALHOFF; Deacon DARYL FORTIN; Rev. DENNIS JUHL; JANET O'MEARA; Sr. CARLA POPES, P.B.V.M.; CATHY SCHMITZ; Rev. Msgr. W. DEAN WALZ.

American Martyrs Retreat House Advisory Board—Rev. DANIEL J. KNIPPER, Dir. ROGER KEUTER, Chm. JOAN GLAZ, Sec. BETTIE FERGUSON; EDWARD J. GALLAGHER, JR.; RON LEIBOLD.

Archdiocesan Medical-Moral Commission—JANINE MARIE IDZIAK, Ph.D., Chm.; Rev. WILLIAM JOENSEN; Very Rev. DANIEL A. KRAPFL; RICHARD V. MCKAY, M.D.; GERALD ODEFEY, Ph.D.; Sr. MARY CLARE O'TOOLE, O.S.F.; Sr. DOLORES ULLRICH, O.S.F.; BETTY WEBER, R.N.; RICHARD WHITTY, J.D.

Archdiocesan Pastoral Council—Most Rev. JEROME HANUS, O.S.B., Pres. THOMAS MCGREAL, Chm. CARLOS LEDESMA, Vice Chm.; Sr. MARY MONTGOMERY O.P., Exec. Sec. MARIE THOME, Sec.; Rev. Msgr. W. DEAN WALZ; Rev. Msgr. JAMES O. BARTA; Rev. Msgr. DAVID A. WHEELER; Deacon MICHAEL BLOUIN; Bro. RODNEY BOWERS, S.V.D.; Revs. PATRICK GEARY; RICHARD MIHM; Sr. LOUANN DOERING, P.B.V.M.; Sr. SUSAN DUNNWALD, R.S.M.; Sr. NORMA JEAN HOLTHAUS, O.S.F.; TOM BOCK; JULIE BYBEE; PATRICIA HAMILTON; CHARLES MAZUR; Sr. PATRICIA MCNAMARA, B.V.M.; RICHARD REDING; PHYLLIS REITER; RON SMITH; DICK PITZENBERGER; JON MUNKEL; PEGGY SWIFT; JOYCE MERRITT.

Archdiocesan Personnel Advisory Board—Revs. JOSEPH V. O'BRIEN, Chm. JAMES L. MILLER, Sec.; Rev. Msgr. RUSSELL M. BLEICH; Revs. JAMES E. HAYES; WAYNE RESSLER.

Archdiocesan Permanent Diaconate Formation Board—Deacon LEN FROYEN, Chm.; Deacons IRV FROST; GERALD JORGEN; MAUREEN OATES; MARY JENNEY; Rev. JOHN S. HAUGEN.

Archdiocesan Church Vocation Board (APVB)—Sr. JENNIFER RAUSCH, P.B.V.M; WILMA BILLHORN; MARY CLEMEN; JOE FEATHERSTON; BETTY HUMPAL; LEROY WESTEMEIER; CLETUS SCHMIT; CATHERINE QUINT.

Archdiocesan Priests' Council—Most Rev. JEROME HANUS, O.S.B., Pres.; Rev. JAMES DUSTER, Chm. Episcopal Vicars: Rev. Msgr. DAVID A. WHEELER; Rev. Msgr. W. DEAN WALZ; Rev. Msgr. JAMES O. BARTA.

Appointed—Rev. Msgr. JOSEPH SLEPICKA; Revs. DONALD BRUGGEMAN; DONALD L. KLEIN.

Age Group Representatives—Age Group 1- Rev. Msgr. ROBERT R. VOGL,Age Group 2- Rev. HERBERT L. TEGELER,Age Group 3- Rev. Msgr. WALTER L. BRUNKAN,Age Group 4- Rev. RICHARD J. AMENT,Age Group 5- Rev. MARK OSTERHAUS.

Religious Priests Representative—Rev. PAUL CONNORS, S.V.D.

Deanery Representatives—Bellevue Deanery: Rev. DAVID O'CONNOR, Cedar Rapids Deanery: Rev. JAMES J. DUSTER, Charles City Deanery: Rev. JOHN A. MOSER, Decorah Deanery: Rev. HENRY W. CHARIPAR, Dubuque Deanery: Rev. LYLE L. WILGENBUSCH, Dyersville Deanery: Rev. LOUIS M. JAEGER, Elkader Deanery: Rev. RICHARD G. GAUL, Independence Deanery: Rev. ALOYSIUS J. VORWALD, Loras College Deanery: Rev. DOUGLAS O. WATHIER, Marshalltown Deanery: Rev. RONALD G. FRIEDELL, Mason City Deanery: Rev. STEPHEN L. MEYER, New Hampton Deanery: Rev. MARVIN C. SALZ, Waterloo Deanery: Rev. DONALD P. SCHMITT, Webster City Deanery: Rev. WAYNE J. DROESSLER. Consultors Ex-Officio: Rev. Msgr. WALTER BRUNKAN; Rev. DONALD KLEIN; Rev. Msgr. JOSEPH SLEPICKA.

Archdiocesan Seminary Board—Rev. JOSEPH L. HAUER, Chm.; Revs. JOHN GOSSMAN; DOUGLAS J. LOECKE; JON M. SEDA; LYLE WILGENBUSCH; Sr. JENNIFER RAUSCH, P.B.V.M.; Rev. DENNIS J. COLTER, Ex-Officio.

Archdiocesan Worship Commission—Rev. NEIL MANTERNACH, Exec. Sec.; Sr. KATE HENDEL, B.V.M., Chm. BOB BURKE, Vice Chm.; Revs. ROBERT R. BECK; JAMES J. DUSTER; EVERETT HEMANN; DANIEL J. KNEPPER; Deacon TIM LOBIANCO; LORRAINE LOECHER, O.S.F.; MICHAEL KELLOGG; MARY BETH SIEMANN; TERRY SLADE; Sr. MARJORIE STAUDT, O.S.F.

Archdiocesan Young Adult Advisory Board—BOB BURKE; KRIS EGAN; Rev. PHILLIP GIBBS; STEVE HILL; Rev. LOUIS JAEGER; CHARLOTTE MCCOY; DIANNE MCDERMOTT; CHRIS MILLER; JULIE MODDE; JOHN MOSHER; Sr. CARLA POPES, P.B.V.M.; MARCIA REILLY; SUE SCHLADER.

Archdiocesan Youth Commission—SHARON BAINBRIDGE, Chm. DAN STERENCHUK, Vice Chm. Adult Members: D'LYNN BUCK; JOYCE CONNORS; BRENDA DUSTER; DIANE FLAHERTY; THERESA HARVEY; Rev. CLAYTON LANDHERR; JOAN LEONARD; GENE MEALHOW; LYNN MEALHOW; Rev. RICHARD J. MIHM; JOHN MOSHER; SUE SCHLADER; KIM VOGEL. Youth Members: MATT FELDMAN; BRIDGET HARTZ; CHRIS LESTER; KATIE MACKEY; LIZ NICHOLS; CARA MOOTHART; KELLY PLEIN; CHAD SCHAWL; AMBER THIBODEAUX; DENISE WHITE; PETER YURKO.

Catholic Charities and St. Mary's Home Boards of Directors—Most Rev. JEROME HANUS, O.S.B., Pres.; Rev. Msgr. DAVID A. WHEELER, Vice Pres. JAMES YEAST, Treas. ALFRED HUGHES, Sec. JUDY BOWLING; ROBERT BRUNKAN; JAMES CAMPBELL; JEFFREY FITZPATRICK; FRITZ GANSHIRT; ELDON HERRIG; MICHAEL HOUSER; CONNIE MAHONEY; Deacon JOHN MCCULLY; LAWRENCE MCGRATH; LARRY MURPHY; CLEM SCHEMMEL; MARGARET SCHMOLKE-FANGMAN; ANNETTE SIMONSON.

CLERGY, PARISHES, MISSIONS AND PAROCHIAL SCHOOLS

CITY OF DUBUQUE
(Dubuque County)

1—ST. RAPHAEL'S CATHEDRAL (1833), Rev. Joseph V. O'Brien, Rector; Barbara Gatch, Pastoral Assoc.; Sr. Ruth Jackson, S.V.M., Music Dir. & Liturgist; Sr. Eileen Bergen, B.V.M., Health Ministry. In res., Rev. James E. Hayes.
Res., 231 Bluff St., 52001-6999. Tel: 319-582-7646. [JC]
Catechesis/Religious Programs—Barbara Gatch, D.R.E.
Students 82.

2—ST. ANTHONY'S (1867), Rev. Eugene C. Kutsch. Pastoral Assocs.: Sr. Anne Sedgwick, O.S.F.; Sr. Barbara Rastatter, P.B.V.M.; Deacon William Mauss. Res., 1870 St. Ambrose St., 52001-4196. Tel: 319-588-0571. [JC]
School—Tel: 319-556-2820. Lori Hermsen, Prin.
Lay Teachers 22; Students 420.
Catechesis/Religious Programs—Carol A. Witry, D.R.E.
Students 250.

3—ST. COLUMBKILLE'S (1887), Rev. Msgr. Richard P. Funke; Deacon William Biver; Diane Kramer, Pastoral Assoc.
Res., 1240 Rush St., 52003-7598. Tel: 319-583-9117. [JC]
School—Kate Kleeman, Prin. (Elementary). Sisters 1; Lay Teachers 18; Students 373.
Catechesis/Religious Programs—Linda Frommelt, D.R.E.
Students 108.

4—ST. MARY'S (1850), Rev. Florian J. Schmidt. In res., Revs. Wilfred W. Schmidt; Maurice J. Lynch.
Res., 1584 White St., 52001. Tel: 319-582-5469. [JC]
School—St. Mary-St. Patrick Consolidated. See separate listing under Institutions Located in the Archdiocese for details.
Catechesis/Religious Programs—Patti Steuer, D.R.E.
Students 82.

5—ST. PATRICK'S (1862), Very Rev. Daniel A. Krapfl; Rev. Richard L. Schaeffer; Deacon Leo Brustkern, Pastoral Admin.; Sr. Rita Clare McDonald, B.V.M., Pastoral Assoc.
Res., 1425 Iowa St., 52001-4890. Tel: 319-583-9749. [JC]
School—St. Mary-St. Patrick Consolidated. See separate listing under Institutions Located in the Archdiocese for details.
Catechesis/Religious Programs—Patti Steuer, D.R.E.
Students 18.

6—CHURCH OF THE RESURRECTION (1857), Rev. Msgr. Joseph P. Herard; Rev. Clayton R. Landherr; Sr.

Eileen Brynda, O.P., Pastoral Assoc.; Deacon Gerald Jorgensen.
Res., 4300 Asbury Rd., 52002-0414. Tel: 319-556-7511. [CEM]
School—Sr. Mary Elizabeth Presseler, P.B.V.M., Prin. Sisters of the Presentation 3; Lay Teachers 22; Students 518.
Catechesis/Religious Programs—Marilyn Kraus, D.R.E.
Students 379.

7—SACRED HEART (1879), Rev. James T. Chappell.
Res., 2215 Windsor Ave., 52001-1698. Tel: 319-583-1709. [JC]
School—Holy Trinity-Sacred Heart Consolidated. See separate listing under Institutions Located in the Archdiocese for details.
Catechesis/Religious Programs—Sr. Mary Kivlahan, O.S.F., D.R.E.
Students 65.

8—HOLY GHOST (1896), Revs. Paul J. Jotting; Ray E. Atwood; Sr. Susan Ivis, O.S.F., Pastoral Min.
Res., 2917 Central Ave., 52001-1999. Tel: 319-582-5443. [JC]
School—Carol Streif, Prin. Priests 1; Sisters of St. Francis of the Holy Family 1; Lay Teachers 22; Students 408.
Catechesis/Religious Programs—Joseph N. White, D.R.E.
Students 110.

9—HOLY TRINITY (1910), Very Rev. Daniel A. Krapfl.
Res., 1700 Lincoln Ave., 52001-2104. Tel: 319-556-0733. [JC]
School—Holy Trinity-Sacred Heart Consolidated. See separate listing under Institutions Located in the Archdiocese for details.
Catechesis/Religious Programs—Sr. Mary Kivlahan O.S.F., D.R.E.
Students 51.

10—NATIVITY (1923), Rev. Wayne A. Ressler; Deacon David McGhee.
Office: 1225 Alta Vista St., 52001-4398. Tel: 319-582-1839. [JC]
Res., 1075 University, 52001. Tel: 319-582-1714.
School—Tel: 319-582-7236. Lynn Devaney, Prin. Sisters 1; Lay Teachers 21; Students 403.
Catechesis/Religious Programs—Sr. Nancy Miller, O.S.F., D.R.E.
Students 117.

11—ST. JOSEPH THE WORKER (1949), Revs. Lyle L. Wilgenbusch; David J. Ambrosy; Deacons Timothy LoBianco; Stephen MacDonald.
Res., 90 S. Algona St., 52001-5605. Tel: 319-588-2934. [JC]
60 S. Algona, 52001-5605. Tel: 319-588-1433.
School—Tel: 319-588-4194. Steven P. Cornelius, Prin.
Lay Teachers 23; Students 460.
Catechesis/Religious Programs—Sr. Kathleen Long, O.P., D.R.E.
Students 238.

OUTSIDE THE CITY OF DUBUQUE

Ackley, Franklin Co., St. Mary's (1891), Rev. Rick D. Dagit.
Res., 614 N. Washington St., Eldora, 50627-1257. Tel: 515-858-5666. [CEM]
Catechesis/Religious Programs—Luella Scallon, D.R.E.
Students 92.

Allison, Butler Co., Immaculate Conception. Closed. For inquiries for parish records contact St. Mary's, Greene.

Alta Vista, Chickasaw Co., St. Bernard (1897), Rev. Roger R. Rethamel.
Res., 203 Seventh St., P.O. Box 38, Elma, 50628-0038. Tel: 515-393-2520. [CEM]
Church—114 E. Washington.
Catechesis/Religious Programs—Irene Huegel, D.R.E.
Students 60.

Ames, Story Co., St. Cecilia (1899), Revs. Terrence Rasmussen, O.F.M.Conv.; John Elmer, O.F.M.Conv.; Bro. Randy Kin, O.F.M.Conv., Pastoral Assoc.; Deacons Gary Aitchison; John McCully; Kenneth Simmons; Richard Tondra.
Res., 2900 Hoover Ave., 50010-4498. Tel: 515-233-3092; Fax: 515-233-6423.
School—Tel: 515-232-5290. Loretta Tracy, Prin. Lay Teachers 6; Students 173.
Catechesis/Religious Programs—Tel: 515-232-5290. JoAnne G. Dalhoff, D.R.E.
Students 517.

St. Thomas Aquinas Church (and Catholic Student Center) (1947), Revs. Everett Hemann; Jon M. Seda; Deacon Steve VanKerckvoorde. Campus Ministry: Mr. John Donaghy; Crystal Caruana. In res., Rev. Msgr. James Supple, (Retired).
Res., 2210 Lincoln Ave., 50014. Tel: 515-292-3810.
Catechesis/Religious Programs—Ernest Bayer, D.R.E.
Students 238.

Anamosa, Jones Co., St. Patrick's (1861), Very Rev. Charles E. Lang; Rev. Michael L. Tauke, Sacramental Min.; Regina Bonifazi, Pastoral Assoc.; Sr. Patricia McNamara, B.V.M., Pastoral Admin.
Res., 215 N. Garnavillo St., 52205-1122. Tel: 319-462-2141. [CEM]
School—Tel: 319-462-2688. Linda Vaughn, Prin. & D.R.E.
Lay Teachers 8; Students 98.
Catechesis/Religious Programs—Students 129.
Oratory—Stone City, St. Joseph.

Andrew, Jackson Co., St. John (1914), Rev. Michael L. Tauke.
Res. and Mailing—St. John Rectory, 507 Elm St., P.O. Box 26, Lamonte, 52054-0026. Tel: 319-773-2323.
Church—204 Main St.
Catechesis/Religious Programs—D.R.E.: Phyllis Gerlach; Tammy Sommers.
Students 90.

Balltown, Dubuque Co., St. Francis of Assisi (1891), Rev. Melvin D. Hemann; Sr. Mildred Leuenberger, O.S.F., Pastoral Admin.
Res. and Mailing Address—5131 Sherrill Rd., Sherrill, 52073-9612. Tel: 319-552-2611.
Church—468 Balltown Rd.
School—Balltown-Sherrill Consolidated School. See separate listing under Institutions Located in the Archdiocese for details.
Catechesis/Religious Programs—Mary Anne Manternach, D.R.E.
Students 29.

Bankston, Dubuque Co., St. Clement's (1859), Rev. Linus E. Rasing.
Res., 24287 New Vienna Rd., Epworth, 52045-9801. Tel: 319-744-3314. [CEM]
School—Seton Catholic Elementary School, Epworth. See separate listing under Institutions Located in the Archdiocese for details.
Catechesis/Religious Programs—Betty Puis, D.R.E.
Students 72.

Barclay, Blackhawk Co., St. Francis (1862), Rev. Donald P. Schmitt.
Res., 7837 E. Airline Hwy., Dunkerton, 50626-9715. Tel: 319-822-4614. [CEM]
Catechesis/Religious Programs—D.R.E.: Margaret Miller; Debra Thurman.
Students 97.

Belle Plaine, Benton Co., St. Michael (1885), Very Rev. Charles Lang; Rev. Steven G. O'Brien; Deacon J.C. Otto, Pastoral Admin.
Mailing Address: 1304 Ninth Ave., 52208-1614. Tel: 319-444-3106.
Catechesis/Religious Programs—Debbie Drahos, D.R.E.
Students 142.

Bellevue, Jackson Co., St. Joseph's (1841), Rev. Daniel J. Knepper. In res., Rev. Msgr. Ernest P. Ament.
Res., 405 Franklin St., 52031-1596. Tel: 319-872-3234. [CEM]
School—Bellevue Area Catholic Elementary School. See separate listing under Institutions Located in the Archdiocese for details.
Catechesis/Religious Programs—Carol Scott Feller, D.R.E.
Students 154.

Belmond, Wright Co., St. Francis Xavier (1870), Rev. Thomas F. Currier; Deacon Nick Schmit.
Res., 1207 Third St. N.E., 50421-1608. Tel: 515-444-3249. [CEM]
Catechesis/Religious Programs—Julie M. Jonas, D.R.E.
Students 127.

Blairstown, Benton Co., St. John (1948), Rev. Louis C. Zee; Sr. Nora Rochford, O.S.F., Pastoral Assoc.; Deacon James Naso.
Mailing Address: 105 West St. N.W.; P.O. Box E, 52209-0340. Tel: 319-454-6431.
Res., 405 4th Ave., Van Horne, 52346-0250.
Catechesis/Religious Programs—Patricia Angerman, D.R.E.
Students 76.

Blessing, Blackhawk Co., Immaculate Conception (1875), Revs. Lloyd Reuten; Douglas Loecke.
Res. and Mailing Address—1435 E. Eagle Rd., R.R. 4, Waterloo, 50701-9447. Tel: 319-342-2481.
Church—14004 S. Hudson Rd.
Catechesis/Religious Programs—Rita Schmidt, D.R.E.
Students 57.

Bluffton, Winneshiek Co., St. Bridget (1858), Rev. Michael Fitzgerald.
Res. and Mailing Address—116 Third St. E., Cresco, 52136. Tel: 319-547-3565.
Church—3094 253 Ave., Ridgeway.
Catechesis/Religious Programs—Marie O'Shea, D.R.E.
Students 47.

Britt, Hancock Co., St. Patrick's (1880), Rev. Marvin J. Bries.
Res., 139 Third St. S.E., 50423-1726. Tel: 515-843-3215. [CEM]
Catechesis/Religious Programs—Kathryn Smith, D.R.E.
Students 119.

Buffalo Center, Winnebago Co., St. Patrick's (1899), Rev. Craig E. Steimel.
Res. and Mailing Address—St. James Rectory, Bancroft Rd., P.O Box 310, Forest City, 50436-0310. Tel: 515-582-4856.
Church—115 5th Ave. N.W.
Catechesis/Religious Programs—Jody Smith, D.R.E.
Students 47.

Calmar, Winneshiek Co., St. Aloysius (1875), Rev. Robert M. Hirsch.
Res., 304 S. Maryville, P.O. Box 819, 52132-0819. Tel: 319-562-3603. [CEM]
School—Calmar-Festina-Spillville (CFS) Catholic Elementary School. See separate listing under Institutions Located in the Archdiocese for details.
Catechesis/Religious Programs—Tracy Elsbernd, D.R.E.
Students 108.

Cascade, Dubuque Co., St. Matthias, Rev. Philip E. Thompson; Deacon Joseph D. Hayes; Sr. Marlene McDonnell, S.F.C.C., Pastoral Assoc.
Res., 206 Grant St. S.W., P.O. Box 699, 52033-0699. Tel: 319-852-3524.
School—Aquin Educational System. See separate listing under Institutions Located in the Archdiocese for details.
Catechesis/Religious Programs—Richard Bronson, D.R.E.
Students 258.

Castle Grove, Jones Co., Immaculate Conception (1877), Rev. Msgr. Neil W. Tobin; Sr. M. Damian O'Brien, P.B.V.M., Pastoral Assoc.
Mailing Address: 22178 County Rd. D-62, Monticello, 52310-7827. Tel: 319-465-5570.
Res., Sacred Heart, 328 N. Sycamore St., Monticello, 52310. Tel: 319-465-5944.
Catechesis/Religious Programs—Sr. M. Damian O'Brien, P.B.V.M., D.R.E.
Students 20.

Cedar Falls, Blackhawk Co., St. Patrick (1855), Rev. Msgr. Paul T. Steimel; Rev. Douglas J. Loecke; Deacons Michael Oates; Daryl Fortin; Michael Moetsch.
Res., 122 W. Seventh St., 50613-2902. Tel: 319-266-3523. [CEM]
School—Tel: 319-277-6781. Sr. Mary Louise Scieszinski, P.B.V.M., Prin.
Sisters 3; Lay Teachers 22; Students 356.
Catechesis/Religious Programs—D.R.E.: Marie Lemka; Jean Ripplinger; Diane Flaherty.
Students 275.

Cedar Rapids, Linn Co.,

1—IMMACULATE CONCEPTION, (1858), Rev. Karl L. Glovik; Deacon Gerald D. Pettit. In res., Revs. Steven O'Brien; Dwayne Thoman.
Res., 857 Third Ave. S.E., Box 1247, 52406-1247. Tel: 319-362-7181. [JC]
Catechesis/Religious Programs—Mary Ann McEniry, D.R.E.
Students 57.

2—ALL SAINTS, (1947), Very Rev. Charles E. Lang; Rev. James L. Blocklinger; Deacon Mike Blouin.
Res., 720 29th St. S.E., 52403-3099. Tel: 319-363-6130. [JC]
School—Tel: 319-363-4110. Cindy Machado, Prin. Sisters 1; Lay Teachers 21; Students 386.
Catechesis/Religious Programs—Elaine Collins, D.R.E.
Students 227.

3—ST. JUDE, (1962), Revs. Donald R. Bruggeman; Dennis J. Quint. Pastoral Assocs.: Mark McDermott; Sr. Phyllis Heble, N.D.
Res., 3601 First Ave. S.W., 52405. Tel: 319-396-8827. [JC]
Church—50 Edgewood Rd. N.W., 52405-4598. Tel: 319-390-3520.
School—Holy Family Consolidated Catholic School. See separate listing under Institutions Located in the Archdiocese.
Catechesis/Religious Programs—D.R.E.: Mary Beth Siemann; Diane Morse.
Students 369.

4—ST. LUDMILA'S, (1922), Rev. Harry A. Koelker; Deacons Richard Manning; James Berger; William Cisler.
Res., 2107 J St. S.W., 52404-3615. Tel: 319-362-7282. [JC]
School—Holy Family Consolidated Catholic School.
Catechesis/Religious Programs—Sue Berger, D.R.E.
Students 170.

5—ST. MATTHEW'S, (1922), Rev. Msgr. Robert G. Hogan; Roseann Wiley, Pastoral Assoc.; Deacons Phil Saunders; John Malone.

Res., 2310 First Ave. N.E., 52402-4999. Tel: 319-363-8269; Fax: 319-362-8260. [JC]
School—Tel: 319-362-3021. Joe Wolf, Prin.
Lay Teachers 16; Students 306.
Catechesis/Religious Programs—Betsy Schmuck, D.R.E.
Students 209.

6—St. Patrick's, (1886), Rev. Steven J. Rosonke; Sr. Lucy Kurt, O.S.F., Pastoral Assoc.; Deacon Daniel Hoeger.
Parish Office: 516 A Ave. N.W., 52405-3935. Tel: 319-362-7966; 366-5369. [JC]
Catechesis/Religious Programs—Unita Schliemann, D.R.E.
Students 87.

7—St. Pius X, (1959), Rev. Donald L. Klein; Deacons Albert Scharosch; Paul Zimmerman. Pastoral Assocs.: Sr. Karen Luecy, F.S.P.A.; Sr. Eileen Schoenherr, O.S.F.
Office: 4949 Council St. N.E., 52402-2492. Tel: 319-393-4445; Fax: 319-393-9424. [JC]
School—Tel: 319-393-4507. Candace Kent, Prin.
Lay Teachers 21; Students 437.
Catechesis/Religious Programs—D.R.E.: Julie Johnson; Liz Pollard.
Students 673.

8—St. Wenceslaus, (1874), Rev. Karl L. Glovik; Sr. Rosemary Riesberg, F.S.P.A., Pastoral Assoc.; Deacon William Cisler.
Mailing Address: 510 16th Ave. S.E., 52401-2697. Tel: 319-362-8061. [JC]
Catechesis/Religious Programs—Sr. Rosemary Riesberg, F.S.P.A., D.R.E.
Students 36.

Central City, Linn Co., St. Stephen's (1932), Rev. Richard J. Ament; Sr. Anne Kisting, O.S.F., Pastoral Assoc.
Res. and Mailing Address—410 Terrance Dr., Box S, 52214-0619. Tel: 319-438-6625.
Catechesis/Religious Programs—Monica Carpenter, D.R.E.
Students 119.

Charles City, Floyd Co., Immaculate Conception (1857), Rev. Msgr. Stanley J. Hayek; Sr. M. Jeanine Kuhn, P.B.V.M., Pastoral Assoc.; Deacon James Sinnwell.
Res., 106 Chapel Ln., 50616-2898. Tel: 515-228-1071. [CEM]
School—Tel: 515-228-1225. Sr. M. Dianne Michels, P.B.V.M., Prin.
Sisters of the Presentation 2; Lay Teachers 14; Students 238.
Catechesis/Religious Programs—Patricia Rottinghaus, D.R.E.
Students 274.

Chelsea, Tama Co., St. Joseph's (1867), Very Rev. Charles E. Lang; Rev. Steven G. O'Brien; Deacon J.C. Otto, Pastoral Admin.
Mailing Address: 307 Station St., P.O. Box 98, 52215-0098. Tel: 319-444-3106. [CEM]
Catechesis/Religious Programs—Skip Ledvina, D.R.E.
Students 44.

Cherry Mound, Allamakee Co., St. Pius (1863), Rev. Robert J. Levenhagen.
Res. and Mailing Address—St. Mary's Rectory, 311 7th St., McGregory, 52157-9999. Tel: 319-586-2150. [CEM]
Religious Education Office: 699 State Forest Rd., Harper's Ferry, 52146.
Catechesis/Religious Programs—Mary Ann Kelly, D.R.E.
Students 44.

Chester, Howard Co., St. Stephen's (1916), Rev. Robert J. Ament.
Res. and Mailing Address—Our Lady of Lourdes Rectory, 17536 Lourdes Rd., Elma, 50628-8083. Tel: 515-393-2115.
Church—406 Main St.
Catechesis/Religious Programs—Debra Meyer, D.R.E.
Students 39.

Clarion, Wright Co., St. John's (1883), Rev. Wayne J. Droessler; Deacon Michael Whitters; Sr. Mary K. Doughan, R.S.M., Pastoral Assoc.
Mailing Address: 608 Second Ave. N.E., P.O. Box 26, 50525-0026. Tel: 515-532-3586. [CEM]
Res., Sacred Heart, 204 S. Jackson, Eagle Grove, 50533. Tel: 515-448-4765.
Catechesis/Religious Programs—Sue Moss, D.R.E.
Students 118.

Clear Lake, Cerro Gordo Co., St. Patrick's (1901), Rev. Msgr. Joseph J. Slepicka; Deacon Leo W. Stattelman.
Res., 1001 Ninth Ave. S., 50428-2615. Tel: 515-357-3214.
Catechesis/Religious Programs—D.R.E.: Christine & Van Carrier; Virginia Copas; Delores Orozco.
Students 187.

Clermont, Fayette Co., St. Peter's (1855), Rev. Leo P. Riley.
Mailing Address: 608 Larrabee, 52135-0025. Tel: 319-423-7293.
Res., St. Bridget, 135 W. Williams, P.O. Box 369, Potsville, 52162. Tel: 319-864-3138. [CEM]
Catechesis/Religious Programs—Robert Fassbinder, D.R.E.
Students 103.

Clutier, Tama Co., Immaculate Conception (1900), Rev. John R. Tilp.
Res. and Mailing Address—1102 Walnut St., Traer, 50675-1440. Tel: 319-478-2222.
Church—501 5th St.
Catechesis/Religious Programs—Jane Svoboda, D.R.E.
Students 61.
Oratory—Carroll Township, St. Wenceslaus.

Coggon, Linn Co., St. John the Evangelist (1912), Rev. Richard J. Ament; Sr. Anne Kisting, O.S.F., Pastoral Assoc.
Mailing Address: P.O. Box 47, 52218. Tel: 319-435-2236.
Res., 410 Terrace Dr., Central City, 52214. Tel: 319-438-6625.
Church—211 Third St. N., 52218.
Catechesis/Religious Programs—Pamela Klima, D.R.E.
Students 34.

Colesburg, Delaware Co., St. Patrick's (1862), Rev. John J. Friederick.
Res., St. Mark Rectory, 205 S. Locust, P.O. Box 345, Edgewood, 52042-0345. Tel: 319-853-2265. [CEM]
Church—Delaware St.
Catechesis/Religious Programs—Gene Kruse, D.R.E.
Students 96.

Colo, Story Co., St. Mary's, Rev. John M. Herzog; Sr. Jeanne Marie Roche, R.S.M., Pastoral Assoc.
Res., 410 Bailey, P.O. Box 236, 50056-0236. Tel: 515-377-2710. [CEM]
Church—422 Fourth St.

Corwith, Hancock Co., St. Mary's (1912), Rev. Marvin J. Bries.
Mailing Address: 139 Third St. S.E., Britt, 50423. Tel: 515-843-3215.
Church—404 Wayne St.
Catechesis/Religious Programs—Judy Weber, D.R.E.
Students 14.

Cresco, Howard Co., Assumption of the Blessed Virgin Mary (1858), Rev. Michael C. Fitzgerald; Sr. Mary Hargrafen, O.S.F., Pastoral Assoc.
Office: 116 Third St. E., Box 198, Crecso, 52136-1699. Tel: 319-547-3243.
Res., 221 Third Ave. W., 52136. Tel: 319-547-3243. [JC]
Church—229 Third Ave. W.
School—Notre Dame System of Education. See separate listing under Institutions Located in the Archdiocese for details.
Catechesis/Religious Programs—Bruce Kingsley, D.R.E.
Students 325.

St. Joseph's (1870), Rev. Michael C. Fitzgerald; Sr. Mary Hargrafen, O.S.F., Pastoral Assoc.
Office: 116 Third St. E., Box 198, 52136-1699. Tel: 319-547-3565.
Res., 221 Third St. W., 52136. Tel: 319-547-3243. [JC]
Church—223 Second Ave. E.
School—Notre Dame System of Education. See separate listing under Institutions Located in the Archdiocese for details.
Catechesis/Religious Programs—Bruce Kingsley, D.R.E.
Students 325.

Decorah, Winneshiek Co., St. Benedict's (1864), Very Rev. Gary Krapfl. In res., Rev. John McTarsney.
Res., 307 W. Main St., 52101. Tel: 319-382-9631. [CEM]
School—Tel: 319-382-4668. Sr. Francesca Oldham, R.S.M., Prin.
Sisters of Mercy 1; Lay Teachers 12; Students 178.
Catechesis/Religious Programs—Colleen Wetli, D.R.E.
Students 413.

Delhi, Delaware Co., St. John's (1872), Rev. Paul L. Weis.
Res., 307 South St., P.O. Box 187, 52223-0187. Tel: 319-922-2251. [CEM]
Catechesis/Religious Programs—D.R.E.: Randy Thuman; Lynn Lechtenberg.
Students 150.

Dike, Grundy Co., St. Mary (1880), Rev. Daniel J. Knipper.
Res. and Mailing Address—2209 N. Union Rd., P.O. Box 605, Cedar Falls, 50613. Tel: 319-266-3543.
Church—680 Main St.
Catechesis/Religious Programs—Janine Whipps, D.R.E.
Students 57.

Dorchester, Allamakee Co., St. Mary's (1865), Rev. Henry W. Charipar; Sr. Erma Rottinghaus, O.S.F., Pastoral Assoc.
Mailing Address: P.O. Box 21, 52140-0021.
Parish Office: 114 Third St. N.E., P.O. Box D, New Albin, 52160. Tel: 319-544-4855.
Church—590 Waterloo Creek Rd., Dorcester.
Catechesis/Religious Programs—Sr. Erma Rottinghaus, D.R.E.
Students 61.

Dougherty, Cerro Gordo Co., St. Patrick's (1870), Rev. Stephen L. Meyer; Deacon Victor Groh.
Church and Mailing Address—410 Patrick St., P.O. Box 208, 50433-0288.
Res., Sacred Heart Rectory, P.O. Box 30, 305 Elm St. E., Rockwell, 50469-0030. Tel: 515-822-4957. [CEM]
Catechesis/Religious Programs—Dolores Marzen, D.R.E.
Students 55.

Dumont, Butler Co., St. Francis (1890), Very Rev. Gerald A. Condon.
Res. and Mailing Address—St. Patrick, 1405 N. Federal St., Hampton, 50441-1005. Tel: 515-456-4857; 456-3406.
Church—720 Pine St., 50625.
Catechesis/Religious Programs—Judy Nelson, D.R.E.
Students 21.

Duncan, Hancock Co., St. Wenceslaus (1900), Rev. John W. Hemann.
Res. and Mailing Address—St. Bonafice Rectory, 660 Bush Ave., Garner, 50438-1513. Tel: 515-923-2329.
Church—2343 Navy Ave.
Catechesis/Religious Programs—Esther Hadacek, D.R.E.
Students 50.

Dyersville, Dubuque Co., Basilica of St. Francis Xavier (1859), Revs. Edward C. Petty; Gabriel C. Anderson. Pastoral Assocs.: Sr. Mary Clare Miller, O.S.F.; Sr. Marian Einck, O.S.F.; Mr. Gerald C. Dolan.
Res., 104 Third St. S.W., 52040-1696. Tel: 319-875-7325. [CEM]
School—Tel: 319-875-7376. Ralph Pauly, Prin.
Sisters of St. Francis of the Holy Family 2; Lay Teachers 21; Students 329.
Catechesis/Religious Programs—D.R.E.: John F.E. Steger; Jennifer Rahe.
Students 160.

Dysart, Tama Co., St. Joseph (1878), Rev. Joseph E. McGuire.
Mailing Address: P.O. Box 116, Vinton, 52349-0116. Tel: 319-472-4448. [CEM]
Church—101 Clark St.
Catechesis/Religious Programs—Peg Hennings, D.R.E.
Students 53.

Eagle Center, Blackhawk Co., St. Mary of Mt. Carmel (1859). Unassigned. Rev. Lloyd E. Reuter.
Mailing Address: 1435 E. Eagle Rd., Rte. 4, Waterloo, 50701-9447. Tel: 319-342-2481. [CEM]
Catechesis/Religious Programs—Sr. Betty Tranel, S.Sp.S., D.R.E.
Students 108.

Eagle Grove, Wright Co., Sacred Heart (1882), Rev. Wayne J. Droessler; Louise Russell, Pastoral Assoc.
Res., 204 S. Jackson St., 50533. Tel: 515-448-4765. [CEM]
Catechesis/Religious Programs—Jacquelyn Zigrang, D.R.E.
Students 143.

Earlville, Delaware Co., St. Joseph's (1887), Rev. Frank M. Benda; Sr. Lenore Gardner, R.S.M., Pastoral Assoc.; Deacon James Steger.
Res. and Mailing Address—307 Mary St., P.O. Box 187, 52041-0187. Tel: 319-923-3135.
School—Sandra Klaus, Prin. Lay Teachers 6; Students 81.
Catechesis/Religious Programs—Joan Steger, D.R.E.
Students 98.

Edgewood, Delaware Co., St. Mark's (1916), Rev. John J. Friederick.
Res., 205 S. Locust St., P.O. Box 345, 52042-0340. Tel: 319-928-6938; 928-7200. [CEM]
Catechesis/Religious Programs—Judith Kintzle, D.R.E.
Students 157.

Eldora, Hardin Co., St. Mary's (1868), Rev. Rick D. Dagit; Deacon Wayne Cashatt.
Res., 614 Washington St., 50627-1257. Tel: 515-858-5666. [CEM]
Catechesis/Religious Programs—Mary Reede, D.R.E.
Students 87.

Elkader, Clayton Co., St. Joseph's (1844), Rev. Thomas W. Rhomberg; Sr. Rosanna Gleason, O.P., Pastoral Assoc.
Res., 330 First St., 52043-0626. Tel: 319-245-2548.

[CEM]
Catechesis/Religious Programs—D.R.E.: Patty Engelhardt; Kathy Schutte.
Students 159.
Oratory—Wadena, St. Joseph.

Elma, Howard Co., Immaculate Conception (1887), Rev. Roger R. Rethamel.
Res., 203 Seventh St., P.O. Box 38, 50628-0038. Tel: 515-393-2520. [CEM]
Catechesis/Religious Programs—Eleanor Burke, D.R.E.
Students 115.

Epworth, Dubuque Co., St. Patrick's (1879), Rev. Louis M. Jaeger.
Res., 104 First St. S.E., 52045-0286. Tel: 319-876-5540. [CEM]
School—Seton Catholic Elementary School, Epworth. See separate listing under Institutions Located in the Archdiocese for details.
Catechesis/Religious Programs—D.R.E.: Lori Kramer; Diane McDermott.
Students 207.

Evansdale, Blackhawk Co., St. Nicholas (1951), Rev. Msgr. Cletus J. Hawes; Deacon William Jenney.
Res., 443 S. Roosevelt Rd., 50707-1259. Tel: 319-232-9737. [JC]
School—St. John-St. Nicholas Consolidated. See St. John, Waterloo for details.
Catechesis/Religious Programs—Dave Cushing, D.R.E.
Students 51.

Fairbank, Buchanan Co., Immaculate Conception (1858), Rev. Mark J. McGovern.
Res., 302 W. Main St., P.O. Box 505, 50629-0505. Tel: 319-635-2211. [CEM]
Catechesis/Religious Programs—Kim Weepie, D.R.E.
Students 181.

Fairfax, Linn Co., St. Patrick's (1875), Rev. Thomas J. Schwinn; Mr. Jerry Corrigan, Pastoral Assoc.
Parish Office: 620 Church St., Tel: 319-846-2025.
Res., 324 Church St., P.O. Box 219, 52228-0219. Tel: 319-846-2025. [CEM]
Catechesis/Religious Programs—Karen Swindler, D.R.E.
Students 137.

Farley, Dubuque Co., St. Joseph's (1914), Rev. John P. Ptacek.
Res., 204 Second Ave. S.E., P.O. Box 67, 52046-0067. Tel: 319-744-3715. [CEM]
School—Seton Catholic Elementary School, Epworth. See separate listing under Institutions Located in the Archdiocese for details.
Catechesis/Religious Programs—D.R.E.: Joanne Dardis; Deb Jasper; Monica Lynch.
Students 230.

Fayette, Fayette Co., St. Francis of Assisi (1879), Rev. Dale J. Rausch.
Mailing Address: P.O. Box 276, 52142-0276. Tel: 319-425-3228.
Res., 128 N. Walnut St., West Union, 52175-1347. Tel: 319-422-3184. [CEM]
Church—205 Lovers Lane.
Catechesis/Religious Programs—Patricia Burghardt, D.R.E.
Students 108.

Festina, Winneshiek Co., Our Lady of Seven Dolors (1843), Rev. Jacob P. Roth.
Res. and Mailing Address—202 Second St. S.E., c/o St. John Nepomucene, Fort Atkinson, 52144-0157. Tel: 319-534-7298.
Church—2348 County Rd. B32.
School—Calmar-Festina-Spillville (CFS) Elementary. See separate listing under Institutions Located in the Archdiocese for details.

Fillmore, Dubuque Co., Sacred Heart (1890), Rev. Neil J. Manternach.
Res., 19661 Sacred Heart Ln., Bernard, 52032-9722. Tel: 319-879-3103. [CEM]
School—Aquin Elementary School. See separate listing under Institutions Located in the Archdiocese for details.

Forest City, Winnebago Co., St. James (1870), Rev. Craig E. Steimel; Sr. Mary Dolores Moes, P.B.V.M., Pastoral Assoc., Tel: 515-582-3336.
Res., Bancroft Rd., P.O. Box 310, 50436-0310. Tel: 515-582-4856. [CEM]
Catechesis/Religious Programs—Rita Kleemeier, D.R.E.
Students 148.

Fort Atkinson, Winneshiek Co., St. John Nepomucene's (1875), Rev. Msgr. Jacob P. Roth.
Res., 202 Second St. S.E., 52144-0157. Tel: 319-534-7298. [CEM]
School—Fort Atkinson-St. Lucas Consolidated. See separate listing under Institutions Located in the Archdiocese for details.
Catechesis/Religious Programs—Trudy Smith, D.R.E.
Students 58.

Garber, Clayton Co., St. Michael's (1917), Rev. Richard G. Gaul.
Res. and Mailing Address—St. Joseph Rectory, 402 S. Washington, P.O. Box 7, Garnavillo, 52049-0007. Tel: 319-964-2168.
Church—800 Main.
Catechesis/Religious Programs—Ann Armstrong, D.R.E.
Students 33.

Garnavillo, Clayton Co., St. Joseph's (1846), Rev. Richard G. Gaul.
Res., 402 S. Washington St., P.O. Box 7, 52049-0007. Tel: 319-964-2168. [CEM]
Church—204 W. Oak St.
Catechesis/Religious Programs—Darlene Wille, D.R.E.
Students 84.

Garner, Hancock Co., St. Boniface (1883), Rev. John W. Hemann.
Res., 660 Bush Ave., 50438-1513. Tel: 515-923-2329. [CEM]
Catechesis/Religious Programs—Rebecca Rolling, D.R.E.
Students 229.

Garryowen, Jackson Co., St. Patrick's (1840), Rev. Thomas R. Bisenius.
Res., 28914 46th Ave., Bernard, 52032-9289. Tel: 319-879-3303. [CEM]
School—Aquin Elementary School. See separate listing under Institutions Located in the Archdiocese for details.
Catechesis/Religious Programs—Joanne Harry, D.R.E.
Students 53.

Garwin, Tama Co., St. Boniface (1884), Rev. Lloyd Paul Ouderkirk.
Office and Mailing Address—306 4th St., 50632. Tel: 515-499-2180.
Res., St. Mary Church, 9 W. Linn St., Marshalltown, 50158. Tel: 515-753-6278. [JC]
Catechesis/Religious Programs—Diane Jones, D.R.E.
Students 42.

Geneva, Franklin Co., St. Paul. Closed. Sacramental records are located at St. Mary, Ackley.

Gilbert, Story Co., SS. Peter and Paul (1882). Conventual Franciscan Friars. Revs. Terrence Rasmussen, O.F.M.Conv.; John Elmer, O.F.M.Conv.
Res., St. Cecilia Rectory, 2900 Hoover, Ames, 50010-4498. Tel: 515-233-3092. [CEM]
Church—County Line Rd., Rte. 38.

Gilbertville, Blackhawk Co., Immaculate Conception (1875), Rev. James L. Secora.
Res., 311 15th Ave., 50634-0136. Tel: 319-296-1092. [CEM]
School—Immaculate Conception-St. Joseph. (Gilbertville-Raymond Consolidated). See separate listing under Institutions Located in the Archdiocese for details.
Catechesis/Religious Programs—Dessie Rottinghaus, D.R.E.
Students 39.

Greeley, Delaware Co., St. Joseph's (1870), Rev. Frank M. Benda; Deacon Jim Steger; Sr. Charmaine Plotz, O.S.F., Pastoral Assoc.
Mailing Address—307 Mary St., P.O. Box 187, Earlville, 52041-0187. Tel: 319-923-3135.
Church—208 E. 2nd Ave.
Catechesis/Religious Programs—Sr. Charmaine Plotz, O.S.F., D.R.E.
Students 68.

Greene, Butler Co., St. Mary's (1872), Rev. Msgr. Walter L. Brunkan.
Res., 105 N. Main, P.O. Box 480, 50636-0480. Tel: 515-823-4146. [CEM]
Catechesis/Religious Programs—Sherilyn Backer, D.R.E.
Students 127.

Grundy Center, Grundy Co., Sacred Heart (1885), Rev. John M. Kissling.
Res., 204 G Ave., 50638-1939. Tel: 319-824-3571. [CEM]
Catechesis/Religious Programs—D.R.E.: Sharon Davidson; Cheryl Osterhaus.
Students 48.

Guttenberg, Clayton Co., St. Mary's (1851), Rev. Paul R. Peters.
Res., 520 S. Second, P.O. Box 847, 52052-0847. Tel: 319-252-1247. [CEM]
School—Guttenberg-North Buena Vista Consolidated. See separate listing under Institutions Located in the Archdiocese for details.
Catechesis/Religious Programs—Julie Rastetter, D.R.E.
Students 155.

Hampton, Franklin Co., St. Patrick's (1870), Very Rev. Gerald A. Condon.
Res., 1405 N. Federal, 50441-1005. Tel: 515-456-3406; 456-4857.
Catechesis/Religious Programs—Judy Nelson, D.R.E.
Students 156.

Hanover, Allamakee Co., St. Mary's (1875), Rev. Henry W. Charipar; Sr. Erma Rottinghaus, O.S.F., Pastoral Assoc.
Mailing Address: P.O. Box 21, Dorchester, 52140-0021.
Res., 114 3rd N.E., Box D, New Albin, 52160-0404. Tel: 319-544-4855. [CEM]
Church—2096 Hwy. 76.
Catechesis/Religious Programs—Mary Teresa Klauke, D.R.E.
Students 26.

Harpers Ferry, Allamakee Co., St. Ann-St. Joseph (1855), Rev. Louis J. Trzil.
Res. and Mailing Address—Immaculate Conception (Wexford), 1416 Great River Rd., Lansing, 52151-7519.
Church—307 W. Orange, Harper's Ferry.
Catechesis/Religious Programs—Bernadine Heffern, D.R.E.
Students 32.

Haverhill, Marshall Co., Immaculate Conception (1877), Rev. William D. O'Brien.
Res., 101 Second Ave., 50120-5009. Tel: 515-475-3341. [CEM]
School—Marshalltown Area Consolidated Catholic. See separate listing under Institutions Located in the Archdiocese for details.
Catechesis/Religious Programs—Rev. William O'Brien, D.R.E.
Students 21.

Hawkeye, Fayette Co., St. Francis Xavier (1891), Rev. John J. Purtell.
Res. and Mailing Address—Immaculate Conception, 413 W. First St., Sumner, 50674-9802. Tel: 319-578-5366.
Church—304 E. Main.
Catechesis/Religious Programs—Donna Scholbrock, D.R.E.
Students 15.

Hazleton, Buchanan Co., St. Mary's (1881), Rev. Dennis Juhl; Mr. Robert Burke, Pastoral Assoc.
Mailing Address: 305 Worth St., P.O. Box 146, Lamont, 50650. Tel: 319-924-2691.
Church—209 Benton.
Catechesis/Religious Programs—Julie Dettbarn, D.R.E.
Students 28.

Hiawatha, Linn Co., St. Elizabeth Ann Seton Parish (1989), Rev. John A. Gossman; Marlene Myers, Pastoral Assoc.
Res., 1045 Eisenhower Rd., 52233-1927. Tel: 319-393-3778. [JC]

Holy Cross, Dubuque Co., Holy Cross (1845), Rev. Donald J. Plamondon.
Res., 875 Church St., P.O. Box 398, 52053-0398. Tel: 319-870-2155. [CEM]
School—Rickardsville-Holy Cross-Luxemburg (RHCL) Catholic. See separate listing under Institutions Located in the Archdiocese for details.

Hopkinton, Delaware Co., St. Luke's (1922), Rev. Harold J. Drexler; Patricia Hucker, Pastoral Assoc.
Mailing Address: P.O. Box 159, 52237-0159.
Res. and Parish Office—202 First St. S.E., 52237. Tel: 319-926-2613.
Church—206 First St. S.E.
Catechesis/Religious Programs—Patricia Hucker, D.R.E.
Students 132.

Independence, Buchanan Co., St. John Evangelist (1856), Rev. Aloysius Vorwald. Pastoral Assocs.: Deacon Paul J. Carroll; Sharon Bainbridge; Michael Kellogg.
Res., 209 Fifth Ave. N.E., 50644-1998. Tel: 319-334-7191. [CEM]
School—Christine Beumer, Prin. Lay Teachers 9; Students 124.
Catechesis/Religious Programs—Christine Beumer, D.R.E.
Students 203.

Ionia, Chickashaw Co., St. Boniface's (1899), Rev. Francis J. Perry.
Mailing Address: 200 E. Prairie, P.O. Box 160, 50645-0160. Tel: 515-394-2078.
Res., 114 N. Wapsil, North Washington, 50661. Tel: 515-394-2078. [CEM]
Catechesis/Religious Programs—Bonnie Boggess, D.R.E.
Students 81.

Iowa Falls, Hardin Co., St. Mark's (1855), Rev. Phillip E. Schmitt.
Res., 415 Main St., P.O. Box 368, 50126-0368. Tel: 515-648-9547. [CEM]
Catechesis/Religious Programs—Judith Connell, D.R.E.
Students 117.

Jesup, Buchanan Co., St. Athanasius (1880), Rev. Donald P. Schmitt; Sr. Donna Burke, O.S.F., Pastoral Assoc.
Res., 634 Stevens St., P.O. Box 316, 50648-0316. Tel: 319-827-6682. [CEM]
School—Gladys Oppold, Prin. Lay Teachers 8; Students 136.
Catechesis/Religious Programs—Lynda Westemeier, D.R.E.
Students 160.

Jewell, Hamilton Co., Good Shepherd (1915), Rev. Philip F. Recker.
Res., St. Mary, 404 Fourth St., P.O. Box 157, Williams, 50271-0157. Tel: 515-827-5612.
Church—503 Edwards St.
Catechesis/Religious Programs—Students 46.

Key West, Dubuque Co., St. Joseph's (1872), Rev. James J. Goedken.
Res., 10234 Key West Dr., Dubuque, 52003-8000. Tel: 319-582-7392.
Church—10280 Key West Dr., Dubuque, 52003.
School—10244 Key West Dr., Dubuque, 52003. Tel: 319-582-2866. Connie Kessler, Prin.
Sisters 1; Lay Teachers 11; Students 219.
Catechesis/Religious Programs—Maurna E. Stover, D.R.E.
Students 117.

Lake Mills, Winnebago Co., St. Patrick (1870), Rev. Craig E. Steimel; Sr. Mary Dolores Moes, P.V.B.M., Pastoral Assoc.
Res. and Mailing Address: 906 West St., P.O. Box 310, Forest City, 50436-0310. Tel: 515-582-4856. [CEM]
Church—406 S. Grant St.
Catechesis/Religious Programs—Regina Adams, D.R.E.
Students 67.

Lamont, Buchanan Co., St. Mary's (1894), Rev. Dennis A. Juhl.
Res. and Mailing Address—305 Worth St., P.O. Box 180, 50650-0180. Tel: 319-924-2691.
Church—845 Pearl St.
Catechesis/Religious Programs—Linda Paris, D.R.E.
Students 112.

La Motte, Jackson Co., Holy Rosary (1893), Rev. Michael L. Tauke.
Res., 507 Elm St., P.O. Box 26, 52054-0026. Tel: 319-773-2323. [CEM]
School—Bellevue Area Catholic Elementary. See separate listing under Institutions Located in the Archdiocese for details.
Catechesis/Religious Programs—Marla Kilburg, D.R.E.
Students 33.

Lansing, Allamakee Co., Immaculate Conception (1855), Rev. Herbert L. Tegeler; Sr. Catherine Schmitz, F.S.P.A., Pastoral Assoc.
Res., 648 Main St., 52151-9685. Tel: 319-538-4171. [CEM]
Catechesis/Religious Programs—Karen Weber, D.R.E.
Students 166.

La Porte City, Blackhawk Co., Sacred Heart (1887), Rev. Lloyd E. Reuter.
Res., 1021 Poplar St., 50651-1732. Tel: 319-342-2991.
Catechesis/Religious Programs—Barb Oberhauser, D.R.E.
Students 137.

Lawler, Chickasaw Co., Our Lady of Mt. Carmel (1869), Rev. Marvin C. Salz; Sr. Lois Erpelding, O.S.F., Pastoral Assoc.
Res., 2940 Iowa Hwy. 24, Box 119, 52154. Tel: 319-238-3444. [CEM]
Catechesis/Religious Programs—Leslie Cuvelier, D.R.E.
Students 164.

Little Turkey, Chickasaw Co., Assumption of the B. V. M. (1902), Rev. Allen M. Schmitt.
Res. and Mailing Address—110 Commercial Ave., P.O. Box 205, Protivin, 52163-0205. Tel: 319-569-8259. [CEM]
Church—3303 160th St., Lawler.
Catechesis/Religious Programs—Kathy Ball, D.R.E.
Students 41.
Oratory—Reilly Settlement, Sacred Heart.

Lourdes, Howard Co., Our Lady of Lourdes (1875), Rev. Robert J. Ament.
Res. and Mailing Address—17536 Lourdes Rd., Elma, 50628-8083. Tel: 515-393-2115. [CEM]
Church—14068 175th St., Elma, 50628.
Catechesis/Religious Programs—Bernadette Voves, D.R.E.
Students 53.

Luxemburg, Dubuque Co., Holy Trinity (1865), Rev. Donald J. Plamondon.
Res. and Mailing Address—875 Church St., P.O. Box 398, Holy Cross, 52053-0398. Tel: 319-870-2155. [CEM]
Church—103 S. Audres.
School—Rickardsville-Holy Cross-Luxemburg (RHCL) Catholic. See separate listing under Institutions Located in the Archdiocese for details.
Catechesis/Religious Programs—Students 22.

Lycurgus, Allamakee Co., St. Mary's (1859), Rev. Msgr. Edward W. Lechtenberg; Sr. Margaret Anne Kramer, P.B.V.M., Pastoral Assoc.
Res. and Mailing Address—109 Second St. S.W., P.O. Box 158, Waukon, 52172-0158. Tel: 319-568-3671. [CEM]
Church—1831 Lycurgus Rd., Waukon, 52172-0146.
Catechesis/Religious Programs—Rita Whalen, D.R.E.
Students 41.

Manchester, Delaware Co., St. Mary's (1872), Rev. Ralph P. Simington; Deacon Tom Lang; Sr. Mary Klisart, O.S.F., Pastoral Assoc.
Res., 119 W. Fayette St., 52057-1596. Tel: 319-927-4710. [CEM]
School—Sr. Marilou Irons, P.B.V.M., Prin. Sisters 1; Lay Teachers 11; Students 224.
Catechesis/Religious Programs—Dianne Larsen, D.R.E.
Students 400.

Manly, Worth Co., Sacred Heart (1883), Rev. Thomas McAndrew; Deacon Robert Mega.
Res., 120 E. North, 50456-2586. Tel: 515-454-2586. [CEM]
Catechesis/Religious Programs—Betty Benjegerdes, D.R.E.
Students 87.

Maquoketa, Jackson Co., Sacred Heart (1873), Very Rev. Dennis R. Cain; Sr. Nancy Anderson, O.S.B., Pastoral Assoc.
Res., 200 S. Vermont St., 52060. Tel: 319-652-6931. [CEM]
School—Sr. Rita Green, O.S.F., Prin. Sisters 1; Lay Teachers 8; Students 143.
Catechesis/Religious Programs—Karen Steffan, D.R.E.
Students 251.
Oratory—Baldwin, Holy Trinity.

Marion, Linn Co., St. Joseph's (1890), Rev. Msgr. John R. McClean; Rev. Phillip G. Gibbs; Barbara McGrane, Pastoral Assoc.; Deacons Leo Schmall; Ed Pantaloni.
Res., 1790 14th St., 52302-2267. Tel: 319-377-4869; Fax: 319-377-9043. [JC]
School—Sr. Margaret Weigel, R.S.M., Prin. Sisters of Mercy 1; Lay Teachers 21; Students 376.
Catechesis/Religious Programs—D.R.E.: Ruth Ard; Mary Hauschildt.
Students 555.

Marshalltown, Marshall Co., St. Henry's (1959), Rev. Thomas Braak; Toni Waters, Pastoral Assoc.; Deacon Irvin Vaske.
Parish Center: 221 W. Olive St., 50158-4248. Tel: 515-753-7374; Fax: 515-753-4178. [JC]
Res., 212 Huisman Cir., 50158. Tel: 515-752-2043.
School—Marshalltown Area Consolidated Catholic. See separate listing under Institutions Located in the Archdiocese for details.
Catechesis/Religious Programs—Connie Murray, D.R.E.
Students 297.

St. Mary's (1869), Rev. Jerry F. Kopacek; Deacon Edward J. Mead. In res., Rev. Lloyd Paul Ouderkirk.
Res., 9 W. Linn St., P.O. Box 642, 50158-0642. Tel: 515-753-6278. [JC]
School—Marshalltown Area Consolidated Catholic. See separate listing under Institutions Located in the Archdiocese for details.
Catechesis/Religious Programs—Sr. Sheila Geraghty, R.S.M., D.R.E.
Students 195.

Mason City, Cerro Gordo Co., St. Joseph's (1873), Rev. Carl A. Ries; Margaret Hugo, Pastoral Assoc.; Deacon Jack Barlow.
Res., 302 Fifth St. S.E., 50401-4005. Tel: 515-423-5001.
School—Newman Catholic. See separate listing under Institutions Located in the Archdiocese for details.
Catechesis/Religious Programs—Ginny Verstegen, D.R.E.
Students 161.

Holy Family (1908), Revs. John R. Kremer; David M. Beckman; Deacons Charles Cooper; Matthew Berry.
Res., 714 N. Adams St., 50401-2124. Tel: 515-423-7301. [JC]
School—Newman Catholic. See separate listing under Institutions Located in the Archdiocese for details.
Catechesis/Religious Programs—Ginny Verstegen, D.R.E.
Students 260.

Masonville, Delaware Co., Immaculate Conception (1883), Rev. Ivan R. Nienhaus; Sr. Mary Valentine Smith, O.S.F., Pastoral Assoc.
Res. and Mailing Address—555 First St., P.O. Box 236, Winthrop, 50682-0236. Tel: 319-935-3523.
Church—Bernhardt St., 50654.
Catechesis/Religious Programs—Julie Francois, D.R.E.
Students 86.

McGregor, Clayton Co., St. Mary's (1873), Rev. Robert J. Levenhagen.
Res., 311 Seventh St., 52157-9999. Tel: 319-873-2287. [CEM]
Catechesis/Religious Programs—Mary Young, D.R.E.
Students 68.

Meyer, Mitchell Co., Sacred Heart (1900), Rev. Joseph M. Schneider.
Mailing Address: 2697 480th St. W., McIntire, 50455-9718.
Res., 604 N. Broad St., Stacyville, 50476-5019. Tel: 515-737-2262. [CEM]
School—Visitation (Stacyville-Meyer) Consolidated. See separate listing under Institutions Located in the Archdiocese for details.
Catechesis/Religious Programs—Annette Adams, D.R.E.
Students 48.

Monona, Clayton Co., St. Patrick's (1856), Rev. John W. Moran.
Res., 403 East St. S., P.O. Box U, 52159-0557. Tel: 319-539-4442. [CEM]
Catechesis/Religious Programs—D.R.E.: Marilyn Ryan; Don Montgomery.
Students 209.

Monti, Buchanan Co., St. Patrick's (1855), Rev. John W. Carpender.
Res. and Mailing Address—615 Howard St., P.O. Box 219, Ryan, 52330-0219. Tel: 319-932-2151.
Church—2856 Washington Ave., Masonville, 50654.
Catechesis/Religious Programs—Linda Dolan, D.R.E.
Students 61.

Monticello, Jones Co., Sacred Heart (1868), Rev. Msgr. Neil W. Tobin.
Office and Res.—328 N. Sycamore, 52310-1213. Tel: 319-465-5944. [CEM]
Church—302 N. Sycamore.
School—(Grades PreK-6). David E. Bertling, Prin. Lay Teachers 8; Students 162.
Catechesis/Religious Programs—Guy E. Woodward, D.R.E.
Students 172.

Mount Vernon, Linn Co., St. John's the Baptist (1843), Rev. James J. Duster. In res., Rev. Ernest Evgler.
Res., 212 7th St. S.E., P.O. Box 169, 52314-0169. Tel: 319-895-6246. [CEM]
Catechesis/Religious Programs—Sue Schettler, D.R.E.
Students 229.

Nashua, Chickasaw Co., St. Michael's (1870), Rev. Msgr. Robert L. Spaight.
Res., 612 Cedar St., P.O. Box 308, 50658-0308. Tel: 515-435-2070. [CEM]
Catechesis/Religious Programs—Kendra Gilbert, D.R.E.
Students 145.

Nevada, Story Co., St. Patrick's (1870), Rev. John M. Herzog; Sr. Carole Freking, O.S.F., Pastoral Assoc.
Mailing Address: 1127 10th St., 50201-1708. Tel: 515-382-2974. [CEM]
Res., St. Mary, 410 Bailey St., Colo, 50056. Tel: 515-377-2710.
Catechesis/Religious Programs—Belinda Hanson, D.R.E.
Students 163.

New Albin, Allamakee Co., St. Joseph's (1910), Rev. Henry W. Charipar; Sr. Erma Rottinghaus, O.S.F., Pastoral Assoc.
Res., 114 3rd N.E., Box D, 52160-0404. Tel: 319-544-4855. [CEM]
Catechesis/Religious Programs—Rita Kyzbietke, D.R.E.
Students 45.

Newhall, Benton Co., St. Paul's (1914), Rev. Louis C. Zee; Sr. Nora Rochford, O.S.F., Pastoral Assoc.; Deacons Robert F. Hurych; James Naso.
Mailing Address: P.O. Box 447, 52315-0447. Tel: 319-223-5576.
Res., Immaculate Conception, 405 Fourth Ave., P.O. Box 250, Van Horne, 52346. Tel: 319-228-8131.
Church—303 Third St. E.
Catechesis/Religious Programs—Sr. Nora Rochford, O.S.F., D.R.E.
Students 140.

New Hampton, Chickasaw Co., St. Joseph's (1870), Very Rev. Carl L. Schmitt. Pastoral Assocs.: Sr. Lorraine Loecher, O.S.F.; Sr. Phyllis Ann Hackman, F.S.P.A.; Deacon Robert Baltes.
Res., 202 N. Broadway, 50659-1111. Tel: 515-394-2105. [CEM]
School—Alice Conlon, Prin. Sisters 1; Lay Teachers

13; Students 224.
Catechesis/Religious Programs—Gladys Christoph, D.R.E.
Students 180.
St. Mary's (1894), Rev. Marvin C. Salz.
Res., 239 S. Walnut Ave., P.O. Box 66, 50659-0066. Tel: 515-394-2195. [CEM]
Catechesis/Religious Programs—Sr. Lois Erpelding, O.S.F., D.R.E.
Students 156.
Oratory—Reilly Settlement, Sacred Heart.

New Haven, Mitchell Co., St. Peter's (1876), Rev. John A. Moser.
Mailing Address: 2985 360th St., Osage, 50461-8517.
Office: 209 E. Main St., Riceville, 50466-0146. Tel: 515-985-2028. [CEM]
Church—2985 360th St., Osage.
Catechesis/Religious Programs—Pat Wickham, D.R.E.
Students 33.

New Melleray, Dubuque Co., Holy Family (1850), Rev. Carl J. Manternach.
Res., St. John the Baptist, 10761 Sundown Rd., Peosta, 52068-9507. Tel: 319-582-4217.
Church—16500 Holy Family Ln., Peasta.
Catechesis/Religious Programs—Kay Goedken, D.R.E.
Students 65.

New Vienna, Dubuque Co, St. Boniface's (1845), Rev. John J. O'Connor.
Mailing Address: P.O. Box 200, 52065-0114. Tel: 319-921-2465.
Res., SS. Peter and Paul, 1625-300th Ave., Petersburg, 52040-8736. Tel: 319-875-7992. [CEM]
Church—7401 Columbus St.
School—Archbishop Hennessy Catholic. See separate listing under Institutions Located in the Archdiocese for details.

North Buena Vista, Clayton Co., Immaculate Conception (1898), Rev. Paul R. Peters.
Mailing Address: P.O. Box 847, Guttenberg, 52052. Tel: 319-252-1247. [CEM]
Church—218 Main St.N., Buena Vista.

North Washington, Chickasaw Co., Immaculate Conception (1868), Rev. Francis J. Perry.
Res., 114 N. Wapsi, 50661. Tel: 515-394-2078. [CEM]
Catechesis/Religious Programs—Mary Roethler, D.R.E.
Students 56.

Norway, Benton Co., St. Michael's (1867), Rev. Walter J. Kleinfehn.
Res., 512 Evergreen, P.O. Box 09, 52318-9998. Tel: 319-227-7169. [CEM]
Catechesis/Religious Programs—Cathy Maile, D.R.E.
Students 109.

Oelwein, Fayette Co., Sacred Heart (1876), Rev. Frederick C. Fangmann; Carol Hamilton, Pastoral Assoc.
Res., 628 S. Frederick Ave., 50662-2818. Tel: 319-283-3743. [CEM]
School—(Grades K-6). Sr. Benjamin Duschner, P.B.V.M., Prin.
Sisters of Mercy 2; Lay Teachers 7; Students 197.
Catechesis/Religious Programs—Bonnie O'Brien, D.R.E.
Students 279.

Osage, Mitchell Co., Sacred Heart (1878), Rev. Dennis H. Cahill; Sr. Rosanne Rottinghaus, P.B.V.M., Pastoral Assoc.
Res., 1209 State St., 50461-1844. Tel: 515-732-4342. [CEM]
School—(Grades PreK-6). Sr. Lenore Ostdiek, O.S.F., Prin.
Lay Teachers 4; Students 119.
Catechesis/Religious Programs—D.R.E.: Eve Kenny; Jane Krabbe.
Students 211.

Ossian, Winneshiek Co., St. Francis de Sales (1876), Rev. Richard W. Kuhn.
Res., 418 E. Main St., 52161-9998. Tel: 319-532-9366. [CEM]
School—Mae Becker, Prin. Lay Teachers 8; Students 147.
Catechesis/Religious Programs—Jennifer Shimek, D.R.E.
Students 65.

Otter Creek, Jackson Co., St. Lawrence (1854), Rev. Msgr. Thomas J. Ralph.
Res., 17486 Bellevue-Cascade Rd., Zwingle, 52079-9688. Tel: 319-686-4228. [CEM]
Catechesis/Religious Programs—Mary Gansen, D.R.E.
Students 67.

Oxford Junction, Jones Co., Sacred Heart (1890), Rev. William E. Reynolds.
Res. and Mailing Address—301 Hwy. 136, P.O. Box 127, Lost Nation, 52254-0127. Tel: 319-678-2200.
Church—309 Church St.

Parkersburg, Butler Co., St. Patrick's (1889), Rev. Kenneth C. Stecher.
Res., P.O. Box E, 50665-0035. Tel: 319-346-1411. [CEM]
Church—702 Grant St.

Peosta, Dubuque Co., St. John the Baptist (1874), Rev. Carl J. Manternach.
Res., 10761 Sundown Rd., 52068-9507. Tel: 319-582-4217. [CEM]
School—Seton Catholic Elementary School, Epworth. See separate listing under Institutions Located in the Archdiocese for details.
Catechesis/Religious Programs—Sr. Mary Kent Pearson, O.P., D.R.E.
Students 114.
Oratories—Lattnerville, Annunciation; Prairie, St. Joseph.

Petersburg, Delaware Co., SS. Peter and Paul (1867), Rev. John J. O'Connor.
Res. and Mailing Address—1625 300th Ave., 52040-8736. Tel: 319-875-7992.
School—Archbishop Hennessy Catholic, New Vienna. See separate listing under Institutions Located in the Archdiocese for details.

Placid, Dubuque Co., St. John's (1874), Rev. Joseph L. Hauer.
Res., 22453 E. Pleasant Grove Rd., Epworth, 52045-9603. Tel: 319-876-5501. [CEM]
School—Seton Catholic Elementary School, Epworth. See separate listing under Institutions Located in the Archdiocese for details.
Catechesis/Religious Programs—Joann Koopmann, D.R.E.
Students 54.

Plymouth, Cerro Gordo Co., St. Michael (1872), Rev. Thomas F. McAndrew.
Res., Sacred Heart, 120 E. North, Manly, 50456-2586. Tel: 515-454-2586.

Plymouth Rock, Winneshiek Co., St. Agnes (1857), Rev. Michael C. Fitzgerald.
Res. and Mailing Address—116 Third S.E., Cresco, 52136. Tel: 319-547-3565. [CEM]
Church—2875 County Rd. A 18, 50464.
Catechesis/Religious Programs—Dorothy Hovey, D.R.E.
Students 25.

Postville, Allamakee Co., St. Bridget's (1872), Rev. Leo P. Riley.
Res., 135 W. Williams, P.O. Box 369, 52162-0369. Tel: 319-864-3138.
Catechesis/Religious Programs—Mary Koopmann, D.R.E.
Students 118.

Prairieburg, Linn Co., St. Joseph's (1874), Rev. Richard J. Ament; Sr. Anne Kisting, O.S.F., Pastoral Assoc.
Mailing Address: P.O. Box 4248, 52219-9999.
Parish Office: 410 Terrace Dr., Central City, 52214. Tel: 319-438-6625. [CEM]
Church—300 West Ave.
Catechesis/Religious Programs—Bette Holub, D.R.E.
Students 20.

Preston, Jackson Co., St. Joseph's (1881), Rev. Donald V. Bakewell; Sr. Susan Dunnwald, R.S.M., Pastoral Assoc.
Res. and Mailing Address: 250 S. Faith St., P.O. Box 309, 52069-0309. Tel: 319-689-5161. [CEM]
Catechesis/Religious Programs—D.R.E.: Irene Entsminger; Rosemary Sievers.
Students 223.

Protivin, Howard Co., Holy Trinity (1878), Rev. Allen M. Schmitt.
Res. and Mailing Address—110 Commercial Ave., P.O. Box 205, 52163-0205. Tel: 319-569-8259.
School—Julie Franzen, Prin. Lay Teachers 4; Students 94.
Catechesis/Religious Programs—Students 59.
Oratory—Schely, Holy Cross.

Raymond, Blackhawk Co., St. Joseph's (1905), Rev. John R. Flaherty.
Res. and Mailing Address—313 E. Central St., P.O. Box 158, 50667-0158. Tel: 319-233-5395.
School—Immaculate Conception-St. Joseph (Gilbertville-Raymond Consolidated Elementary). See separate listing under Institutions Located in the Archdiocese for details.

Reinbeck, Grundy Co., Queen of Heaven (1958), Rev. John M. Kissling.
Res., Sacred Heart, 204 G Ave., Grundy Center, 50638-1939. Tel: 319-824-3571.
Church—1006 Blackhawk St., 50669.
Catechesis/Religious Programs—Gloria Rickert, D.R.E.
Students 48.

Riceville, Howard Co., Immaculate Conception (1879), Rev. John A. Moser.
Res. and Mailing Address: 209 Main St., Box 146, 50466-0146. Tel: 515-985-2028. [CEM]
Catechesis/Religious Programs—Deborah Oulman, D.R.E.
Students 158.

Rickardsville, Dubuque Co., St. Joseph's (1840), Rev. Melvin D. Hemann.
Res., 20245 St. Joseph Dr., 52039-9757. Tel: 319-552-2233. [CEM]
School—Rickardsville-Holy Cross-Luxemburg (RHCL) Catholic. See separate listing under Institutions Located in the Archdiocese for details.
Catechesis/Religious Programs—Mary Ann Manternach, D.R.E.
Students 45.

Rockford, Floyd Co., Holy Name (1910), Rev. Roger L. Katz.
Res., 507 First Ave. N.W., 50468-1132. Tel: 515-756-3769.
Catechesis/Religious Programs—Brenda Schmitt, D.R.E.
Students 136.

Rockwell, Cerro Gordo Co., Sacred Heart (1878), Rev. Stephen L. Meyer; Deacon Victor Groh.
Res. and Mailing Address: 305 Elm St. E., P.O. Box 30, 50469-0030. Tel: 515-822-4957. [CEM]
Catechesis/Religious Programs—Eleanor Nelson, D.R.E.
Students 113.
Oratory—Cartersville, St. John.

Roseville, Floyd Co., St. Mary (1867), Rev. Msgr. Walter L. Brunkan.
Res., 105 N. Main, P.O. Box 480, Greene, 50636-0480. Tel: 515-823-4146. [CEM]
Church—2397 Hwy. 14, Marble Rock.
Catechesis/Religious Programs—Betty Jo Staudt, D.R.E.
Students 51.

Rowley, Buchanan Co., All Saints (1896), Rev. Aloysius J. Vorwald; Michael Kellog, Pastoral Assoc.
Mailing Address: 3103 Michael, 52329-0206.
Res., 209 Fifth Ave. E., Independence, 50644-1998. Tel: 319-334-7191. [CEM]
Church—219 Park Ave.
Catechesis/Religious Programs—Brenda Corkery, D.R.E.
Students 49.

Ryan, Delaware Co., St. Patrick's (1882), Rev. John W. Carpender.
Res. and Mailing Address: 615 Howard St., P.O. Box 219, 52330-0219. Tel: 319-932-2151. [CEM]
Church—606 Franklin St.
Catechesis/Religious Programs—Kathy Zimmerman, D.R.E.
Students 124.

Sabula, Jackson Co., St. Peter (1840), Rev. Donald V. Bakewell; Sr. Susan Dunnwald, R.S.M., Pastoral Admin.
Res., 504 Elk St., P.O. Box 325, 52070-0325. Tel: 319-687-2525. [CEM]
Catechesis/Religious Programs—Sr. Susan Dunnwald, R.S.M., D.R.E.
Students 25.

St. Ansgar, Mitchell Co., St. Ansgar (1951), Rev. Joseph M. Schneider.
Mailing Address: P.O. Box 396, 50472-0396.
Parish Office: 604 N. Broad St., Stacyville, 50476-5019. Tel: 515-737-2262.
Church—704 E. Fourth St.
Catechesis/Religious Programs—Mary Wilder, D.R.E.
Students 67.

St. Anthony, Marshall Co., Sacred Heart (1878), Rev. Richard J. Hess.
Res., 418 Main St., P.O. Box 300, 50239. Tel: 515-477-8227. [CEM]
Catechesis/Religious Programs—Rev. Richard J. Hess, D.R.E.
Students 22.

St. Catherine, Dubuque Co., St. Catherine's (1887). Unassigned.
Res., 5177 St. Catherine Rd., Dubuque, 52003-9566. Tel: 319-583-0092. [CEM]
School—Bellevue Area Catholic Elementary. See separate listing under Institutions Located in the Archdiocese for details.
Catechesis/Religious Programs—Sr. Dolores McAllister, O.S.F., D.R.E.
Students 63.

St. Cecilia, Howard Co., St. Patrick's. Closed. Sacramental records are located at Immaculate Conception, Elma.

St. Donatus, Jackson Co., St. Donatus (1853), Sr. Dolores McAllister, O.S.F., Pastoral Assoc.
Res. and Mailing Address—5177 St. Catherine Rd., Dubuque, 52003-9566. Tel: 319-583-0092.
Church—E. First. St.
School—Bellevue Area Catholic Elementary. See separate listing under Institutions Located in the Archdiocese for details.

St. Lucas, Fayette Co., St. Luke's (1855), Rev. Raphael A. Ludwig.
Res., 215 E. Main St., P.O. Box 186, 52166-0186. Tel: 319-778-2370. [CEM]
School—Fort Atkinson-St. Lucas Consolidated. See separate listing under Institutions Located in the Archdiocese for details.
Catechesis/Religious Programs—D.R.E.: Trudy Smith; Deb Dietzenbach.
Students 71.

St. Theresa, Jackson Co., St. Theresa's (1853), Rev. Mark R. Nemmers.
Res., 34257 230th Ave., LaMotte, 52054-9794. Tel: 319-773-2341. [CEM]
Catechesis/Religious Programs—Patricia Puetz, D.R.E.
Students 45.

Sand Springs, Delaware Co., Immaculate Conception (1884), Rev. Harold J. Drexler; Patricia Hucker, Pastoral Assoc.
Res., St. Luke, P.O. Box 28, Hopkinton, 52237-0028. Tel: 319-926-2613.
Church—Hwy. 38, 52237.

Schley, Howard Co., Holy Cross (1928). Closed. Sacramental records are located at Holy Trinity, Protivin.

Shell Rock, Butler Co., Holy Name. Closed. Sacramental records are located at St. Mary's, Waverly.

Sherrill, Dubuque Co., SS. Peter and Paul (1852), Rev. Melvin D. Hemann; Sr. Mildred Leuenberger, O.S.F., Pastoral Admin.
Res., 5131 Sherrill Rd., 52073-9612. Tel: 319-552-2611. [CEM]
School—Balltown-Sherrill Catholic. See separate listing under Institutions Located in the Archdiocese for details.
Catechesis/Religious Programs—Mary Ann Manternach, D.R.E.
Students 71.

Spillville, Winneshiek Co., St. Wenceslaus (1860), Rev. Daniel J. Keppler.
Res., 207 Church St., Box 128, 52168-0128. Tel: 319-562-3637. [CEM]
School—Calmar-Festina-Spillville (CFS) Catholic Elementary. See separate listing under Institutions Located in the Archdiocese for details.
Catechesis/Religious Programs—Lois Meyer, D.R.E.
Students 10.

Springbrook, Jackson Co., SS. Peter and Paul (1864), Rev. Donald V. Bakewell; Sr. Susan Dunnwald, R.S.M., Pastoral Assoc.
Mailing Address: 105 E. Main St., 52075. Tel: 319-872-3875.
Res., 205 Faith St., Preston, 52069-0309. Tel: 319-689-5161. [CEM]
School—Bellevue Area Catholic Elementary. See separate listing under Institutions Located in the Archdiocese for details.

Springville, Linn Co., St. Isidore's (1961), Rev. Msgr. John R. McClean; Rev. Phillip G. Gibbs.
Res. and Mailing Address—St. Joseph Rectory, 1790 14th St., Marion, 52302-2267. Tel: 319-377-4860.
Church—603 6th St. S.
Catechesis/Religious Programs—Marilyn Anderson, D.R.E.
Students 67.

Stacyville, Mitchell Co., Church of the Visitation (1894), Rev. Joseph M. Schneider.
Res., 601 N. Broad St., 50476-5019. Tel: 515-737-2262. [CEM]
School—Visitation (Stacyville-Meyer) Consolidated. See separate listing under Institutions Located in the Archdiocese for details.
Catechesis/Religious Programs—Julie Brumm, D.R.E.
Students 33.

State Center, Marshall Co., St. Joseph's (1870), Rev. Ronald G. Friedell.
Res., 607 Third St. S.W., P.O. Box 694, 50247-0694. Tel: 515-483-2464. [CEM]
Catechesis/Religious Programs—Judy Eggers, D.R.E.
Students 58.

Strawberry Point, Clayton Co., St. Mary's (1876), Rev. Dennis D. Juhl; Deacon Bob Burke, Pastoral Assoc.
Mailing Address: 314 W. Mission St., 52076-9432. Tel: 319-933-6166. [CEM]
Catechesis/Religious Programs—Bonnie Hayes, D.R.E.
Students 198.

Sumner, Bremer Co., Immaculate Conception (1894), Rev. John J. Purtell; Eloyce Munk, Pastoral Assoc.
Res., 413 W. First St., 50674-1313. Tel: 319-578-5366. [CEM]
Catechesis/Religious Programs—Barbara Hennessey, D.R.E.
Students 132.
Oratory—St. Bridget (Pinhook), St. Bridget.

Sylvia, Dubuque Co., Assumption (1896), Rev. Mark R. Nemmers.
Res., 34257 230th Ave., La Motte, 52054-9794. Tel: 319-773-2341. [CEM]
Catechesis/Religious Programs—Patricia Puetz, D.R.E.
Students 39.

Tama-Toledo, Tama Co., St. Patrick's (1864), Rev. Keith L. Birch; Patti Hoffman, Pastoral Assoc.
Res., 900 Park St., Tama, 52339-1238. Tel: 515-484-3039; 484-4242. [CEM]
Catechesis/Religious Programs—Patricia Green, D.R.E.
Students 163.

Temple Hill, Jones Co., St. Peter's (1852), Rev. Thomas E. Toale.
Res., 20189 Temple Hill Rd., 52033-9802. Tel: 319-852-3448. [CEM]
School—Aquin Elementary School. See separate listing under Institutions Located in the Archdiocese for details.
Catechesis/Religious Programs—Linda Greenwood, D.R.E.
Students 74.

Traer, Tama Co., St. Paul's (1912), Rev. John R. Tilp.
Res., 1102 Walnut St., 50675-1440. Tel: 319-478-2222. [CEM]
Catechesis/Religious Programs—Cecilia Podhajsky, D.R.E.
Students 121.
Oratory—Carroll Township, St. Wenceslaus.

Urbana, Benton Co., St. Mary (1872), Rev. Paul C. McManus.
Res. and Mailing Address—Sacred Heart, 516 Rowley St., P.O. Box 116, Walker, 52352. Tel: 319-448-4316.
Church—401 Ash Ave.
Catechesis/Religious Programs—Laverne Dolphin, B.V.M., D.R.E.
Students 106.

Van Horne, Benton Co., Immaculate Conception (1869), Rev. Louis C. Zee; Deacon James Naso.
Res., 405 Fourth Ave., P.O. Box 250, 52346-0250. Tel: 319-228-8131. [CEM]
Catechesis/Religious Programs—Sr. Nora Rochford, O.S.F., D.R.E.
Students 115.

Vining, Tama Co., St. Mary's (1874), Rev. John R. Tilp.
Res. and Mailing Address—1102 Walnut St., Traer, 50675-1440. Tel: 319-478-2222.
Church—405 2nd Ave.
Catechesis/Religious Programs—Barbara Cibula, D.R.E.
Students 31.

Vinton, Benton Co., St. Mary's (1878), Rev. Joseph E. McGuire.
Res., 2200 S. Second Ave, P.O. Box 116, 52349-0116. Tel: 319-472-4448. [CEM]
Catechesis/Religious Programs—Lynn Mealhow, D.R.E.
Students 177.

Volga, Clayton Co., Sacred Heart (1889), Rev. Thomas W. Rhomberg; Sr. Rosanna Gleason, O.P., Pastoral Assoc.
Mailing Address: 330 First St. P.O. Box 135, El Kader, 52043-0626. Tel: 319-245-2548.
Church—304 White St.
Catechesis/Religious Programs—Sr. Rosanna Gleason, O.P., D.R.E.
Students 17.

Walford, Linn Co., Holy Trinity (1890), Rev. Thomas J. Schwinn; Jerry Corrigan, Pastoral Assoc.
Mailing Address: 110 First St. S., 52351-0126. Tel: 319-846-2270.

Walker, Linn Co., Sacred Heart (1885), Rev. Paul C. McManus.
Res., 516 Rowley St., P.O. Box 116, 52352-0116. Tel: 319-448-4316. [CEM]
Catechesis/Religious Programs—Sr. Laverne Dolphin, B.V.M., D.R.E.
Students 95.

Waterloo, Blackhawk Co.,

1—St. Joseph's, (1868), Very Rev. Donald J. Hawes, Admin.; Rev. Robert E. Hilmer; Deacon Clarence Gram.
Res., 320 Mulberry St., 50703-3598. Tel: 319-234-4439. [JC]

2—St. Mary's, (1898), Very Rev. Donald J. Hawes; Rev. Robert Hilmer.
Res., 2127 E. Fourth St., 50703-2699. Tel: 319-232-1326. [JC]
School—Tel: 319-232-2418. Patricia Powell, Prin. Lay Teachers 9; Students 160.
Catechesis/Religious Programs—Bev Byford, D.R.E.
Students 39.

3—Sacred Heart, (1909), Rev. Michael Mescher; Sr. Louann Doerning, P.B.V.M., Pastoral Assoc.
Res., 627 W. Fourth St., 50702-1501. Tel: 319-234-4996. [JC]
School—Julie Niemeyer, Prin. Lay Teachers 16; Students 342.
Catechesis/Religious Programs—Pamela Johnston, D.R.E.
Students 106.

4—St. Edward's, (1945), Rev. Msgr. Russell M. Bleich; Rev. Raymond A. Burkle; Karol Rae Hoth, Pastoral Assoc.; Deacon John Baker.
Res., 1423 Kimball Ave., 50702-3896. Tel: 319-233-8060. [JC]
School—Joan Leonard, Prin. (Elementary). Sisters 1; Lay Teachers 23; Students 460.
Catechesis/Religious Programs—Mary Ann Helie, D.R.E.
Students 122.

5—St. John's, (1923), Rev. George W. Karnik; Sr. JoAnn O'Connell, B.V.M., Pastoral Assoc.
Res., 1701 Mulberry St., 50703-4991. Tel: 319-233-5241. [JC]
School—St. John-St. Nicholas Consolidated. Sr. Barbara Emerson, Prin.
Sisters of Mercy (Cedar Rapids) 2; Lay Teachers 15; Students 370.
Catechesis/Religious Programs—Dave Cushing, D.R.E.
Students 33.

6—Blessed Sacrament, (1947), Revs. Patrick G. Geary; Paul E. Lippstock; Sr. Madonna M. Friedman, O.S.F., Pastoral Assoc.; Deacons John Herman; James Freet.
Res., 650 Stephan Ave., 50701-2099. Tel: 319-233-6179. [JC]
School—Tel: 319-233-7863. Georgine Hurt, Prin. Lay Teachers 11; Students 244.
Catechesis/Religious Programs—Ann Phillips, D.R.E.
Students 74.

Watkins, Benton Co., St. Patrick's (1880), Rev. Walter J. Kleinfehn.
Res. and Mailing Address—St. Michael, 512 Evergreen St., P.O. Box 9, Norway, 52318-9998. Tel: 319-227-7169.
Church—2nd St., 52354.
Catechesis/Religious Programs—Yvonne Brecht, D.R.E.
Students 31.

Waucoma, Fayette Co., St. Mary's (1898), Rev. Raphael A. Ludwig.
Res. and Mailing Address—215 E. Main, P.O. Box 186, St. Lucas, 52166-0186. Tel: 319-778-2370.
218 3rd St. N.W.
Catechesis/Religious Programs—Shirley Riha, D.R.E.
Students 74.

Waukon, Allamakee Co., St. Patrick's (1851), Rev. Msgr. Edward W. Lechtenberg; Sr. Margaret Anne Kramer, P.B.V.M., Pastoral Min. & D.R.E.
Res., 109 Second St. S.W., Box 146, 52172-0146. Tel: 319-568-3671. [CEM]
School—Tel: 319-568-2415. Peter Smith, Prin. Lay Teachers 12; Students 177.
Catechesis/Religious Programs—Sr. Margaret Anne Kramer, P.B.V.M., D.R.E.
Students 257.
Oratory—West Ridge, St. John the Baptist.

Waverly, Bremer Co., St. Mary's (1856), Rev. James L. Miller. Pastoral Assocs.: Sr. Bernadette Engelhaupt; Sr. Dorlores Schmitz.
Res., 112 Second Ave. S.E., 50677-3404. Tel: 319-352-2493. [CEM]
Catechesis/Religious Programs—Sue Hinderlider, D.R.E.
Students 381.

Webster City, Hamilton Co., St. Thomas Aquinas (1870), Rev. John J. Walsh.
Res., 1010 Des Moines St., 50595-2147. Tel: 515-832-1190. [CEM]
School—Tel: 515-832-1346. Michael Whittlesey, Prin. Lay Teachers 8; Students 127.
Catechesis/Religious Programs—D.R.E.: Betsy McGlynn; Mary Mechem.
Students 163.

West Union, Fayette Co., Holy Name (1870), Rev. Dale J. Rausch.
Res., 128 N. Walnut St., 52175-1347. Tel: 319-422-3184. [CEM]
Catechesis/Religious Programs—Mike Woodson, D.R.E.
Students 227.

Wexford, Allamakee Co., Immaculate Conception (1851), Rev. Louis J. Trzil.
Res. and Mailing Address—1416 Great River Rd., Lansing, 52151-7519. Tel: 319-586-2150.
Catechesis/Religious Programs—Patty Manning, D.R.E.
Students 35.

Williams, Hamilton Co., St. Mary's (1875), Rev. Philip F. Recker.

Res., 404 Fourth St., P.O. Box 157, 50271-0157. Tel: 515-854-2241. [CEM]
Catechesis/Religious Programs—Marty Doerning, D.R.E.
Students 38.

Winthrop, Buchanan Co., St. Patrick's (1894), Rev. Ivan R. Nienhaus; Sr. Mary Valentine Smith, O.S.F., Pastoral Assoc.
Res., 555 First St., P.O. Box 236, 50682-0236. Tel: 319-935-3523. [CEM]
Catechesis/Religious Programs—Roger Decker, D.R.E.
Students 168.

Woden, Hancock Co., Sacred Heart (1900), Rev. Marvin J. Bries.
Res. and Mailing Address—139 Third St. S.E., Britt, 50423-1726. Tel: 515-843-3215.
Church—147 Howard Ave., 50484.
Catechesis/Religious Programs—Kathryn Smith, D.R.E.
Students 25.

Worthington, Dubuque Co., St. Paul's (1875), Rev. Mark Osterhaus.
Res., 314 Third Ave. S.W., P.O. Box 38, 52078-0038. Tel: 319-855-2405. [CEM]
School—Sandra Klaus, Prin. Lay Teachers 7; Students 90.
Catechesis/Religious Programs—Julie Bries, D.R.E.
Students 94.

Zearing, Story Co., St. Gabriel (1904), Rev. Richard J. Hess.
Res. and Mailing Address—Sacred Heart, 418 Main St., St. Anthony, 50239. Tel: 515-477-8227.
Church—302 N. Center.
Catechesis/Religious Programs—D.R.E.: Rev. Richard Hess; Rex Goherty.
Students 40.

Chaplains of Public Institutions

ANAMOSA. *Iowa State Men's Reformatory*. Vacant.

INDEPENDENCE. *Mental Health Institute*. P.O. Box 505, 302 W. Main St., Fairbanks, 50629. Tel: 319-635-2211. Rev. Mark J. McGovern, Part-Time Chap.

MARSHALLTOWN. *Veterans' Home*. St. Joseph Rectory, 607 Third St. S.W., State Center, 50247. Tel: 515-483-2464. Rev. Ronald G. Friedell, Chap.

On Special or Other (Arch)Diocesan Assignment:
Reverend Monsignors—
Barta, James O., Episcopal Vicar
Walz, W. Dean, Episcopal Vicar

On Duty Outside the Archdiocese:
Reverend Fathers—
Burke, Clement, 2321 Aldrich Ave. S., #315, Minneapolis, MN 55405
Connolly, Leon L., Misioneros de Maryknoll, Guatemala, Central America
Flanagan, James W., Dept. of Religion, Mather House, Case Western Reserve Univ., Cleveland, OH 44106
Grady, Bernard C., Padres San Columbano, Lima, 100, Peru.SA.

Military Chaplains:
Reverend Fathers—
Remy, David P., U.S.N., C.H.C., L.C.D.R., PSNS (Code 801), 1400 Farragut Ave., Bremerton, WA 98314
Schueller, La Verne L., Ch. Col., 96 ABW/HC, 202 N. Eighth St., Ste. 1, Eglin AFB, FL 32542-5651

Graduate Studies:
Reverend Fathers—
Bullock, Scott E., St. Jane Frances de Chantal, 9701 Georgetown Rd., Bethesda, MD 20814
Joensen, William, St. Bernadette Parish, 70 University Blvd., E., Silver Springs, MA 20901
Zinkula, Thomas R., Ediface Deschatelets, 175, Rue Main, Ottawa, ONT. KISIC3

Unassigned:
Reverend Fathers—
Purtell, Thomas W.
Wild, Alexander

On Leave of Absence:
Reverend Fathers—
Barta, Ardel H.
Devenney, Timothy L.
McTarsney, John F.
Mihm, Richard L.

Retired:
Reverend Monsignors—
Ament, Ernest P., 405 Franklin St., Bellevue, IA 52031
Blessington, William H., Villa Raphael, 1235 Mt. Loretta, Dubuque, IA 52003-8785
Chihak, John P., 420 W. Lyon St., Garner, IA 50438
Collins, Bernard G., 3160 E. Main St., Village Grove #8, Mesa, AZ 85213
Dalton, John W., 1301 Rhodes, Naperville, IL 60540
Ferring, Robert L., 3400 Dana Dr., #4, Dubuque, IA 52002
Friedl, Francis P., 3400 Dana Dr., #3, Dubuque, IA 52002
Halbach, A. A., Stonehill Care Center, 3485 Windsor Ave., Dubuque, IA 52001-1312
Heineman, Donald P., 108 3rd St., SE, P.O. Box 187, Fort Atkinson, IA 52144-0187
Heles, Frederic G., 107 Martin Dr., Apollo, PA 15613
Heuring, Alvan P., 3458 Edison St., San Mateo, CA 94403-3401
Kress, Justin A., Villa Raphael, 1235 Mt. Loretta Ave., Dubuque, IA 52003-8785
Kurt, Edgar J., Villa Raphael, 1235 Mt. Loretta, Dubuque, IA 52003-8785
Leonard, William P., 971 Mt. Loretta Ave., Dubuque, IA 52003
Manternach, Albert V., 617 1st Ave., W., Cascade, IA 52033
McAvoy, Ambrose A., Stonehill Care Center, 3485 Windsor Ave., Dubuque, IA 52001-1312
O'Brien, Roger E., Villa Raphael, 1235 Mt. Loretta, Dubuque, IA 52003-8785
Raker, Clarence J., Stonehill Care Center, 3485 Windsor Ave., Dubuque, IA 52001-1312
Reicks, Leander H., 105 E. Rural St., P.O. Box 223, St. Lucas, IA 52166
Sullivan, Joseph A., 2245 Chaney Rd., #1, Dubuque, IA 52001
Supple, James A., 129 Ash St., #2, Ames, IA 50010
Sweeney, Donald F., Villa Raphael, 1235 Mt. Loretta Ave., Dubuque, IA 52003-8785
Vogl, Robert R., Loras College, 1450 Alta Vista, Dubuque, IA 52004-0178
Zachar, Albert L., 3031 Sixth St., S.W., Apt. 12, Cedar Rapids, IA 52404

Reverend Fathers—
Arquitt, William A., 1715 Edgewood Dr., NW, Apt. 3, Cedar Rapids, IA 52405
Auer, Robert F., 1027 N. Third St., Guttenberg, IA 52052
Axen, Ronald J., St. Francis Village, 105 Trinity Cir., Crowley, TX 76036
Bahning, Frederick C., Windsor Park, # 408, 801 Davis St., Dubuque, IA 52001
Barnes, John G., 114 Sheakley, New Hampton, IA 50659
Bierie, Elwyn L., P.O. Box 198, Bullshoals, AR 72619
Bodensteiner, Peter C., 108 W. Spring St., Apt. A-1, Lawler, IA 52154
Brickley, John J., Villa Raphael, 1235 Mt. Lorette Ave., Dubuque, IA 52003-8785
Brosius, Alfred G., Villa Raphael, 1235 Mt. Loretta Ave., Dubuque, IA 52003-8785
Carpender, Thomas J., Brookwood, 1320 E. 48th Pl., Tulsa, OK 74105
Cross, Vern F., Stonehill Care Center, 3485 Windsor Ave., Duguque, IA 52001-1312
Currier, Thomas F., 925 N. Harrison Ave., Mason City, IA 50401
Devine, William P., 22623 V Ave., Eldora, IA 50627-8012
Dunkel, Henry N., Lourdes R.F.D. 1, Elma, IA 50628
Einck, Gregory J., Windsor Park Apartments, No. 109, 801 Davis Ave., Dubuque, IA 52001
Engler, Ernest J., St. John Rectory, 212 Seventh St. S.E., Mt. Vernon, IA 52314-0169
Evans, Paul J., 400 Blunt St., Charles City, IA 50616
Frana, Clarence L., 3031 Sixth St., S.W., Apt. 9, Cedar Rapids, IA 52404
Goedken, Nestor B., Windsor Park, 801 Davis, Dubuque, IA 52001
Goltz, William A., P.O. Box 675, Guttenberg, IA 52052-0675
Griffin, Joseph F., Villa Rafael, 1235 Mount Loretta Ave., Dubuque, IA 52003-8785
Guter, Lawrence, Stonehill Care Center, 3485 Windsor Ave., Dubuque, IA 52001-1312
Hamilton, Philip A., 12 Padgett Ct., Bluffton, SC 29910
Heimerman, Francis D., 151 Main St., P.O. Box 623, Nashua, IA 50658
Holzer, Wm., 292 Northpointe Dr., N.E. 118, Cedar Rapids, IA 52405-6215
Hussmann, John R., Villa Raphael, 1235 Mt. Loretta Ave., Dubuque, IA 52003-8785
Kalb, Bertram J., Stonehill Care Center, 3485 Windsor Ave., Dubuque, IA 52001-1312
Kane, Justin J., 3709 W. Ninth, Apt. 8, Waterloo, IA 50702
Karal, John W., Maple View, 603 E. Main St., Apt. 1, Marshalltown, IA 50158-1973
Kissling, Joseph L., Stonehill Care Center, 3485 Windsor Ave., Dubuque, IA 52001-1312
Klein, Karl J., Cedar River Tower, Apt. 905, 100 First Ave., N.E., Cedar Rapids, IA 52401
Kruse, Clarence, Villa Raphael, 1235 Mt. Loretta Ave., Dubuque, IA 52003
Kunsch, William C., Villa Raphael, 1235 Mt. Loretta Ave., Dubuque, IA 52003-8785
Kurt, Allan J., P.O. Box 479, Dubuque, IA 52004-0479
LaBarge, Charles F., 1538 Kehl Ct., Dubuque, IA 52003
Laughlin, Martin T., St. Francis by the Sea, PO Box 22239, Hilton Head Island, SC 29925
Maichen, Richard F., 1112 E. Main, Troy, OH 45373
McDonald, J. Robert, 2123 Buckingham Dr., N.W., Cedar Rapids, IA 52405
McDonald, Paul F., U.S.A.F., 8915 Willmon Way, San Antonio, TX 78239
Menster, William J., 703 Bluff St., Dubuque, IA 52001
Merfeld, Vincent C., U.S.A.F., 4536 Wilshire Blvd., #4, Los Angeles, CA 90010
Most, William G., 9210 Park Ave., Manassas, VA 22110
Norton, Claude B., Villa Raphael, 1235 Mt. Loretta Ave., Dubuque, IA 52003-8785
Otting, Loras C., Villa Raphael, 1235 Mt. Loretta Ave., Dubuque, IA 52003-8785
Palen, Robert L., 19 W. 230 Governors Trail, Oak Brook, IL 60521
Pepper, David J., 102 W. Spring, Box 200, Lawler, IA 52154
Peters, John M., 6841 E. Fourth St., Tucson, AZ 85710
Pitzen, John J., 215 Vanderbilt St., Fairfax, IA 52228
Raftis, J. Duane, Stonehill Care Center, 3485 Windsor Ave., Dubuque, IA 52001-1312
Reiss, Robert J., P.O. Box 479, Dubuque, IA 52004-0479
Rogers, Daniel J., 3839 St. Catherine Rd., Bellevue, IA 52031
Ruhland, Carl J., 3955 Creston St., Dubuque, IA 52002
Saunders, Robert J., 710 Anderson St., Manchester, IA 52057
Schmidt, Wilfred W., 1584 White St., Dubuque, IA 52001
Schroeder, Karl G., Loras College, 1450 Alta Vista St., Dubuque, IA 52001-0178
Schwartz, William T., 6421 S. Oakmont Dr., Chandler, AZ 85249
Sigwarth, Reynold J., Villa Raphael, 1235 Mt. Loretta Ave., Dubuque, IA 52003
Simon, Vincent J., 100 South St., P.O. Box 304, Ossian, IA 52161
Smith, John P., 203 First St. E., Cresco, IA 52136
Stark, John W., 3312 Carlton Dr., Cedar Falls, IA 50613
Weydert, Donald D., 2249 Del Monaco Dr., Dubuque, IA 52002
Whalen, Charles W., 2245 Chaney Rd., #4, Dubuque, IA 52001-2939
White, Norman R., 1025 Hill Dr. SE, Cedar Rapids, IA 52403

Permanent Deacons:
Aitchison, Gary, St. Cecilia, Ames
Ayers, John, Clear Lake
Baker, John, St. Edward, Waterloo
Baltes, Robert, St. Joseph, New Hampton
Barlow, Jack, St. Joseph, Mason City
Bassler, Eugene, Retired
Berger, James, St. Ludmila, Cedar Rapids
Berry, Matthew, Holy Family, Mason City
Biver, William, St. Columbkille, Dubuque
Blouin, Mike, All Saints, Cedar Rapids
Brustkern, Leo J., St. Patrick, Dubuque
Carroll, Paul J., St. John Evangelist, Independence
Cashatt, Wayne, St. Mary, Eldora
Cisler, William, St. Ludmila, St. Wenceslaus, Cedar Rapids
Cooper, Charles, Holy Family, Mason City
DiPietre, Dennis, Columbia, MO
Dutcher, Frank, (Retired), St. Louis, MO
Fessler, Ray, (Retired), Dubuque
Fortin, Daryl, St. Patrick, Cedar Falls
Freet, James, Blessed Sacrament, Waterloo
Frost, Irwin, (Retired), Waterloo
Froyen, Leonard, St. Stephen The Witness Student Center, Cedar Falls
Gehrke, Richard, St. Mary, Hazleton
Gram, Clarence, St. Joseph, Waterloo
Groh, Victor, Sacred Heart, Rockwell; St. Patrick, Dougherty
Hayes, Joseph, St. Matthias, Cascade
Herman, John, Blessed Sacrament, Waterloo
Hoeger, Daniel, St. Patrick, Cedar Rapids
Hurych, Robert F., St. Paul, Newhall
Jenney, William, St. Nicholas, Evansdale

Jorgensen, Gerald, Resurrection, Dubuque
Karsten, Thomas M., (Retired)
Knepper, Walter, (Retired), Cascade
Lang, Thomas, St. Mary, Manchester
LoBianco, Timothy, St. Joseph The Worker, Dubuque
MacDonald, Stephen, St. Joseph the Worker, Dubuque
Malone, John, St. Matthew, Cedar Rapids
Manning, Richard, St. Ludmila, Cedar Rapids
Mauss, William, St. Anthony, Dubuque
McCully, John, St. Cecilia, Ames
McGhee, David, Nativity, Dubuque
Mead, Edward, St. Mary, Marshalltown
Mega, Robert, Sacred Heart, Manly
Moetsch, Michael, St. Patrick, Cedar Falls
Naso, James, Immaculate Conception, Van Horne; St. Paul, Newhall; St. John, Blairstown
Oates, Michael, St. Patrick, Cedar Falls
Otto, J. C., St. Michael, Belle Plaine; St. Joseph, Chelsea
Pantaloni, Ed, St. Joseph, Marion
Pettit, Gerald, Immaculate Conception, Cedar Rapids
Saunders, Phil, St. Matthew, Cedar Rapids
Scharosch, Albert, St. Pius X, Cedar Rapids
Schmall, Leo, St. Joseph, Marion
Schmit, Nick, St. Francis Xavier, Belmond
Simmons, Kenneth, St. Cecilia, Ames
Sinnwell, James E., Immaculate Conception, Charles City
Stattelman, Leo W., St. Patrick, Clear Lake
Steger, James, St. Joseph, Earlville; St. Joseph, Greeley
Tondra, Richard, St. Cecilia, Ames
Van Kerckvoorde, Steve, St. Thomas Aquinas, Ames
Vaske, Irvin, St. Henry, Marshalltown
Whitters, Michael, St. John, Clarion
Wilson, James, (Retired), Waterloo
Zimmerman, Paul, St. Pius X, Cedar Rapids

INSTITUTIONS LOCATED IN THE ARCHDIOCESE

[A] SEMINARIES, ARCHDIOCESAN

DUBUQUE. *Seminary of St. Pius X*, Loras College, 1450 Alta Vista St., 52001. Tel: 319-588-7782. Revs. Dennis J. Colter, Rector; Mark A. Ressler, Vice Rector; Douglas O. Wathier, Spiritual Dir. Students for Archdiocese of Dubuque 9; Seminarians 12.

[B] SEMINARIES, RELIGIOUS OR SCHOLASTICATES

EPWORTH. *Divine Word College*, 102 Jacoby Dr., 52045-0380. Tel: 319-876-3353. Society of the Divine Word (S.V.D.). Very Rev. William Shea, S.V.D., Rector; Revs. Michael Hutchins, S.V.D., Pres.; Kenneth Anich, S.V.D., Vice Pres. & Vice Pres. for Academic Affairs; Bros. Dennis Newton, S.V.D., Vice Pres. of Recruitment & Admissions; Leonard Bauer, S.V.D.; Rev. James Heiar, S.V.D., Vice Pres. for Devel.; Bros. Daniel Holman, S.V.D.; Brian McLauchlin, S.V.D.; Rev. Joseph McDermott, S.V.D.; Bro. Henry Oeser, S.V.D.; Rev. John Tra, S.V.D.; Bros. Rodney Bowers, S.V.D.; Tony Kreinus, S.V.D.; Rogers Hannan, S.V.D.; Revs. Quang Duc DinhShea, S.V.D., Vice Pres. for Formation & Dean of Students; John-Hue Tran, S.V.D., Assoc. Development Dir.; Joseph Dang, S.V.D.; Walter Bunofsky, S.V.D.; Francis Kuttikattukunnel, S.V.D.; Gus Wall, S.V.D. Priests 12; Brothers 8; Sisters 2; Lay Teachers 26; Students 115.

[C] COLLEGES AND UNIVERSITIES

DUBUQUE. *Clarke College*, 1550 Clarke Dr., 52001. Tel: 319-588-6300; Fax: 319-588-6789.
For a complete listing, refer to the Colleges and Universities section.
Loras College, 1450 Alta Vista St., 52004-0178. Tel: 319-588-7100; Fax: 319-588-7964.
For a complete listing, refer to the Colleges and Universities section.

CEDAR RAPIDS. *Mount Mercy College*, 1330 Elmhurst Dr., N.E., 52402. Tel: 319-363-8213; Fax: 319-363-5270.
For a complete listing, refer to the Colleges and Universities section.

[D] HIGH SCHOOLS, INTERPAROCHIAL

DUBUQUE. *Wahlert High School*, 2005 Kane St., 52001. Tel: 319-583-9771. Mr. Donald Miller, Prin.; Revs. Maurice J. Lynch, Spiritual Dir. & Student Counselor; James E. Hayes. Priests 2; Sisters 2; Lay Teachers 67; Students 965.
Serving all Parishes in Dubuque; Holy Family, New Melleray; St. Joseph's, Key West; SS. Peter and Paul, Sherrill.

BELLEVUE. *Marquette High School*, 502 Franklin St., 52031. Tel: 319-872-3356. Rev. Donald V. Bakewell, Exec. Coord. Priests 1; Sisters 1; Lay Teachers 8; Students 129.
Serving St. John's, Andrew; St. Joseph's, Bellevue; St. Catherine's, St. Catherine; St. Donatus, St. Donatus; Holy Rosary, LaMotte; St. Peter's, Sabula; SS. Peter and Paul, Springbrook.

CEDAR RAPIDS. *LaSalle High School*. (Coed), 3700 First Ave., N.W., 52405. Tel: 319-396-7791. Rev. Donald R. Bruggeman, Exec. Coord.; Jeff Henderson, Chief Admin.; Joe Steepleton, Prin.; Rev. Steven G. O'Brien. Priests 1; Sisters 1; Lay Teachers 15; Students 212.
Serving Holy Trinity, Walford; St. Patrick's, Fairfax; St. Jude's, St. Ludmila's and St. Patrick's, Cedar Rapids.
Metropolitan Office of Catholic Education, Cedar Rapids Metro Office, 516 A Ave. N.W., 52405. Tel: 319-366-2517. Sr. Jean Brady, B.V.M., Assoc. Dir.
Regis High School, 735 Prairie Dr., N.E., 52402. Tel: 319-365-6991. Rev. Donald R. Bruggeman, Exec. Coord.; Mr. Jeff Henderson, Chief Admin.; Mr. Justin Kramer, Guidance Dir.; Mr. Richard Breitbach, Prin.; Mr. David Glynn, Asst. Prin.; Rev. Steven G. O'Brien. Priests 1; Lay Teachers 35; Students 477.
Serving the following parishes in Cedar Rapids: Immaculate Conception, St. Wenceslaus, St. Matthew, All Saints, St. Pius X, St. Joseph, Marion; St. Elizabeth Ann Seton, Hiawatha.
Regis LaSalle Foundation, 516 A Ave. N.W., P.O. Box 1394, 52406. Tel: 319-366-0491. Anne Cunningham, Exec. Dir.; Rev. Msgr. Robert G. Hogan, Exec. Coord.

DYERSVILLE. *Beckman High School*. (Grades 7-12). (Coed), 1325 Ninth St. SE, 52040. Tel: 319-875-7188. Steve Schute, Prin. Asst. Principals: Mr. Terry Scherbring; Mr. Wayne Wilgenbusch. Priests 1; Sisters 1; Lay Teachers 34; Students 496.
Serving the following Parishes: St. Francis Xavier, Dyersville; St. Joseph, Earlville; St. Boniface, New Vienna; Ss. Peter and Paul, Petersburg; St. Paul, Worthington.

GILBERTVILLE. *Don Bosco High School*, 405 16th Ave., 50634. Tel: 319-296-1692. Rev. James L. Secora, Exec. Coord.; James Hrabe, Prin.; Rev. John Flaherty, Spiritual Dir. Guidance Counselors: Joseph Oppold; Nicole Wee. Priests 1; Lay Teachers 19; Students 226.
Serving St. Francis, Barclay, Dunkerton; Immaculate Conception, Gilbertville; St. Athanasius, Jesup; Sacred Heart, LaPorte City; St. Joseph's, Raymond; St. Mary of Mt. Carmel, Eagle Center.

WATERLOO. *Columbus High School*, 3231 W. Ninth St., 50702. Tel: 319-233-3358. Rev. Msgr. Russell M. Bleich, Exec. Coord.; Mr. D. Michael Palmer, Prin.; Todd Dirth, Assoc. Prin.; Rev. Paul E. Lippstock. Sisters 1; Lay Teachers 50; Students 621.
Serving all parishes in Waterloo; St. Nicholas, Evansdale; St. Patrick's, Cedar Falls.

[E] SCHOOLS OF RELIGION

CALMAR. *Christian Family School*, 52312. Tel: 319-562-3045. Rev. Richard W. Kuhn, Exec. Coord.; Jennifer Shimek, Youth Min. Priests 1; Lay Teachers 1; Students 175.

CASCADE. *Aquin Religious Education Center*, 608 Third Ave. NW, 52033-0460. Tel: 319-852-3005. Rev. Philip E. Thompson, Exec. Coord.; Richard J. Bronson, D.R.E. Lay Teachers 2; Students 100.

LANSING. *Lansing School of Religion*, 52151. Tel: 319-538-4668; 538-4360. Rev. Herbert L. Tegeler; Karen Weber, Dir. Students 145.

MANCHESTER. *St. Paul's School of Religion*, 408 Clara Ave., 52057. Tel: 319-927-2900. Rev. Ralph Simington, Exec. Coord.; Wilma Billhorn, Dir. Priests 1; Lay Teachers 2; Students 474.

NEW HAMPTON. *St. John's School*, Box 108, 50659. Tel: 515-394-3171. Rev. Marvin C. Salz, Dir.; Elizabeth J. Boehmer, Coord. Lay Teachers 3; Students 185.

[F] CONSOLIDATED PARISH SCHOOLS

DUBUQUE. *Holy Trinity-Sacred Heart Consolidation*. (Grades PreK-8), 2222 Queen St., 52001. Tel: 319-588-4657. Jean Burgmeier, Prin. Lay Teachers 17; Students 301.
St. Mary-St. Patrick Catholic School. Martha Wightman, Prin., St. Patrick Attendance Center, 180 W. 15th St., 52001. Tel: 319-582-2127. St. Mary's Attendance Center, 1600 White St., 52001. Tel: 319-582-1053. Sisters 1; Lay Teachers 12; Students 168.

BALLTOWN. *Balltown-Sherrill Catholic School*. (Grades PreK-6). 5135 Sherrill Rd., Sherrill, 52073. Tel: 319-552-2166. Sr. Ruth Elsbernd, O.S.F., Prin.; Sr. Mildred Leuenberger, O.S.F., Pastoral Admin.; Rev. Melvin D. Hemann, Exec. Coord.
Consolidation of the following parishes: St. Francis, Balltown; SS. Peter & Paul, Sherrill. Lay Teachers 5; Students 77.

BELLEVUE. *Bellevue Area Catholic Elementary School*. (Grades K-8), 403 Park St., 52031. Tel: 319-872-3284. Jim Squires, Prin.; Rev. Donald V. Bakewell, Exec. Sec.
Consolidation of the following parishes: St. Donatus, St. Donatus; St. Peter Springbrook; St. Joseph, Bellevue (School location); Holy Rosary, LaMotte. Lay Teachers 22; Students 285.

CALMAR. *Calmar-Festina-Spillville (CFS) Catholic Elementary School*, Box 815, 52132. Tel: 319-562-3291; Fax: 319-562-3292. Michael Ward, Prin.; Rev. Robert M. Hirsch, Exec. Sec.
Consolidation of the following parishes: Our Lady of Seven Dolors (St. Marys), Festina; St. Wenceslaus, Spillville; St. Aloysius, Calmar; St. Wenceslaus (Grades 1-4); St. Aloysius (Grades 5-8). Lay Teachers 10; Students 141.

CASCADE. *Aquin Elementary School*, 608 Third Ave., N.W., 52033-0460. Tel: 319-852-3331. Rev. Philip E. Thompson, Exec. Coord.; Sr. Bertha Bonert, O.S.F., Prin.
Consolidation of the following parishes: St. Matthias, Cascade; Sacred Heart, Fillmore; St. Patrick, North Garryowen; St. Peter, Temple Hill. Sisters of St. Francis of the Holy Family 2; Lay Teachers 19; Students 266.

CEDAR RAPIDS. *Holy Family Catholic Consolidated School*. Rev. Harry Koelker, Exec. Sec. Lay Teachers 45; Students 694.
St. Ludmila Center. (Grades PreK-5), 215 21st Ave., S.W., 52404. Tel: 319-362-1943. Mike Welch, Prin.
St. Jude Center. (Grades PreK-5), 50 Edgewood Rd., N.W., 52405. Tel: 319-396-7818. Jack Luensman, Prin.
St. Patrick Center. (Grades 6-8), 509 A Ave., N.W., 52405. Tel: 319-363-1027. John Krumbholz, Prin.

CRESCO. *Notre Dame System of Education*. (Grades PreK-6), 221 Second Ave., E., 52136. Tel: 319-547-4513. Rev. Michael C. Fitzgerald, Exec. Coord.; Alice M. Barton, Prin. Lay Teachers 12; Students 229.

EPWORTH. *Seton Catholic Elementary School*, 52045. Gary Fortney, Prin.; Rev. John P. Ptacek, Exec. Sec.
Consolidation of the following parishes: St. Patrick, Epworth; St. John, Peosta; St. John, Placid; St. Joseph, Farley; St. Clement, Bankston. Sisters of the Presentation 1; Lay Teachers 24; Students 363.

GILBERTVILLE. *Immaculate Conception-St. Joseph School*. (Gilbertville-Raymond Consolidated Elementary School), 311 16th Ave., 50634. Tel: 319-296-1089. Ruth Palmer, Prin.
Consolidation of the following parishes: St. Joseph, Raymond; Immaculate Conception, Gilbertville; St. Joseph (Grades K-2); Immaculate Conception (Grades 3-8). Sisters 1; Lay Teachers 19; Students 347.

GUTTENBERG. *Guttenberg-North Buena Vista Consolidated School*. (Grades K-8), 502 S. Second St., 52052. Tel: 319-252-1577. Sr. Suzanne Gallagher, Prin.; Rev. Paul R. Peters, Exec. Sec.
Consolidation of the following parishes: St. Mary's, Guttenberg; Immaculate Conception, North Buena Vista. Lay Teachers 11; Students 154.

HOLY CROSS. *Rickardsville-Holy Cross-Luxemburg (RHCL) Catholic School*, 835 Church St., P.O. Box 368, 52053. Tel: 319-870-2405. Rev. Donald Plamondon, Exec. Coord.; Mary Smock, Prin.
Consolidation of the following parishes: St. Joseph, Rickardsville; Holy Cross, Holy Cross; Holy Trinity, Luxemburg (Grades K-3); Holy Cross (Grades 4-8). Sisters 2; Lay Teachers 12; Students 194.

MARSHALLTOWN. *Marshalltown Area Consolidated Catholic School*, 10 W. Linn St., P.O. Box 512, 50158. Tel: 515-753-7977. Mrs. Patricia Fox, Prin.; Rev. Thomas E. Braak, Exec. Sec.
Consolidation of the following parishes: St. Mary, Marshalltown; St. Henry, Marshalltown; Immaculate Conception, Haverhill; St. Henry, 310 Columbus (Grades K-2); St. Marys, 10 W. Linn St. (Grades 3-6). Lay Teachers 18; Students 285.

NEW VIENNA. *Archbishop Hennessy Catholic School*, Box 210, 52065. David Gross, Prin.; Rev. John J. O'Connor, Exec. Sec.
Consolidation of the following parishes: St. Boniface Center (Grades K-3), New Vienna; SS. Peter & Paul (Grades 4-6), Petersburg. Sisters 1; Lay Teachers 6; Students 112.

ST. LUCAS. *Fort Atkinson-St. Lucas Catholic School*, Box 249, 52166. Tel: 319-778-2340. Julie Franzen, Prin.; Rev. Raphael A. Ludwig, Exec. Sec.
Consolidation of the following parishes: St. John Nepomucene, Fort Atkinson; St. Luke, St. Lucas. Lay Teachers 7; Students 88.

STACYVILLE. *Visitation School*. (Grades 1-8), 603 N. Broad St., 50476. Tel: 515-737-2380. Sr. Lenore Ostdiek, O.S.F., Prin.
Consolidation of the following parishes: Church of the Visitation, Stacyville; Sacred Heart, Meyer. Sisters 2; Lay Teachers 8; Students 78.

[G] CONSOLIDATED K-12 SYSTEMS

MASON CITY. *Newman Catholic.* Newman High and Middle Schools. (Grades 5-12), 2445 19th St., S.W., 50401. Tel: 515-423-6939. St. Joseph Center. (Grades K-4), 320 Fifth St., S.E., 50401. Tel: 515-423-3101. Holy Family Day Care Center, 713 N. Adams, 50401. Tel: 515-423-0168. Revs. John R. Kremer, Exec. Coord.; David Beckman; Vicki Steil, Secondary Prin.; Kathy Lloyd, Early Childhood Dir. Parishes served: Holy Family, St. Joseph, Mason City; St. Patrick, Clear Lake; Sacred Heart, Manly; St. Michael, Plymouth; Sacred Heart, Rockwell; St. Patrick, Dougherty. Priests 1; Sisters 3; Lay Teachers 47; Elementary 511; High School 212.

[H] GENERAL HOSPITALS

DUBUQUE. *Mercy Health Center-St. Joseph's Unit,* Mercy Dr., 52001. Tel: 319-589-8000; Fax: 319-589-8073.
For a complete listing, refer to the Hospitals section.

CEDAR RAPIDS. *Mercy Care Management, Inc.,* P.O. Box 786, 52406. Tel: 319-398-6144.
For a complete listing, refer to the Hospitals section.
Mercy Medical Center, Cedar Rapids, Iowa, 701 Tenth St., S.E., 52403. Tel: 319-398-6011.
For a complete listing, refer to the Hospitals section.
Mercy Medical Center, Cedar Rapids, Iowa, Endowment Foundation, Inc., 701 Tenth St., S.E., 52403. Tel: 319-398-6519.
For a complete listing, refer to the Hospitals section.
Mercycare Service Corporation, 701 10th St., S.E., 52403. Tel: 319-398-6011.
For a complete listing, refer to the Hospitals section.

DYERSVILLE. *Mercy Health Center-St. Mary's Unit,* 1111 Third St., S.W., 52040. Tel: 319-875-7101; Fax: 319-875-2957.
For a complete listing, refer to the Hospitals section.

MASON CITY. *North Iowa Mercy Health Center,* 84 Beaumont Dr., 50401. Tel: 515-424-7211; Fax: 515-424-7827.
For a complete listing, refer to the Hospitals section.

NEW HAMPTON. *St. Joseph Community Hospital,* 308 N. Maple Ave., 50659. Tel: 515-394-4121; Fax: 515-394-5628.
For a complete listing, refer to the Hospitals section.

OELWEIN. *Mercy Hospital of Franciscan Sisters,* 50662. Tel: 319-283-6000; Fax: 319-283-6004.
For a complete listing, refer to the Hospitals section.

WATERLOO. *Covenant Medical Center,* 3421 W. Ninth St., 50702. Tel: 319-236-4111.
For a complete listing, refer to the Hospitals section.

[I] SPECIAL HEALTH CENTERS

DUBUQUE. *Holy Family Hall Infirmary,* 3340 Windsor Ave., 52001-1300. Tel: 319-583-9786; Fax: 319-583-3250.
For a complete listing, refer to the Special Care Facilities section.
Marian Hall Infirmary, 1050 Carmel Dr., 52003. Tel: 319-556-5474.
For a complete listing, refer to the Special Care Facilities section.
St. Dominic Villa, Cardiff St. and Mazzuchelli Heights, 52001-7399.
For a complete listing, refer to the Special Care Facilities section.

[J] HOMES FOR AGED

DUBUQUE. *Padre Pio Health Care Center, Inc. dba Stonehill Care Center,* 3485 Windsor Ave., 52001-1312. Tel: 319-557-7180; Fax: 319-557-8934.
For a complete listing, refer to the Special Care Facilities section.
Villa Raphael, 1235 Mt. Loretta Ave., 52003. Tel: 319-583-4904.
For a complete listing, refer to the Special Care Facilities section.

CEDAR RAPIDS. *Hallmar-Mercy Medical Center,* 701 Tenth St., S.E., 52403.
For a complete listing, refer to the Special Care Facilities section.

CRESCO. *Elder Hospitality of Iowa, Inc.,* Heritage Haven, 301 First Ave., 52136. Tel: 319-547-3325.
For a complete listing, refer to the Special Care Facilities section.

DYERSVILLE. *Mercy Health Center St. Mary's Unit-Oakcrest Manor,* 1111 Third St., S.W., 52040. Tel: 319-875-7101; Fax: 319-875-2957.
For a complete listing, refer to the Special Care Facilities section.

[K] MONASTERIES AND RESIDENCES OF PRIESTS AND BROTHERS

PEOSTA. *New Melleray Abbey, Order of Cistercians of the Strict Observance,* 6500 Melleray Cir., 52068. Tel: 319-588-2319. Legal Title: *Corporation of New Melleray.* Rt. Revs. Brendan J. Freeman, O.C.S.O., Abbot; David R. Bock, O.C.S.O., Retired Abbot; James J. Kerndt, O.C.S.O., Retired Abbot; David L. Wechter, O.C.S.O., Retired Abbot; Philip J. O'Connor, O.C.S.O., Retired Abbot; Revs. Timothy L. Welsh, O.C.S.O.; Bernard J. Cullen, O.C.S.O.; Daniel F. Lenihan, O.C.S.O.; Kenneth F. Tietjen, O.C.S.O.; Thomas J. McCarty, O.C.S.O.; James E. O'Connor, O.C.S.O.; Thaddeus J. Kennedy, O.C.S.O.; Xavier L. Dieter, O.C.S.O.; Joseph P. Bauwens, O.C.S.O.; Thomas A. MacMaster, O.C.S.O., Prior; Joseph G. Knapp, O.C.S.O.; James B. Henderson, O.C.S.O.; Neil Paquette, O.C.S.O. Total Residents 37; Priests 18; Brothers 19; Scholastics 1.

[L] CONVENTS AND RESIDENCES FOR SISTERS

DUBUQUE. *Mt. Loretto Convent.* Motherhouse and Novitiate of the Sisters of the Presentation of the B.V.M. 2360 Carter Rd., 52001-2997. Tel: 319-588-2008. Sr. Mary Jacqueline Quillin, P.B.V.M., Major Supr.; Sr. Mary Sharon Kelchen, P.B.V.M., Dir.; Rev. Douglas O. Wathier, Chap. Professed Sisters 77; Novices 1.
International Presentation Association.
Mt. St. Francis, 3390 Windsor Ave., 52001-1311. Tel: 319-583-9786; Fax: 319-583-3250. Motherhouse and Novitiate of the Sisters of St. Francis of the Holy Family. Sr. Margaret Jungers, O.S.F., Pres.; Sr. Marge Staudt, O.S.F., Dir. Sister Support Svcs.; Rev. Dennis J. Colter, Chap. Professed Sisters 133.
Sisters of St. Francis of the Holy Family Charitable Trust.
Our Lady of the Mississippi Abbey, 8400 Abbey Hill, 52003. Tel: 319-582-2595; Fax: 319-582-5511. The Cistercian Nuns of the Strict Observance. (Monastery of Trappistine Nuns). Rev. Mother Gail Marie Fitzpatrick, O.C.S.O., Abbess; Rt. Rev. James Kerndt, O.C.S.O., Chap. Professed Nuns 24; Novices 2.
St. Joseph's Convent, Mount Carmel, 1150 Carmel Dr., 52003. Tel: 319-556-3240. Motherhouse of the Sisters of Charity of the Blessed Virgin Mary. Sr. Floria Shannon, B.V.M., Admin.; Sr. Donard Collins, B.V.M., Admin.; Sr. Eileen Healy, B.V.M., Pastoral Care; Rev. Msgr. David A. Wheeler, Chap. Professed Sisters 130.
Sisters of Charity of the Blessed Virgin Mary, BVM Center, Mount Carmel, 1100 Carmel Dr., 52003. Tel: 319-588-2351. Sr. Dolores Marie McHugh, B.V.M., Pres. Congregation; Sr. Mary McCauley, B.V.M., 1st Vice Pres.; Sr. Mary Joellen McCarthy, B.V.M., 2nd Vice Pres.; Sr. Mary Ellen Schulte, B.V.M., Admin., B.V.M. Center.
Sisters of Charity of the Blessed Virgin Mary: Retirement Trust Plan and Charitable Trust.
Visitation Convent, 2950 Kaufmann Ave., 52001-1655. Tel: 319-556-2440. Sisters of the Visitation of the Congregation of the Immaculate Heart of Mary. Sr. Ruth Jackson, S.V.M., Pres.; Rev. Robert Beck, Chap. Professed Sisters 9.

CEDAR RAPIDS. *Sacred Heart Convent,* 1125 Prairie Dr., N.E., 52402-4737. Tel: 319-364-5196; Fax: 319-364-7383. Motherhouse of the Sisters of Mercy (Cedar Rapids Regional Community). Sr. Susan O'Connor, R.S.M., Pres.; Sr. Delores Marie Hannon, R.S.M., Vice Pres.; Marianne Arndorfer, Admin. Sacred Heart Convent; Rev. Dwayne J. Thoman, Chap. Professed Sisters 115; Total Staff 3. Sisters of Mercy, Cedar Rapids.
Sisters of Mercy Charitable Trust.
Catherine McAuley Center for Women, Cedar Rapids.
Mount Mercy College, Cedar Rapids.

HIAWATHA. *Central Region of Franciscan Sisters of Perpetual Adoration,* Box 190, 52233-0190. Tel: 319-393-6092. Sr. Karen Flottmeier, F.S.P.A., Reg. Supr. Tel: 319-393-5982. Professed Sisters 178; Temporary Profession 2.

[M] RETREAT HOUSES

DUBUQUE. *New Melleray Guest House,* 6500 Melleray Cir., 52068. Tel: 319-588-2319.
Shalom Retreat Center, 1001 Davis Ave., 52001. Tel: 319-582-3592. Sr. Marie Therese Kalb, O.S.F., Dir. Total Staff 8; Retreatants 5,450.

CEDAR FALLS. *American Martyrs Retreat House,* 2209 North Union Rd., P.O. Box 605, 50613-0605. Tel: 319-266-3543. Rev. Daniel J. Knipper, Dir. Total Staff 13.

[N] NEWMAN CENTERS

AMES. *St. Thomas Aquinas Church and Catholic Student Center (Iowa State University),* 2210 Lincoln Way, 50014. Tel: 515-292-3810. Revs. Everett Hemann; Jon M. Seda; Rev. Msgr. James A. Supple, (Retired); Deacon Steve Vankerckvoorde; Dee McConnell, Parish Family Life; John Donaghy, Dir. Campus Ministry & Charity, Justice and Peace Coord.; Robert LeBlanc, Church Business Admin.; Karri Kerns, Marriage Preparation; Jack Alexander, Coord. of Order of Christian Initiation of Adults & Liturgist; Crystal Caruana, Campus Min. & Liturgist; Ernest Bayer, D.R.E.; Janine Greenwood, Youth Min.; Karen Piconi, Development Dir.

CEDAR FALLS. *St. Stephen the Witness Catholic Student Center, University of Northern Iowa,* 1019 W. 23rd St. Tel: 319-266-9863; Fax: 319-266-3706. Rev. John S. Haugen, Dir. Pastoral Assocs.: Lynne Vaske, Coord. Student Svcs.; Deacon Leonard Froyen, Marriage Preparation, Alumni Director; Joan E. Farstad, Coord. Education & Worship.

WEST UNION. *Upper Iowa University,* c/o St. Francis of Assisi Church of Fayette, 128 N. Walnut, 52175. Tel: 319-422-3184. Rev. Dale J. Rausch, Chap., Holy Name Parish, 52175.

[O] MISCELLANEOUS

DUBUQUE. *Archdiocese of Dubuque Deposit and Loan Fund,* 1229 Mt. Loretta, 52003-7800. Richard L. Runde, Finance Officer.
Archdiocese of Dubuque Education Fund, 1229 Mt. Loretta, 52003-7800. Richard L. Runde, Finance Officer.
Archdiocese of Dubuque Perpetual Care Fund, 1229 Mt. Loretta, 52003-7800. Richard L. Runde, Finance Officer.
Archdiocese of Dubuque Seminarian Education Fund, 1229 Mt. Loretta, 52003-7800. Richard L. Runde, Finance Officer.
Heartland Housing Initiative, 696 Central Ave., 52001. Tel: 319-583-9653; Fax: 319-583-6490. (A member of the Mercy Housing System, Heartland Housing Initiative.). Sr. Mary Martensen, R.S.M., Regional Pres. Total Staff 3; Total Assisted 121.
Hennessy Charitable Trust, 2360 Carter Rd., 52001-2297. Tel: 319-588-2008. Sr. Mary Jacqueline Quillin. Sponsored by the Sisters of the Presentation.
National Communicators Network for Women Religious, Sisters of the Presentation/NCNWR Office, 2360 Carter Rd., 52001. Tel: 319-588-2008. Sr. Beth Kress, P.B.V.M., Contact Person. Sponsor: Communication personnel of congregations of Women Religious who are members. Purpose: NCNWR is organized to promote and assist in the understanding of women religious and specifically, to enhance their image and advance their mission. The organization is also organized to provide a network of professional support and education for its members.
St. Vincent de Paul Society of the Archdiocese of Dubuque.
Dubuque Council, 1351 Iowa St., 52001. Tel: 319-583-8701. Paul Hoppman, Natl. Trustee & Pres.
Waterloo Council, 4114 Heritage Rd., Cedar Falls, 50613. Tel: 319-232-8662. Richard McGrane, Pres.
Cedar Rapids Council, 339 22nd Ave. S.W., Cedar Rapids, 52404. Tel: 319-364-0748. Robert Crawford, Pres.

WATERLOO. *Ridgeway Place, Inc.,* 155 E. Ridgeway Ave., 50702.. Ms. Cindi Herrera, Pres.
Sponsored by the Wheaton Franciscan Sisters, Wheaton, IL and a corporation of Wheaton Franciscan System. Purpose: to provide economical housing and related services, for elderly people and individuals.

RELIGIOUS INSTITUTES OF MEN REPRESENTED IN THE ARCHDIOCESE

For further details refer to the corresponding bracketed number in the Religious Institutes of Men or Women section.

[1180]—*Brothers of Saint Pius X.*—C.S.P.X.

[0350]—*Cistercians Order of the Strict Observance-Trappists.* (Our Lady of New Melleray).—O.C.S.O.

[0480]—*Conventual Franciscans.* (Prov. of Our Lady of Consolation).—O.F.M.Conv.

[0430]—*Order of Preachers-Dominicans.* (Prov. of St. Albert the Great).—O.P.

[0420]—*Society of the Divine Word.* (Northern Prov.).—S.V.D.

RELIGIOUS INSTITUTES OF WOMEN REPRESENTED IN THE ARCHDIOCESE

[0230]—*Benedictine Sisters of Pontifical Jurisdiction.* (Yankton, SD).—O.S.B.

[0670]—*Cistercian Nuns of the Strict Observance.*—O.C.S.O.

[2100]—*Congregation of the Humility of Mary.* (Davenport, IA).—C.H.M.

[1780]—*Congregation of the Sisters of the Third Order of St. Francis of Perpetual Adoration.*—F.S.P.A.

[1710]—*Congregation of the Third Order of St. Francis of Mary Immaculate, Joliet, IL.*—O.S.F.

[1070-03]—*Dominican Sisters.*—O.P.

[1240]—*Franciscan Sisters, Daughters of the Sacred Hearts of Jesus and Mary.*—O.S.F.

[1820]—*Hospital Sisters of the Third Order of St. Francis.*—O.S.F.

[2575]—*Institute of the Sisters of Mercy of the Americas.* (Cedar Rapids, IA; Omaha, NE; Detroit, MI).—R.S.M.

[3530]—*Missionary Sisters Servants of the Holy Spirit.*—S.Sp.S.
[2960]—*Notre Dame Sisters.* (Omaha).—N.D.
[3130]—*Our Lady of Victory Missionary Sisters.*—O.L.V.M.
[2970]—*School Sisters of Notre Dame.* (Mankato, MN).—S.S.N.D.
[1680]—*School Sisters of St. Francis.* (Milwaukee, WI).—O.S.F.
[0430]—*Sisters of Charity of the Blessed Virgin Mary.*—B.V.M.
[1705]—*The Sisters of St. Francis of Assisi.*—O.S.F.
[3320]—*Sisters of the Presentation of the B.V.M.*.—P.B.V.M.
[1720]—*Sisters of the Third Order Regular of St. Francis of the Congregation of Our Lady of Lourdes.*—O.S.F.
[4200]—*Sisters of the Visitation of the Congregation of the Immaculate Heart of Mary.* (Dubuque, IA).—S.V.M.

CEMETERIES

DUBUQUE. *Mount Calvary.*
Mount Olivet.
CEDAR RAPIDS. *Calvary.*
St. John.
St. Joseph.
CRESCO. *Calvary.*
MARSHALLTOWN. *St. Mary.*
MCINTIRE. *St. Mel.*
St. Patrick.
WATERLOO. *Catholic Cemeteries, Inc.*

NECROLOGY

† Becker, Rev. Msgr. Edmund J., (Retired). —Died Nov. 23, 1996.
† Byrne, Most Rev. James J., (Retired). —Died Aug. 2, 1996.
† Cassidy, Francis P., Corwith, IA St. Mary Parish. —Died June 19, 1996.
† Cizek, Rev. Msgr. Robert W., Greene, IA St. Mary Parish. —Died April 27, 1996.
† Cooney, Robert E., Marion, IA St. Joseph Parish. —Died May 12, 1996.
† Lana, Francis A., Cascade, IA St. Mary Parish. —Died June 14, 1996.
† Lukan, Kenneth J., (Retired). —Died Feb. 18, 1996.
† Matt, Irwin H., LaMotte, IA Holy Rosary Parish. —Died Dec. 4, 1995.
† May, Alois B., Waterloo, IA St. Edward Parish. —Died Aug. 1, 1996.
† McBride, James J., Peosta, IA St. John the Baptist Church. —Died Dec. 27, 1995.
† Schulte, Rev. Msgr. George N., Dubuque, IA Loras College. —Died April 23, 1996.
† Walbaum, Dean L., Andrew, IA St. John Parish. —Died April 4, 1996.
† White, Norman R., (Retired). —Died Aug. 28, 1996.

Diocese of Duluth

(Dioecesis Duluthensis)

Most Reverend

ROGER L. SCHWIETZ, O.M.I., D.D.

Bishop of Duluth; ordained December 20, 1967; appointed Bishop of Duluth December 12, 1989; consecrated and installed February 2, 1990. *Res., 2830 E. Fourth St., Duluth, MN, 55812.* Tel.: 218-724-9111; Fax: 218-724-1056.

Corporate title: *Diocese of Duluth.*

ESTABLISHED OCTOBER 3, 1889.

Square Miles 22,354.

Comprises the counties of Aitkin, Carlton, Cass, Cook, Crow Wing, Itasca, Koochiching, Lake, Pine and St. Louis in the State of Minnesota.

For legal titles of parishes and diocesan institutions, consult the Chancery Office.

Pastoral Center: 2830 E. Fourth St., Duluth, MN, 55812. Tel.: 218-724-9111; Fax: 218-724-1056.

STATISTICAL OVERVIEW

Personnel	
Bishop	1
Priests: Diocesan Active in Diocese	57
Priests: Active Outside Diocese	4
Priests: Retired, Sick or Absent	22
Number of Diocesan Priests	83
Religious Priests in Diocese	16
Extern Priests in Diocese	2
Ordinations:	
Permanent Deacons in Diocese	19
Total Sisters	178
Parishes	
Parishes	95
With Resident Pastor:	
Resident Diocesan Priests	50
Resident Religious Priests	11
Without Resident Pastor:	
Administered by Priests	34
Missions	3
Closed Parishes	4
Welfare	
Catholic Hospitals	2
Total Assisted	171,785
Homes for the Aged	2
Total Assisted	370
Special Centers for Social Services	1
Total Assisted	700
Educational	
Diocesan Students in Other Seminaries	9
Total Seminarians	9
Colleges and Universities	1
Total Students	2,000
Elementary Schools, Diocesan and Parish	13
Total Students	1,689
Catechesis/Religious Education:	
High School Students	4,605
Elementary Students	5,385
Total Students Under Catholic Instruction	13,688
Teachers in the Diocese:	
Priests	1
Sisters	8
Lay Teachers	136
Vital Statistics	
Receptions into the Church:	
Infant Baptism Totals	1,195
Adult Baptism Totals	43
Received into Full Communion	195
First Communions	1,243
Confirmations	1,135
Marriages:	
Catholic	289
Interfaith	310
Total Marriages	599
Deaths	1,564
Total Catholic Population	82,175
Total Population	378,000

Former Bishops—Rt. Rev. JAMES MCGOLRICK, D.D., cons. Dec. 27, 1889; died Jan. 23, 1918.—Rt. Rev. JOHN T. MCNICHOLAS, O.P., S.T.D., cons. Sept. 8, 1918; appt. Archbishop of Cincinnati July 8, 1925.—Most Rev. THOMAS A. WELCH, D.D., cons. Feb. 3, 1926; died Sept. 9, 1959.—Most Rev. FRANCIS J. SCHENK, D.D., cons. May 24, 1945; appt. to Duluth Jan. 19, 1960; resigned April 30, 1969; died Oct. 28, 1969.—Most Rev. PAUL F. ANDERSON, D.D., appt. Titular Bishop of Polignando and Co-adjutor Bishop with right of succession July 19, 1968; cons. Oct. 17, 1968; succeeded to See April 10, 1969; resigned Aug. 7, 1982; appt. Apostolic Administrator Aug. 7, 1982; appt. Auxiliary Bishop of Sioux Falls, SD March 25, 1983; died Jan. 4, 1987.—Most Rev. ROBERT H. BROM, D.D., cons. May 23, 1983; appt. Coadjutor Bishop of San Diego, CA, May 9, 1989.

Vicar General—Rev. DAVID TUSHAR.

Chancellor—Rev. DALE NAU, J.C.L.

Pastoral Center—2830 E. Fourth St., Duluth, 55812. Tel: 218-724-9111; Fax: 218-724-1056. Office Hours: Mon.-Fri. 8:30-12 & 1-4:30.

Deans—Brainerd: Very Rev. PAUL FRUTH; Cloquet: Very Rev. JAMES SCHEUER; Duluth: Very Rev. GERALD LAPATKA; Hibbing: Very Rev. JOHN O'DONNELL; Virginia: Very Rev. LLOYD MUDRAK.

Diocesan Tribunal—2830 E. Fourth St., Duluth, 55812. Tel: 218-724-9111.

Judicial Vicar—Rev. JAMES BISSONETTE, J.C.L.

Associate Judge and Vicar for Canonical Affairs—Rev. DALE NAU, J.C.L.

Defenders Of Bond—Rev. PATRICK MORAN, J.C.L.

Advocate—BETTE DAMBERG.

Notary—ROSE MARIE EICHMUELLER.

College of Consultors—Most Rev. ROGER SCHWIETZ, O.M.I.; Revs. DAVID TUSHAR; RONALD GAGNE; MICHAEL HAYES; ANDREW KNOP, O.M.I; FREDICK METHOD; KENTON SAILSTAD; JEROME WEISS.

Priests' Pension Board—Most Rev. ROGER L. SCHWIETZ, O.M.I.; Revs. DAVID TUSHAR, V.G.; PATRICK MORAN; JERRY WEISS; DALE NAU; FREDRICK METHOD; Mr. ROBERT MILLER.

Presbyteral Council—Rev. FREDICK METHOD, Chm.

Corporate Board—Most Rev. ROGER L. SCHWIETZ, O.M.I.; Revs. DALE NAU; DAVID TUSHAR; Mr. ROBERT MILLER.

Finance Council—Most Rev. ROGER L. SCHWIETZ, O.M.I.; Revs. DALE NAU; LAWRENCE O'SHEA; DAVID TUSHAR, V.G.; Mr. ROBERT MILLER; Bro. CRAIG BONHAM, O.M.I.; JOHN R. RYAN; JAMES BARTKOWSKI.

Finance Officer—Rev. LAWRENCE O'SHEA.

Diocesan Offices and Directors

Archivists—Rev. PATRICK J. MORAN, J.C.L., *2830 E. Fourth St., Duluth, 55812.* Tel: 218-724-9111.

Boy Scouts—Deacon GREGORY HUTAR, *604 E. Boundary St., Ely, 55731.* Tel: 218-365-5906.

Campus Ministry—Rev. DALE NAU, Dir., *421 W. Ste. Marie, Duluth, 55811.* Tel: 218-728-3757.

Cemeteries—Rev. DALE NAU, Dir., *2830 E. Fourth St., Duluth, 55812.* Tel: 218-724-9111.

Censor of Books—Rev. J. W. EVANS, Ph.D.

Continuing Formation of Priests—Rev. DAVE TUSHAR.

Coordinators of Catechesis—KRISTIN RUHLAND, (Jr-Sr High/Youth Ministry); DENISE MACIEJ, (Preschool-Elementary), *2830 E. Fourth St., Duluth, 55812.* Tel: 218-724-9111.

Council of Catholic Women—Vacant, Moderator, *3 N. Sixth Ave., Proctor, 55810.* Tel: 218-624-0007.

Cursillo Movement—Rev. ROMAN SPORS, Spiritual Advisor, *Box 266, Emily, 56477.* Tel: 218-763-2101. BRYON HARKER, Lay Dir., *Rte. 1, Box 245, Longville, 56655.* Tel: 218-363-2567.

Diocesan Pastoral Council—Most Rev. ROGER L. SCHWIETZ, O.M.I., Pres.; ROSE EICHMUELLER, Sec.

Ecumenical and Inter-faith Affairs—Sr. CLAUDIA RIEHL, O.S.B., *2830 E. Fourth St., Duluth, 55812.* Tel: 218-724-9111.

Finance Officer—Rev. LAWRENCE O'SHEA, *2830 E. Fourth St., Duluth, 55812.* Tel: 218-724-9111.

Health Affairs—Rev. JOHN WHITNEY EVANS, *1200 Kenwood Ave., Duluth, 55811.* Tel: 218-723-6000.

Liturgy and Spirituality—Rev. KENT SAILSTAD, S.T.L., Dir., *2830 E. Fourth St., Duluth, 55812.* Tel: 218-724-9111.

Mission Outreach and Propagation of the Faith—Rev. LAWRENCE O'SHEA, Dir., *2830 E. Fourth St., Duluth, 55812.* Tel: 218-724-9111.

Newspaper "Catholic Outlook"—Rev. WILLIAM FOURNIER, Editor, *2830 E. Fourth St., Duluth, 55812.* Tel: 218-724-9111.

Office of Indian Ministry—Sr. MARIE ROSE MESSINGSCHLAGER, C.D.P., Dir., *2830 E. Fourth St., Duluth, 55812.* Tel: 218-724-9111.

Office for Clergy Vocations—Rev. STEVEN DAIGLE, *2830 E. Fourth St., Duluth, 55812.* Tel: 218-724-9111.

Office for Communications—Rev. WILLIAM FOURNIER, Dir., *2830 E. Fourth St., Duluth, 55812.* Tel: 218-724-9111.

Office for Education (Evangelization and Catechesis)—Rev. DAVID TUSHAR, Coord.; Mr. TERRY CHURCHILL, (Schools), *2830 E. Fourth St., Duluth, 55812.* Tel: 218-724-9111.

Office for Marriage and Family Life—Rev. DALE NAU, *2830 E. Fourth St., Duluth, 55812.* Tel: 218-724-9111.

Office for Development—MICHAEL MARRIN, Dir., *2830 E. Fourth St., Duluth, 55812.* Tel: 218-724-9111.

Office for the Permanent Diaconate—Deacon DAVID CRAIG, Dir., *2830 E. Fourth St., Duluth, 55812.* Tel: 218-724-9111.

Office for the Social Apostolate of the Church—KENT PETERS, S.T.L., *2830 E. Fourth St., Duluth, 55812.* Tel: 218-724-9111.

Rural Life—Rev. MICHAEL HAYES, Dir., *112 Cedar, Moose Lake, 55767.* Tel: 218-485-5909.

CLERGY, PARISHES, MISSIONS AND PAROCHIAL SCHOOLS

CITY OF DULUTH
(St. Louis County)

1—CATHEDRAL OF OUR LADY OF THE ROSARY, Revs. David Tushar, Rector; Timothy Deutsch. In res., Rev. James Crossman.
Res., 2801 E. Fourth St., 55812. Tel: 218-728-3646.
School—Sisters 4; Lay Teachers 16; Students 346.
Catechesis/Religious Programs—D.R.E.: Mrs. Tina Marie Hoban; Mrs. Bernadette Larson.
Students 186.
Convent—443 Lakeview Ave., 55812. Tel: 218-724-4370. Sisters of the Third Order of St. Dominic (Springfield, IL)

2—GOOD SHEPHERD, Revs. Charles Flynn; Vincent Arimond.
Res., 109 S. 59th Ave., W., 55807. Tel: 218-624-0823.

3—HOLY FAMILY,. Consolidated with Ss. Peter and Paul, and Ss. Clement. Revs. Andrew Knop, O.M.I.; Anthony Wroblewski, O.M.I.
Parish Office: 518 N. 24th Ave., 55806. Tel: 218-722-4445.
Res., 2423 W. Third St., 55806. Tel: 218-722-0730.
Church—2401 W. Fifth St., 55806.
Catechesis/Religious Programs—Desiree Taylor, D.R.E.
Students 134.

4—OUR LADY OF MERCY, Rev. Patrick McDowell. In res., Rev. John C. Petrich.
Res., 325 E. Third St., 55805. Tel: 218-722-3078.
Church—2002 Minnesota Ave., 55805.

5—ST. ANTHONY. Closed. Sacramental records are located at St. Benedict.

6—ST. BENEDICT'S, Rev. Jon Wild; Deacon Dennis Anderson.
Office: 1419 St. Benedict St., 55811. Tel: 218-728-4325; 724-4828.
Res., 1419 Arrowhead Rd., 55811. Tel: 218-724-8926.
Catechesis/Religious Programs—Bob Huot, D.R.E.
Students 340.
Stations—Duluth, Chris Jensen Home; Duluth, Aftenro Home.

7—ST. ELIZABETH'S, Rev. Patrick J. Moran.
Res., 610 99th Ave. W., Duluth, 55808. Tel: 218-626-2283.
Catechesis/Religious Programs—Mrs. Ann Menart, D.R.E.
Students 59.

8—ST. JAMES, Rev. Charles Flynn.
Res., 721 N. 57th Ave. W., Duluth, 55807. Tel: 218-624-0125.
School—Catherine Clark, Prin. Lay Teachers 8; Students 102.
Catechesis/Religious Programs—Cheryl Foldesi, D.R.E.
Students 144.

9—ST. JOHN'S (Woodland), Rev. Jerome P. Weiss. In res., Rev. Joseph A. Hughes.
Res., 4230 St. John's Ave., 55803. Tel: 218-724-6332.
School—Tel: 218-724-9392. Mrs. Marie McCarthy, Prin.
Lay Teachers 6; Students 182.
Catechesis/Religious Programs—Students 258.
Mission—Gnesen, St. Joseph. [CEM]

10—ST. JOSEPH'S (Duluth Heights), Rev. Noel Stretton.
Res., 151 W. Linden St., 55811. Tel: 218-722-1021.
Catechesis/Religious Programs—Denise Maciej, D.R.E.
Students 120.

11—ST. LAWRENCE'S, Rev. William Fournier.
Res., 2404 Morris Thomas Rd., 55811. Tel: 218-722-1900; 722-2259.
Catechesis/Religious Programs—Shawna Hansen, D.R.E.
Students 215.

12—ST. MARGARET MARY (Morgan Park), Rev. Richard Partika.
Res., 1467 88th Ave. W., 55808. Tel: 218-626-2379.
Catechesis/Religious Programs—Janet Stanley, D.R.E.
Students 55.

13—ST. MARY STAR OF THE SEA, Rev. Patrick McDowell.
Res., 325 E. Third St., 55805. Tel: 218-722-3078.
Catechesis/Religious Programs—Shirley Baker, D.R.E.
Students 68.

14—ST. MICHAEL'S, Revs. William P. Fider; Frank Melovasich.
Office: 4901 E. Superior St., 55804. Tel: 218-525-1902.
Res., 4931 E. Superior, 55804. Tel: 218-525-7513.
School—4924 Pitt St., 55804. Tel: 218-525-1931.
Catechesis/Religious Programs—Anne Case, D.R.E.
Students 447.

15—ST. PETER'S, Rev. Patrick McDowell.
Res., 325 E. Third St., 55805. Tel: 218-722-3078.
Church—Third St. and Eighth Ave. W., 55805.

16—SS. PETER AND PAUL. See seperate listing. Holy Family, Duluth.

17—ST. RAPHAEL'S, Rev. Lawrence O'Shea.
Parish Center: 5779 Seville Rd., 55811. Tel: 218-729-7537.
Res., 4458 Midway Rd., 55811. Tel: 218-729-5546.
Catechesis/Religious Programs—Rachelle Benoit, D.R.E.
Students 263.

18—WEST END CATHOLIC PARISH OF SS. CLEMENT AND JEAN. See seperate listing. Holy Family, Duluth.

OUTSIDE THE CITY OF DULUTH

Aitkin, Aitkin Co., St. James, Rev. Patrick Coyle.
Res., 309 Second St., N.W., 56431. Tel: 218-927-6581. [CEM]
Catechesis/Religious Programs—D.R.E.: Mary Grulke; Mary Ellen Moriarty.
Students 155.

Aurora, St. Louis Co., Holy Rosary, Rev. Joseph Sirba.
Res., 16 W. Fifth Ave., N., 55705. Tel: 218-229-3210.
Catechesis/Religious Programs—Students 108.

Babbitt, St. Louis Co., St. Pius X, Rev. John Sustarsic.
Res., 15 Ash Blvd., 55706. Tel: 218-827-2291.
Catechesis/Religious Programs—Jane Holm, D.R.E.
Students 71.

Ball Club, Itasca Co., St. Joseph's, Rev. Athanase Fuchs, O.S.B.
Res., HC4 Box 104, Deer River, 56636. Tel: 218-246-1805. [CEM]
Missions—Federal Dam, Sacred Heart; Bena, St. Anne's.

Beroun, Pine Co., St. Joseph's, Rev. James W. Scheuer.
Res. and Mailing Address—203 Lawler Ave. S., P.O. Box 490, Hinckley, 55037. Tel: 320-384-6313.
Church—250 Praha Ave., 55063. [CEM]

Bigfork, Itasca Co., Our Lady of the Snows, Rev. Stephen Solors; Deacon Jerome Sura.
Res., P.O. Box 11, 56628. Tel: 218-743-3255.
Chapel—Squaw Lake, St. Catherine's.

Biwabik, St. Louis Co., St. John's, Rev. Frank Perkovich; Deacon Herb Riley.
Res., Box 569, 55708. Tel: 218-865-6774.

Brainerd, Crow Wing Co., St. Andrew's, Rev. Cornelius Kelleher.
Res., 1122 11th St., S.E., 56401. Tel: 218-829-0723; 829-8932 (Office).
Catechesis/Religious Programs—D.R.E.: Veronica Besmehn; Cheryl Hawkinson.
Students 383.

St. Francis, Revs. Roland J. Antus; Mark Coen.
Office: 412 N. Eighth St., 56401. Tel: 218-829-8753.
Res., 1-913 Juniper St., 56401. Tel: 218-829-3833;
Res., 2-921 Juniper St., 56401. Tel: 218-829-0184.
School—817 Juniper St., 56401. Tel: 218-829-2344. Sandra Opheim, Prin.
Lay Teachers 13; Students 179.
Catechesis/Religious Programs—Kim Koning, D.R.E.
Students 561.
Convent—625 N. Third St., 56401. Tel: 218-829-2437. Sisters of St. Benedict
Chapel—Pine Beach, St. Thomas of the Pines. [CEM]

Carlton, Carlton Co., St. Francis, Rev. James Bissonette.
Res., 509 Sunrise Dr., 55718. Tel: 218-384-4563. [CEM]
Mission—Cromwell-Wright, Immaculate Conception. [CEM]

Cass Lake, Cass Co., St. Charles, Rev. Bogumil Kosciesza.
Res., 308 Central Ave., N., Box 368, 56633. Tel: 218-335-2359.
Catechesis/Religious Programs—Students 85.
Mission—Pennington, St. Charles.

Chisholm, St. Louis Co., St. Joseph's, Rev. Steven Daigle. In res., Rev. Clement Gustin, O.S.C.
Res., 113 S.W. Fourth St., 55719. Tel: 218-254-5703. [CEM]
Catechesis/Religious Programs—D.R.E.: Deanne Hildenbrand; Kathy Gregorich.
Students 425.
Mission—Buhl, Our Lady of the Sacred Heart, Tel: 218-258-3279.

Cloquet, Carlton Co., Holy Family, Rev. Eugene Francis Lyttle.
Res., 280 Reservation Rd., 55720. Tel: 218-879-9047. [CEM]
Mission—Sawyer, SS. Mary & Joseph.

Queen of Peace. Consolidated from the following two parishes: St. Casimir and Our Lady of the Sacred Heart. Rev. Kenton Sailstad.
102 4th St., 55720. Tel: 218-879-6958. [CEM]
Office: Tel: 218-879-6793.
School—Tel: 218-879-8516. Mother Colleen Kimbro, F.S.E., Prin.
Sisters 2; Lay Teachers 6; Students 123.
Catechesis/Religious Programs—Irene McKay, D.R.E.
Students 510.
Convent—5613 Lilac Hill Rd., Duluth, 55810. Tel: 218-624-9038. Franciscan Sisters of the Eucharist

Coleraine, Itasca Co., Mary Immaculate, Rev. Paul J. Larson.
Res., Box 290, 55722. Tel: 218-245-1684.

Cook, St. Louis Co., St. Mary's, Rev. Lawrence T. Antus, O.M.I.
Res., Box 107, 55723. Tel: 218-666-5334. [CEM]

Crosby, Crow Wing Co., St. Joseph's, Rev. Howard P. Eisel, S.S.C.
Res., 619 Poplar St., 56441. Tel: 218-546-6559.
Mission—Deerwood, St. Joseph.

Crosslake, Crow Wing Co., Immaculate Heart, Rev. Paul Fruth.
Res., Box 155, 56442. Tel: 218-692-3731.
Catechesis/Religious Programs—Students 95.

Deer River, Itasca Co., St. Mary's, Rev. Anselm Thevarkunnel.
Res., Box 98, 56636. Tel: 218-246-8582.
Catechesis/Religious Programs—Students 113.

Ely, St. Louis Co., St. Anthony's, Rev. Dennis H. Hoffman; Deacon Gregory Hutar.
Res., 231 E. Camp St., 55731. Tel: 218-365-4017.
Catechesis/Religious Programs—Barbara Condor, D.R.E.
Students 260.

Emily, Crow Wing Co., St. Emily's, Rev. Roman Spors.
Res., Box 25, 56447. Tel: 218-763-2101.

Eveleth, St. Louis Co., Resurrection, Rev. Eamonn Boland.
Res., Box 586, 55734. Tel: 218-744-3277.
Catechesis/Religious Programs—D.R.E.: Pam Rapacz, (Grades K-6); Mary Dosan, (Grades 7-12).
Students 230.

Floodwood, St. Louis Co., St. Louis, Rev. John Doyle.
Res., Box 378, 55736. Tel: 218-476-2367.
Mission—Meadowlands, St. Mary's.
Chapel—Elmer, St. Joseph's.

Garrison, Crow Wing Co., Our Lady of Fatima, Rev. Vincent Ott, O.M.I.; Deacon Roger Marks.
Res., St. Therese Church, Onamia, 56359. Tel: 612-532-3614; 692-4466.

Gilbert, St. Louis Co., St. Joseph's, Rev. Frank Perkovich.
Res., Box 788, 55741. Tel: 218-741-9551.
Catechesis/Religious Programs—Students 173.

Grand Marais, Cook Co., St. John's, Rev. Walter O'Connell, O.P.
Res., Box 549, 55604-0549. Tel: 218-387-1409. [CEM]
Catechesis/Religious Programs—Students 70.
Mission—Grand Portage, Holy Rosary. [CEM]

Grand Rapids, Itasca Co., St. Joseph's, Revs. Thomas Radaich; Michael Cotone, O.S.C.
Parish Center: 613 First Ave., N.W., 55744. Tel: 218-326-2843.
Res., 726 Second Ave. N.W., 55744. Tel: 218-326-3959.
School—Sr. Mary Rochefort, O.S.B., Prin. Lay Teachers 10; Students 169.
Catechesis/Religious Programs—D.R.E.: Mary Gunderson; Mary Prudhomme; Lori Dowling; Edna Trunt.
Students 504.
Mission—Cohasset, St. Augustine's.

Hibbing, St. Louis Co., Blessed Sacrament, Rev. John O'Donnell.
Res., 2328 Seventh Ave., E., 55746. Tel: 218-263-3681.
School—Assumption.
Benedictine Sisters 1; Lay Teachers 6; Students 133.
Catechesis/Religious Programs—Becky Adams, D.R.E.
Students 330.
Convent—718 E. 23rd St., 55746.
Station—Side Lake, Blessed Sacrament Chapel.

Immaculate Conception, Rev. John O'Donnell, Admin.
Res., 1928 Fifth Ave., E., 55746. Tel: 218-263-4319.

St. Leo's, Rev. Fredrick Method.
Res., 218 E. 39th St., 55746. Tel: 218-262-5541.
School—Rita Perry, Prin. Lay Teachers 10; Students 122.
Catechesis/Religious Programs—Students 454.
Convent—(Duluth) 2503 W. Third Ave., 55746. Sisters of St. Benedict

Hill City, Aitkin Co., St. John, Rev. Edward Buczynski.

Res., Box 156, 55748. Tel: 218-697-2465.
Catechesis/Religious Programs—Students 58.
Mission—Warba, St. Paul's.

Hillman, Crow Wing Co., Holy Family, Rev. Vincent Ott, O.M.I.
Res., Rte. 1, Box 188, 56338. Tel: 612-277-3386.

Hinckley, Pine Co., St. Patrick's, Rev. James W. Scheuer.
Res., Box 490, 55037-0490. Tel: 320-384-6313.
Catechesis/Religious Programs—Students 102.

Hoyt Lakes, St. Louis Co., Queen of Peace, Rev. Joseph Sirba.
Res., 513 Hampshire Dr., P.O. Box 211, 55750. Tel: 218-225-2867.
Catechesis/Religious Programs—Students 125.

International Falls, Koochiching Co., St. Thomas Aquinas, Revs. Louis Sondgeroth, O.M.I.; Raymond Kirtz, O.M.I.; Wilfrid Upson, O.M.I.
Res., 810 Fifth St., 56649. Tel: 218-283-3293.
School—Rev. Louis Songeroth, O.M.I., Admin. Lay Teachers 10; Students 110.
Catechesis/Religious Programs—D.R.E.: Dawn Fausz; Jo McLaughlin.
Students 316.

Keewatin, Itasca Co., St. Mary's, Rev. Ronald Gagne.
Res., Box 219, 55753. Tel: 218-778-6379.

Littlefork, Koochiching Co., St. Columban, Rev. Louis Sondgeroth, O.M.I.
Res., Box C, 56653. Tel: 218-278-6638.

Longville, Cass Co., St. Edward's, Rev. Thomas J. Kisting.
Res., Box 38, 56655-0038. Tel: 218-363-2799.
Mission—Remer, St. Paul.

McGregor, Aitkin Co., Holy Family, Rev. John J. Fleischhacker, O.S.C.
Res., 55760. Tel: 218-768-2702.
Catechesis/Religious Programs—Students 62.
Chapel—McGrath, Our Lady of Fatima.

Marble, Itasca Co., St. Mary's, Rev. Paul Larson, Admin.
Res., Box 411, 55764. Tel: 218-247-7368.
Mission—Taconite, St. Joseph's.

Moose Lake, Carlton Co., Holy Angels, Rev. Michael T. Hayes.
Res., P.O. Box 487, 55767. Tel: 218-485-4909.
Catechesis/Religious Programs—D.R.E.: Peggy Rosera; Mary Rose Rosc.
Students 196.

Nashwauk, Itasca Co., St. Cecilia's, Rev. Ronald Gagne.
Res., 326 Second St., 55769. Tel: 218-885-1126.
Catechesis/Religious Programs—Students 238.
Mission—Pengilly, St. Kevin.

Northome, Koochiching Co., St. Michael's. (Under the jurisdiction of the Duluth Diocese; administered by the Crookston Diocese.). Rev. Alcuin Henger, O.M.I.
Res., St. Ann, P.O. Box G, Blackduck, 56630. Tel: 218-835-6673.

Orr, St. Louis Co., Holy Cross, Rev. Lawrence T. Antus, O.M.I.
Res., Box 218, 55771. Tel: 218-757-3273.
Chapel—Buyck, St. Joseph's.

Pequot Lakes, Crow Wing Co., St. Alice's, Rev. James Walsh; Deacon David Craig.
Res., Box 159, 56472. Tel: 218-568-4760.
Catechesis/Religious Programs—Deacon Mike Knuth, D.R.E.
Students 276.
Mission—Nisswa, St. Christopher's.

Pine City, Pine Co., Immaculate Conception, Rev. Michael J. Lyons; Deacon Eugene Biever.
Res., 535 Eighth St., 55063. Tel: 612-629-2935. [CEM]
School—St. Mary's, 815 W. Sixth Ave., 55063. Tel: 612-629-3953. Mary Beth Badowich, Prin.
Lay Teachers 4; Students 73.
Catechesis/Religious Programs—Students 140.

Pine River, Cass Co., Our Lady of Lourdes, Rev. Edward M. Foster.
Res., Box 44, 56474. Tel: 218-587-4163; 587-4203.

Proctor, St. Louis Co., St. Rose Catholic Church, Rev. Peter Muhich.
Res., 3 Sixth Ave., 55810. Tel: 218-624-0007.
School—Tel: 218-624-0818. Peggy Frederickson, Prin.
Lay Teachers 7; Students 67.
Catechesis/Religious Programs—Janice Rohweder, D.R.E.
Students 197.
Mission—Saginaw, St. Philip Neri.

St. Mathias, Crow Wing Co., St. Mathias, Rev. Henry A. Miller, O.S.C.
Res., 9988 Co. Rd. 121 S.W., Fort Ripley, 56449. Tel: 218-829-4061.
Station—St. Mathias, Crow Wing State Park.

Sandstone, Pine Co., St. Luke's, Rev. Jerome Datko, O.M.I.
Res., P.O. Box 644, 55072. Tel: 320-245-5175.
Catechesis/Religious Programs—Students 108.
Missions—Finlayson, St. Joseph's. [CEM]
Bruno, Sacred Heart. [CEM]

Silver Bay, Lake Co., St. Mary's, Rev. Francis Paquette; Deacon Fred Wright.
Res., 57 Horn Blvd., 55614. Tel: 218-226-3100.
Catechesis/Religious Programs—Students 54.

Tower, St. Louis Co., St. Martin's, Rev. Rudolph Pakiz.
Res., Box 757, 55790. Tel: 218-753-4310.
Catechesis/Religious Programs—Students 80.

Two Harbors, Lake Co., Holy Spirit, Rev. George Zeck.
Res., 227 Third St., 55616. Tel: 218-834-4313.
Catechesis/Religious Programs—Students 270.

Virginia, St. Louis Co., Holy Spirit, Rev. Lloyd Mudrak.
Res., 306 S. Second St., 55792. Tel: 218-741-6344.
School—Marquette, 311 3rd St. S., 55792. Tel: 218-741-6811.
Catechesis/Religious Programs—Linda Strukel, D.R.E.
Students 250.

Sacred Heart, Rev. Brian Schultz.
Res., 603 12th St., N., 55792. Tel: 218-741-2322.
Catechesis/Religious Programs—Cora Culbert, D.R.E.
Students 331.
Mission—Mountain Iron, Sacred Heart.

Walker, Cass Co., St. Agnes, Rev. Bruce Engen.
Res., Box 874, 56484. Tel: 218-547-1054.
Mission—Hackensack, Sacred Heart.
Station—Walker, Ah-Gwah Ching State Nursing Home.

Willow River, Pine Co., St. Mary's, Rev. Norman Pahl, O.M.I.
Res., Box 97, 55795. Tel: 218-372-3446. [CEM]
Mailing Address: Box 38, Sturgeon Lake, 55783. Tel: 218-372-3208.
Mission—Sturgeon Lake, St. Isidore's.
Station—Willow River, Youth Conservation Camp.

INDIAN MISSIONS

Duluth, St. Louis Co., Indian Missions,
c/o Chancery Office: 2830 E. Fourth St., 55812. Sr. Marie Rose Messingschlager, C.D.P.
Missions—Cloquet, Carlton Co., Holy Family Church, Reservation Rd., P.O. Box 280, Cloquet, 55720. Tel: 218-879-9047. [CEM]
Rev. Eugene Lyttle.
Sawyer, Carlton Co., SS. Mary and Joseph, 280 Reservation Rd., Cloquet, 55720. Rev. Eugene Lyttle; Ball Club, Itasca Co., St. Joseph's. [CEM]
Federal Dam, Sacred Heart, HC4 Box 104, Deer River, 56636. Rev. Athanase Fuchs, O.S.B.; Grand Portage, Holy Rosary, P.O. Box 549, Grand Marais, 56604. [CEM]
Rev. Ronald Gagne.
Walker, Ah-Gwah-Ching State Nursing Home, Box 874, Walker, 56484. Rev. Bruce Engen; Nett Lake, St. Louis Co., Immaculate Conception. (Indian Apostolate) Holy Cross, Box 218, Orr, 55771.

Chaplains of Public Institutions

Hospitals

DULUTH. *Miller Dwan Hospital*. Rev. John C. Petrich, Chap., Tel: 218-727-1089.
St. Luke's Hospital, 2002 Minnesota Ave., 55802. Tel: 218-727-1089. Rev. John C. Petrich, Chap.

BRAINERD. *Brainerd Regional Human Services Center*. Vacant.

MOOSE LAKE. *Moose Lake State Hospital,* 112 Cedar, 55767. Tel: 218-485-4909. Rev. Michael T. Hayes, Chap., Tel: 218-485-4411.

Correctional Institutions

DULUTH. *Duluth Federal Prison*. Rev. Noel Stretton.

SAGINAW. *Northeast Regional Correctional Institution*. Rev. John C. Petrich, Chap., Tel: 218-727-1089.

WILLOW RIVER. *Youth Conservation Camp*. Rev. Norman Pahl, O.M.I., Chap., Tel: 218-372-3446.

Special Assignment:
Reverend Fathers—
Evans, John Whitney, College of St. Scholastica, 1200 Kenwood Ave., Duluth, MN 55811. Tel: 218-723-6000

On Duty Outside the Diocese:
Reverend Fathers—
Graham, William C., 47 E. 129th St., New York City, NY 10035
Johnson, Lawrence P., 7752 Clarmont Dr., No. 1634, San Diego, CA 92122
Kaster, Alfred D., St. Patrick, 235 Chapel St., Grass Valley, CA 95945
Kottiry, Alphonsus, Ramapuran Bazaar, P.O. Box Kattayam Dist., Kerala State S., India

Military Chaplains:
Reverend Fathers—
Lambert, Peter, Chap., U.S.A.F.

On Leave Without Assignment:
Reverend Fathers—
Klein, Robert W., Albuquerque Villa, Albuquerque, NM 87150

Retired:
Reverend Monsignors—
Hogan, Michael, Rte. 1, Box 577, Longville, MN 56655. Tel: 218-363-2386
Popesh, Bernard, 609 E. Chapman St., Ely, MN 55731. Tel: 218-365-6085
Reverend Fathers—
Bouchard, Thomas, Box 38, Remer, MN 56672. Tel: 218-566-2954
Cossette, Raymond, 1599 County Rd. 8 SE., Brainerd, MN 56401. Tel: 218-764-2941
Dolsina, Stanley, 2423 Morris Thomas Rd., Duluth, MN 55811
Faith, Rudolph, 330 E. 3rd. St., Duluth, MN 55805. Tel: 218-733-0988
Fox, Fredrick, 1711 E. First St., #103, Duluth, MN 55812. Tel: 218-724-9228
Gaber, Francis, 250 Praha, Beroun, MN 55004. Tel: 612-629-3342
Golden, James, 204-4th Ave., Keewatin, MN 55753. Tel: 218-778-6949
Golobich, John, 524 N.Oak Bend Drive, #102, Duluth, MN 55811. Tel: 218-723-1566
Hughes, Joseph A., 4230 St. John's Ave., Duluth, MN 55803. Tel: 218-728-3068
Kuras, Felix, 330 E. 3rd St., Duluth, MN 55805. Tel: 218-723-7125
Marincel, Frank, 8521 Park Villa Drive, #105 W, Mt. Iron, MN 55768. Tel: 218-749-6750
McEnery, Dennis, Abbeyfeale, Co. Limerick, Ireland
O'Doherty, Dermot, 5840 31st Ave. N., St. Petersburg, FL 33710
Vovk, Joseph, 16 W. Fifth Ave. N., Aurora, MN 55705. Tel: 218-229-3210
Zorichak, William, 330 E. Third St., Duluth, MN 55805

Permanent Deacons:
Anderson, Dennis, St. Benedict, Duluth
Anderson, H. L., St. John, Duluth
Beier, Walter, St. John's, Duluth
Biever, Eugene, Immaculate Conception Church, Pine City
Birkland, Roger, St. Joseph, Gnesen
Christensen, Robert, (Retired)
Craig, David, St. Alice, Pequot Lakes
Griffiths, James, St. Leo's, Hibbing
Hume, Michael, Central City Parishes, Duluth
Hutar, Gregory, St. Anthony, Ely
Knuth, Michael, St. Alice, Pequot Lakes
Laumeyer, Richard, St. Michael's, Duluth
Marks, Roger, Holy Family, Hillman
Mayer, Philip, St. Joseph's, Crosby
Olson, Barry, Immaculate Heart, Cross Lake
Riley, Herbert, St. John, Biwabik
Sura, Jerome, Our Lady of the Snows, Bigfork
Szyman, Robert, Queen of Peace, Cloquet
Woznick, Gregory, St. Paul, Remer
Wright, Fred, St. Mary's, Silver Bay

INSTITUTIONS LOCATED IN THE DIOCESE

[A] COLLEGES AND UNIVERSITIES

DULUTH. *College of St. Scholastica,* 1200 Kenwood Ave., 55811. Tel: 218-723-6000; Fax: 218-723-6290.
For a complete listing, refer to the Colleges and Universities section.

[B] ELEMENTARY SCHOOLS, INTERPAROCHIAL

VIRGINIA. *Marquette Catholic School,* 311 Third St. S., 55792. Tel: 218-741-6811. Serving the parishes of Holy Spirit & Sacred Heart. Marianne Runkle, Prin. Lay Teachers 8; Students 119.

[C] GENERAL HOSPITALS

DULUTH. *St. Mary's Medical Center,* 407 E. Third St., 55805. Tel: 218-726-4000; Fax: 218-726-4383.
For a complete listing, refer to the Hospitals section.

BRAINERD. *St. Joseph's Medical Center*, 523 N. Third St., 56401. Tel: 218-829-2861; Fax: 218-828-3103.
For a complete listing, refer to the Hospitals section.

[D] HOMES FOR AGED

DULUTH. *Benedictine Health Center*, 935 Kenwood Ave., 55811. Tel: 218-723-6408; Fax: 218-723-6449.
For a complete listing, refer to the Special Care Facilities section.
St. Ann's Senior Residence, 330 E. Third St., 55805. Tel: 218-727-8831; Fax: 218-727-8833.
For a complete listing, refer to the Special Care Facilities section.

[E] CONVENTS AND RESIDENCES FOR SISTERS

DULUTH. *Benedictine Sisters Benevolent Association.* (Minnesota Corporation), 1200 Kenwood Ave., 55811. Tel: 218-728-1817; Fax: 218-723-5902. Sr. Danile Lynch, O.S.B., Pres.
Motherhouse and Novitiate of the Sisters of Saint Benedict, St. Scholastica Monastery, 1200 Kenwood Ave., 55811. Tel: 218-723-6555. Sr. Aelred Roehl, O.S.B., Archivist.
In community: Professed Sisters 172.

[F] NEWMAN CENTERS

DULUTH. *University of MN-Duluth*, 421 W. Ste. Marie St., 55811. Tel: 218-728-3757. Rev. Dale Nan, Dir.; Deacon Chico Anderson, Assoc. Dir.
College of St. Scholastica, 1200 Kenwood Ave., 55811. Tel: 218-723-6000. John O'Connor, Campus Ministry Dir.; Mary O'Connor, Campus Ministry Dir.
Brainerd Community College, 921 Juniper St., Brainerd, 56401. Tel: 218-829-8753.
Itasca Community College, St. Joseph's, Box 110, Grand Rapids, 55744.
Hibbing Community College, 2328 Seventh Ave., E., Hibbing, 55746. Tel: 218-263-3681. Rev. John O'Donnell.
Mesabi Community College, 603 12th St. N., Virginia, 55792. Tel: 218-741-2322. Rev. Brian Schultz.
Vermilion Community College, St. Anthony's Catholic Church, 231 E. Camp St., Vermilion, 55731. Rev. Dennis H. Hoffman.

[G] MISCELLANEOUS LISTINGS

DULUTH. *Benedictine Sisters Benevolent Association.* (Parent Co.), 1200 Kenwood Ave., 55811. Tel: 218-728-1817; Fax: 218-723-5902. Sr. Danile Lynch, O.S.B., Pres.
Benedictine Health System. (Sub. of Benedictine Sisters Benevolent Association), 503 E. Third St., Suite 400, 55805. Tel: 218-720-2370; Fax: 218-720-2373. Barry J. Halm, Pres. & COO.
St. Mary's Medical Center. (Sub. of Benedictine Health System), 407 E. Third St., 55805. Tel: 218-726-4000; Fax: 218-726-4383. Sr. Kathleen Hofer, O.S.B., Pres./CEO.
St. Joseph's Medical Center, Brainerd. (Sub. of Benedictine Health System), 323 N. Third St., Brainerd, 56401. Tel: 218-829-2861; Fax: 218-828-3103. Thomas Prusak, Pres./CEO.
Benedictine Foundation, Inc. (Sub. of Benedictine Health System), 407 E. Third St., 55805. Tel: 218-720-2396; Fax: 218-726-4018. Steve Yorde, Pres./CEO.
Benedictine Health Center. (Sub. of Benedictine Health System), 935 Kenwood Ave., 55811. Tel: 218-723-6408; Fax: 218-723-6449. Joseph Devore, Admin.
St. Francis Regional Medical Center. (Sub. of Benedictine Health System), 1455 St. Francis Ave., Shakopee, 55379. Tel: 612-403-3000; Fax: 612-403-3820. Venetia Kudrle, Pres.
St. Mary's Regional Health Center. (Sub. of Benedictine Health System), 1027 Washington, Detroit Lakes, 56501. Tel: 218-847-5611; Fax: 218-847-7674. John Solheim, Pres./CEO.
Polinsky Medical Rehabilitation Center, (Sub. of St. Mary's Medical Center), 530 E. Second St., 55805. Tel: 218-727-5083.
St. Mary's/Polinsky Center for Personal Fitness. (sub of Polinsky Medical Rehabilitation Center), 5th Ave. E. & 2nd St., Daluth, 55805. Tel: 218-725-5400. David Ross, Pres.
BHS Long Term Care, Inc. (Sub. of Benedictine Health System), 503 E. Third St., Suite 400, 55805. Tel: 218-720-2370; Fax: 218-720-2373. Dennis Acrea, Pres./CEO.
St. Mary's Hospital. (Sub. of Benedictine Health System), P.O. Box 137, Cottonwood, ID, 83522. Tel: 208-962-3251; Fax: 208-962-3722. Mrs. Casey Uhling, Admin.
Madonna Towers of Rochester, Inc. (sub of Benedictine Health System), 4001 19th Ave. NW, Rochester, 55901. Tel: 507-288-3911; Fax: 507-288-0393. Mark Cairns, Admin.
Tekawitha Nursing Center, Inc. (sub of Benedictine Health System), 6 E. Chestnut, Sisseton, SD, 57262. Tel: 605-698-7693; Fax: 605-698-3091. Robert Faehn, Admin.
The Blessed Nuno Society, P.O. Box 3484, 55803.
Holy Rosary Parish Endowment Fund, 2801 E. Fourth St., 55812.
The Human Life and Development Fund of the Diocese of Duluth, 2830 E. Fourth St., 55812. Tel: 218-724-9111; Fax: 218-724-1056. Most Rev. Roger Schwietz, O.M.I., Pres.; Revs. David Tushar, V.G., Vice Pres.; Dale Nau, Chancellor, Sec./Treas.
John S. Duss Memorial Music Conservatory, 2211 Greysolon Rd., 55812. Tel: 218-724-2052. Franciscan Sisters of the Eucharist. Part of Franciscan Life Center Network, Inc.
McCabe Renewal Center, 2125 Abbotsford Ave., 55803. Tel: 218-724-5266. Sr. Mary Stephen Eckes, O.S.B., Dir.
Port Area Catholic Education (PACE), 2830 E. Fourth St., 55812. PACE is a consortium of Catholic parish elementary schools (St. Rose, Proctor; Holy Rosary, St. Michael, St. John, & St. James, Duluth; Queen of Peace, Cloquet).
St. Vincent de Paul Society, 109 W. Fourth St., 55806. Tel: 218-727-9145.
WALKER. *S.W. Deanery Chapter of Magnificat of the Diocese of Duluth*, P.O. Box 1030, 56484. Rosemary Ellis, Incorporator; Betty Garoutte, Incorporator.

RELIGIOUS INSTITUTES OF MEN REPRESENTED IN THE DIOCESE

For further details refer to the corresponding bracketed number in the Religious Institutes of Men or Women section.

[0200]—*Benedictine Monks.*—O.S.B.
[0400]—*Canons Regular of the Order of Holy Cross.*—O.S.C.
[0430]—*Dominican Fathers.* (Northern Prov.).—O.P.
[0910]—*Oblates of Mary Immaculate.* (Central Prov.).—O.M.I.
[0370]—*Society of St. Columban.*—S.S.C.

RELIGIOUS INSTITUTES OF WOMEN REPRESENTED IN THE DIOCESE

[0230]—*Benedictine Sisters of Pontifical Jurisdiction.* (St. Joseph, MN; Watertown, SD; St. Paul, MN; Duluth, MN).—O.S.B.
[1070-10]—*Dominican Sisters.*—O.P.
[1070-13]—*Dominican Sisters.*—O.P.
[1250]—*The Institute of the Franciscan Sisters of the Eucharist.* (Meriden, CT).—F.S.E.
[2970]—*School Sisters of Notre Dame.* (Mankato Prov.).—S.S.N.D.
[0430]—*Sisters of Charity of the Blessed Virgin Mary.*—B.V.M.
[]—*Sisters of Divine Providence of KY.*—C.D.P.
[1990]—*Sisters of the Holy Names of Jesus and Mary.*—S.N.J.M.
[1720]—*Sisters of the Third Order Regular of St. Francis of the Congregation of Our Lady of the Lourdes.*—O.S.F.
[2150]—*Sisters Servants of the Immaculate Heart of Mary.*—I.H.M.

DIOCESAN CEMETERIES

DULUTH. *Calvary Cemetery*, 1312 Howard Gnesen Rd., 55803. Tel: 218-724-3376. Rev. Dale Nau, Dir.; Mr. Eric Hillman, Supt.

NECROLOGY

(No Deaths)

Diocese of El Paso

(Dioecesis Elpasensis)

Most Reverend

ARMANDO X. OCHOA, D.D.

Bishop of El Paso; ordained May 23, 1970; appointed Titular Bishop of Sitifi and Auxiliary of the Archdiocese of Los Angeles December 29, 1986; ordained Bishop February 23, 1987; appointed Bishop of El Paso April 1, 1996; installed June 26, 1996.

ERECTED MARCH 3, 1914.

Square Miles 26,686.

Comprises in Texas, the Counties of El Paso, Brewster, Culberson, Hudspeth, Jeff Davis, Loving, Presidio, Reeves, Ward and Winkler.

For legal titles of parishes and diocesan institutions, consult the Chancery Office.

Chancery Office: 499 St. Matthews St., El Paso, TX, 79907. Tel.: 915-595-5000; Fax: 915-595-5095.

STATISTICAL OVERVIEW

Personnel	
Bishop	1
Priests: Diocesan Active in Diocese	62
Priests: Active Outside Diocese	2
Priests: Retired, Sick or Absent	28
Number of Diocesan Priests	92
Religious Priests in Diocese	43
Ordinations:	
Diocesan Priests	1
Transitional Deacons	1
Permanent Deacons in Diocese	17
Total Brothers	16
Total Sisters	243
Parishes	
Parishes	58
With Resident Pastor:	
Resident Diocesan Priests	40
Resident Religious Priests	15
Without Resident Pastor:	
Administered by Priests	2
Administered by Women Religious	1
Missions	22
Professional Ministry Personnel:	
Brothers	1
Sisters	11
Lay Ministers	20
Welfare	
Health Care Centers	1
Total Assisted	18,500
Homes for the Aged	2
Total Assisted	101
Day Care and Extended Day Care Centers	2
Total Assisted	185
Specialized Homes	1
Total Assisted	55
Special Centers for Social Services	5
Total Assisted	74,200
Educational	
Seminaries, Diocesan	1
Students from This Diocese	3
Diocesan Students in Other Seminaries	4
Seminaries, Religious	2
Students Religious	20
Total Seminarians	27
High Schools, Diocesan and Parish	1
Total Students	677
High Schools, Private	2
Total Students	325
Elementary Schools, Diocesan and Parish	9
Total Students	3,380
Elementary Schools, Private	3
Total Students	841
Catechesis/Religious Education:	
High School Students	4,963
Elementary Students	12,437
Total Students Under Catholic Instruction	22,650
Teachers in the Diocese:	
Priests	13
Brothers	10
Sisters	35
Lay Teachers	273
Vital Statistics	
Receptions into the Church:	
Infant Baptism Totals	8,307
Adult Baptism Totals	121
Received into Full Communion	250
First Communions	5,326
Confirmations	3,571
Marriages:	
Catholic	1,141
Interfaith	96
Total Marriages	1,237
Deaths	1,780
Total Catholic Population	579,766
Total Population	776,724

Former Bishops—Most Rev. JOHN J. BROWN, S.J., preconized Bishop of El Paso, Jan. 22, 1915; resigned June 16, 1915.—Most Rev. ANTHONY J. SCHULER, S.J., D.D., cons. Oct. 28, 1915; died June 3, 1944.—Most Rev. SIDNEY M. METZGER, S.T.D., J.C.D., cons. April 10, 1940; succeeded to See, Nov. 29, 1942; retired May 29, 1978; died April 12, 1986.—Most Rev. PATRICK F. FLORES, D.D., cons. May 5, 1970; installed Bishop of El Paso, May 29, 1978; appt. Archbishop of San Antonio, Aug. 28, 1979.—Most Rev. RAYMUNDO J. PENA, D.D., cons. Dec. 13, 1976; appt. Bishop of El Paso, April 29, 1980; appt. Bishop of Brownsville, May 23, 1995.

Diocesan Pastoral Staff—Rev. RICHARD A. MATTY, Chancellor; Sr. HELEN SANTAMARIA, S.L., Assoc. Chancellor.

Diocesan Pastoral Center—499 St. Matthews St., El Paso, 79907. Tel: 915-595-5000; Fax: 915-595-5095. Refer all official business to this address.

Diocesan Tribunal—499 St. Matthews St., El Paso, 79907. Tel: 915-595-5038. Rev. JOSE C. GUERRERO, J.C.L., Judicial Vicar. Adjutant Vicars: Revs. STEPHEN PETERS; ROBERT S. KOBE.

Judges—Revs. JOSE C. GUERRERO, J.C.L.; STEPHEN PETERS; ROBERT S. KOBE; JAMES W. HALL.

Defenders of the Bond—Rev. Msgr. DAVID G. FIERRO; Rev. TRINI FUENTEZ; Deacon GEORGE LEVY.

Advocates—Rev. Msgr. FRANCIS J. SMITH; Revs. JUVENTINO CELINO; RICHARD ZAMORANO; FRANCISCO LOPEZ; Deacon GUS RODRIGUEZ, SR.

Lay Advocates—CARMEN RODRIGUEZ; SUE KURITA; OUISA DAVIS.

Tribunal Ecclesiastical Notary—YOLANDA RUIZ.

Peritus—RICHARD B. PATTERSON, Ph.D.; Dr. CHESTER L. REYNOLDS, M.D.

Vicar for Clergy and Religious—Vacant.

Vicars-Vicariates—St. Peter: Rev. TRINDAD FUENTEZ, *Queen of Peace Parish, 1551 Belvidere, El Paso, 79912.* Tel: 915-584-5817. St. Paul: Rev. HECTOR CRUZ, S.M., *Santa Lucia Parish, 519 Gallagher, El Paso.* Tel: 915-592-5245. St. John: Rev. SANTOS PEREZ, O.F.M., *Our Lady of Guadalupe Parish, 2709 Alabama, El Paso, 79930.* Tel: 915-562-4304. St. Mark: Rev. JOHN TELLES, *St. Thomas - St. Joseph Parish, 838 Bellaire, Kermit, 79745.* Tel: 915-586-4694. St.Luke: Rev. RAUL TRIGUEROS, *Cristo Rey Parish, 8011 Williamette, El Paso, 79907.* Tel: 915-591-0688.

Diocesan Master of Ceremonies—Rev. MARCUS MCFADIN.

Finance Council—Most Rev. ARMANDO X. OCHOA; Rev. Msgr. FRANCIS J. SMITH; STEVE EGGER; ANTONIO VERA; PHILLIP MULLIN; HECTOR HOLGUIN; Mr. E. H. BAEZA; PHYLIS ARMIJO; Rev. JOSEPH HERMOSO; TED HOUGHTON, JR.; ALBERTO SANCHEZ.

Future Parish Sites Committee—Rev. JUVENTINO CELINO; NAT CAMPOS; GREG CHAVARRIA.

Diocesan Building Committee—Most Rev. ARMANDO X. OCHOA; Rev. JUVENTINO CELINO; FRANK ALDERETE; ERNESTO ARMENDARIZ; RICARDO BACA; PEDRO HERRERA.

Priests' Personnel Advisory Committee—Revs. RICHARD A. MATTY; TRINI FUENTEZ; HECTOR CRUZ, S.M.; SANTOS PEREZ, O.F.M.; JOHN TELLES; RAUL TRIGUEROS.

Catholic Ministry in Hospitals & Nursing Homes—Rev. ANTHONIO CONCHA, S.J., Dir. Tel: 915-532-5447.

Laity, Office of the—Rev. Msgr. ARTURO BANUELAS, *Youth Services, 499 St. Matthew St., El Paso, 79907.* Tel: 915-595-5020; Youth: 915-595-5000. The following associations are under the direction of the Office of the Laity:

Adoracion Nocturna (Nocturnal Adoration)—Rev. SANTOS PEREZ, O.F.M.

Apostolado de la Cruz (Apostolate of the Cross)—Vacant.

Blue Army—Rev. RICHARD WAIWOOD.

Catholic Daughters of America—Rev. BENJAMIN FLORES-RUIZ.

Catholic Knights of America—Rev. BENJAMIN FLORES-RUIZ.

Cursillos de Cristianidad—Rev. Msgr. JOSE GOMEZ.

Franciscans, Secular Order of Franciscans—Rev. SANTOS PEREZ, O.F.M.

Knights of Columbus—Rev. Msgr. FRANCIS J. SMITH.

Knights of the Holy Sepulchre—Rev. Msgr. FRANCIS J. SMITH.

Knights of St. Gregory—Vacant.

Ladies of Charity; Daughters of Charity; Ladies of the Holy Sepulchre—Rev. Msgr. FRANCIS J. SMITH.

Legion of Mary—Rev. VINCENT ASCHERL.

Serra Club—Rev. BENJAMIN FLORES-RUIZ.

St. Vincent de Paul Society—Mr. TOM WALTERS.

Young Adults-Singles—Vacant.

Catholic Communications Ministry—Rev. RAUL TRIGUEROS, *499 St. Matthews St., El Paso, 79907.* Tel: 915-595-5056.

Diocesan Newspaper—"Rio Grande Catholic," 499 St. Matthews St., El Paso, 79907. Tel: 915-595-5056.

Persons with Disabilities—Vacant.

Evangelization & Renewal Center—Sr. ASUNTA LABRADO, C.D.P., *499 St. Matthews St., El Paso, 79907.*

Tel: 915-595-5063.

Villa Maria - Home for Aged Women & Men—Sr. MARY ANN HAMOR, C.S.J., Dir., *920 S. Oregon, El Paso, 79901.* Tel: 915-533-5152.

Catholic Charities—Sr. MARIAN KLUESNER, F.S.P.A., *1013 E. San Antonio, El Paso, 79901.* Tel: 915-532-9532.

Campaign for Human Development—JOSE G. MORENO, J.D., *1117 N. Stanton, El Paso, 79907.* Tel: 915-532-3975.

Office of Marriage and Family Life—Rev. JAMES W. HALL, *499 St. Matthews St., El Paso, 79907.* Tel: 915-595-5032.

Historical Archives & Diocesan Museum—Rev. RICHARD A. MATTY, *499 St. Matthews St., El Paso, 79907.* Tel: 915-595-5007; 915-595-5000.

Campus Ministry—Sr. ANN FRANCIS MONADERO, O.S.F., *400 E. Robinson, El Paso, 79902.* Tel: 915-544-3888.

Permanent Diaconate Office—Deacon JAMES SPRINGER, Dir., *499 St. Matthews St., El Paso, 79907.* Tel: 915-595-5000.

Priests' Retirement and Disability Plan—Rev. Msgr. FRANCIS J. SMITH, Pres.; Rev. Msgr. WILLIAM RYAN; Mr. YAZBIK DAW; ROBERT ORTEGA.

Missions Office—Sr. HELEN SANTAMARIA, S.L., *499 St. Matthews St., El Paso, 79907.* Tel: 915-595-5007.

Office of Education—Sr. ELIZABETH SWARTZ, S.S.N.D., Supt., *499 St. Matthews St., El Paso, 79907.* Tel: 915-595-5026.

Tepeyac Institute—Rev. Msgr. ARTURO BANUELAS, S.T.D., Dir.; Sr. ESTHER ORTEGA, O.P., Assoc. Dir.; Sr. DONNA KUSTUSCH, O.P., Teacher, *499 St. Matthews St., El Paso, 79907.* Tel: 915-595-5020.

Retreat House—*499 St. Matthews St., El Paso, 79907.* Tel: 915-595-5006.

Reverence for Life Ministry—Rev. RAFAEL GARCIA, S.J., *499 St. Matthews St., El Paso, 79907.* Tel: 915-595-5046.

Vocations & Seminarians—Rev. BENJAMIN FLORES, *499 St. Matthews St., El Paso, 79907.* Tel: 915-595-5003.

Jail Ministry—Rev. WILSON CUEVAS, *499 St. Matthews St., El Paso, 79907.* Tel: 915-595-5000.

West Texas Ministry—Team Ministry: Sr. MARGIE SILGUERO, M.J.M.J.; Sr. LUZ DONEZ, M.J.M.J., *Box 1118, Marfa, 79843.* Tel: 915-729-3385. Sr. FLORA CARILLO, O.P., *P.O. Box 1747, Pecos, 79772.* Tel: 915-445-3208.

Cursillo—Rev. Msgr. JOSE GOMEZ, *St. Patrick Cathedral, 1118 N. Mesa, El Paso, 79902.* Tel: 915-533-4451.

Movimiento Familiar Cristiano—Rev. Msgr. JOSE GOMEZ, Dir., *St. Patrick Cathedral, 1118 N. Mesa, El Paso, 79902.* Tel: 915-533-4451.

CLERGY, PARISHES, MISSIONS AND PAROCHIAL SCHOOLS

CITY OF EL PASO
(El Paso County)

1—ST. PATRICK'S CATHEDRAL, Rev. Msgr. David G. Fierro, Rector; Rev. Alfred Villanueva; Deacon Ken Flynn. In res., Rev. Wilson Cuevas.
Res., 1118 N. Mesa St., 79902. Tel: 915-533-4451; Fax: 915-532-8761.
School—(Grades K-8) 1111 N. Stanton St., 79902. Sisters 1; Brothers 1; Lay Teachers 22; Students 404.

2—ALL SAINTS, Rev. Kennon Y. Ducre, S.T.L.
Res., 1415 Dakota St., 79930. Tel: 915-566-9711.

3—BLESSED JUAN DIEGO PARISH, Rev. Edward G. Roden-Lucero, Administrator.
Res., 14520 E. Montana, 79938. Tel: 915-855-2217.

4—BLESSED SACRAMENT, Revs. Stephen Peters; Jose F. Molina.
Res., 9025 Diana Dr., 79924. Tel: 915-755-7658; Fax: 915-755-6310.
School—(Grades PreK-8). Tel: 915-755-2711. Ms. Guadalupe Varela.
Franciscan Sisters of Our Lady of Perpetual Help 3; Lay Teachers 15; Students 255.
Catechesis/Religious Programs—Teri Valdez, D.R.E. Students 615.

5—CHRIST THE SAVIOR, Rev. Robert S. Kobe; Deacon Paul Andrade.
Res., 5301 Wadsworth Ave., 79924. Tel: 915-821-3766.

6—CORPUS CHRISTI, Rev. Wilson Cuevas, Admin.
Res., 9205 N. Loop Dr., 79907. Tel: 915-858-0488.
Catechesis/Religious Programs—Students 783.

7—CRISTO REY CHURCH, Revs. Raul Trigueros; Jose Martinez-Mata (Mexico).
Res., 8011 Williamette, 79907. Tel: 915-591-0688.

8—GUARDIAN ANGEL, Revs. Thomas Devine; Jesus Maria P. Arrilucea, O.A.R.
Res., 3021 Frutas Ave., 79905. Tel: 915-533-2077; Fax: 915-533-3649.

9—HOLY FAMILY, Rev. Msgr. David G. Fierro, Admin. In res., Rev. Jose Velasquez.
Res., 104 Fewel St., 79902. Tel: 915-532-8462.

10—IMMACULATE CONCEPTION, Rev. Msgr. William H. Ryan.
Res., 118 N. Campbell St., 79901-2404. Tel: 915-533-3427.

11—LA PURISIMA, Rev. Rafael Farrera, S.M.
Res., 328 S. Nevarez St., 79927. Tel: 915-859-7718.

12—SAINT THERESE OF THE LITTLE FLOWER PARISH, Rev. Francisco Siguenza, O.A.R.
Church—171 Polo Inn, 79915.
Res., 3021 Frutas, 79901. Tel: 915-772-1285.

13—MOST HOLY TRINITY, Rev. Msgr. Robert S. Calles; Rev. Fidel Cervantes; Deacon Donald L. Gale.
Res., 10,000 Pheasant Rd., 79924. Tel: 915-751-6416; Fax: 915-751-3242.
School—(Grades K-8).
Lay Teachers 15; Students 225.

14—OUR LADY OF ASSUMPTION, Rev. Msgr. Carlos G. Frias; Rev. Daniel G. Benito.
Res., 4800 Byron St., 79930. Tel: 915-566-4040.
School—(Grades K-8). Tel: 915-565-3411.
Sisters 1; Lay Teachers 10; Students 128.

15—OUR LADY OF GUADALUPE, Revs. Santos Perez, O.F.M.; Ricardo Rodriguez, O.F.M.; Jorge Frausto, O.F.M.; Bro. Bernardo Alvarado, O.F.M.
Res., 2709 Alabama St., 79930. Tel: 915-562-4304; Fax: 915-562-3509.
Catechesis/Religious Programs—Mrs. Zenaida Servin, D.R.E.
Students 350.

16—OUR LADY OF THE LIGHT, Rev. Jose C. Guerrero. In res., Rev. Rodolfo Lacerna.
Res., 4700 Delta Dr., 79905. Tel: 915-532-1757.

17—OUR LADY OF MT. CARMEL, Revs. Donald J. Adamski, O.F.M.Conv.; Mark Tegmeyer, O.F.M.Conv.; John Stowe, O.F.M.Conv.
Res., 131 S. Zaragoza, 79907. Tel: 915-859-9848; Fax: 915-860-9340. [CEM]
School—(Grades K-8) 9101 Socorro Rd., 79907. Tel: 915-859-9812.
Sisters 2; Lay Teachers 20; Students 189.

18—OUR LADY OF SORROWS, Revs. Ruben M. Torres, O.S.M., Admin.; Andres Ponso, O.S.M.; Daniel M. Sierra, O.S.M.
Res., 7712 Rosedale St., 79915. Tel: 915-772-4834; Fax: 915-772-9078.

19—OUR LADY OF THE VALLEY, Revs. John Rini; Miguel Meneses.
Res., 8600 Winchester, 79907. Tel: 915-859-7939.
School—Tel: 915-859-6448. Sr. Caroline Vasquez, O.S.F., Prin.
Lay Teachers 14; Students 213.

20—QUEEN OF PEACE, Rev. Trinidad Fuentez.
Res., 1551 Belvidere, 79912. Tel: 915-584-5817; Fax: 915-584-7761.
Catechesis/Religious Programs—Pat Fowler, D.R.E. Students 560.

21—SACRED HEART, Revs. Rafael Garcia, S.J.; Eduardo Fernandez, S.J.; John Paul, S.J.; Louis J. Lambert, S.J.; Antonio Concha, S.J. In res., Revs. Edward Schott, S.J.; Michael Gallagher, S.J.; Bro. Manuel Cabral, S.J.
Res., 602 S. Oregon St., 79901. Tel: 915-532-5447; Fax: 915-533-0013.

22—ST. FRANCES XAVIER CABRINI PARISH, Rev. Frank Lopez; Sr. Julia Donez, Pastoral Assoc.
Res., 12037 Picasso, 79936. Tel: 915-857-1263.

23—ST. FRANCIS XAVIER, Rev. Esteban Sescon; Deacon Luis Montes.
Res., 519 S. Latta St., 79905. Tel: 915-532-2761; Fax: 915-544-5103.

24—ST. IGNATIUS OF LOYOLA, Revs. Francisco De'Tomasi, O.S.M.; Federico Franco, O.S.M.; Angel M. Maldonado, O.S.M.
Res., 408 Park St., 79901. Tel: 915-532-9534.

25—ST. JOSEPH'S, Revs. Francisco Herrera; Joseph Hermoso.
Res., 1315 Travis St., 79903. Tel: 915-566-9396; Fax: 915-566-5606.
School—(Grades K-8) 1300 Lamar, 79903. Tel: 915-566-1661. Bro. Edwin Gallagher, Prin.
Brothers 3; Lay Teachers 23; Students 473.

26—ST. LUKE, Rev. Msgr. John Peters.
Res., 930 E. Redd Rd., 79912. Tel: 915-585-0255.

27—ST. MARK, Rev. Leonides Rivero.
Res., 11609 John Weir, 79936. Tel: 915-857-2955.
Church—11700 Pebble Hills, 79936.

28—ST. MATTHEW, Rev. Msgr. Dixon Hartford; Rev. Miguel Luna.
Res., 400 W. Sunset Rd., 79922. Tel: 915-584-3461; Fax: 915-584-2107.
Catechesis/Religious Programs—D.R.E.: Mrs. Alice Teran; Mrs. Rachel Pineda.
Students 425.

29—ST. PAUL THE APOSTLE, Rev. Emanuel Alcazar; Deacon Vicente Aguirre.
Res., 7424 Mimosa, 79915. Tel: 915-778-5304.

30—ST. PIUS X, Rev. Msgr. Arturo Banuelas; Revs. Victor Lopez; Marcus McFadin; Juan Narez; Deacon Jim Szostek.
Res., 1050 N. Clark Rd., 79905. Tel: 915-772-3226; Fax: 915-771-6665.
School—(Grades PreK-8). Tel: 915-772-6598.
Sisters 3; Lay Teachers 29; Students 503.
Catechesis/Religious Programs—Students 332.

31—ST. RAPHAEL, Rev. Msgr. Francis J. Smith, P.A.; Revs. Vicente Calderon, Jr.; Roberto Alvarado; Paul Garcia; Deacons George Levy; Frank Mares; John Paddenburg; Henry Padilla; Bernard Rulong.
Res., 2301 Zanzibar Rd., 79925. Tel: 915-598-3431; 3432; Fax: 915-598-0944.
School—(Grades PreK-8) 2310 Woodside, 79925. Tel: 915-598-2241; Fax: 915-598-3002. Elizabeth Wiehe, Prin.
Lay Teachers 46; Students 580.
Catechesis/Religious Programs—Students 1,270.

32—ST. STEPHEN, DEACON AND MARTYR, Rev. Juventino C. Celino; Deacons Gus Rodriquez, Sr.; Gustavo J. Rodriguez.
Res., 1651 Janet Coles Ln., 79936.
Church—1700 George Dieter, 79936. Tel: 915-855-1661; Fax: 915-857-5800.

33—ST. THOMAS AQUINAS, Rev. James W. Hall.
Church—10970 Bywood, 79936. Tel: 915-592-1313.
Catechesis/Religious Programs—Sr. Carmen Moreno, A.S.C., D.R.E.
Students 585.

34—STS. PETER AND PAUL, Rev. Saul de Jesus Uribe. In res., Rev. Celimo Osorio.
Res., 673 Old Hueco Tanks Rd., 79927. Tel: 915-859-3758.

35—SAN ANTONIO, Revs. Luis Martin; Santiago Alonso.
Res., 503 Hunter, 79915. Tel: 915-598-1457; Fax: 915-590-1312.

36—SAN JOSE, Rev. Jose Alcocer.
Res., 8100 San Jose Rd., 79907. Tel: 915-598-6285.

37—SAN JUAN BAUTISTA, Revs. Richard Waiwood; Jose Ignacio Echave.
Res., 5649 Dailey Ave., 79905. Tel: 915-779-1583.

38—SAN JUDAS TADEO, Rev. Msgr. Rafael Miranda.
Res., 4006 Hidden Way, 79922. Tel: 915-584-1095.
Mission—El Paso, El Paso Co., Santa Teresita, 3400 Lomont Dr., 79912. Rev. Richard Weiss.

39—SANTA LUCIA, Revs. Hector J. Cruz, S.M. (Mexico); J. Trinidad Morales, S.M.
Res., 518 Gallagher St., 79915. Tel: 915-592-5245.

40—SANTO NINO DE ATOCHA, Rev. J. Alfredo Olivas.
Res., 210 S. Clark, 79905. Tel: 915-779-3164; Fax: 915-779-1811.

OUTSIDE THE CITY OF EL PASO

Alpine, Brewster Co., Our Lady of Peace, Revs. Kim Van Nam; Ricardo Ruiz.
Res., Box 89, 79831. Tel: 915-837-3304. [CEM]
Missions—Lajitas, Big Bend National Park; Marathon, Brewster Co., St. Mary, P.O. Box 268, Marathon, 79842.; Fort Davis, Jeff Davis Co., St. Joseph's, P.O. Box 787, Fort Davis, 79734. Tel: 915-426-3284.

Balmorhea, Reeves Co., Christ the King. Unassigned.
Res., Rte. 1, Box 3, 79718. Tel: 915-375-2347.
Mission—Saragosa, Our Lady of Guadalupe, Tel: 915-375-2636.

Canutillo, El Paso Co., St. Patrick, Rev. Benjamin S. Mones.
Res., 7065 Second St., P.O. Box 10, 79835. Tel: 915-877-3997.
Mission—Westway, El Paso Co., Immaculate Heart of Mary, 8701 Joplin Rd., 79835. Tel: 915-886-3539.

Clint, El Paso Co., San Lorenzo, Rev. Isaac Vaquero, M.Des.
Res., P.O. Box 215, 79836. Tel: 915-851-2255.

Fabens, El Paso Co., Our Lady of Guadalupe, Rev. Carlos San Jose, M.Des.
Res., P.O. Box 356, 127 W. Main St., 79838. Tel: 915-764-3942. [CEM]
Missions—Cuadrilla, San Jose; Tornillo, Santa Rita; La Isla, San Luis.

Fort Davis, Jeff Davis Co., St. Joseph, Rev. Nam Van Kim, Admin.
Res., P.O. Box 787, 79734. Tel: 915-426-3284. [CEM]

Fort Hancock, Hudspeth Co., Santa Teresa, Sr. Maureen Jerkowski, O.S.F., Admin., Tel: 915-769-3711.
Res., P.O. Box 215, 79839.

Horizon City, Holy Spirit. (Independent Mission). Rev.

Pablo Matta; Sr. Terese Wente; Sr. Maureen Jerkowski.
Res., 1608 McMahon St., El Paso, 79927. Tel: 915-852-3582.

Kermit, Winkler Co., St. Thomas & St. Joseph, Rev. John Telles.
Res., 838 Bellaire Rd., 79745. Tel: 915-586-3922.
St. Joseph the Worker. Consolidated with St. Thomas in 1990.

Marfa, Presidio Co., St. Mary's, Rev. Demetrio Ponce.
Res., Box 356, 79843. Tel: 915-729-4694. [CEM]
Mission—Valentine, Sacred Heart.

Monahans, Ward Co., St. John the Apostle and Evangelist, Rev. John Lucido.
Res., 5th & S. Ike St., 79756. Tel: 915-943-5114. [JC]
Mission—Grandfalls, Ward Co., St. Gertrude, P.O. Box 181, Grandfalls, 79742. Tel: 915-547-2484.

Pecos, Reeves Co., St. Catherine, Deacon George Vasquez.
Res., P.O. Box 1660, 79772. Tel: 915-447-9231.
Mission—Toyah, St. Emily.
Santa Rosa Church, Revs. Antonio Mena; Richard Zamorano; Edward C. Carpenter, Jr.
Res., 620 E. 4th St., Box 686, 79772. Tel: 915-445-2309. [CEM]
Mission—Barstow, Our Lady of Refuge.

Presidio, Presidio Co., Santa Teresa de Jesus, Revs. Arturo Bustamante, O.F.M.; Ricardo Arroyo, O.F.M.
Res., P.O. Box 949, 79845. Tel: 915-229-3235. [CEM]
Missions—Shafter, Sgdo. Corazon de Jesus; Redford, San Jose; Candelaria, Our Lady of Peace; Lajitas, Lajitas Mission; Big Bend, Big Bend Mission.

San Elizario, El Paso Co., San Elceario, Rev. Lorenzo Lucero.
Res., P.O. Drawer 910, 79849. Tel: 915-851-2333. [JC]
San Felipe de Jesus, Rev. Celimo Osorio.
Res., P.O. Box 1070, 79849. Tel: 915-851-3039.

Van Horn, Culberson Co., Our Lady of Fatima, Rev. Ralph Solis, Jr.
Res., 308 Almond St., P.O. Box 398, 79855. Tel: 915-283-2042.
Missions—Sierra Blanca, Our Lady of Miracles, P.O. Box 1, Sierra Blanca, 79851.; Dell City, San Isidro.

Chaplains of Public Institutions

El Paso. *El Paso County Jail*. Rev. Wilson Cuevas.
El Paso Juvenile Detention Center. Vacant.

Anthony. *La Tuna Federal*. Vacant. 7045 Second St., P.O. Box 10, Canutillo, 79835.

On Duty Outside of Diocese:
Reverend Fathers—
Aguilera, Sal, U.S. Navy
Day, Ed, Veterans Administration, 46 Brookside, Jamaica Plain, MA 02130
Islas, Mario, St. Anthony Parish, 419 W. First St., Liberal, KS 67901
Lopez, Jairo
Rowland, Thomas, Madonna House, Ontario, Combermere K0J 1L0 Canada
Soria, Manuel, Sacred Heart Church, 515 Main St., Red Bluff, CA 96080

Absent on Leave:
Reverend Fathers—
Bengert, Anthony L.
Galvan, Alfred
Kleinworth, Robert
Knopp, John
Madrid, Jaime
Maraya, Felipe
Ramirez, Jose Nieves

Retired:
Reverend Fathers—
Acevedo, Luis H.
Ascherl, Vincent
Bertasius, Anthony
Burkus, John
Camacho, Gilbert
Finochietto, Arnold
Lafrenz, James
Perera, Paul
Saez, Jose
Stegman, Leonard F.

Permanent Deacons:
Aguirre, Vicente G., St. Paul, El Paso
Andrade, Paul, Christ the Saviour, El Paso
Flynn, Ken, St. Patrick's Cathedral, El Paso
Gale, Donald L., Most Holy Trinity, El Paso
Guerrero, Teofilo, Prison Ministry
Holbritter, Milton A., (Retired)
Levy, George, St. Raphael, El Paso
Mares, Frank J., St. Raphael, El Paso
Montes, Louis A., St. Francis Xavier, El Paso
Paddenburg, John A., St. Raphael, El Paso
Padilla, Henry, St. Raphael, El Paso
Rodriguez, Gus J., St. Stephen, El Paso
Rulong, Bernard, St. Raphael, El Paso
Schuffer, George M., Jr., William Beaumont Army Medical Center, El Paso
Solis, Ralph, St. Joseph, El Paso
Springer, James, St. Patrick's Cathedral, El Paso
Szostek, James T., St. Pius X, El Paso
Vasquez, George, St. Catherine, Pecos
Wauson, Thomas J., Christ the Saviour, El Paso

INSTITUTIONS LOCATED IN THE DIOCESE

[A] SEMINARIES, DIOCESAN

El Paso. *St. Charles Seminary College Program*, P.O. Box 17548, 79917. Tel: 915-591-9821. Very Rev. Juan Garcia, Rector; Rev. Cristian Mier, Spiritual Dir. Priests 2; Students 6.

[B] SEMINARIES, RELIGIOUS OR SCHOLASTICATES

El Paso. *Roger Bacon College* (1940), 2400 Marr St., 79903. Tel: 915-565-2921. Minor Seminary of the Franciscan Fathers, Province of the Holy Gospel. Revs. Alberto Hernandez, O.F.M.; Romeo Rojas Arriaga, O.F.M.; Most Rev. Raimundo Lopez Mateo, O.F.M., (Retired). Priests 4; Brothers 1.
St. Anthony's School of Theology, Hastings St. and Crescent Dr., 79903. Tel: 915-566-2261. Franciscan Fathers of St. Peter and St. Paul Province, Michoacan, Mexico. Revs. Alejandro Juarez, O.F.M.; Martin Arriage, O.F.M., Guardian; Jaime Yanez, O.F.M.; Hugo Cordova, O.F.M.; Jorge Rivas, O.F.M.; Fernando Mendoza, O.F.M.; Joaquin Acevedo, O.F.M. Priests 7; Scholastics 20; Brothers 3.

[C] HIGH SCHOOLS, DIOCESAN

El Paso. *Cathedral High School*. (Boys), 1309 N. Stanton St., 79902. Tel: 915-532-3238. Brothers of the Christian Schools (de La Salle Christian Brothers). Bro. Brendan Hayden, F.S.C., Pres.; Mr. Leo Cancellare, Prin. Sisters 2; Brothers 6; Lay Teachers 35; Students 677.

[D] HIGH SCHOOLS, PRIVATE

El Paso. *Father Yermo High School*, 250 Washington St., 79905. Tel: 915-533-3185. Servants of the Sacred Heart of Jesus and of the Poor. Sisters 4; Lay Teachers 9; Students 150.
Loretto Academy, 1300 Hardaway, 79903. Tel: 915-564-0211. Sisters of Loretto at the Foot of the Cross. Sisters 8; Lay Teachers 60; Students 851; Priests 1.

[E] ELEMENTARY SCHOOLS, PRIVATE

El Paso. *Father Yermo Elementary School*. (Grades K-8), 237 Tobin Pl., 79905. Tel: 915-533-4693. Servants of the Sacred Heart and of the Poor. Sisters 4; Lay Teachers 10; Students 169.
Loretto Academy Middle School, 1300 Hardaway, 79903. Tel: 915-566-5453. Sisters of Loretto at the Foot of the Cross. Sr. Patricia Williams, S.L., Prin. Sisters 2; Lay Teachers 9; Students 105.
Loretto Elementary School-Loretto Academy. (Grades PreK-5), 4625 Clifton, 79903. Tel: 915-565-2765. Sisters of Loretto at the Foot of the Cross. Mrs. Karla Onick, Prin. Lay Teachers 16; Students 208.
St. Michael School, 616 S. Virginia, 79901. Tel: 915-542-1253; Fax: 915-564-0563. Servants of the Sacred Heart of Jesus and of the Poor. Sr. Maria Angelica Omana, S.S.H.J.P. Sisters 5; Lay Teachers 3; Students 35.

[F] CLINICS

El Paso. *Centro San Vicente*, 8061 Alameda, 79915. Tel: 915-859-7545.
For a complete listing, refer to the Hospitals section.
La Clinica Guadalupana, Inc., 901 Ascencion, 79927. Tel: 915-852-3328.
For a complete listing, refer to the Hospitals section.

[G] AGENCIES AND INSTITUTIONS OF THE CHARITIES OF THE DIOCESE

El Paso. *Catholic Charities*, 1013 E. San Antonio St., 79901. Tel: 915-532-9532. Sr. Marian Kluesner, F.S.P.A., Dir.

[H] DAY CARE CENTERS

El Paso. *St. Joseph of the Valley*, 7681 Barton, 79915. Tel: 915-778-3407. Sisters 3; Lay Teachers 7; Students 65.

[I] HOMES FOR AGED

El Paso. *Nazareth Hall*, 4614 Trowbridge, 79903. Tel: 915-565-4677; Fax: 915-566-7530.
For a complete listing, refer to the Special Care Facilities section.
Villa Maria, 920 S. Oregon St., 79901. Tel: 915-533-5152.
For a complete listing, refer to the Special Care Facilities section.

[J] MONASTERIES & RESIDENCES FOR PRIESTS & BROTHERS

El Paso. *Christian Brothers*, 1204 N. Mesa, 79902-4012. Tel: 915-532-9314.

[K] CONVENTS AND RESIDENCES FOR WOMEN

El Paso. *Adorers of the Blood of Christ (A.S.C.)*, 2209 Pittsburg, 79930. Tel: 915-566-5855. Sr. Darlene Stoecklein, A.S.C., Contact Person. Sisters 2.
Adrian Dominican Sisters (O.P.), 1011 E. Nevada, 79902. Tel: 915-533-4744. Sr. Donna Kustusch, O.P., Contact Person. Sisters 4.
Association of Mary Immaculate (A.I.M.), 3900 La Luz St., 79903. Tel: 915-566-0447. Sr. Sue Castaneda, A.I.M., Contact Person.
Daughters of Charity of St. Vincent De Paul (D.C.), 1020 N. Campbell St., 79902. Tel: 915-533-9013; Fax: 915-859-9862. Sisters 4.
Franciscan Sisters of Our Lady of Perpetual Help (O.S.F.), Blessed Sacrament Convent, 9005 Diana Dr., 79904. Tel: 915-755-4871. Sisters 4.
Hermanas Contemplativas del Buen Pastor (H.B.P.). (Cloistered), Good Shepherd Convent, 8824 Old County Rd., P.O. Box 17254, 79917. Tel: 915-859-3683. Sr. Ernestina Estrada, Supr. Sisters 11.
Hermanas del Servicio Social, 6372 Saint Lo Dr., 79925-1807. Tel: 915-771-0780. Sr. Carmen Aurora Gomez.
Hermanas Dominicas de la Doctrinia Cristiana (O.P.), San Alberto Magno Convent, P.O. Box 17391, 79917. Sr. Celia Gonzalez, Provincial Supr.; Sr. Teresa Martin, Local Supr. Sisters 11.
Hermanas Josefinas - St. Charles Seminary, 8330 Park Haven Ave., 79907. Tel: 915-591-9821. Sr. Margarita Ayala, Supr. Sisters 5.
Missionary Sisters of Jesus, Mary & Joseph (M.J.M.J.), 7681 Barton Dr., 79915. Tel: 915-778-3407. Sr. Gloria Rodriquez, Supr. Sisters 6.
North American Union Sisters of Our Lady of Charity, 415 N. Glenwood Dr., 79905. Tel: 915-772-0737. Sr. Yolanda Martinez, Supr. Sisters 12.
San Juan Day Care Center, 5636 Frutas St., 79905. Tel: 915-772-1681. Sr. Cruz Celia Gomez, Admin.
School Sisters of St. Francis (O.S.F.), 124 Bauxite, 79932. Tel: 915-581-2776. Sr. Imelda Kaufman, Contact Person, 431 Riverside, 79915. Tel: 915-778-7016. Sr. Bernadette Halbur, Contact Person, 793 #A Horizon Blvd., 79927. Tel: 915-852-2049. Sr. Maureen Jerkowski. Sisters 3.
Servants of the Sacred Heart of Jesus and of the Poor (S.S.H.J.P.), Father Yermo Convent, 237 Tobin Pl., 79905. Tel: 915-533-3338. Sr. Marie Enedina Tirres, Supr. Sisters 14.
Queen of Peace Convent, 3119 Pera Ave., 79905. Tel: 915-533-0590. Sr. Maria de la Luz Fernandez, Supr. Sisters 17.
Sisters of Loretto at the Foot of the Cross (S.L.), Loretto Academy, 1400 Hardaway St., 79903. Tel: 915-566-1628. Sr. Agnes Ann Schum, S.L., Coord. Sisters 16.
Sisters of Our Lady of Charity of the Good Shepherd (R.G.S.), Good Shepherd Convent, 8824 Old County Rd., P.O. Box 17635, 79917. Tel: 915-859-6004. Sr. Ma. Emanuel Galvan, Supr. Sisters 10.
Sisters of Perpetual Adoration (A.P.). (Cloistered), Corpus Christi Monastery, 451 Mockingbird Ln., 79907. Tel: 915-591-5662. Mother Maria Sagrario Perez, A.P., Supr. Sisters 15; Novices 1; Postulants 3.
Cristo Rey Monastery of Perpetual Adoration, 145 Cotton St., 79901. Tel: 915-533-5323. Mother Maria de Jesus Armendariz, A.P., Supr. Sisters 13; Novices 2; Postulants 1.
Sisters of St. Joseph of Carondelet (C.S.J.), 4704 Caples, 79903. Tel: 915-566-7635. Sr. Jacqueline Lawson, C.S.J.; Sr. J. Sue Smith, C.S.J.; Sr. Kate Forbes, 4904 Gary Owen, 79903. Tel: 915-565-1258. Sisters 4.

Marfa. *Missionary Sisters of Jesus, Mary & Joseph*, P.O. Box 1118, 79843. Tel: 915-729-3385. Sisters 2.

Presidio. *Sisters of the Most Precious Blood of O'Fallen, Missouri*, P.O. Box 893, 79845. Tel: 915-229-3409; 915-229-4246.

Sierra Blanca. *School Sisters of St. Francis, (S.S.S.F.)*, P.O. Box 303, 79851. Tel: 915-369-2062;369-2651.

[L] RESIDENCES FOR WOMEN

EL PASO. *Queen of Angels Residence for College Girls and Business Women*, 119 W. Nevada Ave., 79902. Tel: 915-533-3173; Fax: 915-541-1123. Sr. Grace I. Vargas, R.J.M., Supr. Residence for Ladies conducted by the Religious of Jesus and Mary. Sisters 13; Residents 25.

[M] NEWMAN CENTERS

EL PASO. *University of Texas at El Paso Catholic Campus Ministry*, Archbishop Oscar Romero Center, 400 E. Robinson, 79902-2619. Tel: 915-544-3883. Sr. Ann Francis Monedero, O.S.F., Dir.

ALPINE. *Sul Ross State University Newman Center*, P.O. Box C 78, 79832. Tel: 915-837-2905. Dr. Paul Lister.

[N] MISCELLANEOUS LISTINGS

EL PASO. *Annunciation House*, 1003 E. San Antonio, 79901. Tel: 915-545-4509. Mr. Ruben Garcia, Dir.

Casa Vides. (Shelter for Refugees), 325 Leon St., 79901. Mr. Ruben Garcia, Dir.

Catholic Counseling Services, Inc., 499 St. Matthews St., 79907. Tel: 915-595-5096; Fax: 915-595-5098. Mr. Jose Castrellon, Exec. Dir.

The Catholic Diocese of El Paso Foundation, 499 St. Matthews, 79907. Tel: 915-595-5054; Fax: 915-595-5095. Mr. Gilber Morales.

Catholic Legal Immigration Network, Inc. (CLINIC). U.S. Catholic Conference Southwestern Regional Office: 1205 N. Oregon, 79902. Tel: 915-533-3971; Fax: 915-533-3974. Lily Gutierrez, S.W. Reg. Clinic Coord. Services: National immigration support network to the Catholic Dioceses throughout the U.S. Southwest regional CLINIC office provides technical assistance, basic organizational program services, management assessments, and immigration law training for its diocesan affiliates. CLINIC assists dioceses in applying for agency recognition and staff accreditation before the Immigration Board of Appeals. CLINIC assists dioceses and religious congregations in obtaining legal status for foreign clergy as non-immigrant and legal permanent residents.

Catholic Properties of El Paso, Inc., 499 St. Matthews St., 79907. Tel: 915-595-5006; Fax: 915-595-5095. Mr. Jorge Virgen, Exec. Dir.

Christ Child Society, 8317 Hopewell, 79925.

Historic Missions Restoration, Inc., 499 St. Matthews St., 79907.

La Posada Home, 248 Francis St., 79905-4416. Tel: 915-544-4595. Shelter for Displaced Women. Sisters 3.

The Office of Migrant and Refugee Services, 1117 N. Stanton, 79902. Tel: 915-532-3975; 3976; Fax: 915-533-4106. Jose Moreno, J.D., Dir.

Our Lady's Youth Center, 515 S. Kansas, P.O. Box 1422, 79948. Tel: 915-533-5260. Rev. Richard M. Thomas, S.J., Dir. The Lord's Ranch & The Lord's Food Bank.

Progress for the Diocese of El Paso, 499 St. Matthews St., 79907. Tel: 915-585-5054; Fax: 915-595-5095. Mr. Gilberto Morales, Exec. Dir.

RELIGIOUS INSTITUTES OF MEN REPRESENTED IN THE DIOCESE

For further details refer to the bracketed number in the Religious Institutes of Men or Women section.

[0330]—*Brothers of the Christian Schools*. (New Orleans and Santa Fe Provs.).—F.S.C.

[0460]—*Brothers of the Poor of St. Francis*.—C.F.P.

[0480]—*Conventual Franciscan Friars*. (Custody of Our Lady of Guadalupe).—O.F.M.Conv.

[]—*Diocesan Laborer Priests*.—D.L.P.

[0520]—*Franciscan Friars*. (Holy Gospel Prov. and St. Peter & Paul Province Prov.).—O.F.M.

[0690]—*Jesuit Fathers and Brothers*. (Prov. of New Orleans).—S.J.

[0780]—*Marist Fathers*.—S.M.

[]—*Mercedarios* Descalzos.—M.Des.

[0150]—*Order of the Augustinian Recollects*. (Prov. of San Nicolas of Tolentino, Italy).—O.A.R.

[1070]—*Redemptorist Fathers*.—C.SS.R.

[1240]—*Servites*. (Province of Mexico).—O.S.M.

RELIGIOUS INSTITUTES OF WOMEN REPRESENTED IN THE DIOCESE

[0100]—*Adorers of the Blood of Christ*.—A.S.C.

[]—*Association of Mary Immaculate*.—A.I.M.

[1010]—*Congregation of Divine Providence of San Antonio, Texas*.—C.D.P.

[1780]—*Congregation of the Sisters of the Third Order of St. Francis of Perpetual Adoration*. (Central Region).—F.S.P.A.

[0760]—*Daughters of Charity of St. Vincent de Paul*.—D.C.

[1070-13]—*Dominican Sisters*.—O.P.

[1070-14]—*Dominican Sisters*.—O.P.

[1430]—*Franciscan Sisters of Our Lady of Perpetual Help*.—O.S.F.

[]—*Franciscan Sisters of the Sorrowful Mother*.—F.S.S.M.

[]—*Hermanas Contemplativas del Buen Pastor*.—H.B.S.

[]—*Hermanas del Buen Pastor*.—S.G.S.

[]—*Hermanas del Servico Social*.—H.S.S.

[]—*Hermanas Dominicanas de la Doctrina Cristiana*.—O.P.

[1910]—*Hermanas Josefinas*.—H.J.

[2770]—*Missionaries of Jesus, Mary and Joseph*.—M.J.M.J.

[3070]—*North American Union of the Sisters of Our Lady of Charity*.—N.A.U.-O.L.C.

[3190]—*Nuns of the Perpetual Adoration of the Blessed Sacrament*.—A.P.

[3450]—*Religious of Jesus and Mary*.—R.J.M.

[1680]—*School Sisters of St. Francis*.—S.S.S.F.

[3660]—*Servants of the Sacred Heart of Jesus and of the Poor*.—S.S.H.J.P.

[2360]—*Sisters of Loretto at the Foot of the Cross*.—S.L.

[4090]—*Sisters of Social Services*.—S.S.S.

[3830-15]—*Sisters of St. Joseph*.—C.S.J.

[3840]—*Sisters of St. Joseph of Carondelet*. (Prov. of St. Paul).—C.S.J.

[1830]—*The Sisters of the Good Shepherd*. (St. Louis Province).—R.G.S.

[3270]—*Sisters of the Most Precious Blood (O'Fallon, MO)*.—C.PP.S.

[4100]—*Sisters of the Sorrowful Mother (Third Order of St. Francis)*.—S.S.M.

DIOCESAN CEMETERY

EL PASO. *Mount Carmel*, Box 17655, 79917. Tel: 915-859-7734.

NECROLOGY

† Fearson, Alexander, El Paso, TX, Nazareth Hall. —Died Dec. 30, 1995.

† LaPiezo, Rev. Msgr. Francisco, El Paso, TX, Holy Family. —Died Jan. 1, 1996.

Diocese of Erie

(Dioecesis Eriensis)

Most Reverend

DONALD W. TRAUTMAN, S.T.D., S.S.L.

Bishop of Erie; ordained April 7, 1962; appointed Titular Bishop of Sassura and Auxiliary Bishop of Buffalo February 27, 1985; consecrated April 16, 1985; appointed to Erie June 12, 1990; installed July 16, 1990. *Res., 205 West 9th St., Erie, PA, 16501.* Tel.: 814-824-1120; Fax: 814-824-1124.

Most Reverend

MICHAEL J. MURPHY, D.D., S.T.L.

Retired Bishop of Erie; ordained February 28, 1942; appointed Titular Bishop of Arindela and Auxiliary Bishop of Cleveland April 20, 1976; consecrated June 11, 1976; appointed Coadjutor Bishop of Erie November 28, 1978; succeeded to See July 16, 1982; retired July 16, 1990. *Mailing Address: St. Patrick/St. Hedwig Parish Cluster, 130 East 4th St., Erie, PA, 16507.* Tel.: 814-454-8085.

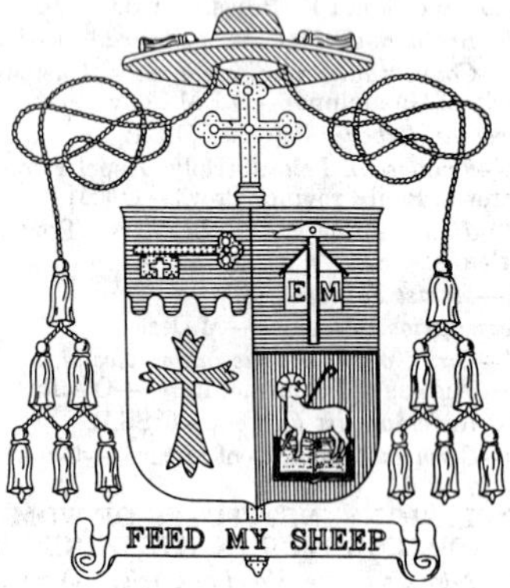

ESTABLISHED 1853.

Square Miles 9,936.

Comprises the following Counties in Northwestern Pennsylvania: Erie, Crawford, Mercer, Venango, Forest, Clarion, Jefferson, Clearfield, Cameron, Elk, McKean, Potter and Warren.

For legal titles of parishes and diocesan institutions, consult the Chancery Office.

Chancery: St. Mark Catholic Center, P.O. Box 10397, Erie, PA, 16514. Tel.: 814-824-1111; Fax: 814-824-1128.

Web site address: http://www.erienet/~eriercd

E-mail address: cprehoda@erie.net

STATISTICAL OVERVIEW

Personnel	
Bishop	1
Retired Bishops	1
Priests: Diocesan Active in Diocese	182
Priests: Active Outside Diocese	9
Priests: Diocesan in Foreign Missions	1
Priests: Retired, Sick or Absent	59
Number of Diocesan Priests	251
Religious Priests in Diocese	14
Extern Priests in Diocese	3
Ordinations:	
Diocesan Priests	3
Transitional Deacons	3
Permanent Deacons in Diocese	2
Total Brothers	2
Total Sisters	570
Parishes	
Parishes	127
With Resident Pastor:	
Resident Diocesan Priests	108
Resident Religious Priests	6
Without Resident Pastor:	
Administered by Priests	13
Missions	27
Pastoral Centers	1
Professional Ministry Personnel:	
Sisters	23
Lay Ministers	41
Welfare	
Catholic Hospitals	1
Total Assisted	225,000
Homes for the Aged	4
Total Assisted	678
Day Care and Extended Day Care Centers	1
Total Assisted	175
Specialized Homes	2
Total Assisted	237
Special Centers for Social Services	9
Total Assisted	114,651
Other Institutions	1
Total Assisted	598
Educational	
Seminaries, Diocesan	1
Students from This Diocese	13
Diocesan Students in Other Seminaries	5
Total Seminarians	18
Colleges and Universities	2
Total Students	6,027
High Schools, Diocesan and Parish	6
Total Students	1,779
High Schools, Private	2
Total Students	1,410
Elementary Schools, Diocesan and Parish	44
Total Students	10,801
Elementary Schools, Private	1
Total Students	380
Catechesis/Religious Education:	
High School Students	7,398
Elementary Students	13,467
Total Students Under Catholic Instruction	41,280
Teachers in the Diocese:	
Priests	10
Sisters	36
Lay Teachers	777
Vital Statistics	
Receptions into the Church:	
Infant Baptism Totals	2,534
Adult Baptism Totals	275
Received into Full Communion	266
First Communions	3,027
Confirmations	2,667
Marriages:	
Catholic	797
Interfaith	577
Total Marriages	1,374
Deaths	2,583
Total Catholic Population	235,195
Total Population	874,244

Former Bishops—Rt. Rev. MICHAEL O'CONNOR, cons. Bishop of Pittsburgh, Aug. 15, 1843; transferred from Pittsburgh as first Bishop of Erie in 1853; transferred back to Pittsburgh in 1854; died Oct. 18, 1872.—Rt. Rev. JOSUE M. YOUNG, cons. April 23, 1854; died Sept. 18, 1866.—Rt. Rev. TOBIAS MULLEN, D.D., cons. Aug. 2, 1868, Bishop of Erie; resigned Aug. 10, 1899, and appt. to Titular See of Germanicopolis; died April 22, 1900.—Rt. Rev. JOHN E. FITZMAURICE, D.D., cons. Feb. 24, 1898; died June 18, 1920.—Most Rev. EDWARD P. MCMANAMAN, S.T.D., Titular Bishop of Floriana and Auxiliary Bishop of Erie; cons. Oct. 28, 1948; died July 18, 1964.—Most Rev. JOHN MARK GANNON, D.D., Archbishop-Bishop of Erie; ord. Dec. 21, 1901; appt. Titular Bishop of Nilopolis, Nov. 13, 1917; cons. Feb. 6, 1918; transferred to Erie, Aug. 26, 1920; installed Dec. 16, 1920; appt. Assistant at the Pontifical Throne Nov. 4, 1944; appt. Archbishop "ad personam" Nov. 25, 1953; resigned Sept. 21, 1966 and transferred to Titular See of Tacarata, Dec. 14, 1966; died Sept. 5, 1968.—Most Rev. JOHN F. WHEALON, D.D., appt. Titular Bishop of Andrapa and Auxiliary Bishop of Cleveland, June 2, 1961; cons. July 6, 1961; transferred to the See of Erie, Dec. 14, 1966; transferred to the Archdiocese of Hartford; died Aug. 2, 1991.—Most Rev. ALFRED M. WATSON, D.D., Bishop of Erie; ord. May 10, 1934; Titular Bishop of Nationa and Auxiliary Bishop of Erie; appt. May 17, 1965; cons. June 29, 1965; succeeded to See, March 19, 1969; retired July 16, 1982; died Jan. 4, 1990.—Most Rev. MICHAEL J. MURPHY, D.D., S.T.L., Titular Bishop of Arindela and Auxiliary Bishop of Cleveland; appt. April 20, 1976; cons. June 11, 1976; Coadjutor Bishop of Erie; appt. Nov. 28, 1978; succeeded to See, July 16, 1982; retired July 16, 1990.

Vicar General—Rev. Msgr. ROBERT J. SMITH, J.C.L., *St. Mark Catholic Center, P.O. Box 10397, Erie, 16514.* Tel: 814-824-1130.

Office of the Bishop—NANCY HAMILTON, Sec. to the Bishop, *St. Mark Catholic Center, P.O. Box 10397, Erie, 16514.* Tel: 814-824-1120.

Chancery—*St. Mark Catholic Center, P.O. Box 10397, Erie, 16514.* Tel: 814-824-1135; Fax: 814-824-1124.

Chancellor—Rev. Msgr. LAWRENCE E. BRANDT, J.C.D., Ph.D.

Vice Chancellor—Rev. GREGORY KIRSCH.

Diocesan Archivist and Historian—Rev. ROBERT G. BARCIO, Ph.D. All Diocesan Offices and Personnel listed in Directory can be reached at: *St. Mark Catholic Center, 429 E. Grandview Blvd., P.O. Box 10397, Erie, 16514-0397.* Tel: 814-824-1111 unless otherwise indicated.

Episcopal Vicars—
Northern Vicariate—Rev. Msgr. ROBERT J. SMITH, J.C.L., *St. Mark Catholic Center, P.O. Box 10397, Erie, 16514.* Tel: 814-824-1130.
Eastern Vicariate—Rev. Msgr. CHARLES A. KAZA, *1100 Hewett St., Brockway, 15824.* Tel: 814-265-1374.
Western Vicariate—Rev. Msgr. ROBERT L. BRUGGER, *967 Chancery Ln., Meadville, 16335.* Tel: 814-333-6382.

Administrative Coordinator—FRANK E. HAKEL, *St. Mark Catholic Center, P.O. Box 10397, Erie, 16514.* Tel: 814-824-1245.

Vicar for Religious—Sr. MARY RITA KUHN, S.S.J., *St. Mark Catholic Center, P.O. Box 10397, Erie, 16514-0397.* Tel: 814-824-1125.

Director of Planning—WALTER SPILLER, *St. Mark Catholic Center, P.O. Box 10397, Erie, 16514-0397.* Tel: 814-824-1116.

Mission Office and Society for the Propagation of the Faith—Sr. THERESA ZOKY, O.S.B., *St. Mark Catholic Center, P.O. Box 10397, Erie, 16514-0397.* Tel: 814-824-1230.

Advisory To Bishop

Administrative Cabinet—Rev. Msgr. ROBERT J. SMITH, J.C.L., V.G.; Rev. Msgr. CHARLES A. KAZA; Sr. MARY RITA KUHN, S.S.J.; Rev. Msgr. ANDREW H. KARG; Rev. Msgr. LAWRENCE E. BRANDT, J.C.D., Ph.D.; Mr. FRANK HAKEL; Rev. Msgr. MICHAEL D. MCGRAW, L.S.W., M.Ss.A.; Rev. CONRAD KRAUS; DAVID MURPHY; Rev. Msgr. ROBERT A. BRUGGER. Special Consultants: WALTER SPILLER; GARY LONCKI.

Consultors—Rev. Msgr. WILLIAM C. KARG; Rev. Msgr. ROBERT L. BRUGGER; Rev. Msgr. HENRY A. KRIEGEL; Rev. Msgr. ROBERT W. COHAN, V.F.; Rev. Msgr. LOUIS J. HEBERLEIN; Rev. Msgr. ROBERT J. SMITH, J.C.L.

Finance Council—PAUL C. ROCHE, JR.; WILLIAM P. BOLASH; Most Rev. DONALD W. TRAUTMAN; THOMAS GUELCHER; HAROLD LANZEL; PATRICIA LIEBEL; Sr. LEONELLA GINGENBACH, S.S.J.; Rev. NORBERT G. WOLF; Rev. Msgr. JOHN R. SNYDER. Ex-Officios: Rev. Msgr. ROBERT J. SMITH, J.C.L.; FRANK HAKEL; DAVID MURPHY.

Deans—Erie East: Rev. Msgr. ROBERT W. COHAN, V.F.; Erie West: Rev. Msgr. WILLIAM E. BIEBEL, V.F.; Gannon University: Very Rev. CHARLES H. DREXLER; Sharon: Rev. Msgr. EDWARD J. ZEITLER, V.F.; Oil City: Very Rev. THOMAS L. TYLER, V.F.; Bradford: Very Rev. THOMAS M. ALEKSA, V.F.; Clearfield: Rev. Msgr. JOSEPH K. BOBAL, V.F.; Meadville: Rev. Msgr. JOHN J. LUCAS, V.F.; Dubois: Rev. Msgr. HENRY L. KREBS; St. Marys: Vacant; Warren: Rev. Msgr. EDWARD J. KOSIK, V.F.

Presbyteral Council—Most Rev. DONALD W. TRAUTMAN, Chm.; Rev. Msgr. DANIEL ARNOLD, Chm.; Rev. WILLIAM LASKA, Sec.

Priest Personnel Board—Rev. Msgr. ROBERT BRUGGER, Chm.; Rev. Msgr. RICHARD MAYER, Vice Chm.; Rev. JEFF NOBLE, Sec.

Priest Retirement Board—Most Rev. DONALD W. TRAUTMAN, Chm. Members: WILLIAM BOLASH; Sr. JEAN BAPTISTE DILUZIO, S.S.J.; JAMES HOLLAND; Rev. Msgr. JOHN J. SLATER; JAMES TOOHEY, Attorney. Ex-Officio: Rev. Msgr. LAWRENCE E. BRANDT; Rev. DANIEL K. ARNOLD. Staff: DAVID J. MURPHY; Rev. Msgr. ROBERT L. BRUGGER.

Pennsylvania Catholic Conference—Rev. Msgr. LAWRENCE E. BRANDT, J.C.D., Ph.D., Personal Rep. of the Bishop, *St. Mark Catholic Center, P.O. Box 10397, Erie, 16514.*

The Bishop's Theological Advisory Committee—Rev. Msgr. GERALD L. ORBANEK, M.A., Chm.; Revs. JOHN P. SCHANZ, Ph.D.; CHARLES H. DREXLER, S.T.D.; EDWARD KRAUSE, Ph.D.; CASIMIR J. WOZNIAK, Ph.D.; RICHARD J. SULLIVAN, M.A.; SCOTT P. DETISCH, M.A.; Mr. PATRICK O'CONNELL, Ph.D.; Sr. MICHELLE HEALY, S.S.J., M.A.

Lake Shore Visitor Advisory Board—Most Rev. DONALD W. TRAUTMAN; GINA ADAMS; GARY LONCKI, Editor; Rev. Msgr. WILLIAM E. BIEBEL; JOSEPH MASSA, District Attorney; PATRICK C. BOYLE; DAVID SLOMSKI; JILL T. SLOMSKI; Rev. Msgr. LAWRENCE BRANDT, Chancellor; Sr. MARY LOUIS EICHENLAUB, O.S.B.; TOM BRENNAN.

Matrimonial Concerns

All requests for marriage dispensations, permissions, and rogatory commissions should be sent to this office.

Diocesan Tribunal—*St. Mark Catholic Center, P.O. Box 10397, Erie, 16514.* Tel: 814-824-1140.
Judicial Vicar—Rev. MARK L. BARTCHAK, J.C.D.
Adjutant Judicial Vicar—Rev. SCOTT T. STROUPE, J.C.L.
Promoter of Justice—Rev. Msgr. LAWRENCE E. BRANDT, J.C.D., Ph.D.

Defenders of the Bond—Rev. Msgr. LAWRENCE E. BRANDT, J.C.D., Ph.D.; Revs. CHARLES MURCKO; JOSEPH RICCARDO.

Matrimonial Judges—Rev. Msgr. ROBERT J. SMITH, J.C.L.; Rev. Msgr. RICHARD J. STACK, J.C.L.; Revs. MARK L. BARTCHAK, J.C.D.; JOHN P. BEAL, J.C.D.; CHARLES SCHMITT, M.A.; L. THOMAS SNYDERWINE, Ph.D.; Sr. CARLOTTA BARTONE, S.H.C.J., J.C.L.; Rev. SCOTT T. STROUPE, J.C.L.

Auditors—Rev. JAMES P. RUHLING; Sr. RAPHAEL BAKER, O.S.B.; Sr. REBECCA ANN COSTA, S.S.J.; Sr. JEAN BAPTISTE DILUZIO, S.S.J.; Sr. CHRISTINE QUIRK, S.S.J.

Secretary/Notary—BARBARA ALWARD; CAROL GRYGIER.

Office of Conciliation & Arbitration—*St. Mark Catholic Center, P.O. Box 10397, Erie, 16514.* Tel: 814-824-1140. Rev. MARK L. BARTCHAK, J.C.D., Dir.

Catholic Education

Episcopal Vicar for Catholic Education—Rev. Msgr. ANDREW H. KARG, *St. Mark Catholic Center, P.O. Box 10397, Erie, 16514-0397.*

Superintendent for Catholic Schools—Sr. MARY ARNOLD TANN, S.S.J., *St. Mark Catholic Center, P.O. Box 10397, Erie, 16514-0397.*

Coordinator of Secondary Schools—FRANK HAKEL, *St. Mark Catholic Center, P.O. Box 10397, Erie, 16514-0397.*
Directors—CHARLES BANDUCCI, School Finance; JANICE WHITEMAN, Curriculum; MAUREEN DUNN, Spec. Prog & Pub. Rels.; Sr. MARY ANN BADER, R.S.M., Teacher Personnel; NED SMITH, Community Rels. & Educational Opportunity Grants; J. WILLIAM JONES, Youth Athletic Programs, *St. Mark Catholic Center, P.O. Box 10397, Erie, 16514-0397.*
Youth Athletic Director—J. WILLIAM JONES, *St. Mark's Catholic Center, P.O. Box 10397, Erie, 16514-0397.* Tel: 814-824-1213.
Religious Education—Mr. JOSEPH STREETT, Dir., Religious Education, Curriculum & Catechist Formation; Sr. NANCY FISCHER, S.S.J., Dir., Community Formation & Ministry Training; GERARD WHITE, Dir., Youth Ministry; KAREN LESLIE, Media Resource Coord. Mktg., *St. Mark Catholic Center, P.O. Box 10397, Erie, 16514-0397.*

Campus Ministry—Diocesan Co-Dirs.: RENEE J. LABAKI, *Gannon University, University Sq., Erie, 16541.* Tel: 814-871-7435. Sr. ANNA MAE KUZMA, O.S.F., *Penn State Erie, The Behrend College, Sta. Rd., Erie, 16563.* Tel: 814-898-6245. See separate listing in the institution section for details on Campus Ministry and Newman Centers.

Catholic Charities, Affiliated Offices, Agencies and Institutions Central Administration

Office of Catholic Charities—Rev. Msgr. MICHAEL D. MCGRAW, M.Ss.A., L.S.W., Exec. Dir., *St. Mark Catholic Center, P.O. Box 10397, Erie, 16514-0397.*

Catholic Charities of the Diocese of Erie, Inc.—Rev. Msgr. MICHAEL D. MCGRAW, M.Ss.A., L.S.W., Exec. Dir., *St. Mark Catholic Center, P.O. Box 10397, Erie, 16514-0397.* Charities program and fiscal development organization.

Development and Grantwriting

STEVEN C. DEHART, Dir., *St. Mark Catholic Center, P.O. Box 10397, Erie, 16514-0397.* Rev. MICHAEL G. BARLETTA, Devel. & Pub. Rels. Assoc., *St. Mark Catholic Center, P.O. Box 10397, Erie, 16514-0397*

Parish Social Services

Family Ministries—MARY MAXWELL, M.A., Dir., *St. Mark Catholic Center, P.O. Box 10397, Erie, 16514-0397.* Office includes Marriage Preparation and Enrichment Programs, Divorced Ministry, Retrouvaille, Parenting and Rainbows.

Respect Life/Justice and Peace—RITA M. SCRIMENTI, M.S.W., Dir., *St. Mark Catholic Center, P.O. Box 10397, Erie, 16514-0397.* Office includes advocacy, parish-based social justice education programs and respect life efforts.

Heart and Soul Programs—GREGORY SCHLUETER, Dir., *St. Mark Catholic Center, P.O. Box 10397, Erie, 16514-0397.* Office includes chastity education.

Parish Social Ministry—Sr. ANN AMEN, S.S.J., Ph.D., Dir., *St. Mark Catholic Center, P.O. Box 10397, Erie, 16514-0397.* Consultant for Parish Care and Concern model and training program for volunteers.

Natural Family Planning—Diocesan Coords.: EDWARD BURKETT; BARBARA BURKETT, *St. Mark Catholic Center, P.O. Box 10397, Erie, 16514-0397.* Natural Family Planning training and education, Teen Chastity educational programs.

Rainbows-Services to Children of Separation/Divorce—MARY ALICE DOOLIN, M.S., Dir., *St. Mark Catholic Center, P.O. Box 10397, Erie, 16514-0397.*

Campaign for Human Development—RITA M. SCRIMENTI, M.S.W., Dir., *St. Mark Catholic Center, P.O. Box 10397, Erie, 16514-0397.*

Persons with Disabilites Ministries—Sr. MARY REGIS SCHROCK, S.S.J., Coord.

Clinical Services

Catholic Charities Counseling and Adoption Services—NANCY MONICATTI, A.C.S.W., L.S.W., Agency Dir. ROSEMARIE RADOMSKI, M.A., M.S., Clinical Dir.
Northern Vicariate - Erie Office—*329 W. Tenth St., Erie, 16502.* Tel: 814-456-2091., Satellite Office - Warren: *213 W. Third Ave., Office 105, Warren.* Tel: 814-726-9799.
Western Vicariate - Sharon Office—MARTHA CONSLA, M.Ed., Reg. Supvr., *786 E. State St., Sharon, 16146.* Tel: 412-346-4142., Satellite Office - Meadville: *967 Chancery Ln., Meadville, 16335.* Tel: 814-337-5551.
Eastern Vicariate - DuBois Office—Vacant, *90 Beaver Dr., DuBois, 15801.*

Institutional Care of Elderly

John XXIII Home—ROBERTA T. LAMONT, Admin., *2250 Shenango Fwy., Hermitage, 16148.* Tel: 814-981-3200.

Christ the King Manor—Rev. Msgr. JOHN W. MIGNOT, Admin., *1100 W. Long Ave., Du Bois, 15801.* Tel: 814-371-3180.

Community Services

* *St. Martin Center*—CHERYL WEBER, M.A., Dir., *1701 Parade St., Erie, 16503.* Tel: 814-452-6113.

Harborcreek Youth Services—JAMES E. HENRY, A.C.S.W., L.S.W., Dir., *5712 Iroquois Ave., Harborcreek, 16421.* Tel: 814-899-7664.

Prince of Peace Center—Sr. CLARE MARIE BEICHNER, S.S.J., Dir., *502 Darr Ave., Box 89, Farrell, 16121.* Tel: 412-346-5777.

Better Housing for Erie, c/o H.A.N.D.S.—CHARLES SCALISE, SR., Dir., *139 E. 12th St., Erie, 16501.* Tel: 814-459-1047.

Ministry for the Marginalized—Rev. Msgr. JAMES W. PETERSON, Dir., *1218 French St., Erie, 16501-2030.* Tel: 814-454-0891.

Good Samaritan Center—Rev. JAMES C. MCKEE, S.J., Dir., *Clearfield.* Tel: 814-236-1896; 814-768-7229.

Other Charitable/Social Agencies and Institutions

Gannondale Residential Center for Girls—LOUIS J. GRANDE, A.C.S.W., Exec. Dir., *4635 E. Lake Rd., Erie, 16511.* Tel: 814-899-7659.

St. Mary's Home—Sr. ANASTASIA VALIMONT, S.S.J., Admin., *607 E. 26th St., Erie, 16504.* Tel: 814-459-0621.

Mercy Center For Women—PATRICIA DONZE, Dir., *1039 E. 27th St., Erie, 16507.* Tel: 814-455-4577.

Young People Who Care—Sr. THERESE DUSH, C.A., Dir., *Frenchville, 16836.* Tel: 814-263-4177.

Maria House Projects—Rev. Msgr. JAMES PETERSON, Dir., *1701 Parade St., Erie, 16503.* Tel: 814-454-0891.

Emmaus Ministries—Sr. MARY MILLER, O.S.B., Dir., *218 E. 11th St., Erie, 16501.* Tel: 814-459-8754.

St. Patrick Haven—Sr. MARY EILEEN MOYER, S.S.J., Dir., *147 E. 12th St., Erie, 16501.* Tel: 814-454-7219.

Parish Services

Liturgy & Worship—Rev. CONRAD KRAUS, Dir., *St. Mark Catholic Center, P.O. Box 10397, Erie, 16514-0397.*

Community Formation—Sr. NANCY FISCHER, S.S.J., Dir., *St. Mark Catholic Center, P.O. Box 10397, Erie, 16514-0397.*

Lay Ministry Training—Sr. NANCY FISCHER, S.S.J., Dir. JOSEPH STREETT, *St. Mark Catholic Center, P.O. Box 10397, Erie, 16514-0397.*

Rite of Christian Initiation for Adults—Rev. GERARD H. KREBS, *St. Mark Catholic Center, P.O. Box 10397, Erie, 16514-0397.* Tel: 814-824-1272.

Finance and Development

Director—DAVID J. MURPHY, *St. Mark Catholic Center, P.O. Box 10397, Erie, 16514-0397.*

Finance Office—DAVID J. MURPHY, Dir. JAMES L. BOGNIAK, Mgr., Accounting & Budgeting; THOMAS E. BURIK, Parish Accountant & Auditor, *St. Mark Catholic Center, P.O. Box 10397, Erie, 16514-0397.* Tel: 814-824-1180.

Development Office—WILLIAM F. GRANT, II, Dir., *St. Mark Catholic Center, P.O. Box 10397, Erie, 16514-0397.* Consultants: JACK DWYER; Rev. Msgr. ERNEST J. DALEY. Tel: 814-824-1193.

Diocesan Attorney—FRANK L. KROTO, JR., ESQ., *Quinn, Buseck, Leemhuis, Toohey & Kroto, Inc., 2222 W. Grandview Blvd., Erie, 16506.* Tel: 814-833-2222.

Erie Diocesan Cemeteries—Board of Members: Most Rev. DONALD W. TRAUTMAN; Rev. Msgr. ROBERT J. SMITH, J.C.L.; Rev. Msgr. LAWRENCE E. BRANDT, J.C.D., Ph.D.; DAVID J. MURPHY; THOMAS L. COPECK, Dir. JOHN HROMYAK, Operations Mgr., *3325 West Lake Rd., Erie, 16505.* Tel: 814-838-7724.

Clergy Formation

Clergy Personnel—Rev. Msgr. ROBERT L. BRUGGER, Dir.

Clergy Continuing Education and Formation—Rev. THOMAS J. WHITMAN, Dir., *St. Mark Catholic Center, P.O. Box 10397, Erie, 16514-0397.*

Seminary Program

Vocation Office—Rev. EDWARD M. LOHSE, Dir., *St. Mark Catholic Center, P.O. Box 10397, Erie, 16514-0397.*

St. Mark's College Formation Program—Rev. Msgr. LAWRENCE T. SPEICE, Rector, *St. Mark Catholic Center, P.O. Box 10397, Erie, 16514-0397.*

Continuum Program & Spiritual Formation—Rev. NICHOLAS J. ROUCH, Dir., *St. Mark Catholic Center, P.O. Box 10397, Erie, 16514-0397.*

Special Apostolates

Spiritual Apostolates—Rev. JOHN T. CARTER, Dir., *5145 Peach St., Erie, 16509.* Tel: 814-864-0622.

Black Apostolate—Rev. EDWARD C. KRAUSE, C.S.C., *233 E. 16th St., Erie, 16503.* Tel: 814-454-1615.

Hispanic Apostolate—Rev. JORGE VILLEGAS, Dir., *1237 W. 21st St., Erie, 16502.* Tel: 814-459-0543.

Apostleship of the Sea and Chaplain to the Port of Erie—Rev. L. THOMAS SNYDERWINE, Dir., *c/o St. Paul Church, 1617 Walnut St., Erie, 16502.* Tel: 814-459-3173.

Blue Army of Our Lady of Fatima—Rev. OTTO B. PISONI, Dir., *502 Peach St., Erie, 16501-1104.* Tel: 814-454-6494.

Cursillo Movement—Rev. JOHN J. HILBERT, Dir., *695 Smithson Ave., Erie, 16511.* Tel: 814-899-3000.

Legion of Mary—Rev. JOHN T. CARTER, Dir., *5145 Peach St., Erie, 16509.* Tel: 814-864-0622.

Charismatic Movement—MICHAEL VEHEC, Diocesan Liaison, *St. Mark Catholic Center, P.O. Box 10397, Erie, 16514-0397.*

Bread of Life Community—Rev. DAVID L. POULSON, Moderator, *830 W. 9th St., Erie, 16502.* Tel: 814-456-5698. GENE KOBAL, Pres.

Word of Life Charismatic Renewal—St. Mark Catholic Center, 429 E. Grandview Blvd., P.O. Box 10397, Erie, 16514-0397. Tel: 814-824-1286.

Ecumenism

Pennsylvania Conference on Inter-Church Cooperation—Rev. Msgr. LAWRENCE E. BRANDT, J.C.D., Ph.D., Diocesan Rep.

Ecumenical Officers—

Eastern Vicariate—Rev. DENNIS C. HADBERG.

Western Vicariate—Rev. Msgr. WILLIAM C. KARG, *St. Joseph, 79 Case Ave., Sharon, 16146.* Tel: 412-981-3232.

Northern Vicariate—Rev. Msgr. WILLIAM E. BIEBEL, *St. Peter Cathedral, 230 W. 10th St., Erie, 16501.* Tel: 814-453-6677.

Communication

Office of Communications—GARY C. LONCKI, Dir., *P.O. Box 10668, Erie, 16514-0668.* Tel: 814-824-1160; Fax: 814-824-1128.

"Lake Shore Visitor" - Diocesan Newspaper—GARY C. LONCKI, Editor; ANDREA BARAN, Asst. Editor, *P.O. Box 10668, Erie, 16514-0668.* Tel: 814-824-1160; Fax: 814-824-1128.

CLERGY, PARISHES, MISSIONS AND PAROCHIAL SCHOOLS

CITY OF ERIE
(Erie County)

1—ST. PETER CATHEDRAL (1893), Rev. Msgr. William E. Biebel, V.F., Rector; Rev. Barry Hudock; Sr. Mary McCarthy, R.S., D.R.E. In res., Rev. Msgr. Edward H. Latimer, (Retired); Revs. Gregory A. Kirsch, Vice Chancellor; Robert Barcio, Archivist; Joseph P. Reigel.
Res., 230 W. 10th St., 16501. Tel: 814-453-6677; Fax: 814-456-1351.
Church—10th St. & Sassafras St., 16501.
School—Tel: 814-452-4276.
Sisters 1; Lay Teachers 20; Students 356.

2—BLESSED SACRAMENT (1938), Rev. Msgr. Daniel K. Arnold; Rev. John J. Detisch; Sr. Mary Rose Romeo, S.S.J., Music Dir.; Sr. Rose Kuzma, O.S.F., D.R.E.
Res., 1626 W. 26th St., 16508. Tel: 814-454-0171; Fax: 814-459-6832.
School—Tel: 814-455-1387.
Sisters of St. Joseph 2; Lay Teachers 19; Students 487.

3—HOLY FAMILY/ST. ANN/ST. CASIMIR (1902) (Slovak), Rev. James T. O'Hara; Sr. Marilyn Zimmerman, S.S.J.; Sr. Susan Doubet.
Office: 913 Fulton St., 16503. Tel: 814-452-4832.
School—Tel: 814-452-4720.
Lay Teachers 9; Students 176.

4—HOLY ROSARY (1927), Very Rev. Richard D. Lynch; Rev. William M. Laska.
Res., 2701 East Ave., 16504. Tel: 814-456-4254; Fax: 814-456-4255.
School—Tel: 814-456-7212.
Lay Teachers 13; Students 224.

5—HOLY TRINITY (1903) (Polish), Rev. David J. Maciukiewicz; Sr. Teresita Langowski, C.S.S.F., Pastoral Min.
Res., 2220 Reed St., 16503. Tel: 814-456-0671.
School—Tel: 814-455-8240.
Felician Sisters 1; Lay Teachers 9; Students 89.

6—IMMACULATE CONCEPTION (1946) (African American), Rev. Edward Krause, C.S.C., Admin.
Res., 1237 W. 21, 16502.
Church—233 E. 16th St., 16503. Tel: 814-454-1615.

7—MOUNT CALVARY (1951), Rev. Msgr. Daniel E. Magraw.
Res., 2004 East Lake Rd., 16511. Tel: 814-454-0061; Fax: 814-454-7177.
School—Tel: 814-455-1268.
Lay Teachers 10; Students 201.

8—OUR LADY OF MERCY (1946), Rev. Gerald T. Ritchie; Sr. Rosemary O'Brien, S.S.J., Pastoral Min.; Sr. Irene Lucas, O.S.B., D.R.E.; Sr. Mary Daniel Meahl, O.S.B., Dir. Music.
Res., 837 Bartlett Rd., Harborcreek, 16421. Tel: 814-899-5342.

9—OUR LADY OF MT. CARMEL (1960), Rev. Thomas M. Fialkowski; Rev. Msgr. Joseph V. Reszkowski; Sr. Carol Wilcox, S.S.J.
Res., 1553 E. Grandview Blvd., 16510. Tel: 814-825-7313.
School—Tel: 814-825-2822.
Sisters 1; Lay Teachers 17; Students 340.

10—OUR LADY OF PEACE (1955), Rev. Msgr. Ernest J. Daley; Rev. Dennis J. Veltri; Sr. Elizabeth Bauer, O.S.F., Pastoral Assoc. In res., Rev. Msgr. Andrew H. Karg; Rev. James Ruhling.
Res., 2401 W. 38th St., 16506. Tel: 814-833-7701; Fax: 814-833-7702.
School—Tel: 814-838-3548.
Sisters 1; Lay Teachers 21; Students 461.

11—SACRED HEART (1894), Revs. David Findlay; Thomas M. Brooks; Sr. Ricarda Vincent, S.S.J., Pastoral Assoc. In res., Rev. James S. Simmions.
Res., 816 W. 26th St., 16508. Tel: 814-456-6256.
School—Tel: 814-459-7247; Fax: 814-459-8838.
Sisters 2; Lay Teachers 18; Students 441.

12—ST. ANDREW (1871), Rev. Richard J. Sullivan; Sr. Nancy Sonnenfeld, S.S.J. In res., Revs. Scott T. Stroupe; John E. Santor.
Res., 1116 W. Seventh St., 16502. Tel: 814-454-2486.
School—Tel: 814-454-2454.
Sisters 1; Lay Teachers 10; Students 188.

13—ST. ANN (1887). (See Holy Family for Ministry Team.). Rev. James T. O'Hara. In res., Revs. Chester J. Gawronski; Gerald J. Koos; Edward Feeney, (Retired).
Church—921 East Ave., 16503. Tel: 814-453-4681.

14—ST. BONIFACE (1857), Rev. Leo J. Gallina. In res., Rev. Raymond W. Hahn.
Res., 7615 Wattsburg Rd., 16509. Tel: 814-825-4439; Fax: 814-825-4430. [CEM]
School—Tel: 814-825-4238.
Lay Teachers 15; Students 268.

15—ST. CASIMIR (1914) (Polish), Rev. James T. O'Hara. In res., Rev. Leon T. Muroski.
Church—629 Hess Ave., 16503. Tel: 814-459-7361.

16—ST. GEORGE (1922), Rev. Msgr. Jan C. Olowin; Revs. Stephen L. Vileo; John P. Malthaner; John T. Carter; Sr. Maria O'Connor, R.M.S., Pastoral Min.; Sr. Regina Przestrzelski, R.M.S., D.R.E.
Res., 5145 Peach St., 16509. Tel: 814-864-0622; Fax: 814-866-7532.
School—Tel: 814-864-4821.
Sisters 2; Lay Teachers 28; Students 574.

17—ST. HEDWIG/ST. PATRICK (1910), Rev. Msgr. John M. Dollinger.
Res., 521 E. 3rd St., 16507. Tel: 814-454-8096.

18—ST. JAMES (1921), Rev. Msgr. Robert W. Cohan, V.F.; Sr. Colette Hilow, C.D.S D.R.E. In res., Rev. James McCormick.
Res., 2635 Buffalo Rd., 16510. Tel: 814-899-6178; 899-7681.
School—Tel: 814-899-3429.
Sisters of the Congregation of the Divine Spirit 8; Lay Teachers 8; Students 282.

19—ST. JOHN THE BAPTIST (1870), Rev. Philip M. Oriole.
Res., 509 E. 26th St., 16504. Tel: 814-454-2873; Fax: 814-456-7073.
School—Tel: 814-452-6874.
Sisters 1; Lay Teachers 12; Students 220.

20—ST. JOSEPH (1867) (German), Rev. Jeffery J. Lucas. In res., Rev. Msgr. John M. Gannon, (Retired); Rev. Gerard H. Krebs.
Res., 147 W. 24th St., 16502. Tel: 814-452-2982.
School—Tel: 814-452-3119.
Lay Teachers 10; Students 151.

21—ST. JUDE THE APOSTLE (1955), Rev. Msgr. Henry A. Kriegel. In res., Rev. Thomas J. Whitman.
Res., 2801 W. 6th St., P.O. Box 8408, 16505. Tel: 814-833-0927; Fax: 814-833-9692.
School—Our Lady's Christian, 814-838-7676.
Sisters 2; Lay Teachers 19; Students 491.

22—ST. JULIA (1938), Rev. Msgr. Richard J. McGuire.
Res., 638 Roslyn Ave., 16505. Tel: 814-833-4347; Fax: 814-833-4347.
School—Our Lady's Christian. (See St. Jude the Apostle for details.).

23—ST. LUKE (1954), Rev. Msgr. Richard J. Stack; Rev. Lawrence Richards; Sr. Margaret Mary Wagner, C.D.P., Pastoral Min. & D.R.E. In res., Rev. Msgr. Robert D. Goodill; Rev. David E. Prenatt.
Res., 421 East 38th St., 16504. Tel: 814-825-6920.
School—Tel: 814-825-7105.
Lay Teachers 22; Students 435.

24—ST. MARK THE EVANGELIST (Lawrence Park) (1938), Rev. John J. Hilbert.
Res., 695 Smithson Ave., 16511. Tel: 814-899-3000; Fax: 814-899-5212.

25—ST. MARY (1840) (German), Rev. Msgr. Robert J. Reilly; Sr. Mary Louis Eichenlaub, O.S.B., Pastoral Min.; Sr. Lucia B. Serrano, R.M.S.
Res., 315 E. 9th St., 16503. Tel: 814-452-2410.

26—ST. MATTHEW IN THE WOODS (1966), Rev. Richard E. Powers; Sr. Bernadine Gehringer, Pastoral Min.
Res., 1290 Townhall Rd. West, 16509. Tel: 814-866-6248.

27—ST. PATRICK/ST. HEDWIG (1834), Rev. William E. Sutherland, Admin.; Rev. Msgr. Joseph V. Wardanski; Revs. Michael G. Barletta; Thomas E. Smith; Sr. Mary Pascal Gray, S.S.J., Food Bank; Sr. Marie Stephen Kebort, S.S.J., D.R.E. In res., Most Rev. Michael J. Murphy.
Res., 130 E. 4th St., 16507. Tel: 814-454-8085; Fax: 814-459-8685.

28—ST. PAUL (1891) (Italian), Rev. L. Thomas Snyderwine; Sr. Martha Howick, S.S.J., Pastoral Min. In res., Rev. James Tachuah.
Res., 1617 Walnut St., 16502. Tel: 814-459-3173.

29—ST. STANISLAUS (1885) (Polish), Rev. Msgr. Bernard J. Urbaniak; Sr. Elizabeth Oettel, O.S.B., D.R.E.; Sr. Rosemary Modzelewski, C.S.F.N., Parish Min. In res., Rev. Mark L. Bartchak.
Res., 516 E. 13th St., 16503. Tel: 814-452-6606. [CEM]
School—Tel: 814-452-4825.
Lay Teachers 9; Students 188.

30—ST. STEPHEN (1917), Rev. Jorge C. Villegas; Sr. Teresa Gomez.
Res., 1237 W. 21 St., 16502. Tel: 814-459-0543.

OUTSIDE THE CITY OF ERIE

Albion, Erie Co., St. Lawrence (1914), Rev. John M. Fischer.
Res., 180 E. State St., 16401. Tel: 814-756-3623.
St. Lawrence Catechetical Center—129 E. Pearl St., 16401. Tel: 814-756-4840.

Anita, Jefferson Co., St. Joseph (1898), Rev. Paul Schill.
Res., Box 24, Walston, 15781.

Bradford, McKean Co., St. Bernard (1880), Very Rev. Thomas M. Aleksa, V.F. In res., Rev. Christopher C. Merry.
Res., 98 E. Corydon St., 16701. Tel: 814-362-6825; Fax: 814-362-1479. [CEM]
School—Tel: 814-368-5891.
Lay Teachers 18; Students 330.

St. Francis of Assisi (1846), In res., Rev. W. Desmond McGee; Bro. Michael W. Hicks, D.R.E.
Res., 574 E. Main St., 16701. Tel: 814-368-6959; Fax: 814-368-6959.

Brandy Camp, Elk Co., Holy Cross (1908) (Italian), Rev. Msgr. Louis Heberlein, Admin.; Rev. John R. Neff; Sr. Helen Herbstritt.
Mailing Address: P.O. Box 65, 15822. Tel: 814-265-4331.
Res., 287 Treasure Lake, Du Bois, 15821. Tel: 814-371-2899. [CEM]

Brockway, Jefferson Co., St. Tobias (1898), Rev. Msgr. Louis J. Heberlein; Rev. Msgr. Charles A. Kaza; Deacon Thomas Jackson.
Res., 1100 Hewett St., 15824. Tel: 814-268-3655. [CEM]

Brookville, Jefferson Co., Immaculate Conception (1852), Rev. Joseph A. Ciaiola; Sr. M. Judith Uzzo, R.M.S., D.R.E.
Res., 129 Graham Ave., 15825. Tel: 814-849-8697. [CEM]
Missions—Corsica, Jefferson Co., St. Ann; Sigel, Jefferson Co., St. Dominic.

Cambridge Springs, Crawford Co., St. Anthony (1899), Rev. Robert F. Bower, Admin. In res., Revs. Mark A.

Nowak; Robert G. Craig.
Res., 165 Beach Ave., 16403. Tel: 814-398-4234.

Clarion, Clarion Co., Immaculate Conception (1855), Revs. Frank J. Przepierski; Brian E. Vossler; Sr. Virginia Cummings, O.S.F.
Res., 720 Liberty St., 16214. Tel: 814-226-8433; Fax: 814-226-1090. [CEM]
School—Tel: 814-226-9690.
Lay Teachers 8students133.
Catechesis/Religious Programs—Students 395.

Clearfield, Clearfield Co., St. Francis (1830), Rev. Dennis C. Hadberg.
Res., 212 S. Front St., 16830. Tel: 814-765-9671; Fax: 814-765-9489. [CEM]
School—Tel: 814-765-2618.
Lay Teachers 11; Students 188.

Coalport, Clearfield Co., St. Basil the Great (1887), Rev. Alexander D. Amico.
Res., Box 395, 16627. Tel: 814-672-5561; Fax: 814-672-5954. [CEM]

Conneaut Lake, Crawford Co., Our Lady Queen of the Americas (1958), Rev. Msgr. John J. Lucas, V.F.
Res., 9th & Water Sts., Box 110, 16316. Tel: 814-382-7252. [CEM]

Conneautville, Crawford Co., St. Peter (1853) (Irish), In res., Rev. Robert P. Fedor.
Res., 626 Washington St., P.O. Box F, 16406. Tel: 814-587-3435. [CEM]
Convent—High St., P.O. Box 305, 16406. Tel: 814-587-2011. Sacred Heart

Corry, Erie Co., St. Thomas The Apostle (1856), Rev. Msgr. John B. Hagerty; Mr. Richard J. Allen.
Res., 203 W. Washington St., 16407. Tel: 814-663-3041; Fax: 814-663-0505. [CEM]
School—Tel: 814-665-7375.
Lay Teachers 9; Students 153.

St. Elizabeth (1876), Rev. Joseph F. Finucane.
Res., 26 W. Pleasant St., 16407. Tel: 814-664-7105. [CEM]
Mission—Spartansburg, Crawford Co., Our Lady of Victory, Spartansburg, 16434. Tel: 814-664-7105.

Coudersport, Potter Co., St. Eulalia (1891), Rev. John F. Weibel.
Res., 16915. Tel: 814-274-8646. [CEM]
Mission—Austin, Potter Co., St. Augustine. [CEM]

Crossingsville, Crawford Co., St. Philip (1840), Rev. Thaddeus T. Kondzielski.
Res., Crossingville, R.D. 2, Edinboro, 16412. Tel: 814-734-7395. [CEM]

Crown, Clarion Co., St. Mary (1848), Rev. Thomas S. Hoderny.
Res., 16220. Tel: 814-744-9919; Fax: 814-744-8624. [CEM 2]
Mission—Marienville, Forest Co., St. Anne.

Curwensville, Clearfield Co., St. Timothy (1915), Rev. James C. McKee, S.J. In res., Rev. James C. McKee, S.J.
Res., 306 Walnut St., 16833. Tel: 814-236-1845. [JC]

Daguscahonda, Elk Co., St. Benedict. Closed. Effective April 30, 1995, St. Benedict in Daguscahonda became a Public Oratory (Cannon 1223).

Delancey, Jefferson Co., St. Adrian, Rev. Paul A. Schill, Jr., Admin.
Res., Box 24, Walston, 15781. Tel: 814-938-9687.

Du Bois, Clearfield Co., St. Catherine (1877), Rev. Richard R. Siefer. In res., Revs. Edward J. Walk; James G. Faluszczak.
Res., 116 S. State St., 15801. Tel: 814-371-8556; Fax: 814-371-0592. [CEM]
School—Tel: 814-371-2570. Joseph Ryan, Prin.
Lay Teachers 15; Students 258.

St. Joseph (1893) (Lithuanian), Rev. James J. Kennelley.
Res., 15 South Ave., 15801. Tel: 814-371-7956; 371-7604. [CEM]

St. Michael (1912), Rev. Msgr. Henry L. Krebs, V.F. In res., Revs. Mark S. Swoger; Michael G. DeMartinis.
Res., 15 Robinson St., 15801. Tel: 814-371-5773. [CEM]

East Brady, Clarion Co., St. Eusebius (1877), Rev. Joseph J. Kalinowski.
Res., R.D. 1, Box 747, 16028. Tel: 412-526-3366. [CEM]
Mission—Rimersburg, Clarion Co., St. Richard.

Edinboro, Erie Co., Our Lady of the Lake (1950), Rev. John B. Jacquel; Sr. Mary Francis Humenay, S.S.J., D.R.E.
Res., Box 838, 128 Sunset Dr., 16412. Tel: 814-734-3113; Fax: 814-734-3085.

Eldred, McKean Co., St. Raphael (1847), Rev. Samuel B. Slocum.
Res., 22 First St., Box No. 252, 16731. Tel: 814-225-4231; Fax: 814-225-4298. [CEM]
Mission—Sartwell, McKean Co., St. Mary. [CEM]

Emlenton, Venango Co., St. Michael (1867), Rev. Mark E. Rusnak, Admin.
Res., Chestnut St., P.O. Box 177, 16373. Tel: 412-867-2422. [CEM]

Emporium, Cameron Co., St. Mark (1888), Sr. Mercedes Muskovish, O.S.B., Parish Min.
Res., 235 E. 4th St., 15834. Tel: 814-486-0569; Fax: 814-486-3298. [CEM]
Mission—Driftwood, Cameron Co., St. James.

Fairview, Erie Co., Holy Cross (1963), Rev. J. Thomas Dugan.
Res., 3627 Shauna Ave., P.O. Box 10, 16415. Tel: 814-474-2605; Fax: 814-474-1256.

Falls Creek, Jefferson Co., St. Bernard (1952), Rev. Stanley J. Swacha.
Res., 205 Taylor Ave., 15840. Tel: 814-371-7419.

Farrell, Mercer Co.,

1—Holy Trinity, (1915) (Hungarian), Rev. William A. Rice, Admin.
Res., 1132 Fruit Ave., 16121. Tel: 412-342-0794; Fax: 412-342-0831. [CEM]

2—Our Lady of Fatima, (1952), Rev. Donald E. Berdis.
Res., 601 Roemer Blvd., 16121. Tel: 412-346-3359. [CEM 2]
School—Monsignor Geno Monti School, Tel: 412-347-1440.
Lay Teachers 10; Students 106.
Mission—Farrell, Mercer Co., St. Paul.

3—St. Adalbert, (1913), Rev. William A. Rice.
Res., 1035 Fruit Ave., 16121. Tel: 412-346-5379; Fax: 412-342-0831. [CEM]

4—St. Ann, (1904) (Slovak), Rev. Charles S. Murcko.
Res., 1035 Fruit Ave., 16121. Tel: 412-346-5979. [CEM]

Force, Elk Co., St. Joseph (1906), Rev. Donald J. Cooper.
Res., 15841. Tel: 814-787-4151. [CEM]

Franklin, Venango Co., St. Patrick (1867), Revs. John J. Herbein; Gregory Passauer; Sr. M. Felice Duska, R.M.S., Pastoral Min.
Res., 949 Liberty St., 16323. Tel: 814-437-5763; Fax: 814-437-6326. [CEM]
School—Tel: 814-432-8689.
Lay Teachers 9; Students 191.

Frenchtown, Crawford Co., St. Hippolyte (1838), Rev. Monty Sayers.
Res., R.D. 2, Guys Mills, 16327. Tel: 814-789-2022.
Mission—Cochranton, Crawford Co., Our Lady of Lourdes.

Frenchville, Clearfield Co., St. Mary of the Assumption (1840), Rev. Samuel Bungo; Sr. Therese Dush, C.A.
Res., P.O. Box 159, 16836. Tel: 814-263-4354; Fax: 814-263-4219. [CEM]
Missions—Karthaus, Clearfield Co., SS. John & Paul; Grass Flats, Clearfield Co., SS. Peter & Paul; Drifting, Clearfield Co., St. Severin.

Fryburg, Clarion Co., St. Michael (1846), Rev. John A. Walsh.
Res., P.O. Box 46, Main St., Rte. 208, 16326. Tel: 814-354-2467. [CEM]
School—Tel: 814-354-2523.
Lay Teachers 5; Students 65.

Galeton, Potter Co., St. Bibiana (1888) (Italian), Rev. Thomas E. Brown.
Res., 111 Germania, 16922. Tel: 814-435-2303. [CEM]
Mission—Germania, Potter Co., St. Germain.

Girard, Erie Co., St. John the Evangelist (1853), Rev. Glenn R. Whitman; Sr. Geraldine Kasper, O.S.F., D.R.E. In res., Rev. Conrad L. Kraus.
Res., 142 E. Main St., Box 336, 16417. Tel: 814-774-4108. [CEM]
School—Lay Teachers 10; Students 198.

Grampian, Clearfield Co., St. Bonaventure (1833), Rev. James C. McKee, S.J.
Res., P.O. Box 127, 16838. Tel: 814-236-0364. [CEM]

Greenville, Mercer Co., St. Michael (1850), Rev. Msgr. A. Joseph Book; Rev. John R. Boeckman; Sr. Mary Gertrude McElhinny, S.C., Pastoral Min.
Res., 85 N. High St., 16125. Tel: 412-588-9800; Fax: 412-588-7053. [CEM]
School—Tel: 412-588-7050.
Lay Teachers 15; Students 265.
Mission—Jamestown, Mercer Co., St. Margaret.

Grove City, Mercer Co., Beloved Disciple (1925), Revs. John B. Bicsey; James A. Wiley.
Res., 321 N. Broad St., 16127. Tel: 412-458-7145. [CEM]

Hermitage, Mercer Co., Church of Notre Dame (1960), Rev. Msgr. Edward J. Zeitler, V.F.; Rev. James F. Bird.
Res., 2325 Highland Rd., 16148. Tel: 412-981-5566; Fax: 412-981-3215.
School—Tel: 412-342-2205.
Lay Teachers 11; Students 263.

Houtzdale, Clearfield Co., Christ the King (1970), Rev. Msgr. Joseph K. Bobal, V.F.; Rev. John G. Chaplin, C.S.C. In res., Rev. Ronald E. Gmerek.
Res., 123 Good St., 16651. Tel: 814-378-7653. [CEM]
Mission—Madera, Clearfield Co., Immaculate Conception.

Johnsonburg, Elk Co., Holy Rosary (1896), Rev. Joseph Czarkowski; Sr. Joanne Crawford, S.S.J., D.R.E. In res., Sr. Angela Marie Serviden, S.S.J.
Res., 606 Penn St., 15845. Tel: 814-965-2819; Fax: 814-965-5528. [CEM]
School—Tel: 814-965-2812.
Sisters of St. Joseph 1; Lay Teachers 9; Students 124.

Kane, McKean Co., St. Callistus (1878), Rev. William M. Kuba.
Res., 342 Chase St., 16735. Tel: 814-837-6694. [CEM]
Convent—116 Haines St., 16735.
Mission—James City, Elk Co., SS. John and Stephen.

Kersey, Elk Co., St. Boniface (1832), Rev. John A. Kuzilla; Sr. Laura Vallimont, O.S.B., Prin.
Res., 355 Main St., 15846. Tel: 814-885-8941. [CEM]
School—Tel: 814-885-8093.
Sisters of St. Benedict 1; Lay Teachers 6; Students 83.

Lewis Run, McKean Co., Our Mother of Perpetual Help (1946), Rev. Howard J. King.
Res., 31 Lafayette, 16738. Tel: 814-368-6355.

Linesville, Crawford Co., St. Philip (1957), Rev. William J. Driscoll.
Res., R.D. 1, Box 1C, 16424. Tel: 814-683-5313. [CEM]

Lucinda, Clarion Co., St. Joseph (1840), Rev. Joseph P. Staszewski.
Res., 16235. Tel: 814-226-7288. [CEM]
School—Tel: 814-226-8018. Sr. Monica Steiner, O.S.B., Prin., D.R.E.
Sisters 2; Lay Teachers 5; Students 90.

McKean, Erie Co., St. Francis Xavier (1838), Rev. Msgr. John A. Kirk; Sr. Jane Matheis, S.S.J., Pastoral Min.
Res., 16426. Tel: 814-476-7657. [CEM]

Meadville, Crawford Co., St. Agatha (1849), Rev. Msgr. Henry J. Schauerman; Rev. Philip A. Pinczewski.
Res., 353 Pine St., 16335. Tel: 814-336-1112. [CEM]
School—Seton School. Consolidation of St. Agatha Elementary and St. Brigid Elementary. Tel: 814-336-2320; Fax: 814-336-2328.
Lay Teachers 15; Students 261.
Mission—Saegertown, Crawford Co., St. Bernadette, 222 Renner Ln., Saegertown, 16433. Tel: 814-763-2831.

St. Brigid (1865), Rev. Msgr. Richard E. Butryn; Rev. James E. Piszker. In res., Rev. Msgr. Robert L. Brugger.
Res., 967 Chancery Ln., 16335. Tel: 814-336-4459. [CEM]

St. Mary (1909), Rev. Msgr. Casimir A. Bogniak.
Res., 1085 Water St., 16335. Tel: 814-333-6161.

Mercer, Mercer Co., Immaculate Heart (1838), Rev. Richard C. Tomasone.
Res., 16137. Tel: 412-662-2999. [CEM]
Mission—Pardoe, Mercer Co., St. Hermenegild.

Morrisdale, Clearfield Co., St. Agnes (1891), Rev. Mark R. Anderson; Sr. Therese Dush, D.R.E.
Res., 16858. Tel: 814-342-2583; Fax: 814-342-6377. [CEM]
Mission—Hawk Run, Clearfield Co., SS. Peter & Paul.

Mount Jewett, McKean Co., St. Joseph (1898), Rev. John G. Barwin.
Res., P.O. Box 520, 17 Division St., 16740. Tel: 814-778-5520.

New Bethlehem, Clarion Co., St. Charles (1872), Very Rev. Thomas L. Tyler, V.F.
Res., 201 Washington St., 16242. Tel: 814-275-3446. [CEM]
Missions—Crates, Clarion Co., St. Nicholas; Seminole, Clarion Co., SS. Cosmas and Damian.

North East, Erie Co., St. Gregory Thaumaturgus (1875), Revs. Michael T. Gaines; Regis J. Meenihan.
Res., 136 W. Main St., 16428. Tel: 814-725-9691; Fax: 814-725-1225. [CEM]

School—140 W. Main St., 16428. Tel: 814-725-4571. Sisters of St. Benedict 1; Lay Teachers 10; Students 184.

Oil City, Venango Co.,

1—ASSUMPTION OF THE BLESSED VIRGIN MARY, (1899) (Polish), Rev. F. Thomas Suppa.
Res., 210 Emerald St., 16301. Tel: 814-677-2032.
Mission—Rouseville, Venango Co., St. Venantius.

2—OUR LADY HELP OF CHRISTIANS, (1914), Rev. William J. O'Brien, Admin.
Res., 69 Willow St., 16301. Tel: 814-677-3078.

3—ST. JOSEPH, (1865), Revs. William C. Miller; Mark J. Mastrian. In res., Rev. John M. Schultz.
Res., 35 Pearl Ave., 16301. Tel: 814-677-4004; Fax: 814-677-5977. [CEM]

4—ST. STEPHEN, (1898), Rev. Jeffrey Noble.
Res., 210 Reed St., 16301. Tel: 814-677-3020. [CEM]
School—Tel: 814-677-2053.
Lay Teachers 17; Students 264.

Osceola Mills, Clearfield Co., Immaculate Conception (1866), Very Rev. Joseph K. Bobal.
Res., 123 Good St., Houtzdale, 16651. Tel: 814-339-7321; Fax: 814-339-7176. [CEM]
Church—408 Stone St., 16666.

Port Allegany, McKean Co., St. Gabriel the Archangel (1876), Rev. Charles R. Schmitt.
Res., 203 Arnold Ave., 16743. Tel: 814-642-2847. [CEM]
Mission—Roulette, Potter Co., St. Mary.

Punxsutawney, Jefferson Co., SS. Cosmas and Damian (1885), Rev. Joseph J. Riccardo.
Res., 616 W. Mahoning St., 15767. Tel: 814-938-6540; Fax: 814-938-7439. [CEM]
School—Tel: 814-938-4224.
Lay Teachers 9; Students 142.

Ramey, Clearfield Co., Holy Trinity (1937), Rev. Killian E. Shuman, T.O.R.
Res., Box 196, 16671. Tel: 814-378-7193. [CEM]

Reynoldsville, Jefferson Co., St. Mary (1872), Rev. Msgr. John W. Mignot.
Res., 607 Main St., 15851. Tel: 814-653-8586. [CEM]

Ridgway, Elk Co., St. Leo the Great (1874), Revs. Robert Horgas; Paul S. Siebert; Sr. Frances Therese Matia, S.S.J., D.R.E.; Sr. Mary Joan Beauseigneur, S.S.J., Prin.
Res., 111 Depot St., 15853. Tel: 814-772-3135; Fax: 814-772-3225. [CEM]
School—Tel: 814-772-9775.
Lay Teachers 11; Students 176.
Convent—117 Depot St., 15853.

Rouseville, Venango Co., St. Venantius (1870), Rev. F. Thomas Suppa, Admin.
Res., 210 Emerald St., Oil City, 16301. Tel: 814-677-2032. [CEM 2][JC 2]
Church—403 Main St., 16344.

St. Marys, Elk Co., St. Mary (1842) (German), Revs. Jude W. Brady, O.S.B.; Alfred Patterson, O.S.B.; Bro. Edward Alton; Sr. Josephine DePetro, S.S.J., D.R.E.
Res., 144 Church St., St. Mary, 15857. Tel: 814-781-1019. [CEM]
School—Tel: 814-834-2665.
Lay Teachers 18; Students 293.

Queen of the World (1954), Revs. Leon Hont, O.S.B.; Jeremy Bolha, O.S.B.; Sr. Josephine DiPetro, S.S.J., D.R.E.
Res., 134 Queens Rd., 15857. Tel: 814-834-4701; Fax: 814-834-3422.
School—Tel: 814-834-4169.
Lay Teachers 19; Students 393.

Sacred Heart of Jesus (1876), Revs. Chad R. Ficorilli, O.S.B.; Ananius G. Butch, O.S.B.; Mark A. Hoffman; Scott W. Jabo.
Res., 323 Center St., 15857. Tel: 814-834-7861; Fax: 814-834-1376.
School—Tel: 814-834-4017.
Lay Teachers 17; Students 273.

Sharon, Mercer Co.,

1—SACRED HEART, (1864), Rev. Daniel J. Kresinski; Rev. Msgr. Donald J. Scully.
Res., 40 S. Irvine Ave., 16146. Tel: 412-346-3567. [CEM]

2—ST. ANTHONY, (1924) (Croatian), Rev. Matthew Ruyechan, O.F.M.
Res., 804 Idaho St., 16146. Tel: 412-342-7391. [CEM]

3—ST. JOSEPH, (1892), Rev. Msgr. William C. Karg; Revs. Jerry S. Priscaro; Patrick J. Damond. In res., Rev. Msgr. Raymond O. Meier, (Retired).
Res., 79 Case Ave., 16146. Tel: 412-981-3232. [JC]
School—Tel: 412-938-8382.
Lay Teachers 17; Students 327.

4—ST. STANISLAUS KOSTKA, (1931) (Polish), Revs. Victor Maksimovich, O.F.M.; Justin Ratajczak, O.F.M.Conv.
Res., 370 Spruce Ave., 16146. Tel: 412-347-7526. [CEM]
Catechesis/Religious Programs—Rose DeSantis, D.R.E.
Students 180.

Sharpsville, Mercer Co., St. Bartholomew (1874), Rev. John S. Lynch.
Res., 311 W. Ridge Ave., 16150. Tel: 412-962-7130; Fax: 412-962-1771.

Sheffield, Warren Co., St. Anthony (1878), Rev. John F. Bauer.
Res., P.O. Box 518, Four Mile Rd., 16347. Tel: 814-968-5915.

Shinglehouse, Potter Co., St. Theresa (1901), Rev. Joseph J. Olsen.
Res., P.O. Box 277, 16748. Tel: 814-697-6900.
Mission—Genesee, Potter Co., Sacred Heart. [CEM]

Smethport, McKean Co., St. Elizabeth (1875), Rev. Theodore B. Marconi, Admin.
Res., 307 Franklin St., 16749. Tel: 814-887-9254; Fax: 814-887-1930. [CEM]

Stoneboro, Mercer Co., St. Columbkille (1874), Rev. Henry C. Andrae, Admin.
Res., Franklin St., P.O. Box 206, 16153. Tel: 412-376-3393. [CEM]

Sykesville, Jefferson Co., Assumption of Blessed Virgin Mary (1923), Rev. William F. Presley.
Res., 20 Shaffer St., 15865. Tel: 814-894-2772; Fax: 814-894-7981. [CEM]

Tidioute, Warren Co., St. John (1866), Rev. V. David Foriadori.
Res., 25 First St., 16351. Tel: 814-484-7747; Fax: 814-484-7231. [CEM]
Mission—Tionesta, Forest Co., St. Anthony.

Titusville, Crawford Co., St. Titus (1962), Rev. James G. Gutting; Sr. Mary David Callahan, O.S.B., Music Min.; Sr. Edith Hirsch, R.M.S., Pastoral Min.
Res., 513 W. Main St., 16354. Tel: 814-827-4636. [JC]
School—Tel: 814-827-3312.
Lay Teachers 7; Students 120.
Christian Activities Center—505 W. Walnut St., 16354. Tel: 814-827-7223.
Mission—Mageetown, Crawford Co., Immaculate Conception, Tel: 814-827-2075.

St. Walburga (1872) (German), Rev. Rocco A. Tito.
Res., 120 Brook St., 16354. Tel: 814-827-3958. [CEM]

Union City, Erie Co., St. Teresa of Avila (1906), Rev. Daniel J. Prez.
Res., 9 Third Ave., 16438. Tel: 814-438-2924. [CEM]
Mission—Canadohta Lake, Crawford Co., Our Lady of Fatima.

Walston, Jefferson Co., St. Anthony (1898), Rev. Paul A. Schill, Admin.
Res., Box 24, 15781. Tel: 814-938-9687. [JC]

Warren, Warren Co., Holy Redeemer (1912), Rev. Msgr. Edward J. Kosik, V.F.
Res., 11 Russell St., 16365. Tel: 814-726-3360.

St. Joseph (1858), Revs. David J. Wilson; Walter E. Packard.
Res., 600 Penna. Ave. W., 16365. Tel: 814-723-2090; Fax: 814-723-6042. [JC]
School—Tel: 814-723-2030.
Lay Teachers 10; Students 203.

Waterford, Erie Co., St. Cyprian (1878), Rev. Richard E. Powers.
Church—12775 Donation Rd., Box 535, 16641. Tel: 814-796-4329.

West Middlesex, Mercer Co., Good Shepherd (1955), Rev. Msgr. Richard G. Mayer.
Res., P.O. Box 226, 16159. Tel: 412-528-3539. [JC]

Wilcox, Elk Co., St. Anne (1890), Revs. Joseph Czarkowski; Norbert K. Wolf.
Res., P.O. Box 65, Clarion St., 15870. Tel: 814-929-5577. [JC]
Mission—Rasselas, Elk Co., Holy Cross. [CEM]

Winburne, Clearfield Co., SS. Cyril and Methodius (1904) (Slovak-Hungarian), Rev. Msgr. Michael E. Tutokie, Admin.
Res., 16879. Tel: 814-345-5674. [JC]

Youngsville, Warren Co., St. Luke (1958), Rev. John W. Swoger, Admin.
Res., 420 N. Main St., 16371. Tel: 814-563-4432.

Chaplains of Public Institutions

ERIE. *Erie County Geriatric Center Annex,* St. Paul, 1617 Walnut St. Rev. L. Thomas Snyderwine.
Erie County Geriatrics Center. Vacant.
Erie County Prison. Rev. Msgr. John M. Dollinger.
Hamot Medical Center, 201 State St., 16550. Rev. Gerald J. Koos.
St. Vincent's Health Center, 232 W. 25th St., 16544. Revs. Dennis A. Martin, Chap.; Raymond Gramata, Chap.
Shriners Hospital for Crippled Children. Vacant. 1116 W. 7th St., 16550.
Soldiers and Sailors Home. Rev. James Ruhling.
Veterans Administration Hospital. Rev. Thomas M. Fialkowski, Chap.

ALBION. *Albion State Correctional Facility.* Vacant.

BRADFORD. *Federal Correction Institution,* P.O. Box 5000, 16701-0950. Rev. John G. Barwin.

CAMBRIDGE SPRINGS. *Cambridge Springs Correction Institution.* Rev. Robert G. Craig.

DU BOIS. *Du Bois Regional Hospital,* 100 Hospital Ave., 15801. Rev. John Neff, Chap.

LEWIS RUN. *Federal Correction Institution.* Vacant. P.O. Box 5000, 16738.

MEADVILLE. *Crawford Country Home,* 967 Chancery Ln., 16335. Rev. Richard E. Butryn, Chap.

MERCER. *State Correctional Facility,* Box 530, 16137. Rev. Patrick J. Healy, Chap.

POLK. *Polk Center,* Box 94, 16342. Rev. Mark J. Mastrian.

WARREN. *Warren State Hospital.* Rev. John F. Bauer.

Special or Diocesan Assignment:
Reverend Fathers—
Fischer, G. William, O.S.F.S. Tel: 814-774-9655

On Duty Outside Diocese:
Reverend Monsignors—
Sanner, James E., Army
Reverend Fathers—
Beal, John P., Washington, DC
Burke, John R., Mexico
Fischer, G. William, O.S.F.S. Tel: 814-774-9655
Gmerek, Ronald E.
Humenay, Robert, WY
Jeselnick, Stephen, AFB
Kelley, Thomas, TX
Kesecki, Michael T., Rome
Malene, Robert, AZ
Milewski, Robert, Navy

On Leave of Absence:
Reverend Fathers—
Collins, Stephen L., III
Haas, Francis
Toven, Ronald D.
Weiss, James F.

Retired:
Reverend Monsignors—
Daniszewski, John D.
Enright, Vincent L.
Gannon, James J.
Gannon, John M.
Goodill, Robert D.
Latimer, Edward H.
Martin, Daniel J.
Meier, Raymond O.
Mitchell, Salvatore P.
Ritchie, G. Carlton
Schriefer, Robert F.
Slater, John J.
Sperry, James E.
Tutokie, Michael E.
Reverend Fathers—
Anderson, Emil
Barcio, Robert G.
Capozzlli, Anthony M.
Cici, William
Cray, Kevin, S.D.S.
Dobosiewicz, Stephen J.
Donovan, Edmund J.
Feeney, J. Edward
Fin, Robert G.
Groucutt, George L.
Jerge, Joseph W.
Kacprowicz, Joseph A.
Kotyuk, Stephen
Kozlowski, Louis
Levis, Robert J.
Lohse, Walter H.
Maloney, William J.
Maryland, Joseph A.
Murray, John L.
Obenrader, Paul F.
Pisoni, Otto B.
Sharpe, Patrick F.
Skinner, Charles D.
Somers, Eldon K.
Stutz, Edward J.
Varga, George
Weber, James H.
Wiley, Joseph
Wilson, Edward M.

INSTITUTIONS LOCATED IN THE DIOCESE

[A] SEMINARIES, DIOCESAN

ERIE. *St. Mark's Seminary*. Mailing Address: 429 E. Grandview Blvd., P.O. Box 10397, 16514. Tel: 814-824-1200. Rev. Msgr. Lawrence T. Speice, Rector & Dir. Seminarians; Revs. Nicholas J. Rouch, Dir. Spiritual Formation & Continuum Office; Edward M. Lohse, Vocation Dir.

[B] COLLEGES AND UNIVERSITIES

ERIE. *Gannon University*, University Square, 16541. Tel: 814-871-7000.
For a complete listing, refer to the Colleges and Universities section.
Mercyhurst College, 501 E. 38th St. Blvd., 16546. Tel: 814-824-2000.
For a complete listing, refer to the Colleges and Universities section.

[C] HIGH SCHOOLS, DIOCESAN

ERIE. *Cathedral Preparatory School*, 225 W. Ninth St., 16501. Tel: 814-453-7737. Rev. Msgr. Bruce Allison, Headmaster; Mrs. Joann Mullen, Prin.
Faculty: Rev. Raymond W. Hahn; Rev. Msgr. Bruce Allison, (Retired); Revs. Lawrence Richards; James McCormick; Regis Meenihan; William Fischer; Sr. Rachael McGuire; Rev. Lawrence Spiece; Sr. James Francis Mulligan. Priests 7; Sisters 2; Laymen 26; Laywomen 9; Students 632.

BRADFORD. *Bradford Central Christian High School*, 450 W. Washington St., 16701. Tel: 814-362-3815. Rev. H. Desmond McGee, Jr., Prin. Priests 1; Brothers 1; Lay Teachers 14; Students 95.

DU BOIS. *Du Bois Area Catholic Schools*, 204 Hospital Ave., 15801. Tel: 814-371-3060. Revs. Edward J. Walk, Prin.; Mark S. Swoger; James Bird.
Central Christian High School.
Central Christian Middle School. Priests 2; Sisters 1; Lay Teachers 26; Students 357.

HERMITAGE. *Kennedy Christian High School*, 2120 Fwy., 16148. Tel: 412-346-5531. Mr. Peter Iacino, Headmaster; Rev. Richard Tomasone, Asst. Headmaster; Mrs. Christine Perry, Asst. Headmaster/Curriculum. Priests 2; Lay Teachers 22; Students 367.

OIL CITY. *Venango Christian High School*, 1505 W. 1st St., 16301. Tel: 814-677-3098. Revs. John M. Schultz, Headmaster; William O'Brien, Campus Min. Priests 2; Lay Teachers 11; Students 76.

SAINT MARYS. *Elk County Christian High School*, 600 Maurus St., 15857. Tel: 814-834-7800; Fax: 814-781-3441. Mr. John W. Kowach, Headmaster. Campus Ministers: Revs. Mark Hoffman; Scott W. Jabo. Priests 2; Sisters 1; Lay Teachers 28; Students 396.

[D] HIGH SCHOOLS, PRIVATE

ERIE. *Mercyhurst Preparatory School*, 538 E. Grandview Blvd., 16504. Tel: 814-824-2210; Fax: 814-824-2116. Georgia C. Johnson, Pres.; Edward Zenewichz, Prin. Sisters 3; Lay Teachers 58; Students 843.
Villa Maria Academy, 2403 W. 8th St., 16505. Tel: 814-838-2061. Sr. Ann Marie Joint, S.S.J., Prin.; Mrs. Kathleen DiNicola, Asst. Admin.; Mr. John Gardner, Asst. Admin. Sisters 5; Lay Teachers 40; Students 565.

[E] ELEMENTARY SCHOOLS, PRIVATE

ERIE. *Villa Maria Elementary School*, 2551 W. 8th St., 16505. Tel: 814-838-5451. Sr. Margaret Frank, S.S.J., Prin. Sisters of St. Joseph 4; Lay Teachers 23; Students 380.

[F] SPECIAL MINISTRY

ERIE. *Erie East Coast Migrant Programs*, 345 E. 9th St., 16503. Tel: 814-454-4514. Benedictine Sisters of Erie. Sr. Diane Rabe, O.S.B., Dir. Students 30.
L'Arche Community, 523 W. 8th, 16502. Tel: 814-452-4616. Rev. George E. Strohmeyer, Pastoral Min., Eastern U.S. Communities.
Mercy Center of the Arts, 444 E. Grandview Blvd., 16504. Tel: 814-824-2519.
St. Benedict Child Development Center, 345 E. 9th St., 16503. Tel: 814-454-4515. Sr. Diane Rabe, O.S.B., Admin.
St. Benedict Education Center, 330 E. 10th St., 16503. Tel: 814-452-4072; Fax: 814-454-2686. Sr. Miriam Mashank, O.S.B., Dir. Students 90.
Villa Maria Center, 2551 W. 8th St., 16505. Tel: 814-838-5514. Sr. Leonie Shanley, S.S.J., Admin.

[G] GENERAL HOSPITALS

*ERIE. *Saint Vincent Health Center*, 232 W. 25th St., 16544. Tel: 814-452-5000.
For a complete listing, refer to the Hospitals section.

[H] PROTECTIVE INSTITUTIONS

ERIE. *Gannondale Residential Center for Girls*, 4635 E. Lake Rd., 16511. Tel: 814-899-7659.
For a complete listing, refer to the Special Care Facilities section.

HARBORCREEK. *Harborcreek Youth Services*, 5712 Iroquois Ave., 16421. Tel: 814-899-7664; Fax: 814-899-3075.
For a complete listing, refer to the Special Care Facilities section.

[I] APARTMENTS FOR SENIOR CITIZENS

ERIE. *Mercy Terrace Apartments*, 430 E. Grandview Blvd., 16504. Tel: 814-825-6791.
For a complete listing, refer to the Special Care Facilities section.

*HARBORCREEK. *Benetwood Apartments for Persons Elderly and Handicapped*, 641 Troupe Rd., 16421-1048. Tel: 814-899-0088.
For a complete listing, refer to the Special Care Facilities section.

[J] RESIDENCES FOR RETIRED PRIESTS

ERIE. *Bishop Michael J. Murphy Residence for Retired Priests*, 400 E. Gore Rd., 16509. Tel: 814-825-0680.
For a complete listing, refer to the Special Care Facilities section.

[K] NURSING HOMES

ERIE. *St. Mary's Home of Erie*, 607 E. 26th St., 16504. Tel: 814-459-0621; Fax: 814-454-0909.
For a complete listing, refer to the Special Care Facilities section.

DU BOIS. *Christ the King Manor, Inc.*, 1100 W. Long Ave., 15801. Tel: 814-371-3180.
For a complete listing, refer to the Special Care Facilities section.

HERMITAGE. *John XXIII Home*, 2250 Shenango Fwy., 16148. Tel: 412-981-3200.
For a complete listing, refer to the Special Care Facilities section.

[L] SHELTERS FOR MEN AND WOMEN

ERIE. *Community House Inc.*, 521 W. 7th St., 16502. Tel: 814-459-5853.
For a complete listing, refer to the Special Care Facilities section.
Mercy Center for Women, 1039 E. 27th St., 16504. Tel: 814-453-3668.
For a complete listing, refer to the Special Care Facilities section.
St. Patrick Haven, Inc., 147 E. 12th St., 16501. Tel: 814-454-7219; 814-838-5430.
For a complete listing, refer to the Special Care Facilities section.

[M] CONVENTS AND RESIDENCES FOR SISTERS

ERIE. *Congregation of the Divine Spirit*, 409 W. 6th St., 16507. Tel: 814-455-3590; Fax: 814-454-8899. Mother Patricia O'Connor, C.D.S., Supr. Gen.; Rev. John E. Santor. Members 47.
Erie Dawn, 330 E. 10th St. Tel: 814-454-8488. Sr. Phyllis Hilbert, S.S.J., Admin.
Gannondale Residential Center for Girls, 4635 E. Lake Rd., 16511.
Holy Family Monastery, 510 E. Gore Rd., 16509-3799. Mother Emmanuel of the Mother of God, O.C.D., Prioress; Rev. Msgr. James Peterson, Chap. Discalced Carmelites 7.
Kraus House Priory, 436 E. 9th St., 16503. Sisters of St. Benedict. Sisters 4.
Mount Saint Benedict Monastery, 6101 E. Lake Rd., 16511. Tel: 814-899-0614; Fax: 814-898-4004. Sr. Phyllis Schleicher, O.S.B., Prioress. Sisters of St. Benedict of Erie. Professed Sisters in Community 138; Sisters in Formation 9.
North American Union Sisters of Our Lady of Charity, 4635 E. Lake Rd., 16511. Tel: 814-899-1052. Sr. Carol Pregno, Local Supr.
Om Shanti, 1239 W. 7th St., 16502. Tel: 814-459-3215. Sr. Diane Cook, O.S.B. Sisters of St. Benedict 2.
St. Scholastica Priory, 355 E. 9th St., 16503. Tel: 814-454-4052.
Sisters of Mercy Motherhouse, 444 E. Grandview Blvd., 16504. Tel: 814-824-2516; Fax: 814-824-2127. Sr. Joanne Courneen, R.S.M. Professed Sisters 88.
Villa Maria, 5031 W. Ridge Rd., 16506-1249. Tel: 814-838-4100; Fax: 814-838-5167. Sr. Mary Fromknecht, S.S.J., Congregational Admin.; Rev. Msgr. Gerald L. Orbanek, Chap. The Sisters of St. Joseph of Northwestern PA. Professed Sisters in Community 190.
World of Life Catholic Charismatic Renewal, St. Mark Catholic Center, 429 E. Grandview Blvd., P.O. Box 10397, 16514-0397. Tel: 814-824-1286.

ST. MARYS. *Benedictine Sisters of Elk County O.S.B. St. Joseph Monastery*, 303 Church St., 15857. Tel: 814-834-2267. Sr. Mariella Hathorn, O.S.B., Prioress; Sr. M. Raphael Baker, Prioress. Professed Sisters 54.

[N] SOCIOLOGICAL

ERIE. *Emmaus Ministries*, 345 E. 9th St., 16503. Tel: 814-459-8349. Sr. Mary Miller, O.S.B., Dir.
Mercy Center for Women, 1039 E. 27th St., 16504. Tel: 814-453-3668. Tish Donze, Exec. Dir.
Mercy Center on Aging, 444 E. Grandview Blvd., 16504-2604. Tel: 814-824-2214; Fax: 814-824-2127. Sr. Mary Dolores, R.S.M., Exec. Dir.
Pax Priory, 345 E. 9th St., 16503. Tel: 814-452-6318. Benedictine Sisters of Erie 5.

[O] RETREAT & RENEWAL CENTERS

ERIE. *Ecclesia Center*, 9101 Ridge Rd., 16417-9625. Tel: 814-774-9691. Rev. Jerome Simmons.
Glinodo Center, 6270 E. Lake Rd., 16511. Tel: 814-899-4584; Fax: 814-898-4004. Sr. Carolyn Gorny-Kopkowski, O.S.B., Admin. Benedictine Sisters of Erie.
Office of the Marginalized, 1218 Parade St., 16503. Tel: 814-456-0891. Rev. Msgr. James W. Peterson, Dir.
Theophilus, Theophilus House, 4115 Royal Ave., 16509-1428. Tel: 814-866-6891. Rev. Anthony M. Capozzelli, Dir.

DU BOIS. *Nazareth In The Woods, Inc.*, R.D. #2, Box 23, 15801. Tel: 814-375-0268. Rev. F. Thomas Suppa, 814-677-2032. A center of renewal and the Spirituality of the Hidden Life of Nazareth.

FRENCHVILLE. *Young People Who Care Center, Caritas Mission*, 16836. Tel: 814-263-4177. Sr. Theresa Dush, Dir.

UNION CITY. *Avila House Retreat Center*, 61 E. High St., 16438. Tel: 814-438-7020. Mr. & Mrs. John Merkle, Dir.

[P] CAMPUS MINISTRY

ERIE. *Newman Centers and Campus Ministry*. Office of Education, P.O. Box 10397, 429 E. Grandview Blvd., 16514-0397.
Allegheny College, 147 Crimson Dr., R.D. 1, Meadville, 16335. Tel: 814-332-2800. Mr. David Roncolato, Dir.
Bradford Extension. (University of Pittsburgh), St. Bernard Parish, 98 E. Corydon St., Bradford, 16701. Tel: 814-362-6825. Rev. Chris Merry.
Clarion University of Pennsylvania, 720 Liberty St., Clarion, 16214. Tel: 814-226-6869. Rev. Brian Vossler, Dir.
Clearfield Extension. (Lockhaven University), St. Francis Parish, 212 S. Front St., 16830. Tel: 814-765-9671.
Du Bois Extension. (Penn State University), St. Catherine Parish, 116 State St., DuBois, 15801. Tel: 814-371-8556. Rev. Richard Siefer.
Edinboro University of PA, P.O. Box 820, Edinboro, 16412. Tel: 814-734-1651. Rev. Mark A. Nowak, Dir.
Gannon University, University Sq., 16541. Tel: 814-871-7547. Rev. Nicholas Rouch, Dir.; Ms. Renee Boltri, Diocesan Co-Dir.; Barb Lindstrom, Graduate Asst.; Jerry Hayes, Graduate Asst.
Grove City College, Beloved Deciple Parish, 321 N. Broad St., Grove City, 16127. Tel: 412-458-7145. Rev. James A. Wiley.
Mercyhurst College, 501 E. 38th St., 16546. Tel: 814-824-2301. Sr. Elisabeth Lintsen, M.S.O.L.A., Dir.; Rev. Stephen A. Anderson, Chap. & Dir. Tel: 814-824-2467; Yvonne Parker, Graduate Asst.
Oil City Extension. (Clarion State University of PA), St. Stephen Parish, 210 Reed St., Oil City, 16301. Tel: 814-677-3020. Rev. Jeffrey J. Noble.
Penn State University, The Behrend College, Station Rd., 16563-0901. Tel: 814-898-6245. 1113 Brewster St., 16503-1522. Tel: 814-455-9985. Rev. Lawrence Richards, Chap. Tel: 814-825-4850; Sr. Anna Mae Kuzma, O.S.F., Diocesan Co-Dir.
Punxsutawney Extension. (Indiana University of PA), S.S. Cosmos & Damian Parish, 616 W. Mahoning St., Punxsutawney, 15767. Tel: 814-938-6540. Rev. Brian Vossler.
Sharon Extension. (Penn State University), St. Joseph Parish, 74 Case Ave., Sharon, 16146. Tel: 412-981-3232.
Thiel College, St. Michael Parish, 85 N. High St., Greenville, 16125. Tel: 412-588-9800.
Titusville Extension. (University of Pittsburgh), St. Titus Parish, 513 W. Main St., Titusville, 16354. Tel: 814-827-4636.

[Q] MISCELLANEOUS

ERIE. *Alliance for International Monasticism (AIM)*, 355 E. 9th St., 16503. Tel: 814-453-4724. AIM is an organization founded to assist Benedictine and Cistercian monasteries in the Third World. Sr. Mary Lou Kownacki, O.S.B., Exec. Dir.
St. Thomas More Society, 429 E. Grandview Blvd., 16514.

ST. MARYS. *Opportunity for Parochial Education Network (OPEN)*, 575 Charles St., 15857. Tel: 814-834-6181. Richard J. Reuscher, Trustee.

RELIGIOUS INSTITUTES OF MEN REPRESENTED IN THE DIOCESE

For further details refer to the corresponding bracketed number in the Religious Institutes of Men or Women section.

[0200]—*Benedictine Monks.* (St. Vincent's Archabbey).—O.S.B.

[1330]—*Congregation of the Mission.*—C.M.

[0480]—*Conventual Franciscans.* (Anthony of Padua Prov.).—O.F.M.Conv.

[0520]—*Franciscan Friars.*—O.F.M.

[0690]—*Jesuit Fathers and Brothers.*—S.J.

[0610]—*Priests of the Congregation of Holy Cross.*—C.S.C.

[1070]—*Redemptorist Fathers.* (Baltimore Prov.).—C.SS.R.

[1200]—*Society of Divine Savior.*—S.D.S.

[0560]—*Third Order Regular of Saint Francis.* (Most Sacred Heart Prov.).—T.O.R.

RELIGIOUS INSTITUTES OF WOMEN REPRESENTED IN THE DIOCESE

[0230]—*Benedictine Sisters of Elk Co.*—O.S.B.

[0160]—*Benedictine Sisters of Erie.*—O.S.B.

[]—*Congregation of Divine Providence.* (Pittsburgh).—C.D.P.

[]—*Congregation of the Divine Providence.*—C.D.P.

[]—*Congregation of the Divine Spirit.*—C.D.S.

[0420]—*Discalced Carmelite Nuns.*—O.C.D.

[1170]—*Felician Sisters.*—C.S.S.F.

[1840]—*Gray Nuns of the Sacred Heart.*—G.N.S.H.

[2720]—*Mission Helpers of the Sacred Heart.*—M.H.S.H.

[2820]—*Missionary Sisters of Our Lady of Africa.*—M.S.O.L.A.

[3530]—*Missionary Sisters Servants of the Holy Spirit.*—S.Sp.S.

[3070]—*North American Union of Sisters of Our Lady of Charity.*—N.A.U.-O.L.C.

[1690]—*School Sisters of the Third Order of St. Francis.*—O.S.F.

[0507]—*Sisters of Charity of Seton Hill, Greenburg, PA.*—S.C.

[2570]—*Sisters of Mercy.*—R.S.M.

[1620]—*Sisters of St. Francis of Millvale, PA.*—O.S.F.

[3830]—*Sisters of St. Joseph.*—S.S.J.

[1970]—*Sisters of the Holy Family of Nazareth.*—C.S.F.N.

[]—*Society of the Holy Child of Jesus.* (New Jersey).—S.H.C.J.

DIOCESAN CEMETERIES

ERIE. *Queen of Peace.*

Trinity, Calvary & Gate of Heaven.

NECROLOGY

† Cizmar, John S., (Retired). —Died July 16, 1996.

† Griffin, Rev. Msgr. W. Robert, (Retired). —Died May 18, 1996.

† Niebling, Howard V., Curwensville, PA, St. Timothy Church. —Died Sept. 14, 1996.

† Webber, Bernard F., (Retired). —Died Aug. 15, 1996.

Diocese of Evansville

(Dioecesis Evansvicensis)

Most Reverend

GERALD ANDREW GETTELFINGER

Bishop of Evansville; born October 20, 1935; ordained May 7, 1961; appointed Fourth Bishop of Evansville March 11, 1989; ordained and installed April 11, 1989. *Res., 3980 Woodcastle, Evansville, IN, 47711. Mailing Address: Catholic Center, 4200 N. Kentucky Ave., P.O. Box 4169, Evansville, IN, 47724-0169.*

Catholic Center: 4200 N. Kentucky Ave., P.O. Box 4169, Evansville, IN, 47724-0169. Tel.: 812-424-5536; Fax: 812-421-1334.

ESTABLISHED NOVEMBER 11, 1944.

Square Miles 5,010.

Comprises twelve Counties in the Southwestern part of Indiana: Daviess, Dubois, Gibson, Greene, Knox, Martin, Pike, Posey, Spencer (except township of Harrison), Sullivan, Vanderburgh, Warrick.

The Diocese of Evansville was established by decree of Pope Pius XII, November 11, 1944, and the See was fixed at Evansville.

For legal titles of parishes and diocesan institutions, consult the Chancery.

STATISTICAL OVERVIEW

Personnel	
Bishop	1
Priests: Diocesan Active in Diocese	72
Priests: Active Outside Diocese	5
Priests: Retired, Sick or Absent	29
Number of Diocesan Priests	106
Religious Priests in Diocese	10
Ordinations:	
Diocesan Priests	1
Permanent Deacons in Diocese	22
Total Brothers	2
Total Sisters	318
Parishes	
Parishes	73
With Resident Pastor:	
Resident Diocesan Priests	59
Resident Religious Priests	3
Without Resident Pastor:	
Administered by Priests	7
Administered by Permanent Deacons	1
Administered by Women Religious	3
Pastoral Centers	6
Professional Ministry Personnel:	
Sisters	22
Lay Ministers	45
Welfare	
Catholic Hospitals	2
Total Assisted	332,475
Health Care Centers	1
Total Assisted	60
Homes for the Aged	3
Total Assisted	251
Day Care and Extended Day Care Centers	1
Total Assisted	436
Special Centers for Social Services	15
Total Assisted	23,000
Educational	
Diocesan Students in Other Seminaries	9
Total Seminarians	9
High Schools, Diocesan and Parish	4
Total Students	1,722
High Schools, Private	1
Total Students	101
Elementary Schools, Diocesan and Parish	24
Total Students	5,745
Non-residential Schools for the Disabled	1
Total Students	17
Catechesis/Religious Education:	
High School Students	1,929
Elementary Students	8,049
Total Students Under Catholic Instruction	17,572
Teachers in the Diocese:	
Priests	2
Brothers	2
Sisters	36
Lay Teachers	440
Vital Statistics	
Receptions into the Church:	
Infant Baptism Totals	1,596
Adult Baptism Totals	122
Received into Full Communion	143
First Communions	1,558
Confirmations	1,305
Marriages:	
Catholic	369
Interfaith	284
Total Marriages	653
Deaths	859
Total Catholic Population	89,203
Total Population	475,953

Former Bishops—Most Rev. HENRY JOSEPH GRIMMELSMAN, D.D., appt. Nov. 11, 1944; cons. Dec. 21, 1944; retired and named Titular Bishop of Tabla Oct. 20, 1965; died June 26, 1972.—Most Rev. PAUL F. LEIBOLD, D.D., appt. Titular Bishop of Trebenna and Auxiliary of Cincinnati April 10, 1958; cons. June 17, 1958; appt. to Evansville April 6, 1966 translated to Archbishop of Cincinnati July 23, 1969; died June 1, 1972.—Most Rev. FRANCIS R. SHEA, appt. Dec. 10, 1969; retired; died Aug. 18, 1994.

Catholic Center—4200 N. Kentucky Ave., P.O. Box 4169, Evansville, 47724-0169. Tel: 812-424-5536; Fax: 812-421-1334. Office Hours: Mon.-Fri. 8-5.

Vicar General—Rev. Msgr. KENNETH R. KNAPP, A.C.S.W., M.S.

Chancellor—JUDITH A. NEFF.

Executive Director of Diocesan Services—KENNETH W. KRASAVAGE.

Secretary to the Bishop—DEANNA RUSTON.

Treasurer—ROBERT J. COX.

Associate Treasurer—SCOTT BRITT.

Senior Consultant to the Treasurer—Rev. Msgr. OMER MEYER.

Assistant Treasurer—MARY KIRSCH.

Diocesan Tribunal—P.O. Box 4169, Evansville, 47724-0169.

Director of Operations—Rev. JAMES R. ENDRESS.

Judicial Vicar—Rev. Msgr. CHARLES J. KOCH, S.T.L., J.C.L.

Adjutant Judicial Vicar—Rev. J. KENNETH WALKER, B.A., M.Div., M.C.L., J.C.L.

Promoter Justitiae—Rev. Msgr. CHARLES SCHOETTELKOTTE, M.S., M.S.W.

Defender of the Bond—Rev. Msgr. CLINTON F. HIRSCH, J.C.L.; Rev. JAMES ENDRESS, S.T.L., M.S., M.A.

Judges—Rev. Msgr. THOMAS J. CLARKE, J.C.D.; MARY GEN BLITTSCHAU, M.A., M.C.L., J.C.L.

Advocates—Revs. JOHN H. SCHIPP; MICHAEL MADDEN.

Secretary and Notary—CHARLEEN HEBERT; JUDITH KNAPP; SHERYL SEIBERT, Sec.

Archivist—JUDITH A. NEFF.

Diocesan Consultors—Rev. Msgr. KENNETH R. KNAPP; Rev. Msgr. CHARLES KOCH; Revs. DAVID NUNNING; JOSEPH ZILIAK; JAMES ENDRESS; DAVID FLECK; FRANCIS SCHROERING.

Diocesan Council of Priests—Rev. Msgr. KENNETH R. KNAPP; Rev. Msgr. CHARLES J. KOCH; Revs. DAVID H. NUNNING; JOSEPH ZILIAK; GREGORY CHAMBERLIN, O.S.B.; DAVID FLECK; JACK DURCHHOLZ; JAMES ENDRESS; HENRY KUYKENDALL; LOWELL WILL; JOHN SCHIPP; BERNARD LUTZ.

Personnel Board—Revs. FRANCIS SCHROERING; JAMES KORESSEL; DAVID MARTIN; HENRY KUYKENDALL; PATRICK FOSTER; JAMES BLESSINGER.

Deans—Evansville, East: Rev. KENNETH R. KNAPP; Evansville, West: Rev. DAVID NUNNING; Jasper: Rev. PATRICK FOSTER; Newburgh: Rev. JOSEPH ZILIAK; Princeton: Rev. FRANCIS SCHROERING; Vincennes: Rev. DONALD K. ACKERMAN; Washington: Rev. LEO KIESEL.

Censors Of Books—Rev. Msgr. CHARLES J. KOCH, J.C.L., S.T.L.; Rev. JOSEPH ZILIAK, S.T.L.

Diocesan Offices And Directors

Apostleship Of Prayer—Rev. FRANCIS BAUER, Dir.

Boy Scouts—JACK THOMPSON, Chap.

Campus Ministry—MICHAEL H. EPPLER, Coord.

Catholic Charities—JAMES F. COLLINS, Exec. Dir., *Court Building, Suite 603, 123 N.W. Fourth St., Evansville, 47708.* Tel: 812-423-5456.

Catholic Diocese of Evansville, Inc.—Most Rev. GERALD A. GETTELFINGER.

Catholic Education Endowment, Inc. (Washington)—ROBERT GRAHAM, JR.

Catholic Education Foundation, Inc. (Evansville)—JOHN MICHAEL O'LEARY, Pres.

The Catholic Foundation of Southwestern Indiana, Inc.—ROBERT L. KOCH, II, *P.O. Box 4169, Evansville, 47724-0169.*

Holy Family Catholic School Foundation, Inc.—WILFRED WEINZAPFEL, Pres., *950 Church Ave., Jasper, 47546.*

Catholic Education, Office of—PHYLLIS BESHEARS, Dir. Schools; VICKI KIESEL, Admin. Asst. MARYLOU ULRICH, Coord. Media Svcs. MARY GARRETT, Media Clerk.

Catholic Communication Office—PAUL LEINGANG, Dir., *P.O. Box 4169, Evansville, 47724-0169.*

Catholic Hospitals, Diocesan Representative for—Rev. RALPH SCHIPP, *St. Mary's Medical Center, 3700 Washington Ave., Evansville, 47750.* Tel: 812-479-4342.

Catholic Relief Services—JAMES F. COLLINS, *Court Building, Suite 603, 123 N.W. Fourth St., Evansville, 47708.* Tel: 812-423-5456.

Cemeteries—Rev. EUGENE SCHROEDER, Dir., *725 Wedeking, Evansville, 47711.* Tel: 812-422-8211.

Christian Educational Foundation of Vincennes, Inc.—Dr. DAVID GRUNDMAN, Pres.

Continuing Education of Clergy—Revs. JAMES SAUER;

JAMES KORESSEL, *P.O. Box 4169, Evansville, 47724-0169.*

Cursillos in Christianity—JOANN SCHLACHTER, Lay Dir., *1337 Thompson, Evansville, 47715.* Tel: 812-476-1980.

Deaf Ministry—Rev. HENRY KUYKENDALL, *3635 Pollack, Evansville, 47714.* Tel: 812-476-4646.

Diocesan Finance Council—Ex-Officio: Most Rev. GERALD A. GETTELFINGER; Rev. Msgr. KENNETH R. KNAPP; KEN KRASAVAGE; ROBERT COX; GARY BECKMAN; ALAN HOFFMAN; MARGARET CONWAY; CHRIS MELTON; KEN ELLSPERMANN.

Diocese of Evansville Retirement Trust Agreement and Plan for Priests—Office of the Vicar General, 4200 N. Kentucky Ave., P.O. Box 4169, Evansville, 47724-0169. Tel: 812-424-5536.

Ecumenism—4200 N. Kentucky Ave., P.O. Box 4169, Evansville, 47724-0169. Tel: 812-424-5536.

Evangelization, Office of—4200 N. Kentucky Ave., P.O. Box 4169, Evansville, 47724-0169. Tel: 812-424-5536.

Girl Scouts—JACK THOMPSON, Chap.

Spanish Speaking Apostolate—Rev. EUGENE HEERDINK.

Propagation of the Faith and Holy Childhood Association—Rev. Msgr. CLARENCE A. SCHLACHTER, Dir., *4200 N. Kentucky Ave., P.O. Box 4169, Evansville, 47724-0169.* Tel: 812-424-5536.

Justice and Peace—(Please refer to Catholic Charities for further information).

Legion of Mary—Vacant.

Message, The—Catholic Press of Evansville; Publisher, Most Rev. GERALD A. GETTELFINGER; PAUL LEINGANG, Editor.

National Shrine of the Immaculate Conception Washington, D.C.—Vacant.

Permanent Diaconate Program—Deacon THOMAS HOLSWORTH, *1066 W. Tenth, Jasper, 47546.*

Adult Formation—Sr. GERALDINE HEDINGER, O.S.B., Dir.

Rural Life Conference—Rev. JOHN BOEGLIN, Dir., *Holy Family Church, 950 E. Church Ave., Jasper, 47546-3797.*

St. Vincent De Paul Society—Rev. RAYMOND BRENNER, Diocesan Chap.; Deacon CHARLES SEIFERT, Spiritual Dir., Jasper District Council; Rev. DONALD ACKERMAN, Spiritual Dir., Vincennes District Council.

Sarto Retreat House—GEORGE ANNE RYDER, Dir. CAROLYN SINGER, Sec.

Secretariat for Charismatic Renewal—CAROL VOLLMAN, *771 Tulip Ave., Evansville, 47711.*

Stewardship/Development, Office of—JUSTIN CLEMENTS, Dir., *P.O. Box 4169, Evansville, 47724-0169.* Tel: 812-424-5536.

Vocation Office—Rev. BERNARD ETIENNE, Vocation Dir., *P.O. Box 4169, Evansville, 47724-0169.* Tel: 812-424-5536.

Worship/RCIA—Rev. WILLIAM DEERING, Dir., *4200 N. Kentucky, P.O. Box 4169, Evansville, 47724-0169.* Tel: 812-424-5536.

Youth and Young Adult Ministry—MICHAEL H. EPPLER, Dir., *4200 N. Kentucky, P.O. Box 4169, Evansville, 47724-0169.* Tel: 812-424-5536.

CLERGY, PARISHES, MISSIONS AND PAROCHIAL SCHOOLS

CITY OF EVANSVILLE
(Vanderburgh County)

1—PRO-CATHEDRAL OF THE MOST HOLY TRINITY, Rev. Msgr. Michael O.J. Wolf, Rector.
Res., 305 Court St., 47708-1233. Tel: 812-422-5150.

2—ASSUMPTION CATHEDRAL. Closed. For inquiries for parish records contact Holy Trinity Pro-Cathedral.

3—CHRIST THE KING, Rev. Msgr. Kenneth R. Knapp.
Res., 3109 Bayard Park Dr., 47714-2602. Tel: 812-476-3061; Fax: 812-476-3062.
School—Lay Teachers 22; Students 301.

4—CORPUS CHRISTI, Rev. John Breidenbach; Deacon David A. Franklin.
Res., 5528 Hogue Rd., 47712-3298. Tel: 812-422-2027; Fax: 812-421-8316.
School—Lay Teachers 13; Students 180.

5—GOOD SHEPHERD, Rev. Theodore G. Tempel; Deacons Edward Wilkerson; Cyril Will.
Res., 2301 N. Stockwell, 47715. Tel: 812-477-5405; Fax: 812-476-4495.
School—Lay Teachers 18; Students 283.

6—HOLY REDEEMER, Rev. William Wargel.
Res., 918-A W. Mill Rd., 47710. Tel: 812-424-8344.
School—Lay Teachers 20; Students 281.

7—HOLY ROSARY, Revs. James Sauer; Brian Holtz; Rev. Msgr. Maurilius Bilskie, Pastor Emeritus; Deacons Richard Preske; Robert Thurgood.
Res., 1301 S. Green River Rd., 47715. Tel: 812-477-8923; Fax: 812-471-7226.
School—Lay Teachers 24; Students 432.

8—HOLY SPIRIT, Rev. Thomas Kessler; Sr. Joan Scheller, O.S.B., Pastoral Assoc.
Res., 1800 S. Lodge Ave., 47714. Tel: 812-477-1738.
School—Lay Teachers 15; Students 189.
Convent—Sisters of St. Benedict 4.

9—NATIVITY, Rev. Henry Kuykendall; Sr. Jane McConnell, O.S.F., Pastoral Assoc.
Res., 3635 Pollack, 47714. Tel: 812-476-7186; Fax: 812-476-7956.
Catholic Ministry of the Deaf Office—Tel: 812-476-4646.

10—RESURRECTION, Rev. Raymond A. Brenner; Deacon Joseph Schapker.
Res., 5301 New Harmony Rd., 47720-1774. Tel: 812-963-3121; Fax: 812-963-1141.
School—Sisters of St.Benedict 1; Lay Teachers 13; Students 282.

11—SACRED HEART, Rev. Eugene Dewig; Rev. Msgr. Omer F. Meyer.
Res., 2701 W. Franklin St., 47712. Tel: 812-425-5505.
School—Westside Catholic Consolidated, (Grades PreK-K).
Sisters of St. Benedict 1; Lay Teachers 6; Students 124.

12—ST. AGNES, Rev. Raymond L. Kuper; Deacon Richard Grannan.
Res., 1600 Glendale Ave., 47712. Tel: 812-425-9140.
School—Westside Catholic Consolidated, (Grades 1-4).
Lay Teachers 9; Students 129.

13—ST. ANTHONY, Rev. John Davidson; Lucille Pierpont, Pastoral Assoc. In res., Revs. James Lex; Earl Rohleder.
Res., 704 First Ave., 47710. Tel: 812-423-5209; Fax: 812-424-5498.

14—ST. BENEDICT, Rev. Gregory D. Chamberlin, O.S.B.; Sr. Mary Agnes Semersheim, Pastoral Assoc.
Parish Center—1328 Lincoln Ave., 47714-1598. Tel: 812-425-3369; Fax: 812-425-3378.
Res., 1312 Lincoln Ave., 47714.
School—530 S. Harlan Ave., 47714-1598. Tel: 812-425-4596.
Lay Teachers 18; Students 263.

15—ST. BONIFACE, Rev. William M. Schwenk. In res., Rev. Robert Wannemuehler.
Res., 418 N. Wabash Ave., 47712. Tel: 812-425-8375.
School—Westside Catholic Consolidated, (Grades 5-8). Serves St Agnes, St. Boniface and Sacred Heart Parishes. 2031 W. Michigan St., 47712.
Lay Teachers 12; Students 140.

16—ST. JOHN, Rev. Kenneth Herr; Sr. Jane Nesmith, S.B.S., Pastoral Life Coord.
Church—617 Bellemeade Ave., 47713-1707. Tel: 812-424-9261.

17—ST. JOHN THE EVANGELIST, Rev. Robert A. Deig; Robert Vollmer, Pastoral Assoc.
Church—5301 Daylight Dr., 47711. Tel: 812-867-3718.
Res., 4020 E. Boonville-New Harmony Rd., 47711. Tel: 812-867-3987.

18—ST. JOSEPH, Rev. Wilfred Englert. Pastoral Staff: Jeffrey T. Ward; Sr. Agnes Marie Dauby, O.S.B.
Res., 600 E. Virginia St., 47711. Tel: 812-422-5668; Fax: 812-422-6779.

19—ST. MARY, Rev. Stephen P. Lintzenich. Pastoral Assocs.: Sr. Darlene Boyd, S.F.C.C.; Sr. Mary Mundy, S.P.; Deacon James Cavera.
Res., 609 Cherry St., 47713. Tel: 812-425-1577; Fax: 812-426-1416.

20—ST. THERESA, Rev. Eugene Schroeder; Sr. Annette Langenderfer, O.S.F., Pastoral Assoc.
Mailing Address: 725 Wedeking Ave., 47711-3897.
Res., 600 Herndon Dr., 47711-3897. Tel: 812-422-8211.
School—Sisters of St. Benedict 1; Lay Teachers 14; Students 260.
Convent—Sisters of St. Benedict 5.

OUTSIDE CITY OF EVANSVILLE

Bicknell, Knox Co., St. Philip Neri, Rev. Timothy A. Tenbarge.
Res., 605 W. Fourth St., 47512. Tel: 812-735-4069.

Bloomfield, Greene Co., Holy Name, Sr. Diane Fischer, O.S.B., Pastoral Life Coord.; Rev. Hilary F. Vieck, Pastoral Moderator.
Res., R.R. 5, 700 Lincoln Dr., 47424-0124. Tel: 812-384-8415.

Boonville, Warrick Co., St. Clement, Rev. James Koressel; Deacon Tom Lambert; Mrs. Mary Ann Miles, Pastoral Assoc.
Res., 216 N. Seventh St., 47601. Tel: 812-897-2631; 897-4652; Fax: 812-897-4653.
Religious Education Center—Tel: 812-897-1843.
Convent—Sisters 2.

Cannelburg, Daviess Co., All Saints, Rev. Frank G. Renner.
Res., P.O. Box 98, 47519. Tel: 812-486-3375; Fax: 812-486-3375.

Celestine, Dubois Co., St. Celestine, Rev. Robert S. Bultman.
Res., 6864 E. State Rd. 164, P.O. Box 1, 47521-0001. Tel: 812-634-1875; Fax: 812-634-1875. [CEM]

Chrisney, Spencer Co., St. Martin, Rev. Gordon Mann.
Res., P.O. Box 147, 47611-0147. Tel: 812-362-7313. [CEM]

Dale, Spencer Co., St. Joseph, Rev. Eugene Heerdink.
Res., 8 E. Maple St., R.R. 1, Box 308, 47523. Tel: 812-937-2200; Fax: 812-937-4349.

Dubois, Dubois Co., St. Raphael, Rev. Donald E. Spaulding.
Res., 5564 E. St. Raphael St., 47527. Tel: 812-678-2011. [CEM]

Ferdinand, Dubois Co., St. Ferdinand, Revs. Philip J. Kreilein; Jack J. Durchholz; Sr. Ruth Ellen Doane, S.P., Pastoral Assoc.
Res., 840 Maryland, P.O. Box 156, 47532. Tel: 812-367-1212; Fax: 812-367-1066.
Spiritual Life Center—Tel: 812-367-1092.

Fort Branch, Gibson Co., Holy Cross, Rev. Bernard A. Lutz; Rev. Msgr. Charles Kaiser, Pastor Emeritus; Deacon Stephen Hall.
Res., 305 E. Walnut St., 47648. Tel: 812-753-3548. [CEM]
School—Sisters 1; Lay Teachers 10; Students 106.

Haubstadt, Gibson Co., SS. Peter and Paul, Rev. Francis A. Schroering.
Res., 201 Vine St., 47639. Tel: 812-768-6457.
School—(Grades PreK-5).
Lay Teachers 9; Students 174.

Huntingburg, Dubois Co., Visitation of the Blessed Virgin Mary, Rev. Pius Klein, O.S.B.
Res., 313 Washington St., 47542. Tel: 812-683-2372.
Convent—Daughters of Charity 3.

Ireland, Dubois Co., Annunciation of the Blessed Virgin Mary. (St. Mary's). Rev. Kenneth Betz.
Res., P.O. Box 67, 47545. Tel: 812-482-7041. [CEM]

Jasonville, Greene Co., St. Joan of Arc. Attended by St. Mary, Sullivan, Tel: 812-268-4088.

Jasper, Dubois Co., Holy Family, Rev. John Boeglin; Deacon Charles Seifert.
Res., 950 E. Church Ave., 47546-3797. Tel: 812-482-3076; Fax: 812-634-6998.
School—Sisters of St. Benedict 3; Lay Teachers 19; Students 293.
Convent—Sisters of St. Benedict 7.

Precious Blood, Rev. Joseph E. Kane; Sr. Mildred Giesler, S.P., Pastoral Assoc.
Res., 1458 Gregory Ln., 47546.
Church—1385 W. Sixth St., 47546. Tel: 812-482-3589; Fax: 812-482-7762.
School—(Grades PreK-5).
Sisters 4; Lay Teachers 10; Students 191.
Convent—Sisters of Providence 5.

St. Joseph, Revs. Patrick Foster; Michael Allen; Kenneth Steckler. Pastoral Staff: Sr. Mary Jane Kiesel, O.S.B.; Sr. Therese Mary Rebstock, S.S.N.D.
Res., 1020 Kundek St., 47546. Tel: 812-482-1805; Fax: 812-482-1814. [CEM]

Linton, Greene Co., St. Peter, Rev. Hilary F. Vieck.
Res., 489 E St. N.E., 47441. Tel: 812-847-7821.

Loogootee, Martin Co., St. John, Rev. Leo C. Kiesel.
Res., 408 Church St., 47553. Tel: 812-295-2225; Fax: 812-295-2031. [CEM]

Mariah Hill, Spencer Co., Mary, Help of Christians, Rev. Paul Roos.
Church—Spaeth Rd., 47556. Tel: 812-937-4326.

Montgomery, Daviess Co., St. Peter, Rev. Lowell C. Will.
Res., P.O. Box 38, 47558. Tel: 812-486-3149. [CEM]
Convent—Sisters of St. Benedict 3.

Mount Vernon, Posey Co., St. Matthew, Rev. Joseph Swartz.
Res., 421 Mulberry St., 47620. Tel: 812-838-2535. [CEM]
School—Sr. Christine Kempf, O.S.B., Prin. Sisters 2; Lay Teachers 10; Students 115.

Convent—Sisters 4.

New Boston, Spencer Co., St. John Chrysostom, Rev. Micheas Langston, O.S.B.
Mailing Address: R.R. 1, Box 156, Evanston, 47531. Tel: 812-357-6485.

Newburgh, Warrick Co., St. John the Baptist, Rev. Joseph L. Ziliak. Pastoral Assocs.: Sr. Jeanne Voges, O.S.B.; Lynda Provence. In res., Rev. J. Kenneth Walker; Deacon Joseph Siebert.
Res., 625 Frame Rd., 47630. Tel: 812-853-6181; Fax: 812-853-6182.
School—Lay Teachers 10; Students 307.
Convent—Sisters of St. Benedict 1.

New Harmony, Posey Co., Holy Angels, Rev. Earl Rohleder.
Mailing Address: 423 South St., P.O. Box 548, 47631. Tel: 812-682-4224.

Oakland City, Gibson Co., Blessed Sacrament. Attended by St. Bernard, St. Bernard.
Res., Rte. 1, Box 72-A, 47660. Tel: 812-749-4474.

Petersburg, Pike Co., SS. Peter and Paul, Rev. Edward Schneider; Deacon Donald Haag.
Res., 711 Walnut St., 47567. Tel: 812-354-6942.

Poseyville, Posey Co., St. Francis Xavier, Rev. William Dietsch; Sr. Leta Zeller, O.S.B., Pastoral Assoc.
Res., 10 N. St. Francis Ave., 47633. Tel: 812-874-2258. [CEM]

Princeton, Gibson Co., St. Joseph, Rev. Bernard Etienne; Sr. Melanie Rauh, P.H.J.C., Pastoral Assoc.
Res., 410 S. Race St., P.O. Box 47, 47670. Tel: 812-385-2617; Fax: 812-385-2603. [CEM]
School—Lay Teachers 10; Students 89.

Red Brush, Warrick Co., St. Rupert, Rev. Sylvester Loehrlein.
Church—1244 Red Brush Rd., Newburgh, 47630. Tel: 812-853-3040.

Rockport, Spencer Co., St. Bernard, Rev. Edward C. Schnur.
Res., 547 Elm St., 47635. Tel: 812-649-4811. [CEM]
School—Lay Teachers 11; Students 97.

St. Anthony, Dubois Co., St. Anthony, Rev. Joseph F. Erbacher.
Res., P.O. Box 98, 4444 S. Ohio St., 47575-0098. Tel: 812-326-2777; 634-0617. [CEM]

St. Bernard, Gibson Co., St. Bernard, Rev. William Deering; Deacon Stephen Hall, Jr.
Res., R.R. 2, Box 115, Fort Branch, 47648. Tel: 812-753-4568. [CEM]

St. Henry, Dubois Co., St. Henry, Rev. Camillus Ellspermann, O.S.B., (St. Meinrad Archabbey); Sr. Edith Hohl, O.S.B., Pastoral Assoc.
Res., 1311 W. 1100 S., Ferdinand, 47532-9710. Tel: 812-367-2731. [CEM]

St. James, Gibson Co., St. James, Rev. Michael T. Madden.
Res., R.R. 1, Box 280, Haubstadt, 47639. Tel: 812-867-5175. [CEM]
School—Sisters of St. Benedict 1; Lay Teachers 9; Students 135.
Convent—Sisters of St. Benedict 3.

St. Joseph, Martin Co., St. Joseph's, Rev. Gregory Spencer.
Res., 408 Church St., Loogootee, 47553. Tel: 812-295-2225.

St. Joseph's, Vanderburgh Co., Rev. Richard J. Wildeman; Deacons Gilbert Fehrenbacher; Francis Hillenbrand.
Res., 6202 W. St Joseph Rd., Evansville, 47720. Tel: 812-963-3273. [CEM]
School—Sisters 2; Lay Teachers 10; Students 158.
Convent— Sisters of St. Benedict
Sisters 3.

St. Martin, Martin Co., St. Martin's, Rev. Msgr. Carl Shetler.
Res., R.R. 4 (Whitfield), Loogootee, 47553. Tel: 812-295-2830; Fax: 812-295-2830. [CEM]

St. Mary, Daviess Co., St. Mary's. Attended by All Saints, Cannelburg.
P.O. Box 98, Cannelburg, 47519. Tel: 812-486-3375.

St. Michael, Daviess Co., St. Michael's. Attended by St. Peter, Montgomery.
c/o St. Peter: P.O. Box 38, Montgomery, 47558. Tel: 812-486-3149.

St. Patrick, Daviess Co., St. Patrick's. Attended by St. Peter, Montgomery.
c/o St. Peter: P.O. Box 38, Montgomery, 47558. Tel: 812-486-3149.

St. Philip, Posey Co., St. Philip's, Rev. David Fleck; Sr. Shirley Warner, O.S.U., Pastoral Assoc.
Res., 3500 S. St. Philip Rd., Mt. Vernon, 47620. Tel: 812-985-2275; Fax: 812-985-2590. [CEM]
School—Lay Teachers 13; Students 279.

St. Wendel, Posey Co., St. Wendel, Rev. David H. Nunning; Deacon Joseph Blankenberger.
Res., 10542 W. Boonville-New Harmony Rd., Evansville, 47720-7901. Tel: 812-963-3733; Fax: 812-963-3835. [CEM]
School—Sisters of the Third Order of St. Francis 1; Lay Teachers 11; Students 168.
Convent—Sisters of St. Francis 2.

Santa Claus, Spencer Co., St. Nicholas, Rev. Gordon Mann, Pastoral Moderator; Sr. Mary Terence Knapp, Pastoral Life Coord.
Res., P.O. Box 351, 181 Balthazar, 47579. Tel: 812-544-2381.

Schnellville, Dubois Co., Sacred Heart, Rev. Firmus Dick.
Res., 2504 Walnut St., 47580. Tel: 812-389-2535. [CEM]

Shoals, Martin Co., St. Mary's. Attended by St. Joseph, St.Joseph.

Sullivan, Sullivan Co., St. Mary, Rev. Kenneth Graehler.
Res., 105 E. Jackson St., P.O. Box 506, 47882. Tel: 812-268-4088.

Vincennes, Knox Co.

1—SACRED HEART, Rev. James C. Blessinger.
Res., 2004 N. Second St., 47591. Tel: 812-882-8382.
School—Vincennes Schools Consolidated. See St. John the Baptist for details.

2—BASILICA OF ST. FRANCIS XAVIER, Revs. John H. Schipp; Robert Nemergut.
Res., 205 Church St., 47591. Tel: 812-882-5638. [JC]
School—Vincennes Schools Consolidated. See St. John the Baptist for details.

3—ST. JOHN THE BAPTIST, Rev. Donald K. Ackerman. In res., Rev. Robert Nemergut.
Res., 803 Main St., 47591. Tel: 812-882-1762; Fax: 812-886-9151. [JC]
Parish Center—828 Vigo St., 47591.
School—Vincennes Schools Consolidated.
Lay Teachers 16; Students 288.

4—ST. THOMAS, Revs. Donald Ackerman, Pastoral Mod.; Mark Kurzendoerfer, Sacramental Min.; Deacon Joseph Sturgis, Pastoral Life Coord.
Res., R.R. 5, Box 102, 47591. Tel: 812-882-2478. [CEM]

5—ST. VINCENT DE PAUL, Rev. Albert J. Scheller.
Res., R.R. 3, Box 267, 47591. Tel: 812-882-8968. [CEM]

Washington, Daviess Co., Immaculate Conception, Rev. Ronald S. Zgunda; Yvonne Evans, Pastoral Assoc.
Res., 114 W. Van Trees St., 47501. Tel: 812-254-3187; Fax: 812-257-1133.
School—Elementary & Middle - Washington Catholic Interparochial Schools. See St. Simon Parish for details.
High School—Washington Catholic Interparochial Schools. See High Schools, Diocesan under Institutions Located in the Diocese for details.

St. Simon, Rev. David A. Martin; Sr. Rose Anne Muller, O.S.U., Pastoral Assoc.; Deacon Michael Morris.
Res., 315 N.E. Third St., 47501. Tel: 812-254-2883.
Schools—Schools Operated jointly by St. Mary & St. Simon Parishes. Washington Catholic Interparochial Schools Elementary. 310 N.E. Second St., 47501.
Lay Teachers 18; Students 271; Washington Catholic Interparochial Schools Middle, (Grades 6-8) 200 W. Main St., 47501.
Sisters 1; Lay Teachers 11; Students 104.
High School—See High Schools, Diocesan under Institutions Located in the Diocese for details.

Special Assignment:
Reverend Monsignors—
Knapp, Kenneth R., Vicar General, 3109 Bayard Pk. Dr., Evansville, IN 47714
Koch, Charles J., Judicial Vicar, P.O. Box 4169, Evansville, IN 47724-0169
Meyer, Omer, 2701 W. Franklin, Evansville, IN 47712
Schlachter, Clarence A., Dir., Propagation of the Faith & Holy Childhood Association, 1508 Greenfield Rd., Evansville, IN 47715
Reverend Fathers—
Deering, William, R.R. 2, Box 115, Fort Branch, IN 47648
Endress, James R., 600 Cullen Ave., Apt. 510, Evansville, IN 47715
Herr, Kenneth, Faculty Residence, 1500 Lincoln Ave., Evansville, IN 47714
Kurzendoerfer, Mark A., 1500 Lincoln Ave., Evansville, IN 47714
Schipp, Ralph, 856 S. Lombard, Evansville, IN 47714
Walker, J. Kenneth, 625 Frame Rd., Newburgh, IN 47630

On Duty Outside the Diocese:
Reverend Monsignors—
Kissel, Anthony, P.O. Box 321, San Antonio, FL 33576
Neufelder, Jerome M., St. Meinrad School of Theology, St. Meinrad, IN 47577
Reverend Fathers—
Kress, Robert, 2845 Hikes Ln., Apt. 102, Louisville, KY 40218
O'Brien, Christopher, 5850 Cameron Run Ter., Apt. 1415, Alexandria, VA 22303
Traylor, William A., Our Lady of Mercy, Belgium

On Leave of Absence:
Reverend Fathers—
Verkamp, Bernard J.
Vogler, Jean

Retired:
Reverend Monsignors—
Bilskie, Maurilius, 1301 S. Green River Rd., Evansville, IN 47715
Clarke, Thomas J., Little Sisters of the Poor, 1236 Lincoln Ave., Evansville, IN 47714
Conti, Leo J., P.O. Box 2485, Evansville, IN 47728
Hirsch, Clinton F., Villa Maria, 1640 Lincoln Ave., Apt. 102, Evansville, IN 47714
Kaiser, Charles, 305 E. Walnut St., Fort Branch, IN 47648
Kilfoil, Patrick, 6161 Sunset Ln., North Crow's Nest, Indianapolis, IN 46208
Lautner, William A., 1236 Lincoln Ave., Evansville, IN 47714
Lindauer, Clarence, 1236 Lincoln Ave., Evansville, IN 47714
Schoettelkotte, Charles T., Little Sisters of the Poor, 1236 Lincoln Ave., Evansville, IN 47714
Vollmer, Roman, Regina Continuing Care, 3900 Washington, Evansville, IN 47714
Reverend Fathers—
Bauer, Francis, P.O. Box 396, Owensville, IN 47665
Brosmer, Donald
Brune, James, Villa Maria, 1640 Lincoln Ave., Apt. 101, Evansville, IN 47714
Busch, August, 3119 Bayard Park Dr., Evansville, IN 47714
Clauss, Joseph, Guadalupe Retreat Center, 39100 Orchard Ave., Cherry Valley, CA 92223
Dilger, Donald, 6621 Smith Diamond Rd., Evansville, IN 47712
Egloff, Adolph, 2017 N. Second St., Vincennes, IN 47591
Emge, John P., Villa Maria, 1640 Lincoln Ave., Apt. 205, Evansville, IN 47714
Finis, John, R.R. 2, Box T 42, Taswell, IN 47175
Hoffman, Richard L., 3943 Aspen Dr., Evansville, IN 47711
Hut, Clemens, 1711 E. Grandview, Mesa, AZ 85203
Lefler, John, 7788 Taylorville Rd., Tennyson, IN 47637
Lex, James, St. Anthony Church, 704 First Ave., Evansville, IN 47710
Reising, Raymond, Villa Maria, 1640 Lincoln Ave., Apt. 202, Evansville, IN 47714
Rogers, James, 801 N. Shortridge Rd., Apt. F4, Indianapolis, IN 46219
Schroering, Raymond A., Villa Maria, 1640 Lincoln Ave., Apt. 201, Evansville, IN 47714
Wannemuehler, Robert, 418 N. Wabash, Evansville, IN 47712

Permanent Deacons:
Blankenberger, Joseph V., St. Wendel Parish, Evansville
Cavera, James, St. Mary Parish, Evansville
Dow, Lancaster, Jr., Unassigned
Fehrenbacher, Gilbert, St. Joseph Parish, Vanderburgh County
Franklin, David, Corpus Christi Parish, Evansville
Grannan, Richard, St. Agnes Parish, Evansville
Haag, Donald, SS. Peter & Paul Parish, Petersburg
Hall, Stephen, St. Bernard Parish & Holy Cross, Fort Branch
Hayden, Robert, Unassigned
Hillenbrand, Francis, St. Joseph Parish, Vanderburgh County
Holsworth, Thomas, Permanent Deacon Coord.
Lambert, Thomas, St. Clement, Boonville
McFall, Gerald D., Unassigned
Morris, Michael, St. Simon, Washington
Preske, Richard, Holy Rosary, Evansville
Schapker, Joseph, Resurrection Parish, Evansville
Seibert, Joseph S., St. John, Newburgh
Seifert, Charles, Holy Family Parish, Jasper
Sturgis, Joseph V., St. Thomas Parish, Vincennes
Thurgood, Robert, Holy Rosary Parish, Evansville
Wilkerson, Edward, Good Shepherd, Evansville
Will, Cyril, Good Shepherd, Evansville

INSTITUTIONS LOCATED IN THE DIOCESE

[A] HIGH SCHOOLS, DIOCESAN

EVANSVILLE. *Mater Dei High School*, 1300 Harmony Way, 47712. Tel: 812-426-2258; Fax: 812-421-5717. Mr. Herb Neighbors, M.A., Prin.; Rev. Mark Kurzendoerfer, Chap. Priests 1; Sisters 2; Lay Teachers 41; Students 619.

Reitz Memorial High School, 1500 Lincoln Ave., 47714. Tel: 812-476-4973; Fax: 812-474-2941. Mr. Gerry Adams, M.A., Ed.S., Prin.; Miss Linda Eberhard, M.A., Asst. Prin.; Del Schiavone, Asst. Prin.; Rev. Kenneth Herr, Chap. Brothers 2; Lay Teachers 54; Students 865.

VINCENNES. *Jean Francois Rivet High School*. (Vincennes Area), 210 Barnett St., 47591. Tel: 812-882-6215. Richard Kapiszka, Prin. Lay Teachers 15; Students 222.

WASHINGTON. *Washington Catholic Interparochial Schools*, 201 N.E. Second St., 47501. Tel: 812-254-2050. Lay Teachers 16; Students 122.

[B] HIGH SCHOOLS, PRIVATE

FERDINAND. *Marian Heights Academy*, 812 E. Tenth St., 47532. Tel: 812-367-1431. High School for Girls. Sisters of St. Benedict. Sr. Jane Ann Breen, Prin. Sisters 12; Lay Teachers 8; Students 101.

[C] SCHOOLS OF SPECIAL EDUCATION

EVANSVILLE. *Marian Day School*, 700 Herndon Dr., 47711. Tel: 812-422-5346. Bev Williamson, Dir. Lay Teachers 2; Students 17.

[D] DAY CARE CENTERS

EVANSVILLE. *St. Vincent Day Care Center*, 611 First Ave., 47710. Tel: 812-424-4780. Sr. Patricia Dunne, D.C., Admin.; Sr. Evelyn Boyd, Supr. Daughters of Charity of St. Vincent de Paul 6; Children 436.

[E] GENERAL HOSPITALS

EVANSVILLE. *St. Mary's Medical Center of Evansville, Inc.*, 3700 Washington Ave., 47750. Tel: 812-485-4000.

For a complete listing, refer to the Hospitals section.

JASPER. *Memorial Hospital and Health Care Center, Little Company of Mary of Indiana, Inc.*, 800 W. Ninth St., 47546. Tel: 812-482-2345.

For a complete listing, refer to the Hospitals section.

Memorial Hospital Foundation, Inc., 47546.

For a complete listing, refer to the Hospitals section.

[F] HOMES FOR AGED

EVANSVILLE. *The Regina Continuing Care Center*, 3900 Washington Ave., 47714. Tel: 812-479-4226.

For a complete listing, refer to the Special Care Facilities section.

St. John's Home for the Aged, 1236 Lincoln Ave., 47714. Tel: 812-464-3607.

For a complete listing, refer to the Special Care Facilities section.

Seton Residence, 9200 New Harmony Rd., 47720-8918. Tel: 812-963-7600.

For a complete listing, refer to the Special Care Facilities section.

JASPER. *Providence Home, Nursing Home for the Needy*, 520 W. Ninth St., 47546. Tel: 812-482-6603.

For a complete listing, refer to the Special Care Facilities section.

[G] RETREAT HOUSES

EVANSVILLE. *Sarto Retreat House*, 4200 N. Kentucky Ave., P.O. Box 4169, 47724-0169. Tel: 812-424-5536. Mrs. George-Anne Ryder, Dir.; Mrs. Carolyn Singer, Sec.

FERDINAND. *Kordes Enrichment Center*, 841 E. 14th St., 47532-9216. Tel: 812-367-2777. Sr. Karlene Sensmeier, O.S.B., Dir.

[H] CONVENTS AND RESIDENCES FOR SISTERS

EVANSVILLE. *Daughters of Charity of St. Vincent de Paul of Indiana, Inc.*, 9400 New Harmony Rd., 47720. Tel: 812-963-3341. Sr. Catherine Madigan, D.C., Visitatrix; Rev. Patrick Harrity, C.M., Prov. Dir. Legal Title: *Daughters of Charity of St. Vincent de Paul of Indiana, Inc., Mater Dei Provincialate, Inc.*

Monastery of St. Clare, 6825 Nurrenbern Rd., 47712. Tel: 812-425-4396. Franciscan Poor Clare Nuns. Sr. Anna Scheessele, O.S.C., Supr. Solemnly Professed Cloistered Nuns 17.

FERDINAND. *Sisters of St. Benedict of Ferdinand, IN, Inc., Monastery Immaculate Conception*, 802 E. Tenth St., 47532. Tel: 812-367-1411. Sisters of St. Benedict. Sr. Kathryn M. Huber, O.S.B., Prioress; Rev. Matthias Neuman, O.S.B., Chap., St. Meinrad Chaplain Team. Professed Sisters in Community 215; Temporary Commitment 12; Novices 7; Postulants 5.

[I] NEWMAN CENTERS & CAMPUS MINISTRY

EVANSVILLE. *Newman Center for the University of Evansville*, 1901 Lincoln Ave., 47714. Tel: 812-477-6446. Joe Cook, Dir.

University of Southern Indiana Newman Center, 8113-A O'Daniel Ln., 47712. Tel: 812-464-1810; 464-1871. Chris Hoehn, Dir.

OAKLAND CITY. *Oakland City College Newman Center*, Blessed Sacrament Church, R.R. 1, Box 72-A, 47660. Tel: 812-749-4474.

VINCENNES. *Vincennes University-Newman Center*, 1002 N. First St., 47591-1504. Tel: 812-888-5394. Diane Vonderhaar, Dir.

[J] MISCELLANEOUS

EVANSVILLE. *Catholic Education Foundation, Inc.*, P.O. Box 4169, 47724-0169. Linda Montejano, Dir.

Daughters of Charity National Health System-East Central, Inc., 9404 New Harmony Rd., 47720. Sr. Xavier Ballance, D.C., Board Chm.; Lawrence D. Prybil, Regional Exec., CEO.

Seton Health Corporation of Southern Indiana, 3700 Washington Ave., 47750. Sr. Veronica Ann Brown, D.C., Chm.

LOOGOOTEE. *American-Innsbruck Alumni Association*, St. John Parish Church, 408 Church St., 47553. Tel: 812-295-2225. Rev. Leo C. Kiesel, Contact Person.

SANTA CLAUS. *The Outpost*, P.O. Box 64, 47579. Tel: 812-937-2723. Michael H. Eppler; John "Jack" Thompson, Camp Dir.

VINCENNES. *Old Cathedral Library & Museum, Inc.*, 205 Church St., 47591. Tel: 812-882-7016. Revs. John H. Schipp, Registered Agent; Steve Cochran, Librarian & Conservator.

RELIGIOUS INSTITUTES OF MEN REPRESENTED IN THE DIOCESE

For further details refer to the corresponding bracketed number in the Religious Institutes of Men or Women section.

[0200]—*Benedictine Monks*.—O.S.B.

[0600]—*Brothers of the Congregation of Holy Cross*. (Midwest Prov.).—C.S.C.

[1330]—*Congregation of the Mission*.—C.M.

[0410]—*Sons of Divine Providence*.—F.D.P.

RELIGIOUS INSTITUTES OF WOMEN REPRESENTED IN THE DIOCESE

[0230]—*Benedictine Sisters of Pontifical Jurisdiction*.—O.S.B.

[1730]—*Congregation of the Third Order of St. Francis*.—O.S.F.

[0760]—*Daughters of Charity of St. Vincent de Paul*.—D.C.

[2340]—*Little Sisters of the Poor*.—L.S.P.

[3760]—*Order of St. Clare*.—O.S.C.

[3230]—*Poor Handmaids of Jesus Christ*.—P.H.J.C.

[2970]—*School Sisters of Notre Dame*.—S.S.N.D.

[]—*Sisters for Christian Community*.—S.F.C.C.

[3360]—*Sisters of Providence of Saint Mary-of-the-Woods, Indiana*.—S.P.

[0260]—*Sisters of the Blessed Sacrament for Indian & Colonel People*.—S.B.S.

[2270]—*Sisters of the Little Company of Mary*.—L.C.M.

[1760]—*Sisters of the Third Order of St. Francis, of Penance and Charity*.—O.S.F.

[4120]—*Ursuline Nuns of the Congregation of Paris*. (Louisville, KY).—O.S.U.

[4120-04]—*Ursuline Nuns of the Congregation of Paris*. (Cleveland, OH).—O.S.U.

JOINT CEMETERIES

EVANSVILLE. *St. Joseph*, 2500 Mesker Park Dr., 47712.

JASPER. *Fairview*, 1215 Newton St., 47546.

VINCENNES. *Calvary*, P.O. Box 4, 47591.

WASHINGTON. *St. John*, 101 N. Meridian St., 47501-2931.

NECROLOGY

(No Deaths)

Diocese of Fairbanks

Most Reverend

MICHAEL J. KANIECKI, S.J., D.D.

Bishop of Fairbanks; ordained June 5, 1965; appointed March 8, 1984; consecrated May 1, 1984; installed July 28, 1985. *Office: 1316 Peger Rd., Fairbanks, AK, 99709.* Tel.: 907-474-0753.

Most Reverend

ROBERT LOUIS WHELAN, S.J., D.D.

Retired Bishop of Fairbanks; ordained June 17, 1944; appointed Titular Bishop of Sicilibba and Coadjutor Bishop of Fairbanks, *"cum jure successionis"* December 6, 1967; consecrated February 22, 1968; succeeded to See November 30, 1968; retired July 28, 1985. *Mailing Address: Regis Community, 1107 N. Astor, Spokane, WA, 99202.*

Chancery Office: 1316 Peger Rd., Fairbanks, AK, 99709. Tel.: 907-474-0753; Fax: 907-474-8009.

Web site address: http://www2.polarnet.com/~cbna

E-mail address: chancelr@cbna.org.

Corporate Title: "Catholic Bishop of Northern Alaska."

ESTABLISHED AS THE PREFECTURE APOSTOLIC OF ALASKA, JULY 27, 1894.

ERECTED INTO THE VICARIATE OF ALASKA, DEC. 22, 1916; ELEVATED TO A DIOCESE, AUG. 8, 1962.

Square Miles 409,849.

Comprises all of the State of Alaska, north of the old Territorial Third Judicial Division whose boundary extended in a northwesterly direction from the Canadian Border along the crest of the Alaska range to Mount McKinley, thence southwesterly to Cape Newenham and west along the 58 parallel north of the Pribilof Islands.

For legal titles of parishes and diocesan institutions, consult the Chancery Office.

STATISTICAL OVERVIEW

Personnel	
Bishop	1
Retired Bishops	1
Priests: Diocesan Active in Diocese	8
Priests: Active Outside Diocese	1
Number of Diocesan Priests	9
Religious Priests in Diocese	23
Ordinations:	
Permanent Deacons	5
Permanent Deacons in Diocese	42
Total Brothers	4
Total Sisters	19
Parishes	
Parishes	41
With Resident Pastor:	
Resident Diocesan Priests	8
Resident Religious Priests	5
Without Resident Pastor:	
Administered by Priests	10
Administered by Permanent Deacons	5
Administered by Professed Men Religious	1
Administered by Women Religious	5
Administered by Lay People	15
Missions	7
Pastoral Centers	1
Professional Ministry Personnel:	
Brothers	2
Sisters	19
Lay Ministers	16
Welfare	
Special Centers for Social Services	1
Total Assisted	4,400
Educational	
Diocesan Students in Other Seminaries	1
Total Seminarians	1
High Schools, Diocesan and Parish	1
Total Students	225
Elementary Schools, Diocesan and Parish	1
Total Students	261
Catechesis/Religious Education:	
High School Students	381
Elementary Students	1,542
Total Students Under Catholic Instruction	2,410
Teachers in the Diocese:	
Priests	1
Sisters	2
Lay Teachers	36
Vital Statistics	
Receptions into the Church:	
Infant Baptism Totals	519
Adult Baptism Totals	19
Received into Full Communion	38
First Communions	399
Confirmations	141
Marriages:	
Catholic	37
Interfaith	35
Total Marriages	72
Deaths	139
Total Catholic Population	17,181
Total Population	152,194

Former Bishops—Most Rev. JOSEPH RAPHAEL CRIMONT, S.J., D.D., Vicar-Apostolic of Alaska; ord. Aug. 26, 1888; appt. Prefect-Apostolic March 28, 1904; appt. Vicar-Apostolic of Alaska Feb. 15, 1917; preconized Titular Bishop of Ammaedera, March 22, 1917; cons. July 25, 1917; died May 20, 1945.—Most Rev. WALTER J. FITZGERALD, S.J., D.D., Vicar-Apostolic of Alaska; ord. May 16, 1918; appt. Coadjutor Vicar-Apostolic of Alaska *cum jure successionis,* Dec. 14, 1938; cons. Titular Bishop of Tymbrias, Feb. 24, 1939; succeeded to as Vicar-Apostolic of Alaska, May 20, 1945; died July 19, 1947.—Most Rev. GEORGE T. BOILEAU, S.J., D.D., appt. Coadjutor Bishop *cum jure successionis,* April 21, 1964; cons. Titular Bishop of Ausuccura, July 31, 1964; died Feb. 25, 1965.—Most Rev. FRANCIS D. GLEESON, S.J., D.D., ord. July 29, 1926; appt. Titular Bishop of Cotenna and Vicar-Apostolic of Alaska Jan. 8, 1948; cons. April 5, 1948; appt. First Bishop of Fairbanks Aug. 8, 1962; retired Nov. 30, 1968; transferred to Titular See of Cuicul in Numidia and Assistant at the Pontifical Throne by Pope Paul VI, Feb. 3, 1969; died April 30, 1983.—Most Rev. ROBERT LOUIS WHELAN, S.J., D.D., retired Bishop of Fairbanks; ord. June 17, 1944; appt. Titular Bishop of Sicilibba and Coadjutor Bishop of Fairbanks, *cum jure successionis* Dec. 6, 1967; cons. Feb. 22, 1968; succeeded Nov. 30, 1968; retired July 28, 1985.

Vicar General—Vacant, *1316 Peger Rd., Fairbanks, 99709.*

Superior Regular—Rev. THEODORE E. KESTLER, S.J., *Bro. Joe Prince Jesuit Community, St. Mary's Mission Center, St. Marys, 99658.*

Chancery Office—1316 Peger Rd., Fairbanks, 99709. Tel: 907-474-0753; Fax: 907-474-8009.

Chancellor—Sr. MARILYN MARX, S.N.J.M.

Secretary to Bishop—THERESE BURIK.

Treasurer—GEORGE W. BOWDER.

Matrimonial Tribunal—Sr. CAROLYN ROEBER, O.P., Tribunal Dir.

Judicial Vicar—Rev. FRANCIS E. MUELLER, S.J., J.C.D.

Defender of the Bond—Rev. JOSEPH E. LAUDWEIN, S.J.

Promotor of Justice—Rev. RICHARD L. MCCAFFREY, S.J.

Notaries—BARBARA THIEME TOLLIVER; Sr. CAROLYN ROEBER, O.P.; Sr. MARILYN MARX, S.N.J.M.

Bishop's Council; Diocesan Consultors—Bro. KIRBY BOONE, C.F.X.; Revs. JAMES M. KOLB, C.S.P.; AL LEVITRE; Sr. MARILYN MARX, S.N.J.M.; Revs. RICHARD MCCAFFREY, S.J.; Bro. ROBERT RUZICKA, O.F.M.

Diocesan Archivist—Sr. MARILYN MARX, S.N.J.M.; BECKY MESSINA, Sec.

Diocesan Offices and Directors

Apostleship of Prayer—Rev. J. ALBERT LEVITRE, JR., Dir.

"Alaskan Shepherd" Office—Rev. LOUIS L. RENNER, S.J., Editor, *1312 Peger Rd., Fairbanks, 99709.* Tel: 907-474-9649.

Campaign for Human Development—Sr. MARILYN MARX, S.N.J.M.

Campus Ministry—Rev. JAMES M. KOLB, C.S.P., *1265 Deborah St., Fairbanks, 99701.* Tel: 907-479-3994.

Catholic Community Resources—Vacant, *1316 Peger Rd., Fairbanks, 99709.* Tel: 907-474-0656.

Fairbanks Counseling and Adoption—NANCY DEWITT, Dir., *912 Barnette, P.O. Box 1544, Fairbanks, 99707.* Tel: 907-456-4729.

Beginning Experience—Rev. TIMOTHY SANDER, O.S.B., Dir., *626 Second St., Ste. 302, Box 74401, Fairbanks, 99707.* Tel: 907-452-1215.

Ecumenical Commission—Revs. RICHARD L. MCCAFFREY, S.J.; JAMES M. KOLB, C.S.P.

Communications, Radio and TV—THOMAS BUSCH, Dir., KNOM Radio Station, *P.O. Box 988, Nome, 99762.* Tel: 907-443-5221.

Cursillo Movement—PEGGY MANTEI, Lay Dir.; Rev. J. ALBERT LEVITRE, Spiritual Dir.
The Children and Family Life Center—MADELINE NANCE.
Construction Committee—GEORGE W. BOWDER; Revs. RICHARD L. MCCAFFREY, S.J., Chm.; Mr. WILLIAM A. PIKE; GEORGE SUNDBORG, JR.
Engaged Encounter—KELLY HUGHES; CRAIG HUGHES, *Fairbanks.* Tel: 907-479-6402.
Finance Advisory Board—Most Rev. MICHAEL J. KANIECKI, S.J., Chm. DONALD HOOVER; JAMES LYNCH; Rev. RICHARD L. MCCAFFREY, S.J.; JOAN OSTERKAMP; Sr. MARILYN MARX, S.N.J.M.; MICHAEL KELLIHER; JOSEPH PASKVAN; PAUL MCCARTHY.
Hispanic Ministry—Rev. NORMAND PEPIN, S.J.
Native Alaskan Ministries Coordinators—Bro. KIRBY BOONE, C.F.X., *St. Aloysius, Tanana, 997777.* Vacant, *St. Mary's Conf. Ctr., P.O. Box 172, St. Marys, 99658.*
Marriage Encounter—Vacant.
Ministry of Sick, Aged and Imprisoned—Rev. JOSEPH LAUDWEIN, S.J.; Sr. MARITA SOUCY, C.S.J.
Office of Religious Education—GERALD FINKLER, Dir., *1316 Peger Rd., Fairbanks, 99709.* Tel: 907-474-0753.
Office of Native Permanent Diaconate—Rev. RICHARD D. CASE, S.J., Dir., *Jesuit Community, P.O. Box 173, St. Marys, 99658.* Tel: 907-438-2536.
Office of Urban Permanent Diaconate—Sr. ALITA LISBETH, O.P., Dir., *1316 Peger Rd., Fairbanks, 99709.* Tel: 907-474-0753; Fax: 907-474-8009.
Office of Worship—Sr. ALITA LISBETH, O.P.
Personnel—Sr. MARILYN MARX, S.N.J.M.
Pontifical Association of the Holy Childhood—Chancery Office.
Pontifical Society for Propagation of the Faith—Sr. MARILYN MARX, S.N.J.M.,Chancery Office.
Schools—NANCY COOK, Supt., *615 Monroe St., Fairbanks, 99701.* Tel: 907-456-8571.
Vocations—Ordained Ministries Formation Board: Most Rev. MICHAEL J. KANIECKI, S.J.; Rev. AL LEVITRE; Sr. MARILYN MARX, S.N.J.M.
Vocation Director—Rev. JOHN HINSVARK.

CLERGY, PARISHES, MISSIONS AND PAROCHIAL SCHOOLS

CITY OF FAIRBANKS NORTH STAR BOROUGH

1—SACRED HEART CATHEDRAL (1966), Rev. Patrick Bergquist; Deacon Paul Perreault.
Res., 1316 Peger Rd., 99709. Tel: 907-474-0836; Fax: 907-479-3327.
Church—2501 Airport Way, 99709. Tel: 907-474-9032.
Catechesis/Religious Programs—Tel: 907-474-9033; Fax: 907-479-3327. Gigi Martinez, D.R.E. Students 243.

2—IMMACULATE CONCEPTION (1904). Consolidated with St. Michael's, Hanover. Rev. Andrew L. Maddock, S.J.; Deacon Robert Mantei.
Res., 115 N. Cushman St., 99701. Tel: 907-452-3533; Fax: 907-456-3336. [JC]
Catechesis/Religious Programs—Kathleen Kohler-Balko, D.R.E.
Students 314.

3—ST. MARK UNIVERSITY PARISH (1977), Rev. James M. Kolb, C.S.P.
Res., 1265 Deborah St., 99709. Tel: 907-479-3994.
Catechesis/Religious Programs—Tel: 907-474-6776. Joan Soutar, D.R.E.
Students 50.
Mission—Harding Lake, North Star Borough, St. Mary's of the Lake. Salcha Dr.

4—ST. RAPHAEL'S (1991), Mrs. Betty Johnson, Admin.; Rev. James Kolb, C.S.P.
Res., P.O. Box 10508, 99710. Tel: 907-457-6603; Fax: 907-457-6603.
Catechesis/Religious Programs—Students 85. D.R.E.: Richelle Schruf, (Grades K-6); Karen Schauer.

OUTSIDE CITY OF FAIRBANKS

Alakanuk, St. Ignatius (1954) (Yup'ik), Rev. Thomas G. Provinsal, S.J.; Deacons Joseph Phillip, (Retired); Emmanuel Stanislaus; Denis Sheldon; Charles Clyde Smith.
Res., P.O. Box 53, 99554. Tel: 907-238-3914. [CEM][JC]
Mission—Sheldon Point, St. Peter's, P.O. Box 45, 99666.

Aniak, St. Theresa (1935) (Yup'ik), Rev. William E. Cardy, O.F.M.
Res., P.O. Box 308, 99557. Tel: 907-675-4448. [CEM]
Mission—Kalskag, Box 11, Kalskag, 99607. Tel: 907-471-2298. Sr. Ann Hogan, S.S.G., Pastoral Min.

Barrow, North Slope Borough, St. Patrick (1954), Rev. Francis E. Mueller, S.J.
Mailing Address: P.O. Box 389, 99723. Tel: 907-852-3515. [JC]

Bethel, Immaculate Conception (1942), Rev. Richard L. McCaffrey, S.J.; Deacons Bob Aloysius; Peter Aluska.
Res., 790 River St., P.O. Box 428, 99559. Tel: 907-543-2464.
Catechesis/Religious Programs—Susan Murphy, D.R.E.
Students 134.

Chefornak, St. Catherine (Yup'ik), Rev. Paul Cochran, S.J.; Agnes Kairaiuak, Admin.; Deacons David Panruk; Cyril Alexie; David Erik, (Retired).
Res., 99561. Tel: 907-867-8702. [CEM]
Catechesis/Religious Programs—Students 159.

Chevak, Sacred Heart (1952) (Cup'ik), Rev. Gregg D. Wood, S.J.; Doris A. Atchak, Acting Parish Admin.; Deacons Frank Smart; David Boyscout.
Res., 99563. Tel: 907-858-7826; 858-7265. [CEM]
Catechesis/Religious Programs—Tel: 907-858-7265.
Students 409.

Delta Junction, Our Lady of Sorrows (1959), Rev. Don M. Balquin.
Res., 2565 Deborah St., Box 446, 99737. Tel: 907-895-5232.
Catechesis/Religious Programs—Students 53.
Mission—Tok, Holy Rosary, P.O. Box 369, Tok, 99780. Tel: 907-883-4111. Sr. Linda Hogan, C.S.J., Pastoral Admin.
Stations—Northway, St. Ann.; Eagle, St. Francis Xavier.

Emmonak, Sacred Heart (1961), Rev. Thomas Provinsal, S.J.; Mr. Patrick C.W. Tam, Dir. Youth Ministry; Deacons Bart Agathluk, Sr.; Raymond Waska.
Res., P.O. Box 190, 99581. Tel: 907-949-1012. [JC]
Catechesis/Religious Programs—Students 179. D.R.E.: Virginia Kassock; Nora Westlock.

Galena, St. John Berchman (1923) (Athabascan), Rev. Edward J. Hartmann; Bro. Robert Ruzicka, O.F.M.
Res., P.O. Box 131, 99741. Tel: 907-656-1240; Fax: 907-656-1240.
Catechesis/Religious Programs—Students 68.
Station—Huslia, St. Francis Regis, Tel: 907-829-2234.

Healy, Holy Mary of Guadalupe (1984), Rev. Jack de Verteuil.
Mailing Address: P.O. Box 32, 99743.
Church—P.O. Box 32, 99743. Tel: 907-683-2535; 683-1018 (Rectory).
Mission—Cantwell, Denali National Park. [JC]

Holy Cross, Holy Cross (1888), Rev. William Cardy, O.F.M.
Res., P.O. Box 101, 99602. Tel: 907-476-7144.
Catechesis/Religious Programs—Students 40.

Hooper Bay, Little Flower of Jesus (1928) (Yup'ik), Rev. Gregg D. Wood, S.J.; Deacon James Gump; Jerry Moses, Pastoral Admin.
Res., 99604. Tel: 907-758-4620. [JC]
Catechesis/Religious Programs—Students 90.

Kaltag, St. Teresas (Athabaskan), Rev. Joseph Hemmer, O.F.M.
Res., 99748. Tel: 907-534-2218. [JC]
Catechesis/Religious Programs—Students 72.

Kotlik, St. Joseph (1949) (Yup'ik), Rev. Eugene Delmore, S.J.; Deacons Henry Teeluk, (Retired); David Mike; Raymond Teeluk; Aloysius Wasuli; Mary Ann Mike, Acting Parish Admin.
Church—99620. Tel: 907-899-4715.
Catechesis/Religious Programs—Della Hunt, D.R.E. Students 144.

Kotzebue, Northwest Arctic Borough, St. Francis Xavier (1929), Rev. John B. Martinek (CHI).
Res., Box 358, 99752. Tel: 907-442-3239; Fax: 907-442-2217. [JC]

Koyukuk, St. Patrick (Athabascan), Rev. James E. Falsey.
Res., P.O. Box 10, 99754. Tel: 907-927-2240.

Marshall, Immaculate Heart of Mary (Yup'ik), Rev. Charles Peterson, S.J.; Deacon Alvin Owleyuk; Ms. Clara Shorty, Acting Parish Admin.
Mailing Address:99585. Tel: 907-679-6639.
Mission—Our Lady of Guadalupe Russian Mission.

McGrath, St. Michael (1960), Rev. Thomas Gallagher, S.J.; Sr. Frances McCarron, I.B.V.M., Pastoral Minister.
Res., P.O. Box 141, 99627. Tel: 907-524-3928.
Station—Takotna, Tel: 907-298-2328.

Mountain Village, Northwest Arctic Borough, St. Lawrence (1918) (Yup'ik), Rev. Eugene Delmore, S.J.; Deacon Elmer Beans; Susie Luke, Parish Admin.
Res. & Mailing Address—P.O. Box 32205, 99632. Tel: 907-591-2348; 549-3231 (Pilot Station).

Nenana, St. Theresa (1922). Served out of Healy, AK. Sr. Agnes Anne Wilcox, S.M.S.M., Pastoral Admin.; Rev. Jack deVerteuil, Visiting Priest.
P.O. Box 312, 99760. Tel: 907-832-5617. [JC]
P.O. Box 32, Healy, 99743.

Newtok, Holy Family (1950) (Yup'ik), Rev. Paul Cochran, S.J.; Deacons Larry Charles; Mark Tom; Katherine Charles, Admin.
Res., 99559. Tel: 907-237-2427. [CEM]
Catechesis/Religious Programs—Sophie John, D.R.E.
Students 90.

Nightmute, Our Lady of Perpetual Help (1950), Rev. Henry Hargreaves, S.J.; Cecilia Anthony, Acting Parish Admin.; Deacons Thomas Jumbo; Camillus Tulik.
Res., 99690. Tel: 907-647-6428. [CEM]
Catechesis/Religious Programs—Students 60.

Nome, St. Joseph (1901), Rev. John Hinsvark; Bro. Philip Drouin, (Retired).
Res., P.O. Box 1010, 99762. Tel: 907-443-5527.
Catechesis/Religious Programs—Tel: 907-443-2725.
Students 89. D.R.E.: Bernadette Alvanna-Stimpfle; Marilyn Koezuna-Irelan.
Missions—Teller, St. Ann; Diomede, St. Jude.

North Pole, North Star Borough, St. Nicholas (1975), Rev. J. Albert Levitre, Jr.; Deacon Walt Gelinas.
Res., 707 St. Nicholas Dr., 99705. Tel: 907-488-2595; Fax: 907-488-2595.
Catechesis/Religious Programs—Students 130.
Station—Manley Hot Springs.

Nulato, Our Lady of the Snows (1877) (Athabascan), Rev. James E. Falsey (SAG).
Res., P.O. Box 89, 99765. Tel: 907-898-2242.

Pilot Station, St. Charles Spinola (Yup'ik), Rev. Richard D. Case, S.J.
Mailing Address: P.O. Box 5120, 99650. Tel: 907-549-3231. [JC]
Station—Russian Mission, Our Lady of Guadalupe.

Ruby, St. Peter-in-Chains (1912) (Athabascan), Rev. Joseph Hemmer, O.F.M.
Res., P.O. Box 45, 99768. Tel: 907-468-4482; 468-4413. [JC]

St. Marys, Church of the Nativity, Revs. Theodore E. Kestler, S.J.; Richard Case, S.J.; Charles J. Peterson, S.J.; Deacon Patrick L. Beans, Sr., (Retired); Natalia Leuhmann, Pastoral Admin.
Res., P.O. Box 105, 99658. Tel: 907-438-2133; Fax: 907-438-2536. [CEM]
Catechesis/Religious Programs—Students 60.

St. Michael, St. Michael (Yup'ik), Rev. Thomas F. Carlin, S.J.
Res., P.O. Box 29, 99659. Tel: 907-923-3151. [JC]
Catechesis/Religious Programs—Students 38.

Scammon Bay, Blessed Sacrament (Yup'ik), Sr. Darlene Cholok, Admin.; Rev. Gregg D. Wood, S.J., Itinerant Min.; Deacon Francis Charlie.
Res., P.O. Box 133, 99662. Tel: 907-558-5229. [JC]

Stebbins, St. Bernard (1897) (Yup'ik), Rev. Thomas F. Carlin, S.J.; Margaret Marlin, Acting Admin.
Res., 99671. Tel: 907-934-3151. [JC]
Catechesis/Religious Programs—Students 61.

Tanana, St. Aloysius (1887) (Athabascan), Bro. Kirby Boone, C.F.X., Pastoral Admin.; Rev. Joseph Laudwein, S.J.
Res., P.O. Box 6, 99777. Tel: 907-366-7238.

Teller, St. Ann, Rev. John Hinsvark.
Res., P.O. Box 529, 99778.
Mission—Little Diomede, St. Jude, Box 7999, 99762-7999.

Toksook Bay, St. Peter the Fisherman (1964) (Central Yup'ik), Deacon James Charlie, Admin.; Revs. Henry Hargreaves, S.J.; Paul Cochran, S.J.; Deacons Joseph Asuluk, Sr.; Nick Therchik, Sr.; Gregory Charlie; Maggie John, Acting Parish Admin.
P.O. Box 37046, 99637. Tel: 907-427-7813. [CEM]
Catechesis/Religious Programs—Tel: 907-427-7826; Fax: 907-427-7820. Maggie John, D.R.E.
Students 135.
Station—Umkumute.

Tununak, Northwest Arctic Borough, St. Joseph, Rev. Henry Hargreaves, S.J.; Sophie Oscar, Admin.; Deacons Dick Lincoln; Mike Angaiak, (Retired).
Res., P.O. Box 113, 99681. Tel: 907-652-6214. [CEM]
Catechesis/Religious Programs—Tel: 907-652-6237.
Students 75.

Unalakleet, Northwest, Church of the Holy Angels, Rev. Thomas F. Carlin, S.J.
Res., 99684.

Chaplains of Public Institutions

Leave of Absence:
Reverend Fathers—
Wallner, Gerhard

Permanent Deacons:
Agathluk, Bart, Sacred Heart, Emmonak
Alexie, Cyril, St. Catherine's, Chefornak
Aloysius, Bob, Immaculate Conception, Bethel
Altsik, Maxie, Our Lady of Perpetual Help, Nightmute
Aluska, Peter, Sr., Immaculate Conception, Bethel
Angaiak, Michael, St. Joseph Church, Tununak
Asuluk, Joe, St. Peter Fisherman, Toksook Bay
Beans, Elmer, St. Lawrence Church, Mountain Village
Beans, Patrick L., Church of the Nativity, St. Mary
Boyscout, David, Sacred Heart Church, Chevak
Charles, Larry, Holy Family Church, Newtok
Charles, Nick, Immaculate Conception Church, Bethel
Charlie, Francis, Blessed Sacrament, Scammon Bay
Charlie, Gregory, St. Peter the Fisherman, Toksook Bay
Charlie, James, St. Peter the Fisherman, Toksook Bay
Edwards, Patrick, St. Charles Spinola, Pilot Station
Eric, David, St. Catherine's, Chefornak
Gelinas, Walt, St. Nicholas, North Pole
Gump, James, Little Flower Mission, Hooper Bay
Jumbo, Thomas, Our Lady of Perpetual Help, Nightmute
Kelly, Norman, St. Charles Spinola Church, Pilot Station
Lincoln, Dick, St. Joseph's, Tununak
Mantei, Robert, Immaculate Conception, Fairbanks
Mike, David, St. Joseph, Kotlik
Owletuk, Alvin, Immaculate Heart of Mary Church, Marshall
Panruk, David, St. Catherine, Chefornak
Perreault, Paul, Sacred Heart Cathedral, Fairbanks
Phillip, Joseph, St. Ignatius, Alakanuk
Sheldon, Dennis, St. Ignatius, Alakanuk
Sinka, Joe, St. Joseph, Kotlik
Smart, Frank, Sacred Heart Church, Chevak
Smith, Clyde, St. Ignatius, Alakanuk
Stanislaus, Emmanuel, Alakanuk
Steve, Charlie, St. Bernard Church, Stebbins
Teeluk, Henry, St. Joseph Church, Kotlik
Teeluk, Raymond, St. Joseph, Kotlik
Therchik, Nick, St. Peter the Fisherman, Toksook Bay
Tom, Mark, Holy Family, Newtok
Tommy, Nicholas, Holy Family, Newtok
Tulik, Camillus, Our Lady of Perpetual Help, Nightmute
Waska, Ray, Sacred Heart, Emmonak
Wasuli, Aloysius, St. Joseph, Kotlik

INSTITUTIONS LOCATED IN THE DIOCESE

[A] HIGH SCHOOLS, DIOCESAN

FAIRBANKS. *Monroe Catholic Junior-Senior High School*, 615 Monroe St., 99701. Tel: 907-452-2044. Mr. John Hoffman, Prin.; Rev. Normand Pepin, S.J. Priests 1; Lay Teachers 20; Religious 1; Students 225.

[B] GRADE SCHOOLS, DIOCESAN

FAIRBANKS. *Immaculate Conception Grade School*, 715 Monroe St., 99701. Tel: 907-456-4574; Fax: 907-456-7481. Mr. Ron Bates, Prin. Sisters 1; Lay Teachers 16; Students 261.

[C] RESIDENCES FOR PRIESTS AND BROTHERS

FAIRBANKS. *Jesuit Residence*, 2890 N. Kobuk Ave., 99709. Tel: 907-474-9320. Very Rev. Theodore E. Kestler, S.J., Alaska Jesuit Supr.; Revs. Francis E. Mueller, S.J., Local Supr.; Joseph Laudwein, S.J.; Normand A. Pepin, S.J.; Louis L. Renner, S.J.; Andrew L. Maddock, S.J.; Vincent Kelliher, S.J.; William C. Dibb, S.J.; Bro. Ignatius Jakes, S.J.

[D] CONVENTS AND RESIDENCES OF SISTERS

FAIRBANKS. *Diocesan Convent*, 1316 Peger Rd., 99709. Tel: 907-474-9538. Sr. Alita Lisbeth, O.P.; Sr. Marilyn Marx, S.N.J.M.; Sr. Carolyn Roeber, O.P. Sisters 3.

Immaculate Conception Convent, 615 Betty St., 99701. Tel: 907-452-2750. Sisters 4.

Xavier Hall, 417 Monroe St., 99701. Tel: 907-452-1322.

NOME. *Little Sisters of Jesus*, Box 845, 99762. Sr. Odette, L.S.J.; Sr. Damiene, L.S.J. Sisters 2.

[E] MISCELLANEOUS LISTINGS

FAIRBANKS. *Bishop's Attic, III*, 3670 Geraghty St., 99709. Tel: 907-474-0209. Ronnell Jonas, Dir.

House of Prayer, 1310 Peger Rd., 99709. Tel: 907-474-9379. Rev. Normand A. Pepin, S.J., Dir.; Sr. Marie Teresa Boulet, O.P.

**Monroe Foundation, Inc.*, P.O. Box 71620, 99707. Tel: 907-456-7970; Fax: 907-456-7481. Rev. Francis W. McGuigan, S.J., Exec. Dir., 718 Betty St., 99701.

Voice in the Wilderness Prayer Community, 2501 Airport Rd., 99709.

NOME. *Alaska Radio Mission, Station KNOM*, Box 988, 99762. Tel: 907-443-5221. Thomas Busch, Gen. Mgr. Total Staff 9; Total in Residence 5.

ST. MARYS. *Brother Joe Prince Jesuit Community*, P.O. Box 173, 99658. Tel: 907-438-2536. Very Rev. Theodore E. Kestler, S.J., Alaska Jesuit Supr. & Asst. in Native Ministry Program; Revs. Charles Peterson, S.J., Local Supr. & Asst. Ministry Training Program; Richard D. Case, S.J., Dir. of Native Deacon Program.

Native Ministry Training Program, P.O. Box 172, 99658. Tel: 907-438-2832; Fax: 907-438-2536. Very Rev. Theodore E. Kestler, S.J.; Rev. Charles Peterson, S.J.; Sr. Angela Fortier, C.S.J., Dir.; Mrs. Lilly Afcan; Mr. Bradly Kehoe. Total Staff 5; Total in Residence 4.

St. Marys Conference Center, P.O. Box 172, 99658. Tel: 907-438-2712. Erik Weingarth, Admin.

RELIGIOUS INSTITUTES OF MEN REPRESENTED IN THE DIOCESE

For further details refer to the corresponding bracketed number in the Religious Institutes of Men or Women section.

[0200]—*Benedictine Monks*.—O.S.B.
[0320]—*Brothers of Christian Instruction*.—F.I.C.
[0520]—*Franciscan Friars*.—O.F.M.
[0690]—*Jesuit Fathers and Brothers*.—S.J.
[1030]—*Paulist Fathers*.—C.S.P.
[1350]—*Xaverian Brothers*.—C.F.X.

RELIGIOUS INSTITUTES OF WOMEN REPRESENTED IN THE DIOCESE

[1070-03]—*Dominican Sisters*.—O.P.
[1070-21]—*Dominican Sisters*.—O.P.
[2370]—*Institute of the Blessed Virgin Mary*.—I.B.V.M.
[2330]—*Little Sisters of Jesus*.—L.S.J.
[2420]—*Missionary Sisters Society of Mary*.—S.M.S.M.
[0590]—*Sisters of Charity of Saint Elizabeth, Convent Station*. (Northern Prov.).—S.C.
[3830]—*Sisters of St. Joseph*.—S.S.J.
[3840, 3850, 3870]—*Sisters of St. Joseph of Carondelet*.—C.S.J.
[1990]—*Sisters of the Holy Names of Jesus and Mary*.—S.N.J.M.

NECROLOGY

(No Deaths)

Diocese of Fall River

(Dioecesis Riverormensis)

Most Reverend

SEAN O'MALLEY, O.F.M.CAP., PH.D.

Bishop of Fall River; ordained August 29, 1970; named Coadjutor May 30, 1984; appointed Bishop of St. Thomas, Virgin Islands; ordained August 2, 1984; installed October 16, 1985; appointed Bishop of Fall River June 16, 1992; installed August 11, 1992.

ESTABLISHED MARCH 12, 1904.

Square Miles 1,194.

Comprises Bristol, Barnstable, Dukes and Nantucket Counties, and the Towns of Marion, Mattapoisett and Wareham in Plymouth County, Massachusetts.

For legal titles of parishes and diocesan institutions, consult the Chancery Office.

Chancery Office: Box 2577, Fall River, MA, 02722. Tel.: 508-675-1311; Fax: 508-679-9220.

STATISTICAL OVERVIEW

Personnel	
Bishop	1
Priests: Diocesan Active in Diocese	140
Priests: Active Outside Diocese	3
Priests: Diocesan in Foreign Missions	1
Priests: Retired, Sick or Absent	35
Number of Diocesan Priests	179
Religious Priests in Diocese	113
Extern Priests in Diocese	1
Ordinations:	
Diocesan Priests	4
Transitional Deacons	5
Permanent Deacons in Diocese	36
Total Brothers	39
Total Sisters	387
Parishes	
Parishes	112
With Resident Pastor:	
Resident Diocesan Priests	97
Resident Religious Priests	11
Without Resident Pastor:	
Administered by Priests	3
Missions	13
Professional Ministry Personnel:	
Brothers	1
Sisters	23
Lay Ministers	48
Welfare	
Catholic Hospitals	1
Total Assisted	124,334
Health Care Centers	1
Total Assisted	120
Homes for the Aged	5
Total Assisted	969
Residential Care of Children	1
Total Assisted	130
Day Care and Extended Day Care Centers	2
Total Assisted	56
Special Centers for Social Services	4
Total Assisted	2,400
Educational	
Diocesan Students in Other Seminaries	26
Total Seminarians	26
Colleges and Universities	1
Total Students	2,882
High Schools, Diocesan and Parish	4
Total Students	2,467
Elementary Schools, Diocesan and Parish	24
Total Students	5,857
Elementary Schools, Private	1
Total Students	161
Catechesis/Religious Education:	
High School Students	5,563
Elementary Students	32,456
Total Students Under Catholic Instruction	49,412
Teachers in the Diocese:	
Priests	15
Brothers	4
Sisters	30
Lay Teachers	552
Vital Statistics	
Receptions into the Church:	
Infant Baptism Totals	5,695
Adult Baptism Totals	103
Received into Full Communion	125
First Communions	5,307
Confirmations	4,351
Marriages:	
Catholic	1,703
Interfaith	382
Total Marriages	2,087
Deaths	4,062
Total Catholic Population	345,940
Total Population	715,000

Former Bishops—Rt. Rev. WILLIAM STANG, D.D., cons. May 1, 1904; died Feb. 2, 1907.—Most Rev. DANIEL F. FEEHAN, D.D., cons. Sept. 19, 1907; died July 19, 1934.—Most Rev. JAMES E. CASSIDY, D.D., appt. Titular Bishop of Ibora and Auxiliary, March 21, 1930; cons. May 27, 1930; succeeded to the See, July 28, 1934; died May 17, 1951.—Most Rev. JAMES L. CONNOLLY, D.D., D.Sc.H., ord. Dec. 21, 1923; appt. Titular Bishop of Mylasa and Coadjutor "cum jure successionis," April 18, 1945; cons. May 24, 1945; succeeded to See, May 17, 1951; retired Oct. 30, 1970; died Sept. 12, 1986.—Most Rev. DANIEL A. CRONIN, D.D., S.T.D., ord. Dec. 20, 1952; appt. Titular Bishop of Egnatia and Auxiliary Bishop of Boston, June 10, 1968; cons. Sept. 12, 1968; transferred Fall River, Oct. 30, 1970; installed Dec. 16, 1970; transferred Hartford, Dec. 9, 1991.

Vicar-General—Rev. Msgr. GEORGE W. COLEMAN, V.G., *1335 N. Main St., Fall River, 02720.*

Episcopal Vicars of Diocese Fall River—Rev. Msgr. JOHN J. OLIVEIRA, P.A., V.E., *106 Illinois St., New Bedford, 02745.* Rev. Msgr. HENRY T. MUNROE, P.A., V.E., *230 S. Main St., Centerville, 02632.* Rev. Msgr. DANIEL F. HOYE, J.C.L., V.E., *155 N. Main St., Attleboro, 02703.* Rev. Msgr. JOHN J. SMITH, V.E., *5 Barbara St., S. Yarmouth, 02664.*

Cabinet Secretaries—

Secretary for Community Service—Rev. JOSEPH M. COSTA, *2425 Highland Ave., Fall River, 02720.* Tel: 508-679-8511; Fax: 508-672-2558.

Secretary for Health Care—Rev. EDMUND J. FITZGERALD, *386 N. Main St., Fall River, 02720.* Tel: 508-679-8154; Fax: 508-679-1422.

Secretary for Spiritual Development/Apostolates—Rev. Msgr. THOMAS J. HARRINGTON, J.C.L., *121 Mt. Pleasant St., New Bedford.* Tel: 508-992-3184.

Secretary for Youth—Rev. GEORGE E. HARRISON, *984 Taunton Ave., Seekonk, 02771.* Tel: 508-336-9022; Fax: 508-336-9010.

Secretary for Temporalities—Rev. MICHAEL K. MCMANUS, *P.O. Box 2577, Fall River, 02722.* Tel: 508-675-1311; Fax: 508-679-9220.

Secretary for Communications—Rev. JOHN F. MOORE, *P.O. Box 7, Fall River, 02720.* Tel: 508-675-0211; Fax: 508-675-7048.

Secretary for Education/Evangelization—Rev. Msgr. JOHN J. OLIVEIRA, P.A., V.E., *106 Illinois St., New Bedford, 02745.* Tel: 508-995-3593; Fax: 508-995-2453.

Secretary for Ministerial Personnel—Rev. JOHN A. PERRY, *P.O. Box 718, E. Freetown, 02717.* Tel: 508-763-2240; Fax: 508-763-3040.

Vicar for Clergy—Very Rev. FRANCIS L. MAHONEY, *709 Hanover St., Fall River, 02720.*

Chancery Office—410 Highland Ave., Fall River, 02720., Mailing Address: Box 2577, Fall River, 02722-2577. Tel: 508-675-1311; Fax: 508-679-9220.

Chancellor—Rev. MICHAEL K. MCMANUS.

Secretary to the Bishop—Rev. STEPHEN J. AVILA, *394 Highland Ave., Fall River, 02720.*

Diocesan Tribunal—887 Highland Ave., Fall River, 02720. Tel: 508-675-7150; Fax: 508-675-7295.

Judicial Vicar—Rev. JAY T. MADDOCK, J.C.L.

Adjutant Judicial Vicar—Rev. PAUL F. ROBINSON, O.Carm., J.C.D.

Promotor Justitiae—Rev. Msgr. DANIEL F. HOYE, V.E., J.C.L.

Judges—Revs. RICHARD W. BEAULIEU; THOMAS L. RITA; GERARD A. HEBERT, J.C.L.; MARK R. HESSION, J.C.L.; THOMAS E. MCGLYNN, J.C.L.; Rev. Msgr. HENRY T. MUNROE, P.A., V.E.; Rev. JOSE M. SOUSA, J.C.L.

Defenders of the Bond—Rev. ROLAND BOUSQUET, S.T.L.; Rev. Msgr. THOMAS J. HARRINGTON, J.C.L.; Rev. Msgr. DANIEL F. HOYE, V.E., J.C.L.

Advocates—Revs. MARC H. BERGERON; BRUCE M. NEYLON; Rev. Msgr. JOHN J. OLIVEIRA, P.A., V.E.; Revs. LUCIO B. PHILLIPINO; HORACE J. TRAVASSOS.

Advocate/Auditor—Rev. DAVID M. ANDRADE.

Auditors—Revs. DANIEL W. LACROIX; JOHN J. PERRY; Deacons PAUL FOURNIER; ROBERT LEMAY; ROBERT PELLAND; THOMAS J. SOUZA; THOMAS SURPRENANT.

Notaries—DENISE BERUBE; HELEN BEAUDOIN.

Diocesan Consultors—Rev. Msgr. GEORGE W. COLEMAN, V.G.; Very Rev. PETER N. GRAZIANO, V.F.; Rev. Msgr. THOMAS J. HARRINGTON, J.C.L.; Rev. Msgr. DANIEL F. HOYE, J.C.L., V.E.; Rev. Msgr. HENRY T. MUNROE, P.A., V.E.; Rev. Msgr. JOHN J. OLIVEIRA, P.A., V.E.; Rev. Msgr. JOHN J. SMITH, V.E.

Presbyteral Council—Revs. JOHN J. OLIVEIRA, Chm. JOHN J. STEAKEM, Vice Chm. DOUGLAS H. SOUSA, Sec., *P.O. Box 2577, Fall River, 02722.* Members: Rev. MARC H. BERGERON; Rev. Msgr. GEORGE W. COLEMAN, V.G.; Revs. ANDRE H. FARIA; THOMAS A. FRECHETTE; Very Revs. BENTO R. FRAGA, V.F.; PETER N. GRAZIANO, V.F.; Rev. Msgr. DANIEL F. HOYE, V.E.; Very Rev. FRANCIS L. MAHONEY, V.F.; Rev. MICHAEL K. MCMANUS; Rev. Msgr. HENRY T. MUNROE, P.A., V.E.; Rev. BRUCE M. NEYLON; Rev. Msgr. JOHN J. OLIVEIRA, P.A., V.E.; Revs. JOHN A. PERRY; RICHARD M. ROY; STEPHEN B. SALVADOR; Rev. Msgr. JOHN J. SMITH, V.E.; Rev. RONALD A. TOSTI.

Deans—Fall River Deanery: Very Rev. FRANCIS L. MAHONEY, V.F., *709 Hanover St., Fall River, 02720.* Taunton Deanery: Very Rev. BENTO R. FRAGA, V.F., *261 Tremont St., Taunton, 02780.* Attleboro Deanery: Very Rev. PETER N. GRAZIANO, V.F., *105 Stanley St., Attleboro Falls, 02763.* Cape Cod Deanery: Very Rev. GERALD T. SHOVELTON, V.F., *246 Main St., West Harwich, 02671.* New Bedford Deanery: Very Rev. HENRY S. ARRUDA, V.F., *230 Bonney St., New Bedford, 02744.*

Diocesan Offices and Directors

Apostolate for Persons with Disabilities—Rev. JOSEPH VIVEIROS, Dir., *243 Forest St., Fall River, 02721.* Tel: 508-679-8373; 674-5741, Ext. 2270.

Campus Ministry—Rev. RICHARD W. BEAULIEU, Dir., *529 Eastern Ave., Fall River, 02723.* Tel: 508-679-1991; Fax: 508-676-5276.

Bristol Community College—Sr. ANNETTE BIBEAU, S.S.A., *777 Elsbree St., Fall River, 02720.* Tel: 508-678-2811, Ext. 301.

University of Massachusetts Dartmouth—Rev. MICHAEL CARVILL; Sr. MADELEINE TACY, O.P. Tel: 508-999-8872.

Wheaton College—Rev. THOMAS M. FEELEY, C.S.C.

Massachusetts Maritime Academy—Rev. VINCENT NAGLE, *420 Bradford Ave., Fall River, 02721.*

Cape Cod Community College—Vacant.

Catholic Youth Organization—Rev. JAY T. MADDOCK, Dir., *403 Anawan St., Fall River, 02720.*

Catholic Charities Appeal—Rev. Msgr. THOMAS J. HARRINGTON, Dir., Office: *344 Highland Ave., Fall River, 02720.* Rev. GEORGE B. SCALES, Asst. Dir.

Diocesan Apostolate to Hispanics—Rev. PAUL E. CANUEL, Diocesan Dir., *P.O. Box 40605, New Bedford, 02744.* Area Offices, Fall River: Rev. EDUARDO COLL, I.V.E., Dir., *327 2nd St., Fall River, 02721.* Tel: 508-672-9303. Attleboro: Rev. KEVIN J. HARRINGTON, Dir., *208 S. Main St., Attleboro, 02703.* Tel: 508-266-1115. Taunton: Rev. WILLIAM M. COSTELLO, Dir., *14 St. Mary's Square, Taunton, 02780.* Tel: 508-822-7116. New Bedford: Rev. PAUL E. CANUEL, Dir., *P.O. Box 40605, New Bedford, 02744.*

Director of Ministry to Sick, Retired, and Senior Priests—Rev. JOHN P. CRONIN, *818 Middle St., Fall River, 02721.*

Director of Portuguese Ministry—Rev. JOHN J. OLIVEIRA, *344 Country St., New Bedford, 02740.*

Diocesan Archives—Rev. MICHAEL K. MCMANUS, *Chancery, P.O. Box 2577, Fall River, 02722.*

Diocesan Office of Communications—Rev. JOHN F. MOORE, Dir. JOHN E. KEARNS, JR., Asst. to the Dir., *887 Highland Ave., Fall River, 02720.* Tel: 508-675-7151., *Mailing Address: P.O. Box 7, Fall River, 02722.*

Diocesan Director of Cemeteries—Rev. JOHN P. CRONIN, *818 Middle St., Fall River, 02721.* Tel: 508-673-0377.

Diocesan Education Center—Rev. WILLIAM T. GARLAND, O.S.A., Dir., Schools; JAMES A. MCNAMEE, Supt., Schools; Sr. ANNE M. LANDRY, C.N.D., Supt., Elementary Schools; Deacon BRUCE J. BONNEAU, Dir., Religious Education; LISA M. GULINO, Dir., Adult Education, *Office, 423 Highland Ave., Fall River, 02720.* Tel: 508-678-2828; Fax: 508-674-4218.

Diocesan Department of Pastoral Care for the Sick—Rev. GEORGE C. BELLENOIT, Dir.; Sr. SHIRLEY AGNEW, R.S.M., Asst. Dir.; Rev. DOUGLAS H. SOUSA, Asst. to the Dir., Office: *330 Pratt St., Mansfield, 02048.* Tel: 508-339-2981.

Diocesan Department of Catholic Social Services and Special Apostolates—ARLENE A. MCNAMEE, Exec. Dir., Office: *783 Slade St., Box M, S. Station, Fall River, 02724.* Tel: 508-674-4681; Fax: 508-675-2224.

Diocesan Finance Council—Most Rev. SEAN O'MALLEY, O.F.M.Cap., Chm.; Rev. Msgr. HENRY T. MUNROE, P.A., V.E.; Rev. Msgr. JOHN J. OLIVEIRA, P.A., V.E.; FREDERIC J. TORPHY, ESQ.; LAURENCE T. FLYNN, C.P.A., Consultant, *P.O. Box 2577, Fall River, 02722.* Tel: 508-675-1311.

Diocesan Guild for the Blind—Rev. BRUCE M. NEYLON, *385 Central Ave., Seekonk, 02771.* Tel: 508-399-8440.

Diocesan Health Facilities—Rev. EDMUND J. FITZGERALD, Dir., Office: *368 N. Main St., Fall River, 02720.* Tel: 508-679-8154; Fax: 508-679-1422.

Diocesan Insurance Department—Rev. MICHAEL K. MCMANUS; JOSEPH A. FIGLOCK, *P.O. Box 2577, Fall River, 02722.* Tel: 508-675-3850; Fax: 508-672-3802.

Diocesan Newspaper, "The Anchor"—Rev. JOHN F. MOORE, Editor, Office: *887 Highland Ave., Fall River, 02722.* Tel: 508-675-7151., *Mailing Address: P.O. Box 7, Fall River, 02722.*

Episcopal Representative for Religious—Sr. MARY NOEL BLUTE, R.S.M., *500 Slocum Rd., N. Dartmouth, 02747.* Tel: 508-992-9921.

Family Ministry—Rev. HORACE J. TRAVASSOS, Dir., *Family Life Center, 500 Slocum Rd., N. Dartmouth, 02747.* Tel: 508-999-6420.

Holy Childhood Association, The—Rev. Msgr. JOHN J. OLIVEIRA, P.A., V.E., Dir., *106 Illinois St., New Bedford, 02745.* Tel: 508-995-3593.

Missionary Cooperative Plan—Rev. Msgr. JOHN J. OLIVEIRA, P.A., V.E., Dir., *106 Illinois St., New Bedford, 02745.* Tel: 508-995-3593.

Office for Divine Worship—Rev. JON-PAUL GALLANT, S.L.L., Dir., *311 Somerset Ave., Taunton, 02780.* Tel: 508-823-2521.

Permanent Diaconate Program—Rev. JOHN F. MOORE, Dir.; Deacon LAWRENCE A. ST.ONGE, Asst. Dir., *500 Slocum Rd., N. Dartmouth, 02747.* Tel: 508-993-9935; 993-9938.

Propagation of the Faith—Rev. Msgr. JOHN J. OLIVEIRA, P.A., V.E., Dir., Office: *106 Illinois St., New Bedford, 02745.* Tel: 508-995-3593; Fax: 508-995-2453.

St. Vincent De Paul Society—Vacant.

Vocations—Rev. Msgr. JOHN J. SMITH, V.E., Dir., *5 Barbara St., S. Yarmouth, 02664.* Tel: 508-398-2248. Rev. CRAIG A. PREGANA, Asst. Dir., *160 Seabury St., Fall River, 02720.* Tel: 508-673-0852.

Commissions and Councils

Campaign for Human Development—ARLENE A. MCNAMEE, *P.O. Box M, S. Station, Fall River, 02724.* Tel: 508-674-4681; Fax: 508-675-2224.

Catholic Scouting Program—Rev. STEPHEN B. SALVADOR, Dir., *71 Linden St., Attleboro, 02703.* Tel: 508-222-3266.

Continuing Education of the Clergy—Rev. MARK R. HESSION, Dir., *327 2nd St., Fall River, 02721.* Tel: 508-673-2833.

Diocesan Council of Catholic Nurses—Rev. MARK R. HESSION, Moderator, *327 2nd St., Fall River, 02721.* Tel: 508-673-2833.

Diocesan Council of Catholic Women—Rev. Msgr. DANIEL F. HOYE, V.E., Moderator, *155 N. Main St., Attleboro, 02703.*

Diocesan Ecumenical Commission—Rev. HORACE J. TRAVASSOS, Chm., *327 2nd St., Fall River, 02721.*

Diocesan Liaison to the Committee on Evangelization—Rev. Msgr. JOHN J. OLIVEIRA, P.A., V.E., *106 Illinois St., New Bedford, 02745.* Tel: 508-995-3593.

Diocesan Liaison with Marriage Encounter—Vacant.

Diocesan Liaison with Charismatic Groups—Rev. ROBERT S. KASZYNSKI, Dir., *36 Rockland St., Fall River, 02724.* Tel: 508-672-0423.

Diocesan Liaison with Cursillo—Rev. EDMUND J. FITZGERALD, *945 Main Rd., P.O. Box 3328, Westport, 02790.* Tel: 508-636-2251.

Diocesan Pastoral Council—Rev. Msgr. GEORGE W. COLEMAN, V.G., Sec., *P.O. Box 2577, Fall River, 02722.*

Legion of Mary—Rev. BARRY W. WALL, *22 Barstow St., Mattapoisett, 02739.* Tel: 508-758-3719.

Pastoral Ministry to the Sick—Rev. GEORGE C. BELLENOIT, Dir., *330 Pratt St., Mansfield, 02048.* Sr. SHIRLEY AGNEW, R.S.M., Asst. Dir.; Revs. DOUGLAS H. AGNEW, Asst. to the Dir. ROBERT A. ROCHON; RICHARD G. ANDRADE; Sr. CAROLE V. M. MELLO, O.P.; Sr. LORNA RIORDAN, O.P.; Sr. PATRICIA ANNE CONLAN, R.S.M.; Deacon MICHAEL E. MURRAY, *St. Anne's Hospital, 795 Middle St., Fall River, 02721.* Revs. STEVEN R. FURTADO; MARK R. HESSION; HERBERT T. NICHOLS; Sr. JACQUELINE DUBOIS, S.S.A.; Sr. LUCILLE SOCCIARELLI, R.S.M.; Sr. MARCELINE VELASQUEZ, F.M.M.,*Charlton Memorial Hospital, Fall River.* Rev. JOHN M. SULLIVAN,Sturdy Memorial Hospital, Attleboro. Rev. EDWARD J. HEALEY; Sr. DYMPNA SMITH, R.S.M.,*Cape Cod Hospital, Hyannis.* Revs. FRANCIS J. MCMANUS, S.J.; JOHN F. DIAS, C.S.C.; Sr. ROBERTA O'CONNELL, F.C.J.; Sr. KATHLEEN SCHMITH, R.S.M.; Sr. M. HOPE HUGHES, R.S.M.,*St. Luke's Hospital, New Bedford.* Rev. DAVID J. LANDRY; Bro. RONALD CHRISTENSON, C.S.C.,*Morton Hospital, Taunton.*

Divine Worship Commission—Rev. JON-PAUL GALLANT, S.L.L., Chm., *311 Somerset Ave., Taunton, 02780-4822.* Tel: 508-823-2521.

Pro-Life-Respect Life Program—Rev. STEPHEN A. FERNANDES, Dir., *SS. Peter and Paul, 500 Slocum Rd., N. Dartmouth, 02747.* Tel: 508-997-2290.

Television Apostolate—Rev. STEPHEN J. AVILA, Coord., *394 Highland Ave., Fall River, 02720.*

Diocesan Office of Youth Ministry—Rev. DAVID A. COSTA, Dir. LOUIS MILLER, Coord., *P.O. Box 1167, Fall River, 02722.* Tel: 508-676-6503.

CLERGY, PARISHES, MISSIONS AND PAROCHIAL SCHOOLS

CITY OF FALL RIVER
(Bristol County)

1—CATHEDRAL OF ST. MARY OF THE ASSUMPTION (1838), Rev. Horace J. Travassos, Rector. In res., Rev. Mark R. Nession.
Res., 327 Second St., 02721. Tel: 508-673-2833.
Catechesis/Religious Programs—467 Spring St., 02721. Tel: 508-672-5531.
Students 86.

2—BLESSED SACRAMENT (1902) (French), Rev. Gerald P. Barnwell.
Res., 2492 S. Main St., 02724. Tel: 508-672-5473.
Catechesis/Religious Programs—Students 82.

3—ESPIRITO SANTO (1904) (Portuguese), Rev. James Ferry. In res., Rev. Steven R. Furtado, Chap.
Res., 311 Alden St., 02723. Tel: 508-672-3352.
School—143 Everett St., 02723. Tel: 508-672-3362; Fax: 508-672-7724. Mrs. Patricia Benoit, Prin.
Lay Teachers 13; Students 243.
Catechesis/Religious Programs—Diane Rego Pacheco, D.R.E.
Students 435.

4—HOLY CROSS (1916) (Polish), Revs. Walter Mruk, O.F.M.Conv.; Charles Porada, O.F.M.Conv.
Res., 69 Pulaski St., 02721. Tel: 508-672-2093.

5—HOLY NAME (1923), Very Rev. Francis L. Mahoney.
Res., 709 Hanover St., 02720. Tel: 508-679-6732; Fax: 508-675-4755.
School—850 Pearce St., 02720. Tel: 508-674-9131; Fax: 508-679-0571.
Religious Sisters of Mercy 1; Lay Teachers 12; Students 225.
Catechesis/Religious Programs—Tel: 508-679-6732.
Students 525.

6—NOTRE DAME DE LOURDES (1874) (French), Revs. Richard W. Beaulieu; Michael S. Racine. In res., Rev. Daniel Gamache.
Res., 529 Eastern Ave., 02723. Tel: 508-679-1991; Fax: 508-676-5276.
School—34 St. Joseph St., 02723. Tel: 508-672-5461.
Lay Teachers 12; Students 240.
Catechesis/Religious Programs—Students 180.

7—OUR LADY OF THE ANGELS (1915) (Portuguese), Rev. Evaristo Tavares; Deacon John F. Branco.
Res., 221 Kilburn St., 02724. Tel: 508-676-8883; Fax: 508-677-9078.
Catechesis/Religious Programs—Tel: 508-679-8292. Marion Carrier, D.R.E.
Students 332.

8—OUR LADY OF HEALTH (1924) (Portuguese), Rev. Jose A.F. dos Santos.
Res., 642 Cambridge St., 02721. Tel: 508-672-2793.
Catechesis/Religious Programs—49 Somerset St., 02721. Tel: 508-673-8987.
Students 400.

9—OUR LADY OF THE HOLY ROSARY (1904) (Italian), Rev. Vincent F. Diaferio.
Res., 120 Beattie St., 02723. Tel: 508-672-7232; Fax: 508-672-1506.
Catechesis/Religious Programs—84 Beattie St., 02723. Tel: 508-672-7267. Ernest DiGiammo, D.R.E.
Students 154.

10—OUR LADY OF THE IMMACULATE CONCEPTION (1882), Rev. Kenneth J. Delano.
Res., 15 Thomas St., P.O. Box 4127, 02723. Tel: 508-673-2122; Fax: 508-730-1694.
Catechesis/Religious Programs—Tel: 508-672-3254. Mrs. Colleen Laliberte, D.R.E.
Students 185.

11—SACRED HEART (1872), Rev. John C. Ozug; Sr. Eugenia Margaret Ready, S.U.S.C., Pastoral Asst.
In res., Rev. Craig A. Pregana.
Res., 160 Seabury St., 02720. Tel: 508-673-0852; Fax: 508-678-0873.
Catechesis/Religious Programs—Tel: 508-673-0852; Fax: 508-678-0873. Sr. Virginia Vierling, S.S.D., D.R.E.
Students 128.

12—ST. ANNE'S (1869) (French), Revs. Marc H. Bergeron; Pierre E. Lachance, O.P.; Jean Dominique Pare, O.P.
Res., 818 Middle St., 02721. Tel: 508-674-5651; 678-5322; Fax: 508-672-0939.
School—Tel: 508-678-2152; Fax: 508-674-5190. Mrs. Denise Gagne, Prin.
Sisters 2; Lay Teachers 24; Students 435.
Catechesis/Religious Programs—Tel: 508-678-1510. Susan Chapdelaine, D.R.E.
Students 274.

13—ST. ANTHONY OF PADUA 1911 (Portuguese), Rev. John C. Martins.
Res., 48 Sixteenth St., 02723. Tel: 508-673-2402.
Catechesis/Religious Programs—Tel: 508-764-1986.
Students 440. D.R.E.: Jorgelina B. Krupa; Deborah Polselli.

14—ST. ELIZABETH'S (1915) (Portuguese), Rev. Raymond Cambra.
Res., 515 Tucker St., 02721. Tel: 508-679-6903; Fax: 508-675-8983.

Catechesis/Religious Programs—Tel: 508-672-6602.
Students 69.

15—ST. JEAN BAPTISTE 1901 (French), Rev. Rene G. Gauthier. In res., Rev. Louis R. Boivin.
Res., 951 Stafford Rd., 02721. Tel: 508-672-6552; Fax: 508-673-5518.
School—Lamphor St., 02721. Tel: 508-673-6772; Fax: 508-730-1864. Kathleen Barboza, Prin.
Lay Teachers 9; Students 219.
Catechesis/Religious Programs—Students 107.

16—ST. JOSEPH'S (1874), Rev. John J. Perry, Admin. In res., Rev. Msgr. George W. Coleman, V.G.
Res., 1335 N. Main St., 02720. Tel: 508-673-1123; Fax: 508-646-1060.
Catechesis/Religious Programs—Students 199.

17—ST. LOUIS 1885, Revs. Michael Carvill; Vincent Nagle; Antonio Lopez.
Res., 420 Bradford Ave., 02721. Tel: 508-676-8603; Fax: 508-324-1702.
Catechesis/Religious Programs—Students 135.

18—ST. MICHAEL'S (1902) (Portuguese), Revs. Luis A. Cardoso; Michael M. Camara, O.F.M.; Deacon John A. Moniz. In res., Rev. Manuel T. Faria.
Res., 189 Essex St., 02720. Tel: 508-672-6713; Fax: 508-679-1841. [CEM]
School—Tel: 508-678-0266.
Religious of the Holy Union of the Sacred Hearts 1; Lay Teachers 9; Students 170.
Catechesis/Religious Programs—Tel: 508-678-0266.
Students 355.

19—ST. PATRICK'S 1873, Rev. John F. Andrews.
Res., 1598 S. Main St., 02724-2596. Tel: 508-672-2302; Fax: 508-673-1280.
Catechesis/Religious Programs—John J. Fortin, D.R.E.
Students 208.

20—SS. PETER AND PAUL (1882), Rev. Stephen A. Fernandes.
Res., 250 Snell St., 02721. Tel: 508-676-8463; Fax: 508-678-8070.
School—240 Dover St., 02721. Tel: 508-672-7258; Fax: 508-674-6042.
Sisters of Mercy 1; Lay Teachers 12; Students 217.
Catechesis/Religious Programs—Tel: 508-672-3720.
Students 161.

21—ST. STANISLAUS (1898) (Polish), Rev. Robert S. Kaszynski; Deacon Franciszek W. Mis.
Res., 36 Rockland St., P.O. Box 111, 02724. Tel: 508-672-0423; Fax: 508-677-1378.
School—37 Rockland St., 02724. Tel: 508-674-6771; Fax: 508-677-1622. Mrs. Denita Tremblay, Prin.
Lay Teachers 11; Students 200.
Catechesis/Religious Programs—Students 95.

22—ST. WILLIAM'S (1905), Rev. Jay T. Maddock. In res., Rev. David M. Andrade.
Res., 42 Chicago St., 02721. Tel: 508-675-7503; Fax: 508-676-5567.
Catechesis/Religious Programs—Tel: 508-675-0695.
Students 133.

23—SANTO CHRISTO (1891) (Portuguese), Revs. Gastao A. Oliveira; Maurice O. Gauvin.
Res., 185 Canal St., 02721. Tel: 508-676-1184.
Catechesis/Religious Programs—Tel: 508-675-3007. Mr. Osvaldo Pacheco, D.R.E.
Students 876.

OUTSIDE THE CITY OF FALL RIVER

Acushnet, Bristol Co., St. Francis Xavier's (1915), Rev. Paul A. Caron.
Res., 125 Main St., 02743. Tel: 508-995-7600; Fax: 508-995-1794.
School—223 Main St., 02743. Tel: 508-995-4313. Dr. Ludovico Perella, Prin.
Dominican Sisters 2; Lay Teachers 11; Students 224.
Catechesis/Religious Programs—Tel: 508-998-7445.
Students 360.

Assonet, Bristol Co., St. Bernard's (1938), Rev. Timothy J. Goldrick; Deacon Lawrence A. St. Onge.
Res., 32 S. Main St., P.O. Box 370, 02702. Tel: 508-644-5585.
Catechesis/Religious Programs—Tel: 508-644-2032. John G. Lanctot, D.R.E.
Students 493.

Attleboro, Bristol Co.,

1—ST. JOHN THE EVANGELIST, (1883), Rev. Msgr. Daniel F. Hoye, V.E.; Rev. David A. Pregana.
Res., 155 N. Main St., 02703-2251. Tel: 508-222-1206; Fax: 508-226-6461. [CEM]
School—13 Hodges St., 02703. Tel: 508-222-5062; Fax: 508-223-1737. Sr. Ann Therese Connolly, C.D.P., Prin.
Congregation of Divine Providence 1; Lay Teachers 10; Students 265.
Catechesis/Religious Programs—Tel: 508-222-0707.
Students 665.

2—ST. JOSEPH'S, (1905), Rev. Kevin J. Harrington.
Res., 208 S. Main St., 02703. Tel: 508-226-1115; Fax: 508-226-0234.
Catechesis/Religious Programs—10 Maple St., Tel: 508-222-1730.
Students 215.

3—ST. STEPHEN'S, (1875), Rev. William L. Boffa; Deacon Robert W. Pelland.
Res., 683 S. Main St., 02703-6397. Tel: 508-222-0641; Fax: 508-222-1815. [CEM]
Catechesis/Religious Programs—Mrs. Irene Pelland, D.R.E.
Students 295.

4—HOLY GHOST, 1921, Rev. Stephen B. Salvador; Deacon Paul M. Fournier.
Res., 71 Linden St., 02703. Tel: 508-222-3266; Fax: 508-222-3292.
Catechesis/Religious Programs—Tel: 508-222-6756. Jacqueline DaSilva, D.R.E. & Coord.
Students 180.

5—ST. THERESA OF THE CHILD JESUS, (1925), Rev. Robert F. Kirby; Deacon Robert E. Nicholson, D.R.E.
Res., 18 Baltic St., S. Attleboro, 02703. Tel: 508-761-8111; Fax: 508-761-5475.
Catechesis/Religious Programs—Tel: 508-761-5367.
Students 500.

Attleboro Falls, Bristol Co., St. Mark's (1967), Revs. Peter N. Graziano; Thomas A. Frechette.
Res., 105 Stanley St., Box 1240, 02763. Tel: 508-699-7566; Fax: 508-643-0103.
Catechesis/Religious Programs—Tel: 508-695-7773; Fax: 508-643-0103. Mrs. Elaine Corvese, D.R.E.
Students 903.

Brewster, Barnstable Co., Our Lady of the Cape (1961), Revs. Richard Lavoie, M.S.; Raymond Vaillancourt, M.S.; Deacons Francis J. Camacho; Loren King, Jr.; R. Donald Biron.
Res., Stony Brook Rd., P.O. Box 1799, 02631. Tel: 508-385-3252.
Catechesis/Religious Programs—Tel: 508-385-2115. Elizabeth M. McCullough, D.R.E.
Students 586.
Mission—East Brewster, Barnstable Co., Immaculate Conception, Rte. 6A, 02631.

Buzzards Bay, Barnstable Co., St. Margaret (1915), Rev. James C. Tuxbury, O.F.M.
Res., 141 Main St., 02532. Tel: 508-759-7777; Fax: 508-759-3920.
Catechesis/Religious Programs—Tel: 508-759-2065. Roberta Smolinsky, D.R.E.
Students 505.
Mission—Onset, St. Mary Star of the Sea.

Centerville, Barnstable Co., Our Lady of Victory (1957), Rev. Msgr. Henry T. Monroe, P.A., V.E.; Revs. Andre H. Faria; Marek Chmurski; Deacon Joseph P. Stanley.
Res., 230 S. Main St., 02632. Tel: 508-775-5744; Fax: 508-771-0170.
Catechesis/Religious Programs—Tel: 508-771-1614; Fax: 508-771-0170. D.R.E.: Jessie duMont; Claudia Anderson.
Students 1,193.
Mission—West Barnstable, Barnstable Co., Our Lady of Hope, Rte. 6A, West Barnstable, 02668.

Chatham, Barnstable Co., Holy Redeemer (1955), Rev. James F. Buckley.
Res., 57 Highland Ave., Box 687, 02633. Tel: 508-945-0677; Fax: 508-945-3186.
Catechesis/Religious Programs—Students 133.
Mission—South Chatham, Barnstable Co., Our Lady of Grace, 02633.

Dighton, Bristol Co., St. Peter's (1904), Rev. Francis Allen, S.M.M.
Res., 2039 County St., 02715. Tel: 508-669-6463; Fax: 508-669-6463.
Catechesis/Religious Programs—Tel: 508-669-6925.
Students 200.

East Falmouth, Barnstable Co., St. Anthony's (1923), Rev. Leonard Mullaney.
Res., 167 E. Falmouth Hwy., 02536. Tel: 508-548-0108. [CEM]
Catechesis/Religious Programs—Tel: 508-548-3515.
Students 510.

East Freetown, Bristol Co., St. John Neumann (1984), Rev. John A. Perry; Deacon Robert L. Surprenant.
Res., Middleboro Rd., Box 718, 02717. Tel: 508-763-2240; Fax: 508-763-3040.
Catechesis/Religious Programs—Tel: 508-763-8122. D.R.E.: Dr. Doris Thibault; Mrs. Madeleine Oliver.
Students 532.

East Taunton, Bristol Co., Holy Family (1908), Rev. George F. Almeida; Deacon John J. Fitzpatrick.
Res., 370 Middleboro, P.O. Box 619, 02718. Tel: 508-824-5707; Fax: 508-824-5665.
Catechesis/Religious Programs—Tel: 508-824-4207. Sr. Anita Marie, M.S.B.T., D.R.E.
Students 531.

Edgartown, Dukes Co., St. Elizabeth (1925), Revs. Michael R. Nagle, D.Min.; Michael O'Hearn.
Res., 86 Main St., P.O. Box 156, 02539. Tel: 508-627-5017; Fax: 508-627-6021.
Catechesis/Religious Programs—Pease Point Way, 02539. Tel: 508-627-5871.
Students 106.

Fairhaven, Bristol Co., St. Joseph's (1905), Revs. William Heffron, SS.CC.; Frederick Meyers, SS.CC. In res., Rev. Leo King, SS.CC.; Bro. Chris Santangelo, SS.CC., Pastoral Assoc.
Res., 41 Walnut St., 02719. Tel: 508-994-9714; Fax: 508-979-4659.
School—Spring St. and Homestead Ave., 02719. Tel: 508-996-1983. Sr. Muriel Ann Lebeau, SS.CC., Prin.
Sisters 1; Lay Teachers 10; Students 255.
Catechesis/Religious Programs—Tel: 508-994-8679. Sr. Dolores Pavao, SS.CC., D.R.E.
Students 447.

St. Mary's (1933), Rev. Robert Charlton, SS.CC. In res., Rev. Alphonsus McHugh, SS.CC.
Res., 41 Harding Rd., 02719. Tel: 508-992-7300; Fax: 508-992-8721.
Catechesis/Religious Programs—Tel: 508-992-7300. Sr. Eleanor Cyr, SS.CC., D.R.E.
Students 375.

Falmouth, Barnstable Co., St. Patrick's (1899), Rev. Msgr. John J. Regan; Rev. George B. Scales; Deacon Patrick J. Mahoney.
Res., 511 E. Main St., P.O. Box 569, 02541. Tel: 508-548-1065; Fax: 508-495-0875. [CEM]
Catechesis/Religious Programs—Tel: 508-548-2306. D.R.E.: Ellen Driscoll; Cynthia O'Connor.
Students 390.
Chapel—Falmouth Heights, St. Thomas, Tel: 508-548-8539.

Hyannis, Barnstable Co., St. Francis Xavier's (1904), Revs. Edward J. Byington; James M. Fitzpatrick. In res., Deacon Richard M. Dresser.
Res., 347 South St., 02601. Tel: 508-775-0818.
Catechesis/Religious Programs—Tel: 508-775-6200. Mrs. Mary Offiler, D.R.E.
Students 275.
Mission—Yarmouth Port, Barnstable Co., Sacred Heart Chapel, Summer St., Yarmouth Port, 02675.

Mansfield, Bristol Co., St. Mary's (1894), Revs. George C. Bellenoit; Daniel W. Lacroix; Sr. Ann William Publicover, M.S.B.T., Pastoral Min.
Res., 330 Pratt St., 02048-1581. Tel: 508-339-2981; Fax: 508-339-0612. [CEM]
Catechesis/Religious Programs—Tel: 508-339-4621. Mrs. Ellen Westlund, D.R.E.
Students 1,582.

Marion, Plymouth Co., St. Rita's (1972), Rev. William G. Campbell.
Res., 113 Front St., Box 902, 02738. Tel: 508-748-1497; Fax: 508-748-0604.
Catechesis/Religious Programs—Tel: 508-748-2196.
Students 176.

Mashpee, Barnstable Co., Christ The King (1984), Rev. Ronald A. Tosti; Deacon Robert D. Lemay. In res., Rev. Edward J. Healey.
Res., The Commons, P.O. Box 1800, 02649. Tel: 508-477-7710; Fax: 508-477-8158.
Catechesis/Religious Programs—Tel: 508-477-6565. Margaret Rich, D.R.E.
Students 809.

Mattapoisett, Plymouth Co., St. Anthony's (1908), Rev. Barry W. Wall; Deacon Louis A. Bousquet.
Mailing Address: P.O. Box 501, 02739-0501. Fax: 508-758-3019.
Res., 22 Barstow St., 02739. Tel: 508-758-3719. [CEM]
Catechesis/Religious Programs—Tel: 508-758-3735. Mrs. Natalie Taber, D.R.E.
Students 344.

Nantucket, Nantucket Co., St. Mary's, Our Lady of the Isle (1903), Rev. Thomas C. Lopes.
Res., 6 Orange St., P.O. Box 1168, 02554. Tel: 508-228-0100; Fax: 508-325-7991. [CEM]
Catechesis/Religious Programs—Tel: 508-228-4852.
Students 256.
Station—Siasconset.

New Bedford, Bristol Co.,

1—HOLY NAME, Rev. Msgr. Thomas J. Harrington.
Res., 121 Mt. Pleasant St., 02740. Tel: 508-992-3184; Fax: 508-984-3406.
Catechesis/Religious Programs—Tel: 508-996-8654. D.R.E. Mrs. Nancy Davis; Mrs. Heidi Kuliga.

Students 200.

2—NUESTRA SENORA DE GUADALUPE, (1993) (Hispanic), Rev. Paul E. Canuel.
Mailing Address: P.O. Box 40605, 02744-0006. Tel: 508-996-5862; Fax: 508-992-2208.
Res., 344 County St., 02740. Tel: 508-994-2521; Fax: 508-997-1462.
Catechesis/Religious Programs—Tel: 508-997-8729. Sr. Candelaria Hernandez, M.G.Sp.S., D.R.E. Students 55.

3—OUR LADY OF THE ASSUMPTION, (1905) (Cape Verdean), Revs. David P. Reid, SS.CC.; Richard Lifrak, SS.CC.
Res., 54 S. 6th St., 02740.
Parish Center—47 S. 6th St., 02740. Tel: 508-994-7602.
Catechesis/Religious Programs—Tel: 508-994-7602.
Students 237.

4—OUR LADY OF FATIMA, (1966), Rev. James F. Greene.
Res., 4254 Acushnet Ave., 02745. Tel: 508-995-7351; Fax: 508-995-4401.
Catechesis/Religious Programs—Tel: 508-995-6685. Mrs. Pearl Enos, D.R.E.
Students 190.
Parish Center—980 Tobey St., New Bedord, 02745.

5—OUR LADY OF THE IMMACULATE CONCEPTION, (Portuguese), Revs. Daniel O. Reis; Brian E. Albino.
Res., 136 Earle St., 02746. Tel: 508-992-9892; Fax: 508-992-9907.
Catechesis/Religious Programs—Immaculate Conception School of Religious Education, 156 Davis St., 02746. Tel: 508-990-0249.
Students 947.

6—OUR LADY OF MT. CARMEL, (1902) (Portuguese), Very Rev. Henry S. Arruda; Revs. Jose M. Sousa; Antonino C. Tavares, (Retired); Deacon Paul Macedo.
Res., 230 Bonney St., 02744. Tel: 508-993-4704; Fax: 508-991-5536.
School—103 Crapo St., 02744. Tel: 508-997-9612. Mrs. Rosemary da Silva, Prin.
Lay Teachers 11; Students 160.
Catechesis/Religious Programs—Tel: 508-984-7097.
Students 900.
Convent—238 Bonney St., 02744. Tel: 508-993-0529.

7—OUR LADY OF PERPETUAL HELP, (1905) (Polish), Revs. Roman Chwaliszewski, O.F.M.Conv.; Sebastian Slesinski, O.F.M.Conv. In res., Rev. Isidore Kowalski, O.F.M.Conv.
Res., 235 N. Front St., 02746. Tel: 508-992-9378; Fax: 508-993-4881.
Catechesis/Religious Programs—Students 61.

8—SACRED HEART, (1874) (French), Rev. Clement E. Dufour.
Res., 341 Summer St., 02740. Tel: 508-993-1204.
Catechesis/Religious Programs—Tel: 508-999-4140.
Students 74.

9—ST. ANNE, (1908) (French), Rev. Martin L. Buote; Deacon Marcel Morency.
Res., 890 Brock Ave., 02744. Tel: 508-997-9271.

10—ST. ANTHONY OF PADUA'S, (1895) (French), Rev. Edmond R. Levesque.
Res., 1359 Acushnet Ave., 02746. Tel: 508-993-1691; Fax: 508-999-4775.
School—109 Ashley Blvd., 02746. Tel: 508-994-5121; Fax: 508-979-5923. Sr. Elizabeth Lavigne, Prin.
Lay Teachers 15; Students 325.
Catechesis/Religious Programs—Students 125.
Convent—106 Bullard St., 02746. Mother of God Sisters of Capuchin Recollect 8.

11—ST. CASIMIR, (1927) (Polish), Rev. Henry K. Kropiwnicki.
Res., 2048 Acushnet Ave., 02745-6139. Tel: 508-995-0345.

12—ST. FRANCIS OF ASSISI CHURCH, (1928) (Italian), Rev. Albert J. Ryan.
Res., 247 North St., 02740. Tel: 508-997-7732; Fax: 508-991-6630.
Catechesis/Religious Programs—Students 60.

13—ST. HEDWIG, 1908 (Polish), Rev. Paul E. Canuel.
Mailing Address: P.O. Box 40605, New Bedord, 02744-0006. Tel: 508-996-8703; Fax: 508-992-2208.
Res., 344 County St., 02740. Tel: 508-994-2521; Fax: 508-997-1462.

14—ST. JAMES, (1888), Rev. Edward E. Correia. In res., Rev. Francis J. McManus, S.J., Chap.
Res., 233 County St., 02740. Tel: 508-992-9408.
School—St. James-St. John, 180 Orchard St., 02740. Tel: 508-996-0534; Fax: 508-996-0534.
Sisters of Mercy 1; Lay Teachers 10; Students 250.
Catechesis/Religious Programs—Tel: 508-992-7122.
Students 225.

15—ST. JOHN THE BAPTIST, (1871) (Portuguese), Revs. John J. Oliveira; Christopher Stanibula; Deacon Antonio M. daCruz. In res., Rev. Paul E. Canuel.
Res., 344 County St., 02740. Tel: 508-992-7727; Fax: 508-997-1462. [CEM]
School—See listing for St. James, New Bedford.
Catechesis/Religious Programs—Tel: 508-996-3087. Ms. Marge Ferreira, D.R.E.
Students 331.

16—ST. JOSEPH'S, (1910) (French), Rev. Roger J. Levesque; Deacon Maurice Lavallee.
Res., 51 Duncan St., 02745-6108. Tel: 508-995-5235; Fax: 508-998-8490.
School—35 Kearsarge St., 02745-6117. Tel: 508-995-2264. Mr. Anthony W. Lopes, Prin.
Lay Teachers 11; Students 240.
Catechesis/Religious Programs—Students 125.

17—ST. KILIAN, (1896), Revs. Benito M. Lagos, I.V.E.; Eduardo Coll, I.V.E.
Res., 306 Ashley Blvd., 02746. Tel: 508-992-7587.
Catechesis/Religious Programs—Students 130.

18—ST. LAWRENCE MARTYR, (1821), Revs. John P. Driscoll; Thomas E. O'Dea.
Res., 110 Summer St., 02740. Tel: 508-992-4251; Fax: 508-993-8277.
School—Holy Family-Holy Name, 91 Summer St., 02740. Tel: 508-993-3547. Ms. Cecilia Felix, Prin. & D.R.E.
Sisters 2; Lay Teachers 15; Students 265.
Catechesis/Religious Programs—Tel: 508-993-3577.
Students 246.

19—ST. MARY'S, Rev. Msgr. John J. Oliveira, P.A., V.E.; Rev. Charles A. Jodoin; Deacon Claude A. Leblanc.
Res., 106 Illinois St., 02745. Tel: 508-995-3593; Fax: 508-995-2453.
School—115 Illinois St., 02745.
Sisters 1; Lay Teachers 11; Students 220.

20—ST. THERESA, (1926) (French), Rev. Roland Bousquet, S.T.L.
Res., 2693 Acushnet Ave., 02745. Tel: 508-995-0403; Fax: 508-998-2957.
Catechesis/Religious Programs—Students 149.

North Attleboro, Bristol Co., St. Mary's (1890), Rev. Robert A. Oliveira. In res., Revs. John M. Sullivan; William T. Babbitt.
Mailing Address: P.O. Box 1027, 02761-1027. Tel: 508-695-6161; Fax: 508-695-5248.
Res., 14 Park St., 02760. Tel: 508-695-6161. [CEM]
School—See St. Mary-Sacred Heart. Tel: 508-695-3072.
Catechesis/Religious Programs—14 Park St., P.O. Box 1027, 02761-1027. Tel: 508-695-3823.
Students 419.
Convent—125 Broad St., 02760. Tel: 508-695-7989. Sisters of the Holy Union 14.

Sacred Heart (1904) (French), Rev. Richard E. Degagne.
Res., 58 Church St., P.O. Box 470, 02761-0894. Tel: 508-699-8383; Fax: 508-699-7016.
School—St. Mary's-Sacred Heart Consolidated School, 57 Richards Ave., 02760. Tel: 508-695-3072. Mrs. Denise M. Peixoto, Prin.
Lay Teachers 16; Students 236.
Catechesis/Religious Programs—Tel: 508-643-9009.
Students 194.

North Dartmouth, Bristol Co., St. Julie Billiart (1969), Revs. Brian J. Harrington; James S. Medeiros; Deacon Bruce J. Bonneau.
Res., 494 Slocum Rd., 02747. Tel: 508-993-2351; Fax: 508-993-2437.
Catechesis/Religious Programs—Tel: 508-990-0287. Sr. Theresa Sparrow, D.R.E.
Students 835.

North Dighton, Bristol Co., St. Joseph's (1913), Revs. James McLellan; David Costa.
Res., 499 Spring St., P.O. Box 564, 02764-0564. Tel: 508-822-1425; Fax: 508-822-3886.
Catechesis/Religious Programs—Tel: 508-824-6581. Sr. Judith Costa, S.S.D., D.R.E.
Students 423.

North Easton, Bristol Co., Immaculate Conception (1871), Rev. Lucio B. Phillipino.
Res., 193 Main St., 02356. Tel: 508-238-3232; Fax: 508-238-7849. [CEM]
Catechesis/Religious Programs—Tel: 508-238-3230; Fax: 508-238-7849. Maryann Dziekiewicz, D.R.E.
Students 289.

North Falmouth, Barnstable Co., St. Elizabeth Seton (1977), Rev. John F. Moore; Deacon Paul K. Roma.
Res., 481 Quaker Rd., Box 861, 02556. Tel: 508-563-7770; Fax: 508-563-7794.
Catechesis/Religious Programs—Tel: 508-563-7774.
Students 275.

Norton, Bristol Co., St. Mary's (1925), Revs. Arnold R. Medeiros; Gregory A. Mathias.
Res., 133 S. Worcester St., Box 430, 02766-0430. Tel: 508-285-4462; Fax: 508-285-5589.
Catechesis/Religious Programs—Tel: 508-285-3237. Mrs. Rose E. Collette, D.R.E.
Students 940.

Oak Bluffs, Dukes Co., Sacred Heart (1880), Revs. Michael R. Nagle; Michael O'Hearn.
Res., 259 Circuit Ave., P.O. Box 1565, 02557. Tel: 508-693-0342. [CEM]
Catechesis/Religious Programs—Tel: 508-693-3995.
Students 100.

Orleans, Barnstable Co., St. Joan of Arc (1947), Revs. Richard M. Roy; Joseph Mauritzen.
Res., 61 Canal Rd., P.O. Box 336, 02653. Tel: 508-255-0170; Fax: 508-240-6741.
Catechesis/Religious Programs—Tel: 508-255-7442.
Students 245.
Mission—North Eastham, Barnstable Co., Church of the Visitation, Masasoit Rd., North Eastham, 02651. Tel: 508-255-6588.

Osterville, Barnstable Co., Our Lady of the Assumption (1906), Rev. Thomas L. Rita.
Res., 76 Wianno Ave., P.O. Box E., 02655. Tel: 508-428-2011.
Catechesis/Religious Programs—Students 134.

Pocasset, Barnstable Co., St. John the Evangelist (1969), Rev. Robert C. Donovan; Deacon James Marzelli, Jr.
Res., 15 Virginia Rd., P.O. Box 1558, 02559. Tel: 508-563-3121; 563-5887; Fax: 508-563-3102.
Catechesis/Religious Programs—841 Shore Rd., P.O. Box 1558, 02559. Tel: 508-563-5536. Bette Songer, D.R.E.
Students 303.

Provincetown, Barnstable Co., St. Peter the Apostle (1874), Rev. John A. Raposo.
Res., 11 Prince St., 02657. Tel: 508-487-0095. [CEM]
Catechesis/Religious Programs—Students 100.

Raynham, Bristol Co., St. Ann (1961), Revs. Philip A. Davignon; Pawel Swiercz; Deacon John Welch.
Res., 660 N. Main St., P.O. Box 247, 02768. Tel: 508-823-9833; 823-9834; Fax: 508-823-8935.
Catechesis/Religious Programs—725 N. Main St. Box 247, Raynham Center, 02768. Tel: 508-824-9021. Donna Martyniak, D.R.E.
Students 757.

Sandwich, Barnstable Co., Corpus Christi (1830), Revs. Marcel H. Bouchard; Henry J. Dahl; Felician Plichta, O.F.M.Conv.; Deacons Richard J. Murphy, Sr.; John J. Emmert.
Res., 251 Service Rd., P.O. Box 1170, East Sandwich, 02537-2170. Tel: 508-888-0209; Fax: 508-888-8961. [CEM]
Parish Center—324 Quaker Meetinghouse Rd., East Sandwich, 02537.
Catechesis/Religious Programs—Tel: 508-888-8267. Sr. Doreen Donegan, D.R.E.
Students 1,200.
Mission—Sagamore, Barnstable Co., St. Theresa.

Seekonk, Bristol Co., Our Lady of Mt. Carmel (1922), Revs. George E. Harrison; Timothy P. Reis.
Res., 984 Taunton Ave., 02771. Tel: 508-336-9022; Fax: 508-336-9010.
Catechesis/Religious Programs—1040 Taunton Ave., 02771. Tel: 508-336-8608. Sr. Irene Rivard, F.C-.S.C.J., D.R.E.
Students 779.

St. Mary's (1906), Rev. Bruce M. Neylon.
Res., 385 Central Ave., 02771. Tel: 508-399-8440; Fax: 508-399-7398.
Catechesis/Religious Programs—Tel: 508-399-7534.
Students 772.

Somerset, Bristol Co., St. John of God (1928) (Portuguese), Rev. Raul M. Lagoa. In res., Rev. Luciano J. de M. Pereira, (Retired).
Res., 996 Brayton Ave., Box 113, 02726. Tel: 508-678-5513; Fax: 508-678-6458.
Catechesis/Religious Programs—1036 Brayton Ave., 02726. Tel: 508-678-5139. Edward Medeiros, D.R.E.
Students 364.

St. Thomas More (1949), Revs. John J. Steakem; John J. Murphy. In res., Rev. Michael K. McManus.
Res., 386 Luther Ave., 02726. Tel: 508-673-7831; Fax: 508-730-1396.
Catechesis/Religious Programs—Tel: 508-679-1236. Mrs. Patricia Pasternak, M.A., D.R.E.
Students 407.

St. Patrick's (1883), Rev. Marc P. Tremblay.
Res., 306 South St., 02726-5617. Tel: 508-672-1523; Fax: 508-646-3726. [CEM]
Catechesis/Religious Programs—Tel: 508-675-1073.
Students 310.

South Dartmouth, Bristol Co., St. Mary's (1930), Revs. Walter A. Sullivan; Thomas E. McGlynn.

Res., 783 Dartmouth St., 02748. Tel: 508-992-7163; Fax: 508-992-5209.
Catechesis/Religious Programs—Tel: 508-992-7505. Sr. Joan Blazevich, C.J.C., D.R.E.
Students 563.

South Easton, Bristol Co., Holy Cross (1967), Revs. Richard C. Hochman, C.S.C.; Francis E. Grogan, C.S.C.; Deacons Daniel Kayajan, C.S.C.; George H. Zarella.
Res., 225 Purchase St., 02375. Tel: 508-238-2235; Fax: 508-230-7455.
Catechesis/Religious Programs—Tel: 508-238-2131. D.R.E.: Lorraine Gryniuk; Kathy Hohl; Janet Merriam.
Students 945.

South Yarmouth, Barnstable Co., St. Pius Tenth (1954), Rev. Msgr. John J. Smith, V.E.; Revs. Hugh J. McCullough, S.J.B.; Joseph J. Blyskosz; Deacons Richard J. Hasey; Thomas Bailey.
Res., 5 Barbara St., 02664. Tel: 508-398-2248; Fax: 508-398-7233.
Catechesis/Religious Programs—Station Ave., 02664. Tel: 508-394-0709; 0708. D.R.E.: Mrs. Joan Robinson; Mrs. Jean Kelly.
Students 606.
Chapel—Bass River, Our Lady of the Highway.

Swansea, Bristol Co.,

1—St. Dominic's, (1911), Revs. Joseph F. Viveiros; Bernard Vanasse.
Res., 1277 Grand Army Hwy., P.O. Box 205, 02777. Tel: 508-675-7206.
Catechesis/Religious Programs—Tel: 508-675-7002.
Students 263.

2—St. Louis de France, (1928), Rev. Roger D. LeDuc; Deacon Robert G.L. Normandin.
Res., 56 Buffington St., 02777. Tel: 508-674-1103; Fax: 508-674-1103.
Catechesis/Religious Programs—66 Buffington St., 02777. Tel: 508-672-0615. Mrs. Lucia C. Marcille, D.R.E.
Students 516.

3—St. Michael's, (1922), Rev. Richard R. Gendreau; Deacon Thomas F. Prevost.
Res., 270 Ocean Grove Ave., 02777. Tel: 508-673-2808; Fax: 508-672-1642.
Catechesis/Religious Programs—Tel: 508-674-0024.
Students 215.

4—Our Lady of Fatima, (1958), Rev. Terence F. Keenan.
Res., 530 Gardner Neck Rd., 02777. Tel: 508-676-1541; Fax: 508-676-0289.
Catechesis/Religious Programs—Tel: 508-678-7011. Sr. Mary Denisita Sullivan, R.S.M., D.R.E.
Students 275.

Taunton, Bristol Co.,

1—Our Lady of the Holy Rosary, (1909) (Polish), Revs. Cyril Augustyn, O.F.M.Conv.; Joseph Grzybowski, O.F.M.Conv.
Res., 80 Bay St., 02780. Tel: 508-823-3046; Fax: 508-823-0585.
Catechesis/Religious Programs—Tel: 508-824-3910.
Students 84.

2—Our Lady of the Immaculate Conception, (1883), Rev. William P. Blottman; Deacon Michael Murray. In res., Rev. David J. Landry.
Res., 387 Bay St., 02780-1718. Tel: 508-824-8794; Fax: 508-821-7616.
Catechesis/Religious Programs—Tel: 508-824-4545.
Students 271.

3—Our Lady of Lourdes, (1905) (Portuguese), Rev. John A. Gomes.
Res., 49 First St., 02780. Tel: 508-822-0357; Fax: 508-823-4999.
School—52 First St., 02780. Tel: 508-822-3746. Sr. Mary Margretta, R.S.M., Prin.
Sisters of Mercy 2; Lay Teachers 5; Students 200.
Catechesis/Religious Programs—Students 230.
Convent—55 First St., 02780. Tel: 508-822-9206.

4—Sacred Heart, (1873), Rev. Jon-Paul Gallant.
Res., 311 Somerset Ave., 02780. Tel: 508-823-2521; Fax: 508-823-2522.
Catechesis/Religious Programs—29 First St., 02780. Tel: 508-824-6791.
Students 300.

5—St. Anthony's, (1910) (Portuguese), Revs. Manuel P. Ferreira; Douglas H. Sousa; Deacon Thomas J. Souza.
Res., 126 School St., 02780. Tel: 508-822-0714.
Catechesis/Religious Programs—Students 354.

6—St. James, (1904) (French), Rev. Thomas E. Morrissey.
Res., 249 Whittenton St., 02780. Tel: 508-824-7794.
Catechesis/Religious Programs—Tel: 508-824-7808.
Students 81.
Convent—279 Whittenton St., 02780. Tel: 508-824-8946.

7—St. Joseph's, (1896), Rev. Joseph D. Maguire; Sr. M. Elizabeth Mahoney, C.S.C., Pastoral Assoc.
Res., 19 Kilmer Ave., 02780. Tel: 508-824-5435; Fax: 508-880-1903.
Catechesis/Religious Programs—Tel: 508-823-6819. Margaret Borden, D.R.E.
Students 400.

8—St. Mary's, (1828), Rev. William M. Costello.
Res., 14 St. Mary's Square, 02780. Tel: 508-822-7116; Fax: 508-822-7117.
School—Tel: 508-822-9480; Fax: 508-822-7164.
Lay Teachers 26; Students 488. Co-Principals: Mrs. Martina Grover; Mr. Brian Cote.
Catechesis/Religious Programs—Tel: 508-880-5062.
Students 181.
Dolan Parish Center—Tel: 508-880-5062.

9—St. Paul's, (1904), Very Rev. Bento R. Fraga, V.F.; Deacon John M. Schondek.
Res., 261 Tremont St., 02780. Tel: 508-824-7166; Fax: 508-822-9618.
Catechesis/Religious Programs—Tel: 508-822-9672.
Students 317.

Vineyard Haven, Dukes Co., St. Augustine (1962), Revs. Michael R. Nagle, D.Min.; Michael O'Hearn.
Res., 56 Franklin St., P.O. Box 1058, 02568. Tel: 508-693-0103; Fax: 508-693-8517.
Catechesis/Religious Programs—Students 132.

Wareham, Plymouth Co., St. Patrick's (1911), Revs. Ralph D. Tetrault; Freddie Babiczuk, Jr.; Deacon William A. Martin.
Res., 82 High St., P.O. Box 271, 02571-0271. Tel: 508-295-2411; Fax: 508-295-2417. [CEM]
Catechesis/Religious Programs—Tel: 508-295-0780; Fax: 508-295-2417. Mrs. Ann MacDonald, D.R.E.
Students 793.
Mission—West Wareham, Plymouth Co., St. Anthony, 02571-0271.

Wellfleet, Barnstable Co., Our Lady of Lourdes (1910), Rev. Bernard R. Kelly.
Res., 355 Main St., P.O. Box 1414, 02667-1414. Tel: 508-349-2222. [CEM]
Catechesis/Religious Programs—Students 54.
Missions—North Truro, Barnstable Co., Our Lady of Perpetual Help, Pond Rd., North Truro, 02652.; Truro, Barnstable Co., Sacred Heart, 40 Truro Center Rd., Truro, 02666.

Westport, Bristol Co., Our Lady of Grace (1954), Rev. Richard L. Chretien.
Res., 569 Sanford Rd., 02790. Tel: 508-674-6271.
Catechesis/Religious Programs—Tel: 508-675-5857. Teresa Alexander, D.R.E.
Students 488.
St. George's (1914), Rev. Gerard A. Hebert.
Res., 12 Highland Ave., P.O. Box 1530, 02790. Tel: 508-636-4965; Fax: 508-636-4188.
Catechesis/Religious Programs—Tel: 508-636-4909.
Students 263.
St. John the Baptist (1930), Rev. Edmund J. Fitzgerald.
Res., 945 Main Rd., Box 3328, 02790. Tel: 508-636-2251; Fax: 508-636-8306.
Catechesis/Religious Programs—924 Main Rd., P.O. Box 3328, 02790. Tel: 508-636-5506.
Students 231.

West Harwich, Barnstable Co., Holy Trinity (1918), Very Rev. Gerald T. Shovelton, V.F.; Rev. Paul T. Lamb. In res., Rev. Oscar Clemente (Brazil); Deacon Ralph F. Cox.
Res., S. Main St., 02671. Tel: 508-432-4000; Fax: 508-432-3494.
Catechesis/Religious Programs—Tel: 508-432-2898. Marie Mann, D.R.E.
Students 340.
Mission—Dennis Port, Barnstable Co., Our Lady of the Annunciation, P.O. Box 428, Dennis Port, 02639. [CEM]

Woods Hole, Barnstable Co., St. Joseph's (1882), Rev. William W. Norton.
Res., 33 Millfield St., P.O. Box 3, 02543. Tel: 508-548-0990.
Catechesis/Religious Programs—Tel: 508-540-3723.
Students 59.

Chaplains of Public Institutions

Barnstable. *Barnstable County House of Correction.* Deacon Richard J. Murphy, Coord., 347 South St., Hyannis, 02601.

New Bedford. *Bristol Co. House of Correction & Eastern Massachusetts Correctional Alcohol Center.* Rev. Matthew Sullivan, SS.CC., 3 Adams St., P.O. Box 111, Fairhaven, 02719. Tel: 508-993-2442.

Special Assignment:
Reverend Fathers—
Bowen, Donald J., St. James Society Latin America
Morse, James H.

Absent on Leave:
Reverend Fathers—
Boulet, Norman J., 2402 Highland Ave., Fall River, MA 02720
Hamel, Philip N.
Robillard, Raymond A., 2402 Highland Ave., Fall River, MA 02720
Simoes, Gilbert, Box 706, Falmouth, MA 02541
Tripp, Kevin F.

Military Chaplains:
Reverend Fathers—
Fahey, James W., U.S.N.

Absent on Sick Leave:
Reverend Fathers—
de Mello, Arthur T., P.O. Box 40905, New Bedford, MA 02744-0005

Retired:
Reverend Monsignors—
Mendonca, Luiz G., P.O. Box 561, Somerset, MA 02726
Reverend Fathers—
Babbitt, William, P.O. Box 1027, North Attleboro, MA 02761
Bessette, Ernest, 71 Center St., Fairhaven, MA 02719
Boivin, Louis R., 951 Stafford Rd., Fall River, MA 02721
Boule, Roland B., 375 Elsbree St., Fall River, MA 02720
Burns, Edward J., 418-21 Quinaquisset Ave., Mashpee, MA 02649
Chabot, Bertrand R., 57 Wilfin Rd., South Yarmouth, MA 02135
Clark, James W., P.O. Box 139, Monument Beach, MA 02635-0169
Connors, Francis B., 9 Bayside Ln., Pocasset, MA 02559
d'Entremont, Clarence J., Middle West Pubnico, Yarmouth County, Nova Scotia B0W 1M0 Canada
Dalzell, James P., 161 Clark Ave., Hyde Park, MA 02136
Denehy, John F., 460 Grant Ave., Satellite Beach, FL 32937
Freitas, Daniel L., P.O. Box 411154, Melbourne, FL 32941-1154
Gamache, Daniel, 529 Eastern Ave., Fall River, MA 02723
Joseph, Louis, 2022 San Angelo St., Fairfield, CA 94533
Jussaume, Andre P., 32 Churchill Rd., Lakeville, MA 02347
Jussaume, Lucien, 2400 S. Main St., Fall River, MA 02724
Levesque, Rene R., P.O. Box 169, Cotuit, MA 02635-0169
Lyons, James F., 287 Cory St., Fall River, MA 02720
McCarthy, James, P.O. Box 3176, Pocasset, MA 02559
McIsaac, Edward F., 2446 Highland Ave., Fall River, MA 02720
Murphy, Clarence, 900 VFW Pkwy., West Roxbury, MA 02132
Murphy, John J., 386 Luther Ave., Somerset, MA 02726
O'Neill, Cornelius J., 375 Elsbree St., Fall River, MA 02720
Oliveira, Joseph, 2446 Highland Ave., Fall River, MA 02720
Pereira, Luciano J., 996 Brayton Ave., Somerset, MA 02721
Powers, Joseph L., 15 Widgeon Rd., Falmouth, MA 02540
Robida, Raymond A., 375 Elsbree St., Fall River, MA 02720
Shovelton, William J., P.O. Box 1284, Harwich, MA 02645
Tavares, Antonino, 230 Bonney St., New Bedford, MA 02744
Wallace, Francis X., P.O. Box 3737, Pocasset, MA 02559

Permanent Deacons:
Bailey, Thomas, St. Pius the Tenth, South Yarmouth
Bonneau, Bruce J., St. Julie Billiart, North Dartmouth
Bousquet, Louis A., St. Anthony, Mattapoisett
Branco, John F., Our Lady of the Angels, Fall River

Camacho, Francis J., Our Lady of the Cape, Brewster
Cwiekowski, John W., (Retired)
daCruz, Antonio, Our Lady of the Assumption, New Bedford
Dresser, Richard M., St. Francis Xavier, Hyannis
Drinkwater, Oscar T., (Retired)
Emmert, John J., Corpus Christi, East Sandwich
Faria, Robert A., Our Lady of Health, Fall River
Fitzpatrick, John J., Holy Family, East Taunton
Fournier, Paul M., Holy Ghost, Attleboro
Lavallee, Maurice, St. Joseph, New Bedford
LeBlanc, Claude A., St. Mary, New Bedford
Lemay, Robert D., Christ the King, Mashpee
Martin, William A., St. Patrick, Wareham
Marzelli, James, Jr., St. John the Evangelist, Pocasset
Meloni, James J., Jr., St. Mary's, North Attleboro
Mis, Franciszek W., St. Stanislaus Church, Fall River
Moniz, John de A., St. Michael, Fall River
Morency, Marcel G., St. Anne, New Bedford
Murphy, Richard J., Corpus Christi, East Sandwich
Murray, Michael E., Immaculate Conception, Taunton
Nasser, Andre P.
Normandin, Robert G.L., St. Louis de France, Swansea
Pelland, Robert W., St. Stephen, Attleboro
Prevost, Thomas F., St. Michael, Swansea
Racine, Leo W., St. Theresa, New Bedford
Roma, Paul K., St. Elizabeth Seton, North Falmouth
Schondek, John H., St. Paul, Taunton
Souza, Thomas J., St. Anthony, Taunton
St. Onge, Lawrence A., St. Bernard, Assonet
Stanley, Joseph P., Our Lady of Victory, Centerville
Surprenant, Robert L., St. John Neumann, East Freetown
Welch, John, St. Ann, Raynham
Zarella, George H., Holy Cross, South Easton

INSTITUTIONS LOCATED IN THE DIOCESE

[A] SEMINARIES, RELIGIOUS OR SCHOLASTICATES

WAREHAM. *Sacred Hearts Retreat Center*, Great Neck Rd., 02571. Tel: 508-295-0100; 295-1450. Congregation of the Sacred Hearts of Jesus and Mary and of the Perpetual Adoration of the Most Blessed Sacrament. Rev. Thomas McElroy, SS.CC., Dir.; Bro. Joseph Fandel, SS.CC. In res., Rev. William Mitchell, SS.CC. Priests 2; Brothers 1; Sisters 1.

[B] COLLEGES AND UNIVERSITIES

NORTH EASTON. *Holy Cross Fathers Religious*, 480 Washington St., 02356. Tel: 508-238-6089.
For a complete listing, refer to the Colleges and Universities section.

Stonehill College, 02357. Tel: 508-238-1081; Fax: 508-230-3732.
For a complete listing, refer to the Colleges and Universities section.

[C] HIGH SCHOOLS, DIOCESAN

FALL RIVER. *Bishop Connolly High School*, 373 Elsbree St., 02720. Tel: 508-676-1071. Mr. Anthony S. Nunes, Prin.; Bro. Richard J. Lunny, C.F.X., Academic Vice Prin. Priests 2; Brothers 3; Lay Teachers 30; Students 438.

ATTLEBORO. *Bishop Feehan High School*, 70 Holcott Dr., 02703. Tel: 508-226-6223; Fax: 508-226-7696. Mr. George Milot, Prin.; Rev. Thomas A. Frechette, Chap. Priests 1; Sisters 8; Lay Teachers 53; Students 778.

Our Lady of Mercy Convent, 70 Holcott Dr., 02703. Tel: 508-226-4608. Sr. Rose Angela McLellan, R.S.M., Supr. Sisters 28.

NORTH DARTMOUTH. *Bishop Stang High School*, 500 Slocum Rd., 02747-2999. Tel: 508-996-5602; Fax: 508-994-6756. Theresa E. Dougall, President; Mary Ann Miskel, Academic Prin.; Robert Zukowski, Prin. of Students; Rev. James S. Medeiros, Chap. Priests 1; Sisters 1; Lay Teachers 44; Support Staff 18; Students 520.

TAUNTON. *Coyle and Cassidy High School*, 2 Hamilton St., 02780. Tel: 508-823-6164. Mr. Michael J. Donly, Headmaster; Rev. John Denning, C.S.C. Priests 2; Sisters 4; Lay Teachers 52; Students 715.

[D] ELEMENTARY SCHOOLS, DIOCESAN

TAUNTON. *Taunton Catholic Middle School*, 61 Summer St., 02780. Tel: 508-822-0491. Kathleen A. Simpson, Prin.; Rev. Pawel A. Swiercz. Lay Teachers 17; Students 310.

[E] ELEMENTARY SCHOOLS, PRIVATE

FALL RIVER. *Dominican Academy*, 37 Park St., 02721. Tel: 508-674-6100. Sr. Diane Dube, R.J.M., Prin. Sisters 2; Lay Teachers 16; Girls 161.

[F] RESIDENTIAL CHILD CARE FACILITIES

FALL RIVER. *St. Vincent's Home Corp.*, 2425 Highland Ave., 02720. Tel: 508-679-8511; Fax: 508-672-2558. Rev. Joseph M. Costa, Exec. Dir. Sisters 8; Total Staff 275; Children Residents 130.

[G] NURSERIES

NEW BEDFORD. *St. Saviour's Day Nursery*, 405 County St., 02740-4935. Tel: 508-997-0233. Sr. Marcella Rostkowski, C.R., Supr. Congregation of the Resurrection 5; Students 30.

[H] GENERAL HOSPITALS

FALL RIVER. *Saint Anne's Health Care Management Services, Inc.*, 795 Middle St., 02721-1798.
For a complete listing, refer to the Hospitals section.

Saint Anne's Health Care System, Inc., 795 Middle St., 02721-1798.
For a complete listing, refer to the Hospitals section.

Saint Anne's Hospital, 795 Middle St., 02721-1798. Tel: 508-674-5741.
For a complete listing, refer to the Hospitals section.

[I] SPECIAL HOSPITALS AND SANATORIA FOR INVALIDS

FALL RIVER. *Rose Hawthorne Lathrop Home*, 1600 Bay St., 02724. Tel: 508-673-2322; Fax: 508-679-5830.
For a complete listing, refer to the Special Care Facilities section.

[J] HOMES FOR AGED

FALL RIVER. *Catholic Memorial Home Inc.*, 2446-2474 Highland Ave., 02720. Tel: 508-679-0011; Fax: 508-672-5858.
For a complete listing, refer to the Special Care Facilities section.

FAIRHAVEN. *Our Lady's Haven of Fairhaven Inc.*, 71 Center St., 02719. Tel: 508-999-4561.
For a complete listing, refer to the Special Care Facilities section.

NEW BEDFORD. *Sacred Heart Home*, 359 Summer St., 02740. Tel: 508-996-6751.
For a complete listing, refer to the Special Care Facilities section.

NORTH ATTLEBORO. *Madonna Manor Inc.*, 85 N. Washington St., 02760. Tel: 508-699-2740; Fax: 508-699-0481.
For a complete listing, refer to the Special Care Facilities section.

TAUNTON. *Bethany House Adult Day Care*, 72 Church Green, 02780. Tel: 508-822-9200.
For a complete listing, refer to the Special Care Facilities section.

Marian Manor Inc., 33 Summer St., 02780. Tel: 508-822-4885.
For a complete listing, refer to the Special Care Facilities section.

[K] MONASTERIES AND RESIDENCES OF PRIESTS AND BROTHERS

FALL RIVER. *Brothers of Christian Instruction*, 555 Eastern Ave., 02723. Tel: 508-672-5763. Bros. Daniel Caron, Supr.; Raymond Berube, Asst. Supr.; Walter Zwierchowski; Roger Millette; Norman Simoneau; Roger Monfette. Brothers 6; Faculty of Bishop Connolly High 3.

Cardinal Medeiros Residence-Retirement Facility for Priests, 375 Elsbree St., 02720. Tel: 508-675-1050; Fax: 508-675-2181.

Dominican House, 818 Middle St., 02721. Tel: 508-678-5322. Rev. Pierre Lachance, O.P., Supr.

Priests' Hostel, 2402 Highland Ave., 02720. Tel: 508-672-1632; Fax: 508-679-1422. In res., Revs. Raymond A. Robillard; Normand J. Boulet; Herbert T. Nichols.

St. John Vianney House, 818 Middle St., 02721-1734. Tel: 508-673-0377. Revs. John P. Cronin; Richard G. Andrade. Priests 5; Total Staff 3.

Vincentian Fathers Mission House, 601 June St., 02720. Tel: 508-672-1122.

ATTLEBORO. *La Salette Missionary Association*, 947 Park St., 02703. Tel: 508-222-0027. Very Rev. Gilles Genest, M.S., Dir.

La Salette Provincial House, 947 Park St., P.O. Box 2965, 02703-0965. Tel: 508-222-6682. Immaculate Heart of Mary Province. Very Rev. Gilles Genest, M.S., Prov. Supr.; Revs. Ronald Beauchemin, M.S.; Andre Patenaude, M.S.; William Slight, M.S. Priests 4; Brothers 2.

Priests of the Province serving outside the U.S.: Rev. Gerald Baril, M.S., 85 Archambault Blvd., Pointe Gatineau, Canada, PQ J8T-2N2. Rev. Gerard Comeau, M.S., Sanctuario de Nuestra Senora de LaSalette Siador-Silleda, Ponte Vedra, Espana. Rev. Camille Doucet, M.S., 3535 Park Ave., Montreal, Canada, PQ H2X 2H8. Rev. George Dube, M.S., Our Lady of LaSalette, 3535 Park Ave., Quebec H2Z-2H8, Canada. Rev. Andre Lussier, M.S., La Salette Fathers, P.O. Box AC 59, Quezon City 1100, Philippines. Rev. Paul Belhumeur, M.S., 229 Cadillac St., Ontario N8Y-2S8, Canada. Rev. Fernand Langevin, M.S., 270 Deragon St., Granby, Canada, PQ J2G 5J5. Rev. Paul M. Roy, M.S., 490 Charles St., Buckingham, PQ J8L-2K5, Canada. Rev. Robert Vachon, M.S., 4917 St. Urbain, Montreal, PQ H2T-2W1, Canada. Rev. Theodule Richard, M.S., 97, rue Laval Sud, Granby, Quebec J2G 7G6, Canada. Rev. Roland Vandal, M.S., 3535 Park Ave., Montreal, Quebec H2X-2H8, Canada.

La Salette Shrine, 947 Park St., 02703. Tel: 508-222-5410; Fax: 508-222-6770. Revs. Rene Gelinas, M.S., Gen Counselor, Vicar Prov., Supr.; Ernest J. Corriveau, M.S., Dir. In res., Revs. George Brennan, M.S.; Paul Dalbec, M.S.; Richard Delisle, M.S.; Gerald Forest, M.S.; Albert Fredette, M.S.; Joseph Fredette, M.S.; Armand Giroux, M.S.; Joseph P. Gosselin, M.S.; Armand Gonthier, M.S.; Richard Landry, M.S.; Leo Maxfield, M.S.; Raymond Moquin, M.S.; Thomas Paris, M.S.; Manuel Pereira, M.S.; Joseph Ross, M.S.; Normand Theroux, M.S.; Bros. Armand Binette, M.S.; Lucien Brodeur, M.S.; Charles Caillouette, M.S.; David Dumaine, M.S.; Roger Moreau, M.S.; Leonard Melanson, M.S.; Robert Nichols, M.S.; Ronald Taylor, M.S.; Raymond Tetreault, M.S. Priests 18; Brothers 9.

FAIRHAVEN. *National Center of the Enthronement*, 42 1/2 Adams St., 02719. Tel: 508-999-2680. Total Staff 2.

Sacred Hearts Provincial House, 77 Adams St., P.O. Box 111, 02719-0111. Tel: 508-993-2442; Fax: 508-996-5499. Congregation of the Sacred Hearts of Jesus and Mary. Very Rev. Columban Crotty, SS.CC.; Revs. William T. Penderghest, SS.CC., Treas.; Gabriel Healy, SS.CC., Mission Procurator & Dir. Devel.; Robert Charlton, SS.CC., Vocation Dir.; Matthew Sullivan, SS.CC.; James Nickel, SS.CC. Fathers 3. Damien Residence, 73 Adams St., P.O. Box 111, 02719-0111. Tel: 508-999-0500. Congregation of the Sacred Hearts of Jesus and Mary. Revs. William Davis, SS.CC., Dir.; Albert Dagnoli, SS.CC.; Albert Evans, SS.CC.; Harold Whelan, SS.CC.; Roy Yurco, SS.CC.; Rene Gaudin, SS.CC.; Owen Goodwin, SS.CC.; Henry Creighton, SS.CC.; Bros. Damien O'Hare, SS.CC.; William Keane, SS.CC. Fathers 8; Brothers 2.

Priests of the Province Serving Abroad - In Japanese Missions: Very Rev. Michael Narita, SS.CC., Vice Prov.; Revs. Michael Coleman, SS.CC.; Cornelius Biffar, SS.CC.; John Yamada, SS.CC.; Lawrence Craig, SS.CC.; William Donegan, SS.CC.; William Ducey, SS.CC.; Louis Kawamata, SS.CC.; Edward Keeney, SS.CC.; Augustine Kobayashi, SS.CC.; Peter Kusunoki, SS.CC.; James E. McDonough, SS.CC.; Philip Murphy, SS.CC.; Daniel Perry, SS.CC.; Kenji Honma, SS.CC.; Bro. Francis Nakazawa, SS.CC.

In the Philippines: Rev. Andrew Healey, SS.CC.

In Nassau, Bahamas: Revs. Martin Gomes, SS.CC.; Michael Kelly, SS.CC.; Brian Marggraf, SS.CC.

In Abaco, Bahamas: Rev. Stanley Kolasa, SS.CC.

In Eleuthera, Bahamas: Revs. Patrick Killilea, SS.CC.; Patrick Fanning, SS.CC.

In India: Revs. William Petrie, SS.CC.; Michael Shanahan, SS.CC.; Bro. James Rukavina, SS.CC.

In Rome, Italy: Rev. Richard McNally, SS.CC., General Councillor.

Chaplains in Military Facilities: Rev. James Keefe, SS.CC., William Beaumont Army Medical Center, Chaplains Office, P.O. Box 70005, El Paso, TX, 79920-0005. Rev. Jude Morgan, SS.CC., V.A. Medical Center, First Ave., at 24th. St., New York, NY, 10010-5050. Rev. Austin Nagle, SS.CC., V.A. Hospital, Belmont St., Brockton, 02401-5599.

NEW BEDFORD. *Marian Friary of Our Lady, Queen of the Seraphic Order*, 600 Pleasant St., 02740-6299. Tel: 508-996-8274. Mailing Address: P.O. Box 3003, 02741-3003. Martin Mary of the Crucified Jesus (Fonte), F.F.I. Revs. Francis Mary of the Angels Pimental, F.F.I., Guardian; Peter Damian Mary of the Sacred Fehlner, F.F.I.; Martin Mary of the Crucified Jesus Fonte, F.F.I. Priests 3; Brothers 15.

NORTH DARTMOUTH. *Holy Cross Mission House*, 824 Tucker Rd., 02747. Tel: 508-993-2238. Residence for Religious Priests and Brothers. Revs. Charles L. Wallen, C.S.C., Dir.; Thomas L. Campbell, C.S.C.; Mortimer A. Ferrick, C.S.C.; J. Marc Herbert; Thomas J. Tobin; John F. Dias, C.S.C.; Bro. Joseph L. Morris, C.S.C.

St. Joseph's Hall, 800 Tucker Rd., 02747-3599. Tel: 508-996-2413. Revs. J. Robert Rioux, C.S.C., Dir. of Province Dev.; Lawrence Jerge, C.S.C. Tel: 508-996-2410; Bro. Thomas Mahon, C.S.C. Priests 2; Brothers 1.

ONSET. *St. Joseph Novitiate-Franciscan Friars*, P.O.

Box 63, Robinwood Rd., 02558. Tel: 508-759-7280. Revs. Regis Gallo, O.F.M., Supr., Dir. of Novices; Gilbert J. Silverio, O.F.M., Assoc. Dir. of Novices; Bros. Juniper O'Connor, O.F.M., Cook; Costa Adamopolous, O.F.M., Novice; Peter Penten, O.F.M., Novice. Total Staff 2; Total in Residence 5.

[L] CONVENTS AND RESIDENCES FOR SISTERS

FALL RIVER. *Bishop's Residence Convent*, 394 Highland Ave., 02720. Tel: 508-675-1311. Sisters of Ste. Jeanne d'Arc. Sisters 3.

Convent of Dominican Sisters of Hope, 37 Park St., 02721. Tel: 508-676-3096. Sr. Catherine Walsh, O.P., Prioress Gen.

Convent of the Sacred Hearts, 47 Prospect Pl., 02720. Tel: 508-679-1044; 1045. Sisters of the Holy Union of the Sacred Hearts 20.

Franciscan Missionaries of Mary, Mary of Nazareth Novitiate, 621 2nd St., 02721. Tel: 508-673-2892. Franciscan Missionaries of Mary 8.

Holy Union Provincialate, 550 Rock St., 02720-3436. Tel: 508-678-3616; Fax: 508-324-0686. Sr. Theresa M. Horvath, S.U.S.C., Prov. Sisters of the Holy Union, Fall River Prov.

Other Convents: Our Lady of Mercy Convent, 70 Holcott Drive, Attleboro, 02703. 116 Cory St., 02720. 18 Pear St., 02720. 161 Shawmut St., 02720. Sisters 3. Sacred Hearts Convent, 47 Prospect Place, 02720-5403. Sisters 20. Catholic Memorial Home, 2446 Highland Ave., 02720. Sisters 6. 527 Rock St., 02720. Sisters 2. 570 Rock St., 02720. Sisters 7. St. Patrick's Convent, 55 Tuttle St., 02720. 601 King Philip St., Apt. #37, Raynham, 02767. Sisters 2. 12 Woodridge Rd., Sandwich, 02563. 7 Bradford St., Taunton, 02780. Sisters 2. 34 Mitchell Dr., Apt. 71H, 02724. St. Anthony Convent, Taunton. Sisters 7. 82 Eldridge St., Taunton, 02780.

Residence of the Sisters of the Sacred Hearts, 491 Hood St., 02720. Tel: 508-675-7716. Congregation of the Sacred Hearts of Jesus and Mary and of Perpetual Adoration. Sisters 4.

Other Convents: 35 Huttleston Ave., Fairhaven, 02719. Tel: 508-994-9341. Sisters 3. 44 Adams St., Fairhaven, 19027. Tel: 508-994-5917. Sisters 4.

St. Patrick's Convent, 55 Tuttle St., 02724. Tel: 508-673-0796. Sr. M. Romana Murphy, R.S.M., Coord. Sisters 9.

Sisters of Mercy, 2425 Highland Ave., 02720. Tel: 508-679-8511, Ext. 319. Sr. M. Lourdette Harrold, Contact. Sisters of Mercy of the Americas 5; Total Assisted 103; Total Staff 250.

ATTLEBORO. *Our Lady of Mercy Convent*, 70 Holcott Dr., 02703. Tel: 508-226-4608. Sr. Rose Angela McLellan, R.S.M., Local Coord. Sisters 24.

DIGHTON. *Dominican Sisters of Charity of the Presentation of the Blessed Virgin*, 3012 Elm St., 02715. Tel: 508-669-5425; 669-5023 (Novitiate); Fax: 508-669-6521. Sr. Joanna Fernandes, O.P., Prov. Supr. Provincial House-Residence, Residence for Aged Sisters, Novitiate. Sisters 23.

FAIRHAVEN. *Franciscan Sisters of the Immaculate*, 382 Main St., 02719. Tel: 508-992-0482.

Sisters of the Sacred Hearts of Jesus and Mary and of Perpetual Adoration, SS.CC, 35 Huttleston Ave., 02719. Tel: 508-994-9341. Sr. Dolores Paveo, SS.CC., Regional Supr.

44 Adams St., 02719. Tel: 508-994-5917. Sr. Lillian Cookson, SS.CC., Supr.

NEW BEDFORD. *Misioneras Guadalupanas del Espiritu Santo*, 2 Acushnet Ave., 02744. Tel: 508-997-8729. Sr. Gloria Rodriguez, M.G.Sp.S., Supr.; Sr. M. Candelaria Hernandez; Sr. Soledad Mendoza; Sr. Ladivel Diaz; Sr. Obdulia Olivar. Sisters 5.

Sisters of Mercy, 15 Lemos St., 02740. Tel: 508-992-4947. Sr. M. Nathan Doherty, R.S.M., Contact Person. Sisters 3.

NORTH DARTMOUTH. *Diocesan Family Life Center*, 500 Slocum Rd., 02747. Tel: 508-999-4620; Fax: 508-999-6430. Total Staff 3.

Dominican Sisters of Hope, 856 Tucker Rd., 02747. Tel: 508-996-1305. Sisters 7.

TAUNTON. *Our Lady of Lourdes Convent*, 55 First St., 02780. Tel: 508-822-9206. Sr. M. Margretta Sol, Contact Person. Sisters of Mercy of the Union 3.

Villa Fatima, 90 County St., 02780. Tel: 508-822-6282. Sisters of St. Dorothy. Sr. Rosalie Patrello, S.S.D., Local Coord. Professed Sisters 10.

WAREHAM. *St. Patrick's Missionary Cenacle*, 86 High St., 02571. Tel: 508-295-0780. Missionary Servants of the Most Blessed Trinity 1.

[M] RETREAT HOUSES

ATTLEBORO. *La Salette Center for Christian Living*, 947 Park St., 02703-0965. Tel: 508-222-8530; Fax: 508-222-8558. Revs. Richard Landry, M.S., Dir.; Fern Cassista, M.S.; Mrs. Karen Laroche; Mr. Mark Moitoza; Bros. David Dumaine, M.S.; Roger A. Moreau, M.S. In res., Rev. Normand Theroux, M.S. Priests 2; Total Staff 12; Total Assisted 4,200.

EAST FREETOWN. *Cathedral Camp Retreat Center*, 167 Middleboro Rd., P.O. Box 428, 02717-0428. Tel: 508-763-3994. Sr. Joseph Marie Levesque, O.P., Dir. Total Staff 6; Total in Residence 1.

NORTH EASTON. *Holy Cross Fathers Retreat House*, 490 Washington St., Rte. 138, 02356-1294. Tel: 508-238-2051. Revs. Thomas E. Lawton, C.S.C., Dir.; Richard H. Sullivan, C.S.C., Asst. Dir. Priests 2.

[N] DEPARTMENT OF CATHOLIC SOCIAL SERVICES AND SPECIAL APOSTOLATES

FALL RIVER. *Catholic Social Services of Fall River*, 783 Slade St., P.O. Box M-S, Station, 02724. Tel: 508-674-4681; Fax: 508-675-2224. Arlene A. McNamee, Exec. Dir. Program Directors: Mary Lou Mancini, M.Ed., L.C.S.W., Pregnancy & Adoption Services; Maria C. Pereira, M.S.W., L.I.C.S.W., Counseling Services; Susan E. Desrosiers, M.S.W., L.S.W., Sexual Abuse Prevention.

Catholic Social Services of Attleboro, 10 Maple St., Attleboro, 02703. Tel: 508-226-4780.

Catholic Social Services of New Bedford, 59 Rockland St., New Bedford, 02740. Tel: 508-997-7337.

Catholic Social Services of Cape Cod, 261 South St., Hyannis, 02601. Tel: 508-771-6771.

Catholic Social Services of Taunton, 78 Broadway, Taunton, 02780. Tel: 508-824-3264.

Reaching Out, 311 Hooper St., Tiverton, RI, 02878. Tel: 401-624-9270.

St. Mathieu's Residence for Women, 189 Wellington St., 02720. Tel: 508-675-1868.

Special Apostolates, Department of, 783 Slade St., P.O. Box M-S, Station, 02724. Tel: 508-674-4681. Arlene A. McNamee, Executive Dir.

Campaign For Human Development Apostolate. Craig Gaspard, Commmunity Organizer.

Apostolate for Persons with Developmental Disabilities, 243 Forest St., 02721. Tel: 508-679-8373 (Voice); 679-4277 (TTY). Rev. Joseph F. Viveiros, Dir.

Spanish Apostolate, 2 Acushnet Ave., New Bedford, 02744. Tel: 508-997-8729. Gloria Rodriquez; Rev. Paul E. Canuel, Dir., P.O. Box 40605, New Bedford, 02744-0006. Tel: 508-997-8729.

[O] CAMPS AND COMMUNITY CENTERS

FALL RIVER. *Diocesan Catholic Youth Organization*, 42 Chicago St., 02721. Tel: 508-675-7503. Rev. Jay T. Maddock, Diocesan & Area Dir.

Fall River Area Catholic Youth Organization, 403 Anawan St., 02720. Tel: 508-672-9644.

New Bedford Area Catholic Youth Organization, Kennedy Youth Center, 377 County St., New Bedford, 02740. Tel: 508-996-0536. Rev. Andre H. Faria, Area Dir.

Taunton Area Catholic Youth Organization, 61 Summer St., Taunton, 02780. Tel: 508-822-5218. Deacon Thomas J. Souza, Area Dir.

[P] NEWMAN CENTERS AND CAMPUS MINISTRY

FALL RIVER. *Bristol Community College Newman Center*, 777 Elsbree St., 02720-7395. Sr. Annette Bibeau, S.S.A., (Full Time). Total Staff 1.

Diocesan Education Center, 423 Highland Ave., 02720. Tel: 508-678-2828; Fax: 508-674-4218. Rev. William T. Garland, Dir. of Education; Mr. James A. McNamee, Supt. of Secondary Schools; Deacon Bruce Bonneau, Dir. Religious Education; Rev. Mark R. Hession, Dir. Continuing Formation of Clergy; Sr. Anne M. Landry, C.N.D., Supt. of Elementary Schools; Lisa M. Gulino, Dir. of Adult Education.

BUZZARDS BAY. *Massachusetts Maritime Academy Newman Center*, 141 Main St., 02532. Rev. Vincent Nagle, Chap.

NORTH DARTMOUTH. *University of Massachusetts Dartmouth Catholic Campus Ministry*, 285 Old Westport Rd., 02747-2300. Tel: 508-999-8872. Campus Ministers: Rev. Michael Carvill; Sr. Madeleine Tacy, O.P. Total Staff 2.

NORTON. *Wheaton College Newman Center*. Rev. Thomas M. Feeley, C.S.C., Chap., Holy Cross Residence, 480 Washington St., N. Easton, 02356.

TAUNTON. *Paul A. Dever State School (For Retarded) Newman Center*, Box 631, 02780. Tel: 508-824-5881. Rev. William J. Beston, C.S.C., Chap.

WEST BARNSTABLE. *Cape Cod Community College Newman Center*.

[Q] MISCELLANEOUS LISTINGS

FALL RIVER. *Carmelite Convent of Dartmouth, Inc.*, c/o P.O. Box 2577, 02722.

Community Action for Better Housing, Inc., 783 Slade St., P.O. Box M, S. Station, 02724.

Diocesan Facilities Self-Insurance Group, Inc., P.O. Box 1110, 02722.

Office of AIDS Ministry, Inc., 243 Forest St., Clemence Hall, Rm. 225, 02721. Total Assisted 500.

Priestly Fraternity of the Missionaries of St. Charles Borromeo, Inc., 420 Bradford Ave., 02721. Tel: 508-676-8603. Revs. Michael Carvill; Vincent Nagle; Antonio Lopez.

St. Francis' Residence. A program of Catholic Social Services. 166, 182 and 196 Whipple St., 02721. Tel: 508-676-9332. Arlene A. McNamee, Executive Dir.; Susan E. Desrosiers, Coord.; Mrs. Zilda Fagundes, House Mgr. Residence for women. Boarders 34.

Saint Mary's Education Fund, Inc., P.O. Box 2577, 02722. Tel: 508-675-1311.

Youth Apostles, c/o David Sharland, 327 2nd St., 02721-2007. Tel: 508-672-2755. Deacon David Sharland, Dir. Total in Residence 4.

NEW BEDFORD. *The Institute of the Incarnate Word, Inc.*, 306 Ashley Blvd, 02746. Tel: 508-672-9303. Revs. Benito Lagos, I.V.E.; Eduardo Coll, I.V.E.

Missionaries of Charity, 556 County St., 02740. Shelter for homeless women. Total in Residence 4; Total Assisted 54.

St. Mary's Home of New Bedford, Inc. c/o P.O. Box 2577, Fall River, 02722. Tel: 508-675-1311.

RELIGIOUS INSTITUTES OF MEN REPRESENTED IN THE DIOCESE

For further details refer to the corresponding bracketed number in the Religious Institutes of Men or Women section.

[0320]—*Brothers of Christian Instruction.*—F.I.C.
[0330]—*Brothers of the Christian Schools.*
[0600]—*Brothers of the Congregation of Holy Cross.*
[]—*Capuchin Recollects Friars.*
[1330]—*Congregation of the Mission.*—C.M.
[1140]—*Congregation of the Sacred Hearts of Jesus and Mary.*—SS.CC.
[0480]—*Conventual Franciscans.* (Buffalo, NY).—O.F.M.Conv.
[0470]—*Franciscan (Order of Friars Minor Capuchin).* (St. Augustine Prov.).—O.F.M.Cap.
[0520]—*Franciscan Friars.* (Immaculate Conception Prov.).—O.F.M.
[0533]—*Franciscan Friars of the Immaculate.*—F.F.I.
[]—*The Institute of the Incarnate Word.*—I.V.E.
[0690]—*Jesuit Fathers and Brothers.*—S.J.
[0720]—*The Missionaries of Our Lady of La Salette.*—M.S.
[0870]—*Montfort Missionaries.*—S.M.M.
[0430]—*Order of Preachers (Dominicans).*—O.P.
[]—*Priestly Fraternity of the Missionaries of St. Charles Borromeo Order.*—C.S.
[0610]—*Priests of the Congregation of the Holy Cross.* (Eastern Prov.).—C.S.C.

RELIGIOUS INSTITUTES OF WOMEN REPRESENTED IN THE DIOCESE

[]—*Capuchin Recollects Sisters.*
[0330]—*Carmelite Sisters of the Aged and Infirm.*—O.Carm.
[3815]—*Congregation of the Sisters of St. Joan of Arc.*—S.J.A.
[0750]—*Daughters of the Charity of the Sacred Heart of Jesus.* (Sacred Heart Prov.).—F.C.S.C.J.
[1070-23]—*Dominican Sisters.*—O.P.
[1100]—*Dominican Sisters of Charity of the Presentation of the Blessed Virgin.*—O.P.
[]—*Dominican Sisters of Hope.*—O.P.
[1370]—*Franciscan Missionaries of Mary.*—F.M.M.
[]—*Franciscan Sisters of the Immaculate.*—F.S.I.
[2580]—*Institute of the Sisters of Mercy of the Americas.* (Hartford, CT; Manchester, NH).—R.S.M.
[3790]—*Institute of the Sisters of St. Dorothy.*—S.S.D.
[2790]—*Missionary Servants of the Most Blessed Trinity.*—M.S.B.T.
[]—*Missioneras Guadalupanas del Espirito Santo.*
[3240]—*Poor Sisters of Jesus Crucified and the Sorrowful Mother.*
[3410]—*Religious of Christian Education.*—R.C.E.
[3450]—*Religious of Jesus and Mary.*—R.J.M.
[2070]—*Religious of the Holy Union of the Sacred Hearts.* (Immaculate Heart and Sacred Heart Provs.).—S.U.S.C.
[3650]—*Servants of Our Lady, Queen of the Clergy.*—S.R.C.
[0560]—*Sisters of Charity of Quebec (Grey Nuns).*—S.C.Q.
[0590]—*Sisters of Charity of Saint Elizabeth (Convent Station).*—S.C.
[0640]—*Sisters of Charity of St. Vincent de Paul (Halifax).*—S.C.
[3000]—*Sisters of Notre Dame De Namur.*—S.N.D.deN.
[3720]—*Sisters of Saint Anne.*—S.S.A.
[1705]—*The Sisters of St. Francis of Assisi.*—O.S.F.
[3830-16]—*Sisters of St. Joseph.*—S.S.J.
[3860]—*Sisters of St. Joseph of Cluny.*—S.J.C.
[2980]—*Sisters of the Congregation of Notre Dame.*—C.N.D.
[3180]—*Sisters of the Cross and Passion.*—C.P.

[1830]—*Sisters of the Good Shepherd.*—R.G.S.
[]—*Sisters of the Holy Cross.*
[]—*Sisters of the Holy Cross and of the Seven Dolors.*—C.S.C.
[3480]—*Sisters of the Resurrection.*—C.R.
[3690]—*Sisters of the Sacred Hearts of Perpetual Adoration.*—SS.CC.
[4048]—*Society of the Sisters, Faithful Companions of Jesus.*—F.C.J.

DIOCESAN CEMETERIES

FALL RIVER. *Notre Dame.*
St. John.
St. Mary.
St. Patrick.
ATTLEBORO. *St. John.*
St. Stephen.
EAST FALMOUTH. *St. Anthony.*
HYANNIS. *St. Francis.*
MANSFIELD. *St. Mary.*
MATTAPOISETT. *St. Anthony.*
NANTUCKET. *St. Mary.*
NEW BEDFORD. *St. John Sacred Heart.*
St. Mary.
NORTH ATTLEBORO. *St. Mary.*
NORTH EASTON. *Immaculate Conception.*
OAK BLUFFS. *Sacred Heart.*
PROVINCETOWN. *St. Peter.*
SANDWICH. *St. Peter.*
SOMERSET. *St. Patrick.*
TAUNTON. *St. Francis.*
St. James.
St. Joseph.
St. Mary.
TRURO. *Sacred Heart.*
WAREHAM. *St. Patrick.*
WELLFLEET. *Our Lady of Lourdes.*
WEST HARWICH. *Holy Trinity.*

NECROLOGY

† Andrade, Manuel, (Retired). —Died Dec. 27, 1995.

† Considine, Rev. Msgr. Raymond T., P.A., (Retired). —Died Oct. 15, 1996.

† D'Amico, Joseph, (Retired). —Died May 1, 1996.

† Gendreau, Rev. Msgr. Alfred J., (Retired). —Died April 12, 1996.

† Lamontagne, Maurice H., (Retired). —Died July 2, 1996.

† McCarrick, Paul F., Fall River, MA, Saint Joseph's Church. —Died Dec. 12, 1996.

† Monty, Raymond P., (Retired). —Died Feb. 8, 1996.

† Pegnam, John W., (Retired). —Died April 16, 1996.

† Quinn, Justin J., (Retired). —Died June 14, 1996.

† Souza, Rev. Msgr. Maurice, (Retired). —Died Aug. 17, 1996.

Diocese of Fargo

(Dioecesis Fargensis)

Most Reverend

JAMES S. SULLIVAN, D.D.

Bishop of Fargo; ordained June 4, 1955; consecrated Auxiliary Bishop of Lansing September 21, 1972; appointed Bishop of Fargo April 2, 1985; installed May 30, 1985. *Res., Bishop's House, 608 Broadway, P.O. Box 1750, Fargo, ND, 58107.*

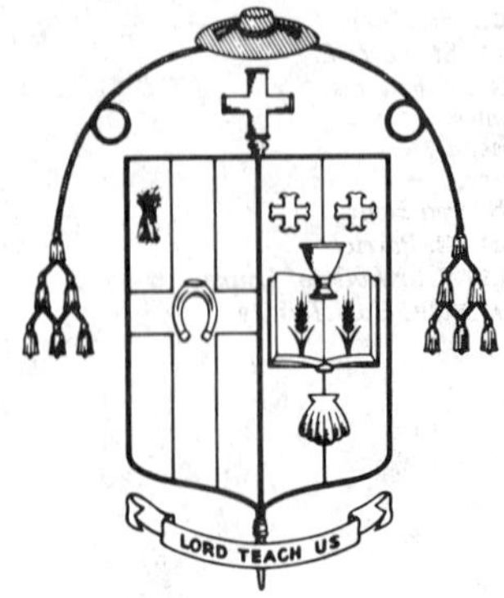

Chancery Office: 1310 Broadway, Box 1750, Fargo, ND, 58107. Tel.: 701-235-6429; Fax: 701-235-0296.

Corporate title: *The Diocese of Fargo.*

FORMERLY DIOCESE OF JAMESTOWN.

ESTABLISHED NOVEMBER 12, 1889. TRANSFERRED TO FARGO, APRIL 6, 1897.

Square Miles 35,786.

Comprises the Counties of Barnes, Benson, Bottineau, Cass, Cavalier, Dickey, Eddy, Foster, Grand Forks, Griggs, Kidder, LaMoure, Logan, McHenry, McIntosh, Nelson, Pembina, Pierce, Ramsey, Ransom, Richland, Rolette, Sargent, Sheridan, Steele, Stutsman, Towner, Traill, Walsh and Wells in the State of North Dakota.

For legal titles of parishes and diocesan institutions, consult the Chancery Office.

STATISTICAL OVERVIEW

Personnel	
Bishop	1
Priests: Diocesan Active in Diocese	82
Priests: Active Outside Diocese	13
Priests: Diocesan in Foreign Missions	1
Priests: Retired, Sick or Absent	40
Number of Diocesan Priests	136
Religious Priests in Diocese	10
Extern Priests in Diocese	7
Ordinations:	
Diocesan Priests	4
Transitional Deacons	6
Permanent Deacons in Diocese	35
Total Brothers	15
Total Sisters	220
Parishes	
Parishes	160
With Resident Pastor:	
Resident Diocesan Priests	71
Resident Religious Priests	6
Without Resident Pastor:	
Administered by Priests	83
Welfare	
Catholic Hospitals	8
Total Assisted	60,798
Homes for the Aged	8
Total Assisted	662
Educational	
Seminaries, Diocesan	1
Students from This Diocese	17
Students from Other Diocese	7
Diocesan Students in Other Seminaries	23
Seminaries, Religious	1
Students Religious	5
Total Seminarians	45
Colleges and Universities	1
Total Students	24
High Schools, Diocesan and Parish	1
Total Students	340
High Schools, Private	1
Total Students	19
Elementary Schools, Diocesan and Parish	12
Total Students	1,518
Catechesis/Religious Education:	
High School Students	5,225
Elementary Students	10,597
Total Students Under Catholic Instruction	17,768
Teachers in the Diocese:	
Brothers	4
Sisters	9
Lay Teachers	184
Vital Statistics	
Receptions into the Church:	
Infant Baptism Totals	1,570
Adult Baptism Totals	68
Received into Full Communion	107
First Communions	1,558
Confirmations	1,646
Marriages:	
Catholic	309
Interfaith	278
Total Marriages	587
Deaths	905
Total Catholic Population	98,915
Total Population	390,400

Former Bishops—Rt. Rev. JOHN SHANLEY, D.D., ord. 1874; cons. Dec. 27, 1889; died July 16, 1909.—Most Rev. JAMES O'REILLY, D.D., ord. June 24, 1880; cons. May 19, 1910; installed June 1, 1910; died Dec. 19, 1934.—His Eminence ALOISIUS CARDINAL MUENCH, ord. June 8, 1913; appt. Bishop of Fargo, Aug. 10, 1935; cons. Oct. 15, 1935; installed Nov. 6, 1935; appt. Apostolic Visitator for Germany, July 8, 1946 granted personal title of Archbishop, Nov. 1, 1950; appt. Papal Nuncio to Germany, March 10, 1951; created Cardinal Priest and elevated to the Roman Curia, Dec. 14, 1959; died Feb. 15, 1962.—Most Rev. LEO F. DWORSCHAK, ord. May 29, 1926; appt. Coadjutor Bishop of Rapid City, June 23, 1946; cons. August 22, 1946; appt. Auxiliary Bishop of Fargo, April 10, 1947; succeeded to See, May 10, 1960; resigned and retired Sept. 8, 1970; died Nov. 5, 1976.—Most Rev. JUSTIN A. DRISCOLL, ord. July 28, 1945; appt. Bishop of Fargo, Sept. 8, 1970; ord. Bishop of Fargo and installed Oct. 28, 1970; died Nov. 19, 1984.

Chancery Office—1310 Broadway, Box 1750, Fargo, 58107. Tel: 701-235-6429; Fax: 701-235-0296.

Vicar General—Rev. Msgr. WENDELYN VETTER, V.G.

Moderator of the Curia—Rev. T. WILLIAM COYLE, C.SS.R.

Chancellor—Rev. T. WILLIAM COYLE, C.SS.R.

Vice-Chancellor—Rev. DANIEL PILON, J.C.L.

Vice-Chancellor / Priest Secretary to the Bishop—Rev. STEVEN REISKE.

Special Assistant to the Bishop & Vice-Chancellor for Research & Grants—J. RITTER HARSY.

Archivist—Sr. MARY JAMES MERRICK, O.S.F.

Fiscal Manager—SCOTT HOSELTON, C.P.A.

Diocesan Tribunal—2537 S. University Dr., Fargo, 58103. Tel: 701-235-7279.

Officialis—Rev. Msgr. WENDELYN VETTER, V.G.

Vice-Officialis—Rev. DANIEL PILON, J.C.L., Adjutant Judicial Vicar.

Promotor Justitiae—Very Rev. VALERIAN PACZEK, J.C.D.

Defensor Vinculi—Very Rev. VALERIAN PACZEK, J.C.D.

Judges—Rev. ALBERT H. BINDER; Very Rev. JOHN D. ANDERSON; Rev. Msgr. WENDELYN VETTER, V.G.; Very Rev. VAL GROSS; Revs. AL M. BITZ; LEONARD BURCKHARD; DANIEL PILON.

Advocates—MARILYN BITTNER; Sr. CELINE FOY, P.B.V.M.; ELLEN O'CONNOR; Deacon DONALD TINGUELY; IONE NIELAND.

Notaries—SCOTT HOSELTON, C.P.A.; J. RITTER HARSY; Rev. T. WILLIAM COYLE, C.SS.R.; SUSAN M. FEAKES.

Diocesan College of Consultors—Rev. Msgr. WENDELYN VETTER, V.G.; Revs. DONALD LEIPHON; BRIAN DONAHUE; FRANKLIN MILLER; Very Rev. VAL GROSS; Revs. DALE KINZLER; GERALD MCCARTHY; PETER HUGHES, C.S.Sp.

Deans—Southeast: Very Rev. JOHN D. ANDERSON; Hankinson; East Central South: Very Rev. VAL GROSS; West Fargo; East Central North: Very Rev. ROMAN E. LUDWIG, Larimore; North East: Very Rev. GERALD MYERS, Walhalla; North Central: Very Rev. ROBERT SKAROHLID, Lakota; North West: Very Rev. GEORGE SCHNEIDER, Rolla; West Central: Very Rev. JOSEPH P. SENGER, Velva; South Central: Very Rev. BERNARD PFAU, Jamestown; South West: Very Rev. ADAM HASEY, Oakes.

Diocesan Pastoral Council—Most Rev. JAMES S. SULLIVAN, Pres. Priest Representatives: Area 1, Rev. DONALD A. LEIPHON; Area 2, Very Rev. ROMAN LUDWIG; Area 3, Rev. LEO KINNEY; Area 4, Rev. CHAD WILHELM. Deacon Representatives: Deacon GEORGE ETHIER. Sister Representatives: Sr. PAULA RINGUETTE, P.B.V.M.; Sr. MARLYSS DIONNE, S.M.P. Lay Representatives: Deanery 1, KATHLEEN SKROCH; Deanery 2, STUART LONGTIN; Deanery 3, SUSAN SPICER; Deanery 4, JEFFREY BATES; Deanery 5, LINDA CULLMER; Deanery 6, JAMIE BRADLEY; Deanery 7, BETTY REGSTAD; Deanery 8, DARLENE WESHNEVSKI; Deanery 9, GARY HORSAGER; FRANCIS MLARNIK, Lay Member at Large; Deacon DAVID EBLEN, Chm. Ex-Officio Members: Rev. Msgr. WENDELYN VETTER, V.G.; Revs. T. WILLIAM COYLE, C.SS.R., Moderator of the Curia; TIMOTHY SCHROEDER; JO RITTER HARSY, Vice Chancellor & DPC Sec. SCOTT HOSELTON, Fiscal Mgr.; Rev. GREGORY SCHLESSELMANN; Dr. SHERRYL HOUDEK; TERRY KNOEPFLE. Emeritus Members: ROBERT ARTZ; Revs. PETER HUGHES, C.S.Sp.; JAMES MEYER; Sr. MARY JAMES MERRICK, O.S.F.; BERNIE WAGNER; RALPH ERICKSON.

Diocesan Offices and Directors

Corporate Board—Most Rev. JAMES S. SULLIVAN; Rev. Msgr. WENDELYN VETTER, V.G.; Rev. T. WILLIAM COYLE, C.SS.R.; Rev. Msgr. ALLAN F. NILLES; Very Rev. JOHN D. ANDERSON; TERRY W. KNOEPFLE; SCOTT HOSELTON, C.P.A.; ROY WASCHE.

Administration Board of Minor Seminary—Rev. Msgr. ANTHONY R. PESCHEL; Rev. Msgr. WENDELYN VETTER, V.G.,Consilium pro Re Temporali; Very Rev. VAL GROSS, Oeconomus.

Apostleship of Prayer—Rev. ROMAN LUDWIG, Dir.

Diocesan Finance Council—Most Rev. JAMES S. SULLIVAN, Pres.; Rev. Msgr. WENDELYN VETTER, V.G.; Rev. T. WILLIAM COYLE, C.SS.R., Moderator of the Curia; GERALD F. HAMERLIK; GARY DIETZ; MICHAEL FIX; RAY SIMON; SCOTT A. HOSELTON, C.P.A.; Very Rev. VAL GROSS; TERRY W. KNOEPFLE; DWAYNE SHELTON; Rev. FRANKLIN MILLER; JOHN FLAKES.

The Catholic Church Expansion Fund of the Diocese of Fargo—Most Rev. JAMES S. SULLIVAN; Rev. Msgr.

WENDELYN VETTER, V.G.; Revs. T. WILLIAM COYLE; RICHARD M. GOELLEN; Rev. Msgr. ALLAN F. NILLES; Very Rev. JOHN D. ANDERSON; SCOTT A. HOSELTON, C.P.A.; TERRY W. KNOEPFLE; ROY WASCHE.

Censor Librorum—Rev. ROBERT LALIBERTE.

Catholic Family Service—ROGER E. SCHWINGHAMMER, Dir., *2537 S. University Dr., Fargo, 58103.* Tel: 701-235-4457; Fax: 701-239-8266., Grand Forks Office: *505 University Ave., Ste. 1, Grand Forks, 58203.* Tel: 701-775-4196; Fax: 701-775-0129.

Office of Liturgy and Worship—Rev. JAMES A. LEITH, J.C.D., Dir. Tel: 701-235-6429.

Continuing Education of Priests—Rev. ROBERT LALIBERTE, Chm.

Due Process Board Members (Conciliators)—Rev. Msgr. ALLAN F. NILLES, Chm.; Revs. EDWARD SHERMAN; GERALD MCCARTHY; JOSEPH AXTMANN; PETER GRADY; Sr. MARY JANE REIBER, O.S.F.; Sr. LEONIDA SCHMIDT, O.S.F.; Sr. ELIZABETH ROSE MUSCHA, S.M.P.; JOHN D. KELLY; PAUL CRARY; JOSEPH BLACK.

Ecumenical Commission—Rev. C. RICHARD RUDD.

Vicar for Diocesan Development—Very Rev. VAL GROSS. *Director of Development*—DOUG TOLLEFSON. Tel: 701-235-6429.

Director of God's Gift Appeal—DOUG TOLLEFSON.

Catholic School Network Office—Dr. SHERRYL HOUDEK, Acting Prin. MICHAEL HOGEN, Pub. Rels. for enrollment, *705 13th Ave. N., P.O. Box 7100, Fargo, 58109.* Tel: 701-293-3780.

Villa Nazareth—Sr. PAULA RINGUETTE, P.B.V.M., Pres., *3004 11th St. S., Fargo, 58103.* Tel: 701-235-8217.

Holy Childhood Association—Rev. JOSEPH J. SENGER, Dir., *St. Cecilia's Church, 201 Second Ave., W. Velva, 58790.* Tel: 701-338-2663.

Migrant Workers Apostolate—Rev. C. JAMES JEFFREY, Dir., All mail to go to: *Church of St. Bridget, 201 1st St. S., Box 280, Cavalier, 58220.*

Media Office—CHARLES ELDREDGE; ANGIE PERGANDE.

The "New Earth"-Diocesan Newspaper—CHARLES ELDREDGE.

North Dakota Catholic Conference—CHRISTOPHER DODSON, *227 W. Broadway, Ste. 2, Bismarck, 58501.*

Permanent Diaconate—Deacon MATT PROM, Dir.

Priests Mutual Aid Fund—Most Rev. JAMES S. SULLIVAN, Chm.; Very Rev. VAL GROSS, Sec. & Treas.

Priests Eucharistic League—Rev. JOSEPH R. HUEBSCH, Dir.

Priests Personnel Board—Very Rev. JOHN D. ANDERSON, Chm.; Revs. PHILLIP ACKERMAN; FRANKLIN MILLER; MATT LANZ; GERALD MYERS.

Presbyteral Council—Rev. TIMOTHY SCHROEDER, Chm., All mail to go to: *Church of St. Mary, Box 175, Forman, 58032.*

Propagation of the Faith—Rev. JOSEPH SENGER, Dir., *St. Cecilia's Church, 201 Second Ave. W., Velva, 58790.*

Retreats—GEORGE LACHER, Bldg. Dir., *Queen of Peace Retreat Center, 1310 Broadway, Fargo, 58102.* Tel: 701-293-9286.

Rural Life Conference—Coords.: Deacon JAMES WEST, *Reynolds;* Rev. WILLIAM C. SHERMAN, *St. Michael's Church, 520 N. Sixth St., Grand Forks, 58201.*

St. Vincent de Paul Society—ORVILLE KELLY, Pres., *1425 First Ave. S., Fargo, 58102.* Tel: 701-235-5944.

Office for Evangelization—*P.O. Box 1750, Fargo, 58107.* Tel: 701-235-6429.

Department for Catholic Education and Formation—Rev. GREGORY SCHLESSELMANN.

Catechesis-Evangelization-Youth—KURT GUNWALL, B.A.; Deacon DAVID EBLEN.

Resource Center-Office Secretary—JACINTA GOERING, B.S.

Technology-Promotions—WILLIAM LAGE.

Department for Catholic Schools—Dr. SHERRYL HOUDEK, Supt. THOMAS FREI, Education Asst.

Vicar for Religious—Rev. DONALD A. LEIPHON, All mail to: *Church of St. Anthony, 204 2nd St. N., Fairmount, 58030.*

Vocation Coordinator—Revs. JEFFREY WALD; JAMES MEYER, *Cardinal Muench Seminary, 100-35th Ave. N.E., Fargo, 58102.*

Office of Priestly Formation—Rev. JEFFREY WALD.

Diocesan Pension Plan for Lay Employees—SCOTT A. HOSELTON, C.P.A.

Pro-Life—RACHELLE SAUVAGEAU, Coord. Tel: 701-235-6429.

Catholic Cemeteries—Rev. T. WILLIAM COYLE, C.SS.R.

Diocesan Planning and Survey Board—Very Revs. JOHN D. ANDERSON; VAL GROSS; JOSEPH T. SENGER; DALE LAGODINSKI; ROBERT SKAROHLID; GEORGE SCHNEIDER; ROMAN LUDWIG; BERNARD PFAU; ADAM HASEY.

Diocesan Building Committee—Rev. LEONARD LOEGERING, Chm.

World Apostolate of Fatima (Blue Army)—Rev. DAMIAN HILS.

Cursillo Movement—Very Rev. JOHN D. ANDERSON.

Engaged Encounter—Rev. GERALD A. MCCARTHY.

Marriage Encounter—Rev. DALE KINZLER.

Catholic Scouting—Rev. GREG SMITH.

Apostolate for Spanish Speaking—Rev. C. JAMES JEFFREY, *St. Bridget Church, Box 280, Cavalier, 58220.*

Beginning Experience Apostolate—Rev. Msgr. WENDELYN VETTER, V.G.

Clergy Credit Union at Carmel of Mary, Wahpeton—Rev. DONALD LEIPHON.

Prison Apostolate—Very Rev. JOSEPH SENGER.

Liaison with Charismatic Movement—Rev. ADAM J. HASEY.

CLERGY, PARISHES, MISSIONS AND PAROCHIAL SCHOOLS

CITY OF FARGO
(Cass County)

1—ST. MARY'S CATHEDRAL (1880). Also serving Argusville and Merit Care Hospital. Revs. Peter Hughes, C.S.Sp.; Fernando Sayasaya; Matthew Pamplaniyil; Deacon Julian Mrozla.
Office: 619 7th St. N., 58102. Tel: 701-235-4289; 235-4280; Fax: 701-235-6354.
Res., 679 6th Ave., N., 58102. [JC]
Mission—Argusville, St. William.

2—HOLY SPIRIT (1951). Also serving Vets' Hospital. Revs. Phillip Ackerman; Damien Schill; Deacon James Perius.
Res., 1420 N. 7th St., 58102. Tel: 701-232-5900; Fax: 701-232-5902. [JC]
School—1441 8th St. N., 58102. Mr. Tim Jacobson, Prin.
Lay Teachers 11; Students 138.

3—NATIVITY (1960). Also serving Riverview, Dakota Heartland Hospital. Revs. Dale Kinzler; Kazimierz Kopacz; Sr. Ruth Gerates, P.B.V.M., Pastoral Assoc.; Deacon Maurice Van Houtte.
Res., 1825 11th St. S., 58103. Tel: 701-232-2414; Fax: 701-232-4491. [JC]
School—Tel: 701-232-7461. Cindy Hutchins, Prin.
Lay Teachers 22; Students 274.

4—SS. ANNE & JOACHIM (1995), Very Rev. Val Gross.
3329 S. University Dr., 58103. Tel: 701-235-5757; Fax: 701-235-0651.
Res., 2501 58th Ave. S.W., 58104. Tel: 701-235-1514.

5—ST. ANTHONY OF PADUA (1917). Also serving Heartland Medical Center (formerly St. John Hospital), and Cass County Jail. Rev. Msgr. Wendelyn Vetter, V.G.; Revs. Damien Hils; Jude F. Vos; Deacon Math Prom. In res., Rev. Leonard Burckhard.
Res., 710 S. 10th St., 58103. Tel: 701-237-6063; Fax: 701-237-6064. [JC]
School—St. Anthony's Junior High, 719 9th St., 58103. Tel: 701-232-3296. Mr. Bob Dignan, Prin.
Lay Teachers 15; Students 246.
Mission—Kindred, St. Maurice.

6—ST. PAUL NEWMAN CENTER, N.D.S.U. (1957), Rev. Paul Duchschere. In res., Rev. Steven Reiske, Sec. to the Bishop.
Res., 1129 N. University Dr., 58102. Tel: 701-298-9775.
Church—1141 N. University Dr., 58102. Tel: 701-235-0142. [JC]

OUTSIDE THE CITY OF FARGO

Alice, Cass Co., St. Henry (1902). Served from Enderlin.
c/o 302 Bluff St., Enderlin, 58027.
Church—58003. [CEM]

Anamoose, McHenry Co., St. Francis Xavier (1899). Also serving Balfour, Drake and Esmond. Rev. Leo Kinney.
Res., Box 49, 58710. Tel: 701-465-3780. [CEM]
Missions—Drake, St. Margaret Mary. [CEM]
Balfour, St. Joseph; Esmond, St. Boniface.

Aneta, Nelson Co., Sacred Heart. Served from Cooperstown.
c/o P.O. Box 217, Cooperstown, 58425. Tel: 701-797-2624.

Ardoch, Walsh Co., St. John the Baptist (1883). Served from Minto.
c/o 629 3rd St., Box 316, Minto, 58261.

Argusville, Cass Co., St. William (1942). Served from St. Mary's Cathedral, Fargo.
c/o 619 7th St., N., Fargo, 58102. Tel: 701-235-4289.
Church—107 Drake Ave., 58005. Tel: 701-484-5211. [JC]

Ashley, McIntosh Co., St. David (1960). Served from Zeeland.
c/o P.O. Box 1, Zeeland, 58581. Tel: 701-423-5494.

Balfour, McHenry Co., St. Joseph's (1906). Closed. For inquiries for parish records contact the Chancery.

Balta, Pierce Co., Our Lady of Mount Carmel (1902). Also serving Fulda and Orrin. Rev. Vincent J. Tuchscherer.
Res., Box 428, 58313. Tel: 701-542-3326. [CEM]
Missions—Fulda, McHenry Co., St. Anselm. [CEM]
Orrin, Pierce Co., Sacred Heart. [CEM]

Bathgate, Pembina Co., St. Anthony (1883). Served from Walhalla.
c/o 801 Central Ave., Box 228, Walhalla, 58282. Tel: 701-549-2729. [CEM]

Bechyne, SS. Peter & Paul. Served from Michigan, ND.
c/o P.O. Box 332, Michigan, 58259. Tel: 701-259-2248.

Belcourt, Rolette Co., St. Ann (1885), Revs. Jacques Dolbec, S.O.L.T.; Robert J. Cronin, S.O.L.T.; Bro. John DeMay, S.O.L.T.
Res., Box 2000, 58316. Tel: 701-477-5601; Fax: 701-477-5602. [CEM]
Mission—Belcourt, Rolette Co., St. Anthony Indian Mission. [CEM]
St. Anthony (1895). Attended by St. Ann, Belcourt.
c/o P.O. Box 2000, 58316. Tel: 701-477-5601. [CEM]

Bisbee, Towner Co., Holy Rosary (1889). Served from Rolette.

Bottineau, Bottineau Co., St. Mark's (1905). Also serving Westhope. Rev. Kevin J. Boucher.
Res., 322 Sinclair St., 58318. Tel: 701-228-3164. [CEM]
Mission—Westhope, Bottineau Co., St. Andrew.

Bremen, Wells Co., St. Joseph (1896). Served from Fessenden.
c/o P.O. Box 325, Fessenden, 58438. Tel: 701-547-3430.

Brocket, Ramsey Co., St. Joseph's (1910). Served from Lakota.
c/o 109 East Ave., E., P.O. Box 509, Lakota, 58344. Tel: 701-247-2594. [CEM]

Buchanan, Stutsman Co., St. Margaret. Served from Jamestown.
c/o 622 1st Ave. S., Box 347, Jamestown, 58402. Tel: 701-252-0119.

Buffalo, Cass Co., St. Thomas (1900). Served from Casselton.
c/o 712 2nd St. N., Box 340, Casselton, 58012.

Burnstad, Logan Co., St. Clara (1915). Served from Napoleon.
c/o 401 Broadway, P.O. Box 305, Napoleon, 58561-9701. Tel: 701-754-2860.

Cando, Towner Co., Sacred Heart (1893), Rev. John Sutton.
Res., 310 3rd Ave., P.O. Box 399, 58324. Tel: 701-968-3462. [CEM]

Carrington, Foster Co., Sacred Heart (1887). Also serving Kensal, St. John's. Rev. Lawrence Haas.
Res., 663 1st St., S., P.O. Box 420, 58421. Tel: 701-652-2519. [CEM]
Mission—Kensal, Stutsman Co.

Casselton, Cass Co., St. Leo (1880). Also serving Buffalo. Rev. Al Bitz; Deacons Donald Tinguely; George Loegering.
Res., 712 2nd St., N., P.O. Box 340, 58012. Tel: 701-347-4609. [CEM]
Mission—Buffalo, St. Thomas. St. Leo's Religious Education Center, 152 8th Ave., N., 58012. Tel: 701-347-4611.

Cavalier, Pembina Co., St. Bridget's (1881). Also serving Neche. Rev. C. James Jeffrey.
Res., 201 First St., S., P.O. Box 280, 58220. Tel: 701-265-8877. [CEM]
Mission—Neche, Pembina Co., SS. Nereus and Achilleus. [CEM]

Cayuga, Sargent Co., SS. Peter and Paul (1916). Served from Forman.
c/o Box 175, Forman, 58032-0175. Tel: 701-724-3319.

Cogswell, Sargent Co., Our Lady of Mercy (1903). Served from Forman.
c/o Box 175, Forman, 58032-0175. Tel: 701-724-3319.

Conway, Walsh Co., St. Mark. Served from Pisek.
c/o Box 27, Pisek, 58273. Tel: 701-284-6060; Fax: 701-284-6331.

Cooperstown, Griggs Co., St. George's (1939). Also serving Aneta, Jessie. Rev. Luke Odor.
Res., P.O. Box 217, 58425. Tel: 701-797-2624. [CEM]
Missions—Jessie, Griggs Co., St. Lawrence. [CEM]
Aneta, Nelson Co., Sacred Heart. [CEM]

Courtenay, Stutsman Co., St. Mary's. Served from Sanborn.
c/o 1324 95 Ave. S.E., Sanborn, 58426. [CEM]

Crow Hill, St. Jerome. Served from Fort Totten.

Crystal, Pembina Co., St. Patrick (1892). Served from Park River.
c/o Hwy. 17 E., P.O. Box 110, Park River, 58270. Tel: 701-284-6165.

Dazey, Barnes Co., St. Mary (1899). Served from Sanborn.
Church—c/o P.O. Box 35, Sanborn, 58480.

Devils Lake, Ramsey Co., St. Joseph's (1884). Also serving Rutten (sometimes called Crary). Revs. Jeffrey Wald; Jude Vos; James Cheney; Deacon Lawrence Lange.
Res., 515 Fourth St., Box 898, 58301. Tel: 701-662-7558. [CEM]
School—Tom Burckhard, Prin. Lay Teachers 11; Students 189.
Missions—Rutten, Ramsey Co., St. Benedict. [CEM]
Starkweather, Ramsey Co., Assumption of the Blessed Virgin Mary. [CEM]

Dickey, LaMoure Co., Assumption (1909). Served from LaMoure.
c/o 209 First St., S.E., Box 217, La Moure, 58458. Tel: 701-883-5987.

Drake, McHenry Co., St. Margaret Mary's (1910). Attended by St. Francis Xavier, Anamoose.
Res., 600 Main St., P.O. Box 197, 58736. [CEM]

Drayton, Pembina Co., St. Edward's (1889). Also serving St. Thomas, St. Thomas and Pembina, Assumption. Rev. Charles Fisher.
Res., 211 N. Main St., P.O. Box 215, 58225. Tel: 701-454-6171. [CEM]
Mission—St. Thomas, Pembina Co., St. Thomas. [CEM]

Dunseith, Rolette Co., St. Louis (1882). Also serving Immaculate Heart of Mary (Rolette Co.). Rev. Joseph H. Zimmer, S.A.C.
Res., 112 First St., N.W., Box 160, 58329. Tel: 701-244-5738. [CEM]
St. Louis and St. Mary's Catechetical and Mission Center—58329.
Mission—Indian, Rolette Co., Immaculate Heart of Mary, (1948).

Edgeley, LaMoure Co., Transfiguration (1915). Also serving Nortonville, Manor St. Joseph. Rev. Duaine M. Cote; Deacon Thurston Ham.
Res., 205 Second St., P.O. Box 347, 58433. Tel: 701-493-2387. [CEM]
Mission—Nortonville, LaMoure Co., Holy Spirit.

Ellendale, Dickey Co., St. Helena's (1888). Also serving Fullerton. Rev. Gary Luiten.
Res., 421 Second St. N., P.O. Box 796, 58436. Tel: 701-349-3297. [CEM]
Mission—Fullerton, Dickey Co., St. Patrick. [CEM]

Enderlin, Ransom Co., St. Patrick's (1908). Also serving Alice, Sheldon. Rev. Raymond Courtright.
Res., 302 Bluff St., 58027. Tel: 701-437-2791. [CEM]
Missions—Alice, St. Henry. [CEM]
Sheldon, St. Mary & Our Lady of the Scapular. [CEM]

Esmond, Benson Co., St. Boniface (1909). Served from Anamoose.
c/o Box 49, Anamoose, 58710.

Fairmount, Richland Co., St. Anthony's (1909). Also serving Carmel Convent. Rev. Donald A. Leiphon.
Res., 204 Second St. N., Box 292, 58030. Tel: 701-474-5518. [CEM]

Fessenden, Wells Co., St. Augustine's (1896). Also serving Bremen and Maddock. Rev. George B. Billman.
Res., P.O. Box 325, 58438. Tel: 701-547-3430.
Missions—Bremen, Wells Co., St. Joseph. [CEM]
Maddock, Benson Co., St. William.

Fingal, Barnes Co., Holy Trinity (1889). Attended by St. Bernard, Oriska.
c/o 606 Fifth St., Oriska, 58063. Tel: 701-845-3713.

Finley, Steele Co., St. Olaf. Served from Hope.
c/o P.O. Box 99, Hope, 58046. Tel: 701-945-2652.

Forman, Sargent Co., St. Mary's (1913). Also serving Cayuga, Cogswell, and Milnor. Rev. Timothy C. Schroeder; Deacons Richard Biss; David Gates.
Res., Box 175, 58032-0175. Tel: 701-724-3319. [CEM]
Missions—Cayuga, Sts. Peter & Paul. [CEM]
Cogswell, Our Lady of Mercy. [CEM]
Milnor, Sargent Co., St. Arnold. [CEM]

Fort Totten, Benson Co., Seven Dolors (1875). Also serving Crow Hill, Tokio. Rev. Charles J. Leute, O.P.; Deacon Anthony McDonald.
Res., P.O. Box 299, 58335. Tel: 701-766-4314.
Mission—Tokio, Benson Co., Christ the King.
Memorial Station, Crow Hill, St. Jerome—.

Fried, Stutsman Co., Sacred Heart (1888). Served from Jamestown.
c/o 622 First Ave. S., Box 347, Jamestown, 58402. Tel: 701-252-0119.

Fulda, McHenry Co., St. Anselm (1901). Served from Balta.
c/o Box 428, Balta, 58313.

Fullerton, Dickey Co., St. Patrick (1921). Served from Ellendale.
c/o 421 Second St. N., P.O. Box 796, Ellendale, 58436. Tel: 701-349-3297.

Gackle, Logan Co., St. Anne. Served from Windsor.
Mailing Address: c/o 207 Washington Ave., Cleveland, 58424. Tel: 701-763-6192.

Geneseo, Sargent Co., St. Martin's (1907). Served from Lidgerwood.
c/o 118 Second Ave. N.W., Box 449, Lidgerwood, 58053. Tel: 701-538-4608.
Church—58037. [CEM]

Grafton, Walsh Co., St. John the Evangelist's (1881). Also serving State School. Rev. Bert Miller; Sr. Donna Jean Chaput, Pastoral Assoc.
Res., 344 15th St. W., P.O. Box 636, 58237. Tel: 701-352-1648; Fax: 701-352-0499. [CEM]
St. John's Catechetical Center—58237. John W. Flakes, Admin. & Pastoral Assoc.; Linda Flakes, D.R.E.
Lay associates and workers 11.

Grand Forks, Grand Forks Co.,

1—Holy Family, (1960), Revs. Leonard Loegering; Samuel Ezeibekwe; Sr. Joanne Heim, Pastoral Assoc.; Deacon Samuel Pupino.
Res., 1122 18th Ave. S., 58201. Tel: 701-746-1454. [JC]
School—Mr. Charles Scherr, Prin. Sisters 1; Lay Teachers 10; Students 140.

2—St. Mary's, (1915), Rev. Jerald L.C. Finnestad; Deacon Don Litzinger.
216 Belmont Rd., 58201. Tel: 701-775-9318; Fax: 701-775-7568. [JC]
School—Dixie Klein, Prin. Lay Teachers 9; Students 105.

3—St. Michael's, (1872), Revs. William C. Sherman; James F. McKinney; Anthony J. Dudzinski; Deacon Albert Schmisek.
Res., 520 N. Sixth St., 58203. Tel: 701-772-2624; Fax: 701-772-0211. [JC]
School—Tel: 701-772-1822. Sharon Litchy, Prin. Sisters 1; Lay Teachers 14; Students 148.
St. James Religious Center—414 University Ave., 58203. Tel: 701-775-4261. Sr. M. Beata Seil, O.S.F., Admin.; Lois Stoltman, Dir.

4—St. Thomas Aquinas Parish, UND, (1951). Also serving Manvel. Revs. H. Gerard Braun; Paul Schuster; Bill Serb, Pastoral Assoc.
Res., 410 Cambridge St., 58201. Tel: 701-775-7129; Fax: 701-777-8905. [JC]

Granville, McHenry Co., Our Lady of Perpetual Help. Served from Towner.
c/o 503 First St., SW., Box 267, Towner, 58788. Tel: 701-537-5133.

Gwinner, Sargent Co., St. Vincent (1984). Served from Lisbon.
707 Oak St., P.O. Box 226, Lisbon, 58054-0226. Tel: 701-683-4620.

Hankinson, Richland Co., St. Philip's (1889), Very Rev. John D. Anderson.
Res., 612 S. Main, P.O. Box 419, 58041. Tel: 701-242-7327. [CEM]
St. Philip's Religious Education Center—(Grades K-12) St. Francis Convent, Hankison, 58041. Tel: 701-242-7800. Mr. William Hrdlicka, Prin.; Sr. Edwardine O.S.F., D.R.E.
Lay Teachers 29; Students 138.

Hansboro, Towner Co., Sacred Heart. Closed. For inquiries for parish records contact the Chancery.

Harvey, Wells Co., St. Cecilia's (1895). Also serving St. Aloysius Hospital and Selz, St. Anthony's. Rev. Vernon Smith.
Res., 413 E. Brewster St., 58341. Tel: 701-324-2144; Fax: 701-324-2640. [CEM]
St. Cecilia Religious Education Center—413 E. Brewster St., 58341. Tel: 701-324-2637.
Teachers 20; Students (Grades 1-8) 144; Students (Grades 9-12) 69.
Mission—Selz, Pierce Co.

Hillsboro, Traill Co., St. Rose of Lima (1892), Rev. C. Richard Rudd.
Res., 503 Third St. S.E., Box 459, 58045. Tel: 701-436-4541. [CEM]

Hope, Steele Co., St. Agatha's (1907). Also serving Finley and Page. Rev. Steven Meyer.
Res., P.O. Box 99, 58046. Tel: 701-945-2652. [CEM]
Missions—Finley, Steele Co., St. Olaf; Page, Cass Co., St. James. [CEM]

Hunter, Cass Co., St. Agnes (1898). Attended by Our Lady of Peace, Mayville.
c/o 435 E. Main St., Mayville, 58257. Tel: 701-874-2226. [CEM]

Hurdsfield, Wells Co., St. Patrick (1969). Served from Sykeston.
c/o P.O. Box 397, Sykeston, 58486. Tel: 701-984-2266.

Jamestown, Stutsman Co., The Basilica of St. James (1881). Also serving Buchanan, Fried, and Pingree. Very Rev. Bernard A. Pfau; Rev. John Lewandowski; Sr. Michaeleen Jantzer, O.S.B., Pastoral Min.; Deacon Tim Marcy.
Res., 622 First Ave. S., Box 347, 58402. Tel: 701-252-0119; Fax: 701-252-4453. [CEM]
School—St. John's Grade School. Sr. Dorothy Zeller, Prin.
Lay Teachers 10; Students (Grades PreK-6) 169.
St. James Religious Education—622 First Ave. S., P.O. Box 2093, 58042. Rita Kenna, D.R.E., Tel: 701-252-3397.
Lay Teachers 53.
Missions—Fried, Sacred Heart; Buchanan, St. Margaret; Pingree, St. Michael. [CEM]
Deacon Timothy Marcy.

Jessie, Griggs Co., St. Lawrence (1888). Served from Cooperstown.
c/o P.O. Box 217, Cooperstown, 58425. Tel: 701-797-2624.

Karlsruhe, McHenry Co., SS. Peter and Paul's (1903). Served from Velva.
c/o 201 Second Ave., W., Box K, Velva, 58790. [CEM]

Kensal, Stutsman Co., St. John's (1917). Served by Carrington.
c/o P.O. Box 420, Carrington, 58421.
Church—58455. Tel: 701-435-2876.

Kindred, Cass Co., St. Maurice (1965). Served from St. Anthony's, Fargo.
5313 165 Ave. N.E., 58081. Tel: 701-237-6063.

Kintyre, Logan Co., St. Boniface's (1906), Rev. John A. Bacevicius.
Res., 7103 26th Ave. S.E., 58549. Tel: 701-332-6636. [CEM]

Knox, Benson Co., St. Mary's (1936). Served from Leeds.
Mailing Address: Box 97, 58343. Tel: 701-538-2808.

Lake Williams, Kidder Co., Our Lady of the Lake (1946). Served from Tappen.
c/o P.O. Box 98, Tappen, 58487. Tel: 701-327-8344.

Lakota, Nelson Co., St. Mary's (1902). Also serving Brocket and Tolna. Rev. Robert F. Skarohlid.
Res., 109 East Ave., E., P.O. Box 509, 58344. Tel: 701-247-2594. [CEM]
Missions—Brocket, Ramsey Co., St. Joseph. [CEM]
Tolna, Nelson Co., St. Joseph.

La Moure, La Moure Co., Holy Rosary (1890). Also serving Dickey and Marion. Rev. Kevin Willis.
Res., 209 First St., S.E., Box 217, 58458. Tel: 701-883-5987. [CEM]
Missions—Marion, LaMoure Co., St. Francis, (1910); Dickey, LaMoure Co., Assumption. [CEM]

Langdon, Cavalier Co., St. Alphonsus (1888). Also serving Nekoma. Revs. Michael Schommer; Joseph Allen.
Res., 1010 Third St., 58249. Tel: 701-256-5966; Fax: 701-256-2358. [CEM]
School—Tel: 701-256-2354. Mr. Randy Hill, Prin. Sisters 1; Lay Teachers 11; Students 96.
Mission—Nekoma, Cavalier Co., St. Edwards, (1907).

Lankin, Walsh Co., St. Joseph's (1906). Attended by St. John Nepomucene, Pisek.
Church—Box 216, 58250. Tel: 701-593-6212. [CEM]
Box 27, Pisek, 58273.

Larimore, Grand Forks Co., St. Stephen's (1885), Very Rev. Roman E. Ludwig.
Res., 311 W. Front St., P.O. Box 778, 58251. Tel: 701-343-2377. [CEM]

Leeds, Benson Co., St. Vincent de Paul (1897). Also serving Knox and Minnewaukan. Rev. Mathias F. Lanz.
Res., 315 Central Ave., P.O. Box 307, 58346. Tel: 701-466-2777. [CEM]
Missions—Minnewauken, Benson Co., St. James. [CEM]
Knox, Benson Co., St. Mary. [CEM]

Leroy, Pembina Co., St. Joseph's (1873). Served from Walhalla.
c/o 801 Central Ave., Box 228, Walhalla, 58282. Tel: 701-549-3750.
Church—58252. [CEM]

Lidgerwood, Richland Co., St. Boniface's (1887). Also serving Geneseo. Rev. Eugene Gilles, S.A.C.
Res., 118 Second Ave., N.W., P.O. Box 449, 58053. Tel: 701-538-4608. [CEM]
Mission—Geneseo, Sargent Co., St. Martin. [CEM]

Lisbon, Ransom Co., St. Aloysius (1884). Also serving

Gwinner. Rev. John L. Evans, II.
Res., 707 Oak, P.O. Box 226, 58054-0226. Tel: 701-683-4620. [CEM]
Mission—Gwinner, Sargent Co., St. Vincent. [CEM]

Lomice, Walsh Co., St. Catherine (1936). Served from Michigan, ND.
c/o P.O. Box 332, Michigan, 58259. Tel: 701-259-2248. [CEM]

Maddock, Benson Co., St. William (1954). Served from Fessenden.
c/o P.O. Box 325, Fessenden, 58438. Tel: 701-547-3430.

Mantador, Richland Co., SS. Peter and Paul's (1906). Served from Mooreton.
c/o 204 Mooreton Ave., N., Mooreton, 58061. Tel: 701-274-8259.
Church—58058. [CEM]

Manvel, Grand Forks Co., St. Timothy's (1882). Served from St. Thomas Aquinas Newman, Grand Forks. Rev. Paul Schuster.
Church—511 Eighth St. W., P.O. Box 28, 58256. Tel: 701-696-2219. [CEM]

Marion, La Moure Co., St. Francis (1910). Served from LaMoure.
c/o 209 First St., S.E., Box 217, LaMoure, 58458.
Church—58466. [CEM]

Mayville, Traill Co., Our Lady of Peace (1945). Also serving Hunter. Rev. Bernard R. Schneider.
Res., 435 E. Main St., 58257. Tel: 701-786-3234. [CEM]
Missions—Hunter, Cass Co., St. Agnes. [CEM]
Mayville, State University Newman Club.

McClusky, Sheridan Co., Holy Family (1932). Served from Sykeston.
c/o P.O. Box 397, Sykeston, 58486. Tel: 701-984-2266. [CEM]

McHenry, Foster Co., SS. Peter & Paul (1912). Served from New Rockford.
c/o 116 First Ave., N., New Rockford, 58356. Tel: 701-947-5325. [CEM]

Medina, Stutsman Co., St. Mary. Served from Windsor.
c/o 207 Washington Ave., Cleveland, 58424. Tel: 701-763-6192. [CEM]

Michigan, Nelson Co., St. Lawrence O'Toole (1883). Also serving Bechyne and Lomice. Rev. Alfred Allmaras.
Res., P.O. Box 332, 58259. Tel: 701-259-2248. [CEM]
Missions—Bechyne, Walsh Co., SS. Peter & Paul. [CEM]
Lomice, Walsh Co., St. Catherine. [CEM]

Milnor, Sargent Co., St. Arnold's (1905). Attended by St. Mary, Forman.
c/o Box 175, Forman, 58032-0175.
Church—Box 295, 58060. Tel: 701-427-9288. [CEM]

Milton, Cavalier Co., St. Clotilde. Served from Wales.
Mailing Address: c/o P.O. Box 127, Wales, 58281. Tel: 701-283-5352. [CEM]

Minnewaukan, Benson Co., St. James (1899). Served from Leeds.
c/o 315 Central Ave., P.O. Box 307, Leeds, 58346. Tel: 701-466-2777. [CEM]

Minto, Walsh Co., Sacred Heart (1905). Also serving Ardoch. Rev. Feliks Lubas.
Res., 629 Third St., P.O. Box 316, 58261. Tel: 701-248-3589. [CEM]
Mission—Ardoch, Walsh Co., St. John the Baptist. [CEM]

Mooreton, Richland Co., St. Anthony's (1885). Also serving Mantador. Very Rev. Albert H. Binder.
Res., 204 Mooreton Ave., N., 58061. Tel: 701-274-8259. [CEM]
Mission—Mantador, Richland Co., Sts. Peter & Paul. [CEM]

Mount Carmel, Cavalier Co., Our Lady of Mount Carmel (1888). Served from Wales.
c/o P.O. Box 127, Wales, 58281. Tel: 701-283-5352. [CEM]

Munich, Cavalier Co., St. Mary's (1916), Rev. Joseph S. Axtmann.
Res., P.O. Box 159, 58352. Tel: 701-682-5178. [CEM]

Napoleon, Logan Co., St. Philip Neri (1906), Rev. James P. Lauerman, M.R.E.; Deacon Howard Hunkler.
Res., 401 Broadway, P.O. Box 305, 58561-9701. Tel: 701-754-2860. [CEM]
Mission—Burnstad, Logan Co., St. Clara. [CEM]

Neche, Pembina Co., SS. Nereus and Achilleus (1884). Attended by St. Bridget, Cavalier.
c/o 201 First St. S., Box 280, Cavalier, 58220. Tel: 701-886-7471. [CEM]

Nekoma, Cavalier Co., St. Edward (1907). Served from Langdon.
c/o 1010 Third St., Langdon, 58249. Tel: 701-256-5966. [CEM]

New Rockford, Eddy Co., St. John's (1896). Also serving McHenry. Rev. Jerome Hunkler.
Res., 116 First Ave. N., P.O. Box 389, 58356. Tel: 701-947-5325. [CEM]
Mission—McHenry, Foster Co., SS. Peter & Paul. [CEM]

Nortonville, LaMoure Co., Holy Ghost (Spirit) (1912). Served from Edgeley.
c/o 205 Second St., P.O. Box 347, Edgeley, 58433. Tel: 701-493-2387.

Oakes, Dickey Co., St. Charles Borromeo (1905). Also serving Oakes Community Hospital, Verona. Very Rev. Adam J. Hasey.
Res., 410 N. Seventh St., 58474. Tel: 701-742-2418. [CEM]
Mission—Verona, LaMoure Co., St. Raphael. [CEM]

Oakwood, Walsh Co., Sacred Heart (1881). Unassigned.
Res., R.R. No. 3, Box 151, Grafton, 58237. Tel: 701-352-1392. [CEM]

Olga, Cavalier Co., Our Lady of the Sacred Heart (1882). Served from Walhalla.
Res., H.C. 2, Box 102, Langdon, 58249. Tel: 701-549-3465. [CEM]

Oriska, Barnes Co., St. Bernard's (1908). Also serving Fingal. Rev. Gregory Schlesselmann.
Res., 606 Fifth St., 58063. Tel: 701-845-3713. [CEM]
Mission—Fingal, Barnes Co., Holy Trinity.

Orrin, Pierce Co., Sacred Heart (1903). Served from Balta.
c/o Box 428, Balta, 58313.
Church—58368. [CEM]

Osnabrock, Cavalier Co., St. Joseph (1909). Served from Wales.
c/o P.O. Box 127, Wales, 58281. Tel: 701-282-5352. [CEM]

Page, Cass Co., St. James (1909). Served from Hope.
c/o Box 99, Hope, 58046. Tel: 701-945-2652.
Church—58064. [CEM]

Park River, Walsh Co., St. Mary's (1888). Also serving St. Ansgar Hospital, Crystal. Rev. Msgr. Allan F. Nilles; Deacon Gerald F. Sobolik.
Res., Hwy. 17 E., P.O. Box 110, 58270. Tel: 701-284-6165. [CEM]
Mission—Crystal, Pembina Co., St. Patrick. [CEM]

Pembina, Pembina Co., Assumption of the Blessed Virgin Mary (1818). Served from Drayton.
Church—143 Hayden St., Box 151, 58271. Tel: 701-825-6266. [CEM]

Penn, Ramsey Co., Immaculate Conception. Closed. For inquiries for parish records contact St. Vincent de Paul, Leeds.

Pingree, Stutsman Co., St. Michael's (1905). Served from Jamestown.
c/o 622 First Ave. S., Box 347, Jamestown, 58402. Tel: 701-252-0119.
Church—58476. [CEM]

Pisek, Walsh Co., St. John Nepomucene (1886). Also serving Conway and Lankin. Rev. John Fallon.
Res., Box 27, 58273. Tel: 701-284-6060; Fax: 701-284-6331. [CEM]
Missions—Conway, Walsh Co., St. Marks. [CEM]
Lankin, Walsh Co., St. Joseph. [CEM]

Reynolds, Grand Forks Co., Our Lady of Perpetual Help (1895). Also serving Thompson. Rev. Kenneth F. Knoke.
Res., 424 Fifth St., Box 96, 58275. Tel: 701-847-2371. [CEM]
Mission—Thompson, Grand Forks Co., St. Jude. [CEM]

Rock Lake, Towner Co., Immaculate Heart of Mary. Served from Rolla.
c/o P.O. Box 788, Rolla, 58367. Tel: 701-656-3307.

Rolette, Rolette Co., Sacred Heart (1918). Also serving Willow City and Bisbee. Rev. Thomas Graner; Deacon Conrad Schuster.
Res., Box 127, 58366. Tel: 701-246-3449; Fax: 701-246-3449. [CEM]
Missions—Willow City, Bottineau Co., Notre Dame. [CEM]
Bisbee, Towner Co.
Immaculate Heart of Mary (1948). Attended by St. Louis, Dunseith.
c/o 112 First St., N.W., Box 160, Dunseith, 58329. Tel: 701-244-5738.

Rolla, Rolette Co., St. Joachim's (1894). Also serving Rock Lake and Rolla Community Hospital. Very Rev. George D. Schneider.
Res., 207 Second Ave. N.E., P.O. Box 788, 58367. Tel: 701-477-5277. [CEM]
St. Joachim Religious Education Center—P.O. Box 788, 58367. Tel: 701-477-3568.
Mission—Rock Lake, Towner Co.

Rugby, Pierce Co., St. Therese, Little Flower (1910), Rev. Daniel Miho Mrnarevic, Admin.; Deacon Edward Eberle.
Res., 218 Third St. S.E., 58368. Tel: 701-776-5327. [CEM]
School—306 Third Ave., S.E., 58368. Tel: 701-776-6740. Sr. Donna Welder, Admin.
Sisters of St. Francis of the Immaculate Heart of Mary (Hankinson, ND) 3; Lay Teachers 7; Students 104.
Little Flower Parish School of Religious Education—306 Third Ave. S.E., 58368. Tel: 701-776-6258. Joan Marie Scheet, D.R.E.
Lay Teachers 25.

Rutten, Ramsey Co., St. Benedict. Served from Devils Lake.
c/o 515 Fourth St., Box 898, Devils Lake, 58301. Tel: 701-662-7558. [CEM]

St. John, Rolette Co., St. John the Baptist (1882). Also serving St. Benedict Indian Mission (Rolette Co.). Rev. Gerald McCarthy.
Church—Box 170, 58369. Tel: 701-477-3081. [CEM]
Mission—Belcourt, Rolette Co., St. Benedict. [CEM]

St. Michael, Benson Co., St. Michael's (1874), Rev. Edward Sherman; Sr. Francis Marie Voight, S.M.P.
Res., P.O. Box 84, 58370. Tel: 701-766-4151. [CEM]

St. Thomas, Pembina Co., St. Thomas (1886). Served from Drayton.
c/o 211 N. Main St., P.O. Box 215, Drayton, 58225. Tel: 701-454-6171.
Church—58276. Tel: 701-257-6492. [CEM]

Sanborn, Barnes Co., Sacred Heart (1904). Also serves Dazey, Courtenay and Wimbledon. Rev. Chad Wilhelm.
Res., P.O. Box 35, 58480. Tel: 701-646-6306. [CEM]
Missions—Dazey, Barnes Co., St. Mary. [CEM]
Courtenay, Stustman Co.,; Wimbledon, Barnes Co.

Selz, Pierce Co., St. Anthony's (1917). Served from Harvey.
c/o 29 Girard St., Harvey, 58341-7316.

Sheldon, Ransom Co., St. Mary, Our Lady of the Scapular (1884). Served from Enderlin.
c/o 302 Bluff St., Enderlin, 58027. Tel: 701-437-2791.
Church—58068.

Starkweather, Ramsey Co., Assumption of the Blessed Virgin Mary (1905). Served from Devils Lake.
c/o 515 Fourth St., Box 898, Devils Lake, 58301. Tel: 701-662-7558.
Church—58377. Tel: 701-292-4301. [CEM]

Steele, Kidder Co., St. Francis de Sales (1958). Served from Tappen.
c/o P.O. Box 98, Tappen, 58487. Tel: 701-327-8344. [CEM]

Stirum, Sargent Co., St. Vincent. Closed. 1986. For inquiries for parish records contact St. Aloysius, Lisbon.

Sykeston, Wells Co., St. Elizabeth's (1905). Also serving Hurdsfield and McCluskey. Rev. Julian F. Kupisz.
Res., P.O. Box 397, 58486. Tel: 701-984-2266. [CEM]
Missions—Hurdsfield, Wells Co., St. Patrick; McClusky, Sheridan Co., Holy Family.

Tappen, Kidder Co., St. Paul's (1908). Also serving Lake Williams and Steele. Rev. Thomas J. Krupich.
Res., P.O. Box 98, 58487. Tel: 701-327-8344.
Missions—Lake Williams, Kidder Co., Our Lady of the Lake. [CEM]
Steele, Kidder Co., St. Francis de Sales. [CEM]

Thompson, Grand Forks Co., St. Jude's (1895). Served from Reynolds.
c/o 424 Fifth St., Box 96, Reynolds, 58275.
Church—58278. [CEM]

Tokio, Benson Co., Christ the King (Indian Mission). Served from Fort Totten.
c/o P.O. Box 299, Fort Totten, 58335. Tel: 701-766-4314.

Tolna, Nelson Co., St. Joseph's (1911). Served from Lakota.
c/o 109 E. E Ave., Box 509, Lakota, 58344.
Church—58380. [CEM]

Towner, McHenry Co., St. Cecilia's (1906). Also serving Granville. Rev. Ronald Yee Mon.
Res., 503 First St., S.W., Box 267, 58788. Tel: 701-537-5133. [CEM]
Mission—Granville, McHenry Co., Our Lady of Perpetual Help.

Valley City, Barnes Co., St. Catherine's (1882). Also serving Newman Center. Deacons Arlie Braunberger; Raphael Grim; Eugene Klein.
524 Third Ave., N.E., 58072. Tel: 701-845-0354. [CEM]
School—(Grades K-6). Tel: 701-845-1453. Mr. Ralph Dyrness, Prin.
Lay Teachers 5; Students 63.
St. Catherine's Parish Education Center—540 Third

Ave. N.E., 58072. Ralph Dyrness, Parish Education Dir.
Lay Teachers 22.

Velva, McHenry Co., St. Cecilia's (1906). Also serving Karlsruhe. Very Rev. Joseph P. Senger.
Res., 201 Second Ave. W., P.O. Box K, 58790. Tel: 701-338-2663. [CEM]
Mission—Karlsruhe, McHenry Co., Sts. Peter & Paul. [CEM]

Verona, LaMoure Co., St. Raphael (1898). Served from Oakes.
c/o 410 N. Seventh St., Oakes, 58474. Tel: 701-742-2418. [CEM]

Veseleyville, Walsh Co., St. Luke (1880). Served from Warsaw. Rev. Joseph F. Gregory, S.J.
Mailing Address: R.R. 1, Box 99, Minto, 58261. Tel: 701-248-3981. [CEM]

Wahpeton, Richland Co., St. John's (1876), Rev. Dale Lagodinski; Deacons Gene Hoefs; George Ethier; Ignatz Zach.
Office: 115 Second St. N., 58075. Tel: 701-642-6982. [CEM]
Res., 222 Dakota Ave., 58075. Tel: 701-642-4985.
School and Religious Education Office—122 Second St., N., 58075. Tel: 701-642-6116. Wilfred Sauer, Prin.
Lay Teachers 11; Students 156.
St. John Day Care Center—Tel: 701-642-4922. Bobbi Jo Neiber, Dir.
Staff 24; Students 111.

Newman Student Parish (1968), Rev. Dale Lagodinski, Campus Min. North Dakota State College of Science.
Office: 701 N. Seventh St., 58075. Tel: 701-642-3410.

Wales, Cavalier Co., St. Michael's (1889). Also serving Mount Carmel, Milton, and Osnabrock. Rev. Vincent Fitzpatrick.
Res., P.O. Box 127, 58281. Tel: 701-283-5352. [CEM]
Missions—Mount Carmel, Cavalier Co., Our Lady of Mount Carmel. [CEM]
Milton, Cavalier Co., St. Clothilde. [CEM]
Osnabrock, Cavalier Co., St. Joseph. [CEM]

Walhalla, Pembina Co., St. Boniface's (1848), Rev. Gerald Myers; Deacons Jim Carpenter; Alan Storey.
Res., 801 Central Ave., Box 228, 58282. Tel: 701-549-2729. [CEM]
Missions—Bathgate, Pembina Co., St. Anthony. [CEM]
Leroy, Pembina Co., St. Joseph. [CEM]
Olga, Cavalier Co., Our Lady of the Sacred Heart. [CEM]

Warsaw, Walsh Co., St. Stanislaus (1882). Also serves Veselyville. Rev. Joseph Gregory, S.J.
Rt. 1, Box 99, Minto, 58261. Tel: 701-248-3981. [CEM]

West Fargo, Cass Co., Blessed Sacrament (1945), Rev. John Cavanaugh; John Normandin, Pastoral Assoc. & D.R.E.
Res., 210 Fifth Ave. W., 58078. Tel: 701-282-4554; Fax: 701-282-6503. [JC]

Holy Cross (1981), Rev. James A. Leith, J.C.D.; Sr. Ruth Wirtzfield, Pastoral Assoc.; Deacons James Uline; Jack Lane.
Res., 1420 Cross Way, 58078. Tel: 701-282-7217; Fax: 701-277-9337. [JC]

Westhope, Bottineau Co., St. Andrew's (1904). Served from Bottineau.
Mailing Address: Box 365, 58793. Tel: 701-245-6171.

Wild Rice, Cass Co., St. Benedict's (1870), Rev. Daniel J. Pilon; Sr. Ann O'Brien, Pastoral Assoc.
Res., 11705 38th St., S., Horace, 58047. Tel: 701-588-4288. [CEM]

Willow City, Bottineau Co., Notre Dame des Victoires (1895). Attended by Sacred Heart, Rolette.
c/o Box 127, Rolette, 58366.
Church—R.R. 1, Box 167, 58384. Tel: 701-366-4771. [CEM]

Wimbledon, Barnes Co., St. Boniface's (1886). Unassigned. Served from Sanborn.
P.O. Box 9, 58492. Tel: 701-435-2310. [CEM]

Windsor, Stutsman Co., St. Mathias (1910). Also serving Gackle and Medina. Rev. Andrew Roehrich.
Res., 207 Washington Ave., Cleveland, 58424. Tel: 701-763-6192. [CEM]
Missions—Medina, Stutsman Co., St. Mary. [CEM]
Gackle, Logan Co., St. Anne.

Wishek, McIntosh Co., St. Patrick (1952). Served from Zeeland.
c/o Box 1, Zeeland, 58581. Tel: 701-423-5494. [CEM]

Wyndmere, Richland Co., St. John the Baptist (1912), Rev. James A. Meyer.
Res., 630 Sixth St., Box 68, 58081. Tel: 701-439-2200. [CEM]

Zeeland, McIntosh Co., St. Andrew's (1906). Also serving Ashley and Wishek. Rev. Franklin Miller.
Res., P.O. Box 1, 58581. Tel: 701-423-5494. [CEM]
Missions—Ashley, McIntosh Co., St. David; Wishek, McIntosh Co., St. Patrick. [CEM]

INDIAN MISSIONS

Turtle Mountain Reservation, (Chippewa Indians), *Missions*—Belcourt, St. Ann. Revs. Jaques Dolbec, S.O.L.T.; Robert J. Cronin, S.O.L.T.; Bro. John DeMay, S.O.L.T.; St. Anthony, Rolette Co., St. Anthony. Served from Belcourt. Revs. Jacques Dolbec, S.O.L.T.; Robert J. Cronin, S.O.L.T.; Bro. John DeMay, S.O.L.T.

Fort Totten Reservation, (Sioux Indians), *Missions*—Tokio, Christ the King. Rev. Charles Leute, O.P.; Fort Totten Reservation, Benson Co., Seven Dolors Indian Mission. Also serving Crow Hill, Tokio. Seven Sorrows Dr., Box 299, 58335. Tel: 701-766-4314. Rev. Charles Leute, O.P.

St. Michael, St. Michael's Indian Mission, Rev. Edward Sherman; Bro. Roman Sleger, O.S.B.

Chaplains of Public Institutions

FARGO. *Meritcare Hospital in Fargo*. Served from St. Mary Cathedral, Fargo. 619 N. Seventh St., 58102.
Veterans Administration Facility. Rev. Phillip Ackerman, Res., Holy Spirit Church, 1420 N. Seventh St., 58102.

DEVILS LAKE. *School for the Deaf*. Rev. Jeffrey Wald, Res., St. Joseph's Rectory, 515 Fourth St., Box 898, 58301.

GRAFTON. *Grafton State School*. Rev. Burt Miller, Res., St. John the Evangelist Church, 344 15th St. W., P.O. Box 636, 58237.

GRAND FORKS. *Grand Forks Air Force Base*. Rev. David Krogmann, Res., 1699 J. St., GFAFB, 58205.
School for the Blind. Rev. William C. Sherman, Res., St. Michael Church, 520 N. 6th St., 58203.

JAMESTOWN. *State Hospital*. Judith Poquette.

LISBON. *Soldier's Home*. Rev. John L. Evans, Res., St. Aloysius Church, 707 Oak St., Box 226, 58054.

Special Assignment:
Reverend Fathers—
Coyle, T. William, C.SS.R., Moderator of the Curia, 608 Broadway, Fargo, ND 58102
Donahue, Brian, Cardinal Muench Seminary, 100 35th Ave. N.E., Fargo, ND 58102
Gross, Richard J., Chap., United Hospital, 1220 S. Columbia Rd., Grand Forks, ND 58201
Laliberte, Robert L., Cardinal Muench Seminary, 100 35th Ave. N.E., Fargo, ND 58102
Potter, Gerald L., U.N.D., Box 7128 University Station, Grand Forks, ND 58202
Reiske, Steven, 1129 N. University Dr., Fargo, ND 58102
Skonseng, Dennis, Cardinal Muench Seminary, 100 35th Ave. NE, Fargo, ND 58102

On Duty Outside the Diocese:
Reverend Fathers—
Bachmeier, Bernard A., Mercy Hospital & Medical Center, 4077 Fifth Ave., San Diego, CA 92103
Bushy, Timothy F., Immaculate Conception Church, 702 Summit Ave., Crookston, MN 56716-2736
Cosentino, Jack A., St. Ambrose, P.O. Box 999, Deerfield Beach, FL 33441
Davis, John E., Apartado 134, Chimbote, Peru
Ermer, James R., Casa Santa Maria, Via Dell 'umilta' 30, Rome, 00187 Italy
Graven, John P., St. Polycarp Church, 8100 Chapman Ave., Stanton, CA 90680
LaCorte, Richard P., St. John the Cross Rectory, 950 82nd Ave., Vero Beach, FL 32966
McCauley, David, 475 University Ave., St. Paul, MN 55103

Military Chaplains:
Reverend Fathers—
Herron, Jack B. (CPT), Chap., USACHCS, CHOAC, 95-001, Fort Manmouth, NJ 07703-5612
Kawczynski, Ronald (LT), Chap., Asst. Regt Chaplains, 3942 Roebling Ln., Virginia Beach, VA 23452

Absent on Leave:
Reverend Fathers—
Feltis, Jerome
Haenke, Roger, 5501 Queens Ave. S., Minneapolis, MN 55410
Pietrus, Henryk

Retired:
Reverend Monsignors—
McNamee, William J., 715 Washington, Larimore, ND 58251
Peschel, Anthony R., 150 County Rd. 34 #210B, Arthur, ND 58006
Reverend Fathers—
Aleksonis, Vladas, Riverview Pl., 5300-12th St. S. # 303A, Fargo, ND 58104
Bolte, George, Holy Trinity, 417 First Ave., Fingal, ND 58031
Campbell, Joseph, 4 Lakeview Ave., Bella Vista, AR 72714
Conway, John, 3500 Dupont Ave. S., #203, Minneapolis, MN 55408
Cote, Donald J., RR #1, Hatton, ND 58240
Cullen, Martin T., R.R. 2, Box 271, Lake Park, MN 56554
Dickinson, Stephen, P.O. Box 667, Valley City, ND 58072-0667
Duda, Stanislaus J., 2911 Manitoba Ln., Bismarck, ND 58501
Duffy, Patrick, Box 63, Neche, ND 58265
Engelhardt, Adam J., Good Samaritan Center, 1414 20 St., N.W., E. Grand Forks, MN 56721
Filteau, Jerome E., Riverview Pl., 5320-12th St. S., Box 318E, Fargo, ND 58104
Grady, Peter W., Riverview Pl., 5220-12th St. S #206C, Fargo, ND 58104
Gregory, Joseph F., S.J., Rt. 1, Box 99, Minto, ND 58261
Huebsch, Joseph R., 514 First Ave. S.W., P.O. Box 98, Hankinson, ND 58041
King, Stephen D., Good Samaritan Nursing Home, Hwy. 18, Arthur, ND 58006
Koehler, Paul L., St. Gerard Nursing Home, P.O. Box 279, Hankinson, ND 58041
Krile, George F., Brentwood West, 3104 E. Broadway #211, Mesa, AZ 85204
Lang, Julius, P.O. Box 126, Naples, FL 33939
Lommel, George D., 509 Almeron Ave., Drayton, ND 57225
Mehok, William J., S.J., Riverview Place, 5320 12th St. S., #218, Fargo, ND 58104
Mentel, Joseph C., 912 27th St. N., Bismarck, ND 58501
Moore, John E., Riverview Pl., 5320 12th St. S. #322, Fargo, ND 58104
Mueller, Maurice M., Riverview Pl., 5320 12th St. S., #217E, Fargo, ND 58104
Mullins, Robert J., 1451 Third St., S.E., Apt. 306B, St. Cloud, MN 56301
Neva, Roman G., 417 Second St., N., Wahpeton, ND 58078
Paczek, Valerian, 24 Third Ave. S.W., Lidgerwood, ND 58053
Proeller, Ulric, Padua Place, 100 Peter Baque Rd., San Antonio, TX 78209
Richard, Antonio J., Riverview Place, 5300 12 St. S., #328E, Fargo, ND 58104
Scheller, Raymund B., 101 28th Ave., #15, San Mateo, CA 94403
Schill, Victor J., P.O. Box 12, Walhalla, ND 58282
Schue, Dennis L., Mercy Hospital, 1031 Seventh St., Devils Lake, ND 58301
Sinner, Richard W., 625 21st St.,#1, Fargo, ND 58103
Snell, Roger K., 404 Fourth Ave., Edgeley, ND 58433
Stelten, Leo F., Rt. 2, Box 651, Frazee, MN 54544
Studzinski, Lambert V., Riverview Place, 5320 12th St. S., #127E, Fargo, ND 58104
Walz, Julius J., 29259 Elias Ct., Chicago, IL 60608
Wild, David D.

Permanent Deacons:
Biss, Richard, St. Arnold, Milnor
Braumberger, Arlie, St. Catherine, Valley City
Buresh, Leonard, St. John the Evangelist, Grafton
Carpenter, Stanley, St. Boniface, Walhalla
Davis, Francis R., St. Ann, Belcourt
Didier, Harry, Jr., Sacred Heart, Sanborn
Eberle, Edward, St. Therese Little Flower, Rugby
Eblen, David, St. Rose of Lima, Hillsboro
Ethier, George, St. John, Wahpeton
Faul, Jeffrey, St. Cecilia, Harvey
Gates, David, St. Arnold, Milnor
Grim, Raphael, St. Catherine, Valley City
Ham, Thurston, Transfiguration, Edgeley
Hoefs, Gene, St. John, Wahpeton
Hunkler, Howard, St. Philip Neri, Napolean
Klein, Eugene, St. Catherine, Valley City
La Rocque, Dorian, St. Boniface, Walhalla
Lange, Lawrence, St. Joseph's, Devils Lake
Litzinger, Donald, St. Mary, Grand Forks
Loegering, George, St. Leo, Casselton
Marcy, Timothy, Sacred Heart, Fried
McDonald, Anthony, Seven Dolors, Fort Totten
Mrozla, Julian, St. Mary Cathedral, Fargo
Perius, James, Holy Spirit, Fargo
Prom, Mathias, St. Anthony, Fargo
Pupino, Samuel, Holy Family, Grand Forks
Schmisek, Albert, St. Michael, Grand Forks
Schuster, Conrad, Notre Dame, Willow City
Sobolick, Gerald, St. Mary, Park River

Storey, Alan, St. Boniface, Walhalla
Tinguely, Donald, St. Leo, Casselton
Uline, James, Holy Cross, West Fargo
Van Houtte, Maurice, Nativity, Fargo
West, James, St. Jude, Thompson
Zach, Ignatz, St. John, Wahpeton

INSTITUTIONS LOCATED IN THE DIOCESE

[A] SEMINARIES, DIOCESAN

FARGO. *Cardinal Muench Seminary*, 100 35th Ave., N.E., 58102. Tel: 701-232-8969.
Corporate Title: The Cardinal Muench Seminary. Revs. James E. Ermer, Rector & Pres.; Brian G. Donahue, Vice Rector; Dennis A. Skonseng; Robert L. Laliberte. Sisters 1; Priests 4; Lay Teachers 4; 4-year College Students 16.

[B] HIGH SCHOOLS, DIOCESAN

FARGO. *Fargo Catholic Schools Network*, 705 13th Ave. N., P.O. Box 2085, 58107. Dr. Sherry Houdek, Supt.; Michael Hogen, Bus. Mgr.; Andree Horst, Admin. Asst.; Greg Straus, Transportation Supr.; Barry Anderson, Athletic Dir.
Shanley High School, 705 13th Ave. N., 58102. Tel: 701-235-5581; Fax: 701-293-3613. Sherryl Houdek, Prin.; Patricia A. Neuharth, Admin. Asst. Priests 1; Lay Teachers 23; Students 340.

[C] PROTECTIVE INSTITUTIONS

FARGO. *Friendship, Inc. dba Villa Nazareth*, 3004 S. 11th St., 58103. Tel: 701-235-8217.
For a complete listing, refer to the Special Care Facilities section.

[D] GENERAL HOSPITALS

BOTTINEAU. *St. Andrew's Health Center*, 316 Ohmer St., 58318. Tel: 701-228-2255.
For a complete listing, refer to the Hospitals section.

CARRINGTON. *Carrington Health Center*, 800 N. Fourth St., 58421. Tel: 701-652-3141.
For a complete listing, refer to the Hospitals section.

DEVILS LAKE. *Mercy Hospital*, 1031 Seventh St., 58301. Tel: 701-662-2131; Fax: 701-662-4862.
For a complete listing, refer to the Hospitals section.

HARVEY. *St. Aloisius Medical Center*, 325 E. Brewster St., 58341. Tel: 701-324-4651.
For a complete listing, refer to the Hospitals section.

OAKES. *Oakes Community Hospital*, 314 S. Eighth St., 58474. Tel: 701-742-3291.
For a complete listing, refer to the Hospitals section.

PARK RIVER. *St. Ansgar's Health Center*, 115 Vivian St., 58270. Tel: 701-284-7500.
For a complete listing, refer to the Hospitals section.

ROLLA. *Presentation Medical Center*, 213 N.E. Third St., 58367. Tel: 701-477-3161.
For a complete listing, refer to the Hospitals section.

VALLEY CITY. *Mercy Hospital*, 570 Chautauqua Blvd., 58072. Tel: 701-845-0440.
For a complete listing, refer to the Hospitals section.

[E] HOMES FOR AGED

FARGO. *Riverview Place, Inc.*, 5300 12th St., S., 58103. Tel: 701-237-4700.
For a complete listing, refer to the Special Care Facilities section.

EDGELEY. *Manor St. Joseph*, 404 Fourth Ave., 58433. Tel: 701-493-2477.
For a complete listing, refer to the Special Care Facilities section.

ELLENDALE. *Ellendale Nursing Center*, 201 8th St. N., 58436. Tel: 701-349-3312; Fax: 701-349-3944.
For a complete listing, refer to the Special Care Facilities section.

GRAND FORKS. *St. Anne's Guest Home*, 524 N. 17th St., 58203. Tel: 701-746-9401.
For a complete listing, refer to the Special Care Facilities section.

HANKINSON. *St. Gerard Community Nursing Home*, 613 First Ave. S.W., 58041. Tel: 701-242-7891.
For a complete listing, refer to the Special Care Facilities section.

LA MOURE. *La Moure Healthcare Manor*, Hwy. 13, P.O. Box 627, 58458. Tel: 701-883-5363; Fax: 701-883-5711.
For a complete listing, refer to the Special Care Facilities section.

ROLETTE. *Presentation Care Center*, 304 John St., 58366. Tel: 701-246-3786.
For a complete listing, refer to the Special Care Facilities section.

WAHPETON. *Wahpeton Health Care Center*, 1307 N. Seventh St., 58075. Tel: 701-642-6667.
For a complete listing, refer to the Special Care Facilities section.

[F] CONVENTS AND RESIDENCES FOR SISTERS

FARGO. *Prairieland Home Health Agency, Inc.*, 1102 Page Dr., P.O. Box 10007, 58106-0006. Tel: 701-237-9290. Margaret A. Kaltefleiter, Pres.
Presentation Center-Sacred Heart Convent, 1101 32nd Ave. S., 58103. Tel: 701-237-4857; Fax: 701-237-9822. Sr. Paula Ringuette, Pres.; Rev. Maurice Mueller. Sisters 63. Sisters of Mary of the Presentation Health Corporation, 1102 Page Dr., P.O. Box 10007, 58106-0006. Tel: 701-237-9290. Sr. Aaron Alton, Pres.
Sisters Minor of Mary Immaculate, 1131 N. University Dr., 58102. Tel: 701-239-4669. Sr. Donna Marie, S.M.M.I., Supr. Sisters 1; Postulants 1.

BELCOURT. *Queen of Peace Monastery*. Sisters of St. Benedict, P.O. Box 370, 58316. Tel: 701-477-6167. Sr. Maura Schnur, O.S.B., Prioress. Sisters 7.

HANKINSON. *Sisters of St. Francis of the Immaculate Heart of Mary*, P.O. Box 447, 58041-0447. Sr. Ann Marie Friederichs, O.S.F., Prov. Sisters 76.

VALLEY CITY. *Sisters of Mary of the Presentation*, 11550 River R. Rd., 58072. Sr. Margaret Rose Pfeifer, S.M.P., Prov. Supr.; Rev. John Odermann, O.S.B., Chap. Sisters 68.

WAHPETON. *Carmel of Mary*, 17765 78th St. S.E., 58075. Tel: 701-642-2360. Carmelite Nuns of the Ancient Observance. Mother Rose of the Sacred Heart, O.Carm., Prioress; Rev. Donald Leiphon, Chap. Solemn Professed Nuns 12; Junior Professed Nuns 2; Postulants 1; Novices 2.

[G] RETREAT HOUSES

FARGO. *Presentation Prayer Center*, 1101 32nd Ave. S., 58103. Tel: 701-237-4857. Sr. Andrea Arendt, P.B.V.M., Dir. Sisters 2.
Queen of Peace Retreat Center, 1310 Broadway, 58102. Tel: 701-293-9286. Diocesan sponsored retreat house operated by the Diocese of Fargo. George Lacher, Bldg. Dir.

[H] NEWMAN FOUNDATIONS

FARGO. *St. Paul's Catholic Chapel*, 1141 N. University Dr., 58102. Rev. Paul Duchschere, Dir. Campus Ministry. Staff 3.

GRAND FORKS. *Univ. of North Dakota Newman Center*, St. Thomas Aquinas Parish, UND. St. Thomas Aquinas Newman Center, UND. Also serving Manvel. 410 Cambridge St., 58201. Revs. H. Gerard Braun; Paul Schuster; Bill Serb, Pastoral Asst. Staff 12; Catholic Students 2,500.

MAYVILLE. *Mayville State University Newman Center*. c/o Our Lady of Peace, 435 E. Main St., 58257. Rev. Bernard R. Schneider. Catholic Students 180.

WAHPETON. *State College of Science Newman Student Parish*, 701 N. Seventh St., 58075. Rev. Dale Lagodinski.

[I] MISCELLANEOUS LISTINGS

FARGO. *Catholic Development Foundation*. c/o Chancery, 1310 Broadway, Box 1750, 58107. A non-profit foundation for religious charitable and educational purposes.
Catholic Family Service, 2537 S. University Dr., 58103. Tel: 701-235-4457.
Catholic School Network Foundation, Office, 705-13th Ave. N., P.O. Box 2085, 58107-2085. A non-profit foundation for religious charitable and educational purposes.
Ministry Potential Discerner, Cardinal Muench Seminary, 100 35th Ave. N.E., 58102. Tel: 701-280-1755. Mr. Greg Smith, Exec. Dir. A self-assessment evangelizing vocational tool designed to aid vocation recruitment in discerning individuals for service to the church as priest or religious.
The Presentation Foundation, Sacred Heart Convent, 1101 32nd Ave. S., 58103. Sr. Paula Ringuette, Supr. & Pres.

BOTTINEAU. *Minot State University-Bottineau*, c/o St. Mark, 322 Sinclair St., 58318. Rev. Kevin J. Boucher. Catholic Students 70.

DEVILS LAKE. *UND-Lake Region*, c/o St. Joseph's, 515 Fourth St., P.O. Box 898, 58301. Rev. Jeffrey Wald. Catholic Students 90.

GRAND FORKS. *Air Force Base*, 319BW-HC, 58205. Tel: 701-594-3074. Rev. David J. Krogmann, Chap.
Grand Forks Catholic Schools Association, 216 Belmont Rd., 58201. Pamela Neppel, Sec. A non-profit organization developing, curriculum study, scholarship, transportation, personnel and fund raising.

JAMESTOWN. *Jamestown College*, 6052 College Ln., 58405. Rev. Bernard A. Pfau; Sr. Michaeleen Jantzer, O.S.B., Pastoral Min. & Campus Min. Catholic Students 250.

VALLEY CITY. *Valley City State University*, St. Catherine's, 58072. Ralph Dyrness. Catholic Students 314.

RELIGIOUS INSTITUTES OF MEN REPRESENTED IN THE DIOCESE

For further details refer to the corresponding bracketed number in the Religious Institutes of Men or Women section.

[0200]—*Benedictine Monks*. (Marvin, SD; Collegeville, MN).—O.S.B.
[]—*Bethlehem Community*. RR 1 Box 137-A, Minto, ND 58261.
[]—*Franciscan Brothers of the Sacred Heart*.—O.S.F.
[]—*Franciscan Friars of Mary Immaculate*.—O.F.M.I.
[]—*Franciscan Monks of the Conventional*.—O.F.M.Conv.
[0650]—*Holy Ghost Fathers*.—C.S.Sp.
[0690]—*Jesuit Fathers and Brothers*. (Wisconsin Prov.).—S.J.
[0430]—*Order of Preachers-Dominicans*.—O.P.
[1070]—*Redemptorists*. (St. Louis Prov.).—C.SS.R.
[]—*Society of Our Lady of the Most Holy Trinity*.—S.O.L.T.
[0990]—*Society of the Catholic Apostolate*. (Mater Dei Prov.).—S.A.C.

RELIGIOUS INSTITUTES OF WOMEN REPRESENTED IN THE DIOCESE

[0230]—*Benedictine Sisters of the Pontifical Jurisdiction*. (Belcourt, ND).—O.S.B.
[0300]—*Calced Carmelites*.—O.Carm.
[2575]—*Institute of the Sisters of Mercy of the Americas*. (Omaha, NE).—R.S.M.
[]—*Sisters Minor of Mary Immaculate*. (Fargo, ND).—S.M.M.I.
[2450]—*Sisters of Mary of the Presentation*. (Maryvale, R.F.D. 1).—S.M.P.
[1590]—*Sisters of St. Francis of the Immaculate Heart of Mary*. (Hankinson, North Dakota).—O.S.F.
[3320]—*Sisters of the Presentation of the B.V.M.*. (Fargo, ND).—P.B.V.M.

NECROLOGY

† Bellerose, Joseph A., San Antonio, TX, Padua Place. —Died Jan. 9, 1996.
† Hogan, James P., (Retired). —Died Nov. 11, 1996.
† Kostrzewski, Daniel, O.F.M. Conv, Grafton, ND, Sacred Heart of Oakwood. —Died Oct. 6, 1996.
† Preske, Felix J., (Retired). —Died July 25, 1996.
† Svetinsky, Ludvik F., (Retired). —Died Jan. 6, 1996.

Diocese of Fort Wayne - South Bend

(Dioecesis Wayne Castrensis-South Bendensis)

Most Reverend

JOHN M. D'ARCY, D.D., M.A., S.T.D.

Bishop of Fort Wayne-South Bend; ordained February 2, 1957; appointed Auxiliary Bishop of Boston and Titular Bishop of Mediana December 31, 1974; consecrated February 11, 1975; appointed Bishop of Fort Wayne-South Bend February 26, 1985; installed May 1, 1985. *Mailing Address: P.O. Box 390, Fort Wayne, IN, 46801.*

Chancery Office: 1103 S. Calhoun St., P.O. Box 390, Fort Wayne, IN, 46801. Tel.: 219-422-4611; Fax: 219-423-3382.

Most Reverend

JOSEPH R. CROWLEY, D.D.

Retired Auxiliary Bishop of Fort Wayne-South Bend; ordained May 1, 1953; appointed Titular Bishop of Maraguia June 16, 1971; consecrated August 24, 1971; retired July 15, 1990. *Mailing Address: 1240 Honan Dr., South Bend, IN, 46614.* Tel.: 219-299-9155.

Most Reverend

LEO ALOYSIUS PURSLEY, D.D.

Retired Bishop of Fort Wayne-South Bend; appointed Titular Bishop of Hadrianopolis and Auxiliary July 22, 1950; consecrated September 19, 1950; appointed Bishop February 26, 1957; retired October 19, 1976. *Res., 2 Northway Dr., Huntington, IN, 46750.*

Most Reverend

JOHN R. SHEETS, S.J.

Auxiliary Bishop of Fort Wayne-South Bend; completed theological studies at St. Mary Jesuit School in Kansas and was ordained in 1953; received his Doctorate in Theology in 1957 in Innsbruck, Austria; ordained to the Episcopacy for the Diocese of Fort Wayne-South Bend on June 25, 1991; and Titular Bishop of Murkona, Province of Maurtitania Cesariense. *Res., St. Matthew Cathedral, 1701 Miami St., South Bend, IN, 46613.* Tel.: 219-289-5539.

Most Reverend

WILLIAM E. MCMANUS, D.D.

Retired Bishop of Fort Wayne-South Bend; ordained April 15, 1939; appointed Auxiliary Bishop of Chicago June 21, 1967; appointed Titular Bishop of Mesarfelta; appointed Bishop of Fort Wayne-South Bend August 31, 1976; installed as Seventh Bishop of Fort Wayne-South Bend October 19, 1976; retired February 25, 1985. *Mailing Address: 409 S. SeeGwun, Mt. Prospect, IL, 60056.* Tel.: 708-255-3624.

ESTABLISHED SEPT. 22, 1857.

Square Miles 5,792.

REDESIGNATED DIOCESE OF FORT WAYNE-SOUTH BEND ON JULY 22, 1960.

Comprises the Counties of Adams, Allen, Dekalb, Elkhart, Huntington, Kosciusko, La Grange, Marshall, Noble, St. Joseph, Steuben, Wabash, Wells, Whitley in the State of Indiana.

For legal titles of parishes and diocesan institutions, consult the Chancery Office.

STATISTICAL OVERVIEW

Personnel	
Bishop	1
Auxiliary Bishops	1
Retired Bishops	2
Priests: Diocesan Active in Diocese	78
Priests: Active Outside Diocese	1
Priests: Retired, Sick or Absent	25
Number of Diocesan Priests	104
Religious Priests in Diocese	159
Ordinations:	
Religious Priests	1
Permanent Deacons in Diocese	25
Total Brothers	129
Total Sisters	697
Parishes	
Parishes	88
With Resident Pastor:	
Resident Diocesan Priests	49
Resident Religious Priests	39
Without Resident Pastor:	
Administered by Priests	6
Pastoral Centers	2
Professional Ministry Personnel:	
Brothers	129
Sisters	697
Welfare	
Catholic Hospitals	5
Total Assisted	361,160
Health Care Centers	1
Total Assisted	20,000
Homes for the Aged	4
Total Assisted	547
Day Care and Extended Day Care Centers	2
Total Assisted	600
Specialized Homes	3
Total Assisted	20,000
Special Centers for Social Services	6
Other Institutions	6
Educational	
Diocesan Students in Other Seminaries	9
Seminaries, Religious	11
Students Religious	33
Total Seminarians	42
Colleges and Universities	5
Total Students	13,805
High Schools, Diocesan and Parish	4
Total Students	3,045
Elementary Schools, Diocesan and Parish	40
Total Students	11,542
Catechesis/Religious Education:	
High School Students	1,601
Elementary Students	7,875
Total Students Under Catholic Instruction	37,910
Teachers in the Diocese:	
Brothers	2
Sisters	23
Lay Teachers	694
Vital Statistics	
Receptions into the Church:	
Infant Baptism Totals	2,534
Adult Baptism Totals	440
Received into Full Communion	455
First Communions	2,956
Confirmations	2,532
Marriages:	
Catholic	571
Interfaith	429
Total Marriages	1,000
Deaths	1,404
Total Catholic Population	159,659
Total Population	1,960,876

Former Bishops—Rt. Rev. JOHN HENRY LUERS, D.D., cons. Jan. 10, 1858; died June 29, 1871.—Rt. Rev. JOSEPH DWENGER, C.PP.S., D.D., cons. April 14, 1872; died Jan. 27, 1893.—Rt. Rev. JOSEPH RADEMACHER, D.D., cons. Bishop of Nashville, June 24, 1883; transferred to Fort Wayne, July 14, 1893; died Jan. 12, 1900.—Rt. Rev. HERMAN JOSEPH ALERDING, D.D., cons. Nov. 30, 1900; died Dec. 6, 1924.—Most Rev. JOHN FRANCIS NOLL, D.D., cons. June 30, 1925; promoted to rank of Archbishop "ad personam," Sept. 2, 1953; died July 31, 1956.—Most Rev. LEO A. PURSLEY, D.D., cons. Sept. 19, 1950; retired Oct. 19, 1976.—Most Rev. WILLIAM E. MCMANUS, D.D., ord. April 15, 1939; appt. Auxiliary Bishop of Chicago, June 21, 1967; appt. Bishop of Fort Wayne, Aug. 31, 1976; installed as 7th Bishop of Fort Wayne, Oct. 19, 1976; retired Feb. 25, 1985.

Diocese of Fort Wayne-South Bend, Inc.—(Incorporated Aug. 29, 1955). *Board of Directors:* Most Rev. JOHN M. D'ARCY, Pres.; Rev. Msgr. J. WILLIAM LESTER P.A., Vice Pres.; Rev. Msgr. JAMES J. WOLF, Sec. *Finance Council:* JOHN BRELL; ARTHUR DECIO; LOUIS PACH; Sr. M. THERESA SOLBACK, O.S.F.; Mr. JERRY HAMMES; JOSEPH DAHM; MICHAEL HAMMES; THOMAS BLEE; RICHARD DOERMER; VINCENT TIPPMANN; Mr. JERRY KEARNS.

Chancery Office—1103 S. Calhoun St., P.O. Box 390, Fort Wayne, 46801. Tel: 219-422-4611; Fax: 219-423-3382. Office Hours: Mon.-Fri. 8:30-4:30. Other times by appointment.

Vicar General-Chancellor—Rev. Msgr. JAMES J. WOLF; Rev. Msgr. J. WILLIAM LESTER, P.A.

Episcopal Vicar for Education—Rev. Msgr. J. WILLIAM LESTER, P.A., *1103 S. Clinton St., Box 390, Fort Wayne, 46801.* Tel: 219-422-4611.

South Bend Chancery—114 W. Wayne St., S. Bend, 46624. Tel: 219-234-0687; Fax: 219-232-8483.

Diocesan Tribunal—1103 S. Calhoun St., P.O. Box 390, Fort Wayne, 46801. Tel: 219-422-4611., South Bend Office: *114 W. Wayne St, P.O. Box 1432, S. Bend, 46624.* Tel: 219-287-6531.

Judicial Vicar—Rev. BRUCE PIECHOCKI.

Defenders of the Bond—Deacon LOUIS B. MCDOUGALL; MARILYN DWIRE.

Pro-Synodal Judges—Revs. PHILIP DEVOLDER; LAWRENCE KRAMER; BRUCE PIECHOCKI; ROBERT SCHULTE.

Court Consultants—JEROME HENRY, A.C.S.W.; PATRICIA CROSSEN, Ph.D.; PHIL SUTTON, Ph.D.

Fort Wayne Office Secretary—JANICE BRELL. Office Auditors: MARILYN DWIRE; LINDA O'DONNELL; VICKI FERRIER; MONICA KLUESNER; JAMES SHERRON.

Notary—MARIE MCMAHON; JANICE BRELL.

South Bend Office Secretary—DIANA HEIDT. Office Auditor: SANDRA LAVIOLETTE.

Consultors—Most Rev. JOHN R. SHEETS, S.J.; Rev. Msgr. J. WILLIAM LESTER, P.A.; Rev. Msgr. JAMES J. WOLF; Rev. Msgr. JOHN N. SUELZER; Revs. BRUCE PIECHOCKI; WILLIAM HODDES; RAYMOND BALZER; BERNARD GALIC.

Diocesan Offices and Directors

Business Administration Office—JOHN BRELL, Chief Fin. Officer; MARCY ERNST, Controller, *P.O. Box 390, Ft. Wayne, 46801.* Tel: 219-422-4611.

Buildings and Improvements—Advisory Board: Rev. Msgr. JAMES WOLF; Rev. Msgr. J. WILLIAM LESTER, P.A.; Rev. Msgr. ROBERT CONTANT; Revs. ANTHONY LETKO; LAURENCE TIPPMANN; DAVID CARKENORD; ROBERT YAST; ELDEN J. MILLER; Mr. JOHN BRELL; JAMES SCHENKEL.

Budget Committee—Rev. Msgr. J. WILLIAM LESTER, P.A.; Rev. Msgr. JAMES J. WOLF; Rev. JOHN PFISTER; Rev. Msgr. JOHN SUELZER; Rev. BERNARD GALIC; JOHN BRELL.

Diocesan Services Agency—JOHN KLEIN; MARY LOU O'KEEFFE, Purchasing, *P.O. Box 390, Fort Wayne, 46801.* Tel: 219-422-4611; 800-856-4611.

Diocesan Office of Development—JOHN BARRETT, *1103 S. Calhoun St., P.O. Box 390, Fort Wayne, 46801.* Tel: 219-422-4611.

Campus Ministry—LINDA FURGE, Dir., *1330 E. Washington Center Rd., Fort Wayne, 46825.* Tel: 219-483-3661.

Campaign for Human Development—Rev. THOMAS O'CONNOR, *430 E. Jefferson St., Fort Wayne, 46802.* Tel: 219-424-8231.

Catholic Charities—KATHLEEN DONNELLAN, Dir., *315 E. Washington, Fort Wayne, 46802.* Tel: 219-422-7511.

Censor Librorum—Rev. JOHN KUZMICH, *8669 Auburn Rd., Ft. Wayne, 46825.* Tel: 219-489-3537.

Cemeteries—Rev. Msgr. ROBERT W. CONTANT, Dir., *11337 Old U.S. No. 27 S., Fort Wayne, 46806.* Tel: 219-639-3748.

Catholic Cemetery Association of Fort Wayne, Inc.—3500 Lake Ave., Fort Wayne, 46805. Tel: 219-426-2044.

Charismatic Movement—Rev. GEORGE KAMINSKI, *St. Vincent de Paul, 8669 Auburn Rd., Fort Wayne, 46825.* Tel: 219-489-3537. Deacon KEVIN RANAGHAN, *1003 St. Vincent, South Bend, 46617.* Tel: 219-234-2465.

Clergy Relief Association—Revs. PHILLIP WIDMANN, Pres. KENNETH SARRAZINE, Vice Pres. EDWARD J. KRASON, Treas. DANIEL LEEUW, Sec. Dirs.: Revs. STEPHEN COLCHIN; JAMES J. WOLF.

Communications—CHRISTINE BONAHOOM, *150 Doan Dr., Fort Wayne, 46816.* Tel: 219-744-0012; Fax: 219-744-1473.

Continuing Education of the Clergy—Rev. Msgr. J. WILLIAM LESTER, P.A., *P.O. Box 390, Fort Wayne, 46801.* Tel: 219-422-4611.

Council of Priests—Most Rev. JOHN SHEETS, S.J.; Rev. Msgr. J. WILLIAM LESTER, P.A.; Rev. Msgr. JAMES J. WOLF; Revs. RAYMOND BALZER; BRUCE PIECHOCKI; Rev. Msgr. JOHN SUELZER; Revs. BERNARD GALIC; THOMAS JONES, C.S.C.; WILLIAM HODDE; WILLIAM SULLIVAN, C.S.C.; DAVID VOORS; RICHARD HIRE; DAVID CARKENORD; KENNETH SARRAZINE; RONALD RIEDER, O.F.M.Cap.

Cursillo—Rev. PAUL BUETER, *114 W. Monroe, Goshen, 46526.* Tel: 219-533-3385.

Hispanic Ministry Services—Rev. PAUL BUETER, Diocesan Coord., *114 W. Monroe, Goshen, 46526.* Tel: 219-533-3385.

Fort Wayne—Rev. GLENN KOHRMAN; Sr. ELIZABETH GARCIA, S.N.D., *St. Paul, 416 W. Washington Blvd., Fort Wayne, 46858.* Tel: 219-744-1450.

Milford—Rev. PAUL R. BUETER; Sr. M. VICTOR KERCHER, O.S.B., *Our Lady of Guadalupe, 4th & Main St., Milford, 46542.* Tel: 219-658-9384; 658-9594.

South Bend—Rev. THOMAS LEMOS, C.S.C., *St. Stephen, 1102 W. Thomas St., South Bend, 46625.* Tel: 219-287-7681.

La Casa de Amistad, Inc.—CHRIS NANNI, Dir., *746 S. Meade St., S. Bend, 46619.* Tel: 219-233-2120.

Diocesan Council of Catholic Women—Rev. EDWARD NARCOWICH, *55756 Tulip Rd., New Carlisle, 46552.* Tel: 219-654-3781. BETTY LOMONT, Pres., *15412 State Rd. 14, New Haven, 46774.* Tel: 219-749-9396.

Diocesan Family Life—FRED EVERETT; LISA EVERETT, *114 W. Wayne St., S. Bend, 46601.* Tel: 219-234-0687.

Ecumenical Affairs—Rev. Msgr. J. WILLIAM LESTER, P.A., Chm., *P.O. Box 390, Fort Wayne, 46801.* Tel: 219-422-4611.

Human Development Commission—Rev. THOMAS O'CONNOR, *430 E. Jefferson St., Fort Wayne, 46802.* Tel: 219-424-8231.

Liturgical Commission—Rev. WILLIAM SCHOOLER, Chm.

Environment and Art—Dr. ROBERT AMICO; Dr. JAIME BELLATA; Revs. JOSE MARTELLI, C.S.C.; JAMES FLANIGAN, C.S.C.

Liturgy—Revs. WILLIAM SCHOOLER; WILLIAM KUMMER.

Music—JUDY THROM; Dr. EDWARD KLINE; STEVE WARNER.

R.C.I.A.—Ms. GERVAISE BASTIAN; Sr. BETTY KORESSEL, S.P.

Office of Worship—Sr. AGNES MARIE REGAN, O.S.F., Dir., *1103 S. Calhoun St., Box 390, Fort Wayne, 46801.* Tel: 219-422-4611.

Official Publication "Today's Catholic"—JOHN ANKENBRUCK, Editor; MURRAY HUBLEY, JR., News Editor, *150 Doan Dr., Fort Wayne, 46816., Mailing Address: P.O. Box 11169, Fort Wayne, 46856.* Tel: 219-456-2824; Fax: 219-744-1473.

Permanent Diaconate—Rev. WILLIAM KUMMER, *St. John, 4525 Arlington Ave., Fort Wayne, 46807.* Tel: 219-744-4393.

Priests' Eucharistic League—Vacant, *P.O. Box 390, Fort Wayne, 46801.* Tel: 219-422-4611.

Pro-Life—FRED EVERETT; LISA EVERETT, *114 W. Wayne St., S. Bend, 46601.* Tel: 219-234-0687., Birthline phones: Tel: 219-422-1818 (Fort Wayne); 356-3322 (Huntington); 289-1034 (South Bend).

Propagation of the Faith and Holy Childhood Association—Rev. PHILLIP WIDMANN, *641 N. Main, P.O. Box 358, Roanoke, 46783.* Tel: 219-672-2838.

Religious Education, Office of—Sr. M. JANE CAREW, C.S.J., Diocesan Dir., Religious Education; Vacant; Assoc. Dir., *P.O. Box 390, Fort Wayne, 46801.* Tel: 219-422-4611.

South Bend-Mishawaka Area Office of Religious Education—CAROL CONE, Assoc. Dir. MARY ANN MCGWIN, Resource Asst., *1328 W. Dragoon Trail, Mishawaka, 46554.* Tel: 219-259-9994.

Refugee Resettlement Program—BRIDGET SERRANI MOE, Dir., *315 E. Washington, Fort Wayne, 46802.* Tel: 219-422-7511.

Retired Clergy Committee—Revs. WILLIAM GIERANOWSKI, Pres. BARRY ENGLAND; JAMES WOLF; JOHN SUELZER; Rev. Msgr. J. WILLIAM LESTER, P.A.

Retired Senior Volunteer Program (RSVP)—Auburn: PATTI SHEPPARD, Coord., *500 E. 7th St., Auburn, 46706.* Tel: 219-925-0917.

Serra International—Revs. GLENN KOHRMAN, *Sacred Heart Parish, 1020 Capitol Ave., Fort Wayne, 46806.* Tel: 219-744-2519. BERNARD GALIC, *Holy Family Parish, 56405 Mayflower Rd., S. Bend, 46619.* Tel: 219-282-2317.

Single Catholic Adult Club—Rev. GEORGE KAMINSKI, *1103 S. Calhoun St., P.O. Box 390, Fort Wayne, 46801.* Tel: 219-422-4611.

Schools—Dr. JEANETTE KAM, Supt. CANDACE SCHEIDT, Assoc., *1102 S. Clinton St., Box 390, Ft. Wayne, 46801.* Tel: 219-422-4611. South Bend Office: LARRY BARTEK, Assoc. Supt.; Sr. ESTHER BLACK, Psychometrist, *1328 W. Dragoon Trail, Mishawaka, 46544.* Tel: 219-255-1387.

School Board, Diocesan—

Vicariate A, B, C—Rev. BERNARD GALIC; MARY JANE STANLEY; THOMAS SLAMKOWSKI; JIM BANKOWSKI.

Vicariate D, E, F—Rev. LAURENCE TIPPMANN; DANIEL ARNOLD; CATHY KROUSE; JOHN WOENKER.

At-Large Representatives—MICHAEL RYAN; STEPHEN SMITH; Sr. ELAINE BROTHERS, O.S.F.

Catholic Schools Office—Dr. JEANETTE KAM; CANDACE SCHEIDT; KATHLEEN BARRETT-JONES; JOHN GAUGHAN.

Ex Officio Members—Most Rev. JOHN M. D'ARCY; Most Rev. JOHN R. SHEETS, S.J.; Rev. Msgr. J. WILLIAM LESTER, P.A.

Scouting—Fort Wayne: Rev. TIMOTHY WROZEK, *4916 Trier Rd., Fort Wayne, 46815.* Tel: 219-482-2186. South Bend: Rev. ELDEN J. MILLER, *Queen of Peace, 4508 Vistula Rd., Mishawaka, 46555.* Tel: 219-255-9674.

St. Vincent de Paul Society—Rev. THOMAS O'CONNOR, *430 E. Jefferson St., Fort Wayne, 46802.* Tel: 219-424-8231.

Spiritual Development—Fort Wayne: Sr. CAROLINE CLARK, D.C., Dir.; Sr. ANN KIHSLINGER S.S.N.D., Assoc. Dir.; South Bend: Sr. MARY BROOKS, *114 W. Wayne St., S. Bend, 46601.* Tel: 219-234-0687.

Office of Youth Ministry and Spiritual Development—STEVEN J. WEIGAND, Assoc., *P.O. Box 390, Fort Wayne, 46801.* Tel: 219-422-4611; Fax: 219-420-6306.

Vocations—Rev. BERNARD GALIC, Dir., *114 W. Wayne St., South Bend, 46601.* Tel: 219-234-0687.

Youth Organizations—Rev. GEORGE KAMINSKI, Moderator, *8669 Auburn Rd., Fort Wayne, 46825.* Tel: 219-489-3537.

CLERGY, PARISHES, MISSIONS AND PAROCHIAL SCHOOLS

CITY OF FORT WAYNE
(Allen County)

1—CATHEDRAL OF THE IMMACULATE CONCEPTION (1836). (Calhoun, between Lewis and Jefferson Sts.). Rev. Msgr. James J. Wolf, Co-Rector; Rev. Msgr. J. William Lester, Co-Rector; Sr. Sally Soules, S.F.C.C., Pastoral Min.; Deacon Joseph R. Zickgraf. In res., Rev. Joseph Lawrence (India).
Res., 1122 Clinton St., P.O. Box 10898, 46854. Tel: 219-424-1485.
Catechesis/Religious Programs—Students 116.
Chapel—MacDougall Memorial Chapel.

2—ST. ANDREW (1910), Rev. John H. Delaney, Admin. 518 E. DeWald, 46803. Tel: 219-744-2765; Fax: 219-744-1972.
Res., 2610 New Haven Ave., 46803. Tel: 219-422-0380. Sr. Rose Clare Ehrlich, C.S.A., Pastoral Assoc.

3—ST. CHARLES BORROMEO (1957), Rev. Msgr. John N. Suelzer; Revs. Ronald Ramenaden, O.M.I. (Sri Lanka); Michael Heintz; Rev. Msgr. Edward I. Hession, Pastor Emeritus, (Retired); Sr. Kathleen Morrissey, O.P., Pastoral Assoc.; Deacon Louis B. McDougall.
Res., 4916 Trier Rd., 46815. Tel: 219-482-2186; Fax: 219-471-2144.
School—3700 Reed Rd., 46815. Tel: 219-484-3392; Fax: 219-482-2006. Mrs. Michelle Hittie, Prin.
Franciscan Sisters of the Sacred Heart 2; Lay Teachers 33; Students 715.
Catechesis/Religious Programs—Tel: 219-484-7322. Kathy Monagle, D.R.E.
Students 500.

4—ST. ELIZABETH ANN SETON (1988), Revs. Robert Schulte; Nimal George Fernando (Sri Lanka).
Office: 10700 Aboite Center Rd., 46804. Tel: 219-432-0268; Fax: 219-436-5851.
Res., 10517 Unita Dr., 46804. Tel: 219-436-9819.
Catechesis/Religious Programs—Tel: 219-432-0268. Mary Ann Welling, D.R.E.
Students 820.

5—ST. HENRY (1956), Rev. Kenneth Sarrazine.
Res., 2929 E. Paulding Rd., 46816. Tel: 219-447-4100.

6—ST. HYACINTH (1910). Closed. For inquiries for parish records contact the Chancery.

7—ST. JOHN BAPTIST (1929), Revs. William Kummer; James Sapp; John Benedict Adde-Nweah (Ghana); Mary L. Glowaski, Pastoral Assoc.; Deacon Michael J. Doehrman.
Res., 4525 Arlington Ave., 46807. Tel: 219-744-4393; Fax: 219-456-3072.
School—4500 Fairfield Ave., 46807. Tel: 219-456-3321. Mr. J. Mark Mugg, Prin.
Sisters 1; Lay Teachers 23; Students 376.
Catechesis/Religious Programs—4501 Arlington Ave., 46807. Tel: 219-744-3578.
Students 58.

8—ST. JOSEPH (1914) (Italian), Revs. Laurence Tippmann; Adam Schmitt.
Res., 1910 Hale Ave., 46802. Tel: 219-432-5113; Fax: 219-432-4711.
School—2213 Brooklyn Ave., 46802. Tel: 219-432-4000; Fax: 219-432-8642. Ms. Mary Schreiber, Prin.
Sisters of St. Agnes 2; Lay Teachers 14; Students 324.

9—ST. JUDE (1929), Revs. William C. Schooler; Robert Van Kempen; Mary Pohlman, Pastoral Assoc.; Deacon Fred J. Larson. In res., Rev. Robert L. Traub.
Res., 2101 Pemberton Dr., 46805. Tel: 219-484-6609.
School—2110 Pemberton Dr., 46805. Tel: 219-484-4611. Sr. Alice Marie Willman, S.N.D., Prin.
Sisters of Notre Dame 4; Lay Teachers 34; Students 600.
Catechesis/Religious Programs—Tel: 219-484-6609. Mary Barnes, D.R.E.
Students 257.

10—ST. MARY (1849), Rev. Thomas P. O'Connor.
Res., 430 E. Jefferson St., 46802. Tel: 219-424-8231; Fax: 219-426-2406.

11—MOST PRECIOUS BLOOD (1897), Revs. Kenneth G. Alt, C.PP.S.; Werner F. Verhoff, C.PP.S.
Res., 1515 Barthold St., 46808. Tel: 219-424-5535.
School—1529 Barthold St., 46808. Tel: 219-424-4832. Corinne Tessman, Prin.
Lay Teachers 12; Students 100.

12—OUR LADY OF GOOD HOPE (1969), Rev. Lawrence A. Kramer.
Res., 7215 St. Joe Rd., 46835. Tel: 219-485-9615; Fax: 219-486-9000.
Catechesis/Religious Programs—Tel: 219-485-3732. D.R.E.: Mary Kay Matasky, (Elementary); Rev. Larry Kramer, (High School).

Students 225.

13—ST. PATRICK (1889), Rev. James W. Koons. In res., Rev. Matthew S. Kafka.
Res., 2120 S. Harrison St., 46802. Tel: 219-744-1450.

14—ST. PAUL (1865) (Hispanic), Rev. Glenn Kohrman, Admin.; Sr. Elizabeth Garcia, S.N.D., Pastoral Assoc.; Deacon Justo Donias.
Office & Res.: St. Patrick, 2120 S. Harrison, 46805. Tel: 219-744-1450.

15—ST. PETER (1872), Rev. John Delaney. Pastoral Assocs.: Sr. Eva Maria Sanchez, O.L.V.M.; Sr. Grace Golenberke, O.L.V.M.
Res., 518 E. De Wald St., 46803. Tel: 219-744-2765; Fax: 219-744-1972.

16—QUEEN OF ANGELS (1947), Revs. John F. Pfister; Rohan DeAlwis (Sri Lanka); Sr. Joan Bakle, S.S.N.D., Pastoral Min. In res., Rev. Bruce Piechocki.
Res., 1500 W. State St., 46808. Tel: 219-482-9411; Fax: 219-471-0005.
School—1600 W. State Blvd., 46808. Tel: 219-483-8214. Mrs. Sandra Koziol, Prin.
Lay Teachers 15; Students 330.
Catechesis / Religious Programs—Students 86.

17—SACRED HEART (1947), Rev. Glenn Kohrman.
Res., 1020 Capitol, 46806. Tel: 219-744-2519; Fax: 219-744-2519.
School—Julian Benoit Academy, 3029 E. Paulding Rd., 46816. Tel: 219-447-5121.
Catechesis / Religious Programs—Early Childhood Program, 4643 Gaywood Dr., 46808. Tel: 219-744-4261.
Students 327.

18—ST. THERESE (1947), Rev. Michael J. Rosswurm.
Res., 2304 Lower Huntington Rd., 46819. Tel: 219-747-9139.
School—2222 Lower Huntington Rd., 46819. Tel: 219-747-2343; Fax: 219-747-4767. Charles A. Grimm, Prin.
Lay Teachers 12; Students 243.
Catechesis / Religious Programs—Tel: 219-747-9139.
Students 115.

19—ST. VINCENT DE PAUL (1846), Revs. John M. Kuzmich; George Kaminski; Deacon Mark Gurtner. Pastoral Assocs.: Sr. Joetta Huelsmann, P.H.J.C.; Mrs. Judy Mockenhaupt.
Res., 8669 Auburn Rd., 46825. Tel: 219-489-3537; Fax: 219-489-3697. [CEM]
School—8905 Auburn Rd., 46825. Tel: 219-489-4591; Fax: 219-489-5318. Mrs. Barbara McClure, Prin.
Sisters 1; Lay Teachers 30; Students 700.
Catechesis / Religious Programs—Tel: 219-489-1684. Elizabeth Balbo, D.R.E.
Students 570.

CITY OF SOUTH BEND
(St. Joseph County)

1—ST. MATTHEW CATHEDRAL, Most Rev. John R. Sheets, S.J., D.D.; Rev. Thomas R. Shoemaker.
Res., 1701 Miami St., 46613. Tel: 219-289-5539.
School—1015 E. Dayton, 46613. Tel: 219-289-4535. Ms. Mary Ann Retseck, Prin.
Lay Teachers 21; Students 411.

2—ST. ADALBERT (1910) (Polish), Revs. Daryl Rybicki; John Klimczyk. In res., Rev. James Fahey, C.S.C.
Res., 2420 W. Huron St., 46619. Tel: 219-288-5708.
School—519 S. Oliver St., 46619. Tel: 219-288-6645. Sr. M. Edwardine Stoppa, C.S.S.F., Prin.
Felician Sisters 2; Lay Teachers 9; Students 175.

3—ST. ANTHONY DE PADUA (1949), Revs. Barry England; Joseph Gaughan; Deacon Brian Miller.
Res., 2120 E. Jefferson Blvd., 46617. Tel: 219-282-2308; Fax: 219-288-8877.
School—2310 E. Jefferson Blvd., 46615. Tel: 219-233-7169; Fax: 219-288-8877. Ms. Martha Lewallen, Prin.
Lay Teachers 22; Students 459.
Catechesis / Religious Programs—Tel: 219-282-2308.
Students 96.

4—ST. AUGUSTINE (1928) (African American), Rev. Daryl Rybicki; Deacon Paul Baumgartner.
Mailing Address: P.O. Box 3198, 46619-0198. Tel: 219-234-6334.
Res., 1130 W. Thomas St., 46601. Tel: 219-234-0295.

5—ST. CASIMIR (1899) (Polish), Revs. Thomas F. Lemos, C.S.C.; William A. Pifher, C.S.C.
Res., 1308 W. Dunham St., 46619. Tel: 219-287-9551.

6—CHRIST THE KING (1933), Revs. Thomas J. Jones, C.S.C.; John P. Riley, C.S.C.; Bro. Paul Loos, C.S.C; Sr. Diane C. Jamison, O.S.F., (Dir. of Christian Formation); Mr. Gary Chamberland, C.S.C.
Res., 52473 U.S. 33 N., 46637. Tel: 219-272-3113; Fax: 219-273-6702.
School—Tel: 219-272-3922. Jacqueline M. Klaybor, Prin.
Lay Teachers 25; Students 517.
Catechesis / Religious Programs—Students 174.

7—CORPUS CHRISTI (1961), Rev. Camillo Tirabassi. In res., Rev. Walter J. Bly.
Res., 2822 Corpus Christi Dr., 46628. Tel: 219-272-9982.
School—2817 Corpus Christi Dr., 46628. Tel: 219-272-9868; Fax: 219-272-9894. Sr. M. Marcia, F.D.C., Prin.
Daughters of Divine Charity 2; Lay Teachers 23; Students 560.

8—ST. HEDWIG (1877) (Polish), Rev. Leonard F. Chrobot; Ms. Jessica Ziembroski, Pastoral Minister.
Res., 331 S. Scott St., 46601. Tel: 219-287-8932.

9—HOLY CROSS (1929), Revs. Michael Belinski, C.S.C.; Richard Conyers, C.S.C.; John Donato, C.S.C.
Res., 1520 Vassar Ave., 46628. Tel: 219-233-2179; Fax: 219-237-6736.
School—(Grades PreK-8) 1020 Wilber St., 46628. Tel: 219-234-3422. Mrs. Karen Van Meter, Prin.
Lay Teachers 20; Students 499.

10—HOLY FAMILY (1945), Revs. Bernard J. Galic; Paul Butler (Ireland); Deacon Eugene Szynski, Pastoral Assoc. In res., Rev. Paul Miller.
Res., 56405 Mayflower Rd., 46619. Tel: 219-282-2317; Fax: 219-282-2318. [JC]
School—Tel: 219-289-7375. Sr. Joan Marie Shillinger, C.S.S.F., Prin.
Felician Sisters of Livonia, MI 2; Lay Teachers 17; Students 393.
Catechesis / Religious Programs—Tel: 219-289-7375. Ann Schramm, D.R.E.
Students 195.

11—ST. JOHN THE BAPTIST (1956), Rev. Terry E. Place.
Res., 3526 St. John Way, 46628. Tel: 219-233-5414.
School—3616 St. John Way, 46628. Tel: 219-232-9849. Sr. Connie Bach, Prin.
Lay Teachers 10; Students 195.

12—ST. JOSEPH (1853), Revs. Anthony V. Szakaly, C.S.C.; Donald W. Dilg, C.S.C.; Regina Wilson, Pastoral Assoc. In res., Rev. James Gunshinan, C.S.C.; Bro. Steve Nani, C.S.C.
Res., 226 N. Hill St., 46617. Tel: 219-234-3135.
Parish Office: 211 N. St. Louis Blvd., 46617. Tel: 219-234-3134; Fax: 219-234-2822.
School—216 N. Hill St., 46617. Tel: 219-234-0451. Mrs. Suzanne Wiwi, Prin.
Lay Teachers 20; Students 314.

13—ST. JUDE (1948), Revs. James Stoyle; Robert Muhiirwa, C.S.C. (Uganda).
Res., 19704 Johnson Rd., 46614. Tel: 219-291-0570; Fax: 219-299-3051.
School—19657 Hildebrand St., 46614. Tel: 219-291-3820. Ms. Judi Cole, Prin.
Lay Teachers 10; Students 224.
Catechesis / Religious Programs—Tel: 219-291-2797.
Students 108.

14—ST. MARY OF THE ASSUMPTION (1882) (German), Rev. Paul McCarthy.
Res., 3501 S. Locust Rd., 46614. Tel: 219-287-0225.
School—3402 S. Locust Rd., 46614. Tel: 219-287-1472.
Lay Teachers 10; Students 190.

15—OUR LADY OF HUNGARY (1921), Rev. Thaddeus Kwak; Deacon Ervin Kuspa. In res., Rev. Anthony Molnar.
Res., 829 W. Calvert St., 46613. Tel: 219-287-1700. [CEM]
School—735 W. Calvert St., 46613. Tel: 219-289-3272. Mr. Clem Wroblewski, Prin.
Lay Teachers 10; Students 180.

16—ST. PATRICK (1858), Rev. Charles J. Lavely, C.S.C. In res., Revs. Richard A. Laurick, C.S.C.; Donald J. Bielby, C.S.C. (Canada).
Res., 309 S. Taylor St., 46625. Tel: 219-232-5839.
Catechesis / Religious Programs—Tel: 219-289-3700.
Students 73.

17—FAITH & HOPE & CHARITY CHAPEL (1975), Revs. James Blaes, C.S.C.; Raymond Cour, C.S.C.; William Botzum, C.S.C.
Res., 114 W. Wayne St., P.O. Box 143, 46624. Tel: 219-289-4263.

18—ST. STANISLAUS (1899) (Polish), Revs. David J. Porterfield, C.S.C.; Ronald R. Tripi, C.S.C.; Daniel C. Coughlin, C.S.C.; Sr. Linda Bellemore, C.S.C., Pastoral Assoc.
Res., 415 N. Brookfield St., 46628. Tel: 219-233-1217; 233-5490.

19—ST. STEPHEN (1909) (Hispanic), Revs. Thomas Lemos, C.S.C.; William Pifher, C.S.C.
Res., 1102 W. Thomas St., 46601. Tel: 219-287-7681.
Catechesis / Religious Programs—Tel: 219-287-7681. Sr. Clare Alfred, C.S.C., D.R.E., Pastoral Min.
Students 215.

20—ST. THERESE, LITTLE FLOWER (1937), Revs. Paul LeBrun, C.S.C.; Michael E. Alcoser, C.S.C.
Res., 54191 N. Ironwood Dr., 46635. Tel: 219-272-7070; Fax: 219-273-9722.
Catechesis / Religious Programs—Fax: 219-243-3434.
Students 256.

OUTSIDE THE CITIES OF FORT WAYNE AND SOUTH BEND

Albion, Noble Co., Blessed Sacrament (1875), Rev. Dale Bauman; Deacon Ramiro Reyes.
Res., 300 Ravine Park Dr., Ligonier, 46767. Tel: 219-894-4946. [JC]
Church—State Rd. 9 S., Box 102, 46701-0102. Tel: 219-636-2072.

Angola, Steuben Co., St. Anthony (1926), Rev. Robert St. Martin, O.F.M.Conv. In res., Revs. Conrad Schweibold, O.F.M.Conv.; Philip Schneider, O.F.M.Conv.
Res., 700 W. Maumee St., 46703. Tel: 219-665-2259.
Catechesis / Religious Programs—Tel: 219-665-6129. Kathy Dowe, D.R.E.
Students 190.
Mission—Clear Lake, Steuben Co., St. Paul Chapel, 46703.

Arcola, Allen Co., St. Patrick (1846), Rev. Eugene A. Koers.
Res., 12305 Arcola Rd., Fort Wayne, 46818. Tel: 219-625-4151. [CEM]
Catechesis / Religious Programs—Students 95.

Auburn, De Kalb Co., Immaculate Conception (1872), Rev. Raymond J. Balzer.
Res., 500 E. 7th St., 46706. Tel: 219-925-3930. [CEM]
Catechesis / Religious Programs—Tel: 219-925-1621. D.R.E.: Phyllis Gurtner; Karen Wrona.
Students 283.

Avilla, Noble Co., St. Mary of the Assumption (1853), Rev. Daniel Durkin. In res., Rev. Herman J. Schnurr.
Res., 228 N. Main St., Box 700, 46710-0700. Tel: 219-897-3261; Fax: 219-897-3261. [CEM]
School—232 N. Main St., 46710. Tel: 219-897-3481. Sr. Theresa Renninger, O.S.F., Prin.
Franciscan Sisters of the Sacred Heart 2; Lay Teachers 7; Students 171.
Catechesis / Religious Programs—Students 91.

Besancon, Allen Co., St. Louis, Rev. Thomas Lombardi.
Res., 15535 Lincoln Hwy. E., New Haven, 46744. Tel: 219-749-4525. [CEM]
School—15529 Lincoln Hwy. E., New Haven, 46744. Tel: 219-749-5815. Ms. Agnes Hart, Prin.
Lay Teachers 6; Students 75.

Big Long Lake, LaGrange Co., St. Mary of the Angels (1937), Rev. Conrad L. Schweibold, O.F.M.Conv.
Res., St. Anthony Rectory, 700 W. Maumee, Angola, 46703. Tel: 219-665-2259. [JC]
Church—Hudson, 46747. Tel: 219-351-2404.

Bluffton, Wells Co., St. Joseph (1875), Rev. Stephen E. Colchin.
Res., 1700 N. Main St., 46714. Tel: 219-824-1380. [JC]
Catechesis / Religious Programs—Students 181.

Bremen, Marshall Co., St. Dominic (1947), Rev. Robert J. Dombrowski.
Church—212 N. Maryland St., 46506. Tel: 219-546-3601; Fax: 219-423-3382.

Bristol, Elkhart Co., St. Mary of the Annunciation (1942), Rev. James F. Seculoff.
Res., 411 W. Vistula St., Box 245, 46507. Tel: 219-848-4305; Fax: 219-848-4305.
Catechesis / Religious Programs—Students 241.

Churubusco, Whitley Co., St. John Bosco (1971), Rev. Danny Pinto (Sri Lanka).
Res., 216 N. Main St., 46723. Tel: 219-693-9578.
Catechesis / Religious Programs—Students 177.

Clear Lake, Steuben Co., St. Paul Chapel (1941), Rev. Philip Schneider, O.F.M.Conv., Admin.
Res., St. Anthony Rectory, 700 W. Maumee, Angola, 46703. Tel: 219-665-2259; Fax: 219-848-4305.
Church—8780 E. 700 N., 46703. Tel: 219-495-9913.
Catechesis / Religious Programs—Students 56.

Columbia City, Whitley Co., St. Paul of the Cross (1860), Rev. Melvin J. Herber.
Res., 307 S. Line St., 46725. Tel: 219-244-5723. [CEM]
Catechesis / Religious Programs—Students 282.

Culver, Marshall Co., St. Mary of the Lake, Rev. Jeffery Largent.
Res., 124 College Ave., 46511. Tel: 219-842-2522.

Decatur, Adams Co., St. Mary (1840), Revs. Philip DeVolder; Susil Fernando (Sri Lanka); Sr. Margaret Rose Donnelly, S.S.N.D., Pastoral Assoc.; Deacon Edward M. Hilger.
Res., 414 W. Madison St., P.O. Box 207, 46733. Tel:

219-724-9159; Fax: 219-724-8948. [CEM]
School—St. Joseph, 127 N. Fourth St., 46733. Tel: 219-724-2765; Fax: 219-724-4953. Mr. Daniel Swygart, Prin.
Lay Teachers 17; Students 361.
Catechesis/Religious Programs—Tel: 219-724-9159; Fax: 219-724-9380. Roberta Lemke, D.R.E.
Students 179.

Ege, Noble Co., Immaculate Conception (1876). Attended by St. John Bosco, Churubusco. Rev. Danny Pinto (Sri Lanka).
216 N. Main St., Churubusco, 46723. Tel: 219-693-9578. [CEM]
Catechesis/Religious Programs—Students 107.

Elkhart, Elkhart Co., St. Thomas the Apostle (1949), Revs. Richard P. Hire; Thomas Ryan (Ireland); Sr. Marcianne Targonski, C.S.S.F., Pastoral Assoc.
Res., 1405 N. Main St., 46514. Tel: 219-262-1505. [JC]
School—1331 N. Main St., 46514. Tel: 219-264-4855; Fax: 219-262-8477. Robert J. Sikorski, Prin.
Felician Sisters 2; Lay Teachers 24; Students 352.
Catechesis/Religious Programs—Tel: 219-264-0491.
Students 325.

St. Vincent de Paul (1868), Revs. Joseph A. Rulli; James R. Myers (Ghana).
Res., 1108 S. Main St., 46516. Tel: 219-293-8231; Fax: 219-293-1105. [CEM]
School—(Grades PreK-6) 1114 S. Main St., 46516. Tel: 219-293-8451; Fax: 219-293-1105. Mr. A. Gerald Strabley, Prin.
Lay Teachers 9; Students 183.
Catechesis/Religious Programs—Tel: 219-293-8071. D.R.E.: Miss Lisa Kloska; Mrs. Nancy DeMarco; Mrs. Kristi Ward.
Students 430.

Garrett, De Kalb Co., St. Joseph (1876), Deacon Harris Hoeffel.
Office: 300 W. Houston, 46738. Tel: 219-357-3122.
Res., 307 S. Ijams St., 46738. Tel: 219-357-3122. [CEM]
School—(Grades K-6) 301 W. Houston, 46738. Tel: 219-357-5137. Ms. Linda Speer, Prin.
Lay Teachers 7; Students 130.

Geneva, Adams Co., St. Mary of the Presentation (1883), Rev. Edward Narowich.
Res., 5790 E. 1100 S., 46740-9132. Tel: 219-997-6558; Fax: 219-997-6558. [CEM]
Catechesis/Religious Programs—Students 93.

Goshen, Elkhart Co., St. John the Evangelist (1840), Rev. Edward J. Krason; Deacon N. Arthur Bleau. In res., Revs. Paul Bueter; Martin A. Horvath.
Res., 114 W. Monroe St., 46526. Tel: 219-533-3385.
School—117 W. Monroe, 46526. Tel: 219-533-9480. Mrs. Diane Gorman, Prin.
Sisters 1; Lay Teachers 9; Students 137.
Catechesis/Religious Programs—Tel: 219-533-0020. Mr. James Finnigan, D.R.E.
Students 195.

Granger, St. Joseph Co., St. Pius X (1955), Revs. Peter A. Jarret, C.S.C.; William J. Neidhart, C.S.C.; Deacon William G. Gray. In res., Rev. James G. Karaffa, C.S.C.
Res., 52553 Fir Rd., 46530. Tel: 219-272-8462; Fax: 219-272-8493.
Catechesis/Religious Programs—Tel: 219-277-5760; Fax: 219-272-8493.
Students 1,300.

Hessen Cassel, Allen Co., St. Joseph (1851), Rev. Msgr. Robert W. Contant.
Res., 11337 Old U.S. 27 S., Fort Wayne, 46816. Tel: 219-639-3748. [CEM]
School—11521 Old U.S. 27 S., Fort Wayne, 46816. Tel: 219-639-3580. Miss Lois Widner, Prin.
Lay Teachers 9; Students 196.
Catechesis/Religious Programs—Students 43.

Huntington, Huntington Co., St. Mary (1896), Rev. Gary L. Sigler.
Res., 903 N. Jefferson St., 46750. Tel: 219-356-4398. [JC]
School—Huntington Catholic School. (Consolidated with SS. Peter and Paul) Primary Building, 820 Cherry St., 46750. Tel: 219-356-2320.
Sisters 4; Lay Teachers 10; Students 219.
Middle Building: 960 Warren St., 46750. Tel: 219-356-1926. Sr. Moira McGinley, O.S.F., Prin.

SS. Peter and Paul (1843), Revs. Ronald Rieder, O.F.M.Cap.; Thomas Zelinski, O.F.M.Cap.
Res., 860 Cherry St., 46750. Tel: 219-356-4798; Fax: 219-356-7154. [CEM]
School—Huntington Catholic School. (See St. Mary for details). Tel: 219-356-2320.
Catechesis/Religious Programs—Sr. Miriam Gill, S.S.N.D., D.R.E.
Students 275.

Kendallville, Noble Co., Immaculate Conception (1867), Rev. Jacob M. Gall.
Res., 319 E. Diamond St., 46755. Tel: 219-347-2522.

LaGrange, LaGrange Co., St. Joseph (1934), Rev. Paul Paroh, O.F.M.Conv.
Res., 100 E. 50 N., P.O. Box 69, 46761. Tel: 219-463-3472. [JC]

Lagro, Wabash Co., St. Patrick (1838), Rev. Gary L. Sigler.
Res., St. Mary Rectory, 903 N. Jefferson, Huntington, 46750. Tel: 219-356-4398. [CEM]

Lakeville, St. Joseph Co., Sacred Heart (1932), Rev. Richard J. Smith.
Res., 63568 U.S. 31 S., South Bend, 46614. Tel: 219-291-2826. [CEM]
Catechesis/Religious Programs—Students 68.

Ligonier, Noble Co., St. Patrick (1860), Rev. Dale Bauman.
Res., 300 Ravine Park Dr., 46767-1301. Tel: 219-894-4946. [JC]

Milford, Kosciusko Co., Our Lady of Guadalupe (1972) (Hispanic), Rev. Paul Bueter; Sr. Dolores Carlos, O.L.V.M., Pastoral Assoc.
Res. & Church: P.O. Box 605, 46542. Tel: 219-658-9594.

Mishawaka, St. Joseph Co.,

1—St. Bavo, (1903), Rev. James A. Shafer; Gus Zuehlke, Pastoral Assoc.; Deacon Kevin M. Ranaghan.
Res., 511 W. 7th St., 46544. Tel: 219-255-1437.
School—513 W. 7th St., 46544. Tel: 219-259-4214. Dr. Susan Bryant, Prin.
Lay Teachers 13; Students 230.
Catechesis/Religious Programs—Students 105.

2—St. Joseph, (1848), Rev. Robert A. Yast; Deacon Ronald Moser.
Res., 225 S. Mill St., 46544. Tel: 219-255-6134. [CEM]
School—220 W. 4th St., 46544. Tel: 219-255-5554. Mrs. Mary Geist, Prin.
Lay Teachers 13; Students 245.
Catechesis/Religious Programs—Students 100.

3—St. Monica, (1915), Rev. William Sullivan; Sr. Eileen Daudlin, S.S.N.D., Pastoral Assoc.; Deacon Carl Lenzo.
Res., 222 W. Mishawaka Ave., 46545. Tel: 219-255-2247; Fax: 219-255-8375.
Parish Center: 214 W. Mishawaka Ave., 46545. Tel: 219-255-1957.
School—223 W. Grove St., 46545. Tel: 219-255-0709. Sr. Pat Gavin, S.S.N.D., Prin.
Sisters 1; Lay Teachers 13; Students 256.
Catechesis/Religious Programs—Jane Cors Smith, D.R.E.
Students 115.

4—Queen of Peace, (1957), Rev. Elden J. Miller; Deacon Eugene Egendoerfer; Carol Cone, Pastoral Assoc.
Res., 4508 Vistula Rd., 46544. Tel: 219-255-9674; Fax: 219-255-1029.
Catechesis/Religious Programs—Tel: 219-255-0392. Betty S. Whitson, D.R.E.
Students 304.

5—St. Michael's Byzantine Ukrainian Catholic Church, (1916) (Ukrainian), Rev. John Hritzko.
Res., 712 E. Lawrence St., 46545. Tel: 219-259-7173.

Monroeville, Allen Co., St. Rose of Lima (1888), Rev. Babasino Fernandes (India).
Res., P.O. Box 406, 46773. Tel: 219-623-6437. [CEM]
School—St. Joseph, 209 Mulberry St., 46773. Tel: 219-623-3447. Ms. Carolyn Kirkendall, Prin.
Lay Teachers 4; Students 78.
Catechesis/Religious Programs—Students 61.

Napanee, Elkhart Co., St. Isidore. Closed. For inquiries for parish records contact the Chancery.

New Carlisle, St. Joseph Co., St. Stanislaus Kostka (1884) (Polish), Rev. Eugene J. Kazmierczak.
Res., 55756 Tulip Rd., 46552. Tel: 219-654-3781.
Catechesis/Religious Programs—Tel: 219-654-8738. Barbara Mireles, D.R.E.
Students 196.

New Haven, Allen Co., St. John the Baptist (1859), Revs. Derrick Sneyd; Anthony Gillespie, Assoc.
Res., 943 Powers St., 46774. Tel: 219-493-4553; Fax: 219-749-6164. [CEM]
School—206 Rufus St., 46774. Tel: 219-749-9903; Fax: 219-749-6047. Robert Sordelet, Prin.
Lay Teachers 15; Students 355.
Catechesis/Religious Programs—Students 205.

Nix Settlement, Whitley Co., St. Catharine (1850), Rev. Phillip A. Widmann.
Res., St. Joseph Rectory, 641 N. Main St., P.O. Box 358, Roanoke, 46783. Tel: 219-672-2838.
Church—Ind. Hwy. 9 & Whitley Co. Rd., 1,000 S., 46783. Tel: 219-672-2838. [CEM]

North Manchester, Wabash Co., St. Robert Bellarmine (1963), Rev. Robert J. Hammond.
Res., 1203 State Rd., 114 E., 46962. Tel: 219-982-4404.

Notre Dame, St. Joseph Co., Sacred Heart (1842), Revs. Jose Martelli, C.S.C.; James W. Thorton, C.S.C.; Christoper Miller, Pastoral Assoc.
Res., Presbytery, 46556. Tel: 219-631-7511; 7512; Fax: 219-631-9687. [CEM][JC]

Pierceton, Kosciusko Co., St. Francis Xavier (1841), Rev. Bruce Piechocki; Deacon H. Dean Tucker.
Mailing Address: P.O. Box 376, 46562. Tel: 219-594-5750.
Church—408 W. Catholic St., 46562. [CEM]
Catechesis/Religious Programs—Students 87.

Plymouth, Marshall Co., St. Michael (1862), Rev. David W. Voors; Deacon Ed Lyczak.
Res., 612 N. Walnut St., 46563. Tel: 219-936-4935; Fax: 219-936-9293. [CEM]
School—(PreK-5) 612 N. Center St., 46563. Tel: 219-936-4329. Ms. Martha Strickler, Prin.
Lay Teachers 7; Students 157.
Catechesis/Religious Programs—Therese Mitchell, D.R.E.
Students 225.

Roanoke, Huntington Co., St. Joseph (1867), Rev. Phillip A. Widmann.
Res., 641 N. Main St., P.O. Box 358, 46783. Tel: 219-672-2838. [CEM]
Catechesis/Religious Programs—Tel: 219-672-3069. Dr. Kathleen Schneider, D.R.E.
Students 113.

Rome City, Noble Co., St. Gaspar del Bufalo (1957), Rev. Charles F. Mullen, C.PP.S.
Res., 10871 N. State Rd. 9, 46784. Tel: 219-854-3100. [CEM]
Catechesis/Religious Programs—Students 70.

Syracuse, Kosciusko Co., St. Martin de Porres (1966), Rev. Edward Erpelding.
Res., 6941 E. Waco Dr., 46567-9496. Tel: 219-457-3528.

Wabash, Wabash Co., St. Bernard (1864), Rev. Timothy A. Wrozek; Deacon Ted Krizman.
Res., 207 N. Cass St., 46992. Tel: 219-563-4750; Fax: 219-563-4750.
School—191 N. Cass St., 46992. Tel: 219-563-5746. Ms. Jean Scech, Prin.
Lay Teachers 8; Students 100.
Catechesis/Religious Programs—Tel: 219-563-4495.
Students 101.

Walkerton, St. Joseph Co., St. Patrick (1856), Rev. Michael J. Winkowski, C.PP.S.
Res., 801 Tyler St., 46574. Tel: 219-586-7404.
School—811 Tyler St., 46574. Tel: 219-586-7405. Sr. Dian Majsterek, S.S.J.-T.O.S.F., Prin.
Sisters of St. Joseph of the Third Order of St. Francis 2; Lay Teachers 4; Students 70.
School Annex—807 Tyler St., 46574.
Catechesis/Religious Programs—Students 80.

Warsaw, Kosciusko Co., Sacred Heart (1852), Rev. Terry A. Fisher; Michelle Kriss, Pastoral Minister.
Res., 125 N. Harrison St., 46580. Tel: 219-267-5842; Fax: 219-267-2589. [JC]
School—135 N. Harrison, 46590. Tel: 219-267-5874. Mrs. Cheryl Zale, Prin.
Lay Teachers 11; Students 230.
Catechesis/Religious Programs—Students 225.

Waterloo, DeKalb Co., St. Michael the Archangel (1880), Rev. David Carkenord.
Res., 1098 County Road 39, 46793-9779. Tel: 219-837-7115. [CEM]
Catechesis/Religious Programs—Students 202.

Yoder, Allen Co., St. Aloysius (1859), Rev. William G. Hodde.
Res., 14623 Bluffton Rd., 46798-9741. Tel: 219-622-4491. [CEM]
School—14607 Bluffton Rd., 46798-9741. Tel: 219-622-7151. Mr. Robert Kelty, Prin.
Lay Teachers 5; Students 79.

Chaplains of Public Institutions

Fort Wayne. *Lutheran Hospital,* 3024 Fairfield Ave., 46807. Tel: 219-458-2117; 458-2001. Sr. Adele Mann, S.P.; Deacon Thomas Doell.
Parkview Memorial Hospital. Tel: 219-484-6636, Ext. 26311. Roseann Bloomfield, Chap.
Veterans Administration Hospital. Rev. Daniel Leeuw.

On Special Assignment:
Reverend Fathers—
Doriot, Thomas E., 2637 Fulton Ave., #232, Sacramento, CA 95821
McNulty, Patrick J., Madonna House, Combermere, Ontario K0J 1L0
Piechocki, Bruce, Officialis of Diocese, Chancery

Retired:
Reverend Monsignors—
Faber, William, Summer, 728 S. Main, Kendallville, IN 46755. Tel: 219-347-5041
Voors, William J., 4837 Greenfield, Fort Wayne, IN 46815. Tel: 219-485-5587

Reverend Fathers—
Bell, Milford C., Rte. 1, P.O. Box 171, Kearnysville, WV 25430. Tel: 304-725-44329
Cardinali, Fred, 4520 S. Hanna St., Fort Wayne, IN 46806. Tel: 219-456-6889
Cis, James, 6930 Whiteoak Ave., Apt. 216, Hammond, IN 46324. Tel: 219-845-5091
Gieranowski, William, Parliament House, 405 N. Ocean Blvd., Apt. 1004, Pompano Beach, FL 33062-5116. Tel: 954-784-1455
Gillig, John, 612 N. Second St., Decatur, IN 46733. Tel: 219-724-3545
Hayes, James E., St. Paul's Retirement Community, 3602 S. Ironwood, South Bend, IN 46614. Tel: 219-291-8205
Hession, Edward, 4827 Woodmark Ct., Fort Wayne, IN 46815. Tel: 219-483-2567
Hinckley, Christopher, 4924 S. Wayne, Fort Wayne, IN 46807. Tel: 219-456-7785
Hoevel, Robert J., 1104 New England Dr., Fort Wayne, IN 46815. Tel: 219-749-8245
Horvath, Joseph P., R.R. No. 4, Box 136 B, Walkerton, IN 46574. Tel: 219-586-3678
Horvath, Martin A., 114 W. Monroe, Goshen, IN 46526. Tel: 219-533-3385
Jacobs, Joseph A., 2722 Rock Maple Ct., South Bend, IN 46628. Tel: 219-271-1288
Lange, Matthew, 1149 Co. Rd. 39, Waterloo, IN 46793. Tel: 219-837-7766
Letko, Anthony, R.R. No. 5, Box 155A, Walkerton, IN 46574. Tel: 219-586-7644
Molnar, Anthony, 829 W. Calvert, South Bend, IN 46613. Tel: 219-289-6704
O'Connor, James J., 6006 Chapel Pines Run, Fort Wayne, IN 46804. Tel: 219-436-1703
Peil, William, 1841 N. Anthony, Fort Wayne, IN 46805. Tel: 219-422-1950
Rose, James, 2781 Huycks, Coldwater, MI 49036
Schnurr, Herman J., St. Mary Parish, 228 N. Main St., Avilla, IN 46710-0700
Urbine, Richard, 510 S. Harkless, P.O. Box 365, Syracuse, IN 46567
Zenz, Louis, St. Anne Home, 1900 Randallia, Fort Wayne, IN 46805

Permanent Deacons:
Bamgartner, Paul E., 417 Howard St., South Bend, IN 46617
Bleau, N. Arthur, 64429 Pleasant Pl., Goshen, IN 46526
Crowder, Richard E., 2005 Camelot Dr., Las Cruces, NM 88005
Dits, Paul, 17433 Battles Rd., Mishawaka, IN 46544
Doehrman, Michael J., 902 Lake, Ft. Wayne, IN 46805
Egendoerfer, Eugene, 1302 Cantondale Ln., Mishawaka, IN 46544
Folds, Milton, 3286 West, #50, Columbia City, IN 46725
Gizzi, Emilio, 238 Eckman, South Bend, IN 46614
Hilger, Edward, 5321 Yorkshire Dr., Fort Wayne, IN 46816
Hoeffel, Harris H., 401 S. Harrison, Garrett, IN 46738
Krizman, Ted, Box 134 W. Sinclair, Wabash, IN 46992
Kuspa, Ervin, 434 S. Liberty, South Bend, IN 46619
Larson, Fred J., 1001 Bell, New Haven, IN 46774
Lyczak, Edward, 4460 Pleasant Point Ln., Bremen, IN 46506
Madey, Robert T., 5217 Country Trail, Raleigh, NC 27609
McDougall, Louis, 3419 Sanibel Dr., Fort Wayne, IN 46815
Miller, Brian L., 1115 N. St. Peter St., South Bend, IN 46617
Moser, Ronald J., 51793 Whitestable, South Bend, IN 46637
Ranaghan, Kevin, 1003 St. Vincent, South Bend, IN 46617
Salinas, Rogelio, 30492 Co. Rd. 38, Wakarusa, IN 46573
Sanborn, Phillip J., R.R. 2, 814 Apple Hill, Angola, IN 46703
Tucker, H. Dean, 8378 E. 350 North, Pierceton, IN 46562
Walsh, Francis, 1722 Rosemont Dr., Fort Wayne, IN 46808
Walsh, James M., 2222 Broadmoor Dr., Elkhart, IN 46514
Zickgraf, Joseph R., 289 N. Columbia Pkwy, Columbus City, IN 46725

INSTITUTIONS LOCATED IN THE DIOCESE

[A] SEMINARIES, RELIGIOUS, OR SCHOLASTICATES

NOTRE DAME. *Moreau Seminary*, P.O. Box 668, 46556. Tel: 219-631-7735; Fax: 219-631-9233. This is a college level and Theological Seminary run by the Indiana Province of the Congregation of Holy Cross for Religious Priesthood and Brotherhood candidates.
Formation Staff: Revs. John F. Lahey, C.S.C., Supr.; David L. Guffey, C.S.C., Asst. Supr.; Andre E. Leveille, C.S.C.; Robert H. Moss, C.S.C.; Peter Rocca, C.S.C.; Patrick Neary, C.S.C.; James Rigert, C.S.C. In res., Bros. James E. Gormley, C.S.C.; James Lakofka, C.S.C.; John Platte, C.S.C.; Chester Ziemba, C.S.C.; Robert Ewald, C.S.C.; Richard Kyle, C.S.C.; Joseph Dougherty, F.S.C.; Revs. John I. Jenkins, C.S.C.; Robert A. Kreig, C.S.C.; Anthony J. Lauck, C.S.C.; James Trepanier, C.S.C.; Anthony Zachary Rweza (Uganda); Jerome Wilson, C.S.C.; Arokisamy Arul, C.S.C. (Province of India); Michael Sherwin, O.P.; James T. Rahilly, C.S.C.; Charles Gordon, C.S.C.; Andrew Guljas, C.S.C.; Bimal Rozario, C.S.C. (Bangladesh).
Vocations Office: Revs. John E. Conley, C.S.C., Dir.; Patrick Neary, C.S.C., Asst. Dir., Mailing Address: Moreau Seminary, Box 541, 46556. Priests 7; Sisters 3; Seminarians 36.
Old College. Mailing Address: Box 638, 46556. Tel: 219-631-8403. College candidates study here for up to three years before entering Moreau Seminary. Rev. Robert Moss, C.S.C., Dir..Priests 2; Sisters 1; Candidates for the Priesthood in the First Three Years of Undergraduate Formation 14.

[B] COLLEGES AND UNIVERSITIES

FORT WAYNE. *Saint Francis College of Fort Wayne, Inc.*, 2701 Spring St., 46808-3994. Tel: 219-434-3100; Fax: 219-434-3183; 434-3194.
For a complete listing, refer to the Colleges and Universities section.

DONALDSON. *Ancilla Domini College*. Mailing Address: P.O. Box 1, 46513.
For a complete listing, refer to the Colleges and Universities section.

NOTRE DAME. *Holy Cross College, Holy Cross College, Inc.*, 1801 N. Michigan, P.O. Box 308, 46556-0308. Tel: 219-239-8400; Fax: 219-233-7427.
For a complete listing, refer to the Colleges and Universities section.
Saint Mary's College, 46556. Tel: 219-284-4000; Fax: 219-284-4716.
For a complete listing, refer to the Colleges and Universities section.
**University of Notre Dame Du Lac*, (1842) Corby Hall, 46556. Tel: 219-631-5000.
For a complete listing, refer to the Colleges and Universities section.

[C] HIGH SCHOOLS, DIOCESAN

FORT WAYNE. *Bishop Dwenger High School*, 1300 E. Washington Center Rd., 46825. Tel: 219-483-1108. Mr. J. Fred Tone, Prin.; Mr. Eva Merkel, Asst. Prin. Lay Teachers 54; Students 942.
Bishop Luers High School, 333 E. Paulding Rd., 46816. Tel: 219-456-1261; Fax: 219-456-1262. Mary Keefer, Prin.; Jo Ann Roscoe, Asst. Prin. Chaplains: Revs. Lawrence Tippmann; Glenn Kohrmann; Anthony Gillespe. Lay Teachers 37; Students 560.

SOUTH BEND. *Saint Joseph's High School*, 1441 N. Michigan St., 46617. Tel: 219-233-6137; Fax: 219-232-3482. Mrs. Barbara Jemielity, Prin.; Mrs. Kathleen Ratliff, Vice Prin.; Rev. Walter Bly. Priests 1; Brothers of Holy Cross 4; Sisters of the Holy Cross 4; Lay Teachers 65; Students 864.

MISHAWAKA. *Marian High School*, 1311 S. Logan St., 46544. Tel: 219-259-5257. Mr. Joseoh Brettnacher, Prin.; Jennifer Tindell, Pastoral Min. Priests 2; Sisters 5; Lay Teachers 44; Students 702.

[D] DIOCESAN ELEMENTARY SCHOOLS

FORT WAYNE. *Monsignor Julian Benoit Academy*, 3029 E. Paulding Rd., 46816. Tel: 219-447-5121. Sr. Joellen Flynn, C.S.A., Prin. Consolidation of Sacred Heart, St. Patrick's & St. Henry's Schools. Lay Teachers 14; Students 320.

[E] CONSOLIDATED SCHOOL DAY CARE CENTER RESIDENTIAL TREATMENT CENTER

FORT WAYNE. *Catholic Charities Children's Services*, 2820 Reed St., 46806. Tel: 219-745-4929. Lora Heerschе, Dir. Lay Teachers 11; Enrollment 110.
The Children's Cottage, 2820 Reed St., 46806. Tel: 219-745-4929. Licensed day care facility with a capacity for 82 children, ages 2 to 12. Serves families of all faiths. Lay Teachers 9.

[F] GENERAL HOSPITALS

FORT WAYNE. *St. Joseph Medical Center*, 700 Broadway, 46802. Tel: 219-425-3000; Fax: 219-425-3222.
For a complete listing, refer to the Hospitals section.

SOUTH BEND. *Saint Joseph's Medical Center, Inc.*, 801 E. LaSalle St., 46617. Tel: 219-237-7111.
For a complete listing, refer to the Hospitals section.
St. Mary Community Hospital, 2515 E. Jefferson Blvd., 46615. Tel: 219-288-8311.
For a complete listing, refer to the Hospitals section.

*MISHAWAKA. *St. Joseph Community Hospital*, 215 W. 4th St., 46544. Tel: 219-259-2431.
For a complete listing, refer to the Hospitals section.

PLYMOUTH. *Saint Joseph's Hospital of Marshall County, Inc.*, 1915 Lake Ave., P.O. Box 670, 46563. Tel: 219-936-3181.
For a complete listing, refer to the Hospitals section.

[G] SPECIAL HOSPITALS

NOTRE DAME. *University Health Services*, 46556. Tel: 219-239-8013.
For a complete listing, refer to the Special Care Facilities section.

[H] HOMES FOR THE AGED

FORT WAYNE. *Saint Anne Home & Retirement Community*, 1900 Randallia Dr., 46805. Tel: 219-484-5555.
For a complete listing, refer to the Special Care Facilities section.

AVILLA. *LaVerna Terrace Apartments*, 517 N. Main St., 46710. Tel: 219-897-2093.
For a complete listing, refer to the Special Care Facilities section.
Sacred Heart Home, 515 N. Main St., 46710-9602. Tel: 219-897-2841.
For a complete listing, refer to the Special Care Facilities section.

[I] PERSONAL PRELATURES

SOUTH BEND. *Prelature of the Holy Cross and Opus Dei*, Windmoor Center, 1121 N. Notre Dame Ave., 46617. Tel: 219-232-0550. Legal Title: *The Work of God, Inc.* Rev. Gerry Kolf. Staff 10.

[J] MONASTERIES AND RESIDENCES OF PRIESTS AND BROTHERS

SOUTH BEND. *Congregation of Holy Cross Indiana Province Provincial House*, 1304 E. Jefferson Blvd., 46617. Tel: 219-289-6850. Legal Title: *Priests of Holy Cross, Indiana Province, Inc.* Revs. Carl F. Ebey, C.S.C., Prov.; Robert L. Epping, C.S.C., Asst. Prov.; James E. McDonald, C.S.C., Prov. Steward. Councilors: Revs. William D. Dorwart, C.S.C.; David L. Guffey, C.S.C.; M. Terrance Lally, C.S.C.; Thomas F. Lemos, C.S.C.; Kenneth M. Molinaro, C.S.C.; Mark L. Poorman, C.S.C.; Anthony V. Szakaly, C.S.C.; Richard V. Warner, C.S.C.; Bro. John J. Platte, C.S.C.
Holy Cross Priests Serving in Foreign Countries:
Chile:
Congregacion de Santa Cruz, Casilla 1271, Santiago 1, Chile. Revs. Jorge A. Canepa, C.S.C., District Supr.; Jose E. Ahumanda, C.S.C.; Thomas V. Bednar, C.S.C.; Sergio E. Concha, C.S.C.; Charles A. Delaney, C.S.C.; Joseph M. Doherty, C.S.C.; Fermin J. Donoso, C.S.C.; Joseph A. Dorsey, C.S.C.; Erwin A. Fonseca, C.S.C.; Roberto M. Gilbo, C.S.C.; Christopher P. Johnson, C.S.C.; Malcolm D. Johnson, C.S.C.; Gerald T. Papen, C.S.C.; Bro. Joaquin R. Parada, C.S.C.; Revs. Robert L. Plasker, C.S.C.; Francis A. Provensano, C.S.C.; Robert G. Simon, C.S.C.; Jorge Urtubia, C.S.C.; Romulo E. Vera, C.S.C.; Gerald J. Whelan, C.S.C.
Peru: Rev. Diego J. Yrarrazaval, C.S.C.
Instituto de Estudios Aymaras, Apartado 295, Puno, Peru. Rev. Philip T. Devlin, C.S.C., Apartado 3872, Lima 100, Peru. Rev. Gerald R. Barmasse, C.S.C., Apartado 317, Chimbote, Peru.
On Leave for Higher Studies: Rev. Robert A. Dowd, C.S.C.
St. Monica's Parish, 725 California Ave., Santa Monica, CA, 90403. Rev. Jeffrey A. Cooper, C.S.C., Oxford College 311, 50 S. College Ave., Notre Dame, 46556. Rev. John J. Donato, C.S.C.
Holy Cross Parish, 1520 Vassar Ave., 46628. Rev. James K. Foster, C.S.C.
St. Thomas the Apostle Church, 5472 S. Kimbark Ave., Chicago, IL, 60615. Rev. Charles B. Gordon, C.S.C.
Queen of Apostles Philosophy Center, P.O. Box 798, Jinga, Uganda. Rev. William M. Lies, C.S.C., 4720 Fifth Ave., Pittsburgh, PA, 15213. Rev. Russell K. McDougall, C.S.C.
Via Framura 85, 00168 Rome, Italy. Rev. Francis J. Murphy, C.S.C.
Loyola House Ontario, Box 245, Guelph, Canada, N1H6J9. Rev. Mark B. Thesing, C.S.C., 211 McCauley St., Chapel Hill, NC, 27516.
Military Chaplains: Rev. S. Douglas Smith, C.S.C., Office of the Chaplain, USS Blue Ridge (LCC-19), 96628-3300. Rev. Robert E. Roetzel, C.S.C., HHT, 3-4 Calvary Squadron, 25th Infantry Division (L),

Wheeler AAF, Hawaii, 96854.

Priests of the Province in Residences Not Listed Elsewhere: Rev. Maurice E. Amen, C.S.C., College of Comparative Culture, Sophia University, 4 Yonbancho Chiyoda-Ku, Tokyo 102, Japan. Rev. Robert C. Antonelli, C.S.C., Congregazione di Santa Croce, Via Framura, 85, 00168 Rome, Italy. Rev. James T. Burtchaell, C.S.C., Our Lady of Princeton, Great Rd. at Drakes Corner, 08540. Rev. LeRoy E. Clementich, C.S.C., 225 Cordova St., Anchorage, AK, 99501. Rev. Charles W. Corso, C.S.C., Box 3908, Fremont, CA, 94539. Rev. Ralph F. Dunn, C.S.C., 655 W. Irving Park Rd., Apt. 3916, Chicago, IL, 60613. Rev. Thomas Elliott, C.S.C., St. Vincent's Medical Center, P.O. Box 6016, Bridgeport, CT, 06606. Rev. John T. Ford, C.S.C., Mailing Address: Catholic University, Cardinal Station, Box 236, Washington, DC, 20064. Rev. William W. Faiella, C.S.C., 73-955 Santa Rosa Way, Palm Desert, CA, 92260. Rev. Thomas E. Hewitt, C.S.C., 5714 Prentiss St., San Antonio, TX, 78240. Rev. James W. Irwin, C.S.C., c/o Calle Puebla 844 Norte, Ciudad Obregon, Mexico. Rev. George G. Kahle, C.S.C., St. Paul's Retirement Community, 3602 S. Ironwood Dr., 46614. Rev. Edward C. Krause, C.S.C., Gannon University, Erie, PA, 16541. Rev. Robert J. Lochner, C.S.C., 325 Arthur Ave., Cocoa Beach, FL, 32931. Rev. John W. Lubbers, C.S.C., Our Lady of the Lake University, San Antonio, TX, 78285. Rev. Walter L. McInerney, C.S.C., 51 Joan Rd., Centerville, MA, 02632. Rev. John M. Mulcahy, C.S.C., Morris Camp, Box 550, Ontario, Canada. Rev. Edward J. Reidy, C.S.C., 73441 Fred Waring Dr., Palm Desert, CA, 92260. Most Rev. Charles A. Schleck, C.S.C., Piazza di Spagna 48, Rome, Italy. Rev. Norbert J. Sinski, C.S.C., 319 Ave. C, Apt. 2B, New York, NY, 10009. Rev. Thomas G. Streit, C.S.C., Hospital Sainte Croix, Leogane, Haiti, c/o Lynx Air Service, P.O. Box 40719, Ft. Lauderdale, FL, 33340. Rev. John A. Struzzo, C.S.C., Mission Hospital Regional Medical Center, 27700 Medical Center Rd., Mission Viejo, CA, 92691. Rev. David H. Verhalen, C.S.C., LeMans Academy, Rolling Prairie, 46371. Rev. James N. Watzke, C.S.C., 400 E. Randolph St., Apt. 3230, Chicago, IL, 60601. Rev. Herbert C. Yost, C.S.C., Solitude of the Savior, 9033 N. County Rd., 600E, Rolling Prairie, 46371. Rev. Richard P. Zang, C.S.C., Congregazione di Santa Croce, Via Framura, 85, Roma, Italy, 00168.

Holy Cross House, Notre Dame, 46556. Revs. Joseph F. O'Donnell, C.S.C., Supr.; Patrick J. Sullivan, C.S.C., Asst. Supr.; Lawrence T. Bauer, C.S.C.; Paul E. Beichner, C.S.C.; James F. Blaes, C.S.C.; Claude L. Boehm, C.S.C.; Ferdinand L. Brown, C.S.C.; Edward A. Buenger, C.S.C.; John C. Burke, C.S.C.; Jeremiah R. Buttomer, C.S.C.; Allen Cormier, C.S.C.; David H. Fosselman, C.S.C.; Arthur S. Harvey, C.S.C.; William F. Hickens, C.S.C.; Albin L. Hosinski, C.S.C.; Joseph F. Houser, C.S.C.; Joseph A. Kehoe, C.S.C.; Joseph M. Kmiecik, C.S.C.; Roman S. Ladewski, C.S.C.; Gregory J. Lombardo, C.S.C.; John P. Lucey, C.S.C.; Charles J. Mahoney, C.S.C.; Peter F. Mueller, C.S.C.; Edmund J. Murray, C.S.C.; Alfred F. Neff, C.S.C.; Michael G. O'Brien, C.S.C.; Paul B. Rankin, C.S.C.; Bernard E. Ransing, C.S.C.; Joseph A. Rogusz, C.S.C.; George E. Schidel, C.S.C.; Chester A. Soleta, C.S.C.; Edgar S. Szymanski, C.S.C.; John V. VandenBossche, C.S.C.; Andrew B. Wohman, C.S.C.; Bros. Remy Aydt, C.S.C.; Clarence J. Breitenbach, C.S.C.; Thomas J. Combs, C.S.C.; Orlando Gozdowski, C.S.C.

NOTRE DAME. *Columba Hall*, 46556. Tel: 219-239-6187. Bros. James Newberry, C.S.C., Supr.; Martinus Bombardier, C.S.C., Asst. Supr. This is the residence of the Brothers employed in various appointments at the University of Notre Dame and is also a house of retirement for Holy Cross Brothers, Midwest Prov. Brothers 32.

Congregation of Holy Cross, Midwest Province, Provincial House, 1801 N. Michigan St., Box 460, 46556. Tel: 219-239-8311; Fax: 219-289-0487. Legal Title: *Brothers of Holy Cross, Inc.* Bros. William Geenen, C.S.C., Prov. Supr.; Donald Gibbs, C.S.C., Asst. Prov. & Vicar; Donald Bailer, C.S.C., Prov. Steward; Robert Fillmore, C.S.C., Prov. Sec.; Richard Gilman, C.S.C., Councilor. Total in Residence 85.

Holy Cross Brother Center, Mailing Address: P.O. Box 716, 46556. Tel: 219-239-8330. Bro. Joseph F. Fox, C.S.C., Supr. & Dir.; Rev. Kenneth Grabner, C.S.C., Chap. Brothers 32.

Dujarie House. Infirmary for Brothers. Tel: 219-287-1838. Bro. Thomas M. Shaughnessy, C.S.C., Dir. Tel: 219-287-1838. Brothers 20.

Holy Cross Community, Corby Hall, University of Notre Dame, 46556. Tel: 219-631-7325. Revs. Robert J. Austgen, C.S.C.; Nicholas Ayo, C.S.C.; Leonard N. Banas, C.S.C.; Ernest J. Bartell, C.S.C.; E. William Beauchamp, C.S.C.; Thomas E. Blantz, C.S.C.; William A. Botzum, C.S.C.; Richard Bullene, C.S.C.; David B. Burrell, C.S.C.; Bro. John Campbell, C.S.C.; Revs. Charles M. Carey, C.S.C.; Joseph H. Carey, C.S.C.; Austin I. Collins, C.S.C.; John E. Conley, C.S.C.; Michael Connors, C.S.C.; Raymond F. Cour, C.S.C.; Alfred F. D'Alonzo, C.S.C.; Robert A. Dowd, C.S.C.; Paul F. Doyle, C.S.C., Religious Supr.; John S. Dunne, C.S.C.; Clarence R. Durbin, C.S.C.; Joseph Fey; Mark J. Fitzgerald, C.S.C.; James F. Flanigan, C.S.C.; Patrick Gaffney, C.S.C.; David A. Garrick, C.S.C.; Thomas E. Gaughan, C.S.C.; Mark R. Ghyselinck; Edmund N. Goedert, C.S.C.; Bro. Francis J. Gorch, C.S.C.; Rev. Gregory A. Green, C.S.C.; Bro. Valery Greenwell, C.S.C.; Rev. Carl G. Hager, C.S.C.; Bro. Edward Hagus, C.S.C.; Revs. Michael J. Heppen, C.S.C.; Theodore M. Hesburgh, C.S.C.; Bro. Louis F. Hurcik, C.S.C.; Revs. Daniel R. Jenky, C.S.C.; Edmund P. Joyce, C.S.C.; Thomas P. King, C.S.C.; Jerome E. Knoll, C.S.C.; John F. Lahey, C.S.C.; William M. Lewers, C.S.C.; Terence H. Linton, C.S.C.; Bro. Edward C. Luther, C.S.C.; Revs. Donald McNeill, C.S.C.; Edward A. Malloy, C.S.C.; Patrick H. Maloney, C.S.C.; Jose M. Martelli, C.S.C.; James J. McGrath, C.S.C.; Most Rev. Mark G. McGrath, C.S.C.; Rev. Leon J. Mertensotto, C.S.C.; Bro. Dennis Meyers, C.S.C.; Revs. Matthew M. Miceli, C.S.C.; Wilson D. Miscamble, C.S.C.; Robert Moss, C.S.C.; Michael J. Murphy, C.S.C.; Patrick M. Neary, C.S.C.; Stephen Newton, C.S.C.; Martin Lam Nguyen, C.S.C.; Edward D. O'Connor, C.S.C.; John H. Pearson, C.S.C.; Robert S. Pelton, C.S.C.; Mark L. Poorman, C.S.C.; Herman R. Reith, C.S.C.; James L. Riehle, C.S.C.; James A. Rigert, C.S.C.; Joseph D. Ross, C.S.C.; George A. Rozum, C.S.C.; David J. Scheidler, C.S.C.; Bro. Beatus Schlenker, C.S.C.; Revs. Timothy Scully, C.S.C.; William D. Seetch, C.S.C.; Thomas G. Streit, C.S.C.; Michael B. Sullivan; Thomas Tallarida, C.S.C.; Merwyn J. Thomas, C.S.C.; Bro. Thomas P. Tucker, C.S.C.; Revs. Joseph L. Walter, C.S.C.; Richard V. Warner, C.S.C.; Charles F. Weiher, C.S.C.; Oliver F. Williams, C.S.C.; George C. Wiskirchen, C.S.C.

[K] CONVENTS AND RESIDENCES OF SISTERS

FORT WAYNE. *Daughters of Charity of St. Vincent de Paul, D.C.*, 522 E. Madison St., 46802. Tel: 219-424-1034. Sisters 2.

Marian Convent. (St. Joseph Medical Center Convent, P.H.J.C.), 4138 S. Harrison, 46807. Tel: 219-745-4041. Sr. Marybeth Martin; Sr. Mary Conrad Kirchhoff; Sr. Julienne Smith; Sr. Laura Banet; Sr. Rose Boddie. Poor Handmaids of Jesus Christ 5.

Sisters of Providence Residences, 813 1-2 Kinnaird St., 46807. Tel: 219-744-0780. Other Location: 612 Meyer Ave., 46807. Tel: 219-744-5586.

Sisters of St. Benedict, St. Jude Convent, 2130 Pemberton Dr., 46805-4628. Tel: 219-484-4985. Mailing Address: 802 E. Tenth St., Ferdinand, 47532-9239. Other Residences: 210 S. East St., P.O. Box 605, Milford. Tel: 219-658-9594. 2115 Schomburg Dr. Tel: 219-483-7495. 631 Tennessee Ave., Apt. 105, 46805. Tel: 219-424-7987.

Sisters of St. Joseph of the Third Order of St. Francis Residences S.S.J.-T.O.S.F., 2425 Chestnut St., 46803. Tel: 219-422-6675. Sisters 3. Other Location: 2419 Chestnut St., 46803. Tel: 219-424-5084. Sisters 2.

SOUTH BEND. *Handmaids of the Most Holy Trinity Monastery-Hermitage*, 23089 Adams Rd., 46628-9674. Tel: 219-272-9425. Sr. Mary Emmanuel Baggoo, H.T., Rep.; Sr. Mary Magdalene Sladicka, H.T. Contemplative Community; Prayer Ministry; Prayer Witness which includes Retreats and Spiritual Direction.

Our Lady of Holy Cross Convent, 1300 E. Erskine Manor Hill Dr., 46614. Tel: 219-291-2522; 291-6961. Sr. Virginia MacNeil, C.S.C., Supr. Sisters 5. Convent for retired sisters. Legal Title: *Sisters of the Holy Cross, Inc.*

St. Joseph Hall, 1300 E. Erskine Manor Hill Dr., 46614. Tel: 219-291-9391. Sisters 4.

St. Joseph High School Convent, 1445 N. Michigan, 46617. Tel: 219-234-0149. Sisters 5.

Sisters of the Holy Cross Convents, 821 N. Blaine Ave., 46617. Tel: 219-287-6703. Sisters 4. 1104 N. Notre Dame Ave., 46617. Tel: 219-288-2665. Sisters 5. Legal Title: *Sisters of the Holy Cross, Inc.*, 919 St. Vincent St., 46617. Tel: 219-232-6084. Sisters 3. 52700 Shellbark Ave., 46628. Tel: 219-277-1877; 277-1646. Sisters 3. 2558 Flint Ct., #5. Tel: 219-273-5289. Sisters 2. La Casa de Amistad, 746 S. Meade St., 46619. Tel: 219-287-0531. 303 Waterfall Dr., Elkhart, 46514. Tel: 219-262-0336. 190 Village Dr., 46545. Tel: 219-258-5974. St. Paul's Retirement Community, 3602 S. Ironwood Dr., 46614. Tel: 219-291-9667. Sisters 2. St. Joseph's Towers, 316 S. St. Joseph's St., #116, 46601-2342. Tel: 219-232-8170.

The Sisters of St. Joseph of the Third Order of St. Francis Central Offices, S.S.J.-T.O.S.F.

Sisters of St. Joseph of the Third Order of St. Francis Residences, 2419 Chestnut St., Fort Wayne, 46806. Tel: 219-744-5773. Sisters 2. 2425 Chestnut St., Fort Wayne, 46803. Tel: 219-422-6675. Sisters 3. 1208 Thomas St., 46601. Tel: 219-287-7341. 1042 Patty Ln., 46615. Tel: 219-289-2735. 617 W. Wayne St., 46601-9998. Tel: 219-232-6573. Sisters 3. 1445 N. Michigan St., 46617. Tel: 219-234-0149. Sisters 2. 1043 Thomas St., 46601. Tel: 219-288-5071. Sisters 2.

Chiara Home, Inc., 1105 W. Jefferson St., 46601-2618. Tel: 219-287-3184. Sisters 2.

AVILLA. *St. Mary Convent*, 226 N. Main St., P.O. Box 109, 46710. Tel: 219-897-3484. Franciscan Sisters of the Sacred Heart. Sr. M. Debrah, Funfsinn; Sr. Theresa Renninger. Sisters 3.

DONALDSON. *Convent Ancilla Domini*, 46513. Tel: 219-936-9936; Fax: 219-935-1785. Provincialate, Poor Handmaids of Jesus Christ (The Ancilla Domini Sisters). Sr. Annemarie Kampwerth, P.H.J.C., Prov. Professed Sisters 45.

Catherine Kasper Home. Retired Sisters 65.

Ancilla Domini Hospitals Insurance Trust.

Maria Center. Senior Apartments (Efficiency and Singles), 46513. Apartments 15.

Poor Handmaids of Jesus Christ Community Support Trust.

Ancilla College.

Lindenwood, Retreat & Conference Center.

ELKHART. *Sisters of the Holy Cross*, 303 Waterfall Dr., 46514. Tel: 219-262-0336. 303 Waterfall Dr., 46516.

HUNTINGTON. *Victory Noll—Motherhouse of Our Lady of Victory Missionary Sisters*, 1900 W. Park Dr., Box 109, 46750. Tel: 219-356-0628; Fax: 219-356-0628, ext. 157. Rev. Thomas C. Fahey, Chap.; Sr. Lucy Regalado, O.L.V.M., Pres.

Legal Holding: Victory Noll Sisters Community Support Trust. Sr. Mary Elise Allmaras, O.L.V.M.; Sr. Margarita Aragon, O.L.V.M.; Sr. Joan Arnold, O.L.V.M.; Sr. Helen Marie Beall, O.L.V.M.; Sr. Jean Brosnan, O.L.V.M.; Sr. Marie Jean Chettle, O.L.V.M.; Sr. Helen Collis, O.L.V.M.; Sr. Camilla Cray, O.L.V.M.; Sr. Kathleen Cummings, O.L.V.M.; Sr. Marjorie Curran, O.L.V.M.; Sr. Adriana Daskoski, O.L.V.M.; Sr. Evelyn Marie Davis, O.L.V.M.; Sr. Denise Dean, O.L.V.M.; Sr. Madeline DeGroot, O.L.V.M.; Sr. Mary Barbara Desch, O.L.V.M.; Sr. Mary Ellen Descourouez, O.L.V.M.; Sr. Mary Ellen Dooley, O.L.V.M.; Sr. Theresa Egidy, O.L.V.M.; Sr. Marie Celine Ernst, O.L.V.M.; Sr. Sharon Rose Eshleman, O.L.V.M.; Sr. Celestine Feik, O.L.V.M.; Sr. Catherine Marie Ganse, O.L.V.M.; Sr. Mary Eva Geiskopf, O.L.V.M.; Sr. Agatha Gerlits, O.L.V.M.; Sr. Mary Joan Ginsterblum, O.L.V.M.; Sr. Monica Gogin, O.L.V.M.; Sr. Antoinette Golabowski, O.L.V.M.; Sr. Victoria Grabler, O.L.V.M.; Sr. Beatrice Haines, O.L.V.M.; Sr. Virginia Hamilton, O.L.V.M.; Sr. Elizabeth Hann, O.L.V.M.; Sr. Mary Magdelan Heim, O.L.V.M.; Sr. Veronica Hirjak, O.L.V.M.; Sr. Rose Elizabeth Hohner, O.L.V.M.; Sr. Mary Lucille Huegel, O.L.V.M.; Sr. Carolyn Issenmann, O.L.V.M.; Sr. Mary Karl, O.L.V.M.; Sr. Isabelle Kestler, O.L.V.M.; Sr. Justine Kiefer, O.L.V.M.; Sr. Josephine Konrad, O.L.V.M.; Sr. Mary Dolores Kotas, O.L.V.M.; Sr. Frances Kowalewski, O.L.V.M.; Sr. Vivian Lembeck, O.L.V.M.; Sr. Dorothy Anne Lengerich, O.L.V.M.; Sr. Mary Rosella Lengerich, O.L.V.M.; Sr. Callista Ley, O.L.V.M.; Sr. Florentine Lohr, O.L.V.M.; Sr. Madelon LoRang, O.L.V.M.; Sr. Florence Luechtefeld, O.L.V.M.; Sr. Trinidad Luna, O.L.V.M.; Sr. William Ann Maloney, O.L.V.M.; Sr. Clarice May, O.L.V.M.; Sr. Barbara McCord, O.L.V.M.; Sr. Lurlien McCoy, O.L.V.M.; Sr. Frances Meyer, O.L.V.M.; Sr. Susanna Michels, O.L.V.M.; Sr. Mary Middendorf, O.L.V.M.; Sr. Anna Rita Matoya, O.L.V.M.; Sr. Carolyn Louise Neff, O.L.V.M.; Sr. Mary Cecelia Niehaus, O.L.V.M.; Sr. Marcella Poydock, O.L.V.M.; Sr. Mary Isabel Quinn, O.L.V.M.; Sr. John Francis Radler, O.L.V.M.; Sr. Lucy Regaldo, O.L.V.M.; Sr. Cecilia Marie Richter, O.L.V.M.; Sr. Mary Lawrence Rochel, O.L.V.M.; Sr. Mary Helen Rogers, O.L.V.M.; Sr. Mary Esther Rosenbeck, O.L.V.M.; Sr. Gertrude Salitrik, O.L.V.M.; Sr. Grace Marie Samblanet, O.L.V.M.; Sr. Marie Schene, O.L.V.M.; Sr. Clare Marie Schnedecker; Sr. Marguerite Sheilds, O.L.V.M.; Sr. Martha Sijota, O.L.V.M.; Sr. Rita Snyder, O.L.V.M.; Sr. Gertrude Spetter, O.L.V.M.; Sr. Mary Matilda Spetter, O.L.V.M.; Sr. Germaine Stadler, O.L.V.M.; Sr. Joachim Stetar, O.L.V.M.; Sr. Janet Thill, O.L.V.M.; Sr. Regina Torzewski, O.L.V.M.; Sr. Monica Ulibarri, O.L.V.M.; Sr. Margaret Urhausen, O.L.V.M.; Sr. Amelia Villanueva, O.L.V.M.; Sr. Genevieve Whitehead, O.L.V.M.; Sr. Henrietta Wilke, O.L.V.M.; Sr. Mary Rita Windolph, O.L.V.M.; Sr. Barbara Marie Witt, O.L.V.M.; Sr. Dorothy Louise Wortmann, O.L.V.M.

MILFORD: Sr. Dolores Carlos, O.L.V.M.

FORT WAYNE: Sr. Grace Golenberke, O.L.V.M.; Sr. Rita Musante, O.L.V.M.; Sr. Eva Maria Sanchez, O.L.V.M.; Sr. Judith Ann Turnock, O.L.V.M.; Sr.

Angeline Walczyk, O.L.V.M.; Sr. Martha Wordeman, O.L.V.M. Professed Sisters 98.

MISHAWAKA. *Our Lady of the Angels Convent*, 1515 Dragon Tr., P.O. Box 766, 46546-0766. Tel: 219-259-5427. Convent for retired and infirm sisters. Sr. M. Julitta, O.S.F., Supr.; Rev. Maynard Kolodziej, O.F.M., Chap. Sisters 61.

St. Francis Provincialate, Box 766, 46546-0766. Tel: 219-259-5427. Sisters of St. Francis of Perpetual Adoration, Inc. St. Francis Convent and Novitiate of Immaculate Heart of Mary Province. Sr. M. Rose Agnes Pfautsch, O.S.F., Prov.; Revs. George Dubowski, O.F.M., In Res. Tel: 219-255-4068; Francis Affelt, O.F.M., Chap. Sisters 42; Novices 4.

Sisters of St. Francis of Perpetual Adoration, Inc. Capital Improvements Trust, 1515 Dragoon Tr., Box 766, 46546-0766. Tel: 219-256-3935.

Sisters of St. Joseph of Medaille, 3510 N. Main St., 46545. Tel: 219-259-6953. Sr. Eleanor Bernstein, C.S.J., Contact Person.

NOTRE DAME. *Saint Mary's of the Immaculate Conception*, Bertrand Hall, 46556. Tel: 219-284-5550; Fax: 219-284-5779. Sr. Catherine O'Brien, C.S.C., Pres.; Sr. Aline Marie, C.S.C., Councilor; Sr. M. Genevra, C.S.C., General Sec.; Sr. Joan Marie Steadman, C.S.C., Councilor; Sr. Kathleen Moroney, C.S.C., Councilor Fin.; Sr. M. Veronique, C.S.C., Councilor. Professed Sisters in Congregation 666; Temporarily Incorporated 30; Novices 12. Generalate, Candidate Program, Associate Program. Legal Title: *Sisters of the Holy Cross, Inc.; Sisters of the Holy Cross, Inc. dba CSC Consultation Services; Holy Cross Health System Corporation; The Corporation of Saint Mary's College, Notre Dame; Holy Cross Services Corporation.*

Sisters of the Holy Cross Other Residences and Programs:

Andre House-East. Tel: 219-284-5644. Sisters 4.

Andre House-West. Tel: 219-254-5645. Sisters 4.

Holy Cross Hall. Tel: 219-284-4520.

Immaculata Hall Convent. Tel: 219-284-5676. Sisters 12.

Lourdes Convent. Tel: 219-284-5589. Sisters 24.

Marian Convent. Tel: 219-284-5614. Sisters 4.

Mary's Solitude. Tel: 219-284-5599.

Moreau Convent. Tel: 219-284-5663. Sisters 7.

Queen of Peace Convent. Tel: 219-284-5579. Sisters 13.

Rosary Convent. Tel: 219-284-5845. Sr. John Margaret, Supr. Sisters 33.

Shalem House. Tel: 219-284-5358. Sisters 2.

St. Bridget's Convent. Tel: 219-232-2683. Sisters 2.

St. John's Convent. Tel: 219-284-5695. Sisters 5.

St. Joseph's Convent. Tel: 219-284-5719. Sisters 5.

Bethany House. Tel: 219-284-3674. Sisters 6.

Saint Mary's Convent. Tel: 219-284-5688; 5689; 284-5736. Sr. Patricia Mulvaney, C.S.C., Supr. Sisters 82.

The Guest House. Tel: 219-284-5667. Sisters 7.

Siegfried Hall, Notre Dame. Tel: 219-631-5158.

University Health Services, Notre Dame. Tel: 219-631-6358. Sisters 3.

University of Notre Dame, 46556. Sisters 3.

WALKERTON. *St. Patrick School Annex*, 807 Tyler St., 46574.

[L] MISSION HOUSES

NOTRE DAME. *Holy Cross Mission House*, 46556. Tel: 219-232-6005. Revs. William B. Simmons, C.S.C., Supr.; William G. Blum, C.S.C., Asst. Supr.; Arnold A. Fell, C.S.C.; Stephen Gibson, C.S.C.; Casimir Grabarz, C.S.C.; Charles W. Kohlerman, C.S.C.; William P. Melody, C.S.C.; Adrien J. Ste. Marie, C.S.C.; William M. Schreiner, C.S.C.; Paul G. Wendel, C.S.C., Asst. Supr.; John H. Wilson, C.S.C.

[M] RETREAT HOUSES & EDUCATIONAL CENTERS

DONALDSON. *Lindenwood Retreat and Ministry Center*. Mailing Address: P.O. Box 1, 46513. Tel: 219-935-1780; Fax: 219-935-1728. Carole Wielosinski, Dir. Overnight facilities for 100, Conference rooms for 250, Handicapped accessibility. Total Staff 12.

NOTRE DAME. *Mary's Solitude-Prayer Center*, 46556. Tel: 219-284-5599. Sr. Arlene Kniola, Dir. Center for spiritual direction, days and evenings of recollection, weekend retreats, individually-directed retreats, private & group retreats, scripture & special interest programs, 30-day retreat. Rooms 15. Total Staff 8.

Our Lady of Fatima Retreat Center, 46556. Tel: 219-234-1067. Directors: Revs. Michael Connors, C.S.C.; Stephen C. Gibson, C.S.C.; Charles W. Kohlerman, C.S.C.; Paul G. Wendel, C.S.C., Spiritual Dir. in Res.; Sr. Rose Edward Goodrow, C.S.C. Retreats for men, women, husbands and wives, special interest groups, professional groups, youth groups and religious.

[N] CATHOLIC SOCIAL SERVICES

FORT WAYNE. *Catholic Charities*, 315 E. Washington Blvd., 46802. Tel: 219-439-0240; Fax: 219-439-0250. Kathleen Donnellan, M.S.W., Exec. Dir. Total Staff 98; Total Assisted 11,369.

SOUTH BEND. *Catholic Charities*, 425 N. Michigan, Suite 222, 46601. Tel: 219-234-3111; Fax: 219-289-1034. Sr. Joanne Clavel, O.S.F., Admin. Total Staff 17; Total Assisted 3,400.

ELKHART. *Catholic Charities*, 201 S. 2nd St., 46516. Tel: 219-295-5284. Cheryl Murphy, M.S.W., Contact Person.

[O] MISCELLANEOUS

FORT WAYNE. *Crosier Fathers of Fort Wayne*, 1721 Magnavox Way, 46802. William G. Niezer, Registered Agent. Total Staff 1.

The Diocese of Fort Wayne-South Bend, Endowment Trust, Inc., 1103 S. Calhoun Street, P.O. Box 390, 46801. Tel: 219-422-4611. Most Rev. John M. D'Arcy, Contact Person.

Foundation For Catholic Secondary Schools of Fort Wayne, Inc., Mailing Address: P.O. Box 11632, 46859-1632. Tel: 219-424-8112. Donald J. Mauch, Pres.; Michael E. Millikan, Contact Person-Dir.

Institute for the Study of Bibliotherapy, Don Bosco Triple "T" Center, Inc., 1671 Spy Run Ave., 46805. Tel: 219-422-4228. Sr. Miriam Schultheis, O.S.B., Dir. Ed. & Counseling. Private tutoring for special needs students and home schooling. Sisters 2.

St. Joseph Medical Center of Fort Wayne, Inc., 700 Broadway, 46802. Tel: 219-425-3000. John T. Farrell, Sr., Contact Person-Pres. & CEO.

St. Joseph's Health Foundation, Inc., 700 Broadway, 46802. Meg Distler, Exec. Dir.

St. Vincent de Paul Society Store, 1600 S. Calhoun St., 46802. Tel: 219-456-3561. Steve R. App, Mgr. Total Assisted 500.

Villa of the Woods-Catholic Charities Residential Living, 5610 Noll Ave., 48606. Tel: 219-745-7039. Cheryl Smith, Admin. Residential facilities for the elderly including housing, meals, laundry services and planned activities. Total Staff 10; Residents 27.

SOUTH BEND. *Chiara Home, Inc.*, 1105 W. Jefferson Blvd., 46601-2618. Tel: 219-287-5435. Contact Persons: Sr. Sharon E. Dillon, S.S.J.-T.O.S.F.; Sr. Gretchen Clark, S.S.J.-T.O.S.F. Respite Care for people with special needs. Total Staff 2; Total Assisted 507.

Christ Child Society of South Bend. Tel: 219-288-6028. Mailing Address: P.O. Box 1286, 46624. Mrs. Rose Acklin, Res. Agent.

The Foundation of Ancilla Health Care, 316 S. St. Joseph St., 46601; Fax: 219-239-4908. Edward Newman, Pres. Housing for the elderly 202; Residents 84.

Holy Cross Care Services, Inc., 105 Jefferson Ctr., Ste. 700, 46601-1916. Tel: 219-232-3512. Edward B. Newman, Pres. & CEO.

Holy Cross Community Services, Inc., 610 N. Michigan, Ste. 310, 46601. Tel: 219-232-9534. Bro. Christopher J. Dreyer, C.S.C., Pres./Contact Person. Total Staff 12; Total Assisted 450.

Holy Cross Health System Corporation, 3606 E. Jefferson Blvd., 46615. Tel: 219-233-8558; Fax: 219-233-8891. Sr. Patricia Vandenberg, C.S.C., Pres. & CEO. Sponsored by Congregation of the Sisters of the Holy Cross, St. Mary's, Notre Dame.

Saint Joseph's Care Foundation, Inc., 801 E. LaSalle, P.O. Box 1935, 46634-1935.

Saint Joseph's Care Group, Inc., 801 E. LaSalle, 46617. Dennis W. Heck, President & CEO.

St. Vincent de Paul Referral Services, 230 E. Sample St., 46601. Tel: 219-234-6211. Mrs. Joan Eash, Exec. Dir. Total Staff 6; Volunteers 186.

St. Vincent de Paul Society of St. Joseph County, Inc., 230 E. Sample St., 46601. Tel: 219-234-6211. Total Staff 6; Volunteers 180; Total assisted 20,000.

St. Vincent de Paul Thrift Shop, 230 E. Sample St., 46601. Tel: 219-234-6009. Alicia McMurtrie, Mgr.

GRANGER. *Jesuit Community*, 16203 Candlewycke Ct., 46530. Tel: 219-243-0601. Rev. Jerome H. Neyrey, S.J., Contact Person.

St. Joseph's Farm, 52682 Current Rd., 46530. Tel: 219-272-0962. Brothers of the Congregation of Holy Cross, South-West Province. Bro. Donald Dunleavy, C.S.C., Supr. This farm is operated in the interests of the Congregation of Holy Cross, South-West Province. Brothers 1; Total Staff 2.

HUNTINGTON. *Our Sunday Visitor, Inc.*, 200 Noll Plaza, 46750. Tel: 219-356-8400. Publishers of Catholic Periodicals, Books and Religious Education Materials. Robert P. Lockwood, Pres. & CEO; Most Rev. John M. D'Arcy, Chm. Bd.

MISHAWAKA. *Alverno Administrative Services, Inc.*, 1515 Dragoon Tr., P.O. Box 1290, 46546-1290.

Alverno Health Corporation, 1515 Dragoon Tr., P.O. Box 1290, 46546-1290.

Alverno-Louisville Corporation, 1515 Dragoon Tr., P.O. Box 1290, 46546-1290. Tel: 219-256-3935.

Alverno Memphis Corporation, 1515 Dragoon Tr., P.O. Box 1290, 46546-1290.

Sisters of St. Francis Health Services, Inc. Mailing Address: P.O. Box 1290, 46546-1290.

St. Anthony Medical Center Foundation, 1515 Dragoon Tr., P.O. Box 1290, 46546-1290. Tel: 219-256-3935.

Ancilla Health Care, Incorporated.

dba St. Joseph Community Hospital of Mishawaka.

dba St. Mary Community Hospital, South Bend. 215 W. Fourth St., 46544. Tel: 219-259-2431.

St. Joseph Hospital of Mishawaka Foundation, Inc., 215 W. Fourth St., 46544. William B. Killilea, Foundation Dir.

Sisters of St. Francis of Perpetual Adoration, Inc., Mailing Address: P.O. Box 766, 46546-0766.

Sisters of St. Francis of Perpetual Adoration, Inc., Medical Benefits Trust.

**St. Margaret Mercy Health Care Center, Inc.*, 1515 Dragoon Tr., 46544. Tel: 219-256-3935.

Yves R. Simon Institute, 508 Travers Cir., 46545. Tel: 219-259-1864. Mr. Anthony O. Simon, Dir. & Contact Person. Catholic academic institute.

NOTRE DAME. *Association of St. Joseph*, Mailing Address: P.O. Box 985, 46556. Tel: 219-631-7830. Bro. Flavius Ellison, C.S.C., Contact Person.

Ave Maria Press, Inc., P.O. Box 428, 46556. Tel: 219-287-2831; Fax: 219-239-2904. Frank J. Cunningham, Pres. & Publisher. Owned and operated by the Congregation of Holy Cross, Indiana Province, Inc.

Brothers of Holy Cross Life Development Trust, Mailing Address: P.O. Box 460, 46556. Tel: 219-239-8300; Fax: 219-289-0487. Trustees: Bros. Donald Bailer; William Dygert; Paul Kelly; Stanley Olszowka; Lawrence Skitzki.

Holy Cross Associates, Mailing Address: Moreau Seminary, P.O. Box 668, 46556. Tel: 219-631-5521. John Pinter, Contact Person-Dir.

Holy Cross Services Corp., Bertrand Hall, St. Mary's, 46556. Tel: 219-284-5779. Sisters of the Holy Cross.

Midwest Hispanic Catholic Commission, N.C.C.B. Regions VI and VII, 18965 Douglas Rd., P.O. Box 703, 46556. Tel: 219-271-7459; 271-7593; Fax: 219-631-6947.

PLYMOUTH. *Earthworks, Inc.*, 9805 Union Rd., 46563. Tel: 219-936-9936. Sr. Janis Yaekel, A.S.C., Coord. An environmental education center; a sponsored entity of the Poor Handmaids of Jesus Christ (P.H.J.C.) affiliated with Convent Ancilla Domini, Donaldson, IN.

RELIGIOUS INSTITUTES OF MEN REPRESENTED IN THE DIOCESE

For further details refer to the corresponding bracketed number in the Religious Institutes of Men or Women section.

[0600]—*Brothers of the Congregation of Holy Cross.* (Midwest Province).—C.S.C.

[0470]—*The Capuchin Friars.* (Prov. of St. Joseph).—O.F.M.Cap.

[0480]—*Conventual Franciscans.* (Prov. of Our Lady of Consolation).—O.F.M.Conv.

[0520]—*Franciscan Friars.* (Prov. of St. John the Baptist).—O.F.M.

[0690]—*Jesuit Fathers and Brothers.*—S.J.

[0610]—*Priests of the Congregation of Holy Cross.* (Indiana Province).—C.S.C.

[1060]—*Society of the Precious Blood.* (Cincinnati Province).—C.PP.S.

RELIGIOUS INSTITUTES OF WOMEN REPRESENTED IN THE DIOCESE

[0230]—*Benedictine Sisters of Pontifical Jurisdiction.* (Ferdinand, IN).—O.S.B.

[3710]—*Congregation of the Sisters of Saint Agnes.*—C.S.A.

[1920]—*Congregation of the Sisters of the Holy Cross.*—C.S.C.

[1710]—*Congregation of the Third Order of St. Francis of Mary Immaculate.* (Joliet, IL).—O.S.F.

[0760]—*Daughters of Charity of St. Vincent de Paul.* (East Central Province).—D.C.

[0790]—*Daughters of Divine Charity.* (Holy Trinity Province).—F.D.C.

[1070-03]—*Dominican Sisters.*—O.P.

[1070-13]—*Dominican Sisters.*—O.P.

[1170]—*Felician Sisters.* (Presentation of the B.V.M. Province).—C.S.S.F.

[1450]—*Franciscan Sisters of the Sacred Heart.*—O.S.F.

[]—*Handmaids of the Most Holy Trinity.*—H.T.

[3130]—*Our Lady of Victory Missionary Sisters.*—O.L.V.M.

[3230]—*Poor Handmaids of Jesus Christ.*—P.H.J.C.

[2970]—*School Sisters of Notre Dame.*—S.S.N.D.

[2990]—*Sisters of Notre Dame.* (Province of Toledo).—S.N.D.

[3000]—*Sisters of Notre Dame de Namur.* (Chesapeake Province).—S.N.D.deN.

[3360]—*Sisters of Providence of Saint Mary-Of-The-Woods, Indiana.*—S.P.

[1640]—*Sisters of St. Francis of Perpetual Adoration.* (Province of the Immaculate Heart of Mary).—O.S.F.

[3830]—*Sisters of St. Joseph.*—C.S.J.

[3880]—*Sisters of St. Joseph of Medaille.* (New Orleans).—C.S.J.

[3930]—*Sisters of St. Joseph of the Third Order of St. Francis.*—S.S.J.-T.O.S.F.

[2110]—*Sisters of the Humility of Mary.*—H.M.

[3260]—*Sisters of the Precious Blood.* (Dayton, Ohio).—C.PP.S.

DIOCESAN CEMETERY

FORT WAYNE. *Catholic,* 3500 Lake Ave., 46805. Tel: 219-426-2044.

NECROLOGY

† Hoffman, Rev. Msgr. Leo A., (Retired). —Died July 28, 1996.

† Keever, Edward T., (Retired). —Died July 8, 1996.

† Kopsca, Andrew, (Retired). —Died Nov. 3, 1996.

† Vrabely, John A., Garrett, IN, St. Joseph. —Died Sept. 18, 1996.

Diocese of Fort Worth

(Dioecesis Arcis-Vorthensis)

Most Reverend

JOSEPH P. DELANEY, D.D.

Bishop of Fort Worth; ordained December 18, 1960; appointed Bishop of Fort Worth July 10, 1981; ordained Bishop September 13, 1981. *Mailing Address: 800 West Loop 820 S., Fort Worth, TX, 76108.* Tel.: 817-560-3000.

ESTABLISHED AUGUST 22, 1969.

Square Miles 23,950.

Comprises the following twenty-eight Counties in the State of Texas: Archer, Baylor, Bosque, Clay, Comanche, Cooke, Denton, Eastland, Erath, Foard, Hardeman, Hill, Hood, Jack, Johnson, Knox, Montague, Palo Pinto, Parker, Shackleford, Stephens, Somervell, Tarrant, Throckmorton, Wichita, Wilbarger, Wise and Young.

For legal titles of parishes and diocesan institutions, consult the Chancery Office.

The Catholic Center: 800 West Loop 820 S., Fort Worth, TX, 76108. Tel.: 817-560-3300; Fax: 817-244-8839.

STATISTICAL OVERVIEW

Personnel	
Bishop	1
Priests: Diocesan Active in Diocese	46
Priests: Active Outside Diocese	2
Priests: Diocesan in Foreign Missions	1
Priests: Retired, Sick or Absent	9
Number of Diocesan Priests	58
Religious Priests in Diocese	53
Extern Priests in Diocese	5
Ordinations:	
Diocesan Priests	1
Transitional Deacons	1
Permanent Deacons in Diocese	58
Total Brothers	14
Total Sisters	99
Parishes	
Parishes	88
With Resident Pastor:	
Resident Diocesan Priests	38
Resident Religious Priests	23
Without Resident Pastor:	
Administered by Priests	23
Administered by Permanent Deacons	3
Administered by Women Religious	1
Missions	2
New Parishes Created	2
Professional Ministry Personnel:	
Brothers	3
Sisters	25
Lay Ministers	97
Welfare	
Catholic Hospitals	1
Total Assisted	60,000
Health Care Centers	1
Total Assisted	622
Homes for the Aged	4
Total Assisted	801
Day Care and Extended Day Care Centers	6
Total Assisted	221
Special Centers for Social Services	16
Total Assisted	22,416
Educational	
Diocesan Students in Other Seminaries	15
Total Seminarians	15
High Schools, Diocesan and Parish	4
Total Students	1,930
Elementary Schools, Diocesan and Parish	15
Total Students	6,109
Elementary Schools, Private	1
Total Students	216
Catechesis/Religious Education:	
High School Students	6,013
Elementary Students	18,045
Total Students Under Catholic Instruction	32,328
Teachers in the Diocese:	
Priests	2
Brothers	9
Sisters	16
Lay Teachers	375
Vital Statistics	
Receptions into the Church:	
Infant Baptism Totals	4,663
Adult Baptism Totals	296
Received into Full Communion	650
First Communions	3,691
Confirmations	2,013
Marriages:	
Catholic	771
Interfaith	427
Total Marriages	1,198
Deaths	955
Total Catholic Population	192,890
Total Population	2,263,399

Former Bishops—Most Rev. JOHN J. CASSATA, D.D., ord. Dec. 8, 1932; Titular Bishop of Bida and Auxiliary of Dallas-Fort Worth; appt. March 20, 1968; cons. June 5, 1968; first Bishop, Fort Worth; appt. Aug. 22, 1969; retired Sept. 16, 1980; died Sept. 8, 1989.

Vicar General—Rev. Msgr. JOSEPH A. SCHUMACHER.

Chancellor and Moderator of the Curia—Rev. ROBERT WILSON.

Deans—North: Rev. THOMAS CRAIG, Southwest: Rev. RAY MULLAN, Northwest: Rev. WILLIAM WINASKI, East: Rev. PHILIP JOHNSON, Central: Rev. TIMOTHY THOMPSON.

Diocesan Pastoral Advisory Council—(Includes Presbyteral Council listed below). Lay Persons: Ms. JAMES GAGLIARDO; Ms. JOSIE HERNANDEZ; Ms. MARGARITA LUNA; Mr. GARY MICHELS; Ms. LINDA RAINOSEK; Ms. OFELIA TAFOLLA. Career Ministers: Mr. ANDRES ARANDA; Sr. DOROTHY EGGERING, S.S.N.D.; Sr. BERNICE KNAPEK, S.S.M.N.; Mr. RALPH MCCLOUD; Ms. MARY PESQUEDA; Deacon JAMES POOLE; Ms. KAREN ROACH; Ms. LEONA SCHWARTZ; Ms. CHARMAINE WILLIAMS, Facilitator.

Presbyteral Council and Consultors—Revs. WILLIAM HOPKINS; ESTEBAN JASSO, T.O.R.; JAMES O'TOOLE; JONATHAN SCALONE; JOSEPH SCANTLIN; JOSEPH A. SCHUMACHER; TIMOTHY THOMPSON; ROBERT WILSON; WILLIAM WINASKI.

Diocesan Finance Council—Mr. CHUCK BARTUSH, JR.; Mr. JOHN HERNANDEZ; Rev. Msgr. CHARLES KING; Mr. DENNIS MAUNDER; Mr. DAVID MORITZ; Ms. ELAINE PETRUS; Mr. ROBERT SCHUMACHER; Mr. EARLE SHIELDS, JR.; Mr. PETER FLYNN, Staff; Rev. ROBERT WILSON, Ex-Officio; Rev. Msgr. JOSEPH A. SCHUMACHER, Chm./Ex-Officio.

Catholic Foundation of North Texas—Mr. PETER FLYNN, Dir.; Mr. ROBERT V. DOCHERTY, C.F.R.E., Planned Giving.

Catholic Schools Trust—

Catholic Cemeteries Trust—

Division Directors, Diocesan Offices

Christian Formation—Dr. DAN LUBY.

Clergy and Religious Personnel Services—Rev. Msgr. JOSEPH A. SCHUMACHER.

Executive Services—Rev. ROBERT WILSON.

Financial Services—Mr. PETER FLYNN.

Pastoral and Community Services—Mr. RALPH MCCLOUD.

Pastoral Planning and Human Resources—Mrs. CHARMAINE WILLIAMS.

Schools—Sr. MARGUERITE CONNORS, S.H.Sp.

The Catholic Center—800 West Loop 820 S., Fort Worth, 76108. Tel: 817-560-3300; Fax: 817-244-8839. Departments and programs below, which are part of one of the divisions above, are listed alphabetically. Unless specifically noted the address and phone numbers are as above.

Boards and Associations

Association of Priests—Rev. GERARD SCHOLL.

Board of Arbitration and Conciliation—Mr. PHIL RECORD, Chm.; Ms. SANDRA LEIGHTON; Mr. STEVE WILCOX; Mr. CLE ROYAL; Ms. MARIA EZELA BAZAN.

Building Commission—Rev. Msgr. HUBERT NEU, Chm.; Rev. Msgr. JOSEPH A. SCHUMACHER; Mr. WILLIAM PETRELLI; Mr. CREIGHTON PICKETT; Mr. PETER FLYNN, Staff.

Diocesan Pastoral Finance Council (Budgets)—Rev. ROBERT WILSON, Chm.

Diocesan School Board—Mr. HOWARD NEEB, Pres.

Priests' Personnel Board—Rev. JOSEPH SCANTLIN, Chm., *2100 N. Davis Dr., Arlington, 76102-1803.* Tel: 817-460-2751.

Priests' Retirement Board—Rev. Msgr. JOSEPH A. SCHUMACHER, Chm.; Rev. JAMES O'TOOLE; Mr. EARLE SHIELDS; Rev. Msgr. HUBERT NEU; Mr. FRANKLIN MOORE.

Diocesan Programs

Christian Formation—Dr. DAN LUBY, Div. Dir.

Adult Formation—Dr. DAN LUBY, Dir.

Campus Ministry—Mr. PAUL COMBEST, Contact Person.

Children's Catechesis—Ms. NANCY RISTUCCIA, Dir.

Cursillo—Rev. ERIC AZCONA, O.F.M.Cap., *Cursillo Center, 2221 N.W. 26th St., Fort Worth, 76106.* Tel: 817-624-9411.

Hispanic Pastoral Services—Mr. ANDRES ARANDA, Dir.

Light of Christ Institute for Lay Ministry Development—Dr. ANN HEALEY, Dir.

Media Library—Ms. SARA BARON, Librarian.

Scouting—Rev. JOHN GREMMELS, *2016 Willis Ln., Keller, 76248.* Tel: 817-431-3857.

Worship—Ms. MARY MCLARRY, Dir.

Young Adult Ministry—Mr. PAUL COMBEST, Dir.

Youth Ministry and Adolescent Catechesis—Mr. KEVIN

PREVOU, Dir.
Clergy and Religious Personnel Services—Rev. Msgr. JOSEPH A. SCHUMACHER, Div. Dir.
Clergy Relief Association—Rev. Msgr. JOSEPH A. SCHUMACHER.
Continuing Pastoral Formation—Rev. WILLIAM HOPKINS.
Permanent Diaconate, Office of—Deacon JOSEPH MILLIGAN, Dir.
Seminarians—Sr. DONNA FERGUSON, S.S.M.N., Dir.
Vicar for Religious—Sr. THERESA KHIRALLAH, S.S.N.D.
Vocations—Rev. WILLIAM HOPKINS, Dir.
Executive Services—Rev. ROBERT WILSON, Div. Dir.
Development Office—Mr. JERRY KRAMER, Dir.
Foundation Relations—Ms. BARBARA M. SHELTON, Dir.
Parish Stewardship—Ms. MARY RALEY, Dir.
Newspaper "North Texas Catholic"—Mr. JEFF HENSLEY, Editor; Mr. JORDAN MCMORROUGH, Assoc. Editor.
Propagation of the Faith—Rev. ROBERT WILSON, Acting Dir.
Tribunal—Rev. TIMOTHY THOMPSON, Judicial Vicar; Mrs. SANDRA LEIGHTON, Dir.
Financial Services—Mr. PETER FLYNN, Div. Dir.
Accounting/Budgeting—Ms. CAROLYN JONES.
Construction and Property Management—Mr. GARY FRAGOSSO, Dir.
Cemeteries—Ms. CAROLYN JONES, Dir.
Catholic Center/Central Services—Ms. CAROL WATSON.
Data Processing—Mr. RICHARD NIMZ.
Planning and Human Resources—Ms. CHARMAINE WILLIAMS, Div. Dir.
Pastoral Planning Office—Ms. CHARMAINE WILLIAMS, Dir.
Benefits Coordinator—Ms. SHARON FIELDER.
Parish Pastoral Planning—Ms. MARY RALEY, Dir.
Personnel Officer—Mrs. MARY MILLS.
Pastoral and Community Services—Mr. RALPH MCCLOUD, Div. Dir.
African American Ministries—Mr. RALPH MCCLOUD, Dir.
Catholic Women, Council of—Rev. IVOR KOCH, *Sacred Heart Parish, 1504 10th St., Wichita Falls, 76301.* Tel: 817-723-5288.
Campaign for Human Development—Mr. RALPH MCCLOUD.
Ecumenism, Office of—Rev. Msgr. CHARLES KING, *St. John the Apostle, 7341 Glenview Dr., Fort Worth, 76180.* Tel: 817-284-4811.
Family Life and Pre-Cana—Ms. ALICE MORRIS, Dir.
Hospital Chaplaincy—Rev. RAPHAEL EAGLE, T.O.R., *St. Mary of the Assumption, 509 W. Magnolia Ave., Fort Worth, 76104.* Tel: 817-923-1911. Sr. TERESA NASCHE, S.H.Sp., *3416 Brady, Fort Worth, 76109.* Tel: 817-926-7180.
Jail Ministry—Mr. RALPH MCCLOUD, Dir.
Laotian Pastoral Center—3508 Maurice Ave., Fort Worth, 76111. Tel: 817-831-4404.
Peace and Justice Office—Mr. RALPH MCCLOUD, Coord.
Prolife—Ms. ALICE MORRIS.
Rural Life—Mr. RALPH MCCLOUD, Contact Person.
St. Vincent de Paul—Deacon JOE RAETZ, *5013 Emerald Dr., Fort Worth, 76103.* Tel: 817-457-6948.
Wichita Falls-Bethania Hospital-Chaplin—Rev. AIDAN DONLON, S.A.C., *1600 11th St., Wichita Falls, 76301.* Tel: 817-723-4111.
Schools—Sr. MARGUERITE CONNORS, S.H.Sp., Div. Dir./Supt., Catholic Schools.
Associate Superintendent—Sr. BERNICE KNAPEK, S.S.M.N.
Holy Childhood Association—Sr. MARGUERITE CONNORS, S.H.Sp., Dir.
New Schools Coordinator—Ms. GRACE MESSINA.

CLERGY, PARISHES, MISSIONS AND PAROCHIAL SCHOOLS

CITY OF FORT WORTH
(Tarrant County)

1—ST. PATRICK CATHEDRAL (1870), Rev. Msgr. Hubert Neu; Revs. Dennis Smith; Albert Tyl; Robert Strittmatter.
Res., 1206 Throckmorton St., 76102. Tel: 817-332-4915; Fax: 817-338-1988.
Catechesis/Religious Programs—Tel: 817-338-4441.
Students 436.

2—ALL SAINTS (1902) (Hispanic), Revs. Stephen Jasso, T.O.R.; Bernardo Nicolau, T.O.R. (Spain); Amando Trujillo, T.O.R. (Mexico).
Res., 214 N.W. 20th St., 76106. Tel: 817-626-3055; Fax: 817-626-3056.
School—2006 N. Houston St., 76106-8195. Tel: 817-624-2670; 624-3471; Fax: 817-624-1221.
Sisters 1; Lay Teachers 11; Students 174.
Catechesis/Religious Programs—2022 Houston St., 76106. Tel: 817-626-1711.
Students 725.

3—HOLY FAMILY (1942), Rev. Joseph Pemberton; Deacon Joseph L. Milligan, Jr.
Res., 6150 Pershing Ave., 76107. Tel: 817-737-6768; Fax: 817-737-6876.
School—Tel: 817-737-4201.
Lay Teachers 13; Students 225.
Catechesis/Religious Programs—Students 280.

4—HOLY NAME OF JESUS (1952), Rev. Lawrence Breedlove.
Res., 2637 Avenue L., 76105. Tel: 817-536-9604.
Catechesis/Religious Programs—Tel: 817-535-8495.
Students 390.

5—IMMACULATE HEART OF MARY (1961), Revs. Francisco X. Fernandez, O.F.M.Cap. (Spain); Francis Garces, O.F.M.Cap. (PH); Jose Maria Oroquieta, O.F.M. (Spain).
Res., 100 E. Pafford St., 76110. Tel: 817-923-6323.
Catechesis/Religious Programs—Tel: 817-923-8582.
Students 1,312.

6—OUR LADY OF GUADALUPE (1977) (Hispanic), Revs. Claudio Zudaire, O.F.M.Cap.; Ignacio Martinez, O.F.M.Cap. In res., Rev. Eric Azcona, O.F.M.Cap.
Res., 3301 Clinton, 76106. Tel: 817-626-7421; Fax: 817-625-8032.
Catechesis/Religious Programs—Tel: 817-624-3240.
Students 878.

7—OUR MOTHER OF MERCY (1929) (African American), Rev. Vincent B. Inametti, M.S.P. (Nigeria).
Res., 1007 E. Terrell Ave., 76104-3788. Tel: 817-335-1695.
School—1003 E. Terrell Ave., 76104-3799. Tel: 817-336-2880.
Sisters of the Holy Spirit 3; Lay Teachers 8; Students 212.

8—ST. ANDREW (1953), Revs. Warren Murphy, T.O.R.; Joseph Janiszeski, T.O.R.; Damian-Vincent Amantia, T.O.R. In res., Revs. Benjamin Medeiros, T.O.R.; Theodore J. Bradower, T.O.R.
Res., 3717 Stadium Dr., 76109. Tel: 817-927-5383; Fax: 817-927-8507.
School—St. Andrew Catholic School, 3304 Dryden Rd., 76109. Tel: 817-924-8917; Fax: 817-927-8507.
Lay Teachers 37; Students 704.
Catechesis/Religious Programs—Students 663.

9—ST. BARTHOLOMEW (1969), Revs. Richard Beaumont; Gary Geurtz; Deacon Gerald M. Barry.
Res., 3601 Altamesa Blvd., 76133. Tel: 817-292-7703; Fax: 817-292-2568.
Catechesis/Religious Programs—Students 390.

10—ST. GEORGE (1941), Rev. Ken Robinson; Deacon Ruben Curiel.
Res., 825 Karnes, 76111. Tel: 817-831-4404; Fax: 817-834-0121.
School—824 Hudgins St., 76111. Tel: 817-838-5685; Fax: 817-834-0121.
Lay Teachers 9; Students 150.
Catechesis/Religious Programs—Tel: 817-831-4404.
Students 325.

11—ST. JOHN THE APOSTLE (North Richland Hills) (1964), Rev. Msgr. Charles B. King; Revs. Phillip Magaldi; Danny Kelley; Deacon Tom Giovannetti.
Res., 7341 Glenview Dr., 76180. Tel: 817-284-4811; Fax: 817-284-1729.
School—7421 Glenview Dr., 76180. Tel: 817-284-2228.
Lay Teachers 37; Students 610.
Catechesis/Religious Programs—Tel: 817-590-0915.
Students 1,015.

12—ST. MARY OF THE ASSUMPTION (1909), Rev. Paul Neumann, S.M.; Bro. Robert Minges, S.M. In res., Rev. Raphael Eagle, T.O.R.; Bros. Paul Galantowicz, S.M.; Richard Villa, S.M.
Res., 509 W. Magnolia Ave., 76104. Tel: 817-923-1911; Fax: 817-923-0769.
Catechesis/Religious Programs—Ben Garcia D.R.E.
Students 293.

13—ST. PAUL (1952), Rev. Ellsworth T. Wigginton; Deacon Ron Aziere.
Res., 925 Yale St., 76114. Tel: 817-738-9925; Fax: 817-735-8579.
Church—5508 Black Oak Ln., 76114.
Catechesis/Religious Programs—Students 150.

14—ST. PETER THE APOSTLE (1952), Rev. D. Timothy Thompson; Mrs. Fran Bresler, Pastoral Assoc.; Deacons Louis Poth; Pat Bresler.
Office: 1201 S. Cherry Ln., 76108. Tel: 817-246-3622; Fax: 817-246-4900.
Res., 7828 Abbott, 76108. Tel: 817-246-3442.
School—Tel: 817-246-2032. Mrs. Deborah Herrera, Prin.
Lay Teachers 12; Students 171.
Catechesis/Religious Programs—Students 245.

15—ST. RITA (1910), Revs. Richard Flores; Mark Bau, C.M.C.
Res., 5550 E. Lancaster, 76112. Tel: 817-451-9395; Fax: 817-451-9421.
School—712 Weiler Blvd., 76112. Tel: 817-451-9383.
Lay Teachers 20; Students 235.
Catechesis/Religious Programs—Students 170.

16—ST. THOMAS (1937), Revs. Salvator Stefula, T.O.R.; George Thennattil, T.O.R.
Res., 2920 Azle Ave., 76106. Tel: 817-624-2184; Fax: 817-624-9688.
Catechesis/Religious Programs—Students 572.
Mission—Azle, Tarrant Co., Holy Trinity, 800 Highcrest, Azle, 76020.
Mailing Address: P.O. Box 136038, Forth Worth, 76136.

17—ST. THOMAS MORE, Rev. Edward James Hart.
Res., 2728 Merida Ave., 76109. Tel: 817-927-2414.

18—SAN MATEO (1939) (Hispanic), Sr. Felipa Guadalupe Lara, M.C.
Rectory—2909 Photo Ave., 76107. Tel: 817-737-5470.
Res., 2640 Avenue L., 76105. Tel: 817-535-8495.
Catechesis/Religious Programs—Students 118.

19—CHRIST THE KING. (Quasi-Parish). Rev. Matthias Tinh An Tran Man.
Res., 1112 Eagle Dr., 76111. Tel: 817-831-7200.

OUTSIDE THE CITY OF FORT WORTH

Abbott, Hill Co., Immaculate Heart of Mary (1946), Rev. Reinhard J. Sternemann, O.S.A. In res., Rev. James G. Ryan, O.S.A.
Res., Rte. 2, Box 82A, 76621. Tel: 817-582-3092. [CEM]
Catechesis/Religious Programs—Students 83.

Albany, Shackelford Co., Jesus of Nazareth (1970), Deacon Ruben L. Castaneda.
Res., P.O. Box 1584, 76430. Tel: 915-762-2632. [JC]
Catechesis/Religious Programs—Students 56.

Arlington, Tarrant Co.,

1—CHURCH OF ST. MARY THE VIRGIN, (1994), Rev. Allan R.G. Hawkins.
Res., 1408 N. Davis Dr., 76012. Tel: 817-460-2278; Fax: 817-277-9927.

2—MOST BLESSED SACRAMENT, (1978), Rev. Joseph S. Scantlin.
Res., 2100 N. Davis Dr., 76012. Tel: 817-460-2751; Fax: 817-460-2761.
Catechesis/Religious Programs—Students 290.

3—ST. JOSEPH'S, (1988), Rev. James Miller.
Office: 1927 S.W. Green Oaks Blvd., 76017-2734. Tel: 817-472-5181; Fax: 817-467-9319.
Res., 5108 Winterberry, 76018. Tel: 817-468-7521.

4—ST. MARIA GORETTI, (1941), Revs. James Gigliotti, T.O.R.; Joseph Lehman, T.O.R.; Richard Eldredge, T.O.R.
Res., 1200 S. Davis Dr., 76013. Tel: 817-274-0643; Fax: 817-277-4193.
School—Tel: 817-275-5081.
Lay Teachers 26; Students 459.
Catechesis/Religious Programs—Tel: 817-460-0048.
Students 361.

5—ST. MATTHEW, (1964), Rev. Msgr. Joseph A. Schumacher; Rev. Hilary M. Tran-cong-Ly, C.M.C.; Deacons Eduardo Garcia; Benito Serenil.
Res., 2021 New York Ave., 76010-6097. Tel: 817-860-0130; Fax: 817-277-7159.
Catechesis/Religious Programs—Students 830.

6—ST. VINCENT DE PAUL, (1976), Rev. Philip L. Johnson; Deacons George R. Nicklas, Jr.; Phil Christian; Charles Castleberry.
Res., 5819 W. Pleasant Ridge Rd., 76016. Tel: 817-478-8206; Fax: 817-478-8513.
Catechesis/Religious Programs—Tel: 817-478-8208.
Students 1,325.

Bedford, Tarrant Co., St. Michael (1977), Revs. James O'Toole; Michael Olson; E. James Hart; Deacons Richard Griego; Harry Heinz; Lonnie Weaver.
Res., 3713 Harwood, 76021-4097. Tel: 817-283-8666; Fax: 817-283-9306.
Catechesis/Religious Programs—Students 1,450.

Bowie, Montague Co., St. Jerome (1986). Attended by St. Mary, Henrietta. Rev. John S. Stasiowski.
Mailing Address: 105 S. Barrett, Henrietta, 76365. Tel: 817-538-4214.
Catechesis/Religious Programs—Students 67.

Breckenridge, Stephens Co., Sacred Heart (1920), Rev. Anh Q. Tran.
Res., 208 S. Miller St., 76424. Tel: 817-559-2860.

Catechesis / Religious Programs—Students 91.

Bridgeport, Wise Co., St. John the Baptizer (1889), Rev. Gonzalo Morales.
Res., 1801 Irvin, 76426. Tel: 817-683-2743; Fax: 817-683-2743.
Catechesis / Religious Programs—Tel: 817-627-2743.
Students 135.

Burkburnett, Wichita Co., St. Jude Thaddeus (1965), Rev. Severius Blank.
Res., 600 Davey Dr., 76354. Tel: 817-569-1222.
Catechesis / Religious Programs—Students 58.

Burleson, Tarrant Co., St. Ann (1971), Rev. John Hennessy.
Res., 100 S.W. Alsbury Blvd., 76028. Tel: 817-295-5621.
Catechesis / Religious Programs—Students 308.

Carrollton, Denton Co., St. Catherine of Siena (1981), Rev. Thomas J. Craig; Deacons Philip Webb; Robert Stuart. In res., Rev. Jovian Lang, O.F.M. Tel: 972-394-2945.
Mailing Address: 1705 Peters Colony, 75007-3704. Tel: 972-492-3237; Fax: 972-394-0676.
Catechesis / Religious Programs—Students 845.

Cisco, Eastland Co., Holy Rosary (1920). Attended by St. Rita, Ranger. Rev. Robert D. Edwards.
1109 Blackwell St., Ranger, 76470. Tel: 817-647-3167.

Cleburne, Johnson Co., St. Joseph (1888), Rev. Sergio Rizo.
Mailing Address: 807 N. Anglin St., 76031. Tel. 817-645-4478.
Catechesis / Religious Programs—Students 245.

Clifton, Bosque Co., Holy Angels (1954), Rev. Salvador Perez, O.S.A.
Church—Box 431, 76634. Tel: 817-675-8877.
Catechesis / Religious Programs—Students 70.

Colleyville, Good Shepherd (1992), Rev. Robert Wilson. Administrators: Sr. Dorothy Eggering, S.S.N.D.; Sr. Theresa Khirallah, S.S.N.D.
1000 Tinker Rd., 76034. Tel: 817-421-1387; Fax: 817-421-4709.
Catechesis / Religious Programs—Students 862.

The Colony, Denton Co., Holy Cross (1981), Rev. Publius Xuereb.
Church—7000 Morning Star, P.O. Box 560156, 75056. Tel: 972-625-5252; Fax: 972-370-5524.
Catechesis / Religious Programs—Students 465.

Comanche, Comanche Co., Sacred Heart (1964). Attended by St. Brendan, Stephenville. Rev. Philip McNamara, S.A.C.
Church—1444 W. Washington Ave., Stephenville, 76401. Tel: 817-965-5693.
Catechesis / Religious Programs—Students 78.

Crowell, Foard Co., St. Joseph (1910). Attended by Holy Family, Vernon. Rev. Oren W. Key, S.J.
Church—2200 Roberts, P.O. Box 1377, Vernon, 76384. Tel: 817-552-2895; Fax: 817-552-6084.

Decatur, Wise Co., Assumption of the Blessed Virgin Mary (1938), Rev. Gonzalo Morales.
Res., 1305 Deer Park Rd., 76234-9701. Tel: 817-627-3307; Fax: 817-683-2743.
Church Rectory: 1801 Irvin, Bridgeport, 76426. Tel: 817-627-2561.
Catechesis / Religious Programs—Students 175.

De Leon, Comanche Co., Our Lady of Guadalupe (1975). Attended by St. Brendan, Stephenville. Rev. Philip McNamara, S.A.C.
Mailing Address: c/o St. Brendan, 1444 W. Washington, Stephenville, 76401. Tel: 817-965-5693.
Church—Hwy. 16, 2 miles S. of Hwy. 6, 76444. Tel: 817-893-5511.
Catechesis / Religious Programs—Students 75.

Denton, Denton Co., Immaculate Conception (1894), Rev. Juan Rivero; Deacon Popo Gonzalez. In res., Rev. Robert Lewandowski, S.M.
Res., 1215 N. Elm St., 76201. Tel: 817-565-1770; Fax: 817-382-7939.
Catechesis / Religious Programs—Sr. Helen Stejskal, S.S.N.D., D.R.E.
Students 360.

St. Mark (1995), Rev. Eugene Sweeney, S.M.
2800 Pennsylvania, 76205. Tel: 817-387-6223; Fax: 817-382-1641.

Dodson Prairie, Palo Pinto Co., St. Boniface (1913). Attended by Sacred Heart, Breckenridge. Rev. Anh Q. Tran.
Mailing Address: 208 S. Miller, Breckenridge, 76424. Tel: 817-559-2860.

Dublin, Erath Co., St. Mary (1916). Attended by St. Brendan, Stephenville. Rev. Philip McNamara, S.A.C.
1444 W. Washington Ave., Stephenville, 76401. Tel: 817-965-5693.
Catechesis / Religious Programs—Students 112.

Eastland, Eastland Co., St. Francis Xavier (1920). Attended by St. Rita, Ranger. Rev. Robert Dale Edwards.
1109 Blackwell St., Ranger, 76470. Tel: 817-647-3167; Fax: 817-647-3167.

Electra, Wichita Co., St. Paul (1966), Deacon Patrick Burke, Admin.
Mailing Address: P.O. Box 991.
Res., 709 W. Rebecca St., Iowa Park, 76367. Tel: 817-592-2930. [JC]
Church—500 N. Bailey, 76360. Tel: 817-495-3464; 592-2802.

Gainesville, Cooke Co., St. Mary (1879), Rev. Jack Dowling, O.S.A. In res., Rev. David Petraitis, O.S.A., Hispanic Min.
Res., 805 N. Weaver St., 76240. Tel: 817-665-2413; Fax: 817-665-0957.
School—931 N. Weaver St., 76240. Tel: 817-668-7898; Fax: 817-668-1881.
Sisters of St. Mary of Namur 1; School Sisters of Notre Dame 2; Lay Teachers 17; Students 200.
Catechesis / Religious Programs—Tel: 817-665-5395.
Students 199.
Convent—825 N. Weaver St., 76240.

Glen Rose, Somervell Co., St. Rose of Lima (1969). Attended by St. Frances Cabrini. Rev. Lawrence Gould, S.A.C.
P.O. Box 757, Granbury, 76048. Tel: 817-326-2131. [JC]

Graford, Palo Pinto Co., St. Francis of Assisi (1949). Attended by Sacred Heart, Breckenridge. Rev. Anh Q. Tran.
Res., P.O. Box 404, 76449. Tel: 817-779-2023.

Graham, Young Co., St. Mary (1922), Rev. Raymund Mullan.
Res., 1218 Rodgers Dr., Box 547, 76450. Tel: 817-549-4314. [JC]
Catechesis / Religious Programs—Students 147.

Granbury, Hood Co., St. Frances Cabrini (1976), Rev. Lawrence Gould, S.A.C.; Deacon Ed Bevers.
Res., F.M. 4 South, P.O. Box 757, 76048. Tel: 817-326-2131. [JC]
Catechesis / Religious Programs—812 Shady Grove Dr., 76048. Tel: 817-326-2131.
Students 205.

Grapevine, Tarrant Co., St. Francis of Assisi (1949), Rev. B. S. Szarka, O.Cist.
Res., P.O. Box 56, 76099-0056. Tel: 817-481-2685; Fax: 817-488-3169.
Catechesis / Religious Programs—Students 1,098.

Henrietta, Clay Co., St. Mary (1879), Rev. John S. Stasiowski.
Res., 105 S. Barrett St., 76365. Tel: 817-538-4214. [CEM]

Hillsboro, Hill Co., Our Lady of Mercy (1887), Rev. Alfred LaFleur, O.S.A.
Res., Interstate 35, P.O. Box 567, 76645. Tel: 817-582-5640.
Catechesis / Religious Programs—Students 65.

Iowa Park, Wichita Co., Christ the King (1980), Deacon Patrick Burke, Admin.
Mailing Address: P.O. Box 239, 76367.
Office: 1008 First St., 76367. Tel: 817-592-2802.
Res., 709 W. Rebecca St., 76367. Tel: 817-592-2930; Fax: 817-592-2802.
Catechesis / Religious Programs—Students 51.

Jacksboro, Jack Co., St. Mary (1911), Rev. Gonzalo Morales.
Mailing Address: c/o St. John the Baptizer, 1801 Irvin St., Bridgeport, 76426. Tel: 817-683-2743; Fax: 817-683-2743.
Church—Hwy. 148 N., 76458.

Keller, Tarrant Co., St. Elizabeth Ann Seton (1985), Rev. John Gremmels.
Office: 2016 Willis Ln., 76248. Tel: 817-431-3857; Fax: 817-431-9568.
Catechesis / Religious Programs—Tel: 817-431-6023.
Students 800.

Knox City, Knox Co., Santa Rosa (1948). Attended by St. Joseph, Rhineland. Rev. Kevin Fagan.
Mailing Address: Rte. 2, Box 15, Munday, 76371. Tel: 817-422-4994.
Church—N. 3rd and Ave. G, 79521. Tel: 817-658-5062. [JC]
Catechesis / Religious Programs—Students 100.

Lewisville, Denton Co., St. Philip the Apostle (1976), Rev. Jonathan Scalone.
Office: 1773 Canterbury Ln., 75067. Tel: 972-436-9581; Fax: 972-436-5302.
Catechesis / Religious Programs—1897 W. Main, 75067.
Students 1,003.

Lindsay, Cooke Co., St. Peter (1902), Rev. Eugene Luke, O.S.B.
Res., 424 Main St., P.O. Box 148, 76250. Tel: 817-668-7609; Fax: 817-668-7723. [CEM]
Catechesis / Religious Programs—P.O. Box 95, 76250.
Students 320.

Mansfield, Tarrant Co., St. Jude (1898), Rev. Karl Schilken.
Res., 500 E. Dallas St., 76063. Tel: 817-473-6709; Fax: 817-477-2088. [CEM]
Catechesis / Religious Programs—Tel: 817-473-0768.
Students 376.
Parish Hall: Tel: 817-473-9463.

Megargel, Archer Co., St. Mary (1909). Attended by Sacred Heart. Rev. Bart J. Landwermeyer.
205 N. Cedar, Seymour, 76380. Tel: 817-888-5252; Fax: 817-888-2136. [CEM]

Mineral Wells, Palo Pinto Co., Our Lady of Lourdes (1960), Rev. John Nagle, S.A.C.
Res., 108 N.W. 4th Ave., P.O. Box 1327, 76068. Tel: 817-325-4789.
Catechesis / Religious Programs—Students 227.

Montague, Montague Co., St. William (1899). Attended by St. Mary, Henrietta. Rev. John S. Stasiowski.
Mailing Address: 105 S. Barrett, Henrietta, 76365. Tel: 817-538-4214. [CEM]
Catechesis / Religious Programs—Students 63.

Morgan, Bosque Co., Our Lady of Guadalupe (1987), Rev. Salvador Perez.
Mailing Address: P.O. Box 431, Clifton, 76634. Tel: 817-675-8877.
Church—Jessup St.

Muenster, Cooke Co., Sacred Heart (1889), Revs. David Bellinghausen, O.S.B.; Frowin Schoech, O.S.B.
Res., 714 N. Main St., 76252. Tel: 817-759-2511. [CEM]
Pre-School—.
Lay Teachers 2; Students 25.
School—Tel: 817-759-4121.
Benedictine Sisters 1; Lay Teachers 14; Students 175.
High School—Benedictine Sisters 2; Priests 1; Lay Teachers 10; Students 96.
Catechesis / Religious Programs—Tel: 817-759-2511 #37.
Students 231.

Nocona, Montague Co., St. Joseph (1948). Attended by St. Mary, Henrietta. Rev. John S. Stasiowski.
105 S. Barrett, Henrietta, 76365. Tel: 817-538-4214.

Olney, Young Co., St. Theresa of the Infant Jesus (1935). Attended by St. Mary, Graham. Rev. Raymund A. Mullan.
Mailing Address: P.O. Box 547, Graham, 76450. Tel: 817-549-4314. [JC]
Church—Oak & Avenue E, 76374. Tel: 817-564-5426.

Penelope, Hill Co., Nativity of the Blessed Virgin Mary (1909), Rev. Reinhard Sternemann, O.S.A.
Mailing Address: P.O. Box 98, 76676. Tel: 817-533-2325. [CEM 2]
Catechesis / Religious Programs—Students 78.

Pilot Point, Denton Co., St. Thomas Aquinas (1891), Rev. Donald Brennan, O.S.A.
Res., 925 N. Charcut, 76258. Tel: 817-686-2088. [CEM]
Catechesis / Religious Programs—400 E. Gibbons, 76258. Tel: 817-686-2360.
Students 257.

Quanah, Hardeman Co., St. Mary (1914). Attended by Holy Family, Vernon. Rev. Oren Key, S.J.
2200 Roberts, P.O. Box 1377, Vernon, 76384. Tel: 817-552-2895; Fax: 817-552-6084. [JC]

Ranger, Eastland Co., St. Rita (1919), Rev. Robert D. Edwards.
Res., 1109 Blackwell St., 76470. Tel: 817-647-3167.

Rhineland, Knox Co., St. Joseph (1895), Rev. Kevin Fagan.
Res., Rte. 2, P.O. Box 15, Rhineland, Munday, 76371. Tel: 817-422-4994. [CEM]
Catechesis / Religious Programs—Students 134.

Scotland, Archer Co., St. Boniface (1911). Attended by St. Mary, Windthorst. Rev. David Kraeger, T.O.R.
Church—76379. Tel: 817-423-6687; Fax: 817-423-6657. [CEM]

Seymour, Baylor Co., Sacred Heart (1910), Rev. Bart J. Landwermeyer.
Res., 205 N. Cedar St., 76380. Tel: 817-888-3902. [CEM]
Sacred Heart Pastoral Center—207 W. Pecan, 76380. Tel: 817-888-5252; Fax: 817-888-2136.
Catechesis / Religious Programs—Students 139.

Stephenville, Erath Co., St. Brendan (1958), Rev. Philip McNamara, S.A.C.
Res., 1444 W. Washington Ave., 76401. Tel: 817-965-5693.
Catechesis / Religious Programs—Students 230.

Strawn, Palo Pinto Co., St. John (1912). Attended by St. Rita. Rev. Robert Dale Edwards.
Res., 1109 Blackwell Rd., Ranger, 76470. Tel: 817-647-3167.

Throckmorton, Throckmorton Co., San Patricio (1964). Attended by Sacred Heart, Breckenridge. Rev. Anh Q. Tran.

Mailing Address: 208 S. Miller, Breckenridge, 76024. Tel: 817-559-2860.

Valley View, Cooke Co., St. John (1946), Rev. Harry W. Fisher.
Res., 709 Lee St., 76272. Tel: 817-726-3524. [JC]

Vernon, Wilbarger Co., Holy Family (1891), Rev. Oren Key, S.J.
Res., 2200 Roberts, P.O. Box 1377, 76384. Tel: 817-552-2895; Fax: 817-552-6084.
Catechesis/Religious Programs—Students 180.

Weatherford, Parker Co., St. Stephen (1882), Rev. Michael McCormack, S.A.C.
Mailing Address: P.O. Box 1743, 76086.
Office: 1802 Bethel Rd., 76086. Tel: 817-596-9585.
Res., 105 E. Columbia St., 76086. Tel: 817-596-9586.
Catechesis/Religious Programs—Students 520.

Wichita Falls, Wichita Co., Our Lady of Guadalupe (1927) (Hispanic), Rev. Hector Medina.
Res., 421 Marconi, 76301. Tel: 817-766-2735. [JC]
Parish Hall: Tel: 817-322-0143.
Catechesis/Religious Programs—Students 307.

Our Lady Queen of Peace (1956), Rev. William Winaski; Deacons Richard A. Arndt; Larry W. Bills.
Res., 4040 York Ave., 76309. Tel: 817-696-1253; Fax: 817-696-1216. [JC]
Catechesis/Religious Programs—Students 254.

Sacred Heart (1891), Revs. Ivor Koch; John Vu Quang Huy, C.M.C.
Mailing Address: 1504 Tenth St., 76301. Tel: 817-723-5288; Fax: 817-767-0160.
Res., 1505 Ninth St., 76301. Tel: 817-723-5288; Fax: 817-767-0160.
Catechesis/Religious Programs—Students 378.
Mission—Wichita Falls, Wichita Co., The Assumption of Mary, 909 Lincoln St., 76304. Tel: 817-322-2500. [CEM][JC]

Windthorst, Archer Co., St. Mary (1892), Rev. David Kraeger, T.O.R.
Res., P.O. Drawer 230, 76389. Tel: 817-423-6687; Fax: 817-423-6657. [CEM]
Catechesis/Religious Programs—Students 305.

Chaplains of Public Institutions

DENTON. *State School* 1215 E. Elm St., 76201. Tel: 817-387-1755. Rev. Juan Rivero.

GAINESVILLE. *Texas Youth Council Youth Facility*. Vacant. 805 N. Weaver, 76240. Tel: 817-665-2413.

WICHITA FALLS. *State Hospital* Tel: 817-723-4111. Rev. Aidan Donlon, S.A.C.

On Duty Outside the Diocese:
Reverend Fathers—
Renteria, Rudy, 4050 Glenridge Rd., Dallas, TX 75220
Spong, William, Ogdensburg, NY
Thames, Robert, Residencia Episcopal, C.P. 34, Trinidad, Bolivia

Absent on Leave:
Reverend Fathers—
Miranda, Luke
Owen, David

Retired:
Reverend Monsignors—
Hartnett, Donald, Retirement Inn, 8000 Calmont Apt. 113, Fort Worth, TX 76116
Reilly, James J., 321 W. Butler Ave., Chalfont, PA 18914
Wolf, Vincent J., 330 W. Camp Wisdom Rd., Ducanville, TX 75116
Reverend Fathers—
Boyle, James A., Wildwood Springs, 305 Springdale Village, Bradenton, FL 34207
Cooney, Gerald, c/o 1824 Clark Rd., Crowley, TX 76036-9714
Curtsinger, George, 3015 Lubbock #5, Fort Worth, TX 76109
Stephens, Gerald, 208 Martin St., Wylie, TX 75098

Permanent Deacons:
Amos, Clarence
Armknecht, William
Arndt, Richard
Aziere, Ronald
Barry, Gerald
Bell, James
Bevers, Eddy
Bills, Larry
Bolf, William
Bowden, Edgar
Bressler, Patrick
Burke, Patrick
Casias, Arturo
Castaneda, Ruben
Castellon, Damaso
Castleberry, Charles
Christian, Phil
Curiel, Ruben
Detwiler, Russell
Firth, John
Friedman, William
Garcia, Eduardo
Garcia, Raul
Giovannitti, Thomas
Gonzalez, Emilio
Greene, Clifford
Griego, Richard
Gutbier, Klaus
Guzman, John
Hatch, Larry
Heinz, Harry
Junginger, George
Konar, Albert
Kunath, Wolfgang
Lamarre, Raymond
Luna, Andres
Marquez, Mario
McDermott, John
Metzinger, Clarence
Milligan, Joseph
Nicklas, George
Novak, Jim
Perez, Anastasio
Poole, James
Poth, Louis
Raetz, Joseph
Salva, Hector
Serenil, Benito
Stojak, Richard
Stuart, Robert
Tassin, Terry
Torrez, Simon
Vicroy, Clarence
Warner, Don
Weaver, Lonnie
Webb, Philip
Wolf, George
Wuenschel, Douglas

INSTITUTIONS LOCATED IN THE DIOCESE

[A] HIGH SCHOOLS, DIOCESAN

FORT WORTH. *Cassata Learning Center*. (Coed Secondary). 1400 Hemphill St., 76104-4796. Tel: 817-926-1745; Fax: 817-926-3132. Ms. Cynthia Morton, Exec. Dir. Teachers 9; Students 458.

Nolan Catholic High School. (Grades 7-12). (Coed), 4501 Bridge St., 76103. Tel: 817-457-2920; Fax: 817-496-9775. Society of Mary. Bro. Eugene Meyerpeter, S.M., Prin.; Revs. James Young, S.M.; Robert Hackel, S.M. Priests 1; Brothers 9; Sisters 3; Lay Teachers 72; Students 1,118.

Nolan School Trust.

WICHITA FALLS. *Notre Dame Middle-High School*, 2821 Lansing Blvd., 76309. Tel: 817-692-6041; Fax: 817-692-2811. Mr. Joe Cluley, Prin. Lay Teachers 24; Students 257.

[B] HIGH SCHOOLS, PAROCHIAL

MUENSTER. *Sacred Heart School*. (Grades Prek-12), 141 E. Sixth, Box 588. Mr. Jack Murdock, Prin. Priests 1; Olivetan Benedictine Sisters 3; Lay Teachers 20; Students 297.

**Sacred Heart Teachers Trust Fund*.

[C] ELEMENTARY AND SECONDARY SCHOOLS, PAROCHIAL

ARLINGTON. *South Arlington Catholic School*, 2021 New York Ave., 76010-6097. Tel: 817-459-2922; Fax: 817-459-3690. Total Staff 23; Students 159.

DENTON. *Immaculate Conception Catholic School*, 1212 Bolivar, 76201. Tel: 817-381-1155; Fax: 817-381-1837. Lay Teachers 5; Students 92.

GRAPEVINE. *Holy Trinity Catholic School*. Mailing Address: P.O. Box 3338, 76099-3338. 3450 William D. Tate Blvd., 76051. Tel: 817-283-8834; Fax: 817-283-7977. Lay Teachers 19; Students 300.

WICHITA FALLS. *Notre Dame Elementary School*, 4060 York Ave., 76309. Sisters 2; Lay Teachers 19; Students 288.

[D] ELEMENTARY SCHOOLS, PRIVATE

FORT WORTH. *Our Lady of Victory Elementary*, 3320 S. Hemphill St., 76110. Tel: 817-924-5123; Fax: 817-922-6598. Lay Teachers 10; Students 216.

[E] CHILDREN'S GROUP CARE

FORT WORTH. *Catholic Charities, Inc*. An Independent Corporation Founded by the Diocese of Fort Worth, 2701 Burchill Rd.,N., 76105-3012. Tel: 817-534-0814; Fax: 817-535-8779. Karen Spicer, LMSW-ACP, Exec. Dir.

Emergency Financial Assistance, 1404 Hemphill, 76104. Tel: 817-921-5381. Carolyn Henry, Dept. Dir. Provides direct financial and material assistance to families in financial crisis.

Office Sites: 401 W. Sanford, Arlington, 76011. Tel: 817-274-2560. 349 N.W. Renfro, Burleson, 76028. Tel: 817-295-6252. 6201 Camp Bowie Blvd., 76116. Tel: 817-737-9338. 208 Miller, 76105. Tel: 817-534-5610.

Special Services Department: 2701 Burchill Rd., N., 76105-3012. Tel: 817-534-0814; Fax: 817-535-8779. Ann Tucker, Ph.D., Dept. Dir. Administers residential programs for the elderly, disabled, and additional programs for special populations.

Program Sites: Nuestro Hogar, Inc., 709 Magnolia St., Arlington, 76012. Tel: 817-216-0608; Fax: 817-861-6178. CASA, Inc., 3201 Sondra Dr., 76107. Tel: 817-332-7276; Fax: 817-877-0487. CASA Brendan and CASA II, Inc., 1300 Hyman St., Stephenville, 76401. Tel: 817-965-6964; Fax: 817-968-3072.

Department of Family & Children's Services, 2701 Burchill Rd., N., 76105. Tel: 817-534-0814; Fax: 817-535-8779. Johnny Wright, LMSW-ACP. Provides a wide range of clinical and supportive services.

Program Sites: St. Teresa's Group Home, 2701 Burchill Rd., N., 76105-3012. Tel: 817-534-0814. Assessment Center of Tarrant County (children's shelter), 2000 McKenzie, 76105. Extended Day Treatment, 3600 Fossill, 76111. Tel: 817-834-0044. Therapeutic Foster and Respite Care, 2701 Burchill Rd., N., 76105. Tel: 817-534-0814. Family Preservation Unit, 1208 W. Magnolia, 76104. Anne Simon Reeves Children's Center, 2641 Ave. L, 76105. Tel: 817-536-1160.

Outpatient Clinical Services Department, 1216 W. Magnolia, 76104. Tel: 817-536-6857; Fax: 817-923-8211.

Immigration and Refugee Services Department, 1216 W. Magnolia, 76104. Tel: 817-338-0774; Fax: 817-335-9749. Katy Burns, LMSW-ACP, Dept. Dir. Immigration Counseling, Refugee Resource Center and Refugee Resettlement. Assistance in migration matters: family reunification, adjustment of status, naturalization, ESL, and employment services.

Community Support Services Department, 1404 Hemphill, 76104. Carolyn Henry, LMSW-AP, Dept. Dir. Coordinates the Emergency Assistance Association of Tarrant County, Social Concerns, Holiday Network, Disaster Relief, Public Relations.

[F] GENERAL HOSPITALS

WICHITA FALLS. *Bethania Regional Health Care Center*, 1600 Eleventh St., 76301. Tel: 817-723-4111.
For a complete listing, refer to the Hospitals section.

[G] RETIREMENT & DISABILITY HOUSING

FORT WORTH. *Casa del Cor, Inc.*, 2701 Burchill Rd., N., 76105. Tel: 817-534-0814; Fax: 817-535-8779.
For a complete listing, refer to the Special Care Facilities section.

Casa, Inc. Housing for the Elderly and Handicapped, 3201 Sondra Dr., 76107. Tel: 817-332-7276.
For a complete listing, refer to the Special Care Facilities section.

ARLINGTON. *Nuestro Hogar, Inc. Catholic Charities*, 709 Magnolia St., 76012. Tel: 817-261-0608.
For a complete listing, refer to the Special Care Facilities section.

CROWLEY. *St. Francis Village, Inc.*, 1 Chapel Plaza, 76036. Tel: 817-292-5786.
For a complete listing, refer to the Special Care Facilities section.

STEPHENVILLE. *CASA Brendan and CASA II, Inc. Catholic Charities*, 1300 Hyman, 76401. Tel: 817-965-6964.
For a complete listing, refer to the Special Care Facilities section.

[H] MONASTERIES AND RESIDENCES OF PRIESTS AND BROTHERS

CROWLEY. *St. Maximilian Kolbe Friary* (Fort Worth), 1 Marquard Cir. & 2 Marquard Cir., St. Francis Village, 76036. Tel: 817-370-9747; Fax: 817-294-2989. Revs. Peter Fritz, O.F.M., Guardian; Raymar Bobber, O.F.M.; John Ostdiek, O.F.M.; Vincent Elsen, O.F.M; Jovian Lang, O.F.M; Armand Lubanski, O.F.M; Raymond Nytes, O.F.M.; Cal Giesen, O.F.M.; Donald Werr, O.F.M.; Mathias Kiemen, O.F.M; Bros. Earl Benz, O.F.M.; Allan Haiar, O.F.M.

[I] CONVENTS AND RESIDENCES FOR SISTERS

FORT WORTH. *Hermanas Catequistas Guadalupanas*, 3203 Clinton, 76106. Tel: 817-740-0038. Sr. Maria Martinez, H.C.G., Supr. Sisters 4.

Missionary Catechists of the Sacred Hearts of Jesus and Mary, 2640 Avenue L., 76105. Tel: 817-535-8495. Sr. Felipa Guadalupe Lara, Supr. Sisters 4.

Provincialate, Our Lady of Victory Center, 909 W. Shaw St., 76110. Tel: 817-923-8393; Fax: 817-921-5064. Provincial House of the Western Province, Sisters of St. Mary of Namur. Sr. Joan Markey, S.S.M.N., Prov. Supr.; Rev. James Young, S.M., Chap.

Sisters of St. Mary Namur, 3233 College Ave., 76110. Tel: 817-921-0305; 923-8393. Sisters of St. Mary of Namur.

ARLINGTON. *Monastery of the Most Holy Trinity, Discalced Carmelites*, 5801 Mt. Carmel Dr., 76017. Tel: 817-468-1781. Mother Anne Teresa Kulinski, O.C.D., Prioress. Solemn Professed Nuns 9; Novices 1.

LINDSAY. *Congregation of Divine Providence*, P.O. Box 95, 76250. Tel: 817-665-6763. Sisters 4.

WICHITA FALLS. *Mercy Convent*, 3000 Lansing Blvd., 76309. Sisters 2; Associates 1.

Notre Dame Convent, 2820 Lansing Blvd., 76309. Sisters 3.

[J] RETREAT HOUSES

LAKE DALLAS. *Montserrat Jesuit Retreat House*, P.O. Box 398, 75065. Tel: 817-321-6020; 321-6030; Fax: 817-321-6040. Rev. John J. Heaney, S.J., Dir. Associate Directors: Revs. Walter C. McCauley, S.J.; Joseph P. McGill, S.J.; Charles G. Coyle, S.J. In res., Rev. John P. Koeplin, S.J.

[K] RENEWAL CENTERS

FORT WORTH. *The Catholic Renewal Center of North Texas, Inc.*, 4503 Bridge St., 76103. Tel: 817-429-2920 (Metro).

Beginning Experience.
Retorno.
Special Days for Special People.
National Marriage Encounter of North Texas.
Engaged Encounter of North Texas.
Stepping Stones.

[L] SOCIETY OF ST. VINCENT DE PAUL

FORT WORTH. *St. Vincent de Paul Diocesan Council of Fort Worth*, 6336 Genoa, 76116. Tel: 817-737-9167. Mr. Robert Churchill, Contact Person.

WICHITA FALLS. *Particular Council of Wichita Falls, St. Vincent de Paul Society*, 4516 Lake Park Dr., 76302. Tel: 817-322-2920. Mr. Walter Brady.

[M] NEWMAN CENTERS

FORT WORTH. *Texas Christian University Catholic Community*, TCU Station, P.O. Box 297310, 76129-0001. Tel: 817-921-7830, Ext. 5100; Fax: 817-921-7333. Rev. Charles L. Calabrese (STU). E-mail:c.calabrese@tcu.edu.

ARLINGTON. *University of Texas at Arlington*, 303 Lampe, 76010. Tel: 817-460-1155. Rev. Robert Lewandowski, S.M., Chap.; Mr. Tuyen Nguyen, Campus Min. Legal Title: *University of Texas at Arlington University Catholic Community.*

DENTON. *University of North Texas and Texas Woman's University*, 1303 Eagle Dr., 76201. Tel: 817-566-0004. Rev. Robert M. Lewandowski, S.M., Chap.; Mr. Tuyen Nguyen, Campus Min. Legal Title: *University of North Texas and Texas Woman's University.*

HILLSBORO. *Hill College Newman Center*. Attended from Our Lady of Mercy as United Christian Fellowship. P.O. Box 567, 76645. Tel: 817-582-5640. Deacon Jim Poole, Campus Min.

WICHITA FALLS. *Catholic Campus Ministry*, Midwestern State University, 3410 W. Campus Dr., 76308. Tel: 817-692-9778. Rev. Christopher Davis, O.S.B.

[N] MISCELLANEOUS

FORT WORTH. *Community Hospice of Texas*, 1000 Summit Ave., 76102. Tel: 817-870-2795; Fax: 817-878-3713. Ms. Andrea Green.

Loaves and Fishes, The Metroplex Food Bank, 3200 Yuma St., 76119. Tel: 817-924-FEED; Fax: 817-924-3210.

Soup Kitchen, 1709 E. Hattie, 76104. Tel: 817-536-9100.

Sister of St. Mary of Namur Marion House, 3353 College Ave., 76110.

RELIGIOUS INSTITUTES OF MEN REPRESENTED IN THE DIOCESE

For further details refer to the corresponding bracketed number in the Religious Institutes of Men or Women section.

[0140]—*The Augustinians.*—O.S.A.
[0200]—*Benedictine Monks.*—O.S.B.
[0470]—*The Capuchin Friars.*—O.F.M.Cap.
[0340]—*Cistercian Fathers.*—O.Cist.
[0520]—*Franciscan Friars.*—O.F.M.
[0690]—*Jesuit Fathers and Brothers.*—S.J.
[]—*Missionaries of St. Paul.*—M.S.P.
[0897]—*Paris Foreign Mission Society.*—M.E.P.
[]—*Priests and Brothers of the Mother Coredemptrix.*—C.M.C.
[0760]—*Society of Mary (Marianists).*—S.M.
[0990]—*Society of the Catholic Apostolate.*—S.A.C.
[0560]—*Third Order Regular of Saint Francis.*—T.O.R.

RELIGIOUS INSTITUTES OF WOMEN REPRESENTED IN THE DIOCESE

[0100]—*Adorers of the Blood of Christ.*—A.S.C.
[0230]—*Benedictine Sisters of Pontifical Jurisdiction.*—O.S.B.
[]—*Congregation of Missionary Catechists of the Sacred Heart of Jesus and Mary.*—M.C.
[0420]—*Discalced Carmelite Nuns.*—O.C.D.
[1170]—*Felician Sisters.*—C.S.S.F.
[1900]—*Hermanas Catequistas Guadalupanas.*—H.C.G.
[2970]—*School Sisters of Notre Dame.*—S.S.N.D.
[1010]—*Sisters of Divine Providence of San Antonio, Texas.*—C.D.P.
[3950]—*Sisters of Saint Mary of Namur.*—S.S.M.N.
[1970]—*Sisters of the Holy Family of Nazareth.*—C.S.F.N.
[2050]—*Sisters of the Holy Spirit and Mary Immaculate.*—S.H.Sp.
[1110]—*Cabra Dominican Sisters.*—O.P.
[0460]—*Congregation of Sisters of Charity of the Incarnate Word.*—C.C.V.I.
[2150]—*Servants of the Immaculate Heart of Mary.*—I.H.M.

NECROLOGY

† Hoover, William R., (Retired). —Died Oct. 19, 1996.
† Mitchell, John E., St. Antonio, TX, St. Henry's Church. —Died Oct. 1, 1996.
† Wiewell, Rev. Msgr. John M., (Retired). —Died April 1, 1996.

Diocese of Fresno

(Dioecesis Fresnensis)

Most Reverend

JOHN T. STEINBOCK, D.D.

Bishop of Fresno; ordained May 1, 1963; appointed Titular Bishop of Midila and Auxiliary Bishop of Orange May 29, 1984; consecrated July 14, 1984; installed as Bishop of Santa Rosa March 31, 1987; installed as Bishop of Fresno November 24, 1991. *Office: 1550 N. Fresno St., Fresno, CA, 93703-3788.* Tel.: 209-488-7400; Fax: 209-488-7464.

ESTABLISHED DECEMBER 15, 1967.

FORMERLY DIOCESE OF MONTEREY-FRESNO.

Square Miles 35,239.

Comprises the Counties of Fresno, Inyo, Kern, Kings, Madera, Mariposa, Merced and Tulare in the State of California.

Diocesan Patroness: St. Therese of the Child Jesus.

Legal titles of parishes and institutions, the Roman Catholic Bishop of Fresno, a Corporation Sole, Diocese of Fresno Education Corporation (for schools).

Chancery Office: 1550 N. Fresno St., Fresno, CA, 93703-3788. Tel.: 209-488-7400; Fax: 209-488-7464.

STATISTICAL OVERVIEW

Personnel	
Bishop	1
Priests: Diocesan Active in Diocese	83
Priests: Active Outside Diocese	2
Priests: Retired, Sick or Absent	29
Number of Diocesan Priests	114
Religious Priests in Diocese	38
Extern Priests in Diocese	14
Ordinations:	
Diocesan Priests	1
Transitional Deacons	3
Permanent Deacons	1
Permanent Deacons in Diocese	6
Total Brothers	10
Total Sisters	127
Parishes	
Parishes	84
With Resident Pastor:	
Resident Diocesan Priests	69
Resident Religious Priests	10
Without Resident Pastor:	
Administered by Priests	4
Administered by Permanent Deacons	1
Missions	40
Closed Parishes	1
Professional Ministry Personnel:	
Brothers	1
Sisters	127
Lay Ministers	160
Welfare	
Catholic Hospitals	3
Total Assisted	513,646
Health Care Centers	2
Homes for the Aged	1
Total Assisted	105
Specialized Homes	1
Total Assisted	100
Special Centers for Social Services	5
Total Assisted	561,742
Educational	
Diocesan Students in Other Seminaries	16
Total Seminarians	16
High Schools, Diocesan and Parish	1
Total Students	727
High Schools, Private	1
Total Students	699
Elementary Schools, Diocesan and Parish	23
Total Students	5,715
Catechesis/Religious Education:	
High School Students	6,193
Elementary Students	22,393
Total Students Under Catholic Instruction	35,743
Teachers in the Diocese:	
Brothers	5
Sisters	36
Lay Teachers	333
Vital Statistics	
Receptions into the Church:	
Infant Baptism Totals	16,818
Adult Baptism Totals	507
Received into Full Communion	348
First Communions	10,275
Confirmations	3,687
Marriages:	
Catholic	1,926
Interfaith	438
Total Marriages	2,364
Deaths	3,134
Total Catholic Population	323,191
Total Population	2,171,617

Former Prelates of Diocese of Monterey-Fresno—Most Rev. JOHN B. MACGINLEY, ord. June 8, 1895; cons. May 10, 1910; First Bishop of Monterey-Fresno, July 31, 1924; resigned Sept. 30, 1932; died Oct. 19, 1969.—Most Rev. PHILIP G. SCHER, ord. June 6, 1903; appt. April 28, 1933; cons. June 29, 1933; died Jan. 3, 1953.—Most Rev. ALOYSIUS J. WILLINGER, C.Ss.R., ord. July 2, 1911; cons. Bishop of Ponce, Puerto Rico, Oct. 28, 1929; Coadjutor Bishop of Monterey/Fresno *"cum jure successionis,"* Dec. 17, 1946; succeeded to the See, Jan. 3, 1953; resigned Oct. 25, 1967; died July 25, 1973.—Most Rev. HARRY ANSELM CLINCH, D.D., ord. June 6, 1936; appt. Auxiliary to the Bishop of Monterey-Fresno, Dec. 5, 1956; transferred to the See of Monterey, Dec. 14, 1967.

Former Bishops of Fresno—His Eminence TIMOTHY CARDINAL MANNING, D.D., appt. Titular Bishop of Lesvi and Auxiliary of Los Angeles, Aug. 3, 1946; cons. Oct. 15, 1946; installed as First Bishop of Fresno, Dec. 15, 1967; elevated to Coadjutor Archbishop of Los Angeles *"cum jure successionis,"* June 11, 1969; succeeded to the See, Jan. 21, 1970; created Cardinal, March 5, 1973; died June 23, 1989.—Most Rev. HUGH A. DONOHOE, D.D., ord. June 14, 1930; appt. Auxiliary in San Francisco, Aug. 2, 1947; cons. Oct. 7, 1947; appt. Bishop of Stockton, Feb. 21, 1962; appt. Second Bishop of Fresno, Aug. 28, 1969; resigned July 1, 1980; died Oct. 26, 1987.—His Eminence ROGER CARDINAL MAHONY, D.D., ord. May 1, 1962; appt. Auxiliary, Jan. 7, 1975; ord. Bishop, March 19, 1975; transferred to Diocese of Stockton, CA April 17, 1980; appt. Archbishop of Los Angeles, July 16, 1985; created Cardinal, June 28, 1991.—Most Rev. JOSEPH J. MADERA, D.D., cons. March 4, 1980 and; succeeded to the See on July 1, 1980; transferred to Archdiocese for the Military Services, Washington, DC May 28, 1991.

Vicar General and Moderator of the Curia—Rev. SERGIO P. NEGRO, V.G.

Vicar for Insurance and Retirement Matters—Rev. Msgr. J. WAYNE HAYES, P.A.

Chancellor—Sr. SANDRA ANN SILVA, S.H.F.

Chancery Office—1550 N. Fresno St., Fresno, 93703-3788. Tel: 209-488-7400; Fax: 209-488-7464.

Diocesan Tribunal—Rev. DAVID A. BRUM, J.C.L., Dir. Tribunal, *1550 N. Fresno St., Fresno, 93703-3788.* Tel: 209-488-7490; Fax: 209-488-7464.

Judicial Vicar—Rev. Msgr. HERBERT ELMLINGER.

Adjutant Judicial Vicars—Rev. Msgr. STEPHEN A. FROST, J.C.L.; Rev. DAVID A. BRUM, J.C.L.

Promoter of Justice—Rev. Msgr. SEAMUS MCMULLAN.

Defensores Vinculi—Rev. Msgr. PATRICK G. DOHERTY; Rev. Msgr. HERBERT ELMLINGER; Rev. Msgr. JOHN O'FRIEL; Rev. Msgr. MICHAEL R. BRAUN; Rev. Msgr. STEPHEN A. FROST, J.C.L.; Rev. Msgr. THOMAS G. KLEINHANS; Rev. PATRICK MCCORMICK.

Judges—Rev. Msgr. RICHARD RYAN, J.C.D.; Rev. Msgr. HERBERT ELMLINGER; Revs. STEPHEN A. FROST, J.C.L.; DAVID A. BRUM, J.C.L.; THOMAS FRANSISCUS, C.SS.R., J.C.L.

Notaries—Revs. PERRY KAVOOKJIAN; THOMAS M. TIMMINGS; Mrs. NANCY CLEMONS; GLORIA MARSCHALL.

Approved Advocates—Rev. Msgr. JOHN ESQUIVEL; Rev. Msgr. WALTER MINHOTO; Rev. Msgr. STEPHEN A. FROST, J.C.L.; Rev. Msgr. THOMAS G. KLEINHANS; Revs. JOHN GRIESBACH; PATRICK MCCORMICK; CHARLES F. SMITH; RICHARD URIZALQUI; DAVID A. BRUM, J.C.L.

Diocesan Consultors—Rev. Msgr. ED POSCHEN; Rev. Msgr. JOHN HARGUINDEGUY; Rev. Msgr. RONALD SWETT; Rev. Msgr. THOMAS KLEINHANS; Rev. Msgr. FRANCIS G. TASY; Revs. JEAN-MICHAEL LASTIRI; SERGIO P. NEGRO, V.G.

Vicars Forane—Rev. Msgr. JOHN HARGUINDEGUY, V.U.; Rev. Msgr. RONALD SWETT, V.F.; Rev. Msgr. THOMAS KLEINHANS, V.F.; Rev. Msgr. FRANCIS G. TASY, V.F.; Rev. JEAN-MICHAEL LASTIRI, V.F.

Diocesan Offices and Directors

Catholic Charities—Dir. Vacant, *149 N. Fulton, Fresno, 93701.* Tel: 209-237-0851; Fax: 209-237-7144.

Channel 49 (KNXT)—MARV HARRISON, Gen. Mgr., *1550 N. Fresno St., Fresno, 93703-3788.* Tel: 209-488-7440; Fax: 209-488-7444.

Continuing Formation of Priests—Rev. SERGIO P. NEGRO, *1550 N. Fresno St., Fresno, 93703.* Tel: 209-488-7400. Rev. JEAN-MICHAEL LASTIRI, *P.O. Box 2087, Merced, 95344.* Tel: 209-383-3924.

Cursillo Movement—Rev. RONALD ALVES, C.M.F., *P.O. Box 97, Laton, 93242.* Tel: 209-923-4935.

Diocese of Fresno Education Corporation—1550 N. Fresno St., Fresno, 93703-3788.

Diocesan Newspaper—BILL LUCIDO, Editor, *"Central California Catholic Life," 1550 N. Fresno St., Fresno, 93703-3788.*

Ecumenical Affairs—Rev. DAVID J. NORRIS, *1572 E. Barstow Ave., Fresno, 93710.* Tel: 209-436-3434.

Finance Committee—Rev. SERGIO P. NEGRO, V.G.; Rev. Msgr. MICHAEL BRAUN; Rev. JOSEPH HEFFERNAN; Mr. JOSEPH ZIEMANN; LEROY GILSDORF; GARY BETHKE; LARRY STEFANI; GARY RENNER, *1550 N. Fresno St., Fresno, 93703-3788.* Tel: 209-488-7400.

Health and Hospitals—Rev. SERGIO P. NEGRO, V.G.

Hispanic Apostolate—Mr. ZEFERINO GONZALES, Coord.

Migrant Prog., *1530 N. Fresno St., Fresno, 93703-3788.* Tel: 209-488-7455.

Holy Childhood, Pontifical Association—Rev. SERGIO NEGRO, V.G., Dir., *1550 N. Fresno St., Fresno, 93703-3788.* Tel: 209-488-7400; Fax: 209-488-7464.

Italian Catholic Federation—Rev. Msgr. J. WAYNE HAYES, P.A., Diocesan Chap.

Legion of Mary—Rev. Msgr. LASERIAN BYRNE, Diocesan Dir., *5770 N. Maroa, Fresno, 93704.* Tel: 209-439-0124.

Marian Federation of Guadalupe—Rev. Msgr. DANIEL LOPEZ, Diocesan Chap., *213 Orange Ave., Chowchilla, 93610.*

Ministry to Priests—Rev. SERGIO P. NEGRO, V.G.

Newman Apostolate—Rev. PERRY KAVOOKJIAN, *1572 E. Barstow Ave., Fresno, 93710.*

Office of Development—BILL LUCIDO, *1550 N. Fresno St., Fresno, 93703-3788.* Tel: 209-488-7414.

Office of Diocesan Properties—TIM TILLMAN, *1550 N. Fresno St., Fresno, 93703-3788.* Tel: 209-488-7470.

Office of Finances—GARY BETHKE, Fiscal Mgr., *1550 N. Fresno St., Fresno, 93703-3788.* Tel: 209-488-7476.

Office of Personnel and Insurance—GARY BETHKE, *1550 N. Fresno St., Fresno, 93703-3788.*

Office of Ministries—JAMES GRANT, Dir. PAUL MENTLEWSKI, Admin. Asst.

Campesino and Youth Ministry (Spanish)—Mr. ZEFERINO GONZALEZ.

Youth Ministry (English)—CHARISE HANSEN.

Family Life and Social Justice (Bi-lingual)—PATRICIA RODRIGUEZ, Dir.

Ministry Formation Coord.—Deacon MAURY MCCAFFREY. Tel: 209-488-7474.

Office of Worship—Rev. PATRICK MCCORMICK, Dir., *4636 W. Dakota, Fresno, 93722.* Tel: 209-275-2022.

Pastoral Center—TIM TILLMAN, *1530 N. Fresno St., Fresno, 93703.* Tel: 209-488-7470.

Personnel Committee—Rev. Msgr. JOHN HARGUINDEGUY, V.U.; Rev. Msgr. RONALD SWETT, V.F.; Rev. Msgr. LASERIAN BYRNE; Rev. Msgr. THOMAS KLEINHANS, V.F.; Rev. Msgr. FRANCIS TASY, V.F.; Rev. Msgr. JOSEPH BARNES; Revs. SERGIO P. NEGRO, V.G.; JEAN-MICHAEL LASTIRI; JOHN GRIESBACH; MYRON COTTA.

Priests' Council—Rev. Msgr. JOHN HARGUINDEGUY, V.U.; Rev. Msgr. FRANCIS TASY, V.F.; Rev. Msgr. RONALD SWETT, V.F.; Rev. Msgr. THOMAS KLEINHANS, V.F.; Rev. Msgr. JEAN-MICHAEL LASTIRI, V.F.; Rev. Msgr. JOHN MORETON; Rev. Msgr. JOHN ESQUIVEL, Chm.; Rev. Msgr. JOHN STEPHEN FROST, J.C.D.; Rev. Msgr. ED POSCHEN; Revs. SERGIO P. NEGRO, V.G.; JERRY AMERANDO; JAMES STUMP, O.F.M.Cap.; Sr. SANDRA ANN SILVA, S.H.F.

Propagation of the Faith and St. Peter Society—Rev. SERGIO NEGRO, V.G., *1550 N. Fresno St., Fresno, 93703-3788.*

Retreats—Rev. LOREN BLESSING, O.F.M., Dir.; Bro. TIM ARTHUR, O.F.M., Admin. Retreat Masters: Revs. JUAN LEON, O.F.M.; DAVID JOHNSON, O.F.M., *P.O. Box 249, Three Rivers, 93271.* Tel: 209-561-4595.

Schools—RICHARD SEXTON, Supt.; Miss ADRIENNE LOPES, Asst. Supt.

Diocesan Advisory Board of Education—Miss KAY ANTONGIOVANNI, Pres., *1510 N. Fresno St., Fresno, 93703.* Tel: 209-488-7420; Fax: 209-488-7422.

Vicar for Insurance and Retirement Affairs—Rev. Msgr. J. WAYNE HAYES, P.A., *2850 N. Crystal, Fresno, 93705.* Tel: 209-226-1163.

Vicar for Religious—Sr. SANDRA SILVA, S.H.F., *1550 N. Fresno St., Fresno, 93703.* Tel: 209-488-7473.

Vocations—Rev. ROD CRAIG, Dir., *1550 N. Fresno St., Fresno, 93703-3788.* Tel: 209-488-7400.

CLERGY, PARISHES, MISSIONS AND PAROCHIAL SCHOOLS

CITY OF FRESNO
(Fresno County)

1—ST. JOHN CATHEDRAL, Rev. Msgr. John Harguindeguy, Rector; Rev. Rodrigo Ortiz, O.F.M. In res., Rev. Umberto Nespolo, O.M.I., (Hmong Ministry); Rev. Msgr. Walter Minhoto, (Retired).
Res., 2814 Mariposa St., 93721. Tel: 209-485-6210; Fax: 209-485-8409.
Catechesis/Religious Programs—Students 566.
Mission—Fresno, St. Francis, Ninth & Lowe, 93702. Tel: 209-485-9467. Rev. Joseph Cong Hoan, (Vietnamese Ministry).

2—HOLY SPIRIT (1981), Rev. Msgr. James T. Logan; Stephanie Hacnik, Business Mgr.
Mailing Address: 355 E. Champlain Dr., 93720-1273.
Res., 8781 N. Millbrook, 93720-1718. Tel: 209-434-7701 (Office); 435-2278 (Rectory); Fax: 209-434-7734.
Catechesis/Religious Programs—Judy Bedrosian. Students 464.
Mission—Pinedale, Fresno Co., St. Agnes, 111 W. Birch St., Pinedale, 93650. Tel: 209-439-2100.
Stations—Tollhouse, Shaver Lake, Tel: 209-841-3524; Tollhouse, Auberry, Tel: 209-855-5011.

3—THE CATHOLIC COMMUNITY OF MT. CARMEL/ST. ALPHONSUS (1955) (Spanish). Merged Our Lady of Mt. Carmel merged with St. Alphonsus. Revs. Phil Van Linden, C.M.; Jeff Harvey, C.M.; Deacon Arnold Hernandez, C.M.
Res., 816 Pottle Ave., 93706. Tel: 209-264-2587; Fax: 209-264-2539.
Catechesis/Religious Programs—847 Waterman Ave., 93706. Tel: 209-497-1416.
Students 180.

4—OUR LADY OF VICTORY (1950), Rev. Msgr. J. Wayne Hayes, P.A.
Res., 1215 W. Michigan Ave., 93705. Tel: 209-226-1163.
Parish Center—2850 N. Crystal, 93705. Fax: 209-229-2093.
School—1626 W. Princeton Ave., 93705. Tel: 209-229-0205. Ms. Patricia Baldwin, Prin.
Lay Teachers 11; Students 245.
Catechesis/Religious Programs—Tel: 209-229-0024.
Students 371.

5—SACRED HEART (1947), Rev. Charles F. Smith.
Res., 2240 N. Cedar Ave., 93703-2668. Tel: 209-237-4121.
School—4460 E. Yale, 93703. Tel: 209-251-3171; Fax: 209-237-0122. Connie McGhee, Prin.
Sisters of the Love of God 3; Lay Teachers 6; Students 168.
Catechesis/Religious Programs—Tel: 209-237-4365.
Students 450.
Convent—4305 E. Union, 93703. Tel: 209-454-1864.

6—ST. ALPHONSUS. Merged See The Catholic Community of Mt. Carmel/St. Alphonsus.
Catechesis/Religious Programs—Students 130.
Mission—Easton, Fresno Co., St. Jude, 208 W. Jefferson, 93706. Tel: 209-485-3879. Rev. David Brum, J.C.L.

7—ST. ANTHONY OF PADUA (1953), Rev. Msgr. Laserian Byrne; Revs. John Fluetsch; Patrick Joel Davadilla, S.V.D.
Res., 5770 N. Maroa St., 93704. Tel: 209-439-0124; Fax: 209-439-3050.
School—Tel: 209-437-0700; Fax: 209-435-6749. Mr. Shawn Carey, Prin.
Lay Teachers 23; Students 640.
Catechesis/Religious Programs—5680 N. Maroa St., 93704. Tel: 209-431-8512.
Students 725.

8—ST. ANTHONY CLARET (Calwa Area) (1952), Revs. Arturo S. Gomez, C.M.F.; Ronald Alves, C.M.F. In res., Revs. Fernando Vega, C.M.F.; Cecil Barron, C.M.F.
Res., 2494 S. Chestnut Ave., 93725. Tel: 209-255-4260; Fax: 209-255-4274.
Catechesis/Religious Programs—Students 433.
Mission—Malaga, Fresno, Christ the King, 3565 Calvin St., 93725.

9—ST. GENEVIEVE, Rev. Vincent Lau (Hong Kong).
Res., 1127 Tulare St., 93706. Tel: 209-486-2988. [CEM]

10—ST. HELEN (1955), Rev. Eric Swearingen. In res., Revs. Stephen Frost; Joseph Hoan (Vietnam).
Res., 4870 E. Belmont, 93727. Tel: 209-255-3871; Fax: 209-255-7625.
School—4888 E. Belmont, 93727. Tel: 209-251-5855; Fax: 209-251-5948. Toni Amodio, Prin.
Franciscan Hospitalers of the Immaculate Conception 1; Lay Teachers 10; Students 253.
Catechesis/Religious Programs—Tel: 209-251-4978; Fax: 209-255-7625.
Students 215.

11—ST. MARY (1967), Rev. Patrick Joseph McCormick.
Res., 4636 W. Dakota, 93722. Tel: 209-275-2022; Fax: 209-275-2040. [CEM]

12—ST. PAUL (1964), Rev. Perry Kavookjian.
Church—California State University, St. Paul Newman Center, 1572 E. Barstow St., 93710. Tel: 209-436-3434; Fax: 209-436-3430.

13—ST. THERESE (1927), Rev. Msgr. Edward Poschen.
Mailing Address: 1444 N. Wishon, 93728. Tel: 209-268-6388; Fax: 209-268-6389.
Res., 855 E. Floradora Ave., 93728. Tel: 209-485-2199.
Catechesis/Religious Programs—Tel: 209-268-6388; Fax: 209-268-6389.
Students 150.

OUTSIDE THE CITY OF FRESNO

Arvin, Kern Co., St. Thomas (1939) (Mexican), Rev. Lucas Ezpericueta, Admin.
Res., 350 E. Bear Mountain, 93203. Tel: 805-854-6150; Fax: 805-854-2564. [JC]
Catechesis/Religious Programs—Students 317.

Atwater, Merced Co., St. Anthony (1909), Rev. Thomas Timmings.
Office: 1799 Winton Way, 95301. Tel: 209-358-5743.
Res., 1999 Juniper Ave., 95301. Tel: 209-358-5743.
School—Tel: 209-358-3341. Miss Dianne Silva, Prin.
Lay Teachers 9; Students 125.
Catechesis/Religious Programs—Tel: 209-358-3382.
Students 650.
Mission—Buhach, Merced Co., Immaculate Conception, 1799 Winton Wy., Atwater 95301. Tel: 209-358-5743.

Avenal, Kings Co., St. Joseph (Spanish), Rev. Gregory Kareta, O.F.M. Con.
Res., P.O. Box 219, 93204. Tel: 209-386-9523.
Mission—Kettleman City, St. Cecilia.

Bakersfield, Kern Co.,

1—OUR LADY OF GUADALUPE, (1925), Revs. James Catalano, O.S.J.; Chummar Chirayath, O.S.J.
Res., 601 E. California Ave., 93307. Tel: 805-323-3148; Fax: 805-323-6016.
School—609 E. California Ave., 93307. Tel: 805-323-6059. Sr. Teresa Juarez, S.J.S., Prin.
Sisters 3; Lay Teachers 6; Students 169.
Catechesis/Religious Programs—Tel: 805-637-0601; Fax: 805-323-6016. Sofia Mendez, D.R.E.
Students 431.
Missions—Bakersfield, Kern Co., Holy Spirit, 720 E. Belle Terrace, 93307. Tel: 805-834-7095; Bakersfield, Kern Co., St. Jude, 825 Chapman, 93307. Tel: 805-323-2347.

2—OUR LADY OF PERPETUAL HELP, (1948), Rev. Msgr. Michael R. Braun.
Res., 124 Columbus St., 93305. Tel: 805-323-3108; Fax: 805-325-7067.
School—Tel: 805-327-7741. Mrs. Elenor Etcheverry, Prin.
Lay Teachers 15; Students 272.
Catechesis/Religious Programs—Students 400.
Mission—Bakersfield, Kern Co., San Clemente, 1305 Water St., 93305. Tel: 805-871-9190. Rev. Msgr. Ralph Belluomini.

3—SACRED HEART, (1952), Rev. Dan Coyle.
Res., 9915 Ramos St., 93307. Tel: 805-831-8905; Fax: 805-837-8075.
Catechesis/Religious Programs—Tel: 805-831-6223.
Students 235.

4—ST. FRANCIS, (1881), Revs. A. Joseph Hetternan; Leonard J. Trindade.
Res., 900 H St., 93304. Tel: 805-327-4734; Fax: 805-327-4930.
School—2516 Palm St., 93304. Tel: 805-326-7955; 326-7958 (PreSchool); Fax: 805-327-0395. Mrs. Fabienne Esparza, Prin.
Sisters 2; Lay Teachers 24; Students 477; PreSchool 53.
Catechesis/Religious Programs—Tel: 805-323-8800. Mrs. Alice Fry, D.R.E.
Students 543.

5—ST. JOSEPH, (1907) (English-Spanish), Rev. Robert D. Wenzinger.
Res., 1515 Baker St., 93305. Tel: 805-327-2744; Fax: 805-327-0133.

6—ST. PHILIP THE APOSTLE, (1968), Rev. Msgr. Ronald J. Swett; Rev. John Gracey.
Mailing Address: 7100 Stockdale Hwy., 93309-1399. Tel: 805-834-7483; Fax: 805-834-2214.
Catechesis/Religious Programs—Tel: 805-834-6930. D.R.E.: Leila Hunzman, (Elementary); Joan Lund.
Students 1,050.

Bass Lake, Madera Co., St. Dominic Savio (1961), Rev. Herman O. Bezunartea.
Res., P.O. Box 410, 93604. Tel: 209-642-3452.
Mission—North Fork, Madera Co., St. Joseph the Worker.

Bishop, Inyo Co., Our Lady of Perpetual Help (1947), Rev. Gerald F. Chavez.
Res., 849 N. Home St., 93514. Tel: 619-872-7231; Fax: 619-872-7231.
Catechesis/Religious Programs—Tel: 619-873-8862.
Students 210.
Mission—Big Pine, Inyo Co., St. Stephen, 461 S. Main St., Bishop 93513. Tel: 619-938-2724.

Boron, Kern Co., St. Joseph (1969), Rev. Robert E. Gamel.
Mailing Address: Drawer D, 93596. Tel: 619-762-5453.
Catechesis/Religious Programs—Judy Hibbs, D.R.E. (California City).
Students 177.
Station—California City, Our Lady of Lourdes, Tel:

619-373-2256; Fax: 619-373-1265.

Buttonwillow, Kern Co., St. Mary (1941), Rev. Msgr. Loydell J. Marth, Admin.
Res., 420 N. Main St., Box 875, 93206. Tel: 805-764-5486.

Chowchilla, Madera Co., St. Columba (1921) (Anglo-Saxon-Spanish), Rev. Msgr. Daniel M. Lopez.
Res., 213 Orange Ave., 93610. Tel: 209-665-3376. [JC]
Catechesis/Religious Programs—Tel: 209-665-5104.
Students 279.

Clovis, Fresno Co., Our Lady of Perpetual Help (1929), Rev. Msgr. Raymond C. Dreiling; Rev. Gregory J. Beaumont.
Res., 929 Harvard, 93612. Tel: 209-299-4270; Fax: 209-299-7126.
Church—Ninth & DeWitt.
School—836 DeWitt, 93612. Tel: 209-299-7504.
Immaculate Conception Sisters 4; Lay Teachers 7; Students 266.
Catechesis/Religious Programs—Tel: 209-297-8506.
Students 521.

Coalinga, Fresno Co., St. Paul The Apostle (1907) (English), Rev. John B. Farao, O.F.M.Conv.
Res., 637 Sunset St., P.O. Box 812, 93210. Tel: 209-935-1872; Fax: 209-935-3763. [JC]

Corcoran, Kings Co., Our Lady of Lourdes (1939) (Hispanic), Rev. Richard D. Magdaleno.
Res., 1404 Hanna, 93212. Tel: 209-992-4414; Fax: 209-992-2512.
Catechesis/Religious Programs—Tel: 209-992-4698; Fax: 209-992-2512.
Students 560.

Cutler, Tulare Co., St. Mary (1953), Rev. Jose Luis Vega.
Res., 12588 Avenue 407, P.O. Box 6, 93615. Tel: 209-528-3566.
Catechesis/Religious Programs—Tel: 209-528-3077.
Students 112.

Delano, Kern Co., St. Mary's of the Miraculous Medal (1920), Rev. Rick Fierros, M.Div.
Res., 916 Lexington St., 93215. Tel: 805-725-8456; Fax: 805-725-8485.
School—Tel: 805-725-9055; Fax: 805-725-3224. Marie Macedo, Prin.
Sisters 1; Lay Teachers 8; Students 205.
Catechesis/Religious Programs—Tel: 805-725-9041. Mrs. Alex Guerrero, D.R.E.
Students 710.
Mission—Richgrove, Tulare Co., St. Vincent.

Our Lady of Guadalupe (1954) (Mexican-American-Filipino), Rev. Emerito Gomez, O.F.M.
Res., 1015 Clinton St., 93215. Tel: 805-725-9087; 725-9115.
Catechesis/Religious Programs—Students 500.

Del Rey, Fresno Co., St. Katherine. (Quasi-parish included with St. Mary, Sanger). Rev. John Bruno, R.C.J.
Res., 828 "O" St., P.O. Box 335, Sanger, 93657. Tel: 209-888-2889; 875-2025.

Dinuba, Tulare Co., St. Catherine (1948), Rev. Msgr. Anthony Janelli.
Res., 356 N. Villa Ave., 93618. Tel: 209-591-0931.
Catechesis/Religious Programs—Tel: 209-591-2988. D.R.E.: Keri Douglass; Tomi Castilleja; Anita Betancourt; Robert Garcia; Efrain Orjuela.
Students 700.

Dos Palos, Merced Co., Sacred Heart (1924), Rev. Robert R. Vanoncini.
Res., 1650 Lucerne, 93620. Tel: 209-392-2724; Fax: 209-392-1037.

Earlimart, Tulare Co., St. Jude (1968), Rev. Victor Villegas Piansay.
Res., P.O. Box 2, 93219. Tel: 805-849-3170.

Easton, Fresno Co., St. Jude Mission. See St. Alphonsus, Fresno for details.

Exeter, Tulare Co., Sacred Heart (Hispanic) (1950), Rev. Msgr. Nicolas Herrero.
Res., 417 North E St., 93221. Tel: 209-592-2465.
Catechesis/Religious Programs—Tel: 209-592-1020.
Students 502.
Mission—Farmersville, Tulare Co., St. Anthony of Egypt, 821 W. Visalia Rd., Farmersville, 93223. Tel: 209-747-0234.

Firebaugh, Fresno Co., St. Joseph (1950) (Hispanic), Rev. Craig F. Harrison.
Res., 1558 12th St., 93622. Tel: 209-659-2225; Fax: 209-659-0408.
School—1900 Saipan, 93622. Tel: 209-659-2841.
Sisters 4; Lay Teachers 5; Students 195.
Catechesis/Religious Programs—Students 375.

Fowler, Fresno Co., St. Lucy (1965), Rev. Msgr. John Esquivel; Rev. Raul Sanchez; Deacons Maury McCaffrey; Ed Harmon, III.
Res., P.O. Box 295, 93625. Tel: 209-834-2624.
Catechesis/Religious Programs—Tel: 209-834-9124; Fax: 209-896-3975.
Students 87.

Goshen, Tulare Co., St. Thomas the Apostle (1963), Rev. Rafael E. Garcia; Deacon Julian Ponce.
Res., 1908 N. Court, Visalia, 93291. Tel: 209-732-8089; Fax: 209-732-0969. [CEM]

Gustine, Merced Co., Our Lady of Miracles (1919) (Portuguese), Rev. Myron Cotta.
Res., 370 Linden Ave., 95322. Tel: 209-854-6692; Fax: 209-854-1344.
School—Tel: 209-854-3180. Sarah Howard, Prin.
Lay Teachers 10; Students 197.
Catechesis/Religious Programs—Students 221.

Hanford, Kings Co., St. Brigid (1886), Rev. Daniel C. Avila.
Office & Mailing Address: 200 E. Florinda, 93230. Fax: 209-582-9193.
Res., 1005 N. Douty St., 93230. Tel: 209-582-2533. [CEM]
School—St. Rose-McCarthy Catholic School, 1000 N. Harris St., 93230. Tel: 209-584-5218; Fax: 209-584-5273. Ms. Debra Cabral, Prin.
Sisters of Our Lady of Nazareth 1; Lay Teachers 10; Students 202.
Catechesis/Religious Programs—Students 471.

Immaculate Heart (1948) (Mexican-Portuguese), Rev. Antonio Gonzalez.
Res., 10355 Hanford Armona Rd., 93230. Tel: 209-584-8576; Fax: 209-584-0436.
Catechesis/Religious Programs—Students 317.

Hilmar, Merced Co., Holy Rosary (1948) (Portuguese), Rev. David J. Norris.
Res., P.O. Box 429, 95324. Tel: 209-667-8961; Fax: 209-667-5239.
Catechesis/Religious Programs—Tel: 209-632-7163.
Students 300.
Mission—Stevinson, Merced Co., St. Mary.

Huron, Fresno Co., St. Frances Cabrini (1961) (Hispanic), Rev. Stephen M. Devine.
Res., 36986 Los Angeles St., P.O. Box 939, 93234. Tel: 209-945-2507.
Catechesis/Religious Programs—Students 259.

Kerman, Fresno Co., St. Patrick (1943), Revs. John Griesbach; Gregory DeSilva.
Mailing Address: P.O. Box 375, 93630. Tel: 209-846-8190; Fax: 209-846-7705.
Res., 567 S. Sixth St., 93630.
Catechesis/Religious Programs—Students 320.

Kingsburg, Fresno Co., Holy Family, Rev. Kenneth J. Bozzo.
Res., 1301 Smith St., P.O. Box 798, 93631. Tel: 209-897-5953. [JC]
Catechesis/Religious Programs—Tel: 209-897-7620.
Students 200.
Missions—London, Tulare Co., Santa Cruz, 5625 Ave. 378, 93631; Traver, Tulare Co., St. John the Baptist Educational Center, 4204 Merritt Dr., Traver, 93673. Tel: 209-897-2716.

Lamont, Kern Co., St. Augustine (Mexican), Rev. John Schmoll.
Res., 10601 Myrtle Ave., 93241-2198. Tel: 805-845-0003.
Catechesis/Religious Programs—Tel: 805-845-3622.
Students 588.
Mission—Frazier Park, Our Lady of the Snows, P.O. Box 995, Frazier Park, 93225. Tel: 805-245-3741. Rev. Msgr. Michael O'Connor.

Laton, Fresno Co., Shrine of Our Lady of Fatima (1953), Rev. Timothy A. Gallemore.
Res., P.O. Box 97, 93242. Tel: 209-923-4935.
Catechesis/Religious Programs—Students 240.

Lemoore, Kings Co., St. Peter (1912), Rev. Msgr. John O'Friel.
Res., P.O. Box 100, 93245. Tel: 209-924-2562.
School—884 N. Lemoore Ave., 93245. Tel: 209-924-3424; Fax: 209-924-7848. Sr. Marion Abraham, C.S.S.T., Prin.
Carmelite Sisters of St. Teresa 4; Lay Teachers 6; Students 257.
Catechesis/Religious Programs—Tel: 209-924-2826. Cathy Hammond, D.R.E.
Students 225.
Missions—Stratford, Kings Co., St. Joseph; Tache Indian Reservation, Kings Co., St. Rosa. [CEM]

Lindsay, Tulare Co., Sacred Heart (1925), Rev. Alex C. Ignacio.
Res., 217 Lindero Ave., 93247. Tel: 209-562-4008.
Catechesis/Religious Programs—Tel: 209-562-2082.
Students 350.
Mission—Tonyville, St. Anthony.
Stations—Plainview; Strathmore.

Livingston, Merced Co., St. Jude Thaddeus (1937) (American-Portuguese), Rev. Harvey Fonseca.
Res., 330 Franci St., 95334. Tel: 209-394-7512.
Catechesis/Religious Programs—Rosa Maria Mercado, D.R.E.
Students 602.

Lone Pine, Inyo Co., Santa Rosa (1919), Deacon John Burns, Admin.
Res., P.O. Box 246, 93545. Tel: 619-876-4350.
Missions—Shoshone-Tecopa, Inyo Co., St. John the Baptist, Lone Pine 92384; Independence, Inyo Co., St. Vivian, P.O. Box 192, Lone Pine 93526.
Station—Lone Pine, Death Valley.

Los Banos, Merced Co., St. Joseph (1905), Rev. Msgr. J. Wayne Hayes, P.A.; Rev. Jim Kudilil.
Res., 1109 Fifth St., 93635. Tel: 209-826-4246; Fax: 209-826-5335.
School—Tel: 209-826-2709. Ms. Kathy Nerell, Prin.
Franciscan Sisters 4; Lay Teachers 7; Students 269.
Catechesis/Religious Programs—1625 Center Ave., 93635. Tel: 209-826-1512.
Students 534.

Madera, Madera Co., St. Joachim (1881), Revs. Arnold Ortiz, O.S.J.; Guadalupe Sanchez, O.S.J.; Xavier Thyppadth, O.S.J.
Res., 401 W. Fifth St., 93637. Tel: 209-673-3290; Fax: 209-673-6471.
School—Tel: 209-674-7628. Sr. Encarnacion Ortega, R.C.M., Prin.
Immaculate Conception Sisters 2; Lay Teachers 7; Students 306.
Catechesis/Religious Programs—Tel: 209-674-5871.
Students 1550.
Missions—Madera, Madera Co., St. Agnes, 7308 Hwy 145, 93637; Raymond, Madera Co., St. Anne, Raymond-Knowles, Raymond, 93653.

Mariposa, Mariposa Co., St. Joseph (1857), Rev. Stephen C. Bulfer.
Mailing Address: P.O. Box 215, 95338-0215. Tel: 209-966-2522.
Res., 4985 Bullion St. [CEM 3]
Mission—Hornitos, Mariposa Co., St. Catherine of Sienna.

McFarland, Kern Co., St. Elizabeth (1966), Rev. Jose Luis Varo, O.F.M., (Spain) Admin.
Res., 835 E. Perkins, 93250. Tel: 805-792-3225.
Catechesis/Religious Programs—Tel: 805-792-3429. Rosa Carmona, D.R.E.
Students 458.

Mendota, Fresno Co., Our Lady of Guadalupe (1953) (Hispanic), Rev. Msgr. Ricardo Barajas.
Res., P.O. Box 248, 93640. Tel: 209-655-3631.
Mission—Three Rocks, Fresno Co., Our Lady of Lourdes, 161015 S. Derrick, Three Rocks, 93608. Tel: 209-829-3358.

Merced, Merced Co., Our Lady of Mercy/St. Patricks, Revs. Jean-Michael Lastiri; Michael Burchfield.
Mailing Address: P.O. Box 2087, 95344.
Churches—Our Lady of Mercy, 435 W. 21st St., 95340. Tel: 209-383-3930 (Mass Recording). [JC]
St. Patrick, 671 E. Yosemite, 95340. Tel: 209-726-3216.
Res., 610 Rambler Rd., 95348. Tel: 209-383-3924; Fax: 209-723-6510.
School—Our Lady of Mercy Elementary, 1400 E. 27th St., 95340. Tel: 209-722-7496; Fax: 209-722-7532. Mrs. Brenda Feehan, Prin.
Lay Teachers 21; Students 484.
Catechesis/Religious Programs—Tel: 209-723-8888. Sr. Mary Kinsinger, D.R.E.
Students 574.
Mission—Hopeton, St. John the Baptist.

Sacred Heart (1945) (English-Hispanic), Rev. Jose M. Montiel.
Res., 1220 M St., 95340. Tel: 209-383-6604; Fax: 209-383-6147.
Catechesis/Religious Programs—Tel: 209-383-1528. Sr. Gabriel Ann Tamayo, D.R.E.
Students 803.
Mission—Merced, Merced Co., El Nido, 95340.

Mojave, Kern Co., St. Francis, Rev. Leslie F. Shenoy.
Mailing Address: 15380 Myer Rd., P.O. Box 790, 93502. Tel: 805-824-2073; Fax: 805-824-1720.
Res., 3100 15th St., Rosamond, 93560. Tel: 805-256-4505; Fax: 805-256-7127.
Catechesis/Religious Programs—Students 177.
Mission—Rosamond, St. Mary of the Desert.

Oildale, Kern Co., Christ the King (1952), Rev. Dan Coyle, Admin.
Res., 1711 Bedford Way, 93308. Tel: 805-399-0046.

Orange Cove, Fresno Co., St. Isidore the Farmer (1978), Rev. Angel L. Sotelo, Admin.
Mailing Address: P.O. Box 309, 93646. Tel: 209-626-4943; Fax: 209-626-4648.
Res., 404 Adams Ave., 93646.
Catechesis/Religious Programs—Tel: 209-626-4648; Fax: 209-626-4648.
Students 244.
Mission—Squaw Valley, Fresno Co., St. Rita.

Parlier, Fresno Co., Our Lady of Sorrows (1963), Rev.

Rodolfo Orozco.
Res., 830 Tulare St., 93648. Tel: 209-646-2161.

Planada, Merced Co., Sacred Heart (1939) (Hispanic-Italian), Rev. Thomas J. Fransiscus, C.SS.R., J.C.L.
Res., 9317 Amistad, P.O. Box 278, 95365. Tel: 209-382-0459; Fax: 209-382-0459. [JC]
Catechesis/Religious Programs—Students 400.
Mission—Le Grand, Merced Co., Our Lady of Lourdes.

Porterville, Tulare Co., St. Anne (1896), Revs. Scott Daugherty; Miguel A. Sepulveda.
Res., 378 North F St., 93257. Tel: 209-784-2800; Fax: 209-784-4338.
School—369 North F St., 93257. Tel: 209-784-4096. Sr. Rosario Mediavilla, R.A.D., Prin.
Sisters of the Love of God 4; Lay Teachers 8; Students 175.
Catechesis/Religious Programs—Students 580.
Missions—Porterville, Our Lady of Guadalupe, 217 S. Wallace, 93257; Tule Indian Reservation, Tulare Co., Mater Dolorosa; Terra Bella, Blessed Miguel Agustin Pro, 9120 Rd. 236, Terra Bella, 93270.
Station—At Methodist Church, 35725 Hwy 190, Springville, 93265.

Reedley, Fresno Co., St. Anthony (1906), Rev. Msgr. Francis G. Tasy, V.S.; Rev. Angel Gonzalez, S.P.
Res., P.O. Box 188, 93654. Tel: 209-638-2012.
School—St. La Salle Grammar School, 404 E. Manning Ave., 93654. Tel: 209-638-2621; Fax: 209-638-5542.
Sisters 2; Lay Teachers 12; Students 221.
Catechesis/Religious Programs—Tel: 209-638-5608. D.R.E.: Sr. Sandra Ann Silva, S.H.F.; Laura Rivera.
Students 574.

Ridgecrest, Kern Co., St. Ann (1946), Rev. Msgr. Kevin Cleary.
Res., 446 W. Church St., P.O. Box 127, 93556. Tel: 619-375-2110; Fax: 619-375-6345. [JC]
School—(Grades K-5). Tel: 619-375-4713.
Lay Teachers 6; Students 173.
Catechesis/Religious Programs—Students 326.
Mission—Randsburg, Kern Co., Santa Barbara, Randsburg, 93554.

Riverdale, Fresno Co., St. Ann (1928), Revs. Raymond J. Duffy; Pedro M. Mancilla.
Res., P.O. Box 335, 93656. Tel: 209-867-3035. [JC]
Catechesis/Religious Programs—Tel: 209-867-4996.
Students 326.
Missions—Diener Ranch At Five Points, Fresno Co., Holy Family Chapel; Caruthers, Fresno Co., Our Lady of the Assumption, West & Herndon, P.O. Box 26, Caruthers, 93609.

Sanger, Fresno Co., St. Mary (1922), Revs. Salvatore Ciranni, R.C.J.; John Bruno, R.C.J.; Loji Pilones, R.C.J.
Res., 828 O St., P.O. Box 335, 93657. Tel: 209-875-2025; Fax: 209-875-1281. [JC]
Catechesis/Religious Programs—2590 North Ave., 93657. Tel: 209-875-6340.
Students 780.
Mission—Del Rey, St. Katherine's.

Selma, Fresno Co., St. Joseph (1913), Rev. Msgr. John Esquivel; Rev. Raul Sanchez; Deacons Maury McCaffrey; Ed Harmon.
Res., 2441 Dockery Ave., P.O. Box 179, 93662. Tel: 209-896-1052; Fax: 209-896-3975.
Catechesis/Religious Programs—Tel: 209-896-2620.
Students 400.

Shafter, Kern Co., St. Therese (1952), Rev. Thomas O'Neill.
Res., 300 W. Lerdo, P.O. Box 1355, 93263. Tel: 805-746-4471.
Catechesis/Religious Programs—Students 328.

Taft, Kern Co., St. Mary (1918), Rev. Msgr. Loydell J. Marth.
Res., 110 E. Woodrow St., 93268. Tel: 805-765-4292.

Tehachapi, Kern Co., St. Malachy (1887), Rev. Msgr. Joseph C. Barnes; Rev. Msgr. Seamus O. McMullan, Pastor Emeritus; Rev. Msgr. Francis J. Pointek, Pastor Emeritus; Revs. Neil Adolfo (Philippines) Prison Chap.; Godfrey Raffel, (Retired).
Res., P.O. Box 618, 93581. Tel: 805-822-3060; Fax: 805-822-3159.
Catechesis/Religious Programs—Tel: 805-822-6327.
Students 400.

Tipton, Tulare Co., St. John (1945) (Portuguese), Rev. Warren Hengel, Jr.
Res., 232 S. Adams Rd., Box 159, 93272. Tel: 209-752-4544; Fax: 209-752-1409.
Catechesis/Religious Programs—Students 375.
Mission—Woodville, Tulare Co., St. Francis of Assisi, 16410 Ave. 168, Woodville, 93258.
Station—Tipton, Pixley.

Tranquillity, Fresno Co., St. Paul (1924), Revs. John Griesbach; Gregory Bede DeSilva.
Res., P.O. Box 575, 93668. Tel: 209-698-7429.
Catechesis/Religious Programs—Students 155.
Mission—San Joaquin, Fresno Co., St. Vincent de Paul.

Tulare, Tulare Co., St. Aloysius (1905), Revs. Richard Urizalqui; Raul Marta.
Res., 125 E. Pleasant Ave., 93274. Tel: 209-688-1796; 1797; Fax: 209-688-0948.
School—Tel: 209-686-6250; Fax: 209-686-0479. Sr. Kay O'Brien, O.P., Prin.
Dominican Sisters of Tacoma, WA 1; Lay Teachers 9; Students 274.
Catechesis/Religious Programs—Students 600.
St. Rita (1967), Rev. Timothy N. Cardoza.
Res., 954 S. O St., 93274. Tel: 209-686-3847; Fax: 209-686-9672.

Visalia, Tulare Co., Holy Family (1950), Rev. Rafael E. Garcia; Deacon Julian Ponce.
Res., 1908 N. Court St., 93291. Tel: 209-732-8089; Fax: 209-732-0969. [JC]
Catechesis/Religious Programs—Tel: 209-732-9651.
Students 634.
St. Mary (1861), Rev. Msgr. Thomas G. Kleinhans; Rev. Jerry Amerando.
Res., 608 N. Church St., P.O. Box 287, 93279. Tel: 209-734-9522; Fax: 209-734-3435.
School—George McCann Memorial School, 200 E. Race St., 93291. Tel: 209-732-5831; Fax: 209-741-1562. Mr. Victor Suarez, Prin.
Lay Teachers 9; Students 242.
Catechesis/Religious Programs—Tel: 209-733-3929. Mrs. Joan Bell, D.R.E.
Students 871.

Wasco, Kern Co., St. John the Evangelist (1919) (Hispanic), Rev. Msgr. Dino F. Riccomini.
Res., 1300 Ninth Pl., 93280. Tel: 805-758-6688.
School—Tel: 805-758-6467. Mrs. Joanne Todd, Prin.
Lay Teachers 4; Students 57.
Catechesis/Religious Programs—Students 430.
Mission—Blackwell's Corner, Kern Co., Nuestra Senora de la Paz, Blackwell's Corner, 93279.

Wofford Heights, Kern Co., St. Jude (1969), Rev. Charles B. Casale.
Res., 86 Nellie Dent Dr., 93285. Tel: 619-376-2416.

Woodlake, Tulare Co., St. Frances Cabrini (1963) (Spanish), Rev. Jesse C. Venzor.
Res., 599 N. Valencia Blvd., P.O. Box 459, 93286. Tel: 209-564-2647.
Catechesis/Religious Programs—Students 277.
Mission—Three Rivers, Tulare Co., St. Clair, Alta Acres Dr., Three Rivers, 93271.

Yosemite National Park, Mariposa Co., Our Lady of the Snows (1963), Rev. Dennis M. Alvernaz.
Res., P.O. Box 457, 95389. Tel: 209-372-4729.
Station—Yosemite National Park, Wawona.

Chaplains of Public Institutions

FRESNO. *Community Hospital, Veterans' Hospital.* Attended by Capuchin Fathers. Revs. David LaPierre, O.F.M.Cap., Supr.; Alejandro Magallanes, O.F.M.Cap.; James Stump, O.F.M.Cap.

AVENAL. *California State Prison, Kings Co.* Rev. Perera, O.S.B., Chap.

BAKERSFIELD. *Kern Medical Center, Bakersfield Memorial Hospital & San Joaquin Community Hospital.* Rev. John Geary, S.J.

CHOWCHILLA. *Department of Corrections, Central California Women's Facility.* Rev. Dominic T. Pontolillo, O.F.M.Cap.

COALINGA. *Pleasant Valley State Prison.* Vacant. 601 C Washington, 93210.

CORCORAN. *Calif. State Prison.* Tel: 209-992-8800. Rev. John J. Moore.

DELANO. *North Kern State Prison.* Vacant. Tel: 805-721-2345, Ext. 6862.

PORTERVILLE. *State Hospital.* Vacant. P.O. Box 2000, 93258.

TEHACHAPI. *California Correctional Institution,* P.O. Box 6005, 93581. Tel: 209-822-3911. Rev. Hermengildo Adolfo, Chap.

WASCO. *Prison Facility,* P.O. Box 8800, 93280-8800. Tel: 805-758-8400. Rev. Paul L. Manzano.

On Special Assignment:
Reverend Fathers—
Craig, Rod, Vocations Dir., 1550 N. Fresno St., Fresno, CA 93703-3788
Frost, Stephen A., J.C.L., Adjutant Judicial Vicar & Dir. of Tribunal, 1550 N. Fresno St., Fresno, CA 93703-3788
McCormick, Patrick, Dir., Office of Liturgical Worship, 4636 W. Dakota, Fresno, CA 93722
Negro, Sergio P., Vicar Gen., 1550 N. Fresno St., Fresno, CA 93703-3788
Nespolo, Umberto, Asian Ministry in Fresno, 2814 Mariposa, Fresno, CA 93721

Faculties Only:
Reverend Fathers—
Becerra, Alfred
Da Costa, Joseph Dinis, O.F.M.
Drieci, Pat, C.SS.R.
Harris, Edward, S.J.
Olmos, Pedro
Peters, Noel, O.M.I.
Schindler, Robert
Vespa, Bauttista
Vogt, William

On Duty Outside the Diocese:
Reverend Monsignors—
Petersen, E. James, Dir., California Catholic Conference, 1010 11 St., Ste. 200, Sacramento, CA 95814
Reverend Fathers—
Flickinger, Don D., 15333 Woodard Rd., San Jose, CA 95124

Absent on Sick Leave:
Reverend Fathers—
Bray, Kevin
Nacauili, John

Retired:
Reverend Monsignors—
Balker, Joseph W., 2401 N. Kaweah, Exeter, CA 93221
Doherty, Patrick G., P.O. Box 348, Visalia, CA 93279
Elmlinger, Herbert, 188A W. Barstow, Fresno, CA 93704
Flood, Patrick, 2550 W. Clinton, Fresno, CA 93705
Gallagher, Francis J., 2121 N. First St., Fresno, CA 93703
Herdegen, Anthony, 5660 N. River Forrest Dr., Milwaukee, WI 53209
Lahey, Maurice, 378 N. F St., Porterville, CA 93257
Lee, Howard T.
McHugh, Martin, Knock Inverin, County Galway, Ireland
McMullan, Seamus O., St. Malachy, 542 Jacobson Ct., Tehachapi, CA 93581
Meyer, Gilbert, P.O. Box 117, Olancha, CA 93548
Minhoto, Walter F., 2934 R St., Merced, CA 95340
O'Connor, Michael, 4963 N. Harrison, Fresno, CA 93704
Pointek, Francis J., P.O. Box 1240, Tehachapi, CA 93581
Ryan, John F.C., 2121 N. First St., Fresno, CA 93703
Reverend Fathers—
Alabart, Francis X., 722 Dover Pl., Delano, CA 93215
Costabile, George, 200 E. Florinda, Hanford, CA 93230
Cummins, Timothy, 2121 N. First St., Fresno, CA 93703
Grupa, Henry, 2121 First St., Fresno, CA 93703
Leitheiser, Douglas, P.O. Box 639, Lindsay, CA 93247
McGagh, Martin, P.O. Box 52, Porterville, CA 93258
McKee, John, 228 Sword Rd., Dublin, Ireland
Pascual, Manuel, 4701 S. Mooney Blvd., Sp.R7, Visalia, CA 93277
Raffel, Godfrey, P.O. Box 387, Tehachapi, CA 93581
Sancho-Boyles, Anthony

INSTITUTIONS LOCATED IN THE DIOCESE

[A] HIGH SCHOOLS, PRIVATE

FRESNO. *The San Joaquin Memorial High School of Fresno, Inc.,* 1406 N. Fresno St., 93703. Tel: 209-268-9251; Fax: 209-268-1351. Bros. Raphael Philip, F.S.C., Dir./ Prin.; Ricardo Palacio, F.S.C., Campus Ministry Dir.; John Montgomery, F.S.C., Dir. of Student Activities; Austin Gili, FSC - Instructor; Robb Wallace, FSC - Instructor; Dennis Bava, Pres.
Brothers of the Christian Schools 5; Sisters 3; Lay Teachers 36; Students 699.

[B] HIGH SCHOOLS, INTERPAROCHIAL

BAKERSFIELD. *Garces Memorial High School,* 2800 Loma Linda Dr., 93305. Tel: 805-327-2578. John Kvasnicka, Prin.; David West, Campus Ministry Coord.
Lay Teachers 40; Students 727.

[C] GENERAL HOSPITALS

FRESNO. *Saint Agnes' Medical Center,* 1303 E. Herndon, 93720. Tel: 209-449-3000.
For a complete listing, refer to the Hospitals section.

BAKERSFIELD. *Mercy Healthcare Bakersfield,* 2215 Truxtun Ave., 93301. Tel: 805-632-5000; Fax: 805-327-2592.
For a complete listing, refer to the Hospitals section.
MERCED. *Mercy Hospital & Health Services,* 2740 M St., 95340. Tel: 209-384-6444; Fax: 209-722-2902.
For a complete listing, refer to the Hospitals section.

[D] HOMES FOR INVALID AND AGED

FRESNO. *Nazareth House,* 2121 N. First St., 93703. Tel: 209-237-2257.
For a complete listing, refer to the Special Care Facilities section.

[E] CATHOLIC CHARITIES

FRESNO. *Catholic Charities of the Diocese of Fresno.* Vacant. 149 N. Fulton St., 93701. Tel: 209-237-0851.
Catholic Social Services, 149 N. Fulton St., 93701. Tel: 209-264-6414. Anita Tomlinson, Dir.
Francis X. Singleton Emergency Food Assistance Program, 149 N. Fulton St., 93701. Tel: 209-233-3663. Peter P. Hagel, Dir.
Immigration & Refugee Services, 149 N. Fulton St., 93701. Tel: 209-264-6400. Tam Nguyen, Dir. Total Staff 6; Total Assisted 800.
Infant of Prague Adoption and Counseling Services, 6059 N. Palm, 93704. Tel: 209-447-3333; Fax: 209-447-3322. Judith Casson, M.S.W., Dir.
Office of Senior Affairs. Vacant. 149 N. Fulton St., 93701. Tel: 209-485-2244.
Senior Companion Program. Tel: 209-498-6377. Patricia A. Strahl, Dir.
BAKERSFIELD. *Bakersfield Big Brothers,* 415 E. 19th St., 93305. Tel: 805-323-3025. George San Miguel, Dir.
Catholic Social Services, 310 Baker St., 93305. Tel: 805-323-2941. Joan Garabaldi, Prog. Chm.
Health Services, Homemaker Program, Cabrini League. Vacant. 310 Baker St., 93305. Tel: 805-323-2941.
Immigration & Refugee Services, 415 E. 19th St., 93305. Tel: 805-325-7751. Delfina Granados, Dir.
Junipero Serra Inn-Half Way House, 700 19th St., 93301. Tel: 805-324-6125; 323-4646. Stella Greenhalgh, Dir. Halfway/Work Furlough Community Correctional Re-entry Center (CCRC). Total Staff 17; Total Assisted 100.
Kaleidoscope. Vacant. (Drug Counseling Program), 310 Baker St., 93305. Tel: 805-323-2941.
FARMERSVILLE. *St. Vincent de Paul Center,* 468 E. Visalia Rd., P.O. Box 106, 93223. Tel: 209-594-4932. Mary G. Flores.
MERCED. *Catholic Social Services,* 1810 Canal St., 95340. Tel: 209-383-2494; 383-5220. Ramiro Coronado, Dir.
Direct Services, 1810 Canal St., 95340. Tel: 209-383-2494. Ramiro Coronado, Dir.
Migrant and Refugee Services, 1810 Canal St., 95340. Tel: 209-383-0283. Ramiro Coronado, Dir. Tel: 209383-5220.
PORTERVILLE. *Catholic Social Services,* 1309 S. Main, Bldg. B, 93257. Tel: 209-781-5778. Mary Meisel, Dir. Patients assisted annually 35,778.
VISALIA. *Catholic Social Services,* 1638 N. Dinuba Blvd., 93291. Tel: 209-734-1572; Fax: 209-234-4921. Sr. Kenneth Quinn, D.C., M.S.W., Dir.
Good News Medical Clinic, 1638 N. Dinuba Blvd., 93291. Tel: 209-734-1572.
Good News Center (Sr. Ursula's Kitchen & Thrift Store), 1724 N. Dinuba Blvd., 93291. Tel: 209-738-8922.
Good News Inn (Shelter), 1718 & 1722 N. Dinuba Blvd., 93291. Tel: 209-734-6470. Total Staff 15; Total Assisted 92,664.

[F] CONVENTS AND RESIDENCES FOR SISTERS

FRESNO. *Franciscan Hospitallers,* 6020 N. Flora Ave., 93722. Tel: 209-261-1782. Sisters 3.
Poor Sisters of Nazareth, 2121 N. First St., 93703. Tel: 209-237-2257. Sr. Teresa Grant, P.S.N., Supr. Sisters 6.
St. Agnes Hospital Convent, 1261 E. Los Altos Ave., 93710. Tel: 209-431-3376. Sisters of the Holy Cross, Inc. 8.
San Joaquin Memorial Convent, 1402 N. Fresno St., 93703-3789. Tel: 209-485-2900. Sisters of the Holy Cross 4.
Sister Disciples of the Divine Master, 3700 N. Cornelia Ave., 93722. Tel: 209-275-1656. Sr. Mary Michelle Hernandez, P.D.D.M., Supr. Sisters 12.
ATWATER. *Our Lady of the Atonement Convent,* 1694 Grove Ave., 95301. Tel: 209-358-2109. Sr. Helena Horwood, S.A. Franciscan Sisters of the Atonement 4.
MERCED. *Sisters of the Third Order of St. Dominic,* 2635 Piedmont Dr., 95340. Tel: 209-723-6564. Sisters 3.

[G] RETREAT HOUSES

THREE RIVERS. *St. Anthony's Retreat House,* P.O. Box 249, 93271. Tel: 209-561-4595. Revs. Loren Blessing, O.F.M., Dir. & Supr.; David Johnson, O.F.M.; Juan Leon, O.F.M.; Bros. Joseph Brand, O.F.M.; Nicholas Heinrich, O.F.M. Priests 3; Brothers 2.

[H] NEWMAN CENTERS

FRESNO. *St. Paul Newman Center,* 1572 E. Barstow Ave., 93710. Tel: 209-436-3434. Rev. Perry Kavookjian; Ms. Suzanne Ortez, Campus Min.
California State University at Fresno.
Fresno City College.
BAKERSFIELD. *Bakersfield College Newman Center,* 124 Columbus, 93305. Tel: 805-323-3108. Rev. Msgr. Michael Braun, Chap.

[I] SOCIETY OF ST. VINCENT DE PAUL

FRESNO. *St. Vincent's Thrift Store,* 149 N. Fulton St., 93701. Tel: 209-268-3362; 264-6414 (Office). Anita Tomlinson, Dir.
Society of St. Vincent de Paul, 149 N. Fulton St., 93701. Tel: 209-237-0851. Parish Conferences are located in parishes throughout the Diocese.
Fresno District Council, 149 N. Fulton St., 93701. Alice M. Thoms, Trustee.
Kern District Council, 310 Baker St., 93305. Tel: 805-323-7340.
Merced-Mariposa District Council, 131 W. Main St., Merced, 95340. Tel: 209-723-5077. Legal Title: *Merced-Mariposa District Council of St. Vincent de Paul Society.* Dolores Schwerdferger, Pres.
BAKERSFIELD. *Bakersfield St. Vincent de Paul Thrift Store,* 300 Baker St., 93305. Tel: 805-323-7340.

[J] MISCELLANEOUS & AGENCIES

FRESNO. *Apostolate of Christian Action,* P.O. Box 24, 93707. Tel: 209-291-0400; Fax: 209-291-1650. Roger Oraze, Pres.; Rev. Msgr. James T. Logan, Spiritual Dir.
Catholic Truth International, 5654 E. Westover, Suite 103, 93727. Tel: 209-291-0400; Fax: 209-291-1650. Christopher Knuffke, Pres.; Rev. Stephen A. Frost, Spiritual Dir.
St. Anthony's Bread Basket, Inc., P.O. Box 6045, 93703. Tel: 209-252-4929. James R. Johnson, Pres.
CLOVIS. *Catholic Fraternity for Restoration,* P.O. Box 807, 93613.
Catholic Professional & Business Breakfast Club of the Fresno Diocese, c/o Our Lady of Perpetual Help, Ninth and DeWitt Ave. Mailing Address: 929 Harvard Ave., 93612. Tel: 209-299-4270. Rev. Msgr. Raymond C. Dreiling, Contact Person.
SANGER. *Fr. Hannibal House Social Service Center,* 1501 14th St., P.O. Box 37, 93657. Tel: 209-875-0564; Fax: 209-875-1281.

RELIGIOUS INSTITUTES OF MEN REPRESENTED IN THE DIOCESE

For further details refer to the corresponding bracketed number in the Religious Institutes of Men or Women section.
[0200]—*Benedictine Monks.*—O.S.B.
[0330]—*Brothers of the Christian Schools.* (San Francisco Prov.).—F.S.C.
[0470]—*The Capuchin Friars.*—O.F.M.Cap.
[0360]—*Claretian Missionaries.* (Western Prov.).—C.M.F.
[0480]—*Conventual Franciscans.* (St. Joseph Cupertino Prov.).—O.F.M.Conv.
[0520]—*Franciscan Friars.* (St. Barbara Prov.).—O.F.M.
[0650]—*Holy Ghost Fathers.* (Western Prov.).—C.S.Sp.
[0690]—*Jesuit Fathers and Brothers.*—S.J.
[0910]—*Oblates of Mary Immaculate.*—O.M.I.
[0930]—*Oblates of St. Joseph.* (Asti, Italy).—O.S.J.
[0430]—*Order of Preachers.*—O.P.
[1070]—*Redemptorists.*—C.SS.R.
[1090]—*Rogationist Fathers.*—R.C.J.
[1200]—*Society of the Divine Savior.*—S.D.S.
[0420]—*Society of the Divine Word.*—S.V.D.
[1330]—*Vincentians (Congragation of the Mission).*—C.M.

RELIGIOUS INSTITUTES OF WOMEN REPRESENTED IN THE DIOCESE

[0230]—*Benedictine Sisters of Pontifical Jurisdiction.* (Mt Angel, OR & Grand Terrace, CA).—O.S.B.
[]—*Carmelite Sisters of St. Teresa.* (Gidellahalli, Bangalore-India).—C.S.S.T.
[1920]—*Congregation of the Sisters of the Holy Cross.* (Notre Dame, IN).—C.S.C.
[0760]—*Daughters of Charity of St. Vincent de Paul.* (Los Altos Hills, CA) (Western Prov.).—D.C.
[0820]—*Daughters of the Holy Spirit.* (France) (Putnam, CT Prov. House).—D.H.S.
[1070-20]—*Dominican Sisters.* (Congregation of St. Thomas Aquinas, Marymount, Tacoma, Washington).—O.P.
[1070-25]—*Dominican Sisters.* (Congregation of the Dominican Sisters of St. Catherine of Siena of Kenosha).—O.P.
[1270]—*Franciscan Hospitaller Sisters of the Immaculate Conception.* (San Jose, CA).—F.H.I.C.
[1190]—*Franciscan Sisters of the Atonement.* (Graymoor, NY).—S.A.
[2180]—*Immaculate Heart Community.* (Los Angeles, CA).—I.H.M.
[2570]—*Institute of the Sisters of Mercy of the Americas.* (Burlingame, CA).—R.S.M.
[2580]—*Institute of the Sisters of Mercy of the Americas.* (Omaha, NE).—R.S.M.
[2690]—*Missionary Catechists of Divine Providence.* (San Antonio, TX).—M.C.D.P.
[0980]—*Pious Disciples of the Divine Master.* (Staten Island, NY).—P.D.D.M.
[3242]—*Poor Sisters of Nazareth.* (Los Angeles, CA).—P.S.N.
[2970]—*School Sisters of Notre Dame.* (St. Louis, MO).—S.S.N.D.
[3580]—*Servants of Mary.* (Omaha, NE).—O.S.M.
[3499]—*Servants of the Blessed Sacrament.* (El Secondo, CA).—S.J.S.
[0430]—*Sisters of Charity of Blessed Virgin Mary.* (Dubuque, IA).—B.V.M.
[1010]—*Sisters of Divine Providence of San Antonio, Texas.*—C.D.P.
[]—*Sisters of Korean Martyrs.*—S.K.M.
[2560]—*Sisters of Mercy.*—S.M.
[]—*Sisters of Our Lady of Nazareth.* Fiji, South Pacific.—S.O.L.N.
[1540]—*Sisters of Saint Francis, Clinton, Iowa.*—O.S.F.
[3840]—*Sisters of St. Joseph of Carondelet.* (Los Angeles, CA & Baden, PA).—C.S.J.
[1960]—*Sisters of the Holy Family.* (Mission San Jose, CA).—S.H.F.
[2130]—*Sisters of the Immaculate Conception.* (San Francisco, CA).—R.C.M.
[]—*Sisters of the Love of God.* (La Puenta, CA).—R.A.D.
[4120-06]—*Ursuline Nuns of the Congregation of Paris.* (Toledo, OH).—O.S.U.

DIOCESAN CEMETERIES

FRESNO. *Fresno Catholic Cemeteries,* 264 N. Blythe, 93706. Tel: 209-488-7449; Fax: 209-488-7466. Michael Orlando, Dir.

NECROLOGY

† Cariglia, Michael W., (Retired). —Died June 3, 1996.
† Higgins, Clement, (Retired). —Died Feb. 18, 1996.
† Lima, Rev. Msgr. Joseph, (Retired). —Died April 11, 1996.
† Montano, Benjamin, Delano, CA, St. Mary's. —Died Oct. 19, 1996.
† Sypneski, John, (Retired). —Died June 8, 1996.

Diocese of Gallup

(Diocesis Gallupiensis)

Established December 16, 1939.

Square Miles 55,468.

Comprises Apache, Navajo and those parts of the Navajo and Hopi Reservations in Coconino Counties in the State of Arizona; San Juan, McKinley, Catron, Cibola and those parts of Rio Arriba, Sandoval, Bernalillo and Valencia Counties lying west of 106, 52', 41" meridian in the State of New Mexico.

Legal Title: New Mexico: Roman Catholic Church of the Diocese of Gallup. Arizona: Bishop of the Roman Catholic Church of the Diocese of Gallup.

For legal titles of parishes and diocesan institutions, consult the Chancery Office.

Most Reverend

DONALD E. PELOTTE, S.S.S., D.D., PH.D.

Bishop of Gallup; ordained September 2, 1972; appointed Coadjutor Bishop of Gallup February 24, 1986; consecrated May 6, 1986; succeeded to See, March 20, 1990. *Office: P.O. Box 1338, Gallup, NM, 87305. Res., 433 Camino Del Sol, P.O. Box 1317, Gallup, NM, 87305.* Tel.: 505-722-3047.

STRENGTHEN ONE ANOTHER

Chancery: 711 S. Puerco Dr., P.O. Box 1338, Gallup, NM, 87305. Tel.: 505-863-4406; Fax: 505-722-9131.

STATISTICAL OVERVIEW

Personnel	
Bishop	1
Priests: Diocesan Active in Diocese	30
Priests: Active Outside Diocese	19
Priests: Diocesan in Foreign Missions	1
Priests: Retired, Sick or Absent	8
Number of Diocesan Priests	58
Religious Priests in Diocese	31
Extern Priests in Diocese	8
Ordinations:	
Permanent Deacons in Diocese	33
Total Brothers	12
Total Sisters	155
Parishes	
Parishes	58
With Resident Pastor:	
Resident Diocesan Priests	28
Resident Religious Priests	19
Without Resident Pastor:	
Administered by Priests	9
Completely Vacant	2
Missions	41
Pastoral Centers	38
Welfare	
Homes for the Aged	1
Total Assisted	42
Specialized Homes	2
Total Assisted	180
Special Centers for Social Services	1
Total Assisted	44,931
Educational	
Diocesan Students in Other Seminaries	2
Total Seminarians	2
High Schools, Private	3
Total Students	201
Elementary Schools, Diocesan and Parish	2
Total Students	272
Elementary Schools, Private	8
Total Students	1,337
Catechesis/Religious Education:	
High School Students	803
Elementary Students	3,335
Total Students Under Catholic Instruction	5,950
Teachers in the Diocese:	
Sisters	26
Lay Teachers	115
Vital Statistics	
Receptions into the Church:	
Infant Baptism Totals	886
Adult Baptism Totals	246
Received into Full Communion	69
First Communions	847
Confirmations	569
Marriages:	
Catholic	149
Interfaith	65
Total Marriages	214
Deaths	515
Total Catholic Population	41,181
Total Population	355,640

Former Bishop—Most Rev. Bernard T. Espelage, O.F.M., D.D., ord. May 16, 1918; appt. Bishop of Gallup, July 20, 1940; cons. Oct. 9, 1940; resigned Sept. 3, 1969; died Feb. 19, 1971.—Most Rev. Jerome J. Hastrich, D.D., ord. Feb. 9, 1941; cons. Auxiliary Bishop of Madison and Titular Bishop of Gurza, July 31, 1963; transferred to the See of Gallup, Sept. 3, 1969; installed Dec. 3, 1969; retired March 20, 1990; died May 12, 1995.

Vicar General—Rev. Msgr. Leo Gomez, V.G.

Vicar for Indian Affairs—Rev. Caron Vollmer, O.F.M.

Office of the Bishop—711 S. Puerco Dr., P.O. Box 1338, Gallup, 87305. Tel: 505-863-4406.

Chancery—711 S. Puerco Dr., P.O. Box 1338, Gallup, 87305. Tel: 505-863-4406; Fax: 505-722-9131. Office Hours: Mon.-Thurs. 8:30-12 & 1-4:30; Fri. 8:30-12.

Chancellor—Bro. Duane A. Torisky, O.F.M.

Vice Chancellor—Deacon Daniel Resendes, Ph.D.

Financial Secretary—Mrs. Anna J. DiGregorio.

Diocesan Tribunal (First Instance)—711 S. Puerco Dr., P.O. Box 1338, Gallup, 87305. Tel: 505-863-4406; Fax: 505-722-9324.

Judicial Vicar—Rev. Lawrence J. O'Keefe, J.C.D.

Adjutant Judicial Vicar—Rev. Alfred A. Tachias, J.C.L.

Judges—Revs. Alfred A. Tachias, J.C.L.; Deacon Paul Dooley; Rev. Msgr. Leo Gomez; Rev. Msgr. James Lindenmeyer.

Defenders of the Bond—Revs. Meldon Hickey, O.F.M.; Michael Vigil; Thomas Maikowski, Ph.D.; Emeric Nordmeyer, O.F.M.

Notary—Mary Alice Salaz.

Episcopal Vicars—McKinley Vicariate: Very Rev. Diego Mazon, O.F.M., V.F.; Apache Vicariate: Very Rev. Martan Rademaker, O.F.M., V.F.; Navajo Vicariate: Very Rev. Michael Vigil, V.F.; Lower Arizona Vicariate: Very Rev. Jose Rodriquez, V.F.; San Juan Vicariate: Very Rev. Timothy Farrell; Cibola Vicariate: Very Rev. Emeric Nordmeyer, O.F.M.

Vicaress for Religious—Sr. Mary Louise Hoelscher, C.PP.S., *P.O.Box 120, Manuelito, 87318-0120.* Tel: 505-863-1918.

Presbyteral Council—Most Rev. Donald E. Pelotte, S.S.S., Ph.D.; Rev. Msgr. Leo Gomez, V.G.; Very Revs. Lawrence O'Keefe, Moderator; Diego Mazon, O.F.M.; Emeric Nordmeyer, O.F.M.; Rev. Edward Fronske, O.F.M.; Very Revs. Louis Franz, C.M.; Timothy Farrell; Revs. Thomas Maikowski; Michael Vigil; Jose Rodriquez; Very Rev. Martan Rademaker, O.F.M.; Bro. Duane Torisky O.F.M., Sec., *P.O. Box 1338, Gallup, 87305.*

Diocesan Consultors—Rev. Msgr. Leo Gomez, V.G.; Revs. Lawrence O'Keefe; Jose Rodriguez; Edward Fronske, O.F.M.; Thomas Maikowski; Very Revs. Diego Mazon, O.F.M.; Louis Franz, C.M.

Diocesan Navajo Mission Board—Most Rev. Donald E. Pelotte, S.S.S.; Very Rev. Martan Rademaker, O.F.M.; Revs. Caron Vollmer, O.F.M.; Davin Von Hagel, O.F.M.

Diocesan Offices and Directors

Archivist—Bro. Duane Torisky, O.F.M.

Boys Scouts—Rev. Thomas Maikowski, Ph.D., Dir. & Chap., *P.O. Box 1028, Gallup, 87305.* Tel: 505-863-3563.

Budget and Finance—Deacon James P. Hoy, Dir.

Cemeteries—Rev. Msgr. James Lindenmeyer, *Box 2840, Farmington, 87401.*

Catholic Charities—Sr. Betty Marie Dunkel, D.C., Dir., *Main Office, Gallup, P.O. Box 1589, Gallup, 87305.* Tel: 505-722-5272. Chinle: *P.O. Box 417, Chinle, AZ, 86053.* Tel: 520-674-3238. Grants-Milan: *2595 W. Hwy. 66, P.O. Box 124, Grants, 87020.* Tel: 505-285-5451. Farmington: *119 W. Broadway, Farmington, 87401.* Tel: 505-325-3724. Holbrook: *P.O. Box 41, Holbrook, AZ, 86025.* Tel: 520-524-9720. White Mountain: *P.O. Box 600, McNary, AZ, 85930.* Tel: 520-334-2219.

Cursillos—Rev. Meldon Hickey, O.F.M., *P.O. Drawer 60, Fort Defiance, AZ, 86504.* Tel: 520-729-5068.

Diocesan Pastoral Council—Most Rev. Donald E. Pelotte, S.S.S.; Bro. Duane Torisky, O.F.M.; Kathleen Beaton, Chm. Mary Ann Montoya, Vice Chm.; Sr. Francella Mary Griggs, Sec. Roger Ridgeway, Consultant; Revs. Thomas Maikowski; Walter Opalewski; Michael Vigil; Deacon Jorge Campos; Bro. Duane Torisky, O.F.M.; Sr. Sarah Page, O.S.F.; Pauline Baca; Judy Davis; Julia Gorman; Barbara Kozeliski; Jerry Lindsay; Francis J. Pawlowski; Sam Rotolo.

Director of Education, (Catholic Schools and Religious Education)—Rev. Thomas Maikowski, Ph.D., Director of Education, *P.O. Box 1028, Gallup, 87305.* Tel: 505-863-3563.

Ecumenical Affairs in Arizona, Arizona Ecumenical Council—Rev. Alberto Avella, *P.O. Box 1449, Showlow, 85901.* Tel: 520-537-2543.

Ecumenical Affairs in New Mexico, New Mexico Council of Churches—Rev. Daniel Daley, *307 N. Church St., Bloomfield, 87413.* Tel: 505-632-2014.

Newspaper—"Voice of the Southwest"; Rev. Timothy Farrell, *P.O. Box 1338, Gallup, 87305.* Tel: 505-863-4406.

Permanent Deacon Program—Most Rev. Donald E. Pelotte, S.S.S.; Deacon Timoted P. Lujan, Deacon Dir.

Priests' Retirement Fund—William Day, Chm.; Revs. Jose Rodriquez; Patrick Wedeking; Oliver Curran; Frank Chacon.

Propagation of the Faith—Rev. Michael Mack, *P.O. Box 1338, Gallup, 87305.*

Radio and Television—Rev. Cormac Antram, O.F.M., *P.O. Box 517, Kayenta, AZ, 86033.*

Search—Ted Gomez, Dir., *2103 Lynwood Dr., Farmington, 87401.*

Serra Club—Rev. Francis Buck, S.J., Dir., *P.O. Box 208, Fort Wingate, 87305.*

Social Justice and Outreach—FRANCIS J. PAWLOWSKI, *P.O. Box 1338, Gallup, 87305.*

Vocations—For Priesthood: Rev. JOACHIM BLONSKI, *414 N. Allen Ave., Farmington, 87401.* Deacon Vocations: Deacon TIMOTED LUJAN, *P.O. Box 2612, Milan, 87021-2612.* MAGDA GARCIA, H.N.S.G., *217 E. Wilson, Gallup, 87301.*

Youth Ministry—DOUGLAS CLAPPER; LENA CLAPPER, *P.O. Box 1615, Aztec, 87410.*

CLERGY, PARISHES, MISSIONS AND PAROCHIAL SCHOOLS

CITY OF GALLUP (McKinley County)

1—CATHEDRAL OF THE SACRED HEART. (Dedicated June 19, 1955). Rev. Msgr. Leo Gomez, V.G., Rector; Deacon Joseph Krikawa.
Mailing Address: P.O. Box 1029, 87305.
Res., 415 E. Green Ave., 87301. Tel: 505-722-6644; Fax: 505-722-6645.
Catechesis/Religious Programs—Barbara Kozeliski, D.R.E.
Students 327.

2—ST. FRANCIS OF ASSISI, Revs. Diego Mazon, O.F.M.; Ulric Pax, O.F.M.; Bro. George Ward, O.F.M. In res., Bro. Duane Torisky, O.F.M.
Res., 411 N. Second, 87301. Tel: 505-863-3033.
School—215 W. Wilson, 87301. Tel: 505-863-3145. Rev. Thomas Maikowski, Prin.
Sisters 2; Lay Teachers 6; Students 87.
Catechesis/Religious Programs—Sr. Annette O'Donnell, D.R.E.
Students 400.
Mission—Gamerco, St. Joseph the Worker.

3—ST. JEROME. Closed. For inquiries for parish records contact the Chancery.

4—ST. JOHN VIANNEY, Rev. Walter Opalewski; Deacon Timothy Kelley.
Res., 3408 Zia Dr., 87301. Tel: 505-722-3361.
Catechesis/Religious Programs—Students 96.
Mission—Bluewater, Risen Savior.

OUTSIDE THE CITY OF GALLUP, NEW MEXICO

Acoma, Cibola Co., San Esteban, Indian Mission, Rev. Antonio Trujillo, O.F.M.
Res., P.O. Box 448, Pueblo of Acoma, 87034-0448. Tel: 505-552-6403.
Catechesis/Religious Programs—Students 120.
Missions—Acomita, St. Anne; McCartys, Santa Maria de Acoma.

Aragon, Catron Co., Santo Nino, Rev. Patrick C. Wedeking; Deacon Juan Aragon.
Res., P.O. Box 493, 87830. Tel: 505-533-6240.
Missions—Lower San Francisco, San Isidro; Reserve, St. Francis; Horse Springs, St. Anne.
Station—Apache Creek.

Aztec, San Juan Co., St. Joseph, Rev. Luis J. Garcia, J.C.L.; Deacons Charles Peterson; Frank Chavez.
Res., 500 N. Mesa Verde St., 87410. Tel: 505-334-6535; Fax: 505-334-6535.
Catechesis/Religious Programs—Sr. Sara M. Gomez, O.S.U., D.R.E.
Students 257.

Blanco, San Juan Co., St. Rose, Rev. Daniel P. Daley.
Res., P.O. Box 417, 87412. Tel: 505-632-2064.
Catechesis/Religious Programs—Ms. Monique Bryant, D.R.E.
Students 87.
Mission—Los Martinez, Our Lady of Guadalupe.

Bloomfield, San Juan Co., St. Mary, Rev. Dan Daley.
Res., 307 N. Church St., 87413. Tel: 505-632-2014.
Catechesis/Religious Programs—Sr. Edith Stichler, D.R.E.
Students 290.

Chichiltah, McKinley Co., St. Patrick Navajo Mission, Rev. Jeffrey King.
Res., P.O. Box 267, Vanderwagon, 87326. Tel: 505-778-5410.

Church Rock, McKinley Co., St. Philip Benizi, Rev. Francis C. Buck, S.J.
Res., P.O. Box 310, 87311. Tel: 505-488-5515.
Station—Pinedale.

Crownpoint, McKinley Co., St. Paul, Rev. Patrick J. Universal.
Res., P.O. Box 268, 87313. Tel: 505-786-7110; Fax: 505-786-5376.
Catechesis/Religious Programs—Sr. Barbara Smith, A.S.C., D.R.E.
Students 41.
Mission—Star Lake, San Ignacio.
Station—Lake Valley.

Cuba, Sandoval Co., Immaculate Conception (Nacimiento), Rev. Jerry T. Mesley.
Res., P.O. Box 40, 87013. Tel: 505-289-3803.
Missions—La Jara, Santo Nino; San Luis, Saint Aloysius Gonzaga; Cabezon, San Jose; Guadalupe, Sacred Heart of Mary.
Station—Torrcon, Counselors.

Farmington, San Juan Co., Sacred Heart, Revs. Timothy Farrell; Joachim Blonski.
Res., 414 N. Allen Ave., 87401. Tel: 505-325-9743; Fax: 505-325-8860.
Catechesis/Religious Programs—Sr. Rene Backe, C.S.A., D.R.E.
Students 350.
St. Mary's, Rev. Msgr. James Lindenmeyer; Deacon Paul Berhost. In res., Rev. Raymond Mahlmann.
Res., P.O. Box 2840, 87499-2840. Tel: 505-325-0287.
Catechesis/Religious Programs—James Hornecker, D.R.E.
Students 210.

Flora Vista, San Juan Co., Holy Trinity, Rev. Luis J. Garcia, J.C.L.; Deacons Frank Chavez; Charles Peterson.
Mailing Address: 500 N. Mesa Verde St., Aztec, 87410. Tel: 505-334-6535.
Res., 42 Road 3520, P.O. Box 459, 87415. Tel: 505-334-3885.

Fort Wingate, McKinley Co., St. Eleanor, Rev. Francis C. Buck, S.J.
Res., P.O. Box 208, 87316. Tel: 505-488-5515.
Station—Iyanbito.

Grants, Cibola Co., St. Teresa, Rev. Emeric Nordmeyer, O.F.M. In res., Rev. Maurus Pax, O.F.M.; Bro. Arthur Puthoff, O.F.M.; Deacons Larry Chavez; Paul Sanchez; Elie Calonge.
Res., 213 Smith St., P.O. Box 668, 87020. Tel: 505-285-6646; Fax: 505-285-6646.
Catechesis/Religious Programs—Dina Calonge, D.R.E.
Students 146.

Laguna, Cibola Co., St. Joseph (Indian Pueblo), Rev. Matthias Crehan, O.F.M.
Res., P.O. Box 1000, 87026. Tel: 505-552-9330.
Catechesis/Religious Programs—D.R.E.: Sr. Marcia Huber, S.M.I.C., (Youth); Sr. Virginia Adler, C.S.A, (Adult).
Students 175.
Missions—Encinal, Nativity of the Blessed Virgin Mary; Mesita, Sacred Heart; Paguate, St. Elizabeth; Paraje, St. Mary Margaret; Seama, St. Anne.

Lumberton, Rio Arriba Co., St. Francis of Assisi, Rev. Stephan Perzan (PH).
Res., P.O. Box 68, 87547. Tel: 505-759-3498.
Catechesis/Religious Programs—Sr. Carmelita Erdman, D.R.E.
Students 55.
Mission—Dulce, St. Anthony.

Milan, Cibola Co., St. Vivian, Rev. William Day; Deacon Timoteo P. Lujan.
Res., P.O. Box 2938, 87021. Tel: 505-287-9327.
Catechesis/Religious Programs—Sr. Miriam Becerre, H.N.S.G., D.R.E.
Students 142.

Navajo, McKinley Co., St. Berard, Rev. Niles E. Kraft, O.F.M.; Deacon Wilson Gorman.
Res., P.O. Box 1284, 87328. Tel: 505-777-2251.
Catechesis/Religious Programs—Sr. Dorothy Dowd, S.B.S., D.R.E.
Students 50.
Mission—Sawmill, Apache Co., St. Francis Mission, P.O. Box 41, Sawmill, AZ 86549. Tel: 602-729-5224.
Station—Crystal.

Pinehaven, McKinley Co., Good Shepherd Catholic Mission, Rev. Jeffrey King.
Res., P.O. Box 2170, Gallup, 87305. Tel: 505-778-5658.
Convent—Box 267, Vanderwagen, 87326. Tel: 505-778-5740. Missionaries of Charity
Sisters 4.

Quemado, Catron Co., Sacred Heart, Rev. Thomas Coleman.
Res., P.O. Box 338, 87829. Tel: 505-773-4631.
Mission—Datil, Nativity of the Blessed Virgin Mary.

San Fidel, Cibola Co., St. Joseph. Unassigned.
Res., P.O. Box 370, 87049. Tel: 505-552-6236.
Mission—Cubero, Our Lady of Light.

San Mateo, Cibola and McKinley Cos., San Mateo, Rev. William Day.
Mailing Address: P.O. Box 14, 87050.
Res., P.O. Box 2938, Milan, 87021.

San Rafael, Cibola Co., San Rafael, Rev. William Da
Res., P.O. Box 145, 87051. Tel: 505-287-8164.
Catechesis/Religious Programs—Sr. Ana Zuniga, H.N.S.G., D.R.E.
Students 73.

Seboyeta, Cibola Co., Our Lady of Sorrows, Rev. John Boland.
Res., P.O. Box 13, 87055. Tel: 505-552-6301.
Missions—Bibo, Our Lady of Loretto; Moquino, Santa Rosalia.
Station—Marquez.

Shiprock, San Juan Co., Christ the King, Rev. John Sauter; Deacon Bob Gouladdle.
Res., P.O. Box 610, 87420. Tel: 505-368-4532.

Thoreau, McKinley Co., St. Bonaventure. Unassigned.
Res., P.O. Box 1389, 87323. Tel: 505-862-7449.
Station—Smith Lake, Holy Spirit.

Tinaja, Cibola Co., San Lorenzo, Rev. Steve Pispeky.
Res., State Rte. 2, Box 47, Ramah, 87321. Tel: 505-783-4301.
Mission—Fence Lake, El Morro.

Tohatchi, McKinley Co., St. Mary Church, Revs. John Mittelstadt, O.F.M.; Pacian Meyer, O.F.M.; Bro. Michael Haag, O.F.M.; Deacon Sherman Manuelito.
Res., Box 39, 87325. Tel: 505-733-2243. [CEM]
Catechesis/Religious Programs—Sr. Patricia Bietsch, O.S.F., D.R.E.
Students 120.
Mission—Naschitti, St. Anthony.
Stations—Coyote Canyon; Mexican Springs; Twin Lakes; Sheep Springs; Chuska.

Waterflow, San Juan Co., Sacred Heart, Rev. Arley Downie.
Res., Rte. 1, Box 10, 87421. Tel: 505-598-5454.
Catechesis/Religious Programs—Gretchen Hohenberg, D.R.E.
Students 89.
Mission—Kirtland, San Juan Catholic Center Ojo Amarillo Mission.

Zuni, McKinley Co., St. Anthony Indian Mission, Our Lady of Guadalupe (Indian Pueblo), Revs. Dale Jamison, O.F.M.; Terence Rhodes, O.F.M.; Richard Maguire, Pastoral Min.
Res., P.O. Box 486, 87327. Tel: 505-782-2888.
School—St. Anthony Indian School, Tel: 505-782-4596. Sr. Patricia Glynn, F.S.P., Prin.
Sisters 4; Lay Teachers 10; Students 215.

ARIZONA

Alpine, Apache Co., St. Helena, Rev. Msgr. Arthur F. MacDonald.
Res., P.O. Box 229, 85920. Tel: 520-339-4363.
Missions—Glenwood, Catron Co., Santo Nino, P.O. Box 284, Glenwood, NM 88039.; Mogollon, Our Lady.

Chinle, Apache Co., Our Lady of Fatima, Indian Mission, Revs. Blane Grein, O.F.M.; Pio O'Connor, O.F.M.; Eugene Bowski.
Res., P.O. Box 2119, 86503. Tel: 520-674-5413.
Missions—Many Farms, St. Anthony, Tel: 520-781-6350; Pinon, Navajo Co., St. Mary of the Rosary, P.O. Box 432, Pinon, AZ 86510. Tel: 520-725-3365
Stations—Salina Springs; Rough Rock; Black Mo tain; Canyon Del Muerto; Cotton Wood; Nazl

Cibecue, Navajo Co., St. Catherine, Rev. Green, S.D.S.
Res., P.O. Box 156, 85911. Tel: 520-332
Mission—Cedar Creek, St. Anthony.

Concho, Apache Co., San Rafael, Rev.
Church—P.O. Drawer C, 85924.

Fort Defiance, Apache Co., O Sacrament, Revs. Martan R don Hickey, O.F.M.; Deac
Res., P.O. Box 60, 8650
Catechesis/Religious P S.B.S., D.R.E.
Students 98.

Ganado, Apache C O.F.M.
Res., P.O. B
Catechesi Moreau
Stude
Mis st

Kayenta, Davin
Res., P.O.
Catechesis/

C.D.P., D.R.E.
Students 74.
Stations—Chilchinbito; Shonto.

Keams Canyon, Navajo Co., St. Joseph's Indian Mission, Rev. Clayton F. Kilburn, C.M.
Res., P.O. Box 128, 86034. Tel: 520-738-2325.
Stations—Kykotsmovi Hopi Indian Reservation, Tel: 520-734-2283; Toyei.

Lukachukai, Apache Co., St. Isabel Mission for Navajo Indians, Rev. Caron Vollmer, O.F.M.
Res., P.O. Box 128, 86507. Tel: 520-787-2322.
Missions—Round Rock, Our Lady of Guadalupe; Tsaile, St. Ann; Wheatfields, Our Lady of the Lake.

McNary, Apache Co., St. Anthony, Rev. Cyril Levy.
Res., P.O. Box 628, 85930. Tel: 520-334-2394.
Stations—Hawley Lake; The Ranch (Summer); Sunrise Ski Lodge (Winter).

Overgaard, Navajo Co., Our Lady of Assumption, Rev. Jose Rodriguez.
Res., P.O. Box 628, 85933. Tel: 520-535-5329.

Page, Coconino Co., Immaculate Heart of Mary, Revs. Mark Ford, C.M.; Louis Franz, C.M.; Deacon Roy Stringfellow.
Res., P.O. Box 1387, 86040. Tel: 520-645-2301.
Catechesis/Religious Programs—Students 124.

Pinetop, Apache Co., St. Mary of the Angels, Rev. Oliver Curran; Sr. M. Daria Herbella, O.P., Pastoral Assoc. & D.R.E.
Res., Box 819, 85935. Tel: 520-367-2080; Fax: 520-367-2085.
Catechesis/Religious Programs—Students 115.

Pinon, Navajo Co., St. Mary of the Rosary. Attended by Chinle, AZ.
Res., P.O. Box 432, 86510. Tel: 520-725-3365.
Stations—Tachee; Blue Gap; Forest Lake; Whippoorwill Spring; Hardrock; Kits'iiLi.

Show Low, Navajo Co., St. Rita, Rev. Alberto Avella; Deacon John Heal.
Res., P.O. Box 1449, 85901. Tel: 520-537-2543.
Catechesis/Religious Programs—D.R.E.: Mary Sexton; Lucy Coen.
Students 94.

Snowflake, Navajo Co., Our Lady of the Snows, Rev. Jose Rodriguez; Deacon William J. Rogers.
Res., P.O. Box 1060, 85937. Tel: 520-536-4559.
Catechesis/Religious Programs—Mrs. John M. Heal, D.R.E.
Students 68.

Springerville, Apache Co., St. Peter, Rev. Robert Mathieu; Deacons George Campos; Russel Majesky.
Res., P.O. Box 1566, 85938. Tel: 520-333-4423.

St. Johns, Apache Co., St. John the Baptist, Rev. Frank Chacon.
Res., P.O. Box 309, 85936. Tel: 520-337-4390.
Catechesis/Religious Programs—Students 240.

St. Michaels, Apache Co., St. Michael, Rev. Simon Conrad, O.F.M. In res., Revs. Cormac Antram, O.F.M.; Lorenzo Ruiz, O.F.M.; Bros. John Friebel, O.F.M.; Francis Evans, O.F.M.; Gerald Grantner, O.F.M.; Maynard Shurley, O.F.M.
Res., P.O. Box 680, 86511-0680. Tel: 520-871-4171.
Catechesis/Religious Programs—D.R.E.: Sr. Josephine Geoble; Sr. Frances Rose Dickel.
Students 90.
Mission—St. Michaels, St. Michael's Mission for Navajo Indians.

City, Coconino Co., St. Jude, Revs. Mark Ford, M.; J. Godden Menard, C.M.
s., P.O. Box 248, 86045. Tel: 520-283-5391.

Whiteriver, Navajo Co., St. Francis Apache Indian, Rev. Edward Fronske, O.F.M.; Bro. Ernest LuVisi, O.F.M., Pastoral Assoc.
Res., P.O. Box 778, 85941. Tel: 520-338-4432.
Catechesis/Religious Programs—Sr. Mary Hottenroth, S.B.S., D.R.E.
Students 100.

Winslow, Navajo Co., St. Joseph's, Rev. Michael A. Vigil.
Res., 300 W. Hillview St., 86047. Tel: 520-289-2350.
Catechesis/Religious Programs—Students 213.
Stations—Leupp; Dilcon; Seba Dalkai.
Madre de Dios, Rev. William Welch.
Res., 1015 Central St., 86047. Tel: 520-289-2010.
Catechesis/Religious Programs—J. Lopez, D.R.E.
Students 68.

Chaplains of Public Institutions

GALLUP. *Gallup Area Hospitals & Nursing Homes.* Vacant. 506 W. 66 Ave., 87301. Tel: 505-722-0999.

Special Assignment:
Reverend Fathers—
Maikowski, Thomas, Dir. of Education

On Duty Outside of Diocese:
Reverend Fathers—
Bezzina, Benjamin, St. Mary's Catholic Church, 56 Burton St., Concord, New South Wales 2137 Australia
Casimano, Santino, Chap., Navsubase Nlon, Groton, CT 06349-5013
Coutu, Joseph, Most Holy Trinity Monastery, Dugway Rd., Petersham, MA 01366
DeGante, Adalberto, St. Anthony Parish, 327 South St., Sterling, CO 80751. Tel: 303-522-6422
Hussey, Daniel, CHC, USNR, 779-229 East Shore Terrace, Chula Vista, CA 91913
Llano, Isidoro
Mangampo, Gil, 2901 E. Yorba Linda Blvd., Fullterton, CA 92631. Tel: 714-985-1463
Morello, Peter, VA Medical, 650 E. Indian School Rd., Phoenix, AZ 85012
Perez, Rafael, St. Joseph Parish, 416 E. Second St., Lordsburg, NM 88045
Richardson, Donald, Mision Catolica, Puerto Cabezas, Nicaragua
Sanchez, Raul, Ch. Capt., USAF, 6933 Borderbrook Dr., Apt. 1313, San Antonio, TX. Tel: 210-670-7373
Turner, Robert, Blessed Sacrament Parish, 3100 S. 41st St., Milwaukee, WI 53215

Absent on Leave:
Reverend Fathers—
Buckley, James, P.O. Box 71037, Sanger, TX 76266
Finnegan, Kevin, St. Paul University Seminary, 249 Main St., Ottawa, Ontario, K1S 1C5 Canada
Kassis, Daniel, P.O. Box 4742, Laguna Beach, CA 92652-4742
Kugler, Michael, 304 N. 74th St., Milwaukee, WI 53213
Lopez, Adolfo
McConvey, Michael, 3 Argyll Ave., Bustin Brae Larne, Co. Antrim, Ireland
McNeill, Douglas, 488 7th Ave., Brooklyn, NY 11215
Obersteiner, Ernest, 67-918 Arden Dr., Cathedral City, CA 92234
Wollersheim, David, 1222 A Washington St., Apt. 1, Manitowoc, WI 54220

Retired:
Reverend Fathers—
Brackett, Joseph, Good Shepherd Manor, P.O. Box 10248, Albuquerque, NM 87184-0284
Budai, Frank A., 149530 Seneca Tr., P.O. Box 2709, Big River, CA 92242
Burns, James, P.O. Box 2155, Wickenburg, AZ 85378
Doyle, Gerald, P.O. Box 2131, Swansboro, NC 28584
Hart, William, P.O. Box 413, Castine, ME 04421
Manero, Ismael, Eladio Perlado 26-8C, Burgos, 09007
Quintana, Edward, 193 E. 2nd South St., Snowflake, AZ 85937
Smith, Norman, Mullen Home, 3629 W. 29th Ave., Denver, CO 80211
Stanfield, Francis E., 309 E. Logan Ave., Gallup, NM 87301

Permanent Deacons:
Aragon, Juan, Gen. Del., Aragon, NM
Aragon, Vidal, 324 Jane N.E., Albuquerque, NM 87123
Berhost, Paul, 2104 E. 17th St., Farmington, NM 87020
Bloomfield, John, P.O. Box 5024, Gallup, NM 87305
Calonge, Elie, 206 Smith St., Grants, NM 87020
Campos, George, P.O. Box 1254, Eagar, AZ 85925
Chavez, Frank, 341 Arnold Dr., Aztec, NM 87410
Chavez, Larry, P.O. Box 1883, Grants, NM 87020
Dooley, Paul, P.O. Box 2954, Gallup, NM 87301
Droessler, Cyril J., 1790 Garfield St., Dubuque, IA 52001
Gorman, Wilson C., P.O. Box 218, Fort Defiance, AZ 86504-0218
Guoladdle, Bobby, HC61, Box 240, Winslow, NM 86047
Heal, John, P.O. Box 1429, Snowflake, AZ 85937
Hernandez, Arnold, St. Edwards Church, 610 W. Stevens, Carlsbad, NM 88220
Hoy, James, P.O Box 1084, Gallup, NM 87305
Kelley, Timothy, 416 Valentina Dr., Gallup, NM 87301
Krikawa, Joseph, P.O. Box 1029, Gallup, NM 87305
Lane, John F., P.O. Box 1750, Fargo, ND 58107-1750
Lucero, Levy, 414 San Andreas, Alamogordo, NM 88310
Lujan, Timoteo, P.O. Box 2612, Milan, NM 87021-2612
Majesky, Russel, P.O. Box 139, Greer, AZ 85927
Manuelito, Sherman, P.O. Box 296, Tohatchi, NM 87325-0296
Martin, Daniel Nez, P.O. Box 724, Window Rock, AZ 86515
Moffett, Stephen, P.O. Box 4383, North Las Vegas, NV 89036
Peterson, Charles, 28 Rd. 3009, Aztec, NM 87410
Resendes, Daniel, 412 LaCima Rd., Gallup, NM 87301
Rogers, William, P.O. Box 217, Taylor, AZ 85939-0217
Sanchez, Paul, 203 N. Nimitz, Grants, NM 89020
Scarabino, Anthony, P.O. Box 1278, Taylor, AZ 85939
Stando, Matthew, 2446 Harlem Rd., Cheektowaga, NY 14225
Starrs, William, 4580 N. Aqua Fria Dr., #A, Prescott Valley, AZ 86314
Stringfellow, Roy, P.O. Box 2559, Page, AZ 86040
Valencia, Ernest, P.O. Box 461, Blanco, NM 87412

INSTITUTIONS LOCATED IN THE DIOCESE

[A] SEMINARIES, DIOCESAN

ocesan Diaconate Formation Program, P.O. 38, 87305. Tel: 505-863-4406. Most Rev. E. Pelotte; Deacons Timoteo Lugan, Dir.; ley, Asst. Dir.; Daniel Resendes, Ph.D., Coord. Faculty: Revs. Alfred A. Tachias; O'Keefe; Berard Doerger, O.F.M.; Meldon M.; Dr. Emerine Glowienka, Ph.D.; Sr. ht, O.S.F.; Sr. Ruth Battaglia, C.S.A.; e, C.S.A.; Sr. Dolores Marr. Diaconate

American Lay Ministry and Diacon- O. Box 2119, 86503. Rev. Blane Dir. Faculty: Rev. Pio O'Connor, een Farrar, A.S.C.; Sr. Barbara Maria Sarto Moreau, O.P.; Sr. F.; Sr. Barbara Hileman, O.S.F.; S.B.S. Students 57.

OOLS, PRIVATE

ael High School, P.O. Box eilly, Prin. Sisters 8; Lay 4.

witha Academy. (Grades O. Box 909, 87323. Tel: 505-862-7466. Steve Ward, Prin. Lay Teachers 12; Students 67.

[C] ELEMENTARY SCHOOLS, PRIVATE

GALLUP. *Gallup Catholic School.* (Grades PreK-11), 515 Park Ave., 87301. Tel: 505-863-6652. Donald Sparks, Prin. Lay Teachers 17; Students 265.

CUBA. *Immaculate Conception School.* (Grades K-8), P.O. Box 218, 87013. Tel: 505-289-3749. Robert Gutierrez, Prin. Sisters 1; Lay Teachers 6; Students 97.

FARMINGTON. *Sacred Heart School.* (Grades K-6), 404 N. Allen Ave., 87401. Tel: 505-325-7152. William Francis, Prin. Lay Teachers 14; Students 163.

GRANTS. *St. Teresa of Avila School.* (Grades K-8), P.O. Box 729, 87020. Tel: 505-287-2261. Marcia Lackey, Prin. Lay Teachers 12; Students 144.

LUMBERTON. *St. Francis School.* (Grades K-8), P.O. Box 26, 87528. Tel: 505-759-3252. Sr. Rose Marie Deibel, S.N.D.deN., Prin. Sisters 1; Lay Teachers 10; Students 98.

ST. MICHAELS, AZ. *St. Michael Indian School*, P.O. Box 650, 86511. Tel: 520-871-4636. Sr. Kathleen Kajer, Prin. (Elementary). Sisters 7; Lay Teachers 6; Students 279.

SAN FIDEL. *St. Joseph School.* (Grades K-6), P.O. Box 370, 87049. Tel: 505-552-6362. Sr. Michelle Geerken, Prin. Sisters 4; Lay Teachers 5; Students 57.

THOREAU. *Blessed Kateri Tekakwitha Academy.* (Grades PreK-6), 200 Central Ave., P.O. Box 909, 87323. Tel: 505-862-7465. Sr. Natalie Bussiere, S.N.D.deN., Prin. Sisters 2; Faculty 18; Students 230.

[D] CONVENTS AND RESIDENCES FOR SISTERS

GALLUP. *Carmelite Monastery*, P.O. Box 690, 191 Twin Buttes Rd., 87305-0690. Tel: 505-722-4516. Discalced Carmelite Nuns. Mother Mary Angels, O.C.D., Prioress; Rev. Louis D. Konechne, Chap. Sisters 6.
Casa Reina, 217 E. Wilson, 87301. Tel: 505-722-5511. Sisters of Guadalupe and St. Joseph. Mother Magda, H.N.S.G., Supr.
Perpetual Adoration Chapel. Immigration and Naturalization Services, Hispanic Ministry. Sisters 12.
Our Lady of Mt. Carmel, 208 Cedar Ave., 87301. Tel: 505-722-9411; Fax: 505-863-5017. Sr. Rose Marie Holden, O.S.F., Dir. Residence for Indian girls.
St. Valerians Catholic Indian Center, 506 W. 66th Ave., 87301. Deacon James Hoy, Dir. Tel: 505-722-0999.

[E] HOMES FOR THE AGED

GALLUP. *Villa Guadalupe Home for the Aged*, 1900 Mark Ave., 87301. Tel: 505-863-6894. Sr. Celine Therese, L.S.P.; Rev. Alfred A. Tachias, Chap. Little Sisters of the Poor 8.

[F] MISCELLANEOUS LISTINGS

GALLUP. *Blue Army*. (Fatima Apostolate), 217 E. Wilson Ave, 87301. Tel: 505-722-5511. Mrs. Lillie Yepez, Pres.; Sr. Magda Leticia Garcia, Spiritual Dir.

Casa San Martin, 411 W. Wilson St., 87301. Tel: 505-722-5156. Soup Kitchen & Shelter for Native American Clients. Missionaries of Charity. Sr. M. Crispina, M.C., Supr. Convent, 207 E. Wilson Ave., 87301. Tel: 505-722-5261.

Sacred Heart Retreat, Zuni Hwy. S., P.O. Box 1989, 87305. Tel: 505-722-6755. Sr. Sarah Page, O.S.F. Sisters 2.

Southwest Indian Foundation, 100 W. Coal Ave., P.O. Box 307, 87305. Tel: 505-863-9568. Mr. William McCarthy, Exec. Dir. Board of Directors: Mr. John Dowling, Pres.; Mr. James Mason, Vice Pres.; Mrs. Fred Melton, Sec.; Rev. Conall P. Lynch, O.F.M.; Hon. Judge Homer Bluehouse; Hon. Judge Marie Nezwood; Mrs. Mary Constant; Rev. Francis Stanfield; Mr. Daniel Deschiney; Sr. Beata Maria Stones, S.B.S.; Rev. Caron Vollmer, O.F.M.

CHINLE, AZ. *Talbot House-Catholic Charities*, P.O. Box 417, 86503. Tel: 520-674-3238. Sr. Adelaide Link, S.F.P., C.I.S.W., Dir. (Affiliated with Catholic Charities).

GRANTS-MILAN. *Casa San Jose*, 2595 W. Hwy. 66, P.O. Box 124, 87020. Tel: 505-285-5451. Sr. Francine Schuster, A.S.C., Admin. Residence of Pregnant teenagers. Operated by Catholic Charities. Sisters Adorers of the Blood of Christ 4.

PINETOP, AZ. *St. Vincent DePaul Society*. Thrift Shop & Emergency Aid Office. St. Mary of the Angels, P.O. Box 819, 85935. Tel: 520-367-2029; 3057. Ann C. Schultz, Pres.; Bill Schultz, Shop Mgr.; Lani Kilm, Emergency Aid Contact Person.

THOREAU. *St. Bonaventure Indian Mission & School*, 25 Navarre Blvd. W., P.O. Box 610, 87323. Tel: 505-862-7847; Fax: 505-862-7029. Hubert O'Reilly, Pres.; Barbara Morales; Dr. Franklin Freeland, Sec.; George Kearney, Treas.

WINSLOW, AZ. *La Casa de Nuestra Senora*. Mission of Madonna House Apostolate Combermere, Ontario, Canada. 213 Jefferson St., 86047. Tel: 520-289-3007. Mariann Dunsmore, Dir.
Prayer and Social Service Center.

RELIGIOUS INSTITUTES OF MEN REPRESENTED IN THE DIOCESE

For further details refer to the corresponding bracketed number in the Religious Institutes of Men or Women section.

[1100]—*Brothers of the Sacred Heart*.—S.C.
[1330]—*Congregation of the Mission*.—C.M.
[0520]—*Franciscan Friars*. (Provs. of Our Lady of Guadalupe & St. Barbara).—O.F.M.
[0690]—*Jesuit Fathers and Brothers*.—S.J.
[1200]—*Society of the Divine Savior*.—S.D.S.

RELIGIOUS INSTITUTES OF WOMEN REPRESENTED IN THE DIOCESE

[0100]—*Adorers of the Blood of Christ*.—A.S.C.
[]—*Auxiliaries of the Blessed Sacrament*.—A.B.S.
[0230]—*Benedictine Sisters*.—O.S.B.
[1810]—*Bernardine Sisters of the Third Order of St. Francis*.—O.S.F.
[3710]—*Congregation of the Sisters of Saint Agnes*.—C.S.A.
[0420]—*Discalced Carmelite Nuns*.—O.C.D.
[1070-03]—*Dominican Sisters*.—O.P.
[1070-06]—*Dominican Sisters*.—O.P.
[1070-13]—*Dominican Sisters*.—O.P.
[1070-09]—*Dominican Sisters*.—O.P.
[1070-14]—*Dominican Sisters*.—O.P.
[1120]—*Dominican Sisters of the Roman Congregation*.—O.P.
[1390]—*Franciscan Missionary Sisters of Our Lady of Sorrow*.—O.S.F.
[1350]—*Franciscan Missionary Sisters of the Immaculate Conception*.—O.S.F.
[1425]—*Franciscan Sisters of Peace*.—F.S.P.
[2340]—*Little Sisters of the Poor*.—L.S.P.
[2470]—*Maryknoll Sisters of St. Dominic*.—M.M.
[2720]—*Mission Helpers of the Sacred Heart*.—M.H.S.H.
[2710]—*Missionaries of Charity*.—M.C.
[2790]—*Missionary Servants of the Most Blessed Trinity*.—M.S.B.T.
[2760]—*Missionary Sisters of the Immaculate Conception of the Mother of God*.—S.M.I.C.
[2850]—*Missionary Sisters of the Precious Blood*.—C.P.S.
[1640]—*Poor Sisters of St. Francis Seraph of the Perpetual Adoration*.—O.S.F.
[2970]—*School Sisters of Notre Dame*.—S.S.N.D.
[]—*Sisters for Christian Community*.—S.F.C.C.
[2360]—*Sisters of Loretto at the Foot of the Cross*.—S.L.
[2570]—*Sisters of Mercy*. (Erie, PA).—R.S.M.
[3000]—*Sisters of Notre Dame de Namur*.—S.N.D.deN.
[]—*Sisters of Our Lady of Guadalupe and St. Joseph, Inc.*.
[1510]—*Sisters of St. Francis*.—O.S.F.
[1705]—*Sisters of St. Francis of Assisi*.
[1730]—*Sisters of St. Francis of Oldenburg*.—O.S.F.
[1650]—*The Sisters of St. Francis of Philadelphia*.—O.S.F.
[1550]—*Sisters of St. Francis of the Holy Cross*.—O.S.F.
[1660]—*Sisters of St. Francis of the Providence of God*.—O.S.F.
[0260]—*Sisters of the Blessed Sacrament for Indians and Colored People*.—S.B.S.
[2980]—*Sisters of the Congregation of Notre Dame*.—C.N.D.
[1100]—*Sisters of the Divine Providence of Kentucky*.—C.D.P.
[1030]—*Sisters of the Divine Savior*.—S.D.S.
[1830]—*The Sisters of the Good Shepherd*.—R.G.S.
[1990]—*Sisters of the Holy Names of Jesus and Mary*.—S.N.J.M.
[2940]—*Sisters of the Most Holy Sacrament*.—M.H.S.
[1440]—*Sisters of the Poor of St. Francis*.—S.F.P.
[3260]—*Sisters of the Precious Blood (Dayton, Ohio)*.—C.PP.S.
[1800]—*Sisters of the Third Order Regular*.—O.S.F.
[4120-05]—*Ursuline Nuns of the Congregation of Paris*.—O.S.U.

NECROLOGY

† Paulmichi, John, (Retired). —Died Jan. 8, 1996.

Diocese of Galveston—Houston

(Dioecesis Galvestoniensis Houstoniensis)

Most Reverend

JOSEPH A. FIORENZA, D.D.

Bishop of Galveston-Houston; ordained May 29, 1954; appointed Bishop of San Angelo September 4, 1979; consecrated and installed October 25, 1979; appointed Bishop of Galveston-Houston December 18, 1984; installed February 18, 1985. *Office: 1700 San Jacinto, Houston, TX, 77002-8291. Mailing Address: P.O. Box 907, Houston, TX, 77001-0907.* Tel.: 713-659-5461.

Most Reverend

CURTIS JOHN GUILLORY, S.V.D., D.D.

Auxiliary Bishop of Galveston-Houston; ordained December 16, 1972; appointed Titular Bishop of Stagno and Auxiliary Bishop of Galveston-Houston December 29, 1987; consecrated February 19, 1988. *Mailing Address: P.O. Box 907, Houston, TX, 77001-0907. Office: 1700 San Jacinto, Houston, TX, 77002-8291.* Tel.: 713-659-5461.

Most Reverend

JAMES A. TAMAYO, D.D.

Auxiliary Bishop of Galveston-Houston; ordained June 11, 1976; appointed Titular Bishop of Ita and Auxiliary Bishop of Galveston-Houston January 26, 1993; consecrated March 10, 1993. *Mailing Address: P.O. Box 907, Houston, TX, 77001-0907. Office: 1700 San Jacinto, Houston, TX, 77002-8291.* Tel.: 713-659-5461.

Chancery Office: P.O. Box 907, Houston, TX, 77001-0907. Tel.: 713-659-5461; Fax: 713-759-9151.

ESTABLISHED IN 1847.

Square Miles 9,354.

REDESIGNATED DIOCESE OF GALVESTON-HOUSTON ON JULY 25, 1959.

Comprises the Counties of Madison, Walker, San Jacinto, Galveston, Grimes, Montgomery, Waller, Harris, Fort Bend, Brazoria and Austin in the State of Texas.

For legal titles of parishes and diocesan institutions, consult the Chancery Office.

STATISTICAL OVERVIEW

Personnel	
Bishop	1
Auxiliary Bishops	2
Priests: Diocesan Active in Diocese	146
Priests: Active Outside Diocese	9
Priests: Diocesan in Foreign Missions	1
Priests: Retired, Sick or Absent	38
Number of Diocesan Priests	194
Religious Priests in Diocese	223
Extern Priests in Diocese	36
Ordinations:	
Diocesan Priests	5
Religious Priests	1
Transitional Deacons	3
Permanent Deacons in Diocese	231
Total Brothers	17
Total Sisters	553
Parishes	
Parishes	149
With Resident Pastor:	
Resident Diocesan Priests	94
Resident Religious Priests	54
Without Resident Pastor:	
Administered by Priests	1
Missions	10
Pastoral Centers	8
Welfare	
Catholic Hospitals	4
Total Assisted	270,285
Health Care Centers	2
Total Assisted	60,463
Homes for the Aged	3
Total Assisted	1,576
Residential Care of Children	2
Total Assisted	215
Day Care and Extended Day Care Centers	30
Total Assisted	2,656
Specialized Homes	5
Total Assisted	4,418
Special Centers for Social Services	7
Total Assisted	483,661
Educational	
Seminaries, Diocesan	1
Students from This Diocese	13
Students from Other Diocese	41
Diocesan Students in Other Seminaries	18
Seminaries, Religious	6
Students Religious	28
Total Seminarians	59
Colleges and Universities	1
Total Students	2,504
High Schools, Diocesan and Parish	2
Total Students	1,215
High Schools, Private	6
Total Students	2,300
Elementary Schools, Diocesan and Parish	45
Total Students	11,410
Elementary Schools, Private	6
Total Students	1,885
Catechesis/Religious Education:	
High School Students	14,631
Elementary Students	60,450
Total Students Under Catholic Instruction	94,454
Teachers in the Diocese:	
Priests	35
Brothers	4
Sisters	59
Lay Teachers	1,422
Vital Statistics	
Receptions into the Church:	
Infant Baptism Totals	16,913
Adult Baptism Totals	1,363
Received into Full Communion	885
First Communions	13,778
Confirmations	6,721
Marriages:	
Catholic	2,653
Interfaith	1,106
Total Marriages	3,759
Deaths	3,302
Total Catholic Population	854,653
Total Population	4,231,599

Former Bishops—Rt. Rev. J. M. ODIN, C.M., D.D., cons. Bishop of Claudiopolis and Vicar-Apostolic of Texas, March 6, 1842; transferred to Galveston 1847; promoted to New Orleans in 1861; died in Ambierle, France, May 25, 1870; Rt. Rev. C. M. DUBUIS, D.D., cons. Nov. 23, 1862; resigned 1881 remained Titular Bishop of Galveston till 1892, when he was promoted to an Archbishopric *i.p.i.; died May 21, 1895* at Vernaison, France; Rt. Rev. P. DUFAL, C.S.C., D.D., cons. Nov. 25, 1860; Bishop of Delcon, and Vicar-Apostolic of Eastern Bengal; transferred to Galveston as Coadjutor of Rt. Rev. C. M. DUBUIS, *cum jure successionis,* May 14, 1878; resigned 1880; died in Paris 1898; Rt. Rev. NICHOLAS A. GALLAGHER, D.D., cons. Titular Bishop of Canopus, April 30, 1882; succeeded to Galveston, Dec. 16, 1892; died Jan. 21, 1918; Most Rev. CHRISTOPHER E. BYRNE, D.D., appt. July 18, 1918; cons. Nov. 10, 1918 made Assistant at the Pontifical Throne, May 8, 1941; died April 1, 1950.—Most Rev. WENDELIN J. NOLD, S.T.D., appt. Nov. 29, 1947; cons. Feb. 25, 1948; died Oct. 1, 1981; Most Rev. JOHN L. MORKOVSKY, S.T.D., ord. Dec. 5, 1933; Titular Bishop of Hieron and Auxiliary Bishop of Amarillo; appt. Dec. 22, 1955; cons. Feb. 22, 1956; succeeded to See Aug. 18, 1958; transferred to Galveston-Houston as Titular Bishop of Tigava and Coadjutor and Apostolic Administrator *"cum jure successionis"*April 1963; installed June 11, 1963; succeeded to the See of Galveston-Houston, April 22, 1975; retired Aug. 16, 1984; died March 24, 1990.

Chancery Office—1700 San Jacinto St., Houston, 77002-8291., P.O. Box 907, Houston, 77001-0907. Office Hours: Mon.-Fri. 8:30-4:30. Tel: 713-659-5461; Fax: 713-759-9151.

Chancellor and Moderator of the Curia—Rev. FRANK H. ROSSI, S.T.L., *1700 San Jacinto St., Houston, 77002-8291., P.O. Box 907, Houston, 77001-0907.* Tel: 713-659-5461.

Vice Chancellor—Rev. R. TROY GATELY, *1700 San Jacinto St., Houston, 77002-8291., P.O. Box 907, Houston, 77001-0907.* Tel: 713-659-5461., *Christ the King Rectory, 4419 N. Main, Houston, 77009-5199.* Tel: 713-869-1440; 863-3140.

Vicars General—Most Rev. CURTIS JOHN GUILLORY, S.V.D., *1700 San Jacinto St., Houston, 77002-8291., P.O. Box 907, Houston, 77001-0907.* Tel: 713-659-5461. Most Rev. JAMES A. TAMAYO, D.D., *1700 San Jacinto St., Houston, 77002-8291., P.O. Box 907, Houston, 77001-0907.* Tel: 713-659-5461. Rev. Msgr. VINCENT M. RIZZOTTO, *11720 Joan of Arc, Houston, 77024-2602.* Tel: 713-465-3414.

Ethnic Vicars—Most Rev. CURTIS JOHN GUILLORY, S.V.D., Vicar of African American Catholics; Most Rev. JAMES A. TAMAYO, D.D., Vicar of Hispanic Catholics; Rev. ANTHONY CHINH QUANG DAO, O.P., Vicar of Vietnamese Catholics; Rev. Msgr. SETH HERMOSO, Vicar of Filipino Catholics.

Vicar for Religious—Sr. M. ADELINE O'DONOGHUE,

C.C.V.I., *6510 Lawndale, Houston, 77023.* Tel: 713-928-6053.

Spiritual Director for Priests—Vacant.

Parish Priest Consultor—Rev. Msgr. JOSEPH H. CROSTHWAIT, *P.O. Box 1302, New Ulm, 78950.* Tel: 409-992-3821.

Finance Officer and Business Manager—Mr. THOMAS B. O'TOOLE, *1700 San Jacinto St., Houston, 77002-8291. P.O. Box 907, Houston, 77001-0907.* Tel: 713-659-5461.

Diocesan Tribunal—1700 San Jacinto St., Houston, 77002-8291. P.O. Box 907, Houston, 77001-0907. Tel: 713-659-5461.

Judicial Vicar—Rev. STEPHEN P. ZIGRANG, J.C.L., *Chancery Bldg., P.O. Box 907, Houston, 77001-0907.* Tel: 713-659-5461.

Adjutant Judicial Vicar—Rev. FRED CHALUPA, J.C.L., *P.O. Box 907, Houston, 77001-0907.* Tel: 713-659-5461.

Diocesan Judges—Rev. Msgr. T. JOSEPH CULVER; Rev. Msgr. PHILIPPE LE-XUAN THUONG, J.C.D.; Revs. ROBERT BARRAS; ERIC PITRE; ANTON SHELTZ; LAWRENCE JOZWIAK, J.C.L.

Promotor of Justice—Rev. Msgr. VINCENT M. RIZZOTTO, J.C.L.

Defender of the Bond—Rev. FRED CHALUPA, J.C.L.

Censor Librorum—Rev. TERENCE BRINKMAN, S.T.D., *2302 Oak Shores Dr., Kingwood, 77339-1801.* Tel: 281-358-6637.

Deans and Vicariates—

Central Vicariate—Episcopal Vicar: Most Rev. CURTIS J. GUILLORY, S.V.D., V.G. Tel: 713-659-5461. Central Dean: Rev. ISIDORE GARCIA, O.M.I., V.F. Tel: 713-224-5291. Northeast Dean: Rev. GARY F. WANZONG, V.F. Tel: 713-631-3681. Southeast Dean: Rev. JOHN N. MORFIN, V.F. Tel: 281-497-1500.

Northern Vicariate—Episcopal Vicar: Rev. Msgr. WILLIAM P. ROBERTSON, E.V. Tel: 281-376-6831. Northern Dean: Rev. Msgr. DAVID W. KENNEDY, V.F. Tel: 409-756-8186. Eastern Dean: Rev. JOHN A. ZABELSKAS, V.F. Tel: 281-843-2422. San Jacinto Dean: Rev. GEORGE A. SHELTZ, V.F. Tel: 281-469-2686.

Southern Vicariate—Episcopal Vicar: Rev. Msgr. T. JOSEPH CULVER, E.V. Tel: 409-938-7000. Galveston-Mainland Dean: Rev. Msgr. MILAM E. KLEAS, V.F. Tel: 281-337-4112. Bay Area Dean: Rev. THOMAS J. HUHN, V.F., M.S. Tel: 281-482-1391. Southern Dean: Rev. Msgr. LEO WLECZYK, V.F. Tel: 409-297-3041.

Western Vicariate—Episcopal Vicar: Rev. Msgr. WILLIAM M. PICKARD, E.V. Tel: 713-774-7475. Western Dean: Rev. DANIEL WARDEN, V.F. Tel: 281-342-3089. Southwest Dean: Rev. Msgr. EDWARD RANDALL, V.F. Tel: 713-789-1250. Northwest Dean: Rev. ADAM S. MCCLOSKEY, V.F. Tel: 281-955-7324. Bluebonnet Dean: Rev. Msgr. BOLESLAUS ZIENTEK, V.F. Tel: 409-885-3868.

Secretariat Directors—

Secretariat For Christian Formation—Sr. MARY GRACE O'BRIEN, C.V.I., Dir., *2403 E. Holcombe Blvd., Houston, 77021-2099.* Tel: 713-741-8786.

Secretariat for Family and Social Concerns—Mrs. SUSAN STROMATT, Dir., *2403 E. Holcombe Blvd., Houston, 77021-2099.* Tel: 713-741-8769.

Secretariat For Administration and Communication—Mr. THOMAS B. O'TOOLE, Dir., *1700 San Jacinto St., Houston, 77002-8291. P.O. Box 907, Houston, 77001-0907.* Tel: 713-659-5461.

Secretariat For Special Services—Rev. FRANK H. ROSSI, Dir., *1700 San Jacinto St., Houston, 77002-8291. P.O. Box 907, Houston, 77001-0907.* Tel: 713-659-5461.

Diocesan Councils, Commissions and Committees—

Diocesan Presbyteral Council—Rev. DAN WARDEN, Chm., *1700 San Jacinto St., Houston, 77002-8291. P.O. Box 907, Houston, 77001-0907.* Tel: 281-446-8211.

Presbyteral Council—Most Rev. CURTIS J. GUILLORY, S.V.D.; Most Rev. JAMES A. TAMAYO, D.D.; Revs. DREW WOOD; JOHN N. MORFIN; Rev. Msgr. EUGENE CARGILL; Rev. BILL COUGHLIN, C.S.B.; Rev. Msgr. WILLIAM M. PICKARD, E.V.; Rev. Msgr. WILLIAM P.ROBERTSON; Rev. HUBERT KEALY; Rev. Msgr. T. JOSEPH CULVER; Revs. DAVID CARDENAS; DON KUDER, C.S.B.; PAUL PROCELLA; Rev. Msgr. VINCENT M. RIZZOTTO; Rev. FRANK H. ROSSI; Rev. Msgr. DANIEL SCHEEL; Revs. DAN WARDEN; WILLIAM YOUNG, C.S.B.

College of Consultors—Most Rev. CURTIS J. GUILLORY, S.V.D.; Most Rev. JAMES A. TAMAYO, D.D.; Rev. Msgr. JOSEPH H. CROSTHWAIT; Rev. Msgr. DANIEL SCHEEL; Rev. Msgr. CHESTER L. BORSKI; Rev. Msgr. T. JOSEPH CULVER; Rev. Msgr. VINCENT M. RIZZOTTO, J.C.L.; Rev. FRANK H. ROSSI, S.T.L.

Priests Personnel Committee—Rev. Msgr. VINCENT M. RIZZOTTO, J.C.L., Chm., *11720 Joan of Arc, Houston, 77024-2602.* Tel: 713-465-3414. Rev. Msgr. GENE FRANCIS; Revs. DENNIS PETERSON; STEVE TIEMANN; FRANK H. ROSSI; GEORGE A. SHELTZ, V.F.; PHILIP WILHITE.

Building Commission—Rev. Msgr. CHARLES C. DOMEC, Chm., *26777 Glen Loch Rd., The Woodlands, 77381-2921.* Tel: 281-367-9885. Rev. Msgr. T. JOSEPH CULVER; Rev. Msgr. EDWARD RANDALL; Mr. TONY ROURKE; Mr. BILL MAREK; Rev. ANTON SHELTZ.

Board of Education—Mr. JAMES MCLAIN, Pres., *Chancery Bldg., at St. Dominic Center.* Tel: 713-741-8786.

Ecumenism and Interreligious Affairs Commission—Mrs. GARLAND POHL, Chm., *8003 Mobud, Houston, 77036-6403.* Tel: 713-774-0097.

Liturgical Commission—Rev. WILLIAM OLIVER, Coord. Tel: 409-922-1240.

Diocesan Departments and Offices

Archives—Ms. LISA MAY, Dir., *1700 San Jacinto St., Houston, 77002-8291. P.O. Box 907, Houston, 77001-0907.* Tel: 713-659-5461.

Accounting Department—Mrs. NANCY HEISLER, Dir., *1700 San Jacinto St., Houston, 77002-8291. P.O. Box 907, Houston, 77001-0907.* Tel: 713-659-5461.

African American Ministry—Ms. CHAROLETTE DAVIS, Dir., *2403 E. Holcombe Blvd., Houston, 77021-2098.* Tel: 713-741-8733.

Aging Ministry—Sr. DOROTHY SACHNIK, C.V.I., Dir., *2403 E. Holcombe Blvd., Houston, 77021-2098.* Tel: 713-741-8712.

Apostleship of Prayer—Vacant.

Apostleship of the Sea (Port Ministry)—Rev. RIVERS PATOUT, Houston Dir., *9217 E. Ave. L., Houston, 77012-2727.* Tel: 713-923-5843; 926-7669 (Rectory)., *Houston International Seaman's Center, P.O. Box 9506, Houston, 77261.* Tel: 713-672-0511. Galveston: Mrs. KAREN LAI, *2002 Mechanic, Galveston, 77550.* Tel: 409-762-0021.

Boy and Girl Scouts—Rev. Msgr. T. A. WENDLAND, Dir., *3600 Brinkman Rd., Houston, 77018-6329.* Tel: 713-692-9123.

Campus Ministry—Sr. MARY GRACE O'BRIEN, Sec.-Dir., *2403 E. Holcombe Blvd., Houston, 77021-2098.* Tel: 713-741-8786.

Catholic Cemeteries—Mr. TERRANCE D. MULCANE, Dir., *P.O. Box 965 (Gulf Frwy. at Hughes Rd.), Dickinson, 77539.* Tel: 281-337-1641; 409-948-1455.

Catholic Chaplain Corps (Hospital Chaplains)—Rev. ALCUIN E. GREENBURG, Dir., *4206 MacGregor Way S., Houston, 77021-1598.* Tel: 713-526-6438.

Associated Catholic Charities—Mrs. ANNA BABIN, Dir., *3520 Montrose Blvd., Houston, 77006-4387.* Tel: 713-526-4611; Fax: 713-526-1546.

Associate Executive Director Program Services—YOLANDA SANTOS, P.H.

Associate Executive Director Finance and Support Services—MICHAEL J. PIERI, C.P.A.

Director, Fund Development/Marketing—JULIE PLATEK, M.S.W.

Children Services—VALERIE PERALES, L.M.S.W.-A.C.P., Admin.

Children Placement Services Adoption and Foster Care—SHARON JORGESON, L.M.S.W., Supvr., *St. Joseph Inn, P.O. Box 8275, Galveston, 77553.* ELLEN HANLEY, Prog. Coord. Tel: 409-765-5343.

Services to Pregnant Adolescents and Their Families—SYLVIA ALANIS, L.M.S.W.-A.C.P., A.C.S.W., Supvr.

Post Adoption Services—MARY LOU KELLY, L.M.S.W., Supvr.

Community Outreach Services—KATHERINE BINGHAM, M.P.H.

Diocesan AIDS Ministry—THERESA GOMEZ, Prog. Coord.-Interim Dir., *3400 Montrose #400, Houston, 77006.* Tel: 713-524-0182.

Guadalupe Area Social Services—YOLANDA GUTIERREZ, L.M.S.W., Supvr., *326 S. Jensen, Houston, 77003-1599.* Family Assistance Program, La Casita, Villa Guadalupe-Transitional Housing for Women.

Parish Social Ministry—ESMERALDA CERVANTES, Coord.

Serenity House—Temporary housing for medical center patient's families. KATHERINE BINGHAM, M.P.H.

Services to the Alone and Frail Elderly—KATHERINE BINGHAM, M.P.H., In Formation:: Tel: 713-520-7835.

Family Counseling—CAROL KELLEHER, Ph.D., Admin. CAROL KELLEHER, Ph.D., Supvr., Prevention Services; DAVID QUIROZ, L.M.S.W.-A.C.P., L.P.C., Supervising Family Counseling. Tel: 713-668-5763; 526-4611 ext. 3500 (Appointments); Fax: 713-527-9198 (Family Counseling).

Immigration Services—JANET WAITES, Admin.

Texas Center for Immigrant Legal Assistance—SUSIE MAXWELL, Supvr. Tel: 713-529-9382.

Parish Social Ministry—

St. Joseph's Inn—

Project Learn—JANET WAITES, Supvr. Tel: 713-229-0220.

Refugee Resettlement Services—JANET WAITES, Supvr. Tel: 713-526-5812.

Undocumented and Unaccompanied Juvenile Foster Care—CONNIE HIDALGO, Supvr. Tel: 713-526-4611.

Outreach Services—KATHY BINGHAM. Tel: 713-520-7835.

Needy Family Services—YOLANDA GUITIERREZ, Supvr. Tel: 713-520-9561.

Services to the Elderly—KATHY BINGHAM, Supvr. Tel: 713-520-9561.

Serenity House—KATHY BINGHAM. Tel: 713-526-4611, Ext. 3268.

Direct Services: Counseling, Adoption, Foster Care, Services to Young Parents—SHARON JORGESON, Admin.

Catholic Charities Galveston—Mrs. JANE AYALA, Dir., *4418 Ave. M, Galveston, 77550-3726.* Tel: 409-762-2062.

Catholic Relief Services—Mrs. HILDA HERNANDEZ, Dir., *Chancery Bldg., 1700 San Jacinto St., Houston, 77002-8921. P.O. Box 907, Houston, 77001-0907.* Tel: 713-659-5461.

Computer Network Manager—Mr. ED HERRERA, *Chancery Bldg., 1700 San Jacinto St., Houston, 77002-8921. P.O. Box 907, Houston, 77001-0907.* Tel: 713-659-5461.

Community Relations—Mrs. SUSAN STROMATT, *2403 E. Holcombe Blvd., Houston, 77021-2099.* Tel: 713-741-8731.

Continuing Christian Education—Mrs. JOANNE SANDERS, Dir., *2403 E. Holcombe Blvd., Houston, 77021-2099.* Tel: 713-741-8730.

Construction/Preventative Maintenance—Mr. TONY ROURKE, Dir., *Chancery Bldg., 1700 San Jacinto St., Houston, 77002-8291. P.O. Box 907, Houston, 77001-0907.* Tel: 713-659-5461. Mr. RANDY ALLEN, Preventive Maintenance.

Correctional Ministries (Jail Chaplains)—Rev. RONALD F. CLOUTIER, Dir. (Chaplain Office at Harris County Jail), Office and Mailing Address: *2403 E. Holcombe Blvd., Houston, 77021-2098.* Tel: 713-869-1449., *215 E. 10th St., Houston, 77008-7025.* Tel: 713-864-2653.

Council of Catholic Women—Rev. Msgr. THOMAS A. WENDLAND, Dir., *3600 Brinkman Rd., Houston, 77018-6329.* Tel: 713-692-9123. Rev. Msgr. LEO WLECZYK, Assoc. Moderator, *100 Oak Dr., S., Lake Jackson, 77566-5630.* Tel: 409-297-3041.

Cursillos in Christianity—Rev. JOSE MARIA FERNANDEZ, Dir., *4419 N. Main, Houston, 77009-5199.* Tel: 713-869-1449., *St. Paul Cursillo Center, 4000 Belk St., Houston, 77087.* Tel: 713-643-7682.

Deaf Apostolate—Rev. ROBERT BEK, C.SS.R., Dir., *St. Dominic Center, 2401 E. Holcombe Blvd., Houston, 77021-2099.* Tel: 713-741-8721.

Development Office—Mr. HAROLD TEAGLE, Dir., *1700 San Jacinto St., Houston, 77002-8291. P.O. Box 907, Houston, 77001-0907.* Tel: 713-659-5461.

Diaconal Formation/Diaconal Ministry—Rev. Msgr. JACK M. DINKINS, Dir., *1530 Norwalk Dr., Katy, 77450-4999.* Tel: 281-578-0707.

Permanent Deacons—Mr. FRED SHETZ, Dir., *1700 San Jacinto St., Houston, 77002-8291. P.O. Box 907, Houston, 77001-0907.* Tel: 713-659-5461.

Diocesan Services Fund—Mrs. BARBARA SCIONEAUX, Dir., *Lock Box 200562, Houston, 77216. 1700 San Jacinto St., Houston, 77002-8291.* Tel: 713-659-5461.

Disaster Relief—Rev. REGINALD PETRASH, Dir., *St. Mary, Star of the Sea Church, 1019 W. 6th St., Freeport, 77541-5423.* Tel: 409-233-5271.

Evangelization Office—Rev. CARL TENHUNDFELD, Dir., *215 E. 10th St., Houston, 77021-2024.* Tel: 713-864-5786.

Family Life Ministry—Mrs. WINIFRED HONEYWELL, Dir., *St.Dominic Center, 2403 E. Holcombe Blvd., Houston, 77021-2099.* Tel: 713-741-8710.

Hispanic Ministry—Mr. PEDRO MORENO, Dir., *2403 E. Holcombe Blvd., Houston, 77021-2099.* Tel: 713-741-8727.

Risk Manager—Mr. TOM BESONG, Dir., *Chancery Bldg., 1700 San Jacinto St., Houston, 77002-8291. P.O. Box 907, Houston, 77001-0907.* Tel: 713-659-5461.

Internal Auditor—Mr. CHARLES ROBINSON, Dir., *1700 San Jacinto St., Houston, 77002-8291. P.O. Box 907, Houston, 77001-0907.* Tel: 713-659-5461.

Land Specialist—Mr. KEN SYKES, *1700 San Jacinto St., Houston, 77002-8291. P.O. Box 907, Houston, 77001-0907.* Tel: 713-659-5461.

Marian Activities—Rev. Msgr. FRANCIS G. WEARDEN, Spiritual Dir., *1100 Parthenon Pl., New Caney, 77357-3039.* Tel: 281-399-0270.

Media Center—Mrs. GALE HANKS, Dir., *2403 E. Holcombe Blvd., Houston, 77021-2099.* Tel: 713-741-8781.

Mission Office—Mrs. HILDA HERNANDEZ, Dir., *Chancery Bldg., 1700 San Jacinto St., Houston, 77002-8291. P.O. Box 907, Houston, 77001-0907.* Tel: 713-659-5461. Holy Childhood, Propagation of the Faith.

Oremus Pro Invicem—Rev. Msgr. FRANCIS G. WEARDEN, Dir., *1100 Parthenon Pl., New Caney, 77357-3039.* Tel: 281-399-0270.

Parish Accounting Services (PAS)—Mrs. PAT MITCHELL, Dir., *1700 San Jacinto St., Houston, 77002-8291.*

P.O. Box 907, Houston, 77001-0907. Tel: 713-659-5461.

Parish Social Ministry/(CHD)—AWANDA WHITWORTH, Supvr., *Chancery at St. Dominic's Diocesan Center, 2403 E. Holcombe Blvd., Houston, 77021-2099.* Tel: 713-741-8730.

Personnel—Mr. FRED SHETZ, Dir.

Benefits—Mrs. DAWN GIBLIN, Dir.

Parish Development—Mr. THOM JONES, Dir., *1700 San Jacinto St., Houston, 77002-8291. P.O. Box 907, Houston, 77001-0907.* Tel: 713-659-5461.

Radio—Mrs. MADELINE JOHNSON, Dir., *1700 San Jacinto St., Houston, 77002-8291. P.O. Box 907, Houston, 77001-0907.* Tel: 713-659-5461.

Records—Miss MARY ANN ACOSTA, Dir., *1700 San Jacinto St., Houston, 77002-8291. P.O. Box 907, Houston, 77001-0907.* Tel: 713-659-5461.

Respect Life Office—Mrs. MARCELLA COLBERT, Dir., *2403 E. Holcombe Blvd., Houston, 77021-2098.* Tel: 713-225-5826; 741-8730 (Main Tel.).

Claims Risk Manager—Mr. JAMES QUATTRINI, Dir., *2403 E. Holcombe Blvd., Houston, 77021-2099.* Tel: 713-741-8758; 800-856-4040; Fax: 713-748-3205.

Rural Life Bureau—Rev. FRANK H. ROSSI, *1700 San Jacinto St., Houston, 77002-8291. P.O. Box 907, Houston, 77001-0907.* Tel: 713-659-5461.

Seminarian Support—Rev. STEPHEN E. TIEMANN, Dir., *1700 San Jacinto St., Houston, 77002-8291. P.O. Box 907, Houston, 77001-0907.* Tel: 713-659-5461.

Catholic School Office—Sr. COLLEEN HENNESSEY, S.S.N.D., Supt., *2403 E. Holcombe Blvd., Houston, 77021-2099.* Tel: 713-741-8704.

School of Environmental Education - Camp Kappe—Sr. THOMAS ANN LACOUR, O.P., Dir., *Rte. 2, Box 3197, Navasota, 77868.* Tel: 409-894-2141.

St. Dominic Diocesan Center—Mr. JIM HORSTMAN, Mgr., *2401 E. Holcombe Blvd., Houston, 77021-2024.* Tel: 713-741-8741.

St. Vincent de Paul Society—Sr. YVONNE WUENSCHE, Dir., *2403 E. Holcombe Blvd., Houston, 77021-2099.* Tel: 713-741-8783.

Stewardship—Mr. ADAM MARTINEZ, Dir., *1700 San Jacinto St., Houston, 77002-8291.* Tel: 713-659-5461. *P.O. Box 907, Houston, 77001-0907.*

Texas Catholic Herald—Mr. MARION ZIENTEK, Editor, *1700 San Jacinto St., Houston, 77002-8291. P.O. Box 907, Houston, 77001-0907.* Tel: 713-659-5461. Saturdays & Holidays. Tel: 713-659-3702; Fax: 713-659-3444.

Vocations Office—Rev. STEPHEN E. TIEMANN, Dir., *1700 San Jacinto St., Houston, 77002-8291. P.O. Box 907, Houston, 77001-0907.* Tel: 713-659-5461.

Worship—Mrs. PAT KERWIN, Dir., *2403 E. Holcombe Blvd., Houston, 77021-2099.* Tel: 713-741-8760.

Youth Ministry—Bro. JIM BARRETTE, S.M., Dir., *2403 E. Holcombe Blvd., Houston, 77021-2099.* Tel: 713-741-8723.

Special Youth Services (Juvenile Detention Ministry)—MARILU BALLOW, Dir., *2403 E. Holcombe Blvd., Houston, 77021-2099.* Tel: 713-527-1894; 762-7192 (Pager).

CLERGY, PARISHES, MISSIONS AND PAROCHIAL SCHOOLS

CITY OF GALVESTON
(Galveston County)

1—ST. MARY'S CATHEDRAL BASILICA (1847), In res., Revs. Charles J. Coffey, C.S.Sp.; Edward Baur, S.V.D.; Gerald Lewis, S.V.D.; Deacon John S. Pistone.
Res., 2011 Church St., 77550-2091. Tel: 409-762-9611; Fax: 409-765-8585.

2—HOLY ROSARY (1888), Rev. Paul H. Banet, S.S.J. In res., Revs. Robert DeGrandis, S.S.J.; Charles H. Banet, C.PP.S.
Res., 1420 31st St., 77550-4399. Tel: 409-762-2478; Fax: 409-762-8383.

3—OUR LADY OF GUADALUPE. Closed. August 1992. Contact Chancery for further information.

4—ST. PATRICK (1870), Revs. Page E. Polk, O.F.M.; Larry Dunham, O.F.M.; Deacon Tom Hunter.
Church—1010 35th St., 77550. Fax: 409-765-7636.
Res., 3420 Avenue K, 77550-4091. Tel: 409-762-9646.
Catechesis/Religious Programs—Jo Anita Jefferies, D.R.E.
Students 277.
Mission—Galveston, Galveston Co., Queen of Peace Mission, 706 51st St., 77551. Tel: 409-762-2833; Fax: 409-765-9747. Rev. Serafin Cejudo.

5—ST. PETER THE APOSTLE (1967), Rev. William D. Bartniski; Deacon William J. Bobb.
Res., 1805 Driftwood Ln., 77551-1399. Tel: 409-744-3561; Fax: 409-744-4286.
Catechesis/Religious Programs—Tel: 409-744-7250. Randy Adams.
Students 175.
Mission—Jamaica Beach, Galveston Co., Mary, Star of the Sea.

6—SACRED HEART (1884), Rev. Frank T. Fabj.
Res., 1302 Broadway, 77550-6198. Tel: 409-762-6374; Fax: 409-762-0919.

CITY OF HOUSTON
(Harris County)

1—SACRED HEART CO-CATHEDRAL (1896), Rev. Msgr. Philippe Xuan Le Thuong, J.C.D., S.T.L.; Rev. Lawrence Jozwiak, J.C.L.; Deacons Robert Brueggerhoff; Marvin R. Fikac.
Res., 1111 Pierce St., 77002-8195. Tel: 713-659-1561; 1562; Fax: 713-739-1306.
Catechesis/Religious Programs—Sr. Sabrina D.R.E.
Students 200.

2—ALL SAINTS (1908), Rev. Carl Tenhundfeld; Deacon Frank Matula. In res., Rev. Ronald F. Cloutier.
Res., 215 E. 10th St., 77008-7025. Tel: 713-864-2653; Fax: 713-864-0761.
Catechesis/Religious Programs—Natalia Pena, D.R.E.
Students 248.

3—ST. ALBERT OF TRAPANI (1907), Revs. Mark J. Schaffner, O.Carm.; Sylvan Boyle, O.Carm.
Res., 11027 S. Gessner Dr., 77071-3599. Tel: 713-771-3596; Fax: 713-270-0441.
Catechesis/Religious Programs—Peggy Popkey, D.R.E.
Students 276.

4—ST. ALPHONSUS (1968) (Hispanic), Rev. Rivers A. Patout, Coord. Port Min.; Sr. Lucinda Gonzalez, Admin. & Pastoral Assoc.
Res., 9217 E. Ave. L, 77012-2299. Tel: 713-923-5843; Fax: 713-923-5843.
Catechesis/Religious Programs—Tel: 713-644-7008. Ophelia Martinez, D.R.E.
Students 182.

5—ST. AMBROSE (1958), Revs. Joseph A. Gietl; Miguel A. Solorzano.
Res., 4213 Mangum Rd., 77092-5599. Tel: 713-686-3497; Fax: 713-686-6604.
School—Tel: 713-686-6990; Fax: 713-686-6902. Mrs. Mary Kay Volker, Prin.
Sisters 2; Lay Teachers 29; Students 494.
Catechesis/Religious Programs—Tel: 713-686-3857. Alicia I. Perez, D.R.E.
Students 590.

6—ST. ANDREW KIM, Rev. Paul Chun-Ho Kim.
Res., 1706 Bingle Rd., 77055-2336. Tel: 713-465-5974.

7—ST. ANNE (1925), Revs. Charles A. Christopher, C.S.B.; Thomas B. Mailloux, C.S.B.; Thomas J. McReavy, C.S.B.; David J. Zapalac, C.S.B.
Res., 2140 Westheimer, 77098-1496. Tel: 713-526-3276; Fax: 713-526-3079.
School—Tel: 713-526-3279.
Sisters 1; Lay Teachers 32; Students 361.
Catechesis/Religious Programs—Tel: 281-286-2369. D.R.E.: Arlene Holm; Marisa Loredo.
Students 584.

8—ST. ANNE DE BEAUPRE (1948), Rev. Michael J. Farrell, S.S.J.
Res., 2810 Link Rd., 77009-1196. Tel: 713-869-1319; Fax: 713-869-1319.

9—ANNUNCIATION (1869), Rev. Msgr. James L. Golasinski; Deacons Joseph Jachimcyk; David Adame.
Mailing Address: P.O. Box 214, 77001-0214. Tel: 713-222-2289; Fax: 713-222-2280.
Res., 1618 Texas Ave., 77003.

10—ASCENSION CHINESE MISSION (1988) (Chinese), Rev. Francis X. Chang-Lei, S.J.
Res., 4605 Jetty Ln., 77072-1222. Tel: 281-575-8855; Fax: 281-575-8866.

11—ASSUMPTION (1948), Revs. Italo Dell'Oro, C.R.S. (Italy); Narciso Bordignon, C.R.S.; John Peter Borsari; Deacon Albert Bottijer.
Res., 901 Rose Ln., 77037. Tel: 281-447-6381; Fax: 281-447-6382. [CEM]
Catechesis/Religious Programs—Tel: 281-445-1268. Betty Blazek, D.R.E.
Students 950.

12—ST. AUGUSTINE (1955) (Spanish), Rev. Msgr. Seth Hermoso, Admin. (Vicar for Filipinos); Rev. J.B. Nuynh Ngoc Tran; Deacons James Bart; Joe Zamora.
Res., 5560 Laurel Creek Way, 77017-6729. Tel: 713-946-8968; Fax: 713-946-0080.
School—Terry Smith, Prin. Sisters 1; Lay Teachers 25; Students 333.
Catechesis/Religious Programs—Tel: 713-946-7636. Mrs. Bea Zamora, D.R.E.
Students 348.

13—ST. BENEDICT THE ABBOT (1963), Revs. Nicholas Pasadilla; Tin Cosmas Kim Pham; Deacon Marcelino Villarreal.
Office: 4025 Grapevine, 77045-6320. Tel: 713-433-9836; Fax: 713-433-3949.
Catechesis/Religious Programs—Tel: 713-433-2436. Brenda Wade, D.R.E.
Students 517.

14—ST. BERNADETTE SOUBIROUS (1977), Revs. Joseph J. McCarthy, O.Carm.; Sebastian Meyer, O.Carm.; Joseph Joyce, O.Carm.; Deacon Cyril Hodapp.
Mailing Address: 15500 El Camino Real, 77062. Tel: 281-486-0337; Fax: 281-486-7664.
Catechesis/Religious Programs—Tel: 281-486-0337. June Mergen, D.R.E.
Students 1,224.

15—CHURCH OF THE BLESSED SACRAMENT (1910) (Hispanic), Rev. Jose Isidore Garcia, O.M.I., V.F.; Deacon Pedro Lerma.
Res., 4015 Sherman Ave., 77003-2695. Tel: 713-224-5291; Fax: 713-224-5292.
Catechesis/Religious Programs—Tel: 713-947-2515. Mary T. Martinez, D.R.E.
Students 334.

16—ST. CATHERINE OF SIENA (1975), Rev. Robert S. Barras; Deacon John Stanley.
Mailing Address: 10688 Shadow Wood, 77043-2826. Tel: 713-467-8170; Fax: 713-467-7149.
Catechesis/Religious Programs—Tel: 713-467-8170. Dorris Desroche, D.R.E.
Students 160.

17—ST. CECILIA (1956), Rev. Msgr. Vincent M. Rizzotto, J.C.L., Vicar Gen.; Revs. Oscar Cantu; Guido Anthony Fregeau; Deacons Don Bradley; Gregg Elliott; Cade Nelms.
Res., 11720 Joan of Arc, 77024-2602. Tel: 713-465-3414; Fax: 713-465-1305.
School—Tel: 713-468-9515; Fax: 713-468-4695. Angelina Karpinski, Prin.
Lay Teachers 31; Students 550.
Catechesis/Religious Programs—Lee Renaud, D.R.E.
Students 880.

18—ST. CHARLES BORROMEO (1962), Revs. John E. Cahoon; Edwin Coreas; Deacon Rodrigo Lozano.
Res., 501 Tidwell, 77022. Tel: 713-692-6303; Fax: 713-692-6314.
School—Tel: 713-692-4898. Kathleen Martin, Prin.
Sisters 1; Lay Teachers 15; Students 266.
Catechesis/Religious Programs—Tel: 281-442-1334. Linda Schulle, D.R.E.
Students 750.

19—CHRIST THE KING (1928), Rev. Stephen B. Reynolds. In res., Revs. R. Troy Gately, Vice Chancellor; Jose Maria Fernandez.
Res., 4419 N. Main St., 77009-5199. Tel: 713-869-1449; Fax: 713-869-1491.
Catechesis/Religious Programs—Tel: 713-869-3140. Daniel Schwieterman, D.R.E.
Students 700.

20—CHRIST THE REDEEMER (1980), Revs. Dominic A. Peluse, S.C.J.; Robert Naglich, S.C.J.; Deacon Barry L. Beckmann.
Res., 12402 Bexhill, 77065.
Church—11507 Huffmeister, 77065-1051. Tel: 281-469-5533; Fax: 281-469-8441.
Catechesis/Religious Programs—Tel: 281-469-5533. Mary Lou Lietzau, D.R.E.
Students 933.

21—ST. CHRISTOPHER (1924), Revs. Paul R. Chovanec, B.S., M.Th.; Jader de Jesus Cardenas. In res., Rev. Denis A. Osuagwu, C.M.F.; Deacons Peter J. Kelleher; Jose Aranda; Merce C. Leal, Jr.; Henry T. Gramann; Terrance D. Mulcare.
Res., 8150 Park Place Blvd., 77017-3033. Tel: 713-645-6614; Fax: 713-640-1640.
School—8134 Park Place Blvd., 77017. Tel: 713-649-0009. Therese Cutrer, Prin.
Sisters 3; Lay Teachers 21; Students 406.
Catechesis/Religious Programs—D.R.E.: Gloria Leal; Tammy Juarez.
Students 766.

22—ST. CLARE OF ASSISI (1990), Rev. John H. Kappe; Deacons Wilfred J. Hargraves; Daniel Q. Guerra.
Res., 15922 Hillside Falls Tr., 77062.
Mailing Address: 3131 El Dorado Blvd., 77059-5100. Tel: 281-286-7729; Fax: 281-286-1256.
Catechesis/Religious Programs—Tel: 281-486-0874. Celia Guadiano, D.R.E.
Students 545.

23—ST. CYRIL OF ALEXANDRIA (1963), Rev. Msgr. Edward Randall, V.F.; Revs. Jesus Bahena; Niall Nolan. In res., Rev. Jacques Weber., S.J., S.T.L., M.S.; Deacon Woods Martin.
Res., 10503 Westheimer, 77042-3502. Tel: 713-789-1250; Fax: 713-780-0967.

Catechesis/Religious Programs—Tel: 713-789-1250. Margaret McDermott, D.R.E.
Students 569.

24—CORPUS CHRISTI (1956), Rev. Roger C. Prefontaine, S.S.S.; Deacon Joseph Bourgeois. In res., Revs. Robert P. Rousseau, S.S.S.; Donald J. Jette, S.S.S.
Res., 9900 Stella Link Rd., 77025-4798. Tel: 713-667-0497; Fax: 713-668-4742.
School—4005 Cheena St., 77025. Tel: 713-664-3351; Fax: 713-664-6095. Dr. Marty Webb, Prin.
Lay Teachers 30; Students 257.
Catechesis/Religious Programs—Tel: 713-667-1911. Peggy Marroquin, D.R.E.
Students 280.

25—ST. DOMINIC (1965), Rev. Anton R. Sheltz, M.Th.; Deacon Philip Arlen Wiles.
Res., 8215 Reservoir Ave., 77049-1728. Tel: 281-458-2910; Fax: 281-458-7114.
Catechesis/Religious Programs—George T. McDonald, D.R.E.
Students 174.

26—ST. ELIZABETH ANN SETON (1977), Revs. Frank Wittouck, S.C.J.; Richard DiLeo, S.C.J.; Leonard Elder, S.C.J.; Deacons Francis Adams; Ben Vigil; Charles G. Pennell.
Res., 6646 Addicks-Satsuma Rd., 77084-1599. Tel: 281-463-7878; Fax: 281-463-4822.
Catechesis/Religious Programs—Tel: 281-463-7356. Mrs. Pam Krinock, D.R.E.
Students 2,078.

27—ST. FRANCES CABRINI (1962), Revs. Dennis L. Peterson, M.A., L.M.S.W.; Joseph Thanh Vu; Deacons John Rooney; Frank Moreno; Robert Gregory Stevens; Fernando Ramirez.
Mailing Address: 10727 Hartsook St., 77034-3523. Tel: 713-946-5768; Fax: 713-946-3282.
Res., 10726 Bessemer, 77034.
Catechesis/Religious Programs—Patricia Weimer, D.R.E.
Students 803.

28—ST. FRANCIS DE SALES (1962), Rev. Msgr. William M. Pickard, J.C.D., E.V.; Rev. Michael Peter Berlowski; Deacons Albert G. Bothe; Frank Comer; Hugo Klein.
Res., 8200 Roos Rd., 77036. Tel: 713-774-7475; Fax: 713-774-6591. [JC]
School—8100 Roos Rd., 77036. Tel: 713-774-4447; Fax: 713-271-6744.
Lay Teachers 37; Students 529.
Catechesis/Religious Programs—Tel: 713-774-9631. Janet Pitcaithly, D.R.E.
Students 740.

29—ST. FRANCIS OF ASSISI (1950), Rev. Patrick R. Wells; Deacons Emmanuel Okonmah; Ignatius Joseph.
Res., 5102 Dabney St., 77026-3015. Tel: 713-672-7773; Fax: 713-673-1913.
School—5100 Dabney St., 77026. Tel: 713-631-3681; Fax: 713-631-6114.
Sisters 4; Lay Teachers 14; Students 241.
Catechesis/Religious Programs—Tel: 713-674-5314. Shirley M. Rene, D.R.E.
Students 131.

30—ST. FRANCIS XAVIER (1952), Revs. Brian Fox, S.S.J.; Alfred Umagu, M.S.P.; Deacons Daniel W. Gilbert; Albert Henry; Michael V. Jenkins.
Res., 9202 Cullen Blvd., 77051-3399. Tel: 713-738-2311; Fax: 713-738-2312.
Catechesis/Religious Programs—Tel: 281-495-7458. Grenda Williams, D.R.E.
Students 251.

31—ST. GREGORY THE GREAT (1962), Revs. Gary F. Wanzong, V.F.; J. Jesus Godinez, Pro Tem; Deacon Julio Ramirez.
Res., 10500 Nold Dr., 77016-2921. Tel: 713-631-3681; Fax: 713-631-6114.
Catechesis/Religious Programs—Tel: 713-631-0058. D.R.E.: Raquel Castillo; Jessica Dargin.
Students 179.

32—HOLY CROSS CHAPEL (Downtown), Rev. Msgr. Albert J. Beck, Dir.; Rev. Msgr. George A. Beck.
Chapel—905 Main St., 77002. Tel: 713-650-1323; Fax: 713-650-8836.

33—HOLY GHOST (1946), Revs. Alton T. Carr, C.Ss.R.; John M. Farnik, C.Ss.R.; Peter H. Voelker, C.Ss.R.; Edward Glebe, C.Ss.R. In res., Revs. A. J. Chandonnet, C.Ss.R.; Robert Bek, C.Ss.R.; Deacon Robert Brueggerhoff.
Res., 6921 Chetwood Dr., 77081-5697. Tel: 713-668-0463; Fax: 713-661-4645.
School—6920 Chimney Rock, 77081. Tel: 713-668-5327. Susan Sanchez, Prin.
Lay Teachers 18; Students 253.
Catechesis/Religious Programs—Tel: 713-668-8001. Anne W. Brown, D.R.E.
Students 218.

34—HOLY NAME (1920) (Hispanic), Revs. Charles Kelly, S.C.J.; Vincent McDonald, S.C.J.; Michael Ortiz, S.C.J.
Res., 1917 Cochran St., 77009-8497. Tel: 713-222-1255; Fax: 713-222-1260.
School—1912 Marion St., 77009-8649. Tel: 713-227-9529. Sr. Angelica Garza, S.S.C.J., Prin.
Sisters 3; Lay Teachers 12; Students 184.
Catechesis/Religious Programs—Tel: 713-223-4059. Mrs. Alicia Bernal, D.R.E.
Students 647.

35—HOLY ROSARY (1913), Revs. Joseph D. Konkel, O.P.; William H. Brenda, O.P.; Joseph Nguyen Ngoc Tu, O.P.
Res., 3600 Travis St., 77002-9591. Tel: 713-529-4854; Fax: 713-522-3967.

36—IMMACULATE CONCEPTION (1911), Revs. Charles Borski, O.M.I.; James Miller, O.M.I.; Deacon Joseph G. Morin.
Res., 7250 Harrisburg Blvd., 77011-4791. Tel: 713-921-1261; Fax: 713-921-2304.
Catechesis/Religious Programs—Tel: 713-923-4780. Ms. Teresa Martinez, D.R.E.
Students 658.

37—IMMACULATE HEART OF MARY (1926) (Hispanic), Revs. Adolph Kaler, O.M.I.; William Davis, O.M.I.; Deacon Paul G. Navarro.
Res., 7539 Ave. K, 77012-1033. Tel: 713-923-2394; Fax: 713-923-2395.
School—7535 Ave. L, 77012-1098. Tel: 713-921-5431; Fax: 713-923-2395. Sr. Juana Olivarez Villescas, S.S.C.J., Prin. & D.R.E.
Sisters 2; Lay Teachers 5; Students 70.
Catechesis/Religious Programs—Tel: 713-928-5238. Sr. Juana Olivarez Villescas, D.R.E.
Students 549.

38—ST. JEROME (1960), Rev. Msgr. Daniel Scheel, S.T.L., M.Ch.A.; Revs. Douglas Smith, O.F.M.Cap.; Lee Flores. In res., Rev. Dominic Trinh The Huy, O.P.; Deacons Alden Knobloch; Jim Rutledge; Joseph Chuong Nguyen Do.
Res., 8825 Kempwood, 77080-4199. Tel: 713-468-9555; Fax: 713-464-0325.
School—Tel: 713-468-7946.
Lay Teachers 18; Students 329.
Catechesis/Religious Programs—Tel: 713-464-5029. Sr. Oralia Arzola, M.C.M., D.R.E.
Students 1,049.

39—ST. JOHN NEUMANN (1980), Rev. Msgr. Eugene G. Francis, M.R.E.; Revs. John Prill; Francis Huan Ton Ngo; Deacons Klaus W. Petereit; Richard L. Leach.
2703 Nelwood Drive, 77038-1025.
Res., 2715 Nelwood Dr., 77038-1025. Tel: 281-931-0684; Fax: 281-931-5363.
Catechesis/Religious Programs—Tel: 281-931-0684. Mrs. Kathy Kimich, D.R.E.
Students 461.

40—ST. JOHN VIANNEY (1966), Revs. John N. Morfin; John C. Upton; Doakim Nguyen; Deacons Dale Steffes; A. G. Aiuvalasit; John Coussirat; Hector Komeu; Albert Vacek, Jr.
Res., 625 Nottingham Oaks Tr., 77079-6299. Tel: 281-497-1500; Fax: 281-584-2024.
Catechesis/Religious Programs—Tel: 281-497-6665. Marilyn Corbin, D.R.E.
Students 1,737.

41—ST. JOSEPH (1880), Revs. Ferdinand Derrera, S.J., Spiritual Dir. for Priests; Donald G. Bahlinger, S.J.; Bro. Walter A. Eckler, S.J.; Deacons Mariano Salaazar; Geronimo Flores; Martin Sanchez.
Res., 1505 Kane St., 77007-7711. Tel: 713-222-6193; Fax: 713-222-6195.
Catechesis/Religious Programs—Marina Ramirez, D.R.E.
Students 238.

42—ST. JUSTIN MARTYR (1982), Revs. John T. Keller, M.Th., M.R.E.; Francis Pham, C.Ss.R.; Deacons Robert C. Keller; Gene Festa; Cornelius C. Llorens.
Res., 13350 Ashford Point Dr., 77082-5100. Tel: 281-556-5116; Fax: 281-556-6932.
Rectory: 12809 Sunset Dunes, 77082.
Catechesis/Religious Programs—Carole Polzer, D.R.E.
Students 910.

43—ST. LEO THE GREAT (1973), Revs. Richard Zanotti, C.S.; Rafael Becera, C.S.; Deacon Chuck Butler.
Res., 2131 Lauder Rd., 77039-3199. Tel: 281-449-2344; Fax: 281-449-3664.
Catechesis/Religious Programs—Julie Korniewicz, D.R.E.
Students 504.

44—ST. LUKE THE EVANGELIST (1975), Revs. Stephen R. Horn, M.Div.; Thu Ngoc Nguyen; Deacons John E. Devine, Jr.; James Sharpless; Paul J. Robison, Jr.
11011 Hall Rd., 77089-2999.
Res., 10914 Sagemeadow, 77089. Tel: 281-481-6816; Fax: 281-481-8969.
Catechesis/Religious Programs—Tel: 281-481-4735.
Students 900.

45—ST. MARK THE EVANGELIST (1974), Rev. Roosevelt Martin, Admin.
Res., 5302 Castlecreek Ln., Houston, 77053. Tel: 281-437-9114; 437-4828; Fax: 281-835-6303.
Church—5430 W. Ridgecreek Dr., Houston, 77053-3211.
Catechesis/Religious Programs—Tel: 281-438-0350. Zulema Perez, D.R.E.
Students 266.

46—ST. MARY OF THE PURIFICATION (1929), Revs. Michael J. Fritzen, S.V.D.; John Duah Prempeh, S.V.D. In res., Rev. Stanley J. Gootee, S.V.D.
Res., 3006 Rosedale Ave., 77004-6199. Tel: 713-528-0571; Fax: 713-528-0572.
School—3002 Rosedale, 77004. Tel: 713-522-9276; Fax: 713-522-1879. Mae Smith, Ed.D., Prin.
Lay Teachers 21; Students 201.
Catechesis/Religious Programs—Tel: 281-437-4110. Mrs. Evelyn Hunter, D.R.E.
Students 117.

47—ST. MATTHEW THE EVANGELIST (1974), Revs. Richard Johnston, S.C.J.; James R. Schifano, S.C.J.; Deacons John Adams; Adolph Zuk.
Res., 9915 Hollister Dr., 77040-1702. Tel: 713-466-4030; Fax: 713-896-7235.
Catechesis/Religious Programs—Virginia Diehl, D.R.E.
Students 620.

48—ST. MAXIMILIAN KOLBE CATHOLIC COMMUNITY (1983), Rev. Adam S. McClosky; Deacon Ronald J. Frazier.
Res., 10218 Great Plains, 77064.
Church—10135 West Rd., 77064-5361. Tel: 281-955-7324; Fax: 281-850-7328.
Catechesis/Religious Programs—Ginger Tamborello, D.R.E.
Students 790.

49—ST. MICHAEL (1925), Revs. Laurence Connelly; Fred P. Valone; Stephen V. Cooley, O.Carm.
Res., 1801 Sage Rd., 77056-3598. Tel: 713-621-4370; Fax: 713-850-8341.
School—1833 Sage Rd., 77056-3599. Tel: 713-621-6847; Fax: 713-877-8812. Dean Karns, Prin.
Lay Teachers 40; Students 480.
Catechesis/Religious Programs—Tel: 713-840-8213. Patricia Jantz, D.R.E.
Students 567.

50—ST. RAPHAEL THE ARCHANGEL (1995), Rev. James C. Arrambide, C.Ss.R.
Mailing Address: P.O. Box 630787, 77263. Tel: 713-781-9511.
Res., 3915 Ocee, 77063-5417.
Catechesis/Religious Programs—Ana Oliva, D.R.E.
Students 170.

51—ST. MONICA (1960), Rev. Alphonsus Bakyil, S.O.L.T.
Res., 8421 W. Montgomery Rd., 77088-7116. Tel: 281-447-5837; Fax: 281-447-8410.
Catechesis/Religious Programs—Students 180.

52—ST. NICHOLAS, Rev. Gabre-Tinsaye Adhana, S.T.L.
Res., 2508 Clay Ave., 77003-4498. Tel: 713-223-5210; Fax: 713-223-5210.

53—NOTRE DAME (1969), Revs. Hubert J. Kealy; John Hoang Minh Toan; Charles J. Samperi; Deacons Elie Calonge; Arturo M. Gomez; Bach Si Nguyen.
Res., 11226 Pompano Ln., 77072-3595.
Church—7720 Boone Rd., 77072-3595. Tel: 281-498-4653; Fax: 281-879-1527.
Catechesis/Religious Programs—Robby Lantz, D.R.E.
Students 519.

54—OUR LADY OF CZESTOCHOWA (1982) (Polish), Rev. Jerzy Frydrych, S.Ch.
Res., 1712 Oak Tree, 77080-7240. Tel: 713-973-1081; Fax: 713-973-1081.

55—OUR LADY OF GUADALUPE (1912) (Hispanic), Revs. James D. Steffes, S.C.J.; Francis Strafalace, S.C.J.
Res., 2405 Navigation Blvd., 77003-1599. Tel: 713-222-0203; Fax: 713-225-2235. [JC]
School—Tel: 713-224-6904. Chris Skoron, Prin.
Sisters 3; Lay Teachers 21; Students 204.
Catechesis/Religious Programs—Sr. Lelia Martinez, M.C.D.P., D.R.E.
Students 767.

56—OUR LADY OF LAVANG CHURCH (Vietnamese), Revs. Anthony Chinh Quang Dao, O.P., Vicar for Vietnamese; Anthony Hung Ngoc Tran, O.P.; Bro. Peter Mai Van To, O.P.; Deacon Michael Nguyen K. Khanh.
Res., 12320 Old Foltin Rd., 77086-3513. Tel: 281-999-1672; Fax: 281-999-1670.
Catechesis/Religious Programs—Nam Loang Luong, D.R.E.
Students 550.

57—OUR LADY OF MT. CARMEL (1952), Rev. Roy Ontiveros, O.Carm.
Res., 6723 Whitefriars Dr., 77087-6598. Tel: 713-645-6673; Fax: 713-645-6674.
School—6703 Whitefriars Dr., 77087. Tel: 713-643-0676. Sr. Alberta Novosad, I.W.B.S., Prin.
Sisters 1; Lay Teachers 15; Students 228.
Catechesis/Religious Programs—Tel: 713-645-6010. Sr. Cecelia Nguyen, D.R.E.
Students 244.

58—OUR LADY OF ST. JOHN (1957), Rev. Armando J. Rodriguez.
Res., 7500 Hirsch Rd., 77016-6215. Tel: 713-631-0810; Fax: 713-631-0781.
Catechesis/Religious Programs—Students 257.

59—OUR LADY OF SORROWS, Rev. Norberto Conde, Admin.
Res., 3006 Kashmere St., 77026-5999. Tel: 713-673-5622; Fax: 713-673-5667.
Catechesis/Religious Programs—Diana Ruiz, D.R.E. Students 215.

60—OUR LADY OF WALSINGHAM (1984), Rev. James T. Moore; Deacon James M. Barnett.
Mailing Address & Res.: Dorrington Blvd., 77030. Tel: 713-661-0235; Fax: 713-661-0235.

61—OUR MOTHER OF MERCY (1929), Revs. Kenneth J. Howard, S.S.J.; Eugene R. Moynihan, S.S.J. In res., Rev. John E. Hardman, S.S.J.; Deacon Charles J. Allen, Sr.
Res., 4000 Sumpter St., 77020-2497. Tel: 713-672-0026; Fax: 713-672-2031.
School—Sr. Benjamin Auzenne, Prin. Sisters 3; Lay Teachers 18; Students 221.
Catechesis/Religious Programs—D.R.E.: Sr. Theresa Healy; Tom Davis.
Students 214.

62—OUR LADY STAR OF THE SEA (1958), Rev. Louis R. Saporito, S.S.J.
Res., 1401 Fidelity St., 77029. Tel: 713-674-9206; Fax: 713-675-7842.

63—ST. PATRICK (1880), Rev. Salvatore F. DeGeorge, O.M.I.
Res., 4918 Cochran St., 77009-2117. Tel: 713-695-0631; Fax: 713-695-6255.
Catechesis/Religious Programs—Students 460.

64—ST. PAUL (1964), Revs. Dominic J. Pistone, Jr.; Walter N. Sheffield; Deacons Ray Sanders; Richard Labrecque.
Church—18223 Point Lookout Dr., 77058. Tel: 281-333-3891; Fax: 281-333-3815.
Rectory: 18326 Point Lookout Dr., 77058.
Catechesis/Religious Programs—Students 570.

65—ST. PETER THE APOSTLE, Revs. Raymond A. Woodka, S.S.J.; Paschal Nwachukwu; Deacon Clarence Johnson.
Res., 6220 La Salette Dr., 77021-1399. Tel: 713-747-7800; Fax: 713-747-9671.
School—Tel: 713-747-9484; Fax: 713-747-8754. Mr. Lucius M. Guillory, Prin.
Lay Teachers 12; Students 161.

66—ST. PETER CLAVER (1964), Rev. Larry A. Gutierrez, S.S.J.
Mailing Address: 6005 N. Wayside Dr., 77028-4494. Tel: 713-674-3338; Fax: 713-674-6524.
Catechesis/Religious Programs—Students 148.

67—ST. PHILIP NERI (1961), Rev. Tom Byrne, C.S.Sp., D.Min.; Bro. Robert Hassel, C.S.Sp.; Deacon Ronald Simon.
Res., 10950 Martin Luther King Blvd., 77048-1815.
Mailing Address: P.O. Box 330190, 77233-0190. Tel: 713-733-0320; Fax: 713-734-0331.
School—Tel: 713-733-2343. Melina G. Harris, Prin. Lay Teachers 12; Students 92.
Catechesis/Religious Programs—Mrs. Joan Graham, D.R.E.
Students 165.

68—ST. PHILIP OF JESUS (1958), Rev. Timothy Gray, S.C.J., (Hispanic Ministry Hechos Program); Deacon Roy Breaux.
Res., 3526 La Retama Dr., 77013-3818. Tel: 713-672-6141; Fax: 713-672-8675.
Catechesis/Religious Programs—Tel: 713-674-1664. Leticia Davila, D.R.E.
Students 165.

69—PRINCE OF PEACE (1971), Revs. George A. Sheltz, V.F.; Thomas V. Ponzini.
Res., 8300 Dorrcrest Ln., 77070-3510. Tel: 281-469-2686; Fax: 281-469-8418.
Church—19222 Tomball Pkwy., 77070-3510.
Catechesis/Religious Programs—Marion Joyce, D.R.E.
Students 1,251.

70—QUEEN OF PEACE (1942), Rev. Joseph A. Limanni. In res., Rev. Stephen E. Tiemann, Dir. Office of Vocations; Deacons Jose Liendo; John Sullivan.
Res., 3011 Telephone Rd., 77023-5395. Tel: 713-921-6127; Fax: 713-921-6128.
School—Tel: 713-921-1558. Sr. M. Alberta Novosad, Prin.
Sisters 3; Lay Teachers 10; Students 131.
Catechesis/Religious Programs—Tel: 713-921-1917. Sr. Gisela Rivera, C.M.S.T., D.R.E.
Students 672.

71—RESURRECTION (1920), Revs. David J. Cardenas; Blas P. Herrador; Deacons Leopold R. Moreno; Gregory Garcia; Jose J. Ramirez.
Res., 915 Zoe St., 77020-6898. Tel: 713-675-5333; Fax: 713-673-3605.
School—916 Majestic St., 77020. Tel: 713-674-5545. Philomena Morgan, Prin.
Sisters 3; Lay Teachers 11; Students 163.
Catechesis/Religious Programs—Tel: 713-674-2151. Gloria Hewitt, D.R.E.
Students 250.
Station—Port Houston, La Divina Providencia.

72—ST. ROSE OF LIMA (1947), Rev. Msgr. Thomas A. Wendland; Rev. Patrick John Cummings. In res., Rev. Franklin Simmons, (Chaplain Corps).
Res., 3600 Brinkman, 77018-6329. Tel: 713-692-9123; Fax: 713-692-5638.
School—Ms. Judy Johnson, Prin. Lay Teachers 22; Students 391.
Catechesis/Religious Programs—Mary Jo Wilt, D.R.E.
Students 300.

73—OUR LADY OF LOURDES (1994) (Vietnamese), Rev. Dominic Trinh The Huy, O.P.; Deacon Joseph Chuong Nguyen Do.
Mailing Address: c/o St. Jerome Church, 8825 Kempwood Dr., 77080-4199. Tel: 713-468-9555; Fax: 713-464-0325.

74—ST. STEPHEN (1932) (Hispanic), Revs. Antonio Rivera, M.J.; Angel Montano, M.J.
Mailing Address: 2019 Center St., 77007-6106.
Res., 1910 Center St., 77007. Tel: 713-864-4075; Fax: 713-880-8611.
Catechesis/Religious Programs—Tel: 281-445-8830. Sr. Ruth Martinez, C.M.S.T., D.R.E.
Students 227.

75—ST. THERESA, Revs. Benjamin Smaistrla; James M. Burkart; Deacons Larry A. Vaclavik; Jay Vocelka, D.R.E.
Res., 6622 Haskell St., 77007-2097. Tel: 713-869-3783; Fax: 713-869-3784.
School—Tel: 713-864-4536. Mrs. Ellen Hughes, Prin.
Lay Teachers 18; Students 258.
Social Service Office—6712 Durford, 77007. Tel: 713-869-2176.
Catechesis/Religious Programs—Tel: 713-869-9725.
Students 238.

76—ST. THOMAS MORE (1963), Revs. William L. Young, III; Stanislaus Bieniek. In res., Revs. Joseph T. O'Malley; Joseph Meledom; Rev. Msgr. Thomas A. Donovan; Deacons Anthony Alessi; Edwin Gosline; Thomas Newhouse; Edward Stoessel.
Res., 10330 Hillcroft, 77096-4795. Tel: 713-729-0221; Fax: 713-729-3294.
School—5927 Wigton, 77096. Tel: 713-729-3434. Mrs. Nadine Mouser, Prin.
Lay Teachers 39; Students 613.
Catechesis/Religious Programs—Tel: 713-729-3435. Mrs. Chris Twardowski, D.R.E.
Students 712.

77—ST. VINCENT DE PAUL (1941), Rev. Msgr. James A. Jamail; Revs. Howard Drabek; Richard Barker. In res., Most Rev. James A. Tamayo; Deacons Dr. Joseph Lorino; George Sheltz.
Res., 6800 Buffalo Speedway, 77025-1499. Tel: 713-667-9111; Fax: 713-667-3453.
School—6802 Buffalo Speedway, 77025. Tel: 713-666-2345. Virginia Malloy, Prin.
Sisters 2; Lay Teachers 32; Students 531.
Catechesis/Religious Programs—Tom Wells, D.R.E.
Students 525.

78—VIETNAMESE MARTYRS (1986) (Vietnamese), Rev. Peter Thanh Ngoc Chu; Deacon Joseph Nguyen Pham.
Res., 10610 Kingspoint Rd., 77075-4114. Tel: 713-941-0521; Fax: 713-941-0521.
Catechesis/Religious Programs—Students 350.

OUTSIDE THE CITIES OF GALVESTON AND HOUSTON

Alvin, Brazoria Co., St. John the Baptist (1954), Revs. Daniel McKenna, O.M.I.; Stanley Guzik, O.M.I.; Deacons Bart Hock; Robert Kacz; Diego Gutierrez, Sr.
Res., 110 E. South St., 77511-3500. Tel: 281-331-3751; Fax: 281-331-5430.
Catechesis/Religious Programs—Tel: 281-331-0181. Sr. Charles Marie Flores, S.S.C.J., D.R.E.
Students 844.

Anderson, Grimes Co., St. Stanislaus (1866), Rev. Louis S. Sikorski, D.R.E.; Deacons Anton Sicinski; Peter Sechelski.
Res., P.O. Box 210, 77830-0210. Tel: 409-873-2291; Fax: 409-873-2291. [CEM]
Catechesis/Religious Programs—Students 143.

Angleton, Brazoria Co., St. Basil (1960), Revs. Vincent Dulock, C.S.B.; James F. Blocher, C.S.B.; Gerald F. Dillon, C.S.B.; Deacon Andrew J. Shefts.
Res., 1713 N. Tinsley, 77515-3598. Tel: 409-849-2421; Fax: 409-849-2425.
Catechesis/Religious Programs—Tel: 409-849-1764. D.R.E.: Bernetta Cook; Norma Mata.
Students 628.

Barrett Station, Harris Co., St. Martin de Porres (1944), Rev. Joseph Uko, M.S.P., Mission Devel. Dir. In res., Rev. Matthias Selemobri, M.S.P.; Deacon Steve Arceneaux, Jr.
Mailing Address: P.O. Box 3459, 77532-2459. Tel: 281-328-4451; Fax: 281-328-7306.
Res., 12606 Crosby-Lynchburg Rd., 77532.
Missionary Society of St. Paul—Tel: 281-328-8931. Rev. Anthony Afangide, M.S.P., (Nigeria) Provincial Supr.
Mailing Address: P.O. Box 3200, 77532-2200.
Catechesis/Religious Programs—Mrs. Jude Arceneaux, Jr., D.R.E.
Students 232.

Beasley, Ft. Bend Co., St. Wenceslaus Mission (1916). (Independent Mission). Rev. Henry C. Rachunek.
Res., P.O. Box 121, Hungerford, 77448-0121. Tel: 409-532-4767; Fax: 409-532-8713. [CEM]

Baytown, Harris Co., St. John the Evangelist (1974), Rev. Stephen P. Laliberte. In res., Rev. John Nijenhuis, O.Carm.; Deacon Justin Wewer.
Res., 800 W. Baker Rd., 77521-2311. Tel: 713-837-8180; Fax: 713-837-8181.
Catechesis/Religious Programs—Jan Allison, D.R.E.
Students 325.

St. Joseph (1924), Rev. Stephen A. Mandry, S.T.D.; Deacon John William Singer, Jr.
Res., 1907 Carolina St., 77520-6098. Tel: 281-420-3588; Fax: 281-420-3044.
School—1811 Carolina St., 77520. Tel: 281-422-9749. Joe W. Connealy, Prin.
Lay Teachers 15; Students 135.
Catechesis/Religious Programs—Fax: 281-427-5720. Judy Arceneaux.
Students 162.

Our Lady of Guadalupe (1958), Revs. Ramon Martinez, O.S.A.; Jose Luis Rivera, O.S.A.; Deacons Fernando Gonzalez; Rudy Venegas; George Rincon.
Res., 1124 Beech St., 77520-4198. Tel: 281-428-1507; Fax: 281-422-4554.
Catechesis/Religious Programs—Tel: 281-427-5836. Dahlia & Hector Meza, D.R.E.
Students 455.

Bellville, Austin Co., SS. Peter & Paul (1860) (Slavic), Rev. Roger K. Duffy, C.S.Sp.
Res., P.O. Box 176, 77418-0176. Tel: 409-865-2368; Fax: 409-865-9929. [CEM]
Catechesis/Religious Programs—Tel: 409-836-1492. Wava Jackson, D.R.E.
Students 191.
Mission—Industry, Austin Co., Immaculate Conception.

Brazoria, Brazoria Co., St. Joseph (1840), Rev. Michael J. Carmody; Deacons Raul A. Castillo; Jimmy Smith.
Res., Rte. 4, Box 4100, 77422-8699. Tel: 409-798-2288; Fax: 409-798-4702. [CEM]
Catechesis/Religious Programs—Betty Castillo, D.R.E.
Students 243.

Channelview, Harris Co., St. Andrew (1970), Rev. John-Vincent Rouse; Deacons Jack Rook; John Santos; Steve Miller; Javier Gomez.
Res., 827 Sheldon Rd., 77530-3511. Tel: 281-452-9865; Fax: 281-452-2157. [JC]
Catechesis/Religious Programs—Tel: 281-452-0618. Sr. Helen Spanos, D.R.E.

Clute, Brazoria Co., St. Jerome (1969), Rev. James F. Lynes.
Mailing Address: 107 N. Lazy Ln., 77531.
Res., 204 Wayne Dr., 77531. Tel: 409-265-5179; Fax: 409-265-4601. [JC]
Catechesis/Religious Programs—Tel: 409-233-0520. Dina Tonche, D.R.E.
Students 330.

Conroe, Montgomery Co., Sacred Heart (1916), Rev. Msgr. David W. Kennedy, V.F.; Rev. Jhon J. Arroyave.
Res., 109 N. Frazier St., 77301-2889. Tel: 409-756-8186; Fax: 409-756-8105.
School—105 N. Frazier, 77301. Tel: 409-756-3848. Margaret Looper, Prin.
Sisters 2; Lay Teachers 11; Students 524.
Spanish Ministry—Tel: 409-756-8288.
Catechesis/Religious Programs—Becki Lipari, D.R.E.
Students 524.

Crosby, Harris Co., Sacred Heart (1936), Rev. Msgr. Fred P. O'Connor; Deacon Charles F. Roessler, Jr.
Res., 915 Runneburg Rd., 77532-5826. Tel: 281-328-4871; Fax: 281-328-1075. [CEM]
School—907 Runneberg Rd., 77532. Tel: 281-328-6561.
Lay Teachers 12; Students 127.
Catechesis/Religious Programs—Tel: 409-756-8186. Margaret Benham, D.R.E.
Students 197.

Damon, Brazoria Co., SS. Cyril and Methodius (1925) (Czech), Rev. James Ramsey.

Mailing Address: & Res.—P.O. Box 309, 77430-0309. Tel: 409-742-3383; Fax: 409-742-3383.
Church—603 Parrot Ave., 77430.

Danbury, Brazoria Co., St. Anthony de Padua (1911), Rev. William A. Oliver; Deacon Gerald Peltier.
Res., P.O. Box 288, 77534-0288. Tel: 409-922-1240; Fax: 409-922-8643. [CEM]
Catechesis/Religious Programs—Tel: 409-922-1241. Catine Peltier, D.R.E.
Students 173.

Deer Park, Harris Co., St. Hyacinth (1965), Rev. Msgr. Elmer T. Quinters; Rev. Antonio A. Castro; Deacons Dennis M. Hickey; Richard F. Camunez.
Res., 2921 Center St., 77536-4997. Tel: 281-479-4298; Fax: 281-479-4132.
Catechesis/Religious Programs—Tel: 713-479-8832. Mary Wilson, D.R.E.
Students 928.

Dickinson, Galveston Co., Shrine of the True Cross (1909), Rev. Msgr. Milam E. Kleas; Rev. Marco Guzman; Deacon Sam Ausmus, III.
Mailing Address: P.O. Box 687, 77539.
Res., 3720 Spruce, 77539. Tel: 713-337-4112; Fax: 713-337-5779.
Church—300 Pine Dr., 77539-0687.
School—400 Pine Dr., 77539. Tel: 713-337-5212. Susan Callaway, Prin.
Lay Teachers 17; Students 274.
Catechesis/Religious Programs—Tel: 713-337-3130. Pattie Courtin, D.R.E.
Students 545.

Freeport, Brazoria Co., St. Mary: Star of the Sea (1926), Rev. Reginald F. Petrash; Deacon Wallace Shaw.
Res., 914 W. 7th St., 77541. Tel: 409-233-5271; Fax: 409-233-5272.
Catechesis/Religious Programs—Tel: 409-233-2771. Marilyn Saccomanno, D.R.E.
Students 350.

St. Henry (1938) (Hispanic), Rev. Jose M. Sanchez.
Res., 318 E. 5th St., 77541-0857. Tel: 409-233-2887; Fax: 409-233-2887.

Friendswood, Galveston Co., Mary, Queen (1969), Revs. Francis Fitzsimmons, M.S.; Paul Mandziuk, M.S.; Phil M. Negley, M.S.; Bro. Roman Wilbers, M.S.; Deacons Darrell Moulton; Robert George Alexander.
Res., P.O. Box 207, 77549. Tel: 281-482-1391; Fax: 281-482-4886.
Catechesis/Religious Programs—Tel: 713-482-5875. Donna Patlach, D.R.E.
Students 980.
Students 1,007.

Frydek, Austin Co., St. Mary's (1908), Rev. Bernard C. Snock.
Res., 124 Zaruba Rd., Sealy, 77474-0337. Tel: 409-885-3131; Fax: 409-885-4555. [CEM]

Galena Park, Harris Co., Our Lady of Fatima (1946), Revs. Robert D. Carlson; Faustino Maramot.
Res., 1705 Eighth St., P.O. Box 644, 77547-0644. Tel: 713-675-0981; Fax: 713-675-0982.
School—1702 Ninth St., 77547. Tel: 713-674-5832.
Lay Teachers 11; Students 163.
Catechesis/Religious Programs—Sr. Martina Hoare, D.R.E.
Students 495.

Hempstead, Waller Co., St. Mary (1897), Rev. Edward C. Kucera, Jr., M.Th., B.A.
Mailing Address: P.O. Box 576, 77445. Tel: 409-826-2275; Fax: 409-826-2275.
Res., 604 14th St., 77445.
Catechesis/Religious Programs—Barbara Bezub, D.R.E.
Students 148.

Highlands, Harris Co., St. Jude Thaddeus (1946), Rev. John A. Zabelskas. In res., Rev. Luis Chia.
Res., 800 S. Main St., 77562-4236. Tel: 281-843-2422; Fax: 281-426-3671.
Catechesis/Religious Programs—Tel: 713-426-6800. Theresa A. Cashion, D.R.E.
Students 207.

Hitchcock, Galveston Co., Our Lady of Lourdes (1954), Rev. John C. DeForke.
Res., 10114 Hwy. 6, 77563-4515. Tel: 409-925-3579; Fax: 409-925-5094.
School—Joseph Meli, Prin. Sisters 2; Lay Teachers 8; Students 163.
Catechesis/Religious Programs—Sr. Mary Anne C.V.I., D.R.E.
Students 294.

Huffman, Harris Co., St. Philip the Apostle (1977), Rev. George J. Olsovsky, M.Th.
Mailing Address: P.O. Box 292, 77336-0292. Tel: 281-324-1478; Fax: 281324-2775.
Res., 2308 Third St., 77336.
Catechesis/Religious Programs—Tel: 281-334-4401. Maureen Schuster, D.R.E.
Students 156.

Humble, Harris Co., St. Mary Magdalene (1911), Revs. Paul Procella; Octavio Miguerza; Deacons James N. Caruso; Martin Davies.
Mailing Address: 527 S. Houston Ave., 77338-4763.
Res., 525 S. Houston Ave., 77338-4763. Tel: 281-446-8211; Fax: 281-446-8213.
Catechesis/Religious Programs—Tel: 281-446-2933. Jean Johnson, D.R.E.
Students 1,162.

Huntsville, Walker Co., St. Thomas the Apostle (1963), Rev. Stephen J. Payne. In res., Rev. Robert P. Zawacki, S.S.J.
Res., 1323 16th St., 77340-4431. Tel: 409-295-8159; Fax: 409-295-3543.
Catechesis/Religious Programs—Tel: 409-295-2298. Janet Johnson, D.R.E.
Students 205.

Katy, Harris Co., St. Bartholomew (1965), Rev. Alberto A. Maullon, Jr.; Deacon William C. Wagner.
Res., 5356 11th St., 77493-1797. Tel: 713-391-4758; Fax: 713-391-3978.
Catechesis/Religious Programs—Tel: 281-391-0839. Bill Wagner, D.R.E.
Students 1,021.

Epiphany of the Lord (1981), Rev. Msgr. Jack M. Dinkins; Rev. Anthony A. Castro; Deacons Don Kish; Leonard Broussard; Steve Harper.
Res., 1530 Norwalk Dr., 77450-4999. Tel: 281-578-0707; Fax: 281-578-9161.
Catechesis/Religious Programs—Tel: 281-578-8271. Bonnie Caruso, D.R.E.
Students 1,650.

Kingwood, Harris Co., St. Martha (1979), Revs. Terence Brinkman, S.T.D.; Jimmy B. Hababag. In res., Rev. Romanus O. Muoneke.
Res., 2302 Oak Shores Dr., 77339-1801. Tel: 713-358-6637; Fax: 713-358-7973.
School—P.O. Box 6354, 77325-6354. Tel: 713-358-5523. Roger L. Larson, Prin.
Lay Teachers 6; Students 51.
Catechesis/Religious Programs—Tel: 713-358-1959. Francine Puglia, D.R.E.
Students 2,066.

Lake Jackson, Brazoria Co., St. Michael (1966), Rev. Msgr. Leo Wleczyk, V.F.
Res., 100 Oak Dr., S., 77566-5630. Tel: 409-297-3041; Fax: 409-297-7895.
Catechesis/Religious Programs—Tel: 409-297-3043. Marsha Jacklitsch, D.R.E.
Students 1,052.

La Marque, Galveston Co., Our Lady Queen of Peace (1951), Rev. Msgr. T. Joseph Culver, E.V.; Deacons James Bonura; Earl Llewellyn.
Res., 626 Laurel, 77568. Tel: 409-938-7000; Fax: 409-935-9791.
Church—1224 Cedar Dr., 77568.
Catechesis/Religious Programs—Tel: 409-935-3535. Maira Compean, D.R.E.
Students 204.

La Porte, Harris Co., St. Mary of the Immaculate Conception (1954), Rev. Thomas F. Rafferty; Deacons Hector Cantu; Thomas Lewis.
Res., 816 Park Ave., 77571-5811. Tel: 281-471-2000; Fax: 281-471-9365. [JC]
Catechesis/Religious Programs—Joan Westbeld, D.R.E.
Students 394.

League City, Galveston Co., St. Mary (1965), Rev. Msgr. Eugene Cargill; Deacons Robert Garza; Jerome McAllister.
Res., 1612 E. Walker St., 77573-4137. Tel: 281-332-3031; Fax: 281-332-8328.
School—Lay Teachers 19; Students 182.
Catechesis/Religious Programs—Tel: 281-332-4014. Santos Flores, D.R.E.
Students 590.

McNair, Harris Co., Holy Family (1945), Rev. Lawrence A. Ebuk, M.S.P. (Nigeria).
Mailing Address: P.O. Box 307, Highlands, 77562-0307. Tel: 281-426-8448; Fax: 281-426-8449.
Res., 7122 Whiting Rock Dr., Baytown, 77521. [JC]

Madisonville, Madison Co., St. Elizabeth Ann Seton (1974), Rev. Joseph Phiet The Nguyen, Admin.; Deacon Burke J. Landry.
Res., 209 S. Tammye Ln., 77864-3011. Tel: 409-348-5570.

Magnolia, Montgomery Co., St. Matthias the Apostle (1978), Rev. Frank W. Jones; Deacon Theodore Otis Baker.
Res., 302 S. Magnolia Blvd., 77355-8535. Tel: 713-356-2000; Fax: 713-356-7818.
Catechesis/Religious Programs—Barbara Bezub, D.R.E.
Students 152.

Manvel, Brazoria Co., Sacred Heart of Jesus (1945), Revs. James J. Gaunt, C.S.B.; John S. Broussard, C.S.B.
Res., 6502 Co. Rd. 48, 77578-2902. Tel: 281-489-8720; Fax: 281-489-8727.
Catechesis/Religious Programs—Tel: 281-489-7603. Diane Arsola, D.R.E.
Students 386.

Missouri City, Ft. Bend Co., Holy Family (1915), Revs. William E. Coughlin, C.S.B.; Frederick L. Clay, C.S.B.; Hugh J. Curran, C.S.B.; Thaddeus T. Valencia, C.S.B.; Deacons Jesse Santiago; Leonard Ramirez; William Seifert.
Res., 1510 Fifth St., 77489-1298. Tel: 713-499-9688; Fax: 713-499-9680.
Catechesis/Religious Programs—Tel: 281-499-4612.
Students 820.

Navasota, Grimes Co., Christ Our Light (1869), Rev. Norbert J. Maduzia, Jr., D.Min.; Deacons Grant E. Holt; Gregory N. Jelinek, M.D.; William Leonard Sheffield.
Mailing Address: 510 Manley St., 77868-3926.
Res., 615 Church St., 77868-3905. Tel: 409-825-3920; Fax: 409-825-7612.
Church—1705 S. Loop 6, 77868.
Catechesis/Religious Programs—Mrs. Lucille Pavlock, D.R.E.
Students 402.

Needville, Fort Bend Co., St. Michael (1912), Rev. James Ramsey.
Res., P.O. Box 95, 77461-0095. Tel: 409-793-4477; Fax: 409-793-7456. [CEM]
Catechesis/Religious Programs—Lynn Sury, D.R.E., Tel: 281-232-4006 (Res.).
Students 520.

New Caney, Montgomery Co., St. John of the Cross (1989), Rev. Robert Ramon, Admin., Pro Tem.
Catechesis/Religious Programs—Students 188.

New Waverly, Walker Co., St. Joseph (1869), Rev. Joseph K. Kalladan.
Res., P.O. Box 188, 77358-0188. Tel: 409-344-6104; Fax: 409-344-2818. [CEM 2]
Mission—Point Blank, St. Stephen the Martyr.

Pasadena, Harris Co., St. Pius the Fifth (1941), Revs. Mario J. Arroyo; Philip A. Wilhite, S.T.L.; Deacons Don Hart; Leon Arceneaux.
Res., 824 S. Main St., 77501-0188. Tel: 713-473-9484; Fax: 713-473-2731.
School—Tel: 713-472-5172.
Lay Teachers 21; Students 241.
Catechesis/Religious Programs—D.R.E.: Sr. Felice Mojica, M.C.D.P.; Sr. Frances Jean Terrazas, M.C.D.P.
Students 1,081.

Blessed Juan Diego (1954) (Hispanic). (Formerly Guardian Angel). Revs. J. Francisco Leon, O.S.A.; Leonel Martinez, O.S.A. (Mexico); Deacon Valeriano Leija.
Res., 3301 Pasadena Blvd., 77503-3201. Tel: 713-477-6693; Fax: 713-477-0523.
Catechesis/Religious Programs—Tel: 713-472-0356. Beatrice Canas, D.R.E.
Students 447.

Pattison/Brookshire, Waller Co., Sacred Heart (1914), Rev. Timothy P. Bucek.
Mailing Address: P.O. Box 300, Pattison, 77466-0300.
Res., 4445 F.M. 359 N., Pattison, 77466. Tel: 281-934-2888; Fax: 281-375-5799.
Catechesis/Religious Programs—Tel: 713-375-6638. Mrs. Marie Pattison, D.R.E.
Students 156.

Pearland, Brazoria Co., St. Helen (1966), Rev. Msgr. Leroy H. Braden; Rev. Trung Nguyen; Deacons John Housholder; Gilbert Villarreal; Darvin Bordelon.
Catechesis/Religious Programs—Tel: 713-991-3486. Patsy Morales, D.R.E.
Students 1,500.

Plantersville, Grimes Co., St. Mary (1894), Rev. James F. Burke, C.S.Sp.
Res., Rte. 2, Box 3160, Navasota, 77868-9604. Tel: 409-894-2223; Fax: 409-894-2223. [CEM]

Port Bolivar, Galveston Co., Our Mother of Mercy, Rev. John J. Connolly.
Mailing Address: P.O. Drawer C, 77650-0703.
Res., 1313 18th St., 77650-0703. Tel: 409-684-8962; Fax: 409-684-8962.
Mission—Crystal Beach, Galveston Co., St. Therese of Lisieux, 2400 Hwy. 87, 77650-0703.

Prairie View, Waller Co., St. Martin de Porres (1962), Rev. Bernard C. Keller, S.V.D.
Res., P.O. Box 3027, 77446-3027. Tel: 409-857-3351; Fax: 409-857-3351. [CEM]

Richmond, Fort Bend Co., Sacred Heart (1935), Rev. Eric J. Pitre; Deacons Don Ries; Lou Endris.
Res., 507 S. Fourth St., 77469-3599. Tel: 713-342-3609; Fax: 713-342-9833.
Catechesis/Religious Programs—Tel: 281-342-8371. Virginia Ewald, D.R.E.
Students 861.

St. John Fisher (1952) (Hispanic), Rev. Wencil Pavlovsky, C.S.B.; Deacon Guillermo F. Castaneda, Jr.

Mailing Address: 410 Clay St., 77469-1708.
Res., 106 Fifth St., Sugar Land, 77487. Tel: 713-342-5092; Fax: 281-232-2607.
Catechesis/Religious Programs—Tel: 281-232-0348. Frank Trevino, D.R.E.
Students 291.

Rosenberg, Fort Bend Co., Holy Rosary (1911) (Czech), Rev. Daniel L. Warden, V.F.; Deacon David D. Mitchell.
Res., 1416 George St., 77471-3198. Tel: 713-342-3089; Fax: 713-342-7688.
School—1408 James St., 77471. Tel: 713-342-5813. Mrs. Elizabeth Anthony, Prin.
Lay Teachers 15; Students 260.

Our Lady of Guadalupe (1936), Revs. Jamie M. Abercrombie, C.S.B.; Charles E. Lynch, C.S.B.
Catechesis/Religious Programs—Tel: 281-232-4322. Dolores Yanz, D.R.E.
Students 540.

Sealy, Austin Co., Immaculate Conception (1889), Rev. Msgr. Boleslaus J. Zientek; Deacon Frank Laredo.
Mailing Address: P.O. Box 337, 77474.
Res., 517 Fifth St., 77474. Tel: 409-885-3868; Fax: 409-885-2246. [CEM]
Parish Center—605 Fifth St., 77474. Tel: 409-885-6902.
Catechesis/Religious Programs—Donna Brown, D.R.E.
Students 349.

South Houston, Harris Co., Our Lady of Grace, Rev. Jose Maria Asenjo.
Res., 1204 Michigan St., 77582. Tel: 713-946-6461; Fax: 713-946-0647.
Catechesis/Religious Programs—Tel: 281-333-4174. Amailia D. Parra, D.R.E.
Students 317.

Spring, Harris Co.,

1—CHRIST THE GOOD SHEPHERD, (1978), Rev. Msgr. William P. Robertson, E.V.; Rev. Francisco Quezada, (Retired). In res., Rev. Clifton J. Natho; Deacons Steve La Bonte; Pat Camerino.
Res., 18511 Klein Church Rd., 77379-4998. Tel: 713-376-7319; Fax: 713-376-8945.
Catechesis/Religious Programs—D.R.E.: Judy Lawyer; Lorelei Guerin; K. Kelly.
Students 975.

2—ST. EDWARD, (1969), Rev. Msgr. Al R. Doga; Revs. Paul Felix; Joe Mignogna; Deacon Kenneth Martin.
Res., 2601 Spring Stuebner Rd., 77389-4824. Tel: 713-353-9774; Fax: 713-353-9786.
School—Tel: 713-353-4570; Fax: 713-353-8255. Ann Henthorn, Prin.
Lay Teachers 20; Students 335.
Catechesis/Religious Programs—Tel: 713-353-4930. Joe Wappelhorst, D.R.E.
Students 663.

3—ST. IGNATIUS OF LOYOLA, (1985), Revs. Francis X. Pistorius, S.J.; Paul B. Patin, S.J.; Joseph M. Nasser, S.J.; Deacon Glen Cupier.
Church—7810 Cypresswood Dr., 77379-7101. Tel: 281-370-3401 (Office); Fax: 281-370-9306.
Catechesis/Religious Programs—Deacon James L. Hite, D.R.E.
Students 1,700.

4—ST. JAMES THE APOSTLE, (1976), Revs. John Francis Ulm; William P. Somerville; Deacons Steven Griesmyer; Michael Schmidt.
Res., 22800 Aldine Westfield Rd., 77373-6500. Tel: 713-353-5053; Fax: 713-355-8847.
Catechesis/Religious Programs—Tel: 281-353-3497. D.R.E.: Nancy Tomczak; Nicky St. Cyr.
Students 711.

Sugar Land, Fort Bend Co., St. Laurence (1985), Revs. John T. Weyer, B.A., M.Th.; Al Walsh; Deacons Lee Tollett; Bob Dunham.
Res., 3100 Sweetwater Blvd., 77479-2630. Tel: 281-980-9812; Fax: 281-980-0686.
School—Tel: 281-980-0550; Fax: 281-980-0026.
Lay Teachers 25; Students 353.
Catechesis/Religious Programs—Tel: 281-265-5774. Eleanor Notz, D.R.E.
Students 1,684.

St. Theresa (1924), Revs. Robert J. Matzinger, C.S.B.; Roy J. Oggero, C.S.B.; Robert G. Ritz, C.S.B.; George E. Silvester, C.S.B.; Deacons Gerald DuPont; Don Burns.
Res., 115 Seventh St., P.O. Box 968, 77487-0968. Tel: 281-494-1156; Fax: 281-242-1393.
Catechesis/Religious Programs—Tel: 281-494-2717. Kathleen Barnosky, D.R.E.
Students 1,622.

St. Thomas Aquinas (1978), Rev. Kevin C. Thissen, O.P.; Deacon Thomas Saucier, O.P.
Res., 10415 Huntington Wood Dr., Houston, 77099-3721. Tel: 281-240-6721; Fax: 281-240-6733.
Catechesis/Religious Programs—Christy Wright, D.R.E.
Students 707.

Sweeny, Brazoria Co., Our Lady of Perpetual Help (1954), Rev. Peter Mastrobuono, S.C.J.
Res., 310 N. McKinney St., 77480-2899. Tel: 409-548-2020; Fax: 409-548-2020.
Catechesis/Religious Programs—Tel: 409-548-4470. Mary Wooderson, D.R.E.
Students 115.
Mission—West Columbia, Brazoria Co., St. John the Apostle, 807 Loggins, West Columbia, 77486-3843. Tel: 409-345-3600.

Texas City, Galveston Co., St. Mary (1911), Rev. Ralph G. Schmidt, Jr. In res., Rev. Msgr. Thomas J. Cullen (Mobile); Deacons Michael Satterwhite; Jose Duplan, Jr.
Mailing Address: 1604 Ninth Ave., N., 77590-5468.
Res., 722 Third Ave. N., 77590. Tel: 409-948-8448; Fax: 409-945-8662.
School—Our Lady of Fatima, 1600 Ninth Ave., N., 77590. Tel: 409-945-3326.
Lay Teachers 23; Students 258.
Catechesis/Religious Programs—Joe Hensley, D.R.E.
Students 537.

The Woodlands, Montgomery Co., Sts. Simon and Jude (1979), Rev. Msgr. Charles C. Domec; Rev. Peter Ferguson; Deacons Ken Carlson; Robert Flynn; Fred Shetz; Sid Sandiford; John Charnisky.
Res., 26777 Glen Loch Dr., 77381-2921. Tel: 713-367-9885; Fax: 713-367-9888.
Catechesis/Religious Programs—Tel: 281-292-9801. Robin Walker, D.R.E.
Students 1,883.

Tomball, Harris Co., St. Anne (1953), Rev. David J. DuBois; Deacon J. R. (Bob) Crawford.
Res., 1111 S. Cherry St., 77375-6675. Tel: 713-351-8106; Fax: 713-351-8142.
School—Tel: 713-351-0093. Nina Edwards, Prin.
Lay Teachers 15; Students 220.

Wallis, Austin Co., Guardian Angel (1892), Rev. Kenneth E. Mikulik, Pro Tem.
Res., 5610 Demel St., P.O. Box 487, 77485-0487. Tel: 409-478-6532; Fax: 409-478-7275. [CEM]
Catechesis/Religious Programs—Tel: 409-478-6843.
Students 237.

Chaplains of Public Institutions

Prison Chaplains

GALVESTON. *Galveston County Jail*. Vacant. 715 19th St., 77550. Tel: 409-766-2315.

ANGLETON. *Retrieve Unit*. Deacon Earl Llewellyn, Rte. 4, Box 1500, 77515. Tel: 713-595-3465.

BRAZORIA. *Clemens Unit*. Vacant. Rte. 1, Box 1077, 77422. Tel: 409-798-2188.

GATESVILLE. *Gatesville Unit*. Ms. Marie Bonville, 1401 State School Rd., 76599. Tel: 817-865-8431.
Hilltop Unit. Ms. Marie Bonville, 1500 State School Rd., 76598. Tel: 817-865-8431.
Mountainview Unit. Ms. Marie Bonville, Rte. 4, Box 800, 76528. Tel: 817-865-7226.

HUNTSVILLE. *Diagnostic Unit*. Deacon Frank Ortego, Box 77340, 76054. Tel: 409-295-8159.
Ellis I Unit. Deacon Richard Lopez, Rte. 6, 77343. Tel: 409-295-5756, Ext. 155.
Ellis II Unit. Rev. Robert Zawacki, S.S.J., Tel: 409-295-8159.
Goree Unit. Deacon Frank Ortego, Box 38, 77340. Tel: 409-295-8159.
Walls Unit. Rev. Robert Zawacki, S.S.J., Box 32, 77340. Tel: 409-295-8159.
Wynne Unit. Rev. Robert Zawacki, S.S.J., Rte. 1, Box 1, 77340. Tel: 409-295-8159.

MIDWAY. *Ferguson Unit*. Vacant. Rte. 2, Box 20, 75852. Tel: 409-348-3751; 295-8159.

NAVASOTA. *Pack I Unit*. Deacon Peter Sechelski, Rte. 3, Box 300, 77686. Tel: 409-825-3728.
Pack II Unit. Deacon Peter L. Sechelski, Rte. 1, Box 1000, 77686. Tel: 409-825-7548.

RICHMOND. *Jester I Unit*. Vacant. Rte. 2, 77469.
Jester II Unit. Vacant. Rte. 2, 77469.
Jester III Unit. Vacant. Rte. 2, 77469.
Jester IV Unit Rte. 2, 77469. Tel: 713-277-3700. Rev. Donald McNally, O.M.I.

ROSHARON. *Darrington Unit*. Deacon Earl Llewellyn, Rte. 3, Box 59, 77583. Tel: 713-595-2465.
Ramsey I Unit. Vacant. Rte. 4, Box 1100, 77583.
Ramsey II Unit. Vacant. Rte. 4, Box 1200, 77583.
Ramsey III Unit, Rte. 4, Box 1300, 77583. Deacon Robert Kacz.

SUGAR LAND. *Central Unit*. Deacon Emilio Gonzales, One Circle Dr., 77478. Tel: 713-491-2146.

Jail Chaplains

HOUSTON. *Harris County Jail*. Bro. John Cosgrove, O.P. Tel: 713-755-8562; Rev. Ron F. Cloutier. Tel: 713-755-5326, Res., 215 E. 10th St., 77008.
Juvenile Detention Center. Bro. Mike Gillespie, S.M. Tel: 713-527-1894; Ms. Marilu Ballow. Tel: 713-762-7192.

On Special Assignment:
Reverend Fathers—
Beck, Albert J., Downtown Chapel, 906 Main St., Houston, TX 77002
Gately, R. Troy, Vice Chancellor
Rossi, Frank H., Chancellor
Zigrang, Stephen P., Tribunal

On Duty Outside the Diocese:
Reverend Monsignors—
Broussard, William L., Texas Catholic Conference
Fruge, Donald J., P.O. Box 13327, Capitol Station, Austin, TX 78711
Reverend Fathers—
Burns, Malcolm J., St. Brigid Church, 50 Post Ave., Westbury, NY 11590
Cahill, Brendan J., Casa Santa Maria, Via dell'Umilta, 30 00187, Rome, Italy. Tel: (06)68-69-441
Corrigan, Michael T., St. Anne, 300 Ashton Ave., Kingstree, SC 29556. Tel: 803-354-7798
Guenter, Frank, St. James Society, Parroquia Fatima, Casilla 919, Santa Cruz, Bolivia S.A.
Hughes, Royce, 745 E. U.S. Hwy. 90, Schulenburg, TX 78956-5233. Tel: 409-743-3722
Perez, Joseph, The Chancery, P.O. Box 907, Houston, TX 77001

Military Chaplains:
Reverend Fathers—
Edelin, Richard A., Leave of Absence
Schwarting, J. Donald, Pastoral Care Services, National Naval Medical Center, Bethesda, MD 20889

Retired:
Reverend Monsignors—
Alleman, C. J., 501 13th St., Galveston, TX 77550-5034. Tel: 409-763-2588
Barzyk, Robert R., 212 Oakdale, Shoreacres, TX 77571-7347
Beck, George A., 8045 Holiday, Houston, TX 77075
Crosthwait, Joseph H., P.O. Box 1302, New Ulm, TX 78950. Tel: 409-992-3821
Donovan, Thomas A., Pope John XXIII Residence, 2407 E. Holcombe Blvd., Houston, TX 77021-2023. Tel: 409-748-4608
Fuchs, Sylvester, Lost Prairie Villa, 9901 FM 2086, Temple, TX 76501-3528. Tel: 817-984-2312
Jones, John B., Pope John XXIII Residence, 2407 E. Holcombe Blvd., Houston, TX 77021-2023. Tel: 713-747-1746
Lagana, Frank A., Pope John XXIII Residence, 2407 E. Holcombe Blvd., Houston, TX 77021-2023. Tel: 713-748-4608
Madden, James J., Pope John XXIII Residence, 2407 E. Holcombe Blvd., Houston, TX 77021-2023. Tel: 713-748-3115
Peguero, Lawrence, Pope John XXIII Residence, 2407 E. Holcombe Blvd., Houston, TX 77021-2023. Tel: 713-748-4608
Pekar, Gilbert F., P.O. Box 425, Damon, TX 77430. Tel: 409-742-3345
Price, Leo J., 1101 Parthenon Pl., New Caney, TX 77357. Tel: 713-689-7228
Rhein, George V., 2407 E. Holcombe Blvd., Houston, TX 77021-2023. Tel: 713-747-7308
Schoppe, Charles K. Tel: 713-748-4596
Wearden, Francis G., 1100 Parthenen Pl., New Caney, TX 77357-3039. Tel: 713-399-0270
Reverend Fathers—
Antle, Nicholas C., Pope John XXIII Residence, 2407 E. Holcombe Blvd., Houston, TX 77021-2023. Tel: 713-748-1553
Banet, Charles, C.PP.S., Holy Rosary Church, 1420 31st St., Galveston, TX 77550-4399. Tel: 409-762-2478
Brumleu, Ernest J., Pope John XXIII Residence, 2407 E. Holcombe Blvd., Houston, TX 77021-2023. Tel: 713-748-3115
Burns, Charles E., 343 Bobolink, New Braunfels, TX 78130-3868
Burns, David E.
Carreon, Albert S., P.O. Box 15836, Santa Ana, CA 92705
Chandonnet, A. J., C.SS.R., Holy Ghost, 6921 Chetwood, Houston, TX 77081-5697. Tel: 713-668-0463
Clemens, Norbert, C.S.B., Dillon House, 1302 Kipling St., Houston, TX 77006-4297. Tel: 713-529-3994; 529-3970
Daigle, Robert E., 6505 O'Bannon Dr., Las Vegas, NV 89102-0854
del Val, Feliciano, Pope John XXIII Residence, 2407 East Holcombe Blvd., Houston, TX 77021-2023. Tel: 713-748-4608
Dougherty, George Patrick, 7228 Comanche Trail, Austin, TX 78732-1011. Tel: 512-266-2186
Ferguson, Carlos, c/o Chancery
Freret, Warren Joseph, P.O. Box 850, Hawthorne,

NV 89415. Tel: 702-945-2020
Gillece, Alfred F., 630 N. Via Lucia, Tucson, AZ 85745. Tel: 602-792-0122
Gillgannon, Patrick, P.O. Box 300923, Houston, TX 77230-0923. Tel: 713-799-8350
Greenwald, Alfred F., 630 N. Via Lucia, Tucson, AZ 85745. Tel: 602-792-0122
Guillermo, Rodrigo J., M.S.Ch.E., M.B.A., c/o Chancery
Hebert, Marvin A., c/o Mr. Jude C. Hebert, 415 Jeannette Dr., Bridge City, TX 77611-3742
Horacek, Mark, Notre Dame, 7720 Boone Rd., Houston, TX 77072-3595. Tel: 713-498-4653
Hosko, George H., C.S.B., Supr., Dillon House, 1302 Kipling St., Houston, TX 77006-4297. Tel: 713-529-3994; 529-3970
Joubert, Gerard, O.P., 9946 Village Bell, Houston, TX 77038-2612. Tel: 713-820-3871
Kellick, John W., 6517 Burdock Dr., Santa Fe, TX 77510-9340. Tel: 409-925-6817
Lee, Lawrence, Pope John XXIII Residence, 2407 E. Holcombe Blvd., Houston, TX 77021-2023. Tel: 713-748-3115
Leonard, Lawrence J., C.M., Pope John Paul XXIII Residence, 2407 E. Holcombe Blvd., Houston, TX 77021-2023. Tel: 713-747-4844
Lynch, Denis
Madden, John F., C.S.B., Campus Ministry, Dillon House, 1302 Kipling St., Houston, TX 77006-4297. Tel: 713-529-3994; 529-3970
Murphy, Joseph R., S.S.J., 100 Ferol Ln., Highlands, TX 77562-3934 7. Tel: 713-426-3433
Natho, Clifton J., Christ the Good Shepherd Church, 18511 Klein Church Rd., Spring, TX 77379. Tel: 713-376-6831
O'Loughlin, Raphael, C.S.B., Dillon House, 1302 Kipling St., Houston, TX 77006-4297. Tel: 713-529-3994; 529-3970
Posluszny, Sylvester, Hospice Ste. Elizabeth, BP. 143, Freyming-Merlebach, 57804 France
Roussel, Joseph P., C.S.B., 1302 Kipling St., Houston, TX 77006-4297. Tel: 713-529-3994; 529-3970
Stredny, Anthony G., B.A.
Tran, John Chinh Chan, 8138 Lynn St., Houston, TX 77017-3050. Tel: 713-645-2834
Van Der Peet, Michael, S.C.J., Aids Ministry Support Group, St. Matthew Church, Scotland Yard Apts., 8450 Cambridge, #1174, Houston, TX 77054-3919. Tel: 713-797-1830
Volpe, C. Rocco, C.S.B., Dillon House, 1302 Kipling St., Houston, TX 77006-4297. Tel: 713-529-3994; 529-3970
Walker, Anselm, 1817 Parker, Houston, TX 77093. Tel: 713-697-7109
Weihrer, John A., Pope John XXIII Residence, 2407 East Holcombe Blvd., Houston, TX 77021-2023. Tel: 713-748-3130

Permanent Deacons:
Abram, Alfred, Sr., Harris County Jail, Houston
Acosta, Angel R., St. Mary, Texas City
Adame, David, Annunciation & St. Joseph Hospital, Houston
Adams, Francis E., St. Elizabeth Anne Seton, Houston
Adams, John W., St. Matthew the Evangelist, Houston
Aiuvalasit, Anthony George, St. John Vianney, Houston
Alessi, Anthony V., St. Thomas More, Houston
Alexander, Robert George, Mary Queen, Friendswood
Allen, Charles J., Sr., Our Mother of Mercy, Houston
Aranda, Jose Francisco, St. Christopher, Houston
Arceneaux, Leon M., Jr., St. Pius V, Pasadena
Arceneaux, Steve, Jr., St. Martin de Porres, Barrett Station
Arellano, Jose, Immaculate Heart of Mary, Houston
Arnold, Daniel, Diocese of Palm Beach, FL
Ausmus, Sam, III, Shrine of the True Cross, Dickinson
Baker, John M., St. Michael, Houston
Baker, Theodore Otis, St, Matthias the Apostle, Magnolia
Barnett, James, Our Lady of Walsingham, Houston
Bart, James, St. Augustine, Houston
Beckmann, Barry L., Transfer to D/Tyler
Betancourt, Manuel, Unassigned
Bobb, William J., St. Peter the Apostle, Galveston
Bonura, James L., Sr., TDC/Queen of Peace, La Marque
Bordelon, Darvin A., St. Helen, Pearland
Bothe, Albert G., St. Francis de Sales, Houston
Bottjer, Albert, Assumption, Houston
Bradley, Donald E., St. Cecilia, Houston
Breaux, Roy, St. Phillip of Jesus, Houston
Brinkman, Fred H., TDC-Ramsey Units/Drug Rehab. Ctr., Houston
Broussard, Leonard J., Epiphany of the Lord, Katy
Brueggerhoff, Robert T., Holy Ghost/Sacred Heart Co-Cathedral, Houston
Burns, Don, St. Theresa, Sugar Land
Cabler, Paul Stephen, Unassigned
Calonge, Elie, Transfer to Grants NM (D/Gallup)
Calvo, Clement S., Hispanic Ministry Office, Houston
Camerino, Pat W., Christ the Good Shepherd, Spring
Camunez, Richard F., St. Hyacinth, Deer Park
Cantu, Hector, St. Mary, La Porte
Carlson, Kenneth D., Sts. Simon & Jude, Woodlands
Carranza, Joe M., A/D St. Paul, MN
Caruso, James, St. Mary, Humble
Castaneda, Guillermo F., Jr., St. John Fisher, Richmond
Castillo, Raul A., St. Joseph, Brazoria
Charnisky, John E., Jr., Sts. Simon & Jude, Woodlands
Cooper, Leslie F., Christ the Good Shepherd, Spring
Coussirat, John F., St. John Vianney, Houston
Cox, Ralph, Diocese of Fall River, MA
Crawford, J. R., St. Anne, Tomball
Cromer, Frank P., St. Francis de Sales, Houston
Cuiper, Glen H., St. Ignatius of Loyola, Spring
D'Agnolo, Louis A., Diocese of Phoenix, AZ
Dalecki, Robert, Prince of Peace, Houston
Davies, Martin Henry, St. Mary Magdalene, Humble
Despania, Raymond L., Sr., St. Peter Claver, Houston
Devine, John E., Jr., St. Luke the Evangelist, Houston
Do, Joseph Chuong Nguyen, St. Jerome & Our Lady of Lourdes, Houston
Duck, Charles, Prince of Peace, Houston
Dunham, Robert K., Holy Name Retreat Center, Houston
Duplan, Jose, Jr., St. Mary's, Texas City
Dupont, Gerald W., St. Theresa, Sugar Land
Duron, Jose, St. Alphonsus, Houston
Ehrman, John W., Jr., Sacred Heart, Conroe
Elliott, W. Gregg, St. Cecelia Church, Houston
Embry, Robin, Diocese of Austin
Endris, Lou, Sacred Heart, Richmond
Evon, William J., Sr., St. Ignatius of Loyola, Spring
Festa, Gene, St. Justin Martyr, Houston
Fikac, Marvin R., Sacred Heart Co-Cathedral, Houston
Flores, Geronimo, St. Joseph, Houston
Floyd, Ivy C., St. Thomas the Apostle, Huntsville
Flynn, Robert E., Sr., Sts. Simon & Jude, Woodlands
Foreman, Boyce, Diocese of Austin
Fraser, Ronald J., St. Maximilian Kolbe, Houston
Garcia, Gerardo J., Christ the King, Houston
Garcia, Gregory C., Resurrection, Houston
Garza, Robert, St. Mary, League City
Gilbert, Daniel W., St. Francis Xavier, Houston
Glor, Richard J.L., Unassigned
Godinez-Galvan, Jorge, Diocese of Nuevo Laredo
Gomez, Arturo M., Notre Dame, Houston
Gomez, Javier, St. Andrew, Channelview
Gonzales, Emiliano, TDC Prison Chaplain, Houston
Gonzalez, Enrique, St. Charles Borromeo, Houston
Gonzalez Bangs, Fernando, Our Lady of Guadalupe, Baytown
Gosline, Edwin F., St. Thomas More, Houston
Graham, Michael G., St. John the Evangelist, Baytown
Gramman, Henry T., St. Christopher, Houston
Granado, Alfred E., Jr., Leave of Absence
Griesmyer, Steven, Sr., St. James the Apostle, Spring
Guajardo, Fredrico, Our Lady of Mt. Carmel, Houston
Guerra, Daniel, Sr., St. Clare of Assisi, Houston
Gutierrez, Diego, Sr., St. John the Baptist, Alvin
Hall, Raymond J., St. James the Apostle, Spring
Hamilton, L. William, Unassigned
Hargraves, Wilfred J., Jr., St. Clare of Assisi, Houston
Harper, Stephen Edwin, Epiphany of the Lord, Katy
Hart, Donald J., St. Pius V, Pasadena; Catholic Charismatic Center, Houston
Henry, Albert, St. Francis Xavier, Houston
Herrera, Rolando, Unassigned
Hickey, Dennis, St. Hyacinth, Deer Park
Hill, Russell, Diocese of Wheeling, Chareston, WV
Hite, James, St. Ignatius Loyola, Spring
Hock, Leslie Bart, Immaculate Conception, Houston
Hodapp, Cyril J., St. Bernadette, Houston
Holt, Grant E., Christ Our Light, Navasota
Horbowy, Thaddeus J., Federal Detention Center, Oakdale, LA
Horr, Louis Eugene, St. Jerome, Houston
Housholder, John, St. Helen, Pearland
Hubisz, John Lawrence, Jr., Raleigh, NC
Hunsucker, Paul David, St. Thomas the Apostle, Canyon Lake
Hunter, Thomas Alexander, Hospital/Port/St.Patrick, Galveston
Husch, John M., St. Michael, Lake Jackson
Jachimczyk, Joseph Alexander, Annunciation, Houston
Jackson, Clifford X., Our Lady of Sorrows, Houston
Jelinek, Gregory N., M.D., Christ Our Light, Navasota
Jenkins, Michael V., St. Francis Xavier, Houston
Johnson, Clarence B., St. Peter the Apostle, Houston
Joseph, Ignatius, St. Francis of Assisi, Houston
Kacz, Robert, TDC; St. John the Baptist, Alvin
Kelleher, Peter J., St. Christopher, Houston
Keller, Robert C., St. Justin Martyr, Houston
Kelly, Alfred John, Dr., Covington, LA
Kelly, Joseph R., Sr., Sacred Heart, Richmond
Kish, Don, Epiphany of the Lord, Katy
Klein, Hugo L., St. Francis de Sales, Houston
Knobloch, Alden J., St. Jerome, Houston
Koch, William E., Sr., Leave of Absence
Krupa, Joe, Archdiocese of San Antonio
Kulhanek, Jerry Peter, Sr., Our Lady of Fatima Church, Galena Park
Kutach, Emil W., Leave of Absence
LaBonte, Stephen L., Christ the Good Shepherd, Spring
Labrecque, Richard, St. Paul, Houston
Landry, Burke J., St. Elizabeth Ann Seton, Madisonville
Lansch, John, St. Justin Martyr, Houston
Laredo, Frank, Immaculate Conception, Sealy
Laugermann, Frank J., Jr., St. Benedict the Abbot & County Jail, Houston
Leach, Richard L., Christ the Redeemer; St. John Neumann, Houston
Leal, Merce C., Jr., St. Christopher, Houston
Leblanc, Irvin, St. Mary of the Purification, Houston
Leicht, Robert, Ramsey III TDC
Leija, Valeriano, Blessed Juan Diego, Pasadena
Lerma, Pedro, Sr., Blessed Sacrament, Houston
Lewis, Edward Thomas, St. Mary, La Porte
Liendo, Jose L., Queen of Peace, Houston
Llewellyn, Earl, Jr., TDCJ Hospital Chaplain, Galveston
Llorens, Cornelius C., St. Justin Martyr, Houston
Lopez, Richard, St. Thomas the Apostle, Huntsville
Lorino, Joseph E., St. Vincent de Paul, Houston
Loving, Peter, Diocese of Fort Wayne-South Bend, IN
Lozano, Rodrigo, St. Charles Borromeo, Houston
Lugo, Loni G., Holy Family, Missouri City
Lynch, Philip F., Unassigned
Marquez, Antonio, St. Raphael Mission, Houston
Martin, Henry Woods, St. Cyril of Alexandria, Houston
Martin, Kenneth, St. Edward, Spring
Matula, Francis L., All Saints, Houston
McAllister, Jerome, St. Mary, League City
McKinney, Thomas, Atoscosita Jail Facility
Mignogna, Joe, St. Edward, Spring
Miller, Arthur, Harris Co. Psychiatric Center, Houston
Miller, Stephen, St. Andrew, Channelview
Mitchell, David D., Holy Rosary, Rosenberg
Morales, Hector Hernando, Our Lady of Fatima, Galena Park
Moreno, Aurelio Frank, Jr., St. Frances Cabrini, Houston
Moreno, Leopold R., Resurrection, Houston
Morin, Joseph G., Immaculate Conception, Houston
Motley, John M., Unassigned
Moulton, Darrell, Mary Queen, Friendswood; Covenant House, Houston
Mulcare, Terrance D., St. Christopher, Houston
Navarro, Raul G., Immaculate Heart of Mary, Houston
Nelms, D. Cade, St. Cecilia, Houston
Newhouse, Thomas C., St. Thomas More, Houston
Nguyen Kim Khanh, Michael, Our Lady of Lavang, Houston
Nguyen Pham, Joseph, Vietnamese Martyrs, Houston
Nguyen Si Bach, Joseph, Our Lady of Lavang, Houston
O'Brien, Alfred J., TDC Stiles Unit, Beaumont
Ortego, Frank P., St. Thomas the Apostle, Huntsville
Osterhaus, James H., Christ the Redeemer, Houston
Ostrand, Gerard, St. Martha, Kingwood
Pareja, Juan Francisco, St. Jerome, Houston
Parr, Kenneth, Catholic Charismatic Center, Houston
Payne, George, Leave of Absence
Peltier, Gerald, St. Anthony, Danbury
Pennell, Charles G., St. Elizabeth Ann Seton, Houston

Petereit, Klaus, St. John Newmann, Houston
Pistone, John Salvadore, St. Mary's Cathedral Basilica, Galveston
Poth, Louis J., Diocese of Fort Worth
Ramirez, Fernando, St. Frances Cabrini, Houston
Ramirez, Jose J., Resurrection, Houston
Ramirez, Julio M., St. Gregory the Great, Houston
Ramirez, Leonard, Holy Family, Missouri City
Ries, Donald G., Sacred Heart, Richmond
Rincon, George, Our Lady of Guadalupe, Baytown
Risk, Ralph F., Archdiocese of San Antonio
Robison, Paul L., Jr., St. Luke the Evangelist, Houston
Rodriquez, Damian, Diocese of San Angelo
Roessler, Charles F., Jr., St. Frances Cabrini, Houston
Romeu, Hector J., St. John Vianney, Houston
Rook, R. Jack, St. Andrew, Channelview
Rooney, John, St. Frances Cabrini, Houston
Rowan, Vincent A., St. Michael, Lake Jackson
Rutledge, James E., St. Jerome, Houston
Salazar, Mariano, St. Joseph, Houston
Saltzmann, Peter, Catholic Charismatic Center, Houston
Sanchez, Martin G., St. Joseph, Houston
Sanders, Raymond L., Jr., St. Paul, Houston
Sandiford, Sid, Sts. Simon & Jude, The Woodlands
Sandoval, Alberto, Archdiocese of Santa Fe, NM
Santos, John, St. Andrew, Channelview
Satterwhite, Michael, St. Mary, Texas City
Schmidt, Glendon Michael, St. James, Spring; Sacred Heart, Conroe
Sechelski, Peter, TDC/St. Stanislaus, Anderson
Seifert, William E., Jr., Holy Family, Missouri City
Sharpless, James, St. Luke the Evangelist, Houston
Shaw, Wallace, St. Mary Star of the Sea, Freeport
Sheffield, William L., Christ Our Light, Navasota
Shefts, Andrew, St. Basil, Angleton
Sheltz, George A., Sr., St. Joseph Hospital/St. Vincent de Paul, Houston
Shetz, Fred T., Dir. Perm. Deacons, Sts. Simon & Jude, The Woodlands
Sicinski, Anton, St. Stanislaus, Anderson
Simon, Ronald, St. Philip Neri, Houston
Singer, John William, Jr., St. Joseph, Baytown
Smaistrla, Denis J., St. Mary's Seminary, Houston
Smith, Jimmy, St. Joseph, Brazoria
St. Aubin, Leo F., Sacred Heart, Conroe
Stanley, John, Terrell Unit, Livingston
Stasiulis, Stan, Diocese of Jackson, MS
Steffes, Dale W., St. John Vianney, Houston
Stevens, Robert Gregory, St. Francis Cabrini, Houston
Stoessel, Edward T., St. Thomas More, Houston
Stubbs, Peter, Holy Ghost Hall, Houston
Suriano, Julio S., Sacred Heart Co-Cathedral, Houston
Tassin, Terry, Diocese of Fort Worth
Tollett, Lee Joseph, St. Laurence, Sugar Land
Trosclair, George, Prince of Peace, Houston
Vacek, Albert E., Jr., St. John Vianney, Houston
Vaclavik, Larry A., St. Theresa, Houston
Vanderslice, Ron, Leave of Absence
Venegas, Rudy, Our Lady of Guadalupe, Baytown
Vicknair, Tom Jude, Catholic Charismatic Center, Houston
Villarreal, Gilbert R., St. Helen, Pearland
Villarreal, Marcelino, St. Benedict the Abbot, Houston
Vocelka, Frank Jay, Jr., St. Theresa, Houston
Wagner, William C., St. Bartholomew, Katy
Watkins, Rollo J., Christ the King, Houston
Weaver, Lonnie, Diocese of Fort Worth
Weaver, William A., St. Elizabeth Ann Seton, Houston
Welsh, James L., Diocese of Dallas
Werner, Robert Martin, Diocese of Amarillo
Wewer, Justin J., St. John the Evangelist, Baytown
Wiles, Philip Arlen, St. Dominic, Houston
Wright, Jim, St. Thomas Aquinas, Sugar Land
Wuenschel, Cyril, Diocese of Orlando, FL
Zamora, Joe, St. Augustine, Houston
Zuk, Adolph J., St. Matthew the Evangelist, Houston

INSTITUTIONS LOCATED IN THE DIOCESE

[A] SEMINARIES, DIOCESAN

HOUSTON. *St. Mary's Seminary*, 9845 Memorial Dr., 77024-3498. Tel: 713-686-4345. Rev. Msgr. Chester L. Borski, Rector; Rev. Msgr. Reginald Nesvadba, Vice Rector; Revs. Leon Strieder (AUS), Formation Dir.; Michael Howell (CC), Formation Dir.; John Kha Tran, Formation Dir.; Drew Wood, Spiritual Dir.; Edward Abell, Spiritual Dir.; Anthony Dao, O.P., Formation Dir.; Sr. Barbara Tovar, M.C.D.P., Dir., Cultural Formation; Deacon Denis J. Smaistrla, Treas.-Plant Mgr.; Revs. Louis T. Brusatti, C.M., Dean, School of Theology; James B. Anderson, Asst. Prof., Systematic Theology; Dr. Frances Panchok, Prof., Church History; Dr. Michael Prokurat, Asst. Prof., Sacred Scripture; Dr. Sandra Magie, Asst. Prof., Moral Theology; Dr. Richard Gaillardetz, Asst. Prof. Systematic Theology; Dr. Margaret Ayers, Asst. Prof., Pastoral Theology; Rev. Sean Martin, Asst. Prof. Sacred Scripture. Lay Teachers 4; Diocesan Seminarians 54; Religious Seminarians 8; Total Enrollment 158.

[B] SEMINARIES, RELIGIOUS, OR SCHOLASTICATES

HOUSTON. *Casa San Basilio*, 1910 W. Alabama, 77098. Tel: 713-522-1736. Rev. Alvin A. Sinasac, C.S.B., Dir.
Purpose: House of formation for Hispanic men in Religious life discernment (Spanish language). Apostolate of the Basilian Fathers. Total Enrollment 2.

Holy Ghost Fathers, Holy Ghost Seminary, 4410 Yoakum Blvd., 77006-5820. Tel: 713-529-0405. Rev. John J. Walsh, C.S.Sp.; Deacon Peter Stubbs, C.S.Sp., Dir. of House Formator; Mrs. Judy Stubbs, Bursar Formator; Revs. Frankie L. G. Santos, C.S.Sp., Vocation/Formation Dir.; Binh The Quach, C.S.Sp., Vocation Co-Director; Anton Morgenroth, C.S.Sp., (Retired).

St. Basil Novitiate, 106 Fifth St., 77478-2631. Tel: 713-491-8700.

[C] COLLEGES AND UNIVERSITIES

HOUSTON. *University of St. Thomas*, 3800 Montrose Blvd., 77006-4696. Tel: 713-522-7911.
For a complete listing, refer to the Colleges and Universities section.

[D] HIGH SCHOOLS, DIOCESAN

GALVESTON. *O'Connell High School*, 1320 Tremont St., 77550-4513. Tel: 409-765-5534; Fax: 409-765-5536. Sr. Mary Frances Heins, O.P., Prin.; Ms. Cathy Ford, Business Mgr. Sisters 3; Lay Teachers 18; Students 182.

HOUSTON. *Mt. Carmel High School*, 6700 Mt. Carmel Dr., 77087. Tel: 713-649-2745; Fax: 713-649-6851. Mr. Anthony M. Durso, Prin. Priests 1; Lay Teachers 20; Students 228.

[E] JUNIOR HIGH SCHOOLS, DIOCESAN

HOUSTON. *Seton Catholic Jr. High School*, 801 Rose Ln., 77037-4696. Tel: 713-447-2132; Fax: 713-447-1825. Miss Mary Jo Smith, Prin. Sisters 2; Principals 1; Assistant Principals; 1; Counselors 1; Development Directors 1; Lay Teachers 16; Total Staff 21; Students 313.

[F] HIGH SCHOOLS, PRIVATE

HOUSTON. *Academy of the Incarnate Word*, 609 Crawford St., 77002-3668. Tel: 713-227-3637; Fax: 713-227-1014. Sisters of the Incarnate Word and Blessed Sacrament. Ms. Mary Welch, Prin. Sisters 2; Lay Teachers 19; Girls 250.

Duchesne Academy of the Sacred Heart, 10202 Memorial Dr., 77024-3299. Tel: 713-468-8211. Religious of the Sacred Heart. Sr. Paula Toner, R.S.C.J., Headmistress. Sisters 1; Lay Teachers 31; Girls 201.

St. Agnes Academy, 9000 Bellaire Blvd., 77036-4683. Sr. Mary Joseph Roach, O.P., Pres. Tel: 713-219-5401; Sr. Jane Meyer, O.P., Prin. Tel: 713-219-5450. Dominican Sisters 3; Lay Teachers 59; Girls 743.

St. Pius X High School, Inc., 811 W. Donovan, 77091-5699. Tel: 713-692-3581. Sr. Donna M. Pollard, O.P., Prin. Dominican Sisters 3; Lay Teachers 50; Total Staff 66; Students 615.

St. Thomas High School, 4500 Memorial Dr., 77007-7332. Tel: 713-864-6348 (School); 868-9209 (Residence); Fax: 713-864-5750. Basilian Residence, Basilian Fathers. Revs. Jack H. Hanna, C.S.B., Supr.; Michael P. Cerretto, C.S.B., Prin.; Carl L. Belisch, C.S.B.; Edward A. Doser, C.S.B.; William Vela, C.S.B.; Norbert C. Reuss, C.S.B. Priests 6; Lay Teachers 54; Boys 650.

Strake, Jesuit College Preparatory Inc., 8900 Bellaire Blvd., 77036-4699. Tel: 713-774-7651; Fax: 713-774-6427. Rev. Brian F. Zinnamon, S.J., Pres.; Mr. Richard Nevle, Prin.; Revs. Christopher A. Billac, S.J.; Edward T. Coles, S.J.; John N. Folzenlogen, S.J.; Douglas J. Hypolite, S.J., Rector; Joseph B. Leininger, S.J.; Vincent A. Orlando, S.J.; D. Richard Toye, S.J.; Bros. Castenzio A. Ferlita, S.J.; Gerald J. Landry, S.J. Scholastics: Harlan W. Fails. Teachers: Priests 8; Brothers 1; Lay Teachers 49; Boys 697.

[G] ELEMENTARY SCHOOLS, PRIVATE

HOUSTON. *Duchesne Academy of the Sacred Heart*, 10202 Memorial Dr., 77024-3299. Tel: 713-468-8211. Sr. Jan Dunn, R.S.C.J., Headmistress. Lay Teachers 29; Total Staff 52; Girls 405.

John Paul II Catholic School, 1400 Parkway Plaza, 77077. Tel: 713-496-1500; Fax: 713-496-2943. Clarice Franke, Prin. Sisters 1; Lay Teachers 29; Students 502.

The Regis School, 7330 Westview Dr., 77055-5122. Tel: 713-682-8383; Fax: 713-682-8388. Catholic School for Boys. Anne Storey Carty, Headmistress. Lay Teachers 15; Students 124.

St. Catherine's Montessori, 2510 Westridge, 77054. Tel: 713-665-2195. Mailing Address: P.O. Box 20728, 77225-0728. Sisters 3; Lay Teachers 6; Students 191.

[H] ELEMENTARY SCHOOLS, CONSOLIDATED

GALVESTON. *Galveston Catholic School*, 2601 Ursuline Ave., 77550-4398. Tel: 409-765-6607. Mr. Dennis Pennington, Prin. Lay Teachers 27; Students 383. Serving the parishes of Holy Rosary, Sacred Heart, St. Mary Cathedral Basilica, St. Patrick, Queen of Peace Mission, St. Peter the Apostle.

NAVASOTA. *School of Environmental Education - Camp Kappe.* (Grade 5), Rte. 2, Box 3197, 77868-9604. Tel: 409-894-2141. Sr. Thomas Ann LaCour, O.P., Prin. Lay Teachers 2.

RICHWOOD. *Our Lady Queen of Peace*, 1600 Hwy. 2004, 77531. Tel: 409-265-3909. Mr. Jack Hawthorne, Prin. Sisters 1; Lay Teachers 20; Students 294. Serving the parishes of St. Basil; St. Thomas Aquinas Mission, Angleton; St. Joseph, Brazoria; St. Jerome, Clute; St. Anthony, Danbury; St. Henry; St. Mary, Star of the Sea, Freeport; St. Michael, Lake Jackson; Our Lady of Perpetual Help, Sweeney; St. John the Apostle Mission, West Columbia.

[I] SOCIAL AGENCIES CATHOLIC CHARITIES

HOUSTON. *Associated Catholic Charities of the Diocese of Galveston-Houston*, 3520 Montrose Blvd., P.O. Box 66508, 77266. Tel: 713-526-4611; Fax: 713-526-1546. Anna M. Babin, Exec. Dir.
Diocesan AIDS Ministry.
Catholic Charities, Galveston.
St. Joseph's Inn, Galveston.
Guadalupe Area Social Services.
Children's Placement Services.
Services to Pregnant Adolescents and Their Families.
Post Adoption Services.
Family Counseling.
Prevention Services.
Texas Center for Immigrant Legal Assistance.
Refugee Resettlement Program.
Unaccompanied Juvenile Foster Care Program.
Services to the Alone and Frail Elderly.
Serenity House.
Parish Social Ministry.

[J] HEALTH AND HOSPITALS

HOUSTON. *St. Joseph Hospital*, 1919 LaBranch, 77002. Tel: 713-757-1000.
For a complete listing, refer to the Hospitals section.
Sisters of Charity of the Incarnate Word, Houston, Texas, 2600 N. Loop W., 77092. Tel: 713-681-8877.
For a complete listing, refer to the Hospitals section.

NASSAU BAY. *St. John Hospital*, 2050 Space Park Dr., 77058. Tel: 713-333-5503; Fax: 713-333-8891.
For a complete listing, refer to the Hospitals section.

[K] CATHOLIC CHAPLAIN CORPS

HOUSTON. *The Catholic Chaplain Corps*, 4206 S. MacGregor Way, 77021-1598. Tel: 713-526-6438; Fax: 713-747-3642. Rev. Alcuin E. Greenburg, Dir. Houston Hospitals: St. Luke's Episcopal, Texas Heart Institute, Texas Children's Hospital, Methodist, M. D. Anderson Cancer Center - Hospital of University of Texas, Diagnostic, Shriners Hospital for Crippled Children, The Institute of Rehabilitation and Research, Ben Taub Hospital, Hermann Hospital, Diagnostic Center Hospital, Vencor Hospital.

Catholic Chaplain Corps, Texas Medical Center. Revs. Alcuin E. Greenburg; Joseph Bang; Elias E. Doroin; Joseph Haley; Bruce H. Noble; David H. Noble; Don A. Neumann; Donald E. Kuder, C.S.B.; Teodoro Tim Y. Prado.

Chaplain Corps, Southwest Memorial Center Complex, 10330 Hillcroft, 77096-4795. Rev. Joseph T. O'Malley.

Chaplain Corps, Lyndon B. Johnson Hospital. Tel: 713-526-6438 (24-hour paging).

Chaplain Corps, 3600 Brinkman, 77018-6329. Tel: 713-526-6438 (24 hour paging). Rev. Franklin Simmons.
Memorial City/Spring Branch Medical Complexes: Memorial City Medical Center Hospital.

Chaplain Corps: John Sealy Medical Center, U.T.M.B. Hospital, 2011 Ave. F (Church St.), Galveston, 77550-2091; Fax: 409-762-9612. Revs. Gerald Lewis, S.V.D.; Edward Baur, S.V.D.

[L] CLINICS

HOUSTON. *San Jose Clinic*, 301 Hamilton St., 77002. Tel: 713-228-9411; Fax: 713-228-6371. Sr. Margaret Bulmer, C.C.V.I., Exec. Dir. Sisters of Charity of the Incarnate Word 1; Patients assisted annually 21,570; Lay Staff 32.

[M] PROTECTIVE INSTITUTIONS

HOUSTON. *Casa de Esperanza, De Los Ninos, Inc.*, Mailing Address: P.O. Box 66581, 77006. Tel: 713-529-0639.
For a complete listing, refer to the Special Care Facilities section.

Casa Juan Diego, 4818 Rose, 77007. Tel: 713-869-7376.
For a complete listing, refer to the Special Care Facilities section.

Casa Maria de Guadalupe Medical Clinic and Social Service Center, 6101 Edgemoor, 77081. Tel: 713-995-9414.
For a complete listing, refer to the Special Care Facilities section.

Covenant House Texas, 1111 Lovett Blvd., 77006. Tel: 713-523-2231.
For a complete listing, refer to the Special Care Facilities section.

Santa Maria Hostel, 807 Paschall St., 77009. Tel: 713-228-0125.
For a complete listing, refer to the Special Care Facilities section.

[N] HOMES FOR THE AGED

HOUSTON. *Pope John XXIII Priest Residence*, 2407 E. Holcombe Blvd., 77021-2023. Tel: 713-748-4608.
For a complete listing, refer to the Special Care Facilities section.

St. Dominic Nursing Home, St. Dominic Center, 2409 E. Holcombe Blvd., 77021-2023. Tel: 713-741-8701.
For a complete listing, refer to the Special Care Facilities section.

St. Dominic Residence Hall, St. Dominic Diocesan Center, 2401 E. Holcombe Blvd., 77021-2023. Tel: 713-741-8700.
For a complete listing, refer to the Special Care Facilities section.

[O] RESIDENTIAL TREATMENT AND RENEWAL CENTERS

SPLENDORA. *Shalom Center, Inc.*, 13516 Morgan Dr., 77372-3121. Tel: 713-399-0520; Fax: 713-399-0520. A residential treatment center for clergy and religious. Sr. Gina Marie Iadanza, M.S.C., Exec. Dir.

[P] PERSONAL PRELATURES

HOUSTON. *Opus Dei.* (Prelature of the Holy Cross and Opus Dei), 5505 Chaucer Dr., 77005. Tel: 713-528-4081. Very Rev. Michael J. Barrett, Delegate Vicar; Revs. Jose Gomez; George W. Crafts.

[Q] MONASTERIES AND RESIDENCES OF PRIESTS AND BROTHERS

HOUSTON. *Carmelite Priory*, Casa Santa Teresita, 6725 Reed Rd., 77087-6830. Tel: 713-644-5561. Rev. Sean O'Leary, O.Carm., Dir. & Prior; Bro. Matthew Deffains, O.Carm. College level pre-novitiate house and program of formation for Hispanic candidates seeking admission to the Most Pure Heart of Mary Province of the Carmelite Order (O.Carm.). Students 6.

Congregation of the Mother Coredemptrix, Holy Family House, Rte. 4, Box 265 B (Oak Shadow), 77357. Tel: 713-354-4764. Rev. Anselm Dinh Vuong Can, C.M.C.

Dillon House, 1302 Kipling, 77006-4297. Tel: 713-529-3994; 529-3970 (Ans. machine); Fax: 713-942-7623. Basilian Fathers. Revs. George H. Hosko, C.S.B., Supr.; Norbert H. Clemens, C.S.B., (Retired); John F. Madden, C.S.B., (Retired); S. Raphael O'Loughlin, C.S.B., (Retired); Wilfred S. Canning, C.S.B., (Retired); Joseph B. Courtney, C.S.B., (Retired); Rocco C. Volpe, C.S.B., (Retired).

Dominican Fathers and Brothers, St. Mark Priory, Inc., 1702 Bolsover Rd., 77005-1726. Tel: 713-526-6411. Revs. Richard Martin Patrick, O.P., Prior; Joseph Ngoc Tu Nguyen, O.P.; Thomas D. Sheehan, O.P.; Isidore V. Vicente, O.P.; Daniel Ulloa, O.P.; Wilfred S. Canning, C.S.B., (Retired); Joseph B. Courtney, C.S.B., (Retired); Rocco C. Volpe, C.S.B., (Retired).
Assigned to St. Mark Priory, Residing Elsewhere: Rev. Terence A. Holachek, O.P., Corpus Christi, TX; Bro. John M. Cosgrove, O.P.; Rev. Stephen T. Smithers, O.P., Houston, TX. Total Assisted 100; Total Staff 10.

Franciscan Friars, 2508 Wilshire St., 77023-5246. Tel: 713-921-0259; Fax: 713-526-6010. Rev. Jeffrey Scheeler, O.F.M.

Franciscan Friars, 1508 Hyde Park Blvd., 77006. Tel: 713-524-7566. Mailing Address: P.O. Box 66669, 77266-6669. Bro. Robert Hozie, O.F.M., Supr.; Rev. Loren Connell, O.F.M.; Bro. David Crank, O.F.M.

Marianist Community, 6409 Brookside Dr., 77023-3323. Tel: 713-926-5925. Society of Mary. Bros. James E. Barrette, S.M.; Michael H. Gillespie, S.M.

Maryknoll Fathers and Brothers, 2360 Rice Blvd., 77005-2652. Tel: 713-529-1912; Fax: 713-529-0372. Revs. Rafael R. Davila, M.M., Dir.; Edward E. Schoellmann, M.M.; Paul R. Masson, M.M., Catholic Charismatic Center, 2500 Bell St., 77003. Tel: 713-236-9977. Rev. Richard E. Paulissen, M.M. Total in Residence 3; Total Staff 4.

Residence of the Basilian Fathers of the University of St. Thomas, 4019 Yoakum Blvd., 77006-4696. Tel: 713-525-3515; Fax: 713-529-0844. Revs. John C. Gallagher, C.S.B., Supr.; Dennis M. Andrews, C.S.B.; Edward A. Bader, C.S.B.; Edward J. Baenziger, C.S.B.; Patrick O. Braden, C.S.B.; Victor B. Brezik, C.S.B.; Robert W. Crooker, C.S.B.; Mark R. Gazin, C.S.B.; James J. Keon, C.S.B.; John E. McManus, C.S.B.; Joseph L. Meyers, C.S.B.; Harold V. O'Leary, C.S.B.; Joseph P. Roussel, C.S.B.; Richard J. Schiefen, C.S.B.; Frederick H. Sohn, C.S.B., Treas.; T. Patrick Warden, C.S.B.; William J. Young, C.S.B.; Janusz Ihnatowicz (Poland).

Western Province of the Congregation of the Holy Ghost, 1700 West Alabama St., 77098-2808. Tel: 713-522-2882; Fax: 713-522-8063. Very Rev. Donald S. Nesti, C.S.Sp., Supr.

BARRETT STATION. *Missionary Society of St. Paul, Inc. - U.S. Region*, 12606 Crosby-Lynchburg Rd., P.O. Box 3200, 77532-2200. Tel: 713-328-8931; Fax: 713-328-7306. Rev. Paul N. Ofoha, M.S.P., Local Supr.

MANVEL. *The Basilian Fathers' Monastery of Citeaux*, Mailing Address: 6502 County Rd. 48, 77578-2908. Rev. James J. Gaunt, C.S.B., Dir.

SUGAR LAND. *Basilian Mission Center*, 414 Main St., P.O. Box 708, 77487-0708. Tel: 713-242-3148. Revs. John R. Whitley, C.S.B., Supr., Mission Procurator, Treas.; Robert J. Klem, C.S.B.; W. Maximus Murphy, C.S.B.; Joseph P. Shannon, C.S.B. In res., Revs. Frederick L. Clay, C.S.B.; Wencil C. Pavlovsky, C.S.B.
Priests Serving in Foreign Missions: Revs. Francis A. Amico, C.S.B.; John L. Boscoe, C.S.B.; M. Marciano Dominguez, C.S.B.; Thomas P. Dugan, C.S.B.; Rene J. Espejel, C.S.B.; William J. Frankenberger, C.S.B.; Marco A. Hernandez, C.S.B.; Leonard A. Kennedy, C.S.B.; Francis J. Launtrie, C.S.B.; Rafael I. Lopera, C.S.B.; W. Hodgson Marshall, C.S.B.; W. Lawrence Moran, C.S.B.; Francois J. Morfin, C.S.B.; Jesse Owens, C.S.B.; W. Wallace Platt, C.S.B.; A. John Ruth, C.S.B.; Robert J. Seguin, C.S.B.; Thomas W. Sepulveda, C.S.B.; J. Vincent Thompson, C.S.B.; Clarence E. Watrin, C.S.B. Associates 18; Scholastics 14; Novices 5.

[R] CONVENTS AND RESIDENCES FOR SISTERS

HOUSTON. *Carmelite Sisters of the Sacred Heart (O.C.D.)*, 22 Farrell, 77022. Tel: 713-697-6020. Sr. Maria Esther Alonso; Sr. Antonia Albarron; Sr. Rosa Maria Diaz; Sr. Gloria Diaz; Sr. Aurora Gonzalez. Total Staff 5.

Casa de Esperanza, Mailing Address: P.O. Box 66581, 77266-6581. Tel: 713-529-0639. Sisters 10; Total Assisted 125; Total Staff 36.

Congregation of Divine Providence (C.D.P.), 2008 Southgate, 77030. Tel: 713-659-5461.
Other Addresses: 2800 West T.C. Jester, No. 15, 77018. Tel: 713-683-9762. 6427 Pinehurst, 77023. Tel: 713-926-2829. 2425 Sage, #174, 77056. Tel: 713-621-5269.

Congregation of the Incarnate Word & Blessed Sacrament (C.V.I.) (Houston), Incarnate Word Convent, 3400 Bradford Pl., 77025-1398. Tel: 713-668-0423. Casa Pacis Convent, 3428 Bradford Pl., 77025. Tel: 713-661-3785. Sisters 2. Incarnate Word Academy, 609 Crawford St., 77002. Tel: 713-223-4143. Sisters 6. St. Christopher Convent, 8711 Glen Loch, 77061. Tel: 713-649-4700. Sisters 2. Visitation Convent, 3702 Maroneal, 77025. Tel: 713-664-8370. Sisters 4. Our Lady of Lourdes Convent, 10114 Hwy 6, Hitchcock, 77563. Tel: 409-925-7237. Sisters 3. Sacred Heart Convent, 1015 N. Frazier, Conroe, 77301. Tel: 409-756-3051. Sisters 2. St. Joseph Convent, 1811 Carolina, Baytown, 77520. Tel: 713-422-7700. St. Michael Convent, 5515 W. 43rd, 77092. Tel: 713-682-2242. Sisters 40.

Congregation of the Lovers of the Cross of Thaibinh Diocese, N. Vietnam, 1919 Runnels, No. 268, 77003. Tel: 713-224-7233. Sisters 4.

Congregation of the Sisters of Charity of the Incarnate Word (CCVI), 6510 Lawndale, P.O. Box 230969, 77223-0969. Tel: 713-928-6053; Fax: 713-928-8148. Total Sisters in Congregation 261. St. Jeanne Convent. Sisters 2. Caritas Convent. Sisters 6. Marian Convent. Sisters 25. St. Anne Convent. Sisters 21. Ruah Community. Sisters 4. Villa de Matel. Sisters 10. St. Placidus Convent, 1500 S. Wayside Dr., P.O. Box 230969, 77223-0969. Tel: 713-928-6053. Sisters 33. Shalom Hermitage, 6510 Lawndale, P.O. Box 230969, 77223-0969. Tel: 713-921-5305. Sisters 2. Edith Stein Convent, 6405 Pinehurst, 77023. Tel: 713-926-6024. Sisters 3. Dubuis Convent, 6510 Lawndale Ave., P.O. Box 230696, 77223-0969. Tel: 713-748-8814. Sisters 3. St. Joseph Convent, 1919 La Branch St., 77002. Tel: 713-757-7485. Sisters 20. St. John Convent, 1623 Antigua Ln., 77058. Tel: 713-333-9363. Sisters 3. St. Mary's Convent, 4400 Ave. N., Galveston, 77550. Tel: 409-763-1971. Sisters 2.

Evelyn Malloy Education Fund for The Sisters of Charity of the Incarnate Word, 6510 Lawndale Ave., P.O. Box 230969, 77223-0969. Tel: 713-928-6053. Sr. John Marie Crowley, C.C.V.I.

Incarnate Word Charitable Trust, 6510 Lawndale, P.O. Box 230969, 77223-0969. Sr. John Marie Crowley, Chairperson.

Congregation of the Sisters of Charity of the Incarnate Word (C.C.V.I.), Mailing Address: P.O. Box 230969, 77223-0969. Villa de Matel, 6510 Lawndale Ave., 77023. Tel: 713-928-6053.

Incarnate Word Charitable Trust.

Evelyn Malloy Education Fund for the Sisters of Charity of the Incarnate Word, 6510 Lawndale Ave., P.O. Box 230969, 77023-0969. Tel: 713-928-6053. Sr. John Marie Crowley, C.C.V.I.

Dominican Sisters of Houston, Motherhouse Complex & Administrative Offices: 6501 Almeda Rd., 77021-2095. Tel: 713-747-3310; Fax: 713-747-4707. Legal Title: *Dominican Sisters of Houston (Congregation of the Sacred Heart) (O.P.) Dominican Convent.* The Sacred Heart Convent Retirement Trust.
Other Addresses: Aquinas House, 7400 Bellerive, No. 1306, 77036. Tel: 713-266-5106. Sisters 2. Gannon House Community, 2604 White Oak Dr., 77009. Tel: 713-868-5124. Sisters 3. Genesis House (Formation), 6505 Almeda Rd., 77021. Tel: 713-741-8298; 665-2195. Sisters 4. Magevney Convent, 6509-B Almeda Rd., 77021. Tel: 713-741-8342. Sisters 5. Queen of Peace Convent, 2330 Oakcliff, 77023. Tel: 713-923-8255. Sisters 4. Rose Lynch Convent, 6509-A Almeda Rd., 77021. Tel: 713-741-8369. Sisters 5. St. Benedict Convent, 3927 Grapevine, 77045. Tel: 713-433-8368. St. Catherine Convent, 6503 Almeda Rd., 77021. Tel: 713-748-8649. Sisters 5. St. Dominic Villa, 6504 Almeda Rd., 77021. Tel: 713-747-9425. Sisters 39. St. Francis de Sales Convent, 8018 Roos, 77036. Tel: 713-774-3674. Sisters 3. St. Joseph Convent, 6507 Almeda Rd., 77021. Tel: 713-741-8310; 747-3310. Sisters 5. Seton Convent, 801 Rose Ln., 77037. Tel: 713-447-2617. Sisters 3. Siena House, 1509 Hyde Park, 77006. Tel: 713-522-8416. Sisters 3. Sojourner House, 1039 LeGreen, 77009. Tel: 713-861-3870. Sisters 4. Dominican Convent, 2210 Avenue M, Galveston, 77550. Tel: 409-762-4878. Sisters 2. Camp Kappe, Rte. 2, Box 3197, 77868. Tel: 409-894-2141. Sisters 2. Wellsprings, P.O. Box 66463, 77266. Tel: 713-529-6559. Sisters 2. 3809 N. Braeswood, #11, 77025. Tel: 713-661-1534. 2800 W. T.C. Jester, #18, 77018. Tel: 713-957-0239. Charis House, 3233 Mangum Rd. #283, 77092. Tel: 713-688-3573. Sisters 2. 7447 Cambridge #101, 77054. Tel: 713-790-0230. 3809 N. Braeswood #8, 77025. Tel: 713-665-6457. 4102 Cherry Oak Cir., 77088. Tel: 713-847-9263. 109 N. Frazier, Conroe, 77301. Tel: 409-756-3051; 756-8186. 1660 W. T.C. Jester #623, 77008. Tel: 713-864-1905; 686-4345, Ext. 269. Dominican Sisters Convent, 8791 Hammerly Blvd. #248, 77080. Tel: 713-973-7817; 686-6990. Sisters 2. 5440 Braesvalley #142, 77096. Tel: 713-721-0998; 665-2195. 7992 Locke Ln. #8, 77063. Tel: 713-784-5447; 771-8392. Benincasa, 1802 Rosedale, 77004-5631. Tel: 713-521-9623. Sisters 3. Circle Lake Retreat, P.O. Box 1408, Pinehurst, 77362-1408. Tel: 713-356-6764. 9988 Windmill Lakes #1607, 77075. Tel: 713-910-5227.
St. Agnes Academy; St. Agnes Academy Foundation; St. Pius X High School; St. Pius High School Foundation, Inc.; The Sacred Heart Convent Retirement Trust.

Dominican Sisters-Vietnamese (O.P.), Inc., St. Catherine Convent, 5250 Gasmer Dr., 77035. Tel: 713-723-8250. Sisters 57. Vietnamese Dominican Sisters Novitiate & House of Study, 5250 Gasmer Dr., 77035. Tel: 713-723-8250. Mary Immaculate Convent, 5900 Chippewa Blvd., 77086. Tel: 713-445-9574. Sisters 7.

Eucharistic Missionaries of St. Theresa-Mexico (M.E.S.T.), St. John of the Cross Convent, 430 Bunker Hill, 77024. Tel: 713-461-8337. Sr. Olegaria Romero, M.E.S.T., Supr. Sisters 4.

Handmaids of the Sacred Heart of Pohang (H.S.H.), St. Andrew Kim Convent, 1706 Bingle Rd., 77055. Tel: 713-465-1196. Rev. Benedict Yong Tae Kim (Korea). Sisters 2.

Incarnate Word Convent, 3400 Bradford Pl., 77025-1398. Tel: 713-668-0423.

Maryknoll Sisters of St. Dominic (M.M.), 7490 Brompton, No. 265, 77025. Tel: 713-793-2480 (Office); 666-5245 (Home). 14515 Wunderlick Rd., No. 1603, 77069. Tel: 713-376-6831 (Office); 440-9994 (Home). Total in Residence 2.

Missionary Carmelites of St. Teresa (C.M.S.T.), Holy Family Provincial House, 9548 Deer Trail Dr., 77038. Tel: 713-445-5520; Fax: 713-445-5748. Divine Providence Convent, 9600 Deer Trail Dr., 77038. Tel: 713-847-3328. Sisters 6. Mt. Carmel House of Prayer, 9600 Deer Trail Dr., 77038. Tel: 713-445-8830. Sisters 10. Pre-Postulancy M. Margarita Dieguez, 9600 Deer Trail Dr., 77038. Tel: 713-820-3732. Sisters 2; Candidates 3.

Missionary Catechists of Divine Providence (M.C.D.P.) Casa Providencia, Blessed Sacrament Convent, 201 Hunt St., 77003. Tel: 713-223-2275. Our Lady of Sorrows Convent, 4703 Lelia St., 77026. Tel: 713-676-2630. 3907 Rotman, 77003. Tel: 713-227-2555. 5102 Irvington Blvd., 77009. Tel: 713-692-8266. St. Pius V Convent, 812 S. Main, 77506. St. Mary's Convent, 1400 Wilkins St., 77445. Tel: 409-826-2275. 1719 Knightwick, 77008. Tel: 713-862-2376.

Missionary Catechists of the Sacred Hearts of Jesus and Mary (M.C.S.H.S.M.). Our Lady of Guadalupe Convent, 502 Carlisle St., Rosenberg, 77471. Tel: 713-232-5500. Sisters 3.

Missionary Sisters of the Immaculate Conception (S.M.I.C.), 6414 Ludington, 77035. Tel: 713-729-6971. Total Assisted 151; Total Staff 2.

Our Lady of the Cenacle (R.C.), Cenacle Retreat House, 420 N. Kirkwood, 77079. Tel: 713-497-3131. Sr. Lois Dideon, Supr.; Sr. Mary Dennison; Sr. Thressa Heard; Sr. Emily Katz; Sr. Margaret Byrne; Sr. Elizabeth Mozina; Sr. Catherine Quinn. Sisters 30.

Religious of the Sacred Heart (R.S.C.J.), Duchesne Community, 10204 Memorial Dr., 77024. Tel: 713-467-5312; Fax: 713-468-8211. 1830 Arlington, 77008. Tel: 713-880-5230. Sisters 4. 2020 Harvard, 77008. Tel: 713-868-9607. Sisters 5. Sisters 5.

School Sisters of Notre Dame (S.S.N.D.) Community, 4010 Linkwood Dr., #902, 77025. Tel: 713-660-9317. Sisters 2.

Sisters for Christian Community (S.F.C.C.). SFCC Community, 109 N. Frazier, Conroe, 77301. Tel: 409-756-3051. Sacred Heart Convent, 105 N. Frazier St., 77301. Tel: 409-756-3051. St. Gregory the Great Convent, 5123 Calgary, 77016. Sr. Natalia Adame, S.F.C.C., 2200 Fountainview, #60, 77057. Sr. Ginny Braniff, S.F.C.C., 510 Manley St., Navasola, 77868-3905. Sr. Josefina Gutierrez, S.F.C.C., Sacred Heart Convent, 105 N. Frazier, Conroe, 77301. Sr. Isidra Hernandez, S.F.C.C., 3709 Lila, 77026. Sr. Juanita Martinez, S.F.C.C., 502 29th Ave. N., Texas City, 77590. Sr. Laurine Murragh, S.F.C.C.

Sisters of Loretto (S.L.), 2425 Sage Rd., No. 150, 77056. Tel: 713-623-2713; 468-8211.

Sisters of Providence of St. Mary of the Woods (Indiana) (S.P.), 4727 Oakshire, No. 2, 77027. Tel: 713-850-1687.

Sisters of St. Francis of the Providence of God (O.S.F., Whitehall, PA), P.O. Box 66581, 77266. Tel: 713-529-0639 (Work); 713-528-2940 (Res.).

Sisters of St. Francis-Our Lady of Lourdes (O.S.F.), Casa de Esperanza, 1801 Wichita, 77004. Tel: 713-529-0639.

Sisters of St. Mary of Namur (S.S.M.N.), Casa de Esperanza, 1807 Wichita, 77004. Tel: 713-529-0639. Sisters of St. Mary, 4119 Graustark, #3, 77006. Tel: 713-526-8175. Sisters of St. Mary, 3822 Braeswood, #135, 77025. Tel: 713-349-8901. Sisters 3.

Sisters of the Holy Family (S.S.F.), Our Mother of Mercy Convent, 2000 Benson St., 77020. Tel: 713-674-6560. St. Philip Neri Convent, 5503 Greylog, 77048. Tel: 713-733-5757. Sisters 6.

Sisters of the Holy Spirit and Mary Immaculate (S.H.Sp.), St. Charles Borromeo Convent, 9601 McGallon, 77076. Tel: 713-694-4264. Sr. Anne Finnerty, S.H.Sp., Gen. Supr. Tel: 210-533-5149; 533-5522; Fax 210-533-3434; Sr. Muriel Clarke; Sr. Pauline Hynes; Sr. Hilda Mangan, Our Lady of Fatima Convent, 1701 Ninth St., 77547. Tel: 713-674-1811. Sr. Martina Hoase, S.H.Sp. Sisters 3.

Sisters of the Sacred Heart (S.S.C.J.), Holy Name Convent, 1217 Hogan, 77009. Tel: 713-228-4500. Sisters 3. Immaculate Heart of Mary Convent, 7535 Ave. L, 77012. Tel: 713-921-5431. Sisters 4; Total Staff Both Addresses 5.

Vietnamese Carmelite Sisters of Our Lady of Mt. Carmel (O.C.A.), 1602 Adams St., 77489. Tel: 713-499-4281. Legal Title: *Vietnamese Carmelite Sisters of Our Lady of Mt. Carmel (O.C.A.) Vietnamese Carmelite Sisters*. Sisters 14; Novices 1.

DANBURY. *Incarnate Word and Blessed Sacrament Sisters*, St. Anthony Convent, 1603 N. Main St., 77534. Tel: 409-922-8533.

MISSOURI CITY. *Schoenstatt Sisters of Mary (I.S.S.M.)*, Holy Family Church, 1510 Fifth St., 77489. Tel: 713-499-6246.

NEW CANEY. *Discalced Carmelite Nuns (O.C.D.) Carmel of the Holy Trinity*, 1100 Parthenon Pl., 77357-3039. Tel: 713-399-0270; Fax: 713-689-3615. Sisters 12.

[S] RETREAT HOUSES

HOUSTON. *Cenacle Retreat House*, 420 N. Kirkwood, 77079. Tel: 713-497-3131. Congregation of Our Lady of the Retreat in the Cenacle. Sr. Lois Dideon, R.C., Supr.; Sr. Thressa Heard, R.C., Coord. of Ministry. Sisters 7.

Holy Name Retreat Center, 430 Bunker Hill Rd., 77024-6399. Tel: 713-464-0211; Fax: 713-464-0671. Revs. John Schork, C.P., Retreat Dir.; John P. Conley, C.P.; David Colhour, C.P., Assoc. Dir. Total in Residence 1; Total Staff 5.

Shalom House of Prayer, 6510 Lawndale Ave., P.O. Box 230969, 77223. Tel: 921-5305. Sr. Genevieve Marheineke, Hermit. Total in Residence 2.

DICKINSON. *Christian Renewal Center*, 1515 Hughes Rd., P.O. Box 635, 77539-0635. Tel: 713-337-1312 (Center); 337-7359 (OMI Res.). Rev. Edward W. Couch, O.M.I., Dir.; D. Drue Pollan, M.T.S., Exec. Admin. Associate Directors: Rev. Maurice Lange, O.M.I. In res., Rev. John Ward, O.M.I. Total in Residence 2; Total Staff 19.

[T] NEWMAN CENTERS

GALVESTON. *Newman Apostolate Center*, 1402 Broadway, 77550. Tel: 409-762-4202.

Texas A & M, University of Galveston, University of Texas, Medical Branch of Galveston College, College of the Mainland. Mr. James Bonura.

HOUSTON. *Rice University / Texas Medical Center Schools; Catholic Student Center*, 1703 Bolsover Rd., 77005. Tel: 713-526-3809; Fax: 713-526-6010. Co-Directors: Rev. Daniel Ulloa, O.P.; Sr. Kitty Carter, O.P. Total Staff 2.

San Jacinto Community College North Campus Newman Center, 5800 Uvalde, 77049. Tel: 713-458-2398. Ms. Delores Fischer.

San Jacinto Community College South Campus, Catholic Newman Association, 13735 Beamer Rd., 77089. Tel: 713-484-1900, Ext. 3509. Ms. Kathleen Doran Wood.

Texas Southern University Catholic Newman Hall, 3535 Wheeler, 77004. Tel: 713-747-9595. Rev. John J. Walsh, C.S.Sp. Total in Residence 1; Total Staff 4.

University of Houston Central Campus Catholic Newman Association, 203 A.D. Bruce Religion Center, 77204-3621. Catholic Center. Tel: 713-748-2529; 748-2342. Rev. Paul Gallagher, O.F.M. Campus Ministers: Rev. Isidore V. Vicente; Pamela Krinock.

University of Houston Downtown Catholic Campus Ministry, 1 Main St., Room 280 S., 77002. Tel: 713-221-8592.

University of Houston, Clear Lake City Newman Center. 1515 Hughes Rd., P.O. Box 635, Dickinson, 77539. Student Activities, 18519 Egret Bay, No. 1609, 77058. Tel: 713-488-9466. Rev. John Ward, O.M.I.

University of St. Thomas Campus Ministry, 3800 Montrose Blvd., 77006. Tel: 713-525-3589. Rev. Mark R. Gazin, C.S.B., Dir., Campus Ministry. Total Assisted (Centers) 100; Total in Residence 20; Total Staff (All Facilities) 12.

ALVIN. *Alvin Community College Newman Center*, 3110 Mustang Rd., 77511. Tel: 713-388-4646. Gillian Callen.

BAYTOWN. *Lee College Newman Center*, Mailing Address: P.O. Box 818, 77522. Tel: 713-427-5611. Mr. Ben Meese.

HUNTSVILLE. *Catholic Student Center, S.H.S.U.*, 1310 17th St., 77340-4415. Tel: 409-291-2620. Total Assisted 500.

LAKE JACKSON. *Brazosport College Newman Club*, 500 College Dr., 77566. Tel: 409-297-1821; 265-6131, Ext. 33F. Ms. Nelda Thrash.

PRAIRIE VIEW. *Prairie View A & M University Catholic Center*, P.O. Box 3027, 77446-3027. Tel: 409-857-3351. Rev. Robert B. Fisher, S.V.D. Total Staff 3.

SPRING. *North Harris College Newman Center*, 2700 W. Thorne Dr., 77073. Tel: 713-443-5546. Mrs. Bertha Parle.

[U] MISCELLANEOUS

HOUSTON. *A.I.I.L.S.* (Adult Institute of Independent Living Skills), 2403 E. Holcombe Blvd., 77021-2024. Tel: 713-741-8725.

Asociacion Nacional de Sacerdotes Hispanos, 2471 Bolsover, Ste. #442, 77005. Tel: 713-528-6517. Rev. Jose H. Gomez, Pres.

Berakah Alternative Investment Fund, 2476 Bolsover #272, 77005. Tel: 713-522-8028; Fax: 713-529-8411. Paul Degler, Exec. Dir. The Berekah Fund makes loans to spur economic development in low-income neighborhoods.

Catholic Charismatic Center, 2501 Leeland, P.O. Box 230287, 77223. Tel: 713-236-9977; 921-2736 (Res.). Rev. Richard E. Paulissen, M.M., Dir.

Catholic Clerical Student Fund, 9845 Memorial, 77024. Most Rev. Joseph A. Fiorenza, Chm.; Pat Salvat, Pres. Higher learning for the priesthood.

Charity Guild of Catholic Women, 1203 Lovett Blvd., 77006. Tel: 713-529-0995.

Charity Guild of St. Joseph, 3802 Piping Rock, 77027. Tel: 713-626-9788. Mrs. Catherine Cash, Pres., 4234 Whitman, 77027. Tel: 713-623-2935.

Education Foundation of the Diocese of Galveston-Houston, 1700 San Jacinto, 77002-8291. Tel: 713-659-5461. Thomas B. O'Toole, Treas.

Equestrian Order of the Holy Sepulchre of Jerusalem, 309 Knipp Rd., 77024. Tel: 713-468-5602. Mr. F. Russell Kendall, Knight of the Collar, Vice Gov. Gen., Member of the Grand Magisterium.

Southwestern Lieutenancy, Equestrian Order of the Holy Sepulchre of Jerusalem, 2121 Kirby #46, 77019. Tel: 713-520-7646; 222-2505. Mr. Andrew J. Layden, Lieutenant.

Jesuit Volunteer Corps: South, P.O. Box 3126, 77253-3126. Tel: 713-756-5095; Fax: 713-756-8928. Mr. Kevin O'Brien, Dir. Volunteer service organizations.

Kolbe Project, Inc., 1509 Fairview St., P.O. Box 66669, 77266-6669. Tel: 713-522-8182; Fax: 713-527-0439. Pastoral Staff: Rev. Loren Connell, O.F.M.; Bro. David Crank, O.F.M.

Sacred Military Constantinian Order of Saint George, American Delegation, 3731 Olympia, 77019-3029. Tel: 713-888-0242; Fax: 713-888-0345. Mr. David L. Garrison, Delegate.

St. Dominic Center, Inc., 2401 E. Holcombe, 77021. Tel: 713-741-8741. Jim Horstman, Admin.

St. Francis de Sales School Foundation, 8100 Roos, 77036. Tel: 713-774-7474.

St. Mary's Orphanage Board, Chancery Bldg., 1700 San Jacinto, P.O. Box 907, 77001. Tel: 713-659-5461. Most Rev. Joseph A. Fiorenza, Pres.; Rev. Msgr. Frank A. Lagana, Vice Pres.

St. Pius X High School Foundation, Inc., 811 W. Donovan, 77091-5699. Tel: 713-692-3581. Jim Clepper, Pres.

Sociedad San Martin de Porres, P.O. Box 7788, 77270-7788. Tel: 713-880-0091; Fax: 713-880-0091.

Southern Dominican Volunteer Program, 6501 Almeda Rd., 77021-2095. Tel: 713-747-3310. Sr. Elizabeth Ferguson, O.P., Pres.; Sr. Katie Gaspard, O.P., Prog. Admin.

CONROE. *Dogwood Foundation, Inc.*, P.O. Box 2774, 77305-2774. Tel: 409-588-2078. Ben J. Petru, Pres.

RELIGIOUS INSTITUTES OF MEN REPRESENTED IN THE DIOCESE

For further details refer to the corresponding bracketed number in the religious Institutes of Men or Women section.

[0140]—*The Augustinians*.—O.S.A.
[0170]—*Basilian Fathers*. (Toronto, Canada).—C.S.B.
[0470]—*The Capuchin Friars*.—O.F.M.Cap.
[0270]—*Carmelite Fathers & Brothers*. (Prov. of Most Pure Heart of Mary).—O.Carm.
[0350]—*Cistercians of the Strict Observance-Trappists*.—O.C.S.O.
[0220]—*Congregation of the Blessed Sacrament*.—S.S.S.
[1330]—*Congregation of the Mission*. (Southern Prov.).—C.M.
[]—*Congregation of the Mother Coredemptrix*.—C.M.C.
[1000]—*Congregation of the Passion*. (Chicago).—C.P.
[1130]—*Congregation of the Priests of the Sacred Heart*.—S.C.J.
[0520]—*Franciscan Friars*.—O.F.M.
[0650]—*Holy Ghost Fathers*. (Western Prov.).—C.S.Sp.
[0690]—*Jesuit Fathers and Brothers*. (New Orleans Prov.).—S.J.
[0800]—*Maryknoll*.—M.M.
[0720]—*The Missionaries of Our Lady of La Salette*. (Prov. of Mary Queen).—M.S.
[]—*Missionaries of St. Joseph*. (Mexico).—M.J.
[]—*Missionaries of St. Paul*.—M.S.P.
[0910]—*Oblates of Mary Immaculate*.—O.M.I.
[0430]—*Order of Preachers-Dominicans*. (Prov. of St. Albert the Great).—O.P.
[1310]—*Order of the Holy Trinity*.—O.SS.T.
[1030]—*Paulist Fathers*.—C.S.P.
[0610]—*Priests of the Congregation of Holy Cross*. (Houston).—C.S.C.
[1070]—*Redemptorist Fathers*. (New Orleans Vice Prov.).—C.SS.R.
[0700]—*St. Joseph's Society of the Sacred Heart*. (Baltimore, MD).—S.S.J.
[]—*Scalabrinians*.—C.S.

[1260]—*Society of Christ.*—S.Ch.
[0420]—*Society of the Divine Word.*—S.V.D.
[1250]—*Somascan Fathers.*—C.R.S.

RELIGIOUS INSTITUTES OF WOMEN REPRESENTED IN THE DIOCESE

[]—*Adrian Dominican Sisters.*—O.P.
[]—*Benedictine Sisters of the Sacred Heart.*—O.S.B.
[]—*Carmelite Missionaries of St. Teresa.*—C.M.S.T.
[]—*Carmelite Sisters of the Sacred Heart.*—C.S.C.
[]—*Congregation of Divine Providence.*—C.D.P.
[]—*Congregation of Our Lady of the Retreat in the Cenacle.*—R.C.
[]—*Congregation of St. Joseph.* (Cleveland, OH).—C.S.J.
[]—*Congregation of the Lovers of the Cross.* (N. Vietnam).—H.C.L.
[]—*Congregation of the Sisters of St. Joseph of Boston.*—C.S.J.
[]—*Cordi-Marian Missionary Sisters.*—M.C.M.
[]—*Daughters of Divine Love.*—D.D.L.
[0420]—*Discalced Carmelite Nuns.*—O.C.D.
[]—*Dominican Sisters.* Adrian, MI.—O.P.
[]—*Dominican Sisters.* (Congregation of the Sacred Heart).—O.P.
[]—*Eucharistic Missionaries of St. Theresa.* (Mexico).—M.E.S.T.
[]—*Handmaids of the Sacred Heart.* (N. Korea).—H.S.H.
[2470]—*Maryknoll Sisters of St. Dominic.*—M.M.
[]—*Missionary Catechists of Divine Providence.*—M.C.D.P.
[2700]—*Missionary Catechists of the Sacred Hearts of Jesus and Mary.*—M.C.
[]—*Missionary Sisters of the Immaculate Conception.*—S.M.I.C.
[]—*Missionary Sisters of the Sacred Heart.*—M.S.C.
[]—*Religious of the Sacred Heart*R.S.C.J.
[]—*Roman Union of the Order of St. Ursula.*—O.S.U.
[]—*Schoenstatt Sisters.* (Rockport, TX).—I.S.S.M.
[2970]—*School Sisters of Notre Dame.* (South Central Prov.).—S.S.N.D.
[]—*Sisters for the Christian Community.*—S.F.C.C.
[]—*Sisters of Charity.* Cincinnati, OH.—S.C.
[]—*Sisters of Charity of St. Elizabeth.*—S.C.
[]—*Sisters of Charity of the Incarnate Word.*—C.C.V.I.
[]—*Sisters of Charity of the Incarnate Word.* (San Antonio).—C.C.V.I.
[]—*Sisters of Our Lady of Mt. Carmel.* (Vietnamese).—O.C.A.
[]—*Sisters of Providence.* (St. Mary of the Woods, IN).—S.P.
[]—*Sisters of St. Francis.* (Sylvania, OH).—O.S.F.
[3840]—*Sisters of St. Joseph of Carondelet.*—C.S.J.
[3950]—*Sisters of St. Mary of Namur.*—S.S.M.N.
[]—*Sisters of the Holy Family.*—S.S.F.
[]—*Sisters of the Holy Spirit and Mary Immaculate.*—S.H.Sp.
[]—*Sisters of the Immaculate Heart of Mary.*—I.H.M.
[]—*Sisters of the Incarnate Word and Blessed Sacrament.*—C.V.I.
[]—*Sisters of the Incarnate Word and Blessed Sacrament.* (Corpus Christi).—I.W.B.S.
[]—*Sisters of the Incarnate Word and Blessed Sacrament.* (Victoria).—I.W.B.S.
[]—*Sisters of the Presentation of Mary.*—P.M.
[]—*Sisters of the Sacred Heart of Jesus.*—S.S.C.J.
[]—*Vietnamese Dominican Sisters.*—O.P.
[]—*Whitehall Franciscan Sisters.*—O.S.F.

DIOCESAN CEMETERIES

GALVESTON. *Old Catholic, Calvary.*
HOUSTON. *Holy Cross.*
St. Vincent.
DICKINSON. *Mount Olivet.*

NECROLOGY

† Aranda, Sofronio A., Houston, TX, Catholic Chaplain Corps, Texas Medical Center. —Died March 24, 1996.
† Flynn, Rev. Msgr. Cornelius P., (Retired). —Died Feb. 9, 1996.
† Fos, Rev. Msgr. John L., (Retired). —Died March 13, 1996.
† Krol, Michael F., (Retired). —Died Sept. 18, 1996.
† Missenda, Rev. Msgr. Edward S., Crosby, TX, Sacred Heart Church. —Died Dec. 19, 1995.
† Perhach, Ernest, (Retired). —Died Oct. 14, 1996.
† Price, Rev. Msgr. L. J., (Retired). —Died Sept. 29, 1995.
† Tinney, Rev. Msgr. William L., (Retired). —Died April 3, 1996.

Diocese of Gary

(Dioecesis Gariensis)

Most Reverend

DALE J. MELCZEK, D.D.

Bishop of Gary; ordained June 6, 1964; appointed Auxiliary Bishop of Detroit and Titular Bishop of Trau December 3, 1982; consecrated January 27, 1983; appointed Apostolic Administrator of Gary August 19, 1992; appointed Coadjutor Bishop of Gary October 20, 1995; succeeded to the See of Gary June 1, 1996. *Office: 9292 Broadway, Merrillville, IN, 46410.* Tel.: 219-769-9292; Fax: 219-769-2066.

Most Reverend

NORBERT F. GAUGHAN, D.D., PH.D.

Retired Bishop of Gary; ordained November 4, 1945; appointed Auxiliary Bishop of Greensburg and Titular Bishop of Taraqua April 2, 1975; consecrated June 26, 1975; appointed Bishop of Gary July 9, 1984; retired June 1, 1996. *The Chancery: 9292 Broadway, Merrillville, IN, 46410.*

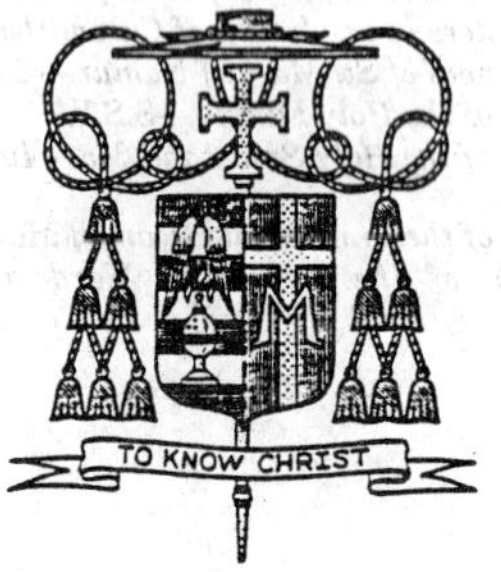

ESTABLISHED DECEMBER 17, 1956.

Square Miles 1,807.

Comprises the Counties of Lake, LaPorte, Porter and Starke in the State of Indiana.

For legal titles of parishes and diocesan institutions, consult the Chancery.

Chancery: 9292 Broadway, Merrillville, IN, 46410. Tel.: 219-769-9292; Fax: 219-738-9034.

STATISTICAL OVERVIEW

Personnel	
Bishop	1
Retired Bishops	1
Priests: Diocesan Active in Diocese	97
Priests: Active Outside Diocese	5
Priests: Diocesan in Foreign Missions	1
Priests: Retired, Sick or Absent	28
Number of Diocesan Priests	131
Religious Priests in Diocese	50
Extern Priests in Diocese	7
Ordinations:	
Diocesan Priests	2
Transitional Deacons	2
Permanent Deacons in Diocese	30
Total Brothers	20
Total Sisters	137
Parishes	
Parishes	79
With Resident Pastor:	
Resident Diocesan Priests	74
Resident Religious Priests	4
Without Resident Pastor:	
Administered by Priests	1
Missions	3
Pastoral Centers	7
Professional Ministry Personnel:	
Brothers	1
Sisters	16
Lay Ministers	37
Welfare	
Catholic Hospitals	6
Total Assisted	401,469
Homes for the Aged	3
Total Assisted	478
Residential Care of Children	4
Total Assisted	184
Day Care and Extended Day Care Centers	1
Total Assisted	200
Educational	
Diocesan Students in Other Seminaries	8
Seminaries, Religious	1
Students Religious	5
Total Seminarians	13
Colleges and Universities	1
Total Students	1,022
High Schools, Diocesan and Parish	3
Total Students	2,093
High Schools, Private	1
Total Students	105
Elementary Schools, Diocesan and Parish	30
Total Students	7,911
Elementary Schools, Private	1
Total Students	110
Catechesis/Religious Education:	
High School Students	948
Elementary Students	10,996
Total Students Under Catholic Instruction	23,198
Teachers in the Diocese:	
Priests	6
Brothers	3
Sisters	20
Lay Teachers	504
Vital Statistics	
Receptions into the Church:	
Infant Baptism Totals	2,638
Adult Baptism Totals	181
Received into Full Communion	282
First Communions	2,336
Confirmations	2,134
Marriages:	
Catholic	557
Interfaith	323
Total Marriages	880
Deaths	1,824
Total Catholic Population	184,516
Total Population	759,673

Former Bishops—Most Rev. ANDREW GREGORY GRUTKA, D.D., ord. Dec. 5, 1933; appt. Bishop of Gary Dec. 29, 1956; cons. February 25, 1957; retired July 9, 1984; died Nov. 11, 1993.—Most Rev. NORBERT F. GAUGHAN, D.D., Ph.D., ord. Nov. 4, 1945; appt. Auxiliary Bishop of Greensburg April 2, 1975; cons. June 26, 1975; appt. Bishop of Gary July 9, 1984; retired June 1, 1996.

Vicars General—Revs. JOSEPH M. PAWLOWSKI; GERALD H. SCHWEITZER.

Deans—Gary-Hobart Deanery: Rev. ROBERT P. GEHRING; Northlake County Deanery: Rev. STANLEY J. DOMINIK; SouthLake County Deanery: Rev. DAVID H. GOSNELL; Porter-Starke County Deanery: Rev. Msgr. RICHARD F. ZOLLINGER; LaPorte County Deanery: Rev. RICHARD H. AMELING.

Chancery—9292 Broadway, Merrillville, 46410. Tel: 219-769-9292; Fax: 219-738-9034.

Chancellor/Moderator of the Curia—Rev. GERALD H. SCHWEITZER.

Bishop's Delegate for Sexual Abuse Matters—Rev. Msgr. JOHN J. SIEKIERSKI, J.C.L.

Director of Finance and Administration—KARL DYTRYCH.

Secretary to the Bishop—VALERIE D. MCMANUS. Tel: 219-769-9181; Fax: 219-769-2066.

Diocesan Tribunal—9292 Broadway, Merrillville, 46410. Tel: 219-769-9292.

Judicial Vicar—Rev. JOSEPH F. GAZARKIEWICZ, J.C.L.

Adjutant Judicial Vicar—Rev. MATTHEW C. IWUJI, J.U.D.

Judges—Rev. JAMES W. MEADE, J.D., S.T.L., J.C.L.; Sr. THERESE GUERIN SULLIVAN, S.P., D.Min., J.C.L.

Defenders of the Bond—Revs. JAMES P. MCGROGAN; SAMMIE L. MALETTA, J.D., J.C.L.

Auditor-Advocate—Rev. THOMAS T. TIBBS.

Advocates—DONNA V. CALLAWAY; LINDA PLANER.

Promoter of Justice—Rev. JAMES P. MCGROGAN.

Notaries—VALERIE MCMANUS; MARY LESKO; DONNA CALLAWAY; MARY ANN O'CONNELL; JENNIFER POTCHEN.

Bishop's Council of Priests—Rev. Msgr. JOHN J. CHARLEBOIS; Rev. Msgr. RICHARD F. ZOLLINGER; Rev. Msgr. F. J. MELEVAGE; Rev. Msgr. DON C. GRASS; Revs. RICHARD H. AMELING; WILLIAM E. CREED, S.J.; ALFRED J. DETTMER; STANLEY J. DOMINIK; ROBERT P. GEHRING; DAVID H. GOSNELL; JOSEPH V. MURPHY; JOSEPH M. PAWLOWSKI; WALTER J. RAKOCZY; SAMMIE L. MALETTA; PATRICK J. KALICH; GERALD H. SCHWEITZER; DOMINIC V. BERTINO; MICHAEL J. YADRON; ROBERT J. TOKARZ.

Consultors—Rev. Msgr. RICHARD F. ZOLLINGER; Revs. ROBERT P. GEHRING; STANLEY J. DOMINIK; JOSEPH M. PAWLOWSKI; RICHARD H. AMELING; GERALD H. SCHWEITZER; DAVID H. GOSNELL.

Priests' Personnel Board—Rev. Msgr. JOSEPH F. SEMANCIK, M.S.W., Ph.D.; Rev. Msgr. RICHARD F. ZOLLINGER; Rev. Msgr. DON C. GRASS; Revs. JOSEPH M. PAWLOWSKI; JOSEPH F. GAZARKIEWICZ; RICHARD H. AMELING; STANLEY J. DOMINIK; ROBERT P. GEHRING; GERALD H. SCHWEITZER; DAVID H. GOSNELL; PATRICK J. CONNOLLY; STEPHEN J. TITKO.

Diocesan Offices and Directors

African American Catholic Ministry—Rev. CHARLES A. MOSLEY, Dir., *P.O. Box 436, Gary, 46402.* Tel: 219-882-3738.

Blue Army—Rev. MARK G. MAZZA, Chap., *303 Keller Ave., North Judson, 46366.* Tel: 219-896-2195.

Boy Scouts Liaison—Deacon WILLIAM E. JONES, *9542 McKinley, Crown Point, 46307.* Tel: 219-663-2112.

Campaign for Human Development—Rev. DERRICK F. DUDASH, Dir., *302 N. Madison, Hebron, 46341.* Tel: 219-996-4611.

Campus Ministry—See Catholic Student Center - St. Teresa of Avila and Indiana University Northwest.

Catholic Marriage Preparation Course—RITA MAYER, *Catholic Family Service, 973 W. 6th Ave., Gary, 46402.* Tel: 219-882-2759.

Catholic Student Center-St. Teresa of Avila (Valparaiso University)—Rev. DOUGLAS J. MAYER, Dir., *1511 LaPorte St., Valparaiso, 46383.* Tel: 219-464-4042.

Catholic Youth Organization (CYO) Office—FRANK R. KONTOR, Dir., *7725 Broadway, Ste. G, Merrillville, 46410.* Tel: 219-736-8931; Fax: 219-736-9457.

Cemeteries—Rev. STANLEY J. DOMINIK, Dir., *7113 Columbia Ave., Hammond, 46324.* Tel: 219-844-9027.

Charismatic Apostolate—Rev. JOHN V. SCOTT, Dir., *2949 Willowcreek Rd., Portage, 46368.* Tel: 219-762-4858.

Charities—Rev. Msgr. JOSEPH F. SEMANCIK, M.S.W., Ph.D., Dir., *973 W. Sixth Ave., Gary, 46402.* Tel: 219-882-2720.

Communications Office—BRIAN T. OLSZEWSKI, Dir., *9292 Broadway, Merrillville, 46410.* Tel: 219-769-9292.

Council of Catholic Women—Rev. ROY T. BEECHING, Diocesan Moderator, *5304 Hohman Ave., Hammond, 46320.* Tel: 219-932-0702.

Cursillos in Christianity—Revs. JUAN GONZALEZ, C.PP.S., Dir. (Spanish); EDWARD J. KENNEDY, *1445 Hoffman St., Hammond, 46327.* Tel: 219-931-5229.

Diaconate—Rev. J. PATRICK GAZA, Dir., *9292 Broadway, Merrillville, 46410.* Tel: 219-769-9292.

Ecumenical Officer—Rev. DOUGLAS J. MAYER, *356 W. Seven Mile Rd., Valparaiso, 46383.* Tel: 219-759-2400.

Education Department—Sr. ROSEMARY HICKMANN, O.P., Dir., *9292 Broadway, Merrillville, 46410.* Tel: 219-769-9292.

Family Life Ministry—RITA MAYER, Coord., *973 W. Sixth Ave., Gary, 46402.* Tel: 219-882-2720.

Finance Council—JOSEPH ALVARADO; DENNIS BIELFELDT; CALVIN E. BELLAMY; T. CLIFFORD FLEMING; JOSEPH F. GLOTZBACH, C.P.A.; KARL DYTRYCH; FELICIA FLOWERS SMITH; Revs. JOSEPH M. PAWLOWSKI; GERALD H. SCHWEITZER.

Girl Scout Liaison—Rev. THEODORE A. NORDQUIST, *109 C St., LaPorte, 46350.* Tel: 219-362-9595.

Health Care, Bishop's Representative—Rev. SAMMIE L. MALETTA, *200 E. 78th Ave., Merrillville, 46410.* Tel: 219-769-1973; Fax: 219-769-9056.

Heartland Project—Revs. THOMAS GANNON, S.J.; JAMES SCHULZ, S.J., *7128 Arizona Ave., Hammond, 46323.* Tel: 219-844-7515; Fax: 219-844-7566.

Holy Childhood Association—cf. Mission Office.

Hispanic Diocesan Ministries—ANGEL TORRES, Dir.; Sr. CONSUELO COVARRUBIAS, P.B.V.M., *4012 Elm St., East Chicago, 46312.* Tel: 219-397-2125.

Indiana Catholic Conference—Diocesan Co-Coordinators: Revs. JAMES W. SCHULTZ, S.J.; GERALD H. SCHWEITZER, *9292 Broadway, Merrillville, 46410.* Tel: 219-769-9292.

Indiana University Northwest—Rev. ROBERT P. GEHRING, *St. Mark Parish, 501 W. Ridge Rd., Gary, 46408.* Tel: 219-887-0514.

Lay Ministry Formation Office—Sr. HELEN HAYES, O.P., Dir., *9292 Broadway, Merrillville, 46410.* Tel: 219-769-9292.

Legal Counsel—Rev. SAMMIE L. MALETTA, *200 E. 78th Ave., Merrillville, 46410.* Tel: 219-769-1973; Fax: 219-769-9056.

Liturgy Office—Rev. MARTIN J. DOBRZYNSKI, Dir. JULIE VOLKMANN, Admin. Asst., *9292 Broadway, Merrillville, 46410.* Tel: 219-769-9292.

Ministry with the Physically and Mentally Challenged—Rev. JOHN J. ZEMELKO, Dir., *638 N. Calumet Rd., Chesterton, 46304.* Tel: 219-926-1282.

Mission Office—Rev. J. PATRICK GAZA, S.T.L., Dir., *9292 Broadway, Merrillville, 46410.* Tel: 219-769-9292.

Newspaper—"Northwest Indiana Catholic", BRIAN T. OLSZEWSKI, Editor; CAROL MACINGA, Circulation Mgr., *9292 Broadway, Merrillville, 46410.* Tel: 219-769-9292.

Peace and Social Justice, Office of—Rev. THOMAS GANNON, S.J., Dir., *7128 Arizona Ave., Hammond, 46323.* Tel: 219-844-7515; Fax: 219-844-7566.

Priestly Life Coordinator—Rev. Msgr. WILLIAM L. MARTIN, *11000 W. 133rd Ave., Cedar Lake, 46303.* Tel: 219-374-7160.

Pro-Life Activities—Rev. THEODORE J. MENS, Diocesan Dir., *525 N. Broad St., Griffith, 46319.* Tel: 219-924-4163.

Propagation of the Faith and Holy Childhood Association—cf. Mission Office.

Religious Education Office—Sr. CAROLINE CERVENY, S.S.J.-T.O.S.F., Dir., *9292 Broadway, Merrillville, 46410.* Tel: 219-769-9292.

Religious, Liaison for—Sr. THERESE G. SULLIVAN, S.P., J.C.L., *9292 Broadway, Merrillville, 46410.* Tel: 219-769-9292.

Retirement Plan of the Diocese of Gary, Indiana—JOSEPH F. GLOTZBACH, C.P.A., *9292 Broadway, Merrillville, 46410.* Tel: 219-769-9292.

Rural Life Conference—Rev. ANTHONY L. SPANLEY, *P.O. Box 230, Hamlet, 46532.* Tel: 219-867-2461.

Schools Office—Dr. JOHN M. SHIELDS, Supt. of Schools; ROSEMARY B. BRATTON, Assoc. Supt. Schools, *9292 Broadway, Merrillville, 46410.* Tel: 219-769-9292.

Sisters' Council—Sr. PHILOTHEA FABIAN, S.S.C.M., Chm., *5959 Broadway, Merrillville, 46410.* Tel: 219-887-5287.

Spiritual Life Center—Rev. WILLIAM E. CREED, S.J., Dir., *1441 Hoffman St., Hammond, 46327.* Tel: 219-932-8321.

Stewardship—Rev. JOSEPH V. MURPHY, *509 W. Division Rd., Valparaiso, 46383.* Tel: 219-464-1624.

Vocations—Rev. STEPHEN G. GIBSON, Dir., *812 W. 144th St., East Chicago, 46312.* Tel: 219-398-2409.

Youth Ministry—FRANK J. ZOLVINSKI, Dir., *9292 Broadway, Merrillville, 46410.* Tel: 219-769-9292.

CLERGY, PARISHES, MISSIONS AND PAROCHIAL SCHOOLS

CITY OF GARY
(Lake County)

1—CATHEDRAL OF HOLY ANGELS (1907), Rev. Matthew C. Iwuji.
Res., 640 Tyler St., 46402-2299. Tel: 219-882-6079.

2—BLESSED SACRAMENT (1947), Rev. Robert J. Tokarz.
Res., 1775 W. 41st Ave., 46408. Tel: 219-980-3081.
School—Tel: 219-980-5635.
Poor Handmaids of Jesus Christ 2; Lay Teachers 13; Students 213.
Catechesis/Religious Programs—Mrs. Lucille Highsmith, D.R.E.
Students 40.
Convent—6001 W. 25th Ave., 46406. Tel: 219-844-3212.

3—HOLY FAMILY (1926) (Polish), Rev. Stanley J. Milewski.
Res., 416 E. Ridge Rd., 46409. Tel: 219-884-1733.

4—HOLY ROSARY (1931), Rev. Ferdinand De Cristobal; Deacons Martin Gomez; Frederick Romanski.
Res., 719 Clark Rd., 46406. Tel: 219-944-1084.
Catechesis/Religious Programs—Sr. Rose Ann Kaiser, O.L.V.M., D.R.E.
Students 84.

5—HOLY TRINITY (1911) (African American), Rev. Charles A. Mosley.
Res., 410 W. 13th Ave., 46407. Tel: 219-885-2282.

6—SACRED HEART (1918) (Polish). Closed. For inquiries for parish records contact Cathedral of Holy Angels, Gary.

7—ST. ANN (1942), Rev. Stephen D. Kosinski.
Res., 6025 W. 25th Ave., 46406. Tel: 219-844-2448.

8—ST. ANTHONY (1918). Closed. For inquiries for parish records contact Cathedral of Holy Angels, Gary.

9—ST. CASIMIR (1916) (Lithuanian), Rev. Msgr. Ignatius L. Urbonas.
Res., 1390 W. 15th Ave., 46407. Tel: 219-882-1171.

10—ST. EMERIC (1911). Closed. For inquiries for parish records contact Holy Trinity (Hungarian), East Chicago.

11—ST. HEDWIG (1908) (Polish),
Serviced by Salvatorian Fathers. 1746 Pennsylvania St., 46407. Tel: 219-882-2584.; 5755 Pennsylvania St., Merrillville, 46410. Tel: 219-884-0714.

12—ST. JOSEPH THE WORKER (1912) (Croatian), Revs. Benedict Benakovic, O.F.M.Conv.; Stephen Loncar, O.F.M.Conv.
Res., 330 E. 45th Ave., 46409. Tel: 219-980-1846.

13—ST. LUKE (1917). See St. Monica, Gary.

14—ST. MARK (1921), Rev. Robert P. Gehring; Sr. Rose Ann O.L.V.M., Pastoral Assoc.
Res., 501 W. Ridge Rd., 46408. Tel: 219-887-0514.
School—3880 Jackson St., 46408. Maria E. Vazquez, Prin.
Lay Teachers 8; Students 150.

15—ST. MARY OF THE LAKE (1929), Rev. Joseph M. Pawlowski.
Res., 6060 Miller Ave., 46403. Tel: 219-938-1373.
Catechesis/Religious Programs—Tel: 219-938-9115. Mary K. Mauer, D.R.E.
Students 58.

16—SS. MONICA-ST. LUKE (1927; 1917), Rev. J. Patrick Gaza; Deacons Melvin Clark; Michael Richardson.
Res., 645 Rhode Island, 46402. Tel: 219-883-1861.
Catechesis/Religious Programs—Students 60.

OUTSIDE THE CITY OF GARY

Beverly Shores, Porter Co., St. Ann (1956), Rev. Charles E. Doyle.
Res., P.O. Box 727, 46301. Tel: 219-879-7565; Fax: 219-874-4349.

Cedar Lake, Lake Co., Holy Name (1859), Rev. Msgr. William L. Martin.
Res., 11000 W. 133rd Ave., 46303. Tel: 219-374-7160; Fax: 219-374-7165. [CEM]
Parish Center—13209 Schneider St., 46303. Tel: 219-374-8798.
Catechesis/Religious Programs—Tel: 219-374-8798.
Students 260.

Chesterton, Porter Co., St. Patrick (1858), Revs. Lawrence S. Heeg; John J. Zemelko; Deacon Nicholas Juracevich.
Parish Office & Mailing Address—638 N. Calumet Rd., 46304. Tel: 219-926-1282.
Res., 642 N. Calumet Rd., 46304. Tel: 219-926-9633. [CEM]
School—640 N. Calumet Rd., 46304. Tel: 219-926-1707. Ruth McCullough, Prin.
Lay Teachers 19; Students 182.
Catechesis/Religious Programs—Tel: 219-926-1265. Norma Dvorscak, D.R.E.
Students 580.

Crown Point, Lake Co., St. Mary (1865) (German), Rev. Msgr. Don C. Grass; Rev. Patrick J. Kalich.
Res., 321 E. Joliet St., 46307. Tel: 219-663-0044; Fax: 219-663-0676. [CEM]
School—405 E. Joliet St., 46307. Tel: 219-663-0676. Carole Bacon, Prin.
Lay Teachers 23; Students 577.
Catechesis/Religious Programs—Mrs. Jan Mucha, D.R.E.
Students 253.
Convent—22 E. Walnut St., 46307. Tel: 219-663-0420.

St. Matthias (1967), Rev. Terrence J. Steffens; Deacon Gregory Fabian.
Mailing Address: 2449 W. 125th Ave., 46307.
Res., 12505 Marshall St., 46307. Tel: 219-663-2201; Fax: 219-663-2567.
Catechesis/Religious Programs—Carol Mikuta, D.R.E.
Students 340.

Dyer, Lake Co., St. Joseph (1867), Rev. Mark S. Pavlina.
Res., 440 Joliet St., 46311. Tel: 219-865-2271. [CEM]
School—Tel: 219-865-2750; Fax: 219-865-2750. Mrs. Shirley Cyzon, Prin.
Lay Teachers 11; Students 175.
Catechesis/Religious Programs—430 Joliet St., 46311. Tel: 219-865-2355.
Students 302.

St. Maria Goretti (1977), Rev. Alfred Dettmer.
Res., 500 Northgate Dr., 46311. Tel: 219-865-8956; Fax: 219-322-1670.
Catechesis/Religious Programs—Tel: 219-322-6124. Joyce Peterson, D.R.E.
Students 362.

East Chicago, Lake Co.,

1—ASSUMPTION, (1915) (Slovak), Rev. Larry J. Kew.
Res., P.O. Box I, 46312. Tel: 219-398-0420.

2—HOLY TRINITY, (1916) (Croatian), Rev. Msgr. Paul P. Bogovich.
Res., 4754 Carey St., 46312. Tel: 219-398-3061.

3—HOLY TRINITY, (1906) (Hungarian), Rev. Alphonse Skerl.
Res., 4759 McCook Ave., 46312. Tel: 219-397-1907.

4—IMMACULATE CONCEPTION, (1933) (Italian). Closed. For inquiries for parish records contact St. Stanislaus, East Chicago.

5—OUR LADY OF GUADALUPE, (1927) (Hispanic), Revs. Juan Gonzalez, C.PP.S.; Diego J. Getting, C.PP.S.; Bro. Jerry Schwieterman, C.PP.S., Pastoral Assoc.
Office: 3510 Deodar St., P.O. Box 3400, 46312. Tel: 219-398-0253.
Res., 4001 Fir St., 46312. Tel: 219-398-5640.
School—Interparochial Consolidated, Tel: 219-397-1122; Fax: 219-397-1972.
Catechesis/Religious Programs—Tel: 219-398-1983. Sr. Irene DeMeulenaere, O.L.V.M., D.R.E.
Students 325.

6—SACRED HEART, (1926) (Slovak), Rev. Msgr. Joseph F. Semancik.
Res., 4423 Olcott Ave., 46312. Tel: 219-397-5857.

7—ST. FRANCIS, (1913) (Lithuanian). Closed. For inquiries for parish records contact St. John Cantius, East Chicago.

8—St. John Cantius, (1906) (Polish), Rev. Joseph R. Niezgoda. In res., Rev. Matthew Kish.
Res., 3903 Main St., P.O. Box C, 46312. Tel: 219-398-1370.
School—Indiana Catholic Elementary School, Tel: 219-397-1122.

9—St. Joseph, (1916) (Polish). Closed. For inquiries for parish records contact St. John Cantius, East Chicago.

10—St. Jude, (1933). Closed. For inquiries for parish records contact Our Lady of Guadalupe, East Chicago.

11—St. Mary, (1890), Revs. Stephen G. Gibson; Frank D. Torres.
822 W. 144th St., 46312. Tel: 219-398-2409.
School—Tel: 219-397-4404. Mr. Donald Domsich, Prin.
Lay Teachers 10; Students 198.
Catechesis/Religious Programs—Students 200.

12—St. Patrick, (1902), Rev. John T. Ambre.
Res., 3810 Grand Blvd., 46312. Tel: 219-398-1036; Fax: 219-398-1036.
School—Interparochial, Tel: 219-397-1122.
Catechesis/Religious Programs—3814 Grand Blvd., 46312. Tel: 219-398-1983.
Students 81.

13—St. Stanislaus, (1896) (Polish), Rev. Msgr. John J. Siekierski; Rev. Stanley Witek.
Res., 808 W. 150th St., 46312. Tel: 219-398-2341.
School—4930 Indianapolis Blvd., 46312. Tel: 219-398-1316. Patricia Panozzo, Prin.
Sisters of St. Joseph of the Third Order of St. Francis 4; Lay Teachers 13; Students 242.
Convent—4940 Indianapolis Blvd., 46312. Tel: 219-397-7059.

East Gary, Lake Co., (Name change - refer to Lake Station, Lake Co., IN, for all information.).

Fish Lake, La Porte Co., St. Anthony (1948), Rev. Michael G. Heimer.
Res., (Fish Lake) 7732 E. State Rd. 4, Walkerton, 46574. Tel: 219-369-1210.

Griffith, Lake Co., St. Mary (1928), Revs. Theodore J. Mens; James W. Meade. In res., Rev. Jon J. Plavcan.
Res., 525 N. Broad St., 46319. Tel: 219-924-4163; Fax: 219-922-2291.
School—Tel: 219-924-8633. Sr. Helen Minich, Prin.
Sisters of St. Francis of Perpetual Adoration 3; Lay Teachers 18; Students 358.
Catechesis/Religious Programs—Tel: 219-922-2277. Mrs. Laura Mathews, D.R.E.
Students 425.
Convent—508 N. Lafayette St., 46319. Tel: 219-922-2278.

Hamlet, Starke Co., Holy Cross (1888), Rev. Anthony L. Spanley.
Res., P.O. Box 230, 46532. Tel: 219-867-2461. [CEM]
Mission—Koontz Lake, Starke Co., St. Dominic, (1981) P.O. Box 230, 46532.

Hammond, Lake Co.,

1—All Saints, (1896), Rev. J. Antonio Valtierra.
Res., 570 Sibley St., P.O. Box 836, 46325-0836. Tel: 219-932-0204; Fax: 219-932-4507.
Catechesis/Religious Programs—Josephine Perez, D.R.E.
Students 126.

2—Our Lady of Perpetual Help, (1937), Revs. John R. Winterlin; Andrew Corona. In res., Deacon Thomas Kreidler.
Res., 7132 Arizona St., 46323. Tel: 219-844-3438; Fax: 219-844-3580.
Catechesis/Religious Programs—7128 Arizona St., 46323. Tel: 219-844-8722. Deborah Ormechea, D.R.E.
Students 80.

3—St. Casimir, (1890) (Polish), Revs. Vladimir Janeczek; Richard M. Penczynski.
Res., 4340 Johnson St., 46327. Tel: 219-931-2589.
School—4329 Cameron St., 46327. Tel: 219-932-2686. Mrs. Stasia Krempa, Prin.
Lay Teachers 7; Students 164.
Catechesis/Religious Programs—Students 50.

4—St. Catherine of Siena, (1956), Rev. Richard A. Orlinski.
Res., 6605 Kentucky Ave., 46323. Tel: 219-845-1939.
School—6525 Kentucky Ave., 46323. Tel: 219-845-1217. Christine Nielsen, Prin.
Poor Handmaids of Jesus Christ 1; Lay Teachers 8; Students 197.
Catechesis/Religious Programs—Tel: 219-845-2207. Susan Bates, D.R.E.
Students 125.
Convent—Tel: 219-845-5341.

5—St. John Bosco, (1934), Revs. Stanley J. Dominik; Peter J. Muha; Deacon Robert DeVore.
Res., 7113 Columbia Ave., 46324. Tel: 219-844-9027.
Pastoral Center: 1247-171st Pl., 46324. Tel: 219-844-6986.
School—(Grades K-8) 1231-171st Pl., 46324. Tel: 219-845-6226. James O'Donnell, Prin.
Lay Teachers 17; Students 257.
Catechesis/Religious Programs—Tel: 219-844-7874. Mrs. Kathy Hocker, D.R.E.
Students 245.

6—St. Joseph, (1879), Rev. Roy T. Beeching; Deacon James F. Etter.
Res., 5304 Hohman Ave., 46320. Tel: 219-932-0702; Fax: 219-932-0702.
Catechesis/Religious Programs—Tel: 219-932-7294. Sr. Barbara Koza, S.S.J.-T.O.S.F., D.R.E.
Students 132.

7—St. Margaret Mary, (1947), Deacon Gilbert Perez.
Res., 1445 Hoffman St., 46327. Tel: 219-931-5229; Fax: 219-937-4357.
Catechesis/Religious Programs—Students 120.

8—St. Mary, (1912) (Polish). Unassigned.
Res., 931 Merrill St., 46320. Tel: 219-932-2511.
Church—Morris & Tapper Aves., 46320.

Hebron, Porter Co., St. Helen (1946), Rev. Derrick F. Dudash.
Res., 302 N. Madison St., 46341. Tel: 219-996-4611.
Catechesis/Religious Programs—Tel: 219-996-4612. Teresa Barone, D.R.E.
Students 135.

Highland, Lake Co., Our Lady of Grace (1949), Revs. Edward J. Moszur; Edward J. Kennedy.
Office: 3005 Condit St., 46322. Tel: 219-838-0395; Fax: 219-972-6372.
School—3025 Highway Ave., 46322. Tel: 219-838-2901. Marilyn Tomko, Prin.
Sisters 1; Lay Teachers 17; Students 306.
Catechesis/Religious Programs—Tel: 219-838-6790. Mrs. Diane Foster, D.R.E.
Students 255.

St. James the Less (1967), Revs. Francis M. Lazar; Joseph A. Angotti; Deacons Martin Denkhoff; Raymond Dec.
Mailing Address: 9640 Kennedy Ave., 46322.
Res., 2703 45th St., 46322. Tel: 219-924-4220; Fax: 219-924-4295.
Catechesis/Religious Programs—Ruth Ann Rossi, D.R.E.
Students 420.

Hobart, Lake Co., St. Bridget (1873), Revs. Dominic V. Bertino; Andrew Malarz.
Res., 568 E. Second St., 46342. Tel: 219-942-6441; Fax: 219-942-4573.
School—107 Main St., 46342. Tel: 219-942-1894. Miss Dorothy Murphy, Prin.
Lay Teachers 15; Students 272.
Catechesis/Religious Programs—Students 250.

Kingsford Heights, La Porte Co., Immaculate Heart of Mary (1953), Rev. Walter M. Ciesla.
Res., Wayland Rd., 46346. Tel: 219-393-5061.
Catechesis/Religious Programs—Students 47.

Knox, Starke Co., St. Thomas Aquinas (1923), Rev. Msgr. Richard F. Zollinger.
Res., 406 E. Washington St., 46534. Tel: 219-772-4134.
Catechesis/Religious Programs—Students 58.

Kouts, Porter Co., St. Mary (1884), Rev. Thomas T. Tibbs.
Res., P.O. Box 663, 46347. Tel: 219-766-3680.
Catechesis/Religious Programs—Mary Martin, D.R.E.
Students 110.

Lake Station, Lake Co., St. Francis Xavier (1930), Rev. Robert B. Evers; Deacon Leonard Holland.
Res., 2447 Putnam St., 46405. Tel: 219-962-8626. [CEM]
School—2453 Putnam St., 46405. Tel: 219-962-4507. Carol Brendza, Prin.
Lay Teachers 4; Students 92.
Catechesis/Religious Programs—Kenneth Mayner, D.R.E.
Students 236.

La Porte, La Porte Co., St. Joseph (1858), Rev. Ted Nordquist; Deacon Robert Bucheit.
Res., 109 C St., 46350. Tel: 219-362-9595. [CEM]
School—101 C St., 46350. Tel: 219-362-6472. Sr. M. James Kuzell, Prin.
Sisters of St. Francis of Perpetual Adoration 2; Lay Teachers 11; Students 188.
Catechesis/Religious Programs—Sr. M. Robertann, D.R.E.
Students 120.
Convent—102 B St., 46350. Tel: 219-362-2587.

St. Peter (1853), Rev. George M. Vrabely.
Res., 1104 Monroe St., 46350. Tel: 219-362-6186.
Catechesis/Religious Programs—1110 Monroe St., 46350. Tel: 219-362-2509. Sr. Gloria Jean Kozlowski, D.R.E.
Students 365.

Sacred Heart (1912) (Polish), Rev. John J. Strebig.
Res., 128 Bach St., 46350. Tel: 219-362-2815.
Catechesis/Religious Programs—Tel: 219-362-9541. Joan Kowalczyk, D.R.E.
Students 136.

Lowell, Lake Co., St. Edward (1870), Rev. Thomas E. Mischler.
Res., 216 S. Nichols St., 46356. Tel: 219-696-7307; Fax: 219-696-3525. [CEM]
School—210 S. Nichols St., 46356. Tel: 219-696-9876; Fax: 219-696-2524.
Lay Teachers 11; Students 140.
Catechesis/Religious Programs—Tel: 219-696-4282. Veronica Grubb, D.R.E.
Students 249.
Mission—Shelby, Lake Co., St. Theresa, 23315 Shelby Rd., Shelby, 46377.

Merrillville, Lake Co.,

1—Our Lady of Consolation, (1947), Rev. Joseph E. Vamos; Deacon Robert E. Gill.
Res., 8303 Taft St., 46410. Tel: 219-769-2785; Fax: 219-769-2785.
Catechesis/Religious Programs—Tel: 219-769-1755. Bridget Bowman, D.R.E.
Students 387.

2—St. Andrew, (1965), Rev. David H. Gosnell.
Res., 801 W. 73rd Ave., 46410. Tel: 219-769-8534; Fax: 219-769-8543.
School—Tel: 219-769-2049. June Kachur, Prin.
Lay Teachers 9; Students 145.
Catechesis/Religious Programs—Tel: 219-769-2049.
Students 233.

3—St. Joan of Arc, (1968), Rev. Sammie L. Maletta.
Res., 200 E. 78th Ave., 46410. Tel: 219-769-1973; Fax: 219-769-9056.
Catechesis/Religious Programs—Tel: 219-769-2037. Anita Zolondz, D.R.E.
Students 100.
St. Joan of Arc Center—.

4—Ss. Peter and Paul, (1850), Rev. Dennis J. Teles.
Res., 5885 Harrison St., 46410. Tel: 219-980-2693. [CEM]
Catechesis/Religious Programs—Tel: 219-887-2940. Pat Parker, D.R.E.
Students 94.

5—St. Stephen, Martyr, (1968), Rev. David G. Nowak; Deacon Joseph Codespoti.
Res., 5920 Waite St., 46410. Tel: 219-980-9348.
Catechesis/Religious Programs—5885 Harrison, 46410. Tel: 219-887-2940.
Students 68.

Michigan City, La Porte Co.,

1—St. Mary of the Immaculate Conception, (1849), Rev. James P. McGrogan. In res., Rev. John B. Barasinski.
Res., 411 W. 11th St., 46360. Tel: 219-874-7231.
School—321 W. 11th St., 46360. Tel: 219-873-1321. James L. Faroh, Sr., Prin.
Lay Teachers 8; Students 193.

2—Notre Dame, (1953), Rev. Richard H. Ameling.
Res., 1010 Moore Rd., 46360. Tel: 219-872-4844.
School—Tel: 219-872-6216. Paul Cress, Prin.
Lay Teachers 12; Students 289.
Catechesis/Religious Programs—Students 70.

3—Queen of All Saints, (1950), Revs. Michael J. Yadron; William F. O'Toole; Alfred J. Dettmer.
Res., 526 S. Woodland Ave., 46360. Tel: 219-872-9196; Fax: 219-872-9176.
School—1715 E. Barker Ave., 46360. Tel: 219-872-4420. Larry E. Gondek, Prin.
Sisters of Holy Cross 1; Lay Teachers 20; Students 483.
Catechesis/Religious Programs—Tel: 219-878-9348. Theresa Glowacki, D.R.E.
Students 210.
Convent—606 S. Woodland Ave., 46360. Tel: 219-872-5401.

4—St. Stanislaus Kostka, (1891) (Polish), Rev. Msgr. Michael J. Tomaszewski; Deacon Daniel Bowmar.
Res., 109 Ann St., 46360. Tel: 219-879-9281.
School—1506 Washington St., 46360. Tel: 219-872-2258. Margaret Clifford, Prin.
Lay Teachers 9; Students 174.
Catechesis/Religious Programs—Tel: 219-879-6561. Antoinette Sajewski, D.R.E.
Students 100.

5—Sacred Heart, (1915) (Lebanese), Rev. Dennis J. Blaney.
Res., 1001 W. Eighth St., 46360. Tel: 219-874-3491.

Munster, Lake Co., St. Thomas More (1945), Revs. Richard A. Emerson; Keith M. Virus; Ian J. Williams; Deacon Joseph Sobek.
Res., 8501 Calumet Ave., 46321. Tel: 219-836-8610; Fax: 219-836-0945.
School—Tel: 219-836-9151; Fax: 219-836-0982. Patricia Carnahan, Prin.
Lay Teachers 30; Students 505.
Catechesis/Religious Programs—Tel: 219-836-9152. Mrs. Marietta Duray, D.R.E.

Students 863.

New Chicago, Lake Co., Assumption of the Blessed Virgin Mary (P.O. Hobart) (1917) (Polish), Rev. Martin J. Dobrzynski.
Res., 3530 Illinois St., Hobart, 46342. Tel: 219-962-1073.
Catechesis/Religious Programs—Tel: 219-962-6678.
Students 54.

North Judson, Starke Co., Ss. Cyril and Methodius (1881), Rev. Mark G. Mazza.
Res., 303 Keller Ave., 46366. Tel: 219-896-2195. [CEM]
Catechesis/Religious Programs—Students 81.

Otis, La Porte Co., St. Mary (1873), Rev. Joseph E. Pusateri.
Res., 101 N. Church St., 46391. Tel: 219-785-2212; Fax: 219-785-4743. [CEM]

Portage, Porter Co., Nativity of Our Savior (1964), Revs. John V. Scott; Kevin P. McCarthy; Deacons Robert J. Bonta; Alexander A. Saims.
Res., 2949 Willowcreek Rd., 46368. Tel: 219-762-4858.
School—2929 Willowcreek Rd., 46368. Tel: 219-763-2400. Jo Ann Abbott, Prin.
Lay Teachers 10; Students 222.
Catechesis/Religious Programs—Students 512.

Rolling Prairie, Laporte Co., St. John Kanty (1888) (Polish), Rev. Leonard J. Kronkowski.
Res., 6988N 600 E., 46371. Tel: 219-778-2935. [CEM]

Saint John, Lake Co., St. John Evangelist (1839), Revs. Stephen J. Titko; Kevin R. Huber.
Mailing Address: P.O. Box 360, 46373.
Res., 11211 W. 93rd St., 46373. Tel: 219-365-5678; Fax: 219-365-2703. [CEM]
Parish Office: 11350 School St., P.O. Box 360, St. John, 46373.
School—9400 Wicker Ave., St. John, 46373. Tel: 219-365-5451; Fax: 219-365-6173. Sr. Angela Mellady, Prin.
Sisters of St. Francis of Perpetual Adoration 3; Lay Teachers 16; Students 354.
Catechesis/Religious Programs—Tel: 219-365-3709. Arlene Crilley, D.R.E.
Students 335.
Convent—11340 School St., 46373. Tel: 219-365-3882.

San Pierre, Starke Co., All Saints (1858), Rev. William J. Spranger.
Res., P.O. Box 56, 46374. Tel: 219-828-4281. [CEM]

Schererville, Lake Co., St. Michael (1874), Rev. Patrick J. Connolly. In res., Revs. Joseph F. Gazarkiewicz; Terrence R. Chase.
Res., One Wilhelm St., 46375. Tel: 219-322-4505; Fax: 219-322-4508. [CEM]
School—16 W. Wilhelm St., 46375. Tel: 219-322-4531.
Franciscan Sisters of the Sacred Heart 1; Lay Teachers 18; Students 365.
Catechesis/Religious Programs—Tel: 219-322-3077.
Students 620.

Shelby, Lake Co., St. Theresa (1939), Rev. Thomas Mischler.
Res., 216 S. Nichols St., Lowell, 46356. Tel: 219-696-7307; Fax: 219-696-3525.

Valparaiso, Porter Co., Our Lady of Sorrows (South Haven) (1967), Rev. Douglas J. Mayer; Deacon Sherman Brown.
Res., 356 W. Seven Mile Rd., 46383. Tel: 219-759-2400; Fax: 219-759-6076.
Catechesis/Religious Programs—Tel: 219-759-2286.
Students 158.

St. Paul (1858), Rev. Msgr. John J. Charlebois; Deacon John McGuckin.
Mailing Address: P.O. Box 1475, 46384-1475.
Res., 452 W. Chicago St., 46383. Tel: 219-465-3723. [CEM]
Church—1855 Harrison Blvd., 46383. Tel: 219-464-4831; Fax: 219-464-4833.
School—352 W. Chicago St., 46383. Tel: 219-462-3374. Patricia Kohl, Prin.
Lay Teachers 12; Students 200.
Catechesis/Religious Programs—Tel: 219-464-8502.
Students 640.
Child Development Center—Tel: 219-465-0882. Janet McCorkle, Dir.

St. Elizabeth Seton (1978), Rev. Gerald A. Sroka; Deacon James J. Keough.
Res., 509 W. Division Rd., 46383. Tel: 219-464-1624; Fax: 219-465-7673.
Catechesis/Religious Programs—Tel: 219-462-2202. MaryAnn Kelley, D.R.E.
Students 638.

Wanatah, La Porte Co., Sacred Heart (1887), Rev. Gerald H. Schweitzer.
Res., 202 N. Ohio St, P.O. Box 386, 46390. Tel: 219-733-2955. [CEM]
Catechesis/Religious Programs—Tel: 219-733-2315.
Students 160.
Mission—LaCrosse, LaPorte Co., St. Martin, (1860) Lowell & Dominic Sts., LaCrosse, 46348.

Whiting, Lake Co.,

1—Immaculate Conception, (1922) (Slovak), Rev. Anthony D. Ficko.
Res., 2006 Schrage Ave., 46394. Tel: 219-659-0724.

2—Sacred Heart, (1889), Rev. Msgr. F. Raymond Fowerbaugh.
Res., 1731 Laporte Ave., 46394. Tel: 219-659-0733.
School—1723 Laporte Ave., 46394. Tel: 219-659-0705. James Repko, Prin.
Lay Teachers 7; Students 148.
Convent—1717 Laporte Ave., 46394. Tel: 219-659-1648.

3—St. Adalbert, (1902) (Polish), Rev. Walter J. Rakoczy.
Res., 1340 121st St., 46394. Tel: 219-659-3848.

4—St. John the Baptist, (1897) (Slovak), Revs. John E. Kalicky, C.PP.S.; Edward C. Homco, C.PP.S.; Matthew W. Jozefiak, C.PP.S.; Deacons David Hajduch; Joseph Manchak.
Res., Tel: 219-659-0023; Fax: 219-473-7551.
School—1844 Lincoln Ave., 46394. Tel: 219-659-3042. Thomas J. Puplava, Prin.
Lay Teachers 23; Students 450.
Catechesis/Religious Programs—Tel: 219-659-1889. Miss Lenore R. Lazur.
Students 140.

5—Sts. Peter and Paul, (1910), Rev. Charles W. Niblick.
Res., 1709 Center St., 46394. Tel: 219-659-1291.
Catechesis/Religious Programs—Students 70.

Chaplains of Public Institutions

Michigan City. *Indiana State Prison.* Revs. Joseph Lanzalaco, C.S.B.; Joseph Ross, C.S.C., 5959 Broadway, Merrillville, 46410. Tel: 219-887-5281; 887-5284.

Westville. *Westville Correctional Center.* Rev. Walter M. Ciesla, P.O. Box 190, Kingsford Heights, 46346. Tel: 219-393-5061.

On Duty Outside the Diocese:
Reverend Monsignors—
Charlebois, Robert L., 161 E. Chicago Ave., Chicago, IL 60611
Reverend Fathers—
Coriden, James A., Washington Theological Union, 9001 New Hampshire Ave., Silver Spring, MD 20903
Hand, Dennis M., Parroquia de lost Santos Inocentes, Apartado Postal #102, La Libertad, El Salvador
Hendricks, Clare, P.O. Box 8066, Columbia, TN 38401

Military Chaplains:
Reverend Fathers—
Nondorf, Aloysius J.

Graduate Studies:
Reverend Fathers—
Danforth, Clarence E., Convitto San Tommaso, Via degli Ibernesi, 20, Rome, 00184 Italy

Absent on Leave:
Reverend Fathers—
Montoro, Joseph J.
Murzyn, John A., Sick Leave, P.O. Box 817, Flager Beach, FL 32136

Retired:
Reverend Monsignors—
Doody, Timothy F., 1501 Hoffman St., Hammond, IN 46327
Hoffmann, Ralph G., 2103 Hawthorne Ln., Chesterton, IN 46304
Lengerich, Vincent L., 301 S. Main St., Knox, IN 46534
Litot, Edward F., 317 Waverly Rd., La Porte, IN 46350
Melevage, F. J., 3214 Milestone Creek Ct., Valparaiso, IN 46383
Morales, John F., 333 N. Palm Dr., #305, Beverly Hills, CA 90210
Senderak, Casimir E., 4330 Cameron Ave., Hammond, IN 46327
Van Nevel, Albert H., 11652 Patterson St., Cedar Lake, IN 46303
Witte, John C., 3713 S. State Rd. 104, La Porte, IN 46350
Reverend Fathers—
Bargielski, John C., Albertine Home, 1501 Hoffman St., Hammond, IN 46327
Daniels, John W., 425 Birch St., N.W., DeMotte, IN 46310
Fusco, Philip N., 3132 100th Pl., Highland, IN 46322
Kashmer, George B., 2501 Chelwood, N.E., Albuquerque, NM 87112
Kish, Matthew J., P.O. Box C, East Chicago, IN 46312
Lukaszewski, Leonard, 21-163rd St., Calumet City, IL 60409
Madejczyk, Louis S., 3599 Kingsway Dr., Crown Point, IN 46307
Mastey, Walter S., 235 Lawndale Dr., Munster, IN 46321
McGinnity, Ambrose T., 6450 S. State Rd. 10, Knox, IN 46534
Meneghello, Serafino, Via Oliosi, 13 San Massimo, Verona, Italy
Minnich, John F., P.O. Box 537, Georgetown, IN 47122
Peil, William L., 1841 N. Anthony Blvd., Fort Wayne, IN 46805
Pogorzelski, Eugeniusz, 1501 Hoffman St., Hammond, IN 46327
Shank, Bernard F., 2231 Hampton Dr., Apt. 8, Highland, IN 46322
Till, Joseph E., 317 W. 10th St., Michigan City, IN 46360
Vogt, William E., 4700 N. Pebble Ct., Muncie, IN 47304
Wozniak, Louis B., 1501 Hoffman St., Hammond, IN 46327
Zimmerman, Albert J., Albertine Home, 1501 Hoffman St., Hammond, IN 46327

Permanent Deacons:
Bonta, Robert J.
Bowmar, Daniel L.
Brah, Eugene
Brown, Sherman W.
Bucheit, Robert J.
Clark, Melvin
Codespoti, Joseph
Dec, Raymond
Denkhoff, Martin J.
DeVore, Robert S.
Etter, James F.
Fabian, Gregory G.
Gill, Robert E.
Gomez, Martin
Hajduch, David A.
Holland, Leonard D.
Jones, William E., Jr.
Jurasevich, Nicholas J.
Keough, James J.
Kreidler, Thomas
Maldonado, Felipe
Manchak, Joseph C.
McGuckin, John D.
Modrak, George V.
Perez, Gilberto
Richardson, Michael E.
Romanski, Frederick J., Sr.
Roscoe, John D., Sr.
Saims, Alexander A.
Sobek, Joseph J., Sr.

INSTITUTIONS LOCATED IN THE DIOCESE

[A] COLLEGES AND UNIVERSITIES

Whiting. *Calumet College of St. Joseph,* 2400 New York Ave., 46394. Tel: 219-473-7770.
For a complete listing, refer to the Colleges and Universities section.

[B] HIGH SCHOOLS, DIOCESAN

Hammond. *Bishop Noll Institute,* 1519 Hoffman St., 46327. Tel: 219-932-9058; Fax: 219-853-1736. Suzan LaPeer, Prin.; Rev. Andrew Corona. Priests 3; Lay Teachers 66; Students 987.

Merrillville. *Andrean High School,* 5959 Broadway, 46410. Tel: 219-887-5281. Rev. Paul E. Quanz, C.S.B., Prin.; Sr. Fabian Philothea, S.S.C.M., Asst. Prin.; Revs. John J. Fiore, C.S.B.; Ralph C. Koehler, C.S.B.; Joseph M. Lanzalaco, C.S.B. Basilian Fathers 4; Sisters of Sts. Cyril and Methodius 3; Lay Teachers 59;; Students 827.

Michigan City. *Marquette Catholic High School,* 306 W. Tenth St., 46360. Tel: 219-873-1325. Jim White, Prin. Sisters of the Holy Cross 1; Priests 1; Lay Teachers 14; Students 242.

[C] HIGH SCHOOLS, PRIVATE

LA PORTE. *LaLumiere School*, P.O. Box 5005, 46352. Tel: 219-326-7450. Coed College prep boarding and day school. Faculty 20; Students 105.

[D] ELEMENTARY SCHOOLS, DIOCESAN

GARY. *Sr. Thea Bowman Elementary School*, 975 W. Sixth Ave., 46402-1799. Tel: 219-883-1331. Mrs. Hazel Holmes, Prin. Lay Teachers 14; Total Staff 32; Students 386.

[E] ELEMENTARY SCHOOLS, PRIVATE

ROLLING PRAIRIE. *Le Mans Academy*. (Grades 5-9), 46371. Tel: 219-778-2521. Private boarding school for boys. Bro. William Dygent, C.S.C., Pres.; Rev. David H. Verhalen, C.S.C. Priests 1; Brothers 4; Lay Teachers 15; Total Staff 50; Enrollment 110.

[F] ELEMENTARY SCHOOLS, INTERPAROCHIAL

EAST CHICAGO. *Indiana Harbor Catholic Elementary School*, 3916 Pulaski St., 46312. Tel: 219-397-1122. Mrs. Francisca C. Phelps, Prin. Lay Teachers 8; Students 180. Serving the parishes of Assumption, Our Lady of Guadalupe, St John Cantius, and St. Patrick in East Chicago.

[G] GENERAL HOSPITALS

CROWN POINT. *St. Anthony Medical Center, Inc.*, 1201 S. Main St., 46307-8483. Tel: 219-738-2100.
For a complete listing, refer to the Hospitals section.

DYER. *St. Margaret Mercy Healthcare Centers, South Campus*, 24 Joliet, 46311. Tel: 219-932-2300.
For a complete listing, refer to the Hospitals section.

EAST CHICAGO. *St. Catherine Hospital*, 4321 Fir St., 46312. Tel: 219-392-1700; Fax: 219-392-7002.
For a complete listing, refer to the Hospitals section.

HAMMOND. *St. Margaret Mercy Healthcare Centers - North Campus*, 5454 Hohman Ave., 46320. Tel: 219-932-2300.
For a complete listing, refer to the Hospitals section.

HOBART. *St. Mary Medical Center*, 1500 S. Lake Park Ave., 46342. Tel: 219-942-0551; Fax: 219-947-6037.
For a complete listing, refer to the Hospitals section.

MICHIGAN CITY. *St. Anthony Hospital and Health Centers*, 301 W. Homer St., 46360. Tel: 219-879-8511.
For a complete listing, refer to the Hospitals section.

[H] PROTECTIVE INSTITUTIONS

EAST CHICAGO. *Carmelite Home for Girls*, 4840 Grasselli Ave., 46312. Tel: 219-397-1085; Fax: 219-392-3574.
For a complete listing, refer to the Special Care Facilities section.

HAMMOND. *Carmelite Home for Boys*, 4007 Sheffield Ave., 46327. Tel: 219-931-6451.
For a complete listing, refer to the Special Care Facilities section.

SCHERERVILLE. *Hoosier Boys' Town*, 7403 Cline Ave., 46375. Tel: 219-838-7723.
For a complete listing, refer to the Special Care Facilities section.

[I] HOMES FOR THE AGED

CROWN POINT. *St. Anthony Home, Inc.*, 203 Franciscan Dr., 46307-4824. Tel: 219-757-6281.
For a complete listing, refer to the Special Care Facilities section.

HAMMOND. *Albertine Home*, 1501 Hoffman St., 46327. Tel: 219-937-0575.
For a complete listing, refer to the Special Care Facilities section.

SAN PIERRE. *Holy Cross Care Services dba Little Company of Mary Health Facility, Inc.*, 7520 S. U.S. Hwy. 421, 46374-4275. Tel: 219-828-4111; Fax: 219-828-4172.
For a complete listing, refer to the Special Care Facilities section.

[J] PERSONAL PRELATURES

VALPARAISO. *Opus Dei*, 359 West 200 North, 46383. Tel: 219-462-6594; 462-0931. Prelature of the Holy Cross and Opus Dei, Shellbourne Conference Center. Legal Title: *The Work of God, Inc.*

[K] MONASTERIES AND RESIDENCES OF PRIESTS AND BROTHERS

CEDAR LAKE. *Our Lady of Lourdes Friary*, 12915 Parrish St., P.O. Box 156, 46303. Tel: 219-374-5931. Franciscan Friars of the Assumption of the B.V.M. Province (Order of Friars Minor). Revs. Anthony F. Janik, O.F.M., Guardian; Francis Appelt; George Dubowski, O.F.M.; Bede Hepnar, O.F.M.; Bronislaus Jaskulski, O.F.M.; Maynard Kolodziej; Andrew Meronek; Bert Pepowski; Clarence Mazur, O.F.M.; Patrick Szemla, O.F.M.; Carmen Scuderi, O.F.M. Priests 12; Brothers 3.

San Damiano Friary, 12921 Parrish St., P.O. Box 500, 46303. Tel: 219-374-5741; Fax: 219-374-9650. Cedar Lake Franciscan Friars (Order of Friars Minor). Interprovincial Novitiate. Revs. Donald P. Blaeser, O.F.M., Guardian; Thomas W. Luczak, O.F.M., Dir. Novices; Ronald F. Walters, O.F.M., J.C.L., Treas.; Bro. Edward Demyanovich, Vicar. Priests 3; Brothers 1; Novices 5.

EAST CHICAGO. *Roque Gonzalez Residence-Jesuit Fathers*, 3905 Fir St., 46312. Tel: 219-397-1885; 397-3906. Revs. William E. Creed, S.J.; Thomas M. Gannon, S.J.; James W. Schulz, S.J.

MERRILLVILLE. *Basilian Fathers Residence*, 5959 Broadway, 46410. Tel: 219-887-5284. Revs. John J. Fiore, C.S.B., Rector; Paul E. Quanz, C.S.B., First Councillor; Ralph C. Koehler, C.S.B., Treas.; Joseph M. Lanzalaco, C.S.B.; Michael P. Cerretto, C.S.B.; John Murphy, C.S.B.; Edward A. Zemelko, C.S.B. Associates: Bill May; David Savage. Priests 7; Associates 2.

Salvatorian Fathers (Society of the Divine Savior), 5755 Pennsylvania St., 46410. Tel: 219-884-0714. Mission House for Polish Priests and Brothers. Revs. Joseph R. Zuziak, S.D.S., Supr.; Waclaw Jamroz, S.D.S., Vice Supr.; Emil Jarco, S.D.S., Treas.; Wladyslaw Pawlik, S.D.S.; Norbert Stawowy, S.D.S.; Edward Kawa, S.D.S.; Bronislaw Jakubiec, S.D.S.; Bros. Marek Miazga, S.D.S.; Marian Tomasiak, S.D.S. Priests 7; Brothers 2.

MUNSTER. *Discalced Carmelite Fathers Monastery*, 1628 Ridge Rd., 46321. Tel: 219-838-7111; Fax: 219-838-7214. Revs. Thomas I. Balys, O.C.D., Prior; Bronislaw F. Socha, O.C.D., Subprior; Casimir Adalbert Borcz, O.C.D., Second Consultor; Michael G. Veneklase, O.C.D., Master of Novices; Waclaw L. Lech, O.C.D., Treas.; John Baptista Kolaczek, O.C.D.; Edward C. Spyrka, O.C.D.; Joseph Ivans, O.C.D.; Mark Nojek, O.C.D. Priests 9; Postulants 2.

[L] CONVENTS AND RESIDENCES OF SISTERS

EAST CHICAGO. *St. Catherine Convent*, 4325 Elm St., 46312. Tel: 219-398-0403. Poor Handmaids of Jesus Christ 5; Franciscan Sisters of Green Bay 1; Sisters of St. Joseph 1.

Saint Patrick Convent, 3814 Grand Blvd., 46312. Tel: 219-398-1983. Teaching and Parish Ministry, Our Lady of Victory Missionary Sisters; Health Ministry and Home Nursing, Poor Handmaids of Jesus Christ. Sisters 3.

HAMMOND. *Albertine Sisters (Prov. of Krakow, Poland)*, 1501 Hoffman St., 46327. Tel: 219-937-0575. Sr. Sigmunda Wojtusiak, Supr. Sisters 11.

MERRILLVILLE. *Convent of Sts. Cyril and Methodius*, 5959 Broadway, 46410. Tel: 219-887-5287. Teaching at Andrean High School. Sisters 4.

[M] RETREAT HOUSES

EAST CHICAGO. *Bethany Retreat House*, 2202 Lithuanica Ave., 46312. Tel: 219-398-5047. Sr. Joyce Diltz, P.H.J.C. Total Staff 3.

MICHIGAN CITY. *Angela House*, 412 W. 10th St., 46360. Tel: 219-873-1324. Sr. Anna Clare O'Connor, C.S.C., Dir.; Sr. Cyril Dubala, C.S.C. Total Staff 2; Total in Residence 2.

[N] DIOCESAN CHARITIES

GARY. *Catholic Charities*, 973 W. Sixth Ave., 46402. Tel: 219-882-2720; Fax: 219-886-2428. Rev. Msgr. Joseph F. Semancik, M.S.W., Ph.D., Dir. Coordination and supervision of social welfare program; Francis M. Moynihan, M.A., Admin.

Catholic Family Service, 973 W. Sixth Ave., 46402. Tel: 219-882-2723. Marcella Walters, M.S.W., Exec. Dir.

St. Mark's Center, 509 W. Ridge Rd., 46408. Tel: 219-980-1318. 3901 Fir St., East Chicago, 46312. Tel: 219-397-5803. 6919 Indianapolis Blvd., Hammond, 46324. Tel: 219-844-4883. 2967 Willowcreek Rd., Portage, 46368. Tel: 219-762-1177. 1501 Franklin St., Michigan City, 46360. Tel: 219-879-9312. 166 S. West St., Crown Point, 46307. Tel: 219-662-7677.

Family Life Ministry. Legal Title: *Family Life Ministry, Immigrant Documentation Program, Refugee Assistance Program, Rainbows For All God's Children, Caretaker Program, and Pastor's Emergency Fund*. 973 W. Sixth Ave., 46402. Tel: 219-882-2720.

Services to the Aging, Retired Senior Volunteer Program. LaPorte & Starke Co., 1501 Franklin St., Michigan City, 46360. Tel: 219-874-8195. Lake Co., 973 W. Sixth Ave., 46402. Tel: 219-882-2737.

Senior Companion Program. Lake Co., 973 W. Sixth Ave., 46402. Tel: 219-882-7331.

Society of St. Vincent DePaul.

Particular Council of Gary, 973 W. Sixth Ave., 46402. Tel: 219-882-2720. Rev. Theodore A. Nordquist, Moderator.

[O] NEWMAN APOSTOLATES

GARY. *Indiana University Northwest*, 501 W. Ridge Rd., 46408. Tel: 219-887-0514. Rev. Robert P. Gehring. For Catholic students attending Indiana University, Northwest. Students 5,000.

VALPARAISO. *Newman Apostolate-Valparaiso University*, 1511 La Porte Ave., 46383-5818. Tel: 219-464-4042. St. Teresa, Catholic Student Center of Avila. Chapel and Center for Catholic Students attending Valparaiso University. Rev. Douglas J. Mayer, Chap. Students 738.

[P] MISCELLANEOUS

DYER. *Amicare Home Health Services, Inc.*, 24 Joliet St., 46311. Tel: 219-322-1323. Mr. Gary Baum, Pres.

EAST CHICAGO. *Hispanic Ministry Office*, 4012 Elm St., 46312. Tel: 219-397-2125; Fax: 219-397-2168. Angel Torres, Dir.

Hispanic Catholic Center, 4012 Elm St., 46312. Tel: 219-397-3220.

Lakeshore Health System Incorporated (the "Corporation"). dba St. Catherine Hospital of East Chicago; dba St. Mary Medical Center (Hobart), 4321 Fir St., 46312. Tel: 219-392-7004; Fax: 219-392-7037. Affiliate of Ancilla Systems, Inc. Sponsored by the Poor Handmaids of Jesus Christ.

HAMMOND. *Alverno-Hammond Corporation*. 1515 Dragoon Tr., P.O. Box 1290, Mishawaka, 46546-1290.

Heartland Center, 7128 Arizona Ave., 46323. Tel: 219-844-7515; Fax: 219-844-7566. Office of Peace and Social Justice of the Diocese of Gary. Revs. Thomas M. Gannon, S.J.; James W. Schulz, S.J.

Seimetz Center, 1441 Hoffman, 46327. Tel: 219-933-0226. Rev. William Creed, S.J.

Spiritual Life Center, 1441 Hoffman St., 46327. Tel: 219-932-8321. Rev. William E. Creed, S.J., Dir. Total Staff 6.

HOBART. *Ancilla Systems, Inc.*, 1000 S. Lake Park Ave., 46342.

Ancilla Medical Foundation, Inc.

Ancilla Systems Foundation, Inc.

MICHIGAN CITY. *Alverno-Michigan City Corp*. 1515 Dragoon Tr., P.O. Box 1290, Mishawaka, 46546-1290.

VALPARAISO. *Camp Lawrence*. Diocesan Spiritual Center and Youth Camp. 68 E. 700 N., 46383. Tel: 219-462-8243; 462-5261. Catholic Youth Organization, 5284 Broadway, Merrillville, 46410. Tel: 219-887-9581.

RELIGIOUS INSTITUTES OF MEN REPRESENTED IN THE DIOCESE

For further details refer to the corresponding bracketed number in the Religious Institutes of Men or Women section.

[0170]—*Basilian Fathers*. (Toronto).—C.S.B.
[0600]—*Brothers of the Congregation of Holy Cross*.—C.S.C.
[0275]—*Carmelites of Mary Immaculate*. (India).—C.M.I.
[1130]—*Congregation of the Priests of the Sacred Heart*.—S.C.J.
[0480]—*Conventual Franciscans*. (Croatia).—O.F.M.Conv.
[0260]—*Discalced Carmelite Friars*. (Holy Ghost Prov., Poland).—O.C.D.
[0520]—*Franciscan Friars*. (Prov. of Assumption of B.V.M.; Prov. of St. John the Baptist; Prov. of the Sacred Heart).—O.F.M.
[0690]—*Jesuit Fathers and Brothers*.—S.J.
[0610]—*Priests of the Congregation of Holy Cross*.—C.S.C.
[1200]—*Society of the Divine Savior*.—S.D.S.
[1060]—*Society of the Precious Blood*.—C.PP.S.

RELIGIOUS INSTITUTES OF WOMEN REPRESENTED IN THE DIOCESE

[]—*Albertine Sisters*. (Prov. of Krakow, Poland).—C.S.A.
[0230]—*Benedictine Sisters of the Pontifical Jurisdiction*.—O.S.B.
[0360]—*Carmelite Sisters of the Divine Heart of Jesus*.—Carmel D.C.J.
[3710]—*Congregation of the Sisters of Saint Agnes*.—C.S.A.
[1920]—*Congregation of the Sisters of the Holy Cross*.—C.S.C.
[1070-03]—*Dominican Sisters*.—O.P.
[1070-13]—*Dominican Sisters*.—O.P.
[1210]—*Franciscan Sisters of Chicago*.—O.S.F.
[1450]—*Franciscan Sisters of the Sacred Heart*.—O.S.F.
[3130]—*Our Lady of Victory Missionary Sisters*.—O.L.V.M.
[3230]—*Poor Handmaids of Jesus Christ*.—P.H.J.C.
[2970]—*School Sisters of Notre Dame*.—S.S.N.D.
[3340]—*Sisters of Providence*.—S.P.
[3780]—*Sisters of Saints Cyril and Methodius*.—SS.C.M.

[]—*Sisters of St. Anne of Bangalore.*—S.A.B.

[1640]—*Sisters of St. Francis of Perpetual Adoration.*—O.S.F.

[3930]—*Sisters of St. Joseph of the Third Order of St. Francis.* (Immaculate Conception Prov.).—S.S.J.-T.O.S.F.

DIOCESAN CEMETERIES

HAMMOND. *Saint John-Saint Joseph,* 1547 167th St., 46324. Tel: 219-844-9475.

MICHIGAN CITY. *Saint Stanislaus,* 1015 Greenwood, 46360. Tel: 219-874-4310.

NECROLOGY

† Beckmann, John M., (Retired). —Died Feb. 4, 1996.

† Suelzer, Anthony J., (Retired). —Died Dec. 5, 1996.

† Viater, Rev. Msgr. John J., Hammond, IN, St. Margaret Mary Parish. —Died Nov. 7, 1996.

Diocese of Gaylord

(Dioecesis Gaylordensis)

Most Reverend

PATRICK R. COONEY, S.T.D., S.T.L.

Bishop of Gaylord; ordained December 20, 1959; appointed Titular Bishop of Hodelm and Auxiliary Bishop of Detroit December 3, 1982; consecrated January 27, 1983; appointed Bishop of Gaylord November 21, 1989; installed January 28, 1990. *Res., 1665 W. M-32, Seton Building, Gaylord, MI, 49735.*

ESTABLISHED JULY 20, 1971.

Square Miles 11,171.

Comprises the following 21 Counties in the State of Michigan: Alcona, Alpena, Antrim, Benzie, Charlevoix, Cheboygan, Crawford, Emmet, Grand Traverse, Iosco, Kalkaska, Leelanau, Manistee, Missaukee, Montmorency, Ogemaw, Oscoda, Otsego, Presque Isle, Roscommon and Wexford.

For legal titles of parishes and diocesan institutions, consult the Chancery Office.

Diocesan Pastoral Center: 1665 W. M-32, Gaylord, MI, 49735. Tel.: 517-732-5147; Fax: 517-732-1706.

STATISTICAL OVERVIEW

Personnel	
Bishop	1
Priests: Diocesan Active in Diocese	46
Priests: Active Outside Diocese	2
Priests: Retired, Sick or Absent	25
Number of Diocesan Priests	73
Religious Priests in Diocese	15
Extern Priests in Diocese	13
Ordinations:	
Diocesan Priests	2
Transitional Deacons	3
Permanent Deacons in Diocese	11
Total Brothers	3
Total Sisters	71
Parishes	
Parishes	82
With Resident Pastor:	
Resident Diocesan Priests	45
Resident Religious Priests	11
Without Resident Pastor:	
Administered by Priests	21
Administered by Women Religious	5
Professional Ministry Personnel:	
Sisters	20
Lay Ministers	30
Welfare	
Catholic Hospitals	3
Total Assisted	189,779
Health Care Centers	1
Total Assisted	774
Specialized Homes	2
Total Assisted	30
Special Centers for Social Services	16
Total Assisted	10,168
Educational	
Diocesan Students in Other Seminaries	8
Total Seminarians	8
High Schools, Diocesan and Parish	4
Total Students	632
Elementary Schools, Diocesan and Parish	18
Total Students	2,549
Catechesis/Religious Education:	
High School Students	1,406
Elementary Students	5,527
Total Students Under Catholic Instruction	10,122
Teachers in the Diocese:	
Sisters	10
Lay Teachers	188
Vital Statistics	
Receptions into the Church:	
Infant Baptism Totals	1,170
Adult Baptism Totals	126
Received into Full Communion	226
First Communions	1,268
Confirmations	1,418
Marriages:	
Catholic	321
Interfaith	256
Total Marriages	577
Deaths	836
Total Catholic Population	82,302
Total Population	437,375

Former Bishops—Most Rev. EDMUND C. SZOKA, J.C.L., D.D., First Bishop of Gaylord; ord. June 5, 1954; cons. July 20, 1971; installed July 20, 1971; appt. Archbishop of Detroit March 28, 1981; installed May 17, 1981; named Cardinal Priest May 29, 1988; elevated June 28, 1988 Assigned to the Vatican, 1990—Most Rev. ROBERT J. ROSE, S.T.L., D.D., ord. Dec. 21, 1955; appt. Bishop of Gaylord Oct. 13, 1981; installed Dec. 6, 1981; transferred to Diocese of Grand Rapids July 11, 1989; installed Aug. 30, 1989.

Vicar General—Rev. JAMES L. BRUCKSCH.

Diocesan Offices and Departments

Diocesan Pastoral Center—1665 W. M-32, Gaylord, 49735. Tel: 517-732-5147; Fax: 517-732-1706. Office Hours: 8-4:30 Mon.-Fri. All business should be directed to this office.

Consultors, Diocesan Board of—Revs. JAMES L. BRUCKSCH; ANDREW G. BUVALA, O.F.M.; FRANCIS J. MURPHY; RAYMOND C. MULKA; THOMAS A. NEIS; DENNIS R. Stilwell.

Members of the Presbyteral Council—

Elected Members—Revs. ALEXANDER BORUTA, O.F.M.; ANDREW G. BUVALA, O.F.M.; CHARLES DONAJKOWSKI; GERALD F. MICKETTI; ISADORE J. MIKULSKI; FRANCIS J. MURPHY; THOMAS A. NEIS; FRANCIS C. PARTRIDGE; DENNIS R. STILWELL; CASIMIR J. ZAWACKI.

Appointed Members—Revs. JAMES L. BRUCKSCH; WALTER W. DERYLO; RAYMOND C. MULKA.

Vicars (by region)—Alpena: Rev. JOSEPH P. GRAFF; Gaylord: Rev. ROBERT W. NALLEY; Manistee: Rev. MICHAEL P. CONNER; Petosky: Rev. DONALD PAULUS, O.F.M.; Traverse City: Rev. EDWIN A. THOME; West Branch: Rev. JOHN O. LADD.

Administrative Services, Secretariat for—MICHAEL E. STEFFEL, Dir., *1665 W. M-32, Gaylord, 49735.* Tel: 517-732-5147.

Audio-Visual Resource Center—JAMES C. MCLAUGHLIN, *1665 W. M-32, Gaylord, 49735.* Tel: 517-732-5147.

Archivist—Rev. GERALD F. MICKETTI, *1665 W. M-32, Gaylord, 49735.* Tel: 517-732-5147.

Catechesis—(See Education-Formation.).

Communications, Secretariat for—SAM BARBARO, Dir., *1665 W. M-32, Gaylord, 49735.* Tel: 517-732-5147.

Council of Catholic Women, Diocesan—GENEVIEVE SIETING, Pres., *5739 Sieting Rd. S.W., South Boardman, 49680.* Tel: 616-369-4123.

Cursillo—Rev. ANTHONY CITRO, *P.O. Box 40, Cheboygan, 49721.* Tel: 616-627-2105.

Ecumenical Apostolate—Rev. JOSEPH P. GRAFF, Dir., *322 W. Chisholm, Alpena, 49707.* Tel: 517-354-2676.

Education-Formation, Secretariat for—Miss MARLENE PEPLINSKI, Dir.; Rev. JOHN E. MCCRACKEN, Assoc. Dir. (Includes Catechesis, Ministries and Schools). *1665 W. M-32, Gaylord, 49735.* Tel: 517-732-5147.

Finance Council, Diocesan—Most Rev. PATRICK R. COONEY; Rev. JAMES L. BRUCKSCH; SHARON R. STACK; JANICE SMOLINSKI; MARY LOU NADON; CHARLES BREITHAUPT; BERNARD BAK; RENE HOENSCHEID; WILLIAM CORBETT.

Financial Development and C.S.A., Secretariat for—RALPH SORENSEN, Dir., *1665 W. M-32, Gaylord, 49735.* Tel: 517-732-5147.

Holy Childhood Pontifical Association—Rev. Msgr. GERARD F. GUZIKOWSKI, *371 Fifth St., Manistee, 49660.* Tel: 616-723-2165.

Native American Apostolate—Rev. ANDREW G. BUVALA, O.F.M., Coord., *Blessed Kateri Tekakwitha Parish, P.O. Box 369, Suttons Bay, 49682.* Tel: 616-271-6651.

Knights of Columbus—ROBERT S. SLUSARSKI, Eastern Diocesan Prog. Dir., *1901 Deeter Rd., Luzerne, 48636.* Tel: 517-826-5088. FRANK KRAMER, Western Diocesan Prog. Dir., *403 E. Nelson St., Cadillac, 49601.* Tel: 616-775-3408; 779-2845.

Liturgy and Evangelization, Secretariat for—Sr. ARLENE BENNETT R.S.M., Dir., *1665 W. M-32, Gaylord, 49735.* Tel: 517-732-5147.

Migrant Apostolate—Contact the Bishop's Office: *1665 W. M-32, Gaylord, 49735.* Tel: 517-732-5147.

Parish Social Ministries, Secretariat for—Sr. T. J. SEMMERLING, S.C.S.C., Dir., *1665 W. M-32, Gaylord, 49735.* Tel: 517-732-5147.

Pastoral Support Services for Priests and Pastoral Administrators—Rev. ROBERT W. NALLEY, Dir., *1665 W. M-32, Gaylord, 49735.* Tel: 517-732-5147.

Priests' Retirement Fund—Most Rev. PATRICK R. COONEY, Chm. Board of Directors. Elected Members: Revs. THOMAS M. DOMINIAK; RAYMOND C. MULKA; EDWIN J. FREDERICK; JOHN C. GREENE; MARGE WAGNER, Appointed Member.

Priestly Vocations—Rev. JAMES P. HAYDEN, Dir., *Diocese of Gaylord, 1665 W. M-32, Gaylord, 49735.* Tel: 517-732-5147.

Propagation of the Faith—Rev. Msgr. GERARD F. GUZIKOWSKI, Dir., *Guardian Angels Parish, 317 Fifth St., Manistee, 49660.* Tel: 616-723-2165.

St. Vincent De Paul, Society of—Particular Council of Tawas, *115 First St., Tawas City, 49763.* Roscommon County, *Box 644, Prudenville, 48651.* Tel: 517-366-7613. *1028 Hannah, Traverse City, 49684.* Also particular councils in Cheboygan, Hillman, Hale, Prescott, Mikado and Alpena.

Tribunal Diocesan—Rev. WILLIAM L. ZWIEFKA, Judicial Vicar; Revs. DENNIS R. STILWELL; R. DALE MAGOON; ROBERT W. NALLEY. Judges: Revs. JAMES A. HOLTZ; ROBERT W. NALLEY. Defenders of the Bond: Revs. JOHN C. GREENE; JAMES P. HAYDEN; CHARLES G.DONAJKOWSKI. Procurators-Advocates: RHONDA KLEE, Auditor; MARY DICKERSON, Notary Inquiries may be made through the local pastors or directed to this office., *1665 W. M-32, Gaylord, 49735.* Tel: 517-732-5147.

CLERGY, PARISHES, MISSIONS AND PAROCHIAL SCHOOLS

CITY OF GAYLORD
(Otsego County)

1—ST. MARY CATHEDRAL, Revs. Francis J. Murphy, Rector; Wayne H. Dziekan; Sr. Cecilia Faber, O.P., Pastoral Min.
Res., 606 N. Ohio Ave., 49735. Tel: 517-732-5448. [CEM]
Catechesis/Religious Programs—Diana Pefffers, D.R.E.
Students 149.
Convent—211 N. Otsego, 49735. Tel: 517-732-4989.

OUTSIDE THE CITY OF GAYLORD

Acme, Grand Traverse Co., Christ the King, Rev. Edwin A. Thome.
Res., P.O. Box 95, 49610. Tel: 616-938-9214; Fax: 616-938-3266.
Church—3801 Shore Rd., 49610.
School—Grand Traverse Area Schools. See separate listing under Institutions Located in the Diocese.
Catechesis/Religious Programs—Patricia Cesere, D.R.E.
Students 390.

Afton, Cheboygan Co., St. Monica, Rev. R. Dale Magoon.
Res., P.O. Box 130, Onaway, 49765. Tel: 517-733-6053. [CEM]
Church—M-68, 49705.

Alpena, Alpena Co.,

1—ST. ANNE, Rev. John C. Greene.
Res., 203 S. Ninth Ave., 49707. Tel: 517-356-0622; Fax: 517-354-3918. [JC]
Church—201 S. Ninth Ave., 49707.
Catechesis/Religious Programs—Jeri Standen, D.R.E.
Students 266.

2—ST. BERNARD, Rev. Joseph P. Graff; Sylvia Owens, Pastoral Min.
Res., 322 Chisholm St., 49707. Tel: 517-354-2676; Fax: 517-354-6087. [JC]
Catechesis/Religious Programs—Tel: 517-354-8018. Geraldine LaCross, D.R.E.
Students 94.

3—ST. JOHN THE BAPTIST, Rev. Kenneth R. Stachnik; Patricia Przeslawski, Pastoral Assoc.
Res., 2425 Frederick St., 49707. Tel: 517-354-3019.
Catechesis/Religious Programs—2550 S. First, 49707. Tel: 517-354-3292. Judith H. Burns, D.R.E.
Students 240.

4—ST. MARY, Rev. Walter W. Derylo.
Res., 516 N. Second Ave., 49707. Tel: 517-354-2322; Fax: 517-356-9637. [JC]
Catechesis/Religious Programs—Tel: 517-354-8655. Mrs. Cherie Smigelski, D.R.E.
Students 278.
Convent—120 E. Miller St., 49707.

Alverno, Cheboygan Co., St. Francis of Assisi. Closed. For sacramental records contact St. Mary-St. Charles Parish, Cheboygan.

Atlanta, Montmorency Co., Jesus the Good Shepherd, Rev. Raymond J. Pilarski.
Res., P.O. Box 216, Hillman, 49746. Tel: 517-742-4542.
Church—4521 County Rd. 491, 49746.

Bay Shore, Emmet Co., St. Francis Solanus, Rev. Andre Schludecker, O.F.M.
Res., 415 State St., Petoskey, 49770. Tel: 616-347-4133.
Church—Townline Rd., 49770.

Beaver Island, Charlevoix Co., Holy Cross. Unassigned.
Res., P.O. Box 145, St. James, 49782. [CEM]
Church—St. James, Bonner St., 49782. Tel: 616-448-2230.

Bellaire, Antrim Co., St. Luke, Sr. Celine Goessl, S.C.S.C., Admin.
Res., 3078 M-88, P.O. Box 799, 49615-0799. Tel: 616-533-8121.

Black River, Alcona Co., St. Gabriel, Rev. Lawrence A. Kelleher.
Res., 2188 W. Nicholson Hill Rd., Ossineke, 49766-9736. Tel: 517-471-2556. [CEM]
Church—Black River Rd., 48721.

Boyne City, Charlevoix Co., St. Matthew, Rev. Francis C. Partridge.
Res., 1303 Boyne Ave., 49712. Tel: 616-582-7718. [JC]
Catechesis/Religious Programs—Tel: 616-582-6589. Suzanne Dzwik, D.R.E.
Students 134.

Boyne Falls, Charlevoix Co., St. Augustine, Rev. Francis C. Partridge.
Res., 1303 Boyne Ave., Boyne City, 49712. Tel: 616-582-7718. [CEM]
Church—Grove St., 49713.
Catechesis/Religious Programs—Frank Wasylewski, D.R.E.
Students 49.

Burt Lake, Cheboygan Co., Assumption of St. Mary, Rev. Sylvester Micek, O.F.M.
Res., P.O. Box 122, Pellston, 49769. Tel: 616-539-8805.

Cadillac, Wexford Co., St. Ann, Rev. Robert H. Bissot; Sr. Hilda Sucher, R.S.M., Pastoral Min.
Res., 800 W. 13th St., 49601-9281. Tel: 616-775-2471. [CEM]

Cedar, Leelanau Co., Holy Rosary. Unassigned.
Res., 3919 E. Gatzke Rd., 49621. Tel: 616-228-5429. [CEM]

Charlevoix, Charlevoix Co., St. Mary, Rev. Thomas A. Neis.
Res., 102 W. Garfield, 49720. Tel: 616-547-6652.
Catechesis/Religious Programs—Students 150.

Cheboygan, Cheboygan Co., St. Mary-St. Charles, Revs. Anthony M. Citro, Admin.; Donald R. Geyman. Pastoral Assocs.: Mrs. Patricia Watson; Mr. Joseph T. Fortin.
Mailing Address: P.O. Box 40, 49721. Tel: 616-627-2105; Fax: 616-627-5362. [JC]
Catechesis/Religious Programs—Mrs. Deby Frato, D.R.E.
Students 187.

Copemish, Manistee Co., St. Raphael, Rev. Richard A. Kosterman.
Res., P.O. Box 204, 49625. Tel: 616-378-2984. [CEM]
Church—M-115, 49765.

Cross Village, Emmet Co., Holy Cross, Rev. Albert Langheim, O.F.M.
Res., 6624 N. Lake Shore, 49740-9745. Tel: 616-526-2030. [CEM]

East Jordan, Charlevoix Co., St. Joseph, Rev. William McKeon.
Res., P.O. Box 379, 49727. Tel: 616-536-2934. [CEM]
Catechesis/Religious Programs—Students 79.

East Tawas, Iosco Co., St. Joseph, Rev. Ronald V. Gronowski, Admin.
Res., 516 W. Lincoln St., 48730. Tel: 517-362-3162. [CEM]
Catechesis/Religious Programs—Students 80.

Elk Rapids, Antrim Co., Sacred Heart, Rev. James E. Coke.
Res., 143 Charles St., 49629. Tel: 616-264-8087. [CEM]
Catechesis/Religious Programs—Roberta L. Cornelissen, D.R.E.
Students 157.

Elmira, Antrim Co., St. Thomas Aquinas, Rev. Richard T. Hannon, Admin.
Res., P.O. Box 128, 49730. Tel: 616-546-3326. [CEM]
Church—M-32, 49730.

Empire, Leelanau Co., St. Philip Neri, Rev. John B. Tupper.
Res., P.O. Box 257, 49630. Tel: 616-326-5255. [CEM]
Church—11411 La Core Ave., 49630.
Catechesis/Religious Programs—Millie Allen, D.R.E.
Students 43.

Fife Lake, Grand Traverse Co., St. Aloysius, Rev. James A. Holtz.
Res., P.O. Box 668, Kalkaska, 49646. Tel: 616-258-5021. [CEM]
Church—Merritt St., 49633.

Frankfort, Benzie Co., St. Ann, Rev. Msgr. David W. Gemuend.
Res., P.O. Box 1168, 508 Crystal Ave., 49635. Tel: 616-352-4421; Fax: 616-352-9940.
Catechesis/Religious Programs—Teresa Bieszka, D.R.E.
Students 52.

Gills Pier, Leelanau Co., St. Wenceslaus, Rev. Charles G. Donajkowski.
Mailing Address: P.O. Box 136, Lake Leelanau, 49653. Tel: 616-256-9676; Fax: 616-256-7812.
Res., 8500 E. Kolarik, Suttons Bay, 49682. Tel: 616-271-3574. [CEM]
Church—County Rds. 637 & 626, 49682.

Glennie, Alcona Co., St. Francis of Assisi. Closed. For inquiries for parish records contact the Chancery.

Good Hart, Emmet Co., St. Ignatius, Rev. Albert Langheim, O.F.M.
Res., 6624 N. Lake Shore Dr., Cross Village, 49740. Tel: 616-526-2030. [CEM]

Grayling, Crawford Co., St. Mary, Rev. Robert W. Nalley.
Res., 702 Peninsular St., 49738. Tel: 517-348-7291; 348-7657 (Office).
Catechesis/Religious Programs—Tel: 517-348-8669.
Students 117.

Hale, Iosco Co., St. Pius X, Rev. J. August Franczek.
Res., P.O. Box 428, 48739. Tel: 517-728-2278.
Church—3900 M-65, 48739.
Catechesis/Religious Programs—Karol Shellenbarger, D.R.E.
Students 42.

Hannah, Grand Traverse Co., St. Mary, Rev. Albin J. Gietzen.
Res., 2962 M-113 West Rd., Kingsley, 49649. Tel: 616-263-5640. [CEM]
Catechesis/Religious Programs—Sr. Geneva Marie Schaub, O.P., D.R.E.
Students 67.
Convent—2912 M-113 West Rd., Kingsley, 49649. Tel: 616-263-5287.

Harbor Springs, Emmet Co., Holy Childhood of Jesus, Rev. Frank Kordek, O.F.M.; Bro. Patrick Kendrick, O.F.M.
Res., 150 W. Main St., 49740. Tel: 616-526-2017. [CEM]
Catechesis/Religious Programs—Tel: 616-526-7181. Sr. Corinne Smollar, O.P., D.R.E.
Students 152.

Harietta, Wexford Co., St. Edward, Rev. Robert H. Bissot.
Res., 800 W. 13th St., Cadillac, 49601-9281. Tel: 616-775-2471.
Church—207 W. Gaston, 49638.

Harrisville, Alcona Co., St. Anne, Rev. Lawrence E. Boks.
Res., P.O. Box 345, 48740. Tel: 517-724-6713. [CEM]
Church—110 State St., 48740.

Herron, Alpena Co., St. Rose of Lima, Sr. Carmelita Switzer, O.P., Pastoral Admin.
Church—3439 Herron Rd., 49744. Tel: 517-379-4316.
Catechesis/Religious Programs—Vicki Cook, D.R.E.
Students 80.

Higgins Lake, Roscommon Co., St. Hubert, Sr. Ann Christopher Herald, O.P., Pastoral Admin.
Res., P.O. Box 75, 48627. Tel: 517-821-5591.
Church—7612 W. Higgins Lake Dr., 48627.

Hillman, Montmorency Co., St. Augustine, Rev. Raymond J. Pilarski.
Res., P.O. Box 216, 49746. Tel: 517-742-4542. [CEM]
Church—24140 Veterans Memorial Hwy., 49746.
Catechesis/Religious Programs—Jean Davis, D.R.E.
Students 116.

Houghton Lake, Roscommon Co., St. James, Sr. Ann Christopher Herald, O.P., Pastoral Admin.
Res., P.O. Box 75, Higgins Lake, 48627. Tel: 517-821-5591.
Church—7878 E. Houghton Lake Dr., 48629.

Indian River, Cheboygan Co., Cross in the Woods Catholic Shrine, Revs. Donard Paulus, O.F.M.; Flavius Czuba, O.F.M.; Elstan Coghill, O.F.M.; Deacon John B. Wallace.
Res., 7078 M-68, 49749. Tel: 616-238-8973; Fax: 616-238-7012. [CEM]
Catechesis/Religious Programs—49749. Tel: 616-238-8542. Mrs. Kenya Swiss, D.R.E.
Students 80.

Kalkaska, Kalkaska Co., St. Mary of the Woods, Rev. James A. Holtz.
Res., P.O. Box 668, 49646. Tel: 616-258-5021. [CEM]
Church—County Rd. 612, 49646.
Catechesis/Religious Programs—Donalda Barrett, D.R.E.
Students 109.

Klacking Creek, Ogemaw Co., Holy Family, Rev. Miro Wiese, O.F.M.
Res., 402 W. Peters Rd., West Branch, 48661. Tel: 517-345-3422. [CEM]
Catechesis/Religious Programs—Rose Quackenbush, D.R.E.
Students 70.

Lake City, Missaukee Co., St. Stephen, Rev. Theron E. Pelky.

Res., P.O. Box 379, 49651. Tel: 616-839-2121.
Church—506 Union St., 49651.
Catechesis/Religious Programs—Joan Boomgaard, D.R.E.
Students 66.

Lake Leelanau, Leelanau Co., St. Mary, Rev. Charles G. Donajkowski.
Mailing Address: P.O. Box 136, 49653. Tel: 616-256-9676; Fax: 616-256-7812.
Res., 8500 E. Kolarik, Suttons Bay, 49682. Tel: 616-271-3574. [CEM]

Larks Lake, Emmet Co., St. Nicholas, Rev. Albert Langheim, O.F.M.
Res., 6624 N. Lake Shore Dr., Cross Village, 49740. Tel: 616-526-2030. [CEM]

Lewiston, Montmorency Co., St. Francis of Assisi, Rev. Gregory Kurutz, O.F.M.
Res., P.O. Box 182, 49756. Tel: 517-786-2235. [CEM]
Church—4086 Salling Ave., 49756. Tel: 517-786-3081.
Catechesis/Religious Programs—Eva Claeys, D.R.E.
Students 62.

Mackinaw City, Emmet Co., St. Anthony of Padua, Rev. Leonard Jocys. In res., Rev. John J. Adomaitis.
Res., P.O. Box 460, 49701. Tel: 616-436-5561; 436-5601. [CEM]
Church—600 W. Central Ave., 49701.
Catechesis/Religious Programs—Eileen Raymond, D.R.E.
Students 51.

Mancelona, Antrim Co., St. Anthony, Rev. William L. Zwiefka.
Mailing Address: P.O. Box 677, 49659-0677.
Church—209 Jefferson St., 49659. Tel: 616-587-8401. [CEM]

Manistee, Manistee Co., Guardian Angels, Rev. Msgr. Gerard Guzikowski.
Res., 371 Fifth St., 49660. Tel: 616-723-2165. [JC]
Convent—501 Michael St., 49660. Tel: 616-723-6332.

St. Joseph, Rev. Robert J. Zuchowski.
Res., 254 Sixth St., 49660. Tel: 616-723-2619; Fax: 616-723-3711. [JC]
Catechesis/Religious Programs—Tel: 616-723-3732. Shirley Skiera, D.R.E.
Students 131.

St. Mary of Mt. Carmel Shrine, Rev. Gabriel Fox.
Res., 260 St. Mary Pkwy., 49660. Tel: 616-723-3345. [JC]
Catechesis/Religious Programs—Sr. Ann Porter, O.P., D.R.E.
Students 60.

Manton, Wexford Co., St. Theresa, Rev. Theron E. Pelky.
Res., P.O. Box 379, Lake City, 49651. Tel: 616-839-2121.
Church—9475 14th & 1/4 Rd., 49663.

Maple City, Leelanau Co., St. Rita-St. Joseph. Unassigned.
Res., 3919 Gatzke Rd., Cedar, 49621. Tel: 616-228-5429. [CEM]
Church—8707 Hill St., 49664. Tel: 616-228-5823.
Catechesis/Religious Programs—Rita Wilson, D.R.E.
Students 125.

Mapleton, Grand Traverse Co., St. Joseph, Rev. Patrick J. Barrett.
Mailing Address: 13400 Center Rd., Traverse City, 49686. Tel: 616-223-4303. [CEM]
Catechesis/Religious Programs—Connie Wood, D.R.E.
Students 75.

McBain, Missaukee Co., St. Rita. Closed. For inquiries for parish records contact the Chancery.

Metz, Presque Isle Co., St. Dominic, Sr. Rita Epple, R.S.M., Pastoral Admin.
Res., 9269 County Rd. 441, Posen, 49776. Tel: 517-766-2694. [CEM]
Catechesis/Religious Programs—Carolyn Haske, D.R.E.
Students 48.

Mikado, Alocona Co., St. Raphael, Rev. Lawrence E. Boks.
Res., P.O. Box 345, Harrisville, 48740. Tel: 517-724-6713. [CEM]
Church—2531 E. Mikado Rd., 48745. Tel: 517-736-6071.

Mio, Oscoda Co., St. Mary, Rev. Roy Zebrowski, O.F.M.
Res., P.O. Box 189, 48647. Tel: 517-826-5509.
Ministry Office—200 Pearl, 48647. Tel: 517-826-6057.

North Port, Leelanau Co., St. Gertrude, Rev. Gerard A. Hunko.
Res., P.O. Box 9, Suttons Bay, 49682. Tel: 616-271-3744.
Church—701 Warren, Northport, 49670.

Onaway, Presque Isle Co., St. Paul, Rev. R. Dale Magoon.
Res., 3856 Oak St., P.O. Box 130, 49765. Tel: 517-733-4043. [CEM]

Onekama, Manistee Co., St. Joseph, Rev. Michael P. Conner.
Res., P.O. Box 150, 49675. Tel: 616-889-4254. [CEM]
Church—8380 Fifth St., 49675.
Catechesis/Religious Programs—Students 86.

Oscoda, Iosco Co., Sacred Heart, Rev. James L. Brucksch.
Res., 5300 N. U.S.-23, 48750. Tel: 517-739-9511. [CEM]
Catechesis/Religious Programs—Mrs. Jackie Welles, D.R.E.
Students 36.

Ossineke, Alpena Co., St. Catherine, Rev. Lawrence A. Kelleher.
Res., 2188 W. Nicholson Hill Rd., 49766-9736. Tel: 517-471-2556. [CEM]
Catechesis/Religious Programs—Tel: 517-471-5121. D.R.E.: Mary Kay Lee; Cynthia Prevo.
Students 202.

Pellston, Emmet Co., St. Clement, Rev. Sylvester Micek, O.F.M.
Res., P.O. Box 122, 49769. Tel: 616-539-8805. [CEM]
Church—202 Maple, 49769.

Peshabestown, Leelanau Co., Blessed Kateri Tekakwitha, Rev. Andrew Buvala, O.F.M.
Res., P.O. Box 369, Suttons Bay, 49682. Tel: 616-271-6651.

Petoskey, Emmet Co., St. Francis Xavier, Revs. Andre Schludecker, O.F.M.; Wilbert Hegener, O.F.M.; Robert Dentzman, O.F.M.; Bros. Daniel Badsing, O.F.M.; Wolfe Price, O.F.M.
Res., 513 Howard St., 49770. Tel: 616-347-4133. [CEM]
School—414 Michigan St., 49770. Tel: 616-347-3651. Sr. Paula Blank, Prin.
Students 260.
Catechesis/Religious Programs—Tel: 616-347-2681. Sr. Maryl Gardner, D.R.E.
Students 260.

Posen, Presque Isle Co., St. Casimir, Rev. Stanislaw J. Bereda.
Res., P.O. Box 217, 49776. Tel: 517-766-2660. [CEM]
Church—10075 M-65 North, 49776-0217.
Catechesis/Religious Programs—Joan Chappa, D.R.E.
Students 135.

Praga, Antrim Co., St. John Nepomucene, Rev. William McKeon.
Res., P.O. Box 379, East Jordan, 49727. Tel: 616-536-2934. [CEM]

Prudenville, Roscommon Co., Our Lady of the Lake, Rev. John O. Ladd.
Res., 1037 W. Houghton Lake Dr., P.O. Box 800, 48651. Tel: 517-366-5533.
Catechesis/Religious Programs—D.R.E.: Vernon Anderson; Fern Anderson.
Students 109.
Convent—1039 W. Houghton Lake Dr., 48651. Tel: 517-366-5592.

Riggsville, Cheboygan Co., Sacred Heart, Rev. Leonard Jocys.
Mailing Address: P.O. Box 460, Mackinaw City, 49701-0460.
Res., St. Anthony of Padua, P.O. Box 460, Mackinaw City, 49701. Tel: 616-436-5561.
Church—Polish Line Rd., Cheboygan, 49721.

Rogers City, Presque Isle Co., St. Ignatius, Rev. Thomas M. Dominiak.
Res., 175 W. Ira Ave., 49779. Tel: 517-734-3388. [CEM]
Catechesis/Religious Programs—Robert Chapdelaine, D.R.E.
Students 74.
Convent—585 S. Third St., 49779. Tel: 517-734-3605.

Roscommon, Roscommon Co., St. Michael, Rev. John E. McCracken.
Res., 104 N. 6th St., P.O. Box 248, 48653. Tel: 517-275-5212.
Catechesis/Religious Programs—Kathleen Butler, D.R.E.
Students 160.

St. Helen, Roscommon Co., St. Helen, Rev. Albert Couturier.
Res., 737 N. M-76, 48646. Tel: 517-389-3495; 389-4959 (Office); 389-3441 (Church).

Skidway Lake, Ogemaw Co., St. Stephen of Hungary, Rev. Alexander Boruta, O.F.M.
Res., 2811 E. Greenwood Rd., Prescott, 48756. Tel: 517-873-3340.
Catechesis/Religious Programs—Students 67.

Suttons Bay, Leelanau Co., St. Michael the Archangel, Rev. Gerard A. Hunko.
Res., P.O. Box 9, 49682. Tel: 616-271-3744. [CEM]
Church—315 Broadway, 49682.
Catechesis/Religious Programs—Tel: 616-271-3733. Nita Send, D.R.E.
Students 250.

Tawas City, Iosco Co., Immaculate Heart of Mary, Rev. Ronald V. Gronowski.
Res., 501 Lake St., 48763. Tel: 517-362-5076. [CEM]
Catechesis/Religious Programs—Tel: 517-362-7877. Sr. Nancy Ribble, O.P., D.R.E.
Students 57.

Traverse City, Grand Traverse Co., Immaculate Conception, Revs. Dennis R. Stilwell; Chad W. Zielinski.
Res., 720 W. Second, 49684. Tel: 616-946-4211.
Catechesis/Religious Programs—Tel: 616-946-2782. Dannie Brzezinski, D.R.E.
Students 240.

St. Francis of Assisi, Rev. James K. Gardiner; Sr. Katherine Murphy, R.S.M., Pastoral Assoc.
Res., 1025 S. Union St., 49684. Tel: 616-947-4620; Fax: 616-947-4693.

St. Patrick, Rev. Gerald F. Micketti.
Res., 630 W. Silver Lake Rd., S., 49684-8526. Tel: 616-943-4633.
Catechesis/Religious Programs—Sr. Jean Williams, O.P., D.R.E.
Students 275.

Vanderbilt, Otsego Co., Holy Redeemer, Rev. Richard T. Hannon; Mrs. Carolyn Zecchin, Admin. & D.R.E.
Res., 606 N. Ohio St., Gaylord, 49735. Tel: 517-732-5448.
Catechesis/Religious Programs—Students 32.

West Branch, Ogemaw Co., St. Joseph, Rev. Richard R. Seifferly.
Res., 907 Houghton Ave., 48661. Tel: 517-345-0064. [CEM]
School—Tel: 517-345-0220.
Catechesis/Religious Programs—Tel: 517-345-0670.
Students 115.
Convent—961 W. Houghton, 48661. Tel: 517-345-0221.

Whittemore, Iosco Co., St. James, Rev. Regis Burzynski, O.F.M.
Res., P.O. Box 206, 48770. Tel: 517-756-2591; Fax: 517-756-3255. [CEM]
Church—202 E. Sherman, 48770.

Special Assignment:
Reverend Fathers—
Hayden, James P., Dir. Priestly Vocations, 1665 W. M-32, Gaylord, MI 49735
Nalley, Robert W., Tribunal Judge & Dir. Pastoral Support Svcs. for Priests & Pastoral Admin., 1665 W. M-32, Gaylord, MI 49735
Suchocki, James A., Special assignment

Absent on Leave:
Reverend Fathers—
Cotter, Raymond C.
Kaiser, Thomas A
Klingshirn, Charles
McLaughlin, James C., II
Messing, Arnold A.
Schaub, Martin R.

Retired:
Reverend Fathers—
Adomaitis, John J., St. Anthony Parish, P.O. Box 460, Mackinaw City, MI 49701-0460
Dieninis, Lionginas, 3016 Risdale, Lansing, MI 48911
Gaj, Zygmut, 2733 Bullock Rd., Bay City, MI 48708
Harnish, Lionel, 4039 26th St., Dorr, MI 49323
Kluonius, Joseph V., 2013 Hess, Holiday, FL 34691
Machcinski, Anthony J., 7826 Homer Ave., Hudson, FL 34667
Marciulonis, Benedict J., 1407 Chilean Ln., Winter Park, FL 32792
Marek, Walter, P.O. Box 203, Whitehall, MI 49461
Mausolf, James H., 703 W. Seventh St., Traverse City, MI 49684
Mikulski, Isadore J., 7718 Westwood Dr., Oscoda, MI 48750
Mulka, Arthur C., 2388 Emmett, Alpena, MI 49707
Mulka, Raymond C., 300 Washington, Alpena, MI 49707
Reitz, Joseph A., 52 Marble Rd., Lowell, MI 49331
Rushman, John, P.O. Box 646, East Tawas, MI 48730
Sarosiek, John H., 4468 Lincoln, Dearborn Heights, MI 48125
Sitar, Richard T., 1484 Spring Lake Rd., Fruitland, FL 34731
Smolinski, Clarence D., 14692 Lakeside Dr., Presque Isle, MI 49777
Tamulis, John J., 1189 S. 35 Mile Rd., Cadillac, MI 49601
Thomas, Fred J., 11 Hawaiian Way, Malokai Park,

Leesburg, FL 34788
Wiekierak, Joseph F., 1470 West Norton, Apt. H-5, Muskegon, MI 49441-4362
Zawacki, Casimir J., 305 Fifth Ave., #8, Manistee, MI 49660

Permanent Deacons:
Barbaro, Sam, Unassigned
Bousmara, Thomas, Immaculate Conception, Traverse City
Friend, Harry, St. Philip, Empire
LePain, Andrew, Unassigned
LoVetere, Arthur, Jesus the Good Shepherd, Atlanta
Nelson, Joseph B., Unassigned
Szczepanski, Stanley T., St. Anthony of Padua, Mackinaw City
Trapp, Richard, Unassigned
Vondra, Edward, Unassigned
Wallace, John, Catholic Shrine, Indian River
Wendell, Max, Unassigned

INSTITUTIONS LOCATED IN THE DIOCESE

[A] INTERPAROCHIAL SCHOOLS

CHEBOYGAN. *Bishop Baraga Elementary.* (Grades K-6), 421 State St., 49721. James Leinbach, Prin. Lay Teachers 7; Students 187.

Bishop Baraga Preschool, 120 C St., 49721. Lay Teachers 1; Students 71.

MANISTEE. *Manistee Catholic Central Schools.* (Grades PreK-12), 1200 U.S. 31 South (at 12th St.), 49660. Tel: 616-723-2529. Michael Buell, Prin. Sisters 1; Lay Teachers 16; Students 203; Preschool 20.

TRAVERSE CITY. *Grand Traverse Area Catholic Schools,* 123 E. 11th St., 49684. Tel: 616-946-8100. Mary Oosterhouse, Admin. Sisters 2; Lay Teachers 51; Students 984.

Immaculate Conception Middle School. (Grades 5-8), 218 Vine, 49684. Tel: 616-947-1252. Kenneth J. Knudsen, Prin. Lay Teachers 13; Students 292.

St. Francis Elementary. (Grades K-4), 130 E. 10th, 49684. Tel: 616-946-5961. Mr. William J. Gorney, Prin. Sisters 1; Lay Teachers 21; Students 426.

St. Francis High School, 123 E. 11th St., 49684. Tel: 616-946-8038; Fax: 616-946-1878. Mark Esper, Prin. Sisters 1; Lay Teachers 17; Students 266.

[B] PAROCHIAL SCHOOLS

GAYLORD. *St. Mary Cathedral Elementary School.* (Grades K-6), 321 N. Otsego Ave., 49735. Sr. Jean Karen Woloszyk, O.P., Prin. Lay Teachers 15; Students 266.

St. Mary Cathedral High School. (Grades 7-12), 310 W. Mitchell, 49735. Mr. James Kerfoot, Prin. Sisters 1; Lay Teachers 10; Students 183.

ALPENA. *St. Anne Elementary.* (Grades K-8), 205 S. 9th, 49707. Mr. William Morford, Jr., Prin. Lay Teachers 10; Students 199.

St. Mary Elementary. (Grades PreK-6), 500 N. Second, 49707. Sr. Mary Gloria Ertman, C.S.S.F., Prin. Sisters 1; Lay Teachers 7; Students 106.

CADILLAC. *St. Ann Elementary.* (Grades K-5), 800 W. 13th, 49601. Mary Ann Palacios, Prin. Lay Teachers 6; Students 120.

CEDAR. *Holy Rosary Elementary.* (Grades K-6), 6982 Schomberg, 49621. Heidi Sleder, Prin. Lay Teachers 6; Students 43.

CHARLEVOIX. *St. Mary Elementary.* (Grades PreK-5), 1005 Bridge St., 49720. Sr. Margaret Schneider, O.P., Prin. Sisters 2; Lay Teachers 8; Students 92.

EAST TAWAS. *St. Joseph Elementary.* (Grades K-6), 411 N. Wilkinson, 48730. Sr. Monica Meyer, O.P., Prin. Sisters 1; Lay Teachers 4; Students 80.

HANNAH. *St. Mary's Hannah School.* (Grades K-6), 2912 M-113, 49649. Deanna Couture, Prin. Sisters 1; Lay Teachers 4; Students 66.

LAKE LEELANAU. *St. Mary's Schools.* (Grades PreK-12), 303 S. St. Mary St., 49653. Mailing Address: P.O. Box 340, 49653. Therese Lichty, Prin. Lay Teachers 16; Students 206.

PETOSKEY. *St. Francis Xavier Elementary.* (Grades K-8), 414 Michigan, 49770. Sr. Paula Blank, Prin. Sisters 2; Lay Teachers 21; Students 255.

POSEN. *St. Casimir Elementary.* (Grades 1-8), 10053 M-65 North, 49776. Judy Leginza, Prin. Lay Teachers 4; Students 44.

PRUDENVILLE. *Our Lady of the Lake Elementary.* (Grades K-8), 1039 W. Houghton Lake, 48651. Sr. Mary Lourdes Campbell, R.S.M., Prin. Lay Teachers 5; Students 85.

ROGERS CITY. *St. Ignatius Elementary.* (Grades 1-8), 545 S. Third, 49779. David Giles, Prin. Lay Teachers 10; Students 145.

WEST BRANCH. *St. Joseph Elementary.* (Grades K-8), 935 W. Houghton Ave., 48661. Lorrene Spaulding, Prin. Lay Teachers 9; Students 212.

[C] GENERAL HOSPITALS

CADILLAC. *Mercy Hospital,* 400 Hobart St., 49601. Tel: 616-779-7200.
For a complete listing, refer to the Hospitals section.

GRAYLING. *Mercy Hospital,* 1100 Michigan Ave., 49738. Tel: 517-348-5461; Fax: 517-348-4839.
For a complete listing, refer to the Hospitals section.

*TAWAS CITY. *Saint Joseph Huron Home Health and Hospice,* 716 German St., Ste. B, P.O. Box 208, 48764. Tel: 517-362-4611.
For a complete listing, refer to the Hospitals section.

Tawas St. Joseph Hospital, 200 Hemlock, M-55, 48764-0659. Tel: 517-362-3411; Fax: 517-362-7277.
For a complete listing, refer to the Hospitals section.

[D] CONVENTS AND RESIDENCES FOR SISTERS

CONWAY. *Sacramentine Monastery of Perpetual Adoration,* 49722. Tel: 616-347-0447. Sr. Mary Rosalie, O.S.S., Prioress. Sacamentine Sisters 4.

TRAVERSE CITY. *Infant Jesus of Prague Monastery,* 3501 Silver Lake Rd., 49684-8949. Tel: 616-946-4960. Mother Teresa Margaret, O.C.D., Prioress; Rev. Valerian J. Rykowski, Chap. Tel: 616-947-6935. Carmelite Nuns. Solemn Vows 8.

[E] CHILD CARE FACILITIES

ALPENA. *Huron House / Boysville of Michigan, Inc.,* 4761 U.S. 23 N., 49707. Tel: 517-356-3573; Fax: 517-356-4910. Residential and community-based treatment programs for troubled youth and families, with facilities located throughout the state of Michigan and one in the state of Ohio under the auspices of the Brothers of the Holy Cross at Notre Dame. Parent company, Boysville of Michigan, Inc. Bro. Francis Boylan, C.S.C., Exec. Dir.; Joseph Martinus, Pastoral Min.; Rick Boone, Regional Dir. Boys 11.

Boysville's Family & Community Support Program. Includes specialized foster care, supervised independent living, in-home family treatment, Families First and Nokomis Challenge.

TRAVERSE CITY. *Non-Secure Detention / Boysville of Michigan, Inc.,* 207 W. Grandview Pkwy., Ste. 200, 49684. Tel: 616-922-9664; 800-235-9664. Bro. Francis Boylan, C.S.C., Exec. Dir.; Rick Boone, Regional Dir. Youth 19.

[F] RETREAT HOUSES

CONWAY. *Augustine Center,* P.O. Box 84, 49722-0084. Tel: 616-347-3657. Sr. Barbara Hubeny, O.P., Dir.

ST. JAMES. *Brother Damian Lodge* (Beaver Island), 49782. Tel: 616-448-2204. Open June, July and August. Bro. Kevin Mackey, F.S.C., Dir.

[G] CATHOLIC SOCIAL SERVICE AGENCIES

GAYLORD. *Catholic Human Services,* 111 S. Michigan Ave., Ste. A, 49735. Tel: 517-731-2877. Mr. Clement C. Veeser, Pres. & CEO; Mrs. Anita Lawnichak, Dir. Accounting & Financial Svcs.
Area Offices: 154 S. Ripley Blvd., Alpena, 49707. Tel: 517-356-6385. Mr. Thomas LaCross, Admin., 140 W. River St., #7, Cadillac, 49601. Tel: 616-775-6581. Mr. David Martin, Admin., 111 S. Michigan, 49735. Tel: 517-732-6761. Mr. Thomas LaCross, Admin., 1000 Hastings St., Traverse City, 49686. Tel: 616-947-8110. Mr. David Martin, Admin.

[H] MISCELLANEOUS

GAYLORD. *Camp Sancta Maria.* (Sponsored by the Archdiocese of Detroit), P.O. Box 338, 49735. Mike Hickey, Mgr., 3002 N. Connecticut, Royal Oak, 48073. Tel: 810-589-2306.

ALPENA. *Madonna House Apostolate,* 309 Lockwood, 49707. Tel: 517-354-4073. Rosemary Horan, Dir.

HARBOR SPRINGS. *Christ Child Society,* P.O. Box 132, 49740-0132. Tel: 616-526-2711. Diane Conn, Treas.

JOHANNESBURG. *Stella Maris Hermitage,* 19920 Black River Rd., 49751-9622. Tel: 517-732-9580. Rev. Richard Kropf.

PRESCOTT. *House of the Holy Shroud,* 1629 Beach Rd., 48756. Tel: 517-873-4000. Bro. Michael W. Whitman, Dir.

RELIGIOUS INSTITUTES OF MEN REPRESENTED IN THE DIOCESE

For further details refer to the corresponding bracketed number in the Religious Institutes of Men or Women section.

[0520]—*Franciscan Friars.* (Assumption, Sacred Heart Provs.).—O.F.M.

RELIGIOUS INSTITUTES OF WOMEN REPRESENTED IN THE DIOCESE

[0420]—*Discalced Carmelite Nuns.*—O.C.D.
[1070-03]—*Dominican Sisters.*—O.P.
[1070-13]—*Dominican Sisters.*—O.P.
[1070-14]—*Dominican Sisters.*—O.P.
[1070-26]—*Dominican Sisters.*—O.P.
[1170]—*Felician Sisters.*—C.S.S.F.
[1230]—*Franciscan Sisters of Christian Charity.* (Manitowac, WI).—O.S.F.
[2580]—*Institute of the Sisters of Mercy of the Americas.*—R.S.M.
[3490]—*Sacramentine Nuns.*—O.S.S.
[3560]—*Servants of Jesus.*—S.J.
[3580]—*Servants of Mary (Servite Sisters).*—O.S.M.
[0440]—*Sisters of Charity of Cincinnati, Ohio.*—S.C.
[2630]—*Sisters of Mercy of the Holy Cross.* (Merill, WI).—S.C.S.C.
[3830-11]—*Sisters of St. Joseph.*—S.S.J.

NECROLOGY

† Roczen, Edward A., (Retired). —Died Jan. 2, 1996.

Diocese of Grand Island

(Dioecesis Insulae Grandis)

Most Reverend

LAWRENCE J. McNAMARA, D.D., S.T.L.

Bishop of Grand Island; ordained May 30, 1953; appointed January 10, 1978; consecrated and installed March 28, 1978. *Mailing Address: Box 1531, Grand Island, NE, 68802.*

Most Reverend

JOHN L. PASCHANG, D.D., PH.D., J.C.D.

Retired Bishop of Grand Island; ordained June 12, 1921; appointed July 28, 1951; consecrated October 9, 1951. *Res., 320 E. Decatur St., West Point, NE, 68788.*

Chancery Office: 311 W. 17th St., P.O. Box 996, Grand Island, NE, 68802. Tel.: 308-382-6565; Fax: 308-382-6569.

ERECTED AT KEARNEY, MARCH 8, 1912; SEE TRANSFERRED TO GRAND ISLAND, APRIL 11, 1917.

Square Miles 40,000.

Comprises the Counties of Arthur, Banner, Blaine, Box Butte, Brown, Buffalo, Cherry, Cheyenne, Custer, Dawes, Deuel, Garden, Garfield, Grant, Greeley, Hooker, Howard Keyapaha, Kimball, Logan, Loup, McPherson, Morrill, Rock, Scotts Bluff, Sheridan, Sherman, Wheeler, Sioux, Thomas, Valley, and those portions of Dawson, Hall, Lincoln and Keith lying north of the South Platte River in the State of Nebraska.

For legal titles of parishes and diocesan institutions, consult the Chancery Office.

STATISTICAL OVERVIEW

Personnel	
Bishop	1
Retired Bishops	1
Priests: Diocesan Active in Diocese	49
Priests: Active Outside Diocese	3
Priests: Retired, Sick or Absent	29
Number of Diocesan Priests	81
Religious Priests in Diocese	1
Ordinations:	
Diocesan Priests	1
Total Sisters	94
Parishes	
Parishes	44
With Resident Pastor:	
Resident Diocesan Priests	44
Without Resident Pastor:	
Missions	42
Professional Ministry Personnel:	
Sisters	22
Lay Ministers	16
Welfare	
Health Care Centers	2
Total Assisted	142,646
Homes for the Aged	1
Total Assisted	79
Educational	
Diocesan Students in Other Seminaries	3
Total Seminarians	3
High Schools, Diocesan and Parish	4
Total Students	959
Elementary Schools, Diocesan and Parish	7
Total Students	792
Catechesis/Religious Education:	
High School Students	2,478
Elementary Students	5,609
Total Students Under Catholic Instruction	9,841
Teachers in the Diocese:	
Sisters	9
Lay Teachers	115
Vital Statistics	
Receptions into the Church:	
Infant Baptism Totals	1,012
Adult Baptism Totals	132
Received into Full Communion	189
First Communions	1,061
Confirmations	796
Marriages:	
Catholic	212
Interfaith	220
Total Marriages	432
Deaths	523
Total Catholic Population	53,841
Total Population	290,429

Former Bishops—Most Rev. JAMES ALBERT DUFFY, D.D., cons. April 16, 1913; resigned See, May 7, 1931; appt. Titular Bishop of Silando; died Feb. 12, 1968.—Most Rev. STANISLAUS V. BONA, D.D., appt. Bishop of Grand Island, Dec. 18, 1931; cons. Feb. 25, 1932; appt. Coadjutor Bishop of Green Bay and Titular Bishop of Mela, Dec. 2, 1944; succeeded to See, March 3, 1945; died Dec. 1, 1967.—Most Rev. EDWARD J. HUNKELER, D.D., ord. June 14, 1919; appt. March 10, 1945; cons. May 1, 1945; transferred to Kansas City in Kansas, March 31, 1951; died Oct. 1, 1970.—Most Rev. JOHN L. PASCHANG, D.D., Ph.D., J.C.D., ord. June 12, 1921; appt. July 28, 1951; cons. October 9, 1951; resigned July 25, 1972.—Most Rev. JOHN J. SULLIVAN, D.D., ord. Sept. 23, 1944; appt. July 25, 1972; cons. Sept. 19, 1972; transferred to Kansas City-St. Joseph in Missouri, Aug. 17, 1977.

Vicar General—Rev. JAMES D. O'KANE, *St. Agnes, Scottsbluff, 69363.* Tel: 308-632-3541.

Chancery Office—*311 W. 17th St., P.O. Box 996, Grand Island, 68802.* Tel: 308-382-6565; Fax: 308-382-6569. Office Hours: 9-5.

Chancellor and Moderator of the Curia—Rev. RICHARD L. PIONTKOWSKI, JR., S.T.L., J.C.L.

Diocesan Tribunal—*P.O. Box 996, Grand Island, 68802.* Tel: 308-382-6364.

Vicar-Judicial—Rev. MICHAEL F. MCDERMOTT, J.C.L.

Adjutant Vicars-Judicial—Revs. RICHARD L. PIONTKOWSKI, JR., S.T.L., J.C.L.; CHARLES L. TORPEY, S.T.L., J.C.L.

Defenders of the Bond—Revs. THOMAS RYAN; DONALD E. LARMORE, J.C.D.

Promoter Justitiae—Rev. DONALD E. LARMORE, J.C.D.

Judges—Revs. CHARLES L. TORPEY, S.T.L., J.C.L.; RICHARD PIONTKOWSKI, JR., S.T.L., J.C.L.; MICHAEL F. MCDERMOTT, J.C.L.

Procurator—Rev. JAMES M. HUNT.

Advocates—Rev. JAMES M. HUNT; RUTH NOZICKA; CONNIE RUHLMAN.

Associate Director-Notary—JOYCE M. PROUTY.

Diocesan Consultors—Revs. JOHN E. SCHLAF; DON BUHRMAN; CHARLES L. TORPEY, S.T.L., J.C.L.; JOSEPH HANNAPPEL; RICHARD L. PIONTKOWSKI, JR., S.T.L., J.C.L.; ROBERT B. ROONEY; JAMES D. O'KANE.

Vicar for Religious Communities of Women—Rev. FRANK L. HOELCK, Chadron.

Diocesan Offices and Directors

Apostleship of Prayer—Rev. FREDERICK SNYDER, Dir.

Building Committee—Revs. ANDREW GONDA; STANLEY GORAK; JOHN SCHLAF; JAMES D. O'KANE.

Charismatic Renewal—Rev. HAROLD KURTENBACH, Dir., *Box 405, Broken Bow, 68822.* Tel: 308-872-5716.

Charities—Rev. JOSEPH M. WALSH, Dir., Catholic Soc. Svc. Bureau; JAMES R. BLUE, Asst. Dir., Catholic Soc. Svcs., *335 N. 27th St., Lincoln, 68503.* Tel: 402-474-1600.

Communications—Rev. DONALD E. LARMORE, Dir., *1724 N. Walnut, Grand Island, 68801.* Tel: 308-384-0532.

Continuing Education for the Clergy—Revs. ARTHUR FAESSER, *4110 Cannon Rd., Grand Island, 68803.* ROBERT ROONEY.

Council of Catholic Women, Diocesan—Rev. STEPHEN F. DEAVER, Diocesan Moderator.

Family Life—EUGENE GILSDORF, Dir., *214 W. 5th, P.O. Box 1064, North Platte, 69103.* Tel: 308-532-2707.

Hispanic Ministry—Rev. ADOLFO BARROS, Dir., *Box 651, North Platte, 69103.* Tel: 308-532-2707.

Holy Childhood Association—Rev. REGINALD URBAN, Dir.

Liturgical Commission—Revs. CHARLES L. TORPEY, S.T.L., J.C.L., Chm. JAMES D. O'KANE, Vice Chm.

Marriage Encounter—Rev. WALTER W. PHILLIPS, *701 Student Dr., Ogallala, 69153.* Tel: 308-284-2458.

Newspaper—*"The West Nebraska Register".* Co-Editors: MARY PARLIN; MARILYN ZASTROW. Address all correspondence to: *P.O. Box 608, Grand Island, 68802.* Tel: 308-382-4660; Fax: 308-382-4746.

Personnel Board—Revs. THOMAS J. DILLON; BRYAN D. ERNEST; JAMES C. SCHMITT; FRANK L. HOELCK; JOHN E. SCHLAF; BERNARD M. BERGER; HAROLD KURTENBACH; ROBERT KARNISH.

Priests' Advisory Board (Presbyteral Council)—Revs. DON BUHRMAN; RICHARD L. PIONTKOWSKI, JR., S.T.L., J.C.L.; JOSEPH HANNAPPEL; RAYMOND M. KOSMICKI; RODNEY L. PRUSS; PAUL J. COLLING; DAVID L. RYKWALDER; JOHN E. SCHLAF; ROBERT B. ROONEY; LOUIS NOLLETTE; EDWARD CORTNEY; JAMES O'KANE.

Catholic Relief Services—Rev. FRANCIS T. CURRAN, Dir.

Priests' Pension and Welfare Board—Address all mail

to: Rev. JAN SMUTNY, *P.O. Box 194, Pleasanton, 68866.*

Propagation of the Faith—Rev. MICHAEL D. MCDONALD, Dir., *P.O. Box 667, Burwell, 68823.* Tel: 308-346-4190.

Remex-Media Center—214 W. 5th St., P.O. Box 1617, North Platte, 69103. Tel: 308-532-2707.

Religious Education—DONALD KURRE, Dir.; Sr. MARIETTA SPENNER, O.S.F., Assoc. Dir., *214 W. 5th St., P.O. Box 1617, North Platte, 69103.* Tel: 308-532-2707.

Rural Life Conference—Rev. NEAL P. NOLLETTE, Dir., *Box 530, Elm Creek, 68836.*

Schools—Rev. THOMAS A. RYAN, Diocesan Supt. of Schools, *311 W. 17th, P.O. Box 996, Grand Island, 68802.* Tel: 308-682-6565; Fax: 308-382-6569.

Sisters Council, Administrative Team—Sr. PAULETTE KUTA; Sr. ROBERTA ANN SEMPER; Sr. CLARE SCHERR.

Vocations—Rev. BRYAN D. ERNEST, Dir., *1104 Cheyenne Ave., Alliance, 69301.* Tel: 308-762-1418.

Youth—LISA CALDERONE-STEWART, *P.O. Box 1721, Grand Island, 68802.* Tel: 308-382-4660; Fax: 308-382-4746.

CLERGY, PARISHES, MISSIONS AND PAROCHIAL SCHOOLS

CITY OF GRAND ISLAND
(Hall County)

1—CATHEDRAL OF THE NATIVITY OF THE BLESSED VIRGIN MARY (1864), Revs. Thomas A. Ryan; Mark A. Maresh.
Res., 207 S. Elm St., 68801. Tel: 308-384-2523.
Catechesis/Religious Programs—502 West Division, 68801. Tel: 308-382-1198. Sr. Barbara Bader, C.S.J., D.R.E.
Students 480.

2—BLESSED SACRAMENT (1949), Revs. Donald E. Larmore; Martin Egging.
Res., 1724 N. Walnut, 68801. Tel: 308-384-0532.
Catechesis/Religious Programs—518 W. State St., 68801. Tel: 308-384-2086. Ms. Mary Jane Terrell, D.R.E.
Students 414.
Chapel—Geer-Sterne, 801 Stoeger Dr., 68803.

3—RESURRECTION (1973), Rev. James C. Schmitt.
Res., 4110 Cannon Rd., 68803. Tel: 308-382-8644.
Catechesis/Religious Programs—Therese Stump, D.R.E.
Students 210.

4—ST. LEO (1972), Rev. John R. Rademacher; Sr. Leona Augustyn, Pastoral Min.
Res., 2410 S. Blaine, 68801. Tel: 308-382-4753.
Catechesis/Religious Programs—D.R.E.: Beata Nabity, (Grades K-6); Mary Lynne McNeil, (Grades 7-12).
Students 310.

OUTSIDE THE CITY OF GRAND ISLAND

Ainsworth, Brown Co., St. Pius X, Rev. James M. Hunt.
Res., P.O. Box 7, 69210. Tel: 402-387-1275.
Catechesis/Religious Programs—Tel: 402-387-2260. D.R.E.: Lorraine Pozehl; Mary Kaup.
Students 150.
Mission—Bassett, Rock Co., Holy Cross.

Alliance, Box Butte Co., Holy Rosary (1894), Revs. Bryan D. Ernest; Timothy L. Stoner.
Parish Offices: 1104 Cheyenne Ave., 69301. Tel: 308-762-2009; Fax: 308-762-7474.
Res., 916 Cheyenne Ave., 69301. Tel: 308-762-1418. [CEM]
School—St. Agnes Academy.
Sisters 2; Lay Teachers 14; Students 145.
Catechesis/Religious Programs—Shari Harris, D.R.E.
Students 375.

Anselmo, Custer Co., St. Anselm's, Rev. Lawrence W. Coulter.
Res., P.O. Box 157, 68813. Tel: 308-749-2254. [CEM]
Catechesis/Religious Programs—D.R.E.: Charles McGinn, (High School); Peggy Anderson, (Elementary).
Students 80.
Mission—Merna, Custer Co., St. Paul. [CEM]

Ashton, Sherman Co., St. Francis, Rev. Frederick N. Snyder.
Res., 245 Howells Ave., P.O. Box 147, 68817. Tel: 308-738-2198.
Catechesis/Religious Programs—Mrs. Eddy Krzycki, D.R.E.
Students 55.
Mission—Paplin, Howard Co., Our Lady of Mt. Carmel.

Bridgeport, Morrill Co., All Souls (1919), Rev. Christopher R. Keith.
Res., P.O. Box 250, 69336-0250. Tel: 308-262-0709. [CEM]
Catechesis/Religious Programs—D.R.E.: Sheri Hopkins; Michelle Lempke; Janet Dailey.
Students 140.
Missions—Broadwater, Cheyenne Co., St. Dominic; Dalton, Cheyenne Co., St. Mary; Bayard, Morrill Co., Sacred Heart.

Broken Bow, Custer Co., St. Joseph's (1888), Rev. Robert Rooney.
Res., 1407 S. E St., 68822. Tel: 308-872-5716. [CEM]
Catechesis/Religious Programs—Tel: 308-872-5809; Fax: 308-872-5809.
Students 176.
Missions—Ansley, Custer Co., Sacred Heart, Ansley, 68814; Mason City, Custer Co., St. Thomas, Mason City, 68855.

Burwell, Garfield Co., Sacred Heart (1910), Rev. Michael D. McDonald.
Res., 747 I St., P.O. Box 667, 68823. Tel: 308-346-4190.
Catechesis/Religious Programs—Betty Kovorik, D.R.E.
Students 242.
Missions—Ericson, St. Theresa of the Child Jesus; Sargent, Assumption of the Blessed Virgin Mary.

Chadron, Dawes Co., St. Patrick's (1886), Rev. Edward P. Cortney.
Office: 340 Cedar St., P.O. Box 231, 69337. Tel: 308-432-2626. [CEM]
Catechesis/Religious Programs—Linda Yeradi, D.R.E.
Students 125.

Chappell, Deuel Co., St. Joseph's (1909), Rev. Joseph A. Hannappel.
Office: Tel: 308-874-3407.
Res., 1049 2nd St., P.O. Box 586, 69129. Tel: 308-874-3221. [CEM]
Catechesis/Religious Programs—Students 150.
Missions—Lodgepole, Sacred Heart; Oshkosh, St. Elizabeth; Lisco, St. Gall.

Cozad, Dawson Co., Christ the King (1951), Rev. Donald J. O'Brien; Sr. Juana O'Brien, O.P., Pastoral Assoc., Tel: 308-537-3364.
Res., 1220 Ave. M, 69130. Tel: 308-784-3959.
Catechesis/Religious Programs—Donna Kolbo, D.R.E.
Students 245.
Mission—Gothenburg, Dawson Co., Our Lady of Good Counsel, Gothenburg, 69138.

Crawford, Dawes Co., St. John the Baptist (1896), Rev. Todd K. Philipsen.
Res., 808 4th St., 69339. Tel: 308-665-1584. [CEM]
Catechesis/Religious Programs—D.R.E.: Linda Moloney; Jackie Rapier.
Students 77.
Mission—Harrison, Sioux Co., Church of the Nativity of the Blessed Virgin Mary.

Elm Creek, Buffalo Co., Immaculate Conception (1879), Rev. Neal P. Nollette.
Res., P.O. Box 530, 68836. Tel: 308-856-4375. [CEM]
Catechesis/Religious Programs—Vickie Sullwold, D.R.E.
Students 154.
Missions—Overton, Dawson Co., Holy Rosary, Overton, 68863; Amherst, Buffalo Co., St. John Capistran, Amherst, 68812; Eddyville, St. Patrick.

Elyria, Valley Co., St. Mary's. Closed. For inquiries for parish records contact the Chancery.

Farwell, Howard Co., St. Anthony of Padua (1877), Rev. David L. Rykwalder.
Res., 103 Kearns St., Box 156, 68838. Tel: 308-336-3323.
Catechesis/Religious Programs—D.R.E.: Kathy Gorecki; Tami Morrow.
Students 118.
Missions—Elba, St. Joseph; Geranium, St. Wenceslaus. [CEM]

Gering, Scotts Bluff Co., Christ the King (1958), Rev. Gerald J. Harr.
Res., 1730 N St., P.O. Box 33, 69341. Tel: 308-436-4000. [CEM]
Catechesis/Religious Programs—18th & N St., P.O. Box 33, 69341. Tel: 308-436-2923. Pat Schumacher, D.R.E. & Dir. Youth Ministry.
Students 305.
Mission—Minatare, St. Mary.

Gordon, Sheridan Co., St. Leo's (1887), Rev. Robert A. Karnish.
Res., 228 N. Maverick, 69343. Tel: 308-282-0427. [JC]
Catechesis/Religious Programs—Students 170.
Missions—Rushville, Immaculate Conception; Hay Springs, St. Columbkille; Merriman, St. Elizabeth.

Greeley, Greeley Co., Sacred Heart (1893) (Irish), Rev. Loren G. Pohlmeier.
Res., 302 W. Wicklow, P.O. Box 99, 68842. Tel: 308-428-2855. [JC]
Catechesis/Religious Programs—Students 88.
Missions—Scotia, St. Patrick; O'Connor, Our Lady of the Visitation.

Hemingford, Box Butte Co., St. Bridget (1888), Rev. Hubert J. Spanel.
Res., 801 Niobrara Ave., P.O. Box 67, 69348. Tel: 308-487-3617. [CEM]
Catechesis/Religious Programs—Judy Gonzalez, D.R.E.
Students 100.
Mission—Hay Springs, Sacred Heart.

Kearney, Buffalo Co., St. James (1881), Revs. Charles L. Torpey; James R. Golka.
Res., 7 Sioux Ln., P.O. Box 128, 68848. Tel: 308-234-5536; 234-5354.
High School—Kearney Catholic, (Grades 7-12). Mr. Terrence Torson, Admin.
Sisters 2; Lay Teachers 22; Students 309.
Catechesis/Religious Programs—Tel: 308-234-9695. Deb Kratochvil, D.R.E.
Students 524.

Prince of Peace (1986), Rev. Gerald J. Carlson; Sr. Roberta Ann Semper, O.P., Pastoral Min.
Res., 1210 E. 11th St., 68847. Tel: 308-236-9171.
Catechesis/Religious Programs—Ms. Carolyn Smallcomb, D.R.E.
Students 151.

Kimball, Kimball Co., St. Joseph's (1921), Rev. Francis T. Curran.
Res., 507 S. Howard, 69145. Tel: 308-235-2162.
Catechesis/Religious Programs—Students 78.

Lexington, Dawson Co., St. Ann's (1883), Rev. Donald A. Buhrman; Sr. Clara Scherr, S.C.L., Pastoral Ministry, Tel: 308-324-4647.
Res., 303 E. 6th St., P.O. Box 578, 68850. Tel: 308-324-4647. [CEM]
Catechesis/Religious Programs—St. Ann's Parish Center, 10th & Taft St., 68850. Tel: 308-324-2616. D.R.E.: Joan Karre, (Grades K-12); Lisa Baughman, Youth Min.
Students 349.

Loup City, Sherman Co., St. Josaphat's, Rev. Reginald A. Urban.
Res., Rte. 2, P.O. Box 38A, 68853. Tel: 308-745-0315. [CEM]
Catechesis/Religious Programs—Students 207.

Mitchell, Scotts Bluff Co., St. Theresa's, Rev. Stephen F. Deaver.
Res., 1715 17th St., 69357. Tel: 308-623-1745.
Catechesis/Religious Programs—Students 82.
Missions—Morrill, St. Ann; Lyman, Sacred Heart.

Mullen, Hooker Co., St. Mary's, Rev. Louis A. Nollette.
Res., 302 S. Blaine, P.O. Box 191, 69152. Tel: 308-546-2250; Fax: 308-546-2327.
Catechesis/Religious Programs—Students 107.
Missions—Brownlee, Cherry Co., St. Joan of Arc; Hyannis, Grant Co., All Saint's; Thedford, Thomas Co., St. Thomas of Canterbury.

North Platte, Lincoln Co., Holy Spirit (1973), Rev. James H. Heithoff.
Res., P.O. Box 427, 69103. Tel: 308-534-4334; 534-7906.
Catechesis/Religious Programs—Kathy Schroeder, D.R.E.
Students 225.

St. Patrick (1875), Rev. Bernard M. Berger.
Res., 415 N. Chestnut, P.O. Box 399, 69103. Tel: 308-532-0942. [CEM]
School—(Grades K-6). Mr. Tom Rhodes, Prin.
Lay Teachers 18; Students 227.
High School—(Grades 7-12). Mr. William McGahan, Jr., Supt.
Lay Teachers 18; Students 216.
Catechesis/Religious Programs—Tel: 308-532-6388. Rebecca Wing, D.R.E.
Students 199.

Ogallala, Keith Co., St. Luke's (1887), Rev. John E. Schlaf.
Res., 417 E. Third, 69153. Tel: 308-284-3196. [JC]
School—Ursuline Sisters 1; Lay Teachers 3; Students 67.
Catechesis/Religious Programs—Lay Teachers 22; Students 165.

Ord, Valley Co., Our Lady of Perpetual Help, Rev. James L. Warner.
Res., P.O. Box 123, 68862. Tel: 308-728-3351. [CEM]
School—Tel: 308-728-5389.
Sisters 1; Lay Teachers 7; Students 78.
Catechesis/Religious Programs—Students 137.

Pleasanton, Buffalo Co., St. Mary's (1909) (German), Rev. Harold R. Kurtenbach.
Res., 504 N. Sycamore St., Box 134, 68866. Tel: 308-388-2181. [CEM]
Catechesis/Religious Programs—Tel: 308-388-3062. D.R.E.: Delores Paitz; Karen Flamig; Darlene Schulte.
Students 165.
Missions—Hazard, Sherman Co., St. Gabriel; Prairie Center, Buffalo Co., St. Mary. [CEM]

Ravenna, Buffalo Co., Our Lady of Lourdes (1887) (German), Rev. Rodney Lee A. Pruss.
Res., 515 Sicily Ave., Box 90, 68869. Tel: 308-452-3314.
Catechesis/Religious Programs—Students 106.
Mission—Rockville, Sherman Co., St. Mary's, 406 Fair St., Rockville, 68871.

St. Libory, Howard Co., St. Libory's (1884), Rev. Richard L. Piontkowski.
Res., P.O. Box 7, 68872. Tel: 308-687-6276. [CEM]

St. Paul, Howard Co., SS. Peter and Paul (1878), Rev. Michael F. McDermott.
Res., 405 7th St., 68873. Tel: 308-754-4649. [JC]
Catechesis/Religious Programs—713 Elm St., 68873. Tel: 308-754-4002. Sr. Maria del Rey Mangan, O.P., D.R.E.
Students 199.
Mission—Wolbach, St. Joseph.

Scottsbluff, Scotts Bluff Co., St. Agnes (1912), Rev. James D. O'Kane.
Res., 2314 3rd Ave., P.O. Box 349, 69363. Tel: 308-632-2541.
School—Lay Teachers 9; Students 95.
Catechesis/Religious Programs—Kathleen Roehl, D.R.E.
Students 212.

Our Lady of Guadalupe (1955) (Hispanic), Rev. Paul J. Colling.
Res., 1103 12th Ave., 69361. Tel: 308-632-2845. [CEM]
Catechesis/Religious Programs—Tel: 308-783-2548. Elesio Guadarrama, Jr., D.R.E.
Students 151.

Sidney, Cheyenne Co., St. Patrick's (1978), Rev. Ted A. Nekoliczak; Sr. Esther Fehringer, Pastoral Assoc.
Res., 1039 14th Ave., P.O. Box 99, 69162. Tel: 308-254-2828.
Catechesis/Religious Programs—D.R.E.: Kay Kahl, (Grades K-6); Jack Mertz, (Grades 7-12).
Students 308.

Spalding, Greeley Co., St. Michael's (1887), Rev. Frank Hoelck.
Res., 68665. Tel: 308-497-2662. [CEM 2]
Schools—Spalding Academy.
Sisters of St. Dominic 2; Lay Teachers 16; Students 88; (Grades K-6).
Lay Teachers 5; Students 46.
High School—Lay Teachers 9; Students 42.
Catechesis/Religious Programs—Students 108.

Stapleton, Logan Co., St. John the Evangelist (1913), Rev. James E. Novakowski.
Res., P.O. Box 309, 69163. Tel: 308-636-2421. [CEM]
Catechesis/Religious Programs—Students 90.
Missions—Arnold, St. Agnes; Callaway, St. Boniface; Oconto, St. Mary.

Sutherland, Lincoln Co., Sacred Heart, Rev. Thomas J. Dillon.
Res., 69165. Tel: 308-386-4300.
Catechesis/Religious Programs—Students 92.
Missions—Paxton, St. Patrick; Hershey, Our Lady of Guadalupe.

Valentine, Cherry Co., St. Nicholas, Rev. James J. Janovec.
Res., 69201. Tel: 402-376-1672. [JC]
Catechesis/Religious Programs—Mary Lou Stauffer, D.R.E.
Students 210.
Mission—Nenzel, St. Mary. [CEM]

Wood River, Hall Co., St. Mary's (1884), Rev. Raymond M. Kosmicki.
Res., P.O. Box 37, 68883. Tel: 308-583-2464. [CEM]
Catechesis/Religious Programs—Students 208.
Mission—Shelton, Sacred Heart.

Chaplains of Public Institutions

GRAND ISLAND. *Nebraska Veterans Home*. Rev. James C. Schmitt.
U.S. Veterans' Hospital. Rev. Walter M. Phelan.

KEARNEY. *Youth Development Center*, W. Hwy. 30, 68847. Tel: 308-237-3181. Rev. Arthur A. Faesser, Chap.

On Duty Outside the Diocese:
Reverend Fathers—
Fenton, Lawrence E., Holy Name of Jesus Church, 345 S. Military Trail, West Palm Beach, FL 33415
Whalen, Joseph E., 512 Gibson Ave., Lexington, KY 40517

Military Chaplains:
Reverend Fathers—
Borzych, Alexander J.

Retired:
Reverend Monsignors—
Hayden, Carl T., 111 Emerson #1225, Denver, CO 80218
Portrey, Lawrence A., 816 W. First, North Platte, NE 69101
Reverend Fathers—
Abele, Joseph P., Box 168, Oshkosh, NE 69154
Augustyn, Andrew M., 2517 W. Phoenix, Grand Island, NE 68803
Bauer, Jacob F., 2106 W. Cottage, Grand Island, NE 68803
Chamberlain, Robert F., Box 803, Sutherland, NE 69165
Cook, John N., Box 242, Greeley, NE 68842
Cortney, Kevin J., 510 Centennial Circle, Rm 110, North Platte, NE 69101
Dennett, John A., Box 1323, Lusk, WY 82225
Dowd, Thomas M., 2516 Commerce Ave., Grand Island, NE 68801
Ferris, Carl A., Valentine, NE 69201
Foster, Robert L., P.O. Box 241, Greeley, NE 68842
Gonda, Andrew, 1111 E. Nebraska Ave., Grand Island, NE 68801
Gorak, Stanley C., 318 E. 22nd St., Kearney, NE 68847
Guevara, Miguel H., Box 399, North Platte, NE 69103
Hargarten, Joseph F., No. 12 Pinewood Grove, Gering, NE 69341
Koprowski, Mitchell J., Mullen, NE 69152
Kremeier, James, 200 Swink Ave., Rocky Ford, CO 81067
Krystosek, Robert, Box 425, Clara City, MN 56222
McSweeney, James, P.O. Box 100A, Rte. 1, Stapleton, NE 69163
Mullowney, Thomas E., 110 E. 39th St., E7, Kearney, NE 68847
Murphy, James E., Rte. 1, Box 131, Spalding, NE 68665
Phelan, Walter M., 1111 E. Nebraska Ave., Grand Island, NE 68801
Phillips, Walter W., 701 Student Dr., Ogallala, NE 69153
Smutny, Jan, Box 194, Pleasanton, NE 68866
Szczesny, Michael S., 1405 W. Koenig, No. 307, Grand Island, NE 68801
Valdez, Max E., 3010 Ave. D, Scottsbluff, NE 69361
Whalen, James R., 314 East E, Ogallala, NE 69153
Wiest, Robert E., 2111 Bantam, Grand Island, NE 68801

INSTITUTIONS LOCATED IN THE DIOCESE

[A] HIGH SCHOOLS, DIOCESAN

GRAND ISLAND. *Central Catholic Junior Senior High School*. (Grades 7-12), 1200 N. Ruby, 68803. Tel: 308-384-2440. Dr. R. L. Ripp, Supt.; John Golka, Prin.; Howard Schumann, Asst. Prin.; Rev. Martin L. Egging. Lay Teachers 30; Students 441.

[B] GENERAL HOSPITALS

GRAND ISLAND. *Saint Francis Medical Center*, 2620 W. Faidley Ave., P.O. Box 9804, 68802. Tel: 308-384-4600; Fax: 308-389-5589.
For a complete listing, refer to the Hospitals section.

KEARNEY. *Good Samaritan Health Systems dba Good Samaritan Hospital*, 10 E. 31st St., 68847-2926. Tel: 308-236-8511.
For a complete listing, refer to the Hospitals section.

[C] HOMES FOR THE AGED

KEARNEY. *Mount Carmel Home-Keens' Memorial*, 412 W. 18th St., 68847. Tel: 308-237-2287.
For a complete listing, refer to the Special Care Facilities section.

[D] NEWMAN CENTERS

CHADRON. *Chadron State College-Newman Club*, 907 Main St., 69337. Tel: 308-432-4286; 432-3846. Mr. Gregory Golka.

KEARNEY. *University of Nebraska at Kearney Newman Apostolate*, 821 W. 27th St., 68847. Tel: 308-234-1539. Rev. Arthur A. Faesser.

RELIGIOUS INSTITUTES OF WOMEN, REPRESENTED IN THE DIOCESE

For further details refer to the corresponding bracketed number in the Religious Institutes of Men or Women section.

[0350]—*Carmelite Sisters (Corpus Christi)*.—O.Carm.

[1070-01]—*Dominican Sisters*.—O.P.

[1070-13]—*Dominican Sisters*.—O.P.

[3580]—*Servants of Mary*. (Omaha, NE).—O.S.M.

[0480]—*Sisters of Charity of Leavenworth, Kansas*.—S.C.L.

[3710]—*Sisters of St. Agnes*.—C.S.A.

[1630]—*Sisters of St. Francis of Penance and Christian Charity*.—O.S.F.

[1640]—*Sisters of St. Francis of Perpetual Adoration*.—O.S.F.

[3830]—*Sisters of St. Joseph*.—C.S.J.

[2110]—*Sisters of the Humility of Mary*.—H.M.

[4120-03]—*Ursuline Nuns of the Congregation of Paris*. (Louisville, KY).—O.S.U.

NECROLOGY

(No Deaths)

Diocese of Grand Rapids

(Dioecesis Grandormensis)

Most Reverend

ROBERT J. ROSE, S.T.L., D.D.

Bishop of Grand Rapids; ordained December 21, 1955; appointed Bishop of Gaylord October 13, 1981; consecrated December 6, 1981; appointed Bishop of Grand Rapids July 11, 1989; installed August 30, 1989. *Office: 660 Burton St., S.E., Grand Rapids, MI, 49507.* Tel.: 616-243-0491.

Most Reverend

JOSEPH M. BREITENBECK, D.D.

Retired Bishop of Grand Rapids; ordained May 30, 1942; appointed Titular Bishop of Tepelta and Auxiliary of Detroit October 18, 1965; consecrated December 20, 1965; appointed Bishop of Grand Rapids October 15, 1969; installed December 2, 1969; retired August 3, 1989. *Mailing Address: 660 Burton St., S.E., Grand Rapids, MI, 49507.*

Most Reverend

JOSEPH C. McKINNEY, D.D.

Titular Bishop of Lentini and Auxiliary of Grand Rapids; ordained December 20, 1953; appointed Auxiliary July 24, 1968; consecrated September 26, 1968. *Res., 4865 Eleven Mile Rd., Rockford, MI, 49341.* Tel.: 616-866-0931.

ESTABLISHED MAY 19, 1882.

Square Miles 6,795.

Comprises the following Counties of the Lower Peninsula of the State of Michigan: Ionia, Kent, Lake, Mason, Mecosta, Montcalm, Muskegon, Newaygo, Oceana, Osceola, Ottawa.

For legal titles of parishes and diocesan institutions, consult the Chancery Office.

Administrative Office of Diocese of Grand Rapids: 660 Burton St., S.E., Grand Rapids, MI, 49507. Tel.: 616-243-0491; Fax: 616-243-4910.

STATISTICAL OVERVIEW

Personnel	
Bishop	1
Auxiliary Bishops	1
Retired Bishops	1
Priests: Diocesan Active in Diocese	92
Priests: Active Outside Diocese	6
Priests: Retired, Sick or Absent	33
Number of Diocesan Priests	131
Religious Priests in Diocese	23
Extern Priests in Diocese	5
Ordinations:	
Diocesan Priests	3
Permanent Deacons in Diocese	20
Total Brothers	3
Total Sisters	321
Parishes	
Parishes	90
With Resident Pastor:	
Resident Diocesan Priests	87
Resident Religious Priests	3
Without Resident Pastor:	
Missions	12
Professional Ministry Personnel:	
Brothers	1
Sisters	26

Lay Ministers	78
Welfare	
Catholic Hospitals	2
Total Assisted	295,263
Homes for the Aged	1
Total Assisted	135
Specialized Homes	1
Total Assisted	271
Special Centers for Social Services	12
Total Assisted	18,715
Residential Care of Disabled	1
Total Assisted	71
Other Institutions	2
Total Assisted	1,254
Educational	
Seminaries, Diocesan	1
Students from This Diocese	2
Diocesan Students in Other Seminaries	9
Total Seminarians	11
Colleges and Universities	1
Total Students	2,385
High Schools, Diocesan and Parish	4
Total Students	1,839
Elementary Schools, Diocesan and Parish	41

Total Students	9,404
Catechesis/Religious Education:	
High School Students	2,383
Elementary Students	14,307
Total Students Under Catholic Instruction	30,329
Teachers in the Diocese:	
Brothers	1
Sisters	32
Lay Teachers	655
Vital Statistics	
Receptions into the Church:	
Infant Baptism Totals	3,006
Adult Baptism Totals	420
Received into Full Communion	547
First Communions	3,242
Confirmations	2,191
Marriages:	
Catholic	636
Interfaith	494
Total Marriages	1,130
Deaths	1,390
Total Catholic Population	146,205
Total Population	1,167,900

Former Bishops—Most Rev. HENRY JOSEPH RICHTER, D.D., cons. April 22, 1883; died Dec. 26, 1916.—Most Rev. MICHAEL JAMES GALLAGHER, D.D., ord. March 19, 1893; appt. titular Bishop of Tipasa and Coadjutor Bishop of Grand Rapids July 5, 1915; cons. Sept. 8, 1915; succeeded to the Diocese of Grand Rapids, Dec. 26, 1916; transferred to the See of Detroit, July 18, 1918; died Jan. 20, 1937.—Most Rev. EDWARD D. KELLY, ord. June 16, 1886; cons. auxiliary Bishop of Detroit, Jan. 26, 1911; transferred to the See of Grand Rapids, Jan. 16, 1919; died March 26, 1926.—Most Rev. JOSEPH G. PINTEN, D.D., ord. Nov. 1, 1890; cons. Bishop of Superior May 3, 1922; transferred to See of Grand Rapids June 25, 1926; resigned and appt. Titular Bishop of Sela Nov. 1, 1940; died Nov. 6, 1945.—Most Rev. JOSEPH CASIMIR PLAGENS, ord. July 5, 1903; cons. Sept. 30, 1924, Auxiliary Bishop of Detroit and Titular Bishop of Rhodiopolis; transferred to See of Marquette Nov. 16, 1935; transferred to See of Grand Rapids Dec. 16, 1940; installed as Bishop of Grand Rapids Feb. 18, 1941; died March 31, 1943.—Most Rev. FRANCIS J. HAAS, D.D., ord. June 11, 1913; appt. Sept. 26, 1943; cons. and installed as Bishop of Grand Rapids, Nov. 18, 1943; died Aug. 29, 1953.—Most Rev. ALLEN J. BABCOCK, D.D., ord. March 7, 1925; appt. Titular Bishop of Irenopolis and Auxiliary of Detroit Feb. 15, 1947; cons. March 25, 1947; appt. to Grand Rapids March 23, 1954; died June 27, 1969.

Administrative Office of Diocese of Grand Rapids—660 Burton St., S.E., Grand Rapids, 49507. Tel: 616-243-0491; Fax: 616-243-4910. Office Hours: Mon.-Fri. 8-4:30 All official communications to be directed to this office.

Moderator of the Curia—Rev. Msgr. TERRENCE L. STEWART.

Chancellor—Sr. PATRICE KONWINSKI, O.P.

Director of Finance—JOHN S. CZACHORSKI.

Vicars General—Most Rev. JOSEPH C. McKINNEY, *4865 Eleven Mile Rd., Rockford, 49341.* Tel: 616-866-0931. Rev. Msgr. TERRENCE L. STEWART, *660 Burton St., S.E., Grand Rapids, 49507.* Tel: 616-243-0491.

Clergy Fund—Rev. DONN TUFTS, *10224 Maple Island Rd., Fremont, 49412-9116.* Tel: 616-924-3389.

Deans—Big Rapids: Rev. ROCK BADGEROW, Grand Haven: Rev. JOHN F. PORTER, *12285 Heights Ravenna Rd., Ravenna, 49451-0216.* Tel: 616-853-6222. Grand Rapids North: Rev. ROBERT A. HART, *2275 Diamond, N.E., Grand Rapids, 49505.* Tel: 616-361-7339. Grand Rapids South: Rev. ROBERT L. PINKSTON, C.S.P., *246 Ionia N.W., Grand Rapids, 49583.* Tel: 616-459-7267. Grand Rapids East: Rev. Msgr. ERNEST SCHNEIDER, *6477 Ada Dr. P.O. Box 369, Ada, 49301.* Tel: 616-676-9111. Grand Rapids West: Rev. JOHN J. WISNESKI, *1200 Alpine Church Rd., Comstock Park, 49321.* Tel: 616-458-3065. Ionia: Rev. THOMAS F. BOUFFORD, *531 Jordan Lake St., Lake Odessa, 48849.* Tel: 616-374-7253. Ludington: Rev. KENNETH H. SCHICHTEL, *702 E. Bryant Rd., Ludington, 49431.* Tel: 616-842-8606. Montague: Rev. RICHARD J. VAN LENTE, *510 Iroquois, Fremont, 49412.* Tel: 616-924-0160. Muskegon: Rev. JAMES WYSE, *1292 Jefferson St., Muskegon, 49441-2027.* Tel: 616-722-2793.

Presbyteral Council—Rev. JOHN J. WISNESKI, *1200 Alpine Church Rd., Comstock Park, 49321.* Tel: 616-458-3065.

Finance Council—Most Rev. ROBERT J. ROSE, *660 Burton St., S.E., Grand Rapids, 49507.* Tel: 616-243-0491.

Vicar For Religious—Vacant.

Catholic Services Appeal—660 Burton St., S.E., Grand Rapids, 49507. Tel: 616-243-0491.

Tribunal Office—Rev. DENNIS A. WAGNER, Officialis, *265 Sheldon Ave., S.E., Grand Rapids, 49503.* Tel: 616-459-4509.

Vicar For Priests—Rev. Msgr. JOHN A. NAJDOWSKI, *3937 S. Wilson, Grandville, 49418.* Tel: 616-532-9344. Rev. DONALD E. WEBER, *1630 Godfrey S.W., Wyoming, 49509.* Tel: 616-241-6489.

Moderator of the Curia—Rev. Msgr. TERRENCE L. STEWART, *660 Burton St., S.E., Grand Rapids, 49507.* Tel: 616-243-0491.

Secretariat for Pastoral Formation

Secretary—Rev. DANIEL R. DEPEW, *Res., 723 Rosewood Ave., S.E., East Grand Rapids, 49506.* Tel: 616-243-6538.

Christopher House—Rev. DANIEL R. DEPEW, *Res., 723 Rosewood Ave., S.E., East Grand Rapids, 49506.* Tel: 616-243-6538.

Permanent Diaconate—Rev. RICHARD LAWIE.

Vocation Director—Rev. MICHAEL DANNER.

Continuing Formation of Priests—Rev. MICHAEL DANNER, Dir.

Secretariat for Parish Formation

Secretary—DANIEL J. PIERSON, Sec., *600 Burton St., S.E., Grand Rapids, 49507-3278.* Tel: 616-243-0491; Fax: 616-243-1442.

Religious Education and Youth Ministry—DANIEL J. PIERSON, Dir.

Worship and Christian Initiation—Rev. RICHARD LAWIE, Dir.

Bishop Baraga Bookstore and Religious Education Resource Center—MARGARET A. DEVITO, Coord. Tel: 616-245-2251.

Family Ministry (Education & Formation)—DANIEL J. PIERSON.

Pastoral Councils—Rev. DENNIS A. WAGNER, Dir.

Ministry Formation—DANIEL J. PIERSON.

Catechetical Ministry with Persons with Disabilities—DANIEL J. PIERSON.

Young Adult Ministry—DANIEL J. PIERSON.

Spiritual Development—Rev. PHILIP A. SHANGRAW, Coord.

Secretariat of Diocesan Schools

Secretary—JAMES O'DONNELL.

Supt. of Schools—JAMES O'DONNELL, *660 Burton St., S.E., Grand Rapids, 49507.* Tel: 616-243-0491.

Associate Supt.—CHRISTINE BURNS.

Secretariat for Social Justice

Secretary—JANET VOSS, Dir., *650 Burton St., S.E., Grand Rapids, 49507.* Tel: 616-243-0491.

Catholic Social Services, Grand Rapids—RICHARD V. LIBERATORE, Exec. Dir., *1152 Scribner N.W., Grand Rapids, 49504.* Tel: 616-456-1443.

Catholic Social Services, Muskegon—ROBERT H. MILLS, Dir., *Suite 125, 1095 Third St., Muskegon, 49441.* Tel: 616-726-4735.

Catholic Human Development Office—JOHN OTT, Dir., *650 Burton St., S.E., Grand Rapids, 49507.* Tel: 616-248-3030.

Christian Community Center—540 E. Hackley, Muskegon, 49444. Tel: 616-725-7579.

Good Shepherd Advocacy Program—660 Burton S.E., Grand Rapids, 49507. Tel: 616-246-6445.

Office of Social Justice—650 Burton St., S.E., Grand Rapids, 49507. Tel: 616-243-0491.

Bishops Overseas Appeal—

Catholic Relief Services—

Project Rachel—650 Burton St., S.E., Grand Rapids, 49507.

Indian & Negro Mission Fund—650 Burton St., S.E., Grand Rapids, 49507. Tel: 616-248-3030.

Black Catholic Ministry—650 Burton St., S.E., Grand Rapids, 49507. Tel: 616-248-3030.

Native American Ministry—650 Burton St., S.E., Grand Rapids, 49507. Tel: 616-248-3030.

Hispanic Ministry—LUIS BETETA, *650 Burton S.W., Grand Rapids, 49507.* Tel: 616-243-0491.

Vietnamese Parish—Rev. PETER NGHIEM, *1630 Godfrey, S.W., Grand Rapids, 49509.* Tel: 616-241-0131.

Prison/Jail Ministry—GERTRUDE STAWICK, Dir., *650 Burton St., S.E., Grand Rapids, 49507.* Tel: 616-243-0491.

Secretariat for Administration

Secretary—Sr. PATRICE KONWINSKI, O.P., *660 Burton St., S.E., Grand Rapids, 49507.* Tel: 616-243-0491.

Archivist—Rev. DENNIS W. MORROW, *660 Burton St., S.E., Grand Rapids, 49507.* Tel: 616-243-0491.

Building and Planning Committee—Sr. PATRICE KONWINSKI, O.P., *660 Burton St., S.E., Grand Rapids, 49507.* Tel: 616-243-0491.

Cemeteries—Rev. JAMES C. CUSACK, *660 Burton St., S.E., Grand Rapids, 49507.* Tel: 616-243-0491. Resurrection Cemetery: ROBERT R. MENZEL, Mgr., *Res., 4100 Clyde Park, S.W., Grand Rapids, 49509.* Tel: 616-531-9320.

Communications Coordinator—THOMAS JUREK, *660 Burton St., S.E., Grand Rapids, 49507.* Tel: 616-243-0491.

Director of Finance—JOHN S. CZACHORSKI, *660 Burton St., S.E., Grand Rapids, 49507.* Tel: 616-243-0491.

Self-Insurance Program—Sr. PATRICE KONWINSKI, O.P., *660 Burton St., S.E., Grand Rapids, 49507.* Tel: 616-243-0491.

Tribunal—Rev. DENNIS A. WAGNER, Officialis, *265 Sheldon, S.E., Grand Rapids, 49503.* Tel: 616-459-4509.

Council of Catholic Women—ARLENE THOMAS, *650 Burton St., S.E., Grand Rapids, 49507.* Tel: 616-243-0491.

Ecumenical Commission—Rev. CHARLES R. DAUTREMONT, *150 E. Summit St., Muskegon Hts., 49444.* Tel: 616-733-2440.

Hospital Apostolate—Rev. EUGENE S. GOLAS, Chap., *Res., 2110 Leonard, N.E., Grand Rapids, 49505.* Tel: 616-242-4832. Rev. MARK E. MITCHELL, Assoc. Chap., *Res., 628 Diamond N.E., Grand Rapids, 49503.* Tel: 616-242-4832.

Director of Stewardship Development—FRANK LANESEY, *660 Burton St., S.E., Grand Rapids, 49507.* Tel: 616-243-0491.

CLERGY, PARISHES, MISSIONS AND PAROCHIAL SCHOOLS

CITY OF GRAND RAPIDS
(Kent County)

1—CATHEDRAL OF ST. ANDREW, Rev. M. Thomas Bolster. Res., 267 Sheldon Ave., S.E., 49503. Tel: 616-456-1454. [CEM]
School—305 Sheldon Ave., S.E., 49503.
Sisters 9; Lay Teachers 14; Students 222.
Catechesis/Religious Programs—Karen Noguera, D.R.E.
Students 150.

2—BASILICA OF ST. ADALBERT (Polish), Rev. Thomas J. DeYoung.
Res., 671 Davis, N.W., 49504. Tel: 616-458-3065. [JC]
School—640 Fifth St., N.W., 49504. Tel: 616-459-7988.
Sisters 1; Lay Teachers 9; Students 120.

3—ST. ALPHONSUS, Revs. Daniel L. Lowery, C.SS.R.; Bernard Rooney, C.SS.R.; Bernie Carlin, C.SS.R.; Rudy Papes, C.SS.R.; Thomas O'Connor, C.SS.R.; Robert Balser, C.SS.R.; Patrick Grile, C.SS.R.
Res., 224 Carrier St., N.E., 49505. Tel: 616-451-3043. [JC]
School—228 Carrier St., N.E., 49505. Tel: 616-454-4904.
Sisters 1; Lay Teachers 20; Students 375.
Catechesis/Religious Programs—Lucio Caruso, D.R.E.
Students 240.

4—ST. ANTHONY OF PADUA, Revs. Bernard Zajdel, O.F.M.Conv.; John Raphael Hadnagy, O.F.M. Conv.; Sr. Eileen Golos, O.S.F., Pastoral Min. In res., Rev. Raymond Oosdyke, O.F.M.Conv.
Res., 1776 Acacia Dr., N.W., 49504. Tel: 616-453-8229; Fax: 616-453-8053.
School—2510 Richmond, N.W., 49504. Tel: 616-453-4062.
Lay Teachers 13; Students 282.
Catechesis/Religious Programs—Cecilia Rinkevich, D.R.E.
Students 207.

5—BLESSED SACRAMENT, Rev. Robert A. Hart; Deacon George LeMire.
Res., 2275 Diamond Ave. N.E., 49505-4313. Tel: 616-361-7339. [JC]
School—2233 Diamond N.E., 49505-4313. Tel: 616-364-9453.
Lay Teachers 26; Students 452.

6—ST. FRANCIS XAVIER, Rev. Charles R. Antekeier.
Res., 250 Brown St. S.E., 49507. Tel: 616-241-2485. [JC]
School—240 Brown St. S.E., 49507. Tel: 616-241-5474. Sr. Winifred Wheeler, S.J., Prin.
Lay Teachers 13; Students 202.
Convent—(Detroit Prov.) 245 Griggs S.E., 49507. Tel: 616-241-0198. Sisters of Mercy

7—HOLY NAME, Rev. Donald E. Weber.
Res., 1630 Godfrey Ave. S.W., 49509. Tel: 616-241-6489. [JC]
School—1650 Godfrey Ave. S.W., 49509. Tel: 616-243-1126. Sr. Adele Labiotka, Prin.
Sisters 1; Lay Teachers 12; Students 192.

8—HOLY SPIRIT, Revs. David E. LeBlanc; Mark C. Przybysz; Daryl E. Nowicki, Business Mgr.
Res., 2230 Lake Michigan Dr. N.W., 49504. Tel: 616-453-6369.
School—Lay Teachers 27; Students 564.
Catechesis/Religious Programs—Patricia Frisk, D.R.E.
Students 260.

9—IMMACULATE HEART OF MARY, Revs. Joseph Ferraioli, O.M.I.; Arthur King, O.M.I.; Bro. James Lucas.
Res., 1935 Plymouth Rd. S.E., 49506. Tel: 616-241-4477.
School—Lay Teachers 20; Students 489.
Catechesis/Religious Programs—Teri D'Orazio, D.R.E.
Students 150.

10—ST. ISIDORE'S (Polish), Rev. Donald E. Lomasiewicz.
Res., 628 Diamond Ave. N.E., 49503. Tel: 616-459-4731. [JC]
School—625 Spring Ave. N.E., 49503.
Lay Teachers 12; Students 160.

11—ST. JAMES, Rev. Steven D. Cron; Norm Szubinski, Pastoral Assoc.
Res., 733 Bridge St. N.W., 49504. Tel: 616-458-3213.
School—751 First St. N.W., 49504.
Lay Teachers 16; Students 209.

12—ST. JOHN VIANNEY, Revs. Larry King; Chris Rouech.
Res., 4135 Clyde Park S.W., 49509. Tel: 616-534-5449. [JC]
School—Michaek Duffy, Prin. Lay Teachers 25; Students 523.
Catechesis/Religious Programs—Tel: 616-530-8224. Mark Kranenberg, D.R.E.
Students 460.

13—ST. JOSEPH THE WORKER, Rev. Pedro V. Garcia.
Res., 333 Rumsey St., S.W., 49503-4935. Tel: 616-456-7982.

14—ST. DOMINIC, Rev. Charles R. Dautremont.
Office: 50 Bellevue, S.W., 49548-3144. Tel: 616-531-1480; Fax: 616-531-0759.
Res., 59 Thurston, S.W., 49548-3163.
Catechesis/Religious Programs—Tel: 616-531-1480.
Students 211.

15—ST. JUDE, Rev. Thomas S. Vesbit.
Office: 1120 Four Mile N.E., 49505. Tel: 616-363-6885.
School—Lay Teachers 19; Students 255.
Catechesis/Religious Programs—1110 Four Mile N.E., 49505. Tel: 616-363-6897.
Students 335.

16—ST. MARY'S, Rev. Dick Host.
Res., 423 First St., N.W., 49504. Tel: 616-459-7390.
Catechesis/Religious Programs—Dick Bulkowski, D.R.E.
Students 46.

17—ST. MARY MAGDALEN, Revs. Louis L. Anderson; Loc Trinh; Sr. Beverly Pety, O.P., Pastoral Assoc.; Deacon Michael L. Wood.
Res., 1213 52nd St., S.E., 49508. Tel: 616-455-9310.

18—OUR LADY OF SORROWS (Italian), Rev. Theodore Kozlowski.
Res., 101 Hall St., S.E., 49507. Tel: 616-243-0222.
Catechesis/Religious Programs—Joseph Amante, D.R.E.
Students 75.

19—ST. PAUL THE APOSTLE, Rev. R. Louis Stasker.
Res., 2750 Burton St., S.E., 49546. Tel: 616-949-4170.
School—Tel: 616-949-1690.
Lay Teachers 16; Students 272.
Catechesis/Religious Programs—Beth Kolenda, D.R.E.
Students 165.

20—SS. PETER AND PAUL'S (Lithuanian), Rev. Dennis Morrow. In res., Rev. Joseph J. Pettit, (Retired).
Res., 520 Myrtle St., N.W., 49504. Tel: 616-454-6000. [CEM]
School—1433 Hamilton Ave., N.W., 49504. Mrs. Nancy Kryger, Prin.
Sisters of St. Francis of the Providence of God 2; Lay Teachers 10; Students 183.
Catechesis/Religious Programs—Students 55.

21—SACRED HEART, Rev. Edward A. Hankiewicz; Sr. Marie Bernarde Salazar, O.P., Pastoral Assoc.; Sr. Marjorie Vangness, O.P., Ministry to Elderly.
Res., 156 Valley Ave., S.W., 49504. Tel: 616-459-8362. [JC]
School—Tel: 616-459-0948. Richard E. Kosla, Prin.
Sisters 1; Lay Teachers 15; Students 203.
Catechesis/Religious Programs—Mrs. Mary Ann Cichewicz, D.R.E.

Students 100.

22—ST. STEPHEN'S, Rev. Mark C. Przybysz.
Res., 750 Gladstone Ave., S.E., 49506. Tel: 616-243-8998. [JC]
School—740 Rosewood Ave., S.E., 49506. Tel: 616-243-9013. Nannette Swanson, Prin.
Lay Teachers 12; Students 270.
Catechesis/Religious Programs—Tel: 616-243-9012. Mrs. Ann Aikens, D.R.E.
Students 261.

23—ST. THOMAS THE APOSTLE, Rev. James A. Chelick.
Res., 1449 Wilcox Park Dr., S.E., 49506. Tel: 616-459-4662. [JC]
School—David A. Faber, Prin. Sisters of the Third Order of St. Dominic 4; Lay Teachers 10; Students 327.

OUTSIDE THE CITY OF GRAND RAPIDS

Ada, Kent Co., St. Robert, Rev. Msgr. Ernest P. Schneider; Rev. David L. Harpe. Pastoral Assocs.: Sr. Joan Brown, O.P.; Dorothy Powell.
Res., 49301. Tel: 616-676-9111.
Catechesis/Religious Programs—Tel: 616-676-1488. Mary Ann Snyder, D.R.E.
Students 1,413.

Alpine, Kent Co., Holy Trinity, Rev. John J. Wisneski.
Res., 1200 Alpine Church Rd., N.W., 49321. Tel: 616-784-0677.
School—Comstock Park, 49321. Tel: 616-784-0696. Julie Whelan, Prin.
Lay Teachers 8; Students 200.
Catechesis/Religious Programs—Eric Egeler, D.R.E.
Students 235.

Baldwin, Lake Co., St. Ann's, Rev. Joseph J. Fix.
Res., 740 E. Ninth St., 49304. Tel: 616-745-7997.
Mission—Luther, St. Ignatius.

Belding, Ionia Co., St. Joseph's, Rev. George E. Darling.
Office: 409 S. Bridge St., 48809. Tel: 616-794-2145. [CEM]
School—St. Joseph-St. Mary, Tel: 616-794-1910. Christine Dallos, Prin.
Lay Teachers 4; Students 72.

Belmont, Kent Co., Assumption of the Blessed Virgin Mary, Rev. James M. Bozung, Admin.
Res., 49306. Tel: 616-361-5126. [CEM]
School—6393 Belmont Ave., 49306. Tel: 616-361-5483. Sr. Rosemary Smith, R.S.M., Prin.
Sisters 2; Lay Teachers 8; Students 220.

Big Rapids, Mecosta Co., St. Mary's, Rev. Michael G. McKenna.
1009 Marion Ave., 49307. Tel: 616-796-5202. [CEM 2]
School—Robert C. King, Prin. Sisters 2; Lay Teachers 9; Students 137.
Catechesis/Religious Programs—Students 68.
St. Paul's Campus Parish, Rev. Thomas P. Page.
Res., One Damascus Rd., 49307. Tel: 616-796-7393.

Brunswick, Newaygo Co., St. Michael's, Rev. Donn P. Tufts.
Res., 10224 Maple Island Rd., R.R. #5, Fremont, 49412. Tel: 616-924-3389; 924-9803. [CEM]
School—Tel: 616-924-0268. Sr. M. Theresa Pelky, R.S.M.
Sisters 4; Lay Teachers 1; Students 82.
Catechesis/Religious Programs—Students 102.
Mission—Hesperia, Christ the King.

Byron Center, Kent Co., St. Sebastian's, Rev. Msgr. Gaspar F. Ancona.
Res., 9408 Wilson, 49315. Tel: 616-878-1893. [CEM]
Catechesis/Religious Programs—Theresa Dekker, D.R.E.
Students 125.

Caledonia, Kent Co., Holy Family, Rev. Raymond Bruce.
Res., 9669 Kraft Ave., S.E., 49316. Tel: 616-891-1160; 891-9259 (Office). [CEM]
Catechesis/Religious Programs—Judy France, D.R.E.
Students 495.

Carson City, Montcalm Co., St. Mary's, Rev. William J. Reitz.
Res., 404 N. Division St., 48811. Tel: 517-584-3553. [CEM]
Catechesis/Religious Programs—Kathleen Copp, D.R.E.
Students 70.

Conklin, Ottawa Co., St. Francis Xavier, Rev. John F. Porter.
Res., 2044 Gooding Rd., 49403. Tel: 616-899-2471.

Coopersville, Ottawa Co., St. Michael's, Rev. Mark F. Bauer.
Res., 17151 88th Ave., 49404. Tel: 616-837-8792; 837-8158 (Parish Office).
School—Tel: 616-837-6346. Wendy Sipka, Prin.
Sisters 1; Lay Teachers 5; Students 85.

Custer, Mason Co., St. Mary's, Rev. William F. McKnight.
Res., 49405. Tel: 616-757-4709. [CEM]
Catechesis/Religious Programs—Roberta Edel, D.R.E.
Students 86.
Mission—Round Lake, St. Joseph.

Edmore, Montcalm Co., St. Margaret Mary, Rev. Vincent Bryce, O.P.
Res., 1051 E. Howard City Rd., 48829. Tel: 517-427-5645.

Evart, Osceola Co., Sacred Heart, Rev. Rock J. Badgerow.
Res., 9878 E. US 10, P.O. Box 778, 49631. Tel: 616-734-3171.

Free Soil, Mason Co., St. John Cantius, Rev. Isidro T. Gargantiel.
Res., 49411. Tel: 616-464-5672. [CEM]
Catechesis/Religious Programs—Mary Kovalcik, D.R.E.
Students 70.

Fremont, Newaygo Co., All Saints, Rev. Richard J. Van Lente.
Res., 510 Iroquois Dr., P.O. Box 248, 49412. Tel: 616-924-0160; Fax: 616-924-0996.

Grand Haven, Ottawa Co., St. Patrick's, Rev. William A. Langlois.
Res., 920 Fulton St., 49417. Tel: 616-842-0001.
Catechesis/Religious Programs—William Dunn, D.R.E.
Students 303.
Mission—Robinson Township, St. Anthony.

Grandville, Kent Co., St. Pius X, Rev. Msgr. John A. Najdowski.
Res., 3937 Wilson Ave., S.W., 49418. Tel: 616-532-9344.
Catechesis/Religious Programs—Linda Vanden Berg, D.R.E.
Students 574.

Greenville, Montcalm Co., St. Charles, Rev. Thomas A. McKinney.
Res., 102 W. Oak, 48838. Tel: 616-754-4194. [CEM]
School—501 S. Franklin St., 48838. Tel: 616-754-3196. Sr. David Therese Korson, O.P., Prin.
Sisters of St. Dominic, Grand Rapids, MI 1; Lay Teachers 7; Students 118.
Catechesis/Religious Programs—Diane Hamel, D.R.E.
Students 147.
Mission—Harvard, Kent Co., St. Margaret. [CEM]

Hart, Oceana Co., St. Gregory's, Rev. Ronald F. Schneider.
Res., 316 Peach St., 49420. Tel: 616-873-2660.
Catechesis/Religious Programs—Linda Foster, D.R.E.
Students 113.
Mission—Elbridge, St. Joseph Church.

Holland, Ottawa Co., St. Francis de Sales, Revs. Stephen S. Dudek; Jose Luis Quintana; Sr. M. Therese Harum, I.H.M., Pastoral Assoc.; Deacon Juan Garcia.
Office: 195 W. 13th St., 49423. Tel: 616-396-7641; Fax: 616-392-2474.
Res., 284 Maple Ave., 49423. Tel: 616-392-3985.
School—183 W. Thirteenth St., 49423. Tel: 616-396-4725. Mitre Zainea, Prin.
Lay Teachers 13; Students 233.
Catechesis/Religious Programs—195 1/2 W. 13th St., 49423. Tel: 616-392-6700. Marilyn Torborg, D.R.E.
Students 671.
Our Lady of the Lake, Rev. William H. Duncan.
Res., 557 Scarlet Oak Ct., 49424. Tel: 616-355-0256.
Catechesis/Religious Programs—Mark E. Peacock, D.R.E.
Students 713.

Howard City, Montcalm Co., Christ the King, Rev. Phong Q. Pham.
Res., 9596 Reed Rd., 49329. Tel: 616-937-5757.
Catechesis/Religious Programs—Ruth Lovelace, D.R.E.
Students 93.

Hubbardston, Ionia Co., St. John the Baptist, Rev. William J. Reitz.
Res., 404 N. Division, Carson City, 48811. Tel: 517-584-3553. [CEM]
Catechesis/Religious Programs—Kathleen Copp, D.R.E.
Students 70.

Ionia, Ionia Co., SS. Peter and Paul, Rev. Charles D. Hall; Deacon Zenon Cardenas, Sr.
Parish Office: 434 High St., 48846. Tel: 616-527-3610. [CEM]
School—317 Baldie, 48846. Tel: 616-527-3561. Lisa Francisco, Prin.
Lay Teachers 10; Students 228.

Irons, Lake Co., St. Bernard's, Rev. Thomas C. Niedzwicki.
Res., One Oak St., P.O. Box 155, 49644. Tel: 616-266-5155.
Catechesis/Religious Programs—Students 16.

Jenison, Ottawa Co., Holy Redeemer, Rev. Denis P. Nash.
Res., 2700 Baldwin Dr., 49428. Tel: 616-669-9220.
Catechesis/Religious Programs—Therese Carroll, D.R.E.
Students 612.

Lake Odessa, Ionia Co., St. Edward's, Rev. Thomas F. Boufford.
Res., 531 Jordan Lake St., 48849-6200. Tel: 616-374-7253.
Catechesis/Religious Programs—Dee Manshum, D.R.E.
Students 108.

Lakeview, Montcalm Co., St. Francis de Sales, Rev. Phong Q. Pham.
Res., 9596 N. Reed Rd., Howard City, 49329.
Church—829 E. Richardson, 48850. Tel: 517-352-7293.
Catechesis/Religious Programs—Ruth Lovelace, D.R.E.
Students 80.

Lakewood Club, Muskegon Co., St. Mary of the Woods, Rev. Henry J. Dondzila.
Res., 150 Church St., Twin Lake, 49457. Tel: 616-894-5887.

Lowell, Kent Co., St. Mary's, Rev. George J. Fekete; Deacon John Paroff.
Res., 402 Amity St., 49331-1308. Tel: 616-897-9820. [CEM]
Catechesis/Religious Programs—Maggie Walsh, D.R.E.
Students 120.

Ludington, Mason Co., St. Simon's, Rev. Kenneth H. Schichtel.
Res., 702 E. Bryant Rd., 49431. Tel: 616-843-8606. [CEM]
School—Cindy Bollman. Lay Teachers 10; Students 190.
St. Stanislaus, Rev. Dennis O'Donnell.
Res., 503 Third St., 49431. Tel: 616-845-7666. [JC]

Marion, Osceola Co., St. Agnes, Rev. Rock J. Badgerow.
Res., P.O. Box 778, Evart, 49631. Tel: 616-734-3171.
Church—Tel: 616-743-6401.

Marne, Ottawa Co., St. Mary's, Rev. Msgr. Terrence L. Stewart; Sr. Bernadine Gazda, S.S.J., Pastoral Assoc.
Res., 15164 Juniper Dr., 49435. Tel: 616-677-3934. [CEM]
Catechesis/Religious Programs—Students 165.

Miriam, Ionia Co., St. Mary's, Rev. George E. Darling.
Office: 409 S. Bridge St., Belding, 48809. Tel: 616-794-2145. [CEM]
School—St. Joseph-St. Mary. See St. Joseph, Belding. 616-794-1910.

Montague, Muskegon Co., St. James, Rev. Thomas A. Schiller.
Res., 5179 Dowling St., 49437. Tel: 616-893-3085. [CEM]
School—Tel: 616-893-2972. Geraldine Tutak, Prin.
Lay Teachers 5; Students 74.
Catechesis/Religious Programs—Tel: 616-894-8771. Joyce Richards, D.R.E.
Students 200.
Mission—Claybanks, St. John.

Muskegon, Muskegon Co.,

1—OUR LADY OF GRACE, Rev. G. Fredrick Brucker.
Res., 451 S. Getty St., 49442. Tel: 616-722-2803; Fax: 616-722-3622. [JC]
Catechesis/Religious Programs—Sr. Mary Middendorf, O.L.V.M., D.R.E.
Students 85.

2—ST. FRANCIS DE SALES, Revs. Thomas G. Simons; Ronald Hutchinson; Deacon William McCabe.
Res., 2929 McCracken St., 49441. Tel: 616-755-1953; Fax: 616-759-7074.
Catechesis/Religious Programs—Suzanne Southworth, D.R.E.
Students 387.

3—ST. JEAN BAPTISTE, Rev. James B. Wyse; Michael Stacy, Pastoral Assoc.
Res., 1292 Jefferson St., 49441. Tel: 616-722-2793. [JC]
Catechesis/Religious Programs—Barbara Miles, D.R.E.
Students 130.

4—ST. JOSEPH'S, Rev. John A. Johnson; Theresa Secord, D.R.E.
Res., 1224 Fifth St., 49441. Tel: 616-722-2556. [CEM]
Catechesis/Religious Programs—Students 80.

5—ST. MARY'S, Rev. John A. Johnson.
Res., 239 W. Clay Ave., 49440-1213. Tel: 616-722-2844. [JC]

6—ST. MICHAEL'S, Rev. Thomas J. Hack.

Res., 1716 Sixth St., 49441. Tel: 616-722-3071. [JC]
Catechesis/Religious Programs—Sr. Agnes Mary Wojtkowiak, O.P., D.R.E.
Students 480.

7—ST. THOMAS THE APOSTLE, Rev. Phillip J. Witkowski; Deacon David Kasprzyk.
Res., 3252 Apple Ave., 49442. Tel: 616-773-3160.

Muskegon Heights, Muskegon Co., Sacred Heart, Rev. Norman P. Droski.
Res., 150 E. Summit Ave., 49444. Tel: 616-733-2440.
School—Lay Teachers 5; Students 105.
Convent—2900 Leahy St., 49444.

Newaygo, Newaygo Co., St. Bartholomew's, Rev. Paul A. Milanowski; Sr. Helen Battle, S.S.J., Pastoral Min.
Res., 599 Brooks St., 49337. Tel: 616-652-1286. [CEM]
Catechesis/Religious Programs—Janet Vile, D.R.E. Students 230.
Mission—Grant, Our Lady of Guadalupe Church.

North Muskegon, Muskegon Co., Prince of Peace, Rev. Melvin E. Fox. Pastoral Assocs.: Sr. Judie Schuett, S.J.; Deacon Wesley Hewitt.
Res., 1110 Dykstra, 49445. Tel: 616-744-3321.
Catechesis/Religious Programs—Sandra Finkelstein, D.R.E.
Students 422.

Parnell, Kent Co., St. Patrick's, Rev. Wayne B. Wheeler, Jr.
Res., 4351 Parnell Ada, 49301. Tel: 616-691-8541. [CEM]
School—Mr. Thomas O'Brien, Prin. Students 138.

Pewamo, Ionia Co., St. Joseph's, Rev. Charlon O. Mason, Admin.
Res., 106 East St., 48873. Tel: 517-593-3440. [CEM]
School—Tel: 517-593-3400. George Heckman, Prin. Lay Teachers 5; Students 90.

Portland, Ionia Co., St. Patrick's, Revs. Julian Reginato; Troy Nevins.
Res., 140 Church St., 48875. Tel: 517-647-6505.
School—122 West St., 48875. Tel: 517-647-7551. Lay Teachers 16; Students 280.
High School—Lay Teachers 14; Students 202.
Catechesis/Religious Programs—Nancy Gleason, D.R.E.
Students 212.

Ravenna, Muskegon Co., St. Catherine, Rev. John F. Porter.
Res., 49451. Tel: 616-853-6222. [CEM]
School—Sr. Peter Mary Korson, O.P., Prin. Sisters 1; Lay Teachers 3; Students 58.
Catechesis/Religious Programs—Students 69.

Reed City, Osceola Co., St. Philip Neri, Rev. Daniel C. Aerts.
Res., 831 S. Chestnut, 49677. Tel: 616-832-5544. [CEM]
Catechesis/Religious Programs—Elizabeth Marek, D.R.E.
Students 136.
Mission—Paris, Mecosta Co., St. Anne.

Remus, Mecosta Co., St. Michael's, Rev. William F. Zink.
Res., 5045 Nine Mile Rd., 49340. Tel: 517-967-3520. [CEM]
School—(Grades PreK-6). Mr. Robert Cathcart, Prin.
Sisters 4; Lay Teachers 7; Students 180.
Catechesis/Religious Programs—Tel: 517-967-3681.
Students 120.

Rockford, Kent Co., Our Lady of Consolation, Most Rev. Joseph C. McKinney; Mary Ellen Koziol, Pastoral Assoc.
Office: 5001 Eleven Mile Rd., 49341. Tel: 616-866-0931.
School—(Grades PreK-6). Tel: 616-866-2427. Carolyn Hardy, Prin.
Lay Teachers 8; Students 166.
Catechesis/Religious Programs—Tammy Graves, D.R.E.
Students 480.

Rothbury, Oceana Co., Our Lady of the Assumption, Rev. John F. Vallier.
Res., 1372 S. Oceana Dr., Shelby, 49455. Tel: 616-861-2620.
Church—3000 Winston Rd., 49452. Tel: 616-893-0905.

Sand Lake, Kent Co., Mary Queen of Apostles, Rev. Joseph W. Kenshol.
Res., P.O. Box 140, 49343. Tel: 616-636-5671. [CEM]
Catechesis/Religious Programs—Pat Patin, D.R.E. Students 236.
Mission—Coral, St. Clara.

Saranac, Ionia Co., St. Anthony, Rev. Norbert L. Leyrita.
Res., 3927 Jackson Rd., 48881. Tel: 616-642-6119.
Catechesis/Religious Programs—Tel: 616-642-6402. D.R.E.: Janice Diaz; Monty Simpson; Sharon Basset.
Students 107.

Scottville, Mason Co., St. Jerome, Rev. Isidro T. Gargantiel.
Res., 203 W. State St., 49454. Tel: 616-757-2855.
Catechesis/Religious Programs—Kathy Papes, D.R.E.
Students 84.

Shelby, Oceana Co., Our Lady of Fatima, Rev. John F. Vallier.
Res., 1372 S. Oceana Dr., 49455. Tel: 616-861-2620.
Catechesis/Religious Programs—Paula Michalko, D.R.E.
Students 60.

Sparta, Kent Co., Holy Family, Rev. Martin S. Kurylowicz.
Res., 425 S. State St., 49345. Tel: 616-887-8222.
Catechesis/Religious Programs—Students 263.

Spring Lake, Ottawa Co., St. Mary's, Rev. Anthony C. Vainavicz.
Res., 406 E. Savidge, 49456. Tel: 616-842-1702; Fax: 616-842-3392.
School—Sr. Mary Lou Houghton, O.P., Prin. Dominican Sisters 3; Lay Teachers 11; Students 218.
Catechesis/Religious Programs—Peggy Secory, D.R.E.
Students 370.
Convent—421 E. Exchange St., 49456.

Stanton, Montcalm Co., St. Bernadette of Lourdes, Rev. Vincent Bryce, O.P.
Res., 1051 E. Howard City, Edmore, 48829. Tel: 517-427-5645.

Weare Twp., Oceana Co., St. Joseph's, Rev. Msgr. John J. Giammona.
Res., 2380 W. Jackson Rd., Hart, 49420. Tel: 616-873-2683. [CEM]
Mission—Pentwater, St. Vincent, Tel: 616-869-2601.

White Cloud, Newaygo Co., St. Joseph's, Rev. John Truong Au.
Res., 965 Newell St., 49349. Tel: 616-689-6061. [CEM]

Wright Township, Ottawa Co., St. Joseph's, Rev. Leo S. Rosloniec.
Res., 18876 Eighth Ave., Conklin, 49403. Tel: 616-899-2286.
School—Mrs. Ann Rutowski, Prin. Dominican Sisters 2; Lay Teachers 3; Students 100.

CHAPELS

GRAND RAPIDS. *Chapel of Our Lady of Aglona, Latvian Apostolate,* 507 Broadway Ave., N.W., 49504. Tel: 616-454-5921.
Chapel of St. Paul-Catholic Information Center, 246 Ionia, N.W., 49503. Tel: 616-459-7267. Revs. Robert L. Pinkston, C.S.P.; Robert Sirico, C.S.P.; Joseph W. Gallagher, C.S.P.; Michael Martin, C.S.P.; Deacon Elmer Zinn; Sr. Carmen Rostar, O.P.
Michigan Veterans' Facility Catholic Chapel, 3000 Monroe Ave., N.E., 49505. Tel: 616-363-2691.

On Special Assignment:
Reverend Monsignors—
Stewart, Terrence L., Moderator of the Curia & Vicar Gen., 660 Burton, S.E., Grand Rapids, MI 49507. Tel: 616-243-0491
Reverend Fathers—
Danner, Michael A., Assoc. Dir., Dir. Continuing Formation of Priests & Dir. Vocations, Christopher House, 723 Rosewood, S.E., Grand Rapids, MI 45906. Tel: 616-243-6538
DePew, Daniel R., Dir., Christopher House, 723 Rosewood, S.E., Grand Rapids, MI 49506. Tel: 538616-243-6
Dudek, Stephen S., Assoc. Dir. Hispanic Apostolate, Res., 3252 Apple Ave., Muskegon, MI 49442. Tel: 616-777-1621
Golas, Eugene S., Chap., Blodgett & Butterworth Hospitals, 2110 Leonard, N.E., Rm. 416, Grand Rapids, MI 49505. Tel: 616-242-4732
Heydens, Donald J., Tribunal Office. Tel: 616-459-4509
Kowalski, James C., Parish Pastoral Ministry Coordinator, Saint Mary's Health Services. Tel: 616-752-6338
LaGoe, John P., Muskegon Christian Community Center, 540 E. Hackley, Muskegon Heights, MI 49444. Tel: 616-725-7579
Lawie, Richard J., Diocesan Dir. Planning, Spiritual Moderator Permanent Deacons & Acting Dir. Worship, 660 Burton, S.E., Grand Rapids, MI 49507. Tel: 616-243-0491
Mitchell, Mark E., Assoc. Chap., Blodgett & Butterworth Hospitals, 628 Diamond N.E., Grand Rapids, MI 49503. Tel: 616-242-4832
Nghiem, Peter Hoan-Xuan, Dir. Vietnamese Apostolate, 1630 Godfrey, S.W., Grand Rapids, MI 49509
Page, Thomas P., Diocesan Coord. Campus Ministry, One Damascus Rd., Big Rapids, MI 49307
Shangrow, Philip A., 660 Burton S.E., Grand Rapids, MI 49507. Tel: 616-243-0491
Wagner, Dennis A., Officialis, Diocesan Tribunal Office, 265 Sheldon, S.E., Grand Rapids, MI 49503. Tel: 616-459-4509

On Duty Outside the Diocese:
Reverend Fathers—
Brucker, Frederick G.
Cook, Daniel
Hartwig, Lawrence N.
Nguyen, Phillip D.
Turner, Robert

Retired:
Reverend Monsignors—
Brophy, Charles D., 1247 Rennslaer, N.W., Grand Rapids, MI 49504
Jude, Walter F., R.R. #2, Box 76-1, Irons, MI 49644
Moran, James P., 156 Valley S.W., Grand Rapids, MI 49504
Powers, William E., 3033 N.W. 33rd Ave., Fort Lauderdale, FL 33311
Sniegowski, Thaddeus R., 17885 Apple Ave., Casnovia, MI 49318
Zerfas, Herman H., 3888 44th St., S.W., Grandville, MI 49418
Reverend Fathers—
Allen, Joseph A., 1631 Ferdinand, Detroit, MI 48209
Alvesteffer, Eugene
Baudone, Louis
Bernott, Albert R., 1409 Quarry, N.W., Grand Rapids, MI 49504
Bernott, Ernest J.
Bielskas, Edward J., 4101 Clyde Park, S.W., Wyoming, MI 49509
Branigan, Francis H., 2110 E. Leonard, Apt. 214, Grand Rapids, MI 49505
Cawley, Patrick
Cusack, James C.
Farrell, Edmund J., 307 57th St. Ct., West Bradenton, FL 34209
Feltman, Harold R., 504 S.E. 14 Ter., Cape Coral, FL 33990
Flynn, Francis J., 1060 Becker Rd., North Muskegon, MI 49445
Gillespie, Robert B., 1305 Walker, N.W., Apt. 5315, Grand Rapids, MI 49504
Hall, Bernard
Hoogterp, M. James, 3278 Roosevelt Rd., Muskegon, MI 49442
Kubiak, Edward J., 437 First St., N.W., Grand Rapids, MI 49504
Malewitz, Joseph M., 17444 A Dunewood Ct., Spring Lake, MI 49456
Ostrowski, Max J., 2044 Gooding Rd., Conklin, MI 49403
Pattok, Raymond J., 3843 Oakhurst Dr., Zephyrhills, FL 33541
Pettit, Joseph
Plewka, Edwin J., 2161 Leonard, N.W., Grand Rapids, MI 49504
Sikorski, Andrew, P.O. Box 191, White Hall, MI 49461
Statkus, Edward, 541 Broadway, Grand Rapids, MI 49504
Toolis, Martin, 3028 Piney Ridge Rd., Ludington, MI 49431
Wing, Kenneth A., 625 Lake Forest Ln., Apt. A5, Muskegon, MI 49441
Yager, James P., 3062 W. Leonard St., Grand Rapids, MI 49504
Zvirblis, John, 501 Broadway, N.W., Grand Rapids, MI 49504

Permanent Deacons:
Cardenas, Zenon, SS. Peter and Paul, Ionia
Fett, Richard, (applying for faculties)
Garcia, Juan, St. Francis de Sales, Holland
Glocheski, Virgil, (applying for faculties)
Herrera, Manuel E., SS. Peter and Paul, Grand Rapids
Hewitt, Wesley, Prince of Peace, North Muskegon
Hollern, Dale, St. Stephen, Grand Rapids
Jankowski, Leon, Holy Name, Grand Rapids
Jurek, Thomas, Holy Name, Grand Rapids
Kasprzyk, David, St. Mary of the Woods, Lakewood Club
LeMire, George, Blessed Sacrament, Grand Rapids
Mauer, Michael J., St. James, Grand Rapids
McCabe, William, St. Mary, Muskegon

Paroff, John, St. Mary, Lowell
Radecki, Richard, St. Paul the Apostle, Grand Rapids
Riksen, Norman, St. Pius X, Grandville
Rodriguez, Simon, St. Jean, Muskegon
Scheid, Howard, St. Joseph, Belding
Wood, Michael, St. Mary Magdalen, Grand Rapids
Zinn, Elmer, Catholic Information Center, Grand Rapids

INSTITUTIONS LOCATED IN THE DIOCESE

[A] SEMINARY, DIOCESAN

GRAND RAPIDS. *Christopher House-College Department of St. Joseph's Seminary*, 723 Rosewood Ave., S.E., 49506. Tel: 616-243-6538. Revs. Daniel R. DePew, Dir.; Michael Danner, Assoc. Dir. Students 2. Students attend area colleges.

[B] COLLEGES AND UNIVERSITIES

GRAND RAPIDS. *Aquinas College*, 1607 Robinson Rd., S.E., 49506. Tel: 616-459-8281.
For a complete listing, refer to the Colleges and Universities section.

[C] HIGH SCHOOLS, DIOCESAN

GRAND RAPIDS. *Catholic Central High School*, 319 Sheldon Ave., S.E., 49503. Tel: 616-459-4559. Paul Guild, Prin.; Mr. Kevin Pearson, Asst. Prin. Sisters of St. Dominic 3; Lay Teachers 45; Students 874.
West Catholic High School, 1801 Bristol, N.W., 49504. Tel: 616-453-4467. Mr. Bernard T. Stanko, Prin.; Mr. John Kolassa, Asst. Prin. Lay Teachers 32; Students 560.
MUSKEGON. *Muskegon Catholic Central Junior High and High School*. Greater Muskegon Catholic Schools. 1145 W. Laketon, 49441. Tel: 616-755-2201. Thomas Powers, Chief School Officer & Exec. Dir.; Patricia O'Toole, Prin. Lay Teachers 27; High School Students 276; Junior High Students 140.

[D] GRADE SCHOOL INTERPAROCHIAL

MUSKEGON. *St. Francis de Sales Elementary School*. (Grades PreK-6). Greater Muskegon Consolidated School. 2947 McCracken Ave., 49441. Tel: 616-755-1045. Mrs. Marcy Henehan, Prin. Lay Teachers 12; Students 251.
St. Michael Elementary School. (Grades PreK-6). Greater Muskegon Consolidated School. 215 W. Dale Ave., 49441. Tel: 616-722-4666. Elaine Bertram, Prin. Lay Teachers 8; Students 245.

[E] GENERAL HOSPITALS

GRAND RAPIDS. *St. Mary's Health Services*, 200 Jefferson, S.E., 49503. Tel: 616-774-6090.
For a complete listing, refer to the Hospitals section.
MUSKEGON. *Mercy Hospital*, 1500 E. Sherman Blvd., P.O. Box 358, 49443. Tel: 616-739-9341; Fax: 616-733-0957.
For a complete listing, refer to the Hospitals section.

[F] PROTECTIVE INSTITUTIONS

GRAND RAPIDS. *Contemplative Sisters of the Good Shepherd*, 1355 Walker Ave., N.W., 49504. Tel: 616-454-6268.
For a complete listing, refer to the Special Care Facilities section.

[G] HOMES FOR THE AGED

GRAND RAPIDS. *St. Ann's Home*, 2161 Leonard St., N.W., 49504. Tel: 616-453-7715; Fax: 616-453-7359.
For a complete listing, refer to the Special Care Facilities section.

[H] MONASTERIES AND RESIDENCES OF PRIESTS AND BROTHERS

MUSKEGAN. *Dominican Friars*, 1145 West Laketon, 49441. Tel: 616-755-5238. Dominicans Province of St. Albert the Great, U.S.A. Bros. Benedict Baer, O.P.; Joachim M. Thiel, O.P.

[I] CONVENTS AND RESIDENCES FOR SISTERS

GRAND RAPIDS. *Aquinata Hall*, 153 Lakeside, N.E., 49503-3894. Tel: 616-456-5038. Ms. Jacqueline Ghysels, Admin. Sisters 44; Beds 54.
Contemplative Sisters of the Good Shepherd, 1400 Morgan St., N.W., 49504. Tel: 616-453-4315. Sr. Genevieve Heart of Mary, C.G.S., Supr. Sisters 6.
Dominican Center, 2025 E. Fulton St., 49503-3895. Tel: 616-454-1241; Fax: 616-454-2861. Mark Clarke, Dir.
Motherhouse of the Dominican Sisters, Marywood, 2025 E. Fulton St., 49503-3895. Tel: 616-459-2910. Motherhouse and Novitiate for the Sisters of the Order of St. Dominic of the Congregation of Our Lady of the Sacred Heart. Legal Titles: *Sisters of St. Dominic of the Congregation of Our Lady of the Sacred Heart (The Religious Institute)*; *Sisters of the Order of St. Dominic of Grand Rapids, Michigan (The Corporation)*. Sr. Barbara Hansen, O.P., Prioress; Rev. Paul Colloton, O.P., Coord. Pastoral Life; Sr. Diane Zerfas, O.P., Coord. Pastoral Life. Sisters 356; Novices 1.
ADA. *Discalced Carmelite Nuns, Monastery of Our Lady of Guadalupe*, 4300 Mount Carmel Dr., N.E., 49301-9740. Mother Agnes Therese, O.C.D., Prioress. Professed Carmelite Nuns 20; Extern Sisters 3.
BELMONT. *Motherhouse of the Consolata Missionary Sisters*, 6801 Belmont Rd., P.O. Box 371, 49306. Tel: 616-361-2072; Fax: 616-361-2049. Sr. Felicia Bertaina, M.C., Supr. Consolata Sisters 22.

[J] RETREAT HOUSES

SPRING LAKE. *St. Lazare Retreat House*, 18600 W. Spring Lake Rd., 49456-0462. Tel: 616-842-3370. Revs. Michael J. Shea, C.M.; Alfred Pehrsson, C.M.

[K] NEWMAN CENTERS

COOPERSVILLE. *Grand Valley State University Catholic Campus Ministry*, Allendale Campus, 17151-88th Ave., 49404. Tel: 616-837-8158. Rev. Mark F. Bauer, Campus Priest; Deacon Dale Holleran, Campus Min.
EDMORE. *Montcalm Community College Newman Center*, 1051 E. Howard City Rd., 48829. Rev. Isidro Gargantiel.

[L] MISCELLANEOUS LISTINGS

GRAND RAPIDS. *Bishops' Housing Corporation*, 660 Burton St., S.E., 49507.
The Catholic Foundation of West Michigan, 660 Burton, S.E., 49507. Tel: 616-243-0491; Fax: 616-243-4910. Sr. Patrice Konwinski, O.P.
**Dominican Land Company*, 2025 E. Fulton St., 49503-3895. Tel: 616-459-2910; Fax: 616-454-6105. Sr. Ann Walters, O.P.
Educational Foundation of St. Francis Xavier School, Inc., 240 Brown St., S.E., 49507.
The Foundation for Catholic Education of Greater Grand Rapids, Inc., 410 Bridge St., N.W., 49504.
Fund for Faith, 660 Burton St., S.E., 49507. Foundation established in 1976 for various apostolic works.
Marywood Academy, 2025 E. Fulton St., 49503-3895. Tel: 616-454-2910; Fax: 616-454-6105. Sr. Ann Walters, O.P.
SS. Peter and Paul Parish Education Endowment Fund, 520 Myrtle St., N.W., 49504. Tel: 616-454-6000.
Sisters of St. Dominic Charitable Trust, 2025 E. Fulton Rd., 49503-3895. Tel: 616-459-2910; Fax: 616-454-6105. Sr. Barbara Hansen, O.P. Legal Title: *Sisters of St. Dominic of the Congregation of Our Lady of the Sacred Heart Charitable Trust (The Trust)*.
Steepletown Neighborhood Services, Inc., 423 First St., N.W., 49504.
West Michigan Catholic Education Foundation Funds, Inc., 660 Burton St., S.E., 49507. Tel: 616-243-0491.
LOWELL. *Franciscan Life Process Child Development Center*, 11650 Downes St., 49331-9489. Tel: 616-897-7842; Fax: 616-897-7054. Sr. Colleen Ann Nagle, F.S.E., Dir.
MUSKEGON HEIGHTS. *Christian Community Center*, 540 E. Hackley, 49444. Tel: 616-725-7579. Rev. John P. LaGoe, Dir.
Madonna House Apostolate, 3201 Peck St., 49444. Tel: 616-733-1129. Theresa Marsey, Dir.
PORTLAND. *The Father Flohe Foundation*, 140 Church St., 48875.

RELIGIOUS INSTITUTES OF MEN REPRESENTED IN THE DIOCESE

For further details refer to the corresponding bracketed number in the Religious Institutes of Men or Women section.

[1330]—*Congregation of the Mission*. (Eastern Prov.).—C.M.
[0480]—*Conventual Franciscans*. (Louisville).—O.F.M.Conv.
[0910]—*Oblates of Mary Immaculate*. (Eastern Prov.).—O.M.I.
[0430]—*Order of Preachers-Dominicans*. (Central Prov.).—O.P.
[1030]—*Paulist Fathers*.—C.S.P.
[]—*Priests of the Holy Cross*. (Indiana Prov.).—C.S.C.
[1070]—*Redemptorist Fathers*. (Prov. of St. Louis).—C.SS.R.

RELIGIOUS INSTITUTES OF WOMEN REPRESENTED IN THE DIOCESE

[0360]—*Carmelite Sisters of the Divine Heart of Jesus*.—Carmel.D.C.J.
[0720]—*Consolata Missionary Sisters*.—M.C.
[1830]—*Contemplative Sisters of the Good Shepherd*.—C.G.S.
[0420]—*Discalced Carmelite Nuns*.—O.C.D.
[1070-14]—*Dominican Sisters*.—O.P.
[1250]—*Institute of the Franciscan Sisters of the Eucharist*.—F.S.E.
[2575]—*Institute of the Sisters of Mercy of the Americas*.—R.S.M.
[3130]—*Our Lady of Victory Missionary Sisters*.—O.L.V.M.
[2970]—*School Sisters of Notre Dame*.—S.S.N.D.
[3830-11]—*Sisters of St. Joseph of Nazareth*.—S.S.J.
[1830]—*Sisters of the Good Shepherd*.—R.G.S.
[2150]—*Sisters of the Immaculate Heart of Mary*.—I.H.M.
[3260]—*Sisters of the Precious Blood*.—C.PP.S.

NECROLOGY

† Chmielewski, Edward A., (Retired). —Died Sept. 24, 1996.
† Popell, Rev. Msgr. Charles W., (Retired). —Died Sept. 18, 1996.

Diocese of Great Falls - Billings

(Dioecesis Magnocataractensis-Billingensis)

Most Reverend

ANTHONY M. MILONE, D.D.

Bishop of Great Falls-Billings; ordained December 15, 1957; appointed Titular Bishop Plestia and Auxiliary of Omaha November 10, 1981; Episcopal ordination January 6, 1982; appointed Bishop of Great Falls-Billings December 14, 1987; installed February 23, 1988. *Office: 121-23rd St. S., Great Falls, MT, 59401.* Tel.: 406-727-6683.; (Corporation title: "Roman Catholic Bishop of Great Falls, Montana A Sole Corporation.")

Most Reverend

ELDON BERNARD SCHUSTER, D.D.

Former Bishop of Great Falls; ordained May 27, 1937; appointed Titular Bishop of Amblada October 30, 1961; consecrated December 21, 1961; appointed Bishop of Great Falls December 2, 1967; resigned December 27, 1977. *Res., 1325 Smelter Ave., Black Eagle, MT, 59414.* Tel.: 406-453-8425.

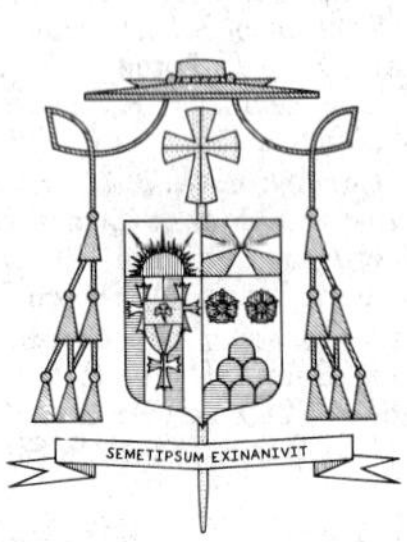

ERECTED MAY 18, 1904.

Square Miles 94,158.

Comprises the eastern part of the State of Montana and is made up of the following Counties: Big Horn, Blaine, Carbon, Carter, Cascade, Chouteau, Custer, Daniels, Dawson, Fallon, Fergus, Garfield, Golden Valley, Hill, Judith Basin, Liberty, McCone, Musselshell, Park, Petroleum, Phillips, Powder River, Prairie, Richland, Roosevelt, Rosebud, Sheridan, Stillwater, Sweet Grass, Treasure, Valley, Wibaux, Yellowstone and parts of Teton and Toole.

For legal titles of parishes and diocesan institutions, consult the Pastoral Office .

Pastoral Office: 121 23rd St. S., P.O. Box 1399, Great Falls, MT, 59403. Tel.: 406-727-6683; 800-332-9998 (Toll Free Montana Only); Fax: 406-454-3480.

E-mail address: lmc@mcn.net

STATISTICAL OVERVIEW

Personnel	
Bishop	1
Retired Bishops	1
Retired Abbots	1
Priests: Diocesan Active in Diocese	36
Priests: Active Outside Diocese	7
Priests: Retired, Sick or Absent	35
Number of Diocesan Priests	78
Religious Priests in Diocese	15
Extern Priests in Diocese	3
Ordinations:	
Permanent Deacons in Diocese	3
Total Sisters	78
Parishes	
Parishes	54
With Resident Pastor:	
Resident Diocesan Priests	32
Resident Religious Priests	11
Without Resident Pastor:	
Administered by Priests	5
Administered by Women Religious	6
Missions	72
Closed Parishes	1
Professional Ministry Personnel:	
Sisters	23
Lay Ministers	56
Welfare	
Catholic Hospitals	2
Total Assisted	106,271
Health Care Centers	1
Total Assisted	15,897
Day Care and Extended Day Care Centers	6
Total Assisted	664
Special Centers for Social Services	2
Total Assisted	63,350
Educational	
Diocesan Students in Other Seminaries	3
Total Seminarians	3
Colleges and Universities	1
Total Students	1,299
High Schools, Diocesan and Parish	1
Total Students	393
High Schools, Private	1
Total Students	154
Elementary Schools, Diocesan and Parish	9
Total Students	1,889
Elementary Schools, Private	3
Total Students	576
Catechesis/Religious Education:	
High School Students	2,505
Elementary Students	4,667
Total Students Under Catholic Instruction	11,486
Teachers in the Diocese:	
Priests	4
Sisters	6
Lay Teachers	273
Vital Statistics	
Receptions into the Church:	
Infant Baptism Totals	924
Adult Baptism Totals	115
Received into Full Communion	153
First Communions	1,045
Confirmations	638
Marriages:	
Catholic	209
Interfaith	144
Total Marriages	353
Deaths	743
Total Catholic Population	56,384
Total Population	392,900

Former Bishops—Most Rev. MATHIAS C. LENIHAN, D.D., ord. Dec. 20, 1879; cons. First Bishop of Great Falls, Sept. 21, 1904; resigned Jan. 18, 1930; created Titular Archbishop of Preslavo, Feb. 14, 1930; died Aug. 19, 1943.—Most Rev. EDWIN V. O'HARA, D.D., ord. June 10, 1905; appt. Aug. 1, 1930; cons. Oct. 28, 1930; appt. Bishop of Kansas City April 15, 1939 made asst. at the Pontifical Throne Jan. 5, 1949; appt. Archbishop "Ad Personam" June 29, 1954; died Sept. 11, 1956, Milan, Italy.—Most Rev. WILLIAM J. CONDON, D.D., ord. Oct. 14, 1917; appt. Aug. 5, 1939; cons. Oct. 18, 1939 asst. at the Pontifical Throne Dec. 9, 1964; died Aug. 17, 1967.—Most Rev. ELDON BERNARD SCHUSTER, D.D., ord. May 27, 1937; appt. Titular Bishop of Amblada; cons. Dec. 21, 1961; appt. Bishop of Great Falls Dec. 2, 1967; resigned Dec. 27, 1977.—Most Rev. THOMAS JOSEPH MURPHY, S.T.D., D.D., appt. Bishop of Great Falls July 5, 1978 Episcopal ordination and installation Aug. 21, 1978; appt. co-adjutor Archbishop of Seattle May 26, 1987.

Vicars General—Very Rev. DAVID F. DWYER; Very Rev. GILBERT HEMAUER, O.F.M.Cap.; Very Rev. EUGENE P. HRUSKA.

Pastoral Office—121 23rd St. S., P.O. Box 1399, Great Falls, 59403. Tel: 406-727-6683; 800-332-9998 (Montana Toll Free Number Only); Fax: 406-454-3480. All applications for dispensations and official communications should be addressed to this office.

Chancellor—Rev. ROBERT D. GROSCH, J.C.L.

Moderator of the Curia—Rev. EUGENE P. HRUSKA, V.G.

Business Manager—JOSEPH LONCKI.

Diocesan Tribunal—121 23rd St. S., P.O. Box 1399, Great Falls, 59403. Tel: 406-727-6683; 800-332-9998 (Montana Toll Free Number Only).

Judicial Vicar—Rev. ROBERT D. GROSCH, J.C.L.

Promoter of Justice—Rev. JOHN W. ROBERTSON, J.C.L.

Defenders of the Bond—Rev. DALE MCFARLANE; MARGARET ROMANO-HOGAN.

Tribunal Director—TERRYAL ANN REAVLEY.

Notaries—TERRYAL ANN REAVLEY; Rev. DALE MCFARLANE.

Diocesan Consultors—Most Rev. ELDON B. SCHUSTER; Revs. DAN CROSBY, O.F.M.Cap.; ROBERT J. FOX; ROBERT GROSCH; THOMAS HARNEY; DAN O'ROURKE; DALE YURKOVIC; PATRICK ZABROCKI; STEPHEN ZABROCKI.

Personnel Board—Revs. DICK SCHLOSSER, Chm. PETER E. GUTHNECK; KIRK C. MORGAN; ANTHONY J. SCHUSTER; GREGORY R. STAUDINGER; RICHARD OSTERMAN; ROGER VEIK, O.F.M.Cap., Vicar of Clergy Personnel (Ex Officio).

Regional Deans & Vicar Delegates—Billings: Rev. STEPHEN L. TOKARSKI; Great Falls: Rev. JAY PETERSON; Havre: Rev. PATRICK ZABROCKI; Miles City: Rev. KIRK MORGAN; Wolf Point: Rev. STEPHEN ZABROCKI.

Cemetery Board—Revs. EUGENE HRUSKA, V.G., Great Falls: JOSEPH LONCKI.

Vicar of Clergy Personnel—Rev. ROGER VEIK, O.F.M.Cap., *1122 N. 30th St., Billings, 59101.* Tel: 406-259-9902.

Vicar for Cum Christo Movement—Rev. KIRK C. MORGAN.

Vicars for Ministry to Native Americans—Revs. PETER E. GUTHNECK, *Rocky Boy CPU-Box 3009, Box Elder, 59521.* Tel: 406-395-4380.

Diocesan Offices and Directors

Apostleship of Prayer—Vacant.

Care & Share Committee—STELLA ZIEGLER, Chm.

Catechesis—PAUL F. KAISER, Dir., *Pastoral Center, P.O. Box 1399, Great Falls, 59403.* Tel: 406-727-3386. Sr. BARBARA BROWN, O.P., Assoc. Dir., *1109 Orr St., Miles City, 59301.* Tel: 406-232-2116.

Catholic Relief Services—JOSEPH LONCKI, Dir., Pastoral Center.

Catholic University, Friends of—Rev. ROBERT J. FOX, S.T.L., Ph.D., *Our Lady of Lourdes, P.O. Box 53, Poplar, 59255.*

Clerical Benefit Association—Most Rev. ANTHONY M. MILONE, Ex Officio; Revs. ANTHONY SCHUSTER, Chm. STEPHEN ZABROCKI; JAMES E. BIRKMAIER; THEODORE F. SZUDERA, Sec. LOTHAR KRAUTH; TERRANCE REGAN; JOSEPH LONCKI, Consultant; Rev. MICHAEL GUINAN, Retired Priests' Rep.

Continuing Education for Clergy—Rev. JOHN J. HOULIHAN, *St. Patrick's Co-Cathedral, 215 N. 31st St., Billings, 59101-9920.*

Diocesan Pastoral Council—Sr. PAT CORMACK, S.C.S.C., Exec. Dir., *121-23rd St. S., P.O. Box 1399, Great Falls, 59403-1399.* Tel: 406-727-6683; Fax: 406-454-3480.

D.C.C.W.—TONI DEMPSEY, Pres.; Most Rev. ANTHONY M. MILONE, Episcopal Moderator; Rev. JOHN J. HOULIHAN, Priest Moderator.

Ecumenical Officer—PAUL F. KAISER.

Education—Sr. KATHERINE FRANCHETT, S.C.L., Diocesan School Supt., *P.O. Box 31158, Billings, 59107.* Tel: 406-252-9595; 800-682-2218 (Montana Toll Free Number Only); Fax: 406-252-9875.

Finance Council—Most Rev. ANTHONY M. MILONE; JOSEPH LONCKI, Consultant; WILLIAM ARTZ; Rev. DAVID F.DWYER, V.G.; Sr. KATHERINE FRANCHETT, S.C.L.; MARILYN HARMON; Rev. EUGENE P. HRUSKA, V.G.; THOMAS LANE; JOHN NELSON; Most Rev. ELDON B. SCHUSTER; ALBERT MARTENS; THOMAS PELATT; MARILYN ROSE; ELLEN SOLEM; Rev. PATRICK ZABROCKI.

Holy Childhood Association—Vacant.

Lay Ministry Program—Sr. PAULINE SCHWANDT, O.S.F., Pastoral Center.

Liturgy Commission—REGINA GABRIEL; Sr. MARGARET MARY O'DOHERTY, O.P.; DIANA O'HARA; Rev. TERRANCE REGAN; JOE SULLIVAN; MICHAEL PRENDERGAST, Chm. JAN WOOD; Rev. STEPHEN ZABROCKI; ANN O'BRIEN; Most Rev. ANTHONY MILONE.

Liturgy Office—MICHAEL PRENDERGAST.

Missions—Vacant.

Newspaper—*"Harvest"*; Rev. EUGENE HRUSKA, V.G.

Office of Peace and Justice—BRUCE DAY, Dir., *121-23rd St. S., P.O. Box 1399, Great Falls, 59403-1399.* Tel: 406-727-6683; Fax: 406-454-3480.

RCIA—MICHAEL PRENDERGAST, Consultant, Pastoral Center.

Pastoral Outreach—PAUL F. KAISER, Coord.; Sr. BARBARA BROWN, O.P.; Sr. PAT CORMACK, S.C.S.C.; BRUCE DAY; Rev. EUGENE HRUSKA; SHEILA MOOS; MICHAEL PRENDERGAST; Sr. PAULINE SCHWANDT, O.S.F.

Priests' Council—Revs. DAN CROSBY, O.F.M.Cap., Chm. ROBERT GROSCH, Vice Chm. DAN O'ROURKE; ANTHONY GREGORI; DALE YURKOVIC; PATRICK ZABROCKI; STEPHEN ZABROCKI; THOMAS HARNEY; EUGENE P. HRUSKA, V.G.; GILBERT HEMAUER, O.F.M.Cap., V.G.; DAVID F. DWYER, V.G.

Sister's Council—Sr. CLAVER EHREN, O.S.F., Pres.; Sr. LAURITA WYDRA, S.S.S., Vice Pres.; Sr. JUDITH MAENDER, O.P., Sec.; Sr. VALERIE MCGEOUGH, R.S.M., Treas.; Sr. BARBARA BROWN, O.P., 5th Member.

Social Justice Commission—BRUCE DAY, Chm., *Pastoral Office, P.O. Box 1399, Great Falls, 59403.*

Director of Vocations—Rev. DALE E. YURKOVIC, *St. Mary's Church, P.O. Box 646, Livingston, 59047.* Tel: 406-222-1393.

Inter-Diocesan Organizations

Montana Catholic Conference—SHARON HOFF, Dir., *P.O. Box 1708, Helena, 59624.* Tel: 406-442-5761; Fax: 406-442-9047.

Montana Catholic Social Services—MARILYN MCKIBBEN, Dir., *P.O. Box 907, Helena, 59624.* Tel: 406-442-4130. Provides adoption and counseling services for families, children and infants.

Billings Office—BECKY HUBBERT, *1222 N. 27th St., Ste. 101, Billings, 59101.* Tel: 406-252-3399.

Great Falls Office—KYLA KALANICK, *P.O. Box 7410, Great Falls, 59403.* Tel: 406-771-7805.

Helena Office—Sr. NOEL BRUCH; KIM DALE, *P.O. Box 907, Helena, 59601.* Tel: 406-442-4130.

Missoula Office—BETSY ROBEL-GOMEZ, *St. Patrick's Hospital, 554 W. Broadway, Missoula, 59802.* Tel: 406-329-5629, Ext. 2029.

Montana Association of Churches—RUSTY CRAIG, Pres. MARGUERITE E. MCDONALD, Exec. Dir., *Andrew Square, Ste. G, 100 24th St. W., Billings, 59102.* Tel: 406-656-9779.

CLERGY, PARISHES, MISSIONS AND PAROCHIAL SCHOOLS

CITY OF GREAT FALLS
(Cascade County)

1—ST. ANN'S CATHEDRAL, Most Rev. Anthony M. Milone, D.D.; Rev. William A. Hogan, Rector; Sr. M. Genevieve Garvin, S.M., Pastoral Min.
Res., 715 Third Ave. N., P.O. Box 1708, 59403. Tel: 406-761-5456.

2—EASTSIDE CATHOLIC COMMUNITIES, Rev. Richard Schlosser; Rev. Msgr. Joseph Gluszek, (Retired).
Office: 2816 Central Ave., 59401-3498. Tel: 406-452-6491; Fax: 406-452-6493.
Churches—St. Gerard Majella, 2211-5th Ave. N., 59401.; Holy Family, 2800 Central Ave., 59401.; Sts. Peter & Paul, 200-44th St. S., 59405.
Catechesis/Religious Programs—Kathy Malby, D.R.E.
Students 218.

3—ST. JOSEPH'S, Rev. Anthony J. Shuster.
Res., 420-22nd Ave. N.E., 59404. Tel: 406-453-5558.
Church—420-2nd Ave. S.W., 59404.
Catechesis/Religious Programs—Tel: 406-453-9331. Jean Sobolik, D.R.E.
Students 145.

4—OUR LADY OF LOURDES, Rev. Lothar Krauth; Sr. Marian Lorang, O.S.U., Pastoral Assoc.
Res., 409 13th St. S., 59405. Tel: 406-452-6464.
School—(Grades PreK-8) 1305 Fifth Ave. S., 59405. Tel: 406-452-0551. Mrs. Adele Meister, Prin.
Ursuline Nuns 1; Lay Teachers 15; Students 260.
Catechesis/Religious Programs—Betty Ehman, D.R.E.
Students 120.

5—ST. LUKE THE EVANGELIST, Rev. Anthony J. Schuster. Pastoral Assocs.: Mary Anne Sladich-Lantz; LaVonne Pidcock.
Res., 420 22nd Ave. N.E., 59404. Tel: 406-453-6546; Fax: 406-453-0323.
Catechesis/Religious Programs—Suzanne Johnson, D.R.E.
Students 370.

CITY OF BILLINGS
(Yellowstone County)

1—ST. PATRICK'S CO-CATHEDRAL, Revs. John J. Houlihan; Leo George McDowell; Richard J. Hopkins; Sr. Lillian Maguire, S.C.L., Pastoral Assoc.
Res., 215 N. 31st St., 59101. Tel: 406-259-3389; Fax: 406-248-1185.
Catechesis/Religious Programs—Jean Ott, D.R.E.
Students 114.

2—HOLY ROSARY, Sr. Eileen Hurley, S.C.L., Pastoral Admin.; Virginia Jeanotte, Pastoral Assoc.; Deacon Melvin A. Melius. Sacramental Ministers: Revs. John Houlihan; Leo McDowell.
Office: 521 Custer Ave., 59101. Tel: 406-259-7611.
Catechesis/Religious Programs—Jean Ott, D.R.E.
Students 64.

3—LITTLE FLOWER, Rev. Paul Reichling, O.F.M.Cap.
Res., 209 S. 35th St., 59101. Tel: 406-245-4717.
Catechesis/Religious Programs—Jean Ott, D.R.E.
Students 80.

4—ST. BERNARD'S, Rev. David Reichling, O.F.M.Cap.
Office: 226 Wicks Ln., 59105. Tel: 406-259-4350; Fax: 406-259-0443.
Catechesis/Religious Programs—D.R.E.: Nora Nichols; Mary Newpower.
Students 490.
Mission—Ballantine, Sts. Cyril & Methodius.

5—OUR LADY OF GUADALUPE, Rev. Paul Reichling, O.F.M.Cap.
Res., 209 S. 35th St., 59101. Tel: 406-245-4717.
Catechesis/Religious Programs—Students 80.

6—ST. PIUS X, Rev. Stephen L. Tokarski; Sr. Mary Dostal, O.S.U., Pastoral Assoc.; Deacon Robert W. Daem.
Parish Center: 717 18th St. W., 59102. Tel: 406-656-2522; Fax: 406-656-2584.
Catechesis/Religious Programs—Cheryl Daem, D.R.E.
Students 286.

7—ST. THOMAS THE APOSTLE, Rev. Nathaniel J. Bourke; Jim Downs, Pastoral Assoc.
Res., 2101 24th St., 59102. Tel: 406-656-5578.
Church—2055 Woody Dr., 59102. Tel: 406-656-5800.
Catechesis/Religious Programs—Joyce Hollowell, D.R.E.
Students 386.

OUTSIDE THE CITIES OF GREAT FALLS AND BILLINGS

Ashland, Rosebud Co., St. Labre's, Rev. Paschal Siler, O.F.M.Cap.
Res., Tongue River Rd., 59003. Tel: 406-784-2755.
Station—Ashland, Birney Post.

Baker, Fallon Co., St. John the Evangelist, Rev. Thomas Tobin.
Res., Drawer K, 59313. Tel: 406-778-2297.
Catechesis/Religious Programs—Norma Losing, D.R.E.
Students 161.
Missions—Ekalaka, St. Joan of Arc; Plevna, St. Anthony. [CEM]

Belt, Cascade Co., St. Mark the Evangelist, Rev. Theodore F. Szudera.
Res., P.O. Box 213, 59412. Tel: 406-277-3537.
Catechesis/Religious Programs—Patty Kolar, D.R.E.
Students 103.
Missions—Highwood, St. Jane Frances; Monarch, St. Clement; Raynesford, St. Mary.

Big Sandy, Chouteau Co., St. Margaret Mary, Rev. Peter E. Guthneck; Sr. Margaret Mary O'Doherty, O.P., Pastoral Assoc. & D.R.E.
Res., St. Mary's Rocky Boy Indian Reservation, Rocky Boy CPU-Box 3009, Box Elder, 59521. Tel: 406-395-4380.
Catechesis/Religious Programs—Students 75.
Missions—Box Elder, St. Anthony; Rocky Boy Indian Reservation, St. Mary.

Big Timber, Sweet Grass Co., St. Joseph, Sr. Catherine Kinsella, O.P., Pastoral Admin.
Res., P.O. Box 871, 59011. Tel: 406-932-4728.

Black Eagle, Cascade Co., Most Blessed Sacrament, Rev. Raymond J. Nyquist. In res., Most Rev. Eldon B. Schuster, D.D., (Retired).
Res., 1325 Smelter Ave., Great Falls, 59414. Tel: 406-453-8425; Fax: 406-453-8425.

Bridger, Carbon Co., Sacred Heart, Sr. Mary Lou Mendel, S.C.L., Pastoral Admin.
Res., P.O. Box 309, 59014-0309. Tel: 406-662-3550.
Catechesis/Religious Programs—Students 133.
Missions—Fromberg, St. Joseph; Joliet, St. John.

Broadus, Powder River Co., St. David's, Rev. Chester Poppa, O.F.M.Cap.
Mailing Address: P.O.Box 52, 59317. Tel: 406-436-2348. [CEM]
Mission—Alzada.

Centerville, Cascade Co., Holy Trinity, Sr. Laurita Wydra, S.S.S., Pastoral Admin.
Res., 692 Stockett Rd., P.O. Box 125, Stockett, 59480-0125. Tel: 406-736-5491.
Catechesis/Religious Programs—Tel: 406-736-5114. D.R.E.: Bev Pepos; Cynthia Ingman.
Students 58.

Chester, Liberty Co., St. Mary's, Rev. Joseph Marmion.
Res., P.O. Box 647, 504 Main, 59522. Tel: 406-759-5377.
Catechesis/Religious Programs—D.R.E.: Natalie Ghekiere; Dianne Folk.
Students 171.
Missions—Hingham, Our Lady of Ransom; Inverness, Sacred Heart; Rudyard, Holy Family Center.

Chinook, Blaine Co., St. Gabriel's, Sr. Bernadette Helfert, S.C.L., Pastoral Admin.
Res., 152 Eighth St., P.O. Box 1089, 59523. Tel: 406-357-2073; Fax: 406-357-2073.
Catechesis/Religious Programs—D.R.E.: Mrs. Ellen Pyette, (Elementary); Mrs. Norma Fritz, (High School).
Students 110.
Missions—Harlem, St. Thomas the Apostle; Hogeland, St. Thomas Aquinas.

Circle, McCone Co., St. Francis Xavier, Rt. Rev. Robert West, O.S.B.
Res., P.O. Box 160, 59215-0160. Tel: 406-485-3520.
Missions—Jordan, St. John the Baptist; Richey, St. Francis de Sales.

Colstrip, Rosebud Co., St. Margaret Mary, William Medved, Pastoral Admin.
Res., P.O. Box 305, 59323. Tel: 406-748-2234; Fax: 406-748-2234.
Catechesis/Religious Programs—Students 46.

Columbus, Stillwater Co., St. Mary's, Rev. Thomas Harney; Sr. Mary Francis Kirkpatrick, S.C.L., Pastoral Admin.
Res., 243 N. Fifth St., P.O. Box 956, 59019. Tel:

406-322-5541.
Catechesis/Religious Programs—D.R.E.: Teresa Kaiserski; Jeanne Harsha; Beverly Kovanda; Jeanne Babcock.
Students 75.
Mission—Absarokee, St. Michael.

Crow Agency, Big Horn Co., St. Dennis, Rev. Charles Robinson, O.F.M.Cap.; Sr. Loretta Sedlmayer, R.S.M., Pastoral Assoc.
Res., P.O. Box 57, 59022. Tel: 406-638-2641.
Catechesis/Religious Programs—Students 55.
Mission—St. Xavier, St. Francis Xavier. Sr. Claver Ehren, O.S.F., Pastoral Assoc.

Culbertson, Roosevelt Co., St. Anthony's, Rev. Lawrence G. Manion.
Res., P.O. Box 30, 59218. Tel: 406-787-6666; Fax: 406-787-6183.
Catechesis/Religious Programs—Lynn Finnicum, D.R.E.
Students 95.
Missions—Bainville, Sacred Heart; Froid, Immaculate Conception; Medicine Lake, St. Patrick.

Forsyth, Rosebud Co., Immaculate Conception, Rev. Gilbert Hemauer, O.F.M.Cap., V.G.
Res., 591 N. 12th Ave. N., P.O. Box 166, 59327. Tel: 406-356-2101 (Church); 356-9239 (Parish Center).
Catechesis/Religious Programs—Renee Steinberger, D.R.E.
Students 91.
Mission—Hysham, St. Joseph.

Fort Benton, Chouteau Co., Immaculate Conception, Rev. Denis J. Keane.
Res., P.O. Box 868, 59442. Tel: 406-622-3726.
Catechesis/Religious Programs—Tel: 406-622-5288.
Students 96.
Mission—Geraldine, St. Margaret.

Fort Shaw, Cascade Co., St. Ann, Rev. Eugene P. Hruska, V.G.
Res., P.O. Box 99, 59443. Tel: 406-264-5554.
Catechesis/Religious Programs—D.R.E.: JoAnn Holmes, (St. Ann), Tel: 406-264-5495; Debbie Smith, (Sacred Heart), Tel: 406-468-9281.
Students 105.
Mission—Cascade, Sacred Heart.

Glasgow, Valley Co., St. Raphael's, Rev. Thad Kozikowski.
Office: 412 Third Ave. N., P.O. Box 1047, 59230. Tel: 406-228-4651.
Catechesis/Religious Programs—Tel: 406-228-4651. Bernardine Sullivan, D.R.E.
Students 240.
Missions—Fort Peck, Our Lady of the Lake; Hinsdale, St. Albert; Nashua, Queen of the Angels.

Glendive, Dawson Co., Sacred Heart, Revs. Joseph Ponessa; Benjamin Lobo; Gene Fitzpatrick, Pastoral Assoc.
Res., 316 W. Benham St., P.O. Box 36, 59330. Tel: 406-365-2585; Fax: 406-365-4033.
Catechesis/Religious Programs—Tel: 406-365-4569. Monica Christianson, D.R.E.
Students 325.
Missions—Savage, St. Michael; Wibaux, St. Peter; Wibaux, St. Philip; Circle, St Francis Xavier; Richey, St Francis de Sales.

Hardin, Big Horn Co., St. Joseph's, Rev. Fabian Fehring, O.F.M.Cap.
Res., 710 N. Custer, P.O. Box 510, 59034. Tel: 406-665-1432. [JC]
Catechesis/Religious Programs—Students 95.
Mission—Custer, St. Mary.

Havre, Hill Co., St. Jude Thaddeus, Revs. Robert D. Grosch; Patrick Zabrocki.
Res., 624 Fourth St., P.O. Box 407, 59501. Tel: 406-265-4261; Fax: 406-265-4408.
School—(Grades K-8). Tel: 406-265-4613. Mrs. Therese Cowdery, Prin.
Lay Teachers 13; Students 212.
Catechesis/Religious Programs—Timothy Maroney, D.R.E.
Students 200.
Mission—Cottonwood, St. John.

Hays, Blaine Co., St. Paul's Indian Mission, Rev. Joseph R. Retzel, S.J.
Res., P.O. Box 40, 59527. Tel: 406-673-3300.
School—Sr. Helen Durso, O.P., Prin. Sisters 6; Lay Teachers 4; Students 127.
Catechesis/Religious Programs—Sr. Nora McCarthy, O.P., D.R.E.
Students 200.
Missions—Zortman, St. Joseph; Lodge Pole, St. Thomas. Sr. Laura Fucito, O.P., Pastoral Assoc.; Fort Belknap Agency, Sacred Heart. Pastoral Assocs.: Sr. Nancy Maclean, S.P.; Sr. Mary Eileen Boyle, O.S.U.

Lame Deer, Rosebud Co., Blessed Sacrament, Rev. Daniel Crosby, O.F.M.Cap. Pastoral Assocs.: Mary K. Manger; Sr. Mary Ann Stoffregen, O.S.F.
Res., P.O. Box 100, 59043. Tel: 406-477-6384.
Catechesis/Religious Programs—Students 30.
Mission—Busby, Christ the King.

Laurel, Yellowstone Co., St. Anthony's, Rev. Thomas C. Harney.
Res., P.O. Box 955, 59044. Tel: 406-628-7182. [CEM]
Catechesis/Religious Programs—Barb Hoppel, D.R.E.
Students 280.

Lewistown, Fergus Co., St. Leo's, Rev. Jay H. Peterson; Sr. Anne Walch, O.S.F.; Rene M. Kay, Pastoral Assoc.
Res., P.O. Box 421, 59457. Tel: 406-538-9306; Fax: 406-538-7624. [CEM]
Catechesis/Religious Programs—D.R.E.: Judy Marxer, (Grades K-6); Denise Goodwyn, (Grades 7-12).
Students 238.
Missions—Hobson, Sacred Heart; Moore, St. Mathias; Winifred, Holy Family.
Chapels—Danvers, St. Wenceslaus.; Hilger, St. Victor.; Roy, Sacred Heart.

Livingston, Park Co., St. Mary's, Rev. Dale E. Yurkovic; Joannie Lee, Pastoral Assoc. & D.R.E.
Res., S. F St., P.O. Box 646, 59047. Tel: 406-222-1393; Fax: 406-222-1405. [CEM]
School—(Grades PreK-8). Tel: 406-222-3303. Michelle Moore, Prin.
Lay Teachers 10; Students 117.
Catechesis/Religious Programs—Students 62.
Missions—Clyde Park, St. Margaret; Gardiner, St. William; Cooke City, St. John.

Lodge Grass, Big Horn Co., Our Lady of Loretto, Rev. James Antoine, O.F.M.Cap.
Res., P.O. Box N, 59050. Tel: 406-639-2254; Fax: 406-639-2254.
Catechesis/Religious Programs—Rosaline Old Bear, D.R.E.
Students 35.
Mission—Wyola, Blessed Kateri Tekakwitha.

Malta, Phillips Co., St. Mary's, Rev. James O'Neil, Supt.
Res., 27 S. Seventh St. W., P.O. Box 70, 59538. Tel: 406-654-1446; Fax: 406-654-1446.
School—(Grades K-6) 101 S. Seventh St. W., 59538. Tel: 406-654-1311.
Lay Teachers 4; Students 37.
Catechesis/Religious Programs—Jean Niebur, D.R.E.
Students 118.
Missions—Dodson, Sacred Heart; Saco, St. Francis of Assisi; Whitewater, St. John.

Miles City, Custer Co., Sacred Heart, Rev. Kirk Morgan. Pastoral Assocs.: Sr. Janice Steiger, S.C.L.; Mrs. Carol Green.
Res., P.O. Box 1016, 59301. Tel: 406-232-1691; Fax: 406-232-5687.
School—(Grades K-8). Tel: 406-232-3850. Mrs. Kay Plummer, Prin.
Lay Teachers 7; Students 54.
Catechesis/Religious Programs—Mrs. Janice Wood, D.R.E.
Students 190.
Mission—Terry, Sacred Heart.
Stations—Pine Hills School.; Custer County Rest Home.; Holy Rosary Hospital.; Veterans' Administration Hospital.; Miles City, Friendship Villa Rest Home.

Plentywood, Sheridan Co., St. Joseph's, Rev. Jerry P. Connolly; Kordelia French, Admin. Asst.
Res., P.O. Box 6, 59254. Tel: 406-765-2250.
Catechesis/Religious Programs—Kathleen Jensen, D.R.E.
Students 164.
Missions—Outlook, St. Boniface; Wesby, St. Elizabeth. [CEM]

Poplar, Roosevelt Co., Our Lady of Lourdes, Rev. Michael Schneider; Sr. Mary Hourigan, O.P., Pastoral Assoc.
Res., P.O. Box 187, 59255. Tel: 406-768-3244 (Rectory); 768-3305 (Office).
Catechesis/Religious Programs—Yvonne Shields, D.R.E.
Students 84.
Missions—Brockton, St. Thomas; Brockton, Roosevelt Co., St. Anthony, P.O. Box 86, Fort Kipp, 59213. Tel: 406-786-3265.

Pryor, Big Horn Co., St. Charles Borromeo Mission, Rev. Randolph Graczyk, O.F.M.Cap.
Res., P.O. Box 29, 59066. Tel: 406-259-9747; Fax: 406-259-7092.
School—(Grades K-8). Tel: 406-259-9976; Fax: 406-259-7092. Larry Cunningham, Prin.
Sisters 1; Lay Teachers 12; Students 138.

Red Lodge, Carbon Co., St. Agnes, Rev. Richard D. Osterman.
Res., P.O. Box 1067, 59068. Tel: 406-446-1237; Fax: 406-446-1237.
Catechesis/Religious Programs—Students 63.
Mission—Roberts, St. Thomas Aquinas.

Roundup, Musselshell Co., St. Benedict's, Rev. Wayne Pittard.
Res., 503 Main St., 59072. Tel: 406-323-1019.
Catechesis/Religious Programs—Ann Newell, D.R.E.
Students 125.
Missions—Melstone, Our Lady of Mercy; Musselshell, St. Honorata; Winnett, St. Aloysius; Broadview, Little Flower; Lavina, St Joseph; Ryegate, St Mathias.

Scobey, Daniels Co., St. Philip Bonitus, Rev. Daniel J. O'Rourke.
Res., P.O. Box 827, 59263. Tel: 406-487-5525; Fax: 406-487-5566.
Catechesis/Religious Programs—D.R.E.: Diana Carney; Terry Risa; Ronnalee Harrold.
Students 119.
Missions—Flaxville, St. Louis; Glentana, Holy Family; Peerless, St. Ann. [CEM]

Sidney, Richland Co., St. Matthew, Rev. Greg Staudinger.
Res., 219 Seventh St. S.E., 59270. Tel: 406-482-1068. [CEM]
Catechesis/Religious Programs—D.R.E.: Barbara Olson; Valerie Wentz; Yvonne Volkman; Leslie Bieber.
Students 360.
Missions—Fairview, St. Catherine; Lambert, St. Theresa; Charley Creek, St. Bernard's.

Stanford, Judith Basin Co., St. Rose of Lima, Rev. Terrence P. Regan.
P.O. Box 250, 59479. Tel: 406-566-2531.
Catechesis/Religious Programs—Students 106.
Missions—Denton, St. Anthony; Geyser, St. Cyril.

Wolf Point, Roosevelt Co., Immaculate Conception, Rev. Stephen J. Zabrocki.
Res., 500 Fifth Ave. S., P.O. Box 789, 59201. Tel: 406-653-2610. [CEM]
Catechesis/Religious Programs—Linda Johnson, D.R.E.
Students 200.
Missions—Frazer, St. Joseph; Vida, St. Ann; Riverside, Sacred Heart.

Special Assignment:
Reverend Fathers—
Decker, Douglas, 341 MW/HC, 315 72nd St. N., Malmstrom AFB, MT 59402
Sikora, James R., University of Great Falls, 1302 20th St. S., Great Falls, MT 59405
Taylor, Jon, University of Great Falls, 1302 20th St. S., Great Falls, MT 59405

On Duty Outside of the Diocese:
Reverend Fathers—
Cawley, William, St. Patrick Rectory, 231 S. Beaver St., York, PA 17403
Dobbin, Jay D., P.O. Box 27084 GMF, Barrigada, Guam 96921
Kirkness, Michael D., 136 N G St., Lompoc, CA 93436
Krier, John P., Immaculate Conception Church, P.O. Box 910, Davenport, WA 99122-0910
Moore, John J., 1520 Wigdal Ave., Corcoran, CA 93212-2378
Papes, Joseph T., 5201 Raubinger Rd., Swartz Creek, MI 48473

Military Chaplains:
Reverend Fathers—
Munsell, Richard F., 114 Patrick Drive, Biloxi, MS 39531

Absent on Leave:
Reverend Fathers—
Gunville, Gary M., c/o Pastoral Center, P.O. Box 1399, Great Falls, MT 59403
Rutan, Albert E., P.O. Box 50, Liberty Center, IA 50145-0050
Struckman, Timothy W., c/o Pastoral Center, P.O. Box 1399, Great Falls, MT 59403

Retired:
Reverend Monsignors—
Gluszek, Joseph, Mailing Address: P.O. Box 7204, Great Falls, MT 59403
Werner, Martin E., Mailing Address: 1609 Sand Court, Apt. 8, Great Falls, MT 59405
Reverend Fathers—
Arbanas, Harold P., P.O. Box 14011, San Francisco, CA 94114-0011
Beggin, Thomas M., Regina Cleri, 2003 Woody Dr., No. 2, Billings, MT 59102
Berther, Patrick, O.F.M.Cap., St. Labre's Mission, P.O. Box 216, Ashland, MT 59003
Bezdicek, Valerian V., Regina Cleri, 2003 Woody Dr., No. 3, Billings, MT 59102
Bofto, Robert C., 3001 S. 28th St., #230, Federal Way, WA 98003
Clausen, Kenneth J., 3729 Second Ave. N., Billings, MT 59101

Coady, John, 5734 E.19th St., Tucson, AZ 85711
Dwyer, David F., 1701 26th St. S., #3, Great Falls, MT 59405
Fisher, Martin, 507 Parkhill Dr., Billings, MT 59102
Fox, Robert J., P.O. Box 53, Poplar, MT 59255
Galour, Joseph L., 4630 S. Lakeshore, #116, Tempe, AZ 85282
Gedvila, Izidorius, 426 Randolph, Sunny Hills, FL 32428
Geisen, Bernard S., c/o Beverly Nielson, 502 Jay Vee, Kingsville, TX 78363
Reverend Fathers—
Gorman, Charles L., Moate, Ballinakill, Portlaois, Laois, Ireland
Reverend Fathers—
Gregori, Anthony F., 1711 1/2 Smelter Ave., Great Falls, MT 59414
Guinan, Michael, 1701 26th St. S., #4, Great Falls, MT 59405
Hanrahan, John A., 1701 26th St. S., #2, Great Falls, MT 59405
Heretick, Joseph S., c/o Diocese of Great Falls-Billings, P.O. Box 1399, Great Falls, MT 59403
Hoffman, Emmett G., Golden Sun Estates, 40-985 Sun Estates, Palm Desert, CA 92211
Hopkins, Richard J., St. Patrick's Co-Cathedral, 215 N. 31st St., Billings, MT 59101
Janson, Leo F., Regina Cleri, 2003 Woody Dr., No. 1, Billings, MT 59102
Kaminski, Joseph M., 649 21st St., Black Eagle, MT 59414
Kelly, Frank F., 1701 26th St. S., #1, Great Falls, MT 59405
McFarlane, Dale F., Eagles Manor, 1501 Ninth St. S., #418, Great Falls, MT 59405
McInnis, Francis L., 4126 3rd Ave. S., Great Falls, MT 59405
McTague, Thomas, P.O. Box 225, Hysham, MT 59038
Mears, Charles T., 1430 E. El Parque, Tempe, AZ 85282
Moran, Patrick A., 1464 Green Trails Dr., No. 1, Naperville, IL 60540
O'Hanlon, Michael A., Danesfort, Dromahane Mallow, County Cork, Ireland
O'Reilly, Patrick J., 823 Leisure World, Mesa, AZ 85206
Powers, Thomas F., Regina Cleri, Aspen Meadows, 3155 Ave. C., #421, Billings, MT 59102
Sampson, Patrick, 596 Acorn Pl., Billings, MT 59102
Shinnick, Edward P., RR 2 - Box 156A, Savage, MT 59262
Tarrant, Patrick J., P.O. Box 275, Yarmouth Port, MA 02675

Permanent Deacons:
Birkle, Timothy J., 1216 Claim Jumper, Billings, MT 59101
Daem, Robert W., 220 34th St. W., Billings, MT 59102
Melius, Melvin A., 1437 Avenue D, Billings, MT 59102

INSTITUTIONS LOCATED IN THE DIOCESE

[A] COLLEGES AND UNIVERSITIES

GREAT FALLS. *University of Great Falls*, (1932) 1301 20th St. S., 59405. Tel: 406-761-8210.
For a complete listing, refer to the Colleges and Universities section.

[B] HIGH SCHOOLS, DIOCESAN

BILLINGS. *Central Catholic High School*, 3 Broadwater Ave., 59101. Tel: 406-245-6651. Mr. Ronald Nistler, Prin.; Mr. Donald Dundas, Asst. Prin. Sisters 2; Lay Teachers 32; Students 393.

[C] HIGH SCHOOLS, PRIVATE

ASHLAND. *St. Labre Indian Catholic High School*, Mission Rd., 59003. Tel: 406-784-2347; Fax: 406-784-2199. Dr. Russell Alexander, Dir. of Schools; Mr. Sean Flynn, Prin. Priests 2; Sisters 1; Lay Teachers 18; Students 154.

[D] ELEMENTARY SCHOOLS, DIOCESAN

GREAT FALLS. *Blessed Trinity School*, 2820 Central Ave., 59401. Tel: 406-761-5775. Mrs. Patricia Scotson, Prin. Lay Teachers 22; Students 327.

BILLINGS. *St. Francis Intermediate School*. (Grades 3-5), 1734 Yellowstone Ave., 59101. Tel: 406-656-2300. Ed Rachac, Prin. Lay Teachers 12; Students 193.
St. Francis Primary School. (Grades PreK-2), 511 Custer Ave., 59101. Tel: 406-259-6421. Sr. Elizabeth Youngs, S.C.L., Head Prin.; Karen Peterman, Assoc. Prin. Lay Teachers 10; Students 277.
St. Francis Upper School. (Grades 6-8), 205 N. 32nd St., 59101. Tel: 406-259-5037. Martha Zauher, Prin. Lay Teachers 13; Students 231.

[E] ELEMENTARY SCHOOLS, PRIVATE

ASHLAND. *St. Labre Indian Catholic Elementary School*, Mission Rd., 59003. Tel: 406-784-2746; Fax: 406-789-2199. Dr. Russell Alexander, Dir. of Schools; Scott Gion, Prin. Lay Teachers 36; Students 306.

PRYOR. *St. Charles Mission School*, 59066. Tel: 406-259-9976; Fax: 406-259-7092. Larry Cunningham, Prin. Sisters 1; Lay Teachers 16; Students 134.

ST. XAVIER. *Pretty Eagle Catholic School*, 59075. Tel: 406-666-2215; Fax: 406-666-2245. Veronica Small, Prin. Sisters 3; Lay Teachers 17; Students 136.

[F] CHILD CARE & YOUTH SERVICES

GREAT FALLS. *St. Thomas Child and Family Center*, 416 23rd St. N., 59401. Tel: 406-761-6538. Sisters of Providence. Ms. Crystalle Ebbinga, Admin.
Child Care Center; Family Life Education; Prevention and Treatment of Child Abuse; Education, Information, and Referral Service; Summer Food Program for Low-Income Children; Before- and After-School Care Programs. Lay Staff 62; Child Care & Nursery Children 550.

BILLINGS. *Little Flower Day Care*, 120 S. 34th St., P.O. Box 31158, 59107. Tel: 406-252-5697. Sr. Anita Sullivan, S.C.L., Dir.
St. Francis Day Care, 511 Custer Ave., 59101. Tel: 406-259-6421. Sr. Anita Sullivan, S.C.L., Dir.
Saint Francis Day Care West, 2821 Augusta Ln., 59102. Tel: 406-256-3562. Sr. Anita Sullivan, S.C.L., Dir.

[G] GENERAL HOSPITALS

GREAT FALLS. *Benefis Health Care*, 500-15th Ave. S., P.O. Box 5013, 59403. Tel: 406-727-3333.
For a complete listing, refer to the Hospitals section.

BILLINGS. *Saint Vincent Hospital and Health Center*, 1233 N. 30th St., P.O. Box 35200, 59107-5200. Tel: 406-657-7000.
For a complete listing, refer to the Hospitals section.

MILES CITY. *Holy Rosary Health Center*, 2600 Wilson St., 59301. Tel: 406-233-2600; Fax: 406-233-2601.
For a complete listing, refer to the Hospitals section.

[H] CONVENTS AND RESIDENCES FOR SISTERS

GREAT FALLS. *Our Lady of Lourdes Convent*, 319 14th St. S., 59405. Tel: 406-761-6443. Ursuline Nuns 2.
Ursuline Convent, 2300 Central Ave., 59401. Tel: 406-452-8585. Sr. Daniel Ryan, OSU, Supr. Ursuline Sisters 10.

BILLINGS. *Mercy Convent*, 2420 Elm St., 59101. Tel: 406-259-2550. Sisters of Mercy 3.
Sisters of Charity of Leavenworth, 1134 N. 31st St., 59101. Tel: 406-252-0395. Sisters 2.

[I] RENEWAL CENTERS

BILLINGS. *Sacred Heart Retreat Center*, 26 Wyoming Ave., P.O. Box 153, 59103-0153. Tel: 406-252-0322. Val King, Admin.; Polly Eaton, Spiritual Dir.

[J] RETREAT HOUSES

GREAT FALLS. *Ursuline Retreat Centre*, 2300 Central Ave., 59401. Tel: 406-452-8585. Harry J. Tholen, Dir.

[K] MISCELLANEOUS LISTINGS

GREAT FALLS. *Big Sky Cum Christo*. P.O. Box 1248, 59403. Tel: 406-965-2235. John Ball, Pres.
Cascade County Council of the St. Vincent de Paul Society, P.O. Box 1562, 500 Central Ave. W., 59403. Tel: 406-761-0870; 761-0966. Mr. Alan Reavley, Exec. Dir.
Eastside Catholic Community of Great Falls, 2820 Central Ave., 59401. Tel: 406-761-5775. Education Trust for Blessed Trinity Catholic School. Katherine Willett-Gold, Pres.
Frank & Isabell Stites Memorial Center. (Retired Priests Living). Mailing Address: Pastoral Center, P.O. Box 1399, 59403. Tel: 406-727-6683. 1701 26th St. S. Joseph Loncki, Contact Person.
Great Falls City-Wide Ministry to Native Americans, 121 23rd St. S., P.O. Box 1399, 59403. Tel: 406-727-6683. Linda Kovar, Dir.
Heisey Memorial Trust Fund, 313 Seventh St. N., 59401. Tel: 406-453-1211. Mr. Kirby Crosley, Dir.
Heisey Memorial Youth Center, 313 Seventh St. N., 59401. Tel: 406-453-1211. Mr. Kirby Crosley, Dir. Recreation center serving the adults and youth of the community.
St. Joseph's Education Trust, 500-2nd Ave. S.W., 59404. Tel: 406-453-5558. Rev. Anthony J. Schuster, Chm.
Tekakwitha Conference, P.O. Box 6768, 59406. Tel: 406-727-0147; Fax: 406-452-9845. Richard L. King, Dir.

BILLINGS. *Billings Area Catholic Education Trust*. (BACET), P.O. Box 1746, 59103. Tel: 406-252-0997. Ms. Patte Paquette, Chairperson; Mr. Robert Brown, Treas.
Kateri Indian Ministry, 1015 Broadwater, #12, 59102. Tel: 406-256-5142. Sr. Catherine A. Dorsey, O.P., Dir.
Mayfair Auction, Billings Catholic Schools. Mailing Address: P.O. Box 31158, 59107. Tel: 406-245-5463. Joni Harman, Exec. Dir.
Ministry to Nursing Homes, 3729 Second Ave. S., 59101. Tel: 406-259-3141. Rev. Kenneth J. Clausen.
Newman Center, 1500 N. 30th St., Box 55 MSU-Billings, 59101. Tel: 406-657-2276.
Regina Cleri. Pastoral Center, P.O. Box 1399, Great Falls, 59403. Tel: 406-727-6683. 2003 Woody Dr., 59102. (Retired Priests Living). Joseph Loncki, Contact Person.
St. Vincent de Paul Society of Yellowstone County, 2610 Montana Ave., 59101. Tel: 406-252-1855. Harold W. Merchant, Exec. Dir.; Rev. Anthony Ozimek, OSM, Spiritual Advisor.
Saint Vincent Foundation, P. O. Box 35200, 59107-5200. Tel: 406-657-7997. Carolyn K. Ennis, Exec. Dir.; Mike Gustafson, Chm., Board of Trustees.

ASHLAND. *St. Labre Home for Indian Children and Youth*, P.O. Box 458, 59003. Tel: 406-784-2746; Fax: 406-784-2217. Mr. Curtis Yarlott, Pres. & Exec. Dir.; Mr. Randal Widdicombe, Acting Program Dir. Children 23.
St. Labre Indian School Educational Association, P.O. Box 216, 59003. Tel: 406-784-2746; Fax: 406-784-6161. A nonprofit Corporation. Mr. Curtis Yarlott, Pres & Exec. Dir.; Rev. Emmett G. Hoffmann, (Retired). Four Catholic schools for Native Americans: St. Labre Indian School at Ashland (Grade School Students 335); (High School Students 148); Pretty Eagle School, St. Xavier (Students 138); St. Charles Mission School, Pryor (Students 137).

GLENDIVE. *Sacred Heart Educational Endowment Trust*, P.O. Box 36, 59330. Tel: 406-365-2585. Rev. Joseph Ponessa.

HAVRE. *St. Jude's Education Trust*, 811-6th St., 59501. Tel: 406-265-9445. M. F. Clancey, Chm.

LEWISTOWN. *St. Leo's Catholic Education Trust*, P.O. Box 421, 59457. Tel: 406-538-9306. Rev. Jay H. Peterson, Chm.

MALTA. *St. Mary's Catholic Education Trust*, P.O. Box 70, 59538. Rev. Jim O'Neil.

MILES CITY. *Custer County Conference of the Society of Saint Vincent de Paul and Thrift Store*, 407 Main St., 59301. Tel: 406-232-3011. Dorothy Buck, Co-Pres.; Regina White, Co-Pres. Store Managers: Mathel Jager; Marcia Rudolph; Mrs. Marjorie Shipp.

MONARCH. *Thieltges-St. Thomas Camp*, P.O. Box 46, 59463. Tel: 406-236-5385.

RELIGIOUS INSTITUTES OF MEN REPRESENTED IN THE DIOCESE

For further details refer to the corresponding bracketed number in the Religious Institutes of Men or Women section.

[0200]—*Benedictine Monks*. (Assumption Abbey, Richardton, ND).—O.S.B.
[0470]—*The Capuchin Friars*. (Prov. of St. Joseph, Detroit).—O.F.M.Cap.
[0690]—*Jesuit Fathers and Brothers*. (Oregon Prov.).—S.J.

RELIGIOUS INSTITUTES OF WOMEN REPRESENTED IN THE DIOCESE

[0230]—*Benedictine Sisters of Pontifical Jurisdiction*. (Rapid City, SD and St. Paul, MN).—O.S.B.
[2100]—*Congregation of the Humility of Mary*. (Davenport, IA).—C.H.M.
[1730]—*Congregation of the Sisters of the Third Order of St. Francis*. (Oldenburg, IN).—O.S.F.
[1070-11]—*Dominican Sisters, Congregation of Our Lady of the Rosary*. (Sparkill, NY).—O.P.
[1070-03]—*Dominican Sisters, Sinsinawa Dominican Congregation of the Most Holy Rosary*. (Sinsinawa, WI).—O.P.
[1430]—*Franciscan Sisters of Our Lady of Perpetual Help*. (St. Louis, MO).—O.S.F.
[1680]—*School Sisters of St. Francis*. (Milwaukee, WI).—S.S.S.F.
[0480]—*Sisters of Charity of Leavenworth, Kansas*.—S.C.L.
[]—*Sisters of Mercy of Ballyshannon*. (Ballyshannon, Ireland).—R.S.M.
[2575]—*Sisters of Mercy of the Americas*. (Omaha, NE).—R.S.M.
[2630]—*Sisters of Mercy of the Holy Cross*. (Merrill, WI).—S.C.S.C.
[3350]—*Sisters of Providence*. (Spokane, WA).—S.P.

[4080]—*Sisters of Social Service.* (Los Angeles, CA).—S.S.S.

[3930]—*Sisters of St. Joseph of the Third Order of St. Francis.* (South Bend, IN).—S.S.J.-T.O.S.F.

[3320]—*Sisters of the Presentation of the B.V.M..* (Aberdeen, SD).—P.B.V.M.

[1720]—*Sisters of the Third Order Regular of St. Francis of the Congregation of Our Lady of Lourdes.* (Rochester, MN).—O.S.F.

[4110]—*Ursuline Nuns.* (Santa Rosa, CA).—O.S.U.

[4120-04]—*Ursuline Nuns.* (Cleveland, OH).—O.S.U.

DIOCESAN CEMETERIES

GREAT FALLS. *Calvary.*

Mount Olivet.

BILLINGS. *Calvary.*

Holy Cross.

NECROLOGY

† Kelly, Michael Joseph, (Retired). —Died May 4, 1996.

Diocese of Green Bay

(Dioecesis Sinus Viridis)

Most Reverend

ROBERT J. BANKS, D.D.

Bishop of Green Bay; ordained December 20, 1952; consecrated September 19, 1985; appointed Auxiliary Bishop to the Archbishop of Boston and Titular Bishop of Taraqua on June 26, 1985; appointed to Green Bay October 16, 1990. *Office: 1910 S. Webster Ave., P.O. Box 23066, Green Bay, WI, 54305-3066.* Tel.: 414-435-4406.

Most Reverend

ALOYSIUS J. WYCISLO, D.D.

Retired Bishop of Green Bay; ordained April 7, 1934; appointed Titular Bishop of Stadia and Auxiliary of Chicago October 17, 1960; consecrated December 21, 1960; appointed to Green Bay March 8, 1968; retired May 10, 1983; appointed Apostolic Administrator of Green Bay Diocese June 16, 1983. *Res., 1825 Riverside Dr., Green Bay, WI, 54301.* Tel.: 414-435-3685.

Most Reverend

ROBERT F. MORNEAU, D.D.

Auxiliary Bishop of Green Bay and Titular Bishop of Massa Lubrense; ordained May 28, 1966; appointed December 19, 1978; consecrated February 22, 1979. *Res., St. Margaret Mary Parish, 666 Division St., Neenah, WI, 54956-3397. Office: 1910 S. Webster, P.O. Box 23066, Green Bay, WI, 54305-3066.* Tel.: 414-435-4406.

Chancery: 1910 S. Webster Ave., P.O. Box 23066, Green Bay, WI, 54305-3066. Tel.: 414-435-7531; Fax: 414-435-1330.

ESTABLISHED MARCH 3, 1868.

Square Miles 10,728.

Incorporated January 16, 1907.

Legal Title: Catholic Diocese of Green Bay.

Comprises these 16 Counties: Brown, Calumet, Door, Florence, Forest, Kewaunee, Langlade, Manitowoc, Marinette, Menominee, Oconto, Outagamie, Shawano, Waupaca, Waushara and Winnebago in the State of Wisconsin.

For legal titles of parishes and diocesan institutions, consult the Chancery Office.

STATISTICAL OVERVIEW

Personnel	
Bishop	1
Auxiliary Bishops	1
Retired Bishops	1
Abbots	1
Retired Abbots	2
Priests: Diocesan Active in Diocese	160
Priests: Active Outside Diocese	9
Priests: Diocesan in Foreign Missions	5
Priests: Retired, Sick or Absent	63
Number of Diocesan Priests	237
Religious Priests in Diocese	143
Extern Priests in Diocese	5
Ordinations:	
Diocesan Priests	1
Transitional Deacons	3
Permanent Deacons	3
Permanent Deacons in Diocese	78
Total Brothers	49
Total Sisters	714
Parishes	
Parishes	201
With Resident Pastor:	
Resident Diocesan Priests	121
Resident Religious Priests	32
Without Resident Pastor:	
Administered by Priests	42
Administered by Permanent Deacons	1
Administered by Women Religious	5
Missions	4
Pastoral Centers	19
New Parishes Created	1
Closed Parishes	4
Professional Ministry Personnel:	
Sisters	123
Lay Ministers	161
Welfare	
Catholic Hospitals	8
Total Assisted	508,448
Homes for the Aged	11
Total Assisted	1,191
Day Care and Extended Day Care Centers	2
Total Assisted	100
Specialized Homes	4
Total Assisted	607
Special Centers for Social Services	9
Total Assisted	200,481
Residential Care of Disabled	1
Total Assisted	8
Educational	
Diocesan Students in Other Seminaries	15
Seminaries, Religious	1
Students Religious	9
Total Seminarians	24
Colleges and Universities	2
Total Students	4,100
High Schools, Diocesan and Parish	5
Total Students	1,436
High Schools, Private	1
Total Students	820
Elementary Schools, Diocesan and Parish	80
Total Students	13,659
Catechesis/Religious Education:	
High School Students	9,418
Elementary Students	20,479
Total Students Under Catholic Instruction	49,936
Teachers in the Diocese:	
Priests	4
Brothers	1
Sisters	44
Lay Teachers	897
Vital Statistics	
Receptions into the Church:	
Infant Baptism Totals	9,262
Adult Baptism Totals	432
Received into Full Communion	705
First Communions	10,048
Confirmations	6,611
Marriages:	
Catholic	3,171
Interfaith	976
Total Marriages	4,147
Deaths	6,503
Total Catholic Population	582,681
Total Population	836,600

Former Bishops—Rt. Rev. JOSEPH MELCHER, D.D., cons. July 12, 1868; died Dec. 20, 1873.—Rt. Rev. FRANCIS XAVIER KRAUTBAUER, D.D., cons. June 29, 1875; died Dec. 17, 1885.—Rt. Rev. FREDERICK XAVIER KATZER, D.D., appt. July 13, 1886; cons. Sept. 21, 1886; appt. Archbishop of Milwaukee, Jan. 30, 1891; died July 20, 1903.—Rt. Rev. SEBASTIAN GEBHARD MESSMER, D.D., cons. Bishop of Green Bay, March 27, 1892; appt. Archbishop of Milwaukee, Nov. 28, 1903; died Aug. 4, 1930.—Rt. Rev. JOSEPH J. FOX, D.D., cons. Bishop of Green Bay, July 25, 1904; resigned Dec. 4, 1914; appt. Titular Bishop of Ionopolis; died March 14, 1915.—Most Rev. PAUL P. RHODE, D.D., ord. June 17, 1894; cons. Titular Bishop of Barca and Auxiliary to the Archbishop of Chicago, July 29, 1908; transferred to the See of Green Bay, July 5, 1915; died March 3, 1945.—Most Rev. STANISLAUS V. BONA, D.D., ord. Nov. 1, 1912; appt. Bishop of Grand Island, NE Dec. 18, 1931; cons. Feb. 25, 1932; appt. Coadjutor Bishop of Green Bay, Dec. 2, 1944; succeeded to See, March 3, 1945; died Dec. 1, 1967.—Most Rev. ALOYSIUS J. WYCISLO, D.D., ord. April 7, 1934; appt. Titular Bishop of Stadia and Auxiliary Bishop of Chicago Oct. 17, 1960; cons. Dec. 21, 1960; appt. to Green Bay, March 8, 1968; retired May 10, 1983.—Most Rev. ADAM J. MAIDA, J.C.L., J.D., S.T.L., Bishop of Green Bay; ord. May 26, 1956; appt. to Green Bay, Nov. 8, 1983; cons. Jan. 25, 1984.

Vicars General—Most Rev. ROBERT F. MORNEAU, D.D.; Rev. JOHN B. DEWANE, M.A., S.T.L., D.Min.

Chancery—1910 S. Webster Ave., P.O. Box 23066, Green Bay, 54305-3066. Tel: 414-437-7531; Fax: 414-435-1330. Office Hours: Mon.-Fri. 9-5; other times by appointment only.

Vicar for Administration—Rev. JOHN B. DEWANE, M.A., S.T.L., D.Min.

Chancellor—Sr. LISA LUCHT, O.P., M.M., D.Min.

Vice-Chancellor—Rev. Msgr. JOHN H. SCHUH.

Assistant Chancellor—Rev. ROBERT J. KABAT, J.C.L.

Archivist—Sr. ELLA KASTER, C.S.J., M.A., , Ext. 8186.

Secretary to Bishop—TERRI WICKMAN, , Ext. 8194.

Chancery Secretary—MARY JO KRUEGER, , Ext. 8188.

Diocesan Tribunal—Mailing Address: *1910 S. Webster Ave., P.O. Box 23066, Green Bay, 54305-3066.* Tel: 414-437-7531.

Presiding Judge and Officialis—Rev. Msgr. BRIAN P. COLEMAN, J.C.L.
Vice-Officialis and Assoc. Presiding Judge—Rev. RICHARD GETCHEL, J.C.L.
Defenders of the Bond—Revs. LEE J. KAHRS; PHILIP HOFFMANN.

Prosynodal Judges—Rev. Msgr. DENNIS M. LALLY; Revs. DENNIS M. BURKE, O.Praem, S.T.D., J.C.D.; ARTHUR J. DANKS; ROBERT KABAT, J.C.L.; RICHARD C. SHAFER, M.A.; WILLIAM L. VAN DE KREEKE, J.C.L.
Notaries—MARGIE GANTZ; RITA VANDEN AVOND; KATHLEEN SCHUMACHER.

Diocesan Consultors—Most Rev. ROBERT F. MORNEAU, V.G.; Rev. JOHN B. DEWANE, M.A., S.T.L., D.Min.; Revs. C. TERRENCE LACOMBE; MICHAEL BETLEY; PAUL DEMUTH; DENNIS DRURY; DAVID BAETEN; EARL BROUCHOUD; Rev. Msgr. ROY KLISTER.
Secretary to Consultors—Sr. LISA LUCHT, O.P.

Pastor Consultors—Rev. Msgr. PETER N. KLAUCK; Rev. Msgr. CARL E. STEINER; Revs. JOHN P. BERGSTADT; JAMES A. HABLEWITZ; JOSEPH A. MATTERN; PAUL A. SCHUMACHER; WILLARD J. VAN DE LOO.

Regional Vicars—Revs. RALPH GILLIS, Vicariate I; LEONARD M. EVERS, Vicariate II; PAUL J. RADETSKI, Vicariate III; DENNIS L. BERGSBAKEN, Vicariate IV; DENNIS M. RYAN, Vicariate V; JAMES A. HABLEWITZ, Vicariate VI; DEAN DOMBROSKI, Vicariate VII; DAVID SCHMIDT, Vicariate VIII; JOHN T. MULLARKEY, Vicariate IX; MICHAEL KOCH, Vicariate X; WILLIAM O'BRIEN, Vicariate XI; RALPH C. MERKATORIS, Vicariate XII.

Presbyteral Council—Revs. DAVID BAETEN, Chm.
Appointed Representatives—Rev. Msgr. ROY M. KLISTER; Rev. Msgr. BRIAN COLEMAN; Revs. DAVID HOFFMAN; LOREN NYS, S.D.S.; JOHN ZICKERT, O.F.M.Cap.; DAVID BAETEN; EARL BROUCHOUD; JOHN HARPER.
Elected Representatives—Vicariate I: Rev. GERALD SCHMIDT, O.F.M.Cap; Vicariate II: Rev. MICHAEL CARROLL; Vicariate III: Rev. JOHN GALLAGHER; Vicariate IV: Rev. MICHAEL BETLEY; Vicariate V: Rev. GARY DANTINNE; Vicariate VI: Rev. JOHN BERGSTADT; Vicariate VII: Rev. DENNIS DRURY; Vicariate VIII: Rev. JAMES GILSOUL; Vicariate IX: Rev. ELROY REIMER; Vicariate X: Rev. MARTIN CARR; Vicariate XI: Rev. GARY NEW, S.D.S.; Vicariate XII: Rev. JOHN PUODZIUNAS, O.F.M. Ex-Officios: Most Rev. ROBERT F. MORNEAU; Rev. JOHN B. DEWANE.

Bishop's Finance Council—Rev. ROBERT K. FINNEGAN, O.Praem.; MARY STAUDENMAIER; MICHAEL ARIENS; JAMES LIETHEN; JOHN F. BERGSTROM; ROBERT C. GALLAGHER.

Resource—Most Rev. ROBERT F. MORNEAU; THOMAS KURKOWSKI.

Ministry Personnel

Vicar for Religious—Rev. Msgr. JOHN H. SCHUH, *P.O. Box 23066, Green Bay, 54305-3066.* Tel: 414-437-7531, Ext. 8179.

Representative for Religious—Sr. MARY JO KIRT, *P.O. Box 23825, Green Bay, 54305-3825.* Tel: 414-437-7531, Ext. 8292.

Vicar for Priests—Rev. WILLARD J. VAN DELOO, *P.O. Box 23825, Green Bay, 54305-3825.* Tel: 414-437-7531, Ext. 8322.

Vicar for Senior Priests—Rev. PHILIP HOFFMANN, *P.O. Box 23066, Green Bay, 54305-3066.* Tel: 414-437-7531, Ext. 8183.

Ministry to Priests Program—Rev. WILLARD J. VAN DELOO, Dir., *P.O. Box 23825, Green Bay, 54305-3825.* Tel: 414-437-7531, Ext. 8322.

Department of the Permanent Diaconate—Deacon MAURICE REED, Dir., Prog. Coord. & Vicar for Deacons, *P.O. Box 23825, Green Bay, 54305-3825.* Tel: 414-437-7531, Ext. 8290.

Vocations—P.O. Box 23825, Green Bay, 54305-3825. Tel: 414-437-7531. Rev. DOUGLAS LECAPTAIN, Dir.; Sr. MARY JO KIRT, Assoc. Dir.

Department for Parish Ministers—Sr. FLORENCE YOUNGWIRTH, A.N.G., Dir., *P.O. Box 23825, Green Bay, 54305-3825.* Tel: 414-437-7531, Ext. 8268.

Education

Education—1825 Riverside Dr., P.O. Box 23825, Green Bay, 54305-3825. Tel: 414-437-7531; Fax: 414-437-0694.

Total Catholic Education Department—Mr. LELAND NAGEL, Dir., , Ext. 8269.
Consultants—
Youth and Young Adult Ministry—TONY PICHLER, Ext. 8270.
Staff Development Services—Sr. PAT MCCORMICK, Ext. 8271.
Personnel Services—Sr. THEA MCQUISTION, Ext. 8273.
Curriculum and Instructional Services—Sr. JANE RIHA, Ext. 8284.
Educational Programs—CHRIS BROSLAVICK, Ext. 8283.
Adult Education and Human Sexuality—RICHARD REICHERT, Ext. 8281.
Religious Education (K-6)—JEANNINE GOGGIN, Ext. 8274.
Catechist Formation—Sr. STEPHANIE SPENCE, Ext. 8277.

Liaisons-Office of Education—
Priests Eucharistic League—Rev. DONALD FELLER, *2496 Mary Jo Dr., Green Bay, 54301.* Tel: 414-465-3460.
The Diocesan Charismatic Renewal Center—Rev. Msgr. JAMES VANDEN HOGEN, *Res., St. John Parish, 323 S. Pine St., Little Chute, 54140.* Tel: 414-788-9061.
Serra Clubs—Rev. DOUGLAS LECAPTAIN, *P.O. Box 23825, Green Bay, 54305-3825.* Tel: 414-437-7531.
Blue Army - World Apostolate of Fatima—Rev. ARTHUR DANKS, *2616 He-Nis-Ra Ln., Green Bay, 54304.* Tel: 414-499-9309.
Cursillo—Rev. WILLIAM O'BRIEN, *215 Center St., Brillion, 54110-1222.* Tel: 414-756-2535.
Xavier Guild—Rev. DENNIS M. RYAN, Chap., *St. Nicholas Parish, N4088 Cty. Tr. E., P.O. Box 1006, Freedom, 54131-1006.* Tel: 414-788-1492.
Diocesan Council of Catholic Women—ROSALYN BOUGEOIS, Pres., *963 Laduron Dr., Mishicot, 54228.* Tel: 414-755-2645.

Pastoral Services

Pastoral Services—1825 Riverside Dr., P.O. Box 23825, Green Bay, 54305-3825. Tel: 414-437-7531; Fax: 414-437-0694. MARK MOGILKA, Dir., Ext. 8297.

Family Life Department (Voice & TDD)—TOM RINKOSKI, Dir., Ext. 8304.
Consultants—
Evangelization—JACKIE STALEY, Ext. 8316.
Ministry with Persons with Disabilities—SUE PERRAULT, Ext. 8306.
Marriage Preparation, Parenting, Aging—MARY STUBLER, Ext. 8315.
Pastoral Care—MARK MITCHELL, Ext. 8300.
Respect Life-Natural Family Planning, Family & Social Concerns—HELEN URBAN, Ext. 8308.
Rural Life—Deacon ORVELL DEBRUIN, Dir., *2121 Culbertson Rd., Seymour, 54165.* Tel: 414-833-2279.
Native American Urban Ministry—Rev. DEAN W. DOMBROSKI, Coord. Tel: 414-863-2593.

Worship Department—DIANN WIMMER, Dir., Ext. 8311.
RCIA—CINDE BECKER, Consultant, Ext. 8301.

Campus Ministry—Rev. JEFFREY VANDEN HEUVEL, Dir., *717 W. Irving, Oshkosh, 54901.* Tel: 414-233-5555.

Department of World Mission Services—CLAIRE THOMAS, Dir., *P.O. Box 23066, Green Bay, 54305-3066.* Tel: 414-437-7531, Ext. 8192; Fax: 414-435-1330.
Agencies—Propagation of the Faith, St. Peter Apostle, Holy Childhood Association, Catholic Relief Services.

Holy Name Retreat House—MICHAEL CHERF, Co-Admin. MARY CHERF, Co-Admin.; Rev. Msgr. JAMES B. FEELY, Spirtual Dir.

Evangelization Commission—JACKIE STALEY.
Liturgical Commission—DIANN WIMMER.
Ecumenism Commission—Rev. PHILIP HOFFMAN.
Justice & Peace Commission—HELEN URBAN.
Family Life Commission—MARK MOGILKA; TOM RINKOSKI.

Community Services

Community Services—PAUL GRIMM, Dir., *1825 Riverside Dr., P.O. Box 23825, Green Bay, 54305-3825.* Tel: 414-437-7531, Ext. 8226; Fax: 414-437-0694.

Department of Catholic Social Services—PAUL GRIMM, Dir. JANE KOEFERL, Clinical Svcs. Coord., Ext. 8242.

Department of Refugee, Migration and Hispanic Services—BARBARA B. BIEBEL, Dir., Ext. 8252.
Apostleship of the Sea—Deacon GLENN TESKE, Dir., *2839 S. Broadway, Green Bay, 54304-5309.* Tel: 414-499-0035.

Diocesan Health Services—Rev. DAVID BEAUDRY, Coord., *8109 Northeim Rd., Newton, 53063-9630.* Tel: 414-726-4228.

McCormick Memorial Home for the Aged—212 Iroquois St., Green Bay, 54301. Tel: 414-437-0883. Rev. THADDEUS J. KOSZAREK, Chap.

Liaisons - Community Services—
Sign of God Deaf Ministry—Rev. ANTHONY WIECZOREK, O.Praem., Chap. MARY E. ZUPANSIC, Pastoral Assoc., *1016 N. Broadway, De Pere, 54115.* Tel: 414-337-9454.
Society of St. Vincent de Paul—JOHN J. LORITZ, Pres. & Trustee; Rev. ARTHUR J. DANKS, Spiritual Dir. (Council of the Green Bay Diocesan, Society of St. Vincent de Paul, Inc.), *P.O. Box 400, Green Bay, 54305.* Tel: 414-432-1413.
Knights of Columbus—DON BETTINE, District Deputy, Council 5382, *1243 Valley View Rd., Green Bay, 54304.* Tel: 414-499-2811. Rev. STANLEY BROWNE, Chap.
Our Lady of Charity Center, Inc.—Sr. BARBARA JEAN ARNSMEYER, O.L.C., *2640 West Point Rd., P.O. Box 11737, Green Bay, 54307-1737.* Tel: 414-494-8708.
Daughters of Isabella—ELEANORE WENNESHEIMER, Local Regent, *220 Trout Creek Dr., Oneida, 54155.* Tel: 414-869-2591.
Catholic Veterans of War—RAYMOND WOZNICK, Commander, *418 Forrest Ave., Fond du Lac, 54935.* JOSEPH RICKERT, District 3 Commander, *936 W. Marquette St., Appleton, 54911.* Tel: 414-734-9684.
Menominee Pastoral Program—Rev. DAVID S. BARRETT, *St. Michael Church, P.O. Box 610, Keshena, 54135-0160.* Tel: 715-799-3811.

Support Services

Support Services—1910 S. Webster Ave., P.O. Box 23066, Green Bay, 54305-3066. Tel: 414-437-7531; Fax: 414-435-1330. Rev. JOHN B. DEWANE, M.A., S.T.L., D.Min., Vicar for Admin., , Ext. 8171.

Annual Bishop's Appeal—CINDI BRAWNER, , Ext. 8173.

Benefits—MARY VANKAUWENBERG, *Box 23825, Green Bay, 54305-3825.* Tel: 414-437-7531, Ext. 8265.

Bishop's Charities Game—JAMES HOGAN, *P.O. Box 23825, Green Bay, 54305-3825.* Tel: 414-437-7531, Ext. 8219.

Camp Tekawitha—ROBERTA LARSON, *112 N. 8th Ave., Winneconne, 54986.* Tel: 414-582-7727.

Cemeteries—JOHN C. NELSON, *1825 Riverside Dr., P.O. Box 23825, Green Bay, 54305-3825.* Tel: 414-437-7531, Ext. 8229.

Communications—P.O. Box 23825, Green Bay, 54305-3825. Tel: 414-437-7531. TONY KUICK, Dir., Ext. 8214. SUSAN MEDD, Pub. Rels. Coord., Ext. 8213.
Diocesan Newspaper—"The Compass", P.O. Box 23825, Green Bay, 54305-3825. Tel: 414-437-7531. Appleton Area: Tel: 414-233-5555. TONY KUICK, Dir., Ext. 8214. ANTON STALEY, Editor, Ext. 8210.

Computer Services—TONY KUICK, Dir. BEA SEIDL, Database Admin. DAN LEE, P.C. Specialist, *Box 23825, Green Bay, 54305-3825.* Tel: 414-437-7531, Ext. 8255.

Financial Services—THOMAS KURKOWSKI, Dir., Ext. 8267. MIKE SPEEL, Sr. Acct., Ext. 8259., *P.O. Box 23825, Green Bay, 54305-3825.* Tel: 414-437-7531.

Insurance and Pensions—GLORIA GIESE, Benefits Coord., *P.O. Box 23825, Green Bay, 54305-3825.* Tel: 414-437-7531, Ext. 8253.

Personnel—JAMES HOGAN, Dir., *P.O. Box 23825, Green Bay, 54305-3825.* Tel: 414-437-7531, Ext. 8219.

Property Management and Real Estate—JOHN C. NELSON, Dir. Temporalities, *P.O. Box 23825, Green Bay, 54305-3825.* Tel: 414-437-7531, Ext. 8229.

Sacred Heart Seminary, Inc.—P.O. Box 23066, Green Bay, 54305-3066. Tel: 414-437-7531.

Sacrificial Giving Program—CINDI BRAWNER, Dir., *P.O. Box 23066, Green Bay, 54305-3066.* Tel: 414-437-7531, Ext. 8173.

St. Joseph Corporation and Central Services—VINCE PELLETIER, *P.O. Box 23825, Green Bay, 54305-3825.* Tel: 414-437-7531, Ext. 8246.

Stewardship and Development—CINDI BRAWNER, *P.O. Box 23066, Green Bay, 54305-3066.* Tel: 414-437-7531, Ext. 8173.
Priests' Personnel Board—Revs. JOHN H. VAN DEUREN, Chm. RONALD COLOMBO; RALPH MERKATORIS; MICHAEL BETLEY; WILLIAM SPALDING; JOHN MULLARKEY; Rev. Msgr. JOHN H. SCHUH; Rev. WILLARD J. VAN DELOO, Resource Person.
Conciliation and Arbitration Board—Rev. JOHN T. MULLARKEY, Chm. ROBERT J. KABAT, Clerk, *P.O. Box 23066, Green Bay, 54305-3066.* Tel: 414-437-7531.

Liaisons—Personnel—
Association of Pastoral Associates—Sr. FLORENCE YOUNGWIRTH, *P.O. Box 23825, Green Bay, 54305-3825.* Tel: 414-437-7531.
Leo Benevolent Association—Rev. WILLIAM J. SPALDING, Chm., *310 Alpine Dr., Apt. 9, Shawano, 54166.* Tel: 715-524-5904.
Clergy Credit Union—Rev. CHARLES W. MOCCO, Treas., *Res., UWGB Ecumenical Center, 2420 Nicolet Dr., Green Bay, 54311-7001.* Tel: 414-465-5133.
Community of Our Lady—Rev. REGIS N. BARWIG, Prior, *2804 Oakwood Ln., Oshkosh, 54901.* Tel: 414-233-5633.
Sisters of A New Genesis—Sr. BARBARA LOCH, Moderator, *2777 He-Nis-Ra Ln., Green Bay, 54304.* Most Rev. ALOYSIUS J. WYCISLO, Chap.

CLERGY, PARISHES, MISSIONS AND PAROCHIAL SCHOOLS

CITY OF GREEN BAY (Brown County)

1—St. Francis Xavier Cathedral, Rev. Msgr. Peter N. Klauck; Deacon Paul Plantico.
Res., 139 S. Madison St., 54301-4588. Tel: 414-432-4348.
School—St. Thomas More. Consolidated with St. Mary and Ss. Peter & Paul.
Catechesis/Religious Programs—Students 77.

2—Nativity of Our Lord, Revs. James A. Hablewitz; W. Thomas Long; Sr. Louise Kwaterski, Pastoral Assoc.
Res., 2270 S. Oneida St., 54304-4796. Tel: 414-499-5156.
Catechesis/Religious Programs—Lorraine Cann, D.R.E.
Students 1,433.

3—St. Agnes, Revs. Richard Getchel; Thomas K. Pomeroy; Deacon Robert Arnold.
Res., 1484 9th St., 54304-3098. Tel: 414-494-2534.
School—Holy Family. Serving the parishes of St. Elizabeth Seton and St. Agnes. 1204 S. Fisk St., 54304. Tel: 414-494-1931. Sr. Kathryn Klackner, O.S.F., Prin.
Franciscan Sisters of Christian Charity 4; Lay Teachers 26; Students 477.
Catechesis/Religious Programs—Students 377.
Convent—1208 S. Fisk St., 54304.

4—Annunciation of the Blessed Virgin Mary, Rev. Joseph R. Coopmans, O.Praem.
Res., 401 Gray St., 54303-3099. Tel: 414-499-2333.
School—1087 Kellogg St., 54303. Tel: 414-499-1919. Alice Jaques, Prin.
Lay Teachers 12; Students 221.
Catechesis/Religious Programs—Students 111.

5—St. Bernard, Revs. John P. Bergstadt; Michael Seis; Sr. Pauline Feiner, S.D.S., Pastoral Assoc.; Deacons Robert Jacqmin; John Laurant; Lawrence Mastalish.
Res., 2040 Hillside Ln., 54302-4098. Tel: 414-468-4811. [CEM]
School—St. Bernard, 2020 Hillside Ln., 54302. Tel: 414-468-5026; Fax: 414-468-1396. Mrs. Pat Ford, Prin.
Sisters 1; Lay Teachers 20; Students 488.
Catechesis/Religious Programs—Sr. Mary Ramone Blahnik, D.R.E.
Students 752.

6—St. John, Rev. Msgr. James B. Feely.
Res., 413 St. John St., 54301-4195. Tel: 414-436-6380.

7—St. Joseph, Revs. Stanley T. Browne; John F. Blaha.
Res., 936 Ninth St., 54304-3499. Tel: 414-497-7042.
School—1224 12th Ave., 54304. Tel: 414-497-7085. Ms. Carol Schevers, Prin.
Lay Teachers 13; Students 174.
Catechesis/Religious Programs—Eugene Mailhiot, D.R.E.
Students 128.

8—St. Jude, Rev. Ronald C. Belitz; Ann Froelich, Pastoral Min.
Res., 1423 Kellogg St., 54303-3197. Tel: 414-496-2160.
School—1420 Division St., 54303-3113. Tel: 414-496-2162; Fax: 414-496-2167. Jane Schueller, Prin.
Religious 1; Lay Teachers 14; Students 259.
Catechesis/Religious Programs—Carolyn Whitcomb, D.R.E.
Students 246.

9—Holy Martyrs of Gorcum, Rev. Robert E. Rhyner; Deacon William Burkel.
Res., 3562 Finger Rd., 54311-7733. Tel: 414-468-5718. [CEM]
School—Holy Martyrs, 3542 Finger Rd., 54311-7733. Tel: 414-468-7262; Fax: 414-468-5713. Sr. Therese Kulas, Prin.
Lay Teachers 9; Students 141.
Catechesis/Religious Programs—Tim Younk, D.R.E.
Students 138.

10—St. Mary, Revs. Finian Zaucha, O.F.M.; Joachim Swarick, O.F.M.
Res., 645 S. Irwin Ave., 54301-3397. Tel: 414-437-1979.
School—St. Thomas More, (Grades PreK-8). Consolidated with Cathedral and Ss. Peter & Paul. 650 S. Irwin, 54301. Tel: 414-432-8242. Miss Joan Faltynski, Prin.
Religious 1; Lay Teachers 22; Students 255.
Catechesis/Religious Programs—Students 105.

11—St. Matthew, Rev. David Baeten.
Res., 130 St. Matthew St., 54301-2999. Tel: 414-435-6811.
School—2575 S. Webster Ave., 54301. Tel: 414-432-5223; Fax: 414-435-0065. Sr. Carmelyn Gentrap, Prin.
Religious 1; Lay Teachers 15; Students 198.
Catechesis/Religious Programs—Mike Westenberg, D.R.E.
Students 275.

12—St. Patrick, Rev. John F. O'Brien; Sr. Jeanne Vander Boomen, O.S.F., Pastoral Assoc.
Res., 211 N. Maple Ave., 54303-2783. Tel: 414-437-3911; Fax: 414-437-3356.
Catechesis/Religious Programs—Marge Vander Steeg, D.R.E.
Students 165.

13—SS. Peter and Paul, Rev. Msgr. Roy M. Klister; Revs. Joseph E. Dorner; John G. Van Der Horst; Earl J. Schuh, Pastor Emeritus; Sr. Lucy Andre, O.S.F., Pastoral Assoc.; Deacon Kenneth D. Kopydlowski.
Res., 710 N. Baird St., 54302-1997. Tel: 414-435-7548. [CEM]
Schools—St. Thomas More Elementary. Consolidation of SS. Peter & Paul,St. Mary,& Cathedral. Tel: 414-432-8242. Ms. Joan Faltynski, Prin.
Sisters 1; Lay Teachers 24; SSPP Students 81; St. Thomas More School System, (Grades PreK-8) 650 S. Irwin St., 54301. Ms. Jeanne Pischke, Prin.
Lay Teachers 7; SSPP Students 42.
Catechesis/Religious Programs—Associated with Holy Martyrs (for Confirmation). Mike & Doris Vincent, D.R.E.
Students 234.

14—St. Philip the Apostle, Revs. Lawrence J. Canavera; Paul E. Du Charme; Sr. Dorothy Wagner, Pastoral Assoc.
Res., 312 Victoria St., 54302-2818. Tel: 414-468-7848.
School—Tel: 414-468-7755; Fax: 414-468-7755. Sr. Mary Ann Hart, Prin.
Sisters 2; Lay Teachers 14; Students 279.
Catechesis/Religious Programs—D.R.E.: Mary Terrien; Sandy Mangin.
Students 354.
Convent—312 Victoria St., 54302. Franciscan Sisters of Christian Charity

15—Resurrection, Revs. Paul E. Demuth; Douglas LeCaptain; Sr. Helen Plum, S.S.N.D., Pastoral Assoc. & Liturgist; Deacon Timothy Reilly.
Res., 333 Hilltop Dr., 54301-2799. Tel: 414-336-7768; Fax: 414-336-1949.
School—Tel: 414-336-3230; Fax: 414-336-1949. Doris Schoultz, Vice Prin.; Brian Jones, Educ. Dir.
Lay Teachers 18; Students 229.
Catechesis/Religious Programs—Brian Jones, D.R.E.
Students 374.

16—St. Elizabeth Ann Seton. Unassigned. Sr. Madonna Schmelzle, O.S.F., Pastoral Assoc.
Res., 2771 Oakwood Dr., 54304-1699. Tel: 414-499-1546.
School—Holy Family. Consolidated with St. Agnes. 1204 Fisk St., 54304. Tel: 414-494-1931. Sr. Kathryn Klackner, Prin.
Religious 5; Lay Teachers 26; Students 259.
Catechesis/Religious Programs—Carol Vanden Bush, D.R.E.
Students 675.

17—St. Willebrord, Revs. Kenneth J. DeGroot, O.Praem.; Albin V. Veszelovszky, O.Praem.; Harvey H. Toonen, O.Praem. In res., Rev. Willard Van De Loo. Pastoral Assocs.: Sr. Melanie Maczka, S.S.C.; Sr. Sharon Stecker, S.S.N.D.; Sr. Elizabeth Koszarek, S.S.J., T.O.S.F.; Mary Funk.
Res., 209 S. Adams St., 54301-4584. Tel: 414-435-2016; Fax: 414-435-2039.

OUTSIDE THE CITY OF GREEN BAY

Abrams, Oconto Co., St. Louis. Attended by St. John Cantius Parish, Sobieski. Rev. Gerald Prusakowski, O.F.M.
Res., 6051 Noble St., Sobieski, 54171-9724. Tel: 414-822-5255. [JC]
Catechesis/Religious Programs—Associated with St. John Cantius, Sobieski.
Students 65.

Algoma, Kewaunee Co., St. Mary, Rev. Michael Flanary.
Res., 118 Church St., 54201-1098. Tel: 414-487-5001; Fax: 414-487-5002. [CEM]
School—214 Church St., 54201. Tel: 414-487-5004; Fax: 414-487-5002. Mrs. Mary Mayheu, Prin.
Lay Teachers 9; Students 115.
Catechesis/Religious Programs—Students 130.

Alverno, Manitowoc Co., St. Joseph, Rev. David Beaudry.
Mailing Address: 8109 Northeim Rd., Newton, 53063-9630. Tel: 414-726-4228. [CEM]
Church—2413 S. Alverno Rd., Manitowoc, 54220-9340. [CEM]
School—(Also serves St. Casimir, Northeim.). Mrs. Mary Recheck, Prin.
Lay Teachers 6; Students 52.
Catechesis/Religious Programs—Students 131.

Amberg, Marinette Co., St. Agnes. Attended by St. Augustine, Wausaukee. Rev. John F. McLaughlin.
Mailing Address: P.O. Box 375, Wausaukee, 54177-0375. Tel: 715-856-5276. [JC]

Aniwa, Shawano Co., St. Boniface. Attended by St. Philomena, Birnamwood. Rev. Everard S. Scesney, O.F.M.
Res., P.O. Box K, Birnamwood, 54414-0911. Tel: 715-449-2104. [CEM]
Catechesis/Religious Programs—Students 84.

Antigo, Langlade Co., St. John, Rev. Charles G. Hoffmann.
Res., 426 Hudson St., 54409-2197. Tel: 715-623-2024. [JC]
School—420 Fulton St., 54409. Tel: 715-623-4835; Fax: 715-627-2969. John Cerny, Prin.
Lay Teachers 12; Students 261.
Catechesis/Religious Programs—Gerald Bahar, D.R.E.
Students 249.

St. Hyacinth, Rev. Msgr. Paul P. Koszarek.
Res., 819 3rd Ave., 54409-1930. Tel: 715-623-2425. [JC]
Catechesis/Religious Programs—Students 74.

St. Mary, Rev. Jeremiah F. Worman; Deacon Thomas J. Hanley.
Res., 735 Deleglise St., 54409-1497. Tel: 715-623-2522. [JC]
School—723 Deleglise St., 54409. Tel: 715-623-5629. Vicki Koeppel, Prin.
Sisters of Mercy of the Holy Cross 1; Lay Teachers 5; Students 71.
Catechesis/Religious Programs—Students 94.

Appleton, Outagamie Co.,

1—St. Bernadette, Rev. Harold Berryman; Deacon Michael Rovella.
Office & Mailing Address: 2331 E. Lourdes Dr., 54915-3698. Tel: 414-739-4157.
Church—2331 E. Lourdes Dr., 54915-3698. Tel: 414-739-4157.
School—1810 W. Prospect Ave., 54914. Tel: 414-735-9380. Donald Geenen, Prin.
Lay Teachers 26; Students 218.
Catechesis/Religious Programs—D.R.E.: Lorna Davel; Donna Cherry.
Students 510.

2—St. Bernard, Revs. Orville H. Janssen; Thomas Farrell; Deacon Maurice Reed. In res., Rev. Orville Catuso, S.J.
Parish Center: 1617 Pine St., 54914-5118. Tel: 414-739-0331; Fax: 414-749-9771.
Catechesis/Religious Programs—Students 697.

3—St. Joseph, Revs. John Holly, O.F.M.Cap.; William Frigo, O.F.M.Cap.; Sr. Lynne Marie Simonich, O.S.F., Pastoral Assoc.; Deacon Roy Baumruk. In res., Rev. Kurt Gessner, O.F.M.Cap.
Res., 404 W. Lawrence St., 54911-5855. Tel: 414-734-7195. [CEM]
School—Appleton Catholic Education System, 1810 W. Prospect Ave., 54914. Tel: 414-735-9380.
Catechesis/Religious Programs—Associated with St. Mary's, Appleton. D.R.E.: Sr. Maxine Bauer, S.S.N.D., (Grades K-5); Peter Reinl, Dir.; Doug Lynott, (Grades 6-10).
Students 167.

4—St. Mary, Rev. Michael K. O'Rourke. Pastoral Assocs.: Sr. Joanne Goessl; Ms. Barbara Kratz; Deacon William Burke.
Church—312 S. State St., 54911-5926. Tel: 414-739-5119; 731-2001 (Res.); Fax: 414-739-5111. [CEM]
School—Catholic Central. Member of Appleton Catholic Education System. 313 S. State St., 54911. Tel: 414-733-3709; Fax: 414-733-8142. Rosemary Perrino, Prin.
Religious 1; Lay Teachers 23; Students 226.
Catechesis/Religious Programs—Associated with St. Joseph-St. Mary Interparish. Peter Reinl, D.R.E.
Students 307.

5—St. Pius X, Revs. David R. Schmidt; Robert Stegmann; Donald M. Zuleger.
Office: 500 W. Marquette, 54911-1997. Tel: 414-733-0575.
School—Tel: 414-733-4918. Sr. Mary Shawn Fagan, Prin.
Lay Teachers 16; Students 332.
Catechesis/Religious Programs—Students 726.

6—Sacred Heart, Rev. William M. Kuhr; Deacon Donald Gigure.
Res., 222 E. Fremont St., 54915-1890. Tel: 414-739-3196.
School—Member of Appleton Catholic Education System. 1810 W. Prospect Ave., 54914. Tel: 414-735-9380.
Lay Teachers 3; Students 29.
Catechesis/Religious Programs—Students 304.

7—St. Therese, Rev. Daniel C. Gilsdorf; Deacon Patrick Whitcomb, Pastoral Min.
Res., 216 E. Summer St., 54911-4864. Tel: 414-733-8568; Fax: 414-054-5727. [CEM]

Rectory: 213 E. Wisconsin Ave., 54911. Tel: 414-738-0376.
School—Member of Appleton Catholic Education System. 1810 W. Prospect Ave., 54914. Tel: 414-735-9380.
Catechesis/Religious Programs—Tel: 414-739-0794. Marie Loberger, D.R.E.
Students 156.

8—ST. THOMAS MORE, Rev. Gerald R. Falk; Sr. Betty Reinders, Pastoral Assoc.; Deacons Paul Klein; Donald Wetzel; Reinhart Wessing.
Res., 1825 N. McDonald St., 54911-3499. Tel: 414-739-7758.
School—Appleton Catholic Education System, 1810 N. McDonald St., 54911. Tel: 414-739-7826; Fax: 414-739-2376. Sr. Mary Barbara Loch, Prin.
Sisters 2; Lay Teachers 19; Students 229.
Catechesis/Religious Programs—Peggy LeClair, D.R.E.
Students 415.
Convent—1226 E. Pauline St., 54911.

Argonne, Forest Co., St. Mary. Attended by St. Joseph, Crandon. Rev. Ralph J. Gillis.
Res., 208 N. Park Ave., Crandon, 54520-1351. Tel: 715-478-3396. [CEM]

Armstrong Creek, Forest Co., St. Stanislaus Kostka. (Also serves St. Joan of Arc, Goodman). Rev. Edward S. Nowakowski.
Mailing Address: P.O. Box 39, 54103-0039. Tel: 715-336-2334.
Catechesis/Religious Programs—Associated with St. Joan of Arc, Goodman.
Students 67.

Askeaton, Brown Co., St. Patrick, Rev. Allen Geiser.
Res., 7815 St. Patrick Church Rd., Greenleaf, 54126-9611. Tel: 414-532-6665. [CEM]

Aurora, Florence Co., Sacred Heart. Attended by Immaculate Conception, Florence. Rev. Leo R. Lessard.
Mailing Address: P.O. Box 85, Florence, 54121-0085.
Res., 308 Florence Ave., Florence, 54121-0085. Tel: 715-528-3310.
Catechesis/Religious Programs—Students 63.

Baileys Harbor, Door Co., St. Mary of the Lake, Rev. Chester Cappucci, O.M.I.
Mailing Address: P.O. Box 405, 54202-0405. Tel: 414-839-2041. [CEM]
Station—Washington Island, Door Co., St. Michael. (Also serves St. Rosalia, Sister Bay.).

Bay Settlement, Brown Co., Holy Cross, Rev. Timothy D. Shillcox, O.Praem.
Res., 3009 Bay Settlement Rd., Green Bay, 54311-7301. Tel: 414-468-0595; Fax: 414-468-0625. [CEM 2]
School—3002 Bay Settlement Rd., Green Bay, 54311-7301. Tel: 414-468-0625; Fax: 414-468-0625. Mrs. Jane Wicker, Prin.
Lay Teachers 10; Students 193.
Catechesis/Religious Programs—Students 195.

Bear Creek, Outagamie Co., St. Mary. Attended by St. Rose Parish, Clintonville. Rev. Msgr. Mark Schommer.
Mailing Address: P.O. Box 27, 54922-0027. Tel: 715-752-4177. [CEM]
School—P.O. Box 216, 54922-0027. Tel: 715-752-4168. Sr. Jane Resop, Prin.
Sisters 1; Lay Teachers 2; Students 35.
Convent—Tel: 715-752-3585.
Catechesis/Religious Programs—Associated with St. Rose, Clintonville.
Students 68.

Birnamwood, Shawano Co., St. Philomena, Rev. Everard S. Scesney, O.F.M.
Res., (Also serves St. Boniface, Aniwa.) Box K, 54414-0911. Tel: 715-449-2104. [CEM]
Catechesis/Religious Programs—Students 170.

Black Creek, Outagamie Co., St. Mary, Rev. Robert F. Sladek.
Res., 301 E. Burdick St., P.O. Box 217, 54106-0217. Tel: 414-984-3319. [CEM]
Catechesis/Religious Programs—Rita Theobald, D.R.E.
Students 202.

Brillion, Calumet Co., St. Mary, Rev. William G. O'Brien.
Res., 215 Center St., 54110-1222. Tel: 414-756-2535. [CEM]
School—209 N. Custer St., 54110. Tel: 414-756-2502. Mrs. Kathy VanVonderen, Prin.
Lay Teachers 11; Students 115.
Catechesis/Religious Programs—Mrs. Roberta Whittaker, D.R.E.
Students 228.

Brussels, Door Co., St. Francis and St. Mary Parish. (Worship sites in Brussels and Namur.). Rev. Pius Cotter, O.F.M.Cap., Admin.
Res., 9716 Cemetery Rd., 54204-9749. Tel: 414-825-7555. [CEM 3]
Catechesis/Religious Programs—Sue Johnson, D.R.E.
Students 247.

Casco, Kewaunee Co., Holy Trinity, Rev. Richard W. Gilsdorf.
Res., 506 Church Ave., 54205-9709. Tel: 414-837-7234. [CEM]
School—504 Church Ave., 54205. Tel: 414-837-7531. Kaye Jacobs, Prin.
Lay Teachers 7; Students 111.
Catechesis/Religious Programs—Students 152.

Cecil, Shawano Co., St. Martin. Attended by Sacred Heart, Shawano. Rev. Leonard M. Evers; Deacon Charles Daily.
Mailing Address: 321 S. Sawyer St., Shawano, 54166-2437. Tel: 715-526-2023.
Church—107 S. Warrington, P.O. Box 157, 54111. [CEM]

Champion, Brown Co., St. Joseph. Attended by St. Killian, New Franken. Rev. Florian Resheske.
Mailing Address: Rte. 1, P.O. Box 83, New Franken, 54229-0083. Tel: 414-866-2285. [CEM]
Catechesis/Religious Programs—Mrs. Bonnie Agahaite, D.R.E.
Students 125.

Charlesburg, Calumet Co., St. Charles Borromeo. (Catholic Inter-Parish Ministry in Chilton.). Revs. Gary New, S.D.S.; Fred Peters, S.D.S.
Mailing Address: 62 E. Main St., Chilton, 53014-1499.
School—Chilton Catholic. Consolidated with all 6 Chilton area parishes. See St. Mary, Chilton. Chilton, 53014. Tel: 414-849-4141. Sr. Betty Ann Heegman, O.P.

Charlestown, Calumet Co., St. Martin. (Catholic Inter-Parish Ministry in Chilton.). Revs. Gary New, S.D.S.; Fred Peters, S.D.S.
Mailing Address: 62 E. Main St., Chilton, 53014-1499. Tel: 414-849-9363.
School—Chilton Catholic. Consolidated with all 6 Chilton area parishes. See St. Mary, Chilton. Chilton, 53014. Tel: 414-849-4141. Sr. Betty Ann Heegman, O.P.

Chase, Oconto Co., St. Joseph. Attended by St. John Cantius, Sobieski. Rev. Gerald Prusakowski, O.F.M.
Res., 6051 Noble St., Sobieski, 54171-9724. Tel: 414-822-5255. [CEM]

Chilton, Calumet Co., St. Augustine. (Catholic Inter-Parish Ministry in Chilton.). Revs. Gary New, S.D.S.; Fred Peters, S.D.S.
Mailing Address: 62 E. Main St., 53014-1499.
School—Chilton Catholic. Consolidated with all 6 Chilton parishes. See St. Mary, Chilton. 53014. Tel: 414-849-4141. Sr. Betty Ann Heegman, O.P.

St. Mary. (Catholic Inter-Parish Ministry of Chilton.). Revs. Gary New, S.D.S.; Fred Peters, S.D.S.
Res., 62 E. Main St., 53014-1499. Tel: 414-849-9363. [CEM]
School—Chilton Catholic School. Consolidated with all 6 Chilton parishes. 53041. Tel: 414-849-4141. Sr. Betty Ann Heegman, O.P., Prin.
Sisters 1; Lay Teachers 10; Students 155.
Catechesis/Religious Programs—Consolidated with all area parishes.
Students 574.
Convent—(Catholic Inter-Parish Ministry of Chilton includes the following parishes: St. Charles, Charlesburg; St. Martin, Charlestown; St. Elizabeth, Kloten; Holy Trinity, Jericho; and St. Augustine and St. Mary, Chilton.) 38 E. Washington St., 53014. School Sisters of St. Francis

Clarks Mills, Manitowoc Co., Immaculate Conception, Rev. John F. Conrad.
Res., 15 S. County Hwy. J, Cato, 54206-9612. Tel: 414-775-4365. [CEM]
School—19 S. CTH J, Cato, 54206. Tel: 414-775-4366. Sr. Marie Bernadette Dorn, Prin.
Franciscan Sisters of Christian Charity 4; Lay Teachers 5; Students 88.
Catechesis/Religious Programs—Students 116.

Cleveland, Manitowoc Co., St. Wendel, Rev. Gilbert H. Jacobs, O.Praem., Admin.
Res., 701 Westview St., P.O. Box 236, 53015-0236. Tel: 414-693-8552. [CEM 2][JC 2]
Catechesis/Religious Programs—Associated with grades 1-12 w/Osman & grades 9-12 w/Alverno,& Northeim. Janice Batchelder, D.R.E.
Students 128.

Clintonville, Waupaca Co., St. Rose, Rev. Msgr. Mark J. Schommer; Deacon Thomas Jozwiak.
Res., 24-7th St., 54929-1733. Tel: 715-823-3416. [CEM]
School—140 Auto St., 54929. Fax: 714-823-7160. Robert Bootz, Prin.
Lay Teachers 9; Students 77.
Catechesis/Religious Programs—Associated with St. Mary, Bear Creek. D.R.E.: Dawn Kratzke; Gemma Niemuth.
Students 149.

Coleman, Marinette Co., Ss. Francis of Assisi and Wenceslaus. St. Francis of Assisi, Coleman, merged with St. Wenceslaus, Klondike. Rev. Michael J. Clifford, Admin.; Sr. Carleen Peters, S.S.N.D., Pastoral Assoc.
Res., 228 E. Main St., 54112-9407. Tel: 414-897-3226. [CEM 2][JC]
Catechesis/Religious Programs—Students 221.

Combined Locks, Outagamie Co., St. Paul, Rev. Robert H. Vandenberg; Deacon George Schraufnagel, D.R.E.
Res., 410 Wallace St., 54113-1128. Tel: 414-788-4553. [CEM]
Catechesis/Religious Programs—Ms. Mary Ann Jasiak, D.R.E.
Students 254.

Cooperstown, Manitowoc Co., St. James, Rev. Ronald A. Colombo, Admin.
Res., 18228 County Rd., Denmark, 54208-9519. Tel: 414-863-2585. [CEM]
Catechesis/Religious Programs—Jean Schleis, D.R.E.
Students 224.

Crandon, Forest Co., St. Joseph, Rev. Ralph J. Gillis.
Res., 208 N. Park Ave., 54520-1351. Tel: 715-478-3396.
Catechesis/Religious Programs—Students 155. (Also serves St. Mary, Argonne, and Station of St. Michael at Hiles).

Crivitz, Marinette Co., St. Mary, Rev. Donald R. Burkart.
Mailing Address: P.O. Box 159, 54114-0159. Tel: 715-854-2501. [CEM]
Catechesis/Religious Programs—Students 265.
Station—Caldron Falls.

Darboy, Outagamie Co. (Appleton P.O.), Holy Angels, Rev. Donald F. Fuller.
Res., W. 5831 KK, Appleton, 54915-9345. Tel: 414-733-6214. [CEM]
School—W2796 KK, Appleton, 54915-9407. Tel: 414-733-2651. Doris Vincent, Prin.
Religious 1; Lay Teachers 16; Students 280.
Catechesis/Religious Programs—Sr. Elise Cholewinski, D.R.E.
Students 311.

Denmark, Brown Co., All Saints, Rev. Msgr. Robert F. Gulig; Mary Burns, Pastoral Assoc. & D.R.E.
Res., 125 St. Claude St., P.O. Box 787, 54208-0787. Tel: 414-863-2357. [CEM]
Office: Tel: 414-863-5256.
School—Tel: 414-863-2449. Jo Martin Boss, Prin.
Lay Teachers 8; Students 112.
Catechesis/Religious Programs—Associated with Holy Trinity, New Denmark. Tel: 414-863-5256.
Students 191.
Mission—New Denmark, Holy Trinity.

De Pere, Brown Co.,

1—ST. FRANCIS XAVIER, Rev. V. Anthony Dolski; Kenneth Trinkner, Admin. Asst. In res., Rev. Msgr. Brian P. Coleman.
Res., 220 S. Michigan St., 54115-2794. Tel: 414-336-1813. [JC]
School—Notre Dame. Consolidated with St. Mary, De Pere. 221 S. Wisconsin St., 54115. Tel: 414-337-1100. William Matchefts, Prin.
Religious 1; Lay Teachers 26; Students 243.
Catechesis/Religious Programs—Students 274.

2—ST. MARY, Rev. John H. Harper; Deacon Frank W. Kremer.
Res., 121 S. Superior St., 54115-2895. [JC]
Office: 120 S. Huron St., 54115-2819. Tel: 414-337-2330.
School—Notre Dame School. Consolidated with St. Francis Xavier, De Pere. 100 S. Huron St., 54115. Tel: 414-337-1100. William Matchefts, Prin.
Sisters of St. Francis of the Holy Cross 1; Lay Teachers 26; Students 484.
Catechesis/Religious Programs—Marge Frase, D.R.E.
Students 266.

3—ST. JOSEPH. Merged with St. Boniface, De Pere to form Our Lady of Lourdes, De Pere.

4—ST. BONIFACE. Merged with St. Joseph, De Pere to form Our Lady of Lourdes, De Pere.

5—OUR LADY OF LOURDES, (1996),
Res., 1307 Lourdes Ave., 54115-1018. Tel: 414-336-4033; Fax: 414-336-3910. Revs. Conrad J. Kratz, O. Praem.; James T. Baraniak, O. Praem.; Deacons Harvey Quinette; Glenn Teske; Robin Cribb, Pastoral Assoc.
School—1305 Lourdes Ave., 54225-1099. Tel: 414-336-3091.
Lay Teachers 25; Students 311.
Catechesis/Religious Programs—Students 407.

6—ST. NORBERT COLLEGE PARISH, Rev. Gery G. Meehan, O.Praem.; Tami Schmitz, Pastoral Assoc.
Res., Grant St., 54115-2099. Tel: 414-337-3010.
Catechesis/Religious Programs—Students 78.

Dyckesville, Kewaunee Co., St. Louis, Rev. Richard Mauthe.

Res., N8726 County Line Rd., Luxemburg, 54217-8629. Tel: 414-866-2410. [CEM]
School—N8710 Cty. Line Rd., Luxemburg, 54217. Tel: 414-866-2611. Mrs. Georgie Leeming, Prin.
Lay Teachers 6; Students 60.
Catechesis/Religious Programs—Students 125.

Eaton, Brown Co., SS. Cyril and Methodius, Rev. Dean W. Dombroski.
Res., 3041 S. County Rd. T, Green Bay, 54311-9429. Tel: 414-863-2593. [CEM]
Catechesis/Religious Programs—Students 169.

Egg Harbor, Door Co., St. John the Baptist. (Also serves St. Paul, Fish Creek, and St. Michael, Jacksonport). Rev. William Hagan, O.M.I.
Mailing Address: P.O. Box 49, 54209-0049. Tel: 414-868-3241. [CEM]
Catechesis/Religious Programs—Students 60.

Eland, Shawano Co., St. William. Attended by Holy Family, Wittenberg. Rev. Claude Zabinski, O.F.M.
Res., 106 N. Ellms, Wittenberg, 54499-9099. Tel: 715-253-2050.

Elcho, Langlade Co., Holy Family, Rev. Joseph C. Bauschka.
Mailing Address: P.O. Box 128, 54428-0128. Tel: 715-275-3750. [CEM][JC]
Mission—Pickerel, St. Mary.

Fish Creek, Door Co., St. Paul. Attended by St. John the Baptist, Egg Harbor. Rev. William Hagan, O.M.I.
Mailing Address: P.O. Box 49, Egg Harbor, 54209-0049. Tel: 414-868-3241.

Flintville, Brown Co., SS. Edward and Isidore, Rev. David D. Kasperek; June Ingold, Pastoral Assoc.; Deacon Earl Kunzer.
Res., 3667 Flintville Rd., Green Bay, 54313-8330. Tel: 414-865-7677. [CEM]
Rectory: 3752 Elm Tree Rd., Green Bay, 54313. Tel: 414-865-7019.
Catechesis/Religious Programs—D.R.E.: Nancy Nelson; Mary Neckuty; June Ingold.
Students 656.

Florence, Florence Co., Immaculate Conception. (Also serves Sacred Heart, Aurora). Rev. Leo R. Lessard.
Res., 308 Florence Ave., Box 166, 54121-0166. Tel: 715-528-3310. [CEM]
Catechesis/Religious Programs—Students 139.

Francis Creek, Manitowoc Co., St. Anne. (Also serves St. Augustine, Kossuth.). Rev. Theodore J. Hendricks.
Res., 126 Packer Dr., P.O. Box 217, 54214-0217. Tel: 414-682-6640. [CEM]
School—202 Packer Dr., 54214. Tel: 414-682-1454. Mr. Charles Vaughan, Prin.
Franciscan Sisters of Christian Charity 4; Lay Teachers 4; Students 95.
Catechesis/Religious Programs—Students 109.

Freedom, Outagamie Co., St. Nicholas, Rev. Dennis M. Ryan; Deacon Donald Newhouse.
Res., N4088 Co. Tr. E., P.O. Box 1006, 54131-1006. Tel: 414-788-1492. [CEM]
School—P.O. Box 1022, 54131-1022. Tel: 414-788-9371. Phyllis Techlin, Prin.
Lay Teachers 12; Students 189.
Catechesis/Religious Programs—Sr. Charlene Hockers, D.R.E.
Students 355.

Gillett, Oconto Co., St. John, Rev. John M. Gallagher.
Res., 127 Garden St., P.O. Box 377, 54124-0377. Tel: 414-855-2542. [CEM][JC]
Catechesis/Religious Programs—Students 122.

Glenmore, Brown Co., Immaculate Conception. (Also serves St. Mary, Stark.). Rev. David J. Pleier, Admin.
Res., 5840 Big Apple Rd., DePere, 54115-9766. Tel: 414-864-7641. [CEM]
Catechesis/Religious Programs—Judy Hoida, D.R.E.
Students 172.

Goodman, Marinette Co., St. Joan of Arc. Attended by St. Stanislaus Kostka, Armstrong Creek. Rev. Edward S. Nowakowski.
Mailing Address: P.O. Box 39, Armstrong Creek, 54103-0039. Tel: 715-336-2334.
Catechesis/Religious Programs—Associated with St. Stanislaus Kosta, Armstrong Creek.
Students 50.

Greenleaf, Brown Co., St. Mary, Rev. Robert J. Kabat.
Res., 2212 Day St., 54126-9200. Tel: 414-864-2550. [CEM 2]
School—2218 Day St., 54126. Tel: 414-864-2586. Sr. Margaret Mary Halbach, Prin.
Religious 1; Lay Teachers 6; Students 64.
Catechesis/Religious Programs—Lois Trad, D.R.E.
Students 159.

Greenville, Outagamie Co., St. Mary, Rev. Justin N. Werner.
Mailing Address: N2385 Municipal Dr., P.O. Box 195, 54942-0195. Tel: 414-757-6555. [CEM]
Res., N2343 Municipal Dr., 54942. Tel: 414-757-6333.
School—(Grades PreK-8) N2387 Municipal Dr., 54942. Tel: 414-757-5516. Mary Lou Kalaus, Prin.
Lay Teachers 5; Students 146.
Catechesis/Religious Programs—Jane Angha, D.R.E.
Students 305.

Gresham, Shawano Co., St. Francis Solanus. Attended by St. Mary, Leopolis. Rev. Harry Hafeman; Deacon Paul Boucher.
Mailing Address: P.O. Box 177, 54128-0177. Tel: 715-787-3250. [CEM]
Catechesis/Religious Programs—Students 63.

Hilbert, Calumet Co., St. Mary, Rev. Rallen H. Stencil.
Res., 108 S. 6th St., P.O. Box 386, 54129-0386. Tel: 414-853-3252. [CEM]
School—154 S. 6th St., P.O. Box 249, 54129-0249. Tel: 414-853-3216. Sr. Elise Zettel, Prin.
Religious 1; Lay Teachers 4; Students 51.
Catechesis/Religious Programs—Students 155.

Hofa Park, Shawano Co., St. Stanislaus, Rev. Vianney Sipulski, O.F.M.
Res., N1302 Maple Rd., Seymour, 54165-9506. Tel: 414-822-5512. [CEM]
Catechesis/Religious Programs—Students 69.

Hollandtown, Brown Co., St. Francis, Rev. William J. Rickert.
Res., 439 County Rd. CE, Kaukauna, 54130-8964. Tel: 414-766-1222. [CEM]
School—Rte. 4, Kaukauna, 54130. Tel: 414-766-3469. Sr. Marcelyne Prin.
Franciscan Sisters of Christian Charity 2; Lay Teachers 5; Students 54.
Catechesis/Religious Programs—Associated with St. Aloysius, Kaukauna.
Students 58.

Hortonville, Outagamie Co., SS. Peter and Paul, Rev. Dennis L. Bergsbaken.
Res., 108 E. Cedar St., P.O. Box 238, 54944-0238. Tel: 414-779-6133; Fax: 414-779-4425. [CEM]
School—107 N. Olk St., 54944. Tel: 414-799-4425; Fax: 414-799-4425. Ms. Donna Koeller, Prin.
Sisters of St. Agnes 1; Lay Teachers 8; Students 110.
Catechesis/Religious Programs—Ms. Catherine Benoy, D.R.E.
Students 214.

Howard, Brown Co., St. John the Baptist, Revs. Gregory J. Smith, Co-Pastor; William Swichtenberg, Co-Pastor; Deacon David LeMere.
Res., 2597 Glendale Ave., Green Bay, 54313-6899. Tel: 414-434-2145; Fax: 414-434-5015. [CEM]
School—2561 Glendale Ave., Green Bay, 54313. Fax: 414-434-5016. Sherilyn M. Moon, Prin.
Lay Teachers 21; Students 342.
Catechesis/Religious Programs—D.R.E.: Patricia A. Vanden Boogaard, (Grades 1-6); Mary A. Vanden Busch, (Grades 7-12).
Students 652.

Humboldt, Brown Co., Our Lady Queen of Peace, Rev. Dean H. Dombroski; Sr. Marlene Dimmerling, O.P., Pastoral Assoc.
Res., 5930 Humboldt Rd., Luxemburg, 54217-9325. Tel: 414-863-6113; 845-5180. [CEM 3]
Catechesis/Religious Programs—Associated with Ss. Cyril & Methodius, Eaton.
Students 229.

Institute, Door Co., SS. Peter and Paul, Rev. Nicholas Prickel, S.C.J.; Deacon Roger Madsen.
Res., 4767 Dunn Rd., Sturgeon Bay, 54235-8822. Tel: 414-743-4842; Fax: 414-743-3885. [CEM]
School—4761 Dunn Rd., Sturgeon Bay, 54235. Tel: 414-743-6335; Fax: 414-743-3885. Kathryn LaChapell, Prin.
Sisters of St. Francis of the Holy Cross 1; Lay Teachers 6; Students 119.

Isaar, Outagamie Co., St. Sebastian, Rev. David Ashbeck.
Res., N9269 Isaar Rd., Seymour, 54165-9428. Tel: 414-833-2558. [CEM]
Catechesis/Religious Programs—Students 161.

Jacksonport, Door Co., St. Michael. Attended by St. John the Baptist, Egg Harbor. Rev. William Hagan, O.M.I.
Mailing Address: P.O. Box 49, Egg Harbor, 54209-0049. Tel: 414-868-3241. [CEM]

Jericho, Calumet Co., Holy Trinity. (Catholic Inter-Parish Ministry in Chilton). Revs. Gary New, S.D.S.; Fred Peters, S.D.S.
Mailing Address: 62 E. Main St., Chilton, 53014-1499. Tel: 414-849-9363.
School—Chilton Catholic. Consolidated with all 6 Chilton area parishes. See St. Mary, Chilton. Tel: 414-849-4141. Sr. Betty Ann Heeggan, O.P., Prin.

Kaukauna, Outagamie Co., Holy Cross, Revs. John T. Mullarkey; Paul Paider; David Hoffman.
Res., 309 Desnoyer St., 54130-2187. Tel: 414-766-3773. [CEM]
School—Kaukauna Catholic Schools System, Tel: 414-766-0186. Sr. Camilla Wolfgram, Prin. (Grades PreK-5).
Sisters 5; Lay Teachers 14; Students 237.
Catechesis/Religious Programs—Elaine Huss, D.R.E.
Students 502.

St. Aloysius, Rev. John J. Hephner.
Res., 134 W. Ann St., 54130-3499. Tel: 414-766-2966.
School—Kaukauna Catholic Schools System, 2401 Main Ave., 54130. Tel: 414-766-5199. Jennifer Rohlf, Prin.
Franciscan Sisters of Christian Charity 3; Lay Teachers 12; Students 125.
Catechesis/Religious Programs—Maxine Geiger, D.R.E.
Students 309.

St. Mary of the Annunciation, Rev. Robert Udulutsch, O.F.M.Cap. Pastoral Assocs.: Sr. Mary Rose O'Connell.
Res., 119 W. 7th St., 54130-2356. Tel: 414-766-1445; Fax: 414-766-1476. [JC]
School—Kaukauna Catholic Schools System, 112 W. 8th St., 54130. Tel: 414-766-1545; Fax: 414-766-1476. Mrs. Susan Knier, Prin.
Sisters 1; Lay Teachers 13; Students 153.
Catechesis/Religious Programs—Students 369.
Convent—Tel: 414-766-2952. Franciscan Sisters of Christian Charity

Kellnersville, Manitowoc Co., St. Joseph, Rev. Ronald Colombo; Deacon Richard Meidl; Sr. Marlene Greatens, Dir.
Res., 522 Tower Ave., 54215-0027. Tel: 414-732-3770. [CEM 2]
Catechesis/Religious Programs—Students 68.

Keshena, Menominee Co., St. Michael (Indian), Rev. David S. Barrett; Sr. Kathleen Walli, O.P., Pastoral Assoc.
Mailing Address: P.O. Box 610, 54135-0610. Tel: 715-799-3811. [CEM 3]
Catechesis/Religious Programs—Students 113.
Mission—Keshena, Menominee Co., St. Joseph of the Lake, South Branch, P.O. Box 610, 54135-0610.

Kewaunee, Kewaunee Co., Holy Rosary, Rev. Daniel Dewane; Deacon Dana Gallenberger.
Res., 521 Juneau St., 54216-1397. Tel: 414-388-2285. [CEM]
School—519 Kilbourn St., 54216. Mrs. Nancy Leifer, Prin.
Lay Teachers 11; Students 175.
Catechesis/Religious Programs—D.R.E.: Phylis Gencius; Evy Walecka; Barbara Puzdera.
Students 178.

Kiel, Manitowoc Co., SS. Peter and Paul, Rev. Loren G. Nys, S.D.S. In res., Rev. Cletus E. La Mere, S.D.S.
Res., 413 Fremont St., 53042-1398. Tel: 414-894-3553. [CEM]
School—423 Fremont St., 53042. Fax: 414-894-4462. Sr. Rosalyn Geenen, F.S.O.L., Prin.
Sisters 2; Lay Teachers 9; Students 135.
Catechesis/Religious Programs—D.R.E.: Barb Graf; Kathy Pritzl.
Students 254.

Kimberly, Outagamie Co., Holy Name of Jesus, Revs. John Zickert; Frank Weber.
Res., 602 E. Kimberly Ave., 54136-1599. Tel: 414-788-7640 (Office). [CEM]
School—614 E. Kimberly Ave., 54136. Tel: 414-788-7650. Sr. Mary Barbieur, Prin.
Lay Teachers 24; Students 276.
Catechesis/Religious Programs—Students 436.

King, Waupaca Co., St. George, Rev. Paul A. Vanden Hogen.
Res., Wisconsin Veteran's Home, P.O. Box 152, 54946-0152. Tel: 715-258-5586.

Klondike, Oconto Co., St. Wenceslaus. Merged with St. Francis of Assisi, Coleman, to form Ss. Francis of Assisi and Wenceslaus.

Kloten, Calumet Co., St. Elizabeth. (Catholic Inter-Parish Ministry in Chilton). Revs. Gary New, S.D.S.; Fred Peters, S.D.S.
Mailing Address: 62 E. Main St., Chilton, 53014-1499. [CEM]
School—Chilton Catholic. Consolidated with all 6 Chilton area parishes. See St. Mary, Chilton. Tel: 414-849-4141.

Kossuth, Manitowoc Co., St. Augustine. Attended by St. Anne, Francis Creek. Rev. Theodore Hendricks.
Mailing Address: 126 Packer Dr., P.O. Box 217, Francis Creek, 54214-0217. Tel: 414-682-6640. [CEM]

Krakow, Shawano Co., St. Casimir, Rev. James J. Esser, O.F.M.
Mailing Address: P.O. Box 66, 54137-0066. Tel: 414-899-3621. [CEM]
Catechesis/Religious Programs—Students 106.

Krok, St. John. Merged with St. Joseph, Monteplier to form St. Joseph-St. John, Luxemberg.

Lakewood, Oconto Co., St. Mary of the Lake. Attended by St. Ambrose, Wabeno.
Res., 15232 Co. Rd. F, P.O. Box 219, 54138-0219.

Tel: 715-276-7364. [CEM]
Stations—Crooked Lake; Silver Cliff. Rev. Gerald Schmidt, O.F.M.Cap.; Deacon Harold Orlowski.
Catechesis / Religious Programs—Students 75.

Langlade, Langlade Co., St. Stanislaus Kostka. Merged with St. James, White Lake.

Laona, Forest Co., St. Leonard, Rev. John W. Cerkas.
Res., Rte. 1, Box 344, 54541-9641. Tel: 715-674-3241. [JC]
Catechesis / Religious Programs—Students 137.
Mission—Newald, Argonne Co., St. Hubert. (Also serves St. Norbert, Long Lake).

Lebanon Township, Waupaca Co., St. Patrick, Rev. Msgr. Dennis Lally, Admin.
Res., N. 5705 County Rd. T, New London, 54961-9559. Tel: 414-982-5475. [CEM]
Catechesis / Religious Programs—Students 99.

Lena, Oconto Co., Holy Cross, Rev. Harold A. Beerntsen.
Res., 209 E. Main St., P.O. Box 30, 54139-0030. Tel: 414-829-5222. [CEM 2][JC 2]
School—221 E. Main St., 54139. Tel: 414-829-6027. Carol Hoard, Prin.
Lay Teachers 4; Students 68.
Catechesis / Religious Programs—Students 211.

Leopolis, Shawano Co., St. Mary. (Also serves St. Francis Solanus, Gresham.). Rev. Harry G. Hafeman; Deacon Paul Boucher.
Res., W. 2242 Third St., P.O. Box 38, 54948-0038. Tel: 715-787-3377. [CEM]
Catechesis / Religious Programs—Students 64.

Lincoln, Kewaunee Co., St. Peter. Merged with St. Hubert, Rosiere.

Little Chute, Outagamie Co., St. John Nepomucene, Rev. Msgr. James Vanden Hogen; Rev. David C. Ruby; Deacon Vincent M. DeGroot, Pastoral Assoc.
Res., 323 Pine St., 54140-1896. Tel: 414-788-9061. [CEM]
School—328 Grand Ave., 54140. Tel: 414-788-9082. Susan Sands, Prin.
Sisters 4; Lay Teachers 25; Students 584.
Catechesis / Religious Programs—Colleen Mitchell, D.R.E.
Students 533.

Little Suamico, Oconto Co., St. Pius. Attended by St. Benedict, Suamico. Rev. Gary J. Dantinne.
Mailing Address: P.O. Box 66, Suamico, 54173-0066. Tel: 414-434-2024.
Catechesis / Religious Programs—Students 80.

Long Lake, Florence Co., St. Norbert. Attended by St. Leonard, Laona. Rev. John W. Cerkas.
Res., R.R.1, Box 344, Laona, 54541-9641. Tel: 715-674-3241.

Luxemburg, Kewaunee Co., St. Joseph-St. John. Unassigned.
Res., E. 860 State Hwy. 29, 54217-7462. Tel: 414-845-2565. [CEM]
Immaculate Conception, Rev. Milton M. Suess.
Res., 1412 Main St., 54217-1308. Tel: 414-845-2056. [CEM]
School—St. Mary, 1406 Main St., 54217-1308. Tel: 414-845-2224. Linda Gerlach, Prin.
Lay Teachers 8; Students 161.
Catechesis / Religious Programs—Students 232.

Mackville, Outagamie Co., St. Edward, Rev. Charles Brooks.
Res., N2921 State Rd. 47, Appleton, 54915-9564. Tel: 414-733-2887 (Rectory); 733-9266 (Office). [CEM]
School—N2944 St. Rd. 47, Appleton, 54915. Tel: 414-733-6276. Jaclyn Behnke, Prin.
Lay Teachers 6; Students 45.
Catechesis / Religious Programs—Students 232.

Manawa, Waupaca Co., Sacred Heart. Unassigned.
Res., 614 S. Bridge St., P.O. Box 10, 54949-0010. Tel: 414-596-3323. [CEM][JC]
Catechesis / Religious Programs—Students 118.

Manitowoc, Manitowoc Co.,

1—St. Boniface, Rev. Carl Meulemans, M.M., Admin.; Sr. Mary Kevin, Pastoral Assoc. In res., Rev. Richard H. Klingeisen.
Res., 1110 S. 10th St., 54220-5212. Tel: 414-684-3718. [CEM][JC]
School—See Consolidated Schools under Institutions Located in the Diocese. 1418 Grand Ave., 54220. Tel: 414-683-6888. Barbara Heil, Prin. & Admin.
Religious 2; Lay Teachers 9; Students 40.
Catechesis / Religious Programs—Associated with St. Paul,St. Mary, & St. Andrew.
Students 60.
Convent— Franciscan Sisters of Christian Charity *Holy Family Conservatory*—1015 S. 11th St., 54220.

2—Holy Innocents, Revs. Gerald J. Foley; David M. Zimmerman, O.F.M.Cap.; Sr. Connie Wavrunek, O.S.F., Pastoral Assoc.; Deacons Paul Kieffer; Ken Nelesen.
Res., 1121 N. 14th St., 54220-3298. Tel: 414-682-0031. [CEM]
School—St. Francis de Sales. See Consolidated Schools under Institutions Located in the Diocese. 1408 Waldo Blvd., 54220. Tel: 414-683-6892.
Religious 1; Lay Teachers 22; Students 381.
Catechesis / Religious Programs—Claudia Maly, D.R.E.
Students 354.

3—St. Mary, Revs. Roman Zbieranski, O.F.M.; John Puodziunas, O.F.M.; Deacons Robert Drobka; Phillip Andrastek.
Res., 1114 S. 21st St., 54220-4994. Tel: 414-684-3558.
School—St. Frances Cabrini. See Consolidated Schools under Institutions Located in the Diocese. 2109 Marshall St., 54220. Tel: 414-683-6884. James Clark, Prin.
Lay Teachers 20; Students 229.
Catechesis / Religious Programs—Associated with St. Boniface, Manitowoc.
Students 210.

4—Sacred Heart, Rev. William H. Zimmer.
Res., 520 N. 7th St., 54220-4099. Tel: 414-684-8692. [JC]
School—Manitowoc Area Catholic System (MACS). See Consolidated Schools under Institutions Located in the Diocese.
Catechesis / Religious Programs—Sr. Rose Marie Buscemi, D.R.E.
Students 220.

5—St. Andrew, Rev. James J. Stamborski.
Res., 1416 Grand Ave., 54220-6199. Tel: 414-682-0023. [JC]
School—St. Francis Xavier. See Consolidated Schools under Institutions Located in the Diocese. 1418 Grand Ave., 54220. Tel: 414-683-6888. Mrs. Linda Bender, Prin.
Religious 2; Lay Teachers 11; Students 216.
Catechesis / Religious Programs—Associated with St. Boniface,St. Paul,St. Mary, & St. Andrew.
Students 60.

6—St. Paul, Rev. Ronald P. Reimer; Deacons Alan Boeldt; William D. Klein.
Res., 712 S. 24th St., 54220-4498. Tel: 414-684-6714. [JC]
School—Manitowoc Area Catholic System (MACS). See Consolidated Schools under Institutions Located in the Diocese.
Catechesis / Religious Programs—Associated with St. Boniface.
Students 72.

Maple Grove, Manitowoc Co., St. Patrick. Merged St. Mary, Reedsville. Rev. Nicholas A. Johannes; Deacon Donald Schneider.
Mailing Address: P.O. Box 248, Reedsville, 54230-0248. Tel: 414-754-4665. [CEM]

Maplewood, Door Co., St. Mary, Rev. Wilbert L. Buhl.
Mailing Address: P.O. Box 308, 54226-0308. Tel: 414-856-6440. [CEM 2]
Catechesis / Religious Programs—D.R.E.: Sharon McNulty; Joan Schley.
Students 209.

Marchand, Door Co., St. Francis de Paul (Duvall). Closed. For inquiries for parish records contact St. Louis, Dyckesville.

Marinette, Marinette Co.,

1—Holy Family. (Includes the combined parishes of Our Lady of Lourdes, St. Anthony, Sacred Heart, and St. Joseph). Revs. Lawrence T. Marto; Donald Everts; Sr. Donna Marie Botz, S.S.N.D., Pastoral Assoc.; Deacons Byron Otradovec; Jerry Thetreau.
Office: 1223 Carney Blvd., 54143-2599. Tel: 715-735-9100. [CEM 2]
School—1232 Garfield Ave., 54143. Tel: 715-735-7174. Mrs. Judith Urbanski, Prin.
Students 210.
Catechesis / Religious Programs—D.R.E.: Kathryn Lieburn; Sabrina Schmidt; Charlotte Duran.
Students 470.

2—Our Lady of Lourdes. Merged with Holy Family Parish.

3—St. Joseph. Merged with Holy Family Parish.

4—Sacred Heart Congregation. Merged with Holy Family Parish.

5—St. Anthony. Merged with Holy Family Parish.

Marion, Waupaca Co., St. Mary. Attended by St. Anthony, Tigerton. Rev. Michael R. Carroll, Admin.
Mailing Address: Box 106, Tigerton, 54486-0106. Tel: 715-535-2571; 754-2116 (Office). [CEM]
Catechesis / Religious Programs—Students 87.

Mattoon, Shawano Co., Holy Family. Attended by St. Anthony, Neopit. Rev. R. David Kiefer; Deacon Tom Hartman.
Mailing Address: P.O. Box 21, 54450-0021. Tel: 715-756-2361. [CEM]

Menasha, Winnebago Co., St. Patrick, Rev. Roy J. Geenen; Mary Doverspike, Pastoral Assoc.; Deacon Howard Bricco.
Res., 320 Nicolet Blvd., 54952-3394. Tel: 414-725-8381; Fax: 414-727-1215. [JC]
School—Seton Catholic Middle School, 312 Nicolet Blvd., 54952. Tel: 414-727-0279; Fax: 414-727-1215. Ms. Monica Bausom, Prin.
Lay Teachers 16; Students 160.
Catechesis / Religious Programs—Barb Mauthe, D.R.E.
Students 205.
St. Mary, Revs. William O'Halloran, S.S.S.; Robert Lussier, S.S.S.; Michael Noreika, S.S.S. In res., Bros. Michael Galligan, S.S.S.; Anthony Ornelas, S.S.S.
Res., 212 Appleton St., 54952-3189. Tel: 414-725-7714; Fax: 414-725-7612. [CEM]
School—(Grades PreK-5) 540 Second St., 54952. Tel: 414-725-5351; Fax: 414-722-5940. Michael Buss, Prin.
Lay Teachers 17; Students 187.
Catechesis / Religious Programs—Mary Gyrion, D.R.E.
Students 175.
St. John, Rev. R. Thomas Golden.
Res., 516 De Pere St., 54952-2899. Tel: 414-722-8922. [CEM]
School—628 Fifth St., 54952. Tel: 414-722-9370. Mrs. Suzanne P. Mathias, Prin.
Lay Teachers 15; Students 168.
Catechesis / Religious Programs—Patricia Jakubek, D.R.E.
Students 163.

Mishicot, Manitowoc Co., Holy Cross, Rev. John Neuser.
Res., 423 S. Main St., 54228-9777. Tel: 414-755-2550. [CEM]
School—423 Church St., 54228. Tel: 414-755-2487. Patricia Brault, Prin.
Lay Teachers 6; Students 102.
Catechesis / Religious Programs—Corrine Duffek, D.R.E.
Students 180.

Montpelier, Kewaunee Co., St. Joseph. Merged with St. John's, Krok to form St. Joseph/St.John, Luxemberg.

Namur, Door Co., St. Mary. Closed. See St. Frances and St. Mary, Brussels, for details.

Navarino, Shawano Co., St. Lawrence, Rev. John P. Kastenholz, O.Praem.; Sr. Judith Miller, C.S.J., Dir.
Res., W. 5125 State Hwy. 156, Bonduel, 54107-8614. Tel: 715-758-8161. [CEM]
Catechesis / Religious Programs—Students 90.

Neenah, Winnebago Co., St. Margaret Mary, Rev. David J. Koch; Joan Bartman, Pastoral Assoc.; Deacon Norman Spielbauer. In res., Rev. William Van Oss.
Res., 439 Washington Ave., 54956-3398. Tel: 414-729-4560. [JC]
Church—666 Division St., 54956-3398.
School—610 Division St., 54956. Tel: 414-729-4565; Fax: 414-729-4572. Sr. Gretchen Schaeffer, Prin.
Lay Teachers 18; Students 169.
Catechesis / Religious Programs—D.R.E.: Cathy Poirier; Peggy Lemberg; Kathy Kellerman.
Students 230.
St. Gabriel the Archangel, Revs. Richard L. Allen; Robert Lexa.
Res., 151 Andrew Ave., 54956-2289. Tel: 414-722-4914. [JC]
School—900 Geiger St., 54956. Tel: 414-725-4161. Selene Finch, Prin.
Lay Teachers 18; Students 224.
Catechesis / Religious Programs—Kurt Grube, D.R.E.
Students 688.

Neopit, Menominee Co., St. Anthony. (Also serves St. Joseph, Phlox, and Holy Family, Mattoon). Rev. R. David Kiefer; Sr. Michael Ann O'Donnel, Pastoral Assoc.; Deacon Thomas Hartman.
Mailing Address: P.O. Box 241, 54150-0241. Tel: 715-756-2361. [CEM]
Catechesis / Religious Programs—Students 104.

Neva, Langlade Co., St. Wenceslaus. Attended by St. Mary, Antigo. Rev. Jeremiah F. Worman; Deacon Thomas Hanley.
Mailing Address: 735 Deleglise St., Antigo, 54409-1497. Tel: 715-623-2522.
Res., N5340 Church Rd., Deerbrook, 54424-9413. Tel: 715-623-7019. [CEM]
Catechesis / Religious Programs—Tina Bures, Co-ord.
Students 160.

New Franken, Brown Co., St. Kilian. (Also serves St. Joseph, Champion). Rev. Florian Resheske.
Res., Rte. 1, P.O. Box 83, 54229-0083. Tel: 414-866-2285. [CEM]
Catechesis / Religious Programs—Mrs. Nancy Meltzer, D.R.E.
Students 122.

New Holstein, Calumet Co., Holy Rosary. (Also serves St. Ann, St. Anna). Rev. Patrick J. Lloyd, S.C.J.

Res., 1724 Madison St., 53061-1389. Tel: 414-898-4884. [CEM]
School—1814 Madison St., 53061-1347. Tel: 414-898-4210. Sr. Anna Tisler, Prin.
Sisters 4; Lay Teachers 10; Students 150.
Catechesis/Religious Programs—Mrs. Gail Welter, D.R.E.
Students 158.

New London, Waupaca Co., Most Precious Blood, Rev. Tito Sammut; Deacon Dave De Young.
Res., 808 S. Pearl St., 54961-1863. Tel: 414-982-2346. [CEM]
School—120 E. Washington St., 54961. Tel: 414-982-2134.
Lay Teachers 12; Students 156.
Catechesis/Religious Programs—Mary Kleist, D.R.E.
Students 332.

Niagara, Marinette Co., St. Anthony. (Also serves St. Margaret, Pembine). Rev. Patrick A. Bernardy; Deacon Al Klenovich.
Res., 1432 River St., 54151-1599. Tel: 715-251-4515; 251-3879 (Office). [CEM]
Catechesis/Religious Programs—D.R.E.: Mary Ann Brasure, (Grades K-8); Joetta Bartolac, (Grades 9-12).
Students 251.

Norman, Kewaunee Co., St. Joseph, Rev. Lawrence S. Gerend, Admin.
Res., E3295 County Rd. G, Kewaunee, 54216-9538. Tel: 414-776-1600. [CEM]

Northeim, Manitowoc Co., St. Casimir. Attended by St. Joseph, Alverno. Rev. David Beaudry.
Res., 8109 Northeim Rd., Newton, 53063-9630. Tel: 414-726-4228. [CEM]
Catechesis/Religious Programs—Students 50.

Oconto, Oconto Co., Holy Trinity (1996). Unassigned.
Res., 716 Madison St., 54153.
St. Joseph. Merged with St. Peter, Oconto to form Holy Trinity Parish, Oconto.
St. Peter. Merged with St. Joseph, Oconto to form Holy Trinity Parish, Oconto.

Oconto Falls, Oconto Co., St. Anthony. Attended by St. Patrick, Stiles. Rev. Msgr. Carl E. Steiner.
Church—239 N. Franklin St., 54154-1042. Tel: 414-846-2152. [CEM]
School—253 N. Franklin St., 54154. Tel: 414-846-2276. Ms. Rosemary Marifke, Prin.
Lay Teachers 5; Students 48.
Catechesis/Religious Programs—Mary Holtzberger, D.R.E.
Students 191.

Omro, Winnebago Co., St. Mary, Rev. Joseph A. Mattern.
Res., 233 E. Scott, 54963-1705. Tel: 414-685-2258.
Catechesis/Religious Programs—Beth Winkel, D.R.E.
Students 218.

Oneida, Brown Co., St. Joseph, Rev. George G. Lenzner.
Res., 145 St. Joseph Dr., 54115-8914. Tel: 414-869-2244. [CEM]
Catechesis/Religious Programs—Andrea Sabor, D.R.E.
Students 258.

Oneida Township, Outagamie Co., Immaculate Conception, Rev. Richard L. Thomas, Admin.
Res., N5589 County Rd. E., De Pere, 54115-8529. Tel: 414-869-2626; 788-9840. [CEM]
Catechesis/Religious Programs—Students 83.

Oshkosh, Winnebago Co.,

1—St. Peter, Rev. John J. Becker; Sr. Diane Faust, Pastoral Assoc.; Deacon Gerald Kuborn.
Res., 435 High Ave., 54901-4796. Tel: 414-231-9782; Fax: 414-231-9808. [JC]
School—St. John Neumann Middle School, (Grades 6-8). Part of the Oshkosh Area Catholic Educational System. Includes St. Vincent, St. Mary & St. Raphael. 449 High St., 54901-4796. Tel: 414-235-6156; Fax: 414-231-9808.
Lay Teachers 13; Students 156.
Catechesis/Religious Programs—Students 274.

2—St. Mary. Unassigned.
Res., 442 Monroe St., 54901-5198. Tel: 414-231-5317. [JC]
School—St. Francis Cabrini Elementary School. Part of the Oshkosh Area Catholic Educational System. Includes St. Vincent, St. Peter & St. Raphael. 619 Merritt Ave., 54901-5100. Tel: 414-235-0637. Rosemary Perrino, Prin.
Lay Teachers 12; Students 227.
Catechesis/Religious Programs—Students 150.
Convent—441 Boyd St., 54901-5135. Tel: 414-231-3388.

3—St. Josaphat, Rev. Stanley F. Kolbusz.
Res., 1333 Walnut St., 54901-3699. Tel: 414-235-1564. [JC]
Catechesis/Religious Programs—Mrs. M. Wichmann, D.R.E.
Students 173.

4—St. Vincent de Paul. Unassigned. Deacon Raymond Brandenstein.
Res., 216 W. South Park Ave., 54901-6598. Tel: 414-231-8855. [JC]
School—St. Elizabeth Seton Elementary School. (Part of the Oshkosh Area Catholic Educational System. Includes St. Vincent, St. Peter, St. Raphael, and St. Mary) 1207 Oregon St., 54901. Tel: 414-235-4060. Sr. Colleen Walsh, Prin.
Religious 1; Lay Teachers 10; Students 233.
Catechesis/Religious Programs—Students 109.

5—St. John, Rev. William L. Van De Kreeke.
Res., 434 W. South Park Ave., 54901-6569. Tel: 414-231-8596. [JC]
Catechesis/Religious Programs—Students 232.

6—Sacred Heart, Rev. Martin Fox.
Res., 1020 W. 6th Ave., 54901-5794. Tel: 414-235-2073. [CEM]
School—505 Knapp, 54901-5794. Tel: 414-235-7412. Mary Jo Winter, Prin.
Sisters 1; Lay Teachers 16; Students 251.
Catechesis/Religious Programs—Students 112.

7—St. Raphael the Archangel, Rev. Daniel J. Felton. In res., Rev. Jeffrey M. Vanden Heuvel.
Mailing Address: 2355 W. Ninth Ave., 54904. Tel: 414-235-7158. [JC]
Church—830 Westhavan Dr., 54904-7977. Tel: 414-233-8044 (Office); Fax: 414-233-2360.
School—P.O. Box 1513, 54902-1513. Tel: 414-426-3626.
Catechesis/Religious Programs—Lee Vanden Heuvel, D.R.E.
Students 785.

Osman, Manitowoc Co., St. Isidore, Rev. Lee J. Kahrs.
Res., 10707 Hwy. 42, Newton, 53063-9783. Tel: 414-726-4754. [CEM 2]

Pembine, Marinette Co., St. Margaret. Attended by St. Anthony, Niagara. Rev. Patrick A. Bernardy.
Res., 1432 River St., Niagara, 54151-1599. Tel: 715-251-4515.

Peshtigo, Marinette Co., St. Mary, Rev. Paul J. Radetski.
Res., 600 Thompson St., 54157-1430. Tel: 715-582-3876. [CEM]
School—141 S. Wood, 54157. Tel: 715-582-4041. Mr. Frank C. Kotecki, Prin.
Sisters 1; Lay Teachers 7; Students 89.
Catechesis/Religious Programs—Mrs. Janice Vande Hei, D.R.E.
Students 251.

Phlox, Langlade Co., St. Joseph. Attended by St. Anthony, Neopit. Rev. R. David Kiefer; Deacon Tom Hartman.
Mailing Address: P.O. Box 73, 54464-0073. Tel: 715-489-3330. [CEM]
Catechesis/Religious Programs—Students 83.

Pine Grove, Brown Co., Holy Trinity, Rev. Ralph C. Merkatoris.
Res., 4767 Stagecoach Rd., Denmark, 54208-9181. Tel: 414-863-2545. [CEM]
Catechesis/Religious Programs—D.R.E.: Jane Lyon; Tammy Vanderloop.
Students 340.

Plainfield, Waushara Co., St. Paul, Rev. Michael E. Betley.
Res., 622 Beach St., 54966-9637. Tel: 715-335-4314. [CEM]
Catechesis/Religious Programs—Students 200.

Poy Sippi, Waushara Co., Sacred Heart of Jesus. Attended by St. Mark, Redgranite. Rev. Francis Reinke, Admin.
Mailing Address: P.O. Box 273, Redgranite, 54970-0273. Tel: 414-566-4442. [CEM]

Pulaski, Brown Co., Assumption of the Blessed Virgin Mary, Revs. Albert Lis, O.F.M.; Edward Tlucek, O.F.M.; Michael Vincent, Pastoral Min.; Deacon William Doran.
Res., 124 E. Pulaski St., P.O. Box 379, 54162-0379. Tel: 414-822-3279. [CEM]
School—109 E. Pulaski St., 54162. Tel: 414-822-5650. Mrs. Mary Terrien, Prin.
Sisters 2; Lay Teachers 10; Students 125.
Catechesis/Religious Programs—Robert Berchmans, D.R.E.
Students 290.

Redgranite, Waushara Co., St. Mark. (Also serves Sacred Heart, Poy Sippi). Rev. Francis Reinke, Admin.
Mailing Address: P.O. Box 273, 54970-0273. Tel: 414-566-4442. [CEM]
Catechesis/Religious Programs—Students 72.

Reedsville/Maple Grove, Manitowoc Co., St. Mary-St. Patrick. St. Mary, Reedsville, and St. Patrick, Maple Grove, merged to become St. Mary-St. Patrick. Rev. Ronald Guillette, Admin.; Deacon Donald Schneider.
Res., 613 Menasha St., P.O. Box 248, Reedsville, 54230-0248. Tel: 414-754-4665. [CEM 3]
School—628 Menasha St., Reedville, 54230. Tel: 414-754-4124. Daniel O'Rourke, Prin.
Lay Teachers 8; Students 118.
Catechesis/Religious Programs—Students 152.

Rosiere, Kewaunee Co., St. Peter and St. Hubert. Merged with St. Peter, Lincoln. Rev. Dennis G. Drury.
Res., E3085 Rd. X, Casco, 54205-9757. Tel: 414-837-2852. [CEM 4][JC 4]
Catechesis/Religious Programs—Students 279.

St. Anna, Calumet Co., St. Ann. Attended by Holy Rosary, New Holstein. Rev. Patrick J. Lloyd, S.C.J.
Res., 1724 Madison St., New Holstein, 53061-1389. Tel: 414-898-4884. [CEM]
Catechesis/Religious Programs—Students 54.

St. John, Calumet Co., St. John the Baptist Parish. Merged with Sacred Heart, Sherwood, to form St. John-Sacred Heart, Sherwood/St. John.

St. Nazianz, Manitowoc Co., St. Gregory, Rev. Gerald Sirois, S.D.S. In res., Rev. Melvin Tracy, S.D.S.
Res., 208 Church St., 54232-9999. Tel: 414-773-2511. [CEM]
School—212 School St., 54232. Tel: 414-773-2530. Mrs. Judy Phillip, Prin.
Lay Teachers 10; Students 90.
Catechesis/Religious Programs—Fran Durkee, D.R.E.
Students 154.

School Hill, Manitowoc Co., Holy Trinity, Rev. Cyril Dickrell, S.D.S., Admin.; Deacon James Steffen.
Res., 11928 Marken Rd., Kiel, 53042-9750. Tel: 414-773-2380. [CEM]
Catechesis/Religious Programs—Mrs. Barbara Graf, D.R.E.
Students 168.

Seymour, Outagamie Co., St. John, Rev. Francis R. Kerscher; Deacon Orvell DeBruin.
Mailing Address: 915 Ivory St., 54165-1629.
Res., 904 S. Main St., 54165. Tel: 414-833-6140. [CEM]
School—928 S. Main St., 54165. Tel: 414-833-2122. Barbara G. Schneider, Prin.
Lay Teachers 8; Students 109.
Catechesis/Religious Programs—Theresa Hebert, D.R.E.
Students 222.

Shawano, Shawano Co., Sacred Heart. (Also serves St. Martin, Cecil). Revs. Leonard M. Evers; Peter W. Mastalir; Sr. Evelyn Antoine, O.P., Pastoral Assoc.; Deacon Charles Daily.
Mailing Address: Office, 321 S. Sawyer St., 54166-2437. Tel: 715-526-2023.
Res., 325 S. Main St., 54166. Tel: 715-526-4106. [CEM 2]
School—124 E. Center St., 54166. Tel: 715-526-5328. Darren Petschar, Prin.
Lay Teachers 13; Students 220.
Catechesis/Religious Programs—Mrs. Mary Ellen Waldvogel, D.R.E.
Students 350.

Sherwood/St. John, Calumet Co., St. John-Sacred Heart, Rev. Kenneth R. Frozena.
Res., N341 Military Rd., P.O. Box 58, Sherwood, 54169-0058. Tel: 414-989-1515. [CEM]
School—N361 Military Rd., Sherwood, 54169. Tel: 414-989-1373. Kerry Sievert, Prin.
Lay Teachers 9; Students 125.
Catechesis/Religious Programs—Students 113.

Shiocton, Outagamie Co., St. Denis, Rev. Joseph L. Bestler; Luanne Vandenberg, Pastoral Assoc.
Res., N5591 Second St., P.O. Box 146, 54170-0146. Tel: 414-986-3369. [CEM]
Catechesis/Religious Programs—Jennifer Nooker, D.R.E.
Students 166.

Sister Bay, Door Co., St. Rosalia. Attended by St. Mary of the Lake, Baileys Harbor. Rev. Chester Cappucci, O.M.I.
Mailing Address: P.O. Box 405, Baileys Harbor, 54202-0405. Tel: 414-839-2041. [CEM]
Catechesis/Religious Programs—Students 95.

Slovan, Kewaunee Co., St. Adalbert. Merged with Holy Trinity, Casco.

Sobieski, Oconto Co., St. John Cantius. (Also serves St. Joseph, Chase, and St. Louis, Abrams). Rev. Gerald Prusakowski, O.F.M.
Res., 6051 Noble St., 54171-9742. Tel: 414-822-5255. [CEM 2]
Catechesis/Religious Programs—Students 101.

South Branch, Menominee Reservation, St. Joseph of the Lake. (Mission of St. Michael, Keshena.). Rev. David S. Barrett; Sr. Kathleen Walli, O.P., Pastoral Assoc.
Mailing Address: P.O. Box 610, Keshena, 54135-0610. Tel: 715-799-3811. [CEM]

Spruce, Oconto Co., Sacred Heart of Jesus. Merged with St. Charles Borromeo, Lena.

Stangelville, Kewaunee Co., St. Lawrence. Attended by St. Hedwig, West Kewaunee. Rev. Alexis Lukasik, O.F.M.

Res., E3306 Krok Rd., Kewaunee, 54216-9687. Tel: 414-863-8747. [CEM]
Catechesis/Religious Programs—Students 50.

Stark, Brown Co., St. Mary. Attended by Immaculate Conception, Glenmore. Rev. David J. Pleier, Admin.
Res., 5840 Big Apple Rd., De Pere, 54115-9746. Tel: 414-864-7641. [CEM]

Stephensville, Outagamie Co., St. Patrick, Sr. Mary Bride Grubbs, A.N.G.; Rev. Joseph Bestler.
Res., N3686 State Rd. 76, Hortonville, 54944-9707. Tel: 414-757-5090. [CEM]
Catechesis/Religious Programs—Students 120.

Stiles, Oconto Co., St. Patrick. (Also serves St. Anthony, Oconto Falls). Rev. Msgr. Carl E. Steiner.
Res., 5246 St. Patrick Rd., Lena, 54139-9105. Tel: 414-834-2575. [CEM][JC]
Catechesis/Religious Programs—Associated with St. Anthony, Oconto Falls.
Students 51.

Stockbridge, Calumet Co., St. Mary, Rev. Leander F. Nickel.
Res., 120 Davis St., P.O. Box 8, 53088-0008. Tel: 414-439-1515. [CEM]
Catechesis/Religious Programs—Students 125.

Sturgeon Bay, Door Co., St. Joseph, Rev. Robert J. Karuhn; Sr. Sandra Peterson, S.S.N.D., Pastoral Assoc.; Deacon Kenneth Hunsader.
Res., 526 Louisiana St., 54235-1796. Tel: 414-743-2062.
School—130 N. 5th Ave., 54235. Tel: 414-743-9219; Fax: 414-743-9297. Michael Taylor, Prin.
Lay Teachers 11; Students 112.
Catechesis/Religious Programs—Students 263.

Corpus Christi, Rev. Anthony J. Birdsall; Deacon Paul Zenefski.
Mailing Address: 25 N. Elgin Ave., 54235-2963. Tel: 414-743-4716.
Res., 722 W. Maple St., 54235. [JC]
School—731 W. Juniper, 54235. Tel: 414-743-4144. Sr. Mary Kabat, Prin.
Lay Teachers 9; Students 171.
Catechesis/Religious Programs—Karen Stookinger, D.R.E.
Students 169.

Suamico, Brown Co., St. Benedict. (Also serves St. Pius, Little Suamico). Rev. Gary J. Dantinne; Deacon John Maloney.
Mailing Address: P.O. Box 66, 54173-0066. Tel: 414-434-2024. [CEM]
Catechesis/Religious Programs—Students 143.

Suring, Oconto Co., St. Michael, Rev. Frank D. Melchior.
Mailing Address: P.O. Box 248, 54174-0248. Tel: 414-842-2580. [CEM]
Catechesis/Religious Programs—Students 128.
Station—Chute Lake.

Thiry Daems, Kewaunee Co., St. Odile. Closed. For inquiries for parish records contact the Chancery.

Tigerton, Shawano Co., St. Anthony. (Also serves St. Mary, Marion). Rev. Michael Carroll, Admin.; Deacons Ken Sambs; Hilary Hayek.
Mailing Address: P.O. Box 106, 54486-0106. Tel: 715-535-2571. [CEM]
Catechesis/Religious Programs—Students 70.

Tisch Mills, Manitowoc Co., Nativity of the Blessed Virgin Mary, Rev. Gerald B. Kempen, O.Praem., Admin.
Mailing Address: 18424 Tisch Mills Rd., Denmark, 54208-9508. Tel: 414-776-1555. [CEM]
Catechesis/Religious Programs—Students 145.

Tonet, Kewaunee Co., St. Martin. Closed. For inquiries for parish records contact the Chancery.

Two Rivers, Manitowoc Co.,

1—St. Luke, Rev. Larry J. Seidl, Admin.; Deacon Kenneth Coenen.
Res., 1814 Jefferson St., 54241-2699. Tel: 414-793-2236. [JC]
School—Two Rivers Catholic Central. Consolidated with St. Mark, Two Rivers. 1800 Jefferson St., 54241. Tel: 414-794-7266. Mrs. Kay Franz, Prin.
Lay Teachers 16; Students 255.
Catechesis/Religious Programs—Students 93.

2—Sacred Heart, Rev. Donald F. Marquardt.
Res., 2208 Washington St., 54241-2241. Tel: 414-794-7869.

3—St. Mark, Rev. Larry J. Seidl, Admin.
2214-11th St., 54241-3718. Tel: 414-794-1717. [JC]
School—Two Rivers Catholic Central. Consolidated with St. Luke, Two Rivers. 2203 12th St., 54241. Tel: 414-794-7622.
Students 95.
Catechesis/Religious Programs—Associated with Most Holy Redeemer, Two Rivers.
Students 128.

4—Most Holy Redeemer, Rev. Paul A. Schumacher; Donna Treml, Pastoral Assoc.; Deacon James E. Sustman.
Church—3210 Tannery Rd., 54241-1648. Tel: 414-793-1755. [CEM]
Catechesis/Religious Programs—Associated with St. Luke,St. Mark,& Sacred Heart, Two Rivers. Sr. Maria Casetta, O.S.F., D.R.E.
Students 684.

Wabeno, Forest Co., St. Ambrose. (Also serves St. Mary of the Lake, Lakewood). Rev. Gerald Schmidt, O.F.M.Cap.
Mailing Address: P.O. Box 219, Lakewood, 54138-0219. Tel: 715-473-2511. [CEM]
Catechesis/Religious Programs—Students 67.

Wagner, Marinette Co., St. Edward. Attended by St. Joseph, Walsh. Rev. Roger Strebel, Admin.
Res., W3308 Hwy. G, Porterfield, 54159-9736. Tel: 715-789-2254. [CEM]
Catechesis/Religious Programs—Students 37.

Walhain, Kewaunee Co., St. Amand. Closed. For inquiries for parish records contact the Chancery.

Walsh, Marinette Co., St. Joseph. (Also serves St. Edward, Wagner). Rev. Roger Strebel, Admin.
Res., W3308 Hwy. G, Porterfield, 54159-9736. Tel: 715-789-2254. [CEM]
Catechesis/Religious Programs—Students 106.

Waupaca, Waupaca Co., St. Mary Magdalene, Rev. James F. Vennix.
Office and Mailing Address: 223 S. Division St., 54981-1594. Tel: 715-258-3000. [CEM]
Res., E. 1277 Cleghorn Rd., 54981. Tel: 715-258-4928.
Catechesis/Religious Programs—Students 440.

Wausaukee, Marinette Co., St. Augustine. (Also serves St. Agnes, Amberg). Revs. John F. McLaughlin; William Stengel, Pastoral Assoc.
Mailing Address: P.O. Box 375, 54177-0375. Tel: 715-856-5276. [JC]
Catechesis/Religious Programs—Mrs. Joy Duhey, D.R.E.
Students 170.

Wautoma, Waushara Co., St. Joseph, Rev. Philip Dinh-Van-Thiep; Deacon Steve Rocchi. Pastoral Assocs. & D.R.E.: Sr. Mary Ellen Doherty; Sr. Veronica Horvat, S.S.N.D.
Res., Rtc. 1, Box 426, 54982-9581. Tel: 414-787-3848. [CEM]
Catechesis/Religious Programs—Students 236.

West Kewaunee, Kewaunee Co., St. Hedwig. (Also serves St. Lawrence, Stangelville). Rev. Alexis Lukasik, O.F.M.
Res., E3306 Krok Rd., Kewaunee, 54216-9687. Tel: 414-388-3471. [CEM]

Weyauwega, Waupaca Co., SS. Peter and Paul, Rev. Bertin L. Samsa, O.F.M.Cap.
Res., 105 N. Lincoln St., P.O. Box 548, 54983-0548. Tel: 414-867-2179. [CEM]
Catechesis/Religious Programs—Shirley Sexton, D.R.E.
Students 175.

White Lake, Langlade Co., Ss. James and Stanislaus Congregation, Deacon Thomas Craig, Dir.; Rev. Omer Kelley.
Mailing Address: P.O. Box 36, 54491-0036. Tel: 715-882-2551. [CEM 2]
Res., 252 Bissell St., 54491.

Whitelaw, Manitowoc Co., St. Michael, Rev. Richard H. Heymen.
Mailing Address: P.O. Box 206, 54247-0206. Tel: 414-732-3901. [CEM]
School—132 W. Menasha Ave., 54247. Tel: 414-732-4442. Mrs. Arlene Rhein, Prin.
Lay Teachers 5; Students 53.
Catechesis/Religious Programs—Students 124.

Winneconne, Winnebago Co., St. Mary, Rev. Leroy R. Smet.
Res., 205 Pleasant Dr., 54986-0640. Tel: 414-582-4246.
Church—210 Pleasant Dr., P.O. Box 640, 54986-0640. Tel: 414-582-7712. [CEM][JC]
Catechesis/Religious Programs—Students 291.

Wittenberg, Shawano Co., Holy Family. (Also serves St. William, Eland). Rev. Claude A. Zabinski, O.F.M.
Res., 106 N. Ellms St., 54499-9065. Tel: 715-253-2050. [CEM]
Catechesis/Religious Programs—D.R.E.: Sr. Therese Lukas; Joyce Zaverorsky.
Students 116.

Wrightstown, Brown Co., St. Paul, Rev. Elroy Reimer.
Res., 437 Main St., P.O. Box 187, 54180-0187. Tel: 414-532-4374. [CEM][JC 2]
School—425 Main St., 54180. Tel: 414-532-4833. Ms. Ann Fox, Prin.
Lay Teachers 8; Students 105.
Catechesis/Religious Programs—Students 131.

Chaplains of Public Institutions

Green Bay. *Green Bay Correctional Institution.* Rev. Jerome Taddy, 2615 Washington St., Two Rivers, 54241-2140. Tel: 414-794-7273.

King. *Wisconsin Veterans Home,* P.O. Box 152, 54946-0152. Tel: 715-258-5586, Ext. 381. Rev. Paul Vanden Hogen.

Special Assignment:
Reverend Monsignors—
Coleman, Brian P., P.O. Box 23066, Green Bay, WI 54305-3066
Maufort, Richard A., Charlestown Pointe I, 1975 Ridgeway Dr., Apt. 30, De Pere, WI 54115
Schuh, John H., P.O. Box 23066, Green Bay, WI 54305-3066
Reverend Fathers—
Carr, Martin P., 1965 Oshkosh Ave., Oshkosh, WI 54901-2659
Dewane, John B., P.O. Box 23066, Green Bay, WI 54305-3066
Gilsdorf, Gordon J., Notre Dame de la Baie Academy, 610 Maryhill Dr., Green Bay, WI 54303-2092
Groher, Robert C., 6202 Dogwood Ln., Oconto, WI 54153
Hoffmann, Philip A., P.O. Box 23066, Green Bay, WI 54305-3066
Koch, Michael R., Chap. for Sisters of the Sorrowful Mother, Oshkosh, 890 Graceland Dr., Apt. 8, Oshkosh, WI 54904
Krutzik, Norman, 622 E. Pershing St., Appleton, WI 54911-8270
Massart, James, 910 E. Cedar Ave., Unit 403, Manitowoc, WI 54220-1352
Mocco, Charles, UW-Green Bay Ecumenical Center, 2420 Nicolet Dr., Green Bay, WI 54311-7001
Samter, James, P.O. Box 23825, Green Bay, WI 54305-3825. Tel: 414-437-7531
Smith, Ivan E., 3416 County Rd. V, Sturgeon Bay, WI 54235-8832
Van De Loo, Willard, P.O. Box 23825, Green Bay, WI 54305-3825
Vanden Heuvel, Jeffrey, Newman Center, 717 W. Irving, Oshkosh, WI 54901-4319
Ver Bust, Richard, Faculty St. Norbert College, 824 Voelker St., De Pere, WI 54115-3618

On Duty Outside the Diocese:
Reverend Monsignors—
Dewane, Frank J., Pontificio Consiglio Cor Unum, 00120 Vatican City, Rome, Italy. Tel: 011-396-6988-7331
Polc, Jaroslav, Bibliotecario Generale, Pontificia Universita Lateranense, Piazza Giovanni in Laterano 4, 00120 Vatican City, Rome, Italy
Reverend Fathers—
Conard, Raymond J., Apartado Postal 13, San Juan de la Maguana, Dominican Republic
Doerfler, John, St. Joseph Seminary, 1200 Varnum St., N.E., Washington, D.C. 20017
Dowling, Raymond G., 9707 Kingsley Rd., Apt. 514, Dallas, TX 75238
Hoffmann, William A., Casa Curiel, Parroquia Santa Teresa, Elias Pina, Dominican Republic
Mayefske, Thomas, 6041 Sequoia A-18NW, Albuquerqe, NM 87120
Rank, Robert F., 203 Dunne St., Robstown, TX 78380
Reuter, John F., Apartado 46, Tlaxiaco, Oaxaca Mexico
Schiavone, Robert W., 10430 W. Plum Tree Cir., #203, Hales Corners, WI 53130-2670
Seis, Michael, Casa Curiel, Pannoquia Santa Teresa, Elius Pina, Dominican Republic
Taylor, Peter, 18225 N. 35th Dr., Glendale, AZ 85308
Vander Heyden, William F., Chap. V.A. Medical Center, 1616 Hinman Ave., #4-D, Evanston, IL 60201-4525

Military Chaplains:
Reverend Fathers—
Dory, Michael, Lt. Cmdr., 2907 Shelter Island Dr., Ste. 105-216, San Diego, CA 92106

Absent on Leave:
Reverend Monsignors—
Witczak, Edward
Reverend Fathers—
Eberhardy, William
Pawelski, John
Resheske, Florian
Reynebeau, Thomas
Scherer, Steven J.
Schneider, Ronald
Shebuski, Charles
Somers, Michael
Stocker, Thomas
Thompson, Robert

Retired:
Reverend Monsignors—
Hotchkiss, Eugene, 1400 S. Park Ave., Neenah, WI 54956-4651

Rose, Donald, 865 Mill Rd., Sturgeon Bay, WI 54235-9267
Schneider, Alfred A., 2214 Paul Rd., Manitowoc, WI 54220-1122

Reverend Fathers—
Bablitch, Michael A., 3100 Ellis St., Apt. #8, Stevens Point, WI 54481
Barcome, Earl W., 1326 S. Fisk, Green Bay, WI 54304-3055
Bedessem, Henry W., 1851 Eldorado Dr., Apt. 6, Green Bay, WI 54302-5554
Bestler, Joseph, 1524 Schaefer Cir., #1, Appleton, WI 54915
Brouchoud, Earl R., 1136 S. Lake St., Manitowoc, WI 54220-5328
Danks, Arthur J., 2616 He Nis Ra Ln., Green Bay, WI 54304-1308
Feeney, John P., 3333 W. 2nd St., 56/123, Los Angeles, CA 90004-6149
Feller, Donald J., 2496 Mary Jo Dr., Green Bay, WI 54311-5208
Flatley, Eugene T., 2153 Calle Buena Ventura, Oceanside, CA 92054-3216
Gartska, Joseph A., N8778 Forest Rd., Deerbrook, WI 54424-9613
Geigel, Francis G., Rte. 1, Box 396, Wabeno, WI 54566-9742
Gitter, Aloysius A., P.O. Box 98, Harper, TX 78631-0098
Gomulka, Henry J., Alvernia Manor, 1598 Main St., Lemont, IL 60439-3701
Hemauer, William G., 307 Seidl St., Luxemburg, WI 54217-1106
Hietpas, Raymond W., 224 Iroquois Ave., #7, Green Bay, WI 54301-1918
Hogan, Leroy, 220 W. 4th St., Kaukauna, WI 54130
Jacobs, James T., P.O. Box 86, Crandon, WI 54520-0086
Janssen, Orville, 1500 Oakcrest Ct., Appleton, WI 54914
Johanek, John G., 1137 Edgewood Dr., Green Bay, WI 54311-5524
Kelly, Omer, 1215 Spanish Fort Ave., Antigo, WI 54409-1566
Kerch, Rudolph S., 1331 Bellevue, Lot 225 Huguet, Green Bay, WI 54302-2145
Kilsdonk, Edward P., 2249 W. Cortland Dr., Appleton, WI 54914-1932
Kleiber, Richard J., 3920 Libal St., Green Bay, WI 54301-1048
Knier, Aloysius M., 224 Iroquois Ave., #2, Green Bay, WI 54301-1918
Koehne, David, 1051 Main St., Wrightstown, WI 54180-1007
Koszarek, Thaddeus J., 224 Iroquois Ave., #1, Green Bay, WI 54301-1918
Kutiuk, Casimir R., 259 Westhaven Dr., Apt. 101, OshKosh, WI 54904-7858
Laux, Donald J., P.O. Box 219, Birnamwood, WI 54414-0219
Loehr, Alfred M., 425 Memory Ct., Green Bay, WI 54301-2275
Marquardt, Donald, 224 Iroquois Ave., #3, Green Bay, WI 54301-1918
Melchoir, Frank, E. 2783 Rockledge Rd., Casco, WI 54205
Peeters, R. Thomas, 224 Iroquois Ave., #6, Green Bay, WI 54301-1918
Rickert, William, 224 Iroquois Ave., #5, Green Bay, WI 54301-1918
Rodgers, Kenneth W., 441 St. Mary Blvd., Green Bay, WI 54301-2607
Scanlan, Lambert D., 1499 Capitol Dr., Apt. 105, Green Bay, 54303-2244
Schmidt, Eugene, 2650 Vinland Rd., Oshkosh, WI 54901-1524
Schmitt, John P., 2819 35th St., Two Rivers, WI 54241-1521
Schmitt, Leo J., 8635 Beach Rd., Two Rivers, WI 54241-9069
Schneider, Donald A., 509 Laurel Dr., P.O. Box 163, Francis Creek, WI 54214-0163
Schreiter, Daniel A., 4616 Basswood St., Land O'Lakes, FL 34639-5603
Schuh, Earl J., 2470 Mary Jo Dr., Green Bay, WI 54311-5207
Shafer, Richard, 1515 Capitol Dr., #105, Green Bay, WI 54303-2246
Sladek, Robert, 520 S. Kensington Dr., Appleton, WI 54915
Spalding, William, 310 Alpine Dr., #9, Shawano, WI 54166-2011
Staudenmaier, Wilbert N., 214 E. Summer St., Appleton, WI 54911-4814
Steckbauer, Linus J., 1411 N. Superior St., Antigo, WI 54409-2359
Stingle, Lawrence A., 2777 He Nis Ra Ln., Green Bay, WI 54304-1357
Watry, Jerome R., c/o Judy Dern, P.A., W2918 Co. Rd. E, Chilton, WI 53014
Worzalla, Dennis, 800 4th Ave., Stevens Point, WI 54481

Permanent Deacons:
Andrastek, Phillip, 1607 Hamilton St., Manitowoc, WI 54220
Arnold, Robert, St. Agnes Church, Green Bay
Asmuth, James, 1615 Nicolet Blvd., Neenah, WI 54956
Baumruk, Roy, St. Joseph Church, Appleton
Beaudry, Glenn, 221 E. Fairview, Green Bay, WI 54301
Boeldt, Alan, St. Paul Church, Manitowoc
Boucher, Paul, St. Francis Solanus Church, Gresham and St. Mary Church, Leopolis
Brandenstein, Raymond, St. Vincent de Paul Church, Oshkosh
Bricco, Howard, St. Patrick Church, Menasha
Burke, William, St. Mary Church, Appleton
Burkel, William, St. Philip the Apostle Church, Green Bay
Charlier, Earl, 733 S. Clay St., Green Bay, WI 54301
Coenen, Kenneth, St. Luke Church, Two Rivers
Craig, Thomas, Ss. James & Stanislaus Church, White Lake/Langlade
Daily, Charles, Sacred Heart Church, Shawano and St. Martin Church, Cecil
De Bruin, Orvell, St. John Church, Seymour
DeGroot, Vincent M., St. John Nepomucene Church, Little Chute
DeYoung, David, Most Precious Blood Church, New London
Doran, William, Assumption of the Blessed Virgin Mary Church, Pulaski
Drobka, Robert, St. Mary Church, Manitowoc
Ellis, Robert, 1372 Nienhaus Dr., De Pere, WI 54115-9802
Gallenberger, E. Dana, Holy Rosary Church, Kewaunee
Garcia, Ben, 612 E. Smith St., Iron Mountain, MI 49801-1954
Gauthier, James, St. Elizabeth Ann Seton Church, Green Bay
Gigure, Donald, Sacred Heart Church, Appleton
Goetz, Claude, 538 N. 8th St., Manitowoc, WI 54220-1906
Hanley, Thomas, St. Mary's Church, Antigo; St. Wenceslaus, Neva
Hartman, Thomas, St. Joseph Church, Phlox; Holy Family Church, Mattoon; St. Anthony Church, Neopit
Hayek, Hilary, St. Anthony Church, Tigerton
Hunsader, Kenneth, St. Joseph Church, Sturgeon Bay
Jacqmin, Robert, St. Bernard Church, Green Bay
Jozwiak, Thomas, St. Rose Church, Clintonville
Kaszynski, Walter, Holy Trinity, Oconto
Kieffer, Paul, Holy Innocents Church, Manitowoc
Klein, Paul L., St. Thomas More Church, Appleton
Klein, William D., St. Paul Church, Manitowoc
Koehler, Dan, 1302 W. Ajo Way, Unit 14, Tucson, AZ 85713-5704
Kopydlowski, Kenneth, SS. Peter & Paul Church, Green Bay
Kostichka, James, Holy Cross Church, Lena/Spruce
Kremer, Frank, St. Mary Church, DePere
Kuborn, Gerald, St. Peter Church, Oshkosh
Kunzer, Earl, Ss. Edward and Isidore Church, Flintville
Laurant, John, St. Bernard Church, Green Bay
LeMere, David, St. John the Baptist Church, Howard
Lowe, Russell E., N2280 Country Ln., Waupaca, WI 54981
Ludke, David, 3518 Glasscock Ave., Bossier City, LA 71112
Madsen, Roger, Ss. Peter and Paul Church, Institute
Maloney, John, St. Benedict Church, Suamico
Mastalish, Lawrence, St. Bernard Church, Green bay
Meidl, Richard, St. Joseph Church, Kellnersville
Nass, Donald, 945 Debbie Ln., Redgranite, WI 54970
Nelesen, Ken, Holy Innocents Church, Manitowoc
Newhouse, Donald, St. Nicholas Church, Freedom
Orlowski, Harold, St. Mary of the Lake Church, Lakewood
Otradovec, Byron, Holy Family Church, Marinette
Paulick, Donald P., 915 N. Locust St., Green Bay, WI 54303
Penzenstadler, Robert, St. Mary Church, Oshkosh
Peronteau, Bernard, 1787 Cecil Ave., Wabeno, WI 54566
Plantico, Paul G., St. Francis Xavier Cathedral, Green Bay
Proulz, Rahlf, Holy Innocents Church, Manitowoc
Quinette, Harvey, Our Lady of Lourdes Church, DePere
Reed, Maurice, Dir. Office of Permanent Diaconate, Vicar for Deacons, St. Bernard Church, Appleton
Reilly, Timothy, Resurrection Church, Green Bay
Rocchi, Steve, N4297 Cty. WW, Wild Rose, WI 54984-9418
Sambs, Kenneth, St. Anthony Church, Tigerton
Sauve, Willard, 107 Park Rd., Two Rivers, WI 54241
Schneider, Donald, Sr., St. Mary-St. Patrick Church, Reedsville/Maple Grove
Schraufnagel, George, St. Paul Church, Combined Locks
Siebers, David, 5321 2nd Ave., Great Falls, MT 59405-1509
Spielbauer, Norman, St. Margaret Mary Church, Neenah
Steffen, James, Holy Trinity Church, School Hill
Sustman, James, Most Holy Redeemer Church, Two Rivers
Swinford, Norval, N1764 C. Rd. D, Hortonville, WI 54944
Teske, Glenn, Our Lady of Lourdes, DePere
Thetreau, Jerome, Holy Family Church, Marinette
Vande Hey, Steven, St. Mary Church, Kaukauna
Wessing, Reinhart, St. Thomas More Church, Appleton
Wetzel, Donald, St. Thomas More Church, Appleton
Whitcomb, Patrick, St. Theresa Church, Appleton
Wildenberg, Clay, 115 Professional Plaza, Apt. 138, Neenah, WI 54956-4064
Williams, Nick, St. John the Baptist, Howard
Zenefski, Paul, Corpus Christi Church, Sturgeon Bay

INSTITUTIONS LOCATED IN THE DIOCESE

[A] SEMINARIES, RELIGIOUS OR SCHOLASTICATES

GREEN BAY. *St. Mary of the Angels Friary*, 645 S. Irwin Ave., 54301-3303. Tel: 414-437-7411. Rev. Joachim Swarick, O.F.M., Guardian.

DE PERE. *St. Norbert Abbey*, 1016 N. Broadway, 54115-2697. Tel: 414-337-4300; Fax: 414-337-4328. Rt. Revs. E. Thomas De Wane, O.Praem., Abbot; Benjamin T. Mackin, O.Praem., Abbot Emeritus; Sylvester M. Killeen, O.Praem., Abbot Emeritus; Jerome G. Tremel, O.Praem., Abbot Emeritus; Very Rev. Eugene E. Gries, O.Praem., Prior; Revs. Robert K. Finnegan, O.Praem., Provisor, Sec. & Treas.; James T. Baraniak, O.Praem., Vocation Coord.; Ambrose J. Peeters, O.Praem., Subprior & House Supr.; Anthony J. Wieczorek, O.Praem., Dir. Formation & Novice Master; Thomas O. Meulemans, O.Praem., Mission Procurator.

[B] COLLEGES AND UNIVERSITIES

DE PERE. *St. Norbert College*, 54115-2099. Tel: 414-337-3181.
For a complete listing, refer to the Colleges and Universities section.

MANITOWOC. *Silver Lake College of the Holy Family*, 2406 S. Alverno Rd., 54220-9340. Tel: 414-684-6691; Fax: 414-684-7082.
For a complete listing, refer to the Colleges and Universities section.

[C] HIGH SCHOOLS, DIOCESAN

APPLETON. *Xavier High School*. Coed, 1600 W. Prospect Ave., 54914. Tel: 414-733-6632. Mr. Matt Reynebeau, Prin.; Mrs. Donna Fahrenkrug, Assoc. Prin.; Andrew Mahoney, Dir. Guidance Dept.; Ms. Sarah Simon, Minister. Priests 1; Lay Teachers 42; Students 538.

MANITOWOC. *Roncalli High School*, 2000 Mirro Dr., 54220-6799. Tel: 414-682-8801. Christian Brothers and Franciscan Sisters of Christian Charity. Bro. Patrick Conway, Pres.; Sr. Adrianna Schouten, Prin.; Mr. Ron Klestinski, Dean of Students.
Campus Ministers: Bro. Larry Zeman; Mrs. Jennifer Nooker. Brothers 4; Sisters 7; Lay Teachers 28; Students 399.

MARINETTE. *Marinette Catholic Central High School*, 1200 Main St., 54143. Tel: 715-735-7481. Sr. Rose Adler, Prin. Lay Teachers 15; Students 103.

MENASHA. *St. Mary Central High School*, 528 2nd St., 54952-3194. Tel: 414-722-7796. Mrs. Sue Simonsen, Prin. Sisters 2; Lay Teachers 17; Students 201.

OSHKOSH. *Lourdes Academy*. Coed. 110 N. Sawyer St., 54901-5696. Tel: 414-235-5670. Bro. Roger Betzold, F.S.C., Prin.; Mr. Tom Baum, Vice Prin.; Carol Staszkiewicz, Dev. Dir. Lay Teachers 22; Students 195.

[D] HIGH SCHOOLS, PRIVATE

GREEN BAY. *Notre Dame de la Baie Academy*, 610 Maryhill Dr., 54303-2092. Tel: 414-498-6464. Sr. Patricia Clement, C.S.J., Prin. Priests 2; Lay Teachers 49820.

[E] CONSOLIDATED SCHOOLS

APPLETON. *Appleton Catholic Educational System (ACES)*, 1810 W. Prospect Av., 54914. Tel: 414-735-9380. William O'Brien, Exec. Dir.

MANITOWOC. *Manitowoc Area Catholic System (MACS)*, 1418 Grand Ave., 54220. Tel: 414-683-6880. Linda Bender, Contact Person & Prin.
St. Francis de Sales School. (Grades K-5), 1408 Waldo Blvd., 54220.
St. Francis Xavier School. (Grades PreK-5), 1418 Grand Ave., 54220.
St. Frances Cabrini Middle School. (Grades 6-8), 2109 Marshall St., 54220. Consolidation of Holy Innocents, Sacred Heart, St. Andrew, St. Paul, St. Mary and St. Boniface grade schools in Manitowoc.

MENASHA. *Twin Cities Catholic Educational System (TCCES)*, 528 Second St., 54952. Tel: 414-722-7922; Fax: 414-722-1838. Michelle Uitenbroek, Contact Person. Consolidation of St. Gabriel, St. Margaret Mary, St. Mary Elementary, Seton Catholic Middle School and St. Mary Central High School.

OSHKOSH. *OACES-Oshkosh Area Catholic Educational System*, 110 N. Sawyer St., P.O. Box 1513, 54902-1513. Tel: 414-426-3626.

[F] GENERAL HOSPITALS

GREEN BAY. *Libertas Treatment Center for Chemically Dependent*, 1701 Dousman St., 54303-3282. Tel: 414-498-8600.
For a complete listing, refer to the Hospitals section.
St. Mary's Hospital-Medical Center, 1726 Shawano Ave., 54303-3282. Tel: 414-498-4200.
For a complete listing, refer to the Hospitals section.
St. Vincent Hospital, P.O. Box 13508, 54307-3508. Tel: 414-433-0111; 433-8162.
For a complete listing, refer to the Hospitals section.

ANTIGO. *Langlade Memorial Hospital*, 112 E. 5th Ave., 55409. Tel: 715-623-2331.
For a complete listing, refer to the Hospitals section.

APPLETON. *Kaukauna Community Hospital*. Mailing Address: c/o St. Elizabeth Hospital, 1506 S. Oneida St., 54915-1305.
For a complete listing, refer to the Hospitals section.
St. Elizabeth Hospital, 1506 S. Oneida St., 54915-1305. Tel: 414-738-2665; Fax: 414-738-0949.
For a complete listing, refer to the Hospitals section.

KEWAUNEE. *St. Mary Kewaunee Area Memorial Hospital*, 810 Lincoln St., P.O. Box 217, 54216. Tel: 414-388-2210.
For a complete listing, refer to the Hospitals section.

MANITOWOC. *Holy Family Memorial, Inc.*, 2300 Western Ave., P.O. Box 1450, 54221-1450. Tel: 414-684-2011; Fax: 414-684-2522.
For a complete listing, refer to the Hospitals section.

OSHKOSH. *Mercy Medical Center*, 631 Hazel St., P.O. Box 1100, 54902-1100. Tel: 414-236-2000; Fax: 414-231-5677.
For a complete listing, refer to the Hospitals section.

[G] PROTECTIVE INSTITUTIONS

GREEN BAY. *McClosky Program, Inc.*, Our Lady of Charity Center, 2640 West Point Rd., P.O. Box 10357, 54307-0357. Tel: 414-494-8747.
For a complete listing, refer to the Special Care Facilities section.
Our Lady of Charity Center, Inc., 2640 West Point Rd., P.O. Box 10357, 54307-0357. Tel: 414-494-8747.
For a complete listing, refer to the Special Care Facilities section.

OSHKOSH. *The Convent Project, Inc.*, 435 High Ave., 54901. Tel: 414-235-6002.
For a complete listing, refer to the Special Care Facilities section.

TWO RIVERS. *Sisters Treatment Group Home*, 3904 Martin Ln., 54241. Tel: 414-794-1524.
For a complete listing, refer to the Special Care Facilities section.

[H] HOMES FOR AGED

GREEN BAY. *The McCormick Memorial Home for the Aged*, 212 Iroquois Ave., 54301-1918. Tel: 414-437-0883.
For a complete listing, refer to the Special Care Facilities section.

APPLETON. *Franciscan Care Center, Inc.*, 2915 N. Meade St., 54911-1598. Tel: 414-731-3184; Fax: 414-731-3206.
For a complete listing, refer to the Special Care Facilities section.
McKinnon Manor, 2525 E. Lourdes Dr., 54915. Tel: 414-733-0234.
For a complete listing, refer to the Special Care Facilities section.

KAUKAUNA. *St. Paul Home, Inc.*, 1211 Oakridge Ave., 54130-9961. Tel: 414-766-6020; Fax: 414-766-9161.
For a complete listing, refer to the Special Care Facilities section.

MANITOWOC. *Felician Village Inc.*, 1700 S. 18th St., 54220.
For a complete listing, refer to the Special Care Facilities section.
St. Mary's Home for the Aged, 2005 Division St., 54220-5699. Tel: 414-684-7171; Fax: 414-684-0240.
For a complete listing, refer to the Special Care Facilities section.

NEENAH. *Assisi Homes of Neenah, Inc.*, 210 Byrd Ave., 54946. Tel: 414-821-0336.
For a complete listing, refer to the Special Care Facilities section.
Villa Saint Clare, Inc., 130 Byrd Ave., 54952.
For a complete listing, refer to the Special Care Facilities section.

NEW LONDON. *St. Joseph Residence, Inc., New London*, 107 E. Beckert Rd., 54961. Tel: 414-982-5354.
For a complete listing, refer to the Special Care Facilities section.

NIAGARA. *Maryhill Manor Nursing Home (SNF)*, 501 Madison Ave., 54151. Tel: 715-251-3178; Fax: 715-251-1200.
For a complete listing, refer to the Special Care Facilities section.

[I] MONASTERIES AND RESIDENCES OF PRIESTS AND BROTHERS

GREEN BAY. *St. Mary of the Angels Friary*, 645 S. Irwin Ave., 54301-3303. Tel: 414-437-7411. Franciscan Friars, Assumption of the Blessed Virgin Mary Province (Order of Friars Minor). Revs. Finian Zaucha, O.F.M.; Joachim Swarick, O.F.M., Guardian; Campion Kluczynski, Chap. St. Vincent's Hospital; Lawrence Karcz, O.F.M., Preaching Ministry; Bros. James Buda, O.F.M., Vicar; Columban Sokolowski, O.F.M.; Joseph Krymkowski, O.F.M.; Theodore Tokarz, O.F.M. Priests 4; Brothers 4.

APPLETON. *St. Fidelis Friary*, 1100 N. Ballard Rd., 54911-5100. Tel: 414-954-8954. Revs. Simeon Keogh, Guardian; Donald Brody; Ambrose De Groot; Silas Baumann; William Lulloff; Pius Pulvermacher; Ambrose Simon; Giles Soyka; Jerome Tuller; Joel Tuller; Vianney Thibedeau; Anthony Thoma; Grigion Wenning; Bros. Thomas Heegeman; Carmel Labadie; Cyrus Toschik; Richard McDaniel; Conrad Heinen. Priests 13; Brothers 5; Staff 3.
St. Joseph Friary, 404 W. Lawrence St., 54911-5855. Tel: 414-734-7195. Order of Friars Minor Capuchin. Revs. John Holly, O.F.M.Cap.; Kurt Gessner, O.F.M.Cap.

DE PERE. *St. Joseph Priory*, 103 Grant St., 54115-2001. Tel: 414-403-3258. Residence for Norbertine Community. Revs. James T. Baraniak; Dennis M. Burke, O.Praem.; Robert J. Cornell, O.Praem.; Rowland C. De Peaux, O.Praem.; George J. Feldman, O.Praem.; David Komatz, O.Praem.; Brendan J. McKeough; Gilbert Mihayli, O.Praem.; Gery G. Meehan, O.Praem.; Thomas O. Meulemans; Joseph Rekasi; Harvey H. Toonen, O.Praem.; Louis J. Vande Castle, O.Praem.; John Bostwick, O.Praem., House Supr.; Conrad Kratz; Mark Payne; Allan Scheible; Timothy Shillcox; Robert Vande Hey; Bro. Robert Craanen. Priests 19; Brothers 1.
St. Norbert Abbey, 1016 N. Broadway, 54115-2697. Tel: 414-337-4300; Fax: 414-337-4328. Canons Regular of Premontre. Legal Titles: *The Premonstratensian Fathers; NORBERT & CO., a nominee of The Premonstratensian Fathers, Norbertine Fathers; St. Norbert Abbey, Inc.; Augustine Stewardship Fund Trust; Norbertine Retirement Fund Trust; St. Norbert Abbey Seminarian and Education Fund Trust; The Walnut Markets, Inc.; Los Amigos del Peru, Inc.* Rt. Revs. E. Thomas De Wane, O.Praem., Abbot; Benjamin T. Mackin, O.Praem., Abbot Emeritus; Sylvester M. Killeen, O.Praem., Abbot Emeritus; Jerome G. Tremel, O.Praem., Abbot Emeritus; Very Rev. Eugene E. Gries, O.Praem., Prior; Revs. Robert K. Finnegan, O.Praem., Provisor & Sec.-Treas.; Ambrose J. Peeters, O.Praem., Subprior & House Supr.; Anthony J. Wieczorek, O.Praem., Dir. Formation and Novice Master; Thomas O. Meulemans, O.Praem., Mission Procurator; Bartholomew A. Agar, O.Praem.; Jordan R. Blecha, O.Praem.; Robert E. Carson, O.Praem.; Angelo J. Feldkamp, O.Praem.; Isadore M. Gosz, O.Praem.; Guy E. Guyon, O.Praem; Gabriel A. Hinkes, O.Praem.; Robert L. Hyde, O.Praem.; Fabian A. Jolicoeur, O.Praem.; Stanislaus N. Joppe, O.Praem; John P. Kastenholz, O.Praem.; Alfred A. McBride, Weston, MA; Francis B. McHugh, O.Praem.; Laurence A. Mayer, O.Praem.; Gilbert E. Mihalyi, O.Praem., (Szombathely, Hungary); Emmanuel F. Mulhall, O.Praem.; Conan P. Mulrooney, O.Praem.; Richard D. Mulroy, O.Praem.; James P. Nielsen, O.Praem.; Gary J. Neville, O.Praem.; Donald C. Noel, O.Praem.; Peter J. Renard, O.Praem.; Robert B. Reppen, O.Praem.; Julian C. Resch, O.Praem.; Joseph A. Rohlinger, O.Praem; Stephen J. Rossey, O.Praem.; Glen F. Siebers, O.Praem; Milton C. Strebel, O.Praem.; Roman R. Vanasse, O.Praem.; Achilles E. Van Hoof, O.Praem., (Tongerlo, Belgium); Albin V. Veszelovszky, O.Praem., (Godollo, Hungary); Michael J. Weber, O.Praem., (Chap., United States Air Force, Tucson, AZ); Bros. Gerlac J. Riess, O.Praem.; Clement G. Tourangeau, O.Praem. Brothers 6; Priests 85; Priests at St. Norbert Abbey 36; Seminarians 9.
Retreats, Missions and Renewals: Rev. Robert E. Carson, O.Praem.; Rt. Rev. Jerome G. Tremel, O.Praem.
Priests serving in foreign Countries: Archdiocese of Lima, Peru, South America, Padres Norbertinos, Correo Las Flores, Lima 36. Tel: 011-511-992-4323 (Cellular); 011-511-458-0715 (Regular); Fax: 011-511-459-5905. Revs. Roderick R. Fenzl, O.Praem.; William J. Fischer, O.Praem.; Sebastian R. Schalk, O.Praem.; David F. Strenski, O.Praem., Archidiocese of Iquitos, Peru, South America, Santa Clotilde, Rio Napo, Apartado 216. Tel: 011-51-94-25-1932; Fax: 011-51-94-25-1932. Revs. Lambert C. Baeten, O.Praem.; John P. MacCarthy, O.Praem.

NEW HOLSTEIN. *Salvatorian Center Residence*, 53061-0001. Tel: 414-898-5635. Brothers 6.
Salvatorian Public Relations, Salvatorian Center, 53062. Tel: 414-898-4201. Rev. Gregory Coulthardt, S.D.S.
Salvatorian Mission Warehouse, 53061. Tel: 414-898-5898. Bro. Regis Fust, S.D.S., Dir. Mission Supply Program.

OSHKOSH. *Community of Our Lady*. (Diocesan Pious Union), 2804 Oakwood Ln., 54904-8406. Tel: 414-233-5633; Fax: 414-233-5604. Very Rev. Regis N. Barwig, Prior; Revs. Eugene E. Kalinski; Augustine Serafini.

PULASKI. *Assumption of B.V.M. Friary*, 143 E. Pulaski St., P.O. Box 100, 54162-0100. Tel: 414-822-5422; Fax: 414-822-5423. Headquarters of the Assumption of the Blessed Virgin Mary Province, Franciscan Friars (Order of Friars Minor). Revs. Paul Reczek, O.F.M., Minister Prov.; Thomas Luczak, O.F.M., Vicar Prov.; John Puodziunas, O.F.M., Treasurer; Richard Tulko, O.F.M., Prov. Sec.
Friary, 54162. Tel: 414-822-8125. Revs. Edward Tlucek, O.F.M., Guardian; Melvin Wierzbicki, O.F.M.; Jesse Zajac, O.F.M.; Adalbert Kalenty, O.F.M.; De Paul Sobotka, O.F.M.; Bros. Herman-Joseph Peplinski, O.F.M.; Anthony Gancarz, O.F.M.; Peter Rydza, O.F.M.; Gregory Stasinski, O.F.M.; David Typek, O.F.M.; Henry Kolbok, O.F.M.; Austin Mysliwiec, O.F.M.; Andrew Brophy, O.F.M.; Michael Janiak, O.F.M.
Retired-Infirm - Elsewhere: St. Mary's Home, Manitowoc: Revs. Thomas Wojciechowski, O.F.M., Chap.; Herman J. Ziembla, O.F.M.; Josaphat Ledwon, O.F.M.; Gerard Kotula, O.F.M.; Damien Rybka, O.F.M.; Sylvester Makarewicz, O.F.M.; Bros. Eugene Lacny, O.F.M.; Miles Brainer, O.F.M.; Martinian Babiarz, O.F.M.; Lambert Gorczycki, O.F.M.
Outside of Diocese: Revs. Ladislaus Szepe, S.F.O., Sarasota, FL; Lazarus Macior, O.F.M., Univ. of Akron, Biology Dept., 44325.
Priests of the Province Serving Abroad: Revs. Lyle Chrobak, O.F.M., Guaymas, Mexico; Arcadius Smolinski, O.F.M., Europe; Henry Howaniec, O.F.M., Kazakstan.
Military Chaplains: Revs. Conrad Targonski, O.F.M.; Adam E. Szufel, O.F.M.; Randall Roberts, O.F.M.
Franciscan Publishers. Tel: 414-822-5833.

ST. NAZIANZ. *Religious House of the Society of the Divine Savior S.D.S.* Salvatorian Community. 206 Church, 54232. Tel: 414-773-2794. Bros. Thaddeus Huebner, S.D.S.; Florian Schueth, S.D.S. Brothers 2.

[J] CONVENTS AND RESIDENCES FOR SISTERS

GREEN BAY. *Hospital Sisters of the Third Order of St. Francis*, 304 David Dr., 54303. Tel: 414-497-1882. Sisters 4. 1015 S. Webster St., 54305. Tel: 414-432-1337. Sisters 2.
St. Francis Convent of Sisters of St. Francis of the Holy Cross, 3025 Bay Settlement Rd., 54311-7301. Tel: 414-468-1828; Fax: 414-468-1207. Sr. Paulette Hupfauf, Pres. Sisters 99; In Diocese 86.
Sisters of Our Lady of Charity of the North American Union, Inc., 2640 West Point Rd., P.O. Box 10357, 54307-0357. Tel: 414-494-8747. Sr. Barbara Jean Arnsmeyer, Supr. Sisters 30.

MANITOWOC. *Holy Family Convent of Franciscan Sisters of Christian Charity*. Motherhouse and Novitiate dedicated to the Holy Family, 2409 S. Alverno Rd., 54220-9320. Tel: 414-682-7728; Fax: 414-682-4195. Revs. Louis Fronczek, O.F.M., Chap.; Samuel D. Jadin, O.Praem.; Sr. Paula Vanden Hogen, Community Dir. Sisters 565; In Diocese 384; Novices 1; Postulants 1; Total in Residence 195.

St. Clare Convent, 3 Riverview Dr., 54220. Tel: 414-682-5145. Sr. Mary Noel Brown, Dir. Franciscan Sisters of Christian Charity. Sisters 8.

St. Francis Convent, 6835 Hwy. 151, 54220. Tel: 414-684-7884. Sr. Debra Shepeck, Sec. Franciscan Sisters of Christian Charity. Sisters 43.

NEW FRANKEN. *Monastery of the Holy Name of Jesus, Ltd.*, Carmelite Monastery, 4047 Chapel Dr., 54229-9768. Tel: 414-866-2571. Sr. Mary Elizabeth. Total 13.

OSHKOSH. *SSM Franciscan Courts*, 815 Westhaven Dr., 54904-7978. Tel: 414-426-2440; Fax: 414-426-3196. Sisters of the Sorrowful Mother. Mrs. Pat Sinn, Facility Mgr.; Rev. Michael R. Koch, Chap. Sisters 48.

ST. NAZIANZ. *St. Mary's Convent-Sisters of the Divine Savior.* (Home for retired sisters), 300 S. 2nd Ave., 54232. Tel: 414-773-2515. Sr. Jane Barman, S.D.S., Coord. Sisters 13.

[K] CAMPS AND COMMUNITY CENTERS

SHAWANO. *Camp Tekawitha*, W5248 Lake Dr., 54166. Tel: 715-526-2316. Mailing Address: 112 N. 8th Ave., Winneconne, 54986. Tel: 414-582-7727. Mrs. Roberta Larson, Dir. (Boys & Girls ages 7 to 14) Located on Loon Lake, Shawano. Capacity 160.

[L] SHRINES

ROBINSONVILLE. *The Chapel of Our Lady of Good Help (Diocesan Shrine)-Robinsonville*, 4047 Chapel Dr., 54229-9768. Tel: 414-866-2571. Sr. Mary Elizabeth.

[M] RETREAT HOUSES

APPLETON. *Monte Alverno Retreat Center*, 1000 N. Ballard Rd., 54911-5148. Tel: 414-733-8526. The Province of St. Joseph of the Capuchin Order, Inc. Revs. Gabriel Diefenbach, O.F.M.Cap.; Werner Wolf, O.F.M.Cap., Dir.; Lester Bach, O.F.M.Cap.; Timon Costello, O.F.M.Cap.; Ellis Zimmer, O.F.M.Cap.; Mel Hermanns, O.F.M.Cap; Bro. John Kocian, O.F.M.Cap. Priests 4; Brothers 6; Retreatants Annually 2,500; Total in residence 7; Total Staff 13.

BAILEYS HARBOR. *St. Joseph Retreat Center*, 3035 O'Brien Rd., 54202-9132. Tel: 414-839-2391. Sr. Mary Anne Albert, S.S.S.F., Dir.; Rev. Byron Haaland, S.C.J., Admin. Retreats & Coord. Community; Sr. Lorraine Aspenleiter, S.S.S.F.; Sr. Mary Louise Schramer, O.S.F.; Bros. John Monek, S.C.J.; Andrew Lewandowski, S.C.J. Lay Missioners: Priests of the Sacred Heart. Ms. Maria Galang; Ms. Karen Powers. In res., Rev. Joseph Dean, S.C.J. Priests 2; Brothers 2; Sisters 3; Total in residence 9; Total staff 11.

CHAMBERS ISLAND. *Holy Name Retreat House.* 1825 Riverside Dr., P.O. Box 23825, Green Bay, 54305-3825. Tel: 414-437-7531; Fax: 414-437-0694. Conducted by Diocese of Green Bay. Rev. Msgr. James B. Feely, Spiritual Dir.; Michael & Mary Cherf, Admin.

DE PERE. *Ministry and Life Retreat Center.* (An Apostolate of the Norbertine Fathers), St. Norbert Abbey, 1016 N. Broadway, 54115-2697. Tel: 414-337-4315. Rev. Anthony J. Wieczorek, O.Praem., Dir. Total in residence 1; Total staff 5.

MENASHA. *LaSalle Center*, 522 2nd St., 54952. Tel: 414-722-8918. Bro. Richard D. Roller, F.S.C., Dir. of Dev.; Mrs. Jennifer A. Plath, Admin.

OSHKOSH. *Jesuit Retreat House*, 4800 Fahrnwald Rd., Hwy. 45, 54901-7598. Tel: 414-231-9060. Society of Jesus. Revs. Richard F. McCaslin, S.J., Dir.; Cornelius Carr, S.J.; Robert Dufford, S.J.; Orville J. Catuso, S.J.; Sr. Marie Schwan, C.S.J. In res., Bro. Anthony Simon, S.J.

[N] NEWMAN CENTERS

GREEN BAY. *University of Wisconsin Ecumenical Center*, 2420 Nicolet Dr., 54311-7001. Tel: 414-465-5133. Rev. Charles W. Mocco, Catholic Campus Min.

Lawrence University Newman Center. (Appleton).

University of Wisconsin Manitowoc Campus Newman Center. (Manitowoc).

University of Wisconsin Marinette Campus Newman Center. (Marinette).

University of Wisconsin Fox Valley Campus Newman Center. (Menasha).

University of Wisconsin Newman Center, 717 W. Irving Ave., Oshkosh, WI, 54901. Tel: 414-233-5555. Rev. Jeffrey Vanden Heuvel, Dir. & Chap.

[O] MISCELLANEOUS LISTINGS

GREEN BAY. *The Diocesan Charismatic Renewal Center*, 405 Grant St., 54115. Tel: 414-337-6161. Rev. Msgr. James Vanden Hogen, Liaison; Mrs. Karen Wautlet, Pres.; Judy Goolsbey, Office Mgr.

Green Bay Area Catholic High School Foundation, L.T.D., P.O. Box 23066, 54305-3066. Tel: 414-435-4406. Mr. Dick White, Pres.; Rev. Edward J. Smith, O.Praem., Exec. Dir.

Sacred Heart Seminary, Inc., P.O. Box 23066, 54305-3066. Rev. John B. Dewane, Admin.; Sr. Lisa Lucht, Chancellor.

St. Joseph Corporation, Diocesan Central Offices, P.O. Box 23825, 54305-3825. Tel: 414-437-7531; Fax: 414-437-0694. Mr. Vincent Pelletier, Admin.

Sisters of A New Genesis (ANG). An Association of the Faithful, 1825 S. Riverside Dr., P.O. Box 23825, 54305-3825. Sr. Mary Barbara Loch, Pres., St. Joseph Home Chapel; Most Rev. Aloysius J. Wycislo.

Teens Encounter Christ (TEC), Green Bay Chapter, P.O. Box 23825, 54305. Tel: 414-437-7531; Fax: 414-437-0694. Mr. Tony Pichler, Diocesan Liaison.

APPLETON.

**First Care North, Inc.*, 1506 S. Oneida St., 54915. Tel: 414-738-2000. Judy Westphal, Pres.; Rosemary Dorachek, Dir.

St. Elizabeth Hospital Community Foundation, Inc., 1506 S. Oneida, 54915-1305. Tel: 414-738-2365; Fax: 414-738-0949. Franciscan Sisters, Daughters of the Sacred Heart of Jesus and Mary (Wheaton, IL). Mr. Otto Cox, Pres.; Lisa Weiner, Dir. of Devel.

DE PERE. *Augustine Stewardship Fund Trust*, 1016 N. Broadway, 54115-2697. Tel: 414-337-4300; Fax: 414-337-4328.

Canons Regular of Magnovarad, Ltd., 1016 N. Broadway, 54115-2697. Tel: 414-337-4300; Fax: 414-337-4328. Rev. Albin V. Veszelovszky, O.Praem., Pres.; Rt. Rev. Jerome G. Tremel, O.Praem., Vice Pres.; Revs. Joseph S. Rekasi, O.Praem.; Robert K. Finnegan, O.Praem., Sec. & Treas.

Los Amigos del Peru, Inc., 1016 N. Broadway St., 54115-2697. Tel: 414-337-4300; Fax: 414-337-4328.

NORBERT & CO. A nominee of The Premonstratensian Fathers, 1016 N. Broadway, 54115-2697. Tel: 414-337-4300; Fax: 414-337-4328. Rt. Rev. E. Thomas DeWane, O.Praem.; Very Rev. Eugene E. Gries, O.Praem.; Rev. Robert K. Finnegan, O.Praem.

Norbertine Generalate, Inc., 1016 N. Broadway, 54115-2697. Tel: 414-337-4300; Fax: 414-337-4328. Most Rev. Hermenegild J. Noyens, O.Praem., Pres., Rome, Italy; Rt. Rev. Benjamin T. Mackin, O.Praem., Vice Pres.; Rev. Robert K. Finnegan, O.Praem., Sec. & Treas.

Norbertine Retirement Fund Trust, 1016 N. Broadway, 54115-2697. Tel: 414-337-4300; Fax: 414-337-4328.

St. Norbert Abbey Seminary and Education Fund Trust, 1016 N. Broadway, 54115-2697. Tel: 414-337-4300; Fax: 414-337-4328.

MANITOWOC. *Franciscan Sisters of Christian Charity Healthcare Ministry, Inc.*, 2409 S. Alverno Rd., 54220-9320. Tel: 414-684-7071; Fax: 414-684-6417. Sr. Laura J. Wolf, O.S.F., Pres.

MENASHA. *St. Mary High School Foundation, Inc.*, 528 2nd St., 54952-3194.

NEENAH. *Global Outreach, Inc.*, 433 Hawthorne St., 54956. Tel: 414-727-1207. James Catlin, Pres.; Gary Elmer, Vice Pres. & Treas.; Barbara Bartz, Sec.; Mary Piette, Dir.

OSHKOSH. *Affinity Health System*, P.O. Box 1100, 54902. Tel: 414-738-2757; Fax: 414-738-0949. Mr. Otto Cox, Pres. & CEO. Sponsored by Franciscan Sisters, Daughters of the Sacred Hearts of Jesus and Mary, Wheaton, IL.

RELIGIOUS INSTITUTES OF MEN REPRESENTED IN THE DIOCESE

For further details refer to the corresponding bracketed number in the Religious Institutes of Men or Women section.

[0140]—*The Augustinians.*—O.S.A.
[0330]—*Brothers of the Christian Schools.*—F.S.C.
[0900]—*Canons Regular of Premontre.*—O.Praem.
[0470]—*The Capuchin Friars.* (Province of St. Joseph).—O.F.M.Cap.
[0220]—*Congregation of the Blessed Sacrament.*—S.S.S.
[1130]—*Congregation of the Priests of the Sacred Heart.*—S.C.J.
[0690]—*Franciscan Friars.*—O.F.M.
[0690]—*Jesuit Fathers and Brothers.* (Wisconsin Province).—S.J.
[0800]—*Maryknoll Fathers and Brothers.*—M.M.
[0910]—*Oblates of Mary Immaculate.*—O.M.I.
[1200]—*Society of the Divine Savior.*—S.D.S.

RELIGIOUS INSTITUTES OF WOMEN REPRESENTED IN THE DIOCESE

[3710]—*Congregation of the Sisters of St. Agnes.*—C.S.A.
[0420]—*Discalced Carmelite Nuns.*—O.C.D.
[1070-03]—*Dominican Sisters.*—O.P.
[1070-09]—*Dominican Sisters.*—O.P.
[1070-13]—*Dominican Sisters.*—O.P.
[1070-14]—*Dominican Sisters.*—O.P.
[1170]—*Felician Sisters.*—C.S.S.F.
[1230]—*Franciscan Sisters of Christian Charity.*—O.S.F.
[1240]—*Franciscan Sisters, Daughters of the Sacred Hearts of Jesus and Mary.*—O.S.F.
[1820]—*Hospital Sisters of the Third Order of St. Francis.*—O.S.F.
[3070]—*North American Union Sisters of Our Lady of Charity.*—N.A.U.-O.L.C.
[3440]—*Religious Hospitallers of Saint Joseph.*—R.H.S.J.
[2970]—*School Sisters of Notre Dame.*—S.S.N.D.
[1680]—*School Sisters of St. Francis.*—O.S.F.
[3510]—*Sister Servants of Christ the King.*—S.S.C.K.
[]—*Sisters of Charity of the B.V.M.*—B.V.M.
[0500]—*Sisters of Charity of Nazareth.*—S.C.N.
[2630]—*Sisters of Mercy of the Holy Cross.*—S.C.S.C.
[3800]—*Sisters of St. Elizabeth.*—S.S.E.
[1705]—*The Sisters of St. Francis of Assisi.*—O.S.F. - S.S.S.F.
[1550]—*Sisters of St. Francis of the Holy Cross.*—O.S.F.
[3840]—*Sisters of St. Joseph of Carondelet.* (Prov. of St. Louis).—C.S.J.
[3880]—*Sisters of St. Joseph of Medaille.*—C.S.J.
[3930]—*Sisters of St. Joseph of the Third Order of St. Francis.*—S.S.J.-T.O.S.F.
[1030]—*Sisters of the Divine Savior.*—S.D.S.
[4100]—*Sisters of the Sorrowful Mother (Third Order of St. Francis).*—S.S.M.

DIOCESAN CEMETERIES

GREEN BAY. *Diocesan Cemeteries*, P.O. Box 23825, 54305-3825. Tel: 414-437-7531, Ext. 8229. Mr. John C. Nelson, Diocesan Dir.

Allouez, 2121 Riverside Dr., 54301.

Allouez Chapel Mausoleum, 2121 Riverside Dr., 54301.

Queen of Peace Cemetery & Mausoleum, Box 535, Antigo, 54409.

St. Joseph, P.O. Box 2676, Appleton, 54913-2676.

Mount Calvary, 1307 Lourdes Ave., De Pere, 54115.

Mount Olivet, S. Erie St., De Pere, 54115.

Calvary Cemetery & Calvary Chapel Mausoleum, 2601 S. 14th St., Manitowoc, 54220-6467.

Oconto, c/o 716 Madison St., Oconto, 54153. Tel: 414-834-5750.

Oshkosh, 1905 Roosevelt Ave., Oshkosh, 54901.

St. Joseph Cemetery & Mausoleum, 25 N. Elgin, Sturgeon Bay, 54235.

NECROLOGY

† Baum, John, (Retired). —Died Oct. 20, 1996.
† Bujarski, Edward, (Retired). —Died Dec. 8, 1995.
† Ebel, Alfred, (Special Assignment). —Died May 2, 1996.
† Haen, John, (Retired). —Died Oct. 23, 1996.
† Stamborski, James, Manitowoc, WI, St. Andrew. —Died Dec. 31, 1995.
† Stern, Sylvester, (Retired). —Died April 13, 1996.

Diocese of Greensburg

(Dioecesis Greensburgensis)

Most Reverend

ANTHONY G. BOSCO, D.D., J.C.L.

Bishop of Greensburg; ordained June 7, 1952; appointed Auxiliary Bishop of Pittsburgh and Titular Bishop of Labico May 14, 1970; consecrated June 30, 1970; appointed Bishop of Greensburg April 14, 1987; installed June 30, 1987. *Office: 723 E. Pittsburgh St., Greensburg, PA, 15601.*

ESTABLISHED MARCH 10, 1951.

Square Miles 3,334.

Comprises the Counties of Armstrong, Fayette, Indiana and Westmoreland in the State of Pennsylvania.

For legal titles of parishes and diocesan institutions, consult the Chancery Office.

Chancery Office: 723 E. Pittsburgh St., Greensburg, PA, 15601. Tel.: 412-837-0901; Fax: 412-837-0857.

STATISTICAL OVERVIEW

Personnel	
Bishop	1
Abbots	1
Retired Abbots	1
Priests: Diocesan Active in Diocese	114
Priests: Active Outside Diocese	11
Priests: Retired, Sick or Absent	29
Number of Diocesan Priests	154
Religious Priests in Diocese	96
Ordinations:	
Diocesan Priests	3
Religious Priests	1
Transitional Deacons	7
Permanent Deacons in Diocese	1
Total Brothers	38
Total Sisters	322
Parishes	
Parishes	107
With Resident Pastor:	
Resident Diocesan Priests	85
Resident Religious Priests	10
Without Resident Pastor:	
Administered by Priests	12
Professional Ministry Personnel:	
Brothers	1
Sisters	27
Lay Ministers	43
Welfare	
Catholic Hospitals	1
Total Assisted	79,287
Homes for the Aged	2
Total Assisted	134
Residential Care of Disabled	1
Total Assisted	83
Other Institutions	5
Total Assisted	4
Educational	
Diocesan Students in Other Seminaries	15
Seminaries, Religious	1
Students Religious	11
Total Seminarians	26
Colleges and Universities	2
Total Students	2,144
High Schools, Diocesan and Parish	2
Total Students	837
Elementary Schools, Diocesan and Parish	27
Total Students	5,804
Elementary Schools, Private	3
Total Students	229
Catechesis/Religious Education:	
High School Students	1,242
Elementary Students	10,183
Total Students Under Catholic Instruction	20,465
Teachers in the Diocese:	
Priests	2
Brothers	5
Sisters	39
Lay Teachers	366
Vital Statistics	
Receptions into the Church:	
Infant Baptism Totals	2,273
Adult Baptism Totals	115
Received into Full Communion	358
First Communions	2,306
Confirmations	2,460
Marriages:	
Catholic	685
Interfaith	471
Total Marriages	1,156
Deaths	2,518
Total Catholic Population	195,582
Total Population	688,501

Former Bishops—Most Rev. HUGH L. LAMB, S.T.D., First Bishop of Greensburg; ord. May 29, 1915; appt. Titular Bishop of Helos and Auxiliary of Philadelphia December 19, 1935; cons. March 19, 1936; promoted to Greensburg May 28, 1951; installed Jan. 16, 1952; died Dec. 8, 1959.—Most Reverend WILLIAM G. CONNARE, D.D., ord. June 14, 1936; appt. Feb. 23, 1960; cons. May 4, 1960; retired Jan. 20, 1987; died June 12, 1995.

Chancery Office—723 E. Pittsburgh St., Greensburg, 15601. Tel: 412-837-0901; Fax: 412-837-0857. Office Hours: Mon.-Fri. 8:45-5.

Vicar General / General Executive Director, Moderator of the Curia—Rev. ROGER A. STATNICK, V.G., S.T.L., Ph.D. Tel: 412-837-9521.

Chancellor / Associate General Executive Director—Rev. LAWRENCE T. PERSICO, J.C.L. Tel: 412-837-9522.

Executive Director of Finance—MICHAEL J. MCGEE.

Deaneries—Deanery 1-Alle Kiski: Rev. THADDEUS J. KACZMAREK, V.F., Deanery 2-Indiana: Rev. Msgr. WILLIAM G. CHARNOKI, V.F., Deanery 3-Westmoreland West: Rev. Msgr. JOHN L. CONWAY, V.F., Deanery 4-Westmoreland East: Rev. LAWRENCE R. KINIRY, V.F., Deanery 5-Mon Yough: Rev. JOHN R. CINDRIC, V.F., Deanery 6-Fayette: Rev. JOHN A. REGOLI, V.F.

Director for Religious—Vacant, Office: *723 E. Pittsburgh St., Greensburg, 15601.*

Tribunal—Address all correspondence to, *723 E. Pittsburgh St., Greensburg, 15601.* Tel: 412-837-9523.

Judicial Vicar—Rev. WILLIAM R. RATHGEB, J.C.L.

Defender of Bond—Rev. LAWRENCE T. PERSICO, J.C.L.

Judges—Revs. LAWRENCE T. PERSICO, J.C.L.; WILLIAM R. RATHGEB, J.C.L.; RICHARD J. KOSISKO, J.C.L.; Rev. Msgr. WILLIAM G. CHARNOKI, V.F.

Advocates—Rev. Msgr. ROBERT J. SHUDA, V.F.; Rev. DANIEL C. MAHONEY; Sr. MARY HALLORAN, S.C.

Notaries—CINDY J. OZZELLO; KATHLEEN POLOSKY.

Advisory Bodies

Board of Consultors—Most Rev. ANTHONY G. BOSCO, Presider; Revs. ROGER A. STATNICK, V.G.; THADDEUS J. KACZMAREK, V.F.; Rev. Msgr. JOHN L. CONWAY, V.F.; Revs. LAWRENCE R. KINIRY, V.F.; THOMAS J. BERTOLINA; MICHAEL J. BEGOLLY; JAMES D. TRINGHESE; GEORGE W. SWAST.

Diocesan Pastoral Council—In process of restructuring.

Bishop's Priests Council—Rev. ROGER A. STATNICK, V.G.; Rev. Msgr. JOHN L. CONWAY, V.F.; Revs. LAWRENCE R. KINIRY, V.F.; THADDEUS J. KACZMAREK, V.F.; Rev. Msgr. WILLIAM G. CHARNOKI, V.F.; Revs. JOHN A. REGOLI, V.F.; GEORGE W. SWAST; Rev. Msgr. DAVID L. FISHER; Revs. RICHARD G. CURCI; THOMAS J. BERTOLINA; JOHN R. CINDRIC, V.F.; ALEXANDER L. PLEBAN; RICHARD E. MACKIEWICZ; RONALD L. SIMBOLI; LARRY J. KULICK.

Finance Council—Most Rev. ANTHONY G. BOSCO; Rev. ROGER A. STATNICK, V.G.; JOSEPH G. KLOCEK; JOHN A. ROBERTSHAW, JR.; Mrs. BERNARD F. SCHERER; MICHAEL J. MCGEE; Rev. Msgr. JOHN L. CONWAY; ADOLPH BARTOLOMUCCI; CHARLES A. FAGAN, III; JACK L. HADLEY; Sr. GERTRUDE FOLEY, S.C.

Diocesan Offices, Commissions and Special Programs

The Catholic Foundation Trust for the Diocese of Greensburg—Under Declaration of Trust dated 1st day of November, 1988, as amended 2nd day of November 1992 having as its purpose the support of any Roman Catholic benevolent, charitable, educational or missionary undertaking. Most Rev. ANTHONY G. BOSCO, D.D., J.C.L., Chm. Board of Trustees; Revs. ROGER A. STATNICK, V.G., S.T.L., Ph.D., Vice Chm. LAWRENCE T. PERSICO, J.C.L., Assoc. Vice Chm. JOHN A. ROBERTSHAW, JR., Pres. CHARLES A. FAGAN, III, Sec. MICHAEL J. MCGEE, Treas., *723 E. Pittsburgh St., Greensburg, 15601.*

The Catholic Institute of Greensburg—A Corporation, not-for-profit, incorporated under the law of the Commonwealth of Pennsylvania on the 4th day of June, 1954 having as its purpose the support of any Roman Catholic benevolent, charitable, educational or missionary undertaking. Most Rev. ANTHONY G. BOSCO, D.D., J.C.L., Pres.; Revs. ROGER A. STATNICK, V.G., Vice Pres. LAWRENCE T. PERSICO, Sec. MICHAEL J. MCGEE, Treas., *723 E. Pittsburgh St., Greensburg, 15601.*

Greensburg Catholic Accent and Communications, Inc.—A corporation, not-for-profit, under the laws of the Commonwealth of Pennsylvania having as its purpose the support of any Roman Catholic benevolent, charitable, educational or missionary undertaking. Most Rev. ANTHONY G. BOSCO, D.C., J.C.L., Chief Exec. Officer; Rev. ROGER A. STATNICK, V.G., Vice Pres. MICHAEL J. MCGEE, Treas., *723 E. Pittsburgh St., Greensburg, 15601.* Tel: 412-837-0901.

Catholic Charities of the Diocese of Greensburg, PA, Inc.—A corporation not-for-profit incorporated under the law of the Commonwealth of Pennsylvania on the 27th day of August, 1954, having as its purpose, the support of any Roman Catholic benevolent, charitable, educational or missionary undertaking. Most Rev. ANTHONY G. BOSCO, D.D., J.C.L.,

Chm. of the Members of the Corp. CHARLES DELUZIO, Pres. Bd. of Trustees; Rev. RAYMOND E. RIFFLE, Exec. Dir., *115 Vannear Ave., Greensburg, 15601.* Tel: 412-837-1840.

Archives—ALBINA GUERRIERI, Sec.

Catholic Charities—Rev. RAYMOND E. RIFFLE, M.S.W., M.P.A., Exec. Dir. ROBERT MCHENRY, Dir. Operations & Finance, *115 Vannear Ave., Greensburg, 15601.* Tel: 412-837-1840; Fax: 412-837-4077.

Catholic Relief Services Representative—Rev. Msgr. DAVID L. FISHER, *723 E. Pittsburgh St., Greensburg, 15601.* Tel: 412-837-0901.

Communications—Ms. ANGELA J. BURROWS, Exec. Dir. DAVID MALONEY, Mgr. Television & Radio, *723 E. Pittsburgh St., P.O. Box 850, Greensburg, 15601.* Tel: 412-834-4010; Fax: 412-836-5650.

Services and Facilities—EDWARD J. BLASZKOWSKI, Assoc. Exec. Dir., *723 E. Pittsburgh St., Greensburg, 15601.*

Department of Education and Spiritual Formation—Rev. JAMES T. GASTON, Exec. Dir., *723 E. Pittsburgh St., Greensburg, 15601.* Tel: 412-837-9543.

Office of Catholic Schools—Dr. PHILIP BOGGIO, Supt.; Sr. MARGUERITE COYNE, C.S.J., Assoc. Supt. REYNOLD A. PEDUZZI, Coord. Secondary & Government Programs; THERESE TELEPAK, Coord. Drug & Alcohol Prevention, *723 E. Pittsburgh St., Greensburg, 15601.* Tel: 412-836-1281.

Office of Initiation and Spiritual Formation—MICHAEL J. GRAMMER, Dir. THERESE TELEPAK, Assoc. Dir. for Youth Formation; SALLY LOUGHRAN, Coord. Marriage Formation; ANGELO DIPPOLITO, Coord. Athletics; Rev. LAWRENCE L. MANCHAS, Coord. Scouts, *723 E. Pittsburgh St., Greensburg, 15601.* Tel: 412-837-9543.

Office of Parish Life and Ministry—MARY ANN GUBISH, Dir.; Sr. SUSAN JENNY, S.C., Assoc. Dir., *723 E. Pittsburgh St., Greensburg, 15601.* Tel: 412-837-9543.

Office of Worship—Rev. MICHAEL J. BEGOLLY, Dir. MARIE KONOPKA, Diocesan Liturgy Coord., *723 E. Pittsburgh St., Greensburg, 15601.* Tel: 412-837-0901.

Office of Vocations / Clergy Formation—Rev. JOSEPH P. MADDALENA, Dir.; Rev. JAMES S. HAGEDER, Asst. Dir. Vocations, *723 E. Pittsburgh St., Greensburg, 15601.* Tel: 412-837-0901.

Diocesan Commission for Human Life and Justice—Rev. WILLIAM C. MCGUIRK, Chm., *497 Athena Dr., Delmont, 15626.* Tel: 412-468-4221.

Missions—Society for the Propagation of the Faith and Holy Childhood, Rev. Msgr. DAVID L. FISHER, *723 E. Pittsburgh St., Greensburg, 15601.* Tel: 412-837-0901.

Newspaper—"The Catholic Accent", 723 E. Pittsburgh St., P.O. Box 850, Greensburg, 15601. Tel: 412-834-4010; Fax: 412-836-5650. VINCENT A. CAPOZZI, Editor.

Parish Facilities Management Office—EDGAR R. TURNER, Dir. Engrg. & Parish Facilities Mgmt., *723 E. Pittsburgh St., Greensburg, 15601.*

Stewardship—ROBERT P. MUELLER, Dir. Stewardship & Devel. JAMES A. SCHUCOLSKY, Assoc. Dir. Stewardship & Devel. JOSEPH W. HOAG, Dir. Devel. for Catholic Schools, *723 E. Pittsburgh St., Greensburg, 15601.*

SPECIAL PROGRAMS:

Apostleship of Prayer—Rev. J. EDWARD MCCULLOUGH, Dir., *R.D.#1, Ranch Road, Dunbar, 15431.*

Apostolate for the Deaf—Rev. JOSEPH P. TRAYNOR, Dir., *47 Morris St., Clymer, 15728.*

Catholic Business and Professional Women's Association—Rev. JOSEPH P. MADDALENA, Chap., *723 E. Pittsburgh St., Greensburg, 15601.*

Catholic Daughters of America—Rev. Msgr. DAVID L. FISHER, Dir., *P.O. Box 398, 201 Church St., Penn, 15675.* Tel: 412-523-3450.

Cemeteries—Rev. ALEXANDER L. PLEBAN, Dir., *St. Joseph Church, R.D.#4, Walnut Hill Rd., Uniontown, 15401.*

Charismatic—Sr. ANN INFANGER, S.C., Moderator, *Seton Hill College, Greensburg, 15601.*

Cursillo—Vacant.

Diocesan Council of Catholic Women—Rev. DONALD J. MONDELLO, Dir., *1204 Ligonier St., Latrobe, 15650.*

Holy Childhood Association—Rev. Msgr. DAVID L. FISHER, Dir., *723 E. Pittsburgh St., Greensburg, 15601.*

Holy Name Society—Rev. GEORGE K. ALDERSON, Dir., *50 Jefferson St., Uniontown, 15401.*

Legion of Mary—Rev. HENRY P. DINICCO, Dir., *216 Spruce St., Mt. Pleasant, 15666.*

Pilgrimages—Rev. J. EDWARD MCCULLOUGH, Dir., *R.D.#1, Ranch Road, Dunbar, 15431.*

Priests' Eucharistic League—Rev. J. EDWARD MCCULLOUGH, *R.D. 1, Ranch Rd., Dunbar, 15431.*

St. Thomas More Guild for Lawyers—723 E. Pittsburgh St., Greensburg, 15601.

St. Vincent de Paul Society—Rev. JOHN A. SEDLAK, Spiritual Dir., *St. Hedwig Church, P.O. Box 251, Smock, 15480.*

CLERGY, PARISHES, MISSIONS AND PAROCHIAL SCHOOLS

CITY OF GREENSBURG (Westmoreland County)

1—BLESSED SACRAMENT CATHEDRAL, Rev. Msgr. Robert J. Shuda; Rev. Michael P. Sikon. In res., Rev. James S. Hageder.
Res., 300 N. Main St., 15601. Tel: 412-834-3710; Fax: 412-834-1518. [CEM]
Convent—350 N. Main St., 15601. Tel: 412-834-0894. Sisters of Charity
School—Aquinas Academy. See separate listing under Elementary Schools in the Institution section.

2—ST. BRUNO, Rev. Richard Ulam, O.S.B.
Res., 1707 Poplar St., 15601. Tel: 412-836-0690.
School—Aquinas Academy. See separate listing under Elementary Schools in the Institution section.

3—OUR LADY OF GRACE, Revs. Lawrence R. Kiniry; Salvatore Lamendola. In res., Rev. James T. Gaston.
Res., 1001 Mount Pleasant Rd., 15601. Tel: 412-838-9480; Fax: 412-838-1842.
School—Aquinas Academy. See separate listing under Elementary Schools in the Institution section.

4—ST. PAUL, Rev. Leonard W. Stoviak. In res., Revs. Daniel L. Blout; Raymond E. Riffle.
Res., 820 Carbon Rd., 15601. Tel: 412-834-6880; Fax: 412-834-1492.
School—Aquinas Academy. See separate listing under Elementary Schools in the Institution section.

OUTSIDE THE CITY OF GREENSBURG

Apollo, Armstrong Co., St. James the Greater, Rev. Ronald L. Simboli.
Res., 109 Owens View, 15613. Tel: 412-478-4958; Fax: 412-478-1802.
School—109 Owens View, 15613. Tel: 412-478-4851; Fax: 412-478-1802. Mr. Thomas J. Shearon, Prin.
Sisters 1; Lay Teachers 4; Students 116.
Convent—715 Rte. 56 E., 15613. Tel: 412-478-3287. Sisters of Charity

Arnold, Westmoreland Co., All Saints (Slovak), Richard G. Curci, Admin.
Res., 1700 Leishman Ave., 15068. Tel: 412-335-8232.

Avonmore, Westmoreland Co., St. Ambrose, Rev. William J. Homolak.
Res., P.O. Box 617, 505 Cambria Ave., 15618. Tel: 412-697-4129.

Belle Vernon, Westmoreland Co., St. Sebastian, Revs. John R. Cindric, V.F.; E. George Saletrik.
Res., 801 Broad Ave., 15012. Tel: 412-929-9300; Fax: 412-930-7611.
School—815 Broad Ave., 15012. Tel: 412-929-5143; Fax: 412-929-3038. Sr. Mildred Minosky, V.S.C., Prin.
Sisters of St. Francis Millvale 1; Lay Teachers 10; Students 204.
Chapel—Belle Vernon, Newell Chapel of St. Sebastian.

Blairsville, Indiana Co., SS. Simon and Jude, Rev. Chester J. Raimer.
Res., 155 N. Brady St., 15717. Tel: 412-459-7103; Fax: 412-459-5314.

Bovard, Westmoreland Co., St. Bede, Rev. Brinstan G. Takach, O.S.B.
Res., c/o St. Vincent Archabbey, 300 Fraser Purchase Rd., Latrobe, 15650. Tel: 412-532-6629; 837-3690.

Brady's Bend, Armstrong Co., St. Patrick, Rev. Thomas A. Federline.
Res., R.D. 1, Box 78, 16028. Tel: 412-526-5079. [CEM]
Chapel—Sugar Creek, Chapel of St. Patrick, Brady's Bend. [CEM]

Brownsville, Fayette Co., St. Peter, Rev. Vincent J. Gigliotti.
Res., 304 Shaffner Ave., 15417. Tel: 412-785-7781; Fax: 412-785-8161. [CEM]
School—Brownsville Catholic School. See separate listing under Elementary Schools in the Institution section.
Convent—302 Shaffner Ave., 15417. Tel: 412-785-7172.
St. Mary, Rev. John S. Szczesny.
Res., 118 Church St., 15417. Tel: 412-785-5932. [CEM]
School—Brownsville Catholic School. See separate listing under Elementary Schools in the Institution section.

Cadogan, Armstrong Co., St. Lawrence, Rev. Edward Volz, O.S.P.P.E.
Res., Box 114, 16212. Tel: 412-763-1089. [CEM]
Chapel—Nicholson Run, Chapel of St. Lawrence, Cadogan.

Calumet, Westmoreland Co., St. Stanislaus (Polish), Rev. John M. Foriska, Admin.
Res., P.O. Box 56, 15621. Tel: 412-423-4052. [CEM]

Cardale, Fayette Co., Madonna of Czestochowa, Rev. Ronald J. Rutkowski.
Res., P.O. Box 8, 15420. Tel: 412-246-9657. [CEM]

Clymer, Indiana Co., Church of the Resurrection, Revs. Micah E. Kozoil; Joseph P. Traynor; Stephen R. Bugay.
Administration Center: 47 Morris St., 15728. Tel: 412-254-3041; Fax: 412-254-3045. [CEM]
Chapel—Camerons Bottom,Chapel of Church of the Resurrection,Clymer.

Connellsville, Fayette Co.,

1—IMMACULATE CONCEPTION, Rev. Michael J. Sciberras.
Res., 148 E. Crawford Ave., 15425. Tel: 412-628-8550; Fax: 412-628-3410. [CEM]
School—Conn-Area Catholic School. See separate listing under Elementary Schools in the Institution section.
Chapel—Dawson, Chapel of Immaculate Conception, Connellsville.

2—HOLY TRINITY, (Polish), Rev. Benjamin S. Babula, Admin.
Res., 109 N. Seventh St., 15425. Tel: 412-628-7061. [CEM]
School—Conn-Area Catholic School. See seperate listing under Elementary Schools in the Institution section.

3—ST. JOHN THE EVANGELIST, (Slovak), Rev. John M. Butler.
Res., 908 W. Crawford Ave., 15425. Tel: 412-628-2112. [CEM]
School—Conn-Area Catholic School. See separate listing under Elementary Schools in the Institution section.

4—ST. RITA, (Italian), Rev. Francis A. Lesniowski.
Res., 116 S. Second St., 15425. Tel: 412-628-4015. [CEM]
School—Comm-Area Catholic School. See separate listing under Elementary Schools in the Institution section.

Coral, Indiana Co., St. Francis, Rev. Elmer A. Kacinko.
Res., Box G, 15731. Tel: 412-479-9161; Fax: 412-479-0449. [CEM]
Chapel—Blacklick, Chapel of St. Francis, Coral.

Crabtree, Westmoreland Co., St. Bartholomew, Rev. Augustine Flood O.S.B.
Res., P.O. Box A, 15624. Tel: 412-834-0709. [CEM]

Delmont, Westmoreland Co., St. John Baptist de La Salle, Rev. William C. McGuirk.
Res., St. John Square, 497 Athena Dr., 15626. Tel: 412-468-4221; Fax: 412-468-4221.

Derry, Westmoreland Co., St. Joseph, Rev. Kenneth G. Zaccagnini. In res., Rev. Roger A. Statnick, V.G., S.T.L., Ph.D.
Res., 117 S. Ligonier St., 15627. Tel: 412-694-5359. [CEM]
St. Joseph Residence: 209 Broad St., 15627. Tel: 412-694-0320; Fax: 412-694-0320.

Donegal, Westmoreland Co., St. Raymond, Rev. Leonard J. McAlpin.
Res., P.O. Box D, 15628. Tel: 412-593-7479. [CEM]

Dunbar, Fayette Co., St. Aloysius, Rev. J. Edward McCullough.
Res., R.D. 1, Ranch Rd., 15431. Tel: 412-277-4236; Fax: 412-277-0192. [CEM]

East Vandergrift, Westmoreland Co., Our Lady, Queen of Peace, Rev. Joseph Minsterman.
Res., 400 Kennedy Ave., 15629. Tel: 412-567-7603.

Ernest, Indiana Co., Church of the Assumption. Closed. For inquiries for parish records contact Church of the Resurrection, Clymer.

Everson, Fayette Co., St. Joseph, Rev. Joseph L. Sredzinski, M.Div.
Res., 201 Painter St., 15631. Tel: 412-887-6714. [CEM]

Export, Westmoreland Co., St. Mary, Rev. Dismas Young, O.F.M.Cap. In res., Revs. John Carey, O.F.M.Cap.; Angelus Shaughnessey, O.F.M.Cap.; Gabriel Giles, O.F.M.Cap.; Bro. John Donatelli, O.F.M.Cap.

Res., 5900 Kennedy Ave., 15632. Tel: 412-327-0647; Fax: 412-325-3784.

Fairchance, Fayette Co., SS. Cyril and Methodius, Rev. Anthony A. Wozniak.
Res., 50 Morgantown St., 15436. Tel: 412-564-7436. [CEM]
Chapel—Shoaf, Chapel of SS. Cyril & Methodius, Fairchance.

Farmington, Fayette Co., St. Joan of Arc, Rev. Paul A. Whalen.
Res., P.O. Box 92, 15437. Tel: 412-329-4522. [CEM]

Fayette City, Fayette Co., Holy Spirit, Rev. Richard E. Mackiewicz.
Res., P.O. Box 639, 139 S. High St., 15438. Tel: 412-326-4352.

Footedale, Fayette Co., St. Thomas (Polish), Rev. James L. Popochock, Admin.
Res., P.O. Box 636, New Salem, 15468. Tel: 412-245-9244; Fax: 412-245-9289. [CEM]

Forbes Road, Westmoreland Co., St. Mary, Rev. Anthony J. Burlas, O.S.B.
Res., c/o St. Vincent Archabbey, 300 Fraser Purchase Rd., Latrobe, 15650. Tel: 412-539-9761; 532-6648.

Ford City, Armstrong Co., St. Mary, Rev. Terry A. Hercik.
Res., 718 Fourth Ave., 16226. Tel: 412-763-1631. [CEM]
School—Ford City Catholic School. See separate listing under Elementary Schools in the Institution section.

St. Francis of Paola (Polish), Rev. Lawrence L. Hoppe, Admin.
Res., P.O. Box 327, 736 Fifth Ave., 16226. Tel: 412-763-1196. [CEM]
School—Ford City Catholic School. See separate listing under Elementary Schools in the Institution section.

Holy Trinity (Slovak), Rev. Robert E. Feeney.
Res., 1008 Sixth Ave., 16226. Tel: 412-763-9141. [CEM]
School—Ford City Catholic School. See separate listing under Elementary Schools in the Institution section.
Convent—1016 Sixth Ave., 16226. Tel: 412-763-1109. Vincentian Sisters of Charity

Freeport, Armstrong Co., St. Mary, Rev. Denis R. Sweeney, M.Div., M.S.W.
Res., 608 High St., 16229. Tel: 412-295-2281; Fax: 412-295-3090. [CEM]
School—610 High St., 16229. Tel: 412-295-3003; Fax: 412-295-3003. Mrs. Adrienne Ofcharsky, Prin.
Lay Teachers 7; Students 101.

Glen Campbell, Indiana Co., St. Michael. Closed. For inquiries for parish records contact Church of the Resurrection, Clymer.

Grindstone, Fayette Co., St. Cecilia (Slovak), Rev. John A. Sedlak, Admin.
c/o P.O. Box 251, Smock, 15480. Tel: 412-677-2110; Fax: 412-677-0146.

Harrison City, Westmoreland Co., St. Barbara, Revs. V. Paul Fitzmaurice; Edward J. Lewis.
Res., 34 Raymaley Rd., 15636. Tel: 412-744-7474; Fax: 412-744-3056.

Heilwood, Indiana Co., St. John the Baptist. Closed. For inquiries for parish records contact Church of the Resurrection, Clymer.

Herminie, Westmoreland Co., St. Edward, Revs. Lawrence L. Manchas; Anthony W. Ditto.
Res., 87 Sixth St. Ext., 15637. Tel: 412-446-5197; Fax: 412-446-1433.
School—89 Sixth St., 15637. Tel: 412-446-5381. Sr. MaryLou Witkowski, S.H.S., Prin.
Sisters of the Holy Spirit 2; Lay Teachers 9; Students 180.
Convent—87 Sixth St., 15637. Tel: 412-446-5359. Sisters of the Holy Spirit

Indiana, Indiana Co., St. Bernard, Rev. Msgr. William G. Charnoki, J.C.L., V.F.; Rev. Paul R. Stivason.
Res., 200 Clairvaux Dr., 15701. Tel: 412-465-2210; Fax: 412-465-0422. [CEM]
School—300 Clairvaux Dr., 15701. Tel: 412-465-7139; Fax: 412-465-0803. Mrs. Lucinda Copeland, Prin.
Lay Teachers 8; Students 176.
Convent—470 Clairvaux Dr., 15701. Tel: 412-349-1778. Sisters of St. Joseph

St. Thomas More University Parish. (Newman Center). Rev. Michael J. Begolly.
Res., Indiana University of PA, 1200 Oakland Ave., 15701. Tel: 412-463-2277; Fax: 412-463-7116.

Irwin, Westmoreland Co., Immaculate Conception, Rev. Msgr. John L. Conway, V.F.; Rev. Larry J. Kulick.
Res., 305 Second St., 15642. Tel: 412-863-9550; Fax: 412-863-9552. [CEM]
School—Queen of Angels Regional Catholic School. See separate listing under Elementary Schools in the Institution section.

Iselin, PA, Indiana Co., Holy Cross. Closed. For inquiries for parish records contact Church of the Good Shepherd, Kent.

Jeannette, Westmoreland Co., Sacred Heart, Revs. William A. Beaver, O.S.B.; Mark Wenzinger, O.S.B.; Bro. James Cartwright, O.S.B., Parish Min. In res., Rev. Dominic J. Petroy, O.S.B.
Res., 504 Cowan Ave., 15644. Tel: 412-523-2560. [CEM]

Ascension (Italian), Rev. Msgr. Nicholas A. Mitolo.
Res., 615 Division Ave., 15644. Tel: 412-523-6567; 6568.

Kent, Indiana Co., Church of the Good Shepherd, Rev. Michael W. Matusak.
Res., P.O. Box 99, 15752. Tel: 412-479-3881; Fax: 412-479-3882.

Kittanning, Armstrong Co., St. Mary, Our Lady of Guadalupe, Rev. William J. Kiel.
Res., 101 W. High St., 16201. Tel: 412-548-7649; 548-7640; Fax: 412-545-3262. [CEM]
Convent—348 N. Water St., 16201. Tel: 412-543-4518. Sisters of St. Joseph

Maxwell, Fayette Co., St. James, Rev. George R. Pierce.
Res., Box 247, LaBelle, 15450. Tel: 412-785-3617.
Chapel—Isabella, Chapel of St. James, Maxwell.

Latrobe, Westmoreland Co.,

1—Holy Family, Revs. Donald J. Mondello; Alan W. Grote; Paul E. Rubadue, O.S.B.
Res., 1204 Ligonier St., 15650. Tel: 412-539-9751; Fax: 412-539-8044. [CEM]
School—Christ the Divine Teacher School. See separate listing under Elementary Schools in the Institution section.

2—St. Vincent Basilica, Revs. Mario A. Fulgenzi, O.S.B., Admin.; Vincent E. Zidek, O.S.B.; Stanley T. Markiewicz, O.S.B.
Res., 300 Fraser Purchase Rd., 15650. Tel: 412-539-8629; Fax: 412-539-3810. [CEM]
School—Christ the Divine Teacher School. See separate listing under Elementary Schools in the Institution section.

3—St. John the Evangelist, Rev. Thomas M. Lukac. In res., Rev. Stephen C. West.
Res., 306 St. John Dr., 15650. Tel: 412-537-8909.
School—Christ the Divine Teacher School. See separate listing under Elementary Schools in the Institution section.
Convent—310 St. John Dr., 15650. Tel: 412-537-7580.

4—St. Rose, Rev. William P. Donahue.
Res., 1112 Hillview Ave., 15650. Tel: 412-537-3709. [CEM]
School—Christ the Divine Teacher School. See separate listing under Elementary Schools in the Institution section.

5—St. Boniface. (Chestnut Ridge). Rev. Simon J. Toth, O.S.B. Tel: 412-593-7869.
Res., c/o St. Vincent Archabbey, 300 Fraser Purchase Rd., 15650. Tel: 412-532-6600.
School—Christ the Divine Teacher School. See separate listing under Elementary Schools in the Institution section.

Leckrone, Fayette Co., Our Lady of Perpetual Help (St. Mary), Rev. Andrew M. Kawecki.
Res., P.O. Box 248, 15454. Tel: 412-737-5736. [CEM]

Leechburg, Armstrong Co., St. Catherine of Alexandria, Rev. Dominic G. Pozzuoli.
Res., 612 Second St., 15656. Tel: 412-845-8191. [CEM]
Chapel—Hyde Park, Chapel of St. Catherine, Leechburg.

Church of the Assumption, Rev. Robert R. Byrnes.
Res., R.D. 5, Box 1235, 15656. Tel: 412-842-3521; 845-6593 (Church Hall).

St. Martha (Slovak), Rev. Richard P. Karenbauer.
Res., 368 Third St., 15656. Tel: 412-842-1791. [CEM]

Leisenring, Fayette Co., St. Vincent de Paul, Rev. Peter L. Peretti.
Res., Box 24, 15455. Tel: 412-628-7361. [CEM]
Chapel—West Leisenring, Chapel of St. Vincent de Paul, Leisenring.

Ligonier, Westmoreland Co., Holy Trinity, Rev. James F. Petrovsky.
Res., 342 W. Main St., 15658. Tel: 412-238-6434; Fax: 412-238-6688. [CEM]
School—327 W. Vincent St., 15658. Tel: 412-238-6430. Sr. Lorilee Ufolla, S.C., Prin.
Lay Teachers 9; Students 141.
Chapel—Wilpen, Chapel of Holy Trinity, Ligonier.

Lower Burrell, Westmoreland Co., St. Margaret Mary, Revs. John T. Sweeney; Michael E. Ripple.
Res., 201 Park Dr., 15068. Tel: 412-335-2336.
School—3055 Leechburg Rd., 15068. Tel: 412-335-6700. Dr. Dennis M. Spinella, Ph.D.
Lay Teachers 9; Students 203.
Chapel—Braeburn, Chapel of St. Margaret Mary, Lower Burrell.

Lucernemines, Indiana Co., St. Louis, Rev. James M. Goldberg.
Res., P.O. Box 197, 15754. Tel: 412-479-9542; Fax: 412-479-0983. [CEM]

Marguerite, Westmoreland Co., St. Benedict, Rev. Stephen R. Honeygosky, O.S.B.
Res., R.D. 8, Box 560, Greensburg, 15601. Tel: 412-834-9045.

Masontown, Fayette Co., All Saints, Rev. Edward C. Tajc.
Res., 101 W. Church Ave., 15461. Tel: 412-583-7866; Fax: 412-583-0373. [CEM]
School—100 S. Washington St., 15461. Tel: 412-583-2141; Fax: 412-583-2141. Sr. Maria Estelle Chopnak, V.S.C., Prin.
Vincentian Sisters 1; Lay Teachers 9; Students 150.
Convent—100 S. Washington St., 15461. Tel: 412-583-9891.
Chapel—McClellandtown, Chapel of All Saints, Masontown.

Monessen, Westmoreland Co., The Epiphany of Our Lord, Revs. Paul A. Lisik; James W. Clark.
Res., 618 Knox Ave., 15062. Tel: 412-684-7661; Fax: 412-684-8981. [CEM 2]
School—701 Schoonmaker Ave., 15062. Tel: 412-684-5610. Mrs. Kathleen Warfield, Prin.
Lay Teachers 10; Students 175.

Mount Pleasant, Westmoreland Co., St. Pius X, Rev. Henry P. Dinicco.
Res., 216 Spruce St., 15666. Tel: 412-547-3533. [CEM]
School—Holy Trinity Catholic School. See separate listing under Elementary Schools in the Institution section.

Transfiguration (Polish), Rev. Robert M. Washko.
Res., 35 N. Hitchman St., 15666. Tel: 412-547-2556. [CEM]
School—Holy Trinity Catholic School. See separate listing under Elementary Schools in the Institution section.
Convent—409 Smithfield St., 15666. Tel: 412-547-8112. Felician Sisters

Visitation of the Blessed Virgin Mary (Slovak), Rev. Gregory F. Premoshis. In res., Rev. Nicholas Trongo.
Res., 740 Walnut St., 15666. Tel: 412-547-5735. [CEM]
School—Holy Trinity Catholic School. See seperate listing under Elementary Schools in the Institution section.

Murrysville, Westmoreland Co., Mother of Sorrows, Revs. Daniel C. Mahoney; John A. Moineau.
Res., 4200 Old William Penn Hwy., 15668. Tel: 412-733-8870; Fax: 412-733-8108.
School—3264 Evergreen Dr., 15668. Tel: 412-733-8840. Dr. Patricia Sheahan, Ph.D., Prin.
Lay Teachers 19; Students 315.

New Alexandria, Westmoreland Co., St. James, Rev. Patrick J. O'Connor.
Res., R.D. 3, Box 400, 15670. Tel: 412-668-2829; Fax: 412-668-7327.

New Derry, Westmoreland Co., St. Martin, Rev. Arthur Holtz, O.S.B.
Res., R.D. 1, Box 100, 15671. Tel: 412-694-5716. [CEM]

New Kensington, Westmoreland Co., St. Mary of Czestochowa (Polish), Rev. Thaddeus J. Kaczmarek, V.F.
Res., 857 Kenneth Ave., 15068. Tel: 412-335-8212; 335-2626; Fax: 412-335-1314. [CEM]
Convent—837 Kenneth Ave., 15068. Tel: 412-339-9868. Felician Sisters

St. Joseph, Revs. George W. Swast; Anthony J. Carbone.
Res., 1125 Leishman Ave., 15068. Tel: 412-337-6412; Fax: 412-337-4022.
School—1129 Leishman Ave., 15068. Tel: 412-339-4411. Sr. Marie Corde Denny, C.S.J., Prin.
Sisters 5; Lay Teachers 10; Students 217.
Convent—1129 Leishman Ave., 15068. Tel: 412-335-7433. Sisters of St. Joseph

Mt. St. Peter (Italian), Revs. Richard G. Curci; Robert T. Lubic.
Res., 100 Freeport Rd., 15068. Tel: 412-335-9877; Fax: 412-335-9138.
School—100 Freeport Rd., 15068. Tel: 412-335-5911. Sr. Rita Marie Fritzen, O.S.F., Prin.
Sisters of St. Francis of the Providence of God (Mt. Providence) 1; Lay Teachers 14; Students 340.

New Salem, Fayette Co., St. Procopius, Rev. James L. Popochock.
Res., 20 Church St., P.O. Box 535, 15468. Tel: 412-245-9244; Fax: 412-245-9289. [CEM]

North Huntingdon, Westmoreland Co., St. Agnes, Revs. Thomas J. Bertolina; David J. Nazimek.
Res., 11400 St. Agnes Ln., 15642. Tel: 412-863-2626; 863-2630.
School—Queen of Angels Catholic School. See

separate listing under Elementary Schools in the Institution section.
Convent—1190 Clay Pike, 15642. Tel: 412-863-1670. Sisters of St. Joseph

St. Elizabeth Ann Seton, Rev. Michael J. Crookston. Res., 200 Leger Rd., 15642. Tel: 412-864-6364.

Palmer, Fayette Co., St. Albert, Rev. Ronald J. Rutkowski.
Res., Box 295, Adah, 15410. Tel: 412-737-6720.

Parker, Armstrong Co., St. Mary, Our Lady of the Snows, Rev. Thomas A. Federline, Admin.
Res., c/o R.D. 1, Box 78, Brady's Bend, 16028. Tel: 412-526-5079.

Penn, Westmoreland Co., St. Boniface, Rev. Msgr. David L. Fisher.
Res., 201 Church St., Box 398, 15675. Tel: 412-523-3450. [CEM]

Perryopolis, Fayette Co., St. John the Baptist, Rev. John T. Euker.
Res., P.O. Box 606, 15473. Tel: 412-736-4442. [CEM]

Point Marion, Fayette Co., St. Hubert, Rev. Dennis A. Bogusz.
Res., 9 Sadler St., 15474. Tel: 412-725-3655.

Republic, Fayette Co., Holy Rosary, Rev. Mark E. Purnell.
Res., Main St., P.O. Box 400, 15475. Tel: 412-246-9639; Fax: 412-246-8081. [CEM]
School—Abigail St., P.O. Box 797, 15475. Tel: 412-246-9083; Fax: 412-246-2500. Sr. Corrine Giel, V.S.C., Prin.
Sisters 2; Lay Teachers 8; Students 182.
Convent—P.O. Box 797, 15475. Tel: 412-246-2500. Vincentian Sisters of Charity

Rossiter, Indiana Co., St. Francis of Assisi. Closed. For inquiries for parish records contact the Church of the Resurrection, Clymer.

Rostraver, Westmoreland Co., St. Anne, Rev. Thomas W. Rogers.
Res., R.D. 2, Box 240, Rostraver Rd. (Rte. 201) & Willowbrook Rd., 15012. Tel: 412-929-9599.
Chapel—Webster, Chapel of St. Anne, Rostraver.

Sagamore, Armstrong Co., Sacred Heart, Rev. Robert E. Moslener, Admin.
Res., P.O. Box 75, 8 W. Church St., 16250. Tel: 412-783-7451. [CEM]

Saltsburg, Indiana Co., St. Matthew, Rev. Gregory J. Flohr.
Res., 703 Indiana Ave., 15681. Tel: 412-639-3690. [CEM]

Scottdale, Westmoreland Co., St. John the Baptist, Rev. Emil S. Payer.
Res., 416 S. Broadway, 15683. Tel: 412-887-6321; Fax: 412-887-6324. [CEM]
School—504 S. Broadway, 15683. Tel: 412-887-9550; Fax: 412-887-9553. Joseph Dreliszak, Prin.
Benedictine Sisters 4; Lay Teachers 11; Students 157.
Convent—408 S. Broadway, 15683. Tel: 412-887-6612. Benedictine Sisters

Seward, Westmoreland Co., Holy Family, Rev. John E. Wilt.
Res., Box 336, 15954. Tel: 814-446-5759; Fax: 814-446-4481. [CEM]
Chapels—New Florence, Chapel of Holy Family, Seward.; Bolivar, Chapel of Holy Family, Seward.

Slickville, Westmoreland Co., St. Sylvester, Rev. Richard J. Kosisko, J.C.L.
Res., Box 307, 15684. Tel: 412-468-5794; Fax: 412-468-5765.

Smithton, Westmoreland Co., St. Timothy, Rev. James D. Vasil.
Res., Peer & Third St., Box 776, 15479. Tel: 412-872-8070. [CEM]

Smock, Fayette Co., St. Hedwig. Unassigned.
Res., Box 251, 15480. Tel: 412-677-2110; Fax: 412-677-0146. [CEM]
Chapel—Keisterville, Chapel of St. Hedwig, Smock.

Starford, Indiana Co., St. Elizabeth. Closed. For inquiries for parish records contact Church of the Resurrection, Clymer.

Sutersville, Westmoreland Co., St. Charles Borromeo, Rev. James F. Bump.
Res., Fifth Ave., P.O. Box 413, 15083. Tel: 412-872-5286.

Trafford, Westmoreland Co., St. Regis, Rev. James D. Tringhese.
Res., 517 Homewood Ave., Ste. 100, 15085. Tel: 412-372-4577; Fax: 412-373-5979.
Convent—424 Edgewood Ave., 15085. Tel: 412-372-3198. Sisters of Charity

Trauger, Westmoreland Co., Forty Martyrs, Rev. Joel R. Lieb, O.S.B.
Res., c/o St. Vincent Archabbey, 300 Fraser Purchase Rd., Latrobe, 15650. Tel: 412-423-3282; 532-6725. [CEM]

Uniontown, Fayette Co.,

1—St. John The Evangelist, Revs. George K. Alderson; John J. Harrold.
Res., 50 Jefferson St., 15401. Tel: 412-437-7569; Fax: 412-437-6277.
School—88 Pennsylvania Ave., 15401. Tel: 412-438-8598. Sr. M. Kevin Berdis, O.S.F., Prin.
Sisters 2; Lay Teachers 14; Students 251.
Convent—88 Pennsylvania Ave., 15401. Tel: 412-438-5271. School Sisters of St. Francis

2—St. Joseph, (Polish), Rev. Alexander L. Pleban, S.T.L.
Res., R.D. 4, Walnut Hill Rd., 15401. Tel: 412-437-3927; Fax: 412-437-5354. [CEM]

3—Nativity of the Blessed Virgin Mary, (Slovak), Rev. Msgr. Andrew A. Chupela.
Res., 61 N. Mount Vernon Ave., 15401. Tel: 412-437-1512; Fax: 412-437-7482. [CEM]
School—17 Gilmore St., 15401. Tel: 412-438-8471; Fax: 412-438-8338. Sr. Mary Jean Kubilus, V.S.C., Prin.
Sisters 1; Lay Teachers 11; Students 235.
Convent—7 Gilmore St., 15401. Tel: 412-437-5478; Fax: 412-439-9328. Vincentian Sisters of Charity
Chapel—Lemont Furnace, Chapel of St. Mary, Uniontown.

4—St. Therese, the Little Flower of Jesus, (Italian), Revs. John A. Regoli; Joseph E. Bonafed.
Res., 61 Mill St., 15401. Tel: 412-438-2341; Fax: 412-438-2361.

United, Westmoreland Co., St. Florian, Rev. John M. Foriska.
Res., P.O. Box 187, 15689. Tel: 412-423-4431. [CEM]
School—P.O. Box 188, 15689. Tel: 412-423-4437. Sr. Mary Rosaire Sedory, V.S.C., Prin.
Sisters 1; Lay Teachers 7; Students 137.
Convent—P.O. Box 188, 15689. Tel: 412-423-5087. Vincentian Sisters of Charity

Vandergrift, Westmoreland Co., St. Gertrude, Rev. Thaddeus E. Rettger, O.S.B.
Res., 303 Franklin Ave., 15690. Tel: 412-568-2331. [CEM]
School—315 Franklin Ave., 15690. Tel: 412-568-3304. Mr. Thomas J. Kazmeraski, Prin.
Lay Teachers 9; Students 121.

West Newton, Westmoreland Co., Holy Family, Rev. Robert F. Brannon.
Res., 225 N. Second St., P.O. Box 216, 15089. Tel: 412-872-6123; Fax: 412-872-6133.

Whitney, Westmoreland Co., St. Cecilia, Rev. Mark M. Peters, O.S.B.
Res., P.O. Box 80, 15693. Tel: 412-423-3777;2289.

Yatesboro, Armstrong Co., St. Mary, Rev. Robert E. Moslener.
Res., P.O. Box 327, 16263. Tel: 412-783-7191. [CEM]

Youngstown, Westmoreland Co., Sacred Heart, Rev. Aelred J. Beck, O.S.B.
Res., P.O. Box 328, 15696. Tel: 412-537-7358.
School—P.O. Box 328, 15696. Tel: 412-539-5561; Fax: 412-539-5561. Sr. Grace Marie Spera, C.S.S.F., Prin.
Felician Sisters 3; Lay Teachers 5; Students 146.
Convent—Main St., P.O. Box 328, 15696. Tel: 412-537-8958. Felician Sisters

Youngwood, Westmoreland Co., Holy Cross, Rev. Angelo G. Ciuffoletti.
Res., 701 Depot St., 15697. Tel: 412-925-7811.
School—S. Eighth St., 15697. Tel: 412-925-7253. Mrs. Sally Hurrianko, Prin.
Lay Teachers 8; Students 147.
Chapel—Hunker, Chapel of Holy Cross, Youngwood.

Yukon, Westmoreland Co., Seven Dolors, Rev. Dennis E. Sheehy.
Res., Center & Hill St., P.O. Box 308, 15698. Tel: 412-722-3141; 722-3140 (Hall). [CEM]

Chaplains of Public Institutions

Greensburg. *Westmoreland Hospital.* Tel: 412-832-4000. Rev. Jacques DePaul Daley, O.S.B., Chap., Assoc. Chaplains: Rev. Justin Withrow, O.S.B.; Sr. Mary Ann Thimons, C.S.J.

Brownsville. *Brownsville General Hospital.* Attended by St. Peter, Brownsville, Tel: 412-785-7200; 785-7781 (Res.).

Connellsville. *Highlands Hospital & Health Center.* Tel: 412-628-1500. Rev. Nicholas Trongo, Chap., Tel: 412-547-5735 (Res.).

Indiana. *Indiana Hospital.* Attended by St. Bernard, Indiana, Tel: 412-357-7000; 412-465-2210 (Res.). Tel: 412-357-7000.

Jeannette. *Jeannette District Memorial Hospital.* Tel: 412-527-3551. Revs. Dominic J. Petroy, O.S.B., Chap., Tel: 412-523-2560 (Res.); Justin Withrow, O.S.B., Assoc. Chap., Tel: 412-539-9761 (Res.).
Monsour Medical Center. Tel: 412-527-1511. Revs. Dominic J. Petroy, O.S.B., Chap., Tel: 412-523-2560 (Res.); Justin Withrow, O.S.B., Assoc. Chap., Tel: 412-539-9761 (Res.).

Kittanning. *Armstrong County Hospital.* Tel: 412-543-8500. Rev. Raphael Glinkowski, O.S.P.P.E., Chap., Tel: 412-763-1375 (Res.).

Latrobe. *Latrobe Area Hospital.* Tel: 412-537-1000. Rev. Ermin R. Smith, O.S.B., Chap., Assoc. Chaplains: Revs. Justin Withrow, O.S.B.; Michael McIlwain, O.S.B. Tel: 412-539-9761 (Res.).

Mount Pleasant. *Frick Community Health Center.* Tel: 412-547-1500. Rev. Nicholas Trongo, Chap., Tel: 412-547-5735 (Res.).

New Kensington. *Citizens General Hospital.* Attended by St. Mary, New Kensington, Tel: 412-335-8212 (Res.); St. Joseph, New Kensington, Tel: 412-337-6412 (Res.); Mount St. Peter, New Kensington, Tel: 412-335-9877 (Res.). Tel: 412-337-3541.

Torrance. *Torrance State Hospital.* Tel: 412-459-8000. Rev. Chester J. Raimer, Chap., Tel: 412-459-7103 (Res.).

Uniontown. *Uniontown Hospital.* Tel: 412-430-5000. Rev. Marion L. Herrick, O.F.M., Chap., Tel: 412-438-0500 (Res.).

On Duty Outside the Diocese:
Reverend Monsignors—
DeAndrea, Joseph A., Villa Stritch, Via della Nocetta 63, 00164 Rome, Italy. Tel: 011-39-6-66162662
McCarren, Stephen A., Chap., Rte. 2, Box 390, Kearneysville, WV 25430. Tel: 304-263-3456
Reverend Fathers—
Boley, Edward J., Marian Hall, 529 Martin Luther King Ave., Flint, MI 48532. Tel: 313-235-8574
Conroy, Donald B., Dir., Nat'l. Institute for Family, 3019 4th St., N.E., Washington, DC 20017. Tel: 202-269-3461
Dylag, Michael R., One Kenberton Dr., Pleasant Ridge, MI 48069. Tel: 810-547-2006
Marzilli, Raphael, Chap. to the Franciscan Missionaries of Mary, 399 Fruit Hill Ave., North Providence, RI 02911-2898. Tel: 401-354-4254
Preneta, Henry S., St. Paul Church, 128 N. McKean St., Butler, PA 16001
Survil, Bernard, Convento Santo Domingo, Primer Ave. 1-31, Zona 3, 16001 Coban Ave., Guatemala C.A.
Waczula, Michael F., HC 33 Box 4, Tilly, AR 72679

Military Chaplains:
Reverend Fathers—
Koser, Rudolph J., Jr., Maj. CH., 694 IG/HC 9829 Love Rd., Fort George Meade, MD 20755-5260. Tel: 301-688-7605
Mandock, Patrick H., CH. (LTC), HQ, 19th TAACOM, Unit 15015, Box 2023, APO, AP 96218-0171
Sinclair, Roger A., 150 S. Huntington Ave., Boston, MA 02130

Retired:
Reverend Monsignors—
Garred, John L., Neumann House, 2900 Seminary Dr., Greensburg, PA 15601
Hanicak, Robert A., Neumann House, 2900 Seminary Dr., Greensburg, PA 15601
Ramellini, P. Lino, 19 Rex Blvd., Monessen, PA 15062
Reverend Fathers—
Bahleda, Aloysius J., Neumann House, 2900 Seminary Dr., Greensburg, PA 15601
Bienia, Michael A., Neumann House, 2900 Seminary Dr., Greensburg, PA 15601
Borkowski, Aloysius J., R.D. 3, Box 138D, Derry, PA 15627
Bratus, Walter N., 723 East Pittsburgh St., Greensburg, PA 15601
Bucci, Michael J., 1319 Walnut St., South Connellsville, PA 15425
Casaliggi, John R., Neumann House, 2900 Seminary Dr., Greensburg, PA 15601
Charnoki, Andrew J., St. Anne Home, 685 Angela Dr., Greensburg, PA 15601
Cheatham, Louis W., Neumann House, 2900 Seminary Dr., Greensburg, PA 15601
Curry, Edward V., Neumann House, 2900 Seminary Dr., Greensburg, PA 15601
Drab, Stephen J., R.D. 1, Box 228-N, Connellsville, PA 15425
Gearing, Edward P., 1088 Greentree Rd., Apt. #101, Pittsburgh, PA 15220
Higgins, Edward F., St. Benedict the Abbot Church, 120 Abington Dr., McMurray, PA 15317
Hirt, Edwin H., St. Anne Home, 685 Angela Dr., Greensburg, PA 15601
Horvath, Andrew B., 735 Mace St., Greensburg, PA 15601
Murawski, Apolinary, Neumann House, 2900 Seminary Dr., Greensburg, PA 15601
Murphy, Harry J., Nazareth House-St. Michael's,

Rancho Mission Rd., San Diego, CA 92108-2099
Oris, Fabian G., 133 Walnut St., Uniontown, PA 15401
Ott, Francis M., Neumann House, 2900 Seminary Dr., Greensburg, PA 15061
Pirulli, Francis D., Neumann House, 2900 Seminary Dr., Greensburg, PA 15601
Rivi, Geno G., Sailwind Condo #416, 1200 Shoreline Dr., Gulf Breeze, FL 32561
Stofcik, John A., 304 Stacey Dr., Mount Pleasant, PA 15666
Vallor, Robert, 9 Third St., Rossiter, PA 15772
Weiksner, Jerome M., West Hill Dr., Apt. F-9, Greensburg, PA 15601

INSTITUTIONS LOCATED IN THE DIOCESE

[A] SEMINARIES, RELIGIOUS OR SCHOLASTICATES

LATROBE. *St. Vincent Seminary*, 300 Fraser Purchase Rd., 15650. Tel: 412-537-4592; Fax: 412-532-5052. Very Rev. Thomas Acklin, O.S.B., Rector; Revs. Justin Matro, O.S.B., Dir. Spiritual Life; William J. Fay, Vice Rector & Dean of Students; Sr. Cecilia Murphy, R.S.M., Academic Dean; Rev. Richard Michel, O.S.B., Dir. of Field Education. Professors 27; Theology Students 92; Seminarians 62; Benedictines 12; Oratorians 1.

[B] COLLEGES AND UNIVERSITIES

GREENSBURG. *Seton Hill College*, 15601. Tel: 412-834-2200; Fax: 412-830-4611.
For a complete listing, refer to the Colleges and Universities section.

LATROBE. *St. Vincent College*, 300 Fraser Purchase Rd., 15650-2690. Tel: 412-539-9761.
For a complete listing, refer to the Colleges and Universities section.

[C] HIGH SCHOOLS, DIOCESAN

GREENSBURG. *Greensburg Central Catholic High School*, 901 Armory Dr., 15601. Tel: 412-834-0310; Fax: 412-834-2472. Sr. Brigid Marie Grandey, S.C., Prin.; Mr. James N. Farrell, Asst. Prin.; Rev. Daniel L. Blout, Chap. Priests 1; Sisters 3; Lay Teachers 28; Students 425.

CONNELLSVILLE. *Geibel Catholic High School*, 611 E. Crawford Ave., 15425. Tel: 412-628-5600; Fax: 412-626-5700. Mr. Stephen Fusco, Prin.; Mr. Joseph V. Shigle, Vice Prin.; Rev. Gregory F. Premoshis, Chap. Priests 1; Sisters 1; Lay Teachers 30; Students 417.

[D] ELEMENTARY SCHOOLS, INTER-PAROCHIAL

GREENSBURG. *Aquinas Academy*, 330 N. Main St., 15601. Tel: 412-834-7940; Fax: 412-836-0497. Sr. Brycelyn Eyler, S.C., Prin.; Mr. Daniel Mahoney, Vice-Prin. Sisters 1; Lay Teachers 39; Students 599.

CONNELLSVILLE. *Conn-Area Catholic School*, 110 N. Prospect St., 15425. Tel: 412-628-5090. Sr. Catherine Meinert, S.C., Prin. Lay Teachers 11; Students 197.

FORD CITY. *Ford City Catholic*, 726 Fourth Ave., 16226. Tel: 412-763-3761. Sr. Mary Ann Kropilak, V.S.C., Prin. Sisters 1; Lay Teachers 9; Students 255.

LATROBE. *Christ the Divine Teacher School*. (Grades PreK-8), 323 Chestnut St., 15650. Tel: 412-539-1561. Sr. Donna Marie Palya, V.S.C., Prin. Sisters 4; Lay Teachers 22; Students 360.

MOUNT PLEASANT. *Holy Trinity Catholic*, 222 Summit St., 15666. Tel: 412-547-9871; 547-9474. Sr. Kathleen McCauley, S.C., Prin. Sisters 1; Lay Teachers 9; Students 100.

NORTH HUNTINGDON. *Queen of Angels Regional Catholic School*, 11410 St. Agnes Ln., 15642. Tel: 412-863-2628; 863-9581; Fax: 412-861-8858. Sr. Grace Hartzog, S.C., Prin. Sisters 2; Lay Teachers 22; Students 489.

[E] SPECIAL EDUCATION

GREENSBURG. *Clelian Heights School for Exceptional Children*, R.D. 9, Box 607, 15601. Tel: 412-837-8120. Apostles of the Sacred Heart of Jesus. Sr. M. Adrianne DiLonardo, A.S.C.J., Dir.; Sr. Linda Pettinella, A.S.C.J., Prin.; Sr. Maria Battaglia, A.S.C.J., Asst. Dir.; Sr. Benjamin Merlotti, A.S.C.J., Devel. Dir.; Rev. William R. Rathgeb, J.C.L., Chap. Sisters 14; Lay Teachers 6; Students 83.

Elizabeth Seton Montessori School of Westmoreland County, Inc., R.D. 7, P.O. Box 268, 15601. Tel: 412-837-8500. Sisters of Charity. Sr. Anita Schulte, S.C., Dir. Sisters 1; Lay Teachers 3; Students 52.

MOUNT PLEASANT. *Verna Montessori School*, R.D. 2, Box 348, 15666. Tel: 412-887-8810; Fax: 412-887-0220. Ivrea Sisters of Charity of the Immaculate Conception. Sr. M. Letizia Tribuzio, S.C.I.C., Prin. Sisters 6; Lay Teachers 3; Students 145.

[F] GENERAL HOSPITALS

JEANNETTE. *Jeannette District Memorial Hospital*, Jefferson Ave., 15644. Tel: 412-527-3551.
For a complete listing, refer to the Hospitals section.

[G] HOMES FOR AGED

GREENSBURG. *Neumann House*, 2900 Seminary Dr., 15601 Fax: 412-834-7351.
For a complete listing, refer to the Special Care Facilities section.

St. Anne Home, 685 Angela Dr., 15601. Tel: 412-837-6070; Fax: 412-837-6099.
For a complete listing, refer to the Special Care Facilities section.

[H] MONASTERIES AND RESIDENCES OF PRIESTS AND BROTHERS

KITTANNING. *Pauline Fathers Monastery*, Bunker Hill Rd., Box 66, 16201. Tel: 412-763-1375. Revs. Edward Volz, O.S.P.P.E., Prior; Raphael K. Glinkowski, O.S.P.P.E., Admin. Priests 2.

LATROBE. *Saint Vincent Archabbey*, 300 Fraser Purchase Rd., 15650-2686. Tel: 412-539-9761; 532-6600; Fax: 412-539-2110. Legal Titles: *The Benedictine Society of Westmoreland County*; *Saint Vincent College Corporation*; *The Wimmer Corporation*; *The Saint Vincent Cemetery Corporation*. Rt. Revs. Douglas R. Nowicki, O.S.B., Archabbot; Paul R. Maher, O.S.B., Archabbot (Retired); Egbert H. Donovan, O.S.B., Archabbot (Retired); Very Rev. Albert C. Bickerstaff, O.S.B., Prior; Bro. David A. Kelly, O.S.B., Subprior; Revs. Warren D. Murrman, O.S.B., Master of Novices; Reginald G. Bender, O.S.B., Procurator; Thomas Acklin, O.S.B., Rector of the Seminary; Martin R. Bartel, O.S.B., Pres. of the College; Aelred J. Beck, O.S.B.; Kurt J. Belsole, O.S.B.; Joseph P. Bronder, O.S.B.; Gilbert J. Burke, O.S.B.; Godfrey F. Burkhardt, O.S.B.; Anthony J. Burlas, O.S.B.; Julian F. Burt, O.S.B.; Aaron N. Buzzelli, O.S.B.; Andrew S. Campbell, O.S.B.; Athanasius C. Cherry, O.S.B.; Richard Chirichiello, O.S.B.; Wulfstan F. Clough, O.S.B.; Vincent de Paul Crosby, O.S.B.; Jacques de Paul Daley, O.S.B.; Thomas W. Devereux, O.S.B.; Alvin T. Downey, O.S.B.; Demetrius R. Dumm, O.S.B.; Bertrand H. Dunegan, O.S.B.; Bertin L. Emling, O.S.B.; Marion J. Emling, O.S.B.; John R. Erickson, O.S.B.; Mauro de Souza Fernandes, O.S.B.; Mario A. Fulgenzi, O.S.B.; Clair F. Gannon, O.S.B.; Campion P. Gavaler, O.S.B.; David R. Griffin, O.S.B., Dir. of College Campus Ministry; Alfred L. Grotzinger, O.S.B.; Mark F.X. Gruber, O.S.B.; Thomas M. Hart, O.S.B.; Bede J. Hasso, O.S.B.; Clement J. Heid, O.S.B.; Roland L. Heid, O.S.B.; Earl J. Henry, O.S.B.; Lawrence H. Hill, O.S.B.; Vernon A. Holtz, O.S.B.; Cuthbert A. Jack, O.S.B.; Myron M. Kirsch, O.S.B.; Omer U. Kline, O.S.B., Admin. Asst. to the Archabbot; Rene M. Kollar, O.S.B.; Joel R. Lieb, O.S.B.; Stanley T. Markiewicz, O.S.B.; Justin M. Matro, Spiritual Dir. (Seminary); Michael A. McIlwain, O.S.B.; Michael McKay, O.S.B.; Alphonse H. Meier, O.S.B.; Richard B. Michel, O.S.B.; Xavier R. Mihm, O.S.B.; Method J. Mraz, O.S.B.; Jonathan J. Murrman, O.S.B.; Giles L. Nealen, O.S.B.; Justin Nolan, O.S.B.; Daniel Paul O'Keefe, O.S.B.; Emeric J. Pfiester, O.S.B.; James Podlesny, O.S.B.; Donald Raila, O.S.B.; Emmeran A. Rettger, O.S.B.; Roland R. Ripoli, O.S.B.; Noel H. Rothrauff, O.S.B., Dir. of Foreign Missions; Norbert A. Rupprecht, O.S.B.; Sebastian A. Samay, O.S.B.; Chrysostom V. Schlimm, O.S.B.; Louis S. Sedlacko, O.S.B.; Paulinus J. Selle, O.S.B.; Brendan L. Smetana, O.S.B.; Ermin R. Smith, O.S.B.; Brinstan G. Takach, O.S.B.; Paul R. Taylor, O.S.B.; Simon J. Toth, O.S.B.; Herman F. Ubinger, O.S.B.; Remigius B. Verostko, O.S.B.; Eric T. Vogt, O.S.B.; Damian J. Warnock, O.S.B.; Charles A. Weber, O.S.B.; Canice T. Welsh, O.S.B.; Justin Withrow, O.S.B.; William Wurm, O.S.B.; Flavian G. Yelinko, O.S.B.; Vincent E. Zidek, O.S.B.; Frank E. Ziemkiewicz, O.S.B., Dean of Students at the College.
On Leave for Study and Teaching: Revs. Millard S. Cook, O.S.B., Fordham Univ.; Patrick T. Cronauer, O.S.B., Pontifical Biblical Institute, Rome; Nathan Munsch, O.S.B.; Ralph M. Tajak, O.S.B., University of Toronto, School of Theology, Toronto.
Priests of the Archabbey Serving Abroad: Very Rev. Cristiano Brito, O.S.B., Prior; Revs. Fernando Henrique Lima, O.S.B.; Leo P. Rothrauff, O.S.B.; Claudio Moraes, O.S.B.; Luiz Antonio Carqueijo Se, O.S.B.
Priests on Leave: Revs. Ambrose G. Eberz, O.S.B.; Becket G. Senchur, O.S.B.; Anthony St. Pierre, O.S.B.; Daniel-Zachary Waldspurger, O.S.B.
Priests on Loan: Revs. Cornelius P. Chang, O.S.B., Archdiocese of New York; Cyprian G. Constantine, O.S.B. (DEN); Christian G. Le Frois, O.S.B., Diocese of Savannah. Priests in Archabbey 87; Community: Priests 147; Deacons 4; Solemn Professed Choir-Monks 24; Junior Professed Monks 7; Choir Novices 9; Brothers 7.

NEW FLORENCE. *Mount Carmel Hermitage*, Pineland, R.D. No. 3, Box 36, 15944. Tel: 412-235-2157. Revs. Bede J.K. Mulligan, O.Carm.; Simeon D. Marro, O.Carm. Priests 2.

UNIONTOWN. *St. Anthony Friary*, 115 Oakland Ave., 15401-2818. Tel: 412-438-0500; Fax: 412-438-4251. Friars Richard A. Portasik, O.F.M., Local Min.; Joseph L. Portasik, O.F.M., Vicar; Marion J. Herrick, O.F.M., Hospital Chap.; Paul Wild, O.F.M.; Bro. Damien Murkley, O.F.M., Assistance.

[I] CONVENTS AND RESIDENCES FOR SISTERS

GREENSBURG. *Apostles of the Sacred Heart of Jesus*, Clelian Heights Convent, R.D. 9, Box 607, 15601. Tel: 412-837-8120. Sr. M. Adrianne DiLonardo, A.S.C.J., Local Supr.; Rev. William R. Rathgeb, J.C.L., Chap. Sisters 14.

Benedictine Sisters (Eichstatt, Bavaria), St. Emma Monastery, 1001 Harvey Ave., 15601-1494. Tel: 412-834-3060; Fax: 412-834-5772. Mother Mary Anne Noll, O.S.B., Prioress; Rev. Lawrence T. Persico, J.C.L., Chap. Sisters 20; Postulants 1.

House of Welcome, Ennis Hall, 447 Mount Thor Rd., 15601. Tel: 412-836-7940. Sisters of Charity 12.

Regina House (Sisters of Charity Generalate), DePaul Center, Administrative Offices, Mount Thor Rd., 15601. Tel: 412-836-0406. Sr. Gertrude Foley, S.C., Major Supr. Sisters 505; Novices 36; Postulants 16.

Sisters of Charity, Sisters of Charity Center, Mount Thor Rd., 15601. Tel: 412-837-8645. Sr. Annette Frey, S.C., Sister Servant; Sr. Vincent Marie Sidick, S.C., Admin.; Rev. Stephen C. West, Chap. Sisters 77.

Sisters of Charity Formation House, Marian Hall, 451 Mount Thor Rd., 15601. Tel: 412-837-5863. Sisters of Charity 3.

Sisters of Mary Immaculate (Krishnagar, India), St. Joseph Center Convent, 2900 Seminary Dr., 15601. Tel: 412-836-0449. Sr. Tracy Vattakuzhiyil, S.M.I., Local Supr. Sisters 3.

LATROBE. *Discalced Carmelite Nuns*, Carmel of the Assumption, R.D. 6, Box 28, Center Dr., 15650. Tel: 412-539-1056. Sr. Barbara Sitter, O.C.D., Prioress; Rev. Giles Nealen, O.S.B., Chap. Professed Nuns of Solemn Vows 14; Extern 1.

LEECHBURG. *Sisters of Mary Immaculate (West Bengal, India)*, R.D. 5, Box 1231, 15656. Tel: 412-845-2828. Sr. Tracy Vattakuzhiyil, S.M.I., Local Supr. Sisters 3.

MOUNT PLEASANT. *Ivrea Sisters of Charity of the Immaculate Conception*, Immaculate Virgin of Miracles Convent, R.D. 2, Box 348, 15666. Tel: 412-887-6753; Fax: 412-887-0220. Sr. Letizia Garruba, S.C.I.C., Local Supr. Sisters 9.

[J] RETREAT HOUSES

GREENSBURG. *Doran Hall*, 443 Mount Thor Rd., 15601. Tel: 412-837-8645; Fax: 412-836-0766. Sisters of Charity. Sr. Mary Jude McColligan, S.C., Sr. Servant.

St. Emma Retreat House, 1001 Harvey Ave., 15601. Tel: 412-834-3060; Fax: 412-834-5772. Benedictine Sisters (Eichstatt, Bavaria). Mother Mary Anne Noll, O.S.B., Prioress.

[K] MISCELLANEOUS LISTINGS

GREENSBURG. *Gilbert Straub Plaza*, 620 Reamer Ave., 15601. Tel: 412-832-2280; Fax: 412-836-8280. Sisters of Charity. Co-Managers: Sr. Isabelle Jorden, S.C.; Sr. Miriam David Volker, S.C. Sisters 2.

St. Joseph Center, 2900 Seminary Dr., 15601. Tel: 412-834-7350; Fax: 412-834-7351. Mr. Gerald R. Bertig, Dir. Facilities Mgmt.

INDIANA. *Clairvaux Commons*, 100 Clairvaux Dr., 15701. Tel: 412-349-2920; Fax: 412-349-2921. Sisters of St. Joseph 2.

LEECHBURG. *Bishop Morrow Personal Care Home*, R.D. #5, Box 1231, 15656. Sisters of Mary Immaculate. Sr. Tracy Vattakuzhiyil, S.M.I., Dir.

SMOCK. *Ladies of Charity*, Box 251, 15480. Tel: 412-677-2110. Rev. John A. Sedlak, Spiritual Dir.

RELIGIOUS INSTITUTES OF MEN REPRESENTED IN THE DIOCESE

For further details refer to the corresponding bracketed number in the Religious Institutes of Men or Women section.

[0200]—*Benedictine Monks*. (St. Vincent Archabbey).—O.S.B.
[0270]—*Carmelite Fathers and Brothers*.—O.Carm.
[0520]—*Franciscan Friars*.—O.F.M.
[1010]—*Pauline Fathers*.—O.S.P.P.E.

RELIGIOUS INSTITUTES OF WOMEN REPRESENTED IN THE DIOCESE

[0130]—*Apostles of the Sacred Heart of Jesus*.—A.S.C.J.

[0190]—*Benedictine Sisters.*—O.S.B.
[0230]—*Benedictine Sisters of Pontifical Jurisdiction.*—O.S.B.
[0420]—*Discalced Carmelite Nuns.*—O.C.D.
[1070]—*Dominican Sisters, St. Mary of the Springs.* (Columbus, OH).—O.P.
[1170]—*Felician Sisters.*—C.S.S.F.
[2575]—*Institute of the Sisters of Mercy of the Americas.* (Pittsburgh, PA).—R.S.M.
[1690]—*School Sisters of the Third Order of St. Francis.*—O.S.F.
[0570]—*Sisters of Charity of Seton Hill, Greensburg, Pennsylvania.*—S.C.
[0450]—*Sisters of Charity of the Immaculate Conception of Ivrea.*—S.C.I.C.
[0990]—*Sisters of Divine Providence.* (St. Peter Prov.).—C.D.P.
[2440]—*Sisters of Mary Immaculate.*—S.M.I.
[1660]—*Sisters of Saint Francis of the Providence of God.*—O.S.F.
[1620]—*Sisters of Saint Francis, Millvale, Pennsylvania.*—O.S.F.
[3830-13]—*Sisters of St. Joseph.*—C.S.J.
[2040]—*Sisters of the Holy Spirit.*—S.H.S.
[3730]—*Sisters of the Order of St. Basil the Great.*—O.S.B.M.
[4160]—*Vincentian Sisters of Charity.*—V.S.C.

NECROLOGY

† Podowski, Rev. Msgr. Henry A., (Retired). —Died Sept. 19, 1996.

Diocese of Harrisburg

(Dioecesis Harrisburgensis)

Most Reverend

NICHOLAS C. DATTILO, D.D.

Bishop of Harrisburg; ordained May 31, 1958; appointed Eighth Bishop of Harrisburg November 21, 1989; consecrated January 26, 1990. *Res., 4800 Union Deposit Rd., P.O. Box 2153, Harrisburg, PA, 17105.* Tel.: 717-657-4804.

LOVE LIFE AND DO GOOD

ESTABLISHED MARCH 3, 1868.

Square Miles 7,660.

Comprises the Counties of Dauphin, Lebanon, Lancaster, York, Adams, Franklin, Cumberland, Perry, Juniata, Mifflin, Snyder, Northumberland, Union, Montour and Columbia in the State of Pennsylvania.

PATRON OF DIOCESE: St. Patrick, Bishop and Confessor.

For legal titles of parishes and diocesan institutions, consult the General Secretariat.

Diocesan Center: P.O. Box 2153, Harrisburg, PA, 17105-2153. Tel.: 717-657-4804; Fax: 717-657-7673.

STATISTICAL OVERVIEW

Personnel	
Bishop	1
Priests: Diocesan Active in Diocese	131
Priests: Active Outside Diocese	9
Priests: Retired, Sick or Absent	28
Number of Diocesan Priests	168
Religious Priests in Diocese	44
Extern Priests in Diocese	9
Ordinations:	
Diocesan Priests	3
Religious Priests	1
Transitional Deacons	2
Permanent Deacons in Diocese	59
Total Brothers	1
Total Sisters	571
Parishes	
Parishes	89
With Resident Pastor:	
Resident Diocesan Priests	74
Resident Religious Priests	12
Without Resident Pastor:	
Administered by Priests	3
Missions	7
Welfare	
Catholic Hospitals	2
Total Assisted	212,530
Homes for the Aged	4
Total Assisted	410
Residential Care of Children	1
Total Assisted	136
Day Care and Extended Day Care Centers	2
Total Assisted	82
Specialized Homes	3
Total Assisted	226
Special Centers for Social Services	9
Total Assisted	4,857
Educational	
Diocesan Students in Other Seminaries	11
Total Seminarians	11
High Schools, Diocesan and Parish	7
Total Students	3,693
High Schools, Private	1
Total Students	37
Elementary Schools, Diocesan and Parish	40
Total Students	10,751
Catechesis/Religious Education:	
High School Students	2,247
Elementary Students	20,724
Total Students Under Catholic Instruction	37,463
Teachers in the Diocese:	
Priests	2
Sisters	105
Lay Teachers	924
Vital Statistics	
Receptions into the Church:	
Infant Baptism Totals	3,312
Adult Baptism Totals	350
Received into Full Communion	470
First Communions	3,565
Confirmations	2,170
Marriages:	
Catholic	570
Interfaith	645
Total Marriages	1,215
Deaths	1,890
Total Catholic Population	230,000
Total Population	1,940,954

Former Bishops—Rt. Rev. JEREMIAH F. SHANAHAN, D.D., cons. July 12, 1868; died Sept. 24, 1886.—Rt. Rev. THOMAS MCGOVERN, D.D., cons. March 11, 1888; died July 25, 1898.—Rt. Rev. JOHN W. SHANAHAN, D.D., cons. May 1, 1899; died Feb. 19, 1916.—Most Rev. PHILIP R. MCDEVITT, D.D., cons. Sept. 21, 1916; died Nov. 11, 1935.—Most Rev. GEORGE L. LEECH, D.D., J.C.D., appt. Auxiliary of Harrisburg July 6, 1935; cons. Oct. 17, 1935; succeeded to See Dec. 19, 1935; retired Oct. 19, 1971; died March 12, 1985.—Most Rev. JOSEPH T. DALEY, D.D., cons. Jan. 7, 1964; appt. Coadjutor Bishop July 31, 1967; succeeded to See Oct. 19, 1971; died Sept. 2, 1983.—Most Rev. WILLIAM H. KEELER, ord. July 17, 1955; cons. Sept. 21, 1979; appt. Bishop of Harrisburg, Nov. 10, 1983; succeeded to See Jan. 4, 1984; transferred Baltimore May 23, 1989.

Diocese of Harrisburg Officials

Bishop—Most Rev. NICHOLAS C. DATTILO, D.D., *P.O. Box 2153, Harrisburg, 17105-2153.* Tel: 717-657-4804.

Vicar General—Very Rev. JAMESM. LYONS, M.Div., M.Ed., *4800 Union Deposit Rd., Box 2153, Harrisburg, 17105-2153.* Tel: 717-657-4804.

General Secretary—Very Rev. JAMESM. LYONS, M.Div., M.Ed., *P.O. Box 2153, Harrisburg, 17105-2153.*

Secretary for Canonical Services—Very Rev. WILLIAM J. KING, J.C.L., *P.O. Box 2557, Harrisburg, 17105-2557.* Tel: 717-657-4804.

Secretary for Catholic Charities—Rev. Msgr. FRANCIS M. KUMONTIS, M.S.W., M.B.A., Ph.D., *P.O. Box 3551, Harrisburg, 17105-3551.* Tel: 717-657-4804.

Secretary for Clergy and Religious Life—Very Rev. PAUL C. HELWIG, M.Div., *P.O. Box 2161, Harrisburg, 17105-2161.*

Secretary for Communications—Very Rev. THOMAS R. HANEY, M.A., *4800 Union Deposit Rd., P.O. Box 2555, Harrisburg, 17105-2555.* Tel: 717-657-4804.

Secretary for Education—Rev. Msgr. ROBERT E. LAWRENCE, M.Div., *4800 Union Deposit Road, Box 3553, Harrisburg, 17105-3553.* Tel: 717-657-4804; 939-6485 (Res.).

Secretary for Parish and Special Ministries—Very Rev. JOSEPH F. GOTWALT, M.Ed., S.T.B., *4800 Union Deposit Road, Box 3557, Harrisburg, 17105-3557.* Tel: 717-657-4804.

Judicial Vicar—Very Rev. WILLIAM J. KING, J.C.L., *P.O. Box 2557, Harrisburg, 17105-2557.* Tel: 717-657-4804.

Chancellor—CAROL HOUGHTON, S.T.D., J.C.D., *P.O. Box 2557, Harrisburg, 17105-2557.* Tel: 717-657-4804.

Diocesan Offices, Commissions, Boards and Programs

Adult Religious Formation, Department for—Dr. MARY ANN BOYARSKI, Dir., *P.O. Box 2161, Harrisburg, 17105-2161.*

Archives—KATHLEEN SIGNOR, Archivist, *4800 Union Deposit Rd., P.O. Box 2153, Harrisburg, 17105-2153.* Tel: 717-657-4804.

Black Catholic Ministry—GWEN SUMMERS, Coord., *4800 Union Deposit Rd., P.O. Box 3557, Harrisburg, 17105.* Tel: 717-657-4804.

Buildings and Properties—LES ZIMMERMAN, Dir., *4800 Union Deposit Rd., P.O. Box 3651, Harrisburg, 17105.* Tel: 717-657-4804.

Campus Ministry—Very Rev. JOSEPH F. GOTWALT, Coord., *P.O. Box 3557, Harrisburg, 17105.* Tel: 717-657-4804.

Catholic Charities Administration, Department for—THOMAS J. D'ANNUNZIO, Dir., *P.O. Box 3551, Harrisburg, 17105.*

Catholic Charities Counseling/Field Services, Department for—Reg. Directors: PETER BIASUCCI, L.S.W.; FRANK KOEBER, M.S., M.F.; THOMAS THORPE, *P.O. Box 3551, Harrisburg, 17105.*

Catholic Schools, Department for—Sr. MARILOU MCDONALD, I.H.M., Supt., *P.O. Box 3553, Harrisburg, 17105.*

The "Catholic Witness"—Very Rev. T. RONALD HANEY, Exec. Editor, *4800 Union Deposit Road, Box 2555, Harrisburg, 17105.* Tel: 717-657-4804.

Catholic Women, Diocesan Council of—LOUISE CONDON, *1205 Livingston Rd., York, 17404.* Tel: 717-848-6444.

Cemeteries—EDWARD G. FARADAY, Dir., *4800 Union Deposit Road, Box 3651, Harrisburg, 17105.* Tel: 717-652-0539.

Charismatic Movement—Rev. Msgr. ROBERT E. LAWRENCE, Liason, *P.O. Box 3553, Harrisburg, 17105.*

Consultors, College—Rev. Msgr. THOMAS R. BRENNER, V.F.; Very Rev. PHILIP G. BURGER, V.F.; Very Rev. PATRICK A. DEVINE, V.F.; Very Rev. PAUL C. HELWIG; Rev. LAWRENCE J. HEMLER; Very Rev. KENNETH F. LAWRENCE, V.F.; Very Rev. JAMES M. LYONS, V.G.; Rev. J. MICHAEL MCFADDEN; Rev. Msgr. HUGH A. OVERBAUGH; Revs. CHESTER A. SNYDER; ALLAN F. WOLFE; Rev. Msgr. RICHARD A. YOUTZ, V.F.

Cursillo Movement—Rev. Msgr. THOMAS H. SMITH, Moderator.

Deans—Adams Deanery: Very Rev. JOSEPH C. HILBERT, V.F., Cumberland/Perry Deanery: Very Rev. RICHARD P. WALDRON, V.F., Dauphin Deanery: Rev. Msgr. WILLIAM M. RICHARDSON, V.F., Franklin Deanery:

Rev. Msgr. THOMAS R. BRENNER, V.F., North Lancaster Deanery: Very Rev. KENNETH F. LAWRENCE, V.F., South Lancaster Deanery: Very Rev. WILLIAM J. SULLIVAN, V.F., Lebanon Deanery: Very Rev. DAVID T. MCANDREW, V.F., Northern Deanery: Very Rev. PATRICK A. DEVINE, V.F., York Deanery: Very Rev. THOMAS R. HOKE, V.F.

Diocesan Center—LES ZIMMERMAN, Coord., *4800 Union Deposit Rd., P.O. Box 3651, Harrisburg, 17105.* Tel: 717-657-4804.

Ecumenical and Interreligious Affairs—Rev. LAWRENCE J. MCNEIL, Dir., *P.O. Box 3557, Harrisburg, 17105.*

Family Ministries, Department for—VICTORIA LASKOWSKI, J.D., Dir., *P.O. Box 3557, Harrisburg, 17105.* Tel: 717-657-4804.

Finance Council—

Financial Administration, Department for—EDWARD G. FARADAY, Dir., *4800 Union Deposit Rd., P.O. Box 3651, Harrisburg, 17105.* Tel: 717-657-4804.

Health Care Ministry—*P.O. Box 3557, Harrisburg, 17105.*

Holy Name Societies—NORMAND RABOIN, Liaison, *334 Frederick St., Hanover, 17331.* Tel: 717-637-6491.

Knights of Columbus—PATRICK MONAGHAN, Pres., *1304 Foerster Dr., New Cumberland, 17070.* Tel: 717-774-3489.

Ministry Development, Department for—MARY ANN O'DONNELL, Dir., *4800 Union Deposit Rd., P.O. Box 3557, Harrisburg, 17105.* Tel: 717-657-4804.

Lay Personnel, Department for—Very Rev. JAMES M. LYONS, M.Div., M.Ed., *Box 2153, Harrisburg, 17105.* Tel: 717-657-4804.

Legion of Mary—Rev. WALTER SEMPKO, Moderator, *1051 Avila Rd., Harrisburg, 17109.* Tel: 717-652-5900.

Missions, Office of (Home and Foreign)—Rev. Msgr. GEORGE V. LENTOCHA, S.T.L., Dir., *P.O. Box 3657, Harrisburg, 17105.* Tel: 717-657-4804.

Pastoral Council, Diocesan—ANNA BIANCO; DANIEL P. ERNST; VERONICA FABIAN; LAWRENCE P. GEMMELL; Rev. ARTHUR P. GILDEA, C.SS.R.; Very Rev. JOSEPH F. GOTWALT; Deacon MICHAEL A. GRELLA; Dr. CAROL L. HOUGHTON; SARAH C. KANASKIE; ERNEST P. KLINE; JOSEPH C. LAMONT; NINH V. LE; BLANDINA LECCE; Very Rev. JAMES M. LYONS; Dr. HUGH F. MCKEEGAN; LORRAINE MITRICK; ALBERTA COSTA NORTON; MARY ANN O'DONNELL; Rev. EDWARD J. QUINLAN, III; THOMAS ROBEL; Dr. WALTER SEVERS; Rev. ROBERT F. SHARMAN; Sr. MARY AGNES SHURER, S.C.C.

Permanent Diaconate, Office for—Very Rev. PAUL C. HELWIG, Dir., *P.O. Box 2161, Harrisburg, 17105.* Tel: 717-657-4804.

Presbyteral Council—Rev. Msgr. FRANCIS J. HUDAK; Rev. CHESTER P. SNYDER; Rev. Msgr. HUGH A. OVERBAUGH; Rev. Msgr. THOMAS R. BRENNER, V.F.; Rev. J. MICHAEL MCFADDEN; Very Rev. KENNETH F. LAWRENCE, V.F.; Very Rev. BERNARDO PISTONE; Rev. JOSEPH A. CELIA; Very Rev. PHILIP J. BURGER, V.F.; Rev. LAWRENCE J. HEMLER; Very Rev. PATRICK A. DEVINE, V.F.; Revs. SAMUEL E. HOUSER; EDWARD R. LAVELLE; EDWARD C. MALESIC; WILLIAM J. NESSEL, O.S.F.S.; Rev. Msgr. VINCENT J. TOPPER; Rev. ALLEN F. WOLFE; Rev. Msgr. RICHARD A. YOUTZ.

Prison Ministry—*P.O. Box 3557, Harrisburg, 17105.*

Project: Head, Elder Council—VICTORIA LASKOWSKI, Coord., *P.O. Box 3557, Harrisburg, 17105.*

Respect Life/Human Growth and Development, Office for—MARY SHRIVER, M.A., Dir., *P.O. Box 3553, Harrisburg, 17105.*

Public Relations, Department for—Very Rev. T. RONALD HANEY, M.A., Dir., *P.O. Box 2555, Harrisburg, 17105.*

Research and Planning, Office of—EDMUND J. GLABUS, Dir., *P.O. Box 2153, Harrisburg, 17105.* Tel: 717-657-4804.

Religious Education (CCD), Department for—TERRY KLUGH, Dir., *P.O. Box 3553, Harrisburg, 17105.*

Religious Life, Department for—Sr. MARION DOLORES, Dir., *P.O. Box 2161, Harrisburg, 17105.*

Saint Thomas More Society—JOHN NANORTA Esq., *17 Spring Creek Manor, Hershey, 17033.* Tel: 717-787-8491.

Saint Vincent de Paul Society—JOSEPH MERLINA, Pres., *40 Hickorytown Rd., Carlisle, 17013.* Tel: 717-243-1090.

Spanish Speaking Ministry—Very Rev. BERNARDO PISTONE, Vicar, *Assumption B.V.M., 119 S. Prince St., Lancaster, 17603.* Tel: 717-392-2578.

Special Ministries, Department for—Very Rev. JOSEPH F. GOTWALT, Dir., *P.O. Box 3557, Harrisburg, 17105.*

Telecommunications—JOSEPH APONICK, Dir., *4800 Union Deposit Rd., Box 2555, Harrisburg, 17105.* Tel: 717-657-4804.

Tribunal—

Judicial Vicar—Very Rev. WILLIAM J. KING, J.C.L., *4800 Union Deposit Rd., P.O. Box 2557, Harrisburg, 17105.* Tel: 717-657-4804.

Diocesan Judges—Rev. Msgr. DAMIEN E. MCGOVERN, J.C.L.; Revs. MICHAEL F. BARRETT; DAVID M. O'CONNELL, C.M., J.C.L.; CAROL HOUGHTON, S.T.D., J.C.D.; Rev. Msgr. RICHARD A. YOUTZ, J.C.L.

Defender of the Bond—Rev. EDWARD R. LAVELLE, S.T.L.

Notaries—BARBARA ROTH; KATHRYN GOULDY; RITA PATACKIS.

Vietnamese Ministry—Rev. JOSEPH HOA VAN NGUYEN, Coord., *St. Paul the Apostle, 125 S. Spruce St., Annville, 17003.* Tel: 717-867-1525.

Vocations, Office for—Rev. THOMAS J. ROZMAN, S.T.B., Dir., *P.O. Box 2161, Harrisburg, 17105.* Tel: 717-657-4804.

World Apostolate of Fatima—Rev. JOHN A. SZADA, JR., Spiritual Moderator, *309 S. George St., York, 17403.* Tel: 717-845-7629.

Worship, Office of—Rev. THOMAS J. ROZMAN, S.T.B., Dir., *P.O. Box 2161, Harrisburg, 17105.* Tel: 717-657-4804.

Youth and Young Adult Ministry, Department for—LUCILLE SMITH, Dir., *4800 Union Deposit Rd., Box 3551, Harrisburg, 17105.* Tel: 717-657-4804.

CLERGY, PARISHES, MISSIONS AND PAROCHIAL SCHOOLS

CITY OF HARRISBURG
(Dauphin County)

1—CATHEDRAL PARISH OF ST. PATRICK (1995), Rev. Msgr. William M. Richardson, V.F.; Rev. John Schmalhofer; Margaret Danner, Pastoral Assoc.; Deacons J. Leo Dunn; Charles W. Clark. In res., Very Rev. Joseph F. Gotwalt; Rev. Thomas J. Rozman.
Res., 212 State St., 17101. Tel: 717-232-2169; Fax: 717-232-2799.

2—ST. CATHERINE LABOURE (1948). (Shrine of the Miraculous Medal). Rev. Msgr. Hugh A. Overbaugh; Rev. Ignatius Madumere, O.P. (Nigeria); Deacons Thomas H. Flannery; William E. Whale; Thomas A. Fedor. In res., Very Rev. James M. Lyons, V.G.
Res., 4000 Derry St., 17111. Tel: 717-564-1321.
School—4020 Derry St., 17111. Tel: 717-564-1760; Fax: 717-564-3010. Sr. Suzanne Duzen, SS.C.M., Prin.
Sisters of SS. Cyril and Methodius 3; Lay Teachers 25; Students 485.
Catechesis/Religious Programs—Sr. Carol Marie, SS.C.M., D.R.E.
Students 480.
Convent—4010 Derry St., 17111. Tel: 717-564-0721.

3—ST. FRANCIS OF ASSISI (1901), Revs. Daniel C. Mitzel; John Bateman; Hilda Gomez, Pastoral Assoc.; Deacon Miguel Marroquin.
Res., 1439 Market St., 17103. Tel: 717-232-1003; Fax: 717-232-1003.
Catechesis/Religious Programs—Tel: 717-233-7912.
Students 113.

4—HOLY FAMILY (1958), Rev. Bernard P. McGinley, M.A.
Church—555 S. 25th St., 17104. Tel: 717-232-4237.
Rectory: 2501 Barkley Ln., 17104. Tel: 717-561-8250.
School—Tel: 717-232-2551. Sr. Mary Sue Carwile, I.H.M., Prin.
Sisters Servants of the Immaculate Heart of Mary 2; Lay Teachers 9; Students 234.
Catechesis/Religious Programs—Students 294.
Convent—2473 Adrian St., 17104. Tel: 717-564-7236.

5—HOLY NAME OF JESUS (1960), Revs. Daniel J. Mahoney; Alfred Sceski; Deacons Jerome Foerster; Joseph J. Wrabel.
Res., 6150 Allentown Blvd., Harrisburg, 17112. Tel: 717-652-4211; Fax: 717-652-6941.
School—(Lower Paxton Twp.) 6190 Allentown Blvd., Harrisburg, 17112. Tel: 717-657-1704; Fax: 717-697-8834. Tom Nissley, Prin.
Sisters of St. Joseph 1; Lay Teachers 54; Students 852.
Catechesis/Religious Programs—Evelyn Alviani, D.R.E.
Students 1,042.
Convent—Tel: 717-545-4357.
Pastoral Associates 3; Teachers 1; Diocesan Administrators 2.

6—ST. LAWRENCE (1859) (German). Closed. See St. Patrick Cathedral, Harrisburg.

7—ST. MARGARET MARY ALACOQUE (1948), Revs. John G. Allen; Michael M. Laicha; Mrs. Karen Hurley, Pastoral Assoc. In res., Rev. Edward C. Malesic.
Res., 2848 Herr St., Harrisburg, 17103-1817. Tel: 717-233-3062.
School—Tel: 717-232-3771. Mrs. Kathleen McKenna, Ph.D., Prin.
Sisters of Mercy 2; Lay Teachers 19; Students 370.
Catechesis/Religious Programs—Tel: 717-232-3800. Mrs. Suzanne Fonner, D.R.E.
Students 159.

8—OUR LADY OF THE BLESSED SACRAMENT (1906), Rev. Paul R. Shuda; Deacon John Mowery. In res., Rev. Edward R. Lavelle.
Res., 2121 N. Third St., 17110-1812. Tel: 717-233-1014.
Catechesis/Religious Programs—Students 80.
Convent—2900 N. Green St., 17110. Tel: 717-236-3354. Sisters of Mercy
Sisters 2.

9—SACRED HEART OF JESUS (1901). Closed. See St. Patrick Cathedral, Harrisburg.

OUTSIDE THE CITY OF HARRISBURG

Abbottstown, York Co., Immaculate Heart of Mary (1809), Rev. Thomas F. Langan; Deacon Raymond J. Smith; Karen Kreller, Pastoral Assoc. & D.R.E.
Res., R.D. 1, Box 343, Canal Rd., 17301-9051. Tel: 717-259-0611. [CEM]
Catechesis/Religious Programs—Tel: 717-259-9426.
Students 324.

Annville, Lebanon Co., St. Paul the Apostle (1928), Rev. John D. Hoke; Deacon Richard A. Ryan. In res., Rev. Dennis M. Young (STA).
Res., 125 S. Spruce St., 17003. Tel: 717-867-1525.
Catechesis/Religious Programs—Tel: 717-867-7471.
Students 227.
Stations—Fort Indiantown Gap, Our Lady of Victory, Tel: 717-861-2241; Lebanon Valley College, Miller Chapel, Tel: 717-867-6135.

Berwick, Columbia Co., Immaculate Conception of the Blessed Virgin Mary (1906), Rev. Joseph H. Fennessy.
Res., 1730 Fowler Ave., 18603-1462. Tel: 717-759-8113; Fax: 717-759-6637. [CEM]
School—Holy Family Consolidated School, Tel: 717-752-2021; Fax: 717-752-2914.
Catechesis/Religious Programs—Tel: 717-759-9225.
Students 239.

St. Joseph's (1928), Rev. Dominick A. Mammarella; Sr. M. Carmelina, D.M., Pastoral Assoc.
Res., 721 Monroe St., 18603. Tel: 717-752-5684.
School—Holy Family Consolidated School, Tel: 717-752-2021. Sr. M. Ambrogina, D.M., Prin.
Catechesis/Religious Programs—Students 163.
Convent—728 Washington St., 18603. Tel: 717-752-2112. Daughters of Mercy
Sisters 3.

Bloomsburg, Columbia Co., St. Columba (1882) (Irish), Revs. Patrick A. Devine; Ronald J. Moratelli.
Mailing Address: P.O. Box 829, 17815.
Res., 42 E. Third St., 17815. Tel: 717-784-0801; Fax: 717-387-2604. [CEM]
School—40 E. Third St., 17815. Tel: 717-784-5932. Sr. Rita Polchin, S.S.C.M., Prin.
Sisters 3; Lay Teachers 5; Students 171.
Catechesis/Religious Programs—Tel: 717-387-4068.
Students 372.
Convent—342 Iron St., 17815. Tel: 717-784-1385.
Mission—Benton, Columbia Co., Christ the King, Mendenhall Ln., Benton, 17814. Tel: 717-925-6969.

Blue Ridge Summit, Franklin Co., St. Rita (1919), Revs. Michael A. Messaro, M.SS.CC.; Antony Attumaly, M.SS.CC.
Immaculate Conception:Fairfield, 17320. Tel: 717-642-8815. [JC]

Bonneauville, Adam Co., St. Joseph (1859), Revs. Brian P. Conrad; Paul N. Miller; Deacon Richard J. Weaver.
Res., 12 E. Hanover St., Gettysburg, 17325-7750. Tel: 717-334-2510. [CEM]
Catechesis/Religious Programs—Students 108.

Buchanan Valley, Adams Co., St. Ignatius Loyola (Orrtanna) (1817), Rev. Carl J. Steffen.
Res., 1095 Church Rd., Orrtanna, 17353. Tel: 717-677-8012. [CEM]
Catechesis/Religious Programs—Tel: 717-677-8012.
Students 83.

Camp Hill, Cumberland Co., Good Shepherd (1951), Rev. Msgr. Vincent J. Smith; Rev. Robert S. Panza; Deacon Francis Gorman. In res., Rev. Daniel P. O'Brien.
Res., 3435 Trindle Rd., 17011. Tel: 717-761-1167; Fax: 717-761-5313.
School—Tel: 717-737-7261. Mr. Ultan J. Oman, Prin.
Lay Teachers 16; Students 303.
Catechesis/Religious Programs—3400 Market St., 17011. Tel: 717-737-8216.
Students 329.

Carlisle, Cumberland Co., St. Patrick (1779), Revs. Andrew J. Fontanella; Joseph T. Scanlin; William M. Keary; Deacon Gerard J. Kole. In res., Rev.

Daniel J. Menniti.
Res., 140 E. Pomfret St., 17013. Tel: 717-243-4411. [CEM 2]
School—87 Marsh Dr., 17013. Tel: 717-249-4826. Sr. Karen Washabaugh, S.S.J., Prin.
Lay Teachers 15; Students 380.
Catechesis/Religious Programs—Tel: 717-243-4891. Mrs. Helen Richards, D.R.E.
Students 510.
Chapel—Pine Grove Furnace, St. Eleanor Regina.

Centralia, Columbia Co., St. Ignatius (1869). Closed. See Our Lady of Mount Carmel, Mount Carmel.

Chambersburg, Franklin Co., Corpus Christi (1792), Rev. Msgr. Thomas R. Brenner, V.F.; Revs. Daniel F. Lawler, S.J.; Jude Dawson-Amoah, O.P.
Res., 320 Philadelphia Ave., 17201. Tel: 717-264-6317; Fax: 717-264-1787. [CEM]
School—305 N. Second St., 17201. Tel: 717-263-5036; Fax: 717-263-6079. Mr. Thomas F. Yurkovic, Prin.
Lay Teachers 17; Students 330.
Catechesis/Religious Programs—Tel: 717-263-9541. Mrs. Jean M. Brigham, D.R.E.
Students 295.
Mission—Doylesburg, Franklin Co., Our Lady of Refuge, 21169 Cross Rd., Doylesburg, 17219. Tel: 717-349-7953. Rev. John Campion, Admin.
Station—Scotland School for Veterans' Children, Tel: 717-264-7187.

Coal Township, Our Lady of Hope, Very Rev. Philip G. Burger, V.F.; Rev. Edward J. Keating.
Res., 863 W. Chestnut St., 17866-1995. Tel: 717-648-4432.

St. Stephen Protomartyr, Northumberland Co., (1898) (Polish). Closed. See Our Lady of Hope, Coal Township.

Columbia, Lancaster Co., St. Peter (1828), Rev. John F. Smith; Sr. George Ann Biscan, A.S.C., Pastoral Assoc.; Deacon Michael J. Lydon.
Res., 217 Maple St., Wrightsville, 17368. Tel: 717-252-3806; Fax: 717-684-3102. [CEM 2]
School—121 S. Second St., 17512. Tel: 717-684-2433; Fax: 717-684-5039. Mrs. Theresa M. Burg, Prin.
Lay Teachers 9; Students 176.
Catechesis/Religious Programs—Mr. John J. Campbell, III, D.R.E.
Students 92.
Convent—Tel: 717-684-2707.
Mission—Wrightsville, York Co., Mother of Holy Purity, 217 Maple St., 17368.

Holy Trinity (1860), Rev. Kenneth F. Lawrence; Sr. Anna Cosgrave, O.S.F., Pastoral Assoc.
Res., 409 Cherry St., 17512. Tel: 717-684-2711; Fax: 717-684-9612. [CEM]
School—404 Cherry St., 17512. Tel: 717-684-2664. Shirley A. Meley, Prin.
Lay Teachers 9; Students 180.
Catechesis/Religious Programs—Students 127.
Convent—548 Cherry St., 17512. Tel: 717-684-2232. Sisters of St. Francis of Philadelphia

Conewago Township, Adams Co., Basilica of the Sacred Heart of Jesus (1730), Rev. Msgr. George W. Rost.
Res., 30 Basilica Dr., Hanover, 17331-8924. Tel: 717-637-2721. [CEM]
School—Tel: 717-632-8715. Sr. Eileen Kean, Prin.
Sisters of St. Joseph 3; Lay Teachers 8; Students 236.
Convent—55 Basilica Dr., Hanover, 17331. Tel: 717-637-3370. Sisters of St. Joseph
Sisters 4.

Cornwall, Lebanon Co., Sacred Heart of Jesus (1886), Rev. Andrew P. Marinak.
Res., 2596 Cornwall Rd., P.O. Box 136, 17016-0136. Tel: 717-273-1574. [CEM]
Parish Center—Tel: 717-274-3239.
Catechesis/Religious Programs—Tel: 717-273-2160. Sr. Helen Ann Gaidos, D.R.E.
Students 108.

Dallastown, York Co., St. Joseph (1850), Revs. Matthew Casey, O.M.I.; Michael J. Amesse, O.M.I.; Robert Leising, O.M.I.; Matthew Casey, O.M.I.; Deacon John Weaver.
Res., 251 E. Main St., 17313. Tel: 717-246-3007. [CEM]
School—271 E. Main St., 17313. Tel: 717-244-9386. Donna Phillips, Prin.
Lay Teachers 12; Students 170.
Catechesis/Religious Programs—Tel: 717-244-6279.
Students 450.

Danville, Montour Co., St. Joseph (1849), Revs. Edward J. Quinlan; Lawrence C. Gross.
Res., 18 E. Center St., 17821. Tel: 717-275-2512; Fax: 717-275-6840. [CEM 3]
School—511 Ferry St., 17821. Tel: 717-275-2435. Sisters 1; Lay Teachers 7; Students 155.
Catechesis/Religious Programs—Students 380.
Convent—9 Bloom St., 17821. Tel: 717-275-0562.

Dauphin, Dauphin Co., St. Matthew, Apostle and Evangelist (1976), Rt. Rev. John E. Neitzel, O.Praem., Abbot; Deacon Richard Aull.
Res., 420 Stony Creek Rd., P.O. Box 459, 17018. Tel: 717-921-2363.

Doylesburg, Franklin Co., Our Lady of Refuge Mission (1802), Rev. John R. Campion, Admin.
Res., 21169 Cross Rd., 17219. Tel: 717-349-7953. [CEM]

Elizabethtown, Lancaster Co., St. Peter (1752), Rev. Joseph D. Blascovich. In res., Rev. Thomas J. Kujovsky.
Res., 127 N. Cherry Alley, 17022-1956. Tel: 717-367-1255. [CEM]
School—61 E. Washington St., 17022. Tel: 717-367-1678. Mrs. Paula Fish, Prin.
Lay Teachers 7; Students 83.
Catechesis/Religious Programs—Tel: 717-367-5538.
Students 265.

Elysburg, Northumberland Co., Queen of the Most Holy Rosary (1950), Rev. Charles R. Slough.
Res., 103 W. Center St., 17824. Tel: 717-672-2302; Fax: 717-672-3310. [JC]
Catechesis/Religious Programs—Tel: 717-672-9930.
Students 200.

Enhaut, Dauphin Co., St. John the Evangelist (1902). Closed. See Prince of Peace, Steelton.

Enola, Cumberland Co., Our Lady of Lourdes (1926), Rev. John A. Acri; Ms. Celeste Hamilton, Pastoral Assoc.; Deacon Edwin L. Fitzpatrick.
Res., 225 Salt Rd., 17025. Tel: 717-732-9642; Fax: 717-732-8184.
Catechesis/Religious Programs—Students 392.

Ephrata, Lancaster Co., Mother of Perpetual Help (1914), Very Rev. Arthur P. Gildea, C.SS.R.; Revs. Edward W. Jackson, C.SS.R.; William F. Rosner, C.SS.R.; John J. Dorff, C.SS.R.
Res., 300 Pine St., P.O. Box 209, 17522-0209. Tel: 717-733-6596; Fax: 717-733-0502.
School—Tel: 717-738-2414; Fax: 717-738-3280. Sr. Ann Damien, O.S.F., Prin.
Bernardine Sisters of the Third Order of St. Francis 4; Lay Teachers 10; Students 340.
Catechesis/Religious Programs—Tel: 717-738-4517; Fax: 717-733-2119.
Students 430.
Convent—310 Church Ave., 17522. Tel: 717-733-1291.

Fairfield, Adams Co., Immaculate Conception of the Blessed Virgin Mary (1823), Revs. Michael A. Messaro, M.SS.CC.; Antony Attumaly, M.SS.CC.
Res., 17320. Tel: 717-642-8815. [CEM][JC]
Catechesis/Religious Programs—Students 105.

Gettysburg, Adams Co., St. Francis Xavier's (1831), Very Rev. Joseph C. Hilbert, V.F.; Rev. Caesae A. Belchez; Deacon James Sneeringer.
Res., 22 W. High St., 17325. Tel: 717-334-3919; 334-7711; Fax: 717-338-0831. [CEM]
School—45 W. High St., 17325. Tel: 717-334-4221. Sr. Phyllis R.S.M., Prin.
Sisters of Mercy 8; Lay Teachers 15; Students 241.
Catechesis/Religious Programs—Tel: 717-334-1221.
Students 187.
Convent—Tel: 717-334-4310.

Greencastle, Franklin Co., St. Mark the Evangelist (1965), Rev. Joseph L. Stahura.
Res., 395 S. Ridge Ave., P.O. Box 218, 17225. Tel: 717-597-2705. [JC]
Catechesis/Religious Programs—Students 167.
Mission—Mercersburg, St. Luke the Evangelist.

Hanover, York Co., St. Joseph (1864), Rev. Msgr. Robert C. Gribbin; Revs. Robert M. Gillelan; Norman C. Hohenwarter, Jr.
Res., 244 Baltimore St., 17331. Tel: 717-637-5236; Fax: 717-637-6615. [CEM]
School—236 Baltimore St., 17331. Tel: 717-632-1335. Sr. Dorothy Kelm, Prin.
Sisters of St Joseph 4; Lay Teachers 10; Students 270.
Catechesis/Religious Programs—Students 465.
Convent—252 Baltimore St., 17331. Tel: 717-637-4233.

St. Vincent (1904), Rev. Bernard Quinn.
Res., 220 Third St., 17331. Tel: 717-637-4625. [CEM]
School—224 Third St., 17331. Tel: 717-637-5190. Lay Teachers 8; Students 228.
Catechesis/Religious Programs—Students 76.

Hershey, Dauphin Co., St. Joan of Arc (1920), Rev. Msgr. Leo N. Bierster; Rev. John Trigilio, Jr.; Deacon Thomas S. Oliver. In res., Rev. Stephen D. Weitzel; Rev. Msgr. Francis M. Kumontis.
Res., 359 W. Areba Ave., 17033. Tel: 717-533-7168; Fax: 717-520-0526.
School—305 W. Areba Ave., 17033. Tel: 717-533-2854. Sr. Eileen M. McGowan, Prin.
Daughters of Our Lady of Mercy 4; Lay Teachers 24; Students 325.
Catechesis/Religious Programs—Students 421.
Convent—Tel: 717-533-2864.
Sisters 4.

Kulpmont, Northumberland Co., Assumption of the Blessed Virgin Mary (1909). Closed. See Holy Angels, Kulpmont.

St. Casimir (1915). Closed. See Holy Angels, Kulpmont.

Holy Angels (1995), Rev. Raymond J. Orloski.
Res., 855 Scott St., 17834. Tel: 717-373-1221; Fax: 717-373-1226. [CEM 3]
Catechesis/Religious Programs—863 Scott St., Kulpont, 17834. Tel: 717-373-1512.
Students 205.

Lancaster, Lancaster Co.,

1—St. Anne, (1923), Rev. Gerald A. Lytle; Deacons Frank Eckman; Joseph L. Anders.
Res., 929 N. Duke St., 17602. Tel: 717-392-2225.
School—Cherry & Liberty St., 17602. Tel: 717-394-6711; Fax: 717-394-8628.
Lay Teachers 11; Students 263. Principals: Donna Power, (Elementary); Dermot Garrett, (High School).
Catechesis/Religious Programs—Tel: 717-397-8755. Mrs. Suzanne Ganse, D.R.E.
Students 110.

2—St. Anthony of Padua, (1870), Revs. Charles McDonald, C.SS.R.; James Small, C.SS.R.; William Geiger, C.SS.R.
Res., 501 E. Orange St., 17602. Tel: 717-394-0669; Fax: 717-394-4507. [CEM]
School—Resurrection. See Assumption of the Blessed Virgin Mary, Lancaster, and report of Resurrection School for details. Tel: 717-392-3083.
Catechesis/Religious Programs—Tel: 717-392-2930. Patricia Meyer, D.R.E.
Students 280.
Convent—533 E. Orange St., 17602. Tel: 717-397-1043. Sisters of the Holy Cross
Stations—Lancaster, Lancaster County Prison, Tel: 717-299-7800; Conestoga View Nursing Home, Tel: 717-299-7850.

3—Assumption of the Blessed Virgin Mary, (1741), Very Rev. Bernardo Pistone; Revs. Thomas J. Gralinski; Ignacio Palomino (Peru); Mrs. Frances Sescilla, Pastoral Assoc.; Deacon Manuel Velazquez.
Res., 119 S. Prince St., 17603. Tel: 717-392-2578; Fax: 717-394-6549.
School—Resurrection. Consolidation of St. Anthony, St. Joseph and St. Mary. 32 W. Vine St., 17603. Tel: 717-397-3136. Mary Jo Moczulski, Prin.
Religious 2; Lay Teachers 17; Students 370.
Catechesis/Religious Programs—Ann Bleistine, D.R.E.
Students 302.

4—St. John Neumann, (1978), Rev. Msgr. Richard A. Youtz, J.C.L.; Rev. David L. Danneker, Ph.D.; Sr. Helen E. McCormac, Pastoral Assoc.; Deacon William J. Jordan.
Res., 601 E. Delp Rd., 17601. Tel: 717-569-8531; Fax: 717-569-2135.
Catechesis/Religious Programs—Tel: 717-569-8533; Fax: 717-569-9156.
Students 933.

5—St. Joseph, (1849), Rev. Msgr. Thomas H. Smith; Rev. Msgr. Cletus H. Wagman, Senior Priest; Mrs. Patricia Weaver, Pastoral Assoc. In res., Revs. James Muthuplakel; Michael F. Barrett.
Res., 440 St. Joseph St., 17603-5298. Tel: 717-397-6921. [CEM]
School—Resurrection. See Assumption of the Blessed Virgin Mary, Lancaster, for details.
Catechesis/Religious Programs—Students 118.

6—Sacred Heart of Jesus, (1900), Rev. Msgr. Damian E. McGovern; Rev. Allen F. Wolfe; Sr. Anne Hodgson, S.N.D., Pastoral Assoc.
Res., 558 W. Walnut St., 17603. Tel: 717-394-0757; Fax: 717-394-3589.
School—235 Nevin St., 17603. Tel: 717-393-8433. Sr. Ellen Thomas, I.H.M., Prin.
Servants of the Immaculate Heart of Mary 2; Lay Teachers 10; Students 233.
Catechesis/Religious Programs—Sr. Mary Canavan, I.H.M., D.R.E.
Students 82.
Convent—565 W. Walnut St., 17603. Tel: 717-392-4522.

Lebanon, Lebanon Co.,

1—Assumption of the Blessed Virgin Mary, (1810), Very Rev. David T. McAndrew, V.F.; Rev. Martin O. Moran, III; Deacon Richard Wentzel. In res., Rev. Walter A. Halaburda.
Office: 12 N. Eighth St., 17046. Tel: 717-272-5674.
Res., 202 Hathaway Park, 17042. [CEM][JC]
Catechesis/Religious Programs—Tel: 717-272-6223. Mrs. Julie Shuyler, D.R.E.
Students 154.
Mission—Jonestown, Lebanon Co., Our Lady of Fatima, Tel: 717-865-4456.

2—ST. BENEDICT THE ABBOT, (1995), Rev. Msgr. Mercurio A. Fregapane.
Res., 1300 Lehman St., 17042. Tel: 717-272-0623; Fax: 717-270-6926.
Catechesis/Religious Programs—Tel: 717-272-1242.
Students 162.

3—ST. CECILIA, (1995), Rev. J. Michael McFadden.
Res., 202 E. Lehman St., 17046. Tel: 717-272-4412; Fax: 717-272-3206.
Catechesis/Religious Programs—Students 329.

4—ST. GERTRUDE, (1906). Closed. See St. Cecilia, Lebanon.

5—ST. GREGORY THE GREAT, (1965). Closed. See St. Cecilia, Lebanon.

6—SS. CYRIL AND METHODIUS, (1905) (Slavonic). Closed. See St. Benedict the Abbot, Lebanon.

Lewisburg, Union Co., Sacred Heart of Jesus (1935), Revs. William J. Nessel, O.S.F.S.; Patrick J. Shannon.
Res., 814 St. Louis St., 17837. Tel: 717-523-3104; Fax: 717-524-5156.
Catechesis/Religious Programs—Sr. Karen Wilson, SS.C.M., D.R.E.
Students 350.
Station—Laurelton, Laurelton Center, Tel: 717-922-5100.

Lewistown, Mifflin Co., Sacred Heart of Jesus (1830), Revs. Thomas C. Marickovic; Thaddeus B. Strzelec.
Res., 106 N. Dorcas St., 17044. Tel: 717-242-2781. [CEM]
School—110 N. Dorcas St., 17044. Tel: 717-248-5351.
Lay Teachers 7; Students 120.
Convent—Tel: 717-248-0260.
Mission—Burnham, Mifflin Co., Mary Queen of All Saints.

Lititz, Lancaster Co., St. James (1977), Revs. Gerard J. Szymkowiak, C.SS.R.; John Creaven, C.SS.R.; Deacon Donald Hackman.
Res., 505 Woodcrest Ave., 17543. Tel: 717-733-6596.
Catechesis/Religious Programs—Kathy Trusz, D.R.E.
Students 426.

Littlestown, Adams Co., St. Aloysius (1884), Rev. James M. Sterner.
Res., 29 S. Queen St., 17340. Tel: 717-359-4513. [CEM]
Catechesis/Religious Programs—Faith Redding, D.R.E.
Students 174.

Locustdale, Columbia Co., St. Joseph (1913). Closed. See Our Lady of Mount Carmel, Mount Carmel.

Locust Gap, Northumberland Co., St. Joseph (1870). Closed. See Our Lady of Mount Carmel, Mount Carmel.

Lykens, Dauphin Co., Our Lady Help of Christians (1853), Rev. Francis J. Karwacki, M.Ed., M.Div.
Res., 732 E. Main St., 17048. Tel: 717-453-7895. [CEM 2][JC 3]
Catechesis/Religious Programs—Tel: 717-453-9931.
Students 151.
Mission—Williamstown, Dauphin Co., Sacred Heart of Jesus, 140 E. Market St., Williamstown, 17098. Tel: 717-647-2645.

McSherrystown, Adams Co., Annunciation of the Blessed Virgin Mary (1899), Rev. Andre J. Meluskey; Deacon Joseph F. Lawrence.
Res., 26 N. Third St., 17344. Tel: 717-637-1191. [CEM]
School—316 North St., 17344. Tel: 717-637-3135; Fax: 717-637-1715. Sr. Ann Marie Wierman, S.S.J., Prin.
Lay Teachers 18; Students 300.
Catechesis/Religious Programs—Students 97.

Manheim, Lancaster Co., St. Richard (1978), Rev. Raymond J. Christ, O.S.F.S. In res., Rev. John F. Kenny, O.S.F.S.
Res., 201 Adele Ave., 17545. Tel: 717-665-2465.
Catechesis/Religious Programs—Mary Schreiner, D.R.E. (Grades K-12).
Students 113.

Marietta, Lancaster Co., Presentation of the Blessed Virgin Mary (1869). Closed. See Mary, Mother of the Church, Mount Joy.

Marion Heights, Northumberland Co., Our Lady of Perpetual Help (1905). Closed. See Holy Angels, Kulpmont.

Marysville, Perry Co., Our Lady of Good Counsel (1956), Rev. John F. Greaney.
Res., 121 William St., 17053. Tel: 717-957-2662.
Catechesis/Religious Programs—Tel: 717-834-4519. Sally Rebert, D.R.E.
Students 177.
Mission—Duncannon, Perry Co., St. Bernadette, 901 High St., Duncannon, 17020. Tel: 717-834-4519.

Mechanicsburg, Cumberland Co., Blessed Katharine Drexel (1988), Rev. James R. O'Brien.
Res., One Clover Ln., 17055. Tel: 717-697-8716.
Mailing Address: 1 Peter Dr., 17055.
Catechesis/Religious Programs—Tel: 717-795-8572. Carolyn Keffer, D.R.E.
Students 445.

St. Elizabeth Ann Seton (1977), Very Rev. Richard P. Waldron, V.F.; Rev. Robert F. Sharman.
Res., 310 Hertzler Rd., 17055. Tel: 717-697-2614; Fax: 717-795-0800.
Catechesis/Religious Programs—Tel: 717-697-3545. D.R.E.: Carol Holder; Judy Olinger.
Students 455.

St. Joseph (1952), Revs. Chester P. Snyder; Daniel F. X. Powell; Cyril Orsi, O.P.; Rose Baker, Pastoral Assoc.; Deacons Andrew Fine; Jack Paruso. In res., Very Rev. William J. King.
Res., 200 S. Filbert St., P.O. Box 2012, 17055. Tel: 717-766-9433.
Church—400 E. Simpson St., 17055.
School—410 E. Simpson St., 17055. Tel: 717-766-2564; Fax: 717-766-1226.
Sisters of SS. Cyril and Methodius 3; Lay Teachers 19; Students 478.
Catechesis/Religious Programs—Tel: 717-766-2472.
Students 533.
Convent—302 S. Chestnut St., 17055. Tel: 717-766-6221.

Middletown, Dauphin Co., Seven Sorrows of the Blessed Virgin Mary (1855), Rev. Msgr. George V. Lentocha; Rev. Louis P. Ogden.
Res., 280 N. Race St., 17057. Tel: 717-944-3133; Fax: 717-944-1170. [CEM]
School—(Grades PreK-8) Race & Conewago St., 17057. Tel: 717-944-5371; Fax: 717-944-5419. Mr. Thomas Frey, Prin.
Lay Teachers 12; Students 220.
Catechesis/Religious Programs—Students 275.

Mifflintown, Juniata Co., St. Jude (1959), Rev. Thomas C. Marickoviic; Deacon John A. Rocco.
Res., Box 187, 17059. Tel: 717-436-6722.

Millersburg, Dauphin Co., Queen of Peace (1952), Rev. Joseph A. Kelly, O.Praem.
Res., 202 Zimmerman, 17061. Tel: 717-692-3504.
Catechesis/Religious Programs—Tel: 717-692-3504. Mrs. Cynthia Miskinis, D.R.E.
Students 157.

Millersville, Lancaster Co., St. Philip the Apostle (1965), Revs. Michael E. Homola; Stephen A. Sheetz; Deacons Martin C. Light, Sr.; Ross Beighley.
Res., 2111 Millersville Pike, Lancaster, 17603. Tel: 717-872-2166.
Catechesis/Religious Programs—Tel: 717-872-9892. Sr. Charlotte O.S.F., D.R.E.
Students 421.

Milton, Northumberland Co., St. Joseph (1805), Rev. Thomas A. Scala.
Res., 109 Broadway, 17847. Tel: 717-742-4356; Fax: 717-742-9171. [CEM]
Catechesis/Religious Programs—Tel: 717-742-4481. Belinda Stefl, D.R.E.
Students 9.

Mount Carmel, Northumberland Co.,

1—DIVINE REDEEMER, Revs. Joseph M. Pease; Robert A. Yohe.
Res., 438 West Ave., 17851. Tel: 717-339-3450.

2—HOLY CROSS, (1892) (Lithuanian). Closed. See Divine Redeemer, Mount Carmel.

3—ST. JOHN THE BAPTIST, (1892) (Slovak). Closed. See Divine Redeemer, Mount Carmel.

4—ST. JOSEPH, (1875) (Polish). Closed. See Our Lady of Mount Carmel, Mount Carmel.

5—OUR LADY OF MOUNT CARMEL, (1886), Rev. Msgr. Lawrence R. Overbaugh; Revs. Robert Strome; Charles Procopio, (Retired).
Res., 47 S. Market St., 17851. Tel: 717-339-1031. [JC 4]
Catechesis/Religious Programs—Students 285.

6—OUR MOTHER OF CONSOLATION, (1895) (Polish). Closed. See Divine Redeemer, Mount Carmel.

7—ST. PETER, (1905) (Italian). Closed. See Divine Redeemer, Mount Carmel.

Mount Joy, Lancaster Co., Assumption of B.V.M. (1979). Closed. See Mary, Mother of the Church, Mount Joy.

Mary, Mother of the Church (1995), Rev. Paul T. Rindos.
Res., 625 Union School Rd., 17552-9712. Tel: 717-653-4903.

Myerstown, Lebanon County, Mary, Gate of Heaven (1926), Rev. Robert F. Berger.
Res., 188 W. McKinley Ave., P.O. Box 227, 17067. Tel: 717-866-5640.
Catechesis/Religious Programs—Students 152.

New Bloomfield, Perry Co., St. Bernard (1942), Rev. Anthony J. Larry, O.S.F.S.
Res., W. McClure St., P.O. Box 25, 17068. Tel: 717-582-4113; Fax: 717-582-3797.
Catechesis/Religious Programs—Alice Vilk, D.R.E.
Students 230.

New Cumberland, Cumberland Co., St. Theresa of the Infant Jesus (1928), Rev. Msgr. Francis J. Taylor; Revs. Lawrence R. Coakley; Luis R. Rodriguez; Deacon Joseph J. Kramer. In res., Very Rev. Thomas R. Haney.
Res., 1300 Bridge St., 17070. Tel: 717-774-5918.
School—1210 Bridge St., 17070. Tel: 717-774-7464; Fax: 717-774-3154.
Sisters of Mercy 4; Lay Teachers 20; Students 479.
Principals: Sr. Bernadette Bergen, R.S.M., (Elementary); Sr. Francine Gagne, I.H.M., (High School).
Catechesis/Religious Programs—Tel: 717-774-7296.
Students 395.
Convent—1200 Bridge St., 17070. Tel: 717-774-6583. Sisters of Mercy
Sisters 4.

New Freedom, York Co., St. John the Baptist (1841), Revs. Sylvan P. Capitani; Robert J. Kobularik.
Res., 315 N. Constitution Ave., 17349. Tel: 717-235-2156; Fax: 717-235-2223. [CEM]
Catechesis/Religious Programs—Tel: 717-235-2439.
Students 606.

New Holland, Lancaster Co., Our Lady of Lourdes (1972), Rev. Patrick McGarrity, C.SS.R.
Res., 737 Walnut St., 17557. Tel: 717-354-2540; Fax: 717-354-4170.
Catechesis/Religious Programs—Tel: 717-354-4686.
Students 241.

New Oxford, Adams Co., Immaculate Conception of the Blessed Virgin Mary (1852), Rev. Msgr. Francis J. Hudak.
Res., 106 Carlisle St., 17350. Tel: 717-624-4121; Fax: 717-624-9711. [CEM]
School—101 N. Peter St., 17350. Tel: 717-624-2061. Sr. Ann Leonard, Prin.
Lay Teachers 9; Students 174.
Catechesis/Religious Programs—Sr. Paula Mary D.R.E.
Students 141.
Convent—5 Carlisle St., 17350. Tel: 717-624-7531.

Northumberland, Northumberland Co., St. Thomas More (1955). Closed. See St. Monica, Sunbury.

Palmyra, Lebanon Co., Holy Spirit (1955), Rev. George J. Koychick.
Res., 245 W. Pine St., 17078. Tel: 717-838-3369.
Catechesis/Religious Programs—Mrs. Helen Remington, D.R.E.
Students 144.

Quarryville, Lancaster Co., St. Catherine of Siena (1843), Rev. Joseph C. Coyne; Deacon Ed Leszczynski.
Res., 15 E. Third St., 17566-1255. Tel: 717-786-2695. [CEM]
Catechesis/Religious Programs—Mrs. Diane Dalgaard, D.R.E.
Students 260.

Ranshaw, Northumberland Co., St. Anthony of Padua (1919). Closed. See Mother Cabrini, Shamokin.

Roaring Creek, Columbia Co., Our Lady of Mercy (1923), Rev. Thomas Ignatius Mannion.
Res., R.R. #1, Box 56, Catawissa, 17820. Tel: 717-799-5642. [CEM]
Catechesis/Religious Programs—Mrs. Margaret Jessick, D.R.E.
Students 67.

Rohrerstown, Lancaster Co., St. Leo the Great (1964), Very Rev. William J. Sullivan, V.F.; Rev. Kenneth G. Smith; Deacon Eugene Vannucci.
Res., 2427 Marietta Ave., Lancaster, 17601. Tel: 717-394-1742; Fax: 717-394-1779.
School—Tel: 717-392-2441. Mrs. Joyce Redington, Prin.
Lay Teachers 18; Students 286.
Catechesis/Religious Programs—Tel: 717-394-7354.
Students 631.

Selinsgrove, Snyder Co., St. Pius X (1964), Rev. Joseph A. Celia; Deacon Samuel A. Sica.
Res., 610 University Ave., 17870. Tel: 717-374-4113; Fax: 717-374-4113.
Catechesis/Religious Programs—Students 218.
Missions—Susquehanna, Snyder Co., Susquehanna University; Selinsgrove, Snyder Co., Selinsgrove Center.

Shamokin, Northumberland Co.,

1—ASSUMPTION OF THE BLESSED VIRGIN MARY, (1892) (Slovak). Closed. See Mother Cabrini, Shamokin.

2—ST. EDWARD, (1866). Closed. See Mother Cabrini, Shamokin.

3—ST. JOSEPH, (1913). Closed. See Our Lady of Hope,

Coal Township.

4—St. Michael Archangel, (1894) (Lithuanian). Closed. See Mother Cabrini, Shamokin.

5—Mother Cabrini, (1955), Rev. David Grumsey, O.F.M.Conv.
Res., 214 N. Shamokin St., 17872. Tel: 717-648-4512; Fax: 717-648-1209. [CEM]

6—St. Stanislaus Kostka, (1874) (Polish). Closed. See Mother Cabrini, Shamokin.

Shippensburg, Cumberland Co., Our Lady of the Visitation (1950), Rev. Lawrence W. Sherdel; John Boyle, Pastoral Assoc.
Res., 305 N. Prince St., 17257. Tel: 717-532-2912.
Catechesis/Religious Programs—Students 157.

South Mountain, Franklin Co., Most Holy Rosary. Closed. See St. Ignatius, Buchannon Valley.

Spring Grove, York Co., Sacred Heart (1976), Rev. Hugh J. McLaughlin.
Res., 152 N. Main St., Box 42, 17362. Tel: 717-225-1704.
Catechesis/Religious Programs—Tel: 717-225-6404. Peggy Rizzuto, D.R.E.
Students 128.

Steelton, Dauphin Co.,

1—St. Ann, (1901) (Italian). Closed. See Prince of Peace, Steelton.

2—Assumption of the Blessed Virgin Mary, (1898) (Croatian). Closed. See Prince of Peace, Steelton.

3—St. James, (1878). Closed. See Prince of Peace, Steelton.

4—St. Peter, (1909) (Slovenian). Closed. See Prince of Peace, Steelton.

5—Prince of Peace, (1995), Revs. Samuel E. Houser; William Waltersheid; Deacon Michael Grella. In res., Very Rev. Paul C. Helwig.
Res., 815 S. Second St., 17113. Tel: 717-985-1330; Fax: 717-985-1333.
School—245 Reynders St., 17113. Tel: 717-939-6357. Ms. Anna Mae Muryasz, Prin.

Sunbury, Northumberland Co., St. Michael Archangel (1863). Closed. See St. Monica, Sunbury.
St. Monica (1995), Rev. William T. Haviland.
Res., 20 N. Front St., 17801. Tel: 717-286-0761; Fax: 717-286-8566.
School—109 Market St., 17801. Tel: 717-286-5983. Mary P Reinhard, Prin.
Lay Teachers 10; Students 224.
Catechesis/Religious Programs—Fax: 717-286-8588. Mrs. Peggy Walker, D.R.E.
Students 180.

Trevorton, Northumberland Co., St. Patrick (1850), Revs. Philip G. Burger; Edward Keating; Ramon Rivera-Lopez.
Res., 331 W. Shamokin St., 17881. Tel: 717-797-8251. [CEM]
Catechesis/Religious Programs—Tel: 717-797-1882. Mrs. Bernadette Dry, D.R.E.
Students 66.

Waynesboro, Franklin Co., St. Andrew (1893), Rev. Thomas J. Hemler.
Res., 12 N. Broad St., P.O. Box 167, 17268. Tel: 717-762-1914; Fax: 717-762-0697. [CEM]
School—213 E. Main St., 17268. Tel: 717-762-3221. Mrs. Eileen M. Sullivan, Prin.
Sisters of SS. Cyril & Methodius 3; Lay Teachers 7; Students 135.
Catechesis/Religious Programs—219 E. Main St., 17268. Tel: 717-762-5958.
Students 173.
Convent—Tel: 717-762-4935.

Williamstown, Dauphin Co., Sacred Heart of Jesus (1875), Rev. Francis J. Karwacki.
Res., 140 E. Market St., 17098. Tel: 717-647-2645. [CEM][JC]
Catechesis/Religious Programs—Tel: 717-647-2447. Sr. Carlotta R.S.M., D.R.E.
Students 95.

York, York Co.,

1—Immaculate Conception of the Blessed Virgin Mary, (1852), Revs. Lawrence J. Hemler; Michael C. Letteer. Pastoral Assocs.: Deacons Stephen J. Bankos; Catalino Gonzalez; Mrs. Marilynn Trauger. In res., Rev. Michael Grab.
Res., 309 S. George St., 17403. Tel: 717-845-7629. [CEM][JC]
Catechesis/Religious Programs—Tel: 717-846-6001.
Students 352.
Convent—26 E. College Ave., 17403. Tel: 717-848-1232.

2—St. Joseph, (1913), Revs. John Daya, O.F.M.Cap.; Victor Kriley, O.F.M.Cap.; Reginald Russo, O.F.M.Cap.; Dermot Rodgers, O.F.M.Cap. In res., Rev. Andrew Wong, O.F.M.Cap. (Singapore).
Res., 2935 Kingston Rd., 17402-4003. Tel: 717-755-1797; Fax: 717-757-1900.
School—2945 Kingston Rd., 17403. Tel: 717-755-1797; Fax: 717-757-1900. Sr. Dorita Slaughter, O.S.F., Prin.
Sisters 3; Lay Teachers 21; Students 363.
Catechesis/Religious Programs—Tel: 717-757-1707. Sr. Jean Holtz, S.S.J., D.R.E.
Students 497.
Convent—405 Quaker Dr., 17402. Tel: 717-757-3667. Sisters of St. Francis Missionary Sisters of the Sacred Heart.
Sisters 3.

3—St. Patrick, (1776), Revs. C. Anthony Miller; Tri M. Luong; Sr. Monica Imgrund, R.S.M., Pastoral Assoc.; Deacon Sam Moschella. In res., Rev. William M. Cawley (GF).
Res., 231 S. Beaver St., 17403. Tel: 717-848-2007; Fax: 717-843-4533. [CEM]
School—219 S. Beaver St., 17403. Tel: 717-854-8263. Sr. Ann Harrison, I.H.M., Prin.
Sisters, Servants of the Immaculate Heart of Mary 2; Lay Teachers 10; Students 180.
Catechesis/Religious Programs—Tel: 717-854-6653. Mrs. Paula Koch, D.R.E.
Students 235.
Convent—Tel: 717-848-1911. Sisters, Servants of the Immaculate Heart of Mary
Sisters 5.

4—St. Rose of Lima, (1907), Revs. Thomas J. Hoke; Leo M. Goodman, III; Sr. Mary Corbett, S.S.J., Pastoral Assoc.; Deacon Joseph Sferrella. In res., Rev. Carl T. Tancredi.
Res., 950 W. Market St., 17404. Tel: 717-846-4935; Fax: 717-843-4391. [JC]
School—944 W. Market St., 17404. Tel: 717-854-7979. Sr. Kathleen White, Prin.
Sisters of St. Joseph 3; Lay Teachers 10; Students 221.
Catechesis/Religious Programs—Tel: 717-843-3043. D.R.E.: Patricia Drawbaugh; Sr. Jane Keller.
Students 410.
Convent—Tel: 717-854-0378. Sisters of St. Joseph
Sisters 10.

York Haven, York Co., Holy Infant (1972), Rev. Clarence A. Olszewski.
Res., 34 Third St., 17370. Tel: 717-266-5286.
Catechesis/Religious Programs—Tel: 717-266-1643.
Students 183.

Chaplains of Public Institutions

Harrisburg. *Community General Osteopathic Hospital.* Vacant.
Harrisburg Hospital. Tel: 717-782-3333. Rev. John A. Szada, Jr. Tel: 717-233-1014.
Polyclinic Medical Clinic. Tel: 717-782-4141. Rev. John A. Szada Tel: 717-233-1014.
State Hospital, Pouch A, 17105. Tel: 717-787-9232. Deacon Frank Parr.

Camp Hill. *State Correctional Institution,* P.O. Box 200, 17011. Tel: 717-737-4531, Ext. 307. Deacon Manuel Velazquez.

Danville. *Geisinger Medical Center.* Tel: 717-275-2512. Rev. William M. Weary.
State Hospital, P.O. Box 219, 17821. Tel: 717-275-7011. Rev. Thomas Ignatius Mannion Tel: 717-799-5642.

Hershey. *Milton J. Hershey Medical Center,* 500 University Blvd., 17033. Tel: 717-534-8177. Rev. Stephen D. Weitzel Tel: 717-533-7168.

Lancaster. *Lancaster County Prison,* 625 E. King St., 17602. Tel: 717-534-8177. Deacon William J. Jordan.
Lancaster General Hospital and Lancaster Community Hospital. Rev. James Muthuplakel.

Lebanon. *Veterans Administration Hospital,* R.D. No. 1, 17042. Tel: 717-272-6621. Rev. Dennis Young.

Lewisburg. *U.S. Penitentiary.* Vacant. Tel: 717-523-1251.

Selinsgrove. *Selinsgrove Center,* Box 500, 17870. Tel: 717-374-2911, Ext. 425. Rev. Joseph A. Celia; Deacon Samuel Sica.

South Mountain. *Restoration Center.* Tel: 717-749-5773. Rev. Joeseph C. Carolin.

York. *York Hospital.* Vacant. 1001 S. George St., 17405. Tel: 717-771-2345.

On Duty Outside the Diocese:
Reverend Fathers—
Barrett, Edward J., Wadsworth VA Hospital, Los Angeles, CA 90073
Blackwell, Edward, 520 N.E. 20th St., #408, Fort Lauderdale, FL 33305-2195
Kemper, John C., S.S., Sts. Cyril & Methodius Seminary, 3535 Indian Tr., Orchard Lake, MI 48324
McLernon, Thomas M., Sacred Heart University, 5151 Park Ave., Fairfield, CT 06432-1000
Sperber, Timothy (MIA), St. Gregory Church, 200 N. University Dr., Plantation, FL 33324-2085
Topper, Charles J., 467 Bloomfield Ave., Bloomfield, CT 06002

Absent on Leave:
Reverend Fathers—
Bennett, Michael X.

Retired:
Reverend Monsignors—
Kujovsky, Thomas
McGough, Thomas J., Misericordia Convalescent Home, 998 S. Russell St., York, PA 17402. Tel: 717-757-3455
Topper, Vincent J., 915 S. Lincoln Ave., Lebanon, PA 17042. Tel: 717-273-1295
Reverend Fathers—
Aurentz, John W.
Beeman, James W.
Burakowski, Anthony E., 13 Pratt St., Fairfield, CT 06430
Farace, Frederick A., P.O. Box 276, Mount Carmel, PA 17851
McGinley, Anthony J.
Sawdy, Wallace E., 222 Herr St., Harrisburg, PA 17102
Zangari, Salvatore V.

Permanent Deacons:
Anders, Joseph L., St. Anne, Lancaster
Aull, Richard H., St. Matthew's, Dauphin
Bahn, Michael P., St. Joseph, York
Bankos, Stephen, St. Mary, York
Beighley, Ross W., St. Catherine of Siena, Quarryville
Bertollo, Edward L., Jr., Immaculate Conception BVM, Berwick
Clark, Charles W., St. Patrick, Harrisburg
Colonell, Arthur W., Our Mother of Perpetual Help, Ephrata
Culley, Matthew P., St. John Neumann, Lancaster
Dunn, J. Leo, St. Patrick, Harrisburg
Eckman, Frank M., St. Anne, Lancaster
Fedor, Thomas A., Holy Family, Harrisburg
Fine, Andrew V., St. Joseph, Mechanicsburg
Fitzpatrick, Edwin L., Our Lady of Lourdes, Enola
Flannery, Thomas H., St. Catherine, Harrisburg
Foerster, Jerome T., Holy Name of Jesus, Harrisburg
Gonzales, Catalino, Spanish-Speaking Apostolate, Harrisburg; Cristo Salvador, York
Gorman, Francis, Good Shepherd, Camp Hill
Grella, Michael A., St. Peter, Steelton
Hackman, Donald D., St. James, Lititz
Hayes, Arthur Hull, Jr.
Jordan, William J., Lancaster County Prison & St. Anthony of Padua, Lancaster
Kenski, Francis G., Holy Spirit Hospital, Camp Hill; Our Lady of Good Counsel, Marysville
Kole, Gerard J., Chap., County Nursing Home, Cumberford; County Prison, Carlisle
Kramer, Joseph J., St. Theresa, New Cumberland
Lawrence, Joseph F., Annunciation BVM, McSherrystown
Leszczynski, Edward A., St. Catherine of Siena, Quarryville
Light, Martin C., St. Philip, Millersville
Lydon, Michael, St. Peter, Columbia
MacAdam, Morris D., Sacred Heart of Jesus, Harrisburg
Mack, Robert P., St. Edward, Shamokin
Marroquin, Miguel, Spanish-Speaking Apostolate, Harrisburg
Miller, Gene R., Immaculate Conception BVM, New Oxford
Mordecai, Philip B.
Moschella, Sabino E., St. Patrick, York
Mowery, John, Our Lady of the Blessed Sacrament, Harrisburg
Oliver, Thomas S., St. Joan of Arc, Hershey
Parr, Frank J., Harrisburg State Hospital, Harrisburg
Paruso, John L., St. Joseph, Mechanicsburg
Ramos, Felix, San Juan Bautista, Lancaster
Rocco, John, St. Jude Thaddeus, Mifflintown; Sacred Heart, Lewistown
Runkle, Ralph H., St. Patrick, York
Ryan, Richard A., St. Paul the Apostle, Annville
Sahd, Joseph A., St. Joseph Hospital, Lancaster
Santiago, Expidito, San Juan Bautista, Lancaster
Sferrella, Joseph, St. Rose of Lima, York
Sica, Samuel A., St. Pius X & Selinsgrove Center, Selinsgrove
Smith, Raymond, Immaculate Heart, Abbottstown
Sneeringer, James, St. Francis Xavier, Gettysburg
Vannucci, Eugene D., St. Leo the Great, Rohrerstown
Velazquez, Manuel, Camp Hill State Correctional

Institution, Camp Hill
Weaver, John A., St. Joseph, Dallastown
Weaver, Richard J., St. Joseph, Bonneauville
Weaver, Robert E., St. Joseph Hospital, Lancaster
Wentzel, Richard W., Assumption BVM & Lebanon Catholic High School, Lebanon
Whale, William E., St. Catherine Laboure, Harrisburg
Wrabel, Joseph J., Holy Name, Harrisburg

INSTITUTIONS LOCATED IN THE DIOCESE

[A] HIGH SCHOOLS

HARRISBURG. *Bishop McDevitt High School*, 2200 Market St., 17103-2499. Tel: 717-236-7973. Mr. John D. Brixius, Prin. Sisters 5; Lay Teachers 42; Students 709.

CAMP HILL. *Trinity High School*, 3601 Simpson Ferry Rd., 17011. Tel: 717-761-1116; Fax: 717-761-7309. Sr. Francine Gagne, I.H.M., Prin. Sisters 4; Lay Teachers 36; Students 534.

COAL TOWNSHIP. *Our Lady of Lourdes Regional High School*, 2001 Clinton Ave., 17866-1699. Tel: 717-644-0375; Fax: 717-644-7655. Sr. Rita O'Leary, I.H.M., Prin.
E-mail:lourdes@postoffice.ptd.net
Sisters 6; Lay Teachers 23; Students 305.

DANVILLE. *St. Cyril Academy*, 17821. Tel: 717-275-1505. Sr. Donna Marie, SS.C.M., Prin. Sisters of SS. Cyril & Methodius 8; Lay Teachers 6; Girls 45.

LANCASTER. *Lancaster Catholic High School*, 650 Juliette Ave., 17601. Tel: 717-393-0454. Mr. Dermot Garrett, Prin. Sisters 2; Lay Teachers 39; Students 670.

LEBANON. *Catholic Junior-Senior High School*, 1400 Chestnut St., 17042. Tel: 717-273-3731. Mr. Mark J. Freund, Prin. Sisters of St. Joseph 2; Lay Teachers 24; Students 341; Total Staff 7.

MCSHERRYSTOWN. *Delone Catholic High School*, 140 S. Oxford Ave., 17344. Tel: 717-637-5969; Fax: 717-637-0442. Mrs. Maureen C. Thiec, Ed.D., Prin. Sisters 2; Lay Teachers 33; Students 518.

YORK. *York Catholic High School*, 601 E. Springettsbury Ave., 17403. Tel: 717-846-8871. Revs. Michael J. Grab, Prin.; William M. Cawley (GF), Teacher. Priests 1; Sisters 7; Lay Teachers 34; Total Staff 49; Students 646.

[B] CONSOLIDATED ELEMENTARY SCHOOLS

HARRISBURG. *Cathedral School*, 212 State St., 17101. Tel: 717-234-3797. Sr. Mary Agnes Shurer, S.C.C., Prin.
Upper School. (Includes Kindergarten). Sisters 1; Lay Teachers 5.
Lower School. Sisters 1; Lay Teachers 3.

LEBANON. *Our Lady of the Valley School*, 740 Willow St., 17042. Tel: 717-272-8961. Sr. Catherine Thibault, Prin. Sisters 1; Lay Teachers 19; Total Staff 32; Students 428.

MOUNT CARMEL. *Holy Spirit Consolidated School*, 250 West Ave., 17851. Tel: 717-339-3823. Sr. Mary Rene Procopio, Prin. Sisters 3; Lay Teachers 12; Students 245.

SHAMOKIN. *Queen of Peace Consolidated School*. (Grades PreK-8), 201 N. Shamokin St., 17872. Tel: 717-648-6672; 648-0182 (Convent). Sr. Ann McCurdy, Prin. Serves the parishes of St. Joseph, St. Stanislaus, St. Edwards, St. Mary, St. Michael, St. Stephen, Shamokin; Queen of the Most Holy Rosary, Elysburg; St. Anthony, Ranshaw; St. Mary, St. Casimir, Kulpmont; and St. Patrick, Trevorton. Sisters 6; Lay Teachers 19; Students 435.

[C] PRESCHOOLS AND DAY NURSERIES

MCSHERRYSTOWN. *St. Joseph Academy*. (Preschool), Main St., 17344. Tel: 717-637-2227. Sisters of St. Joseph. Sr. Alma Bernadette Hurley, S.S.J., Dir. Sisters 1; Students 30.

YORK. *Holy Child Nursery*, 1141 E. Market St., 17403. Tel: 717-848-1691. Daughters of Our Lady of Mercy. Sr. M. Clare, D.M., Admin. Sisters 5; Lay Aides 5; Students 65.

[D] RELIGIOUS RESOURCE CENTERS

CAMP HILL. *Trinity High School*, 17011. Tel: 717-761-1116; Fax: 717-761-7309.

COLUMBIA. *Religious Education Resource Center*, St. Joseph Convent, 3950 Columbia Ave., 17512-9714. Tel: 717-285-3217. Sr. Hilda Marie, A.S.C.

DANVILLE. *Villa Sacred Heart*, 17821-1698. Tel: 717-275-7513; Fax: 717-275-5997.

MCSHERRYSTOWN. *Delone Catholic High School*, 140 S. Oxford Ave., 17344. Tel: 717-632-7510. Religious Education Resource Center. Sr. Ann Vincentia Snyder, S.S.J.

[E] CATHOLIC CHARITIES COUNSELING & FIELD SERVICES

HARRISBURG. *Department for Catholic Charities Counseling/Field Services*, P.O. Box 3551, 17105.
Adoption Services, 4800 Union Deposit Rd., P.O. Box 3551, 17105. Tel: 717-657-4804. Kay Eisenhour, M.S.W., L.S.W., Prog. Dir.
Capital Region Office, 223 North St., 17101. Tel: 717-233-7978. Larry Belmont, M.S.W., District Dir.
Cenacle Youth Shelter, 1611 Boas St., 17103. Tel: 717-236-8211. Tim Wolfe, B.A., Prog. Dir.
Evergreen House and Day Care Program, 100 Evergreen St., 17104. Tel: 717-238-6343. Program Directors: Willamae Williams; Sr. Marie Aimee Finnegan, R.S.M.
Specialized Foster Care, 806-C South 29th St., 17111. Tel: 717-654-7115. Nancy Jamison, M.S.W., Prog. Dir.
Immigration and Refugee Services, 900 N. 17th St., 17103. Tel: 717-232-0568. Beverly Smith, Ed.D., Prog. Dir.
Interfaith Shelter for Homeless Families, Harrisburg St. Hospital, Hemlock Bldg. #26, 17105. Tel: 717-236-6783. Debra Strohecker, M.S., Prog. Dir.
Lourdeshouse Maternity Services, 100 B. Livingston St., Enhaut, 17113. Tel: 717-986-9510. Deborah Weik, Prog. Dir.
Paradise School, R.D. 1, Box 341, Abbottstown, 17301. Tel: 717-259-9537. Michael Langley, M.S., Prog. Dir.
Chambersburg Office, 336 Philadelphia Ave., Chambersburg, 17201. Tel: 717-263-3765. Carolyn George, M.Div., District Dir.
Chambersburg Family Outreach, 336 Philadelphia Ave., Chambersburg, 17201. Tel: 717-264-2332. Wendy Mellott, M.S., Prog. Dir.
Lancaster Office, 925 N. Duke St., Lancaster, 17602. Tel: 717-299-3659. Kirk Reider, A.C.S.W., L.S.W., District Dir.
Intensive Day Treatment, 47 S. Mulberry St., Lancaster, 17603. Tel: 717-295-9630. Joe Paskovich, M.S., Prog. Dir.
Lancaster In-Home Intensive Services, 417 Poplar St., Lancaster, 17603. Tel: 717-392-3619. Chris Vandenberg, M.H.S., Prog. Dir.
Lebanon Office, 1431 Walnut St., Lebanon, 17042. Tel: 717-273-8514. Kirk Reider, A.C.S.W., L.S.W., District Dir.
Lebanon Family FOCUS, 1431 Walnut St., Lebanon, 17042. Tel: 717-273-3011. D.J. Dunlap, M.S.W., Prog. Dir.
Northern Office, 900 N. Shamokin St., Shamokin, 17872. Tel: 717-648-6431. Loretta Stefanovage, M.S.W., L.S.W., District Dir.
York Office, 253 E. Market St., York, 17403. Tel: 717-845-2696. Donna Dillon, M.S.W., District Dir.
York Intensive Family Services, 253 E. Market St., York, 17403. Tel: 717-845-2696. Connie Krout, M.H.S., Prog. Dir.
HOPE House, 1509 Cresent Ave., Lancaster, 17601. Tel: 717-293-9089. Judy Wendler, L.P.N.A.P., Coord. Total Assisted 600; Total Staff 6.

[F] GENERAL HOSPITALS

CAMP HILL. *Holy Spirit Hospital and Community Mental Health Center*, 503 N. 21st St., 17011-2288. Tel: 717-763-2100; Fax: 717-763-2183.
For a complete listing, refer to the Hospitals section.

LANCASTER. *St. Joseph Hospital*, 250 College Ave., P.O. Box 3509, 17604. Tel: 717-291-8211; Fax: 717-291-8516.
For a complete listing, refer to the Hospitals section.

[G] CONVALESCENT & RETIREMENT HOMES

HARRISBURG. *Villa Teresa Nursing Home*, 1051 Avila Rd., 17109. Tel: 717-652-5900; Fax: 717-652-5941.
For a complete listing, refer to the Special Care Facilities section.

COLUMBIA. *St. Anne's Home*, 3952 Columbia Ave., 17512-9715. Tel: 717-285-5443.
For a complete listing, refer to the Special Care Facilities section.

DANVILLE. *Holy Family Convent and Infirmary*, One Montour St., 17821. Tel: 717-275-3141.
For a complete listing, refer to the Special Care Facilities section.
Maria Hall, Maria Hall Dr., 17821. Tel: 717-275-1120.
For a complete listing, refer to the Special Care Facilities section.
Maria Joseph Manor, 875 Montour Blvd., 17821. Tel: 717-275-4221; Fax: 717-275-4711.
For a complete listing, refer to the Special Care Facilities section.

LEBANON. *Villa Vianney*, 915 S. Lincoln Ave., 17042. Tel: 717-273-1295.
For a complete listing, refer to the Special Care Facilities section.

YORK. *Misericordia Convalescent Home*, 998 S. Russell St., 17402. Tel: 717-755-1964.
For a complete listing, refer to the Special Care Facilities section.

[H] MONASTERIES AND RESIDENCES OF PRIESTS AND BROTHERS

EPHRATA. *St. Clement's Mission House*, P.O. Box 209, 17522-0209. Tel: 717-733-6596; Fax: 717-733-0502. Redemptorist Fathers and Brothers. Very Rev. Arthur P. Gildea, C.SS.R.; Revs. Edward W. Jackson, C.SS.R.; John J. Creaven, C.SS.R.; William F. Rosner, C.SS.R.; Patrick J. McGarrity, C.SS.R.; Gerard J. Szymkowiak, C.SS.R.; John J. Dorff, C.SS.R.; Daniel T. Bowen; John H. Wright.
Mission Preaching Band: Revs. Arthur J. Mahoney, C.SS.R.; John W. Kelly, C.SS.R.; Pasquale T. Tremonte, C.SS.R.

[I] CONVENTS AND RESIDENCES FOR SISTERS

HARRISBURG. *Bishops' Residence*, 4800-A Union Deposit Rd., 17105. Tel: 717-671-9323. Sr. M. Patricia Bonner, A.S.C., Supr. Adorers of the Blood of Christ 2.
Immaculate Heart of Mary Convent, 603 N. Second St., 17101. Tel: 717-236-4821. Sr. Regina M. Havens, I.H.M. Sisters, Servants of the Immaculate Heart of Mary 10.
St. Joseph Convent, 605 N. Second St., 17101. Tel: 717-232-0204. Sisters of Christian Charity. Sr. Mary Agnes Shurer, S.C.C., Supr. Total in Residence 6; Total Staff 6.
Saint Margaret Mary Convent, 2836 Herr St., 17103. Tel: 717-232-0204. Adorers of the Blood of Christ. Total in Residence 4; Total Staff 4.

COLUMBIA. *Adorers of the Blood of Christ*, 3950 Columbia Ave., 17512-9714. Tel: 717-285-4536; Fax: 717-285-9789. Motherhouse of the Adorers of the Blood of Christ. Sr. Agatha Marie Groft, A.S.C., Prov. Supr.; Rev. Francis B. Sullivan, C.PP.S., Chap.
The Precious Blood Spiritual Center, 3950 Columbia Ave., 17512-9714. Tel: 717-285-2215; Fax: 717-285-9789. S. Constance Sophy, R.S.M., Dir. Provincial Sisters 85.

DANVILLE. *Villa Sacred Heart*, 17821-1698. Tel: 717-275-3581; 275-4929; Fax: 717-275-5997. Motherhouse of the Sisters of SS. Cyril and Methodius. Sr. M. Paracleta Amrich, SS.C.M., Gen. Supr.; Rev. Frederick A. Farace, Chap. Sisters 42.
Villa Sacred Heart Novitiate. Tel: 717-275-3702. Sr. Jeanne Ambre, SS.C.M., Dir.
Villa Sacred Heart Music Conservatory, 17821-1698. Tel: 717-275-5185. Sr. M. Michaelette, SS.C.M.
Villa Preschool and Kindergarten, 17821-1698. Tel: 717-275-1667; 275-7513 (Religious Education Resource Center). This building houses the Diocesan Religious Education Resources Center. Sr. M. Michaelette, SS.C.M., Prin.; Sr. Virginia Zapotocky, SS.C.M., Dir.

ELYSBURG. *Carmelite Monastery*, 70 Monastery Rd., 17824-9697. Tel: 717-672-2935. Discalced Carmelite Nuns. Sr. Christine O'Brien, O.C.D., Prioress. Nuns in Solemn Vows 18.

LANCASTER. *Monastery of the Dominican Nuns of the Perpetual Rosary*, 1834 Lititz Pike, 17601-6585. Tel: 717-569-2104. Mother Mary Veronica, O.P., Prioress; Rev. Francis R. Mullin, O.P., Chap. Solemnly Professed Nuns 13; Novices 2; Postulants 1.
St. Francis Convent, 903 W. Walnut St., 17603. Tel: 717-392-1740. Sisters of St. Francis of Philadelphia 5.

LEBANON. *Assumption-Hill Convent*, 1430 Chestnut St., 17042. Tel: 717-272-8262. Sr. S. Loretta Marchetti, S.S.J., Supr. Sisters of St. Joseph 6.

MCSHERRYSTOWN. *Annunciation Convent*, 9 N. Third St., 17344. Tel: 717-632-3123.

[J] QUASI-PARISHES

LANCASTER. *Iglesia de San Juan Bautista*, 425 S. Duke St., 17602. Tel: 717-392-4118. Very Rev. Bernardo Pistone, Diocesan Vicar for the Hispanics; Rev. Ignacio Palomino; Deacons Expedito Santos; Manuel Velazquez; Felix Ramos.

[K] NEWMAN CENTERS

HARRISBURG. *Catholic Campus Ministry*, P.O. Box 3557, 17105. Tel: 717-657-4804. Very Rev. Joseph F. Gotwalt, Coord.
Lebanon Valley College, 125 S. Spruce St., Annville, 17003. Tel: 717-867-1525. Rev. John D. Hoke.
Bloomsburg University of Pennsylvania, 353 College Hill, Bloomsburg, 17815. Tel: 717-784-3123. Rev. Lawrence J. McNeil; Anita McGowan.
Dickinson School of Law, 140 E. Pomfret St., Carlisle, 17013. Tel: 717-243-4411. Rev. Joseph T. Scanlin.
Wilson College Chambersburg, 320 Philadelphia Ave., Chambersburg, 17201. Rev. Msgr. Thomas R. Brenner. Tel: 717-264-6317.

Elizabethtown College, Park St. & Cherry Ave., Elizabethtown, 17022. Tel: 717-367-1255. Rev. Joseph D. Blascovich.
Gettysburg College, 12 E. Hanover St., Gettysburg, 17325-0136. Tel: 717-334-2510. Rev. Brian Conrad.
Hershey Medical Center, 359 W. Areba Ave., 17033. Tel: 717-533-7168. Rev. Stephen D. Weitzel.
Franklin and Marshall College, Lancaster, 227 N. George St., Millersville, 17551. Tel: 717-291-3880. Mr. Richard Groff.
Bucknell University, Newman Center, 610 St. George St., Lewisburg, 17837. Tel: 717-524-7951. Rev. John J. Kelly, O.S.F.S.
Penn State University, Harrisburg Campus, 401 Conewago St., Middletown, 17057. Tel: 717-944-3133.
Millersville University, Newman Center, 227 N. George St., Millersville, 17551. Tel: 717-872-3350. Rev. William C. Forrey.
Susquehanna University Catholic Campus Ministry, 610 University Ave., Selinsgrove, 17870. Tel: 717-374-4113. Rev. Joseph A. Celia.
Shippensburg University, 305 N. Prince St., Shippensburg, 17257. Tel: 717-532-1244. Rev. Lawrence Sherdel.
Penn State University, Mont Alto Campus, South Mountain, Campus Ministry Office, Mont Alto, 17237. Tel: 717-749-6135. Roxanne Dennis.
Penn State University, York Campus, 850 E. Princess St., York, 17403. Tel: 717-848-1797. Rev. Carl Tancredi, D.Min.
York College, 950 W. Market St., York, 17404. Tel: 717-846-4935. Rev. Carl Tancredi, D.Min.

[L] MISCELLANEOUS LISTINGS

HARRISBURG. *Pennsylvania Catholic Conference*, 223 North St., P.O. Box 2835, 17105. Tel: 717-238-9613; Fax: 717-238-1473.
Pennsylvania Catholic Health Association, 223 North St., P.O. Box 2835, 17105. Tel: 717-238-9613; Fax: 717-238-1473. Sr. Clare Christi Schiefer, O.S.F., Pres.

LANCASTER. *Neumann Services, Inc.*, 830 Marietta Ave., 17603. Tel: 717-291-8395. Miss Karen M. Leque, Dir.

SHIREMANSTOWN. *Trinity Spiritual Center*, 3609 Simpson Ferry Rd., 17011. Tel: 717-761-7355. Mrs. Mary Ann O'Donnell, Admin.; Mrs. Esther Fitzgerald, Facility Mgr. Total in Residence 1; Total Staff 3.

RELIGIOUS INSTITUTES OF MEN REPRESENTED IN THE DIOCESE

For further details refer to the corresponding bracketed number in the Religious Institutes of Men or Women section.

[0200]—*Benedictine Monks*.—O.S.B.
[0470]—*The Capuchin Friars*.—O.F.M.Cap.
[0480]—*Conventual Franciscans*. (Buffalo, NY).—O.F.M.Conv.
[0650]—*Holy Ghost Fathers*. (Eastern Prov.).—C.S.Sp.
[0690]—*Jesuit Fathers and Brothers*.—S.J.
[1120]—*Missionaries of the Sacred Hearts of Jesus and Mary*.—M.SS.CC.
[0910]—*Oblates of Mary Immaculate*. (Boston, MA).—O.M.I.
[0920]—*Oblates of St. Francis De Sales*. (American Prov.).—O.S.F.S.
[0430]—*Order of Preachers (Dominicans)*.—O.P.
[1070]—*Redemptorist Fathers*. (Baltimore Prov.).—C.SS.R.
[0700]—*St. Joseph's Society of the Sacred Heart*.—S.S.J.
[1060]—*Society of the Precious Blood*. (Cincinnati Prov.).—C.PP.S.
[0560]—*Third Order Regular of Saint Francis*. (Prov. of the Most Sacred Heart).—T.O.R.

RELIGIOUS INSTITUTES OF WOMEN REPRESENTED IN THE DIOCESE

[0100]—*Adorers of the Blood of Christ*.—A.S.C.
[1810]—*Bernardine Sisters of the Third Order of St. Francis*.—O.S.F.
[1920]—*Congregation of the Sisters of Holy Cross*.—C.S.C.
[0890]—*Daughters of Our Lady of Mercy*.—D.M.
[0420]—*Discalced Carmelite Nuns*.—O.C.D.
[1050]—*Dominican Contemplative Nuns*.—O.P.
[1170]—*Felician Sisters*.—C.S.S.F.
[1470]—*Franciscan Sisters of St. Joseph*.—F.S.S.J.
[2575]—*Institute of the Sisters of Mercy of the Americas*.—R.S.M.
[2970]—*School Sisters of Notre Dame*.—S.S.N.D.
[0660]—*Sisters of Christian Charity*.—S.C.C.
[3780]—*Sisters of Saints Cyril and Methodius*.—SS.C.M.
[1650]—*The Sisters of St. Francis of Philadelphia*.—O.S.F.
[3830-13]—*Sisters of St. Joseph*.—C.S.J.
[2110]—*Sisters of the Humility of Mary*.—H.M.
[2170]—*Sisters, Servants of the Immaculate Heart of Mary*.—I.H.M.

NECROLOGY

† Adams, Rev. Msgr. Donald E., (On Special Assignment). —Died April 18, 1996.
† Barrett, Michael F., Lancaster, PA, St. Joseph Church. —Died Nov. 1, 1996.
† D'Alessandro, Patrick A., (Retired). —Died April 28, 1996.

Archdiocese of Hartford

(Archidioecesis Hartfortiensis)

Most Reverend

DANIEL A. CRONIN, S.T.D.

Archbishop of Hartford; ordained December 20, 1952; appointed Titular Bishop of Egnatia and Auxiliary Bishop of Boston June 10, 1968; consecrated September 12, 1968; transferred to Fall River October 30, 1970; installed December 16, 1970; transferred to Hartford December 10, 1991; installed January 28, 1992. *Office: 134 Farmington Ave., Hartford, CT, 06105-3784.* Tel.: 860-541-6491; Fax: 860-541-6293.

Most Reverend

PETER A. ROSAZZA, D.D., V.G.

Auxiliary Bishop of Hartford and Titular Bishop of Oppido Nuovo; ordained June 29, 1961; appointed February 28, 1978; consecrated June 24, 1978. *Office & Res.: 1450 Chapel St., New Haven, CT, 06511.* Tel.: 203-789-5970.

Chancery Office: 134 Farmington Ave., Hartford, CT, 06105-3784. Tel.: 860-541-6491; Fax: 860-541-6309.

ESTABLISHED NOVEMBER 28, 1843.

CREATED ARCHDIOCESE AUGUST 6, 1953.

Square Miles 2,288.

Corporate Title: *"The Hartford Roman Catholic Diocesan Corporation."*

Comprises the Counties of Hartford, Litchfield and New Haven in the State of Connecticut.

For legal titles of parishes and archdiocesan institutions, consult the Chancery Office.

STATISTICAL OVERVIEW

Personnel	
Archbishop	1
Auxiliary Bishops	1
Priests: Diocesan Active in Diocese	332
Priests: Active Outside Diocese	15
Priests: Diocesan in Foreign Missions	1
Priests: Retired, Sick or Absent	84
Number of Diocesan Priests	432
Religious Priests in Diocese	146
Extern Priests in Diocese	21
Ordinations:	
Diocesan Priests	4
Religious Priests	1
Transitional Deacons	2
Permanent Deacons in Diocese	333
Total Brothers	78
Total Sisters	1,069
Parishes	
Parishes	222
With Resident Pastor:	
Resident Diocesan Priests	197
Resident Religious Priests	17
Without Resident Pastor:	
Administered by Priests	8
Missions	4
Closed Parishes	1
Professional Ministry Personnel:	
Brothers	6
Sisters	59
Lay Ministers	98
Welfare	
Catholic Hospitals	3
Total Assisted	498,190
Homes for the Aged	8
Total Assisted	999
Residential Care of Children	2
Total Assisted	164
Day Care and Extended Day Care Centers	10
Total Assisted	894
Specialized Homes	2
Total Assisted	1,168
Special Centers for Social Services	6
Total Assisted	37,401
Residential Care of Disabled	1
Total Assisted	23
Other Institutions	1
Total Assisted	245
Educational	
Seminaries, Diocesan	1
Diocesan Students in Other Seminaries	21
Seminaries, Religious	1
Students Religious	123
Total Seminarians	144
Colleges and Universities	3
Total Students	2,833
High Schools, Diocesan and Parish	4
Total Students	1,751
High Schools, Private	7
Total Students	3,116
Elementary Schools, Diocesan and Parish	70
Total Students	19,183
Elementary Schools, Private	3
Total Students	388
Catechesis/Religious Education:	
High School Students	8,827
Elementary Students	47,744
Total Students Under Catholic Instruction	83,986
Teachers in the Diocese:	
Priests	5
Brothers	8
Sisters	117
Lay Teachers	1,181
Vital Statistics	
Receptions into the Church:	
Infant Baptism Totals	11,561
Adult Baptism Totals	373
Received into Full Communion	489
First Communions	10,133
Confirmations	6,738
Marriages:	
Catholic	3,175
Interfaith	692
Total Marriages	3,867
Deaths	8,779
Total Catholic Population	778,856
Total Population	1,814,610

Former Bishops—Rt. Rev. WILLIAM TYLER, D.D., first Bishop; cons. March 17, 1844; died June 18, 1849.—Rt. Rev. BERNARD O'REILLY, D.D., second Bishop; cons. Nov. 10, 1850 perished at sea, Jan., 1856.—Rt. Rev. FRANCIS P. MCFARLAND, D.D., third Bishop; cons. March 14, 1858; died Oct. 12, 1874.—Rt. Rev. THOMAS GALBERRY, D.D., fourth Bishop; cons. March 19, 1876; died Oct. 10, 1878.—Rt. Rev. LAWRENCE S. MCMAHON, D.D., fifth Bishop; cons. Aug. 10, 1879; died Aug. 21, 1893.—Rt. Rev. MICHAEL TIERNEY, D.D., sixth Bishop; cons. Feb. 22, 1894; died Oct. 5, 1908.—Most Rev. JOHN J. NILAN, D.D., seventh Bishop; cons. April 28, 1910; died April 13, 1934.—Most Rev. MAURICE F. MCAULIFFE, D.D., eighth Bishop; ord. July 29, 1900; appt. Auxiliary to the Bishop of Hartford, Dec. 17, 1925; cons. April 28, 1926; appt. Bishop of Hartford, April 25, 1934; installed May 29, 1934; died Dec. 15, 1944.—Most Rev. HENRY J. O'BRIEN, D.D., ninth Bishop, first Archbishop; ord. July 8, 1923; appt. Titular Bishop of Sita and Auxiliary to Bishop of Hartford, March 19, 1940; cons. May 14, 1940; appt. Bishop of Hartford, April 7, 1945; appt. Archbishop of Hartford, Aug. 6, 1953; appt. at Pontifical Throne, April 29, 1955; resigned and appt. Titular Archbishop of Utina, Nov. 20, 1968 Given title "Former Archbishop of Hartford", Nov. 14, 1970; died July 23, 1976.—Most Rev. JOHN F. WHEALON, D.D., S.T.L., S.S.L., tenth Bishop, second Archbishop; ord. May 26, 1945; appt. Titular Bishop of Andrapa and Auxiliary of Cleveland, June 2, 1961; cons. July 6, 1961; appt. Bishop of Erie, Nov. 30, 1966; installed March 7, 1967; appt. Archbishop of Hartford, Dec. 28, 1968; installed March 19, 1969; died Aug. 2, 1991.

Vicar General—Most Rev. PETER A. ROSAZZA, D.D.

Episcopal Vicars—Hartford Vicariate: Rev. Msgr. CHRISTIE A. MACALUSO, New Haven Vicariate: Rev. Msgr. JAMES G. COLEMAN, Waterbury Vicariate: Rev. Msgr. JOSEPH A. DEVINE.

Chancery Office—134 Farmington Ave., Hartford, 06105-3784. Tel: 860-541-6491; Fax: 860-541-6293 (Bishop's Office); Fax: 860-541-6309 (Chancery). All applications for dispensations and correspondence on diocesan business should be sent to this address. Office Hours: Mon.-Fri. 8:30-4:30.

Moderator of the Curia / Chancellor—Rev. Msgr. DANIEL J. PLOCHARCZYK.

Canonical Advisor to the Moderator of the Curia / Chancellor—Rev. ROBERT B. VARGO, J.C.L.

Archbishop's Delegate for Special Needs—Sr. HELEN MARGARET FEENEY, C.S.J.

Chief Financial Officer—MICHAEL R. ST. DENIS C.P.A.

Accounts Manager—THERESA MROCZKOWSKI.
Accounts Payable—ROBERT D. NEWBERY.
Accounts Receivable—MARIE C. LUTHER.
Group Benefits—KATHLEEN A. ANDERSON.
Archivist—Sr. MARJORIE FALLON, R.S.M.
Historians—Sr. DOLORES LIPTAK, R.S.M., Ph.D.; JOSEPH W. DUFFY.
Secretary to the Archbishop—Rev. Msgr. THOMAS M. GINTY.
Metropolitan Tribunal—134 Farmington Ave., Hartford, 06105-3784. Tel: 860-541-6491.
Judicial Vicar (Officialis)—Rev. JOHN J. MCCARTHY, J.C.L., J.D.
Adjutant Judicial Vicar (Vice Officialis)—Rev. ALVIN J. LEBLANC, J.C.L.
Defenders of the Bond—Revs. CHRISTOPHER M. FORD, J.C.L.; ROBERT B. VARGO, J.C.L.
Promoter of Justice—Rev. ROBERT B. VARGO, J.C.L.
Judges—Rev. Msgr. WILLIAM J. MULLEN, J.C.D.; Revs. LAWRENCE G. WRENN, J.C.D.; JAMES F. KINNANE, J.C.L.; THOMAS J. BARRY, J.C.L.; MICHAEL H. GOSSELIN, S.T.M., J.C.L.
Case Instructors (part-time)—Revs. LAWRENCE R. BOCK; BRADFORD COLTON; WILLIAM E. DUDACK; JOHN F. EDWARDS; RONALD A. FERRARO; GENE E. GIANELLI; VITTORIO GUERRERA; BERNARD KILLEEN; LEONARD KVEDAS; THOMAS E. PTASZYNSKI; THOMAS J. SAS; BRIAN A. SHAW; RONALD T. SMITH; ADAM C. SUBOCZ; ROBERT F. TUCKER; WILLIAM C. WHALEN; PETER J. ZIZKA; Deacon PAUL B. LAUER; Sr. IRENE FORTIER, D.H.S.; Mr. ANTHONY SYLVESTER; Ms. DIAN GRANT.
Secretary—CAROLE BERTRAND.
College of Consultors—Most Rev. PETER A. ROSAZZA, D.D., V.G.; Rev. Msgr. DANIEL J. PLOCHARCZYK; Rev. Msgr. JOSEPH A. DEVINE; Revs. CHRISTOPHER M. TIANO; HOWARD M. NASH; EDMUND M. O'BRIEN; WILLIAM P. PRZYBYLO.
Deans—Hartford Vicariate: Farmington Valley: Rev. LAWRENCE R. BOCK, New Britain: Rev. FRANCIS T. CARTER, Hartford: Rev. NICHOLAS J. CESARO, Suburban Hartford: Rev. HENRY P. CODY, Manchester: Rev. JOHN S. GOLAS, Enfield: Rev. ROBERT T. RUSSO, New Haven Vicariate: Hamden-North Haven: Rev. DAVID J. BARANOWSKI, East Shore Line: Rev. VINCENT A. BROWN, Meriden: Rev. ARTHUR J. DUPONT, West Shore Line: Rev. THOMAS A. SIEVEL, New Haven: Rev. HOWARD J. NASH, Waterbury Vicariate: Suburban Waterbury: Rev. JOHN M. COONEY, Ansonia-Derby: Rev. LEONARD J. KVEDAS, Waterbury: Rev. JOSEPH E. LOONEY, Litchfield: Rev. JAMES F. PILON, Bristol: Rev. ROBERT J. ROUSSEAU, Naugatuck-Cheshire: Rev. PHILIP A. SHERIDAN.
Ecumenical Affairs Commission for—Rev. KENNETH H. SHINER, Ecumenical Officer, *St. Elizabeth Rectory, 65 Burban Dr., Branford, 06405.* Tel: 203-488-1661.
Evangelization Office—Rev. MICHAEL J. MOTTA, Dir., *650 Willard Ave., Newington, 06111.* Tel: 860-667-0891.
Holy Childhood Association—Rev. BRIAN W. MONNERAT, Dir., *467 Bloomfield Ave., Bloomfield, 06002.* Tel: 860-243-9184; Fax: 860-243-9460.
Office for Divine Worship—Rev. Msgr. THOMAS M. GINTY, Dir. LUCY ZOCCO, Sec., *467 Bloomfield Ave., Bloomfield, 06002.* Tel: 203-242-4020.
Newspaper—"The Catholic Transcript"; Rev. CHRISTOPHER M. TIANO, Exec. Editor, *785 Asylum Ave., Hartford, 06105.* Tel: 860-527-1175; 1-800-726-2391; Fax: 860-947-NEWS (6397); Most Rev. DANIEL A. CRONIN, D.D., Pres. & Publisher; CAROLE CRONSELL, Business Mgr. DANA DREZEK, Asst. Editor; ROY J. ROWLAND, Advertising Mgr.
Office for AIDS Ministries—Sr. DOROTHY STRELCHUN, S.N.D.deN., *Catholic Charities, 467 Bloomfield Ave., Bloomfield, 06002-2999.* Tel: 860-242-9816.
Office for Black Catholics—Vacant Contact office of the Moderator of the Curia/Chancellor. *134 Farmingdale Ave., Hartford, 06105-3784.* Tel: 860-541-6491; Fax: 860-541-6309.
Office for Continuing Education of Priests—Rev. GERALD G. SCHMITZ, Dir., *134 Farmington Ave., Hartford.* Tel: 860-541-6491.
Office of Radio and Television—Rev. JOHN P. GATZAK, Exec. Dir., *785 Asylum Ave., Hartford, 06105.* Tel: 860-246-7295; Fax: 860-246-9455.
Office of Family Life, Marriage and Family Apostolate—Co-Dirs.: DONALD PAGLIA; CHRISTINE PAGLIA, *412 Ridge Rd., Hamden, 06517.* Tel: 203-230-2460; Fax: 203-230-2472.
Archbishop's Annual Appeal—Rev. DOUGLAS P. CLANCY, Exec. Dir. BERNADETTE EGAN, Sec., *134 Farmington Ave., Hartford.* Tel: 860-541-6268; Fax: 860-541-6289.
Office of Religious Education (CCD)—Rev. MICHAEL J. MOTTA, Dir., *650 Willard Ave., Newington, 06111.* Tel: 860-667-0891; Fax: 860-667-2595.
Priests Eucharistic League—Rev. THOMAS E. MCCARTHY, Dir., *St. Ann, 289 Arch Rd., Avon, 06001.* Tel: 860-673-9858.
Commission for Priests' Retreats—Revs. FREDERICK M. ANIELLO, Chm. TERENCE KRISTOFAK, C.P.; GERARD G. SCHMITZ; DANIEL JEREMIAH SULLIVAN.
Office of Ministry for Priests—Rev. JOHN P. CONTE, Minister for Priests, *St. Thomas Seminary, 467 Bloomfield Ave., Bloomfield, 06002.* Tel: 860-286-8644.
Mission Cooperative Planning Office—Sr. HELEN MARGARET FEENEY, C.S.J., *Chancery, 134 Farmington Ave., Hartford, 06105-3784.* Tel: 860-541-6491.
Pro-Life Activities—Rev. JAMES J. CRONIN, Dir., *70 Gulf St., P.O. Box 230, Milford, 06460-0230.* Tel: 203-878-3571.
Propagation of the Faith, Society for—(The Catholic Mission Aid Society of Hartford)—Rev. BRIAN W. MONNERAT, Dir., *467 Bloomfield Ave., Bloomfield, 06002.* Tel: 860-243-9184; Fax: 860-243-9460.
Radio Apostolate—Radio Station WJMJ—JOHN L. ELLINGER, Station Mgr., *467 Bloomfield Ave., Bloomfield, 06002.* Tel: 860-242-8800. Licensed by St. Thomas Seminary, Bloomfield. (Hartford).
Office of Catholic Schools—Rev. ZIGFORD J. KRISS, Supt.; Dr. JOSEPH A. BOUND, Asst. Supt., Spec. Svcs. and Secondary Schools; Sr. LORETTA FRANCIS MANN, O.S.F., Asst. Supt., Elementary Education; JEANNINE V. DASH, Dir., Devel., *467 Bloomfield Ave., Bloomfield, 06002.* Tel: 860-242-4362; Fax: 860-242-8683.
Diocesan Labor Institute—Rev. DANIEL E. JOHNSON, Dir., *115 Pond Hill Rd., Wallingford, 06492.* Tel: 203-265-1694.
Social Service—PATRICK J. JOHNSON, Dir., *467 Bloomfield Ave., Bloomfield, 06002.* Tel: 860-242-9577.
Office for Catholic Relief Services—PATRICK J. JOHNSON, Coord., *467 Bloomfield Ave., Bloomfield, 06002.* Tel: 860-242-9577.
Vocations—Rev. JOHN J. DIETRICH, Dir., *St. Thomas Seminary, 469 Bloomfield Ave., Bloomfield, 06002.* Tel: 860-286-7670.
Office of the Permanent Diaconate—Deacon JOSEPH G. GABRIELE, Dir., *467 Bloomfield Ave., Bloomfield, 06002.* Tel: 860-243-8005.
Office for Religious—Rev. JAMES F. KINNANE, Vicar, *134 Farmington Ave., Hartford, 06105-3784.* Tel: 860-541-6491.
Office of Vicar For Priests—Rev. Msgr. CHARLES B. JOHNSON, *467 Bloomfield Ave., Bloomfield, 06002.* Tel: 860-242-2510.
Censor Librorum—Rev. DAVID Q. LIPTAK.

Archdiocesan Offices and Directors

Archdiocesan Dispute Resolution Office—Rev. Msgr. DANIEL J. PLOCHARCZYK, Moderator of the Curia/ Chancellor, *134 Farmington Ave., Hartford, 06105-3784.* Tel: 860-541-6491.
Archdiocesan Office of Urban Affairs—P. JOSEPH SMYTH, Exec. Dir., *81 Saltonstall Ave., New Haven, 06513.* Tel: 203-777-7279; Fax: 203-776-3233.
Pastoral Hispana (Hispanic Pastoral Office)—Sr. ROSAMARIE ELIAS, M.S.B.T., Centro de Evangelizacion, *467 Bloomfield Ave., Bloomfield, 06002.* Tel: 860-243-0940; 243-3083.
Cana Conferences—DONALD PAGLIA; CHRISTINE PAGLIA, *412 Ridge Rd., Hamden, 06517.* Tel: 203-230-2460; Fax: 203-230-2472.
Catholic Cemeteries Association—Rev. DAVID M. WALKER, Dir. ROBERT S. MAREK, Exec. Dir., *700 Middletown Ave., P.O. Box 517, North Haven, 06473-0517.* Tel: 203-239-2557; Fax: 203-239-5035.
Catholic Deaf Apostolate—Rev. ROBERT D. BERGIN, Dir.; Sr. MAURA JOSEPH, R.S.M., Coord., *243 Steele Rd., W. Hartford, 06117.* Tel: 860-523-7530 (TDD or Voice); 236-3503.
Catholic Library and Information Center—Rev. EDWARD J. MCLEAN, Dir., *125 Market St., Hartford, 06103.* Tel: 860-522-0602; 246-5628; 800-308-3300; Fax: 860-247-3490.
Connecticut Catholic Conference—Rev. THOMAS J. BARRY, J.C.L., Exec. Dir., *134 Farmington Ave., Hartford, 06105-3784.* Tel: 860-524-7882; Fax: 860-525-0750.
Office for People with Disabilities—GEORGE DUCHARME, Ph.D., Dir.; MARY ANN LANGTON, Co-Dir., *467 Bloomfield Ave., Bloomfield, 06002.* Tel: 860-242-3304; Fax: 860-521-3688.
Small Christian Communities—Bro. ROBERT K. MORIARTY, S.M., Coord., *467 Bloomfield Ave., Bloomfield, 06002.* Tel: 860-243-9642; Fax: 860-242-4886.
Cursillo Movement, Archdiocesan Director of—Rev. JOHN M. COONEY, Dir., *St. John the Evangelist, 21 Academy Hill, Watertown, 06795-2101.* Tel: 860-274-8836.
Computer Services, Ministry of—Rev. EUGENE J. CHARMAN, Archdiocesan Consultant, *Computer Learning Center, 50 Knowles Ave., P.O. Box 455, Plantsville, 06479.* Tel: 860-628-7385; Fax: 860-276-0722.

CLERGY, PARISHES, MISSIONS AND PAROCHIAL SCHOOLS

CITY OF HARTFORD
(Hartford County)

1—CATHEDRAL OF ST. JOSEPH (1872), Rev. Msgr. Christie A. Macaluso; Rev. Dennis J. Vincenzo. In res., Rev. John J. McCarthy.
Res., 140 Farmington Ave., 06105-3783. Tel: 860-249-8431; Fax: 860-249-5910.
School—Cathedral Regional, 809 Asylum Ave., 06105. Tel: 860-522-2678. Sr. Carol Kozek, S.N.D., Prin.
Sisters of Mercy 1; Lay Teachers 13; Students 203.

2—HOLY TRINITY (1900) (Lithuanian), Rev. Christopher M. Tiano, Admin.
Res., 53 Capitol Ave., 06106-1798. Tel: 860-246-4162.

3—IMMACULATE CONCEPTION (1899), Revs. James M. Weeks, M.S., Co-Pastor; James Aherne, M.S., Co-Pastor; Bros. Benedict Roy, S.C.; Marcus Turcotte, S.C.; Deacons Carmelo Hernandez; Adolfo G. Carrero.
Res., 574 Park St., Box 6610, 06106. Tel: 860-525-1522; Fax: 860-728-6995.
Catechesis/Religious Programs—Tel: 860-525-1522; Fax: 860-728-6995.
Students 245.

4—OUR LADY OF FATIMA (1957) (Portuguese), Revs. Jose D. Silva; Rui M. Carrico.
Res., Fatima Sq., 06106-2042. Tel: 860-236-1443.

5—OUR LADY OF SORROWS (1895), Revs. Joseph M. O'Neil, M.S., Co-Pastor; Francis C. Cooney, M.S., Co-Pastor; Deacons Domingo Delgado; Rafael Lopez; Peter J. Klimanowski. In res., Rev. Stephen G. Dressell, M.S.
Res., 16 Greenwood St., 06106-2109. Tel: 860-233-4424; Fax: 860-236-0149.
Church—79 New Park Ave., 06106-2109. Tel: 860-233-4424.
Catechesis/Religious Programs—Students 79.

6—SACRED HEART (1872) (Spanish), Revs. Albert Zanatta, C.R.S., Admin.; Franco Cecchini, C.R.S.; Deacons Isidro DeJesus; Edwin Ortiz.
Res., 49 Winthrop St., 06103-1030. Tel: 860-527-6459; Fax: 860-527-6450.
Catechesis/Religious Programs—Tel: 860-527-6459; Fax: 860-527-6450.
Students 165.

7—ST. ANNE (1889) (French), Revs. James Weeks, M.S., Co-Pastor; James Aherne, M.S., Co-Pastor.
Res., 820 Park St., 06106-2388. Tel: 860-728-7445.

8—ST. AUGUSTINE (1902), Revs. Nicholas J. Cesaro; Charles E. Jacobs; Deacons Jose A. Morales; John F. Dempsey.
Res., 10 Campfield Ave., 06114-1800. Tel: 860-522-7128; Fax: 860-246-1753.
School—20 Clifford St., 06114. Tel: 860-249-5661. Sr. Joan Crowley, C.S.J., Prin.
Priests 1; Sisters 4; Brothers 1; Lay Teachers 15; Students 366.
Catechesis/Religious Programs—Tel: 860-249-3430.
Students 100.

9—SS. CYRIL AND METHODIUS (1902) (Polish), Revs. William P. Przybylo; Kazimierz Heisig (Poland); Ronald P. Zepecki.
Res., 55 Charter Oak Ave., 06106-1998. Tel: 860-522-9157.
School—35 Groton St., 06106. Tel: 860-522-8490.
Sisters 5; Lay Teachers 8; Students 200.
Catechesis/Religious Programs—Tel: 860-522-8490.
Students 220.
Convent—45 Groton St., 06106. Tel: 860-527-3775. Felician Sisters

10—ST. JUSTIN (1924) (African American), Rev. Michael C. DeVito. In res., Rev. John P. Hannon.
Res., 230 Blue Hills Ave., 06112-1836. Tel: 860-246-6897.

11—ST. LAWRENCE O'TOOLE (1885), Revs. John P. Tracy; Paul F. Kenefick; Deacons Robert H. Godlewsky; Pedro S. Rivera.
Res., 494 New Britain Ave., 06106-3797. Tel: 860-522-1129; Fax: 860-549-4261.
Catechesis/Religious Programs—Tel: 860-522-1120; Fax: 860-549-4261.
Students 256.

12—ST. LUKE (1930), Rev. John J. Peruti; Deacon James E. Hickey, Jr. In res., Rev. Msgr. Charles W. Daly.
Res., 66 Bolton St., 06114. Tel: 860-296-8681.
Catechesis/Religious Programs—Students 143.

13—ST. MICHAEL (1900) (African American-Hispanic), Rev. Alfred J. Jaenicke; Deacon Valentine Perez, (Spanish Apostolate).

Res., 98 Capen St., 06120-2075. Tel: 860-522-6184; Fax: 860-278-8410.
Catechesis/Religious Programs—Tel: 860-522-6184; Fax: 860-278-8410.
Students 232.

14—ST. PATRICK-ST. ANTHONY (1829), Revs. Jerome Massimino, O.F.M.; John Ullrich, O.F.M.; John Murphy, O.F.M.; Andrew Giardino, O.F.M.; Cornelius Conti, O.F.M.; Bro. Kevin McGoff, O.F.M.; Sr. Regina Whalen, S.N.D., Pastoral Assoc.
Franciscan Center for Urban Ministry: 285 Church St., 06103. Tel: 860-246-6874; Fax: 860-249-6487.

15—ST. PETER (1859) (Irish), Rev. Michael S. Galasso; Deacon Bruce Thompson.
Res., 160 Main St., 06106-1894. Tel: 860-525-2683.
Catechesis/Religious Programs—Students 350.
Convent—11 Charter Oak Pl., 06106. Tel: 860-522-8428. Sisters of Mercy Mercedarian Missionary Sisters (Spanish).

OUTSIDE THE CITY OF HARTFORD

Ansonia, New Haven Co.,

1—ASSUMPTION, (1870), Team Ministry: Revs. George P. Burnett; Robert F. Condron; Deacons John F. Brady, Jr.; Joseph L. DiPiro; Robert C. Johnson. In res., Rev. Albert J. Zanavich.
Res., 61 N. Cliff St., 06401-1698. Tel: 203-735-7857; Fax: 203-734-5521.
School—Tel: 203-734-0855; Fax: 203-734-5521. Mrs. Kathleen Molner, Prin.
Lay Teachers 11; Students 275.
Catechesis/Religious Programs—51 N. Cliff St., 06401. Tel: 203-735-2701.
Students 255.

2—HOLY ROSARY, (1908) (Italian), Revs. Ronald L. Genua; Raymond F. Paul; Deacons Ralph A. Aconfora; Michael Impellitteri; Victor M. Lembo.
Res., Fr. Salemi Dr., 06401-2396. Tel: 203-735-7875; Fax: 203-732-2212.
Catechesis/Religious Programs—Tel: 203-736-0242. Sr. Carmela DiMauro, D.R.E.
Students 443.

3—ST. ANTHONY'S, (1915) (Lithuanian), Rev. Lee W. Hellwig, Admin.
Res., 199 N. Main St., 06401-1696. Tel: 203-734-4759.

4—ST. JOSEPH'S, (1925) (Polish), Revs. Marek W. Sobczak; Joseph Szpilski, C.M.
Res., 32 Jewett St., 06401-2499. Tel: 203-734-0402.
School—36 Jewett St., 06401. Tel: 203-734-3821. Sr. M. Adrianne, C.S.F.N., Prin.
Lay Teachers 10; Students 176.
Catechesis/Religious Programs—Students 89.
Convent—Tel: 203-736-9573. Sisters of the Holy Family of Nazareth

Avon, Hartford Co., St. Ann's (1917), Revs. Thomas E. McCarthy; Kevin G. Donovan; Deacons Donald L. Battiston; William A. Farrell; John E. Thayer; Alan D. Campbell.
Res., 289 Arch Rd., 06001-4209. Tel: 860-673-9858; Fax: 860-675-4350. [CEM]
Catechesis/Religious Programs—Tel: 860-673-2137; Fax: 860-675-4350. Patricia Piano, D.R.E.
Students 820.

Bantam, Litchfield Co., Our Lady of Grace (1949), Rev. John H. McCann, S.M.M., Admin.
Res., P.O. Box 427, Rte. 202, 06750. Tel: 203-567-9522. [CEM]
Catechesis/Religious Programs—Students 99.
Mission—Morris, Litchfield Co., Our Lady of Hope, Rte. 109, 06750. Tel: 860-567-5717.

Beacon Falls, New Haven Co., St. Michael's (1899), Rev. Leonard J. Kvedas; Deacon Frank J. Krasnicki. In res., Rev. James F. O'Dea.
Res., 25 Maple Ave., 06403-1145. Tel: 203-729-2504.
Catechesis/Religious Programs—Tel: 203-729-2504.
Students 307.

Bethlehem, Litchfield Co., Church of the Nativity (1921), Rev. Richard L. Shellman; Deacon William McGrath.
Res., 48 East St., Box 192, 06751-0192. Tel: 203-266-5211.
Catechesis/Religious Programs—Tel: 203-266-5212.
Students 202.

Bloomfield, Hartford Co., Christ the King (1936). Closed. For inquiries for parish records contact the Chancery.

Sacred Heart (1878), Revs. Joseph C. Gengras; Joseph V. DiSciacca; Bro. Paul Gauvin, S.C., Pastoral Assoc.; Sr. Rosemary Ryan, Pastoral Assoc.; Deacon Joseph Whittel.
Res., 25 Foothills Way, 06002-2488. Tel: 860-242-1942.
Church—26 Wintonbury Ave., 06002. Tel: 860-242-4142; Fax: 860-286-0044.
Catechesis/Religious Programs—Students 141.

Branford, New Haven Co., St. Elizabeth (1966), Rev. Kenneth H. Shiner; Deacon Joseph F. Coyne.
Res., 65 Burban Dr., 06405. Tel: 203-488-1661; Fax: 203-483-9248.
Catechesis/Religious Programs—Tel: 203-488-1661; Fax: 203-483-9248.
Students 240.

St. Mary (1868), Revs. Vincent A. Brown; Shawn T. Daly; Deacons Paul V. Prete; Robert P. Tartaris.
Res., 731 Main St., 06405-3693. Tel: 203-488-1607; Fax: 203-488-1608. [CEM 2]
School—(Grades PreK-8). Tel: 203-488-8386.
Lay Teachers 16; Students 277.
Catechesis/Religious Programs—Tel: 203-488-7412.
Students 741.

St. Therese (1947), Revs. Raymond J. Barry; Paul Shamsher; Deacons Paul C. Eschrich, (Retired); Gerald S. Walton.
Res., 82 Thimble Island Rd., 06405. Tel: 203-488-2998; Fax: 203-488-8542.
Catechesis/Religious Programs—Students 272.

Bristol, Hartford Co.,

1—ST. ANN, (1908) (French), Rev. Robert J. Rousseau; Deacons Joseph E. Levesque; Albert Lozier.
Res., 215 West St., 06010-5754. Tel: 860-582-8169; Fax: 860-585-7139.
Catechesis/Religious Programs—Tel: 860-582-3524. Carol Gignac, D.R.E.
Students 232.

2—ST. ANTHONY'S, (1920) (Italian), Revs. Nicholas P. Melo; Louis Paturzo; Deacon Laurent J. Cote.
Res., 111 School St., 06010-6078. Tel: 860-583-1349; Fax: 860-582-3861.
School—30 Pleasant St., 06010. Tel: 860-582-7874.
Lay Teachers 12; Students 275.
Catechesis/Religious Programs—20 Pleasant St., 06010. Tel: 860-583-4495.
Students 211.

3—ST. GREGORY'S, (1957), Revs. Charles R. Mullins; Joseph H. Keating; Daniel H. Connaghan; Deacon Roy Dungan.
Res. & Mailing Address: St. Gregory Rectory, Maltby St., 06010-3892. Tel: 860-589-2295; Fax: 860-589-6692.
Catechesis/Religious Programs—1043 Stafford Ave., 06010. Tel: 860-589-4232; Fax: 860-584-4786.
Students 1,112.

4—ST. JOSEPH, (1864), Revs. James F. Leary; Louis S. Paturzo; Deacon Robert M. Pallotti.
Res., 149 Goodwin St., 06010-5115. Tel: 860-583-1369; Fax: 860-583-1360. [CEM]
School—335 Center St., 06010. Tel: 860-582-8696. Mark J. Monnerat, Prin.
Lay Teachers 21; Students 447.
Catechesis/Religious Programs—Tel: 860-582-2888.
Students 355.

5—ST. STANISLAUS, (1919) (Polish), Rev. Brian A. Shaw; Rev. Msgr. John Wodarski, (Retired). In res., Rev. Lech Kuna (Poland).
Res., 510 West St., P.O. Box 1860, 06011-1860. Tel: 860-583-4242; Fax: 860-583-9464.
Catechesis/Religious Programs—Students 218.

Broad Brook, Hartford Co., St. Catherine's (1886), Rev. David Q. Liptak; Deacons Vincent Motto; John Abdalla.
Res., 6 Windsorville Rd., 06016-0359. Tel: 860-623-4636; Fax: 860-623-4636. [CEM]
Catechesis/Religious Programs—7 Rye St., 06016. Tel: 860-623-1974.
Students 393.

Canaan, Litchfield Co., St. Joseph's (1920), Rev. Francis T. Butler. In res., Rev. Michael A. Malley.
Res., 4 Main St., P.O. Box 845, 06018-2459. Tel: 860-824-7078; Fax: 860-824-7078. [CEM][JC]
Mission—Falls Village, Litchfield Co., St. Patrick, (1851) Beebe Hill Rd. [CEM][JC]
Catechesis/Religious Programs—Students 160.

Cheshire, New Haven Co., Church of the Epiphany (1967), Rev. Norman L. Brockett, Admin.; Deacons Vincent F. Cusano; Edward J. Pantalena.
Res., 1777 Old Waterbury Rd., 06410-1399. Tel: 203-272-4355.
Church & Parish Center—1750 Huckins Rd., 06410. Tel: 203-272-4355; Fax: 203-272-4878.
Catechesis/Religious Programs—Tel: 203-271-0112.
Students 213.

St. Bridget's (1871), Revs. James B. Gunnoud; John J. Cook, S.T.D., Pastor Emeritus; John K. Lynch; Deacons Wesley Baxter; Burdon Lowe.
Res., 175 Main St., 06410-2446. Tel: 203-272-3531; Fax: 203-271-3356. [CEM]
Parish Center—Tel: 203-271-9994.
Catechesis/Religious Programs—Tel: 203-272-6504.
Students 1,009.

St. Thomas Becket (1971), Rev. Kenneth J. Frisbie.
Res., 511 Sharon Dr., 06410-4244. Tel: 203-272-3324.
Catechesis/Religious Programs—Tel: 203-272-5777.
Students 460.

Collinsville, Hartford Co., St. Patrick's (1856), Rev. Ronald P. May, Admin.; Deacon Robert N. Blair.
Res., 7 Burlington Ave., P.O. Box 287, 06022-0287. Tel: 860-693-8727; Fax: 860-693-4538. [CEM][JC 2]
Catechesis/Religious Programs—Tel: 860-693-1068.
Students 356.

Cornwall Bridge, Litchfield Co., St. Bridget (1883), Rev. James F. Pilon.
Res., 7 River Rd., P.O. Box 52, 06754-1903. Tel: 203-672-6515. [CEM]

Derby, New Haven Co., St. Jude (1961), Rev. William J. Killeen; Deacon Robert Fitzgerald.
Res., 71 Pleasant View Rd., 06418-2455. Tel: 203-735-8725; Fax: 203-735-4402.
Catechesis/Religious Programs—Students 124.

St. Mary's (1851), Rev. James H. Smith; Deacon Frederick M. Grant.
Res., 212 Elizabeth St., 06418-1834. Tel: 203-735-3341; Fax: 203-736-6492.
School—St. Mary-St. Michael, (Grades K-8) St. Mary Campus, 14 Seymour Ave., P.O. Box 397, 06418. Tel: 203-735-6471.
Lay Teachers 13; Students 298.
Catechesis/Religious Programs—Students 151.

St. Michael (1905) (Polish), Revs. Ronald A. Wiktor, C.M.; Walenty Pieczka, C.M.; John Kuczynski, C.M.; Deacon Louis Canaveri.
Res., 75 Derby Ave., 06418-2098. Tel: 203-734-0005. [CEM]
School—St. Mary-St. Michael, (Grades 4-8) St. Michael Campus, 73 Derby Ave., P.O. Box 397, 06418. Tel: 203-734-2017.
Lay Teachers 14; Students 313.
Catechesis/Religious Programs—Students 124.

East Berlin, Hartford Co., Sacred Heart (1896), Rev. Thomas C. Culotta.
Res., 92 Oak Ridge Dr., Berlin, 06037-3712. Tel: 860-828-0154; Fax: 860-828-5305.
Church—66 Cottage St., 06023.
Catechesis/Religious Programs—Tel: 860-828-0519.
Students 240.

East Hartford, Hartford Co.,

1—BLESSED SACRAMENT, (1948), Rev. John A. Zalonis.
Res., 36 Cambridge Dr., 06118-2699. Tel: 860-568-2747.

2—OUR LADY OF PEACE, (1971), Rev. James J. Nock.
Res., 370 May Rd., 06118-3496. Tel: 860-568-4414.

3—ST. CHRISTOPHER, (1965), Revs. James G. Fanelli; William E. McGrath, Pastor Emeritus.
Res., 538 Brewer St., 06118-2399. Tel: 860-568-5240.
School—570 Brewer St., 06118. Tel: 860-568-4100. Sr. Valerie Noone, O.P., Prin.
Lay Teachers 14; Students 270.
Catechesis/Religious Programs—Students 325.

4—ST. ISAAC JOGUES, (1964), Rev. Emilio P. Padelli.
Res., 1 Community St., 06108-2808. Tel: 860-528-6749.
Catechesis/Religious Programs—Tel: 860-528-7976.
Students 127.

5—ST. MARY'S, (1873), Revs. Martin J. Scholsky; Frank E. Papa, S.O.L.T.; Deacon Ronald R. Daigle.
Res., 15 Maplewood Ave., 06108-4021. Tel: 860-289-7916.
Parish Center—30 Maplewood Ave., 06108. Tel: 860-289-7510.
Catechesis/Religious Programs—Tel: 860-528-3967; Fax: 860-289-3966.
Students 173.

6—ST. ROSE'S, (1920), Revs. Ronald J. Osborne; Robert P. Ricciardi; Deacon William J. Brown.
Res., 33 Church St., 06108-3794. Tel: 860-289-8616; Fax: 860-289-3966.
School—Tel: 860-528-4169; Fax: 860-528-4160.
Lay Teachers 13; Students 235.
Catechesis/Religious Programs—Tel: 860-528-3967.
Students 211.

East Haven, New Haven Co., Our Lady of Pompeii (1947), Revs. Dennis R. Hussey; Matthew R. Shanley; Deacons Nicholas DelCorte; Joseph LaPierre; Henry Lotto; Pasquale Villecco.
Res., Foxon Rd., 06513. Tel: 203-469-0764.
Catechesis/Religious Programs—Students 650.

St. Clare (1947), Rev. William A. Bray; Deacon Wayne E. Sandford.
Res., 234 Coe Ave., 06512-4112. Tel: 203-467-5136.
Catechesis/Religious Programs—Tel: 203-467-0600.
Students 335.

St. Vincent de Paul's (1915), Revs. Gary F. Simeone; Robert J. Burbank, Pastor Emeritus; Deacons Norman H. Singer; William Eyles.
Res., 80 Taylor Ave., 06512. Tel: 203-467-6394; Fax: 203-467-6716.
School—35 Bishop St., 06512. Tel: 203-467-1606; 467-1607; Fax: 203-467-8851.
Lay Teachers 11; Students 247.
Catechesis/Religious Programs—Students 589.

East Windsor, Hartford Co., St. Philip's (1959), Rev. Robert T. Russo.
Res., 150 S. Main St., 06088-9760. Tel: 860-623-0408; Fax: 860-623-8937.
Catechesis/Religious Programs—Students 108.

Enfield, Hartford Co.,

1—HOLY FAMILY, (1965), Rev. Francis T. Kerwan; Deacons Robert Linehan; Raymond J. McGivney; Donald H. Pond, Jr.; Arthur J. Dickman.
Res., 23 Simon Rd., 06082-5903. Tel: 860-741-2101.
Catechesis/Religious Programs—Tel: 860-745-1018. Elizabeth McGivney, D.R.E.
Students 1,031.

2—ST. ADALBERT'S, (1915) (Polish), Rev. Adam Subocz. In res., Rev. Anthony J. Bruno Tel: 860-745-9966.
Res., 90 Alden Ave., 06082-2865. Tel: 860-745-4837; Fax: 860-745-1787. [CEM]
School—Tel: 860-745-6135.
Sisters 1; Lay Teachers 11; Students 224.
Catechesis/Religious Programs—Students 94.
Convent—82 Alden Ave., 06082. Tel: 860-745-4169. Felician Sisters.

3—ST. BERNARD'S, (1870), Revs. Brian W. Monnerat; Dennis C. Gingras. In res., Rev. William F. O'Keefe; Deacons Joseph J.G. Mon; Hobart T. Stadtlander; Suzanne O. Cannon, Pastoral Assoc.
Res., 426 Hazard Ave., 06082-4719. Tel: 860-749-8353; Fax: 860-749-6456. [CEM]
School—Tel: 860-749-8182.
Sisters 3; Lay Teachers 18; Students 363.
Catechesis/Religious Programs—Tel: 860-749-2993.
Students 312.
Convent—376 Hazard Ave., 06082. Tel: 860-749-4214. Felician Sisters.

4—ST. MARTHA'S, (1961), Revs. John B. O'Connell; Stanley Smolenski; Deacons Rene Kieda; Robert Lambert; Robert Bernd.
Res., 214 Brainard Rd., 06082-2609. Tel: 860-745-5616.
School—Tel: 860-745-3833.
Felician Sisters 1; Lay Teachers 9; Students 260.
Catechesis/Religious Programs—Tel: 860-745-5616.
Students 325.

5—ST. PATRICK'S, (1866), Revs. Francis J. Browne, C.Ss.R.; Thomas G. Sullivan, C.Ss.R.; Sr. Mary O'Neill, R.S.M., Pastoral Assoc.; Deacon Joseph Sloan.
Res., 64 Pearl St., 06082-3594. Tel: 860-745-2411; Fax: 860-253-9483. [CEM]
Catechesis/Religious Programs—Tel: 860-741-0572.
Students 300.

Farmington, Hartford Co., St. Patrick's (1871), Revs. Thomas P. Quinn; James V. Hickey; Deacon Joseph E. Kane.
Res., 110 Main St., P.O. Box 523, 06034-0523. Tel: 860-677-2639.
Catechesis/Religious Programs—Students 618.

Forestville, Hartford Co., St. Matthew (1891), Revs. Robert J. Lysz; Joseph H. Pettit, Pastor Emeritus; Arthur J. Audet; Deacons John E. Pahl; Richard J. O'Day; Sr. Barbara Bamberger, I.H.M., Pastoral Assoc.
Res., 120 Church Ave., Box 9216, 06011-9216. Tel: 860-583-1833; Fax: 860-582-6152.
School—Welch Dr., 06010. Tel: 860-583-5214.
Sisters 6; Lay Teachers 9; Students 296.
Parish Resource Center—101 Church Ave., 06010. Tel: 860-583-1241.
Catechesis/Religious Programs—Tel: 860-583-7806.
Students 588.
Convent—119 Church Ave., 06010. Tel: 860-583-2004. Sisters, Servants of the Immaculate Heart of Mary.

Glastonbury, Hartford Co., St. Dunstan (1971), Rev. Thomas J. Barry; Deacon William J. Gilles.
Res., Manchester Rd., 06033-2604. Tel: 860-633-3317; Fax: 860-659-8611.
Catechesis/Religious Programs—Tel: 860-633-6876; Fax: 860-659-8611.
Students 641.

St. Paul's (1954), Revs. L. Randall Blackall; John P. Gwozdz; Deacon John W. McKaig.
Res., 2577 Main St., 06033-2023. Tel: 860-633-9419; Fax: 860-633-0040.
Catechesis/Religious Programs—Tel: 860-659-3029; Fax: 860-633-0040. Joan Flannery, D.R.E.
Students 698.

Goshen, Litchfield Co., St. Thomas of Villanova (1880), Rev. Raymond G. Proulx; Deacon Nick Diorio.
Res., 71 North St., P.O. Box 177, 06756-0177. Tel: 860-491-2756. [CEM]
Catechesis/Religious Programs—Students 155.

Granby, Hartford Co., St. Therese's (1958), Rev. Ronald R. Yelle; Deacon Robert D. Newbery.
Res., 120 W. Granby Rd., 06035-2907. Tel: 860-653-3371.
Catechesis/Religious Programs—Students 375.

Guilford, New Haven Co., St. George (1870), Rev. Msgr. James G. Coleman; Revs. John W. McHugh; Michael J. Dolan; Deacons Joseph Castaldi; James F. O'Neill.
Res., 33 Whitfield St., 06437-2698. Tel: 203-453-2788; Fax: 203-453-4985. [CEM]
Catechesis/Religious Programs—Tel: 203-453-3496.
Students 945.

Hamden, New Haven Co.,

1—ASCENSION, (1964), Rev. Thomas J. O'Rourke; Deacon Kenneth McCusker.
Res., 1040 Dunbar Hill Rd., 06514-1410. Tel: 203-288-7516.
Catechesis/Religious Programs—Tel: 203-288-5761.
Students 166.

2—BLESSED SACRAMENT, (1939), Revs. David M. McDonald; Stuart H. Pinette; Deacon James A. Tripp, Sr.
Res., 321 Circular Ave., 06514-3428. Tel: 203-288-1652.
Catechesis/Religious Programs—306 Circular Ave., 06514. Tel: 203-288-5228.
Students 370.

3—OUR LADY OF MT. CARMEL, (1869), Revs. Neil F. Fitzgerald; Daniel James Sullivan; Deacon John O'Donovan.
Res., 2819 Whitney Ave., 06518-2598. Tel: 203-248-0141. [CEM]
Parish Center—2809 Whitney Ave., 06518. Tel: 203-287-9017.
Catechesis/Religious Programs—Tel: 203-287-9017. Sr. Ann O'Neill, R.S.M., D.R.E.
Students 915.

4—ST. ANN'S, (1919) (Italian), Rev. Kenneth P. Bonadies.
Res., 930 Dixwell Ave., 06514-4990. Tel: 203-865-0886.

5—ST. JOAN OF ARC, (1971), Rev. Robert G. Heffernan; Deacon John P. Twerago.
Res., 450 W. Todd St., 06518. Tel: 203-288-4543.
Catechesis/Religious Programs—Tel: 203-230-1926.
Students 232.

6—ST. RITA'S, (1928), Revs. David M. Walker; Robert M. Kwiatkowski; Deacon Joseph E. Rolando.
Res., 1620 Whitney Ave., 06517. Tel: 203-248-5513; Fax: 203-248-2684.
School—1601 Whitney Ave., 06517. Tel: 203-248-3114.
Priests 1; Dominican Sisters of St. Mary of the Springs 2; Apostles of the Sacred Heart 3; Lay Teachers 16; Students 503.
Catechesis/Religious Programs—Tel: 203-281-7522; Fax: 203-248-2684. Dianne Breen, D.R.E.
Students 379.

7—ST. STEPHEN'S, (1953), Rev. David J. Baranowski; Deacon Adam J. Michaele.
Res., 400 Ridge Rd., 06517-2941. Tel: 203-288-6439; Fax: 203-288-4152.
School—Tel: 203-288-6792.
Sisters of Mercy 2; Lay Teachers 10; Students 213.

Harwinton, Litchfield Co., Immaculate Heart of Mary (1956), Rev. Allan J. Hill; Deacons Jose L. Dlugokinski; John L. Dembishack. In res., Rev. Philip L. Blaney.
Res., 78 Litchfield Rd., 06791-2230. Tel: 860-485-1588; Fax: 860-485-1004.
Catechesis/Religious Programs—Tel: 860-485-9264. Christine Rousseau, D.R.E.
Students 451.

Kensington, Hartford Co., St. Paul's (1878), Team Ministry: Revs. Herman Czaster; Herbert Obijiski; Thomas Lavin, O.F.M.Conv.; Deacons Oral Talbot; Carmen Guzzardi.
Res., 479 Alling St., 06037-2100. Tel: 860-828-0331; Fax: 860-828-7620.
School—(Grades PreK-8). Tel: 860-828-4343; Fax: 860-828-1226.
Daughters of Mary of the Immaculate Conception 3; Lay Teachers 16; Students 304.
Catechesis/Religious Programs—Tel: 860-828-1934. Louann Warren, D.R.E.
Students 1,149.

Kent, Litchfield Co., Sacred Heart (1970), Revs. William R. Metzler; Allan J. Hill; Deacon Roland Miller.
Res., 90 Cobble Rd., P.O. Box 186, 06757-0186. Tel: 860-927-3003; Fax: 860-927-3985. [CEM]
Church—Bridge St., 06757.
Catechesis/Religious Programs—Students 83.

Lakeville, Litchfield Co., St. Mary's (1874), Rev. Edmund M. O'Brien; Deacon Wayne F. Griffin.
Res., 76 Sharon Rd., 06039-0466. Tel: 860-435-2659. [CEM]
Catechesis/Religious Programs—Students 132.

Litchfield, Litchfield Co., St. Anthony's (1882), Rev. Robert F. Tucker; Deacon Kenneth DosSantos.
Res., 49 South St., P.O. Box 97, 06759-0097. Tel: 860-567-5209. [CEM]

Madison, New Haven Co., St. Margaret (1937), Rev. Gerard G. Schmitz; Deacon Joseph M. Regan; Rev. Francis R. Fador; Deacons John J. Brotz; William A. Elder.
Res., 24 Academy St., P.O. Box 814, 06443-2647. Tel: 203-245-7301; Fax: 203-245-8568.
Catechesis/Religious Programs—Tel: 203-245-7971.
Students 784.

Manchester, Hartford Co.,

1—ASSUMPTION, (1955), Rev. John S. Golas; Deacons J. Fernand Chamberland; Leo R. LaRocque.
Res., 285 W. Center St., 06040-4898. Tel: 860-643-2195.
School—Tel: 860-649-0889. Sr. Martin Prin.
Sisters 3; Lay Teachers 5; Students 137.
Catechesis/Religious Programs—Students 245.
Convent—21 S. Adams St., 06040. Tel: 860-643-0452. Sisters of Charity of Our Lady, Mother of the Church.

2—ST. BARTHOLOMEW'S, (1958), Rev. Peter J. Zizka.
Res., 45 Ludlow Rd., 06040-4542. Tel: 860-646-1613; Fax: 860-646-7121.
Catechesis/Religious Programs—Tel: 860-643-9178.
Students 382.

3—ST. BRIDGET'S, (1870), Rev. Joseph T. Donnelly.
Res., 80 Main St., 06040-3180. Tel: 860-643-2403; Fax: 860-646-6936.
School—74 Main St., 06040. Tel: 860-649-7731; Fax: 860-646-6936.
Sisters 1; Lay Teachers 10; Students 288.
Catechesis/Religious Programs—Tel: 860-643-5454; Fax: 860-646-6936.
Students 483.

4—ST. JAMES, (1874), Revs. Douglas P. Clancy; William F. Lynch; Louis D. Cremonie; Deacon Edward Giard.
Res., 896 Main St., 06040-6079. Tel: 860-643-4129.
School—Tel: 860-643-5088. Sr. Louise Kelly, R.S.M., Prin.
Sisters 4; Lay Teachers 16; Students 498.
Catechesis/Religious Programs—73 Park St., 06040. Tel: 860-643-9605.
Students 400.

Marlborough, Hartford Co., St. John Fisher (1972), Rev. Mario P. Pepe; Deacons Peter Klein; Ray Parenteau.
Res., 24 Cheney Rd., 06447-1327. Tel: 860-295-0067.
Catechesis/Religious Programs—Tel: 860-295-0067.
Students 351.

Meriden, New Haven Co.,

1—OUR LADY OF MOUNT CARMEL, (1894) (Italian), Rev. David J. Borino; Deacon Robert Gale.
Res., 109 Goodwill Ave., 06451-3094. Tel: 203-235-6381; Fax: 203-237-6225.
School—Tel: 203-235-2759; Fax: 203-237-6225.
Sisters 1; Lay Teachers 8; Students 170.
Catechesis/Religious Programs—Tel: 203-235-6381; Fax: 203-237-6225.
Students 160.
Convent—109 Goodwill Ave., Apt. 2, 06450. Tel: 203-235-3622; Fax: 203-237-6225. Apostles of the Sacred Heart of Jesus
Sisters 3.

2—ST. JOSEPH, (1900), Revs. Mark R. Jette; Robert P. Roy; Deacon John J. Suzio. In res., Rev. Daniel G. Keefe.
Res., 22 Goodwill Ave., 06451. Tel: 203-237-5593.
School—Tel: 203-237-6800. Sr. Georgeann Vumbaco, Prin.
Sisters of Mercy 5; Lay Teachers 8; Students 240.
Catechesis/Religious Programs—Tel: 203-237-5593.
Students 325.

3—ST. LAURENT, (1880) (French), Rev. Maurice P. Soucy.
Res., 121 Camp St., 06450-3279. Tel: 203-634-1583.
School—Tel: 203-235-3192. Mrs. Rita Barry, Prin.
Sisters 1; Lay Teachers 9; Students 157.
Catechesis/Religious Programs—Students 157.

4—ST. MARY, (1890) (German), Revs. Mark R. Jette; Robert P. Roy.
Res., 5 Sherman Pl., 06451. Tel: 203-235-0519.

[CEM]
School—Tel: 203-237-2931.
Lay Teachers 7; Students 80.

5—ST. ROSE OF LIMA, (1848), Revs. Joseph E. Vujs; Luis Jaramillo; Deacons Raul Cardona; Charles E. Cunniff, Jr.; Jacinto Ortiz.
Res., 35 Center St., 06450-1504. Tel: 203-235-1644; Fax: 203-235-1360.
Catechesis/Religious Programs—Tel: 203-235-6887.
Students 430.

6—ST. STANISLAUS, (1891) (Polish), Revs. Edmund S. Nadolny; Joseph K. Parzymies. In res., Revs. Joseph C. Paciorek, C.M.; Walter Kaminski.
Res., 82 Akron St., 06450-5796. Tel: 203-235-6341; Fax: 203-235-6342. [CEM]
School—Tel: 203-235-1005; Fax: 203-235-6341.
Sisters of St. Joseph of the Third Of St. Francis (Garfield Heights, OH) 4; Lay Teachers 25; Students 456.
Catechesis/Religious Programs—Tel: 203-235-6341; Fax: 203-235-6342.
Students 180.

Middlebury, New Haven Co., St. John of the Cross (1904), Revs. John D. Regan; Robert F. Birmingham; Deacon Neil Culhane.
Res., 1089 Whittemore Rd., P.O. Box 361, 06762-0361. Tel: 203-758-2659; Fax: 203-758-1121.
Catechesis/Religious Programs—Tel: 203-758-1326.
Students 450.

Milford, New Haven Co.,

1—CHRIST THE REDEEMER, (1966), Rev. John T. Moskus; Deacon Edmund J. Ramos.
Res., 325 Oronoque Rd., 06460-1798. Tel: 203-878-7431; Fax: 203-878-0677.
Catechesis/Religious Programs—Students 135.

2—ST. ANN'S, (1924), Rev. Thomas J. Baylis.
Res., 501 Naugatuck Ave., Devon, 06460-5095. Tel: 203-874-0634.
School—Tel: 203-878-2738.
Lay Teachers 10; Students 190.
Catechesis/Religious Programs—Students 349.

3—ST. GABRIEL, (Wildemere Beach) (1946), Rev. Maurice J. Maroney; Deacons Calvin Croll; Henry Doyle.
Res., 26 Shorefront, 06460-5968. Tel: 203-877-6096; Fax: 203-878-9700.
School—(Grades PreK-8) 1 Tudor Rd., 06460. Tel: 203-874-3811; Fax: 203-874-0416.
Religious 1; Lay Teachers 16; Students 261.
Catechesis/Religious Programs—Tel: 203-876-9355; Fax: 203-876-9355.
Students 237.

4—ST. MARY'S, (Wildemere Beach) (1874), Revs. James J. Cronin; Vito C. DeCarolis; Frederick M. Langlois; Deacons John Rigely; George A. Puskas; Paul E. Sabo; Richard M. Sennett; Paul Lauer.
Res., 70 Gulf St., Box 230, 06460-0230. Tel: 203-878-3571; Fax: 203-877-8741. [CEM]
School—Tel: 203-878-6539.
Sisters of Mercy 2; Lay Teachers 22; Students 443.
Catechesis/Religious Programs—Tel: 203-877-5874. Sue Marra, D.R.E.
Students 790.

Naugatuck, New Haven Co., St. Francis of Assisi (1866), Revs. William L. Burns; William O. Seery. In res., Rev. Joseph P. Donahue; Deacon William F. Mingrone.
Res., 318 Church St., 06770. Tel: 203-729-4543.
School—Tel: 203-729-2247. Mrs. Lorraine Hurley, Prin.
Lay Teachers 12; Students 317.
Catechesis/Religious Programs—Students 610. D.R.E.: Mr. Joseph Guarino; Mr. John Paret.

St. Vincent Ferrer (1975), Rev. Jeremiah N. Murasso; Deacon Nicholas J. Iassogna, Jr.; Sr. Susan Carlin, R.S.M., Pastoral Min.
Res., 1006 New Haven Rd., 06770-4731. Tel: 203-723-7497.
Catechesis/Religious Programs—Mrs. Karen Nappo, D.R.E.
Students 530.

New Britain, Hartford Co.,

1—ALL SAINTS, (1918) (Slovak), Rev. Augustine H. Giusani.
Res., 15 Wilcox St., 06051. Tel: 860-229-0135.

2—HOLY CROSS, (1927) (Polish), Revs. Peter S. Sobiecki; Marion I. Krupnick; Darius Goscinak. In res., Rev. Henry P. Fiedorczyk.
Res., 31 Biruta St., 06053-2899. Tel: 860-229-2011.
School—221 Farmington Ave., 06053. Tel: 860-225-4275.
Sisters of St. Joseph of the Third Order of St. Francis 7; Lay Teachers 24; Students 454.
Catechesis/Religious Programs—Students 157.

3—SACRED HEART OF JESUS, (1894) (Polish), Rev. Paul P. Wysocki.
Res., 158 Broad St., 06053-4195. Tel: 860-229-0081; 826-4721; Fax: 860-826-6201. [CEM]
School—Tel: 860-229-7663. Sr. M. Alma Sakowicz, Prin.
Daughters of Mary of the Immaculate Conception 3; Lay Teachers 21; Students 447.
Catechesis/Religious Programs—Students 190.

4—ST. ANDREW'S, (1895) (Lithuanian), Rev. John E. Rikteraitis. In res., Rev. Ronald T. Smith.
Res., 396 Church St., Box 515, 06050-0515. Tel: 860-224-0341; Fax: 860-826-6201.

5—ST. ANN, (1938) (Italian), Revs. Augustine H. Giusani; J. Thomas Walsh; Deacon Carl Lickwar.
Res., 47 Clark St., 06051-1903. Tel: 860-225-7625.
Catechesis/Religious Programs—Tel: 860-223-2370.
Students 199.

6—ST. FRANCIS OF ASSISI, (1941), Rev. Thomas E. Berberich.
Res., 1755 Stanley St., 06053-2099. Tel: 860-225-6449; Fax: 860-225-2315.
Middle School—Tel: 860-225-8729.
School Sisters of Notre Dame 3; Lay Teachers 8; Students 180.
Catechesis/Religious Programs—Students 100.

7—ST. JEROME'S, (1958), Revs. Edward M. LaRose; Joseph Varickamackal; Deacon Reginald Roy.
Res., 1010 Slater Rd., 06053-1698. Tel: 860-224-2411; Fax: 860-224-6838.
Catechesis/Religious Programs—Students 229.

8—ST. JOHN THE EVANGELIST, (1916), Rev. Harold D. Heinrich; Deacon Albert Kristopik.
Res., 655 East St., 06051-2108. Tel: 860-223-3668.
Catechesis/Religious Programs—Students 125.

9—ST. JOSEPH'S, (1896), Rev. Thomas F. Gaffney.
Res., 195 S. Main St., 06051-3199. Tel: 860-229-4851; Fax: 860-225-1403.
School—Tel: 860-223-5959; Fax: 860-225-1403.
Lay Teachers 11; Students 230.
Catechesis/Religious Programs—Tel: 860-229-4851; Fax: 860-225-1403.
Students 164.

10—ST. MARY'S, (1848), Revs. Salvatore J. Rosa; Francis T. Carter; Deacons Chester Roman; Ronald Camden.
Res., 544 Main St., 06051-1814. Tel: 860-229-4894.
Catechesis/Religious Programs—Students 181.

11—ST. MAURICE, (1946), Rev. Joseph V. Napolitano.
Res., 100 Wightman Rd., 06052-1597. Tel: 860-225-8419; Fax: 860-224-1947.
Catechesis/Religious Programs—Tel: 860-225-4477. Linda E. Tower, D.R.E.
Students 162.

12—ST. PETER'S, (1873) (German-French), Rev. Michael H. Gosselin, S.T.M., J.C.L.
Res., 98 Franklin Sq., 06051-2607. Tel: 860-224-1446; Fax: 860-223-8717.

New Hartford, Litchfield Co., Immaculate Conception (1869), Rev. James R. Emerling.
Res., Town Hill Rd., 06057. Tel: 860-379-5215. [CEM]
Catechesis/Religious Programs—Tel: 860-379-0144.
Students 375.

New Haven, New Haven Co.,

1—SACRED HEART, (1876), Revs. Robert V. Newman, S.C.; James Richardson, S.C.
Res., 74 Liberty St., 06519-2299. Tel: 203-562-7592; Fax: 203-562-1737.
School—208 Columbus Ave., 06519. Tel: 203-777-8137.
Apostles of the Sacred Heart 1; Lay Teachers 12; Students 185.

2—ST. AEDAN'S, (1900), Revs. Joseph H. McCann; Cyriac Maliekal; Deacons Edward Taddei; Joseph R. Ryzewski.
Res., 112 Fountain St., 06515-0156. Tel: 203-389-2619.
School—Tel: 203-387-5693; Fax: 203-387-1609. Miss Nancy Bourgoin, Prin.
Lay Teachers 17; Students 247.
Catechesis/Religious Programs—Students 120.

3—ST. ANTHONY'S, (1904) (Italian), Revs. Joseph G. Moffo, C.S.; Salvatore Zocco; Antonio LiCastro.
Res., 25 Gold St., 06519. Tel: 203-624-1418.

4—ST. BERNADETTE'S, (1938), Revs. Howard J. Nash; Stephen A. Krugel; Deacon Gabriel Azzaro.
Res., 385 Townsend Ave., 06512-3998. Tel: 203-467-1007; Fax: 203-467-3719.
School—Tel: 203-469-2271.
Lay Teachers 15; Students 231.
Catechesis/Religious Programs—Tel: 203-467-8763.
Students 247.

5—ST. BONIFACE'S, (1868) (German), Rev. John D. Casey. In res., Rev. J.B. Hari Kustansto, S.J. (Indonesia).
Res., 630 State St., 06511-6599. Tel: 203-865-3365.

6—ST. BRENDAN'S, (1913), Rev. Donald J. French; Deacon Robert Brunell.
Res., 455 Whalley Ave., 06511-3080. Tel: 203-865-0561; Fax: 203-865-0562.
School—342 Ellsworth Ave., 06511. Tel: 203-562-6128.
Sisters 6; Lay Teachers 8; Students 262.
Convent—455 1/2 Whalley Ave., 06511. Tel: 203-787-4631. Sisters of Our Lady of the Garden

7—ST. CASIMIR'S, (1912) (Lithuanian), Rev. John D. Casey. In res., Revs. Ralph M. Colicchio; Geoffrey Smith.
Res., 339 Greene St., 06511-6599. Tel: 203-624-8085.

8—ST. DONATO'S, (1915) (Italian), Rev. Louis A. Evangelisto.
Res., 505 Lombard St., 06513-2910. Tel: 203-789-1576.

9—ST. FRANCIS, (1868), Rev. William J. Brenza.
Res., 397 Ferry St., 06513-3698. Tel: 203-777-5356; Fax: 203-777-5357.
School—Tel: 203-777-5352. Dr. Robert Schreck, Prin.
Religious 3; Lay Teachers 8; Students 260.
Catechesis/Religious Programs—Tel: 203-865-5179.
Students 80.

10—ST. JOHN THE BAPTIST, (1893), Rev. John J. Keane; Deacon Ronald Gurr. In res., Rev. Daniel J. Scott, M.S.
Res., 782 Dixwell Ave., 06511-1098. Tel: 203-624-3097; Fax: 203-562-0433.
Parish Center—20 Elizabeth St., 06511. Tel: 203-562-3908. Sr. Rosalie Shields, O.P., Pastoral Min.
Catechesis/Religious Programs—Students 72.

11—ST. JOHN THE EVANGELIST. Merged with St. Peter, New Haven.

12—ST. JOSEPH'S, (1900), Revs. John P. Sullivan, Temp. Admin.; Robert Struminski, S.M. Tel: 203-497-8637. In res., Rev. Christopher W. Steck, S.J. Tel: 203-777-3547.
Res., 129 Edwards St., 06511-2299. Tel: 203-777-2548.

13—SAINT MARTIN DE PORRES, (1942) (African American), Rev. Joseph M. Elko.
Res., 136 Dixwell Ave., 06511-3400. Tel: 203-624-9944.

14—ST. MARY'S PRIORY, (1832), Very Rev. Carleton Parker Jones, Prior; Revs. Paul J. Keller, O.P.; James C. Sheehan, O.P.; Thomas Q. Shanley, O.P.; Paul A. Bernardin, O.P.; Charles T. Shannon, O.P.; Gabriel O'Donnell, O.P.; Joseph P. Allen, O.P.; Peter M. Girard, O.P.; Bernard T. Confer, O.P.; Bro. Gerard Thayer, O.P.; Deacon Martin J. O'Connor.
Mailing Address: P.O. Box 1202, 06505-1202. Tel: 203-562-9326.
Res., 5 Hillhouse Ave., 06505. Tel: 203-562-6193; Fax: 203-562-1273.
Shrine—The Shrine of the Infant Prague (Inc.), Tel: 203-562-9326; Fax: 203-562-1273.

15—ST. MICHAEL'S, (1889) (Italian), Rev. Francis Minchiatti, C.S.; Deacon John J.M. Conte, Jr.
Res., 29 Wooster Pl., 06511-6998. Tel: 203-562-7178.
Parish Center—Tel: 203-789-9453.

16—ST. PETER, (1902), Revs. Robert V. Newman, S.C.; James Richardson, S.C.; Deacon Jose A. Rivera; Mr. Alonso Villegas, Pastoral Assoc.
Church—164 Kimberly Ave., 06519-2720. Tel: 203-624-3179; Fax: 203-562-1737.
School—208 Columbus Ave., 06519. Tel: 203-777-8137.
Apostles of the Sacred Heart;; Lay Teachers 12; Students 185.

17—ST. ROSE OF LIMA, (1907), Revs. William Burbank; Carlos Garces-Henao; Deacons Julio Vazquez; Julius Marcarelli.
Res., 115 Blatchley Ave., 06513-4298. Tel: 203-865-6149; Fax: 203-865-6140.
School—12 Richard St., 06513. Tel: 203-624-5075; Fax: 203-624-1686. Mary Joy Walsh, Prin.
Lay Teachers 11; Students 210.
Catechesis/Religious Programs—Students 120.

18—ST. STANISLAUS, (1901) (Polish), Revs. Waclaw Hlond, C.M.; George Dabrowski, C.M.; Henry Sawicki, C.M.; Roman Kulczycki, C.M.
Res., 9 Eld St., 06511-3899. Tel: 203-562-2828; Fax: 203-752-0217.
Catechesis/Religious Programs—Students 73.

Newington, Hartford Co., Holy Spirit (1964), Revs. John T. O'Connor; James F. Kinnane; Faron P. Calumba (Philippines); Deacon James A. Fortier. In res., Rev. Raymond S. Smialowski.
Res., 183 Church St., 06111-4898. Tel: 860-666-5671; Fax: 860-666-9784.
Catechesis/Religious Programs—Tel: 860-666-3562. Mary Marsan, D.R.E.
Students 773.

St. Mary (1924), Revs. Thomas J. Lynch; Joseph G. Kurnath; James P. McHugh; Deacons Michael J.

O'Toole; Peter A. Cenci; Barry T. Skipp.
Res., 626 Willard Ave., 06111. Tel: 860-666-1591.
School—Tel: 860-666-3844.
Religious 3; Lay Teachers 13; Students 281.
Maryhouse—(Sisters of Mercy) 21 Hartford Ave., #9, 06111. Tel: 860-666-1085.
Convent—168 Cedar St., 06111. Tel: 203-667-1790. Sisters of Charity
Catechesis/Religious Programs—Tel: 860-666-6347. Susan Skipp, D.R.E.
Students 600.

New Milford, Litchfield Co., St. Francis Xavier's (1871), Revs. Joseph T. Kaminsky; Timothy A. O'Brien.
Res., 26 Chestnut Land Rd., P.O. Drawer 390, 06776-0390. Tel: 860-354-2202; 350-1611; Fax: 860-354-7511.
Catechesis/Religious Programs—Tel: 860-354-5372.
Students 640.

Our Lady of the Lakes (1990), Rev. Thomas E. Ptaszynski; Deacon Robert E. Muro.
Res., 3 Old Town Park Rd., 06776-4212. Tel: 860-354-5239.
Catechesis/Religious Programs—Tel: 860-355-5365.
Students 441.

Norfolk, Litchfield Co., Immaculate Conception (1889), Rev. John S. Ahern; Deacon Michael T. Sponzo.
Res., 4 North St., P.O. Box 583, 06058-1009. Tel: 860-542-5442. [CEM]
Catechesis/Religious Programs—Students 101.

North Branford, New Haven Co., St. Augustine (1941), Rev. Daniel F. McSheffery.
Res., 30 Caputo Rd., 06471-1027. Tel: 203-484-0403; Fax: 203-484-0132.
Catechesis/Religious Programs—Students 548.

Northford, New Haven Co., St. Monica's (1964), Rev. Joseph Parel; Sr. Judith Mulhall, C.S.J., Pastoral Assoc.; Deacons Louis P. Fusco; William B. Bergers.
Res., 1331 Middletown Ave., Box 160, 06472-0160. Tel: 203-484-9226.
Catechesis/Religious Programs—Tel: 203-484-2434.
Students 410.

North Haven, New Haven Co., St. Barnabas (1922), Revs. Hugh J. MacDonald; John J. Daly, Pastor Emeritus; Deacons James Stanley; James Taylor; William Bartlett; Paul T. Koch.
Res., 44 Washington Ave., 06473-1799. Tel: 203-239-5378; Fax: 203-239-3510.
Catechesis/Religious Programs—Tel: 203-239-3804. Karin Tierney, D.R.E.
Students 396.

St. Frances Cabrini (1967), Rev. John J. Georgia; Deacons Eugene Labagnara; George Stephens.
Res., 6 Welch Rd., 06473-2896. Tel: 203-239-5700; Fax: 203-239-6463.
Church & Parish Center—Pond Hill Rd., 06473. Tel: 203-239-5644.
Catechesis/Religious Programs—94 Chapel Hill Rd., 06473. Tel: 203-239-8012.
Students 362.
Convent— Sisters of the Sacred Heart of Jesus
Nursery School—90 Chapel Hill Rd., 06473.

St. Therese's (1925), Revs. Timothy A. Meehan; Alexander J. Cherukarakunnel. In res., Rev. Vincent E. Lyddy, (Retired).
Res., 555 Middletown Ave., 06473-4000. Tel: 203-239-1671; Fax: 203-234-2220.

Oakville, Litchfield Co., St. Mary Magdalen (1900), Revs. William L. Traxl; William O. Seery.
Res., 145 Buckingham St., 06779-1797. Tel: 860-274-9273; Fax: 860-274-2013.
School—Tel: 860-945-0621; Fax: 860-945-6162.
Lay Teachers 10; Students 289.
Catechesis/Religious Programs—Students 407.

Orange, New Haven Co., Holy Infant (1952), Revs. Peter S. Dargan; Bernard D. Killeen, Pastor Emeritus; Deacons Americo Bichi; William Shaffer; Bernard J. Hayden; Elmer Von Feldt, (Retired); Harold J. Hoffman; Joseph D. Sullivan.
Res., 450 Race Brook Rd., 06477. Tel: 203-799-2379; Fax: 203-799-9720.
Catechesis/Religious Programs—Tel: 203-777-2417.
Students 1,044.

Oxford, New Haven Co., St. Thomas the Apostle (1966), Rev. Dominic J. Valla.
Res., 733 Oxford Rd., 06478. Tel: 203-888-2382; Fax: 203-881-5518.
Catechesis/Religious Programs—Students 450.

Plainville, Hartford Co., Our Lady of Mercy (1881), Revs. Richard P. McGann; Edmund K Karwowski; Deacon Gerald Geraci. In res., Rev. Francis E. Martens, C.I.C.M.
Res., 15 S. Canal St., 06062-2799. Tel: 860-793-1399; Fax: 860-747-5407. [CEM]
Parish Center: 19 S. Canal St., 06062. Tel: 860-747-6825; Fax: 860-747-5407.
Catechesis/Religious Programs—Jeanne Gionfriddo, D.R.E.
Students 202.
Convent—26 Bank St., 06062. Tel: 860-747-0811.

Plantsville, Hartford Co., Mary Our Queen (1961), Rev. Arthur J. DuPont; Deacons Frank Casey; Joseph DiMauro; Paul J. Kulas.
Res., 248 Savage St., P.O. Box 46, 06479-0046. Tel: 860-628-4901; Fax: 860-621-0610.
Catechesis/Religious Programs—Tel: 860-628-0437.
Students 500.

St. Aloysius (1961), Rev. John P. Blanchfield. In res., Rev. Donald J. O'Leary.
Res., 254 Burritt St., 06479-1426. Tel: 860-276-9208. [JC]
Catechesis/Religious Programs—Students 395.

Poquonock, Hartford Co., St. Joseph's (1874), Revs. William J. Hilliard; Robert B. Vargo; Deacon Robert D. Navickas.
Res., 1747 Poquonock Ave., P.O. Box 253, 06064-0253. Tel: 860-688-9566; Fax: 860-683-2225. [CEM]
Catechesis/Religious Programs—Tel: 860-683-0366.
Students 437.

Prospect, New Haven Co., St. Anthony's (1939), Revs. Philip J. Cascia; Joseph R. DeCarolis; Deacons Paul Iadarola; George Dinkle.
Res., 4 Union City Rd., P.O. Box 7117, 06712-0117. Tel: 203-758-4056; Fax: 203-758-4594.
Catechesis/Religious Programs—Tel: 203-758-4848; Fax: 203-758-4594.
Students 740.

Rocky Hill, Hartford Co., St. James (1880), Revs. Thomas B. Shepard; Anthony DeFronzo; Deacon Michael Shelto.
Res., 767 Elm St., 06067-1902. Tel: 860-529-8655.
Catechesis/Religious Programs—(Grades K-10). Tel: 860-529-1274. Thomas Sacerdote, D.R.E.
Students 686.

St. Elizabeth Seton (1985), Rev. James A. Shanley; Deacon Stephen L. Weaver.
Res., 280 Brook St., 06067-0485. Tel: 860-529-3222; Fax: 860-529-6421.
Catechesis/Religious Programs—Students 184.

Seymour, New Haven Co., Good Shepherd (1967), Rev. Edward S. Jaksina; Deacons John R. Maffeo; Alan C. Baldwin.
Res., 135 Mountain Rd., 06483-2038. Tel: 203-888-9243.
Catechesis/Religious Programs—Paula DiGiovanni, D.R.E.
Students 440.

St. Augustine's (1866), Rev. Brian E. Jeffries; Deacon John R. Saffo, Sr.
Res., 35 Washington Ave., 06483-3198. Tel: 203-888-2081; Fax: 203-888-9681. [CEM]
Catechesis/Religious Programs—Tel: 203-888-7003.
Students 221.

Sharon, Litchfield Co., St. Bernard's (1885), Rev. James F. Pilon.
Res., 52 New St., Box 218, 06069-0218. Tel: 860-364-5244; Fax: 860-364-9893. [CEM]

Simsbury, Hartford Co., St. Mary's (1921), Team Ministry: Revs. Lawrence R. Bock; William E. Dudack; Deacons Joseph Gabriele; John Sweeney.
Res., 940 Hopmeadow St., P.O. Box 575, 06070-1819. Tel: 860-658-7627; Fax: 860-658-7626.
School—St. Mary School, 946 Hopmeadow St., 06070. Tel: 860-658-9412. Mrs. Maria Maynard, Prin.
Lay Teachers 15; Students 286.
Catechesis/Religious Programs—Tel: 860-658-5919.
Students 1,031.

Southbury, New Haven Co., Sacred Heart (1884), Rev. Mark F. Flynn; Deacons Joseph Lavoie, (Retired); Vincent Cassidy; Michael Kulas.
Res., 68 Georges Hill Rd., 06488-0686. Tel: 203-264-5071; Fax: 203-264-5005. [CEM]
Catechesis/Religious Programs—Tel: 203-264-5065; Fax: 203-264-5005. Eileen Dignazio, D.R.E.
Students 860.
Station—Southbury, Southbury Training School, Tel: 203-264-8231.

South Glastonbury, Hartford Co., St. Augustine (1877), Rev. John F. McDonald.
Res., 55 Hopewell Rd., P.O. Box 175, 06073-0175. Tel: 860-633-9505. [CEM]
Catechesis/Religious Programs—Hopewell School, (Grades K-8). Tel: 860-633-9505.
Students 275.

Southington, Hartford Co., Immaculate Conception (1915) (Polish), Rev. David J. Lewandowski; Deacon Andrew Galiette. In res., Rev. Eugene J. Charman Tel: 203-628-7385.
Res., 130 Summer St., 06489. Tel: 203-628-2181. [CEM]
Catechesis/Religious Programs—Judy Teleshanic, D.R.E.
Students 208.
Father Kolbe Catechetical Center—152 Summer St., Plantsville, 06479. Tel: 860-628-6973.

St. Dominic (1971), Rev. Walter F. Geraghty; Deacons John L. Crowley; Eugene P. Nebiolo.
Res., 1050 Flanders Rd., P.O. Box 48, 06489-0048. Tel: 860-628-0349.
Catechesis/Religious Programs—Jacqueline Marenholz, D.R.E.
Students 600.

St. Thomas (1860), Revs. George F. Lauretti; Joseph F. Keough; Deacons James P. Quinn; Angelo J. Coppola.
Res., 99 Bristol St., 06489-4599. Tel: 860-628-4713; Fax: 860-628-7341. [CEM]
School—Tel: 860-628-2485. Mrs. Joan Murphy, Prin.
Lay Teachers 9; Students 182.
Catechesis/Religious Programs—Tel: 860-628-9679.
Students 752.

South Meriden, New Haven Co., Holy Angels (1887), Rev. Roland M. LaPlante; Deacons Donald H. Smith; George Kraussman.
Res., 915 Main St., 06451-4999. Tel: 203-235-5311; Fax: 203-630-3041.
Catechesis/Religious Programs—585 Main St., 06451. Tel: 203-237-8697. Stephen N. Filippo, D.R.E.
Students 255.

South Windsor, Hartford Co., St. Francis of Assisi (1941), Rev. John P. Rohan; Deacon David F. Dwyer.
Res., 673 Ellington Rd., 06074-4166. Tel: 860-528-8288; Fax: 860-528-1685.
Catechesis/Religious Programs—Tel: 860-289-3671.
Students 476.

St. Margaret Mary (1961), Revs. Daniel Jeremiah Sullivan; Francis V. Krukowski; Deacons Robert R. LaRochelle; Thomas J. Conklin.
Res., 80 Hayes Rd., 06074-1499. Tel: 860-644-2411.
Catechesis/Religious Programs—Tel: 860-644-2549.
Students 1,110.

Suffield, Hartford Co., Sacred Heart (1884), Revs. Theodore T. Raczynski; Stephen Sledesky; Deacons Benedict Winiarski; Valentino Bertolini.
Res., 446 Mountain Rd., 06078-0626. Tel: 860-668-4246; Fax: 860-668-1337. [JC]
Catechesis/Religious Programs—Students 644.

St. Joseph's (1916) (Polish), Rev. William L. Baldyga; Deacon Edward Szewczyk.
Res., 140 S. Main St., 06078-2218. Tel: 860-668-2880. [CEM]
Convent—156 S. Main St., 06078. Tel: 860-668-2503. Felician Sisters

Tariffville, Hartford Co., St. Bernard's (1878), Rev. Thomas A. Flower; Deacons Andrew J. Anthony; Thomas P. Scanlon.
Res., 7 Maple St., P.O. Box 85, 06081-0085. Tel: 860-658-5142; Fax: 860-658-2804. [CEM]
Catechesis/Religious Programs—Students 274.

Terryville, Litchfield Co., Immaculate Conception (1882), Rev. Gerald H. Dziedzic.
Res., 21 Maple St., 06786-1197. Tel: 860-583-4697. [CEM 2]
Catechesis/Religious Programs—Students 70.

St. Casimir (1906), Rev. Daniel J. Karpiey.
Res., 19 Allen St., 06786-1503. Tel: 860-583-4660.

Thomaston, Litchfield Co., St. Thomas (1869), Revs. Harold M. Kearns; John E. Cockayne; Deacons Gerald Wooton; Robert Gordon.
Parish Center—(CEM) 19 Electric Ave., 06787-1651. Tel: 860-283-5817; Fax: 860-283-1009.
School—30 N. Main St., 06787. Tel: 860-283-5955.
Lay Teachers 11; Students 132.
Catechesis/Religious Programs—Tel: 860-283-4296.
Students 421.

Torrington, Litchfield Co.,

1—St. Francis of Assisi, (1877), Revs. Robert W. Ladish; John G. Weaver; Deacon Edward Dickson; Sr. Helen Marie Clark, R.S.M., Pastoral Assoc.
Res., 160 Main St., 06790-5299. Tel: 860-482-5571.
School—Tel: 860-489-4177. Sr. Margaret Mary Kennedy, O.P., Prin.
Sisters 1; Lay Teachers 8; Students 205.
Catechesis/Religious Programs—360 Prospect St., 06790. Tel: 203-482-3121.
Students 430.

2—Sacred Heart, (1910) (Slovak), Rev. A. Leo Spodnik.
Res., 116 Grove St., 06790-5047. Tel: 860-482-8246.
Parish Center—119 Grove St., 06790. Tel: 860-489-4070.
Catechesis/Religious Programs—Students 58.

3—St. Mary's, (1919) (Polish), Rev. Chester A. Bieluch.

Res., 61 Forest Ct., 06790-4698. Tel: 860-482-3583.
Catechesis/Religious Programs—Students 50.

4—St. Peter's, (1910) (Italian), Revs. John P. D'Alonges; Gerard G. Masters.
Res., 107 E. Main St., 06790-5493. Tel: 860-482-4433; Fax: 860-482-1891.
School—Tel: 860-489-8735; Fax: 860-482-9406. Maestre Pie Filippini 2; Lay Teachers 8; Students 175.
Catechesis/Religious Programs—Students 239.

Union City, New Haven Co., St. Hedwig (Naugatuck) (1906) (Polish), Revs. George F. Ziezulewicz; Edward M. Ziemnicki; Deacon Michael Szumigala.
Res., 32 Golden Hill St., 06770-3099. Tel: 203-729-2490; Fax: 203-720-2161.
School—Tel: 203-729-2403; Fax: 203-720-2161. Ms. Patricia Dayner, Prin.
Lay Teachers 6; Students 128.
Catechesis/Religious Programs—Students 118.

St. Mary's (Naugatuck) (1907), Rev. Philip A. Sheridan; Deacon Thomas J. Clifford.
Res., 338 N. Main St., 06770-3235. Tel: 203-729-2279.
Catechesis/Religious Programs—Students 120.

Unionville, Hartford Co., St. Mary's (1874), Rev. Robert J. St. Martin.
Res., 16 Bidwell Sq., 06085-1116. Tel: 860-673-2422; Fax: 860-673-2001. [CEM]
Catechesis/Religious Programs—Students 645.

Wallingford, New Haven Co., Holy Trinity (1869), Revs. Charles J. MacDonald; Nathaniel C. Labarda; John J. Williams; Deacons Joseph Cretella; Efrain DeJesus; Eugene Riotte.
Res., 68 N. Colony St., 06492-3696. Tel: 203-269-8791; Fax: 203-269-0880.
School—11 N. Whittlesey Ave., 06492. Tel: 203-269-4476. Sr. Kathleen Kelly, R.S.M., Prin.
Sisters of Mercy 1; Lay Teachers 9; Students 270.
Catechesis/Religious Programs—Tel: 203-265-6300. Frances Selmecki, D.R.E.
Students 985.

Resurrection (1963), Revs. Dawson D. Trenchard; Daniel E. Johnson, Pastor Emeritus. In res., Rev. Mark J. Bonsignore (Peru).
Res., 115 Pond Hill Rd., 06492-4836. Tel: 203-265-1694; Fax: 203-284-9766.
Catechesis/Religious Programs—Tel: 203-481-8029. Mary Ann Marchitto, D.R.E.
Students 635.

SS. Peter and Paul (1924) (Polish), Rev. Stephen Bzdyra; Deacon Louis P. Sill, Jr.
Res., 139 N. Orchard St., 06492-3617. Tel: 203-269-4617; Fax: 203-265-6751. [CEM]
Catechesis/Religious Programs—Students 114.

Washington Depot, Litchfield Co., Our Lady of Perpetual Help (1893), Rev. Thomas F. Bennett; Deacon George H. Streib.
Res., 34 Green Hill Rd., P.O. Box 303, 06794. Tel: 860-868-2600. [CEM]
Catechesis/Religious Programs—Students 163.
Mission—Roxbury, Litchfield Co., St. Patrick's, Church St., Roxbury 06783.

Waterbury, New Haven Co.,

1—Blessed Sacrament, (1911), Rev. Walter A. Vichas; Deacon George Wilcox.
Res., 192 Robbins St., 06708. Tel: 203-753-3149.
School—Tel: 203-756-5313.
Sisters 3; Lay Teachers 9; Students 275.
Catechesis/Religious Programs—Tel: 203-757-1656.
Students 85.
Convent—407 Robinwood Rd., 06708. Tel: 203-753-1472. Sisters of the Third Order Regular of St. Francis

2—Immaculate Conception, (1848), Revs. John J. Bevins; George White, O.M.I.; Raymond Pitruzzello; John Curry Gay; Maximo Asencios-Pablo, M.Ss.A. In res., Rev. Charles B. Hagerty.
Res., 74 W. Main St., 06721-1670. Tel: 203-574-0017.
School—St. Mary's, Tel: 203-753-2574.
Sisters 2; Lay Teachers 18; Students 512.
Catechesis/Religious Programs—Students 169.
Convent—55 Cole St., 06702. Tel: 203-754-2913. Maryknoll Sisters

3—Our Lady of Fatima, (1971) (Portuguese), Rev. Nelson Ribeiro, C.M.
Res., 2071 Baldwin St., 06706. Tel: 203-753-1424.

4—Our Lady of Loreto, (1971), Rev. Msgr. Joseph A. Devine.
Res., 12 Ardsley Rd., 06708-1825. Tel: 203-757-6112; Fax: 203-756-9656.
Catechesis/Religious Programs—Students 189.

5—Our Lady of Lourdes, (1899) (Italian), Rev. Ronald A. Ferraro; Deacon George M. Pettinico.
Res., 309 S. Main St., 06706-1090. Tel: 203-754-4134.

6—Our Lady of Mt. Carmel, (1923) (Italian), Revs. Carmine B. Raneri; Daniel J. McLearen. In res., Rev. Lawrence J. LeClair; Deacon Daniel A. Sloan.
Res., 785 Highland Ave., 06708-4199. Tel: 203-756-8981.
School—645 Congress Ave., 06708. Tel: 203-755-6809. Sr. Daniella Marie O'Sullivan, S.S.N.D., Prin.
Lay Teachers 10; Students 276.
Catechesis/Religious Programs—Tel: 203-753-1713.
Students 220.
Convent—656 Congress Ave., 06708. Tel: 203-754-1947.

7—Sacred Heart, (1855), Rev. Joseph E. Looney; Deacon Earle Kimball. In res., Rev. Richard C. Bollea.
Res., 13 Wolcott St., 06702-1790. Tel: 203-757-8737; Fax: 203-754-5862.

8—St. Anne, (1886) (French), Rev. Alvin J. LeBlanc; Deacons Francis X. Bandeira; Gaspard D. LeBlanc.
Res., 515 S. Main St., 06706-1089. Tel: 203-756-4439; Fax: 203-754-3244.

9—St. Cecilia's, (1893) (German), Rev. John C. Blackall, (Spanish Apostolate); Deacon Alejandro Lopez.
Res., 83 Cherry St., 06702-1699. Tel: 203-574-5156.
Catechesis/Religious Programs—Students 367.

10—St. Francis Xavier's, (1896), Rev. Paul J. Pace; Deacon Donald E. Cruess.
Res., 625 Baldwin St., 06706-1597. Tel: 203-756-7804.
School—605 Baldwin St., 06706. Tel: 203-753-3197. Mr. John J. McCarthy, Prin.
Lay Teachers 9; Students 249.
Catechesis/Religious Programs—Tel: 203-754-6996.
Students 165.

11—St. Joseph, (1894) (Lithuanian), Rev. Francis V. Karvelis. In res., Rev. Paul P. Sabulis, (Retired).
Res., 46 Congress Ave., 06708. Tel: 203-754-1557.
School—Lay Teachers 10; Students 219.

12—St. Leo the Great, (1974), Rev. Joseph F. Gorman; Deacons Modesto Rosello; Charles Colella.
Res., 14 Bentwood Dr., 06705-3612. Tel: 203-573-0511.
Catechesis/Religious Programs—Tel: 203-573-0511.
Students 220.

13—St. Lucy's, (1926) (Italian), Rev. Paul Mangiafico; Deacon Oreste M. Giusto.
Res., 24 Branch St., 06704-3626. Tel: 203-574-5903.
School—58 Griggs St., 06704. Tel: 203-756-3831. Mr. John J. Petto, Prin.
Lay Teachers 10; Students 240.
Parish Center: 64 Division St., 06704. Tel: 203-755-8420.
Catechesis/Religious Programs—Students 90.

14—St. Margaret's, (1910), Revs. Kevin J. Gray; Daniel Ayala-Rendon (Columbia); Deacon George Hajjar.
Res., 289 Willow St., 06710. Tel: 203-754-6101.
School—Tel: 203-753-3708. Ms. Margaret Sheehy, Prin.
Lay Teachers 11; Students 238.
Catechesis/Religious Programs—Tel: 203-757-7232.
Students 157.

15—St. Michael, (1897), Rev. Ronald Gliatta, O.F.M.; Friar Richard Martignetti, O.F.M.; Deacon Domenic Stolfi.
Res., 62 St. Michael Dr., 06704-1295. Tel: 203-753-0689; Fax: 203-573-9101.
Catechesis/Religious Programs—Students 180.

16—St. Patrick, (1880), Rev. Richard M. Taberski; Deacon Thomas F. Johnson.
Mailing Address: P.O. Box 271, 06720-0271. Tel: 203-756-8837.
Res., 50 Charles St., 06708. Tel: 203-756-8837.
Catechesis/Religious Programs—Students 62.

17—SS. Peter and Paul, (1920), Revs. Edward F. Hyland; Paul J. Halovatch; Kevin V. Walsh (RVC).
Res., 67 Southmayd Rd., 06705. Tel: 203-756-7919; Fax: 203-755-3535.
School—Tel: 203-755-0881. Janet Curry, Prin.
Lay Teachers 12; Students 344.
Catechesis/Religious Programs—114 Beecher Ave., 06705. Tel: 203-753-4242.
Students 216.

18—St. Stanislaus Kostka, (1913) (Polish), Rev. George Ziezulewicz, Admin.
Res., 86 East Farm St., 06704. Tel: 203-574-0871; Fax: 203-575-0107.

19—St. Thomas, (1898), Rev. Ronald Gliatta, O.F.M.
Res., 84 Crown St., 06704-1295. Tel: 203-753-5682; Fax: 203-573-9101.

Watertown, Litchfield Co., St. John the Evangelist (1878), Revs. John M. Cooney; Kevin J. Forsyth; Deacons George Simonin; Daniel Camerota; John Chartes.
Res., 21 Academy Hill, 06795-2101. Tel: 860-274-8836. [CEM]
School—Tel: 860-274-9208. Sr. Eileen Eden, S.S.N.D., Prin.
School Sisters of Notre Dame 5; Lay Teachers 7; Students 196.
Catechesis/Religious Programs—Tel: 860-274-4123. Theresa N. Morgado, D.R.E.
Students 701.

West Hartford, Hartford Co.,

1—St. Brigid's, (1919), Revs. Edward J. McLean; Richard B. Sherer, Pastor Emeritus; Deacon Robert J. Hilliard. In res., Rev. Msgr. Charles B. Johnson.
Res., 1088 New Britain Ave., 06110-2489. Tel: 860-236-5965.
School—100 Mayflower St., 06110. Tel: 860-561-2130.
Sisters 1; Lay Teachers 15; Students 264.
Catechesis/Religious Programs—Tel: 860-521-8523.
Students 320.

2—St. Helena, (1966), Revs. Francis P. Johnson; Eugene M. Kilbride; Deacons Raymond Fugere; James Murphy. In res., Rev. Zigford Kriss.
Res., 30 Echo Ln., 06107-3698. Tel: 860-521-1921.
Catechesis/Religious Programs—Tel: 860-521-3661.
Students 286.

3—St. John the Evangelist, (1942) (Spanish), Revs. John P. Tracy, Admin.; Paul F. Kenefick; Deacon Thomas F. Breen, III.
Res., 251 Newfield Ave., 06106-3630. Tel: 860-953-3147.
Catechesis/Religious Programs—Students 160.

4—St. Mark the Evangelist, (1942), Team Ministry: Rev. Thomas J. Sas; Rev. Msgr. William J. Mullen; Deacon John J. Mylott.
Res., 467 S. Quaker Ln., 06110-1000. Tel: 860-233-1269.
Catechesis/Religious Programs—491 Quaker Ln., 06110. Tel: 860-236-3545. Agnes Allen, D.R.E.
Students 319.

5—St. Peter Claver, (1966), Revs. Joseph P. McGarry; James M. Moran; John J. Kiely.
Res., 47 Pleasant St., 06107-1600. Tel: 860-561-4235.
Catechesis/Religious Programs—Tel: 860-521-2904.
Students 510.

6—St. Thomas the Apostle Church, (1921), Revs. Arthur J. Murphy; Patrick J. Curran (SLC); Edward M. Moran; Deacon Eugene Phaneuf. In res., Rev. John J. Stack.
Res., 872 Farmington Ave., 06119-1499. Tel: 860-233-8269.
School—25 Dover Rd., 06119. Tel: 860-236-6257; Fax: 860-236-8865.
Lay Teachers 27; Students 310.
Catechesis/Religious Programs—Tel: 860-523-4209.
Students 323.

7—St. Timothy's, (1958), Rev. Henry P. Cody; Deacon George Brown. In res., Rev. Alphonse Labieniec.
Res., 1116 N. Main St., 06117-1209. Tel: 860-233-5131; Fax: 860-232-2189.
School—St. Timothy Middle School, 225 King Philip Dr., 06117. Tel: 860-236-0614.
Lay Teachers 13; Students 138.
Catechesis/Religious Programs—Tel: 860-232-3952.
Students 263.

West Haven, New Haven Co.,

1—Our Lady of Victory, (1935), Revs. Mark S. Suslenko; Mathew Kappalumakkel. In res., Rev. John F. Curran, Pastor Emeritus.
Res., 600 Jones Hill Rd., 06516-6399. Tel: 203-934-6357; Fax: 203-932-3315.
School—Tel: 203-932-6457.
Lay Teachers 13; Students 248.
Catechesis/Religious Programs—Tel: 203-933-0044.
Students 657.

2—St. John Vianney, (1965), Rev. John F. Brinsmade; Deacons Frank J. Bevvino, Jr.; Charles W. Parlee, Jr.
Res., 300 Capt. Thomas Blvd., 06516-5974. Tel: 203-934-6000; Fax: 203-934-5677.
Catechesis/Religious Programs—Tel: 203-933-8471.
Students 276.

3—St. Lawrence's, (1886), Team Ministry: Rev. Thomas A. Sievel; Deacons Anthony P. Solli; John E. Wheeler.
Res., 207 Main St., 06516-4599. Tel: 203-934-8351; Fax: 203-937-7858.
School—233 Main St., 06516. Tel: 203-933-2518. Sr. Rosemarie Ryan, S.N.D., Dir.
Lay Teachers 11; Students 273.
Catechesis/Religious Programs—231 Main St., 06516. Tel: 203-933-2519.
Students 227.

4—ST. LOUIS, (1886) (French Territorial), Rev. Peter J. Pinto; Deacons Salvatore DeFilippo; Edward J. Mancini.
Res., 89 Bull Hill Ln., 06516-3998. Tel: 203-934-5249; Fax: 203-934-5240.

5—ST. PAUL'S, (1916), Rev. Lawrence Symolon; Deacons George Schiro; Richard Fournier.
Res., 41 Alling St., 06516-2799. Tel: 203-933-1024.
Catechesis/Religious Programs—Tel: 203-934-1357. Patricia Sastor, D.R.E.
Students 400.
Parish Center: 45 Alling St., 06516. Tel: 203-934-1357.
Mission—West Haven, Our Lady of Mt. Carmel Chapel, Fenwick St., 06516. Tel: 203-389-6384.

West Simsbury, Hartford Co., St. Catherine of Siena (1971), Rev. Richard R. Russell; Deacon Thomas F. Delehanty.
Res., Box 184, 06092. Tel: 203-658-1642.
Catechesis/Religious Programs—Students 256.

Wethersfield, Hartford Co., Corpus Christi (1941), Team Ministry: Revs. Thomas B. Campion, Co-Pastor; David W. Lonergan, Co-Pastor. In res., Rev. Bradford Colton, Pastor Emeritus.
Res., 84 Somerset St., 06109-3031. Tel: 860-529-2545.
School—Tel: 860-529-5487; Fax: 860-257-9106. Mrs. Eileen Sampiere, Prin.
Religious 1; Lay Teachers 22; Students 460.
Catechesis/Religious Programs—581 Silas Deane Hwy., 06109. Tel: 860-721-9419.
Students 543.

Incarnation (1963), Revs. John F. Edwards; Frederick M. Aniello; Deacons Robert J. D'Efemia; Carroll Violette.
Res., 544 Prospect St., 06109-3696. Tel: 860-529-2533.
Catechesis/Religious Programs—Tel: 860-529-6765. Noranne Wamester, D.R.E.
Students 447.

Sacred Heart (1876), Team Ministry: Revs. Thomas B. Campion, Co-Pastor; David W. Lonergan, Co-Pastor; Deacon Seth M. English.
Res., 56 Hartford Ave., 06109-1800. Tel: 860-529-1991.
Catechesis/Religious Programs—Tel: 860-529-0815.
Students 192.

Windsor, Hartford Co., St. Gabriel's (1894), Revs. James C. Rush; Richard J. Neumann; Michael F.X. Hinkley, S.T.D.; Deacons Joseph J. Cooke; Donald E. Norton; Ronald M. Biamomte.
Res., 379 Broad St., 06095-3004. Tel: 860-688-4905.
School—77 Bloomfield Ave., 06095. Tel: 860-688-6401.
Lay Teachers 11; Students 297.
Catechesis/Religious Programs—Students 288.

St. Gertrude's (1947), Rev. Maurice J. Barry; Deacons Francis J. Giunta; Vincent Thorney.
Res., 550 Matianuck Ave., 06095-3599. Tel: 860-522-6163.

Windsor Locks, Hartford Co., St. Mary (1866), Revs. Robert A. O'Grady; Francis P. McDonnell.
Res., 42 Spring St., 06096-2311. Tel: 860-623-2524; Fax: 860-623-2525. [CEM]
Parish Center—45 Church St., 06096. Tel: 860-627-9469.
Catechesis/Religious Programs—Tel: 860-627-9469.
Students 458.

St. Robert Bellarmine (1962), Rev. Thomas F. Farrell.
Res., 52 S. Elm St., P.O. Box 315, 06096-0315. Tel: 860-623-0240; Fax: 860-623-0240.
Catechesis/Religious Programs—Students 151.

Winsted, Litchfield Co., St. Joseph's (1853), Revs. Anthony F. Moore, O.F.M.; Leon Ristuccia, O.F.M.; John W. Rudy, O.F.M.; Deacons William H. Wilcox; Ferdinand Serafini, (Retired).
Res., 31 Oak St., P.O. Box 808, 06098-0808. Tel: 860-379-3369; Fax: 860-379-4194. [CEM]
School—St. Anthony's, 55 Oak St., 06098. Tel: 860-379-7521. Sr. Fidelis Shepherd, F.M.D.M., Prin.
Lay Teachers 9; Students 227.
Catechesis/Religious Programs—Tel: 860-379-5968.
Students 333.

Wolcott, New Haven Co., St. Pius X (1955), Revs. Henry A. Balchunas; Vittorio Guerrera; Deacon Stephen J. Kelly.
Res., 525 Woodtick Rd., 06716-2898. Tel: 203-879-2544; Fax: 203-879-2545.
Catechesis/Religious Programs—Tel: 203-879-9030; Fax: 203-879-2545.
Students 619.

St. Maria Goretti (1973), Rev. William R. Sokolowski; Deacons Leonard R. Lewandoski; Roger Albert.
Res., 1300 Woodtick Rd., P.O. Box 6291, 06716-0291. Tel: 203-879-4608; Fax: 203-879-4609.
Catechesis/Religious Programs—Tel: 203-879-5242.
Students 350.

Woodbridge, New Haven Co., Church of the Assumption (1924), Revs. Gene Gianelli; Robert J. Lord; Deacons Joseph P. Borland; Mario DiRienzo.
Res., 81 Center Rd., 06525-1699. Tel: 203-387-7119; Fax: 203-387-4281.
Catechesis/Religious Programs—Tel: 203-389-9863; Fax: 203-387-4281. Sr. Dorellen Sullivan, R.S.M., D.R.E.
Students 595.

Woodbury, Litchfield Co., St. Teresa's (1902), Rev. George G. Laliberte.
Res., P.O. Box A, 11 Washington Ave., 06798-0417. Tel: 203-263-2008.
Catechesis/Religious Programs—Students 313.

Woodmont, New Haven Co., St. Agnes (1906), Rev. Francis X. Callahan.
Res., 400 Merwin Ave., 06460-7198. Tel: 203-878-1617.
Catechesis/Religious Programs—Students 558.

Yalesville, New Haven Co., Our Lady of Fatima (1960), Revs. Salvatore F. Cavagnuolo; Thomas J. Cieslikowski; Deacon William D. Giordano. In res., Rev. Leo J. Daily, Pastor Emeritus.
Res., 382 Hope Hill Rd., 06492-2270. Tel: 203-265-0961; Fax: 203-269-9386.
Catechesis/Religious Programs—Tel: 203-265-6426; Fax: 203-269-9386. Linda O'Hara, D.R.E.
Students 708.

Chaplains of Public Institutions

HARTFORD. *Hartford Hospital,* 80 Seymour St., 06102-5037. Tel: 860-545-2251. Chaplains: Rev. Hudson R. Richard; Ms. Diane L. Cardinal.

BRISTOL. *Bristol Hospital,* Brewster Rd., 06011-0977. Tel: 860-585-3431. Rev. Donald O. Rackliffe, Chap.

CHESHIRE. *Connecticut Correctional Institution,* 900 Milldale Rd., 06410. Tel: 203-272-2215. Rev. Daniel G. Keefe, Chap.
Manson Youth Institution, 42 Jarvis St., 06510. Tel: 203-272-5391. Rev. Alphonse S. Labieniec, Chap.

ENFIELD. *Carl Robinson Correctional Institution,* P.O. Box 1400, 06083-1400. Tel: 860-763-6200. Deacon Robert P. Gale, Chap.
Connecticut Correctional Institution, 1500 Enfield, Somers (Enfield), 06083-1500. Tel: 203-763-7318. Rev. Anthony J. Bruno, Chap., Res., 90 Alden Ave., 06082. Tel: 203-745-9966.

NEW BRITAIN. *New Britain General Hospital,* 100 Grand St., 06050. Tel: 860-224-5011. Rev. Ronald T. Smith, Chap., Res., 396 Church St., 06051.

NEW HAVEN. *Connecticut Correctional Institution,* 245 Whalley Ave., 06511. Tel: 203-789-7111. Rev. Eugene Bonski, M.S.s.A., Chap.
Yale-New Haven Hospital, 20 York St., 06510-3202. Rev. Ralph M. Coliccio, Coord. Catholic Apostolate, Tel: 203-785-2152.

NEWINGTON. *Department of Veteran Affairs Medical Center,* 555 Willard Ave., 06111. Tel: 860-666-6951. Rev. Francis M. Vella, Chap.

ROCKY HILL. *Veterans' Home and Hospital,* West St., 06067. Tel: 860-529-2571. Rev. James B. Quilty, M.S.

WATERBURY. *Waterbury Hospital,* 64 Robbins St., 06721. Tel: 203-573-6000. Revs. Richard C. Bollea; Lawrence J. LeClair, Chap., 785 Highland Ave., 06708. Tel: 203-756-8070.

WEST HAVEN. *Veterans' Medical Center,* W. Spring St., 06516. Tel: 203-932-5711. Rev. Daniel Scott, M.S.

Special and other (Arch)Diocesan Assignment:
Reverend Monsignors—
Ginty, Thomas M., Sec. to the Archbishop, Dir. Office for Divine Worship, 467 Bloomfield Ave., Bloomfield, CT 06002
Johnson, Charles B., Vicar for Priests, St. Thomas Seminary, 467 Bloomfield Ave., Bloomfield, CT 06002
Plocharczyk, Daniel J., Moderator of the Curia/Chancellor
Reverend Fathers—
Barry, Thomas J., Exec. Dir., Connecticut Catholic Conference, 134 Framington Ave., Hartford, CT 06105-3784
Bergin, Robert D., Dir., Deaf Apostolate, Mercyknoll, 243 Steele Rd., West Hartford, CT 06117
Charman, Eugene J., Archdiocesan Computer Consultant, 50 Knowles Dr., Plantsville, CT 06479
Conte, John P., Min., Office of Ministry for Priests, 467 Bloomfield Ave., Bloomfield, CT 06002
Dietrich, John J., Vocations Dir., St. Thomas Seminary, 469 Bloomfield Ave., Bloomfield, CT 06002
Donohue, Aidan N., Rector & Pres., St. Thomas Seminary, 467 Bloomfield Ave., Bloomfield, CT 06002
Gatzak, John P., Dir., Office of Communications (Radio/Television), 785 Asylum Ave., Hartford, CT 06105
Kinnane, James F., J.C.L., Vicar for Religious, 134 Farmington Ave., Hartford, CT 06105-3784
Kriss, Zigford J., Supt. of Schools, 467 Bloomfield Ave., Bloomfield, CT 06002
LeBlanc, Alvin J., Adjutant Judicial Vicar (Vice Officialis), Chancery Tribunal, 134 Farmington Ave., Hartford, CT 06105
Liptak, David Q., Consulting Editor, "The Catholic Transcript", 785 Asylum Ave., Hartford, CT 06105
McCarthy, John J., Tribunal, Judicial Vicar (Officialis), Chancery, 134 Farmington Ave., Hartford, CT 06105-3784
McLean, Edward J., Dir., Catholic Library and Information Center, 125 Market St., Hartford, CT 06103
Motta, Michael J., Dir., Office of Religious Education
Murasso, Jeremiah N., Exec. Dir., Highland Heights, New Haven, CT
Tiano, Christopher M., Exec. Editor, "The Catholic Transcript", 785 Asylum Ave., Hartford, CT 06105
Wrenn, Lawrence G., Judicial Vicar for the Court of Appeals, Tribunal Office, 134 Farmington Ave., Hartford, CT 06105

On Duty Outside the Archdiocese:
Reverend Monsignors—
Sokolowski, Robert S., Catholic University of America, 401 Michigan Ave., N.E., Washington, DC 20017
Reverend Fathers—
Charbonneau, William R., 4900 Colonel Addison Pl., Upper Marlborough, MD 20772
Cwiekowski, Frederick J., S.S., St. Patrick Seminary, 320 Middlefield Rd., Menlo Park, CA 94025
Eno, Robert B., S.S., Catholic University of America, 401 Michigan Ave., N.E., Washington, DC 20017
Goekler, Thomas F., Maryknoll Technical School, 45 Choi Ha Rd., Jordan Valley, Kowloon, Hong China. Tel: 852-758-3539; Fax: 852-813-7221
Leavitt, Robert F., S.S., St. Mary Seminary, 5400 Roland Ave., Baltimore, MD 21210
Malave, Will-Roger, St. Joseph Rectory, RD #1, P.O. Box 203, Proctor, WV 26055-9705
Matera, Frank J., Catholic University of America, 401 Michigan Ave., N.E., Washington, DC 20017
McBrien, Richard P., University of Notre Dame, Notre Dame, IN 46556
Mitchell, Thomas R., Good Shepherd, (Buen Pastor Parish) Calle San Gerardo, A-1-A Terrace, Mayaguez, PR 00708
Morrison, Douglas A., 540 N. St., S.W., Apt. 703, Washington, DC 20024
Novoa, Dominic E., Chap., St. Mary Hospital, West Palm Beach, FL 33407
O'Keefe, William F., St. Thomas College, St. Paul, MN 55101
Pfnausch, Edward G., Catholic University, 401 Michigan Ave., N.E., Washington, DC 20017
Thayer, David D., S.S., St. Mary Seminary & University, 5400 Roland Ave., Baltimore, MD 21210
Whalen, William C., 130 Springfield Ave., Ottawa, K1S OE5 Canada

---

Military Chaplains:
Reverend Fathers—
Cavanaugh, Kevin P., U.S. Army, 3147 Capstan Way, Colorado Springs, CO 80906
Devine, Joseph T., U.S. Navy, US Naval Station, Box 47, Pearl Harbor, HI 96860-6000
Hanley, Dennis P., U.S. Air Force, 90 MWG/HC, 7000 Randel Ave., F.E. Warren AFB, WY 82005

Retired:
Reverend Monsignors—
Connelly, James A., 182 Washington St., Norwich, CT 06360
Daly, Charles W., St. Luke Rectory, 66 Bolton St., Hartford, CT 06105-3784
Fries, Francis A., 42 Blakeslee St., Bristol, CT 06010
Kennedy, John S., 1213 N. Main St., West Hartford, CT 06117
Wodarski, John P., St. Stanislaus Rectory, 510 West St., Bristol, CT 06010
Reverend Fathers—
Arehambault, James H., 2003 49th St. West, Bradenton, FL 34209
Barlowski, Joseph R., 141 Curtiss St., Bristol, CT 06010
Blaney, Philip L., St. Jerome Rectory, 1010 Slater Rd., New Britain, CT 06053-1698
Boyle, James M., St. Mary Rectory, 16 Bidwell Sq., Unionville, CT 06085-1116
Castellani, John J., 364 Lakeview Dr., Southington, CT 06489
Chagnon, Robert J., 19333 Summerlin Rd., Fort Myers, FL 33908
Colton, Bradford, Corpus Christi Rectory, 84 Somerset St., Wethersfield, CT 06109

Cretella, Biagio, 75 Washington Ave., Bldg. 4, #207, Hamden, CT 06518-3264
Cronin, W. Vincent, St. Mary Home, 2021 Albany Ave., West Hartford, CT 06117
Croteau, Francois A., 88 Scott Swamp Rd. #309, Farmington, CT 06032
Crowley, Stephen L., 156 Circular Ave., Hamden, CT 06514
Curran, John F., Our Lady of Victory Rectory, 600 Jones Hill Rd., West Haven, CT 06516
Daily, Leo J., Our Lady of Fatima Rectory, 382 Hope Hill Rd., Yalesville, CT 06492
DeMuro, S. Patrick, 1229 Winsted Rd., #91, Torrington, CT 06790
Dery, Henry R., 45 Aldea Ave., Dudley, MA 01571
Dilion, Joseph A., 13 Leeway Dr., Westbrook, CT 06498
Donahue, Joseph P., St. Francis Rectory, 318 Church St., Naugatuck, CT 06770
Dyer, George A., St. Mary Home, 2021 Albany Ave., West Hartford, CT 06117
Ferrigno, Denis P., Our Lady of Good Counsel Rectory, 56 Center St., Folly Beach, NC 29439
Fiedorczyk, Henry P., Holy Cross Rectory, 31 Biruta St., New Britain, CT 06053
Flynn, Joseph A., 12 Yankee Peddler Path, Unit 2, Madison, CT 06443
Flynn, Vincent J., P.O. Box 651, Kent, CT 06757
Foran, Edward R., 52 Grove St., Yalesville, CT 06492
Gradeck, A. Edward, St. Mary Home, 2021 Albany Ave., West Hartford, CT 06117
Graziani, Joseph A., 380 Lake Plymouth Blvd., Plymouth, CT 06728
Guandalini, Julius S., 8 Sara Circle, North Haven, CT 06473
Hale, Francis A., 9 Shady Brook Dr., West Hartford, CT 06107
Hannon, John P., 21 Pleasant Rd., Enfield, CT 06082
Hastillo, Stanley E., 425 East Rd., Broad Brook, CT 06016
Hayes, William J., 47 Clark St., New Britain, CT 06051
Hewitt, Charles L., St. Joseph Manor, 6448 Main St., Trumbull, CT 06611
Horgan, John A., 1696 Litchfield Tpke., Woodbridge, CT 06525
Keane, Martin T., St. Mary Home, 2021 Albany Ave., West Hartford, CT 06117
Keeley, Alban F., St. Mary Home, 2021 Albany Ave., West Hartford, CT 06117
Kennedy, Charles T., St. Joseph Manor, 6448 Main St., Trumbull, CT 06117-2701
Killeen, John J., 40 Derbyshire St., Derby, CT 06418
LeClair, Lawrence J.
Lescoe, Francis J., 196 Eddy Glover Blvd., New Britain, CT 06053
Lyddy, Vincent E., St. Therese Rectory, 555 Middletown Ave., North Haven, CT 06473
Maguire, Felix H., 690 Mulberry Rd., Guilford, CT 06437
Malley, Michael A., St. Joseph Rectory, 4 Main St., Canaan, CT 06018
Matutis, Joseph J., 700 Maple Ave., Unit 209, Hartford, CT 06114
Maynard, Leo E., 123 Maple St., Somers, CT 06071
McGrath, Robert D., 873 Durham Rd., Madison, CT 06443
McGrath, William E., St. Christopher Rectory, 538 Brewer St., East Hartford, CT 06118-2399
Muha, Edward J., 236 Fairlawn Dr., Torrington, CT 06790
Murphy, Joseph G., Heritage Cove Condo, 85 River Rd., N1, Essex, CT 06426
Nazzaro, Stanley J., 135 West Ave., Great Barrington, MA 01230
Neveu, Armand A., 72 Castle Rock Rd., Woodstock, CT 06281
O'Connor, John R., St. Joseph Manor, 6448 Main St., Rm. A-310, Trumbull, CT 06611
O'Dea, James F., St. Michael Rectory, 25 Maple Ave., Beacon Falls, CT 06403
O'Leary, Donald J., St. Aloysius Rectory, 254 Burritt St., Plantsville, CT 06479
O'Neill, Francis S., 265 S.W. 14th Ct., Pompano, FL 33060
O'Neill, George T., 265 S.W 14th Ct., Pompano, FL 33060
Otero, Neil, 565 W. 169th St., Apt. 4C, New York, NY 10032
Perreault, Aurele R., 1884 Old Waterbury Rd., Cheshire, CT 06410
Picher, Leo J., 5 Laurel Ln., Bloomfield, CT 06002
Ptaszynski, Stephen F., 90 Wolcott St., Box 1271, Bristol, CT 06011-1271
Quinn, John J., 150 Pheasant Ln., Branford, CT 06405
Riccio, Alexis D., St. Mary Home, 2021 Albany Ave., West Hartford, CT 06117
Sabulis, Paul P., St. Joseph Rectory, 46 Congress Ave., Waterbury, CT 06708-3845
Sanders, Robert E., 224 Elm St., Apt. 214, West Haven, CT 06516
Saunders, Robert E., 328 Meadow Rd., Farmington, CT 06032
Shamsher, Paul, Sacred Heart Rectory, 74 Liberty St., New Haven, CT 06519-2299
Shaw, Charles E., P.O. Box 10158, Phoenix, AZ 85064
Smith, William C., 82 W. Rocks Rd., Norwalk, CT 06851
Speer, Patrick J., St. Joseph Manor, 6448 Main St., Trumbull, CT 06611
Sullivan, James J., Cromwell Crest, 385 Main St., Cromwell, CT 06416
Sullivan, John L., The Canterbury, 45 Highland St., West Hartford, CT 06119
Suppe, Joseph V., c/o Morgado, 471 Willow St., Waterbury, CT 06710
Testa, Genaro J., 5233 S.W. 11th Ct., Cape Coral, FL 33914
Thuer, William J., Visitation Plaza, 100 Jefferson Sq., Apt. 6-A, Waterbury, CT 06706
Toohey, Thomas F., St. Mary Home, 2021 Albany Ave., West Hartford, CT 06117
Toscano, Pasquale A., St. Joseph Residence, 1365 Enfield St., Enfield, CT 06082
Ventresca, A. Andrew, Spring Rd., P.O. Box 413, Bethlehem, CT 06751
Ventura, Anthony C., St. Mary, 5 Clemont Ter., Newport, VT 05855
Vitka, Stephen G., Underhill Rd., P.O. Box 608, Sandy Hook, CT 06482
Wodarski, John P., St. Stanislaus Rectory, 510 West St., P.O. Box 1860, Bristol, CT 06011
Yuse, Raymond B., 3 Wongonk Tr., P.O. Box 1860, East Hampton, CT 06424
Zanavich, Albert J., Assumption Rectory, 61 N. Cliff St., Ansonia, CT 06401

Permanent Deacons:
Abdalla, John, St. Catherine, Broad Brook
Aconfora, Ralph A., Holy Rosary, Ansonia
Albert, Roger R., St. Maria Goretti, Wolcott
Amat, Emiliano A., Unassigned
Angeloni, Carmine, St. Therese, North Haven
Anthony, Andrew, St. Bernard, Tariffville
Arena, Paul, St. Michael the Archangel, Terryville
Azzaro, Gabriel S., St. Bernadette, New Haven
Baldwin, Alan C., Good Shepherd, Seymour
Bandeira, Francis, St. Anne, Waterbury
Bartlett, William, Jr., St. Barnabas, North Haven
Battiston, Donald, (Retired)
Baxter, Wesley F., St. Bridget, Cheshire
Bergers, William, St. Monica, Northford
Bernd, Robert E., St. Martha, Enfield
Bertolini, Valentino H., Sacred Heart, Suffield
Bevvino, Frank J., Jr., St. John Vianney, West Haven
Biamonte, Ronald, St. Gabriel, Windsor
Bichi, Americo, Holy Infant, Orange
Blair, Robert N., St. Patrick, Collinsville
Borland, Joseph P., Assumption, Woodbridge
Brady, John F., Assumption, Ansonia
Breen, Thomas F., III, St. John the Evangelist, West Hartford
Brotz, John J., St. Margaret, Madison
Brown, George S., St. Timothy, West Hartford
Brown, William J., St. Rose, East Hartford
Brunell, Robert J., St. Brendan, New Haven
Camden, Ronald P., St. Mary, New Britain
Camerota, Daniel A., St. John the Evangelist, Watertown
Campbell, Alan D., St. Ann, Avon
Cardona, Raul, St. Rose, Meriden
Carey, Edward J., (Retired)
Carrero, Adolfo G., Immaculate Conception, Hartford
Carroll, Michael E., SS. Peter & Paul, Waterbury
Casey, Francis J., Mary Our Queen, Plantsville
Cassidy, Vincent, Sacred Heart, Southbury
Castaldi, Joseph R., St. George, Guilford
Cenci, Peter A., St. Mary, Newington
Chamberland, J. Fernand, Assumption, Manchester
Charles, John H., St. John the Evangelist, Watertown
Clifford, Thomas J., St. Mary, Union City
Colella, Charles, St. Leo the Great, Waterbury
Colella, Guy A., (Retired)
Conklin, Thomas J., St. Margaret Mary, South Windsor
Conte, John J.M., Jr., St. Michael, New Haven
Cooke, Joseph J., St. Gabriel, Windsor
Coppola, Angelo J., St. Thomas, Southington
Cote, Laurent L., St. Anthony, Bristol
Coyne, Joseph F., St. Elizabeth, Branford
Cretella, Joseph J., Jr., Holy Trinity, Wallingford
Croll, Calvin S., St. Gabriel, Milford
Crowley, John, St. Dominic, Southington
Cruess, Donald E., St. Francis Xavier, Waterbury
Culhane, Neil, St. John of the Cross, Middlebury
Cunniff, Charles E., Jr., St. Rose, Meriden
Cusano, Vincent F., Jr., Epiphany, Cheshire
D'Efemia, Robert J., Incarnation, Wethersfield
Daigle, Ronald R., St. Mary, East Hartford
Dean, Henry A., (Retired)
DeFilippo, Salvatore A., St. Louis, West Haven
DeHippolytis, Albert J., Unassigned
DeJesus, Efrain, (Retired)
DeJesus, Isidiro, Sacred Heart, Hartford
Delaney, Robert, Unassigned
DelCorte, Nicholas, Our Lady of Pompeii, East Haven
Delehanty, Thomas F., St. Catherine of Siena, West Simsbury
Delgado, Domingo, Our Lady of Sorrows, Hartford
Delmonte, Richard F., (Retired)
Dembishack, John L., Immaculate Heart of Mary, Harwinton
Dempsey, John F., St. Augustine, Hartford
Dickman, Arthur J., Holy Family, Enfield
Dickson, Edward, St. Francis of Assisi, Torrington
DiMauro, Joseph, Mary Our Queen, Plantsville
Dinkle, George J., St. Anthony, Prospect
Diorio, Nicholas J., St. Thomas, Goshen
DiPiro, Joseph L., Assumption, Ansonia
DiRienzo, Mario, Assumption, Woodbridge
Dlugokinski, Jose L., Immaculate Heart of Mary, Harwinton
DosSantos, Kenneth, St. Anthony of Padua, Litchfield
Doyle, Henry, St. Gabriel, Milford
Driscoll, Frank M., Unassigned
Dungan, Roy C., St. Gregory, Bristol
Dwyer, David F., St. Francis of Assisi, South Windsor
Elder, William A., St. Margaret, Madison
English, Seth M., Sacred Heart, Wethersfield
Eschrich, Paul C., (Retired)
Eyles, William H., St. Vincent de Paul, East Haven
Farrell, William A., St. Ann, Avon
Fiederlein, Frank H., (Retired)
Fitzgerald, Robert W., (Retired)
Flenke, Richard M., Unassigned
Florio, Louis J., St. Therese, North Haven
Fortier, James A., Holy Spirit, Newington
Fournier, Richard G., St. Paul, West Haven
Fracasso, Robert G., St. Donato, New Haven
Fugere, Raymond J., St. Helena, West Hartford
Fusco, Louis P., St. Monica, Northford
Gabriele, Joseph G., St. Mary, Simsbury
Gale, Robert P., Our Lady of Mt. Carmel, Meriden
Galiette, Andrew S., Immaculate Conception, Southington
Geraci, Gerald S., Our Lady of Mercy, Plainville
Giaimo, Thomas, Our Lady of Pompeii, East Haven
Giard, Edward J., St. James, Manchester
Gilles, William J., St. Dunstan, Glastonbury
Giordano, William D., (Retired)
Giunta, Francis J., (Retired)
Giusto, Oreste M., (Retired)
Godlewsky, Robert H., St. Lawrence O'Toole, Hartford
Gonzalez, Aquilino, St. Joseph, Meriden
Gordon, Robert D., Unassigned
Grant, Frederick M., St. Mary, Derby
Griffin, Wayne F., St. Mary, Lakeville
Gurr, Ronald, St. John the Baptist, New Haven
Guzzardi, Carmelo A., St. Paul, Kensington
Hajjar, George D., St. Margaret, Waterbury
Harla, Francis J., Jr., Unassigned
Hart, John L., Unassigned
Hayden, Bernard J., Holy Infant, Orange
Hernandez, Carmelo, Immaculate Conception, Hartford
Hickey, James E., Jr., St. Luke, Hartford
Hilliard, Robert J., St. Brigid, West Hartford
Hoffman, Harold, Holy Infant, Orange
Iadarola, Paul P., St. Anthony, Prospect
Iassogna, Nicholas J., Jr., St. Vincent Ferrer, Naugatuck
Impellitteri, Michael, Sr., (Retired)
Jacques, J. Martin, (Retired)
Johnson, Robert C., Assumption, Ansonia
Johnson, Thomas F., St. Patrick, Waterbury
Kane, Joseph E., St. Patrick, Farmington
Kelly, Stephen J., St. Pius X, Wolcott
Kieda, Rene J., St. Martha, Enfield
Kimball, Earle A., Sacred Heart, Waterbury
Klein, Peter J., Jr., St. John Fisher, Marlborough
Klimanowski, Peter J., Our Lady of Sorrows, Hartford
Klimas, Vincent A., (Retired)
Koch, Paul T., St. Barnabas, North Haven
Krasnicki, Frank J., St. Michael, Beacon Falls
Kraussman, George A., Holy Angels, South Meriden
Kristopik, Albert P., St. John the Evangelist, New Britain
Kulas, Michael J., Sacred Heart, Southbury

Kulas, Paul J., Mary Our Queen, Plantsville
Labagnara, Eugene A., St. Francis Cabrini, North Haven
Lambert, Robert E., St. Martha, Enfield
LaPierre, Joseph W., Our Lady of Pompeii, East Haven
LaRochelle, Robert R., St. Margaret Mary, South Windsor
LaRocque, Leo R., Assumption, Manchester
Lauer, Paul B., St. Mary, Milford
Lavoie, Joseph V., (Retired)
LeBlanc, Gaspard D., St. Anne, Waterbury
Lembo, Victor M., Holy Rosary, Ansonia
Lepkowski, Henry M., (Retired)
Levesque, Joseph J., St. Ann, Bristol
Lewandoski, Leonard R., St. Maria Goretti, Wolcott
Lickwar, R. Carl, St. Ann, New Britain
Linehan, F. Robert, Holy Family, Enfield
Locorotondo, Frank S., Unassigned
Loffredo, Eugene E., Unassigned
Lopatosky, Thomas J., (Retired)
Lopez, Alejandro, St. Cecilia, Waterbury
Lopez, Rafael, Our Lady of Sorrows, Hartford
Lotto, Henry, Our Lady of Pompeii, East Haven
Lovelace, William, St. Augustine, North Branford
Lowe, Burdon G., (Retired)
Lozier, Albert J., St. Ann, Bristol
Maffeo, John R., Good Shepherd, Seymour
Makara, John W., Immaculate Conception, Terryville
Mancini, Edward J., St. Louis, West Haven
Marcarelli, Julius R., St. Rose of Lime, New Haven
Masucci, Ernest J., (Retired)
McCusker, Kenneth F., Ascension, Hamden
McGivney, Raymond J., Jr., Holy Family, Enfield
McGrath, William M., Nativity, Bethlehem
McInnis, John P., Unassigned
McKaig, John W., St. Paul, Glastonbury
Michaele, Adam J., St. Stephen, Hamden
Miller, Roland G., Sacred Heart, Kent
Mingrone, William F., St. Francis, Naugatuck
Mon, Joseph J.G., St. Bernard, Enfield
Monaco, Daniel G., (Retired)
Morales, Jose A., St. Augustine, Hartford
Motto, Vincent J., St. Catherine, Broad Brook
Muro, Robert E., Sr., Our Lady of the Lakes, New Milford
Murphy, James R., St. Helena, West Hartford
Mylott, John J., St. Mark the Evangelist, West Hartford
Navickas, Robert D., St. Joseph, Poquonock
Nebiolo, Eugene, St. Dominic, Southington
Newbery, Robert D., St. Therese, Granby
Norton, Donald E., St. Gabriel, Windsor
O'Connell, Cornelius D., Corpus Christi, Wethersfield
O'Connor, Martin J., St. Mary Priory, New Haven
O'Day, Richard J., St. Matthew, Forestville
O'Donovan, John, Our Lady of Mt. Carmel, Hamden
O'Neill, James F., St. George, Guilford
O'Toole, Michael J., St. Mary, Newington
Ortiz, Edwin, Sacred Heart, Hartford
Ortiz, Jacinto, St. Rose of Lima, Meriden
Pahl, John E., St. Matthew, Forestville
Pallotti, Robert M., St. Joseph, Bristol
Pantalena, Edward J., Epiphany, Cheshire
Parenteau, Raymond A., St. John Fisher, Marlborough
Parlee, Charles, St. John Vianney, West Haven
Paturzo, Frank X., St. Therese, North Haven
Perez, Valentin, St. Michael, Hartford
Pettinico, George, Our Lady of Lourdes, Waterbury
Phaneuf, Eugene E., St. Thomas the Apostle, West Hartford
Poland, James K., (Retired)
Pond, Donald H., Jr., Holy Family, Enfield
Prete, Paul V., St. Mary, Branford
Probulis, Gerard J., Unassigned
Puskas, George A., St. Mary, Milford
Quinn, James P., St. Thomas, Southington
Ramos, Edmund J., Christ the Redeemer, Milford
Regan, Joseph M., Jr., St. Margaret, Madison
Renker, Richard E., St. John of the Cross, Middlebury
Rigely, John, (Retired)
Riotte, Eugene C., Holy Trinity, Wallingford
Rivera, Jose A., St. Peter, New Haven
Rivera, Pedro L., St. Lawrence O'Toole, Hartford
Rogers, Joseph K., (Retired)
Rogers, Thomas D., Unassigned
Rolando, Joseph E., St. Rita, Hamden
Roman, Chester J., St. Mary, New Britain
Rosello, Modesto A., St. Leo the Great, Waterbury
Roy, Reginald, St. Jerome, New Britain
Ruiz, Candelario, (Retired)
Ryder, Donald A., Unassigned
Ryzewski, Joseph R., St. Aedan, New Haven
Sabo, Paul E., St. Mary, Milford
Saffo, John R., Sr., St. Augustine, Seymour
Sandford, Wayne E., St. Clare, East Haven
Santello, Richard L., Unassigned
Scanlon, Thomas P., St. Bernard, Tariffville
Schiro, George J., St. Paul, West Haven
Sennett, Richard M., St. Mary, Milford
Serafini, Ferdinand T., (Retired)
Shaffer, William B., Holy Infant, Orange
Shelto, Michael A., St. James, Rocky Hill
Shiels, James H., Sacred Heart, East Berlin
Sill, Louis P., Jr., SS. Peter and Paul, Wallingford
Simonin, George A., St. John the Evangelist, Watertown
Singer, Norman H., St. Vincent de Paul, East Haven
Skipp, Barry T., St. Mary, Newington
Sloan, Daniel A., Our Lady of Mt. Carmel, Waterbury
Sloan, Joseph S., St. Patrick, Enfield
Smith, Donald H., Jr., Holy Angels, South Meridan
Solli, Anthony P., St. Lawrence, West Haven
Sponzo, Michael T., Immaculate Conception, Norfolk
St. Jean, Stephen E., Unassigned
Stadtlander, Hobart, St. Bernard, Enfield
Stanley, James H., St. Barnabas, North Haven
Stephens, George R., St. Francis Cabrini, North Haven
Stolfi, Domenic N., St. Michael, Waterbury
Streib, George H., Our Lady of Perpetual Help, Washington Depot
Sullivan, Joseph, Holy Infant, Orange
Sullivan, Michael F., (Retired)
Suzio, John J., St. Joseph, Meriden
Sweeney, John M., St. Mary, Simsbury
Szewczyk, Edward J., St. Joseph, Suffield
Szumigala, Michael P., St. Hedwig, Union City
Taddei, Edward D., St. Aedan, New Haven
Talbot, Oral A., St. Paul, Kensington
Tartaris, Robert P., St. Mary, Branford
Taylor, James P., St. Barnabas, North Haven
Thayer, John E., St. Ann, Avon
Thompson, Bruce R., St. Peter, Hartford
Thorney, Vincent M., St. Gertrude, Windsor
Tomasiello, Frank R., (Retired)
Tripp, James A., Sr., Blessed Sacrament, Hamden
Twerago, John P., St. Joan of Arc, Hamden
Vazquez, Julio, St. Rose of Lima, New Haven
Vecca, Carl M., Immaculate Conception, Waterbury
Violette, Carroll, Incarnation, Wethersfield
VonFeldt, Elmer, (Retired)
Wallin, Robert F., SS. Peter & Paul, Waterbury
Walton, Gilbert E., Jr., St. Therese, Branford
Weaver, Stephen L., St. Elizabeth Seton, Rocky Hill
Weir, John, Sacred Heart, Southbury
Wheeler, John E., St. Lawrence, West Haven
Whittel, Joseph B., Sacred Heart, Bloomfield
Wilber, Richard, Unassigned
Wilcox, George, (Retired)
Wilcox, William H., St. Joseph, Winsted
Winiarski, Benedict L., Sacred Heart, Suffield
Wootton, Gerald R., St. Thomas, Thomaston

INSTITUTIONS LOCATED IN THE ARCHDIOCESE

[A] SEMINARIES, ARCHDIOCESAN

BLOOMFIELD. *St. Thomas Seminary*, 467 Bloomfield Ave., 06002-2999. Tel: 860-242-5573; Fax: 860-242-4886. Mrs. Irene B. Ronan, Registrar. In res., Revs. Stephen C. Foley; Alvin J. LeBlanc; John P. Conte. Fathers 1.

Pope Paul VI House of Formation, 469 Bloomfield Ave., 06002. Rev. John J. Dietrich, Dir. In res., Rev. Aidan N. Donahue. Students 4.

[B] SEMINARIES, RELIGIOUS OR SCHOLASTICATES

CHESHIRE. *Novitiate of the Legion of Christ*, 475 Oak Ave., 06410. Tel: 203-271-0805; Fax: 203-271-3845. Rev. William Meade, L.C., Rector; Bro. Scott Reilly, L.C., Vice Rector; Revs. Juan Jose Garcia, Asst.; Earnest Daly, L.C., Vocation Dir. Instructors of Novices: Revs. Christopher Brackett, L.C.; Eoghan Devlin, L.C. Studies: Revs. Owen Kearns, L.C.; Anthony Rodriguez, L.C.; Tarciscio Samaniego, L.C.; Victor Franco, L.C.; Kevin Meehan, L.C., High School Rector. Priests 11; Religious 14; Juniors 48; Novices 85; High School 61.

[C] COLLEGES AND UNIVERSITIES

HAMDEN. *Mt. Sacred Heart College*, 265 Benham St., 06514. Tel: 203-248-4225; Fax: 203-230-8341.
For a complete listing, refer to the Colleges and Universities section.

NEW HAVEN. *Albertus Magnus College*, 700 Prospect St., 06511-1189. Tel: 203-773-8500; Fax: 203-773-3117.
For a complete listing, refer to the Colleges and Universities section.

WEST HARTFORD. *Saint Joseph College*, 1678 Asylum Ave., 06117. Tel: 860-232-4571; Fax: 860-233-5695.
For a complete listing, refer to the Colleges and Universities section.

[D] HIGH SCHOOLS, ARCHDIOCESAN

BRISTOL. *St. Paul Catholic High School*, 1001 Stafford Ave., 06010-3894. Tel: 860-584-0911. Sr. Joan A. O'Connor, C.S.J., Prin. & Contact; Richard L. Marino, Asst. Prin.; Rev. Robert E. Saunders, Theology Teacher. Faculty: Sisters 1; Lay Teachers 29; Priests 1; Students 378.

MANCHESTER. *East Catholic High School*, 115 New State Rd., 06040. Tel: 860-649-5336; Fax: 860-649-7191. Peggy Siegmund, Prin. Sisters of Notre Dame de Namur 7; Lay Teachers 42; Priests 1; Students 522.

WATERBURY. *Sacred Heart High School*, 142 S. Elm St., 06722. Tel: 203-753-1605. Rev. John Meaney, M.M., Prin.; Mrs. Eileen Regan, Dir. Devel.; Mrs. Jacqueline Jennings, Vice Prin.; Rev. Joseph F. Gorman. Priests 1; Lay Teachers 39; Students 437.

WEST HARTFORD. *Northwest Catholic High School*, 29 Wampanoag Dr., 06117. Tel: 860-236-4221; Fax: 860-586-0911. Dr. Michael S. Griffin, Prin. & Contact; Mrs. Margaret R. Williamson, Vice. Prin.; Mr. Richard Callahan, Vice Prin. Priests 2; Lay Teachers 50; Students 540.

[E] HIGH SCHOOLS, PRIVATE

HAMDEN. *Sacred Heart Academy*, 265 Benham St., 06514-2833. Tel: 203-288-2309; Fax: 203-230-9680. Apostles of the Sacred Heart of Jesus. Sr. Claudia Calzetta, A.S.C.J., Prin. & Contact. Sisters 11; Lay Teachers 32; Students 480.

MILFORD. *Academy of Our Lady of Mercy*, Lauralton Hall, 200 High St., 06460. Tel: 203-877-2786; Fax: 203-876-9760. Sisters of Mercy. Mrs. Karen Yardley, Pres. & Contact. Sisters 5; Lay Teachers 42; Students 430.

NEW BRITAIN. *Mary Immaculate Academy*, Osgood and Corbin Aves., 06053. Tel: 860-229-1747. Daughters of Mary of the Immaculate Conception. Sr. Mary Felicitas, D.M., Prin. & Contact. Sisters 11; Lay Teachers 9; Students 122.

St. Thomas Aquinas High School, 74 Kelsey St., 06051. Tel: 860-225-7847. David P. McCreesh, Prin. & Contact; Rev. Joseph V. Napolitano, Dir. Spiritual Activities. Sisters 2; Priests 1; Lay Teachers 19; Students 150.

NEW MILFORD. *Canterbury School*, Aspetuck Ave., 06776. Tel: 860-355-3103. Coed. Boarding and day students. Thomas J. Sheehy, III, Head-Master; Rev. Sebastian Leonard, O.S.B., Chap. Priests 1; Lay Teachers 48; Students 330.

WATERBURY. *Holy Cross High School*, 587 Oronoke Rd., 06708. Tel: 203-757-9248. Brothers of the Congregation of Holy Cross. Bro. Jerome Donnelly, C.S.C., Chief Admin./Head of School & Contact; Mr. Timothy McDonald, Prin. Brothers 1; Sisters 2; Lay Teachers 61; Students 896.

WEST HAVEN. *Notre Dame High School*, 24 Ricardo St., 06516. Tel: 203-933-1673. Holy Cross Brothers. Bro. James Branigan, C.S.C., Headmaster; Mr. Ralph Proto, Prin.; Mr. Patrick Clifford, Asst. Prin.; Mr. Joseph Ramirez, Dir. of Guidance; Ms. Elizabeth Parker, Dir. Campus Ministry. Brothers 7; Sisters 1; Lay Teachers 50; Students 628.

Notre Dame Loyalty & Endowment Fund, Inc., 24 Ricardo St., 06516.

[F] ELEMENTARY SCHOOLS, PRIVATE

MADISON. *Our Lady of Mercy School, Incorporated*, 149 Neck Rd., 06443-2728. Tel: 203-245-4393. Sr. Jeanne Barry, Prin. & Contact. Sisters of Mercy 2; Lay Teachers 14; Students 215.

WEST HARTFORD. *Cedar Court School, Inc.*, 27 Park Rd., 06119. Tel: 860-523-0060. Sr. Vernice Molinari, Dir. & Contact. Sisters of St. Joseph of Chambery 4; Lay Teachers 4; Children 49.

[G] SPECIALIZED CHILD CARING HOME

NEW BRITAIN. *Marian Educational Clinic*, 314 Osgood Ave., 06053. Tel: 860-223-0501.
For a complete listing, refer to the Special Care Facilities section.

NEW HAVEN. *St. Francis Home for Children, Inc.*, 651 Prospect St., 06511. Tel: 203-777-5513; Fax: 203-777-0644.
For a complete listing, refer to the Special Care Facilities section.

[H] DAY CARE CENTER

HAMDEN. *Clelian Adult Day Center*, 261 Benham St., 06514. Tel: 203-288-0551; 288-4151. Sr. Shawn Lyons, A.S.C.J., Dir. & Contact. Apostles of the Sacred Heart of Jesus. A day health care facility for elderly and disabled adults. Total Assisted 86 per week;

Total Staff 15.
Sacred Heart Manor Nursery and Kindergarten, 261 Benham St., 06514. Tel: 203-230-4889. Sr. Elaine Ann Lattanzi, Contact. Apostles of the Sacred Heart of Jesus 1; Lay Teachers 4; Students 105; Total Assisted 95.

NEW BRITAIN. *Our Lady of Rosehill Day Care Center*, 594 Burritt St., 06053. Tel: 860-223-4846. Sr. Mary Esther, D.M., Contact. Daughters of Mary of the Immaculate Conception 4; Lay Teachers 8; Children 80.

WEST HARTFORD. *Park Village Day Care Center, Inc.*, 27 Park Rd., 06119. Tel: 203-523-1482. Sr. Kathy A. Lombardo, C.S.J., Ed.D., Contact. Sisters of St. Joseph of Chambery 3; Children 30; Total Assisted 60.

[I] GENERAL HOSPITALS

HARTFORD. *Saint Francis Hospital and Medical Center*, 114 Woodland St., 06105-1299. Tel: 714-548-4000; Fax: 714-493-7809.
For a complete listing, refer to the Hospitals section.

NEW HAVEN. *Hospital of St. Raphael*, 1450 Chapel St., 06511. Tel: 203-789-3000; Fax: 203-789-3653.
For a complete listing, refer to the Hospitals section.
Saint Regis Health Center, Inc., 1354 Chapel St., 06511. Tel: 203-867-8300.
For a complete listing, refer to the Hospitals section.

WATERBURY. *St. Mary Hospital*, 56 Franklin St., 06706. Tel: 203-574-6000; Fax: 203-597-3238.
For a complete listing, refer to the Hospitals section.

[J] SPECIAL HOSPITALS

WEST HARTFORD. *Saint Agnes Home, Inc.*, 104 Mayflower St., 06110. Tel: 860-521-7516; Fax: 860-521-6160.
For a complete listing, refer to the Special Care Facilities section.

[K] HOMES FOR AGED

ENFIELD. *The Home for the Aged of the Little Sisters of the Poor*, 1365 Enfield St., 06082-4900. Tel: 860-741-0791.
For a complete listing, refer to the Special Care Facilities section.

NEW BRITAIN. *Monsignor Bojnowski Manor, Inc.*, 50 Pulaski St., 06053 Fax: 860-229-3252.
For a complete listing, refer to the Special Care Facilities section.
St. Lucian's Home for the Aged, 532 Burritt St., 06053. Tel: 860-223-2123.
For a complete listing, refer to the Special Care Facilities section.

WEST HARTFORD. *Saint Mary Home*, 2021 Albany Ave., 06117. Tel: 860-236-1924.
For a complete listing, refer to the Special Care Facilities section.

[L] HEALTH CARE CENTERS FOR AGED

WEST HARTFORD. *McAuley Center, Inc.*, 275 Steele Rd., 06117. Tel: 860-236-6300.
For a complete listing, refer to the Hospitals section.

[M] MONASTERIES AND RESIDENCES OF PRIESTS AND BROTHERS

HARTFORD. *Missionaries of LaSalette Provincial Secretary*, 915 Maple Ave., 06114-2330. Tel: 860-956-8870. Province of Our Lady of Seven Dolors. Legal Title: *Missionaries of La Salette Corp.* Very Rev. Thomas A. Reilly, M.S., Prov. Supr.; Revs. James H. Kuczynski, M.S., Vicar; Joseph G. Bachand, M.S., Asst. & Prov. Sec.; Bro. G. Peter Collins, M.S., Prov. Treas.; Rev. John R. Dolan, Vocation Dir. Priests 4; Brothers 1.
Religious Trust of the Missionaries of Our Lady of LaSalette. Legal Title: *Religious Trust of the Missionaries of Our Lady of LaSalette Province of Our Lady of Seven Dolors (MLS Trust).*
Missionaries of LaSalette, 85 New Park Ave., 06106-2184. Tel: 860-523-8275. Revs. Brian R. Sheridan, M.S., Mission Procurator. Tel: 860-586-0710; Donald D. Simonds, M.S., Local Coord.; Richard R. Boucher, M.S., Treas.; Salvatore D. Altavista, M.S.; Edward F. Barry, M.S.; Michael J. Cox, M.S.; William H. Crane, M.S.; John B. Good, M.S.; Joseph J. Horgan, M.S.; Joseph A. Markowicz, M.S.; William W. Mulcair, M.S.; Armand J. Nadeau, M.S.; Roland A. Nadeau, M.S.; John R. Nuelle, M.S.; Louis M. Perpete, M.S.; James B. Quilty, M.S.; Daniel J. Scott, M.S.; John G. Toner, M.S.; Bros. Joseph F. Bracken, M.S.; Ronald R. Beaudoin, M.S.; David J. Cook, M.S.; Alexander J. Delaney, M.S.; Gabriel Frank, M.S.; Mark L. Gallant, M.S.; Andre J. Hamel, M.S.; Paul Maceyka; Francis X. Smith, M.S.; Alfred D. Tetrault, M.S.; Donald J. Wininski, M.S. Priests 18; Brothers 11.
Priests-Brothers of Province Serving Abroad:
Missionaries in Argentina: Revs. Robert R. Butler, M.S.; Eugene P. Brennan, M.S.; John M. Garvey, M.S.; John F. Higgins, M.S., Region Supr.; James T. Lowery, M.S.; John J. McCarthy, M.S.; John P. Sullivan, M.S.
Bolivia: Rev. Norman O. Butler, M.S.
Immaculate Conception Rectory, 574 Park St., P.O. Box 260610, 06126-0610. Tel: 860-525-1522. Revs. James J. Aherne, M.S.; James M. Weeks, M.S.
Our Lady of Sorrows Rectory, 16 Greenwood St., 06106-2109. Tel: 860-233-4424. Co-Pastors: Revs. Joseph M. O'Neil, M.S.; Francis C. Cooney, M.S. In res., Rev. Stephen G. Dressell, M.S.
North American La Salette Mission Center, 85 New Park Ave., 06106-2184. Rev. John R. Nuelle, M.S., Dir.; Bro. Mark L. Gallant, M.S., Asst.
Sacred Heart Rectory, 49 Winthrop St., 06103-1030. Tel: 860-527-6459; Fax: 860-527-9450. Somascan Fathers. Total in Residence 3; Total Staff 3.
St. Patrick-St. Anthony Friary (Holy Name Prov.), 285 Church St., 06103-1196. Tel: 860-246-6874. Franciscan Friars.
St. Joseph Rectory, 31 Oak St., P.O. Box 808, Winsted, 06098-1715. Tel: 860-379-3369; Fax: 860-379-4194.

BLOOMFIELD. *Brothers of the Sacred Heart*, 1153 Blue Hills Ave., 06002-1901. Tel: 860-242-3342. Total in Residence 5.
Society of Mary (Marianists), 467 Bloomfield Ave., 06002. Tel: 860-243-9642.

CHESHIRE. *Legionaries of Christ*, 475 Oak Ave., 06410. Tel: 203-271-0805.
393 Derby Ave., Orange, 06477. Tel: 203-795-2800.

EAST HARTFORD. *Society of Our Lady of the Most Holy Trinity*, 15 Maplewood Ave., 06108. Tel: 860-289-7916.

ENFIELD. *St. Patrick Rectory*, 64 Pearl St., 06082. Tel: 860-745-2411. Redemptorist Fathers and Brothers. Total in Residence 2.

HAMDEN. *Oblates of Mary Immaculate*, 298 Thornton St., 06517. Tel: 203-288-9968. Rev. Charles Beausoleil, O.M.I.

LITCHFIELD. *Montfort Missionaries*, Montfort Rd., P.O. Box 667, 06759. Tel: 860-567-8434; Fax: 860-567-9670.
Lourdes Shrine. Tel: 860-567-1041. Revs. Thomas Poth, S.M.M., Supr. & Contact; Eugene Lynch, S.M.M.; Donald Lasalle, S.M.M. Priests 3.

MANCHESTER. *DePaul Provincial Residence*. (Vincentian Fathers and Brothers), 234 Keeney St., 06040-7023. Tel: 860-643-2828; Fax: 860-533-9462. Congregation of the Mission, New England Province. Very Revs. Chester R. Mrowka, C.M., Procurator; John S. Sledziona, C.M., Prov. & Contact; Bros. Henry Ziolkowski, C.M.; Henry Wojtkiewicz, C.M.; Joseph S. Zurowski, C.M. Legal Title: *The New England Province of the Congregation of the Mission Incorporated.*
Charitable Trust of the New England Province of the Congregation of the Mission.
Special Assignments: Revs. Martin Cymbrowski, C.M.; Joseph C. Paciorek, C.M.; Stanley Staniszewski, C.M.
St. Joseph Rectory, 32 Jewett St., Ansonia, 06401-2414. Tel: 203-734-0402.
St. Michael the Archangel Rectory, 75 Derby Ave., Derby, 06418-2098. Tel: 203-734-0005.
1365 Enfield St., Enfield, 06082-4900. Tel: 860-741-0791.
St. Stanislaus Rectory, 82 Akron St., Meriden, 06450. Tel: 203-235-6341.
St. Stanislaus Rectory, 9 Eld St., New Haven, 06511-3899. Tel: 203-562-2828.

MILFORD. *The Augustinians*, 26 Shorefront, 06460. Tel: 203-878-9700. Bro. John N. Konwerski, O.S.A. Total in Residence 1.
Brothers of the Congregation of Holy Cross, 400 Merwin Ave., 06460. Tel: 203-816-9355. Brothers of Holy Cross. Bro. Lawrence Lussier, C.S.C.
10 Ricardo St., West Haven, 06516.
56 Brookwood Rd., Bethany, 06524. Tel: 203-393-0109.

NEW BRITAIN. *Conventual Franciscans*, 50 Pulaski St., 06053-3565. Tel: 860-223-3071.
40 Dunlay St., Apt. B-101, 06051. Tel: 860-225-2629.
548 Burritt St., 06053-2869. Tel: 860-225-5786. Rev. Augustine Pilatowski, O.F.M.Conv., Supr.-Delegate. Chaplains: Revs. John Marion Voytek, O.F.M.Conv.; Benedict Fagone, O.F.M.Conv. Daughters of Mary Motherhouse.
St. Paul Friary, 479 Alling St., Kensington, 06037-2100. Tel: 860-828-0331.

NEW HAVEN. *Priests of the Congregation of Holy Cross*, 203 Maple St., 06511. Tel: 203-776-2405.
Sacred Heart Rectory, 74 Liberty St., 06519-2299. Tel: 203-562-7592. Sons of Charity.
St. Anthony Rectory, 25 Gold St., 06519. Tel: 203-624-1418. Missionaries of St. Charles-Scalabrinians.
St. Michael Rectory, 29 Wooster Pl., 06511. Tel: 203-562-7178.
St. Joseph Rectory, 129 Edwards St., 06511. Tel: 203-773-3588. Jesuit Fathers and Brothers.
700 Prospect St., 06511. Tel: 203-497-8672.
Box 2160, 06520. Tel: 203-393-3193.
1365 Enfield St., Enfield, 06082-4900. Tel: 860-745-1381.
120 Retreat Ave., Apt. A-4, Hartford, 06106. Tel: 860-278-8900.
333 Christian St., Wallingford, 06492. Tel: 203-284-1402.
St. Joseph Rectory, 129 Edwards St., 06511. Tel: 203-777-2548. Marist Fathers.
1450 Chapel St., 06511. Tel: 203-789-3245.
St. Mary Priory, 5 Hillhouse Ave., 06505-1202. Tel: 203-562-6193; Fax: 203-562-1273. Order of Preachers (Dominicans). Total in Residence 12.

NEW MILFORD. *Canterbury School*, Aspetuck Ave., 06776. Tel: 860-355-4891. Benedictine Monks.

NORTH GUILFORD. *Our Lady of Grace Monastery*, 11 Race Hill Rd., 06437. Tel: 203-457-1167. Order of Preachers (Dominicans). Total in Residence 45.

PLAINVILLE. *Our Lady of Mercy Rectory*, 15 S. Canal St., 06062. Tel: 860-793-1399.

SUFFIELD. *Congregation of the Holy Redeemer*, St. Alphonsus College, 06078. Tel: 860-668-7393. Redemptorist Fathers and Brothers.

WATERBURY. *Immaculate Conception Rectory*, 74 W. Main St., 06702. Tel: 203-574-0017. Missionaries of the Holy Apostles; Oblates of Mary Immaculate.
St. Michael Rectory (Immaculate Conception Prov.), 62 St. Michael Dr., 06704-1295. Tel: 203-753-0689; Fax: 203-573-9101.

WEST HARTFORD. *Holy Family Monastery/Retreat*, 303 Tunxis Rd., 06107. Tel: 860-521-0440; Fax: 860-521-0883 (Community); 521-1929. Congregation of the Passion of Jesus Christ. Very Rev. Brice Edwards, C.P., Provincial Vicar; Rev. Ronan Callahan, C.P., Asst. Supr.
Monastery Staff: Revs. John Mark Aleckna, C.P.; Quentin Amrhein, C.P.; Camillus Barth, C.P.; Cajetan Bendernagel, C.P.; Victor Donovan, C.P.; Jude Dowling; Gregory Durkin, C.P.; Kiernan Earley, C.P.; Robert Ehrne, C.P.; Joseph Leo Flynn, C.P.; Randall Gilette, C.P.; Alphonsus Grande, C.P.; Peter Hallisy, C.P.; Bennet Kelley, C.P.; Stephen Paul Kenny, C.P.; Cormac Kinkead, C.P.; Gerald Matejune, C.P.; John Francis McLoughlin, C.P.; Luke Missett, C.P.; Julian Morgan, C.P.; Florian Pekar, C.P.; John Baptist Pesce, C.P.; Damian Reid, C.P.; Linus Rottloff, C.P.; Owen Sharkey, C.P.; Basil Trahon, C.P.; Bros. Frederick Barton, C.P.; Gabriel Chilbert, C.P.; Charles Dell; William Drotar, C.P.; Edward Hall; James Johnson; Joseph Rogers, C.P.
Retreat House. Revs. David Cinquegrani, C.P.; Earl Keating, C.P.; Terence Kristofak, C.P., Dir.

WEST HAVEN. *Franciscan Brothers of Brooklyn*, 233 Main St., 06516. Tel: 203-937-5103. Total in Residence 2.

WOLCOTT. *Maryknoll*, 8 S. View St., 06716. Tel: 203-879-3936.

[N] CONVENTS AND RESIDENCES FOR SISTERS

HARTFORD. *Dominican Oblates of Jesus*, 510 New Britain Ave., 06106. Tel: 203-249-2912. Sisters 4.
Medical Mission Sisters, 92 Sherman St., 06105. Tel: 860-233-0875.
St. Peter Convent, 11 Charter Oak Pl., 06106. Tel: 860-522-8428. Mercedarian Missionaries of Berriz, Sisters of Mercy of the Americas of Connecticut, Sisters of Notre Dame de Namur.
SS. Cyril & Methodius Convent, 45 Groton St., 06106. Tel: 860-527-3775. Felician Sisters of the Order of St. Francis of Connecticut. Rev. William P. Przybylo.
Sister of Notre Dame de Namur, 305 Victoria Rd., 06114. Tel: 860-296-5400. Sisters 2.
Sisters of Mercy of the Americas of Connecticut, 117 Wethersfield Ave., 06114. Tel: 860-278-5824. 252 Laurel St. #206, 06105. Tel: 860-293-1764.
St. Joseph Convent, 35 Oxford St., 06105. Tel: 860-236-1494. 80 Girard Ave., 06105. Tel: 860-231-0252. 91 Mansfield St., 06112. Tel: 860-527-5079.
Sisters of Notre Dame de Namur, 305 Victoria Rd., 06114. Tel: 860-296-5400. Sisters 2.
Sisters of Notre Dame de Namur, One Gold St., Apt. 10, 06103. Tel: 860-246-7300. 18 Dover St., 06114. Tel: 860-296-1981. 191 Preston St., 06114. Tel: 860-956-8969. 217 Laurel St., 06105. Tel: 860-246-0678.
Sisters of St. Joseph, 338 Asylum St., 06103. Tel: 860-278-8389. Sisters of St. Joseph of Chambery. 46 Eastview St., 06114. Tel: 860-246-1316. 145 Elizabeth St., 06105. Tel: 860-523-5704. 149 Barker St., 06114. Tel: 860-296-2546.
Shalom Community, 33 Freeman St., 06114. Tel: 860-956-9247. 35B Freeman St., 06114. Tel: 860-956-9248. 35A Freeman St., 06114. Tel: 860-956-8157.
Sisters of the Cross and Passion, 391 Fairfield Ave., 06114. Tel: 860-956-5186.
Spirit of Mercy Community, 410 Campfield Ave., 06114. Tel: 860-956-3030. Daughters of the Holy Spirit, Sisters of Mercy of the Americas of Connecticut.

157 Kenyon St., 06105-2237. Tel: 860-232-6732.
Bethany Community/Formation Center, 7 Charter Oak Pl., 06106-1915. Tel: 860-728-0851.

ANSONIA. *Dominican Sisters.* (Columbus, OH), 60 Francis St., 06401. Tel: 203-736-2351.
Sisters of Holy Family of Nazareth, 36 Jewett St., 06401. Tel: 203-736-9573.

BEACON FALLS. *Sisters of St. Joseph of the Third Order of St. Francis*, 68 Cambridge Ct., 06403. Tel: 203-729-9415.

BETHLEHEM. *Abbey of Regina Laudis*, Flanders Rd., 06751. Tel: 203-266-7727. Bendictine Nuns of the Primitive Observance. Benedictine Nuns (Cloistered). Mothers Benedict Duss, O.S.B., Abbess; David Serna, O.S.B., Prioress & Mailing Contact. In res., Rev. Claude Peifer, O.S.B. Professed Nuns 27; In First Vows 5; Novices 6; Postulants 1.
St. Catherine's Convent of Mercy, 63 Crane Hollow Rd., 06751. Tel: 203-266-5411. Religious Sisters of Mercy (Alma, MI). Sisters 2.

BLOOMFIELD. *Missionary Servants of the Most Blessed Trinity*, 467 Bloomfield Ave., 06002. Tel: 860-243-0940.
Sisters of Mercy of the Americas of Albany, 467 Bloomfield Ave., 06002. Tel: 860-243-2374. Sr. Mary Costello, R.S.M.
Sisters of Mercy of the Americas of Connecticut, 5 Garrison Ter., 06002. Tel: 860-243-8524.
Sisters of Notre Dame de Namur. (Connecticut Province), 5 Garrison Ter., 06002. Tel: 860-243-8524.
Holy Innocents House, 546 Bloomfield Ave., 06002. Tel: 860-243-2542. Total in Residence 4.

BRISTOL. *Queen of Apostles Provincial House*, 474 East Rd., 06010. Tel: 860-584-2138; Fax: 860-582-1119. Religious Teachers Filippini. Sr. Christine Spirito, M.P.F., Prov. Supr.; Sr. Josephine Riccio, M.P.F., Community Archivist & Contact. Sisters in Diocese 20.
Sisters of Mercy of the Americas of Connecticut, 50 South St. Ext., 06010. Tel: 860-584-2418.
Sisters of St. Joseph of Chambery, 89 Putnam St., 06010. Tel: 860-582-3257.

CHESHIRE. *Sisters of St. Joseph of Chambery*, 1123 Waterbury Rd., #2A, 06410. Tel: 203-699-9421.

EAST HARTFORD. *Sisters of Notre Dame de Namur*, 21 Highview St., 06108. Tel: 860-289-5295. 37 Ridgeview Rd., 06118. Tel: 860-569-8794. 41 Applegate Ln., 06118. Tel: 860-569-7183. 50 Larrabee St. #F, 06108. Tel: 860-528-1024. 50 Larrabee St. #G, 06108. Tel: 860-289-2421. 52 Elms Village Rd., 06118. Tel: 860-569-0022. 8 Larrabee St., 06108. Tel: 860-290-8567. 908 Forbes St., 06118. Tel: 860-568-6958.

EAST HAVEN. *Dominican Sisters.* (Columbus, OH), 157 Short Beach Rd., 06512. Tel: 203-468-2280.
Missionary Franciscan Sisters of the Immaculate Conception, 157 Short Beach Rd., 06512. Tel: 203-468-2280. Total in Residence 2.
Provincial House, 520 Thompson Ave., 06512. Tel: 203-469-7872.
87 Gerrish Ave., 06512. Tel: 203-468-9084.
Sisters of Notre Dame de Namur, 157 Short Beach Rd., 06512. Tel: 203-468-2280.

ENFIELD. *Enfield Montessori School*, 1370 Enfield St., 06082. Tel: 203-745-5847. Students 124.
Felician Sisters - Our Lady of the Angels, Provincial House, 1315 Enfield St., 06082-4920. Tel: 860-745-7791; 745-4946; Fax: 860-741-0819. Felician Sisters of the Order of St. Francis of Connecticut. Sr. Joan Marie Swierzb, C.S.S.F., Contact.
Provincial House and Novitiate. Sr. Mary Laureann Alexandrowicz, C.S.S.F., Prov. Min. Felician Sisters. Chaplains: Rev. Adolphe T. Renkiewicz.
In Province: Professed Sisters 154; Postulants 2.
Felician Adult Day Care, 1325 Enfield St., 06082. Tel: 860-745-2542; 745-3484. Total Assisted 22; Total Staff 12. Felician Sisters. Sr. Patricia Marie Iagrosso, C.S.S.F., Dir. A day respite health care facility for Caregivers of the Frail, elderly and Alzheimer Clients.
Felician Sisters Infirmary, 1315 Enfield St., 06082. Tel: 860-745-0217.
Mother Angela Residence, 1333-B Enfield St., 06082. Tel: 860-745-5705.
Child Jesus Convent, 1370 Enfield St., 06082. Tel: 860-745-5847.
Enfield Montessori School, 1370 Enfield St., 06082-4920. Tel: 860-745-5847. Sr. Mary Anastasia, C.S.S.F., Contact. Students 123.
St. Bernard Convent, 376 Hazard Ave., 06082. Tel: 860-749-4214.
St. Adalbert Convent, 82 Alden Ave., 06082. Tel: 860-745-4169.
Little Sisters of the Poor, 1365 Enfield St., 06082-4900. Tel: 860-741-0791.
St. Patrick Convent, 33 Spring St., 06082. Tel: 860-745-5174. Total in Residence 2. Sisters of Mercy of the Americas of Connecticut.

FARMINGTON. *St. Gabriel House*, 31 Colton St., 06032. Tel: 860-678-7274.
Sisters of Mercy of the Americas of Vermont, 33 Two Mile Rd., 06032. Tel: 860-677-0758.
Sisters of the Cross and Passion, St. Gabriel's House, 31 Colton St., 06032. Tel: 860-678-7274.

FORESTVILLE. *Daughters of Wisdom*, 45 Hawthorne St. D-2, 06010.
St. Matthew Convent, 119 Church Ave., 06010. Tel: 860-583-2004. Sisters, Servants of the Immaculate Heart of Mary.
Sisters of St. Joseph of the Third Order of St. Francis, 105 Kenney St., 06010. Tel: 860-582-1635.
82 Kenney St., 06010. Tel: 860-584-2985. Total in Residence 7; Total Staff 18.

GUILFORD. *Sisters of Mercy of the Americas of Connecticut*, 73A Church St., 06437. Tel: 203-453-3496.

HAMDEN. *Daughters of Wisdom*, 95 Kaye Vue Dr. Apt. 2E, 06514. Tel: 203-281-7800. Total in Residence 2.
Dominican Sisters of Hope, 1204 Whitney Ave., #217, 06517. Tel: 203-248-2601.
Franciscan Sisters of the Atonement, 68 N. Lake Dr., 06517. Tel: 203-281-4319.
Mary, Mother of the Church Convent, 115 Denslow Hill Rd., 06514. Tel: 203-407-1042. Sisters 4.
Mount Sacred Heart Provincial House and Novitiate, 265 Benham St., 06514. Tel: 203-248-4225; Fax: 203-230-8341. Mothers Deborah Lopez, Prov. Supr.; Rosemary Zaffuto, Vicaress. Sisters in Province 196.
Residents in Convent: Sisters 24; Postulants 1.
St. Rita Convent, 30 Gillies Rd., 06517. Tel: 203-288-4707. Dominican Sisters (Columbus, OH).
Sisters of Mercy of the Americas of Connecticut, 2809 Whitney Ave., 06518. Tel: 203-287-9017.
St. Stephen Convent, 412 Ridge Rd., 06517. Tel: 203-288-7270. 77 Second St., 06514. Tel: 203-865-4821.

KENSINGTON. *St. Paul Convent*, 467 Alling St., 06037. Tel: 860-828-5223. Daughters of Mary of the Immaculate Conception. Sisters 3.

LITCHFIELD. *Daughters of Wisdom*, 229 E. Litchfield Rd., 06759. Tel: 860-567-3166.
Dominican Sisters of Hope. (Ossining, NY), 106 Clark Rd., 06759. Tel: 860-567-9487.

MADISON. *Sisters of Mercy of the Americas of Connecticut*, 149 Neck Rd., 06443. Tel: 203-245-4261.
167 Neck Rd., 06443. Tel: 203-245-7710.
Sisters of St. Joseph of Brentwood, 62 Kelsey Pl., 06443. Tel: 203-245-1329.

MANCHESTER. *Assumption Convent*, 21 S. Adams St., 06040. Tel: 860-643-0452. Sisters of Charity of Our Lady, Mother of the Church.
Daughters of the Holy Spirit, Case Dr. #44-D, 06040. Tel: 860-649-4755.
Dominican Sisters. (Columbus, OH), 69 Charter Oak St., 06040. Tel: 860-647-1699.
Sisters of Mercy of the Americas of Connecticut, 16 Lyndale St., 06040. Tel: 860-646-5902.
St. James Convent, 85 Park St., 06040. Tel: 860-649-5791.
Sisters of Notre Dame de Namur, 19 Moore St., 06040. Tel: 860-643-8761. 9 Plano Pl., 06040. Tel: 860-647-8544. 1198A Middle Tpke. W., 06040. Tel: 860-528-5091. 18 Winter St., 06040. Tel: 860-649-6891. Total in Residence 4.
Sisters of St. Joseph. (Springfield, MA), 82 Chestnut St., 06040. Tel: 860-647-7065.
Sisters of St. Joseph of Chambery, 241 E. New State Rd., 06040. Tel: 860-645-9750.
41 Florence St., 06040. Tel: 860-649-9791.

MERIDEN. *Generalate and Motherhouse of the Franciscan Sisters of the Eucharist*, 405 Allen Ave., 06451. Tel: 203-238-2243. The Institute of the Franciscan Sisters of the Eucharist. Sr. Suzanne Gross, F.S.E., Contact. Legal Title: *Franciscan Sisters of the Eucharist, Inc.* Mother Rosemae Pender, F.S.E., Mother General. Professed 20; Novices 1; Postulants 3.
275 Finch Ave., 06451. Tel: 203-630-1771.
Mt. Carmel Convent, 109 Goodwill Ave., 06451. Tel: 203-235-3622. Apostles of the Sacred Heart of Jesus.
St. Joseph Convent, 19 Goodwill Ave., 06451. Tel: 203-235-8551.
28 Fourth St., 06450. Tel: 203-237-2989.
St. Stanislaus Convent, 70 Akron St., 06450. Tel: 203-237-1559. Sisters of St. Joseph of the Third Order of St. Francis.
Ursuline Sisters of the Congregation of Tildonk, Belgium, 125 Goodwell Ave., 06451. Tel: 203-686-1702.

MILFORD. *Franciscan Sisters of the Atonement*, 245 Orange Ave., 06460. Tel: 203-876-2902.
Sisters of Mercy of the Americas of Connecticut, 23 Jones Ct., 06460. Tel: 203-877-1170.
St. Mary Convent, 74 Gulf St., 06460. Tel: 203-874-8427.

NAUGATUCK. *Sisters of Mercy of the Americas of Connecticut*, 1006 New Haven Rd., 06770. Tel: 203-723-8735.
53 Clearview Cir., 06770. Tel: 203-729-2143.

NEW BRITAIN. *Cana*, 1190 Slater Rd., 06053. Tel: 860-826-1655. Sisters of St. Joseph of Chambery.
1166 Slater Rd., 06053. Tel: 860-229-9291. Total in Residence 342.
Daughters of the Holy Spirit, 1222 Stanley St., 06050. Tel: 860-223-0445.
Dominican Sisters of Hope. (Ossining, NY), 597 Burritt St., 06053. Tel: 860-827-8511.
Holy Cross Convent, 225 Farmington Ave., 06053-2929. Tel: 860-229-0677.
40 Chestnut St. #307, 06052-2628. Tel: 860-827-1317.
Maryknoll Sisters of St. Dominic, 950 Farmington Ave. C30, 06053. Tel: 860-229-9912.
Motherhouse of Daughters of Mary of the Immaculate Conception, 314 Osgood Ave., 06053. Tel: 860-225-9406. Daughters of Mary of the Immaculate Conception. Mother Mary Mark Pizzotti, D.M., Supr. Gen.; Sr. Mary Christine, D.M., Sec. & Contact; Rev. John Voytek, O.F.M.Conv., Chap. Tel: 860-225-5786. Sisters in Community 73; Residence at the Motherhouse 35.
Sacred Heart Convent, 23 Orange St., 06053. Tel: 860-225-3989.
Msgr. Bojnowski Manor, 50 Pulaski St., 06053. Tel: 860-229-0336.
St. Lucian Home, 532 Burritt St., 06053. Tel: 860-223-2123.
Our Lady of Rose Hill Day Care Center, 594 Burritt St., 06053. Tel: 860-223-4846.
Marian Educational Clinic, 314 Osgood Ave., 06053. Tel: 860-223-0501.
St. Ann Convent, 112 North St., 06051. Tel: 860-229-1488. Religious Teachers Filippini. Sisters 5.
St. Francis of Assisi Convent, School Sisters of Notre Dame, 1757 Stanley St., 06053. Tel: 860-225-7143.
Sisters of Mercy of the Americas of Connecticut, 1214 Stanley St. #203, 06051. Tel: 860-826-7328.
1218 Stanley St. #202, 06051. Tel: 860-225-3154.
37 Carlton St., 06053. Tel: 860-229-7575.
The Sisters of St. Francis of Philadelphia, 607 Burritt St. #102, 06053. Tel: 860-229-0463.
Sisters of the Cross and Passion, 33 Kim Dr., 06053. Tel: 860-225-1470; 229-1817.
25 Streamside La., 06052. Tel: 860-224-1193.

NEW HARTFORD. *Missionary Servants of the Most Blessed Trinity*, 595 Town Hill Rd., 06057. Tel: 860-379-4329. Total in Residence 3.

NEW HAVEN. *Missionary Franciscan Sisters of the Immaculate Conception*, 904 Howard Ave., 06512. Tel: 203-468-2280.
St. Brendan Convent, 455 1/2 Whalley Ave., 06511. Tel: 203-787-4631. Sisters of Our Lady of the Garden.
St. Joseph Convent, 135 Edwards St., 06511. Tel: 203-562-9202. Dominican Sisters (Columbus, OH).
15 Lincoln St., 06511. Tel: 203-865-7305.
1914 Chapel St., 06515. Tel: 203-389-9428.
Albertus Magnus College, 790 Prospect St., 06511. Tel: 203-777-7484.
Sisters of Charity of St. Elizabeth, Convent Station, 1450 Chapel St., 06511. Tel: 203-789-3377.
450 Central Ave., 06515. Tel: 203-397-5243.
80 Whittier Ave., 06515. Tel: 203-389-4400.
Sisters of Mercy of the Americas of Connecticut, 355 Ferry St. #713, 06513. Tel: 203-773-1060.
510 Lombard St., 06513. Tel: 203-562-9361.
Sisters of Notre Dame de Namur, 180 Howard Ave., 06519. Tel: 203-782-2258.
311 Eastern St. #901E, 06513. Tel: 203-469-5093.
311 Eastern St. #917E, 06513. Tel: 203-469-8385.
311 Eastern St. #1704, 06513. Tel: 203-469-9934.
83 Porter St., 06519. Tel: 203-498-7011.
Sisters of St. Joseph of Chambery, 83 Porter St., 06519. Tel: 203-498-9569.

NEWINGTON. *Maryhouse*, 21 Hartford Ave. #9, 06111. Tel: 860-666-1085. Sisters of Mercy of the Americas of Connecticut.
St. Mary Convent, 168 Cedar St., 06111. Tel: 860-667-1790. Sisters of Charity of St. Elizabeth, Convent Station. Total in Residence 3.
Sisters of Notre Dame de Namur, 42 E. Robbins Ave., 06111. Tel: 860-667-4826.

NORTH BRANFORD. *Sisters of Mercy of the Americas of Detroit*, 1739 Foxon Rd., 06471-1566. Tel: 203-488-0692.

NORTH GUILFORD. *Monastery of Our Lady of Grace*, 11 Race Hill Rd., 06437. Tel: 203-457-0599. Dominican Nuns. A contemplative community with solemn vows and papal enclosure. Perpetual Adoration. Sr. Mary Ann, O.P., Prioress; Rev. Thomas B. Confer, O.P., Chap. Tel: 203-457-0595. Professed Sisters 40. Dominican Contemplative Nuns (Cloistered). Sr. Mary Ann, O.P., Prioress; Rev. Thomas B. Confer, O.P., Chap. Professed Sisters 40; Novices 5.

NORTH HAVEN. *St. Francis Cabrini Convent*, 94 Chapel Hill Rd., 06473. Tel: 203-239-8012. Sisters of the Sacred Heart of Jesus of Ragura. Total in Residence 3.

NORTHFORD. *Sisters of St. Joseph of Chambery*, 30 Mansfield Dr. #1603, 06472. Tel: 203-484-7018.

OXFORD. *Ursuline Sisters of the Congregation of Tildonk, Belgium*, 733 Oxford Rd., 06478. Tel: 203-888-4902.

SOUTHINGTON. *Congregation of Notre Dame*, 96 Summer St., 06489. Tel: 860-628-4506. Total in Residence 3.

SUFFIELD. *St. Joseph Convent*, 156 S. Main St., 06078. Tel: 860-668-2503.

TERRYVILLE. *Daughters of Wisdom*, 25 Allen St., 06786-1503. Tel: 860-583-8786.
41 Allen St., 06786-1503. Tel: 860-582-7676.
Maryknoll Sisters of St. Dominic, 10 Agney Ave. #2E, 06786. Tel: 860-589-4768.

TORRINGTON. *St. Francis of Assisi Convent*, 93 Marcia Dr., 06790. Tel: 860-489-7405. Dominican Sisters (Columbus, OH), Sisters of Mercy of the Americas of Connecticut, Sisters of Notre Dame de Namur.
St. Peter Convent, 25 St. John Pl., 06790. Tel: 860-489-4035. Religious Teachers Filippini.
School Sisters of Notre Dame, 106 Mill Ln., 06790. Tel: 860-489-1741.

WALLINGFORD. *Holy Trinity Convent*, 25 N. Whittlesey Ave., 06492. Tel: 203-265-6999. Sisters of Mercy of the Americas of Connecticut, Sisters of Notre Dame de Namur.
Sisters of Mercy of the Americas of Connecticut, 1043 North Farms Rd., 06492. Tel: 203-265-6624.

WATERBURY. *Anawim Community*, 25 State St., 06702. Tel: 203-753-0867. Daughters of the Holy Spirit.
234 Pine St., 06710. Tel: 203-756-2931.
27 State St., 06702. Tel: 203-754-0844.
44 Kramer Ave., 06705. Tel: 203-754-4825.
Franciscan Sisters of Allegheny, NY, 407 Robbinwood Rd., 06708. Tel: 203-753-1472.
Holy Land Convent, 60 Slocum St., 06706. Tel: 203-755-2456. Religious Teachers Filippini.
Maryknoll Sisters of St. Dominic, 55 Cole St., 06706. Tel: 203-754-2913. Total in Residence 8.
Notre Dame Convent, 119 Southmayd Rd., 06705. Tel: 203-753-4431; 753-1095. Sisters of the Congregation of Notre Dame. Sr. Rita Corley, C.N.D., Contact; Sr. Kathleen Reid, C.N.D.; Sr. Lena Mastroianni, C.N.D.; Sr. Edith Laflamme, C.N.D.; Sr. Pauline Dufresne, C.N.D.; Sr. Jewel Renna, C.N.D. Sisters 6.
156 Beech St., 06704. Tel: 203-756-8201.
587 Oronoke Rd., 06708. Tel: 203-755-8828. Sisters 6.
109 Highland Ave., 06708. Tel: 203-753-3073. Sisters 2.
St. Mary Hospital, 56 Franklin St., 06706. Tel: 203-574-6455. Sisters of St. Joseph of Chambery.
284 Windy Dr., 06705. Tel: 203-574-6374.
31 Marita Dr., 06705. Tel: 203-753-4503.
Sisters of Charity of St. Elizabeth, Convent Station, 100 Jefferson Sq. #31, 06706. Tel: 203-757-5685.
100 Jefferson Sq. #6H, 06706. Tel: 203-596-1331.
Sisters of Mercy of the Americas of Connecticut, 131 Norton St., 06708. Tel: 203-754-7251.
1054 Meriden Rd., 06705-3137. Tel: 203-753-3507.
Visitation Plaza, 100 Jefferson Sq., 06706. Tel: 203-755-7236.
36 Irving St. #2, 06710. Tel: 203-753-4503.
Sisters of Notre Dame de Namur, 131 Herschel Ave., 06708. Tel: 203-757-1444.
38 Summer St., 06704. Tel: 203-755-0012.

WATERTOWN. *St. John the Evangelist Convent*, 9 Academy Hill, 06795. Tel: 203-274-1820. School Sisters of Notre Dame. Sisters 5.
Sisters of Charity of St. Elizabeth, Convent Station, 100 North St., 06795. Tel: 203-274-9893.

WEST HARTFORD. *Convent of Mary Immaculate, Provincial House of the Sisters of St. Joseph of Chambery*. (North American Province), 27 Park Rd., 06119. Tel: 860-233-5126; 232-8252. Sisters of St. Joseph of Chambery. Legal Title: *The Sisters of St. Joseph Corporation*. Sr. Suzanne Brazauskas, C.S.J., Prov. Supr.; Sr. Presentation Hoye, C.S.J., Contact. In Community: Professed Sisters 201.
Religious Trust of the Sisters of St. Joseph of Chambery (the "Trust").
104 Flagg Rd., 06117. Tel: 860-523-7446.
Canticle Hall, 27 Park Rd., 06119. Tel: 860-232-2797.
Caritas, 27 Park Rd., 06119. Tel: 860-233-5126, Ext. 249.
Euphrasia Hall, 27 Park Rd., 06119. Tel: 860-233-1697.
Holy Family Monastery/Retreat, 303 Tunxis Rd., 06107. Tel: 860-521-1477. Feminine Congregation of the Passion.
Mercyknoll, Incorporated, 243 Steele Rd., 06117. Tel: 203-236-3503. Sisters of Mercy of the Americas of Connecticut. A retirement and health care facility of the Sisters of Mercy. Sr. Irene Holowesko, R.S.M., Admin. & Contact; Rev. Robert D. Bergin, Chap. Bed Capacity 84; Skilled Nursing 38; RHNS 10; HFA 36.
St. Mary Home, 2021 Albany Ave., 06117. Tel: 860-236-1924. Sisters of Mercy of the Americas of Connecticut.
Sisters of Charity of Our Lady, Mother of the Church, 1109 Prospect St., 06105. Tel: 860-233-2378.
Sisters of Mercy of the Americas of Albany, 2021 Albany Ave., 06117. Tel: 860-236-1924. Sisters of Mercy of the Americas of Connecticut.
Administrative Office, 249 Steele Rd., 06117. Tel: 860-232-8602. Sr. Judith A. Carey, R.S.M., Regl. Pres. Sisters in Community 289.
Sisters of Mercy of the Americas of Connecticut, 102 Dover Rd., 06119. Tel: 860-232-7981.
104 Dover Rd., 06119. Tel: 860-232-7929.
132 Milton St., 06119. Tel: 860-523-0707.
St. Joseph College, Lourdes Hall, 1678 Asylum Ave., 06117. Tel: 860-232-6730.
Convent of the Holy Spirit, 243 Steele Rd., 06117. Tel: 860-236-7805.
Catherine McAuley Unit, 243 Steele Rd., 06117. Tel: 860-236-3503.
St. Paul Convent, 243 Steele Rd., 06117. Tel: 860-232-7745.
Trocaire, 243 Steele Rd., 06117. Tel: 860-233-2195.
Sacred Heart Convent, 243 Steele Rd., 06117. Tel: 860-236-3503.
Maranatha, 243 Steele Rd., 06117. Tel: 860-236-9448.
25 Beechwood Rd., 06107. Tel: 860-561-5997.
27 Park Rd., 06119. Tel: 860-236-5626.
54 Boulanger Ave. #1, 06110. Tel: 860-231-8472.
54 Boulanger Ave. #2, 06110. Tel: 860-233-6679.
98 Caya Ave., 06110. Tel: 860-236-2051.
Sisters of Mercy of the Americas of Vermont, 25 Beechwood Ave., 06107. Tel: 860-561-5997.
Sisters of Notre Dame de Namur, 21 Prescott St., 06110. Tel: 860-231-7979.
Sisters of St. Joseph. (Springfield, MA), 50 Crescent St., 06119. Tel: 860-233-8708.
Vietnamese Dominican Sisters, 78 Westpoint Ter., 06107. Tel: 860-521-8296.

WEST HAVEN. *Our Lady of Victory Convent*, 634 Jones Hill Rd., 06516. Tel: 203-934-8601. Ursuline Sisters of the Congregation of Tildonk, Belgium.
St. Paul Convent, 45 Alling St., 06516. Tel: 203-934-1357.
Sisters of the Assumption, 491 Washington Ave. #3W, 06516. Tel: 203-932-6449.

WETHERSFIELD. *Daughters of Wisdom*, 78 Fairlane Dr., 06109. Tel: 860-529-8419.
Maryknoll Sisters of St. Dominic, 547 Goff Rd., 06109. Tel: 860-529-1483.
96 Victoria Rd., Hartford, 06114. Tel: 860-296-1826.
Sisters of Notre Dame de Namur, 98-1 Folly Brook Blvd., 06109. Tel: 860-257-7091.

WINCHESTER CENTER. *Villa Ferretti, Religious Teachers Filippini*, 438 Winchester Rd., Box 55, 06094. Tel: 860-379-3279.

WINDSOR. *Sisters of Notre Dame de Namur*, Province Center, 468 Poquonock Ave., 06095-2473. Tel: 860-688-1832. Administrative Team: Sr. Joan Farley, S.N.D. Tel: 860-285-0554; Sr. Elizabeth McLaughlin, S.N.D. Tel: 860-285-8901; Sr. Marilyn Pechillo, S.N.D. Tel: 860-285-8441.
Community, 468 Poquonock Ave., 06095. Tel: 860-285-0038.
Millbrook Village Senior Citizens Development, 35 Mack St., A-5, 06095. Tel: 860-688-0256.
Julie House, 425 Poquonock Ave., 06095. Tel: 860-298-8320. Assisted living home for S.N.D.'s only. Residents 16; Staff 2.
Sisters of St. Joseph of Chambery, 67 Bloomfield Ave., 06095. Tel: 860-285-0890.

WINDSOR LOCKS. *Sisters of Notre Dame de Namur*, 34 Ellis St., 06096-1704. Tel: 860-627-8002. Total in Residence 5.

WINSTED. *St. Anthony Convent*, 66 Oak St., 06098. Tel: 860-379-8375. Franciscan Missionaries of the Divine Motherhood. Sisters 2.

WOLCOTT. *Daughters of Wisdom*, 18 Munson Rd. #2, 06716. Tel: 203-879-3432.

[O] COUNSELING CENTERS

MERIDEN. *Franciscan Life Center*, 271 Finch Ave., 06451. Tel: 203-237-8084. Legal Title: *Franciscan Life Center Network, Inc.* Sr. Shaun Vergauwen, F.S.E., Dir. Franciscan Sisters of the Eucharist 7; Total Assisted 1,045; Total Staff 16.

[P] ADOPTION SERVICES-HOME CARE

MERIDEN. *Franciscan Family Care Center*, 267 Finch Ave., 06450. Tel: 203-237-8084.
For a complete listing, refer to the Special Care Facilities section.

[Q] RETREAT HOUSES-RENEWAL CENTERS

FARMINGTON. *Holy Family Retreat House*, 303 Tunxis Rd., 06107. Tel: 860-521-0440. For laymen and laywomen. Conducted by the Passionist Community. Very Rev. Terence Kristofak, C.P., Retreat Dir./Prov. Consultor. Assoc. Directors: Revs. David Cinquegrani, C.P.; Earl Keating, C.P.; Sr. Eileen Fucito, C.P.; Mr. William Walsh. Priests 2; Sisters 2; Lay Staff 1.
Our Lady of Calvary Retreat House. Conducted by the Sisters of the Cross and Passion for Religious and Lay Persons, 31 Colton St., 06032. Tel: 860-677-8519; Fax: 860-677-2873. Retreat Team: Sr. Joanne Fahey, C.P., Admin. & Contact; Sr. Ann Rodgers, C.P., Prog. Dir.; Sr. Anna Marie Becker, C.P.; Joanne Ceccarelli-Egan; Marie D. Benedetto; Beverly Montana; Sr. Mary O'Brien, C.P.

LITCHFIELD. *Wisdom House Retreat Center*, 229 E. Litchfield Rd., 06759-3002. Tel: 860-567-3163; Fax: 860-567-3166. A retreat center for spiritual and human development programs. Use of space is available for educational and spiritual programs and for non-profit organizations when their purpose corresponds to the Mission of Wisdom House. The Center is a ministry of the Daughters of Wisdom. Sr. Rosemarie Greco, D.W., Admin.

MADISON. *Mercy Center, Incorporated*, 167 Neck Rd., P.O. Box 191, 06443. Tel: 203-245-0401. Sisters of Mercy. Sr. Eugenie Guterch, R.S.M., Admin. & Contact. Sisters 9; Total in Residence 7; Total Staff 25.

NEW HARTFORD. *Trinita*, 595 Town Hill Rd., Rte. 219, 06057. Tel: 860-379-4329. Total in Residence 3; Total Staff 5. Mailing Address: 3501 Solly Ave., Philadelphia, PA, 19136. Missionary Servants of the Most Blessed Trinity.

[R] NEWMAN CENTERS

HARTFORD. *University of Hartford Newman Center*, 200 Bloomfield Ave., 06117. Tel: 860-768-4899. Rev. Raymond S. Smialowski, Chap., Holy Spirit Rectory, 183 Church St., 06111. Trinity College Chapel, 300 Summit St., 06106. Tel: 860-297-2015. Rev. Raymond S. Smialowski, Chap.

HAMDEN. *Catholic Community at Quinnipac College*, P.O. Box 340, 06518. Rev. Louis Anthony Evangelisto, Chap. & Contact.

NEW BRITAIN. *Central Connecticut State University Newman House*, 145 Paul Manafort Dr., 06053-2552. Tel: 860-832-3795. Rev. George M. Couturier. Total in Residence 1; Total Staff 1.

NEW HAVEN. *Southern Connecticut State University Newman Center*, 129 Edwards St., 06511. Tel: 203-392-5331; 624-5297. Rev. John P. Sullivan.
Yale University-St. Thomas More Catholic Center and Chapel, 268 Park St., 06511. Tel: 203-777-5537; Fax: 203-777-0144. Rev. Robert L. Beloin, Ph.D., Chap. & Contact; Sr. Jo-Ann Veillette, S.A.S.V., Assoc. Chap.

[S] ORGANIZED CHARITIES

HARTFORD. *Catholic Charities-Catholic Family Services (Archdiocese of Hartford)*. Central Office. Archdiocesan Center, 467 Bloomfield Ave., Bloomfield, 06002-2999. Tel: 860-242-9577. Patrick J. Johnson, Jr., A.C.S.W., Dir. Charities & Exec. Dir.; Sr. Dorothy Strelchum, Assoc. Dir.; Linda S. Smith, C.I.S.W., Asst. Exec. Dir. Programs; Edgar Bernier, C.P.A., Controller; Francis Laffin, Dir. Group Home Svcs.
Hartford, 896 Asylum Ave., 06105. Tel: 203-522-8241. John R. Morrison, Regl. Dir.
Corpus Christi Child Development Center, 595 Silas Deane Hwy., 06109. Tel: 203-563-3747. Elizabeth Went, Contact Person.
Family Counseling Service, St. Bernard Church, 426 Hazard Ave., Enfield, 06082. Tel: 860-745-1727.
Institute for the Hispanic Family, 80 Jefferson St., 06105. Tel: 860-527-1124. Ramon Rojono, M.D., Dir.
The Hispanic Child Guidance Clinic, 80 Jefferson St., 06105. Tel: 860-524-8974. Peter Arroyo, Dir.
Travelers Aid, 896 Asylum Ave., 06105. Tel: 860-522-8241.
Lower Naugatuck Valley, 205 Wakelee Ave., P.O. Box 364, Ansonia, 06401. Tel: 203-735-7483. Patricia Nere, A.C.S.W., Regl. Dir.
Meriden, 220 Colony St., Meriden, 06450. Tel: 203-235-2707. Raymond S. Shocki, Jr., A.C.S.W., District Exec. Dir.
Outreach Office, 201 W. Main St., Plantsville, 06479.
Milford, 203 High St., P.O. Box 147, Milford, 06460. Tel: 203-874-6270. Wayne Crossman, M.S.W., District Exec. Dir.
New Britain, 90 Franklin Sq., New Britain, 06051. Tel: 860-225-3561. Gregory Paleologos, A.C.S.W., Regl. Dir.
New Haven, 478 Orange St., New Haven, 06502. Tel: 203-787-2207. Guilford Office, 57 Whitfield St., Guilford, 06437. Patricia Nere, A.C.S.W., Regl. Dir.
Torrington, 132 Grove St., Torrington, 06790. Tel: 860-482-5558. Jack Doyle, District Exec. Dir.
Waterbury, 56 Church St., Waterbury, 06702. Tel: 203-755-1196. Jack Doyle, A.C.S.W., District Exec. Dir.
Bristol Office, 300 Main St., Bristol, 06010. Tel: 860-589-8662.
Southbury Office, 88 Main St., Southbury, 06488.
Migration and Refugee Service, 125 Market St., 06103. Tel: 860-548-0059. Stephanie Morton, Dir.

[T] SOCIAL SERVICE CENTERS FOR SPANISH-SPEAKING AND BLACK PEOPLE

BLOOMFIELD. *Pastoral Hispana Office (Hispanic Pastoral Ministry)*, 467 Bloomfield Ave., 06002-2999. Tel: 860-243-0940; 243-3083. Sr. Rosamaria Elias, M.S.B.T., Office of Hispanic Pastoral Ministry (Pastoral Hispana) and Evangelization Center (Centro de Evangelizacion).

NEW HAVEN. *Centro San Jose, Inc.*, 290 Grand Ave., 06513. Tel: 203-562-3135. Peter A. Noble, Exec. Dir.

WATERBURY. *Spanish-Speaking Center*, 83 Cherry St., 06702. Tel: 203-574-5156. Rev. John C. Blackall, Contact. Total Assisted 350; Total Staff 1.

[U] SOCIETY OF ST. VINCENT DE PAUL

HARTFORD. *Particular Council of the St. Vincent de Paul Society*. Greater Hartford, 134 Farmington Ave., 06105-3784. Tel: 860-541-6491. Legal Title: *Particular Council of the St. Vincent de Paul Society of the Archdiocese of Hartford*.

[V] MISCELLANEOUS

HARTFORD. *Counterpoint Communications, Inc.*, 785 Asylum Ave., 06105-2813. Tel: 860-246-7295; Fax: 860-246-9455. Licensee and operators of WTXX TV, Channel 20, Waterbury, CT. Producers of religious/family values-oriented radio and television programming. David L. Brewer, Jr., Pres.; Rev. John P. Gatzak, Coord. of Education; Scott K. Parmelee, Sec., Treas. & Contact.

Mercy Housing & Shelter Corporation, 45 Wyllys St., 06106. Lucy Callahan, Pres. & Exec. Dir.; Amy Lynn Silverman, Contact. Total Assisted 10,000; Total Staff 65.

Religious Trust of the Missionaries of Our Lady of LaSalette. Province of Our Lady of Seven Dolors, (MLS Trust), 915 Maple Ave., 06114-2330. Tel: 860-956-8870. Bro. Peter Collins, M.S., Contact.

BLOOMFIELD. *Archdiocesan Spiritual Life Center*, 467 Bloomfield Ave., 06002-2999. Tel: 860-243-2374. Sr. Barbara Flynn, S.S.A., Contact; Cathleen Murtha, D.W., Assoc. Dir.

Foundation for the Advancement of Catholic Schools, 467 Bloomfield Ave., 06002-2999. Tel: 860-242-4362. Philip J. Schulz, Pres.; Jeannine V. Dash, Exec. Dir. & Contact.

CHESHIRE. *Logos, Inc.*, 475 Oak Ave., 06410. Tel: 203-271-0805. Bro. Juan Sabadell, L.C., Contact.

HAMDEN. *Horizons Institute, Inc.*, 53 Rossotto Dr., 06514. Bro. Guillermo Villanueva, Contact.

The Pastoral Theological Institute Inc., 2 Broadway, Ste. 6, 06518. Tel: 203-281-6593. Mr. William K. Larkin, Th.D., Pres. & Contact.

Rossotto, Inc., 53 Rossotto Dr., 06514. Tel: 203-281-4798. Bro. Guillermo Villanueva, Contact.

MERIDEN. *Franciscan Life Center Network, Incorporated*, 405 Allen Ave., 06450.

Franciscan Life Center, 271 Finch Ave., 06451.

Franciscan Life Process Center, 11650 Downes St., Lowell, MI, 49331.

Franciscan Montessori Earth School, 14750 S.E. Clinton St., Portland, OR, 97236.

Franciscan Northwoods Computer Center, 5601 Lilac Hill Rd., Duluth, MN, 55810.

John S. Duss Memorial Music Center, 2211 Greysolon Rd., Duluth, MN, 55812.

Franciscan Cre-Act School, 526 Grant St., P.O. Box 723, Pocatello, ID, 83204.

Franciscan Family Life Center, 1745 Pocatello Creek Rd., Pocatello, ID, 83201.

Creative Acting, 526 S. Grant St., Pocatello, ID, 83204.

NEW HAVEN. *Angelicum Fund*, L'Ecole Biblique et Archeologique Francaise de Jerusalem, 5 Hillhouse Ave., 06505. Tel: 203-562-6193; Fax: 203-562-1273. Rev. John P. McGuire, O.P., Dir.; Elaine Mello, Asst. Dir.

NEW MILFORD. *Our Lady of the Lakes Corporation*, 3 Old Town Park Rd., 06776-4212.

ORANGE. *Helping Hand Investments, Inc*, 393 Derby Ave., 06477. Tel: 203-795-2800. Bro. Juan Sabadell, L.C., Contact.

Horizons Institute, Inc., 393 Derby Ave., 06477. Bro. Juan Sabadell, L.C., Contact.

Legion of Christ, Inc., 393 Derby Ave., 06477. Tel: 203-795-2800; Fax: 203-795-2808. Revs. Anthony Bannon, L.C., Territorial Dir.; Patrick Langan, L.C., Devel.; Jeffrey Bowker, L.C., Devel.; John Curran, L.C., Secretary. Assistants: Revs. Emilio Diaz Torre, L.C.; Anthony Bailleres, L.C. Priests 6; Religious 16.

LUX ET VITA, INC., 393 Derby Ave., 06477. Tel: 203-795-2800. Bro. Juan Sabadell, L.C., Contact.

Racebrook, Inc., 393 Derby Ave., 06477. Tel: 203-281-4798. Bro. Juan Sabadell, L.C., Contact.

WEST HARTFORD. *Dominican Sisters*, 78 Westpoint Ter., 06107. Tel: 860-521-8296. Sr. Magdalene Nguyen, O.P., Supr. & Contact. Total in Residence 3.

Project Hope, Inc Business Office & Mailing Address, 27 Park Rd., 06119. Tel: 860-233-5126. Center Location, 873 New Britain Ave., Hartford, 06106. Tel: 860-953-2443. Sr. Helen Hart, C.S.J. Total Enrollment 72; Total Staff 3. Sisters of St. Joseph of Chambery.

WINDSOR. *The Connecticut Province of the Sisters of Notre Dame de Namur, Inc.*, 468 Poquonock Ave., 06095-2473. Tel: 860-688-1832. Sr. Elizabeth McLaughlin, S.N.D.deN., Contact.

RELIGIOUS INSTITUTES OF MEN REPRESENTED IN THE ARCHDIOCESE

For further details refer to the corresponding bracketed number in the Religious Institutes of Men or Women section.

[0140]—*The Augustinians*.—O.S.A.
[0170]—*Basilian Fathers*.—C.S.B.
[0200]—*Benedictine Monks*.—O.S.B.
[0600]—*Brothers of the Congregation of Holy Cross*. (Notre Dame, IN).—C.S.C.
[1100]—*Brothers of the Sacred Heart*.—S.C.
[1330]—*Congregation of the Mission (Vincentian Fathers)*.—C.M.
[1000]—*Congregation of the Passion*. (Prov. of St. Paul of the Cross).—C.P.
[0480]—*Conventual Franciscans*. (St. Anthony of Padua Prov.).—O.F.M.Conv.
[0515]—*Franciscan Brothers / Third Order*.—O.S.F.
[0520]—*Franciscan Friars*. (Immaculate Conception, Holy Name Provs.).—O.F.M.
[0690]—*Jesuit Fathers and Brothers*.—S.J.
[0730]—*Legionaries of Christ*.—L.C.
[0780]—*Marist Fathers*.—S.M.
[0800]—*Maryknoll*.—M.M.
[0720]—*The Missionaries of Our Lady of La Salette*. (Prov. O.L. of Seven Dolors).—M.S.
[1210]—*Missionaries of St. Charles-Scalabrinians*.—C.S.
[0590]—*Missionaries of the Holy Apostles*.—M.Ss.A.
[0860]—*Missionhurst Congregation of the Immaculate Heart of Mary*.—C.I.C.M.
[0870]—*Montfort Missionaries*.—S.M.M.
[0910]—*Oblates of Mary Immaculate*.—O.M.I.
[0430]—*Order of Preachers-Dominicans*. (Eastern Prov.).—O.P.
[0610]—*Priests of the Congregation of Holy Cross*.—C.S.C.
[1070]—*Redemptorist Fathers*. (Baltimore Prov.).—C.SS.R.
[1260]—*Society of Christ*.—S.Ch.
[0760]—*Society of Mary (Marianists)*.—S.M.
[0975]—*Society of Our Lady of the Most Holy Trinity*.—S.O.L.T.
[1250]—*Somascan Fathers*.—C.R.S.
[]—*Sons of Charity*.—S.C.

RELIGIOUS INSTITUTES OF WOMEN REPRESENTED IN THE ARCHDIOCESE

[0130]—*Apostles of the Sacred Heart of Jesus*.—A.S.C.J.
[0180]—*Benedictine Nuns of the Primitive Observance*.—O.S.B.
[0860]—*Daughters of Mary of the Immaculate Conception*.—D.M.
[0820]—*Daughters of the Holy Spirit*.—D.H.S.
[0960]—*Daughters of Wisdom*.—D.W.
[1050]—*Dominican Contemplative Nuns*.—O.P.
[]—*Dominican Oblates of Jesus*. (Madrid, Spain).—J.S.O.P.
[1070-02]—*Dominican Sisters (Congregation of St. Mary of the Springs)*.—O.P.
[]—*Dominican Sisters (Vietnamese Congregation of St. Catherine of Siena)*.—O.P.
[1070-15]—*Dominican Sisters of Hope*.—O.P.
[1070-06]—*Dominican Sisters of Newburgh*.—O.P.
[1170]—*Felician Sisters*. (Our Lady of the Angels Province).—C.S.S.F.
[]—*Feminine Congregation of the Passion*.—C.F.P.
[]—*Franciscan Missionaries of the Divine Motherhood*.—F.M.D.M.
[1180]—*Franciscan Sisters of Alleghany, New York*.—O.S.F.
[1190]—*Franciscan Sisters of Atonement*.—S.A.
[1250]—*Institutes of the Franciscan Sisters of the Eucharist*.—F.S.E.
[2340]—*Little Sisters of the Poor*.—L.S.P.
[2470]—*Maryknoll Sisters of St. Dominic*.—M.M.
[2490]—*Medical Mission Sisters*.—M.M.S.
[2510]—*Mercedarian Missionaries of Berriz*.—M.M.B.
[1360]—*Missionary Franciscan Sisters of the Immaculate Conception*.—O.S.F.
[2790]—*Missionary Servants of the Most Blessed Trinity*.—M.S.B.T.
[3160]—*Parish Visitors of Mary Immaculate*.—P.V.M.I.
[2519]—*Religious Sisters of Mercy of Alma*. (MI).—R.S.M.
[3430]—*Religious Teachers Filippini*.—M.P.F.
[2970]—*School Sisters of Notre Dame*.—S.S.N.D.
[0520]—*Sisters of Charity of Our Lady, Mother of Mercy*.—S.C.M.M.
[0530]—*Sisters of Charity of Our Lady, Mother of the Church*.—S.C.M.C.
[0590]—*Sisters of Charity of Saint Elizabeth, Convent Station*.—S.C.
[2575]—*Sisters of Mercy of the Americas*. (Albany, Vermont, Detroit & Connecticut).—R.S.M.
[3000]—*Sisters of Notre Dame de Namur*. (Connecticut, Boston, California & Base Community).—S.N.D.deN.
[]—*Sisters of Our Lady of the Garden*.—O.L.G.
[1650]—*Sisters of St. Francis of Philadelphia*.—O.S.F.
[3830-16]—*Sisters of St. Joseph*. (Springfield).—S.S.J.
[3830-05]—*Sisters of St. Joseph of Brentwood*.—C.S.J.
[3850]—*Sisters of St. Joseph of Chambery*.—C.S.J.
[3930]—*Sisters of St. Joseph of the Third Order of St. Francis*.—S.S.J.-T.O.S.F.
[0150]—*Sisters of the Assumption B.V.*—S.A.S.V.
[2980]—*Sisters of the Congregation de Notre Dame*.—C.N.D.
[3180]—*Sisters of the Cross and Passion*.—C.P.
[1970]—*Sisters of the Holy Family of Nazareth*.—C.S.F.N.
[]—*Sisters of the Sacred Heart of Jesus of Ragura*.—S.S.H.J.
[2170]—*Sisters, Servants of the Immaculate Heart of Mary*.—I.H.M.
[4130]—*Ursuline Sisters of The Congregation of Tildonk, Belgium*.—O.S.U.
[4190]—*Visitation Nuns*.—V.H.M.

ARCHDIOCESAN CEMETERIES

HARTFORD. *Catholic Cemeteries Association of the Archdiocese of Hartford, Inc.* 700 Middletown Ave., P.O. Box 517, North Haven, 06473-0517. Tel: 203-239-2557. Rev. Arthur J. DuPont, Dir.; Robert Marek, Exec. Dir.
Holy Trinity.
St. Patrick.

ANSONIA. *Old St. Mary*.
St. Mary.

BLOOMFIELD. *Mount Saint Benedict*.

DERBY. *Mount St. Peter*.
Old St. Mary.

EAST HARTFORD. *St. Mary*.

MANCHESTER. *St. Bridget*.
St. James.

MERIDEN. *Sacred Heart*.
St. Patrick.

NAUGATUCK. *St. Francis*. (New Haven Region).
St. James.

NEW BRITAIN. *Old St. Mary*.
St. Mary.

NEW HAVEN. *St. Bernard*.
St. Lawrence.

NORTH HAVEN. *All Saints*.

TORRINGTON. *Old St. Francis*.
St. Francis.
St. Peter.

WALLINGFORD. *Holy Trinity*.
St. John.

WATERBURY. *Calvary*.
Old St. Joseph.
St. Joseph.

WATERTOWN. *Mount Olivet*.

NECROLOGY

† Daly, Joseph M., (Retired). —Died March 30, 1996.
† Hurley, John D., (Retired). —Died April 21, 1996.
† Iannetta, Vincent T., (Retired). —Died Sept. 8, 1996.
† Keen, Robert J., (Medical Leave). —Died Nov. 12, 1996.
† Kerwan, Rev. Msgr. James P., (Retired). —Died July 4, 1996.
† Kiely, John J., West Hartford, CT, St. Peter Claver. —Died Dec. 7, 1996.
† Las Heras, Segundo, Poquonock, CT, St. Joseph Church. —Died Feb. 12, 1996.
† Maco, Joseph P., (Retired). —Died July 15, 1996.
† Shea, Thomas F., (Retired). —Died Feb. 11, 1996.
† Toner, Richard J., (Retired). —Died Oct. 28, 1996.
† Zalonis, John A., East Hartford, CT, Blessed Sacrament Rectory. —Died June 14, 1996.

Diocese of Helena

(Dioecesis Helenensis)

Most Reverend

ALEXANDER J. BRUNETT, PH.D.

Bishop of Helena; ordained July 13, 1958; appointed April 19, 1994; consecrated and installed July 6, 1994. *Office: P.O. Box 1729, Helena, MT, 59624.* Tel.: 406-442-5820; Fax: 406-442-1085.

Chancery and Diocesan Pastoral Office: 515 North Ewing, P.O. Box 1729, Helena, MT, 59624. Tel.: 406-442-5820; Fax: 406-442-5191.

ERECTED MARCH 7, 1884.

Square Miles 51,922.

Comprises the western part of the State of Montana, and is made up of the following Counties: Lewis and Clark, Glacier, Pondera, Flathead, Lake, Lincoln, Missoula, Mineral, Sanders, Powell, Granite, Ravalli, Deer Lodge, Silver Bow, Jefferson, Broadwater, Gallatin, Madison, Beaverhead, Meagher, Wheatland and parts of Teton and Toole.

Diocesan Legal Title—*Roman Catholic Bishop of Helena, Montana, a Corporation Sole.*

For legal titles of parishes and diocesan institutions, consult the Chancery Office.

STATISTICAL OVERVIEW

Personnel	
Bishop	1
Priests: Diocesan Active in Diocese	55
Priests: Active Outside Diocese	10
Priests: Diocesan in Foreign Missions	1
Priests: Retired, Sick or Absent	23
Number of Diocesan Priests	89
Religious Priests in Diocese	9
Extern Priests in Diocese	3
Ordinations:	
Transitional Deacons	2
Permanent Deacons	1
Permanent Deacons in Diocese	29
Total Brothers	1
Total Sisters	70
Parishes	
Parishes	58
With Resident Pastor:	
Resident Diocesan Priests	43
Resident Religious Priests	3
Without Resident Pastor:	
Administered by Priests	8
Administered by Women Religious	4
Missions	39
Pastoral Centers	14
Professional Ministry Personnel:	
Brothers	1
Sisters	25
Lay Ministers	27
Welfare	
Catholic Hospitals	3
Total Assisted	173,111
Day Care and Extended Day Care Centers	2
Total Assisted	150
Educational	
Seminaries, Diocesan	1
Students from This Diocese	2
Students from Other Diocese	1
Diocesan Students in Other Seminaries	8
Total Seminarians	10
Colleges and Universities	1
Total Students	1,418
High Schools, Diocesan and Parish	2
Total Students	396
Elementary Schools, Diocesan and Parish	4
Total Students	784
Catechesis/Religious Education:	
High School Students	1,650
Elementary Students	6,100
Total Students Under Catholic Instruction	10,358
Teachers in the Diocese:	
Priests	10
Sisters	10
Lay Teachers	196
Vital Statistics	
Receptions into the Church:	
Infant Baptism Totals	915
Adult Baptism Totals	203
Received into Full Communion	150
First Communions	1,050
Confirmations	850
Marriages:	
Catholic	209
Interfaith	211
Total Marriages	420
Deaths	820
Total Catholic Population	66,500
Total Population	424,372

Former Bishops—Rt. Rev. JOHN B. BRONDEL, cons. Bishop of Victoria, V.I., Dec. 14, 1879; appt. Vicar Apostolic of Montana, April 17, 1883; Bishop of Helena, March 7, 1884; died Nov. 3, 1903.—Rt. Rev. JOHN P. CARROLL, D.D., cons. Bishop of Helena, Dec. 21, 1904; died Nov. 4, 1925.—Most Rev. GEORGE J. FINNIGAN, C.S.C., D.D., cons. Bishop of Helena, Aug. 1, 1927; died Aug. 14, 1932.—Most Rev. RALPH L. HAYES, D.D., cons. Bishop of Helena, Sept. 21, 1933; transferred to Rectorship North American College, Rome, Italy, September 11, 1935; transferred to Titular See of Hierapolis, Oct. 26, 1935; transferred to Davenport, Nov. 16, 1944; appt. Assistant at the Pontifical Throne, April 30, 1958; transferred to Titular See of Naraggara and retired, Oct. 20, 1966; died July 4, 1970.—Most Rev. JOSEPH M. GILMORE, S.T.D., cons. Bishop of Helena, Feb. 19, 1936; died April 2, 1962.—Most Rev. RAYMOND G. HUNTHAUSEN, ord. June 1, 1946; appt. July 8, 1962; cons. Bishop of Helena, Aug. 30, 1962; transferred to Archdiocese of Seattle, Feb. 25, 1975; installed Archbishop of Seattle, May 22, 1975; retired Aug. 21, 1991.—Most Rev. ELDEN F. CURTISS, D.D., ord. May 24, 1958; appt. March 4, 1976; cons. Bishop of Helena, April 28, 1976; transferred to Archdiocese of Omaha, May 4, 1993; installed Archbishop of Omaha, June 25, 1993.

Vicar General—Very Rev. JOHN J. DARRAGH, *P.O. Box 1729, Helena, 59624.* Tel: 406-442-5825; Fax: 406-442-5191.

Episcopal Vicar for Carroll College—Rev. JOSEPH D. HARRINGTON, *Carroll College, Helena, 59625.* Tel: 406-447-4459.

Episcopal Vicar for Senior Status Priests—Rev. BERNARD J. SULLIVAN, *311 9th Ave., Apt. 3, Helena, 59601.* Tel: 406-449-8839.

Chancery and Diocesan Pastoral Office—515 N. Ewing St., P.O. Box 1729, Helena, 59624. Tel: 406-442-5820; Fax: 406-442-5191.

Moderator of the Curia—Rev. JOHN W. ROBERTSON.

Chancellor—Rev. JOHN W. ROBERTSON.

Director of Pastoral Office—Sr. RITA MCGINNIS, S.C.L.

Archivist—Rev. WILLIAM DORNBOS.

Business Administration Office—PETER MCNAMEE, Diocesan Finance Officer, *515 N. Ewing St., P.O. Box 1729, Helena, 59624.* Tel: 406-442-5820.

Development Office—GERALD KUHL, Dir., *P.O. Box 1729, Helena, 59624.* Tel: 406-442-5820.

Western Montana Catholic Foundation—DONALD ST. PETER, Pres. GERALD KUHL, Contact Person, *P.O. Box 1729, Helena, 59624.* Tel: 406-442-5820.

Diocesan Tribunal—515 N. Ewing St., P.O. Box 1729, Helena, 59624. Tel: 406-442-5820.

Judicial Vicar—Rev. JOHN W. ROBERTSON.

Associate Judges—Revs. RAYMOND V. GILMORE; THOMAS HAFFEY; MATTHEW HUBER; PATRICK MCGURK.

Promoter of Justice—Rev. ROBERT GROSCH, J.C.L.

Defenders of the Bond—Revs. EMMETT KELLY; KEVIN O'NEILL; GARY RELLER.

Notaries—NADINE MCCURDY; GERALDINE ROBINSON.

Tribunal Consultants—Revs. JAMES PROVOST, J.C.D.; JOHN WANG, J.U.D., Ph.D.

Diocesan Consultors and Priests' Council—Revs. KEVIN CLARKE, S.J.; JOHN J. DARRAGH, V.G.; JEFFREY M. FLEMING; WILLIAM J. GREYTAK; THOMAS P. HAFFEY; JOSEPH D. HARRINGTON; KEVIN S. O'NEILL; GARY W. RELLER, Chm. JOHN W. ROBERTSON; MICHAEL M. SMITH; BERNARD J. SULLIVAN; JOSEPH P. SULLIVAN.

Vicariates—Conrad: Rev. THOMAS HAFFEY, Helena: Rev. WILLIAM J. GREYTAK, Missoula: Rev. MICHAEL M. SMITH, Kalispell: Rev. JOSEPH P. SULLIVAN, Butte: Rev. KEVIN S. O'NEILL.

Personnel Board—Revs. JOHN J. DARRAGH, V.G.; WILLIAM J. GREYTAK; THOMAS P. HAFFEY; JOHN F. HUNTHAUSEN, Chm. EDWARD G. KOHLER; JOSEPH P. MORAN.

Inter-Diocesan Organizations

Montana Catholic Conference—SHARON HOFF, *P.O. Box 1708, Helena, 59624.* Tel: 406-442-5761; Fax: 406-442-9047.

Board of Directors—Most Rev. ALEX J. BRUNETT, (Helena); Most Rev. ANTHONY MILONE, (Great Falls); JULIE FRENCH, (Great Falls); MYLES GROTBO, (Helena); Rev. EUGENE HRUSKA, (Great Falls); Rev. JEREMIAH LOWNEY, (Helena); Sr. MARY JOE MCDONALD, S.C.L., (Butte); JOSEPH P. "PETE" MALIN, (Helena); EDWARD WAMBOLT.

Catholic Social Services for Montana, Inc.—MARILYN MCKIBBEN, Dir., *22 S. Ewing St., P.O. Box 907, Helena, 59601.* Tel: 406-442-4130; Fax: 406-442-4192. Coordinates and supervises all Catholic Social welfare in the State of Montana.

Board of Directors—Most Rev. ALEX J. BRUNETT, (Helena); Most Rev. ANTHONY MILONE, (Great Falls); JULIE FRENCH, (Great Falls); MYLES GROTBO, (Helena); Rev. EUGENE HRUSKA, (Great Falls); Rev. JEREMIAH LOWNEY, (Helena); Sr. MARY JO MCDONALD, S.C.L., (Butte); JOSEPH P. "PETE" MALIN, (Helena); EDWARD WAMBOLT.

Helena Office—MARILYN MCKIBBEN, Dir., Adoptions; Sr. MARY NOEL BRUCH, S.C.L., Social Worker, *22 S. Ewing, P.O. Box 907, Helena, 59624.* Tel: 406-442-4130.

Billings Office—St. Vincent's Hospital, 1222 N. 27th St., Billings, 59101. Tel: 406-252-3399.

Great Falls Office—1601 Second Ave. N., P.O. Box 7410, Great Falls, 59406. Tel: 406-771-7805.
Missoula Office—St. Patrick Hospital, 554 W. Broadway, Missoula, 59801. Tel: 406-542-0001, Ext. 2029.

Montana Association of Churches—MARGARET MACDONALD, Exec. Dir., *100 24th St. W., Suite G, Billings, 59102.* Tel: 406-656-9779. Rev. GARY W. RELLER, Diocesan Ecumenical Officer, *P.O. Box 1477, Polson, 59860.* Tel: 406-883-4607.

Diocesan Offices and Organizations

Borromeo Pre-Seminary Program—Rev. LEO PROXELL, *Carroll College, Helena, 59625.* Tel: 406-447-4336.

Campaign for Human Development—Sr. RITA MCGINNIS, S.C.L., *P.O. Box 1729, Helena, 59624.* Tel: 406-442-5820.

Catholic Committee on Scouting—JAMES TUCKER, Contact, *P.O. Box 1729, Helena, 59624.* Tel: 406-442-5820.

Catholic Youth Coalition—Deacon DAN MCGRATH, *P.O. Box 1729, Helena, 59624.* Tel: 406-442-5820.

Cemetery Director—SCOTT FITZPATRICK, *P.O. Box 1729, Helena, 59624.* Tel: 406-442-5820.

Charismatic Renewal—Rev. CYRIL HUNKLER, Liaison, *P.O. Box 745, Plains, 59859.* Tel: 406-826-5602.

Christian Family Movement—Diocesan Pastoral Office, P.O. Box 1729, Helena, 59624.

Clergy Senior Status and Security Trust Board—Most Rev. ALEX J. BRUNETT; Revs. ERNEST BURNS; JOSEPH HARRINGTON; EMMETT KELLY; PATRICK MCGURK; JOSEPH OBLINGER; KEVIN O'NEILL.

Continuing Formation of the Clergy—Rev. THOMAS P. HAFFEY, Dir., *106 S. Maryland, Conrad, 59425.* Tel: 406-278-7517.

Assembly of Women Religious—Sr. MARY JO MCDONALD, S.C.L., Pres., *2100 Farragut, Butte, 59701.* Tel: 406-723-4303.

Cursillo Movement, Journey and Search—Diocesan Pastoral Office, P.O. Box 1729, Helena, 59624. Tel: 406-442-5820.

Daughters of Isabella—CAROLYN SMITH, State Regent, *5128 Hwy. 200, Ovando, 59854.*

Diocesan Attorney—WARD SHANAHAN, *Gough, Shanahan, Johnson & Waterman, P.O. Box 1715, Helena, 59624.* Tel: 406-442-8560.

Diocesan Council of Catholic Women—LILLIAN JUDGE, Pres., *219 Central Ave., Whitefish, 59937.* Tel: 406-777-5833.

Diocesan Ecumenical Officer—Rev. GARY W. RELLER, *PO Box 1477, Polson, 59860.* Tel: 406-883-4607.

Friends of The Catholic University—Rev. JOSEPH HARRINGTON, Chm., *Carroll College, Helena, 59625.* Tel: 406-447-4459.

Guatemala Missions—Rev. JOHN W. ROBERTSON, Dir., *P.O. Box 1729, Helena, 59624.* Tel: 406-442-5820.

Holy Childhood Association—Rev. JOSEPH L. BYRNE, Dir., *P.O. Box 610, Townsend, 59644.* Tel: 406-266-3973.

Legendary Lodge (Diocesan Summer Camp)—WILLIAM PENA, Dir. & Supvr., *HC 31, Box 900 S., Seeley Lake, 59868.* Tel: 406-677-2211; 677-2577.

Marriage Encounter—DALE BOESPFLUG; PAM BOESPFLUG, *2014 Fifth Ave. S.W., Great Falls, 59404.*

Office of Due Process—Contact Judicial Vicar, *P.O. Box 1729, Helena, 59624.* Tel: 406-442-5820.

Program of Formation for Lay Ministry—Rev. J. EUGENE PEOPLES, Dir., *Carroll College, Helena, 59625.* Tel: 406-447-4334.

Program of Formation for the Permanent Diaconate—Deacon JAMES CURRY, Coord., *102 S. Washington, Butte, 59701.* Tel: 406-723-5407.

Office of Worship—Rev. EDWARD HISLOP, Liturgy Consultant; Sr. MARY JO QUINN, Liturgical Music Consultant, *1700 Missoula Ave., Helena, 59601.* Tel: 406-442-5268.

Priestly Formation—Rev. JOHN W. ROBERTSON, *P.O. Box 1729, Helena, 59624.* Tel: 406-442-5820.

Propagation of the Faith—Rev. JOSEPH L. BYRNE, Diocesan Dir., *P.O. Box 610, Townsend, 59644.* Tel: 406-266-3973.

Religious Education—JIM TUCKER, Dir., *515 N. Ewing St., P.O. Box 1729, Helena, 59624.* Tel: 406-442-5820.
Resource Center—KATHY WARD, Mgr., *515 N. Ewing St., P.O. Box 1729, Helena, 59624.* Tel: 406-442-5820.

Superintendent of Schools—Sr. KATHERINE FRANCHETT, S.C.L., *P.O. Box 31158, Billings, 59107.* Tel: 406-252-9595; Fax: 406-252-9875.

Third Order of St. Francis—KATHY POELMAN, S.F.O., *1702 Peosta, Helena, 59601.*

Vocations Office—P.O. Box 1729, Helena, 59624. Tel: 406-442-5820. Rev. THOMAS O'DONNELL, Dir., *P.O. Box 1110, East Helena, 59635.* Tel: 406-227-5334. Rev. VICTOR LANGHANS, Assoc. Dir., *P.O. Box 329, Frenchtown, 59834.* Tel: 406-626-4492. Rev. KEVIN O'NEILL, Assoc. Dir., *102 S. Washington, Butte, 59701.* Tel: 406-723-5407. Rev. JEFF FLEMING, Assoc. Dir., *530 N. Ewing, Helena, 59601.* Tel: 406-442-5825. Rev. GREG SMITH, Assoc. Dir., *1502 Shirley Rd., Helena, 59602.* Tel: 406-458-9866.

"Montana Catholic" (Diocesan Newspaper)—GERALD KORSON, Editor; M. CATHERINE TILZEY, Asst. Editor, *515 N. Ewing St., P.O. Box 1729, Helena, 59624.* Tel: 406-442-5820; Fax: 406-442-5191.

CLERGY, PARISHES, MISSIONS AND PAROCHIAL SCHOOLS

CITY OF HELENA
(Lewis and Clark County)

1—CATHEDRAL OF ST. HELENA (1866), Revs. John Darragh, Rector; Jeffrey Fleming; Deacon Fritz Roos. Pastoral Assocs.: Bro. Stephen Hale, C.F.C.; Sr. Nancy Svetlecic, S.C.L.; Lorraine Tucker.
Office: 530 N. Ewing St., 59601. Tel: 406-442-5825; 442-7094 (after hours); Fax: 406-449-5113.
Good Samaritan Thrift Store—(Assistance to those in need.) 1403 N. Cooke, 59601. Tel: 406-442-0780.

2—ST. MARY (1910), Rev. Edward J. Hislop. Pastoral Assocs.: Sr. Mary Agnes Hogan, S.C.L.; Sr. Mary Jo Quinn, S.C.L.; Helen Beausoleil; Janice Nankivel.
Office: 1700 Missoula Ave., 59601. Tel: 406-442-5268; Fax: 406-449-0860.

3—OUR LADY OF THE VALLEY, Rev. D. Gregory Smith; Deacon Richard Miller.
Office: 1502 Shirley Rd., 59601. Tel: 406-458-6114.
Res., 1510 Easy Rd., 59601. Tel: 406-458-9866.
Missions—Wolf Creek, Lewis and Clark Co., Sacred Heart; Marysville, Lewis and Clark Co., Our Lady of Lourdes.

OUTSIDE THE CITY OF HELENA

Anaconda, Deer Lodge Co.,

1—ST. JOSEPH'S, (1957). Closed 1977. For inquiries for parish records contact Anaconda Catholic Community, Anaconda.

2—ST. PAUL'S, (1888). Closed 1980. For inquiries for parish records contact Anaconda Catholic Community, Anaconda.

3—ST. PETER'S, (1898). Closed 1980. For inquiries for parish records contact Anaconda Catholic Community, Anaconda.

4—ANACONDA CATHOLIC COMMUNITY, (1980). Serves the entire community of Anaconda. Revs. John E. Murray; Daniel Driscoll. Pastoral Assocs.: Sr. Eileen Johnson, S.C.L.; Sr. Constance Howe, R.S.M.; Mr. John McKenna, Admin.
Office: 217 W. Pennsylvania, 59711. Tel: 406-563-8406; Fax: 406-563-5912.
Res., 405 Alder St., 59711. Tel: 406-563-6633.
Churches—Holy Family.; St. Peter, 401 Alder St., 59711.
Station—Anaconda, Georgetown Lake.

Bigfork, Flathead Co., St. Catherine (1958), Rev. Richard H. Sodja.
Res., P.O. Box 277, 59911. Tel: 406-837-4846.
Church—105 Oliver Ln., 59911.
Mission—Somers, St. Ann.

Bonner, Missoula Co., St. Ann (1940), Rev. Michael Smith.
Res., P.O. Box 1008, 59823. Tel: 406-258-6815.
Mission—Seeley Lake, Missoula Co., Living Water Mission.

Boulder, Jefferson Co., St. Catherine (1894), Rev. William Greytak.
Res., Box 205, 59632. Tel: 406-225-3222.
Mission—Boulder Valley, Jefferson Co., St. John the Evangelist.

Bozeman, Gallatin Co., Holy Rosary (1885), Rev. Robert J. Beaulieu. Pastoral Assocs.: Sr. Patricia Toeckes, S.C.L.; Mary Fuller.
Office: 220 W. Main St., P.O. Box 96, 59771-0096. Tel: 406-587-4581; Fax: 406-582-0248.
Resurrection (1965). (Newman Parish). Rev. Robert Hall; Deacon Michael Certalic. Pastoral Assocs.: Marge O'Leary; Diane Dwyer.
Office: 1725 S. 11th, 59715. Tel: 406-586-9243.
Res., 905 S. Fifth, 59715. Tel: 406-587-8667.
Mission—Big Sky.

Browning, Glacier Co., Church of the Little Flower (1904), Revs. Edward Kohler; Michael McHugh, S.J.; Sr. Edna Hunthausen, S.C.L., Pastoral Assoc.; Deacons Robert Bremner; Melvin Rutherford; John Gobert.
Office: P.O. Box 519, 59417. Tel: 406-338-5775.
Church—204 First St. N.E., 59417.
Missions—Babb, St. Mary, Queen of the World; Starr School, Sacred Heart; East Glacier, Church of the Ascension.

Butte, Silver Bow Co.,

1—BUTTE CATHOLIC COMMUNITY NORTH. Includes Immaculate Conception, St. Joseph, and St. Patrick Parishes. See individual listings. Revs. Kevin O'Neill, Moderator; Harry Butori; Deacons James Curry; Ronald Fournier.
Office and Res.: 102 S. Washington St., 59701. Tel: 406-723-5407 (Office); 782-8082 (Res.); Fax: 406-782-5408.

2—HOLY SAVIOR, (1904). Closed 1974. For inquiries for parish records contact Butte Catholic Community North, Butte.

3—HOLY SPIRIT, (1978), Sr. Sharon Smith, S.C.L., Pastoral Admin.; Deacon Dan McGrath.
Office: 3930 East Lake, 59701. Tel: 406-494-5078.

4—IMMACULATE CONCEPTION, (1907). (Butte Catholic Community North). Rev. Kevin S. O'Neill.
Office and Res.: 102 S. Washington, 59701. Tel: 406-723-5407 (Office), 782-8082 (Res.); Fax: 406-782-5408.
Church—Western & Caledonia St., 59701.

5—SACRED HEART PARISH, (1903). Closed 1970. For inquiries for parish records contact Butte Catholic Community North, Butte.

6—ST. ANN, (1917), Rev. Gregory Burke; Sr. Mary Jo McDonald, S.C.L., Admin.; Deacon H. J. Johnson.
Res., 2100 Farragut, 59701. Tel: 406-723-4303.

7—ST. HELENA, (1921). Closed 1966. For inquiries for parish records contact Butte Catholic Community North, Butte.

8—ST. JOHN THE EVANGELIST, (1917), Rev. Edward Courtney. Pastoral Assocs.: John McPherson; Kathy Walter.
Office: 1500 Cobban Ave., 59701.
Res., 2040 Whitman, 59701. Tel: 406-782-8349.
Church—1500 Majors Ave., 59701.

9—ST. JOSEPH, (1905). (Butte Catholic Community North). Rev. Harry Butori.
Office and Res.: 102 S. Washington, 59701. Tel: 406-723-5407 (Office), 782-8668 (Res.); Fax: 406-723-5408.
Church—Utah & Second St., 59701.

10—ST. MARY, (1903). Closed 1986. For inquiries for parish records contact Butte Catholic Community North, Butte.

11—ST. PATRICK, (1881). (Butte Catholic Community North). Rev. Kevin O'Neill.
Office and Res.: 102 S. Washington St., 59701. Tel: 406-723-5407 (Office), 782-8082 (Res.).
Church—Mercury & Washington St., 59701.

Choteau, Teton Co., St. Joseph (1898), Rev. Robert C. Noonan, Pastor.
Res., P.O. Box 640, 59422. Tel: 406-466-2961.
Church—320 Main St., 59422.

Columbia Falls, Flathead Co., St. Richard (1941), Rev. Joseph P. Sullivan; Sr. Lorane Coffin, O.S.B., Pastoral Assoc.; Deacon Robert Pearce.
Res., P.O. Box 2073, 59912. Tel: 406-892-5142.
Church—1210 Ninth St. W., 59912.
Mission—West Glacier, Flathead Co.
Station—Columbia Falls, Apgar.

Conrad, Pondera Co., St. Michael (1909), Rev. Thomas P. Haffey; Sr. Mary Agnes Koenig, O.P., Pastoral Assoc.
Res., 106 S. Maryland St., 59425. Tel: 406-278-7517.
Station—Conrad, Stations Brady Ledger.

Cut Bank, Glacier Co., St. Margaret (1914), Rev. Stanley Popowski; Deacon James E. Hayes.
Res., 207 Second St., S.E., 59427. Tel: 406-873-4413.

Deer Lodge, Powell Co., Immaculate Conception (1911), Rev. Patrick McGurk.
Res., 605 Clark St., P.O. Box 786, 59722. Tel: 406-846-1444.
Mission—Avon, Powell Co., St. Theodore.

Dillon, Beaverhead Co., St. Rose of Lima (1901), Rev. John F. Hunthausen; Elaine Collins, Pastoral Assoc.
Office: 226 S. Atlantic St., 59725. Tel: 406-683-4391; 683-6753 (Rectory).
Missions—Melrose, Silver Bow Co., St. John The Apostle; Wisdom, Beaverhead Co., Our Lady of Wisdom.

Drummond, Granite Co., St. Michael (1919), Rev. Jacob Vadakkekudy (India) Admin.
Res., P.O. Box 329, 59832. Tel: 406-288-3847.
Mission—Goldcreek, Powell Co., St. Mary.

Dutton, Teton Co., St. William (1962), Rev. Thomas P. Haffey, Sacramental Min.; Sr. Johanna Rickl, C.H.M., Pastoral Admin.
Res., 20 First Ave. N.E., Box 117, 59433. Tel: 406-476-3429.
Mission—Power, Guardian Angel.

East Helena, Lewis and Clark Co., SS. Cyril and Methodius (1907), Rev. Thomas M. O'Donnell; Deacon Gerald Kuhl.

Res., 214 W. Riggs St., P.O. Box 1110, 59635. Tel: 406-227-5334.
Missions—Canyon Ferry, Our Lady of the Lake; Clancy, St. John's.
Station—East Helena, Alhambra.

Eureka, Lincoln Co., Our Lady of Mercy (1916), Rev. Henry Steinhoff (B).
Res., 500 Dewey Ave., Box 626, 59917. Tel: 406-296-2118.

Fairfield, Teton Co., St. John (1941), Rev. Robert C. Noonan.
Res., 514 First Ave. S., P.O. Box 397, 59436. Tel: 406-467-2481.
Mission—Augusta, Clark Co., St. Matthias.

Frenchtown, Missoula Co., St. John the Baptist (1884), Rev. Victor Langhans.
Res., P.O. Box 329, 59834. Tel: 406-626-4492. [CEM]
Missions—Superior, St. Mary Queen of Heaven; Alberton, Mineral Co., St. Albert the Great.

Hamilton, Ravalli Co., St. Francis (1896), Rev. Raymond Gilmore; Sr. Margaret Hogan, S.C.L., Pastoral Assoc.; Deacon Roland Peterson.
Res., 411 S. Fifth St., 59840. Tel: 406-363-1385.
Mission—Darby, Mount Ravalli Co., St. Philip Benizi.

Harlowton, Wheatland Co., St. Joseph (1909), Rev. Kenneth E. Fortney.
Res., 26 Third St., N.W., Box 286, 59036. Tel: 406-632-5538.
Missions—Judith Gap, Wheatland Co., Immaculate Conception; Shawmut, Wheatland Co., Blessed Sacrament.

Heart Butte, Glacier Co., St. Anne (1911), Rev. Daniel Powers, S.J. Pastoral Assocs.: Sr. Marion McCrickard, O.S.U.; Bev Bullshoe; Deacon Melvin Rutherford.
Res., Blackfeet Reservation, P.O. Box 160, 59448. Tel: 406-338-2312.
Mission—Heart Butte, Mount Glacier Co., Holy Family Mission. [CEM]

Helmville, Powell Co., St. Thomas (1889), Rev. Thomas Fenlon, (Retired); Kathy Daniels, Pastoral Assoc.
Res., P.O. Box 90, 59843. Tel: 406-793-5697. [CEM]
Mission—Lincoln, Lewis and Clark Co., St. Jude's.

Kalispell, Flathead Co., St. Matthew (1895), Revs. Robert C. Noonan; Carl Deitchman. Pastoral Assocs.: Deacon Fred Topp; Sr. Celine Regan, O.P.
Office: 602 S. Main St., 59901. Tel: 406-752-6788; Fax: 406-756-8248.
Res., 644 First Ave., W., 59901.
Risen Christ (1978), Rev. James Connor; Deacon Jack Pelowitz.
Res., 65 W. Evergreen Dr., 59901. Tel: 406-752-4219; 752-4226; Fax: 406-752-4226.

Libby, Lincoln Co., St. Joseph (1911), Rev. Raymond J. Hannigan.
Res., 719 Utah Ave., P.O. Box 1467, 59923. Tel: 406-293-4322; Fax: 406-293-7231.
Mission—Troy, Immaculate Conception.

Madison, Madison County Catholic Community. Comprised of St. Mary of the Assumption, Laurin; St. Joseph, Sheridan; and St. Patrick, Ennis. Rev. Edward L. Stupca. Pastoral Assocs.: Laurie Bartoletti; Kathy Miller; Roberta McKay.
Res., 105 Poppleton, P.O. Box 17, Sheridan, 59749. Tel: 406-842-5588.

Missoula, Missoula Co.,

1—Christ the King, (1966). (Newman Parish). Rev. James J. Hogan; Sr. Nancy Davis, C.S.J., Pastoral Assoc.; Dianne Peterson, Campus Min.
Office: 1400 Gerald Ave., 59801. Tel: 406-728-3845.

2—Holy Family, (1972), Rev. Matthew Huber; Deacon Thomas McCarthy; Sr. Ursula Keough, C.H.M, Pastoral Assoc.
Res., 4616 Gharrett St., 59803. Tel: 406-251-2692.
Mission—Lolo, Missoula Co., Spirit of Christ, 4200 Farm Ln., P.O. Box 743, Lolo, 59847. Tel: 406-273-2748.

3—Pope John XXIII, (1971), Rev. Frank McCormick. Pastoral Assocs.: Beckie Hasse; Chris Kappes; Sr. Alice Ann Byrne, O.P.
Office: 1475 Eaton St., 59801. Tel: 406-721-2405.

4—St. Anthony, (1921), Rev. John P. Miller. Pastoral Assocs.: Terry Jimmerson; Linda McKnight; Maggie Hommond.
Office: 217 Tremont St., 59801. Tel: 406-543-3129.

5—St. Francis Xavier, (1881), Revs. Kevin T. Clarke, S.J.; Thomas F. Healy, S.J.; Deacon Carlton Quamme. In res., Rev. Roger E. Blanchette, S.J.; John S. Harrington, S.J.
Res., 420 W. Pine St., 59802. Tel: 406-542-0321.

Philipsburg, Granite Co., St. Philip (1892), Rev. Jacob Vadakkekudy (India) Admin.
Res., P.O. Box 329, Drummond, 59832. Tel: 406-288-3847.
Church—307 W. Kearney, P.O. Box 397, 59858. Tel: 406-859-3908.

Plains, Sanders Co., St. James (1889), Rev. Cyril Hunkler; Deacon Lynn F. McAtee.
Res., 107 Meany St., P.O. Box 745, 59859. Tel: 406-826-3668.
Mission—Hot Springs, Sacred Heart.

Polson, Lake Co., Immaculate Conception (1909), Rev. Gary W. Reller; Deacons Wesley Vert; Daniel Gullotta.
Res., 908 Fifth Ave. E., P.O. Box 1477, 59860. Tel: 406-883-4607; 883-2506 (Office). [CEM 3]
Church—1002 Fourth Ave. E., 59860.

Ronan, Lake Co., Sacred Heart (1911), Rev. Bernard J. Koenig.
Res., 325 Round Butte W., 59864. Tel: 406-676-4511.
Mission—Charlo, Mount Lake Co., St. Joseph's.

St. Ignatius, Lake Co., St. Ignatius (1854), Rev. Gustav H. Schmidt, S.J. Pastoral Assocs.: Sr. Dolores Shortal, O.P.; Sr. Joan Bartin, O.P.; Deacon Daniel Swoney.
Res., P.O. Box 667, 59865. Tel: 406-745-2768.
Missions—Arlee, Lake Co., Sacred Heart; Jocko, Lake Co., St. John Berchman's.

Shelby, Toole Co., St. William (1924), Rev. Joseph P. Moran.
Res., 531 Main St., 59474. Tel: 406-434-2988.
Mission—Sunburst, St. Thomas Aquinas, (1917).

Stevensville, Ravalli Co., St. Mary (1842), Rev. Stephen Tallman.
Res., 333 Charlos St., 59870. Tel: 777-5574. [CEM]
Mission—Florence, Ravalli Co., St. Joseph.

Swan Valley, Lake Co., Swan Valley Catholic Community, Rev. Dusan Okorn, Admin.; Michelle Jenkins, Pastoral Assoc.
Res., The Sycamore Tree, Swan Lake, 59911. Tel: 406-754-2429.

Thompson Falls, Sanders Co., St. William (1955), Rev. Cyril Hunkler; Deacons Ronald Kazmierezak; Robert W. Kelley.
Res., Spruce & Preston St., P.O. Box 186, 59873. Tel: 406-827-4433.
Mission—Noxon.

Three Forks, Gallatin Co., Holy Family (1886), Rev. John F. Ward; Deacons Francis Finnegan; Robert Lane.
Res., 104 Birch St., P.O. Box 99, 59752. Tel: 406-285-3592.
609 Quaw Blvd., Belgrade, 59714. Tel: 406-388-1290.
Mission—Belgrade, Valley of Flowers.

Townsend, Broadwater Co., Holy Cross (1903), Rev. Joseph L. Byrne; Deacon Donald Marks.
Res., 101 S. Walnut, P.O. Box 610, 59644. Tel: 406-266-3973.
Mission—Toston, Broadwater Co., Immaculate Conception.
St. Joseph's Historical Church—Canton.

Valier, Pondera Co., St. Francis (1909), Sr. Anne Marie Burke, S.C.L., Pastoral Admin.; Rev. Stanley Popowski.
Res., 701-4th St., P.O. Box 338, 59486. Tel: 406-279-3327.
Mission—Dupuyer, Pondera Co., Holy Cross.

Walkerville, Silver Bow Co., St. Lawrence O'Toole (1896). Closed 1986. For inquiries for parish records contact Butte Catholic Community North, Butte.

West Yellowstone, Gallatin Co., Our Lady of the Pines, Rev. Joseph B. Oblinger, (Retired), Admin.
Res., Madison Ave. & Geyser St., P.O. Box 577, 59758. Tel: 406-646-7755.

Whitefish, Flathead Co., St. Charles (1890), Rev. Charles Roman.
Res., 230 Baker, Box 128, 59937. Tel: 406-862-2051.

Whitehall, Jefferson Co., St. Teresa (1911), Rev. Francis J. Wiegenstein; Al Feldsheim, Pastoral Assoc.
Res., 109 Second Ave. E., Box 430, 59759. Tel: 406-287-3893.
Mission—Twin Bridges, Jefferson Co., Notre Dame.

White Sulphur Springs, Meagher Co., St. Bartholomew (1916), Sr. Patricia Sullivan, S.C.L., Pastoral Admin.
Res., 407 Second Ave. S.E., P.O. Box 422, 59645. Tel: 406-547-3737.

DIOCESAN MISSIONS

Guatemala, Santo Tomas La Union,
10017 Departmento Suchitepequez. Rev. James Hazelton; Sr. Mary Waddell, B.V.M., Clinic Dir.; Sr. Anna Priester, B.V.M., D.R.E.

Helena, Guatemala Mission Medical Fund,
Supplies for needs of mission personnel, medicines, medical supplies, and health care needs to people in the mission area in Guatemala. Donations may be forwarded to the Fund at P.O. Box 1729, Helena, MT 59624. P.O. Box 1729, 59624.

Chaplains of Public Institutions

Helena. *U.S. Veteran's Hospital*. Served by Helena Area Parishes. Fort Harrison.

Boulder. *Boulder River School and Hospital*. Attended from St. Catherine, Boulder. Rev. William Greytak.

Deer Lodge. *Montana State Prison*. Rev. Honorato Cabaong. Tel: 406-846-1320.

Warm Springs. *Warm Springs State Hospital*, P.O. Drawer D, 59756. Tel: 406-693-2000; 693-2294. Rev. Honorato Cabaong.

Special Assignments:
Reverend Fathers—
Dornbos, William, Diocesan Archivist, Mailing Address: P.O. Box 1729, Helena, MT 59624
Dumais, George J., S.J., Dir., Rochmont, Inc., 1700 Madeline, Missoula, MT 59801
Finnegan, Joseph, Mailing Address: P.O. Box 503, Whitehall, MT 59759
Malnar, Stan, 4220 W. Fremont Rd., Spokane, WA 99204
O'Neill, Michael, Mailing Address: P.O. Box 1729, Helena, MT 59624
Robertson, John W., Chancellor & Moderator of the Curia, Mailing Address: P.O. Box 1729, Helena, MT 59624

On Duty Outside the Diocese:
Reverend Monsignors—
McCarthy, John F., Catholic Near East Association, Rome
Reverend Fathers—
Driscoll, Michael, Notre Dame University, Department of Theology, Notre Dame, IN 46556
Flynn, Thomas, Emory University, 1278 Oakdale Rd., N.E., Atlanta, GA 30307
Hazelton, James, Santo Tomas La Union, 10017 Departmento Suchitepequez, Guatemala
Provost, James H., Department of Canon Law, The Catholic University of America, Washington, DC 20064
Sullivan, James M., Creighton University, 2500 California St., Omaha, NE 68178

Military Chaplains:
Reverend Monsignors—
Shea, Donald W., U.S. Army
Reverend Fathers—
Diphe, Juan, U.S. Air Force
Hightower, O. Lee., U.S. Army
Patton, Patrick G., U.S. Army

Retired:
Reverend Monsignors—
Brown, Anthony M., 30 Penny Ln., Butte, MT 59701
Harrington, D. B., 35 Wells St., Butte, MT 59701
Marsar, Joseph, P.O. Box 1110, East Helena, MT 59635
Reverend Fathers—
Burns, Ernest, 100 E. Broadway #601, Butte, MT 59701
Chilton, Michael, 1616 E. 30th, #107, Spokane, WA 99203
Courtney, Humphrey, Carroll College, Helena, MT 59625
Fabing, Charles, Carroll College, Helena, MT 59624
Fenlon, Thomas J., Mailing Address: P.O. Box 90, Helmville, MT 59843
Kaparich, Albert N., 100 E. Broadway, #701, Butte, MT 59701
Kelly, Emmett, 4309 Ghurrett, Missoula, MT 59801
Kirsch, John B., P.O. Box 893, Sheridon, MT 59749
Lynam, Gerald J., Carroll College, Helena, MT 59625
McCarthy, Bernard, 1325 W. Quartz, #306, Butte, MT 59701
Moran, Edward F., 410 Rosalie Manor, Butte, MT 59701
O'Sullivan, Sarsfield, 410 N. Western Ave., Butte, MT 59701
Oblinger, Joseph B., P.O. Box 577, West Yellowstone, MT 59758
Okorn, Dusan, Sycamore Tree, Swan Lake, MT 59701
Plummer, J. Bruce, 261 Half Circle Way, Polson, MT 59860
Simons, Lawrence D., P.O. Box 696, Honaunau, HI 96726
Strom, Charles W., 341 Lupfer Ave., Whitefish, MT 59937
Sullivan, J. Bernard, 31 Ninth Ave., #3, Helena, MT 59601
Waggenor, William L., 3033 Busch St., #19, Whitehall, MT 59701
Wang, John, 425 Ford St., Missoula, MT 59801

Permanent Deacons:
- Bremner, Robert, Sr., Little Flower, Browning
- Britton, Michael, (Retired)
- Certalic, Michael, Resurrection, Bozeman
- Curry, James, Catholic Community North, Butte
- Finnegan, Francis R., Holy Family, Three Forks
- Fournier, Ronald, Catholic Community North, Butte
- Gobert, John, Little Flower, Browning
- Gullotto, Daniel, Immaculate Conception, Polson
- Hayes, James E., St. Margaret, Cut Bank
- Johnson, H. J., St. Ann's, Butte
- Kazmierczak, Ronald, St. William, Thompson Falls
- Kelley, Robert, St. William, Thompson Falls
- Kuhl, Gerald, Sts. Cyril and Methodius, East Helena
- Lane, Robert, Holy Family, Three Forks
- Marks, Donald, Holy Cross, Townsend
- McAtee, Lynn F., St. James, Plains
- McCarthy, Thomas, Leave of Absence
- McGrath, Daniel, Holy Spirit, Butte
- Miller, Richard, Our Lady of the Valley, Helena
- Pearce, Robert, St. Richard, Columbia Falls
- Pelowitz, Jack, Risen Christ, Kalispell
- Peterson, Roland, St. Francis Parish, Hamilton
- Quamme, Carlton, St. Francis, Missoula
- Roos, Fritz, Cathedral of St. Helena, Helena
- Rutherford, Melvin, Little Flower, Browning
- Swoney, Daniel, St. Ignatius, Mission
- Topp, Frederick, St. Matthew, Kalispell
- Vert, Wesley, Immaculate Conception, Polson

INSTITUTIONS LOCATED IN THE DIOCESE

[A] SEMINARIES, DIOCESAN

HELENA. *Carroll College*. Rev. Leo G. Proxell, Dir. Diocesan Pre-Seminary Program. Tel: 406-447-4336. Students 3.

[B] COLLEGES AND UNIVERSITIES

HELENA. *Carroll College*, (1909). Tel: 406-447-4300; Fax: 406-447-4533.
For a complete listing, refer to the Colleges and Universities section.

[C] HIGH SCHOOLS, DIOCESAN

BUTTE. *Central High School*, 9 S. Idaho St., 59701. Tel: 406-782-6761; Fax: 406-723-3873. Patrick Prendergast, Prin.; Dr. Thomas E. Hart, Ph.D., Dir. Butte Central Schools. Lay Teachers 16; Students 164.

MISSOULA. *Loyola Sacred Heart High School*, 320 Edith St., 59801. Tel: 406-549-6101; Fax: 406-542-1432. Judith A. Giglio, Prin. Priests 1; Sisters 1; Lay Teachers 21; Students 232.

[D] SCHOOLS, ELEMENTARY

BUTTE. *Central Elementary School*. (Grades PreK-5), 1100 Delaware, 59701. Tel: 406-782-4500. Sr. Mary Jane Schmitz, S.C.L., Prin. Sisters 3; Lay Teachers 13; Students 245.

Central Junior High School. (Grades 6-8), 400 W. Park, 59701. Tel: 406-782-1233. Jacqueline M. Dogel, Prin. Lay Teachers 11; Students 125.

KALISPELL. *St. Matthew School*, 602 S. Main St., 59901. Tel: 406-752-6303. Mary Grace Galvin, Administrative Assoc.

Day Care Center. (Ages 2-6). Ginger Jay, Dir. Sisters 3; Lay Teachers 12; Students 196.

MISSOULA. *St. Joseph Elementary School*, 430 W. Pine St., 59802. Tel: 406-549-1290. Tomas Anderson, Prin.

Child Care Center. (Ages 2-12). Evalie Hawkinson, Dir. Sisters 1; Lay Teachers 12; Students 218.

[E] GENERAL HOSPITALS

BUTTE. *St. James Community Hospital, Inc.*, 400 S. Clark St., 59701.
For a complete listing, refer to the Hospitals section.

MISSOULA. *St. Patrick Hospital Corporation*, 500 W. Broadway, 59802.
For a complete listing, refer to the Hospitals section.

POLSON. *St. Joseph Hospital Corporation*, Skyline Dr., P.O. Box 1010, 59860. Tel: 406-883-5377; Fax: 406-883-4388.
For a complete listing, refer to the Hospitals section.

[F] CONVENTS AND RESIDENCES OF SISTERS

COLUMBIA FALLS. *Epiphany Monastery*, P.O. Box 121, 59912. Tel: 406-892-4670. Monastery dependent upon Benedictine Convent of St. Martin, Rapid City, SD. Sisters 3.

[G] HOUSES OF PRAYER

SWAN LAKE. *The Sycamore Tree Contemplative Prayer Center*, 59911. Tel: 406-754-2429. Rev. Dusan A. Okorn, Dir.; Michelle Jenkins, Asst.

[H] NEWMAN CHAPLAINS

BOZEMAN. *Montana State University*. (Resurrection Parish), Office: 1725 S. Eleventh, 59715-4218. Tel: 406-586-9243. Rev. Robert Hall; Deacon Michael Certalic, Campus Min., Res., 905 S. Fifth, 59715.

BUTTE. *Montana College of Mineral Science and Technology*, 102 S. Washington St., 59701. Tel: 406-723-5407; Fax: 406-723-5408. Deacon James F. Curry, Chap.

DILLON. *Western Montana College*, 226 S. Atlantic St., 59725. Tel: 406-683-4391. Rev. John F. Hunthausen; Jeannette Stewart, Campus Min.

MISSOULA. *University of Montana*. (Christ the King Parish), 1400 Gerald Ave., 59801-4230. Tel: 406-728-3845. Rev. James J. Hogan; Diane Peterson, Campus Min.

[I] MISCELLANEOUS

HELENA. *The St. Helena Cathedral Foundation, Inc.*, 530 N. Ewing St., 59601-4001. Tel: 406-442-5825; Fax: 406-449-5113. Marty Heller, Pres.

BUTTE. *Central Education Foundation*, P.O. Box 634, 59703-0634. Tel: 406-723-6706; Fax: 406-723-3873. Don Peoples, Jr., Exec. Dir.

St. Vincent de Paul Thrift Store, 123 E. Park St., 59701. Tel: 406-782-0233. Wayne Thomas, Mgr.

MISSOULA. *Loyola-Sacred Heart High School Foundation*, 300 Edith, 59801-3916. Tel: 406-728-2367; 728-2353; Fax: 406-542-9900. Sr. Rita Mudd, S.P., Alumni Dir.; Jim Royan, Pres.; Bob Kelly, Dir. Devel.

STEVENSVILLE. *Historic St. Mary's Mission*, P.O. Box 211, 59870-0211. Tel: 406-777-5734. Lucylle H. Evons, Pres.

RELIGIOUS INSTITUTES OF MEN REPRESENTED IN THE DIOCESE

For further details refer to the corresponding bracketed number in the Religious Institutes of Men or Women sections.

[0200]—*Benedictine Monks (Swiss-American Congregation, St. Meinrad Archabbey)*.—O.S.B.

[0690]—*Jesuit Fathers and Brothers*. (Oregon Prov.).—S.J.

RELIGIOUS INSTITUTES OF WOMEN REPRESENTED IN THE DIOCESE

[0230]—*Benedictine Sisters of Pontifical Jurisdiction*. (Rapid City).—O.S.B.

[2100]—*Congregation of the Humility of Mary*.—C.H.M.

[1730]—*Congregation of the Sisters of the Third Order of St. Francis*. (Oldenburg, IN).—O.S.F.

[1780]—*Congregation of the Sisters of the Third Order of St. Francis of Perpetual Adoration*. (Western Prov.).—F.S.P.A.

[1070-03]—*Dominican Sisters*.—O.P.

[1070-11]—*Dominican Sisters*.—O.P.

[1070-13]—*Dominican Sisters*.—O.P.

[2575]—*Institute of the Sisters of Mercy of the Americas*. (Cedar Rapids, IA).—R.S.M.

[0440]—*Sisters of Charity of Cincinnati, Ohio*.—S.C.

[0480]—*Sisters of Charity of Leavenworth, Kansas*.—S.C.L.

[0430]—*Sisters of Charity of the Blessed Virgin Mary*.—B.V.M.

[3350]—*Sisters of Providence*.—S.P.

[3360]—*Sisters of Providence of Saint Mary-of-the-Woods, Indiana*.—S.P.

[3840]—*Sisters of St. Joseph of Carondelet*.—C.S.J.

[3960]—*Sisters of St. Mary of Oregon*.—S.S.M.O.

[1990]—*Sisters of the Holy Names of Jesus and Mary*.—S.N.J.M.

[3320]—*Sisters of the Presentation of the B.V.M.*—P.B.V.M.

[1720]—*Sisters of the Third Order Regular of St. Francis of the Congregation of Our Lady of Lourdes*.—O.S.F.

[4110]—*Ursuline Nuns*.—O.S.U.

DIOCESAN CEMETERIES

HELENA. *Resurrection*, 515 N. Ewing St., P.O. Box 1729, 59624. Tel: 406-442-5820; Fax: 406-442-5191. Mr. Scott Fitzpatrick, Dir. Cemeteries; Laura Disney, Office Mgr.

BUTTE. *Holy Cross*. (St. Patrick's Cemetery), Office: 4700 Harrison Ave., 59701. Tel: 406-494-3812.

MISSOULA. *St. Mary*, Office: 641 Turner St., 59802. Tel: 406-543-7951.

NECROLOGY

† Hartman, Robert J., (Retired). —Died Aug. 12, 1996.

† O'Neill, Emmet P., (Retired). —Died July 26, 1996.

Diocese of Honolulu

(Dioecesis Honoluluensis)

Most Reverend

FRANCIS X. DiLORENZO, D.D., S.T.D.

Bishop of Honolulu; ordained May 18, 1968; appointed Titular Bishop of Tigia and Auxiliary Bishop of Scranton January 26, 1988; consecrated March 8, 1988; appointed Apostolic Administrator October 12, 1993; succeeded to See November 29, 1994. *Mailing Address: Chancery Office, 1184 Bishop St., Honolulu, HI, 96813; Fax: 808-537-1860.*

Most Reverend

JOHN J. SCANLAN, D.D.

Retired Bishop of Honolulu; ordained June 22, 1930; appointed Titular Bishop of Cenae and Auxiliary July 8, 1954; consecrated September 21, 1954; appointed Apostolic Administrator November 10, 1967; succeeded to See March 6, 1968; appointed Apostolic Administrator June 27, 1981. *Res., Nazareth House, 245 Nova Albion Way, San Rafael, CA, 94903.*

Most Reverend

JOSEPH A. FERRARIO, D.D.

Retired Bishop of Honolulu; ordained May 19, 1951; appointed Titular Bishop of Cuse and Auxiliary November 8, 1977; ordained Bishop January 13, 1978; succeeded to See June 25, 1982; retired October 12, 1993. *Mailing Address: Catholic Chancery Office, 1184 Bishop St., Honolulu, HI, 96813-2858.*

Chancery Office: 1184 Bishop St., Honolulu, HI, 96813. Tel.: 808-533-1791; Fax: 808-521-8428.

Corporate Title: *The Roman Catholic Church In The State Of Hawaii.*

Comprises all of the Hawaiian Islands.

The Hawaiian Islands were annexed as a Territory of the United States in 1898. Hawaii became the 50th State of the Union on August 21, 1959.

Square Miles 6,435.

In 1826, a Prefecture-Apostolic was erected for the Hawaiian Islands, then called Sandwich Islands, and entrusted to the Fathers of the Sacred Hearts of Jesus and Mary (Picpus). The Very Rev. ALEXIS BACHELOT, SS.CC., was the first Prefect-Apostolic. He arrived with his companions at Honolulu on the 7th of July, 1827. In 1844, the Islands were erected a Vicariate. Diocese erected Sept. 10, 1941.

For legal titles of parishes and diocesan institutions, consult the Chancery Office.

STATISTICAL OVERVIEW

Personnel	
Bishop	1
Retired Bishops	2
Priests: Diocesan Active in Diocese	43
Priests: Active Outside Diocese	15
Priests: Retired, Sick or Absent	17
Number of Diocesan Priests	75
Religious Priests in Diocese	77
Extern Priests in Diocese	20
Ordinations:	
Permanent Deacons in Diocese	36
Total Brothers	45
Total Sisters	243
Parishes	
Parishes	69
With Resident Pastor:	
Resident Diocesan Priests	38
Resident Religious Priests	27
Without Resident Pastor:	
Administered by Priests	2
Administered by Permanent Deacons	2
Missions	29
Professional Ministry Personnel:	
Brothers	1
Sisters	22
Lay Ministers	139
Welfare	
Catholic Hospitals	2
Total Assisted	343,985
Health Care Centers	3
Total Assisted	38,487
Homes for the Aged	1
Total Assisted	719
Specialized Homes	44
Total Assisted	856
Special Centers for Social Services	13
Total Assisted	5,955
Residential Care of Disabled	2
Total Assisted	16
Other Institutions	99
Total Assisted	309,867
Educational	
Diocesan Students in Other Seminaries	1
Students Religious	1
Total Seminarians	2
Colleges and Universities	1
Total Students	2,528
High Schools, Diocesan and Parish	3
Total Students	1,230
High Schools, Private	4
Total Students	2,445
Elementary Schools, Diocesan and Parish	25
Total Students	6,216
Elementary Schools, Private	1
Total Students	358
Catechesis/Religious Education:	
High School Students	2,123
Elementary Students	7,292
Total Students Under Catholic Instruction	22,194
Teachers in the Diocese:	
Priests	6
Brothers	19
Sisters	83
Lay Teachers	793
Vital Statistics	
Receptions into the Church:	
Infant Baptism Totals	3,603
Adult Baptism Totals	445
Received into Full Communion	488
First Communions	2,725
Confirmations	1,482
Marriages:	
Catholic	684
Interfaith	332
Total Marriages	1,016
Deaths	1,714
Total Catholic Population	232,780
Total Population	1,178,600

Former Prelates—Very Rev. ALEXIS BACHELOT, SS.CC., Pref. Apost. died Dec. 5, 1837.—Very Rev. LOUIS MAIGRET, SS.CC., Pref. Apost. till 1844.—Rt. Rev. VINCENT FERRIER DUBOIZE, SS.CC., resigned before he was consecrated.—Rt. Rev. LOUIS MAIGRET, SS.CC., Titular Bishop of Arathia; cons. at Santiago, Oct. 31, 1847; died June 11, 1882.—Rt. Rev. HERMAN KOECKEMANN, SS.CC., Titular Bishop of Olba; cons. at San Francisco Aug. 21, 1881; died Feb. 18, 1892.—Rt. Rev. GULSTAN ROPERT, SS.CC., Titular Bishop of Panopolis; cons. at San Francisco, Sept. 25, 1892; died Jan. 3, 1903.—Rt. Rev. LIBERT H. BOEYNAEMS, SS.CC., Titular Bishop of Zeugma; cons. at San Francisco, July 25, 1903; died May 13, 1926.—Most Rev. STEPHEN P. ALENCASTRE, SS.CC., Titular Bishop of Arabissus; cons. at Los Angeles, Aug. 24, 1924; died Nov. 9, 1940.—Most Rev. JAMES J. SWEENEY, D.D., ord. June 20, 1925; appt. May 20, 1941; cons. at San Francisco, July 25, 1941; died June 19, 1968.—Most Rev. JOHN J. SCANLAN, D.D., Retired Bishop of Honolulu; ord. June 22, 1930; succeeded to see March 6, 1968; retired June 30, 1981.—Most Rev. JOSEPH A. FERRARIO, D.D., Retired Bishop of Honolulu; ord. May 19, 1951; succeeded to see June 25, 1982; retired Oct. 12, 1993.

Vicar General—Rev. JOHN F. BOLIN, S.M.

Moderator of the Curia—Rev. JOHN F. BOLIN, S.M.

Delegate of the Bishop for Religious—Sr. BEATRICE TOM, O.S.F.

Associate Delegate of the Bishop for Religious—Bro. THOMAS SPRING, S.M.

Chancery Office—1184 Bishop St., Honolulu, 96813. Office Hours: 8-4. Tel: 808-533-1791; Fax: 808-521-8428.

Chancellor—Rev. Msgr. RAYMOND NISHIGAYA, J.C.L.

Assistant Chancellor—Sr. MARIE GERTRUDE ROLDAN, C.S.J., J.C.L.

Diocesan Tribunal—1184 Bishop St., Honolulu, 96813. Tel: 808-533-1791. Address all Tribunal mail to Chancery Office.

Vicar Judicial—Very Rev. JOSEPH BUKOSKI, III, SS.CC., J.C.L.

Administrative Assistant—Sr. MARIE GERTRUDE ROLDAN, C.S.J., J.C.L.

Promotor Justitiae—Rev. Msgr. RAYMOND NISHIGAYA, J.C.L.

Defensor Vinculi—Rev. Msgr. RAYMOND NISHIGAYA, J.C.L.

Tribunal Judges—Rev. ROBERT PHELPS, O.F.M.Cap., J.D.; Very Rev. JOSEPH BUKOSKI, III, SS.CC., J.C.L.; Revs. ROMEO RABUSA; ARTHUR DWYER, M.M., J.C.D.; MATTHEW LOCHS, SS.CC., S.T.L.; Sr. GRACE DOROTHY LIM, M.M., J.C.L.; Sr. MARIE GERTRUDE ROLDAN, C.S.J., J.C.L.

Tribunal Advocate—Rev. MATTHEW LOCHS, SS.CC.

Notaries—ANDREA SAYO; CATHERINE S. WONG.

Diocesan Administrative Council—Most Rev. FRANCIS X. DILORENZO, D.D., S.T.D.; Rev. Msgr. ALAN NAGAI; Rev. JOHN F. BOLIN, S.M., V.G.

Bishop's Administrative Advisory Council—Rev. JOHN

F. BOLIN, S.M., V.G.; Rev. Msgr. TERRENCE WATANABE; WILLIAM BURTON; PATRICIA S. TOSSEY.

Diocesan College of Consultors—Revs. JOHN BOLIN, S.M., V.G.; RUSSELL BECKER, O.F.M.; HALBERT WEIDNER, C.O.; CLYDE GUERREIRO, SS.CC.; ANTHONY BOLGER; GEORGE DECOSTA; GARY SECOR; RAYMOND MALLEY, S.M.

Diocesan Finance Committee—Most Rev. FRANCIS X. DILORENZO, D.D.; Rev. Msgr. TERRENCE A.M. WATANABE; Rev. JOHN F. BOLIN, S.M., V.G.; GEORGE FREITAS; MANUEL SYLVESTER; LAURA CHUN; PHILLIP CHING; ROBERT HASTINGS; ROBERT BRUCE GRAHAM; JAMES WATTS; CREIGHTON ARITA; JAMES SEVERSON; JAMES VENTURA.

Diocesan Business Office—WILLIAM BURTON, Business Mgr.

Diocesan Office of Development—DON MCKENNE, Dir.

Diocesan Development Committee—GEORGE E. BATES; JOAN BICKSON; CHARLES BOCKEN; JOHN BROGAN, Chm. BRUCE GRAHAM; STANLEY HONG; PATRICIA ROBERTI; JON THOMAS HUNTER.

Diocesan Liturgical Commission—Rev. RUSSELL BECKER, O.F.M.; JOE CAMACHO; WENDELL APOSTOL; Sr. MARY LANGE, S.H.F.; BARBARA ISODA; ROBERT MONDOY; MITSU PAPAYOANOU; Sr. MARIE GERTRUDE ROLDAN, C.S.J.; Revs. THOMAS SPLAIN, S.J.; MARVIN SAMIANO; FRANK PHILLIPS.

Diocesan Presbyteral Council—Revs. JOHN BOLIN, S.M., V.G.; GEORGE DECOSTA; GARY SECOR; ANTHONY BOLGER; HERMAN GOMES, SS.CC.; ROBERT PHELPS, O.F.M.Cap.; JOHN KUHN, SS.CC.; HALBERT WEIDNER, C.O.; CLYDE GUERREIRO, SS.CC.; RUSSELL BECKER, O.F.M.; RANDALL ROCHE, S.J.; MARC R. ALEXANDER, S.T.D.; JOVEN JUNIO, M.S.; RAYMOND MALLEY, S.M.; SCOTT BUSH; NATHAN MAMO.

Vicars—East Honolulu: Rev. HALBERT WEIDNER, C.O.; West Honolulu: Rev. RUSSELL BECKER, O.F.M.; Leeward: Rev. GARY SECOR; Windward: Rev. ANTHONY BOLGER; Hawaii: Rev. GEORGE DECOSTA; Kauai: Rev. CLYDE GUERREIRO, SS.CC.; Maui-Lanai-Molokai: Rev. RAYMOND MALLEY, S.M.

Diocesan Theologian—Rev. MARC R. ALEXANDER, S.T.D.

Diocesan Offices and Directors

Diocesan Pastoral Council—Members: Mrs. TINA ANDRADE; Dr. MARIA BRAULT; Mr. TONY BOQUER; Mr. EUGENE BRENNAN; Mr. DAVID CAVACO; Ms. CLEMENTINA CERIA; Mrs. ESTRELLA ESTILLORE; Mr. FREDERICK FARRELL; Mrs. MARJORIE FUJIMUTO; Mrs. ANN HANNAN; Deacon HARVEY KAWAIHAE; Rev. ALAPAKI KIM, C.S.P.; Mrs. MARTHA KRUSE; Mr. STEPHEN KULA; Rev. PAUL MCLEOD, SS.CC.; Mr. DEREK NORDSTROM; Rev. JAMES ORSINI; Mrs. MITSU PAPAYOANOU; Mr. WILLIAM QUINN; Mrs. EHUKAI SAKO; Bro. FRANK SPAETH, S.M.; Rev. JOHN SULLIVAN.

Aina Kupaa 'O Maili—Rev. JOHN BOLIN, S.M., Pres.

Apostleship of Prayer—Rev. ELI CARTER.

Apostleship of the Sea—Rev. JOHN G. NEWTON.

Beginning Experience-Hawaii—Rev. FRANCIS DIFFLEY, M.M., Spiritual Dir. PETER KINOLAU, Coord.

Building Commission—Rev. TERRANCE A.M. WATANABE; WILLIAM BURTON; Rev. GORDIAN CARVALHO; PAT SULLIVAN; LUKE YASAKA; RICHARD LEUNG; GARY BATCHELLER; MARK LIVELY; WALTER YOSHIMITSU; Revs. GEORGE DECOSTA; JOHN BOLIN; Sr. MARY LANGE.

Catholic Charities Inc.—JEROME E. RAUCKHORST, Diocesan Dir. Tel: 808-537-6321, Ext. 301.

Catholic Charities Board of Trustees—Most Rev. FRANCIS X. DILORENZO, D.D., Pres.; Rev. JOHN BOLIN, S.M., V.G.; Sr. GRACE DOROTHY LIM, M.M., Chancellor; BILL BURTON, Chief Financial Officer; ROSE DOMONDON; GINO GABRIO; WILLIAM POWELL.

Board of Directors—Most Rev. FRANCIS X. DILORENZO, Pres. WILLIAM POWELL; LILA MARANTZ, Vice Pres. GINO L. GABRIO, Chm. CATHY SEKIGUCHI, Sec. MARY LOU BROGAN; BRANDT FARIAS; BOB JAWORSKI; STEPHEN YIM; DAVID COLEMAN; Rev. JOHN BOLIN, S.M., V.G.; ROSE DOMONDON; Rev. CLARENCE L. FISHER; PATTI J. LYONS; Sr. GRACE DOROTHY LIM, M.M.; WILLIAM GILARDY; BILL BURTON; ALEXANDER MARRACK; CLIFF CISCO; Rev. CLYDE GUERREIRO, SS.CC.; SANDRA OHARA; MICHAEL PEARING; Sr. RUTH MARGARET RAUPP, C.S.J.; ALEX SANTIAGO; Rev. RAYMOND MALLEY, S.M.; Rev. Msgr. TERRENCE A.M. WATANABE; ART YAMAMOTO, Treas. MARIANITA LOPEZ; CALVIN PANG; THOMAS PAPANDREW; KENNETH SPRAGUE.

Catholic Charities Community Services—MORRIS MASUDA, Exec. Dir.

Catholic Charities Immigrant Services—Sr. EARNEST CHUNG, M.M., Exec. Dir., *712 N. School St., Honolulu, 96817.* Tel: 808-528-5233; Fax: 808-531-1970.

Catholic Charities Elderly Services—STELLA WONG, Exec. Dir.

Catholic Charities Family Services—ANA ROSAL-SILVA.

Catholic Daughters of America—Rev. MARK A. CONSALVI, SS.CC., State Chap. Regents:: GERTRUDE YEE; MARGIE GOOLSBY.

Catholic Relief Services—CAROL IGNACIO, Diocesan Dir., *140 B Holomua St., Hilo, 96720.*

Catholic Women's Guild—Rev. FRANCIS PETERSON, Chap. JULIE BRAIG, Pres.

Diocesan Social Ministry—CAROL IGNACIO, Dir., *140 B Holomua St., Hilo, 96720.* Tel: 808-935-3050; Fax: 808-935-3794.

Hawaii Social Ministry—CAROL IGNACIO, Dir.

Maui Social Ministry—Sr. ROSELANI ENOMOTO, C.S.J., Dir., *54 Kuhinia St., Waihe'e, 96793.*

Oahu Social Ministry—SHARON CHIARUCCI, Dir., *6301 Pali Hwy., Kaneohe, 96744.*

Hoa 'Aina O Makaha—GIGI COCQUIO, Mgr., *84-166 Lahaina St., Waianae, 96792.* Tel: 808-695-9730.

Campaign for Human Development—Rev. Msgr. TERRENCE WATANABE, Dir.

Censor Librorum—Rev. MARC R. ALEXANDER, S.T.D.

Chinese Catholic Club—WALLACE WONG, Pres.

Cursillo—Rev. GABRIEL VANDEN BROUCKE, SS.CC., Spiritual Dir.

Hawaii Catholic Conference—Revs. MARC ALEXANDER, S.T.D., Exec. Dir.-Coord. DANIEL J. DEVER; Sr. BEATRICE TOM, O.S.F.; WILLIAM GILARDY; PATRICK DOWNES; JEROME E. RAUCKHORST; ANA ROSAL-SILVA; SUE WESSELKAMPER, *St. Stephen Diocesan Center, 6301 Pali Hwy., Kaneohe, 96744-5298.* Tel: 808-263-8844; Fax: 808-261-7022.

Hawaii Respect Life—Deacon GEORGE THORP, Dir.

Engaged Encounter—Exec. Team:: FRED CORPUZ; EILEEN CORPUZ; Sr. MARIE GERTRUDE ROLDAN, C.S.J., Spiritual Dir.

Marriage Encounter—Exec. Team:: MARK RYAN; SANDY RYAN; Rev. FRANCIS PETERSON, Spiritual Dir.

Natural Family Planning—TED BORN; HOLLY BORN.

Filipino Catholic Clubs, Diocesan Congress of—Vacant.

Hawaii Catholic Charismatic Renewal Services—PATRICK GOMES, Chm.

Hawaii Catholic Herald—Most Rev. FRANCIS X. DILORENZO, Publisher; PATRICK DOWNES, Editor, *1184 Bishop St., Honolulu, 96813.* Tel: 808-533-1791.

Holy Childhood Association—Rev. ELI CARTER, Dir.

Holy Name Society—DEREK CONSELVA, Pres.

Hospital Ministry—Rev. PAUL SMITH, Dir.

Knights of Columbus—Dr. JOHN SHEEDY, State Deputy; Most Rev. FRANCIS X. DILORENZO, D.D., State Chap.

Korean Catholic Community—Rev. JOHN KANG, Pastor, *1701 Wilder Ave., Honolulu, 96822.*

Legion of Mary—FRANCES VASQUEZ, Pres.

Missionary Basic Christian Community of Hawaii—Sr. GRACE DOROTHY LIM, M.M., Spiritual Dir.

Newman Center—Rev. RANDALL ROCHE, S.J., *1941 East-West Rd., Honolulu, 96822.* Tel: 808-988-6222.

Office of Clergy (Personnel, Vocations, Deacon Formation, Deacon Council)—Rev. Msgr. ALAN NAGAI, Vicar for Priests. Permanent Diaconate Coordinators: Deacon WILLIAM MCPEEK; FLORENCE MCPEEK; WALTER H. YOSHIMITSU, Episcopal Liaison to Deacon Community.

Office of Ethnic Ministries—Sr. GRACE DOROTHY LIM, M.M., Dir.

Filipino Ministry—Rev. EDGARDO BONGHANOY, Coord.

Hispanic Ministry—Rev. JAMES MCFADDEN, M.M., Coord.

Samoan Ministry—Sr. SEKOLASETIKA KENI, M.S.S.M., Coord., *1035 N. School St., Honolulu, 96817.* Tel: 808-841-0897; 533-1791.

Ministry for Persons with Disabilities—CAROL R. IGNACIO, Diocesan Dir.

Office of Worship—Sr. MARY LANGE, S.H.F., Dir.

Propagation of the Faith—Rev. ELI CARTER.

Religious Education (C.C.D.)—Sr. KATHLEEN MARIE SHIELDS, C.S.J., Dir. Tel: 808-263-8844.

Retirement Board—Rev. JOHN F. BOLIN, S.M., V.G., Chm.; Revs. CLARENCE L. FISHER; ROMEO RABUSA; DANIEL J. DEYER; Rev. Msgr. ALAN NAGAI; Rev. Msgr. TERRENCE A.M. WATANABE.

St. Stephen Diocesan Center—EUGENE POLLOCK, Contact Person. Tel: 808-263-8844.

St. Vincent de Paul Society—HAROLD W. WESTPHALEN, JR., Pres.; Rev. NATHAN MAMO, Spiritual Dir., *46-160 Hinalani St., Kaneohe, 96744.* Tel: 808-247-4784.

Samoan Catholic Clubs, Diocesan Union of—Rev. ETUALE ETUALE, Chap.

Hawaii Catholic Schools—JOSEPH MCHUGH, Supt. CARMEN HIMENES, Assoc. Supt. Curr. & Instruction, *6301 Pali Hwy., Kaneohe, 96744.* Tel: 808-263-8844.

Scouting—Rev. THOMAS CHOO, SS.CC.

Serra Club—Rev. GARY L. SECOR, Chap., Spiritual Dir.

Servant Leadership Education Program—Sr. KATHLEEN MARIE SHIELDS, C.S.J.

Diocesan Board of Concilation—Sr. GRACE DOROTHY LIM, M.M., Dir.

Diocesan Board of Education—Rev. JOHN BOLIN, S.M., V.G., Dir.

Priestly Life and Ministry—Rev. HALBERT WEIDNER, C.O., Chm.

St. Francis Xavier Club—Chaplains: Revs. FRANCIS NAKAGAWA, S.M.; CHARLES OYABU, S.M.

Third Order of Mary—Rev. ELI CARTER, Spiritual Dir.

Diocesan Federation of Tongan Catholic Societies—Rev. MARISI PALEPALE, SS.CC., Spiritual Dir.

Young Ladies' Institute—Rev. Msgr. RAYMOND NISHIGAYA, Chap.

Young Men's Institute—Rev. GARY SECOR, Chap.

CLERGY, PARISHES, MISSIONS AND PAROCHIAL SCHOOLS

ISLAND OF OAHU
CITY OF HONOLULU

1—CATHEDRAL OF OUR LADY OF PEACE (1843) (Filipino), Revs. Nathan Mamo, S.T.L., Rector; Russell C. Becker, O.F.M., M.A.,V.F.; Mrs. Ann Hannan, M.R.E., Pastoral Assoc. & D.R.E.
Res., 1184 Bishop St., 96813-2838. Tel: 808-536-7036; Fax: 808-536-7039.
School—Cathedral School, 1728 Nuuanu Ave., 96817. Tel: 808-533-2069; Fax: 808-533-2069. Mrs. Louise Wong, Prin.
Lay Teachers 15; Students 165.
Catechesis/Religious Programs—Students 75.

2—CO-CATHEDRAL OF ST. THERESA OF THE CHILD JESUS (1931) (Filipino), Revs. Daniel J. McNichol, Rector; Donald Macgregor. In res., Revs. Robert DaPonte; Joseph Ky, S.S.
Res., 712 N. School St., 96817. Tel: 808-521-1700; Fax: 808-599-3629.
School—Tel: 808-536-4703; Fax: 808-524-6861. Sr. John Joseph Gilligan, C.S.J., Prin.
Sisters 8; Lay Teachers 16; Students 634.
Catechesis/Religious Programs—Students 252.
Convent— Sisters of St. Joseph of Carondelet

3—ST. ANTHONY (1916) (Filipino), Rev. Joven Junio, M.S.; Sr. Rosalinda Barrozo, M.M., Pastoral Assoc. In res., Revs. Edgardo Bonghanoy; Edgar Serrano.
Res., 640 Puuhale Rd., 96819. Tel: 808-845-3255; Fax: 808-845-3664.
School—Tel: 808-845-2769. Sr. Concepcion Cambaya, R.V.M., Prin.
Sisters 3; Lay Teachers 8; Students 180.
Catechesis/Religious Programs—Students 139.
Convent—702 Puuhale Rd., 96819. Tel: 808-845-4888.
Religious of the Blessed Virgin Mary (R.V.M.) 4.

4—ST. AUGUSTINE (1920), Revs. Lane Akiona, SS.CC., Admin., Pro Tem; Thomas Choo, SS.CC.
Res., 130 Ohua Ave., 96815. Tel: 808-923-7024; Fax: 808-922-4086.

5—BLESSED SACRAMENT (1938), Rev. Mark Consalvi, SS.CC.; Deacon Ronald Choo.
Res., 2124 Pauoa Rd., 96813. Tel: 808-531-6980.
Catechesis/Religious Programs—Mr. Francis Aiu, D.R.E.
Students 58.

6—HOLY FAMILY, Rev. Maurice McNeely.
Res., 830 Main St., 96818. Tel: 808-422-1135.
School—Tel: 808-422-9612; Fax: 808-422-5030. Antonio J. Boquer, Prin.
Lay Teachers 36; Students 460.
Catechesis/Religious Programs—D.R.E.: Ann Amrich; Deborah Naone.
Students 150.

7—NEWMAN CENTER AT THE UNIVERSITY OF HAWAII, HOLY SPIRIT PARISH (1981), Revs. Randall H. Roche, S.J.; Daniel J. Sullivan, S.J. In res., Revs. Bernard F. Cassidy, S.J.; David C. Schwartz, S.J.
Mailing Address: Newman Center, 1941 East West Center, 96822. Tel: 808-988-6222; Fax: 808-988-7627.
Res., Jesuit House, 2727 Pamoa Rd., 96822-1838. Tel: 808-988-3464; Fax: 808-988-7627.

8—HOLY TRINITY (1939), Revs. Halbert Weidner, C.O.; Vincent Mainelli, C.O.; Deacon Paul Lee.
Res., 5919 Kalanianaole Hwy., 96821. Tel: 808-396-0551; Fax: 808-396-1380.
School—Tel: 808-396-8466; Fax: 808-396-3310. Wendie Wong, Prin.
Sisters 4; Lay Teachers 10; Students 130.
Catechesis/Religious Programs—Deacon Sam Taylor, D.R.E.
Students 185.
Convent—Tel: 808-396-9182. Sisters of St. Joseph of Carondelet

9—ST. JOHN THE BAPTIST (1844), Rev. Karl H. Krause (Samoa) Pro Tem; Sr. Brenda Lau, C.S.J., Assoc. Adm. In res., Rev. James McFadden, M.M., Hispanic Ministry.
Res., 2324 Omilo Ln., 96819. Tel: 808-845-0984; Fax: 808-841-6643. [CEM]

School—Tel: 808-841-5551; Fax: 808-842-6104. Sr. Bernarda Sindol, O.P., Prin.
Dominican Sisters 6; Lay Teachers 9; Students 193.
Catechesis/Religious Programs—Tel: 808-845-3304.
Students 147.
Convent—2330 Omilo Ln., 96819. Tel: 808-845-2622.
Dominican Sisters of the Most Holy Rosary 6.

10—Our Lady of the Mount (1870), Rev. Etuale Etuale. In res., Rev. Paulo Tuugusamusu.
Res., 1614 Monte St., 96819. Tel: 808-845-0828; Fax: 808-845-0828.
Catechesis/Religious Programs—Tel: 808-845-0223.
Students 156.

11—St. Patrick (1929), Revs. John C. Kuhn, SS.CC.; Gerard Leicht, SS.CC.; Bro. Richard Kupo, SS.CC. In res., Rev. Matthew Lochs, SS.CC.
Res., 1124 Seventh Ave., 96816. Tel: 808-732-5565; Fax: 808-737-2477. Please refer to the listing for St. Patrick Monastery under Monasteries and Residences for Priests and Brothers for additional residents.
School—Tel: 808-734-8979; Fax: 808-732-2851. Sr. Rose Miriam Schillinger, C.S.J., Prin.
Sisters 2; Lay Teachers 25; Students 520.
Catechesis/Religious Programs—Tel: 808-735-0252. Ms. Regina Pfeiffer, D.R.E.
Students 123.
Mission—Palolo, Honolulu Co., St. James, 2117 Palolo Ave., 96816.

12—St. Philomena (1942), Rev. Msgr. Terrence A.M. Watanabe. In res., Rev. Patrick Freitas.
Res., 3300 Ala Laulani, 96818-2837. Tel: 808-839-1876; Fax: 808-834-6888.
School—Tel: 808-833-8080; Fax: 808-834-3438. Angeline A.V. Thomas, Prin.
Lay Teachers 8; Teacher Aids 4; Students 129.
Catechesis/Religious Programs—Sandra Beltran, D.R.E.
Students 120.

13—Sacred Heart (1914), Revs. Francis A. Diffley, M.M.; Arthur Dwyer, M.M.; Thomas F. Donnelly, M.M.; John Kang, Korean Ministry; Sandra Campos, Pastoral Assoc.
Res., 1701 Wilder Ave., 96822. Tel: 808-973-2211; Fax: 808-973-2209.
School—Maryknoll Grade School, 1722 Dole St., 96822. Tel: 808-973-1777; Fax: 808-973-1799. Mr. James H. Gahler, Prin.
Teacher Aides 5; Lay Teachers 46; Students 816.
High School—1402 Punahou St., 96822. Tel: 808-973-1888; Fax: 808-973-1799. Mr. Andrew Corcoran, Prin.
Sisters 2; Lay Teachers 49; Students 542.
Catechesis/Religious Programs—Tel: 808-973-1780. Rose Anne Petro, D.R.E.
Students 106.

14—St. Stephen (1932), Rev. Msgr. Raymond J. Nishigaya.
Res., 2747 Pali Hwy., 96817. Tel: 808-595-3105.
Catechesis/Religious Programs—Paula Kurashige, D.R.E.
Students 63.

15—Star of the Sea (1946), Revs. John Sullivan, S.M.; Gerard Timmerman, S.M.; Edward C. Blee, S.M.; Bro. Roy Madigan, S.M.; Deacons Thomas Rienzi; Andrew Gerakas.
Res., 4470 Aliikoa St., 96821. Tel: 808-734-0396; Fax: 808-735-6017.
School—Tel: 808-734-0208; Fax: 808-735-9790. Carola Souza, Prin.
Lay Teachers 28; Students 300.
Early Learning Center—Tel: 808-734-3840; Fax: 808-732-1738. Lisa Foster, Prin.
Lay Teachers 9; Assistants 16; Students 194.
Catechesis/Religious Programs—Tel: 808-735-0259; Fax: 808-735-6017. Darlene Ah Yo, D.R.E.
Students 198.

16—St. Pius X (1958), Rev. Louis H. Yim; Deacon Sidney J. Townsley.
Church—2821 Lowrey Ave., 96822-1644. Tel: 808-988-3308; 988-2651; Fax: 808-988-9313.
Res., 2949 Kahawai St., 96822-1699. Tel: 808-988-3308.
Catechesis/Religious Programs—Tel: 808-988-3308; Fax: 808-988-9313. Maria Minkel, D.R.E.
Students 20.

17—Saints Peter and Paul (1969), Rev. David O. Travers, S.S., Admin.; Rev. Msgr. Roy V. Peters; Deacon Richard Port.
Office: 800 Kaheka St., 96814. Tel: 808-941-0675; Fax: 808-945-0689.
Res., 1561 Kanunu St., #1006, 96814. Tel: 808-955-8830.

OUTSIDE THE CITY OF HONOLULU
County of Honolulu

Aiea, St. Elizabeth (1926), Revs. Andrew Mannetta, O.F.M.Cap.; Paulo Kosaka, O.F.M.Cap. In res., Rev. Gordon Combs, O.F.M.Cap., Chap.
Res., 99-312 Moanalua Rd., 96701. Tel: 808-487-2414; Fax: 808-487-2168.
School—Tel: 808-488-5322; Fax: 808-486-0856. Sr. M. Leonarda Montelto, O.P., Prin. Supr.
Sisters 5; Lay Teachers 7; Students 268.
Catechesis/Religious Programs—Tel: 808-487-7994; Fax: 808-487-2168. M. Kimo Llanos, D.R.E.
Students 228.
Convent—99-310 Moanalua Rd., 96701. Tel: 808-487-3131.
Dominican Sisters of the Most Holy Rosary 5.

Ewa, Immaculate Conception, Rev. Eli K. Carter, Jr.
Res., 91-1298 Renton Rd., 96706. Tel: 808-681-3701; Fax: 808-681-3701.
Catechesis/Religious Programs—Tel: 808-681-6703.
Students 120.

Ewa Beach, Our Lady of Perpetual Help (1969) (Filipino), Rev. Robert Phelps, O.F.M.Cap.
Res., 91-1004 North Rd., 96706-2796. Tel: 808-689-8681; Fax: 808-689-4829.
School—91-1010 North Rd., 96706. Tel: 808-689-0474; Fax: 808-689-4847. Mr. Dennis Sasaki, Prin.
Lay Teachers 9; Students 172.
Catechesis/Religious Programs—Tel: 808-689-8563; Fax: 808-689-4829. Janese Akins, D.R.E.
Students 215.

Kahuku, St. Roch (1928) (Filipino), Rev. William F. Mattimore, Admin.
Res., P.O. Box 295, 96731. Tel: 808-293-5026; Fax: 808-293-1737.
Catechesis/Religious Programs—Students 76.
Mission—Punaluu, St. Joachim, (1917) P.O. Box 295, 96731.

Kailua, St. Anthony (1933), Rev. Anthony J. Bolger; Rev. Msgr. Bernard J. Eikmeier; Rev. Paul Minchak, O.F.M. Cap.; Mrs. Maxine Pollock, Pastoral Assoc.; Deacons James Carroll; Jerome Weaver.
Res., 114 Makawao St., 96734. Tel: 808-266-2222; Fax: 808-266-2229.
School—148 Makawao St., 96734. Tel: 808-261-3331; Fax: 808-263-3518. Mr. Gary Marr, Prin.
Sisters 1; Lay Teachers 22; Students 310.
Catechesis/Religious Programs—Tel: 808-266-2231; Fax: 808-266-2229. D.R.E.: Mrs. Kanani Asing; Mrs. Pam Aqui.
Students 220.
Convent—Tel: 808-262-9170. Sisters of St. Joseph of Carondelet.

St. John Vianney (1962), Rev. Thomas L. Gross; Deacons Clarence DeCaires; Lauren S.F. Wong; Walter H. Yoshimitsu. In res., Rev. Msgr. Alan Nagai.
Res., 920 Keolu Dr., 96734. Tel: 808-262-8317.
School—940 Keolu Dr., 96734. Tel: 808-261-4651. Ms. Jean Flynn, Prin.
Lay Teachers 19; Staff 9; Students 282.
Catechesis/Religious Programs—Maria Brasher, D.R.E.
Students 183.

Kaneohe, St. Ann (1841), Revs. Clarence L. Guerreiro, SS.CC.; Bertram Lock, SS.CC.
Res., 46-129 Haiku Rd., 96744. Tel: 808-247-3092; Fax: 808-235-0717. [CEM]
School and Early Learning Center—46-125 Haiku Rd., 96744. Tel: 808-247-3492 (School); 247-3324 (Early Learning Center); Fax: 808-235-0717. Sr. Anne Clare DeCosta, SS.CC. Tel: 808-235-5682; Mrs. Daphne Kauhane, Prin. (School); Mrs. Frances Vasquez, Prin. (Early Learning Center).
Sisters 1; Lay Teachers 25; Students 420.
Catechesis/Religious Programs—Tel: 808-235-5682. Mrs. Lani Almanza, D.R.E.
Students 329.

Makakilo, St. Jude (1988), Rev. Roland Pacudan.
Res., 92-104 Leipapa Way, Ewa Beach, 96707. Tel: 808-672-8669; Fax: 808-672-3779.
Catechesis/Religious Programs—Tel: 808-672-8669; Fax: 808-672-3779. Caren Argenzia, D.R.E.
Students 130.

Mililani Town, St. John Apostle and Evangelist (1969), Rev. Gary Secor; Karen L. Lee, Pastoral Assoc.; Deacon Wally Mitsui. In res., Rev. Thomas Killackey, M.M.
Res., 95-370 Kuahelani Ave., 96789. Tel: 808-623-3332; Fax: 808-623-3286.
St. John Montessori Center—See Preschool Centers under Institutions Located in the Diocese. Carmella Prose, Prin., Tel: 808-623-7331.
Catechesis/Religious Programs—Tel: 808-623-3661. Jack Bacon, D.R.E.
Students 648.

Nanakuli, St. Rita (Hawaiian), Rev. Robert Schwarzhaupt.
Res., 89-318 Farrington Hwy., 96792. Tel: 808-668-7833; Fax: 808-668-7716.
Catechesis/Religious Programs—Tel: 808-668-7716. Cathy Agor, D.R.E.
Students 110.

Pearl City, Our Lady of Good Counsel (1958), Revs. Michael J. Owens; Alfred Rebuldella; Deacon Thomas Miyashiro. In res., Rev. Aloysius Lou, Chinese Ministry.
Res., 1525 Waimano Home Rd., 96782. Tel: 808-455-3012; Fax: 808-456-9443. [CEM]
School—1530 Hoolana St., 96782. Tel: 808-455-4533; Fax: 808-455-5587. Mrs. Cindy Olaso, Prin.
Lay Teachers 12; Students 372.
Catechesis/Religious Programs—Mrs. Barbara Bremus, D.R.E.
Students 280.
Convent—1530-2 Hoolana St., 96782. Tel: 808-455-2058.

Wahiawa, Our Lady of Sorrows (1939), Rev. Clarence L. Fisher; Deacons Benjamin A. Awana; George Kagehiro.
Res., 1403-A California Ave., 96786-2595. Tel: 808-621-5109; Fax: 808-621-0552.
School—Tel: 808-621-8951. Mrs. Deborah Bee, Prin.
Lay Teachers 11; Students 168.
Catechesis/Religious Programs—Mrs. Janice Vannatta, D.R.E.
Students 144.

Waialua, St. Michael (1853), Revs. Edward C. Martin, SS.CC.; Albert Garcia, SS.CC.
Res., 67-390 Goodale Ave., 96791. Tel: 808-637-4040; Fax: 808-637-4287.
School—67-340 Haona St., 96791. Tel: 808-637-4631; Fax: 808-637-7272. Sr. William Marie Eleniki, O.S.F., Prin. & D.R.E.
Sisters 4; Lay Teachers 5; Students 222.
Catechesis/Religious Programs—Tel: 808-637-4040; Fax: 808-637-4287.
Students 80.
Convent—Tel: 808-637-7772; Fax: 808-637-7272.
Sisters 6.
Mission—Waimea Bay, SS. Peter and Paul, 67-390 Goodale, 96791. Tel: 808-638-7676.

Waianae, Sacred Heart (1838), Revs. Ralph Christman, M.M.; Elias Tederous, M.M.
Res., 85-786 Old Government Rd., 96792. Tel: 808-696-3773; Fax: 808-696-2242. [CEM]
Parish Outreach—Tel: 808-696-3746; Fax: 808-696-2242.
Catechesis/Religious Programs—Tel: 808-696-2242.
Students 156.

Waikane, Our Lady of Mt. Carmel (1850), Rev. Romeo Rabusa, Admin.; Deacon George Thorp, Jr.
Res., 48-422 Kamehaineha Hwy., Kaneohe, 96744. Tel: 808-239-9269; Fax: 808-239-9269.
Catechesis/Religious Programs—Tel: 808-239-9269; Fax: 808-239-9269. Betty Kam, D.R.E.
Students 94.

Waimanalo, St. George (1960), Rev. Henry Sabog.
Res., 41-1323 Kalanianaole Hwy., 96795. Tel: 808-259-7188.
Catechesis/Religious Programs—Students 166.

Waipahu, Resurrection of the Lord (1986), Rev. Ronald J. Burke, Adm.
Mailing Address: 94-1260 Lumikula St., 96797. Tel: 808-676-4700; Fax: 808-676-4534.
Res., 94-1449 Waipio Uka, #K-106, 96797.
Catechesis/Religious Programs—Tel: 808-671-8498. Ellen M. Domingo, D.R.E.
Students 87.

St. Joseph (1940), Revs. Alphonse Larochelle, M.S.; Rene Bisaillon; Antonio Quijano, M.S. In res., Rev. Erwin Dela Cruz, M.S.
Res., 94-675 Farrington Hwy., 96797. Tel: 808-677-4276; Fax: 808-671-3215. [CEM]
School—Tel: 808-677-4475; Fax: 808-677-8937. Miss Beverly Sandobal, Prin.
Sisters 3; Lay Teachers 20; Students 445.
Catechesis/Religious Programs—Mrs. Geraldine Simbahon, D.R.E.
Students 357.
Convent—91-807 Poowai Pl., Ewa Beach, 96706. Tel: 808-681-4610. Sisters of St. Joseph of Carondelet.

ISLAND OF HAWAII
County of Hawaii

Hilo, St. Joseph (1919), Rev. Scott Bush; Deacons Harvey Kawaihae; LeRoy Andrews; A. Jos. Schoemaker.
Res., 43 Kapiolani St., 96720. Tel: 808-935-1465; Fax: 808-969-1665. [CEM]
School—1000 Ululani St., 96720. Tel: 808-935-4935; Fax: 808-969-9019. Sr. Grace Michael Souza, O.S.F., Prin. (Elementary); Deacon Leroy Andrews, Prin. (Junior-Senior High School).
Franciscan Sisters of Third Order 5; Lay Teachers 45; Students 500.
Catechesis/Religious Programs—Tel: 808-935-1202. Sr. Mary Victor Negrete, D.R.E.
Students 193.

Convent—440 Kapiolani St., 96720. Tel: 808-935-1388.

Hawi, Sacred Heart (1926), Rev. Sydney Fernandes.
Res., P.O. Box 220, 96719. Tel: 808-889-6436; Fax: 808-889-5698. [CEM]
Catechesis/Religious Programs—Tel: 808-889-5353. Carol Ching, D.R.E.
Students 133.
Mission—Halaula, Hawaii Co., Our Lady of Grace.

Holualoa, St. Michael The Archangel (1840), Revs. James A. Berry; Jack Ryan.
Res., 75 5769 Alii Dr., Kailua-Kona, 96745-1059. Tel: 808-326-7771; Fax: 808-329-6219. [CEM 4]
Catechesis/Religious Programs—Tel: 808-322-2877. Rev. Jack Ryan, D.R.E.
Students 180.
Missions—Kalaoa, Hawaii Co., Holy Rosary; Holualoa, Hawaii Co., Immaculate Conception, P.O. Box 275, Holualoa, 96725; Kawanui, Hawaii Co., St. Paul; Kahaluu, Hawaii Co., St. Peter.

Honaunau, St. Benedict (1899), Rev. Robert Donnelly, M.M.
Res., Box 209, 96726. Tel: 808-328-2227. [CEM 5][JC 5]
Catechesis/Religious Programs—Marjorie Fujimoto, D.R.E.
Students 85.
Missions—Kealakekua, Hawaii Co., P.O. Box 209, 96726. Tel: 808-323-3711; Milolii, Hawaii Co., P.O. Box 209, 96726.

Honokaa, Our Lady of Lourdes (1870), Rev. Dennis M. Koshko.
Res., 45-5028 Plumeria St., 96727. Tel: 808-775-7715; Fax: 808-775-0912. [CEM 6]
Catechesis/Religious Programs—Students 177.
Missions—Kukuihaele, St. Theresa; Paauilo, St. Joseph.

Kamuela, Church of the Annunciation (1965), Rev. Robert F. Wynne, M.M.
Res., P.O. Box 301, 96743. Tel: 808-885-4196. [CEM]
Catechesis/Religious Programs—Students 70.
Mission—Kalikonani, Church of the Ascension, Puako, Puako, 96743.

Keaukaha, Hilo, Malia Puka'O Kalani (Mary Gate of Heaven) (1929) (Hawaiian), Rev. George De Costa.
Res., 326 Desha Ave., 96720. Tel: 808-935-9338; Fax: 808-935-3865.
Montessori Preschool—Coordinators: Marie Roberts, Prin. & D.R.E.; Joseph Camacho.
Catechesis/Religious Programs—Students 160.

Mountain View, St. Theresa, Rev. Marvin J. Samiano; Sr. M. Yolanda DeFrancesco, S.H.F., Pastoral Assoc. & D.R.E.
Res., P.O. Box 37, 96771. Tel: 808-968-6233. [CEM 3]
Catechesis/Religious Programs—Students 144.
Mission—Keaau, Holy Rosary.

Naalehu, Sacred Heart (1846), Rev. Stephen A. Macedo.
Res., P.O. Box 150, 96772. Tel: 808-929-7474. [CEM]
Catechesis/Religious Programs—Tel: 808-929-7686. Margorie Pedra, D.R.E.
Students 59.

Pahala, Holy Rosary (1885), Rev. Stephen A. Macedo.
Res., P.O. Box 760, 96777. Tel: 808-928-8208; Fax: 808-928-8208. [CEM]
Catechesis/Religious Programs—Tel: 808-928-9054. Mary Ibarra, D.R.E.
Students 95.

Pahoa, Sacred Heart (1882), Rev. Alapaki K. Kim, C.S.P., Pro Tem.
Res., P.O. Box 17, 96778. Tel: 808-965-8202. [CEM]
Catechesis/Religious Programs—Tel: 808-965-7866. Nathan Chang, D.R.E.
Students 235.

Papaaloa, St. Anthony (1926), Rev. George D. DeCosta; Deacon Lawrence J. Ignacio, Pastoral Admin.
Res., P.O. Box 339, Laupahoehoe, 96813. Tel: 808-962-6538; Fax: 808-962-6538. [CEM 2]
Catechesis/Religious Programs—D.R.E.: Kay Lundberg; Carol Mendes.
Students 44.
Mission—Ookala, St. James.

Papaikou, Immaculate Heart of Mary (1950), Rev. Konelio Faletoi.
Church—P.O. Box 79, 96781. Tel: 808-964-1240; 963-5434; Fax: 808-964-1240.
Catechesis/Religious Programs—Cheryl Udovic, D.R.E.
Students 77.
Mission—Honomu, Good Shepherd.

ISLAND OF KAUAI
County of Kauai

Kalaheo, Holy Cross (1909), Rev. Gordian J. Carvalho, Jr.
Res., 2-2370 Kaumualii Hwy., 96741. Tel: 808-332-8011; Fax: 808-332-7749. [CEM]
Catechesis/Religious Programs—Students 179.
Mission—Eleele, Kauai Co., Sacred Heart, P.O. Box 487, 96741.

Kapaa, St. Catherine (1887), Revs. Bruce Lery, S.M.; Edward J. McMonagle, S.M.; Francis Springer, S.M.; Francis Twiss, S.M.
Res., 5021-A Kawaihau Rd., 96746. Tel: 808-822-4804; Fax: 808-822-3014. [CEM 2]
School—Tel: 808-822-4212; Fax: 808-822-0991. Carol West, Prin.
Sisters 4; Lay Teachers 5; Students 178.
Catechesis/Religious Programs—Tel: 808-822-0665. Sr. Raymund Orquejo, D.R.E.
Students 262.
Convent—5021 Kawaihau Rd., 96746. Tel: 808-822-0665.
Dominican Sisters of The Most Holy Rosary 4.
Missions—Kilauea, Kauai Co., St. Sylvester; Hanalei, Kauai Co., St. William.

Kekaha, St. Theresa (1944), Revs. Francois A. Bourgeois, M.S.; Manuel J. Laviste.
Res., P.O. Box 159, 96752. Tel: 808-337-1784.
School—8311 Kaumualii Hwy, 96752. Tel: 808-337-1351. Sr. Valerie Lemansky, O.S.F., Prin.
Sisters 4; Lay Teachers 5; Students 130.
Catechesis/Religious Programs—Tel: 808-337-9992. Sr. Mary Jane Mertens, O.S.F., D.R.E.
Students 85.
Missions—Waimea, Kauai Co., Sacred Hearts of Jesus & Mary, 9500 Kaumualii Hwy., Waimea, 96796; Kaumakani, St. Joseph, Village Main St., 96747.
Convent—P.O. Box 277, 96752. Tel: 808-337-9661. Sr. Janet Rose, Supr.
Franciscan Sisters of Christian Charity 5.

Koloa, St. Raphael (1841), Rev. Felix J. Vandebroek, SS.CC.; Abel Medeiros, Pastoral Assoc.
Res., 3011 Hapa Rd., 96756. Tel: 808-742-1955. [CEM 2]
Catechesis/Religious Programs—Students 83.

Lihue, Immaculate Conception (1884), Rev. Clyde Guerreiro, SS.CC. In res., Rev. Paul McLeod, SS.CC.
Res., 4453 Kapaia Rd., 96766. Tel: 808-245-2432; Fax: 808-245-5628. [CEM 2]
Catechesis/Religious Programs—Tel: 808-639-7195. Sr. Florence Remata, O.S.F., D.R.E.
Students 159.

ISLAND OF LANAI

Lanai City, Maui Co., Sacred Hearts (1930), Rev. Florencio B. Rebebes, Adm. Pastoral Assocs.: Sr. Mary Jerome A. Perlas, O.S.B.; Sr. Mary Lilian E. Carranza, O.S.B.
Res., P.O. Box 784, 96763. Tel: 808-565-6837.
Catechesis/Religious Programs—D.R.E.: Rosita Camero; Priscilla Felipe.
Students 167.

ISLAND OF MAUI
County of Maui

Haiku, St. Rita (1950), Rev. Gary Colton.
Res., 655 Haiku Rd., 96708. Tel: 808-575-2601. [CEM]
Catechesis/Religious Programs—Tel: 808-575-2601. D.R.E.: Celia Fraser; Annette Scognamillo.
Students 82.
Mission—Keanae, Maui Co., St. Gabriel, 655 Haiku Rd., 96708. Tel: 808-248-8369.

Hana, St. Mary, Rev. Paul A. Zegers, SS.CC.
Res., P.O. Box 219, 96713. Tel: 808-248-8030. [CEM]
Catechesis/Religious Programs—Stella Perry, D.R.E.
Students 44.
Missions—Puuiki, Maui Co., St. Peter, P.O. Box 219, 96713; Kipahulu, Maui Co., St. Paul, P.O. Box 219, 96713; Kaupo, Maui Co., St. Joseph, P.O. Box 219, 96713.

Kahului, Christ the King, Rev. Charles Oyabu, S.M.; Deacon Frank R. Singson, Sr., Pastoral Asoc. In res., Rev. Gaudelio Donato.
Res., 20 W. Wakea Ave., 96732. Tel: 808-877-6098; Fax: 808-871-6296.
School—(Grades PreK-6). Tel: 808-877-6618. Isaac Balicanta, Prin.
Sisters 5; Lay Teachers 9; Students 120.
Catechesis/Religious Programs—Tel: 808-877-7783. Sr. Angela Laurenzo, C.S.J, D.R.E.
Students 206.
Convent—211 S. Kaulawahine St., 96732. Tel: 808-877-0790. Sisters of St. Joseph of Carondelet.

Kihei, St. Theresa (1908), Rev. John B. Stawasz. Pastoral Assocs.: Sr. Ann Gertrude Vierra, O.S.F.; Sr. Laura Abat, O.S.F.
Res., 25 W. Lipoa St., 96753. Tel: 808-879-2649; Fax: 808-879-0045. [CEM]
Catechesis/Religious Programs—Students 246.

Kula, Our Lady Queen of the Angels (Portuguese), Rev. Thomas R. Heinzel.
Res., R.R. 2, Box 211, 96790. Tel: 808-878-1261; Fax: 808-878-3105. [CEM 2]
Catechesis/Religious Programs—Mrs. Maureen Rompasky, D.R.E.
Students 60.
Missions—Waiakoa, Maui Co., Holy Ghost, 9 Lower Kula Rd., Waiakoa, 96790. Tel: 808-878-1091; Ulupalakua, Maui Co., St. James the Less.

Lahaina, Maria Lanakila (1846), Revs. Marisi Palepale, SS.CC.; Joseph Hendricks, SS.CC., Pastoral Assoc. In res., Rev. Raphael M. Smulders, SS.CC.
Res., P.O. Box 1680, 96767. Tel: 808-661-0552; Fax: 808-667-6963. [CEM]
School—Tel: 808-661-4720; Fax: 808-661-4720. Sr. Charles Miriam Wong, O.S.F., Prin.
Franciscan Sisters 1; Lay Teachers 9; Students 203.
Catechesis/Religious Programs—Tel: 808-661-6607. Sr. Susan Marie Alconcher, B.V.M., D.R.E.
Students 202.
Mission—Honokahua (Kapalua), Maui Co., Sacred Hearts of Jesus and Mary, Office Rd., Honokahua, 96761. Tel: 808-669-7022.

Makawao, St. Joseph (1851), Revs. Herman Gomes, SS.CC.; Michael W. Hill, O.F.M.; Deacon Albert Phillips, Jr.
Res., 1294 Makawao Ave., 96768. Tel: 808-572-7652; Fax: 808-572-9150. [CEM]
School—(Grades PreK-6) 57 Dominican Ln., 96768. Tel: 808-572-8675. Sr. Mary Matthew Brasil, O.P., Prin.
Sisters 6; Lay Teachers 6; Students 140.
Catechesis/Religious Programs—Tel: 808-572-2050. Tina Andrade, D.R.E.
Students 208.
Convent—57 Dominican Ln., 96768. Tel: 808-572-8454.
Dominican Sisters of the Most Holy Rosary 7.

Paia, Holy Rosary (1915), Rev. Gary Colton; Deacon Patrick Constantino.
Church—954 Baldwin Ave., 96779-9605. Tel: 808-579-9551. [CEM]
Catechesis/Religious Programs—Mrs. Clara Pico, D.R.E.
Students 40.

Waihee, St. Ann (1935), Rev. Rogelio S. Quibuyen (Phillipines) Admin.
Res., 40 Kuhinia St., 96793-9216. Tel: 808-244-3284. [CEM][JC]
Missions—Waikapu, Maui Co., St. Joseph, 96793. [CEM][JC]
Kahakuloa, Maui Co., St. Francis Xavier, 96793. [CEM][JC]

Wailuku, St. Anthony, Revs. Raymond Malley, S.M.; Thomas Hogan, S.M.; Joseph Napierkowski, S.M.; Deacons Joseph Borges; James Ronald Gonsalves.
Res., 1627 B Mill St., 96793-1999. Tel: 808-244-4148; Fax: 808-242-9375. [CEM]
School—(Grades PreK-6). Tel: 808-244-4976; 242-9024 (PreK); Fax: 808-242-9375. Mrs. Winona Martinez, Prin.; Mrs. Carlene Santos, Dir. (PreK).
Lay Teachers 11; Students 203.
Catechesis/Religious Programs—Tel: 808-242-6040. Kay Stone, D.R.E.
Students 275.

ISLAND OF MOLOKAI

Kalaupapa, Maui Co., St. Francis (1873), Rev. Arsene Daenen, SS.CC.
Res., 96742. Tel: 808-567-6238.
Mission—Kalawao, Kalawao Co., St. Philomena, P.O. Box 9, 96742.

Kaunakakai, Molokai Co., Molokai Catholic Community (1874). Attended by Our Lady of Sorrows, Kalua'aha; St. Joseph, Kamalo; St. Sophia, Kaunakakai; and St. Vincent, Maunaloa. Rev. James Orsini.
Mailing Address: P.O. Box 1948, 96748-1948. Tel: 808-553-5220. [CEM 2]
Office: 115 Ala Malama St., 96748.
Catechesis/Religious Programs—Students 144.

On Duty Outside the Diocese:
Reverend Fathers—
Butler, John
Coughlin, Thomas
DeOtero, Roberto
Drew, James F.
Halloran, John, Los Angeles, CA
Lee, William, Chicago, IL
Rozycki, George

Military Chaplains:
Reverend Fathers—
Blazek, Eugene E., U.S. Air Force
Evers, Paul, U.S. Navy
Gervacio, Adrian R., U.S. Navy
Lanuevo, Victor, U.S. Navy
Santry, Robert, U.S. Army

Retired:
Reverend Monsignors—
Caraballo, Benito, 819 Puunani Pl., Honolulu, HI 96817
Eikmeier, Bernard, 78 Kaikaina St, Kailua, HI 96734
Marzen, Francis A., P.O. Box 4935, Kaneohe, HI 96744
Rossbach, George, 43-315 Lilipuna Rd., #B-202, Kaneohe, HI 96744
Reverend Fathers—
Ching, Herbert, 86-660 Lualualei, Homestead Rd., Waianae, HI 96777
Churchill, Raymond, 1184 Bishop St., Honolulu, HI 96813
Duffy, Edwin J., Alexander Towers, 1226 Alexander St., Apt. 601, Honolulu, HI 96826
Hannon, Robert E., Cathedral of Our Lady of Peace, 1184 Bishop St., Honolulu, HI 96813
Newton, John G., 579-D Keolu Dr., Kailua, HI 96734
O'Brien, Arthur
O'Leary, Bartholomew J., Nazareth House, 245 Nova Albion Way, San Rafael, CA 94903
Pascale, Anthony, 1778 Ala Moana Blvd., #2807, Honolulu, HI 96815
Prestera, Vincent, 1015 Aoloa Pl., #450, Kailua, HI 96734
Siu, Robert K.C., Holy Rosary Church, P.O. Box 503, Lander, WY 82520
Smith, Paul, 1717 Ala Wai Blvd., #1806, Honolulu, HI 96851
Thomas, Donald, P.O. Box 0358, Haleiwa, HI 96712
Turner, Edward, 150 Irving Ave., Floral Park, NY 11001

Permanent Deacons:
Aanavi, Don, On Leave of Absence
Andrews, LeRoy, St. Joseph, Hilo, 136 Ululani St., Hilo, HI 96720
Awana, Benjamin A., Our Lady of Sorrows, Wahiawa, 89-104 A Haleakala Ave., Nannakuli, HI 96792
Borges, Joseph W., St. Anthony, Wailuku, Maui, 299 Liholiho St., Wailuku, HI 96793
Carlbom, Ernest F., St. George, Waimanalo, 41-865 Mahailua St., Waimanalo, HI 96795
Carroll, James L., (Retired), 323 Kuukama St., Kailua, HI 96734
Choo, Ronald T.Y., Blessed Sacrament, 46-144 Hilinama St., Kaneoha, HI 96744
Constantino, Patrick R., Holy Rosary, Paia; St. Rita, Haiku, 3188 Kilani Pl., Pukalani, HI 96734
DeCaires, Clarence, Jr., St. John Vianney, 1131 Kupau St., Kailua, HI 96734
Gerakas, Andrew J., Star of the Sea, Honolulu, 4524 Waikui St., Honolulu, HI 96821
Gonsalves, James R., St. Anthony, Mailuku, Maui, 2534 Main St., Wailuku, HI 96793
Hart, Christopher L., On Leave
Hope, Jack M., On Leave
Ignacio, Lawrence, St. Anthony, Papaaloa, P.O. Box 317, Paauilo, HI 96776
Kawaihae, Harvey, St. Joseph, Hilo, 1838 Kilauea Ave., Hilo, HI 96720
Larcomb, Dwight, Holy Cross, Kalaheo, Kauai, HI 96741
Lee, Paul, Holy Trinity, Honolulu, Honolulu, HI 96821
Matsuo, Roy T., Sacred Hearts, Makiki (St. Louis High School/Kapiolani & Shriner's)
McPeek, William, Anunciation Parish, Kamuela, P.O. Box 278, Kapaau, HI 96755
Miller, Cletus J., (Retired), Holy Trinity, 5371 Opihi St., Honolulu, HI 96821
Mitsui, Wallace M., St. John Apostle & Evangelist, Mililani, 95-690 Lewanuu St., Mililani, HI 97689
Miyashiro, Thomas H., Our Lady of Good Counsel, Pearl City, 2054 Hoohai St, Pearl City, HI 96782
Phillips, Albert C., St. Joseph, Makawao, Maui, 3297 Haleakala Hwy., Pukalani, HI 96788
Port, Richard J., Sts. Peter and Paul, Honolulu, 1600 Ala Moana Blvd., #3100, Honolulu, HI 96815
Rienzi, Thomas M., Star of the Sea, Honolulu, 676 Elepaio St., Honolulu, HI 96819
Schoemaker, Andres J., St. Joseph, Hilo
Seagraves, Veral, Co-Cathedral of St. Theresa, 1755 Mahani Loop, Honolulu, HI 96819
Shuster, St. Michael, Kailua-Kona, Kailua-Kona, HI 96725
Singson, Frank, Christ the King, Kahului, Kahului, HI 96732
Taylor, Sam, Holy Trinity, Honolulu, Honolulu, HI 96821
Thorp, George, Our Lady of Mount Carmel, Honolulu, 1459 Akamai St., Kailua, HI 96734
Townsley, Sidney J., St. Pius X, Honolulu, 2821 Lowrey Ave., Honolulu, HI 96822
Waldemar, St. Catherine, Kapaa, Kauai, HI 96746
Weaver, Jerome M., St. Anthony, Kaulua, 1031 Lunaai Pl., Kailua, HI 96734
Wong, Lauren H., St. John Vianney, Kailua, 1309 Kupau St., Kailua, HI 96734
Yoshimitsu, Walter H., St. John Vianney, Kailua, 681 Akoakoa St., Kailua, HI 96734

INSTITUTIONS LOCATED IN THE DIOCESE

[A] SEMINARIES, DIOCESAN

KANEOHE. *St. Stephen's Diocesan Center*, 6301 Pali Hwy., 96744. Tel: 808-263-8844. In res., Most Rev. Frances X. DiLorenzo, S.T.D., D.D.; Rev. Marc R. Alexander, S.T.D.; Rev. Msgr. Daniel J. Dever.

[B] COLLEGES AND UNIVERSITIES

*HONOLULU. *Chaminade University of Honolulu*, 3140 Waialae Ave., 96816. Tel: 808-735-4711.
For a complete listing, refer to the Colleges and Universities section.

[C] HIGH SCHOOLS, DIOCESAN AND PAROCHIAL

HONOLULU. *Maryknoll Schools*, 1701 Wilder Ave., 96822. Tel: 808-973-1888. Andrew W. Corcoran, Prin. Sisters 2; Lay Teachers 117; Students 1,357.

HILO. *St. Joseph Junior-Senior High School*, 1000 Ululani St., 96720; Fax: 808-969-9019. Deacon LeRoy M. Andrews, Prin. Sisters 1; Deacons 1; Lay Teachers 28; Students 280.

WAILUKU. *St. Anthony Junior-Senior High School*, 1618 Lower Main St., 96793. Bro. James Dods, S.M., Prin. Brothers 3; Sisters 3; Lay Teachers 29; Students 394.

[D] HIGH SCHOOLS, PRIVATE

HONOLULU. *Damien Memorial High School*, 1401 Houghtailing St., 96817. Tel: 808-841-0195. Congregation of Christian Brothers. Legal Title: *Congregation of Christian Brothers of Hawaii, Inc.* Bros. Karl J. Walczak, C.F.C., Prin.; Francis M. Popish, C.F.C., Supr. Brothers 7; Sisters 1; Lay Teachers 36; Boys 500.

Sacred Hearts Academy, 3253 Waialae Ave., 96816. Tel: 808-734-5058. Mrs. Betty White, Prin. Sisters 6; Lay Teachers 52; Girls 929; Support Staff, Counselors, Administrators 18; Lower School (JK-6) 358; Middle & High School (7-12) 636.

St. Francis School. (Grades 6-12), 2707 Pamoa Rd., 96822. Tel: 808-988-4111. Sr. Joan of Arc Souza, O.S.F., Prin. Sisters 12; Lay Teachers 34; Girls 435.

**St. Louis School*, 3142 Waialae Ave., 96816-1578. Tel: 808-739-7777; Fax: 808-739-4853. Rev. John Russi, S.M., Pres. Chaplains: Revs. Mario Pariante, S.M.; John Bolin, S.M. Priests 5; Brothers 6; Sisters 2; Lay Teachers 60; Boys 876.

[E] PRESCHOOL CENTERS

HONOLULU. *St. Philomena Early Learning Center*, 3300 Ala Laulani St., 96818. Tel: 808-833-8080; Fax: 808-834-6888; 808-834-3438. A.V. Thomas, Prin. Lay Teachers 13; Students 115.

HILO. *Hale Kamalii Montessori*, 326 Desha Ave., 96720. Tel: 808-935-9338, Ext. 25. Co-Directors: Marie Roberts; Joe Camacho. Students 11.

MILILANI TOWN. *St. John Montessori Center*, 95-370 Kuahelani Ave., 96789. Tel: 808-623-7331. Carmella Prose, Dir. Total Staff 9; Students 61.

[F] GENERAL HOSPITALS

HONOLULU. *St. Francis Healthcare System of Hawaii*, P.O. Box 30100, 96820. Tel: 808-566-4783.
For a complete listing, refer to the Hospitals section.

[G] SPECIAL HOSPITALS AND SANATORIA FOR INVALIDS

KALAUPAPA, MOLOKAI. *Kalaupapa Settlement*, 96742.
For a complete listing, refer to the Special Care Facilities section.

[H] MONASTERIES AND RESIDENCES OF PRIESTS AND BROTHERS

HONOLULU. *Center Marianist Community*, 3140 Waialae Ave., 96816. Tel: 808-735-2711. Bro. Franklin R. Pao, S.M., Dir.; Rev. John Russi, S.M. Priests 2; Brothers 9.

Chaminade Pohaku Marianist Community, 3140 Waialae Ave., 96816. Tel: 808-735-4857. Rev. Mario Pariante, S.M., Dir. Priests 1; Brothers 3. Total in Residence 11.

Congregation of Christian Brothers, 1401 Houghtailing St., 96817. Tel: 808-845-2330. Bro. Francis M. Popish, C.F.C., Supr. Brothers 11.

Jesuit Fathers House, 2727 Pamoa Rd., 96822-1838. Tel: 808-988-3464. Revs. Randall H. Roche, S.J., Reg. Supr.; Bernard Cassidy, S.J.; Daniel J. Sullivan, S.J.; David C. Schwartz, S.J.

**Marianist Center of Hawaii*, 3140 Waialae Ave., 96816. Tel: 808-739-4738. Bro. Edward L.K. Gomez, S.M., Vice Pres. & Chm.

Marianist Hall Community, 3140 Waialae Ave., 96816. Tel: 808-739-8300; Fax: 808-739-8320. Rev. John F. Bolin, S.M., Dir. Priests 2; Brothers 9.

Maryknoll Fathers House, Honolulu Society House, 1721 Dole St, 96822. Tel: 808-949-7737. Revs. Francis J. Taney, M.M.; Charles W. Schmidt, M.M.; Joseph Matheis, M.M.; Bro. Venard F. Ruane, M.M., Dir.; Rev. Arthur Dwyer, M.M., Unit Coord., Annunciation Church, P.O. Box 301, Kamuela, 96743. Rev. Robert F. Wynne, M.M., Sacred Heart Church, 1701 Wilder Ave., 96822. Revs. Francis A. Diffley, M.M.; Ralph Christman, M.M.; Thomas F. Donnelly, M.M., Sacred Heart Church, 85-786 Old Government Rd., Waianae, 96792. Revs. Arthur J. Dwyer, M.M.; Elias J. Tederous, M.M., St. Benedict's Church, Box 209, 96726. Rev. Robert W. Donnelly, M.M., St. John Apostle and Evangelist, 95-370 Kuahelani Ave., Mililani, 96789. Rev. Thomas B. Killackey, M.M., St. John the Baptist, 2324 Omilo Ln., 96819. Rev. James J. McFadden, M.M., St. Joseph's Church, 43 Kapiolani St., Hilo, 96720. Priests 2; Brothers 1; Total in Residence 2; Total Staff 1.

St. Patrick's Monastery, 1124-A Seventh Ave., 96816. Revs. Gerard Leicht, SS.CC.; Clement Geysen, SS.CC.; Timothy Jacobs, SS.CC.; Lawrence Mampaey, SS.CC.; Albert Miechielsen, SS.CC.; Anthony O'Brien, SS.CC.; Gabriel Vanden Brouke, SS.CC.; Alfred Vann, SS.CC.; Stephen Van den Eynde, SS.CC.; Christopher Keahi, SS.CC., Supr.; Ildephonse Kuntz, SS.CC.; Edward Popish, SS.CC.; Francis Schellemans, SS.CC.; Bros. James Dunn, SS.CC.; Leo Vendiola, SS.CC.; Patrick Hughes, SS.CC; Dominic Stone, SS.CC. Total in Residence 17; Total Staff 6.

Society of the Priests of St. Sulpice (Sulpicians) S.S., 712 North School St., 96817. Tel: 808-536-0046. Vietnamese Catholic Community. Rev. Joseph Cao Ky, S.S.

KANEOHE. *Congregation of the Sacred Hearts of Jesus and Mary (Hawaii Province SS.CC.)*, P.O. Box 797, 96744. Tel: 808-247-5035. Very Rev. Joseph Bukoski, III, SS.CC., Prov. Priests 37; Brothers 7; Temporary Professed 1.

Sacred Hearts Center, P.O. Box 787, 96744. Tel: 808-247-3647. Revs. Joseph Bukoski, III, SS.CC., Prov.; Gaston Diels, SS.CC.; Nobincio Fernandez, SS.CC.; Bros. Charles Kaahanui, SS.CC.; George Apo, SS.CC.

WAIALUA, OAHU. *Benedictine Monastery of Hawaii*, 67-290 Farrington Hwy., P.O. Box 490, 96791. Tel: 808-637-7887; Fax: 808-637-8601. Benedictine Congregation of Our Lady of Mounte Oliveto, O.S.B. Revs. Michael Sawyer, O.S.B.; Timothy Ottman, O.S.B.; David Barfknecht, O.S.B., Supr.; Sr. Mary Jo McEnany, O.S.B.; Bros. Gregory Foret, O.S.B.; Stephen Coffey, O.S.B.

WAILUKU, MAUI. *Wailuku Marianist Community*, 1627 B Mill St., 96793. Tel: 808-244-3152. Revs. Joseph Hartzler, S.M., Supr.; Raymond E. Malley, S.M.; Joseph J. Napierkowski, S.M.; Bro. James A. Dods, S.M.

Waiehu Marianist Community, 828 Analio St., 96793. Tel: 808-242-6874. Rev. Thomas W. Hogan, S.M., Supr.; Bros. Raymond L. Dotzler, S.M.; Charles J. Ehrenfeld, S.M.; Frank T. Spaeth, S.M.

[I] CONVENTS AND RESIDENCES FOR SISTERS

HONOLULU. *Congregation of the Sacred Hearts and of Perpetual Adoration*, 1120 Fifth Ave., 96816. Tel: 808-737-5822; Fax: 808-735-0878. Sisters of the Congregation of the Sacred Hearts of Jesus and Mary of Perpetual Adoration SS.CC. Sr. Regina Mary Jenkins, Pres. & Prov. Supr.; Sr. Katherine Francis Miller, SS.CC., Vice Pres.; Sr. Rose Kathleen Lenchanko, Sec.; Sr. Anne Clare DeCosta, Auditor; Sr. Mary Josephine Araki, Treas.
The following are listings of residences and the number of sisters residing at each:

Paewalani Community, 45-901A Wailele Rd., 96744. Tel: 808-247-3688. Sr. Anne Clare DeCosta, SS.CC., Contact Person. Sisters 3.

Mali O Ka Malu Community, 1117 Fourth Ave., 96816. Tel: 808-734-2048. Sr. Helene Woods, SS.CC., Contact Person. Sisters 18.

Waianae Community, 86-227 Kawili St., 96792. Tel: 808-696-3772. Sr. Jessie Kai, SS.CC., Contact Person. Sisters 2.

Na Leo Ho'onani Community, 2151 Kauhana St., 96816. Tel: 808-739-5566. Sr. Irene Barboza, SS.CC., Contact Person. Sisters 3. Sisters 8.

Maryknoll Sisters of St. Dominic M.M. 125 Ainoni St., Kailua, 96734-2138. Tel: 808-261-0267.
The following are listings of residences and the number of sisters residing at each:

Maryknoll Sisters, 2880 Oahu Ave., 96822-1726. Tel:

808-988-6540. Sisters 6.
Maryknoll Sisters, 125 Ainoni St., Kailua, 96734-2138. Tel: 808-261-6356. Sisters 3.
Maryknoll Sisters, 1570 Mokulua Dr., Kailua, 96734-3254. Tel: 808-261-1674. Sisters 4.
Maryknoll Sisters, 87-204 Holomalia Pl., Nanakuli, 96792-3706. Tel: 808-668-1603. Sisters 4.
Maryknoll Sisters, St. Anthony Convent, 702 Puuhale Rd., 96819. Tel: 808-841-5652.
Maryknoll Sisters, P.O. Box 996, Pepeekeo, 96783. Tel: 808-964-3032. Sisters 2.
Maryknoll Sisters, 1306 Ululani St., Hilo, 96720. Tel: 808-961-6834.
St. Anthony Home, 3351 Kalihi St., 96819. Tel: 808-845-4353; Fax: 808-848-2696. Sisters of the Sacred Hearts of Jesus and Mary and of Perpetual Adoration SS.CC. Sr. Rose Kathleen Lenchanko, SS.CC., Contact Person.
St. Anthony Retreat Center, 3351 Kalihi St., 96819. Tel: 808-845-0065. Sisters 8.
St. Francis Convent, 2715 Pamoa Rd., 96822. Tel: 808-988-4432.
The following are listings of residences and the number of sisters residing at each:
Marianne Cope Convent, 2102 Liliha St., 96817. Tel: 808-538-1526. Sisters 7.
Sacred Hearts Convent, 239 Dickenson St., Lakaina, 96761. Tel: 808-661-0163. Sisters 4.
Franciscan Sisters, 15 Kulanihakoi St., 10-C, Kihei, 96753. Tel: 808-874-1029. Sisters 2.
St. Elizabeth Convent, Bishop Home and Hospital, Kalaupapa, 96742. Tel: 808-567-6079. Sisters 3.
St. Joseph Convent, 440 Kapiolani St., Hilo, 96720. Tel: 808-935-1388. Sr. Grace Michael Souza, O.S.F. Sisters 5.
St. Francis Medical Center - West, St. Clare Convent, 91-1048 A'awa Dr., Ewa Beach, 96706-1830. Tel: 808-687-3420. Sisters 7.
Molokai Catholic Community, P.O. Box 1948, Kaunakakai, 96748-1948. Tel: 80-558-8120.
St. Michael Convent, 67-340 Haona St., Waialua, 96791. Tel: 808-637-5606. Sisters 19.
Sisters of Notre Dame de Namur, 1117 Fourth Ave., 96816. Tel: 808-734-2048. Sr. Maryanne Gorman, S.N.D., Contact Person. Sisters 3.
Sisters of St. Joseph of Carondelet CSJ, Hawaii Vice-Province, 5311 Apo Dr., 96821. Tel: 808-373-2096; Fax: 808-373-5341. Sr. Ruth Margaret Raupp, C.S.J., Vice Prov.
The following are listings of residences and the number of sisters residing at each:
Carondelet Community, 5311 Apo Dr., 96821. Tel: 808-373-3850. Sisters 5.
Hale Medaille Community, 2220 E. Kalaiwa Way #19, 96819. Tel: 808-847-7807. Sisters 2.
Holy Trinity Community, 5919 Kalanianaole Hwy., 96821. Tel: 808-396-9182. Sisters 4.
Ho'omaluhia Community, 1635 Alaneo St., 96817. Sisters 2.
Mana'olana Community, 1046 6th Ave., 96816. Tel: 808-737-2130. Sisters 2.
St. Joseph the Worker Community, 17-202 Palula St., P.O. Box 609, Keaau, 96749. Tel: 808-966-7754. Sisters 2.
St. Theresa Community, 712 N. School St., 96817. Tel: 808-533-3101. Sisters 13.
Christ the King Community, 211 S. Kaulawahine St., 96732. Tel: 808-877-0790. Sisters 7.
Hale lokepa Community, 54 Kuhinia St., Waihe'e, 96793. Tel: 808-244-8123. Sisters 4.
La'ialoha Community, 21 Craigside Pl., #6F, 96817. Tel: 808-537-9223.

KANEOHE. *Carmel of the Holy Trinity (Carmelite Monastery)*, 6301 Pali Hwy., 96744-5224. Tel: 808-261-6542. Sr. Mary Agnes Tse, O.C.D., Prioress. Sisters 7.

MOUNTAIN VIEW. *Sisters of the Holy Family Residences*, P.O. Box 15, 96771. Tel: 808-968-6426.

WAIPAHU. *Dominican Center Hawaii*, 94-1249 Lumikula St., 96797. Tel: 808-676-1452; 845-2622. Dominican Sisters of the Most Holy Rosary. Sr. M. Aurelia Sanchez, O.P., Reg. Supr.
Please refer to the following parish convents for additional residences: St. Elizabeth, Aiea; St. John, Honolulu; St. Catherine, Kapaa; St. Joseph, Makawao; and St. Charles, San Francisco. Sisters 8.
Sisters of Charity of the Blessed Virgin Mary, 94-1031 Kauhahi Pl., Apt. G7, 96797. Tel: 808-676-4433.
Sacred Hearts Convent, 239 Dickenson St., Lahaina, 96761. Tel: 808-661-0163.

[J] MISCELLANEOUS

HONOLULU. *Aina Kupaa O Maili*, 1184 Bishop St., 96813. Tel: 808-533-1791. Most Rev. Francis X. DiLorenzo, Pres.; Rev. John F. Bolin, S.M., V.G., Vice Pres.; Sr. Grace Dorothy Lim, M.M., Sec.; Jerome Rauckhorst, Treas. Total Assisted 1,368; Total Staff 25.
Leadership Association of Religious Congregation (LARC), 2712 Panmoa Rd., 96822. Tel: 808-988-7800. Rev. Halbert Weidner, C.O., Chm. Tel: 808-396-0551.
The Oratory. (Diocesan House), P.O. Box 26113, 96825. Total in Residence 2.
Our Lady of the Mystical Rose Chapel. Oratory. Marianist Center of Hawaii, 3140 Waialae Ave., 96816; Fax: 808-737-5518.
People of Praise, c/o Chancery Office, 1184 Bishop St., 96813-2859.
Lay Covenant Community (Charismatic group). Bob Linczer, Liaison, Branch Coord.
St. Paul Book and Media Center, 1143 Bishop St., 96813. Tel: 808-521-2731; Fax: 808-523-3685. Daughters of St. Paul 5.
Spiritual Life Center, 2880 Oahu Ave., 96822. Tel: 808-988-6540. Sr. Katherine Theiler, M.M., Dir.; Rev. Nancy Conley, Assoc. Dir.

KANEOHE. *The Augustine Educational Foundation*, St. Stephen Diocesan Center, 6301 Pali Hwy., 96744. Tel: 808-263-8844, Ext. 335; 336. Most Revs. Francis X. DiLorenzo, Pres.; Joseph A. Ferrario, D.D., Chm.

RELIGIOUS INSTITUTES OF MEN REPRESENTED IN THE DIOCESE

For further details refer to the corresponding bracketed number in the Religious Institutes of Men or Women section.

[0200]—*Benedictine Monks*. (Olivetan).—O.S.B.
[0470]—*The Capuchin Friars*.—O.F.M.Cap.
[0310]—*Congregation of Christian Brothers*.—C.F.C.
[1140]—*Fathers of the Sacred Hearts*. (Hawaii Prov.).—SS.CC.
[0520]—*Franciscan Friars*.—O.F.M.
[0690]—*Jesuit Fathers and Brothers*.—S.J.
[0780]—*Marist Fathers*.—S.M.
[0800]—*Maryknoll*.—M.M.
[0720]—*The Missionaries of Our Lady of La Salette*. (Pacific Region).—M.S.
[0950]—*Oratorians*.—C.O.
[1030]—*Paulist Fathers*.—C.S.P.
[0760]—*Society of Mary*. (Prov. of the Pacific).—S.M.
[1290]—*Society of the Priest of Saint Sulpice*.—S.S.

RELIGIOUS INSTITUTES OF WOMEN REPRESENTED IN THE DIOCESE

[]—*Benedictine Congregation of Our Lady of Mounte Oliveto*.—O.S.B.
[]—*Congregation of Benedictine Sisters of the Eucharistic King*.—O.S.B.
[1070-01]—*Congregation of St. Catharine of Siena*.—O.P.
[0870]—*Congregation of the Daughters of Mary Immaculate (Marianist Sisters)*.—F.M.I.
[0420]—*Discalced Carmelite Nuns*.—O.C.D.
[1070-03]—*Dominican Sisters of the Most Holy Rosary*.—O.P.
[1230]—*Franciscan Sisters of Christian Charity*.—O.S.F.
[2420]—*Marist Missionary Sisters*.—S.M.S.M.
[2470]—*Maryknoll Sisters of St. Dominic*.—M.M.
[0950]—*Pious Society Daughters of St. Paul*.—D.S.P.
[]—*Religious of the Blessed Virgin Mary*.—R.V.M.
[0430]—*Sisters of Charity of the Blessed Virgin Mary*.—B.V.M.
[3000]—*Sisters of Notre Dame de Namur*.—S.N.D.deN.
[1640]—*Sisters of St. Francis of Perpetual Adoration*.—O.S.F.
[1650]—*Sisters of St. Francis of Philadelphia*.—O.S.F.
[3840]—*Sisters of St. Joseph of Carondelet*.—C.S.J.
[1830]—*Sisters of the Good Shepherd*.—R.G.S.
[1960]—*Sisters of the Holy Family*.—S.H.F.
[2110]—*Sisters of the Humility of Mary*.—H.M.
[3690]—*Sisters of the Sacred Hearts and of Perpetual Adoration*.—SS.CC.
[1490]—*Sisters of the Third Franciscan Order*. (Syracuse, NY).—O.S.F.

NECROLOGY

† Brodeur, Robert, Hana, Maui, HI, St. Mary. —Died May 1, 1996.

Diocese of Houma-Thibodaux

(Dioecesis Humensis-Thibodensis)

Most Reverend

MICHAEL JARRELL, D.D.

Bishop of Houma-Thibodaux; ordained June 3, 1967; appointed December 29, 1992; consecrated and installed March 4, 1993. *Address: Chancery Office, 1801 Hwy. 311, Schriever, LA, 70395. Mailing Address: P.O. Box 9077, Houma, LA, 70361.* Tel.: 504-868-7720.

Most Reverend

WARREN L. BOUDREAUX, J.C.D., D.D.

Retired Bishop of Houma-Thibodaux; ordained May 30, 1942; appointed Titular Bishop of Calynda and Auxiliary of Lafayette May 19, 1962; consecrated July 25, 1962; appointed Bishop of Beaumont June 4, 1971 and installed August 25, 1971; installed Bishop of Houma-Thibodaux June 5, 1977; retired December 29, 1992. *Address: 233 Rienzi Dr., Thibodaux, LA, 70301.*

ERECTED JUNE 5, 1977.

Square Miles 3,440.

Comprises the parishes of Lafourche, Terrebonne, parts of St. Mary and Jefferson.

For legal titles of parishes and diocesan institutions, consult the Chancery Office.

Address all Chancery correspondence to: P.O. Box 9077, Houma, LA, 70361. Tel.: 504-868-7720; Fax: 504-868-7727.

STATISTICAL OVERVIEW

Personnel	
Bishop	1
Retired Bishops	1
Priests: Diocesan Active in Diocese	48
Priests: Active Outside Diocese	1
Priests: Retired, Sick or Absent	24
Number of Diocesan Priests	73
Religious Priests in Diocese	7
Extern Priests in Diocese	1
Ordinations:	
Diocesan Priests	3
Permanent Deacons	3
Permanent Deacons in Diocese	25
Total Brothers	12
Total Sisters	34
Parishes	
Parishes	40
With Resident Pastor:	
Resident Diocesan Priests	34
Resident Religious Priests	2
Without Resident Pastor:	
Administered by Priests	2
Administered by Women Religious	2
Missions	6
Welfare	
Day Care and Extended Day Care Centers	1
Total Assisted	65
Specialized Homes	2
Special Centers for Social Services	3
Total Assisted	8,936
Educational	
Diocesan Students in Other Seminaries	11
Total Seminarians	11
High Schools, Diocesan and Parish	3
Total Students	1,866
Elementary Schools, Diocesan and Parish	10
Total Students	4,162
Catechesis/Religious Education:	
High School Students	3,720
Elementary Students	7,509
Total Students Under Catholic Instruction	17,268
Teachers in the Diocese:	
Brothers	7
Sisters	1
Lay Teachers	323
Vital Statistics	
Receptions into the Church:	
Infant Baptism Totals	1,827
Adult Baptism Totals	55
Received into Full Communion	113
First Communions	1,592
Confirmations	1,400
Marriages:	
Catholic	475
Interfaith	88
Total Marriages	563
Deaths	1,082
Total Catholic Population	109,412
Total Population	208,185

Former Bishops—Most Rev. WARREN L. BOUDREAUX, J.C.D., D.D., Retired Bishop of Houma-Thibodaux; ord. May 30, 1942; retired Dec. 29, 1992.

Chancery, *Address all correspondence to: P.O. Box 9077, Houma, 70361.* Office: *1801 Hwy. 311, Schriever, 70395.* Tel: 504-868-7720; Fax: 504-868-7727. Office Hours: Mon.-Fri. 8-5

Vicar General and Moderator of the Curia—Rev. Msgr. JAMES B. SONGY.

Chancellor—Rev. Msgr. JOSEPH N. LATINO.

Diocesan Tribunal, *Address all correspondence to: P.O. Box 9077, Houma, 70361.* Office: *1801 Hwy. 311, Schriever, 70395.* Tel: 504-850-3126

Judicial Vicar—Rev. VICENTE DELA CRUZ.

Judges—Rev. Msgr. WILLIAM KONINKX; Revs. BRENDAN FOLEY; JOHN A. GALLEN.

Defenders of the Bond—Rev. Msgr. JOSEPH N. LATINO; Revs. DANIEL M. POCHE; ROLANDO TIMBRE; Sr. ETHALEE MULHERN.

Counselor—Sr. KATERI BATTAGLIA, M.S.C.

Priests Council and College of Consultors—Rev. Msgr. JOSEPH N. LATINO; Rev. Msgr. JAMES B. SONGY; Revs. CARL COLLINS; ROCH NAQUIN; DANIEL POCHE; JUSTIN BROWN; LAWRENCE CAVELL; PATRICK O'BRIEN; DEAN DANOS; Very Rev. BRENDAN P. FOLEY, *Mailing Address: P.O. Box 9077, Houma, 70361. 1801 Hwy. 311, Schriever, 70395.*

Deans—Upper Lafourche Deanery: Very Rev. PATRICK O'BRIEN, *720 Talbot Ave., Thibodaux, 70301.* South Lafourche Deanery: Very Rev. BRENDAN P. FOLEY, V.F., *612 Main St., Lockport, 70374.* Terrebonne Deanery: Rev. Msgr. JOSEPH N. LATINO, V.F., *P.O. Box 4014, Houma, 70361.*

Diocesan Finance Council—Rev. WILFREDO DECAL; Rev. Msgr. FREDERIC J. BRUNET; Rev. Msgr. JOSEPH N. LATINO; A. J. CHAMPAGNE, JR.; ROBERT NAQUIN; Mr. LEE RINGEMAN; ANN BARKER.

Diocesan Pastoral Council—JAMES J. DANOS, Pres. RUSSELL DOMANGUE, Sec., *Mailing Address: P.O. Box 9077, Houma, 70361.*

Departments of the Diocesan Curia

Department of Administration Ministries:

Coordinator—DOUGLAS P. TOUPS, *1801 Hwy. 311, Schriever, 70395. Mailing Address: P.O. Box 9077, Houma, 70361.* Tel: 504-868-7720.

Accounting, Business Office, Finance, Insurance—DOUGLAS P. TOUPS, Business Mgr., *1801 Hwy. 311, Schriever, 70395. Mailing Address: P.O. Box 9077, Houma, 70361.* Tel: 504-868-7720.

Archives and Historical Research Center—Rev. Msgr. ROLAND J. BOUDREAUX, Dir., *205 Audubon St., Thibodaux, 70301.* Tel: 504-446-2383.

Building Commission—JAMES J. DANOS, Dir., *1801 Hwy. 311, Schriever, 70395. Mailing Address: P.O. Box 9077, Houma, 70361.* Tel: 504-868-7720.

Cemeteries—GEORGE COOKE, Dir., *949 Menard St., Thibodaux, 70301.* Tel: 504-446-0280.

Legal Services—Rev. Msgr. JAMES B. SONGY, Dir., *1801 Hwy. 311, Schriever, 70395. Mailing Address: P.O. Box 9077, Houma, 70361.* Tel: 504-868-7720. Attorneys: KENNETH WATKINS; LOUIS WATKINS; DANIEL WALKER, *501 Roussell St., P.O. Box 5095, Houma, 70361.* Tel: 504-868-2333.

Stewardship and Development—Mr. J. C. CUNNINGHAM, Dir., *1801 Hwy. 311, Schriever, 70395. Mailing Address: P.O. Box 9077, Houma, 70361.* Tel: 504-868-7720.

Department for Clergy and Religious:

Coordinator—Rev. Msgr. JOSEPH N. LATINO, *1801 Hwy. 311, Schriever, 70395. Mailing Address: P.O. Box 9077, Houma, 70361.* Tel: 504-868-7720.

Clergy Personnel—Rev. Msgr. JOSEPH N. LATINO, *Mailing Address: P.O. Box 9077, Houma, 70361.* Tel: 504-868-7720.

Continuing Education of the Clergy-Ministry to Priests Program—Rev. GLENN LECOMPTE, Chm., *333 Twin Oaks, Raceland, 70394.* Rev. Msgr. FRANCIS LEGENDRE, Vicar for Priests, *15300 W. Main St., Cutoff, 70345.* Tel: 504-632-3858.

Permanent Diaconate—Deacon ROBERT DUSSE, *514 Gaynell Dr., Houma, 70364.* Tel: 504-876-5122. *1801*

Hwy. 311, Schriever, 70395. Mailing Address: P.O. Box 9077, Houma, 70361. Tel: 504-868-7720.

Vocations—Rev. JAY BAKER, *1801 Hwy. 311, Schriever, 70395. Mailing Address: P.O. Box 9077, Houma, 70361.* Tel: 504-868-7720.

Women Religious—Sr. BARBARA NELL LAPEROUSE, O.Carm., *902 Menard St., Thibodaux, 70301.* Tel: 504-447-9283.

Department of Formation Ministries:

Coordinator—LOUIS G. AGUIRRE, *1801 Hwy. 311, Schriever, 70395. Mailing Address: P.O. Box 9077, Houma, 70361.* Tel: 504-868-7720.

Campus Ministry—Rev. ALEXANDER FRANCISCO, Dir., N.S.U., *Box 2051, Thibodaux, 70310.* Tel: 504-446-6201.

Catholic Schools—Sr. IMMACULATA PAISANT, M.S.C., Supt., *1801 Hwy. 311, Schriever, 70395. Mailing Address: P.O. Box 9077, Houma, 70361.* Tel: 504-868-7720.

Communications, Public Relations, Publications, Radio & Television—LOUIS G. AGUIRRE, Dir., *1801 Hwy. 311, Schriever, 70395. Mailing Address: P.O. Box 9077, Houma, 70361.* Tel: 504-868-7720.

Religious Education and Lay Ministry—Dr. MARIAN SCHWAB, Dir., *1801 Hwy. 311, Schriever, 70395. Mailing Address: P.O. Box 9077, Houma, 70361.* Tel: 504-868-7720.

"The Bayou Catholic"—(Diocesan Newspaper)—LOUIS G. AGUIRRE, Editor, *1801 Hwy. 311, Schriever, 70395. Mailing Address: P.O. Box 9077, Houma, 70361.* Tel: 504-868-7720.

Family Ministries—Sr. MARY KATERI BATTAGLIA, M.S.C., *1801 Hwy. 311, Schriever, 70395. Mailing Address: P.O. Box 9077, Houma, 70361.* Tel: 504-868-7720.

Worship—Rev. GLENN LECOMPTE, Dir., *1801 Hwy. 311, Schriever, 70395. Mailing Address: P.O. Box 9077, Houma, 70361.* Tel: 504-868-7720.

Youth Ministry—MADELINE CHERAMIE, Dir., *1801 Hwy. 311, Schriever, 70395. Mailing Address: P.O. Box 9077, Houma, 70361.* Tel: 504-868-7720.

Department of Social Ministries:

Coordinator—Sr. MIRIAM MITCHELL, S.H.G., *1220 Aycock St., P.O. Box 883, Houma, 70361.* Tel: 504-876-0490.

Assisi Bridge House—Sr. MIRIAM MITCHELL, S.H.G., Dir., *Bull Run Rd., Schriever, 70395.* Tel: 504-872-5529. ROBERT GORMAN, Asst. Dir., *1220 Aycock St., P.O. Box 883, Houma, 70361.* Tel: 504-876-0490.

Campaign for Human Development—ROBERT GORMAN, Diocesan Dir., *1220 Aycock St., P.O. Box 3894, Houma, 70361.* Tel: 505-876-0490. Liaison for Catholic Relief Services, Respect Life, Justice and Peace.

Catholic Social Services—Sr. MIRIAM MITCHELL, S.H.G., Dir. ROBERT GORMAN, Asst. Dir., *1220 Aycock St., P.O. Box 3894, Houma, 70361.* Tel: 504-876-0490.

Disaster Relief—Sr. MIRIAM MITCHELL, S.H.G., Dir., *1220 Aycock St., P.O. Box 3894, Houma, 70361.* Tel: 504-876-0490.

St. Lucy's Day Care Center—BRENDA THOMAS, Admin., *1220 Aycock St., P.O. Box 3894, Houma, 70361.* Tel: 504-876-1246.

Other Offices and Commissions

Charismatic Renewal—Deacon ROBERT DUSSE, Dir., *1801 Hwy. 311, Schriever, 70394.* Tel: 504-868-7720.

Cursillo—Rev. ROCH R. NAQUIN, Dir., *5101 Grand Caillou Rd., Dulac, 70353.* Tel: 504-563-2325.

Ecumenism—Rev. WILMER TODD, Dir., *409 Funderburk Ave., Houma, 70364.* Tel: 504-879-1506.

Pontifical Societies for the Propagation of the Faith; Holy Childhood Association; Society of St. Peter the Apostle—Rev. NGUYEN VAN TY, Dir., *1027 Hwy. 308, Thibodaux, 70301.* Tel: 504-446-6663.

Scouting—Rev. SHENAN J. BOQUET, Dir., *1801 Hwy. 311, Schriever, 70395. Mailing Address: P.O. Box 9077, Houma, 70361.* Tel: 504-868-7720.

Organizations

Catholic Daughters of the Americas—Rev. Msgr. DONALD L. LEDET, Diocesan Advisor to State Court Officers, *3500 Hwy. 1, N., Raceland, 70394.* Tel: 504-537-3204.

Diocesan Council of St. Vincent de Paul Societies—AL JACKSON, Pres., *107 Point St., Houma, 70360.* Tel: 504-872-9373.

Knights of Columbus—Rev. Msgr. JOSEPH N. LATINO, Diocesan Chap., *P.O. Box 4014, Houma, 70361.* Tel: 504-876-6904.

Legion of Mary—ROSE M. MARCEAUX, Pres.; Rev. Msgr. JOSEPH N. LATINO, Spiritual Dir.

St. Vincent de Paul Store—Mr. PETER CAVALIER, Pres.; Mr. STERLING CHAISSON, Vice Pres. JAMES LEGARDE, Mgr., *107 Point St., Houma, 70360.* Tel: 504-872-9373.

Serra Club of Houma—JOHN BREAUX, Pres.

Serra Club of Thibodaux—WILLIE ORGERON, Pres.

Serra Club of South Lafourche—Mr. BOBBY CHERAMIE, Pres.

Anawim—EVELYN RUCKSTUHL, Pres., *501 Grinage St., Houma, 70360.* Tel: 504-872-4761.

CLERGY, PARISHES, MISSIONS AND PAROCHIAL SCHOOLS

CITY OF HOUMA
(Parish Terrebonne)

1—CATHEDRAL OF ST. FRANCIS DE SALES (1847), Rev. Msgr. Joseph N. Latino; Rev. Patrick R. Kujawa. In res., Rev. Msgr. Emile Fossier.
Res., P.O. Box 4014, 70361. Tel: 504-876-6904; Fax: 504-851-4204. [CEM 2]
School—300 Verret St., 70361. Tel: 504-868-6646; Fax: 504-851-5896.
Lay Teachers 33; Students 834.
Catechesis/Religious Programs—Students 134.
Convent—501 Grinage St., 70361. Tel: 504-876-7260.

2—ANNUNZIATA (1963), Revs. James R. Morrison; Ronald Henery, O.P.
Res., 2323 Acadian Dr., 70363. Tel: 504-876-2971; Fax: 504-868-6414.
Catechesis/Religious Programs—Tel: 504-876-2865.
Students 345.

3—MARIA IMMACOLATA (1963), Rev. Caesar Silva; Deacon Douglas Authement.
Administration Office: 104 Corporate Dr., 70360. Tel: 504-876-3313; Fax: 504-879-2137.
Res., 326 Estate Dr., 70360. Tel: 504-868-4915.
School—324 Estate Dr., 70360. Tel: 504-876-1631; Fax: 504-876-1608.
Lay Teachers 19; Students 244.
Catechesis/Religious Programs—Students 370.

4—OUR LADY OF THE MOST HOLY ROSARY (1948). (Holy Rosary Church). Revs. Fred Link, O.F.M. (Cincinnati); Curt Lanzrath, O.F.M. (Cincinnati); Robert Seay, O.F.M. (Cincinnati). In res., Rev. Edwin Deane, O.F.M. (Cincinnati); Deacons Raymond LeBouef; Harold Kurtz.
Res., 1900 E. Main St., 70363. Tel: 504-876-7652; Fax: 504-876-7647. [CEM]
Catechesis/Religious Programs—Tel: 504-879-2815. D.R.E.: Kathy Lirette; Debbie Hotard.
Students 360.

5—ST. BERNADETTE (1958), Revs. Wilmer Todd; Robert-Joel Cruz.
Res., 409 Funderburk Ave., 70364. Tel: 504-879-1506; Fax: 504-876-9654.
School—309 Funderburk Ave., 70364. Tel: 504-872-3854.
Lay Teachers 20; Students 443.
Catechesis/Religious Programs—Mrs. Lee Dies, D.R.E.
Students 776.

6—ST. GREGORY BARBARIGO (1963), Rev. Wilfredo G. Decal; Rev. Msgr. William Koninkx, V.G.
Mailing Address: P.O. Box 1066, 70361. Tel: 504-876-2047; Fax: 504-876-0628.
Res., 439 Sixth St., 70364. Tel: 504-876-2003.
Administration Bldg.: 1005 Williams Ave., 70364.
School—441 Sixth St., 70364. Tel: 504-876-2038; Fax: 504-879-2789.
Lay Teachers 9; Students 218.
Catechesis/Religious Programs—Students 226.

7—ST. LOUIS (1965), Rev. Thomas R. Bouterie.
Res., 2226 Bayou Blue Rd., 70364. Tel: 504-876-3449; Fax: 504-876-6810. [CEM]
Catechesis/Religious Programs—Tel: 504-876-6686. Cheryl Griffin, D.R.E.
Students 527.

8—ST. LUCY, Rev. John J. Tyne, S.S.J.
Mailing Address: P.O. Box 3508, 70361. Tel: 504-879-2632; Fax: 504-876-4054.
Res., 1236 Aycock St., 70360.
Church—1222 Aycock St., 70360.
Catechesis/Religious Programs—Students 63.

CITY OF THIBODAUX
(Lafourche Parish)

1—ST. JOSEPH CO-CATHEDRAL (1817), Rev. Msgr. Francis J. Amedee; Revs. Toan Vu; Michael A. Bergeron; Deacon Willie R. Orgeron.
Res., 721 Canal Blvd., P.O. Box 966, 70302. Tel: 504-446-1387; Fax: 504-446-6571.
School—501 Cardinal Dr., 70301. Tel: 504-446-1346; Fax: 504-449-0760.
Lay Teachers 35; Students 723.
Catechesis/Religious Programs—Students 185.
Convent—212 Bayou Ln., 70301. Tel: 504-447-9283.

2—ST. CHARLES BORROMEO (1912), Rev. Nguyen Van Ty.
Res., 1027 Hwy. 308, 70301. Tel: 504-446-6663; Fax: 504-447-3348. [CEM]
Catechesis/Religious Programs—Students 196.

3—CHRIST THE REDEEMER (1983), Rev. Patrick O'Brien.
Res., 720 Talbot Ave., 70301. Tel: 504-447-2013; Fax: 504-447-4422. [CEM]
Catechesis/Religious Programs—Students 379.

4—ST. GENEVIEVE (1959), Revs. Joseph S. Pilola; Florentino Santiago.
Res., 815 Barbier Ave., 70301. Tel: 504-446-5571; Fax: 504-449-1939.
School—807 Barbier Ave., 70301. Tel: 504-447-9291.
Lay Teachers 26; Students 448.
Catechesis/Religious Programs—Tel: 504-446-5127.
Students 259.

5—ST. JOHN THE EVANGELIST (1919), Revs. Patrick O'Brien; Justin G. Brown, O.S.B.
Res., 2085 Hwy. 1, 70301. Tel: 504-447-3995; Fax: 504-447-2092. [CEM]
Catechesis/Religious Programs—Students 251.

6—ST. LUKE, Rev. John J. Tyne, S.S.J.
Res., P.O. Box 1819, 70302. Tel: 504-446-0487; Fax: 504-876-4054.
Catechesis/Religious Programs—Students 55.

7—ST. THOMAS AQUINAS (1970), Rev. Alexander M. Francisco.
Res., Nicholls Sta., Box 2051, 70310. Tel: 504-446-6201; Fax: 504-449-0710.

OUTSIDE THE CITIES OF HOUMA AND THIBODAUX

Amelia, St. Mary Parish, St. Andrew (1965), Rev. Charles J. Perkins.
Res., P.O. Box 310, 70340. Tel: 504-631-2333; Fax: 504-631-2334. [CEM]
Catechesis/Religious Programs—Students 130.

Thanh Gia (1981). Personal Parish for Vietnamese Community. Revs. Joseph Luu; Francis Bui.
Res., 711 Magnolia St., Morgan City, 70380. Tel: 504-631-3194.
Domus Dei Institute, Inc.—Cypress St., Morgan City, 70380. Tel: 504-851-1351.

Bayou Black, Terrebonne Parish, St. Anthony (1876), Rev. Gerard C. Hayes.
Res., 3897 Bayou Black Dr., Houma, 70360. Tel: 504-872-0922; Fax: 504-872-2001.
Catechesis/Religious Programs—Students 272.

Bourg, Terrebonne Parish, St. Ann (1908), Revs. Guy P. Zeringue; Van Constant.
Res., 4355 Hwy. 24, P.O. Box 700, 70343. Tel: 504-594-3548; Fax: 504-594-3570. [CEM]
Catechesis/Religious Programs—Tel: 504-594-5088.
Students 482.

Chacahoula, Terrebonne Parish, St. Lawrence (1848), Sr. Fatima Robichaux, M.S.C., Pastoral Admin.
Res., 114 Carroll St., P.O. Box 229, Gibson, 70356. Tel: 504-575-3087; Fax: 504-575-8243. [CEM]

Chackbay, Lafourche Parish, Our Lady of Prompt Succor (1892), Rev. Roland Timbre.
Res., 529 Hwy. 20, Thibodaux, 70301. Tel: 504-633-2903; Fax: 504-633-9225. [CEM 2]
Catechesis/Religious Programs—Students 420.

Chauvin, Terrebonne Parish, St. Joseph (1948), Rev. Msgr. Frederic J. Brunet; Rev. Robert Sevigny.
Res., 5232 Hwy. 56, 70344. Tel: 504-594-5859; Fax: 504-594-2116. [CEM]
Catechesis/Religious Programs—Sharon Picou, D.R.E.
Students 750.
Missions—Cocodrie, Our Lady of the Gulf; Upper Little Caillou, Our Lady of Prompt Succor.

Cut-Off, Lafourche Parish, Sacred Heart (1923), Rev. Msgr. Francis J. Legendre; Rev. Sabino B. Rebosura, II (Philippines).
Res., 15300 W. Main, 70345. Tel: 504-632-3858; Fax: 504-632-4452. [CEM]
Catechesis/Religious Programs—Tel: 504-632-6322.
Students 564.

Galliano, LaFourche Parish, St. Joseph (1958), Rev. Jerome Weber.
Res., P.O. Box 516, 70354. Tel: 504-632-7321; Fax: 504-632-7345. [CEM]
Catechesis/Religious Programs—Students 313.

Gheens, LaFourche Parish, Community of St. Anthony. (Quasi Parish). Rev. Daniel Poche, Admin.
Res., P.O. Box 12, Mathews, 70375. Tel: 504-532-6497.
Catechesis/Religious Programs—Tel: 504-537-6002; Fax: 504-337-4408.
Students 124.

Gibson, Terrebonne Parish, St. Patrick (1920), Sr. Fatima Robichaux, M.S.C., Pastoral Admin.
Res., P.O. Box 229, 70356. Tel: 504-575-3087; Fax: 504-575-8243. [CEM]

Golden Meadow, LaFourche Parish, Our Lady of

Prompt Succor (1916), Revs. Oscar A. Solis; Nghia Huu Dinh.
Res., 723 N. Bayou Dr., 70357. Tel: 504-475-5428; Fax: 504-475-7699.
Mission—Golden Meadow, Our Lady of La Salette. [CEM]
Catechesis/Religious Programs—Students 347.

Grand Caillou, Terrebonne Parish, Holy Family (1952), Rev. Roch R. Naquin.
Res., 5101 Grand Caillou Rd., Dulac, 70353. Tel: 504-563-2325; Fax: 504-563-4980. [CEM 2]
Catechesis/Religious Programs—Students 225.

Grand Isle, West Jefferson Parish, Our Lady of the Isle (1933), Rev. Warren F. Chassaniol.
Res., P.O. Box 885, 70358. Tel: 504-787-2385; Fax: 504-787-4530. [CEM]
Catechesis/Religious Programs—Students 117.

Kraemer, Lafourche Parish, St. Lawrence the Martyr (1962), Rev. Domingo Cruz.
Res., 1479 Hwy. 307, Thibodaux, 70301. Tel: 504-633-9431; Fax: 504-633-5706. [JC 2]
Mission—Choctaw, St. James, 1278 Choctaw Rd., Thibodaux, 70301. Tel: 504-633-9855. [CEM]
Catechesis/Religious Programs—Tel: 504-633-5714.
Students 194.

Larose, Lafourche Parish, Our Lady of the Rosary (1873), Revs. Dean F. Danos; Jay Baker; Sr. Claire M. Rodrigue, C.I.C., Pastoral Assoc.
Res., Box 10, 70373. Tel: 504-693-3433; Fax: 504-693-7551. [CEM]
School—P.O. Box 40, 70373. Tel: 504-693-3342; Fax: 504-693-3348.
Lay Teachers 14; Students 318.
Catechesis/Religious Programs—Tel: 504-693-3125. Camile Gautreaux, D.R.E.
Students 720.

Lockport, Lafourche Parish, Holy Savior (1850), Revs. Brendan P. Foley; Shenan J. Boquet.
Res., 612 Main St., 70374. Tel: 504-532-3533; Fax: 504-532-2010. [CEM]
School—201 Church St., 70374. Tel: 504-532-2536; Fax: 504-532-2269.
Lay Teachers 19; Students 278.
Catechesis/Religious Programs—Students 378.

Montegut, Terrebonne Parish, Sacred Heart (1864), Rev. Lawrence Cavell.
Res., P.O. Box 2, 70377. Tel: 504-594-5856; Fax: 504-594-8087. [CEM 2]
Catechesis/Religious Programs—Students 120.

Morgan City, St. Mary Parish, Sacred Heart of Jesus (1859), Rev. John A. Gallen.
Res., 415 Union St., P.O. Box 632, 70381. Tel: 504-385-0770; Fax: 504-384-7176.
Catechesis/Religious Programs—Students 227.
Holy Cross (1964), Revs. Etienne LeBlanc; Vicente Dela Cruz; Deacon Andrew Dragna.
Res., P.O. Box 2623, 70381. Tel: 504-384-3551; Fax: 504-384-5790.
School—2100 Cedar St., Unit 2, 70381. Tel: 504-384-1933.
Lay Teachers 17; Students 405.
Catechesis/Religious Programs—Students 259.
Mission—Morgan City, St. Martin Parish, St. Rosalie, 1315 Stephensville Rd., 70380. Tel: 504-385-5713.

Pointe-Aux-Chenes, Terrebonne Parish, St. Charles Borromeo (1971), Rev. John Ruiz.
Res., 531 Hwy. 665, Montegut, 70377. Tel: 504-594-6801; Fax: 504-594-6802. [CEM]
Catechesis/Religious Programs—Students 175.

Raceland, LaFourche Parish, St. Hilary of Poitiers (1965), Revs. Daniel M. Poche; Glenn D. LeCompte.
Res., 333 Twin Oaks, 70394. Tel: 504-537-6002; Fax: 504-537-4408.
Catechesis/Religious Programs—Students 527.
St. Mary's Nativity (1850), Rev. Msgr. Donald L. Ledet; Rev. Robert Rogers. In res., Very Rev. Stanislaus J. Manikowski.
Res., 3500 Hwy. 1, 70394. Tel: 504-537-3204; Fax: 504-537-3235. [CEM]
School—(Grades PreK-6) P.O. Box K, 70394. Tel: 504-537-7544; Fax: 504-537-4020.
Lay Teachers 8; Students 216.
Catechesis/Religious Programs—Students 233.

Schriever, Terrebonne Parish, St. Bridget (1912), Rev. Scott Dugas.
Res., 100 Hwy. 311, 70395. Tel: 504-446-6801; Fax: 504-448-2764. [CEM]
Catechesis/Religious Programs—Students 302.

Theriot, Terrebonne Parish, St. Eloi (1875), Rev. Carl P. Collins; Deacons Glenn Porche; Daniel Bascle.
Res., 1335 Bayou Dularge Rd., 70397. Tel: 504-872-2946; Fax: 504-872-9961.
Catechesis/Religious Programs—Tel: 504-851-6893.
Students 219.

Chaplains of Public Institutions

HOUMA. *Terrebonne Parish General Hospital.* Vacant.
THIBODAUX. *Nicholls State University.* Rev. Alexander M. Francisco.
Thibodaux General Hospital. Rev. Alexander M. Francisco.

Special and other Diocesan Assignment:
Reverend Monsignors—
Songy, James B., V.G.

On Duty Outside the Diocese:
Reverend Fathers—
Cao, John

On Leave:
Reverend Fathers—
Bergeron, Albert G.
Chaisson, Louis
Charpentier, Dale
Coyne, Joseph
Decell, Stephen
McCool, Malachy
Melancon, Robert
Prinz, Gerald
Violette, Tex

Retired:
Reverend Monsignors—
Boudreaux, Roland, 142 Elmo Ln., Thibodaux, LA 70301
Koninkx, William, P.O. Box 1066, Houma, LA 70361
Reverend Fathers—
Brewerton, Peter H., P.O. Box 1404, Thibodaux, LA 70302
Broussard, Hubert C., Chateau Creole, 220 Monarch Dr., Apt. J13, Houma, LA 70360
Daigle, H.C. Paul, 1915 Branard St., Apt.16, Houston, TX 77098
Finnegan, Michael, Malta Park Apt.107-1101Aline, New Orleans, LA 70115
Fossier, Emile, P.O. Box 4014, Houma, LA 70361
Landry, George A., 1016 France St., New Orleans, LA 70117
Manikowski, Stanislaus J., P.O. Box 527, Raceland, LA 70394
Newfield, John L., 2832 Burdette St., Apt. 428, New Orleans, LA 70125-2514
Pol, Dom Te, 3596 Friendswood, Apt.#6, Houma, LA 70363
Richardson, Albert, 3730 Fairfield Ave., Schreveport, LA 71104
Toth, Victor, 57 Marcus Mitchell Rd., Picayune, MS 39466
Whitney, Philip, 1201 Cardinal Dr., Thibodaux, LA 70302

Permanent Deacons:
Authement, Douglas, Maria Immacolata, Houma
Bascle, Daniel, St. Eloi, Theriot
Blanchard, Edward, St. Mary's Nativity, Raceland
Burregi, Sammy, Sacred Heart, Cut Off
Cantrelle, Michael, Holy Rosary, Larose
Didier, James V., St. Bridget Church, Schriever
Domangue, Kurt J., Holy Family Church, Grand Caillou
Dragna, Andrew J., Holy Cross, Morgan City
Dufrene, Roland, St. Hilary of Poitiers, Raceland
Dusse, Robert, St. Bernadette, Houma
Duthu, James, Annunziata, Houma
Fanguy, Bernard A. Harold, Holy Family, Grand Caillou
Giroir, Charles, Christ the Redeemer, Thibodaux
Hopkins, James, Holy Savior, Lockport
Kurtz, Harold, Our Lady of the Most Holy Rosary, Houma
Landry, Alduce, St. Charles, Thibodaux
LeBouef, Raymond, Holy Rosary, Houma
Legendre, Paul Joseph, Jr., St. Genevieve, Thibodaux
Marts, Melvin, St. Joseph, Galliano
Messina, Nick, St. Anthony, Bayou Black
Orgeron, Willie R., St. Joseph Co-Cathedral, Thibodaux
Porche, Glenn, St. Eloi, Theriot
Pujals, Pedro P., St. Thomas Aquinas, Thibodaux
Rabalais, Bertrand A., Annunziata, Houma
Uzee, Dickey, St. Mary's Nativity, Raceland

INSTITUTIONS LOCATED IN THE DIOCESE

[A] HIGH SCHOOLS, DIOCESAN

HOUMA. *Vandebilt Catholic High,* 209 S. Hollywood Rd., 70360. Tel: 504-876-2551; Fax: 504-868-9774. Brothers of the Sacred Heart. Mr. David Keife, Prin.; Bro. Carl Evans, S.C., Chap. Brothers 4; Lay Teachers 57; Junior High Students 397; Senior High Students 509.

THIBODAUX. *Edward Douglas White Catholic High.* (Coed), 555 Cardinal Dr., 70301. Tel: 504-446-8486; Fax: 504-448-1275. Brothers of the Sacred Heart. Mr. Gary Phillips, Prin. Brothers 4; Sisters 1; Lay Teachers 48; Students 777.
E.D. White Catholic High School Foundation, Inc.
E.D. White Catholic High School Alumni Association.

MORGAN CITY. *Central Catholic High,* 2100 Cedar St., 70380. Tel: 504-385-5372; Fax: 504-385-3444. Mr. Jordan Roy, Prin.; Patricia Roland, Guidance Counselor. Lay Teachers 18; Students 183.

[B] DAY CARE CENTERS

HOUMA. *St. Lucy's Day Care and Child Development Center,* P.O. Box 3894, 70361. Tel: 504-876-1246. Staff 10; Children 65.

[C] RETREAT CENTERS

SCHRIEVER. *Lumen Christi Retreat Center,* 100 Lumen Christi Ln., Hwy. 311, 70395. Tel: 504-868-1523; Fax: 504-868-1525. Rev. Duane R. Stenzel, O.F.M., Dir.

[D] CONVENTS

LOCKPORT. *Monastery of the Heart of Jesus,* 155 Church St., 70374. Dominican Contemplative Sisters of the Heart of Jesus of the Diocese of Houma-Thibodaux. Sr. Mary Henry McKanna, O.P., Prioress.

[E] MISCELLANEOUS

THIBODAUX. *Cemeteries Trust,* 949 Menard St., 70301. Tel: 504-446-0280; Fax: 504-446-1341.
The Diocese of Houma-Thibodaux Historical Research Center, 205 Audubon Ave., 70301. Tel: 504-446-2383; Fax: 504-449-0574. Rev. Msgr. Roland J. Boudreaux, Archivist.
Magnificat of the Houma-Thibodaux Diocese, 306 Cherokee Dr., 70301. Bonnie J. Bourg, Coord., Bayou River Chapter.
St. Joseph Manor. (Retirement Center), 1201 Cardinal Dr., 70301. Tel: 504-446-9050. Rev. Msgr. Francis J. Amedee, Exec. Dir.

RELIGIOUS INSTITUTES OF MEN REPRESENTED IN THE DIOCESE

For further details refer to the corresponding bracketed number in the Religious Institutes of Men or Women section.

[1100]—*Brothers of the Sacred Heart.*—S.C.
[0520]—*Franciscan Friars.*—O.F.M.
[0700]—*St. Joseph's Society of the Sacred Heart.*—S.S.J.
[1360]—*Xaverian Missionary Brothers.*—S.X.
[0200]—*Benedictine Monks.*—O.S.B.

RELIGIOUS INSTITUTES OF WOMEN REPRESENTED IN THE DIOCESE

[0400]—*Congregation of Our Lady of Mount Carmel.*—O.Carm.
[2550]—*Sisters of Mercy.*—R.S.M.
[2410]—*Congregation of the Marianites of Holy Cross.*—M.S.C.
[]—*Dominican Contemplative Sisters.*—O.P.
[1140]—*Eucharistic Missionaries of St. Dominic.*—O.P.
[2970]—*School Sisters of Notre Dame.*—S.S.N.D.
[3830]—*Sisters of St. Joseph.*—C.S.J.
[2050]—*Sisters of the Holy Spirit and Mary Immaculate.*—S.H.Sp.
[2120]—*Sisters of the Immaculate Conception.*—C.I.C.

NECROLOGY

† Hemenway, Richard F., Houma, LA, Maria Immaculata. —Died March 30, 1996.
† Mamo, Henry, (Retired). —Died Dec. 8, 1996.

Archdiocese of Indianapolis

(Archidioecesis Indianapolitana)

Most Reverend

DANIEL MARK BUECHLEIN, O.S.B., D.D.

Archbishop of Indianapolis; ordained May 3, 1964; appointed to Memphis January 20, 1987; consecrated Bishop March 2, 1987; installed March 2, 1987; appointed Archbishop of Indianapolis July 13, 1992; installed September 9, 1992.

The Archbishop Edward T. O'Meara Catholic Center: 1400 N. Meridian St., P.O. Box 1410, Indianapolis, IN, 46206. Tel.: 317-236-1400; Fax: 317-236-1401.

E-mail address: chancery@archindy.com

ESTABLISHED A DIOCESE IN 1834; ESTABLISHED AN ARCHDIOCESE DECEMBER 19, 1944 BY DECREE OF POPE PIUS XII.

Square Miles 13,757.7.

Comprises the Counties of Bartholomew, Brown, Clark, Clay, Crawford, Dearborn, Decatur, Fayette, Floyd, Franklin, Hancock, Harrison, Hendricks, Henry, Jackson, Jefferson, Jennings, Johnson, Lawrence, Marion, Monroe, Morgan, Ohio, Orange, Owen, Parke, Perry, Putnam, Ripley, Rush, Scott, Shelby, Switzerland, Union, Vermillion, Vigo, Washington and Wayne, and the township of Harrison in Spencer County, in the southern part of Indiana.

For legal titles of parishes and archdiocesan institutions, consult the Chancery Office.

STATISTICAL OVERVIEW

Personnel	
Archbishop	1
Abbots	1
Retired Abbots	2
Priests: Diocesan Active in Diocese	123
Priests: Active Outside Diocese	7
Priests: Diocesan in Foreign Missions	1
Priests: Retired, Sick or Absent	37
Number of Diocesan Priests	168
Religious Priests in Diocese	127
Extern Priests in Diocese	12
Ordinations:	
Diocesan Priests	1
Religious Priests	1
Total Brothers	60
Total Sisters	806
Parishes	
Parishes	138
With Resident Pastor:	
Resident Diocesan Priests	94
Resident Religious Priests	23
Without Resident Pastor:	
Administered by Priests	13
Administered by Women Religious	8
Missions	13
Professional Ministry Personnel:	
Brothers	2
Sisters	30
Lay Ministers	132
Welfare	
Catholic Hospitals	2
Total Assisted	1,007,174
Health Care Centers	1
Total Assisted	185
Homes for the Aged	5
Total Assisted	622
Day Care and Extended Day Care Centers	5
Total Assisted	202
Specialized Homes	3
Total Assisted	206
Special Centers for Social Services	12
Total Assisted	117,512
Educational	
Diocesan Students in Other Seminaries	34
Seminaries, Religious	1
Students Religious	113
Total Seminarians	147
Colleges and Universities	3
Total Students	2,573
High Schools, Diocesan and Parish	6
Total Students	3,306
High Schools, Private	3
Total Students	1,879
Elementary Schools, Diocesan and Parish	62
Total Students	18,767
Catechesis/Religious Education:	
High School Students	3,256
Elementary Students	10,429
Total Students Under Catholic Instruction	40,357
Teachers in the Diocese:	
Priests	5
Brothers	9
Sisters	48
Lay Teachers	1,576
Vital Statistics	
Receptions into the Church:	
Infant Baptism Totals	4,106
Adult Baptism Totals	650
Received into Full Communion	741
First Communions	3,507
Confirmations	2,379
Marriages:	
Catholic	737
Interfaith	775
Total Marriages	1,512
Deaths	1,963
Total Catholic Population	213,252
Total Population	2,201,503

The Diocese of Vincennes (now Indianapolis) was established by decree of Gregory XVI, May 6, 1834, and the See was fixed at Vincennes. The territory then comprised the entire State of Indiana and the eastern third of Illinois. By decree of Pius IX, January 8, 1857, the northern half of the State became the Diocese of Fort Wayne. The southern half of the State remained the Diocese of Vincennes.

The second Bishop of Vincennes, by Apostolic Brief, was permitted to establish his residence either at Vincennes, Madison, Lafayette or Indianapolis; the See city, however, was to remain at Vincennes. This permission was renewed to the fourth Bishop, with the exception of Lafayette. On the appointment of the fifth Bishop, he was directed to fix his residence at Indianapolis, but the Cathedral and title of the See were continued at Vincennes. By an Apostolic Brief dated March 28, 1898, the title of the Diocese was changed to that of "Diocese of Indianapolis" with the city of Indianapolis as the Episcopal See. By the same Brief the Patron Saint of the Diocese was to remain St. Francis Xavier, the title of the old Cathedral in Vincennes.

On December 19, 1944, Most Reverend Amleto Giovanni Cicognani, Apostolic Delegate to the United States, solemnly proclaimed the Papal Decree of Pope Pius XII in SS. Peter and Paul Cathedral, Indianapolis, elevating Indianapolis to the status of an Archdiocese, the State of Indiana being the Metropolitan Area. The Dioceses of Evansville and Lafayette-in-Indiana were created by the same decree and were made Suffragan Sees of Indianapolis. Upon the establishment of the Diocese of Gary on February 25, 1957, it too became a Suffragan See.

Former Bishops—Rt. Rev. SIMON GABRIEL BRUTE, S.S., D.D., cons. 1834; died 1839.—Rt. Rev. CELESTINE DE LA HAILANDIERE, D.D., cons. 1839; resigned 1847; died in France, 1882.—Rt. Rev. JOHN S. BAZIN, D.D., cons. 1847; died 1848.—Rt. Rev. MAURICE DE ST. PALAIS, D.D., cons. Jan. 14, 1849; died June 28, 1877.—Rt. Rev. FRANCIS SILAS CHATARD, D.D., cons. May 12, 1878; died Sept. 7, 1918.—Most Rev. JOSEPH CHARTRAND, D.D., cons. Titular Bishop of Flavias and Coadjutor Bishop, Sept. 15, 1910; succeeded to the See of Indianapolis, Sept. 7, 1918; died Dec. 8, 1933.—Most Rev. JOSEPH ELMER RITTER, S.T.D., cons. Titular Bishop of Hippo and Auxiliary Bishop, March 28, 1933; succeeded to the See March 24, 1934; installed as Archbishop Dec. 19, 1944; transferred to Metropolitan See of St. Louis, July 20, 1946; created Cardinal, Jan. 16, 1961; died June 10, 1967.—Most Rev. PAUL C. SCHULTE, D.D., cons. Bishop of Leavenworth, Sept. 21, 1937; appt. Archbishop of Indianapolis, July 20, 1946; installed Oct. 10, 1946; resigned Jan. 14, 1970; died Feb. 17, 1984.—Most Rev. GEORGE J. BISKUP, cons. Titular Bishop of Hermeria and Auxiliary of Dubuque, April 24, 1957; transferred to Des Moines Feb. 3, 1965 transferred to Indianapolis "cum jure successionis," July 26, 1967; succeeded to See Jan. 14, 1970; resigned March 20, 1979; died Oct. 17, 1979.—Most Rev. EDWARD T. O'MEARA, S.T.D., appt. Titular Bishop of Thisiduo and Auxiliary of St. Louis Feb. 1, 1972; cons. in the Basilica of St. Peter, Rome, Feb. 13, 1972; appt. Archbishop of Indianapolis Nov. 27, 1979; installed Jan. 10, 1980; died Jan. 10, 1992.

The Archbishop Edward T. O'Meara Catholic Center—1400 N. Meridian St., P.O. Box 1410, Indianapolis, 46206. Tel: 317-236-1400; Fax: 317-236-1401.

Vicar General and Moderator of the Curia—Very Rev. JOSEPH F. SCHAEDEL, M.S., M.Div.

Chancellor—SUZANNE L. MAGNANT.

Assistant Chancellor—Rev. PAUL D. KOETTER, M.Div.

Chief Financial Officer—JOSEPH B. HORNETT.

Board of Consultors—Most Rev. DANIEL M. BUECHLEIN, O.S.B., D.D., Chm.; Very Rev. JOSEPH F. SCHAEDEL, M.S., M.Div.; Rev. Msgr. FRANCIS R. TUOHY; Revs. STANLEY HERBER; J. PETER GALLAGHER; DANIEL MAHAN; DANIEL STAUBLIN; ANTHONY VOLZ; PAUL KOETTER.

Deaneries and Deans—Indianapolis North: Rev. PATRICK DOYLE, Indianapolis East: Rev. JOSEPH RIEDMAN, Indianapolis South: Rev. Msgr. RICHARD LAWLER,

V.F., Indianapolis West: Rev. JOHN RYAN, V.F., Batesville: Rev. WILLIAM FARRIS, O.F.M., V.F., Bloomington: Rev. CHARLES S. CHESEBROUGH, V.F., Connersville: Rev. STANLEY J. HERBER, V.F., New Albany: Rev. JOHN BEITANS, V.F., Seymour: Rev. STEPHEN BANET, V.F., Tell City: Rev. BARNABAS GILLESPIE, O.S.B., V.F., Terre Haute: Rev. ANTHONY R. VOLZ, V.F.

Council of Priests—Most Rev. DANIEL M. BUECHLEIN, O.S.B., D.D., Pres. SUZANNE MAGNANT; Very Rev. JOSEPH F. SCHAEDEL, M.S., M.Div.; Revs. JAMES BONKE; JAMES BYRNE; NOAH CASEY, O.S.B.; FRANK ECKSTEIN; JOHN HALL; J. PETER GALLAGHER; ROBERT GILDAY; STANLEY HERBER; PATRICK KELLY; PAUL KOETTER; DANIEL MAHAN; PAUL SHIKANY, Chm.; Rev. Msgr. FRANCIS R. TUOHY; Revs. ANTHONY VOLZ; MICHAEL WELCH.

Finance Council—Most Rev. DANIEL M. BUECHLEIN, O.S.B., D.D., Chm.; Very Rev. JOSEPH F. SCHAEDEL, M.S., M.Div.; JOSEPH B. HORNETT, C.F.O. L. H. BAYLEY; JAY BREHM; MICHAEL BINDNER; MIKE DILTS; JOSEPH NAUGHTON; DENNIS SCHLICHTE; DONALD WILLIAMS, *The Archbishop Edward T. O'Meara Catholic Center, 1400 N. Meridian St., P.O. Box 1410, Indianapolis, 46206.* Tel: 317-236-1421.

Priests' Personnel Board—Most Rev. DANIEL M. BUECHLEIN, O.S.B., D.D.; Revs. PATRICK DOYLE; WILLIAM ERNSTES; GERALD KIRKHOFF; JOSEPH MCNALLY; PAUL KOETTER; RAYMOND SCHAFER; LARRY VOELKER; JAMES WILMOTH, Chm.

Secretariat for Catholic Charities—THOMAS GAYBRICK, M.S.W., Sec., *The Archbishop Edward T. O'Meara Catholic Center, 1400 N. Meridian St., P.O. Box 1410, Indianapolis, 46206.* Tel: 317-236-1531.

Catholic Social Services of Central Indiana—TOM COLBERT, *The Archbishop Edward T. O'Meara Catholic Center, 1400 N. Meridian St., P.O. Box 1410, Indianapolis, 46206.* Tel: 317-236-1500.

St. Mary's Child Center—Dr. PATRICIA WELCH, Exec. Dir., *901 Dr. Martin Luther King, Jr. St., Indianapolis, 46202.* Tel: 317-635-1491.

St. Elizabeth's—(Pregnancy Services); MARY ROSE NEVITT, Exec. Dir., *2500 Churchman Ave., Indianapolis, 46203.* Tel: 317-787-3412.

St. Elizabeth's Regional Maternity Center—(Pregnancy Services); KEITH E. STORMES, Exec. Dir., *601 E. Market St., New Albany, 47150.* Tel: 812-949-7305.

Bloomington Catholic Social Services—KAREN MCCOLLOUGH, M.S.W., Dir., *3410 W. Third St., Bloomington, 47404.* Tel: 812-332-1262.

New Albany Catholic Charities—BARBARA WILLIAMS, M.S., C.S.W., Dir., *702 E. Market St., New Albany, 47150.* Tel: 812-948-0438.

Tell City Catholic Charities—802 Ninth St., Tell City, 47586. Tel: 812-547-6414.

Terre Haute Catholic Charities—JOHN ETLING, M.S., Dir., *721 Wabash Ave., Ste. 501, Terre Haute, 47807.* Tel: 812-232-1447.

Pro-Life Office—Rev. VINCENT LAMPERT, Dir. Tel: 317-236-1569.

Deanery Counseling Services—

Batesville Deanery—RENEE RUST, M.A., *420 E. Walnut St., Greensburg, 47240.* Tel: 812-663-2113.

Connersville Deanery—BILL STEELE, Ph.D., *5220 E. 74th Pl., Indianapolis, 46250.*

Seymour Deanery—CECILE BEVIN, M.A., *Columbus Counseling Services, 4550 Jonathan Moore Pike, Columbus, 47201.* Tel: 812-342-1900.

Secretariat for Finance and Administrative Services—JOSEPH B. HORNETT, Sec., *The Archbishop Edward T. O'Meara Catholic Center, 1400 N. Meridian St., P.O. Box 1410, Indianapolis, 46206.* Tel: 317-236-1421.

Accounting Services—SCOTT DENARDIN, Controller. Tel: 317-236-1410.

Catholic Cemeteries—GENE HARRIS, Dir., *9001 N. Haverstick Rd., Indianapolis, 46240.* Tel: 317-574-8898.

Human Resources—ED ISAKSON, Dir. Tel: 317-236-1594.

Information Services—JOSEPH RAUH, Dir. Tel: 317-236-1420.

Internal Auditing—JEFFREY STUMPF, Dir. Tel: 317-236-7315.

Management Services—DAVID L. HODDE, Dir. Tel: 317-236-1452.

Roman Catholic Archdiocese of Indianapolis Properties—Most Rev. DANIEL M. BUECHLEIN, O.S.B., Pres.; Very Rev. JOSEPH F. SCHAEDEL, Vice Pres. Secretaries: SUZANNE L. MAGNANT; JOSEPH B. HORNETT. Tel: 317-236-1421.

Secretariat for Leadership, Pastoral Formation and Services—SUZANNE L. MAGNANT, Sec., *The Archbishop Edward T. O'Meara Catholic Center, 1400 N. Meridian St., P.O. Box 1410, Indianapolis, 46206.* Tel: 317-236-7325.

Associate Secretary—DAVID BATHURAM. Tel: 317-236-1596.

Archives—Rev. JACK W. PORTER, Ph.D., Archivist. Tel: 317-236-1429.

Ecumenism—Rev. THOMAS J. MURPHY, Dir., *126 W. Georgia St., Indianapolis, 46225.* Tel: 317-635-2021.

Family Life—DAVID BETHURAM, Dir. Tel: 317-236-1596.

Multicultural Ministry—Rev. KENNETH TAYLOR, Dir. Tel: 317-236-1562.

Pastoral Councils—DAVID BETHURAM, Contact. Tel: 317-236-1596.

Hispanic Apostolate—Rev. MAURO RODAS, Dir., *317 N. New Jersey St., Indianapolis, 46204.* Tel: 317-637-3983.

Youth, Young Adult, Campus Ministry—JULIE SZOLEK-VANVALKENBURGH, Dir. Tel: 317-236-1439.

Secretariat for Planning, Communications and Development—DAN CONWAY, Sec., *The Archbishop Edward T. O'Meara Catholic Center, 1400 N. Meridian St., P.O. Box 1410, Indianapolis, 46206.* Tel: 317-236-1407.

Archdiocesan Newspaper, "The Criterion"—Most Rev. DANIEL M. BUECHLEIN, O.S.B, D.D., Publisher; DANIEL CONWAY, Assoc. Publisher; WILLIAM BRUNS, Exec. Editor. Tel: 317-236-1585.

Catholic Communications Center—WILLIAM BRUNS, Exec. Dir. Tel: 317-236-1585.

Catholic Community Foundation, Inc.—Most Rev. DANIEL M. BUECHLEIN, O.S.B., Chm. SANDRA BEHRINGER, Dir. Endowment Devel. Tel: 317-236-1427.

Mission Office—(formerly Office of Propagation of the Faith); Sr. MARIAN T. KINNEY, S.P., Dir. Tel: 317-236-1485.

Office of Planning—DAN CONWAY, Dir. Tel: 317-236-1407.

Office of Stewardship and Development—MICHAEL HALLORAN, Dir. Tel: 317-236-1415.

Secretariat for Spiritual and Sacramental Life—CHARLES GARDNER, Sec., *The Archbishop Edward T. O'Meara Catholic Center, 1400 N. Meridian St., P.O. Box 1410, Indianapolis, 46206.* Tel: 317-236-1483.

Evangelization Commission—Rev. JOSEPH FOLZENLOGEN, S.J., Coord. Tel: 317-236-1489.

Office of Worship—CHARLES GARDNER, Dir. Tel: 317-236-1483.

Retreat & Renewal Ministries and Fatima Retreat House—KEVIN DEPREY, Dir., *5353 E. 56th St., Indianapolis, 46226.* Tel: 317-545-7681; Fax: 317-545-0095.

Secretariat for Catholic Education—DANIEL J. ELSENER, Sec., *The Archbishop Edward T. O'Meara Catholic Center, 1400 N. Meridian St., P.O. Box 1410, Indianapolis, 46206.* Tel: 317-236-1430.

Office of Catholic Education—DANIEL J. ELSENER, Exec. Dir. Tel: 317-236-1435.

Associate Executive Director of Religious Education—JOSEPH M. KAPPEL. Tel: 317-236-1431.

Associate Director, Religious Education, Administrative Personnel and Catechists—BOB MEANEY. Tel: 317-236-1433.

Associate Executive Director, Catholic Education—G. JOSEPH PETERS. Tel: 317-236-1437.

Associate Director, Religious Education, Sacramental, Childhood and Family Catechesis—KAREN ODDI. Tel: 317-236-1432.

Associate Director, Catholic Education, Administrative Personnel and Professional Development—ANNETTE (MICKEY) LENTZ. Tel: 317-236-1438.

Associate Director, Schools, Educational Personnel and Technology—BARBARA FOX, Ph.D. Tel: 317-236-1437.

Associate Director, Catholic Education, Finance—REX CAMP. Tel: 317-236-1447.

Coordinator, Promise to Keep Program—EVE JACKSON. Tel: 317-236-1478.

Educational Resources—MARGARET KENNEDY. Tel: 317-236-1446.

Associate Director Catholic Education, Curriculum and Assessment—Sr. MICHELLE FALTUS, S.F.C.C. Tel: 317-236-1439.

Catholic Youth Organization—ED TINDER, Dir., *520 Stevens St., Indianapolis, 46203.* Tel: 317-632-9311.

Vicariate for Ministry Personnel—Rev. PAUL KOETTER, Vicar, *The Archbishop Edward T. O'Meara Catholic Center, 1400 N. Meridian St., P.O. Box 1410, Indianapolis, 46206.*

Priest Personnel—Rev. PAUL KOETTER, Dir. Tel: 317-236-1449.

Lay Ministry Personnel—MARY PAT FARNAND, Dir. Tel: 317-236-1495.

Vocations—Rev. PAUL ETIENNE, Dir. Tel: 317-236-1490.

Ministry to Priests—Rev. NOAH CASEY, O.S.B., Dir. Tel: 317-236-1491.

Vicariate Judicial Metropolitan Tribunal—Rev. FRED EASTON, J.C.L., Vicar, *The Archbishop Edward T. O'Meara Catholic Center, 1400 N. Meridian St., P.O. Box 1410, Indianapolis, 46206.* Tel: 317-236-1460.

Vice Vicars Judicial—Revs. ROBERT J. GILDAY, S.T.B.; PAUL M. SHIKANY, J.C.L.

Advocates—REBECCA BARNES; MICHAEL MAXWELL; CATHERINE LOUGH, Assoc. Advocate.

Defender of the Bond—Rev. Msgr. CHARLES E. ROSS, J.C.L., (Emeritus); Revs. JAMES R. BONKE, J.C.L.; NATHANIAL REEVES, O.S.B., J.C.L.; JOSEPH DOOLEY.

Archdiocesan Judges—Revs. CLEMENT DAVIS; JOHN DEDE; BERNARD HEAD; HERMAN LUTZ; RICHARD MUELLER; JOHN SCIARRA; Rev. Msgr. FRANCIS TUOHY.

Judge Instructor—JEAN GALANTI.

Notaries—BARBARA ADAMS; CATHERINE FISLAR; PEGGY FLECKER; LORRAINE KLEMM.

Indiana Provincial Tribunal of Second Instance—Rev. FRED EASTON, J.C.L., Vicar Judicial.

Groups with Liaison to the Archdiocese

Activities for the National Shrine of the Immaculate Conception, Washington, D.C.—Rev. JOHN BEITANS, Archdiocesan Dir., *8310 St. John Rd., Floyds Knob, 47119.* Tel: 812-923-5785.

Archdiocesan Black Catholics Concerned—Bro. HOWARD P. STUDIVANT, O.S.B., *P.O. Box 88078, Indianapolis, 46208-0078.*

Archdiocesan Council of Catholic Women—Mrs. RUTH BURNS, Pres.; Rev. ALBERT AJAMIE, Chap., *814 S. 34th St., Terre Haute, 47803.* Tel: 812-235-2561.

Archdiocesan Deaf Apostolate—Rev. BERNARD COX, Dir., *1711 "I" St., Bedford, 47421.* Tel: 812-275-6539. Rev. JOSEPH W. DOOLEY, *8021 Guion Rd., Indianapolis, 46268.* Tel: 317-872-5485.

Beginning Experience—Family Life Office, P.O. Box 1410, Indianapolis, 46206. Tel: 317-236-1596.

Boy Scouts of America and Girl Scouts of America—Rev. THOMAS L. SCHLIESSMANN, Archdiocesan Chap., *270 S. Bond St., Scottsburg, 47170.* Tel: 812-752-3693. KERRY D. BLANFORD, Chm., Catholic Committee on Scouting, *456 E. Epler Ave., Indianapolis, 46227.* Tel: 317-782-0437.

Catholic Charismatic Renewal of Central Indiana—LEN BIELSKI, State Rep., *2960 N. Meridian St., Indianapolis, 46201.* Tel: 317-547-8100. Rev. PAUL LANDWERLEN, Liaison for Archdiocese, *4218 E. Michigan Rd., Shelbyville, 46176.* Tel: 317-398-4028.

Censor of Books—Very Rev. JOSEPH F. SCHAEDEL; Revs. MATTHIAS NEUMAN, O.S.B.; CONRAD LOUIS, O.S.B., S.T.D., S.S.L.; DANIEL MAHAN.

Catholic Widowed Organization—Family Life Office, P.O. Box 1410, Indianapolis, 46206. Tel: 317-236-1596.

Cursillo—TOM HANAFEE, Lay Dir., *4960 E. 10th St., Indianapolis, 46201.* Tel: 317-353-8488.

Daughters of Isabella—MARY LOU MCELLHINEY, State Regent, *RR 2, P.O. Box 67, Fort Branch, 47648.* Tel: 812-753-3133.

Equiestrian Order of the Holy Sepulchre of Jerusalem—North Central Lieutenancy. GEORGE MALEY, State Rep., *4521 N. Meridian St., Indianapolis, 46208.*

Focolare - New Families Movement—JOHN WELCH; MARY WELCH. Tel: 317-845-8133.

Hibernians, Ancient Order of—JAMES MCGINLEY, Pres.; Rev. GLENN O'CONNOR, Chap., *1121 Roseway Dr., Indianapolis, 46219.* Tel: 317-352-1076.

Holy Childhood Association—Sr. MARIAN KINNEY, S.P., Acting Dir.

Indiana Catholic Conference—Dr. M. DESMOND RYAN, Exec. Sec., *1400 N. Meridian St., P.O. Box 1410, Indianapolis, 46206.* Tel: 317-236-1455.

Indiana Interreligious Commission on Human Equality—1100 W. 42nd St., Indianapolis, 46208. Tel: 317-924-4226. Representatives: Rev. THOMAS MURPHY; LILLIAN STEVENSON.

Knights of Columbus—MARK DIAZ, Pres., Indianapolis Chapter, *110 Rush Ct., Fishers, 46038.* Tel: 317-845-1044.

Knights and Ladies of Peter Claver—Indianapolis Central Committee. CURTISS GWYNN, Pres., *3024 Sutherland Ave., Indianapolis, 46205.*

Knights of St. John—DON SPRINGMEYER, Indiana Grand Commander, *214 W. 2nd St., Greensburg, 47240.* Tel: 812-663-3544.

Latvian Catholic Association—JANIS SVENTECKIS, Pres., *5849 Brouse Ave., Indianapolis, 46220.* Tel: 317-253-4684. Rev. JOHN BEITANS, Chap., *8310 St. John Rd., Floyds Knob, 47119.* Tel: 812-923-5785.

Legatus Society / Indiana—ROBERT C. SMITH, Pres., *Plastic Welding Technology, 6849 E. 32nd, Indianapolis, 46226-6160.* Tel: 317-541-0112. Very Rev. JOSEPH SCHAEDEL, Chap., *1400 N. Meridian, Indianapolis, 46202.*

Marriage Encounter of Central Indiana—DAVE TIMMERMAN; MARY TIMMERMAN, *2014 Jasmine Dr., Indianapolis, 46219.* Tel: 317-897-2052.

Oblates of St. Benedict of Our Lady of Grace Monastery—Sr. ANTOINETTE PURCELL, O.S.B., Dir., *1402 Southern Ave., Beech Grove, 46107.* Tel: 317-787-3287.

Oblates of St. Benedict of St. Meinrad—Rev. MICHAEL KEENE, O.S.B., Dir., *St. Meinrad, 47577.* Tel: 812-357-6752.

St. Thomas More Society—PATRICIA MARSHALL, Pres., *One Indiana Sq., Indianapolis, 46204.* Tel: 317-634-9777. Rev. THOMAS J. MURPHY, Chap., *126 W. Georgia St., Indianapolis, 46225.* Tel: 317-635-2021.

Secular Franciscan Order—Holy Stigmata Fraternity and Sacred Heart Fraternity. Rev. ELIAS KOPPERT, O.F.M., Spiritual Asst., *Sacred Heart Church, 1530 Union St., Indianapolis, 46225.* Tel: 317-638-5551. People of Peace Fraternity. Sr. NORMA ROCKLAGE, O.S.F., Spiritual Asst., *Marion College, 3200 Cold Spring Rd., Indianapolis, 46222.* Tel: 317-929-0229.

Secular Order of Discalced Carmelites—Indianapolis: Sr. JEAN MARIE HESSBURG, Spiritual Advisor, *Monastery of the Resurrection, 2500 Cold Spring Rd., Indianapolis, 46222.* Tel: 317-926-5654. Terre Haute: Sr. THERESA HEWITT, Spiritual Advisor, *Monastery of St. Joseph, 59 Allendale, Terre Haute, 47802.* Tel: 812-299-1410.

Serra Club—Indianapolis: HUGH SULLIVAN, Pres., *7135 Kingswood Cir., Indianapolis, 46256.* Tel: 317-849-0580. Rev. THOMAS MURPHY, Chap.; Terre Haute: ROD BOSLEY, Pres., *219 1/2 S. 19th St., Terre Haute, 47803.* Tel: 812-238-7411. Rev. LAWRENCE J. MORAN, Chap.

Society of St. Raphael - A Catholic Physician's Guild—Very Rev. JOSEPH F. SCHAEDEL, M.S., M.Div., Chap.; Mr. WILLIAM BRUNS, Contact, *The O'Meara Catholic Center, P.O. Box 1410, Indianapolis, 46206.* Tel: 317-236-1585.

Sovereign Military Order of Malta—EUGENE WITCHGER, Archdiocesan Rep., *210 W. 77th St., Indianapolis, 46260.*

Teams of Our Lady—Family Life Office, P.0. Box 1410, Indianapolis, 46206. Tel: 317-236-1596. CARL WEBER. Tel: 317-353-8186. MARIE WEBER. Tel: 317-353-8186.

Tobit—COURTLAND BYRAM, Council Pres., *Fatima Retreat House, 5353 E. 56th St., Indianapolis, 46226.* Tel: 317-545-7681.

Young Widowed Group—Family Life Office, P.O. Box 1410, Indianapolis, 46206. Tel: 317-236-1596.

CLERGY, PARISHES, MISSIONS AND PAROCHIAL SCHOOLS

CITY OF INDIANAPOLIS
(Marion County)

1—SS. PETER AND PAUL CATHEDRAL (1892), Rev. Richard M. Ginther. In res., Revs. James R. Bonke; Paul D. Koetter.
Res., 1347 N. Meridian St., 46202. Tel: 317-634-4519; Fax: 317-634-0151. [JC]

2—ASSUMPTION OF THE BLESSED VIRGIN MARY (1894). Merged with St. Anthony, where sacramental records are kept.

3—CHRIST THE KING (1939), Rev. Msgr. Francis R. Tuohy. In res., Rev. Paul Etienne.
Res., 5884 N. Crittenden, 46220. Tel: 317-475-6582. Office: 5884 Crittenden Ave., 46220. Tel: 317-255-3666; Fax: 317-475-6579.
School—5858 Crittenden Ave., 46220. Tel: 317-257-9366.
Lay Teachers 25; Students 331.
Catechesis/Religious Programs—Students 93.

4—GOOD SHEPHERD (1993). (St. Catherine, 1909, and St. James the Greater, 1951, were closed, merged, and renamed in 1993). Rev. Thomas Clegg; Ed Aken, Pastoral Assoc.
Church & Parish Office: 1109 E. Cameron St., 46203. Tel: 317-783-3158. [JC]
School—Central Catholic School, 1155 E. Cameron St., 46203. Tel: 317-783-7759; Fax: 317-781-5964.
Students 205.
Catechesis/Religious Programs—Students 205.

5—HOLY ANGELS (1903) (African American), Rev. Clarence R. Waldon.
Res., 740 W. 28th St., 46208. Tel: 317-926-3324; Fax: 317-926-3325. [JC]
School—2822 Dr. Martin Luther King, Jr. St., 46208. Tel: 317-926-5211. Sr. Gerry O'Laughlin, Prin.
Sisters of St. Joseph 2; Lay Teachers 9; Students 165.
Catechesis/Religious Programs—Students 50.

6—HOLY CROSS (1895), Rev. Lawrence Voelker.
Church—125 N. Oriental St., 46202. Tel: 317-637-2620.
School—Tel: 317-638-9068.
Lay Teachers 13; Students 218.

7—HOLY ROSARY (1909) (Italian), Sr. Jean Marie Cleveland, O.S.F., Parish Life Coord.; Revs. Lawrence Voelker; Thomas Clegg, Priest Moderator.
Office: 520 Stevens St., 46203. Tel: 317-636-4478; Fax: 317-636-2522. [JC]

8—HOLY SPIRIT (1946), Revs. Joseph G. Riedman; Henry F. Tully. In res., Rev. Peter Gallagher.
Res., 7243 E. 10th St., 46219. Tel: 317-353-9404; Fax: 317-351-1707.
School—7241 E. 10th St., 46219. Tel: 317-352-1243.
Lay Teachers 23; Students 479.
Catechesis/Religious Programs—Tel: 317-357-6915.
Students 346.

9—HOLY TRINITY (1906), Rev. Kenneth E. Taylor; Sr. Anita Eberle, O.S.B., Pastoral Assoc.
Res., 2618 W. St. Clair St., 46222. Tel: 317-631-2939; Fax: 317-631-2921. [JC]
School—All Saints. Consolidated. See St. Anthony listing.

10—IMMACULATE HEART OF MARY (1946), Rev. Jeffery H. Godecker.
Parish Center: 5692 N. Central Ave., 46220. Tel: 317-257-2266; Fax: 317-475-7380. [JC]
Res., 5683 Washington Blvd., 46220. Tel: 317-252-5737.
School—317 E. 57th St., 46220. Tel: 317-255-5468; Fax: 317-475-7379.
Lay Teachers 30; Students 363.

11—NATIVITY OF OUR LORD JESUS CHRIST (1947), Rev. Steven Schwab.
7225 Southeastern Ave., 46239. Tel: 317-357-1200. [JC]
School—3310 S. Meadow Dr., 46239. Tel: 317-357-1459.
Sisters of Providence 2; Lay Teachers 8; Students 198.
Catechesis/Religious Programs—Tel: 317-359-6075.
Students 210.

12—OUR LADY OF LOURDES (1909). Unassigned.
Res., 5333 E. Washington St., 46219. Tel: 317-356-7291.
School—30 S. Downey St., 46219. Tel: 317-357-3316.
Lay Teachers 21; Students 454.

13—SACRED HEART OF JESUS (1875) (German), Revs. Robert Sieg, O.F.M.; Elias Koppert, O.F.M.; Justin Belitz, O.F.M.; Frank Jasper, O.F.M.
Res., 1530 S. Union St., 46225. Tel: 317-638-5551; Fax: 317-637-9741. [JC]
School—Central Catholic Consolidated. See Good Shepherd Listing. Tel: 317-783-7759.

14—ST. ANDREW THE APOSTLE (1946), Sr. Marilyn Herber, S.P., Parish Life Coord.; Revs. Pat Kelly; Mark Svarczkopf, Priest Moderator.
Parish Office: 3922 E. 38th St., 46218-1496. Tel: 317-546-1571; Fax: 317-549-6311. [JC]
School & Daycare: Tel: 317-549-6305; Fax: 317-549-6306.
Lay Teachers 20; Students 285.

15—ST. ANN (1917), Rev. Stephen W. Giannini; Laura Williams, Pastoral Assoc.
Office: 2862 S. Holt Rd., 46241. Tel: 317-244-3750.
Res., 2850 S. Holt Rd., 46241. [JC]
Catechesis/Religious Programs—Students 80.

16—ST. ANTHONY (1891) (Irish-German), Rev. John T. Ryan, V.F. In res., Very Rev. Joseph F. Schaedel.
Res., 379 N. Warman Ave., 46222. Tel: 317-636-4828. [JC]
School—All Saints Consolidated, 337 N. Warman Ave, 46222. Tel: 317-636-3739.
Sisters of Providence 1; Lay Teachers 8; Students 166.
Catechesis/Religious Programs—Students 174.

17—ST. BARNABAS (1965), Revs. Joseph McNally; J. Patrick Mercier. In res., Rev. John N. Sciarra, (Retired).
Res., 8300 Rahke Rd., 46217. Tel: 317-882-0724; Fax: 317-887-8932.
School—Tel: 317-881-7422; Fax: 317-887-8933. Paulette Conner, Prin.
Lay Teachers 23; Students 540.
Catechesis/Religious Programs—Tel: 317-881-0631.
Students 390.

18—ST. BERNADETTE (1952), In res., Rev. Noah Casey, O.S.B.
Church—4826 Fletcher Ave., 46203. Tel: 317-356-5867.

19—ST. BRIDGET (1880). Closed. For inquiries for parish records contact SS. Peter and Paul Cathedral.

20—ST. CATHERINE (1909). Merged with St. James the Greater (1951) and renamed Good Shepherd in 1993.

21—ST. CHRISTOPHER (1937), Rev. D. Michael Welch. Pastoral Assocs.: Sr. Sue Bradshaw, O.S.F.; Sr. Marie Wolf, S.P.; Mr. Bill Szolek Van Valkenburgh; Nancy L. Meyer. In res., Rev. Robert J. Gilday.
Res., 5301 W. 16th St., Indianapolis, 46224. Tel: 317-241-6314; Fax: 317-241-6587.
School—5335 W. 16th St., Indianapolis, 46224. Mrs. Barbara Leek, Prin.
Lay Teachers 12; Students 229.
Catechesis/Religious Programs—Ms. Therese Brennan, D.R.E.
Students 305.

22—ST. FRANCIS DE SALES (1881). Closed. For inquiries for parish records contact St. Rita. Parish territory incorporated by four neighboring parishes: St. Andrew, St. Philip Neri, St. Rita, and St. Therese.

23—ST. GABRIEL THE ARCHANGEL (1963), Rev. William G. Marks; Sr. Mary Timothy Kavanaugh, O.S.F., Pastoral Assoc. In res., Rev. Frederick C. Easton.
Res., 5813 Sunwood Dr., 46224. Tel: 317-291-7014.
School—(Grades K-8) 6000 W. 34th, 46224. Tel: 317-297-1414.
Teachers 21; Students 308.
Catechesis/Religious Programs—Tel: 317-299-9924.
Students 68.

24—ST. JAMES THE GREATER (1951). Merged with St. Catherine (1909) and renamed Good Shepherd in 1993.

25—ST. JOAN OF ARC (1921), Rev. Patrick A. Doyle. In res., Rev. James Chambers, S.J.
Res., 4217 Central Ave., 46205. Tel: 317-283-5508; Fax: 317-283-5511. [JC]
School—500 E. 42nd St., 46205. Tel: 317-283-1518.
Lay Teachers 11; Students 160.
Catechesis/Religious Programs—Students 57.

26—ST. JOHN THE EVANGELIST (1837) (Irish), Rev. Thomas Murphy.
Res., 126 W. Georgia St., 46225. Tel: 317-635-2021. [JC]

27—ST. JOSEPH (1949). (Old St. Joseph, 1873-1949. Closed. Sacramental records are kept at New St. Joseph parish.). Rev. Glenn L. O'Connor. In res., Rev. Mark Tran-Xuan Thanh (Vietnam).
Res., 1375 S. Mickley Ave., 46241. Tel: 317-244-9002. [JC]
School—All Saints Consolidated. See St. Anthony Listing.

28—ST. JUDE (1959), Rev. Gerald J. Kirkhoff.
Res., 5353 McFarland Rd., 46227. Tel: 317-786-4371; 780-7588; Fax: 317-780-7592.
School—5375 McFarland Rd, 46227. Tel: 317-784-6828.
Sisters of Providence 2; Sisters of St. Joseph 1; Lay Teachers 20; Students 515.
Catechesis/Religious Programs—Tel: 317-780-7591.
Students 270.

29—ST. LAWRENCE (1949), Revs. Mark A. Svarczkopf; Thomas Stepanski, S.T.; Jeong Uk Kim, (Korean Community). In res., Rev. Henry Brown.
Office: 6944 E. 46th St., 46226. Tel: 317-546-4065; Fax: 317-543-4926.
Res., 4650 N. Shadeland Ave., 46226. Tel: 317-543-4921.
School—6950 E. 46th St., 46226. Tel: 317-543-4923.
Sisters of St. Francis 1; Lay Teachers 23; Students 433.

30—ST. LUKE (1961), Revs. Daniel J. Mahan; Kenneth J. Ciano.
Res., 7575 Holliday Dr., E., 46260. Tel: 317-259-4373; Fax: 317-254-3210. [JC]
School—7650 N. Illinois St., 46260. Tel: 317-255-3912.
Lay Teachers 30; Students 477.
Catechesis/Religious Programs—Tel: 317-479-7373.
Students 315.

31—ST. MARK THE EVANGELIST (1946), Rev. Msgr. Richard C. Lawler.
Res., 535 E. Edgewood, 46227. Tel: 317-787-8246; Fax: 317-781-6466.
School—541 E. Edgewood Ave., 46227. Tel: 317-786-4013.
Lay Teachers 22; Students 341.
Catechesis/Religious Programs—Students 368.

32—ST. MARY/IMMACULATE CONCEPTION (1858), Rev. Mauro G. Rodas.
Res., 317 N. New Jersey St., 46204. Tel: 317-637-3983. [JC]
Catechesis/Religious Programs—The Marian Center, 311 N. New Jersey St., 46204.
Students 75.

33—ST. MATTHEW THE APOSTLE (1958), Rev. Donald L. Schmidlin. In res., Revs. Patrick J. Kelly; Jack Okon; Bros. Joseph Umile, C.S.C.; Brian Guerrini, S.S.C.C.
Res., 4100 E. 56th St., 46220. Tel: 317-257-4297; 479-2382 (Rectory); Fax: 317-479-2381. [CEM]
School—Tel: 317-251-3997.
Sisters 1; Lay Teachers 28; Students 502.
Catechesis/Religious Programs—Tel: 317-257-9733.

Students 115.

34—ST. MICHAEL THE ARCHANGEL (1948), Rev. James R. Wilmoth.
Res., 3354 W. 30th St., 46222. Tel: 317-926-7359; Fax: 317-921-3282.
School—3352 W. 30th St., 46222. Tel: 317-926-0516.
Lay Teachers 15; Students 306.
Catechesis/Religious Programs—Tel: 317-925-7597.
Students 138.

35—ST. MONICA (1956), Revs. Clement T. Davis; Joseph B. Moriarty.
Res., 6131 N. Michigan Rd., 46228. Tel: 317-253-2193; Fax: 317-253-3342.
School—Tel: 317-255-7153.
Lay Teachers 20; Students 330.
Catechesis/Religious Programs—Tel: 317-257-3043.
Students 423.

36—ST. PATRICK (1865), Revs. Larry Voelker; Thomas Fox, O.F.M., (Hispanic Ministry); Sr. Mary Slattery, S.P., Pastoral Assoc.; Sr. Jean Marie Cleveland, O.S.F., Parish Life Coord.
Church—950 Prospect St., 46203. Tel: 317-631-5824.
School—Consolidated. See Central Catholic Good Shepherd Parish.

37—ST. PHILIP NERI (1909), Rev. Herman G. Lutz; Mr. Tom Bogenschutz, Pastoral Assoc. In res., Rev. Carlton Beever.
Res., 550 N. Rural St., 46201. Tel: 317-631-8746; Fax: 317-632-8161. [JC]
School—545 Eastern Ave., 46201. Tel: 317-636-0134.
Lay Teachers 15; Students 230.
Catechesis/Religious Programs—Students 218.

38—ST. PIUS X (1955), Rev. Martin A. Peter. In res., Rev. David F. Coons.
Res., 7200 Sarto Dr., 46240. Tel: 317-255-4534; Fax: 317-466-3354.
School—Tel: 317-466-3361.
Lay Teachers 24; Students 501.
Catechesis/Religious Programs—Tel: 317-257-1085.
Students 313.

39—ST. RITA (1919), Rev. Anthony Clark, S.V.D. In res., Revs. Charles Smith, S.V.D.; Kenneth Hamilton, S.V.D.; Chester Smith, S.V.D.
Res., 1733 Dr. Andrew J. Brown Ave., 46202. Tel: 317-632-9349; Fax: 317-687-0973. [JC]
School—1850 N. Arsenal Ave., 46218. Tel: 317-636-8580. Kathleen Sadlowski, Prin.
Lay Teachers 15; Students 199.

40—ST. ROCH (1922) (German), Rev. J. Michael Ewert, O.F.M.
Res., 3600 S. Pennsylvania St., 46227. Tel: 317-784-1763; Fax: 317-783-9617. [JC]
School—3603 S. Meridian St., 46217. Tel: 317-784-9144.
Lay Teachers 13; Students 240.

41—ST. SIMON (1961), Rev. Larry P. Crawford; Larry Hembree, Pastoral Assoc. In res., Rev. Ronald Ashmore.
Res., 8400 Roy Rd., 46219. Tel: 317-898-1707; Fax: 317-899-9719.
School—Tel: 317-898-1666.
Sisters 2; Lay Teachers 17; Students 276.
Catechesis/Religious Programs—Tel: 317-899-4997.
Students 158.

42—ST. THERESE OF THE INFANT JESUS (LITTLE FLOWER) (1925), Rev. Kilian Kerwin, O.S.B.
Res., 4720 E. 13th St., 46201. Tel: 317-357-8352; Fax: 317-357-5316. [JC]
School—1401 N. Bosart Ave, 46202. Tel: 317-353-2282.
Lay Teachers 22; Students 485.
Catechesis/Religious Programs—Students 640.

43—ST. THOMAS AQUINAS (1939), Rev. William G. Munshower.
Office: 4625 N. Kenwood Ave., 46208. Tel: 317-253-1461; Fax: 317-253-1461.
Res., 4650 N. Illinois St., 46208. Tel: 317-253-4112.
School—4600 N. Illinois St., 46208. Tel: 317-255-6244.
Lay Teachers 12; Students 213.

OUTSIDE THE CITY OF INDIANAPOLIS

Aurora, Dearborn Co., St. Mary of the Immaculate Conception (1857), Rev. Raymond E. Schafer.
203 Fourth St., 47001. Tel: 812-926-0060; Fax: 812-926-4439.
Res., 254 Decatur St., 47001. Tel: 812-926-0644.
School—211 Fourth St., 47001. Tel: 812-926-1558.
Lay Teachers 9; Students 164.
Catechesis/Religious Programs—Students 80.

Batesville, Ripley Co., St. Louis (1868), Revs. William J. Farris, O.F.M.; Louis Bartko, O.F.M.; Alphonse Hoff, O.F.M., (Retired).
Res., 13 St. Louis Pl., 47006. Tel: 812-934-3204; Fax: 812-933-0667. [CEM]
School—17 St. Louis Pl., 47006. Tel: 812-934-3310; Fax: 812-934-6202.
Lay Teachers 24; Students 440.
Catechesis/Religious Programs—Students 268.

Bedford, Lawrence Co., St. Vincent de Paul (1864), Rev. Bernard Cox.
Res., 1711 I St., 47421. Tel: 812-275-6539; Fax: 812-275-3493.
School—913 18th St., 47421. Tel: 812-279-2540.
Lay Teachers 9; Students 171.
Catechesis/Religious Programs—Students 114.

Beech Grove, Marion Co., Holy Name (1908), Rev. Gerald F. Burkert. In res., Rev. Joseph F. Rautenberg.
Res., 89 N. 17th Ave., 46107. Tel: 317-784-5454; Fax: 317-784-1834. [JC]
School—21 N. 17th Ave., 46107. Tel: 317-784-9078. Jeanette Colburn, Prin.
Lay Teachers 17; Students 277.
Catechesis/Religious Programs—Students 129.

Bloomington, Monroe Co., St. Charles Borromeo (1864), Rev. Charles S. Chesebrough.
Res., 2222 E. Third St., 47401. Tel: 812-336-6846; Fax: 812-331-6732.
School—(Grades PreK-8) 2224 E. Third St., 47401. Tel: 812-336-5853; Fax: 812-349-0300.
Lay Teachers 30; Students 475.
Catechesis/Religious Programs—Tel: 812-334-1664.
Students 190.

St. John the Apostle (1970), Rev. Daniel B. Donohoo.
Res., 3410 W. Third St., 47404. Tel: 812-339-6006; Fax: 812-339-0400.
Catechesis/Religious Programs—Students 144.

St. Paul Catholic Center (1969), Revs. Daniel Atkins; Michael O'Mara.
Res., 1413 E. 17th St., 47408. Tel: 812-339-5561; Fax: 812-333-4846.
Catechesis/Religious Programs—Students 186.

Bradford, Harrison Co., St. Michael (1835), Rev. Bernard V. Koopman.
Mailing Address: P.O. Box 22, 47107. Tel: 812-364-6646; Fax: 812-364-6614. [CEM]
Catechesis/Religious Programs—Tel: 812-364-6173.
Students 234.

Brazil, Clay Co., Annunciation of the Blessed Virgin Mary (1865), Rev. Anthony P. Spicuzza.
Res., 19 N. Alabama St., 47834. Tel: 812-448-1901. [CEM]
School—Tel: 812-448-1394.
Lay Teachers 4; Students 88.
Mission—Diamond, Parke Co., St. Mary.

Brookville, Franklin Co., St. Michael (1845), Rev. Louis E. Schumacher.
Res., 354 High St., P.O. Box J, 47012. Tel: 317-647-5462. [CEM]
School—145 Wallace St., P.O. Box J, 47012. Tel: 317-647-4961.
Sisters of the Third Order Regular of St. Francis 2; Lay Teachers 10; Students 240.

Brownsburg, Hendricks Co., St. Malachy (1869), Rev. Daniel J. Staublin; Very Rev. Joseph F. Schaedel, Vicar Gen.
Parish Center: 326 N. Green St., 46112. Tel: 317-852-3195; Fax: 317-852-8939. [CEM 2]
School—330 N. Green St., 46112. Tel: 317-852-2242; Fax: 317-852-3604.
Lay Teachers 22; Students 391.
Catechesis/Religious Programs—Tel: 317-852-8476.
Students 595.

Brownstown, Jackson Co., Our Lady of Providence (1934). Attended by St. Ambrose, Seymour. Rev. Joseph B. Sheets, Admin.
Res., Hwy. 50, 47220.

Cambridge City, Wayne Co., St. Elizabeth of Hungary (1852), Rev. John H. Luerman.
Res., 333 W. Maple St., 47327. Tel: 317-478-3242.
Catechesis/Religious Programs—Students 158.

Cannelton, Perry Co., St. Michael (1859), Revs. Severin Messick, O.S.B.; Benet Amato, O.S.B.
Parish Office: c/o St. Paul, 802 Ninth St., Tell City, 47586. Tel: 812-547-7994; Fax: 812-547-6985.
Res., 814 Jefferson St., Tell City, 47586.
Church—Eighth St., 47520. [CEM]

Cedar Grove, Franklin Co., Holy Guardian Angels (1874) (German), Rev. Louis Schumacher, Admin.
Res., 405 U.S. Hwy. 52, 47016. Tel: 317-647-6981. [CEM]
Res., 354 High St., Brookville, 47012. Tel: 317-647-5462.
Catechesis/Religious Programs—Students 66.

Charlestown, Clark Co., St. Michael (1860), Rev. Stephen Donahue.
Res., 101 St. Michael Dr., 47111. Tel: 812-256-3200. [CEM]
School—102 St. Michael Dr., 47111. Tel: 812-256-3503.
Lay Teachers 2; Students 17.
Catechesis/Religious Programs—Students 52.
Mission—Henryville, Clark Co., St. Francis Xavier, (1869) Hwy. 31 & 160, P.O. Box 368, Henryville, 47126.

China, Jefferson Co., St. Anthony (1861). Merged with St. Michael, St. Patrick, and St. Mary, Madison, and renamed Prince of Peace, Madison, where sacramental records are kept.

Clarksville, Clark Co., St. Anthony of Padua (1851), Rev. Dismas J. Veeneman, O.F.M.Conv. In res., Revs. James Oberhausen, O.F.M.Conv.; Arnold Dearing, O.F.M.Conv.; Bro. Ray Ramos, O.F.M.Conv.
Res., 310 N. Sherwood Ave., 47129. Tel: 812-282-2290; Fax: 812-283-3924. [CEM]
School—320 N. Sherwood Ave., 47129. Tel: 812-282-2144.
Sisters of St. Benedict 1; Lay Teachers 23; Students 398.
Catechesis/Religious Programs—Students 62.

Clinton, Vermillion Co., Sacred Heart (1891), Rev. Micheal Kelley.
Office: 656 S. Sixth St., 47842.
Res., 558 Nebeker St., 47842. Tel: 317-832-8468; Fax: 317-832-2549.
School—610 S. Sixth St., 47842. Tel: 317-832-3228.
Lay Teachers 6; Students 82.
Mission—Universal, Vermillion Co., St. Joseph, (1920) Universal, 47884.

Columbus, Bartholomew Co., St. Bartholomew (1994). St Bartholomew (1841) and St. Columbus (1963) were closed, merged, and renamed St. Bartholomew, where the sacramental records for both parishes are kept. Revs. Stephen J. Banet; Christopher A. Craig.
St. Bartholomew's Catholic Parish: 845 Eighth St., 47201. Tel: 812-379-9353; Fax: 812-375-0720.
Res., 1302 27th St., 47201. Tel: 812-372-1509.
School—1306 27th St., 47201. Tel: 812-372-6830; Fax: 812-376-0377.
Lay Teachers 22; Students 404.
Catechesis/Religious Programs—Tel: 812-372-2207.
Students 380.

Connersville, Fayette Co., St. Gabriel (1851), Rev. Stanley J. Herber, M.A.
Res., 232 W. Ninth St., 47331. Tel: 317-825-8578; Fax: 317-827-4347. [JC]
School—(Grades PreK-6) 224 W. Ninth St., 47331. Tel: 317-825-7951. Emily Lemming, Prin.
Lay Teachers 11; Students 228.
Catechesis/Religious Programs—220 W. Ninth St., 47331. Tel: 317-825-2944. Beth Luking, D.R.E.
Students 202.

Corydon, Harrison Co., St. Joseph (1896), Rev. Ernest Waechter, O.F.M.Conv.
Res., 312 E. High St., 47112. Tel: 812-738-2742; Fax: 812-738-2718. [CEM]
School—502 N. Mulberry St., 47112. Tel: 812-738-4549.
Lay Teachers 11; Students 139.
Missions—New Middletown, Harrison Co., Most Precious Blood, (1880) 47112. [CEM]
Elizabeth, Harrison Co., St. Peter, (1849). [CEM]

Danville, Hendricks Co., Mary Queen of Peace (1939), Rev. Vincent P. Lampert.
Res., 1005 W. Main St., 46122. Tel: 317-745-4284.
Catechesis/Religious Programs—Tel: 317-745-7090.
Students 242.

Dover, Dearborn Co., St. John the Baptist (1824), Rev. Louis Manna, O.F.M.Conv.
Res., 7525 Church Ln., West Harrison, 47060. Tel: 812-576-3593. [CEM]
Church—25743 State Rte. 1, Guilford, 47022. Tel: 812-576-4302.

Edinburgh, Johnson Co., Holy Trinity (1851), Rev. Paul M. Shikany.
Res., P.O. Box 216, 46124. Tel: 812-526-9460.

Enochsburg, Decatur Co., St. John the Evangelist (1844) (German), Rev. Jonathan Stewart.
Res., 9995 E. Base Rd., Greensburg, 47240. Tel: 812-934-2880. [CEM]

Fortville, Hancock Co., St. Thomas (1869), Rev. Roger B. Gaudet.
Res., 523 S. Merrill St., 46040. Tel: 317-485-5101; Fax: 317-485-4373.
Catechesis/Religious Programs—Students 166.

Franklin, Johnson Co., St. Rose of Lima (1868), Rev. Paul M. Shikany; Jean Martin, Pastoral Assoc., Tel: 317-738-2965.
Res., 114 Lancelot Dr., 46131. Tel: 317-738-3929; Fax: 317-738-3583.
School—(Grades PreK-2). Tel: 317-738-3451. Laura Riley, Prin.
Catechesis/Religious Programs—Tel: 317-736-6754.

Students 229.

French Lick, Orange Co., Our Lady of the Springs (1887), Rev. John M. Hall.
Res., 8796 W. State Rd. 56, 47432. Tel: 812-936-4568.
Mission—Paoli, Orange Co., Our Lord Jesus Christ the King, (1948) 47432.

Frenchtown, Harrison Co., St. Bernard (1849), Rev. Frederick J. Denison.
Res., 7600 Hwy. 337 N.W., Depauw, 47115. Tel: 812-347-2326. [CEM]
Mission—Frenchtown, Crawford Co., St. Joseph, (1855) 47115.

Fulda, Spencer Co., St. Boniface (1847), Rev. Sean Hoppe, O.S.B.
Mailing Address: P.O. Box 1, 47536. Tel: 812-357-2483. [CEM]

Greencastle, Putnam Co., St. Paul the Apostle (1853), Rev. Michael C. Fritsch.
Res., 202 E. Washington St., 46135. Tel: 317-653-5678; Fax: 317-653-4377.

Greenfield, Hancock Co., St. Michael (1860), Rev. Robert E. Mazzola, S.T.B.
Res., 519 Jefferson Blvd., 46140. Tel: 317-462-4240.
School—515 Jefferson Blvd., 46140. Tel: 317-462-6380.
Lay Teachers 9; Students 169.
Catechesis/Religious Programs—Students 415.

Greensburg, Decatur Co., St. Mary (1858), Rev. Stephen Schaftlein.
Res., 302 E. McKee St., 47240. Tel: 812-663-8427; Fax: 812-663-6088. [CEM]
School—(Grades PreK-6) 210 S. East St., 47240. Tel: 812-663-2804.
Lay Teachers 14; Students 321.
Catechesis/Religious Programs—Students 234.

Greenwood, Johnson Co., Our Lady of the Greenwood (1948), Revs. Harold L. Knueven; Samuel Weber, O.S.B.; James Bonke.
Res., 335 S. Meridian St., 46143. Tel: 317-888-2861; Fax: 317-885-5006. [JC]
School—399 S. Meridian St., 46143. Tel: 317-881-1300.
Lay Teachers 25; Students 492.
Catechesis/Religious Programs—Tel: 317-885-5007.
Students 440.

SS. Francis and Clare of Assisi (1993), Rev. Stephen Jarrell.
Res., 5058 Travis Rd., 46143. Tel: 317-422-5058; Fax: 317-422-1046.

Hamburg, Franklin Co., St. Anne (1869), Rev. Jonathan Stewart.
Res., 5267 N. Hamburg Rd., Oldenburg, 47036. Tel: 812-934-5854. [CEM]

Henryville, Clark Co., St. Francis Xavier (1869). Attended by St. Michael's, 101 St. Michael Dr., Charlestown, IN. Tel: 812-256-3200. Rev. Stephen Donahue, Admin.
Church—Hwy 31 & Hwy 160, P.O. Box 368, Henryville, 47126.

Jeffersonville, Clark Co., Sacred Heart (1953), Rev. David J. Groeller. In res., Rev. H. Michael Hilderbrand.
Church & Parish Office: 1840 E. 8th St., 47103. Tel: 812-282-0423; Fax: 812-284-6673.
School—1842 E. 8th St., 47130. Tel: 812-283-3123.
Lay Teachers 16; Students 311.
Catechesis/Religious Programs—Tel: 812-283-6914.
Students 80.

St. Augustine (1853), Rev. Clifford R. Vogelsang.
Res., 315 E. Chestnut St., P.O. Box 447, 47130. Tel: 812-282-2677; Fax: 812-282-8821. [CEM]
Catechesis/Religious Programs—316 E. Maple St., Tel: 812-282-1231.
Students 128.

Knightstown, Henry Co., St. Rose (1872), Revs. Joe Rautenberg; Stanley Herber; Sr. Shirley Gerth, Parish Life Coord.
Mailing Address: P.O. Box 209, 46148. Tel: 317-345-5595.
Church—8144 W. U.S. Hwy. 40, 46148.

Lanesville, Harrison Co., St. Mary (1843) (German), Rev. Harold A. Ripperger.
Res., 2500 St. Mary's Dr., P.O. Box 144, 47136. Tel: 812-952-2853. [CEM]
Catechesis/Religious Programs—Tel: 812-952-2854.
Students 138.

Lawrenceburg, Dearborn Co., St. Lawrence (1842) (German), Rev. John Hartzer.
Res., 542 Walnut St., 47025. Tel: 812-537-3992. [CEM]
School—524 Walnut St., 47025. Tel: 812-537-3690.
Lay Teachers 9; Students 189.
Catechesis/Religious Programs—Tel: 812-537-1112.
Students 225.

Leopold, Perry Co., St. Augustine (1837), Rev. Barnabus Gillespie, O.S.B.
Res., 47551. Tel: 812-843-5143. [CEM]
Catechesis/Religious Programs—Students 180.

Liberty, Union Co., St. Bridget (1854), Rev. John O'Brien, O.S.B., Admin.
Res., 404 E. Vine St., 47353. Tel: 317-458-5412. [CEM]
Catechesis/Religious Programs—Students 82.

Madison, Jefferson Co., Prince of Peace (1993). St. Michael (1837), St. Mary (1851), St. Patrick (1853), Madison, and St. Anthony, China (1861), were closed, merged, and renamed, Prince of Peace, where their sacramental records are now kept. Rev. John A. Meyer.
Mailing Address: Catholic Community Center, 305 W. State St., 47250.
Res., 415 E. Second St., 47250. Tel: 812-265-4166. [CEM 2]
School—Pope John XXIII, (Grades K-6) 221 State St., 47250. Tel: 812-273-3957.
High School—Shawe Memorial Junior-Senior High School. See High Schools, Inter-Parochial, under Institutions Located in the Archdiocese. Tel: 812-273-2150; Fax: 812-273-6694.
Catechesis/Religious Programs—Students 88.

St. Mary. Merged with St. Anthony, China, and St. Patrick and St. Michael, Madison, to form Prince of Peace, Madison.

St. Michael. Merged with St. Anthony, China, and St. Patrick and St. Mary, Madison, to form Prince of Peace, Madison.

Martinsville, Morgan Co., St. Martin of Tours (1848), Rev. Mark Gottemoeller.
Res., 1709 E. Harrison St., 46151. Tel: 317-342-6379. [CEM]
Catechesis/Religious Programs—Tel: 317-342-8028.
Students 188.

Milan, Ripley Co., St. Charles Borromeo (1908), Rev. Msgr. Bernard R. Schmitz. In res., Rev. John J. Minta, (Retired).
Mailing Address: c/o St. Anthony, P.O. Box 2, Morris, 47033. Tel: 812-654-2009.
Church—213 Ripley St., 47031.
Mission—St. Pius, Ripley Co., St. Pius, (1859) 47033. [CEM]

Millhousen, Decatur Co., Immaculate Conception (1834), Revs. William G. Ripperger; Frank Eckstein; Sr. Christine Ernstes, O.S.F., Parish Life Coord.
Mailing Address: 2081 E. County Rd., 820 S., Greensburg, 47240. Tel: 812-591-2362.
Mission—St. Denis, Jennings Co., St. Denis, (1894) 12155 N. County Rd., 600 E., Westport, 47283. [CEM]
Catechesis/Religious Programs—Students 135.

Mitchell, Lawrence Co., St. Mary/Assumption (1869), Rev. Bernard Cox.
Res., 777 S. 11th St., 47446. Tel: 812-849-3570.
Catechesis/Religious Programs—Students 66.

Montezuma, Parke Co., Immaculate Conception (1867). Attended by St. Joseph's, 219 E. Ohio St., Rockville, IN. Tel: 317-569-5406. Rev. Joseph R. Kern, Admin.
Church—Madison & Sycamore St.

Mooresville, Morgan Co., St. Thomas More (1967), Rev. Edward J. Ripperger.
Res., 1200 N. Indiana St., 46158. Tel: 317-831-4142.
Catechesis/Religious Programs—Tel: 317-831-1431.
Students 300.

Morris, Ripley Co., St. Anthony of Padua (1856), Rev. Msgr. Bernard R. Schmitz.
Mailing Address: P.O. Box 3, 47033. Tel: 812-934-6218; Fax: 812-934-5936. [CEM]
Church—4781 E. Morris Church St., 47033.
Mission—Morris, Ripley Co., 500E 800 N., 47033.

Napoleon, Ripley Co., St. Maurice (1848), Rev. William G. Ripperger.
Mailing Address: 8874 Harrison St., P.O. Box 17, 47034. Tel: 812-852-4237. [CEM]
Catechesis/Religious Programs—Students 140.

Nashville, Brown Co., St. Agnes (1940), Rev. Paul D. Koetter, Admin.
Mailing Address: 602 N. State Rd. 135, P.O. Box 577, 47448. Tel: 812-988-2778. [JC]

Navilleton, Floyd Co., St. Mary (1845), Rev. Tony Hubler.
Res., 7500 Navilleton Rd., Floyds Knobs, 47119. Tel: 812-923-5419. [CEM]
Catechesis/Religious Programs—Tel: 812-923-9957.
Students 275.

New Albany, Floyd Co.,

1—Holy Family, (1954), Rev. Wilfred E. Day.
Res., 129 W. Daisy Ln., 47150. Tel: 812-944-8283.
School—217 W. Daisy Ln., 47150. Tel: 812-944-6090; Fax: 812-944-7299.
Lay Teachers 18; Students 410.

2—Holy Trinity, (1836). Merged with St. Mary, New Albany, where the sacramental records are kept.

3—Our Lady of Perpetual Help, (1950), Rev. John L. Fink; Tom Yost, Pastoral Assoc.
Res., 1752 Scheller Ln., 47150. Tel: 812-944-1184.
School—Tel: 812-944-7676.
Lay Teachers 22; Students 450.
Catechesis/Religious Programs—Students 70.

4—St. Mary, (1858) (German), Rev. William W. Ernst, V.F.
Res., 415 E. Eighth St., 47150. Tel: 812-944-0417; Fax: 812-944-9557. [JC]
School—720 E. Elm St., 47150. Tel: 812-944-0888.
Sisters 1; Lay Teachers 8; Students 288.
Catechesis/Religious Programs—Students 66.

New Alsace, Dearborn Co., St. Paul (1833), Rev. William J. Turner; Sr. Janette Gettelfinger, O.S.B., Pastoral Assoc.
Mailing Address: 8044 Yorkridge Rd., Guilford, 47022.
Res., 9789 N. Dearborn Rd., Guilford, 47022. Tel: 812-623-3408; 487-2096. [CEM]
School—(Grades K-6) 9775 N. Dearborn Rd., Guilford, 47022. Tel: 812-623-2631.
Lay Teachers 5; Students 87.
Catechesis/Religious Programs—Students 52.

New Castle, Henry Co., St. Anne (1873), Revs. Joseph F. Rautenberg; Stanley Herber; Sr. Shirley Gerth, O.S.F., Parish Life Coord.
Parish Office: 102 N. 19th St., 47362. Tel: 317-529-0933. [CEM]
Church—1904 Broad St., 47362. Tel: 317-529-7413.
Catechesis/Religious Programs—Students 126.

New Marion, Ripley Co., St. Magdalen (1847). Attended by St. John, Osgood. Rev. Francis Eckstein.
Res., Tel: 812-689-4244.

New Middletown, Harrison Co., Most Precious Blood (1880). Attended by St. Joseph, Corydon. Rev. Ernest Waechter, O.F.M.Conv.
Res., 312 E. High St., Corydon, 47112. Tel: 812-738-2742.

North Vernon, Jennings Co., St. Mary/Nativity of the Blessed Virgin Mary (1861), Rev. John B. Schoettelkotte.
Res., 212 Washington St., 47265. Tel: 812-346-3604. [CEM]
School—209 Washington St., 47265. Tel: 812-346-3445; Fax: 812-346-5930.
Lay Teachers 10; Students 213.

Oak Forest, Franklin Co., St. Cecilia of Rome/Formerly St. Philomena (1844). Attended by St. Mary-of-the-Rock, Franklin Co., where sacramental records are kept.
Res., 17440 St. Mary's Rd., Batesville, 47006. Tel: 812-934-4165.

Oldenburg, Franklin Co., Holy Family (1837), Rev. Sylvester Heppner, O.F.M. In res., Revs. Humbert Moster, O.F.M.; Rick Travnikar, O.F.M.; Raymar Middendorf, O.F.M.
Res., 3027 Pearl St., P.O. Box 98, 47036. Tel: 812-934-3013. [CEM]
Catechesis/Religious Programs—Students 198.

Osgood, Ripley Co., St. John (1867), Rev. Francis Eckstein.
Res., 331 S. Buckeye St., 47037. Tel: 812-689-4244. [CEM]
Mission—New Marion, Ripley Co., St. Mary Magdalen, (1847) 47037.
Catechesis/Religious Programs—349 S. Buckeye St., 47037. Tel: 812-689-6670.
Students 122.

Paoli, Orange Co., Our Lord Jesus Christ the King (1948). Attended by Our Lady of the Springs, French Lick. Rev. John M. Hall.
Res., Hwy. 150 E., 47454. Tel: 812-936-4568.

Plainfield, Hendricks Co., St. Susanna (1953), Rev. Richard I. Zore.
Res., 1210 E. Main St., 46168. Tel: 317-839-3333; Fax: 317-839-0732.
School—(Grades PreK-6) 1212 E. Main St., 46168. Tel: 317-839-3713.
Lay Teachers 13; Students 183.
Catechesis/Religious Programs—Tel: 317-838-7722.
Students 225.

Richmond, Wayne Co., Holy Family (1953), Revs. Todd M. Riebe, Admin.; Gregory Bramlage. In res., Rev. Daniel F. Armstrong.
Office: 240 S. 6th St., 47374. Tel: 317-962-3902.
Res., 720 N. A St., 47374. Tel: 317-962-3569; Fax: 317-966-0820.
Church—815 W. Main St., 47374.
School—St. Elizabeth Ann Seton (West), (Grades 4-8) 801 W. Main St., 47374. Tel: 317-962-4877.
Lay Teachers 11; Students 149.

St. Andrew (1846), Revs. Todd M. Riebe, Admin.;

Gregory Bramlage. In res., Rev. Daniel F. Armstrong.
Office: 240 S. 6th St., 47374. Tel: 317-962-3902.
Res., 720 North St., 47374. Tel: 317-962-3569; Fax: 317-966-0820. [JC]
Church—235 S. 5th St., 47374.
Parish Center—233 S. Fifth St., 47374.
Catechesis/Religious Programs—Tel: 317-966-0916.
Students 186.

St. Mary (1859), Revs. Todd M. Riebe, Admin.; Gregory Bramlage. In res., Rev. Daniel F. Armstrong.
Office: 240 S. 6th St., 47374. Tel: 317-962-3902.
Res., 720 N. A St., 47374. Tel: 317-962-3569; Fax: 317-966-0820. [JC]
School—St. Elizabeth Ann Seton, (Grades K-3) 700 N. A St., 47374. Tel: 317-962-5010.
Lay Teachers 7; Students 144.

Rockville, Parke Co., St. Joseph (1867), Rev. Joseph R. Kern.
Res., 217 E. Ohio St., 47872. Tel: 317-569-5406.
Mission—Montezuma, Parke Co., Immaculate Conception, (1867) Madison & Sycamore St., Montezuma, 47872. Tel: 317-245-0232. [CEM]

Rushville, Rush Co., Immaculate Conception/St. Mary (1857), Rev. Roger G. Rudolf.
Res., 512 N. Perkins St., 46173. Tel: 317-932-2588. [CEM]
School—(Grades K-6) 226 E. 5th St., 46173. Tel: 317-932-3639.
Lay Teachers 7; Students 176.
Catechesis/Religious Programs—Students 247.

St. Anne, Jennings Co., St. Anne (1841). Attended by St. Joseph, Jennings Co.

St. Croix, Perry Co., Holy Cross (1860), Rev. Isaac McDaniel, O.S.B.
Res., State Rd. 62, Gen. Delivery, 47576. Tel: 812-843-5701. [CEM]

St. Isidore the Farmer (1968). St. John, (1875), and St. Joseph, (1891), Perry Co., were closed, merged, and renamed, St. Isidore, in 1968 where sacramental records are kept. Rev. Isaac McDaniel, O.S.B.
Res., HC 64, Box 265, Bristow, 47515. Tel: 812-843-5713. [CEM]
Catechesis/Religious Programs—Students 96.

St. Denis, Jennings Co., St. Denis (1894). Attended by Immaculate Conception, Millhousen.
Church—12155 N. County Rd. 600E, Westport, 47283.
Mailing Address: 2081 E. County Rd. 820S, Greensburg, 47240. [CEM]

St. Joseph, Crawford Co., St. Joseph (1855). Attended by St. Bernard, Frenchtown.
Mailing Address: 7600 Hwy. 337 N.W., Depauw, 47115. Tel: 812-347-2326.
Church—State Rd. 66, Marengo, 47140.

St. Joseph, Jennings Co., (1850), Rev. John Schoettelkotte, Admin.
Res., 1875 S. County Rd. 700 W., North Vernon, 47265. Tel: 812-346-4783. [CEM]
Mission—St. Anne, Jennings Co., St. Anne, (1841).

St. Joseph Hill, Clark Co., St. Joseph (1853), Rev. Richard Kaley, O.F.M.Conv., Admin.
Res., 2605 St. Joe Rd., W., Sellersburg, 47172. Tel: 812-246-2512; Fax: 812-246-2671. [CEM]
Catechesis/Religious Programs—Tel: 812-246-3969.
Students 91.

St. Leon, Dearborn Co., St. Joseph (1841), Rev. Louis Manna.
Res., 7536 Church Ln., West Harrison, 47060. Tel: 812-576-3593. [CEM]
Catechesis/Religious Programs—29060 State Rte. 1, West Harrison, 47060. Tel: 812-576-3234.
Students 150.

St. Mark, Perry Co., St. Mark (1863) (German), Rev. Barnabas Gillespie, O.S.B.
Res., R.R. 1, Box 324, Tell City, 47586. Tel: 812-836-2481. [CEM][JC]
Catechesis/Religious Programs—Students 86.

St. Mary-of-the-Knobs, Floyd Co., St. Mary-of-the-Knobs (1823), Rev. John F. Geis.
Res., 3033 Martin Rd., Floyds Knobs, 47119. Tel: 812-923-3011. [CEM]
Catechesis/Religious Programs—Tel: 812-932-7258; Fax: 812-923-9526.
Students 431.

St. Mary-of-the-Rock, Franklin Co., St. Mary-of-the-Rock (1844) (German), Rev. Humbert Moster, O.F.M.
Res., 17440 St. Mary's Rd., Batesville, 47006. Tel: 812-934-4165. [CEM]
Mission—Oak Forest, Franklin Co., St. Cecilia of Rome.

St. Mary-of-the-Woods, Vigo Co., St. Mary (1837), Rev. Maurice Hayes, O.F.M.Conv.
Mailing Address: P.O. Box 155, 47876. Tel: 812-523-1240. [CEM]
Catechesis/Religious Programs—Students 78.

St. Maurice, Decatur Co., St. Maurice (1859), Rev. Jonathan Stewart.
Mailing Address: 1963 N. St. John St., Greensburg, 47240. Tel: 812-663-4754. [CEM]

St. Meinrad, Spencer Co., St. Meinrad (1854), Rev. Alan R. McIntosh, O.S.B.
Mailing Address: P.O. Box 8, 47577. Tel: 812-357-5533. [CEM]
Catechesis/Religious Programs—Students 182.

St. Nicholas, Ripley Co., St. Nicholas (1836), Rev. Msgr. Bernard R. Schmitz. In res., Rev. William J. Engbers, (Retired).
Res., 6461 E. St. Nicholas Dr., Sunman, 47041. Tel: 812-623-2964; 934-6218. [CEM]
School—(Grades K-8) 6459 E. St. Nicholas Dr., Sunman, 47041. Tel: 812-623-2348.
Lay Teachers 9; Students 183.
Catechesis/Religious Programs—Students 161.

St. Paul, Decatur Co., St. Paul (1895). Closed. Sacramental records available at St. Vincent de Paul, Shelby Co.

St. Peter, Franklin Co., St. Peter (1838), Revs. William Farris, O.F.M.; Humbert Moster, O.F.M.; Sr. Eileen Flavin, C.S.C., Parish Life Coord.
Res., 1207 East Rd., Brookville, 47012. Tel: 812-623-3670. [CEM]
Catechesis/Religious Programs—Students 90.

St. Peter, Harrison Co., (1849). Attended by St. Joseph, Corydon.
Church—Buena Vista Rd., Elizabeth, 47117.

St. Pius, Ripley Co., St. Pius (1859). Attended by St. Charles Borromeo, Milan.

St. Vincent de Paul, Shelby Co., St. Vincent de Paul (1837), Rev. Paul Landwerlen.
Res., 4128 E. Michigan Rd., Shelbyville, 46176. Tel: 317-398-4028. [CEM]
Mission—. [CEM]

Salem, Washington Co., St. Patrick (1942), Rev. Thomas L. Schliessmann.
Res., S. Shelby St., P.O. Box 273, 47167. Tel: 812-752-3693.

Scottsburg, Scott Co., American Martyrs (1938), Rev. Thomas Schliessmann.
Res., 270 S. Bond St., 47170. Tel: 812-752-3693.
Mission—Salem, Washington Co., St. Patrick, (1942).

Seelyville, Vigo Co., Holy Rosary (1908), Rev. Lawrence Moran, Admin.
Mailing Address: 2585 N. Main, P.O. Box 151, 47878. Tel: 812-877-1279.
Res., 1807 Poplar St., Terre Haute, 47803. Tel: 812-232-8518.

Sellersburg, Clark Co., St. Paul (1948), Rev. Paul F. Richart.
Res., 218 Scheller Ave., 47172. Tel: 812-246-3522.
School—(Grades K-6) 105 St. Paul St., 47172. Tel: 812-246-3266; Fax: 812-246-3397.
Lay Teachers 9; Students 240.
Catechesis/Religious Programs—216 Scheller Ave., 47172. Tel: 812-246-5088.
Students 65.

Seymour, Jackson Co., St. Ambrose (1860), Rev. Joseph B. Sheets.
Res., 325 S. Chestnut St., 47274. Tel: 812-522-5304; Fax: 812-522-8959. [CEM]
School—(Grades K-6) 301 S. Chestnut St., 47274. Tel: 812-522-3522.
Lay Teachers 8; Students 106.
Catechesis/Religious Programs—Tel: 812-522-2686.
Students 182.
Mission—Brownstown, Jackson Co., Our Lady of Providence, (1934) 47274.

Shelbyville, Shelby Co., St. Joseph (1868), Rev. John S. Maung.
Res., 125 E. Broadway, 46176. Tel: 317-398-8227. [CEM][JC]
School—(Grades PreK-6) 127 E. Broadway, 46176. Tel: 317-398-4202; Fax: 317-398-0270.
Sisters of the Third Order Regular of St. Francis 1; Lay Teachers 13; Students 248.
Catechesis/Religious Programs—Tel: 317-398-0530.
Students 245.

Siberia, Perry Co., St. Martin of Tours (1869), Rev. Sean Hoppe, O.S.B., Admin.
Mailing Address: P.O. Box 1, Fulda, 47536. Tel: 812-357-2483. [CEM]

Spencer, Owen Co., St. Jude the Apostle (1951), Rev. Paul M. Dede.
Res., 300 W. Hillside Ave., P.O. Box 317, 47460. Tel: 812-829-3082; Fax: 812-829-0888.

Starlight, Clark Co., St. John the Baptist (1861) (German), Rev. John Beitans.
Res., 8310 St. John's Rd., Floyds Knobs, 47119. Tel: 812-923-5785. [CEM]
Catechesis/Religious Programs—Students 109.

Tell City, Perry Co., St. Paul (1859), Revs. Benet Amato, O.S.B.; Severin Messick, O.S.B.
Parish Office: 802 9th St., 47586. Tel: 812-547-7994; Fax: 812-547-6985.
Church—814 Jefferson St., 47586. [CEM]
Catechesis/Religious Programs—Tel: 812-547-7102.
Students 314.

Terre Haute, Vigo Co.,

1—Sacred Heart of Jesus, (1924), Rev. Anthony R. Volz.
Res., 2322 N. 13 1/2 St., 47804. Tel: 812-466-1231; Fax: 812-466-9683. [JC]
School—1330 Lafayette Ave., 47804. Tel: 812-232-8901.
Sisters 4; Lay Teachers 8; Students 117.
Catechesis/Religious Programs—Students 138.

2—St. Ann, (1876), Sr. Constance Kramer, S.P., Parish Life Coord.; Rev. Anthony R. Volz.
Res., 1440 Locust St., 47807. Tel: 812-232-6832; Fax: 812-232-2444. [JC]

3—St. Benedict, (1865) (German), Rev. Ron Borman, O.F.M.Conv.
Res., 118 S. Ninth St., 47807. Tel: 812-232-8421; Fax: 812-238-0002. [JC]
Catechesis/Religious Programs—Students 182.

4—St. Joseph, (1838), Revs. Martin Day, O.F.M.Conv.; Michael Goodavish, O.F.M.Conv.
Res., 113 S. Fifth St., 47807. Tel: 812-232-7011; Fax: 812-232-7012. [JC]
Catechesis/Religious Programs—Students 377.

5—St. Margaret Mary, (1920), Rev. John F. Dede.
Res., 2405 S. Seventh St., 47802. Tel: 812-232-3512. [JC]
Catechesis/Religious Programs—Students 150.

6—St. Patrick, (1881), Rev. Lawrence J. Moran; John Fuller, Pastoral Assoc.
Church—1807 Poplar St., 47803. Tel: 812-232-8518; Fax: 812-234-3312.
School—(Grades PreK-8) 449 S. 19th St., 47803. Tel: 812-232-2157. Sr. Theresa Boland, S.P., Prin.
Lay Teachers 15; Students 317.
Catechesis/Religious Programs—Tel: 812-232-2827. Barbara Black, D.R.E.
Students 201.

Troy, Perry Co., St. Pius (1849), Revs. Severin Messick, O.S.B.; Benet Amato, O.S.B.
Parish Office: 802 9th St., Tell City, 47586. Tel: 812-547-7994; Fax: 812-547-6985. [CEM]
Res., 814 Jefferson St., Tell City, 47586.
Church—State Rd. 66, 47588.

Universal, Vermillion Co., St. Joseph (1920). Attended by Sacred Heart, Clinton. Rev. Micheal Kelley.
Res., 270 E. Wood Ave., 47884.

Vevay, Switzerland Co., Most Sorrowful Mother of God (1876), Rev. John A. Meyer.
Mailing Address: Catholic Community Center, 305 W. State St., Madison, 47250. Tel: 812-265-4166.
Church—Ferry St., 47043.

West Terre Haute, Vigo Co., St. Leonard of Port Maurice (1912), Rev. Maurice Hayes, O.F.M.Conv.
Res., 126 N. Eighth St., 47885. Tel: 812-533-1240.

Yorkville, Dearborn Co., St. Martin (1852), Rev. William J. Turner; Sr. Ann Janette Gettelfinger, O.S.B., Pastoral Assoc.
Res., 8044 Yorkridge Rd., Guilford, 47022. Tel: 812-487-2096; 623-3408. [CEM]
Catechesis/Religious Programs—Students 62.

Chaplains of Public Institutions

Indianapolis. *Community Hospital North*. Rev. Henry Brown.
Indiana University Hospital. Rev. Joseph S. Kos.
Indiana Women's Prison. Rev. Lawrence Voelker.
Indianapolis Fire Department. Rev. James Wilmoth.
Indianapolis International Airport. Rev. Glenn L. O'Connor.
Larue D. Carter Hospital. Rev. Joseph S. Kos.
Marion County Sheriff Department. Rev. James Wilmoth.
Methodist Hospital. Rev. David Lawler.
Veterans' Administration Hospital. Revs. Mathias J. Crehan, O.F.M.; Gordon P. Wagoner; James S. Cantwell, O.F.M.Conv.
Winona Medical Center. Rev. Henry Brown.
Wishard Memorial Hospital. Rev. Joseph S. Kos.

Putnamville. *Indiana State Farm*. Rev. Michael C. Fritsch.

Richmond. *Richmond State Hospital*. Rev. Todd Riebe, M.C.C.J.

Terre Haute. *Regional Hospital*. Rev. Maurice Hayes, O.F.M.Conv.
U.S. Penitentiary, P.O. Box 33, 47808. Rev. Wes Lamb, O.S.S.T.
Union Hospital. Rev. Maurice Hayes, O.F.M.Conv.

On Duty Outside the Archdiocese:
Reverend Fathers—
Evard, Paul A., Casilla 5825, Guayaquil, Ecuador

Happel, Stephen P., Department of Religious Education, The Catholic University of America, Washington, DC 20064
Stumpf, William F., St. Luke Institute, Suitland, MD

Military Chaplains:
Reverend Monsignors—
Wright, John M.
Reverend Fathers—
Buchanan, Donald E.
Murphy, Kenneth J.

Graduate Studies:
Reverend Fathers—
Dant, Nicholas

Leave of Absence:
Reverend Fathers—
Scheidler, Robert E.
Sims, Robert W.
Smith, Myles H.

On Disability Leave:
Reverend Fathers—
Mader, Joseph
Stahl, George

Retired:
Reverend Monsignors—
Kavanagh, Richard T., 6809 E. 77th St., Indianapolis, IN 46250
Ross, Charles E., St. Augustine Home, 2345 W. 86th St., Indianapolis, IN 46260
Sweeney, Kenny C., 8431 E. Fairmont Ave., Scottsdale, AZ 85251
Reverend Fathers—
Ajamie, Albert, Fatima Retreat House, 5353 E. 56th St., Indianapolis, IN 46226
Armstrong, Daniel F., St. Andrew Rectory, 235 E. Fifth St., Richmond, IN 47374
Arneson, James E., 1868 Shore Dr. S., #114, South Pasadena, FL 33707
Beechem, Joseph, 6927 Atrium Boardwalk S., Indianapolis, IN 46250
Berkemeier, Charles A., 6268 Scottsville Navilleton Rd., Floyds Knobs, IN 47119
Burwinkel, Elmer J., M.Ed., M.Div., 3991 W.C.R. 925 S., Madison, IN 47250
Byrne, James F., S.T.L., 1670 1/2 W. 86th St., Indianapolis, IN 46260
Carey, Thomas P., St. Paul Hermitage, 501 N. 17th Ave., No. 107, Beech Grove, IN 46107
Cleary, William D., 874 W. Bauer Dr., Ninevah, IN 46164
Commons, Patrick M., 1868 Shore Dr. S., Apt. 114, South Pasadena, FL 33707
Courtney, Paul J., 8150 Township Line Rd., Apt. 101A, Indianapolis, IN 46260
Dede, James R., 8499 W. U.S. Hwy. 150, Hardensburg, IN 47125
Diezeman, Andrew S., Star Rte., Box 37A, St. Croix, IN 47576
Dooley, Francis B., St. Paul Hermitage, 501 N. 17th Ave., Beech Grove, IN 46107
Dooley, Joseph W., 8021 Guion Rd., Indianapolis, IN 46268
Engbers, William J., 6457 St. Nicholas Dr., Sunman, IN 47041
Gayso, Edward V., 5235 E. Greenbriar Dr., Apt. 5A, Terre Haute, IN 47802
Grogan, Richard P., c/o Rev. John Fink, 1752 Scheller Ln., New Albany, IN 47150
Herold, Carl A., 1650 Overlook Ln., Santa Barbara, CA 93103
Kraeszig, Charles J., 7901 Castle Dr., Lakewood Estates, New Port Richey, FL 34653
Marchino, Louis H., 127 Rossmore Dr., New Albany, IN 47150
Meny, Hilary G., P.O. Box 245, Haubstadt, IN 47639
Minta, John, 213 Ripley, P.O. Box 336, Milan, IN 47031
Mueller, Richard J., 2722 B Marquette Manor W. Dr., Indianapolis, IN 46268
O'Riley, James K., 3388 Rothshire Cir., North Vernon, IN 47265
Sciarra, John N., 8300 Rahke Rd., Indianapolis, IN 46217
Sexton, Charles E., St. Paul Hermitage, 501 N. 17th St., Beach Grove, IN 46107
Stineman, William F., 7432-D Lions Head Dr., Indianapolis, IN 46260
Strahl, Ernest, St. Paul Hermitage, 501 N. 17th Ave., Beech Grove, IN 46107
Terrill, Richard F., 1391 Gardner Ave., Newago, MI 49337

INSTITUTIONS LOCATED IN THE ARCHDIOCESE

[A] SEMINARIES, RELIGIOUS OR SCHOLASTICATES

ST. MEINRAD. *St. Meinrad Seminary*, 47577. Tel: 812-357-6611; Fax: 812-357-6964. School of Theology. Revs. Mark O'Keefe, O.S.B., Pres. & Rector; Justin Duvall, O.S.B., Vice Rector & Provost; Aurelius Boberek, O.S.B.; John J. Buckel; Simeon Daly, O.S.B.; Cyprian Davis, O.S.B.; Damian Dietlein, O.S.B.; Amador Garza (BWN); Harry Hagan, O.S.B.; Eugene Hensell, O.S.B.; Jeremy King, O.S.B.; Keith McClellan, O.S.B.; Guy Mansini, O.S.B.; Godfrey Mullen, O.S.B.; Jerome Neufelder (EVN); Julian Peters, O.S.B.; Nathaniel Reeves, O.S.B.; J. Lawrence Richardt (IND); Thomas Richstatter, O.F.M.; Kurt Stasiak, O.S.B.; Cajetan White, O.S.B. Other Faculty and Staff 25; Students 106.

[B] COLLEGES AND UNIVERSITIES

INDIANAPOLIS. *Marian College*, 3200 Cold Spring Rd., 46222. Tel: 317-929-0123; Fax: 317-929-0263.
For a complete listing, refer to the Colleges and Universities section.

SAINT MARY-OF-THE-WOODS. *Saint Mary-of-the-Woods College*, 47876. Tel: 812-535-5151; Fax: 812-535-4613.
For a complete listing, refer to the Colleges and Universities section.

ST. MEINRAD. *St. Meinrad Seminary-College of Liberal Arts*, 47577. Tel: 812-357-6611; Fax: 812-357-6964.
For a complete listing, refer to the Colleges and Universities section.

[C] HIGH SCHOOLS, INTER-PAROCHIAL

INDIANAPOLIS. *Bishop Chatard High School*, 5885 N. Crittenden Ave., 46220. Tel: 317-251-1451. Rev. David F. Coons. Priests 1; Sisters of St. Benedict 1; Brothers of the Holy Cross 1; Lay Teachers 43; Students 570.

Cardinal Ritter Junior-Senior High School, 3360 W. 30th St., 46222. Tel: 317-924-4333; Fax: 317-927-7822. Dr. David A. Armstrong, Prin. Priests 2; Sisters 7; Lay Teachers 33; Students 429.

Father Thomas Scecina Memorial High School, 5000 Nowland Ave., 46201. Tel: 317-356-6377. Mr. Steve Papesh, Prin.; Rev. Peter Gallagher. Priests 1; Lay Teachers 35; Students 570.

Roncalli High School, 3300 Prague Rd., 46227. Tel: 317-787-8277. Mr. Joseph D. Hollowell, Pres.; Rev. Steve Giannini. Priests 1; Sisters 2; Lay Teachers 63; Students 850.

CLARKSVILLE. *Our Lady of Providence*, 707 W. Hwy. 131, 47129. Tel: 812-945-2538. Mr. Cecil Mattingly, Prin.; Mr. Gerald Wilkinson, Pres.; Mr. Robert Casey, Asst. Prin.; Rev. H. Michael Hilderbrand, Chap. Priests 1; Sisters 1; Lay Teachers 50; Students (Grades 9-12) 628; Students (Grades 7-12) 695.

MADISON. *Shawe Memorial Junior-Senior High School*, 201 W. State St., 47250. Tel: 812-273-2150. Larry Truax, Pres.; Nancy McCabe, Prin. Lay Teachers 12; Priests 1; Sisters 1; Students 162.

[D] HIGH SCHOOLS, PRIVATE

INDIANAPOLIS. *Brebeuf Jesuit Preparatory School, Inc.*, 2801 W. 86th St., 46268. Tel: 317-872-7050. Society of Jesus. 2823 W. 86 St., 46268. Tel: 317-876-4700. Revs. Albert J. Bischoff, S.J., Rector; William P. O'Brien, S.J., Regent; Frederick J. Deters, S.J.; Joseph D. Folzenlogan, S.J.; Walter C. Deye, S.J.; Robert I. Grib, S.J.; Bros. John F. Buchman, S.J.; James K. McCauley, S.J. Priests 5; Brothers 2; Regents 1; Lay Teachers 70; Students 712.

Cathedral High School (Cathedral Trustees, Inc.), 5225 E. 56th St., 46226. Julian Peebles, Pres.; Rev. Patrick J. Kelly, M.S., Prin. Sisters 6; Priests 2; Lay Teachers 67; Students 974.

OLDENBURG. *Oldenburg Academy of the Immaculate Conception*, 47036. Tel: 812-934-4440; Fax: 812-934-4838. Five-day boarding and day school. Sr. Carol Ann Mause, O.S.F., Prin. Sisters 7; Lay Teachers 18; Girls 193.

[E] RELIGIOUS EDUCATION CENTERS

CLARKSVILLE. *Aquinas Center for Continuing Religious Education*, 707 W. Hwy. 131, 47129. Tel: 812-945-0354. Mr. Robert K. Leonard, Dir. Catechetical Ministry & Religious Education; Mr. D. Ray Lucas, Dir. Youth Ministries.

New Albany Deanery / Catholic Youth Ministry.

TERRE HAUTE. *Terre Haute Deanery Pastoral Center*, 2931 Ohio Blvd., 47803. Tel: 812-232-8400. Ms. Diane M. Carver, Dir.; Susan Hall, Admin. Asst. Total Staff 2.

[F] GENERAL HOSPITALS

INDIANAPOLIS. *St. Vincent Hospital and Health Care Center, Inc.*, 2001 W. 86th St., 46260. Tel: 317-338-7000; Fax: 317-338-7005.
For a complete listing, refer to the Hospitals section.

Seton Health Corporation of Central Indiana, 2001 W. 86th St., 46260. Tel: 317-338-7000; Fax: 317-338-7005.
For a complete listing, refer to the Hospitals section.

BEECH GROVE. *St. Francis Hospital and Health Centers*, 1600 Albany St., 46107. Tel: 317-787-3311.
For a complete listing, refer to the Hospitals section.

[G] PROTECTIVE INSTITUTIONS

TERRE HAUTE. *Gibault School for Boys*, 6301 S. U.S. Hwy. 41, P.O. Box 2316, 47802-0316. Tel: 812-299-1156.
For a complete listing, refer to the Special Care Facilities section.

[H] HOMES FOR AGED

INDIANAPOLIS. *St. Augustine Home, Little Sisters of the Poor*, 2345 W. 86th St., 46260. Tel: 317-872-6420.
For a complete listing, refer to the Special Care Facilities section.

BEECH GROVE. *St. Paul Hermitage*, 501 N. 17th Ave., 46107. Tel: 317-786-2261.
For a complete listing, refer to the Special Care Facilities section.

NEW ALBANY. *Mercy Long Term Care Initiatives dba Providence Retirement Home*, 703 E. Spring St., 47150. Tel: 812-945-5221; Fax: 812-945-2614.
For a complete listing, refer to the Special Care Facilities section.

[I] RETREAT HOUSES

INDIANAPOLIS. *Our Lady of Fatima Retreat House, Inc.*, 5353 E. 56th St., 46226. Tel: 317-545-7681; Fax: 317-545-0095. Mr. Kevin V. DePrey, Dir. Brothers of Christian Instruction. Brothers 1; Priests 1.
Used by both clergy and laity.

BEECH GROVE. *Benedict Inn Retreat & Conference Center*, 1402 Southern Ave., 46107. Tel: 317-788-7581; Fax: 317-782-3142. Sr. Carol Falkner, O.S.B., Admin. Sisters 3. Retreats and workshops for clergy, religious, and laity.

MOUNT SAINT FRANCIS. *Mount Saint Francis Friary and Retreat Center*, 47146-9999. Tel: 812-923-8817; Fax: 812-923-0177. Revs. Thomas A. Smith, O.F.M.Conv., Guardian; Kevin Przyblski, O.F.M.Conv., Retreat Dir.; Ronald Bohl, O.F.M.Conv., Retreat Staff; Jim Van Dorn, O.F.M.Conv., Parish Missions; Eliot Comstock, O.F.M.Conv., Treasurer's Office. In res., Revs. Maximilian Korecki, O.F.M. Conv.; Hilary Gottbrath, O.F.M.Conv.; Dunstan Bryan, O.F.M.Conv., (Retired); Kenneth Gering, O.F.M.Conv., de familia; Ernest Waechter, O.F.M.Conv., de familia; Kevin Godfrey, O.F.M.Conv., de familia; Bros. Robert Roddy, O.F.M.Conv., Retreat Staff; Angelo Catania, O.F.M.Conv., Retreat Staff; Lawrence Eberhardt, O.F.M.Conv., Archivist; Jeffry Hines, O.F.M.Conv., Sec. of the Province; Michael Austin, O.F.M.Conv., Vocation Promotion & Youth Min.; Bruno Nemcosky, O.F.M.Conv., Coord. of Medical Program & Mission Appeals; James Worchuck, O.F.M.Conv., Devel. Office Staff; Gabriel Balassone, O.F.M., Liturgy & Music.

Province of Our Lady of Consolation, Inc. (Provincial Office). Tel: 812-923-8444; Fax: 812-923-8145. Revs. Kent Biergans, O.F.M.Conv., Min. Prov.; Richard Kaley, O.F.M.Conv., Vicar; Bro. Jeffrey Hines, O.F.M.Conv., Sec. of Province. Total Staff 4; Total in Residence 16.

ST. MEINRAD. *Archabbey Guest House*, 47577. Tel: 812-357-6585; 800-581-6905; Fax: 812-357-6325. Retreat House for Men, Women, Couples, and Youth Groups. Double Rooms 25.

[J] MONASTERIES AND RESIDENCES OF PRIESTS AND BROTHERS

INDIANAPOLIS. *St. Maur Priory*, 4615 N. Michigan Rd., 46208. Tel: 317-925-9095. Very Rev. Charles Henry, O.S.B., Prior; Revs. Bernardin Patterson, O.S.B.; Robert McElaney, O.S.B. Priests 3; Brothers 4.

MOUNT SAINT FRANCIS. *Provincial Headquarters for the Conventual Franciscan Province*, 101 Anthony Dr., 47146. Tel: 812-923-8444; Fax: 812-923-8145. Very Rev. Kent Biergans, O.F.M.Conv., Minister Prov.; Rev. Richard Kaley, O.F.M.Conv., Vicar Prov.; Bro. Jeffrey Hines, O.F.M.Conv., Sec. of Province. Priests 3. Legal Title: *Provincial Headquarters for the Conventual Franciscan Province of Our Lady of Consolation.*

Vocation Office of the Province. St. Paul Friary, 6901 Dixie Hwy., Pleasure Ridge Park, KY, 40258. Tel: 502-933-4439. Rev. David Lenz, O.F.M.Conv., Vocation Dir.

Priests of the Conventual Franciscan Province of Our Lady of Consolation Teaching or Studying at Universities: Rev. Duane Doherty, O.F.M.Conv., 3695 Lincoln, Birmingham, MI, 48010. Rev. Basil Heiser, O.F.M.Conv., Curia Generalizia, Piazza Ss.

Apostoli, 51, Rome, Italy, 00187.

Chaplains in the Armed Services: Rev. Harold P. Gott, O.F.M.Conv., USAG-CMR, Box 166, Fort McPherson, GA, 30330-5000. Rev. Edward C. Leis, O.F.M.Conv., USN, Command Chap., Building 3, Naval Training Center, Great Lakes, IL, 60088-1500. Tel: 312-688-2288. Rev. Antonio Moreno, O.F.M.Conv., 4504-D, USAF Academy, CO, 80840-5180.

ST. MEINRAD. *St. Meinrad Archabbey*, 47577-1010. Tel: 812-357-6611; Fax: 812-357-6551. Archabbey of the Order of St. Benedict, including School of Theology and College of Liberal Arts, St. Meinrad Seminary. Rt. Rev. Lambert Reilly, O.S.B., Archabbot; Revs. Keith McClellan, O.S.B., Prior; Harry Hagan, O.S.B., Master of Novices & Junior Master; Gavin Barnes, O.S.B.; Alban Berling, O.S.B.; Aurelius Boberek, O.S.B.; Meinrad Brune, O.S.B.; Theodore Brune, O.S.B.; Adelbert Buscher, O.S.B.; Bede Cisco, O.S.B.; Aelred Cody, O.S.B.; Tobias Colgan, O.S.B.; Patrick Cooney, O.S.B. (BEL); Thomas Crouse, O.S.B. (ANC); Simeon Daly, O.S.B.; Cyprian Davis, O.S.B.; Guerric DeBona, O.S.B.; Martin Dusseau, O.S.B.; Justin DuVall, O.S.B.; Gerard Ellspermann, O.S.B.; Jonathan Fassero, O.S.B.; Malachy Fulton, O.S.B.; Rembert Gehant, O.S.B.; Colman Grabert, O.S.B.; Theodore Heck, O.S.B.; Warren Heitz, O.S.B.; Eugene Hensell, O.S.B.; Richard Hindel, O.S.B.; Michael Keene, O.S.B.; Columba Kelly, O.S.B.; Jeremy King, O.S.B.; Micheas Langston, O.S.B.; Alcuin Leibold, O.S.B.; Eric Lies, O.S.B.; Prosper Lindauer, O.S.B.; Conrad Louis, O.S.B.; Ralph Lynch, O.S.B.; Simon McTighe, O.S.B.; Guy Mansini, O.S.B.; Noel Mueller, O.S.B.; Louis Mulcahy, O.S.B.; Godfrey Mullen, O.S.B.; Matthias Neuman, O.S.B.; Austin Newberry, O.S.B.; Mark O'Keefe, O.S.B., Pres. & Rector, School of Theology & College; Rupert Ostdick, O.S.B.; Julian Peters, O.S.B.; David Rabenecker, O.S.B.; Nathaniel Reeves, O.S.B.; Lynn Robinson, O.S.B. (MEM); William Schipper, O.S.B.; Damian Schmelz, O.S.B.; Christopher Shappard, O.S.B.; Stephen Snoich, O.S.B.; Kurt Stasiak, O.S.B.; Germain Swisshelm, O.S.B.; Cyril Vrablic, O.S.B.; Donald Walpole, O.S.B.; Cajetan White, O.S.B. Priests 96; Brothers 36.

Priests of the Archabbey Teaching, Studying at Universities, or on Special Assignment: Rt. Rev. Bonaventure Knaebel, O.S.B., Resigned Archabbot, Corpus Christi Abbey, HCR #2, Box 6300, Sandia, TX, 78383. Rev. Benet Amato, O.S.B., St. Paul Parish, 814 Jefferson St., Tell City, 47586. Rev. Ephrem Carr, O.S.B., Collegio Sant' Anselmo, Piazza Cavalieri di Malta 5, Rome, Italy, I-00153. Rev. Noah Casey, O.S.B., 4826 Fletcher Ave., Indianapolis, 46203. Rev. Gregory D. Chamberlin, O.S.B., St. Benedict Church, 1328 Lincoln Ave., Evansville, 47714-1598. Rev. Augustine Davis, O.S.B., Monaterio Benedictino, Apdo. Postal 296, 58000 Morelia, Michoacan, Mexico. Rev. Camillus Ellspermann, O.S.B., St. Henry Rectory, 1311 W. 1100 S., Ferdinand, 47532. Rev. Cassian Folsom, O.S.B., Collegio Sant' Anselmo, Piazza Cavalieri di Malta 5, Rome, Italy, I-00153. Rev. Barnabas Gillespie, O.S.B., V.F., St. Augustine Church, General Delivery, Leopold, 47551. Rev. Harold Hammerstein, O.S.B., 701 S. Boeke, Evansville, 47714. Rev. Boniface Hardin, O.S.B., 2171 Avondale Pl., P.O. Box 18567, Indianapolis, 46218. Rev. Sean Hoppe, O.S.B., St. Bonafice Parish, Fulda, 47536. Rev. Aidan Kavanagh, O.S.B., 409 Prospect St., Hamden, CT, 06157. Rev. Kilian Kerwin, O.S.B., Little Flower Parish, 4720 E. 13th St., Indianapolis, 46201. Rev. Pius Klein, O.S.B., St. Mary Rectory, 313 Washington St., Huntingburg, 47532. Rev. Sebastian Leonard, O.S.B., Canterbury School, Aspetuck Ave., New Milford, CT, 06776. Rev. Edward Linton, O.S.B., St. Benedict Parish, 1328 Lincoln Ave., Evansville, 47714-1598. Rev. Isaac McDaniel, O.S.B., 2106 Woodriver Dr., #8, Carbandale, IL, 62901. Rev. Alan McIntosh, O.S.B., St. Meinrad Rectory, 47577. Rev. Severin Messick, O.S.B., St. Paul Parish, 814 Jefferson St., Tell City, 47586. Rev. Benedict Meyer, O.S.B., St. John the Baptist Parish, 203 W. Ash, Brinkley, AR, 72021. Rev. Hilary Ottensmeyer, O.S.B., 1414 Southern Ave., Beech Grove, 46107. Rev. Mel Patton, O.S.B., Sacred Heart Monastery, 1005 W. Eighth St., Yankton, SD, 57078. Rev. Kevin Ryan, O.S.B., St. Paul's Hermitage, 501 N. 17th Ave., Beech Grove, 46107. Rev. Raymond Studzinski, O.S.B., Curley Hall, Catholic University of America, Washington, DC, 20064. Rev. Timothy Sweeney, O.S.B., Parish of the Immaculate, 2516 Christie Place, Owensboro, KY, 42301. Rev. Vincent Tobin, O.S.B., Collegio di Sant'Anselmo, Piazza Cavalieri di Malta 5, Rome, Italy, I-00153. Rev. Frederick Walsh, O.S.B., Our Lady Queen Monastery, 50352 Antioch Rd., Tickfaw, LA, 70466. Rev. Joachim E. Walsh, O.S.B., Our Lady Queen Monastery, 50352 Antioch Rd., Tickfaw, LA, 70466. Rev. Marion Walsh, O.S.B., Our Lady Queen Monastery, 50352 Antioch Rd., Tickfaw, LA, 70466. Rev. Samuel Weber, O.S.B., Our Lady of the Greenwood, 335 S. Meridian St., Greenwood, 46143. Rev. Peter Yock, O.S.B., Collegio Sant'Anselmo, P. Cavalieri di Malta, 5, Rome, Italy, I-00153.

[K] CONVENTS AND RESIDENCES FOR SISTERS

INDIANAPOLIS. *Sisters of Our Lady of Mount Carmel Carmelite Monastery*, 2500 Cold Spring Rd., 46222. Tel: 317-926-5654; Fax: 317-926-1492. Sr. Jean Alice McGoff, O.C.D., Prioress. Professed Religious 14; Novices 3; Transfering from an Active Order 1.

BEECH GROVE. *Charitable Trust of the Monastery of Our Lady of Grace*, 1402 Southern Ave., 46107-1197. Legal Title: *Charitable Trust of the Monastery of Our Lady of Grace, Sisters of the Order of St. Benedict.*

Our Lady of Grace Monastery for Sisters of St. Benedict of Beech Grove, IN, Inc., 1402 Southern Ave., 46107-1197. Tel: 317-787-3287. Rev. Hilary Ottensmeyer, O.S.B., Chap., 1414 Southern Ave., 46107-1197. Tel: 317-786-0338. Sisters 89.

OLDENBURG. *Motherhouse of the Congregation of the Sisters of the Third Order of St. Francis*, 47036. Tel: 812-934-2475; Fax: 812-933-6403. Sr. Amy Kistner, O.S.F., Congregational Minister; Revs. Raymar Middendorf, O.F.M.; Sylvester Heppner, O.F.M., Assoc. Chap., Holy Family Friary. Professed Sisters in Congregation 387; Professed Sisters in Archdiocese 233.

Sisters of St. Francis Community Support Trust.

SAINT MARY-OF-THE-WOODS. *Sisters of Providence General Administration*, 47876-1089. Tel: 812-535-4193; Fax: 812-535-4727. Sr. Diane Ris, S.P., Gen. Supr.; Rev. Bernard Head, Chap. Professed in Congregation 693; Professed Residing in Archdiocese 397; Postulants 2.

Sisters of Providence Community Support Trust.

Woods Day Care/Preschool, Inc. Total Staff 20; Children 58.

Providence Self-Sufficiency Ministries, Inc., 225 W. Daisy Ln., New Albany, 47150. Sr. Barbara Ann Zeller, Pres. Total Staff 25; Total Assisted 900.

St. Mary-of-the-Woods College. Total Staff 130; Total Assisted 1,266.

TERRE HAUTE. *Monastery of St. Joseph, Discalced Carmelites*, 59 Allendale, 47802-4751. Tel: 812-299-1410. Mother Joseph of Jesus, Mary, O.C.D., Prioress. Solemnly Professed 12; Simple Professed 1; Postulants 1.

[L] ARCHDIOCESAN CHARITIES

INDIANAPOLIS. *"A Caring Place" - Adult Day Care Center*, 4609 N. Capitol Ave., 46208. Tel: 317-466-0015; Fax: 317-261-3375. Adult Day Care Center; Catholic Social Services. Lula E. Baxter, Prog. Dir.; Sr. Susan Dinnin, S.P., Site Mgr. Total Staff 5; Total Assisted 136.

Catholic Social Services of Central Indiana, The Catholic Center, 1400 N. Meridian St., P.O. Box 1410, 46206. Tel: 317-236-1500; Fax: 317-261-3375. Thomas Colbert, A.C.S.W., Exec. Dir. Total Staff 85; Total Assisted 3,848.

Holy Family Emergency Shelter, 30 E. Palmer St., 46225. Tel: 317-635-7830; Fax: 317-684-9702. Amy Moelhmer, A.C.S.W., C.C.S.W., Dir. Total Staff 15; Total Assisted 1,437.

Holy Trinity Place - Adult Day Care Center, 907 N. Holmes Ave., 46222. Tel: 317-638-8322; Fax: 317-261-3375. Adult Day Care; Catholic Social Services. Lula E. Baxter, Program Dir.; Joan Goote, Site Mgr. Total Staff 7; Total Assisted 136.

St. Ann's Place-East, 6310 E. 10th St., 46219. Tel: 317-261-3378; Fax: 317-261-3375. Lula E. Baxter, Prog. Dir.; Mandy Wright, Prog. Coord. Total Staff 1; Total Assisted 10.

St. Ann's Place-North, 4609 N. Capitol Ave., 46208. Tel: 317-261-3378; Fax: 317-261-3375. Lula E. Baxter, Prog. Dir.; Mandy Wright, Prog. Coord. Total Staff 1; Total Assisted 8.

COLUMBUS. *Seymour Deanery Counseling*, 4550 Jonathan Moore Pike, 47201. Tel: 812-342-1900. Total Staff 1; Total Assisted 62.

GREENSBURG. *Batesville Deanery Counseling & Family Mediations*, 420 E. Walnut St., 47240-1759. Tel: 812-663-2113. C. Renee Rust, D.Min., C.M.F.T., C.S.W., Counselor & Mediator.

NEW ALBANY. *Catholic Charities*, 702 E. Market St., 47150. Tel: 812-948-0438. Barbara K. Williams, M.S., C.S.W., Dir. Total Staff 3; Total Assisted 660.

St. Elizabeth's Regional Maternity Center, 601 E. Market St., 47150. Tel: 812-949-7305. Full-range maternity home and adoption agency offering residential and outreach services. Keith E. Stormes, Dir. Total Staff 15; Total in Residence 36.

NEW CASTLE. *Connersville Deanery Counseling.* 5220 E. 74th Pl., Indianapolis, 46250. Gary DeSutter, A.C.S.W., Counselor.

TELL CITY. *Catholic Charities*, 802 Ninth St., 47586. Tel: 812-547-6414.

Rainbow Cottage Latch Key Program. Total Staff 4; Total Assisted 40.

TERRE HAUTE. *Catholic Charities*, 721 Wabash Ave., Ste. 501, 47807. Tel: 812-232-1447. John Etling, M.A., Dir. Total Staff 3.

Bethany House, 1402 Locust Ave., 47807. Tel: 812-232-4978. Marty Green, Mgr. Total Staff 3; Total Assisted 10,000.

Christmas House, 829 N. 14th St., 47808. Sr. Brendan Harvey, S.P., Dir. Total Staff 1; Total Assisted 2,300.

Household Exchange, 829 N. 14th St., 47807. John Etling, M.A., Dir. Total Staff 3; Total Assisted 960.

Ryves Hall Youth Center, 1356 Locust St., 47807. Tel: 812-235-1261. Jim Edwards, Youth Center Dir. Total Staff 4; Total Assisted 1,200.

Simeon House I (St. Patrick Parish), 1801 Poplar St., 47803. Tel: 812-232-6144. Delores Carbon, Dir. Total Staff 4; Total Assisted 175.

Simeon House II (Sacred Heart Parish), 1322 Lafayette Ave., 47804. Tel: 812-232-6533. Harriett Johnson, Dir. Total Staff 4; Total Assisted 150.

Terre Haute Catholic Charities Foodbank, 1356 Locust St., 47807. Tel: 812-232-1447. Pat Etling, Dir. Total Staff 3; Total Assisted 80,000.

[M] CATHOLIC YOUTH ORGANIZATIONS

INDIANAPOLIS. *Catholic Youth Organization*, Related Ministries, 580 Stevens St., 46208. Tel: 317-632-9311. Mr. Edward J. Tinder, Exec. Dir.; Mr. Gerald R. Ross, Asst. Exec. Dir. Monsignor Downey Athletic Field, Perkins & Raymond St., 46203. Tel: 317-632-9311. Mailing Address: 580 Stevens St., 46203.

NASHVILLE. *C.Y.O. Camp Christina*, R.R. 2, Box 377, 47448. Mailing Address: 580 Stevens St., Indianapolis, 46203. Mr. Kevin Sullivan, Camp Mgr.

C.Y.O. Camp Rancho Framasa, 2230 N. Clay Lick Rd., 47448. Tel: 812-998-2839. Mr. Kevin Sullivan, Camp Mgr.
E-mail: cyocamp@aol.com

[N] NEWMAN CENTERS

INDIANAPOLIS. *Butler University Newman Center*, 4615 Sunset Ave., 46208. Tel: 317-283-7651. Rev. Don Quinn, Dir. Total Staff 2; Total in Residence 1.

Indiana University-Purdue University, Indianapolis Newman Center, Catholic Student Center, 801 N. Dr. Martin Luther King Jr. St., 46202. Tel: 317-632-4378. Rev. Don Quinn, Dir. Total Staff 2; Total in Residence 1.

University of Indianapolis Newman Center, 4615 Sunset Ave., 46208. Tel: 317-283-7651. Rev. Don Quinn, Dir. Total Staff 2; Total in Residence 1.

BLOOMINGTON. *Indiana University, Bloomington Newman Center*, St. Paul's Catholic Center, 1413 E. 17th St., 47408. Tel: 812-339-5561. Revs. Michael O'Mara; Daniel Atkins. Total Staff 2; Total in Residence 5.

FRANKLIN. *Franklin College Newman Center*, 114 Lancelot Dr., 46131. Tel: 317-738-3929. Rev. Paul M. Shikany.

GREENCASTLE. *DePauw Catholic Campus Ministry*, c/o St. Paul Church, 202 E. Washington St., 46135. Tel: 317-653-5678. Rev. Michael C. Fritsch.

MADISON. *Hanover College Newman Center*, 305 W. State St., 47250. Tel: 812-265-4166; 273-1070. Rev. John A. Meyer.

RICHMOND. *Earlham College Newman Center*, 240 S. Sixth St., 47374. Tel: 317-962-3902. Revs. Todd M. Riebe, M.C.C.J., Admin.; Gregory Bramlage. In res., Rev. Daniel F. Armstrong.

TERRE HAUTE. *Indiana State University, Rose Hulman Institute Newman Center*, St. Joseph Campus Center, 113 S. Fifth St., 47807-3577. Tel: 812-232-8088. Rev. Michael J. Goodavish, O.F.M.Conv., Campus Minister.

[O] MISCELLANEOUS

INDIANAPOLIS. *Archdiocesan Black Catholics Concerned*, P.O. Box 88078, 46208-0078. Bro. Howard P. Studivant, O.S.B.

Association of Contemplative Sisters, c/o Carmelite Monastery, 2500 Cold Spring Rd., 46222. Tel: 317-926-5654. Ms. Barbara Scott, Pres. Membership 625.

**Holy Cross Chapter of St. Vincent De Paul Food Pantry, Inc.*, 125 N. Oriental St., 46202. Tel: 317-635-9560. Patrick Janitz, Coord.

International Catholic Deaf Association (Chapter No. 38), c/o Metropolitan Tribunal, P.O. Box 1410, 46206. Tel: 317-236-1460; 872-5485; 800-855-2880 (TDD). Rev. Joseph W. Dooley, Chap.

St. Vincent De Paul Society Archdiocese Council of Indianapolis, Inc., P.O. Box 19133, 46219. Tel: 317-684-1009. Mr. Don Striegel, Pres.

BEECH GROVE. *Alverno Administrative Services, Inc.*, 1300 Albany St., 46107. Tel: 317-783-9341. Mr. William G. Laker, Vice Pres. Information Svcs. Sponsored by Sisters of St. Francis Health Services, Inc.

Alverno-Beech Grove Corp., 1600 Albany St., 46107. Tel: 317-783-8133; Fax: 317-781-2142. Mr. Robert J. Brody, Pres. & CEO.

MADISON. *Prince of Peace Religious Education*, 305 W. State St., 47250. Tel: 812-265-4166. Sr. Alice Marie Gronotte, O.S.B., Parish Admin. of Religious Education.

MOUNT SAINT FRANCIS. *Mount Saint Francis Sanctuary, Inc.*, 101 St. Anthony Dr., 47146-9999. Tel: 812-923-8817; Fax: 812-923-0177. Samuel L. Smith, Pres.; Thomas A. Smith, O.F.M.Conv., Vice Pres. & Treas.; Michelle Sinkhorn, Sec.

NEW ALBANY. *New Albany Deanery-Catholic Youth Ministry*, 707 W. Hwy. 131, 47129. Tel: 812-945-0354; Fax: 812-945-2929.

TERRE HAUTE. *St. Patrick Endowment Trust*, 1807 Poplar St., 47803.

[P] CLOSED PARISHES, SCHOOLS AND OTHER INSTITUTIONS

INDIANAPOLIS. *O'Meara Catholic Center-Xavier Building*. The Archives, 1400 N. Meridian St., 46202. Tel: 317-236-1429. The following list of closed parishes, schools & institutions indicates where the respective records are kept & where inquiries should be directed. Other inquiries may be directed to the above address.

St. John the Evangelist (1855-1936), Acton.
St. Jude Thaddeus (1889-1898), Adyeville.
St. Patrick (1865-1973), Bainbridge.
Queen of the Most Holy Rosary (1919-1942), Blanford.
St. Patrick (1847-1902). Merged with St. Michael, Cannelton, Cannelton.
St. Joseph (1870-1970). Sacramental records in Archdiocesan Archives, Carbon.
St. Anthony (1917-1942), Centenary.
St. Anthony (1861-1993). Merged with Prince of Peace, Madison, where sacramental records are kept, China.
St. Columba (1963-1994). Merged with St. Bartholomew, Columbus, where sacramental records are kept.
Sacred Heart (1868-1918) (1868-1918), Cypress Dale.
St. Mary (1824-1973). Sacramental records kept at St. Augustine, Leopold, Derby.
St. Michael (1820-1928), Dogwood.
Our Lady of Perpetual Help (1911-1982). Sacramental records kept at St. Mary, Sullivan (Evansville Diocese), Dugger.
St. John (1910-1912). Accounts book in Archdiocesan Archives, Ellsworth.
Mattingly Chapel (1874-1886), Eureka.
St. Augustine (1891-1980). Sacramental records in Archdiocesan Archives, Fontanet.
All Souls Chapel (1900-1915), Hovey.
St. Columban (1848-1868), Indian Creek.
Assumption (1894-1994). Merged with St. Anthony where sacramental records are kept.
St. Bridget (1880-1994). Merged with SS. Peter & Paul where sacramental records are kept.
St. Catherine of Sienna (1909-1993). Merged with St. James & renamed Good Shepherd where sacramental records are kept.
St. Francis de Sales (1881-1983). Sacramental records kept at Archdiocesan Archives.
St. James the Greater (1951-1993). Merged with St. Catherine & renamed Good Shepherd where sacramental records are kept.
St. Joseph (1873-1949). Sacramental records kept at "new" St. Joseph parish.
St. Patrick (1868-1890), Knightsville.
Sacred Heart of Mary (1854-1922), Laconia.
St. Raphael (1869-1958). Sacramental records kept at St. Gabriel, Connersville, Laurel.
Mother of God (1854-1941), Lexington.
St. Joachim (c. 1879-1930), Locust Point.
St. Mary (1851-1993). Merged with St. Michael & St. Patrick to form Prince of Peace where sacramental records are kept, Madison.
St. Michael (1837-1993). Merged with St. Mary & St. Patrick to form Prince of Peace where sacramental records are kept, Madison.
St. Patrick (1853-1993). Merged with St. Mary & St. Michael to form Prince of Peace where sacramental records are kept, Madison.
St. Patrick (1842-1881), McCutcheonville.
St. Mary (c. 1905-1936), Mecca.
St. Joseph (1855-1974), Milltown.
St. John the Baptist (c. 1852-c. 1885), Mount Erin.
St. Rose (c. 1821-c. 1883), Mount Pleasant.
St. Bridget (1845-1936), Nebraska.
Holy Trinity (1836-1975). Merged with St. Mary where sacramental records are kept., New Albany.
St. Peter (1868-1885). Sacramental & cemetery records in Archdiocesan Archives, Rome.
St. Catherine (1841-1871). Sacramental records in Archdiocesan Archives.
St. John (1875-1968). Merged with St. Joseph (1891-1968), Perry Co. to form St. Isidore, Perry Co., where sacramental records are kept.
St. Magdalen (1847-1941). After 1941 formed a mission at New Marion. Sacramental records kept at St. John, Osgood.
St. Paul (1859-1996). Sacramental records up to 1905 kept in Archdiocesan Archives; after 1905 kept at St. Vincent, Shelby Co.
St. Rose (c. 1840-1903). Merged with St. Thomas, Knox Co. (Evansville Diocese), where sacramental records are kept.
St. Mary (1871-1902), Salem.
St. Patrick (1841-1958). Sacramental records kept at Archdiocesan Archives, Scipio.
St. Thomas (c. 1845-c. 1875), Selvin.
St. Ann (1909-1978). Sacramental records kept at St. Mary, Sullivan (Evansville Diocese), Shelburn.
Mother of God (1900-1920). Sacramental records kept at Archdiocesan Archives, Shirley.
St. John the Baptist (c. 1855-1903). Sacramental records kept at Archdiocesan Archives, Valley Mills.
Our Lady of Lourdes (1900-1929), West Baden Springs.
St. Stephen (1906-1944), Willow Valley.
All Saints Catholic Grade School, St. Bartholomew Catholic School, 1306 27th St., Columbus, 47201. Tel: 812-372-6830.
St. Bartholomew Grade School, St. Bartholomew Catholic School, 1306 27th St., Columbus, 47201. Tel: 812-372-6830.
St. Columba Grade School, St. Bartholomew Catholic school, 1306 27th St., Columbus, 47201. Tel: 812-372-6830.
Assumption Grade School, All Saints Catholic School, 337 N. Warman Ave., 46222. Tel: 317-636-3739.
Catholic Grade School, Holy Cross Central school, 125 N. Oriental St., 46201. Tel: 317-638-9068.
Holy Rosary Grade School, Holy Rosary Rectory, 520 Stevens St., 46203. Tel: 317-636-4478.
Holy Trinity Grade School, All Saints Catholic School, 337 N. Warman Ave., 46222. Tel: 317-636-3739.
Sacred Heart Grade School, Sacred Heart Rectory, 1530 Union St., 46225. Tel: 317-638-5551.
St. Ann Grade School, St. Ann Rectory, 2862 S. Holt Rd., 46241. Tel: 317-244-3750.
St. Anthony Grade School, All Saints Catholic School, 337 N. Warman Ave., 46222. Tel: 317-636-3739.
St. Bernadette Grade School. Contact Archdiocesan Archives.
St. Bridget Grade School. Contact Archdiocesan Archives.
St. Catherine Grade School, Central Catholic School, 1155 Cameron St., 46203. Tel: 317-783-7759.
St. Francis de Sales Grade School, St. Rita Grade School, 1733 Dr. Andrew J. Brown Ave., 46202. Tel: 317-636-8580.
St. James Grade School, Central Catholic School, 1155 Cameron St., 46203. Tel: 317-783-7759.
St. Joseph Grade School. (Mickley Rd.), All Saints Catholic School, 337 N. Warman Ave., 46222. Tel: 317-636-3739; 3738.
St. Joseph Grade School. (Nobel St.), All Saints Catholic School, 337 N. Warman Ave., 46222. Tel: 317-636-3739.
St. Mary Grade School, Holy Cross Central School, 125 N. Oriental St., 46201. Tel: 317-638-9068.
St. Patrick Grade School, Central Catholic School, 1155 Cameron St., 46203. Tel: 317-783-7759.
St. Mary Grade School, Pope John XXIII Grade School, 221 State St., Madison, 47250.
St. Michael Grade School, Pope John XXIII Grade School, 221 State St., Madison, 47250.
St. Anthony Grade School, St. Anthony Rectory, P.O. Box 3, Morris, 47033. Tel: 812-934-6218.
St. Anne Grade School, St. Anne Church, 102 N. 19th St., New Castle, 47362. Tel: 317-529-0933.
Holy Family Grade School, St. Elizabeth Ann Seton School, 801 W. Main St., Richmond, 47374. Tel: 317-962-4877.
St. Andrew Grade School, St. Elizabeth Ann Seton School, 801 W. Main St., Richmond, 47374. Tel: 317-962-4877.
St. Mary Grade School, St. Elizabeth Ann Seton School, 801 W. Main St., Richmond, 47374. Tel: 317-962-4877.
St. Ann Grade School, Vigo County School Office, 961 Lafayette Ave., Terre Haute, 47808.
St. Benedict School. Contact Archdiocesan Archives, Terre Haute.
St. Joseph School. Contact Archdiocesan Archives, Terre Haute.
St. Margaret Mary Grade School, St. Margaret Mary Parish, 2405 S. Seventh St., Terre Haute, 47802. Tel: 812-232-3512.
Chartrand High School, Roncalli High School, 3300 Prague Rd., 46227. Tel: 317-787-8277.
Kennedy High School, Roncalli High School, 3300 Prague Rd., 46227. Tel: 317-787-8277.
Ladywood Academy & Ladywood-Agnes Academy, General Administration, Office of the Records-Owens Hall, St. Mary of the Woods, 47876. Tel: 812-535-3131.
Latin School. Contact Archdiocesan Archives.
Our Lady of Grace Academy, Our Lady of Grace Monastery, 1402 Southern Ave., Beech Grove, 46107. Tel: 317-787-3287.
Sacred Heart High School, Roncalli High School, 3300 Prague Rd., 46227. Tel: 317-787-8277.
St. Agnes Academy, General Administration, Office of the Records-Owens Hall, St. Mary of the Woods, 47876. Tel: 812-535-3131.
St. John Academy, General Administration, Office of the Records-Owens Hall, St. Mary of the Woods, 47876. Tel: 812-535-3131.
St. Mary Academy, Registrar, Franciscan Motherhouse, Oldenburg, 47036. Tel: 812-934-2475.
Central Catholic High School for Girls (1937-1946). Contact Archdiocesan Archives, Terre Haute.
St. Joseph Academy (1888-1937). Contact Archdiocesan Archives, Terre Haute.
St. Agnes Academy. Contact Archdiocesan Archives, Terre Haute.
St. Patrick High School for Girls (1923-1937; 1946-1953). Contact Archdiocesan Archives, Terre Haute.
St. Vincent Academy, Sisters of Providence (1848-?). Check records at St. Mary of the Woods, Terre Haute.
Schulte High School (1953-1977), Vigo County School Office, 961 Lafayette Ave., Terre Haute, 47808.
Sisters of the Good Shepherd Convent (1873-1967). The following records are at the Archdiocesan Archive: Angel Guardian School For Orphans, entrance records, 1924-1937; Marydale (High) School (for Delinquent Girls), sacramental records, 1953-1975; Other records at 2849 Fischer Pl., Cincinnati, OH 45211, Tel:513-661-1833.
St. Edward Hospital (1901-1960). Poor Sisters of St. Francis Seraph of Perpetual Adoration (O.S.F.), New Albany.
St. Ann Orphanage for Girls (1876-1919). Sisters of Providence. Some baptismal records in Archdiocesan Archives, most probably at St. Mary of the Woods, Terre Haute.
St. Anthony Hospital (1882-1979). Poor Sisters of St. Francis Seraph of Perpetual Adoration (O.S.F.). Baptismal Records (1917-1975) at Archdiocesan Archives. Baptismal records (1917-1975) at St. Joseph Parish, Terre Haute. Tel: 812-232-7011.
St. Mary Orphanage for Girls (1848-1876). Sisters of Providence, Vincennes.
St. Vincent Orphanage for Boys (1851-1972). Sisters of Providence (1851-1922); Sisters of St. Francis of Oldenburg (1922-1972), Vincennes.

RELIGIOUS INSTITUTES OF MEN REPRESENTED IN THE ARCHDIOCESE

For further details refer to the corresponding bracketed number in the Religious Institutes of Men or Women section.

[0200]—*Benedictine Monks of St. Maur & St. Meinrad.*—O.S.B.
[0320]—*Brothers of Christian Instruction (Notre Dame Province).*—F.I.C.
[0600]—*Brothers of the Congregation of Holy Cross (Midwest & Eastern Provinces).*—C.S.C.
[0380]—*Camboni Missionaries of the Heart of Jesus.*—M.C.C.J.
1140*Congregation of the sacred Heart of Jesus & Mary.*—SS.CC.
[0480]—*Conventual Franciscans.*—O.F.M.Conv.
[0520]—*Franciscan Friars (St. John the Baptist & Sacred Heart Province).*—O.F.M.
[0690]—*Jesuit Fathers and Brothers.*—S.J.
[0840]—*Missionary Servants of the Most Holy Trinity.*—S.T.
[0420]—*Society of the Divine Word.* (Chicago Province).—S.V.D.

RELIGIOUS INSTITUTES OF WOMEN REPRESENTED IN THE ARCHDIOCESE

[0230]—*Benedictine Sisters of Pontifical Jurisdiction.* (Ferdinand, IN).—O.S.B.
[1920]—*Congregation of the Sisters of the Holy Cross.*—C.S.C.
[1730]—*Congregation of the Sisters of the Third Order of St. Francis, Oldenburg, IN.*—O.S.F.
[0760]—*Daughters of Charity of St. Vincent De Paul.* (Evansville, IN).—D.C.
[0420]—*Discalced Carmelite Nuns.*—O.C.D.
[1070-01]—*Dominican Sisters.*—O.P.
[1070-03]—*Dominican Sisters.*—O.P.
[2340]—*Little Sisters of the Poor.* (Baltimore, MD).—L.S.P.
[2820]—*Missionary Sisters of Our Lady of Africa.* (American Headquarters, Winooski, VT).—M.S.O.L.A.
[0440]—*Sisters of Charity of Cincinnati, Ohio.* (Central Region).—S.C.
[0430]—*Sisters of Charity of the Blessed Virgin Mary.*

Dubuque, IA.—B.V.M.
[]—*Sisters of Loretto at the Foot of the Cross*. Nerinx, KY.—S.L.
[3360]—*Sisters of Providence of Saint Mary-of-the-Woods, IN.*—S.P.
[]—*Sisters of St. Benedict of Our Lady of Grace Monastery*. (Beech Grove, IN).—O.S.B.
[1640]—*Sisters of St. Francis of Perpetual Adoration*.—O.S.F.
[3840]—*Sisters of St. Joseph Carondelet*. (St. Louis, MO).—C.S.J.
[]—*Sisters of St. Joseph of Tipton*. (Topton, IN).—C.S.J.
[3320]—*Sisters of the Presentation of the Blessed Virgin Mary*. (Dubuque, IA).—P.B.V.M.
[1760]—*Sisters of the Third Order of St. Francis of Penance and of Charity*. (Triffin, OH).—O.S.F.
[1720]—*Sisters of the Third Order Regular of St. Francis of the Congregation of Our Lady of Lourdes*.—O.S.F.
[4120-03]—*Ursuline Nuns of the Congregation of Paris*.—O.S.U.

ARCHDIOCESAN CEMETERIES

INDIANAPOLIS. *Catholic Cemeteries*, 9001 Haverstick Rd., 46240.
Indianapolis Deanery.
Holy Cross.
St. Joseph.
Calvary.
Our Lady of Peace.
St. Malachy, Brownsburg.
St. Malachy, Pittsboro.
BATESVILLE. *Batesville Deanery*.
St. Mary, Greensburg.
St. John, Osgood.
St. Charles, Milan.
St. Maurice, Napoleon.
BLOOMINGTON. *Bloomington Deanery*.
Catholic, Martinsville.
CONNERSVILLE. *Connersville Deanery*.
St. Raphael, Laurel.
St. Michael, Brookville.
Holy Family, Oldenburg.
Holy Family Shrine, Oldenburg.
Cemetery North, Brookville.
Calvary, Rushville.
St. Bridget, Liberty.
St. Mary, Richmond.
NEW ALBANY. *New Albany Deanery*.
St. Joseph, Corydon.
St. Michael, Dogwood.
St. Peter, Taylor Two.
Cemetery South West, Bradford.
St. Bernard, Frenchtown.
St. Joachim, Locust Point.
St. Anthony, Jeffersonville.
Queen of Heaven.
St. Michael.
SEYMOUR. *Seymour Deanery*.
St. Ambrose.
St. Mary, North Vernon.
St. Catherine.
Old St. James.
St. Joseph.
St. Patrick.
St. Magdalen.
TELL CITY. *Tell City Deanery*.
St. Joseph, St. Croix.
St. Croix. (Cemetery on original parish site.), St. Croix.
St. Meinrad, St. Meinrad.
St. Paul.
St. Peter, Cannelton.
TERRE HAUTE. *Terre Haute Deanery*.
Catholic, Brazil.
Calvary.
St. Joseph.

NECROLOGY

† Bankowski, John A., (Retired). —Died May 18, 1996.
† Barthel, Aloysius A., (Retired). —Died Nov. 30, 1996.
† Drewes, Robert F., North Vernon, IN, St. Mary. —Died June 15, 1996.
† Klein, Robert J., (On Disability Leave). —Died Jan. 1, 1997.

Diocese of Jackson

(Dioecesis Jacksoniensis)

Most Reverend

WILLIAM R. HOUCK, D.D.

Bishop of Jackson; ordained May 19, 1951; appointed Auxiliary Bishop of Jackson and Titular Bishop of Allessano on March 28, 1979; consecrated May 27, 1979; appointed Bishop of Jackson April 24, 1984; installed June 5, 1984. *Mailing Address: P.O. Box 2248, Jackson, MS, 39225-2248.*

Chancery Office: 237 E. Amite St., P.O. Box 2248, Jackson, MS, 39225-2248. Tel.: 601-969-1880; Fax: 601-960-8455.

Legal Title: "Catholic Diocese of Jackson."

ESTABLISHED JULY 28, 1837 AS DIOCESE OF NATCHEZ. NAME CHANGED TO DIOCESE OF NATCHEZ-JACKSON, MARCH 7, 1957. NAME CHANGED TO DIOCESE OF JACKSON, JUNE 6, 1977.

Square Miles 37,643.

Comprises 65 Counties in the State of Mississippi, namely: Adams, Alcorn, Amite, Attala, Benton, Bolivar, Calhoun, Carroll, Chickasaw, Choctaw, Claiborne, Clarke, Clay, Coahoma, Copiah, De Soto, Franklin, Grenada, Hinds, Holmes, Humphreys, Issaquena, Itawamba, Jasper, Jefferson, Kemper, Lafayette, Lauderdale, Leake, Lee, Leflore, Lincoln, Lowndes, Madison, Marshall, Monroe, Montgomery, Neshoba, Newton, Noxubee, Oktibbeha, Panola, Pike, Pontotoc, Prentiss, Quitman, Rankin, Scott, Sharkey, Simpson, Smith, Sunflower, Tallahatchie, Tate, Tippah, Tishomingo, Tunica, Union, Warren, Washington, Webster, Wilkinson, Winston, Yalobusha and Yazoo.

STATISTICAL OVERVIEW

Personnel	
Bishop	1
Priests: Diocesan Active in Diocese	50
Priests: Active Outside Diocese	6
Priests: Diocesan in Foreign Missions	2
Priests: Retired, Sick or Absent	13
Number of Diocesan Priests	71
Religious Priests in Diocese	30
Ordinations:	
Transitional Deacons	1
Permanent Deacons in Diocese	11
Total Brothers	11
Total Sisters	286
Parishes	
Parishes	74
With Resident Pastor:	
Resident Diocesan Priests	44
Resident Religious Priests	21
Without Resident Pastor:	
Administered by Priests	3
Administered by Professed Men Religious	1
Administered by Women Religious	3
Administered by Lay People	2
Missions	27
Pastoral Centers	3
Professional Ministry Personnel:	
Brothers	3
Sisters	23
Lay Ministers	17
Welfare	
Catholic Hospitals	1
Total Assisted	65,812
Health Care Centers	1
Total Assisted	8,465
Homes for the Aged	1
Total Assisted	225
Residential Care of Children	2
Total Assisted	168
Day Care and Extended Day Care Centers	2
Total Assisted	200
Specialized Homes	5
Total Assisted	2,000
Special Centers for Social Services	2
Total Assisted	8,050
Residential Care of Disabled	3
Total Assisted	60
Other Institutions	4
Total Assisted	150
Educational	
Diocesan Students in Other Seminaries	5
Total Seminarians	5
Colleges and Universities	1
Total Students	28
High Schools, Diocesan and Parish	4
Total Students	815
Elementary Schools, Diocesan and Parish	15
Total Students	4,380
Catechesis/Religious Education:	
High School Students	1,295
Elementary Students	4,166
Total Students Under Catholic Instruction	10,689
Teachers in the Diocese:	
Sisters	23
Lay Teachers	325
Vital Statistics	
Receptions into the Church:	
Infant Baptism Totals	750
Adult Baptism Totals	103
Received into Full Communion	256
First Communions	685
Confirmations	455
Marriages:	
Catholic	132
Interfaith	248
Total Marriages	380
Deaths	466
Total Catholic Population	44,340
Total Population	1,980,025

Former Bishops—Rt. Rev. JOHN J. CHANCHE, S.S., D.D., cons. March 14, 1841; died July 22, 1852.—Rt. Rev. J. O. VAN DE VELDE, S.J., D.D., transferred from Chicago, July 29, 1853; died Nov. 13, 1855.—Most Rev. WILLIAM HENRY ELDER, D.D., cons. May 3, 1857; transferred to Cincinnati, 1880; died Oct. 31, 1904.—Most Rev. FRANCIS JANSSENS, D.D., cons. May 1, 1881; transferred to New Orleans, Aug. 7, 1888; died June 9, 1897.—Rt. Rev. THOMAS HESLIN, D.D., cons. June 18, 1889; died Feb. 22, 1911.—Rt. Rev. JOHN EDWARD GUNN, S.M., D.D., cons. Aug. 29, 1911; died Feb. 19, 1924.—Most Rev. RICHARD OLIVER GEROW, LL.D., S.T.D., ord. June 5, 1909; appt. June 25, 1924; cons. Oct. 15, 1924; retired Dec. 2, 1967; died Dec. 20, 1976.—Most Rev. JOSEPH B. BRUNINI, D.D., LL.D., J.C.D., ord. Dec. 5, 1933; cons. Jan. 29, 1957; appt. Bishop, Dec. 2, 1967; installed Jan. 29, 1968; retired Jan. 24, 1984; died Jan. 7, 1996.

Chancery Office—237 E. Amite St., P.O. Box 2248, Jackson, 39225-2248. Tel: 601-969-1880; Fax: 601-960-8455. The telephone number for all Diocesan Offices is 601-969-1880, unless otherwise listed. Office Hours: 8:30-4:30.

Office of the Bishop—Most Rev. WILLIAM R. HOUCK, D.D., *237 E. Amite St., P.O. Box 2248, Jackson, 39225-2248.*

Office of Vicar General—Revs. MICHAEL FLANNERY, J.C.L.; FRANCIS J. COSGROVE.

Department of Ecclesiastical Affairs—

Chancellor—Rev. MICHAEL FLANNERY, J.C.L., *237 E. Amite St., P.O. Box 2248, Jackson, 39225-2248.*

Vice Chancellor—Rev. AEDAN MANNING, S.T., J.C.L.

Director of Vocations—Rev. WILLIAM HENRY.

Director of Permanent Diaconate—Deacon FRANK AGOSTA.

Propagation of the Faith—Rev. Msgr. NOEL FOLEY, Dir., *P.O. Box 57, Jackson, 39205.* Tel: 601-969-3125.

Apostleship of Prayer—Rev. Msgr. NOEL FOLEY, Dir., *P.O. Box 57, Jackson, 39205.* Tel: 601-969-3125.

Archivists—JO ANN HAIEN; FRANCES BOECKMAN.

Judicial Vicar—Rev. AEDAN MANNING, S.T., J.C.L.

Ecumenism—Rev. RICHARD SMITH, *St. Michael, P.O. Box 388, Forest, 39074-0388.* Tel: 601-469-1916.

Promoters of Justice—Revs. MICHAEL FLANNERY, J.C.L.; FRANCIS COSGROVE; THOMAS NIEMIRA.

Defenders of the Bond—Revs. MICHAEL FLANNERY, J.C.L.; FRANCIS COSGROVE; THOMAS NIEMIRA; WILLIAM CULLEN; DANIEL GALLAGHER; KEVIN SLATTERY.

Notaries—Rev. ROBERT OLIVIER; TONI THOMAS.

Diocesan Judges—Rev. Msgr. NOEL G. FOLEY, J.C.L.; Revs. PATRICK FARRELL; AEDAN MANNING, S.T., J.C.L.

Approved Advocate and Auditors—Revs. THOMAS DELANEY; CHARLES BUCCIANTINI; MERYL SCHMIT; DON DERIVAUX, S.T.L.

Priests' Council—Most Rev. WILLIAM R. HOUCK, Pres.; Revs. ELVIN SUNDS, Chm.; PATRICK FARRELL, Vice-Chm.; Rev. Msgr. NOEL FOLEY, Treas.; Revs. FRANCIS COSGROVE, Sec.; GEORGE ARTIS, S.V.D.; CHARLES BUCCIANTINI; ALFRED CAMP; BRIAN CARROLL; MICHAEL FLANNERY, J.C.L.; SAMUEL MESSINA; MICHAEL O'BRIEN; ROBERT OLIVER.

Diocesan Consultors—Revs. MICHAEL FLANNERY, J.C.L.; FRANCIS COSGROVE; Rev. Msgr. NOEL FOLEY; Revs. ROBERT OLIVIER; SAM MESSINA; PATRICK FARRELL.

Association of Priests—Most Rev. WILLIAM R. HOUCK, Co-Chm.; Most Rev. JOSEPH L. HOWZE, Co-Chm.; Rev. Msgr. MICHAEL THORNTON, Pres.; Rev. THOMAS MCGING, Sec.-Treas. Trustees: Rev. THOMAS CONWAY; Rev. Msgr. NOEL FOLEY; Revs. LOUIS LOHAN; ELVIN SUNDS.

Personnel Board—Revs. MICHAEL FLANNERY, Personnel Dir. KENT BOWLDS; BRIAN CARROLL; JOSEPH DYER; PATRICK FARRELL; PATRICK NOONAN.

Department of Administration & Finance—WILLIAM P. DUNNING, Dir., Admin. Affairs, *237 E. Amite St., P.O. Box 2248, Jackson, 39225-2248.*

Income Development—GEORGE ROMAN, Dir.

Department of Catholic Charities and Community Services—LINDA RAFF, Dir., *748 N. President St., P.O. Box 2248, Jackson, 39225-2248.* Tel: 601-355-8634; Fax: 601-960-8493.

Family Life—Sr. DOROTHY HEIDERSCHEIT, O.S.F., Dir. Tel: 601-355-8634.

Peace and Justice—LINDA RAFF, Dir., *P.O. Box 2248, Jackson, 39225-2248.*

Department of Educational Services—Rev. WILLIAM CULLEN, Dir., *237 E. Amite St., P.O. Box 2248, Jackson, 39225-2248.* Catholic Schools, Religious Education.

Superintendent of Schools—Rev. WILLIAM CULLEN.

Associate Superintendent—Sr. DEBORAH HUGHES, S.S.J.
Assistant Superintendent—Sr. MARY KAREN O'KELLY, O.P.
Early Child Development, Health and Education Projects—Sr. CYRENA HARKINS, R.S.M.
Director of Religious Education & Assistant of the Superintendant in School Administration—Sr. RITA DEMATTE, S.C.N.
Associate Director of Religious Education—Sr. THERESA BRETTHAUER, M.S.B.T.
Director of Spring Hill Theology Program—Sr. RITA DEMATTE, S.C.N.
Campus Ministry—Rev. WILLIAM CULLEN, Dir.
Department of Evangelization—Miss MARY WOODWARD, Dir.
Youth Ministry—Mr. ALBERT SIMPSON, Diocesan Dir.
Pastoral Planning and Pastoral Councils—Miss MARY WOODWARD, Dir.
"Mississippi Today"—JANNA AVALON, Editor.
Intercultural Awareness / Diocesan Black Catholic Congress Board—Miss MARY WOODWARD, Dir.
Hispanic Ministry—Sr. PATRICIA BROWN, S.S.M.N., Dir.
Catholic Foundation-Diocese of Jackson—GEORGE ROMAN, Dir., *P.O. Box 2248, Jackson, 39225-2248.*
Friends of Catholic University—Rev. Msgr. NOEL FOLEY, Dir.
Holy Childhood, Pontifical Association—Sr. CYRENA HARKINS, R.S.M., Dir., *P.O. Box 2248, Jackson, 39225.*
The National Catholic Office for Motion Pictures—Rev. Msgr. NOEL FOLEY, Dir.

CLERGY, PARISHES, MISSIONS AND PAROCHIAL SCHOOLS

CITY OF JACKSON
(Hinds County)

1—ST. PETER CATHEDRAL, Rev. Msgr. Noel Foley, Rector. In res., Revs. Michael Flannery; Daniel Gallagher.
Res., 123 N. West St., P.O. Box 57, 39205-0057. Tel: 601-969-3125; Fax: 601-969-3130.

2—ST. MARY, Revs. Richard Chiles, O.Praem., Admin.; Andy Cribben, O.Praem., Assoc. Pastor. In res., Rev. Martin Philipsen, O.Praem.
Res., 653 Claiborne, 39209. Tel: 601-353-2292; Fax: 601-944-1606.
School—Tel: 601-353-7357. Sr. Mary Rose Meis, C.S.A., Prin.
Lay Teachers 6; Students 125.

3—ST. RICHARD, Revs. Richard Somers; Habeeb Joseph Tonos, II. In res., Rev. Msgr. Michael Glynn; Rev. Aedan Manning, S.T.
Res., 1242 Lynnwood Dr., P.O. Box 16547, 39236. Tel: 601-366-2335; Fax: 601-366-0438.
School—Tel: 601-366-1157; Fax: 601-366-0439.
Sisters of Mercy 1; Lay Teachers 22; Students 450.

4—ST. THERESE, Rev. Thomas Lalor; Sr. Mary Frances Gorman, O.P., Pastoral Assoc. In res., Rev. Brian Kaskie.
Res., 304 Fairhill Dr., 39204. Tel: 601-372-3441.
Church—309 McDowell Rd., P.O. Box 8642, 39284-8642. Tel: 601-372-4481.
School—Tel: 601-372-3323.
Lay Teachers 8; Students 154.

5—HOLY FAMILY, Rev. Joseph Dyer.
Res., 820 Forest Ave., 39206. Tel: 601-362-1888.

6—HOLY GHOST, Rev. George Artis, S.V.D.; Deacon Sam Baker.
Res., 1151 Cloister St., 39202. Tel: 601-353-1339.

7—CHRIST THE KING, Revs. Richard P. Chiles, O.Praem.; Andrew Cribben, O.Praem.
Res., 2303 J.R. Lynch St., 39209. Tel: 601-948-8867.
School—Preschool and Montessori, Tel: 601-352-5441. Mrs. Jocelyn Lyons, Dir.
Students 132.

OUTSIDE THE CITY OF JACKSON

Aberdeen, Monroe Co., St. Francis of Assisi, Rev. Timothy Murphy, Glmy.
Res., 104 S. James St., P.O. Box 134, 39730-0134. Tel: 601-369-2897.
Missions—Houston, Chickasaw Co., Immaculate Heart of Mary, P.O. Box 309, Houston, 38851. Tel: 601-456-5450; Okolona, Chickasaw Co., St. Theresa, 116 N. Fleming St., Okolona, 38860. Tel: 601-447-3683. Sr. Elizabeth Brown, C.S.J., Mission Coord.

Amory, Monroe Co., St. Helen, Sr. Marie Gilligan, S.C., Res. Pastoral Min.; Sr. Kathleen Quigley, S.C., Pastoral Assoc.
Res., 401 Eighth Ave. S., P.O. Box 97, 38821-0097. Tel: 601-256-8392.
Mission—Fulton, Itawamba Co., Christ the King, 100 E. Main St., Fulton, 38843-1207. Tel: 601-862-2239. Sr. Martha Werner, S.C., Mission Coord.

Batesville, Panola Co., St. Mary, Rev. Thomas Boyce.
Res., P.O. Box 569, 38606-0569. Tel: 601-563-2273.
Mission—Sardis, St. John the Baptist.

Belzoni, Humphreys Co., All Saints, Rev. Samuel Messina.
Res., 200 Bowles St., P.O. Box 3602, 39038. Tel: 601-247-1408.
Mission—Anguilla, Our Mother of Mercy.

Booneville, Prentiss Co., St. Francis of Assisi, Rev. Thomas L. Burns, S.C.J.; Sr. Marian Jochum, O.S.F., Res. Pastoral Min.
Res., P.O. Box 654, 38829. Tel: 601-728-7509.
Mission—Iuka, Tishomingo Co., St. Mary, P.O. Box 651, Iuka, 38852. Tel: 601-423-9358. Sr. Dolores Partsch, C.S.J., Pastoral Min.

Brandon, Rankin Co., St. Paul, Rev. Edward Balser; Deacon Frank Agosta.
Res., 115 Bellegrove Blvd., 39042. Tel: 601-992-9547; Fax: 601-992-9972.
Church—5971 Hwy. 25, 39042.
School—Learning Center, Tel: 601-992-2876. Sr. Terez Gonsoulin, S.S.N.D., Dir.
Students 100.

Brookhaven, Lincoln Co., St. Francis, Rev. Liam Pentony.
Res., 227 E. Cherokee St., P.O. Box 196, 39601. Tel: 601-833-1799.

Bruce, Calhoun Co., Catholic Community of Calhoun County, Mrs. Amy Giorgio, Pastoral Coord.
Res., 204 East Clay, P.O. Box 230, 38915. Tel: 601-983-2790.

Camden, Madison Co., Immaculate Conception, Rev. Joseph P. Keenan, S.T. In res., Rev. Celestine E. Pfannenstial, S.T.; Bro. Finbarr Ray, S.T.
Res., 1363 Hwy. 17, 39045. Tel: 601-468-2354.
School—Tel: 601-468-2324.
Sisters 3; Lay Teachers 5.

Canton, Madison Co., Sacred Heart, Rev. Patrick Noonan; Sr. Mary Ann Grausam, S.L.W., Pastoral Assoc.
Res., 238 E. Center St., P.O. Box 361, 39046. Tel: 601-859-3749.
Holy Child Jesus, Rev. Patrick Noonan, Admin.; Sr. Mary Ann Grausman, S.L.W., Pastoral Assoc.
Res., 315 Garrett St., P.O. Box 366, 39046. Tel: 601-859-2957.
School—Tel: 601-859-4168. Sr. Rose Mary Cousins, C.C.V.I., Prin.
Sisters 2; Lay Teachers 12; Students 184.

Carthage, Leake Co., St. Anne, Rev. Patrick Noonan, Admin.; Sr. Patricia Godri, S.C., Res. Pastoral Min.
Res., 207 Red Dog Rd., 39051. Tel: 601-267-7190.

Charleston, Tallahatchie Co., St. John, Rev. Peter I. Machesky, O.F.M.
Res., 304 W. Cypress St., P.O. Box 30, 38921-0030. Tel: 601-647-3170.
Convent—402 N. Lafayette St., 38921. Tel: 601-647-8692. Daughters of Charity

Chatawa, Pike Co., St. Teresa, Rev. Robert Dore.
Res., P.O. Box 11, 39632-0011. Tel: 601-783-5931; Fax: 601-783-3984.
Mission—Magnolia, St. James.

Clarksdale, Coahoma Co., St. Elizabeth, Rev. Brian Carroll, Admin.
Res., 130 Florence Ave., 38614-2720. Tel: 601-624-4301.
School—109 Clark St., 38614-2720. Tel: 601-624-4239.
Lay Teachers 13; Students 137.
Immaculate Conception, Revs. Brian Carroll; Jake Roth; Sr. Agnes Zaroski, C.S.J., Pastoral Assoc.
Res., 510 Ritchie Ave., 38614-0042. Tel: 601-624-4029.
Early Childhood Center—520 Ritchie Ave., 38614. Tel: 601-627-4823. Mrs. Catherine Fizer, Directress.
Lay Teachers 3; Students 42.

Cleveland, Bolivar Co., Our Lady of Victories, Rev. Charles Bucciantini.
Res., 215 Bishop Rd., P.O. Box 1450, 38732-1450. Tel: 601-846-6273.
Station—Cleveland, Delta State University.

Clinton, Hinds Co., Holy Savior, Rev. Noel Prendergast.
Res., 714 Lyndale St., P.O. Box 85, 39060. Tel: 601-924-6344.
Mission—Raymond, Immaculate Conception.

Columbus, Lowndes Co., Annunciation, Rev. Gerard Hurley.
Res., 808 College St., 39701. Tel: 601-328-2927; Fax: 601-329-8270.
School—223 N. Browder St., 39701. Tel: 601-328-4479; Fax: 601-328-0430.
Lay Teachers 14; Students 153.

Corinth, Alcorn Co., St. James, Rev. Thomas L. Burns, S.C.J.
Res., 3187 Harper Rd., P.O. Box 660, 38834-0660. Tel: 601-287-1385.
Church—3189 Harper Rd., 38834. Tel: 601-287-1051.

Crystal Springs, Copiah Co., St. John, Rev. Frank Corcoran.
Res., 217 E. Georgetown St., P.O. Box 167, 39059. Tel: 601-892-1717.
Mission—Hazlehurst, St. Martin.

Fayette, Jefferson Co., St. Anne, Rev. Alfred A. Dean, S.S.J.
Res., 195 New Harriston Rd., P.O. Box 159, 39069.

Forest, Scott Co., St. Michael, Rev. Richard Smith.
Res., P.O. Box 388, 39074. Tel: 601-469-1916.
Mission—Newton, St. Anne.

Greenville, Washington Co., St. Joseph, Revs. Patrick Farrell; Jeffrey Waldrep.
Res., 410 Main St., P.O. Box 1220, 38702-1220. Tel: 601-335-5251; Fax: 601-332-1178.
School—Our Lady of Lourdes, (Grades K-6). Tel: 601-334-3287; Fax: 601-332-9877. Sr. Marie Elizabeth Alspaugh, S.S.J., Prin.
Sisters 1; Lay Teachers 25; Students 345.
Junior & Senior High School—(Grades 7-12). Tel: 601-378-9711; Fax: 601-378-3496. Bro. Thomas Geraghty, F.S.C., Prin.
Sacred Heart, Rev. August Langenkamp, S.V.D.; Bro. Matthew Connors, S.V.D., Pastoral Min.
Res., 560 E. Gloster St., 38701-3836. Tel: 601-332-0891.

Greenwood, LeFlore Co., Immaculate Heart of Mary, Rev. Msgr. Thaddeus Harkins; Sr. Christiana Hofmann, S.C.N., Pastoral Min.; Deacon Leon S. Kitchin.
Res., 511 W. Washington St., P.O. Box 313, 38935-0313. Tel: 601-453-3980.
Parish Center—310 Henderson St., 38935-0313. Tel: 601-453-9535.
St. Francis of Assisi, Rev. Hilary Brzezinski, O.F.M.; Bros. Adrian Kolanczyk, O.F.M.; Paul West, O.F.M., Supr.; Donald Lucas, O.F.M.
Res., 2613 Hwy. 82 E., 38930-6070. Tel: 601-453-0623.
School—2607 Hwy. 82 E., 38930-6070. Tel: 601-453-9511; Fax: 601-453-9060.
Brothers 1; Daughters of Mary Mother of Mercy 7; Lay Teachers 3; Students 140.
Convent—2603 Hwy 82 E., P.O. Box 938, 38930-6070. Tel: 601-453-1221.

Grenada, Grenada Co., St. Peter, Rev. Thomas Delaney.
Res., 320 College Blvd., 38901. Tel: 601-226-2490.

Hernando, DeSoto Co., Holy Spirit, Revs. James A. Cunniffe, S.C.J.; Charles Yost, S.C.J.; Deacon Everell Van Tassel.
Res., P.O. Box 424, 38632. Tel: 601-429-7851.

Holly Springs, Marshall Co., St. Joseph, Revs. Paul Casper, S.C.J.; Lawrence Rucker, S.C.J., Assoc. Pastor.
Church—305 Van Dorn Ave., P.O. Box 430, 38635-0430. Tel: 601-252-3138; Fax: 601-252-1522.
School—Holy Family School, Tel: 601-252-1612. Sr. Diane Bauknecht, C.S.A., Prin.
Students 350.

Indianola, Sunflower Co., Immaculate Conception, Rev. Anthony Quyet, Admin.
Res., Hwy. 448, P.O. Box 944, 38751-9665. Tel: 601-887-4659.
St. Benedict the Moor, Rev. Anthony Quyet, Admin.
Res., 403 Church Ave., P.O. Box 407, 38751. Tel: 601-887-4608; 887-4659.

Kosciusko, Attala Co., St. Therese, Barbara A. Sturbaum, Ph.D., Pastoral Min.
Res., 108 Bell St., P.O. Box 628, 39090. Tel: 601-289-1193.

Leland, Washington Co., St. James, Rev. Sean Atkinson.
Res., 312 E. Third St., P.O. Box 352, 38756-0352. Tel: 601-686-7352.
Mission—Hollandale, Immaculate Conception.

Lexington, Holmes Co., St. Thomas, Rev. John Rietti, Admin.
Res., 200 Boulevard St., P.O. Box 762, 39095. Tel: 601-834-4443.
Mission—Winona, Sacred Heart, Tel: 601-283-2808.

Louisville, Winston Co., Sacred Heart, Barbara A. Sturbaum, Ph.D., Pastoral Min.
Res., 410 Spring Ave., 39339. Tel: 601-773-6062.

McComb, Pike Co., St. Alphonsus, Rev. Donald F. Derivaux.
Church—507 Delaware Ave., P.O. Box 1105, 39648-1105. Tel: 601-684-5648; Fax: 601-684-5290.
School—Elementary and Preschool, Tel: 601-684-1843. Mr. David Schommer, Dir.
Students 149.

Madison, Madison Co., St. Francis of Assisi, Revs. Francis J. Cosgrove; Robert Kent Bowlds; Deacon John Camara.
Office: 4000 W. Tidewater Ln., 39110-8942. Tel:

601-856-5556; Fax: 601-856-2849.
School—Learning Center, Tel: 601-856-9494. Sr. Paula Blouin, S.S.N.D., Dir.
Students 149.
Mission—Gluckstadt, St. Joseph, Tel: 601-856-2054.

Magee, Simpson Co., St. Stephen, Rev. Robert Goodyear, S.T.
Res., 821 N. Jackson Drive, P.O. Box 427, 39111. Tel: 601-849-3237.
Mission—Raleigh, St. Paul.

Meridian, Lauderdale Co., St. Patrick, Revs. Elvin Sunds; Walter William Brown. In res., Rev. James Brett.
Res., 2614 Davis St., P.O. Box 529, 39301. Tel: 601-693-1321; Fax: 601-484-8953. [CEM]
School—Tel: 601-482-6044.
Lay Teachers 14; Students 238.
Mission—Quitman, Good Shepherd, Hwy. North, 39335.
St. Joseph, Rev. Elvin Sunds, O.S.F., Admin.; Sr. Andre Burkhart, O.S.F., Pastoral Assoc.
Res., 1914 18th Ave., P.O. Box 532, 39302-0532. Tel: 601-485-5349.

Mound Bayou, Bolivar Co., St. Gabriel, Bro. Pius Kamphefner, F.S.C., Pastoral Min.
Res., P.O. Box 53, 38762-0053. Tel: 601-741-2439.
School—Tel: 601-741-2395.
Sisters 3; Lay Teachers 5; Students 70.

Natchez, Adams Co., Assumption of the B.V.M., Rev. John Brock.
Res., 10 Morgantown Rd., 39120-2788. Tel: 601-442-7250.
Mission—Meadville, St. Ann.
Holy Family, Rev. Alfred A. Dean, S.S.J.
Res., 16 Orange Ave., 39120. Tel: 601-445-5700; Fax: 601-442-3973.
School—Tel: 601-442-3947.
Sisters 3; Lay Teachers 12; Students 203.
Convent—8 Orange Ave., 39120. Tel: 601-445-4257. Sisters of the Holy Spirit
Mission—Cranfield, St. John the Baptist.
St. Mary, Revs. Alfred L. Camp; Jerry Alan Mattingly.
Res., 107 S. Union St., P.O. Box 1044, 39121-1044. Tel: 601-445-5616; Fax: 601-445-5616.
School—Cathedral Unit School. See High Schools, Inter-Parochial under Institutions Located in the Diocese. Tel: 601-442-2531.

New Albany, Union Co., St. Francis of Assisi, Rev. Steven P. Pawelk, Glmy.
Res., 209 Sub-Station Rd., P.O. Box 887, 38652-0887. Tel: 601-534-9205.
Church—650 Hwy. 15 S., 38652-0887. Tel: 601-534-4654.
Mission—Pontotoc, Pontotoc Co., St. Christopher, S. Main St., P.O. Box 67, Pontotoc, 38863.

Olive Branch, DeSoto Co., Queen of Peace, Rev. John Young, S.C.J.; Deacon Henry Babin.
Res., 8680 Sandidge Rd., P.O. Box 65, 38654-0065. Tel: 601-895-5007; Fax: 601-895-5007.

Oxford, Lafayette Co., St. John, Rev. Kevin Slattery; Deacon Dr. Theodore Klingen.
Church & Offices: 403 University Ave., 38655-4329. Tel: 601-234-6073; Fax: 601-234-6079.
Res., 803 S. 11th St., 38655-4329. Tel: 601-234-1940.

Paulding, Jasper Co., St. Michael, Rev. Richard Smith. Mailing Address: P.O. Box 388, Forest, 39074-0388.
Church—Star Route, P.O. Box 15, 39348. Fax: 601-469-1916.

Pearl, Rankin Co., St. Jude, Rev. Martin Ruane. In res., Rev. William Cullen.
Res., 399 Barrow St., P.O. Box 5526, 39288-5526. Tel: 601-939-1863; 939-3181 (Office).
Station—Whitfield, Mississippi State Mental Hospital.

Philadelphia, Neshoba Co., Holy Cross, Rev. Kenan Ryan, S.T.
Res., 406 Wilson St., 39350-2906. Tel: 601-656-1841.
Holy Rosary (Tucker Community), Rev. David A. Hamm, S.T.; Deacon Regis E. Brennan, S.T.; Bro. Raphael F. Toner, S.T.
Res., Hwy. 19, P.O. Box 37, 39350. Tel: 601-656-2880.
Missions—Conehatta, St. Catherine, Tel: 601-775-3900; Philadelphia, St. Theresa, Tel: 601-656-6411.

Port Gibson, Claiborne Co., St. Joseph, Rev. Anthony Pudenz, Admin.
Res., 411 Coffee St., P.O. Box 1012, 39150. Tel: 601-437-5790.

Rosedale, Bolivar Co., Sacred Heart, Pastoral Ministry Team: Sr. Marie Genevieve Love, O.P., Delta Dominican Ministries; Sr. Jeroma Day, B.V.M.; Sr. Catherine Leamy, S.N.J.M.; Rev. Charles Bucciantini.
Res., P.O. Box 307, 38769. Tel: 601-759-6341.

Senatobia, Tate Co., St. Gregory the Great, Rev. James A. Cunniffe, S.C.J.
Res., 1360 Nesbit Rd., P.O. Box 38, Nesbit, 38651. Tel: 601-429-8266; Fax: 601-429-8369.
Church—P.O. Box 515, 707 Strayhorn St., 38668-0515. Tel: 601-562-5318 (Office).

Shaw, Bolivar Co., St. Francis of Assisi, In res., Rev. Henry Shelton.
Res., 303 Dean Blvd., P.O. Box 239, 38773. Tel: 601-754-5561.

Shelby, Bolivar Co., St. Mary, Rev. James Carroll.
Res., 700 Second St., P.O. Box 208, 38774-0208. Tel: 601-398-7964.
Station—Shelby, Parchman State Penitentiary, Tel: 601-745-6611.

Southhaven, DeSoto Co., Christ the King, Revs. Dermot J. Twomey, S.C.J.; Francis J. Burshnick, S.C.J.; Deacon Lawrence M. Campbell; Sr. Mary Della Quinn, O.P.
Office: 1090 Stateline Rd., W. Southhaven, 38671. Tel: 601-342-1073; Fax: 601-342-1074.

Starkville, Oktibbeha Co., St. Joseph, Rev. Michael O'Brien. In res., Rev. Francois Pellissier.
Res., 607 University Dr., 39759. Tel: 601-323-2257; Fax: 601-323-2258.
Mission—Macon, Corpus Christi.
Chaplaincy—Mississippi State University.

Tupelo, Lee Co., St. James, Rev. Meyrl E. Schmit.
Res., 820 Lakeshire Dr., P.O. Box 734, 38802-0734. Tel: 601-842-4881.
Mission—Saltillo, St. Thomas Aquinas.

Vicksburg, Warren Co., St. Paul, Rev. Thomas McGing.
Res., 713 Crawford St., P.O. Box 646, 39180-0646. Tel: 601-636-0140.
High School—Vicksburg Catholic School, (Grades K-12). See High Schools, Inter-Parochial under Institutions Located in the Diocese. Tel: 601-636-2256.
St. Mary, Rev. Donald Murrin, S.V.D.
Res., 1512 Main St., 39180. Tel: 601-636-0115.
St. Michael, Rev. James O'Riordan.
Res., 100 St. Michael Pl., 39180. Tel: 601-636-3445.

Walls, DeSoto Co., Sacred Heart, Revs. Dermot J. Twomey, S.C.J.; Francis J. Burshnick, S.C.J.
Office: P.O. Box 131, 38680. Tel: 601-781-0450.
School—Tel: 601-781-0650; Fax: 601-781-9225.
Sisters 5; Lay Teachers 27; Students 305.
Convent—P.O. Box 237, 38680. Tel: 601-781-9233. School Sisters of St. Francis.
Mission—Tunica, Tunica Co., St. Anthony of Padua, E. Edwards St., Tunica, 38676.

West Point, Clay Co., Immaculate Conception. Unassigned. Rev. John Vollor.
Res., 617 E. Main, 39773-3007. Tel: 601-494-3486.
Mission—Europa, Webster Co., St. John, Rte. 2, Box 11B, Europa, 39744. Tel: 601-258-7539.

Woodville, Wilkinson Co., St. Joseph, Rev. Charles Loyacono.
Res., 338 Church St., P.O. Box 668, 39669. Tel: 601-888-3261.
Missions—Fort Adams, St. Patrick; Gloster, Amite Co., Holy Family, P.O. Box 548, Gloster, 39638. Tel: 601-225-4171.

Yazoo City, Yazoo Co., St. Mary, Rev. P. J. Curley.
Res., 129 N. Washington St., P.O. Box 27, 39194-0027. Tel: 601-746-1680.
St. Francis, Rev. P. J. Curley.
Res., 735 E. Powell St., 39194. Tel: 601-746-1680.

Chaplains of Public Institutions

JACKSON. *Institute for the Blind, Institute for the Deaf and Speech Impaired.* Rev. Richard Somers.
University of Mississippi Medical Center. Rev. Msgr. Noel Foley; Sr. Sharon Glumb, S.L.W., Campus Min.
Veterans Administration Hospital. Rev. Daniel Gallagher.

MERIDIAN. *East Mississippi State Hospital.* Rev. Elvin Sunds.

PARCHMAN. *Mississippi State Penitentiary.* Rev. James Carroll; Sr. Marie Genevieve Love, O.P., Chap.

PEARL. *Rankin County Prison.* Rev. Martin Ruane.

SANATORIUM. *Boswell Retardation Center.* Rev. Robert Goodyear, S.T.

WHITFIELD. *Mississippi State Hospital.* Rev. Martin Ruane.

On Duty Outside the Diocese:
Reverend Fathers—
Johnson, Howard
Lopez, Jose
Madden, Paul
Niemira, Thomas
O'Connor, David
Quinn, Patrick
Quinn, Peter
Spadini, Marian

Retired:
Reverend Monsignors—
Glynn, Michael, St. Richard Church, P.O. Box 16547, Jackson, MS 39236-6547
Koury, Joseph A., 105 Abby Oaks Dr., Clinton, MS 39056
Reverend Fathers—
Brett, James G., St. Patrick Church, P.O. Box 529, Meridan, MS 39302
Curley, Patrick J., 113 Sherri Ln., Oceanside, CA 92054
DeMeules, Donald H., 9507 Windsor Club Cir., Fort Myers, FL 33905-5309
Engelhart, William, 515 Laurel St., McComb, MS 39648
Green, Lacy, Myles Retreat Home, 5911 Holmes Cir., Jackson, MS 39213
Leonard, John, Vicksburg Apartments, 801 Clay St., Apt. #10-A, Vicksburg, MS 39180
Maloney, Walter, 200 Dominican Dr. #5108, Madison, MS 39110-8612
Niemeyer, John, 200 Dominican Dr., #5206, Madison, MS 39110-8612
Pudenz, Anthony, St. Joseph Church, P.O. Box 1012, Port Gibson, MS 39150

Permanent Deacons:
Agosta, Frank, St. Paul, Brandon
Babin, Henry, Queen of Peace, Olive Branch
Baker, Sam, Holy Ghost, Jackson
Camara, John, St. Francis of Assisi, Madison
Campbell, Lawrence M., Christ the King, Southaven
Kitchin, Leon S., Immaculate Heart of Mary, Greenwood
Klingen, Dr. Theodore, St. John, Oxford
McCarthy, Kevin J., St. Joseph Mission, Gluckstadt
Pancratz, Arnold, St. Richard, Jackson
Van Tassel, Everell, Holy Spirit, Hernando

INSTITUTIONS LOCATED IN THE DIOCESE

[A] HIGH SCHOOLS, INTER-PAROCHIAL

JACKSON. *St. Joseph Catholic School.* (Grades 7-12). (Coed). 100 Holly Drive, 39206. Tel: 601-982-5000; Fax: 601-982-5001. Sr. Jackie Howard, R.S.M., Prin.; Rev. Msgr. Paul Canonici, Pres. Priests 2; Sisters 4; Lay Teachers 22; Students 272.

GREENVILLE. *St. Joseph Junior-Senior High School.* (Grades 7-12). (Coed), 700 Golf St., 38701. Tel: 601-378-9711; Fax: 601-378-3496. Bro. Thomas Geraghty, F.S.C., Prin. Brothers 1; Lay Teachers 29; Students 370.

NATCHEZ. *Cathedral Unit School.* (Grades PreK-12). (Coed), 701 Martin Luther King, Jr. St., 39120. Tel: 601-442-2531; Fax: 601-445-9844. Mr. Jules Michel, Prin. Sisters 3; Lay Teachers 41; Students 710.

VICKSBURG. *Vicksburg Catholic School.* (Grades K-12). (Coed), 1900 Grove St., 39180. Tel: 601-636-2256. Mr. George Valadie, Prin. Sisters 2; Lay Teachers 49; Students 667.

[B] SPECIAL SCHOOLS

JACKSON. *St. Richard's Special Kids Program,* P.O. Box 16172, 39236. John Tracy, Coord. Lay Teachers 2; Students 21.

[C] GENERAL HOSPITALS

JACKSON. *St. Dominic-Jackson Memorial Hospital,* 969 Lakeland Dr., 39216. Tel: 601-982-0121.
For a complete listing, refer to the Hospitals section.

TUTWILER. *Tutwiler Clinic, Inc.,* 205 Alma St., P.O. Box 462, 38963-0462. Tel: 601-345-8334; Fax: 601-345-8336.
For a complete listing, refer to the Hospitals section.

[D] ORPHANAGES AND INFANT HOMES

JACKSON. *D'Evereaux Hall Home, Inc.,* P.O. Box 2248, 39225. Tel: 601-355-8634.
For a complete listing, refer to the Special Care Facilities section.
St. Mary Orphan Home, Inc., P.O. Box 2248, 39225. Tel: 601-355-8634.
For a complete listing, refer to the Special Care Facilities section.

[E] MONASTERIES AND RESIDENCES OF PRIESTS AND BROTHERS

JACKSON. *Priory of St. Moses the Black,* 653 Claiborne Ave., 39209. Tel: 601-354-3287. Canons Regular of Premontre (The Premonstratensian Fathers). Revs. Richard P. Chiles, O.Praem., Prior; Xavier G. Colavechio, O.Praem.; Martin Philipsen, O.Praem.;

Andrew Cribben, O.Praem.; Bro. Steven Herro, O.Praem. Priests 4; Brothers 1; Novices 3.

GREENVILLE. *Emmanuel House*, 710 Golf St., 38701. Tel: 601-335-4660. Bro. Thomas Geraghty, F.S.C. Brothers 1.

NESBIT. *St. Michael Community House*, 1360 Nesbit Rd., P.O. Box 38, 38651. Tel: 601-429-8424. Revs. Charles Yost, S.C.J., Coord.; Francis J. Burshnick, S.C.J.; James Cunniffe, S.C.J.; Robert Hess, S.C.J.; Thomas Lind, S.C.J.; Dermot Twomey, S.C.J.; Kenneth Stoll, S.C.J.

[F] CONVENTS AND RESIDENCES FOR SISTERS

JACKSON. *Our Lady of Mount Carmel and Little Flower Monastery*, 2155 Terry Rd., 39204. Tel: 601-373-1460. Sr. Margaret Mary Flynn, O.C.D., Prioress. Discalced Carmelites. Nuns with Solemn Vows 3; Temporary Vows 2.

BROOKSVILLE. *The Dwelling Place*, HC 01 Box 126, 39739-9537. Tel: 601-738-5348. Sr. Clare Van Lent, O.S.F., Dir.

CHATAWA. *St. Mary of the Pines*, 39632. Tel: 601-783-3494; Fax: 601-783-3984. Sr. Mary Brian Overfield, S.S.N.D., Admin. Home for the Retired Sisters of the Dallas Province of the School Sisters of Notre Dame. Retreat Center for Lay and Religious Groups. Sisters in Residence 67.

PHILADELPHIA. *Holy Rosary Convent*, P.O. Box 496, 39350. Tel: 601-656-2949. Sister Servants of the Immaculate Heart of Mary 2.

VICKSBURG. *McAuley Home, Sisters of Mercy Retirement Home*, 102 McAuley Dr., 39180-2825. Tel: 601-636-0601. Sisters 12.

Sisters of Mercy, 1625 East Ave., 39180. Tel: 601-638-8636. Sisters of Mercy 3.

Sisters of Mercy Convent, 103 McAuley Dr., 39180-2824. Tel: 601-634-8845. Sisters 6.

[G] NEWMAN CENTERS

JACKSON. *Belhaven College Newman Center*, P.O. Box 57, 39205-0057. Rev. Msgr. Noel Foley; Sr. Sharon Glumb, S.L.W.

Jackson State University Newman Center, 2303 Lynch St., 32909. Revs. Richard P. Chiles, O.Praem.; Andrew Cribben, O.Praem.

Millsaps College Newman Center, P.O. Box 57, 39205-0057. Rev. Msgr. Noel Foley; Sr. Sharon Glumb, S.L.W.

Tougaloo College Newman Center, Holy Ghost Church, 1151 Cloister St., 39202. Rev. George Artis, S.V.D.

University of Mississippi Medical Center - Newman Center, P.O. Box 57, 39205-0057. Rev. Msgr. Noel Foley; Sr. Sharon Glumb, S.L.W.

BOONEVILLE. *Northeast Miss. Community College Catholic Student Center*, St. Francis of Assisi, P.O. Box 654, 38829. Sr. Marian Jochum, O.S.F.

BROOKHAVEN. *Lincoln Junior College Newman Center*, P.O. Box 196, 39601. Rev. Liam Pentony.

CLEVELAND. *Delta State University Newman Center*, Our Lady of Victories, 215 Bishop Rd., P.O. Box 1450, 38732-1450. Rev. Charles Bucciantini.

CLINTON. *Mississippi College Newman Center*, Holy Savior Church, P.O. Box 85, 39060. Rev. Noel Prendergast.

COLUMBUS. *Mississippi State University for Women Student Center*, Annunciation Church, 808 College St., 39701. Rev. Gerard Hurley.

FOREST. *East Central Community College Newman Center*, St. Michael's Church, P.O. Box 388, 39074. Rev. Richard Smith.

FULTON. *Ittawamba Community College Newman Center*, St. Helen, P.O. Box 97, 38821-0097. Sr. Marie Gilligan, S.C.

HOLLY SPRINGS. *Rust College Newman Center*, St. Joseph's, P.O. Box 430, 38635. Revs. Paul Casper, S.C.J.; Lawrence Rucker, S.C.J.

LEXINGTON. *Holmes Community College Newman Center*, St. Thomas Church, 200 Boulevard St., P.O. Box 762, 39095. Rev. John Rietti.

OXFORD. *University of Mississippi Newman Center*, St. John Church, 403 University Ave., 38655; Fax: 601-234-6079. Rev. Kevin Slattery; Deacon Dr. Theodore Klingen; Ms. Lorraine Turgeon, Campus Min.

RAYMOND. *Hinds Community College Catholic Student Organization*, Immaculate Conception, 39154. Rev. Noel Prendergast; Mrs. Denise Scifres.

SENATOBIA. *Northwest Mississippi Community College Newman Center*, St. Gregory Church, P.O. Box 515, 38668. Rev. James A. Cunniffe, S.C.J.

STARKVILLE. *Mississippi State University Catholic Student Association*, St. Joseph Church, 607 University Dr., 39759. Rev. Michael O'Brien.

[H] MISCELLANEOUS

JACKSON. *Nuestra Senora Del Perpetuo Socorro*, P.O. Box 2248, 39225-2248. Rev. Patrick Quinn. Saltillo Mission Sponsored by Dioceses of Jackson and Biloxi. Apdo. 509 Suc. A, Saltillo, Mexico, C.P. 25000. Tel: 001-52-841-48516.

Pax Christi-Franciscan, LaVerna House, 2108 Alta Woods Blvd, 39204. Tel: 601-373-4463. Genevieve Feyen, Pres.; Rhoda Kalscheur, House Dir. A Public Association of the faithful, living a consecrated life, engaged in social and educational works. Consecrated Members 8.

ABERDEEN. *Catholic Committee of the South, Inc.*, St. Francis of Assisi, Box 134, 39730. Tel: 601-369-2897. Sr. Evelyn Dettling, O.S.B., Coord.

GREENWOOD. *Pax Christi-Franciscan*, St. Francis Information Center, 708 Ave. I, 38930. Tel: 601-453-1465. Genevieve Feyen, Pres.; Bessie Willburn, Center Dir. A Public Association of the faithful, living a consecrated life, engaged in social and educational works. Consecrated Members 8.

MARKS. *DePorres Delta Ministries, Inc.*, 217 Locust St., P.O. Box 207, 38646. Tel: 601-326-2323. Sr. Patricia Chaffee, O.P., Devel. Project Mgr.

DePorres Health Center, 411 Poplar St., P.O. Box 376, 38646. Tel: 601-326-9232. Sr. Andrea Balconis, O.P., M.D., Contact Person & Dir.

DePorres Social Services, 217 Locust St., P.O. Box 292, 38646. Tel: 601-326-2323. Sr. Selina Stanaway, O.P., Contact Person & Dir.

San Martin Center, 317 Locust St., P.O. Box 248, 38646. Tel: 601-326-5404. Sr. Joan Dunning, O.P., Contact Person & Dir.

WALLS. *Sacred Heart League*, 6050 Hwy. 61 N., 38686. Tel: 601-781-1360; Fax: 601-781-3340. Rev. Robert Hess, S.C.J., Pres. & Spiritual Dir.; Mr. Roger Courts, Dir. & CEO.

Sacred Heart Missions, Inc., 6473 Hwy. 61 N., P.O. Box 190, 38680-0190. Tel: 601-781-1472; Fax: 601-781-0842. Sr. Maria V. Brocato, S.C.N., Exec. Dir.

Sacred Heart Southern Missions Housing Corporation, P.O. Box 365, 38680-0365. Tel: 601-781-3298; Fax: 601-781-3534. Sr. Mary Anne Guthrie, Coord. of Housing; Mr. Paul Bauer, Pres.; Mr. Morgan Billingsley, Vice Pres. & Treas.; Mr. J. Martin Regan, Jr., Sec.

RELIGIOUS INSTITUTES OF MEN REPRESENTED IN THE DIOCESE

For further details refer to the corresponding bracketed number in the Religious Institutes of Men or Women section.

[1350]—*Brothers of St. Francis Xavier.*—C.F.X.

[0330]—*Brothers of the Christian Schools.* (Prov. of St. Louis, MO).—F.S.C.

[0900]—*Canons Regular of Premontre.*—O.Praem.

[1130]—*Congregation of the Priests of the Sacred Heart.*—S.C.J.

[0520]—*Franciscan Friars.* (Pulaski, WI).—O.F.M.

[0570]—*Glenmary Home Missioners.*—Glmy.

[0840]—*Missionary Servants of the Most Holy Trinity.*—S.T.

[0700]—*St. Joseph's Society of the Sacred Heart.*—S.S.J.

[0420]—*Society of the Divine Word.*—S.V.D.

RELIGIOUS INSTITUTES OF WOMEN REPRESENTED IN THE DIOCESE

[]—*Congregation of Sisters of Charity of St. Charles Borromeo.*—C.B.

[2410]—*Congregation of the Marianites of the Holy Cross.*—M.S.C.

[3710]—*Congregation of the Sisters of Saint Agnes.*—C.S.A.

[1780]—*Congregation of the Sisters of the Third Order of St. Francis of Perpetual Adoration.*—F.S.P.A.

[0760]—*Daughters of Charity of St. Vincent de Paul.*—D.C.

[0420]—*Discalced Carmelite Nuns.*—O.C.D.

[1070-03]—*Dominican Sisters.* (Sinsinawa, WI).—O.P.

[1070-06]—*Dominican Sisters.* (Newburgh, NY).—O.P.

[1070-09]—*Dominican Sisters.* (Racine, WI).—O.P.

[1070-10]—*Dominican Sisters.* (Springfield, IL).—O.P.

[1070-13]—*Dominican Sisters.* (Adrian, MI).—O.P.

[1310]—*Franciscan Sisters of Little Falls, Minnesota.*—O.S.F.

[2575]—*Institute of the Sisters of Mercy of the Americas.* (Rochester, NY; St. Louis, MO).—R.S.M.

[]—*Literary Society of St. Catherine of Sienna Kentucky Dominican.*—O.P.

[2790]—*Missionary Servants of the Most Blessed Trinity.*—M.S.B.T.

[2800]—*Missionary Sisters of the Most Sacred Heart of Jesus.*—M.S.C.

[3530]—*Missionary Sisters Servants of the Holy Spirit.*—S.Sp.S.

[2970]—*School Sisters of Notre Dame.* (Baltimore & Dallas Provs., Mankato).—S.S.N.D.

[1680]—*School Sisters of St. Francis.*—O.S.F.

[0500]—*Sisters of Charity of Nazareth.* (Kentucky).—S.C.N.

[0590]—*Sisters of Charity of Saint Elizabeth, Convent Station.*—S.C.

[0430]—*Sisters of Charity of the Blessed Virgin Mary.* (Dubuque, Iowa).—B.V.M.

[]—*Sisters of Christian Community.*—S.F.C.C.

[]—*Sisters of Humility of Mary.*—C.H.M.

[]—*Sisters of Mercy of Mississippi, Inc.*.—R.S.M.

[3360]—*Sisters of Providence of Saint Mary-of-the-Woods, Indiana.*—S.P.

[1540]—*Sisters of Saint Francis, Clinton, Iowa.*—O.S.F.

[3893]—*Sisters of Saint Joseph of Chestnut Hill, Philadelphia.*—S.S.J.

[]—*Sisters of St. Francis of Sylvania, Ohio.*—O.S.F.

[1550]—*Sisters of St. Francis of the Holy Cross.* (Green Bay).—O.S.F.

[1570]—*Sisters of St. Francis of the Holy Family.* (Dubuque).—O.S.F.

[3830-02]—*Sisters of St. Joseph.* (La Grange Park, IL).—C.S.J.

[3830-15]—*Sisters of St. Joseph.* (Concordia, KS).—C.S.J.

[3840]—*Sisters of St. Joseph of Carondelet.* (St. Louis & St. Paul Provs.).—C.S.J.

[3930]—*Sisters of St. Joseph of the Third Order of St. Francis.* (Marymount Prov.).—S.S.J.-T.O.S.F.

[3950]—*Sisters of St. Mary of Namur.* (Belgium).—S.S.M.N.

[2980]—*Sisters of the Congregation de Notre Dame.* (Ridgefield, CT).—C.N.D.

[1030]—*Sisters of the Divine Savior.*—S.D.S.

[1990]—*Sisters of the Holy Names of Jesus and Mary.* (Albany, NY; Spokane, WA; Los Gatos, CA; Marylhurst, OR; Winnipeg, Canada).—S.N.J.M.

[2050]—*Sisters of the Holy Spirit and Mary Immaculate.*—S.H.Sp.

[2350]—*Sisters of the Living Word.*—S.L.W.

[1760]—*Sisters of the Third Order of St. Francis of Penance and Charity.*—O.S.F.

[2160]—*Sisters, Servants of the Immaculate Heart of Mary.*—I.H.M.

[4120-03]—*Ursuline Nuns, of the Congregation of Paris.*—O.S.U.

NECROLOGY

† Haddican, Bernard Christopher, (Retired). —Died Jan. 28, 1996.

Diocese of Jefferson City

(Dioecesis Civitatis Jeffersoniensis)

Most Reverend

MICHAEL F. McAULIFFE, S.T.D.

Bishop of Jefferson City; ordained May 31, 1945; appointed July 2, 1969; consecrated August 18, 1969. *Res., Bishop's House, P.O. Box 417, Jefferson City, MO, 65102.*

Chancery: 605 Clark Ave., P.O. Box 417, Jefferson City, MO, 65101. Tel.: 314-635-9127; Fax: 314-635-2286.

ESTABLISHED JULY 2, 1956.

Square Miles 22,127.

Comprises the Counties of Adair, Audrain, Benton, Boone, Callaway, Camden, Chariton, Clark, Cole, Cooper, Crawford, Gasconade, Hickory, Howard, Knox, Lewis, Linn, Macon, Maries, Marion, Miller, Moniteau, Monroe, Montgomery, Morgan, Osage, Pettis, Phelps, Pike, Pulaski, Putnam, Ralls, Randolph, Saline, Schuyler, Scotland, Shelby and Sullivan in the State of Missouri.

For legal titles of parishes and diocesan institutions, consult the Chancery Office.

STATISTICAL OVERVIEW

Personnel	
Bishop	1
Priests: Diocesan Active in Diocese	82
Priests: Active Outside Diocese	2
Priests: Diocesan in Foreign Missions	6
Priests: Retired, Sick or Absent	24
Number of Diocesan Priests	114
Religious Priests in Diocese	10
Extern Priests in Diocese	9
Ordinations:	
Diocesan Priests	3
Transitional Deacons	1
Permanent Deacons	7
Permanent Deacons in Diocese	61
Total Brothers	4
Total Sisters	101
Parishes	
Parishes	95
With Resident Pastor:	
Resident Diocesan Priests	65
Resident Religious Priests	7
Without Resident Pastor:	
Administered by Priests	16
Administered by Women Religious	6
Administered by Lay People	1
Missions	16
Closed Parishes	1
Professional Ministry Personnel:	
Brothers	4
Sisters	33
Lay Ministers	13
Welfare	
Catholic Hospitals	1
Total Assisted	99,202
Health Care Centers	15
Total Assisted	114,821
Homes for the Aged	2
Total Assisted	1,728
Day Care and Extended Day Care Centers	11
Total Assisted	239
Educational	
Seminaries, Diocesan	1
Students from This Diocese	23
Students from Other Diocese	2
Diocesan Students in Other Seminaries	14
Total Seminarians	37
High Schools, Diocesan and Parish	2
Total Students	984
Elementary Schools, Diocesan and Parish	35
Total Students	6,027
Catechesis/Religious Education:	
High School Students	2,878
Elementary Students	4,979
Total Students Under Catholic Instruction	14,905
Teachers in the Diocese:	
Priests	6
Brothers	3
Sisters	32
Lay Teachers	417
Vital Statistics	
Receptions into the Church:	
Infant Baptism Totals	1,333
Adult Baptism Totals	247
Received into Full Communion	295
First Communions	1,542
Confirmations	1,477
Marriages:	
Catholic	358
Interfaith	303
Total Marriages	661
Deaths	752
Total Catholic Population	84,308
Total Population	752,716

Former Bishop—Most Rev. JOSEPH M. MARLING, C.PP.S., D.D., ord. Feb. 21, 1929; appt. Auxiliary of Kansas City, June 9, 1947; cons. Aug. 6, 1947; appt. Bishop of Jefferson City, Aug. 24, 1956; retired July 2, 1969; died Oct. 2, 1979.

Vicar General—Rev. MICHAEL J. WILBERS, *P.O. Box 417, Jefferson City, 65102.*

Chancery Office—605 Clark Ave., P.O. Box 417, Jefferson City, 65101. Tel: 573-635-9127; Fax: 573-635-2286. All offices are at this address unless noted otherwise.

Chancellor—Sr. ETHEL-MARIE BIRI, S.S.N.D., M.R.Ed., M.A.

Vice-Chancellors—Revs. BRENDAN DOYLE; RICHARD CRONIN.

Moderator of the Curia—Rev. MICHAEL J. WILBERS, V.G.

Diocesan Tribunal—613 Clark Ave., Jefferson City, 65101.

Judicial Vicar—Rev. BRENDAN DOYLE.

Adjutant Judicial Vicar—Rev. GREGORY HIGLEY.

Defensors of the Bond—Revs. RICHARD CRONIN; ROBERT W. DUESDIEKER; LEONARD S. MISEY; PAUL M. HARTLEY.

Promoter of Justice—Rev. RICHARD CRONIN.

Judges—Revs. HUGH F. BEHAN; FRANCIS G. GILLGANNON; J. JAMES OFFUTT; MICHAEL F. QUINN.

Notaries—LORETTA NEUNER; CONNIE SCHEPERS.

Diocesan Consultors—Revs. FRED J. BARNETT; JAMES R. FUEMMELER; BRENDAN DOYLE; MICHAEL T. FLANAGAN; JOHN W. GRONER; ROBERT A. KURWICKI; J. DAVID MAHER; MICHAEL J. WILBERS, V.G.

Deans—I. Brookfield: Rev. ROBERT A. KURWICKI, Dean: Brookfield, Brunswick, Clarence, Indian Grove, Macon (Bevier), Marceline (Hurricane Branch/Mendon), Salisbury, Shelbina, Wien; II. Columbia: Rev. CHARLES D. PARDEE, Dean: Boonville, Columbia, Fayette, Moberly, Pilot Grove; III. Hannibal: Rev. KENNETH E. BROCKEL, Dean: Hannibal, Ilasco, Indian Creek (Hunnewell), Louisiana (Clarksville), Monroe City, Palmyra, Perry (Paris), St. Clement; IV. Jefferson City: Rev. EDWIN A. SCHMIDT, Dean: California, Holts Summit, Jefferson City, Osage Bend, Russelville, St. Martins, St. Thomas, Taos, Wardsville; V. Kirksville: Rev. J. DAVID MAHER, Dean: Baring, Canton (LaGrange), Edina, Ewing, Kahoka (Wayland), Kirksville (Novinger), Memphis, Milan (Unionville), St. Patrick; VI. Lake Ozark: Rev. JAMES R. FUEMMELER, Dean: Camdenton, Eldon, Laurie (Versailles), Hermitage (Climax Springs), Lake Ozark, Mary's Home, St. Anthony, St. Elizabeth; VII. Marshall: Rev. PHILLIP M. KANE, Dean: Glasgow, Marshall (Sweet Springs), Sedalia, Slater, Tipton, Warsaw (Cole Camp); VIII. Mexico: Rev. GERALD J. KAIMANN, Dean: Centralia, Fulton, Hermann, Jonesburg, Martinsburg, Mexico, Mokane, Montgomery City, Morrison, Rhineland, Vandalia (Laddonia), Wellsville; IX. Osage: Rev. Msgr. CHARLES H. PATTERSON, Dean: Argyle (Koeltztown), Bonnots Mill, Chamois, Folk, Frankenstein, Freeburg, Linn, Loose Creek, Meta, Rich Fountain, Westphalia; X. Rolla: Rev. DONALD L. WALLACE, Dean: Belle, Bourbon, Brinktown, Crocker, Cuba, Dixon, Owensville, Richland, Rolla, Rosati, St. James, Steelville, Vienna, Waynesville.

Masters of Ceremonies—Revs. ROBERT A. KURWICKI; JOHN J. SCHUTTY; ROBERT W. DUESKIEKER; ROBERT H. FIELDS; JOSEPH HOI.

Personnel Board—Most Rev. MICHAEL F. MCAULIFFE, S.T.D.; Revs. THOMAS J. DUGGAN; JOHN W. GRONER; CHARLES D. PARDEE; EDWIN A. SCHMIDT; MICHAEL J. WILBERS, V.G.

Priests Senate—Revs. FRED J. BARNETT; RICHARD A. COLBERT, C.PP.S.; MICHAEL T. FLANAGAN; JAMES R. FUEMMELER; JOHN W. GRONER; GERALD J. KAIMANN; PHILLIP M. KANE; ROBERT A. KURWICKI; J. DAVID MAHER; MARION J. MAKAREWICZ; CHARLES D. PARDEE; Rev. Msgr. CHARLES H. PATTERSON; Rev. Msgr. GERARD L. POELKER; Revs. EDWIN A. SCHMIDT; DONALD W. WALLACE; MICHAEL J. WILBERS, V.G.; J. JAMES OFFUTT, Consultant.

Diocesan Offices and Directors

Apostleship of Prayer—Rev. Msgr. RALPH G. KUTZ, Dir.

Campus Ministry—Rev. MICHAEL F. QUINN.

Catholic Relief Overseas Fund—ALICE J. WOLTERS.

Charismatic Renewal Program—Deacon ROBERT WATSON.

Communication—MARK D. SAUCIER, Dir.

Cursillo Movement—Rev. PATRICK J. SHORTT, Spiritual Dir. ART BOECKMAN, Dir.

Diocesan Pastoral Council—ANNETTE SMITH, Chm. MARIE LUEBBERING, Exec. Sec.

Diocesan Excellence in Education Fund, Inc.—Most Rev. MICHAEL F. MCAULIFFE, S.T.D., Chm.; Mr. LOUIS J. LEONATTI, Pres.; Sr. ETHEL-MARIE BIRI, S.S.N.D.; Sr. ANN MARIE BONVIE, S.S.N.D.; WILLIAM J. CARR; LORETTA CLINE; Deacon DONALD W. ORSCHELN; Deacon GEORGE T. SPALDING; NORMAN P. STUCKENSCHNEIDER; Rev. MICHAEL J. WILBERS, V.G.

Diaconate Office—Rev. FRED J. ELSKAMP, Vicar; Deacon ROBERT RACKERS.
Ecumenical Commission—Rev. HUGH F. BEHAN, Dir.
Engaged Encounter—Coords.: RICHARD SPORLEDER; BERNICE SPORLEDER, *Rte. 3, Box 249, Moberly, 65270.* Rev. MICHAEL F. QUINN, Spiritual Dir.
Evangelization Office—Rev. HUGH F. BEHAN, Dir.
Family Life—MICHAEL A. VAN GUNDY.
Finance and Development—STEPHEN J. KOMAROMI, Dir.
Finance Committee—Most Rev. MICHAEL F. MCAULIFFE, S.T.D.; Sr. ETHEL-MARIE BIRI, S.S.N.D.; OLIVIA BUERSMEYER; Rev. MICHAEL T. FLANAGAN; Mr. CHRIS HERMANN; RICHARD KAMPETER; PAUL KANAGO; Rev. Msgr. RALPH G. KUTZ; Rev. Msgr. DONALD ORSCHELN; RONALD W. VESSEL; HELEN VOSSEN; Rev. MICHAEL J. WILBERS, V.G.
Historical Diocesan Archivist—Rev. ROBERT A. KURWICKI, *409 S. Kansas, Marceline, 64658.* Tel: 816-376-3239.
Holy Childhood—(See Mission Office).
Human Development Campaign—BARBARA ROSS.
Information Office—MARK D. SAUCIER, Dir.
Leadership Services—Dr. STEPHANA J. LANDWEHR; Sr. ETHEL-MARIE BIRI, S.S.N.D.
Legion of Mary—Rev. WILLIAM KORTE, *Rte. 1, Eugene, 65032.* Tel: 573-498-3820.
Liturgical Commission—Rev. LOUIS E. DORN, Chm., *P.O. Box 220, Marshall, 65340.* Tel: 816-886-7960.
Mediation and Arbitration Board—Rev. LOUIS E. DORN, Vicar, *P.O. Box 220, Marshall, 65340.* Tel: 816-886-7960.
Ministry Formation—Rev. GEORGE KRAMER, Dir., *Bonnots Mill, 65016.* Tel: 573-897-2061.
Ministry to Priests—Rev. J. JAMES OFFUTT, Dir.; Most Rev. MICHAEL F. MCAULIFFE, S.T.D.; Sr. ETHEL-MARIE BIRI, S.S.N.D.; Revs. DONALD J. ANTWEILER; RICHARD CRONIN; FREDERICK J. ELSKAMP; RICHARD W. FRANK; DONALD W. LAMMERS; PATRICK L. PIERCEALL.
Mission Office (Peru Missions, Propagation of the Faith, Holy Childhood)—ALICE J. WOLTERS, Dir. MARK D. SAUCIER, *P.O. Box 551, Jefferson City, 65102.*
Newspaper—"Catholic Missourian"—Rev. HUGH BEHAN, Editor, *P.O. Box 1107, Jefferson City, 65102.*
Peruvian Development Foundation—Vacant, *P.O. Box 551, Jefferson City, 65102.*
Planning Commission—Rev. J. JAMES OFFUTT, Dir. & Exec. Sec.; Sr. EHTEL-MARIE BIRI, S.S.N.D.; Mr. LOUIS HOLROYD.
Priestly and Religious Vocations—Dir.; Sr. JEAN GREENWALD, S.C.C., *P.O. Box 417, Jefferson City, 65102.*
Priests' Eucharistic League—Rev. FRED J. ELSKAMP, Dir.
Priests' Mutual Benefit Society—Board of Trustees: Revs. RICHARD CRONIN; MICHAEL T. FLANAGAN; Rev. Msgr. RALPH G. KUTZ, Sec./Treas.; Rev. J. JAMES OFFUTT; Rev. Msgr. GERARD L. POELKER; Rev. Msgr. JOHN H. DREISOERNER, Consultant.
Priests' Purgatorial Society—Vacant.
Propagation of Faith & Holy Childhood—ALICE J. WOLTERS, Dir., *P.O. Box 551, Jefferson City, 65102.*
Religious Education Office—Mr. JAMES M. KEMNA, Dir. RANDY H. KOLLARS; CAROLYN A. SAUCIER; MICHAEL A. VAN GUNDY.
Research Assistant—Dr. STEPHANA LANDWEHR.
Resettlement Office—ALICE J. WOLTERS, Dir.
Residents Encounter Christ—BARBARA ROSS, Diocesan Liaison.
School Office—Sr. ANN MARIE BONVIE, S.S.N.D., Supt. BARBARA SWANSON, Assoc. Supt.
Scouting—Rev. GREGORY C. MEYSTRIK, Chap., *509 N. Main, Edina, 63537.* Tel: 816-397-2183.
Diocesan Sisters' Organization—Sr. BERNADETTE GOESSLING, S.S.N.D., *1700 Forum, #2006, Columbia, 65203.* Tel: 573-445-4085.
Social Concerns Dept.—BARBARA ROSS, Dir.; Sr. JUDITH KLUMP, C.S.J.; Dr. STEPHANA LANDWEHR; Sr. VIRGINIA GRUMICH, S.S.N.D.
Spiritual Renewal for the Laity—BETH CRAVEN, Dir. PEGGY VAN GUNDY, Assoc.
Vigilance Council—The Rt. Rev. and Very Rev. Deans.
Youth Ministry—RANDY H. KOLLARS.

CLERGY, PARISHES, MISSIONS AND PAROCHIAL SCHOOLS

JEFFERSON CITY (Cole County)

1—ST. JOSEPH CATHEDRAL, Revs. Michael J. Wilbers, V.G., Rector; Christopher Cordes; Deacons Robert J. Rackers; Fred W. Weisel; Joseph Braddock.
Res., 2301 W. Main St., 65101. Tel: 573-635-7991. [JC]
School—2305 W. Main St., 65101. Tel: 573-635-5024.
Lay Teachers 25; Students 410.
Catechesis/Religious Programs—Students 126.

2—ST. PETER, Revs. Donald W. Lammers; Erwin R. Konrad; Brian J. Driscoll; Deacons Harry M. Agniel; Robert L. Dulle; John C. O'Rourke; Tom Whalen.
Res., 216 Broadway, 65101. Tel: 573-636-8159; Fax: 573-634-6079. [JC]
School—Tel: 573-636-8922.
Sisters 3; School Sisters of Notre Dame 2; Sisters of Charity of the Incarnate Word 1; Lay Teachers 27; Students 506.
Catechesis/Religious Programs—Students 123.

3—IMMACULATE CONCEPTION, Revs. J. James Oftutt; Mark S. Smith; Deacons James R. Butler; Robert C. Osman.
Res., 1206 E. McCarty St., 65101. Tel: 573-635-6143; Fax: 573-635-6036. [JC]
School—Sisters 1; Sisters of Charity of the Incarnate Word 1; Lay Teachers 35; Students 530.
Catechesis/Religious Programs—Students 129.

OUTSIDE JEFFERSON CITY

Argyle, Osage Co., St. Aloysius, Rev. Msgr. Ralph G. Kutz.
Res., 65001. Tel: 573-728-6212. [CEM]
Catechesis/Religious Programs—Students 113.
Mission—Koeltztown, St. Boniface, P.O. Box 36, 65001. Tel: 314-728-6919.

Baring, Knox Co., St. Aloysius. Attended by Edina. Rev. Gregory C. Meystrik.
Res., 509 N. Main St., Edina, 63537-1239. Tel: 816-397-2183.

Belle, Maries Co., St. Alexander. Attended by Immaculate Conception, Owensville. Rev. Paul M. Hartley.
Mailing Address: 400 W. Third St., 65013. Tel: 573-854-6231.
Church—Tel: 573-859-6427.

Bonnots Mill, Osage Co., St. Louis. Attended by Our Lady of Help, Frankenstein. Rev. Peter Walsh.
Res., 65016. Tel: 573-897-2587.
Mailing Address: Rte. 1, Box 201, 65016.

Boonville, Cooper Co., SS. Peter and Paul, Rev. Charles D. Pardee; Deacon David Miller.
Res., 322 7th St., 65233. Tel: 816-882-6468.
School—Tel: 816-882-2589.
Sisters 1; Lay Teachers 10; Students 179.
Catechesis/Religious Programs—Students 137.

Bourbon, Crawford Co., St. Francis, Rev. Robert W. Duesdieker; Sr. Rose Duchesne Ernst, S.S.N.D., Pastoral Admin.
Res., P.O. Box 419, 65441. Tel: 573-732-4494. [CEM 2]

Brinktown, Maries Co., Guardian Angels. Attended by St. Cecilia, Meta. Rev. John J. Schutty.
Res., General Delivery, 65443. Tel: 573-422-3105.

Brookfield, Linn Co., Immaculate Conception, Rev. Thomas Duggan.
Res., 313 N. Livingston St., 64628. Tel: 816-258-2507. [CEM]
Catechesis/Religious Programs—Students 115.

Brunswick, Chariton Co., St. Boniface, Rev. Leonard S. Misey.
Res., 203 E. Vine St., P.O. Box 5, 65236. Tel: 816-548-3267. [CEM]
Catechesis/Religious Programs—Students 53.

California, Moniteau Co., Annunciation, Rev. Francis G. Gillgannon.
Res., 414 W. Patrick St., 65018. Tel: 573-796-4872. [CEM]
Catechesis/Religious Programs—Students 170.

Camdenton, Camden Co., St. Anthony, Revs. James R. Fuemmeler; Donald Powers (KC).
Res., HCR 67, P.O. Box 777, Ruach, 65787. Tel: 573-346-2688.
Church—172 N. Hwy. 5, 65020. Tel: 573-346-2716; Fax: 573-346-2716.
Res., Rte. 2, Box 344 E., 65020. Tel: 573-346-6652.
Catechesis/Religious Programs—Tel: 573-346-7080; Fax: 573-346-2539.
Students 176.

Canton, Lewis Co., St. Joseph, Rev. David D. Cox; Sr. Mildred Loddeke, S.S.N.D., Pastoral Admin.
Res., 812 Lewis St., 63435. Tel: 573-288-3198.
Catechesis/Religious Programs—Students 49.
Mission—La Grange, Lewis Co., Notre Dame, Tel: 573-655-4296.

Centralia, Boone Co., Holy Spirit, Rev. Robert H. Fields.
Res., 404 S. Rollins St., 65240. Tel: 573-682-2815.
Catechesis/Religious Programs—Students 105.

Chamois, Osage Co., Most Pure Heart of Mary, Rev. Eric Schlachter.
Res., 65024. Tel: 573-763-5345. [CEM 2]
Catechesis/Religious Programs—Students 52.

Clarence, Shelby Co., St. Patrick, Rev. Patrick L. Pierceall.
Mailing Address: 32 Grand St., P.O. Box 177, 63437. Tel: 816-699-3805. [CEM]
Res., 307 E. Chestnut, Shelbina, 63468. Tel: 573-588-4458.

Columbia, Boone Co., Our Lady of Lourdes, Revs. Michael T. Flanagan; William D. Debo; Deacon Fred Fritsch.
Res., 903 Bernadette Dr., 65203. Tel: 573-445-7915; Fax: 573-446-7402.
School—817 Bernadette Dr., 65203. Tel: 573-445-6516; Fax: 573-446-7402.
Lay Teachers 29; Students 462.
Catechesis/Religious Programs—Students 510.
Sacred Heart, Rev. Edwin Cole; Deacon Bruce Cox.
Res., 1115 Locust St., 65201. Tel: 573-443-2892; Fax: 573-875-3947.
Catechesis/Religious Programs—Students 150.
Columbia Newman Center, University of Missouri, Revs. Michael F. Quinn, Dir.; Dennis Schmidt.
Res., 701 Maryland, 65201. Tel: 314-445-8068.
Church—Tel: 573-449-5514; 449-5424; Fax: 573-874-2777.
Catechesis/Religious Programs—Students 370.

Crocker, Pulaski Co., St. Cornelius. Attended by Dixon. Rev. Walter Reisinger.
Res., P.O. Box 310, Dixon, 65459. Tel: 573-759-7521.

Cuba, Crawford Co., Holy Cross, Rev. Robert W. Duesdieker; Deacons Earl Horsefield; John O. Phillips; Albert W. Wilmarth.
Res., 415 W. School St., P.O. Box 547, 65453. Tel: 573-885-3520; 885-3291 (Rectory). [CEM]
Catechesis/Religious Programs—Students 75.

Dixon, Pulaski Co., St. Theresa, Rev. Walter J. Reisinger, C.M.
Res., P.O. Box 310, 65459. Tel: 573-759-7521. [CEM]

Edina, Knox Co., St. Joseph, Rev. Gregory C. Meystrik.
Res., 509 N. Main St., 63537-1239. Tel: 816-397-2183. [CEM]
Catechesis/Religious Programs—Students 80.

Eldon, Miller Co., Sacred Heart, Rev. James J. O'Sullivan.
Res., 540 N. Mill St., 65026. Tel: 573-392-5334; Fax: 573-392-3493.
Catechesis/Religious Programs—Students 67.

Ewing, Lewis Co., Queen of Peace, Rev. Daniel I. Lueckenotte; Sr. Catherine Wellinghoff, A.S.C., Pastoral Admin.
Res., 307 N. Main, P.O. Box 347, 63440. Tel: 573-494-3343. [CEM 2]
Catechesis/Religious Programs—Students 52.

Fayette, Howard Co., St. Joseph, Rev. Richard A. Colbert, C.PP.S.
Res., 300 S. Cleveland, 65248. Tel: 816-248-2439.

Folk, Osage Co., St. Anthony of Padua, Rev. John Henderson.
Mailing Address: HCR 65, Box 91, Westphalia, 65085. Tel: 573-455-2888. [CEM]
Catechesis/Religious Programs—Students 51.

Frankenstein, Osage Co., Our Lady of Help, Rev. Peter Walsh.
Res., Rte. 1, Bonnots Mill, 65016. Tel: 573-897-2587. [CEM 2]
School—Tel: 573-897-2567.
Lay Teachers 4; Students 74.

Freeburg, Osage Co., Holy Family, Rev. Richard W. Frank.
Res., P.O. Box 97, 65035. Tel: 573-744-5254. [CEM]
School—Tel: 573-744-5200.
Sisters 1; Lay Teachers 3; Students 58.

Fulton, Callaway Co., St. Peter, Rev. Ignazio C. Medina.
Office: 700 Hwy. Z, 65251. Tel: 573-642-5562.
School—Tel: 573-642-2839.
Sisters 3; Lay Teachers 9; Students 147.
Catechesis/Religious Programs—Sisters of Christian Charity 3; Students 90.

Glasgow, Howard Co., St. Mary, Rev. Philip Kane; Deacons Jerome C. Brucks; Robert L. Himmelberg; Charles Nordmeyer.
Res., 421 Third St., 65254. Tel: 816-338-2053. [CEM]
School—Tel: 816-338-2258.
Sisters of Charity 1; Lay Teachers 10; Students 158.
Catechesis/Religious Programs—Students 15.

Hannibal, Marion Co., Holy Family, Revs. John W. Groner; Mark A. Porterfield; Deacons Lindell P. Shumake; Emmett E. Pierceall.
Res., 2100 Chestnut St., 63401. Tel: 573-221-1078; Fax: 573-221-1079. [JC]

School—Tel: 573-221-0456.
Sisters of Notre Dame 1; Lay Teachers 8; Students 170.
Catechesis/Religious Programs—Students 120.

Hermann, Gasconade Co., St. George, Rev. Ambrose German, O.F.M.
Res., 128 W. 4th St., 65041. Tel: 573-486-2723. [CEM]
School—Tel: 573-486-5914.
Lay Teachers 11; Students 167.
Catechesis/Religious Programs—Tel: 573-486-2157.
Students 75.

Hermitage, Hickory Co., St. Bernadette, Rev. John E. Powers (KC).
Church—Hwy. 254, P.O. Box 277, 65668. Tel: 417-745-6361.
Res., Rte. 2, Box 344 E., Camdenton, 65020.
Mission—Climax Springs, Our Lady of the Snows.

Holts Summit, Callaway Co., St. Andrew, Rev. Frederick J. Elskamp.
Res., 400 St. Andrew Dr., 65043. Tel: 573-896-4309. [CEM]
Catechesis/Religious Programs—Students 110.

Ilasco, Ralls Co., Holy Cross. Closed. Records can be found at Holy Family Church, 2100 Chesnut, Hannibal, MO 63401.

Indian Creek, Monroe Co., St. Stephen, Rev. Charles A. Pfeiffer.
Res., Rte. 3, Box 29, Monroe City, 63456. Tel: 573-735-4033. [CEM 3]
Mission—Hunnewell, Shelby Co., St. John the Evangelist.

Indian Grove, Chariton Co., St. Raphael. Attended by Brunswick. Rev. Leonard S. Misey.
Mailing Address: 203 E. Vine St., P.O. Box 5, Brunswick, 65236-0005. Tel: 816-548-3267. [CEM]

Jonesburg, Montgomery Co., St. Patrick, Rev. Gerald J. Kaimann; Ms. Kristin Roth, Pastoral Admin.
Res., 305 N. First St., 63351. Tel: 314-488-5623. [CEM]
Catechesis/Religious Programs—Students 72.

Kahoka, Clark Co., St. Michael the Archangel, Rev. Michael P. Murphy.
Res., P.O. Box 216, 622 W. Exchange St., 63445. Tel: 816-727-3472.
Catechesis/Religious Programs—Students 68.
Mission—Wayland, St. Martha, 202 S. Main St., Wayland, 63472.

Kirksville, Adair Co., Mary Immaculate, Revs. J. David Maher; William P. Kottenstette; Patricia Lehr, Pastoral Min.
716 E. Washington St., 63501. Tel: 816-665-2466; Fax: 816-665-2466.
School—Tel: 816-665-1006.
Lay Teachers 11; Students 128.
Catechesis/Religious Programs—Tel: 816-665-2466.
Students 199.
Mission—Novinger, Adair Co., St. Rose of Lima, Hwy. D, Novinger, 63559.

Lake Ozark, Miller Co., Our Lady of the Lake, Rev. John Long; Deacon Francis P. Zimmerman.
Res., 2411 Bagnell Dam Blvd., 65049. Tel: 573-365-2241; Fax: 573-365-4458.
Catechesis/Religious Programs—Students 108.

Laurie, Morgan Co., Shrine of St. Patrick, Rev. Fred J. Barnett.
Res., Hwy. 5, Box 17, 65038. Tel: 573-374-7855 (Office); Fax: 573-374-0627. [CEM]
Catechesis/Religious Programs—Tel: 573-372-2497.
Students 88.
Mission—Versailles, Morgan Co., St. Philip Benizi, Hwy. D, Versailles, 65084.
Shrine—Mary Mother of the Church, P.O. Box 1250, 65038. Tel: 573-374-6279; Fax: 573-374-0629.

Linn, Osage Co., St. George, Rev. Brendan Doyle.
Res., P.O. Box 49, 65051. Tel: 573-897-2293. [CEM]
School—Tel: 573-897-3645.
Lay Teachers 11; Students 189.
Catechesis/Religious Programs—Tel: 573-897-2293.
Students 119.

Loose Creek, Osage Co., Immaculate Conception, Rev. Richard Cronin.
Res., 65054. Tel: 573-897-2922. [CEM 2]
School—Tel: 573-897-3516.
School Sisters of Notre Dame 2; Lay Teachers 5; Students 94.
Catechesis/Religious Programs—Students 65.

Louisiana, Pike Co., St. Joseph, Rev. Thomas L. Waickman.
Res., 508 N. 3rd St., 63353. Tel: 573-754-4757. [CEM]
Catechesis/Religious Programs—Students 48.
Mission—Clarksville, Pike Co., Mary Queen of Peace, South Second St., Clarksville, 63336. Tel: 573-242-3730.

Macon, Macon Co., Immaculate Conception, Rev. Russell R. Judge; Deacons Charles Kindle; Leo Prenger; Bernhard Toll.
Res., 402 N. Rollins St., 63552. Tel: 816-385-3792. [CEM]
School—Tel: 816-385-2711.
Sisters 2; Lay Teachers 1; Students 35.
Catechesis/Religious Programs—Students 67.
Mission—Bevier, Sacred Heart.

Marceline, Linn Co., St. Bonaventure, Rev. Robert A. Kurwicki.
Res., 409 S. Kansas Ave., 64658-1301. Tel: 816-376-3239. [CEM]
School—Tel: 816-376-3580.
Lay Teachers 5; Students 77.
Catechesis/Religious Programs—Students 70.
Mission—Hurricane Branch, Chariton Co., St. Joseph.

Marshall, Saline Co., St. Peter, Rev. Louis E. Dorn.
Res., 1801 S. Miami Ave., P.O. Box 220, 65340. Tel: 816-886-7960.
School—Tel: 816-886-6390; Fax: 816-866-6606.
Lay Teachers 10; Students 115.
Catechesis/Religious Programs—Students 112.
Mission—Sweet Springs, Holy Family, 200 Ruby St., Sweet Springs, 65351.

Martinsburg, Audrain Co., St. Joseph, Rev. Wayne M. Boyer.
Res., R.R. 1, Box 4, 65264. Tel: 573-492-6595. [CEM]
School—Tel: 573-492-6283.
Lay Teachers 6; Students 88.

Mary's Home, Miller Co., Our Lady of the Snows, Rev. William L. Korte.
Res., Rte. 1, Eugene, 65032. Tel: 573-498-3820. [CEM]
School—Tel: 573-498-3574.
Lay Teachers 5; Students 78.
Catechesis/Religious Programs—Students 105.

Memphis, Scotland Co., St. John, Rev. William P. Kottenstette.
Rectory: Rte. 3, Box 274, 63555. Tel: 816-465-7130. [CEM]
Res., c/o Mary Immaculate Parish Newman Center, 716 E. Washington, Kirksville, 63501. Tel: 816-665-5269; 665-2466. [CEM]

Meta, Osage Co., St. Cecilia, Rev. John J. Schutty.
Res., P.O. Box 96, 65058-0096. Tel: 573-229-4811. [CEM]
Catechesis/Religious Programs—Students 85.

Mexico, Audrain Co., St. Brendan, Rev. Gregory L. Higley; Sr. Angela Ashbey, S.L.W., Pastoral Min. & D.R.E.
Res., 615 S. Washington St., 65265. Tel: 573-581-4720; Fax: 573-581-8801. [CEM]
School—Tel: 573-581-2443.
School Sisters of Notre Dame 1; Lay Teachers 10; Students 192.
Catechesis/Religious Programs—Students 130.

Milan, Sullivan Co., St. Mary, Rev. Thomas L. Alber; Deacon Terence L. Reibenspies.
Res., 101 W. Baker St., P.O. Box 147, 63556. Tel: 816-265-4110. [CEM]
Catechesis/Religious Programs—Tel: 816-265-4110.
Students 52.
Mission—Unionville, Putnam Co., St. Mary.

Moberly, Randolph Co., St. Pius X, Rev. Patrick J. Shortt; Deacon Donald W. Orscheln.
Res., 217 S. Williams St., P.O. Box 310, 65270. Tel: 816-263-5243; Fax: 816-263-0101. [CEM]
School—Tel: 816-263-5500.
Lay Teachers 14; Students 199.
Catechesis/Religious Programs—Students 144.

Mokane, Callaway Co., St. Jude Thaddeus, Rev. Thomas J. Seifner.
Mailing Address: P.O. Box 128, 65059. Tel: 573-676-3238.
Res., Rte. 1, Box 17, Rhineland, 65069. Tel: 573-236-4390. [CEM][JC]

Monroe City, Monroe Co., Holy Rosary, Rev. William Flanagan; Deacon Harold L. Parn.
Res., 405 S. Main St., 63456. Tel: 573-735-4718.
School—Tel: 573-735-2422.
Sisters of St. Dominic 1; Lay Teachers 10; Students 170.
Catechesis/Religious Programs—Students 135.

Montgomery City, Montgomery Co., Immaculate Conception, Rev. Gerald J. Kaimann.
Res., 307 N. Walker, 63361. Tel: 573-564-2375. [CEM 2]
School—407 W. Third St., 63361. Tel: 573-564-2679.
Sisters 2; Lay Teachers 4; Students 47.
Catechesis/Religious Programs—Students 60.

Morrison, Gasconade Co., Assumption. Attended by Chamois. Rev. Eric A. Schlachter.
Mailing Address:Chamois, 65024. Tel: 573-763-5345. [CEM 2]

Osage Bend, Cole Co., St. Margaret, Rev. Michael Coleman; Sr. Peggy Bonnot, C.C.V.I., Pastoral Admin.; Deacon Larry Hildebrand.
Mailing Address: 12025 Rte. W., Jefferson City, 65101. Tel: 573-496-3404. [CEM]
Catechesis/Religious Programs—Students 42.

Owensville, Gasconade Co., Immaculate Conception, Rev. Paul M. Hartley; Deacon Donald E. Warden.
Res., 404 S. First St., 65066. Tel: 573-437-2494. [CEM]
Catechesis/Religious Programs—Tel: 573-437-3086.
Students 185.

Palmyra, Marion Co., St. Joseph, Rev. Daniel I. Lueckenotte; Sr. Marlene Buese, S.S.N.D., Pastoral Min.
Res., 411 S. Lane St., P.O. Box 606, 63461. Tel: 573-769-3270.
Catechesis/Religious Programs—Tel: 573-769-2837.
Students 170.

Perry, Ralls Co., St. William, Rev. Kenneth E. Brockel.
Res., 63462. Tel: 573-565-2852. [CEM]
Catechesis/Religious Programs—Students 81.
Missions—Perry, Monroe Co., St. Frances Cabrini, P.O. Box 339, 65275; Center, Ralls Co., St. Paul (Historic Church).

Pilot Grove, Cooper Co., St. Joseph, Rev. Leo A. Brand, C.PP.S.; Deacon Ralph V. Reuter.
Res., 407 Harris St., 65276. Tel: 816-834-4251. [CEM]
School—Tel: 816-834-5600.
Lay Teachers 5; Students 82.
Catechesis/Religious Programs—Students 107.
Station—Clear Creek, St. John the Baptist. (Mass).

Rhineland, Montgomery Co., Church of the Risen Savior, Rev. Thomas J. Seifner; Deacons Joseph E. Horton; Gerald W. Korman.
Res., 65069. Tel: 573-236-4390. [CEM]
Catechesis/Religious Programs—Students 67.
Pilgrimage Site—Shrine of Our Lady of Sorrows, Starkenburg, Montgomery Co., Tel: 573-236-4390.

Rich Fountain, Osage Co., Sacred Heart, Rev. James L. Finder.
Res., Rte. 1, Box 118, 65035. Tel: 573-744-5987. [CEM]
School—Tel: 573-744-5898.
Sisters of Notre Dame 1; Lay Teachers 3; Students 80.

Richland, Pulaski Co., St. Jude, Rev. Brendan Lawless.
Res., Old Hwy. 66, Waynesville, 65583. Tel: 573-765-3452.
Church—P.O. Box 8, 65556.

Rolla, Phelps Co., St. Patrick, Rev. Donald L. Wallace; Deacons Michael S. Brooks; William E. Louis; Thomas C. Manion.
Res., 17 St. Patrick Ln., 65401. Tel: 573-364-1435; 364-9055; Fax: 573-364-2073. [CEM]
School—Tel: 573-364-1162; Fax: 573-364-2073.
Lay Teachers 10; Students 151.
Catechesis/Religious Programs—Students 167.

Rosati, Phelps Co., St. Anthony, Rev. Joseph Hoi.
Res., 316 E. Scioto, St. James, 65559. Tel: 573-265-7247. [CEM]
Catechesis/Religious Programs—Students 6.

Russellville, Cole Co., St. Michael, Rev. Michael J. Wilbers, V.G.; Sr. Donna Eggering, O.S.F., Pastoral Admin.; Deacon Gary Christhoff.
Res., 13321 Railroad Ave., 65074-9447. Tel: 573-782-3171. [CEM]
Catechesis/Religious Programs—Tel: 573-782-4503.
Students 50.

St. Anthony, Miller Co., St. Anthony, Rev. Clarence E. Wiederholt.
Church—Rte. 2, Box 501, Iberia, 65486. Tel: 573-793-6550. [CEM]
Catechesis/Religious Programs—Students 103.

St. Clement, Pike Co., St. Clement, Rev. J. Patrick Quinn.
Res., Rte. 3, Box 141, Bowling Green, 63334. Tel: 573-324-5545. [CEM]
School—Tel: 573-325-2166.
Lay Teachers 7; Students 89.
Catechesis/Religious Programs—Students 162.

St. Elizabeth, Miller Co., St. Lawrence, Rev. John F. Degnan.
Res., P.O. Box 128, 65075. Tel: 573-493-2301. [CEM]
Catechesis/Religious Programs—Tel: 573-493-2301.
Students 164.

St. James, Phelps Co., Immaculate Conception, Rev. Joseph Hoi.
Res., 316 E. Scioto, 65559. Tel: 573-265-7250.

Catechesis/Religious Programs—Tel: 573-265-7269.
Students 86.

St. Martins, Cole Co., St. Martin, Rev. Edwin A. Schmidt; Sr. Bermita Wesinger, S.S.N.D., Pastoral Min.; Deacon Francis Butel.
Res., 7148 St. Martins Ave., Jefferson City, 65109. Tel: 573-893-2923. [CEM]
School—Tel: 573-893-3519.
Lay Teachers 12; Students 184.
Catechesis/Religious Programs—Students 55.

St. Patrick, Clark Co., The Shrine of St. Patrick. Attended by Kahoka. Rev. Michael P. Murphy.
Church—P.O. Box 35, 63466. Tel: 816-727-3472. [CEM]

St. Thomas, Cole Co., St. Thomas the Apostle Church, Rev. Donald J. Antweiler.
Res., 14814 Rt. B, P.O. Box 146, 65076. Tel: 573-477-3315.
School—P.O. Box 211, 65076. Tel: 573-477-3322. Sr. Kathleen Donovan, Prin.
Lay Teachers 4; Students 75.
Catechesis/Religious Programs—Students 57.

Salisbury, Chariton Co., St. Joseph, Rev. Patrick G. Dolan.
Res., 301 W. Williams, 65281. Tel: 816-388-5590. [CEM]
School—Tel: 816-388-5518.
Sisters of Charity of Leavenworth 1; Lay Teachers 8; Students 114.
Catechesis/Religious Programs—Students 132.

Sedalia, Pettis Co., St. Patrick, Rev. Thomas L. Albers, C.PP.S. In res., Rev. John M. Behen, C.PP.S.; Deacons Peter K. Anderberg; Jerome Connery.
Res., 415 E. Fourth St., 65301. Tel: 816-826-2062.
Catechesis/Religious Programs—Students 70.
Station—Clifton City, St. Joseph. (Mass).

Sacred Heart, Revs. William Miller, C.PP.S.; Michael Volkmer, C.PP.S.; Deacons Peter K. Anderberg; G. Robert Watson; Jerry Connery.
Res., 421 W. Third St., 65301. Tel: 816-827-2311. [CEM]
School—Tel: 816-827-3800.
Lay Teachers 9; Students 198.
High School—Lay Teachers 12; Students 194.
Catechesis/Religious Programs—Students 168.
Mission—Bahner, Pettis Co., St. John.
Station—Spring Fork, St. Patrick. (Mass).

Shelbina, Shelby Co., St. Mary, Rev. Patrick L. Pierceall.
Res., 307 E. Chestnut St., 63468. Tel: 573-588-4498. [CEM]
Catechesis/Religious Programs—Students 101.

Slater, Saline Co., St. Joseph. Attended by Glasgow. Rev. Philip M. Kane.
Res., 325 W. Emma St., 65349. Tel: 816-529-2588.

Steelville, Crawford Co., St. Michael, Rev. Robert W. Duesdieker; Sr. Rose Duchesne Ernst, S.S.N.D., Pastoral Admin.
Res., P.O. Box 419, Bourbon, 65441. Tel: 573-732-4494.

Taos, Cole Co., St. Francis Xavier, Rev. Kevin P. Clohessy.
Res., 7314 Rte. M, Jefferson City, 65101. Tel: 573-395-4401; Fax: 573-395-4302. [CEM]
School—Tel: 573-395-4612.
Lay Teachers 17; Students 246.
Catechesis/Religious Programs—Students 105.

Tipton, Moniteau Co., St. Andrew, Rev. Henry J. Reichert.
Res., 106 W. Cooper St., P.O. Box 598, 65081. Tel: 816-433-2162. [CEM]
School—Tel: 816-433-2232.
Lay Teachers 9; Students 150.
Catechesis/Religious Programs—Students 85.

Vandalia, Audrain Co., Sacred Heart, Rev. Donald E. Siciliano.
Res., 203 W. Home, 63382. Tel: 573-594-2717.
Catechesis/Religious Programs—Students 73.
Mission—Laddonia, Audrain Co., St. John, 7th and Elm, Laddonia, 63352. Tel: 573-373-5351.

Vienna, Maries Co., Visitation, Rev. John J. Schmitz.
Res., Hwy. 42 & Main St., P.O. Box 171, 65582. Tel: 573-422-3950. [CEM]
School—6th & Coffey St., P.O. Box 171, 65582. Tel: 573-422-3375.
Sisters of Notre Dame 2; Lay Teachers 3; Students 53.

Wardsville, Cole Co., St. Stanislaus, Rev. Michael Coleman.
Res., 6418 Rte. W., Jefferson City, 65101. Tel: 573-636-4925; Fax: 573-636-7802. [CEM]
School—Tel: 573-636-7802.
Lay Teachers 13; Students 236.
Catechesis/Religious Programs—Tel: 573-496-3404.
Students 10.

Warsaw, Benton Co., St. Ann, Rev. Dennis Schaab, C.PP.S.
Res., Rte. 4, P.O. Box 92, 65355. Tel: 816-438-5870. [CEM]
Catechesis/Religious Programs—Students 47.
Mission—Cole Camp, Benton Co., SS. Peter & Paul, Tel: 816-668-3952.

Waynesville, Pulaski Co., St. Robert Bellarmine, Rev. Brendan Lawless.
Res., 367 Old Hwy. 66, 65583. Tel: 573-336-3662. [CEM]
Catechesis/Religious Programs—Students 80.

Wellsville, Montgomery Co., Resurrection, Rev. Wayne M. Boyer; Deacon Vincent Garufi.
409 E. Bates, 63384.
Res., Rte. 1, Box 4, Martinsburg, 65264. [CEM]

Westphalia, Osage Co., St. Joseph, Rev. Msgr. Charles H. Patterson.
Res., Box 116, 65085. Tel: 573-455-2320. [CEM]
School—Tel: 573-455-2339.
Lay Teachers 9; Students 113.
Catechesis/Religious Programs—Students 80.

Wien, Chariton Co., St. Mary of the Angels, Rev. Philip M. Moriarty.
Res., Rte. 1, Box 65, New Cambria, 63558. Tel: 816-226-5243. [CEM]
Catechesis/Religious Programs—Students 80.
Station—Hamden, Immaculate Conception. (Mass).

Chaplains of Public Institutions

Prisons

JEFFERSON CITY. *Central Missouri Correctional Center,* Hwy. 179, 65109. Rev. Hugh F. Behan, Chap.
Jefferson City Correctional Center, P.O. Box 900, 65102. Tel: 573-751-3224. Rev. John H. Henderson, Chap., Tel: 573-455-2888; Sr. Ruth Heaney, O.S.B., Chap., Tel: 573-635-5393.
Missouri Intermediate Reformatory. (Algoa) Algoa Rd., 65101. Tel: 573-751-3911. Rev. Thomas E. McGrath, Chap., Tel: 573-635-0454.
Renz Correctional Facility, P.O. Box 3200, 65102. Tel: 573-751-4748. Rev. Hugh F. Behan, Chap., Tel: 573-635-9127.

BOONEVILLE. *Boonville Correctional Center.* HCR 91, Westphalia, 65085. Tel: 573-455-2888. Rev. John H. Henderson, Chap., Tel: 573-455-2888.

FULTON. *Diagnostic and Reception Center,* P.O. Box 581, 65251. Tel: 573-642-1707. Deacon Frederick Fritsch, Chap., Tel: 573-449-3307.

MOBERLY. *Missouri Training Center For Men,* P.O. Box 7, 65270. Tel: 816-263-3778. Rev. Patrick J. Shortt, Chap., Tel: 816-263-5243.

TIPTON. *State Correctional Pre-Release Center,* 65081. Tel: 816-433-2031. Rev. Henry Reichert, Chap., Tel: 816-433-2162.

Hospitals and Schools

JEFFERSON CITY. *Capital Region Medical Center, Memorial Campus,* 1432 Southwest Blvd., 65109. Tel: 573-635-6811. Rev. Erwin R. Konrad. Tel: 573-636-8159.
Capital Region Medical Center, Still Campus, 1125 Madison St., 65101. Tel: 573-635-7100. Rev. Thomas E. McGrath, Chap., Tel: 573-635-0454.

COLUMBIA. *Boone Hospital Center,* 1600 E. Broadway, 65201. Tel: 573-875-4545.
Charter Hillside Hospital, 200 Portland, 65201. Tel: 573-876-8000.
Columbia Regional Hospital, 404 Keene St., 65201. Tel: 573-875-9000.
Ellis Fischel State Cancer Hospital, 115 Business Loop 70 W., 65201. Tel: 573-882-2100.
Mid-Missouri Mental Health Center, 3 Hospital Dr., 65201. Tel: 573-449-2511.
Rusk Rehabilitation Center, One Hospital Dr., 65201. Tel: 573-882-6106.
University Hospital & Clinics, One Hospital Dr., 65201. Tel: 573-882-4141.
Chaplains for the Columbia Hospitals listed above: Revs. Edwin J. Cole, Dir., Tel: 578-443-2892; Robert H. Fields. Tel: 573-682-2815; William D. Debo. Tel: 573-445-7915; Eleanor Braddock, M.D. Tel: 573-445-6701; Sr. Florence Seib, A.S.C. Tel: 573-499-3810.
Veterans' Administration Medical Center. (Harry S. Truman Memorial) 800 Stadium Rd., 65201. Tel: 573-443-2511. Rev. Eugene J. Robl. Tel: 573-443-0423.

FULTON. *Fulton State Hospital,* Fifth St., 65251. Tel: 573-642-3311. Deacon Frederick Fritsch, Chap., Tel: 573-449-3307.
Missouri School for the Deaf, E. Fifth St., 65251. Tel: 573-642-3301. Deacon Frederick Fritsch, Chap., Tel: 573-449-3307.

MARCELINE. *Pershing Regional Health Care Center.* Attended by St. Boniventure Rectory, 409 S. Kansas, Marceline, 64658. Tel.:816-376-3239. 225 W. Hayden, 64658. Tel: 816-376-3521.

MARSHALL. *Marshall State School-Hospital,* E. Slater St., 65340. Tel: 816-886-2202. Rev. Louis E. Dorn, Chap., Tel: 816-886-7960.

ST. JAMES. *Missouri Veterans' Home,* 620 N. Jefferson St., 65559. Tel: 573-265-3271. Rev. Joseph Hoi, Chap., Tel: 573-265-7250.

Special Assignments:
Reverend Fathers—
Behan, Hugh F., Editor, "Catholic Missourian"
Hunkins, Richard C., Dir. Columbia Nursing Home Ministry
Kramer, George J., Chancery, Ministry Formation

On Duty Outside the Diocese:
Reverend Fathers—
Hereford, Thomas D., 6305 N.W. Hogan, Parkville, MO 64152
Palmieri, Luigi, P.O. Box 5309, Trenton, NJ 08648
Starmann, Joseph, 1434 Gerard Park Ln., St. Louis, MO 63042
Stockman, Gerald, 1000 North Hills, St. Louis, MO 63121

Missionary Assignment in Peru:
Reverend Fathers—
Dowling, Patrick
Griffey, Brendan M.
Keyes, Raphael
Lawlor, Joseph
Niemeyer, James
Ritter, David

Awaiting Assignment:
Reverend Fathers—
Jones, W. Paul, 8CC, Box 536, Pittsburg, MO 65724-9705

Absent on Leave:
Reverend Fathers—
Buescher, David G.
Crosby, Donald W.
Doyle, Edward A.
Faletti, Stephen L.
Gormley, Kevin
Keogh, William
Linnebur, Vincent
McNally, James P.
Starmann, Joseph W.

Retired:
Reverend Monsignors—
Bugler, Joseph T., Salt River Nursing Home, Shelbina, MO 63468
Dreisoerner, John H., Santa Maria Apartments, Apt. 233, Hazelwood, MO 63042-1582. Tel: 314-291-7017
Poelker, Gerard L., P.O. Box 39, Holts Summit, MO 65043. Tel: 573-896-4748
Sommer, Jerome, Regina Cleri, 7850 Kenrick Rd., St. Louis, MO 63119. Tel: 314-961-0271
Reverend Fathers—
Boland, Joseph B., St. Joseph Home, Jefferson City, MO 65101
Bonn, Ferdinand C., 303 Bldg. 5 Racquet Club Rd., Fort Lauderdale, FL 33326. Tel: 305-384-1015
Buhman, Leo T., 5910 York St., St. Joseph, MO 64506. Tel: 816-233-7775
Chenoweth, Robert, 929 Country Club Dr., St. Louis, MO 63121
Donohue, Edward J., St. Joseph Carmelite Home, 723 First Capital Dr., St. Charles, MO 63301
Forst, William, P.O. Box 5, Foristell, MO 63348-0005. Tel: 314-673-1052
Mersinger, Arthur, 7850 Kenrick Rd., Ste. 104, St. Louis, MO 63119-5004. Tel: 314-962-5894
Owens, Edward M., 225 W. Hayden, Marceline, MO 64658
Stanal, Frank J., 151/331 Hammond St., Rocky Mount, NC 27804-5824
Wheeler, Clarence, M.S., 612 Norris Dr., Jefferson City, MO 65109. Tel: 573-635-0648

Permanent Deacons:
Agniel, Harry M.
Anderberg, Peter K.
Berry, Kenneth
Bilgrien, Kenneth D.
Bonnarens, Edwin C.
Braddock, Joseph
Breazile, James E.
Brooks, Michael
Brown, William J.
Brucks, Jerome C.
Butel, Francis J.
Butler, James R.
Capuano, Tom
Chaplin, Mark
Christoff, Gary
Connery, Jerry
Cox, Bruce

Daly, Michael M.
Davis, Howard E.
Dodds, Michael
Dulle, Robert L.
Fritsch, Frederick
Garufi, Vincent E.
Gerling, Thomas J.
Heidlage, Walter F.
Hildebrand, Larry
Himmelberg, Robert L.
Horsefield, Earl R.
Horton, Joseph E.
Houston, John D.
Kindle, Charles C.
Kinney, William J.
Korman, Gerald W.
Louis, William E.
Manion, Thomas C.
McEvoy, Tim
Miller, David
Nordmeyer, Charles
O'Rourke, John C.
Orscheln, Donald W.
Osman, Robert C.
Parn, Harold L.
Phillips, John O.
Pierceall, Eugene E.
Prenger, Leo F.
Rackers, Robert J.
Reibenspies, Terence L.
Reuter, Ralph V.
Rockhold, Jess L.
Shumake, Lindell P.
Snooks, Richard W.
Spalding, George T.
Tebbe, John J.
Toll, Bernhard F.
Visot, Luis R.
Warden, Donald E.
Watson, G. Robert
Weisel, Fred M.
Whalen, Tom
Wilmarth, Albert W.
Zimmerman, Francis P.

INSTITUTIONS LOCATED IN THE DIOCESE

[A] SEMINARIES, DIOCESAN

HANNIBAL. *St. Thomas Aquinas Seminary*, P.O. Box 858, 245 N. Levering Ave., 63401. Tel: 573-221-4330. Very Rev. Marion J. Makerewicz, Rector; Revs. James J. Wenting; Louis W. McCorkle; David D. Cox; Mark A. Porterfield; P. Gregory Oligschlaeger; Mr. Terry Miller; Mr. Robert Catalpa; Mr. Jeff Malone. Students 25.

[B] HIGH SCHOOLS, DIOCESAN

JEFFERSON CITY. *Helias High School*, 1305 Swift's Highway, 65109. Tel: 573-635-6139. Mr. James Rackers, Chief Admin.; Sr. Jean Dietrich, Prin.; Mr. Dennis Hughes, Admin. Asst.; Mr. Ron Vossen, Campus Ministry; Revs. Brendan Doyle; Mark S. Smith; Brian J. Driscoll. Brothers of the Christian Schools 3; School Sisters of Notre Dame 1; Lay Teachers 38; Students 790.

[C] GENERAL HOSPITALS

JEFFERSON CITY. *St. Marys Health Center*, 100 St. Marys Medical Plaza, 65101. Tel: 573-761-7000.
For a complete listing, refer to the Hospitals section.

[D] NURSING HOMES

JEFFERSON CITY. *St. Joseph's Home*, 1306 W. Main St., 65109. Tel: 573-635-0166.
For a complete listing, refer to the Special Care Facilities section.
Villa Marie Skilled Nursing Facility, 1030 Edmonds St., 65109. Tel: 573-761-6700.
For a complete listing, refer to the Special Care Facilities section.

COLUMBIA. *Columbia Nursing Home Ministry*, 65202.
For a complete listing, refer to the Special Care Facilities section.

[E] CONVENTS AND RESIDENCES FOR SISTERS

JEFFERSON CITY. *Discalced Carmelite Monastery*, 2201 W. Main St., 65109. Mother Therese Dubois, O.C.D., Prioress. Professed of Solemn Vows 8; Professed of Temporary Vows 2; Postulants 2.
Franciscan Sisters of Mary, Jericho Community, 202 Binder Dr., 65109-0815. Tel: 573-635-8123. Franciscan Sisters of Mary 4.

BRINKTOWN. *Guardian of Angel Convent*, 65443. Tel: 573-422-3921. Franciscan Sisters of Mary.

COLUMBIA. *Our Lady of Peace Monastery*, 3410 W. Broadway St., 65203. Tel: 573-446-2300. Sr. JoAnn Schmidt, O.S.B., Prioress. Benedictine Sisters of Pontifical Jurisdiction 13.

MARCELINE. *Our Lady of the Rosary*, 200 W. Bigger St., 64658-1070. Tel: 816-376-3969. Franciscan Sisters of Mary 2.

[F] NEWMAN CENTERS

JEFFERSON CITY. *Lincoln University-Newman Center*, 708 Marshall St., 65101. Tel: 573-635-9356. Sr. M. Vincella Lake, S.S.N.D., Dir.

COLUMBIA. *University of Missouri-Columbia, Campus Ministry*, 701 Maryland, 65201. Revs. Michael F. Quinn, Dir.; Dennis Schmidt (STL).

FAYETTE. *Central Methodist College*, c/o St. Joseph Church, 300 Cleveland, 65248. Rev. Richard Colbert, C.PP.S., Dir.

KIRKSVILLE. *Catholic Newman Center, Truman State University*, 709 S. Davis, 63501. Tel: 816-665-4357. Mrs. Bettie Lesczynski, Dir.; Rev. William P. Kottenstette, Chap.

ROLLA. *University of Missouri-Rolla*, 2 Vichy Rd., 65401. Tel: 573-364-2133.

[G] MISCELLANEOUS

JEFFERSON CITY. *Diocesan Excellence in Education Fund, Inc.*, P.O. Box 417, 65102. Tel: 573-635-9127.
Missouri Catholic Conference, 600 Clark Ave., P.O. Box 1022, 65102. Tel: 573-635-7239; Fax: 573-635-7431.
St. Mary's Health Center Foundation, 100 St. Mary's Medical Plaza, 65101. Tel: 573-761-7198. A member of the SSM Health Care System.

ST. LOUIS. *Residents Encounter Christ*, Missouri State Board, 7522 Big Bend Blvd., 63119. Tel: 314-647-7060; Fax: 314-647-8380. Mr. Joseph Hedley, Exec. Dir.

RELIGIOUS INSTITUTES OF MEN REPRESENTED IN THE DIOCESE

For further details refer to the corresponding bracketed number in the Religious Institutes of Men or Women section.

[0330]—*Brothers of the Christian Schools.* (Midwest Prov.).—F.S.C

[]—*Brothers of the Poor of St. Francis.* Burlington, IA.—C.F.P.

[1330]—*Congregation of the Mission.* (Midwest Prov.).—C.M.

[0520]—*Franciscan Friars.* (Sacred Heart Prov.).—O.F.M.

[0720]—*The Missionaries of Our Lady of La Salette.* (Prov. of Mary Queen).—M.S.

[1060]—*Society of the Precious Blood.* (Kansas City Prov.).—C.PP.S.

RELIGIOUS INSTITUTES OF WOMEN REPRESENTED IN THE DIOCESE

[0100]—*Adorers of the Blood of Christ.* (Ruma, IL; Wichita, KS).—A.S.C.

[0230]—*Benedictine Sisters of Pontifical Jurisdiction.* (Columbia, MO).—O.S.B.

[0360]—*Carmelite Sisters of the Divine Heart of Jesus.*—Carmel.D.C.J.

[0460]—*Congregation of the Sisters of Charity of the Incarnate Word.*—C.C.V.I.

[1730]—*Congregation of the Sisters of the Third Order of St. Francis.* (Oldenburg, IN).—O.S.F.

[0420]—*Discalced Carmelite Nuns.*—O.C.D.

[1070-11]—*Dominican Sisters.* (Sparkill, NY).—O.P.

[1415]—*Franciscan Sisters of Mary.* (St. Louis Prov.).—F.S.M.

[]—*Franciscan Sisters of Our Lady of Perpetual Help.*

[2970]—*School Sisters of Notre Dame.* (St. Louis Prov.).—S.S.N.D.

[1680]—*School Sisters of St. Francis.* (Milwaukee, WI).—O.S.F.

[0480]—*Sisters of Charity of Leavenworth, Kansas.* (Leavenworth, KS).—S.C.L.

[0660]—*Sisters of Christian Charity.* (Wilmette, IL).—S.C.C.

[0990]—*Sisters of Divine Providence.* (St. Louis Prov.).—C.D.P.

[2549]—*Sisters of Mercy.* (Co. Sligo, Ireland).—R.S.M.

[1670]—*Sisters of St. Francis of Savannah, MO.* (Savannah, MO).—O.S.F.

[3830-15]—*Sisters of St. Joseph.* (Concordia, KS).—C.S.J.

[3840]—*Sisters of St. Joseph of Carondelet.* (St. Louis Prov.; St. Paul Prov.).—C.S.J.

[2350]—*Sisters of the Living Word.* (Arlington Heights, IL).—S.L.W.

[3270]—*Sisters of the Most Precious Blood.* (O'Fallon, MO).—C.PP.S.

DIOCESAN CEMETERIES

JEFFERSON CITY. *St. Peter's Catholic Cemetery Association*, 427 Crystal View Terrace, 65109. Mr. Nelson Vincent, Pres.

NECROLOGY

† Lamping, Stephen, Wellsville, MO, Church of the Resurrection. —Died Dec. 7, 1995.

† Mullen, Lawrence P., Edina, MO, St. Joseph. —Died March 1, 1996.

† Savage, William D., Slater, MO, St. Joseph. —Died March 11, 1996.

Diocese of Joliet in Illinois

(Dioecesis Joliettensis in Illinois)

Most Reverend

JOSEPH L. IMESCH, D.D.

Bishop of Joliet; ordained December 16, 1956; ordained Auxiliary Bishop of Detroit April 3, 1973; appointed Bishop of Joliet June 30, 1979; installed August 28, 1979. *Res., 425 Summit St., Joliet, IL, 60435.*

Most Reverend

ROGER L. KAFFER, D.D.

Auxiliary Bishop of Joliet; Titular Bishop of Dusa; ordained May 1, 1954; appointed April 25, 1985; consecrated June 26, 1985. *Res., 425 Summit St., Joliet, IL, 60435.*

Chancery: 425 Summit St., Joliet, IL, 60435. Tel.: 815-722-6606; Fax: 815-722-6602.

ESTABLISHED BY BULL DATED DECEMBER 11, 1948.

CANONICALLY ERECTED MARCH 24, 1949.

Square Miles 4,218.

Comprises the Counties of Du Page, Kankakee, Will, Grundy, Ford, Iroquois and Kendall in the State of Illinois.

PATRON OF DIOCESE: St. Francis Xavier.

For legal titles of parishes and diocesan institutions, consult the Chancery.

STATISTICAL OVERVIEW

Personnel	
Bishop	1
Auxiliary Bishops	1
Abbots	1
Retired Abbots	2
Priests: Diocesan Active in Diocese	161
Priests: Active Outside Diocese	9
Priests: Diocesan in Foreign Missions	1
Priests: Retired, Sick or Absent	33
Number of Diocesan Priests	204
Religious Priests in Diocese	113
Extern Priests in Diocese	12
Ordinations:	
Diocesan Priests	3
Permanent Deacons in Diocese	117
Total Brothers	92
Total Sisters	757
Parishes	
Parishes	119
With Resident Pastor:	
Resident Diocesan Priests	100
Resident Religious Priests	17
Without Resident Pastor:	
Administered by Priests	2
Missions	10
New Parishes Created	1
Professional Ministry Personnel:	
Brothers	3
Sisters	68
Lay Ministers	194
Welfare	
Catholic Hospitals	3
Total Assisted	433,605
Homes for the Aged	10
Total Assisted	2,378
Day Care and Extended Day Care Centers	3
Total Assisted	662
Specialized Homes	2
Total Assisted	1,357
Special Centers for Social Services	5
Total Assisted	39,196
Residential Care of Disabled	1
Total Assisted	120
Educational	
Diocesan Students in Other Seminaries	18
Total Seminarians	18
Colleges and Universities	4
Total Students	8,171
High Schools, Diocesan and Parish	4
Total Students	2,474
High Schools, Private	4
Total Students	3,128
Elementary Schools, Diocesan and Parish	63
Total Students	19,372
Catechesis/Religious Education:	
High School Students	6,906
Elementary Students	47,194
Total Students Under Catholic Instruction	87,263
Teachers in the Diocese:	
Priests	14
Brothers	10
Sisters	39
Lay Teachers	1,029
Vital Statistics	
Receptions into the Church:	
Infant Baptism Totals	11,156
Adult Baptism Totals	383
Received into Full Communion	871
First Communions	13,978
Confirmations	6,538
Marriages:	
Catholic	1,935
Interfaith	806
Total Marriages	2,741
Deaths	6,052
Total Catholic Population	512,609
Total Population	1,494,976

Former Bishops—Most Rev. MARTIN D. MCNAMARA, D.D.,first Bishop of Joliet; ord. Dec. 3, 1922; appt. Dec. 17, 1948; cons. March 7, 1949; died May 23, 1966.—Most Rev. ROMEO BLANCHETTE, D.D., appt. Auxiliary Bishop of Joliet and Titular Bishop of Maxita Feb. 8, 1965; cons. April 3, 1965; appt. Bishop of Joliet July 19, 1966; installed Aug. 31, 1966; resigned Jan. 30, 1979; died Jan. 10, 1982.

Chancery—425 Summit St., Joliet, 60435. Tel: 815-722-6606; Fax: 815-722-6602. Office Hours: Mon.-Fri. 8:30-4:30.

Vicar General—Most Rev. ROGER L. KAFFER, D.D., J.C.L.

Chancellor—Sr. JUDITH A. DAVIES, O.S.F.

Moderator of the Curia—Rev. JOSEPH TAPELLA.

Director of Administration—JAMES P. LYNCH.

Director of Finance—GUY A. SELL.

Matrimonial Tribunal—310 Bridge St., Joliet, 60435. Tel: 815-722-2256.

Judicial Vicar—Rev. RICHARD SMITH, J.C.L.

Adjutant Judicial Vicar—Revs. MICHAEL GINTER, J.C.L.; JOSEPH J. TAPELLA, J.C.L.

Notaries—LORRAINE A'HEARN; SYLVIA CARBONI; MARIE SMEETS; BETTY JOUTRAS; HELEN MILCHERSKA.

Defender of the Bond—Sr. MARILYN PHILLIPS, O.S.F., Ph.D., J.C.D.

Judges—Revs. RICHARD L. SMITH, J.C.L.; JOSEPH TAPELLA, J.C.L.; MICHAEL W. GINTER, J.C.L.; Sr. MARILYN PHILLIPS, O.S.F., Ph.D., J.C.D.

Advocates—Revs. RICHARD RUFFALO; JAMES RADEK; Mr. JAMES GILLIGAN.

Diocesan Offices and Directors

Board of Conciliation and Arbitration—425 Summit St., Joliet, 60435.

Campaign for Human Development—ELIZABETH FRANKLIN, *St. Charles Borromeo Pastoral Center, 402 S. Independence Blvd., Romeoville, 60441.* Tel: 815-834-4027.

Catholic Cemeteries—NORMAN SCHALL, Dir., *St. Charles Borromeo Pastoral Center, 402 S. Independence Blvd., Romeoville, 60441.* Tel: 815-838-0395.

Catholic Charities—Legal Title: *Catholic Charities of the Diocese of Joliet.* KATHLEEN MCGOWAN, Exec. Dir., *411 Scott St., Joliet, 60435.* Tel: 815-723-3405.

The Catholic Education Foundation of the Diocese of Joliet—MAME BYRNE, Foundation Dir., *St. Charles Borromeo Pastoral Center, 402 S. Independence Blvd., Romeoville, 60441.* Tel: 815-834-4033.

Catholic Relief Services—TOM GARLITZ, Dir., *St. Charles Center, 402 S. Independence Blvd., Romeoville, 60441.* Tel: 815-834-4026.

Catholic Women, Council of—RUTH BENE, Dir., Office: *St. Charles Borromeo Pastoral Center, 402 S. Independence Blvd., Romeoville, 60441.* Tel: 815-834-4070.

Communications Office—St. Charles Borromeo Pastoral Center, 402 S. Independence Blvd., Romeoville, 60441. Tel: 815-834-4064.

Cursillo Movement—Rev. JOSEPH SHIMANEK, Moderator, *St. Charles Borromeo Pastoral Center, 405 S. Independence Blvd., Romeoville, 60441.* Tel: 815-838-8100.

Deans—East Dupage: Rev. JOHN BARRETT; West Dupage Kendall: Rev. JOEL FORTIER; East Will: Rev. FRANK VITUS; West Will: Rev. JAMES DOUGHERTY; Kankakee-Grundy: Rev. CHARLES WHEELER; Ford-Iroquois: Rev. F. LEE RYAN.

Diocesan Development Office—KEVIN DELABRE, Dir., *St. Charles Borromeo Pastoral Center, 402 S. Independence Blvd., Romeoville, 60441.* Tel: 815-838-8515.

Diocesan Coordinator for Health Affairs—Sr. JUDITH A. DAVIS, O.S.F., *Chancery, 425 Summit St., Joliet, 60435.* Tel: 815-722-6606.

Diocesan Vicar for Religious—Sr. MARY MEEGAN, O.P., *St. Charles Borromeo Pastoral Center, 402 S. Independence Blvd., Romeoville, 60441.* Tel: 815-834-4009.

Diaconate Program—Deacon WILL WORDEN, Dir., *St. Charles Borromeo Pastoral Center, 402 S. Independence Blvd., Romeoville, 60441.* Tel: 815-834-4091.

Divine Worship, Office of—Sr. SHARON MARIE STOLA, O.S.B., Dir., *St. Charles Borromeo Pastoral Center, 402 S. Independence Blvd., Romeoville, 60441.* Tel: 815-834-4010.

Ecumenism—Rev. STANLEY ORLIKIEWICZ, Dir., *St. Raymond Cathedral, 604 N. Raynor Ave., Joliet, 60435.* Tel: 815-722-6653.

Family Ministry, Office of—Dr. JAMES HEALY, Dir., *St. Charles Borromeo Pastoral Center, 402 S. Independence Blvd., Romeoville, 60441.* Tel: 815-838-5334.

Hispanic Ministry, Office of—Sr. JUDY CALLAHAN, B.V.M., Dir., *St. Charles Borromeo Center, 402 S. Independence Blvd., Romeoville, 60441.* Tel: 815-834-4037.

New Catholic Explorer—ALFRED DOBLIN, Editor, Office: *St. Charles Borromeo Pastoral Center, 402 S. Independence Blvd., Romeoville, 60441.* Tel: 815-838-6475; Fax: 815-834-4068.

Life Office—FRAN FORTIER, Dir.; Rev. DENIS WHITE, Moderator, *St. Charles Borromeo Pastoral Center, 402 S. Independence Blvd., Romeoville, 60441.* Tel: 815-834-4048.

Marriage Encounter—Rev. HUGH FULLMER, Diocesan Liaison, *Divine Savior Parish, 1200 67th St., Downers Grove, 60516.* Tel: 708-355-8980.

Marriage Preparation Office—Dr. JAMES HEALY, *St. Charles Borromeo Pastoral Center, 402 S. Independence Blvd., Romeoville, 60441.* Tel: 815-838-5334.

Ministry Formation—Dr. JEAN BOHR, Dir., *St. Charles Borromeo Pastoral Center, 402 S. Independence Blvd., Romeoville, 60441.* Tel: 815-834-4001.

Ministry to College Campuses and Young Adults—Bro. JOHN DORNBOS, C.F.C., *402 S. Independence Blvd., Romeoville, 60446-2264.* Tel: 815-834-4022.

Peace and Social Justice Ministry Office—THOMAS GARLITZ, *St. Charles Borromeo Pastoral Center, 402 S. Independence Blvd., Romeoville, 60441.* Tel: 815-834-4026.

Presbyteral Council—Rev. FRANCIS MCDONALD, Pres., *425 Summit, Joliet, 60435.* Tel: 815-722-6606.

Propagation of the Faith—Rev. DAMIEN GRAZIANO, Dir., *15314 Summit St., Oakbrook Terrace, 60181.* Tel: 708-629-5810.

Religious Education Office—Sr. MARILYN ELLERT, O.S.F., Supt., *430 N. Center St., Joliet, 60435.* Tel: 815-727-6411.

Rural Life—Rev. DENNIS WHITE, *St. Patrick, 119 N. Market St., Momeme, 60954.*

St. Vincent de Paul Society—JOHN BASILETTI, Pres., *213 Main St., West Chicago, 60185.* Tel: 708-293-9420.

Schools—Sr. HELEN JEAN KORMELINK, O.S.B., Supt., *425 Summit St., Joliet, 60435.* Tel: 815-727-4674.

Scouts—Rev. JOHN DOYLE, Office: *St. Anne Parish, 1702 N. Dearborn, Joilet.* Tel: 815-722-3222.

Stewardship Office—MARIANNE MURPHY, Dir., *St. Charles Borromeo Pastoral Center, 402 S. Independence Blvd., Romeoville, 60441.* Tel: 815-834-4030.

Vocations—Rev. JOHN REGAN, Dir., *St. Charles Borromeo, 402 S. Independence Blvd., Romeoville, 60441.* Tel: 815-834-4002.

Youth Ministry—Mrs. HELEN JOHNSON, *Religious Education Office, 430 N. Center, Joliet, 60435.* Tel: 815-727-6411.

CLERGY, PARISHES, MISSIONS AND PAROCHIAL SCHOOLS

CITY OF JOLIET
(Will County)

1—THE CATHEDRAL OF ST. RAYMOND (1917), Revs. Stanley Orlikiewicz; Douglas Martis. In res., Rev. Joseph J. Tapella.
Res., 604 N. Raynor Ave., 60435. Tel: 815-722-6653; Fax: 815-722-6175.
School—713 Douglas St., 60435. Tel: 815-722-6626. Sisters 1; Lay Teachers 24; Students 520.
Catechesis/Religious Programs—Students 230.

2—HOLY CROSS, Rev. Richard M. Ruffalo.
Res., 901 Elizabeth St., 60435. Tel: 815-722-0785. [CEM]

3—HOLY FAMILY (1959), Rev. John L. Dennerlein; Deacon Richard M. Yarshen.
1205 N. Larkin Ave., 60435. Tel: 815-725-6880; Fax: 815-725-8649.
Res., 910 Westminster Rd., 60435. Tel: 815-725-6880.
School—1205 N. Larkin Ave., 60435. Tel: 815-725-8149; Fax: 815-725-8649.
Lay Teachers 14; Students 225.
Catechesis/Religious Programs—Tel: 815-729-2243; Fax: 815-725-8649.
Students 225.

4—MOUNT CARMEL (1939) (Mexican American), Rev. Raymond Corkery, O.Carm.
Res., 409 Irving St., 60432. Tel: 815-726-5208; Fax: 815-727-7225.
Catechesis/Religious Programs—Students 215.

5—SACRED HEART (1886) (African American), Rev. Richard L. Bennett.
Res., 337 S. Ottawa St., 60436. Tel: 815-722-0295; Fax: 815-722-6088.
Catechesis/Religious Programs—Students 50.

6—ST. AMBROSE, Rev. Joseph F. Kilas.
Res., 1711 Burry Cir., Crest Hill, 60435. Tel: 815-722-3748.

7—ST. ANNE, Rev. John J. Doyle.
Res., 1702 N. Dearborn St., Crest Hill, 60435. Tel: 815-722-3222.

8—ST. ANTHONY (Italian), Rev. Arthur LaPore.
Res., 100 Scott St., 60431-1210. Tel: 815-722-1057.

9—ST. BERNARD, Rev. Donald O'Connor.
Res., 1313 Ridgewood Ave., 60432. Tel: 815-726-4474.

10—SS. CYRIL AND METHODIUS (Slovak), Revs. James Pajkos, O.F.M.; Micah Muhlen, O.F.M.
Res., 704 Landau Ave., 60432. Tel: 815-722-3586; Fax: 815-722-7276.
Catechesis/Religious Programs—Students 62.

11—ST. JOHN THE BAPTIST, Revs. Jeffery Salwach; Medard Buvala, O.F.M.; Deacon Jose Lopez. In res., Revs. Louis Davino, O.F.M.; Jeffry Donnelly, O.F.M.
Res., 404 N. Hickory St., 60435. Tel: 815-727-4788; Fax: 815-740-1521. [CEM]
School—Tel: 815-723-7315.
Brothers 1; Lay Teachers 7; Students 170.

12—ST. JOSEPH (1891) (Slovenian), Rev. George F. Klepec.
Res., 416 N. Chicago St., 60432. Tel: 815-727-9378.
School—409 N. Scott St., 60432. Tel: 815-722-1005. Sisters 3; Lay Teachers 6; Students 188.
Catechesis/Religious Programs—Students 55.

13—ST. JUDE (1954), Rev. James A. Schwab; Deacons Raymond Clark; William Hetzel.
Res., 2212 McDonough St., 60436. Tel: 815-725-2209; Fax: 815-741-8844.
School—2204 McDonough St., 60436. Tel: 815-729-0288; Fax: 815-729-0344.
Sisters of St. Francis of Mary Immaculate 2; Lay Teachers 15; Students 308.
Catechesis/Religious Programs—Tel: 815-729-0288; Fax: 815-729-0344.
Students 363.

14—ST. MARY. Closed. For inquiries for parish records contact the Chancery.

15—ST. MARY MAGDALENE, Rev. Richard G. Ross.
Res., 127 S. Briggs St., 60433. Tel: 815-722-7653.
School—Tel: 815-727-9079.
Lay Teachers 8; Students 157.

16—ST. MARY NATIVITY (1906) (Croatian), Revs. David Stalzer; Christopher Groh; Michael Powell.
Res., 706 N. Broadway, 60435. Tel: 815-726-4031; Fax: 815-727-4393.
School—702 N. Broadway, 60435. Tel: 815-722-8518.
Sisters of St. Francis of Christ the King 3; Lay Teachers 14; Students 335.
Catechesis/Religious Programs—Students 160.

17—ST. PATRICK (1838), Rev. James M. Lennon; Deacons Paul Kolodziej; Charles Peterson. In res., Rev. Eugene Bucciferro.
Res., 710 W. Marion St., 60436. Tel: 815-727-4746; Fax: 815-727-4798.
School—110 Willow Ave., 60436. Tel: 815-726-2924; Fax: 815-726-9289.
Lay Teachers 15; Students 330.
Catechesis/Religious Programs—Tel: 815-727-4746.
Students 125.

18—ST. PAUL THE APOSTLE (1950), Revs. James Dougherty; Dennis Paul; Deacons James Bouldin; William Bevan.
Res., 18 Woodlawn Ave., 60435. Tel: 815-725-1527; Fax: 815-725-3393.
School—130 N. Woodlawn Ave., 60435. Tel: 815-725-3390; Fax: 815-725-3393.
Lay Teachers 15; Students 409.
Catechesis/Religious Programs—120 Woodlawn Ave., 60435. Tel: 815-725-6927; Fax: 815-725-3393.
Students 211.

19—ST. THADDEUS, Rev. Edward P. Rowland.
Res., 501 Liberty St., 60432. Tel: 815-727-7212.
School—510 Columbia St., 60432. Tel: 815-727-7806.
Lay Teachers 6; Students 130.

OUTSIDE THE CITY OF JOLIET

Addison, Du Page Co., St. Joseph (1956), Revs. James T. Kempfer; Thomas McGivney; Deacons Dino J. Franch; Gabriel Gamboa.
Res., 330 E. Fullerton, 60101. Tel: 630-279-6553.
School—Tel: 630-279-4211; Fax: 630-279-4925. Mrs. Barbara Tatic, Prin.
Lay Teachers 11; Students 293.
Catechesis/Religious Programs—Tel: 630-832-5514. Sr. Suzanne D.R.E.
Students 522.

St. Philip The Apostle (1963), Revs. Raymond P. Garbin; Philip M. Danaher, S.V.D.; Raymond Stonich.
Res., 1223 W. Holtz Ave., 60101. Tel: 630-628-0900.
School—Tel: 630-543-4130.
Lay Teachers 15; Students 296.
Catechesis/Religious Programs—Students 610.

Ashkum, Iroquois Co., Assumption of the Blessed Virgin Mary, Rev. James Holup.
Res., N. Second St., Box 218, 60911. Tel: 815-698-2262. [CEM]
Mission—L'Erable, Iroquois Co., St. John the Baptist, Box 218, 60911. Tel: 815-698-2262; Fax: 815-698-2262.
Catechesis/Religious Programs—Students 117.

Aurora, Du Page Co., Our Lady of Mercy (1988), Rev. Gerald Tivy. Pastoral Assocs.: Sr. Louise Staszewski, O.S.M.; Sr. Marianne Talian, O.S.M.
Res., 801 S. Eola Rd., 60504. Tel: 630-851-3444; Fax: 630-851-3468.
Catechesis/Religious Programs—Students 804.

Beaverville, Iroquois Co., St. Mary, Rev. Ed Mumper.
Res., 308 St. Charles St., P.O. Box 152, 60912. Tel: 815-435-2432. [CEM]
Catechesis/Religious Programs—Students 63.

Bensenville, Du Page Co., St. Alexis (1926), Revs. William Conway; Andres Balvanera Franco, C.C.R.; Oswald S. Reimann; Sr. Laurina Kahne, C.S.J., Pastoral Assoc. In res., Rev. Raymond Davis.
Res., 400 W. Wood St., 60106. Tel: 708-766-3530; Fax: 708-766-3536.
Catechesis/Religious Programs—410 W. Wood St., 60106. Tel: 708-766-4417. Mrs. Trudy Anderson, D.R.E.
Students 435.

St. Charles Borromeo (1959), Rev. Don E. McLaughlin; Juanita Allen, Pastoral Assoc.; Deacon Michael Principe.
Res., 1135 Daniel, 60106. Tel: 630-860-1120; Fax: 630-860-5029.
School—Tel: 630-766-0116; Fax: 630-766-0181.
Lay Teachers 9; Students 272.
Catechesis/Religious Programs—Tel: 630-766-8822; Fax: 630-766-0181.
Students 286.

Bloomingdale, DuPage Co., St. Isidore (1920), Revs. Joel F. Fortier; William Dewan; Robert Coleman; Sr. Helen Mantovani, O.P., Pastoral Assoc.; Deacon Ken Jackson.
Res., 427 W. Army Trail Rd., 60108. Tel: 630-529-3045; Fax: 630-529-2940. [CEM]
School—Tel: 630-529-9323.
Religious 1; Lay Teachers 16; Students 282.
Catechesis/Religious Programs—Tel: 630-529-9191.
Students 1,770.

Bolingbrook, Will Co., St. Dominic (1964), Revs. James W. Antiporek; Gerald Simonelli; Deacons Thomas Ross; John Knapstein; Robert Wallace; Paul Walen; Robert Erickson; Victor Ruiz.
Res., 440 E. Briarcliff Rd., 60440. Tel: 630-739-5703; Fax: 630-739-2036.
School—420 E. Briarcliff Rd., 60440. Tel: 630-739-1633.
Sisters of St. Francis of Christ the King 2; Lay Teachers 14; Students 310.
Catechesis/Religious Programs—Tel: 630-739-2102.
Students 585.

St. Francis of Assisi, Revs. Paul Hottinger; Michael Pennock; Deacons Raymond Hamilton; Terrance Hanley, Sr.; Rudulfo Molano; Thomas Fricke.
Res., 325 Whitewater Dr., 60440. Tel: 630-759-7588; Fax: 630-759-5257.
Catechesis/Religious Programs—Tel: 630-759-7611. D.R.E.: Sr. Mary Jane Petzel, O.S.F.; Sr. Jeanette Pitts, O.S.F.
Students 525.

Bourbonnais, Kankakee Co., Maternity of the Blessed Virgin Mary (1847), Revs. Lawrence D. Lentz, C.S.V.; John N. Peeters, C.S.V.; Donald F. Lund, C.S.V.; Sr. Aimee Laemmrich, Pastoral Assoc.; Deacons Euchrist J. Marcotte; Francis Chamness.
Res., 308 E. Marsile St., 60914. Tel: 815-933-8285. [CEM]
School—Tel: 815-933-7758; Fax: 815-933-1884.

Sisters of the Congregation of Notre Dame 1; Lay Teachers 13; Students 275.
Catechesis / Religious Programs—Tel: 815-933-8226; Fax: 815-933-1884.
Students 381.

Bradley, Kankakee Co., St. Joseph (1904), Revs. Ronald Hart; Douglas Hauber; Deacons Bob LaMotte; Leon Fritz. In res., Rev. John Antczak.
Res., 211 N. Center Ave., 60915. Tel: 815-939-3573; Fax: 815-939-3138.
School—Tel: 815-933-8013.
Dominican Sisters 2; Lay Teachers 13; Students 274.
Catechesis / Religious Programs—283 N. Center Ave., 60915. Tel: 815-937-9340.
Students 234.
Convent—247 N. Center Ave., 60915. Tel: 815-932-0112.

Braidwood, Will Co., Immaculate Conception, Rev. William M. White.
Res., 34060 S. School St., 60408. Tel: 815-458-2125. [CEM]
Catechesis / Religious Programs—Students 260.

Cabery, Ford Co., St. Joseph, Rev. Richard F. Kostelz.
Res., 112 W. Main St., P.O. Box 77, 60919. Tel: 815-949-1568. [CEM]
Mission—Reddick, St. Mary.

Carol Stream, Du Page Co., Corpus Christi (1989), Rev. Charles A. Gemskie; Sr. M. Laurentia Fenlon, O.P., Pastoral Assoc. In res., Rev. Henry Wilkening, (Retired).
Res., 1415 Lies St., 60188-0453. Tel: 630-483-4673; Fax: 630-483-4679.
Catechesis / Religious Programs—Tel: 630-483-4222.
Students 975.

St. Luke (1963), Rev. Thomas Schutter; Sr. Barbara Rowan, S.S.S.F., Pastoral Assoc.
Res., 421 Cochise Ct., 60188. Tel: 630-668-1325; Fax: 630-668-1356.
Catechesis / Religious Programs—Tel: 630-665-2322.
Students 870.

Channahon, Will Co., St. Ann Parish (1990), Rev. Richard Smith.
Res., 25050 W. Eames St., 60410. Tel: 815-467-6962; Fax: 815-467-2320.
Catechesis / Religious Programs—Students 439.

Chebanse, Iroquois Co., SS. Mary and Joseph's (1869), Rev. Lee F. Bacchi.
Res., 525 S. Chestnut, P.O. Box 5, 60922. Tel: 815-697-2654. [CEM]
Catechesis / Religious Programs—Students 90.

Clarendon Hills, Du Page Co., Notre Dame (1954), Revs. Jess Testa; Robert J. Schuler; Venard Kommer, O.F.M.; Deacons Neill Carson; Frank Foys; David Lifka; Alan Symonanis.
Res., 64 Norfolk Ave., 60514. Tel: 708-654-3365; Fax: 708-654-8701.
School—Tel: 708-323-1642.
Lay Teachers 19; Students 271.
Catechesis / Religious Programs—Tel: 708-325-5387.
Students 390.

Clifton, Iroquois Co., St. Peter's, Rev. Lee F. Bacchi.
Res., 450 E. Third Ave., Box 25, 60927. Tel: 815-694-2027. [CEM]
Catechesis / Religious Programs—Students 125.

Coal City, Grundy Co., Assumption (1889), Revs. Mark Jendersyk; Thomas Corley; James Curtin; Sr. Mary Patricia Peacock, S.P., Pastoral Assoc.
Res., 245 S. Kankakee St., 60416. Tel: 815-634-4171.
Catechesis / Religious Programs—Tel: 815-634-8020.
Students 420.

Darien, Du Page Co., Our Lady of Peace (1970), Revs. Alphonse Micka, M.I.C.; Anthony Kelpsas; William Hayward, M.I.C.; Deacons Frank Bina; Paul Brachle; Walter Schmidt.
Res., 701 Plainfield Rd., 60561. Tel: 630-323-4333; Fax: 630-323-4354.
School—709 Plainfield Rd., 60561. Tel: 630-325-9220; Fax: 630-325-1995.
Sisters of St. Casimir 3; Lay Teachers 25; Students 555.
Catechesis / Religious Programs—Tel: 630-963-3053.
Students 905.

Our Lady of Mount Carmel (1970), Revs. Gavin Quinn, O.Carm.; Michael O'Keefe, O.Carm.; Russell Gavin, O.Carm.; Deacon Marco Lovero.
Res., 8404 Cass Ave., 60561. Tel: 630-852-3303; Fax: 630-852-5227.
Catechesis / Religious Programs—Tel: 630-963-3053; Fax: 630-852-5227.
Students 1,228.

Downers Grove, Du Page Co., Divine Savior (1968), Revs. Robert E. Pietras; Leonard Guz.
Res., 1200 67th St., 60516. Tel: 630-969-1532; Fax: 630-969-1724.
Catechesis / Religious Programs—Tel: 630-969-1673.
Students 668.

St. Joseph (1907), Revs. James Fitzgerald; Edward Grotovsky.
Res., 4824 Highland, 60515. Tel: 630-964-0216; Fax: 630-964-0867.
School—Franklin & Highland, 60515. Tel: 630-969-4306; Fax: 630-969-3946.
Lay Teachers 20; Students 482.
Catechesis / Religious Programs—Tel: 630-971-1740; Fax: 630-964-0867.
Students 781.

St. Mary, Revs. Thomas Paul; Scott McCawley.
Res., 444 Wilson Ave., 60515. Tel: 630-969-1063; Fax: 630-969-1259.
School—444 Prairie Ave., 60515. Tel: 630-968-6155.
Felician Sisters 2; Lay Teachers 25; Students 544.
Catechesis / Religious Programs—Tel: 630-960-3565.
Students 747.

Elmhurst, Du Page Co., Immaculate Conception (1876), Revs. Gerald Riva; Robert Duda; John Balluff.
Res., 134 Arthur St., 60126. Tel: 630-530-8515; Fax: 630-530-9346.
School—Tel: 630-530-3490; Fax: 630-530-7688. Helen Kwasmiewski, Prin.
Sisters 1; Lay Teachers 21; Students 603.
High School—217 Cottage Hill Ave., 60126. Tel: 630-530-3460. Sr. Maureen Field, I.H.M.
Priests 1; Sisters 1; Lay Teachers 17; Students 239.
Catechesis / Religious Programs—Tel: 630-530-3480.
Students 531.

Mary, Queen of Heaven (1957), Rev. John Barrett. In res., Rev. Thomas Wolter; Deacons John Maloney; Charles Nunez.
Res., 426 N. West Ave., 60126. Tel: 630-279-5700; Fax: 630-279-4667.
Catechesis / Religious Programs—442 N. West Ave., 60126. Tel: 630-832-8962; Fax: 630-279-4667.
Students 296.

Visitation (1953), Revs. Michael Lane; William DeSalvo; Stan Fernando (India); Deacons Dominic Cuzzone; Jay Janousek; Anthony Spatafore.
Res., 779 S. York St., 60126. Tel: 630-834-6700; Fax: 630-834-6711.
School—Tel: 630-834-4931; Fax: 630-834-4936.
Sisters of St. Adrian Dominican 2; Lay Teachers 23; Students 440.
Catechesis / Religious Programs—851 S. York, 60126. Tel: 630-279-7058.
Students 600.

Frankfort, Will Co., St. Anthony, Revs. Vytas Memenas; John Onger. In res., Rev. John Regan.
Res., 7659 W. Sauk Trail, 60423. Tel: 815-469-3750; Fax: 815-469-6514.
Catechesis / Religious Programs—Tel: 815-469-6072; Fax: 815-469-6514.
Students 1,200.

Gibson City, Ford Co., Our Lady of Lourdes, Rev. William F. Smith.
Res., 534 N. Wood St., 60936. Tel: 217-784-4671.
Catechesis / Religious Programs—Students 69.
Mission—Melvin, St. George.

Gilman, Iroquois Co., Immaculate Conception, Rev. Robert F. Emerson.
Res., 224 N. Secor St., 60938. Tel: 815-265-7236. [CEM]
Catechesis / Religious Programs—Students 97.
Mission—Onarga, Iroquois Co., Our Lady of Guadalupe, 504 W. Seminary Ave., P.O. Box 1, Onarga, 60955.

Glendale Heights, Du Page Co., St. Matthew, Revs. Franklin R. Tasker, O.Carm.; Norbert G. Piper, O.Carm.; David Dillon, O.Carm.; Deacons Ronald Darschewski; Richard A. Mangen; Vincent C. Rizzo.
Res., 1555 Glen Ellyn Rd., 60139. Tel: 630-469-6300; Fax: 630-469-6302.
School—Tel: 630-858-3112.
Lay Teachers 21; Students 404.
Catechesis / Religious Programs—Students 516.

Glen Ellyn, Du Page Co., Queenship of Mary, Rev. Nguyen Huy Quyen.
Res., 23W371 Armitage, 60137. Tel: 630-469-7494.
Catechesis / Religious Programs—Tel: 630-752-0332.
Students 122.

St. Petronille (1925), Revs. Michael A. O'Keefe; John Sullivan; Augustin Ortega-Ruiz; Deacons Edward Schafer; Ronald Yurcus; Mrs. Vinal Van Benthem, Pastoral Assoc. In res., Rev. Nguyen Huy Quyen.
Res., 420 Glenwood Ave., 60137. Tel: 630-469-0404; Fax: 630-469-0412.
School—Tel: 630-469-5041; Fax: 630-469-5071.
Lay Teachers 28; Students 516.
Catechesis / Religious Programs—458 Hillside, 60137. Tel: 630-858-3796.
Students 1,173.

St. James the Apostle (1965), Revs. John M. Sebahar; Jeff Stoneberg, O.F.M.; Raymond Guthrie; Deacon Emmanuel Scavone.
Res., 480 S. Park Blvd., 60137. Tel: 630-469-7540; Fax: 630-469-7590.
School—Tel: 708-469-8060.
Lay Teachers 20; Students 296.
Catechesis / Religious Programs—490 S. Park Blvd., 60137. Tel: 630-858-5646.
Students 805.

Goodrich, Kankakee Co., Sacred Heart, Rev. Paul F. Jasinski, C.S.V.; Deacon John R. Reville.
Res., 588 S. 10000 W. Road, Bonfield, 60913-7019. Tel: 815-426-2221. [CEM]

Herscher, Kankakee Co., St. Margaret Mary, Rev. John P. Driscoll.
Res., 207 E. Fifth St., 60941. Tel: 815-426-2153. [CEM]
Catechesis / Religious Programs—Students 116.

Hinsdale, Du Page Co., St. Isaac Jogues, Revs. Theodore Weitzel; Douglas A. Martis; Matthew Hughes.
Res., 306 W. Fourth St., 60521. Tel: 630-323-1248; Fax: 630-323-6373.
School—Tel: 630-323-3244.
Religious 1; Lay Teachers 23; Students 571.
Catechesis / Religious Programs—427 S. Clay St., 60521. Tel: 630-323-0265.
Students 746.

Hopkins Park, Kankakee Co., Sacred Heart, Rev. Denis E. White.
Res. & Mailing Address: 119 Market St., Momence, 60954. Tel: 815-944-5562.
Catechesis / Religious Programs—16485 E. Birch, P.O. Box 557, 60944.

Irwin, Kankakee Co., St. James The Apostle, Rev. John P. Driscoll.
Res., 4372 Main St., Kankakee, 60901. Tel: 815-933-8807. [CEM]
Catechesis / Religious Programs—Students 75.

Itasca, Du Page Co., St. Andrew Kim, Rev. Simeon Je Chan-Kyu.
Res., 1275 Arlington Hts. Rd., 60143. Tel: 630-250-0576.

St. Peter the Apostle (1956), Revs. Donald P. Pock; Joseph Stalzer; Deacon Robert J. Anchor.
Res., 524 N. Rush St., 60143-1698. Tel: 630-773-1272; Fax: 630-773-1920.
School—500 N. Cherry St., 60143-1699. Tel: 630-773-1979; Fax: 630-773-2826.
Lay Teachers 10; Students 210.
Catechesis / Religious Programs—Tel: 630-773-1959; Fax: 630-773-2826.
Students 285.

Kankakee, Kankakee Co.,

1—St. Martin of Tours, (1950), Rev. Dennis F. Settles.
Res., 905 S. Eighth Ave., 60901. Tel: 815-933-7177; Fax: 815-933-2171. [JC]
School—907 S. Ninth Ave., 60901. Tel: 815-932-7911; Fax: 815-933-2171.
Lay Teachers 10; Students 177.
Catechesis / Religious Programs—Tel: 815-933-7177; Fax: 815-933-2171.
Students 250.

2—St. Patrick, (1893) (Irish), Revs. Richard Pighini, C.S.V.; Michael P. Keliher, C.S.V.; Sr. Mary Noel Plummer, O.P., Pastoral Min. Pastoral Assocs.: Marilyn Mulcahy; Deacon Joseph Cotugno. In res., Revs. Andrew A. Bialas, C.S.V.; Eugene J. Sullivan, C.S.V.; Francis Gerwronka, C.S.V.
Res., 428 S. Indiana Ave., 60901. Tel: 815-932-6716; Fax: 815-932-6717.
School—Tel: 815-932-8124.
Lay Teachers 13; Students 230.
Catechesis / Religious Programs—Tel: 815-939-3879.
Students 115.

3—St. Rose of Lima, Rev. Charles Wheeler.
Res., 486 W. Merchant St., 60901. Tel: 815-933-9391; Fax: 815-933-9393.
Catechesis / Religious Programs—Students 100.

4—St. Stanislaus, (Polish). Closed. For inquiries for parish records contact the Chancery.

5—St. Teresa, Rev. Anthony Taschetta. Pastoral Assocs.: Barbara Staniszeski; Sr. Mary McElmeel, B.V.M.
Res., 361 N. St. Joseph Ave., 60901. Tel: 815-933-7683; Fax: 815-933-7692.
Lisieux Pastoral Center—371 St. Joseph Ave., 60901. Tel: 815-939-2913.

Kinsman, Grundy Co., Sacred Heart, Rev. Jason Kommer, O.F.M., Admin.
Res., 219 Emmett St., 60437. Tel: 815-392-4245; Fax: 815-392-4307. [JC]

Lisle, Du Page Co., St. Joan of Arc (1924), Revs. Roman S. Galiardi, O.S.B.; Gabriel Baltes, O.S.B.; Kenneth Zigmond, O.S.B.; Deacons Denis Stucko; Joseph Dalpiaz.
Office: 820 Division St., 60532. Tel: 630-963-4500;

Fax: 630-963-4568.
School—Tel: 630-963-9070; Fax: 630-969-1732.
Lay Teachers 31; Students 674.
Catechesis/Religious Programs—Tel: 630-963-4500; Fax: 630-963-4568.
Students 455.

Lockport, Will Co.,

1—ST. BERNARD, (1978), Rev. Richard B. Prodehl; Sr. Mary Carr, O.P., Pastoral Assoc.
Res., 14135 Parker Rd., 60441. Tel: 708-301-3020; Fax: 708-301-0738.
Catechesis/Religious Programs—14724 S. Arboretum Dr., 60441. Tel: 708-301-6952; Fax: 708-301-8870.
Students 1,100.

2—ST. DENNIS, Revs. Robert Maternoski; Thomson Panakal.
Res., 1214 Hamilton St., 60441. Tel: 815-838-0704; Fax: 815-838-2401.
School—223 E. 12th St., 60441. Tel: 815-838-4494.
Sisters 2; Lay Teachers 10; Students 225.

3—ST. JOHN VIANNEY, Rev. Peter B. Thongamphai, Admin.
Res., 401 Brassel, 60441. Tel: 815-723-3291.

4—ST. JOSEPH, Rev. Hugh Fullmer; Deacon Joe Urso; Dr. Jeanne M. Cosgrove, Pastoral Assoc.
Res., 410 S. Jefferson St., 60441. Tel: 815-838-0187; Fax: 815-838-5379.
School—529 Madison, 60441. Tel: 815-838-8173; Fax: 815-838-0504.
Franciscan Sisters of the Sacred Heart 3; Lay Teachers 8; Students 275.
Convent—531 E. Fourth St., 60441. Tel: 815-838-0186.
Catechesis/Religious Programs—529 Madison St., 60441. Tel: 815-838-2112.
Students 260.

Lombard, Du Page Co., Christ the King, Revs. James Dvorscak; David Hankus; Deacon Philip Gavin.
Res., 1501 S. Main St., 60148. Tel: 630-629-1717.
School—Tel: 630-627-0640.
Sisters 2; Lay Teachers 10; Students 115.
Catechesis/Religious Programs—Tel: 630-629-1719.
Students 329.

Sacred Heart (1912), Revs. Arno A. Dennerlein; John Zanoni; Deacon Thomas Bailey. In res., Rev. Raynor E. Richter, Pastor Emeritus.
Res., 114 S. Elizabeth St., 60148. Tel: 630-627-0687; Fax: 630-627-0688.
School—Tel: 630-627-0687; Fax: 630-627-0688.
Lay Teachers 15; Students 237.
Catechesis/Religious Programs—328 W. Maple St., 60148. Tel: 630-495-0843; Fax: 630-627-0688.
Students 441.

St. Pius X (1954), Revs. Herbert Essig; Lester Hochhalter; Sr. Pauline Schutz, O.S.F., Pastoral Assoc.; Deacons Thomas Goebel; Ron Knecht; William Crane.
Res., 1025 E. Madison, 60148. Tel: 630-627-4526; Fax: 630-495-5926.
School—Tel: 630-627-2353. Ellen Herron, Prin.
Lay Teachers 22; Students 488.
Catechesis/Religious Programs—Tel: 630-627-1551. Sr. Helen Susan, D.R.E.
Students 490.

Manhattan, Will Co., St. Joseph, Rev. Edward J. O'Malley.
Res., 235 W. North, P.O. Box 25, 60442. Tel: 815-478-3341; Fax: 815-478-5258. [CEM]
School—Tel: 815-478-3951; Fax: 815-478-5258.
Lay Teachers 6; Students 130.
Catechesis/Religious Programs—Students 330.

Manteno, Kankakee Co., St. Joseph (1855), Rev. Mark Fracaro; Deacons Francis Henrisey; John Hindes.
Res., 207 S. Main St., 60950. Tel: 815-468-3403; Fax: 815-468-7089. [CEM][JC]
Catechesis/Religious Programs—Tel: 815-468-8116.
Students 292.

Martinton, Iroquois Co., St. Martin, Rev. Ed Mumper.
Res., P.O. Box 152, Beaverville, 60912. Tel: 815-435-2432. [CEM]

Minooka, Grundy Co., St. Mary, Rev. Frank K. Vitus.
Res., 303 St. Mary St., 60447. Tel: 815-467-2233; Fax: 815-467-1760. [CEM]
Catechesis/Religious Programs—Students 370.

Mokena, Will Co., St. Mary Church, Revs. Joseph E. Butters; Robert Noesen; Sr. Marilyn Renninger, O.S.F., Pastoral Assoc.; Deacon Jim Fitzgerald.
Res., 19517 S. 115th Ave., P.O. Box 2, 60448. Tel: 708-479-3380; Fax: 708-479-8403.
School—Tel: 708-479-3383; Fax: 708-479-4985.
Franciscan Sisters of the Sacred Heart 2; Lay Teachers 8; Students 309.
Catechesis/Religious Programs—11489 W. 195th St., 60448. Tel: 708-479-3385.
Students 1504.

Momence, Kankakee Co., St. Patrick (1859), Rev. Denis White; Deacons Jeffrey Jacob; Dan Hessling.
Res., 119 Market St., 60954. Tel: 815-472-2864. [CEM]
School—404 W. Second St., 60954. Tel: 815-472-2469.
Lay Teachers 5; Students 115.
Catechesis/Religious Programs—Students 170.
Vicariate—Sacred Heart, Hopkins Park, 60944. Tel: 815-944-5156.

Monee, Will Co., St. Boniface, Rev. Mark Menezes; Deacon Robert Jossey.
Res., 5301 W. Main St., P.O. Box 217, 60449. Tel: 708-534-9682.
Catechesis/Religious Programs—Tel: 708-534-9683.
Students 100.

Morris, Grundy Co., Immaculate Conception of the Blessed Virgin Mary (1852), Rev. Michael Foley.
Res., 516 E. Jackson St., 60450. Tel: 815-942-0620. [CEM]
School—Tel: 815-942-4111; Fax: 815-942-5094.
Lay Teachers 13; Students 256.
Catechesis/Religious Programs—505 E. North St., 60450. Tel: 815-942-4177.
Students 369.

Naperville, Will Co.,

1—ST. ELIZABETH SETON, (1986), Rev. Ernest Norbeck; Deacons Thomas Sheridan; James Dixon; William Murphy; Gregg Lawson.
Res., 2220 Lisson Rd., 60565. Tel: 630-416-3325; Fax: 630-416-3642.
Catechesis/Religious Programs—Tel: 630-416-1992; Fax: 630-416-3642.
Students 1,810.

2—STS. PETER AND PAUL, DuPage Co., (1856), Revs. James Burnett; Thomas A. Milota; Gordon Mahoney; Gregory Rothfuchs. Pastoral Assocs.: Sr. Aniceta Skube, O.P.; Sr. Kathleen Hook, O.S.F.; Deacons William Girard; Manuel J. Solis. In res., Rt. Rev. Thomas J. Havlik, O.S.B.
Res., 26 N. Ellsworth St., 60540. Tel: 630-355-1081. [CEM]
School—201 E. Franklin, 60540. Tel: 630-355-0113; Fax: 630-355-9803. Mr. Frank Glowaty, Prin.
Sisters 2; Lay Teachers 25; Students 593.
Catechesis/Religious Programs—120 E. Franklin, 60540. Tel: 630-357-2436.
Students 1,250.

3—ST. RAPHAEL, DuPage Co., (1963), Revs. William E. Donnelly; Dennis Lewandowski; Deacons William Blessing; John McHugh.
Mailing Address: 1215 Modaff Rd., 60540-7818.
Res., 416 Gartner, 60540. Tel: 630-355-4545; Fax: 630-355-7470.
School—Tel: 630-355-1880; Fax: 630-355-7470.
Lay Teachers 17; Students 328.
Catechesis/Religious Programs—Students 2,278.

4—ST. MARGARET MARY, DuPage Co., (1980), Revs. William J. O'Shea; Richard Dochstader; Sr. Madelyn Gould, S.S.S.F., Pastoral Assoc.; Deacons Kenneth J. Miles; Michael Beckley; Frederick E. Straub.
1450 Green Trails Dr., 60540. Tel: 630-369-0777; Fax: 630-369-1493.
Catechesis/Religious Programs—Tel: 630-369-0833; Fax: 630-369-1493.
Students 1,602.

5—ST. THOMAS THE APOSTLE, DuPage Co., (1984), Revs. Donald Kenny; Richard Lundgren; Raymond Grasso. Pastoral Assocs.: Sr. Ann James Murray, O.S.F.; Sr. Marlene Schemmel, C.S.J.; Deacon William Worden.
Res., 1500 Brookdale Rd., 60563. Tel: 708-355-8980; Fax: 708-355-0521.
Catechesis/Religious Programs—Students 1,437.

New Lenox, Will Co., St. Jude (1934), Revs. Richard T. Allen, O.S.A.; Raymond R. Ryan, O.S.A.; John P. Murphy, O.S.A.; Deacon Robert Fitt. In res., Revs. Thomas Osborne, O.S.A.; John Paul Szura, O.S.A.
Res., 241 W. Second Ave., 60451. Tel: 815-485-8049; Fax: 815-485-7754.
School—Tel: 815-485-2549; Fax: 815-485-7754.
Lay Teachers 12; Students 267.
Catechesis/Religious Programs—Tel: 815-485-4852; Fax: 815-485-7754.
Students 1,102.

Oakbrook Terrace, DuPage Co., Ascension of Our Lord (1967), Rev. Damien Graziano; Jack Bartz, Pastoral Assoc.
Res., 1S314 Summit Ave., 60181. Tel: 630-629-5810; Fax: 630-953-8251.
Catechesis/Religious Programs—Students 293.

Oswego, Kendall Co., St. Anne (1963), Revs. Daniel F. Stempora; John T. McGeean; Deacons David Brockman; William Dunn; Leslie Hancock.
Res., 551 Boulder Hill Pass, P.O. Box 670, 60543. Tel: 630-554-3331; Fax: 630-554-0530.
Catechesis/Religious Programs—(Grades K-8). Tel: 630-554-1425.
Students 1,046.

Park Forest, Will Co., St. Mary, Rev. John Ryan.
Res., 212 Monee Rd., 60466. Tel: 708-747-1600; Fax: 708-748-6907.
School—227 Monee Rd., 60466-2403. Tel: 708-748-6686; Fax: 708-748-6907.
Franciscan Sisters of the Sacred Heart 2; Lay Teachers 10; Students 260.

Paxton, Ford Co., St. Mary, Rev. James Heramb.
Res., 407 W. Pells, 60957. Tel: 217-379-4033.
Mission—Loda, Iroquois Co., St. Joseph, 407 W. Pells, 60957. Tel: 217-379-4033.
Catechesis/Religious Programs—Students 140.

Peotone, Will Co., St. Paul the Apostle (1961), Rev. Michael Ginter.
Res., 501 N. Conrad St., P.O. Box 700, 60468-0700. Tel: 708-258-6917.
Catechesis/Religious Programs—Tel: 708-258-6917.
Students 260.

Piper City, Ford Co., St. Peter, Rev. William L. Slikas.
Res. & Mailing Address: 212 Pine St., 60959. Tel: 815-686-2595.
Mission—Roberts, Immaculate Conception. [CEM]

Plainfield, Will Co., St. Mary Immaculate (1909), Revs. Anthony A. Nugent; Joseph Siegel; Deacons James Sossong; Terry Sakfo; James Walters.
Mailing Address: 129 S. Division St. (Rte. 59), 60544.
Res., 116 Frederick, 60544. Tel: 815-436-2651; Fax: 815-436-5017. [CEM]
School—129 S. Division St., 60544-8806. Tel: 815-436-3953.
Lay Teachers 18; Students 415.
Catechesis/Religious Programs—Tel: 815-436-4501.
Students 1,237.

Plano, Kendall Co., St. Mary (1885), Revs. Jerome Zalonis, M.I.C.; Boniface Vaisnoras, M.I.C.; Deacons Dale Metcalf; Santos Martinez. In res., Rev. John Savukynas, M.I.C.
Res., 901 N. Center St., 60545. Tel: 708-552-3448; Fax: 708-552-3450.
School—817 N. Center Ave., 60545. Tel: 708-552-3345.
Sisters 1; Lay Teachers 8; Students 257.
Catechesis/Religious Programs—810 N. Center Ave., 60545. Tel: 708-552-1505. Sr. Kathryn Frankovich, O.S.F., D.R.E.
Students 475.
Mission—Bristol, Kendall Co., St. Patrick, 406 Walnut St., Yorkville, 60560. Tel: 708-553-6671; Fax: 708-553-6600. [CEM]

Rockdale, Will Co., St. Joseph (1914), Rev. Paul Wittosch.
Res., 1329 Belleview Ave., 60436. Tel: 815-725-4469.
Catechesis/Religious Programs—314 S. Midland Ave., 60436. Tel: 815-729-9149.
Students 64.

Romeoville, Will Co., St. Andrew the Apostle (1959), Rev. Richard Walsh; Deacons David Raskowski; Stephen Clancy.
Res., 219 Arlington Dr., 60446. Tel: 815-886-4165; Fax: 815-886-6119.
School—Tel: 815-886-5953.
Sisters 2; Lay Teachers 11; Students 252.
Catechesis/Religious Programs—505 Kingston Dr., 60446. Tel: 815-886-5962; Fax: 815-886-5962.
Students 402.

Roselle, Du Page Co., St. Walter (1946), Revs. Francis B. McDonald; John Guiney, S.M.A.; Peter Jarosz; Deacon Ron Searls.
Res., 130 W. Pine Ave., 60172. Tel: 630-894-2461; Fax: 630-582-4206.
School—201 W. Maple Ave., 60172. Tel: 630-529-1721; Fax: 630-529-9290.
Lay Teachers 28; Students 705.
Catechesis/Religious Programs—140 W. Pine, 60172. Tel: 630-894-5880; Fax: 630-582-4206. Ms. Barbara Ruments, D.R.E.
Students 1,100.

St. Anne, Kankakee Co., St. Anne, Rev. James Curtin, Parochial Admin.
Res., 230 N. Sixth Ave., 60964. Tel: 815-427-8265.

St. George, Kankakee Co., St. George, Rev. Kenneth Yarno, C.S.V.
Res., 5272 E. 5000 North Rd., Bourbonnais, 60914-9725. Tel: 815-939-1851. [JC]

South Wilmington, Grundy Co., St. Lawrence, Rev. Thomas Fleming; Deacon Joseph Riggi.
Res., 165 Rice St., Box 190, 60474. Tel: 815-237-2230.
Mission—Essex, Kankakee Co., St. Lawrence O'Toole, P.O. Box 190, 60474. Tel: 815-237-2230.

Steger, Will Co., St. Liborius (1901), Revs. Joseph Burns; John Sponder; Len Olszak.
Res., 71 W. 35th St., 60475. Tel: 708-754-1363; Fax: 708-754-0922.
School—(Steger Campus) 3436 Halsted Blvd., 60475.

Tel: 708-754-0192.
Lay Teachers 15; Students 292.
Lay Teachers 15; Students 292.
Catechesis/Religious Programs—Tel: 708-754-3460.
Students 440.

Villa Park, Du Page Co., St. Alexander (1924), Revs. John M. Furdek; Tran V. Nguyen; Deacons Gene Schubert; John Boyle.
Res., 300 S. Cornell Ave., 60181. Tel: 630-833-7730; Fax: 630-833-3127.
School—136 S. Cornell Ave., 60181. Tel: 630-834-3787.
Sisters of Notre Dame de Namur 2; Lay Teachers 12; Students 278.
Catechesis/Religious Programs—130 S. Cornell Ave., 60181. Tel: 630-832-0506.
Students 400.

St. John the Apostle (1959), Rev. James Duffy.
Res., 330 N. Westmore, 60181. Tel: 630-279-7404; Fax: 630-530-9918.
Catechesis/Religious Programs—Tel: 630-832-7588.
Students 217.

Warrenville, Du Page Co., St. Irene, Rev. Thomas A. Corbino; Sr. Roseann Eck, C.S.J., Pastoral Assoc.; Deacon Robert True.
Res., 28 W. 441 Warrenville Rd., 60555. Tel: 630-393-2400; Fax: 630-393-9680.
School—35601 Warren Ave., 60555. Tel: 630-393-9303. Beverly Murphy, Prin.
Lay Teachers 13; Students 210.

Watseka, Iroquois Co., St. Edmund, Rev. F. Lee Ryan; Deacon Lloyd Eastburn.
Res., 219 E. Locust St., 60970. Tel: 815-432-3274.
Mission—Crescent City, St. Joseph.

Wayne, Du Page Co., Resurrection, Rev. Laurian Janicki, O.F.M.
Res., P.O. Box 626, 60184. Tel: 630-289-5400; Fax: 630-289-5407.

West Chicago, Du Page Co., St. Mary (1894) (Hispanic), Revs. Vernon Arseneau; John Bosco Panahal; Peter Jankowski.
Res., 140 N. Oakwood Ave., 60185. Tel: 630-231-0013; Fax: 630-293-2671. [CEM]
School—147 Garden St., 60185. Tel: 630-231-1776; Fax: 630-293-2671.
Lay Teachers 13; Students 196.
Catechesis/Religious Programs—Tel: 630-231-5704.
Students 378.

Westmont, Du Page Co., Holy Trinity (1938), Revs. James A. Nowak; Andrew Buczyna.
Res., 111 S. Cass Ave., 60559. Tel: 630-968-1366; Fax: 630-968-1502.
School—25 E. Richmond, 60559. Tel: 630-971-0184; Fax: 630-971-1175.
Sisters 3; Lay Teachers 16; Students 390.
Catechesis/Religious Programs—Tel: 630-968-5978.
Students 452.

Wheaton, Du Page Co., St. Daniel the Prophet Church, Rev. Thomas J. White. Pastoral Assocs.: Sr. Josephine Sincak; Sr. Mary Potthast; Sr. Margaret Ivers, I.B.V.M.
Res., 231 Danada Dr., 60187. Tel: 630-682-5003; Fax: 630-682-5004.

St. Mark, Rev. John Ducaji.
Res., 303 E. Parkway Dr., 60187. Tel: 630-665-0030.
Catechesis/Religious Programs—300 E. Cole St., 60187. Tel: 630-668-4614.
Students 160.

St. Michael (1884), Revs. Martin Gabel; Steven Bondi; Joseph A. Mundakal, C.M.I.; Deacons John Cozzens; Matthew Van Wallene.
Res., 315 W. Illinois St., 60187. Tel: 630-665-2250. [CEM]
School—314 W. Willow Ave., 60187. Tel: 630-653-1454; Fax: 630-665-1491.
Notre Dame Sisters of Toledo 2; Lay Teachers 27; Students 554.
Catechesis/Religious Programs—Tel: 630-682-3650; Fax: 630-665-6820.
Students 1,110.

Wilmington, Will Co., St. Rose (1844), Rev. Francis Maher; Sr. Ann Ellen Quirk, B.V.M., Pastoral Assoc.; Deacon Don Dyer.
Res., 603 S. Main St., 60481. Tel: 815-476-7491. [CEM]
School—Tel: 815-476-6220.
Lay Teachers 12; Students 256.
Catechesis/Religious Programs—Tel: 815-476-6220.
Students 124.

Wilton Center, Will Co., St. Patrick, Rev. S. C. Giunta.
Res., 14936 Wilmington Peotone Rd., Manhattan, 60442. Tel: 815-478-3440. [CEM]

Winfield, Du Page Co., St. John the Baptist (1867), Revs. Guy Vaccaro, Admin.; Don Cunningham, S.J.; Tony Stockinger; Deacon Don Mathieu. In res., Rev. Michael Valente, O.S.
Res., O.S. 233 Church St., 60190. Tel: 630-668-0918; Fax: 630-668-1074. [CEM]
School—O.S. 259 Church St., 60190. Tel: 630-668-2625; Fax: 630-668-7176. Patricia Walther, Prin.
Lay Teachers 17; Students 327.
Catechesis/Religious Programs—Tel: 630-682-4400; Fax: 630-668-1074. Maureen Brennan, D.R.E.
Students 1,206.

Wood Dale, Du Page Co., Holy Ghost (1946), Revs. Kevin R. Farrell; Robert A. Hoffenkamp.
Res., 254 N. Wood Dale Rd., 60191. Tel: 630-860-2975; Fax: 630-860-9482.
School—Tel: 630-766-4508; Fax: 630-860-9482.
Lay Teachers 16; Students 231.
Catechesis/Religious Programs—Tel: 630-766-1045; Fax: 630-860-9482.
Students 556.

Woodridge, Du Page Co., Christ The Servant Parish (1990), Rev. James Ratigan.
Mailing Address: 2952 Harvest Pl., Darien, 60561. Tel: 630-910-0770.
Catechesis/Religious Programs—Students 103.

St. Scholastica (1962), Revs. Thomas Sularz; James Radek; Sr. Regina Ann Weissmann, O.S.B., Pastoral Assoc.; Deacons Roger Schmith; Michael Salerno.
Res., 7800 S. Janes Ave., 60517. Tel: 630-985-2351; Fax: 630-985-8770.
School—Tel: 630-985-2515; Fax: 630-985-2395. Mary Ann Drandt, Prin.
Lay Teachers 10; Students 290.
Catechesis/Religious Programs—7720 Janes Ave., 60517. Tel: 630-985-9255. Sr. Therese Kane, B.V.M., D.R.E.
Students 1,045.

Chaplains of Public Institutions

JOLIET. *Illinois State Penitentiary,* 404 N. Hickory St., P.O. Box 112, 60435. Jerry Bowman.
Illinois Youth Commission, Reception and Diagnostic Center, McDonough St., 60436. Deacon Joseph O'Connor.
Joliet Correctional Depot, Collins St. Revs. John Doyle; Joseph Kilas.
Silver Cross Hospital, 1200 Maple Rd., 60432. Rev. Peter Thongamphi.

ELMHURST. *Elmhurst Memorial Hospital,* 200 Berteau Ave., 60126. Rev. Thomas Wolter.

HINSDALE. *Hinsdale Hospital,* 120 N. Oak, 60521. Rev. James Walton, O.F.M.

KANKAKEE. *Riverside Medical Center,* 350 N. Wells, 60901. Rev. John Antczak.
Shapiro Development Center, 100 E. Jeffrey, 60901. Rev. Andrew Bialas, C.S.V.

NAPERVILLE. *Edward Hospital,* S. Washington St., 60540. Rev. Raymond Grasso.

WINFIELD. *Central DuPage Hospital,* 0N025 Winfield, 60190. Rev. Tony Stockinger.

On Duty Outside the Diocese:
Reverend Fathers—
Caruso, Carmen A., St. Isabel, 3559 Sanibel-Captiva Rd., Sanibel, FL 33957
Dieter, Thomas, St. Catherine of Siena, 1955 S. Belcher Rd., Clearwater, FL 34624
Hemrick, Eugene F., U.S.C.C., Department of Education, 1312 Massachusetts, N.W., Washington, DC 20005
Howlin, Carroll, Good Shepherd Catholic Services, P.O. Box 550, Whitley City, KS 42653
Moriarty, John, Society of St. James the Apostle, 24 Clark St., Boston, MA 02109
Murphy, James, St. Mary of the Lake Seminary, Mundelein, IL 60060
Schoenstene, Robert L., St. Mary of the Lake Seminary, Mundelein, IL 60060

Graduate Studies:
Reverend Fathers—
Collogan, Robert, Ottawa, Canada

Absent on Sick Leave:
Reverend Fathers—
Best, Richard
DeFilippis, Anthony
Joyce, Edwin
Massacavalo, Bruno

Absent on Leave:
Reverend Fathers—
Blanchette, Michael
Collins, Michael J.

In Residence:
Reverend Fathers—
Maher, Arthur, 1115 Lorraine Rd., #326, Wheaton, IL 60187

Retired:
Reverend Monsignors—
Podesta, John F., 5555 N. Sheridan Rd., Apt. 1412, Chicago, IL 60640
Stenger, Frederick R., 3000 S. Ocean Blvd., Apt. 404, Boca Raton, FL 33432
Reverend Fathers—
Bowden, Lloyd, 115 N. May St., Joliet, IL 60435
Cullen, William, 6267 Trinity Dr., #2D, Lisle, IL 60532
Davis, Raymond, St. Alexis, 400 W. Wood St., Bensenville, IL 60106-2496
Dinan, Paul, 440 E. Pell St., Paxton, IL 60957
Doherty, Eugene, St. John Vianney Villa, 1464 Green Trails Dr., Naperville, IL 60540
Fischer, Lowell, Motherhouse, 9201 W. St. Francis Rd., Frankfort, IL 60423
Flynn, George, 2012E Lincoln, Apt. 210, Bloomington, IL 61701
Formusa, Salvatore, P.O. Box 46010, Chicago, IL 60046
Gryga, S., 3 Wheaton Center, Apt. 318, Wheaton, IL 60187
Hurley, George, 5 Oak Brook Dr., Oakbrook, IL 60521-1314
Kinzig, James, 36 E. Naples, Chula Vista, CA 92011
Kloepfer, John S., Box 1742, Clarksville, VA 23927
Kosmal, John, St. Patrick Residence, 1400 Brookdale, Naperville, IL 60563
Morrissette, Dominic, Most Holy Redeemer Shrine, 55 E. Reno Ave., Las Vegas, NV 89119
Mulloy, Sylvester, St. Patrick Residence, 1400 Brookdale, Naperville, IL 60563-2126
Novak, John, Countryside Villas, Rte. 1, Box 7-1A, Clifton, IL 60927
Richter, Raynor E., Sacred Heart Parish, 114 E. Elizabeth, Lombard, IL 60148
Ryan, William, St. John Vianney Villa, 1464 Green Trails Dr., Naperville, IL 60540
Shimanek, Joseph, 438 N. LaGrange Rd., LaGrange Park, IL 60525
Valentino, Dominic, 1230 E. East St., St. John Rd., Phoenix, AZ 85022
Van Duren, Charles, 2246 N. 4350 Rd., Sheridan, IL 60551-9615
Wilkening, Henry, Corpus Christi, 1415 Lies Rd., Carol Stream, IL 60188-4841

Permanent Deacons:
Accardi, Rodger F., Wheaton Franciscan Service, Wheaton
Anchor, Robert, St. Peter, Itasca
Anderson, Roy D., Residing Outside Diocese
Bailey, Thomas, Sacred Heart, Lombard
Beabout, Norman, On Duty Outside Diocese
Beckley, Michael A., St. Margaret Mary, Naperville
Bevan, William F., III, St. Paul the Apostle, Joliet
Bina, Frank, Our Lady of Peace, Darien
Blessing, William, St. Raphael, Naperville
Borkowicz, Leo M., On Duty Outside Diocese
Bouldin, James, St. Paul the Apostle, Joliet
Boyle, John R., St. Alexander, Villa Park
Brachle, Paul L., Jr., Our Lady of Peace, Darien
Brockman, David, St. Anne, Oswego
Carson, Neill, Notre Dame, Claredon Hills
Chambers, Frank A., On Duty Outside Diocese
Chamness, Francis J., Maternity BVM, Bourbonnais
Christensen, Gerald G., Unassigned
Clancy, Steven, St. Andrew, Romeoville
Clark, Raymond, St. Jude, Joliet
Cook, Michael, Cathedral of St. Raymond, Joliet
Cotugno, Joseph, St. Patrick, Kankakee
Cozzens, John, St. Michael, Wheaton
Crane, William H., St. Pius X, Lombard
Cuzzone, Dominic, Visitation, Elmhurst
Dalpiaz, Joseph C., St. Joan of Arc, Lisle
Darschewski, Ronald, St. Matthew, Glendale Heights
Dixon, James A., St. Elizabeth Seton, Naperville
Donahue, James, St. Mary, Downers Grove
Dougherty, Michael, On Duty Outside Diocese
Dunn, William, St. Anne, Oswego
Dyer, Donald L., St. Rose, Wilmington
Eastburn, Lloyd D., St. Edmund, Watseka
Ellman, Edward, On Duty Outside Diocese
Erickson, Robert, St. Dominic, Bolingbrook
Fitt, Robert, St. Jude, New Lenox
Fitzgerald, James P., Jr., St. Mary, Mokena
Foys, Frank F., Notre Dame, Clarendon Hills
Franch, Dino J., St. Joseph, Addison
Fricke, Thomas E., St. Francis of Assisi, Bolingbrook
Fritz, Leon P., St. Joseph, Bradley
Gamboa, Gabriel, St. Joseph, Addison
Gavin, Philip, Christ the King, Lombard
Girard, William, Sts. Peter and Paul, Naperville
Goebel, Thomas, St. Pius X, Lombard

Hamilton, Raymond, St. Francis of Assisi, Bolingbrook
Hamrlick, James, On Duty Outside Diocese
Hancock, Leslie E., St. Anne, Oswego
Hanley, Terrance R., St. Francis of Assisi, Bolingbrook
Henrissey, Francis R., St. Joseph, Manteno
Hessling, Danny E., St. Patrick, Momence
Hetzel, William, St. Jude, Joliet
Hindes, John T., St. Joseph, Manteno
Jackson, Kenneth, St. Isidore, Bloomingdale
Jacob, Jeffrey, St. Patrick, Momence
Janousek, Jay, Visitation, Elmhurst
Jazdzewski, Melvin J., On Duty Outside Diocese
Jossey, Robert, St. Boniface, Monee
Kelly, William, Immaculate Conception, Morris
Knapstein, John W., St. Dominic, Bolingbrook
Knecht, Ronald, St. Pius X, Lombard
Kolodziej, Paul, St. Patrick, Joliet
LaLonde, James A., St. Joseph, Downers Grove
Lamon, John D., On Duty Outside Diocese
LaMotte, Robert, St. Joseph, Bradley
Lawson, Gregg, St. Elizabeth Seton, Naperville
Lifka, David, Notre Dame, Clarendon Hills
Lopez, Jose L., St. John the Baptist, Joliet
Lovero, Marco, Our Lady of Mount Carmel, Darien
Malloy, William, (Retired)
Maloney, John, Mary Queen of Heaven, Elmhurst
Mangen, Richard, St. Matthew, Glendale Heights
Marcotte, Euchrist, Maternity B.V.M., Bourbonnais
Marrow, Philip J., St. John the Apostle, Villa Park
Martinez, Santos H., St. Mary, Plano
Mathieu, Donulus, Sr., (Retired)
McHugh, John, St. Raphael, Naperville
Metcalfe, Dale R., St. Patrick, Bristol; St. Mary, Plano
Miles, Kenneth J., Jr., St. Margaret Mary, Naperville
Molano, Rodulfo N., St. Francis of Assisi, Bolingbrook
Murphy, William E., St. Elizabeth Seton, Naperville
Murray, John, St. Mary Magdalene, Joliet
Neher, Norman, Sacred Heart, Hopkins Park
Nielo, Andrew, Resurrection, Wayne
Nolan, Thomas J., On Duty Outside Diocese
Nowak, Richard, On Duty Outside Diocese
Nunez, Charles, Mary Queen of Heaven, Elmhurst
O'Connor, James, Resurrection, Wayne
O'Connor, Joseph, Illinois Youth Commission, Joliet
Olszak, Leonard, St. Liborius, Steger
Pecka, Lawrence, St. Mary, Downers Grove
Pellack, Robert J., On Duty Outside Diocese
Pepin, Elmer, St. Joseph, Manteno
Petak, Edwin, Cathedral of St. Raymond, Joliet
Peterson, Charles M., St. Patrick, Joliet
Principe, Michael, St. Charles Borromeo, Bensenville
Raskowski, David, St. Andrew, Romeoville
Renville, John, Sacred Heart, Goodrich
Riggi, Joseph, St. Lawrence, South Wilimington
Rizzo, Vincent C., St. Matthew, Glendale Heights
Ross, Thomas, St. Dominic, Bolingbrook
Ruiz, Victor, St. Dominic, Bolingbrook
Safko, Terry L., St. Mary, Plainfield
Salerno, Michael A., St. Scholastica, Woodridge
Scavone, Emmanuel J., St. James, Glen Ellyn
Schaper, Edward, St. Petronille, Glen Ellyn
Schlund, James, On Duty Outside Diocese
Schmidt, Walter F., Our Lady of Peace, Darien
Schmith, Roger, St. Scholastica, Woodridge
Schneider, Paul A., On Leave
Schubert, Anthony, St. Alexander, Villa Park
Schumacher, Carl N.J., St. Joseph, Downers Grove
Searls, Ronald, St. Walter, Roselle
Sheridan, Thomas, St. Elizabeth Seton, Naperville
Siwek, Raymond, (Retired)
Solis, Joseph, Sts. Peter and Paul, Naperville
Sossong, James R., St. Mary Immaculate, Plainfield
Spatafor, Anthony, Visitation, Elmhurst
Stansberry, Robert T., Jr., Immaculate Conception, Morris
Stevens, Richard R., On Duty Outside Diocese
Straub, Fred, St. Margaret Mary, Naperville
Stucko, Denis, St. Joan of Arc, Lisle
Sullivan, Robert, On Leave
Symonanis, Alan, Notre Dame, Clarendon Hills
Tetrault, Robert L., On Duty Outside Diocese
True, Robert, St. Irene, Warrenville
Urso, Joseph, St. Joseph, Lockfort
Van Dril, William, On Duty Outside Diocese
Van Wallene, Matthew, St. Michael, Wheaton
Walen, Paul J., Sr., St. Dominic, Bolingbrook
Wallace, Robert, St. Dominic, Bolingbrook
Walsh, Thomas, On Duty Outside Diocese
Walters, James C., St. Mary, Plainfield
Wood, Charles, St. Raphael, Naperville
Worden, William, St. Thomas the Apostle, Naperville
Yarshen, Richard, Holy Family, Joliet
Yurcus, Ronald J., St. Petronille, Glen Ellyn

INSTITUTIONS LOCATED IN THE DIOCESE

[A] COLLEGES AND UNIVERSITIES

JOLIET. *College of St. Francis*, 500 N. Wilcox, 60435. Tel: 815-740-3360.
For a complete listing, refer to the Colleges and Universities section.

Saint Joseph College of Nursing, (1988) 290 N. Springfield Ave., 60435 Fax: 815-741-7131.
For a complete listing, refer to the Colleges and Universities section.

LISLE. *Benedictine University*, 5700 College Rd., 60532-0900. Tel: 630-829-6000; Fax: 630-960-1126.
For a complete listing, refer to the Colleges and Universities section.

ROMEOVILLE. *Lewis University*, Rt. 53, 60446. Tel: 815-838-0500.
For a complete listing, refer to the Colleges and Universities section.

[B] HIGH SCHOOLS, DIOCESAN

KANKAKEE. *Bishop McNamara High School*, Brookmont & Entrance Ave., 60901. Tel: 815-932-7413. Revs. Donald R. Lewandowski, O.S.A., Prin.; John Sotak, O.S.A.; Chris Howe, O.S.A.; Bros. Robert Fisher, O.S.A.; Kenneth D. Mehn, O.S.A.; Sr. Madeleine LaMarre, C.N.D. Priests 3; Sisters 1; Brothers 2; Lay Teachers 32; Students 531; Total Staff 61.

[C] HIGH SCHOOLS, PRIVATE

JOLIET. *Joliet Catholic Academy*. (Coed), 1200 Larkin Ave., 60435. Tel: 815-741-0500. Carmelite Fathers & Joliet Franciscan Sisters. Sr. Faith Szambelanczyk, O.S.F., Pres. & CEO; Rev. Bernhard Bauerle, O.Carm., Prin. & COO; Mrs. Susan Fritch, Asst. Prin. Priests 5; Sisters 7; Brothers 2; Lay Teachers 42; Students 830.

ADDISON. *Driscoll Catholic High School*, 555 N. Lombard Rd., 60101. Tel: 630-543-6310. Bro. Thomas Hetland, F.S.C., Pres.; Mr. Rod Molek, Prin.; Mrs. Mary Ann Fennell, Dean; Rev. William Dugal, Chap. Brothers of Christian Schools 5; Lay Teachers 40; Students 550.

LISLE. *Benet Academy*, 2200 Maple Ave., 60532. Tel: 630-969-6550. Rt. Rev. Hugh R. Anderson, O.S.B., Chancellor; Rev. Jude D. Randall, Pres.; Mr. Ernest Stark, Prin.; Bro. Charles Hlava, O.S.B., Asst. Prin.; Mr. William J. Maurer, Dir. Devel.; Rev. Anthony J. Jacob, O.S.B., Business Mgr. Priests 6; Sisters 2; Brothers 5; Lay Teachers 60; Students 1,250.

LOMBARD. *Montini Catholic High School*, 19 W. 070 16th St., 60148. Tel: 708-627-6930. Bro. Thomas A. Harding, F.S.C., Pres. Brothers of the Christian Schools 4; Sisters 1; Lay Teachers 36; Students 498.

NEW LENOX. *Providence Catholic High School*. (Coed), 1800 W. Lincoln Hwy., 60451. Tel: 815-485-2136. Revs. Richard J. McGrath, O.S.A., Pres.; John Merkelis, O.S.A., Prin.; Ms. Judith Legan, Asst. Prin.; Revs. Roland F. Follmann, O.S.A.; Bernard Scianna, O.S.A.; Gerald Nicholas, O.S.A.; Casimir A. Pazera, O.S.A. In res., Rev. Gerald Theis, O.S.A. Priests 7; Brothers 1; Sisters 1; Lay Teachers 65; Students 1,173.

WHEATON. *St. Francis High School*, 2130 W. Roosevelt Rd., 60187. Tel: 708-668-5800. Mr. David Angerer, Prin. In res., Rev. Tony A. Stockinger. Sisters 1; Lay Teachers 33; Students 531.

[D] AGENCIES AND INSTITUTIONS OF THE CHARITIES OF THE DIOCESE

JOLIET. *Catholic Charities*, 411 Scott St., 60432. Tel: 815-723-3405. Kathleen McGowan, Exec. Dir. Diocesan Administrative Office and Regional Office for Will and Grundy Counties.

KANKAKEE. *Catholic Charities*, 657 E. Court St., 60901. Tel: 815-933-7791; Fax: 815-932-3030. Regional Office for Kankakee, Ford, and Iroquois Counties.

LOMBARD. *Catholic Charities*, 26 W. St. Charles Rd., 60148. Tel: 708-495-9850; Fax: 708-495-9854. Regional Office for DuPage and Kendall Counties.

[E] PROTECTIVE INSTITUTIONS

JOLIET. *Guardian Angel Home*, 1550 Plainfield Ave., 60435. Tel: 815-729-0930; Fax: 815-744-6087.
For a complete listing, refer to the Special Care Facilities section.

MOMENCE. *Good Shepherd Manor*, P.O. Box 260, 60954. Tel: 815-472-6492; Fax: 815-472-2160.
For a complete listing, refer to the Special Care Facilities section.

[F] DAY CARE LEARNING CENTERS

JOLIET. *Franciscan Learning Center*, 1734 Theodore St., 60435. Tel: 815-744-7634. Sr. Margaret McGuckin, Dir. Students 84.

Vilaseca Day Care Center, 351 N. Chicago St., 60432. Tel: 815-727-1467. Students 88. Josephine Sisters.

BOURBONNAIS. *Alfred Fortin Villa and Day Care Learning Center*, 615 S. Main St., 60914. Tel: 815-932-8411. Sr. Joan Barbara, O.P., Dir. Day care for preschoolers. Sisters of St. Dominic 2; Staff 11; Students 54.

[G] GENERAL HOSPITALS

JOLIET. *St. Joseph Medical Center*, 333 N. Madison St., 60435. Tel: 815-725-7133.
For a complete listing, refer to the Hospitals section.

KANKAKEE. *St. Mary's Hospital*, 500 West Court St., 60901. Tel: 815-937-2490.
For a complete listing, refer to the Hospitals section.

[H] REHABILITATION CENTERS

WHEATON. *Marianjoy Rehabilitation Hospital & Clinics*, 26 W. 171 Roosevelt Rd., P.O. Box 795, 60189. Tel: 630-462-4000. Franciscan Sisters, Daughters of the Sacred Hearts of Jesus and Mary (Wheaton, IL). Mr. Bruce A. Schurman, Pres.; Sr. Mariette Kalbac, Chap. Bed Capacity 110; Patients assisted annually 3,500. Legal Title: *Marianjoy, Inc.*

[I] HOMES FOR AGED

JOLIET. *Our Lady of Angels Retirement Home*, 1201 Wyoming, 60435. Tel: 815-725-6631.
For a complete listing, refer to the Special Care Facilities section.

St. Elizabeth Home, 704 W. Marion St., 60436. Tel: 815-727-0125.
For a complete listing, refer to the Special Care Facilities section.

Villa Franciscan, Franciscan Sisters Health Care Corp., 210 N. Springfield, 60435. Tel: 815-725-3400; Fax: 815-725-2160.
For a complete listing, refer to the Special Care Facilities section.

BOURBONNAIS. *Our Lady of Victory Nursing Home*, 20 Briarcliff Ln., 60914. Tel: 815-937-2022; Fax: 815-937-2026.
For a complete listing, refer to the Special Care Facilities section.

CLIFTON. *Merkle-Knipprath Countryside Home*, Rte. 1, 60927. Tel: 815-694-2306.
For a complete listing, refer to the Special Care Facilities section.

CRETE. *St. James Manor*, 1251 Richton Rd., 60417. Tel: 708-672-6700.
For a complete listing, refer to the Special Care Facilities section.

DARIEN. *Carmelite Carefree Retirement Village*, 8419 Bailey Rd., 60561-5361. Tel: 630-960-4060.
For a complete listing, refer to the Special Care Facilities section.

LISLE. *Queen of Peace Center*, 1910 Maple Ave., 60532. Tel: 630-852-5360.
For a complete listing, refer to the Special Care Facilities section.

NAPERVILLE. *St. John Vianney Villa*, 1464 Green Trails Dr., 60540-8359. Tel: 630-983-0533.
For a complete listing, refer to the Special Care Facilities section.

St. Patrick's Residence, 1400 Brookdale Rd., 60563-2125. Tel: 630-416-6565.
For a complete listing, refer to the Special Care Facilities section.

OAK BROOK. *Mayslake Village*, 1801 35th St., 60521. Tel: 630-654-3280.
For a complete listing, refer to the Special Care Facilities section.

WHEATON. *Marian Park, Inc.*, 26 W. 171 Roosevelt Rd., P.O. Box 667, 60187. Tel: 630-665-9100.
For a complete listing, refer to the Special Care Facilities section.

[J] MONASTERIES AND RESIDENCES OF PRIESTS AND BROTHERS

JOLIET. *Congregation of Christian Brothers, Brother Rice Provincialate*, 958 Western Ave., 60435. Tel: 815-723-5464; Fax: 815-723-5278. Legal Title: *The Christian Brothers of Ireland, Inc.* Bros. Lawrence J. Mooney, C.F.C., Prov.; Michael D. Lucas, C.F.C., Deputy Prov. Consultors: Bros. Charles D. McKenna, C.F.C.; Donald D. Murray, C.F.C.; Ross E. Wielatz, C.F.C. In res., Bros. John Dornbos, C.F.C.; Richard L. Stanich, C.F.C.

St. Elias Carmelites, 3504 Lake Shore Dr., 60431-8819. Tel: 815-439-8246. Revs. Joseph Maisonneuve, O.Carm.; Bernhard Bauerle, O.Carm.; Emmet Gleeson, O.Carm.; Raymond Foster, O.Carm., Prior; Rocco DiLeonardi, O.Carm.; Louis Rogge, O.Carm.; Timothy Andres, O.Carm.; Bros. Thomas Murphy, O.Carm.; Sean Keefe, O.Carm.; Leonard Gilman, O.Carm. Priests 7; Brothers 2.

St. John the Baptist Friary, 404 N. Hickory St., 60435. Tel: 815-727-4788; Fax: 815-740-1521. Revs. Louis Davino, O.F.M.; Medard Buvala, O.F.M.; Jeffery Salwach, O.F.M.; Gerold Schubert, O.F.M.; Jeffrey Donnelly, O.F.M., Chap.; Bros. Thomas Eaton, O.F.M.; John Sweeney, O.F.M. Priests 5; Brothers 2.

BURR RIDGE. *Christian Brothers Provincial Office (Midwest Province)*, 200 S. Frontage Rd., Ste. 300, 60521-6953. Tel: 630-323-3725; Fax: 630-323-3779. Bros. Thomas Johnson, F.S.C., Prov.; Francis Carr, F.S.C., Auxiliary Prov.; Michael Fehrenbach, F.S.C., Auxiliary Prov.; Ms. Marge Beauvais, Dir. Lasallian Family; Bros. Edwin Dupre, F.S.C., Dir. Devel.; Joseph Saurbier, F.S.C., Dir. Finance; Thomas Sullivan, F.S.C., Dir. Vocations/Formation; Nicholas Schumer, F.S.C., Dir. St. La Salle Auxiliary.

DARIEN. *Carmelite Community*, St. Simon Stock Priory, 8501 Bailey Rd., 60561. Tel: 630-241-1802. Rev. Robert Colaresi, O.Carm., Prior; Bros. Robert Murphy, O.Carm.; Lawrence Fidelus, O.Carm.; Eric Bell, O.Carm.; Revs. Aloysius Sieracki, O.Carm.; Raymond J. Clennon, O.Carm., Midwest Commissary Prov.; Kevin Shanley, O.Carm., Communication Dir.; Robert E. Lee, O.Carm.; Peter Byrth, O.Carm.; John Malley, O.Carm.; Leo McCarthy, O.Carm. Priests 7; Brothers 3.

Carmelite Fathers Provincial Office, 1317 Frontage Rd., 60561. Tel: 630-971-0050; Fax: 630-971-0195. Very Rev. Leo McCarthy, O.Carm., Prior Prov.; Rev. Daniel O'Neill, O.Carm., Prov. Procurator. Military Chaplains: Rev. Joseph Wallroth, O.Carm. Carmelites serving abroad: Rev. Craig Morrison, O.Carm., Basilica Parrocchiale, Rome, Italy, General Motherhouse, Via Giovanni Lanza, 138, Rome, Italy, 00184. Most Rev. John R. Malley, O.Carm., Prior Gen., International College of St. Albert, Rome, Italy; Rev. Joachim Smet, O.Carm. Carmelites serving in Canada: Very Rev. Malachy Smith, O.Carm.; Revs. Roger Bonneau, O.Carm.; Myles Colgan, O.Carm.; Gregory Klein, O.Carm.; Marcel Dube, O.Carm.; Leo Huard, O.Carm.; Felix Prior, O.Carm.; Benedict Hogan, O.Carm.; Murray Phelan, O.Carm.; Stanley Makacinas, O.Carm.; Robert Boley, O.Carm.; Thomas Borkowski, O.Carm.; Thomas Hakala, O.Carm.; Jordon Rooney, O.Carm.; Leonard Broughan, O'Carm.; Bro. Gabriel Murray, O.Carm. Carmelites serving in Peru: Prelate Nullius, Sicuani, Peru. Most Rev. Alban Quinn, O.Carm.; Revs. Salvador Bartolo, O.Carm. (Malta); Joseph Cilia, O.Carm. (Malta); Herbert Jones, O.Carm.; Michael Brown, O.Carm.; Kevin Lafey, O.Carm.; Michael LaFay, O.Carm.; Gerald Payea, O.Carm.; Joseph Lucchesi, O.Carm.; Michael Sgarioto, O.Carm.; Enrique Laguna-Vargas, O.Carm.; Gregory Geaney, O.Carm.; Bros. Miguel Macigalupo-Del Corrall, O.Carm.; Jorge Villegas, O.Carm.; Daniel Salazar, O.Carm.; Carlos Valdez, O.Carm.; Rodolfo Aznaran, O.Carm.; Raul Maravic, O.Carm. Carmelites serving elsewhere: Revs. Devin Griffin, O.Carm.; Edward Adelmann, O.Carm.; Kieran O'Hara, O.Carm.; Henry Ormond, O.Carm.; John F. Donohue, O.Carm.; Blaise McInerney, O.Carm.; Venard Poslusney, O.Carm.; Warren Carlin, O.Carm.; Barry Kremer, O.Carm.; Frank Weil, O.Carm.; Myron Judy, O.Carm.; Francis McCarthy, O.Carm.; David Murphy, O.Carm.; Don Carlos Benjamin, O.Carm.; Rudolph Flanik, O.Carm.; Albert Koppes, O.Carm.; Matthew Sprouffske, O.Carm.; Charles Kurgan, O.Carm.; Anton Kollar, O.Carm.; David Fontaine, O.Carm.; Stephen Cooley, O.Carm.; William Travers, O.Carm.; Paul Robinson, O.Carm.; Guy McPartland, O.Carm.; Robert Primozic, O.Carm.; Michael Flynn, O.Carm.; Jerome Callahan, O.Carm.; Joseph Wallroth, O.Carm.; Timothy Moore, O.Carm.; Patrick Gleeson, O.Carm.; James Lewis, O.Carm. Carmelites serving in Mexico: Revs. Peter Hinde, O.Carm.; Joel Moelter, O.Carm.; John Hertel, O.Carm.; Thomas Jordon, O.Carm.; William Smith, O.Carm.; Frank Sanchez, O.Carm.

LISLE. *St. Procopius Abbey*, 5601 College Rd., 60532. Tel: 630-969-6410; Fax: 630-969-6426. Benedictine Monks. Rt. Rev. Hugh R. Anderson, O.S.B., Abbot; Very Rev. Columban Trojan, O.S.B., Prior; Revs. James Flint, O.S.B., Subprior & Master of Novices & Juniors; Kevin Sheeran, O.S.B., Procurator & Business Mgr.; Gabriel Baltes, O.S.B.; Frederic J. Beller, O.S.B.; Christian W. Ceplecha, O.S.B.; Joseph Chang, O.S.B.; Thomas Chisholm, O.S.B.; Odilo Crkva, O.S.B.; Ivan Dobnikar, O.S.B.; Jerome Dobry, O.S.B.; Julian von Duerbeck, O.S.B.; Terence Fitzmaurice, O.S.B.; Becket Franks, O.S.B.; Roman Galiardi, O.S.B.; Rt. Rev. Thomas J. Havlik, O.S.B., Abbot, (Retired); Revs. Paschal Honner, O.S.B.; Alban Hrebic, O.S.B.; Zachary Hrisko, O.S.B.; Anthony Jacob, O.S.B.; Dismas Kalcic, O.S.B.; Michael Komechak, O.S.B.; Demetrius Kowalchik, O.S.B.; Edward Kucera, O.S.B.; George Kuska, O.S.B.; Timothy Marceau, O.S.B.; Jude Randall, O.S.B., Pres., Benet Academy; Rt. Rev. Valentine Skluzacek, O.S.B., Abbot, (Retired); Revs. James Saul, O.S.B.; Clement Sobr, O.S.B.; Theodore Suchy, O.S.B.; Philip Timko, O.S.B.; David Turner, O.S.B.; Mel R. Uzdrowski, O.S.B.; Stanley Vesely, O.S.B.; Kenneth Zigmond, O.S.B.; Francis Lawrence; Most Rev. Daniel W. Kucera, O.S.B., (Retired) Archbishop of Dubuque, IA. Monks 55; Priests 37; Brothers 14; Bishops 1; Oblates 3.

Benedictine Chinese Mission, 2400 Maple Ave., 60532. Tel: 630-968-4264. Rev. James Saul, O.S.B., Dir.

Slav Missions, 5601 College Dr., 60532. Tel: 708-969-6410.

Benedictine University, 5700 College Rd., 60532. Tel: 630-960-1500.

Benet Academy, 2200 Maple Ave., 60532. Tel: 630-969-6550.

MOMENCE. *Brother Mathia Barrett Inc. of Illinois*, P.O. Box 260, 60954. Tel: 815-472-3131. Brothers 4.

NEW LENOX. *Augustinian Friary*, 1800 W. Lincoln Hwy., 60451.
(See separate listing for Providence High School). In res., Revs. Richard J. McGrath, O.S.A., Pres.; Roland F. Follmann, O.S.A.; John D. Merkelis, O.S.A., Prin.; Bernard C. Scianna, O.S.A.; Gerald A. Nicholas, O.S.A., Prior; Gerald J. Theis, O.S.A.; Casimir A. Pazera, O.S.A.; LaVern Flack, O.S.A.; Bro. John E. Newton, O.S.A.

ROMEOVILLE. *Christian Brothers Center*, 200 De La-Salle Dr., 60441. Tel: 815-838-8903; Fax: 815-838-7189. Bro. Edwin Dupre, F.S.C., Dir. Brothers 21.

De La Salle Hall, Lewis University Student Res., 200 De LaSalle Dr., 60441. Tel: 815-838-8902. Bro. Robert Veselsky, F.S.C., Dir. Student Residents 53; Brothers 1.

La Salle House, Lewis University, Rte. 53, 60446. Tel: 815-838-0500, Ext. 5460; Fax: 815-838-9456. Bro. Tom Dupre, F.S.C., Dir. Brothers 18.

[K] CONVENTS AND RESIDENCES FOR SISTERS

JOLIET. *Josephine Sisters*, 351 N. Chicago St., 60431. Tel: 815-727-1467. Josephine Sisters of Mexico (Hermanas Josefinas). Sisters 9.

St. Francis Convent (Motherhouse), 520 Plainfield Ave., 60435. Tel: 815-727-3686; Fax: 815-727-9435. Congregation of the Third Order of St. Francis of Mary Immaculate, Joliet, IL. Sr. Mary Jean Morris, O.S.F., Pres.; Sr. Joan Clare Wisner, Building Admin. Sisters 66. Legal Title: *Retirement Plan Trust of the Congregation of the Third Order of St. Francis of Mary Immaculate.*

FRANKFORT. *Motherhouse, Novitiate, Sacred Heart Residence, Portiuncula, Center for Prayer*, St. Francis Woods, 9201 W. St. Francis Rd., 60423. Tel: 815-469-4895; Fax: 815-469-4864. Legal Title: *An Association of Franciscan Sisters of the Sacred Heart.* Sr. Karen Marie Lanigan, O.S.F., Gen. Supr.; Sr. Mary Mark Segvich, Admin.; Rev. Lowell Fischer, Chap. Sisters 89.

KANKAKEE. *St. Clare House of Prayer*, 2041 W. Rte. 113, 60901. Tel: 815-933-3945. Sisters of St. Francis of Mary Immaculate 6.

Servants of the Holy Heart of Mary, Provincial Administration, 145 S. Fourth Ave., 60901. Tel: 815-937-2380; Fax: 815-937-5520. Sr. Kathleen Mulchay, Prov. Supr. Professed Sisters 60. Legal Titles: *Servants of the Holy Heart of Mary Charitable Trust; ServantCor—HealthCor—ServiceCor, Inc.—Servants United Foundation.*

LISLE. *Benedictine Sisters of the Sacred Heart, Sacred Heart Monastery*, 1910 Maple Ave., 60532. Sr. Judith Ann Heble, O.S.B., Prioress; Rev. Philip Timko, O.S.B., Chap. Professed Sisters 56. Legal Title: *Benedictine Sisters of the Sacred Heart Charitable Trust.*

NAPERVILLE. *Missionary Oblates of St. Benedict*. St. Scholastica Mission House, 24 W. 350 Maple Ave., 60540. Tel: 630-968-4264. Sisters 9.

PLAINFIELD. *Mantellate Sisters Servants of Mary of Plainfield*, 16949 S. Drauden Rd., 60544-9219. Tel: 815-436-5796. Sr. Francis Gresser, O.S.M., Regional Supr. Sisters 12.
Ministry in the field of Academic Education, Parish Ministry, Social Work, Nursing, Homes for the Aged, and Foreign Missions. Homes for the Aged and Foreign Missions.

WHEATON. *Convent of Our Lady of the Angels Motherhouse and Novitiate*. Franciscan Sisters, Daughters of the Sacred Hearts of Jesus and Mary (Wheaton, IL), P.O. Box 667, 60189-0667. Tel: 630-462-7422; Fax: 630-462-7148. Sr. Mary Ellen McAleese, O.S.F., Prov. Dir. Sisters 75. Legal Title: *Wheaton Franciscan Sisters Corp.*

Loretto Convent, Religious of the Institute of the Blessed Virgin Mary, P.O. Box 508, 60189. Tel: 630-653-4740. Sr. Irene Howell, I.B.V.M. Sisters 35.

Loretto Conference Center.

Wheaton Franciscan Sisters Religious Charitable Trust, 26 W. 171 Roosevelt Rd., P.O. Box 667, 60189-0667. Tel: 630-462-7422; Fax: 630-462-7148.

[L] HOUSES OF RETREAT/PRAYER

DARIEN. *Carmelite Spiritual Center*, 8433 Bailey Rd., 60561. Tel: 630-969-4141. Revs. Kevin Shanley, O.Carm.; Robert E. Colaresi, O.Carm., Dir.; Bro. Lawrence Fidelus, O.Carm. Total Staff 16.

DOWNERS GROVE. *Mayslake Marmion Ministries, Inc.*, 4832 Main St., 60515. Tel: 630-719-1620. Rev. Jonathan D. Foster, O.F.M. Priests 1; Lay Staff 2.

FRANKFORT. *Portiuncula Center for Prayer*, 9263 W. St. Francis Rd., 60423. Tel: 815-464-3880.

PLANO. *La Salle Manor Christian Brothers Retreat House*, 12480 Galena Rd., 60545. Tel: 630-552-3224. Robert Dressel, Pres.

WARRENVILLE. *Congregation of Our Lady of the Retreat in the Cenacle*, 29W012 Batavia Rd., P.O. Box 797, 60555-0797. Tel: 708-393-1231. Sr. Lucille Kunz, R.C., Supr. Sisters 12.

[M] MISCELLANEOUS

JOLIET. *St. Vincent Thrift Shop*, 307 N. Chicago St., 60431. Tel: 815-722-1140. John Basiletti, Contact, 211 Main St., West Chicago, 60185. Tel: 630-293-9420.

DARIEN. *Carmelite Mission Office*, 1317 Frontage Rd., 60561. Tel: 630-969-5220. Rev. John Malley, O.Carm., Dir.

Carmelite Visitor Center (National Shrine & Museum of St. Therese), 8501 Bailey Rd., 60561. Tel: 630-969-3311. Bro. Eric Bell, O.Carm., Dir.

Office of the Carmelite Midwest Commissary Provincial, 8419 Bailey Rd., 60561-5361. Tel: 630-960-4934. Rev. Raymond J. Clennon, O.Carm., Commissary Prov.

Provincial Office of Lay Carmelites and Scapular Confraternity, 8501 Bailey Rd., 60561. Tel: 630-969-5050; Fax: 630-969-5536. Rev. Peter Byrth, O.Carm., Prov. Dir.; Sr. Christina Marie Griggs, O.Carm., Assoc. Dir.; Rev. Robert E. Lee, O.Carm., Assoc. Dir.

Society of the Little Flower, 1313 Frontage Rd., 60561-5341. Tel: 630-968-9400; Fax: 630-968-9542. Rev. Robert E. Colaresi, O.Carm., Dir.

FRANKFORT. *Franciscan Sisters Health Care Corporation*, 9223 W. St. Francis Rd., 60423-8334. Tel: 815-469-4888; Fax: 815-469-4864.

GLEN ELLYN. *Society of St. Francis De Sales*, 3 S. 423 Tamarack Dr., 60137. Tel: 708-858-7574. Mrs. Lester Mellin.

KANKAKEE. *Lisieux Pastoral Center*, 371 N. St. Joseph Ave., 60901.

LISLE. *National Association of Catholic Nurses-U.S.A.*, P.O. Box 3016, 60532-3016. Tel: 630-852-1049. Mary T. Pellizzari, NACN-USA Treas.

MOMENCE. *B.G.S. Charitable Trust*, P.O. Box 736, 60954-0736. Tel: 815-472-3131; Fax: 815-472-6914. Michael F. Mieszala, Esq.

Little Brothers of the Good Shepherd, Inc. of Illinois, 4129 N. Dixie Hwy., P.O. Box 736, 60954. Judy Brinkmann, Dir. of Finance.

NAPERVILLE. *Mercy Chicago Region Healthcare System*, 55 Shuman Blvd., Ste. 150, 60563-8469. Sr. Catherine C. Gallagher, R.S.M., Pres.

OAK BROOK. *Consolidated Catholic Health Care*, 1301 W. 22nd St., Ste. 202, 60521. Roger N. Butler, Exec. Dir.

ROMEOVILLE. *Charitable Trust of the Brothers of the Christian Schools*, 1205 Windham Pkwy., 60446-1697. Tel: 630-378-2900; Fax: 630-378-2501.

Christian Brothers Employee Benefit Trust, 1205 Windham Pkwy., 60446-1694. Tel: 630-378-2900; Fax: 630-378-2501.

Christian Brothers Employee Retirement Plan Trust, 1205 Windham Pkwy., 60446-1692. Tel: 630-378-2900; Fax: 630-378-2501.

Christian Brothers Fund, Inc., 200 De La Salle Dr., 60446-1899. Tel: 815-838-8903. Bro. Edwin Dupre.

Christian Brothers Religious Comprehensive Trust, 1205 Windham Pkwy., 60446-1695. Tel: 630-378-2900; Fax: 630-378-2501.

Christian Brothers Religious Deductible Trust, 1205 Windham Pkwy., 60446-1695. Tel: 630-378-2900; Fax: 630-378-2501.

**Christian Brothers Services*, 1205 Windham Pkwy., 60446-1691. Tel: 630-378-2900; Fax: 630-378-2501. Bro. William Walz, F.S.C.

Religious & Charitable Risk Pooling Trust of the Brothers of the Christian Schools, 1205 Windham Pkwy., 60446-1693. Tel: 630-378-2900; Fax: 630-378-2501.

WEST CHICAGO. *Society of St. Vincent de Paul*, Diocesan Council of Joliet, 211 Main St., 60185. Tel: 708-293-9420; Fax: 708-293-9433. John Basiletti.

WHEATON. *Assisi Homes - Aurora, Inc.*, 26 W. 171 Roosevelt Rd., 60187. Tel: 630-462-9271. Katie Grand, Pres.

Assisi Homes - Batavia Apartments, Inc., 26 W. 171 Roosevelt Rd., 60189. Tel: 708-462-9271. Mr. Ray Wojcik, Pres. Total in Residence 290; Total Staff 5.

Assisi Homes - Colony Park, Inc., 26 W. 171 Roosevelt Rd., 60187. Tel: 630-462-9271. Robert Cisek, Pres.

Assisi Homes - Constitution House, Inc., 26 W. 171 Roosevelt Rd., 60187. Tel: 630-462-9271.

Assisi Homes of Gurnee, Inc., 26 W. 171 Roosevelt Rd., P.O. Box 667, 60189. Tel: 630-462-9271. Robert Cisek, Pres.

Assisi Homes of Illinois, Inc., 26 W. 171 Roosevelt Rd., 60187. Tel: 630-462-9271. Ray Wojcik, Pres.; Garth R. Seehawer, Senior Vice Pres.

Assisi Homes, Dekalb, Inc., 26 W. 171 Roosevelt Rd., P.O. Box 667, 60189. Tel: 630-462-9271. Ray Wojcik, Pres.

Canticle Place, Inc., 26 W. 171 Roosevelt Rd., P.O. Box 667, 60189. Tel: 630-462-7422. Garth Seehawer, Senior Vice Pres., Legal Services.

Clara Pfaender Fund, Inc., 26 W. 171 Roosevelt Rd., P.O. Box 667, 60189. Tel: 630-462-9271. Sr. Rose Mary Pint, O.S.F., Pres.; Garth R. Seehawer, Senior Vice Pres. Franciscan Sisters, Daughters of the Sacred Hearts of Jesus and Mary (Wheaton, IL).

Franciscan Health & Education Corp., Inc., 26 W. 171 Roosevelt Rd., P.O. Box 667, 60189. Tel: 630-462-9271, Ext. 236.

Franciscan Ministries, Inc., P.O. Box 667, 26 W. 171 Roosevelt Rd., 60189. Tel: 630-462-9271. Roger Accardi, Pres.; Garth R. Seehawer, Senior Vice Pres.

Institute of the Blessed Virgin Mary Charitable Trust, P.O. Box 508, 60189. Tel: 630-653-6113; Fax: 630-653-4886.

WFSI-Illinois, 26 W. 171 Roosevelt Rd., P.O. Box 667, 60189. Tel: 630-462-9271. John Oliverio, Pres.; Garth R. Seehawer, Senior Vice Pres.

Wheaton Franciscan Services, Inc., 26 W. 171 Roosevelt Rd., P.O. Box 667, 60189. Tel: 630-462-9271. Sr. Rose Mary Pint, O.S.F., Chm.; Mr. Wilfred F. Loebig, Jr., Pres. & CEO; Garth R. Seehawer, Senior Vice Pres.

RELIGIOUS INSTITUTES OF MEN REPRESENTED IN THE DIOCESE

For further details refer to the corresponding bracketed number in the Religious Institutes of Men or Women section.

[0140]—*The Augustinians*. (Mother of Good Counsel Prov.).—O.S.A.
[0200]—*Benedictine Monks*.—O.S.B.
[0330]—*Brothers of the Christian Schools*. (Midwest Prov.).—F.S.C.
[0580]—*Brothers of the Good Shepherd*.—B.G.S.
[0270]—*Carmelite Fathers & Brothers*. (Prov. of Pure Heart of Mary).—O.Carm.
[0275]—*Carmelites of Mary Immaculate*.—C.M.I.
[1320]—*Clerics of St. Viator*.—C.S.V.
[0310]—*Congregation of Christian Brothers*.—C.F.C.
[0430]—*Dominicans*. (Prov. of Albert the Great).—O.P.
[0520]—*Franciscan Friars*. (Sacred Heart, Assumption Provs.).—O.F.M.
[0540]—*Franciscan Missionary Brothers of the Sacred Heart of Jesus*.—O.S.F.
[0520]—*Franciscans*. (Order of Friars Minor, Sacred Heart Prov.).—O.F.M.
[0740]—*Marian Fathers*. (Prov. of St. Casimer).—M.I.C.
[0520]—*Orders of Friars Minor*. (Prov. of Holy Savior).—O.F.M.
[0610]—*Priests of the Congregation of Holy Cross*.—C.S.C.
[0110]—*Society of African Missions*.—S.M.A.
[0690]—*Society of Jesus*. (Chicago and St. Louis Prov.).—S.J.

RELIGIOUS INSTITUTES OF WOMEN REPRESENTED IN THE DIOCESE

[0230]—*Benedictine Sisters of Pontifical Jurisdiction*. (Lisle, IL; Ferdinand, IN).—O.S.B.
[0330]—*Carmelite Sisters for the Aged and Infirm*. (Germantown, NY).—O.Carm.
[0400]—*Congregation of Our Lady of Mount Carmel*. (Lacombe, LA).—O.Carm.
[3110]—*Congregation of Our Lady of the Retreat in the Cenacle*.—R.C.
[2100]—*Congregation of the Humility of Mary*.—C.H.M.
[0460]—*Congregation of the Sisters of Charity of the Incarnate Word*.—C.C.V.I.
[3710]—*Congregation of the Sisters of Saint Agnes*.—C.S.A.
[1920]—*Congregation of the Sisters of the Holy Cross*.—C.S.C.
[1710]—*Congregation of the Third Order of St. Francis of Mary Immaculate, Joliet, IL*.—O.S.F.
[1070-01]—*Dominican Sisters*. (St. Catharine, KY).—O.P.
[1070-03]—*Dominican Sisters*. (Sinsinawa).—O.P.
[1070-10]—*Dominican Sisters*. (Springfield).—O.P.
[1070-13]—*Dominican Sisters*. (Adrian).—O.P.
[1170]—*Felician Sisters*.—C.S.S.F.
[1780]—*Franciscan Sisters of Perpetual Adoration*. (Woodruff, WI).—F.S.P.A.
[1450]—*Franciscan Sisters of the Sacred Heart*.—O.S.F.
[1240]—*Franciscan Sisters, Daughters of the Sacred Hearts of Jesus and Mary*.—O.S.F.
[1910]—*Hermanas Josefinas*.—H.J.
[2370]—*Institute of the Blessed Virgin Mary (Loreto Sisters)*.—I.B.V.M.
[2575]—*Institute of the Sisters of Mercy of the Americas*. (Chicago, IL).—R.S.M.
[3570]—*Mantellate Sisters, Servants of Mary*. (Plainfield, IL).—O.S.M.
[]—*Missionary Sisters of the Holy Family*. (Komorrow-Warsaw, Poland).—M.S.H.F.
[3760]—*Order of St. Clare*.—P.C.C.
[2970]—*School Sisters of Notre Dame*. (Chicago Prov.).—S.S.N.D.
[1680]—*School Sisters of St. Francis*. (U.S. Prov.).—O.S.F.
[3590]—*Servants of Mary*. (Ladysmith, WI).—O.S.M.
[3520]—*Servants of the Holy Heart of Mary*.—S.S.C.M.
[0430]—*Sisters of Charity of the Blessed Virgin Mary*.—B.V.M.
[2990]—*Sisters of Notre Dame*. (Toledo, OH).—S.N.D.
[3000]—*Sisters of Notre Dame de Namur*. (Cincinnati Prov.).—S.N.D.deN.
[3360]—*Sisters of Providence of Saint Mary-of-the-Woods, IN*.—S.P.
[3740]—*Sisters of St. Casimir*.—S.S.C.
[1540]—*Sisters of St. Francis*. (Clinton, IA).—O.S.F.
[1705]—*The Sisters of St. Francis of Assisi*. (St. Francis).—O.S.F.
[1520]—*Sisters of St. Francis of Christ the King*.—O.S.F.
[1570]—*Sisters of St. Francis of Dubuque*. (Iowa).—O.S.F.
[1640]—*Sisters of St. Francis of Perpetual Adoration*. (Mishawaka).—O.S.F.
[1580]—*Sisters of St. Francis of the Immaculate Conception*.—O.S.F.
[3830-02]—*Sisters of St. Joseph*.—C.S.J.
[3930]—*Sisters of St. Joseph of the Third Order of St. Francis*. (Prov. of Immaculate Conception).—S.S.J.-T.O.S.F.
[2980]—*Sisters of the Congregation de Notre Dame*.—C.N.D.
[2270]—*Sisters of the Little Company of Mary*. (American Prov.).—L.C.M.
[2350]—*Sisters of the Living Word*.—S.L.W.
[1720]—*Sisters of the Third Order Regular of St. Francis of the Congregation of Our Lady of Lourdes*. (Rochester, MN).—O.S.F.
[2150]—*Sisters Servants of the Immaculate Heart of Mary*.—I.H.M.

DIOCESAN CEMETERIES

JOLIET. *Holy Cross*.
Mount Olivet.
St. John the Baptist.
St. Mary Nativity.
St. Patrick.
SS. Cyril and Methodius.
BOURBONNAIS. *All Saints*.
Maternity / BVM.
CAROL STREAM. *St. Stephen*.
DOWNERS GROVE. *St. Bernard*.
St. Mary.
ELMHURST. *St. Mary*.
KANKAKEE. *Mt. Calvary*.
St. Rose.
LOCKPORT. *Calvary*.
LOCKPORT SOUTH. *St. Dennis*.
NAPERVILLE. *SS. Peter & Paul*.
ROMEOVILLE. *Resurrection*.
St. Charles Borromeo, 402 S. Independence Blvd., 60446-2264. Tel: 815-838-0395.
WHEATON. *Assumption*.
WINFIELD. *St. John the Baptist*.

NECROLOGY

† Berst, Theodore, Coal City, IL, Assumption Parish. —Died Aug. 2, 1996.
† Doherty, Thomas, San Pierre, IN, Little Co. of Mary. —Died Aug. 25, 1996.
† Marco, LeRoy, Naperville, IL, St. Patrick Residence. —Died June 22, 1996.
† Murray, James, Clarendon Hills, IL, Notre Dame. —Died April 3, 1996.
† Petz, Norman, Lockport, IL, St. John Vianney. —Died June 20, 1996.
† Rudden, Victor, Elmhurst, IL, Mary Queen of Heaven. —Died March 6, 1996.

Diocese of Juneau

(Dioecesis Junellensis)

Most Reverend

MICHAEL W. WARFEL

Bishop of Juneau; ordained April 26, 1980; appointed November 19, 1996; installed December 17, 1996.

ESTABLISHED JUNE 23, 1951.

Square Miles 37,566.

Corporate Title: "Corporation of the Catholic Bishop of Juneau."

Comprises the entire southeastern part of the State of Alaska known legally as The First Judicial District.

For legal titles of parishes and diocesan institutions, consult the Chancery Office.

Chancery: 419 Sixth St., #200, Juneau, AK, 99801.
Tel.: 907-586-2227; Fax: 907-463-3237.

STATISTICAL OVERVIEW

Personnel	
Bishop	1
Priests: Diocesan Active in Diocese	5
Priests: Active Outside Diocese	4
Priests: Retired, Sick or Absent	7
Number of Diocesan Priests	16
Religious Priests in Diocese	3
Extern Priests in Diocese	1
Ordinations:	
Permanent Deacons in Diocese	9
Total Sisters	7
Parishes	
Parishes	8
With Resident Pastor:	
Resident Diocesan Priests	3
Resident Religious Priests	3
Without Resident Pastor:	
Administered by Priests	1
Missions	4
Welfare	
Catholic Hospitals	1
Total Assisted	70,081
Homes for the Aged	1
Total Assisted	68
Day Care and Extended Day Care Centers	1
Total Assisted	8,628
Special Centers for Social Services	1
Total Assisted	6,030
Other Institutions	1
Total Assisted	6,118
Educational	
Elementary Schools, Diocesan and Parish	1
Total Students	100
Catechesis/Religious Education:	
High School Students	143
Elementary Students	574
Total Students Under Catholic Instruction	817
Teachers in the Diocese:	
Lay Teachers	9
Vital Statistics	
Receptions into the Church:	
Infant Baptism Totals	86
Adult Baptism Totals	15
Received into Full Communion	17
First Communions	111
Confirmations	39
Marriages:	
Catholic	18
Interfaith	34
Total Marriages	52
Deaths	19
Total Catholic Population	5,816
Total Population	86,870

Former Bishops—Most Rev. DERMOT O'FLANAGAN, D.D., ord. Aug. 27, 1929; appt. Bishop July 9, 1951; cons. Oct. 3, 1951; resigned June 19, 1968 and; appt. Titular Bishop of Trecalae; died Dec. 31, 1972.—Most Rev. FRANCIS T. HURLEY, D.D., ord. June 16, 1951; appt. Titular Bishop of Daimlaig and Auxiliary of Juneau, Feb. 4, 1970; cons. March 19, 1970; Ordinary of See, July 20, 1971; appt. Archbishop of Anchorage, May 4, 1976.—Most Rev. MICHAEL H. KENNY, D.D., ord. March 30, 1963; appt. March 20, 1979; cons. May 27, 1979; installed June 15, 1979; died Feb. 19, 1995.

Diocesan Pastoral Center

Chancery—419 Sixth St., #200, Juneau, 99801. Tel: 907-586-2227; Fax: 907-463-3237.

Chancellor—Rev. PATRICK J. TRAVERS, J.C.L., J.D.

Diocesan Consultors—Revs. PETER GORGES; MICHAEL NASH; BERNARD KONDA; PATRICK J. TRAVERS, J.C.L., J.D.; MICHAEL SCHWARTE.

Tribunal—419 Sixth St., #200, Juneau, 99801. Tel: 907-586-2227.

Judicial Vicar—Rev. PATRICK J. TRAVERS, J.C.L., J.D.

Defenders of the Bond—Rev. BERNARD KONDA, M.B.A., J.C.D.

Notary—ROBERTA IZZARD.

Administration—419 Sixth St., #200, Juneau, 99801. Tel: 907-586-2227; Fax: 907-463-3237.

Business Manager and Finance Officer—SKIP ELLIOTT.

Office Manager—ROBERTA IZZARD.

Finance Council—Most Rev. MICHAEL W. WARFEL; Revs. PETER GORGES; MICHAEL NASH; ANNA WENZEL; SKIP ELLIOTT; HUGH GRANT; WIN GERMAIN; JOHN FRANK; THOMAS BRIGGS.

Diocesan Offices and Directors

Apostleship of the Sea—Port Chaplains: Revs. PETER GORGES, *416 Fifth St., Juneau, 99801.* BERNARD KONDA, *433 Jackson St., Ketchikan, 99801.* PAUL WIGHTMAN, *P.O. Box 495, Sitka, 99835.* ED MATTHEWS, *Box 469, Wrangell, 99929.* GARY NORMAN, *P.O. Box 47, Petersburg, 99833.*

Catholic Community Service, Inc.—SHARON REBAR, A.C.S.W., Exec. Dir., *419 Sixth St., CCS Wing, Juneau, 99801.* Tel: 907-463-3933.

Board of Directors—ROSEMARY HAGEVIG, Pres. NATALIE ALTON; BILL CORBUS; KAY DIEBELS; Rev. A. GORDON JOHNSON; SHARON KELLY; MARJORIE MENZI; FRED MORINO; Rev. MICHAEL NASH; KEVIN SULLIVAN; MARIJO TONER; VERN VOSS; Most Rev. MICHAEL W. WARFEL.

Southeast Senior Services—PATRICIA JANIK, Program Dir., *419 Sixth St., CCS Wing, Juneau, 99801.* Tel: 907-586-6233.

Child Care & Family Resources—PATRICIA JANIK, Prog. Dir., *520 Harris St., Juneau, 99801.* Tel: 907-586-1634.

Diocesan Publication "Inside Passage"—LOUISE MILLER, Editor, *419 Sixth St., #200, Juneau, 99801.* Tel: 907-586-2237, Ext. 32.

Holy Childhood Association—Rev. PATRICK J. TRAVERS, J.C.L., J.D., Dir., *419 Sixth St., #200, Juneau, 99801.* Tel: 907-586-2227, Ext. 21.

Office of Ministries—Directors: Sr. JUDITH GOMILA, M.S.C.; Sr. ZITA SIMON, O.P., *419 Sixth St., #200, Juneau, 99801.* Tel: 907-586-2227, Ext. 26.

Family Life Office—KARLA DONAGHEY, Dir., *419 Sixth St., Juneau, 99801.* Tel: 907-586-2227, Ext. 29.

Permanent Deacon Program—Deacon CHARLES SESLAR, *4133 Columbia Blvd., Juneau, 99801.* Tel: 907-789-2262.

School—ROBERT VINCENT, Prin., *Holy Name School, 433 Jackson St., Ketchikan, 99901.* Tel: 907-225-2400.

Shrine of St. Therese—THOMAS FITTERER, *5933 Lund St., Juneau, 99801.* Tel: 907-780-6112. CHUCK AND JOAN GASPAREK, Caretakers, *8695 Short Ct., Juneau, 99801.* Tel: 907-789-7478.

St. Vincent de Paul Society—STAN MILLER; JOANNE MILLER, *8617 Teal St., Juneau, 99801.* Tel: 907-789-5535.

Special Collections and Archivist—Sr. HELENA FOX, P.B.V.M., *419 6th St. #200, Juneau, 99801.* Tel: 907-586-2227, Ext. 36.

Vocations—Rev. MICHAEL NASH, Dir., *419 6th St., #200, Juneau, 99801.* Tel: 907-586-2227, Ext. 34.

Hispanic Ministry—Rev. PATRICK J. TRAVERS, J.C.L., J.D., *419 6th St., #200, Juneau, 99801.* Tel: 907-586-2227, Ext. 21.

CLERGY, PARISHES, MISSIONS AND PAROCHIAL SCHOOLS

CITY AND BOROUGH OF JUNEAU

1—CATHEDRAL OF THE NATIVITY OF THE BLESSED VIRGIN MARY, Rev. Peter Gorges, Rector; Carol J. Crater, S.H.F., Pastoral Assoc.
Res., 416 Fifth St., 99801. Tel: 907-586-1513; Fax: 907-586-8091.
Mission—Pelican.

2—ST. PAUL THE APOSTLE, Rev. Jef Johnson.
Res., 9055 Atlin Ave., 99801. Tel: 907-789-2648; 789-7307 (Office); Fax: 907-790-3430.

OUTSIDE THE CITY AND BOROUGH OF JUNEAU

Craig, St. John by the Sea. (Diocesan Mission). Rev. Jim Blaney, O.M.I.; Sr. Laetitia Lariviere, I.H.M., Admin.
Res., P.O. Box 170, 99921. Tel: 907-755-2345.
Mission—Thorne Bay, P.O. Box 19150, Thorne Bay, 99919. Tel: 907-828-3324.
Stations—Coffman Cove; Hydaburg; Klawock; Thorne Bay; Tolstoi Bay; Whale Pass; Naukati.

Haines, Sacred Heart, Sr. Judith Gomila, M.S.C., Pastoral Assoc. In res., Rev. Msgr. James F. Miller, (Retired).
Res., Box 326, 99827. Tel: 907-766-2241.

Hoonah, Sacred Heart. (Diocesan Mission). Administrators: Rev. Michael Nash; Sr. Carol J. Crater, S.H.F.
Res., P.O. Box 368, 99289. Tel: 907-945-3323.

Ketchikan, Holy Name, Revs. Bernard A. Konda, J.C.D.; Michael Schwarte.
433 Jackson St., 99901. Tel: 907-225-2570; Fax: 907-247-0041.; Rectory: Tel: 907-225-5352; Fax: 907-247-7585.
School—Lay Teachers 9; Students 100.

Metlakatla, Holy Family. (Diocesan Mission). Rev. Michael Schwarte, Admin.
Mailing Address: P.O. Box 228, 99926. Fax: 907-247-0041.
Res., 433 Jackson St., Ketchikan, 99901.

Petersburg, St. Catherine of Siena, Rev. Gary R. Norman, O.M.I.
Res., P.O. Box 508, 99833. Tel: 907-772-3257; Fax: 907-772-3080.
Mission—Hobart.
Station—Kake.

Sitka, St. Gregory of Nazianzen, Rev. Paul Wightman, O.M.I.; Sr. Maggie Butler, S.S.S., Pastoral Assoc.
Res., P.O. Box 495, 99835. Tel: 907-747-8371; 747-6997; Fax: 907-747-6997.

Skagway, St. Therese of the Child Jesus, Rev. Michael Nash; Sr. Judith Gomila, M.S.C., Admin.
Res., Box 496, 99840. Tel: 907-983-2271.

Wrangell, St. Rose of Lima, Rev. Edward Matthews, O.M.I., Admin.
Res., Box 469, 99929. Tel: 907-874-3771; Fax: 907-874-3744.

Yakutat, St. Ann. (Diocesan Mission). Rev. Michael Nash, Admin.; Sr. Judith Gomila, M.S.C., Pastoral Min.
Res., P.O. Box 323, 99689. Tel: 907-784-3406.
Stations—Angoon; Cube Cove; Elfin Cove; Gustavus; Pelican; Tenakee Springs.

Chaplains of Public Institutions

On Duty Outside the Diocese:
Reverend Fathers—
Finn, William, St. Louis Parish, 141 156th Ave., SE, Bellevue, WA 98007
Gutierrez, Javier, P.O. Box 6315, Chula Vista, CA 92011
Saba, Joseph, 5660 W. Placita Del Risco, Tuscon, AZ 85745

Retired:
Reverend Monsignors—
Kekumano, Charles A., 700 Richards St., #2609, Honolulu, HI 96813
Miller, James F., Box 326, Haines, AK 99827
Reverend Fathers—
Cronin, James D., 1870-A Vista del Sur, Sante Fe, NM 87505
Dunfey, Ronald K., 1737 University Ave., G-63, Fairbanks, AK 99709
Fister, Jerome, 4322 Cassanna Way, Apt. #403, Oceanside, CA 92057
Manske, James J., P.O. Box 1672, Juneau, AK 99802
Melbourne, David, 3424 E. 15th Ave., Anchorage, AK 99508
Ryan, James, 2828 Sloat Rd., Pebble Beach, CA 93953

Permanent Deacons:
Benigno, Patrick, On Duty Outside the Diocese
Buck, Jack W., Cathedral of the Nativity BVM, Juneau
Duvernay, Anthony, On Duty Outside the Diocese
Horton, Gary, St. Paul the Apostle, Juneau
Johnson, Charles, St. Gregory's Sitka
Jones, Jerred, St. Paul the Apostle, Juneau
Mackin, Francis, St. Gregory's, Sitka
Michaud, George, On Duty Outside the Diocese
Paradis, Paul, St. Paul the Apostle, Juneau
Seslar, Charles, Cathedral of the Nativity BVM, Juneau

INSTITUTIONS LOCATED IN THE DIOCESE

[A] NURSING HOMES

JUNEAU. *St. Ann's Care Center, Inc.*, 415 Sixth St., 99801. Tel: 907-586-3883.
For a complete listing, refer to the Special Care Facilities section.

[B] HOSPITALS

KETCHIKAN. *Ketchikan General Hospital*, 3100 Tongass, 99901. Tel: 907-225-5171; Fax: 907-225-2173.
For a complete listing, refer to the Hospitals section.

[C] CONVENTS AND RESIDENCES FOR SISTERS

JUNEAU. *St. Josephs Convent*, 2971 Douglas Hwy., 99801. Tel: 907-586-2085. Intercommunity residence of various religious orders of women. Sisters 4.

KETCHIKAN. *Sisters of St. Joseph of Peace*, Ketchikan General Hospital, 3100 Tongass Ave., 99901. Tel: 907-225-5171; Fax: 907-225-2173.

RELIGIOUS INSTITUTES OF WOMEN REPRESENTED IN THE DIOCESE

For further details refer to the corresponding bracketed number in the Religious Institutes of Women section.

[2410]—*Congregation of the Marianites of Holy Cross.*—M.S.C.

[1070]—*Dominican Sisters.*—O.P.

[]—*Sisters of St. Joseph.*—S.S.J.

[3890]—*Sisters of St. Joseph of Peace.*—C.S.J.P.

[]—*Sisters of the Holy Family.*—S.H.F.

[2150]—*Sisters, Servants of the Immaculate Heart of Mary.*—I.H.M.

[3330]—*Union of the Sisters of the Presentation of the Blessed Virgin Mary.*—P.B.V.M.

NECROLOGY

† Dunfey, Kenneth, (Retired). —Died April 13, 1996.

Diocese of Kalamazoo

(Dioecesis Kalamazuensis)

Most Reverend

PAUL V. DONOVAN, D.D.

Former Bishop of Kalamazoo; ordained May 20, 1950; appointed Bishop of Kalamazoo June 15, 1971; ordained and installed July 21, 1971; resigned November 22, 1994. *Mailing Address: 238 Falkirk Ct., Kalamazoo, MI, 49006.*

ESTABLISHED JULY 21, 1971.

Square Miles 5,337.

Comprises the following nine Counties in the State of Michigan: Allegan, Barry, Berrien, Branch, Calhoun, Cass, Kalamazoo, St. Joseph and Van Buren.

For legal titles of parishes and diocesan institutions, consult the Chancery.

(Vacant See)

Chancery: 215 N. Westnedge Ave., Kalamazoo, MI, 49007-3760. Tel.: 616-349-8714; Fax: 616-349-6440.

STATISTICAL OVERVIEW

Personnel	
Bishop	1
Retired Bishops	1
Priests: Diocesan Active in Diocese	39
Priests: Retired, Sick or Absent	21
Number of Diocesan Priests	60
Religious Priests in Diocese	14
Extern Priests in Diocese	9
Ordinations:	
Diocesan Priests	1
Transitional Deacons	1
Permanent Deacons in Diocese	18
Total Brothers	4
Total Sisters	230
Parishes	
Parishes	46
With Resident Pastor:	
Resident Diocesan Priests	35
Resident Religious Priests	7
Without Resident Pastor:	
Administered by Priests	1
Administered by Permanent Deacons	1
Administered by Women Religious	2
Missions	13
Pastoral Centers	1
Closed Parishes	1
Professional Ministry Personnel:	
Brothers	3
Sisters	12
Lay Ministers	40
Welfare	
Catholic Hospitals	3
Total Assisted	511,889
Homes for the Aged	5
Total Assisted	425
Day Care and Extended Day Care Centers	2
Total Assisted	75
Specialized Homes	2
Total Assisted	711
Special Centers for Social Services	4
Total Assisted	25,711
Educational	
Diocesan Students in Other Seminaries	5
Total Seminarians	5
High Schools, Diocesan and Parish	3
Total Students	866
Elementary Schools, Diocesan and Parish	21
Total Students	4,597
Catechesis/Religious Education:	
High School Students	1,203
Elementary Students	6,588
Total Students Under Catholic Instruction	13,259
Teachers in the Diocese:	
Sisters	10
Lay Teachers	298
Vital Statistics	
Receptions into the Church:	
Infant Baptism Totals	1,620
Adult Baptism Totals	246
Received into Full Communion	197
First Communions	1,561
Confirmations	1,371
Marriages:	
Catholic	317
Interfaith	290
Total Marriages	607
Deaths	946
Total Catholic Population	99,922
Total Population	909,236

Former Bishops—Most Rev. PAUL V. DONOVAN, D.D., ord. May 20, 1950; appt. Bishop of Kalamazoo June 15, 1971; installed July 21, 1971; resigned Nov. 22, 1994.—Most Rev. ALFRED J. MARKIEWICZ, D.D., ord. June 6, 1953; appt. Titular Bishop of Afufenia and Auxiliary to the Bishop of Rockville Centre, July 7, 1986; ord. Bishop, Sept. 17, 1986; appt. Bishop of Kalamazoo, Nov. 22, 1994; installed Jan. 31, 1995; died Jan. 9, 1997.

Vicar General—Rev. ROBERT E. CONSANI, *534 W. Kilgore Rd., Kalamazoo, 49008.* Tel: 616-345-4389; Fax: 616-345-5211.

Chancery—*215 N. Westnedge Ave., Kalamazoo, 49007-3760.* Tel: 616-349-8714; Fax: 616-349-6440. Office Hours: 9-5; Address all communications to this office.

Moderator of the Curia—Rev. ROBERT C. MORLINO, S.T.D., *542 W. Michigan Ave., Kalamazoo, 49007.* Tel: 616-349-6523.

Chancellor—Rev. Msgr. DELL F. STEWART, *215 N. Westnedge Ave., Kalamazoo, 49007-3760.* Tel: 616-349-8316.

Diocesan Tribunal—*215 N. Westnedge Ave., Kalamazoo, 49007-3760.* Tel: 616-349-7974; Fax: 616-349-6440.

Judicial Vicar—Rev. LEONARD A. BOGDAN, J.C.D.

Defenders of the Bond—Revs. MICHAEL A. HACK, J.C.D.; THOMAS A. MARTIN, J.C.D.

Promoter of Justice—Rev. THOMAS A. MARTIN, J.C.D.

Judges—Rev. Msgr. WALTER E. MEHM, J.C.D.; Revs. KENNETH W. SCHMIDT, J.C.D.; EDWARD A. HANKIEWICZ, J.C.L.; Sr. JOYCE HOBEN, S.N.D., J.C.L.

Advocates—Revs. THOMAS A. MARTIN, J.C.D.; MICHAEL A. OSBORN.

Chief Notary and Administrative Assistant—MARLENE J. PRANSKATIS.

Notaries—ANNA B. BOWMAN; TERESA R.E. STUTZ.

Archivist—Rev. ROBERT F. CREAGON, *150 Taylor St., Coldwater, 49036.* Tel: 517-278-2650; Fax: 517-278-5800.

Consultant for Administrative Services—Rev. Msgr. DELL F. STEWART.

Diocesan Consultors—Rev. Msgr. DELL F. STEWART; Revs. DAVID C. ADAMS; ROBERT E. CONSANI; WILLIAM J. FITZGERALD; MICHAEL D. HAZARD; JAMES S. O'LEARY; EUGENE A. SEARS.

Theological Consultant—Rev. ROBERT C. MORLINO, S.T.D.

Vicar for Religious—Sr. MARY JOAN WALSH, S.S.J., *215 N. Westnedge Ave., Kalamazoo, 49007-3760.* Tel: 616-349-8714; Fax: 616-349-6440.

Diocesan Offices and Directors

Campaign for Human Development—Sr. SUSAN RIDLEY, O.P., Dir., *215 N. Westnedge Ave., Kalamazoo, 49007-3760.* Tel: 616-349-7260.

Catholic Family Services—FRANCES H. DENNY, Exec. Dir., *1819 Gull Rd., Kalamazoo, 49001.* Tel: 616-381-9800; Fax: 616-381-2932.

Catholic Relief Services—Sr. SUSAN RIDLEY, O.P., Dir., *215 N. Westnedge Ave., Kalamazoo, 49007-3760.* Tel: 616-349-7260.

Cemeteries—Rev. JULIUS L. HENGESBACH, *215 N. Westnedge Ave., Kalamazoo, 49007.* Tel: 616-349-8714; Fax: 616-349-6440.

Children's Catechesis—Sr. MARY LOUISE MATT, C.S.J., Dir., *215 N. Westnedge Ave., Kalamazoo, 49007-3760.* Tel: 616-349-6404.

Christian Service—Sr. SUSAN RIDLEY, O.P., Dir., *215 N. Westnedge Ave., Kalamazoo, 49007-3760.* Tel: 616-349-7260.

Common Ministry—MARY JANE DOERR, Dir. BONNIE ROBINS, Coord., *215 N. Westnedge Ave., Kalamazoo, 49007-3760.* Tel: 616-349-1391; Fax: 616-349-6440.

Communications—Vacant, *215 N. Westnedge Ave., Kalamazoo, 49007-3760.* Tel: 616-349-6707.

Audio-Visual Resources—TERESA R.E. STUTZ, Coord., *215 N. Westnedge Ave., Kalamazoo, 49007-3760.* Tel: 616-349-6707.

Catholic Communications Campaign—Vacant, *215 N. Westnedge Ave., Kalamazoo, 49007-3760.* Tel: 616-349-1391.

Cursillo Movement—Vacant.

Diocesan Council of Catholic Women (D.C.C.W.)—Rev. DONALD P. KLINGER, Spiritual Dir.; Mrs. IRENE RUGA, Pres., *2648 116th Ave., Allegan, 49010.* Tel: 616-673-2850.

Diocesan Development Office—T. EDWARD CAREY, JR., Dir., *215 N. Westnedge Ave., Kalamazoo, 49007-3760.* Tel: 616-349-4677.

Diocesan Pastoral Council—Sr. MARY L. SULLIVAN, O.P., Exec. Sec. & Chm. Exec. Committee, *215 N. Westnedge Ave., Kalamazoo, 49007-3760.* Tel: 616-349-7606.

Diocesan-Parish Council Ministry—Sr. MARY L. SULLIVAN, O.P., Dir., *215 N. Westnedge Ave., Kalamazoo, 49007-3760.* Tel: 616-349-7606.

Education—FRANK C. WIPPEL, Supt. of Schools; Sr. CONSTANCE FIFELSKI, O.P., Assoc. Supt., *215 N. Westnedge Ave., Kalamazoo, 49007-3760.* Tel: 616-349-6427. Rev. WILLIAM J. FITZGERALD, Consultant-Resource Person on Educational Matters, *92 Capital Ave., N.E., Battle Creek, 49017.* Tel: 616-968-6645.

Evangelization—Sr. MARY L. SULLIVAN, O.P., Coord., *215 N. Westnedge Ave., Kalamazoo, 49007-3760.* Tel: 616-349-7606.

Finance Council—Most Rev. ALFRED J. MARKIEWICZ; Rev. Msgr. DELL F. STEWART; Revs. DAVID C. ADAMS; ROBERT C. MORLINO; T. EDWARD CAREY, JR.; ALICE C. KONKEY; ED EDWARDS; JOHN T. GILLESPIE; ED KOWIESKI; DANIEL KUNITZER; JERRY B. LOVE; JAMES MORRISON; JOHN A. PANFIL; LEO A. SWIAT.

Holy Childhood Association—Rev. Msgr. DELL F. STEWART, Dir., *215 N. Westnedge Ave., Kalamazoo, 49007-3760.* Tel: 616-349-8316.

Indian Ministry—Vacant.

Inner City Ministry—Sr. RITA SCHAFER, S.S.J.; Sr. ROSE LAMBERTZ, S.S.J., *Catholic Community Center, 589 Pearl St., Benton Harbor, 49022.* Tel: 616-926-6424.

Jail Ministry—Sr. MARILYN SULLIVAN, S.S.J., Coord., *215 N. Westnedge Ave., Kalamazoo, 49007-3760.* Tel: 616-349-7769.

Knights of Columbus—Rev. LEONARD A. BOGDAN, Diocesan Chaplain, *215 N. Westnedge Ave., Kalamazoo, 49007-3760.* Tel: 616-349-7974.

Marriage and Family Ministry, Office of—JOE SCHMITT, Dir. MARCELLA V. KELEMEN, Admin. Dir., *215 N. Westnedge Ave., Kalamazoo, 49007-3760.* Tel: 616-349-8000.

Ministry Formation—Sr. MARLENE HALPIN, O.P., Dir., *215 N. Westnedge Ave., Kalamazoo, 49007-3760.* Tel: 616-349-1444.

Ministry with Persons with Disabilities—ANN SHERZER, Dir., *215 N. Westnedge Ave., Kalamazoo, 49007-3760.* Tel: 616-349-7276.

Missions—Rev. Msgr. DELL F. STEWART, Dir., *215 N. Westnedge Ave., Kalamazoo, 49007-3760.* Tel: 616-349-8316.

Natural Family Planning Center of Southwestern Michigan—MARY CULP, Exec. Dir., *165 N. Washington St., Battle Creek, 49017.* Tel: 616-964-9474.

Permanent Diaconate—Deacon JOHN DESTAZIO, Chm., *211 Church St., St. Joseph, 49085.* Tel: 616-983-1575; Fax: 616-983-1576.

Presbyteral Council—Rev. Msgr. DELL F. STEWART; Revs. DAVID C. ADAMS; WILLIAM J. FITZGERALD; MICHAEL D. HAZARD; JAMES A. MORRIS; JAMES S. O'LEARY; EUGENE A. SEARS; MARK J. VYVERMAN.

Priestly Life and Ministry Office—Rev. JAMES S. O'LEARY, Dir., *61 N. 23rd St., Battle Creek, 49015.* Tel: 616-962-0165; Fax: 616-962-5937.

Respect Life—Sr. SUSAN RIDLEY, O.P., Dir., *215 N. Westnedge Ave., Kalamazoo, 49007-3760.* Tel: 616-349-7260.

St. Vincent DePaul Society—Rev. LAWRENCE W. KROLL, Spiritual Advisor, *939 Charlotte Ave., Kalamazoo, 49001.* Tel: 616-342-0621.

Scouting Apostolate—Deacon JERRY MIX, Chap., *62012 Bayshore Dr., Sturgis, 49091.* Tel: 616-467-8100.

Spanish-Speaking Apostolate—(Bishop's Committee for Migrant Workers), *215 N. Westnedge Ave., Kalamazoo, 49007-3760.* Tel: 616-349-7769.

Pastoral Team for Spanish-Speaking Residents-Migrants—Sr. RUTH HEYN, S.S.J.; Sr. ROSEMARY TIERNEY, S.S.J., *815 Lay Blvd., Kalamazoo, 49001.* Tel: 616-345-1232.

Vocations—Rev. MICHAEL A. OSBORN, Dir., *215 N. Westnedge Ave., Kalamazoo, 49007-3760.* Tel: 616-349-7722.

Worship, Office of—DAVID J. REILLY, Dir., *215 N. Westnedge Ave., Kalamazoo, 49007-3760.* Tel: 616-349-7721.

Youth and Young Adult Ministry—LISA IRWIN, Dir., *215 N. Westnedge Ave., Kalamazoo, 49007-3760.* Tel: 616-349-4947.

Address communications for all other offices to Chancery, Diocese of Kalamazoo. *215 N. Westnedge Ave., Kalamazoo, 49007-3760;* Fax: 616-349-6440.

CLERGY, PARISHES, MISSIONS AND PAROCHIAL SCHOOLS

CITY OF KALAMAZOO
(Kalamazoo County)

1—ST. AUGUSTINE CATHEDRAL, Revs. Robert C. Morlino; Marian M. Kencik (Poland); Mathew Alapatt, M.S.F.S. (India); Stanley T. Staniszewski (Poland).
Res., 542 W. Michigan Ave., 49007. Tel: 616-345-5147; Fax: 616-349-0166.
School—600 W. Michigan Ave., 49007. Tel: 616-349-1945.
Lay Teachers 21; Students 341.

2—ST. JOSEPH, Rev. Michael D. Hazard.
Res., 936 Lake St., 49001. Tel: 616-343-6256.
School—930 Lake St., 49001. Tel: 616-342-9441; Fax: 616-343-1214.
Lay Teachers 12; Students 200.

3—ST. MARY, Rev. Lawrence W. Kroll.
Res., 939 Charlotte Ave., 49001. Tel: 616-342-0621; Fax: 616-342-0677.
School—929 Charlotte Ave., 49001. Tel: 616-342-2884.
Sisters 1; Lay Teachers 11; Students 188.
Convent—Tel: 616-342-8826.

4—ST. MONICA, Revs. Robert E. Consani; Achilles Van Hoof, O.Praem.; Brian L. Stanley. In res., Rev. Richard G. Valls, Sch.P.
Res., 534 W. Kilgore Rd., 49008. Tel: 616-345-4389; Fax: 616-345-5211.
School—530 W. Kilgore Rd., 49008. Tel: 616-345-2444; Fax: 616-345-8534.
Sisters of St. Joseph 1; Lay Teachers 20; Students 523.

5—ST. THOMAS MORE STUDENT PARISH, Revs. Kenneth W. Schmidt; Kenneth A. Templin, S.M.
Office: 421 Monroe St., 49006. Tel: 616-381-8917; Fax: 616-381-0195.

OUTSIDE THE CITY OF KALAMAZOO

Albion, Calhoun Co., St. John the Evangelist, Rev. Michael W. Glockner, C.S.C.
Office: 879 Finley Dr., 49224-9712. Tel: 517-629-4532; Fax: 517-629-9140. [CEM]
School—1020 Irwin Ave., 49224-1507. Tel: 517-629-6132.
Lay Teachers 9; Students 172.

Allegan, Allegan Co., Blessed Sacrament, Rev. Jerome M. Heyman, O.S.A.
Res., 422 Hubbard St., 49010-1246. Tel: 616-673-4455. [CEM]
Church—110 Cedar St., 49010-1244.

Bangor, Van Buren Co., Sacred Heart of Jesus, Rev. Anthony F. Pantyra, M.S.
Res., 201 S. Walnut St., 49013. Tel: 616-427-7514; Fax: 616-427-5719.
Chapel—Grand Junction, St. Cyril. (Summer).

Battle Creek, Calhoun Co., St. Jerome, Rev. Edwin G. Palmer.
Res., 229 Collier Ave., 49017. Tel: 616-968-2218; Fax: 616-968-2233.
St. Joseph, Rev. James S. O'Leary. In res., Revs. Stanislaus A. Nowakowski; Donn J. Taylor.
Res., 61 N. 23rd St., 49015. Tel: 616-962-0165; Fax: 616-962-5937.
School—63 N. 24th St., 49015. Tel: 616-965-7749; Fax: 616-965-0790.
Lay Teachers 17; Students 313.
St. Philip, Revs. William J. Fitzgerald; Richard L. Altine.
Office: 126 Capital Ave., N.E., 49017. Tel: 616-968-6645; Fax: 616-968-0632.
Res., 92 Capital Ave., N.E., 49017. [CEM]
School—20 Cherry St., 49017. Tel: 616-963-4935; Fax: 616-963-5590.
Lay Teachers 18; Students 284.

Benton Harbor, Berrien Co., St. John-St. Bernard, Rev. David C. Adams.
Res., 600 Columbus Ave., 49022. Tel: 616-925-2425. [CEM]
Catechesis/Religious Programs—220 Church St., St. Joseph, 49085. Tel: 616-983-7797.
Students 61.
St. Bernard. Merged with St. John, Benton Harbor.
St. John the Evangelist. Merged with St. Bernard, Benton Harbor.

Bridgman, Berrien Co., Our Lady Queen of Peace, Rev. Raymond J. Barth.
Res., 3903 Lake St., P.O. Box 747, 49106-0747. Tel: 616-465-6252; Fax: 616-465-4930.

Bronson, Branch Co., St. Mary's, Rev. Richard A. Fritz.
Res., 602 W. Chicago, 49028. Tel: 517-369-2120; Fax: 517-369-5101. [CEM]
School—204 Albers Rd., 49028. Tel: 517-369-4625.
Lay Teachers 9; Students 154.
Mission—Colon, St. Barbara.

Buchanan, Berrien Co., St. Anthony, Rev. Joseph W. Weller.
Res., 509 W. 4th St., 49107. Tel: 616-695-3863; Fax: 616-695-3864.
Mission—Berrien Springs, St. Gabriel, Tel: 616-471-2424.

Byron Center, Kent Co., St. Mary's Visitation, Rev. Gordon L. Greene.
Res., 2459 146th Ave., 49315. Tel: 616-681-9701. [CEM]
School—2455 146th Ave., 49315. Tel: 616-681-9607.
Lay Teachers 6; Students 156.

Cassopolis, Cass Co., St. Ann, Rev. Donald G. Potts.
Res., 313 N. Broadway, P.O. Box 247, 49031. Tel: 616-445-3140.
Church—421 N. Broadway, P.O. Box 247, 49031. Tel: 616-445-3000; Fax: 616-445-5787.

Coldwater, Branch Co., St. Charles, Rev. Robert F. Creagan.
Res., 150 Taylor St., 49036. Tel: 517-278-2650; Fax: 517-278-5800.
Mission—Union City, Our Lady of Fatima, Tel: 517-741-7275.

Decatur, Van Buren Co., Holy Family, Deacon Bartholomew E. Connelly.
Res., 500 W. St. Mary Blvd., 49045. Tel: 616-423-3151; Fax: 616-423-7755.

Delton, Barry Co., St. Ambrose, Rev. William A. Crenner.
Res., 11252 Floria Rd., 49046. Tel: 616-623-2490.
Mission—Lacey, Our Lady of Great Oak, Tel: 616-758-3636.

Dorr, Allegan Co., St. Stanislaus, Rev. James Vinh Le.
Res., 1871 136th Ave., 49323. Tel: 616-793-7268. [CEM]
School—1861 136th Ave., 49323. Tel: 616-793-7204.
Lay Teachers 7; Students 130.
Mission—Watson, Allegan Co., Sacred Heart. [CEM]

Douglas, Allegan Co., St. Peter, Rev. Edward L. Hamel., O.S.A.
Res., St. Peter's Dr., 49406. Tel: 616-857-7951; 857-8175.

Dowagiac, Cass Co., Holy Maternity of Mary, Rev. Leo A. Taubitz.
Res., 210 N. Front St., 49047. Tel: 616-782-2808. [CEM]

Edwardsburg, Cass Co., Our Lady of the Lake, Rev. David C. Otto.
Res., 24832 U.S. 12 E., 49112. Tel: 616-699-5870; Fax: 616-699-5474.

Gobles, Van Buren Co., St. Jude, Sr. Theresa V. MacIntyre, S.S.J., Pastoral Min.
Res., 405 S. State, Apt. 2, P.O. Box 102, 49055. Tel: 616-628-4424.
Church—13809 N. M-40, 49055. Tel: 616-628-2219.

Gull Lake, Kalamazoo Co., St. Ann, Rev. Mark J. Vyverman.
Res., 12648 E. D Ave., Augusta, 49012. Tel: 616-731-4721; Fax: 616-731-4147.

Hartford, Van Buren Co., Immaculate Conception, Rev. Michael A. Osborn.
Res., 63559 60th Ave., P.O. Box 185, 49057. Tel: 616-621-4106; Fax: 616-621-2138.

Hastings, Barry Co., St. Rose of Lima, Rev. Charles H. Fischer.
Res., 805 S. Jefferson Ave., 49058. Tel: 616-945-4246. [CEM]
School—707 S. Jefferson St., 49058. Tel: 616-945-3164.
Sisters of St. Joseph 1; Lay Teachers 6; Students 127.
Mission—Nashville, St. Cyril.

Marshall, Calhoun Co., St. Mary, Rev. James L. Barrett.
Res., 212 Hanover St., 49068. Tel: 616-781-3949; 781-7341; Fax: 616-781-3632. [CEM]

Mattawan, Van Buren Co., St. John Bosco, Rev. Charles T. Page.
Res., 23830 Front Ave., 49071. Tel: 616-668-3312.
Mission—Marcellus, Cass Co., St. Margaret Mary.

Mendon, St. Joseph Co., St. Edward, Rev. Thomas A. Martin.
Res., 332 W. State, 49072. Tel: 616-496-3525; Fax: 616-496-3525. [CEM]

New Buffalo, Berrien Co., St. Mary of the Lake, Rev. Thomas F. DeVita.
Res., 718 W. Buffalo St., 49117. Tel: 616-469-2637; Fax: 616-469-7393.
School—704 W. Merchant St., 49117. Tel: 616-469-1515.
Lay Teachers 8.

Niles, Berrien Co., St. Mark, Rev. Joseph W. Koma, C.S.C.
Res., 3 N. 19th St., P.O. Box 517, 49120. Tel: 616-683-8650; Fax: 616-683-9314.
St. Mary, Rev. Stephen E. Naas.
Res., 211 S. Lincoln Ave., 49120. Tel: 616-683-5087; Fax: 616-683-5089. [CEM]
School—217 S. Lincoln Ave., 49120. Tel: 616-683-9191.
Sisters 2; Lay Teachers 7; Students 150.
Convent—219 S. State St., 49120. Tel: 616-683-8630.

Otsego, Allegan Co., St. Margaret, Rev. Donald P. Klingler.
Res., 245 Court St., 49078. Tel: 616-694-6311; Fax: 616-694-5415. [CEM]
School—736 S. Farmer, 49078. Tel: 616-694-2951.
Lay Teachers 10; Students 143.

Parchment, Kalamazoo Co., St. Ambrose, Rev. John M. Steffey.
Res., 1628 E. G Ave., 49004. Tel: 616-385-4152; Fax: 616-385-2527.

Paw Paw, Van Buren Co., St. Mary, Rev. Robert E. Flickinger.
Res., 209 S. Brown St., 49079. Tel: 616-657-4459; Fax: 616-657-4260. [CEM]
School—500 Paw Paw St., 49079. Tel: 616-657-3750.
Lay Teachers 9; Students 99.

Pearl, Allegan Co., San Felipe de Jesus, Sr. Ruth Heyn, S.S.J., Pastoral Admin.
Mailing Address: P.O. Box 588, Fennville, 49408. Tel: 616-561-5029.

Portage, Kalamazoo Co., St. Catherine of Siena, Revs. John J. Klobuka, S.M.; Lawrence A. Schoettelkotte, S.M.
Res., 1150 W. Centre St., 49002. Tel: 616-327-5962; Fax: 616-327-7266.

St. Joseph, Berrien Co., St. Joseph, Revs. Eugene A. Sears; James A. Morris. In res., Rev. Devasahayam Gudime (India).
Res., 211 Church St., 49085. Tel: 616-983-1575; Fax: 616-983-1576. [CEM]
Annex: Stevensville, 5353 S. Roosevelt Rd., 49085. Tel: 616-489-1074.

Silver Creek, Cass Co., Sacred Heart of Mary, Sr. Monica Marie Ruoff, S.S.J., Pastoral Min.
Mailing Address: 51841 Leach Rd., Dowagiac, 49047. Tel: 616-782-5740; Fax: 616-782-5692. [CEM]

South Haven, Van Buren Co., St. Basil, Rev. John E. Young.
Res., 513 Monroe Blvd., 49090. Tel: 616-637-2404.
School—94 Superior St., 49090. Tel: 616-637-3529; Fax: 616-639-1242.
Lay Teachers 9; Students 196.

Sturgis, St. Joseph Co., Holy Angels, Rev. Leon H. Pohl.
Res., 402 S. Nottawa St., 49091. Tel: 616-651-5200; Fax: 616-659-8366.
School—Tel: 616-651-2088.
Lay Teachers 10; Students 170.

Three Oaks, Berrien Co., St. Mary of the Assumption, Rev. Wilfrid A. Menard, C.S.C.
Res., 28 W. Ash St., 49128. Tel: 616-756-2041; Fax: 616-756-2212.
Mission—Sawyer, St. Agnes.

Three Rivers, St. Joseph Co., Immaculate Conception, Rev. Mathew K. Illikattil.
Res., 645 S. Douglas Ave., 49093. Tel: 616-273-8953; Fax: 616-273-2114.
School—601 S. Douglas Ave., 49093. Tel: 616-273-2085.
Lay Teachers 9; Students 171.
Mission—Centreville, St. Clare.

Vicksburg, Kalamazoo Co., St. Martin, Sr. Marjorie Manning, C.S.C., Pastoral Min.
Res., 5855 E. W Ave., 49097. Tel: 616-649-1629; Fax: 616-649-2877.

Watervliet, Berrien Co., St. Joseph, Rev. Donald A. Wieber.
Res., 179 Lucinda Ln., Box 157, 49098. Tel: 616-463-5470; Fax: 616-463-4642. [CEM]
School—Tel: 616-463-3941; Fax: 616-463-4525.
Lay Teachers 8; Students 214.

Wayland, Allegan Co., St. Therese, Rev. Gary W. Pamment.
Res., 128 Cedar St., 49348. Tel: 616-792-2138; 792-9315; Fax: 616-792-2908.
School—Tel: 616-792-2016.
Felician Sisters 3; Lay Teachers 3; Students 84.

SS. Cyril and Methodius, Sr. Marie Beaulac, S.S.J., Pastoral Min.
Church—150-131st Ave., 49348. Tel: 616-792-2889; Fax: 616-792-6244. [CEM]

White Pigeon, St. Joseph Co., St. Joseph, Sr. Maxine McGee, S.S.J., Pastoral Min.
Res., 16603 E. U.S. 12, P.O. Box 344, 49099-0344. Tel: 616-483-7621; Fax: 616-483-7891.

Chaplains of Public Institutions

BATTLE CREEK. *Veteran's Administration Hospital,* 49016. Tel: 616-966-5600. Chaplains: Revs. Juan Porras-Landeo (Peru); Michael Stafford, O.S.B (PRO).

COLDWATER. *Florence Crane Annex.* Rev. Robert F. Creagan, Volunteer Chap., St. Charles Church, 150 Taylor St., 49036. Tel: 517-278-2650; Fax: 517-278-5800.

Florence Crane Correctional Facility for Women. Rev. Robert F. Creagan, Volunteer Chap.

Lakeland Correctional Facility for Men. Rev. Robert F. Creagan, Volunteer Chap.

Special Assignment:
Reverend Fathers—
Bogdan, Leonard A.

Absent on Sick Leave:
Reverend Fathers—
Sulka, Stanley E., 109 Spruce St., Dowagiac, MI 49047

Absent on Leave:
Reverend Fathers—
Snyder, Daniel L.

Retired:
Reverend Monsignors—
Stewart, Dell F., 705 Regency Sq., #203, Kalamazoo, MI 49008
Reverend Fathers—
Atchison, Donald W, 5021 Gilread Shores, Bronson, MI 49028
Burger, Frank J., P.O. Box 143, Grand Junction, MI 49506
Crowley, Charles J., 3221 Olney St., Kalamazoo, MI 49006
Flynn, Francis J., St. Ann's Home, 2161 Leonard St., Grand Rapids, MI 49504
Ginther, Benjamin H., 1328 E. V.W. Ave., Box 10, Vicksburg, MI 49097
Grathwohl, John M., 2065 Arrowhead, Traverse City, MI 49686
Hengesbach, Julius L., St. Mary Church, 939 Charlotte St., Kalamazoo, MI 49001
Limbert, William G., 11859 Marquette Dr., New Buffalo, MI 49117
Nadrach, Adolph W., Box 69, Watervliet, MI 49098
Nowakowski, Stanislaus A., St. Joseph Church, 61 N. 23rd St., Battle Creek, MI 49015
O'Meara, James J., 2469 Beech Dr., Kawkawlin, MI 48631
Sonefeld, Raymond G., 814 Engleman St., Manistee, MI 49660
Spillane, Walter J., 63 Centennial Dr., #17, Norwood, MA 02062
Taylor, Donn J., 61 N. 23rd St., Battle Creek, MI 49015
Thachet, Joseph, Kerala, India
White, Leroy E., 311 W. Flint St., Davison, MI 48423-1053
Wieber, Elmer F., 3317 N. Stewart, Tucson, AZ 85716
Woods, Lawrence H., 560 Cosmopolitan, Marshall, MI 49068

Permanent Deacons:
Aleman, Eugenio, Immaculate Conception, Hartford
Barbosa, Juan, San Felipe de Jesus, Pearl
Brown, David (GRY)
Cardosa, Abraham, (BWN)
Connelly, Bart, Immaculate Conception, Three Rivers
De Stazio, John F. (TOL), St. Joseph, St. Joseph
Fleckenstein, Richard, Cincinnati, OH
Herrera, Manuel, Grand Rapids
Hubbarth, John (LAN), St. Catherine of Sienna, Portage
Karmon, Douglas, Kalamazoo
Middleton, Allan, St. Mary, Kalamazoo
Mix, Jerome (CHI), Holy Angels, Sturgis
Patrick, Albert W., St. Philip, Battle Creek
Pellack, Robert (JOL), Immaculate Conception, Three Rivers
Ponce, Julian, Fresno, CA
Prendergast, John (RCK), St. Catherine of Siena, Portage
Provot, Alvin (DET), St. Charles, Coldwater
Rauner, James D. (FTW), St. Joseph, Watervliet
Rodriguez, Maximino, San Felipe de Jesus, Pearl
Smoker, Gerald J., St. Mary, Bronson
Van Dril, William (JOL), Blessed Sacrament, Allegan
Whitehouse, Howard (DET), St. Mary, Niles
Wilcox, Harry V., West Melbourne, FL
Zientarski, Raymond S., St. Mary of the Lake, New Buffalo

INSTITUTIONS LOCATED IN THE DIOCESE

[A] HIGH SCHOOLS, DIOCESAN

KALAMAZOO. *Msgr. Hackett Catholic Central High School,* 1000 W. Kilgore Rd., 49008. Tel: 616-381-2646; Fax: 616-381-3363. Mr. Donald T. White, Prin. Lay Teachers 25; Students 510.

BATTLE CREEK. *St. Philip Catholic Central High School,* 20 Cherry St., 49017. Tel: 616-963-4503; Fax: 616-963-5590. Mr. Mike Low, Prin. Sisters 1; Lay Teachers 13; Students 138.

ST. JOSEPH. *Lake Michigan Catholic Junior High and High School.* (Grades 7-12), 915 Pleasant St., 49085. Tel: 616-983-2511; Fax: 616-983-0883. Mr. John F. Brown, Prin. Adrian Dominican Sisters of Immaculate Conception Province 1; Lay Teachers 22; Students 337.

[B] GRADE SCHOOLS, INTERPAROCHIAL

ST. JOSEPH. *Lake Michighan Catholic Schools.* (Grades PreK-6), 3165 Washington Ave., 49085. Tel: 616-429-0227; Fax: 616-429-1461. Mrs. Karla J. Cook, Prin. Lay Teachers 19; Students 390.

[C] CATHOLIC SOCIAL AGENCIES

KALAMAZOO. *Catholic Family Services,* 1819 Gull Rd., 49001. Tel: 616-381-9800; Fax: 616-381-2932. Mrs. Frances H. Denny, A.C.S.W., Exec. Dir.

[D] GENERAL HOSPITALS

KALAMAZOO. *Borgess Medical Center,* 1521 Gull Rd., 49001. Tel: 616-226-7000; Fax: 616-226-7396.
For a complete listing, refer to the Hospitals section.

BATTLE CREEK. *Battle Creek Health System,* 300 North Ave., 49016. Tel: 616-966-8000; Fax: 616-966-8010.
For a complete listing, refer to the Hospitals section.

DOWAGIAC. *Lee Memorial Hospital,* 420 W. High St., 49047. Tel: 616-782-8681; Fax: 616-782-7611.
For a complete listing, refer to the Hospitals section.

[E] RESIDENCES OF PRIESTS AND BROTHERS

DOUGLAS. *Order of St. Augustine.* (Chicago Prov.), St. Peter Dr., 49406. Tel: 616-857-8175. Rev. Edward L. Hamel, O.S.A. Brothers 1.

PORTAGE. *Society of Mary.* (Cincinnati Prov.), 1150 W. Centre St., 49024. Tel: 616-327-6952. Revs. Kenneth A. Templin, S.M., Dir.; Bernard L. Horst, S.M.; John J. Klobuka, S.M.; Lawrence A. Schoettelkotte. Brothers 3.

[F] HOMES FOR SENIOR CITIZENS

KALAMAZOO. *Borgess Nursing Home,* 537 Chicago Ave., 49001. Tel: 616-382-2392; Fax: 616-382-0843.
For a complete listing, refer to the Special Care Facilities section.

BATTLE CREEK. *Mercy Pavilion Skilled Nursing Home and Senior Care Residence,* 80 N. 20 St., 40915. Tel: 616-964-5400; Fax: 616-964-5559.
For a complete listing, refer to the Special Care Facilities section.

DOWAGIAC. *Dowagiac Nursing Home,* 610 Uneta St., 49047. Tel: 616-782-3471.
For a complete listing, refer to the Special Care Facilities section.

NAZARETH. *Dillon Complex for Independent Living, Inc.,* 49074. Tel: 616-342-0263.
For a complete listing, refer to the Special Care Facilities section.

OTSEGO. *Otsego Senior Apts., Inc.,* Baraga Manor, 301 Washington St., 49078. Tel: 616-694-9711.
For a complete listing, refer to the Special Care Facilities section.

[G] CONVENTS AND RESIDENCES FOR SISTERS

NAZARETH. *Motherhouse and Novitiate of the Sisters of St. Joseph,* 49074. Tel: 616-381-6290; Fax: 616-381-4909. Sr. Janet Fleischhacker, S.S.J., Pres. Congregation; Rev. Michael J. Howell, Chap. Sisters in the Community 359.

[H] NEWMAN CENTERS

KALAMAZOO. *Western Michigan University, Kalamazoo College-Kalamazoo Valley Community College,* St. Thomas More Student Parish, 421 Monroe St., 49006. Tel: 616-381-8917; Fax: 616-381-0195. Revs. Kenneth W. Schmidt; Kenneth A. Templin, S.M.; Sr. Sue McCrery, S.S.J., Pastoral Assoc.

[I] MISCELLANEOUS LISTINGS

KALAMAZOO. *Borgess Health Alliance, Inc.,* 1521 Gull Rd., 49001. Tel: 616-226-7001; Fax: 616-226-7396. Integrated Health Care System sponsored by the Sisters of St. Joseph which operates Borgess Ambulatory Care, Inc., Borgess Foundation, Borgess Medical Center, Borgess Nursing Home, Inc., Borgess-Pipp Health Center, Dowagiac Nursing Home, Lee Memorial Hospital Corp., ProMed Healthcare, Inc., and Western Nephrology Services, Inc. Incorporated in the State of Michigan. Mr. Timothy R. Stack, Pres.; Mr. Randall Stasik, Treas.; Sr. Elizabeth Veenhuis, S.S.J., Sec.

Central Council of St. Vincent dePaul, 7959 Deerpath Rd., 49009. Tel: 616-375-3736. James Smolinski, Pres.

Kalamazoo Regional Catholic Schools Foundation, 1000 W. Kilgore Rd., 49008. Tel: 616
616-381-3919.

Secular Franciscan Order, 2903 E. M
Tel: 616-342-0989. Mr. Lawrence V
Asst.

BATTLE CREEK. *BCACS Foundation, I*
St., 49015. Tel: 616-963-1131; Fax:

HASTINGS. *St. Rose Lima Trust Fund*, 805 S. Jefferson St., 49058. Tel: 616-945-4246.

ST. JOSEPH. *Twin-City Area Catholic School Fund, Inc.*, 220 Church St., 49085. Tel: 616-983-5529.

SOUTH HAVEN. *St. Basil Educational Endowment Fund*, 94 Superior St., 49090. Tel: 616-637-3529.

STURGIS.

**Holy Angels School Foundation, Inc.*, P.O. Box 24, 49091-0024. Tel: 616-651-5742.

RELIGIOUS INSTITUTES OF MEN REPRESENTED IN THE DIOCESE

For further details refer to the corresponding bracketed number in the Religious Institutes of Men or Women section.

[0140]—*The Augustinians*.—O.S.A.

[0200]—*Benedictine Monks*.—O.S.B.

[0900]—*Canons Regular of Premontre*.—O.Praem.

[0720]—*The Missionaries of Our Lady of LaSalette*. (Polish Prov.).—M.S.

[]—*Missionaries of St. Francis de Sales*. (India).—M.S.F.S.

[1040]—*Piarist Fathers*.—Sch.P.

[0610]—*Priests of the Congregation of the Holy Cross*. (Indiana Prov.).—C.S.C.

[0760]—*Society of Mary*. (Cincinnati Prov.).—S.M.

RELIGIOUS INSTITUTES OF WOMEN REPRESENTED IN THE DIOCESE

[1920]—*Congregation of the Sisters of the Holy Cross*.—C.S.C.

[1070-05]—*Dominican Sisters*.—O.P.

[1070-13]—*Dominican Sisters*.—O.P.

[1070-14]—*Dominican Sisters*.—O.P.

[1170]—*Felician Sisters*. (Livonia, MI).—C.S.S.F.

[2575]—*Sisters of Mercy of the Americas*.—R.S.M.

[3830-11]—*Sisters of St. Joseph*. (Nazareth, MI).—S.S.J.

[3840]—*Sisters of St. Joseph of Carondelet*. (St. Paul, MN).—C.S.J.

[3930]—*Sisters of St. Joseph of the Third Order of St. Francis*.—S.S.J.-T.O.S.F.

[3260]—*Sisters of the Precious Blood*. (Dayton, Ohio).—C.PP.S.

[2150]—*Sisters, Servants of the Immaculate Heart of Mary*. (Monroe, MI).—I.H.M.

NECROLOGY

✠ Markiewicz, Most Rev. Alfred J., (Retired). —Died Jan. 9, 1997.

Archdiocese of Kansas City in Kansas

(Archidioecesis Kansanopolitana in Kansas)

Most Reverend

JAMES P. KELEHER, S.T.D.

Archbishop of Kansas City in Kansas; ordained April 12, 1958; appointed Bishop of Belleville October 23, 1984; consecrated December 11, 1984; transferred to Kansas City in Kansas September 8, 1993. *Office: 12615 Parallel Pkwy., Kansas City, KS, 66109.* Tel.: 913-721-1570.

Most Reverend

IGNATIUS J. STRECKER, D.D., S.T.D.

Former Archbishop of Kansas City in Kansas; ordained December 19, 1942; appointed Bishop of Springfield-Cape Girardeau April 7, 1962; consecrated June 20, 1962; transferred to Kansas City September 10, 1969; retired September 8, 1993. *Res., 3408 Minnesota Ave., Kansas City, KS, 66101.*

Most Reverend

MARION F. FORST, D.D.

Former Auxiliary Bishop of Kansas City in Kansas; ordained June 10, 1934; consecrated Bishop of Dodge City, March 24, 1960; installed April 5, 1960; resigned from Dodge City; appointed Auxiliary October 16, 1976; retired December 23, 1986. *Res., 759 Vermont Ave., Kansas City, KS, 66101.*

Catholic Church Offices: 12615 Parallel Pkwy., Kansas City, KS, 66109. Tel.: 913-721-1570; Fax: 913-721-1577.

E-mail address: 103620.3704

ESTABLISHED VICARIATE APOSTOLIC JULY 19, 1850. DIOCESE OF LEAVENWORTH ESTABLISHED MAY 22, 1877. SEE CHANGED TO KANSAS CITY IN KANSAS MAY 10, 1947.

CREATED ARCHDIOCESE AUGUST 9, 1952.

Square Miles 12,524.

Comprises the following 21 Counties of Kansas: Anderson, Atchison, Brown, Coffey, Doniphan, Douglas, Franklin, Jackson, Jefferson, Johnson, Leavenworth, Linn, Lyon, Marshall, Miami, Nemaha, Osage, Pottawatomie, Shawnee, Wabaunsee and Wyandotte.

PATRONS OF THE DIOCESE: I. Blessed Virgin Mary (Immaculate Conception); II. St. John Baptist Vianney.

STATISTICAL OVERVIEW

Personnel	
Archbishop	1
Retired Archbishops	1
Retired Bishops	1
Abbots	1
Retired Abbots	2
Priests: Diocesan Active in Diocese	80
Priests: Active Outside Diocese	5
Priests: Diocesan in Foreign Missions	1
Priests: Retired, Sick or Absent	12
Number of Diocesan Priests	98
Religious Priests in Diocese	66
Ordinations:	
Transitional Deacons	1
Total Brothers	20
Total Sisters	840
Parishes	
Parishes	119
With Resident Pastor:	
Resident Diocesan Priests	59
Resident Religious Priests	18
Without Resident Pastor:	
Administered by Priests	42
Welfare	
Catholic Hospitals	3
Total Assisted	327,154
Health Care Centers	2
Total Assisted	13,378
Homes for the Aged	4
Total Assisted	573
Day Care and Extended Day Care Centers	1
Total Assisted	125
Special Centers for Social Services	10
Total Assisted	15,245
Residential Care of Disabled	1
Total Assisted	205
Educational	
Diocesan Students in Other Seminaries	13
Students Religious	2
Total Seminarians	15
Colleges and Universities	3
Total Students	2,430
High Schools, Diocesan and Parish	5
Total Students	3,083
High Schools, Private	2
Total Students	338
Elementary Schools, Diocesan and Parish	39
Total Students	12,097
Elementary Schools, Private	1
Total Students	40
Catechesis/Religious Education:	
High School Students	3,418
Elementary Students	14,790
Total Students Under Catholic Instruction	36,211
Teachers in the Diocese:	
Priests	3
Brothers	1
Sisters	45
Lay Teachers	1,012
Vital Statistics	
Receptions into the Church:	
Infant Baptism Totals	3,678
Adult Baptism Totals	409
Received into Full Communion	588
First Communions	3,487
Confirmations	2,693
Marriages:	
Catholic	737
Interfaith	560
Total Marriages	1,297
Deaths	1,354
Total Catholic Population	181,638
Total Population	952,000

Predecessors—Rt. Rev. J. B. MIEGE, S.J., cons. Bishop of Messenia, Vicar-Apostolic, March 25, 1851 resignation accepted by Pope Pius IX Nov. 8, 1874; died July 21, 1884.—Rt. Rev. LOUIS M. FINK, D.D., O.S.B., cons. Bishop of Eucarpia June 11, 1871; appt. first Bishop of Leavenworth May 22, 1877; died March 17, 1904.—Rt. Rev. THOMAS F. LILLIS, O.D., cons. Bishop of Leavenworth, Dec. 27, 1904; appt. Coadjutor Bishop of Kansas City, with right of succession March 14, 1910; succeeded to the See of Kansas City, Feb. 21, 1913.—Rt. Rev. JOHN WARD, D.D., ord. July 17, 1884; appt. Bishop of Leavenworth Nov. 25, 1910; cons. Feb. 22, 1911; died April 20, 1929.—Most Rev. FRANCIS JOHANNES, D.D., LL.D., cons. May 1, 1928; succeeded to the See, April 20, 1929; died March 13, 1937.—Most Rev. PAUL C. SCHULTE, D.D., ord. June 11, 1915; appt. Bishop of Leavenworth May 29, 1937; cons. Sept. 21, 1937; appt. Archbishop of Indianapolis July 20, 1946; installed Oct. 10, 1946.—Most Rev. GEORGE J. DONNELLY, S.T.D., ord. June 12, 1921; appt. Titular Bishop of Coela and Auxiliary of St. Louis March 19, 1940; cons. April 23, 1940; appt. Bishop of Leavenworth Nov. 9, 1946; died Dec. 13, 1950.—Most Rev. EDWARD J. HUNKELER, D.D., ord. June 14, 1919; appt. Bishop of Grand Island March 10, 1945; cons. May 1, 1945; transferred to Kansas City March 28, 1951; elevated to Archiepiscopal dignity Aug. 9, 1952; retired Sept. 10, 1969; died Oct. 1, 1970.—Most Rev. IGNATIUS J. STRECKER, D.D., S.T.D., ord. Dec. 19, 1942; appt. Bishop of Springfield-Cape Girardeau April 7, 1962; cons. June 20, 1962; transferred to Kansas City Sept. 10, 1969; retired Sept. 8, 1993.

Catholic Church Offices—12615 Parallel, Kansas City, 66109. Tel: 913-721-1570; Fax: 913-721-1577. Office Hours: 9-5.

Vicars General—Revs. CHARLES MCGLINN; THOMAS TANK.

Chancellor—Rev. THOMAS TANK.

Metropolitan Tribunal—12615 Parallel, Kansas City, 66109. Tel: 913-721-1570; Fax: 913-721-1577.

Judicial Vicar—Rev. PHILIP KENDALL, C.S.V., J.C.D.

Pro-Synodal Judges—Revs. PHILIP E. KENDALL, C.S.V., J.C.D.; GEORGE BERTELS, J.C.L.

Defender of the Bond—Rev. GARY APPLEGATE, J.C.L.; Rev. Msgr. ROBERT BERGMAN, J.C.D.

Advocates—Selected priests of the Archdiocese.

Director Notary—ARLENE T. WILSON.

Archdiocesan Consultors—Revs. RAYMOND DAVERN; THOMAS TANK; THOMAS CULHANE; Rt. Rev. BARNABAS SENECAL, O.S.B.; Revs. FRANCIS KRISCHE; CHARLES MCGLINN.

Archdiocesan Council on Finances—Rev. THOMAS TANK, Chancellor; Mr. RICHARD ANDERSON; Mr. JERRY MAYNE; Mr. FRANK SABATINI; Mr. JAMES J. OWENS.

Archdiocesan Foundation—12615 Parallel, Kansas City, 66109.

Regional Pastoral Leaders—Atchison: Rev. GERARD SENECAL, O.S.B., Emporia: Rev. MARK MERTES, Johnson Co.: Rev. CHARLES MCGLINN, Lawrence: Rev. JAMES SHAUGHNESSY, Leavenworth: Rev. TERRENCE CYR, O.Carm., Nortonville: Rev. RONALD CORNISH, Topeka: Rev. NORBERT LICKTEIG, Garnett: Rev. EARL

DEKAT, Nemah-Marshall: Rev. RODERIC GILLER, O.S.B., St. Mary's: Rev. JOHN REYNOLDS, Wyandotte Co.: Rev. RAYMOND DAVERN.

Minister to Priests—Rev. JAMES WHITE, S.J., *12600 Hollingsworth Rd., Kansas City, 66109.* Tel: 913-721-3966.

Archdiocesan Archivist—Rev. LEO COOPER.

Archdiocesan Administrative Team—Mrs. CATHERINE COGHLAN; Rev. CHARLES MCGLINN; Mr. BLAKE MULVANY; Mr. JAMES J. OWENS; Mr. DANIEL POPE; Rev. THOMAS TANK.

Archdiocesan Finance Officer—JAMES J. OWENS.

Archdiocesan Offices and Directors

Savior of the World Pastoral Center—12601 Parallel, Kansas City, 66109. Tel: 913-721-1097.

Office for Black Catholics—REGINA BARGER, Dir., *2203 Parallel, Kansas City, 66104.* Tel: 913-321-1958.

Department of Parish Ministries—Rev. THOMAS TANK, Dir., *12615 Parallel Pky., Kansas City, 66109.* Tel: 913-721-1570.

Adult Spirituality / RCIA—Sr. ELEANOR SUTHER.

Deaf—Sr. ANN ALBRECHT.

Family Life—Mrs. JACKI CORRIGAN.

Liturgy—Rev. FRANCIS HUND; Mr. MICHAEL PODREBAREC.

Peace and Justice—Sr. BARBARA MCCRACKEN.

Religious Education—Mrs. JEANNE BRADY.

Youth—Mr. LAWRENCE LIVINGSTON.

Stewardship and Development Office—CATHERINE COGHLAN, Dir., *12615 Parallel, Kansas City, 66109.* Tel: 913-721-1570.

Apostleship of Prayer—Rev. FRANK SCHEPERS, *St. John the Baptist Parish, Greely, 66033.* Tel: 913-867-3120.

Catholic Youth Organization—DAVE NICK, Athletic Dir., *5041 Reinhardt Dr., P.O. Box 721, Shawnee Mission, 66201.* Tel: 913-384-7377.

Catholic Charities—DANIEL POPE, Dir., *2220 Central Ave., Kansas City, 66102.* Tel: 913-621-1504.

Council for Catholic Charismatic Renewal—Rev. MARK MERTES.

Catholic Community Service—2220 Central Ave., Kansas City, 66102. Tel: 913-621-1504.

Communications—Office of Modern Media, *12615 Parallel, Kansas City, 66109.* Tel: 913-721-1570.

Catholic Scouts—Rev. JOHN REYNOLDS, Chap.

Hispanic Ministry—Revs. DANIEL GARDNER; MICHAEL HERMES; RAMON GAITAN, O.A.R.

Holy Childhood Association—Rev. NORBERT LICKTEIG, *12615 Parallel, Kansas City, 66109.* Tel: 913-721-1570.

Hospitals—Rev. JEREMIAS L. SPENCER, Dir., *16 S. Iowa, Kansas City, 66101.*

Kansas Catholic Conference—ROBERT RUNNELS; Exec. Dir., *6301 Antioch, Shawnee Mission, 66202.* Tel: 913-722-6633.

Legion of Mary—Rev. ROBERT BURGER, Dir., *8311 W. 93rd, Overland Park, 66212.*

Missions—Rev. NORBERT LICKTEIG, *12615 Parallel, Kansas City, 66109.*

Newspaper "The Leaven"—Rev. MARK GOLDASICH, Editor, *12615 Parallel, Kansas City, 66109.* Tel: 913-721-1570; Fax: 913-721-5276.

Nurses Association—Rev. JEREMIAS L. SPENCER, Dir., *16 S. Iowa, Kansas City, 66103.*

Priests' Council—Rev. NORBERT LICKTEIG, Chm.

Propagation of the Faith—Rev. NORBERT LICKTEIG, *12615 Parallel, Kansas City, 66109.*

Respect Life—DANIEL POPE, Coord. REBECCA MESSALL, Dir.

Schools—BLAKE MULVANY, Supt. VINCENT WEISS, Assoc. Supt., *12615 Parallel, Kansas City, 66109.* Tel: 913-721-1570.

Vocations Office—Directors: Revs. DENNIS SCHMITZ; MICHAEL MULLEN, *12615 Parallel, Kansas City, 66109.* Tel: 913-721-1570.

CLERGY, PARISHES, MISSIONS AND PAROCHIAL SCHOOLS

CITY OF KANSAS CITY
(Wyandotte County)

1—CATHEDRAL OF ST. PETER THE APOSTLE, Revs. Thomas Tank; Philip Kendall, C.S.V.; Timothy Haberkorn.
Res., 409 N. 15th St., 66102. Tel: 913-371-0840.
School—422 N. 14th, 66102. Tel: 913-371-8101; Fax: 913-371-1014.
Lay Teachers 20; Students 285.
Child Care Center—424 N. 15th St., 66102. Tel: 913-342-5235.

2—BLESSED SACRAMENT, Rev. William McEvoy.
Res., 2203 Parallel Ave., 66104. Tel: 913-321-1958; Fax: 913-321-1997.

3—CHRIST THE KING, Rev. Raymond J. Davern.
Res., 3024 N. 53rd St., 66104. Tel: 913-287-8823.
School—3027 N. 54th St., 66104. Tel: 913-287-8883; Fax: 913-287-7409.
Sisters 1; Lay Teachers 17; Students 300.

4—HOLY FAMILY (Slovene), Rev. Msgr. Heliodore Mejak.
Res., 274 Orchard Ave., 66101. Tel: 913-371-1561.
School—St. John and Holy Family. (Consolidated). See separate listing under St. John the Baptist. Tel: 913-371-3923.

5—HOLY NAME, Rev. Jeremiah L. Spencer.
Res., 16 S. Iowa St., 66103. Tel: 913-236-9219.
School—1007 S.W. Blvd., 66103. Tel: 913-722-1032; Fax: 913-722-4175.
Lay Teachers 9; Students 131.

6—SACRED HEART. Attended by St. John the Evangelist, Kansas City. Rev. Charles Andalikiewicz.
Res., 2910 Strong Ave., 66106. Tel: 913-677-4621.
School—Our Lady of Unity. See separate listing. Tel: 913-262-7022; Fax: 913-262-7836.

7—OUR LADY AND ST. ROSE. Attended by Blessed Sacrament, Kansas City.
Mailing Address: 2203 Parallel, 66104.
Church—2300 N. Eighth St., 66101. Tel: 913-321-0550; Fax: 913-321-1997.

8—ST. MARY-ST. ANTHONY, Rev. Dennis E. Schmitz. In res., Rev. Dennis Wait.
Res., 615 N. Seventh St., 66101. Tel: 913-371-1408; Fax: 913-281-0446.

9—SS. CYRIL AND METHODIUS (Slovak). Attended by St. Joseph-St. Benedict, Kansas City. Rev. Wilfred Fangman, O.S.B.
Res., 801 Vermont, 66101. Tel: 913-371-3549; Fax: 913-621-2709.

10—ST. JOHN THE BAPTIST (Croatian), Rev. Francis Horvat.
Res., 708 N. Fourth St., 66101. Tel: 913-371-0627.
School—St. John the Baptist and Holy Family. (Consolidated) 515 Ohio, 66101. Tel: 913-321-0649; 371-3923; Fax: 913-321-0649.
Lay Teachers 13; Students 164.

11—ST. JOHN THE DIVINE (Mexican). (Stational Church).

12—ST. JOHN THE EVANGELIST, Rev. Charles Andalikiewicz.
Res., 2910 Strong Ave., 66106. Tel: 913-677-4621.
School—Our Lady of Unity. Consolidated with Sacred Heart. See separate listing for further details.

13—ST. JOSEPH AND ST. BENEDICT, Revs. Wilfred Fangman, O.S.B.; Michael Hermes.
Res., 801 Vermont Ave., 66101. Tel: 913-371-1837; Fax: 913-621-2709.
School—All Saints. (Consolidated). See separate listing.

14—ST. PATRICK'S, Revs. Michael Mullen; Harold Wickey, Senior Assoc.
Res., 1086 N. 94th St., 66112. Tel: 913-299-3370.
School—1066 N. 94th, 66112. Tel: 913-299-8131; Fax: 913-299-2845.
Sisters 1; Lay Teachers 23; Students 335.

15—ST. THOMAS THE APOSTLE. Closed. For inquiries for parish records contact the Chancery.

OUTSIDE THE CITY OF KANSAS CITY

Alma, Wabaunsee Co., Holy Family. Attended by Paxico. Rev. John Reynolds.
Church—66401. Tel: 913-765-3545.

Atchison, Atchison Co., St. Benedict's, Rev. Donald Redmond, O.S.B.
Res., 1001 N. Second St., 66002. Tel: 913-367-0671; Fax: 913-367-0797. [JC]
School—Atchison Catholic Elementary. (Consolidated). See separate listing.
Sacred Heart, Rev. Donald Redmond, O.S.B.
Res., 1503 Kansas Ave., 66002. Tel: 913-367-0387. [JC]
School—Atchison Catholic Elementary. (Consolidated). See separate listing.
St. Joseph's, Rev. Gerard Senecal, O.S.B.
Res., 705 Spring Garden St., 66002. Tel: 913-367-4271. [JC]
School—Atchison Catholic Elementary. (Consolidated). See separate listing.

Axtell, Marshall Co., St. Michael's, Rev. Thomas H. Dolezal.
Mailing Address: P.O. Box K, 66403. Tel: 913-736-2220; Fax: 913-736-2230.
School—Tel: 913-736-2257.
Lay Teachers 3; Students 47.

Baileyville, Nemaha Co., Sacred Heart, Rev. Albert J. Fey, C.PP.S.
Church—Box 36, 66404. Tel: 913-336-6464.

Baldwin, Douglas Co., Annunciation. Attended by Assumption, Edgerton. Rev. Phillip Winkelbauer.
Church—P.O. Box 293, 66006. Tel: 913-594-3700. [CEM]

Basehor, Leavenworth Co., Holy Angels, Rev. Edwin Watson, O.S.B., Admin.
Res., 15440 Leavenworth Rd., Box 295, 66007. Tel: 913-724-3122 (Res.), 913-724-1665 (Church). [CEM]

Beattie, Marshall Co., St. Malachy's. Attended by St. Gregory, Marysville. Rev. George Bertels.
Church—1012 Main St., 66406. Tel: 913-353-2280.

Bendena, Doniphan Co., St. Benedict's. Attended by St. Joseph, Wathena. Rev. Daniel P. McCarthy, O.S.B.
Church—Rte. #1, Box 91, 66008. Tel: 913-359-6725; Fax: 913-989-2313. [CEM]

Blaine, Pottawatomie Co., St. Columbkille. Attended by St. Vincent de Paul, Onaga. Rev. Jude Burbach, O.S.B.
Church—66480.

Blue Rapids, Marshall Co., St. Elizabeth. Attended by Annunication, Frankfort. Rev. Bernard Mullen, C.PP.S.

Bonner Springs, Wyandotte Co., Sacred Heart, Rev. Patrick Jerome.
Res., 103 E. Insley, 66012. Tel: 913-422-5700.
School—216 Alcutt, 66012. Tel: 913-422-5520.
Lay Teachers 8; Students 160.

Burlington, Coffey Co., St. Francis Xavier's, Rev. Kenneth W. Kelly.
Res., 214 Juniatta, 66839. Tel: 316-364-2416. [CEM]

Corning, Nemaha Co., St. Patrick's. Attended by St. Mary's, St. Benedict. Rt. Rev. Msgr. Owen Purcell, O.S.B.
Res., St. Mary, R.R. 1, Box 59, Seneca, 66538. Tel: 913-868-2790.

Delia, Jackson Co., Sacred Heart of Jesus. Unassigned. (Stational Church).

Doniphan, Doniphan Co., St. John's. Unassigned. (Stational Church).

Easton, Leavenworth Co., St. Lawrence's, Rev. Paul E. Hosler.
Res., P.O. Box 129, 66020. Tel: 913-773-5712.

Edgerton, Johnson Co., Assumption of the Blessed Virgin Mary, Rev. Phillip J. Winkelbauer.
Church—P.O. Box 74, 66021. Tel: 913-893-6272.

Effingham, Atchison Co., St. Ann's, Rt. Rev. Ralph Koehler, O.S.B.
Res., 301 William, Box 54, 66023. Tel: 913-833-5660.

Emerald, Anderson Co., St. Patrick's. Attended by St. Francis Xavier, Burlington. Rev. Kenneth Kelly.
Church—Williamsburg P.O., 66095. Tel: 316-364-2416; Fax: 316-364-2416.

Emmett, Pottawatomie Co., Holy Cross. Attended by Immaculate Conception, St. Marys. Rev. Carl M. Dekat.

Emporia, Lyon Co., Sacred Heart, Rev. Peter O'Sullivan.
Res., 101 Cottonwood St., 66801. Tel: 316-342-1061. [CEM]
School—102 Cottonwood St., 66801. Tel: 316-343-7394; Fax: 316-343-7394.
Lay Teachers 11; Students 196.
Rectory—123 Cottonwood St., 66801. Tel: 316-342-3328.
St. Catherine's. Attended by Sacred Heart, Paxico.
Church—205 S. Lawrence St., 66801. Tel: 316-342-1368. [CEM]

Eskridge, Wabaunsee Co., St. John Vianney's. Attended by Sacred Heart, Paxico. Rev. John C. Reynolds.

Eudora, Douglas Co., Holy Family, Rev. Paul W. Miller.
Res., P.O. Box H, 66025-0808. Tel: 913-542-2788. [CEM]

Fidelity, Brown Co., St. Augustine's. Attended by Sacred Heart, Sabetha. Rev. Conrad Pillar, O.S.B.

Flush, Pottawatomie Co., St. Joseph's. Attended by St. Bernard, Wamego. Rev. Thomas Hesse Tel: 913-494-8234.

Fort Leavenworth, Leavenworth Co., St. Ignatius Chapel, Rev. Gregory Sykes, Military Services Army Chap. [Natl. CEM].
Res., 709 Bittersweet Ct., Lansing, 66043. Tel: 913-684-3000.
Church—66027.

Frankfort, Marshall Co., Annunciation, Rev. Bernard Mullen, C.PP.S.
Res., 213 E. Fifth St., 66427. Tel: 913-292-4462.

Gardner, Johnson Co., Sacred Heart, Rev. Gerald E. Sheeds.
Res., 122 E. Warren, 66030. Tel: 913-856-7781. [CEM]

Garnett, Anderson Co., Holy Angels, Rev. George A. Matz.
Res., 514 E. Fourth, 66032. Tel: 913-448-3846.
School—530 E. Fourth, 66032. Tel: 913-448-3423.
Sisters 3; Lay Teachers 3; Students 44.

Greeley, Anderson Co., St. John the Baptist's, Rev. Frank Schepers.
Res., 66033. Tel: 913-867-3120. [CEM]
School—Tel: 913-867-2680.
Ursuline Sisters 1; Lay Teachers 4; Students 42.

Hartford, Lyon Co., St. Mary's. Attended by St. Joseph's, Olpe. Rev. Mark Mertes.

Hiawatha, Brown Co., St. Ann's, Rev. Terence Sullivan, O.S.B.
Res., 800 Hiawatha Ave., 66434. Tel: 913-742-3010.

Holton, Jackson Co., St. Dominic's, Rev. Ronald Cornish.
Res., 416 Ohio Ave., 66436. Tel: 913-364-3262. [CEM]

Horton, Brown Co., St. Leo's, Rev. Dave Coleman.
Res., 1340 First Ave. E., 66439. Tel: 913-486-3971; Fax: 913-486-2402. [CEM 3]

Kelly, Nemaha Co., St. Bede's. Attended by St. Mary, St. Benedict. Rt. Rev. Owen Purcell, O.S.B.
Tel: 913-336-3189. [CEM]

LaCygne, Linn Co., Our Lady of Lourdes. Attended by St. Philip Neri, Osawatomie.
Church—66040.

Lansing, Leavenworth Co., St. Francis de Sales, Rev. Michael C. Stubbs.
Res., 119 Woodland Rd., 66043. Tel: 913-727-3768.
Church—900 Ida St., 66043. Tel: 913-727-3742; Fax: 913-727-2536.

Lapeer, Douglas Co., St. Francis. Attended by St. Patrick, Osage City. Rev. Michael Mulvany. [CEM]

Lawrence, Douglas Co., Corpus Christi, Rev. James E. Shaughnessy.
Church & Office: 1100 Kasold Dr., 66049. Tel: 913-843-6286; Fax: 913-865-3933.
Res., 1201 Jana Dr., 66049. Tel: 913-749-4724.

St. John the Evangelist, Rev. Charles Polifka, O.F.M.Cap.
Res., 1229 Vermont St., 66044. Tel: 913-843-0109; Fax: 913-749-5064. [CEM]
School—Tel: 913-843-9511; Fax: 913-843-7143.
Sisters of Charity of Leavenworth 1; Lay Teachers 16; Students 300.

Leavenworth, Leavenworth Co.,

1—Immaculate Conception. (Old Cathedral). Rev. Terrence Cyr, O.Carm.
Office: 747 Osage, 66048. Tel: 913-682-3953; Fax: 913-682-3965.
Church—Fifth & Kiowa St., 66048. Tel: 913-682-3953.
School—Xavier Elementary. (Consolidated). See separate listing.
Rectory, 300 N. Broadway, 66048. Tel: 913-682-0809.

2—Sacred Heart of Jesus, Rev. William M. Haegelin.
Res., 1401 Second Ave., 66048. Tel: 913-682-1787.
School—Xavier Elementary. (Consolidated). See separate listing.

3—St. Casimir's, (Polish), Rev. William M. Haegelin.
Res., 1401 Second Ave., 66048. Tel: 913-682-1787. [JC]
School—Xavier Elementary. (Consolidated). See separate listing.

4—St. Joseph's, Rev. Terrence Cyr, O.Carm.
Office: 747 Osage, 66048. Tel: 913-682-3953; 682-0809 (Res.); Fax: 913-682-3965.
School—Xavier Elementary. (Consolidated). See separate listing.

5—St. Joseph of the Valley. Attended by St. Lawrence, Easton. Rev. Paul Hosler.
Church—R.R. #3, 66048.

Leawood, Johnson Co., Church of the Nativity, Revs. Alfred Rockers; Keith Lunsford.
Church—3800 W. 119th St., 66209. Tel: 913-491-5017; Fax: 913-491-5065.
School—3700 W. 119th St., 66209. Tel: 913-338-4330; Fax: 913-338-4331.
Lay Teachers 28; Students 591.

Cure of Ars, Revs. Charles McGlinn; William Fisher.
Res., 9401 Mission Rd., 66206. Tel: 913-649-1337; Fax: 913-649-1339.
School—9403 Mission Rd., 66206. Tel: 913-648-2620; Fax: 913-648-3810.
Lay Teachers 31; Students 561.
Vianney Center for Ministries—Tel: 913-649-8625; Fax: 913-649-1339.

Lenexa, Johnson Co., Holy Trinity, Revs. Raymond Burger; Robert Burger.
Office: 13520 W. 92nd St., 66215. Tel: 913-888-2770; Fax: 913-888-4403.
School—13600 W. 92nd St., 66215. Tel: 913-888-3250; Fax: 913-888-4403.
Sisters 1; Lay Teachers 34; Students 673.

Lillis, Marshall Co., St. Joseph's (Frankfort). Attended by St. Vincent de Paul, Onaga. Rev. Jude Burbach, O.S.B.
Tel: 913-889-4896. [CEM]

Louisburg, Miami Co., Immaculate Conception, Rev. Stanley J. Loncarcic.
Res., Box 118, 66053. Tel: 913-837-2295. [CEM]

Marysville, Marshall Co., St. Gregory's, Rev. George Bertels.
Res., 204 N. 13th, 66508. Tel: 913-562-3302; Fax: 913-562-4039.
School—207 N. 14th, 66508. Tel: 913-562-2831.
Lay Teachers 7; Students 138.

Mayetta, Jackson Co., St. Francis Xavier. Attended by St. Dominic, Holton. Rev. Ronald Cornish.
Tel: 913-364-3262.

Meriden, Jefferson Co., St. Aloysius. Attended by St. Theresa, Perry. Rev. Francis Hund.
Res., P.O. Box 364, 66512. Tel: 913-484-3312. [CEM]

Mission, Johnson Co., St. Pius X, Rev. Robert Hasenkamp.
Res., 5601 Woodson Ave., 66202. Tel: 913-432-4808; Fax: 913-432-4855.
School—5500 Woodson, 66202. Tel: 913-432-9355.
Sisters of St. Benedict 1; Lay Teachers 12; Students 268.

Mooney Creek, Jefferson Co., Corpus Christi. Attended by St. Lawrence, Easton. Rev. Paul Hosler.
Mailing Address: R.F.D. No. 3, Atchison, 66002. Tel: 913-774-2385.

Mound City, Linn Co., Sacred Heart Shrine to St. Philippine Duchesne. Attended by St. Philip Neri, Osawatomie. Rev. Joseph Cramer.
Res., 66056. Tel: 913-795-2724.

Nortonville, Jefferson Co., St. Joseph's, Rev. Thomas Cawley, C.M.
Res., 221 N. Sycamore St., 66060. Tel: 913-886-2030. [CEM]
School—Tel: 913-886-3510.
Sisters 1; Lay Teachers 1; Students 31.

Olathe, Johnson Co., St. Paul's, Revs. Gary Applegate, Admin.; Charles T. McGinn. Office: 832 Larkspur, 66061. Tel: 913-764-0323.
Res., 840 Larkspur, 66061. Tel: 913-782-6062; Fax: 913-764-0323. [CEM]
School—Tel: 913-764-0619; Fax: 913-764-0323.
Lay Teachers 13; Students 193.

Prince of Peace, Revs. Frank Burger; Jerry Volz.
Res., 14229 Cottonwood Dr., 66062. Tel: 913-782-8864; Fax: 913-780-9658.
School—16000 W. 143rd St., 66062. Tel: 913-764-0650.
Sisters 3; Lay Teachers 18; Students 510.

Olpe, Lyon Co., St. Joseph's, Rev. Mark Mertes.
Res., P.O. Box 165, 66865. Tel: 316-475-3326. [CEM]
School—Tel: 316-475-3416.
Lay Teachers 6; Students 74.

Onaga, Pottawatomie Co., St. Vincent de Paul, Rev. Jude Burbach, O.S.B.
Res., 66521. Tel: 913-889-4896.

Osage City, Osage Co., St. Patrick's, Rev. Michael Mulvany.
Res., 309 S. Sixth St., 66523. Tel: 913-528-3424. [CEM]

Osawatomie, Miami Co., St. Philip Neri, Rev. Joe Cramer.
Church—514 Parker Ave., 66064. Tel: 913-755-2652.
Chaplaincy—State Hospital for Mentally Ill, 66064. Tel: 913-294-2067.

Ottawa, Franklin Co., Sacred Heart, Rev. Tony Blaufuss.
Res., 409 S. Cedar St., 66067. Tel: 913-242-2174. [CEM]
School—426 S. Cedar, 66067. Tel: 913-242-4297.
Sisters of St. Benedict 2; Lay Teachers 6; Students 99.

Overland Park, Johnson Co.,

1—Church of the Ascension, Revs. Lawrence Albertson; Joseph Lopez.
Res., 9510 W. 127th St., 66213. Tel: 913-681-3348; Fax: 913-681-3517.

2—Holy Cross, Revs. Robert Pflumm; Michael Hawken.
Office: 8311 W. 93rd St., 66212. Tel: 913-381-2755; Fax: 913-381-2766.
Res., 8315 W. 93rd St., 66212. Tel: 913-341-5618.
School—8101 W. 95th, 66212. Tel: 913-381-7408.
Lay Teachers 21; Students 335.

3—Holy Spirit, Revs. Albert Hauser, O.S.B.; William A. Finnerty.
Res., 11300 W. 103rd St., 66214. Tel: 913-492-7318; Fax: 913-492-7370.
School—Tel: 913-492-2582.
Lay Teachers 25; Students 482.

4—Queen of the Holy Rosary, Rev. Thomas Kearns.
Res., 7023 W. 71st St., 66204. Tel: 913-432-4616; Fax: 913-432-0620.
School—6915 W. 71st, 66204. Tel: 913-432-6350; Fax: 913-432-5081.
Lay Teachers 17; Students 255.

Paola, Miami Co., Holy Trinity, Rev. Earl Dekat.
Res., 505 E. Chippewa, 66071. Tel: 913-294-2067; Fax: 913-294-9286. [CEM]
School—Tel: 913-294-3286.
Lay Teachers 8; Students 115.

Paxico, Wabaunsee Co., Sacred Heart, Rev. John C. Reynolds.
Res., 66526. Tel: 913-636-5547. [CEM]

Perry, Jefferson Co., St. Theresa's, Rev. Francis Hund.
Res., 66073. Tel: 913-597-5656. [CEM]

Prairie Village, Johnson Co., St. Ann's, Revs. Thomas Culhane; Steven Beseau.
Res., 7231 Mission Rd., 66208. Tel: 913-362-2817; Fax: 913-362-2678.
School—7241 Mission Rd., 66208. Tel: 913-362-7008; Fax: 913-362-7059.
Lay Teachers 26; Students 502.

Purcell, Doniphan Co., St. Mary's (P.O. Huron, KS). Attended by St. Leo's, Horton. Rev. Dave Coleman
Tel: 913-486-3971, Fax: 913-486-2402.

Reading, Lyon Co., Assumption. Closed. For inquiries for parish records contact the Chancery.

Richmond, Franklin Co., St. Therese. Attended by St. Boniface, Scipio. Rev. Clyde R. Ozminkowski, O.Carm.
Res., Rte. 1, Box 156, Garnett, 66032. Tel: 913-835-6273.

Roeland Park, Johnson Co., St. Agnes, Revs. Donald Cullen; John H. Wisner.
Res., 5250 Mission Rd., 66205. Tel: 913-262-2400; Fax: 913-262-1050.
School—5130 Mission Rd., 66205. Tel: 913-262-1686.
Lay Teachers 26; Students 482.

Rossville, Shawnee Co., St, Stanislaus. Attended by Immaculate Conception, St. Marys. Rev. Carl M. Dekat.

Sabetha, Nemaha Co., Sacred Heart, Rev. Conrad Pillar, O.S.B.
Res., 1042 S. 14th, P.O. Box 244, 66534. Tel: 913-284-3068.

St. Benedict, Nemaha Co., St. Mary's, Rt. Rev. Owen Purcell, O.S.B.
Res., R.R. 1, Box 59, Seneca, 66538. Tel: 913-336-3174. [CEM]

St. Louis, Atchison Co., St. Louis. Attended by St. Ann's, Effingham. Rt. Rev. Ralph Koehler, O.S.B.
Mailing Address: c/o St. Ann's, 301 William, Box 54, Effingham, 66023. Tel: 913-833-5660.
Church—11321 Morton Rd., Atchison, 66002. Tel: 913-847-6849.

St. Marys, Pottawatomie Co., Immaculate Conception, Rev. Carl M. Dekat.
Res., 208 W. Bertrand, 66536. Tel: 913-437-2408. [CEM]

St. Patrick, Atchison Co., St. Patrick's. Attended by St. Joseph. Rev. Gerard Senecal, O.S.B. [CEM]

Scipio, Anderson Co., St. Boniface, Rev. Clyde R. Ozminkowsi, O.Carm.
Res., R.R. No. 1, Box 156, Garnett, 66032. Tel: 913-835-6273.

Scranton, Osage Co., St. Patrick's. Attended by St. Patrick's, Osage City. Rev. Michael Mulvany.
Tel: 913-528-3424. [CEM]

Seneca, Nemaha Co., SS. Peter and Paul's, Revs. Roderic Giller, O.S.B.; Francis Broderick, O.S.B.
Res., 66538. Tel: 913-336-2208.
School—401 Pioneer, 66538. Tel: 913-336-2727.
Benedictine Sisters 2; Lay Teachers 14; Students 202.

Shawnee, Johnson Co., Good Shepherd, Rev. George Seuferling.
Office: 7126 Bond, 66203. Tel: 913-631-7116; Fax: 913-631-7357.
Res., 7124 Bond, 66203. Tel: 913-631-5661.
Parish Center: 11411 W. 71st Ter., 66203.

St. Joseph's, Rev. Msgr. Robert Bergman; Rev. Ronald Livojevich.
Res., 5832 King St., 66203. Tel: 913-631-5983; Fax: 913-631-5973.
School—(Grades 1-8) 5901 Flint St., 66203. Tel: 913-631-7730; Fax: 913-631-3608.
Lay Teachers 40; Students 728.
Early Education Center—(Day Care, Preschool & Kindergarten) 5900 Bond St., 66203.
Auxiliary Teachers 30; Students 587.

Summerfield, Marshall Co., Holy Family. Attended by St. Michael's, Axtell. Rev. Thomas H. Dolezal.
Church—P.O. Box 136, 66541. Tel: 913-736-2220.

Tonganoxie, Leavenworth Co., Sacred Heart, Rev. Mark Goldasich.
Res., 703 E. River, P.O. Box 539, 66086. Tel: 913-845-2851.

Topeka, Shawnee Co.,

1—Assumption, Rev. John F. Rossiter.
Res., 204 S.W. Eighth Ave., 66603. Tel: 913-232-2907.

School—735 S.W. Jackson, 66603. Tel: 913-235-0953.
Sisters 2; Lay Teachers 9; Students 193.

2—CHRIST THE KING, Rev. Norbert Lickteig.
Res., 5972 W. 25th St., 66614. Tel: 913-273-0710; 273-0715; Fax: 913-273-4766.
School—5973 S.W. 25th St., 66614. Tel: 913-272-2220; Fax: 913-273-4766.
Lay Teachers 22; Students 300.

3—HOLY NAME, Rev. Harold Schneider.
Res., 1114 W. 10th Ave., 66604. Tel: 913-232-7744; Fax: 913-232-2341.
School—934 Clay St., 66606. Tel: 913-233-1727; Fax: 913-232-2341.
Sisters of Charity of Leavenworth 2; Lay Teachers 14; Students 222.

4—MOST PURE HEART OF MARY, Revs. Francis Krische; William Bruning; Thomas Melchior.
Church Office: 1800 S.W. Stone, 66604. Tel: 913-272-5590; Fax: 913-272-2801.
School—1750 S.W. Stone, 66604. Tel: 913-272-4313; Fax: 913-272-1138.
Lay Teachers 35; Students 540.

5—OUR LADY OF GUADALUPE, (Mexican), Revs. Daniel L. Gardner; Joseph E. Chontos.
Res., 1008 N.E. Atchison Ave., 66616. Tel: 913-232-5088; Fax: 913-232-5166.
School—210 N.E. Branner St., 66616. Tel: 913-233-9171.
Sisters of Charity of Leavenworth 2; Lay Teachers 12; Students 190.

6—SACRED HEART, Rev. John Erickson.
Res., 333 Freeman Ave., 66616. Tel: 913-234-3338.
School—1733 Seward Ave., 66616. Tel: 913-234-8980.
Lay Teachers 11; Students 163.

7—ST. JOSEPH'S, Rev. Arthur J. Trompeter.
Res., 227 Van Buren St., 66603. Tel: 913-232-2863.

8—ST. MATTHEW, Rev. Patric Riley.
Res., 2700 S.E. Virginia Ave., 66605. Tel: 913-232-5012; Fax: 913-232-0028.
School—Tel: 913-235-2188; Fax: 913-232-0028.
Sisters of St. Benedict 2; Lay Teachers 16; Students 216.

Troy, Doniphan Co., St. Charles. Attended by St. Joseph's, Wathena. Rev. Daniel P. McCarthy, O.S.B.
Church—133 S. Park, 66087. Tel: 913-985-2271.

Valley Falls, Jefferson Co., St. Mary's Immaculate Conception. Attended by St. Joseph's, Nortonville.
Church—Broadway at Linn, 66088. Tel: 913-945-3582.

Wamego, Pottawatomie Co., St. Bernard's, Rev. Thomas N. Hesse.
Res., 66547. Tel: 913-456-7869.

Waterville, Marshall Co., St. Monica's. Attended by Annunciation, Frankfort. Rev. Bernard Mullen, C.PP.S.

Wathena, Doniphan Co., St. Joseph's, Rev. Daniel McCarthy, O.S.B.
Res., P.O. Box 159, 66090. Tel: 913-989-4818; Fax: 913-989-2313. [CEM]

Waverly, Coffey Co., St. Joseph's. Attended by St. Francis Xavier, Burlington. Rev. Kenneth W. Kelly. Tel: 316-364-2416.

Wea, Miami Co., Holy Rosary (Bucyrus P.O.), Rev. Anthony J. Lickteig.
Res., 22779 Metcalf Rd., Bucyrus, 66013. Tel: 913-533-2285. [CEM]

Westphalia, Anderson Co., St. Teresa's. Attended by St. Francis Xavier, Burlington. Rev. Kenneth W. Kelly. Tel: 316-364-2416; Fax: 316-364-2416.

Wetmore, Nemaha Co., St. James, Rev. Alfred G. Koestner, O.S.B.
Res., 66550. Tel: 913-866-2780.

Wheaton, Pottawatomie Co., St. Michael's. Closed. For inquiries for parish records contact the Chancery.

Chaplains of Public Institutions

KANSAS CITY. *K.U. Medical Center and Chapel,* Holy Name Church. Rev. Jeremiah L. Spencer, Chap.

LAWRENCE. *Haskell Institute*. (Government Indian School). Rev. Duane Reinert, O.F.M.Cap.

TOPEKA. *Kansas Neurological Institute and Kansas Reception and Diagnostic Center*. Rev. William Guthman (OM) Chap.
Topeka State Hospital. State Reform School attended from Holy Name Church. Menninger Clinic attended from Holy Name Church. Veterans Administration Hospital.

Special Assignment:
Reverend Fathers—
Cooper, Leo, Archdiocesan Archivist, 12615 Parallel, Kansas City, KS 66109

On Duty Outside the Archdiocese:
Reverend Monsignors—
De Runtz, Clarence, Pontifical College Josephinum, 7625 N. High St., Worthington, KS 43085
Reverend Fathers—
Schwalm, Donald, Minnesota
Tillia, Marc, Bahia, Brazil
Zemites, Joseph, Spokane, WA

Military Chaplains:
Reverend Fathers—
Ludwikoski, James E., U.S.A.F.
Williams, Anthony, U.S.A.F.

Absent on Sick Leave:
Reverend Fathers—
Pecinovsky, Albert

Retired:
Reverend Fathers—
Burger, Robert, Lenexa, KS
Fitzgerald, Patrick, Mound City, KS
Gardner, Maurice, Kansas City, KS
Klasinski, George, Topeka, KS
Nebiolo, Emilio, New York, NY
O'Grady, James, Lawrence, KS
Pool, Robert, LaCygne, KS
Roberts, Edward, Kansas City, KS
Stitz, John, Leavenworth, KS
Wempe, Richard C., Seneca, KS
Yadrich, John B., Kansas City, KS

INSTITUTIONS LOCATED IN THE ARCHDIOCESE

[A] COLLEGES AND UNIVERSITIES

KANSAS CITY. *Donnelly College*, 608 N. 18th St., 66102. Tel: 913-621-6070; Fax: 913-621-0354.
For a complete listing, refer to the Colleges and Universities section.

ATCHISON. *Benedictine College*, 66002. Tel: 913-367-5340; Fax: 913-367-3673.
For a complete listing, refer to the Colleges and Universities section.

LEAVENWORTH. *Saint Mary College*, 66048. Tel: 913-682-5151; Fax: 913-758-6140.
For a complete listing, refer to the Colleges and Universities section.

[B] HIGH SCHOOLS, INTERPAROCHIAL

KANSAS CITY. *Bishop Miege High School*. 5041 Reinhardt Dr., Shawnee-Mission, 66205. Tel: 913-262-2700; Fax: 913-262-3754. Joseph Passantino, Ed.D., Pres.; Stanley Herbic, Prin. Sisters 2; Lay Teachers 51; Students 792.
Bishop Ward High School, 708 N. 18th St., 66102. Tel: 913-371-1201; Fax: 913-371-2145. Mr. Timothy Mulvany, Pres.; Mr. Robert Runnebaum, Prin.; Rev. Timothy Haberkorn, Chap. Sisters of Charity of Leavenworth 2; Lay Teachers 27; Students 390.

LEAVENWORTH. *Immaculata High School*, 66048. Tel: 913-682-3900. Dr. John L. Coakley, Prin. Lay Teachers 19; Students 217.

OVERLAND PARK. *Saint Thomas Aquinas High School*, 11411 Pflumm Rd., 66215. Tel: 913-345-1411. Mr. Jerry Degan, Prin.; Sr. Kathleen Condry, Pres.; Rev. Gerald Volz, Chap. Sisters 3; Lay Teachers 65; Students 1,122.

TOPEKA. *Hayden High School*, 401 Gage Blvd., 66606. Tel: 913-272-5210. Mr. Benno Schluterman, Pres.; Rev. William Bruning, Chap. Religious 4; Lay Teachers 36; Students 562.

[C] ELEMENTARY SCHOOLS, INTERPAROCHIAL

KANSAS CITY. *All Saints School*. Consolidated, 809 Vermont, 66101. Tel: 913-342-3669; Fax: 913-621-2709. Lay Teachers 14; Students 241.
Our Lady of Unity School, 2646 S. 34th, 66106. Sr. Delores Long, Prin. Sisters 2; Lay Teachers 11; Students 155.
St. John/Holy Family School. (Consolidated), 515 Ohio & 420 Barnett, 66101. Mary Staley, Prin. Sisters 1; Lay Teachers 11; Students 160.

ATCHISON. *Atchison Catholic Elementary*, 201 Division, 66002. Tel: 913-367-3503. Mrs. Donna McCloskey, Prin. Lay Teachers 22; Students 334.

LEAVENWORTH. *Xavier Elementary School*, Admin. Office, 721 Osage, 66048. Consolidation of the following parishes: St. Casimir (Grades PreK-K); Sacred Heart (Grades 1-3); St. Joseph (Grades 7-8); and Immaculate Conception (Grades 4-6), St. Ignatius, St. Francis de Sales, St. Lawrence, and St. Joseph of the Valley. Margaret O'Sullivan, Prin. Sisters 3; Lay Teachers 24; Students 485.

[D] ELEMENTARY AND SECONDARY SCHOOLS, PRIVATE

SPRING HILL. *Our Lady of Compassion*. P.O. Box 98, Maple Hill, KS, 66507. Tel: 913-256-4500. Rev. Peter Gee, F.S.S.P., Chap.

[E] HIGH SCHOOLS, PRIVATE

ATCHISON. *Maur Hill Prep School*, 66002. Tel: 913-367-5482. Mr. R. Mark Watson, Headmaster; Mr. Mike McGuire, Resident Dir.; Rev. Camillus Wurtz, O.S.B. Profs. Religious 1; Lay Teachers 24; Students 220.
Domestic Department. Misioneras Guadalupanas de Cristo Rey, O.S.B. Sisters 12.
Mount St. Scholastica Academy, 810 R St., 66002. Tel: 913-367-1334. Sisters of St. Benedict. Girls boarding and day high school. Sr. Dorothy Wolters, O.S.B., Pres. Sisters 2; Lay Teachers 12; Students 118.

[F] GENERAL HOSPITALS

KANSAS CITY. *Providence Medical Center*, 8929 Parallel Pkwy., 66112 Fax: 913-596-4098.
For a complete listing, refer to the Hospitals section.

LEAVENWORTH. *St. John Hospital*, 3500 S. 4th St., 66048. Tel: 913-682-3721.
For a complete listing, refer to the Hospitals section.

TOPEKA. *St. Francis Hospital and Medical Center*, 1700 W. 7th St., 66606. Tel: 913-295-8000.
For a complete listing, refer to the Hospitals section.

[G] NURSING AND REST HOMES

KANSAS CITY. *Marian Hall*, 1920 Tauromee, 66102. Tel: 913-621-4302.
For a complete listing, refer to the Special Care Facilities section.
Providence Place, 8909 Parallel, 66112. Tel: 913-596-4200.
For a complete listing, refer to the Special Care Facilities section.
St. Joseph Care Center, 759 Vermont Ave., 66101. Tel: 913-621-6800.
For a complete listing, refer to the Special Care Facilities section.

OVERLAND PARK. *Villa St. Joseph Nursing Home*, 11901 Rosewood, 66209. Tel: 913-345-1745.
For a complete listing, refer to the Special Care Facilities section.

[H] MONASTERIES AND RESIDENCES FOR PRIESTS AND BROTHERS

ATCHISON. *St. Benedict's Abbey*, 66002. Tel: 913-367-5341; Fax: 913-367-6230. Rt. Revs. Barnabus Senecal, O.S.B., Abbot; Owen Purcell, O.S.B., (Retired Abbot); Ralph Koehler, O.S.B., (Retired Abbot); Very Rev. Michael Santa, O.S.B., Prior; Bro. Meinrad Miller, O.S.B., Sub Prior; Revs. Maurice Haefling, O.S.B., Business Mgr.; Peter Beckman, O.S.B.; Mark Broski, O.S.B.; Eugene Dehner, O.S.B.; James Downey, O.S.B.; Emeric Fletcher, O.S.B.; Thomas Flaherty, O.S.B.; Timothy Fry, O.S.B.; Matthew Habiger, O.S.B.; Hilary Heim, O.S.B.; Venard Helget, O.S.B.; Regis Hickey, O.S.B.; Hugh Keefer, O.S.B.; Bertrand LaNoue, O.S.B.; Benedict J. LaRocque, O.S.B.; Meinrad Miller, O.S.B.; Aaron Peters, O.S.B.; Blaine Schultz, O.S.B.; Paul Steingreaber, O.S.B.; Benjamin Tremmel, O.S.B.; Edwin Watson, O.S.B.; Gilbert Wolters, O.S.B.; Michael Zoellner, O.S.B.; Bros. Lawrence Bradford, O.S.B.; Martin Burkhard, O.S.B.; Mark Cason, O.S.B.; Vincent Fitzgerald, O.S.B.; Bede Healey, O.S.B.; Robert Heiman, O.S.B.; John Kaighin, O.S.B.; Walter Landwehr, O.S.B.; Michael Lyons, O.S.B.; Stephen McCann, O.S.B.; Francis Mutter, O.S.B.; John Peto, O.S.B.; Raymond Pfeiffer, O.S.B.; Brendan Rolling, O.S.B.; Joseph Ryan, O.S.B.; Nicholas Tockert, O.S.B.; Gregory Viscek, O.S.B.; Anthony Vorwerk, O.S.B. Bishops 1; Priests 50; Brothers 18.

LAWRENCE. *St. Conrad's Friary*. (Capuchins), 745 Tennessee, 66044. Tel: 913-843-0188. In res., Revs. James Moster, O.F.M.Cap.; Duane F. Reinert, O.F.M.Cap.; Charles Polifka, O.F.M.Cap.; Bros. Benignus Scarry, O.F.M.Cap.; Francisco Ramirez, O.F.M.Cap.; Joseph McGlynn, O.F.M.Cap. Total in Residence 5.

[I] CONVENTS AND RESIDENCES FOR SISTERS

KANSAS CITY. *Convent of the Sisters, Servants of Mary*, 800 N. 18th St., 66102. Tel: 913-371-3423; Fax: 913-621-4962. Ministers to the Sick, Motherhouse of the Congregation for the United States. Nurses, private duty, and visiting nursing in the homes. Mother Alfonsa Bellido, S.M., Prov. Supr.; Rev. Mother Esther Betancourt, S.M., Local Supr.; Rev. Philip Kendall, C.S.V., Chap., St. Peters Cathedral. Professed 37.

ATCHISON. *Dooley Center, Inc.*, 801 S. Eighth St., 66002. Tel: 913-367-6110; Fax: 913-367-3866. Benedictine Sisters of Mount St. Scholastica, Inc., Atchison, KS.

Nursing care facility for the aged/infirmed members of this religious community.

Mount St. Scholastica, 801 S. 8th St., 66002. Tel: 913-367-6110; Fax: 913-367-3866. Motherhouse of the Sisters of St. Benedict. Sr. Mary Agnes Patterson, O.S.B., Prioress.
In community: Professed Sisters 255; Postulants 1; Novices 1. Attended from St. Benedict's Abbey.

LEAVENWORTH. *Motherhouse of the Sisters of Charity of Leavenworth*, 66048-5054. Tel: 913-758-6501; Fax: 913-682-2128. Sr. Mary Kathleen Stefani, Community Dir.; Sr. Jane Jackson, Local Coord.; Sr. Mary Kevin Hollow, Local Admin.; Rev. Daniel O'Shea, O.S.B., Chap. Sisters 458; Total in Residence 136; Novices 1.

PAOLA. *Our Lady of Lourdes Convent*, 901 E. Miami St., 66071. Tel: 913-294-2349.
Motherhouse of the Ursuline Sisters. Sr. Patricia Lynch, O.S.U., Supr.; Rev. Aaron Peters, O.S.B., Chap. Sisters 43.

[J] CAMPUS MINISTRY

EMPORIA. *Didde Catholic Campus Center, Emporia State University*, Office: 1415 Merchant, 66801. Tel: 316-343-6765. Rev. William B. Porter, Chap., 1102 Neosho St., 66801. Tel: 316-342-8727.

LAWRENCE. *Haskell Catholic Campus Center*, 2301 Barker Ave., 66046-4813. Tel: 913-842-2401. Bro. Joseph McGlynn, O.F.M.Cap., Dir.; Rev. Duane F. Reinert, O.F.M.Cap., Chap. Total Staff 2.

St. Lawrence Catholic Campus Center at the University of Kansas and Residence, 1631 Crescent Rd., 66044. Tel: 913-843-0357. Revs. Vincent E. Krische; Raymond May. Total Staff 14.

TOPEKA. *Catholic Campus Center of Washburn University*, 1633 Jewell, 66604. Tel: 913-233-2204.

[K] MISCELLANEOUS LISTINGS

KANSAS CITY. *Casa Juan Diego Centro de Evangelization*, 229 S. 8th, 66101. Tel: 913-342-1276. Rev. Ramon Gaitan, O.A.R.

Catholic Housing Service, Inc., 2220 Central Ave., 66102. Daniel Pope, Coord.

Community Service Center, 2226 Troup, 66104. Tel: 913-371-3148; Fax: 913-371-0970.

Duchesne Clinic, 636 Tauromee, 66101. Tel: 913-321-2626. A division of Caritas Clinics, Inc., Leavenworth, KS. Sr. Janet Cashman, SCL Mgr. Total Staff 7; Total Patients 5,159.

El Centro, Inc., 1333 S. 27th, 66106. Tel: 913-677-0100; Fax: 913-362-8250. Mr. Richard Ruiz, Dir. Sisters 4. 1330 S. 30th St., 66106. Tel: 913-677-1115.

Providence Medical Center Foundation, 8929 Parallel Pkwy., 66112. Tel: 913-596-4882.

St. Vincent de Paul Society-District Council, 619 Grove Ave., 66012. Paul H. Vagner, Jr., Pres.

Shalom Catholic Worker House, 2100 N. 13th, 66104. Tel: 913-321-2206. Total Staff 3; Total Assisted 375.

ATCHISON. *The Maur Hill Prep School Endowment Association, Inc.*, 1000 Green St., 66002. Tel: 913-367-5482. Rev. Edwin P. Watson, O.S.B., Contact Person.

The Mount Community Center, Inc., 751 S. 8th St., 66002. Tel: 913-367-6110. Sr. Noreen Hurter, O.S.B., Dir. of Programs.

EASTON. *Shantivanam Archdiocesan House of Prayer*, 22019 Meagher Rd., 66020. Tel: 913-773-8255. Revs. Joseph F. Nassal, C.PP.S., Dir.; Edward M. Hays. Total in Residence 3; Total Staff 6.

EMPORIA. *Community Service Center*, 116 W. 12th, 66801. Tel: 316-343-2296; Fax: 316-342-9517. Mr. Ron Scott, Dir.

LAWRENCE. *Community Service Center*, 320 Main St., P.O. Box 342, 66044. Tel: 913-841-0307; Fax: 913-832-1710.

LEAVENWORTH. *Caritas Clinics, Inc.*, 511 S. Fifth St., 66048. Tel: 913-651-8860. Sisters of Charity of Leavenworth. Therese Horvat, Pres.; Sr. Ann McGuire, Exec. Dir. Total Staff 6; Total Patients 3,519.

Catholic School Foundation of the Leavenworth Region, Inc., 320 N. Broadway, 66048. Tel: 913-682-7801. Janice Ryan, Exec. Sec., Office of Devel.

Community Service Center, 320 N. Broadway, 66048. Tel: 913-682-0419. Sr. Jane Albert Mehrens, Dir.

Sisters of Charity of Leavenworth Health Services Corporation, 4200 S. 4th St., 66048. Tel: 913-682-1338. Sr. Marie Damian Glatt, S.C.L., Pres.

MAYETTA. *Our Lady of the Snows Catholic Shrine*, Potawatomi Reservation, 66509.

OLATHE. *Community Service Center*, 333 E. Poplar, 66061. Tel: 913-782-4077; Fax: 913-782-0983. Ms. Shirley Kelso, Dir.

PAOLA. *Lakemary Center, Inc.*, 100 Lakemary Dr., 66071-0449. Tel: 913-294-4361. Ursuline Sisters. Dr. William R. Craig, Pres. Serves children and adults with mental retardation. Total Staff 214; Total Assisted 205.

Ursuline Sisters Charitable Trust, 901 E. Miami, 66071. Tel: 913-294-2349.

TOPEKA. *Catholic Community Services Inc.*, 306 Van-Buren, 66603. Tel: 913-233-6300.

Catholic Health Association of Kansas, P.O. Box 2308, 66601. Tel: 913-233-7436.

El Centro de Servicios Para Hispanos, 216 N.E. Branner, 66616. Tel: 913-232-8207; Fax: 913-232-8207.

Marian Clinic, Inc., Medical Plaza Bldg., 1001 Garfield, 66604. Tel: 913-233-8081. Affiliate of Sisters of Charity of Leavenworth Health Services Corp. Sr. Marie Damian Glatt, S.C.L., Pres.; Patricia Hurley, Exec. Dir. Total Patients 10,000.

St. Francis Hospital Foundation, 1700 W. 7th St., 66606. Tel: 913-295-5356; Fax: 913-295-5584.

RELIGIOUS INSTITUTES OF MEN REPRESENTED IN THE ARCHDIOCESE

For further details refer to the corresponding bracketed number in the Religious Institutes of Men or Women section.

[]—*Augustinian Recollects*.—O.A.R.
[0200]—*Benedictine Monks*.—O.S.B.
[0470]—*The Capuchin Friars*. (Holy Family).—O.F.M.Cap.
[0270]—*Carmelite Fathers & Brothers*. (American Prov.).—O.Carm.
[1320]—*Clerics of St. Viator*.—C.S.V.
[0520]—*Franciscan Friars*. (Cincinnati, OH.).—O.F.M.
[]—*Priestly Fraternity of St. Peter*.—F.S.S.P.
[]—*Society of Jesus*.—S.J.
[1060]—*Society of the Precious Blood*.—C.PP.S.
[]—*Vincentian Fathers*.—C.M.

RELIGIOUS INSTITUTES OF WOMEN REPRESENTED IN THE ARCHDIOCESE

[0100]—*Adorers of the Blood of Christ*.—A.S.C.
[0230]—*Benedictine Sisters of Pontifical Jurisdiction*.—O.S.B.
[1170]—*Felician Sisters*.—C.S.S.F.
[1430]—*Franciscan Sisters of Our Lady of Perpetual Help*.—O.S.F.
[3130]—*Our Lady of Victory Missionary Sisters*.—O.L.V.M.
[0480]—*Sisters of Charity of Leavenworth, Kansas*.—S.C.L.
[1520]—*Sisters of St. Francis of Christ the King*.—O.S.F.
[1570]—*Sisters of St. Francis of the Holy Family*.—O.S.F.
[3840]—*Sisters of St. Joseph of Carondelet*. (St. Louis, MO).—C.S.J.
[3830-18]—*Sisters of St. Joseph of Wichita*.—C.S.J.
[3600]—*Sisters, Servants of Mary*.—S.M.
[4120]—*Ursuline Nuns, of the Congregation of Paris*.—O.S.U.

ARCHDIOCESAN CEMETERIES

KANSAS CITY. *St. John's, Mount Calvary, Resurrection, St. Joseph's, Shawnee, and St. John, Lenexa.*
ATCHISON. *Mount Calvary.*
LEAVENWORTH. *Mount Calvary.*
LENEXA. *Holy Trinity.*
TOPEKA. *Mount Calvary.*

NECROLOGY

† Biehler, Rev. Msgr. Joseph E., Flush, KS, St. Joseph Parish. —Died April 11, 1996.
† Curtin, Rev. Msgr. William T., Kansas City, KS, St. Peter's Cathedral. —Died May 26, 1996.
† Zawacki, Carl E., Overland Park, KS, Queen of Holy Rosary Parish. —Died July 24, 1996.

Diocese of Kansas City-St. Joseph

(Dioecesis Kansanopolitanae Sancti Josephi)

Most Reverend

RAYMOND J. BOLAND, D.D.

Bishop of Kansas City-St. Joseph; born February 8, 1932; ordained June 16, 1957; appointed Bishop of Birmingham February 2, 1988; consecrated March 25, 1988; appointed Bishop of Kansas City-St. Joseph June 22, 1993; installed September 9, 1993. *Mailing Address: P.O. Box 419037, Kansas City, MO, 64141-6037.*

Most Reverend

JOHN J. SULLIVAN, D.D.

Former Bishop of Kansas City-St. Joseph; born July 5, 1920; ordained September 23, 1944; appointed Bishop of Grand Island July 25, 1972; consecrated September 19, 1972; installed Grand Island September 21, 1972; appointed Bishop of Kansas City-St. Joseph June 27, 1977; installed August 17, 1977; retired September 9, 1993. *Res., 1236 W. 66th St., Kansas City, MO, 64113.*

DIOCESE OF KANSAS CITY ESTABLISHED SEPTEMBER 10, 1880; DIOCESE OF ST. JOSEPH ESTABLISHED MARCH 3, 1868.

REDESIGNATED DIOCESE OF KANSAS CITY-ST. JOSEPH AUGUST 29, 1956.

Square Miles 15,429.

Comprises the Counties of Andrew, Atchison, Bates, Buchanan, Caldwell, Carroll, Cass, Clay, Clinton, Daviess, DeKalb, Gentry, Grundy, Harrison, Henry, Holt, Jackson, Johnson, Lafayette, Livingston, Mercer, Nodaway, Platte, Ray, Saint Clair, Vernon and Worth in the State of Missouri.

For legal titles of parishes and diocesan institutions, consult the Chancery Office.

Chancery: P.O. Box 419037, Kansas City, MO, 64141-6037. Tel.: 816-756-1850; Fax: 816-756-0878.

STATISTICAL OVERVIEW

Personnel	
Bishop	1
Retired Bishops	1
Abbots	1
Retired Abbots	1
Priests: Diocesan Active in Diocese	75
Priests: Active Outside Diocese	3
Priests: Diocesan in Foreign Missions	1
Priests: Retired, Sick or Absent	53
Number of Diocesan Priests	132
Religious Priests in Diocese	103
Extern Priests in Diocese	3
Ordinations:	
Diocesan Priests	1
Religious Priests	1
Transitional Deacons	3
Permanent Deacons in Diocese	54
Total Brothers	35
Total Sisters	329
Parishes	
Parishes	84
With Resident Pastor:	
Resident Diocesan Priests	58
Resident Religious Priests	21
Without Resident Pastor:	
Administered by Priests	2
Administered by Permanent Deacons	1
Administered by Women Religious	1
Administered by Lay People	1
Missions	15
Welfare	
Catholic Hospitals	3
Total Assisted	161,692
Homes for the Aged	14
Total Assisted	1,014
Day Care and Extended Day Care Centers	14
Total Assisted	303
Residential Care of Disabled	1
Total Assisted	29
Educational	
Diocesan Students in Other Seminaries	8
Seminaries, Religious	1
Students Religious	9
Total Seminarians	17
Colleges and Universities	2
Total Students	3,850
High Schools, Diocesan and Parish	5
Total Students	1,531
High Schools, Private	3
Total Students	1,564
Elementary Schools, Diocesan and Parish	33
Total Students	10,090
Elementary Schools, Private	1
Total Students	265
Catechesis/Religious Education:	
High School Students	1,039
Elementary Students	10,028
Total Students Under Catholic Instruction	28,384
Teachers in the Diocese:	
Priests	4
Brothers	3
Sisters	33
Lay Teachers	1,020
Vital Statistics	
Receptions into the Church:	
Infant Baptism Totals	2,324
Adult Baptism Totals	514
Received into Full Communion	365
First Communions	2,582
Confirmations	1,454
Marriages:	
Catholic	478
Interfaith	497
Total Marriages	975
Deaths	1,202
Total Catholic Population	150,106
Total Population	1,299,555

Former Bishops—Rt. Rev. JOHN JOSEPH HOGAN, D.D., ord. April 10, 1852; cons. Bishop of St. Joseph, MO, Sept. 13, 1868; transferred to Kansas City, Sept. 10, 1880; died Feb. 21, 1913.—Most Rev. THOMAS F. LILLIS, D.D., ord. Aug. 15, 1885; cons. Bishop of Leavenworth, Dec. 27, 1904; appt. Coadjutor to the Bishop of Kansas City, *"cum jure successionis,"* March 14, 1910 Bishop of Kansas City, Feb. 21, 1913; appt. assistant at the Pontifical Throne, Aug. 19, 1935; died Dec. 29, 1938.—Most Rev. EDWIN V. O'HARA, D.D., ord. June 10, 1905; appt. Bishop of Great Falls, MT, August 1, 1930; cons. Oct. 28, 1930; transferred to the See of Kansas City, April 15, 1939 made assistant at the Pontifical Throne, Jan. 5, 1949; appt. Archbishop "ad personam," June 29, 1954; died Sept. 11, 1956.—His Eminence JOHN CARDINAL CODY, S.T.D., ord. Dec. 8, 1931; appt. Titular Bishop of Appollonia and Auxiliary Bishop of St. Louis, May 14, 1947; cons. July 2, 1947; promoted to coadjutor of St. Joseph *"cum jure successionis,"* Jan. 27, 1954; appt. to Diocese of Kansas City-St. Joseph, Aug. 24, 1956; succeeded to Sept. 11, 1956; transferred to Archdiocese of New Orleans as Coadjutor Archbishop *"cum jure successionis,"* Aug. 10, 1961; acceded the See of New Orleans, Nov. 8, 1964; transferred to the Archdiocese of Chicago, June 16, 1965; created Cardinal Priest, June 26, 1967; died April 25, 1982.—Most Rev. CHARLES H. HELMSING, D.D., ord. June 10, 1933; appt. Titular Bishop of Axomis and Auxiliary Bishop of St. Louis, March 17, 1949; cons. April 19, 1949; appt. Bishop of Springfield-Cape Girardeau, Aug. 24, 1956; transferred to Diocese of Kansas City-St. Joseph, Jan. 27, 1962; retired Aug. 17, 1977; died Dec. 20, 1993.—Most Rev. JOHN J. SULLIVAN, D.D., ord. Sept. 23, 1944; appt. Bishop of Grand Island, July 25, 1972; cons. Sept. 19, 1972; installed Grand Island, Sept. 21, 1972; appt. Bishop of Kansas City-St. Joseph, June 27, 1977; installed Aug. 17, 1977; retired Sept. 9, 1993.

Former Bishops of Diocese of St. Joseph, MO—Rt. Rev. JOHN J. HOGAN, D.D., ord. April 10, 1852; appt. first Bishop of St. Joseph, March 3, 1868; cons. Sept. 13, 1868; transferred to See of Kansas City, Sept. 10, 1880 administrator of St. Joseph until 1893; died Feb. 21, 1913.—Rt. Rev. MAURICE F. BURKE, D.D.,born May 5, 1844; ord. May 22, 1875; appt. first Bishop of Cheyenne, Wyoming, Aug. 9, 1887; cons. Oct. 28, 1887; transferred to St. Joseph, June 19, 1893; died March 17, 1923.—Most Rev. FRANCIS GILFILLAN, D.D.,born Feb. 16, 1872; ord. June 24, 1895; appt. titular Bishop of Spigas and Coadjutor with the right of succession to the See of St. Joseph, July 8, 1922; cons. Nov. 8, 1922; succeeded to to the See of St. Joseph, March 17, 1923; died Jan. 13, 1933.—Most Rev. CHARLES H. LEBLOND, D.D., ord. Oct. 27, 1909; appt. Bishop of St. Joseph, July 21, 1933; cons. Sept. 21, 1933; resigned as Bishop of St. Joseph and appointed Titular Bishop of Orcistus, Aug. 24, 1956; died Dec. 30, 1958.

Vicar General—Rev. PATRICK R. RUSH.

Chancery—P.O. Box 419037, Kansas City, 64141-6037. Tel: 816-756-1850; Fax: 816-756-0878. All official matters should be sent to this address.

Chancellor—GEORGE M. NOONAN.

Vice Chancellor—SR. JEAN BESTE, B.V.M.

Diocesan Finance Officer—DAVID A. MALANOWSKI.

Diocesan Tribunal—P.O. Box 419037, Kansas City, 64141-6037. Tel: 816-756-1850.
Judicial Vicar—Rev. C. MICHAEL COLEMAN, J.C.L.
Adjutant Judicial Vicar—Rev. JOSEPH H. MATT, J.C.L.
Canonical Consultant—Rev. RICHARD F. CARNEY, J.C.D.
Defender of the Bond—Sr. MARY HELEN MCINERNEY, S.C.L.
Procurators—Sr. MARY HELEN MCINERNEY, S.C.L.; DONNA EISENBARTH.
Secretary of the Tribunal—CAROLYN RAMM.

Diocesan Consultors—Rev. Msgr. HENRY G. BAUER; Revs. RICHARD CARNEY; C. MICHAEL COLEMAN; JAMES E. HEALY; ROBERT MURPHY; LLOYD E. OPOKA; ROBERT ROST; NORMAN ROTERT; PATRICK J. RUSH; JOHN C. SCHUELE; GERALD WARIS; THOMAS W. WIEDERHOLT.

Presbyteral Council—Rev. MICHAEL E. TIERNEY, Chm.; Rev. KEN RILEY, Vice Chm.; Rev. CHARLES P. TOBIN, Sec./Treas.

Deans—Deanery I: Rev. DONALD P. FARNAN; Deanery II: Rev. ANDREW MEINERS, C.SS.R.; Deanery III: Rev. JOSEPH POWERS; Deanery IV: Rev. JOHN WEISS; Deanery V: Rev. MICHAEL TIERNEY; Deanery VI: Rev. MICHAEL CLARY; Deanery VII: Rev. ROBERT STONE; Deanery VIII: Rev. KENNETH CIRQUI; Deanery IX: Rev. ROBERT CRIDER; Deanery X: Rev. AUGUSTINE DREILING, O.S.B.; Deanery XI: Vacant; Deanery XII: Rev. A. ROBERT MURPHY; Deanery XIII: Rev. ROBERT STEWART; Deanery XIV: Rev. DENIS DOUGHERTY, O.S.B.

Diocesan Offices and Directors

Archivist—Rev. C. MICHAEL COLEMAN, J.C.L.

Building Commission—Revs. MICHAEL RICE; PATRICK J. RUSH, V.G.; DANIEL KENNALEY; Mr. BERNARD J. GRAM, Chm. WILLIAM TURNER; BERNARD JACQUINOT; DAVID GALLAGHER; STEPHEN F. OBARSKI; DAVID A. MALANOWSKI; Sr. JEAN BESTE, B.V.M.; WILLIAM MARKEY; THOMAS REDMOND; WILLIAM FAGAN, (See Property Mgmt. Office).

The "Catholic Key" Diocesan Newspaper—ALBERT DE ZUTTER, Editor, *P.O. Box 419037, Kansas City, 64141-6037.* Tel: 816-756-1859.

Cemetery (Catholic Cemeteries Associated, Diocese of Kansas City-St. Joseph, Inc.)—Rev. ROBERT M. CAMERON, Diocesan Dir., *7601 Blue Ridge, Kansas City, 64138.* Diocesan Cemeteries: Kansas City, Mt. Olivet; Mt. St. Mary; Resurrection; St. Joseph, Mt. Olivet.

Censor Librorum—Rev. Msgr. WILLIAM J. BLACET, J.C.L.

Catholic Charities of Kansas City-St. Joseph, Inc.—1112 Broadway, Kansas City, 64105. Tel: 816-221-4377; Fax: 816-221-9116. *Executive Director:* NEAL D. COLBY, JR., L.I.C.S.W., A.C.S.W. *Assistant Director:* DAVID G. HOWERY, M.A., L.I.C.S.W. *Comptroller:* LEORY RAAB. *Community & Public Relations:* ELINOR DELAY, M.A. *Mental Health Services:* FLORA BOLDRIDGE, L.I.C.S.W., L.P.C., Supvr. *Child Welfare Services:* Mr. GERI SIMMONS, L.M.S.W., Supvr. *In-Home Health Services:* STEPHANIE ROBINSON, M.B.A., Supvr. *Office of Regulatory Compliance:* KIM SUMMERS, M.Ed. *Parish Social Ministry:* VICKIE RIDDLE, A.C.S.W., L.S.C.S.W., Supvr. *Peace and Justice Office:* Sr. MARY ALICE GUILFOIL, O.S.B., Dir., *1310 Westport Rd., Kansas City, 64111.* Tel: 816-931-9744. *Northern Diocesan Branch Office:* KAREN S. HAUSER, Ed.D., L.P.C., Supvr., *1302 Faraon, St. Joseph, 64501.* Tel: 816-232-2885. *Southern Diocesan Branch Office:* SUSAN LOYD, A.C.S.W., L.I.C.S.W., Supvr., *123 E. Gay St., Ste. 2, Warrensburg, 64093.* Tel: 816-747-2241.

Center for Pastoral Life and Ministry—DENISE SIMEONE, Dir.
Ministry Formation—Catechetical Formation: TONY BUTEL; DENISE SIMEONE. Continuing Education: DENISE SIMEONE; CELE BREEN. Heartland Conference: CELE BREEN; TONY BUTEL. Loyola: CELE BREEN; DENISE SIMEONE. New Wine: CELE BREEN; DENISE SIMEONE. Parish Life Summer Institute: TONY BUTEL; DENISE SIMEONE.
Parish Life Development—Christian Initiation: ROSE MULLEN; BIAGIO MAZZA. Evangelization: DALE MOONEY; ROSE MULLEN. Hispanic Ministry: DALE MOONEY; BIAGIO MAZZA. Pastoral Leadership Councils: ROSE THERESE HUELSMAN; BIAGIO MAZZA. Pastoral Leadership Staff: ROSE MULLEN; DALE MOONEY. Religious Education: BIAGIO MAZZA; ROSE MULLEN. Small Christian Communities: ROSE THERESE HUELSMAN; ROSE MULLEN.

Central City School Fund Office—THOMAS SEVERINO, Dir.

Diocesan Annual Appeal—JAMES W. MILLER, Dir.

Diocesan Community Services, Inc.—NEAL D. COLBY, JR., A.C.S.W., L.I.C.S.W., Exec. Dir. RAY AGEE, M.B.A., Housing Coord., *616 E. 63rd St. #208, Kansas City, 64110.* Tel: 816-363-5140; Fax: 816-363-0868.

Diocesan Development—JAMES MILLER, Dir.

Diocesan Ecumenical Officer—GEORGE M. NOONAN.

Diocesan Finance Council—Rev. GERALD R. WARIS; ROBERT AYLWARD; MICHAEL BROSNAHAN; JAMES STACY; JEANNINE STRANDJORD; MARYELLEN CONNOR; DAVID A. MALANOWSKI; JOHN DESTEFANO; JOHN HOULEHAN; THOMAS MCCULLOUGH; JAMES OLSON; SUSAN STANTON; JAMES W. MILLER.

Diocesan Finance Office—DAVID A. MALANOWSKI, Finance Officer; MARYELLEN CONNOR, Internal Auditor; MONICA ADAMS, Accounting Mgr.

Diocesan Insurance Office—MARYELLEN CONNOR, Risk Mgr. PEGGY MCCARTHY, Benefits Coord.

Diocesan Ministry for Persons With Disabilities—JUDY SHUTE, Exec. Sec., *4101 E. 105th Ter., Kansas City, 64137.* Tel: 816-767-0058.

Education Office—Sr. ANNE SHEPARD, Ph.D., O.S.B., Supt., Schools; Sr. CAROL ANN PETERSON, O.S.B., Assoc. Supt. THOMAS BLAKE, Assoc. Supt. Tel: 816-753-6406; 756-1850.

Family Life Office—(Respect Life Activities)—Marriage and Parenting: KENNETH GREENE, Dir.

Holy Childhood Association—Rev. ROBERT M. CAMERON, Dir.

Legion of Mary—Rev. DONALD STURM, Dir.

Office of the Diaconate—Deacon ROSS BEAUDOIN, Dir. Assoc. Dirs.: Rev. MICHAEL COLEMAN; GEORGE NOONAN.

Office of Personnel and Planning—Sr. JEAN BESTE, B.V.M., Dir.

Priests' Purgatorial Society—Rev. ROBERT M. CAMERON, Sec.

Priests' Pension Plan—Administrative Committee: Rev. Msgr. HENRY G. BAUER; Rev. ROBERT M. CAMERON; DAVID A. MALANOWSKI.

Propagation of the Faith—(Pontifical Society for the Propagation of the Faith, Missionary Union of the Clergy and Religious, The Pontifical Society of St. Peter the Apostle for Native Clergy, and Daily World missionaries); Rev. ROBERT M. CAMERON, Dir.

Property Management—WILLIAM TURNER, Dir. JUDITH LISTON, Office Admin. DANIEL KENNALEY, Construction Mgr. Tel: 816-361-8108.

St. Vincent De Paul Particular Council—Sr. PATRICIA BACHMAN, D.C., Moderator.

Vocations—Revs. MICHAEL ROACH, Dir. JOSEPH CISETTI, Assoc. Dir.

Office of Worship—STEPHEN F. OBARSKI, Dir.

Youth Office—WILLIAM CORDARO, Dir.

CLERGY, PARISHES, MISSIONS AND PAROCHIAL SCHOOLS

KANSAS CITY
(Jackson County)

1—CATHEDRAL OF IMMACULATE CONCEPTION (1882). See listing for Old St. Patrick's. Rev. Msgr. Ernest J. Fiedler; Rev. Mario P. Moscaritolo, Pastoral Assoc.
Res., 416 W. 12th St., 64105. Tel: 816-842-0416; Fax: 816-842-1799.

2—ST. MONICA PARISH, Rev. Philip Egan.
Res., 1616 The Paseo, 64108. Tel: 816-471-3696.

3—ST. ALOYSIUS (1886) (Hispanic), Unassigned.
Res., 2611 E. 11th St., 64127. Tel: 816-231-1886.
Catechesis/Religious Programs—Students 61.

4—ST. ANTHONY (1991), Rev. Joseph A. Mancuso.
Res., 318 Benton Blvd., 64124. Tel: 816-231-5445; Fax: 816-231-5446.

5—ST. BERNADETTE'S (1958), Rev. Donald C. Helfrey; Deacon Emory Corrigan.
Res., 9020 E. 51st Ter., 64133. Tel: 816-356-3700; Fax: 816-356-2874.
School—9020 E. 51st Ter., 64133. Tel: 816-356-3702.
Lay Teachers 14; Students 200.
Catechesis/Religious Programs—Tel: 816-356-2874.
Students 180.

6—BLESSED SACRAMENT. Closed. For inquiries for parish records contact the Chancery.

7—ST. CATHERINE OF SIENA (1926), Rev. John C. Schuele; Deacons William Markey; J. Mark Fountain; Josef Walker, Pastoral Assoc. In res., Rev. John P. Coleman.
Res., 4101 E. 105th Ter., 64137-1649. Tel: 816-761-5483; Fax: 816-761-5489.
School—Our Lady of Peace Consolidated School, 10526 Grandview Rd., 64137-1699. Tel: 816-761-5605.
Catechesis/Religious Programs—Fax: 816-761-5483.
Students 47.

8—ST. CHARLES BORROMEO (1947), Revs. John Wolf, C.PP.S.; Paul E. Sattler, C.PP.S.; Garry Richmeier, C.PP.S.; Bro. Robert Herman, C.PP.S.; Deacons Jerry Williams; Frank Peak; John Koch.
Res., 900 N.E. Shady Lane Dr., 64118. Tel: 816-436-0880; Fax: 816-436-0103.
School—804 N.E. Shady Lane Dr., 64118. Tel: 816-436-1009; Fax: 816-436-6293.
Lay Teachers 31; Students 450.
Catechesis/Religious Programs—Students 347.

9—CHRIST THE KING (1938), Revs. John C. Weiss; J. Matthew Rotert.
Res., 8510 Wornall Rd., 64114. Tel: 816-363-4888; Fax: 816-363-2315.
School—425 W. 85th St., 64114. Tel: 816-363-1113.
Lay Teachers 25; Students 340.
Catechesis/Religious Programs—Students 105.

10—ST. ELIZABETH'S (1917), Revs. Robert S. Gregory; Joseph Hughes; Deacon Donald Schmit. In res., Rev. Martin DeMeulenaere, O.S.B.
Res., 7444 Main St., 64114. Tel: 816-523-2405; Fax: 816-444-9858.
School—Tel: 816-523-7100; Fax: 816-523-2566.
Lay Teachers 32; Students 440.
Catechesis/Religious Programs—Students 72.

11—ST. FRANCIS SERAPH. Closed. For inquiries for parish records contact the Chancery.

12—ST. FRANCIS XAVIER (1910), Revs. Timothy M. McMahon, S.J.; James F. Goeke, S.J.
Res., 1001 E. 52nd St., 64110. Tel: 816-523-5115; Fax: 816-333-0082.
School—5220 Troost Ave., 64110. Tel: 816-523-2258.
Lay Teachers 17; Students 220.
Catechesis/Religious Programs—Students 70.

13—ST. GABRIEL ARCHANGEL (1956), Rev. Denis Dougherty, O.S.B.
Res., 4737 N. Cleveland Ave., 64117. Tel: 816-453-1183; Fax: 816-453-6254.
School—Tel: 816-453-4443.
Lay Teachers 16; Students 219.
Early Childhood Learning Center—Tel: 816-453-4555.
Lay Teachers 29; Students 141.
Catechesis/Religious Programs—Students 265.

14—GUARDIAN ANGELS (1909), Margaret Lima, Pastoral Admin.; Rev. C. Thomas Jost, S.J., Pastoral Assoc.
Parish Office: 1310 Westport Rd., 64111. Tel: 816-931-4351; Fax: 816-531-6396.
Schools—Our Lady of the Angels School, 211 W. Linwood, 64111. Tel: 816-931-1693; Fax: 816-753-3606.; Our Lady of Guadalupe School, 2310 Madison, 64111. Tel: 816-221-2539.
Catechesis/Religious Programs—Students 42.

15—HOLY CROSS (1902), Revs. Joseph B. Powers; Raymond Tu; Deacon Charles DiMartino.
Res., 5106 St. John Ave., 64123. Tel: 816-231-4845.

16—HOLY FAMILY (1981), Rev. Robert H. Stewart.
Res., 919 N.E. 96th St., 64155. Tel: 816-436-9200; Fax: 816-436-8049.
Catechesis/Religious Programs—Students 250.

17—CHURCH OF THE HOLY MARTYRS (1991) (Vietnamese), Revs. Joseph Phan Trong Hanh; Raymond Tu.
Res., 7801 Paseo, 64131. Tel: 816-333-3214.
Catechesis/Religious Programs—Tel: 816-333-5349.
Students 320.

18—HOLY ROSARY (1891) (Italian), Rev. Angelo Carbone, C.S.
Res., 911 Missouri Ave., 64106. Tel: 816-842-5440.

19—HOLY TRINITY. Closed. For inquiries for parish records contact the Chancery.

20—ST. JAMES (1906), Rev. William Hubmann, C.PP.S.
Res., 3909 Harrison St., 64110. Tel: 816-561-8512.
Catechesis/Religious Programs—Students 60.

21—ST. JOHN THE BAPTIST. Closed. For inquiries for parish records contact the Chancery.

22—ST. JOHN FRANCIS REGIS (1964), Rev. Paul Turner; Deacons Joseph Clark; Edwin Bonnarens; Marvin Mason.
Res., 8941 James A. Reed Rd., 64138. Tel: 816-761-1608; Fax: 816-966-1350.
School—Tel: 816-763-5837.
Sisters of Charity of the Blessed Virgin Mary 2; Lay Teachers 20; Students 380.
Catechesis/Religious Programs—Tel: 816-763-1366.
Students 216.

23—NEW CATHOLIC COMMUNITY CHURCH. Closed. For inquiries for parish records contact St. Monica Parish.

24—ST. MONICA PARISH, Rev. Philip Egan.
Res., 1616 The Paseo, 64108.
Consolidation of Church of the Risen Christ and St. Joseph.

25—ST. LOUIS (1919) (African American), Rev. Donald Farnan.
Res., 5930 Swope Pkwy., 64130. Tel: 816-444-6535;

Fax: 816-822-2615.
Catechesis/Religious Programs—Students 15.

26—ST. MATTHEW THE APOSTLE (1964), Rev. James Taranto; Deacon Joseph Ofenloch.
Res., 8001 Longview Rd., 64134. Tel: 816-763-0208; Fax: 816-763-4758.
School—Our Lady of Peace Consolidated School, 10526 Grandview Rd., 64134. Tel: 816-761-5605.
Catechesis/Religious Programs—Students 45.

27—ST. MICHAEL ARCHANGEL. Closed. For inquiries for parish records contact the Chancery.

28—OLD ST. PATRICK'S (1869). Public Oratory associated with Cathedral of the Immaculate Conception. Rev. Msgr. Ernest J. Fiedler.
Res., The Cathedral House, 416 W. 12th St., 64105. Tel: 816-842-0416; Fax: 816-842-1799.

29—OUR LADY OF GOOD COUNSEL (1866), Rev. Msgr. William J. Blacet. In res., Rev. John VanGorder.
Res., 3934 Washington, 64111-2904. Tel: 816-561-0400; Fax: 816-561-1551.

30—OUR LADY OF GUADALUPE. Closed. For inquiries for parish records contact the Chancery.

31—SACRED HEART-GUADALUPE (1887) (Hispanic), Rev. James G. Betzen, C.PP.S.
Res., 907 Cesar Chavez Ave., 64108. Tel: 816-842-6146; Fax: 816-471-7540.
Catechesis/Religious Programs—Students 65.

32—OUR LADY OF PEACE (1991), Rev. Michael J. Walker; Deacons Al Ohmes; Manuel Guerra.
Res., 1029 Bennington Ave., 64126-2299. Tel: 816-231-0953.
School—Consolidated School St. Stephen's Academy. See separate listing. Tel: 816-231-5227.

33—OUR LADY OF PERPETUAL HELP (1878), Revs. Gregory Schmitt, C.SS.R.; Andrew Meiners, C.SS.R.; Richard Quinn, C.SS.R.; Bro. James Burke, C.SS.R. In res., Revs. James Springer, C.SS.R.; Edward Kane, C.SS.R.; Bernard Kramer, C.SS.R.
Res., 3333 Broadway, 64111. Tel: 816-561-3771; Fax: 816-561-3704.
School—Our Lady of the Angels, 211 W. Linwood Blvd., 64111. Tel: 816-931-1693; Fax: 816-753-3606. Mary Kallman, Prin.
Sisters 3; Lay Teachers 12; Students 230.

34—OUR LADY OF SORROWS (1891), Rev. Richard F. Carney, J.C.D.
Res., 2552 Gillham Rd., 64108. Tel: 816-421-2112.

35—ST. PATRICK (1924), Rev. Michael G. Roach; Deacon Michael Lewis.
Res., 1357 N.E. 42nd Ter., 64116. Tel: 816-453-5510; Fax: 816-453-4458.
School—1401 N.E. 42nd Ter., 64116. Tel: 816-453-0971.
Lay Teachers 12; Students 220.
Catechesis/Religious Programs—Students 134.

36—ST. PETER'S (1927), Rev. Gerald R. Waris. In res., Rev. Patrick J. Rush, V.G.
Res., 6415 Holmes St., 64131. Tel: 816-363-2320; Fax: 816-363-2492.
School—6400 Charlotte St., 64131. Tel: 816-523-4899; Fax: 816-523-1248.
Sisters 2; Lay Teachers 25; Students 500.
Catechesis/Religious Programs—Students 50.

37—ST. RAPHAEL THE ARCHANGEL, Rev. Alexander B. Sinclair.
Res., 7952 N.E. 54th St., 64119. Tel: 816-453-7449.
Catechesis/Religious Programs—Students 100.

38—ST. STANISLAUS. Closed. For inquiries for parish records contact the Chancery.

39—ST. THERESE LITTLE FLOWER (1925), Rev. Donald Farnan, Sac. Min.; Sr. Helen Flemington, C.S.J., Pastoral Admin.
Res., 5814 Euclid Ave., 64130. Tel: 816-444-5406; Fax: 816-444-9345.
Catechesis/Religious Programs—Students 55.

40—ST. THERESE PARISH (1949), Revs. James Hart; John McCormack, Pastoral Assoc.; Philip Watanabe, Pastoral Assoc.; Joseph Cisetti, Pastoral Assoc.
Res., 7207 Hwy. 9, N.W., Kansas City, 64152. Tel: 816-741-2800; Fax: 816-741-4959.
School—7277 Hwy. 9 N.W., Kansas City, 64152. Tel: 816-741-5400.
Lay Teachers 26; Students 593.
Catechesis/Religious Programs—Tel: 816-741-3957.
Students 473.

41—ST. THOMAS MORE (1964), Revs. William A. Bauman; Robert Kerr.
Res., 11822 Holmes St., 64131. Tel: 816-942-2492; Fax: 816-942-8803.
School—Tel: 816-942-5581; Fax: 816-941-2450.
Lay Teachers 27; Students 569.
Catechesis/Religious Programs—Students 65.

42—VISITATION OF THE BLESSED VIRGIN (1915), Revs. Norman Rotert; Greg Haskamp, Pastoral Assoc. Pastoral Assocs.: Sr. Alice Smitherman, O.S.B.; Peg Ekerdt; Steve Engler; Anne Mcgwire.
Mailing Address: 5141 Main St., 64112. Tel: 816-753-7442; Fax: 816-753-5505.
Res., 2 E. 51st, 64112. Tel: 816-753-6968.
School—Tel: 816-531-6220; Fax: 816-531-2819.
Lay Teachers 24; Students 400.
Catechesis/Religious Programs—5134 Baltimore, 64118.
Students 400.

CITY OF ST. JOSEPH (Buchanan County)

1—ST. JOSEPH'S CO-CATHEDRAL (1845), Rev. Richard Dierkes; Deacons William Dattilo; Richard W. Snooks.
Res., 519 N. 10th St., 64501. Tel: 816-232-7763.
School—518 N. 11th St., 65401. Tel: 816-232-8486.
Lay Teachers 14; Students 237.

2—OUR LADY OF GUADALUPE (1981), Rev. Robert Murphy; Susan Tally, Office Mgr. Pastoral Assocs.: Elizabeth Barmann, Coord. Music/Liturgical Ministries; Julie Lemon, Coord. of Confirmation Process; Kathryn Powers, Coord. of Ministry Devel.; Ellen Simon, Youth Min. Coord.
Church—4503 Frederick, 64506. Tel: 816-232-2847; Fax: 816-232-0269.
Catechesis/Religious Programs—Linda Powers, D.R.E.
Students 468.

3—ST. FRANCIS XAVIER (1890), Revs. James Urbanic, C.PP.S.; Joseph Bathke, C.PP.S. In res., Rev. Bernard Diekhoff, C.PP.S.
Res., 2618 Seneca St., 64507. Tel: 816-232-8449.
School—2614 Seneca St., 64507. Tel: 816-232-9411.
Lay Teachers 21; Students 420.
Catechesis/Religious Programs—Students 89.

4—ST. JAMES (1900), Rev. Vincent Rogers, Admin.; Deacon Robert Farris.
Res., 5814 King Hill Ave., 64504. Tel: 816-238-0853; Fax: 816-238-1758.
School—120 Michigan Ave., 64504. Tel: 816-238-0281.
Benedictine Sisters 1; Lay Teachers 8; Students 205.

5—ST. MARY'S (1891), Rev. Msgr. Victor G. Moser.
Res., 1606 N. 2nd St., 64505. Tel: 816-279-1154.
Catechesis/Religious Programs—Students 64.

6—ST. PATRICK'S (1869), Rev. Matthew Brumleve, Admin. Pastoral Assocs.: Susan Christensen; Deacon Elmer Hoppins.
Office: 1723 S. 12th St., 64503. Tel: 816-279-2594.
School—1813 S. 12th St., 64503. Tel: 816-232-9001; Fax: 816-232-7904.
Lay Teachers 11; Students 149.
Catechesis/Religious Programs—Students 53.

7—QUEEN OF THE APOSTLES. Closed. For inquiries for parish records contact the Chancery.

OUTSIDE THE CITIES OF KANSAS CITY AND ST. JOSEPH

Belton, Cass Co., St. Sabina's (1944), Rev. Joseph H. Matt; Deacon Louie P. Falcon.
Res., 700 Trevis Ave., 64012. Tel: 816-331-4713; Fax: 816-322-6196.
Catechesis/Religious Programs—Students 298.

Bethany, Harrison Co., Blessed Sacrament (1945), Rev. Alexander Luetkemeyer, O.S.B.
Res., 1208 S. 25th St., 64424. Tel: 816-425-8160.
Mission—Cainsville, Harrison Co., St. Mary's, 1208 S. 69 HWY, 64424.

Blue Springs, Jackson Co., St. John La Lande (1938), Revs. Michael O. Clary; Thomas Holder; Deacon John Maloney.
Res., 805 R.D. Mize Rd., 64015. Tel: 816-229-3378; Fax: 816-229-1362.
School—801 R.D. Mize Rd., 64015. Tel: 816-228-5895.
Lay Teachers 20; Students 330.
Catechesis/Religious Programs—Tel: 816-228-4511.
Students 330.

St. Robert Bellarmine (1983), Rev. Lloyd E. Opoka. In res., Rev. Thomas Cronin.
Res., 4313 S. Highway 7, 64014. Tel: 816-229-5168; Fax: 816-229-3981.
Catechesis/Religious Programs—Students 486.

Buckner, Jackson Co., Church of the Santa Fe (1965), Rev. Ralph L. Kaiser.
Res., P.O. Box 317, 64016. Tel: 816-650-9341.

Butler, Bates Co., St. Patrick's, Rev. Richard Ducate.
Res., 400 W. Nursery St., 64730. Tel: 816-679-4482.
Catechesis/Religious Programs—Students 44.
Mission—Rich Hill, Bates Co., St. Bridget's.

Cameron, Clinton Co., St. Munchin (1867) (German-Irish), Rev. Alvin L. Herber, C.PP.S.; Deacon John Riead.
Res., 316 W. Third St., 64429. Tel: 816-632-2768. [CEM][JC 2]
Catechesis/Religious Programs—Tel: 816-632-6276.
Students 217.
Mission—Maysville, DeKalb Co., St. Aloysius.

Carrollton, Carroll Co., St. Mary's (1867), Rev. Kenneth Criqui.
Res., 211 E. Shanklin St., 64633. Tel: 816-542-1259. [CEM]
Catechesis/Religious Programs—Tel: 816-542-1681.
Students 75.

Chillicothe, Livingston Co., St. Columban's, Rev. Reginald Sander, O.S.B.; Deacons Lawrence Schneider, (Retired); Joseph Crookshanks; Jerry Davis.
Res., 1111 Trenton St., 64601. Tel: 816-646-0190. [CEM]
School—Bishop Hogan Memorial School, 1112 Trenton St., 64601. Tel: 816-646-0705.
Lay Teachers 11; Students 153.
Catechesis/Religious Programs—Students 150.

Clinton, Henry Co., Holy Rosary (1875), Rev. Thomas W. Hermes.
Res., 610 S. 4th St., 64735. Tel: 816-885-4523.
School—400 E. Wilson, 64735. Tel: 816-885-4412.
Sisters 1; Lay Teachers 5; Students 97.
Catechesis/Religious Programs—Students 68.
Missions—Osceola, St. Clair Co., St. Catherine's, Hwy. WW, Osceola, 64776. Tel: 417-646-2217; Windsor, Henry Co., St. Bartholomew, 504 E. Benton, Windsor, 65360. Tel: 816-647-2613.

Conception Junction, Nodaway Co., St. Columba (1860), Rev. Augustine Dreiling, O.S.B.; Deacon Martin Goedken.
Res., 1 St. Columba Pl., 64434. Tel: 816-944-2301. [CEM]

Easton, Buchanan Co., St. Joseph's (1830), Rev. Matthew Brumleve, Admin.; Deacon Elmer E. Hoppins; Susan Christensen, Pastoral Assoc.
Res., P.O. Box 197, 64443. Tel: 816-473-2011. [CEM]
Catechesis/Religious Programs—Students 68.

Excelsior Springs, Clay Co., St. Ann (1889), Rev. William Caldwell, Admin.; Deacon John Lauhoff.
Res., 1503 Tracy, 64024. Tel: 816-630-6659.
Catechesis/Religious Programs—Connie Davis, D.R.E.
Students 235.

Gladstone, St. Andrew the Apostle (1964), Rev. Thomas W. Wiederholt.
Res., 6415 N.E. Antioch Rd., 64119. Tel: 816-453-2089; Fax: 816-453-2442.
Catechesis/Religious Programs—Tel: 816-454-7377.
Students 191.

Grandview, Jackson Co., Coronation of Our Lady (1958), Rev. Michael Tierney.
Res., 13000 Bennington, 64030. Tel: 816-761-8811; Fax: 816-761-8812.
Catechesis/Religious Programs—Students 175.

Hamilton, Caldwell Co., Sacred Heart (1921), Rev. Donald E. Sturm.
Res., 205 E. Middle St., 64644. Tel: 816-583-4413.
Catechesis/Religious Programs—Students 55.
Mission—Gallatin, Daviess Co., Mary Immaculate, Hwy. 13, Gallatin, 64640.

Harrisonville, Cass Co., Our Lady of Lourdes (1941), Rev. Bradley S. Offutt.
Res., 2700 N. Highway 7, 64701. Tel: 816-380-5744.
Mission—Pleasant Hill, Cass Co., St. Bridget, (1884) P.O. Box 247, 64701.

Higginsville, Lafayette Co., St. Mary's (1879), Rev. Msgr. Ron Elliott, Pastoral Admin.
Res., 400 W. 29th, 64037. Tel: 816-584-3038. [CEM]

Hirlingen, Buchanan Co., Seven Dolors (1872), Rev. Thomas Waterman.
Res., 12750 Hurlingen Rd., P.O. Box 115, Easton, 64443. Tel: 816-667-5645. [CEM]

Holden, Johnson Co., St. Patrick's, Rev. Ernest L. Gauthier.
Res., 703 S. Olive St., 64040. Tel: 816-732-4516; Fax: 816-732-5595. [CEM]
Catechesis/Religious Programs—Students 70.

Independence, Jackson Co.,

1—ST. ANN'S, (1917), Rev. Terry Bruce.
Res., 10113 Lexington Ave., 64053. Tel: 816-252-1160.
School—Tel: 816-252-1024; Fax: 816-252-3272.
Sisters of St. Francis of the Holy Eucharist 1; Lay Teachers 8; Students 188.
Catechesis/Religious Programs—Students 188.

2—ST. JOSEPH THE WORKER, (1976), Rev. John E. Leitner.
Res., 2200 N. Blue Mills Rd., 64058. Tel: 816-796-6877; Fax: 816-796-6876.
Catechesis/Religious Programs—D.R.E.: Barbara Ganz; Joan Markley, (Adult).
Students 105.

3—St. Mark, (1965), Revs. James E. Healy; Matthew Brumleve; Deacons Philip R. Beaudoin; John R. Thompson.
Res., 3736 Lee's Summit Rd., 64055. Tel: 816-373-2600; Fax: 816-373-3816.
Catechesis/Religious Programs—Joyce Arthur, D.R.E.
Students 316.

4—St. Mary's, Revs. Charles F. Jones; Joseph Meisburger; Deacon Thomas D. Powell.
Res., 611 N. Liberty St., 64050. Tel: 816-252-0121. [CEM]
School—Holy Family. (Consolidated) See separate listing.

5—Nativity of the Blessed Virgin, (1938), Rev. Robert A. Rost, D.Min.
Res., 10017 E. 36th Ter., 64052. Tel: 816-353-2184; Fax: 816-358-5228.
School—10021 E. 36th Ter., 64052. Tel: 816-353-0284.
Lay Teachers 11; Students 240.
Catechesis/Religious Programs—Tel: 816-353-1638.
Students 310.

Kearney, Clay Co., Church of the Annunciation (1980), Rev. Thomas A. Conway, C.PP.S.
Mailing Address: P.O. Box 599, 64060-0599. Tel: 816-628-5030; Fax: 816-628-4279.
Catechesis/Religious Programs—Students 184.

Lee's Summit, Jackson Co., Our Lady of the Presentation (1896), Revs. Michael D. Rice; Kenneth A. Riley; Deacons Joseph Stueve; Del Wilkinson.
Res., 130 N.W. Murray Rd., 64081. Tel: 816-524-3657; Fax: 816-525-8348.
School—Tel: 816-524-4121.
Lay Teachers 20; Students 302.
Holy Spirit (1979), Rev. Roger F. Miller.
Res., 616 S.W. 36th Ter., 64082. Tel: 816-537-7753.
Catechesis/Religious Programs—Tel: 816-537-6990.
Students 93.

Lexington, Lafayette Co., Immaculate Conception (1842), Rev. Franklin J. Lackamp.
Res., 107 N. 18th St., 64067. Tel: 816-259-3043. [CEM]
Catechesis/Religious Programs—Sr. Joyce McNerney, O.S.B., D.R.E.
Students 90.
Mission—Dover, Lafayette Co., St. John the Baptist, Tel: 816-259-4905.

Liberty, Clay Co., St. James (1840), Revs. Ron Will, C.PP.S.; Thomas Ozanne, C.PP.S. In res., Rev. William Dineen, C.PP.S.
Res., 309 S. Stewart Rd., 64068. Tel: 816-781-4343; Fax: 816-781-0747.
School—Tel: 816-781-4428.
Lay Teachers 18; Students 268.
Catechesis/Religious Programs—Students 458.

Maryville, Nodaway Co., St. Gregory Barbarigo (1860), Revs. Chuck Tobin; Donald S. Miller; Deacons Roy Seipel; Martin Schieber.
Res., 333 S. Davis St., 64468. Tel: 816-582-3833; Fax: 816-582-3832. [CEM 2]
School—315 S. Davis St., 64468. Tel: 816-582-2462; Fax: 816-582-2496.
Lay Teachers 13; Students 212.
Newman Center—606 College Ave., 64468. Tel: 816-582-7373. Rev. Xavier Nacke, O.S.B.
Catechesis/Religious Programs—Tel: 816-582-5914.
Students 262.

Montrose, Henry Co., Immaculate Conception (1876) (German), Rev. Robert Stone.
Res., 606 Kansas Ave., 64770-9601. Tel: 816-693-4651. [CEM][JC 2]
School—St. Mary School, Tel: 816-693-4502.
Lay Teachers 3; Students 45.
Mission—Urich, Henry Co., Holy Trinity, 1372 N.W. Grahm Rd., Urich, 64788. Tel: 816-638-4715.
Catechesis/Religious Programs—Students 69.

Nevada, Vernon Co., St. Mary's (1887), Rev. James H. Schrader, C.PP.S.
Res., 330 N. Main St., 64772. Tel: 417-667-5604. [CEM]
School—Tel: 417-67-7517.
Lay Teachers 3; Students 55.
Catechesis/Religious Programs—Students 90.

Odessa, Lafayette Co., St. George (1882), Rev. Donald Cleary.
Res., 716 S. Third, 64076. Tel: 816-230-4127.
Mission—Oak Grove, Jackson Co., St. Jude the Apostle, 2001 S. Broadway, P.O. Box 590, Oak Grove, 64075. Tel: 816-625-3165.
Catechesis/Religious Programs—Students 116.

Parnell, Nodaway Co., St. Joseph's (1891), Rev. Philip Schuster, O.S.B.
Res., P.O. Box 78, 64475. Tel: 816-986-3305. [CEM]
Catechesis/Religious Programs—Students 99.

Plattsburg, Clinton Co., St. Ann's (1866) (Irish), Rev. Robert E. Crider.
Res., 700 Maple St., 64477. Tel: 816-539-2634. [CEM]
Catechesis/Religious Programs—Students 58.

Raytown, Jackson Co., Our Lady of Lourdes (1948), Rev. John Eldringhoff; Deacon Richard Muraski.
Res., 7009 Blue Ridge Blvd., 64133. Tel: 816-353-2380.
School—8812 E. Gregory Blvd., 64133. Tel: 816-353-7062.
Sisters of St. Joseph 2; Lay Teachers 19; Students 217.
Catechesis/Religious Programs—Tel: 816-356-5070.
Students 116.

Richmond, Ray Co., Immaculate Conception (1869), Rev. Mark A. Honhart.
Res., 602 S. Camden, 64085. Tel: 816-470-2268. [CEM]
Catechesis/Religious Programs—Students 96.
Mission—Norbone, Carroll Co., Sacred Heart, 201 E. Fifth St., Norbone, 64668. Tel: 816-594-3536.

Savannah, Andrew Co., St. Rose of Lima, Rev. Thomas K. Ludwig.
Office: 707 Hall Ave., 64485. Tel: 816-324-5700.
Res., 101 E. Park Ave., 64485. Tel: 816-324-3231.
Catechesis/Religious Programs—Students 91.
Mission—Forest City, Holt Co., St. Patrick.

Smithville, Clay Co., Church of the Good Shepherd (1974), Rev. Bernard E. Branson.
Res., 109 Smith St., P.O. Box 653, 64089. Tel: 816-532-4344; 532-0522.
Catechesis/Religious Programs—Tel: 816-532-4404.
Students 130.

Stanberry, Gentry Co., St. Peter's (1880), Rev. Daniel Petche, O.S.B.
Res., 614 N. Alanthus Ave., 64489. Tel: 816-783-2159. [CEM]
Catechesis/Religious Programs—Students 160.
Mission—Ford City, Gentry Co., St. Patrick's, King City 64463.

Sugar Creek, Jackson Co., St. Cyril (1912) (Croatian-Slovak), Rev. Walter J. Pilecki.
Res., 11231 Chicago Ave., 64054. Tel: 816-252-9564.

Tarkio, Atchison Co., St. Paul the Apostle (1890), Rev. Quentin Kathol, O.S.B.
Res., 908 Elm St., 64491. Tel: 816-736-4342.
Catechesis/Religious Programs—Students 50.
Mission—Burlington Junction, Nodaway Co., St. Benedict Catholic Church, Burlington Junction, 64428. Tel: 816-725-4407.

Trenton, Grundy Co., St. Joseph's (1872), Rev. Edgar Probstfield, O.S.B.
Res., 1728 St. Joseph Ave., 64683. Tel: 816-359-2841. [CEM]
Mission—Trenton, Mercer Co., Immaculate Heart of Mary Church, 1728 St. Joseph Ave., 64683. [JC]
Catechesis/Religious Programs—Students 68.

Warrensburg, Johnson Co., Sacred Heart (1865), Rev. William P. Walter, C.PP.S.
Res., 200 Ming St., P.O. Box 926, 64093. Tel: 816-747-6154.
Catechesis/Religious Programs—Tel: 816-747-5965.
Students 134.

Weston, Platte Co., Holy Trinity (1842), Rev. Thomas Hawkins.
Res., 407 Cherry St., 64098. Tel: 816-640-2206. [JC]
Catechesis/Religious Programs—Students 120.

Special Assignment:
Reverend Fathers—
Cameron, Robert, 7601 Blue Ridge, Kansas City, MO 64138
Coleman, C. Michael, J.C.L., P.O. Box 419037, Kansas City, MO 64141-6037
Jankowski, Marcellus A., 6515 E. 7th St., Kansas City, MO 64612
Karels, Ambrose G., P.O. Box 410834, Kansas City, MO 64141
Mahoney, Robert J., Rockhurst College, Sociology Dept., 5225 Troost Ave., Kansas City, MO 64110
Rush, Patrick J., V.G., P.O. Box 419037, Kansas City, MO 64141-6037

On Duty Outside the Diocese:
Reverend Fathers—
Blais, Roger
Cronin, Thomas
Holloway, David L.

Mission Duty:
Reverend Fathers—
Gillgannon, Michael, Casilla 12162, La Paz, Bolivia

Leave of Absence:
Reverend Fathers—
Arciga, Michael
Savidge, Peter
Townsend, C. Frederick
Turner, Thomas
Verhaeghe, Ronald

Unassigned:
Reverend Fathers—
Deming, Robert N.

Retired:
Reverend Monsignors—
Bauer, Henry, 6425 Woodson, Kansas City, MO 64133
Froeschl, Martin H., P.O. Box 201, Oregon, MO 64473
Harper, James J., P.O. Box 5068, Bella Vista, AR 72714
Huhmann, John F., 10515 Bridlespur Dr., Kansas City, MO 64114-4712
Kearney, Vincent L., 12655 State Line, Kansas City, MO 64145
O'Brien, Thomas J., 11281 Oak, Apt. 101, Kansas City, MO 64114-5446
Summers, R. Emmett, 4114 N.E. Davidson Rd., Apt 314, Kansas City, MO 64116
Reverend Fathers—
Bachnak, Francis J., 705A Maple St., Plattsburg, MO 64477
Blaes, Paul, M.A., Ph.D., 1589 Carrollwood Rd., Sarasota, FL 34232
Boyle, Leo A., Marymount Place, 11960 McCracken Rd., Garfield Heights, OH 44125
Byrne, Robert, 2104 Elm St., Higginsville, MO 64037
Carson, Paul C., 1036 W. Main, Bethany, MO 64424
Coleman, John P., 4101 E. 105th Ter., Kansas City, MO 64137
Faller, Henry E., Jeanne Jugan Center, 8745 James A. Reed Rd., Kansas City, MO 64138
Giacopelli, John A., 494 Clinton St., Brooklyn, NY 11231
Hoppe, Sylvester J., 918 S. Noyes Blvd., St. Joseph, MO 64507
Jakubowski, Joseph J., 1131 Central, Apt. 1110, Kansas City, KS 66102
Link, Linus F., 7030 N. Bales, Apt. 337, Gladstone, MO 64119
Lyons, James P., 9001 James A. Reed Rd., Kansas City, MO 64138
Mahoney, Jeremia W., Jeanne Jugan Center, 8745 James A. Reed Rd., Kansas City, MO 64138
McCarthy, Thomas H., 3303 Urban Crest Dr., San Antonio, TX 78209
McGlynn, Francis, 700 E. Eigth St., #910, Kansas City, MO 64106
McQuinn, Maurice, 115 W. 99th Terrace, No 102, Kansas City, MO 64114
Meisburger, Joseph C., 611 N. Liberty, Independence, MO 64050
Mifkovic, Francis S., P.O. Box 7606, Colorado Springs, CO 80933
Miller, Donald S., 333 S. Davis, Maryville, MO 64468
Mullin, Hugh J., 2100 Nursery Rd., Bldg. A-4, Clearwater, FL 34624
O'Connor, Patrick, Rte. 3, Box 32, Butler, MO 64730
Paa, Donald R., 1500 W. 23rd Ter., Apt. 3, Independence, MO 64050
Pecoraro, James A., 410 W. 104th St., Apt. A., Kansas City, MO 64114
Powell, Harold W., 333-A Front St., Grain Valley, MO 64029
Powers, Donald E., P.O Box 535, Roach, MO 65787
Russ, Francis J., 12900 E. 62nd, Kansas City, MO 64133
Ryan, C. Duane, Rt. 2, Box 335, Sunrise Beach, MO 65079
Ryan, Clarence R., 1901 Forrest Ave., Lexington, MO 64067
Saale, Richard T., 8800 Buckingham Ln., Apt. 14, Kansas City, MO 64138
Speichinger, Lawrence, Rt.3 Box 22, Chillicothe, MO 64601
Van Gorder, John, 3934 Washington, Kansas City, MO 64111
Ward, Thomas, 3600 Poplar, Independence, MO 64052
Whelan, Thomas, 3644 Rocky River Dr., Cleveland, OH 44111

Permanent Deacons:
Barry, James Timothy
Beaudoin, Phillip Ross
Bode, William
Bonnarens, Edwin
Browning, Melvin

Cathers, Calvin
Clark, Joseph P.
Corrigan, Emory S.
Crookshanks, Joseph V.
Dattilo, William
Davis, F. Jerry
DiMartino, Charles
Elliot, Ronald
Ernst, John H.
Falcon, Francis L.
Falcon, Louie P.
Farris, Robert E.
Fountain, Mark J.
Gach, Victor S.
Goedken, Martin J.
Guerra, Manuel P.
Henggeler, Francis J.
Hoppins, Elmer E.
Koch, John J.
Kopp, George C.
Kopp, Harold G., Sr.
Kratofil, Lawrence
Langdon, Harry
Lauhoff, John D.
Lewis, Michael
Lickteig, Wayne A.
MacKinnon, William, III
Madden, Donald
Maloney, John J.
Markey, William R.
Mason, Marvin M.
McArdle, Paul
McCandless, Donald L.
McCoy, Warren W.
McKay, Clarence W.
McMenamy, Justin M.
Muraski, Richard J.
Ofenloch, Joseph C.
Ohmes, Albert J.
Peak, Francis L.
Powell, D. Thomas
Riead, John
Rodman, Harold M.
Sandoval, Antonio J.
Santellan, Alfred M.
Schieber, Martin L.
Schmit, Donald A.
Schneider, Lawrence
Seipel, Leroy
Snooks, Richard W.
Stoetzer, Jerome P.
Stueve, Joseph E.
Thompson, John R.
Wilkinson, Del
Williams, Garen R.
Williams, Jerry

INSTITUTIONS LOCATED IN THE DIOCESE

[A] SEMINARIES, RELIGIOUS OR SCHOLASTICATES

KANSAS CITY. *Precious Blood Mission House*, 5221 Rockhill Rd., 64110. Tel: 816-822-2596. Revs. Mark Miller, C.PP.S., Provincial Dir.; William Hubmann, C.PP.S.; James Betzen, C.PP.S.

CONCEPTION. *Conception Seminary College*, 64433. Tel: 816-944-2218. Rt. Rev. Gregory Polan, O.S.B., Chancellor; Revs. Benedict Neenan, O.S.B., Pres.-Rector; Albert Bruecken, O.S.B.; Roland Carbone, O.S.B.; Patrick Caveglia, O.S.B.; Donald Grabner, O.S.B.; Thomas Greisen (OM); James Jones, O.S.B.; Xavier Nacke, O.S.B.; Daniel Petsche, O.S.B.; James Polich; Kenneth Reichert, O.S.B.; Duane Reinert, O.F.M.Cap.; Samuel Russell, O.S.B.; Alexis Saathoff, O.S.B.; Timothy Schoen, O.S.B.; Hugh Tasch, O.S.B.; Benoit Thivierge, O.S.B.; Isaac True, O.S.B.; Peter Ullrich, O.S.B. Priests 20; Brothers 6; Lay Professors 6; Students 64.

LIBERTY. *Precious Blood Center.* (Kansas City Province), 2110-2140 Hughes Rd., 64068. Tel: 816-781-4344; Fax: 816-781-3639. Bro. Stephan Ohnmacht, C.PP.S., Local Dir. Priests 7; Brothers 2.

Society of the Precious Blood Provincial Offices, 2130 Hughes Rd., P.O. Box 339, 64068. Tel: 816-781-4344; Fax: 816-781-3639. Revs. William Walter, C.PP.S., Prov. Vice; Mark Miller, C.PP.S., Prov. Dir.; Ronald Will, C.PP.S., Prov. Sec.; William Dineen, C.PP.S., Prov. Treas.

[B] COLLEGES AND UNIVERSITIES

KANSAS CITY. *Avila College*, 11901 Wornall Rd., 64145-1698. Tel: 816-942-8400; Fax: 816-942-3362.
For a complete listing, refer to the Colleges and Universities section.

Rockhurst College, 1100 Rockhurst Rd., 64110-2561. Tel: 816-501-4000; Fax: 816-501-4588.
For a complete listing, refer to the Colleges and Universities section.

[C] HIGH SCHOOLS, DIOCESAN

KANSAS CITY. *Archbishop O'Hara High School.* (Coed), 9001 James A. Reed Rd., 64138. Tel: 816-763-4800. Mr. Walter Bowman, Prin. Christian Brothers 3; Lay Teachers 42; Students 491.

Bishop Hogan High School, 1221 E. Meyer Blvd., 64131. Tel: 816-444-3464. Ms. Elizabeth Onik, Prin. Lay Teachers 16; Students 219.

St. Pius X High School, 1500 N.E. 42nd Ter., 64116. Tel: 816-453-3450. Edward P. Carlin, Ph.D., Prin. Sisters of Charity of Leavenworth 2; Lay Teachers 23; Students 287.

ST. JOSEPH. *Bishop LeBlond High School*, 3529 Frederick Ave., 64506. Tel: 816-279-1629. Sr. Corrine Connelly, R.S.M., Prin.; Rev. Thomas K. Ludwig, Chap. Priests 1; Lay Teachers 24; Students 265.

INDEPENDENCE. *St. Mary's Diocesan High School-Bundschu Memorial*, 622 N. Main St., 64050. Tel: 816-252-8733. David Woolwine, Pres.; Joseph Mintner, Prin. Lay Teachers 20; Students 268.

[D] HIGH SCHOOLS, PRIVATE

KANSAS CITY. *De La Salle Academy*, 3732 Paseo, 64109. Tel: 816-531-6561. Christian Brothers, F.S.C. and LaSallian Volunteers.

Notre Dame de Sion High School, 10631 Wornall Rd., 64114. Tel: 816-942-3282. Affiliated with Sisters of Notre Dame de Sion. Alice Munninghoff, Head of School; Michelle Olson, Prin. Lay Teachers 26; Students 283.

Rockhurst High School, 9301 State Line Rd., 64114. Tel: 816-363-2036. Revs. Thomas A. Pesci, S.J., Pres.; Christopher P. Pinne, S.J., Superior; David J. Suwalsky, S.J.; Mark J. Daues, S.J.; Bro. Lawrence W. Eilert, S.J.; Deacon R. Mark Michalski, S.J., Scholastic. Jesuit Priests 4; Lay Teachers 56; Students 839.

St. Teresa's Academy, 5600 Main St., 64113. Tel: 816-523-3522; Fax: 816-523-0232. Affiliated with Sisters of St. Joseph of Carondelet. Dr. Faith Wilson, Ph.D., Pres.; Mary Anne Hoecker, M.A., Assoc. Prin.; Nancy Hand, M.A., Assoc. Prin. Sisters 5; Lay Teachers 31; Students 450.

[E] ELEMENTARY SCHOOLS

KANSAS CITY. *Our Lady of Guadalupe School*, 2310 Madison, 64108. Tel: 816-221-2539. Sr. Eileen Haynes, Prin. Sisters 1; Lay Teachers 5; Students 104.

Our Lady of Peace School, 10526 Grandview Rd., 64137. Tel: 816-761-5605. Mrs. Mary Ann Long, Prin. Lay Teachers 20; Students 433.

St. Monica School. (Grades PreK-8), Elementary: 5809 Michigan, 64130. Tel: 816-444-6736. Sr. Michael Delores Allegri, S.C.L., Prin. Sisters 2; Lay Teachers 23; Students 320.

St. Stephen's School, 1001 Bennington, 64126. Tel: 816-231-5227. Rev. Michael Walker; Sr. Leona Bax, O.S.F., Prin. Sisters 4; Lay Teachers 10; Students 186.

[F] ELEMENTARY SCHOOLS, PRIVATE

KANSAS CITY. *Notre Dame de Sion Elementary & Middle School*, 3823 Locust St., 64109. Tel: 816-753-3810; Fax: 816-753-0806. Affiliated with Sisters of Notre Dame de Sion. Alice Munninghoff, Head of School; Susan Roitman, Elementary Prin.; Barbara Altergott, Middle Prin. Lay Teachers 23; Students 262.

[G] GENERAL HOSPITALS

KANSAS CITY. *Saint Joseph Health Center*, 1000 Carondelet Dr., 64114. Tel: 816-942-4400.
For a complete listing, refer to the Hospitals section.

BLUE SPRINGS. *St. Mary's Hospital of Blue Springs*, 201 W. R.D. Mize Rd., 64014. Tel: 816-228-5900; Fax: 816-228-7555.
For a complete listing, refer to the Hospitals section.

MARYVILLE. *St. Francis Hospital & Health Services*, 2016 S. Main, 64468. Tel: 816-562-2600; Fax: 816-562-2411.
For a complete listing, refer to the Hospitals section.

[H] SPECIAL CARE UNITS

BLUE SPRINGS. *St. Mary's Manor*, 111 Mock Ave., 64014. Tel: 816-228-5655.
For a complete listing, refer to the Special Care Facilities section.

LIBERTY. *Immacolata Manor Foundation*, 2101 Hughes Rd., 64068-9397. Tel: 816-781-4332; Fax: 816-781-8820.
For a complete listing, refer to the Special Care Facilities section.

[I] HOMES FOR THE ELDERLY

KANSAS CITY. *Brighton Place*, 2429 Brighton, 64127. Tel: 816-231-3211.
For a complete listing, refer to the Special Care Facilities section.

Cathedral Square Towers, 444 W. 12th St., 64105. Tel: 816-471-6555.
For a complete listing, refer to the Special Care Facilities section.

Columbus Park Plaza, 801 Pacific, 64106. Tel: 816-472-0887.
For a complete listing, refer to the Special Care Facilities section.

Jeanne Jugan Center, 8745 James A. Reed Rd., 64138. Tel: 816-761-4744; Fax: 816-761-4724.
For a complete listing, refer to the Special Care Facilities section.

Marlborough Manor, 1818 E. 79th St., 64132. Tel: 816-221-4377.
For a complete listing, refer to the Special Care Facilities section.

Red Bridge Place, 11300 Colorado, 64137. Tel: 816-761-4667.
For a complete listing, refer to the Special Care Facilities section.

Redemptorist Retirement Home, 207 W. Linwood, 64111-1327. Tel: 816-561-3025.
For a complete listing, refer to the Special Care Facilities section.

Tremont Place, 6161 N. Chatham, 64151. Tel: 816-587-7707.
For a complete listing, refer to the Special Care Facilities section.

LIBERTY. *Our Lady of Mercy Country Home*, 2205 Hughes Rd., 64068. Tel: 816-781-5711.
For a complete listing, refer to the Special Care Facilities section.

SAVANNAH. *La Verna Heights Retirement Center, Inc.*, 104 E. Park Ave., P.O. Box 488, 64485-0488. Tel: 816-324-3179.
For a complete listing, refer to the Special Care Facilities section.

La Verna Village Apartments, 1000-1005 Hall Ave., 64485. Tel: 816-324-3179.
For a complete listing, refer to the Special Care Facilities section.

La Verna Village Nursing Home, 904 Hall Ave., P.O. Box 279, 64485. Tel: 816-324-3185; Fax: 816-324-4097.
For a complete listing, refer to the Special Care Facilities section.

[J] MONASTERIES AND RESIDENCES OF PRIESTS

KANSAS CITY. *Arrupe Jesuit Community*, 3135 Karnes Blvd., 64111. Tel: 816-531-0806. Revs. C. Thomas Jost, S.J., Supr.; William H. Steiner, S.J.

Redemptorists of Kansas City, 3333 Broadway Blvd., 64111. Tel: 816-561-3771. Very Rev. Gregory Schmitt, C.SS.R., Rector; Revs. Andrew Meiners, C.SS.R.; Richard M. Quinn, C.SS.R.; Edward Kane, C.SS.R.; Bernard Kramer, C.SS.R.; James Springer, C.SS.R.; Bros. James Burke, C.SS.R.; Marvin Hamann, C.SS.R. Priests 6; Brothers 2.

Rockhurst College - Jesuit Community, 5133 Forest Ave., 64110. Tel: 816-926-0012. Revs. Thomas N. Lay, S.J., Rector; Frank L. Pedrotti, S.J., Minister; Peter B. Ely, S.J., Pres. of College; E. Eugene Arthur, S.J.; Jules M. Brady, S.J.; Martin J. Bredeck, S.J.; Edward K. Burger, S.J.; Robert R. Burke, S.J.; Michael P. Caruso, S.J.; Thomas J. Casey, S.J.; Thomas F. Denzer, S.J.; Joseph M. Freeman, S.J.; Joseph E. Gough, S.J.; Wilfred L. LaCroix, S.J.; Frank J. Murphy, S.J.; Walter G. Nesbit, S.J.; Louis J. Oldani, S.J.; Maurice E. Van Ackeren, S.J.; James D. Wheeler, S.J.; Bro. John R. Olson, S.J.; Mr. Gerard A. Schroeder, S.J. Total in Residence 21.

Rockhurst High School - Jesuit Community, 9301 State Line Rd., 64114. Tel: 816-363-2036, Ext. 294. Revs. Christopher P. Pinne, S.J., Sup.; Thomas A. Pesci; David J. Suwalsky, S.J.; Mark J. Dues, S.J.; Bro. Lawrence W. Eilert, S.J.; Deacon R. Mark Michalski, S.J.

St. Francis Xavier - Jesuit Community, 1001 E. 52nd St., 64110. Tel: 816-523-5142. Revs. Timothy M. McMahon, S.J.; James F. Goeke, S.J.

Vincentian Parish Mission Center, 2100 N. Noland Rd., 64050. Tel: 816-254-3000; Fax: 816-836-9922. Revs. Richard Gielow, C.M.; Francis Crowley, C.M.; Richard O'Brien, C.M.; Michael Mulhearn, C.M.; Thomas Cawley, C.M.; Carl G. Schulte, C.M., Supr.

CONCEPTION. *Conception Abbey*, 64433. Tel: 816-944-2211; Fax: 816-944-2800. Very Rev. Kenneth Reichert, O.S.B., Prior; Rt. Revs. Anselm Coppersmith, O.S.B., Retired Abbot; James Jones, O.S.B., Retired Abbot; Revs. Alexis Saathoff; Patrick Caveglia; Samuel Russell; Benoit Thivierge; Luke Becker, O.S.B.; Albert Bruecken, O.S.B., Subprior; Richard J. Cleary, O.S.B.; Martin DeMeulenaere, O.S.B.; Conrad Falk, O.S.B.; Lawrence Gidley, O.S.B.; Donald Grabner, O.S.B.; Placid Immegart, O.S.B.; Quentin Kathol, O.S.B., (Pastor at Tarkio so included there.); Aidan McSorley, O.S.B.; Alfred Meyer,

O.S.B.; Benedict Neenan, O.S.B.; Daniel Petsche, O.S.B.; Regis Probstfield, O.S.B.; Aelred Rosser, O.S.B.; Adam Ryan, O.S.B.; Norbert Schapper, O.S.B.; Timothy Schoen, O.S.B.; Gilbert Stack, O.S.B.; Augustine Stock, O.S.B.; Kilian Sullivan, O.S.B.; Hugh Tasch, O.S.B.; Paschal Thomas, O.S.B.; Isaac True, O.S.B.; Peter Ullrich, O.S.B. Benedictine Monks. Priests 54; Brothers 23.

LIBERTY. *Precious Blood Center*, 2130 Hughes Rd., 64068. Tel: 816-781-4344. Bro. Stephen Ohnmacht, C.PP.S., Supr.; Revs. Ralph Bushell, C.PP.S.; Thomas Conway, C.PP.S.; Thomas Ozanne, C.PP.S.; David Dougherty, C.PP.S.; Edmund Weigel, C.PP.S.; Ronald Will, C.PP.S.; Jack McClure; Bro. Joseph Mary Hrezo.

Precious Blood Society Provincial Office, P.O. Box 339, 64068. Tel: 816-781-4344; Fax: 816-781-3639. Very Rev. Mark Miller, C.PP.S., Prov. Dir.; Revs. Ronald Will, C.PP.S., Prov. Sec.; William Dineen, C.PP.S., Prov. Treas. Priests 7; Brothers 2.

[K] CONVENTS AND RESIDENCES FOR SISTERS

KANSAS CITY. *Mercederian Missionaries of Berriz*, U.S. Regional Headquarters, 1400 N.E. 42nd Ter., 64116. Tel: 816-454-1344. Sr. Delia Gomez, M.M.B. Mercedarian Missionaries of Berriz 11.

Sisters of Notre Dame de Sion, 3627 Gillham Rd. #34, 64111. Tel: 816-531-1374. Sisters 2.

Sisters of the Society of Our Lady of the Most Holy Trinity, 3738 Tracy, 64109. Tel: 816-561-8849. Society of Apostolic Life. Sisters 2.

BLUE SPRINGS. *Our Lady of the Springs Community*, 731 N. 6th St., 64014-2404. Tel: 816-228-3739. Franciscan Sisters of Mary 3.

CLYDE. *Benedictine Convent of Perpetual Adoration*, 64432. Tel: 816-944-2221; Fax: 816-944-2133. Sisters 45. Attended by Conception Abbey.

INDEPENDENCE. *St. Francis Convent Novitiate and Prayer Center*, 2100 N. Noland Rd., 64050. Tel: 816-252-1673; Fax: 816-252-5574. Motherhouse of the Sisters of St. Francis of the Holy Eucharist. Sr. M. Connie Boulch, O.S.F., Supr. Sisters 24.

LIBERTY. *Queen of Angels Monastery - Benedictine Sisters*, 717 Kings Hwy., 64068. Tel: 816-781-6246. Sr. Mary Imelda Koch, O.S.B., Prioress. Sisters 7; Total in Residence 11.

MARYVILLE. *St. Francis Convent*, 2022 S. Main, R.R. 1, Box 135, 64468-2655. Tel: 816-582-4005. Franciscan Sisters of Mary. Franciscan Sisters of Mary 3.

PARKVILLE. *Sisters of the Third Franciscan Order*, 6108 B N.W. Hwy. 9, 64152.

SAVANNAH. *La Verna Heights Provincial House*, 104 E. Park, Box 488, 64485-0488. Tel: 816-324-3179; Fax: 816-324-6512. Sisters of St. Francis of Savannah, MO. Motherhouse and Novitiate. Rev. Walter Heeney, O.S.B., Chap. Sisters 31.

Maintenance and Custodial Care Trust of the Franciscan Sisters of Savannah, MO. Total Assisted 2,543; Total Staff 25.

[L] RETREAT ACTIVITY CENTERS

KANSAS CITY. *St. John's Diocesan Center*, 2015 E. 72nd St., 64132. Tel: 816-363-3585. Sr. Marion Renkens, C.S.J., Dir. Retreat and Conference Center for Groups of all Denominations.

[M] SERVICES

KANSAS CITY.

**Seton Center*, 2816 E. 23 St., 64127. Tel: 816-231-3955. Rachel A. Asaro, Dir. Total Assisted 6,000; Total Staff 19.

[N] NEWMAN CENTERS

KANSAS CITY. *Avila College Campus Ministry*, 11901 Wornall, 64145. Rev. Daniel Torson, C.PP.S., Dir. of Campus Ministry.

MARYVILLE. *Northwest Missouri State University Newman House*, The Newman House, 606 College Ave., 64468. Tel: 816-582-7373. Rev. Xavier Nacke, O.S.B.

WARRENSBURG. *Central Missouri State University Newman Center*, 106 Broad St., 64093. Tel: 816-747-6997. Anthony Caudillo, Dir.

[O] MISCELLANEOUS

KANSAS CITY. *Benedictine Counseling and Consulting Institute*, 4737 N. Cleveland, 64117. Tel: 816-453-1183. Rev. Denis Dougherty, O.S.B., Ph.D., Dir. Total Assisted 200.

**Bishop Sullivan Center*, 6435 Truman Rd., 64126. Tel: 816-231-0984; Fax: 816-231-3096. Rev. Thomas W. Turner, Dir. Total Assisted 10,000; Total Staff 9.

Brighton Place, 2429 Brighton, 64127.

Camp Little Flower, 300 E. 36th St., P.O. Box 419037, 64141. Tel: 816-756-1850.

Catholic Woman's Club, 300 E. 36th St., P.O. Box 419037, 64141. Tel: 816-756-1850. Rev. Thomas Hernes, Diocesan Moderator.

Diocesan Council of Catholic Women, 300 E. 36th St., P.O. Box 419037, 64141. Tel: 816-756-1850. Rev. Joseph A. Mancuso, Diocesan Moderator.

Diocesan Education Endowment Trust Fund, 300 E. 36th St., P.O. Box 419037, 64111. Tel: 816-756-1850. Mr. James W. Miller, Contact Person.

Friends, Inc., 300 E. 36th St., P.O. Box 419037, 64141-6037. Tel: 816-756-1850.

Immacolata Retreat Center, 300 E. 36th St., P.O. Box 419037, 64141-6037. Tel: 816-756-1850.

Knights of St. Peter Claver (K.P.C.). Ladies Auxiliary of St. Peter Claver. 1616 Paseo, St. Monica Parish, 64108. Tel: 816-471-3696.

Ladies of Charity of Metropolitan Kansas City, Seton Center, 2816 E. 23rd St., 64127. Tel: 816-942-5311. Mrs. Helen C. Cooke, Pres.

Marillac Home for Children, P.O. Box 419037, 64141-6037.

Our Lady of Perpetual Help Charitable Trust, 3333 Broadway, 64111. Tel: 816-561-3771. Rev. Gregory Schmitt, Contact Person.

Red Bridge Place, 11300 Colorado, 64137.

St. Anthony's Home, 300 E. 36th St., P.O. Box 419037, 64141-6037. Tel: 816-756-1850.

St. John's Seminary, Inc., P.O. Box 419037, 64141-6037.

Siena Club, 300 E. 36th St., P.O. Box 419037, 64141. Tel: 816-756-1850.

Society of Our Lady of the Most Holy Trinity, 3704 Tracy, 64109. Tel: 816-931-9131. Rev. Eckley Macklin.

CONCEPTION. *Conception Benedictine Trust*, 64433. Tel: 816-944-2580; Fax: 816-944-2800. Very Rev. Kenneth Reichert, O.S.B., Pres.; Revs. Mark Kosiba, O.S.B., Vice Pres.; Albert Bruecken, O.S.B., Sec.-Treas.

Pontifical Institute of Liturgy Foundation, Conception Abbey, 64433. Tel: 816-944-2211; Fax: 816-944-2800. Rt. Rev. Marcel Rooney, O.S.B., Pres.

LEE'S SUMMIT. *Mercy Midwest Properties*, 920 Northeast Ridgeview Dr. #A, 64086. Tel: 816-525-0990; Fax: 816-524-0078. Mercy Housing Midwest: 7262 Mercy Rd., Ste. 102, Omaha, NE, 68124-2348. Tel: 402-398-6614; Fax: 402-398-6370. Sr. Carolyn Coffey, R.S.M., Dir. Affordable Housing for Low-Income Families.

LIBERTY. *Our Lady of Mercy Home*, 2205 Hughes Rd., 64068-9469. Tel: 816-781-5711.

**St. Gaspar Society*, P.O. Box 339, 64068. Tel: 816-781-4344; Fax: 816-781-3639.

MARYVILLE. *St. Francis Hospital Foundation*, 2016 S. Main, 64468. Tel: 816-562-2600.

RELIGIOUS INSTITUTES OF MEN REPRESENTED IN THE DIOCESE

For further details refer to the corresponding bracketed number in the Religious Institutes of Men or Women section.

[0200]—*Benedictine Monks.* (Conception Abbey).—O.S.B.

[0330]—*Brothers of the Christian Schools.* (St. Louis, MO).—F.S.C.

[]—*Christian Brothers of the Midwest, Burr Ridge.—FSC.*

[1330]—*Congregation of the Mission.* (Western Prov.).—C.M.

[1210]—*Congregation of the Missionaries of St. Charles.*—C.S.

[0690]—*Jesuit Fathers and Brothers.* (Missouri Prov.).—S.J.

[0800]—*Maryknoll.*—M.M.

[1070]—*Redemptorist Fathers.* (St. Louis Prov.).—C.SS.R.

[]—*Society of Our Lady of Most Holy Trinity.*—S.O.L.T.

[1060]—*Society of the Precious Blood.* (Kansas City Prov.).—C.PP.S.

RELIGIOUS INSTITUTES OF WOMEN REPRESENTED IN THE DIOCESE

[0100]—*Adorers of the Blood of Christ.*—A.S.C.

[0230]—*Benedictine Sisters of Pontifical Jurisdiction.* (Atchinson, KS; Columbia, MD; Liberty, MO).—O.S.B.

[]—*Congration of Mary Queen, (Springfield, MO).*—CMR.

[2950]—*Congregation of Notre Dame de Sion.*—N.D.S.

[0220]—*Congregation of the Benedictine Sisters of Perpetual Adoration of Pontifical Jurisdiction.*—O.S.B.

[0760]—*Daughters of Charity of St. Vincent de Paul.*—D.C.

[]—*Dominican Sisters.* (Adrian, MI; Sinsinawa, WI).—O.P.

[1415]—*Franciscan Sisters of Mary.*—F.S.M.

[2575]—*Institute of the Sisters of Mercy of the Americas.* (Omaha, NE; Cedar Rapids, IA).—R.S.M.

[2340]—*Little Sisters of the Poor.*—L.S.P.

[2510]—*Mercedarian Missionaries of Berriz.*—M.M.B.

[]—*Notre Dame Sisters.* (Omaha, NE).—N.D.

[3130]—*Our Lady of Victory Missionary Sisters.*—O.L.V.M.

[]—*School Sisters of St. Francis.* (Milwaukee, WI).—O.S.F.

[]—*Sister Servants of Immaculate Heart of Mary.* (Monroe, MI).—I.H.M.

[0480]—*Sisters of Charity of Leavenworth, Kansas.*—S.C.L.

[0430]—*Sisters of Charity of the Blessed Virgin Mary.*—B.V.M.

[2360]—*Sisters of Loretto At the Foot of the Cross.*—S.L.

[1670]—*Sisters of St. Francis of Savannah, MO.*—O.S.F.

[1560]—*Sisters of St. Francis of the Holy Eucharist.* (Independence, MO).—O.S.F.

[]—*Sisters of St. Francis of the Holy Eucharist Foundation.*

[3830-15]—*Sisters of St. Joseph.*—C.S.J.

[3830-18]—*Sisters of St. Joseph.*—C.S.J.

[3840]—*Sisters of St. Joseph of Carondelet.*—C.S.J.

[3260]—*Sisters of the Precious Blood (Dayton, OH).*—C.PP.S.

[]—*Sisters of the Presentation.* (Dubuque, IA).—P.B.V.M.

[]—*Sisters of the Third Franciscan Order (Syracuse, NY).*

[]—*Society of Our Lady of the Most Holy Trinity.*—S.O.L.T.

[4120-02]—*Ursuline Nuns (Paola, KS; Cleveland, OH, Maple Mount, KY.*—O.S.U.

DIOCESAN CEMETERIES

KANSAS CITY. *Mount Olivet & Mount St. Mary.*

ST. JOSEPH. *Mount Olivet.*

KANSAS CITY NORTH. *Resurrection.*

NECROLOGY

† North, Orlis F., (Retired). —Died May 6, 1996.

† Schwartz, James A., (Retired). —Died April 29, 1996.

† VonArx, William A., (Retired). —Died July 6, 1996.

Diocese of Knoxville

Most Reverend

ANTHONY J. O'CONNELL, D.D.

Bishop of Knoxville; ordained 1963; appointed June 7, 1988; ordained and installed September 8, 1988. *Office: 805 Northshore Dr., P.O. Box 11127, Knoxville, TN, 37939-1127.*

Chancery Office: 805 Northshore Dr., P.O. Box 11127, Knoxville, TN, 37939-1127. Tel.: 423-584-3307.

ESTABLISHED SEPTEMBER 8, 1988.

Square Miles 14,242.

Comprises the Counties of Anderson, Bledsoe, Blount, Bradley, Campbell, Carter, Claiborne, Cocke, Cumberland, Fentress, Grainger, Greene, Hamblen, Hamilton, Hancock, Hawkins, Jefferson, Johnson, Knox, Loudon, McMinn, Marion, Meigs, Monroe, Morgan, Pickett, Polk, Rhea, Roane, Scott, Sequatchie, Sevier, Sullivan, Unicoi, Union and Washington in the State of Tennessee.

For legal titles of parishes and diocesan institutions, consult the Chancery Office.

STATISTICAL OVERVIEW

Personnel	
Bishop	1
Priests: Diocesan Active in Diocese	38
Priests: Active Outside Diocese	2
Priests: Retired, Sick or Absent	6
Number of Diocesan Priests	46
Religious Priests in Diocese	15
Extern Priests in Diocese	8
Ordinations:	
Diocesan Priests	1
Permanent Deacons in Diocese	23
Total Brothers	16
Total Sisters	53
Parishes	
Parishes	43
With Resident Pastor:	
Resident Diocesan Priests	28
Resident Religious Priests	6
Without Resident Pastor:	
Administered by Priests	8
Administered by Lay People	1
Missions	1
Professional Ministry Personnel:	
Brothers	1
Sisters	6
Lay Ministers	25
Welfare	
Catholic Hospitals	2
Total Assisted	305,074
Health Care Centers	1
Total Assisted	105
Homes for the Aged	1
Total Assisted	277
Specialized Homes	1
Total Assisted	500
Special Centers for Social Services	6
Total Assisted	25,158
Educational	
Diocesan Students in Other Seminaries	16
Total Seminarians	16
High Schools, Diocesan and Parish	2
Total Students	914
Elementary Schools, Diocesan and Parish	7
Total Students	2,513
Catechesis/Religious Education:	
High School Students	1,260
Elementary Students	3,616
Total Students Under Catholic Instruction	8,319
Teachers in the Diocese:	
Priests	2
Sisters	8
Lay Teachers	243
Vital Statistics	
Receptions into the Church:	
Infant Baptism Totals	777
Adult Baptism Totals	133
Received into Full Communion	269
First Communions	863
Confirmations	546
Marriages:	
Catholic	68
Interfaith	154
Total Marriages	222
Deaths	230
Total Catholic Population	39,714
Total Population	1,860,218

Vicar General (Moderator of the Curia)—Rev. F. XAVIER MANKEL, V.G.

Deans of the Diocese—Revs. WILLIAM H. GAHAGAN, Five Rivers Deanery; T. ALLEN HUMBRECHT, Chattanooga Deanery; CHRIS MICHELSON, Cumberland Mtn. Deanery; JOSEPH J. BRANDO, Smoky Mtn. Deanery.

Chancery Office—805 Northshore Dr., P.O. Box 11127, Knoxville, 37939-1127. Tel: 423-584-3307; Fax: 423-584-7538. Office Hours: Mon-Fri 9-4 All official business should be directed to this office.

Chancellor—Rev. J. VANN JOHNSTON, JR., J.C.L.

Auditors—All priests on assignment in the diocese.

Presbyteral Council—Revs. CHRIS MICHELSON, Chm. GEORGE SCHMIDT, JR., Vice Chm. JOSEPH BRANDO, Recording Sec. and all priests on assignment in the diocese.

Diocesan Consultors—Revs. JOSEPH J. BRANDO; WILLIAM C. CASEY; WILLIAM H. GAHAGAN; T. ALLEN HUMBRECHT; F. XAVIER MANKEL, V.G.; CHRIS MICHELSON; TOM VOS, O.F.M.

Diocesan Finance Council—DORMAN BLAINE; J. MICHAEL CONNOR; LARRY COOL, Ex-Officio, Diocesan Finance Officer; MARY ESBENSHADE; SHARON FOLK; TERRY TORRICELLI, Ex-Officio, Diocesan Dir. Stewardship & Devel.; Rev. F. XAVIER MANKEL, V.G., Ex-Officio; DUGAN MCLAUGHLIN; JOHN O'CONNOR, Ex-Officio, Diocesan Attorney; SOCRATES SABATER; DAVE SANTI; Revs. FRANCIS X. SCHILLING; GEORGE E. SCHMIDT, JR.; SUZANNE SCHRIVER; WILLIAM SWAIN; FRAN THIE; FRANK VARALLO; GEORGE WARNE.

Diocesan Offices and Directors

Adult Christian Living—Rev. EVAN ECKHOFF, O.F.M., Dir., *805 Northshore Dr., Knoxville, 37919.* Tel: 423-584-3307.

Appalachian Community Development—MARIE CIRILLO, Dir., *Rte. 1, Box 146-B, Clairfield, 37715.* Tel: 423-784-6832. Participants in CORE-Appalachian Ministries, a joint project of Dioceses of Covington, Knoxville, Lexington, Nashville, Richmond and Wheeling-Charleston.

Associated Catholic Charities of East Tennessee, Inc.—DAVID DOTSON, Exec. Dir., *119 Dameron Ave., Knoxville, 37917.* Tel: 423-524-9896. The umbrella agency for all Catholic charities of the diocese.

Campaign for Human Development—DAVID DOTSON, Dir., *119 Dameron Ave., Knoxville, 37917.* Tel: 423-524-9896.

Campus Ministries—

East Tennessee State University—Rev. WILLIAM GAHAGAN, Chap. REBECCA QUIGLEY, Dir., *Catholic Center, 734 W. Locust St., Johnson City, 37604.* Tel: 423-926-7061.

University of Tennessee-Chattanooga—Rev. T. ALLEN HUMBRECHT, Dir., *514 Palmetto St., Chattanooga, 37403.* Tel: 423-267-3064.

University of Tennessee-Knoxville—Rev. TERRENCE RYAN, C.S.P., Dir., *1710 Melrose Pl., Knoxville, 37916.* Tel: 423-523-7931.

Catholic Schools Office—AURELIA MONTGOMERY, Supt., *805 Northshore Dr., Knoxville, 37919.* Tel: 423-584-3307.

Catholic Charities (Chattanooga Area)—LYNDA DIPRIMA, Admin., *125 N. Market, Chattanooga, 37405.* Tel: 423-267-1297.

Catholic Charities (Knoxville Area)—VICKIE STOVALL, Admin., *119 Dameron Ave., Knoxville, 37917.* Tel: 423-524-9896.

Catholic Charities (Upper East Tennessee Area)—Sr. JEAN SONSALLA, S.S.J.-T.O.S.F., *703 East Jackson Blvd., P.O. Box 323, Jonesborough, 37659.* Tel: 423-753-3001.

Cemeteries—LARRY COOL, Dir., *805 Northshore Dr., Knoxville, 37919.* Tel: 423-584-3307. Rev. GEORGE E. SCHMIDT, JR., Contact, Mt. Olivet Cemetery in Chattanooga. Tel: 423-266-1618. Rev. THOMAS TAVELLA, C.S.P., Contact, Calvary Cemetery in Knoxville. Tel: 423-522-1508.

Chancellor—Rev. J. VANN JOHNSTON, JR., J.C.L., *805 Northshore Dr., Knoxville, 37919.* Tel: 423-584-3307.

Censor Librorum—Rev. ROBERT J. HOFSTETTER, *930 Ashland Ter., Chattanooga, 37415.* Tel: 423-870-2386.

Deaf Ministry—Rev. MICHAEL CRESON, Dir., *700 Holly Ave., P.O. Box 288, South Pittsburg, 37380.* Tel: 423-837-7068.

Diocesan Council of Catholic Women—Rev. PAUL A. HOSTETTLER, Diocesan Spiritual Moderator, *P.O. Box 566, Copperhill, 37317.* Tel: 423-496-3498.

Ecumenism—Rev. WILLIAM CASEY, Dir., *225 Jamestowne Blvd., Knoxville, 37922.* Tel: 423-966-4540.

Evangelization—Sr. ALBERTINE PAULUS, R.S.M., Dir., *805 Northshore Dr., Knoxville, 37919.* Tel: 423-584-3307.

Finance Office—LARRY COOL, Diocesan Finance Officer, *805 Northshore Dr., Knoxville, 37919.* Tel: 423-584-3307.

Hispanic Ministry—JACK KRAMER, Dir., *119 Dameron Ave., Knoxville, 37917.* Tel: 423-637-4769.

Justice - Peace - Integrity of Creation—Co-Dirs.: MARCUS KEYES; GLENDA STRUSS-KEYES, *119 Dameron Ave., Knoxville, 37917.* Tel: 423-540-8348.

Marriage Tribunal—Rev. DEXTER BREWER, J.C.L. J.V., *2400 21st Ave. S., Nashville, 37212-5387.* Tel: 615-383-6393. Diocesan marriage tribunal is shared with the Diocese of Nashville.

Ministries of the Chattanooga Deanery—Rev. T. ALLEN HUMBRECHT, Dean; PATRICIA APPLETON, Exec. Dir., *501 S. Moore Rd., Chattanooga, 37412.* Tel: 423-622-7232.

Ministries of the Five Rivers Deanery—Rev. WILLIAM GAHAGAN, Dean, *2211 E. Lakeview Dr., Johnson City, 37601.* Tel: 423-282-6367.

Ministries of the Cumberland Mt. Deanery—Rev. CHRIS MICHELSON, Dean, *620 North Cedar Bluff Road, Knoxville, 37923.* Tel: 423-531-0770.

Ministries of the Smoky Mtn. Deanery—Rev. JOSEPH J. BRANDO, Dean, *860 Louisville Rd., Alcoa, 37701.* Tel: 423-982-3672.

Permanent Diaconate—Co-Dirs.: Rev. GREGORY BOISVERT, A.A., *711 Northshore Dr., Knoxville, 37919.* Deacon CARL WUST. Tel: 423-588-4102; 483-8739.

Priestly Life and Ministry—Rev. ROBERT J. HOFSTETTER, Dir., *930 Ashland Ter., Chattanooga, 37415.* Tel: 423-870-2386.

Propagation of the Faith—Rev. F. XAVIER MANKEL, V.G., Dir., *805 Northshore Dr., Knoxville, 37919.* Tel: 423-584-3307.

Religious Education—CATHY QUALLS, Dir., *212 Mt. Bethel Rd., Greeneville, 37745.* Tel: 800-553-0284.

Religious Education Resource Center—CATHY QUALLS, Dir., *212 Mt. Bethel Rd., Greeneville, 37745.* Tel: 800-553-0284.

Scouting—Deacon OTTO PRESKE, Scout Chap., *535 Buckhorn Rd., Gatlinburg, 37738.* Tel: 423-436-5339.

Stewardship and Development—TERRY TORRICELLI, Dir., *805 Northshore Dr., Knoxville, 37919.* Tel: 423-584-3307.

Strategic Pastoral Planning—PAUL TERHAAR, Dir., *805 Northshore Dr., Knoxville, 37919.* Tel: 423-584-3307.

"The East Tennessee Catholic"—(Diocesan Newspaper); EDGAR MILLER, Editor, *805 Northshore Dr., Knoxville, 37919.* Tel: 423-584-3307.

Vocations—Most Rev. ANTHONY J. O'CONNELL, D.D., Dir., *805 Northshore Dr., Knoxville, 37919.* Tel: 423-584-3307. Rev. MICHAEL CRESON, Diocesan Coord., Vocation Promotion. Assoc. Dirs.: Revs. JOSEPH BRANDO; WILLIAM GAHAGAN; T. ALLEN HUMBRECHT; CHRIS MICHELSON. Bishop O'Connell also serves as the Director of Seminarian Formation.

Worship and Liturgy—Rev. CHRIS MICHELSON, Dir., *620 North Cedar Bluff Road, Knoxville, 37923.* Tel: 423-531-0770.

Youth Ministry—Rev. PETER IORIO, *2701 Vermont Ave., Chattanooga, 37404.* Tel: 423-624-4618, Ext. 28. PAT RIECKE, Coord. Chattanooga Deanery, *501 S. Moore Rd., Chattanooga, 37412.* Tel: 423-629-6775. LINDA D. MURASKI, Coord., Five Rivers Deanery, *2211 East Lakeview Drive, Johnson City, 37601.* Tel: 423-282-6367. ANNE MCGAUGH, Coord., Cumberland Mt. Deanery, *327 Vermont Ave., Oak Ridge, 37830.* Tel: 423-483-7519. PATRICK DONOVAN, Coord., Smoky Mtn. Deanery, *711 Northshore Dr., Knoxville, 37919.* Tel: 423-558-8348.

CLERGY, PARISHES, MISSIONS AND PAROCHIAL SCHOOLS

CITY OF KNOXVILLE
(Knox County)

1—CATHEDRAL OF THE SACRED HEART OF JESUS (1956), Revs. Xavier Mankel, V.G.; Gregory Boisvert, A.A.; Sean Poland.
Res., 711 Northshore Dr., 37919. Tel: 423-588-5189; Fax: 423-558-9671. [JC]
School—Tel: 423-588-0415; Fax: 423-558-4139. Pamela Bernards, Prin.
Lay Teachers 51; Students 769.
Catechesis/Religious Programs—Tel: 423-584-4528. Joanne Romeo, D.R.E.
Students 193.

2—ALL SAINTS CATHOLIC CHURCH (1994), Revs. Chris Michelson; Michael E. Cummins.
Mailing Address: 620 N. Cedar Bluff Rd., 37923. Tel: 423-531-0770; Fax: 423-531-1009.
Catechesis/Religious Programs—Students 402.

3—IMMACULATE CONCEPTION (1852) (Irish), Revs. Thomas A. Tavella, C.S.P.; Broderick M. Walsh, C.S.P.
Res., 414 W. Vine Ave., 37902. Tel: 423-522-1508; Fax: 423-524-8514. [CEM]
Catechesis/Religious Programs—Betty Krusenklaus, D.R.E.
Students 135.

4—JOHN XXIII CATHOLIC CENTER (1968). (Non-territorial parish for the University of Tennessee at Knoxville). Revs. Terrence P. Ryan, C.S.P.; Ernesto DeCiccio, C.S.P.
Res., 1710 Melrose Pl., 37916. Tel: 423-523-7931; Fax: 423-523-7979.
Catechesis/Religious Programs—Susan Jones, D.R.E.
Students 74.

5—HOLY GHOST (1908), Revs. Albert J. Henkel; John R. Dowling; J. Vann Johnston, Jr., J.C.L.
Res., 111 Hinton St., 37917. Tel: 423-522-2205.
School—St. Joseph, 1810 Howard Rd., 37918. Tel: 423-689-3424. Joan Turbyville, Prin.
Lay Teachers 31; Students 256.
Catechesis/Religious Programs—Betty Krusenklaus, D.R.E.
Students 220.

6—ST. JOHN NEUMANN (1977), Revs. Patrick P. Brownell; William C. Casey; Deacons William Diesing; Donald Amelse; Marquis Syler.
Church—225 Jamestowne Blvd., 37922. Tel: 423-966-4540; Fax: 423-966-4541.
Res., 300 Dominion Cir., 37922. Tel: 615-966-8924.
Catechesis/Religious Programs—Margaret Fontenot, D.R.E.
Students 636.

OUTSIDE THE CITY OF KNOXVILLE

Alcoa, Blount Co., Our Lady of Fatima (1950), Revs. Joseph J. Brando; Thomas W. Moser; Deacon Michael G. Nestor.
Res., 860 Louisville Rd., 37701. Tel: 423-982-3672; Fax: 423-977-4183.
Catechesis/Religious Programs—Tel: 423-981-2676. LuAnne Zelasko, D.R.E.
Students 261.
Mission—Alcoa, Blount Co., St. Francis of Assisi, 37701. Rev. Joseph W. Julius.

Athens, McMinn Co., St. Mary (1968), Rev. Joseph Fiedorowicz.
Res., 2007 Congress Pkwy., 37303. Tel: 423-745-4277; Fax: 423-745-4277.
Catechesis/Religious Programs—Joyce Spurlin, D.R.E.
Students 123.

Chattanooga, Hamilton Co.,

1—SS. PETER AND PAUL, (1852), Rev. George E. Schmidt, Jr.; Deacons James Wilson; Andrew Wassick.
Res., 214 E. 8th St., 37402. Tel: 423-266-1618. [JC]

2—OUR LADY OF PERPETUAL HELP, (1937), Revs. T. Allen Humbrecht; David Boettner; Deacons Mark Gang, Jr.; William Oleck.
Res., 501 S. Moore Rd., 37412. Tel: 423-622-7232; Fax: 423-624-2686.
School—505 S. Moore Rd., 37412. Tel: 423-622-1481; Fax: 423-622-2016.
Sisters of Charity of the Blessed Virgin Mary 2; Lay Teachers 30; Students 425.
Catechesis/Religious Programs—Lois Colosia, D.R.E.
Students 82.
Convent—511 S. Moore Rd., 37412. Tel: 423-698-3274.

3—ST. JUDE, (1958), Revs. Robert J. Hofstetter; Gilbert M. Diaz. In res., Rev. Pio C. Palad (Philippines).
Res., 930 Ashland Terr., 37415. Tel: 423-870-2386.
School—Tel: 423-877-6022; Fax: 423-875-8920. JoAnne Bollman, Prin.
Lay Teachers 27; Students 436.
Catechesis/Religious Programs—Tel: 423-870-2386.
Students 208.

4—ST. STEPHEN, (1961), Rev. P. J. McGinnity. In res., Rev. Peter Iorio.
Res., 7111 Lee Hwy., 37421. Tel: 423-892-1261.
Catechesis/Religious Programs—Tel: 423-892-2957.
Students 165.

Cleveland, Bradley Co., St. Therese of Lisieux (1914), Rev. Michael Nolan; Sr. Marian Ruede, Pastoral Assoc.
Res., 900 Clingan Ridge Dr., N.W., 37312. Tel: 423-476-8123; Fax: 423-479-3339.
Catechesis/Religious Programs—Darline Pullen, D.R.E.
Students 296.

Clinton, Anderson Co., St. Therese (1974), Rev. Dan G. Whitman; Sr. Yvette Gillen, R.S.M., Pastoral Assoc.
Church—701 S. Main St., 37716. Tel: 423-457-4073.
Res., Tel: 423-457-1317.
Catechesis/Religious Programs—Students 62.

Copperhill, Polk Co., St. Catherine (1977). Attended by St. Mary, Athens. In res., Rev. Paul Hostettler.
Mailing Address: Box 566, 37317. Tel: 423-496-3498.

Crossville, Cumberland Co., St. Alphonsus (1948), Rev. Michael B. Roark; Deacon Ralph Torrelli, Pastoral Assoc. & Business Mgr.
Res., Rte. 21, Box 235, 38555. Tel: 615-484-2358 (Res.); 456-5148 (Office).
Catechesis/Religious Programs—Tel: 615-456-5227. Terry Paradis, D.R.E.
Students 89.

Dayton, Rhea Co., St. Bridget (1969), Rev. Michael J. Linder; Deacon Tom Kiefer.
Res., 320 Walnut Grove Church Rd., 37321. Tel: 423-775-2664; 775-5542 (Rectory).
Catechesis/Religious Programs—Students 75.

Elizabethton, Carter Co., St. Elizabeth (1982), Rev. Stephen K. Smith, O.P.
Res., 510 W. C St., 37643. Tel: 423-543-3412.
Catechesis/Religious Programs—Donna Townsend, D.R.E.
Students 55.

Fairfield Glade, Cumberland Co., St. Francis of Assisi (1983), Rev. Philip F. Thoni; Deacons Mark Frederick; Mark White.
Res., Peavine Rd., P.O. Box 1861, 38558. Tel: 615-484-3628. [CEM]
Mission—Jamestown, Fentress Co., Fentress County Catholic Community, 38558.

Gatlinburg, Sevier Co., St. Mary (1935), Rev. Francis X. Schilling; Deacon Otto Preske.
Res., 304 Airport Rd., 37738. Tel: 423-436-4907.
Mission—Pigeon Forge, Holy Cross, 144 Wears Valley Rd., Pigeon Forge, 37863. Tel: 423-429-5587. Rev. Jay Flaherty, Admin.

Greeneville, Greene Co., Notre Dame (1955), Revs. Alex Waraksa; James Phillip Harvey, II.
Res., 212 Mt. Bethel Rd., 37745. Tel: 423-639-9381.
Catechesis/Religious Programs—D.R.E.: Diana Thompon, (Elementary); Maryann Connell, (Elementary); Laura Nachazel, (High School).
Students 84.

Harriman, Roane Co., Blessed Sacrament (1908), Rev. Michael T. Jennings; Deacon James P. O'Connor.
Res., 535 Margrave St., 37748. Tel: 423-882-9838.
Catechesis/Religious Programs—Sr. Rita Bray, C.S.C., D.R.E.
Students 39.
Stations—Brushy Mountain Prison; Morgan County Regional Correctional Facility.

Helenwood, Scott Co., St. Jude Parish (1982). Attended by St. Therese, Clinton. Rev. Dan G. Whitman; Sr. Patricia Soete, R.S.M., Pastoral Assoc.
Mailing Address: Hwy. 27 S., P.O. Box 555, 37755. Tel: 423-569-3492; 569-9584 (Church).

Jefferson City, Jefferson Co., Holy Trinity Church (1990). Attended by St. Patrick, Morristown. Rev. Michael Sweeney.
Mailing Address: 475 N. Hwy. 92, 37760. Tel: 423-471-0347.

Johnson City, Washington Co., St. Mary (1906), Revs. William H. Gahagan; Steve LaPrad.
Res., 2211 E. Lakeview Dr., 37601. Tel: 423-282-8696.
School—Tel: 423-282-8666; Fax: 423-282-0224. Sr. Beverly Reck, S.S.N.D., Prin.
Lay Teachers 16; Students 202.
Catechesis/Religious Programs—Deacon Joseph McMahon, D.R.E.
Students 222.

Kingsport, Sullivan Co., St. Dominic (1941), Revs. Charles Burton; Ragan Schriver; Sr. Madeline MacDougall, Pastoral Assoc.; Deacon Milton Robelot.
Res., 2517 John B. Dennis Hwy., 37660. Tel: 423-288-2773; Fax: 423-288-7183.
School—Tel: 423-245-0362; Fax: 423-245-2907. Philip Dampf, III, Prin.
Lay Teachers 11; Students 97.
Catechesis/Religious Programs—Tel: 423-288-8101. Shirley Parsons, D.R.E.
Students 314.

LaFollette, Campbell Co., Our Lady of Perpetual Help (1905), Rev. Greg Neuzil.
Mailing Address: 923 E. Elm St., P.O. Box 1704, 37766. Tel: 423-562-0312.

Lancing, Morgan Co., St. Ann (1982). Attended by Blessed Sacrament, Harriman. Rev. Michael Jennings; Sr. Rita Bray, C.S.C., Pastoral Assoc.
Mailing Address: P.O. Box 77, 37770-0077.

Lenoir City, Loudon Co., St. Thomas the Apostle (1973), Rev. George Dyer, O.P.; Deacon Jose Rivera.
Res., 2500 Harrison Rd., 37771. Tel: 423-986-9885.

Madisonville, Monroe Co., Monroe County Catholic Community (1992), Jay Gilchrist, Pastoral Coord.
Mailing Address: 737 Hwy. 411 N., 37354. Tel: 423-442-7273; 337-2714.

Morristown, Hamblen Co., St. Patrick (1959), Rev. Michael Sweeney; Deacon Gerald Fage.
Res., 2518 W. Andrew Johnson Hwy., 37814. Tel: 423-586-9174; Fax: 423-318-7044.
Catechesis/Religious Programs—Tel: 423-586-4091. Patricia Holmes, D.R.E.
Students 220.

Mountain City, Johnson Co., St. Anthony of Padua Catholic Church (1995). (Quasi Parish). Rev. Thomas Vos, O.F.M.; Bro. Justin Huber, O.F.M.
Res., 513 Hickory St., 37683. Tel: 423-727-7870; Fax: 423-727-5156.

Newport, Cocke Co., Good Shepherd (1982). Attended by Notre Dame, Greeneville. Revs. Alex Waraksa;

James Phillip Harvey, II; Sr. Mary Ann Konieski, O.P., Pastoral Assoc.
Mailing Address: 659 E. Broadway, 37821. Tel: 423-623-5051.
School—Students 30.

Norris, Anderson Co., St. Joseph (1949), Rev. Frank X. Brett.
Res., 177 W. Norris Rd., P.O. Box 387, 37828. Tel: 423-494-7746 (Res.); 494-8940 (Office).
Catechesis/Religious Programs—Sue Campbell, D.R.E.
Students 58.

Oak Ridge, Anderson Co., St. Mary (1943), Revs. Michael Woods; John Milewski; Deacons Frank Stoetzel; Carl Wust.
Res., 327 Vermont Ave., 37830. Tel: 423-482-2875.
School—323 Vermont Ave., 37830. Tel: 423-483-9700. Sr. Mary Reginald Lane, O.P., Prin.
Sisters of St. Cecilia Dominican Congregation 3; Lay Teachers 20; Students 229.
Catechesis/Religious Programs—Tel: 423-481-8106.
Students 323.

Rogersville, Hawkins Co., St. Henry (1981), Revs. Alex Waraksa; James Phillip Harvey, II.
Res., 112 Hwy. 70 N., 37857. Tel: 423-272-6897.
Catechesis/Religious Programs—Ellen McCoy, D.R.E.
Students 32.

Seymour, Sevier Co., Holy Family (1984), Rev. G. Patrick Garrity.
Mailing Address: 307 Black Oak Ridge Rd., P.O. Box 817, 37865. Tel: 423-573-1203.
Catechesis/Religious Programs—Tel: 423-577-3881. Connie Bigelow, D.R.E.
Students 61.

Signal Mountain, Hamilton Co., St. Augustine (1938), Rev. Paul Valleroy; Deacon Gordon Kilburn.
Res., 1716 Anderson Pike, P.O. Box 10, 37377. Tel: 423-886-3424. [JC]
Catechesis/Religious Programs—Students 150.

Sneedville, Hancock Co., St. James the Apostle (1982). Attended by St. Dominic, Kingsport. Rev. Charles Burton.
Mailing Address: Rte. 2, Box 52, 37869. Tel: 423-288-8101.

South Pittsburg, Marion Co., Our Lady of Lourdes (1930), Rev. Mike Creson.
Res., P.O. Box 288, 37380. Tel: 423-837-7068.
School—Students 33.
Mission—Marian, Marian Co., Virgin of the Poor Shrine, 37380.

Tazewell, Claiborne Co., Christ The King (1990), Rev. John R. Dowling.
Mailing Address: P.O. Box 404, 37879. Tel: 423-522-2205.

Townsend, Blount Co., St. Francis of Assisi (1961). Attended by Our Lady of Fatima, Alcoa. In res., Rev. Joseph Julius (NSH).
Mailing Address: 7717 River Rd., 37882. Tel: 423-448-6070.
Catechesis/Religious Programs—Students 27.

On Duty Outside the Diocese:
Reverend Fathers—
Winkler, William, Jerusalem

Retired:
Reverend Monsignors—
Siener, Leo C., Alexian Village Health Care Center, 198 James Blvd., Rm. 711, Signal Mtn., TN 37377-1816

Reverend Fathers—
Bowes, David, P.O. Box 9325, Pensacola, FL 32513
Hostettler, Paul A., P.O. Box 566, Copperhill, TN 37317
Junod, Louis, 1414 Continental Dr., Apt. 207, Chattanooga, TN 37405
Prescott, Herbert W., P.O. Box 4102, Chattanooga, TN 37405

Permanent Deacons:
Amelse, Donald, St. John Neumann, Knoxville
Diesing, William, St. John Neumann, Knoxville
Fage, Gerald J., II, St. Patrick, Morristown
Fischer, Robert W., St. Mary, Johnson City
Frederick, Mark A., St. Francis of Assisi, Fairfield Glade
Gang, Mark, Jr., Our Lady of Perpetual Help, Chattanooga
Kiefer, Thomas, St. Bridget, Dayton
Kilburn, Gordon, St. Augustine, Signal Mountain
Lawson, James, Sacred Heart Cathedral
McMahon, Joseph T., St. Mary, Johnson City
Nestor, Michael, St. Francis of Assisi, Townsend
O'Connor, James P., Blessed Sacrament, Harriman
Oleck, William A., Our Lady of Perpetual Help, Chattanooga
Preske, Otto F., St. Mary, Gatlinburg
Rivera, Jose, St. Thomas the Apostle, Lenoir City
Robelot, Milton P., St. Dominic, Kingsport
Stoetzel, Frank C., St. Mary, Oak Ridge
Syler, Marquis E., St. John Neumann, Knoxville
Torrelli, Ralph, St. Alphonsus, Crossville
Wassick, Andrew, SS. Peter and Paul, Chattanooga
White, Mark F., St. Francis of Assisi, Fairfield Glade
Wilson, James E., SS. Peter and Paul, Chattanooga
Wust, Carl J., St. Mary, Oak Ridge

INSTITUTIONS LOCATED IN THE DIOCESE

[A] HIGH SCHOOLS, DIOCESAN

KNOXVILLE. *Knoxville Catholic High School* (1932), 1610 E. Magnolia Ave., 37917. Tel: 423-525-0262; Fax: 423-525-6236.
E-mail: kxchs@aol.com. Rev. Patrick Garrity, Prin. Priests 2; Sisters 1; Lay Teachers 22; Students 381.
Knoxville Catholic High School Development Board of Trust.

CHATTANOOGA. *Notre Dame High School* (1876). (Grades 9-12), 2701 Vermont Ave., 37404. Tel: 423-624-4618; Fax: 423-624-4621. Mr. Perry Storey, Prin. Priests 2; Lay Teachers 47; Students 533.
Notre Dame High School Financial Board of Trustees.

[B] GENERAL HOSPITALS

KNOXVILLE. *St. Mary's Medical Center, Inc.*, (1930) 900 E. Oak Hill Ave., 37917. Tel: 423-545-8000.
For a complete listing, refer to the Hospitals section.

CHATTANOOGA. *Memorial Hospital*, (1952) 2525 DeSales Ave., 37404. Tel: 423-495-2525.
For a complete listing, refer to the Hospitals section.

[C] SPECIAL HOSPITALS

SIGNAL MOUNTAIN. *Alexian Village Health Care Center*, (1938) 100 James Blvd., 37377. Tel: 423-886-0100.
For a complete listing, refer to the Special Care Facilities section.

[D] HOMES FOR THE AGED

SIGNAL MOUNTAIN. *Alexian Village of Tennessee, Inc.*, 100 James Blvd., 37377. Tel: 423-870-0101.
For a complete listing, refer to the Special Care Facilities section.

[E] PROTECTIVE INSTITUTIONS

KNOXVILLE. *Columbus Home, Inc.*, 119 Dameron Ave., 37917. Tel: 423-971-3570; Fax: 423-546-0433.
For a complete listing, refer to the Special Care Facilities section.

[F] MONASTERIES AND RESIDENCES OF PRIESTS AND BROTHERS

KNOXVILLE. *Brothers of Holy Cross*, 816 Creswell Ct., 37919. Bro. Roland Driscoll, C.S.C., (Retired). Total in Residence 1; Total Staff 1.

COPPERHILL. *Monastery of Our Lady of Little Citeaux*, Box 1799 McGee Rd., 37317. Tel: 704-496-7373.

HARRIMAN. *Brothers of Holy Cross*, 582 Fairview Rd., 37748-9632. Tel: 423-435-4196. Bro. Douglas H. Roach, C.S.C.

LANCING. *Brothers of Holy Cross*, 297 Davidson Rd., 37770. Tel: 423-965-3392. Bro. Paul Bray, C.S.C.

MOUNTAIN CITY. *Franciscan Friars*, Alverna Friary, 513 Hickory St., 37683. Revs. Evan Eckhoff, O.F.M.; Thomas Vos, O.F.M.; Justin Huber, O.F.M.

SIGNAL MOUNTAIN. *Alexian Brothers*, 198 James Blvd., 37377. Tel: 423-886-0380. Bros. Lawrence Krueger, Local Supr.; Dominic Walsh, C.F.A., Supr. Gen.; Cajetan Gavranich, C.F.A.; Ewald Herb, C.F.A.; Polycarp Miller, C.F.A.; Francis Provasnik, C.F.A.; Simeon Pytel, C.F.A.; Eugene Ratley, C.F.A.; Jerome Revak, C.F.A.; Eugene Gizzi, C.F.A.; David Sznek, C.F.A.; Rupert Trudel, C.F.A.; Rev. Maro Cannon, C.F.A.

[G] CONVENTS AND RESIDENCES FOR SISTERS

KNOXVILLE. *Sisters of Mercy*. (Cincinnati Region).
St. Mary's Medical Center, 900 E. Oak Hill Ave., 37917. Tel: 423-545-8000. Sisters 12.
Sisters of the Divine Compassion, 601 Peters Rd., Apt. 8, 37922. Mailing Address: 52 N. Broadway, White Plains, NY, 10603.

BUTLER. *Sisters of St. Joseph, Third Order of St. Francis*, 254 Pine Orchard Rd., 37940-9556.

CHATTANOOGA. *Missionary Sisters of the Sacred Heart of Jesus "Ad Gentes"*, 430 Glenwood Dr., 37404. Sisters 3.
Sisters of Charity of Nazareth, 4040 Mountain Creek Rd. #2902, 37415. Sisters 2.
Sisters of Charity of Nazareth, 425 Glenwood Dr., 37404. Sisters 4.
Sisters of Charity of Nazareth, 25 S. Germantown Rd., Apt. 244, 37411. Sisters 2.
Sisters of Charity of the Blessed Virgin Mary, 511 S. Moore Rd., 37412-2949. Tel: 423-698-3274. Sisters 2.

CLEVELAND. *Sisters of Charity of Cincinnati*, 2701 Hilltop Dr., 37312. Tel: 423-476-5972.

CLINTON. *St. Therese Convent*, 701 S. Main St., 37716. Tel: 423-457-4073.

HARRIMAN. *Sisters of the Presentation, B.V.M.*, 582 Fairview Rd., 37748. Sisters 3.

HELENWOOD. *Sisters of Mercy*, P.O. Box 555, 37755. Tel: 423-569-3492. Total Assisted 2,000; Total Staff 15.

JACKSBORO. *Presentation Sisters of B.V.M.*, 2151 W. Central Ave., 37757.

JELLICO. *Sisters of the Presentation of the Blessed Virgin Mary*, Rte. 1, Box 331, 37762. Tel: 423-784-9732. Total Assisted 1,450; Total Staff 3.

JOHNSON CITY. *School Sisters of Notre Dame*, 221 E. Tenth Ave., #2, 37601.

JONESBOROUGH. *Sisters of St. Joseph, Third Order of St. Francis*, 703 E. Jackson Blvd., 37659. Tel: 423-753-3963.

KINGSPORT. *Sisters of Notre Dame de Namur*, 2601 John B. Dennis Hwy. #1004, 37660. Tel: 423-288-8317.

LAKE CITY. *Sisters of Loretto*, 506 Old Lake City Hwy., 37769. Tel: 423-426-9435.

LANCING. *Sisters of Holy Cross*, 641 Island Ford Rd., 37770. Tel: 423-965-3923. Sisters 2.

NEWPORT. *Dominican Sisters*. (Congregation of The Holy Rosary), 659 E. Broadway, 37821. Tel: 423-623-5051.

OAK RIDGE. *Dominican Sisters (St. Cecilia Congregation)*, St. Mary's Convent, 323 Vermont Ave., 37830. Tel: 423-483-0720. Sisters 3.

[H]RETREAT HOUSES

KNOXVILLE, TN. *The Mountaincrest*, 4902 Mountaincrest Dr., 37918. Tel: 423-687-6900. Johanna C. Humphrey.

[I] CAMPS AND COMMUNITY CENTERS

NEWCOMB. *Crazy Quilt Friendship Center*, Rte. 1, Box 47, 37819. Tel: 423-784-6022. Community center, crafts co-op and clothing store. Total Assisted 1,450; Total Staff 3.

[J] NEWMAN CENTERS

KNOXVILLE. *UT-Knoxville, Newman Foundation, Inc.*, John XXIII University Parish/Catholic Center, 1710 Melrose Pl., 37916. Tel: 423-523-7931. Revs. Terrence P. Ryan, C.S.P.; Ernesto DeCiccio, C.S.P.

CHATTANOOGA. *Newman Foundation of Chattanooga, Inc.*, Catholic Student Center, 514 Palmetto St., 37403. Tel: 423-267-3064. Rev. T. Allen Humbrecht; Marian Christiana, Assoc. Campus Min. Total Staff 2.

GREENEVILLE. *Tusculum College Newman Center*. Attended by Notre Dame Church, Greeneville. c/o Notre Dame Church, 212 Mt. Bethel Rd., 37745.

JOHNSON CITY. *ETSU-Catholic Center*, 734 W. Locust St., 37604. Tel: 423-926-7061. Rev. Bill Gahagan, Chap.; Rebecca Quigley, Dir.

[K] MISCELLANEOUS

KNOXVILLE. *The Catholic Diocese of Knoxville Foundation, Inc.*, 805 Northshore Dr., 37919. Tel: 423-584-3307.
Catholic Foundation of East Tennessee, 805 Northshore Dr., 37919. Tel: 423-584-3307.
Diocesan Council of Catholic Women, 805 Northshore Dr., 37919. Rev. Paul A. Hostettler, Diocesan Spiritual Moderator. Deanery Spiritual Moderators: Revs. William H. Gahagan, Five Rivers; Robert J. Hofstetter, Chattanooga; Xavier Mankel, Smoky Mountain; Dan G. Whitman, Cumberland Mountain.
Ladies of Charity, 1031 Central Ave., 37917. Tel: 423-522-6341; 524-0538. Rev. Albert J. Henkel, Spiritual Moderator. Total Assisted 15,158; Total Staff 5.

CHATTANOOGA. *Ladies of Charity*, 1800 E. Main St., 37404. Tel: 423-624-3222. Rev. Louis J. Junod, Spiritual Moderator. Gives emergency assistance in the form of food, medicine, clothing, Lifeline, meals on wheels, layettes to new-born, payment on utilities, rent, glasses, dental work, etc.

RELIGIOUS INSTITUTES OF MEN REPRESENTED IN THE DIOCESE

For further details refer to the corresponding bracketed number in the Religious Institutes of Men or Women section.

[0120]—*Alexian Brothers.*—C.F.A.
[0130]—*Assumptionists.*—A.A.
[0600]—*Brothers of the Congregation of Holy Cross.*—C.S.C.
[0520]—*Franciscan Friars.*—O.F.M.

[0570]—*The Glenmary Home Missioners.*—Glmy.
[0430]—*Order of Preachers-Dominicans.*—O.P.
[1030]—*Paulist Fathers.*—C.S.P.

RELIGIOUS INSTITUTES OF WOMEN REPRESENTED IN THE DIOCESE

[1920]—*Congregation of the Sisters of Holy Cross.*—C.S.C.
[1070]—*Dominican Sisters (Congregation of the Holy Rosary).*—O.P.
[1070-07]—*Dominican Sisters (St. Cecilia Congregation).*—O.P.
[2575]—*Institute of the Sisters of Mercy of the Americas.* (Cincinnati Prov.).—R.S.M.
[]—*Missionary Sisters of the Sacred Heart of Jesus "Ad Gentes."*
[2970]—*School Sisters of Notre Dame.*—S.S.N.D.
[0440]—*Sisters of Charity of Cincinnati, Ohio.*—S.C.
[0500]—*Sisters of Charity of Nazareth.*—S.C.N.
[0430]—*Sisters of Charity of the Blessed Virgin Mary.*—B.V.M.
[2360]—*Sisters of Loretto at the Foot of the Cross.*—S.L.
[3000]—*Sisters of Notre Dame De Namur.*—S.N.D.deN.
[]—*Sisters of St. Joseph, Third Order of St. Francis.*
[0970]—*Sisters of the Divine Compassion.*—R.D.C.
[3320]—*Sisters of the Presentation of the B.V.M.*—P.B.V.M.

INTERPAROCHIAL CEMETERIES

KNOXVILLE. *Calvary*, Martin Luther King Blvd., 37915. Tel: 423-522-1508. Rev. Thomas Tavella, C.S.P.
CHATTANOOGA. *Mount Olivet*, Ringgold Rd., 37412. Tel: 423-266-1618. Rev. George Schmidt, Jr.

NECROLOGY

† Hines, Vincent J., (Retired). —Died Jan. 23, 1996.

Diocese of La Crosse

(Dioecesis Crossensis)

Most Reverend

RAYMOND L. BURKE, D.D., J.C.D.

Bishop of La Crosse; ordained June 29, 1975; appointed to the Residential See of La Crosse December 10, 1994; consecrated January 6, 1995; installed as Eighth Bishop of La Crosse February 22, 1995. *Res., 3720 East Ave., S., La Crosse, WI, 54602-4004. Mailing Address: P.O. Box 4004, La Crosse, WI, 54602-4004.* Tel.: 608-788-7700.

Most Reverend

JOHN J. PAUL, D.D.

Retired Bishop of La Crosse; ordained January 24, 1943; appointed Titular Bishop of Lambese and Auxiliary Bishop of La Crosse May 17, 1977; consecrated August 4, 1977; appointed to the Residential See of La Crosse October 18, 1983; installed as Seventh Bishop of La Crosse December 5, 1983; retired December 10, 1994. *Res., Holy Cross Diocesan Center, P.O. Box 4004, La Crosse, WI, 54602-4004.* Tel.: 608-788-8395; 788-7700.

Most Reverend

FREDERICK W. FREKING, D.D., J.C.D.

Retired Bishop of La Crosse; ordained July 31, 1938; appointed Bishop of Salina October 10, 1957; consecrated November 30, 1957; installed January 7, 1958; transferred to La Crosse December 30, 1964; installed February 24, 1965; retired May 10, 1983. *Res., Holy Cross Diocesan Center, P.O. Box 4004, La Crosse, WI, 54602-4004.* Tel.: 608-788-0668; 788-7700.

ERECTED MARCH 3, 1868. SUBDIVIDED MAY 3, 1905. SUBDIVIDED JANUARY 15, 1946.

Square Miles 15,078.

Comprises the following 19 Counties in the State of Wisconsin: Adams, Buffalo, Chippewa, Clark, Crawford, Dunn, Eau Claire, Jackson, Juneau, La Crosse, Marathon, Monroe, Pepin, Pierce, Portage, Richland, Trempealeau, Vernon and Wood.

For legal titles of parishes and diocesan institutions, consult the Chancery Office.

Chancery Office: 3710 East Ave. S., P.O. Box 4004, La Crosse, WI, 54602-4004. Tel.: 608-788-7700; Fax: 608-788-8413.

E-mail address: diocese@zianet.com

STATISTICAL OVERVIEW

Personnel	
Bishop	1
Retired Bishops	2
Abbots	1
Priests: Diocesan Active in Diocese	127
Priests: Active Outside Diocese	8
Priests: Diocesan in Foreign Missions	3
Priests: Retired, Sick or Absent	60
Number of Diocesan Priests	198
Religious Priests in Diocese	27
Extern Priests in Diocese	7
Ordinations:	
Diocesan Priests	4
Permanent Deacons in Diocese	22
Total Brothers	11
Total Sisters	544
Parishes	
Parishes	180
With Resident Pastor:	
Resident Diocesan Priests	107
Resident Religious Priests	7
Without Resident Pastor:	
Administered by Priests	56
Administered by Permanent Deacons	1
Administered by Women Religious	8
Administered by Lay People	1
Pastoral Centers	2
Closed Parishes	7
Professional Ministry Personnel:	
Sisters	22
Lay Ministers	27
Welfare	
Catholic Hospitals	9
Total Assisted	452,748
Homes for the Aged	12
Total Assisted	895
Day Care and Extended Day Care Centers	1
Total Assisted	150
Specialized Homes	6
Total Assisted	11,155
Special Centers for Social Services	5
Total Assisted	2,046
Residential Care of Disabled	3
Total Assisted	183
Educational	
Seminaries, Diocesan	1
Students from This Diocese	3
Students from Other Diocese	4
Diocesan Students in Other Seminaries	32
Students Religious	1
Total Seminarians	36
Colleges and Universities	1
Total Students	1,637
High Schools, Diocesan and Parish	7
Total Students	1,859
Elementary Schools, Diocesan and Parish	78
Total Students	10,151
Catechesis/Religious Education:	
High School Students	8,762
Elementary Students	17,784
Total Students Under Catholic Instruction	40,229
Teachers in the Diocese:	
Priests	19
Brothers	2
Sisters	31
Lay Teachers	790
Vital Statistics	
Receptions into the Church:	
Infant Baptism Totals	3,239
Adult Baptism Totals	122
Received into Full Communion	359
First Communions	3,761
Confirmations	3,334
Marriages:	
Catholic	1,527
Interfaith	515
Total Marriages	2,042
Deaths	2,166
Total Catholic Population	227,937
Total Population	817,382

Former Bishops—Most Rev. MICHAEL HEISS, D.D., cons. Sept. 6, 1868; appt. Titular Archbishop of Hadrianople, and coadjutor to the Metropolitan of Milwaukee March 14, 1880; promoted to Milwaukee, Sept. 1881; died March 26, 1890.—Rt. Rev. KILIAN CASPAR FLASCH, D.D., cons. Aug. 24, 1881; died Aug. 3, 1891.—Rt. Rev. JAMES SCHWEBACH, D.D., cons. Feb. 25, 1892; died June 6, 1921.—Most Rev. ALEXANDER J. MCGAVICK, D.D., LL.D., cons. Titular Bishop of Marcopolis and Auxiliary Bishop of Chicago, May 1, 1899; transferred to See of La Crosse, Nov. 21, 1921; died Aug. 25, 1948.—Most Rev. JOHN P. TREACY, S.T.D., cons. Titular Bishop of Metelis and Coadjutor of La Crosse "cum jure successionis," Oct. 2, 1945; succeeded to the See, July 23, 1946; died Oct. 11, 1964.—Most Rev. FREDERICK W. FREKING, D.D., J.C.D., cons. Bishop of Salina, KS, November 30, 1957; transferred to the See of La Crosse, Dec. 30, 1964; installed La Crosse, Feb. 24, 1965; retired May 10, 1983.—Most Rev. JOHN J. PAUL, D.D., appt. Titular Bishop of Lambese and Auxiliary Bishop of La Crosse, May 17, 1977; cons. Aug. 4, 1977; appt. to the Residential See of La Crosse, Oct. 18, 1983; installed as Bishop of La Crosse, Dec. 5, 1983; retired Dec. 10, 1994.

Vicar General—Very Rev. JOSEPH J. RAFACZ S.T.L., *Holy Cross Diocesan Center, P.O. Box 4004, La Crosse, 54602-4004.*

Chancery Office—3710 East Ave. S., P.O. Box 4004, La Crosse, 54602-4004. Tel: 608-788-7700; Fax: 608-788-8413. Office Hours: Mon.-Fri. 8-4:30.

Chancellor—Rev. MICHAEL J. GORMAN, J.C.L.

Vice-Chancellor—Rev. LEON A. POWELL.

Moderator of the Curia-Vicar General—Very Rev. JOSEPH J. RAFACZ S.T.L.

Secretary to the Bishop—Rev. MICHAEL J. GORMAN, J.C.L.

Archivist—Rev. MICHAEL J. GORMAN, J.C.L.

Finance Officer—SONDRA RIEDER.

Ecclesiastical Notaries—Revs. MICHAEL J. GORMAN; LEON A. POWELL; SHERYL STAPLETON; SUSAN VLASAK, *P.O. Box 4004, La Crosse, 54602-4004.*

Diocesan Tribunal—3710 East Ave. S., P.O. Box 4004, La Crosse, 54602-4004. Tel: 608-788-7700. (Address all rogatory commissions to the Chancellor).

Judicial Vicar—Very Rev. ROBERT P. HUNDT, J.C.L.

Promoter of Justice—GEORGE E. NIX, J.C.L.

Defensores Vinculi—Sr. MARLENE WEISENBECK, F.S.P.A., J.C.L.; GEORGE E. NIX, J.C.L.

Auditors—GEORGE E. NIX, J.C.L.; Sr. MARLENE WEISENBECK, F.S.P.A., J.C.L.

Diocesan Judge—Rev. MICHAEL J. GORMAN, J.C.L.

College of Consultors—Very Revs. JOSEPH J. RAFACZ, V.G.; ROBERT J. COOK; Revs. WILLIAM N. GREVATCH; EUGENE A. KLINK; JOHN L. PARR; MARK R. PIERCE; ROGER J. SCHECKEL; MICHAEL J. GORMAN, Sec.

Deans—Arcadia: Very Rev. LEONARD G. KAISER; Chippewa Falls: Very Rev. THOMAS E. LANGER; Durand: Very Rev. THOMAS J. DONALDSON; Eau Claire: Very Rev. JOHN A. SCHULTZ; La Crosse: Very Rev. ROBERT J. COOK; Marshfield: Very Rev. JAMES J. LOGAN; Mauston: Very Rev. THOMAS J. STEINERT O.S.Cam; Prairie du Chien: Very Rev. EUGENE J. WOLF; Richland Center: Very Rev. WAYNE R. KIDD; Sparta: Very Rev. JAMES P. MCNAMEE; Stevens Point: Very Rev. DONALD L. PRZYBYLSKI; Thorp: Very Rev. ROMAN F. KAISER; Wausau: Very Rev. WILLIAM N. GREVATCH; Wisconsin Rapids: Very Rev. R. JOHN SWING.

Diocesan Offices and Directors

Apostolate for the Indians—Vacant.

Boy Scouts—Rev. THOMAS F. LINDNER, *530 Main St., La Crosse, 54601.* Tel: 608-782-0322.

Building Commission—Very Rev. J. FLOYD DWYER; Revs. ALLAN L. SLOWIAK; MICHAEL J. GORMAN; SONDRA RIEDER; DONALD NOVOTNEY.

Catholic Women, Council of—Rev. DONALD M. BERG, Moderator, *St. Joachim Parish, P.O. Box 69, Pittsville, 54466-0069.* Tel: 715-884-6815.

Central Wisconsin Hispanic Ministry—*P.O. Box 4004, La Crosse, 54602-4004.* Tel: 608-788-7700.

Department of Catholic Education—ROBERT J. LECHELER, Dir., Catechetics; VIRGINIA HALBUR, Asst. Dir., Catechetics; DONALD F. NOVOTNEY, Dir., Schools; MARIANN HESIK, Asst. Dir., Schools; BOUA NENG YANG, LaCrosse Area Hmong Catechist, *3710 East Ave. S., P.O. Box 4004, La Crosse, 54602-4004.* Tel: 608-788-7707.

Family Life Secretariat—SUE GILBERT, Dir., *P.O. Box 4004, La Crosse, 54602-4004.* Tel: 608-788-7700.

Natural Family Planning—Coords.: JEFF HEINZEN; ALICE HEINZEN, *711 24th St. N.E., Menomonie, 54751.* Tel: 715-235-6226.

Holy Childhood Association—Very Rev. JOSEPH J. RAFACZ, Acting Dir., *P.O. Box 4004, La Crosse, 54602-4004.* Tel: 608-788-7700.

Hospitals and Health Affairs—Co-Coords.: Rev. EDMUND J. KLIMEK, *Sacred Heart Hospital, 900 W. Clairemont Ave., Eau Claire, 54701.* Tel: 715-839-4121. Rev. LAWRENCE G. DUNKLEE, *St. Charles Borromeo Parish, P.O. Box 292, Gonoa, 54632.* Tel: 608-689-2646.

Newman Campus Ministry—Rev. MARK R. PIERCE, Coord., *2108 4th Ave., Stevens Point, 54481.* Tel: 715-345-6500.

Office of Communications—ROSE A. HAMMES, Communications and Pub. Rels. Officer, *P.O. Box 4004, La Crosse, 54602-4004.* Tel: 608-788-7700.

Office of the Consecrated Life—Sr. MARLENE WEISENBECK, F.S.P.A., Dir., *P.O. Box 4004, La Crosse, 54602-4004.* Tel: 608-788-7700.

Office of Ecumenism—Rev. LYLE L. SCHULTE, Diocesan Officer, Ecumenical Questions, *910 Wilson Ave., Menomonie, 54751.* Tel: 715-232-4922.

Office of Justice and Peace—MICHAEL R. BROWN, Dir., *P.O. Box 4004, La Crosse, 54602-4004.* Tel: 608-788-7700. Justice and Peace Commission-confer Office.

Office of Ministries—Rev. JOHN L. PARR, Dir., *P.O. Box 4004, La Crosse, 54602-4004.* Tel: 608-788-7700. Office of Ministries consists of Vocation Office, Permanent Diaconate, Lay Ministries & Clergy Continuing Education.

Office for Pastoral Planning—Vacant, *P.O. Box 4004, La Crosse, 54602-4004.* Tel: 608-788-7700.

Office of Sacred Worship—Vacant, *P.O. Box 4004, La Crosse, 54602-4004.* Tel: 608-788-7700. Sacred Worship Commission-confer Office.

Office of Youth Ministry—DENNIS KURTZ, Dir., *P.O. Box 1062, Eau Claire, 54702-1062.* Tel: 715-834-7079.

Pastoral Council—Most Rev. RAYMOND L. BURKE, Pres.; Very Rev. JOSEPH J. RAFACZ, V.G., Exec. Sec., *P.O. Box 4004, La Crosse, 54602-4004.* Tel: 608-788-7700.

Personnel Council—Most Rev. RAYMOND L. BURKE, Pres.; Rev. WILLIAM G. MENZEL, Chm.; Rev. LYLE L. SCHULTE, Sec.; Very Revs. THOMAS J. DONALDSON; JOSEPH J. RAFACZ, V.G.; Revs. DAVID C. KUNZ; JOHN L. PARR; T. MICHAEL SCHELBLE; CHARLES D. STOETZEL, *P.O. Box 4004, La Crosse, 54602-4004.* Tel: 608-788-7700.

Presbyteral Council—Most Rev. RAYMOND L. BURKE, Pres. Elected Members: Revs. BERNARD D. MCGARTY; ANDREW K. KAROBLIS; DANIEL J. KELLY; DELBERT J. MALIN; A. JOSEPH FOLLMAR; EUGENE A. KLINK; WILLIAM G. MENZEL; ROBERT A. STREVELER; MARK R. PIERCE; EDWARD J. SHUTTLEWORTH; CARL J. DOCKENDORFF; JOHN W. WAMBACH, S.J.

Ex-Officio Members—Very Rev. JOSEPH J. RAFACZ, V.G., Moderator of the Curia; Rev. MICHAEL J. GORMAN, Chancellor. Consultors: Very Revs. ROBERT J. COOK; WILLIAM N. GREVATCH; Revs. JOHN L. PARR; ROGER J. SCHECKEL.

Propagation of the Faith—Very Rev. JOSEPH J. RAFACZ, V.G., Acting Dir., *P.O. Box 4004, La Crosse, 54602-4004.* Tel: 608-788-7700.

Rural Life Conference and Community Development—*P.O. Box 4004, La Crosse, 54602-4004.* Tel: 608-788-7700.

St. Joseph's Priest Fund, Inc., (Benevolent Society)—Rev. MICHAEL J. GORMAN, Exec. Sec., *P.O. Box 4004, La Crosse, 54602-4004.* Tel: 608-788-7700.

"Times Review": Diocesan Newspaper—GERALD RUFF, Editor, *P.O. Box 4004, La Crosse, 54602-4004.* Tel: 608-788-1524.

CLERGY, PARISHES, MISSIONS AND PAROCHIAL SCHOOLS

CITY OF LA CROSSE
(La Crosse County)

1—ST. JOSEPH THE WORKMAN CATHEDRAL, Very Rev. Robert J. Cook, Rector; Rev. Thomas F. Lindner.
Res., 530 Main St., 54601. Tel: 608-782-0322; Fax: 608-782-8228. [CEM 2]
School—1319 Ferry St., 54601. Tel: 608-782-5998; Fax: 608-784-9933. John Stellflue, Prin.
Lay Teachers 10; Students 192.

2—BLESSED SACRAMENT, Rev. Bernard O. McGarty.
Res., 130 Losey Blvd. S., 54601. Tel: 608-782-2953; Fax: 608-782-2770. [CEM 2]
School—(Grades K-6) 225 S. 24th St., 54601. Tel: 608-782-5564. Kay Berra, Prin.
Lay Teachers 21; Students 315.

3—HOLY CROSS. Closed. For inquiries for parish records contact St. Joseph the Workman Cathedral, La Crosse.

4—HOLY TRINITY, Rev. Lawrence B. Berger.
Res., 1333 S. 13th St., 54601. Tel: 608-782-2028. [CEM 2]
School—1417 S. 13th, 54601. Tel: 608-782-1040.
Lay Teachers 10; Students 174.

5—ST. JAMES THE LESS, Rev. Roger J. Scheckel.
Res., 1032 Caledonia St., 54603. Tel: 608-782-7557. [CEM 2]
School—716 Windsor St., 54603. Tel: 608-784-6167.
Lay Teachers 10; Students 135.

6—ST. JOHN THE BAPTIST. Closed. For inquiries for parish records contact St. James, La Crosse.

7—ST. MARY. Closed. For inquiries for parish records contact St. Joseph the Workman Cathedral, La Crosse.

8—ST. PIUS X, Very Rev. Joseph J. Rafacz, V.G.; Deacon Richard Sage.
Res., 3710 East Ave. S., P.O. Box 4004, 54602-4004. Tel: 608-788-1139. [CEM 2]
School—Tel: 608-788-6919.
Lay Teachers 9; Students 135.

9—RONCALLI NEWMAN PARISH, Rev. Leo J. Schneider.
Res., 1732 State St., 54601. Tel: 608-784-4994; Fax: 608-784-0230. [CEM 2]

10—ST. THOMAS MORE, Rev. Richard L. Fliss.
Res., 2006 Weston St., 54601. Tel: 608-788-5483. [CEM 2]
School—Tel: 608-788-5225.
Lay Teachers 10; Students 106.

11—ST. WENCESLAUS. Closed. For inquiries for parish records contact St. Joseph the Workman Cathedral, La Crosse.

OUTSIDE THE CITY OF LA CROSSE

Abbotsford, Clark Co., St. Bernard. Attended by Holy Rosary, Owen. Rev. Allen F. Jakubowski; Sr. Mary Jo Donaldson, O.S.B., Pastoral Assoc.
Res., 101 W. Cedar St., 54405-9558. Tel: 715-223-3331. [JC]

Adams, Adams Co., St. Joseph. Also serves St. Ann, Brooks. Rev. Dennis P. Stanchik; Deacon David Kennedy (MIL).
Res., Box 310, 53910. Tel: 608-339-3485. [CEM]

Alma, Buffalo Co., St. Lawrence. Attended by St. Boniface, Waumandee. Rev. Richard C. Dickman.
Mailing Address: P.O. Box 246, 54610. Tel: 608-685-3253; Fax: 608-685-3253.
Res., Box 962, Waumandee, 54622-0962. Tel: 608-626-2621. [CEM]

Alma Center, Jackson Co., Immaculate Conception. Attended by St. Joseph, Fairview. Rev. David A. Ziegelmaier.
Mailing Address: Box 188, 54611. Tel: 715-964-5201.
Res., N13740 Fairview Rd., Fairchild, 54741-8514. Tel: 715-334-2202. [CEM]

Almond, Portage Co., Holy Guardian Angels. Closed. For inquiries for parish records contact St. Maximilian Maria Kolbe, Southeastern Portage County.

Altdorf, Wood Co., St. Joseph, Rev. Joseph W. Hirsch.
Res., 530 10th Ave. N, Wisconsin Rapids, 54494. Tel: 715-421-5777. [CEM]

Altoona, Eau Claire Co., St. Mary, Rev. Norbert J. Wilger.
Res., 1827 Lynn Ave., 54720. Tel: 715-835-8813. [JC]
School—1828 Lynn Ave., 54720. Tel: 715-835-5334.
Lay Teachers 6; Students 75.

Amherst, Portage Co., St. James. Also serves St. Mary of Mount Carmel, Fancher. Rev. Robert F. Pedretti.
Res., 453 S Main, Box 280, 54406-0280. Tel: 715-824-3455. [CEM]

Arcadia, Trempealeau Co., Our Lady of Perpetual Help, Rev. Raymond J. Pedretti.
Office: 411 S. Washington St., 54612. Tel: 608-323-3178.
Res., 223 E. Maple St., 54612. Tel: 608-323-7116. [CEM 2]
School—Tel: 608-323-3676.

St. Stanislaus, Rev. Raymond J. Pedretti.
Res., 223 E. Maple St., 54612. Tel: 608-323-7116. [CEM]

Arkansaw, Pepin Co., St. Joseph, Rev. Matthew J. Molinaro.
Res., W. 7805 County Rd. Z, 54721. Tel: 715-285-5313. [CEM 2]

Arpin, Wood Co., St. Francis. Attended by St. James, Vesper. Rev. Chester J. Osowski.
Mailing Address: Box 68, Vesper, 54489. Tel: 715-569-4412. [CEM]

Athens, Marathon Co., St. Anthony de Padua. Also serves Holy Family, Poniatowski. Rev. Randy E. Olson.
Res., 417 Caroline St., Box 206, 54411-0206. Tel: 715-257-7684. [JC]
School—Tel: 715-257-7541.
Sisters 2; Lay Teachers 4; Students 90.

Auburndale, Wood Co., Nativity of the Blessed Virgin Mary, Rev. T. Michael Schelble.
Res., Also serves St. Michael, Hewitt. 5866 Main St., P.O. Box 177, 54412-0177. Tel: 715-652-2806. [CEM 2]
School—Tel: 715-652-2196; Fax: 715-652-8020.
Franciscan Sisters of Perpetual Adoration, F.S.P.A. 1; Lay Teachers 6; Students 83.

Augusta, Eau Claire Co., St. Anthony de Padua. Attended by Holy Guardian Angels, Brackett. Rev. Paul R. Gitter.
Mailing Address: 800 W. Brown St., P.O. Box 3, 54722. Tel: 715-286-2547.
Res., S10-444 U.S. Hwy. 53, Fall Creek, 54742. Tel: 715-878-4183.

Babcock, Wood Co., All Saints. Attended by Sacred Heart, Nekoosa. Very Rev. R. John. Swing.
Mailing Address: 711 Prospect Ave., Nakoosa, 54457. Tel: 715-886-3422.

Bakerville, Wood Co., Corpus Christi. Attended by Sacred Heart, Marshfield. Rev. Robert A. Schaller. In res., Rev. Charles P. Schumacher Tel: 715-676-2824.
Mailing Address: 10075 Hwy. BB, Marshfield, 54449. Tel: 715-676-3658.
Res., 112 E. 11th St., Marshfield, 54449-4216. Tel: 715-384-3213. [CEM]

Bangor, La Crosse Co., St. Mary. Attended by St. Leo the Great, West Salem. Rev. Robert S. Hegenbarth. In res., Rev. Paul L. Sankoorikal.
Mailing Address: 210 W. Hamlin St., West Salem, 54669. Tel: 608-786-0610. [CEM]
Res., P.O. Box 290, 54614-0290. Tel: 608-486-2033.

Bear Valley, Richland Co., St. Kilian. Closed. For inquiries for parish records contact Nativity, B.V.M., Keyesville.

Bevent, Marathon Co., St. Ladislaus. Attended by St. Joseph, Galloway. Rev. Rex A. Zimmerman; Sr. Mary Ellen Diermeier, S.S.J.-T.O.S.F., Pastoral Assoc.
Mailing Address: 6455 State Hwy. 153, Hatley, 54440. Tel: 715-446-3060. [CEM]

Big River, Pierce Co., Nativity of the Blessed Virgin Mary, Rev. John W. Beckfelt.
Res., W10137 570th Ave., River Falls, 54022. Tel: 715-425-5806. [CEM 2]

Black River Falls, Jackson Co., St. Joseph, Rev. Michael C. Braun.
Res., 507 Main St., 54615-1699. Tel: 715-284-5613. [CEM]

Blair, Trempealeau Co., St. Ansgar. Attended by St. John the Apostle, Whitehall. Rev. James J. Hagmann.
Mailing Address: P.O. Box 127, Whitehall, 54773-0127. Tel: 715-538-4607; Fax: 715-538-2224.

Blenker, Wood Co., St. Kilian. Attended by St. Wenceslaus, Milladore. Rev. John A. Wisneski.
Mailing Address: Box 100, Milladore, 54454. Tel: 715-457-2314. [CEM]

Bloomer, Chippewa Co., St. Paul. Also serves St. Jude, New Auburn. Very Rev. Thomas E. Langer.
Res., 1222 Main St., 54724. Tel: 715-568-3255; Fax: 715-568-3255. [CEM 3]
School—1210 Main St., 54724. Tel: 715-568-3233. Sisters 2; Lay Teachers 11; Students 167.
Convent—1205 13th Ave., 54724. Tel: 715-568-3266.

Boyceville, Dunn Co., St. Luke. Attended by St. Joseph, Menomonie. Rev. Lyle L. Schulte; Sr. Judith Kramer, O.S.B., Min.
Mailing Address: 605 Center St., P.O. Box 136, 54725. Tel: 715-232-4922.
Res., St. Bede Priory, P.O. Box 66, Eau Claire, 54702-0066. Tel: 715-834-3176; Fax: 715-834-4292.

Boyd, Chippewa Co., Sacred Heart of Jesus-St. Joseph. Attended by Holy Family, Stanley. Rev. Robert W. Nelson. In res., Rev. Eugene P. Smith Tel: 714-667-3038.
Res., 719 Patten St., P.O. Box 10, 54726-0010. Tel: 715-667-3341. [CEM]
School—Tel: 715-667-3346.
Lay Teachers 4; Students 78.

Brackett, Eau Claire Co., Holy Guardian Angels. Also serves St. Anthony, Augusta; and St. John, Fall Creek. Rev. Paul R. Gitter.
Res., S10444 U.S. Hwy. 53, Fall Creek, 54742. Tel: 715-878-4183. [CEM]

Brooks, Adams Co., St. Ann. Attended by St. Joseph, Adams. Rev. Dennis P. Stanchik.
Mailing Address: P.O. Box 132, Oxford, 53952. Tel: 608-584-4900. [CEM]

Buena Vista, Portage Co., St. Martin. Closed. For inquiries for parish records contact St. Maximilian Maria Kolbe, Southeastern Portage County.

Cadott, Chippewa Co., St. Rose of Lima. Also serves St. Anthony, Drywood. Rev. Thomas F. Crowley.
Res., Box 160, 54727. Tel: 715-289-4551. [CEM]
School—Tel: 715-289-4985.
Lay Teachers 6; Students 67.

Camp Douglas, Juneau Co., St. James. Also serves St. Michael, Indian Creek. Very Rev. Thomas J. Steinert, O.S.Cam., Admin.
Res., Box 289, 54618. Tel: 608-427-6762. [CEM]

Cashton, Monroe Co., Sacred Heart of Jesus, Rev. Kevin C. Louis.
Res., 26400 CTH U, 54619-9757. Tel: 608-823-7906; Fax: 823-7272. [CEM 3]
School—Sacred Heart of Jesus School, 1223 Front St., 54619. Tel: 608-654-7733.
Lay Teachers 8; Students 84.
Convent—Tel: 608-654-7413.

Cassel, Marathon Co., Sacred Heart. Attended by Nativity of the Blessed Virgin Mary, Marathon City. Revs. Joseph Diermeier, O.F.M.Cap.; Joseph Jeruzal, O.F.M.Cap.
Mailing Address: 3372 County Rd. S., P.O. Box 68, Marathon City, 54448-0068. Tel: 715-443-2045; Fax: 715-443-3045. [CEM]

Cazenovia, Richland Co., St. Anthony de Padua. Also serves Sacred Heart, Lone Rock; and St. Mary, Keyesville. Rev. Daniel J. Kiedinger.
Res., Rte. 2, Box 175, 53924. Tel: 608-983-2367. [CEM]
School—Rte. 2, P.O. Box 180, 53924. Tel: 608-983-2786.
Lay Teachers 4; Students 34.

Chili, Clark Co., St. Stephen. Attended by St. Mary, Neillsville. Rev. Joseph N. Henseler.
Mailing Address: P.O. Box 58, 54420-0058. Tel: 715-683-2418. [CEM]
Res., 1803 Black River Rd., Neillsville, 54456. Tel: 715-743-3840.

Chippewa Falls, Chippewa Co., Holy Ghost. Also serves St. Bridget, Springfield. Revs. Edmund J. Doerre; Charles J. Scherman, S.J.
Res., 412 S. Main St., 54729. Tel: 715-723-4890. [JC]
School—See Consolidated Elementary Schools, Chippewa Falls.

Notre Dame, Rev. Albert W. Sonnberger; Sr. Florence Domka, S.S.J.-T.O.S.F., Pastoral Assoc. In res., Rev. Richard W. Gilles.
Res., 117 Allen St., 54729-2899. Tel: 715-723-7108. [JC]
School—See Consolidated Elementary Schools, Chippewa Falls.

St. Charles Borromeo. Also serves St. John the Baptist, Cooks Valley; St. Peter, Tilden. Revs. William P. Felix; Daniel B. DuChez, O.S.
Res., 810 Pearl St., 54729. Tel: 715-723-4088; Fax: 715-723-2195. [JC]
School—See Consolidated Elementary Schools, Chippewa Falls.

Colby, Clark Co., St. Mary Help of Christians, Rev. John E. Malik.
Res., 205 S. 2nd St., P.O. Box 436, 54421. Tel: 715-223-3048. [CEM]
School—Tel: 715-223-3033.
Lay Teachers 10; Students 163.

Cooks Valley, Chippewa Co., St. John the Baptist. Attended by St. Charles Borromeo, Chippewa Falls. Rev. William P. Felix.
Mailing Address: 4540 State Hwy. 40, Bloomer, 54724. Tel: 715-568-3778.
Res., 810 Pearl St., Chippewa Falls, 54729. Tel: 715-723-4088. [CEM]

Coon Valley, Vernon Co., St. Mary, Rev. Maryon C. Jordan, O.S.B.
Res., 904 Central Ave., 54623. Tel: 608-452-3841; Fax: 608-452-3841. [CEM]

Cornell, Chippewa Co., Holy Cross. Also serves Sacred Heart, Jim Falls. Rev. Jeremiah Cashman.
Res., 107 S. 8th St., P.O. Box 68, 54732. Tel: 715-239-6826. [CEM 2]

Custer, Portage Co., Immaculate Conception. Attended by St. Adalbert, Rosholt. Rev. Joseph R. Konopacky; Sr. Annette Marie Johnson, S.S.N.D., Pastoral Assoc.
Res., 7176 County Rd. Q, 54423. Tel: 715-592-4330. [CEM]

Czestochowa, Clark Co., St. Mary of Czestochowa. Closed. For inquiries for parish records contact Holy Family, Stanley.

De Soto, Crawford Co., Sacred Heart. Attended by St. Charles Borromeo, Genoa. Rev. Lawrence G. Dunklee.
Mailing Address: St. Charles, P.O. Box 130, Genoa, 54632. Tel: 608-689-2646.

Dilly, Vernon Co., St. John Nepomucene. Closed. For inquiries for parish records contact St. Aloysius, Hillsboro.

Dorchester, Clark Co., St. Louis, Rev. James F. Schaefer.
Res., 133 N. 3rd St., 54425-9577. Tel: 715-654-5089. [JC]
School—134 N. 4th St., 54425. Tel: 715-654-5467.
Lay Teachers 4; Students 34.

Drywood, Chippewa Co., St. Anthony. Attended by St. Rose of Lima, Cadott. Rev. Thomas F. Crowley; Sr. Catherine Kaiser, F.S.P.A., Pastoral Assoc.
Res., P.O. Box 68, Jim Falls, 54748. Tel: 715-382-4422. [CEM]

Durand, Pepin Co., St. Mary's Assumption. Also serves Holy Rosary, Lima. Rev. Edward J. Shuttleworth; Deacon James Weingart.
Res., 911 W. Prospect St., P.O. Box 188, 54736-1049. Tel: 715-672-5640; Fax: 715-672-4193. [CEM]
School—901 W. Prospect St., 54736. Tel: 715-672-5617.
Franciscan Sisters of Perpetual Adoration 2; Lay Teachers 12; Students 188.

Eastman, Crawford Co., St. Wenceslaus, Rev. John V. Cassidy.
Res., P.O. Box 109, 54626. Tel: 608-874-4151. [CEM]

Eau Claire, Eau Claire Co.,

1—IMMACULATE CONCEPTION, Rev. Eugene A. Klink.
Res., 1712 Highland Ave., 54701. Tel: 715-835-9935.
School—(Grades K-8) 1715 Sherwin Ave., 54701. Tel: 715-835-3500.
Franciscan Sisters of Perpetual Adoration 4; Lay Teachers 16; Students 390.

2—NEWMAN COMMUNITY, Revs. George R. Szews; Edmund J. Klimek; Thomas J. Krieg; Deacon Larry Agema.
Res., 110 Garfield Ave., 54701-4042. Tel: 715-834-3399. [JC]

3—SACRED HEART OF JESUS, Rev. John W. Steiner.
Office: 416 N. Dewey St., 54703-3299. Tel: 715-835-9154.
Res., 318 Fulton St., 54703-5399. Tel: 715-832-0925. [CEM]
School—Eau Claire Coordinated Catholic Schools. See Consolidated Elementary Schools under Institutions Located in the Diocese. Tel: 715-835-1609.

4—ST. JAMES THE GREATER, Very Rev. John A. Schultz.
Res., 2502 Eleventh St., 54703-2700. Tel: 715-835-5887; Fax: 715-835-2032. [JC]
School—Eau Claire Coordinated Catholic Schools. See Consolidated Elementary Schools under Institutions Located in the Diocese. Tel: 715-832-8280.

5—ST. OLAF, Rev. Frank Corradi, S.C.; Deacon John Barnum.
Res., 2408 North Ln., 54703-0960. Tel: 715-832-2504. [JC]
School—Eau Claire Coordinated Catholic Schools. See Consolidated Elementary Schools under Institutions Located in the Diocese. Tel: 715-834-4959.

6—ST. PATRICK, Rev. John W. Steiner. In res., Rev. James F. Trempe.
Res., 318 Fulton St., 54703-5399. Tel: 715-832-0925. [CEM]
School—Eau Claire Coordinated Catholic Schools. See Consolidated Elementary Schools under Institutions Located in the Diocese. Tel: 715-835-8931; Fax: 715-835-4658.

Eau Galle, Dunn Co., St. Henry, Rev. James P. Binkowski.
Res., N. 460 CTH D, 54737. Tel: 715-283-4448. [CEM]

Edgar, Marathon Co., St. John the Baptist, Rev. Bernard L. Raschke; Deacon Herman Schulz.
Res., 103 N. Fourth Ave., P.O. Box 35, 54426. Tel: 715-352-3011; Fax: 715-352-3011. [CEM]
School—Tel: 715-352-3000.
Lay Teachers 8; Students 131.

Edson, Chippewa Co., Sacred Heart of Jesus. Attended by Sacred Heart of Jesus-St. Joseph, Boyd. Rev. Arthur S. Redmond.
Res., See Sacred Heart of Jesus-St. Joseph. R.R. 2, Box 284A, Boyd, 54726. Tel: 715-667-3341. [CEM]

Elk Mound, Dunn Co., St. Joseph, Rev. Henry R. Hoerburger.
Res., P.O. Box 275, 54739. Tel: 715-879-5332. [CEM]

Ellsworth, Pierce Co., St. Francis of Assisi, Very Rev. Thomas J. Donaldson.
Res., 264 S. Grant St., P.O. Box 839, 54011. Tel: 715-273-4774; Fax: 715-723-4774. [CEM]
School—Box 250, 54011. Tel: 715-273-4391.
Sisters of St. Benedict 1; Lay Teachers 8; Students 158.

Elmwood, Pierce Co., Sacred Heart. Also serves Sacred Heart of Jesus, Spring Valley. Rev. George A. Becker.
Res., 510 Wilson St., 54740. Tel: 715-639-2741. [CEM]

Elroy, Juneau Co., St. Patrick, Rev. G. Richard Roberts.
Res., 110 Spring St., 53929. Tel: 608-462-5875. [CEM]

Ettrick, Trempealeau Co., St. Bridget. Also serves St. Kevin, Melrose. Rev. Thomas J. McInnis.
Res., 22650 Washington St., 54627. Tel: 608-525-3811. [CEM]

Fairchild, Eau Claire Co., St. John Cantius. Attended by St. Joseph, Fairview. Rev. David A. Ziegelmaier.
Res., N13740 Fairview Rd., 54741-8514. Tel: 715-334-2202.

Fairview, Eau Claire Co., St. Joseph. Also serves Immaculate Conception, Alma Center; and St. John Cantius, Fairchild. Rev. David A. Ziegelmaier.
Res., N13740 Fairview Rd., Fairchild, 54741-8514. Tel: 715-334-2202.

Fall Creek, Eau Claire Co., St. John the Apostle. Attended by Holy Guardian Angels, Brackett. Rev. Paul R. Gitter.
Mailing Address: P.O. Box 322, 54742. Tel: 715-877-3400.
Res., S. 10444 U.S. Hwy. 53, 54742. Tel: 715-878-4183.

Fancher, Portage Co., St. Mary of Mount Carmel. Attended by St. James, Amherst. Rev. Robert F. Pedretti.
Res., P.O. Box 280, 453 S. Main St., Amherst, 54406. Tel: 715-824-3455. [CEM]

Fountain City, Buffalo Co., Immaculate Conception, Rev. J. Thomas Finucan.
Res., One Wall St., P.O. Box 218, 54629-0218. Tel: 608-687-3496. [CEM]

Galesville, Trempealeau Co., St. Mary. Attended by St. Bartholomew, Trempealeau.
Mailing Address: 20354 W. Ridge Ave., P.O. Box 68, 54630-0068. Tel: 608-582-2365.
Res., 11646 South St., Trempealeau, 54461-8238. Tel: 608-534-9760.

Galloway, Marathon Co., St. Joseph. Also serves St. Ladislaus, Bevent. Rev. Rex A. Zimmerman; Sr. Mary Ellen Diermeier, S.S.J.-T.O.S.F., Pastoral Assoc.
Res., 8846 CTH C, Wittenberg, 54499-8936. Tel: 715-454-6431. [CEM]

Gays Mills, Crawford Co., St. Mary. Also serves St. Philip, Rolling Ground. Rev. Leon S. Rausch, S.J.
Res., Box 36, 54631-0036. Tel: 608-735-4420. [JC]

Genoa, Vernon Co., St. Charles Borromeo. Also serves Sacred Heart, DeSoto. Rev. Lawrence G. Dunklee.
Res., P.O. Box 130, 54632. Tel: 608-689-2646. [CEM]
School—Tel: 608-689-2642.
Lay Teachers 6; Students 65.

Germantown, Juneau Co., Our Lady of the Lake. Attended by St. Paul, New Lisbon. Rev. Steven M. Baures.
Res., 408 W. River St., New Lisbon, 53950. Tel: 608-562-3125. [CEM]

Greenwood, Clark Co., St. Mary Help of Christians. Also serves Holy Family, Willard. Rev. A. Joseph Follmar.
Res., 123 N. Main St., P.O. Box 70, 54437. Tel: 715-267-6282. [CEM]
School—Tel: 715-267-6477.
Lay Teachers 4; Students 48.

Halder, Marathon Co., St. Patrick. Attended by Nativity of the Blessed Virgin Mary, Marathon City. Revs. Joseph Diermeier, O.F.M.Cap.; Joseph Jeruzal, O.F.M.Cap.
Mailing Address: 3158 Halder Dr., Mosinee, 54455. Tel: 715-693-2765. [CEM]

Hatley, Marathon Co., St. Florian, Rev. Thomas J. Abraham.
Res., 500 Church Ln., P.O. Box 110, 54440. Tel: 715-446-2252; 446-3085 (Office). [CEM]
School—Tel: 715-446-3950.
Lay Teachers 5; Students 78.

Heffron, Portage Co., St. John the Baptist. Closed. For inquiries for parish records contact St. Maximilian Maria Kolbe, Southeastern Portage County.

Hewitt, Wood Co., St. Michael. Attended by St. Mary, Auburndale. Rev. T. Michael Schelble.
Office: 11086 Main St., 54441. Tel: 715-384-7676.
Res., 5866 Main St., Box 177, Auburndale, 54412. Tel: 715-652-2806; Fax: 715-384-7675. [CEM]

Hillsboro, Vernon Co., St. Aloysius, Rev. James E. Ennis.
Res., 545 Prairie Ave., Box 466, 54634. Tel: 608-489-2580.

Holmen, La Crosse Co., St. Elizabeth Ann Seton, Rev. Delbert J. Malin; Sr. Bridget Donaldson, O.S.B., Pastoral Assoc.
Office: 515 N. Main St., 54636. Tel: 608-526-4424; Fax: 608-526-3177.
Res., 704 Hillcrest Dr., 54636.

Independence, Trempealeau Co., SS. Peter and Paul. Also serves St. Michael, North Creek. Very Rev. Leonard G. Kaiser.
Res., 308 Osseo Rd., P.O. Box 428, 54747-0428. Tel: 715-985-2227. [CEM]
School—Tel: 715-985-3719.
Lay Teachers 10; Students 120.

Indian Creek, Juneau Co., St. Michael. Attended by St. James, Camp Douglas. Very Rev. Thomas J. Steinert, O.S.Cam.
Mailing Address: P.O. Box 289, Camp Douglas, 54618. Tel: 608-427-6762. [CEM]

Jim Falls, Chippewa Co., Sacred Heart. Attended by Holy Cross, Cornell. Rev. Jeremiah Cashman; Sr. Catherine Kaiser, F.S.P.A., Pastoral Assoc.
Res., Box 68, 54748. Tel: 715-382-4422.

Junction City, Portage Co., St. Michael. Attended by St. Wenceslaus, Milladore. Rev. John A. Wisneski.
Res., P.O. Box 100, Milladore, 54454. Tel: 715-457-2314. [CEM]

Kendall, Monroe Co., St. Joseph. Also serves St. John the Baptist, Wilton. Very Rev. James P. McNamee.
Res., 307 Spring St., P.O. Box 155, 54638. Tel: 608-463-7120. [CEM]

Keyesville, Richland Co., Nativity of the Blessed Virgin Mary. Attended by St. Anthony, Cazenovia. Rev. Daniel J. Kiedinger.
Mailing Address: Rte. 2, Box 247, 53581. Tel: 608-585-4846. [CEM]
Res., R.R. 2, Box 175, Cazenovia, 53924. Tel: 608-983-2367.

Knowlton, Marathon Co., St. Francis Xavier. Also serves St. John the Baptist, Peplin. Rev. Joseph A. Grassl.
Res., 651 Mead Ln., Mosinee, 54455. Tel: 715-693-3120. [CEM]

Lanark, Portage Co., St. Patrick. Closed. For inquiries for parish records contact St. Maximilian Maria Kolbe, Southeastern Portage County.

Lima, Pepin Co., Holy Rosary. Attended by St. Mary, Durand. Rev. Edward J. Shuttleworth.
Office: N6235 CTH V, Durand, 54736. Tel: 715-672-5911.
Res., 911 W. Prospect St., Box 188, Durand, 54736-1048. Tel: 715-672-5640. [CEM]
School—Tel: 715-672-4276.
Lay Teachers 4; Students 62.

Lone Rock, Richland Co., Sacred Heart. Attended by St. Anthony, Cazenovia. Rev. Daniel J. Kiedinger.
Mailing Address: Rte. 2, Box 175, Cazenovia, 53924. Tel: 608-983-2367.

Loyal, Clark Co., St. Anthony of Padua, Very Rev. Roman F. Kaiser.
Res., 407 N. Division St., P.O. Box 69, 54446-0069. Tel: 715-255-8017. [CEM]
School—212 W. Spring St., Tel: 715-255-8636.
Lay Teachers 7; Students 94.

Lyndon Station, Juneau Co., St. Mary, Rev. Ronald T. Zinkle, S.J.
Res., 117 Juneau St. N., P.O. Box 303, 53944. Tel: 608-666-2421. [CEM]

Marathon City, Marathon Co., Nativity of the Blessed Virgin Mary. Also serves Sacred Heart, Cassel & St. Patrick, Halder. Revs. Joseph Diermeier, O.F.M.Cap.; Joseph B. Jeruzal, O.F.M.Cap.
Res., 712 Market St., Box 7, 54448-0007. Tel: 715-443-2045. [CEM]
School—Tel: 715-443-3430.
Franciscan Sisters of Perpetual Adoration 2; Lay Teachers 16; Students 260.

Marshfield, Wood Co., Our Lady of Peace, Very Rev. James J. Logan.
Res., 1414 W. 5th St., 54449. Tel: 715-384-9414. [JC]
School—1300 W. 5th St., 54449. Tel: 715-384-5474.
Sisters of Notre Dame 2; Lay Teachers 20; Students 202.

Sacred Heart of Jesus. Also Serves Corpus Christi, Bakerville. Rev. Robert A. Schaller.
Res., 112 E. 11th St., 54449-4216. Tel: 715-384-3213. [JC]
School—School Sisters of Notre Dame, 1117 S. Central Ave., 54449. Tel: 715-384-3939.
Lay Teachers 6; Students 53.

St. John the Baptist. Also serves Christ the King, Spencer. Rev. Charles D. Stoetzel. In res., Rev. Douglas C. Robertson.
Res., 201 W. Blodgett St., P.O. Box 644, 54449-0644. Tel: 715-384-3252; Fax: 715-384-4989. [JC]
School—Tel: 715-384-4989.
Lay Teachers 15; Students 240.

Mauston, Juneau Co., St. Patrick, Rev. Thomas J. Reardon; Very Rev. Thomas J. Steinert, O.S.Cam.
Res., 401 Mansion St., 53948-1393. Tel: 608-847-6054. [CEM 2]
School—325 Mansion St., 53948. Tel: 608-847-5844.
Lay Teachers 12; Students 209.

Melrose, Jackson Co., St. Kevin. Attended by St. Bridget, Ettrick. Rev. Thomas J. McInnis.
Mailing Address: St. Bridget, 22650 Washington, Ettrick, 54627. Tel: 608-525-3811. [JC]

Menomonie, Dunn Co., St. Joseph. Also serves St. Luke, Boyceville. Revs. Lyle L. Schulte; William P. Neis.
Res., 910 Wilson Ave., 54751. Tel: 715-232-4922; Fax: 715-232-4923. [CEM]
School—910 Ninth Ave., 54751. Tel: 715-232-4920; Fax: 715-232-4923.
Lay Teachers 7; Students 190.

Middle Ridge, La Crosse Co., St. Peter. Also serves St. Joseph, St. Joseph Ridge. Very Rev. Robert P. Hundt.
Res., Box 101, W695 Hwy. 33, Rockland, 54653. Tel: 608-486-2180. [CEM]

Milan, Marathon Co., St. Thomas. Attended by St. John the Baptist, Wuerzburg. Rev. Leonard C. Stashek.
Mailing Address: 1506 Wuerzburg Rd., Athens, 54411. Tel: 715-257-7092. [CEM]

Mill Creek, Portage Co., St. Bartholomew. Attended by St. Stephen, Stevens Point. Very Rev. Dennis J. Lynch; Miss Laura J. Kaufmann, Pastoral Assoc.
Res., 2493 CTH. M, Stevens Point, 54481. Tel: 715-344-3003. [CEM]

Milladore, Wood Co., St. Wenceslaus. Also serves St. Kilian, Blenker & St. Michael, Junction City. Rev. John A. Wisneski.
Res., 146 Main St., Box 100, 54454. Tel: 715-457-2314. [CEM]

Mondovi, Buffalo Co., Sacred Heart of Jesus, Rev. William J. Blazewicz.
Res., 503 W. Hudson St., 54755. Tel: 715-926-3619. [CEM 2]
School—227 S. State St., 54755. Tel: 715-926-4407.
Lay Teachers 3; Students 42.
Convent—Tel: 715-926-4418.

Mosinee, Marathon Co., St. Paul, Rev. Jerome G. Hoeser.
Res., 603 Fourth St., 54455. Tel: 715-693-2650; Fax: 715-693-1332. [CEM]
School—404 High St., 54455. Tel: 715-693-2675; Fax: 715-693-1332.
Sisters 1; Lay Teachers 11; Students 137.

Necedah, Juneau Co., St. Francis of Assisi, Rev. James J. Lesczynski.
Res., 202 W. 5th St., 54646-8142. Tel: 608-565-2488. [CEM]
Church—Main at Sixth, 54646.

Neillsville, Clark Co., St. Mary. Also serves St. Stephen, Chili. Rev. Joseph N. Henseler.
Res., 1803 Black River Rd., 54456. Tel: 715-743-3840. [CEM]

Nekoosa, Wood Co., Sacred Heart of Jesus. Also serves All Saints, Babcock; St. Alexander, Port Edwards. Very Rev. R. John Swing.
Res., 711 Prospect Ave., 54457. Tel: 715-886-3422; Fax: 715-886-3954.
School—710 Vilas Ave., 54457. Tel: 715-886-3761.
Lay Teachers 9; Students 148.

New Auburn, Chippewa Co., St. Jude. Attended by St. Paul, Bloomer. Very Rev. Thomas E. Langer.
Mailing Address: 1222 Main St., Bloomer, 54724. Tel: 715-568-3255; Fax: 715-568-3255.

New Lisbon, Juneau Co., St. Paul. Also serves Our Lady of the Lake, Germantown. Rev. Steven H. Baures.
Res., 408 W. River St., 53950. Tel: 608-562-3125. [CEM]

North Creek, Trempealeau Co., St. Michael. Attended by SS. Peter and Paul, Independence. Very Rev. Leonard G. Kaiser.
Mailing Address: 308 Osseo Rd., Independence, 54747. Tel: 715-985-2227. [CEM]

Norwalk, Monroe Co., St. Augustine of Hippo, Rev. Kevin C. Louis. In res., Rev. James W. Genovesi Tel: 608-823-7339.
Res., 26400 CTH U, Cashton, 54619-9757. Tel: 608-823-7906; Fax: 608-823-7272. [CEM]

Onalaska, La Crosse Co., St. Patrick, Rev. William J. Matzek; Deacons J. Michael Koza; Frank Abnet. In res., Rev. Edwin J. Thome.
Res., 1031 Main St., 54650. Tel: 608-783-5535.
School—127 N. 11th Ave., 54650. Tel: 608-783-5483; Fax: 608-783-5483.
Lay Teachers 11; Students 232.

Owen, Clark Co., Holy Rosary. Also serves St. Bernard, Abbotsford. Rev. Allen F. Jakubowski.
Res., 415 W. 3rd St., P.O. Box 309, 54460-0309. Tel: 715-229-2747.
School—Tel: 715-229-2348.
Lay Teachers 5; Students 53.

Peplin, Marathon Co., St. John the Baptist. Attended by St. Francis Xavier, Knowlton. Rev. Joseph A. Grassl. In res., Rev. Wladyslaw J. Kowalski (SUP).
Mailing Address: 651 Mead Ln., Mosinee, 54455. Tel: 715-693-3120. [CEM]

Pine Creek, Trempealeau Co., Most Sacred Heart, Rev. Robert F. Polcyn, O.F.M.Cap., Parochial Admin.
Res., N20555 CTH G, Dodge, 54625-9721. Tel: 608-539-3704.

Pittsville, Wood Co., St. Joachim. Also serves North American Martyrs, Spaulding. Rev. Donald M. Berg.
Res., 5312 Third Ave., P.O. Box 69, 54466-0069. Tel: 715-884-6815. [CEM]

Plover, Portage Co., St. Bronislava, Rev. Patrick A. Umberger.
Res., 3200 Plover Rd., P.O. Box 158, 54467-0158. Tel: 715-344-4326; Fax: 715-344-6121. [CEM]
School—3301 Willow Dr., 54467. Tel: 715-341-6700.

Plum City, Pierce Co., St. John the Baptist, Rev. Ambrose J. Blenker.
Res., 212 Church Rd., P.O. Box 206, 54761-0206. Tel: 715-647-2301. [CEM]
School—Tel: 715-647-2901.
Lay Teachers 5; Students 65.

Polonia, Portage Co., Sacred Heart. Attended by St. Adalbert, Rosholt. Rev. Joseph R. Konopacky. In res., Rev. Steven J. Kachel.
Res., 7375 Church St., Custer, 54423. Tel: 715-592-4221. [CEM]
School—7379 Church St., Custer, 54423. Tel: 715-592-4902.
Lay Teachers 4; Students 80.
Convent—7381 Church St., Custer, 54423. Tel: 715-592-4213.

Poniatowski, Marathon Co., Holy Family. Attended by St. Anthony de Padua, Athens. Rev. Randy E. Olson; Deacon LeRoy Knauf.
Mailing Address: P.O. Box 206, Athens, 54411-0206. Tel: 715-257-7684. [CEM]

Port Edwards, Wood Co., St. Alexander. Attended by Sacred Heart, Nekoosa. Very Rev. R. John Swing.
Office: 880 First St., 54469. Tel: 715-887-3012.
Res., 711 Prospect Ave., Nekoosa, 54457. Tel: 715-886-3422.

Prairie du Chien, Crawford Co., St. Gabriel, Revs. William F. Gerut, S.J.; Burton W. Pratt, S.J.; John W. Wambach, S.J.
Office: 506 N. Beaumont Rd., P.O. Box 176, 53821-0176. Tel: 608-326-2404. [JC]
School—515 N. Beaumont Rd., 53821. Tel: 608-326-8624.
Lay Teachers 16; Students 266.

St. John Nepomucene, Revs. William F. Gerut, S.J.; Burton W. Pratt, S.J.; John W. Wambach, S.J. In res., Rev. Raymond O. Burger, S.J.
Res., 710 S. Wacouta St., P.O. Box 28, 53821-0028. Tel: 608-326-6511.
School—Prairie Catholic Schools, 720 S. Wacouta St., 53821. Tel: 608-326-4400.
Lay Teachers 9; Students 105.

Prescott, Pierce Co., St. Joseph, Rev. Thomas J. Mannion.
Res., 269 Dakota St. S., P.O. Box 245, 54021-0245. Tel: 715-262-5310. [CEM]
School—281 Dakota St. S., 54021. Tel: 715-262-5912.
Franciscan Sisters of Perpetual Adoration 3; Lay Teachers 5; Students 116.
Convent—268 Dakota St. S., 54021. Tel: 715-262-5105.

Richland Center, Richland Co., St. Mary (Assumption of B.V.M.), Very Rev. Wayne R. Kidd.
Res., 160 W. 4th St., P.O. Box 456, 53581. Tel: 608-647-2621. [CEM]
School—155 W. 5th St., 53581. Tel: 608-647-2422.
Sisters 1; Lay Teachers 11; Students 114.
Convent—789 N. Central Ave., 53581. Tel: 608-647-4933.

Rising Sun, Crawford Co., St. James. Closed. For inquiries for parish records contact St. Mary, Viroqua.

Rock Falls, Dunn Co., St. Joseph, Rev. Anton L. Lecheler.
Res., E. 9265 STH 85, Mondovi, 54755-8857. Tel: 715-875-4539. [CEM]

Rolling Ground, Crawford Co., St. Philip. Attended by St. Mary, Gays Mills. Rev. Leon S. Rausch, S.J.
Mailing Address: P.O. Box 36, Gays Mills, 54631-0036. Tel: 608-735-4420. [CEM]

Rosholt, Portage Co., St. Adalbert. Also serves Immaculate Conception, Custer; Sacred Heart, Polonia. Rev. Joseph R. Konopacky.
Res., 3315 St. Adalbert Rd., 54473. Tel: 715-677-4519. [CEM]
School—3314 St. Adalbert Rd., 54473. Tel: 715-677-4517.
Religious 1; Lay Teachers 5; Students 38.

Rothschild, Marathon Co., St. Mark, Rev. Allan L. Slowiak; Deacon Patrick McKeough.
Res., 602 Military Rd., 54474-1523. Tel: 715-359-5206.
School—Wausau Area Catholic Schools. See Consolidated Elementary Schools under Institutions Located in the Diocese.

St. Therese of the Child Jesus, Rev. Robert A. Streveler.
Res., 113 Kort St., 54474-1094. Tel: 715-359-2421. [CEM]
School—Wausau Area Catholic Schools. See Consolidated Elementary Schools under Institutions Located in the Diocese.

Rozellville, Marathon Co., St. Andrew. Attended by St. Joseph, Stratford. Rev. Thomas J. Rudolph. In res., Rev. Arthur S. Redmond Tel: 715-384-3859.
Res., Box 6, Stratford, 54484. Tel: 715-687-2404. [CEM]

Rudolph, Wood Co., St. Philip. Attended by St. Lawrence, Wisconsin Rapids. Rev. John P. Hogan.
Office: 6957 Grotto Ave., Box 165, 54475. Tel: 715-435-3286. [CEM]
Res., 530 Tenth Ave. N., Wisconsin Rapids, 54495. Tel: 715-421-5777.
School—Tel: 715-435-3386.
Lay Teachers 7; Students 69.

Saint Joseph Ridge, La Crosse Co., St. Joseph. Attended by St. Peter, Middle Ridge. Rev. Robert P. Hundt.
Res., W2601 Hwy. 33, La Crosse, 54601. Tel: 608-788-1646. [CEM]

Saint Mary's Ridge, Monroe Co., Nativity of the Blessed Virgin Mary. Also serves St. Augustine, Norwalk; St. John the Baptist, Summit; Sacred Heart of Jesus, Cashton. Rev. Kevin C. Louis.
Res., 26400 CTH U, Cashton, 54619-9157. Tel: 608-823-7906; Fax: 608-823-7272. [CEM]
School—Tel: 608-823-7577.
Lay Teachers 3; Students 30.

Seneca, Crawford Co., St. Patrick. Also serves Sacred Heart, Wauzeka. Very Rev. Eugene J. Wolf; Deacon Fredrick R. Skrade.
Res., Box 18, 54654. Tel: 608-734-3931. [CEM]

Sigel, Wood Co., Holy Rosary. Attended by St. James, Vesper. Rev. Chester J. Osowski.
Mailing Address: 6190 Chapel Rd., Wisconsin Rapids, 54495-9215. Tel: 715-569-4412. [CEM]

Southeastern Portage County, Portage Co., St. Maximilian Maria Kolbe, Rev. Charles J. Hiebl.
Res., 1632 Oak St., Box 66, Almond, 54909-0066. Tel: 715-366-2811; 824-3380. [CEM 4]

Sparta, Monroe Co., St. Patrick, Rev. Mark A. Walljasper.
Res., 319 W. Main St., 54656-2143. Tel: 608-269-2655. [CEM]
School—318 W. Oak St., 54654. Tel: 608-269-4748.
Lay Teachers 11; Students 168.

Spaulding-City Point, Jackson Co., North American Martyrs. Attended by St. Joachim, Pittsville. Rev. Donald M. Berg.
Mailing Address: Box 69, Pittsville, 54466-0069. Tel: 715-884-6815. [CEM 2]

Spencer, Marathon Co., Christ the King. Attended by St. John, Marshfield. Rev. Charles D. Stoetzel.
Res., 101 Wendell St., 54479-0156. Tel: 715-659-4480. [JC]

Spring Valley, Pierce Co., Sacred Heart of Jesus. Attended by Sacred Heart, Elmwood. Rev. George A. Becker; Sr. Karen Freund, O.P., Pastoral Assoc.
Res., S. 105 Sabin Ave., P.O. Box 456, 54767-0456. Tel: 715-778-5519. [CEM]

Springfield, Eau Claire Co., St. Bridget. Attended by Holy Ghost, Chippewa Falls. Revs. Edmund J. Doerre; Charles J. Scherman, S.J.
Office: 412 S. Main, Chippewa Falls, 54729. Tel: 715-723-4890. [CEM]

Stanley, Chippewa Co., Holy Family. Also serves Sacred Heart of Jesus-St. Joseph, Boyd. Rev. Robert W. Nelson.
Office: 226 E. 3rd Ave., P.O. Box 125, 54768. Tel: 715-644-5435.
Res., 239 S. Franklin St., P.O. Box 125, 54768. Tel: 715-644-5435. [CEM]
School—136 3rd Ave., 54768. Tel: 715-644-3602.
Lay Teachers 8; Students 49.
Convent—303 S. Franklin, 54768. Tel: 715-644-5953. Sisters of St. Joseph

Stevens Point, Portage Co.,

1—Newman University Parish, Rev. Mark R. Pierce.
Office: 2108 Fourth Ave., 54481. Tel: 715-345-6500.
Res., 838 Fremont St., 54481. Tel: 715-344-9117. [JC]

2—St. Casimir. Also serves St. Mary, Torun. Rev. Donald J. Walczak; Sr. Catherine Kieliszewski, S.S.J.-T.O.S.F., Pastoral Assoc.
Res., 203 W. Casimir Rd., 54481. Tel: 715-344-9582. [CEM]

3—St. Joseph, Rev. Alan T. Burkhardt.
Res., 1709 Wyatt Ave., 54481-3699. Tel: 715-341-1617. [JC]
School—See Consolidated Elementary Schools, Stevens Point.

4—St. Peter, Rev. Gerald E. Fisher. In res., Rev. Dennis A. Worzalla (Diocese of Green Bay).
Res., 800 4th Ave., 54481-1627. Tel: 715-344-6115. [JC]
School—See Consolidated Elementary Schools, Stevens Point.

5—St. Stanislaus, Very Rev. Donald L. Przybylski; Deacon Hugh Walker. In res., Rev. Mark R. Pierce.
Res., 838 N. Fremont St., 54481. Tel: 715-344-9117; Fax: 715-344-1771. [JC]
School—See Consolidated Elementary Schools, Stevens Point.

6—St. Stephen. Also serves St. Bartholomew, Mill Creek. Rev. Dennis J. Lynch; Deacon Robert Hensen.
Res., 1401 Clark St., 54481. Tel: 715-344-3319. [CEM]
School—See Consolidated Elementary Schools, Stevens Point.

Stratford, Marathon Co., St. Joseph. Also serves St. Andrew, Rozellville. Rev. Thomas J. Rudolph.
Res., 420 Larch St., Box 6, 54484. Tel: 715-687-2404. [CEM 3]
School—P.O. Box 6, 54484. Tel: 715-687-4145.
Lay Teachers 11; Students 110.

Summit, Monroe Co., St. John the Baptist. Attended by Nativity of the Blessed Virgin Mary, St. Mary's Ridge. Rev. Kevin C. Louis.
Mailing Address: 26400 CTH U, Cashton, 54619-9757. Tel: 608-823-7906; Fax: 608-823-7272. [CEM]

Thorp, Clark Co., St. Bernard-St. Hedwig Parish, Rev. John W. Puerner.
Res., Box 329, 54771. Tel: 715-669-5526. [CEM]
School—Box 369, 54771. Tel: 715-669-5530.
Sisters of St. Joseph 1; Lay Teachers 11; Students 140.

Tilden, Chippewa Co., St. Peter. Attended by St. Charles Borromeo, Chippewa Falls. Rev. William P. Felix.
Mailing Address: 11358 CTH Q, Chippewa Falls, 54729-6115. Tel: 715-288-6484; Fax: 715-228-6008.
Res., 11358 CTU Q, Chippewa Falls, 54729-6115. Tel: 715-723-4088; Fax: 715-723-2195. [CEM]
School—(Grades 1-8) 11370 CTH Q, 54729. Tel: 715-288-6250.
Lay Teachers 5; Students 78.

Tomah, Monroe Co., St. Mary (Immaculate Conception). Also serves St. Andrew, Warrens. Rev. Daniel E. Kozlowski.
Res., 303 W. Monroe St., 54660. Tel: 608-372-4516. [CEM]
School—315 W. Monroe St., 54660. Tel: 608-372-5765.
Lay Teachers 14; Students 223.

Torun, Portage Co., St. Mary. Attended by St. Casimir, Stevens Point. Rev. Donald J. Walczak; Sr. Catherine Kieliszewski, S.S.J.-T.O.S.F., Pastoral Assoc.
Res., 5589 Dewey Dr., Stevens Point, 54481. Tel: 715-344-2599. [CEM]

Trempealeau, Trempealeau Co., St. Bartholomew. Also serves St. Mary, Galesville. Rev. Robert J. Wagner.
Res., 11646 South St., 54661-8238. Tel: 608-534-6652. [CEM 2]

Union Center, Juneau Co., St. Theresa of Avila. Closed. For inquiries for parish records contact St. Jerome, Wonewoc.

Vesper, Wood Co., St. James. Also serves St. Francis, Arpin; Holy Rosary, Sigel. Rev. Chester J. Osowski.
Res., 6623 N. Church St., Box 68, 54489. Tel: 715-569-4412. [CEM]

Viroqua, Vernon Co., Annunciation of the Blessed Virgin Mary, Rev. James H. Miller.
Res., 400 Congress Ave., 54665. Tel: 608-637-7711. [CEM]

Warrens, Monroe Co., St. Andrew. Attended by St. Mary (Immaculate Conception), Tomah. Rev. Daniel E. Kozlowski.
Mailing Address: Rte. 2, Box 18, 54666. Tel: 608-378-4813.
Res., 303 W. Monroe St., Tomah, 54660. Tel: 608-372-4516.

Waumandee, Buffalo Co., St. Boniface. Also serves St. Lawrence, Alma.
Res., Box 962, 54622-0962. Tel: 608-626-2621; Fax: 608-685-3253. [CEM 2]
School—Tel: 608-626-2611.
Students 43.

Wausau, Marathon Co.,

1—Holy Name of Jesus, Rev. Norman D. Boneck; Mrs. Patricia Gaska, Pastoral Assoc.
Res., 1104 S. Ninth Ave., 54401. Tel: 715-842-4543; Fax: 715-845-5059. [JC]
School—Wausau Area Catholic Schools. See Consolidated Elementary Schools under Institutions Located in the Diocese. Tel: 715-848-3281.

2—St. Anne, Revs. Steven J. Brice; Woodrow H. Pace.
Res., 710 N. 6th Ave., 54401. Tel: 715-675-9749; Fax: 715-675-4718. [JC]
School—Wausau Area Catholic Schools. See Consolidated Elementary Schools under Institutions Located in the Diocese. Tel: 715-845-5754.

3—St. James the Greater, Rev. Stephen F. Gross.
Res., 621 Second St., 54403. Tel: 715-845-6715; Fax: 715-845-6715. [JC]
School—Wausau Area Catholic Schools. See Consolidated Elementary Schools under Institutions Located in the Diocese.

4—St. Mary (Immaculate Conception), Rev. Stephen F. Gross.
Office: 408 Seymour St., 54403-6266. Tel: 715-845-5379.
Res., 621 Second St., 54403. [JC]
School—Wausau Area Catholic Schools. See Consolidated Elementary Schools under Institutions Located in the Diocese.

5—St. Matthew, Rev. Robert T. Altmann; Deacon Garry Lee Jolliffe.
Res., 2700 Westwood Dr., 54401. Tel: 715-842-3148; 842-3209. [JC]
School—Wausau Area Catholic Schools. See Consolidated Elementary Schools under Institutions Located in the Diocese.
St. Matthew Parish Education Center—221 S. 28th Ave., 54401. Tel: 715-845-2938.

6—St. Michael, Very Rev. William N. Grevatch.
Res., 1315 6th St., 54403-3599. Tel: 715-842-4283; 842-2344; Fax: 715-849-2509. [CEM]
School—Wausau Area Catholic Schools. See Consolidated Elementary Schools under Institutions Located in the Diocese.
Convent—611 Stark, 54403. Tel: 715-845-6885.

Wauzeka, Crawford Co., Sacred Heart. Attended by St. Patrick, Seneca. Very Rev. Eugene J. Wolf; Sr. Donna Weber, F.S.P.A., Pastoral Assoc.
Res., 711 E. Main St., P.O. Box 237, 53826. Tel: 608-875-5401. [CEM]

West Salem, La Crosse Co., St. Leo the Great. Also serves St. Mary, Bangor. Rev. Robert S. Hegenbarth.
Res., 210 W. Hamlin St., 54669. Tel: 608-786-0610.

Weston, Marathon Co., St. Agnes, Rev. William J. Jablonske.
Res., 6101 Zinser St., 54476. Tel: 715-359-5675; Fax: 715-359-4392. [CEM]

Whitehall, Trempealeau Co., St. John the Apostle. Also serves St. Ansgar, Blair. Rev. James J. Hagmann.
Res., 35900 Lee St., P.O. Box 127, 54773-0127. Tel: 715-538-4607.

Willard, Clark Co., Holy Family. Attended by St. Mary Help of Christians, Greenwood. Rev. A. Joseph Follmar.
Res., 123 N. Main St., Greenwood, 54437. Tel: 715-267-6282; 267-6760. [CEM]

Wilson, WI, Eau Claire Co., St. Peter. Closed. For inquiries for parish records contact Sacred Heart-St. Joseph, Boyd.

Wilton, Monroe Co., St. John the Baptist. Attended by St. Joseph, Kendall. Very Rev. James P. McNamee.
Res., Box 155, Kendall, 54638. Tel: 608-463-7120. [CEM]

Wisconsin Rapids, Wood Co.,

1—Our Lady, Queen of Heaven, Rev. Mark A. Doyle.
Res., 750 10th Ave., S., 54494. Tel: 715-423-1251.
School—Tel: 715-423-9350.
Lay Teachers 12; Students 236.

2—St. Lawrence. Also serves St. Philip, Rudolph. Rev. John P. Hogan; Deacon James L. Landry. In res., Rev. Joseph W. Hirsch.
Res., 530 10th Ave., N., 54494. Tel: 715-421-5777; 424-2651. [JC]
School—551 10th Ave. N., 54494. Tel: 715-424-1112; Fax: 715-424-1124.
Lay Teachers 6; Students 64.

3—St. Vincent de Paul, Rev. William G. Menzel.
Res., 820 13 St. S., 54494-5336. Tel: 715-423-2111.
School—831 12th St. S., 54494. Tel: 715-423-6470.
Lay Teachers 13; Students 225.

4—SS. Peter and Paul, Rev. Andrew K. Karoblis.
Res., 1150 2nd St. N., 54494. Tel: 715-423-1351. [CEM]
School—1140 N. 2nd St., 54494. Tel: 715-423-4770.
Lay Teachers 10; Students 92.

Wonewoc, Juneau Co., St. Jerome. Attended by St. Patrick, Elroy. Rev. G. Richard Roberts.
Office: 528 N. Center St., R.R. 2, Box 87A, 53968. Tel: 608-464-7713.
Res., 110 Spring St., Elroy, 53929. Tel: 608-462-5875. [CEM]

Wuerzburg, Marathon Co., St. John the Baptist. Also serves St. Thomas, Milan. Rev. Leonard C. Stashek.
Res., 1506 Wuerzburg Rd., Athens, 54411. Tel: 715-257-7092. [CEM]

Yuba, Richland Co., St. Wenceslaus. Closed. For inquiries for parish records contact St. Aloysius, Hillsboro.

Chaplains of Public Institutions

Oxford. *Federal Correctional Institute,* 53952. Tel: 608-584-5511. Rev. Daniel Kelly, Chap., Res., 406 Thomas St., P.O. Box 162, Westfield, 53964. Tel: 608-296-3170.

Tomah. *Veterans Administration Medical Center,* 54660. Tel: 608-372-3971. Rev. Myles J. Kenny, C.S.Sp., Chap.

Wausau. *Wausau Hospital Center,* 333 Pine Ridge Blvd., 54401. Tel: 715-847-2121; 847-2840. Rev. Michael J. Lynch, Res., 4303 Lake Shore Dr., 54401. Tel: 715-355-4499.

Special Assignment:
Reverend Fathers—
Gorman, Michael J., Chancellor, P.O. Box 4004, La Crosse, WI 54602-4004
McHugh, John T., Dir. of Holy Cross Seminary House of Formation, P.O. Box 4004, Lacrosse, WI 54602-4004. Tel: 608-788-9095
Parr, John L., Dir. of Ministries, P.O. Box 4004, La Crosse, WI 54602-4004
Powell, Leon A., Vice Chancellor, P.O. Box 4004, La Crosse, WI 54602-4004. Tel: 608-788-7700; 788-4625
Rafacz, Joseph J., Moderator of the Curia & Vicar Gen., P.O. Box 4004, La Crosse, WI 54602-4004

On Duty Outside the Diocese:
Reverend Fathers—
Faber, Emmett N., 77 Cynthia Dr., Bastrop, TX 78602-9530
Heagle, John L., Tara Center, 1037 S. 102nd St., Seattle, WA 98168. Tel: 206-763-8721
Mason, James E., 233 S. Kane St., Burlington, WI 53105
Monti, Robert M., 3003 Terramar St., Apt. 201, Fort Lauderdale, FL 33304-4037. Tel: 954-561-5908
O'Lenny, Patrick J., Pastor of Holy Family Chapel, N. Yorkshire, U.K., PSC 45, Box 1503, APO, APE, 09468 U.S.A.

Graduate Studies:
Reverend Fathers—
Berns, Eric R., Pontifical North American College, 00120 Vatican City State, Europe. Tel: 001-396-6849-3377
Wolf, Anthony J., Pontifical North American College, 00120 Vatican City State, Europe. Tel: 011-396-6849-3456

Foreign Missions:
Reverend Fathers—
Flock, Robert H., Parroquia de la Santa Cruz, Casilla 713, Santa Cruz, Bolivia. Tel: 011-591-343-0302
Penchi, Edward J., Parroquia de la Santa Cruz, Casilla 713, Santa Cruz, Bolivia. Tel: 011-591-343-0302
Walijewski, Joseph A., Casa Hogar Juan Pablo II, Lurin 16, Peru. Tel: 011-5114-30-5646

Awaiting Assignment:
Reverend Fathers—
Mish, Roy L.

Absent on Leave:
Reverend Fathers—
Ball, Bruce E.

Suspended:
Reverend Fathers—
Peters, Raymond W.

Retired:
Reverend Monsignors—
Dall, Norbert P., W5735 Timber Trail, New Lisbon, WI 53950. Tel: 608-565-7714
Finucan, James P., Holy Cross Diocesan Center, 3710 E. Ave. S., P.O. Box 4004, La Crosse, WI 54602-4004
Reverend Fathers—
Abts, Cletus, Box 402, Tomahawk, WI 54487
Blecha, Charles A., 420 Heller Rd., Apt. 322, Menomonie, WI 54751
Bofenkamp, Andrew H., 304 Second St., Apt. 5, Spencer, WI 54479
Bornbach, Raymond H., 215 W. Upham St., Marshfield, WI 54449. Tel: 715-384-7571
Coke, James E., 143 Charles St., Elk Rapids, MI 49629
Connolly, Robert V., Holy Cross Diocesan Center, 3710 East Ave. S., P.O. Box 4004, La Crosse, WI 54602-4004
Cosgrove, J. Kelly, 4182 Mt. Vernon Ave., Titusville, FL 32780
Curtiss, John B., 207 Marlbank Dr., Yorktown, VA 23692-4233
Devine, Patrick T., Holy Cross Diocesan Center, 3710 East Ave. S., P.O. Box 4004, La Crosse, WI 54602-4004
Dockendorff, Carl J., 1092 Queensway, Nekoosa, WI 54457
Dwyer, J. Floyd, Holy Cross Diocesan Center, 3710 East Ave. S., P.O. Box 4004, La Crosse, WI 54602-4004
Eichman, Dominic P., Winter Residence, 10343 Oakmont Dr., Sun City, AZ 85351
Ferron, Joseph B., Longwood Building 5, #2C, 11811 Avenue of PGA, Palm Beach Gardens, FL 33418
Fischer, Anthony W., 408 W. Arnold St., Marshfield, WI 54449
Garthwaite, Thomas F., 163 Stanley St. E., West St. Paul, MN 55118
Geissler, Lloyd F., 309 Hwy. 107 N., Marathon, WI 54448
Geissler, Ralph J., 705 Munes St., Athens, WI 54411
Gerum, Jerome G., 1601 N. Palmetto Ave., P.O. Box 673, Marshfield, WI 54449-0673. Tel: 715-387-4783
Hansen, Robert H., Holy Cross Diocesan Center, 3710 East Ave. S., P.O. Box 4004, La Crosse, WI 54602-4004
Hemmersbach, Alfred F., Holy Cross Diocesan Center, 3710 East Ave. S., P.O. Box 4004, La Crosse, WI 54602-4004
Herrmann, Richard J., 309 W. Blodgett St., Marshfield, WI 54449. Tel: 715-384-5039
Kamla, Jerome J., 8316 E. Calypso Ave., Mesa, AZ 85208
Keating, Joseph R., P.O. Box 639, North East, MD 21901-0639
Kelly, Bernard T., W. 7407 CTH Z, R.R. 2, Box 284, Onalaska, WI 54650
King, Norbert E., 135 Charles St., Schofield, WI 54476-1202
Knauf, Edwin L., Loring Apartments, Apt. 3, 648 N. Main, River Falls, WI 54022
Kulovits, Fred A., 221 Scott St., Apt. 412, Wausau, WI 54403
Lee, Henry H., 817 Macomber St., Chippewa Falls, WI 54729
Leinfelder, Philip, Holy Cross Diocesan Center, 3710 East Ave. S., P.O. Box 4004, La Crosse, WI 54602-4004
Leisle, Charles E., 3141 Mayer Rd., Eau Claire, WI 54701
Leketas, Peter J., 109 North Oak Ave., Apt. M, Marshfield, WI 54449. Tel: 715-384-8331
Mauel, John N., 5533 Woodland St., Stevens Point, WI 54481
Mertens, Michael G., Holy Cross Diocesan Center, 3710 East Ave. S., P.O. Box 4004, La Crosse, WI 54602-4004. Tel: 608-788-0311
Moczarny, Chester B., Holy Cross Diocesan Center, 3710 East Ave. S., P.O. Box 4004, La Crosse, WI 54602-4004
Murphy, John T., Winter Residence, 1100 Ponce de Leon Cir., Apt. 208E, Vero Beach, FL 32960
Nikolai, William V., Holy Cross Diocesan Center, 3710 East Ave. S., P.O. Box 4004, La Crosse, WI 54602-4004
Nowak, Bernard J., Keeler Park Apartments, 601 Seneca Manor Dr., Apt. 14L, Rochester, NY 14621
Oberwinder, Robert J., Bethany-St. Joseph Care Center, 2501 Shelby Rd., La Crosse, WI 54601
Papiernik, Roman J., 3460 Woodbridge Ct., La Crosse, WI 54601
Redmond, Arthur S., St. Andrew Rectory, D1876 CTHC, P.O. Box 106, Stratford, WI 54484-0106
Reuter, Arnold F., Holy Cross Diocesan Center, 3710 East Ave. S., P.O. Box 4004, La Crosse, WI 54602-4004. Tel: 608-788-0717
Schreiber, Bernard G., Bethany-St. Joseph Care Center, 2501 Shelby Rd., La Crosse, WI 54601
Schulte, Oswald W., Holy Cross Diocesan Center, 3710 East Ave. S., P.O. Box 4004, La Crosse, WI 54602-4004. Tel: 608-788-1402
Schulz, Raymond B., Heritage Manor, 307 Royal Ave., Elroy, WI 53929. Tel: 608-462-8494
Schumacher, Charles P., Corpus Christi, 10775 Hwy. BB, Marshfield, WI 54449. Tel: 715-676-2824
Simmons, Hilary F., Winter Residence, 2731 S.W. 11th Ct., Fort Lauderdale, FL 33312
Smith, Eugene D., St. Joseph Rectory, P.O. Box 10, Boyd, WI 54726-0010. Tel: 715-667-3038
Szczerbicki, Thaddeus P., 5319 Greenview Ln., Stevens Point, WI 54481
Tetzlaff, Joseph W., 2327 Morningside Dr., Mosinee, WI 54455
Theisen, Donald J., 1025 Pine Beach Rd., Apt. 207, Marinette, WI 54143
Thome, Edwin J., St. Patrick Rectory, 1031 Main St., Onalaska, WI 54650. Tel: 608-783-5535
Trant, John P., 5456 N. Lakewood, Chicago, IL 60640
Wagner, Raymond J., 211 Rincon Loop, Tijeras, NM 87059. Tel: 505-281-9158
Wozniak, Aloysius A., Casilla 713, Santa Cruz, Bolivia. Tel: 011-591-343-0302
Zoromski, Herbert P., 409 Moonlite Rd., Wittenberg, WI 54499. Tel: 715-454-6994
Zvinklys, Antanas, Holy Cross Diocesan Center, 3710 East Ave. S., P.O. Box 4004, La Crosse, WI 54602-4004

Permanent Deacons:
Abnet, Frank, St. Patrick, Onalaska
Agema, Larry, Newman Community, Eau Claire
Barnum, John, St. Olaf, Eau Claire
Beck, Guy, Marshfield
Braski, Raymond, Retired
Ebben, Ronald, St. Anthony Retreat Center, Marathon
Hensen, Robert, St. Stephen, Stevens Point
Hite, James, On Leave
Hurrish, Florian, (Retired)
Jolliffe, Garry, St. Matthew, Wausau
Kennedy, David (MIL), St. Joseph, Adams
Knauf, LeRoy, Holy Family, Poniatowski
Koza, J. Michael, St. Patrick, Onalaska
Landry, James, St. Lawrence, Wisconsin Rapids
McKeough, Patrick, St. Mark, Rothschild
Proulx, Rahlf, Holy Family Medical Center, Manitowoc
Richard, Gordon, On Leave
Sage, Richard, St. Pius X, La Crosse
Schulz, Herman, St. John the Baptist, Edgar
Skrade, Fredrick, St. Patrick, Seneca
Stack, William, On Leave
Walker, Hugh, St. Stanislaus, Stevens Point
Weingart, James, St. Mary's Assumption, Durand; Holy Rosary, Lima

INSTITUTIONS LOCATED IN THE DIOCESE

[A] SEMINARIES DIOCESAN

LA CROSSE. *Holy Cross Seminary House of Formation*, 3710 East Ave. S., P.O. Box 4004, 54602-4004. Tel: 608-788-9095; Fax: 608-788-8413. Revs. John T. McHugh, Dir.; Michael J. Gorman, Asst. Dir.; Mr. Trevor M. Hall, Prefect. Tel: 608-788-4925. Students 7.

[B] COLLEGES AND UNIVERSITIES

LA CROSSE. *Viterbo College*, 815 S. 9th, 54601-4797. Tel: 608-796-3000; Fax: 608-796-3050.
For a complete listing, refer to the Colleges and Universities section.

[C] HIGH SCHOOLS, DIOCESAN

LA CROSSE. *Aquinas High School*, 315 S. 11th St., 54601. Tel: 608-784-0287; Fax: 608-782-8851. Mr. James Vail, Prin.; Rev. John T. McHugh, Chaplain Instructor. Central Catholic Secondary School for the La Crosse Area. Faculty: Priests 2; Lay Teachers 33; Students 465.

CHIPPEWA FALLS. *McDonell Central Catholic High School*, 1316 Bel Air Blvd., 54729. Tel: 715-723-9126; Fax: 715-723-1501. Mr. John Flanagan, Prin.; Rev. Richard W. Gilles, Chap. Instructor. Central Secondary School for Catholics of Chippewa Falls and surrounding parishes. Priests 1; Lay Teachers 20; Students 264.

EAU CLAIRE. *Regis High School*, 2100 Fenwick Ave., 54701-4498. Tel: 715-835-5141. Mr. William Uelmen, Prin. Central Secondary School for Catholics of Eau Claire, Altoona and surrounding parishes. Priests 1; Lay Teachers 21; Students 235.

MARSHFIELD. *Columbus High School*, 710 Columbus Ave., 54449. Tel: 715-387-1177. Revs. Paul Lauzon, S.D.S., Prin.; Douglas C. Robertson, Chap. Instructor. Central Secondary School of Marshfield and surrounding area. Priests 2; Lay Teachers 19; Students 186.

STEVENS POINT. *Pacelli High School*, 1301 Maria Dr., 54481. Tel: 715-341-2442. Bro. John Vietoris, F.S.C., Prin.; Rev. Steven J. Kachel, Chap., Instructor. Priests 1; Christian Brothers 2; Sisters 3; Lay Teachers 23; Students 315.

WAUSAU. *Newman High School*, 1130 W. Bridge St., 54401. Tel: 715-845-8274 Rev. Fax: 715-842-1302. Mr. Donald J. Sisler, Prin.; Rev. Woodrow H. Pace, Chap. Central Catholic Secondary School of Wausau, Marathon, Schofield, Rothschild and Mosinee. Priests 1; Lay Teachers 25; Students 234.

WISCONSIN RAPIDS. *Assumption High School*, 445 Chestnut St., 54494. Tel: 715-423-2920. Mr. James J. Dyer, Prin.; Rev. Joseph W. Hirsch, Chap., Instructor. Central Catholic Secondary School for Wisconsin Rapids and surrounding area. Priests 1; Lay Teachers 15; Students 180.

[D] CONSOLIDATED ELEMENTARY SCHOOLS

LA CROSSE. *Aquinas Middle School*. (Grades 7-8), 315 S. 11th St., 54601. Tel: 608-784-0287; Fax: 608-782-8851. Mrs. Kathleen Forslund, Prin.; Rev. John T. McHugh, Chap. Faculty 21; Students 260.

CHIPPEWA FALLS. *Chippewa Area Catholic Schools*, 1316 Bel Air Blvd., 54729. Tel: 715-723-0538; Fax: 715-723-1501. Mr. Michael Sullivan, Area Admin.
Holy Ghost. (Grades 3-5), 436 S. Main St., 54729. Tel: 715-723-6478. Margaret Glose, Prin. Lay Teachers 13; Students 188.
Notre Dame Middle School. (Grades 6-8), 22 S. Prairie, 54729. Tel: 715-723-4777. Marilyn Joseph, Prin. Lay Teachers 13; Students 201.
St. Charles Borromeo. (Grades PreK-2), 429 W. Spruce St., 54729. Tel: 715-723-5827. Margaret Glose, Prin. Lay Teachers 13; Students 236.

EAU CLAIRE. *Eau Claire Coordinated Catholic Schools*, 322 Fulton St., 54703. Tel: 715-835-8931. Mr. Rob T. Fortener, Area Admin.
Sacred Heart. (Grades PreK-1), 418 N. Dewey St., 54703. Tel: 715-835-1609. Lay Teachers 4; Students 69.
St. James. (Grades K-5), 2502 11th St., 54703-2700. Tel: 715-832-8280. Faculty 8; Students 99.
St. Olaf. (Grades K-5), 2407 North Ln., 54703-0961. Tel: 715-834-4959. Faculty 8; Students 96.
St. Patrick Middle School. (Grades 6-8), 322 Fulton St., 54703. Tel: 715-835-8931. Rev. James F. Trempe, Chap. Faculty 8; Students 76.

MARSHFIELD. *Holy Family Middle School*. (Grades 7-8), 710 Columbus Ave., 54449. Tel: 715-384-7184. Revs. Paul Lanzon, S.D.S., Admin.; Douglas C. Robertson, Chap. Priests 2; Lay Teachers 7; Students 99.

STEVENS POINT. *Stevens Point Area Catholic Schools*, 1408 Ellis St., 54481. Tel: 715-341-2445. Mrs. Joanne Lodzinski, Area Admin.
St. Joseph. (Grades K-2), 1901 Lincoln Ave., 54481. Tel: 715-341-2878. Lay Teachers 6; Students 119.
St. Peter Middle School. (Grades 6-8), 708 First St., 54481. Tel: 715-344-1890. Anne Rogalski, Prin.; Rev. Steven J. Kachel, Chap. Lay Teachers 16; Students 224.
St. Stanislaus. (Grades K-5), 2150 High St., 54481. Tel: 715-344-3086. Lay Teachers 11; Students 183.
St. Stephen. (Grades PreK, 3-5), 1335 Clark St., 54481. Tel: 715-344-3751. Lay Teachers 9; Students 214.
St. Bronislava. (Grades K-3), 3301 Willow Dr., Plover, 54467. Tel: 715-342-2015. Lay Teachers 5; Students 112.

WAUSAU. *Wausau Area Catholic Schools*, 602 Second St., 54401. Tel: 715-845-5735. Marian Wolaver, Area Admin.
Holy Name. (Grades PreK-5), 1122 S. 9th Ave., 54401. Tel: 715-848-3281. Sisters of the Divine Saviour. Lay Teachers 12; Students 147.
St. Anne's. (Grades PreK-5), 604 N. 6th Ave., 54401. Tel: 715-845-5754. Lay Teachers 16; Students 277.
St. Matthew Middle School. (Grades 6-8), 225 S. 28th Ave., 54401. Tel: 715-845-5735. Rev. Woodrow H. Pace, Chap. Lay Teachers 19; Students 242.
St. Michael. (Grades PreK-5), 614 Steuben, 54403. Tel: 715-848-0206. Felician Sisters 1; Lay Teachers 14; Students 171.
St. Mark, Rothschild. (Grades K-3), 602 Military Rd., Rothschild, 54474-1523. Tel: 715-359-5206. Sisters of the Divine Savior. Lay Teachers 13; Students 120.
St. Therese, Schofield. (Grades PreK, 4-6), 113 W. Kort St., Schofield, 54476. Tel: 715-359-2131. Franciscan Sisters of St. Joseph. Lay Teachers 10; Students 113.

[E] GENERAL HOSPITALS

LA CROSSE. *Franciscan Skemp Healthcare, Mayo Health System, La Crosse Campus Medical Center*, 700 West Ave. S., 54601-4796. Tel: 608-785-0940; Fax: 608-791-9429.
For a complete listing, refer to the Hospitals section.

ARCADIA. *Franciscan Skemp Healthcare, Mayo Health System, Arcadia Campus Hospital*, 464 S. St. Joseph Ave., 54612. Tel: 608-323-3341.
For a complete listing, refer to the Hospitals section.

CHIPPEWA FALLS. *St. Joseph's Hospital*, 2661 County Rd. I, 54729. Tel: 715-723-1811.
For a complete listing, refer to the Hospitals section.

EAU CLAIRE. *Sacred Heart Hospital*, 900 W. Clairemont Ave., 54701-5105. Tel: 715-839-4121.
For a complete listing, refer to the Hospitals section.

HILLSBORO. *St. Joseph's Memorial Hospital, Inc.*, 400 Water Ave., P.O. Box 527, 54634. Tel: 608-489-2211.
For a complete listing, refer to the Hospitals section.

MARSHFIELD. *St. Joseph's Hospital*, 611 St. Joseph Ave., 54449. Tel: 715-387-1713.
For a complete listing, refer to the Hospitals section.

SPARTA. *Franciscan Skemp Healthcare, Mayo Health System, Sparta Campus Hospital*, 310 W. Main St., 54656-2142. Tel: 608-269-2132.
For a complete listing, refer to the Hospitals section.

*STANLEY. *Victory Medical Center, Inc.*, 230 E. Fourth Ave., 54768. Tel: 715-644-5571; Fax: 715-644-5665.
For a complete listing, refer to the Hospitals section.

STEVENS POINT. *St. Michael's Hospital and School for Med. Technology*, 900 Illinois Ave., 54481. Tel: 715-346-5000; Fax: 715-346-5077.
For a complete listing, refer to the Hospitals section.

[F] REHABILITATION FACILITIES

LA CROSSE. *St. Francis Community Programs, Inc.*, 700 West Ave. S., 54601-4796. Tel: 608-791-9582.
Gerard Hall. 14 bed home for single mothers.
St. Francis Community Housing, Inc. Apartment units for chronically mentally ill; 8 bed apartment unit in Dodgeville, WI; and 12 bed apartment unit in Prairie du Chien, WI.
St. Francis Housing Alternatives, Inc. Apartment units for the chronically mentally ill; 8 bed apartment unit in Arcadia, WI; 8 bed apartment unit in Black River Falls, WI; and 8 bed apartment unit in Mauston, WI.

CHIPPEWA FALLS. *Libertas-L.E. Phillips Treatment Center for the Chemically Dependent*, 2661 County Rd. I, 54729. Tel: 715-723-5585. Hospital Sisters Health System, Hospital Sisters of the Third Order of St. Francis. David B. Fish, Exec. Vice Pres.; Larry W. Monson, Program Coord. Bed Capacity 44; Patients assisted annually 11,072.
Transitus House, 1830 Wheaton St., 54729. Tel: 715-723-1155. Hospital Sisters of the Third Order of St. Francis. David B. Fish, Chm.; Judith J. Munkholm-Jones, M.S., Program Coord. Transitional living facility for women recovering from chemical dependency. Legal Title: *Hospital Sisters HealthCare-West, Inc.* Beds 20; Assisted annually 83.

[G] HOMES FOR AGED

LA CROSSE. *Bethany-St. Joseph Care Center*, 2501 Shelby Rd., 54601. Tel: 608-788-5700.
For a complete listing, refer to the Special Care Facilities section.
Elder Care of North La Crosse, Inc. (Village Apts. of St. James), 800 St. James St., 54603. Tel: 608-791-9784.
For a complete listing, refer to the Special Care Facilities section.
Franciscan Elder Care, Inc., 800 West Avenue S., 54601-4796. Tel: 608-791-9774.
For a complete listing, refer to the Special Care Facilities section.
Franciscan Skemp Healthcare, Mayo Health System, La Crosse Campus Nursing Home, 620 S. 11th St., 54601. Tel: 608-791-9787.
For a complete listing, refer to the Special Care Facilities section.
St. Joseph's Nursing Home, 2902 East Ave., S., 54601. Tel: 608-788-9870.
For a complete listing, refer to the Special Care Facilities section.

ARCADIA. *Franciscan Skemp Healthcare, Mayo Health System, Arcadia Campus Nursing Home*, 464 S. St. Joseph Ave., 54612. Tel: 608-323-3341.
For a complete listing, refer to the Special Care Facilities section.

EAU CLAIRE. *St. Francis Apartment*, 851 University Dr., 54701. Tel: 715-834-1388.
For a complete listing, refer to the Special Care Facilities section.

HILLSBORO. *St. Joseph's Nursing Home*, P.O. Box 527, 54634.
For a complete listing, refer to the Special Care Facilities section.

ONALASKA. *Franciscan Skemp Healthcare, Mayo Health System, Onalaska Nursing Home*, 1600 Main St., 54650. Tel: 608-783-4681.
For a complete listing, refer to the Special Care Facilities section.

SPARTA. *Elder Care of Sparta, Inc.*, 622 S. Court, 54656. Tel: 608-791-9774.
For a complete listing, refer to the Special Care Facilities section.
Franciscan Skemp Healthcare, Mayo Health System, Sparta Campus Nursing Home, 310 W. Main St., 54656-2142. Tel: 608-269-2132.
For a complete listing, refer to the Special Care Facilities section.

WAUSAU. *Marywood Convalescent Center*, 1821 N. 4th Ave., 54401. Tel: 715-675-9451.
For a complete listing, refer to the Special Care Facilities section.

[H] RETREAT HOUSES

LA CROSSE. *Franciscan Spirituality Center*, 920 Market St., 54601-4782. Tel: 608-791-5295. Franciscan Sisters of Perpetual Adoration. Sr. Mary Kathryn Fogarty, F.S.P.A., Dir.

EAU CLAIRE. *Saint Bede Retreat and Conference Center*, 1190 Priory Rd., P.O. Box 66, 54702-0066. Tel: 715-834-8642. Benedictine Sisters. Co-Directors: Sr. Hildegarde Geraets, O.S.B.; Mary Traynor.

MARATHON CITY. *St. Anthony Retreat Center*, 300 E. 4th St., 54448-9602. Tel: 715-443-2236. The Province of St. Joseph of the Capuchin Order, Inc. Rev. Kenneth W. Reinhart, O.F.M.Cap., Dir. Priests 4; Brothers 2; Sisters 1.

POLONIA. *St. Clare Center for Spirituality*, 7381 Church St., 54423. Tel: 715-592-4680. Felician Sisters. Sr. Mary Therese Lukas, C.S.S.F., Dir.

[I] MONASTERIES AND RESIDENCES OF PRIESTS AND BROTHERS

LA CROSSE. *Holy Cross (Seminary) Diocesan Center*, 3710 East Ave. S., P.O. Box 4004, 54602-4004. Tel: 608-788-7700. Mr. John J. Newman, Dir. In res., Most Revs. Frederick W. Freking. Tel: 608-788-0668; John J. Paul. Tel: 608-788-8395; Rev. Msgr. James P. Finucan. Tel: 608-788-7151; Very Revs. J. Floyd Dwyer. Tel: 608-788-6935; Joseph J. Rafacz. Tel: 608-788-6594; Revs. Robert V. Connolly. Tel: 608-788-1218; Patrick T. Devine; Dominic P. Eichman. Tel: 608-788-4714; Michael J. Gorman. Tel: 608-788-4578; Robert H. Hansen. Tel: 608-788-3918; Alfred F. Hemmersbach. Tel: 608-788-8326; Philip Leinfelder. Tel: 608-787-5833; John T. McHugh. Tel: 608-788-9095; Michael G. Mertens. Tel: 608-788-0311; Chester B. Moczarny. Tel: 608-787-5834; John T. Murphy. Tel: 608-788-9597; William V. Nikolai. Tel: 608-787-1839; John L. Parr. Tel: 608-788-4866; Leon A. Powell. Tel: 608-788-4625; Arnold F. Reuter. Tel: 608-788-0717; Oswald W. Schulte. Tel: 608-788-1402; Thomas J. Smith. Tel: 608-788-4555; Antanas Zvinklys. Tel: 608-788-2539.

DE SOTO. *Brothers of St. Pius X*, P.O. Box 217, 54624-0217. Tel: 608-648-2087. Bro. Charles Bisenius, C.S.P.X., Dir.

MARATHON CITY. *St. Anthony Retreat Center*, 300 E. Fourth St., 54448-9602. Tel: 715-443-2236. The Province of St. Joseph of the Capuchin Order, Inc. Revs. Kenneth W. Reinhart, O.F.M.Cap., Dir.; Peter Hesse, O.F.M.Cap.; John Guimond, O.F.M.Cap.; Loran Miller, O.F.M. Cap. Priests 4; Brothers 2.

PLOVER. *Brothers of the Christian Schools Residence*, 2421 Deepwood Ct., 54467. Tel: 715-344-3853. The Brothers of the Christian Schools. Bro. Gary Smith, F.S.C., Dir.

ST. MARY'S RIDGE. *Immaculate Conception Priory*. 26400 CTH U, Cashton, 54619-9757. Tel: 608-823-7992; Fax: 608-823-7992. Institute of Christ the King-Sovereign Priest. Rev. Timothy E. Svea, Supr.

SPARTA. *Our Lady of Spring Bank, Cistercian Abbey*, Rt. 3, Box 211, 54656-9536. Tel: 608-269-8138; Fax: 608-269-2800. Legal Office for Cistercian Monasteries Auxiliary. Rt. Rev. Blaise J. Fuez, O.Cist., Abbot; Very Rev. Bernard McCoy, O.Cist., Prior; Rev. Gregory Norman, O.Cist. Solemnly Professed 4; Postulants 1; Novices 1.

[J] CONVENTS AND RESIDENCES FOR SISTERS

LA CROSSE. *St. Rose Convent*, 912 Market St., 54601. Tel: 608-782-5610; Fax: 608-782-6301. Motherhouse and Novitiate of the Congregation of the Franciscan Sisters of Perpetual Adoration. Sr. Marla Lang, F.S.P.A., Pres.
In community: Professed 529; Transfers 6.
In Motherhouse: Sisters 90.

Villa St. Joseph, W2658 State Rd. 33, 54601-2625. A Retirement home for aged and convalescent Sisters. Franciscan Sisters of Perpetual Adoration. Sr. Maris Kerwin, F.S.P.A., Admin. Sisters 15; Lay Staff 83; Under Care 100.

CHIPPEWA FALLS. *St. Francis Convent*, 2509 County Rd. I, 54729. Tel: 715-723-7476. Hospital Sisters of the Third Order of St. Francis. Sr. Frances E. Schmitz, O.S.F., Coord. Professed Sisters 6.

St. Joseph Convent, 5085 176th St., 54729. Tel: 715-723-7479. Hospital Sisters of the Third Order of St. Francis.

Sisters of St. Benedict - Lakeside North, 2821 CTH I, 54729. Tel: 715-723-0005. Residence for Sisters of the Order of St. Benedict. Sr. Mary Frances Gebhard, O.S.B., Health Care & House Coord. Sisters 15.

EAU CLAIRE. *Sacred Heart Hospital Franciscan Sisters Convent*, 901 University Ave., 54701. Tel: 715-839-8725. Hospital Sisters of the Third Order of St. Francis. Sr. Augusta Sperl, O.S.F., Coord. Professed Sisters 6.

St. Bede Priory, 1190 Priory Rd., P.O. Box 66, 54702-0066. Tel: 715-834-3176. Motherhouse of Sisters of the Order of St. Benedict. Retreat and Conference Center. Sr. Margaret Michaud, O.S.B., Prioress; Rev. Thomas J. Krieg, Chap. Professed 53.

POLONIA. *St. Clare Convent*, 7381 Church St., 54423. Tel: 715-592-4213. Sr. M. Ursula Myszka, Local Min. Felician Sisters 6.

STEVENS POINT. *St. Joseph Congregational Home*, 1300 Maria Dr., 54481. Tel: 715-344-2830. Residence of the Sisters of St. Joseph of the Third Order of St. Francis. Sr. Marise Zielinski, S.S.J.-T.O.S.F., Coord.; Rev. Robert W. Greatorex, Chap. Tel: 715-344-8346. Sisters 75.

[K] SOCIAL SERVICE AGENCIES

LA CROSSE. *Catholic Charities Inc.*, 128 S. Sixth St., P.O. Box 266, 54602-0266. Tel: 608-784-5323; Fax: 608-782-0702. Ms. Marky Engler, Exec. Dir. Total Staff 50; Patients assisted annually 2,046.

Riverdale Clinic, 128 S. 6th St., P.O. Box 266, 54602-0266. Tel: 608-782-0704.

EAU CLAIRE. *Riverdale Clinic*, 2004 Highland Ave., Suite M, 54701-4380. Tel: 715-832-3483.

STEVENS POINT. *Riverdale Clinic*, 1052 Main St., Box 428, 54482-0428. Tel: 715-344-2500.

WAUSAU. *Northland House*, 102 McClellan St., 54402-0231. Tel: 715-845-4898. Residential Care of Children. Charles Wirtz, Admin.

[L] NEWMAN CAMPUS MINISTRY

LA CROSSE. *Roncalli Newman Parish*. Serving University of Wisconsin-La Crosse and Western Wisconsin Technical College. 1732 State St., 54601. Tel: 608-784-4994. Rev. Leo J. Schneider, Pastor.

EAU CLAIRE. *Newman Parish*. Serving University of Wisconsin-Eau Claire and Chippewa Valley Technical College. 110 Garfield Ave., 54701-4042. Tel: 715-834-3399. Revs. George R. Szews, Pastor; Edmund J. Klimek, Assoc.; Thomas J. Krieg, Assoc.

MENOMONIE. *The Ministry to the University of Wisconsin-Stout*, 108 3rd Ave. W., 54751. Tel: 715-235-4258. Rev. William P. Neis, Chap.; Dee Bernhardt, Campus Minister.

STEVENS POINT. *Newman University Parish*. Serving University of Wisconsin-Stevens Point. 2108 Fourth Ave., 54481. Tel: 715-345-6500. Rev. Mark R. Pierce, Pastor.

[M] FOUNDATIONS, FUNDS & TRUSTS

LA CROSSE. *Aquinas High School and Aquinas Schools Foundation*, 315 S. 11th St., 54601. Tel: 608-784-0287; Fax: 608-782-8851.

Bishop's Education Endowment Trust, P.O. Box 4004, 54602-4004. Tel: 608-788-7700.

Blessed Sacrament Parish Endowment Trust, 130 S. Losey Blvd., 54601. Tel: 608-782-2953; Fax: 608-782-2770.

Cathedral of St. Joseph the Workman Endowment Trust, 530 Main St., 54601.

Franciscan Skemp Foundation, Inc., 700 W. Ave. South, 54601-4796. Tel: 608-784-6449; Fax: 608-791-9799. Peter Grabow, Dir.

Holy Cross Seminary Education Fund Endowment Trust, P.O. Box 4004, 54602-4004. Tel: 608-788-7700; Fax: 608-788-8413.

Holy Trinity Catholic Church Endowment Trust, 1333 S. 13th St., 54601.

La Crosse Deanery Catholic Education Endowment Trust, P.O. Box 4004, 54602-4004.

Roncalli Newman Parish Student Endowment Trust, 1732 State St., 54601.

St. James Parish Endowment Trust, 1032 Caledonia St., 54603.

St. Pius X Parish Endowment Trust, P.O. Box 4004, 54602-4004.

St. Thomas More Parish Endowment Trust, 2006 Weston St., 54601.

ARCADIA. *Arcadia Catholic School Endowment Trust Fund*, 223 E. Maple St., 54612.

Franciscan Skemp Foundation of Arcadia, Inc., 464 S. St. Joseph Ave., 54612. Tel: 608-323-3341. Robert Tracey, Admin.

AUBURNDALE. *St. Mary Education Endowment Trust*, Box 177, 54412-0177.

BIG RIVER. *The St. Mary's-Big River Endowment Trust*. W10139 570th Ave., River Falls, 54022.

BLAIR. *The St. Ansgar Catholic Church Endowment Trust*. 35900 Lee St., P.O. Box 127, Whitehall, 54773-0127.

CADOTT. *St. Rose of Lima Catholic Church Endowment Trust*, Box 160, 54727.

CHIPPEWA FALLS. *The Chippewa Area Catholic Schools Endowment Trust*, 1316 Bel Air Blvd., 54729; Fax: 715-723-1501.

The Education/Sustaining Endowment Trust, 412 Main St., 54729.

Friends of St. Joseph's Foundation, St. Joseph's Hospital, 2661 County Rd. I, 54729. Tel: 715-723-1811.

Notre Dame Children's Endowment Trust, 117 Allen St., 54729-2899.

Notre Dame Parish Endowment Trust, 117 Allen St., 54729-2899.

St. Charles Future Fund Trust, 810 Pearl St., 54729.

DURAND. *St. Mary Catholic School Endowment Trust*, 901 W. Prospect St., 54736-1049.

EAU CLAIRE. *Educational Endowment Trust of Eau Claire Coordinated Catholic Schools*, 322 Fulton St., 54703.

The Newman Parish - Eau Claire Endowment Trust, 110 Garfield Ave., 54701-4042.

Regis High School Foundation, 2100 Fenwick Ave., 54701-4498.

The Sacred Heart Parish Endowment Trust, 416 N. Dewey St., 54701-3299. Tel: 715-835-3299.

The St. James the Greater Catholic Church Endowment Trust, 2502 11th St., 54703-2700.

St. Olaf Parish Endowment Trust, 2408 North Ln., 54703-0960.

St. Patrick Parish of Eau Claire Endowment Trust, 318 Fulton St., 54703-5399.

ELLSWORTH. *The St. Francis Parish Endowment Trust*, 264 S. Grant, Box 839, 54011.

HOLMEN. *St. Elizabeth Ann Seton Endowment Trust*, 515 N. Main St., 54636.

INDEPENDENCE. *The SS. Peter & Paul Catholic Church Endowment Trust*, 308 Osseo Rd., P.O. Box 428, 54747-0428.

LYNDON STATION. *Troy Quasi-Endowment Trust*, P.O. Box 303, 53944.

MARSHFIELD. *Columbus High School Foundation*, 710 S. Columbus Ave., 54449. Tel: 715-387-2444. Ms. Jodi Hansen, Dir. Devel.

Community Foundation of St. Joseph's Hospital of Marshfield, Inc., 611 St. Joseph Ave., 54449.

The Our Lady of Peace Endowment Trust, 1414 W. 5th St., 54449.

St. John the Baptist Educational Endowment Trust, 201 W. Blodgett, Box 644, 54449-0644.

St. John the Baptist Maintenance Endowment Trust, 201 W. Blodgett, Box 644, 54449.

MAUSTON. *St. Patrick's Congregation Trust*, 401 Mansion St., 53948-1393.

MENOMONIE. *The St. Joseph School at Menomonie Endowment Trust*, 910 Wilson Ave., 54747.

MOSINEE. *St. Paul Parish Endowment Trust*, 603 4th St., 54455.

NEILLSVILLE. *The St. Mary's Catholic Church Endowment Trust*, 1803 Black River Rd., 54456.

ONALASKA. *Father John Rossiter and Friends Endowment Trust of St. Patrick Parish*, 1031 Main St., 54650.

PRAIRIE DU CHIEN. *The St. Gabriel's Endowment Trust*, 506 N. Beaumont Rd., P.O. Box 176, 53821-0176.

The St. John's Endowment Trust, 710 S. Wacouta St., P.O. Box 28, 53821-0028.

RICHLAND CENTER. *The Assumption of the Blessed Virgin Mary Parish Endowment Trust*, 160 W. 4th St., Box 456, 53581.

ROTHSCHILD. *The St. Mark Catholic Parish Endowment Trust*, 602 Military Rd., 54474-1523.

St. Therese Catholic Church Endowment Fund, 113 Kort St., 54474.

ST. JOSEPH RIDGE. *St. Joseph Endowment Trust*. W2602 Hwy. 33, Rte. 1, La Crosse, 54601. Tel: 608-788-1646.

ST. MARY'S RIDGE. *Holy Family Endowment Trust Fund*. 26400 CTH U, Cashton, 54619-9757.

SPARTA. *Endowment Trust of the Friends and Parishioners of St. Patrick Parish*, 319 W. Main St., 54656-2143.

Franciscan Skemp Foundation of Sparta, Inc., 310 W. Main St., 54656-2142. Tel: 608-269-2132. William P. Sexton, M.H.A., Exec. Dir.

STEVENS POINT. *Catholic Schools Endowment Trust in Portage County, Wisconsin*, 1408 Ellis St., 54481.

Community Foundation of St. Michael's Hospital, 900 Illinois Ave., 54481. Phyllis A. Devlin, Coord.

Pacelli High School Foundation, 1301 Maria Dr., 54481. Tel: 715-341-2442.

St. Stephen Parish Endowment Trust, 1401 Clark St., 54481.

STRATFORD. *St. Joseph Parish Endowment Trust*, Box 6.

TILDEN. *St. Peter Parish Endowment Trust*, 11358 CTH Q. Chippewa Falls, 54729-6115.

TOMAH. *The St. Mary's Catholic Church Educational Endowment Trust*, 303 W. Monroe St., 54660. Tel: 608-372-4516.

WAUMANDEE. *St. Boniface Parish Catholic School Endowment Trust Fund*, Box 962, 54622-0962.

WAUSAU. *St. Michael Parish Endowment Trust*, 1315 6th St., 54403-3599.

**Wausau Area Catholic Schools Endowment Trust*, 602 Second St., 54403. Tel: 715-845-5735. Marian Wolaver, Admin.

WHITEHALL. *St. John Parish Endowment Trust*, 35900 Lee St., P.O. Box 127, 54773-0127.

[N] ASSOCIATIONS OF THE FAITHFUL

TILDEN. *Institute of St. Joseph*. 11358 CTH Q, Chippewa Falls, 54729-6115. Tel: 715-288-6272; Fax: 715-288-6008. Rev. William P. Felix, Moderator.

[O] SOCIETY FOR APOSTOLIC LIFE

CASHTON. *Institute of Christ the King-Sovereign Priest*, American Hdqrts.: Immaculate Conception Priory, 26400 CTH U, 54619-9757. Tel: 608-823-7992; Fax: 608-823-7992. Rev. Timothy E. Svea, Prior & U.S. Supr.

[P] MISCELLANEOUS LISTINGS

LA CROSSE. *Franciscan Skemp Healthcare, Inc., Mayo Health System*, 700 West Ave. S., 54601-4796. Tel: 608-791-9710. Brian C. Campion, M.D., Pres. & CEO, Integrated Healthcare Delivery System. Sponsored by the Congregation of the Sisters of the Third Order of St. Francis of Perpetual Adoration (Franciscan Sisters of Perpetual Adoration) and Mayo Foundation.

Franciscan Skemp Healthcare, Mayo Health System, La Crosse Campus Clinic, 800 West Ave. S., 54601. Tel: 608-782-9760. Brian C. Campion, M.D., Pres. & C.E.O.

Franciscan Skemp Medical Center, Inc., 700 West Ave. S., 54601-4796. Tel: 608-785-0940. Brian C. Campion, M.D., Pres. & CEO.

CHIPPEWA FALLS. *Northern Wisconsin Center for the Developmentally Disabled*. State Institution for the Developmentally Disabled, East Park Ave., 54729. Tel: 715-723-5542.

EAU CLAIRE. *Hospital Sisters Health Care-West, Inc.*, St. Francis Apartments, 851 University Dr., 54701. Tel: 715-834-1338.

STEVENS POINT. *Saint Michael's Hospital Auxiliary*, 900 Illinois Ave., 54481.

RELIGIOUS INSTITUTES OF MEN REPRESENTED IN THE DIOCESE

For further details refer to the corresponding bracketed number in the Religious Institutes of Men or Women section.

[0330]—*Brothers of Christian Schools*. (Winona Prov.).—F.S.C.

[1180]—*Brothers of Saint Pius X*.—C.S.P.X.

[0600]—*Brothers of the Congregation of the Holy Cross*.—C.S.C.

[0240]—*Camillan Fathers and Brothers.*—O.S.Cam.
[0470]—*The Capuchin Friars.* (St. Joseph's Prov.).—O.F.M.Cap.
[0340]—*Cistercian Fathers.*—O.Cist.
[0650]—*Holy Ghost Fathers.*—C.S.Sp.
[0690]—*Jesuit Fathers and Brothers.* (Missouri Prov. and Wisconsin Prov.).—S.J.
[0800]—*Maryknoll.*—M.M.
[0370]—*Society of St. Columban.*—S.S.C.
[1200]—*Society of the Divine Savior.*—S.D.S.

RELIGIOUS INSTITUTES OF WOMEN REPRESENTED IN THE DIOCESE

[0230]—*Benedictine Sisters of Pontifical Jurisdiction.*—O.S.B.
[1780]—*Congregation of the Sisters of the Third Order of St. Francis of Perpetual Adoration.*—F.S.P.A.
[1070-09]—*Dominican Sisters (Racine, WI).*—O.P.
[1170]—*Felican Sisters.*—C.S.S.F.
[1310]—*Franciscan Sisters of Little Falls, Minnesota.*—O.S.F.
[1240]—*Franciscan Sisters, Daughters of the Sacred Hearts of Jesus and Mary.*—O.S.F.
[1820]—*Hospital Sisters of the Third Order of St. Francis.*—O.S.F.
[3280]—*Presentation of the Blessed Virgin Mary Sisters.*—P.B.V.M.
[2970]—*School Sisters of Notre Dame.*—S.S.N.D.
[3590]—*Servants of Mary (Servite Sisters).*—O.S.M.
[2630]—*Sisters of Mercy of the Holy Cross.*—S.C.S.C.
[1550]—*Sisters of St. Francis of the Holy Cross.*—O.S.F.
[3930]—*Sisters of St. Joseph of the Third Order of St. Francis.*—S.S.J.-T.O.S.F.
[1030]—*Sisters of the Divine Savior.*—S.D.S.
[4100]—*Sisters of the Sorrowful Mother (Third Order of St. Francis).*—S.S.M.
[1705]—*Sisters of the Third Order of St. Francis of Assisi (Sisters of Penance and Charity).*—O.S.F.

DIOCESAN CEMETERIES

LA CROSSE. *Catholic,* 519 Losey Blvd. S., 54601. Tel: 608-782-0238. Jeffrey Reinhart, Supt.
Gate of Heaven Cemetery; French Island Cemetery.
Woodlawn, 3636 Mormon Coulee Rd., 54601. Tel: 608-788-0980. John Reinhart, Supt.

CHIPPEWA FALLS. *Hope Cemetery and Mausoleum,* 418 N. State St., 54729. Tel: 715-723-0792. Walter Hurt, Supt.

EAU CLAIRE. *Calvary Cemetery and Mausoleum,* P.O. Box 755, 54702-0755. Tel: 715-832-1411. Harold Hunt.

MARSHFIELD. *Gate of Heaven,* 1803 S. Maple Ave., 54449. Tel: 715-384-3869. Monica Herman, Sec.

STEVENS POINT. *Stevens Point Area Catholic Cemetery Association, Inc.,* P.O. Box 497, 54481. Tel: 715-341-3236. Jack Hurrish, Supt.

NECROLOGY

† Brickl, Frank C., (Retired). —Died Oct. 12, 1996.
† Brockman, Vaughn W., Menomonie, WI, St. Joseph Parish. —Died Dec. 5, 1995.
† Buchman, William J., (Retired). —Died Sept. 19, 1996.
† Marx, Joseph B., (Retired). —Died Nov. 27, 1996.
† Masalewicz, Edward A., (Retired). —Died Oct. 26, 1996.
† Mathieu, Georges P., (Retired). —Died Feb. 28, 1996.
† Meinen, Myron J., (Retired). —Died May 13, 1996.
† O'Reilly, Daniel J., (Retired). —Died Dec. 20, 1995.
† Stanek, Edwin J., (Retired). —Died Aug. 12, 1996.

Diocese of Las Cruces

(Dioecesis Las Cruces)

Most Reverend

RICARDO RAMIREZ, C.S.B., D.D.

Bishop of Las Cruces; ordained December 10, 1966; appointed Titular Bishop of Vatarba and Auxiliary of San Antonio October 27, 1981; consecrated December 6, 1981; appointed First Bishop of Las Cruces August 31, 1982; installed October 18, 1982. *Res., 455 W. Palmer Rd., Las Cruces, NM, 88005.*

ESTABLISHED OCTOBER 18, 1982.

Square Miles 44,483.

Comprises the Counties of Dona Ana, Hidalgo, Grant, Luna, Sierra, Otero, Lincoln, Chaves, Eddy and Lea in the State of New Mexico.

For legal titles of parishes and diocesan institutions, consult The Pastoral Center.

The Pastoral Center: 1280 Med Park Dr., Las Cruces, NM, 88005. Tel.: 505-523-7577; Fax: 505-524-3874.

STATISTICAL OVERVIEW

Personnel	
Bishop	1
Priests: Diocesan Active in Diocese	20
Priests: Active Outside Diocese	2
Priests: Retired, Sick or Absent	8
Number of Diocesan Priests	30
Religious Priests in Diocese	47
Extern Priests in Diocese	7
Ordinations:	
Diocesan Priests	1
Religious Priests	1
Permanent Deacons	1
Permanent Deacons in Diocese	26
Total Sisters	76
Parishes	
Parishes	44
With Resident Pastor:	
Resident Diocesan Priests	15
Resident Religious Priests	20
Without Resident Pastor:	
Administered by Priests	7
Administered by Permanent Deacons	1
Administered by Women Religious	1
Missions	44
Professional Ministry Personnel:	
Sisters	5
Lay Ministers	14
Welfare	
Health Care Centers	3
Total Assisted	141,420
Day Care and Extended Day Care Centers	1
Total Assisted	40
Special Centers for Social Services	1
Total Assisted	480
Educational	
Diocesan Students in Other Seminaries	2
Total Seminarians	2
Elementary Schools, Diocesan and Parish	5
Total Students	653
Catechesis/Religious Education:	
High School Students	2,601
Elementary Students	7,627
Total Students Under Catholic Instruction	10,883
Teachers in the Diocese:	
Sisters	2
Lay Teachers	44
Vital Statistics	
Receptions into the Church:	
Infant Baptism Totals	2,433
Adult Baptism Totals	104
Received into Full Communion	115
First Communions	2,265
Confirmations	1,170
Marriages:	
Catholic	391
Interfaith	103
Total Marriages	494
Deaths	872
Total Catholic Population	125,309
Total Population	453,500

The Pastoral Center—1280 Med Park Dr., Las Cruces, 88005. Tel: 505-523-7577; Fax: 505-524-3874. Office Hours: Mon.-Fri. 8:00-4:30.

Bishops Administrative Council—Most Rev. RICARDO RAMIREZ, C.S.B.; Very Rev. Msgr. JOHN E. ANDERSON; Revs. ROBERT POWER, C.S.B.; DENIS TEJADA; Sr. MARY ELLEN QUINN, R.S.M.

Vicar General—Very Rev. Msgr. JOHN E. ANDERSON.

Episcopal Vicar for Clergy and Personnel—Very Rev. Msgr. ROBERT L. GETZ.

Chancellor—Sr. MARY ELLEN QUINN, R.S.M.

Director of Clergy Personnel—Very Rev. Msgr. JOHN E. ANDERSON.

Diocesan Tribunal—Rev. JOHN S. WEBER, O.F.M.Conv., J.C.L., Judicial Vicar; Sr. CATHERINE C. DARCY, R.S.M., J.C.D., Admin. Dir., *1280 Med Park Dr., Las Cruces, 88005.*

Promoter of Justice—Very Rev. DANIEL R. BARFIELD, S.J.

Judges—Very Revs. GILES CARIE, O.F.M.Conv.; JOHN M. WILSON, C.S.B., J.C.L.; Revs. THOMAS P. BEGGANE, J.C.L.; ENRIQUE LOPEZ-ESCALERA, J.C.L.; Deacon ALPHONSO F. BOWERS; Sr. CATHERINE C. DARCY, R.S.M., J.C.D.

Defenders of the Bond—Very Rev. DANIEL R. BARFIELD, S.J.; Very Rev. Msgr. JOHN E. ANDERSON, V.G.; Revs. DAVID BERGS; RICHARD CATANACH; MICHAEL LINDSAY; NOEL KRAMER, O.F.M.Conv.

Assesors—JUDITH MONTES; ARTHUR E. JIRON; DANIEL MONTES.

Advocates—Sr. JANE KERNS, S.H.C.J.; JUDY MONTES; DAN MONTES.

Notaries—ARTHUR E. JIRON; IRENE V. PORTILLO; VELIA SALINAS.

Vicars—Revs. CONRADO PYTLIK; RICHARD CATANACH; VALENTINE JANKOWSKI, O.F.M.Conv.; DENNIS FOUNTAIN, O.F.M.Conv.; EDWARD HERRERA; Very Rev. ALFRED GALVAN.

Diocesan Consultors—Very Rev. Msgr. JOHN E. ANDERSON; Very Rev. Msgr. ROBERT L. GETZ; Revs. DENNIS FOUNTAIN, O.F.M.; VALENTINE JANKOWSKI, O.F.M.Conv.; CONRADO PYTLIK; DENIS TEJADA.

Presbyteral Council—Revs. EDWARD HERRERA, Pres. MICHAEL LINDSAY, Vice Pres. RICHARD CATANACH, Sec.; Very Rev. Msgr. ROBERT L. GETZ; Revs. ANDRES ALAVA, O.A.R.; THOMAS HERBST, O.F.M.; RICHARD CATANACH; THOMAS MERRILL, O.F.M.Conv.; FRANKLIN EICHHORST, O.F.M.Cap.; VALENTINE JANKOWSKI, O.F.M.Conv.; DENNIS FOUNTAIN, O.F.M.; MICHAEL LINDSAY; PAULUS KAO; CONRADO PYTLIK; ROBERT POWER, C.S.B.; JOHN WEBER, O.F.M.Conv., J.C.L.; DENIS TEJADA; Very Rev. Msgr. JOHN E. ANDERSON; Revs. ENRIQUE LOPEZ; JOE ZERMENO, O.F.M.; MIGUEL ECHEVERRIA; ART ROBERTS, C.S.B.; ALFRED GALVAN.

Priests Personnel Board—Most Rev. RICARDO RAMIREZ, C.S.B.; Very Rev. Msgr. JOHN E. ANDERSON; Very Rev. Msgr. ROBERT L. GETZ; Revs. DENIS TEJADA; RODERICK NICHOLS; MICHAEL LINDSAY; Deacon DANIEL CHECK; Sr. MARY ELLEN QUINN, R.S.M.

Priestly Life and Ministry Committee—Rev. DAVID BERGS, Chm.; Most Rev. RICARDO RAMIREZ, C.S.B.; Very Rev. Msgr. ROBERT L. GETZ; Revs. FRANKLIN EICHHORST, O.F.M.Cap; VALENTINE JANKOWSKI, O.F.M.Conv.; MICHAEL LINDSAY; ROBERT POWER, C.S.B.; JOHN TICKLE; RICHARD CATANACH; RICARDO HINOJAL, O.A.R.

Lay Personnel Committee—CARLOS CORRAL; DOLORES DIAZ; DEBBIE ISHAM MOORE; Sr. MARY ELLEN QUINN, R.S.M.; MARGARET FLORES; MANUEL LEYVA; ANTONIO LUJAN.

Sisters Council—Sr. JANE MARIE KERNS, S.H.C.J., Chm.

Priests Retirement Fund Committee—Rev. MICHAEL LINDSAY; Very Rev. Msgr. ROBERT L. GETZ; Revs. WILLIAM MCCANN; DAVID BERGS; Mr. DANIEL DOLAN; FELIPE SALCIDO, JR.

Permanent Deacon Council—Rev. DENIS TEJADA, Coord.; Deacons DANIEL CHECK, Pres. JOHNNIE PEREZ; PETE VELOTT; FRANK SCHRETLEN; JOHN LUCERO.

Comptroller—FELIPE SALCIDO, JR.

Finance Council—Most Rev. RICARDO RAMIREZ, C.S.B.; Very Rev. Msgr. JOHN E. ANDERSON; Revs. ROBERT POWER, C.S.B.; EDWARD HERRERA; Sr. MARY ELLEN QUINN, R.S.M.; FELIPE SALCIDO; DAN DOLAN; DON BEASLEY; EDDIE YBARRA; CHARLENE WARD; Mr. SAM ACOSTA; HAROLD GRANDI; EDWARD PILLAR.

Office of Stewardship and Development and United In Ministry Appeal—DAN DOCHERTY, Exec. Dir.

Office of Insurance—MARTA ROMERO, Insurance Dir.

Office of Buildings and Properties—Rev. DENIS TEJADA, Dir. MANUEL LEYVA, Assoc. Dir.

Diocesan Ministries Offices and Directors

Vicar for Ministries—Rev. ROBERT POWER, C.S.B.

Office of Adult Catechesis and Ministerial Development—Rev. ROBERT POWER, C.S.B.

Art and Environment Committee—Sr. LUCY MEISSEN, C.PP.S.

Attorney—DANIEL DOLAN.

Campus Ministry—Revs. MITCHELL DOWALGO, C.S.B.; JON ALEXANDER, O.P.

Judicial Vicar—Rev. JOHN WEBER, O.F.M.Conv., J.C.L.

Office of Catholic Schools—Sr. JOAN BERNINGER, M.M., Supt.

Office of Catholic Social Ministry—ANTONIO LUJAN, Dir. CARLOS CORRAL, Assoc. Dir.

Office of Parish 2000—Rev. ROBERT POWER, C.S.B., Dir.

Cursillo Secretariat—VERA MEIN, Pres. VICTOR RODRIQUEZ, Vice Pres. BLANCA LUNA, Treas. PAULA PEREZ, Sec.

Office of Elementary Catechesis—DAVID MCNAMARA, Dir.

Ecumenical Liaison—Sr. CAMILLA VERRET, R.S.M.
Hispanic Ministry—Rev. ROBERT POWER, C.S.B.
Holy Childhood Association—Very Rev. Msgr. JOHN E. ANDERSON.
Hospital Ministry—Sr. FRANCIS ROYER, C.S.J.
Office of Liturgical Education—Sr. LUCY MEISSEN, C.PP.S.
Propogation of the Faith—Very Rev. Msgr. JOHN E. ANDERSON.
Order of Christian Initiation of Adults—Sr. LUCY MEISSEN, C.PP.S., Co-Chm. DAVID MCNAMARA, Co-Chm.; Sr. JANE MARIE KERN, S.H.C.J.; NORMA SPINA.
Vocation Team—Sr. LUCY MEISSEN, C.PP.S.; Rev. RICHARD CATANACH.
Office of Adolescent Catechesis and Youth Ministry—KEVIN VIGIL.
Pastoral Councils—DAVID MCNAMARA; ANTONIO LUJAN.
Diocesan Resource Center—DAVID MCNAMARA, Coord. DOLORES DIAZ, Librarian.
Diocesan Archives—Rev. JOHN TICKLE, Archivist.
Charismatic Renewal Liaisons—LEO MARRUFO, (East); Mr. SAM TOME, (West); Mrs. SAM TOME, (West).
Agua Viva—CHRISTY ANCHONDO, Editor; DAVID MCNAMARA, Special Projects.
Agua Viva Editorial Advisory Board—Rev. ROBERT POWER, C.S.B.; Mr. ANTONIO LUJAN; PHILIP ALVAREZ; RUBEN ABEYTA; LALA GONZALEZ; MANUEL LEYVA; DAVID MCNAMARA; BETTY MORENO; Sr. MARY ELLEN QUINN, R.S.M.; RICK SENTENO; CHRISTINA ANCHONDO.

CLERGY, PARISHES, MISSIONS AND PAROCHIAL SCHOOLS

CITY OF LAS CRUCES
(Dona Ana County)

1—CATHEDRAL OF IMMACULATE HEART OF MARY, Revs. Thomas P. Beggane; Louis D. Amezaga; Deacon Frank J. Lujan, (Retired).
Office: 1240 S. Espina St., 88001. Tel: 505-524-8563.
School—865 E. Idaho, 88001. Tel: 505-524-8563. Lay Teachers 11; Students 162.

2—HOLY CROSS, Very Rev. Msgr. John E. Anderson; Rev. Enrique Lopez.
Office: 1327 N. Miranda St., 88005. Tel: 505-523-0167; Fax: 505-523-8023.
School—Lay Teachers 16; Students 174.

3—OUR LADY OF HEALTH, Revs. Narciso Rivera, O.A.R.; Antonio Martinez, O.A.R.
Res., 1178 N. Mesquite, 88001. Tel: 505-526-9545; Fax: 505-526-9545.

4—ST. ALBERT THE GREAT NEWMAN PARISH. Serving New Mexico State University. Rev. Mitchell G. Dowalgo, C.S.B.; Deacon Richard R. DeBlassie.
Res., 2615 S. Solano, 88001. Tel: 505-522-6202.

5—ST. GENEVIEVE, Revs. Denis Tejada; Juan Moreno; Deacon LaRue Velott.
Res., 100 S. Espina, 88001. Tel: 505-524-9649. [CEM]

6—SANTA ROSA DE LIMA, Rev. Jesus Espinosa, O.A.R.
Church—5035 Holsome Rd., 88004. Tel: 505-382-9768.

OUTSIDE THE CITY OF LAS CRUCES

Alamogordo, Otero Co., Immaculate Conception, Revs. Bryant Hausfeld, O.F.M.; Gregg D. Petri; Bruce Hausfeld, O.F.M.
Res., 705 Delaware Ave., 88310. Tel: 505-437-3291; Fax: 505-437-3239. [CEM]
School—Fr. James B. Hay Catholic School, 708 Hawaii Ave., 88310. Tel: 505-437-7821. Sr. Margaret Wilson, Prin.
Franciscan Sisters of Our Lady of Perpetual Help 3; Lay Teachers 9; Students 120.
Missions—Boles Acres, Our Lady of the Desert; La Luz, Our Lady of the Light; Cloudcroft, Sacred Heart.
St. Jude, Very Rev. Daniel R. Barfield, S.J.
Office: 1404 College Ave., 88310. Tel: 505-437-0238; Fax: 505-437-0267.

Anthony, Dona Ana Co., St. Anthony's, Revs. Andres Alava, O.A.R.; Juan Almarza, O.A.R.
Res., P.O. Drawer C, 88021. Tel: 505-882-2239; Fax: 505-882-2239. [CEM]
Church—224 Lincoln St., 88021.
Convent—124 Tornillo Dr., Chaparral, 88021. Tel: 505-824-0508. Hermanas Dominicas de la Doctrina Cristiana
Missions—Chaparral, St. Thomas More, 528 E. Paseo, Chaparral, 88021. Tel: 505-824-4433. Rev. Miguel Echeverria, O.A.R.; La Union, Our Lady of Refuge, Rte. 1, Box 484A, La Union, 88021. Tel: 505-874-2967; Berino, Immaculate Conception, San Benito Rd., P.O. Box 155, Berino, 88024.

Artesia, Eddy Co., St. Anthony, Rev. Joseph P. Johnson, S.J.
Res., 502 S. Ninth St., 88210. Tel: 505-746-4471.
Our Lady of Grace, Rev. John W. Curran, O.F.M.Conv.; Deacon Charles Polson, Pastoral Assoc.
Res., 1111 N. Roselawn Ave., 88210. Tel: 505-748-1356.
Catechesis/Religious Programs—Martha Shoemaker, D.R.E.
Students 422.

Bayard, Grant Co., Our Lady of Fatima, Rev. Paulus Kao.
Res., P.O. Box 1425, 88023. Tel: 505-537-2421.
Missions—Fierro, St. Anthony; Hanover, Holy Family; San Lorenzo, San Lorenzo.

Carlsbad, Eddy Co., St. Edward, Revs. Sebastian Cunningham, O.F.M.Conv.; Noel Kramer, O.F.M. Conv.
Res., 610 W. Stevens, 88220. Tel: 505-885-6600.
School—(Grades K-6) 805 Walter St., 88220. Tel: 505-885-4620. William Threlkeld, Prin.
Lay Teachers 6; Students 90.
Convent—206 N. Guadalupe, 88220. Tel: 505-885-2480. Adorers of the Blood of Christ
San Jose, Rev. Thomas J. Merrill, O.F.M. Conv.
Res., 1002 DeBaca, 88220. Tel: 505-885-5792; Fax: 505-887-3553.
Religious Education Center—Tel: 505-887-1346. Patsy Grantner, D.R.E.
Students 525.

Carrizozo, Lincoln Co., St. Rita, Rev. David J. Bergs.
Res., Box 727, 88301. Tel: 505-648-2853.
Missions—Capitan, Sacred Heart; Corona, St. Therese of the Little Flower.

Santa Clara, Grant Co., Santa Clara, Rev. Michael P. Lindsay.
Res., P.O. Box 215, 88026. Tel: 505-537-3713; Fax: 505-537-4929.

Chamberino, Dona Ana Co., San Luis Rey, Rev. Robert Villegas, C.S.C.
Res., P.O. Box 230, 88027. Tel: 505-882-2045.
Convent—275 San Pablo Rd., P.O. Box 149, 88027. Tel: 505-882-5811. Our Lady of Guadalupe Franciscan Missionaries of Mary 4.

Deming, Luna Co., Holy Family, Rev. Joseph K. Anderson, O.S.B.
Res., 612 S. Copper Ave., 88030. Tel: 505-546-9783; Fax: 505-544-3655.
St. Ann's, Rev. Alfred Galvan.
Res., 400 S. Ruby St., 88030. Tel: 505-546-3343.
Catechesis/Religious Programs—901 S. Pearl (Fr. Stangley Hall), 88030. Tel: 505-546-3905. Kitty Jimenez, D.R.E.
Students 475.
Mission—Columbus, Holy Family. In res., Rev. Aloys Ketteler, S.V.D.

Dexter, Chavez Co., Immaculate Conception, Deacon John S. Lucero, Admin.
Res., 400 W. Fifth, P.O. Box 189, 88230. Tel: 505-734-5478.
Missions—Lake Arthur, Our Lady of Guadalupe; Hagerman, St. Catherine.

Dona Ana, Dona Ana Co., Our Lady of the Purification, Rev. Miguel Macaya.
Mailing Address: P.O. Box 385, 88032. Tel: 505-526-2114. [JC]
Mission—San Isidro, San Isidro.

Garfield, Dona Ana Co., San Isidro, Sr. Marie Paule Willem, F.M.M., Parish Life Coord.
Res., H.C. 31, Box 43, 87936-9701. Tel: 505-267-5111.
Missions—San Jose, Arrey; Hillsboro, Our Lady of Guadalupe.

Hatch, Dona Ana Co., Our Lord of Mercy, Revs. Robert E. Power, C.S.B.; Bill McCann, Admin.
Res., Box 321, 87937. Tel: 505-267-4983.
Mission—Rincon, Our Lady of All Nations.

Hobbs, Lea Co., Our Lady of Guadalupe, Rev. Anthony Clark; Deacon Samuel Navarrette.
Office: 914 S. Selman, 88240. Tel: 505-393-4991.
St. Helena, Revs. Valentine Jankowski, O.F.M.Conv.; Jose Reyes, O.F.M.Conv. Pastoral Assocs.: Sr. Margaret McTaggert, S.S.C.; Sr. Maurita Sharko, S.S.C. In res., Rev. Maurus Hauer, O.F.M.Conv.
Res., 100 E. Bender Blvd., 88240. Tel: 505-392-7551; 7552.
School—Tel: 505-392-5405; Fax: 505-392-0128. Lay Teachers 8; Students 93.
Convent—110 E. Bender, 88240. Tel: 505-392-8115.

Hurley, Grant Co., Infant Jesus, Rev. Rafael Perez.
Res., Box 97, 88043. Tel: 505-537-3691; 536-9405.
Missions—San Juan, San Juan; Faywood, San Jose.

Jal, Lea Co., St. Cecilia, Rev. Valentine Jankowski, O.F.M.Conv.
Res., P.O. Box 430, 300 N. Nevada St., 88252. Tel: 505-395-2431.
Mission—Eunice, St. Clare.

La Mesa, Dona Ana Co., San Jose, Rev. Tomas Perez, O.A.R.
Res., P.O. Box 278, 88044. Tel: 505-233-3191.
Mission—Vado, Dona Ana Co., San Pedro Del Cerro, P.O. Box 281, La Mesa 88048.

Lordsburg, Hidalgo Co., St. Joseph, Rev. Virgilio Florez.
Res., 416 E. Second St., 88045. Tel: 505-542-3268.
Missions—Cotton City, St. Jude; Rodeo, San Felipe; Playas, St. Augustine; Hachita, St. Catherine.

Loving, Eddy Co., Our Lady of Grace, Rev. Dominic Manion, O.F.M.Conv.; Deacon Odie Saldivar.
Res., P.O. Box 428, 301 4th St., 88256. Tel: 505-745-3341.
Mission—Malaga, Cristo Rey.

Lovington, Lea Co., St. Thomas Aquinas, Rev. Franklin Eichhorst, O.F.M.Cap.
Res., 1301 N. Ninth St., 88260. Tel: 505-396-4206.
Mission—Tatum, Our Lady of the Holy Rosary.

Mescalero, Otero Co., St. Joseph (Apache Indian Mission), Rev. Thomas Herbst, O.F.M.; Sr. Robert Ann Hecker, O.S.F.
Res., Box 187, 88340. Tel: 505-671-4473.
Missions—Bent, Our Lady of Guadalupe; Three Rivers, St. Patrick.

Mesilla, Dona Ana Co., St. Albino, Rev. Conrad E. Pytlik.
Res., P.O. Box 26, 88046. Tel: 505-526-9349; Fax: 505-647-1619.

Mesilla Park, Dona Ana Co., Shrine and Parish of Our Lady of Guadalupe, Rev. Giles Carie, O.F.M.Conv.
Res., Box 296, 88047. Tel: 505-526-8171.

Roswell, Chaves Co., St. Peter, Revs. Dennis Fountain, O.F.M.; Richard Young, O.F.M. In res., Revs. Ramon Smith, O.F.M.; John Lanzrath, O.F.M.
Res., 105 E. Mathews, 88201. Tel: 505-622-5742.
St. John's, Revs. Dennis Fountain, O.F.M.; Richard Young, O.F.M.
Res., 105 E. Matthews, 88201. Tel: 505-622-7228.
Assumption of the Blessed Virgin Mary, Rev. Msgr. Robert Getz.
Res., 2808 N. Kentucky, 88201. Tel: 505-622-9895; Fax: 505-622-6845.

Ruidoso, Lincoln Co., St. Eleanor, Rev. Richard Catanach.
Res., P.O. Box 8300, 120 Junction Rd., 88345. Tel: 505-257-2330.
Missions—San Patricio, St. Jude Thaddeus; Lincoln, San Juan; Fort Stanton, Sacred Heart; Picacho, St. Joseph.

San Miguel, Dona Ana Co., San Miguel, Rev. Ricardo Hinojal, O.A.R.
Res., Drawer E, 88058. Tel: 505-233-2453; Fax: 505-233-2453.
Augustinian Recollects: P.O. Box 310, Mesilla, 88046. Tel: 505-523-7030; Fax: 505-233-7030.
Mission—Mesquite, Our Lady of Perpetual Help.

Silver City, Grant Co., St. Vincent de Paul, Rev. Rodrick Nichols; Deacon William Holguin.
Res., 414 Bayard St., P.O. Box 1189, 88061. Tel: 505-538-9373; Fax: 505-388-0870.
Missions—Gila, St. Isidore; Pinos Altos, Holy Cross.
St. Francis Newman Center Parish. Serving Western New Mexico University. Rev. Jon Alexander, O.P.
Res., 914 W. 13th St., 88061. Tel: 505-538-3662.

Sunland Park, Dona Ana Co., St. Martin de Porres, Rev. Edward Herrera; Deacon Jesus Favela.
Res., P.O. Box 248, 88063. Tel: 505-589-2106.
Stations—El Naranjo, Shrine of Sierra de Cristo Rey.; El Naranjo, Santo Nino de Atocha.

Tularosa, Otero Co., St. Francis de Paula, Rev. Joseph Zermeno, O.F.M.
Res., 303 Encino, 88352. Tel: 505-585-2793. [CEM]

Truth or Consequences, Sierra Co., Our Lady of Perpetual Help, Rev. Art Roberts, C.S.B.
Res., 103 E. Sixth Ave., 87901. Tel: 505-894-7804; Fax: 505-894-0451.
Missions—Cuchillo, St. Joseph; Las Palomas, San Ysidro; Montecello, St. Ignatius; Placitas, San Lorenzo.
Chapels—St. Gregory, Chapels Chise; San Miguel, Rancho de San Miguel; Winston, St. Jude.

Special Assignment:
Reverend Fathers—
Cruz, Gustavo
Morgan, Arthur

Retired:
Reverend Monsignors—
Chavez, Albert
Lynch, Richard

Milano, James
VonderHaar, Roland
Reverend Fathers—
Griffith, Edwin
Lafrenz, James
Moynahan, Kevin

Permanent Deacons:
Alvarado, Alfonso, Blackrange Stations, San Lorenzo
Andis, John A., Leave of Absence
Bowers, Al, Our Lady of Guadalupe, Mesilla Park
Chavez, Rigoberto, Our Lady of Purification, Dona Ana
Check, Daniel, Our Lady of Purification, Dona Ana
Crowder, Richard, Holy Cross, Las Cruces
DeBlassie, Richard, Leave of Absence
Dickman, Donald, La Luz, Our Lady of the Light
Dougil, Edward, (Retired)
Favela, Jesus, San Martin de Porres, Sunland Park
Gale, Howard, (Retired), Immaculate Heart of Mary, Las Cruces
Holguin, William, St. Vincent de Paul, Silver City
Lehman, James, Leave of Absence
Lucero, John S., Immaculate Conception, Dexter
Lucero, Levy, Immaculate Conception, Alamogordo
Lujan, Frank, (Retired), Immaculate Heart of Mary, Las Cruces
Narvaez, Arthur, (Retired), St. Genevieve, Las Cruces
Navarrette, Sam, Our Lady of Guadalupe, Hobbs
Perez, Johnnie, Leave of Absence
Polson, Charles, Our Lady of Grace, Artesia
Roane, Tom, Our Lady of Guadalupe, Hobbs
Saldivar, Odie, Our Lady of Grace, Loving
Sanchez, Adam L., St. Jude, Alamagordo
Schretlen, Frank, (Retired), Our Lady of the Light, La Luz
Velott, Pete, St. Genevieve, Las Cruces
Vigil, Benjamin, St. Eleanors, Ruidoso

INSTITUTIONS LOCATED IN THE DIOCESE

[A] CLINICS

CARLSBAD. *St. Mary's Health Care Center*, 2330 West Pierce, 88220. Tel: 505-887-0516; Fax: 505-885-8239.
For a complete listing, refer to the Special Care Facilities section.

HOBBS. *St. Mary Medical Center*, 2410 North Fowler, 88240. Tel: 505-392-5572; Fax: 505-392-4848.
For a complete listing, refer to the Special Care Facilities section.
St. Mary's Family Health Care Center, 515 East Main, 88240. Tel: 505-393-1096; Fax: 505-393-3758.
For a complete listing, refer to the Special Care Facilities section.

[B] MONASTERIES & RESIDENCES OF PRIESTS AND BROTHERS

LAS CRUCES. *Basilian Fathers*, 1682 Alta Vista Pl., 88011. Tel: 505-521-4269. Revs. Robert E. Power, C.S.B., Rector; Mitch Dowalgo, C.S.B.

MESILLA. *Augustinian Recollects Fathers*. Province of St. Nicholas of Tolentine, Provincial Delegation in the South of U.S.A. San Alipius House, P.O. Box 310, 88046. Tel: 505-523-7030. Revs. Ricardo Hinojal, O.A.R. (Spain); Benito Suen, O.A.R; Tomas Perez, O.A.R. (Spain).

[C] CONVENTS AND RESIDENCES FOR SISTERS

LAS CRUCES. *Fransiscan Sister*, 1700 Baldwin Dr., 88001. Tel: 505-522-7057.
Maryknoll Sisters, 700 California, Apt. 14, 88001. Tel: 505-525-0807.
Medical Mission Sisters, 3267 Executive Hills Rd., 88001. Tel: 505-521-4087.
Precious Blood Sisters, 1705 Montana, 88001. Tel: 505-522-3857. Sisters 2.
Sisters of St. Francis, 135 Roberts Dr., 88005. Tel: 505-526-3444.
Sisters of St. Joseph, Concordia, KS, 700 California, Apt. 16, 88001. Tel: 505-524-7223.
Society of the Holy Child Jesus, 1412 Gladys, 88001. Tel: 505-522-4873.

ANTHONY. *Sisters of Mercy of the Americas (Omaha Region & Vermont Region)*, 301 Lincoln St., P.O. Box 2411, 88021. Tel: 505-882-5553. Sisters 3.

CARLSBAD. *Adorers of the Blood of Christ*, St. Edwards Convent, 206 N. Guadalupe, 88220. Tel: 505-885-2480.

CHAMBERINO. *Franciscan Missionaries of Mary*, P.O. Box 149, 88027. Tel: 505-882-5811.

CHAPPARAL. *Dominicas De La Doctrina Cristiana*, 124 Tornillo, 88021. Tel: 505-824-0508. Sisters 4; Novices 8.

DEMING. *Daughters of the Heart of Mary*, P.O. Box 1531, 88030. Tel: 505-546-7599.

GARFIELD. *Franciscan Missionaries of Mary*, HC 31, Box 43, State Rd. 436, 87936-9701. Tel: 505-267-5111.

LAUNION. *Sisters of Mercy - New Jersey Region*, Rt. 1, Box 490 A, 88021. Tel: 505-589-0852.

MESCALERO. *Franciscan Sisters of Our Lady of Perpetual Help*, P.O. Box 187, 88340. Tel: 505-671-4893. Sisters 2.

ROSWELL. *Poor Clare Monastery of Our Lady of Guadalupe*, 809 E. 19th St., 88201. Tel: 505-622-0868. Mothers M. Francis, P.C.C., Abbess; Mary Veronica, P.C.C., Vicaress. Professed Nuns 32; Novices 1.
Sisters of St. Francis - Neumann Community, 2813 S. Emerald Dr., 88201. Tel: 505-624-2475.

SILVER CITY. *Sisters of St. Joseph*, St. Mary's Center, 1801 N. Alabama, 88061. Tel: 505-538-3350. 1803 N. Alabama, 88061. Tel: 505-388-3684.

SUNLAND PARK. *Sister of Charity, Franciscan Sister, Sister of the Incarnate Word*, 115 Mesa Verde, P.O. Box 1768, 88063. Tel: 505-589-4412.

TRUTH OR CONSEQUENCES. *Sister of the Sorrowful Mother*, 216 Radium St., 87901.

[D] RETREAT CENTERS

MESILLA PARK. *Holy Cross Retreat and Friary*, P.O. Box 158, 88047. Tel: 505-524-3688; 524-3811 (Friary). Revs. Marcos O. Reyna, O.F.M.Conv., Dir. H.C.R., Vicar of Friary; John S. Weber, O.F.M.Conv., Guardian; Alcuin Hunter, O.F.M.Conv.; Arthur Young, O.F.M.Conv.; Bro. Simon McHugh, O.F.M.Conv.

[E] MISCELLANEOUS

LAS CRUCES. *Catholic Diocese of Las Cruces Foundation, Inc.*, 1280 Med Park Dr., 80005. Dan Docherty, Exec. Dir.
Our Lady of Guadalupe Prayer Center, Inc., P.O. Box 6772, 88006. Tel: 505-522-5250.
The Priests' Retirement Plan of the Catholic Diocese of Las Cruces, Inc., 1280 Med Park Dr., 88005.

RELIGIOUS INSTITUTES OF MEN REPRESENTED IN THE DIOCESE

For further details refer to the corresponding bracketed numbers in the Religious Institutes of Men or Women section.

[0170]—*Basilian Fathers*.—C.S.B.
[0200]—*Benedictine Monks*.—O.S.B.
[0470]—*Capuchin Friars*. (St. Bonaventure).—O.F.M.Cap.
[0480]—*Conventual Franciscans*. (Our Lady of Guadalupe Custody).—O.F.M.Conv.
[0520]—*Franciscan Friars*. (St. John the Baptist, Our Lady of Guadalupe, St. Barbara Provs.).—O.F.M.
[0690]—*Jesuit Fathers and Brothers*. (New Orleans, Wisconsin Provs.).—S.J.
[0430]—*Order of Preachers*. (Province of St. Albert the Great, Chicago, IL).—O.P.
[0150]—*Order of the Augustinian Recollects*.—O.A.R.
[0610]—*Priests of the Congregation of Holy Cross*. (Southwest Prov.).—C.S.C.
[0420]—*Society of the Divine Word*.—S.V.D.
[1290]—*Society of the Priests of Saint Sulpice*.

RELIGIOUS INSTITUTES OF WOMEN REPRESENTED IN THE DIOCESE

[0100]—*Adorers of the Blood of Christ*. (Wichita; Ruma, KS; Columbia, PA).—A.S.C.
[0460]—*Congregation of the Sisters of Charity of the Incarnate Word*.—C.C.V.I.
[0810]—*Daughters of the Heart of Mary*.—D.H.M.
[1070]—*Dominicas de la Doctrina Cristiana*.—O.P.
[1370]—*The Franciscan Missionaries of Mary*.—F.M.M.
[1430]—*Franciscan Sisters of Our Lady of Perpetual Help*.—O.S.F.
[2470]—*Maryknoll Sisters of St. Dominic*.—M.M.
[2490]—*Medical Mission Sisters*.—M.M.S.
[2690]—*Missionary Catechists of Divine Providence*.—M.C.D.P.
[3130]—*Our Lady of Victory Missionary Sisters*.—OWM.
[3760]—*Poor Clares Monastery of Our Lady of Guadalupe*.—P.C.C.
[]—*Sisters for Christian Community*.
[0440]—*Sisters of Charity of Cincinnati, Ohio*.—S.C.
[2575]—*Sisters of Mercy of the Americas*. (Omaha).—R.S.M.
[3740]—*Sisters of St. Casimir*.—S.S.C.
[1570]—*Sisters of St. Francis of the Holy Family*.—O.S.F.
[3830-15]—*Sisters of St. Joseph*.—C.S.J.
[2575]—*Sisters of the Americas (Omaha, Vermont and New Jersey)*.—R.S.M.
[3270]—*Sisters of the Most Precious Blood (O'Fallon, MO)*.—C.PP.S.
[4100]—*Sisters of the Sorrowful Mother (Third Order of St. Francis)*.—S.S.M.
[4060]—*Society of the Holy Child Jesus*.—S.H.C.J.

NECROLOGY

(No Deaths)

Diocese of Las Vegas

(Dioecesis Campensis)

Most Reverend

DANIEL F. WALSH, D.D.

Bishop of Las Vegas; ordained March 30, 1963; appointed Titular Bishop of Tigia and Auxiliary of San Francisco September 24, 1981; appointed Bishop of Reno-Las Vegas June 9, 1987; installed August 6, 1987. *Res., 2809 Cameo Cir., Las Vegas, NV, 89107.*

ERECTED BY HIS HOLINESS POPE PIUS XI MARCH 27, 1931.

REDESIGNATED DIOCESE OF RENO-LAS VEGAS BY POPE PAUL VI, OCTOBER 13, 1976; REDESIGNATED DIOCESE OF LAS VEGAS BY HIS HOLINESS POPE JOHN PAUL II MARCH 21, 1995.

Square Miles 39,688.

For legal titles of parishes and diocesan institutions, consult the Chancery Office.

Chancery Office: 336 Cathedral Way, Las Vegas, NV, 89109. Mailing Address: Mailing Address P.O. Box 18316, Las Vegas, NV, 89114-8316. Tel.: 702-735-3500; Fax: 702-735-8941.

STATISTICAL OVERVIEW

Personnel	
Bishop	1
Priests: Diocesan Active in Diocese	21
Priests: Retired, Sick or Absent	21
Number of Diocesan Priests	42
Religious Priests in Diocese	20
Extern Priests in Diocese	18
Ordinations:	
Permanent Deacons in Diocese	7
Total Brothers	6
Total Sisters	53
Parishes	
Parishes	23
With Resident Pastor:	
Resident Diocesan Priests	18
Resident Religious Priests	5
Without Resident Pastor:	
Missions	8
Welfare	
Catholic Hospitals	1
Total Assisted	77,190
Total Assisted	523,993
Educational	
High Schools, Diocesan and Parish	1
Total Students	1,028
Elementary Schools, Diocesan and Parish	7
Total Students	2,213
Elementary Schools, Private	1
Total Students	211
Catechesis/Religious Education:	
High School Students	1,390
Elementary Students	7,100
Total Students Under Catholic Instruction	11,942
Teachers in the Diocese:	
Priests	2
Brothers	3
Sisters	9
Lay Teachers	173
Vital Statistics	
Receptions into the Church:	
Infant Baptism Totals	3,351
Adult Baptism Totals	277
Received into Full Communion	279
First Communions	1,903
Confirmations	707
Marriages:	
Catholic	401
Interfaith	161
Total Marriages	562
Deaths	579
Total Catholic Population	335,124
Total Population	1,155,600

Chancery Office—336 Cathedral Way, Las Vegas, 89109. Tel: 702-735-3500; Fax: 702-735-8941. Office Hours: Mon.-Fri 8:30-12 & 1-4:30, *Mailing Address: P.O. Box 18316, Las Vegas, 89114-8316.*

Vicar General—Rev. PATRICK LEARY, V.G.

Chancellor—Rev. PATRICK R. LEARY. Tel: 702-735-9605.

Diocesan Tribunal Office-Judicial Vicar—Very Rev. FRANCIS M. VIVONA, S.T.M., J.C.L. Tel: 702-735-1210; Fax: 702-735-5146.

Auditors—Rev. JOSEPH L. ANTHONY; MARY JOE GRETZINGER, J.C.L.; Rev. Msgr. ADRIAN DWYER, J.C.D.; Revs. PETER ROMEO, J.C.L.; STEPHAN WASHKO; MANUEL QUINTERO.

Notary-Secretary—Mrs. SIDNEY MARSH; Mrs. CECELIA CAMMARANO.

Promoter of Justice—Rev. MARK ROBERTS, J.C.L.

Defenders of the Bond—Revs. FRANCIS M. VIVONA; KEVIN MCAULIFFE, J.C.L.

Diocesan Judges—Revs. PETER ROMEO, J.C.L.; MARK ROBERTS, J.C.L.; FRANCIS M. VIVONA, S.T.M., J.C.L.; KEVIN MCAULIFFE, J.C.L.

Advocates—Revs. JOSEPH ANTHONY; STEPHEN WASHKO; MANUEL QUINTERO; ANTHONY VERCELLONE; MARY JO GRETZINGER, J.C.L.; MARY FULLER, J.C.L.; Rev. ROBERT ACQUARO, J.C.L.

Diocesan Offices and Directors

Building Committee—Most Rev. DANIEL F. WALSH, D.D., Chm.; Rev. PATRICK LEARY, V.G.; Bro. JOHN DODD, C.S.V.; Rev. DAVE CASALEGGIO.

Catholic Charities of Southern Nevada—808 S. Main St., Box 1926, Las Vegas, 89125. Tel: 702-385-2662. Mr. MIKE HUSTED, Exec. Dir.

Comptroller—Bro. JOHN DODD, C.S.V.

Development Office—Ms. PATSY VINCENT. Tel: 702-735-1109.

Education Department—

Superintendent of Schools—ELLEN AYOUB.

Office of Catechetical Ministries—Sr. MIRIAM MULLINS, O.P., Dir. Tel: 702-735-6044. Sr. KAREN CROUSE, O.S.F., Dir., Newman Apostolate. Tel: 702-736-0887.

Office of Peace and Social Justice—Rev. CAESAR J. CAVIGLIA.

Home and Foreign Missions—Rev. PATRICK LEARY, V.G. Tel: 702-735-9605.

Hospital Apostolate—Attended from St. Anne Parish. Tel: 702-735-0510.

Information, Communications and Media—Rev. BEDE WEVITA. Tel: 702-870-2767.

Italian Catholic Federation—Vacant.

Native American and Colored People Commission—Rev. PATRICK LEARY, V.G.

Newsletter—DESERT CLARION.

Pontifical Association of the Holy Childhood—Rev. PATRICK LEARY, V.G.

Priests' Pension Board—Revs. PHILIP O'DONNELL; FRANCIS VIVONA; JAMES BEVAN; Bro. JOHN DODD, C.S.V.

Priests' Personnel Board—Revs. DAVE CASALEGGIO; FRANCIS VIVONA; JOSEPH ANTHONY.

Property Management—Bro. JOHN DODD, C.S.V.

Vicar for Oriental Rites—Very Rev. FRANCIS VIVONA, S.T.M., J.C.L.

Vocations—Rev. PATRICK LEARY, V.G.

Youth Activities—Rev. MARK ROBERTS, M.A., J.C.L., *Diocese of Las Vegas: P.O. Box 18316, Las Vegas, 89114.* Tel: 702-735-9605.

CLERGY, PARISHES, MISSIONS AND PAROCHIAL SCHOOLS

CITY OF LAS VEGAS

(Clark County)

1—GUARDIAN ANGEL CATHEDRAL (1963), Revs. James Crilly, C.S.V., Rector; Francis P. White, C.S.V.; Daniel Reardon, C.S.V.; Sr. Timothy Malone, C.H.S., Pastoral Assoc.
Office: 336 Cathedral Way, 89109. Tel: 702-735-5241.

2—CHRIST THE KING (1978), Revs. William J.M. Kenny; Leo Coughlin; Robert Stoeckig.
Office: 4925 S. Torrey Pines, 89118. Tel: 702-871-1904; Fax: 702-251-4935.
Res., 5122 S. Torrey Pines, 89118.
Catechesis/Religious Programs—Beth Summers, D.R.E.
Students 534.
Mission—Sandy Valley, St. Catherine of Siena.

3—HOLY FAMILY (1975), Revs. John McShane; William McDonald (STO); Peter A. Romeo (MET).
Office: 4490 Mountain Vista, 89121. Tel: 702-458-0966.
Res., 4528 E. Harmon Ave., 89121-6548.
Catechesis/Religious Programs—Tel: 702-458-2211; Fax: 702-458-0966.
Students 311.

4—OUR LADY OF LAS VEGAS (1957), Revs. Dave Casaleggio; Bede Wevita; Dionisio Besinga.
Office: 3050 Alta Dr., 89107. Tel: 702-870-2767; Fax: 702-870-1267.
Res., 3104 Alta Dr., 89107.
School—3036 Alta Dr., 89107. Tel: 702-878-6841.
Brothers 1; Sisters 3; Lay Teachers 9; Students 341.

Catechesis/Religious Programs—Tel: 702-870-1882.
Students 341.

5—PRINCE OF PEACE (1981), Revs. Francis Timoney; Clarence Savial.
Office: 5485 E. Charleston Blvd., 89122. Tel: 702-431-2233; Fax: 702-431-2234.
Res., 653 Los Feliz, 89110.
Catechesis/Religious Programs—Tel: 702-431-2233; Fax: 702-431-2234.
Students 615.

6—ST. ANNE (1948), Revs. Robert Votta; Alberto Alzate (Colombia); Jesse Cortes (Philippines) Hospital Chap.
Office & Res.: 1901 Maryland Pkwy., 89104. Tel: 702-735-0510; Fax: 702-894-9237.
School—1813 Maryland Pkwy., 89104. Tel: 702-735-2586. Phyllis Joyce, Prin.
Lay Teachers 13; Students 336.
Catechesis/Religious Programs—Tel: 702-735-2985; Fax: 702-735-2973.
Students 324.

7—ST. BRIDGET (1945), Rev. James L. Swenson.
Office: 220 N. 14th St., 89101-4312. Tel: 702-384-3382.
Res., 215 N. 14th St., 89101.
Catechesis/Religious Programs—Students 95.

8—ST. ELIZABETH ANN SETON (1992), Revs. Anthony T. Vercellone; Raymond Rioux; Jerry Nadine; Deacons Joe Deegan; Frank Pemper; Howard Tigrath.
Office: 1811 Pueblo Vista Dr., 89128. Tel: 702-228-8311; Fax: 702-228-8310.
Res., 2109 Golden Lotus, 89134.
Catechesis/Religious Programs—Tel: 702-228-8311.
Students 684.

9—ST. FRANCIS DE SALES (1964), Revs. James J. Bevan, Jr.; Frank S. Yncierto; Stewart Schramko, C.S.V.
Office: 1111 Michael Way, 89108. Tel: 702-647-3440; Fax: 702-646-3587.
Res., 1628 Desert Fort, 89128.
School—Tel: 702-647-2828. Mrs. Gloria Hagstrom, Prin.
Lay Teachers 11; Students 301.
Catechesis/Religious Programs—Tel: 702-646-2266.
Students 300.

10—ST. JAMES THE APOSTLE (1942) (African American), Rev. Michael Blackburn, O.F.M.; Sr. Deborah Lockwood, O.S.F., Pastoral Assoc. & D.R.E.
Office: 820 N. H St., 89106. Tel: 702-648-6606; Fax: 702-648-0352.
Res., 1420 W. Bartlett, 89106. Tel: 702-648-2798.
Catechesis/Religious Programs—Tel: 702-648-6606.
Students 76.

11—ST. JOAN OF ARC (1908), Rev. Philip O'Donnell.
Office & Res.: 315 S. Casino Center Blvd., 89101. Tel: 702-382-9909; Fax: 702-382-6655.
School—1300 Bridger Ave., 89101. Tel: 702-384-6909; Fax: 702-386-0249. Mrs. Lynda Ballard, Prin.
Lay Teachers 8; Students 282.

12—ST. JOSEPH, HUSBAND OF MARY (1989), Revs. Joseph L. Anthony; Thomas E. Gallenbach; Gary Vollmer; Deacon Michael J. Heidenreich.
Office: 7260 W. Sahara Ave., 89117. Tel: 702-363-1902; Fax: 702-363-7976.
Res., 3759 Barrelwood Dr., 89117.
Catechesis/Religious Programs—Tel: 702-363-3658; Fax: 702-363-0142. Dr. Joan Tansey, D.R.E.
Students 685.

13—ST. MARY THE VIRGIN (1983), Rev. Michael Morrissey, S.S.C. Tel: 702-453-9032.
Office: 5083 Judson Ave., 89115. Tel: 702-438-1960.

14—ST. PAUL JUNG-HA-SANG (1987) (Korean), Rev. Michael Morrissey.
5225 Meikle Ln., 89115. Tel: 702-453-0033.

15—ST. VIATOR (1954), Revs. Thomas Langenfeld, C.S.V.; Wayne Dupuis, C.S.V.; William Haesaert, C.S.V.; Bro. Dale Barth, C.S.V.
Office: 2461 E. Flamingo Rd., 89121. Tel: 702-733-8323; Fax: 702-733-8154.
School—Tel: 702-732-4477; Fax: 702-732-4418. Mr. William C. Langley, Prin.
Sisters 2; Lay Teachers 26; Students 685.
Catechesis/Religious Programs—Tel: 702-732-0459. Carol Russell, D.R.E.
Students 465.

16—SHRINE OF THE MOST HOLY REDEEMER (1991), Revs. Patrick R. Leary, V.G.; Dominic Morrissette.
Office: 55 E. Reno Ave., 89119. Tel: 702-891-8600; Fax: 702-891-0339.
Res., 8222 Skycrest, 89123.

OUTSIDE THE CITY OF LAS VEGAS

Amargosa Valley, Nye Co., Mission of Our Lady Of the Valley (1987), Sr. Jacinta Kaiser, Admin.
Office & Res.: P.O. Box 218, Amargosa, 89020. Tel: 702-372-5337. [JC]

Boulder City, Clark Co., St. Andrew's (1931), Rev. Joseph P. Annese.
Office & Res.: 1399 San Felipe Dr., 89005. Tel: 702-293-7500; Fax: 702-293-4419. [JC]
Catechesis/Religious Programs—Michael Willis, D.R.E.
Students 141.

Caliente, Lincoln Co., Holy Child (1870), Rev. Leo Slatterie.
Res., Monastery of Christ in the Mountains, P.O. Box 708, 89008. Tel: 702-726-3669. [CEM]

Henderson, Clark Co., St. Peter the Apostle (1943), Rev. Mark Roberts.
Res., 204 S. Boulder Hwy., 89015. Tel: 702-565-8406; Fax: 702-565-8731.
St. Thomas More (1986), Revs. Dan Nolan, C.S.V.; Ken Morris, C.S.V.
Res., 130 N. Pecos Rd., 89014. Tel: 702-361-3022; Fax: 702-361-7784.

Ely, White Pine Co., Sacred Heart (1907), Rev. Timothy C. Wehn, S.A.C.
Mailing Address: P.O. Box 26, 89301. Tel: 702-289-2201.
Office & Res.: 501 Murry St., 89301.
School—1100 Park Ave., P.O. Box 278, 89301. Tel: 702-289-4302. Sr. Maura McGarry, R.S.M., Prin.
Sisters of Mercy 4; Lay Teachers 5; Students 100.
Catechesis/Religious Programs—Students 64.
Convent—550 First St., 89301. Tel: 702-289-4733. Mercy Convent
Mission—McGill, St, Michael's.

Laughlin, St. John the Baptist Catholic Mission (1992), Rev. Kevin McAuliffe, Admin.
P.O. Box 31888, 89028.
Res., 3115 Terrace View, 89029.

North Las Vegas, St. Christopher (1953), Revs. Gregory Gordon; Manuel Quintero.
Res., 1840 N. Bruce, 89030. Tel: 702-642-1154; Fax: 702-642-0719.

Overton, Clark Co., St. John, the Evangelist (1959), Rev. Gustavo Cruz.
Mailing Address: P.O. Box 493, 89040. Tel: 702-397-8096; Fax: 702-397-8264.
Office: 150 N. Moapa Valley Blvd., 89040. Fax: 807-397-2846.
Res., 425 W. Joan St., 89040.
Catechesis/Religious Programs—Students 155.
Mission—Bunkerville, Clark Co., La Virgen de Guadalupe, Corner of 1st W. & 1st S., P.O. Box 7309, Bunkerville, 89007. Tel: 702-346-7065.

Pahrump, NYE Co., Our Lady of the Valley (1985), Rev. Joseph Bochenski, C.M.F.
Res., 781 E. Gamebird, 89041.
Mailing Address: P.O. Box 1506, 89041. Tel: 702-727-4044.

Tonopah, Nye Co., St. Patrick (1902), Rev. John H. Lima.
Mailing Address: P.O. Box 325, 89049. Tel: 702-482-6746.
Office & Res.: 144 South St., 89049.
Missions—Round Mountain & Fish Lake, St. Barbara; Our Lady of Guadalupe.

Chaplains of Public Institutions

Special Assignment:
Reverend Fathers—
Richard, Alain, O.F.M., PACE E BENE, 1420 W. Bartlett St., Las Vegas, NV 89106. Tel: 702-648-2798

Military Chaplains:
Reverend Fathers—
Grochowski, Bernard, Our Lady of the Skies, 4302 N. Washington Blvd., Nellis AFB, NV 89191. Tel: 702-644-4969
Hanrahan, William, Our Lady of the Skies, 4302 N. Washington Blvd., Nellis AFB, NV 89191
McNulty, Jerry, Dept. of Veterans Affairs, VAMC - 125, 1703 W. Charleston Blvd., Las Vegas, NV 89102. Tel: 702-426-2813

Retired:
Reverend Fathers—
Caviglia, Caesar
Duff, William
Fanning, Gerard
Franzinell, Benjamin
Lavoy, Elwood
McVeigh, John J.

Permanent Deacons:
Alves, Joshua
Heidenriech, Mike
Moffett, Steve
Pemper, Frank
Stoehr, George
Tirgrath, Howard

INSTITUTIONS LOCATED IN THE DIOCESE

[A] HIGH SCHOOLS, DIOCESAN

LAS VEGAS. *Bishop Gorman High School*, 1801 Maryland Pkwy., 89104. Tel: 702-732-1945; Fax: 702-732-2856. Rev. Thomas R. vonBehren, C.S.V., Pres.; David W. Erbach, Prin.; Rev. Norbert Bibeault, C.S.V. Priests 2; Brothers 2; Sisters 2; Lay Teachers 53; Students 1,025.

[B] GENERAL HOSPITALS

HENDERSON. *St. Rose Dominican Hospital*, 102 Lake Mead Dr., 89015. Tel: 702-564-2622.
For a complete listing, refer to the Hospitals section.

[C] DAY NURSERIES

LAS VEGAS. *Holy Family Day Care Center*, 451 E. Twain, 89109. Tel: 702-735-4358. Connie Johnson, Dir.
Sponsor: Catholic Charities. Boys 62; Girls 68.

Variety Day Home, 990 D St., 89106. Tel: 702-647-4907. Sisters of the Holy Family. Sr. M. Diane Maguire, S.H.F., Dir.; Sr. Marie Julie Casatas, S.H.F., Family Coord. Day Home for infants through kindergarten age; Family Resource Center; Teacher Training Center. Boys 118; Girls 100.

[D] MONASTERIES AND RESIDENCES OF PRIESTS AND BROTHERS

LAS VEGAS. *Clerics of St. Viator*, 1212 E. Oakey Blvd., 89104. Tel: 702-735-4637; Fax: 702-732-2856. Rev. Thomas R. von Behren, C.S.V., Pres. Viatorian priests on facility of Gorman High School. In res., Bros. Corey D. Brost, C.S.V.; Robin L. Robertson, C.S.V. Priests 1; Brothers 2.

Clerics of St. Viator Retirement Home, 4219 Pinecrest Cir. E., 89121. Tel: 702-456-8512. Revs. Robert F. Cooney, C.S.V., Dir.; Edward C. Anderson, C.S.V.; Norbert P. Bibeault, C.S.V.; Patrick J. Hayes, C.S.V. Priests 4.

[E] CONVENTS AND RESIDENCES FOR SISTERS

LAS VEGAS. *Carmelite Monastery of Jesus, Mary and Joseph (O.C.D.)*, 4835 Pearl Ave., 89121. Mother Teresa, Prioress.

Convent of the Franciscan Sisters of Perpetual Adoration, 3315 Yuma Circle, 89109-3230. Tel: 702-735-0640. Sisters 2.

Holy Family Convent, 5276 S. Lookout St., 89120. Tel: 702-435-1526. Sisters of the Holy Family 5.

ELY. *Mercy Convent*, 550 First St., P.O. Box 278, 89301. Tel: 702-289-4733. Sisters 4.

[F] RETREAT HOUSES

CALIENTE. *Monastery of Christ in the Mountains*, P.O. Box 708, 89008.

[G] MISCELLANEOUS LISTINGS

LAS VEGAS. *Catholic Charities Annex, Inc.*, P.O. Box 1926, 89125-1926. Tel: 702-385-2662. Mrs. Mary Boozan Stivers, Sec. & Treas. Total Staff 251; Total Served 523,993.

Catholic Charities Mojave Project, Inc., 551 N. 30th St., 89101. Tel: 702-385-2662. Project known as Monsignor Charles T. Shallow Plaza; Construct & operate low-income senior citizen housing.

Catholic Charities of Southern Nevada, 808 S. Main St., P.O. Box 1926, 89125. Tel: 702-385-2662. Mr. Michael Husted, Exec. Dir.

Crossroads Family Shelter, 1526 N. Main St., 89101. Tel: 702-385-2777.

Diocese of Las Vegas Adoption Services, 808 S. Main St., P.O. Box 1926, 89125. Tel: 702-385-3351. Patricia Gutierrez, L.S.W., M.S.W., Dir. Also provides counseling for birth parents and grandparents, exercise classes, resource referrals and support groups with decision making sessions.

Emergency Assistance, 1501 N. Las Vegas Blvd., 89101. Tel: 702-385-2550. Martha Nedley, Dir.

Migration and Refugee Services, 1501 N. Las Vegas Blvd., 89101. Tel: 702-383-8387; Fax: 702-385-7748. Redda G. Mehari, Dir.

Retired Senior Volunteer Program. (Sponsored by Catholic Charities), Cannon Senior Center, 340 N. 11th St., 89101. Tel: 702-382-0721. Diane Guinn, Dir.

St. Paul Jung-Ha-Sang. (Korean Catholic Community), 5225 Meikle Ln., 89115. Tel: 702-453-0033.
St. Vincent Dining Room, 1501 N. Las Vegas Blvd., P.O. Box 1926, 89101. Tel: 702-385-7801.
St. Vincent Shelter, 1501 N. Las Vegas Blvd., 89101. Tel: 702-384-0409.
St. Vincent Thrift Store, 808 S. Main St., P.O. Box 1926, 89125. Tel: 702-382-4604.
St. Vincent Thrift Store, 1503 N. Main St., 89101. Tel: 702-399-0188.
St. Vincent Thrift Store, 4921 W. Vegas Dr., 89108. Tel: 702-647-6729.
Senior Community Service Employment Program, Cannon Senior Center, 340 N. 11th St., 89101. Tel: 702-382-0721. Ms. Ella Tucker, Dir.
Senior Companion Program, Cannon Senior Center, 340 N. 11th St., Ste. 204, 89101. Tel: 702-382-0721. Ann Mankenberg, Project Dir. Total Staff 14; Total Assisted 86.
Senior Housing (NCWB Housing, Inc.), Stella Fleming Towers, 400 Brush St., 89107. Tel: 702-385-2662.
Senior Nutrition Program, 531 N. 30th St., 89101. Tel: 702-385-5284. Sam Cortes, Dir.

HENDERSON. *Black Mountain Senior Nutrition Program,* 27 E. Texas St., 89015. Tel: 702-565-7980. Sandra Quinnell, Dir.
Regina Hall, 215 Palo Verde, 89015. Tel: 702-565-9925. Total Staff 7; Total in Residence 11.

RELIGIOUS INSTITUTES OF MEN REPRESENTED IN THE DIOCESE

For further details refer to the corresponding bracketed number in the Religious Institutes of Men or Women section.

[0360]—*Claretian Missionaries.*—C.M.F.
[1320]—*Clerics of St. Viator.*—C.S.V.
[0520]—*Franciscan Friars.*—O.F.M.

RELIGIOUS INSTITUTES OF WOMEN REPRESENTED IN THE DIOCESE

[1780]—*Congregation of the Sisters of the Third Order of St. Francis of Perpetual Adoration.*—F.S.P.A.
[0420]—*Discalced Carmelite Nuns.*—O.C.D.
[1070-04]—*Dominican Sisters.*—O.P.
[1190]—*Franciscan Sisters of the Atonement.*—S.A.
[2690]—*Missionary Catechists of Divine Providence.*—M.C.D.P.
[1630]—*Sisters of St. Francis of the Penance and Christian Charity.* (St. Francis Prov.).—O.S.F.
[1960]—*Sisters of the Holy Family.*—S.H.F.

NECROLOGY

(No Deaths)

Diocese of Lafayette in Indiana

(Diocesis Lafayettensis in Indiana)

Most Reverend

WILLIAM L. HIGI, D.D.

Bishop of Lafayette in Indiana; ordained May 30, 1959; appointed Bishop of Lafayette in Indiana April 7, 1984; consecrated and installed June 6, 1984. *Res., 610 Lingle Ave., P.O. Box 260, Lafayette, IN, 47902.*

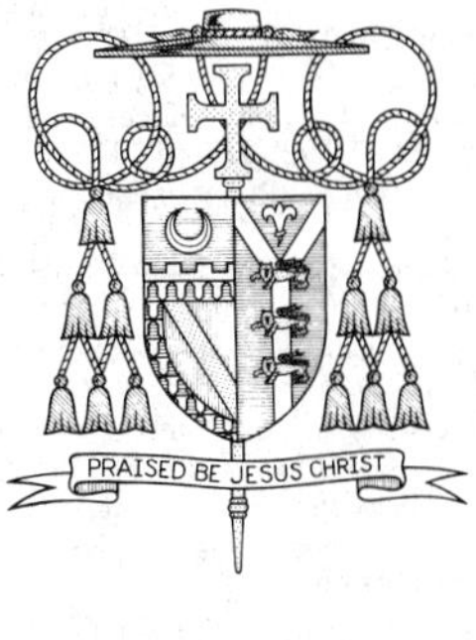

CANONICALLY ERECTED OCTOBER 21, 1944.

Square Miles 9,832.

Comprises the Counties of Benton, Blackford, Boone, Carroll, Cass, Clinton, Delaware, Fountain, Fulton, Grant, Hamilton, Howard, Jasper, Jay, Madison, Miami, Montgomery, Newton, Pulaski, Randolph, Tippecanoe, Tipton, Warren and White in the State of Indiana.

For legal titles of parishes and diocesan institutions, consult the Bishop's Office (Chancery).

Office of Bishop and Chancery: P.O. Box 260, Lafayette, IN, 47902. Tel.: 317-742-0275; Fax: 317-742-7513.

STATISTICAL OVERVIEW

Personnel	
Bishop	1
Priests: Diocesan Active in Diocese	79
Priests: Active Outside Diocese	19
Priests: Retired, Sick or Absent	22
Number of Diocesan Priests	120
Religious Priests in Diocese	19
Extern Priests in Diocese	2
Ordinations:	
Permanent Deacons in Diocese	5
Total Brothers	2
Total Sisters	112
Parishes	
Parishes	62
With Resident Pastor:	
Resident Diocesan Priests	51
Resident Religious Priests	4
Without Resident Pastor:	
Administered by Priests	7
Missions	1
Professional Ministry Personnel:	
Sisters	18
Lay Ministers	73
Welfare	
Catholic Hospitals	4
Total Assisted	501,103
Health Care Centers	2
Homes for the Aged	2
Total Assisted	693
Educational	
Diocesan Students in Other Seminaries	8
Total Seminarians	8
Colleges and Universities	3
Total Students	7,700
High Schools, Diocesan and Parish	1
Total Students	368
Elementary Schools, Diocesan and Parish	18
Total Students	4,013
Catechesis/Religious Education:	
High School Students	2,626
Elementary Students	7,938
Total Students Under Catholic Instruction	22,653
Teachers in the Diocese:	
Lay Teachers	234
Vital Statistics	
Receptions into the Church:	
Infant Baptism Totals	1,893
Adult Baptism Totals	252
Received into Full Communion	310
First Communions	1,804
Confirmations	1,450
Marriages:	
Catholic	303
Interfaith	328
Total Marriages	631
Deaths	792
Total Catholic Population	92,454
Total Population	1,101,765

Former Bishops—Most Rev. JOHN GEORGE BENNETT, D.D., LL.D., ord. June 27, 1914; appt. First Bishop of Lafayette Nov. 11, 1944; cons. Jan. 10, 1945; died Nov. 20, 1957.—His Eminence JOHN CARDINAL CARBERRY, D.D., ord. July 28, 1929; appt. Coadjutor with Right of Succession Aug. 22, 1956; appt. Bishop of Lafayette in Indiana Nov. 20, 1957; transferred to Diocese of Columbus, Jan. 20, 1965; transferred to the Archdiocese of St. Louis Mar. 24, 1968; created Cardinal April 28, 1969; retired July 31, 1979.—Most Rev. RAYMOND J. GALLAGHER, D.D., ord. March 25, 1939; appt. Bishop of Lafayette in Indiana June 23, 1965; cons. August 11, 1965; installed August 23, 1965; resigned October 26, 1982; retired April 13, 1983; died March 7, 1991.—Most Rev. GEORGE A. FULCHER, S.T.D., D.D., ord. Feb. 28, 1948; appt. Auxiliary Bishop of Columbus, OH and Titular Bishop of Morosbido May 24, 1976; cons. July 18, 1976; appt. Bishop of Lafayette in Indiana Feb. 8, 1983; installed April 14, 1983; died Jan. 25, 1984.

Vicar General—Rev. ROBERT L. SELL, III, J.C.L.

Chancellor and Moderator of the Curia—Rev. ROBERT L. SELL, III, J.C.L.

Office of Bishop and Chancery—P.O. Box 260, Lafayette, 47902. Tel: 317-742-0275; Fax: 317-742-7513.

Deans—Lafayette Deanery: Rev. DANIEL B. GARTLAND; Anderson Deanery: Rev. ROBERT L. WILLIAMS; Fowler Deanery: Rev. AMBROSE M. ZIEGLER; Carmel Deanery: Rev. LEO A. PIQUET; Logansport Deanery: Rev. DONALD L. GROSS; Muncie Deanery: Rev. WILLIAM R. GRADY.

Diocesan Consultors—Revs. WILLIAM R. GRADY, V.F.; LEO A. PIGUET, V.F.; ROBERT L. SELL, III, J.C.L., V.G.; DONALD L. GROSS, V.F.; THEODORE D. ROTHROCK; MICHAEL J. MCKINNEY; DOMINIC G. YOUNG.

Diocesan Pastoral Office for Administration—ROBERT H. QUINN, Finance Officer, *P.O. Box 260, Lafayette, 47902.* Tel: 317-742-4852.

Diocesan Pastoral Office for Planning and Communication—THOMAS A. RUSSELL, Dir., *610 Lingle Ave., P.O. Box 1603, Lafayette, 47902.* Tel: 317-742-2050.

Publisher- "The Catholic Moment"—RUSSELL FLYNN, Editorial Asst.-Reporter; MARY MANCHA, Reporter; CAROLYN CASE, Sec.

Diocesan Pastoral Office for Social Ministry—DAVID R. WILSON, Dir., *836 S. Purdum, Kokomo, 46901-5533.* Tel: 317-457-1172. Assists parishes in developing parish social ministry; co-ordinates the work of the Campaign for Human Development and the Indiana Catholic Conference; liaison with St. Elizabeth Home (Indianapolis) relative to adoption services, Pro-Life Service Centers, St. Vincent dePaul and Ladies of Charity, and coordinates the Premarital Evaluation program.

Diocesan Pastoral Office for Formation—Sr. MARILYN WINTER, O.P., Dir., *Catholic Pastoral Center, 2300 S. Ninth St., Lafayette, 47905-2400.* Tel: 317-474-8072; Fax: 317-474-3403. Coordinates marriage preparation conferences and programs, Natural Family Planning, Separated-Divorced Catholic programs, Sacramental preparation with families, implementation of Family Perspective and Family Catechesis. Additional responsibilities include all programs (Catholic Schools, Religious Education, Youth Ministry, Pre-schools, Sacramental Preparation, Scouts, Athletics, etc.) for young people in the Local Church. That responsibility extends to the formation of those who minister to young people as catechists, teachers, coaches, youth leaders and administrators.

Diocesan Tribunal—Catholic Pastoral Center, 2300 S. Ninth St., Lafayette, 47905. Tel: 317-474-0506.

Judicial Vicar—Rev. DAVID L. RASNER, J.C.L.

Adjutant Judicial Vicar—Rev. WILLIAM R. VATH.

—First Instance:

Presiding Judges—Revs. DAVID L. RASNER, J.C.L.; WILLIAM R. VATH.

Defenders of the Bond—Revs. DAVID J. BUCKLES, J.C.L.; DONALD L. GROSS.

Deputy Defenders—Rev. PETER VANDERKOLK; Sr. KATHRYN KIRK.

Ecclesiastical Notary—VERNA S. MEEK.

Full-Time Advocates—BRIDGET O'BRIEN; MAREN SCHERF.

Periti—PHILLIP M. SUTTON, Ph.D.; MICHAEL MILLARD, Ph.D.

—Second Instance:

Presiding Judge—Rev. RICHARD E. MILLER, J.C.L.

Associate Judges—Rev. Msgr. JOHN C. DUNCAN; Rev. Msgr. FRED E. POTTHOFF; Revs. MELVIN BENNETT; GERALD J. BORAWSKI; JAMES R. GOODRUM; FRED H. GSCHWIND; DONALD B. VERNON; EDWARD F. DHONDT; THOMAS J. ZIMMER.

Defender of the Bond—Rev. JOSEPH W. DOOLEY.

Ecclesiastical Notary—PEGGY FLETCHER.

Advocates—Refer to Court of First Instance.

Lay Advocates—Refer to Court of First Instance.

Periti—Refer to Court of First Instance.

Administrative Causes—Rev. ROBERT L. SELL, III, J.C.L.

Diocesan Offices and Directors

Archivist—Vacant.

Building Commission—KEN MCGINITY, Chm.; Revs. THEODORE ROTHROCK; ROBERT SELL; Sr. MARILYN WINTER, O.P.; ROBERT GLOYESKE; ANN MCKEE; Dr. DOUGLAS SUTTON; WILL WRIGHT; ERIC ERNSTBERGER; ROBERT TURNER; DANIEL MADER.

Finance Officer—ROBERT H. QUINN, *P.O. Box 260, Lafayette, 47902.* Tel: 317-742-4852.

Administration—Refer to Diocesan Pastoral Office.

Corporation—Roman Catholic Diocese of Lafayette in Indiana, Inc.(Incorporated, March 21, 1958.); Most Rev. WILLIAM L. HIGI, Pres.; Revs. ROBERT L. SELL, III, J.C.L., Vice Pres.-Sec. RICHARD WEISENBERGER, Treas.

Director of Stewardship—SHARON HUECKEL, *Bishop's*

Office, P.O. Box 1687, Lafayette, 47902. Tel: 317-742-7000; Fax: 317-742-7330.

Director of Planned Giving—CHARLES HOVORKA, *Bishop's Office, P.O. Box 1687, Lafayette, 47902.* Tel: 317-742-7000; Fax: 317-742-7330.

Finance Council—Most Rev. WILLIAM L. HIGI; Rev. ROBERT L. SELL, III, J.C.L., V.G.; ROBERT H. QUINN, Dir. Pastoral Office for Admin. LEON CYR; MARGARET ANDREZJEWSKI; JOAN TRET; DON GOETZ; EDWARD LOPKE; JOHN F. BODLE, Legal Counsel.

Fruitful Harvest Office—P.O. Box 1687, Lafayette, 47902. Tel: 317-742-4852.

Legal Council—JOHN DUFFEY, *Life Building, P.O. Box 1010, Lafayette, 47902.* Tel: 317-423-1561; Fax: 317-742-8175.

Presbyteral Council—Revs. DOMINIC G. YOUNG, Chm. MICHAEL J. MCKINLEY, Vice Chm.

Members—Revs. ROBERT L. SELL, III, J.C.L., V.G.; DENNIS J. GOTH; WILLIAM R. GRADY, V.F.; DONALD L. GROSS, V.F.; PHILIP S. HASLINGER; DOMINIC G. YOUNG; DANIEL B. GARTLAND, V.F.; LEO A. PIGUET, V.F.; THEODORE D. ROTHROCK; ROBERT L. WILLIAMS, V.F.; MICHAEL J. MCKINLEY, V.F.; MICHAEL A. MCKINNEY; PATRICK R. CLICK.

Catholic Relief Services—Vacant.

Censor Librorum—Rev. DAVID L. RASNER, J.C.L., *Catholic Pastoral Center, 2300 S. Ninth St., Lafayette, 47905.* Tel: 317-474-0506.

Aquinas Educational Foundation, Inc.—Rev. PATRICK R. CLICK, Res. Agent, *535 State St., W. Lafayette, 47906.* Tel: 317-743-4653.

Clergy Relief Association—Board of Directors: Revs. LEROY G. KINNAMAN, Pres.; TIMOTHY M. ALKIRE, Vice Pres.; JERRY BORAWSKI, Sec.; THOMAS FOX, Treas.; ALEJANDRO PATERNOSTER, Asst. Treas.

Members—Revs. EDWARD DHONDT; THEODORE ROTHROCK; RICHARD WEISENBERGER.

Catholic Charities Central Office—Refer to Diocesan Pastoral Office.

Social Ministry—DAVID R. WILSON, Diocesan Dir., *Diocesan Catholic Offices, 836 S. Purdum, Kokomo, 46901.* Tel: 317-457-1172.

Society of St. Vincent de Paul—DAVID R. WILSON, Diocesan Dir., *Diocesan Catholic Offices, 836 S. Purdum St., Kokomo, 46901.* Tel: 317-457-1172.

Association of Ladies of Charity—DAVID R. WILSON, Dir., Diocesan Catholic Offices, 836 Purdum St., Kokomo, 46901. Tel: 317-457-1172.

Liturgical Commission—Refer to Diocesan Pastoral Office.

Eucharistic League—The Chancery, P.O. Box 260, Lafayette, 47902.

Greater Lafayette Catholic School Board——Contact; DAVID WORLAND.

Greater Lafayette Catholic School Foundation, Inc.—JERRY MARTIN, *2410 S. Ninth St., Lafayette, 47905.*

Holy Childhood Association—Vacant.

Diocesan Board of Education—In process of reorganization & formation.

D.C.C.W.—Rev. DUANE CRAYCRAFT, Moderator, *1031 Kem Rd., Marion, 46952-2097.*

Ministry to Priests Program—Rev. DONALD L. GROSS, V.F., Dir., *All Saints Church, 112 E. Market St., Logansport, 46947.* Tel: 219-753-3020.

Newman Apostolate, Purdue University—Rev. PATRICK R. CLICK, Dir., *535 State St., West Lafayette, 47906.* Tel: 317-743-4652.

Newman Foundation, Ball State, Inc.—Rev. JOHN J. KEIFER, Dir., *800 Riverside Ave., Muncie, 47303.* Tel: 317-288-6180.

Newman Apostolate, Wabash College—Rev. LEROY KINNAMAN, Dir., *310 S. Grant Ave., Crawfordsville, 47933.* Tel: 317-362-6121.

Newspaper "The Catholic Moment"—THOMAS A. RUSSELL, Editor; RUSSELL FLYNN, Editorial Asst./Reporter; MARY MANCHA, Reporter, Editorial Office, *P.O. Box 1603, Lafayette, 47902.* Tel: 317-742-2050.

Office of the Apostolate to the Spanish Speaking—Deacon DOMINGO CASTILLO, Assoc. Dir., *917 Branson St., Marion, 46952.* Tel: 317-662-3288., *Guadalupe Center.* Tel: 317-664-3710.

Propagation of the Faith—DAVID WILSON. Refer to Pastoral Office for Social Ministry.

Religious Education Dept.—Refer to Pastoral Office for Formation.

RENEW—Rev. THEODORE ROTHROCK, Dir., *St. Patrick Church, 502 S. Michigan St., Oxford, 47971-9731.* Tel: 317-385-2587.

Rural Life Program—Rev. FRED H. GSCHWIND, Dir., *340 N. Mill St., Tipton.* Tel: 317-675-2422. *46072.*

Schools—Refer to Pastoral for Formation.

St. Joseph Memorial Hospital Foundation, Inc.—PEGGY CALDWELL, Exec. Dir., *1907 W. Sycamore St., Kokomo, 46901.* Tel: 317-456-5425.

Vicar for Clergy—Vacant.

Vicar for Religious—Vacant.

Vocation Director—Rev. THEODORE ROTHROCK, Dir., *St. Patrick, 502 S. Michigan St., Oxford, 47971-9731.* Tel: 317-385-2587.

CLERGY, PARISHES, MISSIONS AND PAROCHIAL SCHOOLS

CITY OF LAFAYETTE
(Tippecanoe County)

1—ST. MARY CATHEDRAL (1843), Revs. Richard J. Weisenberger; Jeffrey S. Brambora. In res., Rev. Joseph Bruetsch.
Res., 1207 Columbia St., 47901-1522. Tel: 317-742-4440; Fax: 317-742-8933. [CEM]
School—(Grades PreK-3). Tel: 317-742-6302.
Lay Teachers 11; Students 209.
Catechesis/Religious Programs—Tel: 317-742-8336.
Students 134.

2—ST. ANN (1884), Revs. Ambrose M. Ziegler; Maurice R. Miller.
Res., 612 Wabash Ave., 47905-1096. Tel: 317-742-7031. [JC]
Catechesis/Religious Programs—Tel: 317-423-4635.
Students 268.

3—ST. BONIFACE (1853) (German), Rev. Timothy M. Alkire; Deacon Ron Nevinger. In res., Rev. William R. Vath.
Res., 318 N. Ninth St., 47904-2597. Tel: 317-742-5063; Fax: 317-742-5018. [CEM]
School—Lafayette Catholic Middle School, (Grades 4-6). Tel: 317-742-7913; Fax: 317-423-4988. Sr. M. Lois DeLee, O.S.F., Prin.
Lay Teachers 7; Students 126.
Catechesis/Religious Programs—Tel: 317-742-1351.
Students 260.

4—ST. LAWRENCE (1895), Revs. Daniel B. Gartland; Christopher T. Miller. In res., Rev. Anthony Pogorelc (SAT).
Res., 1916 Meharry St., 47904-1442. Tel: 317-742-2107; Fax: 317-742-1347.
School—1902 Meharry St., 47904-1497. Tel: 317-742-4450. Mrs. Pam Peroutky, Prin.
Lay Teachers 10; Students 225.
Catechesis/Religious Programs—Tel: 317-423-2396. Susan Schmitz, D.R.E.
Students 273.

OUTSIDE THE CITY OF LAFAYETTE

Alexandria, Madison Co., St. Mary (1896), Rev. Philip S. Haslinger.
Res., 820 W. Madison St., 46001-1520. Tel: 317-724-2483; 724-4459.
School—Tel: 317-724-4459.
Sisters 3; Lay Teachers 4; Students 102.
Catechesis/Religious Programs—Students 65.

Anderson, Madison Co., St. Ambrose (1947), Rev. Edward F. Dhondt.
Res., 2801 Lincoln St., 46016-5067. Tel: 317-644-5956; Fax: 317-642-7348.
School—Tel: 317-642-8428; Fax: 317-642-7348.
Lay Teachers 13; Students 203.
Catechesis/Religious Programs—Tel: 317-644-5956.
Students 201.

St. Mary (1858), Rev. Robert L. Williams; Mrs. Mary Pat Marstall, Pastoral Assoc.
Res., 1115 Pearl St., 46016-1789. Tel: 317-644-8467.
School—Tel: 317-642-1848. Mrs. Kris Duncan, Prin.
Lay Teachers 15; Students 145.
Station—Anderson, St. John Medical Center Chapel, Tel: 317-649-2511.
Catechesis/Religious Programs—Tel: 317-642-5339.
Students 125.

Attica, Fountain Co., St. Francis Xavier (1890), Rev. Charles Kline.
Res., 407 S. Perry St., P.O. Box 55, 47918-0001. Tel: 317-762-3330; Fax: 317-762-1810. [CEM]
Catechesis/Religious Programs—Students 99.

Bryant, Jay Co., Holy Trinity (1860) (German), Rev. Robert C. Reinhart, C.PP.S.
Res., R.R. 1, P.O. Box 87, 47326-9724. Tel: 219-997-6450. [CEM]
Catechesis/Religious Programs—Tel: 219-997-6450.
Students 150.

Carmel, Hamilton Co., Our Lady of Mount Carmel (1955), Rev. Msgr. John C. Duncan; Revs. Kevin J. Haines; David J. Newton; Michael A. Ondo; Richard J. Doerr; Deacon William Rahill.
Office: 1045 W. 146th St., 46032-1198. Tel: 317-846-3475; Fax: 317-846-3477.
School—Tel: 317-846-1118.
Sisters of Notre Dame 4; Lay Teachers 34; Students 664.
Catechesis/Religious Programs—Tel: 317-846-3878.
Students 1,040.
Mission—Westfield, Hamilton Co., St. Maria Goretti, (1994) 17104 Springmill Rd., Westfield, 46074.

St. Elizabeth Ann Seton (1981), Revs. Leo A. Piguet; Robert W. Klemme; Fred A. Schroeder.
Res., 10655 Haverstick Rd., 46033-3800. Tel: 317-846-3850; 846-6073; 846-6945; Fax: 317-846-3850.
Catechesis/Religious Programs—Tel: 317-846-3850; Fax: 317-846-3850.
Students 667.

Cicero, Hamilton Co., Sacred Heart (1898) (German-Irish), Rev. W. Michael Kettron.
Res., 429 S. Main St., 46034-9680. Tel: 317-984-5117.
Catechesis/Religious Programs—Tel: 317-984-2115.
Students 80.

Covington, Fountain Co., St. Joseph (1861), Rev. Leroy G. Kinnaman.
Res., 308 Pearl St., 47932-1062. Tel: 317-793-3289. [CEM]
Catechesis/Religious Programs—Tel: 317-793-4961.
Students 63.

Crawfordsville, Montgomery Co., St. Bernard (1859), Rev. Melvin J. Bennett.
Res., 1306 E. Main St., P.O. Box 719, 47933-0719. Tel: 317-362-6121; Fax: 317-361-0796. [CEM]
Catechesis/Religious Programs—Tel: 317-362-5472.
Students 282.

Delphi, Carroll Co., St. Joseph (1859), Rev. Peter J. Vanderkolk.
Res., 207 N. Washington St., 46923-1297. Tel: 317-564-2407. [CEM]
Catechesis/Religious Programs—Tel: 317-564-3439.
Students 136.

De Motte, Jasper Co., St. Cecilia (1952), Rev. Paul R. Wicklum.
Res., 334 Fifteenth St., S.W., 46310-9705. Tel: 219-987-3511; Fax: 219-987-7755. [CEM]
Catechesis/Religious Programs—Tel: 219-987-3514.
Students 156.

Dunkirk, Jay Co., St. Mary (1896), Rev. Dennis J. Goth.
Res., 346 S. Broad St., 47336-1310. Tel: 317-768-6157.
Catechesis/Religious Programs—Students 71.

Dunnington, Benton Co., St. Mary (1876), Rev. Donald B. Vernon, Admin.
Mailing Address: 2961 South SR71, Ambia, 47917. Tel: 317-884-1818. [CEM]

Earl Park, Benton Co., St. John the Baptist (1888), Rev. Robert J. Bernotas, Admin.
Mailing Address: P.O. Box 131, Kentland, 47951-0131. Tel: 219-474-5514. [CEM]

Elwood, Madison Co., St. Joseph (1889) (Irish-German), Rev. Kenneth T. Raczek.
Res., 1306 S. A St., 46036-1941. Tel: 317-552-6753. [CEM][JC]
Catechesis/Religious Programs—Tel: 317-552-6753. Mary Pat Miller, D.R.E.
Students 235.

Fishers, Hamilton Co., Holy Spirit Church (1991), Revs. Phillip T. Bowers; Michael A. McKinney.
Mailing Address: 10350 Glaser Way, 46038. Tel: 317-849-9245; Fax: 317-849-9388.
Res., 10868 Geist Woods Ln., Indianapolis, 46256. Tel: 317-845-0992; Fax: 317-849-9388.
Catechesis/Religious Programs—Tel: 317-849-8016.
Students 731.

St. Louis de Montfort (1978), Rev. Donald J. Eder.
Res., 11441 Hague Rd., 46038-1876. Tel: 317-842-6778; 842-6358; 576-1932; Fax: 317-842-6358.
Catechesis/Religious Programs—Students 1017.

Fowler, Benton Co., Sacred Heart of Jesus (1872), Rev. Donald B. Vernon.
Res., 107 E. Main St., 47944-1148. Tel: 317-884-1818. [CEM]
School—Tel: 317-884-0710. Sr. Helene Seculoff, Prin.
Sisters of St. Francis of Perpetual Adoration 3; Lay Teachers 7; Students 152.
Catechesis/Religious Programs—Students 101.

Francesville, Pulaski Co., St. Francis Solano (1867), Rev. Paul R. White, C.PP.S., Admin.
Res., St. Joseph's College, P.O. Box 852, Rensselaer, 47978. Tel: 219-866-6271.

Frankfort, Clinton Co., St. Mary (1875), Rev. Gerald J. Borawski.
Res., 600 St. Mary's Ave., P.O. Box 265, 46041-0181. Tel: 317-654-5796; Fax: 317-654-6589. [JC]

Gas City, Grant Co., Holy Family (1893), Rev. A.

Leonard Reemmer.
Res., 325 E. North A St., 46933-1431. Tel: 317-674-2605.
Catechesis/Religious Programs—Students 130.

Goodland, Newton, SS. Peter and Paul (1880), Rev. Robert J. Bernotas, Admin.
Res., P.O. Box 131, Kentland, 47951-0131. Tel: 219-474-5514. [JC]
Church—419 S. Newton St., 47948.

Hartford City, Blackford Co., St. John the Evangelist (1865), Rev. Robert E. Moran.
Res., 209 S. Spring St., 47348-2551. Tel: 317-348-3123.
School—Tel: 317-348-3889; Fax: 317-348-4399.
Lay Teachers 5; Students 101.
Catechesis/Religious Programs—Students 67.

Kentland, Newton, St. Joseph (1864), Rev. Robert J. Bernotas.
Res., 409 E. Allen St., P.O. Box 131, 47951-1322. Tel: 219-474-5514. [CEM]
School—Tel: 219-474-5614.
Lay Teachers 8; Students 106.
Convent—501 E. Allen St., 47951. Tel: 219-474-6604.
St. Joseph School Foundation, Inc.—Tel: 219-474-5514.
Catechesis/Religious Programs—Tel: 219-474-5614.
Students 110.

Kewanna, Fulton Co., St. Ann (1857), Rev. John H. Zahn, Admin.
Res., P.O. Box 235, 46939-0181. Tel: 219-653-2520. [CEM]

Kokomo, Howard Co., St. Joan of Arc (1927), Revs. David E. Hellmann; Timothy D. Kroeger.
Res., 900 S. Purdum, 46901-5598. Tel: 317-457-9371; Fax: 317-454-7241.
School—SS. Joan of Arc and Patrick School. (Consolidated School) 824 S. Purdum St., 46901-5500. Tel: 317-452-1610 (St. Joan); 459-4769 (St. Patrick).
Lay Teachers 21; Students 338.
Catechesis/Religious Programs—923 South Jay St., 46901. Tel: 317-457-1375; Fax: 317-454-7241.
Students 376.

St. Patrick (1859), Revs. Francis I. Kilcline; Jack Trippel.
Office—1229 N. Washington St., 46901-2898.
Res., 320 W. Broadway, 46901-2898. Tel: 317-452-6021; Fax: 317-868-8384. [JC]
Schools—(Grades K-7). Tel: 317-459-4769.
Lay Teachers 22; Students 52; SS. Joan of Arc and Patrick School. (South Campus) 824 S. Purdum St., 46901-5500. Tel: 317-459-4769.
(North Campus) 1230 N. Armstrong St., 46901.
Catechesis/Religious Programs—1229 N. Washington, 46901. Tel: 317-452-6021; Fax: 317-868-8384. Rita Ricci, D.R.E.
Students 340.

Lake Village, Newton, St. Augusta (1947), Rev. Michael J. McKinley.
Res., 3228 W. St. Rd. 10, 46349-9706. Tel: 219-992-3220. [JC]
Catechesis/Religious Programs—Students 52.

Lebanon, Boone Co., St. Joseph (1862), Rev. Thomas H. Metzger.
Mailing Address: P.O. Box 309, 46052-0309. Tel: 317-482-5558.
Res., 319 E. South St., 46052-2684. Tel: 317-482-5558. [CEM]
Catechesis/Religious Programs—Tel: 317-482-1581.
Students 244.

Logansport, Cass Co., All Saints (1985). Consolidation of the following three parishes (Legal Titles): St. Bridget (1875); St. Joseph (1868); and St. Vincent de Paul (1838). Revs. Donald L. Gross; Leo J. Haigerty; Sr. Margaret Rose Donnelly, S.S.N.D., Pastoral Assoc.
Parish Office: 111 E. Market St., 46947-2922. Tel: 219-722-4080; Fax: 219-722-5426.
Res., 112 E. Market St., 46947. Tel: 219-753-3020. [JC]
School—All Saints Elementary, 107 Eel River Ave., 46947-3188. Tel: 219-753-3714.
All Saints Middle School—620 Wilkinson St., 46947. Tel: 219-722-5622.
Sisters 1; Lay Teachers 13; Students 283.
Convent—700 Wheatland Ave., 46947. Tel: 219-753-3684.
Catechesis/Religious Programs—Tel: 219-722-4080.
Students 180.

Lucerne, Cass Co., St. Elizabeth (1953), Rev. Donald L. Gross, Admin.
Mailing Address: 112 East Market, Logansport, 46947. Tel: 219-753-3020.
Office: P.O. Box 86, 46950. [CEM]

Marion, Grant Co., St. Paul (1868), Revs. Duane M. Craycraft; C. Alan Funk.
Res., 1031 Kem Rd., 46952-2098. Tel: 317-664-6345; Fax: 317-664-5953.
School—1009 Kem Rd., 46952. Tel: 317-662-2883. Mr. Tom Ray, Prin.
Lay Teachers 6; Students 102.
Catechesis/Religious Programs—Tel: 317-664-6345.
Students 213.

Our Lady of Guadalupe (Hispanic). Closed. For inquiries for parish records contact St. Paul, Marion.

Medaryville, Pulaski Co., St. Henry (1868), Rev. Paul R. White, C.PP.S., Admin.
Res., St. Joseph's College, P.O. Box 852, Rensselaer, 47978. Tel: 219-866-6271. [CEM]

Monterey, Pulaski Co., St. Anne (1851) (German), Rev. Dominic Young.
Res., Church St., P.O. Box 96, 46960-0096. Tel: 219-542-2061. [CEM]
School—Tel: 219-542-4711.
Lay Teachers 4; Students 60.
Catechesis/Religious Programs—Tel: 219-542-4711.
Students 34.

Monticello, White Co., Our Lady of the Lakes (1948), Rev. James R. Goodrum.
Res., 543 S. Main St., 47960-2948. Tel: 219-583-5724.
Catechesis/Religious Programs—Tel: 219-583-6790.
Students 194.

Montpelier, Blackford Co., St. Margaret of Scotland (1864), Rev. Frederick J. Perry.
Res., 207 W. Huntington St., P.O. Box 247, 47359. Tel: 317-728-5757. [CEM]

Muncie, Delaware Co., St. Francis of Assisi (1972). (Ball State University Parish). Revs. John D. Kiefer; Richard J. Doerr.
Res., 1200 W. Riverside Ave., 47303-3650. Tel: 317-288-6180.
Catechesis/Religious Programs—Students 176.

St. Lawrence (1869), Rev. Dennis J. O'Keeffe.
Res., 820 E. Charles St., 47305-2699. Tel: 317-288-9223; Fax: 317-289-9262.
School—2801 E. 16th St., 47302. Tel: 317-282-9353; Fax: 317-282-0457.
Lay Teachers 11; Students 178.
Catechesis/Religious Programs—Students 115.

St. Mary (1930), Revs. William R. Grady; Alejandro Paternoster. In res., Revs. James T. Keane; Anthony Prosen.
Res., 2300 W. Jackson St., 47303-4797. Tel: 317-288-5308.
School—2301 W. Gilbert St., 47303-4797. Tel: 317-288-5878; Fax: 317-284-3685.
Lay Teachers 19; Students 270.
Catechesis/Religious Programs—Students 151.

Noblesville, Hamilton Co., Our Lady of Grace (1944), Revs. James R. Bates; Martin J. Sandhage.
Res., 9900 E. 191st St., 46060-1998. Tel: 317-773-4275; Fax: 317-773-9344.
Catechesis/Religious Programs—Tel: 317-773-0297.
Students 702.

Otterbein, Benton Co., St. Charles (1902), Rev. David L. Rasner.
Res., 108 N. Meadow St., Box 661, 47970-0661. Tel: 317-583-4641. [JC]
Catechesis/Religious Programs—Students 115.

Oxford, Benton Co., St. Patrick (1867) (Irish), Rev. Theodore D. Rothrock.
Res., 502 S. Michigan St., 47971-8562. Tel: 317-385-2587; Fax: 317-385-0225. [CEM]
Catechesis/Religious Programs—Students 111.

Peru, Miami Co., St. Charles Borromeo (1860), Rev. Virgil M. Barker.
Res., 58 W. Fifth St., 46970-2100. Tel: 317-473-5543. [CEM]
School—Tel: 317-473-5669.
Lay Teachers 7; Students 99.
Catechesis/Religious Programs—80 W. Fifth St., 46970. Tel: 317-472-2692.
Students 105.

Portland, Jay Co., Immaculate Conception (1876), Rev. Joseph W. Grace.
Res., 506 E. Walnut St., 47371-1599. Tel: 219-726-7341.
Catechesis/Religious Programs—Tel: 219-726-7055.
Students 292.

Remington, Jasper Co., Sacred Heart (1875), Rev. Thomas E. Fox.
Res., 124 New York St., P.O. Box 159, 47977-0159. Tel: 219-261-2302. [CEM]
Catechesis/Religious Programs—Tel: 317-279-2656.
Students 104.

Rensselaer, Jasper Co., St. Augustine (1883), Revs. Mark R. Peres, C.PP.S.; Leonard I. Kostka, C.PP.S., Pastoral Assoc.
Res., 318 N. McKinley St., 47978-2599. Tel: 219-866-5351. [CEM]
School—Tel: 219-866-5480.
Religious 2; Lay Teachers 5; Students 117.
Catechesis/Religious Programs—Tel: 219-866-5351.
Students 160.

Reynolds, White Co., St. Joseph (1866), Rev. Richard E. Miller.
Res., 601 South Kenton St., 47980-8098. Tel: 219-984-5401. [CEM]
Catechesis/Religious Programs—Students 110.

Rochester, Fulton Co., St. Joseph (1900), Rev. John H. Zahn.
Res., 1310 S. Main St., 46975-2108. Tel: 219-223-2808; Fax: 219-224-2808. [JC]
Catechesis/Religious Programs—Tel: 219-223-3246.
Students 152.
Mission—Kewanna, Fulton Co., St. Ann, P.O. Box 235, Kewanna, 46939. Tel: 219-653-2520.

Star City, Pulaski Co., St. Joseph (1851), Rev. Ronald J. Schiml, C.PP.S.
Res., R.R. 2, P.O. Box 65, 46985-9517. Tel: 219-595-7198. [CEM 2]
Catechesis/Religious Programs—Students 74.

Tipton, Tipton Co., St. John the Baptist (1866), Rev. Fred H. Gschwind.
Res., 340 N. Mill St., 46072-1403. Tel: 317-675-2422. [CEM]
School—(Grades PreK-5). Tel: 317-675-4741; Fax: 317-675-2163.
Lay Teachers 12; Students 157.
Catechesis/Religious Programs—Students 149.

Union City, Randolph Co., St. Mary (1865) (Irish-German), Rev. Dennis J. Goth.
Res., 425 W. Hickory St., 47390-1301. Tel: 317-964-4202. [CEM]
Catechesis/Religious Programs—Students 132.

Westfield, Hamilton Co., St. Maria Goretti (1995), Res., 17104 Springmill Rd., 46074. Tel: 317-896-5582; Fax: 317-867-0783.
School—Sisters of Notre Dame 1; Lay Teachers 7; Students 188.
Catechesis/Religious Programs—Students 125.

West Lafayette, Tippecanoe Co., Blessed Sacrament (1957), Rev. David M. Douglas.
Res., 2224 Sacramento Ave., 47906-1998. Tel: 317-463-5733; Fax: 317-497-7866.
Catechesis/Religious Programs—Students 289.
Stations—Indiana Veterans' Home, Tel: 317-463-1502; Mary Queen of the Universe Chapel.

St. Thomas Aquinas (1951). (Purdue University Parish). Revs. Patrick R. Click; Anthony J. Levi. Pastoral Assocs.: Mrs. Phyllis Scanlon; Mr. Christopher O'Neal. In res., Rev. Frank DeRego (HON).
Office: 535 State St., 47096-3592. Tel: 317-743-4652; Fax: 317-743-0426.
Catechesis/Religious Programs—Linda Koerner, D.R.E.
Students 395.

Wheatfield, Jasper Co., Sorrowful Mother (1887), Rev. Philip A. Mahalic.
Res., P.O. Box 248, 46392-0248. Tel: 219-956-3343. [CEM]
Church Hall: Tel: 219-956-4648.
Catechesis/Religious Programs—Students 131.

Winamac, Pulaski Co., St. Peter (1859), Rev. Herbert Woolson, C.PP.S.
Res., 401 N. Monticello St., 46996-1327. Tel: 219-946-4906. [CEM]
Catechesis/Religious Programs—424 N. Market St., 46996. Tel: 219-946-6804.
Students 196.

Winchester, Randolph Co., St. Joseph (1952), Rev. Louis S. Heitz.
Res., 425 W. North St., 47394-1502. Tel: 317-584-4391.

Zionsville, Boone Co., St. Alphonsus (1945), Rev. Douglas McCormack; Deacon Harold W. Cloud.
Res., 1870 W. Oak, 46077-1894. Tel: 317-873-2885; 873-2700; Fax: 317-873-8746.
Catechesis/Religious Programs—Tel: 317-873-9418.
Students 380.

Chaplains of Public Institutions

LAFAYETTE. *Indiana Veterans' Home, Queen of the Universe Chapel.* Attended from Blessed Sacrament Church, West Lafayette.

GRISSOM. *Grissom Air Force Base, St. Michael's Chapel,* 46971. Tel: 317-688-2191. Rev. Richard E. Miller, Auxiliary Civilian Chap.

LOGANSPORT. *Logansport State Hospital.* Vacant.

MARION. *U.S. Veteran's Hospital.* Rev. James Rose (FTW), Chap., Auxiliary Chaplains: Revs. Joseph W. Grace; A. Leonard Reemmer.

PENDLETON. *Correctional Industrial Complex Ecumenical Chapel,* P.O. Box 601, 46064. Tel: 317-778-8011. Rev. Anthony J. Prosen.

Indiana State Reformatory, St. Christopher Chapel, P.O. Box 28, 46064. Tel: 317-778-2107. Rev. Anthony J. Prosen.

Special Assignment:
Reverend Fathers—
Buckles, David, J.C.L., Diocesan Tribunal, 2300 S. 9th St., Lafayette, IN 47905. Tel: 317-474-0506
Miller, Richard E., J.C.L., Diocesan Tribunal, 2300 S. 9th St., Lafayette, IN 47905. Tel: 317-474-0506
Prosen, Anthony, 1315 W. University St., Muncie, IN 47303. Tel: 317-288-6180
Rasner, David L., J.C.L., Treas., Clergy Relief Association,.
Rothrock, Theodore D., Vocation Dir., 502 S. Michigan St., Oxford, IN 47971-9131. Tel: 317-385-2587
Sell, Robert L., III, J.C.L., Vicar General, Chancellor, Moderator of the Curia, 1128 E. State St., Lafayette, IN 47905. Tel: 317-742-3286
Vath, William R., Diocesan Tribunal, 2300 S. 9th St., Lafayette, IN 47905. Tel: 317-474-0506; 742-4440

On Duty Outside the Diocese:
Reverend Fathers—
Carr, Bernard, Sacred Heart Church, Box 118, Anza, CA 92306. Tel: 714-763-5636
Clegg, Timothy, 56 FW/HC, MacDill AFB, FL 33608
Comeau, Ronald R., 6 Johnson Rd., Aurora, Ontario L4C 2A2. Tel: 416-727-1965
Cover, Phillip B., 808 D St. S.E., Washington, DC 20003. Tel: 202-544-0525
Cox, Alan
Gross, Barry, 1601 Georgia Ave., Wheaton, MD 20902
Holbrook, William M., 6210 W. Bell Plaine, Chicago, IL 60634
Mannion, John H., St. Francis Hospital, Pastoral Care Department, 1600 Albany St., Beechgrove, IN 46107. Tel: 317-787-3311
Plaster, George, 1751 - A Pemberton Ln., Indianapolis, IN 46260. Tel: 317-872-9923
Schultz, John C., P.O. Box 415, Danville, IL 61834. Tel: 217-443-3936
Westfall, Joseph B., 4344 Holly Dr., Apt. 1-N, Kansas City, MO 64111

Military Chaplains:
Reverend Fathers—
Kinney, John M., PSC Box 719, APO, NY 09289

Leave of Absence:
Reverend Fathers—
Bohlinger, Kenneth
Cummings, John J.

Unassigned:
Reverend Fathers—
Colletti, Joseph A.
Courtney, Patrick E.
DiGeronimo, Richard
Hagan, Paul
Lutkenhoff, Bernard

Retired:
Reverend Monsignors—
Foley, Maurice D., Our Lady of the Lakes Parish, 543 S. Main St., Monticello, IN 47960. Tel: 219-583-5023
Klein, Sylvester, R.R. 3, Box 291-A, Tipton, IN 46072. Tel: 317-675-6921
Potthoff, Frederick E., 87 Wea Oakes, Lafayette, IN 47905
Sego, Arthur A., 6476 Eime Rd., Dittmer, MO 63023
Reverend Fathers—
Eckert, Carl, St. Paul Parish, 1031 Kem Rd., Marion, IN 46952
Fosselman, Robert J., R.R. No. 1, P.O. Box 245, Monticello, IN 47690
Funcheon, Gerald A., 6476 Eime Rd., Dittmer, MO 63023
Heilman, Thomas O'Connor, 4511 Columbus Ave., Apt M 89, Anderson, IN 40614. Tel: 317-649-0777
Remaklus, Charles W., 708 Mohee Dr., Hartford City, IN 47348. Tel: 317-348-1998
Scheck, Frances M., 3920 County Rd. E., 200 North, Lafayette, IN 47905. Tel: 317-742-7488
Schiavone, Jeldo, Yuma Lakes, 6233 Ave. 8 1/2E., Yuma, AZ 85364. Tel: 602-726-5800
Weller, Harold E., R.R. 4, Rochester, IN 46975. Tel: 219-223-2305

Permanent Deacons:
Castillo, Domingo, Our Lady of Guadalupe, Marion
Cloud, H. William, St. Alphonsus, Zionsville
Nevinger, Ronald, St. Mary Cathedral, Lafayette
Rahill, William, Our Lady of Mount Carmel, Carmel
Roscoe, John, Holy Spirit, Fishers

INSTITUTIONS LOCATED IN THE DIOCESE

[A] COLLEGES AND UNIVERSITIES

RENSSELAER. *Saint Joseph's College,* 47978. Tel: 219-866-6000.

For a complete listing, refer to the Colleges and Universities section.

[B] HIGH SCHOOLS, INTER-PAROCHIAL

LAFAYETTE. *Central Catholic Junior-Senior High School,* 2410 S. Ninth St., 47905. Tel: 317-474-2496. David L. Worland, Prin.; G. J. Martin, Controller; Miss Helen Klemme, Dir. Religious Studies. Lay Teachers 29; Students 368.

[C] GENERAL HOSPITALS

LAFAYETTE. *St. Elizabeth Hospital Medical Center,* 1501 Hartford St., P.O. Box 7501, 47903. Tel: 317-423-6011.

For a complete listing, refer to the Hospitals section.

ANDERSON. *Saint John's Health System,* 2015 Jackson St., 46016. Tel: 317-649-2511.

For a complete listing, refer to the Hospitals section.

ELWOOD. *St. Vincent Mercy Hospital, Inc.,* 1331 South A St., 46036-1942. Tel: 317-552-3336; Fax: 317-552-6945.

For a complete listing, refer to the Hospitals section.

KOKOMO. *Saint Joseph Hospital & Health Center of Kokomo, Indiana, Inc.,* 1907 W. Sycamore St., 46901. Tel: 317-452-5611.

For a complete listing, refer to the Hospitals section.

[D] NURSING HOMES

LAFAYETTE. *St. Anthony Health Care,* 1205 N. 14th St., 47904. Tel: 317-423-4861; Fax: 317-742-8790.

For a complete listing, refer to the Special Care Facilities section.

DELPHI. *St. Elizabeth Healthcare Center,* 701 Armory Rd., 46923 Fax: 317-564-6384.

For a complete listing, refer to the Special Care Facilities section.

[E] MONASTERIES AND RESIDENCES OF PRIESTS AND BROTHERS

LAFAYETTE. *Emmaus House,* 2500 S. Ninth St., 47905. Tel: 317-477-6441.

[F] CONVENTS AND RESIDENCES FOR SISTERS

LAFAYETTE. *Monastery of the Precious Blood,* 1106 State St., E., 47905-1219. Tel: 317-742-8227. Sr. Jacqueline Hayden, A.P.B., Supr.; Rev. John A. Bach, Chap., Res., 155 Durkee's Run Dr., 47905. Sisters Adorers of the Precious Blood. Professed 9; Postulants 1.

ANDERSON. *Sisters of the Holy Cross,* 1007 Raible Ave., 46011. Tel: 317-642-6117. Sisters 6.

Additional addresses for Sisters of the Holy Cross: 2115 Meridian St., 46016. Tel: 317-642-2427. Sisters 3. St. Joseph College, Box 804, Rensselaer, 47978.

Sisters of the Holy Cross, Inc.

KOKOMO. *Maria Regina Mater Monastery,* 1175 N. County Rd. 300 W., 46901. Tel: 317-457-5743. Monastery of Poor Clares of the Reform of St. Colette. Mother Miriam, Abbess; Rev. Method Wilson, O.F.M., Chap. Solemnly Professed Nuns in Cloister 8; Perpetually Professed Extern Sister 1.

TIPTON. *St. Joseph Center: Sisters of St. Joseph,* 1440 W. Division Rd., 46072-8584. Tel: 317-675-4146; Fax: 317-675-7471. Sr. Dorothy Gall, C.S.J., Pres., Tel: 317-675-6203. Friar Edmund Mundwiller, Chap. Sisters Resident at Motherhouse 29; Total in Residence 25; Total Staff 1.

[G] RETREAT HOUSES

HARTFORD CITY. *John XXIII Center,* 407 W. McDonald St., 47348. Tel: 317-348-4008. Rev. Keith P. Hosey, Dir.; Sr. Maureen Mangen, C.PP.S., Asst. Dir.

[H] NEWMAN CENTERS

CRAWFORDSVILLE. *Newman Center at Wabash College,* 310 S. Grant Ave., 47933. Tel: 317-362-8105. Rev. Leroy G. Kinnaman.

MUNCIE. *St. Francis of Assisi University Church,* Newman Center, 1200 W. Riverside Ave., 47303. Tel: 317-288-6180. Rev. John D. Kiefer.

WEST LAFAYETTE. *St. Thomas Aquinas Parish and Foundation for Catholic Students attending Purdue Univ.,* 535 State St., 47906. Revs. Patrick R. Click, Pastor & Dir., Newman Apostolate; Tony Levi, Assoc. Pastor; Mrs. Phyllis Scanlon, Pastoral Assoc./Admin. Dir.; Mr. Christopher O'neal, Pastoral Assoc. In res., Revs. Frank DeRego (HON); David Buckles.

[I] MISCELLANEOUS

LAFAYETTE. *Catholic Foundation of Northcentral Indiana, Inc.,* P.O. Box 260, 47902-0260. Tel: 317-742-0275; Fax: 317-742-7513.

MISHAWAKA. *Alverno-Lafayette Corporation,* 1515 Dragoon Trail, P.O. Box 1290, 46546-1290.

MT. CARMEL. *Our Lady of Mount Carmel Parochial School Trust,* 1045 W. 146 St., 46032. Tel: 317-846-3475. Rev. Msgr. John C. Duncan, Contact Person.

RELIGIOUS INSTITUTES OF MEN REPRESENTED IN THE DIOCESE

For further details refer to the corresponding bracketed number in the Religious Institutes of Men or Women section.

[0520]—*Order of St. Francis Minors.*—O.F.M.

[1060]—*Society of the Precious Blood.*—C.PP.S.

RELIGIOUS INSTITUTES OF WOMEN REPRESENTED IN THE DIOCESE

[1920]—*Congregation of the Sisters of the Holy Cross.*—C.S.C.

[1070-09]—*Dominican Sisters.*—O.P.

[1780]—*Franciscan Sisters of Peace.*—F.S.P.A.

[4150]—*Irish Ursuline Union.*—O.S.U.

[0240]—*Olivetan Benedictine Sisters.*—O.S.B.

[3230]—*Poor Handmaids of Jesus Christ.*—P.H.J.C.

[2970]—*School Sisters of Notre Dame.*—S.S.N.D.

[0110]—*Sisters Adorers of the Precious Blood.*—A.P.B.

[0430]—*Sisters of Charity of the Blessed Virgin Mary.*—B.V.M.

[2990]—*Sisters of Notre Dame.* (Toledo Prov.).—S.N.D.

[3000]—*Sisters of Notre Dame de Namur.*—S.N.D.deN.

[3360]—*Sisters of Providence of Saint Mary-of-the-Woods, IN.*—S.P.

[]—*Sisters of St. Francis.* (Sylvania, OH).—O.S.F.

[1640]—*Sisters of St. Francis of Perpetual Adoration.*—O.S.F.

[3830-10]—*Sisters of St. Joseph.*—C.S.J.

[3260]—*Sisters of the Precious Blood.* (Dayton, Ohio).—C.PP.S.

NECROLOGY

† Cooley, Richard A., (On Duty Outside the Diocese). —Died June 6, 1996.

† Lanning, George B., (Retired). —Died Oct. 1, 1996.

Diocese of Lafayette

(Dioecesis Lafayettensis)

Most Reverend

EDWARD JOSEPH O'DONNELL, D.D.

Bishop of Lafayette; ordained April 6, 1957; appointed Titular Bishop of Britonia and Auxiliary Bishop of St. Louis December 6, 1983; consecrated February 10, 1984; appointed fifth Bishop of Lafayette November 8, 1994; installed December 16, 1994. *Mailing Address: P.O. Box 3387, Lafayette, LA, 70502.*

Most Reverend

GERARD LOUIS FREY, D.D.

Retired Bishop of Lafayette; ordained April 2, 1938; appointed Bishop of Savannah May 31, 1967; consecrated August 8, 1967; transferred to Lafayette November 7, 1972; installed January 7, 1973; retired May 13, 1989. *Office: 1408 Carmel Ave., Lafayette, LA, 70501.* Tel.: 318-261-5613.

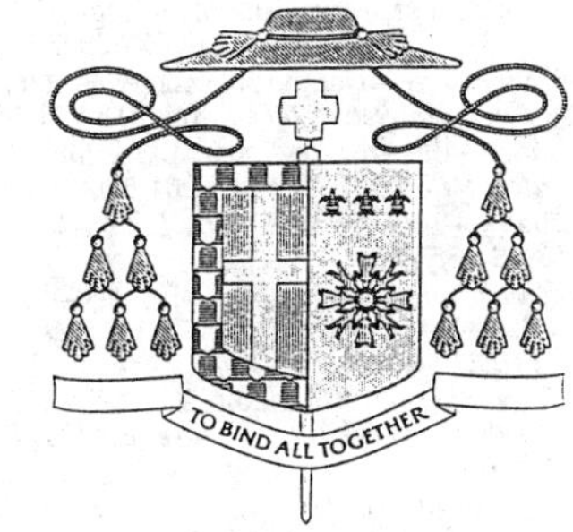

ESTABLISHED JANUARY 11, 1918.

Square Miles 5,777.

Comprises the civil parishes (Counties) of Acadia, Evangeline, Iberia, Lafayette, St. Landry, St. Martin and St. Mary (west of Atchafalaya River) and Vermilion in the south central part of the State of Louisiana.

For legal titles of Diocese, parishes and diocesan institutions, consult the Chancery Office.

Administrative Offices: Diocesan Office Building, 1408 Carmel Ave., Lafayette, LA, 70501. Tel.: 318-261-5500; Fax: 318-261-5635.

STATISTICAL OVERVIEW

Personnel	
Bishop	1
Retired Bishops	1
Priests: Diocesan Active in Diocese	111
Priests: Active Outside Diocese	8
Priests: Diocesan in Foreign Missions	1
Priests: Retired, Sick or Absent	26
Number of Diocesan Priests	146
Religious Priests in Diocese	52
Extern Priests in Diocese	4
Ordinations:	
Diocesan Priests	4
Permanent Deacons in Diocese	52
Total Brothers	30
Total Sisters	175
Parishes	
Parishes	121
With Resident Pastor:	
Resident Diocesan Priests	89
Resident Religious Priests	26
Without Resident Pastor:	
Administered by Permanent Deacons	1
Administered by Women Religious	4
Completely Vacant	1
Missions	35
Welfare	
Catholic Hospitals	1
Total Assisted	81,000
Health Care Centers	1
Total Assisted	16,000
Homes for the Aged	5
Total Assisted	1,200
Specialized Homes	1
Total Assisted	1,000
Special Centers for Social Services	6
Total Assisted	180,000
Educational	
Diocesan Students in Other Seminaries	34
Seminaries, Religious	1
Students Religious	10
Total Seminarians	44
High Schools, Diocesan and Parish	9
Total Students	3,383
High Schools, Private	1
Total Students	130
Elementary Schools, Diocesan and Parish	29
Total Students	10,133
Elementary Schools, Private	2
Total Students	670
Catechesis/Religious Education:	
High School Students	11,131
Elementary Students	26,627
Total Students Under Catholic Instruction	52,118
Teachers in the Diocese:	
Brothers	3
Sisters	23
Lay Teachers	820
Vital Statistics	
Receptions into the Church:	
Infant Baptism Totals	6,084
Adult Baptism Totals	180
Received into Full Communion	205
First Communions	5,306
Confirmations	3,984
Marriages:	
Catholic	1,725
Interfaith	242
Total Marriages	1,967
Deaths	3,416
Total Catholic Population	355,435
Total Population	540,001

Former Bishops—Most Rev. JULES B. JEANMARD D.D., LL.D., ord. June 11, 1903; appt. first Bishop of Lafayette, July 18, 1918; cons. Dec. 8, 1918; installed as first Bishop of Lafayette, Dec. 12, 1918; appt. Assistant at the Pontifical Throne, Dec. 8, 1943; resigned and named Titular Bishop of Bareta, March 13, 1956; died Feb. 23, 1957.—Most Rev. ROBERT E. TRACY, D.D., Auxiliary Bishop of Lafayette, March 18, 1959; appt. first Bishop of Baton Rouge, Aug. 10, 1961.—Most Rev. WARREN L. BOUDREAUX, D.D., J.C.D., Auxiliary Bishop of Lafayette, May 19, 1962; appt. second Bishop of Beaumont, Texas, June 4, 1971.—Most Rev. MAURICE SCHEXNAYDER, D.D., ord. April 11, 1925; appt. Titular Bishop of Tuscamia and Auxiliary of Lafayette, Dec. 11, 1950; cons. Feb. 22, 1951; appt. second Bishop of Lafayette, March 13, 1956; installed May 24, 1956; resigned Nov. 7, 1972; died Jan. 23, 1981.—Most Rev. GERARD L. FREY, D.D., appt. third Bishop of Lafayette, Nov. 7, 1972; installed Jan. 7, 1973; resigned May 13, 1989.—Most Rev. HARRY J. FLYNN, D.D., ord. May 28, 1960; appt. Coadjutor Bishop of Lafayette, April 19, 1986, fourth Bishop of Lafayette, May 13, 1989; appt. Coadjutor Archbishop of St. Paul, Minneapolis, Feb. 22, 1994.

Bishop's Office—Diocesan Office Building, P.O. Box 3387, Lafayette, 70502. Tel: 318-261-5614; Fax: 318-261-5603.

Administrative Offices—Diocesan Office Building, 1408 Carmel Ave., Lafayette, 70501. Tel: 318-261-5500; Fax: 318-261-5635.

Vicars General—Rev, Msgr. H. ALEXANDRE LARROQUE, J.C.D., *P.O. Box 3387, Lafayette, 70502.* Tel: 318-261-5613. Very Rev. RONALD BROUSSARD, *P.O. Box 3387, Lafayette, 70502.* Tel: 318-261-5536.

Chancellor and Director of Administration—Sr. JOANNA VALONI, S.S.N.D., *P.O. Box 3387, Lafayette, 70502.* Tel: 318-261-5611.

Deans—East Lafayette Deanery: Rev. FRANCIS BORGIA AUBESPIN, S.V.D.; West Lafayette Deanery: Rev. Msgr. GLEN J. PROVOST; Evangeline Deanery: Very Rev. J. ROBERT ROMERO; St. Landry Deanery: Rev. MALCOLM O'LEARY, S.V.D.; Iberia Deanery: Rev. THOMAS JAMES, S.V.D.; St. Mary Deanery: Rev. MICHAEL GUIDRY; Acadia Deanery: Very Rev. DONALD N. LEGER; Vermilion Deanery: Rev. DONALD THERIOT.

Vicar for Religious—Sr. MILDRED LEONARDS, C.D.P., *1408 Carmel Ave., Lafayette, 70501.* Tel: 318-261-5634.

Vicar for Priests—Rev. RUSSELL HARRINGTON, *P.O. Drawer V, Lafayette, 70501.* Tel: 318-268-9677; Fax: 318-261-5545.

Tribunal—1408 Carmel Ave., Lafayette, 70501. Tel: 318-261-5623.

Officialis—Very Rev. KENNETH R. MORVANT, J.C.L.

Vice-Officiales—Revs. ROBIE ROBICHAUX, J.C.L.; ARTHUR M. WARREN.

Procurators-Advocates—Mrs. KAROL MEYNARD; Deacon EUGENE WAQUESPACK; Revs. A. REX BROUSSARD; BILL JOHN MELANCON; ROBERT COURVILLE.

Promoter of Justice—Rev. Msgr. H. A. LARROQUE, J.C.D., V.G.

Assessors—Mrs. KAROL MEYNARD; Deacon EUGENE WAGUESPACK.

Pro-Synodal Judges—Rev. Msgr. GLEN JOHN PROVOST; Revs. GRADY ESTILETTE; THOMAS FINLEY; JUDE A. HALPHEN; ARTHUR WARREN; HERBERT MAY.

Defenders of the Bond—Revs. OVERTON JOSEPH BREAUX; J. DOUGLAS COURVILLE, J.C.L.

Coordinator of Cases—BERNARD BEYT, J.D.
Auditors—Mrs. KAROL MEYNARD; Deacon EUGENE WAGUESPACK.
Notaries—EULA B. LANDRY; BERNARD BEYT, J.D.
College of Consultors—Rev. Msgr. ALEXANDER O. SIGUR; Rev. Msgr. H. ALEXANDRE LARROQUE; Rev. Msgr. GLEN PROVOST; Revs. JOSEPH ALEXANDER; MILLARD BOYER; OVERTON JOSEPH BREAUX; JOSEPH BRENNAN; FRED SWENSON.
Diocesan Consultors—Rev. Msgr. H. A. LARROQUE; Rev. Msgr. ALEXANDER O. SIGUR; Revs. JAMES W. DOIRON; L. MICHAEL HERPIN.

Diocesan Offices and Directors

Adult Catechesis—GLORIA CLARK, *1408 Carmel Ave., Lafayette, 70501.* Tel: 318-261-5550.
Alcohol & Drug Abuse—PHYLLIS LUKE, *1408 Carmel Ave., Lafayette, 70501.* Tel: 318-261-5674.
Archives—ANNA JANE MARKS, *1408 Carmel Ave., Lafayette, 70501.* Tel: 318-261-5639; 261-5667.
Auxiliary Services—ELSIE HEBERT, *1408 Carmel Ave., Lafayette, 70501.* Tel: 318-261-5600.
Bishop's Services Appeal—CONNIE KLEINPETER, *1408 Carmel Ave., Lafayette, 70501.* Tel: 318-261-5641.
Black Catholics—Rev. RONALD BROUSSARD, V.G., *1408 Carmel Ave., Lafayette, 70501.* Tel: 318-261-5536.
Catholic Social Services—PAULA MILNER, *1408 Carmel Ave., Lafayette, 70501.* Tel: 318-261-5654.
Catholic Foundation of the Diocese of Lafayette—CONNIE KLEINPETER, *1408 Carmel Ave., Lafayette, 70501.* Tel: 318-261-5641.
Catholic Charismatic—Rev. ALBERT G. NUNEZ, *P.O. Box 40, Carencro, 70520.* Tel: 318-896-7732.
Christian Formation—Sr. LORRAINE LANDRY, S.S.N.D., *1408 Carmel Ave., Lafayette, 70501.* Tel: 318-261-5565.
Clergy Health Care & Retirement—BEVERLY BROUSSARD, *1408 Carmel Ave., Lafayette, 70501.* Tel: 318-261-5629.
Communications—Newspaper—*"Acadiana Catholic,"* BARBARA GUTIERREZ, Editor, *1408 Carmel Ave., Lafayette, 70501.* Tel: 318-261-5513; 261-5511; 261-5518.
Radio-TV—DAVID MERGIST, Producer/Dir., *1408 Carmel Ave., Lafayette, 70501.* Tel: 318-261-5626.
Community Services—J. BERNEL FONTENOT, *1408 Carmel Ave., Lafayette, 70501.* Tel: 318-261-5650.
Data Processing—DARREL DRONET, *1408 Carmel Ave., Lafayette, 70501.* Tel: 318-261-5516.
Deaf Apostolate—MYRA MOUTON, *1408 Carmel Ave., Lafayette, 70501.* Tel: 318-261-5548.
Development—CONNIE KLEINPETER, *1408 Carmel Ave., Lafayette, 70501.* Tel: 318-261-5641.
Education/Communication—GERALD DILL, *1408 Carmel Ave., Lafayette, 70501.* Tel: 318-261-5526.
Family Life—BARBARA WALLEY, M.S.W., Mailing Address: *1408 Carmel Ave., Lafayette, 70501.* Tel: 318-261-5653.
Fiscal Administration—MARY PARKER, *P.O. Box 3387, Lafayette, 70502.* Tel: 318-261-5629.
Hispanic Ministry—Sr. VIVIAN COULON, M.S.C., *1408 Carmel Ave., Lafayette, 70501.* Tel: 318-261-5535; 261-5542.
Institutions—J. BERNEL FONTENOT, *1408 Carmel Ave., Lafayette, 70501.* Tel: 318-261-5650.
Justice and Peace—UNA HARGRAVE, *1408 Carmel Ave., Lafayette, 70501.* Tel: 318-261-5545.
Migration Refugee Services—TINA DAVIS, *1408 Carmel Ave., Lafayette, 70501.* Tel: 318-261-5535.
Office for Persons with Disabilities—MYRA MOUTON, *1404 Carmel Ave., Lafayette, 70501.* Tel: 318-261-5548.
Parish Services—Sr. LORRAINE LANDRY, S.S.N.D., *1408 Carmel Ave., Lafayette, 70501.* Tel: 318-261-5565.
Parish Finances—JEANNINE REYNOLDS, Mgr., *P.O. Box 3387, Lafayette, 70502.* Tel: 318-261-5632.
Permanent Diaconate—Deacon RONALD A. BOREL, *1408 Carmel Ave., Lafayette, 70501.* Tel: 318-261-5609.
Pro-Life Issues—BRENDA DESORMEAUX, *1408 Carmel Ave., Lafayette, 70501.* Tel: 318-261-5607.
Prison Ministry—*1408 Carmel Ave., Lafayette, 70501.* Tel: 318-261-5545.
Religious Education and Pastoral Ministry—Sr. CARMELITA LATIOLAIS, *1408 Carmel Ave., Lafayette, 70501.* Tel: 318-261-5674.
Religious Personnel—Sr. MILDRED LEONARDS, C.D.P., Vicar, *1408 Carmel Ave., Lafayette, 70501.* Tel: 318-261-5634.
Research & Information—A. JAMES BROUSSARD, *1408 Carmel Ave., Lafayette, 70501.* Tel: 318-261-5608.
Schools—RICHARD MEAUX, Supt., *1408 Carmel Ave., Lafayette, 70501.* Tel: 318-261-5529.
Seminarians & Vocations—Rev. W. CURTIS MALLET, *1408 Carmel Ave., Lafayette, 70501.* Tel: 318-261-5690.
Youth Ministry—KATHY STELLY, *1408 Carmel Ave., Lafayette, 70501.* Tel: 318-261-5551.
Worship—Rev. JASON MOUTON, *1408 Carmel Ave., Lafayette, 70501.* Tel: 318-261-5536.

Diocesan Commissions and Boards

Building Review Board—Sr. JOANNA VALONI, S.S.N.D., *1408 Carmel Ave., Lafayette, 70501.* Tel: 318-261-5611.
Campus Ministry—Rev. HAMPTON DAVIS, Dir., *Our Lady of Wisdom Catholic Student Center, P.O. Box 43271, Lafayette, 70504.* Tel: 318-232-8742.
Catholic Daughters of America—Rev. DONALD PELOUS, *St. Bernard Church, 204 N. Main St., Breaux Bridge, 70517.* Tel: 318-332-2159.
Catholic Relief Services—UNA HARGRAVE, *1408 Carmel Ave., Lafayette, 70501.* Tel: 318-261-5545.
Clergy Personnel Advisory Board—Rev. MARTIN BORCHERDING, *St. Ann Church, P.O. Box 410, Youngsville, 70592.* Tel: 318-856-5331.
Clergy Welfare Commission—Rev. Msgr. RICHARD MOUTON, Chm., *P.O. Box 80489, Lafayette, 70598.* Tel: 318-232-4656.
Continuing Formation of the Clergy—Rev. RUSSELL HARRINGTON, *P.O. Drawer V, Lafayette, 70501.* Tel: 318-268-9677.
Credit Union—*116 St. Jules St., Lafayette, 70506.* Tel: 318-261-1151.
Cursillo—Rev. OVERTON JOSEPH BREAUX, *P.O. Box 8, Duson, 70529-0008.* Tel: 318-873-4962.
Diocesan Council of Catholic Women—Rev. Msgr. J. GUY LEMOINE, Diocesan Moderator, *St. Peter Church, P.O. Box 12507, New Iberia, 70562.* Tel: 318-369-3816.
Ecumenism—Rev. HERBERT DELAUNAY, *P.O. Box 40, Carencro, 70520.* Tel: 318-896-9408.
Finance Advisory Board—LEON K. POCHE, K.S.G., *633 W. 17th St., Crowley, 70526.* Tel: 318-783-0650.
Holy Childhood—Sr. MILDRED LEONARDS, C.D.P., *1408 Carmel Ave., Lafayette, 70501.* Tel: 318-261-5634.
Holy Name Society—Rev. Msgr. ALEXANDER O. SIGUR, J.C.D., *P.O. Box 406, Crowley, 70527.* Tel: 318-783-7394.
Hospitals—Rev. M. KEITH LABOVE, Coord., Health Affairs, *P.O. Box 52531, Lafayette, 70505.* Tel: 318-261-7483.
Knights of Columbus—Rev. GEORGE SIMON, Diocesan Chap., *St. Martin de Porres, P.O. Box 728, Scott, 70583.* Tel: 318-232-1968.
Legion of Mary—Vacant.
Parish Boundaries and Future Parish Development Board—Sr. JOANNA VALONI, S.S.N.D., *1408 Carmel Ave., Lafayette, 70501.* Tel: 318-261-5611.
Retreats—Rev. JAMES C. BABB, S.J., *Our Lady of the Oaks Retreat House, P.O. Box D, Grand Coteau, 70541.* Tel: 318-662-5410. Rev. THOMAS MADDEN, S.J., Dir., *Jesuit Spirituality Center, P.O. Box C, Grand Coteau, 70541.* Tel: 318-662-5251.
Scouting—Rev. KENNETH DOMINGUE, Chap., *St. Augustine Church, P.O. Box 696, Basile, 70515.* Tel: 318-432-6817. ROBERT MARCEAUX, Lay Chm., *101 Bellridge Dr., Lafayette, 70506.* Tel: 318-984-1767.
Society for the Propagation of the Faith—Sr. MILDRED LEONARDS, C.D.P., *P.O. Box 3387, Lafayette, 70502.* Tel: 318-261-5634.

CLERGY, PARISHES, MISSIONS AND PAROCHIAL SCHOOLS

CITY OF LAFAYETTE
(Lafayette Parish)

1—ST. JOHN THE EVANGELIST CATHEDRAL, Rev. Msgr. Glen John Provost, Rector; Rev. Russel J. Harrington; Deacon James Oliver. In res., Rev. Kurian Kanat (India).
Res., 515 Cathedral St., P.O. Drawer V, 70502. Tel: 318-232-1322; Fax: 318-232-1379.
School—Cathedral-Carmel Elementary, 848 St. John St., 70502. Tel: 318-235-5577; Fax: 318-261-9493. Mr. Linden Bercegeay, Prin.
Sisters of Mt. Carmel 5; Brothers of the Christian Schools 4; Lay Teachers 48; Students 815.

2—ST. PAUL THE APOSTLE, Rev. Dennet Jung, O.F.M.
Res., 326 S. Washington St., 70501. Tel: 318-235-0272; Fax: 318-235-3100.
Mission—Lafayette, Our Lady of Good Hope.

3—HOLY CROSS, Rev. Martin Borcherding; Deacons Michael Clark; Norbert Luke.
Res., 505 Broadmoor Blvd., 70503. Tel: 318-984-9636; Fax: 318-988-3790.

4—IMMACULATE HEART OF MARY, Revs. Francis Borgin Aubespin, S.V.D.; Antoine G. Leason, S.V.D.; Deacon Anthony Ozene. In res., Rev. Charles Heskamp, S.V.D.
Res., 818-12th St., P.O. Box 2398, 70502. Tel: 318-235-4618; Fax: 318-235-4775. [CEM]
School—800-12th St., 70502. Tel: 318-235-7843; 235-4775. Sr. Mary Joseph Charles, S.S.F., Prin.
Sisters of Holy Family 4; Lay Teachers 8; Students 191.

5—OUR LADY OF FATIMA, Rev. Richard R. Greene.
Res., 2319 Johnston St., 70503. Tel: 318-232-8945; Fax: 318-232-0323.
School—2315 Johnston St., 70503. Tel: 318-235-2464; Fax: 318-235-1320. Mr. Lloyd Guiberteau, Prin.
Lay Teachers 47; Students 899.

6—OUR LADY OF WISDOM, UNIVERSITY OF SOUTHWESTERN LOUISIANA, Rev. Frank Hampton Davis; Deacon Coley Bellamy. In res., Revs. M. Keith Labove; Thomas Finley.
Mailing Address: P.O. Box 42371, 70504. Tel: 318-232-8741; Fax: 318-236-6737.

7—OUR LADY QUEEN OF PEACE, Rev. Thomas Jason Mouton; Deacon Louis J. Lloyd.
Res., 145 Martin Luther King Jr. Dr., 70501. Tel: 318-233-1591; Fax: 318-232-5961.

8—ST. ANTHONY, Rev. Frank A. Charles, S.V.D.; Deacon Alvin Ray Dejean.
Res., 615 Edison St., 70501. Tel: 318-234-5855; Fax: 318-264-1507.

9—ST. EDMOND, Rev. Gary Schexnayder; Deacon Paul D. Matte.
Res., 4131 W. Congress St., 70506. Tel: 318-981-0874; Fax: 318-989-1417.

10—ST. ELIZABETH SETON, Rev. Harold Trahan.
Office: 610 Raintree Tr., 70507. Tel: 318-235-1483; Fax: 318-235-9645.
Res., 603 Raintree Tr., 70507. Tel: 318-232-7365.

11—ST. GENEVIEVE, Revs. Jody Simoneaux; W. Curtis Mallet.
Res., 417 E. Simcoe St., P.O. Box 90307, 70509. Tel: 318-234-5147; Fax: 318-234-8654. [CEM]
School—201 Elizabeth St., 70501. Tel: 318-234-5257; Fax: 318-237-6065. Mrs. Susan Stephen, Prin.
Lay Teachers 22; Students 346.
Mission—Lafayette, Gift of Mary Chapel.

12—ST. JULES, Rev. Wayne J. Duet; Deacon Eugene P. Waguespack.
Res., 116 St. Jules St., 70506. Tel: 318-234-2727; Fax: 318-261-1397.

13—ST. LEO, Rev. Michael J. Arnaud. In res., Rev. Edwin Bourg.
Res., 300 W. Alexander St., 70501. Tel: 318-232-2404; Fax: 318-261-0801.
School—Sts. Leo-Seton, 502 St. Leo St., 70501. Tel: 318-234-5510. Mr. Lester Bourg, Prin.
Sisters 2; Lay Teachers 18; Students 483.

14—ST. MARY, MOTHER OF THE CHURCH, Rev. Msgr. Robert G. Angelle; Rev. Howard Blessing; Deacon Julian Judice.
Res., 419 Doucet Rd., 70503. Tel: 318-981-3379; Fax: 318-981-5445.
School—St. Mary Early Learning Center, (Grades Pre-K). Tel: 318-984-3750. Mrs. Renee McAlister, Prin.
Students 120.

15—ST. PATRICK, Rev. Robie E. Robichaux, J.C.L.
Res., 107 Petro St., 70501. Tel: 318-237-0988; Fax: 318-233-8868.

16—ST. PIUS X, Rev. Msgr. Richard von Phul Mouton.
Res., 200 E. Bayou Pkwy., P.O. Box 80489, 70598. Tel: 318-232-4656; Fax: 318-233-9468.
School—Our Lady of Life Preschool, 201 E. Bayou Pkwy., 70508. Tel: 318-237-3139. Mrs. Shirley Alexander, Dir.

OUTSIDE THE CITY OF LAFAYETTE

Abbeville, Vermilion Parish, St. Mary Magdalen, Revs. Donald C. Theriot; Kenneth Mayne.
Mailing Address: P.O. Box D, 70511. Tel: 318-893-0244; 0245; Fax: 318-893-0427.
High School—Vermilion Catholic, 425 Park Ave., 70511. Tel: 318-893-6636; Fax: 318-893-8718. Mr. William Simon, Prin.
Sisters 1; Lay Teachers 20; Students 245.
St. Therese of the Child Jesus, Rev. Chester Arceneaux; Deacon Samuel Theriot.
Mailing Address: P.O. Box 609, 70511. Tel: 318-893-5631; Fax: 318-893-9168.

Arnaudville, St. Landry Parish, St. Francis Regis, Rev. William Ruskoski.
Mailing Address: P.O. Box 36, 70512. Tel: 318-754-5912. [CEM]
St. Catherine, Rev. William Ruskoski; Sr. Paula Derise, O.Carm., Pastoral Assoc.
Mailing Address: P.O. Box 53, 70512. Tel: 318-754-7754.

Baldwin, St. Mary Parish, Sacred Heart, Rev. Bill John Melancon; Deacons Harold Achee; Gerald Bourg.
Mailing Address: P.O. Box 308, 70514. Tel: 318-923-7781; Fax: 318-923-7781.

Basile, Evangeline Parish, St. Augustine, Rev. Kenneth Domingue.
Res., 2717 Third St., P.O. Box 696, 70515. Tel: 318-432-6817; Fax: 318-432-5203.
Mission—Basile, Assumption.

Bayou Vista, St. Mary Parish, St. Bernadette, Rev. Richard Fabre.
Res., 1112 Saturn Rd., Morgan City, 70380. Tel: 504-395-2470; Fax: 504-395-6514.

Berwick, St. Mary Parish, St. Stephen, Rev. Paul G. Bienvenu.
Res., 3217 Second St., 70342. Tel: 504-385-1280; Fax: 504-385-1279.

Breaux Bridge, St. Martin Parish, St. Bernard, Rev. Donald P. Pelous; Deacons Harold Richard; Marcel P. Hebert, Jr.
Res., 204 N. Main St., 70517. Tel: 318-332-2159; Fax: 318-332-2276. [JC 2]
School—251 E. Bridge St., 70517. Tel: 318-332-5350; Fax: 318-332-5894. Keith Bartlett, Prin.
Sisters 1; Lay Teachers 23; Students 500.
St. Francis of Assisi, Rev. Richard F. Wagner, S.S.J.
Res., 610 N. Main St., 70517. Tel: 318-332-2250; Fax: 318-332-2052. [CEM]

Broussard, Lafayette Parish, Sacred Heart of Jesus, Rev. Msgr. L. Michael Herpin.
Mailing Address: P.O. Box 737, 70518. Tel: 318-837-1864; Fax: 318-837-1703.
School—St. Cecilia, P.O. Box 309, 70518. Tel: 318-837-6363; Fax: 318-837-3688. Mr. Russell Meyer, Prin.
Lay Teachers 23; Students 444.
St. Joseph, Rev. Brendan Murphy, S.V.D.
Mailing Address: P.O. Box 278, 70518. Tel: 318-837-6218; Fax: 318-837-6218.
Mission—Cade, St. Anthony.

Cankton, St. Landry Parish, St. John Berchmans, Rev. Jude A. Halphen.
Res., 552 Main St., 70584-9722. Tel: 318-668-4413; Fax: 318-668-4505.

Carencro, Lafayette Parish, St. Peter, Revs. Gregory Todd Downs; Herbert deLaunay.
Mailing Address: P.O. Box 40, 70520. Tel: 318-896-9408; Fax: 318-896-9414.
School—Carencro Catholic, 200 W. St. Peter St., 70520. Tel: 318-896-8973. Mrs. Julie Breaux, Prin.
Lay Teachers 28; Students 529.
Our Lady of the Assumption, Rev. Paul J. LaFleur; Deacon John Thibodeaux.
Res., 410 N. Michaud St., 70520. Tel: 318-896-8304. [CEM]

Catahoula, St. Martin Parish, St. Rita, Rev. Louis Allen Breaux.
Res., 1006 St. Rita Hwy., St. Martinville, 70582. Tel: 318-394-4679.

Cecilia, St. Martin Parish, St. Joseph, Rev. Lloyd F. Benoit.
Mailing Address: P.O. Box 279, 70521. Tel: 318-667-6344. [JC]
St. Rose of Lima, Rev. Norbert W. Stein, S.S.J.
Mailing Address: P.O. Box 126, 70521. Tel: 318-667-6555; Fax: 318-667-6686. [CEM]

Centerville, St. Mary Parish, St. Joseph, Rev. Oneil A. Landry.
Res., 70522. Tel: 318-836-5659. [CEM]

Charenton, St. Mary Parish, Immaculate Conception, Rev. William Crumley, C.S.C.
Mailing Address: P.O. Box 278, 70523. Tel: 318-923-4281.

Chataignier, Evangeline Parish, Our Lady of Mount Carmel, Deacons Thomas J. Richard, Admin.; Charles Ortego. In res., Rev. T. Alcide Sonnier.
Mailing Address: P.O. Box 100, 70524. Tel: 318-885-3223; Fax: 318-885-3223.

Church Point, Acadia Parish, Our Lady of the Sacred Heart, Rev. A. Rex Broussard; Deacon Ivy J. Miller.
Res., 118 N. Rogers St., P.O. Box 403, 70525. Tel: 318-684-5494; Fax: 318-684-5495. [CEM 3][JC]
School—Our Mother of Peace, 218 N. Rogers St., 70525. Tel: 318-684-5780. Mr. Don Soucy, Prin.
Sisters 1; Lay Teachers 14; Students 319.
Chapel—Lewisburg, St. John.
Our Mother of Mercy, Rev. Francis Butler, S.S.J.
Res., 693 N. Main St., P.O. Box 237, 70525. Tel: 318-684-2319; Fax: 318-684-3086. [JC]

Coteau, Iberia Parish, Our Lady of Prompt Succor, Rev. Paul A. Thibodeaux.
Res., 2409 Coteau Rd., New Iberia, 70560. Tel: 318-369-6993. [CEM]

Coteau Holmes, St. Martin Parish, St. Elizabeth, Rev. Thomas Edapady, C.M.I. (India).
Office: 1006 St. Elizabeth St., St. Martinville, 70582. Tel: 318-394-6684; 394-7530.

Cow Island, Vermilion Parish, St. Anne, Rev. Lloyd Bordelon; Deacon Benedict M. Morello.
Res., 17315 Lionel Rd., Abbeville, 70510. Tel: 318-643-7714; Fax: 318-643-1021. [CEM]
Missions—Forked Island, Immaculate Conception; Pecan Island, Sacred Heart.

Crowley, Acadia Parish, St. Michael Archangel, Rev. Louis J. Richard.
Mailing Address: P.O. Box 406, 70527. Tel: 318-783-7394; Fax: 318-788-0237.
School—805 E. Northern Ave., 70527. Tel: 318-783-1410; Fax: 318-783-8547. Co-Principals: Mrs. Clementine Kirsh; Mrs. Myra Broussard.
Lay Teachers 27; Students 483.
Immaculate Heart of Mary, Revs. Joseph X. Steffes, C.SS.R.; Joseph Greenwell, C.SS.R. In res., Rev. Stephen Plei, C.SS.R.
Res., 901 E. Elm St., 70526. Tel: 318-783-3498; Fax: 318-783-7444.
School—Redemptorist Grade School, 606 South Ave. N., 70526. Tel: 318-783-4466. Mr. Dan Bouillion, Prin.
Lay Teachers 12; Students 301.
St. Theresa, Rev. Raymond P. Carignan, S.S.J.
Res., 417 W. 3rd St., 70526. Tel: 318-783-1880.

Delcambre, Vermilion Parish, Our Lady of the Lake, Rev. Thomas P. Voorhies.
Res., 206 W. Church St., 70528. Tel: 318-685-4426; Fax: 318-685-4426. [CEM]
Saint Martin de Porres, Rev. Thomas P. Voorhies.
Res., 206 W. Church St., 70528. Tel: 318-685-4426; Fax: 318-685-4426.

Duralde, Evangeline Parish, Annunciation of the B.V.M., Sr. Diane Hooley, O.P., Admin.
Res., 4476 Duralde Hwy., Eunice, 70535. Tel: 318-457-4849; Fax: 318-457-4502.

Duson, Lafayette Parish, St. Theresa of the Child Jesus, Rev. O. Joseph Breaux.
Mailing Address: P.O. Box 8, 70529. Tel: 318-873-4962; Fax: 318-873-3023.
St. Benedict the Moor, Very Rev. Ronald Broussard, V.G.
Mailing Address: P.O. Box 127, 70529. Tel: 318-873-6772.

Erath, Vermilion Parish, Our Lady of Lourdes, Rev. J. Douglas Courville.
Res., 700 S. Broadway, 70533. Tel: 318-937-6888. [CEM]

Eunice, St. Landry Parish, St. Anthony of Padua, Revs. Joseph J. Alexander; William J. Gearheard.
Mailing Address: P.O. Box 31, 70535. Tel: 318-457-5285; Fax: 318-457-7904. [CEM][JC]
School—St. Edmund Elementary, 331 N. 3rd St., 70535. Tel: 318-457-5988. Sr. Stephanie Brignac, M.S.C., Prin.
High School—St. Edmund High, 351 W. Magnolia St., 70535. Tel: 318-457-2592. Mr. Harry Summerlin, Prin.
Lay Teachers 34; Students: Elementary 345; High 268.
St. Mathilda, Rev. William F. Tyson, S.S.J.
Mailing Address: P.O. Box 346, 70535. Tel: 318-457-3286. [JC]
St. Thomas More, Rev. Jules M. Arceneaux; Deacon David Guillory.
Mailing Address: P.O. Box 1022, 70535. Tel: 318-457-8107; Fax: 318-457-1735.

Evangeline, Acadia Parish, St. Joseph, Rev. Donald Nicholas Leger.
Mailing Address: P.O. Box 183, 70537. Tel: 318-824-4995; Fax: 318-824-4995. [CEM]
Mission—Petit Mamou, St. Jules.

Four Corners, St. Mary Parish, St. Peter the Apostle, Rev. Tommy Calais.
Res., 1325 Big Four Corners Rd., Franklin, 70538. Tel: 318-276-5256; Fax: 318-276-5256.
Missions—Glencoe, St. Joan of Arc; Cypremort Point, St. Francis, (Independent Mission).

Franklin, St. Mary Parish, Assumption B.V.M., Rev. Michael Russo; Deacon Douglas Hebert.
Mailing Address: 913 Main St., 70538. Tel: 318-828-3869; Fax: 318-828-3872.
School—St. John Elementary, 924 Main St., 70538. Tel: 318-828-2648; Fax: 318-828-2112. Joseph Donald Doucet, Prin.
Lay Teachers 19; Students 344.
High School—Hanson High School, 903 Anderson St., 70538. Tel: 318-828-3487; Fax: 318-828-7431. Mr. Donald Dunbar, Prin.
Lay Teachers 28; Students 370.
St. Jules, Rev. George Thychery (India); Deacons Edward Bodin; Joseph Thomas.
Res., 601 Magnolia St., 70538. Tel: 318-828-1714.
Mission—Verdunville, Immaculate Conception.

Grand Coteau, St. Landry Parish, St. Charles Borromeo, Revs. Warren Broussard, S.J.; John Welsh, S.J.; Deacon Samuel Henry.
Mailing Address: P.O. Drawer A, 70541. Tel: 318-662-5279; Fax: 318-662-5270.
School—St. Ignatius, P.O. Drawer J, 70541. Tel: 318-662-3325. Mr. Ervin Fontenot, Prin.
Brothers 1; Sisters 1; Lay Teachers 14; Students 243.
Mission—Bellevue, Christ the King.

Grand Prairie, St. Landry Parish, St. Peter, Rev. Randall P. Moreau.
Res., 1074 Hwy. 748, Washington, 70589. Tel: 318-826-3870; Fax: 318-826-5635.
Mission—Plaisance, St. Andrew.

Gueydan, Vermilion Parish, St. Peter, Rev. Grady J. Estilette.
Res., 603 Main St., P.O. Box 28, 70542. Tel: 318-536-9258.
School—513 6th St., 70542. Tel: 318-536-9460. Sr. Ann Louise Arno, M.S.C., Prin.
Sisters 4; Lay Teachers 8; Students 125.
Mission—Mulvey, St. David.

Henderson, St. Martin Parish, Our Lady of Mercy, Rev. Jefferson J. DeBlanc; Deacon Roy Melancon.
Res., Henderson Sta., P.O. Box 587, Breaux Bridge, 70517. Tel: 318-228-2352; Fax: 318-228-2352.
Mission—Butte La Rose, Sacred Heart.

Henry, Vermilion Parish, St. John, Rev. Joseph H. Stemmann.
Res., 18534 La. Hwy. 689, Erath, 70533. Tel: 318-937-5108; Fax: 318-937-0002. [CEM]
Mission—Esther, St. James.

Iota, Acadia Parish, St. Joseph, Revs. Denis Blais, C.P.M.; Albert Heidecke, C.P.M.
Mailing Address: P.O. Box 710, 70543. Tel: 318-779-2627.
School—St. Francis, P.O. Box 870, 70543. Tel: 318-779-2527. Mrs. Mary Ann Hadaway, Prin.
Lay Teachers 10; Students 180.
Mission—Egan, Acadia Parish, St. Michael, P.O. Box 298, Egan, 70531. Tel: 318-788-0529.

Jeanerette, Iberia Parish, St. John the Evangelist, Rev. Edward Degeyter; Deacon Theodule Landry.
Res., 1510 Church St., 70544. Tel: 318-276-4576; Fax: 318-276-5804.
School—St. Joseph, 10917 Old Jeanerette Rd., 70544. Tel: 318-276-3615; Fax: 318-276-3616. Mrs. Corinne Hebert, Prin.
Lay Teachers 15; Students 186.
Our Lady of the Rosary, Rev. Joseph E. Detig, S.V.D.
Res., 11200 Old Jeanerette Rd., 70544. Tel: 318-276-6900; Fax: 318-276-6900. [CEM][JC]

Judice, Lafayette Parish, St. Basil, Rev. Henry J. Broussard.
Res., 1803 Duhon Rd. (Judice), Duson, 70529. Tel: 318-984-2179; Fax: 318-988-3793.

Kaplan, Vermilion Parish, Our Lady of the Holy Rosary, Revs. William C. Blanda; Barry F. Crochet; Deacon Paul R. Eleazar.
Mailing Address: P.O. Box 429, 70548. Tel: 318-643-6472; Fax: 318-643-2516. [JC]
School—Maltrait Memorial, 612 N. Hebert St., 70548. Tel: 318-643-7765. Mrs. Renee C. Meaux, Prin.
Lay Teachers 10; Students 138.
Mission—Kaplan, Vermilion Parish, St. Frances Xavier Cabrini.

Krotz Springs, St. Landry Parish, St. Anthony, Rev. Robert W. Courville.
Mailing Address: P.O. Box 425, 70750. Tel: 318-566-3527; Fax: 318-566-2803. [CEM]

Lawtell, St. Landry Parish, St. Bridget, Rev. P. Austin Leger.
Mailing Address: P.O. Box 156, 70550. Tel: 318-543-7591; Fax: 318-543-7593. [CEM]
Mission—Prairie Ronde, Sacred Heart.
Holy Family, Rev. Andrew Peter John (India).
Mailing Address: P.O. Box 310, 70550. Tel: 318-543-2366; Fax: 318-543-8281.
Mission—Plaquemine Point, St. Agnes.

Lebeau, St. Landry Parish, Immaculate Conception, Rev. Bartholomew S. Endslow, S.S.J.
Mailing Address: P.O. Box 415, 71345. Tel: 318-623-4783. [CEM]
Mission—Rideau Settlement, Sacred Heart.

Leonville, St. Landry Parish, St. Leo the Great, Rev. Daniel Schexnayder.
Mailing Address: P.O. Box 8, 70551. Tel: 318-879-2365; Fax: 318-879-3050. [JC]
St. Catherine. Unassigned.
Mailing Address: P.O. Box 147, 70551. Tel: 318-879-2940.
Mission—Prairie Laurent, St. Jules.

Leroy, Vermilion Parish, Our Lady of Perpetual Help, Revs. Mario Romero; Thomas Montelaro.
Res., 12995 Louisiana Hwy. 699, Maurice, 70555. Tel: 318-893-0610; Fax: 318-893-0694. [CEM]

Loreauville, Iberia Parish, St. Joseph, Rev. Charles Thevis.
Mailing Address: P.O. Box 365, 70552. Tel: 318-229-4254; Fax: 318-229-4255. [CEM]
Our Lady of Victory, Rev. John Vianney Choorackunnel, C.M.I. (India).
Mailing Address: P.O. Box 387, 70552. Tel: 318-229-8284; Fax: 318-229-4255. [JC]

Louisa, St. Mary Parish, St. Helen, Rev. Thomas Thanh Nguyen.

Res., 108 St. Helen Church Ln., Franklin, 70538. Tel: 318-276-5256.

Lydia, Iberia Parish, St. Nicholas, Rev. Emmanuel Fernandez; Deacon L. J. Freyou.
Mailing Address: P.O. Box 369, 70569. Tel: 318-364-5228.

Lyons Point, Acadia Parish, St. John the Baptist, Rev. Albert G. Nunez; Deacon Rodless Leleux.
Res., 8021 Lyons Point Highway, Crowley, 70526. Tel: 318-783-2457; Fax: 318-783-9015. [CEM]

Mallet, St. Landry Parish, St. Ann, Rev. Andrew Peter John (India); Deacon Jonas Mason.
Mailing Address: P.O. Box 310, Lawtell, 70550. Tel: 318-543-2385; Fax: 318-543-8281.

Mamou, Evangeline Parish, St. Ann, Revs. Timothy Richard; John Kanjiramkuzhy (India).
Parish Center: 716 Sixth St., 70554. Tel: 318-468-3159; Fax: 318-468-3427.
Mission—Vidrine, Holy Spirit.

Maurice, Vermilion Parish, St. Alphonsus, Rev. Martin C. Leonards.
Res., 8700 Maurice Ave., P.O. Box 190, 70555. Tel: 318-893-4099; Fax: 318-893-2474. [CEM]
St. Joseph, Rev. William R. Oliver, S.V.D.
Mailing Address: P.O. Box 250, 70555. Tel: 318-893-5428; Fax: 318-893-5428.

Melville, St. Landry Parish, St. John the Evangelist, Rev. Jose L.F. Padinjarepeedika, C.M.I. (India).
Mailing Address: 318 First St., P.O. Box 256, 71353-0256. Tel: 318-623-4957.
Mission—Palmetto, St. Thomas.

Mermentau, Acadia Parish, St. John the Evangelist, Rev. Msgr. Paul Metrejean; Deacon Leon Lejeune.
Mailing Address: P.O. Box 176, 70556. Tel: 318-824-2278; Fax: 318-824-9624. [CEM]
Mission—Estherwood, St. Margaret.

Milton, Lafayette Parish, St. Joseph, Rev. Louis J. Richard; Deacon Cody Miller.
Mailing Address: P.O. Box 299, 70558. Tel: 318-856-5997; Fax: 318-856-5955.

Mire, Acadia Parish, Assumption of the Blessed Virgin Mary, Rev. Donald J. Hebert; Deacon J. Douglas Melancon.
Res., 6080 Mire Hwy., Church Point, 70525. Tel: 318-873-6574.

Morrow, St. Landry Parish, St. Peter, Rev. Martin C. Maraist.
Mailing Address: P.O. Box 319, 71356. Tel: 318-346-7010.
Mission—Whiteville, Resurrection.

Morse, Acadia Parish, Immaculate Conception, Rev. Donald Pousson.
Mailing Address: P.O. Box 297, 70559. Tel: 318-783-2968.
Mission—Midland, St. Aloysius.

Mowata, Acadia Parish, St. Lawrence, Rev. George Heffner, S.V.D.
Res., 29031 Crowley-Eunice Hwy., Eunice, 70535. Tel: 318-457-2739; Fax: 318-457-2739. [CEM]

New Iberia, Iberia Parish,

1—St. Peter, Rev. Msgr. J. Guy Lemoine; Rev. William Rogalla; Deacons Carl Conrad; Ronald H. Broussard; James Wilson; Kenneth Waguespack. In res., Rev. Msgr. John H. Disch.
Mailing Address: P.O. Box 12507, 70562. Tel: 318-369-3816; Fax: 318-369-3192.

2—Nativity of Our Lady, Rev. Albert J. Boumans.
Res., Richelieu Circle, 70560. Tel: 318-364-8360; Fax: 318-364-1509. [CEM]

3—Our Lady of Perpetual Help, Revs. Daniel Picard; Charles Langlois; Deacons Ulysse J. Boudreaux; Ronald Borel; Albert A. Woodburn; George Sikes.
Res., 1303 St. Jude Ave., 70560. Tel: 318-365-5481; Fax: 318-365-5483.

4—St. Edward, Revs. Thomas James, S.V.D.; Ryszard Kalinowski, S.V.D. In res., Rev. Gerald Lewis, S.V.D.
Res., 175 Frere St., 70560. Tel: 318-369-3101; Fax: 318-369-3118. [CEM][JC]
School—720 Providence St., 70560. Tel: 318-369-6764. Sr. Michelle Callahan, S.B.S., Prin.
Sisters of the Blessed Sacrament 5; Lay Teachers 14; Students 360.
Mission—Olivier, St. Jude.

5—Sacred Heart of Jesus, Rev. Steven C. LeBlanc.
Res., 2514 Old Jeanerette Rd., 70560. Tel: 318-364-4439; Fax: 318-948-1295.

Opelousas, St. Landry Parish,

1—St. Landry, Rev. Charles Nicholas Trahan; Deacons Carlo Cannatella; John W. Miller. In res., Rev. Viateur Desilets.
Res., 900 N. Union St., 70570. Tel: 318-942-6552. [CEM][JC]

2—Our Lady of Mercy, Rev. F. David Broussard. In res., Rev. James Vellankal.
Res., 150 Camille St., 70570. Tel: 318-942-4174; Fax: 318-942-1476.

3—Our Lady Queen of Angels, Rev. Angelo Cremaldi.
Res., 2136 S. Union St., P.O. Box 508, 70570. Tel: 318-942-5628; Fax: 318-942-9708.

4—Holy Ghost, Revs. Malcolm O'Leary, S.V.D.; Raymond Guidry, S.V.D.
Res., 788 N. Union St., 70570. Tel: 318-942-2732; Fax: 318-948-4108. [JC]

Parks, St. Martin Parish, St. Joseph, Rev. Gregory P. Cormier.
Mailing Address: P.O. Box 2671, 70582. Tel: 318-845-4168; Fax: 318-845-5079.
Mission—Parks, St. Louis, Tel: 318-845-4681.

Patterson, St. Mary Parish, St. Joseph, Rev. Michael S. Guidry.
Res., 1011-1st St., P.O. Box 219, 70392. Tel: 504-395-3616; Fax: 504-395-3616. [CEM]

Pine Prairie, Evangeline Parish, St. Peter, Rev. Leslie T.H. Prescott.
Mailing Address: P.O. Box 230, 70576. Tel: 318-599-2224. [CEM]
Mission—St. Landry, St. Theresa.

Plaisance, St. Landry Parish, St. Joseph, Rev. Michael Moody, S.V.D.
Res., 3283 Hwy. 167, Opelousas, 70570. Tel: 318-826-3395.
Mission—Frilot Cove, St. Ann.

Port Barre, St. Landry Parish, Sacred Heart of Jesus, Rev. Michael Herbert.
Mailing Address: P.O. Box 129, 70577. Tel: 318-585-2279; Fax: 318-585-2276. [CEM]
St. Mary, Sr. Maria Canez, O.P., Admin.
Mailing Address: P.O. Box 338, 70577. Tel: 318-585-2315; Fax: 318-585-2315.

Rayne, Acadia Parish, St. Joseph, Revs. Eugene R. Tremie; Mark Richard; Deacon Adam Sonnier.
Mailing Address: P.O. Box 199, 70578. Tel: 318-334-2193; Fax: 318-334-2199. [CEM][JC]
School—Rayne Catholic Elementary, 407 S. Polk St., 70578. Tel: 318-334-5657; 5658. Mrs. Sherry Cormier, Prin.
Lay Teachers 14; Students 304.
Shrine of Our Mother of Mercy, Rev. Joseph J. Campion, S.S.J.; Deacon Coley Bellamy.
Mailing Address: P.O. Box 468, 70578. Tel: 318-334-3516; Fax: 318-334-4416. [CEM]

Richard, Acadia Parish, St. Edward, Rev. J. Daniel Edwards.
Res., 1463 Charlene Hwy., Church Point, 70525. Tel: 318-684-5816. [CEM][JC]
Mission—Savoy, St. Thomas.

Robert's Cove, Acadia Parish, St. Leo IV, Rev. Francis L. Bourgeois.
Res., 7166 Roberts Cove Rd., Rayne, 70578-8912. Tel: 318-334-5056; 334-5950. [CEM]
Mission—Branch, St. Edmund.

Rynella, Iberia Parish, St. Marcellus, Rev. C. Conley Bertrand.
Res., 6100 Avery Island Rd., New Iberia, 70560. Tel: 318-364-0818; Fax: 318-364-0824.

St. Martinville, St. Martin Parish, St. Martin of Tours, Revs. Keith DeRouen; Kenneth Bienvenu. In res., Rev. Jean-Marie Jammes.
Res., 133 S. Main St., P.O. Drawer 10, 70582. Tel: 318-394-6021; Fax: 318-394-6020. [CEM]
Notre Dame de Perpetuel Secours, Rev. Thomas A. Mullally, S.V.D.; Deacon Carlton Lee.
Res., 240 Gary St., 70582. Tel: 318-394-3084; Fax: 318-394-5380. [CEM][JC]

Scott, Lafayette Parish, SS. Peter and Paul, Revs. Frederick O. Swenson; Matthew Higginbotham; Deacon Robert McDonner.
Mailing Address: P.O. Box 458, 70583. Tel: 318-235-2433; Fax: 318-233-4868. [CEM]
Saint Martin de Porres, Rev. George H. Simon.
Mailing Address: P.O. Box 728, 70583. Tel: 318-232-1968; Fax: 318-232-1968.

Ville Platte, Evangeline Parish, Sacred Heart of Jesus, Revs. J. Robert Romero; Matthew Roussel; Deacon Harris Soileau.
Res., 708 E. Main St., 70586. Tel: 318-363-2989; Fax: 318-363-3500.
School—Sacred Heart Elementary, 532 E. Main St., 70586. Tel: 318-363-3322; Fax: 318-363-2318. Paula Landreneau, Prin.
High School—Sacred Heart High, 114 S. Trojan Ln., 70586. Tel: 318-363-1475; Fax: 318-363-0348. Larry Vidrine, Prin.
Lay Teachers 48; Students: Elementary 584; High 233.
Mission—Belaire Cove, Sacred Heart.
Our Lady Queen of All Saints, Rev. Gilbert J. Dutel; Deacons Paul N. Mayeux; Eugene Le Boeuf.
Res., 211 Parkview St., P.O. Drawer E, 70586. Tel: 318-363-5167; Fax: 318-363-5179.
St. Joseph. Unassigned.
Res., 1107 Martin L. King Dr., 70586. Tel: 318-363-1051.

Washington, St. Landry Parish, Immaculate Conception, Rev. Ralph J. Landry.
Mailing Address: P.O. Box 116, 70589. Tel: 318-826-7396.
Holy Trinity, Sr. Juliana Savoy, O.P., Admin.
Mailing Address: P.O. Box 186, 70589. Tel: 318-826-3376; Fax: 318-826-3376.

Youngsville, Lafayette Parish, St. Anne, Rev. Louis Lam Vu.
Mailing Address: P.O. Box 410, 70592. Tel: 318-856-8212; Fax: 318-856-8277. [CEM]

Chaplains of Public Institutions

On Special Assignment:
Reverend Monsignors—
Larroque, H. Alexandre, Vicar General, 1408 Carmel Ave., Lafayette, LA 70501. Tel: 318-261-5613
Reverend Fathers—
Boyer, Millard G., Chap., Lafayette General Medical Center, 2104 Long Plantation Blvd., Lafayette, LA 70508. Tel: 318-988-4590
Dugas, Willard, 520 Dugas Rd., Lafayette, LA 70507
Dutra, Luiz C., Office for Persons with Disabilities, 1404 Carmel Ave., Lafayette, LA 70501. Tel: 318-261-5548
Labove, M. Keith, Chap., Lafayette General Medical Center, P.O. Box 52531, Lafayette, LA 70505
Morvant, Kenneth R., Office of the Tribunal, P.O. Box 3387, Lafayette, LA 70502-3387
Robichaux, Robie E., Office of the Tribunal, P.O. Box 3387, Lafayette, LA 70502-3387. Tel: 318-261-5623
Vellankal, James, Chap., Opelousas General Hospital and Doctors Hospital, P.O. Box 7067, Opelousas, LA 70570

On Duty Outside the Diocese:
Reverend Monsignors—
Mouton, C. Burton, Basilica of St. Mary Major, Vatican City State, 00120 Europe
Reverend Fathers—
Boudreaux, John S., Corpus Christi Church, 6300 McKenna Dr., Mobile, AL 36608
Meaux, Glenn, Haiti Mission, P.O. Box 46802, Gladstone, MO 64118
Rieboldt, Richard, 726 Kirk St., West Orange, NJ 07052. Tel: 201-669-8480
Voorhies, Bennett J., Santa Maria de La Paz Church, 11 College Ave., Sante Fe, NM 87505. Tel: 505-473-4200

Military Chaplains:
Reverend Fathers—
Ledoux, Louis V., Colonel, USAF, P.O. Box 4026, McCord A.F.B., WA 98438

Absent on Sick Leave:
Reverend Fathers—
Broussard, Paul, 112 Peg Ln., Lafayette, LA 70508. Tel: 318-237-5472
Montelaro, Thomas, P.O. Box 471, Eunice, LA 70535

Absent on Leave:
Reverend Fathers—
Broussard, Kenneth M.
Coupar, David A.
Ganucheau, William R.
Hebert, Lloyd P.

Retired:
Reverend Monsignors—
Barsen, Herman J., 130 N. Richelieu Circle, New Iberia, LA 70560. Tel: 318-365-0616
Benedict, Michael J., 2319 E. Main St., New Iberia, LA 70560
Benefiel, Harry E., 301 Eraste Landry Rd., Lafayette, LA 70506. Tel: 318-235-4373
Disch, John H., P.O. Box 12507, New Iberia, LA 70562
Gremillion, John E., 699 Blairshire Circle, Winter Park, FL 32789. Tel: 407-628-9750
Martin, Ignatius, Rte. 2, Box 785, Maurice, LA 70555. Tel: 318-893-8931
Richard, Wayne R., 317 Guilbeau Rd., Apt. 202-B, Lafayette, LA 70506
Sigur, Alexander O., 719 N. Ave. K, Crowley, CA 70526
Van Boxel, W. H., Apollolaan 454, NL-2324 CG Leiden, The Netherlands
Reverend Fathers—
Bourg, Edwin, 300 W. Alexander St., Lafayette, LA 70501
Calais, Floyd J., 313 Rue Louis XIV, Apt. H, Lafayette, LA 70508. Tel: 318-988-6278
DeLeeuw, John, 526 Raintree Trail, Lafayette, LA 70507. Tel: 318-235-5706
Desilets, Viateur, 900 N. Union St., Opelousas, LA

70570. Tel: 318-942-6552
Edwards, Roy D., P.O. Box 280, Carencro, LA 70520
Fontaine, Edouard, Rt. 4, Box 317, Eunice, LA 70535
Hebert, T. J., 202 Stanford St., Apt. B, Lafayette, LA 70503. Tel: 318-981-8113
Jammes, Jean Marie, P.O. Drawer 10, St. Martinville, LA 70582. Tel: 318-394-6021
Larriviere, Marshall
LeBlanc, J. Whitney, P.O. Box 2576, Parks, LA 70582
Mau, Joseph, 3142 Lambert Dr., Baton Rouge, LA 70805
Millet, John H., S.J., 308 Sidney Martin Rd., Apt. 172, Lafayette, LA 70507. Tel: 318-231-1172
Robitaille, Raymond, 2319 Main St., New Iberia, LA 70560
Sinnige, J. C., Mariahof, 5036 NB Tilburg, Bredaseweg 568, The Netherlands
Spekschate, John, Kapelaanspad, 24, NL-5801 BN Venray, B.N. 5801 The Netherlands
Speyrer, Jules, 105 White St., Basile, LA 70515-0212. Tel: 318-432-5054
Sylvester, J. Wilfred, 749 Prudhomme Ln., Apt. 215, Opelousa, LA 70570
Warren, Arthur

Permanent Deacons:
Achee, Harold L., Sr., Sacred Heart, Baldwin
Bellamy, Coley M., Our Lady of Wisdom, Lafayette
Benedetto, Joseph, Office for Persons with Disabilities, Lafayette
Bodin, Edward J., St. Jules Church, Franklin
Borel, Ronald, Our Lady of Perpetual Help, New Iberia
Boudreaux, Ulysse, Our Lady Perpetual Help, New Iberia
Bourg, Gerald J., Sacred Heart, Baldwin
Broussard, Ronald H., St. Peter, New Iberia
Cannatella, Carlo, St. Landry, Opelousas
Clark, Michael, Holy Cross, Lafayette
Conrad, Carl, St. Peter, New Iberia
Dejean, Alvin Ray, St. Anthony, Lafayette
Eleazar, Paul R., Holy Rosary, Kaplan
Freyou, Leonard J., St. Nicholas Church, Lydia
Guilbeau, James, St. John Cathedral, Lafayette
Guillory, David, St. Thomas More, Eunice
Hanemann, Louis, Fayetteville
Hebert, Douglas J., Assumption, Franklin
Hebert, Marcel, St. Bernard, Breaux Bridge
Henry, Samuel, St. Charles, Grand Coteau
Judice, Julian, St. Mary, Lafayette
Landry, Theodule, St. John, Jeanerette
Lebouef, Eugene J., Queen of All Saints, Ville Platte
Lee, Carlton J., Sr., Notre Dame, St. Martinville
Lejeune, Joseph L., St. John the Evangelist, Mermentau
Leleux, Rodless, St. John the Baptist, Lyons Point
Lloyd, Louis, Our Lady Queen of Peace, Lafayette
Luke, Norbert, Holy Cross, Lafayette
Mason, Jonas E., Holy Family, Lawtell; St. Ann, Mallet
Matte, Paul, St. Edmond, Lafayette
Mayeux, Paul N., Our Lady Queen of All Saints, Ville Platte
McDonner, Robert, Sts. Peter and Paul, Scott
Melancon, J. Douglas, Assumption, Mire
Melancon, Roy, Our Lady of Mercy, Henderson
Miller, Cody, St. Joseph, Milton
Miller, Ivy J., Our Lady of the Sacred Heart, Church Point
Miller, John W., St. Landry, Opelousas
Morello, Benedict, Sacred Heart Chapel, Pecan Island
Mouton, Melvin, Pasadena, TX
Oliver, James R., Cathedral of St. John the Evangelist, Lafayette
Ortego, Charles, Our Lady of Mount Carmel, Chataignier
Ozene, Anthony Leroy, Immaculate Heart of Mary, Lafayette
Perron, Roderick P., St. Joseph, Ville Platte
Richard, Harold, St. Bernard, Breaux Bridge
Richard, Thomas, Our Lady of Mount Carmel, Chataignier
Royston, John
Sikes, George, Our Lady of Perpetual Help, New Iberia
Soileau, Harris, Sacred Heart of Jesus, Ville Platte
Sonnier, Adam, St. Joseph, Rayne
Theriot, Samuel, St. Theresa of the Child Jesus, Abbeville
Thibodeaux, John, Assumption, Carencro
Thomas, Joseph, St. Jules, Franklin
Waguespack, Eugene, St. Jules, Lafayette
Waguespack, Kenneth, St. Elizabeth Mission, Coteau Holmes
Wilson, James, St. Peter, New Iberia
Woodburn, Albert A., M.D., Dauterive & Iberia General Hospitals, New Iberia

INSTITUTIONS LOCATED IN THE DIOCESE

[A] SEMINARIES, RELIGIOUS OR SCHOLASTICATES

GRAND COTEAU. *St. Charles College*, P.O. Box C, 70541-1003. Novitiate of New Orleans Province of the Society of Jesus and Jesuit Spirituality Center. Revs. Edmundo Rodriguez, S.J., Supr. & Dir.; Francis W. Huete, S.J., Novice Dir.; Fred G. Reynolds, S.J.; Norman J. Rogge, S.J.; Henry R. Montecino, S.J.; Francis W. Vanderwall, S.J.; Thomas J. Jenniskens, S.J.; David L. Andrus, S.J.; Albert C. Louapre, S.J.; Louis A. Arceneaux, C.M.; Bros. Michael J. Moore, S.J.; George A. Murphy, S.J.; Raul A. Loya, S.J. Priests 10; Scholastics 10; Brothers 3.

[B] HIGH SCHOOLS, INTERPAROCHIAL

LAFAYETTE. *St. Thomas More*, 450 E. Farrel Rd., 70508. Tel: 318-988-3700. Mr. Ray Simon, Prin. Brothers 2; Sisters 1; Lay Teachers 58; Students 869.
Teurlings Catholic High, 139 Teurlings Dr., 70501. Tel: 318-235-5711; Fax: 318-234-0857. Mr. Bruce Baudier, Prin. Lay Teachers 26; Students 475.
CROWLEY. *Notre Dame High School of Acadia Parish*, 910 N. Eastern Ave., 70526. Tel: 318-783-3519. Mr. John E. Dailey, Prin. Sisters 1; Lay Teachers 20; Students 427.
NEW IBERIA. *Catholic High School*. (Grades 4-12), 1301 DeLaSalle Dr., 70560. Tel: 318-364-5116. Dave J. Cavalier, Jr., Prin. Lay Teachers 60; Students 908.
OPELOUSAS. *Opelousas Catholic School*. (Grades PreK-12), 415 E. Prudhomme Ln., 70570. Tel: 318-942-5404. Mrs. Karen Domengeaux, Prin. Elementary: Sisters of the Holy Family 1; Lay Teachers 24; Students 543. High School: Lay Teachers 24; Students 284.

[C] ELEMENTARY SCHOOLS, INTERPAROCHIAL

LAFAYETTE. *Holy Family School*, 200 St. John St., 70501. Tel: 318-235-0267. Sisters of the Holy Family. Sr. Frances Therese Remi, S.S.F., Prin. Sisters 4; Lay Teachers 11; Students 215.
ST. MARTINVILLE. *Trinity Catholic School*. (Grades PreK-8), P.O. Box 438. Miss Rosemary Pierre, Prin. Sisters 3; Lay Teachers 10; Students 279.

[D] ELEMENTARY SCHOOLS, PRIVATE

ABBEVILLE. *Mt. Carmel Elementary School*, 405 Park, 70510. Tel: 318-898-0859. Sr. Janet LeBlanc, O.Carm., Prin. Sisters of Mt. Carmel 3; Lay Teachers 23; Students 502.

[E] HIGH AND ELEMENTARY SCHOOLS, PRIVATE

GRAND COTEAU. *Academy of the Sacred Heart*. (Grades PreK-12), P.O. Box 310, 70541. Tel: 318-662-5275. Day School for girls. Boarding facilities for girls 8th-12th grade. Sr. Carol Haggarty, R.S.C.J., Prin. Religious of the Sacred Heart 4; Lay Teachers 41; Students 351.

[F] GENERAL HOSPITALS

LAFAYETTE. *Our Lady of Lourdes Regional Medical Center, Inc.*, 611 St. Landry St., P.O. Box 4027, 70502. Tel: 318-234-7381.
For a complete listing, refer to the Hospitals section.

[G] HOMES FOR THE AGED INFIRM

LAFAYETTE. *Bethany M.H.S. Health Care Center*, P.O. Box 2308, 70502. Tel: 318-234-2459.
For a complete listing, refer to the Special Care Facilities section.
Village du Lac, Inc., 1404 Carmel Ave., 70501. Tel: 318-234-5106.
For a complete listing, refer to the Special Care Facilities section.
NEW IBERIA. *Consolata Home*, 2319 E. Main St., 70560. Tel: 318-365-8226.
For a complete listing, refer to the Special Care Facilities section.
OPELOUSAS. *C'est La Vie Center of the Sisters Marianites of Holy Cross*, 749 E. Prudhomme Ln., 70570. Tel: 318-942-8154.
For a complete listing, refer to the Special Care Facilities section.
Our Lady of Prompt Succor Home, 751 E. Prudhomme Ln., 70570. Tel: 318-948-3634.
For a complete listing, refer to the Special Care Facilities section.

[H] MONASTERIES AND RESIDENCES PRIESTS AND BROTHERS

LAFAYETTE. *De La Salle Christian Brothers*, 1522 Carmel Dr., 70501. Tel: 318-235-3576. Retired Brothers Home. Bros. Louis Welker, F.S.C., Dir.; Jerry Vincent, F.S.C., Sub-Dir.; C. Daniel Duplantis, F.S.C., Coord.; Rev. Luiz C. Dutra, Chap. Brothers 22.
De La Salle Christian Brothers Provincialate, 1522 Carmel Dr., 70501. Tel: 318-234-1973; Fax: 318-261-1014. Headquarters for the New Orleans-Santa Fe District. Legal Title: *Brothers of the Christian Schools of Lafayette LA, Inc.* Bros. Clarence Fioke, F.S.C., Prov.; James Brown, F.S.C., Auxiliary Prov. and Finance Dir. Prov. Staff: Mrs. Clara Mouton, F.S.C., Sec. to the Provincial; Bro. Duane Gregory, F.S.C., Prov. Bookkeeper.
OPELOUSAS. *Mother of the Redeemer Monastery*, 168 Monastery Ln., 70570. Tel: 318-543-2237. Rev. James Liprie, O.S.B., Supr. Priests 1; Brothers 2; Candidates 1.

[I] CONVENTS AND RESIDENCES FOR SISTERS

LAFAYETTE. *Discalced Carmelites*. Monastery of Mary, Mother of Grace. 1250 Carmel Ave., 70501. Tel: 318-232-4651. Mother Catherine, O.C.D., Prioress; Rev. Msgr. H. Alexandre Larroque, Chap. Cloistered Nuns 16; Extern Sisters 4; Postulants 2.
Dominican Sisters, P.O. Box 42371, 70504. Tel: 318-269-0324.
Eucharistic Missionaries of St. Dominic, 300 N. Chestnut St., 70501. Tel: 318-235-8345.
Franciscan Missionaries of Our Lady, Our Lady of Lourdes Hospital, P.O. Box 4027-C, 70502. Tel: 318-231-2110 (Convent); 237-7381 (Hospital). Sisters 4.
Marianites of Holy Cross, 1417 St. John St., 70506. Tel: 318-234-5454. Sisters 2.
Missionaries of Charity, 911 St. John St., 70501. Tel: 318-233-3929. Sisters 4.
School Sisters of Notre Dame, 1404 Carmel Ave., Apt. 40-C, 70501. Tel: 318-232-6975. Sisters 2.
Sisters of Divine Providence, 317 Guilbeau Rd., Apt. 101-E, 70506. Tel: 318-984-8520.
Other Addresses: 317 Guilbeau Rd., Apt. 202-H, 70506. Tel: 318-981-4215. 220 Wilkle St., Apt. 863, 70506. Tel: 318-234-4546.
Sisters of Mt. Carmel, 309 Evangeline Dr., 70501. Tel: 318-235-8687. Sisters 2.
Other Addresses: 506 Surrey St., 70501. Tel: 318-235-1837. Sisters 2. 317 Guilbeau Rd., Apt. 206A, 70506. Tel: 318-981-4378.
Sisters of St. Agnes, 609 Mudd Ave., 70501. Tel: 318-234-6768.
Sisters of St. Joseph of Carondelet, 317 Guilbeau Rd., No. 106-J, 70506. Tel: 318-988-0714.
Sisters of the Most Holy Sacrament, Convent Generalate, 313 Corona Dr., 70503-4757. Tel: 318-981-8475. Sr. Anthony Richards, M.H.S., Major Supr. Sisters 2. Administrative Offices, P.O. Box 30727, 70593-0727.
Other Addresses: 104 Beta Dr., 70506-3924. Tel: 318-984-4494. Sisters 2. 317 St. Patrick St., No. 1, 70506-4565. Tel: 318-234-6724. 317 St. Patrick St., No. 3, 70506-4565. Tel: 318-264-1948. 317 St. Patrick St., No. 4, 70506-4565. Tel: 318-232-3443. 317 St. Patrick St., No. 5, 70506-4565. Tel: 318-264-1921. 317 St. Patrick St., No. 6, 70506-4565. Tel: 318-235-1755. Sisters 2. 107 Wisteria Dr., 70506-6858. Tel: 318-989-9817. Sisters 3. St. Anne's Annex, P.O. Box 2308, 70502-2308. Tel: 318-233-8901. Sisters 4. Bethany MHS Health Care Center, P.O. Box 2308, 70502-2308. Sisters 12.
ABBEVILLE. *Sisters of Mt. Carmel*, 108 Petain St., 70510. Tel: 318-898-0140. Sisters 2.
Other Addresses: 2326 Camella, 70510. Tel: 318-898-1807. Sisters 3. 108 W. St. Victor St., 70510. Tel: 318-893-0138. Sisters 2.
ARNAUDVILLE. *Sisters of Divine Providence*, P.O. Box 53, 70512.
BREAUX BRIDGE. *Sisters of the Most Holy Sacrament*, 221 Berard St., 70517. Tel: 318-332-1951.
CHURCH POINT. *Sisters of the Blessed Sacrament*, 695 N. Main St., 70525. Tel: 318-684-2120. Sisters 2.
CROWLEY. *Marianites of the Holy Cross*, 516 N. Ave. E, 70526. Tel: 318-783-1550. Sisters 4.
Sisters of Divine Providence, 516 N. Ave. E, 70526. Tel: 318-783-1550.
Sisters of the Holy Spirit, 211 N. Avenue D, 70526. Tel: 318-783-1311.
Sisters of the Most Holy Sacrament. Other Address: P.O. Box 695, 70527. Tel: 318-783-3675.
DUSON. *Eucharistic Missionaries of St. Dominic*, P.O. Box 725, 70529. Tel: 318-873-4159.
FRANKLIN. *Marianites of the Holy Cross*, 619 Iberia St., 70538. Tel: 318-828-5241.
GRAND COTEAU. *Religious of the Sacred Heart*, P.O. Box 292, 70541. Tel: 318-942-1551. Sisters 4.

Other Addresses: P.O. Box 446, 70541. Tel: 318-662-5526. Sisters 5. P.O. Box 308, 70541. Tel: 318-662-5453. Sisters 7.
Sisters of Mt. Carmel, P.O. Box 534, 70541. Tel: 318-662-7178.

IOTA. *Sisters of Divine Providence*, P.O. Box 870, 70543. Tel: 318-779-2228.

JEANERETTE. *School Sisters of Notre Dame*, 100 Beth St., 70544. Tel: 318-276-5640. Sisters 3.

LEBEAU. *Sisters of the Holy Spirit*, P.O. Box 40, 71345. Tel: 318-623-4405. Sisters 2.

NEW IBERIA. *Dominican Rural Missionaries*, 213 Oak Hill Rd., 70560. Tel: 318-364-3142.
Sisters of Providence, 213 Oak Hill Rd., 70560. Tel: 318-364-3142.

OPELOUSAS. *Sisters of the Holy Family*, 720 N. Union St., 70570. Tel: 318-942-2052. Sisters 3.

RAYNE. *Sisters of Mt. Carmel*, 411 S. Polk St., 70578. Tel: 318-334-3403. Sisters 6.
Sisters of the Blessed Sacrament, 710 Malvern St., 70578. Tel: 318-334-3606. Sisters 2.

ST. MARTINVILLE. *Sisters of Mercy of the Americas*, P.O. Box 674, 70582. Tel: 318-394-14486.
Sisters of the Blessed Sacrament, 201 Gary St., 70582. Tel: 318-394-3036. Sisters 3.

[J] RETREAT HOUSES

GRAND COTEAU. *Our Lady of the Oaks Retreat House*, P.O. Box D, 70541. Tel: 318-662-5410. Preached retreats for men, women, and married couples. Jesuit Fathers. Rev. C. Kirk Mansell, S.J., Dir. Assoc. Directors: Revs. Francis J. Coco, S.J.; John T. Condry, S.J.

[K] CURSILLO CENTERS

OPELOUSAS. *Cursillo Center*, 3651 Hwy. 104, 70570. Tel: 318-873-4962; Fax: 318-873-3023. Rev. O. Joseph Breaux, Spiritual Dir.

[L] NEWMAN CENTERS

LAFAYETTE. *Our Lady of Wisdom Catholic Student Center*, University of Southwestern Louisiana, P.O. Box 43271, 70505. Tel: 318-232-8741; 232-8742. Rev. F. Hampton Davis.

EUNICE. *Catholic Student Center-Louisiana State Univ.*, P.O. Box 1129, 70535. Tel: 318-457-8668.

[M] MISCELLANEOUS

LAFAYETTE. *Brothers of the Christian Schools of Lafayette - Retirement Trust*, 1522 Carmel Ave., 70501. Tel: 318-234-1973; Fax: 318-261-1014.
Community of Jesus Crucified, 421 1/2 Carmel Dr., 70501. Tel: 318-232-7491. Revs. Jerome Frey, Spiritual Dir.; Michael Champagne.
Holy Rosary Institute, P.O. Box 3387, 70501. 421 Carmel Ave., 70501.
St. Augustine Trust Fund, P.O. Box 30727, 70593. Sisters of the Most Holy Sacrament.
St. La Salle Auxiliary, 1522 Carmel Dr., 70501. Tel: 318-234-1973. Brothers of the Christian Schools.
Sisters of the Eucharistic Covenant, P.O. Box 80393, 70508. Sr. Camille Martinez, S.E.C., Pres.

[N] SOCIAL SERVICE CENTERS

LAFAYETTE. *Lafayette Catholic Service Centers, Inc.*, 409 St. John St., 70501. Tel: 318-235-4972.
Service Centers: Dr. Justin Green, Exec. Dir.
Msgr. A. O. Sigur Service Center.
St. Joseph Shelter for Men.
St. Joseph Diner.
Shalom House Family Shelter.
Emmanuel House Family Shelter.
St. Joseph Distribution Center.
The Bishop Harry J. Flynn Hospitality Center. Total Assisted Annually 235,196.

ABBEVILLE. *Christian Service Center*, 701 Chevis St., 70510. Tel: 318-893-9756; 893-3114. Co-Directors: Jackie Taylor; Evelyn Fontenot.
St. Vincent de Paul Center, 507 N. Bailey St., 70510. Tel: 318-898-1830. Sr. Jeanette Bernhardt, Coord.

CROWLEY. *Crowley Christian Care Center*, 825 N. Ave. F, P.O. Box 686, 70527-0686. Tel: 318-783-5811. Mona Istre, Admin.

NEW IBERIA. *Social Service Center*, 432 Bank Ave., 70560. Tel: 318-369-6384. Paul H. DeClouet, Jr., Dir.

OPELOUSAS. *Opelousas Housing Corporation*, P.O. Box 7045, 70571.
dba New Life Center. Operated under the direction of the Lafayette Catholic Services Center, Inc.

VILLE PLATTE. *Christian Care and Share Center*, 129 W. Main St., P.O. Box 901, 70586. Tel: 318-363-8041. Mr. Eugene S. Fontenot, Chm.

RELIGIOUS INSTITUTES OF MEN REPRESENTED IN THE DIOCESE

For further details refer to the corresponding bracketed number in the Religious Institutes of Men or Women section.

[0200]—*Benedictines (Olivetan, Subiaco Congregation)*.—O.S.B.
[0330]—*Brothers of the Christian Schools*. (New Orleans Prov.).—F.S.C.
[]—*Carmelites of Mary Immaculate*.—C.M.I.
[0360]—*Claretian Missionaries*.—C.M.F.
[0220]—*Congregation of the Blessed Sacrament*.—S.S.S.
[0520]—*Franciscan Friars*.—O.F.M.
[0690]—*Jesuit Fathers and Brothers*. (New Orleans Prov.).—S.J.
[]—*Missionaries of St. Paul*. (Nigeria).—M.S.P.
[0610]—*Priests of the Congregation of Holy Cross*.—C.S.C.
[1070]—*Redemptorist Fathers*.—C.SS.R.
[0700]—*St. Joseph's Society of the Sacred Heart*. (Baltimore Prov.).—S.S.J.
[0420]—*Society of the Divine Word*.—S.V.D.

RELIGIOUS INSTITUTES OF WOMEN REPRESENTED IN THE DIOCESE

[0400]—*Congregation of Our Lady of Mount Carmel*.—O.Carm.
[2410]—*Congregation of the Marianites of Holy Cross*.—M.S.C.
[1950]—*Congregation of the Sisters of the Holy Family*.—S.S.F.
[0420]—*Discalced Carmelite Nuns*.—O.C.D.
[1130]—*Dominican Rural Missionaries*.—O.P.
[1070-14]—*Dominican Sisters*.—O.P.
[]—*Dominican Sisters of Carondelet*.—O.P.
[1140]—*Eucharistic Missionaries of St. Dominic*.—O.P.
[1380]—*Franciscan Missionaries of Our Lady*.—O.S.F.
[2575]—*Institute of the Sisters of Mercy of the Americas*.—R.S.M.
[2710]—*Missionaries of Charity*. (Bronx, NY).—M.C.
[3530]—*Missionary Sisters Servants of the Holy Spirit*.—S.Sp.S.
[4070]—*Religious of the Sacred Heart*.—R.S.C.J.
[2970]—*School Sisters of Notre Dame*. (South Central).—S.S.N.D.
[0990]—*Sisters of Divine Providence*.—C.D.P.
[3360]—*Sisters of Providence of Saint Mary-of-the-Woods, Indiana*. (Prov. of St. Joseph).—S.P.
[3880]—*Sisters of St. Joseph of Medaille*.—C.S.J.
[0260]—*Sisters of the Blessed Sacrament for Indians and Colored People*.—S.B.S.
[2050]—*Sisters of the Holy Spirit and Mary Immaculate*.—S.H.Sp.
[2940]—*Sisters of the Most Holy Sacrament*.—M.H.S.

NECROLOGY

† Betrand, Louis N., (Retired). —Died July 19, 1996.
† Bussieres, Francois, (Retired). —Died July 5, 1996.
† Doiron, James Wilson, Lafayette, LA, St. Mary. —Died Jan. 16, 1996.
† Gauthier, Raphael, (Retired). —Died Dec. 30, 1996.
† Sinnige, Joannes Cornelius, (Retired). —Died Oct. 7, 1996.
† Zaunbrecher, Charles, (Retired). —Died June 19, 1996.

Diocese of Lake Charles

Most Reverend

JUDE SPEYRER, D.D.

Bishop of Lake Charles; ordained July 25, 1953; appointed First Bishop of Lake Charles January 29, 1980; ordained and installed April 25, 1980. *Mailing Address: P.O. Box 3223, Lake Charles, LA, 70602.*

ESTABLISHED APRIL 25, 1980.

Square Miles 5,313.

Comprises the civil parishes (or counties) of Allen, Beauregard, Calcasieu, Cameron and Jefferson Davis in the State of Louisiana.

For legal titles of parishes and diocesan institutions, consult the Chancery Office.

Chancery Office: 414 Iris St., P.O. Box 3223, Lake Charles, LA, 70602. Tel.: 318-439-7400; Fax: 318-439-7413.

E-mail address: judespeyrer@juno.com

STATISTICAL OVERVIEW

Personnel	
Bishop	1
Priests: Diocesan Active in Diocese	41
Priests: Active Outside Diocese	5
Priests: Retired, Sick or Absent	4
Number of Diocesan Priests	50
Religious Priests in Diocese	18
Extern Priests in Diocese	7
Ordinations:	
Diocesan Priests	1
Transitional Deacons	1
Permanent Deacons in Diocese	19
Total Brothers	4
Total Sisters	32
Parishes	
Parishes	36
With Resident Pastor:	
Resident Diocesan Priests	25
Resident Religious Priests	11
Without Resident Pastor:	
Missions	25
Professional Ministry Personnel:	
Brothers	1
Sisters	11
Lay Ministers	11
Welfare	
Catholic Hospitals	1
Total Assisted	104,497
Day Care and Extended Day Care Centers	1
Total Assisted	57
Special Centers for Social Services	1
Total Assisted	2,437
Educational	
Diocesan Students in Other Seminaries	8
Total Seminarians	8
High Schools, Diocesan and Parish	1
Total Students	483
Elementary Schools, Diocesan and Parish	8
Total Students	2,353
Catechesis/Religious Education:	
High School Students	3,509
Elementary Students	6,864
Total Students Under Catholic Instruction	13,217
Teachers in the Diocese:	
Priests	1
Brothers	1
Lay Teachers	204
Vital Statistics	
Receptions into the Church:	
Infant Baptism Totals	1,543
Adult Baptism Totals	145
Received into Full Communion	199
First Communions	1,369
Confirmations	1,933
Marriages:	
Catholic	379
Interfaith	133
Total Marriages	512
Deaths	782
Total Catholic Population	81,971
Total Population	259,425

Diocesan Board of Administration (Legal Title - *Society of the Roman Catholic Church of the Diocese of Lake Charles, LA*)—Most Rev. JUDE SPEYRER; Rev. EGIDIO VECCHIO, M.S.; Rev. Msgr. CHARLES J. DUBOIS; Rev. Msgr. VINCENT A. SEDITA; Deacon HARRY E. WAGNER, JR.

Bishop's Office—414 Iris St., P.O. Box 3223, Lake Charles, 70602. Tel: 318-439-7400.

Chancery Office—414 Iris St., P.O. Box 3223, Lake Charles, 70602. Tel: 318-439-7400; Fax: 318-439-7413. Office Hours: Mon.-Fri. 8:30-4:30.

Chennault Office Complex—4029 Avenue G, Lake Charles, 70615. Tel: 318-439-7430; Fax: 318-439-7428. Office Hours: Mon.-Fri. 8:30-4:30.

Vicar General—Rev. Msgr. VINCENT SEDITA, V.G., *P.O. Box 3223, Lake Charles, 70602.* Tel: 318-439-7400.

Chancellor—Deacon GEORGE STEARNS, *P.O. Box 3223, Lake Charles, 70602.* Tel: 318-439-7400.

Assistant Chancellor—Deacon HARRY E. WAGNER, JR., *P.O. Box 3223, Lake Charles, 70602.* Tel: 318-439-7400.

Vicar Judicial—Rev. ANTONIO GARCIA, J.C.L., *4029 Avenue G, Lake Charles, 70601.* Tel: 318-439-7410.

Tribunal—414 Iris St., P.O. Box 3223, Lake Charles, 70602. Tel: 318-439-7410.

Judges—Rev. ANTONIO GARCIA, J.C.L.; Rev. Msgr. VINCENT SEDITA; Rev. Msgr. AMOS VINCENT; Rev. JOHN A. POERIO.

Advocates—Rev. Msgr. VINCENT SEDITA; Rev. Msgr. MURPHY BERNARD; Rev. Msgr. RONALD GROTH; Revs. JAMES DOYLE; JOHN POERIO; MICHAEL BARRAS; MICHAEL BLUM, M.S.; JOSEPH MCGRATH; MILTON P. MILLER; Mr. EDGAR PERKINS; JOHN PATIN; JOSEPH TRITICO; PRESTON SAVOY.

Defenders of the Bond—Rev. Msgr. HARRY GREIG; Rev. JAMES DOYLE.

Notaries—Rt. Rev. HERBERT J. MAY, JR., J.C.L.; Rev. Msgr. RONALD GROTH; Rev. Msgr. VINCENT SEDITA; PATRICIA SIGUR.

Episcopal Vicars—Rev. EGIDIO VECCHIO, M.S., West Deanery; Rev. Msgr. CHARLES J. DUBOIS, East Deanery; Rev. Msgr. A. J. VINCENT, Community Services; Rev. Msgr. IRVING DEBLANC, Spec. Svcs.; Rev. Msgr. VINCENT SEDITA, Vicar Gen.; Rev. JOHN GILES, Christian Formation; Rev. ANTONIO GARCIA, Tribunal.

Vicars—Deacon EDWARD LAVINE, Black Catholics; Sr. ROSE ANN BLAIR, C.D.P., Religious.

Priest's Senate—Rev. HERBERT MAY, Chm.; Rev. Msgr. HARRY GREIG; Revs. KARL FUSELIER; MILTON P. MILLER; AUBREY GUILBEAU.

Diocesan Consultors—Rev. Msgr. LOUIS MELANCON; Rev. Msgr. CHARLES J. DUBOIS; Rev. Msgr. A. J. VINCENT, Social Svcs.; Rev. Msgr. IRVING DEBLANC, Spec. Svcs.; Rev. Msgr. VINCENT SEDITA, Vicar Gen.; Rev. Msgr. HARRY GREIG; Rev. HENRY MANCUSO; Rt. Rev. HERBERT J. MAY, JR., J.C.L.; Revs. ALBERT BOREL; JUAN ALERS.

Offices, Boards, Commissions, Committees

Black Catholics—Deacon EDWARD LAVINE, *2043 11th St., Lake Charles, 70601.* Tel: 318-439-2646.

Calcasieu Center for Catholic Studies—Rev. JOHN GILES JR., *920 7th St., Lake Charles, 70601.* Tel: 318-439-7432.

Charismatic Renewal—Rev. ORIS BROUSSARD, *2409 2nd St., Lake Charles, 70601.* Tel: 318-439-1898.

Christian Formation—Rev. JOHN GILES, *4029 Avenue G, Lake Charles, 70601.* Tel: 318-439-7432.

Clergy Formation—Rev. DON PIRARO, *414 Iris St., Lake Charles, 70601.* Tel: 318-439-7400.

Communications—MORRIS LEBLEU, *4029 Avenue G, Lake Charles, 70601.* Tel: 318-439-7430.

Deaf Apostolate—Rev. AUBREY GUILBEAU, *418 Iris St., Lake Charles, 70601.* Tel: 318-439-4373.

Development Office—MORRIS LEBLEU, *P.O. Box 3223, Lake Charles, 70602.* Tel: 318-439-7434.

Diocesan Building Commission—Deacon GEORGE STEARNS, Chm., *P.O. Box 3223, Lake Charles, 70602.* Tel: 318-439-7400.

Diocesan Pastoral Council—Most Rev. JUDE SPEYRER, Chm., *P.O. Box 3223, Lake Charles, 70602.* Tel: 318-439-7400.

Diocesan Religious Council—Sr. ROSE ANN BLAIR, C.D.P., *P.O. Drawer P, Lake Arthur, 70549.* Tel: 318-774-2614.

Director of Seminarians—Rev. AUBREY GUILBEAU, *4029 Avenue G, Lake Charles, 70601.* Tel: 318-439-7430.

Education—Deacon MICHAEL MATHEWS, Supt., *4029 Avenue G, Lake Charles, 70601.* Tel: 318-439-7418.

Evangelization—GLENN HARMON. Tel: 318-439-7400.

Fiscal Administration—Deacon HARRY E. WAGNER, JR., *P.O. Box 3223, Lake Charles, 70602.* Tel: 318-439-7400.

Hispanic Ministry—Rev. Msgr. JUAN M. ALERS, *207 Meadow Dr., Oakdale, 71463.* Tel: 318-335-3780.

Office For Worship—Rev. JACE ESKIND, *221 Aqua Dr., Lake Charles, 70605.* Tel: 318-477-1434.

Parish Boundaries Commission—Deacon GEORGE STEARNS, Chm., *P.O. Box 3223, Lake Charles, 70602.* Tel: 318-439-7400.

Permanent Diaconate—Deacon EDWARD LAVINE, *P.O. Box 3223, Lake Charles, 70602.* Tel: 318-439-7400.

Personnel Board—Rev. TIMOTHY GOODLY, Chm., *P.O. Box 1029, Lake Charles, 70602.* Tel: 318-439-7400.

Propagation of the Faith & Holy Childhood Association—Deacon HARRY E. WAGNER, JR., Dir., *P.O. Box 3223, Lake Charles, 70602.* Tel: 318-439-7400.

Religious Education—Mrs. SANDY GAY, *4029 Avenue G, Lake Charles, 70601.* Tel: 318-439-7429.

Relief Services Catholic—Deacon H. E. WAGNER, JR., *P.O. Box 3223, Lake Charles, 70602.* Tel: 318-439-7400.

St. Charles Retreat Center—Rev. DON PIRARO, Dir., *2151 Sam Houston Jones Pkwy., Lake Charles, 70611.* Tel: 318-855-1232.

Sea, Apostleship of the—PATRICK BROUSSARD, *160 Marine St., Lake Charles, 70601.* Tel: 318-436-1315.

Social Services, Catholic—Deacon EDWARD LAVINE, Dir., *4029 Ave. G, Lake Charles, 70615.* Tel: 318-439-7439.

Community Services, Catholic—Deacon EDWARD LAVINE, Vicar, *4029 Avenue G, Lake Charles, 70615.* Tel: 318-439-7439.

Scouting—Rev. MAURICE J. MARTINEAU, *11054 Hwy. 384, Lake Charles, 70607.* Tel: 318-598-3101.

Seminary Advisory Board—Rev. AUBREY GUILBEAU, *4029 Avenue G, Lake Charles, 70601.* Tel: 318-439-7430.

Vocation Director—Rev. TIMOTHY GOODLY, *4029 Avenue G, Lake Charles, 70601.* Tel: 318-439-7430.

CLERGY, PARISHES, MISSIONS AND PAROCHIAL SCHOOLS

LAKE CHARLES
(Calcasieu Parish)

1—IMMACULATE CONCEPTION CATHEDRAL (1869), Rev. Msgr. Harry D. Greig, II; Rev. Michael J. Barras; Deacons H. E. Wagner; Milton P. White.
Mailing Address: P.O. Box 1029, 70602. Tel: 318-436-7251; Fax: 318-436-7240.
Church—935 Bilbo, 70601. [CEM]
School—Tel: 318-433-3497; Fax: 318-436-8294. Dr. Linda Lebert, Prin.
Lay Teachers 20; Students 238.

2—IMMACULATE HEART OF MARY (1953) (African American), Rev. Msgr. Ronald C. Groth; Rev. Karl Fuselier.
Res., 2031 Opelousas St., 70601. Tel: 318-436-8093; Fax: 318-436-8033.
School—301 N. Cherry St., 70601. Tel: 318-433-0158. Mrs. Kathleen Dubea, Prin.
Lay Teachers 9; Students 140.
Catechesis/Religious Programs—Tel: 318-436-8513.
Students 380.
Mission—Lake Charles, Calcasieu Parish, Our Lady of Fatima Chapel, 1500 Graham St., 70601.

3—SACRED HEART OF JESUS (1919) (African American), Rev. Raymond A. Jones, S.V.D.; Deacon Ed Lavine. In res., Rev. Alfredo Marco.
Res., 612 Louisiana Ave., 70601. Tel: 318-439-2646; Fax: 318-536-2650. [CEM]
School—Tel: 318-436-3588. Joseph W. Guillory, Prin.
Lay Teachers 17; Students 197.
Catechesis/Religious Programs—Tel: 318-439-3008. Willa Golden, D.R.E.
Students 202.

4—ST. HENRY (1942), Revs. Joseph Kariamadam, C.M.I.; Timothy Goodly; Deacon Ray Granger.
Res., 1021 Eighth Ave., 70601. Tel: 318-436-7223; Fax: 318-436-4614. [JC]
Catechesis/Religious Programs—Tel: 318-433-6119. D.R.E.: Mr. Gussie Pitre, Sr.; Mrs. Cynthia Pitre.
Students 266.

5—ST. MARGARET (1940), Revs. Henry Mancuso; William M. Miller; Deacon Dan Landry. In res., Rev. Al Volpe.
Res., 2500 Enterprise Blvd., 70601. Tel: 318-439-4585; Fax: 318-433-3186.
School—Tel: 318-436-7959. Mrs. Priscilla Courville, Prin.
Sisters 1; Lay Teachers 28; Students 416.
Catechesis/Religious Programs—D.R.E.: Betty Timpa; Joanne Schwem.
Students 415.

6—ST. THEODORE'S (1974), Rev. Msgr. Louis J. Melancon; Rev. Vernon W. LeBleu; Deacon Jack Reynolds. In res., Rev. James Doyle.
Res., 786 Sam Houston Jones Pkwy., 70611. Tel: 318-855-6662; Fax: 318-855-6663.
School—(Grades PreK-5). Tel: 318-855-9465. Mr. Franklin Foote, Prin.
Lay Teachers 11; Students 98.
Catechesis/Religious Programs—Tel: 318-855-6664. Linda Harmon, D.R.E.
Students 527.

7—OUR LADY OF GOOD COUNSEL (1957), Rev. Whitney Miller; Sr. Claire Pellerin, S.E., Pastoral Assoc.
Res., 221 Aqua Dr., 70605. Tel: 318-477-1434; Fax: 318-479-2129.
Catechesis/Religious Programs—Mary Guidroz, D.R.E.
Students 111.

8—OUR LADY QUEEN OF HEAVEN (1957), Rev. Milton Peter Miller; Rev. Msgr. Irving A. DeBlanc, Vicar for Special Svcs.; Revs. John H. Giles, Jr.; Daniel A. Torres.
Mailing Address: P.O. Box 5940, 70606.
Res., 617 W. Claude St., 70605. Tel: 318-477-1236; Fax: 318-478-3451. [CEM]
School—(Grades K-8). Tel: 318-477-7349; Fax: 318-477-7384. Mrs. Mary Ann Moses, Prin.
Lay Teachers 41; Students 698.
Preschool and Day Care—Tel: 318-477-8438.
Students 57.
Catechesis/Religious Programs—3909 Creole St., 70605. Tel: 318-477-3937. D.R.E.: Mrs. Sharon Gaspard, (Grades 7-12); Mary Beth Conner, (Grades 1-6).
Students 1,452.
Missions—Lake Charles, Calcasieu Parish, Christ the King, 7680 Gulf Hwy., 70605. Tel: 318-478-0213; Lake Charles, Calcasieu Parish, St. Martin de Porres, 5326 Elliot Rd., 70605. Tel: 318-478-3845.

OUTSIDE THE CITY OF LAKE CHARLES

Bell City, Calcasieu Parish, St. John Vianney (1939), Rev. John A. Poerio.
Res., Box 10, 70630. Tel: 318-622-3255. [CEM]
Catechesis/Religious Programs—Vicki Leonards, D.R.E.
Students 200.
Mission—Hayes, Calcasieu Parish, St. Daniel Chapel, 70630.

Big Lake, Cameron Parish, St. Mary of the Lake, Rev. Maurice Martineau.
Res., Rte. 2, Box 342, Lake Charles, 70605. Tel: 318-598-3101; Fax: 318-598-3101.
Mission—Sweet Lake, St. Patrick's.

Cameron, Cameron Parish, Our Lady Star of the Sea, Rev. Msgr. Curtis S. Vidrine.
Res., P.O. Box L, 70631. Tel: 318-775-5342.

Creole, Cameron Parish, Sacred Heart of Jesus (1890), Rev. Msgr. M. J. Bernard.
Res., P.O. Drawer 9, 70632. Tel: 318-542-4795. [CEM 3]
Catechesis/Religious Programs—Tel: 318-542-4615. Stephanie Rodrique, D.R.E.
Students 252.
Mission—Cameron, Cameron Parish, St. Rose of Lima, 2267 Trosclair Rd., Cameron, 70631. Tel: 318-542-4795.

De Quincy, Calcasieu Parish, Our Lady of La Salette (1922) (African American), Rev. John L. Blumm, M.S. In res., Rev. Jude Brunnert, M.S.
Res., 203 S. Grand, P.O. Box 236, 70633. Tel: 318-786-3500.
Catechesis/Religious Programs—Tel: 318-786-3205.
Students 278.
Mission—Ragley, Beauregard Parish, St. Pius X, 16816 Hwy. 171, Ragley, 70657. Tel: 318-725-3719.

De Ridder, Beauregard Parish, St. Joseph's (1938), Revs. Roland Bernier, M.S.; Patrick McCarthy, M.S.; Deacon Sumner Kohlhund.
Res., 1125 Blankenship Dr., 70634. Tel: 318-463-6878; Fax: 318-463-6875.
Catechesis/Religious Programs—Sr. Rita Deschenes, S.S.J., D.R.E.
Students 272.
Missions—Merryville, Beauregard Parish, St. Bridget, 1025 Blankenship, 70634; De Ridder, Beauregard Parish, St. Jude, Star Rte. 2, P.O. Box 42A, 70634. Tel: 318-328-8476. Rev. Thomas Panthalani.

Elton, Jefferson Davis Parish, St. Paul's, Rev. Marshall Boulet; Deacon John Eaves.
Res., P.O. Box 129, 70532. Tel: 318-584-2818. [CEM]
Catechesis/Religious Programs—Cathy Hollingsworth, D.R.E.
Students 286.
St. Joseph's (1950) (African American), Rev. Jose Vattakunnel; Deacon John Eaves.
Res., P.O. Box 789, 70532. Tel: 318-584-2038. [CEM]
Catechesis/Religious Programs—Tel: 318-584-2642. D.R.E.: Mary Jane Thomas; Carroll Sue Gobert.
Students 75.

Fenton, Jefferson Davis Parish, St. Charles Borromeo (1980), Rev. Augustine Mulanjanany.
Res., P.O. Box 309, 70640. Tel: 318-756-2529.
Catechesis/Religious Programs—Beverly Cornier, D.R.E.
Students 60.

Grand Chenier, Cameron Parish, St. Eugene (1962), Rev. Vincent Vadakkedath.
Res., 5035 Grand Chenier Hwy., 70643. Tel: 318-538-2245. [CEM]
Catechesis/Religious Programs—Students 89.
Mission—Grand Chenier, Cameron Parish, Immaculate Conception, 70643.

Hackberry, Cameron Parish, St. Peter Apostle, Rev. Eugene F. McKenna, M.S.
Res., 1210 Main St., P.O. Box 236, 70645. Tel: 318-762-3365.
Catechesis/Religious Programs—Tamra Welch, D.R.E.
Students 168.
Mission—Holly Beach, Holy Trinity. Rev. Roland Vaughn.
Res., HC 69, Box 245B, Cameron, 70631. Tel: 318-569-2132.
Mission—Johnson Bayou, Our Lady of the Assumption.

Iowa, Calcasieu Parish, St. Raphael (1931), Revs. Aubrey V. Guilbeau; Carlos Garcia-Cardona (Columbia).
Res., P.O. Drawer 849, 70647. Tel: 318-582-3503; Fax: 318-582-6326. [CEM]
Catechesis/Religious Programs—Students 613.
Missions—Lacassine, Jefferson Davis Parish, St. John the Evangelist, 70647-0849. Tel: 318-588-4606; Le Bleu Settlement, Calcasieu Parish, St. Joseph, 70647-0849. Tel: 318-582-3483.

Jennings, Jefferson Davis Parish, Our Lady Help of Christians (1891), Rev. Msgr. Vincent A. Sedita; Deacon John P. Segura.
Res., 710 State St., P.O. Drawer 1170, 70546. Tel: 318-824-0168; 824-7597. [CEM]
School—600 Roberts Ave., 70546. Tel: 318-824-1743. Mrs. Octavie Koon, Prin.
Lay Teachers 18; Students 316.
Catechesis/Religious Programs—Tel: 318-824-0168. Robert Deville, D.R.E.
Students 348.
Immaculate Conception (1956), Rev. Oris Broussard; Deacon Ed McNally.
Res., 515 Bryan St., P.O. Box 358, 70546. Tel: 318-824-1164; Fax: 318-824-0744.
Catechesis/Religious Programs—Bennett McNeal, D.R.E.
Students 252.
Our Lady of Perpetual Help, Rev. Peter Nleedife. In res., Rev. Scott Desormeaux.
Res., 920 S. Broadway, P.O. Box 1331, 70546. Tel: 318-824-3182; 824-3186. [CEM]
Catechesis/Religious Programs—Harriet Laudins, D.R.E.
Students 90.

Kinder, Allen Parish, St. Philip Neri (1937) (Acadian French), Rev. Msgr. James Gaddy. In res., Rev. Austin Park, S.J.
Res., P.O. Box 146, 70648. Tel: 318-738-5612. [CEM]
Catechesis/Religious Programs—Tel: 318-738-3353. Nancy Burleigh, D.R.E.
Students 388.
Missions—Indian Village, Sacred Heart Parish, Sacred Heart, 70648. Tel: 318-328-8476; Reeves, Sacred Heart Parish, St. Maurice, HC 64 Box 142 A, 70634.

Lake Arthur, Jefferson Davis Parish, Our Lady of the Lake (1922), Rev. Msgr. Charles J. DuBois.
Res., P.O. Drawer P, 70549. Tel: 318-774-2614; Fax: 318-774-3793. [CEM][JC 3]
Catechesis/Religious Programs—701 8th St., 70549. Tel: 318-774-3980.
Students 465.
Missions—Thornwell, Jefferson Davis Parish, St. Francis of Assisi Chapel; Andrus Cove, Jefferson Davis Parish, St. Gertrude Chapel.

Oakdale, Allen Parish, Sacred Heart (1948), Rev. Juan M. Alers (LC). Pastoral Assocs.: Sr. Dora Ramirez, R.F.R.; Sr. Carmen Garcia, R.F.R.
Mailing Address: P.O. Box 926, 71463-0926.
Res., 207 Meadow Dr., 71463. Tel: 318-335-3780; Fax: 318-335-0708. [CEM]
Catechesis/Religious Programs—Students 108.
Convent—1011 E. 7th Ave., 71463. Tel: 318-335-4390.
Mission—Elizabeth, Allen Parish, St. Frances, P.O. Box 926, 71463-0926. Tel: 318-335-3790.

Oberlin, Allen Parish, St. Joan of Arc (1920), Rev. Joseph McGrath; Deacon Norris Chapman.
Res., 110 W. Fifth Ave., P.O. Box 479, 70655. Tel: 318-639-4399; 639-4798. [CEM]
Catechesis/Religious Programs—Gloria Taylor, D.R.E.
Students 258.
Mission—Soileau, Allen Parish, St. Joseph, P.O. Box 479, 70655.

Raymond, Jefferson Davis Parish, St. Lawrence, Rev. Fred F. Russi.
Res., 5505 Pine Island Hwy., Jennings, 70546. Tel: 318-584-2700.

Sulphur, Calcasieu Parish,

1—IMMACULATE CONCEPTION OF THE B.V.M., (1959), Rev. Egidio A. Vecchio, M.S.; Sr. Theresa Croteau, S.S.J., Pastoral Assoc. In res., Rev. Innocent Obiulewu.
Res., 1200 Shasta Dr., 70663. Tel: 318-625-3364; Fax: 318-625-9547.
Catechesis/Religious Programs—Beth Richard, D.R.E.
Students 408.

2—OUR LADY OF LASALETTE, Revs. Joseph A. Decoteau, M.S.; Lawrence A. Kohler, M.S.
Res., 602 N. Claiborne St., 70663. Tel: 318-527-6722.
Catechesis/Religious Programs—Tel: 318-527-8307. Stella Barkate, D.R.E.
Students 505.

3—OUR LADY OF PROMPT SUCCOR, (1919), Revs. Donald Thomas, M.S.; George Repchick, M.S.; Charles A. Gendron, M.S.; William O'Brien, M.S.; Bro. Donald V. Smith, M.S.
Res., 1109 Cypress St., 70663. Tel: 318-527-5261; Fax: 318-528-2991.
School—Tel: 318-527-7828; Fax: 318-528-3778. Mrs. Sharon Tolin, Prin.
Lay Teachers 19; Students 258.
Catechesis/Religious Programs—1029 Lasalette Dr., 70663. Tel: 318-527-9964. D.R.E.: Theresa Cooper; Terry Sittig.
Students 420.
Mission—Sulphur, Calcasieu Parish, St. Peter Claver, 465 Maple St., 70663. Tel: 318-527-5987.

4—ST. THERESA, (1971), Rev. Francis Fitzsimmons, M.S.; Mary Little, Admin.
Res., 4822 Carlyss Dr., 70663. Tel: 318-583-4800.
Catechesis/Religious Programs—Tel: 318-583-4010. Charlotte Giese, D.R.E.
Students 306.

Vinton, Calcasieu Parish, St. Joseph, Rev. Charles L. Soileau.
Res., 1502 Industrial, 70668. Tel: 318-589-7358; Fax: 318-589-7843.
Catechesis/Religious Programs—Students 400.
Missions—Edgerly, St. John Evangelist; Starks, St. Michael.

Welsh, Jefferson Davis Parish, Our Lady of the Seven Dolors (1904), Rev. Herbert May.
Res., P.O. Box 515, 70591. Tel: 318-734-3446; Fax: 318-734-3697. [CEM][JC]
Catechesis/Religious Programs—Tel: 318-734-3848. Betty LaBouve, D.R.E.
Students 324.
Mission—Roanoke, Jefferson Davis Parish, St. Mary, P.O. Box 515, 70581.

St. Joseph (1941) (African American), Rev. Donatus Ugochukwu Anosike, M.S.P.
Res., P.O. Box 607, 70591. Tel: 318-734-3673. [JC]
Mission—Iowa, Calcasieu Parish, St. Peter Claver, 400 W. 2nd St., 70547.

Westlake, Calcasieu Parish, St. John Bosco (1955), Rev. Msgr. Joseph A. Bourque; Deacons Fred Reed, Jr.; Garrett Caraway, Jr. In res., Rev. Msgr. Amos J. Vincent; Rev. Cyprian Eze.
Res., P.O. Box 66, 70669. Tel: 318-433-2467; Fax: 318-436-7766.
Catechesis/Religious Programs—Tel: 318-439-6585; Fax: 318-436-9766. D.R.E.: Fred Reed; Judy Reed.
Students 518.

Chaplains of Public Institutions

LAKE CHARLES. *Lake Charles Memorial Hospital*. Rev. Al Volpe.

DEQUINCY. *Phelps Correctional Center*. Rev. Jude Brunnert, M.S., Chap.

JENNINGS. *American Legion Hospital*. Rev. Scott Desormeaux.

SULPHUR. *West Clacasieu Cameron Hospital*. Rev. William P. O'Brien, M.S., Chap.

On Special Assignment:
Reverend Fathers—
Harris, Whitney G., Dir. Ministry Relations, McNeese State University, Lake Charles, LA 70605. Tel: 318-475-5426

On Duty Outside the Diocese:
Reverend Fathers—
Lopez-Velez, Mauricio, 131 Bank St., San Antonio, TX 78204
Miles, James, 115 Gladys Ave., Lansdowne, MD 21227
Mullen, Thomas, 70 Nutwell Ct., Lothian, MD 20711

Graduate Studies:
Reverend Fathers—
Borel, Albert W., St. Paul University, Ottawa,Canada
Esbind, Jace, St. Paul University, Ottawa, Canada

Retired:
Reverend Monsignors—
Daigle, Jules O., Box 266, Welsh, LA 70591
DeBlanc, Irving A., 1505 Jeff Ln., Lake Charles, LA 70605
Reverend Fathers—
Herlong, Theophilus L., 5635 B Welcome Rd., Lake Charles, LA 70611
Smit, Gerard C., 105 Justice Way, Elkton, MD 21921

Permanent Deacons:
Broussard, Gordon, St. Raphael, IA
Caraway, Julius G., Jr., St. John Bosco Church, Westlake
Chapman, Norris, St. Joan of Arc, Oberlin
Dronet, Manny, Immaculate Conception, Maplewood
Eaves, John, St. Paul, Elton
Granger, James R., St. Henry, Lake Charles
Kohlhund, Sumner, St. Joseph's, De Ridder
Landry, Dan, St. Margaret, Lake Charles
LaPoint, Frederick, St. Philip Neri, Kinder
Lavine, Edward, Sacred Heart, Lake Charles
Mathews, Michael, Supt. of Schools, Diocese of Lake Charles
McNally, Ed, Immaculate Conception, Jennings
Michaels, Richard, Immaculate Conception, Maplewood
Normantowicz, Edmund, Our Lady of the Lake, Lake Arthur
Reed, Frederick, St. John Bosco, Westlake
Reynolds, Jack J., St. Theodore's, Lake Charles
Segura, John, Our Lady Help of Christians, Jennings
St. Mary, Harry, Jr., Immaculate Heart of Mary, Lake Charles
Stearns, George, Our Lady of Good Counsel, Lake Charles
Thompson, Paul, Holy City Community, Lake Charles
Wagner, Harry E., Jr., Immaculate Conception Cathedral, Lake Charles
White, Milton, Immaculate Conception Cathedral, Lake Charles

INSTITUTIONS LOCATED IN THE DIOCESE

[A] HIGH SCHOOLS, INTERPAROCHIAL

LAKE CHARLES. *St. Louis High School*, 1620 Bank St., 70601. Tel: 318-436-7275. Vic Bonnaffee, Prin. Lay Teachers 39; Students 483.
For Catholic Studies: 920 Seventh St. Tel: 318-439-7432. Very Rev. John H. Giles, Jr., Vicar of Christian Formation.

[B] GENERAL HOSPITALS

LAKE CHARLES. *St. Patrick Hospital of Lake Charles*, 524 S. Ryan St., 70601. Tel: 318-436-2511.
For a complete listing, refer to the Hospitals section.

[C] RETREAT HOUSES

LAKE CHARLES. *Holy City Community*, 2409A Second St., 70601. Tel: 318-439-6194. Deacon Ed McNally, Moderator; Mr. Daniel Lowery, Admin.; Rev. Oris Broussard, Chap.

MOSS BLUFF. *St. Charles Center*, 2151 Sam Houston Jones Pkwy., 70611. Tel: 318-855-1232; Fax: 318-855-9062. Rev. Don Piraro, Dir.

[D] MONASTERIES AND RESIDENCES OF PRIESTS AND BROTHERS

ELTON.
Herald of Good News, Inc., P.O. Box 789, 70532. Tel: 318-584-2038.

[E] SPECIAL RESIDENCES

LAKE CHARLES. *Our Lady Queen of Heaven Manor*, Villa Maria, 3905 Kingston St., 70607. Tel: 318-478-4780. Rev. Msgr. Irving A. DeBlanc, Pres. Units 62.

[F] NEWMAN CENTERS

LAKE CHARLES. *Catholic Student Center*, McNeese State University, 221 Aqua Dr., 70605. Rev. Whitney Miller.

[G] SOCIAL SERVICE CENTERS

LAKE CHARLES. *Catholic Service Center*, 1938 E. Broad St., 70601. Kathryn Malveaux, Dir.

[H] MISCELLANEOUS

LAKE CHARLES. *School Food Services of Lake Charles, Inc.*, 4029 Ave. G, 70615.

RELIGIOUS INSTITUTES OF MEN REPRESENTED IN THE DIOCESE

For further details refer to the corresponding bracketed number in the Religious Institutes of Men or Women section.

[0600]—*Brothers of the Congregation of Holy Cross.*—C.S.C.

[0275]—*Carmelites of Mary Immaculate.*—C.M.I.

[]—*Heralds of Good News.*

[0690]—*Jesuit Fathers and Brothers.*—S.J.

[0720]—*The Missionaries of Our Lady of La Salette.* (Prov. of Mary Queen).—M.S.

[]—*Missionaries of St. Paul.*

[0700]—*St. Joseph's Society of the Sacred Heart.*—S.S.J.

[0420]—*Society of the Divine Word.*—S.V.D.

RELIGIOUS INSTITUTES OF WOMEN REPRESENTED IN THE DIOCESE

[1010]—*Congregation of Divine Providence of San Antonio, Texas.*—C.D.P.

[0470]—*Congregation of the Sisters of Charity of the Incarnate Word, Houston, Texas.*—C.C.V.I.

[]—*Daughters of Mary, Mother of Mercy.*

[1140]—*Eucharistic Missionaries of St. Dominic.*—O.P.

[]—*Franciscan Sisters of Our Lady of Refuge.*—R.F.R.

[]—*Sisters of Emanuel.*—S.E.

[3830-16]—*Sisters of St. Joseph.*—S.S.J.

NECROLOGY

† Shreve, Robert, (Retired). —Died Feb. 24, 1996.

Diocese of Lansing

(Dioecesis Lansingensis)

Most Reverend

CARL F. MENGELING, D.D., S.T.D.

Bishop of Lansing; ordained May 25, 1957; appointed Bishop of Lansing November 7, 1995; consecrated and installed January 25, 1996. *Address all communications to Chancery: 300 W. Ottawa St., Lansing, MI, 48933.* Tel.: 517-342-2452; Fax: 517-342-2505.

Most Reverend

KENNETH J. POVISH, D.D.

Retired Bishop of Lansing; ordained June 3, 1950; appointed Bishop of Crookston July 28, 1970; consecrated September 29, 1970; appointed Bishop of Lansing October 8, 1975; installed December 11, 1975; retired November 7, 1995. *Res., 401-A E. Madison, DeWitt, MI, 48820.*

ESTABLISHED MAY 22, 1937.

CANONICALLY ERECTED AUGUST 4, 1937.

Square Miles 6,218.

Comprises the Counties of Clinton, Eaton, Genesee, Hillsdale, Ingham, Jackson, Lenawee, Livingston, Shiawassee and Washtenaw, in the State of Michigan.

For legal titles of parishes and diocesan institutions, consult the Chancery Office.

Chancery: 300 W. Ottawa St., Lansing, MI, 48933. Tel.: 517-342-2440; Fax: 517-342-2515.

STATISTICAL OVERVIEW

Personnel	
Bishop	1
Retired Bishops	1
Priests: Diocesan Active in Diocese	100
Priests: Active Outside Diocese	8
Priests: Retired, Sick or Absent	33
Number of Diocesan Priests	141
Religious Priests in Diocese	28
Extern Priests in Diocese	10
Ordinations:	
Permanent Deacons in Diocese	59
Total Brothers	9
Total Sisters	441
Parishes	
Parishes	93
With Resident Pastor:	
Resident Diocesan Priests	75
Resident Religious Priests	8
Without Resident Pastor:	
Administered by Priests	1
Administered by Women Religious	7
Administered by Lay People	2
Missions	1
Pastoral Centers	1
Professional Ministry Personnel:	
Lay Ministers	400
Welfare	
Catholic Hospitals	7
Total Assisted	1,612,137
Health Care Centers	4
Total Assisted	7,518
Homes for the Aged	2
Total Assisted	258
Residential Care of Children	3
Total Assisted	270
Day Care and Extended Day Care Centers	2
Total Assisted	267
Special Centers for Social Services	5
Total Assisted	11,151
Residential Care of Disabled	1
Total Assisted	65
Educational	
Diocesan Students in Other Seminaries	27
Total Seminarians	27
Colleges and Universities	1
Total Students	2,026
High Schools, Diocesan and Parish	4
Total Students	2,382
High Schools, Private	1
Total Students	136
Elementary Schools, Diocesan and Parish	38
Total Students	10,030
Elementary Schools, Private	1
Total Students	340
Catechesis/Religious Education:	
High School Students	3,190
Elementary Students	20,245
Total Students Under Catholic Instruction	38,376
Teachers in the Diocese:	
Priests	5
Brothers	1
Sisters	18
Lay Teachers	599
Vital Statistics	
Receptions into the Church:	
Infant Baptism Totals	4,222
Adult Baptism Totals	642
Received into Full Communion	851
First Communions	4,256
Confirmations	3,471
Marriages:	
Catholic	964
Interfaith	729
Total Marriages	1,693
Deaths	1,953
Total Catholic Population	223,536
Total Population	1,670,223

Former Bishops—Most Rev. JOSEPH H. ALBERS, D.D., J.C.D., appt. Titular Bishop of Lunda and Auxiliary to the Archbishop of Cincinnati, Dec. 16, 1929; cons. Dec. 27, 1929; appt. first Bishop of Lansing, Aug. 4, 1937; died Dec. 1, 1965.—Most Rev. ALEXANDER M. ZALESKI, D.D., S.S.L., appt. Titular Bishop of Lyrbe and Auxiliary of Detroit, March 28, 1950; cons. May 23, 1950; transferred to Lansing Oct. 7, 1964; acceded See Dec. 1, 1965; died May 16, 1975.—Most Rev. KENNETH J. POVISH, D.D., appt. Bishop of Crookston, July 28, 1970; cons. Sept. 29, 1970; appt. Bishop of Lansing, Oct. 8, 1975; installed Dec. 11, 1975; retired Nov. 7, 1995.

Chancery—300 W. Ottawa St., Lansing, 48933. Tel: 517-342-2440; Fax: 517-342-2515. Office Hours: Mon.-Fri. 8-4:30 Address all communications to this office.

Office of the Bishop—SALLY ELLIS, Admin. Asst. to the Bishop, *300 W. Ottawa St., Lansing, 48933.* Tel: 517-342-2452; Fax: 517-342-2505.

Moderator of the Curia/Chancellor—Rev. Msgr. JAMES A. MURRAY, *300 W. Ottawa St., Lansing, 48933.* Tel: 517-342-2449; Fax: 517-342-2505.

Vicar-General—Rev. SYLVESTER L. FEDEWA, *St. Gerard Parish, 4437 W. Willow, Lansing, 48917-2109.* Tel: 517-323-2379.

Regional Vicars—Lansing: Rev. BERNARD REILLY; Livingston: Rev. THOMAS THOMPSON; Genesee-Owosso: Rev. JOHN KLEIN; Jackson: Rev. JAMES SHAVER; Lenewee: Rev. DANIEL WHEELER; Washtenaw: Rev. CHARLES IRVIN.

Vice Chancellor—Rev. GEORGE C. MICHALEK, (see Chancery Address).

Vicar for Charismatic Communities—Rev. PHILIP DUPUIS, *St. Mary Church, 14200 Old U.S. 12, Chelsea, 48118.* Tel: 313-475-1697.

Vicar for Religious—Rev. MICHAEL D. MURPHY, *St. Thomas Aquinas Parish, 955 Alton Rd., East Lansing, 48823.* Tel: 517-351-7215; 7216.

Vicar for Vietnamese Apostolate—Rev. JOSEPH TRAN, *St. Mary Cathedral, 219 Seymour Ave., Lansing, 48933.* Tel: 517-484-5331.

Ecumenical Officer—Rev. ROBERT T. KERR, *St. Joseph, 9425 Whittaker Rd., Ypsilanti, 48197.* Tel: 313-461-6555; Fax: 313-461-1444.

Commissions and Councils—

Diocesan Consultors—Revs. THOMAS BUTLER; SYLVESTER FEDEWA; PAUL GREHL; MARK INGLOT; ROBERT IRISH; ROBERT KERR; JOHN KLEIN; DAN MCKEAN; ROGER PROKOP; DARIN ROBERT; DONALD RUSCH; ALFRED RUSSELL.

Pastoral Council—Sr. RITA WENZLICK, O.P., Exec. Sec., *300 W. Ottawa St., Lansing, 48933.* Tel: 517-342-2502.

Presbyteral Council—Rev. MARK INGLOT, *606 S. Wisner St., Jackson, 49203.* Tel: 517-783-2748.

Board of Education—MARY MATTHEWS, Pres., *747 Beverly Park, Jackson, 49203.* Tel: 517-789-8798.

Building Commission—Rev. GILBERT O. RAHRIG, *440 E. Washington, Howell, 48843.* Tel: 517-546-0090.

Cursillo Movement—Vacant.

Conciliation/Arbitration—WILLIAM D. PARSLEY, *232 S. Capitol, Ste. 1000, Lansing, 48933.* Tel: 517-482-2400.

Finance Council—Rev. DAVID M. STOTENBUR, *Immaculate Heart of Mary Church, 3815 S. Cedar St.,*

Lansing, 48910-4596. Tel: 517-393-3030.
Priest's Assignment Commission—Contact the Bishop's office at 517-342-2452.

Diocesan Offices And Departments

Office of Moderator of the Curia—Rev. Msgr. JAMES A. MURRAY, J.C.L. Tel: 517-342-2449; Fax: 517-342-2505.
Diocesan Archivist—Rev. GEORGE C. MICHALEK, *300 W. Ottawa St., Lansing, 48933.* Tel: 517-485-9902.
Diocesan Mission Office—(Includes Propagation of the Faith, Holy Childhood Assoc., Inter-Parish Sharing) Rev. PHILIP P. GALLAGHER, Dir., *300 W. Ottawa St., Lansing, 48933.* Tel: 517-342-2451.
Joseph H. Albers Trust Fund for Diocesan Vocations—LOUIS A. CLARK, Chm., *300 W. Ottawa St., Lansing, 48933.* Tel: 517-342-2449.
Legal Advisor—CAMILLE S. ABOOD. Tel: 517-342-2456.
Diocesan Tribunal—
Judicial Vicar—Rev. DAVID M. STOTENBUR, J.C.L., *300 W. Ottawa St., Lansing, 48933.* Tel: 517-484-8870. (Address all rogatory commissions to the Diocesan Tribunal.). Fax: 517-484-9080.
Tribunal Judges—Revs. JAMES A. MURRAY, J.C.L.; STEVEN J. RAICA, J.C.D.
Defender of the Bond—Rev. BENNETT P. CONSTANTINE, J.C.D.
Promoter of Justice, Assessor-Auditor—Rev. STEVEN J. RAICA, J.C.D.
Court-Expert—RICHARD G. STRIFE, Ph.D.
Notaries—VIRGINIA A. DELUCA; WANDA D. MILLER.
Fiscal and Public Affairs—RONALD D. HENDERSON, Chm., *300 W. Ottawa, Lansing, 48933.* Tel: 517-342-2448; Fax: 517-342-2519.
Cemeteries—THOMAS PASTULA, *300 W. Ottawa St., Lansing, 48933.* Tel: 517-342-2442.
Communications—MICHAEL DIEBOLD, *300 W. Ottawa St., Lansing, 48933.* Tel: 517-342-2475.
Development—JAY JOHNSON, *300 W. Ottawa St., Lansing, 48933.* Tel: 517-342-2503.
Finance Officer—RONALD D. HENDERSON, *300 W. Ottawa St., Lansing, 48933.* Tel: 517-342-2448; Fax: 517-342-2519.
Real Estate/Environmental Issues—CHARLES BAKER, *300 W. Ottawa St., Lansing, 48933.* Tel: 517-342-2443.
Catholic Charities—ROBERT J. SMITH, A.C.S.W., Chm., *300 W. Ottawa St., Lansing, 48933.* Tel: 517-342-2462; Fax: 517-342-2446.
Aging Ministry—ELLEN MCKAY, A.C.S.W., Dir., *300 W. Ottawa St., Lansing, 48933.* Tel: 517-342-2467.
Bishop's Council on Alcoholism-Chemical Dependency—SANDRA MILLAR, Dir., *300 W. Ottawa St., Lansing, 48933.* Tel: 517-342-2471.
Campaign for Human Development—VIRGINIA SOVIS, Coord., *300 W. Ottawa St., Lansing, 48933.* Tel: 517-342-2470.
Catholic Relief Services—VIRGINIA SOVIS, Coord., *300 W. Ottawa St., Lansing, 48933.* Tel: 517-342-2470.
Parish Social Ministry—STEPHEN RALL, M.A., Dir., *300 W. Ottawa St., Lansing, 48933.* Tel: 517-342-2469.
Peace and Justice Ministry—Vacant.
Respect Life Ministry—Vacant.
Project Rachel (Post-Abortion Counseling)—TONI ROSSI, Dir., *1500 E. Saginaw, Lansing, 48906.* Tel: 517-484-4449; Fax: 517-484-8880.
Women, Poverty & Age—JOHANNA VANDEN BERG, *300 W. Ottawa St., Lansing, 48933.* Tel: 517-342-2465.
Education and Formation—Sr. DORITA WOTISKA, O.P., Ph.D., Chm., *300 W. Ottawa St., Lansing, 48933.* Tel: 517-342-2479; Fax: 517-342-2515.
Superintendent of Schools—Sr. DORITA WOTISKA, O.P., *300 W. Ottawa St., Lansing, 48933.* Tel: 517-342-2481.
Director of Instructional Programs PreK-12—MARY OLIVE DION, *300 W. Ottawa St., Lansing, 48933.* Tel: 517-342-2483.
Director of Catechesis—PETER RIES, *300 W. Ottawa St., Lansing, 48933.* Tel: 517-342-2486.
Director of Youth Ministry—Vacant.
Director of Lay Ministry—MARY TARDIF, *300 W. Ottawa St., Lansing, 48933.* Tel: 517-342-2512.
Director of Permanent Diaconate—Deacon JOHN CAMERON, *300 W. Ottawa St., Lansing, 48933.* Tel: 517-342-2509.
Priestly Life and Ministry—Rev. LARRY DELANEY, Dir., *300 W. Ottawa St., Lansing, 48933.* Tel: 517-669-8321 or 669-8279; Fax: 517-669-2708.
Director of Seminarians—Rev. J. THOMAS MUNLEY, *300 W. Ottawa St., Lansing, 48933.* Tel: 517-342-2507.
Director of Vocation Services—Sr. CARLA MOEGGENBORG, O.P., *300 W. Ottawa St., Lansing, 48933.* Tel: 517-342-2506.
Formation Houses—
Emmaus House—Rev. J. THOMAS MUNLEY, Dir., *320 M.A.C. Ave., East Lansing, 48823.* Tel: 517-351-1543.
CHIRHO—Rev. ROGER PROKOP, Dir., *St. Thomas the Apostle, 517 Elizabeth St., Ann Arbor, 48104.* Tel: 313-761-8606.
Diocesan Ministries—Sr. RITA WENZLICK, O.P., Chm., *300 W. Ottawa St., Lansing, 48933.* Tel: 517-342-2502; Fax: 517-342-2468.
Campus Ministries—AUDREY BROSNAN, *St. Mary Student Parish, Ann Arbor, 48104-2295.* Tel: 313-663-0557.
Christian Initiation Steering Committee—Sr. RITA WENZLICK, O.P., Chm., *300 W. Ottawa St., Lansing, 48933.* Tel: 517-342-2502.
Ministry with Persons with Disabilities/Deaf Ministry—RICHARD STRIFE, Ph.D., Dir.; Sr. MARLENE TAYLOR, A.D., Outreach Worker, *300 W. Ottawa St., Lansing, 48933.* Tel: 517-342-2497; 342-2500.
Hispanic/Migrant Ministry—SERAPIO C. HERNANDEZ, *300 W. Ottawa St., Lansing, 48933.* Tel: 517-342-2498.
Young Adult Ministry/Criminal Justice Ministry—GARY ASHBY, *300 W. Ottawa St., Lansing, 48933.* Tel: 517-342-2495.
Worship Office—Rev. PHILLIP D. SESSIONS, Dir. RITA THIRON, Assoc. Dir., *300 W. Ottawa St., Lansing, 48933.* Tel: 517-342-2480.
Worship Commission—Sr. LAURENA ALFLEN. Tel: 517-653-2377.
Music Consultant—WILLIAM ROWAN. Tel: 517-484-5332.
Liturigical Commission Publishings—MARY JO GILLILLAND, Mng. Editor, *1500 E. Saginaw St., Ste. #1, Lansing, 48906.* Tel: 517-484-4449; Fax: 517-484-8880.
Black Catholic Ministry—Vacant.

CLERGY, PARISHES, MISSIONS AND PAROCHIAL SCHOOLS

CITY OF LANSING
(Ingham County)

1—ST. MARY CATHEDRAL (1866), Revs. James A. Murray; George C. Michalek; Peter Nickels. In res., Rev. Joseph Tran.
Res., 219 Seymour, 48933. Tel: 517-484-5332; Fax: 517-484-0475.

2—ST. CASIMIR (1921), Rev. Raymond M. Rademacher; Deacon Ronald Henderson. In res., Rev. Steve Raica.
Res., 815 Sparrow Ave., 48910-8003. Tel: 517-482-1347; Fax: 517-482-1313.
Catechesis/Religious Programs—Tel: 517-482-1346.
Students 250.

3—HOLY CROSS (1924), Rev. Cyprian Uline, O.F.M.Conv.; Deacon David L. Purvis. In res., Revs. Timothy Byrnes; Bonaventure Crowley.
Res., 1611 Oakland Ave., 48915. Tel: 517-484-7768; Fax: 517-484-5741.
School—1514 W. Saginaw St., 48915. Tel: 517-487-6079. Michael Marshall, Prin.
Dominican Sister 1; Lay Teachers 10; Students 132.
Catechesis/Religious Programs—Students 51.

4—IMMACULATE HEART OF MARY (1949), Revs. David M. Stotenbur; Patrick Cwik; Deacons William Fudge, III; John Cameron; Oliver G. Washington. In res., Rev. Raymond Goehring.
Office: 3815 S. Cedar, 48910. Tel: 517-393-3030; Fax: 517-393-0855.
School—Tel: 517-882-6631.
Lay Teachers 22; Students 414.
Catechesis/Religious Programs—Tel: 517-393-3033.
Students 570.

5—RESURRECTION (1922), Revs. William J. Koenigsknecht; William J. Turner (Canada).
Res., 1531 E. Michigan Ave., 48912. Tel: 517-482-4749; Fax: 517-484-4740.
School—Tel: 517-487-0439.
Lay Teachers 13; Students 202.
Catechesis/Religious Programs—1527 E. Michigan Ave., 48912. Tel: 517-482-2605.
Students 104.

6—ST. GERARD (Delta Township, Eaton Co.) (1958), Revs. Sylvester L. Fedewa; Brendan J. Walsh; Deacons Edwin Schneider; Robert McPhilamy; Richard Savage. In res., Rev. Michael Rejent, O.S.F.S.
Res., 4437 W. Willow, 48917. Tel: 517-323-2379; Fax: 517-886-1394. [JC]
School—4433 W. Willow, 48917. Tel: 517-323-6126.
Lay Teachers 25; Students 543.
Catechesis/Religious Programs—Tel: 517-321-4179.
Students 471.

7—ST. THERESE (1949), Rev. Michael W. Kuchar; Sr. Margaret Ann Roggenbuck, O.P., Pastoral Min.; Deacon David Borzenski.
Res., 102 W. Randolph St., 48906. Tel: 517-487-3749; Fax: 517-487-3755.
School—2620 N. Turner St., 48906. Tel: 517-482-1634. Mrs. Elissa Greenburg, Prin.
Lay Teachers 14; Students 203.
Catechesis/Religious Programs—Tel: 517-482-4152. Ms. Rita Parisi, D.R.E.
Students 180.

8—CRISTO REY (1961) (Hispanic), Rev. Frederick L. Thelen; Sr. Mercedes Dominguez, C.F.P.; Deacon Rogelio Alfaro.
Office: 5430 S. Washington, 48911. Tel: 517-394-4639; Fax: 517-394-8090.
Res., 820 Mel Ave., 48911. Tel: 517-394-0676.
Catechesis/Religious Programs—Students 135.

OUTSIDE THE CITY OF LANSING

Adrian, Lenawee Co., St. Joseph (1864), Rev. James W. Lothamer, S.S.
Res., 415 Ormsby St., 49221. Tel: 517-265-8938. [CEM]
Catechesis/Religious Programs—Tel: 517-265-3732.
Students 216.
Convent—404 Finch St., 49221. Tel: 517-263-1973.
St. Mary of Good Counsel (1853), Rev. Louis A. Komorowski, O.S.F.S.; Deacons Richard Bayes, Jr.; Calistro Torres; Sr. Regina Albers, C.P.P.S. In res., Revs. Robert Mossett, O.S.F.S.; Robert F. Schramm, O.S.F.S.; Jeffrey L. Persons, O.S.F.S.
Office: 305 Division St., 49221. Tel: 517-263-4681; Fax: 517-263-4682.
Res., 320 Division St., 49221. Tel: 517-265-4160; Fax: 517-263-4682. [CEM]
Catechesis/Religious Programs—Tel: 517-265-4160.
Students 336.

Ann Arbor, Washtenaw Co.,
1—ST. FRANCIS OF ASSISI, (1950), Revs. Charles E. Irvin; John A. Byers.
Res., 2150 Frieze Ave., 48104. Tel: 313-769-2550; Fax: 313-769-2550.
School—(Grades K-8). Tel: 313-665-8082.
Lay Teachers 25; Students 546.
Catechesis/Religious Programs—Tel: 313-663-9663.
Students 747.

2—ST. PATRICK, (1831), Rev. Terrence J. Dumas.
Res., 5671 Whitmore Lake Rd., 48105. Tel: 313-662-8141; 663-1851; Fax: 313-662-8142. [CEM]

3—ST. THOMAS THE APOSTLE, (1835), Revs. Roger Prokop; William Ashbaugh; Deacons James Miles; Warren Hecht. In res., Rev. Richard C. Lobert (BAL).
Res., 517 Elizabeth St., 48104. Tel: 313-761-8606; Fax: 313-997-8432. [CEM]
School—Tel: 313-769-0911; Fax: 313-769-9078.
Sisters 1; Lay Teachers 16; Students 298.
Catechesis/Religious Programs—Tel: 313-761-8606; Fax: 313-665-2484. Joanne McGinnis.
Students 403.

4—ST. MARY STUDENT PARISH, (1915), Rev. William J. Stevenson. Pastoral Assocs.: Rev. William F. Wegher; Sr. Linda R. Lenc; Dr. Audrey M. Brosnan; Grace M. Girvan.
Office: 331 Thompson St., 48104. Tel: 313-663-0557; 0558; Fax: 313-663-2756. (Serving students, faculty, and staff at the University of Michigan.).

Bellevue, Eaton Co., St. Ann (1923). (Independent Mission). Rev. Stephen Raica; Deacon James Mathias.
Res., 312 S. Main St., 49021. Tel: 616-763-9372.

Blissfield, Lenawee Co., St. Peter the Apostle (1910), Rev. Randall J. Miller; Deacon James Martinez.
Res., 309 S. Lane St., 49228. Tel: 517-486-2156.
Catechesis/Religious Programs—Students 100.

Brighton, Livingston Co., St. Mary Magdalen Church (1993),
Res., 2201 Old U.S. 23, 48116. Tel: 810-229-8624; Fax: 810-229-6471. Rev. David Howell; Deacon H. David Scharf.
Catechesis/Religious Programs—Students 445.
St. Patrick (1832) (Irish), Revs. Thomas W. Thompson; Keith L. Horstman; Deacon Patrick A. McDonald. Pastoral Assocs.: Margaret Mullally-Henne; Mary W. Rhadigan. In res., Rev. William J. Carolin.
Res., 711 Rickett Rd., 48116. Tel: 810-229-9863; Fax: 810-220-0730. [CEM]
School—710 Rickett Rd., 48116. Tel: 810-229-7946; Fax: 810-229-6206.
Lay Teachers 16; Students 266.
Catechesis/Religious Programs—Tel: 810-229-4221; Fax: 810-229-6206. Sr. Theresa M. Fifer, D.R.E.
Students 884.

Brooklyn, Lenawee Co., St. Joseph's Shrine (Irish Hills) (1845), Rev. Alfred Russell, O.S.F.S.

Res., 8743 U.S. 12, 49230. Tel: 517-467-2183; Fax: 517-467-4285. [CEM]
Catechesis/Religious Programs—Tel: 517-467-2106.
Students 277.

Burton, Genesee Co., Blessed Sacrament (1957) (Hungarian), Rev. Denis R. Spitzley.
Res., 6340 Roberta, 48509. Tel: 810-742-3151; Fax: 810-742-1409.
Catechesis/Religious Programs—Tel: 810-742-3196. Carol Garbacik, D.R.E.
Students 81.

Holy Redeemer, Rev. Vincent DeLorenzo; Earl Matte, Pastoral Min.
Res., 1227 E. Bristol Rd., 48529. Tel: 810-743-3050; Fax: 810-743-4381.
School—3468 S. Grand Traverse, 48529. Tel: 810-743-2520; Fax: 810-743-9102. Carol Olson, Prin.
Lay Teachers 14; Students 231.
Catechesis/Religious Programs—Tel: 810-742-9460. Susan Kachel, D.R.E.
Students 320.

Charlotte, Eaton Co., St. Mary (1868), Rev. Thomas D. Nenneau.
Res., 812 St. Mary Blvd., 48813. Tel: 517-543-4319; Fax: 517-543-9078.
School—905 St. Mary Blvd., 48813. Tel: 517-543-3460.
Lay Teachers 6; Students 105.
Catechesis/Religious Programs—Tel: 517-543-3460.
Students 217.

Chelsea, Washtenaw Co., St. Mary (1845), Rev. Philip Dupuis; Deacon Richard Shaneyfelt.
Res., 14200 Old U.S. 12, 48118. Tel: 313-475-1697; Fax: 313-475-3207. [CEM]
Catechesis/Religious Programs—Tel: 313-475-8164; Fax: 313-475-3250.
Students 427.

Clarklake, Jackson Co., St. Rita (1916), Rev. Lehr Barkenquest, O.S.F.S.; Deacon Louis Weitzel.
Res., 10720 Hayes Rd., 49234. Tel: 517-592-5470; Fax: 517-592-4098.
Catechesis/Religious Programs—Tel: 517-592-5718.
Students 331.

Clinton, Lenawee Co., St. Dominic's (1853), Rev. Donald P. Rusch.
Res., 220 Brown St., 49236. Tel: 517-456-4559. [CEM]
Catechesis/Religious Programs—Students 84.

Clio, Genesee Co., SS. Charles and Helena (1953), Rev. Paul Guoan. In res., Rev. Eoin Murphy (Ireland).
Res., 230 E. Vienna St., 48420-1423. Tel: 810-686-9861; Fax: 810-686-8070.
Catechesis/Religious Programs—Tel: 810-686-6720.
Students 441.

Concord, Jackson Co., St. Catherine Laboure (1953), Patricia Robertson, Pastoral Coord.
Res., 211 Hanover St., P.O. Box 188, 49237. Tel: 517-524-7578.
Catechesis/Religious Programs—Students 110.

Davison, Genesee Co., St. John (1871), Rev. Andrew A. Czajkowski; Deacons Claude Spencer; Robert Poulson; Neil Huiskens; Dan Fairweather. In res., Rev. Leroy White.
Res., 404 N. Dayton St., 48423-1397. Tel: 810-653-2377; 653-8015; Fax: 810-658-1123. [CEM]
Catechesis/Religious Programs—425 N. Genesee, 48423. Tel: 810-653-4056. D.R.E.: Elaine Davis; Eve Houghtaling.
Students 668.

Deerfield, Lenawee Co., St. Alphonsus (1864), Rev. James F. Eisele.
Church Office: 222 Carey St., 49238. Tel: 517-447-3500; Fax: 517-447-3210. [CEM]
Catechesis/Religious Programs—Students 152.

St. Augustine, Livingston Co., (1843). (Quasi Parish). Rev. Carl A. Simon; Deacon Bernard J. Endebrock.
Res., 6481 Fausset Rd., Howell, 48843. Tel: 517-546-9807. [CEM]
Parish House: Tel: 810-750-0354.
Catechesis/Religious Programs—Students 203.

De Witt, Clinton Co., St. Jude (1971), Rev. Bernard L. Reilly.
Res., 409 N. Wilson, P.O. Box 280, 48820. Tel: 517-669-8335; Fax: 517-669-8343.
Catechesis/Religious Programs—Tel: 517-669-8341.
Students 323.

Dexter, Washtenaw Co., St. Joseph (1840), Rev. Bernard L. Tyler.
Res., 3430 Dover St., 48130. Tel: 313-426-8483; Fax: 313-426-6451. [CEM]
Catechesis/Religious Programs—Tel: 313-426-2674; 426-6451.
Students 360.

Durand, Shiawassee Co., St. Mary (1900), Rev. Joseph Aubin.
Res., 700 Columbia Dr., 48429. Tel: 517-288-6704.
Catechesis/Religious Programs—Tel: 512-288-6704.
Students 240.

East Lansing, Ingham Co., St. John the Evangelist, Student Parish (1958), Rev. Thomas D. McDevitt. In res., Revs. Peter C. Dougherty; Jay Munley. Campus Ministers: Sr. Mary Ann Warner, H.M.; Liz Schweitzer; Al Weilbaecher; Sr. Kathleen Kurta, O.S.F.
Res., 327 MAC, 48823. Tel: 517-337-9778.

St. Thomas Aquinas (1940), Revs. Michael D. Murphy; Michael J. Williams; Deacon Stephen Hilker.
Res., 955 Alton Rd., 48823. Tel: 517-351-7215; Fax: 517-351-7271.
School—915 Alton Rd., 48823. Tel: 517-332-0813.
Lay Teachers 24; Students 490.
Catechesis/Religious Programs—Tel: 517-351-5460.
Students 580.

Eaton Rapids, Eaton Co., St. Peter (1881), Rev. Bennett Constantine.
Res., 515 E. Knight St., 48827. Tel: 517-663-4735; Fax: 517-663-7110.
Catechesis/Religious Programs—Tel: 517-663-1288. Denise Clarke, D.R.E.
Students 151.

Fenton, Genesee Co., St. John (1843), Revs. David W. Harvey; Raymond Urbanek.
Res., 600 N. Adelaide St., 48430. Tel: 810-629-2251; Fax: 810-629-2302. [CEM]
School—514 Lincoln St., 48430. Tel: 810-629-6551; Fax: 810-629-2213. Sr. Patricia Fischer, O.P., Prin.
Lay Teachers 11; Students 249.
Catechesis/Religious Programs—512 N. Adelaide St., 48430. Tel: 810-629-1850. D.R.E.: Sr. Jeanine Boivin, O.P.; Ronald Kenney.
Students 681.

Flint, Genesee Co.,

1—St. Agnes, (1928), Rev. John P. Klein.
Res., 500 W. Pierson Rd., 48505. Tel: 810-785-3483; Fax: 810-785-0637.
Catechesis/Religious Programs—Students 60.

2—All Saints, (1910) (Polish), Rev. Anthony P. Majchrowski.
Res., G-4063 W. Pierson Rd., 48504. Tel: 810-787-0491. [CEM]

3—Christ the King, (1929) (African American), Sr. Joanne Fedewa, S.L.W., Pastoral Coord.
Res., 1832 Seymour St., 48503. Tel: 810-233-0402; Fax: 810-233-0402.

4—St. Francis of Assisi. Closed. For inquiries for parish records contact the Chancery.

5—Holy Rosary, (1951), Rev. Paul Schermer.
Res., 5199 Richfield Rd., 48506. Tel: 810-736-4040; Fax: 810-736-9129.
School—5191 Richfield Rd., 48506. Tel: 810-736-4220; Fax: 810-736-9129.
Lay Teachers 11; Students 260.
Catechesis/Religious Programs—Students 207.

6—Our Lady of Guadalupe, (1957) (Spanish), Rev. Eduardo Lorenzo.
Res., G-2316 W. Coldwater Rd., 48505. Tel: 810-787-5701; Fax: 810-787-3198.

7—St. John Vianney, (1941), Rev. Douglas Osborn.
Res., 2415 Bagley St., 48504. Tel: 810-235-1812; Fax: 810-235-4911.
Catechesis/Religious Programs—Students 386.

8—St. Leo the Great, (1957), Rev. James B. Bettendorf.
Res., 3632 Wyoming Ave., 48506. Tel: 810-736-2150; Fax: 810-736-0122.
Catechesis/Religious Programs—Tel: 810-736-7200.
Students 95.

9—St. Luke, (1951), Sr. Judith A. Blake, S.S.J., Pastoral Coord.
Res., 3202 Forest Hill, 48504. Tel: 810-239-5851.

10—St. Mary, (1919), Rev. Francis Faraci.
Res., 2500 N. Franklin Ave., 48506. Tel: 810-232-4012.
Catechesis/Religious Programs—Tel: 810-232-8784. Frances Pavelich, D.R.E.
Students 45.

11—St. Matthew, (1911), Revs. Frederick H. Taggart, O.S.A.; Edward M. Gorra.
Res., 706 Beach St., 48502. Tel: 810-232-0880.

12—St. Michael, (1843), Rev. William Robert Lugger; Sue Meissner, Pastoral Assoc.
Res., 609 E. Fifth Ave., 48503. Tel: 810-238-2679; Fax: 810-232-6820.
Catechesis/Religious Programs—Tel: 810-238-7981; Fax: 810-232-6820.
Students 137.

13—St. Pius X, (1955), Rev. Richard J. Groshek; Deacon David Pigott.
Res., G-3139 Hogarth Ave., 48532. Tel: 810-235-8574; Fax: 810-235-8580.
School—Tel: 810-235-8572.
Sisters 1; Lay Teachers 11; Students 273.
Catechesis/Religious Programs—Tel: 810-235-8573.
Students 252.

14—Sacred Heart, (1928), Dr. Connie McClanahan, Pastoral Coord.; Deacon Anthony Verdun. In res., Rev. Patrick Isichei (Nigeria).
Res., 719 E. Moore St., 48505. Tel: 810-789-8579.

Flushing, Genesee Co., St. Robert (1875), Revs. Steven F. Makranyi; Vincent Doan Bui; Charles E. Jacobs, (Retired); Deacons Michael Lynch; Gerald Butler.
Res., 310 N. Cherry St., 48433. Tel: 810-659-2501; Fax: 810-659-2564. [CEM]
School—Tel: 810-659-2503; Fax: 810-659-4002.
Lay Teachers 21; Students 446.
Catechesis/Religious Programs—Tel: 810-659-8556.
Students 389.

Fowler, Clinton Co., Most Holy Trinity (1881), Rev. Philip P. Gallagher.
Res., 545 N. Maple St., 48835. Tel: 517-593-2162; Fax: 517-593-2801. [CEM]
School—11144 Kent St., 48835. Tel: 517-593-2616.
Lay Teachers 5; Students 117.
Catechesis/Religious Programs—Tel: 517-593-3774; Fax: 517-593-2801.
Students 294.

Fowlerville, Livingston Co., St. Agnes (1891) (Irish-German-Polish), Rev. Francis M. George.
Res., 855 E. Grand River Ave., 48836. Tel: 517-223-8684; Fax: 517-223-0813. [CEM]
Catechesis/Religious Programs—Tel: 517-223-8684.
Students 282.

Gaines, Genessee Co., St. Joseph (1871), Sr. Ann Marie Petri, O.P., Pastoral Coord.; Deacon Currie Cormier.
Res., 118 E. Lord St., 48436. Tel: 517-271-8434. [CEM]
Catechesis/Religious Programs—Tel: 517-271-8434.
Students 124.

Goodrich, Genesee Co., St. Mark the Evangelist (1979), Rev. John Aduba; Sr. Joan M. May, S.S.J., Pastoral Coord.
Church—7296 Gale Rd. - P.O. Box 131, 48438. Tel: 810-636-2216; Fax: 810-636-7319.
Catechesis/Religious Programs—Students 140.

Grand Blanc, Genesee Co., Holy Family (1946), Revs. James R. Swiat; Mark Dehetre.
Res., 11824 S. Saginaw, 48439. Tel: 810-694-4891; Fax: 810-864-1583.
School—(Grades PreK-8) 215 Orchard St., 48439. Tel: 810-694-9072; Fax: 810-694-9405.
Lay Teachers 34; Students 668.
Catechesis/Religious Programs—Tel: 810-694-3080.
Students 395.

Grand Ledge, Eaton Co., St. Michael (1902), Rev. Robert H. McGraw.
Res., 345 Edwards, 48837. Tel: 517-627-8493; 627-8494; Fax: 517-627-1289.
School—Tel: 517-627-2167; Fax: 517-627-0289.
Lay Teachers 7; Students 145.
Catechesis/Religious Programs—Tel: 517-627-3797.
Students 350.

Hamburg, Livingston Co., Holy Spirit (1979), Rev. Timothy D. Krzyzaniak.
Res., P.O. Box 610, 48139. Tel: 810-231-9199; Fax: 810-231-6129.
Catechesis/Religious Programs—Tel: 810-231-6780.
Students 220.

Hartland, Livingston Co., St. John The Baptist (1843), Rev. David Speicher.
Res., 2099 Hacker Rd., Howell, 48843. Tel: 517-546-7200; Fax: 517-546-0403. [CEM]
Catechesis/Religious Programs—Tel: 517-548-2540; Fax: 517-546-0403.
Students 443.

Hillsdale, Hillsdale Co., St. Anthony (1858), Rev. Thomas W. Butler; Deacon Michael Nunez.
Res., 11 N. Broad St., 49242. Tel: 517-437-3305; Fax: 517-437-0034. [CEM]
Catechesis/Religious Programs—Students 234.

Howell, Livingston Co., St. Joseph (1900), Rev. Gilbert O. Rahrig.
Res., 440 E. Washington, 48843. Tel: 517-546-0090; Fax: 517-546-0090. [CEM]
School—425 E. Washington, 48843. Tel: 517-546-1380; Fax: 517-546-8939.
Lay Teachers 21; Students 258.
Catechesis/Religious Programs—Tel: 517-546-3171.
Students 422.

Hudson, Lenawee Co., Sacred Heart (1846), Rev. H. Paul Ruddy, O.S.F.S.

Res., 207 S. Market St., 49247. Tel: 517-448-3811. [CEM]
School—Tel: 517-448-6405.
Lay Teachers 6; Students 98.
Catechesis/Religious Programs—Students 162.

Jackson, Jackson Co.,

1—ST. JOHN THE EVANGELIST, (1856), Revs. James R. Shaver; Cecilio Reyna; Deacon Joseph A. Kratofil. Pastoral Assocs.: Sr. Eileen Souva, O.P.; Patricia Willson.
Res., 711 Cooper St., 49201. Tel: 517-784-0553; Fax: 517-788-5381. [JC]
School—405 E. North St., 49202. Tel: 517-784-1714; Fax: 517-788-5382.
Lay Teachers 16; Students 353.
Catechesis/Religious Programs—Tel: 517-784-5716.
Students 353.

2—ST. JOSEPH, (1902) (Polish-Lithuanian), Rev. Marian J. Lesniak.
Res., 705 N. Waterloo Ave., 49202. Tel: 517-784-9716. [JC]
School—717 N. Waterloo Ave., 49202. Tel: 517-784-4660.
Felician Sisters 2; Lay Teachers 7; Students 140.

3—ST. MARY, STAR OF THE SEA, (1881), Revs. Phillip Schweda; Joseph Sy Kim; Deacons William Everett; Vincent C. Genco.
Res., 301 S. Mechanic St., 49201. Tel: 517-784-7184; Fax: 517-783-2571.
School—116 E. Wesley St., 49201. Tel: 517-784-8811; Fax: 517-788-3425.
Lay Teachers 11; Students 207.
Catechesis/Religious Programs—Tel: 517-788-6153.
Students 180.

4—QUEEN OF THE MIRACULOUS MEDAL, (1934), Revs. Mark Inglot; Miguel Carlos (Mexico).
Res., 606 S. Wisner, 49203. Tel: 517-783-2748; Fax: 517-788-4528.
School—811 S. Wisner, 49203. Tel: 517-782-2664.
Lay Teachers 13; Students 464.
Catechesis/Religious Programs—Tel: 517-782-3609.
Students 230.

5—ST. STANISLAUS KOSTKA, (1920) (Polish), Rev. Canon Darius W. Wyszynski.
Res., 608 S. Elm Ave., 49203. Tel: 517-784-0551; Fax: 517-784-2639. [CEM]
School—614 S. Elm Ave., 49203. Tel: 517-782-6095. Sr. Mary Thaddea Meyers, C.S.S.F., Prin.
Lay Teachers 4; Students 50.

Laingsburg, Shiawassee Co., St. Isidore (1902), Rev. Duaine H. Pamment.
Res., 310 Crum St., 48848. Tel: 517-651-6617; 651-6722 (Office). [CEM]
Catechesis/Religious Programs—Tel: 517-651-6722.
Students 126.

Leslie, Ingham Co., SS. Cornelius and Cyprian (Bunker Hill) (1863), Rev. Eugene J. Beiter.
Res., 1320 Catholic Church Rd., 49251. Tel: 517-589-8492. [CEM]
Catechesis/Religious Programs—Students 97.

Manitou Beach, Lenawee Co., St. Mary on the Lake (1959), Sr. Helen Walling, I.H.M., Pastoral Coord.
Res., 450 Manitou Rd., 49253. Tel: 517-547-7496.

Manchester, Washtenaw Co., St. Mary (1871), Rev. Francis J. Murray.
Res., 210 W. Main St., P.O. Box 249, 48158. Tel: 313-428-8811. [CEM]
Catechesis/Religious Programs—Students 139.

Mason, Ingham Co., St. James (1942), Rev. Kenneth McDonald; Virginia M. Guarnaccia, Pastoral Assoc.
Res., 1010 S. Lansing St., 48854. Tel: 517-676-9111; Fax: 517-676-1343.
Catechesis/Religious Programs—Rose Robertson, D.R.E.
Students 360.

Michigan Center, Jackson Co., Our Lady of Fatima (1954), Revs. Andrew J. Dunne, O.S.F.S.; Thomas J. Smith, O.S.F.S.
Res., 913 Napoleon Rd., 49254. Tel: 517-764-2088; 764-2112; Fax: 517-764-0461.
School—911 Napoleon Rd., 49254. Tel: 517-764-2563.
Sisters of St. Joseph 1; Lay Teachers 7; Students 152.
Catechesis/Religious Programs—Tel: 517-764-1321.
Students 153.

Milan, Washtenaw Co., Immaculate Conception (1854), Rev. John M. Bosco. In res., Rev. Clair M. Dinger.
Church—420 North St., 48160. Tel: 313-439-2667; Fax: 313-439-2030.
Catechesis/Religious Programs—Tel: 313-439-2030.
Students 192.

Montrose, Genesee Co., Good Sheperd (1979), Sr. Josephine McNamara, Pastoral Coord.
Res., 400 N. Saginaw, P.O. Box 3274, 48457. Tel: 810-636-7600.
Catechesis/Religious Programs—Students 142.

Morrice, Shiawassee Co., St. Mary (1892), Rev. Matthew J. Fedewa; Deacon Gary Edington.
Res., 509 N. Main St., P.O. Box K, 48857. Tel: 517-625-4260; Fax: 517-625-3050.
Catechesis/Religious Programs—Tel: 517-625-6140.
Students 224.

Mount Morris, Genesee Co., St. Mary (1867), Rev. Robert F. McKeon.
Res., 11110 Saginaw St., 48458. Tel: 810-686-3920; Fax: 810-686-4790. [CEM]
School—Tel: 810-686-4790.
Sisters of the Immaculate Heart of Mary 2; Lay Teachers 9; Students 185.
Catechesis/Religious Programs—Fax: 810-686-7640.
Students 177.

Okemos, Ingham Co., St. Martha (1988), Rev. Jonathan Wehrle; Deacon Thomas Quasarano; Barbara McNicol, Pastoral Assoc.
Church—1100 W. Grand River, 48864. Tel: 517-349-1763.
School—Tel: 517-349-3322.
Sisters of Charity 4; Lay Teachers 5; Students 116.
Catechesis/Religious Programs—Students 738.

Otisville, Genesee Co., St. Francis Xavier (1947), Sr. Carol Weber, O.P. (Adrian, Dominican).
Res., 212 Center St., 48463. Tel: 810-631-6305. [JC]
Catechesis/Religious Programs—Tel: 810-631-4237. Rose Nixon, D.R.E.
Students 109.

Ovid, Shiawassee Co., Holy Family (1966). (Mission). Rev. Robert D. Lunsford.
Res., 620 N. Mabbitt Rd., P.O. Box 612, 48866. Tel: 517-834-5855.
Catechesis/Religious Programs—Students 123.

Owosso, Shiawassee Co., St. Paul (1871), Rev. Robert D. Kolenski.
Res., 111 N. Howell St., 48867. Tel: 517-723-4277. [CEM 2]
School—738 W. Main St., 48867. Tel: 517-725-7766.
Lay Teachers 11; Students 192.
Catechesis/Religious Programs—718 W. Main St., 48867. Tel: 517-723-1400.
Students 301.

St. Joseph (1923) (Slavic), Rev. David E. Fisher; Mary Ann Dunn, Pastoral Min.
Res., 915 E. Oliver St., 48867. Tel: 517-725-5215.
School—811 E. Oliver St., 48867. Tel: 517-725-8067; Fax: 517-725-1802.
Students 70.
St. Joseph Child Care Services—Tel: 517-723-2030.
Child Care 165.
Catechesis/Religious Programs—811 E. Oliver St., 48867. Tel: 517-723-4765.
Students 208.

Pinckney, Livingston Co., St. Mary (1857), Rev. Kenneth F. Coughlin.
Res., 551 E. Hamburg St., 48169. Tel: 313-878-3161; Fax: 313-878-2383. [CEM]
School—Tel: 313-878-5616.
Lay Teachers 12; Students 205.
Catechesis/Religious Programs—Tel: 313-878-2217.
Students 250.

St. Johns, Clinton Co., St. Joseph (1874), Rev. Robert D. Lunsford; Deacon Marvin Robertson.
Res., 109 Linden St., 48879. Tel: 517-224-8994; Fax: 517-224-3475.
School—Tel: 517-224-2421.
Lay Teachers 10; Students 311.
Catechesis/Religious Programs—Tel: 517-224-8537.
Students 298.

Saline, Washtenaw Co., St. Andrew (1968), Rev. James McDougall; Deacon Paul Ellis.
Res., 910 Austin Dr., 48176. Tel: 313-429-5210; Fax: 313-429-0680.
Catechesis/Religious Programs—Tel: 313-429-7776.
Students 775.

Swartz Creek, Genesee Co., St. Mary (1912) (Czechoslovakian), Rev. Amos H. Wischmeyer.
Res., 7563 Mary St., 48473. Tel: 810-635-3240. [CEM]
School—4413 Morrish Rd., 48473. Tel: 810-635-4985.
Lay Teachers 8; Students 124; Kindergarten 19; PreK 25.
Catechesis/Religious Programs—Tel: 810-635-3989.
Students 209.

Tecumseh, Lenawee Co., St. Elizabeth (1947), Rev. Daniel Wheeler; Deacons James Nicholson; Ray Pizana.
Res., 506 N. Union St., 49286. Tel: 517-423-2447; Fax: 517-423-3734.
Catechesis/Religious Programs—512 N. Union St., 49286. Tel: 517-423-4501.
Students 290.

Westphalia, Clinton Co., St. Mary (1836) (German), Rev. James M. Novak.
Res., 201 N. Westphalia St., P.O. Box 267, 48894. Tel: 517-587-4201; Fax: 517-587-3838. [CEM]
School—Tel: 517-587-3702.
Sisters of Christian Charity 1; Lay Teachers 13; Students 225.
Catechesis/Religious Programs—Tel: 517-587-4201.
Students 187.

Williamston, Ingham Co., St. Mary (1869), Rev. Dan McKean; Deacon Michael Barrett.
Res., 157 High St., 48895. Tel: 517-655-2620; Fax: 517-655-3933. [CEM]
School—220 Cedar St., 48895. Tel: 517-655-4038. Deborah Belprey, Prin.
Lay Teachers 6; Students 120.
Catechesis/Religious Programs—Tel: 517-655-2520. Bernadette Moline, D.R.E.
Students 310.

Ypsilanti, Washentaw Co.,

1—ST. ALEXIS. Closed. For inquiries for parish records contact the Chancery.

2—ST. JOHN, Washtenaw Co., (1858), Rev. Edmond L. Ertzbischoff; Deacons Wayne Charlton; Robert Chadwick.
Res., 410 W. Cross St., 48197. Tel: 313-483-3360; Fax: 313-483-0712. [CEM]
Catechesis/Religious Programs—Tel: 313-483-6378.
Students 181.
Convent—411 Florence St., 48197. Tel: 313-483-0742.

3—ST. JOSEPH, Washtenaw Co., (1889), Rev. Robert T. Kerr.
Res., 9425 Whittaker Rd., 48197. Tel: 313-461-6555; Fax: 313-461-1444. [CEM]
Catechesis/Religious Programs—Tel: 313-461-6321.
Students 275.

4—ST. URSULA, Washtenaw Co. Closed. For inquiries for parish records contact the Chancery.

5—HOLY TRINITY STUDENT CHAPEL, Washtenaw Co., (1965), Rev. Robert Irish.
Res., 511 W. Forest, 48197. Tel: 313-482-1400; 313-487-9756 (Rectory).

6—TRANSFIGURATION CATHOLIC CHURCH, Washtenaw Co., (1994), Rev. David Franco, O.S.F.S.
Res., 1705 E. Forest Ave., 48198-4160. Tel: 313-482-6240; Fax: 313-482-1547.

Chaplains of Public Institutions

Hospitals

LANSING. *Michigan Capital Medical Center, Sparrow Hospital.* Alice Hill, Chap., Tel: 517-646-6850.

ANN ARBOR. *University of Michigan Hospitals.* Revs. Darin Robert. Tel: 313-936-4041; Vincent Van Doan. Tel: 313-769-0422.
Veterans' Hospital. Rev. Vincent Van Doan, Chap.

Prisons

JACKSON. *Southern Michigan Prison.* Vacant. Tel: 517-788-7560, Ext. 6594.

MILAN. *Federal Correctional Institution.* Tel: 313-439-1511. Rev. Howard Stunek, O.F.M., Chap.

Training Schools

CHELSEA. *Cassidy Lake Tech. School.* Tel: 517-475-1697. Rev. Warren Paulson, Chap.

WHITMORE LAKE. *W.J. Maxey Boys Training School,* P.O. Box 349, 48189. Tel: 313-662-8141. Toni McNamara, Chap.

YPSILANTI. *Huron Valley Womens Correctional Facility,* 3511 Bemis Rd., 48197. Tel: 313-577-4003. Alberta Asmar, Chap.

Special Assignment:
Reverend Fathers—
Dougherty, C. Peter, 319 Charles St., East Lansing, MI 48823
Schmitter, Phillip, 2381 E. Carpenter, Flint, MI 48505
Wakefield, Alan, 4512 Glenberry, Holt, MI 48842

On Duty Outside the Diocese:
Reverend Fathers—
Crowley, Timothy
Gerl, Robert, P.O. Box 117, Bardstown, KY 40004
Goehring, Raymond, The Catholic University of America, Caldwell Hall #222, Cardinal Sta., Washington, DC 20064-0001
Kropf, Richard, Star Rte. 1, P.O. Box 629, Johannesburg, MI 49751

Madey, Louis, 219 18th Ave. S.W., Calgary, AB T2S 0C2 Canada
Taylor, Jon, The College of Great Falls, 1301-20th St. S., Great Falls, MT 59405
Thomas, William, Pfarrgasse 2, 8729 Knetzgau, Germany
Wunderlich, Daniel F., Les Missionnaires Oblats de Marie Immaculee, 175 Rue Main, Ottawa, K1S1C3 Canada

Absent on Leave:
Reverend Fathers—
Pleiness, Gregg
Zipple, Francis

Retired:
Reverend Monsignors—
Howard, Vincent, 1849 Pierce Rd., Chelsea, MI 48118
Mehm, Walter, 465 Ashley, Grand Blanc, MI 48439
Reverend Fathers—
Bednarski, Mitchell J., 14465 Levon, Apt. D, Livonia, MI 48154-5022
Bottazo, Alex, Senior Clergy Village, 14455D Levan St., Livonia, MI 48154
Brakora, Anthony, 2705 Ridgecliffe Dr., Flint, MI 48532
Brennan, Thomas, 460 Egan Hwy., Brooklyn, MI 49230
Bush, John H., 9787 Burning Tree Dr., Grand Blanc, MI 48439
Carolin, William, J., St. Patrick, 711 Rickett Rd., Brighton, MI 48116
Cornelli, Neil, 2501 Via Del Ray, Fernandina Beach, FL 32034
Cummings, Paul, 851 Bassett Lake Rd., Middleville, MI 49333
Eder, Donald, 6290 Oak Creek Dr., Swartz Creek, MI 48473
Fitzgerald, James C., 914 Michigan St., Port Huron, MI 48060
Foglio, John, P.O. Box 4098, East Lansing, MI 48826
Handley, Robert, P.O. Box 147, 4076 Beacon Hill, Port Hope, MI 48468
Immel, Joseph, 1971 Watkins Lake Rd., Waterford, MI 48328
Jacobs, Charles E., 205 Elm St., Flushing, MI 48433
Klauke, Raymond, 6636 Sherbourne, Inkster, MI 48141
Koenigsknecht, William J., 5300 W. Mall Dr., Apt. 2002, Lansing, MI 48917
Ledwidge, Brendan K., 7900 Lange Rd., Fowlerville, MI 48836
Martin, Francis T., St. Gerard Church, 4437 W. Willow, Lansing, MI 48917
McKeon, William J., St. Joseph Parish, Box 379, East Jordan, MI 49727
O'Grady, Edward F., St. Joseph Home, 1000 E. Porter, Jackson, MI 49202
Rademacher, William, 3842 Azalea Dr., Las Cruces, NM 88005-1027
Ramer, Leo, 235 Quebec St., Goderich, ON N7A 2H2 Canada
Schmitt, James, J., 215 Banberry N., Lansing, MI 48906
Sparks, Thomas J., Magdalen College, 511 Kearsage Mountain Rd., Warner, NH 03278
Srebernak, Francis, R.R. 1, Rural Box 82B, Hancock, MI 49930-9705
Stockwell, C. Robert, 335 Walnut St., Mount Morris, MI 48458
Wieber, Joseph E., 860 Gordon Dr., Kingman, AZ 86401
Williams, Francis, 3621 Penbrook Ln., Apt. 12, Flint, MI 48507

Permanent Deacons:
Alfaro, Rogelio R., Cristo Rey, Lansing
Barrett, David P., Queens, Jackson
Barrett, Michael, St. Mary, Williamston
Bayes, Richard B., Jr., St. Mary, Adrian.
Berger, Kenneth, Unassigned
Borzenski, David J., St. Therese, Lansing
Brown, James S., Holy Rosary, Flint
Butler, Gerald, St. Robert, Cleveland
Cameron, John, Immaculate Heart of Mary, Lansing
Ceballos, Santos R., Sr., Office of Hispanics, Lansing
Chadwick, Robert, St. John, Ypsilanti
Charlton, Wayne, St. John the Baptist, Ypsilanti
Cormier, Currie, St. Joseph, Gaines
Doran, Endre, St. Joseph, Howell
Eddington, Gary, St. Mary, Morrice
Ellis, Paul, St. Andrew, Saline
Endebrock, Bernard J., St. Augustine, Deerfield
Everett, William, St. Mary of the Sea, Jackson
Fairweather, Daniel, St. John, Davison
Foley, Daniel R. (BGP), Christ the King Catholic Association, Ann Arbor
Fudge, William H., III, Immaculate Heart, Lansing
Garber, J. Patrick, Senior Status
Genco, Vincent, St. Mary, Jackson
Guajardo, Arturo, Jr., Unassigned
Hecht, Warren Jay, St. Thomas, Ann Arbor
Henderson, Ronald D., St. Casimir, Lansing
Herzog, Robert, Baltimore
Hilker, Stephen, St. Thomas Aquinas, East Lansing
Hubbarth, John A., Kalamazoo
Huiskens, Neil F., St. John, Davison
Igoe, James Gerard, Criminal Justice Ministry, Lansing
Kilburn, Gordon P., Serving Knoxville
Kratofil, Joseph A., St. John, Jackson
Lackney, Robert, Unassigned
Leone, Romolo Joseph, St. Joseph, Dexter
Lynch, Michael T., St. Robert, Flushing
Martinez, James N., Office of Hispanics, Lansing
Mathias, James E., St. Ann, Bellevue
Mattox, William, Jr., Atlanta
Mc Philamy, Robert E., St. Gerard, Lansing
McCarthy, John L., St. Michael, Grand Ledge
McDonald, Patrick A., St. Patrick Church, Brighton
McPeek, Gwynn S., Senior Status
Miles, James J., St. Thomas, Ann Arbor
Nicholson, James R., St. Elizabeth, Tecumseh
Novak, Edwin, Blessed Sacrament, Burton
Nunez, Michael, St. Anthony, Hillsdale
O'Toole, Gerald D., Diocese of Phoenix, AZ
Pigott, David J., Jr., St. Pius, Flint
Pizana, Eulalio (Ray), St. Elizabeth, Tecumseh
Pohl, Bernard J., St. Mary's, Westphalia
Poulson, Robert R., St. John, Davison
Preston, Richard, Serving Charlotte, NC
Purvis, David L., Holy Cross, Lansing
Quasarano, Thomas (DET), St. Martha, Okemos
Robertson, Marvin, St. Joseph, St. Johns
Savage, Richard, St. Gerard, Lansing
Scharf, H. David, St. Mary Magdalene, Brighton
Schneider, Edwin J., St. Gerard, Lansing
Shaneyfelt, Richard, St. Mary, Chelsea
Simmon, Mark C., Most Holy Trinity, Fowler
Simon, Edward, Pago, Pago
Spaulding, Kenneth R., Queens, Jackson
Spencer, Claude S., St. John, Davison
Tardif, Joseph A., St. Michael, Grand Ledge
Torres, Calistro, St. Mary of Good Counsel, Adrian
Verdun, Anthony W., Sacred Heart, Flint
Washington, Oliver G., Immaculate Heart, Lansing
Weitzel, Louis U., St. Rita, Clarklake
Wendell, Max W., Serving Gaylord
Wines, Francis J., Pensacola, Tallahassee

INSTITUTIONS LOCATED IN THE DIOCESE

[A] COLLEGES AND UNIVERSITIES

ADRIAN. *Siena Heights College - President*, 1247 E. Siena Heights Dr., 49221-1796. Tel: 517-263-0731; Fax: 517-264-7702.
For a complete listing, refer to the Colleges and Universities section.

[B] HIGH SCHOOLS, DIOCESAN

LANSING. *Lansing Catholic Central High School*, 501 N. Marshall St., 48912. Tel: 517-267-2100. Rev. Michael Rejent, O.S.F.S., Interim Prin. Lansing Catholic Central Board of Education. Priests 1; Lay Teachers 33; Students 527.

ANN ARBOR. *Father Gabriel Richard High School*, 530 Elizabeth St., 48104. Tel: 313-662-0496. Mr. Richard Bayhan, Prin. Gabriel Richard Board of Education. Lay Teachers 23; Students 283.

CLINTON. *St. Thomas More High-Boysville*, 8744 Clinton-Macon Rd., 49236. Tel: 517-423-7451. Mr. Carl LaGore, Prin. Brothers 1; Total Staff 25.

FLINT. *Luke M. Powers Catholic High School*, G-2040 W. Carpenter Rd., 48505. Tel: 810-785-4741. Mr. Joseph Forlenza, Prin. Powers Catholic Board of Education. Priests 1; Sisters 2; Lay Teachers 51; Students 925.

JACKSON. *Lumen Christi High School*, 3483 Spring Arbor Rd., 49203. Tel: 517-787-0630; Fax: 517-787-1066. Oblates of St. Francis de Sales. Revs. Thomas W. Rieden, O.S.F.S., Prin.; Richard L. McLernan, O.S.F.S.; Thomas J. Helfrich, O.S.F.S.; Paul F. Grehl, O.S.F.S.; John W. Bailey, O.S.F.S. Priests 3; Sisters 2; Lay Teachers 38; Students 649.

[C] ELEMENTARY SCHOOLS, PRIVATE

ADRIAN. *St. Joseph Academy Montessori Children's House*. (Grades PreK-5), 1267 E. Siena Heights, 49221. Tel: 517-263-4898. Sisters of St. Dominic, Congregation of the Most Holy Rosary (Adrian, MI). Mrs. Deborah Keller, Prin. Sisters 2; Lay Teachers 45; Students 342.

BURTON. *St. Thomas More Academy*. (Grades K-12), 6456 E. Bristol Rd., 48519. Tel: 810-742-2411. Mr. Patrick LeBlanc, Prin. Students 120.

FLINT. *Donovan-Mayotte Catholic School*, 2319 Bagley, 48504. Tel: 810-235-5687. Mrs. Sharon A. Cuttitta, Prin. Lay Teachers 17; Students 388.
Dukette Catholic School, 530 W. Pierson Rd., 48505. Tel: 810-785-4743. Mr. Harry A. Plummer, Prin. Lay Teachers 16; Total Staff 25; Students 208.

JACKSON. *Jackson Catholic Middle School*, 915 Cooper, 49202. Tel: 517-784-3385. Mrs. Pamela M. Sullivan, Prin. Lay Teachers 20; Students 334.

[D] CATHOLIC CHARITIES REGIONAL OFFICES

LANSING. *Catholic Social Services-St. Vincent Home for Children, Inc.*, 1900 S. Cedar St., Ste. 306, 48910. Tel: 517-374-9005. Donald Ballentine, A.C.S.W., Dir.
Family Mental Health Clinic, 300 N. Washington, Ste. 301, 48933. Tel: 517-372-4020.
Foster Grandparents Program, 6545 Mercantile Way, Suite 2B1, 48911. Tel: 517-482-7611.
Refugee Service, 1900 S. Cedar, Ste. 302, 48910. Tel: 517-484-1010. St. Vincent Home for Children, 2800 W. Willow St., 48917. Tel: 517-323-4734.
Senior Companion Program, 5815 Wise Rd., 48911. Tel: 517-882-8777.
Intergenerational Daycare Center, 13060 U.S. 27, 48820. Tel: 517-669-1551.
Child Welfare Program, 2800 W. Willow St., 48917. Tel: 517-323-4734.
Ballentine Stepping Stones, 825 N. Pennsylvania, 48906. Tel: 517-485-4644.
Capital Area Interfaith Respite, 501 E. Mt. Hope Rd., 48910. Tel: 517-485-1560.
Parish Social Ministry, 300 N. Washington Ste. 301, 48933. Tel: 517-372-4020.
Retired and Senior Volunteer Program, 6545 Mercantile Way A1-A, 48911. Tel: 517-887-6116.
Cristo Rey Community Center, 1717 N. High St., 48906. Tel: 517-372-4700. Tony Benavides, Dir. Total Assisted 55,253; Total Staff 52.
Migrant Program-Cristo Rey Community Center, 1717 N. High St., 48906. Tel: 517-372-4700. Sylvia Holguin, Dir. Total Assisted 2,000; Total Staff 13.

ADRIAN. *Catholic Social Services of Lenawee County*, 307 E. Church St., 49221. Tel: 517-263-2191. Luanne Reaume, Dir.

ANN ARBOR. *C.S.S. of Washtenaw County*, 4925 Packard Rd., 48108. Tel: 313-971-9781. Mr. John Martin, M.S.W., C.S.W., Pres. Total Assisted 6,000; Total Staff 50.

BRIGHTON. *Livingston County Catholic Social Services*, 10291 E. Grand River, Suite D, 48116. Tel: 810-227-2151. Nancy A. Rosso, Dir. Total Assisted 2,000; Total Staff 13.

FLINT. *Catholic Outreach*, 509 N. Grand Traverse, P.O. Box 815, 48501. Tel: 810-234-4693. Sr. Claudia Burke, S.F.P., Dir. Total Assisted 27,001; Total Staff 12.
Catholic Social Services of Flint, 202 E. Boulevard Dr., Rm. 210, 48503. Tel: 810-232-9950. Deborah J. McCormack, A.C.S.W., Pres.
North End Soup Kitchen. Catholic Social Services, Flint. P.O. Box 114, 48505. Tel: 810-785-6911. Deborah J. McCormack, A.C.S.W., Pres. Total Assisted Daily 750; Total Staff 9.
Shelter of Flint, Inc., 1917 Delaware St., 48506. Tel: 810-233-0689; Fax: 810-233-0850. Patricia A. Motter, Exec. Dir.
Emergency Shelter for Women. 1917 Delaware St., 48506. Tel: 810-233-0689. Mary Gian-Norman, Program Dir.
Hospitality House. 524 W. Pierson Rd., 48505. Tel: 810-789-5715. Mary Gian-Norman, Program Dir.

JACKSON. *Catholic Social Services of Jackson*, 407 S. Mechanic St., 49201. Tel: 517-782-2551. Mr. Keith Krusky, Dir. Total Assisted 7,200; Total Staff 11.

OWOSSO. *Catholic Social Services of Shiawassee County*, 120 W. Exchange, 48867. Tel: 517-723-8239. Harriet Johnson, Dir. Total Assisted 371; Total Staff 6.

[E] CHILD CARE FACILITIES

LANSING. *Boysville of Michigan, Inc., Grants Management Office*, Everett Plaza, 3400 S. Cedar St., Ste. 201, 48910. Tel: 517-887-3022. Bro. Francis Boylan, C.S.C., Exec. Dir.; Adolf Armbruster, Grants Mgr.
St. Vincent Home for Children, 2800 W. Willow St., 48917. Tel: 517-323-4734. Foster Care Program serving 60 youths. Mr. Donald Ballentine, Dir.

CHELSEA. *St. Louis Center for Exceptional Children & Adults*, 16195 Old U.S. 12, 48118. Tel: 313-475-8430. Revs. Enzo Addari, S.C., Admin.; Joseph Rinaldo, S.C., Prov. Operated by the Servants of Charity. Priests 2; Staff 45; Students 70.

CLINTON. *Boysville of Michigan, Inc.*, 8744 Clinton-Macon Rd., 49236. Tel: 517-423-7451; Fax: 517-423-5442. Bro. Francis Boylan, C.S.C., Exec. Dir.; Rev. Philip Hart, C.S.P., Dir. of Mission Effectiveness; Mr. Eugene Hausmann, Pastoral Min.; Bro. Chester Freel, C.S.C., Regl. Dir. Brothers 7; Boys 140. Residential and community based treatment programs for troubled youth and families with facilities located throughout the state of Michigan and one in the state of Ohio under the auspices of the Brothers of Holy Cross & Notre Dame.

Boysville's Family & Community Support Program, 8744 Clinton-Macon Rd., 49236. Tel: 517-423-7451, Ext. 532. Bros. Francis Boylan, C.S.C., Exec. Dir.; Chester Freel, C.S.C., Reg. Dir. Specialized Foster Care Treatment and Supervised Independent Living. Total Staff 6; Total Assisted 30.

JACKSON. *St. Joseph Home for Children, Inc.*, 1000 E. Porter, 49202. Sr. Mary Concepta Mastey, C.S.S.F.; Rev. Edward O'Grady, Chap. Felician Sisters (C.S.S.F.). Day Care Center-Retreat-Conference Center and Kindergarten (ages 2 months-6 years). Children 100.

MOUNT MORRIS. *Corcoran House/Boysville of Michigan, Inc.*, 8212 N. Jennings Rd., 48458. Tel: 810-687-5100. Bro. Francis Boylan, C.S.C., Exec. Dir.; Mr. Rick Boone, Regional Dir. A day treatment program for 12 boys and girls. Total Assisted 33; Total Staff 14.

[F] GENERAL HOSPITALS

LANSING. *St. Lawrence Hospital and Healthcare Services*, 1210 W. Saginaw St., 48915. Tel: 517-372-3610; Fax: 517-377-0382.

For a complete listing, refer to the Hospitals section.

ANN ARBOR. *Catherine McAuley Health Services Corporation*, 5305 E. Huron River Dr., P.O. Box 992, 48106. Tel: 313-712-3789.

For a complete listing, refer to the Hospitals section.

Catherine McAuley Health System, 5305 E. Huron River Dr., Box 992, 48106. Tel: 313-712-4025.

For a complete listing, refer to the Hospitals section.

McAuley Clinic Corporation, 5333 McAuley Dr., Box 994, 48106. Tel: 313-712-3788.

For a complete listing, refer to the Hospitals section.

St. Joseph Mercy Hospital, 5301 E. Huron River Dr., P.O. Box 995, 48106. Tel: 313-712-3456.

For a complete listing, refer to the Hospitals section.

Sisters of St. Joseph Health Services Corp., 455 E. Eisenhower, Ste. 300, 48108. Tel: 313-741-1700.

For a complete listing, refer to the Hospitals section.

Sisters of St. Joseph Health System, Inc., 455 E. Eisenhower, Ste. 300, 48108. Tel: 313-741-1700.

For a complete listing, refer to the Hospitals section.

FLINT. *Center for Gerontology*, 303 W. Water St., 48503. Tel: 810-767-7080.

For a complete listing, refer to the Hospitals section.

Genesys Ambulatory Health Services, Inc., 302 Kensington Ave., 48503. Tel: 810-232-9900.

For a complete listing, refer to the Hospitals section.

Genesys Health System, 302 Kensington Ave., 48503-2000. Tel: 810-762-8899.

For a complete listing, refer to the Hospitals section.

Genesys Home Health & Hospice, 100 S. Dort Hwy., 48503. Tel: 810-762-7500.

For a complete listing, refer to the Hospitals section.

Genesys Regional Medical Center/Flint Osteopathic Campus, 3921 Beecher Rd., 48532-3699. Tel: 810-762-4000.

For a complete listing, refer to the Hospitals section.

Genesys Regional Medical Center/St. Joseph Campus, 302 Kensington Ave., 48503-2000. Tel: 810-762-8000.

For a complete listing, refer to the Hospitals section.

GOODRICH. *Genesys Regional Medical Center/Wheelock Memorial Campus*, 7280 State Rd., 48438. Tel: 810-636-2221.

For a complete listing, refer to the Hospitals section.

GRAND BLANC. *Genesys Convalescent Center, Grand Blanc, Inc.*, 8481 Holly Rd., 48439-1899. Tel: 810-694-1711.

For a complete listing, refer to the Hospitals section.

Genesys Regional Medical Center/Health Park, One Genesys Pkwy., 48439. Tel: 810-606-5000.

For a complete listing, refer to the Hospitals section.

HOWELL. *McPherson Hospital*, 620 Bryon Rd., 48843-1093. Tel: 517-546-1410.

For a complete listing, refer to the Hospitals section.

OKEMOS. *Majorie J. Gardner Wellness Center for Women*, 5100 Marsh Rd., 48864.

For a complete listing, refer to the Hospitals section.

SALINE. *Saline Community Hospital*, 400 W. Russell, 48176. Tel: 313-429-1600.

For a complete listing, refer to the Hospitals section.

[G] HOMES FOR THE AGED

DIMONDALE. *St. Lawrence Dimondale Center*, 4000 N. Michigan Rd. (M-99), 48821. Tel: 517-646-6258.

For a complete listing, refer to the Special Care Facilities section.

FLINT. *Marian Hall*, 529 Martin Luther King Ave., 48502. Tel: 810-238-7646.

For a complete listing, refer to the Special Care Facilities section.

[H] CONVENTS AND RESIDENCES FOR SISTERS

ADRIAN. *Motherhouse of the Sisters of St. Dominic.*

Congregation of the Most Holy Rosary, 1257 Siena Heights Dr., 49221-1793. Tel: 517-265-5135; Fax: 517-265-4733. Sr. Patricia Walter, O.P., Prioress. Chaplains: Revs. Joseph Baraniewicz, O.S.F.S.; Roland Calvert, O.S.F.S. Total Congregation 1,180.

Motherhouse Mission Chapter, 1257 Siena Heights Dr., 49221-1793. Tel: 517-265-5135. Sr. Celestine Dunne, O.P., Chap. Prioress.

Rosa de Lima Mission Chapter. (located in the Dominican Republic), c/o 1257 Siena Heights Dr., 49221-1793. Tel: 809-534-8017. Sr. Rose Ann Schlitt, O.P., Chapter Prioress.

Dominican Life Center, 1277 Siena Heights Dr., 49221-1755. Sr. Janet Capone, O.P., Admin.

ANN ARBOR. *Congregation of the Sisters of the Holy Cross*, 331 Thompson St., 48104-2213.

DE WITT. *St. Albert the Great House of Studies*, 217 Schavey Rd., P.O. Box 309, 48820. Tel: 517-669-2277. Religious Sisters of Mercy, Alma Michigan 4.

[I] RETREAT CENTERS

ADRIAN. *Weber Retreat Center*, 1257 Siena Heights Dr., 49221-1793. Tel: 517-263-7088. Sr. Kathleen Schanz, O.P., Dir.

DE WITT. *St. Francis Retreat Center*, 703 E. Main St., 48820. Tel: 517-669-8321. Revs. Lawrence Delaney, Dir.; Gerald Ploof, Assoc. Dir.; Sr. Suzanne Eichhorn, O.P., Assoc. Dir.

HOWELL.

**Emmaus Ministries*, Kennedy Center, 1875 Eager Rd., 48843. Tel: 517-546-4440. Valerie Catenacci, Admin.

[J] NEWMAN CENTERS

ADRIAN. *Siena Heights College Newman Center*, 1247 E. Siena Heights Dr., 49221. Tel: 517-263-0731. Sr. Marilyn Uline, O.P., Dir. Campus Ministry.

ANN ARBOR. *St. Mary Student Parish*, 331 Thompson St., 48104-2295. Tel: 313-663-0557. Rev. William J. Stevenson. Serving the University of Michigan. (Refer to the parish section for complete campus ministry staff). Total in Residence 10; Total Staff 4.

EAST LANSING. *St. John Student Parish.* Serving Michigan State University, 327 M.A.C. Ave., 48823. Tel: 517-337-9778.
(Refer to the parish section for complete campus ministry staff).

HILLSDALE. *St. Anthony.* (Serving Hillsdale College), 11 Broad St., 49242. Tel: 517-437-3305. Total Assisted 300; Total Staff 1.

YPSILANTI. *Holy Trinity Student Chapel*, 511 W. Forest, 48197. Tel: 313-482-1400. Rev. Robert L. Irish; Sr. Maryanna Pratt, S.S.J., Campus Min.; Scott Wright, D.R.E. Serving Cleary College; Eastern Michigan University; Washtenaw Community College.

[K] ENDOWMENTS AND TRUSTS

LANSING. *Chancery Office*, 300 W. Ottawa, 48933. Tel: 517-342-2440.

Benefit Trust of the Adrian Dominican Congregation (Adrian).

Church of the Resurrection Educational Trust Fund (Church of the Resurrection, Lansing).

Father Al Miller Educational Trust Fund (St. Mary Parish, Westphalia).

Father Gabriel Richard High School Trust Fund (Fr. Gabriel Richard H.S., Ann Harbor).

Greater Lansing Catholic Education Foundation (Lansing).

Immaculate Heart of Mary St. Casimir School Mary Goeddeke Educational Trust Fund. (IHM-St. Casimir School, Lansing).

Luke M. Powers Educational Trust Fund (Flint).

Lumen Christi High School Endowment Fund (Lumen Christi H.S., Jackson).

Most Holy Trinity Educational Trust Fund (Most Holy Trinity Church, Fowler).

Msgr. Lawrence H. Soest Educational Trust Fund (St. Mary Parish, Flint).

Rev. Joseph R. Robb Educational Trust Fund (Holy Rosary Parish, Flint).

Sacred Heart Educational Fund (Sacred Heart Parish, Hudson).

St. Francis of Assisi Educational Trust Fund (St. Francis of Assisi Parish, Ann Harbor).

St. John the Evangelist Parish Educational Trust Fund (St. John the Evangelist Parish, Jackson).

St John School Educational Foundation, Inc. (St. John Parish, Fenton).

St. John Vianney Educational Trust Fund (St. John Vianney Parish, Flint).

St. Joseph Church of Howell Trust Fund (St. Joseph Church, Howell).

St. Joseph Educational Trust Fund (St. Joseph Church, Owosso).

St. Joseph Educational Trust Fund (St. Joseph Church, St Johns).

St. Louis Center for Exceptional Children & Adults Endowment Trust Agreement (St. Louis Center, Chelsea).

St. Mary Educational Trust Fund (St. Mary Parish, Mt. Morris).

St. Mary Parish Educational Trust Fund (St. Mary Parish, Charlotte).

St. Mary Star of the Sea Educational Trust Fund (St. Mary Star of the Sea Parish, Jackson).

St. Michael's School Endowment Fund Policy (St. Michael School, Grand Ledge).

St. Paul's School Education Trust Fund (St. Paul Parish, Owosso).

St. Pius X Church Educational Trust Fund (St. Pius X Church, Flint).

St. Robert Bellarmine/Fr. Jacob Educational Trust Fund (St, Robert Bellarmine Parish, Flushing). (St. Robert Bellarmine Parish, Flushing).

St. Therese Educational Trust Fund (St. Therese Parish, Lansing).

St. Thomas Aquinas Educational Foundation Trust (St. Thomas Aquinas Parish, East Lansing).

St. Thomas Grade School Trust Agreement (St. Thomas the Apostle Parish, Ann Arbor).

St. Patrick Parish Educational Trust Fund (St. Patrick Parish, Brighton). For further information regarding these listings contact the Chancery.

St. Gerard Educational Trust Fund (St. Gerard Parish, Lansing).

Holy Redeemer Educational Trust Fund (Holy Redemer Parish, Burton).

[L] MISCELLANEOUS LISTINGS

LANSING. *Catholic Lawyers Guild*, 300 W. Ottawa St., 48933. Tel: 517-342-2449.

Diocesan Service Committee. (Catholic Charismatic Renewal), 835 Maycroft Rd., 48917. Ralph Stamford, Chm.; Rev. Philip Dupuis, Bishop's Liaison, St. Mary Parish, Chelsea.

Michigan Catholic Conference, 505 N. Capitol Ave., 48933. Tel: 517-372-9310. Sr. Monica Kostielney, R.S.M., Pres. & CEO.

Priestly Life and Ministry, 300 W. Ottawa St., 48933.

St. Vincent de Paul Particular Council, St. Vincent de Paul Store, 1020 S. Washington, 48910. Tel: 517-484-5395. Howard Barrons, Pres.; Peter Ellena, Store Mgr.

Society of St. Vincent de Paul. St. Thomas Conference. 517 Elizabeth St., Ann Arbor, 48104. Sr. Dolora Neumaier, I.H.M., Pres.

ADRIAN. *Adrian Dominican Office of Development*, 1257 E. Siena Hts. Dr., 49221-1793. Tel: 517-265-5135. Adrian Dominican Sisters.

ANN ARBOR. *Ann Arbor Catholic Forum*, P.O. Box 2184, 48106-2184. Tel: 313-482-6619. Mr. Anthony Patti.

CHIRO, St. Thomas the Apostle Church, 517 Elizabeth St., 48104.

Christ the King Catholic Center, 2630 N. Earhart Pl., 48105. Tel: 313-665-5040. Rev. Edward O. Fride (LAN).

The Marnee and John DeVine Foundation, 4925 Packard, 48108. Tel: 313-971-9781. Joanne L. Matika, Contact Person.

Renewal Ministries Inc., 230 Collingwood Blvd., Ste. 250, 48103. Tel: 313-662-1730. Ralph Martin, Pres.

**The Catholic Evidence Guild*, 639 Barber Ave., 48103. Tel: 313-995-3125. Tom O'Brien, Pres. & Dir.

BROOKLYN. *Lake Vineyard Camps, Inc., (Camp de Sales)*, 1150 Ventura Dr., 49230-9078. Tel: 517-592-2074. Ronald Helfrich, Contact Person.

Oblate Fathers of St. Francis De Sales, Inc., 150 N. Main St., 49230. Total in Residence 8.

DAVISON. *Outreach East*, 425 N. Genesee St. - P.O. Box 61, 48423. Tel: 810-653-7711. Rita Berby, S.S.J., Dir.; Total Assisted 1,050; Total Staff 1.

FLINT. *Dukette Intercultural Center for Black Catholic Ministry*, 609 E. Fifth Ave., 48503. Tel: 810-235-4950. Mrs. Peggy Cooper, Admin. Sec.

Particular Council of Flint, Society of St. Vincent DePaul Store 1912 N. Franklin, 48506. Gene R. Myers, Pres.; Richard Twomley, Store Dir.

GRASS LAKE. *The Pious Union of St. Joseph*, 971 E. Michigan Ave., 49240-9210. Tel: 517-522-8017 (Voice/TDD); Fax: 517-522-8387.

"Now and at the Hour" Magazine: Revs. Joseph Rinaldo, S.C., Editor in Chief; Germano Pegoraro, S.C., Dir./Mng. Editor; Estelle M. Humenay, Asst. Dir./Editor.

JACKSON. *Society of St. Vincent de Paul*, St. Vincent de Paul Store, 1509 E. Michigan Ave., 49202. Tel: 517-784-0609. Particular Council of Jackson. O. James Pierce, Particular Council Pres.

RELIGIOUS INSTITUTES OF MEN REPRESENTED IN THE DIOCESE

For further details refer to the corresponding bracketed

number in the Religious Institutes of Men or Women section.

[0140]—*The Augustinians.*—O.S.A.

[0480]—*Conventual Franciscans.*—O.F.M.Conv.

[0920]—*Oblates of St. Francis de Sales.*—O.S.F.S.

[1220]—*Servants of Charity.*—S.C.

RELIGIOUS INSTITUTES OF WOMEN REPRESENTED IN THE DIOCESE

[1920]—*Congregation of Sisters of the Holy Cross.*—C.S.C.

[2110]—*Congregation of the Sisters of the Humility of Mary.*—H.M.

[1070-13]—*Dominican Sisters.*—O.P.

[1070-14]—*Dominican Sisters.* (Grand Rapids).—O.P.

[1170]—*Felician Sisters.*—C.S.S.F.

[1470]—*Franciscan Sisters of St. Joseph.*—F.S.S.J.

[1440]—*Franciscan Sisters of the Poor.*—S.F.P.

[2575]—*Institute of the Sisters of Mercy of the Americas.*—R.S.M.

[]—*Mexican Passionist Sisters.*—C.F.P.

[0440]—*Sisters of Charity of Cincinnati, Ohio.*—S.C.

[0660]—*Sisters of Christian Charity.*—S.C.C.

[1560]—*Sisters of St. Francis of the Holy Eucharist.*—O.S.F.

[3830-11]—*Sisters of St. Joseph.*—S.S.J.

[2110]—*Sisters of the Humility of Mary.*—H.M.

[2350]—*Sisters of the Living Word.*—S.L.W.

[3260]—*Sisters of the Precious Blood (Dayton, OH).*—C.PP.S.

[3320]—*Sisters of the Presentation of the Blessed Virgin Mary.*

[2150]—*Sisters Servants of the Immaculate Heart of Mary.*—I.H.M.

DIOCESAN CEMETERIES

LANSING. *St. Joseph.*

FLINT. *New Calvary.*

NECROLOGY

† Fitzgerald, A. Thomas, (Retired). —Died July 5, 1996.

† Strzelewicz, Joseph, (Retired). —Died May 18, 1996.

† Thompson, Mark, (Retired). —Died Feb. 14, 1996.

Diocese of Lexington

Most Reverend

JAMES KENDRICK WILLIAMS, D.D.

Bishop of Lexington; ordained May 25, 1963; appointed Titular Bishop of Catula and Auxiliary Bishop of Covington on April 15, 1984; consecrated June 19, 1984; transferred to Lexington March 2, 1988. *Res., 1310 Leestown Rd., P.O. Box 12350, Lexington, KY, 40582-2350.*

ESTABLISHED MARCH 2, 1988.

Square Miles 16,423.

Comprises the counties of Anderson, Bath, Bell, Bourbon, Boyd, Boyle, Breathitt, Carter, Clark, Clay, Elliott, Estill, Fayette, Floyd, Franklin, Garrard, Greenup, Harlan, Jackson, Jessamine, Johnson, Knott, Knox, Laurel, Lawrence, Lee, Leslie, Letcher, Lincoln, McCreary, Madison, Magoffin, Martin, Menifee, Mercer, Montgomery, Morgan, Nicholas, Owsley, Perry, Pike, Powell, Pulaski, Rockcastle, Rowan, Scott, Wayne, Whitley, Wolfe and Woodford.

For legal titles of parishes and diocesan institutions, consult the Chancellor.

The Catholic Center: 1310 Leestown Rd., P.O. Box 12350, Lexington, KY, 40582-2350. Tel.: 606-253-1993; Fax: 606-254-6284.

STATISTICAL OVERVIEW

Personnel	
Bishop	1
Priests: Diocesan Active in Diocese	37
Priests: Active Outside Diocese	1
Priests: Retired, Sick or Absent	12
Number of Diocesan Priests	50
Religious Priests in Diocese	21
Extern Priests in Diocese	4
Ordinations:	
Permanent Deacons in Diocese	28
Total Brothers	5
Total Sisters	186
Parishes	
Parishes	61
With Resident Pastor:	
Resident Diocesan Priests	36
Resident Religious Priests	7
Without Resident Pastor:	
Administered by Priests	6
Administered by Permanent Deacons	2
Administered by Professed Men Religious	1
Administered by Lay People	1
Administered by Pastoral Teams, etc.	9
Missions	6
Closed Parishes	1
Professional Ministry Personnel:	
Sisters	36
Lay Ministers	23
Welfare	
Catholic Hospitals	6
Total Assisted	253,840
Health Care Centers	4
Total Assisted	60,002
Homes for the Aged	1
Total Assisted	86
Day Care and Extended Day Care Centers	3
Total Assisted	148
Special Centers for Social Services	1
Total Assisted	8,240
Educational	
Diocesan Students in Other Seminaries	4
Total Seminarians	4
High Schools, Diocesan and Parish	1
Total Students	664
High Schools, Private	2
Total Students	78
Elementary Schools, Diocesan and Parish	14
Total Students	2,975
Elementary Schools, Private	1
Total Students	210
Catechesis/Religious Education:	
High School Students	744
Elementary Students	2,729
Total Students Under Catholic Instruction	7,404
Teachers in the Diocese:	
Priests	2
Sisters	24
Lay Teachers	215
Vital Statistics	
Receptions into the Church:	
Infant Baptism Totals	701
Adult Baptism Totals	143
Received into Full Communion	287
First Communions	707
Confirmations	702
Marriages:	
Catholic	104
Interfaith	159
Total Marriages	263
Deaths	193
Total Catholic Population	41,905
Total Population	1,376,114

The Catholic Center—1310 Leestown Rd., P.O. Box 12350, Lexington, 40582-2350. Tel: 606-253-1993; Fax: 606-254-6284. Office Hours: Mon.-Fri. 8:30-4:30.

Vicar General—Rev. Msgr. JOHN J. ROLF.

Chancellor—Sr. MARY KEVAN SEIBERT, S.N.D.

Executive Secretary To The Bishop—SHEILA STEWART.

Finances—Dr. STUART DUBA, Dir., *1310 Leestown Rd., P.O. Box 12350, Lexington, 40582-2350.*

Diocesan Consultors—Rev. Msgr. JOHN ROLF, V.G.; Revs. WILFRED FRAENZLE; FRANK OSBURG; MICHAEL RAMLER; JOHN CURTIS; STEPHEN GALLENSTEIN; RICHARD EDELEN, *1310 Leestown Rd., P.O. Box 12350, Lexington, 40582-2350.*

Regional Councillors—Fayette Region: Rev. WILFRED FRAENZLE; Bluegrass Region: Rev. MICHAEL RAMLER; Mt. West Region: Rev. JOHN CURTIS; Mt. East Region: Rev. RICHARD EDELEN; Big Sandy-Licking Region: Rev. STEPHEN GALLENSTEIN.

Diocesan Tribunal—1310 Leestown Rd., P.O. Box 12350, Lexington, 40582-2350. Tel: 606-253-1993. Rev. JAMES ZUSY, O.P., J.C.D., Dir.

Judicial Vicar—Rev. JOHN E. LIST, J.C.L.

Associate Judges—Sr. MARGARET STALLMEYER, C.D.P., J.C.L.

Defenders Of The Bond—Revs. THOMAS THAI, Ph.D.; MICHAEL WEGLICKI; MAURICE RAJKOVICH, J.D.; Sr. GAYLE BRABEC, B.V.M.; WILLIAM DAVENPORT, J.D.

Case Instructor—CAROLYN SNOWDEN; Rev. BARRY BURRUS.

Promoter of Justice—Rev. PAUL PRABELL, M.S.

Notary—CAROLYN SNOWDEN.

Ministry Admissions Board—Most Rev. J. KENDRICK WILLIAMS.

Priests' Retirement Board—Revs. LAWRENCE HEHMAN; THEODORE KELLER; RAYMOND STRATMAN; GREGORY SCHULER; Mr. JOSEPH SAULINO; Mr. JOHN D. PRICE; WILLIAM TOZER; JOB D. TURNER; STUART DUBA.

Diocesan Offices And Directors

Archives—Sr. MARY KEVAN SEIBERT, S.N.D., Archivist, *1310 Leestown Rd., P.O. Box 12350, Lexington, 40582-2350.* Tel: 606-253-1993.

Campus Ministry—Newman Center Dir., Contact The Catholic Center, *P.O. Box 12350, Lexington, 40582-2350.* Tel: 606-253-1993.

Catholic Charismatic Prayer Groups—Rev. LOUIS LIPPS, S.J., Liaison.

Catholic Scouting—Rev. MICHAEL WEGLICKI, Diocesan Dir. Tel: 606-289-5502.

Catholic Social Service Bureau—Sr. FRANCES MOORE, C.D.P., Dir., Office: *1310 Leestown Rd., Lexington, 40508.* Tel: 606-253-1993.

Communications—Sr. M. KEVAN SEIBERT, S.N.D., Dir., *1310 Leestown Rd., P.O. Box 12350, Lexington, 40582-2350.* Tel: 606-253-1993.

Conciliation, Arbitration Board—CAROL JACKSON, Chm.

Continuing Formation of Priests—Rev. JOSEPH MUENCH.

Deaf Ministry—J. KEVIN MARTIN, Coord.; Rev. JOHN LIST, Chap., *1310 Leestown Rd., Lexington, 40582-2350.* Tel: 606-253-1993. Tel: TDD: 606-744-7876.

Development Office—J. GRANT CHAPLINE, *1310 Leestown Rd., P.O. Box 12350, Lexington, 40582-2350.* Tel: 606-253-1993.

Ecumenical Liaison—Mr. ARDEN WOLTERMAN, *3 Lansdowne Estates, Lexington, 40582.* Tel: 606-268-9067.

Education—

Secretary of Educational Ministries—Dr. MARGARET RALPH, *1310 Leestown Rd., Lexington, 40508.* Tel: 606-253-1993.

Director Of Instructional Services—Sr. RITA BRINK, O.S.B., *1310 Leestown Rd., Lexington, 40508.* Tel: 606-253-1993.

Director For Catechetical Services, Adult Faith Development—PATRICK GUENTERT, *1310 Leestown Rd., Lexington, 40508.* Tel: 606-253-1993.

Director R.C.I.A., And Evangelization—Dr. MARGARET RALPH, *1310 Leestown Rd., Lexington, 40508.* Tel: 606-253-1993.

Family Ministry—Ms. KATHLEEN TOMAZIC, Diocesan Coord., *P.O. Box 12350, Lexington, 40582-2350.* Tel: 606-253-1993.

Healthcare—Sr. M. KEVAN SEIBERT, S.N.D., Diocesan Coord., *1310 Leestown Rd., Lexington, 40582-2350.* Tel: 606-253-1993.

Hispanic Ministry—Rev. JOSEPH VON HANDORF, Diocesan Dir., *1310 Leestown Rd., Lexington, 40582-2350.* Tel: 606-253-1993.

HIV/AIDS Ministry—Rev. JOHN C. CURTIS, Diocesan Coord.

Justice and Peace—Sr. CLARA FEHRINGER, O.S.U., Diocesan Coord.

Commission for African American Catholic Concerns—Dr. MARIAN SWOPE, Dir., *439 Bourbon Ave., Lexington, 40508.* Tel: 606-254-2154.

Rural Life—The Catholic Center, 1310 Leestown Rd., Lexington, 40508. Tel: 606-253-1993.

Liturgy—Sr. CLARA FEHRINGER, O.S.U., Dir., *1310 Leestown Rd., Lexington, 40582-2350.* Tel: 606-253-1993.

Ministry Formation—Sr. IRIS ANN LEDDEN, S.S.N.D., Dir., *P.O. Box 12350, Lexington, 40582-2350.*

Mission Office, Propagation Of The Faith And The Holy Childhood—Sr. MICHAEL LEO MULLANEY, S.C.N., Diocesan Dir., *1310 Leestown Rd., P.O. Box 12350, Lexington, 40582-2350.* Tel: 606-253-1993.

Newspaper "Cross Roads"—THOMAS F. SHAUGHNESSY, Editor, *1310 Leestown Rd., Lexington, 40508.* Tel: 606-253-1993; Fax: 606-259-0951.

Pastoral Services—Sr. HELEN MAHER GARVEY, B.V.M., Diocesan Dir., *1310 Leestown Rd., Lexington, 40582-2350.* Tel: 606-253-1993.

Permanent Diaconate—BILL REED, Dir., *3510 Danada Dr., Lexington, 40502.* Tel: 606-272-1546.

Persons with Disabilities—Mrs. MARY PETRY, *124 Rolling Hills, Danville, 40422.* Tel: 606-236-5017.

Presbyteral Council—Most Rev. J. KENDRICK WILLIAMS, Pres., Ex-officio; Rev. Msgr. JOHN ROLF, V.G.; Revs. FRANK OSBURG, Chm. RICHARD EDELEN; JOHN CURTIS; STEPHEN GALLENSTEIN; WILFRED FRAENZLE.

Priests' Personnel—Rev. PAUL PRABELL, Dir., *1310 Leestown Rd., P.O. Box 12350, Lexington, 40582-2350.*

Prison Ministry—Rev. JOHN NOE, Diocesan Coord., *Castlewood Apts. #19, Russell, 41169.* Tel: 606-928-6414.

Religious—Sr. HELEN MAHER GARVEY, B.V.M., Dir., *1310 Leestown Rd., Lexington, 40582-2350.* Tel: 606-253-1993.

Respect Life—Sr. MARY KEVAN SEIBERT, S.N.D., Diocesan Coord.

Vocations—Most Rev. J. KENDRICK WILLIAMS, Dir. Assoc. Dirs.: Revs. JOHN MORIARTY; MARK DREVES, *P.O. Box 12350, Lexington, 40582-2350.*

Youth Ministry—BARBARA MURRAY, Dir., *The Catholic Center, P.O. Box 12350, Lexington, 40582-2350.*

CLERGY, PARISHES, MISSIONS AND PAROCHIAL SCHOOLS

CITY OF LEXINGTON
(Fayette County)

1—CATHEDRAL OF CHRIST THE KING (1945), Revs. Gregory Schuler, Rector; Robert J. Murphy, S.J.; Gino Donatelli, S.J.; Deacon Arden Wolterman. In res., Rev. Louis Lipps, S.J.
Res., 299 Colony Blvd., 40502. Tel: 606-268-2861; Fax: 606-268-2861.
School—(Grades K-8) 412 Cochran Rd., 40502. Tel: 606-266-5641.
Lay Teachers 27; Students 530.

2—THE NEWMAN CENTER, HOLY SPIRIT (1963). Parish for Students, Faculty and Staff of the University of Kentucky. Revs. Daniel J. Noll; Walter Bado, S.J.
Res., 320 Rose Ln., 40508. Tel: 606-255-8566; Fax: 606-255-8567.

3—MARY, QUEEN OF THE HOLY ROSARY (1960), Revs. Robert H. Nieberding; Mark D. Dreves; Deacon Jeremiah Noe. In res., Rev. Louis R. Schmidt.
Res., 601 Hill'N Dale Rd., 40503. Tel: 606-278-7432; Fax: 606-278-2453.
Church—2501 Clays Mill Rd., 40503.
School—Fax: 606-277-1784.
Sisters of Notre Dame 3; Lay Teachers 25; Students 532.

4—PAX CHRISTI CATHOLIC CHURCH (1994), Rev. Lawrence W. Hehman.
Res., 1790 Viley Rd., 40504. Tel: 606-252-4259; Fax: 606-223-7960.

5—ST. ELIZABETH ANN SETON (1980), Rev. Wilfred J. Fraenzle; Sr. Eileen Golby, O.S.F., Pastoral Assoc.; Deacon James Horine; Ms. Joan Springer, Pastoral Assoc. In res., Rev. Jay Van Handorf.
Res., 1750 Summerhill Dr., 40515. Tel: 606-273-8131.
Parish Center: Tel: 606-273-1318.; Education Office: Tel: 606-273-2318.

6—ST. PAUL (1865), Rev. Frank C. Osburg; Deacon Louis Fister; Sr. Joann Hayden, C.D.P., Pastoral Assoc. In res., Rev. James Zusy, O.P.
Res., 501 W. Short St., 40507-1254. Tel: 606-252-0738; Fax: 606-225-6127. [JC]
School—Inter-Parish Elementary - Sts. Peter and Paul School. See St. Peter for details.

7—ST. PETER (1812), Rev. Thomas Vu-Minh Thai; Sr. Mary Margene Koester, S.N.D., Pastoral Assoc. In res., Rev. Theodore Keller, (Retired).
Res., 153 Barr St., 40507. Tel: 606-252-7551. [JC]
School—Inter-Parish Elementary - Sts. Peter and Paul School, Tel: 606-254-9257; Fax: 606-254-9050.
Lay Teachers 19; Students 278.

8—ST. PETER CLAVER (1887), Deacon Boyd Marshall, Pastoral Assoc.
Res., 410 Jefferson St., P.O. Box 12307, 40582-2307. Tel: 606-254-0030.

OUTSIDE THE CITY OF LEXINGTON

Ashland, Boyd Co., Holy Family (1860), Rev. John J. Wordeman; Deacons Karl A. Mellenger; Robert Barringer.
Res., 900 Winchester Ave., 41101. Tel: 606-329-1607; Fax: 606-329-1806. [CEM]
School—932 Winchester Ave., 41101. Tel: 606-324-7040.
Lay Teachers 12; Students 208.
Mission—Greenup, St. Lawrence.

Barbourville, Knox Co., St. Gregory (1910), Rev. Stanley Tillman, S.J., Admin.
Church—329 N. Sycamore Dr., 40906. Tel: 606-546-4461.

Beattyville, Lee Co., Queen of All Saints (1965), Rev. Richard D. Edelen. Pastoral Assocs.: Sr. Davida Lund, O.S.F.; Sr. Alice Retzner, O.S.F.
Mailing Address: P.O. Box 563, 41311.
Res., 90 Railroad St., 41311. Tel: 606-464-8695.
Mission—Booneville, Owsley Co., Booneville Catholic Church of the Holy Family, (1984) R.R. 2, Box 221, Booneville, 41314. Tel: 606-593-6948. Pastoral Assocs.: Sr. Marge Eilerman, O.S.F.; Sr. Karen Lindenberger, O.S.F.; Campton, Wolfe Co., Catholic Church of the Good Shepherd, (1987) P.O. Box 742, Campton, 41301. Tel: 606-668-3731. Sr. Margie Zurieck, C.PP.S., Pastoral Assoc.; Heidelberg, Lee Co., St. Therese, (1948) P.O.Box 563, Beattyville, KY 41311. Tel: 606-464-8695.

Berea, Madison Co., St. Clare (1950), Rev. John C. Curtis; Sr. Anne Regina Lannon, S.S.J., Pastoral Assoc.
Res., 622 Chestnut St., 40403. Tel: 606-986-4633.
Mission—McKee, Jackson Co., St. Paul, (1973) P.O. Box 189, McKee 40447. Tel: 606-287-7601.

Carlisle, Nicholas Co., Shrine of Our Lady of Guadalupe (1962), Rev. Thomas Farrell.
Church—617 E. Main St., 40311. Tel: 606-289-5502.
Res., 1007 Main St., Paris, 40361-1709. Tel: 606-987-1571.

Corbin, Knox Co., Sacred Heart (1902), Rev. Roger K. Arnsparger. In res., Rev. Thomas Imfeld, (Retired).
Res., 703 Masters St., P.O. Box 455, 40702. Tel: 606-528-5222; Fax: 606-523-9901.

Danville, Boyle Co., SS. Peter & Paul (1807), Revs. Paul Prabell; J. Richard Sullivan (L).
Res., 117 W. Main St., 40422. Tel: 606-236-2111; Fax: 606-236-2922.
Mission—Junction City, Boyle Co., St. Patrick, (1885).

Cumberland, Harlan Co., St. Stephen (1940), Rev. Edward H. Lammert, O.F.M.; Sr. Margaret Mary Mouch, S.N.D., Pastoral Assoc.; Deacon Michael Daukas. In res., Rev. Maynard Tetreault, O.F.M.
Res., 304 Central St., 40823. Tel: 606-589-5616.

Frankfort, Franklin Co., Good Shepherd (1848), Rev. Michael Ramler; Sr. Mary Clare Windholz, R.S.M., Pastoral Assoc.; Deacons James B. Barton; Joseph Alessio; Thomas Snyder.
Res., 310 Wapping St., 40601. Tel: 502-227-4511; Fax: 502-875-9854.
School—(Grades K-8) 316 Wapping St., 40601. Tel: 502-223-5041.
Lay Teachers 20; Students 325.

Georgetown, Scott Co., St. John's (1869), Rev. John E. List; Deacon John Calandrella.
Res., 604 E. Main St., 40324. Tel: 502-863-3404. [CEM]
School—(Grades K-5) 106 Military St., 40324. Tel: 502-863-2607.
Lay Teachers 5; Students 100.
Mission—White Sulphur, Scott Co., St. Francis de Sales, (1794) 4086 Frankfort Pike, 40324. Tel: 502-863-4516.

Grayson, Carter Co., Ss. John & Elizabeth (1964), Rev. Bruce C. Brylinski, Glmy.
Church—Rte. 4, Box 442, 41143. Tel: 606-474-9979.
Res., P.O. Box 841, 41143. Tel: 606-474-9897.

Harlan, Harlan Co., Holy Trinity (1948), Bro. Mark Ligett, O.F.M., Pastoral Dir.; Rev. Edward Lammert, O.F.M., Pastoral Coord.; Deacon Michael Daukas.
Res., 2536 S. U.S. Highway 421, 40831-1798. Tel: 606-573-6311; Fax: 606-574-0093.
School—Tel: 606-573-3570.
Sisters of Notre Dame 3; Lay Teachers 4; Students 90.

Harrodsburg, Mercer Co., St. Andrew (1858), Rev. Joseph Muench.
Res., 334 S. Chiles, 40330. Tel: 606-734-4270; Fax: 606-733-9770.
Mission—Perryville, Boyle Co., St. Mary, (1949).

Hazard, Perry Co., Mother of Good Counsel (1913), Rev. Michael Chowning, O.F.M.; Ms. Patricia Riestenberg, Pastoral Assoc.
Res., 329 Poplar & Cedar Sts., 41701. Tel: 606-436-2533.

Jackson, Breathitt Co., Holy Cross (1923), Deacon Joseph Schueneman, Pastoral Dir.; Rev. Michael Chowning, O.F.M.
Church—46 Brewers Dr., 41339. Tel: 606-666-7871. [CEM]

Jellico, Whitley Co., KY & Campbell Co., TN, St. Boniface (1886), Rev. Robert Damron.
Res., 76 W. Sycamore St., Williamsburg, 40769. Tel: 606-549-2156. [CEM]

Jenkins, Letcher Co., St. George (1913), Rev. Edward L. Randall, O.M.I.
Res., P.O. Box 787, 41537. Tel: 606-832-2409.
Mission—McRoberts, Letcher Co., Holy Angels, (1960).

Lancaster, Garrard Co., St. William (1951), Rev. Michael Weglicki.
Res., 224 Lexington St., P.O. Box 261, 40444. Tel: 606-792-4009.

Lawrenceburg, Anderson Co., St. Lawrence (1873), Rev. Charles J. McDonald; Deacon Thomas Rohan.
Res., 105 Woodland Park Circle, 40342. Tel: 502-839-6381.

London, Laurel Co., St. William/St. Sylvester (1868), Rev. Jerome F. Stern.
Res., 525 W. 5th St., 40741. Tel: 606-864-7500. [CEM]

Louisa, Lawrence Co., St. Jude (1982), Rev. Msgr. Ralph Beiting.
Res., Rte. 5, Box 1083, 41230. Tel: 606-638-0219; Fax: 606-638-0220.
Mission—Hode, Martin Co., St. John Neumann, (1980) Rte. 292, Hode 41223. Tel: 606-395-5947.

Lynch, Harlan Co., Church of the Resurrection (1917), Rev. Edward H. Lammert, O.F.M.; Sr. Margaret Mary Mouch, S.N.D., Pastoral Assoc.
Res., 304 Central St., Cumberland, 40823. Tel: 606-589-5616.

Manchester, Clay Co., St. Ann (1952), Rev. Arturo Molina.
Res., 222 Town Branch Rd., P.O. Box 411, 40962. Tel: 606-598-2718.

Middlesboro, Bell Co., St. Julian (1890), Rev. John Dane; Deacon Donald Flowers.
Res., 118 E. Chester Ave., 40965-1256. Tel: 606-248-2068; Fax: 606-242-3290.
School—(Grades K-8) 116 E. Chester Ave., 40965. Tel: 606-248-8309.
Sisters 2; Lay Teachers 2; Students 95.
Mission—Pineville, Bell Co., St. Anthony, (1889) P.O. Box 628, Pineville 40977-0628. Tel: 606-337-2189.

Morehead, Rowan Co., Church of Jesus Our Savior (1961), Rev. Stephen Gallenstein; Deacon William T. Buelterman.
Res., 315 Battson, Box 307, 40351. Tel: 606-784-4392.
Chapel—Morehead, St. Claire Medical Center, Tel: 606-783-6500.

Monticello, Wayne Co., St. Peter (1967), Deacon John Tohill, Pastoral Dir.; Rev. John Kieffer, S.J.
Office: P.O. Box 669, 42633. Tel: 606-348-9416.
Res., 109 Cooper Dr., Somerset, 42501. Tel: 606-678-4928.

Mt. Sterling, Montgomery Co., St. Patrick (1868), Rev. Msgr. John Rolf.
Res., 139 W. Main St., 40353. Tel: 606-498-0300; Fax: 606-498-2116. [CEM]

Mt. Vernon, Rockcastle Co., Our Lady of Mt. Vernon (1954), Rev. John C. Curtis. Pastoral Assocs.: Ed & Tricia Cortas.
Res., 622 Chestnut St., Berea, 40403. Tel: 606-256-4170.

Nicholasville, Jessamine Co., St. Luke (1867), Rev. William C. Bush; Deacon Carter Ross, Jr.
Res., 304 S. Main St., 40356. Tel: 606-885-4892.

Ottenheim, Lincoln Co., St. Sylvester (1885), Rev. Michael Weglicki.
Res., 224 Lexington St., P.O. Box 261, Lancaster, 40444. Tel: 606-792-4009. [CEM]

Paintsville, Johnson Co., St. Michael Catholic Church (1941), Rev. William J. Fedders.
Res., 720 Washington Ave., 41240. Tel: 606-789-4455.
School—Our Lady of the Mountains, 405 Third St., 41240. Tel: 606-789-3661.
Sisters 2; Lay Teachers 7; Students 62.

Paris, Bourbon Co., Annunciation of the Blessed Virgin Mary (1856), Rev. Thomas P. Farrell.
Res., 1007 Main St., 40361. Tel: 606-987-1571. [CEM]
School—St. Mary, 1121 Main St., 40361. Tel: 606-987-3815.
Sisters of Charity of Nazareth 1; Lay Teachers 5; Students 75.

Pikeville, Pike Co., St. Francis of Assisi (1949), Revs. Terence E. Hoppenjans; Barry Burrus.

Res., 808 Bryan St.-Keel Addition, 41501. Tel: 606-437-6822.
Church—149 College St., 41501.
School—(Grades K-6) 809 Bryan St., 41501. Tel: 606-437-6117.
Sisters 1; Lay Teachers 3; Students 79.
Missions—Elkhorn City, Pike Co., St. Joseph the Worker, (1985) P.O. Box 55, Elkhorn City, 41522. Tel: 606-754-5225; Phelps, Pike Co., Jesus of the Mountains Catholic Church, (1988) 38 Birch Ct., Phelps, 41553. Tel: 606-456-7909. Pastoral Ministers: Sr. Grace Pasquarello, S.S.J.; Sr. Eleanor McNichol, S.S.J.

Prestonsburg, Floyd Co., St. Martha (1984), Rev. John P. Moriarty.
Res., 75 Martha's Vineyard, 41653. Tel: 606-874-9526.
Mission—Salyersville, Magoffin Co., St. Luke's, (1982) 1221 Parkway Dr., 41240. Tel: 606-349-5320. Sr. Mary Catherine Vukmanic, O.S.U., Pastoral Assoc.
Chapel—Martin, Our Lady of the Way Hospital, Tel: 606-285-5181.

Ravenna, Estill Co., St. Elizabeth (1932), Rev. William G. Poole; Sr. Alice Rohe, O.S.F., Pastoral Assoc.
Res., 316 5th St., 40472. Tel: 606-723-4705.
Mission—Stanton, Powell Co., Our Lady of the Mountains, (1984) 1093 E. College, Stanton, 40380. Tel: 606-663-5919. Sr. Kathleen McMullin, O.S.F., Pastoral Assoc.

Richmond, Madison Co., St. Mark (1867), Rev. Kenneth Waibel; Deacon Richard Jackson.
Res., 608 W. Main St., 40475. Tel: 606-623-2989.
School—Tel: 606-623-9112.
Lay Teachers 8; Students 176.
St. Stephen the Martyr (1977). Eastern Kentucky University, Newman Center. Rev. Kenneth Waibel; Ms. Katherine Schmitt, Pastoral Assoc.
Res., 405 University Dr., 40475. Tel: 606-623-9400.

Somerset, Pulaski Co., St. Mildred (1887), Rev. Patrick F. Stewart; Deacons G. A. Weigel; Vincent E. Cheshire; John Borders; Larry Cranfill.
Res., 203 S. Central Ave., 42501. Tel: 606-678-5051.

Versailles, Woodford Co., St. Leo (1891), Rev. Raymond R. Stratman; Deacon James Cox.
Res., 295 Huntertown Rd., 40383. Tel: 606-873-4573.
School—239 N. Main St., 40383. Tel: 606-873-4591. Sisters of Notre Dame 1; Lay Teachers 10; Students 240.

West Liberty, Morgan Co., Prince of Peace (1963), Rev. Peter Richardson, Glmy.
Res., Pine Acres Dr., P.O. Box 393, 41472. Tel: 606-743-4817; Fax: 606-743-3266.
Mission—Owingsville, Bath Co., St. Julie Billiart, (1969). Deacon William R. Grimes.

Williamsburg, Whitley Co., Our Lady of Perpetual Help (1963), Rev. Robert Damron.
Res., 76 W. Sycamore St., 40769. Tel: 606-549-2156.

Winchester, Clark Co., St. Joseph (1872), Rev. Joseph A. Saulino.
Res., 254 S. Main St., 40391. Tel: 606-744-4917.
School—St. Agatha Academy, (Grades K-6). (Montessori) 244 S. Main St., 40391. Tel: 606-744-6484. Sisters of Divine Providence of Kentucky 2; Lay Teachers 8; Students 187.

Whitley City, Mc Creaky Co., Good Shepherd Chapel (1974), Rev. Carroll Howlin (JOL) Admin.
Res., P.O. Box 350, 42653. Tel: 606-376-5815.

Chaplains of Public Institutions

LEXINGTON. *Federal Medical Center,* 3301 Leestown Rd., 40507. Sr. Marie Anna Stelmach, O.P., Chap.
Veterans Administration Hospital, Leestown Pk., 40511. Tel: 606-233-4511. Rev. George C. Maynard, S.J (DET) Chap.

ASHLAND. *Federal Correctional Institution.* Castlewood Apt., #19, Russell, 41169. Rev. John P. Noe, Chap.

MANCHESTER. *Federal Correctional Institution.* Rev. Arturo Molina, Chap.

Special Assignment:
Reverend Fathers—
Farmer, Matthew P.
Johnson, Carl, Federal Bureau of Prisons, Buckley, WV
Kenney, Henry, S.J., Spiritual Dir., Lexington, KY
Lipps, Louis, S.J., Spiritual Dir. for Women Religious

Retired:
Reverend Monsignors—
Nienaber, Leonard B., Vianney Renewal Center, 6476 Eime Rd., Dittmer, MD 63023
Reverend Fathers—
Blandford, James T., P.O. Box 367, Springfield, KY 40069
Brinker, Maurice J., Taylor Manor, P.O. Box 349, Versailles, KY 40383
Imfield, Thomas J., P.O. Box 455, Corbin, KY 40702
Keller, Theodore, 153 Barr St., Lexington, KY 40507
Moore, Elmer R., P.O. Box 1689, Lexington, KY 40592
Pilger, Joseph J., 1333 Gray Hawk Dr., Lexington, KY 40502
Schmidt, Louis R., 601 Hill'N Dale Rd., Lexington, KY 40503
Spalding, William, 5146 Dixie Hwy., Louisville, KY 40216-1702
Trimbur, Lee Francis, 900 Winchester Ave., Ashland, KY 41101
Wethington, Paul V., 551 Bob-O-Link, Lexington, KY 40503

Permanent Deacons:
Alessio, Joseph J.
Arnold, Paul J., Jr.
Barringer, Robert
Barton, James
Borders, John
Buelterman, William
Calandrella, John
Cheshire, Vincent
Cox, James H.
Cranfill, Larry
Daukas, Michael R.
Fister, Louis
Flowers, Don K.
Grimes, William R.
Hohl, David (COL)
Horine, James
Jackson, Richard
Marshall, Boyd
Mellenger, Karl A.
Noe, Jeremiah, H.
O'Neil, Dennis J.
Rohan, Thomas
Ross, Carter, Jr.
Schueneman, Joseph T.
Snyder, Thomas
Tohill, John J.
Weigel, Gerard A.
Wolterman, Arden J.
Young, Melvin

PARISH PILGRIMAGE SHRINES

CARLISLE. *Our Lady of Guadalupe Shrine,* 617 E. Main St., 40311.

INSTITUTIONS LOCATED IN THE DIOCESE

[A] HIGH SCHOOLS, DIOCESAN

LEXINGTON. *Lexington Catholic High School,* 2250 Clays Mill Rd., 40503. Tel: 606-277-7183. Rev. Robert J. Bueter, S.J., Pres.; Mrs. Sally Stevens, Prin. Priests 2; Sisters 1; Lay Teachers 45; Students 667.

[B] HIGH SCHOOLS, PRIVATE

CORBIN. *All Saints High School,* P.O. Box 435, 40702. Tel: 606-528-7543. Mr. Robert C. Halcomb, Prin.

MARTIN. *The Piarist School.* (Grades 9-12), Rte. 80, P.O. Box 870, 41649. Tel: 606-285-3950. College prep high school. Rev. Thomas R. Carroll, Sch.P., Prin. Priests 3; Lay Teachers 5; Students 44.

[C] ELEMENTARY SCHOOLS, PRIVATE

CORBIN. *St. Camillus Academy.* (Grades PreK-8), 709 E. Center St., 40701. Tel: 606-528-5077. Coed Day School. Sisters of Divine Providence of KY. Sisters 7; Lay Teachers 14; Students 210.

[D] GENERAL HOSPITALS

LEXINGTON. *St. Joseph Hospital,* 1 St. Joseph Dr., 40504. Tel: 606-278-3436.
For a complete listing, refer to the Hospitals section.

ASHLAND. *Our Lady of Bellefonte Hospital, Inc.,* St. Christopher Dr., 41101. Tel: 606-833-3333; Fax: 606-833-3695.
For a complete listing, refer to the Hospitals section.

IRVINE. *Marcum and Wallace Memorial Hospital,* 201 Richmond Ave., 40336. Tel: 606-723-2115; Fax: 606-723-6549.
For a complete listing, refer to the Hospitals section.

LONDON. *London, Marymount dba Marymount Medical Center,* 310 E. Ninth St., 40741. Tel: 606-878-6520.
For a complete listing, refer to the Hospitals section.

MARTIN. *Our Lady of the Way Hospital, Inc.,* Box 910, 41649. Tel: 606-285-5181.
For a complete listing, refer to the Hospitals section.

MOREHEAD. *Saint Claire Medical Center,* 40351. Tel: 606-784-6661.
For a complete listing, refer to the Hospitals section.

[E] PRIMARY HEALTH CARE SERVICES

FRENCHBURG. *Menifee Medical Center,* P.O. Box 49, 40322. Tel: 606-768-2191.
For a complete listing, refer to the Hospitals section.

OLIVE HILL. *Carter County Medical Clinic,* P.O. Box V, U.S. 60 W., 41164. Tel: 606-286-4152.
For a complete listing, refer to the Hospitals section.

OWINGSVILLE. *Bath County Medical Clinic,* 632 Slate Ave., 40360. Tel: 606-674-6386.
For a complete listing, refer to the Hospitals section.

SANDY HOOK. *Elliot County Medical Clinic,* P.O. Box 748, 41171. Tel: 606-738-5155.
For a complete listing, refer to the Hospitals section.

[F] NURSING HOMES

VERSAILLES. *Taylor Manor Nursing Home,* 300 Berry Ave., 40383. Tel: 606-873-4201.
For a complete listing, refer to the Special Care Facilities section.

[G] RESIDENCES OF PRIESTS

PRESTONSBURG. *Piarist Fathers,* 99 Martha's Vineyard, 41653. Tel: 606-874-9594. Rev. Thomas R. Carroll, Sch.P. Priests 3.

[H] MONASTERIES FOR SISTERS

MARTIN. *Sisters of St. Benedict-The Dwelling Place Monastery,* 150 Mt. Tabor Rd., 41649. Tel: 606-886-9624. Sr. Judy Yunker, O.S.B., Supr. Total number in community 5.

[I] SECULAR INSTITUTES

LEXINGTON. *Society of St. Vincent de Paul,* 835 Glendover Rd., 40502. Tel: 606-269-4038. Thomas H. Nowack, Pres. District Council of Lexington; Deacon James Barton, Spiritual Dir.

ASHLAND. *Roman Catholic Daughters of the King,* 2801 Hackworth St., 41101. Tel: 606-329-1249. Mrs. Madonna Fisher, Pres. Chapters: Holy Family Chapter, Ashland; St. Augustine of Canterbury Chapter, Dunwoody, GA; Annunciation Chapter, Columbus, MS.

[J] SOCIAL SERVICES

LIVINGSTON.
**Appalachia Science in the Public Interest,* P.O. Box 298, 40445. Tel: 606-256-0077; Fax: 606-453-2105. Revs. Albert J. Fritsch, S.J.; John L. Kieffer, S.J.

[K] RENEWAL CENTERS

LEXINGTON. *Cliffview Retreat Center,* P.O. Box 12350, 40582-2350. Tel: 606-253-1993.

HAZARD. *Father Farrell Spiritual Life Center,* 329 Poplar at Cedar, 41701. Tel: 606-436-2533. Rev. Michael Chowning, O.F.M., Dir.; Pat Riestenberg, Assoc. Dir.

MARTIN. *Sisters of St. Benedict, Mt. Tabor Retreat Center,* 150 Mt. Tabor Rd., 41649. Tel: 606-886-9624. Staff Sisters 3.

[L] NEWMAN CENTERS

LEXINGTON. *The Newman Center Holy Spirit Parish University of Kentucky,* 320 Rose Ln., 40508. Tel: 606-255-8566. Revs. Daniel J. Noll; Walter Bado, S.J.

BARBOURVILLE. *St. Gregory Church-Union College,* 329 N. Sycamore St., 40906. Tel: 606-546-4461. Rev. Stanley Tillman, S.J.

BEREA. *St. Clare Church-Berea College,* 622 Chestnut St., 40403. Tel: 606-986-4633. Rev. John C. Curtis; Sr. Anne Regina Lannon, S.S.J.

MOREHEAD. *Catholic Student Center-Morehead State University,* P.O. Box 307, 40351. Tel: 606-784-4392. Rev. Stephen Gallenstein, Campus Min.

RICHMOND. *Catholic Newman Center-St. Stephen the Martyr Parish,* Eastern Kentucky University, 405 University Dr., P.O. Box 356, 40475. Tel: 606-623-7291; 623-9400 (Center). Rev. Kenneth Waibel, Pastor & Dir. Campus Ministry; Ms. Katherine A. Schmitt, Pastoral Assoc.

[M] MISCELLANEOUS

ASHLAND. *Franciscan Health System of Kentucky, Inc.,* St. Christopher Dr., 41101. Tel: 606-833-3333. Mr. Robert J. Maher, Pres.

RELIGIOUS INSTITUTES OF MEN REPRESENTED IN THE DIOCESE

For further details refer to the corresponding bracketed number in the Religious Institutes of Men or Women section.

[0520]—*Franciscan Friars.* (St. John Baptist Province).—O.F.M.

[0570]—*Glenmary Home Missioners.*—Glmy.

[0690]—*Jesuit Fathers and Brothers.* (Chicago & Detroit Provs.).—S.J.

[0910]—*Oblates of Mary Immaculate.* (Eastern American Prov.).—O.M.I.

[0430]—*Order of Preachers*.—O.P.
[1040]—*Piarist Fathers*. (U.S. Prov.).—Sch.P.

RELIGIOUS INSTITUTES OF WOMEN REPRESENTED IN THE DIOCESE

[0230]—*Benedictine Sisters of Pontifical Jurisdiction*. (Pittsburgh, PA; Covington, KY; Martin, KY).—O.S.B.
[1810]—*Bernardine Sisters of the Third Order of St. Francis*.—O.S.F.
[2980]—*Congregation de Notre Dame*. Ridgefield, CT.—C.N.D.
[2100]—*Congregation of Humility of Mary*.—C.H.M.
[2230]—*Congregation of the Infant Jesus*.—C.I.J.
[3710]—*Congregation of the Sisters of St. Agnes*. (Bronx, NY).—C.S.A.
[1920]—*Congregation of the Sisters of the Holy Cross*.—C.S.C.
[1730]—*Congregation of the Sisters of the Third Order of St. Francis*. (Oldenburg, IN).—O.S.F.
[1780]—*Congregation of the Sisters of the Third Order of St. Francis of Perpetual Adoration*. (Eastern Region).—F.S.P.A.
[1710]—*Congregation of the Third Order Regular of St. Francis of Mary Immaculate, Joliet, IL*.—O.S.F.
[1070-03]—*Dominican Sisters*. (Sinsinawa, WI).—O.P.
[1070-09]—*Dominican Sisters*. (Racine, WI).—O.P.
[1070-13]—*Dominican Sisters*. (Adrian, MI).—O.P.
[1070-14]—*Dominican Sisters*. (Grand Rapids, MI).—O.P.
[1070-02]—*Dominican Sisters*. (Columbus, OH).—O.P.
[1230]—*Franciscan Sisters of Christian Charity*.—O.S.F.
[1440]—*Franciscan Sisters of the Poor*.—S.F.P.
[2080]—*Home Mission Sisters of America (Glenmary)*.—G.H.M.S.
[2575]—*Institute of the Sisters of Mercy of the Americas*. (Charlotte, NC; Philadelphia, PA; West Hartford, CT).—R.S.M.
[2470]—*Maryknoll Sisters of St. Dominic*.—M.M.
[2710]—*Missionaries of Charity*.—M.C.
[2070]—*Religious of the Holy Union of the Sacred Hearts*.—S.U.S.C.
[2970]—*School Sisters of Notre Dame*. (Milwaukee; Baltimore).—S.S.N.D.
[1680]—*School Sisters of St. Francis*.—O.S.F.
[3580]—*Servants of Mary*.—O.S.M.
[0430]—*Sisters of Charity of Blessed Virgin Mary*. (Dubuque, IA).—B.V.M.
[0440]—*Sisters of Charity of Cincinnati*.—S.C.
[0500]—*Sisters of Charity of Nazareth*.—S.C.N.
[0580]—*Sisters of Charity of St. Augustine*. (Rienfield, OH).—C.S.A.
[0590]—*Sisters of Charity of St. Elizabeth*. Convent Station, NJ.—S.C.
[1000]—*The Sisters of Divine Providence of Kentucky*.—C.D.P.
[1010]—*Sisters of Divine Providence of San Antonio, Texas*.—C.D.P.
[2990]—*Sisters of Notre Dame*. (Covington Prov.).—S.N.D.
[3000]—*Sisters of Notre Dame de Namur*. (Cincinnati Prov.).—S.N.D.deN.
[3360]—*Sisters of Providence of St. Mary-of-the-Woods, Indiana*.—S.P.
[3893]—*Sisters of Saint Joseph of Chestnut Hill, Philadelphia*.—S.S.J.
[1540]—*Sisters of St Francis*. (Clinton, IA).—O.S.F.
[3750]—*Sisters of St. Chretienne*. (Wrentham, MA).—S.S.Ch.
[1650]—*The Sisters of St. Francis of Philadelphia*.—O.S.F.
[3830-05]—*Sisters of St. Joseph*. (Baden, PA; Brentwood, NY; West Hartford, CT).—C.S.J.
[3830-05]—*Sisters of St. Joseph*. (Brentwood, NY).—C.S.J.
[3850]—*Sisters of St. Joseph of Chambery*.—C.S.J.
[3920]—*Sisters of St. Joseph the Worker*.—S.J.W.
[1990]—*Sisters of the Holy Names of Jesus and Mary*.—S.N.J.M.
[3270]—*Sisters of the Most Precious Blood (O'Fallon, MO)*. (Dubuque, IA).—C.PP.S.
[3260]—*Sisters of the Precious Blood (Dayton, Ohio)*.—C.PP.S.
[3320]—*Sisters of the Presentation of the B.V.M.* (Fargo, ND; Dubuque, IA; Staten Island, NY).—P.B.V.M.
[1760]—*Sisters of the Third Order of St. Francis of Penance and Charity*. (Tiffin, OH).—O.S.F.
[1720]—*Sisters of the Third Order Regular of St. Francis of the Congregation of Our Lady of Lourdes*.—O.S.F.
[2150]—*Sisters, Servants of the Immaculate Heart of Mary*.—I.H.M.
[4120-03]—*Ursuline Sisters of the Immaculate Conception*. (Louisville, KY).—O.S.U.
[4170]—*Vincentian Sisters of Charity*. (Bedford, OH).—V.S.C.

DIOCESAN CEMETERIES

LEXINGTON. *Calvary*.
ASHLAND. *Calvary*.
MT. STERLING. *St. Thomas*.

NECROLOGY

† Murray, Edward F., (Retired). —Died April 13, 1996.

Diocese of Lincoln

(Dioecesis Lincolnensis)

Most Reverend

FABIAN W. BRUSKEWITZ, D.D., S.T.D.

Bishop of Lincoln; ordained July 17, 1960; appointed Bishop of Lincoln March 24, 1992; consecrated May 13, 1992. *Mailing Address: Address all communications to P.O. Box 80328, Lincoln, NE, 68501-0328.*

Chancery: P.O. Box 80328, Lincoln, NE, 68501-0328. Tel.: 402-488-0921; Fax: 402-488-3569.

ERECTED AUGUST 2, 1887.

Square Miles 23,844.

Comprises that part of the State of Nebraska south of the Platte River.

Legal Title: "The Catholic Bishop of Lincoln".

For legal titles of parishes and diocesan institutions, consult the Chancery.

STATISTICAL OVERVIEW

Personnel	
Bishop	1
Priests: Diocesan Active in Diocese	108
Priests: Active Outside Diocese	3
Priests: Retired, Sick or Absent	23
Number of Diocesan Priests	134
Religious Priests in Diocese	12
Extern Priests in Diocese	2
Ordinations:	
Diocesan Priests	4
Transitional Deacons	8
Total Brothers	11
Total Sisters	118
Parishes	
Parishes	134
With Resident Pastor:	
Resident Diocesan Priests	84
Resident Religious Priests	3
Without Resident Pastor:	
Administered by Priests	47
Missions	1
Welfare	
Catholic Hospitals	3
Total Assisted	162,814
Homes for the Aged	3
Total Assisted	292
Special Centers for Social Services	4
Total Assisted	51,259
Residential Care of Disabled	1
Total Assisted	11
Other Institutions	2
Total Assisted	9,278
Educational	
Diocesan Students in Other Seminaries	44
Total Seminarians	44
High Schools, Diocesan and Parish	6
Total Students	1,881
Elementary Schools, Diocesan and Parish	25
Total Students	5,583
Non-residential Schools for the Disabled	1
Total Students	11
Catechesis/Religious Education:	
High School Students	2,067
Elementary Students	6,149
Total Students Under Catholic Instruction	15,735
Teachers in the Diocese:	
Priests	9
Sisters	48
Lay Teachers	337
Vital Statistics	
Receptions into the Church:	
Infant Baptism Totals	1,377
Adult Baptism Totals	155
Received into Full Communion	219
First Communions	1,519
Confirmations	1,506
Marriages:	
Catholic	268
Interfaith	211
Total Marriages	479
Deaths	628
Total Catholic Population	86,041
Total Population	516,662

Former Bishops—Most Rev. THOMAS BONACUM, D.D., Bishop of Lincoln; cons. Nov. 30, 1887; died Feb. 4, 1911.—Most Rev. J. HENRY TIHEN, D.D., cons. Bishop of Lincoln, July 6, 1911; transferred to the See of Denver, Sept. 21, 1917.—Most Rev. CHARLES J. O'REILLY, D.D., cons. Bishop of Baker City, Aug. 24, 1903; transferred to the See of Lincoln, March 20, 1918; died Feb. 4, 1923.—Most Rev. FRANCIS J. L. BECKMAN, S.T.D., cons. Bishop of Lincoln, May 1, 1924; elevated to the Metropolitan See of Dubuque, Jan. 17, 1930.—Most Rev. LOUIS B KUCERA, D.D., cons. Bishop of Lincoln, Oct. 28, 1930; died May 9, 1957.—Most Rev. JAMES V. CASEY, D.D., J.C.D., appt. Auxiliary of Lincoln April 5, 1957; cons. April 24, 1957; appt. Bishop of Lincoln June 14, 1957; promoted to Archbishop of Denver, Feb. 18, 1967; died March 14, 1986.—Most Rev. GLENNON P. FLAVIN, D.D., appt. Titular Bishop of Joannina and Auxiliary Bishop of St. Louis April 24, 1957; cons. May 30, 1957; promoted to See of Lincoln, May 29, 1967; retired March 24, 1992; died Aug. 27, 1995.

Chancery—3400 Sheridan Blvd., Lincoln, 68506., Mailing Address: P.O. Box 80328, Lincoln, 68501-0328. Tel: 402-488-0921; Fax: 402-488-3569. Office Hours: 9-5.

Moderator of the Curia—Rev. Msgr. ROBERT F. VASA, J.C.L.

Vicar General—Rev. Msgr. ROBERT F. VASA, J.C.L.

Chancellor—Rev. Msgr. TIMOTHY J. THORBURN, J.C.L.

Diocesan Tribunal—3400 Sheridan Blvd., Lincoln, 68506., Mailing Address: P.O. Box 80328, Lincoln, 68501-0328.

Officialis—Rev. DANIEL J. SEIKER, J.C.L.

Adjutant Judicial Vicars—Rev. Msgr. ROBERT F. VASA,J.C.L.; Rev. MAURICE H. CURRENT, J.C.L.

Promoter Justitiae—Rev. GAROLD L. GABEL, J.C.L.

Defensores Vinculi—Rev. Msgr. TIMOTHY J. THORBURN, J.C.L.

Judices—Rev. Msgr. ROBERT F. VASA, J.C.L.; Revs. MAURICE H. CURRENT, J.C.L.; GAROLD L. GABEL, J.C.L.; DANIEL J. SEIKER, J.C.L.

Advocates—Revs. THOMAS Y. AU; DAVID F. BOUREK; MICHAEL K. HOULIHAN; JAMES W. COOPER; JOHN R. SULLIVAN.

Notaries—Rev. Msgr. MICHAEL O. JACKELS, S.T.D.; Revs. GAROLD L. GABEL, J.C.L.; MARY ANN T. BIGLIN; LOUANNE I. COOK; ROSE M. LE CORGNE.

Diocesan Consultors—Rev. Msgr. JAMES D. DAWSON; Rev. Msgr. LEONARD I. KALIN, M.A.; Very Rev. Msgr. DANIEL J. POHL, B.A.; Rev. Msgr. TIMOTHY J. THORBURN; Rev. Msgr. ROBERT F. VASA; Revs. M. JAMES DIVIS, S.T.L.; JOHN T. FOLDA, S.T.L.

Presbyteral Council—Rev. Msgr. ROBERT F. VASA; Rev. Msgr. TIMOTHY J. THORBURN; Rev Msgr. LEONARD I. KALIN; Rev. Msgr. MYRON J. PLESKAC; Revs. JOHN J. PERKINTON; CHARLES R. TOWNSEND; RUDOLF F. OBORNY; DAVID R. HINTL; MICHAEL R. CHRISTENSEN; PETER J. GADIENT; Very Rev. JAMES G. MOEGLEIN, O.S.C.; Revs. LIAM M. BARR; ROBERT G. TUCKER; MICHAEL G. MCCABE.

Vicars For Religious—Rev. Msgr. MICHAEL O. JACKELS, S.T.D.; Rev. Msgr. TIMOTHY J. THORBURN.

Deaneries and Deans—Crete: Rev. Msgr. THOMAS L. HOLOMAN; David City: Rev. Msgr. ADRIAN F. HERBEK; Fairbury: Very Rev. PATRICK J. LYONS; Falls City: Very Rev. ROBERT A. ROH; Grant: Very Rev. GREGORY P. PAWLOSKI; Hastings: Rev. Msgr. JOHN J. MCCABE; Indianola: Rev. Msgr. DANIEL J. POHL; Lawrence: Very Rev. STANLEY F. SCHIEFFER; Lincoln: Rev. Msgr. JAMES D. DAWSON; Orleans: Very Rev. JAMES M. O'CONNOR; Plattsmouth: Very Rev. PAUL H. YORK; Wahoo: Very Rev. LAWRENCE J. GYHRA; York: Rev. Msgr. IVAN F. VAP.

Diocesan Offices and Directors

Apostleship of Prayer— Revs. JOHN W. KELLY, Dir. BERNARD V. KIMMINAU, Asst.

Apostolate to the Elderly—Rev. EDWIN L. STANDER.

Apostolate to the Spanish Speaking—Revs. JULIUS P. TVRDY, Dir. BERNARD A. LORENZ, Asst. Dir.

Apostolate of Suffering—Rev. STANLEY J. REDMERSKI, Dir.

Archivist—Sr. LORETTA GOSEN, C.PP.S.

Bishop's Lay Committee for Vocations—DOUGLAS C. CAREY, Pres.; Rev. Msgr. LEONARD KALIN, Chap.

Bishop's Pastoral Plan for Pro-Life Activities—GREG SCHLEPPENBACH, State Dir., *215 Centennial Mall S., Ste. 410, Lincoln, 68508.*

Building Commission—Rev. Msgr. ROBERT F. VASA, Chm.; Rev. Msgr. RAYMOND B. HAIN; Rev. Msgr. ADRIAN F. HERBEK; Rev. Msgr. IVAN F. VAP; Rev. Msgr. JAMES D. DAWSON; Rev. PETER J. GADIENT; Very Rev. STANLEY F. SCHIEFFER.

Catholic Relief Services—Rev. Msgr. TIMOTHY J. THORBURN, Dir.

Cemeteries—Revs. RONALD PATTERSON, Dir. DAVID R. HINTZ, Asst. Dir.

Censores Librorum—Rev. M. JAMES DIVIS, S.T.L.; Rev. Msgr. MICHAEL O. JACKELS, S.T.D.

Charities—Rev. JOSEPH M. WALSH, Dir. JOHN KOPETZKY, Vice Pres., Operations, *Catholic Social Services, 123 N. 25th St., Lincoln, 68503.* Tel: 402-474-1600., *Administrative Offices, 237 S. 70th St., Lincoln, 68510.* Tel: 402-489-1834., *Catholic Social Services, 518 East Side Blvd., Hastings, 68901.* Tel: 402-463-2112.

Clergy Relief Society—The Saint John Vianney Association—Rev. Msgr. ROBERT F. VASA, Sec.-Treas., *Mailing Address: P.O. Box 80328, Lincoln, 68501-0328.*

Commission on Alcohol and Drug Abuse—Rev. Msgr. CHARLES J. KEENAN, Dir., *3301 Sheridan Blvd., Lincoln, 68506.* Tel: 402-483-1941.

Commission for Sacred Liturgy and Sacred Music—Rev. WILLIAM D. GRANT, Chm.; Sr. MARY DURR, O.S.U., Exec. Sec.; Rev. Msgr. MICHAEL O. JACKELS, S.T.D.; Revs. ROBERT K. BARNHILL; MAURICE H. CURRENT; M. JAMES DIVIS; JOSEPH J. NEMEC.

Office of Diocesan and Social Development—Rev. LIAM M. BARR, Delegate, *P.O. Box 80328, Lincoln, 68501-0328.* Tel: 402-488-2040.

Office of Religious Education (CCD)—Rev. Msgr. MICHAEL O. JACKELS, S.T.D., Diocesan Dir. Tel: 402-488-0921. Sr. MARY DURR, O.S.U., Asst. Dir. Diocesan Area CCD Directors: Revs. THOMAS Y. AU; JOHN L. COPENHAVER, M.Div.; JOHN T. FOLDA; WILLIAM D. GRANT; DENNIS M. HUNT; JAMES J. MEYSENBURG; THOMAS L. WIEDEL; JAMES F. BENTON, M.Div.; THOMAS D. MCGUIRE; MARK E. SEIKER; SEAN P. REDMOND; THOMAS WALSH, *P.O. Box 80328, Lincoln, 68501-0328.*

Cursillo—Rev. MARK E. SEIKER, M.Div.

Diocesan Council of Catholic Women—Mrs. JEANETTE STENGEL, Pres.; Rev. PETER J. GADIENT, Moderator, *P.O. Box 212, Osceola, 68651.*

Diocesan Director of Liturgy—Rev. WILLIAM D. GRANT.

Bishop Bruskewitz Charity and Stewardship Appeal (DDP)—Rev. STANLEY REDMERSKI, Dir., *5401 South St., Lincoln, 68506.*

Diocesan Finance Council—Most Rev. FABIAN W. BRUSKEWITZ, D.D., S.T.D.; Rev. Msgr. ROBERT F. VASA, Finance Officer; Rev. Msgr. MYRON J. PLESKAC; Rev. JOHN T. FOLDA; Gov. ROBERT B. CROSBY.

Diocesan Health Ministries, Inc.—Most Rev. FABIAN W. BRUSKEWITZ, D.D. S.T.D., Pres.; Rev. Msgr. ROBERT F. VASA, Vice Pres.; Rev. JOHN T. FOLDA, Sec., *P.O. Box 80328, Lincoln, 68501-0328.* Tel: 402-488-0921; Fax: 402-488-3569.

Diocesan Housing Ministries, Inc.—Most Rev. FABIAN W. BRUSKEWITZ, D.D., S.T.D., Pres.; Rev. Msgr. ROBERT F. VASA; Revs. JOHN T. FOLDA; LIAM M. BARR; JOSEPH M. WALSH; Ms. HATON, *P.O. Box 80328, Lincoln, 68501-0328.* Tel: 402-488-2040.

Ecumenical Affairs, Commission for—Rev. M. JAMES DIVIS, Chm.; Very. Rev. Msgr. DANIEL J. POHL; Revs. PAUL K. WITT; MAURICE H. CURRENT.

Engaged Encounter—Rev. ROBERT K. BARNHILL.

Family Life Office—Revs. ROBERT K. BARNHILL, S.T.L., Dir. CHRISTOPHER L. BARAK, S.T.L., Asst. Dir., *P.O. Box 80328, Lincoln, 68501-0328.* Tel: 402-488-2040.

Holy Childhood, Pontifical Association—Rev. RONALD PATTERSON, Dir., *P.O. Box 80328, Lincoln, 68501-0328.*

Health Care Facilities—Revs. STANLEY J. REDMERSKI, Dir. PAUL J. RUTTEN, Assoc., *5401 South St., Lincoln, 68506.*

Office of Information and Media—Rev. KENNETH A. BOROWIAK, Dir., *P.O. Box 80329, Lincoln, 68501.* Tel: 402-488-0090.

Insurance—Rev. Msgr. ROBERT F. VASA, Dir.; Rev. JOHN T. FOLDA, *P.O. Box 80328, Lincoln, 68501-0328.*

Legion of Mary—Rev. PETE J. GADIENT, Spiritual Dir.; Rev. LEO V. SEIKEV, Asst. Spiritual Dir.; Mrs. JACKIE SCOTT, Pres.

Liturgical Ministries—Revs. WILLIAM D. GRANT, Diocesan Dir. MAURICE H. CURRENT; Sr. MARY DURR, O.S.U.

Marriage Encounter—Rev. ROBERT K. BARNHILL, Dir.

Missionary Union of the Clergy—Rev. RONALD PATTERSON.

Natural Family Planning—Rev. ROBERT K. BARNHILL.

Nebraska Catholic Conference—JAMES R. CUNNINGHAM, Exec. Dir., *215 Centennial Mall S., Ste. 410, Lincoln, 68508.* Tel: 402-477-7517; Fax: 402-477-1503.

Newman Center University of Nebraska—Rev. Msgr. LEONARD I. KALIN, Chap.; Rev. LORAS K. GRELL, Asst. Chap., *320 N. 16th St., Lincoln, 68508.* Tel: 402-474-7914.

Newspaper—"The Southern Nebraska Register"; Rev. KENNETH A. BOROWIAK, Editor, *3336 High St., Lincoln, Mailing Address: P.O. Box 80329, Lincoln, 68501.* Tel: 402-488-0090.

Pre Cana—Rev. ROBERT K. BARNHILL.

Priests' Continuing Education Committee—Rev. Msgr. JAMES D. DAWSON; Rev. Msgr. THOMAS L. HOLOMAN; Rev. Msgr. LEONARD I. KALIN; Rev. Msgr. MICHAEL O. JACKELS, S.T.D.; Rev. Msgr. MYRON J. PLESKAC; Rev. Msgr. TIMOTHY J. THORBURN, J.C.L.; Rev. Msgr. ROBERT F. VASA, J.C.L.; Revs. MAURICE H. CURRENT, J.C.L.; JOHN J PERKINTON.

Pro Life—Rev. Msgr. THOMAS L. HOLOMAN.

Propagation of the Faith—Rev. RONALD PATTERSON, Dir., *P.O. Box 80328, Lincoln, 68501-0328.*

Rural Life Conference—Rev. DAVID F. BOUREK, *Saint Michael Church, P.O. Box 331, Hastings, 68902.* Tel: 402-463-1023.

Schools—Rev. JOHN J PERKINTON, M.Div., M.A., Supt.; Sr. COLLETTE, O.S.F., Asst. Supt., *3400 Sheridan Blvd., Lincoln, 68506., Mailing Address: P.O. Box 80328, Lincoln, 68501-0328.*

Scouting—Rev. ROBERT K. BARNHILL.

Society of St. Vincent de Paul - Lincoln Council—Rev. PAUL K. WITT, Spiritual Advisor; Mr. JAMES CONROY, Pres. JOYCE BURGESS, Council Sec./Resident Agent, *Blessed Sacrament Conference, 1720 Lake St., Lincoln, 68502.* Tel: 402-474-4249.

Teens Encounter Christ (TEC)—Rev. ROBERT K. BARNHILL.

Vocations—Rev. Msgr. LEONARD I. KALIN, Dir.; Rev. LORAS K. GRELL, Asst. Dir., *St. Thomas Aquinas Church, 320 North 16th St., Lincoln, 68508.* Tel: 402-474-7914.

CLERGY, PARISHES, MISSIONS AND PAROCHIAL SCHOOLS

CITY OF LINCOLN
(Lancaster County)

1—CATHEDRAL OF THE RISEN CHRIST (1932), Rev. Msgr. James D. Dawson; Revs. Mark D. Huber; Douglas D. Dietrich. In res., Rev. Michael O. Jackels.
Res., 3500 Sheridan Blvd., 68506. Tel: 402-488-0948; Fax: 402-488-7895. [JC]
School—Tel: 402-489-9621.
Benedictine Sisters (Yankton, SD) 1; Lay Teachers 28; Students 408.
Catechesis/Religious Programs—Tel: 402-489-9621.
Students 253.

2—BLESSED SACRAMENT, Rev. Michael K. Houlihan. In res., Rev. John J. Perkinton.
Res., 1720 Lake St., 68502. Tel: 402-474-4249. [JC]
School—Tel: 402-476-6202; Fax: 402-474-4258.
Priests 2; Sisters 4; Lay Teachers 18; Students 257.

3—IMMACULATE HEART OF MARY (1979) (Vietnamese), Rev. Isidore D.T. Bac, C.M.C. (Vietnam).
Res., 2601 P St., 68503. Tel: 402-476-0133.
Catechesis/Religious Programs—Students 200.

4—NORTH AMERICAN MARTYRS (1993), Revs. Garold L. Gabel; Joel S. Panzer.
Res., 931 W. Harvest Dr., 68521. Tel: 402-476-8088. [JC]

5—SACRED HEART (1919), Rev. Ronald E. Patterson. In res., Revs. Edwin L. Stander; Julius Tvrdy.
Res., 3128 S St., 68503. Tel: 402-476-2610. [JC]
School—Tel: 402-476-1783; Fax: 402-476-3040.
Sisters 6; Lay Teachers 5; Students 172.
Catechesis/Religious Programs—Students 48.

6—ST. JOHN THE APOSTLE (1959), Revs. Rudolf F. Oborny; Troy J. Schweiger.
Res., 731 Sky Way Rd., 68505. Tel: 402-489-1946. [JC]
School—Tel: 402-486-1860.
Sisters 2; Lay Teachers 22; Students 396.
Catechesis/Religious Programs—Students 274.

7—ST. JOSEPH (1976), Rev. Msgr. Myron J. Pleskac; Rev. Jeffrey Eickhoff.
Res., 7607 Trendwood Dr., 68506. Tel: 402-483-2288; Fax: 402-489-9729. [JC]
School—(Grades PreK-8). Tel: 402-489-0341.
Sisters 3; Lay Teachers 28; Students 442.
High School—Pius High School.
Students 174.
Catechesis/Religious Programs—Students 395.

8—ST. MARY (1867), Revs. Paul K. Witt; John B. Birkel. In res., Rev. Robert K. Barnhill.
Res., 1420 K St., 68508. Tel: 402-435-2125. [JC]
School—Tel: 402-476-3987.
Sisters 1; Lay Teachers 7; Students 139.
Catechesis/Religious Programs—Students 25.

9—ST. PATRICK'S (1926), Revs. David R. Hintz; John R. Sullivan.
Res., 6126 Morrill Ave., P.O. Box 29106, 68529. Tel: 402-466-2752. [JC]
School—Benedictine Sisters (Yankton, SD) 2; Lay Teachers 10; Students 209.

10—ST. PETER (1990), Revs. Michael R. Christensen; Bernard V. Kimminau.
Res., 4500 Duxhall Dr., 68516. Tel: 402-423-1239; Fax: 402-421-6507.
School—Tel: 402-421-6299.
Priests 2; School Sisters of Christ the King 2; Lay Teachers 18; Students 500.
Catechesis/Religious Programs—Students 295.

11—ST. TERESA'S (1926), Revs. Joseph J. Nemec; Thomas S. Brouillette. In res., Rev. Joseph M. Walsh.
Res., 735 S. 36th St., 68510. Tel: 402-477-3979. [JC]
School—616 S. 36th St., 68510. Tel: 402-477-3358.
Sisters 4; Lay Teachers 12; Students 278.
Catechesis/Religious Programs—Students 88.

12—ST. THOMAS AQUINAS (1958), Rev. Msgr. Leonard I. Kalin; Rev. Loras K. Grell.
Res., 320 N. 16th St., 68508. Tel: 402-474-7914; Fax: 402-476-2620. [JC]

13—BISHOP BONACUM CHANCERY, Rev. Msgr. Robert F. Vasa, V.G., Moderator of the Curia.
Res., 3400 Sheridan Blvd., P.O. Box 80328, 68501. Tel: 402-488-0921; Fax: 402-488-3569.

OUTSIDE THE CITY OF LINCOLN

Alma, Harlan Co., St. Joseph's (1909), Rev. Thomas L. Wiedel.
Res., 810 4th, P.O. Box 764, 68920. Tel: 308-928-2575.
Catechesis/Religious Programs—Students 50.
Missions—Bloomington, Franklin Co., Sacred Heart; Naponee, Franklin Co., St. Mary.

Ashland, Saunders Co., St. Mary's (1900), Rev. Francis J. Murphy.
Res., 1625 Adams St., 68003. Tel: 402-944-3554.
Catechesis/Religious Programs—Students 120.
Mission—Greenwood, Cass Co., St. Joseph's.

Auburn, Nemaha Co., St. Joseph's (1881), Rev. Philip J. Rauth.
Res., 1306 23rd St., P.O. Box 406, 68305. Tel: 402-274-3733. [CEM]
Catechesis/Religious Programs—Students 159.
Mission—Peru, St. Clara.

Aurora, Hamilton Co., St. Mary's (1888), Rev. Christopher L. Barak.
Res., 1419 10th St., P.O. Box 291, 68818. Tel: 402-694-3427.
Catechesis/Religious Programs—Students 154.
Mission—Giltner, Hamilton Co., St. Joseph's. [CEM]

Beatrice, Gage Co., St. Joseph's (1869), Rev. Mark E. Seiker.
Res., 612 High St., 68310. Tel: 402-223-2923. [CEM]
School—Tel: 402-223-5033.
Lay Teachers 9; Students 104.
Catechesis/Religious Programs—Students 124.

Beaver Crossing, Seward Co., Sacred Heart (1890), Rev. Maurice H. Current.
Res., P.O. Box 208, 68313. Tel: 402-532-2545.
Catechesis/Religious Programs—Students 76.
Mission—Utica, Seward Co., St. Patrick's. [CEM]

Bellwood, Butler Co., Presentation (1874), Rev. Leo D. Kosch.
Res., Rte. 1, Box 47, 68624. Tel: 402-367-3666. [JC]
Catechesis/Religious Programs—Students 43.
St. Peter's (1889), Rev. Leo V. Seiker.
Res., Rte. 1, Box 6, 68624. Tel: 402-538-3135. [JC]
Catechesis/Religious Programs—Students 139.
Mission—Bellwood, Butler Co., St. Joseph's.

Benkelman, Dundy Co., St. Joseph's (1911), Rev. Mark S. Pfeiffer.
Res., 817 Cheyenne St., P.O. Box 447, 69021. Tel: 308-423-2329. [CEM]
Catechesis/Religious Programs—Students 66.
Mission—Stratton, Hitchcock Co., St. Joseph's.

Brainard, Butler Co., Holy Trinity (1888), Rev. Stephen A. Cooney.
Res., P.O. Box 39, 68626. Tel: 402-545-2691; Fax: 402-545-2691. [CEM]
Catechesis/Religious Programs—Tel: 402-545-2003.
Students 123.

Bruno, Butler Co., St. Anthony (1899), Rev. Thomas J. Lux.
Res., P.O. Box 145, 68014. Tel: 402-543-2233. [CEM]
Catechesis/Religious Programs—Students 48.
Mission—Abie, Butler Co., SS. Peter and Paul.

Cambridge, Furnas Co., St. John's, Rev. Melvin L. Rempe.
Res., 815 Nelson, P.O. Box F, 69022. Tel: 308-697-3722. [CEM]
Mission—Arapahoe, Furnas Co., St. Germanus.

Campbell, Franklin Co., St. Ann's (1880), Rev. James C. Schrader, Jr.
Res., P.O. Box 156, 68932-0156. Tel: 402-756-8006. [CEM]
Catechesis/Religious Programs—Students 63.
Mission—Blue Hill, Webster Co., Holy Trinity.

Cheney, St. Michael, Rev. Christopher L. Barak.
Res., 330 W. 8th St., Palmyra, 68418-2573. Tel: 402-780-5535. [CEM]

Colon, Saunders Co., St. Joseph's (1919), Rev. Patrick J. O'Byrne.
Res., 68018. Tel: 402-647-4901. [CEM]
Mission—Cedar Bluffs, Saunders Co., St. Mary. [CEM]

Cortland, Gage Co., St. James (1882), Rev. Michael J. Morin.
Res., 255 W. First, P.O. Box 72, 68331. Tel: 402-798-7335; Fax: 402-798-7336. [CEM]
Catechesis/Religious Programs—Students 63.

Crete, Saline Co., Sacred Heart (1873), Rev. Nicholas J. Baker.
Res., 515 E. 14th St., 68333. Tel: 402-826-2044; Fax: 402-826-2318. [CEM]
School—(Grades K-6). Tel: 402-826-2318.
Lay Teachers 5; Students 67.
Catechesis/Religious Programs—Students 135.

Curtis, Frontier Co., St. James (1914), Rev. Gary G. Brethour. In res., Rev. Msgr. Jerome E. Murray.
Res., 313 E. 6th St., P.O. Box 144, 69025. Tel: 308-367-4280.
Catechesis/Religious Programs—Students 102.
Missions—Farnam, Dawson Co., St. Joseph's; Wellfleet, Lincoln Co., St. William's; North Platte, Lincoln Co., St. Elizabeth Ann Seton, (1994) P.O.Box 781, North Platte, 69103-0781. Tel: 308-534-5461.

Davey, Lancaster Co., St. Mary's (1876), Rev. Thomas P. Kuffel, O.S.
Res., 17630 N. 3rd St., P.O. Box 37, 68336. Tel: 402-785-3445. [CEM]
Catechesis/Religious Programs—Students 41.

David City, Butler Co., St. Mary's (1878), Rev. Msgr. Adrian F. Herbek, V.F.; Rev. Casey Porada, O.S.
Res., 580 I St., 68632. Tel: 402-367-3579. [CEM]
School—(Grades K-5). Tel: 402-367-3669.
Priests 1; Sisters 3; Lay Teachers 13; Students 225.
Catechesis/Religious Programs—Students 70.
Mission—David City, Butler Co., Assumption, (1878) 68632.

St. Francis (Center) (1878), Rev. Brian P. Connor.
Res., Rte. 1, Box 93, 68632. Tel: 402-367-4202. [CEM]
Catechesis/Religious Programs—Students 51.

Dawson, Richardson Co., St. Mary's, Rev. Michael G. McCabe.
Res., P.O. Box 96, 68337. Tel: 402-855-3595. [CEM]
Mission—Shubert, Richardson Co., St. Ann's. [CEM]

Denton, Lancaster Co., St. Mary's, Rev. Msgr. Thomas L. Holoman.
Res., 7105 Cass, P.O. Box 406, 68339. Tel: 402-797-2105.

Doniphan, Hall Co., St. Ann's (1888), Rev. John G. Hawkins, O.S.C.
Res., 5th & Cedar, P.O. Box G, 68832. Tel: 402-845-2707. [CEM]
Catechesis/Religious Programs—Students 63.

Dwight, Butler Co., Assumption, Rev. Kenneth A. Borowiak.
Res., P.O. Box 70, 68635. Tel: 402-566-2765. [CEM]
Mission—Bee, Seward Co., St. Wenceslaus. [CEM]

Exeter, Fillmore Co., St. Stephen's (1871), Rev. John J. Glaves.
Res., P.O. Box 57, 68351. Tel: 402-266-5581.
Catechesis/Religious Programs—Students 80.

Fairbury, Jefferson Co., St. Michael's (1885), Rev. William David Grant.
Res., 807 F St., P.O. Box 406, 68352. Tel: 402-729-2058. [CEM]
School—(Grades PreK-6). Tel: 402-729-2151.
Lay Teachers 6; Students 60.
Catechesis/Religious Programs—Students 95.
Mission—Alexandria, Thayer Co., St. Mary's, 511 Amanda, Alexandria, 68303.

Falls City, Richardson Co., SS. Peter and Paul (1871), Very Rev. Robert A. Roh, V.F.
Res., 1820 Fulton St., 68355. Tel: 402-245-3002; Fax: 402-245-3002. [CEM 2]
School—(Grades PreK-12). Tel: 402-245-4151.
Lay Teachers 17; Students 295.
Catechesis/Religious Programs—Students 60.

Friend, Saline Co., St. Joseph's (1874), Rev. James W. Cooper.
Res., 405 Main St., 68359. Tel: 402-947-3651. [CEM]
Catechesis/Religious Programs—Students 70.
Mission—Milligan, Fillmore Co., St. Wenceslaus, (1874).

Geneva, Fillmore Co., St. Joseph's (1898), Rev. Msgr. Ivan F. Vap.
Res., 831 E St., 68361. Tel: 402-759-3225. [CEM]
Catechesis/Religious Programs—Students 121.
Mission—Shickley, Fillmore Co., St. Mary, Tel: 402-627-7395.

Grafton, Fillmore Co., St. Helena's. (Admin. from St. Mary Church, Sutton). Rev. Thaddeus Bryl.
Res., P.O. Box 65, 68365. Tel: 402-773-5346.

Grant, Perkins Co., Mother of Sorrows (1928), Rev. Valerian Bartek.
Res., 729 Garfield Ave., P.O. Box 536, 69140. Tel: 308-352-4803.
Catechesis/Religious Programs—Students 84.

Harvard, Clay Co., St. Joseph's (1878), Rev. Bernard A. Lorenz.
Res., 605 N. Kearney, P.O. Box 70, 68944. Tel: 402-772-3511.
Catechesis/Religious Programs—Students 70.

Hastings, Adams Co., St. Cecilia's, Very Rev. Msgr. John J. McCabe, V.F.; Rev. Robert A. Matya.
Res., 301 W. 7th St., 68901. Tel: 402-463-1336.

St. Michael's (1945), Revs. David F. Bourek; John C. Rooney.
Res., 715 Creighton Ave., P.O. Box 331, 68901. Tel: 402-463-1023.
Catechesis/Religious Programs—Hastings Catholic Schools, 521 N. Kansas, 68901. Tel: 402-462-2105; Fax: 402-462-2106.
Students 335.

Hebron, Thayer Co., Sacred Heart, Rev. Patrick J. Lyons.
Res., 436 N. 3rd St., 68370. Tel: 402-768-6293. [CEM]
Catechesis/Religious Programs—Students 99.

Holdrege, Phelps Co., All Saints (1902), Rev. John A. Zastrow.
Res., 1202 Logan St., 68949. Tel: 308-995-4590.
Catechesis/Religious Programs—Students 161.
Mission—Smithfield, Gosper Co., St. John's.

Imperial, Chase Co., St. Patrick's (1903), Very Rev. Gregory P. Pawloski.
Res., 126 E. 7th St., P.O. Box 96, 69033. Tel: 308-882-4995.
Catechesis/Religious Programs—Students 129.
Mission—Wauneta, Chase Co., St. John's, Tel: 308-394-5440 (Church). [CEM]

Indianola, Red Willow Co., St. Catherine's (1888), Rev. Msgr. Daniel J. Pohl, V.F.
Res., P.O. Box 0, 69034. Tel: 308-364-2428. [CEM]
Catechesis/Religious Programs—Students 98.

Kenesaw, Adams Co., Sacred Heart (1908), Rev. John Hawkins, O.S.C.
Res., P.O. Box 789, Hastings, 68902. Tel: 402-463-3188; Fax: 402-463-5701.
Catechesis/Religious Programs—Tel: 402-752-8102.
Students 25.

Lawrence, Nuckolls Co., Sacred Heart (1893), Rev. Dennis Hunt.
Res., P.O. Box 247, 68957. Tel: 402-756-7393. [CEM]
School—(Grades 1-8). Tel: 402-756-7043.
Lay Teachers 4; Students 74.
Catechesis/Religious Programs—Students 159.
Missions—Deweese, Clay Co., Assumption; Lawrence, Nuckolls Co., St. Stephen's.

Loma, St. Luke's Czech Catholic Shrine (Czech), Mailing Address: c/o Rev. Msgr. Myron J. Pleskac 7607 Trendwood Dr., Lincoln, 68506. Tel: 402-483-2288; Fax: 402-489-9729.

Manley, Cass Co., St. Patrick's (1881), Rev. Msgr. Raymond B. Hain.
Res., P.O. Box 27, 68403. Tel: 402-234-3595. [CEM]
Catechesis/Religious Programs—Students 184.
Mission—Elmwood, Cass Co., St. Mary's. [CEM]

McCook, Red Willow Co., St. Patrick (1886), Revs. Robert G. Tucker; Thomas Walsh.
Res., 612 E. 4th St., P.O. Box 216, 69001. Tel: 308-345-6734. [CEM]
School—(Grades PreK-8) 401 E. F St., 69001. Tel: 308-345-4546.
Priests 2; Sisters 4; Lay Teachers 10; Students 120.
Catechesis/Religious Programs—Students 290.
Convent—1201 W. 4th St., 69001. Tel: 308-345-5142. Franciscan Sisters of Our Lady of Grace
Missions—McCook, Red Willow Co., Sacred Heart; McCook, Red Willow Co., St. Ann's. [CEM]

McCool Junction, York Co., St. Patrick's. (Admin. from St. Joseph Church, York). Rev. M. James Divis.
Tel: 402-362-4595. [CEM]

Mead, Saunders Co., St. James (1882), Rev. Charles P. Townsend.
Res., 112 N. Elm, P.O. Box 91, 68041. Tel: 402-624-3555. [CEM]
Catechesis/Religious Programs—Students 53.

Minden, Kearney Co., St. John's (1882), Very Rev. James M. O'Connor, V.F.
Res., 624 N. Garber Ave., P.O. Box 245, 68959. Tel: 308-832-1245.
Catechesis/Religious Programs—Students 64.
Mission—Heartwell, Kearney Co., Holy Family.

Morse Bluff, Saunders Co., St. George (1945), Rev. Lawrence J. Stoley.
Res., P.O. Box 98, 68648. Tel: 402-666-5280.
Mission—Cedar Hill, Saunders Co., Sacred Heart. [CEM]

Nebraska City, Otoe Co., St. Mary's (1869), Rev. Stephen P. Major. In res., Rev. Matthew F. Eickhoff.
Res., 218 N. 6th St., 68410. Tel: 402-873-3024. [CEM]
Catechesis/Religious Programs—Students 65.

St. Benedict's (1856), Rev. Mak A. Tasler.
Res., 411 5th Rue, 68410. Tel: 402-873-3047. [CEM]

Orleans, Harlan Co., St. Mary's (1878), Rev. Gerald F. Vap.
Res., P.O. Box 446, 68966. Tel: 308-473-3475. [CEM]
Catechesis/Religious Programs—Students 53.
Mission—Oxford, Furnas Co., St. Michael's.

Osceola, Polk Co., St. Vincent's, Rev. Peter J. Gadient.
Res., 751 S. Nance, P.O. Box 212, 68651. Tel: 402-747-3491.
Catechesis/Religious Programs—Students 26.
Mission—Osceola, Polk Co., St. Mary's, (1893).

Palmyra, Otoe Co., St. Leo's, Rev. John T. Folda. In res., Rev. Christopher L. Barak.
Res., 330 W. 8th St., 68418-2537. Tel: 402-780-5535. [CEM]
Mission—Douglas, Otoe Co., St. Martin's.

Paul, Otoe Co., St. Joseph's (1871), Rev. Sean P. Redmond.
Res., Rte. 1, Box 243, Nebraska City, 68410. Tel: 402-873-4569. [CEM]
Catechesis/Religious Programs—Students 16.
Mission—Julian, Nemaha Co., St. Bernard's. [CEM]

Plattsmouth, Cass Co., Church of the Holy Spirit (1862), Very Rev. Paul H. York, V.F.; Rev. Sekar Sagayaraj.
Res., 520 S. 18th St., P.O. Box C, 68048. Tel: 402-296-3139. [CEM]
School—(Grades K-8).
Lay Teachers 12; Students 182.
Catechesis/Religious Programs—Students 116.

Prague, Saunders Co., St. John's, Rev. Ronald G. Homes.
Res., P.O. Box 96, 68050. Tel: 402-663-4615. [CEM]
Catechesis/Religious Programs—Students 67.
Mission—Plasi, Saunders Co., SS. Cyril and Methodius. [CEM]

Red Cloud, Webster Co., Sacred Heart (1893), Rev. Stanley F. Schieffer.
Res., 413 N. Seward St., 68970. Tel: 402-746-3750. [CEM]
Catechesis/Religious Programs—Students 46.
Mission—Riverton, Franklin Co., St. Catherine's.

Roseland, Adams Co., Sacred Heart (1921), Rev. Thomas Y. Au.
Res., P.O. Box 67, 68973. Tel: 402-756-6251.
Catechesis/Religious Programs—Students 66.
Mission—Juniata, Adams Co., Assumption. [CEM]

Rulo, Richardson Co., Immaculate Conception (1863), Rev. James J. Meysenburg.
Res., R.R. 1, Box 89C, 68431. Tel: 402-245-4731. [CEM]
Catechesis/Religious Programs—Students 62.
Mission—Arago, Richardson Co., St. Mary's.

Seward, Seward Co., St. Vincent de Paul (1878), Rev. James F. Benton.
Res., 152 Pinewood, 68434. Tel: 402-643-3421.
Catechesis/Religious Programs—Students 343.

Shelby, Polk Co., Sacred Heart, Rev. John L. Copenhaver.
Res., P.O. Box 340, 68662. Tel: 402-527-5425. [CEM]
Catechesis/Religious Programs—Students 125.

Steinauer, Pawnee Co., St. Anthony, Rev. Bradley J. Zitek.
Res., P.O. Box 98, 68441. Tel: 402-869-2256. [CEM]
Mission—Burchard, Pawnee Co., Sacred Heart. [CEM]

Superior, Nuckolls Co., St. Joseph's (1934), Rev. Frank J. Machovec.
Res., 1415 California, P.O. Box 366, 68978. Tel: 402-879-3735.
Catechesis/Religious Programs—Students 121.
Mission—Nelson, Nuckolls Co., Sacred Heart, Tel: 402-225-3011.

Sutton, Clay Co., St. Mary's, Rev. Thaddeus Bryl, Admin.
Res., P.O. Box 406, 68979. Tel: 402-773-5346.

Syracuse, Otoe Co., St. Paulinus (1906), Rev. Daniel J. Seiker.
Res., 440 Popular St., 68446-0018. Tel: 402-269-3382. [CEM]
Catechesis/Religious Programs—Students 134.
Mission—Avoca, Cass Co., Holy Trinity.

Tecumseh, Johnson Co., St. Andrew's (1866), Rev. John A. Cooper.
Res., 186 N. 5th St., P.O. Box 656, 68450. Tel: 402-335-3742. [CEM]
School—(Grades K-8). Tel: 402-335-2034.
Marian Sisters 2; Lay Teachers 3; Students 47.
Catechesis/Religious Programs—Students 34.

Mission—St. Mary, Johnson Co., St. Mary's. [CEM]

Trenton, Hitchcock Co., St. James (1894), Rev. Philip L Luther.
Res., P.O. Box 488, 69044. Tel: 308-334-5328. [CEM]
Catechesis/Religious Programs—Students 41.
Mission—Palisade, Hitchcock Co., Holy Family.

Ulysses, Butler Co., Immaculate Conception (1915), Rev. Paul E. Sheehy.
Res., P.O. Box 128, 68669. Tel: 402-549-2437. [CEM]
Catechesis/Religious Programs—Students 54.

Valparaiso, Saunders Co., Sts. Mary and Joseph's, Rev. Liam M. Barr.
Res., P.O. Box 248, 68065. Tel: 402-784-2511. [CEM]

Wahoo, Saunders Co., St. Wenceslaus (1877), Very Rev. Lawrence J. Gyhra, V.F.; Rev. Michael S. Stec. In res., Rev. Gary L. Gross.
Res., 214 E. 2nd St., 68066. Tel: 402-443-4235. [CEM]
School—(Grades K-6).
Sisters 2; Lay Teachers 10; Students 285.
Catechesis/Religious Programs—Students 35.

Wallace, Lincoln Co., St. Mary's, Rev. Thomas D. McGuire.
Res., P.O. Box 191, 69169. Tel: 308-387-4441.
Catechesis/Religious Programs—Students 80.
Mission—Elsie, Perkins Co., Resurrection of Our Lord.

Weston, Saunders Co., St. John Nepomucene (1885), Rev. Randall L. Langhorst.
Res., P.O. Box 10, 68070. Tel: 402-642-5245. [CEM]
School—(Grades K-6). Tel: 402-642-5234.
Notre Dame Sisters (Omaha, NE) 3; Lay Teachers 5; Students 111.
Mission—Touhy, Saunders Co., St. Vitus. [CEM]

Wilber, Saline Co., St. Wenceslaus (1878),
Res., 501 N. Wilson, R.R. 1, Box 3, 68465. Tel: 402-821-2689.
Catechesis/Religious Programs—Students 105.
Mission—Tobias, Saline Co., St. Joseph's.

Wymore, Gage Co., St. Mary's (1881), Rev. Dennis W. Hotovy.
Res., 107 N. 11th St., P.O. Box 295, 68466. Tel: 402-645-3051. [CEM]
Catechesis/Religious Programs—Students 70.
Missions—Barneston, Gage Co., St. Joseph's; Odell, Gage Co., St. Mary's.

York, York Co., St. Joseph's (1878), Rev. James Divis. In res., Rev. Charles L. Gergen.
Res., 505 East Ave., 68467. Tel: 402-362-4595. [CEM]
School—(Grades K-8). Tel: 402-362-3021.
Franciscan Apostolic Sisters 4; Lay Teachers 10; Students 180.
Catechesis/Religious Programs—Students 171.

Shrines

Loma, St. Luke's Czech Catholic Shrine.

Chaplains of Public Institutions

LINCOLN. *Nebraska Penal Complex,* 3128 S St., 68503. Tel: 402-435-0251. Rev. Edwin L. Stander, Chap.

DENTON. *U.S. Veterans' Hospital,* 7105 Cass, P.O. Box 406, 68339. Tel: 402-797-2105. Rev. Msgr. Thomas L. Holoman, Chap.

On Duty Outside the Diocese:
Reverend Monsignors—
Olmsted, Thomas J., J.C.D., 7625 N. High St., Columbus, OH 43235-1498
Reverend Fathers—
Fucinaro, Thomas J., Villa Stritch, via Della Nocetta, 63, Rome, 00164 Italy
Johnson, Lyle M., Apartado 407, Barquisimeto, Venezuela
Kalin, William A., Apartado 407, Barquisimeto, Venezuela
Keefe, John J., Apartado 407, Barquisimeto, Venezuela
Reinert, James M., 25 East 39th St., New York, NY 10016-0903

Sick Leave:
Reverend Fathers—
Mika, John M., 5010 S. 41st Ave., Omaha, NE 68017

Retired:
Reverend Monsignors—
Barry, Denis L., Bonacum House, 3301 Sheridan Blvd., Lincoln, NE 68506
Keenan, Charles J., Bonacum House, 3301 Sheridan Blvd., Lincoln, NE 68506
Rezabek, William J., Bonacum House, 3301 Sheridan Blvd., Lincoln, NE 68506
Schuster, George J., Madonna Rehabilitation Hospital, 5401 South St., Lincoln, NE 68506
Wageman, Raymond L., Madonna Rehabilitation Hospital, 5401 South St., Lincoln, NE 68506
Reverend Fathers—
Banach, Walter F., P.O. Box 324, Geneva, NE 68361
Danko, Michael S., 201 N. Gregg Rd., Nixa, MO 65714
Derwinski, Victor A., 806 13th St., P.O. Box 281, Aurora, NE 68818
Halligan, James, Choncaulfield, Moydow, Co. Longford, Ireland
Hebert, John M., 7323 Shirley, Apt. 102, Omaha, NE 68124
Howe, John H., Madonna Rehabilitation Hospital, 5401 South St., Lincoln, NE 68506
Kelly, John W., Bonacum House, 3301 Sheridan Blvd., Lincoln, NE 68506
Kotz, Anthony A., 28680 Aline Dr., Warren, MI 48093
Leiblinger, Frank J., 10111 Snowville Rd., Brechsville, OH 44141-3405. Tel: 216-526-8855
Messman, Gerald C., Box 204, Duncan, NE 68634
Mroczkowski, Joseph A., Box 238, Cedar Creek, NE 68016
Reisdorff, Clarence P., Bonacum House, 3301 Sheridan Blvd., Lincoln, NE 68506
Rydz, Zygmund S., Marianna, Box 25R, Cedar Bluffs, NE 68015
Schnoebelen, Kenneth F., 143-21st St., S.W., Cedar Rapids, IA 52404
Sloup, Ernest O., Bonacum House, 3301 Sheridan Blvd., Lincoln, NE 68506
Smith, Robert H., Calle Acacius, #8, Manz 31 Colonia, Jardin Azteca, Acapulco GRO Mexico
Valasek, Edward A., 3322 Park Lane Dr., Apt. #201, Hastings, NE 68901

INSTITUTIONS LOCATED IN THE DIOCESE

[A] SEMINARIES, RELIGIOUS OR SCHOLASTICATES

HASTINGS. *Crosier Monastery,* Crosier Renewal Center, 223 E. 14th Street, P.O. Box 789, 68902. Tel: 402-463-3188; Fax: 402-463-5701. Very Rev. James G. Moeglein, O.S.C., Prior; Revs. Urban J. Schmitt, O.S.C.; Oscar C. Schoenberg, O.S.C.; John G. Hawkins, O.S.C.; Milton A. Thomas, O.S.C.; Ignatius Lempart, O.S.C.; John J. Vincent, O.S.C. Priests 7; Brothers 10.

WAVERLY. *Lincoln Diocesan Seminary,* 7303 N. 112th, R.R. No. 1, Box 110, 68462. Tel: 402-786-7211.

[B] ELEMENTARY SCHOOLS, INTERPAROCHIAL

HASTINGS. *St. Michael's Elementary, Hastings Catholic Schools,* 314 S. Lincoln, 68901. Tel: 402-462-6310; 462-6035. Priests 6; Lay Teachers 20; Students 375.

NEBRASKA CITY. *Lourdes Elementary.* (Grades 4-6), 412 2nd Ave., 68410. Tel: 402-873-3253. Ursuline Sisters (Maple Mount, KY) 1; Lay Teachers 3; Students 66.
Lourdes Primary. (Grades K-3), 411 5th Rue, 68410. Tel: 402-873-3739. Lay Teachers 4; Students 90.

[C] HIGH SCHOOLS, INTERPAROCHIAL

LINCOLN. *Pius X Central High School,* 6000 A St., 68510. Tel: 402-488-0931. Rev. Michael J. Morin, Supt.; Mr. Gregory B. Logsdon, Prin.; Mr. Thomas Seib, Asst. Prin.; Mrs. Jan Frayser, Dir. of Guidance; Mr. George O'Boyle, Dir. Activities. Priests 11; Sisters 5; Lay Teachers 48; Students 985.

DAVID CITY. *Aquinas/St. Mary's Schools.* (Grades K-12), P.O. Box 149, 68632. Tel: 402-367-3175. Rev. Brian P. Connor, Supt.; Mr. David G. McMahon, Prin. (Aquinas High School); Mr. Terry Crum, Prin. (St. Mary's); Rev. Thomas J. Lux, Guidance Dir. Priests 6; Sisters 6; Lay Teachers 33; Students 538.

FALLS CITY. *Sacred Heart High School/Elementary Schools,* 1820 Fulton St., 68355. Tel: 402-245-4151. Revs. Robert A. Roh, Supt.; James J. Meysenburg, Prin.; Michael McCabe, Dir. Guidance.
High School. Priests 3; Lay Teachers 11; Students 70.
Elementary School. Priests 3; Lay Teachers 18; Students 205.

HASTINGS. *St. Cecilia's Middle School/High School.* (Grades 6-12), 521 N. Kansas, 68901. Tel: 402-462-2105. Rev. John C. Rooney, Supt. Priests 3; Sisters 2; Lay Teachers 26; Students 344.

NEBRASKA CITY. *Lourdes Junior-Senior High School.* (Grades 7-12), 412 2nd Ave., 68410. Tel: 402-873-6154. Rev. Matthew F. Eickhoff, Supt. Priests 4; Lay Teachers 9; Students 96.

WAHOO. *Neumann High School,* 202 S. Linden, 68066. Tel: 402-443-4151. Rev. Gary Gross, Supt.; Sr. Michelle Hayek, N.D., Prin.; Ms. Monica Flakus, Guidance Dir. Priests 6; Sisters 2; Lay Teachers 19; Students 315.

[D] GENERAL HOSPITALS

LINCOLN. *St. Elizabeth Community Health Center,* 555 South 70th St., 68510. Tel: 402-489-7181.
For a complete listing, refer to the Hospitals section.

NEBRASKA CITY. *St. Mary's Hospital,* 1314 Third Ave., 68410. Tel: 402-873-3321.
For a complete listing, refer to the Hospitals section.

[E] HOMES FOR AGED

LINCOLN. *Bonacum House,* 3301 Sheridan Blvd., 68506.
For a complete listing, refer to the Special Care Facilities section.
Madonna Rehabilitation Hospital, 5401 South St., 68506. Tel: 402-489-7102.
For a complete listing, refer to the Special Care Facilities section.

DAVID CITY. *St. Joseph's Villa, Inc.,* 927 7th St., 68632. Tel: 402-367-3045; Fax: 402-367-3730.
For a complete listing, refer to the Special Care Facilities section.

[F] RETREAT HOUSES

WAVERLY. *Our Lady of Good Counsel Retreat House,* R.R. No. 1, Box 110, 68462. Tel: 402-786-2705. Rev. Msgr. Timothy J. Thorburn, Dir. Private Rooms 50. In res., Revs. Peter E. Cops, S.S.S.; Daniel Polzer, L.C.

[G] CONVENTS AND RESIDENCES FOR SISTERS

LINCOLN. *Adoration Convent and Church of Christ the King,* 1040 S. Cotner Blvd., 68510. Tel: 402-489-0765. Sister Servants of the Holy Spirit of Perpetual Adoration. Sr. Mary Catherine, Supr.; Rev. Joseph J. Nemec, Chap. Professed Sisters 9.
Congregation of Mary Queen (Vietnam), 6400 Nebraska Hwy. 2, 68516. Tel: 402-421-1704.
Daughters of the Holy Spirit, Nazareth of the Good Shepherd, Hispanic Apostolate, 110 W "E" St., 68508-3087. Tel: 402-477-7646. Sr. Margarita Iturbide, Supr.
School Sisters of Christ the King, Villa Regina Motherhouse & Novitiate, 4100 S.W. 56th St., 68522-9201. Tel: 402-477-5232. Mother Joan Paul, C.K., Supr. In res., Rev. Msgr. Robert F. Vasa. Tel: 402-477-1768.

MCCOOK. *St. Patrick's Convent,* 1201 W. Fourth St., 69001.

WAVERLY. *Marian Sisters of the Diocese of Lincoln Motherhouse and Novitiate.* Mailing Address: Rte. 1, Box 108, 68462. Tel: 402-786-2750. Sr. Ann Divis, M.S. Professed 34.

[H] SPECIAL EDUCATION

LINCOLN. *Villa Marie School and Home for the Educable Mentally Handicapped,* P.O. Box 80328, 68501. Tel: 402-786-3625. Marian Sisters (Waverly, NE). Sr. Patricia Stoeckinger, M.S., Prin.; Rev. John J. Perkinton, Dir. Sisters 3; Students 11.

[I] NEWMAN CENTERS

LINCOLN. *University of Nebraska, Newman Club,* 320 N. 16th St., 68508. Tel: 402-474-7914. See also: St. Thomas Aquinas, Lincoln, NE. Rev. Msgr. Leonard I. Kalin, Chap., Vocation Dir.; Rev. Loras K. Grell, Asst. Chap. & Asst. Vocation Dir.

[J] FUNDS, FOUNDATIONS AND TRUSTS

LINCOLN. *Chancery,* P.O. Box 80328, 3400 Sheridan Blvd., 68501.
Seminary Burse Fund.
Mass Stipends.
Food for the Starving.

[K] MISCELLANEOUS LISTINGS

LINCOLN. *Calvary Cemetery and Mausoleum Association,* 145 S. 40th St., 68510. Tel: 402-476-8787. Joint cemetery for Lincoln parishes. Revs. Ronald Patterson, Dir.; David R. Hintz, Asst. Dir.
Catholic Social Services, 301 S. 70th St., Ste. 300, 68510. Tel: 402-489-1834. Foster home care for children. Rev. Joseph M. Walsh, Dir.
Chancery Annex, 3325 Sheridan Blvd., 68506. Tel: 402-488-2040.
Cristo Rey Catholic Hispanic Center, 1335 N. 30th, 68503. Tel: 402-474-6201.
Kucera Hall, 5720 A St., 68510.

Pius X Foundation and Pius X Endowment Fund, 6000 A St., 68510. Tel: 402-488-0931. Rev. Michael J. Morin, Sec. & Treas.

DAVID CITY. *Aquinas High School Endowment Fund,* P.O. Box 149, 68632. Tel: 402-367-3175. Rev. Brian P. Connor, Sec. & Treas.

FALLS CITY. *Sacred Heart High School Endowment Fund,* 1820 Fulton St., 68355. Tel: 402-245-4151. Very Rev. Robert A. Roh, Sec. & Treas.

HASTINGS. *St. Cecilia High School Endowment Fund,* 521 N. Kansas, 68901. Revs. John C. Rooney, V.F., Sec.; David F. Bourek, Treas.

NEBRASKA CITY. *Lourdes Central High School Endowment Fund,* 412 Second Ave., 68410. Tel: 402-873-6154. Rev. Matthew Eickhoff, Sec. & Treas.

WAHOO. *Bishop Neumann High School Endowment Fund,* 202 S. Linden, 68066. Tel: 402-443-4151. Rev. Gary Gross, Sec. & Treas.

RELIGIOUS INSTITUTES OF MEN REPRESENTED IN THE DIOCESE

For further details refer to the corresponding bracketed number in the Religious Institutes of Men or Women section.

[0400]—*Canons Regular of the Order of the Holy Cross.* (Prov. of St. Odilia).—O.S.C.

[0220]—*Congregation of the Blessed Sacrament.*—S.S.S.

[]—*Congregation of the Mother Coredemptrix.* (Vietnamese).—C.M.C.

[0730]—*Legionaries of Christ.*—L.C.

[]—*Oblates of Wisdom.*—O.S.

RELIGIOUS INSTITUTES OF WOMEN REPRESENTED IN THE DIOCESE

[0100]—*Adorers of the Blood of Christ.*—A.S.C.

[]—*American Province of the Religious Order of Servants of Mary, Inc.*—O.S.M.

[0230]—*Benedictine Sisters of Pontifical Jurisdiction.*—O.S.B.

[]—*Congregation of Mary, Queen.* (Vietnam).

[]—*Daughters of the Holy Spirit, Nazareth of the Good Shepherd.*—H.Sp.S.

[1070-01]—*Dominican Sisters.*—O.P.

[]—*Franciscan Apostolic Sisters.*—F.A.S.

[2575]—*Institute of the Sisters of Mercy of the Americas.*—R.S.M.

[2400]—*Marian Sisters of the Diocese of Lincoln.*—M.S.

[2960]—*Notre Dame Sisters.*—N.D.

[]—*School Sisters of Christ the King.*—C.K.

[1680]—*School Sisters of St. Francis.*—O.S.F.

[3540]—*Sister Servants of the Holy Spirit of Perpetual Adoration.*—S.Sp.S.de A.P.

[0430]—*Sisters of Charity of the Blessed Virgin Mary.*—B.V.M.

[1600]—*Sisters of St. Francis of Martyr St. George.*—O.S.F.

[1640]—*Sisters of St. Francis of Perpetual Adoration.* (Prov. of St. Joseph).—O.S.F.

[3270]—*Sisters of the Most Precious Blood (O'Fallon, MO).*—C.PP.S.

[4120-05]—*Ursuline Nuns of the Congregation of Paris.*—O.S.U.

DIOCESAN CEMETERIES

LINCOLN. *Calvary.*

NECROLOGY

† Cooper, Rev. Msgr. Daniel E., (Retired). —Died Jan. 30, 1996.

† Kealy, Rev. Msgr. Thomas M., (Retired). —Died May 16, 1996.

Diocese of Little Rock

(Dioecesis Petriculana)

Most Reverend

ANDREW J. MCDONALD, D.D., J.C.D.

Bishop of Little Rock; ordained May 8, 1948; appointed Bishop of Little Rock July 4, 1972; consecrated September 5, 1972; installed September 7, 1972. *Res., 30 Sherrill Rd., Little Rock, AR, 72202.* Tel.: 501-664-6738; 374-2794 (Cathedral); 664-0340 (Office). *Mailing Address: Diocese of Little Rock, 2415 N. Tyler, P.O. Box 7239, Little Rock, AR, 72217.*

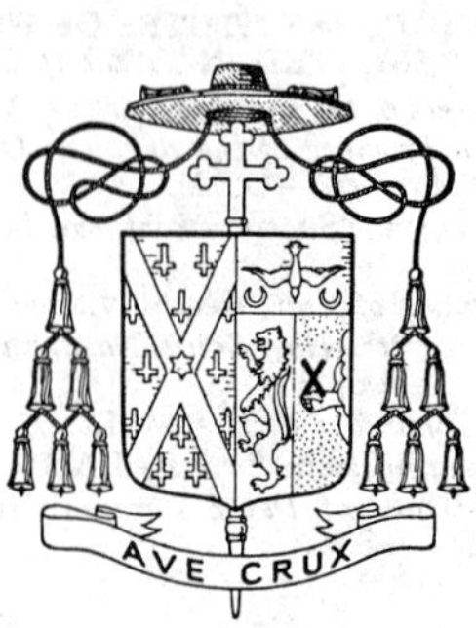

ESTABLISHED NOVEMBER 28, 1843.

Square Miles 53,104.

Comprises the State of Arkansas.

For legal titles of parishes and diocesan institutions, consult the Chancery Office.

Chancery: P.O. Box 7239, 2415 N. Tyler St., Little Rock, AR, 72217. Tel.: 501-664-0340.

STATISTICAL OVERVIEW

Personnel	
Bishop	1
Abbots	1
Retired Abbots	1
Priests: Diocesan Active in Diocese	59
Priests: Active Outside Diocese	1
Priests: Retired, Sick or Absent	27
Number of Diocesan Priests	87
Religious Priests in Diocese	67
Extern Priests in Diocese	14
Ordinations:	
Diocesan Priests	1
Transitional Deacons	1
Permanent Deacons in Diocese	65
Total Brothers	47
Total Sisters	364
Parishes	
Parishes	90
With Resident Pastor:	
Resident Diocesan Priests	56
Resident Religious Priests	30
Without Resident Pastor:	
Administered by Priests	2
Administered by Permanent Deacons	1
Administered by Women Religious	1
Missions	45
Professional Ministry Personnel:	
Brothers	1
Sisters	31
Lay Ministers	47
Welfare	
Catholic Hospitals	10
Total Assisted	694,164
Homes for the Aged	5
Total Assisted	335
Day Care and Extended Day Care Centers	11
Total Assisted	521
Specialized Homes	2
Total Assisted	57
Special Centers for Social Services	25
Total Assisted	13,522
Other Institutions	19
Total Assisted	1,078
Educational	
Diocesan Students in Other Seminaries	12
Students Religious	6
Total Seminarians	18
High Schools, Diocesan and Parish	3
Total Students	996
High Schools, Private	2
Total Students	780
Elementary Schools, Diocesan and Parish	30
Total Students	6,676
Elementary Schools, Private	1
Total Students	82
Catechesis/Religious Education:	
High School Students	2,293
Elementary Students	5,296
Total Students Under Catholic Instruction	16,141
Teachers in the Diocese:	
Priests	9
Brothers	10
Sisters	40
Lay Teachers	516
Vital Statistics	
Receptions into the Church:	
Infant Baptism Totals	1,815
Adult Baptism Totals	255
Received into Full Communion	460
First Communions	1,688
Confirmations	1,349
Marriages:	
Catholic	248
Interfaith	353
Total Marriages	601
Deaths	861
Total Catholic Population	85,992
Total Population	2,483,769

Former Bishops—Rt. Rev. ANDREW BYRNE, D.D., cons. March 10, 1844; died in Helena, June 10, 1862.—Rt. Rev. EDWARD FITZGERALD, D.D., preconized June 22, 1866; cons. Feb. 3, 1867; died in Hot Springs, Feb. 21, 1907.—Most Rev. JOHN B. MORRIS, D.D., ord. June 11, 1892; cons. June 11, 1906; died in Little Rock, Oct. 22, 1946.—Most Rev. ALBERT L. FLETCHER, D.D., ord. June 4, 1920; cons. April 25, 1940; appt. Bishop of Little Rock Dec. 7, 1946; retired July 3, 1972; died Dec. 6, 1979.

Vicar General—Rev. Msgr. J. GASTON HEBERT, V.G.

Chancery—2415 N. Tyler St., P.O. Box 7239, Little Rock, 72217. Tel: 501-664-0340. Office Hours: Mon.-Fri. 8:30-4.

Chancellor for Canonical Affairs—Rev. FRANCIS I. MALONE, J.C.L.

Chancellor for Administration—Mr. GREGORY WOLFE.

Vice Chancellor—Rev. SCOTT L. MARCZUK, J.C.L.

Finance Officer—Mr. WILLIAM HARTMANN.

Diocesan Tribunal—2415 N. Tyler St., P.O. Box 7239, Little Rock, 72217. Tel: 501-664-0340.

Judicial Vicar—Rev. SCOTT L. MARCZUK, J.C.L.

Judges—Rev. Msgr. ROYCE R. THOMAS, J.C.L.; Revs. FRANCIS I. MALONE, J.C.L.; SCOTT L. MARCZUK, J.C.L.

Defender of the Bond—Rev. JOHN KORDSMEIER.

Notaries—Mrs. JANICE BRASS; Mrs. JANIE HIGHTOWER; Mrs. JEANNIE MOORE.

Vicar for Religious—Sr. MAXINE VOGAN, D.L.F., *621 S. Washington, Forrest City, 72335.* Tel: 501-663-1665.

Diocesan Consultors—Rev. Msgr. J. GASTON HEBERT, V.G.; Rev. Msgr. JOHN F. O'DONNELL; Rev. Msgr. BERNARD G. MALONE, V.F.; Revs. FRANCIS I. MALONE; SCOTT MARCZUK; JACK D. Harris.

Deans—Very Rev. Msgr. BERNARD G. MALONE, V.F.; Very Rev. Msgr. JOHN F. O'DONNELL, V.F.; Very Rev. Msgr. LEO RIEDMUELLER, V.F.; Very Revs. ROBERT T. DIENERT, V.F.; ERNEST HARDESTY, V.F.; DAVID JACOBS, V.F.; JOHN KORDSMEIER, V.F.; RICHARD OSWALD, V.F.; JOSEPH L. PALLO; W. ANDREW SMITH, V.F.; FREDERICK ZARRILLI, V.F.; Rt. Rev. JEROME KODELL, O.S.B., V.F.

Diocesan Offices and Directors

Adoption Services—Ms. ANTJE HARRIS, Supvr., *2415 N. Tyler St., P.O. Box 7239, Little Rock, 72217.* Tel: 501-664-0340.

Diocesan Council for Black Catholics—Rev. WARREN HARVEY, *1321 S. Van Buren St., Little Rock, 72204.* Tel: 501-666-5073.

Building Commission—Mr. JAMES DAVIS, Exec. Sec., *2415 N. Tyler St., P.O. Box 7239, Little Rock, 72217.* Tel: 501-664-0340.

Catholic Social Services—Mr. DENNIS LEE, Dir., *2415 N. Tyler St., P.O. Box 7239, Little Rock, 72217.* Tel: 501-664-0340. This office also handles: *Catholic Relief Services.*

Catholic Campus Ministries—See: *Catholic Youth Ministries.*

Catholic Women, Diocesan Council of—Rev. JAMES P. WEST, *589 W. Grand Ave., Hot Springs, 71901.* Tel: 501-623-6201.

Catholic Youth Ministries—PHYLLIS ENDERLIN, Dir., *2500 N. Tyler St., P.O. Box 7565, Little Rock, 72217.* Tel: 501-664-0340. This office also handles: Catholic Campus Ministries; Scouting; Catholic Youth Organization (CYO). Rev. JAMES P. WEST, CYO Moderator, *589 W. Grand Ave., Hot Springs, 71901.* Tel: 501-623-6201.

Cemetery, Greater Little Rock—BARBARA BAKER, Sec., Diocese of Little Rock, *2500 N. Tyler St., Little Rock, 72207.* Tel: 501-664-0340.

Charismatic Movement, Bishop's Liaison—Rev. JAMES E. MANCINI, *St. Patrick's Church, 211 W. 19th St., N. Little Rock, 72114.* Tel: 501-758-1155.

Clergy Welfare Board—Rev. Msgr. J. GASTON HEBERT, V.G., Chm., *2415 N. Tyler St., P.O. Box 7239, Little Rock, 72217.* Tel: 501-664-0340.

Communications Department—Rev. FRANCIS I. MALONE, Dir., *P.O. Box 7417, Little Rock, 72217.* Tel: 501-664-0340.

Continuing Education for the Clergy—Rev. DAVID LESIEUR, Dir., *2500 N. Tyler St., P.O. Box 7565, Little Rock, 72217.* Tel: 501-664-0340.

Cursillo Movement—Rev. JOHN E. MARCONI, Moderator; Mrs. DEBBIE ECKERT, Exec. Dir., *2500 N. Tyler St., P.O. Box 7565, Little Rock, 72217.* Tel: 501-664-0340.

Data Processing—Rev. THOMAS SEBAUGH, Dir., *2500 N. Tyler St., P.O. Box 7565, Little Rock, 72217.* Tel: 501-664-0340.

Development Office—Mr. JOHN HEIRD, Dir., *P.O. Box 7239, Little Rock, 72217.* Tel: 501-664-0340.

Diaconate Program—Sr. YVONNE LERNER, O.S.B., Dir., *2500 N. Tyler St., P.O. Box 7565, Little Rock, 72217.* Tel: 501-664-0340.

Ecumenical and Inter-Religious Affairs Office—Mr. JOHN MARSCHEWSKI, Dir., *P.O. Box 7239, Little Rock, 72217.* Tel: 501-664-0340.

Family Life Office: (Beginning Experience, Pre-Cana, Marriage Encounter, Retrouvaille)—Ms. ELIZABETH REHA, Dir., *2500 N. Tyler St., P.O. Box 7565, Little Rock, 72217.* Tel: 501-664-0340.

Hispanic Ministry—Rev. JAMES BROCKMAN, S.J., Dir., *P.O. Box 7565, Little Rock, 72217.* Tel: 501-664-0340.

Hospitals—*2415 N. Tyler St., P.O. Box 7239, Little Rock, 72217.* Tel: 501-664-0340.

Immigration Services—Mrs. SHEILA GOMEZ, Dir., *2500 N. Tyler St., P.O. Box 7565, Little Rock, 72217.* Tel: 501-664-0340.

Lay Ministry and Parish Renewal—Deacon BO MCALLISTER, Dir., *2500 N. Tyler St., P.O. Box 7565, Little Rock, 72217.* Tel: 501-664-0340.

Liturgical Commission—Rev. FRANCIS I. MALONE, Dir., *2415 N. Tyler St., P.O. Box 7239, Little Rock, 72217.* Tel: 501-664-0340.

Minister to Priests—Rev. DAVID LESIEUR, *P.O. Box 7565, Little Rock, 72217.* Tel: 501-664-0340.

Newspaper "Arkansas Catholic"—Rev. FRANCIS I. MALONE, Mng. Editor; Ms. MALEA WALTERS, Editor, *2500 N. Tyler St., P.O. Box 7565, Little Rock, 72217.* Tel: 501-664-0340.

Presbyteral Council—Rev. Msgr. J. GASTON HEBERT, V.G., Chm., *2415 N. Tyler St., P.O. Box 7239, Little Rock, 72217.* Tel: 501-664-0340.

Priests Personnel Board (Diocesan)—Rev. Msgr. J. GASTON HEBERT, V.G., Chm., *2415 N. Tyler St., P.O. Box 7239, Little Rock, 72217.* Tel: 501-664-0340.

Propagation of the Faith—Mr. DENNIS LEE, Dir., *2415 N. Tyler St., P.O. Box 7239, Little Rock, 72217.* Tel: 501-664-0340.

Refugee Resettlement—Mr. D. DORTCH, Dir., *2500 N. Tyler St., P.O. Box 7565, Little Rock, 72217.* Tel: 501-664-0340.

Religious Education Department—BARB MINCZEWSKI, Dir., *2500 N. Tyler St., P.O. Box 7565, Little Rock, 72217.* Tel: 501-664-0340.

Respect Life Office—ANNE DIERKS, Dir., *2500 N. Tyler St., P.O. Box 7565, Little Rock, 72217.* Tel: 501-664-0340.

Rural Life Department—Vacant, *2500 N. Tyler St., P.O. Box 7565, Little Rock, 72217.* Tel: 501-664-0340.

St. John's Catholic Center—JOHN ROBINETTE, Mgr., *2500 N. Tyler St., P.O. Box 7565, Little Rock, 72217.* Tel: 501-664-0340.

Schools—Mr. MICHAEL ROCKERS, Supt., *2500 N. Tyler St., P.O. Box 7565, Little Rock, 72217.* Tel: 501-664-0340.

Scripture Study—Rev. STEPHEN BINZ, S.S.L., Dir. Associate Directors: LILLY HESS; CACKIE UPCHURCH, *P.O. Box 7565, Little Rock, 72217.* Tel: 501-664-0340.

Seminary Endowment Fund (The Msgr. James E. O'Connell Seminary Burse)—Rev. Msgr. JAMES E. O'CONNELL, Dir., *2500 N. Tyler St., P.O. Box 7565, Little Rock, 72217.* Tel: 501-664-0340.

Social Action Office—Mr. HENRY TUCK, Dir., *2500 N. Tyler St., P.O. Box 7565, Little Rock, 72217.* Tel: 501-664-0340. This office also handles the Campaign for Human Development and Parish Social Ministry.

Vocations—Rev. DAVID LESIEUR, Dir. JOHN HALL, Assoc. Dir., *2500 N. Tyler St., P.O. Box 7565, Little Rock, 72217.* Tel: 501-664-0340. Also serves as Director of Seminarians.

CLERGY, PARISHES, MISSIONS AND PAROCHIAL SCHOOLS

GREATER LITTLE ROCK
(Pulaski County)

1—CATHEDRAL OF ST. ANDREW, Rev. Scott L. Marczuk, J.C.L., Rector; Deacon Gary Dollar.
Res., 617 Louisiana St., 72201. Tel: 501-374-2794; Fax: 501-375-3292. [JC]

2—ST. ANNE (North Little Rock), Revs. James E. Mancini; Clement Kalu; Kevin Murphy, O.S.B.
Mailing Address: 6150 Remount Rd., North Little Rock, 72118. Tel: 501-753-3977.
Res., 211 W. 19th St., North Little Rock, 72114. Tel: 501-758-1155. [JC]

3—ST. AUGUSTINE, Rev. L. Warren Harvey, Admin.
Res., 1421 E. Second, North Little Rock, 72114. Tel: 501-375-9617; Fax: 501-375-9617. [JC]

4—ST. BARTHOLOMEW'S, Rev. Anthony T. Hemphill, S.V.D.; Deacon Kirke Herman.
Res., 1622 Marshall St., 72202. Tel: 501-372-4682.

5—CHRIST THE KING, Rev. Msgr. J. Gaston Hebert, V.G.; Rev. John K. Antony; Deacons Bill Hartmann; Bo McAllister.
Res., 4000 N. Rodney Parham Rd., 72212. Tel: 501-225-6774; Fax: 501-225-8980. [JC]
School—Tel: 501-225-7883. Mrs. Kathy House, Prin.
Lay Teachers 34; Students 735.
Christ the King Endowment Trust Fund for Christ the King Catholic School—Tel: 501-225-7883; Fax: 501-225-1315.

6—ST. EDWARD, Rev. Vincent Flusche; Deacon Ben Rodriquez.
Res., 815 Sherman St., 72202. Tel: 501-374-5767; Fax: 501-374-5839. [JC]
School—E. Ninth & Ferry St., 72202. Tel: 501-374-9166.
Lay Teachers 10; Students 202.
Educational Trust Fund for St. Edward School—.

7—IMMACULATE CONCEPTION, Revs. Francis I. Malone, J.C.L.; Emmanuel Iheaka; Deacon William Nolan.
Res., 7000 John F. Kennedy Blvd., North Little Rock, 72116. Tel: 501-835-4323; Fax: 501-834-5598. [JC]
School—Tel: 501-835-0771.
Lay Teachers 29; Students 495.
Immaculate Conception School Endowment Fund—.

8—IMMACULATE HEART OF MARY (Marche), Very Rev. Msgr. Bernard G. Malone, V.F.; Deacon Brunon Strozyk.
Res., 7006 Jasna Gora Dr., North Little Rock, 72118. Tel: 501-851-2763. [CEM]
School—Tel: 501-851-2760.
Lay Teachers 13; Students 177.
Immaculate Heart of Mary Educational Trust Fund for Immaculate Heart of Mary School—Tel: 501-851-2763.

9—ST. MARY (North Little Rock), Rev. James E. Mancini. In res., Rev. Clement Kalu.
Res., 1516 Parker St., North Little Rock, 72114. Tel: 501-374-7123.
School—1518 Parker St., North Little Rock, 72114. Tel: 501-374-5237.
Lay Teachers 10; Students 208.
St. Mary's School Endowment Fund—.

10—OUR LADY OF GOOD COUNSEL, Revs. Thomas W. Keller; L. Warren Harvey. In res., Rev. Stephen J. Binz.
Res., 1321 S. Van Buren St., 72204. Tel: 501-666-5073; Fax: 501-666-8246.
School—1204 S. Jackson St., 72204. Tel: 501-663-7426; Fax: 501-666-2239.
Lay Teachers 18; Students 256.
Msgr. Scheper Endowment Fund for Our Lady of Good Counsel Catholic School—.

11—OUR LADY OF THE HOLY SOULS, Rev. David LeSieur; Deacon Larry Jegley. In res., Revs. Lawrence Frederick; Victor E. Bertrand, C.S.V.
Res., 1003 N. Tyler St., 72205. Tel: 501-663-8632; Fax: 501-663-8699.
Mailing Address: P.O. Box 250202, 72225.
School—901 N. Tyler St., 72205. Tel: 501-663-4513; Fax: 501-663-1014.
Olivetan Benedictines 2; Lay Teachers 35; Students 512.
Msgr. Allen Trust Fund for Holy Souls School—.

12—ST. PATRICK'S, Revs. James E. Mancini; Clement Kalu; Kevin Murphy, O.S.B.; Deacon George Siebenmorgan. In res., Rev. Do Duy Nho.
Res., 211 W. 19th St., North Little Rock, 72114. Tel: 501-758-1155. [JC]
School—1900 Orange St., North Little Rock, 72114. Tel: 501-758-1508.
Lay Teachers 16; Students 215.
St. Patrick's School Endowment Fund—.

13—ST. THERESA'S, Rev. John M. Connell; Deacons Don Francis; Robert Maes; William R. Wrape, II.
Res., 6219 Baseline Rd., 72209. Tel: 501-565-9198; Fax: 501-565-3949. [JC]
School—Tel: 501-565-3855; Fax: 501-565-9522.
Lay Teachers 17; Students 300.
St. Theresa's Catholic School Endowment Fund—.

OUTSIDE THE CITY OF LITTLE ROCK

Adona, Conway Co., St. Elizabeth's. Attended by St. Boniface Church, New Dixie. Rev. Richard P. Davis.
Mailing Address: Rte. 1, Box 80 Dixie, Bigelow, 72016. Tel: 501-759-2371. [CEM]

Altus, Franklin Co., St. Mary, Rev. Hilary Filiatreau, O.S.B.; Deacon Matthew Post.
Res., 72821. Tel: 501-468-2585. [CEM]

Arkadelphia, Clark Co., St. Mary's. Attended by St. John's Church, Malvern. Sr. Teresa Daly, D.C., Admin.
Church—P.O. Box 26, 71923. Tel: 501-246-7575.

Atkins, Pope Co., Assumption B.V.M., Rev. Edward G. Marley, C.S.Sp.; Deacon Veo J. Condley.
Res., P.O. Box 337, 72823. Tel: 501-641-7179. [CEM]

Barling, Sebastian Co., Sacred Heart of Mary, Rev. William Elser.
Res. and Office: 1301 Frank St., 72923. Tel: 501-452-1795. [CEM]

Batesville, Independence Co., St. Mary's, Rev. Clayton Gould.
Res., 3800 Harrison St., 72501. Tel: 501-793-7717; 793-7464.
512 School St., P.O. Box 926, Mount View, 72560. Tel: 501-269-5194.
Missions—Mount View, Stone Co., St. Mary Mission, Mount Vernon 72560; Newport, Jackson Co., St. Cecilia, Galleria Dr., Newport, 72112.

Bella Vista, Benton Co., St. Bernard, Rev. Joseph J. Enderlin.
Res., 1 St. Bernard Ln., 72715. Tel: 501-855-9060; 855-9069.

Benton, Saline Co., Our Lady of Fatima, Rev. John Marconi; Deacon John Duke.
Res., 900 W. Cross St., 72015. Tel: 501-778-5186; Fax: 501-778-9644.
School—Olivetan Benedictine Sisters 1; Lay Teachers 6; Students 101.
Our Lady of Fatima School Endowment Fund—816 W. Cross St., 72015. Tel: 501-778-3398.
Station—Benton, Benton Services Center, Tel: 501-778-1111.

Bentonville, Benton Co., St. Stephen, Rev. Michael D. Sinkler; Deacon Jerry Becker.
Mailing Address: P.O. Box 1396, 72712. Tel: 501-273-1240; Fax: 501-464-0969.
Res., 1300 N.E. J St., 72712. Tel: 501-273-1240.

Bigelow, Perry Co., St. Boniface's, Rev. Richard P. Davis.
Res., Rte. 1, Box 80 Dixie, 72016. Tel: 501-759-2371. [CEM]
Missions—Little Italy, Pulaski Co., St. Francis; Adona, Conway Co., St. Elizabeth's.

Blytheville, Mississippi Co., Immaculate Conception, Very Rev. Joseph L. Pallo, V.F.; Deacon William G. Brandon.
Res., 1301 W. Main St., 72315. Tel: 501-762-2506.
School—Tel: 501-763-9444.
Lay Teachers 9; Students 102.

Booneville, Logan Co., Church of Our Lady of the Assumption, Rev. Malachy McNerney, O.S.B.
Mailing Address: E. 6th & Cherry St., 72923. Tel: 501-675-3371.
Res., Subiaco Abbey, Subiaco, 72865. Tel: 501-934-4295.

Brinkley, Monroe Co., St. John the Baptist, Rev. Benedict Meyer, O.S.B.
Res., 203 W. Ash, 72021-3201. Tel: 501-734-1202. [CEM]

Camden, Ouachita Co., St. Louis, Rev. Jon McDougal.
Mailing Address: 202 Adams N.W., 71701.
Res., 962 Ridgeview, 71701. Tel: 501-836-2426.
Mission—Magnolia, Columbia Co., Immaculate Heart of Mary, P.O. Box 365, Magnolia, 71753. Tel: 501-234-2710.

Carlisle, Lonoke Co., St. Rose of Lima Church, Rev. Charles Thessing; Deacon William Cunningham, Jr.
Res., Hwy. 70 E., P.O. Box M, 72024. Tel: 501-552-3601.

Center Ridge, Conway Co., St. Joseph's. Attended by Church of Assumption, Atkins. Rev. Edward G. Marley, C.S.Sp.
Mailing Address: 44 Valley Rd., 72027. Tel: 501-893-2887; Fax: 501-354-2711.
Church—Atkins, 72823. Tel: 501-893-2887; 641-7179; Fax: 501-354-2711. [CEM]

Charleston, Franklin Co., Sacred Heart, Rev. Peter Sharum, O.S.B.; Deacon Francis W. Ralston.
Res., Rte. 2, Box 500, 72933-9403. Tel: 501-965-2432. [CEM]

Cherokee Village, Sharp Co., St. Michael's, Rev. Earl Johnson, S.J.; Deacon Michael Cumnock.
Mailing Address: P.O. Box 970, 72525. Tel: 501-257-2850.
Res., 12 Micanopy Circle, 72529. Tel: 501-257-4456.
St. Michael Memorial Garden (Columbarium)—Hwy. 62/167, S. Tekakwitha Dr., 72529.

Clarksville, Johnson Co., Holy Redeemer, Rev. Victor Gillespie, O.S.B.
Res., 103 E. Main St., 72830. Tel: 501-754-3610. [CEM]
Mission—Hartman, Johnson Co., Sacred Heart.

Conway, Faulkner Co., St. Joseph's, Revs. Anthony McKay, C.S.Sp.; Joseph Deniger, C.S.Sp.; Edward T. Crowley, C.S.Sp., (Retired); Deacons David Westmoreland; Richard Bemrich, (Retired).
Res., 1115 College Ave., 72032. Tel: 501-327-6568; Fax: 501-329-6305. [CEM]
Parish Business Office: 375 Harkrider, 72032. Tel: 501-327-5528; Fax: 501-327-6607.

School—(Grades K-6). Tel: 501-327-1204; Fax: 501-327-8350. Daniel Fields, Prin.
Lay Teachers 19; Students 283.
High School—(Grades 7-12). Tel: 501-329-5741; 329-5606; Fax: 501-327-8350.
Lay Teachers 12; Students 206.
St. Joseph School Endowment and Charitable Trust—P.O. Box 1709, 72032.

Crossett, Ashley Co., Holy Cross, Rev. Victor Subb, Glmy.
Res., 808 Maple St., 71635. Tel: 501-364-4847. [JC]
Mission—Hamburg, Ashley Co., Hamburg, 71646.

Dardanelle, Yell Co., St. Augustine. Attended by Russellville.
Mailing Address: 1900 Main St., P.O. Box 308, Russellville, 72801. Tel: 501-967-3699.

De Queen, Sevier Co., St. Barbara's, Rev. R. Scott Friend.
Res., P.O. Box 86, 71832. Tel: 501-642-2256.
Missions—Foreman, Little River Co., Sacred Heart; Nashville, Howard Co., St. Martin's, W. Leslie St., P.O. Box 1039, Nashville, 71857.

El Dorado, Union Co., Holy Redeemer, Rev. Gregory A. Pilcher, O.S.B.
Res., 440 W. Main St., 71730-5757. Tel: 501-863-3620; Fax: 501-863-7537.
School—Ann Finch, Prin. Lay Teachers 9; Students 86.
El Dorado Holy Redeemer School Endowment Fund—1103 W. Cedar St., 71730. Tel: 501-863-8677; Fax: 501-863-7779.
Holy Redeemer Endowment Fund—.

Engelberg, Randolph Co., St. John the Baptist (Pocahontas P.O.), Rev. Leslie A. Farley.
Res., 4650 Engelberg Rd., Pocahontas, 72455. Tel: 501-892-3780. [CEM]
Missions—Corning, Clay Co., St. Joseph, P.O. Box 385, Corning, 72422. Tel: 501-892-3780; Walnut Ridge, Lawrence Co., Immaculate Heart of Mary, 320 Free St., P.O. Box 70, Walnut Ridge, 72176. Tel: 501-886-2119.

Eureka Springs, Carroll Co., St. Elizabeth's, Rev. James M. Fanrak; Deacons Samuel Hilburn; Bill Reuter.
Res., 30 Crescent Dr., 72632. Tel: 501-253-9853.
Mission—Berryville, Carroll Co., St. Anne's, Hwy. 62, P.O. Box 605, Berryville, 72616. Tel: 501-423-3927.

Fairfield Bay, Van Buren Co., St. Francis Assisi, Rev. Francis D. Colavechio.
Res., 250 Woodlawn Dr., 72088. Tel: 501-884-3349.

Fayetteville, Washington Co., St. Joseph's, Rev. Mark Wood; Deacons Paul Cronan; Chuck Marino.
Office: 354 N. Willow Ave., 72701. Tel: 501-442-0890. [CEM]
Church—321 E. Lafayette St., 72701.
School—Tel: 501-442-4554; Fax: 501-442-7887.
Lay Teachers 14; Students 286.
St. Joseph Endowment and Educational Trust Fund—313 E. Lafayette St., 72701. Tel: 501-442-4554.

St. Thomas Aquinas University Parish, Rev. Mark Wood, Sacramental Minister; Deacon Paul Cronan, Pastoral Admin.
Res., 603 N. Leverett Ave., 72701-3220. Tel: 501-444-0223; Fax: 501-442-5371.

Fordyce, Dallas Co., Good Shepherd, Rev. Wilfred C. Okorochukwu.
Res., 410 Oak St., 71742. Tel: 501-352-2328; Fax: 501-352-5037. [CEM]
Mission—Sheridan, Grant Co., Holy Cross.

Forrest City, St. Francis Co., St. Francis of Assisi, Rev. Frederick B. Zarrilli.
Res., 621 S. Washington St., P.O. Box 786, 72336-0786. Tel: 501-633-1665.
Mission—Marianna, Lee Co., St. Andrew's, P.O. Box 724, Marianna, 72360.

Fort Smith, Sebastian Co., Immaculate Conception, Rev. Msgr. John F. O'Donnell, V.F.; Rev. Gregory Luyet.
Mailing Address: P.O. Box 1866, 72902-1866.
Res., 22 North 13th, 72901. Tel: 501-783-7963; Fax: 501-783-7865. [JC]
School—223 South 14th St., 72901. Tel: 501-783-6798; Fax: 501-783-0510.
Sisters of Mercy 1; Lay Teachers 24; Students 355.
Immaculate Conception School Educational Trust—.

St. Boniface, Rev. Placidus Eckart, O.S.B.
Res., 1820 North B St., 72901. Tel: 501-783-6711. [JC]
School—201 N. 19th St., 72901. Tel: 501-783-6601; Fax: 501-783-6605.
Benedictine Sisters 1; Lay Teachers 12; Students 206.
Catholic Education Endowment Trust of Fort Smith, Arkansas—.

Christ the King, Rev. Msgr. Royce R. Thomas.
Res., 1920 S. Greenwood Ave., 72901. Tel: 501-783-7745; Fax: 501-783-2025. [JC]
School—1918 S. Greenwood, 72901. Tel: 501-782-0614; Fax: 501-782-1098.
Lay Teachers 12; Students 199.
Catholic Education Endowment Trust of Fort Smith, Arkansas—.

Hamburg, Ashley Co., Holy Spirit Church. Attended by Holy Cross Church.
808 Maple St., Crossett, 71635. Tel: 501-364-4847.
Church—110 E. Franklin, P.O. Box 188, 71646. Tel: 501-853-8991. [CEM]

Harrison, Boone Co., Mary, Mother of God, Very Rev. John W. Kordsmeier, V.F.
Res., P.O. Box 2150, 72601. Tel: 501-741-5234.

Hartford, Sebastian Co., St. Leo's, Rev. John F. O'Donnell, V.F.
Mailing Address: P.O. Box 1866, Fort Smith, 72902. Tel: 501-783-7963; Fax: 501-783-7865.

Helena, Phillips Co., St. Mary's, Very Rev. C. Edwin Graves, III, V.F.
Res., 123 Columbia St., 72342. Tel: 501-338-6990. [CEM]

Hope, Hempstead Co., Our Lady of Good Hope, Rev. William F. Thomas; Deacon Robert V. Regan.
Office: P.O. Box 517, 71801. Tel: 501-777-3202.
Res., 325 S. Walker St., 71801. Tel: 501-722-2921.
Mission—Ashdown, Little River Co., St. Elizabeth Ann Seton, Hwy. 32 E., P.O. Box 966, Ashdown, 71822. Tel: 501-898-8529.

Horseshoe Bend, Izard Co., St. Mary of the Mount. Attended by Cherokee Village. Rev. Fredrick Schneider, O.F.M.
Mailing Address: P.O. Box 4012, 72512.
Res., 4th & Church St., 72512. Tel: 501-670-5896. [CEM]

Hot Springs National Park, Garland Co., St. Mary's of the Springs, Very Rev. Msgr. Leo A. Riedmueller, V.F.
Res., 100 Central Ave., 71901. Tel: 501-623-3233. [JC]

St. John the Baptist, Rev. James P. West; Deacons David Briselden; Frank Sluppick; John Connell; Joe Harrison.
Res., 589 W. Grand Ave., 71901. Tel: 501-623-6201.
School—583 W. Grand Ave., 71901. Tel: 501-624-3141; Fax: 501-624-3141.
Sisters of Mercy 2; Lay Teachers 9; Students 185.
St. John's School Endowment—.

Hot Springs Village, Garland Co., Sacred Heart of Jesus, Very Rev. Raymond R. Rossi; Deacon Bernard Bauer.
Res., 22 Descollar, 71909. Tel: 501-922-2062.

Huntsville, Madison Co., St. John's, Revs. Stanley Oleksy Salvaturian; Miles Heinen, C.M.; R. Rex Hays, C.M.
Church—Rte. 6, Box 99A, 72740. Tel: 501-738-2709.
Res., 1119 W. Poplar, Rogers, 72756. Tel: 501-636-2548. [JC]

Jacksonville, Pulaski Co., St. Jude the Apostle, Rev. Charles J. Thessing.
Res., 2403 McArthur Dr., P.O. Box 665, 72076. Tel: 501-982-4891; Fax: 501-982-0821.

Jonesboro, Craighead Co., Blessed Sacrament, Rev. Jack D. Harris; Deacon Victor Stepka.
Res., 614 S. Church St., P.O. Box 1735, 72401. Tel: 501-932-2529; Fax: 501-935-4444. [CEM]
School—Tel: 501-932-3684.
Olivetan Benedictine Sisters 2; Lay Teachers 8; Students 122.
Blessed Sacrament Educational Endowment Fund—.

Lake Village, Chicot Co., Our Lady of the Lake, Rev. Henry B. Mischkowiuski.
Res., P.O. Box 272, 71653. Tel: 501-265-5439. [CEM]
School—Tel: 501-265-2921.
Lay Teachers 9; Students 118.
St. Mary's Educational Trust Fund—.

McGehee, Desha Co., St. Mary, Rev. John Eaton, O.F.M.; Bro. Michel LeMier, O.F.M.
Res., 401 N. 3rd St., 71654. Tel: 501-222-3389. [CEM]
Missions—Dumas, Desha Co., Holy Child Church, E. Waterman St., Dumas, 71639; Dermott, Chicot Co., Nativity of the Blessed Virgin Mary, Gaines St., Dermott, 71638.

Malvern, Hot Spring Co., St. John the Baptist, Rev. Stephen J. Binz, Sacramental Min.; Sr. Teresa Daly, D.C., Pastoral Admin.; Deacon Bud Daven.
Res., 1121 McBee St., P.O. Box 6, 72104. Tel: 501-332-6244.; Res., 249 N. 14th St., P.O. Box 26, Arkadelphia, 71923. Tel: 501-246-7575.
Mission—Arkadelphia, Clark Co., St. Mary's, P.O. Box 26, Arkadelphia, 71923. Tel: 501-246-7575.

Mena, Polk Co., St. Agnes, Rev. Kevin Lee.
Res., 203 8th St., P.O. Box 1428, 71953. Tel: 501-394-1017. [CEM]
Missions—Waldron, Scott Co., St. Jude Thaddeus, P.O. Box 1688, Waldron, 72958. Tel: 501-637-2055; Mount Ida, Montgomery Co., All Saints, P.O. Box 724, Mount Ida, 71957. Tel: 501-326-4641.

Monticello, Drew Co., St. Mark, Rev. Daniel Dorsey, Glmy.
Res., 452 W. Jefferson, 71655. Tel: 501-367-5974.
Church—1016 N. Hyatt St., 71655. Tel: 501-367-2848.
Res., 508 W. Pine, Warren, 71671. Tel: 501-226-5284.
Mission—Warren, Bradley Co., St. Luke.

Morrilton, Conway Co., Sacred Heart, Rev. Joseph A. Seiter, C.S.Sp.; Deacon Oscar Rohlman.
Res., 506 E. Broadway, 72110. Tel: 501-354-4181. [CEM]
School—Lay Teachers 11; Students 146.
High School—106 N. St. Joseph, 72110.
Lay Teachers 10; Students 99.
Sacred Heart School Endowment—Tel: 501-354-8113.

Morrison Bluff, Logan Co., SS. Peter and Paul, Rev. Alcuin Kubis, O.S.B.
Mailing Address: Rte. 1, Box 123-A, Scranton, 72863.
Res., Rte. 1, Scranton, 72863. Tel: 501-938-2200. [CEM]

Mountain Home, Baxter Co., St. Peter the Fisherman, Revs. Gregory G. Hart; Stan Swiderski, S.D.S; Deacons Bob Daye; John Krug; Richard Linstad.
Res., 250 S. Dyer St., P.O. Box 298, 72653. Tel: 501-425-2832; Fax: 501-424-5172.
Mission—Yellville, Marion Co., St. Andrew's, P.O. Box 197, Yellville, 72687. Tel: 501-449-4850.

Newport, Jackson Co., St. Cecilia's, Rev. Clayton Gould.
Church—Galeria Subdivision, 72112. Tel: 501-793-7464; 523-6542.
Res., St. Mary's Church, 3800 Harrison St., Batesville, 72501.

Osceola, Mississippi Co., St. Matthew's. Attended by Immaculate Conception, Blytheville. Very Rev. Joseph L. Pallo, V.F.
Church—P.O. Box 583, 72370.
Res., 1301 W. Main St., Blytheville, 72315. Tel: 501-762-2506.

Paragould, Greene Co., St. Mary's, Rev. Joseph Kay, M.Afr., Admin.
Res., 301 W. Highland St., P.O. Box 861, 72450. Tel: 501-236-2568. [CEM]
School—Tel: 501-236-3681.
Lay Teachers 5; Students 60.
Mission—Rector, Clay Co., St. Henry's, 800 Ballard St., Rector, 72461.
St. Mary Educational Trust Fund—.

Paris, Logan Co., St. Joseph's, Rev. Sebastian Beshoner, O.S.B.
Res., 15 S. Spruce St., 72855. Tel: 501-963-2131. [CEM]
School—Tel: 501-963-2119.
Lay Teachers 6; Students 102.
St. Joseph Endowment Fund—.

Pine Bluff, Jefferson Co., St. Joseph's, Very Rev. W. Andrew Smith, V.F.; Deacons Wallace Gieringer; Tim Massanelli.
Res., 412 W. 6th Ave., P.O. Box 7434, 71611. Tel: 501-534-4701; Fax: 501-534-4703. [CEM]
School—St. Joseph's Junior High School, 422 W. 6th, 71611-7434. Tel: 501-534-7545.
St. Joseph's Education Fund—Tel: 501-534-8393. Gertrude Schimmel, Pres.
Mission—Plum Bayou, Jefferson Co., St. Mary's, P.O. Box 7434, 71611.

St. Peter's, Rev. Bernard Keller, S.V.D.; Deacon Elton Harrison.
Res., 207 E. 16th Ave., 71601. Tel: 501-534-6418. [JC]
School—Tel: 501-535-4017; Fax: 501-535-4017.
Sisters of Notre Dame 4; Lay Teachers 6; Students 160.
Convent—Tel: 501-534-2316.
Mission—Pine Bluff, Jefferson Co., St. Raphael's, 71601.
St. Peter Catholic School Foundation—.

Pocahontas, Randolph Co., St. Paul the Apostle, Rev. Michael E. Bass; Deacon George Edwards.
Res., 1002 Convent St., 72455. Tel: 501-892-3319. [CEM]
School—Olivetan Benedictine Sisters 2; Lay Teachers 7; Students 110.
St. Paul School Charitable Trust—311 Cedar St., 72455. Tel: 501-892-5639.

Ratcliff, Logan Co., St. Anthony, Rev. Harold Heiman, O.S.B.
Res., Subiaco Abbey, Subiaco, 72865. Tel: 501-934-4295. [CEM]

Rogers, Benton Co., St. Vincent de Paul, Revs. Richard S. Oswald; Michael D. Sinkler; Deacons Bruce Leach; Clarence Leis; Bill Cook.
Church—1305 W. Cypress St., 72758-4118. Tel:

501-636-4020; Fax: 501-631-2548. [CEM]
School—1315 W. Cypress St., 72758. Tel: 501-636-4421.
Lay Teachers 19; Students 271.
St. Vincent de Paul Endowment Fund—.

Russellville, Pope Co., St. John's, Very Rev. Ernest L. Hardesty, V.F.
Res., 1900 W. Main St., P.O. Box 308, 72801. Tel: 501-967-3699.
School—Tel: 501-967-4644.
Benedictine Sisters 3; Lay Teachers 10; Students 128.
St. John's Educational Trust—1914 W. Main St., 72801.
Mission—Dardanelle, Yell Co., St. Augustine's, 1006 N. 2nd, Dardanelle, 72834. Tel: 501-229-3972.

St. Vincent, Conway Co., St. Mary, Rev. Arthur B. Chiasson, M.Afr.
Res., 11 Kaufman Ln., Hattieville, 72063. Tel: 501-354-3206. [CEM]
Mission—Clinton, Van Buren Co., St. Jude, P.O. Box 526, Clinton, 72031. Tel: 501-745-5716.

Scranton, Logan Co., St. Ignatius, Rev. Raphael DeSalvo, O.S.B.
Church—P.O. Box 87, 72863. Tel: 501-938-2821. [CEM]
Mission—Prairie View, Logan Co., St. Meinrad, 72863.

Searcy, White Co., St. James, Very Rev. Robert T. Dienert, V.F.
Res., 1102 Pioneer Rd., P.O. Box 172, 72143. Tel: 501-268-2418.
Missions—Heber Springs, Cleburne Co., St. Albert, 21 Park Rd., Heber Springs, 72543. Tel: 501-362-2914; Bald Knob, White Co., St. Richard, 72143.

Sheridan, Grant Co., Holy Cross. Attended by Good Shepherd, Fordyce. Rev. Wilfred C. Okorochukwu.
Mailing Address: 921 Vine St., 72150. Tel: 501-942-4532. [CEM]
Mission—Sheridan, Grant Co., Holy Cross.

Shoal Creek, Logan Co., St. Scholastica's (New Blaine), Rev. Paul Hoedebeck, O.S.B.
288 St. Scholastica Rd., New Blaine, 72851. Tel: 501-938-7566.
Res., Subiaco Abbey, Subiaco, 72865. Tel: 501-934-4295. [CEM]

Siloam Springs, Benton Co., St. Mary's, Rev. William H. Moran, S.J.
Res., P.O. Box 118, 72761. Tel: 501-524-8526.

Slovak, Prairie Co., SS. Cyril and Methodius, Rev. Richard M. Strock.
Res., Rte. 1, Box 117, 72160. Tel: 501-241-3359. [CEM]
Mission—England, Lonoke Co., Holy Trinity Church, P.O. Box 243, England, 72046. Tel: 501-842-2460.

Springdale, Washington Co., St. Raphael's, Revs. Joseph M. Correnti; Phillip A. Reaves Tel: 501-361-2312.
Church—P.O. Box 6010, 72766-6010. Tel: 501-756-6711.
Res., P.O. Box 39, Tontitown, 72770.

Stamps, Lafayette Co., St. Vincent de Paul. Closed. For inquiries for parish records contact the Chancery.

Star City, Lincoln Co., St. Justin's. Unassigned.
Res., P.O. Box 128, 71667. Tel: 501-628-3092. [CEM]
Mission—Grady, Lincoln Co., Blessed Sacrament, 71667.

Stuttgart, Arkansas Co., Holy Rosary, Rev. John A. Janesko.
Res., 1815 S. Prairie St., 72160. Tel: 501-673-8351. [CEM]
School—Tel: 501-673-3211.
Benedictine Sisters 2; Lay Teachers 4; Students 85.
Mission—Gillett, Arkansas Co., St. Henry's, 72160.

Subiaco, Logan Co., St. Benedict, Rev. Denis Soerries, O.S.B.
Res., 81 W. Parish Dr., 72865. Tel: 501-934-4321. [CEM]

Texarkana, Miller Co., St. Edward's, Very Rev. David E. Jacobs, V.F.; Deacon Joe Briuck.
Res., 407 Beech St., P.O. Box 1186, 75504. Tel: 501-772-1115; Fax: 501-773-2890. [CEM]
Church—410 Beech St., 71854.

Tontitown, Washington Co., St. Joseph's, Revs. Joseph M. Correnti; Phillip A. Reaves.
Res., P.O. Box 39, 72770. Tel: 501-361-2612. [CEM]

Van Buren, Crawford Co., St. Michael's, Rev. Ralph Esposito; Deacon Al Genna.
Res., 1512 N. 11th, 72956. Tel: 501-474-6402.
Mission—Jenny Lind, Sebastian Co., Sts. Sabina and Mary's Church.

Walnut Ridge, Lawrence Co., Immaculate Heart of Mary. Attended by St. John the Baptist, Engelberg. Rev. Leslie A. Farley; Deacon Marlin Tate.
Res., P.O. Box 70, 72476. Tel: 501-886-2119. [JC]

Weiner, Poinsett Co., St. Anthony's, Rev. Nicholas Fuhrmann, O.S.B.
Mailing Address: P.O. Box 76, 72479. Tel: 501-684-2656.
Res., 415 Kings Hwy., 72479. Tel: 501-684-2656. [CEM]
Mission—Marked Tree, Poinsett Co., St. Norbert's, Marked Tree, 72365.

West Memphis, Crittenden Co., St. Michael's, Rev. Paul F. Worm.
Res., 208 W. Cooper Ave., 72301. Tel: 501-732-3819.
Church—411 Missouri, P.O. Box 899, 72303. Tel: 501-735-1730; 735-7983; Fax: 501-732-4808.
School—405 Missouri, P.O. Box 899, 72303.
Olivetan Benedictine Sisters 2; Lay Teachers 6; Students 121.
St. Michael's School Endowment and Charitable Trust—.
Missions—Crawfordsville, Crittenden Co., Sacred Heart, Main St., Crawfordsville, 72327; Horseshoe Lake, Crittenden Co., St. Mary's of the Lake, Hwy. 131, Horseshoe Lake, 72348.

Winslow, Crawford Co., Our Lady of the Ozarks Shrine, Deacon Dan Daily.
Mailing Address: 22741 N. Hwy. 71, 72959. Tel: 501-634-2181.
Res., 22741 N. Hwy. 71, 72959. Tel: 501-634-2181. [CEM]

Wynne, Cross Co., St. Peter's, Rev. Thomas C. Marks.
Res., P.O. Box 517, 72396. Tel: 501-238-2613.
Mission—McCrory, Woodruff Co., St. Mary's, Tel: 501-731-0048.

Chaplains of Public Institutions

LITTLE ROCK. *U.S. Veterans Administration Hospital*. Vacant. 4300 W. 7th St., 72205. Tel: 501-661-1202, Ext. 1121.

FAYETTEVILLE. *U.S. Veterans Administration Hospital*. Attended from St. Joseph Church.

NORTH LITTLE ROCK. *U.S. Veterans Administration Hospital*, North Little Rock Division, 72114. Tel: 501-661-1202, Ext. 1121. Rev. Victor E. Bertrand, C.S.V., Chap.

On Duty Outside the Diocese:
Reverend Fathers—
Gunti, Frederick W., Springhill College, Mobile, AL 33608

Absent on Leave:
Reverend Fathers—
Eakin, Daniel

Retired:
Reverend Monsignors—
De Clerk, Rainer J., Rte. 1, 506 Elizabeth Ln., Mountain Home, AR 72653
Maus, Rudolph E., 210 N. Vancouver, Russellville, AR 72801
McKee, Francis J., Riley's Oak manor, 8701 Riley Dr., Little Rock, AR 72205
Murphy, John E., St. John Manor, Apt. #304, 2414 N. Tyler St., Little Rock, AR 72207
Scheper, John B., Riley's Oak Hill Manor, 2501 John Ashley Dr., North Little Rock, AR 72114
Stemac, Louis V., St. John Manor, Apt. #307, 2414 N. Tyler St., Little Rock, AR 72207
Reverend Fathers—
Barnes, John E., St. John Manor, 2414 N. Tyler St., Apt. 308, Little Rock, AR 72207
Bauer, Ralph, P.O. Box 1172, Hot springs, AR 71902
Bolds, Bernard L., c/o Little Sisters of the Poor, 3225 N. Florissant Ave., Saint Louis, MO 63107
Booth, Earl J., St. John Manor, 2414 N. Tyler St., Apt. 202, Little Rock, AR 72207
Cheney, Jesse C., St. John Manor, Apt. #201, 2414 N. Tyler St., Little Rock, AR 72207
Dagwell, Robert A., 433 Bluff St., Alton, IL 62002
Donahue, Thomas J., St. John Manor, 2415 N. Tyler, Little Rock, AR 72267. Tel: 501-664-6486
Freyaldenhoven, George P., P.O. Box 123, Pottsville, AR 72858
Hlavacek, John, St. John Manor, Apt. #306, 2414 N. Tyler St., Little Rock, AR 72207
Janesko, Francis J., P.O. Box 730, Rogers, AR 72757
Kane, William, 10 Wadsworth Rd., Arlington, MA 02174
Kepple, Robert, 107 Palm, Hot Springs, AR 71901
Manchino, John, St. Barbara's Nursing Home, P.O. Box 9066, Monogah, WV 26555
McGinnis, N. Charles, Benedictine Manor, P.O. Box 2249, Hot Springs, AR 71901
Preske, Venantius, P.O. Box 4018, Horseshoe Bend, AR 72512
Savary, James, 6720 Brentwood Rd., Little Rock, AR 72205
Strassle, Paul, P.O. Box 1545, Fairfield Bay, AR 72088
Torres, Robert A., 2400 Riverfront Dr. #843, Little Rock, AR 72202. Tel: 501-664-8473; 664-9697
Turner, George F., 10631 Gulf Beach Hwy., Pensacola, FL 32507. Tel: 904-492-5741
Walters, James, 2505 S. 17th St., Paragould, AR 72450

INSTITUTIONS LOCATED IN THE DIOCESE

[A] SEMINARIES, RELIGIOUS OR SCHOLASTICATES

LITTLE ROCK. *Marylake - Carmelite Novitiate*, 5151 Marylake Dr., 72206. Tel: 501-888-3052. Discalced Carmelite Friars of the Province of St. Therese, Little Rock. Revs. Stephen Sanchez, O.C.D., Supr.; Raphael Kitz, O.C.D., Novice Master; Evarist V. Foix, O.C.D.; Felix Da Prato, O.C.D.; Thomas Behnke, O.C.D.; Aloysius Deeney, O.C.D., Prov.; Henry Bordeaux, O.C.D. Priests 7; Novices 5.

SEARCY. *St. Anthony Friary (Formerly Morris School for Boys)*, 285 Morris School Rd., 72143-9649. Tel: 501-268-8145. Bros. Maurus DiSabella; Stanislaus Duran.

SUBIACO. *Subiaco Monastery*, 72865. Tel: 501-934-4295; Fax: 501-934-4328. Rt. Rev. Jerome Kodell, O.S.B., Abbot; Bro. Eric Loran, O.S.B., Prior; Revs. Hugh Assenmacher, O.S.B., Novice Master; Aaron Pirrera, O.S.B., Vocation Dir.; Andrew Wewer; Bernard Schumacher; Brendan Miller; Camillus Cooney; Columbian Kannitzer; Damian Wewers; David Flusche; David McKillin; Felix Fredeman; Harold Heiman; Herbert Vogelpohl; John Walbe; Leo Koesler; Leonard Wangler; Malachy McNerney; Mark Stengel, Novice Master; Meinrad Marbaugh; Paul Hoedebeck; Stephen Eckart; Timothy Donnelly; William Wewers. Abbots 1; Monks 76.

[B] HIGH SCHOOLS, DIOCESAN

LITTLE ROCK. *Catholic High School*, 6300 Lee St., 72205. Tel: 501-664-3939. Revs. George W. Tribou, Rector; Lawrence A. Frederick. Legal Title: *Catholic High School of Little Rock, AR*.
Catholic High School Foundation, Inc. Priests 2; Brothers 1; Lay Teachers 32; Students 743.

CONWAY, AK. *St. Joseph High School*, College & Chestnut St., 72032. Tel: 501-329-5741. Daniel Fields, Prin.; Rita Strause, Asst. Prin. Lay Teachers 16; Students 205.

FORT SMITH. *Trinity Junior High*, 1205 S. Albert Pike, 72903. Tel: 501-782-2451. Rev. Msgr. Royce R. Thomas, J.C.L., Pastor Rep.; Eddie Hauhee, Prin. Sisters of Mercy 2; Lay Teachers 14; Students 229.
Trinity Educational Trust Fund.

MORRILTON. *Sacred Heart High School*, 106 N. St. Joseph St., 72110. Tel: 501-354-8113. Sr. Rachel Auringer, O.S.U., Prin.; Sr. Katherine Etris, Asst. Prin. Lay Teachers 10; Students 99.

[C] HIGH SCHOOLS, PRIVATE

LITTLE ROCK. *Mount St. Mary Academy*. (Girls), 3224 Kavanaugh Blvd., 72205. Tel: 501-664-8006; Fax: 501-666-4382. Sr. Deborah Raye Troillett, R.S.M., Prin.; Sr. Joan Marie Pfauser, R.S.M., Asst. Prin. for Academics; Carolyn Chalmers, Asst. Prin. Student Life. Priests 1; Sisters of Mercy 2; Lay Teachers 33; Students 592.
Mount St. Mary Academy Endowment and Scholarship Fund.

SUBIACO. *Subiaco Academy*. (Boys), 72865. Tel: 501-934-4291. Rt. Rev. Jerome Kodell, O.S.B., Pres.; Rev. Timothy Donnelly, O.S.B., Headmaster. Priests 7; Brothers 9; Lay Teachers 17; Students 185.

[D] DAY CARE CENTERS

LITTLE ROCK. *Little Angel Day Care*, 9111 Auxer Rd., 72209. Olivetan Benedictine Sisters 2.

NORTH LITTLE ROCK. *St. Joseph's Day Care Center*, 6800 Camp Robinson Rd., 72118. Tel: 501-753-1189. Benedictine Sisters 9; Children in day care 105.

[E] GENERAL HOSPITALS

LITTLE ROCK. *St. Vincent Infirmary Medical Center*, No. 2 St. Vincent Circle, 72205. Tel: 501-660-3000; Fax: 501-671-4241.
For a complete listing, refer to the Hospitals section.

FORT SMITH. *Northside Community Health Center*, 3202 North 6th, 72904. Tel: 501-782-1456.
For a complete listing, refer to the Hospitals section.
St. Edward Mercy Medical Center, 7301 Rogers Ave., 72917. Tel: 501-484-6000; Fax: 501-452-1770.

For a complete listing, refer to the Hospitals section.
St. Edward Mercy Medical Center, dba Harbor View Mercy Hospital and Counseling Center, 10301 Mayo Rd., P.O. Box 17000, 72917-7000. Tel: 501-484-5550.
For a complete listing, refer to the Hospitals section.

HOT SPRINGS NATIONAL PARK. *St. Joseph's Regional Health Center*, 300 Werner St., 71913. Tel: 501-622-1000.
For a complete listing, refer to the Hospitals section.

JONESBORO. *St. Bernard's Regional Medical Center*, 224 E. Matthews St., 72401. Tel: 501-972-4100.
For a complete listing, refer to the Hospitals section.

MORRILTON. *Conway County Hospital*, #4 Hospital Dr., 72110-4510.
For a complete listing, refer to the Hospitals section.

OZARK. *St. Edward Health Facilities of Franklin County, dba Mercy Hospital/Turner Memorial*, 801 W. River St., P.O. Box 527, 72949 Fax: 501-667-4751.
For a complete listing, refer to the Hospitals section.

PARIS. *St. Edward Health Facilities of Logan Co., dba North Logan Mercy Hospital*, 500 E. Academy, 72855.
For a complete listing, refer to the Hospitals section.

ROGERS. *St. Mary-Rogers Memorial Hospital*, 72756. Tel: 501-636-0200, Ext. 705; Fax: 501-936-2906.
For a complete listing, refer to the Hospitals section.

WALDRON. *St. Edward Health Facilities of Scott County dba Mercy Hospital*, Hwy. 71 & 80, Box 2230, 72958. Tel: 501-637-4135; Fax: 501-637-3523.
For a complete listing, refer to the Hospitals section.

[F] PROTECTIVE INSTITUTIONS

LITTLE ROCK. *ABBA House*, 1014 S. Oak St., 72204. Tel: 501-666-9718.
For a complete listing, refer to the Special Care Facilities section.
Catherine's House c/o Sisters of Mercy Health System, 1020 W. 14th St., 72202. Tel: 501-370-9100.
For a complete listing, refer to the Special Care Facilities section.

HOT SPRINGS NATIONAL PARK. *Monastery of Our Lady of Charity of Refuge (Good Shepherd)*, 1125 Malvern Ave., 71901. Tel: 501-623-9651.
For a complete listing, refer to the Special Care Facilities section.
St. Michael's School, 1125 Malvern Ave., 71901.
For a complete listing, refer to the Special Care Facilities section.

[G] HOMES FOR AGED

BARLING. *Mercy Crest of Arkansas, Inc.*, 1300 Strozier Ln., 72923. Tel: 501-478-3000.
For a complete listing, refer to the Special Care Facilities section.

HOT SPRINGS. *Benedictine Manor*, 101 Second St., 71913. Tel: 501-623-6308.
For a complete listing, refer to the Special Care Facilities section.

[H] RESIDENCES FOR PRIESTS

LITTLE ROCK. *St. John Manor*, 2414 N. Tyler St., 72207. Bro. Blaise Betley, Mgr.; Rev. Msgr. Francis McKee; Rev. Msgr. John E. Murphy; Rev. Msgr. Louis V. Stemac; Revs. Jesse C. Cheney; John F. Hlavacek; John E. Barnes; Tom Donahue; Earl J. Booth. Priests 7.

[I] CONVENTS AND RESIDENCES FOR SISTERS

LITTLE ROCK. *Discalced Carmelite Nuns*, 7201 W. 32nd St., 72204-4716. Tel: 501-565-5121. Sr. Therese Stewart, Prioress. Legal Title: *Discalced Carmelite Nuns of Little Rock*. Sisters 13; Nuns with solemn vows 10; Nuns with temporary vows 2; Externs 1. Attended from Catholic High School, Little Rock.
Mt. St. Mary's Convent, 3508 Kavanaugh Blvd., 72205. Sr. Ann Hardcastle, R.S.M., Local Coord. Sisters of Mercy of Mount St. Mary Convent of Little Rock, Arkansas, Inc. 8.

BARLING. *Catherine McAuley Convent of Mercy*, 1300 Strozier Ln., 72923. Tel: 501-478-3000. Sisters of Mercy.

FORT SMITH. *St. Edward Convent of Mercy*, 7301 Rogers Ave., P.O. Box 17000, 72917-7000. Tel: 501-484-6098; Fax: 501-452-1770. Sisters of Mercy.
St. Scholastica Monastery-Motherhouse, 1301 S. Albert Pike, P.O. Box 3489, 72913. Tel: 501-783-4147. Sr. Elise Forst, Prioress; Sr. Catherine Markey, Archivist. Benedictine Professed sisters 126; Novices 2; Candidate 2.

HOT SPRINGS. *Monastery of Our Lady of Charity of Refuge*. (Good Shepherd), 1125 Malvern Ave., 71901. Tel: 501-623-9651. Sr. Theresa Marie Lalancette, Supr. Sisters 13; Novices 1.

JONESBORO. *Holy Angels Convent-Motherhouse*, 72403. Tel: 501-935-5810. Olivetan Benedictine Sisters. Rev. Nicholas Fuhrman, O.S.B. Sisters 59.

OZARK. *NAAS House of Mercy*, 1100 Bluff Dr., 72949. Tel: 501-667-4963. Sisters of Mercy.

WALDRON. *Waldron Convent of Mercy*, Rt. 2, Box 14A, 72958. Tel: 501-637-2287. Sisters of Mercy.

[J] NEWMAN CENTERS

LITTLE ROCK. *Catholic Campus Ministries*, 2500 N. Tyler St., P.O. Box 7565, 72217. Tel: 501-664-0340. Phyllis Enderlin, Dir.
Univ. of Arkansas at Little Rock Campus Ministry, Good Counsel Church, 1321 S. Van Buren, 72204.
Henderson State Teachers College and Ouchita Baptist University Campus Ministry. (Arkadelphia), P.O. Box 26, Arkadelphia, 71923. Tel: 501-246-7575.
University of Central Arkansas & Hendrix College Campus Ministry. (Conway), #4 Brierssprings, Conway, 72032. Tel: 501-327-4152. Mrs. Sherry Curran.
University of Arkansas, St. Thomas Aquinas University Parish. (Fayetteville), 603 N. Leverett, Fayetteville, 72701. Tel: 501-444-0223. Deacon Paul Cronan, Pastoral Admin.; Rev. Mark Wood, Sacramental Min.; Esther Breeding, Campus Minister.
Catholic University Parish at Arkansas State University. (Jonesboro), 2800 E. Johnson Ave., Jonesboro, 72401. Tel: 501-972-1888. Rev. Jack Harris; Sr. Mary John Seyler, O.S.B., Campus Min.; Mary Ruth Standt, Dir., Campus Ministry.
Catholic University Parish at Arkansas Tech University. (Russellville), 501 W. "L" St., Russellville, 72801. Tel: 501-968-8249. Pat Buford, Director, Campus Ministry.
Harding University (Searcy) Campus Ministry, 109 Campbell Dr., Beebe, 72012. Flo Fitch, Campus Min.; Denis Kimbrough, Campus Min.; Melodye Stickley, Campus Min.

LAMAR. *University of Ozarks Campus Ministry (Clarksville)*, P.O. Box 111, 72846. Tel: 501-885-3464. Campus Ministers: Denise Kimbrough; Melodye Stickley.

[K] RETREAT CENTERS

EUREKA SPRINGS. *Brothers and Sisters of Charity at Little Portion Hermitage*. (Integrated Monestary), Rte. 7, Box 608, 72632. Tel: 501-253-7710; Fax: 501-253-6640. Legal Title: *Brothers and Sisters of Charity at Little Portion, Inc.* John Michael Talbot, B.S.C., Gen. Min.; Viola Talbot, B.S.C., Vicar Gen. Min.; Bob Denk, Family Minister.
Little Flower Clinic for the Poor.
Little Portion Retreat and Training Center at More Mt., Rte. 4, Box 430, 72632. Tel: 501-253-7379. John Michael Talbot, Exec. Dir.; Tom Fink, Admin. Dir.; Deacon Samuel Hilburn, Spiritual Dir. In Residence 4; Catholic Staff 7.

FORT SMITH. *St. Scholastica Center*, 1205 S. Albert Pike, P.O. Box 3489, 72913. Tel: 501-783-1135. Sr. Cabrini Schmitz, O.S.B., Dir. Center & Program Coord.; Sr. Gertrude Grabber, O.S.B., Dir. Maintenance and Hospitality; Sr. Macrina Wiederkehr, O.S.B., Retreats/Spiritual Dir. Conducted by Benedictine Sisters 10.

SHOAL CREEK. *Hesychia House of Prayer*. 204 St. Scholastica Rd., New Blaine, 72851. Sr. Louise Sharum, O.S.B., Dir. Benedictine Sisters 4. Attended from New Subiaco Abbey, Subiaco, AR.

[L] MISCELLANEOUS LISTINGS

LITTLE ROCK. Sisters of Mercy (Under auspices of St. Edward Mercy Medical Center, Fort Smith, AR).
The "Arkansas Catholic." Published by Arkansas Catholic, Inc. of the Diocese of Little Rock. 2500 N. Tyler St., P.O. Box 7417, 72217. Tel: 501-664-0340; 664-0125; Fax: 501-664-9075. Rev. Francis I. Malone; Ms. Malea Walters, Editor, P.O. Box 7417, 72217.
Adoption Services, Inc., 2415 N. Tyler, P.O. Box 7239, 72217. Tel: 501-664-0340. Ms. Antje Harris, Dir.
Christopher Homes of Arkansas, Inc.
Christopher Homes of Augusta, Inc.
Christopher Homes of Brinkley, Inc.
Christopher Homes of Camden, Inc.
Christopher Homes of Clarendon, Inc.
Christopher Homes of Elaine, Inc.
Christopher Homes of El Dorado, Inc.
Christopher Homes of Forrest City, Inc.
Christopher Homes of Hot Springs, Inc.
Christopher Homes of Jonesboro, Inc.
Christopher Homes of Marianna, Inc.
Christopher Homes of Monette, Inc.
Christopher Homes of North Little Rock, Inc.
Christopher Homes of Palestine, Inc.
Christopher Homes of Paragould, Inc.
Christopher Homes of Parkin, Inc.
Christopher Homes of Searcy, Inc.
Christopher Homes of Strong, Inc.
Christopher Homes of West Helena, Inc.
Christopher Homes of Wynne, Inc. James T. Davis, Exec. Dir.
Cursillo Trust. Mr. John Sweeney, Trustee.
John Gazzola Trust Estate, P.O. Box 7239, 72217. Tel: 501-664-0340. Mr. William Hartmann, Dir.
Priestly Fraternity of St. Peter, 2414 N. Tyler St., #310, 72207-3735. Tel: 501-280-9155; Fax: 501-280-9225. Rev. Pablo D. Alvarez, F.S.S.P.
St. John's Home Missions Seminary, Inc., Endowment Fund, P.O. Box 7565, 72217. Tel: 501-664-0340, Ext. 380. Rev. Msgr. James E. O'Connell, Pres., Dir. of Endowment Funds.

BERRYVILLE. *Martha Mary House for Women and Children*, 301 Shaver St., Box 602, 72616. Tel: 501-423-3572.
St. Vincent de Paul Thrift Shop, 204 S. Main, 72616. Tel: 501-423-3572.

BLYTHEVILLE. *Immaculate Conception Trust Fund*, 1301 W. Main St., 72315. Tel: 501-762-2506. Rev. Joseph L. Pallo, Contact Person.

EUREKA SPRINGS. *St. Vincent de Paul Society*, Rte. 7, Box 700, 72631.

FORT SMITH. *Catholic Youth Ministries of Fort Smith, Inc.*, 1205 S. Albert Pike, 72903. Michael Bushkuhl, Vice Pres. & Treas.; William B. Buergler, Pres.; Bob Bush, Sec.

HORSESHOE BEND. *St. Vincent de Paul Society*, P.O. Box 4012, 72512. St. Mary of the Mount, 72512.

STAMPS. *De Paul Community Development Centers, Inc.*, P.O. Box 116, 71857. Tel: 501-533-2113.

STUTTGART. *Holy Rosary Catholic School "Vision 2000" Educational Trust Fund*, 1815 S. Prairie St., 72160. Tel: 501-673-8351. Rev. John A. Janesko.

RELIGIOUS INSTITUTES OF MEN REPRESENTED IN THE DIOCESE

For further details refer to the corresponding bracketed number in the Religious Institutes of Men or Women section.

[0200]—*Benedictine Monks*. (New Subiaco Abbey).—O.S.B.

[0460]—*Brothers of the Poor of St. Francis*.—C.F.P.

[1330]—*Congregation of the Mission*.—C.M.

[0260]—*Discalced Carmelite Friars*. (St. Therese Prov.).—O.C.D.

[0510]—*Franciscan Brothers of the Holy Cross*.—F.F.S.C.

[0520]—*Franciscan Friars*. (St. John the Baptist Prov.).—O.F.M.

[0570]—*Glenmary Home Missioners*.—Glmy.

[0650]—*Holy Ghost Fathers*. (Western Vice Prov.).—C.S.Sp.

[0690]—*Jesuit Fathers and Brothers*.—S.J.

[0850]—*Missionaries of Africa*. (Prov. of Quebec, Canada).—M.Afr.

[0430]—*Order of Preachers (Dominicans)*. (Southern Prov.).—O.P.

[1065]—*Priestly Fraternity of St. Peter*.—F.S.S.P.

[]—*Public Association of the Faithful - Celibate Brotherhood of the Brothers and Sisters of Charity*.—B.S.C.

[0420]—*Society of the Divine Word*. (Techny, IL).—S.V.D.

RELIGIOUS INSTITUTES OF WOMEN REPRESENTED IN THE DIOCESE

[0230]—*Benedictine Sisters of Pontifical Jurisdiction*. (Fort Smith, AR).—O.S.B.

[0470]—*Congregation of the Sisters of Charity of the Incarnate Word, Houston, Texas*.—C.C.V.I.

[1780]—*Congregation of the Sisters of the Third Order of St. Francis of Perpetual Adoration*. (Central Region).—F.S.P.A.

[0760]—*Daughters of Charity of St. Vincent de Paul*. (West Central Prov.).—D.C.

[]—*Daughters of Our Lady of Fatima*.—D.L.F.

[0420]—*Discalced Carmelite Nuns*. (Little Rock, AR).—O.C.D.

[1070-10]—*Dominican Sisters*.—O.P.

[2575]—*Institute of the Sisters of Mercy of the Americas*. (St. Louis, MO).—R.S.M.

[2490]—*Medical Mission Sisters*.—S.C.M.M.

[2710]—*Missionaries of Charity*.—M.C.

[1360]—*Missionary Franciscan Sisters of the Immaculate Conception*.—O.S.F.

[3070]—*North American Union Sisters of Our Lady of Charity*. (Hot Springs, AR).—N.A.U.-O.L.C.

[0240]—*Olivetan Benedictine Sisters*. (Jonesboro, AR).—O.S.B.

[]—*Public Association of the Faithful - Celibate Sisterhood of the Brothers and Sisters of Charity*.—B.S.C.

[2940]—*School Sisters of Notre Dame*. (Prov. of Dallas).—S.S.N.D.

[0500]—*Sisters of Charity of Nazareth*.—S.C.N.

[4120-03]—*Ursuline Nuns of the Congregation of Paris*.—O.S.U.

CEMETERIES

LITTLE ROCK. *Calvary*.

FORT SMITH. *Calvary*.

NECROLOGY

† Borovec, Peter J., (On Leave). —Died November 25, 1995.

† Bujarski, Paul R., (Retired). —Died Dec. 23, 1995.

† Galvin, Rev. Msgr. William E., Fort Smith, AK, Immaculate Conception. —Died June 1, 1996.

† Kane, William Francis Edward, (Retired). —Died April 19, 1996.

† Maus, Lawrence Dennis, Clinton, AR, St. Mary-St. Vincent. —Died June 9, 1996.

Archdiocese of Los Angeles

(Archidioecesis Angelorum in California)

His Eminence

ROGER CARDINAL MAHONY, D.D.

Archbishop of Los Angeles; ordained May 1, 1962; appointed Titular Bishop of Tamascani and Auxiliary Bishop of Fresno January 7, 1975; consecrated March 19, 1975; appointed Bishop of Stockton February 26, 1980; installed as the third Bishop of Stockton April 17, 1980; appointed Archbishop of Los Angeles July 16, 1985; installed as the fourth Archbishop of Los Angeles September 5, 1985; Created Cardinal June 28, 1991. *Res., 114 E. 2nd St., Los Angeles, CA, 90012. Office: 3424 Wilshire Blvd., Los Angeles, CA, 90010-2241.* Tel.: 213-637-7261.

Archdiocesan Catholic Center Office: 3424 Wilshire Blvd., Los Angeles, CA, 90010-2241. Tel.: 213-637-7000; Fax: 213-637-6607.

Web site address: http://www.LA-Archdiocese.org

Most Reverend

JOHN J. WARD, D.D., J.C.L., V.G.

Auxiliary Bishop and Vicar General; ordained May 4, 1946; appointed Titular Bishop of Bria and Auxiliary October 16, 1963; consecrated December 12, 1963; Assigned Titular Bishop of California, June 15, 1996; retired July 1, 1996. *Office: 3424 Wilshire Blvd., Los Angeles, CA, 90010-2241. Res., 10425 W. Pico Blvd., Los Angeles, CA, 90064.*

Most Reverend

JUAN A. ARZUBE, D.D.

Retired Auxiliary Bishop and Vicar General; ordained May 5, 1954; appointed Titular Bishop of Civitate and Auxiliary February 9, 1971; consecrated March 25, 1971; retired June 1, 1993. *Res., Sacred Heart Church, 2889 N. Lincoln Ave., Altadena, CA, 91001-4598.*

Most Reverend

STEPHEN E. BLAIRE, D.D., V.G.

Auxiliary Bishop and Vicar General; ordained April 29, 1967; appointed Titular Bishop of Lamzella on February 17, 1990; ordained Bishop on May 31, 1990. *Office: Regional Bishop, Our Lady of the Angels Pastoral Region, 2636 S. Mansfield Ave., Los Angeles, CA, 90016.*

Most Reverend

THOMAS J. CURRY, D.D., PH.D.

Auxiliary Bishop and Vicar General; ordained June 18, 1967; appointed Titular Bishop of Ceanannus Mor February 8, 1994. *Office: Regional Bishop, Santa Barbara Pastoral Region, 3240 Calle Pinon, Santa Barbara, CA, 93105.*

Most Reverend

JOSEPH M. SARTORIS, D.D., V.G.

Auxiliary Bishop and Vicar General; ordained May 30, 1953; appointed Titular Bishop of Oliva February 8, 1994; ordained Bishop March 19, 1994. *Office: Regional Bishop, San Pedro Pastoral Region, 3555 St. Pancratius Pl., Lakewood, CA, 90712-1416.*

Most Reverend

GABINO ZAVALA, D.D., J.C.L., V.G.

Auxiliary Bishop and Vicar General; ordained May 28, 1977; appointed Titular Bishop of Tamascani February 8, 1994; ordained Bishop March 19, 1994. *Office: Regional Bishop, San Gabriel Pastoral Region, 16009 E. Cypress Ave., Irwindale, CA, 91706.*

DIOCESE ESTABLISHED 1840; AN ARCHBISHOPRIC JULY 11, 1936.

Square Miles 8,762.

Comprises the Counties of Los Angeles, Santa Barbara and Ventura in the State of California.

PATRONESS OF THE DIOCESE: ST. VIBIANA.

Legal Titles:

The Roman Catholic Archbishop of Los Angeles, a Corporation Sole.

Archdiocese of Los Angeles Education and Welfare Corporation.

Our Lady Queen of Angels Seminary.

St. John's Seminary College.

St. John's Seminary in California.

The Cardinal McIntyre Fund for Charity.

Catholic Charities of Los Angeles, Inc.

Catholic Charities Community Development Corporation.

The Tidings.

Vida Nueva.

For legal titles of parishes and archdiocesan institutions, consult the Chancery Office.

STATISTICAL OVERVIEW

Personnel	
Cardinal	1
Auxiliary Bishops	4
Retired Bishops	2
Abbots	1
Priests: Diocesan Active in Diocese	424
Priests: Active Outside Diocese	16
Priests: Diocesan in Foreign Missions	2
Priests: Retired, Sick or Absent	130
Number of Diocesan Priests	572
Religious Priests in Diocese	593
Extern Priests in Diocese	110
Ordinations:	
Diocesan Priests	15
Religious Priests	5
Permanent Deacons in Diocese	144
Total Brothers	220
Total Sisters	1,980
Parishes	
Parishes	285
With Resident Pastor:	
Resident Diocesan Priests	208
Resident Religious Priests	63
Without Resident Pastor:	
Administered by Priests	12
Administered by Pastoral Teams, etc.	1
Missions	17
Pastoral Centers	1
Professional Ministry Personnel:	
Brothers	11
Sisters	173
Lay Ministers	476

Welfare	
Catholic Hospitals	18
Total Assisted	1,514,263
Health Care Centers	2
Total Assisted	13,200
Homes for the Aged	7
Total Assisted	485
Residential Care of Children	3
Total Assisted	379
Day Care and Extended Day Care Centers	80
Total Assisted	13,189
Specialized Homes	5
Total Assisted	696
Special Centers for Social Services	82
Total Assisted	356,920
Residential Care of Disabled	2
Total Assisted	61
Other Institutions	7
Total Assisted	1,237
Educational	
Seminaries, Diocesan	2
Students from This Diocese	74
Students from Other Diocese	61
Diocesan Students in Other Seminaries	1
Seminaries, Religious	15
Students Religious	24
Total Seminarians	99
Colleges and Universities	6
Total Students	9,977
High Schools, Diocesan and Parish	29

Total Students	17,585
High Schools, Private	22
Total Students	12,892
Elementary Schools, Diocesan and Parish	221
Total Students	67,538
Elementary Schools, Private	9
Total Students	2,586
Catechesis/Religious Education:	
High School Students	24,000
Elementary Students	200,000
Total Students Under Catholic Instruction	334,677
Teachers in the Diocese:	
Priests	69
Brothers	32
Sisters	439
Lay Teachers	3,963
Vital Statistics	
Receptions into the Church:	
Infant Baptism Totals	95,611
Adult Baptism Totals	2,023
Received into Full Communion	2,661
First Communions	40,086
Confirmations	15,180
Marriages:	
Catholic	12,406
Interfaith	1,772
Total Marriages	14,178
Deaths	13,737
Total Catholic Population	3,672,763
Total Population	11,689,801

Former Bishops—Rt. Rev. FRANCIS GARCIA DIEGO Y MORENO, O.F.M., D.D., cons. Oct. 4, 1840; Bishop of both Californias; died at Santa Barbara, April 30, 1846.—Rt. Rev. JOSEPH SADOC ALEMANY, O.P., D.D., cons. June 30, 1850; Bishop of Monterey; transferred to San Francisco, July 29, 1853; died in Valencia, Spain, April 14, 1888.—Rt. Rev. THADDEUS AMAT, C.M., D.D., cons. March 12, 1854; died May 12, 1878.—Rt. Rev. FRANCIS MORA, D.D., cons. Titular Bishop of Mosynopolis and Coadjutor to Bishop Amat, Aug. 3, 1873; resigned May 6, 1896; died Aug. 3, 1905 in Sarria, Barcelona, Spain.—Rt. Rev. GEORGE MONTGOMERY, D.D., cons. April 8, 1894, Bishop of Tmul and Coadjutor-Bishop of Monterey and Los Angeles *cum jure successionis* succeeded to May 6, 1896; appt. Coadjutor-Archbishop of San Francisco, Jan. 1, 1903; died in San Francisco, Jan. 10, 1907.—Rt. Rev. THOMAS JAMES CONATY, D.D., cons. Nov. 24, 1901, Titular-Bishop of Samos; appt. Bishop of Monterey and Los Angeles, March 27, 1903; died at Coronado, CA, Sept. 18, 1915.—Most Rev. JOHN J. CANTWELL, D.D., LL.D., appt. Bishop of Monterey-Los Angeles, Sept. 21, 1917; cons. Dec. 5, 1917; appt. Assistant to the Pontifical Throne, Sept. 30, 1929; transferred to Los Angeles, June 1, 1922; elevated to Archepiscopal dignity, July 11, 1936; installed Dec. 3, 1936; died Oct. 30, 1947, at Los Angeles, CA.—His Eminence JAMES FRANCIS CARDINAL MCINTYRE, D.D., appt. Auxiliary Bishop of New York, Nov. 16, 1940; cons. Jan. 8, 1941; promoted to Coadjutor Archbishop, July 20, 1946; appt. Archbishop of Los Angeles, Feb. 7, 1948; installed March 19, 1948; created Cardinal Priest, Jan. 12, 1953; resigned Jan. 21, 1970; died July 16, 1989.—His Eminence TIMOTHY CARDINAL MANNING, D.D., J.C.D., appt. Titular Bishop of Lesvi and Auxiliary Bishop of Los Angeles, Aug. 3, 1946; cons. Oct. 15, 1946; installed as first Bishop of Fresno, Dec. 15, 1967; appt. Titular Bishop of Capri and Coadjutor Archbishop of Los Angeles, May 26, 1969; appt. Archbishop of Los Angeles, Jan. 21, 1970; created a Cardinal Priest, March 5, 1973; retired Sept. 4, 1985; died June 23, 1989 at Los Angeles, CA.

Archdiocesan Catholic Center Office—3424 Wilshire Blvd., Los Angeles, 90010-2241. Tel: 213-637-7200; Fax: 213-637-6607.

Office of the Cardinal—His Eminence ROGER CARDINAL MAHONY, D.D., *3424 Wilshire Blvd., Los Angeles, 90010-2241.* Tel: 213-637-7288; Fax: 213-637-6510.
- *Priest Secretary*—Rev. Msgr. KEVIN KOSTELNIK. Tel: 213-637-7261.
- *Administrative Assistant*—Sr. MARY BRIGID FITZPATRICK, C.S.J. Tel: 213-637-7384.
- *Cardinal's Director of Special Services*—Sr. MARY JEAN MEIER, S.M. Tel: 213-637-7520.
- *General Counsel*—Sr. JUDY MURPHY, C.S.J. Tel: 213-637-7511.

Auxiliary Bishops-Vicars General—Most Rev. JOHN J. WARD, V.G., *3424 Wilshire Blvd., Los Angeles, 90010-2241.* Tel: 213-637-7264; Fax: 213-637-3510. Most Rev. JUAN A. ARZUBE, (Retired), *Sacred Heart, 2889 N. Lincoln Ave., Altadena, 91001-4598.* Tel: 818-794-2046; Fax: 818-791-7438. Most Rev. STEPHEN E. BLAIRE, Our Lady of the Angels of Region, *2636 S. Mansfield Ave., Los Angeles, 90016.* Tel: 213-936-2588; Fax: 213-938-1190. Most Rev. THOMAS J. CURRY, Santa Barbara Region, *3240 Calle Pinon, Santa Barbara, 93105.* Tel: 805-682-0442; Fax: 805-682-7509. Most Rev. JOSEPH M. SARTORIS, San Pedro Region, Office: *3555 Pancratius Pl., Lakewood, 90712.* Tel: 562-634-0456; Fax: 562-531-4783. Most Rev. GABINO ZAVALA, San Gabriel Region, Office: *16009 E. Cypress Ave., Irwindale, 91706.* Tel: 818-960-9344; Fax: 818-962-0455. Rev. Msgr. GERALD WILKERSON, Episcopal Vicar for the San Fernando Region, *15101 San Fernando Mission Blvd., San Fernando, 91341.* Tel: 818-361-6009; Fax: 818-361-6270.

Moderator of the Curia-Chancellor—Rev. Msgr. TERRANCE L. FLEMING, S.T.D. Tel: 213-637-7255.

Vice Chancellor—Sr. CECILIA LOUISE MOORE, C.S.J. Tel: 213-637-7605.

Secretariat for Administrative Services—Bro. THOMAS FAHY, O.S.F. Tel: 213-251-7608.
- *Archival Center*—Tel: 818-365-1501.
- *Catholic Cemeteries*—Tel: 213-637-7801.
- *Chancery Operations*—Tel: 213-637-7000.
- *Communications*—Tel: 213-637-7312.
- *Construction Department*—Tel: 213-637-7850.
- *Human Resources/Insurance*—Tel: 213-637-7596.
- *Information Services Department*—Tel: 213-637-7271.
- *Media Relations Office*—Tel: 213-637-7215.
- *Purchasing/Mail Center*—Tel: 213-637-7535.
- *Real Estate*—Tel: 213-637-7270.
- *Tribunal*—Tel: 213-637-7245.
- *The Tidings*—Tel: 213-637-7251.
- *Vida Nueva*—Tel: 213-637-7310.

Secretariat for Educational and Formational Services—Sr. CECILIA LOUISE MOORE, C.S.J. Tel: 213-637-7605.
- *Campus Ministry*—Tel: 213-637-7527.
- *Catholic Schools*—Tel: 213-637-7300.
- *Diaconate Formation*—Tel: 213-637-7282.
- *Ministry with Persons with Disabilities*—Tel: 213-637-7252.
- *Mission Office*—Tel: 213-637-7223.
- *Cardinal Manning House of Prayer for Priests*—Tel: 213-662-0092.
- *Religious Brothers Council*—Tel: 213-637-7320.
- *Religious Education*—Tel: 213-637-7335.
- *Spirituality Center*—Tel: 213-747-6508.
- *Vicar for Clergy*—Tel: 213-637-7284.
- *Vicar for Women Religious*—Tel: 213-637-7592.
- *Vocations*—Tel: 213-637-7307.
- *Worship*—Tel: 213-637-7262.

Secretariat for Pastoral and Community Services—Sr. KATHLEEN REILLY, C.S.C. Tel: 213-637-7610.
- *African American Vicariate*—Tel: 213-637-7610.
- *Asian Pacific & Ethnic Ministries*—Tel: 213-637-7540.
- *Cardinal McIntyre Fund for Charity*—Tel: 213-251-3438.
- *Catholic Charities*—Tel: 213-251-3400.
- *Detention Ministries*—Tel: 213-637-7648.
- *Ecumenical/Interreligious Affairs Office*—Tel: 213-637-7555.
- *Family Life Office*—Tel: 213-637-7228.
- *Health Affairs Office*—Tel: 213-637-7531.
- *Hispanic Ministries*—Tel: 213-637-7287.
- *Justice and Peace Office*—Tel: 213-637-7690.
- *Lay Organizations*—
  - *Apostleship of Prayer*—Tel: 213-466-2406.
  - *Catholic Daughters*—Tel: 310-643-9411.
  - *Charismatic Renewal/SCRC*—Tel: 310-371-6433.
  - *Council of Catholic Women*—Tel: 213-637-7394.
  - *Cursillo*—Tel: 213-637-7268.
  - *Holy Name*—Tel: 213-637-7393.
  - *Ladies of Charity*—Tel: 213-382-3659.
  - *Marriage Encounter, Worldwide*—Tel: 805-496-0222.
  - *Ministry with Lesbian & Gay Catholics*—Tel: 213-637-7658.
  - *Pastoral & Parish Councils*—Tel: 213-637-7430.
  - *Respect Life*—Tel: 213-637-7621.

Chief Financial Officer—Mr. JOSE DEBASA. Tel: 213-637-7285.
- *Accounting*—Tel: 213-637-7593.
- *Audit, Internal*—Tel: 213-637-7622.
- *Budget*—Tel: 213-637-7623.
- *Investments*—Tel: 213-637-7292.
- *Payroll*—Tel: 213-637-7594.
- *Pension Plan*—Tel: 213-637-7286.

Archdiocesan Pastoral Regions

Santa Barbara Region—Most Rev. THOMAS J. CURRY, *3240 Calle Pinon, Santa Barbara, 93105-2760.* Tel: 805-682-0442; Fax: 805-682-7509.
- *Deanery 1*—Rev. Msgr. JOHN G. FITZGERALD, V.F. Tel: 805-733-2735.
- *Deanery 2*—Rev. Msgr. STEPHEN DOWNES, V.F. Tel: 805-967-5641.
- *Deanery 3*—Rev. Msgr. PETER D. NUGENT, V.F. Tel: 805-487-3891.
- *Deanery 4*—Rev. Msgr. MICHAEL BUNNY, V.F. Tel: 805-498-3602.

San Fernando Region—Rev. Msgr. GERALD E. WILKERSON, Episcopal Vicar, *15101 San Fernando Mission Blvd., Mission Hills, 91345-2526.* Tel: 818-361-6009; Fax: 818-361-6270.
- *Deanery 5*—Rev. Msgr. GERALD E. WILKERSON, V.F. Tel: 818-342-4686.
- *Deanery 6*—Rev. Msgr. FRANCIS T. WALLACE, V.F. Tel: 818-790-5155.
- *Deanery 7*—Rev. JOHN H. KEESE, V.F. Tel: 818-894-1176.
- *Deanery 8*—Rev. Msgr. TIMOTHY P. O'CONNELL, V.F. Tel: 805-942-7122.

San Gabriel Region—Most Rev. GABINO ZAVALA, V.F., *16009 E. Cypress Ave., Irwindale, 91706-2122.* Tel: 818-960-9344; Fax: 818-962-0455.
- *Deanery 9*—Rev. RICHARD SIEBENAND, V.F. Tel: 213-526-3800.
- *Deanery 10*—Rev. RICHARD PRINDLE, V.F. Tel: 818-797-1167.
- *Deanery 11*—Rev. Msgr. DAVID SORK, V.F. Tel: 818-918-8314.
- *Deanery 12*—Rev. Msgr. JAMES J. LOUGHNANE, V.F. Tel: 909-861-7106.

Our Lady of the Angels Pastoral Region—Most Rev. STEPHEN E. BLAIRE, *2636 S. Mansfield Ave., Los Angeles, 90016.* Tel: 213-936-2588; Fax: 213-938-1190.
- *Deanery 13*—Rev. Msgr. LLOYD A. TORGERSON, V.F. Tel: 310-393-9287.
- *Deanery 14*—Rev. Msgr. JOHN BEATTIE, V.F. Tel: 213-656-4433.
- *Deanery 15*—Rev. Msgr. DENNIS P. O'NEIL, V.F. Tel: 213-737-3325.
- *Deanery 16*—Rev. Msgr. PAUL M. MONTOYA, V.F. Tel: 310-677-2736.

San Pedro Region—Most Rev. JOSEPH M. SARTORIS, *3555 St. Pancratius Pl., Lakewood, 90712-1416.* Tel: 310-634-0456; Fax: 562-531-4783.
- *Deanery 17*—Rev. Msgr. ROBERT W. GIPSON, V.F. Tel: 562-923-4509.
- *Deanery 18*—Rev. Msgr. CHRISTIAN M. VAN LIEFDE, V.F. Tel: 562-942-7300.
- *Deanery 19*—Rev. Msgr. MICHAEL F. LENIHAN, V.F. Tel: 562-540-0329.
- *Deanery 20*—Rev. DOUGLAS W. SAUNDERS, V.F. Tel: 562-594-4657.

Archdiocesan Offices

Unless otherwise listed, all offices are located at 3424 Wilshire Blvd., Los Angeles, CA 90010-2241.

Accounting Department—Mr. ROBERT KEELER, Controller. Tel: 213-637-7593. HENRY NIERODZIK, Accounting Mgr. Tel: 213-637-7297.

African-American Vicariate—Rev. FISHER ROBINSON, S.V.D., Dir. Tel: 213-637-7435.

Alcohol and Substance Abuse—Rev. Msgr. T. TERRENCE RICHEY, Dir. Tel: 213-637-7644.

Annual Catholic Appeal—Mr. CHRISTOPHER MCLAUGHLIN, Dir. Tel: 213-637-7703; Fax: 213-637-6434.

Apostleship of Prayer—Rev. FRANCIS PARRISH, S.J., Dir., *5322 Franklin Ave., Los Angeles, 90027.* Tel: 213-466-2406.

Apostleship of the Sea—Rev. Msgr. PATRICK GALLAGHER, Port Chap.; Rev. SYLVESTER THOMAS, Maritime Chap., *870 W. Eighth St., San Pedro, 90731.* Tel: 310-833-3541.

Archives—Rev. Msgr. FRANCIS J. WEBER, Archivist, *15151 San Fernando Mission Blvd., Mission Hills, 91345.* Tel: 818-365-1501; Fax: 818-361-3276.

Asian Pacific and Ethnic Groups—Sr. LUCIA TU, S.D.S.H., Dir. Tel: 213-637-7540.

Audit Services—SANDRA SMITH. Tel: 213-637-7622.

Brothers Council, Religious—Bro. TIMOTHY MAYWORM, F.S.C., Chm. Tel: 213-637-7320. LUPE A. GARIBAY, Admin. Asst. Tel: 213-637-7320.

Budget—Mrs. JEANNE ZEIND. Tel: 213-637-7623.

Campaign for Human Development—THOMAS A. CHABOLIA, Diocesan Dir. Tel: 213-637-7690. JEFF BONINO-BRITSCH, CHD Prog. Coord. Tel: 213-637-7560.

Campus Ministry (Newman Apostolate)—Mrs. LAURIE W. OESTER, Dir. Tel: 213-637-7527; Fax: 213-637-6527.

Cardinal Manning House of Prayer for Priests—Rev. JOHN D. MCANULTY, S.J., Spiritual Dir., 3441 Waverly Dr.: *Los Angeles, 90027-2597.* Tel: 213-662-0092; Fax: 213-953-4802. Staffed by: Little Brothers of the Good Shepherd; Bro. MALACHY CORBETT, B.G.S., Superior; Bro. DAVID NICKERSON, B.G.S., Residence: *3445 Waverly Dr., Los Angeles, 90027-2597.*

Cardinal McIntyre Fund for Charity—Sr. KATHLEEN REILLY, C.S.C., Exec. Dir. SUSAN V. WEIGHT, Assoc. Dir., *1531 W. Ninth St., Los Angeles, 90015-1194.* Tel: 213-251-3438.

Catholic Charities of Los Angeles—1531 W. Ninth St., Los Angeles, 90015-1194. Tel: 213-251-3400.
- *Chief Executive Officer*—Rev. Msgr. GREGORY A. COX, M.S.W. Tel: 213-251-3464.
- *Chief Administrative Officer*—RONALD LOPEZ, M.S.W. Tel: 213-251-3390.
- *Chief Financial Officer*—Mr. JAMES E. BATHKER. Tel: 213-251-3410.
- *Controller*—PATRICIA GRAVES. Tel: 213-251-3475.
- *Department of Human Resources*—MARILYN KAMERER, Dir. Tel: 213-251-3440.
- *Department of Resource Development*—ALEXANDRIA "SANDI" ARNOLD, Dir. Tel: 213-251-3495.
- *Deputy Assistant*—SUSAN VALERIE WEIGHT. Tel: 213-251-3438.
- *Adeste—Child Development Services*—ARMINE LALAIAN-SANJAR, Dir. Tel: 213-251-3557.
- *C.Y.O. Athletics*—BOB FITZPATRICK, Prog. Dir. Tel: 213-251-3453.
- *Center for Adult Services*—GUADALUPE U. MACKER. Tel: 213-251-3480.
- *Regional Directors*—
  - *Our Lady of the Angels Pastoral Region*—Metro: GREG STUART. Tel: 213-662-4391. O.L.A. Western: JAMES STRATTON. Tel: 310-392-8701.
  - *San Fernando Pastoral Region*—MOEED KHAN. Tel: 818-883-6015.
  - *San Gabriel Pastoral Region*—MARY ROMERO. Tel: 213-266-3130.
  - *San Pedro Pastoral Region*—VANESSA ROMAIN. Tel: 310-591-1351.
  - *Santa Barbara Pastoral Region*—DAVIDA WILLIS. Tel: 805-965-7045. Ventura Co.: A. DIANE MARTELL, M.F.C.C. Tel: 805-643-4694.

Catholic Charities Community Development Corporation, Inc.—His Eminence ROGER CARDINAL MAHONY, D.D., Chm. Bd.; Rev. Msgr. GREGORY A. COX, M.S.W., C.E.O., *Central Office, 1531 W. Ninth St., P.O. Box 15095, Los Angeles, 90015.*

Operations—DAVID FOSTER. Tel: 213-251-3418.
Catholic Relief Services—THOMAS A. CHABOLLA, Diocesan Dir. Tel: 213-637-7690. JEFF BONINO-BRITSCH, Prog. Coord. Tel: 213-637-7560.
Cemeteries, Catholic—Tel: 213-637-7801; Fax: 213-637-6800. Mr. KEITH G. MYERS, Exec. Dir. & Gen. Mgr. Tel: 213-637-7805. Mr. LEWIS J. MCADAMS, Property Devel. - LRP Dir. Tel: 213-637-7809. Deacon SAM FRIAS, Pastoral Rels. Dir. Tel: 213-637-7809. Mr. JAMES M. TIXIER, Admin. Svcs. Dir. Tel: 213-637-7808. Mr. MICHAEL E. WOLNICK, Family Svcs. Dir. Tel: 213-637-7814.
Censor Liborum—Rev. Msgr. CRAIG A. COX. Tel: 213-637-7245.
Clergy, Vicar for—Rev. Msgr. RICHARD A. LOOMIS. Tel: 213-637-7284.
Personnel Board—Rev. GABRIEL GONZALES, Chm.; Rev. Msgr. JOHN KEESE, V.F.; Rev. Msgr. JAMES J. LOUGHNANE, V.F.; Rev. Msgr. PETER D. NUGENT, V.F.; Rev. Msgr. DENNIS P. O'NEIL, V.F.; Rev. Msgr. CHRISTIAN VAN LIEFDE, V.F.; Revs. JOHN W. LOVE; ALLAN ROBERTS; WILLIAM WOLFE.
Communications—DAVID MOORE, Exec. Dir. Tel: 213-637-6215; Fax: 213-637-6360. TERESA GARCIA PEREZ, Office Mgr. Tel: 213-637-7581.
Media Relations—Rev. GREGORY CORIO, O.F.M.Cap., Dir. Tel: 213-637-7215; Fax: 213-385-6586.
Conciliation / Arbitration—Rev. Msgr. TERRANCE FLEMING, S.T.D. Tel: 213-637-7255.
Continuing Formation of Clergy—Rev. RICHARD KREKELBERG, Dir. Tel: 213-637-7571.
Construction—Bro. HILARION O'CONNOR, O.S.F., Dir. Tel: 213-637-7852. JAVIER RODRIGUEZ, Construction Project Supvr. Tel: 213-637-7853.
Earthquake Office—Bro. HILARION O'CONNOR, O.S.F., Dir. Tel: 213-637-7852. CRAIG O. HEARN, Senior Construction Project Supvr. Tel: 213-637-7858. TOM HERWOOD, Construction Project Mgr. Tel: 213-637-7859. CECILIA URIBE, Construction Project Supvr. Tel: 213-637-7855. CHRISTOPHER TRAPP, Oper. Mgr. Tel: 213-637-7862.
Council of Catholic Women—ESTELLE VAUGHN, Pres. Tel: 213-637-7394; Fax: 213-637-6394.
Council of Priests—Rev. DAVID O'CONNELL, Chm. Tel: 213-637-7320.
Cursillo Movement—Revs. MODESTO PEREZ, J.C.D., Spanish Speaking Dir. Tel: 213-637-7268. ENRIQUE PARISI, O.F.M., English Speaking Spiritual Dir. Tel: 213-748-5394.
Deacons—Deacon JOSEPH ORTH, Dir. Deacons. Tel: 213-637-7734.
Detention Ministry—Sr. SUZANNE JABRO, C.S.J., Dir. Tel: 213-637-7648.
Development—KEVIN T. O'CONNER, Chief Devel. Officer. Tel: 213-637-7617.
Archdiocesan Appeals—CHRISTOPHER C. MCLAUGHLIN, Dir. Tel: 213-637-7306.
Parish Stewardship Program—Vacant. Tel: 213-637-7568.
Development Programs / Foundation Relations—Tel: 213-637-7365.
Development Services and Systems—CHRISTOPHER C. MCLAUGHLIN, Dir. Tel: 213-637-7703.
Education Foundation—PHILLIP JORDAN, Exec. Dir. Tel: 213-637-7576.
Research Writer—DAWN DAGUCON. Tel: 213-637-7365.
Trust and Estates Programs—Vacant. Tel: 213-637-7472.
Diaconate, Formation Office—Deacon JOHNNIE HAMMONDS, Dir. Assoc. Dirs.: Rev. FRANK FERRANTE, C.M.F. Tel: 213-637-7536. Sr. CHRIS MACHADO, S.S.S. Tel: 213-637-7747. Deacon CRIS VEGA. Tel: 213-637-7738.
Earthquake—(See Construction).
Ecumenical and Interreligious Affairs—Rev. ALFRED BURNHAM, Dir. Tel: 213-637-7556; Fax: 213-637-6555.
Education Foundation—Tel: 213-637-7576.
Ethnic Ministries—(See African-American, Hispanic, Asian Pacific).
Family Life Office—Mrs. JOAN VIENNA, Dir. Tel: 213-637-7227; Fax: 213-637-7681. Rev. Msgr. CHARLES B. FORTIER, Assoc. Dir. Tel: 213-637-7214.
Coordinator, Marriage Preparation Spanish-Speaking—GRACIELA VILLALOBOS. Tel: 213-637-7561.
Coordinator, Marriage Preparation English Speaking—CANDY METOYER. Tel: 213-637-7250.
Coordinator, Natural Family Planning—Rev. Msgr. CHARLES B. FORTIER. Tel: 213-637-7214.
Coordinator, Parent Education, English—GILDA SILVER. Tel: 213-637-7283.
Coordinator, Parent Education, Spanish—MICAELA REGALADO. Tel: 213-637-7504.
Divorce Recovery Ministry—Tel: 213-637-7283.
Gay and Lesbian Community, Ministry with—Rev. PETER LUIZZI, O.Carm., Dir. Tel: 213-637-7658.
Government Funded Programs—1543 W. Olympic Blvd., Ste. 424, Los Angeles, 90015-3807; Fax: 213-383-1529. LOU CASEY, Dir. Tel: 213-383-0199.
Pre-School Dir.—ETHEL ANTOINE. Tel: 213-388-1291.
Youth Employment Programs Dir.—ROBERT GUTIERREZ. Tel: 213-484-8686.
Health Affairs—Sr. M. CAROLITA HART, C.S.C., Dir. Tel: 213-637-7531.
Hispanic Ministry—Mr. LOUIS VELASQUEZ, Acting Dir. Tel: 213-637-7280.
Pastoral Coordinator, Queen of Angels Region—Sr. ANTONEITA M. ZAPATA, M.G.Sp.S. Tel: 213-932-0998.
Pastoral Coordinator, San Fernando Region—Mr. VICTOR STAFORELLI. Tel: 818-361-9418.
Pastoral Coordinator, San Gabriel Region—Mr. HUMBERTO RAMOS. Tel: 818-960-2805.
Pastoral Coordinator, San Pedro Region—Sr. ISABEL ESCAMILLA, M.G.Sp.S. Tel: 310-531-8155.
Pastoral Coordinator, Santa Barbara Region—Mr. JORGE RODRIGUEZ. Tel: 805-687-5422.
Holy Childhood Association—(See Missions Office).
Holy Name Association, Archdiocesan Union of Parish—Mr. VIC MARCELINO, Pres.; Mr. G. WILLIAM HENDERSON, Exec. Sec.; Rev. Msgr. PAUL MONTOYA, V.F., Moderator; Rev. RAMON MARTI, Sch.P., Assoc. Moderator. Tel: 213-637-7393.
House of Prayer for Priests—(See Cardinal Manning House of Prayer for Priests).
Human Resources / Insurance—WILLIAM HEINEN, Dir. Tel: 213-637-7596. MARGARET M. ANTCZAK, Senior Employee Rels./Training Specialist. Tel: 213-637-7625. Vacant; Senior Employment & Records Specialist. Tel: 213-637-7371. SOFIA SANDRU, H.R. Assoc. Dir./Cemeteries Mgr. Tel: 213-637-7812.
Insurance—Mrs. LEVONTINE TOMACAN, Assoc. Dir. Tel: 213-637-7279. MARTIN HICKS, Benefits Specialist. Tel: 213-637-7671. STEPHEN VAN BUREN, Insurance Risk Mgr. Tel: 213-637-7629. Sr. DILECTA PIERINI, S.S.S., Medical Benefits Consultant. Tel: 213-637-7680.
Information Services—Mr. JAMES R. CELONI, Dir. Tel: 213-637-7271. Rev. ANGUS C. COOPER, O.F.M., Asst. Dir. Tel: 213-637-7699. Mr. DAVID LOPEZ, PC Technician. Tel: 213-637-7611.
Internal Audit—SANDRA SMITH, Dir. Tel: 213-637-7622.
Investments—EDNA CRISTOBAL, Dir. Tel: 213-637-7292.
Justice and Peace—THOMAS A. CHABOLLA, Exec. Dir. Tel: 213-637-7690. JEFF BONINO-BRITSCH, Prog. Coord. Tel: 213-637-7560.
Knights of Columbus-California State Council Office—20280 S. Vermont Ave., Ste. 240, Torrance, 90502. Tel: 310-768-8593; Fax: 310-768-8596.
Ladies of Charity of St. Vincent de Paul—1531 W. Ninth St., Los Angeles, 90015. Tel: 213-382-3659.
Lay Mission Helpers—(See Missions Office).
Liturgy and Worship—(See Worship).
Marriage Encounter—Rev. JOSEPH GEORGE, Dir., *155 E. Janss Rd., Thousand Oaks, 91360.* Tel: 805-496-0222.
Media Relations Office—Rev. GREGORY COIRO, O.F.M.Cap., Dir. Tel: 213-637-7215; Fax: 213-385-6586.
Ministry with Persons with Disabilities—VERONICA GRAY, Dir. Tel: 213-637-7236; 637-7252.
Mission Office—Rev. Msgr. MICHAEL MEYERS, Dir. Tel: 213-637-7223; Fax: 213-637-6223.
Holy Childhood Association—Tel: 213-637-7223.
Lay Mission Helpers—Tel: 213-637-7222.
Mission Circles—Tel: 213-637-7223.
Mission Doctors Assoc.—Dr. TIMOTHY LEFEVRE, Pres. Tel: 213-637-7222.
Propagation of the Faith—Tel: 213-637-7223.
Pastoral Councils—Sr. CLARE REINERT, S.S.N.D., Dir. Tel: 213-637-7430. Vacant; Assoc. Dir. Tel: 213-637-7641. Mrs. MAGGIE STAPP, Reg. Dir., Santa Barbara. Tel: 805-682-0442.
Payroll—FRAN RUSHIE. Tel: 213-637-7594.
Pension Plan—SANDRA PULIDO LENZ. Tel: 213-637-7286.
Priest Pension Plan—LUPE A. GARIBAY. Tel: 213-637-7320.
Propagation of the Faith, Society for—(See Missions Office).
Purchasing / Mail Center—SANDY B. VILLAREAL, Purchasing Agent. Tel: 213-637-7535.
Real Estate—NEAL BLANEY, Dir. Tel: 213-637-7273.
Religious, Vicar for Women—Sr. MARY FAITH CLARKE, S.N.J.M. Tel: 213-637-7592.
Religious Education—Tel: 213-637-7335; Fax: 213-637-6574. Sr. EDITH PRENDERGAST, R.S.C., Dir. Tel: 213-637-7309. Assoc. Dirs.: Mrs. MONICA HUGHES. Tel: 213-637-7350. MARUJA SEDANO. Tel: 213-637-7345. GAIL KRAUSE, Office Coord. Tel: 213-637-7342.
Regional Offices—Our Lady of the Angels Region: Sr. ROSARIO DAVILA, S.D.S.H., *2636 Mansfield, Los Angeles, 90016-3512.* Tel: 213-931-2875; Fax: 213-938-1190. San Fernando Region: LYNN LANG, *15101 San Fernando Mission Blvd., San Fernando, 91345.* Tel: 818-365-5123; Fax: 818-361-6270. San Gabriel Region: EILEEN GATELEY, *San Gabriel Region Pastoral Center, 16009 E. Cypress Ave., Irwindale, 91706.* Tel: 818-962-7707; Fax: 818-962-0455. San Pedro Region: PATRICIA O'BRIEN, *San Pedro Regional Center, 3555 St. Pancratius Pl., Lakewood, 90712.* Tel: 562-630-6272; Fax: 562-531-4783. Santa Barbara Region: MARY BRAITMAN, *Bishop Garcia Diego Center, 4032 La Colina Rd., Santa Barbara, 93110.* Tel: 805-569-1135; Fax: 805-569-2746.
Adult Education—Rev. JAMES J. CLARKE. Tel: 213-637-7654. Sr. ANN DUNN, I.H.M., Santa Barbara Region: Tel: 805-569-2779. MARUJA SEDANO, Spanish Coord. Tel: 213-637-7345. MARY LOU MCGEE, Consultant. Tel: 213-637-7704. MARIA EMILIA MAIRENA, Spanish. Tel: 213-637-7355. Sr. ALINA SPINCEMAILLE, I.C.M., Spanish. Tel: 213-637-7355.
Advanced Cathechetical Ministries and Cathechetical Formation—MONICA HUGHES. Tel: 213-637-7350. LOURDES GONZALES-RUBIO, Spanish. Tel: 213-637-7344.
Asian-Pacific Perspective—IRMA I. ISIP. Tel: 213-637-7669.
Catechesis in a Black Perspective—SHERYL LANGE. Tel: 213-637-7354.
Confirmation—MARIA ALDRETE. Tel: 213-637-7353. JUSTINA PIMENTEL, Spanish. Tel: 213-637-7343.
Early Childhood—NORMA THOMPSON HOLLIS. Tel: 213-637-7352.
Elementary—THELMA DELGADO, Spanish. Tel: 213-637-7351.
Junior High Ministry—RUBEN CASTORENA. Tel: 213-637-7305.
Media—Reservations—YOLANDA ARANDA. Tel: 213-637-7340.
Religious Education Congress—Mrs. ADRIAN WHITAKER. Tel: 213-637-7332.
Young Adult Ministry (18-35)—LEILANI GOECKNER. Tel: 213-637-7498. CAROL SCHMIDT-CLAWSON. Tel: 213-637-7349. Sr. ROSEANNE BELPEDIO, CSJ Spanish. Tel: 213-637-7653. MARTHA NUNEZ, Spanish. Tel: 213-637-7705.
Youth Ministry—MARIA ALDRETE. Tel: 213-637-7353. MICHAEL NORMAN. Tel: 213-637-7674. RUBEN CASTORENA. Tel: 213-637-7305.
Respect Life Office—Mrs. LICIA NICASSIO, Dir. Tel: 213-637-7621.
St. Vincent de Paul Society—HILMAR ROSENAST, Pres., *210 N. Ave. 21, Los Angeles, 90031.* Tel: 213-224-6280. Mr. JOSE J. ROSSIER, Exec. Dir.; Mr. ANTHONY TERRAZAS, Dir., Los Angeles Main Store.
Schools, Dept. of Catholic—Tel: 213-637-7300; Fax: 213-637-6300. Mr. JEROME R. PORATH, Ph.D., Supt. Schools. Tel: 213-637-7313. Sr. JOANNE WITTENBURG, S.N.D., Research Assoc. Tel: 213-637-7324. Assoc. Superintendents of Schools: Sr. MARY ELIZABETH GALT, B.V.M. Tel: 213-637-7315. Ms. BARBARA BROWN. Tel: 213-637-7539.
Elementary School Supervisors—Sr. JOANNE TIERNEY, C.H.F. Tel: 213-637-7318. Sr. JOAN FARAONE, R.J.M. Tel: 213-637-7584. Sr. JILL MARIE NAPIER, C.S.J. Tel: 213-637-7333. Mrs. PAT LIVINGSTON. Tel: 213-637-7323. Mrs. MARION FALCHI. Tel: 213-637-7314. Mrs. SANDRA RANDALL. Tel: 213-637-7322.
Budget Director, Elementary Schools—Sr. JILL MARIE NAPIER, C.S.J. Tel: 213-637-7333.
Consultant for Secondary School Finances / Director of Technology—Sr. GINA MARIE BLUNCK, S.N.D. Tel: 213-637-7368.
Secondary School Supervisors—Sr. PATRICIA BUSSMAN, S.N.J.M. Tel: 213-637-7485. Mrs. DOROTHY PITTELKAU. Tel: 213-637-7325.
Curriculum Director—Mrs. RINO NGO. Tel: 213-637-7311.
Coordinator for Projects & Programs—Sr. PATRICIA SUPPLE, C.S.J. Tel: 213-637-7537.
Director of Certification for High School Religion Teachers—Mrs. LINDA SCHULTZ. Tel: 213-637-7329.
Scouting and Camp Fire Ministry—EILEEN GALLAGHER, Admin. Asst., *P.O. Box 91764, Long Beach, 90809-1764.* Tel: 310-427-2149.
Sisters' Council—Tel: 213-637-7559.
Spirituality Center, Archdiocesan—Sr. THOMAS BERNARD MACCONNELL, C.S.J., Dir., *2 Chester Pl., Los Angeles, 90007.* Tel: 213-747-6508.
Telecommunication Services—DAVE MOORE, Dir. Tel: 213-637-7308. YOSHIO KUMAGAI, Chief Engineer. Tel: 213-637-7399.
Theological Commission—Rev. Msgr. CRAIG A. COX, J.C.D. Tel: 213-637-7204. Sr. KAREN WILHELMY, C.S.J., Sec. Tel: 805-486-7301.
"The Tidings" (Archdiocesan Newspaper)—Tel: 213-637-7360; Fax: 213-637-6360. DAVID MOORE, Gen. Mgr. TOD TAMBERG, Editor. Tel: 213-637-7493. EDWARD ALVAREZ, Advertising Dir. Tel: 213-637-7493. MARY TRUDEAU MOTTOLA, Circulation Mgr. Tel: 213-637-7477. HERMINE LEES, Directory. Tel: 213-637-7392.

Danilo Silverio, Creative Dir. Tel: 213-637-7380. Mr. Polo Diaz, Finance Mgr. Tel: 213-637-7363. Teresa Garcia Perez, Office Mgr. Tel: 213-637-7581.

Tribunal—Tel: 213-637-7245; Fax: 213-637-6245.

Judicial Vicar—Rev. Msgr. Craig A. Cox, J.C.D. Tel: 213-637-7204., *Santa Barbara/Ventura Branch, P.O. Box 2215, Oxnard, 93034.* Tel: 805-486-6553.

Adjutant Judicial Vicar—Rev. Modesto L. Perez, J.C.D. Tel: 213-637-7268.

Canonical Staff—Rev. Thomas C. Anslow, C.M., J.C.L. Tel: 213-637-7268. Rev. Gerald B. Fessard, J.C.L. Tel: 213-637-7201. Sr. Anne Gilbin, R.S.C., J.C.L. Tel: 213-637-7202. Sr. Margaret Ann McCauley, O.P., J.C.L. Tel: 213-637-7205. Sr. Paula K. Modaff, S.P., J.C.L. Tel: 213-637-7203. Deacon Harold Parish, J.C.D., Santa Barbara-Ventura Branch. Tel: 805-486-6553. Sr. Elissa A. Rinere, C.P., J.C.D. Tel: 213-637-7397. Rev. Laurence J. Spiteri, J.C.L. Tel: 213-637-7211.

Judges—Rev. Thomas C. Anslow, C.M., J.C.L.; Rev. Msgr. Arnold Biedermann; Revs. Michael Carcerano, J.C.L.; Jarlath Dolan; Gerald B. Fessard, J.C.L.; Rev. Msgr. Terrance L. Fleming, S.T.D.; Rev. Msgr. William Leser, C.B., S.T.B.; Rev. Msgr. James J. Loughnane; Sr. Margaret Ann McCauley, O.P., J.C.L.; Sr. Paula K. Modaff, S.P., J.C.L.; Rev. Msgr. August Moretti, J.C.D.; Rev. Msgr. Donal Mulcahy; Deacon Harold A. Parish, J.C.D.; Rev. Modesto L. Perez, J.C.D.; Sr. Elissa Rinere, C.P., J.C.D.; Revs. Laurence J. Spiteri, J.C.L.; William P. Wolfe, J.C.L.

Promotors of Justice—Rev. Msgr. Helmut A. Hefner, J.C.L.; Rev. Msgr. Francis T. Wallace, J.C.L.

Defenders of the Bond—Rev. Jerome A. Bouska, M.A.; Sr. Anne Giblin, R.S.C., J.C.L.; Rev. Anselm H. Goosens, C.J.; Rev. Msgr. Helmut A. Hefner, J.C.L.; Rev. Nelson Trinidad, J.C.L.; Rev. Msgr. Francis T. Wallace, J.C.L.

Advocates and Auditors—Rev. Robert Biroschak; Deacon James Henry; Sandra Herrera; Rev. Patrick J. Hill; Deacon John Kunsemiller; Martha Esther Luna; Revs. Dennis P. Mongrain; Peter T. Ngo; Evelyn Ovalles; Rosemary Ramstack; Carlos Venegas.

Notaries and Other Officials—Deacon Emile Adams; Corrie Alvarado; Leticia Ascenio; Dessie Delovino; Deacon James Dillon; Deacon James Farley; Deacon John Gaudin; Ruth Gomez; Alba Gutierez; Bobbie Lopez; Erendira Muro; Anna Parish; Siobhan Prado; Rosemary Ramstack; Merced Salcedo; Tina Santos; Maria Uranga.

Trust and Estate Programs—Tel: 213-637-7472.

"Vida Nueva" (Archdiocesan Spanish Newspaper)—Tel: 213-637-7380; Fax: 213-637-6215. David Moore, Gen. Mgr. Tel: 213-637-7312. Victor Aleman, Editor. Tel: 213-637-7310. Edward Alvarez, Advertising Dir. Tel: 213-637-7232. Mary Trudeau Mottola, Circulation Mgr. Tel: 213-637-7477. Danilo Silverio, Creative Dir. Tel: 213-637-7380.

Vicar for Clergy—Rev. Msgr Richard A. Loomis. Tel: 213-637-7284. Rev. Curtis Bryant, S.J., Staff Consultant. Tel: 213-637-7668. Rev. Richard Krekelberg, Continuing Formation Dir. Tel: 213-637-7571. Rev. Msgr. Terrence Richey, Alcohol/SA Ministry Dir. Tel: 213-637-7644. Rev. Paul Hruby, Ministry to Newly Ordained or Retired Priests. Tel: 213-759-1562. Deacon Joseph Orth, Dir., Deacons. Tel: 213-637-7734. Lucille Miller, Exec. Asst. Tel: 213-637-7204.

Vicar for Women Religious—Sr. Mary Faith Clarke, S.N.J.M. Tel: 213-637-7592.

Vocations—Revs. Richard Martini, Dir. Tel: 213-637-7248. David M. Velazquez, M.Sp.S., Dir., Hispanic Vocations; Sr. Kathleen Bryant, R.S.C., Sister Dir.

Worship—Rev. Richard Albarano, S.S.J., Dir. Tel: 213-637-7262. Kathy A. Lindell, Assoc. Dir. Tel: 213-637-7513. Consultants—Christian Initiation (RCIA); Deni Hayes. Tel: 213-637-7591. Sr. Marilu Covani, S.P., Hispanic Liturgy. Tel: 213-637-7588. Christopher Green, Liturgy Certification. Tel: 213-637-7586. Frank Brownstead, Music. Tel: 213-637-7587.

Women, Archdiocesan Council of Catholic—(See Council of Catholic Women).

Young Adult Ministry (18-35)—(See Religious Education).

Archdiocesan Advisory Boards

Archdiocesan Development Council—His Eminence Roger Cardinal Mahoney, D.D.

Office of Development—Mr. Paul E. Griffin, Jr., Chm.; Mr. Charles F. Smith, Vice Chm. & Chair Elect. Tel: 213-637-7617. Members: Mr. Mario E. Antonini; Rev. Msgr. Michael Bunny; Mr. Louis M. Castruccio; Mrs. Ruby DeVera; Rev. Msgr. Terrance Fleming; Mr. Thomas F. Grojean; Mr. William T. Huston; Rev. Msgr. John J. Kane; Rev. Msgr. Michael Lenihan; Mr. William J. Lyon; Mr. Peter W. Mullin; Rev. Msgr. Dennis P. O'Neil; Rev. Msgr. Patrick Reilly; Mr. John A. Teske.

Archdiocesan Finance Council—His Eminence Roger Cardinal Mahony, D.D.; Mr. Jose Debasa, Chief Financial Officer. Tel: 213-637-7285. Members:: Mr. Robert Arranga; Mrs. Karen Juarez Boyd; Mr. Avis Cheung; Mrs. Ruby B. DeVera; Mr. Robert Erburu; Rev. Msgr. Joseph George; Mr. Mark Granich; Mr. Ruben Jauregui; Mr. Thomas Larkin; Rev. Msgr. Michael Lenihan; Mr. Kenneth Olsen; Mr. J. Steven Rhodes; Mr. Roland Seidler, Jr.; Mr. William E.B. Siart; Rev. Msgr. David Sork; Rev. Msgr. Lloyd Torgerson; Rev. Msgr. Gerald Wilkerson.

Archdiocesan Commission for Catholic Life Issues—Mrs. Licia Nicassio, Dir., Office of Respect Life. Tel: 213-637-7621. Rev. Lawrence Caruso, Co-Chm. Tel: 310-436-6481. Sr. Paula Vandegaer, S.S.S., Co-Chm. Tel: 213-382-2156. Mr. Steve Barbosa; Ms. Marian Burman; Rev. Thomas Cusack, S.S.C.; Dr. Vincent Fortanasce, M.D.; Rev. Msgr. Charles Fortier; Bonifacio Garcia, Esq.; Mrs. Gloria Griffin; Sr. Carolita Hart, C.S.C.; Rev. Msgr. Jeremiah McCarthy; Mrs. Marcella Melendez; Ms. Gloria Miller, R.N.; Rev. Msgr. John Moretta; Mrs. Betty Odello, R.N., M.S.N.; Sr. Carlann Paganelli, S.N.D.; Sr. Kathleen Reilly, C.S.C.; Ms. Mary Sheridan; Alan Shewmon, M.D.; Mrs. Maggie Stapp; Mr. Louis Velasquez; Ms. Germaine Wensley, R.N.; Ms. Marlene Wilson, M.S.W., L.I.C.S.W. Advisory Members: Rev. Msgr. George J. Parnassus; Mrs. Carla Cotti; Ms. Marta M. Fernandez, Esq.; Dr. T. Murphy Goodwin, M.D.; Rev. James McNulty, C.S.P.; Sr. Jane Frances Power, C.S.J.

Archdiocesan Commission for Justice and Peace—Ms. Joan Harper, Chm.; Ms. Saundra Willingham, Vice-Chm.; Mr. Thomas Chabolla, Exec. Dir. Tel: 213-637-7690. Rev. Msgr. Jack Beattie; Raymond T. Bennett; Ms. Ellie Clark; Mr. George Cook; Illegra Evans; Mr. Tom Franklin; Jaime Mendoza; Mr. Fernando Moreno; Marie Alexis Navarro; Mr. Bernardo Perez; Pamela Rector. Ex-Officios: His Eminence Roger Cardinal Mahony, D.D.; Sr. Kathleen Reilly, C.S.C.; Thomas A. Chabolla; Mr. Jeffrey Bonino-Britsch.

Archdiocesan Pastoral Councils—(See Pastoral Councils). Tel: 213-637-7430.

Archdiocesan Catholic School Board—Mrs. Patty Baldwin; Mr. Michael Botello; Dr. Pamela Bourgeois; Mr. William D. Hawkins; Ms. Christine Hanson; Ms. Janice M. Hextall; Ms. Michael Jackman; Rev. Msgr. Anthony Leuer; Sr. Cheryl Milner, S.N.J.M.; Mr. Joey Quinto; Mr. Frank Villalobos; Ms. Christine R. Whelan; Ms. Agnes E. Zelus.

College of Consultors—Most Rev. John J. Ward; Most Rev. Stephen E. Blaire; Most Rev. Thomas J. Curry; Most Rev. Joseph M. Sartoris; Most Rev. Gabino Zavala; Rev. Msgr. Terrance Fleming, S.T.D.; Rev. Msgr. Joseph Cokus; Rev. Msgr. Charles E. Hill; Revs. William Bonner, S.V.D.; Michael Jennett; Alexander Salazar.

Council of Priests—His Eminence Roger Cardinal Mahony, D.D., Pres.; Revs. David O'Connell, Chm. Tel: 213-637-7320. William Bonner, S.V.D., Vice Chm. Jesus A. Parra, Sec. Mark V. Trudeau, Treas.

Members at Large—Rev. Msgr. Charles E. Hill; Revs. Francis R. Colborn; Pedro J. Lopez; Alexander Salazar; David J. Ayotte, Recording Sec.

Age Group—Rev. Msgr. James A. O'Callaghan; Revs. John B. Fitzgerald; Francis R. Colborn; Timothy E. Nichols; Lorenzo Miranda.

Appointees—Revs. Rodel Balagtas; William Bonner, S.V.D.; Edward Dover; Alexander Salazar; Marc V. Trudeau; Albert Vasquez, C.M.F.

Deanery Reps—Deanery 1 - 20: Revs. Richard Vega; Michael J. Jennett; Norman Supancheck; Joseph Cosgrove; James C. Gehl; Lawrence C. Signey; Joseph R. Holguin; Rev. Msgr. Peter L. Amy; Rev. Msgr. John T. Moretta; Revs. Steven Guitron; Pedro J. Lopez; William T. Easterling; Aidan Comerford; Henry L. Hernando; Emille Belletty; David O'Connell; Rev. Msgr. Henry Gomez; Revs. John Woolway; Jesus A. Parra; Jerome C. Elder.

Ex-Officios—Most Rev. John J. Ward; Most Rev. Juan Arzube; Most Rev. Stephen E. Blaire; Most Rev. Thomas J. Curry; Most Rev. Joseph M. Sartoris; Most Rev. Gabino Zavala; Rev. Msgr. Terrance Fleming, S.T.D.; Rev. Msgr. Richard A. Loomis.

Consultants and Liaisons—Revs. Richard Krekelberg; Jeremiah McCarthy; Rev. Msgr. Gerald E. Wilkerson.

Sisters' Council—Tel: 213-637-7559.

Members—Sr. Imelda Alcober, O.P.; Sr. Patricia Arnold, C.S.J.; Sr. Gloria Marie Avila, R.S.M.; Sr. Viola Baca, F.M.I.; Sr. Renee Bauerly, D.M.J.; Sr. Colette Boylan, S.S.L.; Sr. Marie de Montfort Breaux, S.S.F.; Sr. Philomena Breemans, I.C.M.; Sr. Virginia Buchholz, S.C.R.H.; Sr. Rita Callanan, I.H.M.; Sr. Rita Campos, O.S.F.; Sr. Margaret Clare, P.S.N.; Sr. Christina Marie Conroy, C.S.S.F.; Sr. Anne Joseph Crookston, S.S.J.-T.O.S.F.; Sr. Camille Cuadra, D.C.; Sr. Mary Rose Cunningham, C.S.C.; Sr. Lucille Dean, S.P.; Sr. Mary Emily Demuth, C.S.C.; Sr. Julie Drmody, O.S.F.; Sr. Margaret Mary Devine, S.S.C.; Sr. Barbara Dugan, C.S.J.; Sr. Frances Michele Dunaj, O.S.F.; Sr. Marie Celine Enright, S.B.S.; Sr. Martha Leticia Enriquez, S.J.S.; Sr. Theresa Etchegaray, S.M.; Sr. Joan Marie Faraone, R.J.M.; Sr. Marilyn Ficht, R.S.H.M.; Sr. Anne Field, S.S.S.; Sr. Angela Flavin, R.S.C.; Sr. Loretta Flood, C.S.J.; Sr. Vivian Gorman, O.P.; Sr. Mary Bride Gormley, O.S.B.; Sr. Guadalupe Hernandez, O.D.N.; Sr. Catherine Rose Holzman,I.H.M.; Sr. Barbarine Houdek, O.S.F.; Sr. Marian Kozlowski, O.L.V.M.; Sr. Rene Langenecker, O.S.F.; Sr. Angela Lee, I.H.M.; Sr. Matilde Lee, O.S.B.; Sr. Bernita Lindstrom, O.S.F.; Sr. Rosario Lizardi, O.C.D.; Sr. Grace Lopez, E.F.M.S.; Sr. Dolores Madden, C.H.F.; Sr. Helen Markov, S.N.J.M.; Sr. M. Diane Martin, O.S.F.; Sr. Mary McCluskey, C.C.V.I.; Sr. Anne McMullen, C.S.J.; Sr. Joseph Mei, M.J.M.J.; Sr. Patricia Noble, M.M.; Sr. M. Prisca Nwogu, D.M.M.M.; Sr. Eleanor Ortega, C.S.J.; Sr. Eugenia Ortega Quiroga, H.C.J.S.; Sr. Guadalupe Partida, S.H.F.; Sr. Agnes Raday, S.D.S.H.; Sr. Mary Michael Ray, O.C.D.; Sr. Elissa Rinere, C.P.; Sr. Frances Rose Rivers, S.S.N.D.; Sr. Mary Eileen Robinson, R.G.S.; Sr. Mary Ernest Rothe, B.V.M.; Sr. Caroline Sanchez, S.N.D.deN.; Sr. Donna Shanahan, C.S.J.; Sr. Elizabeth Anne Sheehey, C.S.J.P.; Sr. Mary John Shin, I.H.M.; Sr. Gail Tenney, O.S.F.; Sr. Miriam Joseph Teresi, O.S.F.; Sr. Nancy Jean Turner, S.H.C.J.; Sr. Mary Lisette Valenzuela, S.N.D.; Sr. Carol Ward, O.S.F.; Sr. Brendan Watson, S.J.C.; Sr. Margaret Diann Webster, P.B.V.M.; Sr. Catherine White, S.P.; Sr. Rose Marie Wilson, O.S.F.; Sr. Mary Rita Winter, S.C.L.; Sr. Giulii Zobelein, O.P.; Sr. M. Faith Clarke, S.N.J.M., Ex-Officio; Elaine Hritz, Sec.

Spirituality Commission—Rev. James Clarke, Chm. Tel: 213-637-7654. Rev. Austin Doran; Sr. Laura Gormley, S.S.L.; Sr. Thomas Bernard MacConnell, C.S.J. Tel: 213-747-6508. Rev. Kenneth McGuire, C.S.P.; Dr. Patrick Mitchell; Sr. Alice Molina, R.S.H.M.

Theological Commission—Rev. Msgr. Craig A. Xox, J.C.D., Commission Chm. Tel: 213-637-7204. Sr. Karen Wilhelmy, C.S.J., M.A., Commission Sec. Tel: 805-486-7301.

Members:—Rev. Richard B. Benson, C.M., S.T.D.; Rev. John P. Brennan, S.M.A., D.D.; Douglas Burton-Christie, Ph.D.; Rev. Edward William Clark, S.T.D.; Rev. Francis R. Colborn, S.T.D.; Rev. Luke Dysinger, O.S.B., M.D.; Dr. Paul Ford, Ph.D.; Dr. James G. Hannick, Ph.D.; Sr. Maureen Kelly, S.S.L., Ph.D.; Dr. Keith Lewis, Ph.D.; Rev. Jeremiah McCarthy, Ph.D.; Dr. John R. Popiden, Ph.D.; Rev. Thomas P. Rausch, S.J., Ph.D.; Sr. Elissa A. Rinere, C.P., J.C.D.

CLERGY, PARISHES, MISSIONS AND PAROCHIAL SCHOOLS

CITY OF LOS ANGELES
(Los Angeles County)

1—Cathedral of Our Lady of the Angels (1876), Rev. Msgr. Terrance Fleming. In res., His Eminence Roger Mahony; Rev. Msgr. Kevin Kostelnik; Revs. Modesto Perez; Carl Sutphin; Peter T.C. Ngo.

Res., 501 W. Temple, 90012. Tel: 213-624-3941; Fax: 213-680-2399.

Our Lady Chapel—(Catholic Information Center) 809-811 S. Flower St., 90017-4688. Tel: 213-627-4861. Rev. James Kolling, Dir.

2—Cathedral Chapel (1928), Revs. Earl G. Walker; Marcial D. Juan, Admin. In res., Most Rev. Stephen E. Blaire.

Church—927 S. La Brea Ave., 90036.

Res., 922 S. Detroit St., 90036. Tel: 213-935-1128; Fax: 213-935-7308.

School—755 S. Cochran Ave., 90036. Tel: 213-938-9976; Fax: 213-938-9930.
Lay Teachers 12; Students 290.

3—ALL SAINTS (1926) (Hispanic), Revs. Jose L. Vega, O.M.; Gino Vanzillotta, O.M.; Dino Mandarino, O.M.
Rectory—3431 Portola Ave., 90032. Tel: 213-223-1101; Fax: 213-223-9592.
School—3420 Portola Ave., 90032. Tel: 213-225-7264.
Sisters 1; Lay Teachers 8; Students 288.
Catechesis/Religious Programs—Tel: 213-225-5193.
Students 485.

4—ASCENSION (1929) (Hispanic), Revs. Guy B. Wilson, S.T.; John Seymour, S.T. In res., Rev. Gary Michael Banks, S.T.
Res., 517 W. 112th St., 90044. Tel: 213-754-2978; Fax: 213-754-3905.
School—500 W. 111th Pl., 90044. Tel: 213-756-4064. Sr. Judith Flahavan, S.N.D., Prin.
Lay Teachers 9; Students 330.
Catechesis/Religious Programs—Tel: 213-777-6356.
Students 344.
Convent—518 W. 111th Pl., 90044. Tel: 213-754-0020.

5—ASSUMPTION (1926) (Hispanic), Revs. Diosdado Martin; Anthoney Gonzalez.
Res., 2832 Blanchard St., 90033. Tel: 213-269-8171; Fax: 213-269-0106.
School—3016 Winter St., 90063. Tel: 213-269-4319. Ms. Lydia Ortega, Prin.
Lay Teachers 8; Students 250.
Catechesis/Religious Programs—Tel: 213-269-5920.
Students 300.
Mission—Los Angeles, Assumption, 414 N. Fresno St., 90063. Tel: 213-264-6363.

6—BLESSED SACRAMENT (1924), Revs. Anastacio Rivera, S.J.; John J. Brennan, S.J.; James A. Rude, S.J.; Peter Neeley, S.J.; James R. Gallas, S.J.; Deacon Richard Morgan.
Res., 6657 Sunset Blvd., 90028. Tel: 213-462-6311; Fax: 213-462-0113.
School—6641 Sunset Blvd., 90028. Tel: 213-467-4177.
Lay Teachers 9; Students 270.
Catechesis/Religious Programs—Tel: 213-463-9820. Sr. Maria del Socorro Cuevas, E.I.N., D.R.E.
Students 561.

7—CHRIST THE KING (1926), Revs. Alexander George; Roberto F. Jaranilla, Jr.
Res., 624 N. Rossmore Ave., 90004. Tel: 213-465-7605; Fax: 213-463-4895.
School—617 N. Arden Blvd., 90004. Tel: 213-462-4753.
Lay Teachers 9; Students 245.
Catechesis/Religious Programs—Tel: 213-465-7084.
Students 300.

8—CRISTO REY (1954) (Hispanic), Revs. Jose Luis Jimenez, O.A.R.; Juan J. Orobiourritia, O.A.R. In res., Rev. Anthony Iroz, O.A.R.
Res., 4343 Perlita Ave., 90039. Tel: 213-245-4585. [CEM]
Catechesis/Religious Programs—Students 185.

9—DIVINE SAVIOUR (1907) (Hispanic), Revs. Thomas Boudreau; Miguel Plascencia. In res., Rev. Msgr. Charles Fortier.
Res., 610 Cypress Ave., 90065. Tel: 213-225-9181; Fax: 213-225-1099.
School—Tel: 213-222-6077.
Lay Teachers 9; Students 259.
Catechesis/Religious Programs—Alice Perez, D.R.E.
Students 850.

10—DOLORES MISSION (1945) (Hispanic), Revs. Michael E. Kennedy, S.J.; Gregory R. Baumann, S.J.; Gregory R. Bonfiglio, S.J.; Gregory J. Boyle, S.J. In res., Rev. J. Christopher Donahue, S.J.
Res., 171 S. Gless St., 90033. Tel: 213-881-0039 (Church); Fax: 213-881-0034.
School—Tel: 213-881-0001. Mrs. Angelita G. Trevizo, Prin.
Lay Teachers 12; Students 278.
Catechesis/Religious Programs—Sr. Givlii Zobelein, O.P., D.R.E.
Students 145.

11—HOLY CROSS (1906) (African American-Hispanic), Revs. Xavier Colleoni, M.C.C.J. (Italy); Gerardo DeTomasi, M.C.C.J. (Italy); Bartholomew Battirossi, M.C.C.J. (Italy); Bro. Robert Strabla, M.C.C.J. (Italy).
Res., 4705 S. Main St., 90037. Tel: 213-234-5984; Fax: 213-234-0130.
Catechesis/Religious Programs—Students 920.

12—HOLY NAME OF JESUS (1921), Revs. Francis R. Colborn; Emile Bellety; Deacon John Gaudin.
Res., 2190 W. 31st St., 90018. Tel: 213-734-8888; Fax: 213-734-8430.
School—Tel: 213-731-2255. Ms. Christina R. Whelan, Prin.
Lay Teachers 9; Students 308.
Catechesis/Religious Programs—Tel: 213-731-5448.
Students 212.

13—HOLY SPIRIT (1927), Rev. Msgr. Anthony Leuer; Deacon Armando Garcia. In res., Rev. Msgr. Michael W. Meyers.
Res., 1421 S. Dunsmuir Ave., 90019. Tel: 213-935-1333; Fax: 213-935-7741.
School—(Grades K-4) 1418 S. Burnside Ave., 90019. Tel: 213-933-7775.
Sisters of the Holy Faith 2; Lay Teachers 4; Students 138.
Catechesis/Religious Programs—Students 280.

14—HOLY TRINITY (1925), Revs. James E. McElroy; John Daly; Andrew Kim (Korea).
Res., 3722 Boyce Ave., 90039. Tel: 213-664-4723; Fax: 213-664-2581.
School—3716 Boyce Ave., 90039. Tel: 213-663-2064; Fax: 213-663-0732.
Sisters 1; Lay Teachers 9; Students 284.
Catechesis/Religious Programs—Students 170.

15—IMMACULATE CONCEPTION (1908) (Hispanic), Revs. Eduardo Carmona (Mexico); Jose Trinidad Rodriguez (Mexico); Adalberto Jeronimo (Mexico); Rafael Ochoa (Mexico).
Res., 1433 W. Ninth St., 90015. Tel: 213-384-1019; Fax: 213-384-0437.
School—830 Green St., 90017. Tel: 213-382-5931. Ms. Mary Ann Murphy, Prin.
Lay Teachers 9; Students 326.
Catechesis/Religious Programs—832 Green Ave., 90017. Tel: 213-389-7277.
Students 650.

16—IMMACULATE HEART OF MARY (1910), Revs. Henry L. Hernando; Mateo Hicarte.
Res., 4950 Santa Monica Blvd., 90029. Tel: 213-660-0034.
School—1055 N. Alexandria Ave., 90029. Tel: 213-663-4611.
Sisters 1; Lay Teachers 11; Students 319.
Catechesis/Religious Programs—1017 N. Alexandria Ave., 90029. Tel: 213-667-2675.
Students 331.

17—MOTHER OF SORROWS (1923), Revs. Perry D. Leiker; Gilbert J. Cruz.
Res., 114 W. 87th St., 90003. Tel: 213-758-7697; Fax: 213-758-7853.
School—Tel: 213-758-6204. Mr. Brian Tate, Prin.
Lay Teachers 6; Students 151.
Catechesis/Religious Programs—Tel: 213-789-6316.
Students 550.

18—NATIVITY (1920) (Hispanic-African American), Rev. Timothy J. Dyer. In res., Rev. Paul Hruby.
Res., 953 W. 57th St., 90037. Tel: 213-759-1562; Fax: 213-759-7716.
School—Tel: 213-752-0720; Fax: 213-759-7716.
Lay Teachers 8; Students 190.
Catechesis/Religious Programs—Tel: 213-752-1770.
Students 1,080.
Loretto Literary & Benevolent Institution—.

19—NATIVITY OF BLESSED VIRGIN MARY (Ukrainian-Byzantine), Rev. Msgr. Peter Leskiw.
Res., 5134 1/2 De Longpre Ave., 90027. Tel: 213-662-3371.

20—OUR LADY OF SOLITUDE (1925) (Hispanic), Revs. Arnold Gonzalez, C.M.F.; Alberto Domingo, C.M.F.; Manuel Marrufo, C.M.F.; Deacon Fernando Aranda.
Res., 4561 Cesar Chavez Ave., 90022. Tel: 213-269-7248.
School—4545 Dozier St., 90022. Tel: 213-261-1083; Fax: 213-261-5300. Margaret Bestwick, Prin.
Lay Teachers 11; Students 225.
Catechesis/Religious Programs—Tel: 213-269-7248, Ext. 22.
Students 344.

21—OUR LADY HELP OF CHRISTIANS (MARIA AUXILIADORA) (1927), Rev. Juan Santillan, Sch.P. In res., Revs. Raul Palma, Sch.P.; Francis Boronet, Sch.P.
Res., 512 S. Ave. 20, 90031. Tel: 213-223-4153; Fax: 213-223-1427.
School—2024 Darwin Ave., 90031. Tel: 213-222-3913; Fax: 213-222-2561. Sr. Celia Martinez, M.C., Prin.
Poor Clare Missionary Sisters 8; Lay Teachers 7; Students 285.
Catechesis/Religious Programs—Tel: 213-225-2846.
Students 120.

22—OUR LADY OF THE BRIGHT MOUNT (1925) (Polish), Revs. Edward Mroczynski, S.Chr. (Poland); Janusz Zych, S.Chr. (Poland). In res., Rev. Wojciech M. Kania, S.Chr.
Res., 3424 W. Adams Blvd., 90018. Tel: 213-734-5249; Fax: 213-734-0046.
Catechesis/Religious Programs—Students 160.
Convent—Tel: 213-734-0899.
Missionary Sisters of Christ the King (Polonia) 3.

23—OUR LADY OF GUADALUPE (1923) (Hispanic), Revs. Robert Juarez; Thomas E. Baker.
Res., 4018 Hammel St., 90063. Tel: 213-261-8051; Fax: 213-261-1259.
School—436 Hazard Ave., 90063. Tel: 213-269-4998; Fax: 213-261-1259.
Lay Teachers 9; Students 284.
Catechesis/Religious Programs—Tel: 213-262-7957.
Students 450.
Mission—Los Angeles, Los Angeles Co., San Felipe, 738 N. Geraghty Ave., 90063.

24—OUR LADY OF GUADALUPE (Rosehill) (1928) (Hispanic), Revs. David F. Gallardo; Gustavo Lara; Deacon Miguel Arroyo.
Res., 4509 Mercury Ave., 90032. Tel: 213-225-4201; Fax: 213-225-4202.
School—4504 Browne Ave., 90032. Tel: 213-221-8187.
Missionary Sisters of the Immaculate Heart of Mary 2; Lay Teachers 8; Students 284.
Catechesis/Religious Programs—Tel: 213-223-1777.
Students 425.

25—OUR LADY OF LORETTO (1905), Revs. Eamonn Donnelly, S.V.D.; Gerard O'Doherty, S.V.D.; Luc Tram, S.V.D.
Res., 250 N. Union Ave., 90026. Tel: 213-483-3013; Fax: 213-483-3017.
School—258 N. Union Ave., 90026. Tel: 213-483-5251.
Lay Teachers 8; Students 350.
Catechesis/Religious Programs—Students 295.

26—OUR LADY OF LOURDES (1910), Revs. Richard Siebenand; Alfred Hernandez; Angel Mafezzini (Argentina).
Res., 3772 E. Third St., 90063. Tel: 213-526-3800; Fax: 213-526-3807.
School—315 S. Eastman Ave., 90063. Tel: 213-526-3813; Fax: 213-526-3814.
Lay Teachers 9; Students 287.
Catechesis/Religious Programs—Tel: 213-526-3804.
Students 680.

27—OUR LADY OF VICTORY (1966) (Spanish), Revs. Norbert Sharon, S.T.; Edward J. Sittinger, S.T.
Res., 1316 S. Herbert Ave., 90023. Tel: 213-268-9502; Fax: 213-780-3670.
Catechesis/Religious Programs—1317 S. Herbert Ave., 90023. Tel: 213-262-2101.
Students 710.

28—OUR LADY QUEEN OF THE ANGELS (1781) (Spanish), Revs. Albert M. Vazquez, C.M.F.; Joseph M. Gamm, C.M.F.; Domingo Zuniga, C.M.F.
Res., 535 N. Main St., 90012. Tel: 213-629-3101; Fax: 213-629-1951.
Catechesis/Religious Programs—Students 466.

29—OUR LADY OF THE ROSARY OF TALPA (1928) (Mexican), Revs. Francisco Mateos, C.M.; Angel Oyanguren, C.M.; Helios del Cerro, C.M.; Felix Sarachaga, C.M.
Res., 2914 E. Fourth St., 90033. Tel: 213-268-9176; Fax: 213-268-4026.
School—411 S. Evergreen Ave., 90033. Tel: 213-261-0583; Fax: 213-261-0352.
Daughters of Charity of St. Vincent de Paul 2; Lay Teachers 8; Students 270.
Catechesis/Religious Programs—Tel: 213-264-3345.
Students 470.
Convent—427 S. Evergreen St., 90033. Tel: 213-268-7731.
Mission—Los Angeles, Los Angeles Co., La Purisima Chapel, 3236 Inez St., 90033.

30—OUR LADY QUEEN OF MARTYRS (Armenian), Revs. Raphael Minassian, P.I.A.; Basil Ferhatian, C.M.Vd.
Res., 1327 Pleasant Ave., 90033. Tel: 213-261-9898; Fax: 213-261-0522.

31—MOTHER OF GOOD COUNSEL (1925), Revs. Michael J. McFadden, O.S.A.; Anthony J. Wasko, O.S.A.; Kevin C. Mullins, O.S.A.
Res., 2060 N. Vermont Ave., 90027. Tel: 213-664-2111; Fax: 213-664-0556.
School—4622 Ambrose Ave., 90027. Tel: 213-664-2131. Miss Tina Katherine Kipp, Prin.
Sisters 1; Lay Teachers 8; Students 310.
Catechesis/Religious Programs—Students 310.

32—OUR SAVIOUR CATHOLIC CENTER (1957), Rev. William Messenger.
Res., 3207 University Ave., 90007. Tel: 213-749-5341; Fax: 213-749-3475.

33—PRECIOUS BLOOD (1923), Rev. Philip M. Kavanaugh. In res., Rev. Nelson Trinidad.
Res., 435 S. Occidental Blvd., 90057. Tel: 213-389-8439; Fax: 213-389-1951.

School—307 S. Occidental Blvd., 90057. Tel: 213-382-3345.
Lay Teachers 9; Students 200.
Catechesis/Religious Programs—Students 195.

34—PRESENTATION OF THE B.V.M. (1925) (Hispanic), Revs. Charles Ramirez, Admin.; Antonio Garcia (Mexico).
Res., 6406 Parmelee Ave., 90001. Tel: 213-585-0570; Fax: 213-585-8148.
Catechesis/Religious Programs—Students 535.

35—RESURRECTION (1923) (Mexican), Rev. Msgr. John T. Moretta; Revs. Carl Tressler; Rafael Casillas; Deacons Richard Fajardo; Hernando Rodriguez.
Res., 3324 E. Opal St., 90023. Tel: 213-268-1141; Fax: 213-268-1143.
School—3360 E. Opal St., 90023. Tel: 213-261-5750. Mr. Daniel Vidal, Prin.
Franciscan Sisters of Mary Immaculate 2; Lay Teachers 8; Students 300.
Catechesis/Religious Programs—Tel: 213-264-1963.
Students 1,200.

36—SACRED HEART (1887) (Hispanic), Revs. Gabriel Gonzales; Michael D. Guiterrez; Mr. Fred Flores, Admin. In res., Rev. George Horan.
Res., 2210 Sichel St., 90031. Tel: 213-221-3179; Fax: 213-221-3613.
School—2109 Sichel St., 90031. Tel: 213-225-4177; Fax: 213-225-2615.
Sisters of St. Dominic of Mission San Jose 3; Lay Teachers 10; Students 340.
Catechesis/Religious Programs—Tel: 213-223-7571.
Students 530.
Convent—2108 Sichel St., 90031. Tel: 213-222-5157.

37—ST. AGATHA (1923), Revs. Ken Deast; William A. McLean; Deacon Hosea Alexander.
Res., 2610 S. Mansfield Ave., 90016. Tel: 213-935-8127; Fax: 213-939-3547.
Catechesis/Religious Programs—Tel: 213-933-0963.
Students 450.

38—ST. AGNES (1903), Revs. William Delaney, C.PP.S.; John Franck, C.PP.S.; Sae Eul Kim.
Res., 2625 S. Vermont Ave., 90007. Tel: 213-731-2464; Fax: 213-731-6186.
School—Tel: 213-734-6441.
Sisters of the Holy Cross 2; Lay Teachers 8; Students 352.
Catechesis/Religious Programs—Tel: 213-731-0014. Sr. Iris Flores, C.PP.S., D.R.E.
Students 850.

39—ST. ALOYSIUS GONZAGA (1908) (Hispanic), Revs. George Aguilera; Jonathan Atchley.
Res., 7814 Crocket Blvd., 90001. Tel: 213-585-4485; Fax: 213-589-8485.
School—Tel: 213-582-4965. Sr. Anna Marie Law, S.M., Prin.
Lay Teachers 8; Students 225.
Catechesis/Religious Programs—2023 E. Nadeau St., Tel: 213-582-7990.
Students 500.

40—ST. ALPHONSUS (1935) (Hispanic), Revs. Jesse C. Galaz; Joshua Lee; Samuel Rendon; Sr. Catherine Garcia, R.S.H.M., Pastoral Assoc.
Res., 5223 Hastings St., 90022-2699. Tel: 213-264-3353; Fax: 213-264-4858.
School—Tel: 213-268-5165.
Religious of the Sacred Heart of Mary 1; Lay Teachers 8; Students 309.
Catechesis/Religious Programs—552 South Amalia Ave., 90022. Tel: 213-266-0855.
Students 465.

41—ST. AMBROSE (1951), Rev. Msgr. John A. Beattie. In res., Revs. Michael Wempe; Bede Warrington.
Res., 1281 N. Fairfax Ave., 90046. Tel: 213-656-4433; Fax: 213-656-6634.

42—ST. ANASTASIA (1953), Rev. Msgr. Royale M. Vadakin. In res., Rev. Msgr. Gregory Cox.
Res., 7390 W. Manchester Ave., 90045. Tel: 310-670-2243; Fax: 310-670-5052.
School—8631 S. Stanmoor Dr., 90045. Tel: 310-645-8816; Fax: 310-645-6923. Mrs. Rosemary Connolly, Prin.
Lay Teachers 20; Students 300.
Catechesis/Religious Programs—Tel: 310-215-9806.
Students 120.

43—ST. ANN (1937), Rev. Hugh Crowe; Rev. Msgr. John R. Brosnan, Pastor Emeritus.
Office: 1365 Blake Ave., 90031. Tel: 213-221-6368.
Res., 2302 Riverdale Ave., 90031. Tel: 213-221-6968; Fax: 213-276-9351.
Catechesis/Religious Programs—Sr. Eileen Collins, S.H.F., D.R.E.
Students 194.

44—ST. ANSELM (1924), Rev. Lawrence Shelton.
Res., 2222 W. 70th St., 90043. Tel: 213-758-6729; Fax: 213-758-8455.
School—7019 S. Van Ness Ave., 90043. Tel: 213-759-9371; Fax: 213-759-1131.
Lay Teachers 9; Students 280.

45—ST. ANTHONY (1910) (Croatian), Revs. John Segaric; Petar Vuletic (Croatia); Rev. Msgr. Felix Diomartich, Pastor Emeritus.
Res., 712 N. Grand Ave., 90012. Tel: 213-628-2938; Fax: 213-628-1635.

46—SAN ANTONIO DE PADUA (1926) (Hispanic), Rev. Msgr. Joseph Herres.
Res., 555 N. Fairview Ave., 90033. Tel: 213-225-1301; Fax: 213-225-2534.
School—1500 Bridge St., 90033. Tel: 213-221-6970.
Sisters of the Company of Mary 5; Lay Teachers 8; Students 276.
Catechesis/Religious Programs—Tel: 213-225-1086.
Students 200.

47—ST. BASIL'S (1920), Revs. M. Francis Meskill; Abelardo Luistro; Edward Eui Cheol Kim.
Res., 637 S. Kingsley Dr., 90005. Tel: 213-381-6191; Fax: 213-382-5883. [CEM]
Catechesis/Religious Programs—Students 170.

48—ST. BERNADETTE (1947) (African American), Revs. Patrick J. Gorman; Emile Belletty; Deacon Emile Adams.
Res., 3825 Don Felipe Dr., 90008. Tel: 213-293-4877; Fax: 213-293-2838.
School—4196 Marlton Ave., 90008. Tel: 213-291-4284. Sr. Joan Mary O'Dwyer, C.S.J., Prin.
Sisters 3; Lay Teachers 9; Students 291.
Catechesis/Religious Programs—Students 75.

49—ST. BERNARD (1924), Rev. Msgr. Patrick McNulty, Pastor Emeritus; Rev. Gerald McSorley. In res., Rev. Patrick J. Hill.
Res., 2500 W. Ave. 33, 90065. Tel: 213-255-6142; Fax: 213-255-2351.
School—Tel: 213-256-4989.
Sisters of Charity of the Blessed Virgin Mary 2; Lay Teachers 9; Students 289.
Catechesis/Religious Programs—2515 W. Ave. 33, 90065. Tel: 213-256-6242.
Students 400.

50—ST. BRENDAN (1915), Rev. Msgr. Jeremiah T. Murphy. In res., Revs. Timothy Cahalane, M.S.C.; Anthony Page.
Res., 310 S. Van Ness Ave., 90020. Tel: 213-936-4656.
School—238 S. Manhatten Pl., 90004. Tel: 213-382-7401.
Sisters 2; Lay Teachers 10; Students 310.

51—ST. BRIGID'S (1920) (African American-Hispanic), Very Rev. Charles Andrus, S.S.J.; Rev. Fernando Arizti, S.J.; Deacons Gilbert Lanoix; William Hawkins, Jr.
Res., 5214 S. Western Ave., 90062. Tel: 213-292-0781; Fax: 213-290-1254.

52—ST. BRIDGET'S CHINESE CATHOLIC CENTER (1940) (Chinese), Rev. Joseph Cheng, S.D.B. (China).
Res., 445 1/2 Cottage Home St., 90012. Tel: 213-222-5518; Fax: 213-222-0814.
Church—510 Cottage Home, 90012. [JC]

53—ST. CAMILLUS DE LELLIS (1952). (Center for Pastoral Care). Revs. Christopher D. Ponnet; Stephen C. Hernandez; Gustavo Lara, Chap.; Mr. Jorge Manly-Gil, Chap.; Sr. Clara Kelkermans, Chap.; Sr. Dora Hauchecorne, Chap. In res., Rev. Msgr. T. Terrence Richey; Deacon James Dillon.
Res., 1911 Zonal Ave., 90033-1032. Tel: 213-225-4461; Fax: 213-225-9096.

54—ST. CASIMIR (1946) (Lithuanian), Rev. Msgr. Algirdas Olsaukas; Rev. Msgr. John A. Kucingis; Rev. Aloyzas Volskis.
Res., 2718 St. George St., 90027. Tel: 213-664-4660.
School—2716 St. George St., 90027. Tel: 213-661-9200.
Lay Teachers 9; Students 260.
Catechesis/Religious Programs—Students 110.

55—ST. CECILIA (1909), Rev. Thomas J. Peacha; Deacon Jose Caro.
Res., 4230 S. Normandie Ave., 90037. Tel: 213-294-6628; Fax: 213-294-3310.
School—4224 S. Normandie Ave., 90037. Tel: 213-293-4266.
Sisters of St. Joseph of Carondelet 2; Lay Teachers 8; Students 215.
Catechesis/Religious Programs—Tel: 213-295-5283.
Students 300.

56—ST. COLUMBAN (1945) (Filipino), Revs. Robert Conley; Paul O'Malley.
Res., 125 S. Loma Dr., 90026. Tel: 213-250-8818; Fax: 213-250-9476.

57—ST. COLUMBKILLE (1921) (Hispanic-African American), Rev. Severiano Castaneda. In res., Rev. Msgr. Timothy Dyer; Rev. Msgr. Michael Baker.
Res., 6315 S. Main St., 90003. Tel: 213-758-5540; Fax: 213-758-8108.
School—145 W. 64th St., 90003. Tel: 213-758-2284.
Sisters 3; Lay Teachers 6; Students 203.
Catechesis/Religious Programs—Students 460.

58—SAN CONRADO MISSION. Unassigned.
Church—1820 Bouett St., 90012. Tel: 213-223-6581.
Mailing Address: 1039 N. Broadway, 90012-1429.

59—ST. DOMINIC (1921), Revs. Paul Scanlon, O.P.; Martin Diaz, O.P.; Juan Carlos Diaz-Flores, O.P.; Gordon Kalil, O.P. In res., Revs. Aquinas Costello, O.P.; Jude Eli, O.P.; Bro. Frederick Narberes, O.P.
Res., 2002 Merton Ave., 90041. Tel: 213-254-2519; Fax: 213-255-3067.
School—Tel: 213-255-5803; Fax: 213-255-3067.
Dominican Sisters of San Rafael 1; Lay Teachers 18; Students 550.
Catechesis/Religious Programs—Tel: 213-255-6373.
Students 255.

60—ST. EUGENE (1942), Revs. Patrick J. Walsh; Paul F. Menke.
Res., 9505 Haas Ave., 90047. Tel: 213-757-3121; Fax: 213-757-8872.
School—9521 Haas Ave., 90047. Tel: 213-754-9536; Fax: 213-754-0913.
Lay Teachers 16; Students 280.

61—ST. FRANCES XAVIER CABRINI (1946), Rev. David O'Connell; Sr. Teresita Carrillo, R.S.H.M., Pastoral Assoc.
Res., 1440 W. Imperial Hwy., 90047. Tel: 213-757-0271; Fax: 213-757-9267.
School—1428 W. Imperial Hwy., 90047. Tel: 213-756-1354; Fax: 213-756-1157. Sr. Celeste Botello, O.P., Prin.
Dominican Sisters 2; Lay Teachers 7; Students 283.
Catechesis/Religious Programs—Tel: 213-756-8111.
Students 368.

62—SAN FRANCISCO CHURCH (1982) (Mexican), Rev. Juan Romero.
Res., 4800 E. Olympic Blvd., 90022. Tel: 213-262-4253; Fax: 213-268-8246.
Catechesis/Religious Programs—Tel: 213-261-2447.
Students 371.

63—MARYKNOLL JAPANESE CATHOLIC CENTER (1921) (Japanese). Unassigned.
Res., 222 S. Hewitt St., 90012. Tel: 213-626-2279; Fax: 213-628-1757.
Catechesis/Religious Programs—Students 30.

64—ST. FRANCIS OF ASSISI (1921), Revs. Pasquale Vuoso, C.R.I.C.; Charles Lueras, C.R.I.C.; James Garceau, C.R.I.C.
Res., 1523 Golden Gate Ave., 90026. Tel: 213-664-1305; Fax: 213-664-4975.
School—1550 Maltman Ave., 90026. Tel: 213-665-3601; Fax: 213-665-4143.
Sisters of Notre Dame 2; Lay Teachers 8; Students 316.
Catechesis/Religious Programs—Tel: 213-664-9033.
Students 250.

65—ST. GERARD MAJELLA (1952), Revs. William J. Connor; Angel Sagardoy. In res., Revs. Emmanuel Osuji (Nigeria); Pius Itodo.
Res., 4439 Inglewood Blvd., 90066. Tel: 310-390-5034; Fax: 310-397-0964.
School—Tel: 310-397-9489.
Lay Teachers 13; Students 268.
Catechesis/Religious Programs—4419 Inglewood Blvd., 90066. Tel: 310-391-9637.
Students 590.

66—ST. GREGORY NAZIANZEN (1923), Revs. Edward J. Johnson; Charles Carolan, S.S.C.; Paul White, S.S.C.
Res., 900 S. Bronson Ave., 90019. Tel: 213-935-4224; Fax: 213-934-0016.
School—Tel: 213-936-2542; Fax: 213-936-2542. Ellinor Collins, Prin.
Religious 1; Lay Teachers 8; Students 260.
Catechesis/Religious Programs—Tel: 213-935-4701.
Students 148.

67—ST. IGNATIUS OF LOYOLA (1911), Rev. Msgr. Alfred Hernandez; Revs. Chima Eva Nwamadi (Nigeria); Evaristus M. Eshiowu (Nigeria).
Res., 322 N. Ave. 61, 90042. Tel: 213-256-3041; Fax: 213-256-0105.
School—6025 Monte Vista St., 90042. Tel: 213-255-6456; Fax: 213-255-0959.
Dominican Sisters, San Jose Mission 4; Lay Teachers 9; Students 307.
Catechesis/Religious Programs—Tel: 213-254-9073.
Students 600.

68—SANTA ISABEL (1915) (Hispanic), Revs. Luis Eduardo Larrea; Rafael Alvarez, O.F.M.
Res., 918 S. Soto St., 90023. Tel: 213-268-4065; Fax: 213-268-4180.

School—2424 Whittier Blvd., 90023. Tel: 213-263-3716.
School Sisters of Notre Dame 5; Lay Teachers 7; Students 310.
Catechesis/Religious Programs—Tel: 213-268-3019.
Students 329.
Convent—943 S. Soto St., 90023. Tel: 213-262-1711; 264-6556; Fax: 213-526-1655.
Misioneras Eucaristicas Franciscanas 9.

69—ST. JEROME (1949), Revs. James F. Kavanagh; Michael W. Meyer; Deacon Paul Weber. In res., Rev. Donatus I. Ekenachi (Africa).
Res., 5550 Thornburn St., 90045. Tel: 310-348-8212; Fax: 310-417-3577.
School—Tel: 310-670-1678.
Sisters of St. Joseph of Carondelet 3; Lay Teachers 9; Students 300.
Catechesis/Religious Programs—Tel: 310-645-8318.
Students 240.
Convent—5570 Thornburn St., 90045. Tel: 310-670-8838.

70—ST. JOAN OF ARC (1943) (Spanish), Revs. James H. Barnes; John F. Cunningham, Pastor Emeritus; John Higgins; Robert F. Condon, Pastor Emeritus; Frederick Byaruhanga (Uganda).
Res., 11534 Gateway Blvd., 90064. Tel: 310-479-5111; Fax: 310-479-2513.
School—11561 Gateway Blvd., 90064. Tel: 310-479-3607.
Lay Teachers 8; Students 224.
Catechesis/Religious Programs—Students 221.

71—ST. JOHN, THE EVANGELIST (1909) (Mexican-African American), Revs. Melvin P. James, S.V.D.; Stephen Brown, S.V.D.; Deacon Willard Hall. In res., Revs. George Stephan, S.V.D.; Fisher Robinson, S.V.D.; Francisco M. Tinajero, S.V.D.; Bros. Bernard Dorade, S.V.D.; Jeremiah M. Walsh, S.V.D.
Res., 6028 Victoria Ave., 90043. Tel: 213-758-9161; Fax: 213-758-0112.
School—Tel: 213-751-8545. Carla Cotton, Prin.
Lay Teachers 9; Students 260.
Catechesis/Religious Programs—Tel: 213-758-8735. Sr. Guadalupe Partida, S.H.F., D.R.E.
Students 200.

72—ST. JOSEPH (1888) (Hispanic), Revs. Alan McCoy, O.F.M., Supr.; Martial Luebke, O.F.M.; Javier Alvarez, O.F.M.; Enrique Parisi, O.F.M., Pastor & Cursillo; Eugene David Burnett, O.F.M.; Angus C. Cooper, O.F.M.; Bros. Gerald Chumick, O.F.M.; Martin Soto, O.F.M.
Res., 218 E. 12th St., 90015. Tel: 213-748-5394; Fax: 213-748-4793.
School—Tel: 213-749-8894. Sr. Jean Marie Chavez, O.S.F., Prin.
Sisters 2; Brothers 1; Lay Teachers 7; Students 212.
Catechesis/Religious Programs—Students 150.
Mission—Los Angeles, St. Turibius, 1530 Essex, 90021.

73—ST. KEVIN (1923) (Hispanic-Filipino), Rev. Leo Steinbock. In res., Revs. Francis Cullen (Ireland); Ramon Andreu, S.J. (Spain).
Res., 4072 Beverly Blvd., 90004. Tel: 213-383-8206; Fax: 213-386-4390.
Catechesis/Religious Programs—Students 200.

74—ST. LAWRENCE OF BRINDISI (1908) (African American-Hispanic). Capuchin Franciscan Friary. Revs. Edward O'Keefe, O.F.M.Cap.; James L. Cleary, O.F.M.Cap.; Tony Marti, O.F.M.Cap.
Res., 10122 Compton Ave., 90002. Tel: 213-567-1439; Fax: 213-564-4050.
School—10044 Compton Ave., 90002. Tel: 213-564-3051.
Sisters of Notre Dame 3; Lay Teachers 8; Students 243.
Catechesis/Religious Programs—Tel: 213-567-4698.
Students 530.

75—ST. LUCY (1970) (Hispanic), Revs. Vicente Casaus, Sch.P.; Jose Maria Aguilar, Sch.P. In res., Revs. Romualdo M. Gonzalez, Sch.P.; Miguel Campos, Sch.P.
Res., 1419 N. Hazard Ave., 90063. Tel: 213-266-0451; Fax: 213-266-4907. [CEM]

76—ST. MALACHY (1926), Revs. William J. Bonner, S.V.D.; Enrique Huerta, S.V.D. In res., Rev. William Adams, S.V.D.
Res., 1221 E. 82nd St., 90001. Tel: 213-585-1437; Fax: 213-583-5391.
School—1220 E. 81st St., 90001. Tel: 213-582-3112.
Lay Teachers 8; Students 265.
Catechesis/Religious Programs—Tel: 213-582-0203. Sr. Magnolia, D.R.E.
Students 345.
Convent—St. Malachy Convent, 1228 E. 81st St., 90001. Tel: 213-582-0203. Missionaries of Jesus Crucified.
Sisters 4.

77—ST. MARCELLINUS (1957), Rev. Jules A. Mayer.
Res., 2349 Strong Ave., 90040. Tel: 213-269-2733.

78—ST. MARTIN OF TOURS (1946), Rev. Msgr. Lawrence O'Leary; Rev. Donie O'Ceochain.
Res., 11967 Sunset Blvd., 90049. Tel: 310-476-7403; Fax: 310-440-0290.
Church—11967 Sunset Blvd., 90049.
School—Tel: 310-472-7419; Fax: 310-440-2298.
Sisters 2; Lay Teachers 13; Students 287.
Catechesis/Religious Programs—Tel: 310-472-1757.
Students 350.

79—ST. MARY (1886), Revs. James Nieblas, S.D.B.; Cresenciano Salcedo, S.D.B.; J. Francisco Munoz, S.D.B.; Bros. Steve Gomez, S.D.B.; Jesus Hinojosa, S.D.B.
Res., 407 S. Chicago St., 90033. Tel: 213-268-7432; Fax: 213-268-8076.
School—(Grades PreK-8). Tel: 213-262-3395.
Daughters of Mary Help of Christians 2; Lay Teachers 12; Students 360.
Catechesis/Religious Programs—Tel: 213-268-7317.
Students 430.

80—ST. MARY MAGDALEN (1930), Revs. Patrick H. Sullivan; Patrick Adejoh.
Res., 1241 Corning St., LA, 90035. Tel: 213-655-7868.
School—Tel: 310-652-4723.
Sisters of the Holy Faith 1; Lay Teachers 6; Students 105.

81—ST. MICHAEL (1907) (Hispanic-African American), Rev. Bruce Correlo. In res., Revs. John Provenza; Gilbert Cruz.
Res., 1016 W. Manchester Ave., 90044. Tel: 213-753-2696; Fax: 213-753-3475.
School—(Grades K-8) 1027 W. 87th St., 90044. Tel: 213-752-6101.
Dominican Sisters of Mission San Jose 3; Lay Teachers 6; Students 270.
Catechesis/Religious Programs—Tel: 213-753-2976.
Students 250.

82—SAN MIGUEL (1927) (Hispanic), Revs. Alfredo de Dios, O.A.R.; James McGuire, O.A.R.
Res., 2214 E. 108th St., 90059. Tel: 213-569-5951; Fax: 213-567-1850.
School—2270 E. 108th St., 90059. Tel: 213-567-6892.
Lay Teachers 9; Students 194.
Catechesis/Religious Programs—Students 418.

83—ST. ODILIA (1926) (African American-Hispanic), Revs. William F. Drobach, S.A.; Wilfred Tyrrell, S.A. In res., Bro. Marco Raposo, S.A.
Res., 5222 Hooper Ave., 90011. Tel: 213-231-5930; Fax: 213-231-9714.
School—5300 S. Hooper Ave., 90011. Tel: 213-232-5449. Ms. Helen Reneau-Martinez, Prin.
Lay Teachers 7; Students 230.
Catechesis/Religious Programs—Students 440.
Mission—Los Angeles, Los Angeles Co., St. John Bosco, 5516 Duarte St., 90058.

84—ST. PATRICK (1904) (Hispanic), Rev. Francisco X. Ramirez.
Res., 1046 E. 34th St., 90011. Tel: 213-234-5963; Fax: 213-234-6725.
Catechesis/Religious Programs—Tel: 213-232-5460.
Students 283.

85—ST. PAUL (1917), Revs. Eugenio Romo, M.G.; Rafael DeAvila, M.G.
Office: 1920 S. Bronson Ave., 90018. Tel: 213-730-9490.
Res., 4112 W. Washington Blvd., 90018. Tel: 213-730-9491; Fax: 213-734-5266.
School—1908 S. Bronson Ave., 90018. Tel: 213-734-4022. Mrs. Iris Trouillier, Prin.
Lay Teachers 8; Students 285.
Catechesis/Religious Programs—Tel: 213-730-9492.
Students 250.

86—ST. PAUL THE APOSTLE (1928), Revs. William Edens, C.S.P., Supr.; William T. Kenney, C.S.P.; Ellwood E. Kieser, C.S.P.; Harold J. Powers, C.S.P.; James DiLuzio, C.S.P.; Paul A. Lannan; Theodore A. Vierra; Edward D. Wrobleski, C.S.P.; Jeremiah Sullivan, C.S.P.; Robert P. Curtis, C.S.P.; Mark A. Villano; John W. Mulhall, C.S.P.; James McNulty.
Res., 10750 Ohio Ave., 90024. Tel: 310-474-1527; Fax: 310-474-2897.
School—Tel: 310-474-1588; Fax: 310-474-4272.
Daughters of Mary and Joseph 2; Lay Teachers 27; Students 537.
Catechesis/Religious Programs—Students 220.

87—ST. PETER (1904) (Italian), Rev. Angelo Bordignon, C.S.
Res. & Mailing Address: 1039 N. Broadway, 90012-1429. Tel: 213-225-8119; Fax: 213-225-0085.
Mission—Los Angeles, Los Angeles Co., San Conrado, 1821 Bouett St., 90012. Tel: 213-223-6581.

88—ST. RAPHAEL (1924) (Hispanic-African American), Revs. Tracy O'Sullivan, O.Carm.; Felix Rivera, O.Carm.; Mr. Jaime Morales, Pastoral Assoc.; Sr. Brigida Riveros, Dir. of Hispanic Ministry; Mr. Harry Wiley, Dir. of African American Ministry.
Res., 942 W. 70th St., 90044. Tel: 213-758-7100; Fax: 213-758-7134.
School—924 W. 70th St., 90044. Tel: 213-751-2774; Fax: 213-751-1244. Mrs. Helen Reneau-Martinez, Prin.
Religious 1; Lay Teachers 8; Students 257.
Catechesis/Religious Programs—Tel: 213-752-5965.
Students 350.

89—ST. SEBASTIAN (1924), Rev. Aidan Comerford. In res., Rev. Anthony Eze.
Res., 1453 Federal Ave., 90025-2301. Tel: 310-478-0136; Fax: 310-478-0137.
School—1430 Federal Ave. W., 90025. Tel: 310-473-3337.
Sisters Servants of the Blessed Sacrament 4; Lay Teachers 7; Students 235.
Catechesis/Religious Programs—Students 249.
Convent—11607 Ohio Ave., 90025. Tel: 310-473-8627.

90—ST. STEPHEN (1928) (Hungarian-German), Rev. Hermann-Joseph K. Rettig, O.Praem.
Res., 3705 Woodlawn Ave., 90011. Tel: 213-234-9246; Fax: 213-234-2455.
Catechesis/Religious Programs—Students 180.

91—ST. TERESA OF AVILA (1921), Revs. Alexander Salazar; Thomas W. McLaughlin, Pastor Emeritus.
Res., 2216 Fargo St., 90039. Tel: 213-664-8426; Fax: 213-665-3115.
School—(Grades K-8) 2215 Fargo St., 90039. Tel: 213-662-3777; Fax: 213-662-3420.
Lay Teachers 9; Students 285.
Catechesis/Religious Programs—Students 215.
Convent—2223 Fargo St., 90039. Tel: 213-661-4284.

92—SANTA TERESITA (1923) (Hispanic), Revs. Salvadore Cudinach, Sch.P.; Manuel Sanahuja, Sch.P.
Res., 2645 Zonal Ave., 90033. Tel: 213-221-2446; Fax: 213-221-2216.
School—(Grades K-8) 2646 Zonal Ave., 90033. Tel: 213-221-1129.
Dominican Sisters 5; Lay Teachers 8; Students 275.
Catechesis/Religious Programs—Tel: 213-221-2511.
Students 475.

93—ST. THOMAS THE APOSTLE (1903), Revs. Dennis O'Neil; J. Rigoberto Rodriguez; Juan Silva; Jose Perez (Venezuela).
Res., 1321 S. Mariposa Ave., 90006. Tel: 213-737-3325; Fax: 213-737-2665.
School—Tel: 213-737-4730; Fax: 213-737-6348.
Lay Teachers 10; Students 315.
Catechesis/Religious Programs—Tel: 213-737-5624.
Students 1,250.

94—ST. TIMOTHY (1943), Rev. William J. Brelsford.
Res., 10425 W. Pico Blvd., 90064. Tel: 310-474-1216; Fax: 310-475-6047.
School—Tel: 310-474-1811; Fax: 310-470-1391. Dr. Rita Lapple, Ph.D., Prin.
Lay Teachers 13; Students 280.

95—ST. VINCENT DE PAUL (1887), Revs. George E. Stevens, C.M.; Thomas H. Cargo, C.M.; Bro. Anthony B. Wiedemer, C.M., Admin. In res., Rev. Joseph L. Brennan, C.M.
Res., 621 W. Adams Blvd., 90007. Tel: 213-749-8950; Fax: 213-749-9137.
School—2333 S. Figueroa St., 90007. Tel: 213-748-5367.
Sisters 3; Lay Teachers 7; Students 340.
Catechesis/Religious Programs—Tel: 213-741-9347.
Students 310.

96—SANCTUARY OF OUR LADY OF GUADALUPE (1929) (Hispanic), Rev. Leslie N. Delgado (Panama).
Res., 4100 E. Second St., 90063. Tel: 213-261-4365; Fax: 213-261-2735.
Catechesis/Religious Programs—Students 351.

97—TRANSFIGURATION (1923) (African American), Rev. Msgr. Robert E. Howard; Revs. Emile Belletty; Michael Grieco.
Res., 2515 W. Martin Luther King Blvd., 90008. Tel: 213-291-1136; Fax: 213-291-8216.
School—4020 Roxton Ave., 90008. Tel: 213-292-3011; Fax: 213-292-1527.
Lay Teachers 10; Students 310.

98—VISITATION (1943), Rev. James F. O'Grady. In res., Rev. Msgr. Thomas Joseph O'Sullivan; Rev. Laurence Spiteri.
Res., 6561 W. 88th St., 90045. Tel: 310-216-1145; Fax: 310-216-1002.
School—8740 Emerson Ave., 90045. Tel: 310-645-6620.

Sisters 1; Lay Teachers 23; Students 293.
Catechesis/Religious Programs—Tel: 310-568-9085.
Students 130.

OUTSIDE THE CITY OF LOS ANGELES

Alhambra, Los Angeles Co., All Souls (1912), Rev. Msgr. William P. O'Toole; Rev. Steven J. Guitron; Deacon William Aust.
Res., 17 S. Electric Ave., 91801. Tel: 818-281-0466; Fax: 818-281-2163.
Catechesis/Religious Programs—29 S. Electric Ave., 91801. Tel: 818-284-7835.
Students 321.

St. Therese (1924). (Little Flower). Revs. Stephen Watson, O.C.D.; William Fenton, O.C.D.; Paul Keonig, O.C.D.; Deacon Gus Sebenius. In res., Rev. Jerome Lantry, O.C.D.
Res., 510 N. El Molino St., 91801. Tel: 818-282-2744; Fax: 818-282-7560.
School—Tel: 818-289-3364; Fax: 818-284-6700.
Lay Teachers 12; Students 325.
Catechesis/Religious Programs—Tel: 818-284-0020.
Students 160.

St. Thomas More (1948), Revs. Jeremiah O'Neill; Robert E. Butler, S.J.
Res., 2510 S. Fremont Ave., 91803. Tel: 818-284-8333; Fax: 818-282-4459.
School—Tel: 818-284-5778; Fax: 818-284-3303.
Sisters 1; Lay Teachers 10; Students 215.
Catechesis/Religious Programs—Tel: 818-284-0316.
Students 190.

Altadena, Los Angeles Co., St. Elizabeth of Hungary (1918), Revs. Richard G. Prindle; Nelson Trinidad; Bernard J. Jennings, (Retired).
Office: 1879 N. Lake Ave., 91001.
Res., 1849 N. Lake Ave., 91001. Tel: 818-797-1167; Fax: 818-797-9245.
School—Tel: 818-797-7727.
Lay Teachers 9; Students 292.
Catechesis/Religious Programs—Students 150.

Sacred Heart (1935), Rev. Jerome L. Schmit.
Church—2889 N. Lincoln Ave., 91001. Tel: 818-794-2046.
Catechesis/Religious Programs—Students 356.

Arcadia, Los Angeles Co., Holy Angels (1935), Rev. Msgr. Norman F. Priebe; Revs. Mark A. Warnstedt; Richard Patterson; Rev. Msgr. Robert Walsh, Pastor Emeritus.
Res., 370 Campus Dr., 91007. Tel: 818-447-1671; Fax: 818-447-7617.
School—360 Campus Dr., 91007. Tel: 818-447-6312.
Lay Teachers 12; Students 300.
Catechesis/Religious Programs—Tel: 818-445-2967.
Students 450.

Annunciation (1948), Rev. Msgr. Roland G. Zimmerman; Rev. Matthew Di Maria, C.M.F.
Res., 1307 E. Longden Ave., 91006. Tel: 818-447-6202; Fax: 818-447-9834.
School—Tel: 818-447-8262.
Sisters 3; Lay Teachers 9; Students 299.
Catechesis/Religious Programs—Tel: 818-446-1625.
Students 161.

Artesia, Los Angeles Co., Holy Family (1931), Revs. Loreto Gonzales; Peter Ferrer; Leonard Goswitz; Deacons Raul Viramontes; Guadalupe Mejia.
Res., 18708 S. Clarkdale Ave., 90701. Tel: 310-865-2185; Fax: 310-860-0718.
School—Our Lady of Fatima, 18626 S. Clarkdale Ave., 90701. Tel: 310-865-1621; Fax: 310-860-1091.
Lay Teachers 9; Students 325.
Catechesis/Religious Programs—Tel: 310-860-5973.
Students 1,252.

Avalon, Los Angeles Co., St. Catherine of Alexandria (1902), Rev. Paul Alcuin Siebenand.
Res., Box 735, 90704. Tel: 310-510-0192; Fax: 310-510-8360.

Azusa, Los Angeles Co., St. Frances of Rome (1908) (Hispanic), Revs. Edward J. Landreau; Edwin C. Duyshart; Rogue Fernandes.
Res., 501 E. Foothill Blvd., P.O. Box 637, 91702. Tel: 818-969-1829; Fax: 818-815-2755. [CEM]
School—734 N. Pasadena Ave., 91702. Tel: 818-334-2018; Fax: 818-815-2760.
Lay Teachers 10; Students 270.
Catechesis/Religious Programs—508 N. Soldano, 91702. Tel: 818-334-3500.
Students 890.

Baldwin Park, Los Angeles Co., St. John the Baptist (1946) (Hispanic-Filipino), Revs. James R. Forsen; Benigno Antonio Rodriguez; Michael Java; John Montejano.
Res., 3848 Stewart Ave., 91706. Tel: 818-960-2795; Fax: 818-960-5085.
School—3870 Stewart Ave., 91706. Tel: 818-337-1421.
Sisters of the Love of God 5; Lay Teachers 14; Students 530.
Catechesis/Religious Programs—Tel: 818-962-1004.
Students 1,460.
Convent—3963 Baldwin Park Blvd., 91706. Tel: 818-337-0527.

Bellflower, Los Angeles Co., St. Bernard (1923), Revs. Philip J. McGrath; Daniel Fox; Michael O'Shea, Senior Priest; Thomas F. Feltz, Admin.
Res., 9647 E. Beach St., Box 576, 90706. Tel: 310-867-2337; Fax: 310-867-4863.
School—9626 Park St., 90706. Tel: 310-867-9410; Fax: 310-866-2310. Ms. Kathleen M. Flynn, Prin.
Lay Teachers 11; Students 275.
Catechesis/Religious Programs—Tel: 310-925-9886.
Students 450.

St. Dominic Savio (1954), Revs. Harold Danielson, S.D.B.; Paul M. Caporali, S.D.B.; Manuel Fernandez, S.D.B.
Res., 9720 Foster Rd., 90706. Tel: 310-920-7796; Fax: 310-920-0149.
School—9750 Foster Rd., 90706. Tel: 310-866-3617; Fax: 310-804-6738.
Salesian Sisters of St. John Bosco 3; Lay Teachers 10; Students 381.
Catechesis/Religious Programs—Tel: 310-866-6642; Fax: 310-920-0149.
Students 630.

Bell Gardens, Los Angeles Co., St. Gertrude (1938) (Hispanic), Rev. Msgr. Henry Gomez; Rev. Esteban Marquez. In res., Deacon Chris Vega.
Res., 7025 Garfield Ave., 90201. Tel: 310-927-4495; Fax: 310-927-5826.
School—6824 Toler Ave., 90201. Tel: 310-927-1216.
Salesian Sisters of St. John Bosco 3; Lay Teachers 9; Students 289.
Catechesis/Religious Programs—Tel: 310-927-3185.
Students 1,116.

Beverly Hills, Los Angeles Co., Good Shepherd (1924), Rev. Colm O'Ryan. In res., Rev. George O'Brien; Rev. Msgr. Daniel Sullivan, Pastor Emeritus.
Res., 505 N. Bedford Dr., 90210. Tel: 310-285-5425; Fax: 310-285-5433.
School—Tel: 310-275-8601; Fax: 310-275-0366. Sr. Leonella Lynch, Prin.
Sisters 2; Lay Teachers 8; Students 240.
Catechesis/Religious Programs—Students 250.

Burbank, Los Angeles Co., St. Robert Bellarmine (1907), Rev. Msgr. Patrick Reilly; Rev. Msgr. Peter Healy; Rev. John Vogel.
Res., 133 N. Fifth St., 91501. Tel: 818-846-3443; Fax: 818-954-9441.
Church—Fifth St. and E. Orange Grove Ave., 91501.
School—154 N. Fifth St., 91501. Tel: 818-842-5033; Fax: 818-842-9789.
Sisters of Charity of the Blessed Virgin Mary 2; Lay Teachers 10; Students 332.
Catechesis/Religious Programs—Tel: 818-845-3521.
Students 300.

St. Finbar (1938) (Hispanic-Asian), Revs. Jose R. Holguin; John T. Nghi. In res., Rev. Michael Mc Cullough.
Res., 2010 W. Olive Ave., 91506. Tel: 818-846-6251; Fax: 818-846-1703.
School—2120 W. Olive Ave., 91506. Tel: 818-848-0191.
Lay Teachers 12; Students 292.
Catechesis/Religious Programs—Tel: 818-846-8715.
Students 1,000.

St. Francis Xavier (1954), Revs. Michael D. Couhig, C.S.C.; Ronald P. Raab, C.S.C.; William C. O'Connor, C.S.C.
Res., 3801 Scott Rd., 91504. Tel: 818-767-2445; Fax: 818-767-5096.
School—Tel: 818-767-2071, Ext. Z.
Lay Teachers 12; Students 311.
Catechesis/Religious Programs—Tel: 818-767-7000. Lee Jolly, D.R.E.
Students 245.

Camarillo, Ventura Co., Blessed Junipero Serra (1988). Liturgies celebrated at: St. John's Seminary College Chapel, 5118 E. Seminary Rd., Camarillo, CA 93012. Rev. Liam J. Kidney; Deacons John Picard; Ludger Gueringer.
Office: 5205 Upland Rd., 93012. Tel: 805-482-6417; Fax: 805-987-8100.
Res., 5104 Hillridge Dr., 93012.
Catechesis/Religious Programs—Students 503.

St. Mary Magdalen (1940), Rev. Msgr. John C. Hughes; Rev. Marcos Gonzalez; Deacons George Bednar; Johnnie Hammonds; Larry Modugno.
Res., 2532 Ventura Blvd., 93010. Tel: 805-484-0532; Fax: 805-987-2941.
School—2534 Ventura Blvd., 93010. Tel: 805-482-2611; Fax: 805-987-8211.
Sisters of Notre Dame 1; Lay Teachers 13; Students 271.
Catechesis/Religious Programs—Tel: 805-482-1219.
Students 1,080.

Canoga Park, Los Angeles Co., Our Lady of the Valley (1921), Revs. John D. Murray; Olympio D'Mello; Mario de la Torre; Deacon Heriberto Vega.
Pastoral Center—22021 Gault St., 91303-1804. Tel: 818-592-2880; Fax: 818-592-0299.
School—Tel: 818-592-2894; Fax: 818-592-2896.
Lay Teachers 12; Students 262.
Catechesis/Religious Programs—22045 Gault St., 91303. Tel: 818-592-2892.
Students 650.

St. Joseph the Worker (1956) (Hispanic-Vietnamese), Revs. James C. Gehl; R. Dario Miranda; Chanh Nguyen; Deacon William S. Lacy; Judy Kitchen, Admin.; Raymonde Bennett, Pastoral Min.
Res., 19850 Cantlay St., 91306. Tel: 818-341-6634; Fax: 818-341-3875.
School—19812 Cantlay St., 91306. Tel: 818-341-6616. Sr. Eva Bryan, R.S.C., Prin.
Lay Teachers 13; Students 331.
Catechesis/Religious Programs—Tel: 818-998-4166. Elizabeth Mattera Hise, D.R.E.
Students 473.

Canyon Country, Los Angeles Co., St. Clare (1977), Revs. Edmond M. Renehan; William Ustaski; Joseph Quattropane.
Res., 27341 Camp Plenty Rd., 91351. Tel: 805-252-3353; Fax: 805-252-1539.
Catechesis/Religious Programs—Tel: 805-252-6950. Peggy Pigors, D.R.E.
Students 1,696.
Mission—Saugus, Los Angeles Co., Blessed Kateri Tekakwitha Mission, Tamarack & Copper Hill Dr., Tel: 805-296-3180; Fax: 809-252-5842.

Carpinteria, Santa Barbara Co., St. Joseph (1933), Revs. Michael Jennett; Edward Donovan, C.S.P.; Rev. Msgr. Joseph V. Kearney, (Retired).

Carson, Los Angeles Co., St. Philomena (1956), Revs. Riz. J. Carranza; Owen de Souza; Francis K. Kim; Demetrio Bugayong; Cesar Raffo-Rivasplata (Peru); Sr. Teresa Kenny, S.J.C., Pastoral Assoc.
Res., 21900 S. Main St., 90745. Tel: 310-835-7161; Fax: 310-830-5494.
School—Tel: 310-835-4827; Fax: 310-835-1655.
Carmelite Sisters 6; Lay Teachers 7; Students 288.
Catechesis/Religious Programs—Tel: 310-830-6180; Fax: 310-830-6287.
Students 1,306.
Convent—21832 1/2 S. Main St., 90745. Tel: 310-834-9180.

Chatsworth, Los Angeles Co., St. John Eudes (1963), Revs. Robert J. McNamara; Robert Folbrecht; Deacon Chet Holly.
Res., 10001 Mason Ave., 91311. Tel: 818-341-3680; Fax: 818-882-4326.
Church—9901 Mason Ave., 91311.
School—Tel: 818-341-1454.
Sisters of the Pious Schools 4; Lay Teachers 7; Students 272.
Catechesis/Religious Programs—Tel: 818-882-9323.
Students 260.

Claremont, Los Angeles Co., Our Lady of the Assumption (1947), Revs. Thomas Welbers; Charles Ramirez; Huy Nguyen; Benedict Agumanu; Desmond Doherty.
Res., 435 Berkeley Ave., 91711. Tel: 909-626-3596; Fax: 909-624-3680.
School—Tel: 909-626-7135.
Felician Sisters 1; Lay Teachers 25; Students 575.
Catechesis/Religious Programs—Tel: 909-624-1360.
Students 800.

Compton, Los Angeles Co., Our Lady of Victory (1922), Revs. John Clifton Marquis, S.T.; Nicholas Barille, S.T. In res., Rev. Anselm Deehr, S.T.
Res., 500 E. Palmer Ave., 90221. Tel: 310-631-3233; Fax: 310-886-5681.
School—Tel: 310-631-1320.
Sisters of the Holy Family 6.
Catechesis/Religious Programs—409 E. Palmer Ave., 90221. Tel: 310-631-1831.
Students 889.

Sagrado Corazon, Sacred Heart (1956) (Hispanic), Rev. Francisco Vitela.
Res., 1720 North Culver Ave., 90222. Tel: 310-635-5436; Fax: 310-635-2121.
Catechesis/Religious Programs—Tel: 310-635-8483.
Students 600.

St. Albert the Great (1949), Revs. Tesfaldet Asghedom, M.C.C.J. (Eritrean); Tesfamariam Ghebrecristos, M.C.C.J. (Eritrean); Luigi Zanotto, M.C.C.J. (Italy); Deacons Joseph H. Ledoux; Frank Millholland.

Res., 804 E. Compton Blvd., 90220. Tel: 213-321-0240; 310-329-7548; Fax: 310-329-8462.
School—Tel: 213-770-0984.
Sisters of the Holy Family 6; Lay Teachers 21; Students 739.
Catechesis/Religious Programs—Tel: 310-327-4199.
Students 550.

Covina, Los Angeles Co., Sacred Heart (1927), Revs. Brian Cavanagh; Leland Wilson; Mario Pacheco; Deacons Ralph Fry; Eliso Gutierrez.
Res., 314 W. Workman St., 91723. Tel: 818-332-3570; Fax: 818-967-4884.
School—360 W. Workman St., 91723. Tel: 818-332-7222; Fax: 818-967-8836.
Religious 2; Lay Teachers 13; Students 322.
Catechesis/Religious Programs—Tel: 818-331-7914.
Students 900.

St. Louise de Marillac (1963), Rev. Msgr. Robert T. Pierce; Revs. Eugene Herbert; Anthony Prem Raju; Deacon Joseph A. Rivet.
Mailing Address: P.O. Box 4128, 91723-4128.
Res., 1770 E. Covina Blvd., 91724. Tel: 818-915-7873; Fax: 818-332-4431.
School—Tel: 818-966-2317.
Lay Teachers 9; Students 316.
Catechesis/Religious Programs—Tel: 818-332-5822.
Students 640.

Cudahy, Cudahy Mission, Revs. Javier Ochoa, M.S.C.; Juan Pineda, M.S.C.
4235 Clara St., 90201. Tel: 213-562-3356.

Culver City, Los Angeles Co., St. Augustine (1919), Rev. Msgr. Ian E. Holland, Pastor Emeritus; Revs. Alfred S. Burnham, Admin.; John S. Schiavone, Pastoral Assoc.; Andrew G. Encinas; Deacon Rafael Victorin. In res., Rev. Expedit Sserunjogi (Uganda).
Res., 3850 Jasmine Ave., 90232. Tel: 310-838-2477; Fax: 310-838-3070.
School—Tel: 310-838-3144; Fax: 310-838-7479.
Daughters of Mary and Joseph 2; Lay Teachers 8; Students 336.
Catechesis/Religious Programs—Tel: 310-836-6561.
Students 714.

Diamond Bar, Los Angeles Co., St. Denis (1971), Rev. Msgr. James J. Loughnane; Revs. Joel Henson; Charles Gard; Olin W. Mayfield. In res., Rev. Donald W. Potthoff, Pastor Emeritus.
Res., 2151 Diamond Bar Blvd., P.O. Box 4096, 91765. Tel: 909-861-7106; Fax: 909-861-2697.
Catechesis/Religious Programs—Tel: 909-861-8018.
Students 1,600.

Downey, Los Angeles Co., Our Lady of Perpetual Help (1911), Rev. John Moloney; Deacons Charles Denisac; Richard Medina.
Res., 10727 S. Downey Ave., P.O. Box 280, 90241. Tel: 310-923-3246; Fax: 310-862-7020.
School—10441 S. Downey Ave., 90241. Tel: 310-869-9969; Fax: 310-923-0659.
Lay Teachers 12; Students 312.
Catechesis/Religious Programs—Tel: 310-861-3714. Diana Holly, D.R.E.
Students 540.

St. Raymond (1956), Rev. Msgr. Robert W. Gipson; Rev. Stephen V. Davoren; Deacon Joseph Ryan; Sr. Carmel Wright, C.H.F. In res., Rev. Msgr. John Fosselman; Rev. Richard Albarano.
Res., 12348 Paramount Blvd., P.O. Box 2085, 90242. Tel: 310-923-4509; Fax: 310-869-3359.
School—Tel: 310-862-3210.
Sisters of Holy Faith 3; Lay Teachers 11; Students 318.
Catechesis/Religious Programs—Tel: 310-862-6959. Sr. Nancy Hale, C.H.F., D.R.E.
Students 342.
Missions—Downey, Rancho Los Amigos Hospital; Downey, Los Padrinos Juvenile Hall.

El Monte, Los Angeles Co., Nativity (1923), Revs. Pedro J. Lopez; William Dowling; Francis Hoang Dang (Vietnamese).
Res., 3743 N. Tyler Ave., 91731. Tel: 818-444-2511; Fax: 818-443-1417.
School—10907 St. Louis Dr., 91731. Tel: 818-448-2414; Fax: 818-448-2763.
Sisters of St. Louis 3; Lay Teachers 8; Students 309.
Catechesis/Religious Programs—Tel: 818-448-8895.
Students 572.

Our Lady of Guadalupe (1973) (Hispanic), Revs. Pedro Ma. Ciordia; Jesus Castrillo (Spain).
Res., 11359 Coffield Ave., 91731. Tel: 818-448-1795.
Catechesis/Religious Programs—Tel: 818-448-7137.
Students 1,150.

El Segundo, Los Angeles Co., St. Anthony (1925), Revs. James F. O'Grady; Joseph G. Azadian, S.J.; Deacon Theodore A. Goodreau. In res., Revs. Anselm Anukam (Nigeria); Augustine Kalemeera (Uganda).
Res., 710 E. Grand Ave., 90245. Tel: 310-322-4392; Fax: 310-322-0797.
School—233 Lomita St., 90245. Tel: 310-322-4218; Fax: 310-322-2659.
Sisters 2; Lay Teachers 7; Students 275.
Catechesis/Religious Programs—Tel: 310-615-0766.
Students 240.

St. Andrew (1936) (Russian-Greek Catholic), Rev. Alexei Smith.
Res., 538 Concord St., 90245. Tel: 310-322-1892; Fax: 310-322-1919.

Encino, Los Angeles Co., Our Lady of Grace (1945), Rev. Msgr. Gerald E. Wilkerson, V.F.; Rev. Michael J. Sears. In res., Rev. Msgr. Francis M. Osborne, Pastor Emeritus; Rev. Msgr. Craig A. Cox.
Res., 5011 White Oak Ave., 91316. Tel: 818-342-4686; Fax: 818-342-6579.
School—Tel: 818-344-4126.
Sisters 4; Lay Teachers 16; Students 325.
Catechesis/Religious Programs—Tel: 818-342-4505.
Students 292.

St. Cyril (1949), Rev. Msgr. Carl F. Bell; Rev. Msgr. Cyril Navin, Pastor Emeritus.
Res., 4601 Firmament Ave., 91436. Tel: 818-986-8234; Fax: 818-986-3310.
School—4548 Haskell Ave., 91436. Tel: 818-501-4155; Fax: 818-501-8480.
Sisters 1; Lay Teachers 14; Students 301.
Catechesis/Religious Programs—Tel: 818-789-5947.
Students 43.

Fillmore, Ventura Co., St. Francis of Assisi (1926), Revs. Norman A. Supancheck; Paul M. Albee, Admin.; Deacon Gerald Fitzgerald.
Church—1048 West Ventura St., P.O. Box 757, 93016. Tel: 805-524-1306; Fax: 805-524-0784.
Mission—Piru, Ventura Co., San Salvador, 4039 E. Center St., P.O. Box 508, Piru, 93040. Tel: 805-521-1077; Fax: 805-521-1077.
Catechesis/Religious Programs—Tel: 805-524-2865.
Students 455.

Gardena, Los Angeles Co., St. Anthony of Padua (1910), Revs. Peter McGee; Samuel Orellana; Honesto Bismonte.
Res., 1050 W. 163rd St., 90247. Tel: 310-327-5830; Fax: 310-327-6440.
School—1003 W. 163rd St., 90247. Tel: 310-329-7170.
Sisters of Providence of St. Mary-of-the-Woods 3; Lay Teachers 8; Students 264.
Catechesis/Religious Programs—Tel: 310-323-0860.
Students 560.
Convent—St. Gardena, 1050 W. 161 St., 90247. Tel: 213-321-3820.

Maria Regina (1956), Rev. Thomas M. Acton. In res., Rev. Michael J. Carcerano.
Res., 2150 W. 135th St., 90249. Tel: 310-323-0030; Fax: 310-323-8081. [CEM]
School—Tel: 310-327-9133; Fax: 310-327-2636.
Lay Teachers 9; Students 311.

Glendale, Los Angeles Co., Holy Family (1907) (Hispanic-Filipino), Rev. Msgr. Arthur J. Lirette, P.A., Pastor Emeritus; Revs. Joseph Shea; Glenn N. Sequeira; Charles Gard; Deacon Fred Pelletier.
Res., 209 E. Lomita Ave., 91205. Tel: 818-247-2222; Fax: 818-247-4780.
School—(Grades PreK-8). Tel: 818-243-9239; Fax: 818-243-0976.
Sisters 1; Lay Teachers 8; Students 317.
High School—(Girls) 400 E. Lomita Ave., 91205. Tel: 818-241-3178; Fax: 818-241-7753.
Sisters 5; Lay Teachers 19; Students 289.
Catechesis/Religious Programs—400 S. Louise, 91205. Tel: 818-240-6551.
Students 545.

Church of the Incarnation (1927), Rev. Msgr. Eugene Frilot; Rev. Robert Macchler; Deacon Restie Noriega. In res., Rev. Msgr. Laurence O'Brien, Pastor Emeritus.
Res., 1001 N. Brand Blvd., 91202. Tel: 818-242-2579; Fax: 818-507-4976.
School—Tel: 818-241-2269.
Lay Teachers 9; Students 312.
Catechesis/Religious Programs—Tel: 818-241-7045.
Students 200.

Glendora, Los Angeles Co., St. Dorothy (1958), Rev. Msgr. John Acton; Rev. Nestor Rebong (Philippines); Deacon Marv Estey.
Res., 241 S. Valley Center, 91741. Tel: 818-914-3941; Fax: 818-335-0059.
School—215 S. Valley Center, 91741. Tel: 818-335-0772.
Sisters 1; Lay Teachers 10; Students 301.
Catechesis/Religious Programs—Tel: 818-335-2811.
Students 554.

Goleta, Santa Barbara Co., St. Raphael (1896), Rev. Msgr. Stephen N. Downes; Revs. Vaughn Winters; Antonio Cacciapuoti.
Res., 5444 Hollister Ave., Santa Barbara, 93111. Tel: 805-967-5641; Fax: 805-964-2988.
School—160 St. Joseph St., Santa Barbara, 93111. Tel: 805-967-2115; Fax: 805-683-9675. Ellen Manning, Prin.
Lay Teachers 10; Students 288.
Catechesis/Religious Programs—Tel: 805-967-1641.
Students 675.

St. Mark University Parish (1966), Revs. Ruben M. Patino, C.S.P.; Edward C. Nowak, C.S.P.
Res., 6550 Picasso Rd., 93117. Tel: 805-968-1078; Fax: 805-968-3965.

Granada Hills, Los Angeles Co., St. John Baptist de la Salle (1953), Rev. Michael J. Slattery; Rev. Msgr. Peter O'Sullivan, Pastor Emeritus.
Res., 16545 Chatsworth St., 91344. Tel: 818-363-2535; Fax: 818-360-7407.
School—Tel: 818-363-2270; Fax: 818-832-8950.
Lay Teachers 22; Students 580.
Catechesis/Religious Programs—Tel: 818-368-1514.
Students 605.

St. Euphrasia (1963), Revs. Raymond A. Saplis; Daniel A. McGinn, S.S.C.; Deacon Joseph Orth.
Res., 11766 Shoshone Ave., 91344. Tel: 818-360-4611; Fax: 818-360-2755.
School—Tel: 818-363-5515.
Lay Teachers 10; Students 290.
Catechesis/Religious Programs—Tel: 818-368-4512.
Students 115.

Guadalupe, Santa Barbara Co., Our Lady of Guadalupe (1867) (Hispanic), Rev. Abel Suquilvide.
Res., 1164 Obispo St., P.O. Box 897, 93434. Tel: 805-343-2181; Fax: 805-343-6642. [JC]
Catechesis/Religious Programs—Students 220.

Hacienda Heights, Los Angeles Co., St. John Vianney (1965), Rev. Msgr. John T. Kane; Rev. Gordon Chang; Rev. Msgr. James A. O'Callaghan, Pastor Emeritus; Rev. Jose Varela; Deacon Eduardo Delgado.
Res., 1345 Turnbull Canyon Rd., 91745. Tel: 818-330-2269; Fax: 818-330-0220.
Catechesis/Religious Programs—Students 776.

Hawaiian Gardens, Los Angeles Co., St. Peter Chanel (1986) (Mexican-Filipino), Revs. Lawrence T. Darnell, O.M.V.; Edward Broom, O.M.V.; Alan Hall, O.M.V.
Res., 21611 Juan Ave., 90716-1117. Tel: 310-924-7591; Fax: 310-402-9411.
Church—12001 E. 214 St., 90716-1117.
Catechesis/Religious Programs—Tel: 310-860-3637.
Students 570.

Hawthorne, Los Angeles Co., St. Joseph (1915), Revs. Eugene Buhr; Joseph Moniz; Blas Hernandez (Mexico); Rev. Msgr. Patrick J. Redahan, Pastor Emeritus; Rev. Daniel G. Perez-Castaneda.
Res., 11854 Acacia Ave., 90250. Tel: 310-679-1139; Fax: 310-679-3034.
School—11886 Acacia Ave., 90250. Tel: 310-679-1014.
Lay Teachers 15; Students 424.
Catechesis/Religious Programs—Tel: 310-644-1234.
Students 1,000.

Hermosa Beach, Los Angeles Co., Our Lady of Guadalupe (1927), Revs. Gregory J. Gilroy, O.F.M.Conv.; Michael Woznick, O.F.M.Conv.; Maximilian Mallin, O.F.M.Conv. In res., Bro. Michael Zocholl, O.F.M.Conv.
Res., 320 Massey Ave., 90254. Tel: 310-372-7077; Fax: 310-798-4051.
School—340 Massey Ave., 90254. Tel: 310-372-7486. Mrs. Cheryl Hunt, Prin.
Lay Teachers 14; Students 275.
Catechesis/Religious Programs—Tel: 310-374-4649.
Students 320.

Huntington Park, Los Angeles Co., St. Martha (1913) (Hispanic), Revs. Vicente Gutierrez, M.Sp.S.; Jesus Arredondo, M.Sp.S.; Eugenio Cardenas, M.Sp.S.; David Mateo Velazquez, M.Sp.S.; Hilario Cisneros, M.Sp.S.
Res., 6019 Stafford Ave., 90255. Tel: 213-585-5776; Fax: 213-585-4560.
Catechesis/Religious Programs—Students 920.

St. Matthias (1913) (Latino), Revs. Rody I. Gorman; Lucio Juarez; Abelardo Bailon; Mario A. Torres. In res., Rev. Samuel Villegas.
Res., 7125 Mission Pl., 90255. Tel: 213-588-2134; Fax: 213-588-4519.
School—Tel: 213-588-7253; Fax: 213-588-1136.

Sisters 3; Lay Teachers 9; Students 326.
Catechesis/Religious Programs—7105 Mission Pl., 90255. Tel: 213-587-3121; Fax: 213-588-4519.
Students 1,150.

Inglewood, Los Angeles Co., St. John Chrysostom (1923), Rev. Msgr. Paul Montoya; Rev. Msgr. Edward C. Maddox, Senior Priest; Revs. Javier Altuna, S.J.; Luciano Kamienski, S.D.B.; Deacon Roberto Vasquez.
Res., 546 E. Florence Ave., 90301. Tel: 310-677-2736; Fax: 310-677-0584.
School—Tel: 310-677-5868; Fax: 310-677-3429.
Sisters of St. Joseph of Carondelet 2; Lay Teachers 8; Students 300.
Catechesis/Religious Programs—Tel: 310-674-3733.
Students 800.

Irwindale, Los Angeles Co., Our Lady of Guadalupe (1964), Rev. Patrick M. Hughes. In res., Rev. Gerald Walker, Senior Priest.
Res., 16025 Cypress St., 91706. Tel: 818-962-3649; Fax: 818-337-3318. [CEM]
Catechesis/Religious Programs—Tel: 818-960-1310.
Students 498.

La Canada Flintridge, Los Angeles Co., St. Bede the Venerable (1951), Rev. Msgr. Leland Boyer, Pastor Emeritus; Rev. Msgr. Francis T. Wallace; Rev. Lawrence Signey. In res., Rev. Jerome Cummings.
Res., 215 Foothill Blvd., 91011. Tel: 818-790-5155; Fax: 818-790-9520.
School—(Grades K-8) 217 Foothill Blvd., 91011. Tel: 818-790-7884; Fax: 818-790-7887.
Lay Teachers 12; Students 275.
Catechesis/Religious Programs—Tel: 818-790-5094. Sr. Margaret Marso, B.V.M., D.R.E.
Students 379.

La Crescenta, Los Angeles Co., St. James the Less (1955), Rev. Msgr. Thomas Doyle; Rev. Gerard O'Brien.
Res., 4625 Dunsmore Ave., 91214. Tel: 818-248-3442; Fax: 818-248-9332.
School—4635 Dunsmore Ave., 91214. Tel: 818-248-7778; Fax: 818-248-5242.
Sisters 1; Lay Teachers 11; Students 290.
Catechesis/Religious Programs—Tel: 818-957-6168.
Students 169.

La Mirada, Los Angeles Co., Beatitudes of Our Lord (1964), Revs. James F. Williams; David Loftus.
Res., 13013 S. Santa Gertrudes Ave., 90638. Tel: 310-943-1521; Fax: 310-902-7627.
School—Tel: 310-943-3218.
Lay Teachers 9; Students 318.
Catechesis/Religious Programs—Tel: 310-943-5678.
Students 376.

St. Paul of the Cross (1955), Revs. Patrick J. Gannon; William P. Wolfe; Deacon Arthur Fitzpatrick.
Res., 14020 Foster Rd., 90638. Tel: 310-921-2914; Fax: 310-926-1514.
School—14030 Foster Rd., 90638. Tel: 310-921-2118; Fax: 310-802-2048.
Bernardine Sisters 2; Lay Teachers 8; Students 260.
Catechesis/Religious Programs—Tel: 310-921-4911.
Students 288.

La Puente, Los Angeles Co., St. Joseph (1919), Rev. Patrick J. Staunton; Rev. Msgr. Joseph W. Herres; Revs. Carl D. Tresler; William E. Ruther; Deacon Ruben Guerra.
Res., 550 N. Glendora Ave., 91744. Tel: 818-336-2001; Fax: 818-336-6010.
School—551 N. Glendora Ave., 91744. Tel: 818-336-2821; Fax: 818-369-8921.
Carmelite Sisters 5; Lay Teachers 8; Students 286.
Catechesis/Religious Programs—15650 E. Temple Ave., 91744. Tel: 818-336-1191.
Students 597.

St. Louis of France (1955), Revs. David A. Sork; Thomas S. Cook; Jose Luis Ochoa; Deacon Frank R. Guzman. In res., Rev. Msgr. James R. Mulcahy, Pastor Emeritus.
Res., 13935 E. Temple, 91746-2098. Tel: 818-918-8314; Fax: 818-918-2622.
School—Tel: 818-918-6210; Fax: 818-918-9549.
Sisters of St. Louis 1; Lay Teachers 13; Students 322.
Catechesis/Religious Programs—Tel: 818-918-7002.
Students 990.

Lakewood, St. Pancratius (1953), Rev. Msgr. Ronald E. Royer; Rev. Edward Fremgen.
Res., 3519 St. Pancratius Pl., 90712. Tel: 310-634-6111; Fax: 310-634-7817.
School—3601 St. Pancratius Pl., 90712. Tel: 310-634-6310.
Lay Teachers 7; Students 315.
Catechesis/Religious Programs—Tel: 310-634-1611.
Students 345.

Lancaster, Los Angeles Co., Blessed Junipero Serra (Quartz Hill) (1987), Revs. Mariano Biasio, C.S.J.; Ernest Candelaria, C.S.J. In res., Revs. Joseph Scalco, C.S.J.; Angelo Zonta, C.S.J.; Deacon Edward Caputo.
Res., 6122 W. Azalea Dr., 93536-3767. Tel: 805-943-4933; Fax: 805-943-6863.
Office: 42121 60th St. W., 93536-3767.
Catechesis/Religious Programs—Tel: 805-943-9314.
Students 651.
Mission—Quartz Hill, Los Angeles Co., St. Elizabeth, P.O. Box 3307, Quartz Hill, 93586-0307.

Sacred Heart (1886), Rev. Msgr. Timothy O'Connell; Rev. David J. Ayotte; Deacon Donald E. Simanski. In res., Rev. William Caffrey, S.V.D.
Res., 45007 N. Cedar Ave., 93534. Tel: 805-942-7122; Fax: 805-945-4255.
School—45002 N. Date Ave., 93534. Tel: 805-948-3613; Fax: 805-945-4235.
Lay Teachers 13; Students 324.
Catechesis/Religious Programs—45027 N. Cedar Ave., 93534. Tel: 805-948-3011.
Students 1,240.

Lomita, Los Angeles Co., St. Margaret Mary Alacoque (1937), Rev. Msgr. Patrick Thompson; Revs. Mark Choi; Jesus A. Parra. In res., Rev. Sean Cronin; Deacon Dick Corwin.
Res., 25429 Eshelman Ave., 90717. Tel: 310-326-3364; Fax: 310-539-1570.
Parish Center—25511 Eshelman Ave., 90717.
Church—25505 Eshelman Ave., 90717.
School—(Grades K-8) 25515 Eshelman Ave., 90717. Tel: 310-326-9494.
Lay Teachers 12; Students 328.
Catechesis/Religious Programs—Tel: 310-326-3364, Ext. 14.
Students 994.

Lompoc, Santa Barbara Co., La Purisima Concepcion (1787), Rev. Msgr. Andrew McGrath, Pastor Emeritus; Revs. Richard Vega; John Halloran; Deacons John Burke; Charles Hays.
Res., 213 W. Olive Ave., 93436. Tel: 805-735-3068; Fax: 805-735-7649.
School—219 W. Olive Ave., 93436. Tel: 805-736-6210; Fax: 805-735-7649.
Lay Teachers 9; Students 200.
Catechesis/Religious Programs—Tel: 805-735-3068.
Students 493.

Our Lady Queen of Angels (1972), Rev. John G. Fitzgerald.
Res., 3495 Rucker Rd., 93436. Tel: 805-733-2735; Fax: 805-733-1235.
Catechesis/Religious Programs—Tel: 805-733-3155.
Students 222.

Long Beach, Los Angeles Co.,

1—St. Anthony, (1902), Rev. Lawrence Caruso; Rev. Msgr. Ernest J. Gualderon, Pastor Emeritus; Rev. Joseph Canna.
Res., 540 Olive Ave., 90802. Tel: 310-436-6481; Fax: 310-436-1631.
School—855 East 5th St., 90802. Tel: 310-432-5946.
Students 270.
High School—620 Olive Ave., 90802. Tel: 310-432-3300; Fax: 310-437-5415.
Sisters of the Third Franciscan Order of Syracuse, New York 3; Lay Teachers 8; Students 270.
Catechesis/Religious Programs—Tel: 310-432-4266.
Students 520.
Mission—Long Beach, Los Angeles Co., Our Lady of Mt. Carmel, 1851 Cerritos Ave., 90806. Tel: 310-591-8477.

2—St. Athanasius, (1933), Rev. John C. Gutting.
Res., 5390 Linden Ave., 90805. Tel: 310-423-7986; Fax: 310-422-0306.
School—5369 Linden Ave., 90805. Tel: 310-428-7422.
St. Francis Mission Community 2; Lay Teachers 6; Students 200.
Catechesis/Religious Programs—Tel: 310-428-3494.
Students 643.

3—St. Barnabas, (1939), Rev. Msgr. John P. Twomey; Rev. Joseph Kim Dang Nguyen; Rev. Msgr. Christopher J. Kennedy, Pastor Emeritus; Deacon Alden Bohlig.
Res., 3955 Orange Ave., 90807. Tel: 310-424-8595; Fax: 310-595-7875.
School—(Grades K-8). Tel: 310-424-7476; Fax: 310-981-3351.
Lay Teachers 12; Students 288.
Catechesis/Religious Programs—Tel: 310-427-7508.
Students 210.

4—St. Bartholomew, (1937), Rev. Jerome C. Elder. In res., Rev. Msgr. Peter C. Caslin, Pastor Emeritus.
Res., 252 Granada Ave., 90803. Tel: 310-438-3826; Fax: 310-438-2227.

5—St. Cornelius, (1951), Rev. Msgr. John Folliard, Pastor Emeritus; Rev. Michael Reardon; Deacon Alexander Lipski.
Res., 5500 Wardlow Rd., 90808. Tel: 310-421-8966; Fax: 310-421-5096.
School—3330 Bellflower Blvd., 90808. Tel: 310-425-7813; Fax: 310-425-2743.
Lay Teachers 9; Students 330.
Catechesis/Religious Programs—Tel: 310-420-7613.
Students 241.

6—St. Cyprian, (1945), Rev. Peter Foran.
Res., 4714 Clark Ave., 90808. Tel: 310-421-9487; Fax: 310-496-1024.
School—5133 Arbor Rd., 90808. Tel: 310-425-7341.
Sisters of St. Louis (Monaghan) 3; Lay Teachers 10; Students 305.
Catechesis/Religious Programs—Tel: 310-420-6885.
Students 336.

7—Holy Innocents, (1926) (Spanish-Asian), Rev. Antonio P. Astudillo.
Res., 425 E. 20th St., 90806. Tel: 310-591-6924; Fax: 310-591-2164.
School—2556 Pacific Ave., 90806. Tel: 310-424-1018.
Carmelite Sisters of the Most Sacred Heart 6; Lay Teachers 7; Students 264.
Catechesis/Religious Programs—Tel: 310-427-8449.
Students 712.

8—St. Joseph, (1955), Rev. James J. Kelly, Pastoral Assoc.; Rev. Msgr. John J. Reilly, Pastor Emeritus. In res., Rev. Harold L. Ford, Senior Priest.
Res., 6220 E. Willow St., 90815. Tel: 310-594-4657; Fax: 310-431-7424.
School—6200 E. Willow St., 90815. Tel: 310-596-6115.
Lay Teachers 13; Students 298.
Catechesis/Religious Programs—Tel: 310-598-0519.
Students 230.

9—St. Lucy, (1944), Revs. Michael Roebert; Francis T. Bui; William Van Gastel.
Res., 2344 Cota Ave., 90810. Tel: 310-424-9051; Fax: 310-988-0376.
School—2320 Cota Ave., 90810. Tel: 310-424-9062.
Lay Teachers 15; Students 310.
Catechesis/Religious Programs—1731 W. 23rd St., 90810. Tel: 310-997-0511.
Students 275.

10—St. Maria Goretti, (1955), Revs. John B. Fitzgerald; Allan Roberts.
Res., 3954 Palo Verde Ave., 90808-2298. Tel: 310-425-7459; Fax: 310-421-0475.
School—Tel: 310-425-5112; Fax: 310-425-5672.
Lay Teachers 14; Students 315.
Catechesis/Religious Programs—3950 Palo Verde Ave., 90808-2298. Tel: 310-420-1321.
Students 163.

11—St. Matthew, (1920), Revs. Gerald Meisel; Guillermo Rodriguez (El Salvador).
Res., 672 Temple Ave., 90814. Tel: 310-439-0931; Fax: 310-434-7621.
Catechesis/Religious Programs—Tel: 310-434-6402; Fax: 310-434-7621.
Students 550.

12—Our Lady of Refuge, (1948), Rev. William J. O'Keeffe. In res., Revs. Alfonso Scott; Ernest Montoya.
Res., 5195 Stearns St., 90815. Tel: 310-498-6641; Fax: 310-498-3344.
School—5210 Los Coyotes Diagonal, 90815. Tel: 310-597-0819; Fax: 310-597-1419.
Lay Teachers 13; Students 286.
Catechesis/Religious Programs—Tel: 310-597-3102.
Students 260.

Los Nietos, Los Angeles Co., Our Lady of Perpetual Help (1958), Revs. John S. Woolway; Josef Draugialis. In res., Rev. Jose Bellavista.
Res., 8545 S. Norwalk Blvd., 90606. Tel: 310-692-3758; Fax: 310-695-4068.
Catechesis/Religious Programs—Students 790.

Lynwood, Los Angeles Co., St. Emydius (1924), Revs. Donal P. O'Connor; Lorenzo Miranda; David Ochoa (Mexico); Luis Garcia (Mexico). In res., Rev. John C. O'Connor.
Res., 10900 California Ave., 90262-2094. Tel: 310-637-7095; Fax: 310-637-3319.
School—10990 California Ave., 90262. Tel: 310-635-7184; Fax: 310-605-3041.
Sisters of the Holy Faith 2; Lay Teachers 17; Students 508.

Catechesis/Religious Programs—Tel: 310-639-1249.
Students 1,270.
Convent—10950 California Ave., 90262. Tel: 310-635-3264.
Missionaries of Charity 6.

St. Philip Neri (1948) (Hispanic), Rev. Joseph G. Sanchez; Deacon Joe T. Battle. Tel: 310-632-4745.
Res., 4311 Olanda St., 90262. Tel: 310-632-7179; Fax: 310-632-5119.
Pastoral Center—12435 Cookacre Ave., 90262.
School—12522 Stoneacre Ave., 90262. Tel: 310-638-0341; Fax: 310-638-9805.
Lay Teachers 9; Students 300.
Catechesis/Religious Programs—Tel: 310-632-3698.
Students 742.

Malibu, Los Angeles Co., Our Lady of Malibu (1946), Rev. William F. Kerze; Rev. Msgr. John V. Sheridan, Pastor Emeritus.
Res., 3625 S. Winter Canyon Rd., 90265. Tel: 310-456-2361; Fax: 310-456-3942.
School—Tel: 310-456-8071; Fax: 310-456-7767.
Sisters of St. Louis 1; Lay Teachers 12; Students 215.
Catechesis/Religious Programs—Tel: 310-456-8813.
Students 210.

Manhattan Beach, Los Angeles Co., American Martyrs (1930), Rev. Msgr. John F. Barry; Revs. Michael J. Evans; Paul D. Wolkovits.
Res., 624 15th St., P.O. Box 3639, 90266. Tel: 310-545-5651; Fax: 310-546-9209.
School—Tel: 310-545-8559; Fax: 310-546-7219.
Lay Teachers 11; Students 372.
Catechesis/Religious Programs—1701 Laurel Ave., 90266. Tel: 310-546-4734.
Students 660.

Maywood, Los Angeles Co., St. Rose of Lima (1922) (Hispanic), Rev. Msgr. George Duran; Revs. Roberto Pirrone; Edward Soto.
Res., 4450 E. 60th St., 90270. Tel: 213-560-2381; Fax: 213-560-8537.
School—4422 E. 60th St., 90270. Tel: 213-560-3376.
Sisters of Notre Dame 1; Lay Teachers 10; Students 304.
Catechesis/Religious Programs—Tel: 213-560-0187.
Students 1,053.

Mission Hills, Los Angeles Co., San Fernando Rey Mission (1797), Rev. Msgr. Francis J. Weber, Admin.; Deacon Sam Frias.
Res., 15151 San Fernando Mission Blvd., 91345. Tel: 818-361-0186; Fax: 818-361-3276.

Monrovia, Los Angeles Co., Immaculate Conception (1904), Revs. Don R. Kribs; Francis Cassidy; Dennis A. Nobleza, Jr.; Mel Byrne, C.P. (Ireland); Deacon Fred Conrey.
Res., 740 S. Shamrock Ave., 91016. Tel: 818-358-1166; Fax: 818-358-6466.
School—726 S. Shamrock Ave., 91016. Tel: 818-358-5129; Fax: 818-358-3933.
Religious 1; Lay Teachers 10; Students 326.
Catechesis/Religious Programs—Tel: 818-357-3010.
Students 1,130.

Montebello, Los Angeles Co., St. Benedict (1906), Revs. Louis Vanderlay, O.S.B.; Manuel Magallanes, O.S.B.; Timothy P. Maloney, O.S.B.; Brendan Helbing, O.S.B.; Maurus P. Jaeb, O.S.B.; Bro. Dominic Ramirez, O.S.B.; Deacons Jose Lopez; James Dillon.
Res., 1022 W. Cleveland Ave., 90640. Tel: 310-721-1184; Fax: 213-721-5075.
School—Tel: 213-721-3348. Sr. Ann Lawrence Kolbeck, O.S.F., Prin.
Lay Teachers 20; Students 578.
Catechesis/Religious Programs—1009 W. Madison Ave., 90640. Tel: 213-722-6020; Fax: 213-722-6006. Mrs. Helen Arvayo, D.R.E.
Students 669.

Our Lady of the Miraculous Medal (1950) (Hispanic), Rev. Msgr. Juan Matas; Rev. Lawrence J. Beck; Sr. Camille Cuadra, D.C., Pastoral Min.; Deacons Joseph Spada; Fred Rios. In res., Revs. Peter Ling; Brian Delaney.
Res., 820 N. Garfield Ave., 90640. Tel: 213-722-5866; Fax: 213-722-2654.
School—Tel: 213-728-5435; Fax: 213-728-8038.
Daughters of Charity of St. Vincent de Paul 4; Sisters of Providence 1; Lay Teachers 20; Students 601.
Catechesis/Religious Programs—Tel: 213-725-6962. Carol Lazar, D.R.E.
Students 350.
Convent—840 N. Garfield Ave., 90640. Tel: 213-721-4321.

Montecito, Santa Barbara Co., Our Lady of Mount Carmel (1856), Rev. Msgr. Sylvester O'Byrne; Rev. Carrol O'Sullivan.
Res., 1300 E. Valley Rd., Santa Barbara, 93108. Tel: 805-969-6868; Fax: 805-565-5959.
School—530 Hot Springs Rd., 93108. Tel: 805-969-5965; Fax: 805-565-9841.
Lay Teachers 15; Students 240.

Monterey Park, Los Angeles Co., St. Stephen (1921), Rev. Eric Lewis.
Res., 320 W. Garvey Ave., 91754. Tel: 818-573-0427; Fax: 818-288-0260.
School—Tel: 818-573-1716; Fax: 818-573-3251.
Lay Teachers 19; Students 508.
Catechesis/Religious Programs—Tel: 818-573-4517.
Students 224.

St. Thomas Aquinas (1960), Revs. Edward R. Dover; Gabriel Lui; Deacon Jesse Martinez; Sr. Ellen Muldoon; Dr. John Corey.
Res., 1501 S. Atlantic Blvd., 91754. Tel: 213-264-4447; Fax: 213-264-2524.
Catechesis/Religious Programs—Students 286.

Montrose, Los Angeles Co., Holy Redeemer (1925), Revs. John K. Foley; Matthew Quinn, S.S.C.; Robert Rankin.
Res., 2411 Montrose Ave., 91020. Tel: 818-249-2008; Fax: 818-249-5642.
School—2361 Del Mar Rd., 91020. Tel: 818-541-9005; Fax: 818-541-9006.
Lay Teachers 10; Students 254.
Catechesis/Religious Programs—Tel: 818-249-8026.
Students 207.

Moorpark, Ventura Co., Holy Cross (1982), Revs. Joseph Cosgrove; John Love.
Res., 13539 Adlena Pl., 93021. Tel: 805-529-1397; Fax: 805-529-3939.
Parish Church & Administration Bldg.: 13955 Peach Hill Rd., 93021.
Catechesis/Religious Programs—Tel: 805-529-0283; Fax: 805-529-3939.
Students 887.

Newbury Park, Ventura Co., St. Julie Billiart (1969), Rev. Msgr. Michael Bunny; Rev. Cornelius Phelan.
Church—2475 Borchard Rd., 91320. Tel: 805-498-3602; Fax: 805-376-2332.
Catechesis/Religious Programs—Tel: 805-499-0979.
Students 435.

New Cuyama, Ventura and Santa Barbara Cos., Immaculate Conception (1969), Rev. Norbert Rackensperger, O.F.M.Conv.
Res., 4793 Cebrian St., P.O. Box 257, 93254. Tel: 805-766-2741; Fax: 805-766-2919.

North Hollywood, Los Angeles Co.,

1—Jesus Sacred Heart Antiochene Syrian Catholic Mission, (1993). (Syriac Catholic Rite). Rev. Bernard Antouni, Admin.
10837 Collins St., 91601. Tel: 818-766-7001; Fax: 818-766-7254.

2—St. Charles Borromeo, (1921), Rev. Msgr. Thomas Kiefer; Revs. Jospeph Palumbo; Michael Wakefield. In res., Rev. Msgr. Richard Loomis.
Res., 10828 Moorpark St., 91602. Tel: 818-766-3838; Fax: 818-766-2855.
School—10850 Moorpark St., 91602. Tel: 818-508-5359.
Sisters 4; Lay Teachers 14; Students 332.
Catechesis/Religious Programs—Tel: 818-980-1826.
Students 399.

3—St. Jane Frances de Chantal, Revs. Michael Higgins, O.Carm.; Chris Pieklo, O.Carm.
Res., 13001 Victory Blvd., 91606. Tel: 818-985-8600; Fax: 818-985-0606.
School—Tel: 818-766-1714. Mrs. Catherine Doyle, Prin.
Lay Teachers 10; Students 340.
Catechesis/Religious Programs—Tel: 818-985-8272.
Students 315.

4—St. Patrick, (1948), Revs. George J. Markwell, M.Afr.; Rafael Marin, M.Afr.; Sjef Kuppens, M.Afr.
Office: 6153 Cahuenga Blvd., 91606. Tel: 818-752-3240; Fax: 818-769-6174.
Res., 10625 Erwin St., 91606. Tel: 818-752-3240; Fax: 818-769-6174.
School—10626 Erwin St., 91606. Tel: 818-761-7363; Fax: 818-761-6349.
Lay Teachers 13; Students 294.
Catechesis/Religious Programs—Tel: 818-769-0263.
Students 342.

5—St. Paul Assyrian-Chaldean (1980), Rev. Emanuel Isho Shaleta (EST).
Res., 13050 Vanowen St., N. Hollywood, 91605. Tel: 818-765-3665; Fax: 818-765-0493.
Mission—Fullerton, Orange Co., St. George, 706 S. Lemon St., Fullerton, 92632.

Northridge, Los Angeles Co., Our Lady of Lourdes (1958), Rev. Msgr. Peter C. Moran; Revs. Andrew Diviney, S.J.; Charles P. Mayer; Deacon Juan Galido.
Church—18405 Superior St., 91325. Tel: 818-349-1500; Fax: 818-349-2516.
Res., 9800 Canby Ave., 91325.
School—Tel: 818-349-0245.
Sisters 2; Lay Teachers 9; Students 312.
Catechesis/Religious Programs—Tel: 818-349-1285.
Students 273.

Norwalk, Los Angeles Co., St. John of God (1950), Rev. Msgr. Bernard M. Leheny; Revs. Arturo Velasco; Cesar A. Fernandez; Maurice D. Harrington. In res., Rev. Robert Gallagher.
Res., 13819 S. Pioneer Blvd., 90650. Tel: 310-863-5721; Fax: 310-406-3927.
School—13817 S. Pioneer Blvd., 90650. Tel: 310-863-0921.
Sisters of the Holy Faith 2; Lay Teachers 14; Students 365.
Catechesis/Religious Programs—Tel: 310-868-3915.
Students 923.

St. Linus (1961), Revs. Joseph V. Brennan; Michael Mikulski; Kevin A. Kester.
Res., 13915 Shoemaker Ave., 90650. Tel: 310-921-6649; Fax: 310-921-5150.
School—Tel: 310-921-0336; Fax: 310-921-1666.
Sisters of the Holy Faith 2; Lay Teachers 9; Students 326.
Catechesis/Religious Programs—Tel: 310-921-5179.
Students 377.

Oak Park, Ventura Co., St. Maximilian Kolbe (1992), Rev. Msgr. Peter A. O'Reilly.
Res., 638 Lindero Canyon Rd. #325, 91301. Tel: 818-991-3915; Fax: 818-991-7152.
Catechesis/Religious Programs—Tel: 818-991-5604.
Students 300.

Ojai, Ventura Co., St. Thomas Aquinas (1919), Revs. Patrick J. Keane, O.S.A.; James P. Retzner, O.S.A.; Bro. William V. Olivas, O.S.A.; Deacon Allan Doane.
Res., 185 St. Thomas Dr., 93023. Tel: 805-646-4338; Fax: 805-646-5928.
Catechesis/Religious Programs—Tel: 805-646-0307.
Students 190.

Oxnard, Ventura Co.,

1—St. Anthony, (1959), Rev. George Sullivan; Rev. Msgr. Michael J. Condon, Pastor Emeritus; Revs. Jose Mejia; Roger Labonte; Deacons James Henry; Jon McPheeters; Thomas Pina; Oscar Duke.
Res., 2511 S. C St., P.O. Box 2215, 93034. Tel: 805-486-7301; Fax: 805-486-3142.
School—Tel: 805-487-5317; Fax: 805-486-1537.
Sisters 2; Lay Teachers 9; Students 307.
Catechesis/Religious Programs—2421 S. C St., 93033. Tel: 805-486-0784.
Students 1,119.

2—Santa Clara, (1904), Rev. Msgr. Peter D. Nugent; Rev. Msgr. Charles F. O'Gorman, Senior Priest; Revs. Jonathan M. Atchley; Valentine D. Zdilla.
Res., 323 S. E St., 93030. Tel: 805-487-3891; Fax: 805-483-1734.
School—324 S. E St., 93030. Tel: 805-483-6935; Fax: 805-487-6686.
Lay Teachers 11; Students 337.
Catechesis/Religious Programs—Tel: 805-487-6742.
Students 850.
Mission—El Rio, Ventura Co., Santa Clara Chapel, 1333 Ventura Blvd., 93030. Tel: 805-485-7335; Fax: 805-981-1183.

3—Our Lady of Guadalupe Parish, (1958) (Hispanic), Revs. Ricardo de Alba, M.Sp.S.; Enrique Espinosa Ramirez, M.Sp.S.; Jose Natividad Vazquez, M.Sp.S.; Francisco Altamira, M.Sp.S.
Res., 500 N. Juanita Ave., P.O. Box 1091, 93030. Tel: 805-483-0987; 483-1481; Fax: 805-486-2434.
School—530 N. Juanita Ave., 93030. Tel: 805-483-5116; Fax: 805-486-4238.
Sisters of St. Joseph of Carondelet 2; Lay Teachers 7; Students 293.
Catechesis/Religious Programs—Tel: 805-487-4737; Fax: 805-486-2434.
Students 564.
Mission—Oxnard, Ventura Co., Christ the King, 535 Cooper Rd., 93030. Tel: 805-483-3499.

4—Mary Star of the Sea, (1963) (Filipino-Mexican), Revs. Paul Goni, O.A.R.; Rafael Cendejas, O.A.R.; Deacons Harold A. Parish; Fidel Ramirez.
Res., 463 W. Pleasant Valley Rd., 93033. Tel: 805-486-6133; Fax: 805-483-6913.
Catechesis/Religious Programs—Tel: 805-483-9313.
Students 1,000.
Convent—4924 S. "F" St., 93033. Tel: 805-487-8008.

Pacific Palisades, Los Angeles Co., Corpus Christi

(1950), Rev. Msgr. John A. Mihan; Rev. G. Neville Rucker, Pastor Emeritus; Deacon John P. Allen. In res., Revs. Joseph D. Burke, C.S.C.; Richard M. Martini.
Res., 887 Toyopa Dr., 90272. Tel: 310-454-1328; Fax: 310-454-3776.
School—Tel: 310-454-9411.
Sisters of St. Louis (Monaghan) 4; Lay Teachers 13; Students 320.
Convent—875 Toyopa Dr., 90272. Tel: 310-454-6262.

Pacoima, Los Angeles Co., Guardian Angel (1956), Rev. Juan Enriquez.
Res., 10886 Lehigh Ave., 91331. Tel: 818-899-2345; Fax: 818-899-2537.
School—Tel: 818-896-1113.
Religious of Jesus and Mary 4; Lay Teachers 6; Students 309.
Catechesis/Religious Programs—Tel: 818-899-8907.
Students 315.

Mary Immaculate (1957) (Spanish), Revs. Thomas Rush, O.M.I.; Luciano Anton, O.M.I.; Luis Valbuena, O.M.I.
Res., 10390 Remick Ave., 91331. Tel: 818-899-0278; Fax: 818-890-9878.
School—Tel: 818-834-8551; Fax: 818-896-7996.
Lay Teachers 10; Students 230.
Catechesis/Religious Programs—Tel: 818-899-2111.
Students 1,020.

Palmdale, Los Angeles Co., St. Mary (1890), Revs. Richard Miskella; James Gleason; Christopher Cunningham.
Res., 1600 E. Ave., R-4, 93550. Tel: 805-947-3306; Fax: 805-947-8687.
School—P.O. Box 902200, 93590-2200. Tel: 805-273-5555; Fax: 805-273-3845.
Salesian Sisters of St. John Bosco 4; Lay Teachers 9; Students 360.
Catechesis/Religious Programs—Tel: 805-273-5554; Fax: 805-947-8687.
Students 1,660.

Panorama City, Los Angeles Co., St. Genevieve (1950), Rev. Msgr. Charles E. Hill; Revs. Vlatko Poljicak; Christopher Troxell; Michael Ume.
Res., 14061 Roscoe Blvd., 91402. Tel: 818-894-2261; Fax: 818-893-4284.
School—Tel: 818-892-3802; Fax: 818-893-8143.
Sisters 3; Lay Teachers 17; Students 683.
High School—13967 Roscoe Blvd., 91402. Tel: 818-894-6417; Fax: 818-892-9853.
Sisters 1; Lay Teachers 25; Students 506.
Catechesis/Religious Programs—Tel: 818-892-7177.
Students 457.

Paramount, Los Angeles Con., Our Lady of the Rosary (1913) (Hispanic-Tongan), Rev. Msgr. Bernard O'Reilly, (Retired); Revs. Idelfonso Madrigal; Edward J. Dober; Larry Neumeier.
Res., 14815 S. Paramount Blvd., 90723. Tel: 310-633-1126; Fax: 310-633-3192.
School—Tel: 310-633-6360; Fax: 310-633-2641.
Sisters of the Daughters of Mary and Joseph 4; Lay Teachers 10; Students 334.
Catechesis/Religious Programs—Tel: 310-602-0086.
Students 1,370.
Mission—Paramount, Catholic Korean Community of St. Raphael (Downey & Alondra), 15946 Downey Ave., 90723. Tel: 310-630-6168. Rev. Alex Chung.

Pasadena, Los Angeles Co., St. Andrew (1886) (Hispanic), Rev. Msgr. Tobias P. English; Revs. Victor J. Ruvalcaba; Paul A. Sustatya.
Res., 311 N. Raymond Ave., 91103. Tel: 818-792-4183; Fax: 818-792-4456.
School—(Grades K-8). Tel: 818-796-7697.
Sisters of the Holy Names of Jesus and Mary 3; Lay Teachers 8; Students 292.
Catechesis/Religious Programs—42 Chestnut St., 91103. Tel: 818-577-1770.
Students 625.

Assumption of the Blessed Virgin Mary (1950), Rev. Msgr. August Moretti; Rev. Walter Fernando; Rev. Msgr. Timothy J. Crean, Pastor Emeritus.
Res., 2640 E. Orange Grove Blvd., 91107. Tel: 818-792-1343.
School—2660 E. Orange Grove Blvd., 91107. Tel: 818-793-2089; Fax: 818-793-4070. Lou Anne Insprucker, Prin.
Lay Teachers 17; Students 303.
Catechesis/Religious Programs—Tel: 818-792-6844. Elly Dunbar, D.R.E.
Students 193.

St. Philip the Apostle (1921), Rev. Msgr. Gary P. Bauler; Revs. Marc V. Trudeau; Mariano Tomaszewski; Deacon William Landa.
Res., 151 S. Hill Ave., 91106. Tel: 818-793-0693; Fax: 818-793-0733.
School—161 S. Hill Ave., 91106. Tel: 818-795-9691; Fax: 818-795-9946.
Lay Teachers 13; Students 413.
Catechesis/Religious Programs—Students 330.

Pico Rivera, Los Angeles Co., St. Hilary (1950), Rev. Msgr. Christian VanLiefde; Revs. Hugo Neyra; Frank Russo; Deacon Antonio Soto.
Res., 5465 Citronell Ave., 90660. Tel: 310-942-7300; Fax: 310-948-3760.
School—Tel: 310-942-7361.
School Sisters of Notre Dame 3; Lay Teachers 13; Students 360.
Catechesis/Religious Programs—5401 S. Citronell Ave., 90660. Tel: 310-942-7018.
Students 529.
Convent—5333 S. Citronell Ave., 90660. Tel: 310-942-7151.

St. Marianne de Paredes (1951) (Hispanic), Revs. Fernando Iglesias; Martin Slaughter; Manuel Pontones.
Res., 7922 S. Passons Blvd., 90660. Tel: 310-949-8240; Fax: 310-942-2405.
School—7911 Buhman Ave., 90660. Tel: 310-949-1234; Fax: 310-948-3855. Sr. Francis Rose Rivers, S.S.N.D.
School Sisters of Notre Dame 1; Lay Teachers 12; Students 281.
Catechesis/Religious Programs—Tel: 310-949-5653.
Students 450.

St. Francis Xavier (1939), Rev. Jorge Penaloza.
Res., 4245 S. Acacia Ave., 90660. Tel: 310-699-8527; Fax: 310-699-5331.

Pomona, Los Angeles Co., St. Joseph (1886), Revs. Maurice O'Mahony; Richard Carey. In res., Rev. Labib Kobti.
Res., 1150 W. Holt Ave., 91768. Tel: 909-629-4101; Fax: 909-623-0265.
School—Tel: 909-622-3365.
Felician Sisters 5; Lay Teachers 8; Students 332.
Catechesis/Religious Programs—1200 W. Hoet Ave., 91768. Tel: 909-629-1404; Fax: 909-469-5146.
Students 330.

Sacred Heart (1935), Rev. Msgr. Manuel O. Sanchez; Revs. Jose Varela; Joseph F. Hernandez; D. Ignacio Sanchez (Spain).
Res., 1215 S. Hamilton Blvd., 91766. Tel: 909-622-4553; Fax: 909-623-0841.
School—1263 S. Hamilton Blvd., 91766. Tel: 909-622-7170.
Lay Teachers 12; Students 220.
Catechesis/Religious Programs—Tel: 909-622-4716. Edgar Meda, D.R.E.
Students 440.

St. Madeleine (1963), Rev. Msgr. Andrew Tseu.
Res., 931 E. Kingsley Ave., 91767. Tel: 909-629-9495; Fax: 909-623-7148.
Catechesis/Religious Programs—Tel: 909-620-1300.
Students 255.

Rancho Palos Verdes, Los Angeles Co., St. John Fisher (1961), Rev. Msgr. Eugene A. Gilb; Rev. Leo W. Alberg. In res., Rev. Mark Strader.
Res., 5448 Crest Rd., P.O. Box 2249, 90275. Tel: 310-377-5571; Fax: 310-377-6303.
School—Tel: 310-377-2800.
Immaculate Heart of Mary Sisters 2; Lay Teachers 9; Students 274.
Catechesis/Religious Programs—5400 Crest Rd., 90275. Tel: 310-377-4573.
Students 718.

Redondo Beach, Los Angeles Co., St. James (1892), Revs. Timothy Nichols; John Pustaver; Brendan Kearney, S.J.; Deacon Richard Shinkle. In res., Rev. Jim Clarke.
Res., 415 Vincent St., 90277. Tel: 310-372-5228; Fax: 310-379-5552.
School—4625 Garnet St., Torrance, 90503. Tel: 310-371-0416.
Sisters of St. Joseph of Carondelet 2; Lay Teachers 9; Students 289.
Catechesis/Religious Programs—Tel: 310-379-3221.
Students 332.

St. Lawrence Martyr (1955), Rev. Msgr. Michael Lenihan; Revs. John W. Neiman; Paul Vigil; Deacon Frank Dieter.
Res., 1900 S. Prospect Ave., 90277-6099. Tel: 310-540-0329; Fax: 310-540-8999.
School—1950 Prospect Ave., 90277-6003. Tel: 310-540-3049; Fax: 310-316-0888.
Sisters of St. Joseph of Carondelet 1; Lay Teachers 13; Students 311.
Catechesis/Religious Programs—Tel: 310-316-4460.
Students 701.

Reseda, Los Angeles Co., St. Catherine of Siena (1949), Rev. Sean B. Flanagan. In res., Rev. Raul Cortes; Deacon Pedro Lira.
Res., 18115 Sherman Way, 91335. Tel: 818-343-2110.
School—7311 Lindley Ave., 91335. Tel: 818-343-9880; Fax: 818-343-1018.
Lay Teachers 9; Students 332.
Catechesis/Religious Programs—Tel: 818-996-4588.
Students 503.

Rowland Heights, Los Angeles Co., St. Elizabeth Ann Seton (1981), Rev. Msgr. Michael F. Killeen; Revs. Robert Victoria; Peter Tsang; Deacon Steven V. Hillman.
Res., 18090 Via Amorosa, 91748. Tel: 818-964-3629; Fax: 818-913-2209.
Church—1835 Larkvane Rd., 91748.
Catechesis/Religious Programs—Tel: 818-965-5792.
Students 810.

San Dimas, Los Angeles Co., Holy Name of Mary (1957), Revs. Thomas J. Mullen, SS.CC.; William Moore, SS.CC.; Deacon Jack Clinton.
Res., 724 E. Bonita Ave., 91773. Tel: 909-599-1243; Fax: 909-599-4230.
School—Tel: 909-599-1234, Ext. 24.
Sisters 1; Lay Teachers 18; Students 310.
Catechesis/Religious Programs—Students 856.

San Fernando, Los Angeles Co., St. Ferdinand (1902), Rev. Anthony Dummer, O.M.I.
Office: 1109 Coronel St., 91340. Tel: 818-365-3967; Fax: 818-365-0067.
School—1012 Coronel St., 91340. Tel: 818-361-3264; Fax: 818-361-5894.
Sisters of St. Joseph of Carondelet 3; Lay Teachers 10; Students 299.
Catechesis/Religious Programs—Tel: 818-361-1813.
Students 311.

Santa Rosa (1927) (Hispanic), Revs. Paul Wilhelm, O.M.I.; Patrick Thompson, O.M.I.; Edgar Garcia, O.M.I. (Peru).
Res., 668 S. Workman St., 91340. Tel: 818-361-4617; Fax: 818-365-8599.
School—1309 Mott St., 91340. Tel: 818-361-5096; Fax: 818-361-2259.
Franciscan Missionary Sisters of the Immaculate Conception 7; Lay Teachers 4; Students 321.
Catechesis/Religious Programs—Tel: 818-365-5161.
Students 512.

San Gabriel, Los Angeles Co., San Gabriel (1771). (Old Mission). Revs. Valentin Ramon, C.M.F.; Stephen Niskanen, C.M.F.; Brian Culley, C.M.F.; Binh Nguyen, C.M.; Deacon Gil Chavez. In res., Rev. Tobias Romero, C.M.F.; Bro. Cruz Pettinato, C.M.F.
Res., 537 W. Mission Dr., 91776. Tel: 818-457-3035; Fax: 818-282-5308. [CEM]
School—547 W. Mission Dr., 91776. Tel: 818-281-2454; Fax: 818-281-4817.
Dominican Sisters 2; Lay Teachers 8; Students 296.
High School—254 S. Santa Anita St., 91776. Tel: 818-282-3181; Fax: 818-282-4209.
Sisters 7; Lay Teachers 21; Girls 426.
Catechesis/Religious Programs—Tel: 818-457-3041.
Students 800.
Convent—561 W. Mission Dr., 91776. Tel: 818-282-8475.

St. Anthony (1945) (Hispanic), Revs. Michael Gleeson (Ireland); Marco Reyes; Gaspar Bautista (Mexico); Deacon John Messer.
Res., 1901 S. San Gabriel Blvd., 91776. Tel: 818-288-8912; Fax: 818-288-3730.
School—1905 S. San Gabriel Blvd., 91776. Tel: 818-280-7255; Fax: 818-280-3870. Sr. Kathleen Callaway, S.N.J.M., Prin.
Sisters of the Holy Names of Jesus and Mary 2; Lay Teachers 20; Students 615.
Catechesis/Religious Programs—Tel: 818-288-5511. Tommy Mondello, D.R.E.
Students 700.
Convent—626 E. Marshall St., 91726. Tel: 818-288-2200.

San Marino, Los Angeles Co., Saints Felicitas and Perpetua (1938), Rev. Msgr. Lawrence J. Gibson. In res., Rev. Msgr. Paul M. Konoske.
Res., 1190 Palomar Rd., 91108. Tel: 818-796-0432.
School—2955 Huntington Dr., 91108. Tel: 818-796-8223.
Sisters 5; Lay Teachers 9; Students 290.

San Pedro, Los Angeles Co., Mary, Star of the Sea (1889), Rev. Msgr. Patrick J. Gallagher; Revs. Lorenzo De Dominici, (Retired); Mate Bizaca (Croatia); Vivian Ben Lima; Raymond Perez, O.Praem.; Deacon Nino Crisafulli.
Res., 870 W. 8th St., 90731. Tel: 310-833-3541; Fax: 310-833-9254.
School—Tel: 310-831-0875; Fax: 310-831-0877.
Priests 1; Lay Teachers 15; Students 289.
High School—Tel: 310-547-1138; Fax: 310-547-1827.
Priests 5; Lay Teachers 12; Students 316.
Catechesis/Religious Programs—717 S. Cabrillo Ave., 90731. Tel: 310-833-3933.
Students 550.

Holy Trinity (1924), Revs. Thomas J. Glynn; Damian

Fernando; Richard Hoynes.
Parish Center: 209 N. Hanford Ave., 90732. Tel: 310-548-6535; Fax: 310-833-1134.
Church—1292 W. Santa Cruz St., 90732.
School—1226 W. Santa Cruz St., 90732. Tel: 310-833-0703; Fax: 310-833-5219.
Lay Teachers 24; Students 625.
Catechesis/Religious Programs—Tel: 310-833-3500.
Students 485.

St. Peter (1965) (Hispanic), Revs. Claudio De Agostini, C.S.J.; Peter Crema, C.S.J.; Bruno De Santi, C.S.J. In res., Revs. John Trimaglio, C.S.J.; Angelo Zonta, C.S.J.
Res., 338 N. Grand Ave., 90731-2006. Tel: 310-831-5360; Fax: 310-831-0415.
Catechesis/Religious Programs—Tel: 310-832-6731.
Students 660.

Santa Barbara, Santa Barbara Co.,

1—HOLY CROSS, (1973), Rev. Ludo DeClippel, C.J., (Belgium) Admin.; Deacons Nicholas Curran; David Huff.
Res., 1740 Cliff Dr., 93109. Tel: 805-962-0411; Fax: 805-564-6921.

2—OUR LADY OF SORROWS, (1856), Revs. Martin L. Brewer, S.J.; Thomas P. Delaney, S.J.; P. Jeremiah Helfrich, S.J.; Deacons Enrique Sanchez; Manuel Martinez.
Res., 21 E. Sola St., 93101. Tel: 805-963-1734; Fax: 805-965-6461.
School—33 E. Micheltorena St., 93101. Tel: 805-965-1033. Don Huntley, Prin.
Lay Teachers 12; Students 235.
Catechesis/Religious Programs—Tel: 805-966-4941.
Students 307.
Convent—19 E. Micheltorena St., 93101. Tel: 805-966-3089.

3—OUR LADY OF GUADALUPE, (1928) (Hispanic), Revs. Guillermo C. Garcia, C.J.; Timothy P. Lane, C.J.
Res., 801 Jennings Ave., 93103. Tel: 805-965-4060.
Catechesis/Religious Programs—Tel: 805-962-4441.
Students 360.

4—ST. BARBARA, (1786). (Old Mission). Revs. Vincent Mesi, O.F.M.; Maurus Kelly, O.F.M.; Benvenute Bavero, O.F.M.; Deacon Jack Ryan.
Res., Old Mission, 2201 Laguna St., 93105. Tel: 805-682-4151; 682-4713; Fax: 805-687-7841. [CEM]

5—SAN ROQUE, (1953), Rev. James M. Ford; Deacon William B. Sangster. In res., Rev. Msgr. Philip L. Grill, (Retired).
Res., 325 Argonne Circle, 93105. Tel: 805-687-5215; Fax: 805-682-9778. [JC]
School—314 Calle Cedro, 93105. Tel: 805-687-3717; Fax: 805-687-3581. Anne Marie Omweg, Prin.
Lay Teachers 13; Aides 1; Students 250.
Catechesis/Religious Programs—Tel: 805-682-1097.
Students 250.

Santa Clarita, Los Angeles Co., Our Lady of Perpetual Help (1944), Revs. Patrick A. Power; Jeffrey J. Deikel; Sr. M. Jane Mast, S.H.F., Pastoral Min.; Deacon Richard Karl.
Res., 23233 Lyons Ave., 91321-2632. Tel: 805-259-2276; Fax: 805-259-1873.
School—Tel: 805-259-1141; Fax: 805-259-8254.
Franciscan Sisters of the Immaculate Conception 6; Lay Teachers 10; Students 337.
Catechesis/Religious Programs—Tel: 805-259-4266.
Students 997.
Convent—23719 Rotunda Rd., 91355. Tel: 805-259-5591.

Santa Fe Springs, Los Angeles Co., St. Pius X (1954) (Hispanic), Revs. John McHugh; Porfirio Alvarez; Antolin B. Torralba (Philippines); Peter Ha Son Le (Vietnamese); Rev. Msgr. Glen A. Rademacher, Pastor Emeritus.
Res., 10827 S. Pioneer Blvd., 90670. Tel: 310-863-8734; Fax: 310-868-0051.
School—Tel: 310-864-4818; Fax: 310-864-7120.
Lay Teachers 11; Students 378.
Catechesis/Religious Programs—Tel: 310-868-2389.
Students 746.

Santa Maria, Santa Barbara Co., St. Mary of the Assumption (1905), Rev. Msgr. James P. Colberg; Rev. John Wishard, Senior Priest.
Res., 414 E. Church St., 93454. Tel: 805-922-5826; Fax: 805-922-1986.
School—P.O. Drawer 1965, 93454. Tel: 805-925-6713; Fax: 805-922-1986.
Sisters 1; Lay Teachers 9; Students 254.
Catechesis/Religious Programs—Tel: 805-925-1334.
Students 288.

St. Louis de Montfort (Santa Barbara) (1963), Revs. Mark L. Newman, C.J.; Campion W. Aspinall, C.J.; John Mayhew, C.J.; L. Bede Johnson, C.J., (Retired); Deacons Richard Carmody; Douglas Halvorsen.
Res., 5075 Harp Rd., 93455. Tel: 805-937-4555; Fax: 805-934-2805. [JC]
School—Tel: 805-937-5571.
Sisters 2; Lay Teachers 9; Students 292.
Catechesis/Religious Programs—Tel: 805-937-6383.
Students 700.
Mission—Los Alamos, Santa Barbara Co., St. Anthony's Church, 260 Helena St., Los Alamos, 93440.

St. John Neumann (Santa Barbara) (1986) (Hispanic), Revs. Emigdio Herrera; John Higson; Deacons Manuel Liendo; Lyle Goodspeed; Sr. Margaret Bannan, O.S.F., Pastoral Assoc.
Res., 966 W. Orchard, 93454. Tel: 805-922-7099; Fax: 805-346-1747.
Catechesis/Religious Programs—Tel: 805-922-5233.
Students 649.

Santa Monica, Los Angeles Co., St. Monica (1886), Rev. Msgr. Lloyd A. Torgerson; Revs. David Heney; Michael Rocha. In res., Revs. Jon Majarucon; Bernard O'Connor, C.M.F.; Robert A. Dowd, C.S.C (FTW).
Church—725 California Ave., 90403. Tel: 310-393-9287; Fax: 310-319-9758.
School—1039 Seventh St., 90403. Tel: 310-451-9801; Fax: 310-394-6001.
Lay Teachers 12; Students 280.
High School—1030 Lincoln Blvd., 90403. Tel: 310-394-3701; Fax: 310-458-1353.
Sisters of the Holy Names 2; Lay Teachers 33; Students 615.
Catechesis/Religious Programs—Tel: 310-395-8903.
Students 265.

St. Anne (1951) (Hispanic), Rev. Adalberto Blanco.
Res., 2011 Colorado Ave., 90404. Tel: 310-829-4411; Fax: 310-829-9006.
School—2017 Colorado Ave., 90404. Tel: 310-829-2775.
Sisters of St. Louis 1; Lay Teachers 9; Students 213.
Catechesis/Religious Programs—Tel: 310-829-4040.
Students 168.

St. Clement (1904), Rev. Stephen Woodland, Admin. In res., Rev. Richard G. Krekelberg.
Res., 3102 Third St., 90405. Tel: 310-396-2679; Fax: 310-396-4239.
Catechesis/Religious Programs—204 Hampton Dr., Venice, 90291. Tel: 310-392-5769.
Students 150.

Santa Paula, Ventura Co., St. Sebastian (1896), Rev. James A. Rothe.
Res., 235 N. Ninth St., 93060. Tel: 805-525-2149; Fax: 805-933-5520.
School—325 E. Santa Barbara St., 93060. Tel: 805-525-1575.
Lay Teachers 14; Students 250; Pre-School 32.
Catechesis/Religious Programs—Students 160.

Our Lady of Guadalupe (1929) (Hispanic), Rev. Rene Juarez, O.F.M.
Res., 427 N. Oak St., 93060. Tel: 805-525-3716; Fax: 805-525-3788. [CEM]
Catechesis/Religious Programs—Tel: 805-525-2225.
Students 736.
Convent—432 N. Oak St., 93060. Tel: 805-525-9207.

Sepulveda, Los Angeles Co., Our Lady of Peace (1944), Revs. John Keese, Admin.; Sang V. Tran; David Granadino.
Res., 15444 Nordhoff St., 91343. Tel: 818-894-1176; Fax: 818-894-3838.
School—9022 Langdon Ave., 91343. Tel: 818-894-4059.
Lay Teachers 9; Students 286.
Catechesis/Religious Programs—Tel: 818-891-3578.
Students 580.

Sherman Oaks, Los Angeles Co., St. Francis de Sales (1938), Revs. Kevin J. Larkin; Jerome O'Mahony, M.S.C.; James M. Maher; Deacon John Coplen.
Res., 13360 Valleyheart Dr., 91423. Tel: 818-784-0105; Fax: 818-784-4807.
Church—Moorpark St. at Dixie Canyon Ave., 91423.
School—13368 Valleyheart Dr., 91423. Tel: 818-784-9573; Fax: 818-784-9649.
Sisters 2; Lay Teachers 12; Students 312.
Catechesis/Religious Programs—Students 150.

Sierra Madre, Los Angeles Co., St. Rita (1908), Rev. Msgr. Joseph J. Cokus; Rev. Msgr. Robert Gara, Pastor Emeritus; Deacon Ernest Nosari.
Res., 50 E. Alegria Ave., 91024. Tel: 818-355-1292; Fax: 818-355-2290.
School—Tel: 818-355-6114; Fax: 818-355-0713.
Lay Teachers 11; Students 303.
Catechesis/Religious Programs—Tel: 818-355-3841.
Students 220.

Simi Valley, Ventura Co., St. Peter Claver (1972), Revs. Dennis Mongrain; Rock Janowski; Deacon Richard Hamm.
Res., 5649 Pittman St., 93063. Tel: 805-526-6499; Fax: 805-526-7233.
Catechesis/Religious Programs—Tel: 805-526-0680.
Students 506.

St. Rose of Lima (1921), Revs. Michael Carcerano; John W. Sigler; Jerald W. Thompson; Deacon Peter Wilson.
Res., 1305 Royal Ave., 93065. Tel: 805-526-1732; Fax: 805-526-0067.
School—1325 Royal Ave., 93065. Tel: 805-526-5304; Fax: 805-526-0939.
Lay Teachers 11; Students 310.
Catechesis/Religious Programs—Tel: 805-526-5513.
Students 870.

Solvang, Santa Barbara Co., Old Mission Santa Ines (1804) (Spanish), Revs. Ron Talbott, O.F.M.Cap; Miguel Ortiz, O.F.M.Cap. In res., Revs. Cyril Kelleher, O.F.M.Cap.; Timothy O'Sullivan, O.F.M.Cap.
Res., 1760 Mission Dr., P.O. Box 408, 93464. Tel: 805-688-4815; Fax: 805-686-4468.
Catechesis/Religious Programs—Tel: 805-688-4138.
Students 415.

South El Monte, Los Angeles Co., Epiphany (1956), Revs. Joseph F. Greeley; Francisco X. Ramirez; Matthew T. Cumberland.
Res., 10911 Michael Hunt Dr., 91733. Tel: 818-442-6262; Fax: 818-575-1738.
School—10915 Michael Hunt Dr., 91733. Tel: 818-442-6264; Fax: 818-442-6074.
Bernardine Sisters 5; Lay Teachers 6; Students 240.
Catechesis/Religious Programs—Tel: 818-448-3636.
Students 1,125.

South Gate, Los Angeles Co., St. Helen (1931), Revs. Jerome A. Bouska; Francisco Javier Perez.
Res., 8912 South Gate Ave., 90280. Tel: 213-563-3522; Fax: 213-563-0161.
School—Tel: 213-566-5491; Fax: 213-566-2810.
Sisters of Notre Dame 2; Lay Teachers 9; Students 345.
Catechesis/Religious Programs—Tel: 213-563-3536.
Students 535.

South Pasadena, Los Angeles Co., Holy Family (1910), Rev. Msgr. Clement J. Connolly; Revs. Finbarr Devine, SS.CC.; Michael J. Sezzi.
Res., 1301 Rollin St., 91030. Tel: 818-799-8908; Fax: 818-799-0423.
School—1519 Fremont Ave., 91030. Tel: 818-799-8908. Mrs. Anne Murphy, Prin.
Lay Teachers 9; Students 303.
Catechesis/Religious Programs—Tel: 818-799-1037.
Students 340.

Sun Valley, Los Angeles Co., Our Lady of the Holy Rosary (1937), Revs. Pat Murphy, C.S.; Miguel Camarena, C.S. (Mexico); Rodolfo Lache (Columbia).
Res., 7800 Vineland Ave., 91352. Tel: 818-765-3350; Fax: 818-765-3170.
School—7802 Vineland Ave., 91352. Tel: 818-765-4897; Fax: 818-765-5791.
Servant Sisters of the Blessed Sacrament 5; Lay Teachers 8; Students 309.
Catechesis/Religious Programs—Tel: 818-982-4248. Douglas Zuniga, D.R.E.
Students 1,150.
Convent—7757 Cleon St., 91352. Tel: 818-764-9857.
Mission—North Hollywood, Los Angeles Co., Our Lady of Zapopan, 7824 Lankershim Blvd., North Hollywood, 91605. Tel: 818-503-8920.

Sylmar, Los Angeles Co., St. Didacus (1957), Rev. Msgr. Peter L. Amy.
Res., 14339 Astoria St., 91342. Tel: 818-367-6181; Fax: 818-367-0604.
School—14325 Astoria St., 91342. Tel: 818-367-5886.
Lay Teachers 9; Students 326.
Catechesis/Religious Programs—Tel: 818-367-4155.
Students 900.

Temple City, Los Angeles Co., St. Luke the Evangelist (1946), Revs. Thomas King; Michael Carroll; Jeremiah O'Keeffe; Stanislaus Paul.
Res., 9451 E. Broadway, P.O. Box 798, 91780. Tel: 818-291-5900; Fax: 818-287-2332.
Parish Administrative Center—5605 Cloverly, 91780.
School—Tel: 818-291-5959.

Lay Teachers 9; Students 305.
Catechesis/Religious Programs—Tel: 818-291-5925.
Students 455.

Thousand Oaks, Ventura Co., St. Paschal Baylon (1960), Rev. Msgr. Joseph S. George; Revs. Thomas O'Hanlon; Joseph Gaffney; Deacon James Robinson.
Res., 155 E. Janss Rd., 91360. Tel: 805-496-0222; Fax: 805-379-2506.
School—Tel: 805-495-9340.
Sisters of Notre Dame 2; Lay Teachers 11; Students 315.
Catechesis/Religious Programs—Tel: 805-497-2815.
Students 620.

Torrance, Los Angeles Co., Nativity (1924), Revs. Patrick J. McHugh; Miguel Amengual (Spain). In res., Rev. Alexander Hoefler, S.V.D.
Res., 1447 Engracia Ave., P.O. Box 479, 90508. Tel: 310-328-2776; Fax: 310-328-0508.
School—2671 Carson, 90501. Tel: 310-328-5387; Fax: 310-328-5365.
Lay Teachers 12; Students 299.
Catechesis/Religious Programs—2371 Carson Ave., 90501. Tel: 310-320-6673.
Students 289.
Mission—Torrance, Los Angeles Co., St. Joseph, 2314 Del Amo, 90501.

St. Catherine Laboure (1949), Revs. John O'Byrne; John Nguyen; Deacons Matilde Magana; Ralph Ulibarri. In res., Rev. Sal Pilato.
Res., 3846 Redondo Beach Blvd., 90504. Tel: 310-323-8900; Fax: 213-321-0486.
School—Tel: 310-324-8732; Fax: 310-324-2471. Mrs. Kathleen Gorze, Prin.
Lay Teachers 19; Students 568.
Catechesis/Religious Programs—16831 Ainsworth, 90504. Tel: 310-515-6033.
Students 508.

Tujunga, Los Angeles Co., Our Lady of Lourdes (1920), Revs. George R. Brincat; Blaise Brockman; Deacon Paul Chacon.
Res., 10321 Tujunga Canyon Blvd., 91042. Tel: 818-352-3218; Fax: 818-352-2738.
School—Tel: 818-353-1106.
Sisters of Charity of the Blessed Virgin Mary 1; Lay Teachers 8; Students 281.
Catechesis/Religious Programs—Tel: 818-353-3053.
Students 400.

Valinda, Los Angeles Co., St. Martha (1958) (Hispanic-Filipino), Revs. William T. Easterling; Rodel Balagtas; Deacon Jacob Favela. In res., Rev. Msgr. Aidan Carroll.
Res., 444 N. Azusa Ave., 91744-4299. Tel: 818-964-4313; Fax: 818-913-2953.
School—Tel: 818-964-1093; Fax: 818-965-2967.
Sisters of the Love of God 4; Lay Teachers 5; Students 315.
Catechesis/Religious Programs—Tel: 818-912-2581.
Students 1,100.

Van Nuys, Los Angeles Co., St. Elisabeth (1919) (Hispanic), Revs. Kevin Nolan; Luis Martinez; John Brady; Deacon Wesley Balbuena. In res., Rev. Alberto Villalobos.
Res., 6635 Tobias Ave., 91405. Tel: 818-779-1756; Fax: 818-785-4492.
School—Tel: 818-779-1766; Fax: 818-779-1768.
Lay Teachers 9; Students 314.
Catechesis/Religious Programs—Tel: 818-779-1772.
Students 780.

St. Bridget of Sweden (1955), Revs. John C. Kesterson; Raymond Morales; Deacon Ramon Rivera. In res., Rev. Robert Milbauer.
Res., 16711 Gault St., 91406. Tel: 818-782-7180; Fax: 818-782-7184.
School—7120 Whitaker, 91406. Tel: 818-785-4422; Fax: 818-785-0490.
Lay Teachers 13; Students 290.
Catechesis/Religious Programs—Tel: 818-782-7711. Jacinta O'Connor, D.R.E.
Students 160.
Convent—16707 Gault St., 91406. Tel: 818-786-1401.

Venice, Los Angeles Co., St. Mark (1923), Revs. Roderic M. Guerrini; Michael Burns; Mark A. Martinez. In res., Rev. Harry Cronin, C.S.C.
Res., 940 Coeur d'Alene Ave., 90291. Tel: 310-821-5058; Fax: 310-821-7031.
School—912 Coeur d'Alene, 90291. Tel: 310-821-6612; Fax: 310-822-6101.
Lay Teachers 9; Students 318.
Catechesis/Religious Programs—Tel: 310-822-1201.
Students 240.

Ventura, Ventura Co., San Buenaventura Mission (1782) (Hispanic), Rev. Msgr. Patrick J. O'Brien; Rev. Joseph D. Pina; Rev. Msgr. Michael Hughes, (Retired).
Res., 211 E. Main St., 93001. Tel: 805-643-4318; Fax: 805-643-7831.
School—183 E. Main St., 93001. Tel: 805-643-1500.
Lay Teachers 12; Students 246.
Catechesis/Religious Programs—Students 420.

Our Lady of the Assumption (1954), Rev. Msgr. Donal Mulcahy; Revs. Robert V. Biroschak; Lawrence J. Dowdel, Jr.; Deacons James M. Farley; Rodger Adams.
Res., 3175 Telegraph Rd., 93003-3283. Tel: 805-642-7966; Fax: 805-642-7635.
School—3169 Telegraph Rd., 93003-3282. Tel: 805-642-7198.
Sisters 2; Lay Teachers 14; Students 321.
Catechesis/Religious Programs—Tel: 805-642-0568.
Students 530.

Sacred Heart (1966), Revs. Daniel O'Sullivan; Donald F. Grasha; Rev. Msgr. Arnold Biedermann, Pastor Emeritus; Deacon Braden McKinley, Admin.
Res., 10800 Henderson Rd., 93004. Tel: 805-647-3235; Fax: 805-647-8087.
School—(Grades K-8). Tel: 805-647-6174; Fax: 805-647-8087.
Sisters 1; Lay Teachers 9; Students 315.
Catechesis/Religious Programs—Tel: 805-647-6260.
Students 414.
Mission—Camarillo, Ventura Co., Cabrillo Chapel, 2361 Rose Ln., Camarillo, 93012. Tel: 805-491-3972. Rev. Ramon Farre.

Vernon, Los Angeles Co., Holy Angels Parish of the Deaf (1987), Revs. Brian Doran; Tom Schweitzer; Deacon James Dillon; Donald R. Rosenkjar, Pastoral Assoc.
Res., 4433 Santa Fe Ave., 90058. Tel: 213-587-0397 (TDD); Fax: 213-587-7193.

Walnut, Los Angeles Co., St. Lorenzo Ruiz (1991), Rev. Dennis C. Vellucci.
Res., 747 Meadowpass Rd., 91789. Tel: 909-595-9545; Fax: 909-594-3940.
Catechesis/Religious Programs—Tel: 909-468-1812.
Students 450.

West Covina, Los Angeles Co., St. Christopher (1954), Rev. Niall F. O'Leary; Rev. Msgr. John P. Won; Rev. Charles Schwehr; Deacon Douglas Moloney. In res., Rev. Eric A. Lewis.
Res., 629 S. Glendora Ave., 91790. Tel: 818-960-1805; Fax: 818-851-0595.
School—Franciscan Sisters of Christian Charity, 900 W. Christopher St., 91790. Tel: 818-960-3079. Sr. Carol Ward, O.S.F., Prin.
Lay Teachers 10; Students 314.
Catechesis/Religious Programs—Tel: 818-338-2937. Dolores Zavala, D.R.E.
Students 707.
Convent—840 W. Christopher St., 91790. Tel: 818-338-6056. Sr. Carol Ward, O.S.F., Local Dir.

West Hollywood, Los Angeles Co., St. Victor (1906), Rev. Msgr. George J. Parnassus; Rev. Frederick J. Heney, S.J.
Res., 8634 Holloway Dr., 90069. Tel: 310-652-6477; Fax: 310-652-6478.

Westlake Village, Los Angeles Co., St. Jude (1970), Rev. Msgr. William J. Leser, C.B.; Deacons Aloysius Caffrey; Dick Dorman. In res., Rev. Msgr. Thomas O'Connell, Pastor Emeritus.
Res., 32032 W. Lindero Canyon Rd., 91361. Tel: 818-889-1279; Fax: 818-889-3405.
School—32036 W. Lindero Canyon Rd., 91361. Tel: 818-889-9483.
Lay Teachers 15; Students 305.
Catechesis/Religious Programs—32034 W. Lindero Canyon Rd., 91361. Tel: 818-889-0612.
Students 786.

Whittier, Los Angeles Co., St. Mary of the Assumption (1803), Revs. Enrique A. Lopez, C.SS.R.; Joseph Tobin, C.SS.R.; Joseph Elliott, C.SS.R.; Donald Liberty, C.SS.R. In res., Revs. J. Timothy Watson, C.SS.R.; Lionel Sirois, C.SS.R. (Canada); Clarence Bodden, C.SS.R.; Arturo Uribe, C.SS.R.
Res., 7215 S. Newlin Ave., 90602. Tel: 310-698-0107; Fax: 310-696-1617.
School—Tel: 310-698-0253; Fax: 310-698-0206.
Sisters 1; Lay Teachers 22; Students 622.
Catechesis/Religious Programs—Tel: 310-693-3764.
Students 566.

St. Bruno (1955), Revs. Patrick O'Dwyer; Frank Mannion, S.S.C.; Deacon P. Michael Freeman.
Res., 15740 Citrustree Rd., 90603. Tel: 310-947-5637; Fax: 310-943-3193.
School—15700 Citrustree Rd., 90603. Tel: 310-943-8812; Fax: 310-943-2172.
Lay Teachers 13; Students 346.
Catechesis/Religious Programs—Tel: 310-943-2510.
Students 550.
Convent—10734 S. Widener Ave., 90603. Tel: 310-947-1177. Sr. Theresa Thanh Hao Nguyen, L.H.C., Supr.

St. Gregory the Great (1951), Rev. Msgr. Donald J. Ruddy; Revs. Albert Bahhuth; Rolly Jardiniano. In res., Rev. Thomas Stehly.
Res., 13935 Telegraph Rd., 90604. Tel: 310-941-0115; Fax: 310-941-3785.
School—13925 Telegraph Rd., 90604. Tel: 310-941-0750.
Irish Presentation Sisters 3; Lay Teachers 7; Students 349.
Catechesis/Religious Programs—Tel: 310-944-8311.
Students 760.

Wilmington, Los Angeles Co., SS. Peter and Paul's (1866), Revs. Peter Irving; Joaquin Haefeli; Francis Gloudeman, O.Praem.; Deacon Russell Harrison.
Res., 515 W. Opp St., 90744. Tel: 310-834-5215; Fax: 310-834-4685.
School—706 Bayview Ave., 90744. Tel: 310-834-5574.
Sisters 5; Lay Teachers 9; Students 300.
Catechesis/Religious Programs—Tel: 310-549-2048.
Students 600.

Holy Family (1929) (Hispanic), Rev. Msgr. Joseph F. Greeley; Rev. Bernerd Gatlin.
Res., 1220 N. Sanford Ave., P.O. Box 416, 90748. Tel: 310-834-6333; 834-2788; Fax: 310-834-9038.
School—1122 E. Robidoux St., 90748. Tel: 310-518-1440. Ms. Celia Campos, Prin.
Lay Teachers 6; Students 315.
Catechesis/Religious Programs—Tel: 310-549-0011.
Students 320.

Woodland Hills, Los Angeles Co., St. Mel (1955), Rev. Msgr. Padraic Loftus; Rev. Paul Brogan; Rev. Msgr. John T. Naughton, Pastor Emeritus; Rev. Msgr. Michael J. O'Connor, Pastor Emeritus.
Res., 20870 Ventura Blvd., 91364. Tel: 818-340-6020; Fax: 818-340-0261.
School—20874 Ventura Blvd., 91364. Tel: 818-340-1924; Fax: 818-347-4426.
Sisters of St. Louis 2; Lay Teachers 30; Students 595.
Catechesis/Religious Programs—Tel: 818-340-6250.
Students 358.

St. Bernardine of Siena (1962), Rev. Msgr. Paul T. Dotson; Rev. Msgr. Richard H. Murray, Pastor Emeritus; Rev. Alden Sison; Deacons Jerry Cellner; Dan McHugh; Dale Taufer.
Res., 24410 Calvert St., 91367. Tel: 818-888-8200; Fax: 818-888-5046.
School—Tel: 818-340-2130.
Lay Teachers 12; Students 317.
Catechesis/Religious Programs—6061 Valley Circle Blvd., 91367. Tel: 818-340-1440.
Students 388.

Chaplains of Public Institutions

Non-Catholic Hospitals/Institutions

LOS ANGELES. *Cedar Sinai Medical Center,* 8700 Beverly Blvd., Room 2508, 90048. Tel: 310-855-5550. Rev. Michael Wempe, Chap.

L.A. City Fire Dept. Tel: 310-942-7300. Rev. Msgr. Christian M. Van Liefde, Chap., Tel: 310-942-7300.

L.A. County/University of Southern California Hospitals. Tel: 213-226-4715. Chaplains: Revs. Stephen Hernandez; Hugo Neyra; Sr. Dora Hauchecorne, I.C.M.; Sr. Clara Kelkermans, I.C.M.; Ms. Lupe Guzman; Mr. Dennis Apel.

L.A. Police Department, Employee Assistance Unit, 150 N. Los Angeles St., 90012. Tel: 213-485-0703. Rev. Michael P. McCullough. Tel: 213-485-0703.

St. Camillus Center for Pastoral Care, 1911 Zonal Ave., 90033. Tel: 213-225-4561. In res., Rev. Msgr. Terry Richey.

CAMARILLO. *Camarillo State Hospital-Development Center,* P.O. Box 6022-428, 93011. Rev. Hippolyte L. Goossens, C.J., Chap., Tel: 805-484-3661.

DOWNEY. *Rancho Los Amigos Medical Center, L.A. County Facility,* 7601 E. Imperial Hwy., 90242. Rev. Msgr. John Fosselman. Tel: 310-940-7257.

LOMPOC. *Vandenberg Air Force Base,* 587 Utah Ave., Vandenberg AFB, 93437-5000. Rev. Thomas D. Kelly, Chap., 30SPW/HC. Tel: 805-734-8232, Ext. 6-6655.

LONG BEACH. *Veterans Affairs Medical Center,* 5901 E. 7th St., 90822. Tel: 310-494-5418. Rev. Leo Miller, O.M.I., Chap.

NORWALK. *California Youth Authority,* Southern Reception Center and Clinic, 13200 S. Bloomfield Ave., 90650. Tel: 310-868-9979, Ext. 2467. Rev. Leo John Celano, O.Praem., Chap.

Metropolitan State Hospital, 11400 S. Norwalk Blvd., 90650. Tel: 310-863-9509. Rev. Jerome Stack, C.PP.S., Chap., Tel: 310-863-9509.

POINT MUGU. *Naval Air Station,* Code 83G000E NAWS,

93042. Tel: 805-989-7967. Rev. Donald Roy Moss, USNR.

POMONA. *Frank D. Lanterman Development Center*. Vacant. 3035 West Pomona Blvd., 91768. Mailing Address: Chap., P.O. Box 100, 91769. Tel: 909-595-1221, Ext. 2162.

PORT HUENEME. *Naval Construction Battalion Center*, 1000 23rd Ave. (Code 16), 93043. Tel: 805-982-4358. Rev. Gregory S. Pokladowski.

SAN PEDRO. *Fort MacArthur Annex*, 61-ABG/HC, Chaplain's Office, 325 Challenger Way, Ste. 1090, 90245-4677. Tel: 310-363-1956. Rev. Michael O'Neill.

SEPULVEDA. *Veterans Administration Medical Center*, 16111 Plummer St., 91343. Rev. Patrick O'Hagan, SS.CC. Tel: 818-895-9322.

TERMINAL ISLAND. *Federal Correction Institute*, 1299 Seaside Ave., P.O. Box 3007, 90731. Tel: 310-732-5200, Ext. 195. Rev. Frank Tinajero, S.V.D., Chap., Casa Guadalupe, Tel: 213-263-7561.

WEST LOS ANGELES. *Veterans Administration Wadsworth Hospital Center*, Chaplain Service, 11301 Wilshire Blvd. 691/123, 90099-5786. Tel: 310-268-3391. Revs. Edward J. Barrett; Finbar Hall; Francis Kelly Tel: 310-478-3711.

Detention Ministries

LOS ANGELES. *Department of Detention Ministries*, 933 Grattan St., 90015-1194. Tel: 213-251-2648; Fax: 213-251-2675. Bro. Peter Donohue, C.F.X., Dir.; Sr. Suzanne Jabro, C.S.J., Parish Contact Coordinator.
L.A. Juvenile Detention Facilities, Central Juvenile Hall, 1605 Eastlake Ave., 90033. Tel: 213-226-8530. Sr. Janet Harris, P.B.V.M.; Ms. Angelita Hurtado,
MacLaren Hall, Sr. Mary Allyn Ayres, O.P.
Dorothy Kirby Center, Sr. Mary Allyn Ayres, O.P.
Los Angeles County Jails in the City of Los Angeles, Adult Facilities, Biscailuz Center, 1060 Northeastern Ave., Tel: 213-267-2674.
Century Regional Detention Facility, 11705 S. Alameda St., Lynwood, 90262. Tel: 213-357-5114. Deacon Willard J. Hall, Sr.
L.A. Men's Central Jail, 441 Beauchet St., 90012. Tel: 213-974-8081. Rev. George Horan; Bros. Lawrence J. Moen, C.M.F.; Tom Cunningham, C.S.C.; Mr. Pacifico Diaz.
North County Correctional Facility, 29340 The Old Road, Saugus, 91350. Tel: 805-295-7800, Ext. 5217. Mr. William B. McKinley.
Pitchess Honor Rancho, 29300 The Old Road, Saugus, 91350. Bros. Eugene Blee, S.S.S. Tel: 805-257-8830; Gerald T. Chumik, O.F.M. Tel: 805-257-8815; Mr. Jack L. Fithian. Tel: 805-257-8853; Sr. Elizabeth O'Keefe, R.S.H.M. Tel: 805-257-8840.
Sybil Brand Institute, 4500 East City Terrace Drive, LA, 90063. Tel: 213-267-2809. Mrs. Karen E. Brudney; Sr. Mary Leo Grijalva, S.N.J.M.; Sr. Rose Waldron, D.M.J.

DOWNEY. *Los Padrinos Juvenile Hall*. Sr. Teresa Doherty, R.S.C.

LANCASTER. *Challenger Youth Hall*. Mrs. Bertha Maldanado.

SANTA BARBARA. *Juvenile/Adult Facilities*. Tel: 805-685-5326; 681-5334. Mrs. Beth Morales.

SANTA MARIA. *Juvenile Hall*. Beth Morales.

SAUGUS. *Pitchess Honor Rancho*. Bro. Eugene Blee, S.S.S.; Sr. Elizabeth O'Keefe, R.S.H.M.; Bro. Gerald Chumik, O.F.M.; Mr. John Fifthian; Mr. William McKinley.

SYLMAR. *San Fernando Valley Juvenile Hall*. Ms. Doriscia Briceni.

VENTURA. *Ventura County Jail*. Bro. Jerome Schwabe, C.S.C.
Ventura Juvenile Restitution Project. Bro. Jerome Schwabe, C.S.C.
Ventura Juvenile/Adult Facilities. Tel: 805-652-5725; 641-0715. Bro. Jerome Schwabe, C.S.C.

Camps

LOS ANGELES. *Juvenile Probation Camps*.
Camp C.B. Afflerbaugh, La Verne.
Camp Dorothy Kirby Center.
Camp David Gonzales, Calabasas.
Camp Holton.
Camp Glen Rockey, San Dimas.
Camp McLauren Hall.
Camp Miller.
Camp John Munz, Lake Hughes.
Camp Paige.
Camp Kenyon J. Scudder, Saugus.
Camp Joseph Scott, Saugus.
Camp Kilpatrick, Malibu.
Camp Louis Routh, Tujunga.
Camp Wm. V. Mendenhall, Lake Hughes.
Camp Holton Placement Center, San Fernando.
Sierra Conservation Camps, California Department of Correction.
#4 Fransciquito, Saugus. Tel: 805-296-4409.
#11 Acton, Tel: 805-268-0113.
#13 Malibu, Tel: 213-457-2253.
#16 Mount Gleason, Palmdale. Tel: 805-947-7784.
#19 Julius Klein, Azusa. Tel: 818-910-1213.

Other Correctional Institutions

LOS ANGELES. *Metropolitan Detention Center*, 535 N. Alameda, 90053. Tel: 213-485-0439. Rev. Mark Santo, Chap.

LOMPOC. *Federal Correction Institution*, 3600 Guard Rd., 93436. Tel: 805-736-4154, Ext. 645. Rev. William Hoops.
U.S. Penitentiary, 3901 Klein Blvd., 93436. Tel: 805-735-2771, Ext. 450. Rev. Michael Kirkness, Chap.

TERMINAL ISLAND. *Federal Correction Institution*. Rev. Frank Tinajero, S.B.D., Chap.

On Special or Other (Arch)Diocesan Assignment:
Reverend Fathers—
Fessard, Gerald B., J.C.L., Judge, Tribunal Office, 340 Norumbega Dr., Monrovia, CA 91016

On Duty Outside the Archdiocese:
Reverend Fathers—
Brennan, Dennis
Cummins, Charles T.
Fader, John J.
Joy, Laurence
Kane, Brian E.
King, Gerard
King, Gregory
Martin, Diosdado
Murphy, John
O'Shea, Patrick
Palacios, Joseph W.
Parish, John G.
Shine, Cornelius
Tacderas, Joseph
Tucker, James S.
Young, Gerald A.
Zak, Steven B.

Military and VA Chaplains:
Reverend Fathers—
Barrett, Edward J.
Blair, Stephen N.
Collins, John M.
Hall, Finbar
Kelly, Francis
Kelly, Thomas D.
Llanos, Philip S.
Marrell, Dennis P.
McNulty, Gerard J.
Miller, Leo M., O.M.I.
Moss, Donald G.
O'Neill, Michael F.
Pokladowski, Gregory

Graduate Studies:
Reverend Fathers—
Anguiano, James
Cahalane, Timothy
Ramos, Gilbert
Riebe, Gary, S.V.D.
Wilson, Guy, S.T.

Sick Leave:
Reverend Fathers—
Bebek, Dominic L.
Buckley, Michael D.
Cullen, Francis J.
Dawson, John H.
Griffin, Noel
LaNier, Michael L.
Lee, Joseph P.
McDonnell, Anthony
Meskill, Thomas A.
Nuanez, Anthony
O'Connor, John C.
Shimmaly, Edward E.
Thompson, Jerome H.
Warren, Thomas

Retired:
Most Rev.—
Arzube, Juan A., c/o Sacred Heart Church, 2889 N. Lincoln Ave., Altadena, CA 91001-4598
Ward, John J., 3424 Wilshire Blvd., Los Angeles, CA 90010-2241
Reverend Monsignors—
Atwill, William H., 68 Balboa Coves, Newport Beach, CA 92663
Barry, Wiliam J., 68 Balboa Coves, Newport Beach, CA 92663
Biedermann, Arnold, P.O. Box 4037, Ventura, CA 93007
Boyer, Leland J., St. Bede the Venerable, 215 Foothill, La Canada, CA 81001-0809
Brennan, Joseph F., 800 E. Ocean Blvd., #1205, Long Beach, CA 91011-0809
Brosnan, John R., St. Ann Church, 2302 Riverdale Ave., Los Angeles, CA 90031-1133
Caslin, Peter C., St. Bartholomew, 252 Granada Ave., Long Beach, CA 90803
Clark, Laurence E., 15322 Roselle Ave., Lawndale, CA 90260
Clyne, James B., Nazareth House, 3333 Manning Ave., Los Angeles, CA 90064-4804
Collins, Fachtna P., P.O. Box 535, Montrose, CA 91020
Condon, Michael J., St. Anthony, 2511 S. C St., P.O. Box 2215, Oxnard, CA 93034-2215
Condon, Robert, Nazareth House, 3333 Manning Ave., Los Angeles, CA 90064-4804
Crean, Timothy J., Assumption of the B.V.M., 2640 E. Orange Grove Blvd., Pasadena, CA 91107
Dessert, James A., 944 W. Robert Ave., Oxnard, CA 93030
Diomartich, Felix S., St. Anthony, 712 N. Grand Ave., Los Angeles, CA 90012-2299
Doherty, John B., Dana Point Mobile Home Estates, 34202 Del Obispo, Space No. 85, Dana Point, CA 92629
Donnelly, Lawrence E., 1065 W. Lomita Rd., Harbor City, CA 90710
Esutin, Charles E., 16151 Elgenia St., Covina, CA 91722
Folliard, John P., St. Cornelius Church, 5500 E. Wardlow Rd., Long Beach, CA 90808-3698
Gara, Robert, St. Rita, 50 E. Alegrai Ave., Sierra Madre, CA 91024
Grill, Philip L., San Roque, 325 Argonne Cir., Santa Barbara, CA 93105-2798
Gualderon, Ernest J., St. Anthony, 540 Olive Ave., Long Beach, CA 90802-2651
Hayes, Thomas G., Holy Cross, 1740 Cliff Dr., Santa Barbara, CA 93109-1698
Holland, Ian, P.O. Box 11475, Marina Del Rey, CA 90295
Hourihan, James, St. Andrew, 311 N. Raymond Ave., Pasadena, CA 91103-3896
Kearney, Joseph V., St. Joseph, 5048 El Carro Ln., Carpinteria, CA 93013-1450
Kelly, Matthew H., Pinyon Crest, P.O. Box 253, Mountain Center, CA 92361
Kennedy, Christopher J., 3938 Cerritos Ave., Long Beach, CA 90807-3799
Konoske, Paul M., SS. Felicitas and Perpetua, 1190 Palomar Rd., San Marino, CA 91108-2224
Kucingis, John A., St. Casimir, 2718 St. George St., Los Angeles, CA 90027
Lirette, Arthur J., P.A., Holy Family Church, 209 East Lomita Ave., Glendale, CA 91205-1689
McCabe, Vincent, 1270 Franciscan Ct. #8, Carpenteria, CA 93013
McGovern, Thomas, 564 Bellflower Blvd. #3, Long Beach, CA 90814
McGrath, Andrew, 101 South "U" St. #5, Lompoc, CA 93436-7299
McNulty, Patrick, 2501 West Avenue 33, Los Angeles, CA 90065-2892
Mulcahy, James R., St. Louis of France, 13935 E. Temple Ave., La Puente, CA 91746
Murray, Richard H., St. Bernardine of Siena, 24410 Calvert St., Woodland Hills, CA 91367-1099
Naughton, John T., St. Mel Church, 20870 Ventura Blvd., Woodland Hills, CA 91364-2396
Navin, Cyril, St. Cyril of Jerusalem Church, 4601 Firmament Ave., Encino, CA 91436-3108
O'Brien, Kenneth R., P.O. Box 279, Oak View, CA 93022
O'Brien, Thomas L., St. John of God Nursing Home, 2035 West Adams Blvd., Los Angeles, CA 90018
O'Callaghan, James A., St. John Vianney Church, 1345 Turnbull Canyon Rd., Hacienda Heights, CA 91745-2699
O'Connell, Thomas, St. Jude Church, 32032 West Lindero Canyon Rd., Westlake Village, CA 91361-4270
O'Connor, Michael J., St. Mel, 20870 Ventura Blvd., Woodland Hills, CA 91364-2396
O'Reilly, Bernard, 15360 Virginia Ave., Paramount, CA 90723
O'Sullivan, Peter, St. John Baptist, 16545 Chatsworth St., Granada Hills, CA 91344
O'Sullivan, Thomas Joseph, Visitation Church, 6561 W. 80th St., Los Angeles, CA 90045-3716
Osborne, Francis M., Our Lady of Grace, 5011 White Oak Ave., Encino, CA 91316-3799
Rademacher, Glen A., P.O. Box 230357, Encinitas, CA 92023-0357
Ravlic, Cornelius C., 239 Somerset Dr., Kalispell, MT 59901
Redahan, Patrick J., St. Joseph, 11854 Acacia Ave., Hawthorne, CA 90251-3083
Reilly, John J., 16222 Monterey Lane, Space 273, Huntington Beach, CA 92649
Sharpe, Joseph F., P.O. Box 240, Balboa Island, CA 92662
Sheridan, John V., Our Lady of Malibu, 3625 S. Winter Canyon Rd., Malibu, CA 90265

Sullivan, Daniel F., 3333 Manning Ave., Los Angeles, CA 90064-4804
Valle, Fernando, 2nda Avenida A3-44, Zona #1, Guatemala 001, Guatemala
Von Son, Henry A., 11075 S.W. Muirwood, Portland, OR 97225
Walsh, Michael, Monea, Ardmore, Youghal, County Cork, Ireland
Walsh, Robert, Holy Angels, 370 Campus Dr., Arcadia, CA 91006-6917
Young, John M., 4142 Los Padres Dr., Fallbrook, CA 91006-92028

Reverend Fathers—
Bellavista, Jose, 14334 Fallon Ave., P.O. Box 201, Norwalk, CA 90650
Bernardo, Emilio A., 2006 Seventh Ave., Los Angeles, CA 90018
Bradley, Robert M., 202 Cole Rd., Sarver, PA 16055
Bray, Kevin, St. Joseph Convalescent Hospital, 2462 E. Ojai Ave., P.O. Box 760, Ojai, CA 93023
Byrne, Robert P., Nazareth House, 3333 Manning Ave., Los Angeles, CA 90064-4804
Combs, Regis V., Ventura Marina Park, 1215 Anchor Way, Space 74, Ventura, CA 93001. Tel: 805-644-1026
Cooley, John E., 31402 Paseo del Mar, Laguna Niguel, CA 92677-2745
Coronado, Genero, 2505 W. Foothill Blvd., #145, San Bernardino, CA 92410
Coronel, Juan S., 63 Pinagcuruzan, Alitagtag, Batangas Philippines
Cotter, Patrick John, 1854 Hanscom Dr., South Pasadena, CA 91030
Cunningham, John F., 2564 Creston Dr., Los Angeles, CA 90068
Dao, Nhoung V., 5571 Angelus Ave., San Gabriel, CA 91776
DeDominici, Lorenzo, Mary Star of the Sea, 870 W. 8th St., San Pedro, CA 90731-3091
DeJonghe, Harold J., Nazareth House, 3333 Manning Ave., Los Angeles, CA 90064-4804
Delaney, Matthew S., P.O. Box 2007, Seal Beach, CA 90740
Delany, John M., P.O. Box 4083, Seal Beach, CA 90740
Duffy, Eugene J., Bridge St., Louisburgh, County Mayo, Ireland
Eves, John A., P.O. Box 3602, Long Beach, CA 90803
Fallon, John J., Nazareth House, 3333 Manning Ave., Los Angeles, CA 90064-4804
Feeney, John J., Nazareth House, 3333 Manning, Los Angeles, CA 90064-4804
Feeney, Robert J., St. Ignatius Residence, 26 Sea Rd., Galway City, Ireland
Feifel, Eugene, S.V.D., Nazareth House, 3333 Manning Ave., Los Angeles, CA 90064
Gabriel, Vicente S., 3045 N. Gold Star Dr., Long Beach, CA 90810-2708
Gomez, Vicente, 11255 Crossdale Ave., Norwalk, CA 90650
Gubbins, John F., P.O. Box 1205, Hollywood, CA 90078
Han, Andrew, P.O. Box 1081, Encinitas, CA 92024
Hanly, John J., Nazareth House, 3333 Manning Ave., Los Angeles, CA 90064-4804
Harman, Charles W., 261 South Rodeo Dr., Beverly Hills, CA 90212
Hunter, William R., St. John of God Nursing Home, 2035 W. Adams Blvd., Los Angeles, CA 90018
Infuhr, Frank J., St. John of God Nursing Home, 2035 W. Adams, Los Angeles, CA 90018
Jennings, Bernard J., St. Elizabeth, 1849 N. Lake Ave., Altadena, CA 91001-3097
Johnson, Henry J., 1211 North Garsden, Covina, CA 91724
Kass, George, Nazareth House, 3333 Manning Ave., Los Angeles, CA 90064-4804
Kelly, Paul M.
Kennedy, John A., 5 Chester Square, Glenageary, Dublin Ireland
Lee, Peter, 605 South Sefton Ave., Monterey Park, CA 91754-1698
Lichtle, Thomas A., 658 Temple Ave., Long Beach, CA 90814
Luck, Robert O., 388 Thornhill Circle, Henderson, NV 89014
Maechler, Edmund F., 613 California St., Huntington Beach, CA 92648
Maechler, Gerald T., 18401 Delaware Ave., Huntington Beach, CA 92648
McGovern, Martin D., Mulranny, County Mayo, Ireland
McLaughlin, Thomas W., St. Teresa of Avila, 2216 Fargo St., Los Angeles, CA 90039-3198
Meilak, John, 5 Grunju St., Nadur Gozo, Malta-Europe
Merfeld, Vincent, 4536 Wilshire Blvd., #104, Los Angeles, CA 90010-4602
Merino, Santiago, 959 LaDeney Dr., Ontario, CA 91762
Meskill, Patrick A., 63 Ilex Dr., Newbury Park, CA 91320
Murphy, Denis J., Our Lady of the Assumption, 3175 Telegraph Rd., Ventura, CA 93003-3283
Nagy, Joseph, 5037 Navarro St., Los Angeles, CA 90032
Nicolas, Marcos, Avenida de la Paz 120, Logrono (Rioja), 26006 Spain
Nocero, Pascal F., P.O. Box 279, Oak View, CA 93022
O'Sullivan, Thomas C., Our Lady of Mt. Carmel Church, 1300 E. Valley Rd., Santa Barbara, CA 93108-1294
Pisano, Andrew, 6938 Grange Ave., Bell Gardens, CA 90201
Pokladowski, Gregory
Potthoff, Donald W., St. Denis Church, 2151 Diamond Bar Blvd., P.O. Box 4096, Diamond Bar, CA 91765-2860
Raymundo, Gregorio G., 419 Cameron Pl., Glendale, CA 91207
Rodriguez, Lawrence, Soto y Amio, Santoveniada San Marcos, C.P. 24125, (Leon) Spain
Rucker, Neville, Corpus Christi Church, 887 Toyopa Dr., P.O. Box 887, Pacific Palisades, CA 90272-0887
Sanchez, Eliseo, 13308 East Loumont, North Whittier, CA 90601
Spada, Rino CS, St. Charles Residence, 10651 Vinedale St., Sun Valley, CA 91352
Thomas, Sylvester J., Mary Star of the Sea Church, 870 West Eighth St., San Pedro, CA 90731-3091
Vecsey, Stephen N., 1120 Northwood Rd., 186D, Seal Beach, CA 90740
Villa Gomez, Nemorio, Calle Durando 1208, S.H. Guadalajara, Jalisco, CP442-60 Mexico
Villacis, Jose H.
Villegas, Samuel C., 7125 Mission Pl., Huntington Park, CA 90255-5299
Weible, Thomas C., 4234 North Main St. #508, Fall River, MA 02720

Permanent Deacons:
Acquaviva, Dick, Unassigned
Adams, Emile, Jr., St. Bernadette, Los Angeles
Adams, J. Rodger, Our Lady of the Assumption Church, Ventura
Adams, James V., Chaminade College Preparatory, Chatsworth
Alexander, Hosea, Sr., St. Agatha, Los Angeles
Allen, John P., Corpus Christi, Pacific Palisades
Aranda, Fernando, Jr., Our Lady of Solitude, Los Angeles
Arpaia, Frank, St. Elisabeth, Van Nuys
Arroyo, Miguel, Our Lady of Guadalupe, Los Angeles
Aust, William, All Souls, Alhambra
Balbuena, Wesley M., Jr., St. Elisabeth, Van Nuys
Battle, Joe T., St. Philip Neri, Lynwood
Bednar, George J., St. Mary Magdalen, Camarillo
Bohlig, Alden, St. Barnabas, Long Beach
Brandlin, Thomas E., Unassigned
Bravo, Anthony, St. Gerard Majela, Los Angeles
Burke, John, La Purisma Concepcion, Lompoc
Caffrey, Aloysius, St. Jude, Westlake Village
Caputo, Ed, Blessed Junipero Serra, Quartz Hill
Carmody, Richard, St. Louis de Montford, Santa Maria
Caro, Jose, St. Cecilia, Los Angeles
Castorena, John G., Santa Clara, Oxnard
Cellner, Jerry, St. Bernardine of Siena, Woodland Hills
Chacon, Paul, St. Bernard, Los Angeles
Chavez, Gilbert M., San Gabriel Mission, San Gabriel
Clinton, Jack, Holy Name of Mary, San Dimas
Collins, Oscar R., St. Patrick, North Hollywood
Conrey, Fred, Immaculate Conception, Monrovia
Coplen, John, St. Frances de Sales, Sherman Oaks
Corwin, Richard, St. Margaret Mary Alacoque, Lomita
Crisafulli, Nino D., Mary Star of the Sea, San Pedro
Curran, Nicholas P., Holy Cross, Santa Barbara
Delgado, Eduardo, St. John Vianney, Hacienda Hgts.
Denisac, Charles M., Jr., Our Lady of Perpetual Help, Downey
Dieter, Frank, St. Lawrence Martyr, Redondo Beach
Dillon, James, Holy Angels Church of the Deaf, Vernon
Doane, Allan E., St. Thomas Aquinas, Ojai
Dornan, Richard, St. Jude, Westlake Village
Duke, Oscar, St. Anthony, Oxnard
Dumlao, Felix, St. Anthony of Padua, Gardena
Escovedo, Arthur, Our Lady of the Assumption, Claremont
Estey, Marvin, St. Dorothy, Glendora
Fajardo, Richard, Resurrection, Los Angeles
Farley, James, Our Lady of the Assumption, Ventura
Favela, Jacobo M., Jr., St. Martha, Valinda
FitzGerald, Gerald M., St. Francis of Assisi, Fillmore
Fitzgerald, James, St. Mary of the Assumption, Whittier
Fitzpatrick, Arthur, St. Paul of the Cross, La Mirada
Freeman, Mike, St. Bruno, Whittier
Frias, Sam, San Fernando Mission, Mission Hills
Fry, Ralph M., Sacred Heart, Covina
Galido, Juan, Our Lady of Lourdes, Northridge
Garcia, Armando R., St. Joseph, Los Angeles
Gaudin, John, Holy Name of Jesus, Los Angeles
Goodreau, Theodore, St. Anthony, El Segundo
Goodspeed, Lyle, St. John Neumann, Santa Maria
Gueringer, Ludger A., Padre Serra, Camarillo
Guerra, Ruben, St. Joseph, La Puente
Gutierrez, Eliseo, Sacred Heart, Covina
Hall, Willard J., Sr., St. John the Evangelist, Santa Maria
Halley, James, St. Matthew, Long Beach
Halvorsen, Douglas A., St. Louis de Montfort, Santa Maria
Hamm, Richard S., St. Peter Claver, Simi Valley
Hammonds, Johnnie, St. Mary Magdalen, Camarillo
Harrison, Russell J., SS Peter and Paul, Wilmington
Hawkins, Bill, St. Brigid, Los Angeles
Hays, Charles D., La Purisima Concepcion, Lompoc
Henry, James J., St. Anthony, Oxnard
Hillman, Steven, St. Elizabeth Ann Seton, Rowland Heights
Holly, Chester N., St. John Eudes, Chatsworth
Huff, David W., Holy Cross, Santa Barbara
Karl, Richard J., Our Lady of Perpetual Help, Santa Clarita
Kunsemiller, John H., Santa Clara Church, Oxnard
Lacy, William S., St. Joseph the Worker, Canoga Park
Lambey, Alvin S., Mother of Sorrows, Los Angeles
Landa, William, St. Philip the Apostle, Pasadena
Lanoix, Gilbert, St. Brigid, Los Angeles
Ledoux, Joseph, St. Albert the Great, Compton
Lee, Paul D., St. Bruno, Whittier
Liendo, Manuel, St. Mary of the Assumption, Santa Maria
Lipski, Alexander, St. Cornelius, Long Beach
Lira, Pedro, St. Catherine of Siena, Reseda
Lopez, Jose, St. Benedict, Montebello
Magaila, Matilde, St. Catherine Laboure, Torrance
Martinez, Jesse, St. Thomas Aquinas, Monterey Park
Martinez, Manuel J., Our Lady of Sorrows, Santa Barbara
Martinez, Randolph M., Santa Clara, Oxnard
McHugh, Daniel J., St. Bernardine of Siena, Woodland Hills
McKinley, Braden, Sacred Heart, Ventura
McPheeters, Jon C., St. Anthony, Oxnard
Medina, Richard J., Our Lady of Perpetual Help, Downey
Mejia, Guadalupe J., Holy Family, Artesia
Messer, John, St. Anthony, San Gabriel
Millholland, Frank, St. Albert the Great, Compton
Mimiaga, Guillermo, St. Raphael, Los Angeles
Modugno, Larry, St. Mary Magdalen, Camarillo
Moloney, Doug, St. Christopher, West Covina
Morgan, Richard, Blessed Sacrament, Los Angeles
Nawrocik, Zenon L., Marian Medical Center, Santa Maria
Nguyen, Loc, St. Christopher, West Covina
Noriega, Rstie, Incarnation, Glendale
Nosari, Ernest, St. Rita, Sierra Madre
Olivas, William, St. Thomas Aquinas, Ojai
Orth, Joseph, St. Euphrasia, Granada Hills
Parish, Harold A., J.C.D., Mary Star of the Sea, Oxnard
Patlan, Servando, Sr., St. Gregory the Great, Whittier
Patterson, Gary R., Our Lady of Guadalupe, Irwindale
Pelletier, Frederick H., Holy Family, Glendale
Pepe, Joseph, Office of the Catholic Chaplain, NCB, Oxnard
Picard, John B., Blessed Junipera Serra, Camarillo
Pina, Thomas, St. Anthony, Oxnard
Pruitt, Richard, Little Co. of Mary Hospital, Torrance
Ramirez, Fidel M., Mary Star of the Sea, Oxnard
Rascati, Wayne, St. Raphael, Santa Barbara
Rios, Fred, Our Lady of the Miraculous Medal, Montebello
Rivas, Manuel, Santa Clara, Oxnard
Rivera, Raymond, St. Bridget of Sweden, Van Nuys
Rivet, Joseph, St. Louise de Marillac, Covina
Robinson, James M., St. Paschal Baylon, Thousand Oaks
Rodriguez, Hernando, Resurrection, Los Angeles

Ryan, Jack, Santa Barbara Mission, Santa Barbara
Ryan, Joseph M., St. Raymond, Downey
Sanchez, Enrique R., Holy Cross, Santa Barbara
Sangster, William B., San Roque, Santa Barbara
Saucedo, Valentin, St. Aloysius Gonzaga, Los Angeles
Schwerdt, Paul, Blessed Junipero Serra, Quartz Hill
Sebenius, Wayland, "Gus", St. Therese, Alhambra
Sevilla, Rodolfo, Our Lady Queen of Angels, (La Placita) Los Angeles
Shea, Clarke, St. Raphael, Goleta
Shinkle, Richard D., St. James, Redondo Beach
Simanski, Donald E., Sacred Heart, Lancaster
Skupnik, Raymond P., St. Cyprian, Long Beach
Soto, Antonio P., St. Hilary, Pico Rivera
Spada, Joseph D., Our Lady of the Miraculous Medal, Montebello
Suh, Ignatius Jin, Korean Catholic Center (St. Bridget of Sweden), Canoga Park
Taufer, Wm. Dale, St. Bernardine of Siena, Woodland Hills
Torres, Antonio B., San Franciso, Los Angeles
Torres, Pedro M., Our Lady of Loretto, Los Angeles
Ulibarri, Ralph, St. Catherine Laboure, Torrance
Vazquez, Roberto L., St. John Chrysostom, Inglewood
Vega, Cris T., St. Gertrude, Bell Gardens
Vega, Heriberto (Ed), Our Lady of the Valley, Canoga Park
Victorin, Rafael, St. Augustine Church, Culver City
Viramontes, Raul, Holy Family, Artesia
Weber, Paul S., St. Jerome, Los Angeles
Wilson, Peter, St. Rose of Lima, Simi Valley

INSTITUTIONS LOCATED IN THE ARCHDIOCESE

[A] SEMINARIES, ARCHDIOCESAN

CAMARILLO. *St. John's Seminary*, 5012 Seminary Rd., 93012-2598. Tel: 805-482-2755; Fax: 805-484-4074. Major Seminary of the Archdiocese of Los Angeles. Revs. Jeremiah J. McCarthy, Rector & Pres.; Richard Benson, C.M., Vice Rector; Austin Doran, Spiritual Dir.; Leon Hutton, Dir. of Students; Sr. M. Regina Robbins, S.N.D., Dir. of Field Education; Sr. Cecilia Canales, O.P., Dir. of Spiritual Formation; Rev. John D. Stoeger, Assoc. Dir. of Spiritual Formation; Ms. Jacquelein Rotter, Business Mgr.; Mr. Greg Julius, Facilities Mgr.; Dr. Mark F. Fischer, Ph.D., Dir. of Admissions; Mr. Ron Hastings, M.L.S., Librarian; Ms. Rosa Coleman, Registrar; Revs. Richard Benson, C.M.; John P. Brennan, S.M.A.; Jorge Del Valle, M.Sp.S.; Austin Doran; Joseph Duc Minh; Daniel Harris, C.M.; Rev. Msgr. Helmut Heffner; Revs. Leon Hutton; Jeremiah McCarthy; Kevin McCracken, C.M.; Charles E. Miller, C.M.; Edward Owens, O.SS.T.; John Stoeger; Michael F. Walsh, C.M.; Sr. Cecilia Canales, O.P.; Sr. Sheila McNiff, S.H.C.J. Priests 14; Sisters 3; Lay Teachers 5; Students 103.

St. John's Seminary College of the Archdiocese of Los Angeles, 5118 Seminary Rd., 93012-2598. Tel: 805-482-2755; Fax: 805-987-5097.
Staffed by Archdiocesan, Vincentian and Sulpician Priests. Revs. Edward Wm. Clark, President & Rector; Calixto Lopez, C.M., Vice Rector, Dean Formation; James Stehly, Dir. Students & Liturgy; Lawrence Herrera, S.J., Dir. of Spiritual Formation; Sr. Francis Edwards, S.P., Asst. Librarian. Additional Faculty: Mr. Eric Nicolet, Dean Academics; Revs. Gary Landry, C.M., Dir. Admissions; Richard MacDonough, S.S.; Anthony Lobo, S.S.; Joseph Duc-Minh; Sr. Patrice Benson, S.S.L.; Sr. Catherine Foley, S.S.C., Dir. of Apostolic Work Program; Rev. Ramon Farre, Sch.P.; Mr. Jackson Schoos, Dir. of Music. Priests 9; Sisters 3; Lay Teachers 16; Students 74.

[B] SEMINARIES, RELIGIOUS OR SCHOLASTICATES

LOS ANGELES. *Canons Regular of the Immaculate Conception-Novitiate*, 1523 Golden Gate Ave., 90026. Revs. Pasquale Vuoso, C.R.I.C., Supr.; Charles R. Lueras, C.R.I.C.; James G. Garceau, C.R.I.C.; Sergio Garcia, C.R.I.C., St. Clare's, 19606 Calla Way Rd., c/o 27341 Camp Plenty, Canyon Country, 91351. Rev. William B. Ustaski, C.R.I.C., Nazareth House, 3333 Manning Ave., 90064. Rev. John Taggart, C.R.I.C.

St. Joseph's Novitiate, 2035 W. Adams Blvd., 90018; Fax: 213-731-5987. Hospitaller Brothers of St. John of God. Bros. Edward Francis McEnroe, O.H., Prov.; Stephen de la Rosa, O.H., Formation Dir. Brothers 4; Novices 1; Scholastics 3.

BELLFLOWER. *De Sales Hall*. Pre-Novitiate. 13856 Bellflower, 90706. Tel: 310-866-3307; 925-0963; Fax: 310-867-3929. Staffed by Salesians of Don Bosco. Revs. Jerry Bonjean, S.D.B., Dir. of Community & Prog.; Cris Hood-Rosales, S.D.B., Treas.; Bill Bolton, S.D.B., Formation Counselor; Bro. Jack McLinden, S.D.B., Plant Mgr. Priests 3; Brothers 1; Candidates 4.

NORTH HILLS. *Carmel West Community*, 8936 Woodley Ave., 91343. Revs. Dominic Savino, O.Carm.; Peter J. Liuzzi, O.Carm.; Terrence Pfender.

SANTA BARBARA. *College of the Queen of Peace*, P.O. Box 568, 93067-0500. 801 Ladera Ln., 93108-1625. Tel: 805-969-4711. Legal Title: *Jesuit Novitiate of Santa Barbara*.
Jesuit-in-Charge: Treasurer, California Province, Society of Jesus, P.O. Box 519, 95031-0519. Tel: 408-354-8886.

SANTA MARIA. *St. Joseph Seminary (Josephite Fathers' Novitiate)*, 180 Patterson Rd., 93455. Tel: 805-937-5378. Revs. Thomas J. Elewaut, C.J.; Edward Jalbert, C.J.; John A. Mayhew, C.J.; Bede L. Johnson, C.J.; Bro. Christopher Aguilar, C.J. Priests 4; Brothers 1.

SANTA YNEZ. *San Lorenzo Novitiate and Seminary*, 1802 Sky Dr., P.O. Box 247, 93460. Tel: 805-688-5630. Capuchin Fransiscan Friars. Revs. Gerald Barron, O.F.M.Cap., Guardian, Asst. Novice Dir.; Christopher Kearney, Vicar, Postulant Dir.; Sebastian Ward, O.F.M.Cap., Chap.; Bros. Joseph Slominski, O.F.M.Cap.; Pius Higgins, O.F.M.Cap. Prayer Center: Priests 3; Brothers 2; Postulants 2.

[C] COLLEGES AND UNIVERSITIES

LOS ANGELES. *Loyola Marymount University*, 7101 W. 80th St., 90045-2699. Tel: 310-338-2700.
For a complete listing, refer to the Colleges and Universities section.

Mount St. Mary's College. Chalon Campus, 12001 Chalon Rd., 90049. Tel: 310-476-2237; Fax: 310-471-9028.
For a complete listing, refer to the Colleges and Universities section.

RANCHO PALOS VERDES. *Marymount College, Palos Verdes, California*, 30800 Palos Verdes Dr., E., 90275-6299. Tel: 310-377-5501.
For a complete listing, refer to the Colleges and Universities section.

ROSEMEAD. *Don Bosco Technical Institute*, 1151 San Gabriel Blvd., 91770-4299. Tel: 818-307-6500; Fax: 818-280-9316.
For a complete listing, refer to the Colleges and Universities section.

SANTA PAULA. *Thomas Aquinas College*, 10000 N. Ojai Rd., 93060. Tel: 805-525-4417.
For a complete listing, refer to the Colleges and Universities section.

[D] HIGH SCHOOLS, ARCHDIOCESAN

LOS ANGELES. *Bishop Conaty-Our Lady of Loretto High School*. (Girls), 2900 W. Pico Blvd., 90006. Tel: 213-737-0012. Rev. Anthony Page, Chap. Sisters 6; Lay Teachers 12; Students 360.

Bishop Mora Salesian High School. (Boys), 960 S. Soto St., 90023. Tel: 213-261-7124; Fax: 213-261-9474. Salesians of Don Bosco. Mr. Manuel Villarreal, Prin.; Mr. Mark Johnson, Vice Prin.; Revs. Cris Rosales, S.D.B.; James Nieblas, S.D.B. In res., Rev. Carmine Viero, Prov.; Bros. Thomas Keegan, S.D.B.; Philip Mandile, S.D.B.; Robert Hennings, S.D.B. Students 420.

Daniel Murphy Catholic High School. (Boys), 241 S. Detroit St., 90036. Tel: 213-935-1161; Fax: 213-935-1621. Keith T. Murphy, Prin. Priests 1; Lay Teachers 21; Students 429.

Sacred Heart High School. (Girls), 2111 N. Griffin Ave., 90031. Tel: 213-225-2209; Fax: 213-225-5046. Sr. Reina Perea, O.P., Prin. Lay Teachers 20; Students 400.

Verbum Dei High School. (Boys), 11100 S. Central Ave., 90059-1199. Tel: 213-564-6651. Conducted by the Archdiocese of Los Angeles. Mrs. Wilma D. Elbouhnini, Prin.; Bro. Richard Morrill, S.V.D. Brothers 1; Sisters 2; Permanent Deacon 1; Lay Teachers 13; Students 255.

BURBANK. *Bellarmine Jefferson High School*. (Coed), 465 E. Olive Ave., 91501. Tel: 818-972-1400 (Main Office); 972-1401 (Athletic); 972-1402 (Attendance), Ext. 5. Mrs. Mary Ellen Rausch, Prin. Sisters 2; Brothers 2; Lay Teachers 30; Students 530.

COMPTON. *Queen of Angels Academy*. (Girls), 823 E. Compton Blvd., 90220. Tel: 310-515-3891; Fax: 310-515-3894. Conducted by the Archdiocese of Los Angeles. Staffed by the Sisters of the Holy Family. Sr. Henrietta Lazare, S.S.F., Prin. Sisters 6; Lay Teachers 13; Students 204.

DOWNEY. *Pius X - St. Matthias High School*, 7851 E. Gardendale St., 90242.

GARDENA. *Junipero Serra High School*, 14830 S. Van Ness Ave., 90249. Tel: 310-324-6675; Fax: 310-352-4953. Rev. Sabato Pilato, Prin.; Mr. Martin Griffin, Vice Prin. Lay Teachers 25; Students 415.

LA PUENTE. *Bishop Amat Memorial High School*. (Coed), 14301 Fairgrove Ave., 91746. Tel: 818-962-2495. Conducted by the Archdiocese of Los Angeles. Rev. Msgr. Aidan M. Carroll, Prin.; Mrs. Kathleen Wiard, Vice Prin. Sisters 4; Lay Teachers 76; Students 1,655.

LA VERNE. *Damien Boys High School*, 2280 Damien Ave., 91750. Tel: 909-596-1946. Conducted by the Archdiocese of Los Angeles. Revs. Patrick Travers, SS.CC., Prin.; Peadar Cronin, SS.CC., Vice Prin.; Mr. Kenneth Kowalewski, Asst. Prin. & Campus Minister; Mr. Jeffrey Coray, Asst. Prin. Academic Affairs; Mr. Louis Casselle, Asst. Prin. Summer Program; Mr. Timothy Carlson, Asst. Prin. Student Activities; Rev. Donal McCarthy, SS.CC., Asst. Prin. Guidance; Mr. Thomas Carroll, Asst. Prin. Athletic Activities. Legal Title: *Congregation of the Sacred Hearts, Inc.* Faculty Res., 2150 Damien Ave., 91750. Priests 3; Lay Teachers 55; Students 1,100.

LAKEWOOD. *Saint Joseph High School*. (Girls), 5825 N. Woodruff Ave., 90713. Tel: 310-925-5073; Fax: 310-925-3315. Conducted by Archdiocese of Los Angeles. Terri Mendoza, Ph.D., Prin.; Revs. Alfonso Scott; James Henry, S.V.D. Priests 2; Sisters 7; Lay Teachers 42; Students 818.

LANCASTER. *Paraclete High School*. (Coed), 42145 N. 30th St., W., 93536. Tel: 805-943-3255; Fax: 805-722-9455. Conducted by Archdiocese of Los Angeles. Staffed by Divine Word Missionaries and Fathers of St. Joseph. Revs. William J. Caffrey, S.V.D., Prin.; Ernest Candelaria, C.S.J.; Joseph Scalco, C.S.J.; Leonard Petcavage, C.S.J.; Angelo Zonta, C.S.J. Priests 5; Lay Teachers 40; Students 725.

MISSION HILLS. *Alemany High School*, 15101 San Fernando Mission Blvd., 91345. Tel: 818-365-3925. Revs. Robert Milbauer, Prin.; Alberto Villalobos; Patrick Argue, SS.CC. (Ireland), Priests' Res., 15201 Rinaldi St., 91345. Brothers' Res., 15201 Rinaldi St., 91345. Priests 3; Brothers 3; Sisters 6; Lay Teachers 66; Students 1,450.

MONTEBELLO. *Cantwell Sacred Heart of Mary High School*. (Coed), 329 N. Garfield Ave., 90640. Tel: 213-887-2066; Fax: 213-724-4332. Archdiocesan Institution. Rosemary D. Libbon, Prin. Sisters 3; Lay Teachers 26; Students 500.

OXNARD. *Santa Clara High School*, 2121 Saviers Rd., 93033. Tel: 805-483-9502. Mr. Keith Murphy, Prin.; Mrs. Helen Scovell, Vice Prin. and Dean of Studies; Mrs. Kay Brisslinger, Asst. Prin. & Dean of Discipline; Sr. Patrice McGee, C.S.C., Campus Minister; Ms. Robin Fontana, Dir. of Activities; Bros. William Verheyen, C.F.M.M.; Edward Gresnigt, C.F.M.M. Brothers 2; Sisters 2; Lay Teachers 20; Students 380.

PLAYA DEL REY. *St. Bernard High School*. (Coed), 9100 Falmouth Ave., 90293. Tel: 310-823-4651. Conducted by Archdiocese of Los Angeles. Revs. James Anguiano, Prin.; Francis Boronat, Sch.P.; John Provenza. Priests 3; Sisters 4; Lay Teachers 39; Students 781.

POMONA. *Pomona Catholic High School*. (Girls), 533 W. Holt Ave., 91768. Tel: 909-623-5297. Sr. Feliz Gil-Jimenez, C.S.S.F., Prin.; Mrs. Ann Hardman, Dean of Students. Sisters 4; Lay Teachers 22; Students 350.

ROSEMEAD. *Don Bosco Technical Institute*. (Boys), 1151 San Gabriel Blvd., 91770-4299. Tel: 818-307-6500; Fax: 818-280-9316. Secondary Section.
Staffed by Salesians of St. John Bosco. Revs. Nicholas Reina, S.D.B., Pres.; Michael Gergen, S.D.B., Prin./Vice Pres.; Marc Rougeau, S.D.B.; Peter Bui, S.D.B. Priests 4; Brothers 10; Sisters 1; Lay Teachers 70; Students 758.

SANTA BARBARA. *Bishop Garcia Diego High School*. (Coed), 4000 La Colina Rd., 93110. Tel: 805-967-1266; Fax: 805-964-3178. Revs. Charles Hofschulte, C.J., Prin.; Alfred Verstreken, C.J. Priests 2; Sisters 1; Lay Teachers 24; Students 336. (Coed).

SANTA FE SPRINGS. *St. Paul High School*, 9635 S. Greenleaf Ave., 90670. Tel: 310-698-6246; Fax: 310-696-8396. Conducted by Archdiocese of Los Angeles. Rev. Robert J. Gallagher, Prin. Brothers 2; Sisters 4; Lay Teachers 54; Students 1,050.

SANTA MARIA. *St. Joseph High School*. (Coed), 4120 Bradley Rd., 93455. Tel: 805-937-2038. Conducted by Archdiocese of Los Angeles. Revs. Edward Jalbert, C.J.; Thomas Elewaut, C.J., 180 Patterson Rd., 93455. Priests 2; Sisters 1; Lay Teachers 33; Students 650.

TORRANCE. *Bishop Montgomery High School*. (Coed), 5430 Torrance Blvd., 90503. Tel: 310-540-2021. Conducted by the Archdiocese of Los Angeles. James F. Golden, Prin. Priests 3; Friars 1; Lay Teachers 67; Students 1,397.

VENTURA. *St. Bonaventure High School*. (Coed), 3167 Telegraph Rd., 93003-3281. Tel: 805-648-6836; Fax: 805-648-4903. Conducted by Archdiocese of Los

Angeles. Bro. Paulinus Horkan, O.S.F., Prin. Sisters 2; Brothers 1; Lay Teachers 32; Students 625.

[E] HIGH SCHOOLS, PAROCHIAL

LOS ANGELES. High Schools are maintained in the following parishes (for particulars refer to the individual parishes): Glendale: Holy Family; Long Beach: St. Anthony; San Gabriel: San Gabriel Mission; San Pedro: Mary Star of the Sea; Santa Monica: St. Monica; Van Nuys: St. Genevieve.

[F] HIGH SCHOOLS, PRIVATE

LOS ANGELES. *Cathedral High School.* (Boys), 1253 Bishops Rd., 90012. Tel: 213-225-2438; Fax: 213-222-7223. Conducted by the Brothers of the Christian Schools. Bro. J. Jerome Gallegos, F.S.C., Prin. Brothers 9; Sisters 1; Lay Teachers 26; Students 439.

Immaculate Heart High School. (Girls), 5515 Franklin Ave., 90028. Tel: 213-461-3651. Conducted by the Immaculate Heart Community. Sisters 5; Lay Teachers 36; Students 503.

Loyola High School, 1901 Venice Blvd., 90006. Tel: 213-381-5121; Fax: 213-387-0321. Jesuit Fathers. Revs. Gordon D. Bennett, S.J., Pres.; Patrick J. Cahalan, S.J.; Richard E. Cobb, S.J., Rector; J. Philip Conneally, S.J.; Robert T. Walsh, S.J., Prin.; Thomas H. O'Neill, S.J.; David W. MacDonald, S.J.; Lawrence B. Murphy, S.J.; Jerold W. Lindner, S.J.; Louis A. Peinado, S.J.; Kevin A. Leidich, S.J.; Thomas J. Carroll, S.J.; Mark K. Ciccone, S.J.; John I. Geiszel, S.J.; Thomas J. Reilley, S.J.; John P. McGarry, S.J.; Thomas F. McCormick, S.J.; James V. Schaukowitch, S.J. Priests 18; Brothers 2; Scholastics 3; Lay Teachers 66; Students 1,183.

Marymount High School. (Girls), 10643 Sunset Blvd., 90077. Tel: 310-472-1205. Religious of the Sacred Heart of Mary. Dr. Mary Ellen Gozdecki, Head. Priests 1; Sisters 4; Lay Teachers 39; Students 343.

Notre Dame Academy. (Girls), 2851 Overland Ave., 90064. Tel: 310-839-5289. Sr. Marie Paul, S.N.D., Prin. Sisters of Notre Dame of Los Angeles 6; Lay Teachers 35; Students 481.

ALHAMBRA. *Ramona Convent Secondary School, Ramona Convent of the Holy Names.* (Girls Grades 7-12), 1701 W. Ramona Rd., 91803-3099. Tel: 818-282-4151. Sr. Margaret Spiller, S.N.J.M., Prin. Sisters of Holy Names of Jesus and Mary 8; Lay Teachers 37; Students 525.

BELLFLOWER. *St. John Bosco High School*, 13640 S. Bellflower Blvd., 90706. Tel: 310-920-1734. Revs. Richard R. Presenti, S.D.B., Pres.; Frank Ribotta, S.D.B.; John DalMaso, S.D.B.; Michael Baptista, S.D.B.; Joseph Ahn Le, S.D.B.; Bros. Frank Bracchi, S.D.B.; Noel DeBruton, S.D.B.; Barney Hagus, S.D.B.; Timothy Nguyen, S.D.B.; Joseph Vu, S.D.B. Priests 5; Brothers 4; Lay Teachers 53; Students 1,033.

BURBANK. *Providence High School.* (Coed), 511 S. Buena Vista St., 91505. Tel: 818-846-8141; Fax: 818-843-8421. Sr. Lucille Dean, S.P., Prin.; Rafe Vega, Dir. Campus Ministry; C. Victor LeBreton, Vice Prin. Discipline & Student Affairs; Sr. Mary Hawkins, S.P., Vice Prin. Academics. Sisters 6; Lay Teachers 26; Students 526.

CHATSWORTH. *Chaminade College Preparatory*, Office of the President, 10210 Oakdale Ave., 91311-3533. Tel: 818-347-8300. 19800 Devonshire St., 91311. Tel: 818-363-8127. (Coed Grades 6-12). James V. Adams, Pres.; Gary E. Murphy, Prin. West Hills; Ms. Christine Hunter, Prin. Chatsworth. Legal Title: *Chaminade College Preparatory*. Priests 3; Sisters 3; Brothers 2; Lay Teachers 108; Students 1,690.

Marianist Community. Bro. LeRoy Viera, S.M., Dir.; Revs. Lawrence Mann, S.M.; Allen DeLong, S.M.; Edwin Johnson. Priests 3; Brothers 4; Students 1,690.

DOWNEY. *Pius X-St. Matthias High School*, 7851 E. Gardendale St., 90242. Tel: 310-861-2271; Fax: 310-869-8652. Mrs. Nancy Coonis, Prin. Sisters 2; Lay Teachers 31; Students 582.

ENCINO. *Crespi Carmelite High School*, 5031 Alonzo Ave., 91316. Tel: 818-345-1672. Rev. Frederick Tillotson, O.Carm., Prin./Pres.; Ms. Judy Flaherty, Treas.; Revs. Joseph Fitzgerald, O.Carm.; Benjamin Aguilar, O.Carm.; William Wert, O.Carm., Campus Min.; Bro. John Sprissler, O.Carm. In res., Revs. William Heery, O.Carm.; John Coleman, O.Carm. Priests 4; Brothers 1; Lay Teachers 35; Students 480.

GLENDORA. *St. Lucys's Priory High School.* (Girls), 655 W. Sierra Madre Ave., 91741. Tel: 818-335-3322. Conducted by the Benedictine Sisters. Sr. Monica Collins, O.S.B., Prin. Sisters 3; Lay Teachers 39; Students 865.

INGLEWOOD. *St. Mary's Academy.* (Girls), 701 Grace Ave., 90301. Tel: 310-674-8470. Sr. Nancy Munro, C.S.J., Prin. Sisters of St. Joseph of Carondelet 7; Lay Teachers 23; Students 445.

LA CANADA FLINTRIDGE. *Flintridge Sacred Heart Academy.* (Girls), 440 St. Katherine Dr., 91011. Tel: 818-356-1748. Legal Title: *Flintridge Sacred Heart Academy, A Corporation.* Sr. Ramona Bascom, O.P., Prin. Dominican Sisters of Mission San Jose 8; Lay Teachers 30; Students 385.

St. Francis High School. (Boys), 200 Foothill Blvd., 91011. Tel: 818-790-0325. Legal Title: *The Capuchin Franciscan Order of the Western American Province.* Revs. Matthew Elshoff, O.F.M.Cap., Pres. St. Francis High School; Jerome Cummings; Gregory Coiro, O.F.M.Cap.; Matthew Elshoff, O.F.M.Cap.; Chris Thiel, O.F.M.Cap.; Anthony Scannel, O.F.M.Cap.; Bros. Robert Edwards, O.F.M.Cap., Guardian of the Community; Bernard McAllister, Dir. of Vocations; Sr. Barbarine Houdek, O.S.F. Priests 5; Brothers 2; Sisters 1; Lay Teachers 32; Total Teachers 40; Students 620.

OJAI. *Villanova Preparatory School*, 12096 Ventura Ave., 93023-3999. Tel: 805-646-1464; Fax: 805-646-4430. Legal Title: *Villanova Preparatory School of California.* Revs. John P. Pejza, O.S.A., Pres.; John F. Glynn, O.S.A. Conducted by Augustinian Fathers (Order of St. Augustine). Priests 2; Sisters 1; Brothers 1; Lay Teachers 27; Students 270.

PASADENA. *La Salle High School*, 3880 E. Sierra Madre Blvd., 91107. Tel: 818-351-8951; Fax: 818-351-0275. Bro. Philip Clarke, F.S.C., Pres.; Mr. Patrick Bonacci, Prin. Brothers 2; Sisters 1; Lay Teachers 42; Students 696.

Mayfield Senior School of the Holy Child Jesus, 500 Bellefontaine St., 91105-2439. Tel: 818-799-9121; 213-682-2620; Fax: 818-799-8576. Mrs. Jeanne G. Holt, Register; Mrs. Edith Gardener, Business Mgr. Sisters 2; Lay Teachers 28; Students 255.

SHERMAN OAKS. *Notre Dame High School*, 13645 Riverside Dr., 91423. Tel: 818-501-2300; Fax: 818-501-0507. Bro. William C. Nick, C.S.C., Pres.; Mr. David G. Doyle, Prin. Brothers 6; Priests 1; Lay Teachers 58; Students 1,082.

SIERRA MADRE. *Alverno High School.* (Girls), 200 N. Michillinda Ave., 91024. Tel: 818-355-3463; Fax: 818-355-3153. Ann M. Gillick, M.S., Prin. Lay Teachers 18; Students 230.

THOUSAND OAKS. *La Reina High School.* (Girls Grades 7-12), 106 W. Janss Rd., 91360. Tel: 805-495-6494; Fax: 805-494-4966. Sr. Lisa Megaffin, S.N.D., Prin. Sisters of Notre Dame 3; Lay Teachers 38; Students 615.

WOODLAND HILLS. *Louisville High School.* (Girls), 22300 Mulholland Dr., 91364. Tel: 818-346-8812; Fax: 818-346-9483. Sr. Myra McPartland, S.S.L., Prin. Sisters 9; Lay Teachers 36; Students 460.

[G] MIDDLE SCHOOLS, ARCHDIOCESAN

LOS ANGELES. *Holy Cross Middle School*, 104 W. 47th Pl., 90037. Tel: 213-234-9023. Conducted by Archdiocese of Los Angeles. Sr. Daniel Therese, C.S.J., Prin. Sisters 3; Lay Teachers 8; Students 210.

[H] ELEMENTARY SCHOOLS, PRIVATE

LOS ANGELES. *Notre Dame Academy (Elementary)*, 2911 Overland Ave., 90064. Tel: 310-287-3895. Sr. Mary LaReina Kelly, S.N.D., Prin. Sisters of Notre Dame of Los Angeles 2; Lay Teachers 11; Students 314.

PASADENA. *Mayfield Junior School*, 405 S. Euclid Ave., 91101. Tel: 818-796-2774. Sisters of the Society of the Holy Child Jesus 2; Lay Teachers 40; Students 419.

SANTA BARBARA. *Marymount Academy.* (Coed), 2130 Mission Ridge Rd., 93103. Tel: 805-569-1811; Fax: 805-682-6892. Lay Teachers 21; Students 212.

[I] ORPHANAGES AND INFANT HOMES

ROSEMEAD. *Maryvale*, P.O. Box 1039, 91770-1003. Tel: 818-280-6510; 213-283-9311; Fax: 818-288-8903.
For a complete listing, refer to the Special Care Facilities section.

[J] DAY NURSERIES

LOS ANGELES. *Divine Providence Pre-school and Kindergarten*, 2620 Monmouth St., 90007. Tel: 213-747-3074. Sr. Mary Pardo, O.D.M., Dir. Sisters of the Company of Mary 6; Lay Teachers 10; Children 140.

St. Jeanne de Lestonnac Kindergarten and Day Nursery, 4001 Venice Blvd., 90019. Tel: 213-737-1217. (Formerly Little Flower Kindergarten & Day Nursery). Sr. Cecilia Duran, O.D.N., Supervisor. Lay Teachers 13; Children 160.

GARDENA. *St. Anthony's Day Nursery*, 1044 W. 163rd St., 90247. Tel: 310-329-8654. Sr. Maria S. Miranda, M.C., Dir. Sisters 12; Children 90.

SAN FERNANDO. *Poverello of Assisi School*, 1519 Woodworth St., 91340. Tel: 818-361-5864. Franciscan Missionary Sisters of the Immaculate Conception. Sr. Irene San Roman. Sisters 7; Children 190.

[K] GENERAL HOSPITALS

LOS ANGELES. *Queen of Angels-Hollywood Presbyterian Medical Center*, 1300 N. Vermont Ave., 90027.
For a complete listing, refer to the Hospitals section.

St. Vincent Medical Center, 2131 W. 3rd St., 90057. Tel: 213-484-7111.
For a complete listing, refer to the Hospitals section.

Santa Marta Hospital, 319 N. Humphreys Ave., 90022. Tel: 213-266-6500; Fax: 213-260-8641 (Admin.).
For a complete listing, refer to the Hospitals section.

BURBANK. *Providence Health System*, 501 S. Buena Vista St., 91505. Tel: 818-365-8051; Fax: 818-898-4569.
For a complete listing, refer to the Hospitals section.

Providence Saint Joseph Medical Center, 501 S. Buena Vista, 91505. Tel: 818-843-5111; Fax: 818-843-0641.
For a complete listing, refer to the Hospitals section.

DUARTE. *Santa Teresita Hospital*, 819 Buena Vista St., P.O. Box I, 91010. Tel: 818-359-3243; Fax: 818-357-7166.
For a complete listing, refer to the Hospitals section.

*HAWTHORNE. *Hawthorne Community Hospital, Inc.*, 711 Grevilles Ave.
For a complete listing, refer to the Hospitals section.

INGLEWOOD. *Daniel Freeman Memorial Hospital*, 333 N. Prairie Ave., 90301. Tel: 310-674-7050; 678-0361; Fax: 310-419-8273.
For a complete listing, refer to the Hospitals section.

LONG BEACH. *St. Mary Medical Center*, 1050 Linden Ave., 90813.
For a complete listing, refer to the Hospitals section.

St. Mary Medical Center Foundation, P.O. Box 887, 90801.
For a complete listing, refer to the Hospitals section.

St. Mary Professional Building, Inc., 1045 Atlantic Ave., 90813.
For a complete listing, refer to the Hospitals section.

LYNWOOD. *Catholic Health Care West-Southern California*, 3630 E. Imperial Hwy., 90262. Tel: 310-603-6000.
For a complete listing, refer to the Hospitals section.

St. Francis Medical Center, 3630 E. Imperial Hwy., 90262. Tel: 310-603-6000.
For a complete listing, refer to the Hospitals section.

MARINA DEL REY. *Daniel Freeman Marina Hospital*, 4650 Lincoln Blvd., 90292. Tel: 310-823-8911.
For a complete listing, refer to the Hospitals section.

OXNARD. *St. John's Regional Medical Center*, 1600 N. Rose Ave., 93030. Tel: 805-988-2500.
For a complete listing, refer to the Hospitals section.

SAN PEDRO. *San Pedro Peninsula Hospital*, 1300 W. Seventh St., 90732. Tel: 310-832-3311.
For a complete listing, refer to the Hospitals section.

SANTA BARBARA. *St. Francis Medical Center of Santa Barbara*, 601 E. Micheltorena St., 93103. Tel: 805-962-7661; Fax: 805-966-5704.
For a complete listing, refer to the Hospitals section.

SANTA MARIA. *Marian Medical Center*, 1400 E. Church St., 93454. Tel: 805-739-3000.
For a complete listing, refer to the Hospitals section.

SANTA MONICA. *Saint John's Hospital and Health Center*, 1328 22nd St., 90404. Tel: 310-829-5511; Fax: 310-315-6134.
For a complete listing, refer to the Hospitals section.

TORRANCE. *Little Company of Mary Health Services*, 4101 Torrance Blvd., 90503. Tel: 310-540-7676; Fax: 310-540-8408.
For a complete listing, refer to the Hospitals section.

WEST COVINA. *Queen of the Valley Hospital*, 1115 S. Sunset Ave., P.O. Box 1980, 91793. Tel: 818-962-4011; Fax: 818-814-2482.
For a complete listing, refer to the Hospitals section.

[L] SPECIAL HOSPITALS AND SANATORIA FOR INVALIDS

LOS ANGELES. *Franciscan Health Center*, 2859 Glassell St., 90026. Tel: 213-413-1050.
For a complete listing, refer to the Special Care Facilities section.

Knights of Malta Free Clinic, Inc., 2222 W. Ocean View #112, 90057. Tel: 213-384-4323; Fax: 213-384-4097.
For a complete listing, refer to the Special Care Facilities section.

CULVER CITY. *Marycrest Manor, Convalescent Home*, 10664 St. James Dr., 90230-5498. Tel: 310-838-2778.
For a complete listing, refer to the Special Care Facilities section.

NEWBURY PARK. *Mary Health of the Sick Convalescent and Nursing Hospital*, 2929 Theresa Dr., 91320. Tel: 805-498-3644; Fax: 805-498-5112.
For a complete listing, refer to the Special Care Facilities section.

OJAI. *St. Joseph's Health and Retirement Center*, 2464 E. Ojai Ave., P.O. Box 760, 93024. Tel: 805-646-1466.
For a complete listing, refer to the Special Care Facilities section.

[M] HANDICAPPED

LOS ANGELES. *Ministry with Persons with Disabilities*, 3424 Wilshire Blvd., Second Floor, 90010. Tel: 213-637-7236. Veronica Gray, Dir., Marian Homes for the Developmentally and Physically Disabled, Inc., Office of the Admin., 3424 Wilshire Blvd., 2nd Fl., 90010-2241. Tel: 213-637-7236. Katherine Boyet, Prog. Dir.

SANTA MONICA. *Saint John's Child Study Center, Saint John's Hospital & Health Center*, 1339 20th St., 90404. Tel: 310-829-8921; Fax: 310-829-8455. Conducted by Sisters of Charity of Leavenworth. Affiliated with Saint John's Hospital. Rebecca Refuerza, L.C.S.W., Dir. Children Treated Annually 1,800.

SUNLAND.
**Tierra del Sol Foundation*, 9919 Sunland Blvd., 91040. Tel: 818-352-1419; Fax: 818-353-0777. Community Program Supportive Employment for Adults with Disabilities. Stephen J. Miller, Exec. Dir.; Nancy Bissonette-Andrew, Assoc. Dir. Licensed Capacity 200.

VAN NUYS. *Tierra Del Sol West*, 14547 Gilmore St., 91411. Tel: 818-904-9164. Behavior Management Community Program for Adults with Developmental Disabilities. Stephen J. Miller, Exec. Dir.; Cindy Claus-John, Program Dir. Capacity 50.

[N] CHILD ADOPTION SERVICES

PASADENA. *Holy Family Services, Adoption & Foster Care*, 402-A S. Marengo Ave., 91101-3113. Tel: 818-578-1156; Fax: 818-578-7321.
Branch Offices: 1403 South Main St., Los Angeles, 92707. Tel: 714-835-5551; Fax: 714-973-4971. YWCA, 8172 Magnolia Ave., Riverside, 92504. Tel: 800-464-2367. 80 E. Hillcrest #210, Thousand Oaks, 91360. Tel: 800-464-ADOPT.
Holy Family Adoption Foundation, Inc.
Auxiliaries of Holy Family Services: Holy Family's Adoptive Parents Organization, Inc., The Adoption Guild Regents, Adoption Guild of Southern Orange County, Angelique Guild, The 200 Associates. Birthparent unplanned pregnancy counseling 88; Foster care families recruited 10; Children placed in adoptive homes 64.

[O] VISITING NURSE SERVICES

LOS ANGELES. *Sisters Servants of Mary, Ministers of the Sick*, 2131 W. 27th St., 90018-3018. Tel: 213-731-5747. Sr. Theresa Etchegaray, S.M., Supr. Sisters 17; Total Assisted 135; Total Staff 10.

[P] PROTECTIVE INSTITUTIONS

LOS ANGELES. *Convent of the Good Shepherd-Good Shepherd Shelter*, 2561 Venice Blvd., 90019. Tel: 213-737-6111.
For a complete listing, refer to the Special Care Facilities section.
Immaculate Conception Home for Girls, 1923 Micheltorena St., 90039. Tel: 213-664-7070.
For a complete listing, refer to the Special Care Facilities section.
Little Flower Missionary House, 2434 Gates St., 90031. Tel: 213-221-9248.
For a complete listing, refer to the Special Care Facilities section.
Missionary Brothers of Charity, 1345 Alvarado Ter., 90006. Tel: 213-251-9707.
For a complete listing, refer to the Special Care Facilities section.
St. Anne's, 155 N. Occidental Blvd., 90026. Tel: 213-381-2931; Fax: 213-381-7804.
For a complete listing, refer to the Special Care Facilities section.

CHATSWORTH. *Rancho San Antonio*, 21000 Plummer St., 91311. Tel: 818-882-6400.
For a complete listing, refer to the Special Care Facilities section.

SANTA BARBARA. *St. Vincent Residence*, 4200 Calle Real, P.O. Box 669, 93102-0669. Tel: 805-683-6381; Fax: 805-967-7508.
For a complete listing, refer to the Special Care Facilities section.

[Q] HOMES FOR AGED

LOS ANGELES. *Nazareth House*, 3333 Manning Ave., 90064. Tel: 310-839-2361; Fax: 310-839-4204.
For a complete listing, refer to the Special Care Facilities section.
St. John of God Retirement and Care Center, 2035 W. Adams Blvd., 90018. Tel: 213-731-0641.
For a complete listing, refer to the Special Care Facilities section.

SAN FERNANDO. *Mother Gertrude Home for Senior Citizens*, 11320 Laurel Canyon Blvd., 91340. Tel: 818-898-1546; Fax: 818-365-3159.
For a complete listing, refer to the Special Care Facilities section.

SAN PEDRO. *Little Sisters of the Poor*, Jeanne Jugan Residence, 2100 S. Western Ave., 90732. Tel: 310-548-0625.
For a complete listing, refer to the Special Care Facilities section.

SANTA MARIA. *Marian Residence*, 124 S. College Dr., 93454.
For a complete listing, refer to the Special Care Facilities section.

SUN VALLEY. *Villa Scalabrini*, 10631 Vinedale St., 91352. Tel: 818-768-6500; Fax: 818-767-1410.
For a complete listing, refer to the Special Care Facilities section.

[R] MONASTERIES AND RESIDENCES OF PRIESTS AND BROTHERS

LOS ANGELES. *Amat House*, 649 W. Adams Blvd., 90007-2596. Tel: 213-747-1227. Revs. Henry L. van Oudheusden, Supr.; Victor J. Sarrazin; Very Rev. Bernard J. Quinn, Prov.
De Paul Center, 1105 Bluff Rd., Montebello, 90640-6198. Revs. Patrick J. Mullin, Supr.; John J. Casey; Peter J. Diliberto; Robert J. Jones; Thomas J. McIntyre; Jacques J. Nouws; Terence M. O'Donnell; Deacon John P. Kearney. Priests 7; Deacons 1.
St. Mary's Center, 1964 Las Canoas Rd., Santa Barbara, 93105-2351. Revs. James F. McOwen, Supr.; Roy A. Persich, Dir.; James M. Gavin. Priests 3.
Atonement Friars, 4006 Tracy St., 90027. Tel: 213-660-7734. Rev. David L. Doerner, S.A., Moderator.
Brothers of John of God, Inc., The, 2425 S. Western Ave., 90018-2608. Tel: 213-734-0233; Fax: 213-731-5987. Bro. Edward Francis McEnroe, O.H., Prov.
Women's League of St. John of God, Inc.
Helper's Club, Inc.
St. John of God Retirement and Care Center.
St. Joseph's Health and Retirement Center.
Hospitaller Foundation of California, Inc.
Women's League of St. Joseph's Health and Retirement Center.
Grande Apartments-Los Angeles.
Hospitaller Brothers Healthcare, Inc.
St. John of God Health Care Services.
Brothers of Our Lady, Mother of Mercy Inc., 7140 Ramsgate Ave., 90045. Tel: 310-649-3370. Bro. John H. Grever, C.F.M.M., Community Rep. Brothers 3.
Canons Regular of the Immaculate Conception, 1523 Golden Gate Ave., 90026. Tel: 213-664-1305. Revs. James G. Garceau, C.R.I.C.; Charles R. Lueras, C.R.I.C.; Pasquale Vuoso, C.R.I.C., Pastor; Sergio Garcia, C.R.I.C. Priests 4.
Casa Guadalupe, Divine Word Missionaries, 807 N. Fresno, 90063. Tel: 213-263-7561. Revs. Sam Cunningham, S.V.D., Dir. Formation; Joe Miller, S.V.D.; Lloyd Thomas Cunningham, S.V.D.; Lukas Bao Teluma, S.V.D.; Raymundus Bhia Wea, S.V.D. Seminarians 7.
Claretian Retreat Center Community, 1119 Westchester Pl., 90019. Tel: 213-731-9329; Fax: 213-737-0301. Very Rev. Ralph Berg, C.M.F., Provincial Superior; Revs. Carlos C. Castillo, C.M.F., Supr.; Frank J. Ferrante, C.M.F., Dir.; Bro. Rene LePage, C.M.F., Admin.; Revs. Robert Bishop, C.M.F.; George Whedbee, C.M.F.; Gabriel Ruiz, C.M.F.; John Hampsch, C.M.F.; Robert Billett, C.M.F.; Roland Lozano, C.M.F.; Larry Moen, C.M.F.
Columban Fathers, Procure House, 2600 N. Vermont Ave., 90027. Tel: 213-665-4289. Revs. Thomas P. Parker, S.S.C., Supr.; Thomas Cusack, S.S.C.; Seamus Leddy, S.S.C.; Anthony Mortell, S.S.C.; Ernest L. Sullivan, S.C.S.; Denis Bartley, S.S.C.; Jim Shiffer, S.S.C.
Columbiere House. Formerly Connolly House. 5322 Franklin Ave., 90027. Tel: 213-466-3723; Fax: 213-466-3826. Jesuit Fathers. Revs. Francis J. Parrish, S.J.; John D. McAnulty, S.J.; George E. Krivanek, S.J.; John A. Houle, S.J. (China); Allan F. Deck, S.J., Supr.; Charles Prussing, S.J.; Peter Chu, S.J.; George R. Sullivan, S.J. (Wisconsin); John D. Dryden, S.J.; Robert Leonard, S.J.; Patrick Connolly, S.J. (Wisconsin); Frederick J. Heney, S.J. (Japan); Michael J. Mandala, S.J.; Felix A. Maiza, S.J.; Robert E. Griffin, S.J. Priests 15.
Congregation of St. Joseph Casa Nazareth, 2702 Abrigo Ave., 90031. Tel: 213-221-4809. Revs. Giampietro Gasparin, C.S.J.; John Trimaglio, C.S.J., Supr.
Franciscan Brothers of the Third Order Regular, 4522 Gainsborough Ave., 90027. Tel: 213-644-2740. Bro. Hilarion O'Connor, O.S.F., Reg. Supr. Brothers 15.
Franciscan Brothers of the Third Order Regular, 4552 Gainsborough Ave., 90027. Bro. Hilarion O'Connor, O.S.F., Regl. Supr.
Guadalupe Missioners Procure, 4714 W. 8th St., 90005. Tel: 213-937-2780. Revs. Marco A. Martinez, M.G.; Jose Luis Ochoa, M.G., Supr.
Hospitaller Brothers of St. John of God, 2035 W. Adams Blvd., 90018. Tel: 213-731-0641; Fax: 213-731-5987. Formation Community. Bro. Stephen de la Rosa, O.H., Novice Master & Prior. Brothers 13; Novices 1.
Maryknoll Fathers and Brothers. (Catholic Foreign Mission Society of America), 745 W. Adams Blvd., 90007. Tel: 213-747-9676; Fax: 213-747-8923. Revs. Richard R. Fries, M.M.; Michael G. Callanan, M.M., Dir.; Leo J. Melancon, M.M.; Kyungsu Son, M.M.; Joseph A. Klecha, M.M. Priests 5.
Mill Hill Missionaries Procure. (St. Joseph Society for Foreign Missions), 1841 Camino Palmero, 90046. Tel: 213-876-0505; Fax: 213-876-0508. Revs. Theo M. Feldbrugge, M.H.M.; Henk Riesthuis, M.H.M. Priests 2.
Minim Fathers, 3431 Portola Ave., 90032. Tel: 213-223-1101; Fax: 213-223-9592. Revs. Constantino Mandarino, O.M., Supr.; Gino Vanzillotta, O.M., Supr.; Jose L. Vega, O.M. Priests 3.
Missionaries of Charity Brothers, Regional Office: 214 S. Witmer St., 90026. Tel: 213-481-8152; 8153.
House of Formation, 1325 S. Westlake Ave., 90006. Tel: 213-384-6116.
Casa Teresa, 1316 S. Westlake Ave., 90006. Tel: 213-380-5225; 213-390-5356. Hospitality for men and boys.
Nuestro Hogar, 1345 Alvarado Terr., 90006. Tel: 213-251-9707. Daycenter for young adults. Total Assisted 60; Total Staff 5. Brothers 17.
Missionary Sons of the Immaculate Heart of Mary. (Claretian Priests and Brothers). Prov. Headquarters of the Western Prov. of the USA, 1119 Westchecter Place, 90019. Tel: 213-734-1824; Fax: 213-737-0301. Legal Title: *Claretian Missionaries - Western Province, Inc.* Very Rev. Ralph Berg, C.M.F., Prov. Treas.; Rev. Roland Lozano, C.M.F., Prov. Supr.
Claretian Tape Ministry, Inc.
Dominguez Seminary, Inc., Compton.
Claretian Educational and Renewal Center, Inc. This is a non-profit corporation under the laws of the State of California having as its purpose the support of any Roman Catholic benevolent, charitable, educational or missionary undertakings of the Claretian Missionaries - Western Province, Inc.
Mount Carmel Priory, Carmelite Fathers and Brothers, 801 W. 70th St., 90044. Tel: 213-752-3972. Legal Title: *Fathers of the Order of Mount Carmel, Corporation.* Revs. Augustine W. Carter, O.Carm.; Matt J. Ewing, O.Carm., Prior; Bernard Kangley, O.Carm.; Bro. Stephen Diekemper, O.Carm. Priests 3.
Piarist Fathers, 512 S. Avenue 20, 90031. Tel: 213-223-4153. Revs. John Santilian, Sch.P.; Raul Palma, Sch.P.; Francis Boronat, Sch.P.; Jose Margalef, Sch.P. Priests 4.
St. John of God Retirement and Care Center, 2035 W. Adams Blvd., 90018. Tel: 213-731-0641. Bros. Stephen de la Rosa, O.H., Prov. & Chm.; Edward F. McEnroe, O.H., Local Supr.; Paul Hanson, O.H., Novice Master. Brothers 11; Novices 2.
Society of St. Paul. (Mexican Province), 112 Herbert St., 90063. Tel: 213-269-9814. Revs. Valeriano Giachino, S.S.P., Supr.; Jose Estanislao Hernandez, S.S.P., Vice Supr.; Gonzalo Ponce, S.S.P.; Adan Martinez Ruiz, S.S.P.; Tomas Martinez Rayas, S.S.P.; Bro. Agustine G. Castro. Priests 5.
Society of the Divine Word Western Province, Office of the Provincial, 2181 W. 25th St., P.O. Box 77-F, 90007. Tel: 213-731-9982 (Provincial Office); 731-9982 (Community Phone); Fax: 213-735-8122 (Provincial Office). Rev. Eamonn Donnelly, S.V.D., Prov. Supr.; Bro. Jeremiah M. Walsh, S.V.D. In res., Rev. Francis L. Shigo, S.V.D.; Bro. Richard A. Morrill, S.V.D.
Vincentian Fathers and Brothers, Province of the West, Provincial Office, 650 W. 23rd St., 90007-2036. Tel: 213-748-9829. Legal Titles: *Congregation of the Mission in California, a Corporation*; *Vincentian Community Charitable Trust*; *Vincentian Foreign Mission Society*; *DePaul Center Corporation.* (Formerly St. Vincent's Seminary Corporation). Revs. Pedro Villarroya, C.M., Supr.; Thomas C. Anslow, C.M.; Edward F. Danagher, C.M.; Stafford Poole, C.M.; Francis David Pansini, C.M.; Bro. Edward Graham, C.M. Brothers 1; Priests 5.

AZUSA. *Casa Comboni Mission Seminary*, 525 N. Pasadena Ave., 91702. Tel: 818-334-3531. Rev. Giovanni Esti, M.C.C.J. (Italy), Rector & Formation Dir. In res., Rev. Miguel A. Villegas (Mexico). Priests 2; Students 5.

BALDWIN PARK. *Vietnamese Redemptorist Mission*, 3452 N. Big Dalton Ave., 91706. Revs. Vu Minh Nghiem, C.Ss.R.; Ngo Dinh Thoa, C.Ss.R.; Dinh Ngoc Que, C.Ss.R.; Nguyen Thanh Son, C.Ss.R.; Tran Quoc Bao, C.Ss.R.; Trinh Duc Hoa, C.Ss.R.; Pham Quoc Hung, C.Ss.R.; Bros. John M. Viet Hien, C.Ss.R.; Martin Nguyen Van Moi, C.Ss.R.
In Residence Elsewhere: 5404 N.E. Alameda Dr., Portland, OR, 97213. Rev. Hong Phuc, C.Ss.R., 8800 E. 22nd St., Tuscon, AZ, 85710. Rev. Tran Ngoc Bich, C.Ss.R., 318 Leland Ave., San Francisco, 94134. Rev. Tran Dinh Phuc, C.Ss.R., 2458 Atlantic Ave., Long Beach, 90806. Revs. Nguyen Duc Mau, C.Ss.R.; Phan Phat Huon, C.Ss.R.; Ngo Van Dao, C.Ss.R.; Bui quang Tuan, C.Ss.R.; Bro. Vo Thanh Ha, C.Ss.R.

1907 E. Grauwyler Rd., Irving, TX, 75061. Revs. Nguyen Duc Thong, C.Ss.R.; Dinh Minh Hai, C.Ss.R.; Nguyen Duc Thanh, C.Ss.R., 600 Melwood W., Houston, TX, 77009. Revs. Chau Xuan Bau, C.Ss.R.; Le Quang Phung, C.Ss.R.; Tran Tu Nhan, C.Ss.R.; Le Huy Bang, C.Ss.R., 1011 Farm Rd., P.O. Box 1060, Rockport, TX, 78381. Rev. Nguyen Van Phan, C.Ss.R. Priests 23; Brothers 3; Student Clerics 20.

CULVER CITY. *Ignatius House, The Novitiate of the California Province, Society of Jesus*, P.O. Box 5166, 90231-5166. 10775 Deshire Pl., 90230-5017. Tel: 310-815-0166 (Staff); 815-0185 (Novices); Fax: 310-815-0170. Revs. Robert A. Fambrini, S.J., Supr. & Dir. of Novices; John W. Chandler, S.J., Socius, Min. & Asst. to Novice Dir.; George E. Schultze, S.J., Treas. In res., Rev. Steven E. Artiga, S.J.

FILLMORE. *Apostolate of Christian Renewal Holy Family*, 411 First St., P.O. Box 547, 93016-0547. Tel: 805-524-5890. Rev. Luke Zimmer, SS.CC.

LA VERNE. *Congregation of the Sacred Hearts*, 2150 Damien Ave., 91750. Revs. Donal McCarthy, SS.CC.; Patrick Travers, SS.CC.; Peadar Cronin, SS.CC.; Martin P. O'Loghlen, SS.CC. Priests 3.

MISSION HILLS. *Congregation of the Sacred Hearts*, 15201 Rinaldi St., 91345. Tel: 818-361-9152. Revs. Kenneth O. McCabe, SS.CC.; Patrick Argue, SS.CC. Priests 2.

NORTH HILLS. *Rogationist Fathers*, 9815 Columbus Ave., 91343. Tel: 818-894-2546; Fax: 818-895-8934. Revs. Vincenzo Buccheri, R.C.J.; Rodolfo D'Agostino, R.C.J., Rector. Legal Title: *Congregation of Rogationists, Inc.*

OXNARD. *Brothers of Our Lady, Mother of Mercy*, Mother of Mercy Novitiate, 2336 S. C St., 93033. Tel: 805-486-3692. Conducted by the Brothers of Our Lady, Mother of Mercy. Bros. Edward Gresnigt, Reg. Supr.; Edward Gresnigt, C.F.M.M., Local Supr. Brothers 8.

Rogationist Fathers, 548 Glenwood Dr., 93030. Revs. Vito DiMarzio, R.C.J., Dean of Formation; F. Antonio Carlucci, R.C.J., Supr.

St. Augustine Priory, St. Augustine Priory, 400 Sherwood Way, 93033. Tel: 805-486-7433. Prepostulancy & Postulancy Vocation Center.

St. Augustine Priory O.A.R., 400 Sherwood Way, 93033-7510. Tel: 805-486-7433; 486-9651 (Vocations). Prepostulancy and Postulancy Augustinian Recollects & Vocation Center. Revs. John Gruben, O.A.R., Prior; Francisco J. Legarra, O.A.R. (Spain), Prefect of Students & Subprior; Jose Luis Martinez, O.A.R., Dir. of Vocations; Albert Polt, O.A.R., (Retired); Bros. Raymond Fabrin, O.A.R.; Ramiro Munoz, O.A.R.

PASADENA. *Legionaries of Christ*, P.O. Box 61305, 91116. Tel: 818-305-5363. In res., Revs. Brian Wilson, L.C.; Juan Rivas, L.C.; Thomas White, L.C.; Thomas Maher, L.C.

Passionist Community, 651 N. Sierra Madre Blvd., 91107.

Passionist Retreat House, 700 N. Sunnyside Ave., Sierra Madre, 91024. Tel: 818-355-7188; Fax: 818-355-0485. Passionist Residence, 651 N. Sierra Madre Blvd., 91107. Tel: 818-564-1099; Fax: 818-564-1930. Congregation of the Passion, Mater Dolorosa Community. Very Rev. Peter Kumle, C.P., Local Supr.; Revs. Benedict Olson, C.P., Asst. Supr.; Damian McHale, C.P.; Patrick Brennan, C.P., Retreat Dir.; Godfrey Poage, C.P.; Benet Kieran, C.P.; Cyprian Towey, C.P.; Fergus McGuinness, C.P.; Philip Paxton, C.P., Assoc. Retreat Dir. & Vocational Dir.; Bros. John Rockenbach, C.P.; Anthony Mimiaga, C.P. Priests 9; Brothers 2.

RANCHO DOMINGUEZ. *Dominguez Seminary Inc.*, 18127 S. Alameda St., 90220. Tel: 213-636-6030; 310-631-5981; 631-8484; Fax: 310-631-3518. Retirement Center, Ministries Community. Congregation of Missionaries, Sons of the Immaculate Heart of Mary (Claretian Missionaries). Revs. Robert Bishop, C.M.F., Supr.; Patrick McPolin, C.M.F., Supr. Casa Claret Community; Diego Barrios, C.M.F.; John Corominas, C.M.F.; Bernard Stacy, C.M.F.; Albert Connors, C.M.F.; Edward Widmer, C.M.F.; Basil Frison, C.M.F.; Francis X. Hogan, C.M.F.; Celestino de la Iglesia, C.M.F.; Jack Hencier, C.M.F.; Walter Mischke, C.M.F.; Raymond Martinez, C.M.F.; James Overend, C.M.F.; Flavin Willathgamuwa, C.M.F.; Alberto M. Ruiz, C.M.F.; Salvatore Bonano, C.M.F., Vicar; Joseph Daries, C.M.F.; Bros. Paul Roy, C.M.F.; Franklin Stanford, C.M.F. Priests 18; Brothers 2.

SAN GABRIEL. *Claretian Missionaries (Missionary Sons of the Immaculate Heart of Mary)*, 537 W. Mission Dr., 91776. Tel: 818-282-5191. Claretians Old Mission. Revs. Valentin L. Ramon, C.M.F.; Brian Culley, C.M.F.; Steve Niskanen, C.M.F.; Frank Pyka, C.M.F. In res., Bro. Cruz Pettinato, C.M.F.; Rev. Tobias Romero, C.M.F. Priests 5.

SANTA BARBARA. *Franciscan Friary, Order of Friars Minor (Old Mission)*, 2201 Upper Laguna St., 93105. Tel: 805-682-4713. Revs. Ray Tintle, O.F.M., Supr.; Virgil Cordano, O.F.M., Pastor; David Carriere, O.F.M.; Joseph LaRue, O.F.M.; Noel Moholy, O.F.M.; Frederick Bromham, O.F.M.; Benvenute Bavero, O.F.M.; Allan Wolter, O.F.M.; Adrian Erlenheim, O.F.M.; Virgilio Biasiol, O.F.M.; Maurus Kelly, O.F.M., Chap.; Vincent Mesi, O.F.M.; John Flajole, O.F.M.; Leander Laner, O.F.M.; Theophane Robertson, O.F.M.; Berard Weishaar, O.F.M.; Deacon Jack Ryan. Priests 20; Brothers 10.

St. Anthony's Seminary, 2300 Garden St., 93105-3696. Tel: 805-682-4720. Rev. Alberic Smith, O.F.M., Dir. In res., Rev. Nevin Ford, O.F.M.; Bros. Fabian Walker, O.F.M.; Jan Honchosky, O.F.M.; Wenceslaus Farlow, O.F.M.; Damian Byrne, O.F.M. Priests 2; Brothers 4.

TORRANCE. *Franciscan Friars, St. Bonaventure Friary*, 5432 Torrance Blvd., 90503. Tel: 310-540-1452. Conventual Franciscan Friars (St. Joseph Cupertino Province). Legal Title: *Conventual Franciscans of California, Inc.* Revs. Alexander J. Lewis, O.F.M.Conv., Supr.; Gary Klauer, O.F.M.Conv. In res., Revs. Ceaser Inserra, O.F.M.Conv.; Francisco Nahoe, O.F.M.Conv.; Bros. Casimir Roland, O.F.M.Conv.; Patrick Lytell, O.F.M.Conv.; Paul Gawlowski, O.F.M.Conv.; Anthony Tuyen Pham, O.F.M.Conv.

VALYERMO. *St. Andrew's Abbey*, 31001 N. Valyermo Rd., 93563-0040. Tel: 805-944-2178. Benedictine Monks. Rt. Rev. Francis Benedict, O.S.B., Abbot; Very Revs. Isaac Kalina, O.S.B., Prior; Vincent Martin, O.S.B., Subprior; Revs. Eleutherius Winance, O.S.B.; Werner Papeians de Morchoven, O.S.B.; Bro. Peter Zhou Bang-jiu, O.S.B.; Revs. Philip Edwards, O.S.B.; John Borgerding, O.S.B.; Simon O'Donnell, O.S.B.; John Bosco Stoner, O.S.B.; Bro. Dominic Guillen, O.S.B.; Rev. Gregory Elmer, O.S.B.; Bros. Benedict Dull, O.S.B.; Joseph Iarrobino, O.S.B.; Revs. Luke Dysinger, O.S.B.; Martin Yslas, O.S.B.; Paul Pluth, O.S.B.; Bros. Anselmo Taborda, O.S.B.; Andrew Hayes, O.S.B.; Nilo Morand, O.S.B.; Rev. Joseph (Dennis) Brennan, O.S.B.; Bros. Michael Weeks, O.S.B.; Thomas Babusis, O.S.B. Priests 13; Brothers 11.

WHITTIER. *Redemptorist Fathers Mission House*, 7215 Newlin Ave., 40602. Tel: 310-698-0107. Revs. Enrique A. Lopez, C.SS.R., Supr.; Timothy Watson, C.SS.R.; Arturo Uribe, C.SS.R.; Joseph Elliott, C.SS.R.; Joseph Tobin, C.SS.R.; Lionel Sirois, C.SS.R.; Donald Liberty, C.SS.R.; Clarence Bodden, C.SS.R. (Chicago); Bro. Don E. O'Mara, C.SS.R. Priests 8; Brothers 1.

[S] CONVENTS AND RESIDENCES FOR SISTERS

LOS ANGELES. *California Institute of the Sisters of the Blessed Virgin Mary*, Motherhouse, Novitiate, Retreat House: 3431 Waverly Dr., 90027. Tel: 213-664-1124. Legal Title: *California Institute of the Sisters of the Most Holy and Immaculate Heart of the Blessed Virgin Mary*. Sr. Eileen Doherty, I.H.M., Supr. Gen. Sisters 28.

Congregation of the Poor Sisters of Nazareth Motherhouse, U.S.A. and Novitiate, 3333 Manning Ave., 90064. Tel: 310-839-2361; 2362; Fax: 310-839-0648. Mother Margaret Clare, Reg. Supr.; Rev. Paul Peterson, S.S.C., Chap. Sisters 8.

Daughters of Mary and Joseph, 8129 Gonzaga Ave., 90045. Tel: 310-410-4545. Sisters 2.

Eucharistic Franciscan Missionary Sisters, Motherhouse: 943 S. Soto St., 90023. Tel: 213-264-6556; Fax: 213-526-1655. Rev. Mother Gemma de Jesus Aranda, E.F.M.S., Supr. Gen. Sisters 23.

Eucharistic Franciscan Missionary Sisters of Los Angeles, Nativity Convent: 1421 Cota Ave., Torrance, 90501. Tel: 310-328-6725; Fax: 310-328-5248.

Formation Community, Religious of the Sacred Heart of Mary, 2833 Sichel St., 90031. Sisters 4.

Guadalupanas Missionaries of the Holy Spirit. Novitiate. 758 S. Dunsmuir Ave., 90036. Tel: 213-936-0135.

Guadalupanas Missionaries of the Holy Spirit, 5467 W. 8th St., 90036. Tel: 213-936-6565. Formation House. Sisters 5.

Lovers of the Holy Cross Sisters, Good Shepherd Convent, 267 N. Belmont Ave., 90026. Tel: 213-250-5241; Fax: 213-250-5073. Sr. Anne Lanh Tran, L.H.C., Supr. Sisters 4.

Missionary Servants of the Most Blessed Trinity Ascension Missionary Cenacle, 518 W. 111th Pl., 90044. Tel: 213-754-0020.

Missionary Sisters of Christ the King (Poland), 3424 W. Adams Blvd., 90018. Tel: 213-734-6754. Sisters working in Archdiocese of Los Angeles 3.

Monastery of the Angels (Contemplative), 1977 Carmen Ave., 90068. Tel: 213-466-2186; Fax: 213-466-6645. Sr. Mary Raymond, O.P., Prioress; Rev. Armando Ibanez, O.P., Chap. Tel: 213-463-6488. Nuns of the Order of Preachers. Professed Cloistered Nuns 24; Professed Extern Sisters 2.

Pious Disciples of the Divine Master, 215 S. Los Angeles St., 90012; Fax: 213-680-9271. Sr. Peter Mendes, P.D.D.M. Sisters 7.

Provincial House of the Sisters of St. Joseph of Carondelet, 11999 Chalon Rd., 90049-1524. Tel: 213-272-8016; 310-476-5253; Fax: 310-476-8735. Sr. Joyce Marie Gaspardo, Prov. Supr.; Sr. Cecilia Louise, Asst. Prov. Supr.; Sr. Maureen O'Connor, Asst. Prov. Supr. Superiors: Sr. Miriam Joseph Larkin; Sr. Paul Joseph Madden. Sisters 81.

Sisters of St. Joseph in California.

Sisters of St. Joseph Ministerial Services.

Sisters of St. Joseph in Arizona.

Religious Sisters of Charity Regional, 1206 N. Edgemont St., 90029. Sisters 31.

School Sisters of Notre Dame, 638 S. Irving Blvd., 90005. Sisters 6.

Sisters of Our Lady of Perpetual Help, S.O.L.P.H., St. Brendan Convent, 220 S. Manhattan Pl., 90004. Tel: 213-389-6398.

Sisters of Social Service of Los Angeles, General Motherhouse, 2303 S. Figueroa Way, 90007. Tel: 213-746-2117; Fax: 213-747-4499. Legal Titles: *Sisters of Social Service of Los Angeles, Inc.*; *Sisters of Social Service Support Trust Fund*. Sr. Simone Campbell, Gen. Dir. Sisters 104. Sisters of Social Service, Formation, 2303 S. Figeroa Way, 90007. Tel: 213-731-2117. Sr. Deborah Lorentz, S.S.S., Team Co-Chair; Sr. Sarah Nagle, S.S.S., Team Co-Chair. In Formation 6.

Sisters of St. Joseph of Orange, 8000 Regis Way, 90045. Tel: 310-645-2514; 645-0718. Sisters 2.

Sisters of the Company of Mary, 2634 Monmouth Ave., 90007. Tel: 213-747-3542. Sr. Teresa Zapata, O.D.N., Supr. Sisters 9.

Sisters of the Good Shepherd, 2561 Venice Blvd., 90019. Tel: 213-737-6111. Sisters 10.

Sisters of the Guardian Angel, 4529 New York St., 90022. Tel: 213-266-4431.

Sisters of the Immaculate Heart of Mary at Mirinae, I.H.M., P.O. Box 75867, 90075. Tel: 213-381-2481.

Sisters of the Society Devoted to the Sacred Heart, Local Convent: 628 S. Irving Blvd., 90005. Tel: 213-936-8647. Sr. Lucia Tu, S.D.S.H., Supr. Sisters 6.

Sisters of the Society Devoted to the Sacred Heart, 869 S. Rimpau Blvd., 90005. Tel: 213-935-2372. Sisters 3.

ALHAMBRA. *Carmel of St. Teresa*, 215 E. Alhambra Rd., 91801. Tel: 818-282-2387; Fax: 818-282-2053. Discalced Nuns of the Order of Our Blessed Lady of Mt. Carmel. Mother Maria, Prioress. Sisters 15.

Carmelite Sisters of the Most Sacred Heart of Los Angeles, Generalate Motherhouse, Novitiate and Retreat House: 920 E. Alhambra Rd., 91801. Tel: 818-289-1353; Fax: 818-308-1913. Sr. Regina Marie Gorman, O.C.D., Dir. of Novices; Mother Vincent Marie Finnegan, O.C.D., Supr. General. Sisters 17; Postulants 2; Novices 5; Total Professed Sisters 120.

Carmelite Sisters of the Most Sacred Heart of Los Angeles.

ALTADENA. *Franciscan Sisters of the Sacred Heart*, 579 W. Mariposa St., 91001. Tel: 818-791-4359. Sisters 5.

BEVERLY HILLS. *Sisters of Mary Mother of the Church*, 504 N. Roxbury Dr., 90210.

CARSON. *Sisters of the Korean Martyrs, S.K.M.*, 21844 Orrick Ave., 90745. Tel: 310-835-3399.

CULVER CITY. *Daughters of St. Paul*, 3908 Sepulveda Blvd., 90230. Tel: 310-390-4699. Sr. Mary Assumpta, F.S.P., Supr. Sisters 5.

DOWNEY. *Sisters of the Holy Faith in California*, 12322 S. Paramount Blvd., P.O. Box 2085, 90242. Tel: 310-923-4013; Fax: 310-869-4609. Sisters 48.

EL SEGUNDO. *Sisters Servants of the Blessed Sacrament*, U.S. Vice Provincial House, 90245. Tel: 310-615-0766. Sisters 7.

ENCINO. *Sisters of St. Louis*, 5001 White Oak Ave., 91316. Tel: 818-344-7825. Sisters 6. St. Joseph of Carondolet. Holy Names of Jesus and Mary. Ursuline Sisters.

GARDENA. *Poor Clare Missionary Sisters, Inc.*, 1103 W. 164th St., 90247. Tel: 310-323-9942. Sr. Maria S. Miranda, M.C., Supr. Sisters 12.

GLENDORA. *St. Lucy's Priory*, 19045 E. Sierra Madre Ave., 91741. Tel: 818-335-1682. Sr. Elizabeth Brown, Prioress. Legal Title: *St. Lucy's Priory of Glendora California, Inc.* Sisters 27.

LYNWOOD. *Daughters of Mary, Mother of Mercy, D.M.M.M.*, St. Francis Medical Center, 3630 E. Imperial Hwy., 90262. Tel: 310-603-6311. Mailing Address: D.M.M.M. Convent, Mother of Sorrows Parish, 100 W. 87th Pl., Los Angeles, 90003. Tel: 213-753-7805. St. Francis Medical Center, 3630 E. Imperial Hwy., 90262. Sisters 6.

MISSION HILLS. *Sisters of the Holy Cross*, 9933 Woodman Ave., 91345. Tel: 818-365-4659. Legal Title: *Sisters of the Holy Cross of California*. Sisters 5.

MONROVIA. *Convent of the Maryknoll Sisters of St.*

Dominic, 340 Norumbega Dr., 91016-2445. Tel: 818-358-1825. Sr. Andree Normandin, M.M., Coord. Sisters 42.

Convent of the Maryknoll Sisters of St. Dominic, 340 Norumbega Dr., 91016-2445. Tel: 818-358-1825; 1826. Retirement Residence. Sr. Andree Normandin, M.M., Coord. Sisters 45.

MONTEBELLO. *Religious of the Sacred Heart of Mary*, Provincial Center, 441 N. Garfield Ave., 90640-2901. Tel: 213-887-8821; Fax: 213-887-8952.

NORTH HOLLYWOOD. *School Sisters of St. Francis, O.S.F.*, St. Charles Borromeo, 10834 Moorpark St., 91602-2206. Tel: 818-762-0969.

NORTHRIDGE. *Mother of Mercy Convent*, 9329 Crebs Ave., 91324. Tel: 818-882-4095. Sister of Mercy Burlingame.

Sisters of the Society Devoted to the Sacred Heart, Motherhouse: 9814 Sylvia Ave., 91324. Tel: 818-772-9961. Sr. Jane Stafford, S.D.S.H., Supr. Gen.

OXNARD. *Sisters Servants of Mary*, 3779 W. Gonzales Rd., 93030. Tel: 805-486-5502. Sr. Felisa Ripa, S.M., Mistress of Novices. Sisters 13; Novices 10.

PASADENA. *Convent of the Holy Child*, 500 Bellefontaine St., 91105. Tel: 818-799-5312. Sisters 3.

Convent of the Holy Child. Corporate Title: Society of the Holy Child Jesus, American Province, Inc. 443 S. Euclid Ave., 91101. Tel: 818-796-3924.

RANCHO PALOS VERDES. *Daughters of Mary & Joseph, D.M.J.*, Provincial House: 5300 Crest Rd., 90275-5004. Tel: 213-377-9968; 541-0784; Fax: 310-544-0387. Sisters 7.

ROLLING HILLS. *Sisters of Charity of Rolling Hills*, 28600 Palos Verdes Dr. E., 90274. Tel: 310-831-4104. Sr. Dominica Buchholz, S.C.R.H., Supr. Gen. Sisters 14.

SAN FERNANDO. *Franciscan Sisters of the Immaculate Conception*, 11320 Laurel Canyon Blvd., 91340. Tel: 818-365-2582. Legal Title: *Franciscan Sisters of the Immaculate Conception, Province of St. Clare of Assisi Provincial House*. Sisters 93; Novices 11; Postulants 6.

Religious Sisters of Charity, 1608 Eighth St., 91340. Sisters 2.

SAN GABRIEL. *Sisters of the Cross & Passion, C.P.*, 401 E. Live Oak, #23, 91776. Tel: 818-285-5334.

SAN PEDRO. *Little Sisters of the Poor*, 2100 S. Western Ave., 90732. Tel: 310-548-0625. Sr. Mary Anthony, Supr. Sisters 17.

SANTA BARBARA. *Monastery of Poor Clares*, Cloistered Contemplative Monastery, 215 E. Los Olivos St., 93105. Tel: 805-682-7670. Mother Mary Clare of Jesus, Abbess. Professed 15. Attended by Franciscan Fathers of the Old Mission.

St. Francis Convent, 601 E. Micheltorena St., 93103. Tel: 805-962-7661. Sr. Clare Van Vooren, O.S.F., Local Leader. Sisters 5.

SOLVANG. *Carmel of St. Joseph Discalced Carmelite Nuns*, 1883 Ringsted Dr., 93463. Tel: 805-686-4292. Legal Title: *Carmel of St. Joseph Discalced Carmelite Nuns of the Order of Our Blessed Lady of Mt. Carmel*. Mother Mary Veronica, O.C.D., Prioress. Sisters 12.

Sisters of the Society Devoted to the Sacred Heart, 1762 Mission Dr., 93463. Tel: 805-688-6158. Sr. Elizabeth Normanly, S.D.S.H., Supr. Sisters 3.

SYLMAR. *Poor Clare Missionary Sisters*. P.O. Box 227, San Fernando, 91340. Tel: 818-361-0591. Sr. Blanca G. Rivera, M.C., Supr.; Sr. Beatriz Aguilar, M.C. Sisters 7.

THOUSAND OAKS. *Sisters of Notre Dame*, Provincial House, Provincialate, 1776 Hendrix Ave., 91360. Tel: 805-496-3243; Fax: 805-379-3616. Sr. Mary Amy, S.N.D., Supr. Sisters 48.

TORRANCE. *Little Company of Mary Convent*, 20552 Mansel Ave., 90503. Tel: 310-214-3190; 514-5230 (Office); Fax: 310-514-5314. Sr. Mary Babcock, L.C.M. Sisters 4. 20562 Mansel Ave., 90503. Tel: 310-370-3992, 310-540-7676 (Office). Sr. Terrence, Landini, L.C.M. Sisters 3.

VENTURA. *Handmaids of the Sacred Heart of Jesus, Mary and Joseph*, P.O. Box 2957, 93002.

Sisters of the Holy Cross, Saint Catherine-by-the-Sea, 1931 Poli St., 93001. Tel: 805-652-1700. Residence for Retired Sisters. Legal Title: *Sisters of the Holy Cross of California*. Rev. James Gillis, C.S.C.; Sr. M. Gertrude Sullivan, C.S.C., Supr. Sisters 40.

WHITTIER. *Sisters of the Sacred Heart of Jesus, H.C.J.S.*, 11506 Walnut St., 90606. Tel: 310-908-0618.

WOODLAND HILLS. *Sisters of St. Louis, Louisville Convent*, 22300 Mulholland Dr., 91364. Tel: 818-347-2115. Sr. Bernadette Murphy, S.S.L., Reg. Supr. Sisters 14.

[T] SECULAR INSTITUTES

LOS ANGELES. *Society of Our Lady of the Way*, 2339 N. Catalina St., 90027. Tel: 213-665-0333. Legal Title: *Society of Our Lady of the Way of Southern California, Inc.*

[U] RESIDENCES FOR WOMEN

LOS ANGELES. *Bethany House*, 850 N. Hobart Blvd., 90029. Tel: 213-665-6937. Sisters 8; Residents 50.

Estrella del Mar, Inc. dba Regis House, 2303 S. Figueroa Way, 90025. Tel: 310-477-8168. Sr. Georgina Cahill, S.S.S., Dir.; Sr. Jennifer Gaeta, S.S.S., Dir. Sisters of Social Service 2.

Good Shepherd Center for Homeless Women, Languille Residence, 267 N. Belmont Ave., 90026. Tel: 213-250-5241; Fax: 213-250-5073.
(A Division of Catholic Charities). Women in Residence 30; Women Assisted Annually 2,444.

Hawkes Residence, 1039 W. 87th St., 90044. Tel: 213-758-4761; Fax: 213-758-4550. Sr. Monica Phi Tran, L.H.C., Supr. General; Sr. Mary Jo Nga Nguyen, L.H.C.
(A Division of Catholic Charities). Women in Residence 45; Women Assisted Annually 120.

Mother-Child, Transitional Residence, 267 N. Belmont Ave., 90026. Tel: 213-469-6540; Fax: 213-469-0370. Mother-Children in Residence 30; Mother-Children Assisted Annually 150.

St. Anne's. For further details refer to listing in Special Care Facilities section. 155 N. Occidental Blvd., 90026. Tel: 213-381-2931; Fax: 213-381-7804. Group Home for pregnant, parenting teens and their babies.

St. Joseph's Residence, 1124 W. Adams Blvd., 90007. Tel: 213-749-9577. Sisters of the Company of Mary. Women 62.

[V] RESIDENCES FOR MEN

LOS ANGELES. *"Casa Teresa," Missionary Brothers of Charity*, 1316 S. Westlake Ave., 90006. Tel: 213-380-5225; 380-5356. Temporary shelter for sick homeless men and home for Hispanic high school boys. Brothers 7; Novices 2.

"Nuestra Hogar" Missionaries of Charity Brothers, 1345 Alvarado Ter., 90006. Tel: 214-251-9707.

Catholic Kolping House, 1225 S. Union Ave., 90015. Tel: 213-388-9438. Rev. Richard Russell, Spiritual Dir.; Mr. Eddy Coronel, Mgr. Capacity 60.

The Little Brothers of the Good Shepherd BGS, 3441 Waverly Dr., 90027. Tel: 213-662-0092 (Office). Staff for Cardinal Manning House of Prayer.

Missionaries of Charity Brothers, House of Formation, 325 S. Westlake Blvd., 90006. Tel: 213-384-6116.

Missionaries of Charity Brothers, Regional Center and Novitiate, 214 S. Witmer St., 90026. Tel: 213-481-8152.

[W] RETREAT HOUSES

LOS ANGELES. *Claretian Retreat Center (All Groups)*, 1119 Westchester Pl., 90019. Tel: 213-737-8464. Revs. Robert Billett, C.M.F., Supr.; Frank J. Ferrante, C.M.F., Dir.; Bro. Rene Lepage, C.M.F., Admin.

Immaculate Heart Retreat House. (Days of Recollection Only), 3431 Waverly Dr., 90027. Tel: 213-664-1126. Conducted by the Sisters of the Immaculate Heart. Sr. Rita Callanan, I.H.M., Dir. Capacity 48; Sisters 10.

ALHAMBRA. *Retreat House of the Sacred Heart*, 920 E. Alhambra Rd., 91801. Carmelite Sisters of the Most Sacred Heart of Los Angeles. Sr. Rosario Therese, O.C.D., Contact Person. Capacity 89; Sisters 9; Novices 5; Postulants 2.
(See Convents).

ENCINO. *Holy Spirit Retreat Center*, 4316 Lanai Rd., 91436. Tel: 818-784-4515. Sisters of Social Service.

MALIBU. *Serra Retreat*, 3401 Serra Rd., P.O. Box 127, 90265. Tel: 310-456-6631. Franciscan Friars. Revs. Howard Hall, O.F.M., Dir.; Anthony Garibaldi, O.F.M., Guardian; Ralph Weishaar, O.F.M., Retreat Dir.; Bros. Samuel Cabot, O.F.M., Housekeeping Mgr.; Pierre Despres, O.F.M., Gardening Mgr. Priests 3; Brothers 2.

MONTEBELLO. *DePaul Center*, 1105 Bluff Rd., 90640-6198. Tel: 213-721-6060; Fax: 213-887-0765. (Formerly St. Vincent's Seminary). Congregation of the Mission (Vincentians). Retreat and Evangelization Center. Sr. Laura Gormley, S.S.L., Dir.; Rev. Patrick J. Mullin, C.M., Superior; Sr. Grace Briare, S.N.J.M.; Deacon John P. Kearney, C.M., Drug & Alcohol Intervention; Rev. Victor J. Sarrazin, C.M. In res., Revs. John J. Casey, C.M., (Retired); Peter J. Diliberto, C.M., (Retired); Robert J. Jones, C.M.; Thomas J. McIntyre, C.M., (Retired); James J. Nouws, C.M., (Retired); Terence O'Donnell, C.M., (Retired).

RANCHO PALOS VERDES. *Mary and Joseph Retreat Center*, 5300 Crest Rd., 90275-5004. Tel: 310-377-4867. Daughters of Mary and Joseph. Retreat Center Capacity 64; Sisters 5.

ROSEMEAD. *St. Joseph's Salesian Youth Renewal Center*. (Boys and Girls), 8301 Arroyo Dr., P.O. Box 1639, 91770. Tel: 818-280-8622. Conducted by Salesians of St. John Bosco. Rev. Harry Rasmussen, S.D.B., Dir. & Dir. Novices; Bros. George Ghiselli, S.D.B., Treas.; Larry King, S.D.B.; Robert Hennings, S.D.B.; Thien Nguyen; Steve Gomez; Rev. Teodoro Montemayor, S.D.B., Dir. Retreat Center. Priests 2; Brothers 5; Novices 1.

SAN FERNANDO. *Poverello of Assisi Retreat House*, 1519 Woodworth St., 91340. Tel: 818-365-1071. For men and women. Marriage Encounter in Korean. Engaged Encounter in English, Vietnamese and Spanish couples. Other Denominations workshops seminars, staff meetings. Franciscan Missionary Sisters of the Immaculate Conception. Sr. Mary Jesus, O.S.F., Dir. Capacity 112.

SANTA BARBARA. *St. Mary's Seminary Center*, 1964 Las Canoas Rd., 93105. Tel: 805-966-4829. Revs. James F. McOwen, C.M.; Roy Persich, C.M., Dir.; James Galvin, C.M. Priests 3.

SIERRA MADRE. *Mater Dolorosa Retreat Center*, 700 N. Sunnyside Ave., Box 68, 91025. Tel: 818-355-7188; Fax: 818-355-0485. Conducted by the Passionist Community. Lay Retreat League for men and women. Specialized Retreats.
Retreat Team: Revs. Patrick Brennan, C.P., Retreat Dir.; Philip Paxton, C.P., Assoc. Retreat Dir.; Ben Olson, C.P.; Sr. Judy Rinek, S.N.J.M.; Bros. John Rockenbach, C.P.; Anthony Mimiaga, C.P.; Mrs. Mary Lou Butler, Business Admin. Priests 3; Brothers 2.

VALYERMO. *St. Andrew's Abbey Retreat House (All Groups)*, 31001 N. Valyermo Rd., P.O. Box 40, 93563. Conducted by the Benedictine Monks. Revs. Francis Benedict, O.S.B., Retreat Dir. & Abbot. Tel: 805-944-2178; Isaac Kalina, O.S.B., Youth Center Dir. & Prior. Tel: 805-944-2734; Philip Edwards, O.S.B., Guestmaster. Tel: 805-944-2178; Bro. Benedict Dull, O.S.B., Guestmaster.

[X] PERSONAL PRELATURES

LOS ANGELES. *Opus Dei. Prelature of the Holy Cross and Opus Dei*, 655 Levering Ave., 90024. Tel: 310-208-0941. Revs. Rene J. Schatteman; Jose P. Ruisanchez.

[Y] CATHOLIC CHARITIES OF CALIFORNIA

LOS ANGELES. *Catholic Charities of Los Angeles, Inc.* His Eminence Roger Cardinal Mahony, D.D.; Rev. Msgr. Gregory A. Cox, M.S.W., Exec. Dir.; Rev. G. Lopez, M.S.W., Chief Admin. Officer.

Central Office, 1531 W. 9th St., 90015-1194. Tel: 213-251-3400; 251-3464.
Residential Youth Services. Residential & Transitional. Rancho San Antonio, Boys Town of the West, 21000 Plummer St., Chatsworth, 91311. Tel: 818-882-6400. Bro. John Crowe, C.S.C., Exec. Dir.

Child Development Services Department (ADESTE). Schools throughout Archdiocese, Community Centers. 1530 W. Ninth St., P.O. Box 15095, 90015. Tel: 213-251-3557. Armine Lalaian-Sanjar, Quality Assurance Dir.

Youth Services Shelter, Angel's Flight (Runaway Youth Program), 357 S. Westlake, 90057. Tel: 213-413-2311.

CYO Youth Athletics, 1530 W. 9th St., 90015. Tel: 213-251-3453. Mr. Bob Fitzpatrick, Prog. Dir.

Hope in Youth. Mike Clements, Dir. Tel: 213-662-9636.

Center for Adult Services, 1530 W. Ninth St., P.O. Box 15095, 90015. Tel: 213-251-3480. Mrs. Guadalupe U. Macker, Dir.

Psychological Services Department, 1530 W. 9th St., P.O. Box 15095, 90015. Tel: 213-251-3458. Dr. Ed Nelson, Dept. Dir.

Individual, Group, and Family Counseling, 1530 W. 9th St., 90015. Tel: 213-251-3569. 1028 N. Lake Ave., Suite 105, Pasadena, 91001. Tel: 818-398-7067. 7120 Hayvenhurst Ave., Ste. 200, Van Nuys, 91406. Tel: 818-988-2850. 6505 Rosemead Blvd. #108, Pico Rivera, 90660. Tel: 310-949-2496. 2013 Colorado Ave., Santa Monica, 90404. Tel: 310-829-7944. 215 E. Fesler St., Santa Maria, 93455. Tel: 805-348-1627. 609 E. Haley St., Santa Barbara, 93103. Tel: 805-962-2028. 303 N. Ventura Blvd., Ventura, 93001. Tel: 805-643-4780.
Aging Services Department: Spiritual Life Outreach Program, 1530 W. 9th St., 90015. Tel: 213-251-3476. Sr. Marian Gallagher, C.S.J.

OASIS (Older Adult Services & Intervention System), 1150 E. 4th St., Long Beach, 90802. Tel: 310-901-2977. 4032 La Colina Rd. #8, Santa Barbara, 93110. Tel: 805-569-5368. 2532 Ventura Blvd., Camarillo, 93010. Tel: 805-987-2083. 5649 Pittman St., Simi Valley, 93063. Tel: 805-526-3009.

Building Intergenerational Community (BICS)/ Teens Assisting Senior Citizens (TASC), 80 E. Hillcrest #201, Thousand Oaks, 91360. Tel: 805-495-9940.

TASC (Teens Assisting Senior Citizens), 9200 Mines Ave., Pico Rivera, 90660. Tel: 310-801-4304.

Immigration and Refugee Department: Loc Nguyen, Dept. Dir. Tel: 213-251-3489; Jo Marcel, Asst. Dir. Tel: 213-251-3470, Central Administrative Offices, 1530 W. 9th St., 90015.

Immigration Program. Tel: 213-251-3471.

Refugee Resettlement Program. Tel: 213-251-3460.
Regional Offices: 11100 Valley Blvd., Ste. 220, El Monte, 91731. Tel: 818-442-0587. 105 Hawthorne

Blvd., Inglewood, 90304. Tel: 310-672-2208. Central Intake Unit Dept. Tel: 213-251-3478. Joe D. Lee, Dir. Tel: 213-251-3445, Burbank Center, 217 E. Alameda Ave. #211, Burbank, 91502. Tel: 818-841-2430. San Gabriel Center, 11100 Valley Blvd. #100, El Monte, 91731. Tel: 818-582-8073. Long Beach Center, 944 Pacific Ave., Ste. 2, Long Beach, 90813. Tel: 310-437-1399. L.A. Center, 1530 W. 9th St., 90015. Tel: 213-251-3595. Education & Training Department, 1530 W. 9th St., 90015. Tel: 213-251-3547. Mr. Richard Cadena, Dir. Tel: 213-251-3570, Job Training Partnership Act (JTPA), ESL Citizenship Program, 1530 W. 9th St., P.O. Box 15095, 90015. Tel: 213-251-3547.

Santa Monica Youth Employment & Training Program. Tel: 310-829-5451.

Our Lady of the Angels Metro Region. (Inner City, South Central, Hollywood, East Side, Vernon), 4665 Willowbrook Ave., 90029. Tel: 213-662-1462. Greg Stuart, Regional Dir.

Shelters and Housing:

Good Shepherd Center for Homeless Women. Languille Residence, 267 N. Belmont Ave., 90026. Tel: 213-250-5241. The Hawkes Residence, 1039 W. 87th St., 90044. Tel: 213-758-4761. Sr. Julia Mary Farley, Prog. Dir.

Good Shepherd Mother/Child Center. Tel: 213-469-0376. Angel's Flight Shelter & Outreach, 357 S. Westlake, 90057. Tel: 213-413-2311.

Community Centers: El Santo Nino, 601 E. 23rd St., 90011. Tel: 213-748-5246. St. Catherine of Alexandria, 934 W. 70th St, 90044. Tel: 213-752-3786. St. Mary's Center, 4665 Willowbrook Ave., 90029. Tel: 213-662-4391.

Our Lady of the Angels Western Region. (Inglewood, Hawthorne, Lennox, Santa Monica, Venice, Culver City, Mialibu, West Los Angeles), 211 3rd Ave., Venice, 90291. Tel: 310-392-8701. Jim Stratton, Regional Dir.

Community Centers: St. Margaret's, 10505 Hawthorne Blvd., Lennox, 90304. Tel: 310-672-2208. St. Peter Claver, 4202 W. Jefferson, 90016. Tel: 213-737-6036. St. Robert's, 211 3rd Ave., Venice, 90291. Tel: 310-392-8701.

San Fernando Pastoral Region. (Glendale, Burbank, Verdugo Hills, Antelope Valley, San Fernando, Pacoima, Encino, and Van Nuys). 21600 Hart St., Canoga Park, 91303. Tel: 818-883-6015. Moeed N. Khan, L.I.C.S.W., Regl. Dir.

Shelter: Lancaster Community Shelter for the Homeless, 44611 N. Yucca Ave., Lancaster, 93534. Tel: 805-945-7524.

Community Centers: Glendale Community Center, 4322 San Fernando Rd., Glendale, 91204. Tel: 818-409-3080.

Thrift Store: 818-247-8196. Guadalupe Community Center, 21600 Hart St., Canoga Park, 91303. Tel: 818-340-2050. Santa Rosa Community Center, 511 Kalisher St., San Fernando, 91340. Tel: 818-365-3194.

Thrift Stores: 135 1/2 S. Brand Blvd., Glendale, 91204. Tel: 818-956-1857. Loaves and Fishes, 14535 Delano St., Ste. 102, Van Nuys, 91411. Tel: 818-997-0943. Loaves and Fishes, 511 Kalisher St., San Fernando, 91340. Tel: 818-365-3194.

San Gabriel Pastoral Region. (San Gabriel Valley, Mt. Baldy, Pomona Valley, East Los Angeles), 1307 Warren St., 90033. Tel: 213-264-8701. Mary Romero, Regl. Dir.

Community Centers: Brownson House Community Center, 1307 Warren Ave., 90033. Tel: 213-264-8701. 3017 Tyler Ave., #9, El Monte, 91733. Tel: 818-575-7652. Brother Miguel Center, 808 N. Garey Ave., #5, Pomona, 91767. Tel: 909-622-3466.

San Pedro Pastoral Region. (Long Beach, South Bay, Wilmington, Montebello, El Segundo, Lynwood, Pico Rivera, San Pedro, Vernon), 123 E. 14th St., 90813. Tel: 310-591-1351. Vanessa Romain, Regional Dir., Long Beach Family Shelter for the Homeless, 123 E. 14th St., Long Beach, 90813. Tel: 310-591-1351. Community Services Department, 123 E. 14th St., Long Beach, 90813. Tel: 310-591-1351. Pico Rivera Community Services, 9115 Balfour St., Pico Rivera, 90660. Tel: 310-949-2496. Mahar House Community Center, 1115 Mahar Ave., Wilmington, 90744. Tel: 310-834-7265.

Santa Barbara Pastoral Region. (Santa Barbara and Ventura Counties), 609 E. Haley St., 93103. Tel: 805-568-0781. Davida Willis, Regl. Dir.

Community Services Department, 609 E. Haley St., Santa Barbara, 93103. Tel: 805-965-7045. Lompoc Community Center, 1011 N. "A" St., Lompoc, 93436. Tel: 805-736-6226. Carpenteria Community Services, 941 Walnut St., Carpenteria, 93013. Tel: 805-684-8621. Santa Maria Community Services/ Thrift Store, 607 W. Main, Santa Maria, 93454. Tel: 805-922-2059.

Ventura County Region, 303 N. Ventura Ave., Ventura, 93001. Tel: 805-643-4694. A. Diane, Martell, Regional Dir.

Community Services Department: 303 N. Ventura Ave., Ventura, 93001. Tel: 805-643-4694. 77 First St., Moorpark, 93021. Tel: 805-529-0720. 80 E. Hillcrest Dr., Ste. 216, Thousand Oaks, 91630. Tel: 805-496-1113. 402 N. A St., Oxnard, 93030. Tel: 805-486-2900.

[Z] SUMMER CAMPS

LOS ANGELES. *Scouting and Camp Fire Ministry/ Catholic Youth Camps*, 1531 W. Ninth St., 90015. Tel: 310-427-2149. Eileen Gallagher, Contact Person; Al Garcia, Chm. Boy Scouts; Connie Hendry, Chm.; Rev. James J. Maher, Boy Scout Chap.; Sr. Lucille Coulihan, I.H.M., Girl Scout Chap.

St. Vincent dePaul Ranch Camp. (Boys), 210 N. Ave. 21st, 90031. Tel: 213-221-9886. Capacity 100.

Sponsored by St. Vincent de Paul Society.

Camp Mariastella. (Girls). Coed Program for Developmentally Disabled, Ages 7-Adult. 1120 Manchester Pl., 90019. Tel: 213-733-1208.

Owned & Operated by Sisters of Social Service. Capacity 140.

Located in Wrightwood.

Sacred Heart Retreat Camp. Girls & Boys Sessions, Ages 8-17 years. 869 S. Rimpau Blvd., 90005. Tel: 213-935-2372.

Owned and operated by the Sisters of the Society Devoted to the Sacred Heart. Capacity 150.

Located at Big Bear Lake.

Camp Teresita Pines. (Girls), Ages 7-15 years. 1400 W. 9th St., P.O. Box 15095, 90015. Tel: 213-388-5126.

Owned & Operated by Catholic Daughters of the Americas. Capacity 125.

Located in Big Pines Area near Wrightwood.

[AA] ST. VINCENT DE PAUL SOCIETY

LOS ANGELES. *St. Vincent de Paul Society*, 210 N. Avenue 21, 90031. Tel: 213-224-6280. Jose J. Rossier, Exec. Dir.

Stores and Workshops, 210 N. Avenue 21, 90031. Tel: 213-224-6280. Anthony Terrazas, Store Dir.

St. Vincent de Paul Ranch Camp & Retreat Center, 210 N. Avenue 21, 90031. Tel: 213-246-6213. Mario Perez, Camp Coord.

St. Vincent's Cardinal Manning Center, 231 Winston St., 90013. Tel: 213-229-9963; Fax: 213-620-9141. Joan Sotiros, Dir.

St. Vincent de Paul Stores, 210 N. Avenue 21, 90031. Tel: 213-224-6280.

For Pick Up: 213-224-6280; 800-974-3571.

[BB] NEWMAN CENTERS

LOS ANGELES. *Archdiocesan Office for Campus Ministry*, 3424 Wilshire Blvd., 90010-2248. Tel: 213-637-7527; Fax: 213-637-6527. Laurie W. Oester, Archdiocesan Dir.

California State University, Los Angeles, 5151 State Univ. Dr. #220 Health Center, 90032. Tel: 213-343-2571; Fax: 213-343-6407. Rev. Gilbert Romero; Mr. Robert Warren.

Loyola Law School, 1441 W. Olympic Blvd., 90015. Tel: 213-736-1084; Fax: 213-380-3769. Rev. Jim Erps, S.J.

Loyola Marymount University, 7101 W. 80th St., 90045. Tel: 310-338-2860; Fax: 310-338-1805. Mr. Fernando Moreno, Dir.; Revs. John Boyle, S.J.; Thomas P. Higgins, S.J.; Keith Brehob, S.J.; Sr. Cecilia Magladry, C.S.J.; Sr. Peg Dolan, R.S.H.M.; Rev. John Weling, S.J.; Ms. Aimee Loth-Barton; Mr. Will Salvini; Mr. John Flaherty; Ms. Kristi Gonsalves; Ms. Ami McColl; Ms. Debora Garza.

Mount St. Mary College, Chalon Campus, 12001 Chalon Rd., 90049. Tel: 310-471-9837; Fax: 310-476-9296. Ms. Gail Gresser, Dir.

Mount St. Mary College, Doheny Campus, 10 Chester Pl., 90007. Tel: 213-746-0450, Ext. 2152; Fax: 213-744-0833. Sr. Maria Angela Mesa, C.S.J.

Occidental College, Catholic Campus Ministry, 1600 Campus Rd., 90041. Tel: 213-341-4000, Ext. 3426. Ms. Maria Pollia; Rev. Martin Diaz, O.P.

University of California, Los Angeles, University Catholic Center, 840 Hilgard Ave., 90024. Tel: 310-208-5015; Fax: 310-208-6077. Revs. Theodore Vierra, C.S.P., Dir.; Mark Villano, C.S.P.; Terri Pfender, O.Carm.; Ms. Heather Sheridan, University of Southern California, Our Saviour University Parish, 3207 University Ave., 90007. Tel: 213-749-5341; Fax: 213-749-3475. Rev. William Messenger, O.S.M.; Ms. Kay Tallmadge.

University of Southern California, Health Sciences Campus, Catholic Campus Ministry, P.O. Box 61305, Pasadena, 91116. Tel: 818-305-5363; Fax: 818-305-5373. Revs. Thomas White, L.C.; Brian Wilson, L.C.

Claremont Colleges, McAllister Religious Center, 919 N. Columbia, 91711. Tel: 909-621-8825, Ext. 2937; Fax: 909-621-8304.

University of California Santa Barbara. St. Mark University Parish, 6550 Picasso Rd., Goleta, 93117. Tel: 805-968-1078; Fax: 805-968-3965. Revs. Ruben Patino, C.S.P.; Edward Nowak, C.S.P.

University of La Verne (La Verne). Catholic Campus Ministry, 1950 Third St., 91750. Tel: 909-593-3511, Ext. 4322; Fax: 909-593-0965. Ms. Maria Elena Cardena.

California State University - Long Beach. University Interfaith Center, 1250 Bellflower Blvd., USU-116, 90840. Tel: 310-985-7629; Fax: 310-985-5367. Ms. Laurie W. Oester.

California State University - Northridge. CSUN/ CNM, 1811 Nordhoff St., Northridge, 91330. Tel: 818-677-4850; Fax: 818-677-5815. Sr. Patricia Boroughs, S.N.J.M.

California Institute of Technology - Pasadena. Catholic Campus Ministry, P.O. Box 61305, Pasadena, 91116. Tel: 818-305-5363; Fax: 818-305-5373. Revs. Thomas White, L.C.; Brian Wilson, L.C.

California State Polytechnic University (Pomona). Union Plaza Interfaith Center, 3801 West Temple Ave., 91768. Tel: 909-869-3608. Mrs. Jane Kirchner.

Marymount College (Rancho Palos Verdes). Campus Ministry, 30800 Palos Verdes Dr. E., 90274. Tel: 310-377-4240; Fax: 310-377-6223. Rev. Sean Cronin, Dir.

Don Bosco Technical Institute (Rosemead). Campus Ministry, 1151 San Gabriel Blvd., 91770. Tel: 818-307-6551; Fax: 818-280-9316. Rudy Herrera; Mr. Chris Trosclair.

[CC] MISCELLANEOUS LISTINGS

LOS ANGELES. *Archdiocesan Spirituality Center*, 2 Chester Pl., 90007. Tel: 213-747-6508. Sr. Thomas Bernard, C.S.J., Dir.

Catholic Big Brothers, Inc., 3300 W. Temple St., 90026. Tel: 213-251-9800. Ken Martinet, Exec. Dir.; His Eminence Roger Cardinal Mahony, Honorary Chm.

Five branch offices in Los Angeles.

Catholic Charities Community Development Corporation, Inc., 1400 W. Ninth St., 90015.

Catholic Healthcare West Southern California.

Robert F. Kennedy Medical Center.

St. Bernardine Medical Center.

St. Francis Medical Center.

St. Mary Medical Center.

St. Vincent Medical Center.

Charisma in Missions, La Porciuncula, 1059 S. Gage Ave., 90023; Fax: 213-260-7221. Catholic Center of Evangelization and renewal ministries. A service for hispanic people through ongoing affirmation and growth seminars and courses; Catholic evangelizers' formation courses; direct evangelization missions; social service programs; prayer hot-line services; television and radio ministries; and a bookstore providing Catholic books, audio and video cassettes.

Collaborative Project for Aging Religious, 2035 W. Adams Blvd., 90018. Tel: 213-735-3625.

Conrad N. Hilton Fund for Sisters, 10100 Santa Monica Blvd. #760, 90067. Tel: 310-785-0746. Sr. Marcia Sichol, S.H.C.J.

Equestrian Order of the Holy Sepulcher of Jerusalem, 3424 Wilshire Blvd., 90010-2241. His Eminence Roger Cardinal Mahony, K.G.C.H.S., Grand Prior, 994 Rippey St., El Cajon, 92020. Sir George G. Zorn, K.G.C.H.S., Lieutenant.

Filipino Pastoral Ministry (Artesia), 18708 S. Clarkdale Ave., 90701. Tel: 310-402-9226; Fax: 310-860-0178. Rev. Msgr. Loreto Gonzales, Dir.

The Focolare Movement, Men's Branch (California) (Work of Mary), 8016 Cowan Ave., 90045. Tel: 310-670-6736; Fax: 310-670-8036. Formation in the Spirituality of Unity. Mr. Fritz Zuger, Dir. West Coast.

Franciscan Communications, 1229 S. Santee St., 90015. Tel: 213-746-2916, Ext. 202. Kenneth E. Martinet, Pres. & CEO.

(St. Francis Theatre: Winston Press, TeleKETICS, AudioSPOTS, TeleSPOTS).

Friends of John Paul II Foundation of Southern California, 3424 W. Adams Blvd., 90018. Tel: 818-281-0516. Stanislaw K. Cybulski, Pres.

Hospitaller Foundation of California, Inc., The, 2035 W. Adams Blvd., 90018. Tel: 213-731-7141. Bro. Patrick Corr, O.H., Pres., Dir. & Moderator. (Fund raising arm for St. John of God Retirement and Care Center).

Women's League of St. John of God.

Helpers Club of St. John of God.

Korean Catholic Renewal Movement of Southern California, 3422 W. 8th St., 90005.

Luz De Cristo USA. Member of Lumen 2000. 5953 W. 86th Pl., 90045. Tel: 310-641-2000; Fax: 310-641-1127.

National Catholic Council for Hispanic Ministry, Inc. (NCCHM), 8601 Lincoln Blvd., Rm. 430, 90045. Tel: 310-649-4214; Fax: 310-649-4214.

Perpetual Eucharistic Adoration, Inc., 660 Club View Dr., 90024. Tel: 310-273-3856. L. Owen Traynor, Contact Person.

Queen of Angels Hospital, 155 N. Occidental Blvd.,

90026. Tel: 213-381-2931. A California corporation sponsored by the Franciscan Sisters of the Sacred Heart. Tom Owenson, Admin. Mgr.

Rosary Hour Inc., The, 809 S. Flower St., 90017. Tel: 213-627-6863; 6864. Rev. James L. Kolling, Dir.

St. Francis Center, 1203 S. Santee St., 90015. Tel: 213-747-5347; Fax: 213-765-8915. His Eminence Roger M. Mahony, Honorary Pres.; Rev. Joseph Chinnici, O.F.M.Prov.

Provincial Definitors of the Province of Saint Barbara. Legal Title: *Provincial Definitors of the Province of Saint Barbara Franciscan Friars of California*. Mr. Phillip Cunliffe, Executive Dir.

St. Peter Claver Center, 4202 W. Jefferson Blvd., 90016-4113. Tel: 213-737-6036.

St. Vincent Senior Citizen Nutrition Program, Inc., 2131 W. Third St., 90057. Meals served daily 1,987.

Santa Marta Hospital Foundation, 319 N. Humphreys Ave., 90022. Tel: 213-260-8686. Mr. Michael A. O'Flaherty, Chm.; Mr. Ricardo Robles, Vice Chm.; Sr. Catherine Marie Kreta, C.S.J., Sec.; Mr. Michael J. Lightfoot, Treas.

Serra Ancillary Care, 3424 Wilshire Blvd., 90010. Tel: 213-251-3531; Fax: 213-383-0863. Sr. M. Carolita Hart, C.S.C., Pres.

Servants of the Immaculate Child Mary, 5135 Dartsmouth Ave., 90032. Tel: 213-225-3279. Sr. Enedina Cuevas, Contact Person.

Vincentians Province of the West Support Trust Fund, 2131 W. Third St., 90057. Tel: 213-484-5559. Mr. Michael Garko, Contact Person.

BALDWIN PARK. *The Redemptorist Vietnamese Mission Corporation*, 3452 N. Big Dalton Ave., 91706. Revs. Vu Minh Nghiem, C.SS.R., Pres.; Nguyen Duc Thong, C.SS.R., Vice Pres.; Chau Xuan Bau, C.SS.R., Sec. & Treas.

BELLFLOWER. *World Apostolate of Fatima, Los Angeles Archdiocesan Division*. Blue Army of Our Lady of Fatima. 15550 Bellflower Blvd., 90706-3819. Tel: 310-867-8661.

COVINA. *Comboni Missionaries*, 645 S. Aldenville Ave., 91723. Tel: 818-339-1914.

CULVER CITY. *Pauline Book and Media*, 3908 Sepulveda Blvd., 90230. Tel: 310-397-8676. Sr. Mary Assumpta, F.S.P., Supr.

EL MONTE. *Hombre Nuevo*, 12036 Ramona Blvd., 91732. Tel: 818-444-4442. Rev. Juan Rivas, L.C.

FILLMORE. *Apostolate of Christian Renewal/Holy Family Home of Peace*, 411 First St., P.O. Box 547, 93016-0547. Rev. Luke Zimmer, SS.CC., Dir.

GLENDORA. *Serra Institute*, 820 N. Verano Dr., 91771-2275.

GRANADA HILLS. *Chinese Catholic Bishops Conference Vocations Center*, 11459 Hayvenhurst, 91344. Rev. Vincent Mao Men (Taiwan).

HOLLYWOOD. *Family Theater Productions*, 7201 Sunset Blvd., 90046. Tel: 213-874-6635; Fax: 213-874-1168. Sponsored by Congregation of Holy Cross, Eastern Province. Revs. Hugh W. Cleary, C.S.C., Prov.; John P. Phalen, C.S.C., Interim Pres.; Fred Serraino, C.S.C., Natl. Dir.; Mr. Robert P. Klein, Vice Pres. Finance & Admin.

LA CRESCENTA. *Catholic Press Council*, 4919 Ramsdell, 91214. Tel: 818-957-0913. Ms. Sharon Benoit, Pres.

LA VERNE. *Picpus Charitable Trust*, 2150 Damien Ave., 91750.

LANCASTER. *Our Lady of Charity, Inc.*, P.O. Box 412. Tel: 805-942-3222. Ellen Butera. Tel: 805-948-8044.

LONG BEACH. *St. Mary Catholic Housing Corp.*, 1050 Linden Ave., P.O. Box 887, 90801.

St. Mary Medical Center Foundation, 1050 Linden Ave., P.O. Box 887, 90801. Tel: 310-491-9225; Fax: 310-491-9888. Sisters of Charity of the Incarnate Word, Houston, Texas. John T. Wagner, Pres.

MONTEREY PARK. *Congregation of St. John the Baptist*, 220 S. Ynez Ave., 91754. Tel: 818-280-1590; 213-261-3354. Very Rev. Stanislaus Su, C.S.J.B., Contact Person.

Theresian Sisters, 901 W. El Repetto Dr., 91754. Tel: 213-780-1965. Sr. Felicitas Hong, C.S.T., Contact Person.

PACIFIC PALISADES. *Paulist Pictures*, P.O. Box 1057, 90272. Tel: 310-454-0688; Fax: 310-459-6549.

Paulist Productions, (Insight) 17575 Pacific Coast Hwy., 90272. Tel: 310-454-0688; Fax: 310-459-6549. Rev. Ellwood E. Kieser, C.S.P., Pres.

PASADENA. *Journey House, Inc.*, 1232 N. Los Robles Ave., 91104-2814. Tel: 818-798-9478. Bro. Tim Mayworm, F.S.C. Six bed group home for wards of the court helping young people finish high school. Clients have little or no family support.

REDONDO BEACH. *SCRC Renewal Center*, 2810 Artesia Blvd., 90278. Tel: 310-371-6433; Fax: 310-371-8452. Dominic Berardino, Pres.; Donna Ross, Vice Pres.

Host annual summer convention, retreats and year-round seminars & teaching events. Offer Pastoral consultation. Retail operation open Mon.-Sat. features books, gifts, statues, audio, video & jewelry. Book tables available for special events. Call Bookstore, Tel: 310-371-6072.

SAN FERNANDO. *Valley Family Center*, 302 S. Brand Blvd., 91340. Tel: 818-365-8588; Fax: 818-898-3382. Religious Sisters of Charity. Sr. Una Connolly, R.S.C., Exec. Dir.; Sr. Carmel Somers, R.S.C., Dir. of Learning Center. All Services are in English and Spanish. Counseling is available for individual, marriage, family, children/teen, chemical dependency, victims of sexual an physical abuse, and adults molested as children (AMAC). Special Programs include School Counseling; Parent Education; anger management; violence prevention; victims and perpatrators of domestic violence; at risk youth. Learning Center Programs include tutorials; basic skill building for children and adults, and opportunities for gifted students.

SAN PEDRO. *Apostleship of the Sea, Catholic Maritime Ministry*, Mary, Star of the Sea Parish, 870 W. 8th St., 90731. Tel: 310-833-3541. Rev. Msgr. Patrick Gallagher, Port Chap.; Rev. Sylvester J. Thomas, Dir. of Chap. Svcs., Center: Berth 93A, World Cruise Center, Port of Los Angeles, 90731. Tel: 310-521-1041.

SANTA BARBARA. *The Franciscan Sisters of the Sacred Heart in CA*. (A California non-profit corp.), 601 E. Micheltorena, 93103. Tel: 805-568-5816. Franciscan Sisters of the Sacred Heart, (Frankfort). Sr. Karen Marie Lanigan, Supr. Gen.; Mr. Ron Biscaro, Vice Chm. & Pres.

World Wide Marriage Encounter, 1964 Las Canoas Rd., 93105-2351. Tel: 805-882-1942. Rev. James M. Galvin, C.M.

STUDIO CITY. *Association of Christian Therapists*, 3709 Laurel Canyon Blvd., 91604. Tel: 818-762-3329.

VENICE. *St. Joseph Center*, 204 Hampton Dr., 90219. Tel: 310-396-6468. Sr. Mary Allen, Contact Person.

VENTURA. *Buenaventura Interfaith Volunteer CAREGIVERS*, 261 N. Catalina St., 93001. Tel: 805-652-0566; Fax: 805-652-0568. 117 N. 7th St., Santa Paula, 93060. Tel: 805-525-5006.

WEST COVINA. *Fr. Kolbe Missionaries of the Immaculata*, 531 E. Merced Ave., 91790. Tel: 818-917-0040; Fax: 818-917-0900.

WESTLAKE VILAGE. *Veritas Communications, Inc.*, 3114 La Baya Dr., #200, 91362; Fax: 818-991-2024.

WOODLAND HILLS. *West San Fernando Valley Magnificat Chapter Ministry to Catholic Women*, 23211 Collins St., 91367. Tel: 818-347-7144.

[DD] LEGAL TITLES

LOS ANGELES. *Chancery Office*, 3424 Wilshire Blvd., 90010-2241. Tel: 213-837-7000. For further information contact the Chancery. Also see Miscellaneous for additional listings.

Recollect Augustinian Fathers & Brothers, Province of St. Augustine, Inc.

Missionary Oblates of Mary Immaculate, Western Province, Inc.

School Sisters of Notre Dame de Namur of the California Province, Inc.

Congregation of the Sacred Heart of Jesus & Mary and of Perpetual Adoration, Inc.

Sisters of St. Louis Monaghan, Inc.

Ursulines of the Western Province, Inc.

RELIGIOUS INSTITUTES OF MEN REPRESENTED IN THE ARCHDIOCESE

For further details refer to the corresponding bracketed number in the Religious Institutes of Men or Women section.

[0140]—*The Augustinians*.—O.S.A.
[0200]—*Benedictine Monks (Congregation of the Annunciation)*.—O.S.B.
[0980]—*Brothers of Our Lady Mother of Mercy*.—C.F.M.M.
[1350]—*Brothers of San Francis Xavier*.—C.F.X.
[1160]—*Brothers of St. Patrick*.—F.S.P.
[0330]—*Brothers of the Christian Schools*.—F.S.C.
[0900]—*Canons Regular of Premontre*.—O.Praem.
[]—*Canons Regular of the Immaculate Conception*.—C.R.I.C.
[0470]—*The Capuchin Friars (St. Patrick's Custody)*.—O.F.M.Cap.
[0270]—*Carmelite Fathers & Brothers*. (Prov. of the Most Pure Heart of Mary).—O.Carm.
[0360]—*Claretian Missionaries*. (Western Prov.).—C.M.F.
[0380]—*Comboni Missionaries of the Heart of Jesus*. (Verona).—M.C.C.J.
[0310]—*Congregation of Christian Brothers*.—C.F.C.
[]—*Congregation of St. John the Baptist*.—C.S.J.B.
[1150]—*Congregation of St. Joseph*.—C.S.J.
[1330]—*Congregation of the Mission*. (Prov. of the West).—C.M.
[1210]—*Congregation of the Missionaries of St. Charles*.—C.S.
[1000]—*Congregation of the Passion*. (Western Prov.).—C.P.
[1140]—*Congregation of the Sacred Hearts of Jesus and Mary*.—SS.CC.
[0480]—*Conventual Franciscans*. (St. Joseph Cupertino Prov.).—O.F.M.Conv.
[0260]—*Discalced Carmelite Friars*.—O.C.D.
[0520]—*Franciscan Friars*. (St. Barbara Prov.).—O.F.M.
[0530]—*Franciscan Friars of the Atonement*.—S.A.
[]—*Guadalupe Missioners*. (Mexico).—M.G.
[0650]—*Holy Ghost Fathers*.—C.S.Sp.
[0670]—*Hospitaller Brothers of St. John of God*.—O.H.
[0690]—*Jesuit Fathers and Brothers*. (Calif. Prov.).—S.J.
[0710]—*Josephite Fathers*.—C.J.
[0730]—*Legionaries of Christ*.—L.C.
[]—*The Little Brothers of the Good Shepherd*.—B.G.S.
[0780]—*Marist Fathers*.—S.M.
[0800]—*Maryknoll*.—M.M.
[0830]—*Mill Hill Missionaries*.—M.H.M.
[]—*Missionaries of Charity Brothers*.—M.C.
[0660]—*Missionaries of the Holy Spirit*.—M.Sp.S.
[1110]—*Missionaries of the Sacred Heart*.—M.S.C.
[0840]—*Missionary Servants of the Most Holy Trinity*.—S.T.
[0910]—*Oblates of Mary Immaculate*. (Western Prov.).—O.M.I.
[0930]—*Oblates of St. Joseph*.—O.S.J.
[0940]—*Oblates of the Virgin Mary*.—O.M.V.
[]—*Operarios del Reino de Cristo*.—O.R.C.
[0835]—*Order of Minims*.—O.M.
[0430]—*Order of Preachers-Dominicans*. (Western Prov.).—O.P.
[0150]—*Order of the Augustinian Recollects*.—O.A.R.
[1020]—*Pauline Fathers and Brothers, Society of St. Paul*.—S.S.P.
[1030]—*Paulist Fathers*.—C.S.P.
[1040]—*Piarist Fathers*.—Sch.P.
[1050]—*Pontifical Institute for Foreign Missions*.—P.I.M.E.
[0610]—*Priests of the Congregation of Holy Cross*.—C.S.C.
[1070]—*Redemptorist Fathers*. (Oakland Prov.).—C.SS.R.
[1090]—*Rogationist Fathers*.—R.C.J.
[0700]—*St. Joseph's Society of the Sacred Heart*.—S.S.J.
[1190]—*Salesians of Don Bosco*.—S.D.B.
[1240]—*Servites*.—O.S.M.
[0110]—*Society of African Missions*.—S.M.A.
[1260]—*Society of Christ*.—S.Ch.
[0760]—*Society of Mary*.—S.M.
[0850]—*Society of Missionaries of Africa*.—M.Afr.
[0370]—*Society of St. Columban*.—S.S.C.
[0420]—*Society of the Divine Word*.—S.V.D.
[1060]—*Society of the Precious Blood*.—C.PP.S.
[1290]—*Society of the Priests of St. Sulpice*.—S.S.

RELIGIOUS INSTITUTES OF WOMEN REPRESENTED IN THE ARCHDIOCESE

[]—*Armenian Sisters of the Immaculate Conception*.—C.I.C.
[0230]—*Benedictine Sisters of Pontifical Jurisdiction*.—O.S.B.
[1810]—*Bernardine Sisters of the Third Order of St. Francis*.—O.S.F.
[2930]—*California Institute of the Sisters of the Most Holy and Immaculate Heart of the Blessed Virgin Mary*.—I.H.M.
[0370]—*Carmelite Sisters of the Most Sacred Heart of Los Angeles*.—O.C.D.
[3690]—*Congregation of the Sacred Hearts and of Perpetual Adoration*.—SS.CC.
[470]—*Congregation of the Sisters of Charity for the Incarnate Word*.—C.C.V.I.
[3935]—*Congregation of the Sisters of St. Louis, Juilly Monaghan*.—S.S.L.
[1920]—*Congregation of the Sisters of the Holy Cross*.—C.S.C.
[1940]—*Congregation of the Sisters of the Holy Faith*.—C.H.F.
[1950]—*Congregation of the Sisters of the Holy Family*.—S.S.F.
[0760]—*Daughters of Charity of St. Vincent de Paul*. (Prov. of the West).—D.C.
[0880]—*Daughters of Mary and Joseph*.—D.M.J.
[0850]—*Daughters of Mary Help of Christians*.—F.M.A.
[0420]—*Discalced Carmelite Nuns*.—O.C.D.
[1050]—*Dominican Comtemplative Nuns*.—O.P.
[1070-03]—*Dominican Sisters*.—O.P.
[1070-04]—*Dominican Sisters*.—O.P.
[1070-12]—*Dominican Sisters*.—O.P.
[1070-13]—*Dominican Sisters*.—O.P.

[1070-19]—*Dominican Sisters.*—O.P.
[1070-21]—*Dominican Sisters.*—O.P.
[1150]—*Eucharistic Franciscan Missionary Sisters.*—E.F.M.S.
[1170]—*Felician Sisters.*—C.S.S.F.
[1350]—*Franciscan Missionary Sisters of the Immaculate Conception.*—O.S.F.
[1230]—*Franciscan Sisters of Christian Charity.*—O.S.F.
[1310]—*Franciscan Sisters of Little Fall.*—O.S.F.
[1500]—*Franciscan Sisters of Mary Immaculate of the Third Order of St. Francis of Assisi.*—F.M.I.
[1780]—*Franciscan Sisters of Perpetual Adoration.*
[1450]—*Franciscan Sisters of the Sacred Heart.*—O.S.F.
[1845]—*Guadalupan Missionaries.*—M.G.Sp.S.
[]—*Handmaids of the Sacred Heart of Jesus, Mary & Joseph.*—J.M.J.
[2575]—*Institute of the Sisters of Mercy of the Americas.* (Burlingame, CA).—R.S.M.
[2340]—*Little Sisters of the Poor.*—L.S.P.
[2390]—*Lovers of the Holy Cross Sisters.*—L.H.C.
[2470]—*Maryknoll Sisters of St. Dominic.*—M.M.
[2500]—*Medical Sisters of St. Joseph.*—M.S.J.
[2710]—*Missionaries of Charity.*—M.C.
[0210]—*Missionary Benedictine Sisters.*—O.S.B.
[0390]—*Missionary Carmelites of St. Theresa.*—C.M.S.T.
[2790]—*Missionary Servants of the Most Blessed Trinity.*—M.S.B.T.
[2715]—*Missionary Sisters of Christ the King.*—M.S.C.K.
[2880]—*Missionary Sisters of St. Columban.*—S.S.C.
[2750]—*Missionary Sisters of the Immaculate Heart of Mary.*—I.C.M.
[3530]—*Missionary Sisters Servants of the Holy Spirit.*—S.Sp.S.
[3760]—*Order of St. Clare.*—P.C.C.
[3130]—*Our Lady of Victory Missionary Sisters.*—O.L.V.M.
[0980]—*Pious Disciples of the Divine Master.*—P.D.D.M.
[0950]—*Pious Society Daughters of St. Paul.*—F.S.P.
[2840]—*Poor Clare Missionary Sisters.*—M.C.
[3242]—*Poor Sisters of Nazareth.*—P.S.N.
[0930]—*Religious Daughters of St. Joseph.*—F.S.J.
[]—*Religious Missionaries of St. Dominic.*—O.P.
[3450]—*Religious of Jesus-Mary.*—R.J.M.
[3465]—*Religious of the Sacred Heart of Mary.*—R.S.H.M.
[3400]—*Religious Sisters of Charity.*—R.S.C.
[2970]—*School Sisters of Notre Dame.*—S.S.N.D.
[1680]—*School Sisters of St. Francis.*—O.S.F.
[3499]—*Servants of the Blessed Sacrament.*—S.J.S.
[]—*Servants of the Immaculate Child Mary.*—E.I.N.
[]—*Servants of the Love of God.*—R.A.D.
[]—*Servants of the Poor of St. Catherine.*—S.D.P.
[0250]—*Sisters of Bethany.*—C.V.D.
[0480]—*Sisters of Charity of Leavenworth, Kansas.*—S.C.L.
[0570]—*Sisters of Charity of Seton Hill, Greensburg, Pennsylvania.*—S.C.
[0430]—*Sisters of Charity of the Blessed Virgin Mary.*—B.V.M.
[2360]—*Sisters of Loretto At the Foot of the Cross.* (Southern Prov.).—S.L.
[]—*Sisters of Mary, Mother of the Church.*—M.M.C.
[2990]—*Sisters of Notre Dame.* (Prov. of Los Angeles).—S.N.D.
[3000]—*Sisters of Notre Dame de Namur.*—S.N.D.deN.
[3350]—*Sisters of Providence.*—S.P.
[3360]—*Sisters of Providence of Saint Mary-Of-The-Woods, Indiana.*—S.P.
[4080]—*Sisters of Social Service of Los Angeles, Inc.*—S.S.S.
[1705]—*Sisters of St. Francis of Assisi.*—O.S.F.
[1710]—*Sisters of St. Francis of Joliet.*—O.S.F.
[1620]—*Sisters of St. Francis of Millvale, Pennsylvania.*—O.S.F.
[1760]—*Sisters of St. Francis of Oldenburg.*—O.S.F.
[1630]—*Sisters of St. Francis of Penance and Christian Charity.*—O.S.F.
[1650]—*The Sisters of St. Francis of Philadelphia.*—O.S.F.
[1730]—*Sisters of St. Francis of Tiffin.*—O.S.F.
[3830-03]—*Sisters of St. Joseph.*—C.S.J.
[3830-11]—*Sisters of St. Joseph.*—S.S.J.
[3830-18]—*Sisters of St. Joseph.*—C.S.J.
[3840]—*Sisters of St. Joseph of Carondelet.*—C.S.J.
[3860]—*Sisters of St. Joseph of Cluny.*—S.J.C.
[3890]—*Sisters of St. Joseph of Peace.*—C.S.J.P.
[3930]—*Sisters of St. Joseph to the Third Order of St. Francis.*—S.S.J.-T.O.S.F.
[3960]—*Sisters of St. Mary of Oregon.*—S.S.M.O.
[0260]—*Sisters of the Blessed Sacrament for Indians and Colored People.*—S.B.S.
[0700]—*Sisters of the Company of Mary Our Lady.*—O.D.N.
[3180]—*Sisters of the Cross and Passion.*—C.P.
[1830]—*Sisters of the Good Shepherd.*—R.G.S.
[1850]—*Sisters of the Guardian Angel.*—S.A.C.
[1960]—*Sisters of the Holy Family.*—S.H.F.
[1990]—*Sisters of the Holy Names of Jesus and Mary.*—S.N.J.M.
[2270]—*Sisters of the Little Company of Mary.*—L.C.M.
[3200]—*Sisters of the Pious Schools.*—Sch.P.
[3260]—*Sisters of the Precious Blood (Dayton, Ohio).*—C.PP.S.
[3320]—*Sisters of the Presentation of the B.V.M.* (San Francisco CA).—P.B.V.M.
[4050]—*Sisters of the Society Devoted to the Sacred Heart.*—S.D.S.H.
[1490]—*Sisters of the Third Franciscan Order.*—O.S.F.
[3600]—*Sisters Servants of Mary.*—S.M.
[4060]—*Society of the Holy Child Jesus.*—S.H.C.J.
[]—*Theresian Sisters.*—C.S.T.
[3330]—*Union of Sisters of Presentation of the P.B.M.*—P.B.V.M.
[4110]—*Ursuline Nuns (Roman Union).*—O.S.U.

ARCHDIOCESAN CEMETERIES

LOS ANGELES. *Calvary Cemetery and Mausoleum.* Tel: 213-261-3106. Kevin Haynes, Mgr.
CULVER CITY. *Holy Cross Cemetery & Mausoleum & Columbarium.* Tel: 310-670-7697. Philip Birgel, Mgr.
LANCASTER. *Good Shepherd Cemetery & Mausoleum.* Tel: 805-722-0887. Daniel Rejniak, Mgr.
LONG BEACH. *All Souls Cemetery and Mausoleum.* Tel: 213-424-8601. Lillia Sanson, Mgr.
MISSION HILLS. *San Fernando Mission Cemetery & Mausoleum.* Tel: 818-361-7387. Michael Wesner, Mgr.
MONTEBELLO. *Resurrection Cemetery & Mausoleum.* Tel: 213-887-2024. Margaret Hunter, Mgr.
OXNARD. *Santa Clara Cemetery & Mausoleum.* Tel: 805-485-5757. Elizabeth Welsh, Mgr.
POMONA. *Holy Cross Cemetery.* Tel: 909-627-3602. Mary Ann McAdams, Mgr.
ROWLAND HEIGHTS. *Queen of Heaven Cemetery.* Tel: 818-964-1291. Norberta Orta, Mgr.
SANTA BARBARA. *Calvary Cemetery & Mausoleum.* Tel: 805-682-5793. William Sangster, Mgr.
SIMI. *Assumption Cemetery.* Tel: 805-583-5825. Elizabeth Welsh, Mgr.

NECROLOGY

† Lee, Lawrence J., Los Angeles, CA, St. John of God. —Died Dec. 5, 1996.
† Marum, Rev. Msgr. Kieran, Burbank, CA, St. Finbar. —Died Dec. 5. 1995.
† Shine, Cornelius, Los Angeles, CA, Immaculate Heart of Mary Church. —Died Dec. 4, 1996.
† Tamayo, Santiago L., (Unassigned). —Died Jan. 22, 96.

Archdiocese of Louisville

(Archidioecesis Ludovicopolitana)

Most Reverend

THOMAS C. KELLY, O.P., D.D., J.C.D.

Archbishop of Louisville; ordained June 5, 1958; appointed Titular Bishop of Tusuro July 12, 1977; promoted Archbishop of Louisville December 29, 1981. *Office: 212 E. College St., P.O. Box 1073, Louisville, KY, 40201.*

Most Reverend

CHARLES G. MALONEY, D.D.

Auxiliary Bishop Emeritus of the Archdiocese of Louisville; born September 9, 1912; ordained December 8, 1937; appointed Auxiliary December 30, 1954; consecrated February 2, 1955; appointed Titular Bishop of Bardstown February 2, 1995. *Res., 212 E. College St., P.O. Box 1073, Louisville, KY, 40201.*

Most Reverend

THOMAS J. McDONOUGH, D.D., J.C.D.

Retired Archbishop of Louisville; ordained May 26, 1938; appointed Titular Bishop of Thaenae March 10, 1947; consecrated April 30, 1947; transferred as Auxiliary from St. Augustine to Savannah, January 2, 1957; succeeded to See March 2, 1960; promoted Archbishop of Louisville March 1, 1967; resigned September 29, 1981.

Chancery: 212 E. College St., P.O. Box 1073, Louisville, KY, 40201. Tel.: 502-585-3291.

Web site address: http://www.archlou.org

E-mail address: chancery@archlou.org

ESTABLISHED AT BARDSTOWN APRIL 8, 1808; TRANSFERRED TO LOUISVILLE FEB. 13, 1841.

CREATED AN ARCHDIOCESE DEC. 10, 1937.

Square Miles 8,124.

Comprises the following twenty-four Counties in central Kentucky: Adair, Barren, Bullitt, Casey, Clinton, Cumberland, Green, Hardin, Hart, Henry, Jefferson, Larue, Marion, Meade, Metcalfe, Monroe, Nelson, Oldham, Russell, Shelby, Spencer, Taylor, Trimble and Washington.

For legal titles of parishes and archdiocesan institutions, consult the Chancery.

STATISTICAL OVERVIEW

Personnel	
Archbishop	1
Retired Archbishops	1
Retired Bishops	1
Abbots	1
Priests: Diocesan Active in Diocese	131
Priests: Active Outside Diocese	7
Priests: Diocesan in Foreign Missions	1
Priests: Retired, Sick or Absent	58
Number of Diocesan Priests	197
Religious Priests in Diocese	62
Extern Priests in Diocese	1
Ordinations:	
Diocesan Priests	2
Transitional Deacons	2
Permanent Deacons	12
Permanent Deacons in Diocese	103
Total Brothers	94
Total Sisters	1,083
Parishes	
Parishes	113
With Resident Pastor:	
Resident Diocesan Priests	81
Resident Religious Priests	11
Without Resident Pastor:	
Administered by Priests	17
Administered by Permanent Deacons	1
Administered by Women Religious	2
Administered by Lay People	1
Missions	13
Pastoral Centers	3
Closed Parishes	4
Professional Ministry Personnel:	
Sisters	43
Lay Ministers	140
Welfare	
Catholic Hospitals	2
Total Assisted	130,642
Health Care Centers	1
Total Assisted	2,000
Homes for the Aged	5
Total Assisted	577
Residential Care of Children	1
Total Assisted	22
Day Care and Extended Day Care Centers	1
Total Assisted	200
Specialized Homes	1
Total Assisted	378
Special Centers for Social Services	1
Total Assisted	3,521
Educational	
Diocesan Students in Other Seminaries	14
Total Seminarians	14
Colleges and Universities	3
Total Students	3,940
High Schools, Diocesan and Parish	4
Total Students	2,095
High Schools, Private	6
Total Students	3,849
Elementary Schools, Diocesan and Parish	56
Total Students	17,740
Elementary Schools, Private	3
Total Students	540
Non-residential Schools for the Disabled	1
Total Students	74
Catechesis/Religious Education:	
High School Students	1,282
Elementary Students	8,248
Total Students Under Catholic Instruction	37,782
Teachers in the Diocese:	
Priests	12
Brothers	28
Sisters	55
Lay Teachers	1,262
Vital Statistics	
Receptions into the Church:	
Infant Baptism Totals	2,912
Adult Baptism Totals	313
Received into Full Communion	523
First Communions	3,125
Confirmations	2,654
Marriages:	
Catholic	767
Interfaith	492
Total Marriages	1,259
Deaths	1,719
Total Catholic Population	181,570
Total Population	1,139,022

Former Bishops—Rt. Rev. BENEDICT JOSEPH FLAGET, S.S., D.D., cons. Bishop of Bardstown, Nov. 4, 1810; died Feb. 11, 1850.—Rt. Rev. JOHN B. DAVID, S.S., D.D., Coadjutor; cons. Aug. 15, 1819; died July 12, 1841.—Rt. Rev. GUY IGNATIUS CHABRAT, S.S., D.D., Coadjutor; cons. July 20, 1834; died Nov. 21, 1868.—Rt. Rev. MARTIN JOHN SPALDING, D.D., Coadjutor with right of succession; cons. Sept. 10, 1848; transferred to Baltimore, May 6, 1864; died Feb. 7, 1872.—Rt. Rev. PETER JOSEPH LAVIALLE, D.D., cons. Sept. 24, 1865; died May 11, 1867.—Rt. Rev. WILLIAM GEORGE MCCLOSKEY, D.D., cons. May 24, 1868; died Sept. 17, 1909.—Rt. Rev. DENIS O'DONAGHUE, D.D., ord. Sept. 6, 1874; cons. Titular Bishop of Pomario and Auxiliary of Indianapolis on April 25, 1900; transferred to Louisville, Feb. 7, 1910; transferred to the Titular See of Lebedus, July 26, 1924; died Nov. 7, 1925.—Most Rev. JOHN A. FLOERSH, D.D., ord. June 10, 1911; appt. Titular Bishop of Lycopolis and Coadjutor Bishop of Louisville with right of succession, Feb. 6, 1923; cons. April 8, 1923; succeeded to See July 26, 1924; elevated to Archiepiscopal dignity Dec. 10, 1937; resigned and named to Titular See of Sistroniana, March 1, 1967; died June 11, 1968.—Most Rev. THOMAS J. MCDONOUGH, D.D., resigned Sept. 29, 1981.

Vicars General—Very Rev. BERNARD J. BREEN; Most Rev. CHARLES G. MALONEY, D.D.

Chancery—212 E. College St., P.O. Box 1073, Louisville, 40201. Tel: 502-585-3291. Office Hours: 9-12:30 & 1:30-4:30 All applications for dispensations are to be sent to this office.

Archivist - Chancellor—Rev. ROBERT DALE CIESLIK.

Vice Chancellor—FLORENCE M. CRAWFORD.

Secretary to Archbishop—NORMA L. MERRICK.

Chief Administrative Officer—BRIAN B. REYNOLDS.

Chief Financial Officer—JEROME J. PAKENHAM.

Controller—PATRICIA J. MEYER.

Diocesan Tribunal—212 E. College St., P. O. Box 1073, Louisville, 40201. Tel: 502-585-3291.

Judicial Vicar—Very Rev. CHARLES C. THOMPSON.

Associate Director of Tribunal—DONALD M. SWIFT J.C.D.

Promoter of Justice—Rev. JOHN W. HANRAHAN.

Defenders of the Bond—Revs. DONALD R. GOETZ; JOHN J. STOLTZ; ROBERT E. OSBORNE; ANTHONY L. CHANDLER; PATRICK J. DOLAN; Dr. ROBERT L. STENGER; DONALD M. SWIFT.

Associate Judges—Revs. KENNETH R. FORTENER; THOMAS A. HOMMRICH; THOMAS P. CREAGH; T. MICHAEL TOBIN.
Assessor—PATRICIA A. NORRIS.
Notaries—PATRICIA M. SMYTHE; SHARON A. ARCHER; LINDA D. THOMAN.
Interdiocesan Appellate Tribunal-Province of Louisville Tribunal-Director of Tribunal—Very Rev. CHARLES C. THOMPSON.
Judicial Vicar—Very Rev. J. MARK SPALDING.
College of Consultors—Most Rev. CHARLES G. MALONEY; Very Rev. BERNARD J. BREEN; Revs. KEVIN J. BRYAN; WILLIAM D. HAMMER; CLARENCE J. HOWARD; JOHN L. SCHINDLER; J. ROY STILES.
Deans—Bardstown Deanery: Rev. WILLIAM F. MEDLEY, Lebanon Deanery: Rev. IVO E. CECIL, Elizabethtown Deanery: Rev. WILLIAM L. FICHTEMAN.
Clergy Personnel Commission—Revs. ROY E. DENTINGER; JOHN R. BURKE; THOMAS L. BOLAND; CHARLES D. WALKER; J. WAYNE JENKINS, Dir.
Priests' Council—Most Rev. THOMAS C. KELLY, O.P., Presider; Revs. WILLIAM D. HAMMER, Pres., *5505 Hudson Ln., Louisville, 40291.* Very Rev. CHARLES C. THOMPSON, Exec. Sec. Ex Officio: Most Rev. CHARLES G. MALONEY; Very Rev. BERNARD J. BREEN; Revs. JOSEPH H. VOOR; ROBERT E. OSBORNE; THOMAS R. CLARK; H. ANTHONY OLGES; JOSEPH T. GRAFFIS; TRUMIE C. ELLIOTT; BEDE SHIPPS O.P.; JOSEPH T. HERP; ANTHONY L. CHANDLER; THOMAS A. SMITH; JOSEPH DAWSON; J. ROY STILES; G. NICHOLAS RICE; JAMES E. HARGADON; CLARENCE J. HOWARD; MICHAEL D. LOTT; ROBERT M. ABEL; JOHN J. STOLTZ; MICHAEL GREENWELL, O.Carm.; FREDERICK PASCHE O.F.M.Conv.
Archdiocesan Examiners—Revs. JOHN HANRAHAN; JAMES SCHLICH; VINCENT SCHWEIZER; WILLIAM WAGNER.

Archdiocesan Offices and Directors

African American Catholic Ministries Office—M. ANNETTE TURNER, Dir., *Maloney Center, 1200 S. Shelby St., Louisville, 40203.* Tel: 502-636-0296.
Archdiocesan Communications Center—CECELIA PRICE, Chief Communications Officer, *Maloney Center, 1200 S. Shelby St., Louisville, 40203.* Tel: 502-636-0296.
Byzantine Rite Faithful—Rev. JOHN W. BIRK, Chap., *2914 S. Third St., Louisville, 40208.* Tel: 502-637-2058.
Catholic Cemeteries Office—KENNETH POPP, Dir. RICHARD E. STEINMETZ, Coord., *1600 Newburg Rd., P.O. Box 4096, Louisville, 40204.* Tel: 502-451-7710.
Catholic Deaf Office—Sr. THOMASINE DALEY, S.C.N., Dir., *1935 Lewiston Pl., Louisville, 40216.* Tel: 502-448-8937; 589-6766 (TTY).
Catholic Services Appeal—ROSEMARY SMITH, Dir.; Rev. THOMAS E. GENTILE, General Chm., *212 E. College St., P.O. Box 1073, Louisville, 40201.* Tel: 502-585-3291.
Charismatic Renewal—Flaget Center, 1935 Lewiston Pl., Louisville, 40216. Tel: 502-448-8581.
Catholic Charities—Rev. TIMOTHY A. HOGAN, Exec. Dir., *2911 S. 4th St., Louisville, 40208.* Tel: 502-637-9786.
Office of Migration and Refugee Services—
Office for Ministry to the Sick and the Elderly—
Office of Parish Outreach—
Office of Parish Social Ministry—
Office of Catholic Rural Life—
Clergy Personnel Office—Rev. J. WAYNE JENKINS, Dir., *P.O. Box 1073, Louisville, 40201.* Tel: 502-585-3291.
Clerical Aid Society—212 E. College St., P.O. Box 1073, Louisville, 40201. Tel: 502-585-3291.
Commission for the Permanent Diaconate Program—Sr. MARTHA BUSER, O.S.U., *1935 Lewiston Pl., Louisville, 40216.* Tel: 502-448-8581.
Continuing Education for Clergy-Ministry to Priests—Rev. ROBERT E. RAY, Dir. STEVEN WIRTH, Exec. Dir., *1935 Lewiston Pl., Louisville, 40216.* Tel: 502-448-8581.
Cursillo Movement—Deacon BRUCE LINCOLN, Spiritual Dir., *1935 Lewiston Pl., Louisville, 40216.* Tel: 502-448-8581.
Due Process Board—JOHN LAUN, Chm., *Kentucky Home Life Building, 239 S. 5th St., Louisville, 40202.* Tel: 502-587-0330.
Ecumenism, Office of—Rev. JUDE WEISENBECK, S.D.S., *1935 Lewiston Pl., Louisville, 40216.* Tel: 502-448-8581.
Evangelization, Office of—JOAN CUNNINGHAM, Dir., *Flaget Center, 1935 Lewiston Pl., Louisville, 40216.* Tel: 502-448-8581.
Family Ministries, Center for—BARBARA MACDONALD, Dir. THOMAS D. ROBBINS, Ph.D., Clinical Dir., *Maloney Center, 1200 S. Shelby St., Louisville, 40203.* Tel: 502-636-0296; Fax: 502-636-3381.
Respect Life—HELEN ROTHGERBER, Coord.
Holy Childhood Association—Rev. KEVIN CASTER, Dir., *212 E. College St., Box 1073, Louisville, 40201.* Tel: 502-585-3291.
Holy Name Society—MICHAEL HEEB, Pres.; Rev. PAUL J.D. SCANLON, O.P., Spiritual Dir., *2302 Bradford Dr., Louisville, 40218.* Tel: 502-454-7151.
L.A.M.P.—(Louisville Archdiocesan Mission Promoters), Most Revs. THOMAS C. KELLY, O.P.; CHARLES G. MALONEY; Very Rev. BERNARD J. BREEN, *212 E. College St., P.O. Box 1073, Louisville, 40201.* Tel: 502-585-3291.
Legion of Mary—Rev. ROGER A. BOEHMICKE, Spiritual Dir., *3521 Goldsmith Ln., Louisville, 40220.* Tel: 502-451-9300.
Mass of the Air—1930 Bishop Ln., Ste. 1002, Louisville, 40218. Tel: 502-459-5285; Fax: 502-459-5682.
Ministry Formation Program—MARTHA JEWELL, Dir., *1935 Lewiston Pl., Louisville, 40216.* Tel: 502-448-8581.
Office of Lifelong Formation and Education—MATTHEW J. HAYES, Exec. Dir., *Maloney Center, 1200 S. Shelby St., Louisville, 40203.* Tel: 502-636-0296.
Office of Spirituality—STEVE WIRTH, Dir., *1935 Lewiston Pl., Louisville, 40216.* Tel: 502-448-8581.
Office of Worship—JUDY BULLOCK, Dir., *Maloney Center, 1200 S. Shelby St., Louisville, 40203.* Tel: 502-636-0296.
Opportunities for Life—JACKIE CARLSEN, Prog. Dir., *Maloney Center, 1200 S. Shelby St., Louisville, 40203.* Tel: 502-637-5949; 637-5968; 800-822-5824.
Parish Leadership Development Office—Sr. JUSTINA HENEGHAN, R.S.M., Dir., *212 E. College St., P.O. Box 1073, Louisville, 40201.* Tel: 502-585-3291.
Personnel and Planning—BRIAN B. REYNOLDS, Dir., *212 E. College, P.O. Box 1073, Louisville, 40201.* Tel: 502-585-3291.
Priests' Review for Growth in Ministry—Rev. ROBERT E. RAY, Dir., *1935 Lewiston Pl., Louisville, 40216.* Tel: 502-448-8581.
Propagation of the Faith—(Missions Office), Rev. KEVIN CASTER, Dir., *4011 Shelbyville Rd., P.O. Box 1073, Louisville, 40201.* Tel: 502-895-9420.
Respect Life Pastoral Plan—HELEN ROTHGERBER, Dir., *1935 Lewiston Pl., Louisville, 40216.* Tel: 502-448-8581.
Sacred Heart Enthronement Center—Rev. LAWRENCE H. LINDLE, Dir., *8191 New Haven Rd., New Haven, 40051.* Tel: 502-549-3751.
Stewardship and Development Office—ROSEMARY BISIG SMITH, Dir., *212 E. College St., P.O. Box 1073, Louisville, 40201.* Tel: 502-585-3291.
Vicar for Clergy—Rev. JAMES L. SCHLICH, *St. Aloysius Church, 225 W. Third St., Shepherdsville, 40165.* Tel: 502-955-8429.
Vocations—Rev. STEPHEN A. POHL, Dir., *1935 Lewiston Pl., Louisville, 40216.* Tel: 502-448-8581.

CLERGY, PARISHES, MISSIONS AND PAROCHIAL SCHOOLS

CITY OF LOUISVILLE
(Jefferson County)

1—CATHEDRAL OF THE ASSUMPTION, Revs. J. Ronald Knott; Martin A. Linebach; Deacon Joseph P. Wright. In res., Most Rev. Thomas C. Kelly, O.P.
Res., 443 S. 5th St., 40202. Tel: 502-582-2971; Fax: 502-582-3919.

2—ST. AGNES, Revs. John Baptist Ormechea, C.P.; William Browning, C.P.
Res., 1920 Newburg Rd., 40205. Tel: 502-451-2220; Fax: 502-454-8483.
School—Beverly McAuliffe, Prin. Sisters of Charity of Nazareth 1; Lay Teachers 20; Students 419.

3—ST. ALBERT THE GREAT, Revs. Kevin Caster; Theodore R. Sans; Bertrand J. Rapp, Admin.; Deacons Kenneth M. Ward; Vincent G. Stanley.
Res., 1405 Techny Ln., 40222. Tel: 502-425-3940; Fax: 502-394-9896.
School—1301 Techny Ln., 40222. Tel: 502-425-1804. Sheila Marstiller, Prin.
Lay Teachers 43; Students 559.

4—ST. ALOYSIUS. Closed. For inquiries for parish records contact the Chancery.

5—ST. ANN, Rev. Kenneth R. Fortener; Deacon C. Robert Markert.
Res., 1511 Algonquin Pkwy., 40210-2399. Tel: 502-636-0559; Fax: 502-776-7434.

6—ST. ANTHONY, Rev. Leo Kennedy, O.F.M.Conv. In res., Revs. James Cantwell, O.F.M.Conv.; Simon Sauer, O.F.M.Conv., Chap., Veterans Hospital; Alexis Martini, O.F.M.Conv.; Bro. James Fields, O.F.M.Conv.
Res., 2222 W. Market St., P.O. Box 11219, 40212. Tel: 502-778-7413; Fax: 502-776-3599.

7—ASCENSION OF OUR LORD, Rev. John B. Helm; Deacon Lawrence J. Biven.
Res., 4600 Lynnbrook Dr., 40220. Tel: 502-451-3860; Fax: 502-459-9782.
School—Tel: 502-451-2535; Fax: 502-451-2535. Maureen Clerkin, Prin.

8—ST. ATHANASIUS, Revs. Robert L. Huber; James E. Wafzig; Deacon Donald Masterson.
Res., 5915 Outer Loop Dr., 40219. Tel: 502-969-3332; Fax: 502-966-8948.
School—(Grades K-8). Tel: 502-969-2345; Fax: 502-969-8974. Sr. Aidan Hogan, Prin.
Sisters 2; Lay Teachers 22; Students 420.

9—ST. AUGUSTINE, Revs. Joseph T. Graffis; Vernon Robertson; Deacon John Churchill.
Res., 1310 W. Broadway, 40203. Tel: 502-584-4602; Fax: 502-581-0893.
Stations—Blanton House, Tel: 502-587-1259; James Taylor Home, Tel: 502-589-0727.

10—ST. BARNABAS, Revs. Gary G. Davis; Mark M. Hamilton; Deacons James R. Plummer; Robert C. Bryant.
Parish Office: 3042 Hikes Ln., 40220. Tel: 502-459-4251.
Res., 3054 Hikes Ln., 40220. Tel: 502-451-0333.
School—Tel: 502-458-4038; Fax: 502-452-1117. Mary Helen Thompson, Prin.
Lay Teachers 31; Students 441.

11—ST. BARTHOLOMEW, Revs. Terry L. Bradshaw; R. Joseph Hemmerle; Bertrand J. Rapp; Deacon Thomas E. Box, Pastoral Assoc.
Res., 2040 Buechel Bank Rd., 40218. Tel: 502-499-0883; Fax: 502-499-0421.
School—Victoria Davis, Prin. Ursuline Sisters 1; Lay Teachers 10; Students 194.

12—ST. BASIL, Rev. James P. Hendricks, Admin.; Deacon Marvin L. Kruer.
Res., 3901 Wayside Dr., 40216. Tel: 502-772-1017.

13—ST. BENEDICT. Consolidated with St. Charles Borromeo, Louisville, and Holy Cross, Louisville, to form St. Martin de Porres, Louisville.

14—ST. BERNARD, Rev. Joseph E. Vest; Deacon Michael Edwards; Sr. Katharine Hanrahan, S.C.N., Pastoral Assoc.
Res., 7500 Tangelo Dr., 40228. Tel: 502-239-9104; Fax: 502-239-9025.
School—Tel: 502-239-5178. Donald Matlock, Prin.
Sisters 1; Lay Teachers 21; Students 403.

15—ST. BONIFACE, Revs. Sergius H. Scherpenberg, O.F.M.; Stephen V. Schneider, O.F.M.; Edmund R. Moore, O.F.M.
Res., 531 E. Liberty St., 40202-1107. Tel: 502-584-4279.

16—ST. BRIGID, Revs. Donald R. Goetz; Joseph H. Voor.
Res., 1520 Hepburn Ave., 40204. Tel: 502-584-5565.

17—ST. CECILIA, Revs. John Lesousky, C.R.; Charles Schoenbachler, C.R.; Deacons Paul Bissig; Philip Tremblay.
Res., 338 N. 25th St., 40212. Tel: 502-772-3694; Fax: 502-772-3695.
School—Tel: 502-778-1941; Fax: 502-778-9935. Sr. Barbara Van Bokern, Prin.
Lay Teachers 9; Students 130.

18—ST. CHARLES BORROMEO. Consolidated with St. Benedict, Louisville, and Holy Cross, Louisville, to form St. Martin de Porres, Louisville.

19—CHRIST THE KING, Revs. John R. Burke; Dominic Antwi-Bosiako; Deacon Richard Dawson.
Res., 718 S. 44th St., 40211. Tel: 502-778-5055.

20—ST. COLUMBA. Closed. For inquiries for parish records contact the Chancery.

21—ST. DENIS, Rev. James P. Hendricks; Deacons Robert M. Kampschaefer; Marvin L. Kruer.
Res., 4205 Cane Run Rd., 40216. Tel: 502-448-2961; Fax: 502-448-3656.
School—Tel: 502-447-5832. Ann Montgomery, Prin.
Lay Teachers 12; Students 260.

22—ST. ELIZABETH ANN SETON, Rev. Robert M. Abel, Admin.; Deacon James C. Olrich; Sr. Alice Casper, S.C.N., Pastoral Assoc.
Res., 11501 Maple Way, 40229. Tel: 502-966-3164; 966-0661.

23—ST. ELIZABETH OF HUNGARY, Revs. H. Anthony Olges; Robert B. Gray. In res., Rev. Herman J. Naber.
Res., 1020 E. Burnett Ave., 40217. Tel: 502-636-3706; Fax: 502-634-5511.
School—St. Rose Catholic School, (Grades PreK-8) 1016 E. Burnett Ave., 40217. Eileen Soeder, Prin.
Lay Teachers 13; aides 2; Students 217.

24—EPIPHANY, Rev. R. Cass Volpert; Sr. Josette Gocella, S.S.J., Pastoral Assoc.; Deacon Gary E. Becker.
Res., 914 Old Harrods Creek Rd., 40223. Tel: 502-245-9733; Fax: 502-245-7658.

25—ST. FRANCES OF ROME, Rev. John G. Eifler; Sr. Carmelita Dunn, S.C.N., Pastoral Assoc.; Deacon William Mullins.
Res., 2119 Payne St., 40206. Tel: 502-896-8401; Fax: 502-895-0310.

26—ST. FRANCIS OF ASSISI, Revs. Joseph M. Rankin; Donald M. Hill. In res., Rev. Joseph T. Merkt; Deacon Walton G. Jones.
Res., 1960 Bardstown Rd., 40205-1572. Tel: 502-456-6394; Fax: 502-456-9462.
School—1938 Alfresco Pl., 40205-1876. Tel: 502-459-3088. Katherine Schloemer, Prin.
Lay Teachers 15; Students 260.

27—ST. GABRIEL THE ARCHANGEL, Rev. William D. Hammer; Deacon William Skeeters. In res., Rev. R. Dale Cieslik.
Res., 5505 Bardstown Rd., 40291. Tel: 502-239-5481; Fax: 502-239-7717.
School—Tel: 502-239-5535. Alan R. Huelsman, Prin.
Lay Teachers 35; Students 782.

28—ST. GEORGE, Rev. Kenneth R. Fortener.
Res., 1410 Dixie Hwy., 40210-1795. Tel: 502-776-6020; Fax: 502-776-7434.

29—GUARDIAN ANGELS, Rev. James W. Murphy; Deacon Cletus A. Ratterman. In res., Rev. W. Frederick Hendrickson.
Res., 6000 Preston Hwy., 40219. Tel: 502-968-5421; Fax: 502-962-1080.
School—Thomas Merton Academy. (Middle School). Ms. Ann Thompson, Prin.
Lay Teachers 12; Students 226.

30—ST. HELEN, Revs. Thomas E. Gentile; Charles J. Bindner; Deacons Joseph C. Amon; David McGinty.
Res., 4005 Dixie Hwy., 40216. Tel: 502-448-4008; Fax: 502-448-4045.
School—4007 Dixie Hwy., 40216. Tel: 502-447-9671. Diane Smith, Prin.
Lay Teachers 11; Students 225.

31—HOLY CROSS. Consolidated with St. Benedict, Louisville, and St. Charles Borromeo, Louisville, to form St. Martin de Porres, Louisville.

32—HOLY FAMILY, Rev. Anthony L. Chandler; Deacon Lamar Fante.
Res., 3926 Poplar Level Rd., 40213. Tel: 502-459-6066; Fax: 502-459-6066.
School—Tel: 502-458-4531. Rosanne Dillon, Prin.
Lay Teachers 13; Students 213.

33—HOLY NAME, Rev. John W. Birk.
Res., 2914 S. 3rd St., 40208. Tel: 502-637-2058.

34—HOLY SPIRIT, Revs. Thomas L. Boland; J. Randall Hubbard; J. Wayne Jenkins; Frank B. Grauel.
Res., 3345 Lexington Rd., 40206. Tel: 502-893-3982; Fax: 502-893-8287.
School—322 Cannons Ln., 40206. Tel: 502-893-7700; Fax: 502-893-8018. Mrs. Janet Leitner, Prin.
Lay Teachers 25; Students 460.

35—HOLY TRINITY, Revs. Joseph M. Fowler; J. Wayne Jenkins; Deacon John Simpson.
Pastoral Center—501 Cherrywood Rd., 40207. Tel: 502-897-5207; Fax: 502-897-0962.
School—423 Cherrywood Rd., 40207. Tel: 502-897-2785. Mrs. Mary Alice Zettel, Prin.
Lay Teachers 24; Students 486.

36—ST. IGNATIUS, Rev. Thomas P. Creagh; Deacon James R. Young.
Res., 1816 Rangeland Rd., 40219. Tel: 502-964-5904; Fax: 502-964-5905.
Thomas Merton Child Development Center—Tel: 502-969-2336. Ms. Mona Wilkerson, Dir.
Lay Teachers 18; Students 128.

37—IMMACULATE HEART OF MARY, Rev. Louis J. Meiman.
Office: 1545 S. 34th St., 40211. Tel: 502-774-5772.

38—INCARNATION, Rev. Joseph T. Herp.
Res., 2229 Lower Hunters Trace Rd., 40216. Tel: 502-447-2013.

39—ST. JAMES, Rev. Donald R. Goetz; Rev. Msgr. Alfred F. Horrigan; Rev. Joseph H. Voor; Deacon Jerome Fargen.
Res., 1826 Edenside Ave., 40204. Tel: 502-451-1420.
School—Tel: 502-454-0330. Colette Dumstorf, Prin.
Lay Teachers 6; Students 107.

40—ST. JOHN. Closed. For inquiries for parish records contact the Chancery.

41—ST. JOHN VIANNEY, Rev. J. Roy Stiles.
Res., 4839 Southside Dr., 40214. Tel: 502-366-5517.
School—Tel: 502-366-1266. Mrs. Dean Haueter, Prin.
Sisters 1; Lay Teachers 7; Students 149.

42—ST. JOSEPH, Revs. Simeon Cleves, O.F.M.; Alan Heet, O.F.M.; Deacon Perry Carney.
Res., 1406 E. Washington St., 40206. Tel: 502-583-7401.
School—Tel: 502-583-0892. Dottie Clarke, Prin.
Lay Teachers 8; Students 115.

43—ST. LAWRENCE, Rev. Robert L. Stuempel; Sharon A. Benton, Pastoral Assoc.; Deacon James H. Abell.
Res., 1925 Lewiston Dr., 40216. Tel: 502-448-2122.
School—Tel: 502-447-3155. Judy Thomas, Prin.
Religious 1; Lay Teachers 21; Students 415.

44—ST. LEO THE GREAT. Closed. For inquiries for parish records contact St. John Vianney, Louisville.

45—ST. LEONARD, Rev. James F. Hackett; Mr. Robert G. Dever, Pastoral Assoc.
Res., 440 Zorn Ave., 40206. Tel: 502-897-2595; Fax: 502-896-8259.
School—Tel: 502-897-5265. Ms. Lynn Wilt, Prin.
Lay Teachers 14; Students 156.

46—ST. LOUIS BERTRAND, Revs. Charles H. O'Brien, O.P.; George G. Christian, O.P.; Daniel J. Kennedy, O.P.; Robert R. Blais, O.P.; Bro. Fidelis Spalding, O.P.; Rev. Frank B. Shipps, O.P.
Res., 1104 S. 6th St., 40203. Tel: 502-583-4448; Fax: 502-583-6874.
Shrine—Lourdes Rosary Shrine, Inc., Tel: 502-583-1950.

47—ST. LUKE, Rev. Richard P. Berding.
Res., 4211 Jim Hawkins Dr., 40229. Tel: 502-969-3291.

48—ST. MARGARET MARY, Very Rev. Bernard J. Breen; Rev. T. Michael Tobin; Deacon John L. Simpson.
Res., 7813 Shelbyville Rd., P.O. Box 6387, 40206. Tel: 502-426-1588; Fax: 502-426-1503.
School—Tel: 502-426-2635. Ann Kalmey, Prin.
Lay Teachers 25; Students 492.

49—ST. MARTHA, Rev. John D. Deatrick; Senior Deacon James D. Bennett, (Retired); Deacons Raymond G. Kramer, Pastoral Assoc.; Charles K. Brown; John P. Maher.
Res., 2825 Klondike Ln., 40218. Tel: 502-491-8535; Fax: 502-491-8536.
School—Tel: 502-491-3171. Sharon Dutton, Prin.
Lay Teachers 26; Students 516.

50—ST. MARTIN, Rev. Dennis Cousens.
Res., 639 S. Shelby St., 40202. Tel: 502-582-2827; Fax: 502-582-1780.

51—ST. MARTIN DE PORRES. Consolidated with St. Benedict, Louisville, St. Charles Borromeo, Louisville, and Holy Cross, Louisville, parishes. Rev. James Flynn; Deacon James Turner, Pastoral Admin.; Sr. Dorothy Jackson, S.C.N., Pastoral Assoc.; Deacon Frederick Higgins.
Mailing Address: 3112 W. Broadway, 40211. Tel: 502-778-1118.

52—ST. MARY (Bullitt Co.), Rev. Robert Abel; Deacon Paul J. George.
Res., 299 Crestwood Ln., 40229. Tel: 502-957-3385; Fax: 502-957-3385.

53—ST. MARY MAGDALEN. See separate listing under Oratories.

54—ST. MATTHIAS, Gene Scheich; Sr. Joan Riedley, O.S.U., Pastoral Assoc.
Res., 2200 Dixie Hwy., 40210. Tel: 502-776-3250.

55—MOST BLESSED SACRAMENT, Rev. John U. Caskey; Deacons Kenneth J. Mitchell; Harry Prestwood.
Res., 3509 Taylor Blvd., 40215. Tel: 502-361-0149; Fax: 502-375-1076.
School—1128 Berry Blvd., 40215. Tel: 502-361-7103; Fax: 502-367-1513. Michael Rouse, Prin.
Lay Teachers 9; Students 226.
Convent—1126 Berry Blvd., 40215. Tel: 502-368-6634.

56—MOTHER OF GOOD COUNSEL, Rev. John T. Judie; Deacons Patrick Harris; Charles Voll; Joseph Raibert.
Res., 8509 Westport Rd., 40242. Tel: 502-425-2210; Fax: 502-425-0941.
School—Tel: 502-425-2637. Michael J. Doran, Prin.
Lay Teachers 24; Students 452.

57—OUR LADY, Rev. Robert E. Reilly.
Res., 3511 Rudd Ave., 40212. Tel: 502-776-4666.

58—OUR LADY OF LOURDES, Revs. Robert E. Osborne; William Miller; Deacons Norbert Miller; Ben Thornbury, (Retired).
Res., 512 Breckenridge Ln., 40207. Tel: 502-896-0241; Fax: 502-895-5435.
School—Tel: 502-895-5122; Fax: 502-893-5051. Bernadette Ritchey, Prin.
Lay Teachers 25; Students 467.

59—OUR LADY OF MOUNT CARMEL, Revs. Niles J. Gillen, O.Carm.; Thomas Butler, O.Carm.; Bro. Thomas J. Conlon, O.Carm.
Res., 7333 Southside Dr., 40214. Tel: 502-366-5651; Fax: 502-368-9972.
School—Tel: 502-368-8506. Carol Nord, Prin.
Lay Teachers 25; Students 562.

60—OUR MOTHER OF SORROWS, Revs. John W. Hanrahan; Henry C. Stuecker; Deacon Richard E. Steinmetz.
Res., 747 Harrison Ave., 40217. Tel: 502-637-7442.
School—(Grades PreK-8) 770 Eastern Pkwy, 40217. Tel: 502-637-7814; Fax: 502-636-0260. Denise Stead, Prin.
Lay Teachers 14; Students (Grades K-8) 204; Students (Preschool) 31.

61—ST. PATRICK, Revs. John L. Schindler; James W. Graf.
Res., 1000 N. Beckley Station Rd., 40245-4550. Tel: 502-244-6083.

62—ST. PAUL. Closed. For inquiries for parish records contact the Chancery.

63—ST. PETER CLAVER, Rev. Patrick D. Delahanty, Admin.
Res., 526 Lampton St., 40203. Tel: 502-585-3910.

64—ST. PHILIP NERI. Closed. For inquiries for parish records contact St. Elizabeth of Hungary, Louisville.

65—ST. PIUS X, Revs. Charles D. Walker; Roger A. Boehmicke; Sr. Mary Elaine Zehnder, S.C.N., Pastoral Assoc.
Res., 3521 Goldsmith Ln., 40220. Tel: 502-451-4124.
School—Tel: 502-452-1712; Fax: 502-458-7109. Patrice Super, Prin.
Lay Teachers 26; Students 456.

66—ST. RAPHAEL THE ARCHANGEL, Revs. Kevin J. Bryan; Philip L. Erickson; John A. Dalton; Deacon Jim Sturgeon.
Res., 2141 Lancashire Ave., 40205. Tel: 502-458-2500.
School—Tel: 502-456-1541. Paul DeZarn, Prin.
Ursuline Sisters 1; Lay Teachers 40; Students 589.

67—RESURRECTION D.N.J.C., Rev. Raymond Hofmann, C.R.
Res., 4601 Poplar Level Rd., 40213. Tel: 502-968-5483; Fax: 502-969-6375.

68—ST. RITA, Revs. William J. Martin; Emmet Linden, C.P.; Deacon Charles "Mack" Nevitt.
Res., 8709 Preston Hwy., 40219. Tel: 502-969-4579.
School—Laura Glaser, Prin. Lay Teachers 20; Students 430.

69—SS. SIMON AND JUDE, Rev. William F. Wagner; Sr. Ann Carol Mann, S.C.N., Pastoral Assoc.
Res., 4335 Hazelwood Ave., 40215. Tel: 502-368-4887; Fax: 502-375-1988.
School—Tel: 502-366-2424. Sr. M. Michelle Duvall, Prin.
Sisters 1; Lay Teachers 12; Students 215.

70—ST. STEPHEN, MARTYR, Rev. James J. Lichtefeld; Deacon Sylvester Nitzken.
Res., 1000 English Ave., 40217. Tel: 502-635-5813; 635-5888.
School—2931 Pindell, 40217. Tel: 502-635-7141.
Lay Teachers 22; Students 432.

71—ST. THERESE, Revs. H. Anthony Olges; Robert B. Gray; Herman J. Naber.
Res., 1010 Schiller Ave., 40204. Tel: 502-634-3671; Fax: 502-634-3672.

72—ST. THOMAS MORE, Rev. Donald J. Fisher; Deacon Michael A. Tolbert.
Res., 6105 S. Third St., 40214. Tel: 502-366-1463; Fax: 502-363-3719.
School—226 Inverness Ave., 40214. Tel: 502-363-3719. Mrs. Donna Sansone, Prin.
Lay Teachers 11; Students 240.

73—ST. VINCENT DE PAUL. See separate listing under Oratories.

74—ST. WILLIAM, Mr. James J. Butler, Pastoral Admin.
Res., 2650 Six Mile Ln., 40220. Tel: 502-491-0052.
1226 W. Oak St., 40210.

OUTSIDE THE CITY OF LOUISVILLE

Albany, Clinton Co., Emmanuel Catholic, Rev. Lawrence J. Gelthaus.
Res., Hwy. 127 N., P.O. Box 126, 42602. Tel: 606-387-7251.
Mission—Burkesville, Cumberland Co., Holy Cross Catholic, 264 Glasgow Rd., P.O. Box 197, Burkesville, 42717. Tel: 502-864-4107.

Bardstown, Nelson Co., St. Joseph, Revs. William F. Medley; Terry Lee Langford; Deacons Joseph H. Filiatreau; Richard J. Walsh; John Hamilton.
Res., P.O. Box 548, 310 W. Stephen Foster Ave., 40004. Tel: 502-348-3126; Fax: 502-349-0941. [CEM]
School—Tel: 502-348-5994; Fax: 502-348-5994.
Sisters of Charity of Nazareth 2; Lay Teachers 18; Students 430.
High School—Tel: 502-348-8594; Fax: 502-349-1247.
Sisters of Charity 4; Lay Teachers 21; Students 295.

St. Monica, Rev. Stephen A. Pohl; Deacon Samuel R. Filiatreau, Pastoral Admin.
Res., 407 S. Third St., 40004. Tel: 502-348-5250.

Brandenburg, Meade Co., St. John the Apostle, Rev. John A. Barker; Deacon J. Michael Jones.
Res., P.O. Box 565, 40108. Tel: 502-422-2196; Fax: 502-422-2471. [CEM]
School—513 E. Broadway, 40108.
Augustinian Sisters, Servants of Jesus and Mary 4; Lay Teachers 4; Students 202.

Calvary, Marion Co., Holy Name of Mary, Rev. Joseph I. Dawson.
Res., 3265 Hwy. 208, Lebanon, 40033. Tel: 502-692-2298. [CEM]

Missions—Phillipsburg, Marion Co., Our Lady of Fatima; Spurlington, Taylor Co., St. Frances de Sales. [CEM 2]
Station—Lebanon, Calvary Retreat House.

Campbellsville, Taylor Co., Our Lady of Perpetual Help, Rev. John A. Caldwell; Deacon Joseph Ohnemus.
Office: 425 N. Central Ave., 42719. Tel: 502-465-4282. [CEM]

Cecilia, Hardin Co., St. Ambrose, Rev. Stanley L. Osborne, Admin.
Res., c/o 657 St. John Church Rd., Elizabethtown, 42701. Tel: 502-862-9816.

Clementsville, Casey Co., St. Bernard, Rev. Joseph S. Hall.
Res., Rte. 8, Box 244, Liberty, 42539. Tel: 606-787-7570.
Mission—Liberty, Casey Co., Sacred Heart, Tel: 606-787-7324.

Culvertown, Nelson Co., Immaculate Conception, Rev. Lawrence H. Lindle.
Res., 8191 New Haven Rd., New Haven, 40051-6030. Tel: 502-549-3757; Fax: 502-549-7258.
Mission—Bardstown, Nelson Co., St. Mark. Closed. For information contact Immaculate Conception, Culvertown.

Edmonton, Metcalfe Co., Christ the Healer, Rev. John J. Stoltz.
Res., 1610 W. Stockton St., 42129. Tel: 502-432-5024.
Mission—Tompkinsville, Monroe Co., Christ the King, P.O. Box 548, Tompkinsville, 42167. Tel: 502-487-8881.

Elizabethtown, Hardin Co., St. James, Revs. William L. Fichteman; Jeffrey S. Nicolas; Charles E. Reteneller; Deacons Jay Jenkins; Joseph Chathaparampil.
Res., 307 W. Dixie Ave., 42701. Tel: 502-765-6268. [CEM]
School—114 N. Miles St., 42701. Tel: 502-765-7011; Fax: 502-769-5745.
Religious Teachers 1; Lay Teachers 15; Students 350.

Fairdale, Jefferson Co., St. Jerome, Rev. J. Roy Stiles, Admin. In res., Rev. Robert E. Ray.
Res., 903 Fairdale Rd., 40118. Tel: 502-363-9929.

Fairfield, Nelson Co., St. Michael, Revs. Donald L. Ryan; Albert J. Hartlage.
Res., P.O. Box 27, 40020. Tel: 502-252-8308. [CEM]
Mission—Taylorsville, Spencer Co., All Saints Church, 410 W. Main St., P.O. Box 531, 502-477-6676 40071. [CEM] Rev. Donald L. Ryan, Admin.

Finley, Taylor Co., Our Lady of the Hills, Rev. John A. Caldwell.
Office: 425 N. Central Ave., Campbellsville, 42718.
Res., 9259 Old Lebanon Rd., 42736. Tel: 502-465-5280. [CEM]

Flaherty, Meade Co., St. Martin of Tours, Rev. Thomas A. Smith; Deacon John R. Whelan.
Res., 440 Saint Martin Rd., Vine Grove, 40175. Tel: 502-828-2552; Fax: 502-828-2562. [CEM]

Glasgow, Barren Co., St. Helen, Rev. Kenneth Frye, C.P.M.; Deacons Jack Hawkins; Lee Bidwell.
Res., 103 W. Brown St., 42141. Tel: 502-651-5263.
Mission—Horse Cave, Hart Co., Our Lady of the Caves Church, Rte. 31 W., Horse Cave, 42749.

Goshen, Oldham Co., Transfiguration of Our Lord, Rev. Herbert L. Lattis; Deacons J. Pat Ebert; Joseph F. Stuber; David Tomes.
Res., 1620 S. Hwy. 1793, 40026. Tel: 502-228-8665.

Greensburg, Green Co., Holy Redeemer, Rev. John A. Caldwell; Deacon Joseph Ohnemus.
Office: 425 N. Central Ave., Campbellsville, 42719-0484. Tel: 502-465-4282.
Church—110 Industrial Rd., 42743.

Hodgenville, Larue Co., Our Lady of Mercy, Rev. James T. Mudd; Deacon John Kromer.
Res., 208 Walters Ave., 42748. Tel: 502-358-4697. [CEM]

Holy Cross, Marion Co., Holy Cross, Sr. Mary Ellen Curl, R.S.M., Pastoral Admin.; Rev. Thomas A. Hommrich.
Res., 3560 N. Saint Francis Rd., Loretto, 40037. Tel: 502-865-2521. [CEM]

Howardstown, Nelson Co., St. Ann, Rev. James T. Mudd, Admin. In res., Rev. Robert A. Brown.
Res., 7490 Howardstown Rd., 40051. Tel: 502-549-3285. [CEM]
School—(Grades 1-8). Tel: 502-549-7310.
Lay Teachers 3; Students 60.

Jamestown, Russell Co., Holy Spirit, Rev. Daniel L. Lincoln; Sr. Marietta Wethington, O.S.U., Pastoral Assoc.
Res., 406 N. Main St., P.O. Box 247, 42629. Tel: 502-343-3346.
Mission—Columbia, Adair Co., Good Shepherd, P.O. Box 354, Columbia, 42728. Tel: 502-384-4528. Sr. Judith A. Prindiville, C.S.C., Pastoral Assoc.

Jeffersontown, Jefferson Co., St. Edward, Rev. Frank J. Eimer; Deacons Martin Brown; Peter Houck.
Res., 9608 Sue Helen Dr., 40299. Tel: 502-267-7494; Fax: 502-267-7495. [CEM]
School—Tel: 502-267-6633. Susan Jones, Prin.
Lay Teachers 21; Students 486.

St. Michael, Rev. William S. Griner; Agnes Tompkins, Pastoral Assoc.
Res., 12707 Taylorsville Rd., 40299. Tel: 502-266-5611 (Rectory & Parish Office); Fax: 502-267-9550.
Parish Activity Center & Church—Tel: 502-267-9550.

LaGrange, Oldham Co., Immaculate Conception, Rev. Michael D. Lott.
Res., 502 N. Fifth St., 40031. Tel: 502-222-0255; Fax: 502-222-0421.
School—Tel: 502-222-0671. Elizabeth Kenobbie, Prin.
Lay Teachers 9; Students 130.
Mission—Bedford, Trimble Co., St. Matthew, Rte. 2, Bedford, 40006. Tel: 502-255-7369.
Stations—LaGrange, Luther Luckett Correctional Center, Tel: 502-222-0363; Kentucky State Reformatory, Tel: 502-222-9441; Roederer Farm Prison, Tel: 502-222-0173; Cedar Lake Lodge, Tel: 502-222-7157; Tri-County Community Hospital, Tel: 502-222-5388.

Lebanon, Marion Co., St. Augustine, Very Revs. Charles C.E. Thompson; J. Mark Spalding; Deacon Tom Mattingly.
Res., 235 S. Spalding Ave., 40033. Tel: 502-692-4986; Fax: 502-692-5532. [CEM]
School—(Grades 1-8). Tel: 502-692-2063. Mary Gardner, Prin.
Lay Teachers 20; Students 309.

Lebanon Junction, Bullitt Co., St. Benedict, Rev. Kenneth L. Kamber.
Res., 139 N. Brook St., 40150. Tel: 502-833-4886; Fax: 502-833-4420.
School—227 W. Oak St., 40150. Tel: 502-833-4926. Jane M. Crawford, Admin.
Lay Teachers 6; Students 77.
Mission—St. Clare. See separate listing under Oratories. [CEM]

Mount Washington, Bullitt Co., St. Francis Xavier, Rev. James E. Hargadon.
Res., 155 Stringer Ln., 40047. Tel: 502-538-4933; Fax: 502-955-5366. [CEM]

New Haven, Nelson Co., St. Catherine, Rev. Clarence J. Howard; Deacon George B. Clark.
Res., P.O. Box 88, 40051. Tel: 502-549-3152; Fax: 502-549-5410. [CEM]
School—413 First St., P.O. Box 88, 40051. Tel: 502-549-3680.
Sisters 1; Lay Teachers 10; Students 183.

New Hope, Nelson Co., St. Vincent de Paul, Rev. Clarence J. Howard, Admin.; Deacon Edward J. Hutchins.
Res., 101 Church St., 40052. Tel: 502-549-3053. [CEM]

Payneville, Meade Co., St. Mary Magdalen of Pazzi, Rev. James R. Schook.
Res., 110 Hwy. 376, 40157. Tel: 502-496-4333; Fax: 502-496-4790. [CEM]

Pewee Valley, Oldham Co., St. Aloysius, Revs. Vincent J. Schweizer; John W. Dickman; Deacon Francis E. Klosterman.
Res., 202 Mount Mercy Dr., P.O. Box 468, 40056. Tel: 502-241-8452; Fax: 502-241-9550. [CEM]
School—Tel: 502-241-8516.
Lay Teachers 17; Students 288.
Stations—Pewee Valley, Kentucky Correctional Institute for Women; Friendship Manor Nursing Home, Tel: 502-241-8821.

Pleasure Ridge Park, Jefferson Co., St. Paul, Revs. Fred Pasche, O.F.M.Conv.; David Hutt, O.F.M.Conv. In res., Rev. James Kent, O.F.M.Conv.
Res., 6901 Dixie Hwy., 40258. Tel: 502-935-1223; Fax: 502-933-7747.
School—Lay Teachers 11; Students 246.

St. Polycarp, Rev. William P. Burks; Deacons Jon Hosch; Tony Hasson.
Res., 7718 Columbine Dr., 40258. Tel: 502-935-4578; Fax: 502-933-1093.
School—Tel: 502-935-2022. Thomas Boone, Prin.
Lay Teachers 17; Students 361.

Radcliff, Hardin Co., St. Christopher, Rev. B. Leo Craycroft.
Res., 1138 Thomas St., 40160. Tel: 502-351-3706. [CEM]
School—1181 S. Wilson Rd., 40160. Tel: 502-351-3150.
Lay Teachers 9; Students 160.

Raywick, Marion Co., St. Francis Xavier Church, Revs. Vincent P. Dentinger, Admin.; Ernest Schumacher, C.R.
Res., 108 Main St., 40060. Tel: 502-692-2245. [CEM]

Rhodelia, Meade Co., St. Theresa, Rev. James R. Schook, Admin. Pastors Emeriti: Revs. Albert L. Wilson; James Meder.
Res., 9245 Rhodelia Rd., Payneville, 40157. Tel: 502-496-4343. [CEM]
Convent—Tel: 502-496-4314. Sisters of Charity of Nazareth.

St. Francis, Marion Co., St. Francis of Assisi, Sr. Mary Ellen Curl, R.S.M., Pastoral Admin.; Rev. Thomas A. Hommrich.
Res., 6785 Hwy. 52, 40062. Tel: 502-865-2521. [CEM]

St. John, Hardin Co., St. John the Baptist, Rev. Stanley L. Osborne; Deacon Michael Vessels.
Res., 657 St. John Church Rd., Elizabethtown, 42701. Tel: 502-862-9816. [CEM]

St. Joseph, Marion Co., St. Joseph. Closed. For inquiries for parish records contact St. Francis Xavier, Raywick.

St. Mary, Marion Co., St. Charles, Revs. Vincent P. Dentinger; Ernest Schumacher C.R.; Deacon Joseph R. Dant.
Res., 675 Hwy. 327, Lebanon, 40033. Tel: 502-692-4513. [CEM]

St. Thomas, Nelson Co., St. Thomas, Revs. Stephen A. Pohl; J. Irvin Mouser; Deacon David Newton.
Res., 870 Saint Thomas Ln., Bardstown, 40004. Tel: 502-348-3717; Fax: 502-348-1905.
School—(Grades K-8).
Sisters 1; Lay Teachers 8; Students 109.

Samuels, Nelson Co., St. Gregory, Rev. Trumie Culpepper Elliott; Deacon Joseph E. Livers.
Parish Office: 330 Samuels Loop, Cox's Creek, 40013. Tel: 502-348-6337. [CEM]
School—Tel: 502-348-9583.
Lay Teachers 7; Students 101.

Shelbyville, Shelby Co., Annunciation of the Blessed Virgin Mary, Rev. C. Joseph Batcheldor.
Res., 105 W. Main St., 40065. Tel: 502-633-1547.
Mission—Eminence, Henry Co., St. John Chrysostom, Eminence, 40019.

Shepherdsville, Bullitt Co., St. Aloysius, Rev. Gerard L. Bell.
Res., 187 Plum St., 40165. Tel: 502-543-5918; 955-6370.
School—197 Plum St., 40165. Tel: 502-543-6721.
Lay Teachers 11; Students 239.

Springfield, Washington Co.,

1—St. Dominic, Rev. Leon C. Spalding.
Res., 303 W. Main St., 40069. Tel: 606-336-3569. [CEM]
School—Tel: 606-336-7165.
Lay Teachers 10; Students 244.

2—Holy Rosary, Rev. Patrick J. Dolan; Deacon Ernest Cooper.
Mailing Address: Box 146, 40069. Tel: 606-336-3898.

3—Holy Trinity, Rev. Christopher Allegra.
Res., 306 Fredericktown Rd., 40069. Tel: 606-284-5242. [CEM]
Mission—Manton, Washington Co., Holy Rosary. [CEM]

4—St. Rose, Rev. David A. Butler, O.P. In res., Rev. Gerard Arthur Lessard, O.P.
Res., Hwy. 152, P.O. Box 71, 40069. Tel: 606-336-3121; Fax: 606-336-3841. [CEM]

Valley Station, Jefferson Co.,

1—St. Clement, Revs. Harry J. Gelthaus; Thomas Donohue.
Res., 5431 Johnsontown Rd., 40272-3400. Tel: 502-937-5920; Fax: 502-937-5927.
School—Tel: 502-937-1616.
Lay Teachers 12; Students 247.

2—Our Lady Help of Christians, Rev. Thomas R. Clark, Admin.; Deacon Robert L. Burns, Pastoral Assoc.
Res., 13512 Dixie Hwy., 40272. Tel: 502-937-1818.
Mission—West Point, Hardin Co., St. Patrick Church.

3—Our Lady of Consolation, Rev. Donald W. Springman; Deacon Wayne Thieneman.
Res., 10801 Deering Rd., 40272. Tel: 502-937-2100.
School—Tel: 502-937-7400.
Lay Teachers 9; Students 166.

4—St. Timothy, Rev. Thomas R. Clark.
Res., 10300 Lower River Rd., 40272. Tel: 502-937-1238.

Vine Grove, Hardin Co., St. Brigid, Rev. Thomas A. Smith, Admin.; Deacon James Benton.
Res., 306 E. Main St., 40175. Tel: 502-877-2461; Fax: 502-828-2562. [CEM]
School—Tel: 502-877-2451; Fax: 502-877-6864.
Lay Teachers 7; Students 111.

White Mills, Hardin Co., St. Ignatius, Revs. William L. Fichteman; Jeffrey Nicolas; Charles Reteneller;

Deacon Jay Jenkins.
Mailing Address: P.O. Box 64, 42788. Tel: 502-369-6279.
Res., 307 W. Dixie Ave., Elizabethtown, 42701. Tel: 502-765-6268; Fax: 502-765-6268. [CEM]

Oratories

1—ST. MARY MAGDALEN, Jefferson Co. Closed. For inquiries for parish records contact the Chancery.
2—ST. VINCENT DE PAUL, Jefferson Co. Closed. For inquiries for parish records contact St. Elizabeth of Hungary, Louisville.
3—ST. CLARE, Hardin Co. Closed. For inquiries for parish records contact St. Benedict, Lebanon Junction.

Chaplains of Public Institutions

LOUISVILLE. *Alliant Medical Pavillion.* Attended from St. Vincent De Paul.
Audubon Regional Medical Center. Attended by St. Pius X. Rev. Roger Boehmicke.
Baptist Hospital East. Attended by Our Lady of Lourdes. Rev. Robert E. Osborne.
Caritas Medical Center. Rev. Joseph H. Stoltz.
Central State Hospital Lakeland Rd., 40223. Tel: 502-245-4121. Rev. James W. Graf, Chap.
Jewish Hospital. Rev. John B. Gephart.
Kosair-Children's Hospital. Rev. John B. Gephart.
Norton Hospital. Rev. John B. Gephart; Deacon Wheatley, Chap.
Southwest Hospital. Attended by Our Lady of Consolation.
Suburban Hospital. Attended by Ascension.
University Hospital. Rev. James E. Wafzig.
Vencor Veterans Hospital. Revs. Simon Sauer, O.F.M.Conv.; Joseph H. Voor.

On Special Assignment:
Reverend Fathers—
Clark, Daniel C., Passionist Community, 1924 Newburg Rd., Louisville, KY 40205
Covert, James A., 7703 Blue Bonnet Rd., Louisville, KY 40258
Hogan, Timothy A., Catholic Charities, 2911 S. Fourth St., Louisville, KY 40208
Jones, John E., Taylor Wood Rd., Box 352, Finchville, KY 40022
Rice, George N., Pres., National Federation of Priests Council, 214 Eline Ave., Louisville, KY 40207

On Duty Outside the Archdiocese:
Reverend Fathers—
Branch, Edward B., Office of Campus Ministry, Catholic Center at Atlanta University Complex, 1526 Westwood Ave. S.W., Atlanta, GA 30310. Tel: 404-775-9394
Brown, James J., St. Margaret Church, 122 W. Hawk Ave., Pharr, TX 78577
Dittmeier, Charles R., Bishop Ford Center, Tung Tau Tsuen, Kowloon, Hong Kong
Hayden, Joseph F., Apartado 406, Chimbote, Peru
Sullivan, J. Richard, SS. Peter and Paul Church, 117 W. Main St., Lexington, KY 40507
Thornsberry, Michael T., St. Stephen Church, 8030 Bradshaw Rd., Bradshaw, MD 21210
Wimsett, Scott J., Belmont Abbey, 100 Belmont-Mount Holly Rd., Belmont, NC 28012

Graduate Studies:
Reverend Fathers—
Klotter, Frederick W., St. Mary's Seminary & University, 5400 Roland Ave., Baltimore, MD 21210

Military Chaplains:
Reverend Fathers—
Brown, Benedict J., U.S. Navy

Leave of Absence:
Reverend Fathers—
Eve, Paul W.
Schoenbachler, Timothy M.
Vowels, Donald M.

Retired:
Reverend Monsignors—
Horrigan, Alfred F., 1826 Edenside Ave., Louisville, KY 40204
O'Bryan, J. A., Rte. 1, Box 111, McDaniels, KY 40152
Reverend Fathers—
Birkel, Robert C., 7494 Stiles Rd., Howardstown, KY 40051
Boehmicke, Roger A., 3521 Goldsmith Ln., Louisville, KY 40220
Bowling, George K., 15 Audubon Plaza Dr., Louisville, KY 40217
Brennan, William J., St. Margaret Mary Church, P.O. Box 6387, Louisville, KY 40206
Brian, Bertrand J., Nazareth Village II, P.O. Box 2000, #22, Nazareth, KY 40048
Brown, Robert A., St. Ann Church, 7490 Howardstown Rd., Howardstown, KY 40051
Caldwell, William T., 3320 Bardstown Rd., No. 82, Louisville, KY 40218
Cecil, Ivo E., 1080 Optimist Rd., Lebanon Junction, KY 40150
Clark, C. Thomas, 6212 Transylvania Beach, Prospect, KY 40059
Craycroft, George P., 229 N. Main St., New Haven, KY 40051
Creed, C. Patrick, 122 Tom Vittitow Ln., Bardstown, KY 40004
Deddens, Norbert J., Our Lady Queen of the Universe Church, 121 Garrison St., San Benito, TX 78586
Dentinger, Roy E., 1664 Beechwood Ave., Louisville, KY 40204
Dickman, John W., 202 Mount Mercy Dr., Pewee Valley, KY 40056
Diersen, William M., 1695 County Line Rd., N.E., Palmyra, IN 47164
Dollinger, Robert J., P.O. Box 75, Georgetown, PEI C0A 1L0 Canada
Donohue, Thomas E., 9104 Mahoney Dr., Louisville, KY 40258
Gephart, John B., Bishop David Apartments, 5146 Dixie Hwy., Louisville, KY 40216
Giesler, Linus T., Nazareth Home, 2000 Newburg Rd., Louisville, KY 40205
Grauel, Frank B., Holy Spirit Church, 3345 Lexington Rd., Louisville, KY 40206
Hamilton, Joseph K., 16223 Dry Ridge Rd., Louisville, KY 40299
Hannifin, Francis M., 1730 N. Stillwell Rd., Boston, KY 40107
Hardesty, Lindsey Way Apts., 311-C N. 5th St., Bardstown, KY 40004
Hartlage, William C., Bishop David Apartments, 5146 Dixie Hwy., Louisville, KY 40216
Hogan, William E., 3320 Bardstown Rd., Apt. 52, Louisville, KY 40218
Howard, Anthony, 6304 Southside Dr., Louisville, KY 40214
Kelty, Charles J., 800 S. Fourth St., Apt. 2001, Louisville, KY 40203
Kotheimer, Alex L., 2526 Hawthorne Ave., Louisville, KY 40205
Lenahan, John B., #15 Audubon Plaza, Louisville, KY 40217
Lyon, Joseph A., Doe Valley Park, 228 Pine Ridge Pk., Brandenburg, KY 40108
Magel, John E., Royal Arms Apartments, #F-67, 1900 Bashford Manor Ln., Louisville, KY 40218
Maloney, James C., 2301 Goldsmith Ln., Louisville, KY 40218
Meder, James R., 125 Meder Ln., Payneville, KY 40157
Mills, Robert N., Rte. 1, P.O. Box 115, Elizabeth, IN 47117
Moert, Jerome S., Bishop David Apartments, 5146 Dixie Hwy., Louisville, KY 40216
Morgan, John H., 4308 Rudy Ln., Louisville, KY 40207
Nord, Clarence C., 2820 Flora Ave., #15, Louisville, KY 40220
Oyler, George F., 1500 Hurricane Hills, #A3, Boston, KY 40107
Pank, Julian F., 2832 Pomeroy Dr., Louisville, KY 40218
Pank, William H., 2832 Pomeroy Dr., Louisville, KY 40218
Prendiville, Joseph A., 20 Ireta Rd., Shrewsbury, MA 01545
Rapp, Bertrand J., 2040 Buechel Bank Rd., Louisville, KY 40218
Riede, Clifford A., 1516 Hepburn Ave., Apt. 4, Louisville, KY 40204
Robertson, Vernon W., P.O. Box 17408, Louisville, KY 40217
Russell, Paul M., Bishop David Apartments, 5146 Dixie Hwy., Louisville, KY 40216
Scherzer, Edwin J., Bishop David Apartments, 5146 Dixie Hwy., Louisville, KY 40216
Schlich, James J., 503 Lodgson Ct., Louisville, KY 40243
Schmidt, Stanley A., Christopher East Nursing Home, 4200 Browns Ln., Louisville, KY 40220
Schwartz, Clarence J., 1516 Hepburn Ave., #10, Louisville, KY 40204
Smith, F. Harold, 320 Grafton, #10, Dayton, OH 45406
Stuecker, Henry C., 747 Harrison Ave., Louisville, KY 40217
Thompson, James W., Bishop David Apartments, 5146 Dixie Hwy., Louisville, KY 40216
Voor, Joseph H., St. James Church, 1826 Edenside Ave., Louisville, KY 40204
Weyhing, John, 508 Brightwood Pl., A-3, Louisville, KY 40207
Wilson, Albert, 980 Ray Rd., Payneville, KY 40157
Zahner, William M., Bishop David Apartments, 5146 Dixie Hwy., Louisville, KY 40216

Permanent Deacons:
Abell, James H., St. Lawrence, Louisville
Amon, Joseph C., Jr., St. Helen Church, Louisville
Antle, Jerry L., Holy Spirit, Jamestown; Good Shepherd, Columbia
Becker, Gary E., Epiphany
Bennett, James D., (Retired), St. Martha Church, Louisville
Benton, James L., St. Brigid, Vine Grove
Bidwell, Lee G., St. Helen, Glasgow
Bishop, Joseph C., St. Dominic/Holy Rosary, Springfield
Bissig, Paul F., St. Cecilia Church
Biven, Lawrence J., Hospice of Louisville & Ascension Parish, Louisville
Box, Thomas E., Jr., St. Bartholomew, Louisville
Brown, Charles K., St. Martha, Louisville
Brown, Martin J., All Saints, Taylorsville; Hospice of Louisville
Bryant, Robert C., St. Barnabas, Louisville
Burns, Robert L., Our Lady Help of Christians, Valley Station
Carney, Edward P., St. Joseph, Louisville
Caspar, Robert J., St. James, Elizabethtown
Chathaparampil, Joseph, St. James Church, Elizabethtown
Churchill, John R., St. Augustine, Louisville
Clark, George B., St. Catherine, New Haven
Clark, William V., St. James, Elizabethtown
Collard, Paul J., (Retired), Immaculate Conception, La Grange
Cooper, Ernest A., Holy Rosary, Springfield
Dalton, David L., Stann/St. George, Louisville
Dant, Joseph R., (On Leave)
Dawson, Richard L., Christ the King, Louisville
Dever, Robert Glen, St. Leonard
Dew, Joseph M., Fort Knox
Downs, William A., Immaculate Conception, Culvertown
Ebert, John P., Transfiguration of Our Lord, Prospect
Edwards, Michael, St. Bernard, Louisville
Fante, Lamar W., Holy Family, Louisville
Fargen, J. Jerome, (Retired), St. James Church, Louisville
Filiatreau, Joseph H., St. Joseph Church, Bardstown
Filiatreau, Samuel R., St. Monica, Bardstown
George, Paul J., St. Mary, Louisville
Hamilton, John, St. Joseph, Bardstown
Harris, Patrick D., Mother of Good Counsel, Louisville
Hasson, Anthony P., St. Polycarp, Pleasure Ridge Park
Hawkins, Jack W., (Retired), St. Helen, Glasgow
Higgins, Frederick, St. Martin de Porres, Louisville
Hosch, Jon E., St. Polycarp, Pleasure Ridge Park
Houck, Peter L., Chap., Kentucky State Reformatory; St. Edward, Jeffersontown
Hutchins, Joseph E., St. Vincent De Paul, New Hope
Ishmael, Raymond L., On Leave
Jenkins, Jay R., St. James, Elizabethtown
Jones, James M., St. John the Apostle, Brandenburg
Jones, Walton G., St. Francis of Assisi, Louisville
Kampschaefer, Robert M., St. Denis, Louisville
Klosterman, Francis E., (Retired), St. Aloysius Church, Pewee Valley
Klump, William R., St. Louis Bertrand, Louisville
Kramer, Raymond G., St. Martha, Louisville
Kromer, Raymond G., Our Lady of Mercy, Hodgenville; St. Ann, Howardstown
Kruer, Marvin L., St. Basil/St. Denis, Louisville
Lincoln, James Bruce, Spiritual Advisor Cursillo; St. Barnabas, Louisville
Livers, Joseph E., St. Gregory, Samuels
Logsdon, Raymond L., (Retired), St. Michael, Jeffersontown
Maher, John P., St. Martha, Louisville
Markert, Clarence Robert, St. Ann, Louisville
Masterson, Donald E., St. Athanasius, Louisville
Mattingly, Thomas, St. Augustine, Lebannon
McCulloch, Thomas B., (Retired)
McGinty, David L., St. Helen, Louisville
Miller, Norbert F., Our Lady of Lourdes, Louisville
Mitchell, James B., (Retired)
Mitchell, Kenneth J., Most Blessed Sacrament, Louisville
Mullins, William L., St. Francis of Rome, Louisville
Murphy, Howard J., (Retired)
Nevitt, Charles, St. Rita, Louisville
Newton, David W., St. Thomas, Bardstown
Nitzken, Syl J., St. Stephen Martyr, Louisville
Ohnemus, Joseph, Our Lady of Perpetual Help, Campbellsville
Olrich, James Charles, St. Elizabeth Ann Seton

Church, Louisville
Osborne, Kenneth F., On Leave
Padgett, Joseph E., St. Mary Magdalen of Pazzi, Payneville; St. Theresa, Rhodelia
Patterson, Daniel Eugene, St. Luke Church, Louisville
Plummer, James R., St. Barnabas, Louisville
Prestwood, Harry, Most Blessed Sacrament, Louisville
Raibert, Joseph A., Mother of God Counsel & Office of Evangelization, Louisville
Ratterman, Cletus A., Guardian Angels, Louisville
Ronald, Edward R., Jefferson County Department of Corrections, Louisville
Ryan, Thomas, Catholic Deaf Office
Shutts, John F., (Retired), Caritas Medical Center, Louisville
Siers, Ronald R., (Retired)
Simpson, John L., Holy Trinity & St. Margaret Mary, Louisville
Skeeters, William L., St. Gabriel, Louisville
Stanley, Vincent G., St. Albert, Louisville; Catholic Charities
Steinmetz, Richard Earl, Our Mother of Sorrows, Louisville
Stuber, Joseph F., Transfiguration, Goshen
Sturgeon, James C., Sr., St. Raphael, Louisville
Thieneman, C. Wayne, Our Lady of Consolation, Valley Station
Thomas, William A., (Retired), Church of the Resurrection, Louisville
Thornbury, Benjamin, Our Lady of Lourdes, Louisville
Tolbert, Michael A., St. Thomas More, Louisville
Tomes, David R., Transfiguration, Prospect
Turner, James R., St. Martin de Porres, Louisville
Vessels, Michael, St. John the Baptist, Rineyville; St. Ambrose, Cecilia
Voll, Charles Joseph, Mother of Good Counsel, Louisville
Walsh, Richard J., St. Joseph, Bardstown
Walther, Charles F., St. Jerome, Fairdale
Ward, Kenneth M., St. Albert the Great, Louisville
Wheatley, Joseph P., Norton Hospital & Kosair Children's Hospital, Louisville
Whelan, John R., St. Martin of Tours, Flaherty
Wright, J. Patrick, Cathedral of the Assumption, Louisville
Young, R. James, St. Ignatius Martyr, Louisville

INSTITUTIONS LOCATED IN THE ARCHDIOCESE

[A] COLLEGES AND UNIVERSITIES

LOUISVILLE. *Bellarmine College*, 2001 Newburg Rd., 40205-0671. Tel: 502-452-8211.
For a complete listing, refer to the Colleges and Universities section.
Spalding University, 851 S. 4th St., 40203. Tel: 502-585-9911; Fax: 502-585-7158.
For a complete listing, refer to the Colleges and Universities section.

ST. CATHARINE. *St. Catharine College*, 2735 Bardstown Rd., 40061. Tel: 606-336-5082.
For a complete listing, refer to the Colleges and Universities section.

[B] HIGH SCHOOLS, DIOCESAN

LOUISVILLE. *Holy Cross High School*, 5144 Dixie Hwy., 40216. Tel: 502-447-4363. Mrs. Terry Crawley, Prin. Sisters 1; Lay Teachers 22; Students 350.
St. Francis DeSales High School, 425 Kenwood Dr., 40214. Tel: 502-368-6519. Mr. Martin Minogue, Prin. Lay Teachers 28; Students 410.
The Carmelite Community of The St. Francis De-Sales Priory. Tel: 502-368-6553. Revs. Kyrin Caggiano, O.Carm., Faculty, DeSales High School; Michael A. Greenwell, O.Carm., Chap., St. Xavier High School; Nelson Belizario, O.Carm., Campus Min., Bellarmine College; Charles Slobig, O.Carm., (Retired).
Trinity High School, 4011 Shelbyville Rd., 40207. Tel: 502-895-9427. Mr. Peter Flaig, Pres.; Mr. David Winkler, Prin.; Revs. Ronald J. Domhoff; R. Joseph Hemmerle; David H. Zettel. In res., Rev. Kevin Caster. Priests 4; Lay Teachers 64; Students 1,034.

BARDSTOWN. *Bethlehem High School*, 40004. Tel: 502-348-8594. Sisters of Charity of Nazareth. William B. Hart, III, Prin. Sisters 3; Lay Teachers 21; Students 301.

[C] HIGH SCHOOLS, PRIVATE

LOUISVILLE. *Academy of Our Lady of Mercy*, 1176 E. Broadway, 40204. Tel: 502-584-4273. Mr. Michael C. Johnson, Prin.; Melinda C. Ernstberger, Asst. Prin. Sisters of Mercy 1; Lay Teachers 22; Students 270.
Assumption High School, 2170 Tyler Ln., 40205. Tel: 502-458-9551; Fax: 502-454-8411. Sisters of Mercy. Ms. Karen Russ, Prin. Lay Teachers 65; Students 880.
Holy Rosary Academy, 4801 Southside Dr., 40214. Tel: 502-366-4561. Dr. Karen M. Juliano, Prin. Sisters of St. Dominic (St. Catharine, KY) 2; Lay Teachers 18; Girls 199.
Presentation Academy, 861 S. 4th St., 40203. Tel: 502-583-5935; Fax: 502-583-1342.
Spalding University. Stephanie Warren, Prin. Sisters 5; Lay Teachers 24; Students 340.
Sacred Heart Academy, 3175 Lexington Rd., 40206. Tel: 502-897-6097. Ursuline Sisters. Sr. Paula Kleine-Kracht, O.S.U., Prin.; Rev. John J. Butler. Sisters 2; Priests 1; Lay Teachers 45; Students 720.
St. Xavier High School, Xaverian Brothers, 1609 Poplar Level Rd., 40217. Tel: 502-637-4712. Bro. James M. Kelly, C.F.X., Pres.; Mr. Perry E. Sangalli, Prin. Priests 2; Brothers 9; Lay Teachers 80; Students 1,440.

[D] CONSOLIDATED SCHOOLS

LOUISVILLE. *Community Catholic School*, 2530 Slevin St., 40212. Tel: 502-778-1941. Sr. Barbara Von Bokern, S.C.N., Prin. Religious 1; Lay Teachers 8; Students 129. Children from St. Cecilia and Our Lady attend this school.

[E] ELEMENTARY SCHOOLS, PRIVATE

LOUISVILLE. *Holy Angels Academy, Inc.*, 1408 S. Second St., 40208. Tel: 502-634-3223. Joseph M. Norton, Prin. Sisters 4; Lay Teachers 14; Students 142.
Mercy Montessori School, 2181 Tyler Ln., 40205. Tel: 502-459-6545. Sr. Mary Alicia McGinty, R.S.M., Dir. Students 80.
Sacred Heart Model School, 3121 Lexington Rd., 40206. Tel: 502-896-3959. Sr. Jovita, O.S.U., Interim Prin. Lay Teachers 39; Students 333.
Thomas Merton Academy, 4605 Poplar Level Rd., 40213. 6010 Preston Hwy., 40219. Rev. James Murphy; Ann R. Thompson, Prin. Lay Teachers 12; Students 226.
Ursuline Montessori School, 3105 Lexington Rd., 40206. Tel: 502-896-3941. Sr. Delores Kemper, O.S.U., Admin. Students 96.

NAZARETH. *Nazareth Montessori Children's Center*, P.O. Box 44, 40048. Tel: 502-348-1540. Sr. Patricia Marie Hill, S.C.N., Dir. Sisters 2; Lay Teachers 5; Students 62.

[F] SPECIAL SCHOOLS

LOUISVILLE. *Pitt Academy*, 4605 Poplar Level Rd., 40213. Tel: 502-966-6979. Mr. Dennis Firestone, Prin. Sisters 1; Lay Teachers 8; Students 75.
St. Angela Education Center, 1731 Edenside Ave., 40204-1595. Tel: 502-459-9725. Sr. Jean Gertrude Mudd, O.S.U., Dir. Students 7.
St. Joseph Child Development Center, 2823 Frankfort Ave., 40206. Tel: 502-893-0241. Rev. Herman J. Naber, Dir.; Mimi Orr, Assoc. Dir. of Child Devel. Ctr. Students 200.
Ursuline Child Development Center, 3105 Lexington Rd., 40206. Tel: 502-895-7798. Sr. Vera Del Grande, O.S.U., Dir. Students 150.
Ursuline School of Music and Drama, 3105 Lexington Rd., 40206. Tel: 502-897-1816. Anna Jo Paul, Dir. Students 336.

[G] ORPHANAGES AND INFANT HOMES

LOUISVILLE. *St. Joseph Catholic Orphan Society*, 2823 Frankfort Ave., 40206. Tel: 502-893-0241; Fax: 502-896-2394.
For a complete listing, refer to the Special Care Facilities section.
St. Joseph Children's Home, 2823 Frankfort Ave., 40206. Tel: 502-893-0241; Fax: 502-896-2394.
For a complete listing, refer to the Special Care Facilities section.
St. Thomas Orphan Society, Inc., P.O. Box 1073, 40201.
For a complete listing, refer to the Special Care Facilities section.
St. Vincent's Orphan Society, Inc., P.O. Box 1073, 40201.
For a complete listing, refer to the Special Care Facilities section.

[H] GENERAL HOSPITALS

LOUISVILLE. *Caritas Medical Center*, 1850 Bluegrass Ave., 40215. Tel: 502-361-6000.
For a complete listing, refer to the Hospitals section.

BARDSTOWN. *Flaget Memorial Hospital*, 40004. Tel: 502-348-3923, Ext. 242.
For a complete listing, refer to the Hospitals section.

[I] SPECIAL HOSPITALS

LOUISVILLE. *Caritas Health Services, Inc. dba Caritas Peace Center*, 2020 Newburg Rd., 40205. Tel: 502-451-3330.
For a complete listing, refer to the Special Care Facilities section.

[J] PROTECTIVE INSTITUTIONS

LOUISVILLE. *Boys' Haven*, 2301 Goldsmith Ln., 40205. Tel: 502-458-1171; Fax: 502-451-2161.
For a complete listing, refer to the Special Care Facilities section.
Maryhurst, 1015 Dorsey Ln., 40223. Tel: 502-245-1576; Fax: 502-245-4737.
For a complete listing, refer to the Special Care Facilities section.

[K] NURSING HOMES

LOUISVILLE. *Franciscan Health Care Center / Retirement Center*, 3625 Fern Valley Rd., 40219.
For a complete listing, refer to the Special Care Facilities section.
Marian Home, 3105 Lexington Rd., 40206. Tel: 502-893-0121; Fax: 502-896-3925.
For a complete listing, refer to the Special Care Facilities section.
Nazareth Home, 2000 Newburg Rd., 40205. Tel: 502-459-9681; Fax: 502-456-9077.
For a complete listing, refer to the Special Care Facilities section.
St. Joseph Home for the Aged, 15 Audubon Plaza Dr., 40217 Fax: 502-636-2239.
For a complete listing, refer to the Special Care Facilities section.

[L] MONASTERIES AND RESIDENCES OF PRIESTS AND BROTHERS

LOUISVILLE. *Bishop David Apartments*, 5146 Dixie Hwy., 40216. Tel: 502-447-8617. Revs. William C. Hartlage, Dir.; William H. Zahner; Jerome S. Moert; James W. Thompson; John B. Gephart; Edwin J. Scherzer. Priests 6; Sisters 2.
Sacred Heart Retreat. (Corporate Title: Congregation of the Passion, Sacred Heart Community), 1924 Newburg Rd., 40205. Tel: 502-451-2330. Very Rev. Richard L. Parks, C.P., Supr. In res., Revs. Francis W. Cusack, C.P.; Joachim Gemperline, C.P.; Forrest Macken, C.P.; Germain Legere, C.P. (Nova Scotia); Howard Ralenkotter, C.P.; Henry Kielty, C.P. (Ireland); Emmet Linden; Walter Kaelin, C.P.; Kenny Lynch; James DeManuele, C.P.; William Browning, C.P.; John Baptist Ormechea, C.P. Priests 13.
St. Boniface Friary, 531 E. Liberty St., 40202. Tel: 502-584-4279. Revs. Sergius Scherpenberg, O.F.M., Guardian & Pastor; Stephen Schneider, O.F.M.; Edmund R. Moore, O.F.M. Priests 3.

TRAPPIST. *Abbey of Our Lady of Gethsemani, of the Order of Cistercians of the Strict Observance*, 40051. Tel: 502-549-3117; Fax: 502-549-8281. Rt. Revs. Timothy Kelly, O.C.S.O., Abbot; Bernard Murray, O.C.S.O. (Chile); Linus Dodge (Austria); Herbert Seib, O.C.S.O.; Roman Ginn, O.C.S.O.; Paschal Phillips, O.C.S.O.; Chrysogonus Waddell, O.C.S.O.; Gregory Lambing, O.C.S.O.; Bede Kok, O.C.S.O.; Hilarion Schmock, O.C.S.O.; Alan Gilmore, O.C.S.O.; Matthew Kelty, O.C.S.O.; Damien Thompson, O.C.S.O.; Michael Casagram, O.C.S.O. (Venezuela); Jacob Raub, O.C.S.O.; Carlos Rodriguez, O.C.S.O. Priests 16; Brothers 52; Novices 4; Postulants 2.

[M] CONVENTS AND RESIDENCES FOR SISTERS

LOUISVILLE. *Monastery of the Discalced Carmelite Nuns*, 1740 Newburg Rd., 40205. Sr. Francis of the Mother of God, O.C.D., Prioress. Professed Nuns 11.
St. Catherine Convent, 1172 E. Broadway, 40204. Tel: 502-583-7641. Sr. Mary Quentin Barth, R.S.M., Local Coord. Sisters of Mercy in residence 32.
Sisters of the Good Shepherd, 1015 Dorsey Ln., 40223. Sisters 3.
Ursuline Motherhouse of the Immaculate Conception, 3115 Lexington Rd., 40206. Tel: 502-893-0125. Sr. Sarah Stauble, O.S.U., Pres.; Rev. John J. Butler, Chap. Sisters in Motherhouse 56; Total in Congregation 236.
Ursuline Sisters. (Mount St. Joseph), 1731 Edenside Ave., 40204-1595. Tel: 502-451-8685. Sr. Amelia Stenger, Coord. Sisters 8. Attended from St. James.

BARDSTOWN. *Bethlehem Convent*, 40004. Tel: 502-348-3514. Sisters of Charity of Nazareth 4.

COLUMBIA. *Sisters of the Holy Cross*, c/o Good Shepherd Church, 1341 Greensburg Rd., P.O. Box 354, 42728.

NAZARETH. *Generalate, Motherhouse and Novitiate of the Sisters of Charity of Nazareth*, P.O. Box 172, 40048. Tel: 502-348-1555 (SCN Center & Generalate); 348-1500 (Motherhouse); Fax: 502-348-1502. Sr. Mary Collette Crone, S.C.N., Archivist; Revs. C. Patrick Creed, Chap., Motherhouse. Tel: 502-348-1523; Gary Young, C.R., Chap., Motherhouse; Robert A. DeWitt, Chap., Russell Hall. Sisters at Motherhouse 123; Sisters at Russell Hall 32;

Sisters at David Hall 24; Sisters at SCN Center 2; Sisters at Guest House 3; Apt. 2 W, M.H. 3; Apt. 3 N, M.H. 5; Apt. 1 A, R.H. 1.

NERINX. *Motherhouse and Novitiate of the Sisters of Loretto at the Foot of the Cross*, 40049. Tel: 502-865-5811; Fax: 502-865-2200. Sr. Mary Ann Coyle, Pres., Administration Office of the President, 3001 S. Federal Blvd., Denver, CO, 80236-2798. Tel: 303-922-8215. Rev. J. Irvin Mouser, Chap. Sisters in Motherhouse 135; Total in Congregation 440.

ST. CATHARINE. *St. Catharine of Siena Convent*, 2645 Bardstown Rd., 40061. Tel: 606-336-9303; Fax: 606-336-9306. Sr. Joan Scanlon, O.P., Pres. Tel: 606-336-9303; Rev. Charles E. Reteneller, Chap. Motherhouse of Dominican Sisters. Sisters in Motherhouse 48; Total in Congregation 312.

Sansbury Memorial Infirmary, 2645 Bardstown Rd., 40061. Tel: 606-336-3974. Sr. Susan Morris, O.P., Admin.; Rev. George P. Craycroft, Chap. Sisters in Infirmary 63.

TOMPKINSVILLE. *Sisters of the Holy Cross*, P.O. Box 548, 42167. Tel: 502-487-8881. Sr. Judith Anne, C.S.C., Pastoral Assoc.; Sr. Kathleen Moroney, C.S.C., Finance Councilor.

[N] HOMES FOR MEN AND WOMEN

LOUISVILLE. *Sacred Heart Home, Inc.*, 2120 Payne St., 40206. Tel: 502-895-9888; 895-9425; Fax: 502-894-9619.

For a complete listing, refer to the Special Care Facilities section.

[O] RETREAT HOUSES

LOUISVILLE. *Catholic Charismatic Renewal*, Flaget Center, 1935 Lewiston Pl., 40216. Tel: 502-448-8581. Tony Doninger, Contact Person; Rev. James E. Wafzig, Spiritual Advisor.

Flaget Center for Spirituality and Ministry Formation, 1935 Lewiston Dr., 40216. Tel: 502-448-8581; Fax: 502-448-5518. Donna M. McHugh, Admin.

CRESTWOOD. *Lake St. Joseph Center*, 5800 Old LaGrange Rd., 40014. Tel: 502-241-4469.

NAZARETH. *Catherine Spalding Center*, 40048. Tel: 502-348-1515. Sr. Carol Clasgens, S.C.N., Dir. Staff Sisters 4.

NERINX. *Knobs Haven*, 40049. Tel: 502-865-2621. Sr. Elaine Prevallet, S.L., Dir.

NEW HAVEN. *Bethany Spring*, 115 Dee Head Rd., 40051. Tel: 502-549-8277. Sr. Danielle Witt, S.S.N.D., Dir.

[P] ST. VINCENT DE PAUL SOCIETY

LOUISVILLE. *Society of St. Vincent de Paul, Council of Louisville*, P.O. Box 17126, 40217-0126. Tel: 502-584-2480; Fax: 502-587-1977. Dennis A. Shaw, Pres./CEO; Robert L. Dimke, Trustee/Board Chairman.

De Paul Apartments. (Transitional Shelter for Homeless Families).

De Paul Thrift Stores. 1029 S. Preston St., 40203. 248 E. Market St., 40202. 4443 Cane Run Rd., 40210.

Open Hand Kitchen. (Community Kitchen).

Ozanam Inn. (Men's Emergency & Transitional Shelter).

Parish Conferences.

Roberts Hall. (Women's Housing).

St. Jude House. (Women's Recovery).

Simon Hall. (Men's Recovery).

Tranquil House.

[Q] MISCELLANEOUS LISTINGS

LOUISVILLE. *Camp Tall Trees*, 2321 Carolina Ave., 40205.

Cathedral Heritage Foundation, Inc., 429 W. Muhammad Ali Blvd. #100, 40202-2334. Tel: 502-583-3100; Fax: 502-583-8524.

Mass of the Air, 1930 Bishop Ln., Ste. 1002, 40218.

Our Lady's Rosary Makers, 4611 Poplar Level Rd., P.O. Box 37080, 40233. Tel: 502-968-1434. Deacon Harry Prestwood, Pres. & Gen. Mgr.; Rev. Edwin J. Scherzer, Chap.

Perpetual Eucharistic Adoration, P.O. Box 39191, 40233-9191. Tel: 502-637-5309; 583-7641. Rev. Lawrence H. Lindle, Spiritual Dir.

PROJECT AIMM, 1850 Bluegrass Ave., 40215. Sr. Anne Mary Lochner, O.S.U., Exec. Dir.

Publication: "The Record", Maloney Center, 1200 S. Shelby St., 40203-2600. Tel: 502-636-0296; Fax: 502-636-2379. Official newspaper of the Archdiocese of Louisville (Weekly).

Office: Archdiocesan Communications Center. Joseph E. Duerr, Editor & Gen. Mgr.

Sisters of Loretto Charitable Trust. 515 Nerinx Rd., Nerinx, 40049-9999. Tel: 502-865-3414. Sr. Mary Swain, S.L., Treas.

Ursuline Campus Schools, Inc., 3105 Lexington Rd., 40206. Tel: 502-896-3910; Fax: 502-895-0989. Sponsored by Ursuline Sisters.

Ursuline Society and Academy of Education, 3105 Lexington Rd., 40206. Tel: 502-897-1811; Fax: 502-896-3913.

LEBANON. *The Laura*, 1995 Sam Browning Rd., 40033.

LORETTO. *Holy Cross Cemetery Trust, Inc.*, 7945 Loretto Rd., 40037.

NAZARETH. *Nazareth Arts For Life, Inc.*, O'Connell Hall, P.O. Box 14, 40048. Tel: 502-348-1554.

S.C.N. Missions, P.O. Box 9, 40048. Tel: 502-348-1520. Sisters of Charity of Nazareth.

Sisters of Charity of Nazareth Health System, P.O. Box 171, 40048. Tel: 502-349-6250; Fax: 502-349-6258. Mark W. Dundon, Pres.

Owns and operates 6 health care divisions in KY, AR, and TN, 2 of which are in the Louisville Archdiocese. Caritas Health Services and Flaget Memorial Hospital.

NEW HAVEN. *Via Escondida*, 325 Dee Head Rd., 40051. Jacqueline D'Avy, Hermit.

World Apostolate of Fatima (Blue Army), 8191 New Haven Rd., 40051-6030. Tel: 502-549-3757. Rev. Lawrence H. Lindle, Spiritual Dir.

Sacred Heart Apostolate, 8191 New Haven Rd., 40051-6030. Tel: 502-549-3757. Rev. Lawrence H. Lindle, Dir.

NEW HOPE. *St. Martin De Porres Lay Dominican Community*, 40052. Tel: 502-325-3061. Hugh Pimentel, T.O.P., Prior.

PLEASURE RIDGE PARK. *The Franciscan Foundation, Inc.*, 6901 Dixie Hwy., 40258.

RELIGIOUS INSTITUTES OF MEN REPRESENTED IN THE ARCHDIOCESE

For further details refer to the corresponding bracketed number in the Religious Institutes of Men or Women section.

[1350]—*Brothers of St. Francis Xavier*. (American Central Prov.).—C.F.X.

[0600]—*Brothers of the Congregation of Holy Cross*. (Midwest Prov.).—C.S.C.

[0270]—*Carmelite Fathers & Brothers*. (Pure Heart of Mary Prov.).—O.Carm.

[0350]—*Cistercians Order of the Strict Observance-Trappists*.—O.C.S.O.

[0820]—*Congregation of the Fathers of Mercy*.—C.P.M.

[1000]—*Congregation of the Passion*. (Holy Cross Prov.).—C.P.

[1130]—*Congregation of the Priests of the Sacred Heart*.—S.C.J.

[1080]—*Congregation of the Resurrection*. (Rome, Italy).—C.R.

[0480]—*Conventual Franciscans*. (Prov. of Our Lady of Consolation).—O.F.M.Conv.

[0520]—*Franciscan Friars*. (St. John the Baptist Prov.).—O.F.M.

[0430]—*Order of Preachers-Dominicans*. (St. Joseph Prov.).—O.P.

[1070]—*Redemptorist Fathers*.—C.SS.R.

[1060]—*Society of the Precious Blood*.—C.PP.S.

RELIGIOUS INSTITUTES OF WOMEN REPRESENTED IN THE ARCHDIOCESE

[0100]—*Adorers of the Blood of Christ*.—A.S.C.

[2145]—*Congregation of Augustinian Sisters Servants of Jesus and Mary*.—O.S.A.

[1920]—*Congregation of the Sisters of the Holy Cross*.—C.S.C.

[0420]—*Discalced Carmelite Nuns*.—O.C.D.

[1070-01]—*Dominican Sisters*.—O.P.

[1070-13]—*Dominican Sisters*.—O.P.

[2575]—*Institute of the Sisters of Mercy of the Americas*.—R.S.M.

[2470]—*Maryknoll Sisters of St. Dominic*.—M.M.

[2490]—*Medical Mission Sisters*.—S.C.M.M.

[3130]—*Our Lady of Victory Missionary Sisters*.—O.L.V.M.

[0440]—*Sisters of Charity of Cincinnati, Ohio*.—S.C.

[0480]—*Sisters of Charity of Leavenworth, Kansas*.—S.C.L.

[0500]—*Sisters of Charity of Nazareth*.—S.C.N.

[1000]—*Sisters of Divine Providence of Kentucky*.—C.D.P.

[2360]—*Sisters of Loretto At the Foot of the Cross*.—S.L.

[3360]—*Sisters of Providence of Saint Mary-of-the-Woods, IN*. (St. Gabriel Prov.).—S.P.

[1640]—*Sisters of St. Francis of Perpetual Adoration*.—O.S.F.

[3830-16]—*Sisters of St. Joseph of Springfield, MA*.—S.S.J.

[1830]—*Sisters of the Good Shepherd*.—R.G.S.

[1720]—*Sisters of the Third Order Regular of St. Francis of the Congregation of Our Lady of Lourdes*.—O.S.F.

[2150]—*Sisters, Servants of the Immaculate Heart of Mary*.—I.H.M.

[4120-03]—*Ursuline Nuns, of the Congregation of Paris*.—O.S.U.

ARCHDIOCESAN CEMETERIES

Offices for all cemeteries: 1600 Newburg Rd., Louisville, KY 40205; Mailing Address: P.O. Box 4096, Louisville, KY 40204. Tel: 502-451-7710; Fax: 502-456-9270.

LOUISVILLE. *Calvary*, 1600 Newburg Rd., 40205.

St. John, 2601 Duncan St., 40205.

St. Louis, 1215 Barret Ave., 40205.

St. Michael, 1153 Charles St., 40205.

NECROLOGY

† Bowling, Chester B., (Retired). —Died Oct. 26, 1996.

† Daunhauer, Richard J., (Retired). —Died March 6, 1996.

† Waldie, George J., (Retired). —Died June 11, 1996.

† Weiker, Clemens J., (Retired). —Died May 15, 1996.

Diocese of Lubbock

Most Reverend

PLACIDO RODRIGUEZ, C.M.F.

Bishop of Lubbock; ordained May 23, 1968; consecrated December 13, 1983; installed Auxiliary Bishop of Chicago; appointed Second Bishop of Lubbock April 5, 1994; installed June 1, 1994. *Res., Catholic Center, P.O. Box 98700, Lubbock, TX, 79499-8700; Fax: 806-792-2953 (Bishop's Private Line).*

The Catholic Center: P.O. Box 98700, Lubbock, TX, 79499-8700. Tel.: 806-792-3943; Fax: 806-792-8109.

Legal Title: Roman Catholic Diocese of Lubbock.

ESTABLISHED AND CREATED A DIOCESE, JUNE 17, 1983.

Square Miles 23,382.

Comprises the Counties of Bailey, Lamb, Hale, Floyd, Motley, Cottle, Cochran, Hockley, Lubbock, Crosby, Dickens, King, Yoakum, Terry, Lynn, Garza, Kent, Stonewall, Haskell, Gaines, Dawson, Borden, Scurry, Fisher and Jones.

STATISTICAL OVERVIEW

Personnel	
Bishop	1
Priests: Diocesan Active in Diocese	27
Priests: Active Outside Diocese	3
Priests: Retired, Sick or Absent	2
Number of Diocesan Priests	32
Religious Priests in Diocese	9
Extern Priests in Diocese	4
Ordinations:	
Diocesan Priests	1
Transitional Deacons	1
Permanent Deacons in Diocese	23
Total Sisters	32
Parishes	
Parishes	36
With Resident Pastor:	
Resident Diocesan Priests	23
Resident Religious Priests	8
Without Resident Pastor:	
Administered by Permanent Deacons	1
Administered by Women Religious	1
Administered by Lay People	1
Completely Vacant	2
Missions	25
Closed Parishes	2
Professional Ministry Personnel:	
Sisters	8
Lay Ministers	2
Welfare	
Catholic Hospitals	1
Total Assisted	98,982
Health Care Centers	35
Total Assisted	292,665
Special Centers for Social Services	1
Total Assisted	33,000
Educational	
Diocesan Students in Other Seminaries	7
Total Seminarians	7
High Schools, Diocesan and Parish	1
Total Students	78
Elementary Schools, Diocesan and Parish	2
Total Students	331
Catechesis/Religious Education:	
High School Students	2,697
Elementary Students	6,397
Total Students Under Catholic Instruction	9,919
Teachers in the Diocese:	
Vital Statistics	
Receptions into the Church:	
Infant Baptism Totals	1,910
Adult Baptism Totals	70
Received into Full Communion	58
First Communions	1,499
Confirmations	1,012
Marriages:	
Catholic	281
Interfaith	59
Total Marriages	340
Deaths	386
Total Catholic Population	50,378
Total Population	451,995

Former Bishops—Most Rev. MICHAEL J. SHEEHAN, S.T.L., J.C.D., ord. July 12, 1964; cons. and installed as the first Bishop of Lubbock, June 17, 1983; appt. Apostolic Administrator of Santa Fe, April 6, 1993; installed as the 11th Archbishop of Santa Fe, Sept. 21, 1993.

The Catholic Center—4620 Fourth, Lubbock, 79416., Mailing Address: P.O. Box 98700, Lubbock, 79499-8700. Tel: 806-792-3943; Fax: 806-792-8109; 792-2953 (Bishop's Office). Office Hours: Mon.-Fri. 8-5.

Chancellor—Rev. Msgr. ANTONIO G. GONZALEZ.

Moderator of the Curia—Rev. RONALD F. KRISMAN.

Bishop's Secretary—BECKY BARTLEY.

Diocesan Tribunal—P.O. Box 98700, Lubbock, 79499-8700. Tel: 806-792-3943.

Officialis—Rev. MALCOLM NEYLAND, M.C.L., J.C.L.

Advocates—Rev. Msgr. JOSEPH JAMES; Revs. CORNELIO RAMIREZ, S.A.C.; JOHN CASEY, S.A.C.; MARTIN PINA; GEORGE RONEY; MICHAEL MELCHER; JAMES MCCARTNEY.

Administrative Secretary—RITA ORTIZ.

Promoter of Justice—Rev. Msgr. ROLAND BUXKEMPER.

Defenders of the Bond—Rev. BEN KASTEEL, S.M.; Rev. Msgr. CURTIS T. HALFMANN; Rev. EUGENE J. DRISCOLL.

Defender of the Bond-Appeal—Rev. EUGENE J. DRISCOLL.

Notaries—RITA ORTIZ; BECKY BARTLEY.

Presbyteral Council & Diocesan Consultors—Very Rev. BEN KASTEEL, S.M., V.G.; Rev. Msgr. ANTONIO GONZALEZ; Revs. RONALD F. KRISMAN; EUGENE DRISCOLL; JOHN OHLIG; Rev. Msgr. CURTIS T. HALFMAN; Revs. JOHN CASEY; CHARLES HAMMOND, O.M.I.; JAMES O'CONNOR.

Priests Personnel Board—Rev. Msgr. CURTIS T. HALFMANN; Rev. Msgr. ANTONIO GONZALEZ; Most Rev. PLACIDO RODRIGUEZ; Very Rev. BEN KASTEEL, S.M., V.G.

Vicars Forane—Plainview Deanery: Vacant, *Our Lady of Guadalupe Church, P.O. Box 1269, 400 W. 29th, Plainview, 79073.* Tel: 806-296-2753. Brownfield Deanery: Rev. JOHN CASEY, S.A.C., *St. Anthony Church, P.O. Box 671, Brownfield, 79316.* Tel: 806-637-6626. Snyder Deanery: Rev. WILLIAM BRENNAN, S.J., St. Michael's Anson; Lubbock Deanery: Rev. Msgr. ROLAND BUXKEMPER, *Our Lady of Grace Church, 3119 Erskine St., Lubbock, 79415.* Tel: 806-763-4156.

Superintendent of Schools—ROBERTA MEYER, *P.O. Box 98700, Lubbock, 79499.*

Director of Youth—PAUL FLOREZ, *P.O. Box 98700, Lubbock, 79499.*

Campus Ministry—Sr. BETTY PRESTON, *2305 Main St., Lubbock, 79401.* Tel: 806-762-5225.

Director of Scouting—Rev. THOMAS DIEBEL, *P.O. Box 10753, Lubbock, 79408.* Tel: 806-792-3943.

Priests' Pension Fund—Rev. Msgr. JAMES COMISKEY; Revs. GEORGE RONEY; JAMES O'CONNOR; JAMES MCCARTNEY.

Diocesan Building Commission—Rev. BEN KASTEEL, S.M., V.G.; Rev. Msgr. JAMES COMISKEY; JOHN CONNORS; JOHN MOSSER; PAUL MEYER; MAX GARZA; BOB PAIKOWSKI; Rev. Msgr. ROLAND BUXKEMPER.

Diocesan Liturgical Commission—Rev. RONALD F. KRISMAN, *St. Michael's, 316 E. Washington St., Levelland, 79336-2611.* Tel: 806-894-2268.

Office of Christian Formation—Vacant, *P.O. Box 98700, Lubbock, 79499.* Tel: 806-792-3943.

Delegate of Religious—Sr. MARY GERRIOR, O.P., Pres., *3208-B 66th St., Lubbock, 79413-5701.* Tel: 806-792-7940. Rev. Msgr. TIMOTHY SCHWERTNER, Vicar for Religious.

Catholic Family Services, Inc.—STEVE HAY, Dir., *102 Avenue J, Lubbock, 79401.* Tel: 806-765-8475.

Director of Hispanic Affairs—Rev. Msgr. ANTONIO GONZALEZ, *St. Patrick's, 1603 Cherry Ave., Lubbock, 79403-6099.* Tel: 806-765-5123.

Ecumenical Affairs—Sr. MARY GERRIOR, O.P., *3208-B 66th St., Lubbock, 79413-5701.* Tel: 806-792-7940.

Diocesan Council of Catholic Women—Rev. Msgr. ANTONIO GONZALEZ, Moderator, *St. Patrick's, 1603 Cherry Ave., Lubbock, 79403-6099.*

Director of Vocations—Revs. MARTIN PINA, Seminarian Recruitment; EUGENE J. DRISCOLL, Seminarian Formation; RONALD F. KRISMAN, Continuing Education for Priests, *P.O. Box 98700, Lubbock, 79499.* Tel: 806-792-3943.

Diocesan Attorney—MADISON SOWDER, *1703 Ave. K, Lubbock, 79401.* Tel: 806-763-0409.

Diocesan Health Coordinator—Sr. CLAIRE OLIVIER, C.S.J., *St. Mary of the Plains Hospital, 4000 24th St., Lubbock, 79410.* Tel: 806-796-6000.

Propagation of the Faith—P.O. Box 98700, Lubbock, 79499-8100. Tel: 806-792-3943.

Office of Peace & Justice—Deacon DARIO RENDON, *Catholic Family Services, Inc., 102 Ave. J, Lubbock, 79401.* Tel: 806-765-8475.

Campaign for Human Development—Deacon DARIO RENDON, *Catholic Family Services, Inc., 102 Ave. J, Lubbock, 79401.* Tel: 806-765-8475.

Director of the Permanent Diaconate—Rev. Msgr. JOSEPH W. JAMES, *P.O. Box 744, Slaton, 79364-0744.* Tel: 806-828-6428.

Director of Deacon Formation Program—Deacon CLARKE E. COCHRAN, *P.O. Box 98700, Lubbock, 79499.* Tel: 806-792-3943.

Director of Continuing Education of the Clergy—Rev. RONALD F. KRISMAN, *P.O. Box 98700, Lubbock, 79499.* Tel: 806-792-3943.

Cursillo Movement—Rev. Msgr. ANTONIO GONZALEZ, Dir. English & Spanish Cursillo, *P.O. Box 5238, Lubbock, 79217.* Tel: 806-792-4308.

Newspaper—"South Plains Catholic"; Deacon LEROY BEHNKE, Editor, *P.O. Box 98700, Lubbock, 79499.*

Director of Communications—Deacon LEROY BEHNKE.

Office of Evangelization—Vacant.

CLERGY, PARISHES, MISSIONS AND PAROCHIAL SCHOOLS

CITY OF LUBBOCK
(Lubbock County)

1—CATHEDRAL CHRIST THE KING (1958), Rev. Msgr. James A. Comiskey; Rev. John Ohlig.
Res., 4011 54th St., 79413-4699. Tel: 806-792-6168; Fax: 806-792-1417.
School—Tel: 806-795-8283. Mrs. Roberta Meyer, Prin. & D.R.E.
Lay Teachers 18; Students 260.
Middle School—Tel: 806-795-6477.
Lay Teachers 7; Students 75.
Catechesis/Religious Programs—Tel: 806-792-6198.
Students 396.

2—OUR LADY OF GRACE (1960) (Hispanic), Rev. Alfredo Loya; Deacons Alfredo B. Jaime; Benny Brito.
Res., 3111 Erskine St., 79415-1623. Tel: 806-763-4156.
Catechesis/Religious Programs—Tel: 806-763-8727. Sr. Sandra Clark, O.S.F., D.R.E.
Students 570.

3—OUR LADY OF GUADALUPE (1980) (Mexican), Rev. James O'Connor.
Res., 52nd & Ave. L, P.O. Box 3947, 79452-3947. Tel: 806-763-0710.
Catechesis/Religious Programs—Tel: 806-763-0732. Sr. Mechtilde Gogel, O.L.V.M., D.R.E.
Students 722.

4—ST. ELIZABETH UNIVERSITY PARISH (1936), Revs. Eugene Driscoll; Reynaldo Reyes; Deacon Sid Little.
Res., 2305 Main St., 79401-2924. Tel: 806-762-5225; Fax: 806-762-5226.
Catechesis/Religious Programs—Tel: 806-762-1672. Sr. Betty Preston, M.M.B., D.R.E.
Students 450.

5—ST. JOHN NEUMANN (1979), Rev. Msgr. Curtis T. Halfmann; Deacons Thomas F. McCarthy, Pastoral Assoc.; Joe Richard; Richard Flores; Richard Wood; Kyle Broderson; Clarke Cochran.
Res., 5802 22nd, 79407-1721. Tel: 806-799-2649; Fax: 806-799-0037.
Catechesis/Religious Programs—Kathy Ellyson, D.R.E.
Students 369.

6—ST. JOSEPH'S (1924) (Hispanic), Rev. Cornelio C. Ramirez, S.A.C.
Res., 102 N. Ave. P, 79401-1199. Tel: 806-765-9935.
Catechesis/Religious Programs—Tel: 806-763-9695. Sr. Martha Molohon, O.L.V.M., D.R.E.
Students 336.

7—ST. PATRICK (1960) (Spanish), Rev. Msgr. Antonio Gonzales.
Res., 1603 Cherry Ave., 79403-6099. Tel: 806-765-5123.
Catechesis/Religious Programs—Tel: 806-765-6979. Sr. Vianney Martinez, O.S.F., D.R.E.
Students 273.
Mission—New Deal, Lubbock Co., Our Lady Queen of Apostles, Main St. N., 79401. Tel: 806-765-5123.

8—ST. THERESA'S (1961) (Mexican American), Rev. Msgr. Roland Buxkemper.
Res., Rte. 5, Box 285, 79407-9545. Tel: 806-795-2249.
Catechesis/Religious Programs—Tel: 806-866-4413. D.R.E.: Ina Alvarado; Gilbert Alvarado.
Students 102.

OUTSIDE THE CITY OF LUBBOCK

Anson, Jones Co., St. Michael's (1960) (Mexican), Rev. Boniface Riedmann, S.A.
Res., 2010 County Rd. 477, 79501-4732. Tel: 915-823-2777.
Catechesis/Religious Programs—Tel: 915-576-3376. D.R.E.: Mrs. Andrea Ramirez; Mrs. Sylvia Ruiz.
Students 130.
Mission—Hamlin, Jones Co., Holy Trinity.

Brownfield, Terry Co., St. Anthony's (1952) (Hispanic), Rev. John Casey, S.A.C., V.F.
Res., P.O. Box 671, 79316-0671. Tel: 806-637-6626.
Catechesis/Religious Programs—Mrs. Santos Guerra, D.R.E.
Students 350.
Mission—Ropesville, Hockley Co., San Francisco de Asis, P.O. Box 92, Ropesville, 79358. Tel: 806-562-4410.

Denver City, Yoakum Co., St. William (1955) (Hispanic), Rev. Andres Mendoza.
Res., 401 Mustang Ave., 79323-2749. Tel: 806-592-2063; Fax: 806-592-3943.
Catechesis/Religious Programs—D.R.E.: Martha De LaRosa; Alice Espinoza; Alice Gomez.
Students 485.
Mission—Plains, Yoakum Co., Sacred Heart, 1305 11th St., Plains, 79355. Tel: 806-456-7002.

Floydada, Floyd Co., St. Mary Magdalen (1928) (Hispanic), Rev. John Ohlig.
Res., 505 W. Jackson, 79235. Tel: 806-983-5878.
Catechesis/Religious Programs—Tel: 806-983-6553. Ellen Enriquez, D.R.E.
Students 130.
Missions—Matador, Motley Co., Our Lady of Guadalupe, 701 Bundy St., Matador, 79244; Paducah, Cottle Co., St. Elizabeth, Second St. & Clare St., Paducah, 79348. Tel: 806-492-3053.

Hale Center, Hale Co., St. Theresa's (1944) (Hispanic), Rev. Martin Pina.
Res., P.O. Box 570, 79041-0570. Tel: 806-839-2310.
Catechesis/Religious Programs—Tel: 806-839-9938.
Students 88.
Mission—Olton, Lamb Co., St. Peter Apostle, P.O. Box 655, Olton, 79064. Tel: 806-285-2140.

Idalou, Lubbock Co., St. Philip Benizi (1979) (Spanish), Rev. Msgr. Joseph W. James; Deacon Urbano Rodriguez.
Res., Box 1337, 79329-1337. Tel: 806-892-3042.
Mission—Lorenzo, San Lorenzo.

Lamesa, Dawson Co., St. Margaret Mary (1929) (Hispanic), Rev. Charles Hammond, O.M.I.
Res., 908 S. 2nd St, P.O. Box 599, 79331-6104. Tel: 806-872-7100. [CEM]
Catechesis/Religious Programs—Miss Delfina Luna, D.R.E.
Students 425.
Mission—Lamesa, Dawson Co., Our Lady of Guadalupe, P.O.Box 599, 79331.

Levelland, Hockley Co., St. Michael's (1956), Rev. Ronald F. Krisman.
Res., 316 E. Washington St., 79336-2611. Tel: 806-894-2268; Fax: 806-894-3362.
Catechesis/Religious Programs—Sr. Mildred Warminski, C.C.V.I., D.R.E.
Students 631.
Mission—Sundown, Hockley Co., San Isidro, 1306 S. Slaughter, P.O. Box 764, Sundown, 79372-0764.

Littlefield, Lamb Co., Sacred Heart (1921) (Hispanic), Rev. Clarence W. Huber.
Res., Eighth & Sunset, P.O. Box 1347, 79339-4234. Tel: 806-385-6043. [CEM]
Catechesis/Religious Programs—Mary Jane Aguirre, D.R.E.
Students 158.

Morton, Cochran Co., St. Ann (1955) (Hispanic), Rev. Ricardito P. Salditos (Philippines).
Res., 105 N.E. Eighth St., 79346-2719. Tel: 806-266-8693. [CEM]
Catechesis/Religious Programs—Tel: 806-266-5410. D.R.E.: Alfred Franco; Jane Dusterhaus.
Students 85.
Mission—Pep, Hockley Co., St. Philip Neri, Fm. Rd., #303, P.O. Box 395, Pep, 79353. Tel: 806-933-4355.

Muleshoe, Bailey Co., Immaculate Conception (1956) (Hispanic), Rev. Joseph Augustine Chorikavunkal (India).
Res., R.R. 3, Box 247, 79347-2460. Tel: 806-272-4384. [JC]
Catechesis/Religious Programs—Janie Balderas, D.R.E.
Students 172.
Mission—Earth, Lamb Co., St. Mary Magdalen, R.R.3 P.O. Box 247, Muleshoe 79347.
Catechesis/Religious Programs—Janie Fuentes, D.R.E.
Students 36.

O'Donnell, Lynn Co., St. Pius X (1956) (Hispanic), Rev. Todd Arnberg.
Res., P.O. Box 579, 79351-0579. Tel: 806-428-3490. [CEM]
Catechesis/Religious Programs—Tel: 806-428-3497.
Students 60.
Mission—Tahoka, Lynn Co., St. Jude, P.O. Box 128, Tahoka, 79373-0128. Tel: 806-998-4436.

Petersburg, Hale Co., Sacred Heart (1959) (Mexican American), Rev. Louis Dussan, C.M.F.
Mailing Address: P.O. Box 330, 79250-0330. Tel: 806-667-3763.
Res., R.R. 2, Box 159-A, Abernathy, 79311-6921. Tel: 806-298-4278.
Catechesis/Religious Programs—Jessie Flores, D.R.E.
Students 56.
Mission—Abernathy, Hale Co., St Isidore, 510 S. Ave. D, 79311-6921.

Plainview, Hale Co., St. Alice (1911), Rev. Msgr. Timothy Schwetner.
Res., 810 W. 11th, 79072-7124. Tel: 806-293-1903.
Catechesis/Religious Programs—1114 Houston, 79072. Tel: 806-293-2891. Sr. Mary Jane Alaniz, D.R.E.
Students 245.
Mission—Lockney, Floyd Co., San Jose, 303 S.E. Fourth, Lockney, 79241. Tel: 806-652-2321. Sr. Sophie Bonelli, O.S.F., Pastoral Assoc.

Our Lady of Guadalupe (1946) (Mexican), Rev. Ben Kasteel, S.M.
Mailing Address: P.O. Box 1269, 79073-1269. Tel: 806-291-0195.
Church—211 W. Seventh St., 79072-8013. Tel: 806-293-0085; Fax: 806-293-4507. [CEM]
Catechesis/Religious Programs—Tel: 806-293-0086. D.R.E.: Yolanda Gonzales, (Elementary); Yolanda Moreno, (Junior High School & High School).
Students 400.

Sacred Heart (1964) (Hispanic), Rev. Elbert Fadallan.
Mailing Address: P.O. Box 1209, 79073-2399. Tel: 806-296-2753.
Res., 400 W. 29th St., 79072-2399.
Catechesis/Religious Programs—Tel: 806-296-6553.
Students 457.

Post, Garza Co., Holy Cross (1955), Rev. Lawrence Hemp.
Res., Box 190, 79356-0190. Tel: 806-495-2791. [JC]
Catechesis/Religious Programs—Tom Hurley, D.R.E.
Students 90.

Ralls, Crosby Co., St. Michael (1959) (Hispanic), Rev. Gerald Leatham (Ireland).
Mailing Address: P.O. Box 906, 79357-0906. Tel: 806-253-2008. [JC]
Catechesis/Religious Programs—Students 90.
Mission—Crosbyton, Crosby Co., St. Joseph, Tel: 806-675-7017.

Rotan, Fisher Co., St. Joseph (1923) (Hispanic). Unassigned.
Res., 301 E. Lee, 79546-3011. Tel: 915-735-3285. [CEM]
Catechesis/Religious Programs—Tel: 915-735-2935. Frances Zambrano, D.R.E.; Rev. Johnrose H. Hayden.
Students 65.
Missions—Near Hamlin, Fisher Co., Sacred Heart Highway 92; Aspermont, Stonewall Co., St. Mary.

Seminole, Gaines Co., St. James (1958), Rev. William Sweeney, S.A.C. (Ireland).
Res., P.O. Box 898, 79360-0898. Tel: 915-758-2371.
Catechesis/Religious Programs—D.R.E.: Maria Hernandez; Susana Munoz.
Students 388.
Mission—Seagraves, Gaines Co., St. Paul's, P.O. Box 1321, Seagraves, 79359-1321. Tel: 806-546-2950.

Shallowater, Lubbock Co., St. Phillip Benizi (1967) (Mexican American), Deacon Leroy Behnke, Admin.; Rev. Msgr. Roland Buxkemper; Rev. Malcolm Neyland, Sacramental Min.; Deacon Nash Revilla, Pastoral Assoc.
Res., P.O. Box 39, 79363-0039. Tel: 806-832-5915.
Catechesis/Religious Programs—Tel: 806-832-5576. D.R.E.: Yvette Ayala; Julia Escobedo.
Students 120.
Mission—Anton, Hockley Co., St. Anthony, (1966) P.O. Box 545, Anton, 79313. Tel: 806-997-5831.

Slaton, Lubbock Co., Our Lady of Guadalupe (1952) (Mexican), Rev. Lawrence A. Hemp.
Res., 705 S. Fourth, 79363-5406. Tel: 806-828-5108 (Office). [JC]
Catechesis/Religious Programs—Tel: 806-828-4573. Ernestina Perez, D.R.E.
Students 220.

St. Joseph's (1912) (German), Rev. Jim McCartney; Deacon Darris D. Linder.
Res., 205 S. 19th, 79364-3755. Tel: 806-828-3944.
School—20th W. Division, 79364. Tel: 806-828-6761. Mrs. Janet Kitten, Prin.
Lay Teachers 10; Students 76.
Catechesis/Religious Programs—Students 52.
Mission—Wilson, Blessed Sacrament Church, P.O. Box 119, Slaton 79381. Tel: 806-828-6452.

Snyder, Scurry Co., St. Elizabeth's (1952) (Hispanic), Rev. Reynaldo Reyes.
Res., 3005 Ave. A, 79549-3909. Tel: 915-573-2590. [CEM]
Catechesis/Religious Programs—Tel: 915-573-8824. Shirley Pavlik, D.R.E.
Students 297.
Mission—Hermeleigh, Scurry Co., St. John. Hwy. 84.

Our Lady of Guadalupe (1945), Rev. Patrick S. Maher (Ireland).
Res., 1311 Ave. K, Rte. 3, Box 135, 79549-9533. Tel: 915-573-3866.
Catechesis/Religious Programs—Tel: 915-573-2979. D.R.E.: Maria Ramirez; Roberto Ramirez.
Students 255.

Spur, Dickens Co., St. Mary (1948) (Hispanic), Rev. William J. Brennan, S.J.
Res., Box 189, 79370-0189. Tel: 806-271-4385; Fax: 806-271-3606.
Mission—Jayton, Kent Co., Epiphany.

Stamford, Jones Co., St. Ann (1955), Rev. Michael Melcher; Sr. M. Lalemant Pelikan, R.S.M., Pastoral Assoc.
Res., 104 New Braunfels, 79553-6415. Tel: 915-773-2659; Fax: 915-773-3622.
Catechesis/Religious Programs—Students 70.
Mission—Haskell, Haskell Co., St. George, 910 N. 16th St., Haskell, 79521-3340. Tel: 817-864-3171.
Catechesis/Religious Programs—Students 45.

Wolfforth, St. Francis of Assisi Mission. See San Ramon, Woodrow for details.

Woodrow, Lubbock Co., San Ramon (1974), Rev. George Roney.
Church—Rte. 6, Box 356, Lubbock, 79423. Tel: 806-863-2201.
Catechesis/Religious Programs—Tel: 806-863-3435.
Students 164.
Mission—Wolfforth, Lubbock Co., St. Francis of Assisi, P.O. Box 785, Wolfforth, 79382. Tel: 806-866-9007.

Special Assignment:
Reverend Fathers—
Diebel, Thomas, Dir. Scouting, P.O. Box 10753, Lubbock, TX 79408
Furlong, James, Pastoral Care, 1105 Genoa Ave., Lubbock, TX 79416
Thekkedam, George, Pastoral Care, St. Mary's Hospital, 4000 24th St., Lubbock, TX 79410

On Duty Outside the Diocese:
Reverend Fathers—
Cruz, David, The Assumption-St. John Seminary, 2600 W. Woodlawn, San Antonio, TX 78284
Luera, Ruben, 8000 Village Oak, Apt. K63, Live Oak, TX 78233

Military Chaplains:
Reverend Fathers—
Diab, Thomas (ALX), Reese Air Force Base, 64 ABG-HC, TX 79489. Tel: 806-885-3237

Retired:
Reverend Fathers—
Vaze Parampil, Thomas, Corpus Christi Abbey, HCR #2, Box 6300, San Dia, TX 78383-9949

Permanent Deacons:
Acevedo, Miguel, (Retired), St. Mary Magdalen, Earth
Barrera, Salome, Our Lady of Guadalupe, Snyder
Behnke, Leroy, St. Phillip Benizi, Shallowater
Brito, Benny, Our Lady of Grace, Lubbock
Cavazos, Jesus Z., On Duty Outside the Diocese
Cochran, Clarke E., St. John Neumann, Lubbock
DeLeon, Saragosa, (Retired), St. Joseph, Rotan
Flores, Antonio B., St. Michael's, Ralls
Garcia, Doroteo, Sacred Heart, Littlefield
Garcia, Pedro, St. Michael's, Ralls
Jaime, Alfredo B., Our Lady of Grace, Lubbock
King, Edward, St. Michael's, Levelland
Linder, Darris D., St. Joseph's, Slaton
Little, Sidney R., St. Elizabeth's, Lubbock
Martinez, Nasario, (Retired), St. Mary's, Sudan
Moreno, Jesse, (Retired), St. Ann, Stamford
Ortegon, Frank, Our Lady of Guadalupe, Snyder
Peralez, Catarino, (Retired), St. Philip Benizi, Idalou
Ramirez, Robert, Our Lady of Guadalupe, Snyder
Rendon, Dario, (Retired), St. Patrick's, Lubbock
Revilla, Nash, St. Phillip Benizi, Shallowater
Richard, Joseph N., St. John Newmann, Lubbock
Rodriguez, Urbano, St. Philip Benizi, Idalou
Thompson, Richard, Sacred Heart, Littlefield

INSTITUTIONS LOCATED IN THE DIOCESE

[A] CHRISTIAN RENEWAL CENTERS

LUBBOCK. *Christian Renewal Center*, P.O. Box 5238, 79217. Tel: 806-792-1105. Ms. Blanche Arreola, Asst. Dir.
Office of Evangelization. Tel: 806-792-1105.
Office for Cursillo Movement. Tel: 806-792-4308. Rev. Msgr. Antonio Gonzalez, Dir.

[B] GENERAL HOSPITALS

LUBBOCK. *St. Mary of the Plains Hospital*, 4000 24th St., 79410-1894. Tel: 806-796-6000; Fax: 806-796-6081.
For a complete listing, refer to the Hospitals section.

[C] RETREAT HOUSES

SLATON. *Our Lady of Mercy Retreat Center*, P.O. Box 744, 1225 W. Division, 79364-0744. Tel: 806-828-6428. Rev. Msgr. Joseph W. James, Dir.

[D] CONVENTS AND RESIDENCES FOR SISTERS

LUBBOCK. *Casa de San Jose*, 3817 23rd St., 79410. Tel: 806-796-6000; Fax: 806-796-6081. St. Mary of the Plains Hospital Convent. Sisters of St. Joseph of Orange, C.S.J. 4.
Casa Merced, Sisters of Mercy Convent, 4104 68th, 79413-5912. Tel: 806-791-4692. Sisters of Mercy of the Americas 3.
Dominican Sisters, O.P., 3208-B 66th St., 79413-5701. Tel: 806-792-7940.
Our Lady of Grace Convent, 3101 Erskine, 79415. Tel: 806-747-7472. Missionary Catechists of the Sacred Hearts of Jesus and Mary 3.
St. Francis Mission Community Central House (1981), St. Francis Convent, 4305 54th St., 79413-4617. Tel: 806-793-9859. St. Francis Mission Community 9.
St. Joseph Convent, 1602 First St., 79401. Tel: 806-763-9695. Missionary Sisters of Our Lady of Victory 3.
St. Mary Convent, 3820 24th St., 79410. Tel: 806-796-6000. St. Mary of the Plains Hospital Convent. Sisters of St. Joseph of Orange, C.S.J. 3.
Sisters of St. Francis, Millvale, PA, 5430 50th St., Apt. #19, 79414. Tel: 806-793-0331.

LEVELLAND. *Sisters of Charity of the Incarnate Word*, 320 E. Washington, 79336. Tel: 806-894-3424.

PLAINVIEW. *St. Alice Convent*, 1114 Houston, 79072. Tel: 806-296-5426. St. Francis Mission Community Sisters 3; Novices 1; Postulants 1.

SLATON. *Mercedarian Missionaries Convent*, 1035 W. Crosby, 79364. Tel: 806-828-3566. Sisters 4.

[E] MISCELLANEOUS LISTINGS

LUBBOCK. *Catholic Foundation, Diocese of Lubbock*, P.O. Box 98700, 79499-8700.
Christ the King Cathedral School Foundation, 4011 54th St., 79413. Laurel S. Johnson, Chm.

RELIGIOUS INSTITUTES OF WOMEN REPRESENTED IN THE DIOCESE

For further details refer to the corresponding bracketed number in the Religious Institutes of Men or Women section.

[0460]—*Congregation of the Sisters of Charity of the Incarnate Word.*—C.C.V.I.

[]—*Dominican Sisters.*—O.P.

[]—*Mercedarian Missionaries of Berriz.*—M.M.B.

[2700]—*Missionary Cathechists of the Sacred Heart of Jesus and Mary.*—M.C.SS.CC.J.M.

[3130]—*Our Lady of Victory Missionary Sisters.*—O.L.V.M.

[]—*St. Francis Mission Community.* (Amarillo, TX).—O.S.F.

[2575]—*Sisters of Mercy of the Americas.*—R.S.M.

[1620]—*Sisters of Saint Francis of Millvale, PA.*—O.S.F.

[3830]—*Sisters of St. Joseph of Orange.*—C.S.J.

NECROLOGY

† Kolodziejcsyk, Joseph, (Retired). —Died Jan. 22, 1996.

Diocese of Madison

(Dioecesis Madisonensis)

Most Reverend

WILLIAM H. BULLOCK

Bishop of Madison; ordained June 7, 1952; appointed Auxiliary Bishop of St. Paul and Minneapolis and Titular Bishop of Natchez June 3, 1980; consecrated August 12, 1980; appointed Bishop of Des Moines February 10, 1987; installed April 2, 1987; appointed Bishop of Madison April 13, 1993; installed June 14, 1993.

Most Reverend

GEORGE O. WIRZ

Auxiliary Bishop of Madison and Titular Bishop of Municipa; ordained May 31, 1952; appointed December 20, 1977; consecrated March 9, 1978. *Res., St. Patrick Parish, 404 E. Main St., Madison, WI, 53703.*

ESTABLISHED 1946.

Square Miles 8,070.

Corporate Title: "Roman Catholic Diocese of Madison."

Comprises the Counties of Columbia, Dane, Grant, Green, Green Lake, Iowa, Jefferson, Lafayette, Marquette, Rock and Sauk in the State of Wisconsin.

For legal titles of parishes and diocesan institutions, consult the Chancery.

Chancery: 15 E. Wilson St., P.O. Box 111, Madison, WI, 53701. Tel.: 608-256-2677; Fax: 608-256-1006.

STATISTICAL OVERVIEW

Personnel	
Bishop	1
Auxiliary Bishops	1
Priests: Diocesan Active in Diocese	120
Priests: Active Outside Diocese	4
Priests: Retired, Sick or Absent	33
Number of Diocesan Priests	157
Religious Priests in Diocese	23
Ordinations:	
Permanent Deacons in Diocese	1
Total Brothers	9
Total Sisters	427
Parishes	
Parishes	137
With Resident Pastor:	
Resident Diocesan Priests	102
Resident Religious Priests	4
Without Resident Pastor:	
Administered by Priests	31
Professional Ministry Personnel:	
Sisters	34
Lay Ministers	120
Welfare	
Catholic Hospitals	4
Total Assisted	213,742
Health Care Centers	2
Total Assisted	308
Homes for the Aged	6
Total Assisted	780
Day Care and Extended Day Care Centers	14
Total Assisted	878
Special Centers for Social Services	7
Total Assisted	46,297
Residential Care of Disabled	1
Total Assisted	600
Educational	
Diocesan Students in Other Seminaries	24
Total Seminarians	24
Colleges and Universities	1
Total Students	2,109
High Schools, Diocesan and Parish	1
Total Students	93
High Schools, Private	1
Total Students	594
Elementary Schools, Diocesan and Parish	44
Total Students	7,365
Elementary Schools, Private	1
Total Students	252
Catechesis/Religious Education:	
High School Students	11,682
Elementary Students	16,675
Total Students Under Catholic Instruction	38,794
Teachers in the Diocese:	
Brothers	1
Sisters	30
Lay Teachers	546
Vital Statistics	
Receptions into the Church:	
Infant Baptism Totals	3,211
Adult Baptism Totals	408
First Communions	3,138
Confirmations	2,459
Marriages:	
Catholic	765
Interfaith	546
Total Marriages	1,311
Deaths	1,522
Total Catholic Population	256,527
Total Population	866,227

Former Bishops—Most Rev. WILLIAM P. O'CONNOR, D.D., Ph.D., ord. March 10, 1912; appt. Bishop of Superior, Dec. 31, 1941; cons. March 7, 1942; transferred as first Bishop of Madison, Feb. 22, 1946; resigned Feb. 22, 1967; died July 13, 1973.—Most Rev. CLETUS F. O'DONNELL, D.D., J.C.D., ord. May 3, 1941; appt. Titular Bishop of Abrittum and Auxiliary of Chicago, Oct. 26, 1960; cons. Dec. 21, 1960; promoted to Bishop of Madison, Feb. 22, 1967; resigned April 18, 1992; died Aug. 31, 1992.

Vicar-General—Most Rev. GEORGE O. WIRZ, D.D., S.T.L.; Rev. PAUL J. SWAIN, J.D.

Chancery—15 E. Wilson St., P.O. Box 111, Madison, 53701. Tel: 608-256-2677; Fax: 608-256-1006. Office Hours: Mon.-Fri. 8-4.

Moderator of the Curia—Rev. PAUL J. SWAIN, J.D.

Chancellor—Rev. JOSEPH P. HIGGINS, S.T.L.

Director of Finance—GREGORY J. KELLER.

Diocesan Tribunal—15 E. Wilson St., P.O. Box 111, Madison, 53701. Tel: 608-256-7810.

Judicial Vicar—Rev. MICHAEL E. HIPPEE, J.C.L.

Director of the Tribunal—J. MICHAEL RITTY, J.C.L., Ph.D.

Judges—Rev. JAMES W. HINNEN, J.C.L.

Defender of the Bond—RENATO F. AOANAN, J.C.L.

Notary—Rev. BERNARD H. DEITELHOFF; SUSAN STACK.

Diocesan Consultors—Most Rev. GEORGE O. WIRZ; Rev. Msgr. RAYMOND E. KLAAS, J.C.D.; Revs. JOSEPH P. HIGGINS, Sec. WILLIAM A. DEBOCK; DELBERT D. KLINK; JAMES J. UPPENA.

Presbyteral Council—Most Rev. GEORGE O. WIRZ, Ex-Officio. Elected: Revs. THOMAS R. DOHENY; DAVID H. RUNDE; JOHN H. HEDRICK; DOUGLAS DUSHACK; RAYMOND KERTZ; STEPHEN J. UMHOEFER; THOMAS F. BAXTER; JAMES H. MURPHY; WILLIAM A. NOLAN; ROGER G. NILLES; JOHN L. URBAN; MICHAEL C. RICHEL. Appointed: Rev. Msgr. RAYMOND E. KLAAS, P.A.; Revs. MICHAEL L. BURKE; JOSEPH P. HIGGINS; THOMAS M. SEGERSON; PAUL J. SWAIN. Personnel Board: Revs. JOHN M. MEINHOLZ; ELMER J. DIETZEL; THOMAS R. DOHENY; LAWRENCE M. BAKKE; J. DARYL FURLONG; ROGER H. TAYLOR; PAUL J. SWAIN.

Vicars for Religious—Rev. DANIEL T. GANSHERT, *404 E. Main St., Madison, 53703-2891.* Tel: 608-257-5000. Sr. LUCILLE MARIE FROST, *855 Woodrow St., Madison, 53711.*

Deaneries—Columbia Deanery: Rev. RAYMOND J. DISCHLER, East Dane Deanery: Rev. WILLIAM A. DEBOCK, Grant Deanery: Rev. THOMAS F. BAXTER, Iowa Deanery: Rev. DONALD V. MORAN, Jefferson Deanery: Rev. THOMAS P. MARR, Lafayette Deanery: Rev. THOMAS J. COYLE, Madison Deanery: Rev. KENNETH J. FIEDLER, Marquette-Green Lake Deanery: Rev. JEROME J. MAKSVYTIS, Rock Deanery: Rev. EDWARD J. ERBE, Sauk Deanery: Rev. DONALD J. WIECKI, West Dane Deanery: Rev. DELBERT L. SCHMELZER.

Diocesan Offices and Directors

Apostleship of Prayer—Rev. JOSEPH L. HENRY, *432 Maxwell St., Baraboo, 53913.*

Apostolate to the Handicapped—Rev. THOMAS F. CAMPION, *P.O. Box 443, Monroe, 53566.* Tel: 608-324-1000.

Apostolate to the Deaf—Rev. GUY A. BLAIR, S.C.J., *St. Joseph Church, 1905 Beltline Hwy., Madison, 53713.* Tel: 608-278-1980.

Boy Scouts—Rev. BRUCE M. HENNINGTON, *209 South St., Waunakee, 53597-1396.* Tel: 608-849-5121.

Building Commission—Rev. DANIEL T. GANSHERT, Chm.; Revs. MICHAEL E. HIPPEE; DELBERT L. SCHMELZER; Mr. PATRICK GORMAN; Mrs. FRIEDIE CAREY; PAUL

BROWN; ARTHUR MCCLURE.

Camp Gray—JAKE CZARNIK-NEIMEYER, Dir., *E10213 Shady Lane Rd., Reedsburg, 53959.*

Catholic Relief Services—Rev. PAUL J. SWAIN, *P.O. Box 111, Madison, 53701.* Tel: 608-256-2677.

Cemeteries—THOMAS B. HANLON, JR., Diocesan Dir., Central Office: *2705 Regent St., Madison, 53705.* Tel: 608-238-5562.

Charities—Catholic Charities of the Diocese of Madison, Inc., 4905 Schofield St., Madison, 53716. Tel: 608-221-2000. BRIAN CAIN, Dir., *Administrative Office, 4905 Schofield St., Madison, 53716.* Tel: 608-221-2000., *Madison District Office, 30 S. Franklin St., Madison, 53703.* Tel: 608-256-2358., *Beloit District Office, 3311 Prairie Ave., Beloit, 53511.* Tel: 608-365-3665., *Janesville District Office, 2020 E. Milwaukee St., Janesville, 53545.* Tel: 608-752-4906.

Dir. of Clergy Development—Most Rev. GEORGE O. WIRZ, *15 E. Wilson St., Madison, 53701.* Tel: 608-256-2677.

Education—Rev. JAMES J. UPPENA, Dir., Religious Education, *142 W. Johnson St., Madison, 53703.* Tel: 608-255-5108. JACK MCBRIDE, Assoc. Dir., Adult & Special Education; KATHERINE KERKHOF, Assoc. Dir., Youth; JAMES R. SILVER, Supt., Schools, *P.O. Box 1606, Madison, 53701.* Tel: 608-256-0872. JUDY L. PEPPARD, Asst. Supt., *142 W. Johnson St., Madison, 53703.*

Saint Raphael Society Clergy Retirement Plan—Rev. PAUL J. SWAIN, *P.O. Box 111, Madison, 53701.* Tel: 608-256-2677.

Confraternity of the Blessed Sacrament—Rev. JOSEPH HENRY, Dir., *432 Maxwell St., Barab, 53913.* Tel: 608-356-4773.

Council of Catholic Women—Revs. DUANE R. MOELLENBERNDT, Moderator, *St. Joseph Parish, 11 N. 3rd St., Ft. Atkinson, 53538-1801.* Tel: 414-563-3029. LORIN M. BOWENS, Co-Moderator, *St. Boniface Parish, P.O. Box 60, Lime Ridge, 53942.* Tel: 608-986-2101.

Director of Communications—WILLIAM BROPHY. Tel: 608-256-2677.

Holy Childhood, Pontifical Association—Rev. DELBERT L. SCHMELZER, Dir., *301 N. Main St., Verona, 53593.* Tel: 608-845-7323.

Information—Rev. PAUL J. SWAIN, Dir., *P.O. Box 111, Madison, 53701.*

Office of Worship—Dr. PATRICK GORMAN, *Holy Name Catholic Center, 3577 High Pt. Rd., Madison, 53719.* Tel: 608-833-6571.

Office of Family Ministry—Rev. JAMES J. UPPENA, Acting Dir., *142 W. Johnson St., Madison, 53703.* Tel: 608-251-7727.

Office for Justice and Peace—J. MARK BRINKMOELLER, Dir., *Holy Name Catholic Center, 3577 High Pt. Rd., Madison, 53719.* Tel: 608-833-1010.

Newman Apostolate—Madison: Rev. STEVEN J. KORTENDICK, Dir., *St. Paul Univ. Catholic Center, 723 State St., Madison, 53703.* Tel: 608-256-2697. Platteville: Rev. JAMES H. MURPHY, *St. Augustine Newman Center, 135 S. Hickory, Platteville, 53818.* Tel: 608-348-7530.

Newspaper—"Catholic Herald, Madison Edition," MARY UHLER, Editor, *702 N. Blackhawk St., P.O. Box 5913, Madison, 53705.* Tel: 608-233-8060.

Priests' Eucharistic League—Rev. JOSEPH HENRY, Dir., *432 Maxwell St., Baraboo, 53913.* Tel: 608-356-4773.

Office of Hispanic Ministry—MARIO J. DELGADO, Dir., *Holy Name Catholic Center, 3577 High Point Rd., Madison, 53719.* Tel: 608-833-8426.

Centro Pastoral Guadalupano—Sr. ROSEMARY EMPEN, O.P., Dir.; Rev. DANIEL KABAT, O.F.M.Cap., *1862 Beld St., Madison, 53713.* Tel: 608-255-8471. *Our Lady of Guadalupe Migrant Center, Endeavor, and Queen of Americas Migrant Center, Cambria.*

Propagation of the Faith—Rev. DELBERT L. SCHMELZER, Dir., *St. Andrew, 301 N. Main St., Verona, 53593.* Tel: 608-845-7323.

St. Vincent de Paul Society—Rev. FRANCIS J. STEFFEN, *222 W. Main St., Madison, 53703.* Tel: 608-256-5614.

Serra Clubs—Madison: Revs. FRANCIS J. STEFFEN; JOHN G. STILLMANK, Janesville: Rev. RICHARD M. HEILMAN, Beloit: Rev. GARY L. KRAHENBUHL.

Vigilance Council—The Very Rev. Deans.

Vocations—Rev. MICHAEL C. RICHEL, Dir., *Holy Name Catholic Center, 3577 High Pt. Rd., Madison, 53719.* Tel: 608-833-6795.

Wisconsin Catholic Conference—JOHN HUEBSCHER, Exec. Sec., *30 W. Mifflin St., Room 302, Madison, 53703.* Tel: 608-257-0004.

CLERGY, PARISHES, MISSIONS AND PAROCHIAL SCHOOLS

CITY OF MADISON
(Dane County)

1—ST. RAPHAEL CATHEDRAL, Rev. Francis J. Steffen. In res., Revs. Steven J. Kortendick; Steven G. Steele.
Res., 222 W. Main St., 53703. Tel: 608-256-5614. [JC]

2—ST. BERNARD, Rev. Michael E. Hippee.
Res., 2450 Atwood Ave., 53704. Tel: 608-249-9256. [JC]

3—BLESSED SACRAMENT, Revs. Stanley Drongowski, O.P.; Jordan McGrath, O.P. In res., Revs. James Cornelius Hahn, O.P.; Hugh Wreisner, O.P.; Gregory J. Moore, O.P.
Res., 2131 Rowley Ave., 53705. Tel: 608-238-3471. [JC]
School—2112 Holister Ave., 53705.
Lay Teachers 19; Students 306.

4—HOLY REDEEMER, Rev. Kevin D. Holmes. In res., Rev. Lawrence J. Kieffer. In res., St. Paul House, Revs. Daniel Kabat, O.F.M., Cap.; Kenneth Smits, O.F.M., Cap.
Res., 120 W. Johnson St., 53703. Tel: 608-255-1658.

5—IMMACULATE HEART OF MARY, Revs. John M. Meinholz; Eric Nielsen.
Res., 5101 Schofield Ave., 53716. Tel: 608-221-1521. [JC]
School—4913 Schofield Ave., 53716.
Lay Teachers 14; Students 200.

6—OUR LADY, QUEEN OF PEACE, Revs. Kenneth J. Fiedler; Thomas L. Kelley.
Res. and Parish Center: 401 S. Owen Dr., 53711. Tel: 608-231-4600. [JC]
School—418 Holly Ave., 53711.
Lay Teachers 27; Students 483.

7—ST. DENNIS, Revs. Kent A. Schmitt; Randy J. Timmerman; Sr. Ginny Heldorfer, O.S.F., Pastoral Min.
Res., 313 Dempsey Rd., 53714. Tel: 608-246-5124. [JC]
School—Dominican Sisters Sinsinawa 3; Lay Teachers 12; Students 224.

8—ST. JAMES, Rev. Douglas L. Dushack.
Res., 1128 St. James Ct., 53715. Tel: 608-255-1656. [JC]
School—1204 St. James Ct., 53715. Tel: 608-256-3095.
Lay Teachers 16; Students 150.

9—SAINT JOSEPH, Rev. Bernard M. Brunette, O.Praem. In res., Rev. Guy A. Blair, S.C.J., Chap. for the Deaf Community.
Res., 1905 W. Beltline Hwy., 53713. Tel: 608-271-5771.

10—ST. MARIA GORETTI, Rev. Michael L. Burke. In res., Rev. Wilfred J. Schuster.
Res., 10 Maria Pl., 53711. Tel: 608-271-7421. [JC]
School—5405 Flad Ave., 53711. Tel: 608-271-7551.
Oblates to the Blessed Trinity 3; Sisters 3; Lay Teachers 9; Students 195.

11—ST. PATRICK, Rev. Daniel T. Ganshert. In res., Most Rev. George O. Wirz.
Res., 404 E. Main St., 53703. Tel: 608-257-5000. [JC]

12—ST. PAUL UNIVERSITY PARISH, Revs. Steven J. Kortendick; Steven Steele; Faye A. Darnall, M.Div., Pastoral Assoc.; Vincent Pizzuto, Jr., M.Ed., Dir., Catechetical Ministries.
Office: 723 State St., 53703. Tel: 608-258-3140. [JC]

13—ST. PETER, Rev. Roger G. Nilles.
Res., 5001 N. Sherman Ave., 53704. Tel: 608-249-6651. [JC]

14—ST. THOMAS AQUINAS, Rev. Donald J. Murray; Sr. Georgeann Roudebush, Pastoral Assoc.
Res., 602 Everglade Dr., 53717. Tel: 608-833-2600. [JC]

OUTSIDE THE CITY OF MADISON

Argyle, Lafayette Co., St. Joseph, Revs. George M. Hastrich; Bernard H. Deitelhoff.
Res., 313 N. Lafayette St., P.O. Box 76, 53504. Tel: 608-543-3631. [CEM]
Mission—Yellowstone, St. Michael.

Ashton, Dane Co., St. Peter's, Rev. Eugene F. Hollfelder.
Res., 7121 Co. Trunk K, Middleton, 53562. Tel: 608-831-4843. [CEM]
School—Tel: 608-831-4846.
Lay Teachers 4; Students 61.

Baraboo, Sauk Co., St. Joseph, Rev. Gerald P. Vosen.
Res., P.O. Box 70, 53913. Tel: 608-356-4773. [CEM]
School—Lay Teachers 10; Students 152.

Belleville, Dane Co., St. Mary of Lourdes, Rev. Kenneth J. Klink.
Res., 221 Frederick St., P.O. Box 220, 53508. Tel: 608-424-3681. [CEM]
Mission—Dayton, St. James. [CEM]

Belmont, LaFayette Co., St. Philomena, Rev. Monte E. Robinson.
Res., 338 Chestnut St., Box 345, 53510. Tel: 608-762-5446.
Missions—Calamine, St. Michael; Truman, Immaculate Conception. [CEM]

Beloit, Rock Co.,

1—OUR LADY OF THE ASSUMPTION, Rev. Gary L. Krahenbuhl.
Res., 2222 Shopiere Rd., 53511. Tel: 608-362-9066. [JC]
School—Lay Teachers 14; Students 205.

2—ST. JUDE, Rev. William R. Connell.
Res., 747 Hackett St., 53511. Tel: 608-364-2820. [JC]
School—Brother Dutton School.
Lay Teachers 13; Students 183.

3—ST. PAUL. Closed. 1988. For inquiries for parish records contact St. Thomas the Apostle, Beloit.

4—ST. THOMAS THE APOSTLE, Rev. Thomas R. Doheny.
Res., 822 E. Grand Ave., P.O. Box 933, 53512. Tel: 608-362-1034.

Benton, Lafayette Co., St. Patrick, Rev. Richard J. Lenarz.
Res., 53803. Tel: 608-759-2131. [CEM]

Berlin, Green Lake Co., St. Joseph, Rev. Richard D. Lesniak.
Res., 320 S.W. Franklin St., 54923. Tel: 414-361-0940.
Church—246 E. Park Ave., 54923.
School—Consolidated School. See separate listing.

St. Michael, Rev. Richard D. Lesniak.
Res., 320 S.W. Franklin St., 54923. Tel: 414-361-0940. [CEM]
School—Consolidated School. See separate listing.

St. Stanislaus, Rev. Jerome J. Maksvytis.
Res., 167 N. Wisconsin St., 54923. Tel: 414-361-2354. [CEM]
School—Consolidated School. See separate listing.

Bloomington, Grant Co., St. Mary, Rev. David W. Timmerman.
Res., P.O. Box 35, 53804. Tel: 608-994-2526. [CEM 2]
School—Lay Teachers 7; Students 85.
Mission—Patch Grove, St. John.

Boscobel, Grant Co., Immaculate Conception, Rev. John L. Urban.
Res., 405 E. LeGrand St., 53805. Tel: 608-375-4257.

Briggsville, Marquette Co., St. Mary Help of Christians, Rev. August H. Buenzli.
Res., N565 Hwy. A, Box 127, 53920-0127. Tel: 608-981-2282.

Brodhead, Green Co., St. Rose, Rev. Elmer J. Dietzel.
Res., 1005 W. Second Ave., 53520. Tel: 608-897-2666.
Mission—Albany, St. Patrick's. [CEM]

Cambridge, Dane Co., St. Pius X, Rev. William A. Nolan.
Res., 701 W. Water St., P.O. Box 110, 53523. Tel: 608-423-3015.

Cassville, Grant Co., St. Charles Borromeo, Rev. John Norder.
Res., 605 E. Dewey St., 53806. Tel: 608-725-5595. [CEM 2]
School—521 E. Dewey St., 53806. Tel: 608-725-5173.
School Sisters of St. Francis 2; Lay Teachers 9; Students 104.
Mission—Glen Haven, St. Mary Help of Christians.

Clinton, Rock Co., St. Stephen, Rev. Patrick R. Swendrowski.
Res., Box 399, 53525. Tel: 608-676-2241.

Columbus, Columbia Co., St. Jerome, Rev. William J. Hower.
Parish Office—1550 Farnham St., 53925. Tel: 414-623-3753.
Res., 329 Folsom St., 53925. Tel: 414-623-2720. [CEM]
School—Sisters 1; Lay Teachers 11; Students 129.

Cottage Grove, Dane Co., St. Patrick, Rev. David H. Runde.
Res., P.O. Box 400, 53527-0400. Tel: 608-251-7857.

Cross Plains, Dane Co., St. Francis Xavier, Rev. D. Stephen Smith.
Res., 2947 Thinnes St., P.O. Box 35, 53528. Tel: 608-798-3491.
School—Lay Teachers 14; Students 216.

Cuba City, Grant Co., St. Rose of Lima, Rev. Richard A. Jiru.
Res., 53807. Tel: 608-744-2010. [CEM]
School—Dominican Sisters Sinsinawa, WI 2; Lay Teachers 8; Students 136.

Dane, Dane Co., St. Michael, Rev. Alfred J. Kunz.
Res., P.O. Box 170, 53529. Tel: 608-849-5619. [CEM]
School—Lay Teachers 5; Students 90.

Darlington, Lafayette Co., Holy Rosary, Rev. Thomas J. Coyle.
Res., 104 E. Harriet St., P.O. Box 208, 53530. Tel: 608-776-2251. [CEM 2]
School—Lay Teachers 7; Students 77.

De Forest, Dane Co., St. Olaf, Rev. Daniel P. Finnane.
Res., 623 Jefferson St., Box 446, 53532. Tel: 608-846-3812.

Dickeyville, Grant Co., Holy Ghost, Rev. James L. Gunn.
Res., 305 W. Main St., 53808. Tel: 608-568-7519. [CEM]
School—Lay Teachers 7; Students 95.

Dodgeville, Iowa Co., St. Joseph, Rev. Henry N. Kalscheuer.
Res., 310 S. Ellwood St., 53533-1799. Tel: 608-935-3392. [CEM]
School—305 E. Walnut St., 53533.
Lay Teachers 11; Students 160.

Doylestown, Columbia Co., St. Patrick, Rev. George W. Fox.
Res., N4085 Bruce St., P.O. Box 40, 53928. Tel: 414-992-3343. [CEM]
Mission—Rio, St. Joseph's. [CEM]

Durward's Glen, Columbia Co., St. Camillus, Rev. Richard Korzinek, O.S.Cam.
Res., W. 11876 McLeish Rd., Baraboo, 53913. Tel: 608-356-4523. [CEM]
Mission—Merrimac, Sauk Co., St. Mary, Health of the Sick, P.O. Box 41, Merrimac, 53561.

East Bristol, Dane Co., St. Joseph, Rev. William A. DeBock.
Res., 1935 Co. Hwy. V, Sun Prairie, 53590. Tel: 608-837-6159. [CEM]

Edgerton, Rock Co., St. Joseph, Rev. Francis J. Schmidt.
Res., St. Joseph's Circle, P.O. Box 147, 53534. Tel: 608-884-3038. [CEM 2]

Evansville, Rock Co., St. Paul, Rev. Edward J. Erbe.
Res., 35 Garfield Ave., 53536. Tel: 608-882-4138. [CEM]

Fennimore, Grant Co., St. Mary, Rev. George B. Horath.
Res., 930 Jefferson St., 53809. Tel: 608-822-6425. [CEM]
Mission—Mount Hope, St. Lawrence O'Toole.

Footville, Rock Co., St. Augustine, Rev. Bernard J. Pickarts.
Res., P.O. Box 325, 53537. Tel: 608-876-6251.

Fort Atkinson, Jefferson Co., St. Joseph, Rev. Duane R. Moellenberndt.
Res., 11 N. 3rd St., 53538. Tel: 414-563-3029. [CEM]
School—310 N. Main St., 53538. Mrs. Joan Meidl, Prin.
Lay Teachers 15; Students 148.

Gratiot, Lafayette Co., St. Joseph, Rev. Jerold F. Fitzpatrick.
Res., Box 37, 53541. Tel: 608-922-6456. [CEM]
Mission—South Wayne, St. John.

Green Lake, Green Lake Co., Our Lady of the Lake, Rev. John R. Dowd.
Res., 530 Ruth St., P.O. Box 215, 54941. Tel: 414-294-6440.

Hazel Green, Grant Co., St. Francis de Sales, Rev. Cyril O. Weisensel.
Res., 2630 N. Main St., P.O. Box 205, 53811-0205. Tel: 608-854-2391. [CEM]

Highland, Iowa Co., SS. Anthony and Philip, Rev. Kenneth J. Frisch.
Res., 1023 Dodgeville, P.O. Box 306, 53543. Tel: 608-929-7490. [CEM 2]

Hollandale, Iowa Co., St. Patrick, Rev. Leopold Gleissner, O.F.M.Cap.
Res., P.O. Box 37, 53544. Tel: 608-967-2344. [CEM]
Mission—Blanchardville, Immaculate Conception. [CEM]

Janesville, Rock Co.,

1—Nativity of St. Mary, Revs. Raymond N. Kertz; John H. Hedrick.
Res., 313 E. Wall St., 53545. Tel: 608-752-7861. [JC]
School—Sisters 1; Lay Teachers 13; Students 275.

2—St. John Vianney, Revs. Michael J. Doro; Thomas L. Kelley.
Res., 1245 Clark St., 53545. Tel: 608-752-8708. [JC]
School—Lay Teachers 17; Students 221.

3—St. Patrick, Rev. J. Daryl Furlong.
Res., 315 Cherry St., 53545. Tel: 608-754-8193. [JC]
School—Sisters 1; Lay Teachers 9; Students 113.

4—St. William, Rev. Delbert D. Klink.
Res., 1815 Ravine St., 53545. Tel: 608-755-5180. [JC]
School—1822 Ravine St., 53545.
Lay Teachers 12; Students 151.

Jefferson, Jefferson Co., St. John the Baptist, Rev. Terrence L. Connors.
Res., 214 N. Sanborn Ave., 53549. Tel: 414-674-2025. [CEM]
School—Lay Teachers 11; Students 161.
St. Lawrence, Rev. Thomas E. Gillespie.
Res., W. 4926 Hwy. 18, 53549. Tel: 414-674-3217. [CEM]

Kieler, Grant Co., Immaculate Conception, Rev. Philip J. Krogman.
Res., Box 57, 53812. [CEM]
School—Lay Teachers 8; Students 104.

Lake Mills, Jefferson Co., St. Francis Xavier, Rev. John B. Walsh.
Res., 602 College St., P.O. Box 16, 53551. Tel: 414-648-2468.
Mission—Johnson Creek, St. Mary Magdalene. [CEM]

Lancaster, Grant Co., St. Clement, Rev. Thomas F. Baxter.
Res., 135 S. Washington St., 53813. Tel: 608-723-4990. [CEM 2]
School—Sisters 4; Lay Teachers 5; Students 117.

Lime Ridge, Sauk Co., St. Boniface, Rev. Lorin M. Bowens.
Res., 53942. Tel: 608-986-2101. [CEM]
Mission—La Valle, Holy Family. [CEM]

Lodi, Columbia Co., St. Patrick, Rev. Michael C. Richel.
Res., 515 Fair St., 53555. Tel: 608-592-4510. [CEM]

McFarland, Dane Co., Christ the King, Rev. Arthur R. Koth.
Res., 5211 Timber Ln., 53558-9661. Tel: 608-838-8776.

Markesan, Green Lake Co., St. Joseph, Rev. Timothy F. Gericke.
Res., Box 504, 53946-0504. Tel: 414-398-3146.
Mission—Kingston, St. Mary. [CEM]

Marshall, Dane Co., St. Mary's of the Nativity, Rev. Msgr. Raymond E. Klaas, P.A.
Res., P.O. Box 250, 53559-0250. Tel: 608-655-3708. [CEM]

Martinsville, Dane Co., St. Martin, Rev. Thomas H. Schroeder.
Res., 5959 St. Martin Cir., Cross Plains, 53528-9312. Tel: 608-798-2815. [CEM]

Mazomanie, Dane Co., St. Barnabas, Rev. O. Charles Schluter.
Res., 113 E. Division St., P.O. Box 68, 53560. Tel: 608-767-3719. [CEM]
Mission—Mill Creek, St. John the Baptist.

Middleton, Dane Co., St. Bernard, Revs. Joseph P. Higgins; John R. Auby.
Res., 2015 Parmenter St., P.O. Box 620187, 53562-0187. Tel: 608-831-6531. [CEM]

Milton, Rock Co., St. Mary, Rev. James J. McEnery.
Res., 837 Parkview Dr., 53563. Tel: 608-868-3338. [CEM]

Mineral Point, Iowa Co., Congregation of St. Mary-St. Paul, Rev. Thomas M. Segerson.
Res., 224 Davis St., 53565. Tel: 608-987-2026. [JC 2]

Monroe, Green Co., St. Victor, Rev. Stephen J. Umhoefer.
Res., 1760 14th St., 53566. Tel: 608-325-9506. [CEM]
School—Sisters 1; Lay Teachers 9; Students 136.

Montello, Marquette Co., St. John the Baptist, Rev. Gary A. Wankerl.
Res., 277 E. Montello St., 53949. Tel: 608-297-2217. [CEM]
Mission—Westfield, Marquette Co., Good Shepherd, Westfield, 53964. [CEM]

Montfort, Grant Co., St. Thomas, Rev. Laverne G. Meier.
Res., Box 68, 53569. Tel: 608-943-6944. [CEM]
Mission—Castle Rock, St. John Nepomucene. [CEM]

Mount Horeb, Dane Co., St. Ignatius, Rev. Thomas J. Monaghan.
Res., 111 S. Sixth St., 53572. Tel: 608-437-5195. [CEM 2]
Mission—Perry, Holy Redeemer. [CEM]

Muscoda, Grant Co., St. John the Baptist, Rev. Roger H. Taylor.
Res., 341 N. Wisconsin Ave., P.O. Box 35, 53573. Tel: 608-739-3391. [CEM]
Mission—Avoca, St. Joseph. [CEM]

Neshkoro, Marquette Co., St. James, Rev. Joseph H. Schlaefer.
Res., Hwy. 73, P.O. Box 48, 54960. Tel: 414-293-4211. [CEM]

Oregon, Dane Co., Holy Mother of Consolation, Rev. Anthony J. Schumacher.
Res., 651 N. Main St., 53575. Tel: 608-835-5763. [CEM]

Palmyra, Jefferson Co., St. Mary, Rev. Robert E. Buholzer.
Res., 919 W. Main St., P.O. Box P, 53156. Tel: 414-495-2395. [CEM]

Pardeeville, Columbia Co., St. Mary, Rev. Joseph C. Cox.
Res., 318 S. Main St., 53954-0216. Tel: 608-429-3030. [CEM]
Education Center & Hall—Tel: 608-429-3129.
Mission—Buffalo, St. Andrew. [CEM]

Pine Bluff, Dane Co., St. Mary of Pine Bluff, Rev. Felix G. Oehrlein.
Res., 3673 Co. Trunk P, Cross Plains, 53528. Tel: 608-798-2111. [CEM]

Plain, Sauk Co., St. Luke, Rev. Michael A. Resop.
Res., 1240 Nachreiner Ave., 53577. Tel: 608-546-2482. [CEM 2]
School—Lay Teachers 8; Students 109.
Mission—Loreto, St. Patrick. [CEM 2]

Platteville, Grant Co., St. Mary, Rev. Kevin F. Dooley.
Res., 130 W. Cedar St., 53818. Tel: 608-348-9735. [CEM]
School—Lay Teachers 9; Students 167.
St. Augustine University Parish, Rev. James H. Murphy.
Res., 135 S. Hickory St., 53818. Tel: 608-348-7530.

Portage, Columbia Co., St. Mary, Rev. Thomas Fitzgerald.
Res., 307 W. Cook St., P.O. Box 216, 53901-0216. Tel: 608-742-6998. [CEM]
School—315 W. Cook St., 53901. Tel: 608-742-4998.
Lay Teachers 13; Students 180.
Convent—Tel: 608-742-2607.

Poynette, Columbia Co., St. Thomas, Rev. Raymond J. Dischler.
Res., 655 S. Main, P.O. Box 310, 53955-0310. Tel: 608-635-4326.

Princeton, Green Lake Co., St. John the Baptist, Rev. Dale W. Grubba.
Res., 1211 W. Main, 54968. Tel: 414-295-6209. [CEM]
School—Lay Teachers 6; Students 102.

Reedsburg, Sauk Co., Sacred Heart, Rev. Donald J. Wiecki.
Res., 624 N. Willow St., 53959. Tel: 608-524-2412. [CEM 3]
School—545 N. Oak St., 53959. Tel: 608-524-3611.
Lay Teachers 12; Students 221.

Ridgeway, Iowa Co., St. Bridget, Rev. Donald V. Moran.
Res., P.O. Box 127, 53582. Tel: 608-924-2441. [CEM]
Mission—Barneveld, Immaculate Conception.

Roxbury, Dane Co., St. Norbert, Rev. James G. Kuhn.
Res., 8944 County Rd. Y, Sauk City, 53583-9510. Tel: 608-643-3661. [CEM]

Sauk City, Sauk Co., St. Aloysius, Rev. William J. Seipp.
Res., 115 Madison St., 53583. Tel: 608-643-2449. [CEM 2]
School—Tel: 608-643-6868.
Lay Teachers 8; Students 125.

Seymour, Lafayette Co., Our Lady of Hope, Rev. James R. Lins.
Res., Rte. 1, Shullsburg, 53586. Tel: 608-776-2833. [CEM]
Mission—Elk Grove, St. Peter. [CEM]

Shullsburg, Lafayette Co., St. Matthew, Rev. James R. Lins.
Res., 344 Judgement St., 53586. Tel: 608-965-4518. [CEM 2]

Sinsinawa, Grant Co., St. Joseph, Rev. Donald F. Lange.
Res., 780 Hwy. Z, Hazel Green, 53811. Tel: 608-748-4528. [CEM 2]
School—Lay Teachers 5; Students 76.

Spring Green, Sauk Co., St. John the Evangelist, Rev. Kenneth E. Klubertanz.
Res., P.O. Box 628, 53588. Tel: 608-588-2028. [CEM]
School—Lay Teachers 6; Students 80.

Stoughton, Dane Co., St. Ann, Rev. Gerard M. Healy; Sr. Mary Ann Schroedl, O.S.F., Pastoral Assoc.
Res., 320 N. Harrison St., 53589. Tel: 608-873-7633. [CEM]
School—Poor Sisters of Nazareth 3; Students 172.

Sullivan, Jefferson Co., St. Mary Help of Christians, Rev. John H. Hebl.
Res., W. 856 Hwy. 18, 53178. Tel: 414-593-2250. [CEM]

Sun Prairie, Dane Co., Sacred Hearts of Jesus and Mary, Revs. James W. Hinnen; David J. Flanagan; Antonio Rodriguez. Pastoral Assocs.: Sr. Anne Raymond Gasser, S.S.N.D.; Renata Stier.

Res., 221 Columbus St., 53590. Tel: 608-837-7381. [CEM]
School—Lay Teachers 21; Students 458.
St. Albert the Great, Rev. Lawrence M. Bakke.
Res., 2420 St. Albert Dr., 53590. Tel: 608-837-3798.

Tennyson-Potosi, Grant Co., SS. Andrew-Thomas, Rev. Richard J. Leffler.
Res., 101 Church St., Potosi, 53820. Tel: 608-763-2671. [CEM]
School—100 Hwy. 61 N., P.O. Box 160, Potosi, 53820. Tel: 608-763-2120.
Lay Teachers 7; Students 70.

Verona, Dane Co., St. Andrew, Rev. Delbert L. Schmelzer.
Res., 301 N. Main St., 53593. Tel: 608-845-7323.
Mission—Paoli, St. William. [CEM]

Waterloo, Jefferson Co., St. Joseph, Rev. Ronald G. Rank.
Res., 205 W. Milwaukee Ave., 53594-1329. Tel: 414-478-2032. [CEM]
School—Lay Teachers 4; Students 72.

Watertown, Jefferson Co., St. Bernard, Rev. Thomas P. Marr.
Res., 114 S. Church St., 53094-4399. Tel: 414-261-5133. [CEM]
School—Sisters 2; Lay Teachers 12; Students 166.
St. Henry, Rev. Bernard E. Rott.
Res., 412 N. 4th St., 53094. Tel: 414-261-7273. [CEM]
School—300 Cady St., 53094.
Lay Teachers 9; Students 218.

Waunakee, Dane Co., St. John the Baptist, Revs. Bruce M. Hennington; Randy J. Budnar.
Res., 209 South St., 53597. Tel: 608-849-5121. [CEM]
School—Lay Teachers 14; Students 257.

Westport, Dane Co., St. Mary of the Lake, Rev. James G. Kramer.
Res., 5460 Marylake Rd., Waunakee, 53597-9121. Tel: 608-849-4116. [CEM]

Wisconsin Dells, Columbia Co., St. Cecilia, Rev. Kevin W. Cassidy.
Res., 604 Oak St., P.O. Box 436, 53965. Tel: 608-254-8381. [CEM]

Chaplains of Public Institutions

MADISON. *Columbia County Institution*. Attended from St. Mary's Church, Portage.
Dane County Institution. Vacant.
Grant County Institution. Attended from St. Clement's Church, Lancaster.
Green County Institution. Attended from St. Victor's Church, Monroe.
Iowa County Institution. Attended from St. Joseph's Church, Dodgeville.
Madison-Meriter General Hospital. Rev. Laverne G. Meier.
Mendota State Hospital. Rev. Donald Shmauz (MIL), 301 Troy Dr., 53704. Tel: 608-244-2411, Ext. 284.
University Hospitals. Rev. Lawrence J. Kieffer, Chap., 120 W. Johnson, 53703.
Veterans' Administration Hospital. Rev. Lawrence R. Heitke, 8220 Raymond Rd., 53719. Tel: 608-256-1901, Ext. 327.

JANESVILLE. *Jefferson County Institution*. Attended from St. John the Baptist Church, Jefferson.
LaFayette County Institution. Attended from Holy Rosary Church, Darlington.
Mercy Hospital. Attended from Janesville Parishes, Janesville.
Rock County Institution. Attended from Janesville Parishes, Janesville.
Sauk County Institution. Attended from St. Boniface Church, Lime Ridge.
Wisconsin State School for the Blind. Attended from St. Patrick's Church, Janesville.

Military Chaplains:
Reverend Fathers—
Browne, Vincent T.
Hughes, Robert W.
Klarer, Michael E.
Turner, Jerome R.

Leave of Absence:
Reverend Fathers—
Clauder, J. Gibbs
McBride, William F.

Absent on Sick Leave:
Reverend Fathers—
Adams, Archie H.
Doherty, Patrick J.
Dutchoff, C. Robert
Runde, Raymond E.
Sosinski, Thomas P.

Retired:
Reverend Monsignors—
Doherty, Francis E., Rte. 3 W., 11031 Lakeview Dr., Lodi, WI 53555
Mack, Ferdinand A., 7210 Branford Ln., E., Madison, WI 53717
O'Hara, Robert J., 317 N. VanBuren St., Stoughton, WI 53589
Reverend Fathers—
Bauhs, Eugene J., 6209 Mineral Point Rd., #1507, Madison, WI 53705
Beck, Charles L., 502 St. Lawrence Ave., Janesville, WI 53545
Brechtl, Joseph A., 602 N. Segoe Rd., Madison, WI 53705
Brickl, Joseph M., 6130 Century Ave., Apt. 103D, Middleton, WI 53562
Cieciorka, Josef, St. Anthony by the Sea Home, 1200 Surf Rd., Riviera Beach, FL 33404
Conlon, Philip J., 306 Michael Ave., P.O. Box 326, Hollister, MO 65672
Dominic, Francis J., 2029 Brenna Ct., Cuba City, WI 53807
Grasso, Philip A., 211 N. Lincoln, Cuba City, WI 53807
Heindl, Arthur W., N. 7157 Cottage Dr., Westboro, WI 54490
Henry, Joseph L., 432 Maxwell St., Baraboo, WI 53913
Holzer, Ambrose W., 130 N. Main St., Fall River, WI 53932
Marx, Lambert M., 1927 N. Pontiac, Janesville, WI 53545
Mattucci, James J., 502 St. Lawrence Ave., Janesville, WI 53545
Meloy, Bernard F., 6817 Old Sauk Ct., Madison, WI 53717-1128
Mersberger, Jerome, Palmyra, WI 53156
Niglis, Joseph C., 1766 Fordem Ave., Madison, WI 53704
Pierick, Bernard E., P.O. Box 216, Portage, WI 53901
Reddington, Benjamin J., 201 Wallace Ave., Pottsville, PA 17901
Schubiger, Albert B., 424 Prospect Ave., Beloit, WI 53511
Schuster, Wilfred J., 10 Maria Pl., Madison, WI 53711
Stack, William E., 706 Jefferson, Sauk City, WI 53583
Turner, Wayne A., 502 St. Lawrence Ave., Janesville, WI 53545
Young, Anthony J., 2411 Tawhee Dr., Apt. 104, Madison, WI 53711

INSTITUTIONS LOCATED IN THE DIOCESE

[A] SEMINARIES, RELIGIOUS OR SCHOLASTICATES

DURWARD'S GLEN. *St. Camillus Monastery and Retreat Center*, P.O., Baraboo, W 11876 McLeish Rd., 53913. Tel: 608-356-4523. Rev. Richard Korzinek, O.S-.Cam., Supr. Priests 1.

[B] COLLEGES

MADISON. *Edgewood College*, 855 Woodrow St., 53711. Tel: 608-257-4861.
For a complete listing, refer to the Colleges and Universities section.

[C] HIGH SCHOOLS, DIOCESAN

BELOIT. *Catholic High School*, 1221 Henry Ave., 53511. Governed by the Board of Directors. Mr. Tim McKearn, Prin. Lay Teachers 12; Students 92.

[D] HIGH SCHOOLS, PRIVATE

MADISON. *Edgewood High School*, 2219 Monroe St., 53711. Tel: 608-257-1023. Dominican Sisters, Sinsinawa. Mr. Thomas E. Shipley, Pres.; Mr. Kathleen M. Hanlon, Prin. Priests 1; Lay Teachers 55; Students 594.

[E] CONSOLIDATED ELEMENTARY SCHOOLS

BERLIN. *Berlin Catholic School*, 151 S. Grove St., 54923. Tel: 414-361-1781. Jean Inda, Prin. Consolidation of the following parishes: St. Joseph; St. Michael; and St. Stanislaus. Lay Teachers 11; Students 148.

[F] ELEMENTARY SCHOOLS, PRIVATE

MADISON. *Edgewood Campus School*, 2324 Edgewood Dr., 53711. Tel: 608-257-7726. Dominican Sisters, Sinsinawa. Sr. Nancy Rae Reisdorf, O.P., Pres.; Mrs. Donna Jean Gifford, Prin. Sisters 3; Brothers 1; Lay Teachers 20; Students 252.

[G] GENERAL HOSPITALS

MADISON. *St. Marys Hospital Medical Center*, 707 S. Mills St., 53715. Tel: 608-251-6100.
For a complete listing, refer to the Hospitals section.

BARABOO. *St. Clare Hospital and Health Services*, 707 14th St., 53913. Tel: 608-356-5561.
For a complete listing, refer to the Hospitals section.

MONROE. *St. Clare Hospital*, 515 22nd Ave., 53566. Tel: 608-324-1000.
For a complete listing, refer to the Hospitals section.

PORTAGE. *Divine Savior Hospital & Nursing Home, Inc.*, 1015 W. Pleasant St., 53901. Tel: 608-742-4131; Fax: 608-742-6098.
For a complete listing, refer to the Hospitals section.

[H] HOMES FOR THE AGED

MADISON. *St. Marys Care Center*, 1347 Fish Hatchery Rd., 53715. Tel: 608-257-0781.
For a complete listing, refer to the Special Care Facilities section.

BARABOO. *St. Clare Meadows Care Center*, 1414 Jefferson St., 53913. Tel: 608-356-4838; Fax: 608-356-5441.
For a complete listing, refer to the Special Care Facilities section.

JANESVILLE. *St. Elizabeth Home*, 502 St. Lawrence Ave., 53545. Tel: 608-752-6709.
For a complete listing, refer to the Special Care Facilities section.

PORTAGE. *Divine Savior Nursing Home*, 715 W. Pleasant St., 53901. Tel: 608-742-4131.
For a complete listing, refer to the Special Care Facilities section.

STOUGHTON. *Nazareth House*, 814 Jackson St., 53589. Tel: 608-873-6448; Fax: 608-873-0829.
For a complete listing, refer to the Special Care Facilities section.

WATERTOWN. *St. Joseph's Home*, 705 Clyman St., 53094. Tel: 414-261-4283.
For a complete listing, refer to the Special Care Facilities section.

[I] MONASTERIES AND RESIDENCES OF PRIESTS

MADISON. *Holy Name Catholic Center, Inc.*, 3577 High Point Rd., 53719. Tel: 608-833-1010. Revs. John G. Stillmank; Paul J. Swain; James Uppena.

EDGERTON. *Legion of Christ, Inc.*, 432 Liquori Rd., P.O. Box 107, 53534. Tel: 608-884-3428; Fax: 608-884-8175. Revs. Thomas Moylan, L.C., Supr.; Juan G. Guerra, L.C., Chap.; Matthew VanSmoorenburg, L.C., Promotion; Bros. Paul King, L.C.; Michael Lee, L.C.; Alexander Kim, L.C.; Louis Judd, L.C.

[J] CONVENTS AND RESIDENCES FOR SISTERS

MADISON. *Franciscan Sisters of Mary*, 901 High St., 53715-1913. Tel: 608-255-1510. Hilldale Tower, #504 4817 Shebuygan Ave., 53705-2907. Tel: 608-271-7031. Sisters 4.
Monastery of St. Benedict Center, P.O. Box 5070, 53705-0070. Tel: 608-836-1631; Fax: 608-831-5469. Monastery of the Sisters of St. Benedict. Sr. Mary David Walgenbach, O.S.B., Prioress. Sisters 13.
Secular Institute of Schoenstatt Sisters of Mary, 5901 Cottage Grove Rd., 53716. Tel: 608-222-7208; Fax: 608-222-0430. Janice Heyl, Supr. Sisters 9.

BARABOO. *Community of Hope*, 1021 Ash St., 53913-2163. Tel: 608-356-8641. Franciscan Sisters of Mary. Sisters 3.
St. Marys Ringling Convent, 1208 Oak St., 53913-1698. Tel: 608-356-5577. Franciscan Sisters of Mary. Sr. Elizabeth Ruppert, F.S.M., Community Coord.; Rev. Leonard van-Ackeren, O.S.B. (Milwaukee), Chap. Sisters 14.

BELOIT. *Blessed Sacrament Convent*, 916 Bluff St., 53511. Tel: 608-362-3326.
Motherhouse of the Auxiliaries of the Blessed Sacrament. Mother Marie Dufresne, A.B.S., Supr. Gen. Sisters in Residence 6.

PRAIRIE DU SAC. *Valley of Our Lady Monastery*, 53578. Tel: 608-643-3520; (Altar Breads: 608-643-7986); Fax: 608-643-3520. Cistercian Nuns. Mother M. Paula Hannah, O.Cist., Prioress. Solemnly Professed 11; Simply Professed 2; Novices 1.

SINSINAWA. *Dominican Motherhouse*, 53824. Tel: 608-748-4411; Fax: 608-748-4491. Sinsinawa Dominican Congregation of the Most Holy Rosary. Sr. Jean McSweeney, O.P., Prioress of the Congregation. Provincials: Sr. Marise Barry, O.P., Eastern Prov.; Sr. Patricia Caraher, O.P., Southern Prov.; Sr. Carol Coenen, O.P., Western Prov.; Sr. Helen Martin, O.P., Prioress of the Motherhouse; Revs. Joseph Fogarty, O.P.; Brian Bricker, O.P. Sisters in the Congregation 941; Sisters 206.
Dominican Novitiate: Novices 3; Candidates 1.

WISCONSIN DELLS. *North American Union of the Sisters*

of Our Lady of Charity, Inc., Administration Centre, P.O. Box 327, 53965-0327. Tel: 608-254-2070; Fax: 608-254-7744. Administration Office, 154 Edgington Ln., Wheeling, WV, 26003-1535. Tel: 304-242-0042; Fax: 303-242-8981. Sr. Deana Kohlman, Supr. Gen.

[K] CHARITABLE INSTITUTIONS

MADISON. *Catholic Charities, Inc.* Diocese of Madison, Administrative Center, 4905 Schofield St., 53716. Tel: 608-221-2000. Brian Cain, Dir.

Central City Counseling Services, 30 S. Franklin St., 53703. Tel: 608-256-2358.

Beloit District Office, 3311 Prairie Ave., Beloit, 53511. Tel: 608-365-3665.

Janesville District Office, 2020 E. Milwaukee St., Janesville, 53545. Tel: 608-752-4906.

Saint Martin House. (Interracial Center), 1862 Beld St., 53713. Tel: 608-255-1287. Rev. George M. Hastrich, Spiritual Dir. Volunteer Staff.

Society of St. Vincent de Paul. (District Council of Madison, Inc.), 1109 Jonathon Dr., 53713-3230. Tel: 608-278-2920. Rev. Francis J. Steffen, Spiritual Dir.; Mr. Edward B. O'Neill, Council Pres.

JEFFERSON. *St. Coletta School for Exceptional Children*, W. 4955 Hwy. 18, 53549. Tel: 414-674-4330. Sisters of St. Francis of Assisi. Dr. Henry C. Meece, Pres.; Sr. Ruth Marie Soens, O.S.F., Coord.; Rev. Thomas E. Gillespie, Chap. Sisters 30; Brothers 3; Residents 600; Lay Staff 500.

[L] RETREAT HOUSES

MADISON. *St. Benedict Center, Ecumenical Retreat and Conference Center*, P.O. Box 5070, 53705-0070. Tel: 608-836-1631; Fax: 608-831-5469. Sr. Mary David Walgenbach, O.S.B. Sisters 9.

[M] MISCELLANEOUS

MADISON. *Catholic Health Association of Wisconsin, Inc.*, 5721 Odana Rd., Ste. 204, 53719-1222. Tel: 608-274-5588; Fax: 608-274-6872. Sr. Rosemary Sabino, R.S.M., Pres. & CEO; Sr. Louis Bush, S.S.M., Chairperson of the Board.

Edgewood Incorporated, 855 Woodrow St., 53711. Dr. James A. Ebben, Pres. Sponsored by Sinsinawa Dominican Sisters of Sinsinawa, WI. Purpose: The education of individuals in such subjects as are usually taught in high schools, academies, and colleges.

Mid-America Catholic Colleges. (MACC), 15 E. Wilson St., P.O. Box 111, 53701. Membership consists of the following 9 colleges: Clarke College; College of St. Catherine; College of Saint Teresa; College of St. Thomas; Loras College; Mount Mercy College; Saint Mary's College; St. Norbert College; and Viterbo College.

San Damiano Friary, 4123 Monona Dr., 53716. Tel: 608-222-6238. Capuchin Order-Province of St. Joseph. House of Healing and Hospitality. Revs. Leo Petrimoulx, O.F.M.Cap.; Rupert Dorn, O.F.M.Cap; Benedict Adams, O.F.M.Cap.; Joseph Doerfler, O.F.M.Cap.; Gary Keegstra, O.F.M.Cap., Local Min.

Wisconsin Association of Principals of Catholic Secondary Schools, 142 W. Johnson St., 53703-2298. Tel: 608-256-0872. Thomas M. Butler, Exec. Sec.

BARABOO. *Saint Vincent de Paul Society-Baraboo*, 100 S. Boulevard, P.O. Box 233, 53913. Tim Nolden, Contact Person. Sponsored by: Saint Vincent de Paul Society. Purpose: To help the poor and needy in a Vincentian spirit and manner.

EDGERTON. *Oaklawn Academy*, 432 Liguori Rd., 53534.

Oaklawn Incorporated, 432 Liguori Rd., R.R. P.O. Box 107, 53534. Chaplains: Thomas Moylan, L.C.; Rev. Juan Gabriel Guerra, L.C.; Mr. Eduardo Grandio, Prin.

PLATTEVILLE. *St. Augustine Newman Center*, 135 S. Hickory, 53818.
Please refer to St. Augustine University Parish, Platteville.

SINSINAWA. *Sinsinawa Dominican Community Support Trust*, c/o General Delivery, 53824-9999. Sr. Jean McSweeney, O.P., Contact Person. Sponsored by: Sinsinawa Dominicans. Purpose: To provide financial support to retired and invalid vowed members of the Sinsinawa Dominicans.

RELIGIOUS INSTITUTES OF MEN REPRESENTED IN THE DIOCESE

For further details refer to the corresponding bracketed number in the Religious Institutes of Men or Women section.

[0200]—*Benedictine Monks*.—O.S.B.
[0900]—*Canons Regular of Premontre*.—O.Praem.
[0430]—*Order of Preachers-Dominicans*. (Prov. of St. Albert the Great).—O.P.
[0240]—*Order of St. Camillus*.—O.S.Cam.
[0990]—*Society of the Catholic Apostolate*. (Mater Dei Prov.).—S.A.C.

RELIGIOUS INSTITUTES OF WOMEN REPRESENTED IN THE DIOCESE

[]—*Auxiliaries of the Blessed Sacrament*.—A.B.S.
[0230]—*Benedictine Sisters of Pontifical Jurisdiction*.—O.S.B.
[0680]—*Cistercian Nuns*.—O.Cist.
[3735]—*Congregation of St. Brigid*.—C.S.B.
[3710]—*Congregation of the Sisters of Saint Agnes*.—C.S.A.
[1070-03]—*Dominican Sisters*.—O.P.
[1070-09]—*Dominican Sisters*.—O.P.
[1230]—*Franciscan Sisters of Christian Charity*.—O.S.F.
[1310]—*Franciscan Sisters of Little Falls, Minnesota*.—O.S.F.
[1415]—*Franciscan Sisters of Mary*.—F.S.M.
[2575]—*Institute of the Sisters of Mercy of the Americas*.—R.S.M.
[2970]—*School Sisters of Notre Dame*.—S.S.N.D.
[1680]—*School Sisters of St. Francis*.—O.S.F.
[]—*Secular Institute of Schoenstatt Sisters of Mary*.
[3020]—*Sisters Oblates to Divine Love*.—R.O.D.A.
[0530]—*Sisters of Charity of Our Lady, Mother of the Church*.—S.C.M.C.
[3930]—*Sisters of St. Joseph of the Third Order of St. Francis*. (Prov. of St. Joseph).—S.S.J.-T.O.S.F.
[1030]—*Sisters of the Divine Savior*.—S.D.S.
[1705]—*Sisters of the Third Order of St. Francis of Assisi*.—O.S.F.

DIOCESAN CEMETERIES

MADISON. *Resurrection*, 2705 Regent St., 53705. Tel: 608-238-5561.

BELOIT. *Calvary*. 1827 N. Washington, Janesville, 53545. Tel: 608-362-3092.

Mount Thabor. 1827 N. Washington, Janesville, 53545. Tel: 608-362-3092.

DOYLESTOWN. *Rocky Run*, P.O. Box 40, 53928. Tel: 414-992-3343.

JANESVILLE. *Mount Olivet*, 1827 N. Washington St., 53545. Tel: 608-754-3472.

NECROLOGY

† Beckius, Donald J., Baraboo, WI, St. Clare Hospital & Health Services. —Died June 2, 1996.
† Breines, Andrew R., (Retired). —Died May 2, 1996.
† Feyereisen, Nicholas J., (Retired). —Died March 23, 1996.
† Lauters, Harry J., (Retired). —Died Jan. 31, 1996.
† Maier, Raymond P., (Absent On Sick Leave). —Died Feb. 23, 1996.
† Satterlee, John A., (Absent On Sick Leave). —Died June 15, 1996.

Diocese of Manchester

(Dioecesis Manchesteriensis)

Most Reverend

LEO E. O'NEIL, D.D.

Bishop of Manchester; ordained June 4, 1955; appointed Auxiliary Bishop of Springfield and Titular Bishop of Bencenna June 3, 1980; consecrated August 22, 1980; appointed Coadjutor of Manchester October 17, 1989. *Res., 657 North River Rd., Manchester, NH, 03104.*

Most Reverend

ODORE J. GENDRON, D.D.

Retired Bishop of Manchester; ordained May 31, 1947; appointed December 12, 1974; consecrated February 3, 1975. *Res., St. Joseph Cathedral, 145 Lowell St., Manchester, NH, 03104-6135.*

Most Reverend

FRANCIS J. CHRISTIAN, PH.D.

Auxiliary Bishop of Manchester, Titular Bishop of Quincy in Illinois; ordained June 29, 1968; appointed April 2, 1996; consecrated May 14, 1996. *Res., St. Joseph Cathedral, 145 Lowell St., Manchester, NH, 03104-6135.*

ESTABLISHED 1884.

Square Miles 9,305.

Comprises the State of New Hampshire.

For legal titles of parishes and diocesan institutions, consult the Chancery Office.

Chancery Office: 153 Ash St., P.O. Box 310, Manchester, NH, 03105. Tel.: 603-669-3100; Fax: 603-669-0377.

Web site address: http://www.diocesemanch.org

E-mail address: mattmcsorley@grolen.com

STATISTICAL OVERVIEW

Personnel	
Bishop	1
Auxiliary Bishops	1
Retired Bishops	1
Abbots	1
Retired Abbots	1
Priests: Diocesan Active in Diocese	167
Priests: Active Outside Diocese	11
Priests: Retired, Sick or Absent	65
Number of Diocesan Priests	243
Religious Priests in Diocese	84
Extern Priests in Diocese	10
Ordinations:	
Diocesan Priests	4
Transitional Deacons	4
Permanent Deacons in Diocese	21
Total Brothers	41
Total Sisters	823
Parishes	
Parishes	131
With Resident Pastor:	
Resident Diocesan Priests	115
Resident Religious Priests	10
Without Resident Pastor:	
Administered by Priests	5
Missions	34
Professional Ministry Personnel:	
Brothers	1
Sisters	27
Lay Ministers	24
Welfare	
Catholic Hospitals	2
Total Assisted	111,965
Homes for the Aged	6
Total Assisted	433
Residential Care of Children	3
Total Assisted	354
Day Care and Extended Day Care Centers	1
Total Assisted	309
Specialized Homes	1
Special Centers for Social Services	1
Educational	
Diocesan Students in Other Seminaries	18
Students Religious	1
Total Seminarians	19
Colleges and Universities	6
Total Students	6,690
High Schools, Diocesan and Parish	3
Total Students	1,498
High Schools, Private	1
Total Students	782
Elementary Schools, Diocesan and Parish	23
Total Students	6,694
Elementary Schools, Private	3
Total Students	793
Catechesis/Religious Education:	
High School Students	5,346
Elementary Students	28,242
Total Students Under Catholic Instruction	50,064
Teachers in the Diocese:	
Brothers	8
Sisters	61
Lay Teachers	610
Vital Statistics	
Receptions into the Church:	
Infant Baptism Totals	5,530
Adult Baptism Totals	167
Received into Full Communion	184
First Communions	5,102
Confirmations	2,913
Marriages:	
Catholic	1,036
Interfaith	505
Total Marriages	1,541
Deaths	3,166
Total Catholic Population	321,914
Total Population	1,148,000

Former Bishops—Rt. Rev. DENIS M. BRADLEY, D.D., first Bishop of Manchester; cons. June 11, 1884; died Dec. 13, 1903.—Rt. Rev. JOHN B. DELANY, D.D., cons. Sept. 8, 1904; died June 11, 1906.—Most Rev. GEORGE ALBERT GUERTIN, D.D., cons. March 19, 1907; died Aug. 6, 1931.—Most Rev. JOHN B. PETERSON, D.D., cons. Auxiliary Bishop of Boston, Nov. 10, 1927; transferred to See, May 13, 1932; died March 15, 1944.—Most Rev. MATTHEW F. BRADY, D.D., cons. Oct. 26, 1938; transferred to See, Nov. 11, 1944; died Sept. 20, 1959.—Most Rev. ERNEST J. PRIMEAU, S.T.D., appt. Nov. 27, 1959; resigned Jan. 30, 1974; died June 15, 1989.—Most Rev. ODORE J. GENDRON, D.D., ord. May 31, 1947; appt. Dec. 12, 1974; cons. Feb. 3, 1975.

Vicars General—Rev. Msgr. JOHN E. MOLAN, V.G., P.A.; Rev. Msgr. ALBERT W. OLKOVIKAS, V.G., P.A., *153 Ash St., P.O. Box 310, Manchester, 03105.* Tel: 603-669-3100.

Secretary for Pastoral Services—Rev. Msgr. NORMAN P. BOLDUC, S.T.L., J.C.L., *153 Ash St., P.O. Box 310, Manchester, 03105.* Tel: 603-669-3100.

Co-Secretaries for Temporalities—Rev. Msgr. ALBERT W. OLKOVIKAS, S.T.L., J.C.D.; Rev. Msgr. JOHN E. MOLAN, *153 Ash St., P.O. Box 310, Manchester, 03105.* Tel: 603-669-3100.

Associate Secretary for Temporalities—Rev. EDWARD J. ARSENAULT, *153 Ash St., P.O. Box 310, Manchester, 03105.* Tel: 603-669-3100.

Secretary for Christian Formation—Sr. PAULINE LEBEL, C.S.C., *153 Ash St., P.O. Box 310, Manchester, 03105.* Tel: 603-669-3100.

Secretary for Community Services—Rev. Msgr. JOHN P. QUINN, *153 Ash St., P.O. Box 310, Manchester, 03105.* Tel: 603-669-3100.

Controller—Mr. DANA C. HIRST, *153 Ash St., P.O. Box 310, Manchester, 03105.* Tel: 603-669-3100.

Chancery Office—153 Ash St., P.O. Box 310, Manchester, 03105. Tel: 603-669-3100; Fax: 603-669-0377.

Chancellor—Rev. Msgr. NORMAN P. BOLDUC, S.T.L., J.C.L.

Vice Chancellor—Rev. Msgr. PAUL L. BOUCHARD, S.T.L., J.C.L.

Vicar for Clergy—Most Rev. FRANCIS J. CHRISTIAN, Ph.D.

Secretaries to Bishop—HELEN VOLLINGER; LUCILLE CONNOR.

Diocesan Tribunal—153 Ash St., P.O. Box 310, Manchester, 03105. Tel: 603-669-3100.

Judicial Vicar—Rev. Msgr. DONALD J. GILBERT, J.C.L.

Associate Judicial Vicar—Rev. JOHN J. MAHONEY, JR., J.C.L.

Promotor Justitiae—Rev. FRANCIS L. DEMERS, O.M.I., J.C.D.

Canonical Consultant and Judge—Rev. Msgr. RAYMOND O. BLAIR, J.C.D.

Advocates—Revs. KARL E. DOWD; RICHARD P. TETU.

Defensor Vinculi—Rev. FRANCIS DEMERS, O.M.I., J.C.D.; Rev. Msgr. PAUL L. BOUCHARD, S.T.L.,

J.C.L.; Rev. Msgr. NORMAN P. BOLDUC, S.T.L., J.C.L.; Sr. LOUISE TESSIER, P.M., J.C.L.

Associate Judges—Rev. Msgr. NORMAN P. BOLDUC, S.T.L., J.C.L.; Rev. Msgr. JOHN P. QUINN; Revs. GERALD R. DUNN; LEO L. FRECHETTE; DONALD E. LAFOND.

Notaries—JOAN FOX; DEBORAH HARRINGTON.

College of Consultors—Most Rev. FRANCIS J. CHRISTIAN, Ph.D.; Rev. Msgr. ALBERT W. OLKOVIKAS, S.T.L., J.C.D.; Rev. Msgr. JOHN E. MOLAN; Rev. Msgr. THOMAS J. HANNIGAN; Rev. Msgr. JOHN P. QUINN; Rev. Msgr. JOHN F. BURKE; Rev. Msgr. FERNAND L. PICHETTE; Revs. JOSEPH S. KLATKA; TIMOTHY R. O'DONNELL.

Diocesan Administrative Council—Rev. Msgr. ALBERT W. OLKOVIKAS, J.C.D.

Diocesan School Board—Bro. KENNETH HOGAN, Supt., Schools; JOSEPH HORTON; Sr. FRANCES LESSARD, C.S.C.; GUY CHAPDELAINE; JOAN DOBZANSKI; W. JAMES DOYLE; Rev. GEORGE E. HAM; Ms. CHRIS MCMAHON.

Diocesan Building and Real Estate Board—Rev. Msgr. JOHN E. MOLAN, Chm.; Most Rev. FRANCIS J. CHRISTIAN; Rev. Msgr. JOHN P. QUINN; Revs. DONALD GAUTHIER; BERNARD J. CAMPBELL, O.F.M.Cap.; Mr. JOSEPH W. FOBES; ROBERT L. LAFERRIERE; RUSSELL GRADY; PAUL HOUGHTON; JOHN LYONS; THEODORE PAQUETTE, *153 Ash St., Manchester, 03105.* Tel: 603-669-3100.

Deans—Manchester East: Rev. Msgr. THOMAS J. HANNIGAN, Manchester West: Rev. MARC R. MONTMINY, Berlin: Rev. MAURICE R. LACROIX, Concord: Rev. C. PETER DUMONT, Dover: Rev. DANIEL O. LAMOTHE, Franconia: Rev. JOSEPH S. KLATKA, Keene: Rev. W. PIERRE BAKER, Laconia: Rev. WILLIAM J. QUIRK, Lebanon: Rev. BERNARD BARIS, M.S., Nashua: Rev. DANIEL A. ST. LAURENT, Salem: Rev. RICHARD W. CONNORS.

Council of Priests—Most Rev. LEO E. O'NEIL, Pres.; Most Rev. FRANCIS J. CHRISTIAN; Rev. Msgr. ALBERT W. OLKOVIKAS; Rev. Msgr. JOHN E. MOLAN; Rev. Msgr. FERNAND L. PICHETTE; Rev. Msgr. JOHN P. QUINN; Rev. Msgr. JOHN F. BURKE; Rev. Msgr. THOMAS J. HANNIGAN; Rev. Msgr. COLIN E. MACDONALD; Rev. Msgr. NORMAN P. BOLDUC; Revs. RICHARD W. CONNORS; WILFRED H. DESCHAMPS; C. PETER DUMONT, Chm. JOSEPH S. KLATKA; THOMAS HORAN, O.M.I.; GEORGE E. HAM; ROBERT F. COLE; RICHARD T. LOWER; GERALD F. JOYAL; JOHN FORTIN, O.S.B.; ROBERT E. GORSKI; TIMOTHY R. O'DONNELL; W. PIERRE BAKER; ALBION F. BULGER; RICHARD F. CLAVELLE, O.S.B.; A. STEPHEN MARCOUX, III; MARK E. DOLLARD; AGAPIT H. JEAN; LEO A. LEBLANC.

Diocesan Pastoral Council—Most Rev. LEO E. O'NEIL, Pres.; Most Rev. FRANCIS J. CHRISTIAN; MATTHEW CARNEVALE; GERARD ROUTHIER; CAROLE M. WEBBER; DORIS BOUTIN-CYR; PATRICIA BOWERS; DEBORAH REINDERS; ANTHONY POEKERT; MARGARET PLUMER; FRANCIS KUSHI; JENNIFER LAVOIE; PHYLLIS DIPRIZIO; JOSEPH CATANESE; IRENE A. PLOURDE; Sr. CAROL DESCOTEAUX, C.S.C.; Sr. GERMAINE DUCHESNEAU, S.A.S.V.; Sr. ROSINA BECHARD, F.C.S.C.J.; Sr. HARRIET CUTTING, S.N.D.deN.; Sr. MARIA ROSA, P.M.; Sr. FELICIA MCKONE, R.S.M.; Revs. PAUL F. RUZZO; DONALD E. CLINTON; Deacon ALFRED A. LABONTE, JR.; SHARON MARTIN; JOHN DOLAN.

Personnel Board—Most Rev. LEO E. O'NEIL; Rev. Msgr. THOMAS J. HANNIGAN; Rev. Msgr. NORMAN P. BOLDUC; Revs. MARC R. MONTMINY; ROBERT G. BOISVERT; WILLIAM L. QUIRK; PAUL L. GREGOIRE; DENIS F. HORAN; ROBERT F. COLE; GEORGE E. HAM; Rev. Msgr. JAMES P. WATSON.

Apostolate to the Deaf—Rev. BERNARD J. CAMPBELL, O.F.M.Cap., *Blessed Sacrament Church, 14 Elm St., Manchester, 03103.* Tel: 603-622-5445.

Campaign for Human Development—Sr. MARGARET CROSBY, S.N.D.deN., Dir., *153 Ash St., P.O. Box 310, Manchester, 03105.*

Camping—Rev. KARL E. DOWD, Dir., *153 Ash St., P.O. Box 310, Manchester, 03105.* Tel: 603-669-3100.

Censores Librorum—Rev. ROBERT G. BOISVERT, S.T.D.; Most Rev. FRANCIS J. CHRISTIAN, Ph.D.

Commission for Ecumenical Affairs—Rev. Msgr. NORMAN P. BOLDUC, S.T.L., J.C.L., Chm., *153 Ash St., P.O. Box 310, Manchester, 03105.* Tel: 603-669-3100.

Council of Catholic Women—Rev. ROGER A. FORTIER, *St. Peter Rectory, 90 Central St., P.O. Box 565, Farmington, 03835.*

Cursillo Movement—Rev. JOHN M. GRACE, *153 Ash St., Box 310, Manchester, 03105.* Tel: 603-669-3100.

Department of Priestly Life and Ministry—Rev. Msgr. NORMAN P. BOLDUC, S.T.L., J.C.L., Dir., *153 Ash St., P.O. Box 310, Manchester, 03105.* Tel: 603-669-3100.

Department of Faith Development—Sr. BERNADETTE TURGEON S.N.D.deN., Dir.

Office of Adult Education—PATRICIA GABREE, Dir.

Office of Evangelization & Catechumenate—DIANE J. ALLEN, Dir.; Rev. MARC F. GUILLEMETTE, Pastoral Consultant.

Office of Catholic Scouting—Rev. RAYMOND A. BALL, Dir.

Catholic Youth Organization—THERESA ROOT, Dir.

Office of Youth Ministry—Directors: Sr. BERNADETTE TURGEON, S.N.D.deN.; MATTHEW GOODY; ANNE CAVANAUGH, Sec. JACQUELINE ST. HILAIRE, Sec.

Diocesan Bureau of Housing, DBH Shelter, DBH Shelter II, DBH Shelter III, DBH Management—Most Rev. LEO E. O'NEIL, D.D., Pres.; Rev. JOHN P. QUINN, Vice Pres. JOSEPH W. FOBES, Treas. CAROL HAEBLER, Housing Coord., *323 Franklin St., Manchester, 03101.* Tel: 603-625-5422.

Diocesan Moderator for Marian Devotions—Rev. PAUL L. GREGOIRE, *St. Charles Borromeo Rectory, 577 Central Ave., Dover, 03820-3464.*

Diocesan Public Policy Committee—Sr. MARGARET CROSBY, S.N.D.deN., Coord., *153 Ash St., P.O.Box 310, Manchester, 03105.*

Displaced Persons Program—Rev. STANLEY J. PIWOWAR, Dir., *St. Joseph Rectory, Claremont, 03743.* Tel: 603-542-5732.

Holy Childhood, Pontifical Association—Rev. ANTHONY F. DIGIULIO, *153 Ash St., P.O. Box 310, Manchester, 03105.* Tel: 603-669-3100.

Hospitals—Rev. Msgr. JOHN P. QUINN, Diocesan Coord., Health Affairs, *215 Myrtle St., Manchester, 03104.* Tel: 603-669-3030.

Manchester Mission—CLARA BEAULE, *215 Myrtle St., Manchester, 03104.* Tel: 603-669-3030.

Masters of Ceremonies—Revs. MARC F. GUILLEMETTE; ANTHONY R. FRONTIERO, *153 Ash St., P.O. Box 310, Manchester, 03105.* Tel: 603-669-3100.

Ministry for Persons with Disabilities—Rev. BERNARD J. CAMPBELL, O.F.M. Cap.; Sr. PAULINE LAFOND, P.M., *215 Myrtle St., P.O. Box 686, Manchester, 03105.* Tel: 603-668-4572; 669-3030.

Missionary Rosebushes of St. Theresa—Monastery of the Precious Blood—700 Bridge St., Manchester, 03104.

New Hampshire Catholic Charities, Inc.—Rev. Msgr. JOHN P. QUINN, Dir., *215 Myrtle St., Manchester, 03104.* Tel: 603-669-3030.

N.H. Council of Catholic Nurses—ALICE H. MANTEGANI, *160 Calef Rd., Manchester, 03103.* Tel: 603-623-3051.

Office of Charismatic Renewal—Rev. JOHN M. GRACE, *153 Ash St., Box 310, Manchester, 03105.* Tel: 603-669-3100.

Office of Communications—MATTHEW MCSORLEY, Dir. MARY BALON, Admin. Asst. JOHN HAYWOOD, TIDINGS Asst. Editor, *153 Ash St., Box 310, Manchester, 03105.* Tel: 603-669-3100.

Office of the Permanent Diaconate—Rev. MARC F. GUILLEMETTE, Dir., *153 Ash St., P.O. Box 310, Manchester, 03105.* Tel: 603-669-3100.

Office of Pastoral Planning—Most Rev. FRANCIS J. CHRISTIAN, *153 Ash St., P.O. Box 310, Manchester, 03105.*

Office of Worship—Rev. JOHN M. GRACE, Dir. BEVERLY DROLET, Environment & Art; MARY BAGNELL, Music; MARILYN FREESE, Admin. Asst., *153 Ash St., Box 310, Manchester, 03105.* Tel: 603-669-3100.

Priests' Eucharistic League—Rev. Msgr. JOHN F. BURKE, Dir., *153 Ash St., P.O. Box 310, Manchester, 03105.* Tel: 603-669-3100.

Propagation of the Faith—Rev. ANTHONY F. DIGIULIO, Dir., *153 Ash St., P.O. Box 310, Manchester, 03105.* Tel: 603-669-3100.

Rural Life Conference—Rev. GEORGE F. HARVEY, *Assumption Parish, 10 Chestnut St., Tilton, 03276.*

Sacred Liturgy, Art and Music—Rev. JOHN M. GRACE, Chm. MARY BAGNELL, Vice Chm.; Sr. ANITA MARCHESSEAULT, C.S.C., Sec./Treas., *153 Ash St., P.O, Box 310, Manchester, 03105.* Tel: 603-669-3100.

St. Vincent de Paul Society—Rev. Msgr. JOHN P. QUINN, *215 Myrtle St., Manchester, 03104.* Tel: 603-669-3030.

Schools—Bro. KENNETH HOGAN, Supt., Schools, *153 Ash St., P.O. Box 310, Manchester, 03105.* Tel: 603-669-3100.

Social Concerns Office—Sr. MARGARET CROSBY, S.N.D-.deN., Dir., *153 Ash St., P.O. Box 310, Manchester, 03105.*

Spanish Speaking Apostolate—Sr. MARIA LUZ CERVANTES, M.S.C., *St. Anne Church, 231 Merrimack St., Manchester, 03103-5295.* Tel: 603-625-4603. Sr. NANCY BRACELAND, C.S.J., *St. Francis Xavier Church, 41 Chandler St., Nashua, 03060.* Tel: 603-881-8065.

Vigilance Council—The Rt. Rev. Deans.

Vocation Directors—Revs. ANTHONY R. FRONTIERO; MARC F. GUILLEMETTE, *153 Ash St., P.O. Box 310, Manchester, 03105.* Tel: 603-669-3100.

Vocations, Diocesan Board—Most Rev. LEO E. O'NEIL, Pres.; Rev. Msgr. NORMAN P. BOLDUC; Revs. DANIEL L. BERNIER; MARC GUILLEMETTE; ALBION F. BULGER; MARC B. DROUIN; DANIEL O. LAMOTHE; JOHN H. BRYSON; ANTHONY R. FRONTIERO, *153 Ash St., P.O. Box 310, Manchester, 03105.* Tel: 603-669-3100.

CLERGY, PARISHES, MISSIONS AND PAROCHIAL SCHOOLS

CITY OF MANCHESTER (Hillsboro County)

1—ST. JOSEPH CATHEDRAL, Rev. Humbert M. Oliveira, Rector. In res., Most Revs. Francis J. Christian; Odore J. Gendron; Rev. Msgr. Laurence R. Gardner; Rev. Msgr. Charles E. Crosby; Rev. Msgr. John P. Quinn.
Res., 145 Lowell St., 03104-6135. Tel: 603-622-6404; Fax: 603-626-4415. [CEM]
Chapels—Rectory; Convent, Tel: 603-623-2411.
Stations—Kalivas Apartments.; Carpenter Center.; Gallen Apartments.; O'Malley Apartments.

2—ST. ANNE (1848), Revs. Edward J. Arsenault, Admin.; John V. Tiep; Joseph M. Cooper, O.F.M.Cap. Pastoral Assocs.: Sr. Lorraine Cote, R.S.M.; Sr. Maria Luz Cervantes, M.S.C. In res., Rev. Robert J. Densmore.
Res., 231 Merrimack St., 03103. Tel: 603-623-8809.

3—ST. ANTHONY OF PADUA (1899) (French), Rev. Charles E. DesRuisseaux; Dr. Elise B. Tougas, Pastoral Assoc. In res., Revs. Normand A. Fillion, O.M.I.; Raymond Laferriere; William J. Hamilton, S.J.
Res., 172 Belmont St., 03103-4452. Tel: 603-625-6409; Fax: 603-625-0099.

4—ST. AUGUSTIN (1871) (French), Rev. Adrien R. Longchamps.
Res., 383 Beech St., 03103. Tel: 603-625-5655. [CEM]

5—BLESSED SACRAMENT (1907), Rev. Michael E. Sevigny, O.F.M.Cap.; Bro. Paul Crawford, O.F.M.Cap., Pastoral Assoc. In res., Revs. Bernard Campbell, O.F.M.Cap.; Anthony Donahue, O.F.M.Cap.
Res., 14 Elm St., 03103. Tel: 603-622-5445; Fax: 603-627-5983.

6—ST. CATHERINE (1954), Very Rev. Msgr. Thomas J. Hannigan, V.F.; Revs. James P. Walsh; Anthony R. Frontiero.
Res., 207 Hemlock St., 03104. Tel: 603-622-4966.
Catechesis/Religious Programs—Tel: 603-622-2711. Sr. Janet Belcourt, D.R.E.
Students 950.

7—ST. EDMOND (1914) (French), Rev. Msgr. Paul L. Bouchard; Sr. Sally A. Howe, C.S.C., Pastoral Assoc. In res., Rev. John J. Mahoney, Jr.
Res., 55 Edmond St., 03102. Tel: 603-625-6025.
Catechesis/Religious Programs—Tel: 603-623-6820.
Students 222.

8—ST. FRANCIS OF ASSISI (1953), Rev. Paul F. Ruzzo. In res., Rev. Msgr. Colin A. MacDonald.
Res., 3221 Brown Ave., 03103. Tel: 603-623-7306.
School—(Grades K-6) 3223 Brown Ave., 03103. Tel: 603-669-2069.
Sisters of Mercy 1; Lay Teachers 9; Students 136.
Catechesis/Religious Programs—Students 450.

9—ST. GEORGE (1890) (French), Rev. George A. Desjardins. In res., Rev. Roland O. Blais.
Res., 517 Pine St., 03104. Tel: 603-623-6434; Fax: 603-645-1857.

10—ST. HEDWIG, Rev. Msgr. Alfred Daniszewski.
Res., 147 Walnut St., 03104. Tel: 603-623-4835. [CEM]
School—St. Casimir, (Grades K-8) 456 Union St., 03103. Tel: 603-623-6411. Sr. Mary Lawrence Lojko, C.S.S.F., Prin.
Felician Sisters 4; Students 231.

11—ST. JOHN THE BAPTIST (1914) (French), Revs. Leo A. LeBlanc; Raymond A. Ball. In res., Rev. Msgr. James Markham; Rev. Msgr. Roland Tancrede; Rev. Msgr. Wilfrid Paradis; Rev. Leonard Foisy.
Res., 107 Alsace St., 03102. Tel: 603-623-4715.
Catechesis/Religious Programs—Tel: 603-622-0504.
Students 250.

12—ST. MARIE (1880), Revs. Marc R. Montminy, V.F.; Michael E. Gendron; Deacon Frank Gallinaro. In res., Rev. John Grace.
Res., 378 Notre Dame Ave., 03102-3793. Tel: 603-622-4615. [CEM 2]
Chapels—Joseph House Chapel, 279 Cartier St., 03102.; Chapel of North American Martyrs.; St. Joan of Arc.
Catechesis/Religious Programs—D.R.E.: Sr. Doris Bernier, (Elementary); Sean Poza, (Junior & Senior High Schools); Jay Yvars, (Adult).
Students 209.
Convent—133 Wayne St., 03102-3793. Tel: 603-623-0815. Sisters of the Presentation of Mary.

13—OUR LADY OF PERPETUAL HELP (1911) (English), Rev. Maurice D. Lavigne. In res., Rev. Msgr. John F. Burke.
Res., 266 Cypress St., 03103-3700. Tel: 603-622-2535; Fax: 603-668-0356.
Catechesis/Religious Programs—870 Hayward St., 03103-3700. Tel: 603-668-3985.
Students 180.

14—ST. PATRICK (1898) (Irish), Rev. Nicholas P. Rogers; Deacon Harry Kram.
Res., 138 Coolidge Ave., 03102. Tel: 603-624-4115; Fax: 603-624-4115. [CEM]
Catechesis/Religious Programs—100 Coolidge Ave., 03102. Tel: 603-624-0916.
Students 105.

15—ST. PIUS X (1955), Rev. Robert G. Boisvert.
Res., 575 Candia Rd., 03109. Tel: 603-622-6510; Fax: 603-626-1323.
Catechesis/Religious Programs—Tel: 603-669-4547.
Students 453.

16—ST. RAPHAEL, Rev. Bede Camera, O.S.B.
Res., 103 Walker St., 03102. Tel: 603-623-2604.

17—SACRED HEART OF JESUS (1911) (French), Revs. Marc R. Montminy; Michael E. Gendron.
Res., 265 S. Main St., 03102. Tel: 603-625-9525.

18—ST. THERESA, Rev. Robert A. Marchand.
Res., 140 Mitchell St., 03103. Tel: 603-623-5055.

OUTSIDE THE CITY OF MANCHESTER

Alton, Belknap Co., St. Joan of Arc, Rev. Richard H. Wegman.
Res., 03809. Tel: 603-875-7191.
Mission—Center Barnstead, St. Paul, Center Barnstead, 03225.

Ashland, Grafton Co., St. Agnes, Rev. George H. Robichaud.
Res., 6 Hill St., P.O. Box 556, 03217. Tel: 603-968-4433.

Auburn, Rockingham Co., St. Peter (1948), Rev. James W. Haller. In res., Rev. Msgr. Norman Bolduc, Jr.; Rev. Msgr. John E. Molan.
Res., 2345 Candia Rd., 03032-1132. Tel: 603-623-5429.
Catechesis/Religious Programs—Tel: 605-669-5134.
Students 368.

Bedford, Hillsborough Co., St. Elizabeth Seton (1964), Rev. Cornelius J. Goggin; Edward P. Munz, Pastoral Assoc. In res., Rev. Marc Guillemette.
Res., 190 Meetinghouse Rd., 03110-6027. Tel: 603-669-7444; Fax: 603-644-5371.
Catechesis/Religious Programs—Tel: 603-647-1940. James Whittaker, D.R.E.
Students 1,100.

Belmont, Belknap Co., St. Joseph (1899), Rev. Marc B. Drouin.
Res., One High St., P.O. Box 285, 03220. Tel: 603-267-8174; Fax: 603-267-1170.
Catechesis/Religious Programs—Students 174.

Bennington, Hillsborough Co., St. Patrick (1936), Rev. Andre L. Bedard.
Res., 10 Greenfield Rd., P.O. Box 147, 03442-0147. Tel: 603-588-2180. [CEM]
Catechesis/Religious Programs—Students 127.

Berlin, Coos Co.,

1—ST. ANNE, (1885) (French), Rev. Marcel I. Martel.
Res., 58 Church St., 03570-2493. Tel: 603-752-6654; Fax: 603-752-4115. [CEM 2]
Catechesis/Religious Programs—Tel: 603-752-5443.
Students 164.

2—ST. JOSEPH, (1943) (French), Very Rev. Maurice R. Lacroix.
Res., 633 Third Ave., 03570. Tel: 603-752-4280. [JC]
Catechesis/Religious Programs—Tel: 603-752-4556.
Students 120.

3—ST. KIERAN, (1894), Rev. Richard A. Roberge.
Res., 162 Madison Ave., 03570. Tel: 603-752-2880; Fax: 603-752-1855. [CEM]
Catechesis/Religious Programs—140 Blanchard St., 03570. Tel: 603-752-5443.
Students 220.

4—GUARDIAN ANGEL, (1917), Rev. William E. Babineau.
Res., 593 Sullivan St., 03570. Tel: 603-752-1421.
Catechesis/Religious Programs—140 Blanchard St., P.O. Box 518, 03570. Tel: 603-752-5443.
Students 336.

Bristol, Grafton Co., St. Timothy (1900), Rev. William L. Quirk.
Res., School St., P.O. Box 37, 03222. Tel: 603-744-2700.
Mission—Newfound Lake, Grafton Co., Our Lady of Grace, W. Shore Rd., 03222.

Candia, Rockingham Co., St. Paul (1971), Rev. Msgr. Donald J. Gilbert.
Res., 54 Main St., P.O. Box 276, 03034. Tel: 603-483-8481.
Catechesis/Religious Programs—Tel: 603-483-5516.
Students 291.
Station—Chester, St. Jerome.

Cascade, Coos Co., St. Benedict. Closed. For Sacramental records contact St. Kieran, Berlin.

Center Ossipee, Carroll Co., St. Joseph (1965), Rev. Timothy R. O'Donnell.
Res., P.O. Box 248, 03814. Tel: 603-539-5036.
Mission—Chocorua, Carroll Co., Our Lady of Perpetual Help.

Charlestown, Sullivan Co., St. Catherine, Rev. Shawn M. Therrien.
Res., 116 Main St., Box 332, 03603. Tel: 603-826-3359.
Station—Alstead, Holy Spirit.

Claremont, Sullivan Co., St. Joseph (1922) (Polish), Rev. Stanley J. Piwowar.
Res., 58 Elm St., P.O. Box 824, 03743. Tel: 603-542-5732.
Catechesis/Religious Programs—Students 243.

St. Mary (1823), Revs. Arthur Obin, O.M.I.; Gilmond Boucher, O.M.I.; Sr. Pauline Maurier, C.S.C., Pastoral Assoc.
Res., 32 Pearl St., 03743-2552. Tel: 603-542-9518; Fax: 603-542-9614. [CEM]
School—(Grades PreK-8) 18 Central St., 03743. Tel: 603-542-6341. Richard Lizotte, Prin.
Lay Teachers 10; Students 168.
Catechesis/Religious Programs—Students 53.

Colebrook, Coos Co., St. Brendan (1953), Rev. Albert A. Bellefeuille.
Res., 28 Pleasant St., P.O. Box 65, 03576. Tel: 603-237-4342. [CEM]
Catechesis/Religious Programs—Students 147.
Mission—Errol, Coos Co., St. Pius X. [CEM]
Station—Dixville, St. William of York.

Concord, Merrimack Co.,

1—ST. JOHN THE EVANGELIST, (1886), Revs. James P. Watson; Dennis A. Broussard.
Res., 72 S. Main St., 03301. Tel: 603-224-2328. [CEM]
Station—McKerley Home, Tel: 603-224-6561.

2—ST. PETER, Revs. Mitchell J. Wanat, C.M.; Roman Kmiec, C.M.
Res., 135 N. State St., 03301. Tel: 603-225-2131; Fax: 603-228-4580.
Catechesis/Religious Programs—Students 231.

3—SACRED HEART, (1892) (French), Rev. Aime A. Boisselle.
Res., 52 Pleasant St., 03301. Tel: 603-225-6942.
Catechesis/Religious Programs—Tel: 603-225-6942.
Students 97.

4—IMMACULATE HEART OF MARY, (1956), Rev. Marc R. Gagne; Deacon Peter J. Tumulty.
Res., 180 Loudon Rd., 03301. Tel: 603-224-4393; Fax: 603-224-4123.
Catechesis/Religious Programs—176 Loudon Rd., 03301. Tel: 603-225-2026.
Students 225.

Derry, Rockingham Co., Holy Cross, Rev. James A. Riel.
Office: 187 Hampstead Rd., 03038. Tel: 603-437-7550.

St. Thomas Aquinas (1885), Revs. Joseph F. Lorenzo, O.F.M.; Thomas Garone, O.F.M.; Bruce Czapla, O.F.M.
Res., 26 Crystal Ave., 03038. Tel: 603-432-5000; Fax: 603-434-0518.
School—(Grades K-8) 3 Moody St., 03038. Tel: 603-432-2712; Fax: 603-432-2179. Sr. Jacqueline Brodeur, C.S.C., Prin.
Sisters 3; Lay Teachers 11; Students 304.
Catechesis/Religious Programs—16 Rollins Street, 03038. Tel: 603-432-7530. Dr. Jane Dwyer, D.R.E.
Students 660.

Dover, Strafford Co., St. Charles (1893) (French), Rev. Paul L. Gregoire. In res., Rev. Armand J. Provost.
Res., 577 Central Ave., 03820. Tel: 603-742-1354. [CEM]

St. Joseph (1945), Very Rev. Daniel O. Lamothe, V.F.; Rev. John Poirier.
Res., 150 Central Ave., 03820. Tel: 603-742-4837; Fax: 603-749-6779.
Catechesis/Religious Programs—Students 445.
Mission—Barrington, Chapel of the Nativity, Rte. 9, P.O. Box 163, Barrington, 03825. Tel: 603-664-9336.

St. Mary (1833), Rev. Gerald R. Dunn.
Res., 25 Third St., 03820. Tel: 603-742-2619.

Durham, Strafford Co., St. Thomas More, Rev. Patrick F. Irwin.
Res., 6 Madbury Rd., Box 620, 03824. Tel: 603-868-5252; 868-2666 (Office); Fax: 603-868-3765.

Enfield, Grafton Co., St. Helena (1899), Rev. Paul Rainville, M.S.; Deacon John St. George.
Res., South St., R.R. No. 2, Box 26, 03748. Tel: 603-632-4263.
Catechesis/Religious Programs—Students 115.
Mission—Canaan, Grafton Co., St. Mary, 03748. Tel: 603-523-9955.

Epping, Rockingham Co., St. Joseph (1898), Rev. Ronald E. Corriveau.
Res., 14 Church St., 03042-0337. Tel: 603-679-8805. [CEM]
Catechesis/Religious Programs—Tel: 603-679-5724.
Students 239.

Exeter, Rockingham Co., St. Michael (1859), Revs. Maurice J. Rochefort; Agapit H. Jean, Jr.
Res., 9 Lincoln St., 03833. Tel: 603-772-2494; Fax: 603-778-1629.
Catechesis/Religious Programs—Michael House, 11 Linden St., 03833. Tel: 603-772-3916. Julie Hayes, D.R.E.
Students 734.

Farmington, Strafford Co., St. Peter, Rev. Roger A. Fortier.
Res., 90 Central St., P.O. Box 565, 03835. Tel: 603-755-2280.
Catechesis/Religious Programs—Tel: 603-755-3921.

Franklin, Merrimack Co., St. Paul (1884), Rev. Michael Kerper.
Res., 43 W. High St., P.O. Box 490, 03235. Tel: 603-934-5013; Fax: 603-934-6694. [CEM]
Catechesis/Religious Programs—Tel: 603-934-5739.
Students 221.

Goffstown, Hillsborough Co., St. Lawrence (1955), Rev. Donald F. Gauthier, Jr.
Res., 51 Main St., 03045. Tel: 603-497-2651; Fax: 603-497-3668.
Catechesis/Religious Programs—Tel: 603-497-4093.
Students 271.

Gonic, Strafford Co., St. Leo (1989), Rev. Paul D. Montminy.
Res., 59 Main St., 03839. Tel: 603-332-1624. [CEM]
Catechesis/Religious Programs—16 Bridge St., Rochester, 03867. Tel: 603-332-4803.
Students 54.

Gorham, Coos Co., Holy Family, Rev. Wilfred H. Deschamps, Admin.
Res., 5 Church St., 03581-1695. Tel: 603-466-2335. [CEM]

Greenville, Hillsborough Co., Sacred Heart (1888), Rev. Donald E. Clinton.
Res., 15 High St., 03048. Tel: 603-878-1121; Fax: 603-878-4657. [CEM]

Groveton, Coos Co., St. Francis Xavier (1899) (French), Rev. Daniel R. Deveau.
Res., 10 State St., Box 72, 03582. Tel: 603-636-1047; Fax: 603-636-2549. [CEM]
Catechesis/Religious Programs—Students 67.

Hampstead, Rockingham Co., St. Anne, Rev. Florent R. Bilodeau.
Res., P.O. Box 339, 03841. Tel: 603-329-5886.
Station—Sandown, St. Michael.

Hampton, Rockingham Co., Our Lady of the Miraculous Medal (1948), Revs. George E. Ham; Stephen Marcoux; Michael J. Griffin; Deacon Paul Testa.
Res., 289 Lafayette Rd., 03842. Tel: 603-926-2206; Fax: 603-926-8602.
School—Sacred Heart School, (Grades PreK-8). Tel: 603-926-3254; Fax: 603-929-1109. Sr. Mary Joan Walsh, O.L.L., Prin.
Sisters 5; Lay Teachers 14; Students 310.
Catechesis/Religious Programs—(Grades K-12). Tel: 603-926-5573.
Students 524.
Mission—Seabrook Beach, Rockingham Co., St. Elizabeth's, Rte. 1-A, Seabrook Beach, 03874. Tel: 603-474-3839.

Hampton Beach, Rockingham Co., St. Patrick. Closed. Attended from Chancery. For all records contact O.L.M.M. Parish, Hampton.

Hanover, Grafton Co., St. Denis (1907), Rev. Arthur J. Kelliher.

Res., 8 Sanborn Rd., 03755. Tel: 603-643-2166.
Catechesis/Religious Programs—Students 235.

Harrisville, Cheshire Co., St. Denis. Attended by Sacred Heart, Marlborough.
Mission—Dublin, Our Lady of the Snows. [CEM]

Henniker, Merrimack Co., St. Theresa (1945), Rev. Andre M. Thibodeau.
Res., Rush Rd., P.O. Box 557, 03242. Tel: 603-428-3325.
Mission—Contoocook, Merrimack, St. Mary.
Catechesis/Religious Programs—Students 247.

Hillsborough, Hillsborough Co., St. Mary, Rev. John A. Wright.
Res., 38 Church St., P.O. Box 907, 03244. Tel: 603-464-5565.
Parish Hall—Tel: 603-464-6021.

Hinsdale, Cheshire Co., St. Joseph (1884), Rev. Raymond J. Potvin.
Res., 12 Prospect St., P.O. Box 14, 03451. Tel: 603-336-5414. [CEM]
Mission—Chesterfield, Cheshire, Our Lady of the Lake.
Catechesis/Religious Programs—Students 127.

Hooksett, Merrimack Co., Holy Rosary, Rev. Fernand A. Croteau.
Res., 15 S. Main St., 03106. Tel: 603-485-3523. [CEM]

Hudson, Hillsborough Co., St. John the Evangelist, Rev. John C. Horan. In res., Rev. Msgr. Joseph E. Desmond.
Res., 27 Library St., 03051. Tel: 603-882-3603.
Catechesis/Religious Programs—23 Library St., 03051. Tel: 603-882-6541. Mrs. Kathleen Cox, D.R.E.
Students 662.

St. Kathryn (1968), Rev. Gary J. Belliveau; Theresa Gagnon, Pastoral Assoc.
Res., 5 Wason Rd., 03051. Tel: 603-882-7793.
Catechesis/Religious Programs—Sr. Eleanor LaBranche, C.S.C., D.R.E.
Students 675.

Jaffrey, Cheshire Co., St. Patrick (1885), Rev. Richard J. Kelley; Deacon W. Carl Lefleur.
Res., 220 Main St., 03452. Tel: 603-532-6634. [CEM]
School—(Grades K-8) 70 Main St., 03452. Tel: 603-532-7676. David L. O'Connell, Prin.
Sisters 3; Lay Teachers 11; Students 165.
Catechesis/Religious Programs—Tel: 603-532-8831.
Students 260.

Keene, Cheshire Co., St. Bernard (1862), Very Rev. W. Pierre Baker, V.F.; Rev. Aaron J. Pfaff.
Res., 173 Main St., 03431. Tel: 603-352-3525; Fax: 603-352-7472. [CEM]
Catechesis/Religious Programs—St. Joseph School, 92 Wilson St., 03431. Tel: 603-357-4001.
Students 130.

St. Margaret Mary (1955), Rev. Richard M. Giroux.
Res., 35 Arch St., 03431-2297. Tel: 603-352-1311.
Catechesis/Religious Programs—Tel: 603-357-3781.
Students 152.

Laconia, Belknap Co., St. Joseph, Rev. Gary J. Kosmowski.
Res., 30 Church St., P.O. Box 366, 03247. Tel: 603-524-1442; Fax: 603-527-3534. [CEM]
Catechesis/Religious Programs—Tel: 603-524-4196.
Students 138.

Sacred Heart (1891) (French-Canadian), Rev. Eddy N. Bisson. In res., Rev. Nelson Boucher.
Res., 291 Union Ave., 03246. Tel: 603-524-9609. [CEM]

Lakeport, Belknap Co., Our Lady of the Lakes, Rev. George J. Soberick.
Res., 50 Washington St., 03246. Tel: 603-524-1357.
Catechesis/Religious Programs—Students 209.
Mission—Weirs Beach, Belknap, St. Helena.

Lancaster, Coos Co., All Saints (1856), Rev. Maurice R. Larochelle.
Res., 163 Main St., 03584. Tel: 603-788-2083. [CEM]
Mission—Jefferson, Coos, St. Agnes, Rt. 2, 03583.

Lebanon, Grafton Co., Sacred Heart (1875) (French), Very Rev. Bernard Baris, M.S.; Rev. Henry Brodeur, M.S. In res., Rev. John F. Mullin, S.J.; Bro. Claude Rheaume, M.S.
Res., 2 Hough St., P.O. Box 482, 03766. Tel: 603-448-1262.
Catechesis/Religious Programs—Tel: 603-448-1575.
Students 426.

Lincoln, Grafton Co., St. Joseph (1902), Rev. Roger Bilodeau.
Res., Church St., P.O. Box 128, 03251-0128. Tel: 603-745-2266.

Lisbon, Grafton Co., St. Catherine of Siena (1957), Rev. Mark E. Dollard.
Res., c/o 21 Pine St., Woodsville, 03785.

Littleton, Grafton Co., St. Rose of Lima (1882), Very Rev. Joseph S. Klatka, V.F.
Res., 77 Clay St., 03561. Tel: 603-444-2593. [CEM]
Catechesis/Religious Programs—Students 263.
Missions—Bethlehem, Grafton Co., Christ the King, Main St., Bethlehem, 03574; Bethlehem, Grafton, Our Lady of the Snows, Main St., 03580.

Londonderry, Rockingham Co., St. Jude (1962), Rev. W. Timothy Thibeault; Sr. Mary Elizabeth Whalen, S.N.D., Pastoral Assoc.
Res., 435 Mammoth Rd., 03053-2304. Tel: 603-432-3333; Fax: 603-432-1639.

St. Mark the Evangelist (1981), Rev. Thomas J. Bresnahan.
Res., One Griffin Rd., 03053. Tel: 603-432-8711.
Catechesis/Religious Programs—Students 870.

Marlborough, Cheshire Co., Sacred Heart (1886), Rev. Thomas Lierre Duston, Admin.; Sr. Lucie E. Ducas, C.S.C., Pastoral Assoc.
Res., 9 Ling St., 03455. Tel: 603-876-3804; Fax: 603-876-4327. [CEM]

Meredith, Belknap Co., St. Charles (1946), Rev. Msgr. Fernand L. Pichette.
Res., 281A Daniel Webster Hwy., P.O. Box 237, 03253-0237. Tel: 603-279-4403; Fax: 603-279-9924.
Catechesis/Religious Programs—Tel: 603-279-8691.
Students 267.
Mission—Center Harbor, Belknap Co., Our Lady of Victory.

Merrimack, Hillsborough Co., Our Lady of Mercy (1950), Revs. Donald E. Lafond; Daniel I. Sinibaldi.
Res., 16 Baboosic Lake Rd., 03054. Tel: 603-424-3757.
Catechesis/Religious Programs—14 Baboosic Lake Rd., 03054. Tel: 603-424-4477. Elizabeth Lochman, D.R.E.
Students 834.

St. John Neumann (1982), Rev. Robert E. Gorski.
Res., 208 Naticook Rd., 03054. Tel: 603-880-4689; Fax: 603-880-4790.
Catechesis/Religious Programs—Tel: 603-880-0825.
Students 420.

Milford, Hillsborough Co., St. Patrick (1895), Revs. Andrew W. Cryans; Michael Ciullo.
Res., 34 Amherst St., P.O. Box 27, 03055. Tel: 603-673-1311; Fax: 603-673-3687. [CEM]
Catechesis/Religious Programs—Tel: 603-673-4797.
Students 710.
Share Program—(A non-denominational outreach program for the local needy). Tel: 603-673-9898. Mrs. Mariette Facques, Dir.
Mission—Brookline, Hillsborough Co., Infant Jesus, 03055.

Nashua, Hillsborough Co.,

1—St. Aloysius, Rev. Roland P. Cote.
Res., 48 W. Hollis St., 03060. Tel: 603-882-4362. [CEM]

2—St. Casimir, Rev. Francis M. Spencer, M.S.
Res., 119 Temple St., 03060. Tel: 603-882-1313. [CEM]

3—St. Christopher, (1950), Revs. Karl E. Dowd, S.T.L.; James Walsh; John W. Fleming. In res., Rev. Bruce W. Collard.
Res., 62 Manchester St., 03060. Tel: 603-882-0632; Fax: 603-881-8728. [CEM]
School—(Grades K-6) 20 Cushing Ave., 03060. Tel: 603-882-7442. Sr. Joan Marie Messier, R.S.M., Prin.
Students 369.
Catechesis/Religious Programs—Tel: 603-883-2572.
Students 496.

4—St. Francis Xavier, (1885), Rev. Daniel A. St. Laurent; Sr. Nancy Braceland, C.S.J., Pastoral Assoc.
Res., 41 Chandler St., 03060. Tel: 603-882-2333; Fax: 603-594-9648. [CEM]
Catechesis/Religious Programs—Students 121.

5—Immaculate Conception, (1968), Very Rev. Denis F. Horan; Rev. Robert Couto.
Res., 216 E. Dunstable Dr., 03062. Tel: 603-888-0321; Fax: 603-888-8407.
Parish Hall: Tel: 603-888-9841.
Catechesis/Religious Programs—Tel: 603-888-0608.
Students 1,092.

6—Infant Jesus, (1909) (French), Rev. Raymond E. Gagnon. In res., Rev. John E. Healey.
Res., 121 Allds St., 03060. Tel: 603-882-2462; Fax: 603-882-7104.
Catechesis/Religious Programs—Tel: 603-886-9725. Mr. Gerard Bergeron, D.R.E.
Students 234.

7—St. Joseph, (1955), Revs. Gerard R. Desmarais; Daniel L. Bernier.
Res., 265 Lake St., 03060. Tel: 603-883-0757; Fax: 603-883-4587.
Catechesis/Religious Programs—Tel: 603-889-4372.
Students 478.

8—St. Patrick, Rev. Msgr. T. Joseph McDonough; Rev. Martin T. Kelly.
Res., 29 Spring St., 03060. Tel: 603-882-2262. [CEM]

9—Resurrection, (1970), Rev. Albion F. Bulger; Deacon E. Carl Hilston; Ms. Christine Patterson, Pastoral Min.
Pastoral Center: 449 Broad St., 03063-3412. Tel: 603-882-0925; Fax: 603-881-3561.
Catechesis/Religious Programs—Tel: 603-889-0012.
Students 530.

10—St. Stanislaus, (1908) (Polish), Rev. Daniel F. Szopa.
Res., 5 Green St., 03060. Tel: 603-882-0893. [CEM]

New London, Merrimack Co., Our Lady of Fatima (1952), Rev. Richard T. Lower.
Res., Main St., 03257. Tel: 603-526-4484; Fax: 603-526-8055.
Mission—Potter Place, Merrimack Co., Immaculate Conception, Church St., 03216. Tel: 603-735-5821.
Catechesis/Religious Programs—Students 140.

Newmarket, Rockingham Co., St. Mary (1878), Rev. John B. Finnigan. In res., Rev. Joseph E. Shields.
Res., 182 Main St., 03857. Tel: 603-659-3643. [CEM]
Catechesis/Religious Programs—Tel: 603-659-6474.
Students 141.
Mission—Newfields, Rockingham Co., Sacred Heart, 52 Main St., Newfields, 03856. Tel: 603-659-3246.

Newport, Sullivan Co., St. Patrick (1902), Rev. Joseph E. Mahoney.
Res., 32 Beech St., 03773. Tel: 603-863-1422. [CEM]
Catechesis/Religious Programs—Tel: 603-863-7898.
Students 148.
Mission—Sunapee, Sullivan Co., St. Joachim, Rte. 11, Sunapee, 03782. Tel: 603-763-5940.

Newton, Rockingham Co., Mary, Mother of the Church (1967), Rev. Marcel M. Allard.
Res., 12 Amesbury Rd., 03858-0322. Tel: 603-382-6566.
Catechesis/Religious Programs—1 New Boston Rd., Kingston, 03848. Tel: 603-642-8885.
Students 428.
Mission—Kingston, Rockingham Co., St. Frederick, 3 New Boston Rd., Kingston, 03848.

North Conway, Carroll Co., Our Lady of the Mountains (1904), Revs. Edward J.V. Kelley; Louis A. Soucey.
Res., 28 Grove St., 03860. Tel: 603-356-2535; Fax: 603-356-2877. [CEM]
Catechesis/Religious Programs—P.O. Box 593, 03860. Tel: 603-356-3421.
Students 262.
Missions—Bartlett, Carroll, St. Joseph, P.O. Box 189, 03860; North Conway, St. Charles Borromeo, P.O. Box 189, 03860. Tel: 603-356-2535; Fax: 603-356-2877.

North Stratford, Coos Co., Sacred Heart (1888) (French), Rev. Daniel R. Deveau. Pastoral Assocs.: Sr. Marie Mansfield, S.G.M.; Sr. Helene Georges, S.G.M.
Church—121 Main St., P.O. Box C, 03590. Tel: 603-922-3360.
Res., St. Francis Xavier Rectory, Groveton, 03582. Tel: 603-636-1047; Fax: 603-636-2549. [CEM 2]

North Walpole, Cheshire Co., St. Peter (1877), Rev. Anthony DiRusso.
Res., 38 Church St., 03609. Tel: 603-445-5304. [CEM]
Catechesis/Religious Programs—Tel: 603-756-3444.
Students 80.
Mission—Walpole, St. Joseph, Elm St., 03608.

Pelham, Hillsborough Co., St. Patrick (1946), Rev. Edward D. Richard.
Res., 12 Main St., 03076. Tel: 603-635-3525; Fax: 603-635-3919.
School—(Grades K-8) 16 Main St., 03076. Tel: 603-635-2941; 635-9800. Jane A. Gaskell, Prin.
Lay Teachers 13; Students 208.
Catechesis/Religious Programs—Tel: 603-635-1447.
Students 695.

Penacook, Merrimack Co., Immaculate Conception (1880), Rev. Leo P. Lefebvre.
Res., 9 Pleasant St., 03303. Tel: 603-753-4413. [CEM]
Catechesis/Religious Programs—Tel: 603-753-6702.

Students 170.

Peterborough, Hillsborough Co., St. Peter (1900), Rev. William J. Kelley.
Res., 18 Vine St., 03458. Tel: 603-924-3819. [CEM]
Catechesis/Religious Programs—Students 179.

Pittsfield, Merrimack Co., Our Lady of Lourdes (1889), Rev. George Majka.
Res., 20 River Rd., 03263. Tel: 603-435-6242.
Catechesis/Religious Programs—25 Crescent St., 03263. Tel: 603-435-8840.
Students 245.
Mission—Northwood, Rockingham Co., St. Joseph. [CEM]

Plaistow, Rockingham Co., Holy Angels (1892), Rev. Richard B. Thompson. In res., Rev. Gerard A. Boucher.
Res., 8 Atkinson Depot Rd., 03865. Tel: 603-382-8324; Fax: 603-382-8324. [CEM]
Catechesis/Religious Programs—Tel: 603-382-8824. Mrs. Beverly Fisher, D.R.E.
Students 345.

Plymouth, Grafton Co., St. Matthew (1916), Rev. Robert F. Cole.
Res., 46 Langdon St., 03264. Tel: 603-536-4700; Fax: 603-536-4709.
Catechesis/Religious Programs—Students 266.
Station—Campton, Waterville Valley.

Portsmouth, Rockingham Co., Immaculate Conception, Rev. Leo G. Gagnon; Deacon Charles Schladenhauffen.
Res., 98 Summer St., 03801. Tel: 603-436-0048. [CEM]

St. Catherine of Siena (1951), Rev. Msgr. Lawrence E. Burns.
Res., 845 Woodbury Ave., 03801-3294. Tel: 603-436-0344.
Catechesis/Religious Programs—Students 82.

St. James (1958), Rev. Gerald R. Belanger; Sr. Roberta O'Rourke, C.S.J., Pastoral Assoc.
Res., 2075 Lafayette Rd., 03801-5697. Tel: 603-436-4555; Fax: 603-433-4401.
Catechesis/Religious Programs—Students 210.

Rochester, Strafford Co., St. Mary (1868), Rev. Francis E. Kelso.
Res., 38 Charles St., 03867. Tel: 603-332-1869; Fax: 603-332-1869. [CEM]
Catechesis/Religious Programs—Students 318.

Holy Rosary (1883) (French), Revs. Paul D. Montminy; Dennis Audet.
Res., 189 N. Main St., 03867. Tel: 603-332-1863; Fax: 603-330-0865. [CEM]
Catechesis/Religious Programs—16 Bridge St., 03867. Tel: 603-332-4803.
Students 405.

Rollinsford, Strafford Co., St. Mary, Rev. Steven M. Kucharski.
Res., 404 High St., Somersworth, 03878. Tel: 603-692-4367.

Rye Beach, Rockingham Co., St. Theresa (1979), Rev. John V. Moran.
Res., 815 Central Rd., P.O. Box 482, 03871. Tel: 603-964-6440.
Catechesis/Religious Programs—Tel: 603-964-9878.
Students 336.

Salem, Rockingham Co., Mary, Queen of Peace (1966), Rev. Andrew M. Meehan, Admin.
Res., 200 Lawrence Rd., P.O. Box 685, 03079. Tel: 603-893-8661.
Catechesis/Religious Programs—Tel: 603-893-8662. Mrs. Marie Mullen, D.R.E.
Students 500.

St. Joseph (1910), Very Rev. Richard W. Connors; Rev. Gary Lord; Deacons David Costello; George Borkush.
Res., 33 Main St., P.O. Box 938, 03079. Tel: 603-898-4933; Fax: 603-893-9236.
Catechesis/Religious Programs—40 Main St., 03079. Tel: 603-893-9692. Sr. Lorraine LaPete, D.R.E.
Students 610.

Sanbornville, Carroll Co., St. Anthony (1908), Rev. Edmund A. Babicz.
Res., P.O. Box 490, 03872. Tel: 603-522-3304. [CEM]
Catechesis/Religious Programs—Students 153.
Mission—Milton, Strafford Co., Sacred Heart, P.O. Box 647, Milton, 03851. Tel: 603-652-9034.

Seabrook, Rockingham Co., St. Elizabeth. Attended by the Chancery. For all records contact Our Lady of the Miraculous Medal Parish, Hampton.

Somersworth, Strafford Co., Holy Trinity, Rev. Steven M. Kucharski.
Res., 404 High St., P.O. Box 350, 03878. Tel: 603-692-4367. [CEM]

St. Martin (1882) (French), Rev. Robert G. Biron.
Res., 120 Maple St. Ext., 03878-1999. Tel: 603-692-2172. [CEM]
Catechesis/Religious Programs—Tel: 603-692-5878.
Students 220.

Suncook, Merrimack Co., St. John the Baptist (1873), Rev. C. Peter Dumont.
Res., 10 School St., 03275-1917. Tel: 603-485-3113; Fax: 603-485-2113. [CEM 2]
Catechesis/Religious Programs—Tel: 603-485-3972.
Students 309.

Tilton, Belknap Co., St. Mary of the Assumption, Rev. George F. Harvey.
Res., 10 Chestnut St., 03276. Tel: 603-286-4445.

Troy, Cheshire Co., Immaculate Conception, Rev. Thomas L. Duston; Sr. Lucie Ducas, C.S.C., Pastoral Assoc.
Res., 33 School St., 03465. Tel: 603-242-6415; Fax: 603-876-4327. [CEM]
Mission—Fitzwilliam, St. Joseph.

West Lebanon, Grafton Co., Holy Redeemer (1953), Rev. Donald Jeffrey, M.S.
Res., 8 Prospect St. W., Box 5484, 03784. Tel: 603-298-8530.
Catechesis/Religious Programs—Tel: 603-298-5578.
Students 87.

West Stewartstown, Coos Co., St. Albert (1926), Rev. John B. Loughnane, Jr.
Mailing Address: P.O. Box 176, Beecher Falls, VT 05902.
Res., Church St., 03597. Tel: 603-246-8829; Fax: 603-246-7167. [CEM]
School—(Grades 1-8) P.O. Box 177, Beecher Falls, 05902. Tel: 603-246-8631. Sr. Lorraine Trottier, P.M., Prin.
Sisters of Presentation of Mary 4; Students 71.
Station—Coos County Institution.

West Swanzey, Cheshire Co., St. Anthony, Rev. John H. Bryson.
Res., 50 S. Winchester St., Box 117, 03469. Tel: 603-352-6246.
Mission—North Swanzey, St. Stephen.

Whitefield, Coos Co., St. Matthew (1886), Rev. Richard A. Smith.
Res., 9 Jefferson Rd., P.O. Box 246, 03598. Tel: 603-837-2558. [CEM 2]
Catechesis/Religious Programs—Students 60.
Mission—Carroll, St. Patrick, Rte. 3 & 302, Twin Mountain, 03595.
Shrine—Bretton Woods, Our Lady of the Mountains.

Wilton, Hillsborough Co., Sacred Heart, Rev. Donald E. Clinton.
Res., Maple St., P.O. Box 489, 03086. Tel: 603-654-6554. [CEM]

Winchester, Cheshire Co., St. Stanislaus, Rev. Mark A. Rundzio.
Res., 80 Richmond St., 03470. Tel: 603-239-4312.
Mission—Ashuelot, St. Michael.

Windham, Rockingham Co., St. Matthew (1962), Rev. Wilfred G. Demers; Deacon Clarence R. Cummins.
Res., 2 Searles Rd., 03087-1298. Tel: 603-893-3336; Fax: 603-898-4008.
Catechesis/Religious Programs—Tel: 603-898-4818.
Students 869.

Wolfeboro, Carroll Co., St. Cecilia, Rev. Leo L. St. Pierre.
Res., 323 S. Main St., 03894. Tel: 603-569-2548.

Woodsville, Grafton Co., St. Joseph (1896), Rev. Mark E. Dollard.
Res., 21 Pine St., 03785. Tel: 603-747-2038.
Mission—Warren, St. John Vianney.

Chaplains of Public Institutions

MANCHESTER. *Elliott Hospital*. Rev. Robert J. Densmore.
Nursing Homes. Revs. Albert L. Boulanger; Andre J. Gagnon; Gerard J. Dion.
V.A. Hospital. Rev. Francis A. Talbot.

BERLIN. *Androscoggin Valley Hospital*. Sr. Monique Theriault, R.S.M., Chap.

CONCORD. *N.H. State Hospital*. Rev. Normand G. Bordeleau.
N.H. State Prison. Russell Sweeney.

GOFFSTOWN. *Hillsborough County Nursing Home*. Rev. Gerard J. Dion.

HANOVER. *Mary Hitchcock Hospital*. Revs. John F. Mullin, S.J.; Roland Nadeau, M.S.

NASHUA. *Nursing Homes and Memorial Hospital*. Sr. Doris Gagnon, P.M., Chap.; Rev. John E. Healey.

On Duty Outside the Diocese:
Reverend Monsignors—
Blair, Raymond O., Coastal Towers, 309 S., 740 E. Ocean Ave., Boynton Beach, FL 33435
Reverend Fathers—
Barrett, Michael D., Mt. St. Alphonsus, P.O. Box 219, Esopus, NY 12429
Connor, Kevin T., The Saint Paul Seminary, 2260 Summit Ave., St. Paul, MN 55105-1094
Dauphinais, Gerard V., Holy Nativity Monastery, Bethlehem, SD 57708
Simoneau, Norman J., Sacred Heart Rectory, P.O. Box 4861, Eureka, CA 95502-4861

Military Chaplains:
Reverend Fathers—
Cody, Kevin W., 1225 Batson Dr., Charleston AFB, SC 29404
Crowley, Edmund G., 6025A Linden St., Fairchild AFB, WA 99011-2260
Decker, James D., 9204 A Ciarfeo St., Laughlin AFB, TX 78840
Glasgow, Robert K., HHC 44, Eng BN Unit 15391, APO, AP 96251-0117
Lamy, Raymond J., 315 Westover Rd., Goldsboro, NC 27834-5409
Roma, Paul E., Consubgru Two, Code 013, Naval Submarine Base, Groton, CT 06349-5100

Absent on Sick Leave:
Reverend Fathers—
Daneault, Paul W.
Foisy, Leonard R.
Goodwin, Robert T.
LaForest, Conrad V.
Laqueux, Maurice R.
Masterson, Clyde G.
Valliere, Romeo J.

Absent on Leave:
Reverend Fathers—
Croteau, Roger H.
Memolo, Rocco C.
Pollitt, Michael J.
Shea, Leo A.
Wendling, Michael J.

Retired:
Reverend Monsignors—
Burke, John F., Our Lady of Perpetual Help Rectory, 266 Cypress St., Manchester, NH 03103
Chicoine, George D., RFD 4 - 103, Village of Glen Falls, Goffstown, NH 03045
Curran, Francis L., St. Mary Rectory, 182 Main St., P.O. Box 337, Newmarket, NH 03857
Desmond, Joseph E., St. John the Evangelist Rectory, 27 Library St., Hudson, NH 03051
Dumas, Alfred J., Bishop Peterson Residence, 221 Orange St., Manchester, NH 03104
Gardner, Laurence R., Cathedral Rectory, 145 Lowell St., Manchester, NH 03102. Tel: 603-622-6404
Hines, Leo F., St. Agnes Rectory, 1493 Cranston St., Cranston, RI 02920
Kenney, Philip J., 95 Manor Rd., Concord, NH 03303
Lettre, Achille W., 21 Neptune Rd., Ormond Beach, FL 32176
MacDonald, Colin A., St. Francis of Assisi Rectory, 3221 Brown Ave., Manchester, NH 03103
Markham, James J., St. John the Baptist Rectory, 107 Alsace St., Manchester, NH 03102
McGreal, James R., Villa Crest Retirement Center, 1276 Hanover St., Rm. 308, Manchester, NH 03104
Murphy, Eugene, Holy Angels, 8 Atkinson Depot Rd., Plaistow, NH 03865
Nolan, William L., Bishop Peterson Residence, 221 Orange St., Manchester, NH 03104-4324
Paradis, Wilfrid H., 107 Alsace St., Manchester, NH 03102
Tancrede, Roland, St. John the Baptist Rectory, 107 Alsace St., Manchester, NH 03102
Reverend Fathers—
Auger, Gerald E., 235 Alsace St., Manchester, NH 03102
Baillargeon, Albert G., 12 Jacobs Dr., Rochester, NH 03867
Blais, Roland O., St. George Rectory, 517 Pine St., Manchester, NH 03104
Bombardier, Wilfrid F., St. Kieran's Guest House, 158 Madison Ave., Berlin, NH 03570-2065
Boucher, Nelson, Sacred Heart Rectory, 291 Union Ave., Laconia, NH 03246
Bracq, Edward E., 14 Oldfield Rd., Nashau, NH 03060
Cameron, Albert S., Delany Residence #4, P.O. Box 6623, Manchester, NH 03108
Carty, Robert E., P.O. Box 1126, Grantham, NH 03753
Chalifour, Gerald F., Delaney Residence, P.O. Box 6272, Manchester, NH 03108-6272
Desjardins, Raymond S., 51 Partridge Green, Rochester, NH 03867
Frechette, Leo L., P.O. Box 68, West Nottingham, NH 03291
Gallant, Rodrigue J., P.O. Box 428, Belmont, NH 03220
Griffin, Robert F., Bishop Peterson Residence, 221 Orange St., Manchester, NH 03104-4324

Houde, Arthur O., 5626 Marshfield Dr., Port Orange, FL 32127
Hughes, Lawrence J., P.O. Box 462, Rye, NH 03871
Joyal, Gerald F., 106 Mount Delight Rd., P.O. Box 166, Deerfield, NH 03037
Keenan, Thomas E., 39 Hough St., Dover, NH 03820
Kemmery, Robert J., 18 Gull Ln., Orleans, MA 02653
Knott, Edward J., Bishop Peterson Residence, 221 Orange St., Manchester, NH 03104-4324
Lampron, Maurice W., P.O. Box 717, Wolfeboro Falls, NH 03896-0717
MacDonald, Edward J., Bishop Peterson Residence, 221 Orange St., Manchester, NH 03104
Maguire, Joseph T., Knock Nacarra Rd., Salthill, Galway, Ireland
McHugh, Paul F., 17 Picard Rd., Canterbury, NH 03824
Miller, A. Andrew, Bishop Peterson Residence, 221 Orange St., Manchester, NH 03104
Montplaisir, Roland A., 2950 Palm-Aire Dr., Apt. 502, Pompano Beach, FL 33069
O'Connor, Francis J., P.O. Box 704, Hampton, NH 03842
O'Connor, J. Kieran, St. Teresa's Manor, 519 Bridge St., Manchester, NH 03104
Pelletier, Eugene J., 19 S. Blueberry Ln., Box 84, Rochester, NH 03867
Polito, Victor J., 29 Knollwood Ave., Amsterdan, NY 12010
Provost, Armand J., St. Mary Rectory, 182 Main St., P.O. Box 337, Newmarket, NH 03857
Savage, Thomas J., P.O.Box 5531, Manchester, NH 03108
Shields, Joseph E., St. Mary Rectory, 182 Main St., P.O. Box 337, Newmarket, NH 03857
Soucey, Louis A., P.O. Box 222, Tamworth, NH 03886-0222
Tremblay, Jean A., 110 Cilley Rd., Manchester, NH 03103-5638
Turgeon, Armand A., 111 Rochester Ter., Rochester, NH 03867
Vickery, Richard F., P.O. Box 984, Manchester, NH 03105

Permanent Deacons:
Borkush, George J., St. Joseph, Salem
Cloutier, Richard A., St. John Neumann, Merrimack
Costello, David T., St. Joseph, Salem
Cummins, Clarence R., St. Matthew, Windham
Ford, Thomas J.
Gallinaro, Frank, St. Mary, Manchester
Hilston, Edmund C., Resurrection Parish, Nashua
Kayser, Charles Douglas, St. Patrick, Milford
Kram, Harry A., St. Patrick, Manchester
LaBonte, Alfred A., Jr., St. Joseph, Nashua
LaFleur, William Carl, Jr., St. Patrick, Jaffrey
Martin, John J., St. Joseph Hospital, Nashua
Polcari, Joseph A., St. Matthew, Whitefield
Schladenhauffen, Charles D., Immaculate Conception, Portsmouth
St. George, John H., St. Helena, Enfield
St. Laurent, Lionel A., Immaculate Conception, Nashua
Testa, Paul E., Our Lady of the Miraculous Medal, Hampton
Tumulty, Peter J., Immaculate Heart of Mary, Concord

INSTITUTIONS LOCATED IN THE DIOCESE

[A] SEMINARIES, RELIGIOUS OR SCHOLASTICATES

MANCHESTER. *St. Anselm Abbey Seminary*, 100 St. Anselm Dr., 03102. Tel: 603-641-7000; Fax: 603-641-7116. Order of St. Benedict. Rev. Jonathan DeFelice, O.S.B., Dir. Studies. Faculty 4; Students 2.

CENTER HARBOR. *Immaculate Conception Apostolic School*, Plymouth St., P.O. Box 936, 03226. Tel: 603-253-7728. David Steffy, L.C., Prin.; Rev. Patrick Walsh, L.C.; Bros. John Monette, L.C.; Christopher Cross, L.C.; David Consoli, L.C.; Steven Liscinski, L.C.; James Perez, L.C. Priests 2; Brothers 5; Lay Teachers 3; Students 74.

[B] COLLEGES AND UNIVERSITIES

MANCHESTER. *Notre Dame College*, 2321 Elm St., 03104. Tel: 603-669-4298; Fax: 603-644-8316.
For a complete listing, refer to the Colleges and Universities section.

Saint Anselm College, 03102. Tel: 603-641-7000.
For a complete listing, refer to the Colleges and Universities section.

MERRIMACK. *The Thomas More College of Liberal Arts*, 6 Manchester St., 03054. Tel: 603-880-8308; Fax: 603-880-9280.
For a complete listing, refer to the Colleges and Universities section.

NASHUA. *Rivier College*, 03060. Tel: 603-888-1311.
For a complete listing, refer to the Colleges and Universities section.

WARNER. *Magdalen College*, 511 Kearsarge Mountain Rd., 03278-9206. Tel: 603-456-2656.
For a complete listing, refer to the Colleges and Universities section.

WINDHAM. *Castle College*, 21 Searles Rd., 03087-1297. Tel: 603-893-6111.
For a complete listing, refer to the Colleges and Universities section.

[C] HIGH SCHOOLS, DIOCESAN

MANCHESTER. *Trinity High School*, 581 Bridge St., 03104-3595. Tel: 603-668-2910; Fax: 603-668-2913. Mr. Denis Mailloux, Prin.; James Walker, Asst. Prin.; Rev. Raymond Ball, Chap. & Campus Min. Lay Teachers 27; Students 442.

CONCORD. *Bishop Brady High School*, 25 Columbus Ave., 03301. Tel: 603-224-7418. Jean Barker, Prin.; Joy Degnan, Asst. Prin. Sisters of Mercy. Sisters 2; Lay Teachers 33; Students 425.

DOVER. *St. Thomas Aquinas High School*, 197 Dover Point Rd., 03820. Tel: 603-742-3206. Mr. Brian C. Newhall, Prin.; Timothy Hart, Dir. Campus Ministry. Sisters 3; Lay Teachers 43; Students 635.

[D] HIGH SCHOOLS, PRIVATE

NASHUA. *Bishop Guertin High School*, 194 Lund Rd., 03060. Brothers of the Sacred Heart. (Coed). Bros. Leo Labbe, S.C., Headmaster; Paul Demers, S.C., Chap. Brothers 6; Lay Teachers 47; Students 782.

[E] REGIONAL ELEMENTARY SCHOOLS

MANCHESTER. *Mount Saint Mary Early Childhool Center*. (Grades K-2), 147 Laurel St., 03103. Tel: 603-623-3155. Sr. Gloria Morin, R.S.M., Prin. Students 87.

St. Anthony School. (Grades K-6), 148 Belmont St., 03103. Tel: 603-622-0414. Mrs. Evelyn Bernier, Prin. Sisters 4; Lay Teachers 22; Boys 194; Girls 226.

St. Casimir School. (Grades K-8), 456 Union St., 03103. Tel: 603-623-6411. Sr. Mary Lawrence Lojko, C.S.S.F., Prin. Students 211.

St. Catherine School. (Grades K-6), 206 North St., 03104. Tel: 603-622-1711. Sr. Janet Belcourt, C.S.C., Prin. Sisters 6; Lay Teachers 22; Students 419.

St. Francis of Assisi School. (Grades K-6), 3223 Brown Ave., 03103. Tel: 603-669-2069. Jude Chauvette, Prin. Students 135.

St. Joseph Diocesan Regional Junior High Building. (Grades 7-8), 460 Pine St., 03104-6102. Tel: 603-624-4811; Fax: 603-624-6670. Sr. Barbara McLean, R.S.M., Prin. Sisters 1; Lay Teachers 18; Students 242.

West Side Catholic Regional School. (Grades K-6), 85 Third St., 03102. Tel: 603-669-3932. Sr. Maria Rosa, P.M., Prin. Sisters 2; Lay Teachers 6; Students 145.

BERLIN. *Berlin Regional Catholic School*, 140 Blanchard St., 03570. Tel: 603-752-7413. Sr. Cecile Provost, C.S.C., Prin. Lay Teachers 14; Students 138.

CLAREMONT. *St. Mary School*. (Grades K-8), 18 Central St., 03743. Tel: 603-542-6341. Richard Lizotte, Prin. Lay Teachers 10; Students 167.

CONCORD. *St. John Regional School*, 61 S. State St., 03301. Tel: 603-225-3222. Sr. Irene Turgeon, S.N.D., Prin. Sisters 2; Lay Teachers 8; Students 266.

DERRY. *St. Thomas Aquinas School*. (Grades K-8), 3 Moody St., 03038. Tel: 603-432-2712; Fax: 603-432-2179. Sr. Jacqueline Brodeur, C.S.C., Prin. Students 292.

DOVER. *St. Mary Academy*, 222 Central Ave., 03820. Tel: 603-742-3299. Sr. Monica Markey, R.S.M., Prin. Sisters 5; Lay Teachers 26; Students 503.

HAMPTON. *Sacred Heart School*. (Grades P-8), 289 Lafayette Rd., 03842. Tel: 603-926-3254. Sr. Mary Joan Walsh, O.L.L., Prin. Sisters 3; Lay Teachers 14; Students 310.

JAFFREY. *St. Patrick School*. (Grades K-8), 70 Main St., 03452. Tel: 603-532-7676. David L. O'Connell, Prin. Students 164.

KEENE. *St. Joseph School*. (Grades PreK-8), 92 Wilson St., 03431. Tel: 603-352-2720. Carolyn O'Connell, Prin. Lay Teachers 14; Total Staff 25; Students 221.

LACONIA. *Holy Trinity*, 50 Church St., 03246. Tel: 603-524-3156. Mr. Jack Fortier, Prin. Lay Teachers 15; Total Staff 19; Students 175.

NASHUA. *Holy Infant Jesus School*. (Grades PreK-6), 3 Crown St., 03060. Tel: 603-889-2649. Sr. Marie Henault, P.M., Prin. Sisters 3; Lay Teachers 22; Students 330.

Nashua Catholic Regional Junior High. (Grades 7-9), 6 Bartlett Ave., 03060. Tel: 603-883-6707; 882-7011. Mr. George R. LaVoice, Prin. Lay Teachers 21; Total Staff 27; Students 317.

St. Christopher School. (Grades K-6), 20 Cushing Ave., 03060. Tel: 603-882-7442. Sr. Joan Marie Messier, R.S.M., Prin. Students 349.

PELHAM. *St. Patrick School*. (Grades K-8), 16 Main St., 03076. Tel: 603-635-2941; 635-9800. Jane A. Gaskell, Prin. Students 188.

PORTSMOUTH. *St. Patrick*. (Grades PreK-8), 125 Austin St., 03801. Tel: 604-436-0739. Carol Davitt, Prin. Lay Teachers 14; Students 225.

ROCHESTER. *St. Elizabeth Seton School*. (Grades K-8), 16 Bridge St., 03867. Tel: 603-332-4803. Suzanne T. Boutin, Prin. Sisters 1; Lay Teachers 15; Students 302.

SALEM. *St. Joseph Regional School*. (Grades K-8), 40 Main St., 03079. Mr. James Cullen, Prin., Kindergarten. Rev. Richard Connors, Pastor. Lay Teachers 3; Students 87. Lay Teachers 16; Total Staff 31; Students 443.

WEST STEWARTSTOWN. *St. Albert School*. (Grades 1-8). P.O. Box 177, Beecher Falls, 05902. Tel: 603-246-8631. Sr. Lorraine Trottier, P.M., Prin. Sisters 3; Lay Teachers 2; Students 71.

[F] ELEMENTARY SCHOOLS, PRIVATE

MANCHESTER. *Holy Cross Kindergarten*, 357 Island Pond Rd., 03109-4811. Sr. Yvette M. Robert, C.S.C., Prin. & Admin. Sisters 3; Students 30.

St. Augustin Pre-School, 383 Beech St., 03103. Mrs. Mary Tremblay, Dir. Lay Teachers 21; Boys 21; Girls 27.

GOFFSTOWN. *Villa Augustina School*. (Grades K-8), 208 S. Mast St., 03045. Tel: 603-497-2361. Sr. Vivian Patenaude, R.J.M., Prin. Sisters 8; Lay Teachers 22; Students 322.

HUDSON. *Presentation of Mary Academy*. (Grades K-8), 182 Lowell Rd., 03051. Tel: 603-889-6054. Sisters of the Presentation of Mary. Sr. Rachel Morrisette, P.M., Prin. Sisters 2; Lay Teachers 8; Students 353.

[G] CATHOLIC CHARITIES

MANCHESTER. *Catholic Charities Administration*, 215 Myrtle St., 03104. Tel: 603-669-3030; Fax: 603-626-1252. Rev. Msgr. John P. Quinn, Diocesan Dir.; Mr. Robert L. Staniels, Dir. Admin. Svcs.; Mr. Raymond V. Mailloux, Dir. Nursing Home Svcs.; Mr. Robert P. Clohosey, Dir. Family Svcs.; Mr. Timothy Kelly, Dir. Immigration & Refugee Services; Mr. Richard J. Shannon, Dir. Parish Social Ministry; Mr. Denis J. Daigle, Assoc. Dir. Parish Social Ministry; Mrs. Sharon D. Cholette, Dir. Devel.; Dominique A. Rust, Accounting Mgr.; Mr. Robert P. Clohosey, Supvr. Adoption & Maternity Svcs. Total Staff 75; Total Assisted 35,000.

Consultation Services for Church Ministers, 282 Concord St., 03104. Tel: 603-668-0014. Dr. Michael A. Noonan; Sr. Patricia Schmidt, D.W.

New Hampshire Catholic Charities, Manchester District Office, 325 Franklin St., 03101. Tel: 603-624-4717. Joseph P. Naff, M.S.W., A.C.S.W., Supr.

New Hampshire Food Bank, 62 W. Brook St., 03101-1215. Tel: 603-669-9725. Albert J. Tremblay, Sr., Admin.

Office of Family Ministries, 215 Myrtle St., 03104. Jane M. Cosmo, Dir.

BERLIN. *NH Catholic Charities*, 153 Grafton St., 03570. Tel: 603-752-1325.

CONCORD. *NH Catholic Charities*. Parish Social Ministries. Branch Office, 176 Loudon Rd., 03301. Tel: 603-228-1108. Sr. Rosemary Crowley, S.N.D.

KEENE. *NH Catholic Charities*, Monadnock Regional Office, 22 Middle St., 03431. Tel: 603-357-3093. April Geer Fitzgerald, M.S.W., J.D.

LACONIA. *NH Catholic Charities*, Lakes Region Branch Office, 17 Gilford Ave., 03246. Tel: 603-528-3035. Janet O'Connell, A.C.S.W., Counseling Supvr.; Kay E. Smalley, Parish Social Ministry Coord.

LEBANON. *NH Catholic Charities*, Branch Office, 24 Hanover St., # 11, 03766-1334. Tel: 603-448-5151. Marc S. Cousineau, Dir.

LITTLETON. *NH Catholic Charities*, Regional Office, 16 Cottage St., P.O. Box 323, 03561. Tel: 603-444-7727. Anthony F. Poekert, M.S., Coord., Parish Social Min.; Janet O'Connell, A.C.S.W., Counselor (Part Time).

NASHUA. *NH Catholic Charities*, Nashua Regional Office, 261 Lake St., 03060. Tel: 603-889-9431. Mary A. Kenison, Supr.

ROCHESTER. *NH Catholic Charities*, Seacoast Regional Office, 23 Grant St., 03867. Tel: 603-332-7701. Joseph P. Naff, M.S.W., Supr.

SALEM. *NH Catholic Charities*, Branch Office, 130 Main St., Ste. 204, 03079. Tel: 603-893-1971. Mary A. Kenison, Supr.

[H] CHILD CARE INSTITUTIONS

MANCHESTER. *St. Peter's Home*, 03102-3093. Tel: 603-625-9313; Fax: 603-625-1910.
For a complete listing, refer to the Special Care Facilities section.

ALLENSTOWN. *Pine Haven Boys Center*, River Rd., P.O. Suncook, 03275.
For a complete listing, refer to the Special Care Facilities section.

ROCHESTER. *St. Charles Children's Home*, 19 Grant St., 03867.
For a complete listing, refer to the Special Care Facilities section.

[I] GENERAL HOSPITALS

MANCHESTER. *Catholic Medical Center of Manchester, NH, Inc.*, 100 McGregor St., 03102. Tel: 603-668-3545.
For a complete listing, refer to the Hospitals section.

NASHUA. *St. Joseph Hospital*, 172 Kinsley St., 03061. Tel: 603-882-3000.
For a complete listing, refer to the Hospitals section.

[J] HOMES FOR THE AGED

MANCHESTER. *Carpenter Center, Inc.*, 323 Franklin St., 03101.
For a complete listing, refer to the Special Care Facilities section.

Frances Warde House, Inc., 435 Union St., 03103.
For a complete listing, refer to the Special Care Facilities section.

Mt. Carmel Nursing Home, 235 Myrtle St., 03104. Tel: 603-627-3811.
For a complete listing, refer to the Special Care Facilities section.

St. Teresas Manor & Bishop Primeau Apartments, 519 Bridge St., 03104. Tel: 603-668-2373.
For a complete listing, refer to the Special Care Facilities section.

BERLIN. *St. Vincent de Paul Nursing Home*, 29 Providence Ave., 03570. Tel: 603-752-1820.
For a complete listing, refer to the Special Care Facilities section.

DOVER. *St. Ann*, 03820. Tel: 603-742-2612; Fax: 603-743-3055.
For a complete listing, refer to the Special Care Facilities section.

JAFFREY. *Good Shepherd Nursing Home*, 20 Plantation Dr., 03452. Tel: 603-532-8762.
For a complete listing, refer to the Special Care Facilities section.

LACONIA. *Bishop Bradley Apartments*, 406 Court St., 03246.
For a complete listing, refer to the Special Care Facilities section.

St. Francis Home for the Aged, 03246. Tel: 603-524-0466; Fax: 603-527-0884.
For a complete listing, refer to the Special Care Facilities section.

NASHUA. *Marguerite's Place*, 120 Main St., Room 110, 03060. Tel: 603-598-1582.
For a complete listing, refer to the Special Care Facilities section.

WINDHAM. *Warde Health Center*, 21 Searles Rd., 03087 Fax: 603-890-1293.
For a complete listing, refer to the Special Care Facilities section.

[K] MONASTERIES AND RESIDENCES OF PRIESTS AND BROTHERS

MANCHESTER. *St. Anselm Abbey*. of the Order of St. Benedict and St. Anselm College, including Seminary and Formation Program. 100 St. Anselm Dr., 03102-1310. Tel: 603-641-7000; Fax: 603-641-7116. Rt. Revs. Matthew K. Leavy, O.S.B., Abbot and Chancellor; Gerald McCarthy, O.S.B., Resigned Abbot; Very Revs. John R. Fortin, O.S.B., Prior; Peter J. Guerin, O.S.B., Subprior; Revs. Aquinas F. Cafarelli, O.S.B.; Bede G. Camera, O.S.B.; James G. Cassidy, O.S.B.; Ralph G. Cinque, O.S.B.; Richard F. Clavelle, O.S.B.; Mark A. Cooper, O.S.B.; David W. Cotter, O.S.B.; Michael H. Custer, O.S.B.; Jerome J. Day, O.S.B.; Jonathan P. DeFelice, O.S.B.; Daniel G. Dempski, O.S.B.; Cecil J. Donahue, O.S.B.; Brendan P. Donnelly, O.S.B.; Gerard J. Donnelly, O.S.B.; Mathias D. Durette, O.S.B.; Jude J. Gray, O.S.B.; Benedict M. Guevin, O.S.B.; Bernard G. Holmes, O.S.B.; Augustine G. Kelly, O.S.B.; Iain G. MacLellan, O.S.B.; Simon J. O'Donnell, O.S.B.; Finbar P. O'Mahoney, O.S.B.; Benet C. Phillips, O.S.B.; Placidus H. Riley, O.S.B.; Lawrence Schlegel, O.S.B.; Christopher L. Senk, O.S.B.; Patrick M. Sullivan, O.S.B.; Thaddeus W. Ustaszewski, O.S.B. Priests 32; Brothers 6; Novices 2; Joan of Arc Sisters 12; Benedictine Nuns 2.

COLEBROOK. *Shrine of Our Lady of Grace*, 03576. Tel: 603-237-5511. Oblates of Mary Immaculate (Northern U.S. Province). Revs. Roland St. Pierre, O.M.I., Supr.; Myles Cyr, O.M.I.; Roland M. Hamel, O.M.I.; Charles Moreau, O.M.I.; Robert M. Paradis, O.M.I.; Bros. Onil Lauziere, O.M.I.; Joseph Gagne, O.M.I.; Maurice Violette, O.M.I. Priests 5; Brothers 3.

ENFIELD. *Shrine of Our Lady of La Salette*, P.O. Box 420, 03748. Tel: 603-632-4301 (Gift Shop); 632-7087 (Business). Revs. Dennis J. Loomis, M.S., Supr.; Roland S. Nadeau, M.S., Chap.; James Nunes, M.S., Dir. of Pilgrimages; Roger J. Plante, M.S.; Bros. Marc Gelinas, M.S.; Emile Morin, M.S.; Robert Roy, M.S.; Roger St. Germain, M.S.; Jean-Paul Champagne, M.S.; Deacon David Carignan, M.S. Priests 4; Brothers 5; Deacons 1; Total Staff 12.

HUDSON. *Missionary Oblates of Mary Immaculate*, 61 Burns Hill Rd., 03051-4423. Tel: 603-883-3233; Fax: 603-883-6089. Provincial House of the Northern U.S. Province. Very Rev. George G. Capen, O.M.I., Prov.; Revs. Charles Breault, O.M.I., Prov. Treas.; Adhemar Deveau, O.M.I.; Joseph Juaire, O.M.I., (Retired); Real Bourque, O.M.I.; Wilfred Harvey, O.M.I.; George Brown, O.M.I.; Bevil Bramwell, O.M.I.; Norman Comtois, O.M.I.; Joseph Horton, O.M.I.; Bro. Andrew Sensenig, O.M.I. Priests 81; Brothers 11; Total Staff 2; Serving abroad 6; Total in Residence 3; Total Membership 92.

NASHUA. *Brothers of the Sacred Heart*, 28 Berkeley St., 03060. Tel: 603-595-2712. Bro. Roland Champagne, S.C., Dir. Brothers 6. 194 Lund Rd., 03060. Tel: 603-883-3683. Bro. Donald Tardif, S.C., Dir. Brothers 13.

[L] CONVENTS AND RESIDENCES OF SISTERS

MANCHESTER. *Bishop's House*, 661 N. River Rd., 03104. Little Sisters of the Holy Family. Sr. Gabrielle Paille, P.S.S.F., Supr. Sisters 4.

Cathedral Rectory, 145 Lowell St., 03101-6135. Little Sisters of the Holy Family in charge of domestic department. Sr. Theresa Guillemette, P.S.S.F., Supr. Sisters 5.

Monastery of the Precious Blood, 700 Bridge St., 03104. Tel: 603-623-4264. Sisters Adorers of the Precious Blood. Sr. Mary Clare, Supr.; Rev. Msgr. Albert W. Olkovikas, Chap. Sisters 29; Novices 2.

Regional Office of the Sisters of Holy Cross, 377 Island Pond Rd., 03109; Fax: 603-622-9782. Sr. Lucille Cantin, C.S.C., Regional Rep. Total Staff 7.

St. Catherine Convent, 539 N. River Rd., 03104. Sisters of the Holy Cross 2.

St. George Manor, 357 Island Pond Rd., 03109. Tel: 603-624-4557. Sr. Lorraine Paille, C.S.C., Supr.; Rev. Andre J. Gagnon, Chap. (Non-residential). Sisters 82.

Sisters of Holy Cross, 133 Ashland St., 03104. Sisters 4.

Sisters of Holy Cross, 2298 Elm St., 03104. Sr. Kilda Roy, C.S.C., Supr. Sisters 5.

Sisters of Holy Cross, 969 Chestnut St., 03104. Sisters 5. 971 Chestnut St., 03104. Sisters 4.

Sisters of Holy Cross, 2264 Elm St., 03104. Sisters 2.

Sisters of Holy Cross, 454 Island Pond Rd., 03109-4812. Sisters 3.

Sisters of Holy Cross, 136 Lynwood Ln., 03109. Sr. Louise Audette, C.S.C., Supr. Sisters 4.

Sisters of Holy Cross. Queen of Angels Convent, 113 Wedgewood Ln., 03109-4825. Sisters 4.

Sisters of the Presentation of Mary Provincial House, 495 Mammoth Rd., 03104-5494. Tel: 603-669-1080; Fax: 603-622-4953. Sr. Mariette Plante, P.M., Prov. Supr. Sisters in the Diocese 220; Sisters of the Presentation of Mary 243. St. Joseph Residence, 495 Mammoth Rd., 03104-5494. Tel: 603-627-5831. St. Marie Residence, 495 Mammoth Rd., 03104-5494. Tel: 603-623-0671. Bethany House, 25 Garmon St., 03104. Tel: 603-625-1957. St. Marie Convent, 133 Wayne St., 03102. Tel: 603-623-0815. St. Bernard Convent, 161 Main St., Keene, 03431. Tel: 603-357-4472. Rivier College/Florence Hall, 429 Main St., Nashua, 03060. Tel: 603-888-1311, Ext. 8291. Presentation of Mary Academy, 182 Lowell Rd., Hudson, 03051-4987. Tel: 603-883-8192; 883-8054; Fax: 603-889-6362. Presentation of Mary Novitiate, 180 Lowell Rd., Hudson, 03051-4987. Tel: 603-880-8186; Fax: 603-880-0298. Trinity House, 186 Lowell Rd., Hudson, 03051-4908. Tel: 603-882-1347. Presentation of Mary Convent, 58 Church St., Berlin, 03570. Tel: 603-752-1176. St. Albert Covent, P.O. Box 177, Beecher Fall, VT, 05902. Tel: 603-246-3388. Our Lady of Hope House of Prayer, 400 Temple Rd., New Ipswich, 03071. Tel: 603-878-2346. Rivier College/Marywood-Gracewood, 4 Oldfield Rd., Nashua, 03060. Tel: 603-891-5737; 888-3668. Rivier College/Molloy Hall, 429 Main St., Nashua, 03060. Tel: 603-888-1311, Ext. 8294. Rivier College/St. Joseph Hall, 429 Main St., Nashua, 03060. Tel: 603-888-1311, Ext. 8299. Rivier College/Presentation Hall, 429 Main St., Nashua, 03060. Tel: 603-888-1311, Ext. 8296. Holy Angels Convent, 6 Atkinson Depot Rd., Rte 121, Plaistow, 03865. Tel: 603-382-2744.

BEDFORD. *Regina Pacis, Benedictine Srs.*, 333 Wallace Rd., 03102-1808. Tel: 603-472-3239. Benedictine Sisters. Sr. M. Raphaela, O.S.B., Supr. Nursery School. Sisters 4.

CONCORD. *Monastery of Discalced Carmelites*, 275 Pleasant St., 03301-2590. Tel: 603-225-5791. Sr. Thomas Aquinas, O.C.D., Prioress. Professed Sisters 11.

GOFFSTOWN. *Villa Augustina Convent*, 03045. Tel: 603-497-3636; 603-497-3445. Sr. Claire Lebreux, R.J.M., Supr. Religious of Jesus and Mary 24.

LITTLETON. *Provincial House of Daughters of the Charity of the Sacred Heart of Jesus*, Mount Sacred Heart, Grove St., P.O. Box 642, 03561. Tel: 603-444-5346; Fax: 603-444-5348. Local Superiors: Sr. Lucille Grandpre; Sr. Yvette Beloin; Sr. Rosina Bechard, Prov. Supr.; Rev. Roger M. Leroux, M.S., Chap. Sisters 38.

LONDONDERRY. *Sisters of Holy Cross*, Londonderry House, 68 Mammoth Rd., 03053.

NEW IPSWICH. *Our Lady of Hope, House of Prayer*, 400 Temple Rd., 03071. Tel: 603-878-2346. Sr. Jeannette Levasseur, Supr. & Dir. Sisters 6.

PITTSFIELD. *Berakah*. A Place for Blessing, 96 Fairview Rd., 03263-3817. Rev. John Burchill, O.P. Sisters 6.

PORTSMOUTH. *Our Lady of Lourdes Convent*, 11 Fairview Dr., 03801. Tel: 603-436-6612. Sisters of Our Lady of Lourdes (O.L.L.). Sr. Mary Joan Walsh, O.L.L., Supr. Sisters 3.

WEST FRANKLIN. *Our Lady of the Sacred Heart Convent*, 21 Holy Cross Rd., 03235. Sr. Louise M. Tarpey, C.S.C., Supr.; Rev. Anthony DiGiulio, Chap. Sisters 27.

Sisters of Holy Cross, 21 Holy Cross Rd., 03235. Sr. Louise M. Tarpey, C.S.C., Supr. Sisters 27.

WINDHAM. *Sisters of Mercy of the Americas*. Motherhouse of the Sisters of Mercy, Inc., Regional Community of New Hampshire, 21 Searles Rd., 03087. Tel: 603-893-6550 (Admin. Office). Sisters of Mercy of New Hampshire. Sr. Patricia Sullivan, Reg. Community Pres.; Sr. Barbara Joan St. Jean, Coord. Sisters 46.

Mount Saint Mary Corporation of the Sisters of Mercy, Nashua.

Manchester Convent of the Sisters of Mercy, Manchester.

Warde Health Center.

[M] RETREAT HOUSES

MANCHESTER. *Emmaus House*, 286 Concord St., 03104. Tel: 603-624-1173. Sr. Bernadette Turgeon, S.N.D-.deN., Dir.; Matthew Goody, Assoc. Dir. Total Staff 15.

ENFIELD. *La Salette Shrine and Center of Enfield*, Box 420, 03748. Tel: 603-632-7087 (Business); 632-4301 (Gift Shop). Revs. Dennis J. Loomis, M.S., Supr.; Roland S. Nadeau, M.S.; James Nunes, M.S., Shrine Dir.; Roger J. Plante, M.S. Priests 4; Deacons 1; Brothers 5; Total Staff 12.

HUDSON. *Oblates of Mary Immaculate Retreat House*, 200 Lowell Rd., 03051-4934. Tel: 603-882-8141. Revs. Roger Couture, O.M.I., Supr.; Thomas Horan, O.M.I.; Ulric Turcotte, O.M.I.; Gerard Roux, O.M.I. Priests 4.

NEW BOSTON. *Epiphany Monastery*, 96 Scobie Rd., Box 60, 03070. Tel: 603-487-3020; Fax: 603-487-3700. Rev. Romuald Duscher, O.S.B.Cam.; Bros. Jonah Kepfield, O.S.B.Cam.; Zacchaeus Naegele, O.S.B-.Cam. Total Staff 3; Total in Residence 3.

PETERBOROUGH. *The Common-St. Joseph Monastery*, 03458. Tel: 603-924-6060. Discalced Carmelites. Revs. Bruno Cocuzzi, O.C.D., Acting Supr.; Terrence Dougherty, O.C.D.; Bro. Sebastian Reale, O.C.D. Priests 2; Brothers 1.

[N] CAMPUS MINISTRY AND NEWMAN CENTERS

DURHAM. *Campus Ministries*, 6 Madbury Rd., P.O. Box 620, 03824-0620. Tel: 603-862-1310; Fax: 603-868-3765. Rev. Frederick Pennett, Dir., Aquinas House, P.O. Box 147, Hanover, 03755. Tel: 603-643-2154. Revs. Raynold J. Thibodeau; John McHugh, O.F.M.Cap., P.O. Box 557, Henniker, 03242. Tel: 603-428-3325. Rev. Andre M. Thibodeau, 2321 Elm St., Manchester, 03104. Tel: 603-669-4298, Ext. 100. Sr. Kathleen McInnis, R.S.M., 2500 N. River Rd., Manchester, 03104. Tel: 603-668-2211, Ext. 2139. Rev. Bruce Collard, 100 St. Anselm Dr., Manchester, 03102. Tel: 603-641-7130. Revs. Cecil J. Donahue, O.S.B.; Benet C. Phillips, O.S.B., Rivier College, 420 S. Main St., Nashua, 03060. Tel: 603-888-1311, Ext. 8577. Sr. Jacqueline LeBlanc, P.M.; Bro. Paul Demers, S.C. Tel: 603-888-1311 Ext. 8537, Box 200, New London, 03257. Tel: 603-526-2010. Rev. Richard T. Lower, 46 Langdon St., Plymouth, 03264. Tel: 603-535-2673. Sr. Helene Higgins, C.S.J., Catholic Student Center, P.O. Box 620, 03824. Tel: 603-862-1310. Rev. Frederick J. Pennett.

St. Thomas More Catholic Student Center at the University of New Hampshire, 6 Madbury Rd., P.O. Box 620, 03824-0620. Tel: 603-862-1310; Fax: 603-868-3765. Rev. Frederick J. Pennett, Chap; Ms. Jane C. Hall, Assoc. Chap.

HANOVER. *The Catholic Student Center at Dartmouth*,

Aquinas House, Aquinas at Dartmouth, Inc., Occom Ridge & Webster Ave., P.O. Box 147, 03755. Tel: 603-643-2154. Revs. John P. McHugh, O.F.M.Cap., Dir.; Raynold P. Thibodeau, O.F.M.Cap., Assoc. Chap.; Anna Mae Mayer, Assoc. Chap. Total Staff 4; Total in Residence 2.

HENNIKER. *New England College Newman Center*, St. Theresa Rectory, 03242. Tel: 603-428-3325. Rev. Andre M. Thibodeau, Chap.

KEENE. *Keene State College, Catholic Newman Center*, 232 Main St., P.O. Box 491, 03431. Tel: 603-352-7785; 358-2100.

NEW LONDON. *Colby-Sawyer College Newman Center*, Our Lady of Fatima Rectory, 03257. Tel: 603-526-4484. Rev. Richard T. Lower, Chap.

PLYMOUTH. *Plymouth State College Campus Ministry*, St. Matthew Rectory, 46 Langdon St., 03264. Tel: 603-536-4700. Sr. Helene Higgins, C.S.J., Catholic Campus Minister. Tel: 603-535-2673; Rev. Robert F. Cole, Chap.

RINDGE. *Franklin Pierce College Newman Center*, Keene State College, 232 Main St., P.O. Box 491, 03431. Tel: 603-352-7785. Mary Ann Damato, Chap.

[O] MISCELLANEOUS

MANCHESTER. *Diocesan Museum*, 140 Laurel St., 03103. Tel: 603-624-1729; 623-8196. Judith Fosher, Coord.

Holy Cross Health Center, Inc., 357 Island Pond Rd., 03109-4811. Tel: 603-628-3550. Sr. Judith Langevin, C.S.C., N.H.A., Admin.

Sophia Institute Press, P.O. Box 5284, 03108. Tel: 603-641-9344; Fax: 603-641-8108. John L. Barger, Publisher.

CENTER HARBOR. *L.C. Center Harbor, Inc.*, Plymouth St., 03226.

GILFORD. *The Missionary Servants of Pope John Paul I*, 22 Boyd Hill Rd., 03246. Tel: 603-524-4740. The Missionary Servants of Pope John Paul I is a lay missionary association founded to aid established missionaries. Help is mainly given to Mother Teresa's missions in Haiti; however, shipments have also been made to Honduras, the Sudan, British Columbia, areas of the U.S. and to the local poor.

[P] SPECIAL APOSTOLATE CENTERS

BERLIN. *Christian Life Center*, Emery St., P.O. Box 354, 03570. Tel: 603-752-7883. Mrs. Judy J. Rheaume, Coord.

DURHAM. *Christian Life Center*, 6 Madbury Rd., P.O. Box 471, 03824. Tel: 603-868-5514. Sr. Claudette Carisse, S.A.S.V., Dir.

KEENE. *Christian Life Center*, 70 Island St., P.O. Box 293, 03431. Tel: 603-352-7662.

LACONIA. *Christian Life Center*, Box 306, 03247. Tel: 603-524-7503. Janet Leroux, Coord.

NASHUA. *Nashua Deanery Toward Marriage Program*, P.O. Box 3403, 03061-3403. Tel: 603-889-0707.

SALEM. *Christian Life Center*, P.O. Box 314, 03079. Tel: 603-893-5878. Paul J. Donovan, Dir.

[Q] CAMPS AND COMMUNITY CENTERS

CENTER OSSIPEE. *Camp Marist*, Rte. 25 E., 03814. Tel: 603-539-4552; Fax: 603-539-8318 (Summer Address). St. Mary's High School, 51 Clapham Ave., Manhasset, NY, 11030. Tel: 516-627-2711; Fax: 516-627-3209 (Winter Address). Bro. Ken Ward, F.M.S., Dir. Total Staff 90; Total Assisted 300.

GILMANTON IRON WORKS. *Camp Bernadette*. (Girls), Business Office, P.O. Box 206, 03837-0206. Business Office, P.O. Box 206, Wolfeboro, 03837-0206. Mr. Gus Planchet, Dir. Total Staff 80; Total Assisted 800.

Camp Fatima. (Boys), Business Office, P.O. Box 206, 03837-0206. Mr. Gus Planchet, Dir. Total Staff 80; Total Assisted 800.

RELIGIOUS INSTITUTES OF MEN REPRESENTED IN THE DIOCESE

For further details refer to the corresponding bracketed number in the Religious Institutes of Men or Women section.

[0140]—*The Augustinians*.—O.S.A.
[0190]—*Basilian Salvatorian Fathers*.—B.S.O.
[0200]—*Benedictine Monks*. (American Cassinese & Camaldolese Benedictine Congregations).—O.S.B.
[1350]—*Brothers of St. Francis Xavier*.—C.F.X.
[1100]—*Brothers of the Sacred Heart*. (New England Prov.).—S.C.
[0470]—*The Capuchin Friars*. (Prov. of St. Mary).—O.F.M.Cap.
[1320]—*Clerics of St. Viator*.—C.S.V.
[1330]—*Congregation of the Mission*. (New England Prov.).—C.M.
[1000]—*Congregation of the Passion*.—C.P.
[0260]—*Discalced Carmelite Fathers*. (Prov. of Immaculate Heart of Mary).—O.C.D.
[0520]—*Franciscan Friars*. (Prov. of Most Holy Name).—O.F.M.
[0520]—*Franciscan Friars*. (Province of the Immaculate Conception).—O.F.M.
[0690]—*Jesuit Fathers and Brothers*. (Maryland & New England Provinces).—S.J.
[0730]—*Legionaries of Christ*.—L.C.
[0770]—*The Marist Brothers*.—F.M.S.
[0720]—*The Missionaries of Our Lady of La Salette*. (Immaculate Heart of Mary & Our Lady of Seven Dolors Provinces).—M.S.
[0910]—*Oblates of Mary Immaculate*. (Prov. of St. John the Baptist).—O.M.I.
[0920]—*Oblates of St. Francis de Sales*.—O.S.F.S.
[0430]—*Order of Preachers (Dominicans)*.—O.P.
[0610]—*Priests of the Congregation of Holy Cross*.—C.S.C.
[0760]—*Society of Mary (Marianists)*.—S.M.
[1250]—*Somascan Fathers*.—C.R.S.

RELIGIOUS INSTITUTES OF WOMEN REPRESENTED IN THE DIOCESE

[0200]—*Benedictine Sisters*.—O.S.B.
[0230]—*Benedictine Sisters of Pontifical Jurisdiction*. (from Kaunas, Lithuania).—O.S.B.
[0330]—*Carmelite Sisters for the Aged and Infirm*.—O.Carm.
[2410]—*Congregation of the Marianites of Holy Cross*.—M.S.C.
[3815]—*Congregation of the Sisters of St. Joan of Arc*.—S.J.A.
[0750]—*Daughters of the Charity of the Sacred Heart of Jesus*.—F.C.S.C.J.
[0960]—*Daughters of Wisdom*.—D.W.
[0420]—*Discalced Carmelites Nuns*.—O.C.D.
[1110]—*Dominican Sisters of Our Lady of the Rosary and of Saint Catherine of Siena, Cabra*.—O.P.
[1170]—*Felician Sisters*.—C.S.S.F.
[1190]—*Franciscan Sisters of the Atonement*.—S.A.
[2575]—*Institute of the Sisters of Mercy of the Americas*. (Manchester, NH).—R.S.M.
[2320]—*The Little Sisters of the Holy Family*.—P.S.S.F.
[2420]—*Marist Missionary Sisters*.—S.M.S.M.
[2470]—*Maryknoll Sisters of St. Dominic*.—M.M.
[3450]—*Religious of Jesus and Mary*.—R.J.M.
[3465]—*Religious of the Sacred Heart of Mary*.—R.S.H.M.
[2970]—*School Sisters of Notre Dame*.—S.S.N.D.
[1680]—*School Sisters of St. Francis*.—O.S.F.
[3650]—*Servants of Our Lady, Queen of Clergy*.—S.R.C.
[0110]—*The Sisters Adorers of the Precious Blood*.—A.P.B.
[0490]—*Sisters of Charity of Montreal (Grey Nuns)*.—S.G.M.
[0530]—*Sisters of Charity of Our Lady, Mother of the Church*.—S.C.M.C.
[0610]—*Sisters of Charity of St. Hyacinthe (Grey Nuns)*.—S.C.S.H.
[0640]—*Sisters of Charity of St. Vincent De Paul, Halifax*.—S.C.
[1930]—*Sisters of Holy Cross*.—C.S.C.
[3000]—*Sisters of Notre Dame de Namur*.—S.N.D.deN.
[3080]—*Sisters of Our Lady of Christian Doctrine*.—R.C.D.
[]—*Sisters of Our Lady of Lourdes*.—O.L.L.
[3350]—*Sisters of Providence*. (Montreal).—S.P.
[3360]—*Sisters of Providence of Saint Mary-of-the-Woods, IN*.—S.P.
[3718]—*Sisters of St. Ann*.—S.S.A.
[3840]—*Sisters of St. Joseph of Carondelet*. (Prov. of Albany).—C.S.J.
[3850]—*Sisters of St. Joseph of Chambery*.—C.S.J.
[0150]—*Sisters of the Assumption*.—S.A.S.V.
[1990]—*Sisters of the Holy Names of Jesus and Mary*.—S.N.J.M.
[3310]—*Sisters of the Presentation of Mary*.—P.M.
[3320]—*Sisters of the Presentation of the B.V.M.*—P.B.V.M.
[4060]—*Society of the Holy Child Jesus*.—S.H.C.J.

NECROLOGY

† Bordenave, Marius F., (Retired). —Died Jan. 4, 1996.
† Fournier, Roger F., (On Leave of Absence). —Died Nov. 10, 1995.

Diocese of Marquette

(Dioecesis Marquettensis)

Most Reverend

JAMES H. GARLAND, M.A., M.S.W., D.D.

Bishop of Marquette; ordained 1959; appointed Titular Bishop of Garriana and Auxiliary Bishop of Cincinnati June 2, 1984; consecrated July 25, 1984; appointed Bishop of Marquette October 6, 1992; installed November 11, 1992. *Res., 300 Rock St., P.O. Box 550, Marquette, MI, 49855.* Tel.: 906-225-1141.

Most Reverend

MARK F. SCHMITT, D.D.

Retired Bishop of Marquette; ordained May 22, 1948; appointed Titular Bishop of Kells and Auxiliary of Green Bay May 5, 1970; consecrated June 24, 1970; appointed to Marquette March 21, 1978; installed May 8, 1978; retired November 11, 1992. *Res., HCO1 Box 159, Marquette, MI, 49855.*

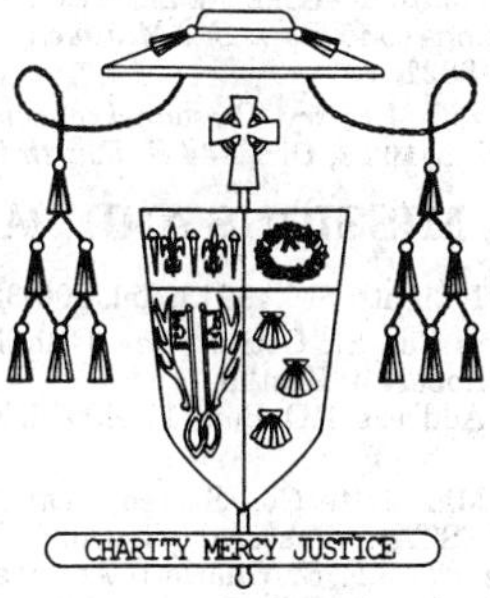

VICARIATE-APOSTOLIC JULY 29, 1853; DIOCESE 1857.

Square Miles 16,281.

Comprises the Upper Peninsula of the State of Michigan.

For legal titles of parishes and diocesan institutions, consult the Pastoral Office.

Pastoral Office: 444 S. Fourth St., P.O. Box 550, Marquette, MI, 49855. Tel.: 906-225-1141; Fax: 906-225-0437.

E-mail address: asample@mail.portup.com

STATISTICAL OVERVIEW

Personnel	
Bishop	1
Retired Bishops	1
Priests: Diocesan Active in Diocese	64
Priests: Active Outside Diocese	4
Priests: Retired, Sick or Absent	42
Number of Diocesan Priests	110
Religious Priests in Diocese	6
Extern Priests in Diocese	3
Ordinations:	
Diocesan Priests	1
Permanent Deacons	2
Permanent Deacons in Diocese	17
Total Sisters	72
Parishes	
Parishes	75
With Resident Pastor:	
Resident Diocesan Priests	62
Resident Religious Priests	5
Without Resident Pastor:	
Administered by Priests	4
Administered by Women Religious	4
Missions	25
Closed Parishes	2
Professional Ministry Personnel:	
Sisters	26
Lay Ministers	24
Welfare	
Catholic Hospitals	1
Total Assisted	63,603
Homes for the Aged	1
Total Assisted	123
Special Centers for Social Services	6
Total Assisted	1,311
Educational	
Diocesan Students in Other Seminaries	9
Total Seminarians	9
Elementary Schools, Diocesan and Parish	10
Total Students	1,802
Catechesis/Religious Education:	
High School Students	3,327
Elementary Students	6,792
Total Students Under Catholic Instruction	11,930
Teachers in the Diocese:	
Sisters	11
Lay Teachers	117
Vital Statistics	
Receptions into the Church:	
Infant Baptism Totals	1,209
Adult Baptism Totals	64
Received into Full Communion	130
First Communions	1,159
Confirmations	927
Marriages:	
Catholic	320
Interfaith	226
Total Marriages	546
Deaths	1,222
Total Catholic Population	74,066
Total Population	318,705

Former Bishops—Rt. Rev. FREDERIC BARAGA, D.D., first Bishop; cons. Nov. 1, 1853; died Jan. 19, 1868.—Rt. Rev. IGNATIUS MRAK, D.D., cons. Feb. 7, 1869; resigned 1878; transferred to Antinoe 1879; died Jan. 2, 1901.—Rt. Rev. JOHN VERTIN, D.D., cons. Sept. 14, 1879; died Feb. 26, 1899.—Rt. Rev. FREDERICK EIS, D.D., cons. Aug. 24, 1899 made Asst. at the Pontifical Throne July 13, 1922; resigned July 8, 1922; appt. Titular Bishop of Bita; died May 5, 1926.—Most Rev. PAUL JOSEPH NUSSBAUM, D.D., cons. Bishop of Corpus Christi May 20, 1913; resigned March 26, 1920; appt. Bishop of Marquette Nov. 14, 1922; died June 24, 1935.—Most Rev. JOSEPH CASIMIR PLAGENS, D.D., LL.D., cons. Sept. 30, 1924, Auxiliary Bishop of Detroit Titular Bishop of Rhodiopolis; appt. to See of Marquette Nov. 16, 1935; transferred to the See of Grand Rapids Dec. 16, 1940; died March 31, 1943.—Most Rev. FRANCIS J. MAGNER, D.D., appt. Dec. 21, 1940; cons. Feb. 24, 1941; died June 13, 1947.—Most Rev. THOMAS L. NOA, D.D., cons. March 19, 1946; Titular Bishop of Salona and Coadjutor Bishop of Sioux City; appt. Bishop of Marquette Aug. 20, 1947; retired March 25, 1968; died March 13, 1977.—Most Rev. CHARLES A. SALATKA, D.D., appt. Titular Bishop of Cariana and Auxiliary of Grand Rapids Dec. 9, 1961; cons. March 6, 1962; appt. Bishop of Marquette Jan. 10, 1968; installed March 25, 1968; appt. Archbishop of Oklahoma City Oct. 11, 1977.—Most Rev. MARK F. SCHMITT, D.D., appt. Titular Bishop of Kells and Auxiliary of Green Bay May 5, 1970; cons. June 24, 1970; appt. Bishop of Marquette March 21, 1978; installed May 8, 1978; retired November 11, 1992.

Pastoral Office—444 S. Fourth St., P.O. Box 550, Marquette, 49855. Tel: 906-225-1141; Fax: 906-225-0437. Office Hours: Mon.-Fri. 9-5.

Vicar General—Very Rev. PETER OBERTO, V.G., J.C.L.

Chancellor—Rev. ALEXANDER K. SAMPLE, J.C.L.

Director For Women Religious—Sr. COLLEEN SWEETING, O.S.F.

Director of Administration & Finance—RICHARD R. SCHAEFER, C.P.A.

Bookkeeper-Accountant—CAROL J. PARKER.

Diocesan Tribunal—444 S. Fourth St., P.O. Box 550, Marquette, 49855. Tel: 906-225-1141.

Judicial Vicar—Very Rev. PETER OBERTO, V.G., J.C.L.

Diocesan Judges—Revs. ALEXANDER K. SAMPLE, J.C.L.; JOSEPH NAGAROOR, J.C.D.

Defensor Vinculi—Rev. JOHN J. SHIVERSKI.

Notary—MARY C. JESKE.

Episcopal Vicars—West Region: Rev. NORMAN A. CLISCH; Central Region: Rev. RICK L. COURIER; East Region: Vacant.

Priests' Council—

Executive Board—Revs. MICHAEL J. STEBER, Chm. NORMAN A. CLISCH, Vice Chm. WILLIAM P. CALLARI, Treas. GREGORY R. HEIKKALA, Sec.

Deans—Marquette: Rev. VINCENT L. OUELLETTE, Escanaba: Rev. CHRISTOPHER B. GARDINER, Houghton: Rev. THOMAS L. POISSON, Iron Mountain: Rev. JOSEPH O. GOUIN, Ironwood: Rev. ALLAN J. MAYOTTE, Menominee: Rev. RICK L. COURIER, Sault Ste. Marie: Rev. THEODORE J. BRODEUR, Iron River: Rev. NORMAN A. CLISCH, Manistique: Rev. TIMOTHY H. DESROCHERS.

Consultors—Revs. RICK L. COURIER; JOHN SHIVERSKI; Very Rev. PETER OBERTO; Revs. GEORGE GUSTAFSON; WAYNE E. MARCOTTE; JOHN E. PATRICK.

Diocesan Offices and Directors

Apostleship of the Sea—Rev. TED BRODEUR, Chap., *Holy Name of Mary Parish, 377 Maple St., Sault Ste. Marie, 49783.* Tel: 906-632-3381.

Bishop Baraga Association Inc.—615 S. Fourth St., P.O. Box 550, Marquette, 49855. Tel: 906-226-7024. An international organization to promote the Cause of the Beatification of the Most Rev. Frederic Baraga.

Revs. ALEX K. SAMPLE, Exec. Dir., Treas., and Vice-Postulator; BRUNO KOROSAK, O.F.M., Postulator; REGIS M. WALLING, Archivist; ELIZABETH J. DELENE, Archivist.

Building Commission, Diocese of Marquette—RICHARD R. SCHAEFER, Sec., *P.O. Box 550, Marquette, 49855.* Tel: 906-225-1141.

Director of Catholic Social Services—STEPHEN J. LYNOTT, M.S.W., *347 Rock St., Marquette, 49855.* Tel: 906-228-8630. Branch Offices: Houghton, Escanaba, Iron Mountain, Sault Ste. Marie, Ironwood.

Catholic Relief Services—Rev. Msgr. DAVID SPELGATTI, Dir., *P.O. Box 550, Marquette, 49855.*

Cemeteries—RICHARD R. SCHAEFER, Bishop's Rep. for Catholic Cemeteries, *444 S. Fourth St., Marquette, 49855.* Tel: 906-225-1141.

Charismatic Prayer Groups—Rev. RAYMOND J. ZEUGNER, Diocesan Liaison, *Precious Blood Parish, Stephenson, 49887.* Tel: 906-753-2562.

Clergy Education—Rev. JAMES C. ZIMINSKI, *P.O. Box 550, Marquette, 49855.* Tel: 906-225-1141.

Council of Catholic Women—Rev. THOMAS L. POISSON, *Sacred Heart Parish, L'Anse, 49946.*

Cursillo—Rev. TIMOTHY DESROCHERS, Diocesan Moderator, *Marygrove, P.O. Box 38, Garden, 49835.* Tel: 906-644-2771.

Education, Board of—JAMES SCHUTTE, Pres. JAMES GHIARDI, Vice Pres., *P.O. Box 280, Marquette, 49855.* Tel: 906-226-3515.

Ecumenical Officer—Deacon DONALD J. GIESEN, *401 Main St., Norway, 49870.*

Superintendent of Schools—CLIFFORD LUFT, *P.O. Box 280, Marquette, 49855.* Tel: 906-226-3515.

Director of Catholic Education—Sr. JOYCE ROSE, O.S.F., *P.O. Box 280, Marquette, 49855.* Tel: 906-226-3515.

Coordinator for Adult and Family Religious Education—DANIEL SPARAPANI, *P.O. Box 280, Marquette, 49855.* Tel: 906-226-3515.

Holy Childhood Association—Rev. LAWRENCE T. GAUTHIER, Dir., *P.O. Box 550, Marquette, 49855.* Tel: 906-225-1141.

Department of Spiritual Development Services—JAMES HANSEN, Dir., *444 S. Fourth St., Marquette, 49855.* Tel: 906-225-1141; 228-4651.

Office of Stewardship—DAVID ADLER, Dir., *444 S. Fourth St., P.O. Box 550, Marquette, 49855.*

Office of Information—LOREENE ZENO KOSKEY, Dir. Communications, *345 Rock St., Marquette, 49855.* Tel: 906-226-8821.

Department of Ministry Personnel Services— ALEXANDER K. SAMPLE, Dir., *444 S. Fourth St., P.O. Box 550, Marquette, 49855.*

Newspaper "The Upper Peninsula Catholic"—JOSEPH ZYBLE, Editor, *P.O. Box 548, Marquette, 49855.* Tel: 906-226-8821; Fax: 906-226-6941.

Panama Mission Fund—Rev. PAUL G. MANDERFIELD, *444 S. Fourth St., Marquette, 49855.* Tel: 906-225-1141.

Permanent Diaconate Program—Rev. JAMES C. ZIMINSKI, Dir., *P.O. Box 550, Marquette, 49855.* Tel: 906-225-1141.

Propagation of the Faith—Rev. LAWRENCE T. GAUTHIER, Diocesan Dir., *P.O. Box 550, Marquette, 49855.* Tel: 906-225-1141.

Family Life Ministry—ROSALYN GROVES, Coord., *8260 23.3 Ln., Rapid River, 49878.* Tel: 906-474-6483.

Retreats—Rev. TIMOTHY DESROCHERS, Dir., *Marygrove Retreat Center, Garden, 49835.* Tel: 906-644-2771.

St. Joseph Association—An Association of the Priests of the Diocese to provide Old Age Benefits. Rev. MICHAEL A. WOEMPNER, Pres., *St. Jude Parish, P.O. Box 427, White Pine, 49971.* Tel: 906-885-5763.

U.P. Catholic Services Appeal—RICHARD R. SCHAEFER, Coord., *444 S. Fourth St., P.O. Box 796, Marquette, 49855.* Tel: 906-225-1378.

Vocation Office—Rev. JAMES C. ZIMINSKI, Dir., *P.O. Box 550, Marquette, 49855.* Tel: 906-225-1141.

CLERGY, PARISHES, MISSIONS AND PAROCHIAL SCHOOLS

CITY OF MARQUETTE
(Marquette County)

1—ST. PETER CATHEDRAL, Revs. Louis C. Cappo; Jan Szczykowski; Deacon David Adler.
Res., 311 Baraga Ave., 49855. Tel: 906-226-6548; Fax: 906-226-8683.
School—Father Marquette Catholic Central Schools System. See Elementary Inter-Parochial Schools under Institutions Located in the Diocese.

2—ST. CHRISTOPHER, Rev. Alexander K. Sample; Sr. Mary Ann Laurin, S.P.C., Pastoral Coord.
Res., 2372 Badger St., 49855. Tel: 906-226-2265.

3—ST. JOHN THE BAPTIST. Closed. 1986. For inquiries for parish records contact St. Peter's Cathedral.

4—ST. LOUIS, Rev. Guy S. Thoren.
Res., 264 Silver Creek Rd., Marquette, 49855. Tel: 906-249-1438; Fax: 906-249-3428.
School—Father Marquette Catholic Central Schools System. See Elementary Inter-Parochial Schools under Institutions Located in the Diocese.

5—ST. MICHAEL, Revs. John E. Patrick; Mariusz Makowski. In res., Rev. James C. Ziminski.
Res., 401 W. Kaye Ave., 49855. Tel: 906-228-8180; Fax: 906-228-5502.
School—Father Marquette Catholic Central Schools System. See Elementary Inter-Parochial Schools under Institutions Located in the Diocese.
Mission—Big Bay, Marquette Co., St. Mary.

OUTSIDE THE CITY OF MARQUETTE

Alpha, Iron Co., St. Edward. Closed. For inquiries for parish records contact the Chancery.

Assinins, Baraga Co., The Most Holy Name of Jesus-Blessed Kateri Tekakwitha, Rev. John S. Hascall, O.F.M.Cap.
Res., Rte. 1, Box 47, Baraga, 49908. Tel: 906-353-6836; Fax: 906-353-6800.
Indian Mission—West & Central Diocese of Marquette.

Baraga, Baraga Co., St. Ann, Rev. Paul G. Manderfield.
Res., 318 Lyons St., P.O. Box 349, 49908. Tel: 906-353-6565.

Bark River, Delta Co., St. Elizabeth Ann Seton. Formerly St. George,Bark River; Sacred Heart of Jesus, Schaffer; & St. Michael, Perronville. Rev. Emmett M. Norden.
Res., 1216 12th Rd., P.O. Box 187, 49807. Tel: 906-466-9938.

Bay Mills, Chippewa Co., Blessed Kateri Tekakwitha. (Formerly St. Catherine).

Bessemer, Gogebic Co., St. Sebastian, Rev. Joseph D. Carne.
Res., 210 E. Iron St., 49911. Tel: 906-667-0952.
School—Tel: 906-667-0322.
Lay Teachers 8; Students 118.

Brimley, Chippewa Co., St. Francis Xavier, Rev. Jeff Johnson.
Mailing Address: P.O. Box 429, 49715. Tel: 906-248-3443.
Missions—Sugur Island, Chippewa Co., Sacred Heart; Sault Ste. Marie, Chippewa Co., St. Isaac Jogues.

Calumet, Houghton Co., Sacred Heart, Rev. Marian Douglas, O.F.M.
Mailing Address: P.O. Box 546, 49913. Tel: 906-337-0810.
St. Paul the Apostle, Rev. Cyprian E. Berens, O.F.M. In res., Rev. Miles Pfalzer, O.F.M.
Res., 301 Eighth St., 49913. Tel: 906-337-2044.

Caspian, Iron Co., St. Cecilia, Rev. Otto J. Sartorelli; Deacon Robert J. Kostka.
Mailing Address: P.O. Box 517, 49915. Tel: 906-265-3777.

Champion, Marquette Co., Sacred Heart, Rev. Gilles Brault (STA). Pastoral Coords: Sr. Margey Schmelzle, O.S.F.; Sr. Charlotte Ann Wagner, O.S.F.
Mailing Address: P.O. Box 155, Republic, 49879. Tel: 906-376-8475.
Mission—Michigamme, Marquette Co., St. Agnes.

Channing, Dickinson Co., St. Rose, Rev. Michael Steber.
Mailing Address: P.O. Box 235, 49815. Tel: 906-542-3215.
Mission—Foster City, Dickinson Co., St. Joseph.

Chassell, Houghton Co., St. Anne, Rev. Bede G. Louzon, O.F.M.Cap.
Mailing Address: P.O. Box 407, 49916. Tel: 906-523-4912.
Missions—Painesdale, Houghton Co., Sacred Heart; Donken, Houghton Co., Immaculate Heart of Mary. Closed. For inquiries for parish records contact Sacred Heart, Painesdale.

Cooks, Schoolcraft Co., St. Mary Magdalene, Rev. John E. Martignon.
Mailing Address: P.O. Box 68, Garden, 49835. [CEM]

Crystal Falls, Iron Co., Guardian Angels, Rev. Norman A. Clisch.
Res., 412 Crystal Ave., 49920. Tel: 906-875-3019; Fax: 906-875-1034.

Daggett, Menominee Co., St. Frederick. Closed. For inquiries for parish records contact Precious Blood Parish, Stephenson.

DeTour, Chippewa Co., Sacred Heart, Rev. Larry Van Damme. Pastoral Coordinators: Sr. Colleen Sweeting, O.S.F.; Sr. Lois Risch, O.S.F.
Mailing Address: P.O. Box 8, 49725. Tel: 906-297-3781.
Mission—Drummond Island, Chippewa Co., St. Florence.

Engadine, Mackinac Co., Our Lady of Lourdes, Rev. Mieczyslaw T. Oniskiewicz.
Mailing Address: P.O. Box 123, 49827. Tel: 906-477-6223.
Missions—Naubinway, Mackinac Co., St. Stephen; Gulliver, Schoolcraft Co., Divine Infant of Prague. Deacon Gilbert G. Sablack.

Escanaba, Delta Co.,

1—ST. ANNE, Rev. Peter A. Minelli; Deacons Bill Hemes; Lewis Vailliencourt.
Res., 817 S. Lincoln Rd., 49829. Tel: 906-786-1421; Fax: 906-786-9346.
School—Holy Name Central Grade School. See Elementary Inter-Parochial Schools under Institutions Located in the Diocese.

2—ST. JOSEPH, Rev. Walter J. Sheedlo.
Res., 709 First Ave. S., 49829. Tel: 906-786-0732; Fax: 906-786-0685.
School—Holy Name Central Grade School. See Elementary Inter-Parochial Schools under Institutions Located in the Diocese.

3—ST. PATRICK, Rev. Ronald J. Skufca.
Res., 212 S. 12th St., 49829. Tel: 906-789-1010; Fax: 906-789-1213.
School—Holy Name Central Grade School. See Elementary Inter-Parochial Schools under Institutions Located in the Diocese.

4—ST. THOMAS THE APOSTLE, Rev. David W. Sedlock.
Res., 1820 Ninth Ave. N., 49829. Tel: 906-786-4627.
School—Holy Name Central Grade School. See Elementary Inter-Parochial Schools under Institutions Located in the Diocese.

Ewen, Ontonagon Co., Sacred Heart, Rev. Francis G. Dobrzenski.
Mailing Address: P.O. Box 169, 49925. Tel: 906-988-2310.
Mission—Sidnaw, Houghton Co., St. Francis Xavier.

Garden, Delta Co., St. John the Baptist, Rev. John E. Martignon.
Mailing Address: P.O. Box 68, 49835. Tel: 906-644-2626.

Gladstone, Delta Co., All Saints, Rev. Arnold J. Grambow.
Res., 715 Wisconsin Ave., P.O. Box 392, 49837. Tel: 906-428-3199.
Holy Family, Rev. Christopher B. Gardiner, Dean of the Escanaba Deanery.
Res., 4011 CO 416-20th Rd., 49837. Tel: 906-786-1209.

Goetzville, Chippewa Co., St. Stanislaus Kostka, Rev. Larry P. Van Damme.
Mailing Address: P.O. Box 207, 49736. Tel: 906-297-5211. [CEM]
Mission—Hessel, Mackinac Co., Our Lady of the Snows, Tel: 906-484-3825.

Grand Marais, Alger Co., Holy Rosary Church, Rev. Pawel J. Mecwel.
Mailing Address: P.O. Box 424, 49839. Tel: 906-494-2589; Fax: 906-494-2589. [CEM]
Missions—Germfask, Schoolcraft Co., St. Therese; Curtis, Mackinac Co., St. Timothy.

Gwinn, Marquette Co., St. Anthony, Rev. David C. Jenner.
Res., 320 Iron St., P.O. Box 1358, 49841. Tel: 906-346-5312.
Mission—Northland, Marquette Co., St. Joseph.

Hancock, Houghton Co., Resurrection, Rev. Wayne E. Marcotte.
Res., 900 Quincy St., 49930. Tel: 906-482-0215. [CEM]
Mission—Dollar Bay, Houghton Co., St. Francis of Assisi.

Hermansville, Menominee Co., St. John Neumann. Formerly St. Mary, Hermansville; St. Francis Xavier, Spalding. Rev. Michael T. Vichich.
Res., P.O. Box 125, 49847. Tel: 906-498-7730.

Houghton, Houghton Co., St. Ignatius Loyola, Rev. Raymond A. Valerio.
Res., 305 Portage St., 49931. Tel: 906-482-0212.
Mission—Atlantic Mine, Houghton Co., St. Mary. Closed. For inquiries for parish records contact St. Ignatius Loyola, Houghton.
St. Albert the Great University Parish. (Michigan Technological University). Rev. William P. Callari; Deacon Paul Lucchesi.
Res., 411 MacInnes Dr., 49931. Tel: 906-482-5530.

Hubbell, Houghton Co., St. Cecilia, Rev. Eric E. Olson.
Mailing Address: c/o 701 Calumet St., Lake Linden, 49945. Tel: 906-296-6851.

Iron Mountain, Dickinson Co., Immaculate Conception of the Blessed Virgin Mary, Rev. Darryl J. Pepin; Deacons Benjamin O. Garcia; Donald R. Christy.
Res., 500 Blaine St., 49801-1840. Tel: 906-774-0511; Fax: 906-779-9953.
School—Dickinson Area Catholic School System. See Elementary Inter-Parochial Schools under Institutions Located in the Diocese.

St. Mary and St. Joseph, Rev. Daniel S. Zaloga.
Res., 411 W. B St., 49801. Tel: 906-774-2046.
School—Dickinson Area Catholic School System. See Elementary Inter-Parochial Schools under Institutions Located in the Diocese.

Iron River, Iron Co., St. Agnes, Rev. Aloysius J. Hasenberg.
Res., 644 N. Fourth St., 49935. Tel: 906-265-4557.

Ironwood, Gogebic Co., Our Lady of Peace. Consolidated Combination of the following three parishes: Holy Trinity, St. Ambrose & St. Michael; 1986. Revs. Norbert B. Landreville; Basil S. Goerner.
Res., 108 S. Marquette St., 49938. Tel: 906-932-0174; Fax: 906-932-1019.
School—Tel: 906-932-3200.
Sisters 2; Lay Teachers 7; Students 141.

St. Ambrose. Consolidated with Holy Trinity & St. Michael to form Our Lady of Peace Parish, 1986.

St. Michael. Consolidated with St. Ambrose & Holy Trinity to form Our Lady of Peace Parish, 1986.

Ishpeming, Marquette Co., St. John the Evangelist, Rev. Peter Oberto, V.G.
Res., 325 S. Pine, 49849. Tel: 906-486-6212.
Religious Education Center—335 S. Pine St., 49849. Tel: 906-486-9361. Sr. Catherine Gleason, C.S.J., Admin.

St. Joseph, Rev. Vincent L. Ouellette.
Office (All Mail): 1889 Prairie Avenue, Ishpeming, 49849-1045.
Res., 1890 Prairie Ave., 49849-1044. Tel: 906-485-4200.

St. Pius X. Closed. For inquiries for parish records contact St. Joseph Church, 1889 Prairie Ave., Ishpeming, MI 49849.

Kingsford, Dickinson Co., American Martyrs, Rev. Joseph O. Gouin.
Res., 908 W. Sagola Ave., 49802. Tel: 906-774-0630.

St. Mary Queen of Peace, Rev. Paul J. Nomellini; Deacon Harold F. Boersma.
Res., 432 Edsel St., 49802. Tel: 906-774-6122.

Lake Linden, Houghton Co., St. Joseph, Rev. Eric E. Olson.
Res., 701 Calumet St., 49945. Tel: 906-296-6851.

L'Anse, Baraga Co., Sacred Heart, Rev. Thomas L. Poisson.
Res., 16 S. Sixth St., 49946. Tel: 906-524-6424.
School—433 E. Baraga Ave., 49946. Tel: 906-524-5157.
Sisters 2; Lay Teachers 7; Students 115.

Mackinac Island, Mackinac Co., Ste. Anne de Michilimackinac (1695), Rev. James M. Williams.
Mailing Address: P.O. Box 537, 49757. Tel: 906-847-3507.

Manistique, Schoolcraft Co., St. Francis de Sales, Rev. George C. Gustafson.
Res., 330 Oak St., 49854. Tel: 906-341-5355.
School—Tel: 906-341-5512.
Sisters 5; Lay Teachers 6; Students 128.

Menominee, Menominee Co., Holy Redeemer (Birch Creek), Rev. Rick L. Courier; Deacon Roland Chaltry.
Res., W-5541 Birch Creek Rd. No. 6, 49858. Tel: 906-863-6920.
School—Menominee Catholic Central. See Elementary Inter-Parochial Schools under Institutions Located in the Diocese.

Holy Spirit, Rev. S. Patrick Wisneske.
Res., 1016 10th Ave., 49858. Tel: 906-863-5239.
School—Menominee Catholic Central. See Elementary Inter-Parochial Schools under Institutions Located in the Diocese.

Resurrection, Rev. Dino F. Silvestrini.
Res., 2607 18th St., 49858. Tel: 906-863-3405.
School—Menominee Catholic Central. See Elementary Inter-Parochial Schools under Institutions Located in the Diocese.

Mohawk, Keweenaw Co., Keweenaw Catholic Missions, Rev. Miles Pfalzer, O.F.M.
Mailing Address: Box 517, 49950. Tel: 906-337-1966.
Missions—Eagle Harbor, Holy Redeemer; Ahmeek, Our Lady of Peace; Copper Harbor, Our Lady of the Pines.

Moran, Mackinac Co., Immaculate Conception, Rev. C. Michael Rhodes.
Res., 120 Church St., St. Ignace, 49781. Tel: 906-643-7671. [CEM]

Munising, Alger Co., Sacred Heart of Jesus, Rev. Raymond F. Moncher; Deacon James E. Anderson.
Office: 110 W. Jewell St., P.O. Box 99, 49862. Tel: 906-387-4900.

Nadeau, Menominee Co., St. Bruno, Rev. Raymond J. Zeugner; Deacon Donald Lobdell.
Res., 49863. Tel: 906-639-2388.

Nahma, Delta Co., St. Andrew, Rev. John E. Martignon.
Mailing Address: P.O. Box 68, Garden, 49864. Tel: 906-644-2626.

Negaunee, Marquette Co., St. Paul, Rev. John J. Shiverski.
Res., 202 W. Case St., 49866. Tel: 906-475-9969.
Mission—Palmer, Marquette Co., Our Lady Perpetual Help, Tel: 906-475-4630.

Newberry, Luce Co., St. Gregory, Rev. George S. Maki; Deacon Dean Hermann.
Office: 212 W. Harrie St., 49868. Tel: 906-293-5511.
Res., 115 W. Harrie St., 49868. Tel: 906-293-5001.
Mission—Paradise, Chippewa Co., Our Lady of Victory.

Norway, Dickinson Co., St. Mary, Revs. Mark A. McQuesten; Benedetto J. Paris.
Res., 401 Main St., 49870. Tel: 906-563-9845.
School—Holy Spirit Central Grade School. See Elementary Inter-Parochial Schools under Institutions Located in the Diocese.

Ontonagon, Ontonagon Co., Holy Family, Rev. John L. Longbucco.
Res., 515 Pine St., 49953. Tel: 906-884-2569; Fax: 906-884-6030. [CEM]

Perkins, Delta Co., St. Joseph, Rev. Joseph Nagaroor.
Res., 5803 Hwy. M-35, P.O. Box 99, 49872. Tel: 906-359-4701.

Perronville, Menominee Co., St. Elizabeth Ann Seton. Formerly St. Michael. Rev. Emmett M. Norden.
Res., 1216 12th Rd., P.O. Box 187, Bark River, 49807. Tel: 906-466-9938.

Quinnesec, Dickinson Co., St. Mary. Closed. For inquiries for parish records contact St. Mary Parish, Norway,MI.

Ramsay, Gogebic Co., Christ the King. Closed. For inquiries for parish records contact St. Sebastian, Bessemer.

Rapid River, Delta Co., St. Charles Borromeo, Rev. Raymond J. Hoefgen; Deacon William Green.
Mailing Address: P.O. Box 247, 49878. Tel: 906-474-6741; Fax: 906-474-9087.

Republic, Marquette Co., St. Augustine, Rev. Gilles Brault (STA). Pastoral Coords: Sr. Margey Schmelzle, O.S.F.; Sr. Charlotte Ann Wagner.
Res., 49879.
Mailing Address: P.O. Box 155, 49879. Tel: 906-376-8475. [CEM]

Rockland, Ontonagon Co., St. Mary, Rev. John L. Longbucco; Deacon Karl L. Wadman.
Mailing Address: Holy Family Parish, 515 Pine St., Ontonagon, 49953. Tel: 906-884-2569.

Rudyard, Chippewa Co., St. Joseph, Revs. Francis J. DeGroot; Jerome A. Nowacki.
Mailing Address: P.O. Box 150, 49780. Tel: 906-478-4331.
Missions—Trout Lake, Chippewa Co., St. Mary; Barbeau, Holy Family.
Stations—Kinross Correctional Facility; Chippewa Correctional Facility; Chippewa Regional Facility; Hiawatha Correctional Facility.

St. Ignace, Mackinac Co., St. Ignatius Loyola, Rev. C. Michael Rhoades.
Res., 120 Church St., 49781. Tel: 906-643-7671. [CEM]

Sault Sainte Marie, Chippewa Co., Holy Name of Mary, Rev. Theodore J. Brodeur.
Res., 377 Maple St., 49783. Tel: 906-632-3381; Fax: 906-632-3390.
School—Tel: 906-635-6141.
Sisters 1; Lay Teachers 4; Students 104.

Nativity of Our Lord. Closed. For inquiries for parish records contact St. Joseph, Sault Ste. Marie.

St. Joseph, Rev. Donald L. Shiroda; Deacon William J. Piche.
Res., 606 E. Fourth Ave., 49783. Tel: 906-632-9625.

Schaffer, Delta Co., St. Elizabeth Ann Seton. Formerly Sacred Heart of Jesus (See Perronville & Bark River). Rev. Emmett M. Norden.
Res., 1216 12th Rd., P.O. Box 187, Bark River, 49807. Tel: 906-466-9938. [CEM]

South Range, Houghton Co., Holy Family, Rev. William P. Callari.
Mailing Address: Box 369, 49963. Tel: 906-482-0684.

Spalding, Menominee Co., St. Francis Xavier. Closed. See St. John Neumann, P.O. Box 125, Hermansville, MI 49847.

Stephenson, Menominee Co., Precious Blood Church, Rev. Raymond Zeugner.
Res., 304 Bluff St., 49887. Tel: 906-753-2562; Fax: 906-753-2811.

Trenary, Alger Co., St. Rita, Rev. Gregory R. Heikkala.
Mailing Address: P.O. Box 207, 49891. Tel: 906-446-3350; Fax: 906-446-3350.
Mission—Autrain, Alger Co., St. Therese.

Vulcan, Dickinson Co., St. Barbara, Revs. Mark A. McQuesten; Benedetto J. Paris.
Mailing Address: P.O. Box 493, 49892. Tel: 906-563-9834.
School—Holy Spirit Central Grade School, Norway. See Elementary Inter-Parochial Schools under Institutions Located in the Diocese.

Wakefield, Gogebic Co., Immaculate Conception of the Blessed Virgin Mary, Rev. Allan J. Mayotte.
Res., 407 Ascherman St., 49968. Tel: 906-224-7851.
Mission—Marenisco, Gogebic Co., St. Catherine, Tel: 906-787-2353.

Watersmeet, Gogebic Co., Immaculate Conception, Rev. Francis G. Dobrzenski.
Mailing Address: Box 398, 49969. Tel: 906-358-4607.

Wells, Delta Co., St. Anthony, Rev. Richard C. Schaefer.
Mailing Address: P.O. Box 280, 49894. Tel: 906-786-5002; Fax: 906-786-8992.
School—Holy Name Central Grade School, Escanaba. See Elementary Inter-Parochial Schools under Institutions Located in the Diocese.

White Pine, Ontonagon Co., St. Jude, Rev. Michael A. Woempner.
Mailing Address: P.O. Box 427, 49971. Tel: 906-885-5763.
Mission—Bergland, Ontonagon Co., St. Ann.

Indian Missions

Assinins, Baraga Co., The Most Holy Name of Jesus-Blessed Kateri Tekakwitha. Indian Missionaries, West & Central. Rev. John S. Hascall, O.F.M.Cap.
Res., Rte. 1, Box 47, Baraga, 49908.

Watersmeet, Gogebec Co., Lac Vieux Desert Reservation, Sr. Joyce Rybarczyk, O.P.
P.O. Box 78, 49969.

Bay Mills, Chippewa Co., Blessed Kateri Tekakwitha, Rev. Jeff G. Johnson.
P.O. Box 429, Brimley, 49715.

Sault Sainte Marie, Chippewa Co., St. Isaac Jogues, Rev. Jeff G. Johnson.
P.O. Box 429, Brimley, 49715.

Sugar Island, Chippewa Co., Sacred Heart. Indian Missionaries, East. Rev. Jeff Johnson.
P.O. Box 429, Brimley, 49715.

Chaplains of Public Institutions

MARQUETTE. *Marquette General Hospital.* Tel: 906-228-9440; 225-3404. Revs. Frank M. Lenz; Gilles Brault (STA) Assoc. Chap.

IRON MOUNTAIN. *Veterans Administration Hospital.* Tel: 906-774-3300; 563-7103. Rev. Patrick E. Murphy.

On Duty Outside the Diocese:
Reverend Fathers—
Challancin, James, St. Joseph College, P.O. Box 984, Rensselaer, IN 47978
Franczek, August, Diocese of Gaylord
Genovesi, James W., Our Lady of the Blessed Sacrament, Hermitage, P.O. Box 260, Norwalk, WI 54648
Timock, Ronald K., Byzantine Catholic Seminary of Sts. Cyril & Methodius, 3605 Perrysville Ave., Pittsburg, PA 15214
Wantland, Thomas, Diocese of Venice, 164 Captain John Smith Loop, North Fort Myers, FL 33917

Special Assignment:
Reverend Fathers—
Sample, Alexander K., Dir., Dept. of Ministry Personnel Service
Schmied, Thomas, O.F.M.Cap., P.O. Box 368, Ahmeek, MI 49901
Ziminski, James C., Pastoral Office; Dir. of Vocations

Military Chaplains:
Reverend Fathers—
Kaczmarek, James, U.S.A.F., PSC 41, Box 607, APO, AE 09464

Awaiting Assignment:
Reverend Fathers—
Hruska, Timothy W.

Leave of Absence:
Reverend Fathers—
Capyak, Michael S.
Craig, Richard T.
Kurtz, Jeffrey A.
Rupp, Daniel N.

Retired:
Reverend Monsignors—
Dunleavy, Joseph J., Bishop Noa Home, 2900 Third St. S., Escanaba, MI 49829
Karol, Bernard A., 550 Warren Ave. #72, Spring Lake Heights, NJ 07762
LaViolette, Matt H., P.O. Box 497, Escanaba, MI 49829
McKevitt, Nolan B., Bishop Noa Home, 2900 Third St. S., Escanaba, MI 49829
Spelgatti, David P., (Winter), 21362 Walling Ct., Port Charlotte, FL 33954

Reverend Fathers—
Andary, Thomas M., 18515 Caminito Pasadero, Apt. 345, San Diego, CA 92128
Beyer, Emil J., Bishop Noa Home, 2900 Third St. S., Escanaba, MI 49829
Bracket, Louis P., 307 Eddy St., Wakefield, MI 49968
Brewer, Gervase, P.O. Box 158, Marquette, MI 49855
Cordy, Robert J., Bishop Noa Home, 2900 Third St. S., Escanaba, MI 49829
Dishaw, Conrad J., 2701 Fifth Ave. S., Apt. 102, Escanaba, MI 49829
Dunleavy, Thomas P., W8079 59, U.S. 2, Iron Mountain, MI 49801
Franczek, Walter J., 5062 S.E. 115th St., Belleview, FL 32620
Gauthier, Lawrence T., P.O. Box 550, Marquette, MI 49855
Gondek, Joseph A., P.O. Box 4, Iron River, MI 49935
Harris, David T., P.O. Box 88, Rockland, MI 49960
Hartman, Donald, 546 Main St., Apt. 529, Roosevelt Island, New York, NY 10044
Hebein, James M., Box 72 Hillside Apartments, #11, Vulcan, MI 49892
Hollenbach, Frank A., 9255 E. Pueblo A, Mesa, AZ 85208
Kichak, Joseph A., 301 W. Oak, Ironwood, MI 49938
LaCosse, Norbert R., 1534A W. Ridge St., Apt. 5, Marquette, MI 49855
LePine, Clement J., 2017 14th St., Menominee, MI 49858
Maloney, John, 917 Woodward Ave., Apt. 5, Kingsford, MI 49801
McArdle, John F., 4305 Sixth St., Menominee, MI 49858
Menapace, James L., Route 1, Box 56, Gulliver, MI 49840
Neurohr, Gilbert N., 5719 Pine 0-25 St., Gladstone, MI 49837
Olivier, John H., S.S., 2600 Hwy. 146, Paicines, CA 95043
Parrotta, Arthur J., St. Francis Hospital, 3401 Ludington St., Escanaba, MI 49829
Paulantonio, Joseph, 89-40 151st Ave., Howard Beach, NY 11414
Polakowski, Joseph, 5948 Country Club Ln., Lake Bluff, Gladstone, MI 49837
Ruppe, Thomas G., E5238 Margaret St., Ironwood, MI 49938
Ryan, John, 1600 N. 19th St., Escanaba, MI 49829
Schiska, Paul A., 6682 D Rd., Bark River, MI 49807
Smith, Neil B., P.O. Box 452, Ramsay, MI 49959
Strelick, Charles J., 4420 Devonshire Ave., Spring Hill, FL 34609
Suda, Conrad P., 100 Pine St., Spalding, MI 49886
Vanitvelt, Milton H., 1524 Seventh St., Menominee, MI 49858
Wenzel, Edward J., Rte. 1, Box 491, Baraga, MI 49908

Permanent Deacons:
Adler, David, St. Peter Cathedral, Marquette
Anderson, James, Sacred Heart of Jesus, Munising
Boersma, Harold, St. Mary, Queen of Peace, Kingsford
Chaltry, Roland, Holy Redeemer, Menominee
Christy, Donald R., Immaculate Conception, Iron Mountain
Garcia, Benjamin O., Immaculate Conception, Iron Mountain
Giesen, Donald, St. Mary, Norway
Green, William, St. Charles Borromeo, Rapid River
Hemes, Dr. Bill D., St. Anne, Escanaba
Hermann, Dean, St. Gregory, Newberry
Kostka, Robert J., St. Cecilia, Caspian
Lobdell, Donald, St. Bruno, Nadeau
Lucchessi, Paul, St. Albert the Great, Houghton
Piche, William J., St. Joseph, Sault Ste. Marie
Sablack, Gilbert G., Divine Infant of Praque, Gulliver
Vailliencourt, Lewis, St. Anne, Escanaba
Wadman, Karl L., St. Mary, Rockland

INSTITUTIONS LOCATED IN THE DIOCESE

[A] ELEMENTARY INTER-PAROCHIAL SCHOOLS

MARQUETTE. *Fr. Marquette Catholic Central Schools System*, 500 S. Fourth St., 49855. Tel: 906-225-1129; Fax: 906-225-1987. James Ghiardi, Supt.
Serving the following parishes: St. Peter's Cathedral; St. Louis; St. Michael. Lay Teachers 28; Students 303.

ESCANABA. *Holy Name Central Grade School*, 409 S. 22nd St., 49829. Tel: 906-786-7550. Barbara Mead, Prin. Lay Teachers 20; Students 359.

IRON MOUNTAIN. *Dickinson Area Catholic School System*, 406 W. B St., 49801. Tel: 906-774-2277. Mr. John Chandler, Prin. Lay Teachers 11; Students 212.

MENOMINEE. *Menominee Catholic Central*, 1406 10th Ave., 49858. Jeanne Pischke, Supt. Lay Teachers 13; Students 224.

NORWAY. *Holy Spirit Central School Educational Fund*, 201 Saginaw St., 49870. Tel: 906-563-8817. Mr. Anthony F. Perrini, Prin. Sisters 1; Lay Teachers 13; Students 98.

[B] CATHOLIC EDUCATION ENDOWMENT FUNDS

MARQUETTE. *Marquette Area Catholic Education Fund*, P.O. Box 550, 49855. Tel: 906-225-1141.
U.P. Catholic Education Endowment Fund, 444 S. Fourth St., P.O. Box 550, 49855. Tel: 906-225-1141. Mr. Richard R. Schaefer.

BESSEMER. *St. Sebastian School Endowment Fund, Inc.*, 210 E. Iron St., 49911. Tel: 906-667-0952.

ESCANABA. *Holy Name Central Endowment Fund, Inc.*, 409 S. 22nd St., 49829. Tel: 906-786-7550.
Holy Name Scholarship Foundation, 409 S. 22nd St., 49829. Tel: 906-786-7550.

IRON MOUNTAIN. *Dickinson Area Catholic School Education Foundation*, 406 W. B St., 49801. Tel: 906-774-2277.

IRONWOOD. *Our Lady of Peace Catholic School Endowment Fund*, 106 S. Marquette St., 49938. Tel: 906-932-3200.

L'ANSE. *Sacred Heart School Endowment Fund*, 16 S. 6th St., 49946.

MANISTIQUE. *St. Francis de Sales Education Foundation, Inc.*, 330 Oak St., 49854. Tel: 906-341-5355.

MENOMINEE.
**Menominee Catholic Education Fund, Inc.*, 1406 Tenth Ave., 49858-2604. Tel: 906-863-2723. Carrie Warren-Wandke, Office Mgr.

NEGAUNEE. *Negaunee St. Paul Endowment Fund*, 202 W. Case St., 49866.

NORWAY. *Holy Spirit Central School Educational Fund*, 201 Saginaw, 49870. Tel: 906-563-8817.

SAULT STE. MARIE. *Holy Family School Endowment Fund, Inc.*, 377 Maple St., 49783. Tel: 906-632-3381.

[C] GENERAL HOSPITALS

ESCANABA. *O.S.F. St. Francis Hospital*, 49829. Tel: 906-786-3311.
For a complete listing, refer to the Hospitals section.

[D] HOMES FOR THE AGED

ESCANABA. *Bishop Noa Home for Senior Citizens*, 2900 3rd Ave., S., 49829. Tel: 906-786-5810; Fax: 906-786-5372.
For a complete listing, refer to the Special Care Facilities section.

[E] CONVENTS AND RESIDENCES OF SISTERS

MARQUETTE. *Provincialate of the Sisters of St. Paul de Chartres*, 1300 County Rd. 492, 49855. Tel: 906-226-3932; Fax: 906-226-8734. Sr. Mary Carol Goodman, District Supr. Sisters 8.

IRON MOUNTAIN. *Monastery of the Holy Cross*, N4028 Hwy. U.S. 2, P.O. Box 397, 49801. Discalced Carmelite Nuns. Mother Pauline Marie, O.C.D., Prioress; Rev. Patrick E. Murphy, Chap. Cloistered Nuns: Professed 14; Extern Professed Sisters 2; Postulants 1.

[F] RETREAT HOUSES

GARDEN. *Marygrove Retreat Center*, 49835. Tel: 906-644-2771. Rev. Timothy H. Desrochers, Dir. Retreats and workshops for priests, religious and laity.

[G] NEWMAN CLUBS

MARQUETTE. *Catholic Campus Ministry-Northern Michigan University*, 1200 Hebard Ct., 49855. Tel: 906-228-3302; Fax: 906-225-0437. Sr. Catherine Mills, S.P.C., Dir.; Rev. James C. Ziminski, Sacramental Min.

HOUGHTON. *St. Albert the Great, University Parish*, 411 MacInnes Dr., 49931. Tel: 906-482-5530. Rev. William P. Callari.

SAULT SAINTE MARIE. *Lake Superior State University, Newman Center*, 517 W. Easterday, 49783. Tel: 906-635-5941. David Orn, Dir.

[H] MISCELLANEOUS

MARQUETTE. *St. Vincent De Paul Society*, 2118 Fitch Ave., Room #101, 49855. Tel: 906-226-2311.

RELIGIOUS INSTITUTES OF MEN REPRESENTED IN THE DIOCESE

For further details refer to the corresponding bracketed number in the Religious Institutes of Men or Women section.

[0470]—*The Capuchin Friars.* (Detroit, MI).—O.F.M.Cap.
[0520]—*Franciscan Friars.* (Cincinnati, OH).—O.F.M.

RELIGIOUS INSTITUTES OF WOMEN REPRESENTED IN THE DIOCESE

[3710]—*Congregation of the Sisters of Saint Agnes.*—C.S.A.
[0420]—*Discalced Carmelite Nuns.*—O.C.D.
[1070-09]—*Dominican Sisters.*—O.P.
[1070-13]—*Dominican Sisters.*—O.P.
[1630]—*Franciscan Sisters of Christian Charity.*—O.S.F.
[2380]—*Institute of the Blessed Virgin Mary (Sisters of Loretto).*—I.B.V.M.
[3130]—*Our Lady of Victory Missionary Sisters.*—O.L.V.M.
[2970]—*School Sisters of Notre Dame.*—S.S.N.D.
[3830-15]—*Sisters of St. Joseph.* (Concordia, Kansas).—C.S.J.
[3840]—*Sisters of St. Joseph of Carondelet.*—C.S.J.
[3980]—*Sisters of St. Paul of Chartres.*—S.P.C.
[2180]—*Sisters of the Immaculate Heart of Mary.*—I.H.M.
[3260]—*Sisters of the Precious Blood.*—C.PP.S.
[3320]—*Sisters of the Presentation of the B.V.M.*—P.B.V.M.
[1770]—*Sisters of the Third Order of St. Francis.* (Peoria, Illinois).—O.S.F.

DIOCESAN CEMETERIES

MARQUETTE. *Holy Cross.*
ESCANABA. *Holy Cross.*

NECROLOGY

† Bares, Elmer J., (Retired). —Died Oct. 17, 1996.
† Bottoni, Samuel A., Watersmeet, MI, Immaculate Conception Church. —Died July 5, 1996.
† Richards, Willaim G., (Retired). —Died April 1, 1996.
† Schick, William F., (Retired). —Died Jan. 9, 1996.
† Smith, Raymond J., South Range, MI, Holy Family Church. —Died Sept. 16, 1996.

Diocese of Memphis

(Memphitana in Tennesia)

Most Reverend

J. TERRY STEIB, S.V.D., D.D.

Bishop of Memphis; ordained January 6, 1967; appointed Titular Bishop of Fallaba and Auxiliary Bishop of St. Louis December 6, 1983; consecrated February 10, 1984; appointed Bishop of Memphis May 5, 1993.

ESTABLISHED JANUARY 6, 1971.

Square Miles 10,682.

Comprises the Counties of Benton, Carroll, Chester, Crockett, Decatur, Dyer, Fayette, Gibson, Hardeman, Hardin, Haywood, Henderson, Henry, Lake, Lauderdale, McNairy, Madison, Obion, Shelby, Tipton and Weakley in the State of Tennessee.

For legal titles of parishes and diocesan institutions, consult the Chancery Office.

Catholic Center: P.O. Box 341669, Memphis, TN, 38184-1669. Tel.: 901-373-1200; Fax: 901-373-1269.

STATISTICAL OVERVIEW

Personnel	
Bishop	1
Priests: Diocesan Active in Diocese	50
Priests: Active Outside Diocese	4
Priests: Retired, Sick or Absent	16
Number of Diocesan Priests	70
Religious Priests in Diocese	11
Extern Priests in Diocese	3
Ordinations:	
Permanent Deacons in Diocese	21
Total Brothers	26
Total Sisters	100
Parishes	
Parishes	42
With Resident Pastor:	
Resident Diocesan Priests	30
Resident Religious Priests	5
Without Resident Pastor:	
Administered by Priests	8
Administered by Permanent Deacons	1
Administered by Women Religious	1
Missions	5
Pastoral Centers	1
Professional Ministry Personnel:	
Brothers	2
Sisters	6
Lay Ministers	24
Welfare	
Catholic Hospitals	1
Total Assisted	47,062
Health Care Centers	1
Total Assisted	64,505
Homes for the Aged	8
Total Assisted	779
Day Care and Extended Day Care Centers	8
Total Assisted	1,442
Specialized Homes	1
Total Assisted	233
Special Centers for Social Services	2
Total Assisted	20,273
Residential Care of Disabled	5
Total Assisted	58
Other Institutions	2
Total Assisted	289
Educational	
Diocesan Students in Other Seminaries	10
Total Seminarians	10
Colleges and Universities	1
Total Students	1,784
High Schools, Diocesan and Parish	4
Total Students	1,295
High Schools, Private	3
Total Students	1,109
Elementary Schools, Diocesan and Parish	11
Total Students	3,563
Elementary Schools, Private	2
Total Students	449
Non-residential Schools for the Disabled	1
Total Students	41
Catechesis/Religious Education:	
High School Students	727
Elementary Students	4,352
Total Students Under Catholic Instruction	13,330
Teachers in the Diocese:	
Priests	2
Brothers	10
Sisters	17
Lay Teachers	440
Vital Statistics	
Receptions into the Church:	
Infant Baptism Totals	1,071
Adult Baptism Totals	203
Received into Full Communion	279
First Communions	1,125
Confirmations	1,031
Marriages:	
Catholic	174
Interfaith	237
Total Marriages	411
Deaths	508
Total Catholic Population	56,885
Total Population	1,426,923

Former Bishops—Most Rev. CARROLL T. DOZIER, D.D., ord. March 19, 1937; appt. Nov. 17, 1970; cons. Jan. 6, 1971; retired July 27, 1982; died Dec. 7, 1985.—Most Rev. J. FRANCIS STAFFORD, D.D., ord. Dec. 15, 1957; cons. Bishop Feb. 29, 1976; appt. Nov. 16, 1982; appt. to Archdiocese of Denver, June 3, 1986.—Most Rev. DANIEL M. BUECHLEIN, O.S.B., D.D., ord. May 3, 1964; appt. Jan. 20, 1987; appt. to Archdiocese of Indianapolis, July 14, 1992.

Vicars General—Rev. J. PETER SARTAIN, V.G., *St. Louis, 203 S. White Station Rd., Memphis, 38117.* Tel: 901-682-6606. Rev. Msgr. PAUL W. CLUNAN, P.A., V.G., (Retired), *38 N. Idlewild #13, Memphis, 38104.*

Catholic Center Offices—Mailing Address: P.O. Box 341669, Memphis, 38184-1669. Tel: 901-373-1200; Fax: 901-373-1269. Office Hours: Mon.-Fri. 7:45-4:45, *5825 Shelby Oaks Dr., Memphis, 38134.*

Chancery

Office of Moderator of the Curia and Chancellor—Rev. ROBERT D. PONTICELLO, J.C.L., *P.O. Box 341669, Memphis, 38184-1669.* Tel: 901-373-1200.

Vice-Chancellor—VERDRUE DOMINIONI.

Notaries—MARIANNA RAMPERSAD; M. TERESA WILTCHER.

Catholic Public Policy Commission of Tennessee—P.O. Box 341669, Memphis, 38184-1669.

Common Sense Diocesan Newspaper—MARY BALTZ, Editor.

Office of Ecumenism—Rev. THOMAS D. KIRK, Dir., *1695 Central Ave., Memphis, 38104.* Tel: 901-725-2700. Rev. GREG SALATA, Assoc. Dir., *203 S. White Station Rd., Memphis, 38117.* Tel: 901-682-6606.

Clergy Personnel Board—Revs. MILTON J. GUTHRIE; WILLIAM R. KANTNER; DANIEL F. MOORE; J. PETER SARTAIN; ROBERT D. PONTICELLO.

Continuing Education for the Clergy—Rev. BRYAN P. TIMBY, Dir., *4851 Park Ave., Memphis, 38117.* Tel: 901-767-6949.

College of Consultors—Revs. J. EDWIN CREARY; J. PETER SARTAIN; Rev. Msgr. PETER P. BUCHIGNANI; Revs. JOACHIM CULOTTA, O.P.; VICTOR P. CIARAMITARO; Rev. Msgr. EDWARD O. HEYMER; Revs. RICHARD M. GANTERT; STEPHEN K. KENNY; ALBERT E. KIRK; DAN F. MOORE; ROBERT D. PONTICELLO; GABRIEL DI-FEDERICO, Dir. Diaconal Formation. Tel: 901-767-6949.

Permanent Deacons Community—Deacon JOHN T. OATES, Dir., *5825 Shelby Oaks Dr., Memphis, 38134.* Tel: 901-373-1216.

Dean of the Jackson Deanery—Rev. VICTOR CIARAMITARO, *Holy Cross Church, 1210 E. Wood St., Paris, 38242.* Tel: 901-642-4681.

Director of Seminarians—Rev. R. BRUCE CINQUEGRANI.

Director of Vocations—Rev. DAVID GRAHAM.

Tribunal

Judicial Vicar—Rev. JOSEPH L. TAGG, III, J.D., J.C.L.

Adjutant Judicial Vicar—Rev. JOACHIM CULOTTA.

Defender of the Bond—Rev. ROBERT D. PONTICELLO, J.C.L.

Promoter of Justice—Rev. ROBERT D. PONTICELLO, J.C.L.

Auditor—Rev. Msgr. WILLIAM J. KLEISER.

Notary—M. TERESA WILTCHER.

Department of Financial Administration

Secretary—JAMES A. KLEISER, JR., *P.O. Box 341669, Memphis, 38184-1669.* Tel: 901-373-1200.

Calvary Cemeteries and All Saints Cemetery—RICHARD B. SMITH, Supt., *1663 Elvis Presley Blvd., Memphis, 38106.* Tel: 901-948-1529.

Controller—EDDIE WALDRUP.

Data Processing—BETTY FURR.

Employee Benefits—KATHY OWINGS.

Facilities and Risk Management—WILLIAM F. HERBERS.

Maintenance—ROBERT PELT.

Department of Catholic Schools

Secretary—Dr. CAROL M. KULPA, *P.O. Box 341669, Memphis, 38184-1669.* Tel: 901-373-1200.

Office of Catholic Schools—Dr. CAROL M. KULPA, Supt. JANET M. DONATO, Asst. Supt.

Department Of Associated Catholic Charities

Secretary—BRIAN J. O'MALLEY, Exec. Dir., *85 N. Cleveland, P.O. Box 41705, Memphis, 38174-1705.* Tel: 901-722-4777.

Catholic Charities, Inc.—Dir. Vacant; LARRY W. COPPOCK, Devel. Dir. CHRISTI SHAW, Communication Dir. JAMES ABERNATHY, Finance Dir.

Community Outreach Services—JOSEPH PFEIFFER, Dir. ALICE HARDY, Parish Liaison.

Parish Social Ministry-Pallotti Center—Vacant.
Ministry to the Sick and Elderly—
Ministry to the Imprisoned—Bro. TALBOT MCSHARRY.
Genesis House—GERALD BETTICE, Dir. Transitional shelter for homeless.
Refugee Resettlement Unit—CAROLYN TISDALE, Dir.
Day Care Services—VIRGINIA DAVENPORT, Dir.
Holy Names Center—LINDA STEED, Dir.
St. Ann-Bartlett Extended Care Program—SUSAN FAUGHN, Prog. Dir.
St. Benedict at Auburndale Extended Care—JOSEPHINE FOLLIN, Site Supvr.
St. John Center—VELTEEN MCGHEE, Program Coord.
St. Louis Extended Care—LORI TUCKER, Site Supvr.
St. Peter Home Day Care Center—BONNIE CARTER, Dir.
St. Michael Extended Care—DEBBIE KALLAHER, Site Supvr.
Diocese of Memphis Housing Corporation—DAVID FIELD, Exec. Dir.
St. Peter Villa Nursing Home—LINDA WARF, Exec. Dir.
St. Peter Home for Children—BRENT ADAMS, Admin.
St. Therese Little Flower Day Care Center—SHARON WEBB, Prog. Dir.
Mid South Caring, Inc.—BRIAN J. O'MALLEY, *85 N. Cleveland St., P.O. Box 41705, Memphis, 38174-1705.*

Department for Worship and Spiritual Life

Secretary—Rev. R. BRUCE CINQUEGRANI, *P.O. Box 341669, Memphis, 38184-1669.* Tel: 901-373-1200.
Office of Worship—MARY MILLER, Assoc. Dir.; Sr. MAUREEN GRINER, O.S.U., Diocesan Dir. of Music.
Commission for Initiation Ministries—PAUL GRAY, Chm.; Rev. R. BRUCE CINQUEGRANI, Liaison.
Cursillo Movement—Rev. GABRIEL J. DIFEDERICO, Spiritual Advisor. Assoc. Spiritual Advisors: Rev. CHARLES BAUER; Mr. ERNIE ALBONETTI, Lay Dir.
Chrismatic Renewal—Rev. JAMES L. MARTELL, Diocesan Liaison; Rev. PAUL CASPER, Assoc. Diocesan Liaison.

Department for Development and Public Relations

Secretary—Vacant, *P.O.Box 341669, Memphis, 38184-1669.* Tel: 901-373-1200.
Planned Giving and Major Donors—LLOYD CROCKETT, Dir.
Communications and Public Relations—JOHN E. MORRIS, Dir.

Department of Evangelization and Pastoral Services

Secretary—EILEEN C. HIVNER, *P.O. Box 341669, Memphis, 38184-1669.* Tel: 901-373-1200.
Diocesan Evangelization Commission—Vacant.
Office of Religious Education—CAROLYN TAMBOLI, Dir.
Resource Library—SARAH COLE.
Office of Christian Formation and Ministries—EILEEN HIVNER, Dir.
Institute for Pastoral Life Liaison—
Professional Ministry Enrichment Programs—
Parish Pastoral Councils—
Diocesan Ministries Training—
Office of Family Ministries—PATRICIA PERRY, Dir.
Diocesan Family Life Commission—JOHN HIVNER, Chm.
Committee for Separated, Divorced, Widowed—
Marriage Encounter—
Retrouvaille—Deacon JOHN HIVNER, Dir.
Natural Family Planning Center—MARY PAT VAN EPPS, Coord. Tel: 901-765-1757.
Programs for the Engaged—
Office of Youth and Young Adult Ministries—CATHERINE MENSI, Dir.; Rev. JAMES MCCARVER, Jackson Deanery.
Search Program—Rev. J. DAVID GRAHAM, JR., Dir.
Catholic Alumni Club—
Scouting—
Campus Ministry—Memphis, GERRY TAULMAN; Rev. FRANK DIXON, O.Carm.; Sr. SUE RUSSELL, R.S.M-.,Martin, Rev. JOSEPH PAOLOZZI, R.S.M.
Office of African American Catholic Ministry and Multi Cultural Ministries—Deacon CURTISS TALLEY, Dir.
African American Catholic Ministry—Deacon CURTISS TALLEY, Dir.
Comunidad Hispana Catolica de Memphis—GABRIEL PAEZ; Rev. DAVID KNIGHT, Chap.
Diocesan Commission for African American Catholics—O. C. PLEASANT, Chm.
Native American Ministry—RUTH ELLEN.
Polish Catholic Mission—BARBARA RYBINSKI; Deacon LARRY HOWELL, Chap.
Vietnamese Community—DOMINIC RAU VAN NGUYEN, Coord.; Sr. MARY PHUC, O.P., D.R.E.

CLERGY, PARISHES, MISSIONS AND PAROCHIAL SCHOOLS

CITY OF MEMPHIS
(Shelby County)

1—CATHEDRAL OF THE IMMACULATE CONCEPTION (1921), Revs. Thomas D. Kirk, Rector; Joseph Kerrigan; Deacon Dick Powelson.
Res., 1695 Central Ave., 38104. Tel: 901-725-2700; Fax: 901-725-2709.
School—1669 Central Ave., 38104. Tel: 901-725-2710. Dr. Maribeth Andereck, Prin.
Priests 2; Lay Teachers 20; Students 325.
High School—See separate category.

2—ST. ANN (1950), Revs. R. Bruce Cinquegrani; J. David Graham; Edward K. Fisher; Deacon James Quinn.
Res., 6529 Stage Rd., Bartlett, 38134. Tel: 901-373-6011; 386-3377; Fax: 901-373-9030.
School—Tel: 901-386-3328.
Sisters 1; Lay Teachers 38; Students 699.

3—ST. ANNE'S (1933), Rev. James L. Pugh.
Res., 706 S. Highland St., 38111. Tel: 901-323-3817.
School—670 S. Highland St., 38111. Tel: 901-323-1344.
Sisters 2; Lay Teachers 10; Students 189.

4—CHURCH OF THE ASCENSION (1974), Rev. Richard L. Mickey; Deacons F. Joseph Mensi; John T. Oates.
Res., 3680 RaMill Rd., 38128. Tel: 901-372-1364.

5—ST. AUGUSTINE (1937), Rev. Frank Coens, O.F.M.; Deacon Curtiss Talley.
Church—1169 Kerr Ave., 38106. Tel: 901-774-2297; Fax: 901-774-3067.

6—ST. BRIGID, Rev. Michael L. Stewart.
Church—7801 Lowrance Rd., 38125-2825. Tel: 901-758-0128.
Res., 4200 Thunderstone Cir. W., 38125-3108. Tel: 901-759-9628.

7—BLESSED SACRAMENT (1912), Rev. Charles A. Bauer.
Church—2564 Hale Ave., 38112. Tel: 901-452-1543.

8—ST. FRANCIS OF ASSISI (1985), Revs. Peter P. Buchignani; Ernie Deblasio; Deacon Max Saller.
Res., 8247 Chimneyrock Blvd., Cordova, 38018. Tel: 901-753-1494; Fax: 901-755-2168.
Church—8151 Chimneyrock Blvd., Cordova, 38018. Tel: 901-756-1213.

9—HOLY NAMES OF JESUS AND MARY (1939), Deacon Fred Brunner, Admin.
Res., 697 Keel Ave., 38107-2599. Tel: 901-525-9870.

10—HOLY ROSARY (1955), Revs. Bryan P. Timby; John A. Aiello; Gabriel DiFederico.
Church and Office: 4851 Park Ave., 38117. Tel: 901-767-6949; Fax: 901-767-8504.
School—4841 Park Ave., 38117. Tel: 901-685-1231.
Sisters 1; Lay Teachers 35; Students 671.

11—HOLY SPIRIT (1975), Revs. Albert E. Kirk; Edward M. Byrnes; Deacon Ned Turner.
Res., 2315 Hickory Crest, 38119. Tel: 901-754-8845; 754-7146; Fax: 901-754-0102.
Church—2300 Hickory Crest, 38119.

12—INCARNATION (1978), Rev. William R. Kantner; Deacon Charles Wells.
Res., 360 Bray Station Rd., Collierville, 38017. Tel: 901-853-7468.

13—ST. JAMES (1956), Rev. Patrick F. Heenan.
Res., 4180 LeRoy, 38108. Tel: 901-767-8672.

14—ST. JOHN'S (1947), Rev. Robert J. Holko, S.C.J.
Res., 2742 Lamar Ave., 38114. Tel: 901-743-4551.

15—ST. JOSEPH'S (1878), Rev. William F. Stelling.
Res., 3825 Neely Rd., 38109. Tel: 901-396-9996.

16—ST. LOUIS (1957), Revs. J. Peter Sartain; Richard Cortese; Gregory Salata; Cyril Wagner, O.F.M.; Deacon Ralph Donati.
Res., 203 S. White Station Rd., 38117. Tel: 901-682-6606; Fax: 901-680-0571.
School—5192 Shady Grove Rd., 38117. Tel: 901-682-9692.
Lay Teachers 26; Aides 3; Students 509.

17—ST. MARY'S (1861), Rev. Maury Smith, O.F.M.; Deacon James Champion.
Church and Office: 155 Market St., 38105. Tel: 901-522-9420; Fax: 901-522-9452.
Res., Franciscan Friary, 1254 S. Lauderdale, 38106. Tel: 901-774-8191.

18—ST. MICHAEL'S (1951), Revs. John V. Atkinson; Alfred Graham.
Office: 3848 Forrest Ave., 38122. Tel: 901-323-0896; 324-6411; Fax: 901-323-3557.
Res., 3867 Summer Ave., 38122. Tel: 901-454-1349; 452-6036.
School—3880 Forrest Ave., 38122. Tel: 901-323-2162.
Lay Teachers 18; Students 158.

19—CHURCH OF THE NATIVITY (1979), Rev. Robert D. Ponticello.
Res., 5955 St. Elmo, Barlett, 38135. Tel: 901-382-2504; Fax: 901-382-3644.

20—ST. PATRICK'S (1866), Revs. Paul Dechant, C.S.P.; Gilbert Martinez, C.S.P.; James F. Fisher, C.S.P., (Retired).
Res., 277 S. Fourth St., 38126. Tel: 901-527-2542; Fax: 901-525-1147.

21—ST. PAUL THE APOSTLE (1944), Revs. John B. McArthur; Michael A. Morgera; Deacon Richard Williams.
Res., 1425 E. Shelby Dr., 38116. Tel: 901-346-2380.
School—Tel: 901-346-0862.
Sisters 3; Lay Teachers 18; Students 304.

22—OUR LADY OF PERPETUAL HELP (1952), Revs. Milton J. Guthrie; Joseph Thinh Nguyen; Marian Spadini; Deacon Walter Chandler.
Res., 8151 Poplar, Germantown, 38138. Tel: 901-754-1204; Fax: 901-753-1181.

23—ST. PETER'S (1840), Rev. Joachim Culotta, O.P.
Res., 190 Adams Ave., 38103. Tel: 901-527-8282; Fax: 901-526-6882.

24—CHURCH OF THE RESURRECTION (1973), Rev. Daniel F. Moore.
Res., 5425 Newberry, 38115-3629. Tel: 901-794-8970; Fax: 901-794-8806.

25—SACRED HEART (1899), Rev. David B. Knight. In res., Rev. Berchmans Kodakal (Kerala).
Res., 1324 Jefferson Ave., 38104. Tel: 901-726-1891; Fax: 901-726-9272.

26—OUR LADY OF SORROWS (1926), Rev. Richard M. Gantert.
Res., 3700 Thomas St., 38127. Tel: 901-353-1530.
School—3690 Thomas St., 38127. Tel: 901-358-7431.
Religious 2; Lay Teachers 6; Students 105.

27—ST. THERESE OF THE INFANT JESUS (1930), Rev. David M. Foley.
Res., 1644 Jackson Ave., 38107. Tel: 901-276-1412.

28—ST. WILLIAM (1951), Rev. J. Edwin Creary.
Res., 4932 Easley Ave., Millington, 38053. Tel: 901-872-4099; 872-2279.

OUTSIDE SHELBY COUNTY

Brownsville, Haywood Co., St. John (1952), Rev. William Parham.
Church—N. Washington St., Hwy. 79, Box 872, 38012.

Bolivar, Hardeman Co., St. Mary, Rev. Carl J. Hood.
Res., 223 Mecklinberg Dr., 38008-1736. Tel: 901-658-4627.

Camden, Benton Co., St. Mary Church (1981), Rev. Stephen K. Kenny.
Res., 220 W. Main St., 38320. Tel: 901-584-6459.
Mission—Huntingdon, Carroll Co., Holy Family Church, 265 Cotham Dr., Huntingdon, 38344. Tel: 901-986-2817.

Covington, Tipton Co., St. Alphonsus (1952), Rev. William J. DeVries.
Res., 1512 Evergreen, 38019. Tel: 901-476-0374.
Church—1225 Hwy. 51 S., P.O. Box 430, 38019. Tel: 901-476-8140.
Mission—Ripley, Lauderdale Co., Ave Maria, 664 S. Washington, Ripley, 38063. Tel: 901-635-8800.

Dyersburg, Dyer Co., Holy Angels (1940), Rev. Elbert Callis.
Res., 526 Charles St., P.O. Box 1929, 38025-1929. Tel: 901-287-8000; Fax: 901-287-7632.

Humboldt, Gibson Co., Sacred Heart (1872), Rev. Peter L. Wiethe.
Res., 2877 E. Main, 38343. Tel: 901-784-3904.
Mission—Crockett Co.

Jackson, Madison Co., St. Mary's (1867), Revs. William J. Parham; J. Keith Stewart.
Res., 1665 Hwy. 45 Byp., 38305. Tel: 901-668-2596; Fax: 901-668-4387.
School—Tel: 901-668-2525; Fax: 901-668-0409.
Sisters 4; Lay Teachers 14; Students 272.
Mission—Brownsville, Haywood Co., St. John Church, P.O. Box 872, Brownsville, 38012. Tel: 901-772-3514.

Lexington, Henderson Co., St. Andrew, Rev. Valentine Handwerker.
Church—311 Elizabeth Circle, 38351. Tel: 901-968-6393.
Res., 311 Elizabeth Cr., 38351. Tel: 901-968-7949.
Mission—Parsons, Decatur Co., St. Regina, 108 Skyline Ln., Parsons 38361. Tel: 901-847-2054.

Martin, Weakley Co., St. Jude's (1968), Rev. Joseph L. Paolozzi.
Res., 104 Hannings Ln., 38237. Tel: 901-587-9777.

Milan, Gibson Co., St. Matthew Mission, Rev. Peter L. Wiethe.
Mailing Address: St. Jude Church, 104 Hannings Ln., Martin, 38237.

Church—9060 Telecom Dr., 38358. Tel: 901-686-8686.

Paris, Henry Co., Holy Cross (1921), Rev. Victor P. Ciaramitaro.
Res., 1210 E. Wood St., 38242. Tel: 901-642-4681; Fax: 901-644-9668.

Savannah, Hardin Co., St. Mary's (1948), Rev. James Joseph Martell.
Res., 1107 Clifton Rd., 38372. Tel: 901-925-4852.

Selmer, McNairy Co., St. Jude (1982), Rev. Carl J. Hood.
Res., Hwy. 45 N., P.O. Box 342, 38375. Tel: 901-645-4188.

Somerville, Fayette Co., St. Philip the Apostle (1981), Rev. Cyril Wagner, O.F.M.; Sr. Jeanne L. Dion, O.P., Pastoral Admin.
Church—11710 Hwy. 64, 38068. Tel: 901-465-8685.

Union City, Obion Co., Immaculate Conception (1891), Rev. Jim McCarver.
Res., 1303 E. Reelfoot Ave., 38261. Tel: 901-885-0963; Fax: 901-885-9960.

Chaplains of Public Institutions

MEMPHIS. *Federal Correctional Institute at Memphis.* Rev. Peter Literal, Chap.

On Special Assignment:
Reverend Monsignors—
Kleiser, William J., Diocesan Tribunal

On Duty Outside the Diocese:
Reverend Fathers—
Henkes, Donald E.
Kelly, Edward, St. Louis University, St. Louis, MO
Nobile, Angelo

Military Chaplains:
Reverend Fathers—
Danner, James L., COMNAVSURFPAC (N01G), 2841 Rendova Rd., San Diego, CA 92155-5490
Lamb, Gary E., Chap., U.S. Navy

Retired:
Reverend Monsignors—
Batson, John R., 2000 S. Ocean Dr. #508, Ft. Lauderdale, FL 33316. Tel: 954-467-1972
Clunan, Paul W., 38 N. Idlewild St., #13, Memphis, TN 38104
Davis, William F., 745 Loeb St., Memphis, TN 38111
Heymer, Edward D., 941 Ivy Rd., Memphis, TN 38117
Lynch, Patrick J., 141 N. McLean Blvd., #317, Memphis, TN 38104
Wiggs, Joel M., 4250 Main St., P.O. Box 306, Humboldt, TN 38343-0306. Tel: 901-784-3233
Reverend Fathers—
Cleary, Edward J., 4776 Childs Dr., Memphis, TN 38116. Tel: 901-397-5997
Elliott, Edward C., Kirby Pines Estates No. N-309, 3535 Kirby Rd., Memphis, TN 38115. Tel: 901-794-5256
Gaffney, James, 108 N. Auburndale #1001, Memphis, TN 38104
Kelly, Edgar M., 38 N. Idlewild St., #3, Memphis, TN 38104
Murphy, James W., Mainstreet Lodge, 909 Mainstreet, N.E., Minneapolis, MN 55413
Oglesby, J. Leonard, Rte. 1, Box 189, Pope, MS 38658
St. Charles, Paul W., 122 Tallwood Dr., Nashville, TN 37211-2711
Stritch, Morris G., Christian Brothers High School, 5900 Walnut Grove Rd., Memphis, TN 38120

Permanent Deacons:
Bass, George
Brunner, Fred
Champion, James
Chandler, Walter
Cranford, William
Donati, Ralph
Finnegan, William
Herbers, Jerome
Hicks, Joseph
Hivner, John
Howell, Larry
Johnson, Eldon
McCarver, Kenneth
Mensi, Joseph
Oates, John
Powelson, Richard
Quinn, Jim
Saller, Max
Schmall, James
Talley, Curtiss
Turner, Ned
Wells, Charles
Williams, Richard

INSTITUTIONS LOCATED IN THE DIOCESE

[A] COLLEGES AND UNIVERSITIES

*MEMPHIS. *Christian Brothers University*, (1871), 650 E. Parkway S., 38104. Tel: 901-321-3000.
For a complete listing, refer to the Colleges and Universities section.

[B] DIOCESAN SCHOOLS

MEMPHIS. *Bishop Byrne High School* (1965), 1475 E. Shelby Dr., 38116; Fax: 901-346-3062. Mrs. Neddy Brookshaw, Prin. Sisters 2; Lay Teachers 26; Students 300.

Memphis Catholic High School and Middle School, 61 N. McLean Blvd., 38104. Tel: 901-276-1221. Mr. Donald Edwards, Prin. Sisters 1; Lay Teachers 26; Students 298.

CORDOVA. *St. Benedict at Auburndale School.* (Grades K-12), 2100 N. Germantown Pkwy., 38018. Tel: 901-388-7321. Special programs for gifted and learning disabled. Dr. Mary C. McDonald, Prin. Lay Teachers 56; Students 715.

[C] HIGH SCHOOLS, PRIVATE AND PAROCHIAL

MEMPHIS.

**Christian Brothers High School*, 5900 Walnut Grove Rd., 38120. Tel: 901-682-7801; Fax: 901-682-7815. Title of Incorporation: Christian Brothers (LaSalle) High School. Bros. Christopher Englert, F.S.C., Prin.; Denis Sutter, F.S.C., Dir. of Brothers' Community; Revs. Morris G. Stritch, (Retired); Eric Burdt, O.SS.T. Priests 2; Brothers 10; Lay Teachers 51; Students 834.

Immaculate Conception Cathedral Middle and High School (1950), 1725 Central Ave., 38104. Tel: 901-276-6341; Fax: 901-726-0141. Mrs. Cheri Kamler, Prin.; Rev. Tom Kirk. Lay Teachers 28; Students 304.

St. Agnes Academy (1851), 4830 Walnut Grove Rd., 38117. Tel: 901-767-1377.
Title of Incorporation: St. Agnes Academy-St. Dominic School, Inc. Sisters of St. Dominic (St. Catharine, KY). Barbara Daush, Pres.; Marian Lehan Swicker, Dean. Lay Teachers 29; Students 243.

[D] ELEMENTARY SCHOOLS, PRIVATE

MEMPHIS. *St. Agnes Academy.* (Grades PreK-8), 4830 Walnut Grove Rd., 38117. Tel: 901-767-1377. Sisters of St. Dominic. (St. Catharine, KY). Barbara Daush, Pres. Lay Teachers 31; Students 220.

St. Dominic Boys School, 30 Avon Rd., 38117. Tel: 901-682-3011. Sisters of St. Dominic. (St. Catherine, KY). Mrs. Barbara Daush, Pres.; Mr. John Murphy, Dean. Lay Teachers 29; Students 226.

[E] CHILD-CARING INSTITUTIONS

MEMPHIS. *St. Peter Home for Children*, (1852), 1805 Poplar Ave., 38104. Tel: 901-725-8240.
For a complete listing, refer to the Special Care Facilities section.

GERMANTOWN. *Madonna Learning Center for Retarded Children*, 7007 Poplar Ave., 38138. Tel: 901-752-5767.
For a complete listing, refer to the Special Care Facilities section.

[F] GENERAL HOSPITALS

MEMPHIS. *St. Joseph Hospital*, (1889), 220 Overton Ave., 38105. Tel: 901-577-2700; Fax: 901-577-3620.
For a complete listing, refer to the Hospitals section.

[G] DAYCARE CENTERS

MEMPHIS. *Holy Names Preschool & After School Program*, 709 Keel, 38107. Tel: 901-525-8443. Legal Title: *Holy Names Center.* Ms. Linda Steed, Coord. & Prog. Dir.

St. Louis Extended, 5192 Shady Grove Rd., 38117. Tel: 901-682-9692. Ms. Lori Tucker, Site Supvr. Children 100.

St. Michael Extended, 3880 Forrest Ave., 38122. Tel: 901-324-6662. Ms. Debbie Kallaher, Site Supvr. Children 100.

St. Therese Little Flower Day Care Center, 1666 Jackson Ave., 38107. Tel: 901-276-5111. Ms. Sharon Webb, Prog. Dir. Children 125.

CORDOVA. *St. Benedict at Auburndale Extended*, 2100 N. Germantown Rd., 38018. Tel: 901-388-7337. Ms. Josephine P. Follin, Site Supvr. Children 112.

[H] PROTECTIVE INSTITUTIONS

MEMPHIS. *DeNeuville Heights School for Girls*, (1875), 3060 Baskin St., 38127.
For a complete listing, refer to the Special Care Facilities section.

[I] ADULT RESIDENCES & HOMES FOR AGED

MEMPHIS. *Diocese of Memphis Housing Corp.*, P.O. Box 41705, 38174-1705. Tel: 901-722-4761; 722-4772.
For a complete listing, refer to the Special Care Facilities section.

Northwood Park Apartments, 1130 N. Breedlove, 38107. Tel: 901-522-9134.
For a complete listing, refer to the Special Care Facilities section.

St. Peter Manor, 108 N. Auburndale, 38104. Tel: 901-278-8200.
For a complete listing, refer to the Special Care Facilities section.

St. Peter Villa, 141 N. McLean, 38104-2644. Tel: 901-276-2021.
For a complete listing, refer to the Special Care Facilities section.

DYERSBURG. *St. Joseph Manor*, 885 Hwy. 51, Byp. W., P.O. Box 151, 38024. Tel: 901-285-8560.
For a complete listing, refer to the Special Care Facilities section.

The Village Apartments, Hwy. 51 Byp. W., P.O. Box 151, 38024. Tel: 901-285-8560.
For a complete listing, refer to the Special Care Facilities section.

Westgate Apartments, 1405-8 Meeks, 38024. Tel: 901-286-4874.
For a complete listing, refer to the Special Care Facilities section.

HUMBOLDT. *St. Matthew Manor*, 2575 Viking Dr., 38343. Tel: 901-784-7229.
For a complete listing, refer to the Special Care Facilities section.

JACKSON. *St. Mary Manor*, 1771 Hwy. 45 By-Pass, 38305. Tel: 901-668-5633.
For a complete listing, refer to the Special Care Facilities section.

MOSCOW. *St. Mark Village Apartments*, 85 St. Mark Cove, 38057. Tel: 901-877-3456.
For a complete listing, refer to the Special Care Facilities section.

[J] RESIDENCES OF PRIESTS AND BROTHERS

MEMPHIS. *Brothers Of The Christian Schools (Prov. of St. Louis)*, 650 E. Parkway, S., 38104. Tel: 901-321-3000; Fax: 901-722-0290. 5900 Walnut Grove Rd., 38119. Tel: 901-682-4704. Brothers 37.

Franciscan Friars (Sacred Heart Prov.) of Memphis, 1254 S. Lauderdale, 38106. Tel: 901-774-8191. Revs. Maury Smith, O.F.M.; Frank Coens, O.F.M.; Cyril J. Wagner, O.F.M.; Bro. Roch Pfeifer, O.F.M. Priests 3; Brothers 1.

Order Of Preachers (Southern Dominican Prov.), 190 Adams Ave., 38103. Tel: 901-527-8282. Revs. Joachim Culotta, O.P.; Edward Everitt, O.P.; Bro. Michael Curtis, O.P.

Order of The Holy Trinity, 5900 Walnut Grove Rd., 38120-2174. Rev. Eric T. Burdt, O.SS.T., Chap., Christian Brothers High School.

Paulist Fathers (New York), St. Patrick Church, 277 S. Fourth St., 38126. Tel: 901-527-2542; Fax: 901-525-1147. Revs. Paul Dechant, C.S.P., Pastor; Gilbert Martinez, C.S.P., Assoc. Pastor; James Fisher, C.S.P., (Retired). Priests 3.

JACKSON. *Brothers Of St. Francis Xavier (Xaverians, Sacred Heart Prov.)*, 611 Burkett St., 38301. Tel: 901-424-5003. Bro. Dan O'Brien, C.F.X.

[K] CONVENTS AND RESIDENCES FOR SISTERS

MEMPHIS. *Dominican Sisters, Congregation of St. Catharine of Siena, KY O.P.*, St. Agnes Convent, 4792 Walnut Grove Rd., 38117. Tel: 901-683-1333. Legal Title: *Dominican Sisters, Congregation of St. Cecilia (Nashville, TN), St. Paul Convent.* Sisters 6.

Dominican Sisters, Congregation of St. Cecila, 1488 Maurine Dr., 38116. Tel: 901-346-0251; Fax: 901-332-3983. Sisters 7.

Medical Mission Sisters of Philadelphia (PA) M.M.S. Mailing Address: 1437 Central Ave. #806, 38104-4830. Tel: 901-272-9932.

Missionaries of Charity, 700 N. 7th St., 38107. Tel: 901-527-4947. Shelter. Tel: 901-526-5456. Sr. M. Sujaya, M.C., Superior. Sisters 4.

Missionary Sisters Of The Society Of Mary (Waltham, MA) S.M.S.M., 60 S. Auburndale, 38104. Tel: 901-272-2808. Sisters 5.

Monastery Of St. Clare O.S.C., 1310 Dellwood Ave., 38127. Tel: 901-357-6662. Sr. Mary Helen, O.S.C., Abbess. Sisters 8; Huehuetenango, Guatamala 3.

Sisters Of Charity Of Nazareth (KY) S.C.N., 904

Hawthorne, 38107. Tel: 901-276-7386.
Sisters Of Charity Of The Blessed Virgin Mary (Dubuque, IA) B.V.M., 286 N. McNeil St., 38112. Tel: 901-274-9015. Sr. Jacquelyn Cramer, B.V.M., Community Rep. Sisters 3.
Sisters of Our Lady of Charity of the Good Shepherd (St. Louis, MO) R.G.S., Convent of the Good Shepherd, 3060 Baskin St., 38127. Tel: 901-357-7316. Sr. Mary Rosalinda Sobremisana, R.G.S., Admin. 13.
Sisters Of St. Benedict (Ferdinand, IN) O.S.B., 5190 Normandy Ave., 38117. Tel: 901-767-7372. Sr. Mary Mark Graf. Sisters 2.
Sisters Of St. Francis (Rochester, MN) O.S.F., 695 S. Barksdale, 38104. Tel: 901-276-8756.
Sisters Of St. Francis Of Perpetual Adoration (Mishawaka, IN) O.S.F. Sr. Elizabeth Ann, O.S.F., St. Joseph Hospital Convent, 220 Overton Ave., 38105. Tel: 901-577-3879; Fax: 901-577-3620. Sisters 5.
Sisters Of St. Joseph Of Pennsylvania (Erie, PA) S.S.J., 931 Ivy, 38117. Tel: 901-821-9907. Sr. Marilyn Terwilliger, S.S.J.

HUNTINGDON. *Franciscan Sisters of Little Falls (Little Falls, MN)*, 257 Cotham Dr., 38344. Tel: 901-986-2817. Sr. Jeanette E. Martell, O.S.F.; Sr. Clara Schroedl, O.S.F.; Sr. Ruth Nistler, O.S.F. Sisters 3.

SOMERVILLE. *Sinsinawa Dominican Sisters*, 305 Charleston St. #6, 38068. Tel: 901-465-6371. Sr. Jeanne Dion, O.P.

[L] NEWMAN CENTERS

MEMPHIS. *Campus Ministry, University of Memphis, Rhodes College*, 3625 Mynders, 38111. Tel: 901-323-3051. UT Center for Health Sciences. Gerry Taulman, Dir.

MARTIN. *Cooperative Ministries Interfaith Center*, 312 Lovelace Ave., 38237. Tel: 901-587-2603. Rev. Joseph Paolozzi.

[M] MISCELLANEOUS

MEMPHIS. *Birthright of Memphis, Inc.*, 115 Alexander, 38111. Tel: 901-327-8109. 1750 Frayser Blvd., Ste. H, 38127. Tel: 901-353-2828. Mrs. Fran Theos, Dir.
Catholic Hispanic Community of Memphis (Comunidad Catolica Hispana de Memphis), Sacred Heart Church, 1324 Jefferson, 38104. Tel: 901-726-1891. Suzanne Martin, Contact.
Cenacle Retreat League, 2265 Tunis Cove, 38104. Tel: 901-274-0438. Ms. Francis Gianotti.
Diocesan Council of Catholic Women, 6659 Fossil Creek, 38120. Tel: 901-753-3751. Mrs. Mary Ann S. Brenner.
Knights of St. Peter Claver (St. Benedict the Black Council No. 188), 5600 Santa Barbara, 38116. Tel: 901-396-8315. Mr. Joseph Randolph, Grand Knight & Vice Pres. Metro Committee S.P.C.
Ladies of Charity of Memphis, 4046 Rhodes, 38111. Tel: 901-323-9076. Mrs. Barbara Singleton, Pres.
**Madonna Circle, Inc.* (Catholic Women's Service Organization), P.O. Box 172174, 38187-2174. Tel: 901-685-7290. Mrs. John F. Presley, Pres.
Marriage Preparation Program, The Catholic Center, 5825 Shelby Oaks Dr., 38134. Tel: 901-373-1235. Mrs. Patricia A. Perry, Coord.
St. Patrick's Center, 277 S. Fourth St., 38126. Tel: 901-527-2542. Rev. Paul Dechant, C.S.P., Dir.
St. Vincent DePaul Society, 3649 Winplace Rd., 38118. Mr. Kenny Bowen, Pres. Tel: 901-365-4830; Rev. Carl J. Hood, Spiritual Dir.
Saint Vincent Palloti Center for Parish Social Ministry, 1325 Jefferson Ave., 38104. Tel: 901-722-4758; Fax: 901-722-4791. P.O. Box 41679, 38174.

CAMDEN. *Good Samaritan Village*, 192 Post Oak Rd., 38320. Mailing Address: Diocese of Memphis Housing Corporation, c/o Mr. David Field, 85 N. Cleveland, Memphis, 38104. Mr. David Field, Dir.

CORDOVA. *Serra Club*, 884 Rocky Hills Cove, 38018. Tel: 901-755-3645. Mr. Werner Rose, Pres.; Rev. J. David Graham, Chap.

JACKSON. *Birthright of Jackson, Inc.*, 273 N. Highland, 38301. Tel: 901-422-3797. Linda Williams, Dir.
Jonah Inc., 416 E. Lafayette, 1st floor, 38301. Tel: 901-427-1630. Mrs. Shirley Richmond, Exec. Dir.

SAVANNAH. *Charismatic Prayer Groups*, 1107 Clifton Rd., 38372. Tel: 901-925-4852. Rev. James J. Martell.

RELIGIOUS INSTITUTES OF MEN REPRESENTED IN THE DIOCESE

For further details refer to the corresponding bracketed number in the Religious Institutes of Men or Women section.

[1350]—*Brothers of St. Francix Xavier.*—C.F.X.
[0330]—*Brothers of The Christian Schools.* (St. Louis Prov.).—F.S.C.
[1130]—*Congregation of the Priests of the Sacred Heart.*—S.C.J.
[0520]—*Franciscan Friars.*—O.F.M.
[0430]—*Order of Preachers (Dominicans).*—O.P.
[1310]—*Order of The Holy Trinity.*—O.S.S.T.
[1030]—*Paulist Fathers.*—C.S.P.

RELIGIOUS INSTITUTES OF WOMEN REPRESENTED IN THE DIOCESE

[0230]—*Benedictine Sisters of the Pontifical Jurisdiction.*—O.S.B.
[1070-01]—*Dominican Sisters.*—O.P.
[1070-03]—*Dominican Sisters.*—O.P.
[1070-07]—*Dominican Sisters.*—O.P.
[1070-13]—*Dominican Sisters.*—O.P.
[1310]—*Franciscan Sisters of Little Falls, Minnesota.*—O.S.F.
[2420]—*Marist Missionary Sisters.*—S.M.S.M.
[2490]—*Medical Mission Sisters.*—S.C.M.M.
[2710]—*Missionaries of Charity.*—M.C.
[1360]—*Missionary Franciscan Sisters of the Immaculate Conception.*—O.S.F.
[3760]—*Order of St. Clare.* (Memphis, TN).—O.S.C.
[0440]—*Sisters of Charity of Cincinnati, Ohio.*—S.C.
[0500]—*Sisters of Charity of Nazareth.*—S.C.N.
[0430]—*Sisters of Charity of the Blessed Virgin Mary.*—B.V.M.
[1640]—*Sisters of St. Francis of Perpetual Adoration.* (Prov. of the Immaculate Heart of Mary).—O.S.F.
[3830-09]—*Sisters of St. Joseph.*—S.S.J.
[3830-13]—*Sisters of St. Joseph.*—C.S.J.
[1830]—*The Sisters of the Good Shepherd.* (St. Louis Prov.).—R.G.S.

DIOCESAN CEMETERIES

MEMPHIS. *All Saints*, c/o Calvary Cemetery, 1663 Elvis Presley Blvd., 38106. Tel: 901-948-1529.
Calvary, 1663 Elvis Presley Blvd., 38106. Tel: 901-948-1529.

JACKSON. *Calvary.*

NECROLOGY

† Donnelly, John R., Memphis, TN, Blessed Sacrament Church. —Died April 19, 1996.
† Doyle, Howard, Memphis, TN, St. Louis Church. —Died Feb. 5, 1996.
† Ewing, Robert J., Memphis, TN, St. Therese Church. —Died Sep. 14, 1996.
† Fuller, Gregory J., Memphis, TN, St. Louis Church. —Died Sep. 10, 1996.

Diocese of Metuchen

Most Reverend

EDWARD T. HUGHES, D.D.

Bishop of Metuchen; ordained May 31, 1947; appointed Auxiliary to Archbishop of Philadelphia and Titular Bishop of Segia June 14, 1976; consecrated July 21, 1976; appointed Second Bishop of Metuchen December 11, 1986; installed February 5, 1987. *Res., 10 Library Pl., Metuchen, NJ, 08840.*

ESTABLISHED NOVEMBER 19, 1981.

Square Miles 1424.55.

Comprises the Counties of Warren, Hunterdon, Somerset and Middlesex in the State of New Jersey.

Legal Corporate Title: The Diocese of Metuchen.

The Diocesan Center: P.O. Box 191, Metuchen, NJ, 08840. Tel.: 732-283-3800; Fax: 732-283-2012.

STATISTICAL OVERVIEW

Personnel	
Bishop	1
Priests: Diocesan Active in Diocese	171
Priests: Active Outside Diocese	17
Priests: Diocesan in Foreign Missions	1
Priests: Retired, Sick or Absent	23
Number of Diocesan Priests	212
Religious Priests in Diocese	45
Extern Priests in Diocese	21
Ordinations:	
Diocesan Priests	4
Transitional Deacons	2
Permanent Deacons	16
Permanent Deacons in Diocese	104
Total Brothers	24
Total Sisters	496
Parishes	
Parishes	108
With Resident Pastor:	
Resident Diocesan Priests	97
Resident Religious Priests	5
Without Resident Pastor:	
Administered by Priests	6
Professional Ministry Personnel:	
Brothers	2
Sisters	45
Lay Ministers	72
Welfare	
Catholic Hospitals	1
Total Assisted	158,798
Health Care Centers	1
Total Assisted	1,723
Homes for the Aged	3
Total Assisted	288
Day Care and Extended Day Care Centers	8
Total Assisted	1,878
Specialized Homes	3
Total Assisted	65
Special Centers for Social Services	9
Total Assisted	18,534
Residential Care of Disabled	1
Total Assisted	10
Other Institutions	2
Total Assisted	38
Educational	
Diocesan Students in Other Seminaries	16
Total Seminarians	16
High Schools, Diocesan and Parish	4
Total Students	2,695
High Schools, Private	2
Total Students	1,107
Elementary Schools, Diocesan and Parish	42
Total Students	14,216
Elementary Schools, Private	1
Total Students	206
Non-residential Schools for the Disabled	1
Total Students	37
Catechesis/Religious Education:	
High School Students	1,255
Elementary Students	37,119
Total Students Under Catholic Instruction	56,651
Teachers in the Diocese:	
Brothers	11
Sisters	91
Lay Teachers	884
Vital Statistics	
Receptions into the Church:	
Infant Baptism Totals	7,407
Adult Baptism Totals	154
Received into Full Communion	280
First Communions	6,738
Confirmations	5,048
Marriages:	
Catholic	1,678
Interfaith	432
Total Marriages	2,110
Deaths	3,865
Total Catholic Population	483,196
Total Population	1,177,058

Former Bishops—Most Rev. THEODORE E. MCCARRICK, ord. May 31, 1958; appt. Titular Bishop of Rusibisir and Auxiliary to the Archbishop of New York, May 24, 1977; cons. June 29, 1977; appt. first Bishop of Metuchen, Nov. 19, 1981; installed Jan. 31, 1982; promoted to the Archdiocese of Newark, June 3, 1986; installed July 25, 1986.

The Diocesan Center—P.O. Box 191, Metuchen, 08840. Tel: 732-283-3800; Fax: 732-283-2012.

Vicar General—Rev. Msgr. JOHN B. SZYMANSKI.

Episcopal Vicars—Rev. Msgr. ANTHONY J. LUISINI; Rev. Msgr. ANTHONY J. GAMBINO; Rev. Msgr. JAMES P. MORAN.

The Diocesan Curia

Moderator—Rev. Msgr. JOHN B. SZYMANSKI, V.G.

The Secretariat for Canonical Affairs

Secretary—Rev. CHARLES T. O'CONNOR, S.T.L.

Delegates for Dispensations—Revs. BRIAN J. NOLAN; CHARLES A. SABELLA; THOMAS J. SERAFIN; THOMAS J. WALSH.

The Center for Counseling and Consultation Svcs.—29 Abeel St., New Brunswick, 08901. Rev. JOSEPH B. SZULWACH, Dir.

The Chancery

Chancellor—Sr. M. MICHAELITA WIECHETEK, C.S.S.F.

Vice Chancellor for Community Affairs—EILEEN A. TABERT, Office of Parish Leadership Services.

The Tribunal

The Diocesan Center—P.O. Box 191, Metuchen, 08840. Tel: 732-283-3800; Fax: 732-283-2012.

Judicial Vicar—Rev. Msgr. WILLIAM BENWELL, J.C.L.

Associate Judicial Vicar—Rev. RICHARD J. LYONS, J.C.L.

Staff—Revs. CHESTER H. CARINA, J.C.L.; NEIL W. DAVIN, C.P., J.C.L.; GEORGE KORYTKOWSKI, O.F.M.Cap., J.C.D.; ROBERT V. MEYERS, J.C.L.; GEORGE M. PISANELLO, J.C.L.; Rev. Msgr. JOHN R. TORNEY, P.A.; Sr. MARY A. KERWIN, R.S.M.; EUGENE F. HORAN; BARBARA J. REAVEY.

Psychological Consultant—FRED J. MCDONALD, Ph.D.

Notaries—MARY JEAN BELSKY; ZENORA LALA-OUTHMAN.

Vicariate for Administration

Vicar for Administration—Rev. Msgr. EUGENE PRUS.

Office of Resource Management—RICHARD P. GERRITY, Exec. Dir.

Department of Finance—RICHARD P. GERRITY, Dir.

Department of Insurance and Pensions—M. BARBARA FRANCFORT, Mgr.

Department of Cemeteries—EUGENE G. BURNS, Dir. THOMAS J. POTENZA, Asst. Dir.; Very Rev. ANDREW L. SZAROLETA, Dir., Pastoral Care.

Department of Management Information Systems—MICHAEL L. GIRASOLI, Mgr.

Department of Property Management—ROGER A. STONE, Supvr., Building Maintenance.

Office of Development—Rev. Msgr. MICHAEL J. CORONA, Dir.; Deacon WILLIAM C. VANZINO, Asst. Dir.; Deacon FRANK J. ENGEL, JR., Development Officer, Bishop's Appeal & Diocesan Projects; DONNA J. KARYCKI, Development Officer, Catholic Charities/Exec. Dir. Flame of Charity Foundation; Mr. AL F. FEMIA, Senior Communications Coord.

"The Catholic Spirit"—RAYANNE DIAMIANO, Editor-in-Chief.

Office of the Missions—Rev. Msgr. RICHARD A. BEHL, Dir.; Sr. MARY JO BURGHDUFF, O.S.F., Assoc. Dir.

Office of Personnel Management—JUDITH H. EICHMAN, Dir.

Commission on Building—Rev. Msgr. EUGENE PRUS, Chm.

Commission for Sites and Boundaries—Rev. STEPHEN H. CONGDON, Chm.

Vicariate for Education

Vicar for Education—Rev. Msgr. GEORGE M. BREMBOS, Ed.D.

Office of the Schools—LORRAINE P. AMENDOLARA, Ed.D., Supt. Assoc. Supts.: Sr. MARY ROSE WATKINS, O.S.F.; Sr. MARYANN JACOBS, S.C.C.; Sr. PATRICIA MCCLURE, S.S.J.; JEAN F. KOLLAR, Admin., Instructional Support Svcs.

Office of Religious Education—MARY KAY CULLINAN, Dir. DOLORES R. NANN, Assoc. Dir.

Office of Youth Ministry—Rev. DAVID J. NICGORSKI, O.M.V., Dir. DIANE DWYER, Admin., Youth Retreat Center.

Commission for Young Adult Ministry—Rev. DAVID J. NICGORSKI, O.M.V., Dir.

Vicariate for Personnel in Ministry

Vicar for Personnel in Ministry—Rev. Msgr. SEAMUS F. BRENNAN.

Office of Ministry to Priests—Rev. CHARLES W. CICERALE, Dir.

Office of the Diaconate—Deacon LUKE J. HALLY, Dir.

Office for Religious—Vacant.

Office of Vocations—Revs. ROBERT G. LYNAM, Dir. JOSEPH M. CURRY, Assoc. Dir. JOSEPH G. CELENO,

Assoc. Dir., College Awareness.
Office of the Health Care Apostolate—Rev. JOSEPH L. DESMOND, Dir.
Commission for the Continuing Education of Priests—Rev. Msgr. WILLIAM BENWELL, Chm.
Board for Seminary Education—Rev. CHESTER H. CARINA.

Vicariate For Pastoral Life

Mailing Address: P.O. Box 6189, E. Brunswick, 08816. Tel: 732-651-8084.
Vicar for Pastoral Life—Rev. Msgr. MICHAEL J. ALLIEGRO.
Office of Family Life Ministry—JUDITH A. PSOTA, Dir.
Office of Evangelization—Revs. GREGORY E.S. MALOVETZ, Dir. GREGORY J. SHORT, O.V.M., Coord., Parish Retreat Ministries.
Office for Shared Ministry—DOROTHY S. HEITZ, Dir.
Office for Multi-Cultural Ministries—Rev. Msgr. ANTHONY J. GAMBINO, Dir.
Commission for African-American Catholic Ministry—JOSEPH J. POWELL, Chm.
Commission for Ecumenical Affairs—Rev. JEROME A. JOHNSON, Chm.
Commission for the Filipino Apostolate—Rev. EDGARDO D. ABANO, Chm.
Commission for Hispanic Ministry—Rev. Msgr. ANTHONY J. GAMBINO, Chm.
Chinese Apostolate—Rev. JOSEPH FU, Chap.
Korean Apostolate—Rev. PETER K. CHOI, Chap.
Portuguese Apostolate—Rev. LAURO C. SEDLMAYER, Chap.
Commission for Pro-Life Action—Rev. Msgr. RICHARD A. BEHL, Chm.
Commission for Ministries with Senior Citizens & People with Disabilities—Rev. ROBERT W. MEDLEY.
Vietnamese Apostolate—Rev. ALFONSO T. NGUYEN, Chap.
Commission for Worship and Preaching—Rev. JOSEPH C. KORNOSKI, Chm.

Diocesan Organizations, Movements and Moderators

Campaign for Human Development—MARY E. NOWACKI, Diocesan Liaison.
Catholic Lawyers Guild—Rev. Msgr. WILLIAM BENWELL, Moderator.
Catholic Scouting Movement—Rev. Msgr. MICHAEL J. CORONA, Moderator.
Catholic League for Religious and Civil Rights—Rev. Msgr. JAMES P. MORAN, Diocesan Liason.
Charismatic Movement—Co-Moderators: Rev. ROBERT L. SANTA BARBARA; DORIS BRENNAN.
Diocesan Council of Catholic Women—Rev. EDWARD M. O'NEILL, Moderator.
Diocesan Eucharistic League—Rev. CHARLES R. PRATS, Dir.
Diocesan Holy Name Society—Rev. THOMAS J. DZURENDA, Moderator.
Diocesan Home School Association—Rev. Msgr. GEORGE M. BREMBOS, Moderator.
Legion of Mary—Rev. Msgr. DOMINIC A. TURTORA, Moderator.
National Shrine of the Immaculate Conception—Rev. Msgr. DOMINIC A. TURTORA, Diocesan Liaison.
St. Vincent de Paul Societies—Rev. THOMAS A. CASELLA, C.M., Moderator.

Vicariate For Charities and Social Ministry

Vicar for Charities and Social Ministry—Rev. Msgr. MICHAEL J. CASHMAN.
Catholic Charities—Sr. FLORENCE EDWARD KEARNEY, D.C., Exec. Dir. MICHAEL LESZCZUK, L.I.C.S.W., Assoc. Exec. Dir. Asst. Exec. Dirs.: MARY E. DAVEY, L.I.C.S.W.; MARIANNE MAJEWSKI, L.I.C.S.W., (See category for Catholic Charities under Institutions Located in the Diocese for the full listing).
HIV Services—DONALD STAGER.

Consultative Bodies

College of Consultors—Rev. Msgr. JOHN B. SZYMANSKI, V.G.; Rev. Msgr. ANTHONY J. LUISINI; Rev. Msgr. JAMES P. MORAN; Rev. Msgr. ANTHONY J. GAMBINO; Rev. Msgr. MICHAEL J. CORONA; Rev. Msgr. EUGENE PRUS; Rev. Msgr. MICHAEL J. CASHMAN; Revs. RAYMOND L. COLE; CHARLES T. O'CONNOR, Sec.
Deans—Cathedral Deanery: Very Rev. MICHAEL A. MCGUIRE; Arthur Kill Deanery: Very Rev. EDMUND J. SHALLOW; Forsgate Deanery: Very Rev. EDWARD J. STRUZIK; Morris Canal Deanery: Very Rev. IGNATIUS H. KUZIEMSKI; Raritan Bay Deanery: Very Rev. TERRANCE M. LAWLER; County Seat Deanery: Very Rev. DANIEL SLOAN; Somerset Hills Deanery: Very Rev. BLAISE R. BARAN; Round Valley Deanery: Very Rev. ANDREW L. SZAROLETA; New Brunswick Deanery: Very Rev. JOSEPH M. CURRY.
Presbyteral Council—Most Rev. EDWARD T. HUGHES, Pres.
Theological Commission—Rev. GLENN J. COMANDINI, Chm.
Administrative Council—Rev. Msgr. JOHN B. SZYMANSKI, V.G., Chm.; Rev. Msgr. GEORGE M. BREMBOS; Rev. Msgr. SEAMUS F. BRENNAN; Rev. Msgr. EUGENE PRUS; Rev. Msgr. MICHAEL J. ALLIEGRO; Rev. Msgr. WILLIAM BENWELL; Rev. Msgr. MICHAEL J. CASHMAN; Rev. CHARLES T. O'CONNOR; Sr. FLORENCE EDWARD KEARNEY, D.C.; Sr. M. MICHAELITA WIECHETEK, C.S.S.F.; LORRAINE P. AMENDOLARA, Ed.D.; ROYANNE DAMIANO; RICHARD P. GERRITY.
Diocesan Pastoral Council—Most Rev. EDWARD T. HUGHES; Rev. Msgr. JOHN B. SZYMANSKI, V.G.; ALINA BANKOWSKI; JOHN BOYLE; BARRY W. CRELIN; JOSEPH DONATO; MATTHEW FRATTEROLO; Rev. Msgr. ANTHONY J. GAMBINO; LORRAINE GERENZA; Rev. DOUGLAS J. HAEFNER; Deacon LUKE J. HALLY; BILL KENNEDY; Mrs. ATTRACTA LYNDON; EDWARD MANSMANN; EDWARD OLEARCZYK; Dr. CHARLES POLOK; JOSEPH QUINLAN; Sr. MARY ANN SPAETTI, I.H.M.; Bro. DONALD SUKANEK, S.C.; RUTH SULLIVAN; CATHERINE SUTLIFF; GYULA VARGA; EILEEN A. TABERT, Exec. Sec.

CLERGY, PARISHES, MISSIONS AND PAROCHIAL SCHOOLS

BOROUGH OF METUCHEN
(Middlesex County)

1—CATHEDRAL OF ST. FRANCIS (1871), Rev. Msgr. Richard A. Behl, Rector; Rev. Msgr. Dominic A. Turtora, Rector Emeritus; Revs. Robert C. Medley; Robert L. Santa Barbara; Deacons Frank J. Cammarano; Robert P. Gellentien; Cornelius S. Smoyak; Paul G. Licameli.
Res., 32 Elm Ave., 08840. Tel: 732-548-0100; Fax: 732-549-1033.
School—45 Library Pl., 08840. Tel: 732-548-3107; Fax: 732-548-5760.
Sisters of Mercy 2; Lay Teachers 19; Students 444.

OUTSIDE THE BOROUGH OF METUCHEN

Alpha, Warren Co., St. Mary (1902), Rev. Msgr. Anthony J. Luisini; Rev. James A. Kyrpczak; Deacon George L. Bolash.
Res., 830 Fifth Ave., 08865. Tel: 908-454-0444; Fax: 908-454-7745.

Avenel, Middlesex Co., St. Andrew (1920), Revs. David B. Kosmoski, O.M.V.; S. Gregory Cleveland, O.M.V.; Bro. James A. Walther, O.M.V. In res., Rev. David J. Nicgorski, O.M.V.
Res., 244 Avenel St., 07001. Tel: 732-634-4355; Fax: 732-750-5905.
Stations—Avenel, Woodbridge State School; Avenel, Woodbridge Emergency Reception Center, Tel: 732-636-4261.

Baptistown, Hunterdon Co., Our Lady of Victories (1973), Rev. David I. Fulton; Deacon John T. Monahan.
Res., P.O. Box 127, 08803. Tel: 908-996-2068; Fax: 908-996-3525.

Basking Ridge, Somerset Co., St. James (1864), Rev. Msgr. William J. Capik; Rev. John F. Primich; Deacons James S. Bell; Luke J. Hally.
Res., 184 S. Finley Ave., P.O. Box 310, 07920. Tel: 908-766-0888; Fax: 908-766-1815.
School—200 S. Finley Ave., P.O. Box 310, 07920. Tel: 908-766-4774; Fax: 908-766-1815.
Felician Sisters 3; Lay Teachers 13; Students 365.

Belvidere, Warren Co., St. Patrick (1892), Rev. Michael A. Driscoll; Deacon John F. Dumschat.
Res., 327 Greenwich St., 07823. Tel: 908-475-2559.

Bernardsville, Somerset Co., Our Lady of Perpetual Help (1898), Revs. Chester H. Carina; Ramiero C. Marincioni; Deacons Joseph E. O'Keefe; Joel R. Livingston.
Res., 111 Claremont Rd., 07924. Tel: 908-766-0079; Fax: 908-766-1185. [CEM]
School—School of St. Elizabeth, Seney Dr., 07924. Tel: 908-766-0244; Fax: 908-766-5372.
Sisters of Christian Charity 2; Lay Teachers 10; Students 260.
Chapel—Bernardsville, Sacred Heart (Chapel of Convenience).

Blairstown, Warren Co., St. Jude (1945), Rev. Michael A. McNulty.
Res., Eisenhower Rd., P.O. Box N, 07825. Tel: 908-362-6444; Fax: 908-362-6862.

Bloomsbury, Hunterdon Co., Church of the Annunciation (1948), Rev. J. Philip Vadakkekara.
Res., 80 Main St., P.O. Box 136, 08804-0136. Tel: 908-479-4905.

Bound Brook, Somerset Co., St. Joseph (1877), Revs. Charles T. O'Connor; Louis A. Mattina; Deacon George D. Coleman.
Office: 124 E. Second St., P.O. Box 72, 08805. Tel: 732-356-0027; Fax: 732-356-8092.
Res., 304 John St., 08805. Tel: 732-356-8936. [CEM]
St. Mary of Czestochowa (1914) (Polish), Revs. Stanley J. Walega; Jude Smith, O.F.M.
Res., 193 W. High St., 08805. Tel: 732-356-0358; Fax: 732-356-1338.

Bridgewater, Somerset Co., Holy Trinity (1948), Revs. John R. Pringle; Sean G. Winters; Deacon Michael A. Forrestall.
Res., 60 Maple St., 08807. Tel: 908-526-2394.
St. Bernard (1843), Revs. John L. Brundage; James W. Hagerman; Deacons Patrick J. Cline; Paul L. Anderson; Gerard C. Sims.
Office: Tel: 908-725-0552; Fax: 908-725-4524.
Res., 500 Rte. 22, 08807. Tel: 908-526-6859; Fax: 908-725-4524. [CEM]

Califon, Hunterdon Co., St. John Neumann (1982), Rev. J. William Mickiewicz; Deacons Thomas J. Gilheany; Dennis K. Webster.
Res., P.O. Box 455, 07830. Tel: 908-832-2513; Fax: 908-832-7618.

Carteret, Middlesex Co.,

1—ST. JOSEPH, (1893), Rev. Edward C. Puleo. In res., Rev. Msgr. Donald M. Endebrock.
Res., 7 Locust St., 07008. Tel: 732-541-8946; Fax: 732-969-2282.
School—865 Roosevelt Ave., 07008. Tel: 732-541-7111.
Sisters 4; Lay Teachers 9; Students 245.

2—HOLY FAMILY, (1907) (Polish), Very Rev. Edmund J. Shallow.
Res., 213 Pershing Ave., 07008. Tel: 732-541-5768; Fax: 732-541-5871.
School—132 Emerson St., 07008. Tel: 732-541-2941.
Bernardine Sisters 1; Lay Teachers 9; Students 178.

3—SACRED HEART, (1910) (Slovak), Rev. Gerald Browne.
Res., 67 Fitch St., 07008. Tel: 732-541-5410.

4—ST. ELIZABETH OF HUNGARY, (1914) (Hungarian), Rev. Patrick H. Barrett.
Res., 119 Washington Ave., 07008. Tel: 732-541-5202.

Clinton, Hunterdon Co., Immaculate Conception (1864), Very Rev. Andrew L. Szaroleta; Rev. Alexander J. Carles; Deacon William R. Bauer.
Res., Rte. 633, Old Allerton Rd., P.O. Box 5400, 08809-0400. Tel: 908-735-7319; Fax: 908-735-4552. [CEM]
Mission—Pittstown, Hunterdon Co., St. Catherine of Siena, 08809.
Stations—Correctional Institution for Women, Tel: 908-735-7111; Hunterdon Developmental Center, Tel: 908-735-4031.

Colonia, Middlesex Co., St. John Vianney (1959), Revs. Edward M. O'Neill; Michael T. Kottar; John R. Butler (RIC); Deacons Joseph A. Vivona; Joseph D. Ragucci. In res., Rev. John D. Murphy.
Res., 420 Inman Ave., 07067. Tel: 732-574-0150; Fax: 732-574-0050.
School—440 Inman Ave., 07067. Tel: 732-388-1662.
Bernardine Sisters 2; Lay Teachers 30; Students 858.

Cranbury, Middlesex Co., Nativity of Our Lord (1992), Rev. Stephen H. Congdon. In res., Rev. Msgr. William J. Haughney.
Res., P.O. Box 583, 08512. Tel: 609-371-0499; Fax: 609-371-0677.

Dunellen, Middlesex Co., St. John the Evangelist (1879), Revs. Richard J. Lyons; Louis J. Eldridge; Deacon Robert F. Reffler.
Res., 317 First St., 08812. Tel: 732-968-2621; Fax: 732-968-2588.

East Brunswick, Middlesex Co., St. Bartholomew (1959), Rev. Msgr. Michael J. Alliegro; Rev. Msgr. J. Morgan Kelly, Pastor Emeritus; Revs. Peter R. Cebulka; Thomas J. Walsh; Deacons Richard R. Kaseta; John P. McShane; Thaddeus C. Raczkowski; Anthony J. Gostkowski.
Res., 460 Ryders Ln., 08816. Tel: 732-257-7722; Fax: 732-257-7723.
School—470 Ryders Ln., 08816. Tel: 732-254-7105.
Felician Sisters 1; Lay Teachers 22; Students 505.

East Millstone, Somerset Co., St. Joseph (1883), Rev. Raymond L. Cole; Deacons George D. LaPolice; Leo F. Clementi; Joseph C. Moseinski; Warren C. Page.
Res., Box 2129, Livingston Ave., 08875. Tel: 908-874-3141; Fax: 908-874-7040.

Edison, Middlesex Co., Guardian Angels (1959), Revs. R. Kevin Crowley; Robert J. Miller.
Res., 37 Plainfield Ave., P.O. Box 1216, 08817. Tel: 732-985-7565.
Mission—Bonhamtown, Middlesex Co., St. Margaret Mary Alacoque, Woodbridge Ave., 08817.
St. Helena (1965), Rev. Msgr. Armando J. Perini; Revs. L. Roger Labonte; Salvatore J. Rossetti, O.P.
Res., 950 Grove Ave., 08820. Tel: 732-494-3399;

Fax: 732-494-2076.
School—930 Grove Ave., 08820. Tel: 732-549-6234. Felician Sisters 3; Lay Teachers 23; Students 390.
Convent—882 Grove Ave., 08820. Tel: 732-321-1462.

St. Matthew (1952), Rev. Msgr. Seamus F. Brennan; Revs. Michael C. Saharic; Thomas J. Serafin; Deacons Barry C. Demarest; Eric S. Massimei; Stephen F. Nemeth. In res., Rev. Neil W. Davin, C.P.
Res., 81 Seymour Ave., 08817. Tel: 732-985-5063; Fax: 732-985-9104.
School—Tel: 732-985-6633; Fax: 732-985-9104.
Sisters of Mercy 3; Lay Teachers 20; Students 465.

Far Hills, Somerset Co., St. Elizabeth (1906), Rev. Msgr. George. M. Brembos.
Res., Box 37, Peapack Rd., 07931. Tel: 908-234-0079; Fax: 908-234-2923.
Mission—Peapack, Somerset Co., St. Brigid, Main St., Peapack, 07977. Tel: 908-234-1265; Fax: 908-234-2923.

Flemington, Hunterdon Co., St. Magdalen de Pazzi (1864), Revs. John J. Barbella; Patrick C. Maccarone; Deacons John H. Purdy; Thaddeus Wislinski; Martin L. Koy.
Res., 105 Mine St., 08822. Tel: 908-782-2922; Fax: 908-782-0952. [CEM]

Fords, Middlesex Co., Our Lady of Peace (1919), Rev. Msgr. Robert J. Zamorski; Revs. Michael J. Bihuniak; Frank W. Fellrath; Deacons Joseph S. Petrovich; Salvatore J. Gagliano.
Res., 26 Maple Ave., P.O. Box 69, 08863. Tel: 732-738-7940; Fax: 732-738-3848.
School—Amboy Ave., 08863. Tel: 732-738-7464.
Dominican Sisters of Divine Providence 1; Lay Teachers 22; Students 365.

Great Meadows, Warren Co., SS. Peter and Paul (1921), Very Rev. Ignatius H. Kuziemski.
Res., Rte. 46, Box 156, 07838. Tel: 908-637-4269; Fax: 908-637-6896.

Hackettstown, Warren Co., Assumption of the Blessed Virgin Mary (1864), Rev. Msgr. Stephen A. Bielen.
Res., 305 High St., 07840. Tel: 908-852-3320; Fax: 908-852-4180.
School—Cook & Liberty Sts., 07840. Tel: 908-852-4791; Fax: 908-852-4180.
Sisters of Christian Charity 2; Lay Teachers 13; Students 356.

Hampton, Hunterdon Co., St. Ann (1859), Rev. William J. Hewitt; Deacon Joseph J. Foldvary.
Res., 6 Church St., P.O. Box 405, 08827. Tel: 908-537-2221. [CEM]
Station—Glen Gardner, NJ Hospital for Geriatrics.

Helmetta, Middlesex Co., Holy Trinity (1911) (Polish), Rev. Stanley Jarosz.
Res., 100 Main St., 08828. Tel: 732-521-0172. [CEM]

High Bridge, Hunterdon Co., St. Joseph (1880), Rev. Laurence H. Smith; Deacon Charles A. Paolino.
Res., 59 Main St., 08829. Tel: 908-638-6211; Fax: 908-638-5802.

Highland Park, Middlesex Co., St. Paul the Apostle (1912), Rev. Sylvester J. Cronin.
Res., 504 Raritan Ave., 08904. Tel: 732-572-0977; Fax: 732-574-7497.
Convent—20 S. 6th Ave., 08904. Tel: 732-572-2362. Franciscan Sisters of Allegany

Hillsborough, Somerset Co., Mary, Mother of God (1948), Revs. Liam A. Minogue; John M. Banko; Joseph F. Hogan; Deacon James P. Walsh.
Res., 157 S. Triangle Rd., 08876. Tel: 908-874-8220; Fax: 908-874-4183.

Iselin, Middlesex Co., St. Cecelia (1923), Rev. Msgr. James P. Moran; Revs. Daniel A. Gomez; David J. Pekola; Deacon Belardino A. Lupini.
Res., 45 Wilus Way, 08830. Tel: 732-283-2300; Fax: 732-283-3326.
School—Tel: 732-283-2824.
Religious Teachers Filippini 4; Lay Teachers 13; Students 340.
Stations—NJ State Home for Disabled Veterans.; Roosevelt Hospital.

Jamesburg, Middlesex Co., St. James the Less (1878), Revs. Louis F. Stingel; Charles P. Scillieri.
Res., 36 Lincoln Ave., 08831. Tel: 732-521-0100; Fax: 732-521-8287. [CEM]
Station—State Home for Boys, Tel: 732-521-0030.

Kendall Park, Middlesex Co., St. Augustine of Canterbury (1952), Revs. Robert G. Lynam; Robert V. Meyers; Charles A. Sabella; Deacons William A. Beirne, Jr.; Richard McCarron.
Res., 51 Henderson Rd., 08824. Tel: 732-297-3000; Fax: 732-940-1746.
School—45 Henderson Rd., 08824. Tel: 732-297-6042.
Brothers of Sacred Heart 2; Lay Teachers 14; Students 367.

Lambertville, Hunterdon Co., St. John the Evangelist (1843), Revs. Leon J. Kasprzyk; John J. Szczepanik; Deacon Joseph J. Masterson.
Res., 44 Bridge St., 08530. Tel: 609-397-3350; Fax: 609-397-8713. [CEM]
Mission—Stockton, Hunterdon Co., St. Agnes, Main St., Stockton, 08559.

Laurence Harbor, Middlesex Co., St. Lawrence (1943), Rev. Raymond V. Attanasio.
Res., 109 Laurence Pkwy., 08879. Tel: 732-566-1093; Fax: 732-566-3252.

Manville, Somerset Co., Sacred Heart of Jesus (1919) (Polish), Revs. Peter G. Suhaka; Stanley G. Gromadzki; Hyacinth M. Dabrowski, O.F.M.Cap.
Res., 136 S. Main St., P.O. Box 924, 08835. Tel: 908-725-0072; Fax: 908-685-3029. [CEM]

Christ the King (1948), Very Rev. Daniel Sloan.
Res., 211 Louis St., 08835. Tel: 908-231-1330.
School—99 N. 13th Ave., 08835. Tel: 908-526-1339.
Lay Teachers 11; Students 246.

Martinsville, Somerset Co., Blessed Sacrament (1968), Rev. Msgr. Eugene Prus; Rev. Richard M. Rusk.
Res., 852 Newmans Ln., P.O. Box 563, 08836. Tel: 732-356-4442; Fax: 732-356-5172.

Middlesex, Middlesex Co., Our Lady of Mount Virgin (1943), Revs. Thomas G. Moore, Admin.; Raymond J. Leonard; Deacon John R. Tietjen.
Res., 650 Harris Ave., 08846. Tel: 732-356-2149.
School—610 Harris Ave., 08846. Tel: 732-356-6560; Fax: 732-356-7860.
Sisters Apostles of the Sacred Heart 4; Lay Teachers 13; Students 272.

Milford, Hunterdon Co., St. Edward the Confessor (1944), Rev. Michael E. Crummy; Deacon James W. Hendrix.
Res., 61 Mill St., P.O. Box 522, 08848. Tel: 908-995-4723; Fax: 908-995-9353.

Milltown, Middlesex Co., Our Lady of Lourdes (1921), Revs. Thomas V. Perunilam; Edward A. Czarcinski.
Res., 233 N. Main St., 08850. Tel: 732-828-0011; Fax: 732-828-3133.
School—43 Cleveland Ave., 08850. Tel: 732-828-1951.
Little Servant Sisters of the Immaculate Conception 4; Lay Teachers 8; Students 252.

Monmouth Junction, Middlesex Co., St. Cecilia (1904), Revs. Thomas A. Piechocinski, Ed.D.; Thomas A. Odorizzi.
Office: 10 Kingston Ln., 08852. Tel: 732-329-2893; Fax: 732-329-3866.
Res., 46 Kingston Ln., 08852. Tel: 732-274-1761.

New Brunswick, Middlesex Co.,

1—St. Peter Apostle, (1829), Very Rev. Joseph M. Curry; Rev. Timothy A. Christy; Deacon Bernard A. Cribbin. In res., Rev. Joseph G. Celano.
Res., 94 Somerset St., 08901. Tel: 732-545-6820; Fax: 732-545-4069. [CEM]
School—165 Somerset St., 08901. Tel: 732-545-1473.
Sisters 3; Lay Teachers 27; Students 390.
High School—175 Somerset St., 08901. Tel: 732-846-8046.
Sisters 3; Lay Teachers 28; Students 233.

2—St. John the Baptist, (1867) (German), Revs. Joseph B. Szulwach, Admin.; Anthony Sirianni.
Res., 29 Abeel St., 08901. Tel: 732-545-5267; Fax: 732-846-6594. [CEM]
Church—Neilson and Carman Sts., 08901.

3—Our Lady of Mt. Carmel, (1977) (Hispanic), Revs. Raymond L. Nacarino; Juan A. Albaladejo.
Res., 86 New St., 07050.
Church—75 Morris St., 08901. Tel: 732-846-5873; Fax: 732-846-5397.

4—St. Joseph, (1924) (Polish), Rev. George Korytkowski, O.F.M.Cap. In res., Revs. John F. Salwowski, O.F.M.Cap.; Joseph M. Kubiak, O.F.M.Cap.
Res., 15 Maple St., 08901. Tel: 732-545-2195.

5—Sacred Heart, (1883), Rev. Jerome A. Johnson; Deacons John R. Czekaj; Luis S. Moral.
Res., 56 Throop Ave., 08901. Tel: 732-545-1681; Fax: 732-545-5059.

6—St. Ladislaus, (1904) (Hungarian), Revs. Paul A. Rotondi, O.F.M.; Capistran Polgar, O.F.M.; Stephen Galambos, O.F.M.
Res., 215 Somerset St., 08901. Tel: 732-545-1427; Fax: 732-545-8501.

7—St. Mary of Mount Virgin, (1905) (Italian), Rev. Msgr. Francis J. Crupi; Rev. Philip A. Higgins, C.S.C.
Res., 190 Sandford St., 08901. Tel: 732-545-5090; Fax: 732-937-9290.
School—192 Sandford St., 08901. Tel: 732-249-7753.
Maestre Pie Filippini Sisters 2; Lay Teachers 8; Students 197.
Mission—Edison, Middlesex Co., St. Therese of the Infant Jesus, Fox Rd., Edison, 08817.

North Brunswick, Middlesex Co., Our Lady of Peace (1969), Rev. John V. Polyak.
Res., 277 Washington Pl., 08902. Tel: 732-297-9680; Fax: 732-297-1024.

North Plainfield, Somerset Co., St. Joseph (1882), Rev. John J. Casey.
Res., 41 Manning Ave., 07060. Tel: 908-756-3383; Fax: 908-756-1155.
School—101 Westervelt Ave., 07060. Tel: 908-756-9539.
Sisters of Mercy 3; Lay Teachers 11; Students 192.

St. Luke (1965), Rev. John C. Giordano; Deacons Albert C. Parenti; Dann C. Rossi.
Res., 300 Clinton Ave., 07063. Tel: 908-754-8811; Fax: 908-754-0120.

Old Bridge, Middlesex Co., St. Ambrose (1961), Revs. Charles F. Kelly; James W. McGuffey; James W. McLaughlin; Deacons Brian F. McIvor; Charles J. Damian; Andrew J. Strus.
Res., 96 Throckmorton Ln., 08857. Tel: 732-679-5666.
School—Tel: 732-679-4700; Fax: 732-679-6062.
Sisters of St. Joseph (Chestnut Hill) 2; Lay Teachers 25; Students 386.
Convent—94 Throckmorton Ln., 08857. Tel: 732-679-5509.

St. Thomas the Apostle (1932), Rev. Msgr. John B. Szymanski, V.G.; Revs. Edward G. Shaner; Kevin M. Casey, C.P.; Deacons John J. Fitzsimmons; Paul E. Featherman.
Res., One St. Thomas Plaza, 08857. Tel: 732-251-4000; Fax: 732-251-4946.
School—22 Barkley Rd., 08857. Tel: 732-251-4812.
Lay Teachers 22; Students 450.

Most Holy Redeemer (1983), Rev. Henry L. Hemmerling; Deacon Robert T. McGovern.
Res., P.O. Box 325, 08857. Tel: 732-566-9334.

Oxford, Warren Co., St. Rose of Lima (1864), Rev. Francis F. Vaz.
Res., Academy St., P.O. Box 88, 07863. Tel: 908-453-2034; Fax: 908-453-4425. [CEM]

Parlin, Middlesex Co., St. Bernadette (1956), Revs. L. Eugene Schellberg; Kenneth D. Brighenti; Deacon Nicholas J. Thornton.
Res., 20 Villanova Rd., 08859. Tel: 732-721-2772; Fax: 732-727-5188.

Perth Amboy, Middlesex Co.,

1—St. Mary, (1845), Rev. Michael P. Scott; Deacon Basilio A. Perez.
Res., 104 Center St., 08861. Tel: 732-442-0039.

2—St. Stephen, (1892) (Polish), Revs. John P. Stec; Pawel Z. Szymanski (Poland).
Res., 490 State St., 08861. Tel: 732-826-1395; Fax: 732-826-4217. [CEM]

3—Holy Trinity, (1899) (Slovak), Rev. John P. Alvarado.
Res., 496 Penn St., 08861. Tel: 732-826-0439. [CEM]

4—Our Lady of Fatima, (1960) (Hispanic), Revs. Leonard J. Brown, C.M.F.; Jesse Carrero, C.M.F.; Benjamin Martinez, C.M.F.; Deacons Angel P. Perez; Herminio Rivera; Daniel Torres.
Res., 380 Smith St., 08861. Tel: 732-442-6634; Fax: 732-826-0958.

5—Our Lady of Hungary, (1902) (Hungarian), Rev. William J. Smith.
Res., 697 Cortlandt St., 08861. Tel: 732-442-0512. [CEM]

6—Most Holy Rosary, (1904) (Italian), Rev. Msgr. Anthony J. Gambino; Deacon Edward Holowienka. In res., Rev. Robert J. Ascolese.
Res., 625 Florida Grove Rd., 08861. Tel: 732-826-2771; Fax: 732-826-0320.

7—Holy Spirit, (1944), Rev. Robert G. Gorman. In res., Revs. George M. Pisanello; J. Michael Venditti.
Res., 580 Hazel Ave., 08861. Tel: 732-826-4859; Fax: 732-697-9380.

8—La Asuncion, (1981) (Hispanic), Rev. Msgr. Anthony J. Gambino, Temporary Admin.; Rev. Thomas F. Ryan; Deacon Corpus V. Perez.
Mailing Address: 777 Cortlandt St., P.O. Box 1335, 08862. Tel: 732-826-4991; Fax: 732-826-6951.

9—Our Lady of the Rosary of Fatima, (1981) (Portuguese), Rev. Lauro C. Sedlmayer (Brazil) Admin.
Res., 188 Wayne St., 08861. Tel: 732-826-4350.

Phillipsburg, Warren Co., SS. Philip and James (1861), Rev. Msgr. Michael J. Corona; Revs. Leonard F.A. Rusay; Kenneth R. Kolibas; Vincent P. Chen (Taiwan); Deacons John F. Flynn; John T. Sheridan.
Res., 430 S. Main St., 08865-3094. Tel: 908-454-0112; Fax: 908-454-0125. [CEM]
Mission—New Village, Warren Co., St. Christopher.

SS. Peter and Paul (1913) (Slovak). Closed. Records at St. Philip & St. James, Phillipsburg.

Piscataway, Middlesex Co., Our Lady of Fatima (1948), Revs. Herbert J. Stab; Thomas R. Ganley; Roberto D. Coruna (Philippines); Deacons Stanley J. Lorenc;

Lawrence P. Reilly.
Res., 501 New Market Rd., 08854. Tel: 732-968-5555; Fax: 732-968-5959.
School—499 New Market Rd., 08854. Tel: 732-968-5017; Fax: 732-968-9259.
Sisters 2; Lay Teachers 15; Students 244.
Convent—50 Van Winkle Pl., 08854. Tel: 732-968-6136. Franciscan Sisters of Allegany.

St. Frances Cabrini (1961), Revs. Edgardo D. Abano; Francis E. Grabowski, Pastor Emeritus; Deacon Michael P. Gleason.
Res., 208 Bound Brook Ave., 08854-4097. Tel: 732-885-5313; Fax: 732-885-9031.
School—2300 Cooper St., 08854. Tel: 732-885-1066.
Sisters of Mercy 2; Lay Teachers 17; Students 250.

Pittstown, Hunterdon Co., St. Catherine of Siena (1992). Closed. Mission parish of Immaculate Conception, Clinton.

Plainsboro, Middlesex Co., Queenship of Mary (1982), Very Rev. Edward J. Struzik; Deacon William C. Vanzino.
Res., P.O. Box 759, 08536. Tel: 609-799-7511; Fax: 609-799-8904.

Port Murray, Warren Co., St. Theodore (1983), Rev. Albert L. Roca; Deacon Donald J. DeLorenzo.
Res., P.O. Box 146, 07865. Tel: 908-689-8318.

Port Reading, Middlesex Co., St. Anthony of Padua (1906), Rev. Michael G. Krull; Deacon Joseph V. Szoke.
Res., 436 Port Reading Ave., 07064. Tel: 732-634-1403; Fax: 732-602-0119.

Raritan, Somerset Co., St. Ann (1903) (Italian), Very Rev. Blaise R. Baran; Deacons John R. Pacifico; James Hewitt, III.
Res., 45 Anderson St., P.O. Box 86, 08869. Tel: 908-725-1008; Fax: 908-707-1915.
School—29 Second Ave., 08869. Tel: 908-725-7787.
Religious Teachers Filippini 4; Lay Teachers 13; Students 299.

St. Joseph (1912) (Slovak), Rev. Kevin A. Kaminski.
In res., Rev. Charles W. Cicerale Tel: 908-253-0630.
Res., 16 E. Somerset St., 08869. Tel: 908-725-0163.

Sayreville, Middlesex Co., Our Lady of Victories (1885), Very Rev. Terrance M. Lawler; Revs. Brian J. Nolan; Ronald J. Jandernoa.
Mailing Address: 42 Main St., 08872.
Res., 24 Main St., 08872. Tel: 732-257-0077; Fax: 732-651-1898.
School—36 Main St., 08872. Tel: 732-254-1676; Fax: 732-254-5066.
Sisters of Mercy 1; Lay Teachers 21; Students 470.

St. Stanislaus Kostka (1914), Rev. Leon S. Aniszczyk.
Res., 225 MacArthur Ave., 08872. Tel: 732-254-0212; Fax: 732-390-2989. [CEM]
School—MacArthur Ave., 08872. Tel: 732-254-5819; Fax: 732-257-2903.
Lay Teachers 11; Students 162.

Skillman, Somerset Co., St. Charles Borromeo (1982), Rev. Gregory E. S. Malovetz.
Res., 376 Burnt Hill Rd., 08558. Tel: 609-466-0300; Fax: 609-466-0602.

Somerset, Somerset Co., St. Matthias (1962), Revs. Douglas J. Haefner; George A. Farrell; Deacon Stephen J. Holzinger, II.
Pastoral Center: 168 J.F. Kennedy Blvd., 08873. Tel: 732-828-1400; Fax: 732-828-0866.
Res., 166 J.F. Kennedy Blvd., 08873.
School—170 J.F. Kennedy Blvd., 08873.
Sisters 4; Lay Teachers 25; Students 552.

Somerville, Somerset Co., Immaculate Conception (1882), Rev. Msgr. J. Nevin Kennedy; Revs. A. Gregory Uhrig; Richard W. Palumbo; Deacons John B. Ivers; Arnold J. De Marco; Frank J. Quinn.
Res., 225 Altamont Pl., 08876. Tel: 908-725-1112. [CEM]
School—Tel: 908-725-6516; Fax: 908-725-3172.
Sisters 6; Lay Teachers 19; Students 565.
High School—Tel: 908-722-0200; Fax: 908-218-7765.
Sisters 13; Lay Teachers 56; Students 858.
Convent—230 Mountain Ave., 08876. Tel: 908-722-6894. Sisters, Servants of the Immaculate Heart of Mary.

South Amboy, Middlesex Co., St. Mary (1864), Revs. William F. Leonard; Dennis R. Weezorak; Deacon Stephen N. Laikowski.
Res., 256 Augusta St., 08879. Tel: 732-721-0179. [CEM]
School—Second St., 08879.
Sisters of Mercy 1; Lay Teachers 17; Students 245.

Sacred Heart (1895) (Polish), Revs. Joseph V. Romanoski; Joseph A. Krajewski; Deacon Robert J. Klein.
Res., 531 Washington Ave., 08879. Tel: 732-721-0040; Fax: 732-721-4448. [CEM]
School—Tel: 732-721-0834; Fax: 732-316-0326.
Felician Sisters 1; Lay Teachers 14; Students 218.

South Bound Brook, Somerset Co., Our Lady of Mercy (1949), Rev. Daniel J. Herlihy.
Res., 122 High St., 08880. Tel: 732-356-1037; Fax: 732-356-1318.

South Plainfield, Middlesex Co., Sacred Heart (1906), Very Rev. Michael A. McGuire; Revs. Joseph C. Kornoski; Anthony M. Dandry; Deacon Joseph J. Stanczak.
Res., 149 S. Plainfield Ave., 07080. Tel: 908-756-0633; Fax: 908-757-5655. [CEM]
School—Sisters 2; Lay Teachers 22; Students 382.

Our Lady of Czestochowa (1943) (Polish), Rev. John M. Skwara.
Mailing Address: P.O. Box 141, South Plainfield, 07080.
Res., 807 Hamilton Blvd., 07080. Tel: 908-756-1333.

South River, Middlesex Co., St. Mary of Ostrabrama (1903) (Polish), Revs. Robert L. Weil; Joseph M. Melaniuk.
Res., 30 Jackson St., 08882. Tel: 732-254-2220. [CEM]
School—22 Holmes Ave., 08882.
Bernardine Sisters 1; Lay Teachers 10; Students 189.

St. Stephen Protomartyr (1907) (Hungarian), Rev. Glenn J. Comandini.
Res., 20 William St., 08882. Tel: 732-257-0100; Fax: 732-257-4646.

Corpus Christi (1944), Revs. Kevin P. Duggan; Maurice T. Carlton.
Res., 100 James St., 08882. Tel: 732-254-1800; Fax: 732-254-8063.
School—80 David St., 08882. Tel: 732-257-5200.
Lay Teachers 20; Students 307.

Spotswood, Middlesex Co., Immaculate Conception (1946), Revs. Harold L. Hirsch; Kenneth R. Murphy; Edward R. Flanagan; Deacon John H. McGuire.
Res., 18 South St., 08884. Tel: 732-251-3110; Fax: 732-251-2407.
School—23 Manalapan Rd., 08884. Tel: 732-251-3446; Fax: 732-251-8270.
Felician Sisters 2; Lay Teachers 18; Students 318.

Three Bridges, Hunterdon Co., St. Elizabeth Ann Seton (1984), Rev. Edward A. Kearns.
Res., 7 Forest Hill Dr., 08887. Tel: 908-782-1475; Fax: 908-782-6230.

Warren, Somerset Co., Our Lady of the Mount (1911), Rev. Msgr. William Benwell; Rev. Joseph M. Holup.
Res., 167 Mount Bethel Rd., 07059. Tel: 908-647-1075; Fax: 908-647-7885.

Washington, Warren Co., St. Joseph (1872), Rev. Michael A. Kochon.
Res., 200 W. Carlton Ave., 07882. Tel: 908-689-0058; Fax: 908-689-3436. [CEM]

Watchung, Somerset Co., St. Mary (1847), Rev. Thomas J. Dzurenda; Deacons Henry F. Albert; Arthur J. Wise.
Res., 225 Mountain Blvd., 07060. Tel: 908-756-6524; Fax: 908-756-2111. [CEM]

Whitehouse Station, Hunterdon Co., Our Lady of Lourdes (1923), Revs. Florian J. Gall; John N. Fell; Deacons Samuel J. Damiano; John H. Hanna.
Res., 390 Rte. 523, 08889. Tel: 908-534-2319; Fax: 908-534-5670.

Woodbridge, Middlesex Co., St. James (1860), Rev. Msgr. Michael J. Cashman; Rev. Sean W. Kenney; Deacon Carl E. Psota. In res., Rev. Alfonso T. Nguyen (Vietnam).
Res., 145 Grove St., 07095. Tel: 732-634-0500; Fax: 732-602-1487. [CEM]
School—341 Amboy Ave., 07095. Tel: 732-634-2090.
Lay Teachers 14; Students 320.
Convent—Tel: 732-634-0176.
Sisters of Mercy 2.

Our Lady of Mt. Carmel (1921) (Hungarian), Rev. Vincent C. Cornejo.
Res., 267 Smith St., 07095. Tel: 732-634-1438; Fax: 732-634-1438.

Chaplains of Public Institutions

ANNANDALE. *Mountainview Youth Correctional Facility*, 08801. Tel: 732-741-6208. Rev. Richard A. Ewing, Chap.

AVENEL. *Woodbridge State School*. Attended by St. Andrew, the Apostle.

BELLE MEAD. *Carrier Clinic*. Rev. Norman R. St. John, S.V.D.

BELVIDERE. *Warren Correctional Center*. Attended by St. Patrick, Belvidere.

CLINTON. *Edna Mahan Correctional Facility for Women*. Attended by Immaculate Conception, Clinton. Tel: 908-741-6208.
Hunterdon State School. Attended by Immaculate Conception. Very Rev. Andrew L. Szaroleta, Chap.

EDISON. *John F. Kennedy Medical Center*. Revs. Patrick F. Holland, C.S.Sp.; Andrew F. Duffy, C.S.Sp.

FLEMINGTON. *Hunterdon Medical Center*. Attended by St. Magdalen de Pazzi.

GLEN GARDNER. *N.J. State Hospital for Geriatrics*. Attended by St. Ann, Hampton.

HACKETTSTOWN. *Hackettstown Community Hospital*. Attended by Assumption of the Blessed Virgin Mary.

JAMESBURG. *N.J. State Home for Boys*. Attended by St. James the Less.

LYONS. *U.S. Veterans Medical Center*. Revs. George F. Kelly, C.Ss.R.; William Warman (BAL).

MENLO PARK. *Roosevelt State Hospital*. Attended by St. Cecelia, Iselin.

NEW BRUNSWICK. *Robert Wood Johnson University Hospital*. Revs. Anthony Sirianni; Joseph Kubiak, O.F.M.Cap.

NORTH BRUNSWICK. *Middlesex County Adult Detention Center*. Attended by Our Lady of Peace.

OLD BRIDGE. *Old Bridge Regional Hospital*. Attended by St. Ambrose.

PERTH AMBOY. *Raritan Bay Medical Center*. Tel: 732-826-2771. Revs. Robert J. Ascolese; J. Michael Venditti Tel: 732-826-4859.

PHILLIPSBURG. *Warren Hospital*. Tel: 908-454-0112. Rev. Vincent P. Chen (Taiwan).

RAHWAY. *East Jersey State Prison*. Attended from St. Andrew Church, Avenel. Tel: 732-634-1438.

SKILLMAN. *NJ State Neuropsychiatric Institute*. Attended by St. Charles Borromeo.

SOMERVILLE. *Somerset Medical Center*. Tel: 908-526-2394. Rev. Sean G. Winters.

SOUTH AMBOY. *South Amboy Memorial Hospital*. Attended by St. Mary and Sacred Heart.

On Duty Outside the Diocese:
Reverend Fathers—
Alvarez, Anthony M., Society of Jesus Christ the Priest, Murcia, Spain
Bochnak, Zenon A., Rome
Carpena, Octavio R., Society of Jesus Christ the Priest, Murcia, Spain
Desmond, Joseph L., Newark
Escribano, Peter E., Society of Jesus Christ the Priest, Murcia, Spain
Gordon, John B., Society of St. James the Apostle,Inc., Ecuador
Lambert, Timothy J., Diocese of Rockville Centre, NY
Marin, John L., Diocese of Arlington, VA
McCord, Kent G., USMC, Guam
Moya, Peter O., Society of Jesus Christ the Priest Murcia, Spain
Muccilli, Sebastian L., 618 Third St., Lake Park, FL 33403
Oterino, Francis L., Society of Jesus Christ the Priest, Ecuador
Pepel, Clement, Diocese of Phoenix, AZ
Romeo, Peter A., Diocese of Las Vegas, NV
Ruiz, Faustino C., Society of Jesus Christ the Priest, Chili
Santillo, Michael P., 2311 Hamlin Tr., Clermont, FL 34711
Scarcella, Philip J., 6300 N. Woodbend Dr., Farmpond Lane, Charlotte, NC 28212
Simon, John A.

Retired:
Reverend Monsignors—
Brzozowski, Joseph R.
Endebrock, Donald M.
Gerety, John L.
Haughney, William J.
Kelly, J. Morgan
Krysztofik, Joseph M.
Torney, John R., P.A.
Turtora, Dominic A.
Reverend Fathers—
Abramowicz, Richard B.
Avery, Raymond
Banach, Joseph S.
Cashioli, Lawrence J.
Egierd, Henry A.
Ewing, Richard A.
Gonsorcik, Joseph
Grabowski, Francis E.
Kapica, Francis A.
Kramarz, Anthony
Laplante, Louis A.
Molloy, William T.
Nester, Edward J.
Neumann, August
Przechacki, Casimir J.
Roos, William A.
Szulecki, Raymond L.
Thul, Joseph T.
Vielgus, Thaddeus A.
Vincze, Michael A.

Permanent Deacons:
Albert, Henry F.
Alexander, Russell C., (Retired)
Anderson, Paul L.
Bauer, William R.
Beirne, William A., (Retired)

Bell, James S.
Bolash, George L.
Cammarano, Frank J.
Clementi, Leo F.
Cline, Patrick J., Brooklyn
Coleman, George D.
Cribbin, Bernard A.
Czekaj, John R.
Daley, James M., (Retired)
Damian, Charles J.
Damiano, Samuel J.
De Blasio, Anthony A., On Leave
De Lorenzo, Donald J.
De Marco, Arnold J.
Demarest, Barry C.
Dumschat, John F.
Featherman, Paul E.
Fitzsimmons, John J.
Flynn, John T.
Foldvary, Joseph J.
Forrestall, Michael J.
Gagliano, Salvatore J.
Gajewski, Stephen J., Sr.
Gellentien, Robert P.
Gilheany, Thomas J., Newark
Gleason, Michael P.
Gostkowski, Anthony J.
Hally, Luke J.
Hanna, John H.
Heissenbuttel, Thomas A., On Leave
Hewitt, James, III
Hoedel, Carl C.
Holowienka, Edward
Holzinger, Stephen J., II
Huether, Vincent E., (Retired)
Ivers, John B.
Janthor, William G.
Kaseta, Richard R.
Klein, Robert J.
Kolasa, Joseph T., (Retired)
Koy, Martin L.
La Police, George D.
Laikowski, Stephen N.
Licameli, Paul G.
Livingston, Joel R.
Lorenc, Stanley J.
Lupini, Belardino A., M.D.
Maksimik, Walter S.
Marano, Francis J., (Retired)
Massimei, Eric S.
Masterson, Joseph J.
Maurer, Joseph S., (Retired)
McCarron, Richard
McGrath, James G., On Leave
McGreevy, Robert A., On Leave
McGuire, John H.
McIvor, Brian F., New York
McShane, John P.
Monahan, John T.
Moral, Luis S.
Morend, Michel, Newark
Moscinski, Joseph C.
Mulroy, Martin B., Brooklyn
Murtha, Michael P.
Nardi, Samuel, On Leave
Nemeth, Stephen F.
O'Keefe, Joseph E.
Pacifico, John R.
Page, Warren C., Syracuse
Paolino, Charles
Parenti, Albert C.
Perez, Angel P.
Perez, Basilio A., Dominican Republic
Perez, Corpus V.
Petrovich, Joseph S.
Psota, Carl E.
Purdy, John H., II
Quinn, Frank J.
Raczkowski, Thaddeus C.
Ragucci, Joseph D.
Reffler, Robert F.
Reilly, Lawrence P.
Rivera, Herminio
Rooney, William R., (Retired)
Rossi, Dann P.
Sheridan, John T.
Sicola, Thomas
Sims, Gerard C.
Smoyak, Cornelius S.
Stanczak, Joseph J.
Strus, Andrew J.
Suswal, Carl S., (Retired)
Szoke, Joseph V.
Thornton, Nicholas J.
Tietjen, John R.
Torres, Daniel
Trimmer, A. Shannon
Vanzino, William C.
Vivona, Joseph A.
Walsh, James P., Trenton
Webster, Dennis K.
Wise, Arthur J.
Wislinski, Thaddeus

INSTITUTIONS LOCATED IN THE DIOCESE

[A] HIGH SCHOOLS, DIOCESAN

EDISON. *Bishop Ahr High School*, 1 Tingley Ln., 08820. Tel: 732-549-1108. Sr. Donna Marie Trukowski, C.S.S.F., Prin.; Rev. Raymond J. Leonard, Chap. Felician Sisters 2; Lay Teachers 62; Students 1,050.

SOUTH AMBOY. *St. Mary Regional High School*, 310 Augusta St., 08879. Tel: 732-721-0748. John T. Gloss, Prin.; Rev. Ronald Jandernoa, Chap. Sisters 6; Lay Teachers 34; Students 525.

[B] HIGH SCHOOLS, PRIVATE

METUCHEN. *St. Joseph High School*, 145 Plainfield Ave., 08840. Tel: 732-549-7600; Fax: 732-549-0664. Bro. Ronald Cairns, S.C., Prin.; Rev. Peter Murphy, S.C., Chap. Brothers of the Sacred Heart 12; Lay Teachers 43; Boys 756.

NEW BRUNSWICK. *Shoreless Lake School*, 75 Morris St., 08901. Tel: 732-725-4879. Rev. Lope D. Pascual (Spain), Headmaster. Students 22.

WATCHUNG. *Mount St. Mary Academy*, 07060. Tel: 908-757-0108; Fax: 908-756-7528. Sr. M. Eloise Claire, R.S.M., Dir.; Rev. William T. Morris (NEW), Chap. Day school for girls. College preparatory only. Sisters of Mercy 17; Lay Teachers 34; Girls 360.

[C] INTER-PAROCHIAL ELEMENTARY SCHOOLS

BOUND BROOK. *Holy Family Academy*, St. Joseph Campus, 120 E. Second St., 08805. Tel: 732-356-1151. Mrs. Donna Kanowitz, Prin.

St. Mary Campus, 08805. Mrs. Roberta Cornyn, Prin., 333 W. Second St., 08805. Tel: 732-469-0055. Sisters 4; Students 420.

PERTH AMBOY. *Holy Spirit Campus*. (Grades PreK-4), Brace & Carlock Aves., 08861. Tel: 732-826-5747.

Perth Amboy Catholic School, 100 Fayette St., P.O. Box 651, 08862. Tel: 732-442-9533. Marie G. Acciani, Admin. Sisters 12; Students 725.

St. Mary Campus. (Grades 5-8), 351 Mechanic St., 08861. Tel: 732-442-1713.

St. Stephen Campus. (Grades K-4), 500 State St., 08861. Tel: 732-826-1598.

PHILLIPSBURG. *All Saints Regional School*, 137 Roseberry St., 08865. Tel: 908-859-1244; Fax: 908-859-1202. Mr. James A. Duris, Prin. Sisters 3; Lay Teachers 19; Students 431.

[D] SPECIAL SCHOOLS, PRIVATE

WATCHUNG. *McAuley School for Exceptional Children*, 1633 U.S. Hwy. 22, 07060. Tel: 908-754-4114. Sr. Lee Ann Amico, R.S.M., Dir. Students 37.

[E] CATHOLIC CHARITIES

METUCHEN. *Catholic Charities Central Office*, 288 Rues Ln., 08816. Tel: 732-257-6677; Fax: 732-651-2685. Sr. Florence Edward Kearney, D.C., M.A., Exec. Dir.; Michael Leszczuk, L.C.S.W., Assoc. Exec. Dir.; Mary E. Davey, L.C.S.W., Asst. Exec. Dir.; Marianne Majewski, L.C.S.W., Asst. Exec. Dir.

BRIDGEWATER. *Family Service Office*, 540-550 U.S. Rte. 22, 08807. Tel: 908-772-1881. Mary Grace Billek, M.S.W., Program Dir.

Somerset County Services, 540-550 U.S. Rte. 22, 08807. Tel: 908-772-1881. Sara Levine, L.C.S.W., Area Dir.

EAST BRUNSWICK. *Mental Health Center*, 288 Rues Ln., 08816. Tel: 732-257-6100; Fax: 732-257-6929. Michael Chenkin, M.S.W., Admin.

EDISON. *Family Service Office*, 26 Safran Ave., 08863. Tel: 732-738-1323. Lu Ann Rufalo, M.S.W., Supvr.

Middlesex County Office, 26 Safran Ave., 08837. Tel: 732-738-1323; Fax: 732-738-3896. Suzanne Siverio, L.I.C.S.W., Dir., Middlesex/Somerset Youth Services; Marilyn Wightman, M.A., Dir. Shelter Svcs.

FLEMINGTON. *Hunterdon County Services*, 6 Park Ave., 08822. Tel: 908-782-7905. Philip Lubitz, M.S.W., Dir.

MANVILLE. *Child Care Service Center*, 210 W. Camplain Rd., 08835. Tel: 908-725-1912.

MILFORD. *Family Service Office*, 69 Water St., 08848. Tel: 908-782-7905.

PERTH AMBOY. *Family Service Office*, 295 Barclay St., 08861. Tel: 732-826-9160; Fax: 732-826-8342. Marge Talbot, L.I.C.S.W., Program Dir.

PHILLIPSBURG. *Family Service Office*, 700 Sayre Ave., 08865. Tel: 908-454-2074. Connie Citro.

Social Service Center, 309 S. Main St., 08865. Tel: 908-454-7986. Sr. M. Michaelita, R.S.M., Program Dir.

Warren County Office, 700 Sayre Ave., 08865. Tel: 908-454-2074. Joan Lorah, Service Area Dir.

WOODBRIDGE. *Social Service Center*, Bunns Ln., 07095. Tel: 732-738-1323.

[F] GENERAL HOSPITALS

NEW BRUNSWICK. *St. Peter's Medical Center*, 254 Easton Ave., 08901. Tel: 732-745-8600; Fax: 732-745-7938.

For a complete listing, refer to the Hospitals section.

[G] HOMES FOR AGED

NORTH PLAINFIELD. *Villa Maria Sanitarium*, 641 Somerset St., 07060-4909. Tel: 908-757-3050; Fax: 908-754-9190.

For a complete listing, refer to the Special Care Facilities section.

SOMERSET. *McCarrick Care Center*, 15 Dellwood Ln., 08873. Tel: 732-545-4200.

For a complete listing, refer to the Special Care Facilities section.

WOODBRIDGE. *St. Joseph Senior Residence*, One St. Joseph Terr., 07095. Tel: 732-634-0004.

For a complete listing, refer to the Special Care Facilities section.

[H] MONASTERIES AND RESIDENCES FOR PRIESTS AND BROTHERS

METUCHEN. *Brothers of the Sacred Heart*, 145 Plainfield Ave., 08840. Tel: 732-548-2292. Bro. Paul Joseph, S.C., Supr. Brothers 14.

Libermann House, 197 Middlesex Ave., 08840. Tel: 732-549-7598. Revs. Patrick F. Holland, C.S.Sp.; Andrew F. Duffy, C.S.Sp.

ASBURY. *Lanteri House*, 668 Mountain View Rd., 08802. Tel: 908-689-5242. Revs. John Lyons, O.M.V.; Andrew Huhtanen, O.M.V.; Gregory J. Short, O.M.V.

BELVIDERE. *Sacred Heart Provincialate*, P.O. Box 68, 07823. Tel: 908-475-4694; Fax: 908-475-2623. Bro. Donald Sukanek, S.C., Prov. Brothers 7.

NEW BRUNSWICK. *De Porres House*, 29 Mine St., 08901. Tel: 732-545-6663. Revs. Ronald A. Stanley, O.P.; Albert A. Caprio, O.P.

NEW VILLAGE. *Society of Jesus Christ the Priest*, 70 Edison Rd., 08886. Tel: 908-213-1447. Rev. Lope A. Pascual, Dir.

PLAINSBORO. *Vincentian Residence*, 65 Mapleton Rd., Box 807, 08536-0807. Tel: 609-452-2144. Revs. William J. Bamber, C.M., Supr.; Donald L. Doyle, C.M.; Walter F. Graham, C.M.; Charles A. Wolbang, C.M.; Bros. Andrew Davis, C.M.; Frank Mallaghan, C.M.

RARITAN. *Clairvaux House*, 52 W. Somerset St., 08869. Tel: 908-526-6232. Revs. Lope A. Pascual; Charles V. Prats.

SOMERSET. *Consolata Society for Foreign Missions*, Provincial Headquarters, 2301 Rt. 27, P.O. Box 5550, 08875. Tel: 732-297-9191; Fax: 732-940-3121. Very Rev. Anthony Bellagamba, I.M.C., Prov. Supr.; Revs. Ivan Callone, I.M.C.; Charles Benelli, I.M.C.; Robert Viscardi, I.M.C.; Jose Salgueiro da Costa, I.M.C.; Aventino Oliveira, I.M.C.; George J. Hickey, I.M.C.; Mario Lecchin, I.M.C.; Vincenzo Salemi, I.M.C.; Bro. Mario Petrino, I.M.C.

Maria Regina Residence, 5 Dellwood Ln., 08873. Tel: 732-828-6800. Rev. Msgr. John R. Torney; Rev. Msgr. Dominic A. Turtora; Revs. Raymond Avery; Edward J. Nester; Francis E. Grabowski; Vincent T. Calderwood. Retirement home for Diocesan priests.

SOUTH RIVER. *Passionist Provincial Office*, 80 David St., 08882. Tel: 732-257-7177; Fax: 732-257-0042. Very Rev. Robert Joerger, C.P., Provincial Staff.

Consultors: Revs. Lucian Clark, C.P.; Paul Ruttle, C.P.; Richard Burke, C.P.; Terence Kristofak, C.P.; Victor Hoagland, C.P.; Paul Fagan, C.P.

Other Staff: Revs. Ambrose Cashman, C.P.; Roger Gannon, C.P.; Bro. Jerome Cowan, C.P. Priests 9; Brothers 1. Rev. James A. Schiffer, Military Chaplain, USAF, 740 Macon St., PSC Box 2202, Robins Air Force Base, GA, 31098-2202.

Religious Service Outside the Province: Bro. Conrad Federspiel, C.P.

67 Lewis St., Toronto, Can., M4M 2H2. Revs. Stephen Dunn, C.P.; John M. Lee, C.P., Holy Cross Center, R.R. 1, Port Burwell, Ontario, Canada, N0J 1T0. Revs. Gabriele Cingolani, C.P.; Paul Cusack, C.P.; John M. Lee, C.P.; Luigi Malorzo, C.P., 10 Red Maple Ct., Willowdale, Ontario, Canada, M2K 2T3.

Religious of the Province in Residences Not Listed Elsewhere: Rev. Michael Brennan, C.P., Mercy Medical Center, P.O. Box 6009, Redding, CA, 90099. Rev. Kevin Casey, C.P., St. Thomas the Apostle, One St. Thomas Plaza, Old Bridge, 08857. Rev. Neil Davin, C.P., St. Mathew's Rectory, 81 Seymour Ave., Edison, 08817. Rev. Norman Demeck, C.P., 391-D Picardy Court, Lakewood, 08701. Rev. Gerald Hynes, C.P., St. Ursula Rectory, 8801

Harford Rd., Baltimore, MD, 21234. Bro. Augustine Paul Lowe, C.P. (ORL), P.O. Box 1800, Orlando, FL, 32802-1800. Revs. Benedict Mawn, C.P.; Wilfred Scanlon, C.P., P.O. Box 946, Londonderry, NH, 03053. Rev. Gerard A. Orlando, C.P., St. Patrick Home, 66 Van Cortlandt Park, Bronx, NY, 10463. Rev. Theodore Vitali, C.P., 5859 Nottingham St., Saint Louis, MO, 63109. Rev. James McHugh, C.P., St. John Seminary, Brighton, MA, 02135. 204 N. Church St., Dublin, GA, 31021. Rev. Salvatore Riccardi, C.P., Church of the Annunciation, 470 W. Chester Ave., Crestwood, NY, 10707. Rev. Paul Vaeth, C.P., P.O. Box 2605, Greenville, NC, 27836. Rev. Conan Conaboy, C.P., St. Joseph's Parish, 312 Davis St., Scranton, PA, 18505. Rev. Emmanuel Gordon, C.P., All Saints Church, 22824 Second St., Hayward, CA, 94541. Rev. Carrol Thorne, C.P., 316 N. 6th St., Apt. 101, Leavenworth, KS, 66048.

[I] CONVENTS AND RESIDENCES FOR SISTERS

METUCHEN. *St. Francis R.C.I.A. Residence*, 44 Elm Ave., 08840.

BOUND BROOK. *Sisters of Jesus Our Hope*, 514 Church St., 08805. Tel: 732-271-5777. Sr. Julia Jamink, Supr. Sisters 5.

CARTERET. *Sisters of Jesus Our Hope*, 55 High St., 07008. Tel: 732-541-4678. Sr. Carlotta LaRocca. Sisters 4.

EAST BRUNSWICK. *DePaul House*, 528 Ryders Ln., 08816. Tel: 732-238-3638. Sisters 4.

EDISON. *St. Thomas Aquinas Convent*, 15 Wren Ct., 08820. Tel: 732-321-0137. Sisters 3.

FLEMINGTON. *The Carmel of Mary Immaculate and St. Mary Magdalen*, Harmony School Rd., P.O. Box 785, 08822. Mother Teresa of Mary Immaculate, O.C.D.; Rev. Sebastian Kaithackal, C.M.I., Chap. Nuns professed with solemn vows 11.

HACKETTSTOWN. *Villa Madonna*. Retirement Home, 1686 Rt. 517, 07840. Tel: 908-852-4551. Daughters of Divine Charity. Sisters 30.

HAMPTON. *Sisters of Jesus Our Hope*, 32 Main St., 08827. Tel: 908-537-6583. Sr. Claire Marie Lessard. Sisters 6.

NEW BRUNSWICK. *Sisters of St. Joseph of Peace*, 61 Jefferson Ave., 08901. Tel: 732-249-5644. Sr. Joanne Rusch, C.S.J.P. Sisters 2.

NORTH PLAINFIELD. *San Damiano Convent*, 99 Harrison Ave., 07060-3606. Tel: 908-769-6498; 757-3050; Fax: 908-754-9190. Sr. M. Antonia Cooper, O.S.F., Supr. Sisters 3.

Villa Maria Regional House, 641 Somerset St., 07060-4909. Tel: 908-757-3050; Fax: 908-754-9190.

Regional House for Congregation of the Servants of the Holy Child of Jesus. Sr. M. Dominic Ritter, O.S.F., Reg. Supr.; Rev. Cyprian M. Sullivan, O.F.M.Conv., Chap., Tel: 908-756-4186. Sisters 35.

PISCATAWAY. *Divine Providence Convent*, 137 Metlars Ln., 08854. Tel: 732-572-3138. Sr. Maria Michele Armato, O.P., Supr. Sisters 4.

SKILLMAN. *Religious of the Sacred Heart*, 54 Robin Dr., 08558. Tel: 609-924-0180. Sr. Kathleen Cox, R.S.C.J.

SOMERSET. *St. Elizabeth Convent*, 13 Renfro Rd., 08873. Tel: 732-247-3697. Sr. M. Carista, O.S.F., Supr. Sisters 4.

SOUTH AMBOY. *Sacred Heart Convent*, P.O. Box 3005, 08879-3005. Tel: 908-727-2094. Sr. M. Anastasia, O.S.F., Supr. Sisters 4.

WASHINGTON. *Handmaids of Mary Immaculate*, Mountain View Rd., 07882. Tel: 908-689-7330. Sr. Mary Joseph Brech, A.M.I., Supr. Sisters 8.

WATCHUNG. *McAuley Hall Inc.*, Health Care Center, 1633 U.S. Hwy 22, 07060. Tel: 908-754-3663; Fax: 908-754-3502. Sr. Irene Gormley, R.S.M.; Rev. Edward Costello, O.F.M.Conv. Retired Sisters 60.

Mount St. Mary, 1645 U.S. Hwy. 22 W., 07060-6587. Tel: 908-756-5348. Sisters of Mercy of the Americas, Regional Community of New Jersey. Sr. Diane Szubrowski, R.S.M., Pres., Reg. Com.; Rev. Edward M. Edwards, O.S.M., Chap. Professed Sisters 336.

Mt. St. Mary House of Prayer, 1651 U.S. Hwy. 22, 07060. Tel: 908-753-2091. Sr. Eileen Smith, R.S.M., Supr. Sisters 3.

WOODBRIDGE. *St. Joseph Convent*, 184 Amboy Ave., 07095. Tel: 732-634-0807. Sr. Mary Lucy, L.S.I.C., Supr. Sisters 8.

[J] RETREAT HOUSES

FLEMINGTON. *Our Lady of Providence*, 31 Britton Dr., 08822. Tel: 908-782-4495. Little Sisters of the Poor. Sr. Christine Marie de St. Joseph, L.S.P., Dir.

HIGHLAND PARK. *Cenacle Retreat House*, (Attn. Cenacle) 411 River Rd., 08904-1999. Tel: 732-249-8100; Fax: 732-249-8101. Sr. Barbara Whittemore. Sisters 6.

LITTLE YORK. *Bethany Ridge*, P.O. Box 241, 08834. Tel: 908-995-9758; Fax: 908-995-7299. Rev. Mark J. Dolak, Dir. Spirituality Center for Priests.

PERTH AMBOY. *Emmaus House*, 101 Center St., 08861. Tel: 732-442-7688. Sr. Susan McGrath, S.M.G., Dir. Sisters 2.

PLAINSBORO. *Vincentian Renewal Center*, 75 Mapleton Rd., P.O. Box 757, 08536. Tel: 609-520-9626; Fax: 609-452-2851. Revs. Thomas A. Casella, C.M., Dir.; Charles F. Krieg, C.M.

[K] SHRINES AND PUBLIC ORATORIES

BERNARDSVILLE. *Sacred Heart Chapel*. (Chapel of Convenience), 111 Claremont Rd., 07924; Fax: 766-1185. Rev. Chester H. Carina, Pastor.

RARITAN. *Shrine Chapel of the Blessed Sacrament*, 50 W. Somerset St., 08869. Tel: 908-722-1489. Rev. Charles V. Prats, Rector.

WASHINGTON. *Shrine of the Immaculate Heart of Mary*. Vacant. Mountain View Rd., 07882. Tel: 908-689-1700.

[L] PUBLIC ASSOCIATIONS OF THE FAITHFUL

BOUND BROOK. *Sisters of Jesus Our Hope*, 514 Church St., 08805. Sr. Julia Jamink, Supr. Sisters 15.

PHILLIPSBURG. *The Anawim Community*, 156 Broad St., 08865. Tel: 908-859-2049. Revs. Francis J. Marino, S.M. (BO), Dir.; Charles A. Sabella; Richard M. Rusk; Richard W. Palumbo.

PISCATAWAY. *Dominican Sisters of Divine Providence*, Divine Providence Convent, 137 Metlars Ln., 08854. Sr. Maria Michele Armato, O.P., Supr. Sisters 4.

WASHINGTON. *Handmaids of Mary Immaculate*, Holy House Convent, Mountain View Rd., 07882. Sr. Mary Joseph Brech, A.M.I., Supr. Sisters 8.

[M] CAMPUS MINISTRY

NEW BRUNSWICK. *Catholic Center at Rutgers University*, 17 Mine St., 08901. Tel: 732-545-6663; Fax: 732-545-6663. Chaplains: Revs. Ronald A. Stanley, O.P.; Albert A. Caprio, O.P.; Joseph G. Celano; Sr. Jeanne Goyette, O.P., Pastoral Asst.

[N] MISCELLANEOUS LISTINGS

METUCHEN. *The Catholic Lawyers Guild of the Diocese of Metuchen, Inc.*, 407 Main St., 08840. Rev. Msgr. William Benwell, Moderator.

The Foundation for Catholic Education, P.O. Box 191, 08840. Most Rev. Edward T. Hughes, D.D., Pres.

The Fund for the Future, Inc., P.O. Box 191, 08840. Most Rev. Edward T. Hughes, Pres.

The Priestly Education Fund, Inc., P.O. Box 191, 08840. Most Rev. Edward T. Hughes, Pres.

EAST BRUNSWICK. *Community House at St. Thomas*, 288 Rues Ln., 08816. Tel: 732-257-6677; Fax: 732-651-2685. Mary E. Davey.

Metuchen Community Services Corporation, 288 Rues Ln., 08816. Tel: 732-257-6677; Fax: 732-651-2685. Michael Leszczuk, L.I.C.S.W.

EDISON. *The Ozanam Shelter for Families and Single Women*, 89 Truman Dr., 08817. Tel: 732-985-0327; Fax: 732-985-2449. Carmen Fernandez, Admin.

St. Paul Book and Media Center, Wick Plaza, 561 Route One S., 08817. Tel: 732-572-1200.

LAMBERTVILLE. *The Jesus School*, Church of St. John the Evangelist, 44 Bridge St., 08530. Tel: 609-397-0593. Sr. Marie Conaughton, Dir. Students 24.

NEW BRUNSWICK. *The Ozanam Shelter for Men*, 155 Memorial Pkwy., 08901. Tel: 732-745-5194; Fax: 732-545-0239. Martin W. Yazgier, Program Dir.

St. John of God Community Health Center, 24 Abeel St., 08901. Tel: 732-745-9800. Steven J. Levin, M.D., Medical Dir.; Sharon Oshatz, M.T. (A.S.C.P.), Dir.

PEAPACK. *Everitt Academy*, Main St., P.O. Box 33, 07977. Tel: 908-234-1524; Fax: 908-234-2923. Rev. Msgr. George M. Brembos; Sr. Madeline Sarli, S.S.J., Dir.

PERTH AMBOY. *Nazareth House*, 301 Barclay St., 08861. Tel: 732-324-0437. Sabrina Myers, Program Dir.

PHILLIPSBURG. *St. Peter and Paul House*, 702 Sayre Ave., 08865. Tel: 908-454-0912. Dominic Romero, Coord.

SOMERSET. *Mission International, Inc.*, 2301 Hwy. 27, 08873. Tel: 732-297-9191; Fax: 732-940-3121. Rev. Mario Lacchin, I.M.C., Dir.

WASHINGTON. *Blue Army of Our Lady of Fatima, U.S.A., Inc.*, P.O. Box 976, 07882. Tel: 908-689-1700.

WATCHUNG. *McAuley Hall Foundation, Inc.*, 1633 U.S. Hwy. 22, 07060.

WOODBRIDGE. *Mt. Carmel Home Nursing Service*, 184 Amboy Ave., 07095. Tel: 732-634-0807. Sr. M. Lucy, L.S.I.C., Dir.

RELIGIOUS INSTITUTES OF MEN REPRESENTED IN THE DIOCESE

For further details refer to the corresponding bracketed number in the Religious Institutes of Men or Women section.

[1100]—*Brothers of the Sacred Heart*.—S.C.

[0470]—*The Capuchin Friars*.—O.F.M.Cap.

[0360]—*Claretian Missionaries*. (Eastern Prov.).—C.M.F.

[0330]—*Congregation of Christian Brothers*. (Philadelphia, PA).—C.F.C.

[1330]—*Congregation of the Mission*.—C.M.

[1000]—*Congregation of the Passion*.—C.P.

[0390]—*Consolata Missionaries*.—I.M.C.

[0520]—*Franciscan Friars*. (Custody of St. John Capistran).—O.F.M.

[0940]—*Oblates of the Virgin Mary*.—O.M.V.

[0430]—*Order of Preacher (Dominicans)*. (Prov. of St. Joseph).—O.P.

RELIGIOUS INSTITUTES OF WOMEN REPRESENTED IN THE DIOCESE

[0130]—*Apostles of the Sacred Heart of Jesus*.—A.S.C.J.

[1810]—*Bernardine Sisters of the Third Order of St. Francis*.—O.S.F.

[3110]—*Congregation of Our Lady of the Retreat in the Cenacle*. (Eastern Prov.).—R.C.

[0760]—*Daughters of Charity of St. Vincent De Paul*. (Albany Prov.).—D.C.

[0790]—*Daughters of Divine Charity*. (Prov. of St. Joseph).—F.D.C.

[0420]—*Discalced Carmelite Nuns*.—O.C.D.

[1070-17]—*Dominican Sisters*. (Philadelphia, PA).—O.P.

[1070-18]—*Dominican Sisters*. (Caldwell).—O.P.

[1070-06]—*Dominican Sisters of Hope*. (Ossining, N.Y.).—O.P.

[1170]—*Felician Sisters*. (Immaculate Conception Prov.).—C.S.S.F.

[1180]—*Franciscan Sisters of Allegany, New York*.—O.S.F.

[1630]—*Franciscan Sisters of Penance and Charity*. (Niagara).—O.S.F.P.C.

[1650]—*Franciscan Sisters of Philadelphia*.—O.S.F.

[2575]—*Institute of the Sisters of Mercy of the Americas*. (New Jersey).—R.S.M.

[2300]—*Little Servant Sisters of the Immaculate Conception*.—L.S.I.C.

[2340]—*Little Sisters of the Poor*. (Brooklyn Prov.).—L.S.P.

[2700]—*Missionary Catechists of the Sacred Hearts of Jesus and Mary*.—M.C.

[2790]—*Missionary Servants of the Most Blessed Trinity*.—M.S.B.T.

[0950]—*Pious Society Daughters of St. Paul*.—F.S.P.

[3640]—*Poor Servants of the Mother of God*.—S.M.G.

[3320]—*Presentation of the Blessed Virgin Mary*. (New Windsor, NY).—P.B.V.M.

[0970]—*Religious of Divine Compassion*. (White Plains, NY).—R.D.C.

[]—*Religious of the Blessed Virgin Mary*.—R.V.M.

[3465]—*Religious of the Sacred Heart of Mary*. Tarrytown, NY.—R.S.H.M.

[3430]—*Religious Teachers Filippini*. (St. Lucy Prov.).—M.P.F.

[3580]—*Servants of Mary*. (American Prov.).—O.S.M.

[1980]—*Servants of the Holy Child of Jesus*.—O.S.F.

[3630]—*Servants of the Most Sacred Heart of Jesus*.—S.S.C.J.

[0590]—*Sisters of Charity of Saint Elizabeth, Convent Station*.—S.C.

[0660]—*Sisters of Christian Charity*. (North American Eastern Prov.).—S.C.C.

[2970]—*Sisters of Notre Dame*. (Baltimore, MD).—S.N.D.

[3893]—*Sisters of Saint Joseph of Chestnut Hill, Philadelphia*.—S.S.J.

[1650]—*Sisters of St. Francis of Philadelphia*.—O.S.F.

[1600]—*Sisters of St. Francis of the Martyr St. George*.—O.S.F.

[3890]—*Sisters of St. Joseph of Peace*.—C.S.J.P.

[1190]—*Sisters of the Atonement*. (Graymoor).—S.A.

[2170]—*Sisters Servants of the Immaculate Heart of Mary*.—I.H.M.

DIOCESAN CEMETERIES

JAMESBURG. *Holy Cross Burial Park*, Cranbury Rd., Box 100, 08831. Tel: 732-521-0770.

PISCATAWAY. *Resurrection Burial Park*, 899 Lincoln Ave., 08854. Tel: 732-545-5966.

NECROLOGY

† MacDonald, John H., (On Leave). —Died July 29, 1996.

† Morris, Edward V., (Retired). —Died Aug. 30, 1996.

Archdiocese of Miami

(Archidioecesis Miamiensis)

Most Reverend

JOHN C. FAVALORA, D.D.

Archbishop of Miami; ordained December 20, 1961; appointed Bishop of Alexandria June 16, 1986; ordained and installed July 29, 1986; appointed Third Bishop of St. Petersburg March 7, 1989; installed May 16, 1989; appointed Third Archbishop of Miami November 3, 1994; installed December 20, 1994. *Office: 9401 Biscayne Blvd., Miami, FL, 33138.*

Most Reverend

AGUSTIN A. ROMAN, D.D., V.G.

Auxiliary Bishop of Miami; ordained July 5, 1959; appointed Titular Bishop of Sertei and Auxiliary of Miami February 6, 1979; consecrated March 24, 1979. *Res., 3605 S. Miami Ave., Miami, FL, 33133.*

Most Reverend

EDWARD A. MCCARTHY, D.D., S.T.D., J.C.D.

Retired Archbishop of Miami; ordained May 29, 1943; appointed Titular Bishop of Tamascani and Auxiliary of Cincinnati April 21, 1965; transferred to Phoenix August 25, 1969; installed December 2, 1969; appointed Coadjutor Archbishop of Miami *"cum jure successionis" September 17, 1976; Archbishop of Miami July 26, 1977; retired November 3, 1994. Office: 9401 Biscayne Blvd., Miami Shores, FL, 33138.*

ESTABLISHED AUGUST 13, 1958.

CREATED AN ARCHBISHOPRIC, JUNE 13, 1968.

Square Miles 4,958.

Comprises the Counties in the southern part of the State of Florida, namely, Broward, Dade and Monroe.

For legal titles of parishes and Archdiocesan institutions, consult the Pastoral Center.

Pastoral Center: 9401 Biscayne Blvd., Miami Shores, FL, 33138. Tel.: 305-757-6241; Fax: 305-754-1897 (Chancery); 758-0356 (Communications Office).

Web site address: http://www.safari.net/~miaarch/

E-mail address: miaarch@safari.net

STATISTICAL OVERVIEW

Personnel	
Archbishop	1
Retired Archbishops	1
Auxiliary Bishops	1
Priests: Diocesan Active in Diocese	218
Priests: Active Outside Diocese	7
Priests: Diocesan in Foreign Missions	1
Priests: Retired, Sick or Absent	27
Number of Diocesan Priests	253
Religious Priests in Diocese	122
Extern Priests in Diocese	88
Ordinations:	
Diocesan Priests	7
Religious Priests	1
Transitional Deacons	2
Permanent Deacons	8
Permanent Deacons in Diocese	113
Total Brothers	56
Total Sisters	346
Parishes	
Parishes	108
With Resident Pastor:	
Resident Diocesan Priests	101
Resident Religious Priests	10
Without Resident Pastor:	
Missions	3
Pastoral Centers	1
Professional Ministry Personnel:	
Brothers	2
Sisters	59
Lay Ministers	143
Welfare	
Catholic Hospitals	2
Total Assisted	527,144
Health Care Centers	3
Total Assisted	35,000
Homes for the Aged	4
Total Assisted	31,755
Residential Care of Children	2
Total Assisted	380
Day Care and Extended Day Care Centers	6
Total Assisted	2,300
Specialized Homes	3
Total Assisted	500
Special Centers for Social Services	31
Total Assisted	528,655
Residential Care of Disabled	2
Total Assisted	11,641
Other Institutions	11
Total Assisted	1,050
Educational	
Seminaries, Diocesan	1
Students from This Diocese	11
Students from Other Diocese	24
Diocesan Students in Other Seminaries	17
Total Seminarians	28
Colleges and Universities	2
Total Students	10,378
High Schools, Diocesan and Parish	7
Total Students	6,706
High Schools, Private	5
Total Students	2,905
Elementary Schools, Diocesan and Parish	49
Total Students	21,705
Elementary Schools, Private	3
Total Students	1,264
Non-residential Schools for the Disabled	2
Total Students	11,641
Catechesis/Religious Education:	
High School Students	2,543
Elementary Students	41,891
Total Students Under Catholic Instruction	99,061
Teachers in the Diocese:	
Priests	10
Brothers	21
Sisters	51
Lay Teachers	1,733
Vital Statistics	
Receptions into the Church:	
Infant Baptism Totals	18,644
Adult Baptism Totals	986
Received into Full Communion	1,256
First Communions	13,003
Confirmations	7,734
Marriages:	
Catholic	3,247
Interfaith	575
Total Marriages	3,822
Deaths	4,856
Total Catholic Population	760,078
Total Population	3,525,351

Former Archbishops—Most Rev. COLEMAN F. CARROLL, D.D., ord. June 15, 1930; appt. Titular Bishop of Pitanae and Auxiliary Bishop of Pittsburgh, Aug. 25, 1953; cons. Nov. 10, 1953; appt. first Bishop of Miami, Aug. 13, 1958; installed Oct. 7, 1958; appt. Archbishop of Miami, March 13, 1968; died July 26, 1977.—Most Rev. EDWARD A. MCCARTHY, D.D., S.T.D., J.C.D., ord. May 29, 1943; appt. Coadjutor Archbishop of Miami "cum jure successionis," Sept. 17, 1976; appt. Archbishop of Miami, July 26, 1977; retired November 3, 1994.

Pastoral Center—9401 Biscayne Blvd., Miami Shores, 33138. Tel: 305-757-6241; Fax: 305-754-1897 (Chancery Office); 754-1797 (Communications Office).

Vicars General—Most Rev. AGUSTIN A. ROMAN, V.G.; Rev. Msgr. WILLIAM J. HENNESSEY, V.G.

Chancellor—Very Rev. TOMAS M. MARIN, J.C.L.

Moderator of the Curia—Rev. Msgr. WILLIAM J. HENNESSEY, V.G.

Secretary to the Archbishop—Rev. MICHAEL CARRUTHERS.

Metropolitan Tribunal—Address all Rogatory commissions and matrimonial matters to the Tribunal (All Pastoral Center searches for information prior to October 7, 1958, should be directed to Diocese of St. Augustine, FL), *9401 Biscayne Blvd., Miami Shores, 33138.* Tel: 305-757-6241, Ext. 360; Fax: 305-758-0178.

Judicial Vicar and Administrator—Very Rev. ANDREW L. ANDERSON, J.C.D.

Adjutant Judicial Vicar—Rev. ERNESTO MOLANO, J.C.L.

Judges—Very Rev. TOMAS MARIN, J.C.L.; Sr. JEANNE-MARGARET MCNALLY, J.C.L., Ph.D.; Revs. JOSE BIAIN, O.F.M.; ERNESTO MOLANO, J.C.L.; MANUEL ORTEGA, J.C.L.; GEORGE PUTHUSSERIL, J.C.D.;

KENNETH SCHWANGER, J.C.L.; MICHAEL THOMAS, J.C.D.; KENNETH WHITTAKER, J.C.L.

Promoters of Justice—Rev. KENNETH WHITTAKER, J.C.L.; J. MICHAEL FITZGERALD, J.C.L., Esq.

Defenders of the Bond—Rev. Msgr. ORLANDO FERNANDEZ; Revs. CARL MORRISON, J.C.L.; MANUEL ORTEGA, J.C.L.; RONALD PUSSAK, J.C.L.; Mr. J. MICHAEL FITZGERALD, J.C.L., Esq.

Notaries—Ms. KATIA ARRIAZA; LILLIAN HUMARA; CONNIE LOFFREDO; CONCHITA VALLE; KATHLEEN CHERRIS, C.P.S.

Assessors—Sr. ISABEL MAZARREDO, O.P.; ROSARIO BERGOUIGNAN.

Counsel-Assistant to the Tribunal—J. MICHAEL FITZGERALD, J.C.L., Esq.

Consultors—Most Rev. AGUSTIN ROMAN, V.G.; Rev. Msgr. WILLIAM J. HENNESSEY, V.G.; Very Rev. TOMAS M. MARIN; Revs. GUSTAVO MIYARES; VINCENT KELLY; ARTHUR DENNISON; ANTHONY MULDERRY.

Deans and Deaneries—Rev. Msgr. JOHN GLORIE, V.F., (Northeast Broward); Rev. Msgr. NOEL FOGARTY, V.F., (Northwest Broward); Very Rev. THOMAS O'DWYER, V.F., (South Broward); Very Rev. JOSE L. HERNANDO, V.F., (East Dade); Very Rev. SEAMUS DOYLE, V.F., (Northeast Dade); Very Rev. LUIS PEREZ, V.F., (Northwest Dade); Very Rev. JAMES FETSCHER, V.F., (South Dade); Very Rev. XAVIER MORRAS, V.F., (West Dade); Very Rev. GERALD MCGRATH, V.F., (Monroe).

Incardination Committee—Most Rev. JOHN C. FAVALORA; Most Rev. AGUSTIN A. ROMAN, V.G.; Rev. Msgr. PABLO A. NAVARRO; Rev. Msgr. WILLIAM J. HENNESSEY, V.G.; Very Rev. TOMAS M. MARIN; Revs. VINCENT KELLY; ARTHUR DENNISON; JAMES MURPHY.

Presbyteral Council—Most Rev. JOHN C. FAVALORA, Pres.; Revs. ARTHUR DENNISON, Vice Pres. MICHAEL HOYER, Sec.

Priests' Personnel Board—Rev. DANIEL KUBALA, Chm. Consultants: Most Rev. AGUSTIN ROMAN, V.G.; Rev. Msgr. WILLIAM J. HENNESSEY, V.G.; Very Rev. TOMAS M. MARIN. Members: Rev. ARTHUR DENNISON; JOSE LUIS HERNANDO; ANTHONY MULDERRY; THOMAS O'DWYER.

Ministry Of General Services

Executive Director—Very Rev. TOMAS M. MARIN.

Chancellor's Office—Very Rev. TOMAS M. MARIN, Chancellor/Exec. Dir.

Coordinator of Special Projects—Rev. PATRICK O'NEILL.

Pastoral Center Services—Mr. TERRY SUNDY.

Legal Services—J. MICHAEL FITZGERALD, *Grand Bay Plaza, Ste. M-103, 2665 S. Bayshore Dr., Miami, 33133.* Tel: 305-854-6666; Fax: 305-856-7634. PATRICK FITZGERALD, *110 Merrick Way, Ste. 3-B, Coral Gables, 33134.* Tel: 305-443-9162; Fax: 305-443-6613.

Communications Dept.—MARY ROSS AGOSTA, Dir. CYNTHIA GUTIERREZ, Coord. MIRIAM MIRANDA, Admin. Asst.

Public and Media Relations—MARY ROSS AGOSTA, Dir.

Community Information—MARY ROSS AGOSTA, Dir., Mailing Address: for Communications, Public and Media Relations and: Community Information *9401 Biscayne Blvd., Miami, 33138.* Tel: 305-757-6241, Ext. 320; 330; Fax: 305-758-0356.

Television and Radio Center—MARY ROSS AGOSTA, Dir. MARIA CLEMENTI MEDINA, Oper. Mgr. ERNESTO GONZALEZ, Staff Dir. CHRISTINE SLOAN, Producer; Revs. JOSE P. NICKSE, Producer & TV Mass Coord. (Spanish); FRANCISCO SANTANA, Producer & TV Mass Coord. (Spanish); THOMAS WENSKI, TV Mass Producer (English), Mailing Address: *9920 N.E. 2nd Ave., Miami, 33138.* Tel: 305-751-0990.

Newspapers—MARY ROSS AGOSTA, Dir.

The Miami edition of "The Florida Catholic"—ROBERT O'STEEN, Editor (English).

The Miami edition of "La Voz Catolica"—Ms. ARACELI CANTERO, Exec. Editor (Spanish), Mailing Address: for Newspapers: *9401 Biscayne Blvd., Miami, 33138.* Tel: 305-757-6241, Ext. 312; 128; Fax: 305-754-1797.

RADIO PEACE / CATHOLIC BROADCASTING, INC.—Rev. FEDERICO CAPDEPON, Pres./Dir.; Deacon RAFAEL DE LOS REYES, V.P./Adm. Tel: 305-368-9729; Fax: 305-636-4571.

Radio Peace - WAXY, 790 AM—20450 N.W. 2nd Ave., Miami, 33169. Tel: 305-525-3193. JOE KEENER, Programming Dir.

Radio Paz - WKAT, 1360 AM—1779 N.W. 28 St., N. Miami, 33142. Tel: 305-638-9729. ISAUL GONZALEZ, Mktg. Dir.

Radio Ke Poze - WKAT, 1360 AM—13499 Biscayne Blvd., N. Miami, 33181. Tel: 305-751-6289. Rev. THOMAS WENSKI, Programming Dir.

Catholic Office for Inter-Faith Activities and Catholic-Jewish Relations Commission—Rev. PATRICK H. O'NEILL, Exec. Dir., *9401 Biscayne Blvd., Miami Shores, 33138.* Tel: 305-754-2444; Fax: 305-754-6649.

Christian Unity Commission—Rev. Dr. PATRICK H. O'NEILL, Ecumenical Officer, *9401 Biscayne Blvd., Miami Shores, 33138.* Tel: 305-757-6241, Ext. 254; Fax: 305-754-1897.

Ministry Of Christian Formation

Executive Director—Rev. VINCENT T. KELLY.

Department of Schools—Rev. VINCENT T. KELLY, Vicar, Christian Formation; Sr. M. NOREEN WERNER, C.S.F.N., Supt.; Bro. FELIX ELARDO, F.M.S.; Sr. CORINNE GMUER, S.S.N.D.; CHRISTINE LAMADRID; Sr. MARY TERZO, F.M.A., Assoc. Supt.; Sr. BARBARA WETTERER, O.P.

Department of Religious Education—Sr. ROSA MONIQUE PENA, O.P., Dir.

Archdiocesan Catechetical Center—Ms. INES EXPOSITO, Mgr.

Archdiocese of Miami Education Endowment Fund, Inc.—PATRICK J. HEFFERNAN, Ph.D., Exec. Dir.

Catholic Charities

Archdiocesan Director—Rev. THOMAS G. WENSKI, M.Div.

Catholic Relief Services—9401 Biscayne Blvd., Miami Shores, 33138. Tel: 305-754-2444; Fax: 305-754-6649.

Campaign for Human Development—9401 Biscayne Blvd., Miami Shores, 33138. Tel: 305-754-2444; Fax: 305-754-6649.

Pierre Toussaint Haitian Catholic Center, Human Services Division—MICHAEL FOULKES, Exec. Dir., *110 NE 62 St., Miami, 33138.* Tel: 305-758-2462; Fax: 305-758-8216.

Legal Services Project—RANDOLPH MCGRORTY, Supervising Attorney; MYRIAM MEZADIEU, Admin., *110 NE 62 St., Maimi, 33138.* Tel: 305-758-3301; Fax: 305-756-6435.

Catholic Community Services—TIMOTHY J. SAWINA, Exec. Dir., *9401 Biscayne Blvd., Miami Shores, 33138.* Tel: 305-754-2444; Fax: 305-754-6649. CARLOS BUSTABAD, Dir., Budget & Mgmt.; Mr. RONALD A. HASSELL, Dir., Personnel & Mgmt. Information Svcs. RICARDO RIESGO, Dir., Accounting Svcs./Data Processing; LLOYDINE MCGUINN, Exec. Asst.

Dade Area Offices—

Miami Shores Office—ALBERT TRICOMI, A.C.S.W., Dir., *9999 N.E. 2nd Ave., Ste. 217, Miami Shores, 33138.* Tel: 305-758-0024; Fax: 305-757-6287.

South Dade Office—GRACIELA PEREZ, M.S.W., Admin., *9245 S.W. 158 Ln., Miami, 33157.* Tel: 305-378-6105; Fax: 305-233-3807.

Little Havana Office—ALICIA DEL TORO, M.S.W., Admin., *970 S.W. 1 St., Ste. 302, Miami, 33130.* Tel: 305-324-1104.

Services for the Elderly—MARY GREEN, Admin., *9900 N.E. 2nd Ave., Miami Shores, 33138.* Tel: 305-751-5203; Fax: 305-758-4972.

Broward Area Offices—VICKI KAUFMAN, M.A., Dir., *1505 N.E. 26 St., Wilton Manors, 33305.* Tel: 954-630-9404; Fax: 954-566-6026.

Catholic Family and Children's Services Trust of Broward County—PAUL A. GORE, Chm.; Rev. THOMAS G. WENSKI, Sec., *9401 Biscayne Blvd., Miami Shores, 33138.* Tel: 305-754-2444; 954-630-9404; Fax: 305-754-6649; 954-566-6026.

Child Welfare Services—MILDRED LUGO, L.C.S.W., Dir., *18601 S.W. 97 Ave., P.O. Box 970143, Miami, 33197.* Tel: 305-238-2381; Fax: 305-232-5421.

Boystown of Florida, Inc.—SALLY ABELLO, L.C.S.W., Admin., *11400 S.W. 137 Ave., Miami, 33186.* Tel: 305-385-1722; Fax: 305-385-8301.

Catholic Home for Children, Inc.—MILDRED LUGO, L.C.S.W., Admin., *18601 S.W. 97 Ave., P.O. Box 970143, Miami, 33197.* Tel: 305-238-2381; Fax: 305-232-5421.

Maternity and Foster Services—MILDRED LUGO, L.C.S.W., Admin., *18601 S.W. 97 Ave., P.O. Box 970143, Miami, 33197.* Tel: 305-238-1447; Fax: 305-232-5421.

Catholic Child Welfare Trust—JOSEPH W. MYRTETUS, Chm.; Rev. THOMAS G. WENSKI, Sec., *9401 Biscayne Blvd., Miami Shores, 33138.* Tel: 305-754-2444; Fax: 305-754-6649.

Substance Abuse Programs—

St. Luke's Addiction Recovery Programs (St. Luke Center, Inc.)—PATRICIA CARTER, Acting Dir. ANDREW CHERY, Acting Dir., *7707 N.W. 2 Ave., Miami, 33150.* Tel: 305-795-0077; Fax: 305-795-0030.

Miami DARE Substance Abuse Prevention Prog.—7707 N.W. 2nd Ave., Miami, 33150. Tel: 305-795-0077; Fax: 305-795-0030.

Child Development Centers—ALICE G. ABREU, Dir., *9401 Biscayne Blvd., Miami, 33138.* Tel: 305-754-2444; Fax: 305-754-6649.

Centro Hispano Child Care Center (Centro Hispano Catolico, Inc.)—LEIANA M. KOURANY-ALVAREZ, Admin., *144 N.W. 26 St., Miami, 33137.* Tel: 305-576-3461; Fax: 305-576-6446.

Centro Mater Child Care and Neighborhood Center (Centro Mater, Inc.)—ANA CRISTINA RODRIGUEZ, M.S.W., Admin., *418 S.W. 4 Ave., Miami, 33130.* Tel: 305-545-6049; 545-7720; Fax: 305-324-6162.

Centro Mater West Child Care Center—MIRIAM ROMAN, M.S.W., Admin., *8420 N.W. 103 St., Miami, 33016.* Tel: 305-827-1050; Fax: 305-827-1079.

Good Shepherd Day Care and Neighborhood Center—ALEIDA BARCENA-CAO, Admin., *18601 S.W. 97 Ave., Miami, 33157.* Tel: 305-235-1756; 235-1330; Fax: 305-255-2788.

Little Havana Child Care Program—MARISABEL CAPOTE, Admin., *970 S.W. 1 St., Room 205, Miami, 33130.* Tel: 305-324-5424;326-8212; Fax: 305-325-0642.

Notre Dame Day Care and Neighborhood Center—MARLENE EVEILLARD, Admin., *130 N.E. 62 St., Miami, 33138.* Tel: 305-751-6778; Fax: 305-751-6959.

Child Care Food Program—CHARIL FELDMAN, Admin., *9401 Biscayne Blvd., Miami Shores, 33138.* Tel: 305-754-2444; Fax: 305-754-6649.

Day Centers for the Elderly—

Miami-Senior Center—MARY GREEN, Admin., *9900 N.E. 2 Ave., Miami Shores, 33138.* Tel: 305-751-5203; Fax: 305-758-4972.

Broward Catholic Senior and Adult Day Care Centers—MIRANDA SGOUROS, Dir., *1505 N.E. 26 St., Wilton Manors, 33305.* Tel: 954-630-9404; Fax: 954-566-6026.

Broward-Central West Senior Day Center—TAMRA TURNER, Coord., *4644 S.W. 64 Ave., Davie, 33314.* Tel: 305-583-6446.

St. Elizabeth Senior Day Center—JOHN CAVOTO, Coord., *801 N.E. 33 St., Pompano Beach, 33064.* Tel: 954-781-0461.

Winton Manors Senior Day Center—KAY SWICORD, Coord., *1505 N.E. 26 St., Wilton Manors, 33305.* Tel: 954-581-7621.

Refugee Resettlement Services—ANITA GAWOR, Acting Admin., *3737 S.W. 8th St., Rm. 200, Coral Gables, 33134.* Tel: 305-567-1655; Fax: 305-567-1177.

Parish Social Ministry—

Dade-Monroe—HUGH CLEAR, Dir., *9401 Biscayne Blvd., Miami Shores, 33138.* Tel: 305-754-2444; Fax: 305-754-6649.

Broward—MURIEL KROLL, Coord., *1505 N.E. 26 St., Wilton Manors, 33305.* Tel: 954-630-9404; Fax: 954-566-6026.

Catholic Hospice, Inc.—Rev. THOMAS G. WENSKI; JANET JONES, Pres., *14100 Palmetto Frontage Rd., Miami Lakes, 33016.* Tel: 305-822-2380; Fax: 305-827-0221.

Services to People with AIDS—

Dade, Genesis Programs, Inc.—Sr. B. EDITA ROJO, M.D., Dir.; Rev. DANIEL DORRITY, Chap., *3675 S. Miami Ave., Miami, 33133.* Tel: 305-856-1043; Fax: 305-856-1633.

Broward, Ministry to People with AIDS—Rev. DENNIS RAUSCH, Admin., *1505 N.E. 26 St., Wilton Manors, 33305.* Tel: 954-630-9404; Fax: 954-566-6026.

Dade, Ministry to People with AIDS—ELIZABETH VERA, Coord., *9245 S.W. 158 Ln., #201, Miami, 33157.* Tel: 305-378-6306; Fax: 305-378-1660.

Foreign Mission Board—ALICIA MARILL, Coord., *9245 S.W. 158 Ln., #201, Miami, 33157.* Tel: 305-378-6306; Fax: 305-378-1660.

The Poverello Ctr., Inc.—Rev. WILLIAM COLLINS, O.F.M., Dir., *2292 Wilton Dr., Wilton Manors, 33305.* Tel: 954-561-3663; Fax: 954-566-7868.

Foundations—

Catholic Health and Rehabilitation Services Foundation—Rev. THOMAS G. WENSKI, Exec. Dir., *9401 Biscayne Blvd., Miami, 33138.* Tel: 305-754-2444; Fax: 305-754-6649.

Catholic Hospice Foundation, Inc.—14100 Palmetto Frontage Rd., Miami Lakes, 33016. Tel: 305-822-2380; Fax: 305-827-0221.

Catholic Commission for Social Advocacy—LEONA COOPER, Chm.; Rev. THOMAS G. WENSKI, Exec. Dir. PETER COATS, Assoc. Dir., *9401 Biscayne Blvd., Miami, 33138.* Tel: 305-754-2444; Fax: 305-754-6649.

Ministry of Catholic Health Services

Archdiocesan Director—Rev. THOMAS HONOLD.

Catholic Health Services, Inc.—Rev. THOMAS HONOLD, Dir. JOSEPH CATANIA, Exec. Dir. MICHAEL A. CASCIATO, Chief Oper. Officer; GLORIA HANSON, Dir., Health Care Svcs., *4740 N. State Rd. 7, Bldg. C, Ste. 100, Lauderdale Lakes, 33319.* Tel: 954-484-1515.

Catholic Housing for the Elderly and Handicapped, Inc.

Catholic Housing Management—Ms. TERE SPRING, Admin., *4740 N. State Rd. 7, Bldg. C, Ste. 106, Lauderdale Lakes, 33319.* Tel: 954-677-8122.

Archbishop Carroll Manor—MARK MERLUCCI, Mgr.,

3667 S. Miami Ave., Miami, 33133. Tel: 305-854-8953.
Archbishop Hurley Hall—LORETTA PALIS, Mgr., *632 N.W. 1st St., Hallandale, 33009.* Tel: 954-454-0855.
Marian Towers—Mr. FAUSTO FERNANDEZ, Mgr., *17505 N. Bay Rd., Miami Beach, 33160.* Tel: 305-932-1300.
Archbishop McCarthy Residence—ROSLYN WILLIAMS, Mgr., *13201 N.W. 28 Ave., Opa Locka, 33054.* Tel: 305-688-2700.
Palmer House—MARIO YANES, Mgr., *1225 S.W. 107 Ave., Miami, 33174.* Tel: 305-221-9566.
St. Andrew Towers—ILBA I. DONNELLY, Mgr., *2700 N.W. 99 Ave., Coral Springs, 33065.* Tel: 954-752-3960.
St. Dominic Gardens—MARIO YANES, Mgr., *5849 N.W. 7th St., Miami, 33126.* Tel: 305-262-0962.
St. Elizabeth Gardens—Mrs. JOHN CAMERON, Mgr., *801 N.E. 33rd St., Pompano Beach, 33064.* Tel: 954-941-4597.
St. Joseph Towers—DEBRA HAMELRATH, Mgr., *3475 N.W. 30th St., Lauderdale Lakes, 33311.* Tel: 954-485-5150.
St. Mary Towers—LORETA PALIS, Mgr., *7615 N.W. 2nd Ave., Miami, 33150.* Tel: 305-757-3190.
Stella Maris—ANNE H. SMITH, Mgr., *8638 Harding Ave., Miami Beach, 33141.* Tel: 305-865-6841.

Nursing and Retirement Centers—
BROWARD:
St. Joseph Residence, Inc.—GLORIA HANSEN, Admin., *3485 N.W. 30 St., Lauderdale Lakes, 33311.* Tel: 954-739-1483.
St. John's Rehabilitation Hospital and Nursing Center, Inc.—DIANE DUBE, Admin., *3075 N.W. 35 Ave., Lauderdale Lakes, 33311.* Tel: 954-739-6233.
Catholic Hospice of Broward, Inc.—4740 N. State Rd. 7, Bldg. C, Ste. 100, Lauderdale Lakes, 33319. Tel: 954-484-1515.
Catholic Home Health Services of Broward, Inc.—BEVERLY IVES, Admin., *3075 N.W. 35 Ave., Lauderdale Lakes, 33311.* Tel: 954-486-3660.
DADE:
St. Anne's Catholic Nursing Center and St. Anne's Residence, Inc.—CYNTHIA PALERMO, Admin. LAVERNE KOONTZ, A.C.L.F., Admin., *11855 Quail Roost Dr., Miami, 33177.* Tel: 305-252-4000.
Villa Maria Nursing and Rehabilitation Center, Inc.—JACK RUTENBERG, Admin., *1050 N.E. 125 St., N. Miami, 33161.* Tel: 305-891-8850.
Villa Maria Health Care Services, Inc.—GLORIA HANSEN, Admin., *1050 N.E. 125 St., N. Miami, 33161.* Tel: 305-899-0400.
Villa Maria Foundation, Inc.—MARY ANN POLIZZI, Dir., *1050 N.E. 125 St., N. Miami, 33161.* Tel: 305-891-8850, Ext. 4315.
Special Education—(Developmentally handicapped and mentally retarded) Marian Center Services. MARIA CONSUEGRA, Dir., *15701 N.W. 37 Ave., Opa Locka, 33054.* Tel: 305-625-8354; Fax: 305-625-3696.

Catholic Cemeteries—JOHN KISSELL, Admin., *11411 N.W. 25th St., Miami, 33172.* Tel: 305-592-0521.
Archdiocesan Cemeteries—Our Lady of Mercy Cemetery, 11411 N.W. 25th St., Miami, 33172. Tel: 305-592-0521., *Our Lady Queen of Heaven Cemetery, 1500 S. State Rd. 7, N. Lauderdale, 33068.* Tel: 954-972-1234.
Catholic Elderly Services, Inc.—4740 N. State Rd. 7, Bldg. C, Ste. 100, Lauderdale Lakes, 33319. Tel: 954-484-1515.

Ministry of Pastoral Services

Ministry of Pastoral Services—Most Rev. AGUSTIN A. ROMAN, Exec. Dir.
Campus Ministry—PATRICIA STOCKTON, Dir., *9401 Biscayne Blvd., Miami, 33138.* Tel: 305-757-6241, Ext. 193.
Barry University—Sr. CORINNE SANDERS, O.P., Dir.; Rev. EMILIANO ZAPATA, O.P., Assoc. Dir.; Sr. MARY CAROL HURLEY, O.P.; ELSIE MIRANDA; FRANK VEGA, *11300 N.E. 2nd Ave., Miami Shores, 33161.* Tel: 305-899-3650.
FIU-North Miami—Revs. KENNETH SCHWANGER, J.C.L., Chap. LUIS PEREZ, Chap. ROLANDO CASTILLO, Chap. PETER T. CAREY, *N.E. 151st St. & Biscane Blvd., N. Miami, 33181.* Tel: 305-940-5609.
FIU-University Park—Revs. FELIPE ESTEVEZ; CHRIS MARINO; CARMEN VILLAFANE; GUILLERMINA DAMAS, *St. Agatha Church, 111 S.W. 107th Ave., Miami, 33174.* Tel: 305-222-1506; 348-3900.
Miami Dade CC-South—Rev. MICHAEL KISH; ANGEL ANTONIO RODRIGUEZ, *7270 S.W. 120 St., Miami, 33156.* Tel: 305-238-7562.
Florida Memorial College—Rev. JOHN MADIGAN, O.M.I., Chap. VINCENT MCGREGOR, *15800 N.W. 42nd Ave., Miami, 33054.* Tel: 305-626-3714; 626-3719; Fax: 305-626-3769.
St. Thomas University—Rev. EDWARD BLACKWELL, JR., Dir. MICHAELA ECKER, *16400 N.W. 32nd Ave., Miami, 33054.* Tel: 305-628-6525.
University of Miami—TOM CORDARO, Dir. JOHN KELLY, Assoc. Dir., *St. Augustine Church, 1400 Miller Rd., Coral Gables, 33146.* Tel: 305-661-1648.
Miami Dade CC-North—Rev. JOHN V. KENNEDY, C.M., Chap. ANGEL ANTONIO RODRIGUEZ, *2000 N.W. 103rd St., Miami, 33147.*
Miami Dade CC-Downtown Wolfson Campus—Rev. THOMAS MADDEN, S.J.; ANGEL ANTONIO RODRIGUEZ, *Gesu Church, 118 N.E. 2 St., Miami, 33132.* Tel: 305-379-1424; 347-3000.
Broward CC-Central and NOVA University—SANDY BOUDEWYNS, *Pastoral Center, 9401 Biscayne Blvd., Miami, 33138.* Tel: 305-757-6241, Ext. 193 (Dade). Tel: 305-525-5157, Ext. 193 (Broward).
Catholic Daughters of America—Court 634, Vice-Regent: NORMA FARRALDO, *St. Mary Star of the Sea Church, 1010 Windsor Ln., Key West, 33040.* Tel: 305-294-1018. Local Chaplain: Rev. GERALD MCGRATH.
Evangelization—MARSHA WHELAN, Dir.; Ms. ROSA MARIA MONTENEGRO, Coord., Evangelization for Hispanics; Ms. MARIA HORTENSIA SAN PELAYO, Sec., *9401 Biscayne Blvd., Miami, 33138.* Tel: 305-757-6241, Ext. 188; 189; 227; Fax: 305-758-2027.
Family Life Ministry—CAROL A. FARRELL, Dir. GLORIA MASMAN, Coord., Divorced & Separated; ELAINE M. SYFERT, Coord., Hispanic Ministry; DAWNE FLERI, Coord., Ministry to Engaged & Married Couples, *9401 Biscayne Blvd., Miami, 33138.* Tel: 305-757-6241.
Lay Apostolic Movements and Associations—
Agrupacion Catolica Universitaria (ACU)—Rev. AMANDO LLORENTE, S.J., Spiritual Dir., *720 N.E. 27 St., Miami, 33137.* Tel: 305-573-1418.
Archdiocesan Council of Catholic Women—Very Rev. LAURENCE J. CONWAY, V.F., Dir., *17775 N. Bay Rd., Miami Beach, 33160.* Tel: 305-931-0600. JOAN WICHMAN, Pres. Spiritual Moderators: Rev. GERALD MORRIS, (Monroe Deanery); Vacant, (North Broward Deanery); Revs. FRANCIS MCCARTHY, (South Broward Deanery); MICHAEL GREER, (South Dade Deanery); Very Rev. ANDREW ANDERSON, (North East Dade Deanery).
Camino (Spanish)—Deacon JORGE GONZALEZ, Dir., *P.O. Box 524160, Miami, 33152-4170.* Tel: 305-226-4664.
Charismatic Renewal—Rev. Msgr. WILLIAM MCKEEVER, Archdiocesan Liaison; Rev. DANIEL DOYLE, S.M., Assoc. Archdiocesan Liaison Charismatic Services: *P.O. Box 816128, Hollywood, 33081.* Tel: 305-925-8464. *Spanish:* Assoc. Dirs.: Rev. JORDI RIVERO; Mr. ABELARDO MENDIZABAL, *Centro Carismatico Catolico—P.O. Box 557302, Miami, 33255-7302.* Tel: 305-592-6333.
Christian Family Movement—Rev. JOSEPH CARNEY, Dir., *4020 Curtiss Pkwy., Miami Springs, 33166.* Tel: 305-871-5780. *Spanish:* Rev. ANGEL VILLARONGA, O.F.M., Spiritual Dir., *Casa Cana, 480 E. 8 St., Hialeah, 33010.* Tel: 305-888-4819.
Cofradia Nuestra Senora de la Caridad (Spanish)—Most Rev. AGUSTIN A. ROMAN, V.G., Dir., *3609 S. Miami Ave., 33133.* Tel: 305-854-2404.
Comunidad de Vida Cristiana (CVX) Regina Mundi—Rev. VICTOR HERNANDEZ, S.J., Ecclesiastical Asst., *Belen Jesuit Prep. School, 500 S.W. 127 Ave., Miami, 33184.* Tel: 305-223-8600.
Cursillo—Rev. DAVID SMITH, Spiritual Dir., *8670 S.W. 27 Ln., Miami, 33155.* Tel: 305-291-6611 (Beeper).; Deacon ROBERT BINDER, Assoc. Dir. *Spanish:* Rev. IGNACIO BLASCO, T.C., Dir., *12525 S.W. 42 St., Miami, 33175.* Tel: 305-223-0633.
Encuentros Familiares (Spanish)—Rev. FLORENTINO AZCOITIA, S.J., Dir., *Casa Manresa, P.O. Box 651512, Miami, 33265.* Tel: 305-596-0001.
Encuentros Juveniles (Spanish)—Rev. MARCOS SOMARRIBA, Dir., *Youth Center, 3333 S. Miami Ave., Miami, 33133.* Tel: 305-856-3404.
Impacto (Spanish)—Deacon MANUEL PEREZ, *Youth Center, 3609 S. Miami Ave., Miami, 33133.* Tel: 305-854-2404.
Knights of Columbus (English and Spanish)—Rev. XAVIER MORRAS, Archdiocesan Chap., *2711 Indian Mound Trail, Coral Gables, 33134.* Tel: 305-446-9950.
Legion of Mary (English Speaking)—Rev. RICHARD SOULLIERE, Dir., *2700 N.E. 36 St., Lighthouse Point, 33064.* Tel: 954-943-9154. (Spanish Speaking); JUDITH PADRON. Tel: 305-821-3693.
Marian Movements & Devotions—Rev. RICHARD SOULLIERE, Coord., *2700 N.E. 36th St., Lighthouse Point, 33064.* Tel: 954-943-9154.
Ministry to Cultural Groups—Rev. THOMAS WENSKI, Dir.
St. Martin de Porres Assoc.—LEONA COOPER, Pres., *P.O. Box 330102, Miami, 33133.* Tel: 305-754-2444; 443-9466; Fax: 305-754-6649.
Brazilian Apostolate(Portuguese)—Rev. SERGIO DALL'AGNESE, Dir., *St. Paul the Apostle Church, 2700 N.E. 36 St., Lighthouse Point, 33064.* Tel: 954-943-9154; Fax: 954-943-9155.
Filipino Apostolate—Ms. ROSA MARIA MONTENEGRO, *Evangelization Office, 9401 Biscayne Blvd., Miami Shores, 33138.* Tel: 305-757-6241, Ext. 189.
French-Canadians—Rev. LEO DIONNE, O.M.I., Coord., *Christ the King Church, 16000 S.W. 112 Ave., Miami, 33157.* Tel: 305-238-2485.
Haitians—Rev. THOMAS WENSKI, Dir., *Notre Dame d'Haiti Mission, 110 N.E. 62 St., Miami, 33138.* Tel: 305-751-6289., *St. Joseph Haitian Catholic Mission, 1210 N.W. 6th Ave., Pompano Beach, 33060.* Tel: 305-941-3095. Divine Mercy Haitian Catholic Mission; Rev. ROLAND LAMY, *1105 N.W. 6th Ave., Ft. Lauderdale, 33311.* Tel: 954-764-8519.
Hispanic—Most Rev. AGUSTIN A. ROMAN, V.G., Dir.
Native Americans—Rev. THOMAS WENSKI, Dir.
Indians—Rev. JAMES PARAPPALLY, (India), Chap., *St. Gabriel Church, 731 N. Ocean St., Pompano Beach, 33062.* Tel: 954-943-3684.
Korean—Rev. JULIAN (JAEHY) NAM, *1051 W. Fairway Rd., Pembroke Pines, 33026.* Tel: 954-433-1824.
Polish - (Our Lady of Czestochowa)—Rev. JAN FIEDUREK, S.Ch., Dir., *123 N.W. 6 Ave., Hallandale, 33009.* Tel: 954-458-1914.
Vietnamese—Rev. ISIDORE BAKY, Coord., *St. Helen Church, 3033 N.W. 33 Ave., Ft. Lauderdale, 33311.* Tel: 954-731-7314.
Ministry to the Deaf and Disabled—Rev. JAMES VITUCCI, Pastoral Dir. JACK GREEN, Exec. Dir.; Sr. CONLETH BRANNAN, C.S.J., Asst. Dir. NERY RODRIGUEZ, Pastoral Worker; IAN ROBERTSON, D.R.E. & Advocate Program Dir., *Schott Memorial Center, 6591 S.W. 124 Ave., Fort Lauderdale, 33330.* Tel: 954-434-3306; 7447.
Ministry to Sea—(serving Seafarers); Rev. JOSE M. PAZ, Dir./Chap., Port of Miami; Deacon VIDAL CAMACHO, Dir., *Stella Maris Seamen's Center, 1275 S. America Way, Miami, 33132.* Tel: 305-371-6272. Rev. ARMANDO PEREZ, Chap., *Stella Maris Seamen's Center, Amman Bldg. No. 7, Port Everglades, 33316.* Tel: 954-527-0467.
Ministry to the Sick—Rev. CHARLES CLEMENTS, Health Care Coord.(South Dade Area).
Prison Ministry—FRANK VEGA, Dir.
Respect Life Office—Rev. JORDI RIVERO, Dir. JOAN CROWN, Assoc. Dir., *18340 N.W. 12 Ave., Miami, 33169.* Tel: 305-653-2921.
Respect Life Branch Offices-Emergency Pregnancy Services—
—N. Dade Central Office, 18340 N.W. 12 Ave., Miami, 33169. Tel: 305-653-2921.
—Coral Springs Office, 10141 W. Sample Rd., Ste. B, Coral Springs, 33065. Tel: 954-753-0770.
—Hialeah Office, 2024 E. 4th Ave., Hialeah, 33011. Tel: 305-883-2229.
—Hollywood Office (S. Broward), 6151 Washington St., Hollywood, 33023. Tel: 954-963-2229.
—Ft. Lauderdale Office, 2907 N. Andrews Ave., Wilton Manors, 33311. Tel: 954-565-8506.
—Coral Way Office, 2075 Coral Way, Miami, 33145. Tel: 305-856-5870.
Rural Life Ministry—Rev. PEDRO GARCIA, Dir.
Centro Catolico Tepeyac, Everglades Community Assoc.-Andrew Ctr.—19200 S.W. 380th St., Florida City, 33030.
Youth and Young Adult Ministry—Sr. ONDINA CORTES, R.M.I., Dir., *Pastoral Center, 9401 Biscayne Blvd., Miami Shores, 33138.* Tel: 305-757-6241.
Scouting—Rev. SERGIO CARRILLO, Archdiocesan Scout Chap.

Ministry of Temporalities

Executive Director—Rev. Msgr. WILLIAM J. HENNESSEY, V.G.
Office of Temporalities—Rev. Msgr. WILLIAM J. HENNESSEY, V.G., Archdiocesan Finance Admin.; Rev. Msgr. JOHN J. VAUGHAN, Assoc. Archdiocesan Finance Admin.
Management—Rev. Msgr. WILLIAM J. HENNESSEY, V.G., Archdiocesan Finance Admin.; Rev. Msgr. JOHN J. VAUGHAN, Assoc. Archdiocesan Finance Admin.
Business Office—JOSEPH CATANIA, Treas.
Data Processing—CARLOS FERNANDEZ.
Building Commission—Most Rev. JOHN C. FAVALORA; GEORGE KAPLAN, Chm.; Rev. Msgr. WILLIAM J. HENNESSEY, V.G.; Rev. Msgr. JOHN J. VAUGHAN; Revs. FREDERICK J. BRICE; GABRIEL O'REILLY; EDMOND WHYTE; XAVIER MORRAS; EMILIO MARTIN; Very Rev. GUSTAVO MIYARES; JAMES DETRICK.
Archdiocesan Fund-Raising & Assessments Committee—Rev. Msgr. WILLIAM J. HENNESSEY, V.G.; Rev. Msgr. JOHN J. VAUGHAN; Rev. Msgr. PATRICK MCDONNELL; Very Rev. SEAMUS DOYLE, V.F.; Very Rev. XAVIER MORRAS, V.F.; Very Rev. JAMES FETSCHER, V.F.; Revs. TIMOTHY HANON; JOSEPH FERRAIOLI, O.M.I.; EDMOND WHYTE; JOSE NICKSE; GEORGE GARCIA; DAVID RUSSELL; ARNALDO LOPEZ; WILLIAM CONROY; JOSEPH CATANIA.
Finance Council—Rev. Msgr. WILLIAM J. HENNESSEY,

V.G.; Rev. Msgr. NOEL FOGARTY; Rev. Msgr. JOHN J. VAUGHAN; Revs. FREDERICK J. BRICE; IGNACIO MORRAS; JAMES CONNAUGHTON; J. PATRICK FITZGERALD; FRANK MCDONOUGH; RAUL MASVIDAL; THOMAS PENNEKAMP; JOSEPH CATANIA.

Lay Personnel—TERRY SUNDY.

Health and Welfare—Very Rev. TOMAS M. MARIN.

Pension—Most Rev. JOHN C. FAVALORA, Chm.; Rev. Msgr. NOEL FOGARTY, Vice Chm.

Real Estate Board—Rev. Msgr. WILLIAM J. HENNESSEY, V.G., Dir.; Rev. Msgr. JOHN J. VAUGHAN; Revs. FREDERICK J. BRICE; ANTHONY MULDERRY; Mr. FRANK MCDONOUGH; HENRY BEZOLD.

Society for the Propagation of the Faith—Rev. FREDERICK J. BRICE.

Plant Operations—DAVID PYLE.

Ministry Of Worship And Spiritual Life

Executive Director—Rev. JUAN SOSA.

Worship & Spiritual Life Commission—Chms.: Rev. MICHAEL GREER; MYRNA GALLAGHER.

Celebration and Rite Committee—Rev. JUAN SOSA, Chm.

Spiritual Life Committee—BARBARA RIETBERG.

Sacred Art & Architecture—Rev. PAUL VUTURO.

Liturgical Music—MICHAEL DERRICK.

Committee on Popular Piety—Most Rev. AGUSTIN A. ROMAN, V.G.; Revs. JUAN SOSA, Chm.; Mr. ROGELIO ZELADA.

Ministry of Persons

Ministry of Persons—Vacant.

Vocations—Rev. PEDRO CORCES, Dir., *9401 Biscayne Blvd., Miami, 33138.* Tel: 305-757-6241, Ext. 273.

Archdiocesan Vocations Review Board—Very Rev. JOHN NOONAN, Rector, St. John Vianney College Seminary, Miami; Very Rev. GUSTAVO MIYARES, Chm.; Revs. FEDERICO CAPDEPON; NEIL DOHERTY; THOMAS ENGBERS; JAMES MURPHY; PEDRO CORCES.

Seminary—St. John Vianney College Seminary, Miami, Very Rev. JOHN NOONAN, Rector.

Office for Religious—Sr. MARY CHRISTINE ZIMORSKI, S.S.J.

Priestly Life and Ministry—Rev. ARTHUR DENNISON, Dir., *9401 Biscayne Blvd., Miami, 33138.* Tel: 305-757-6241, Ext. 225.

Permanent Diaconate—Most Rev. JOHN C. FAVALORA, Dir.; Rev. ALFRED CIOFFI, Coord.; Deacons JOHN AVERY, Asst. Coord. ANTONIO MACEO, Dir. Selection; CARL CARIERI, Dir. Formation; IAN TAYLOR, Dir. Deacon Rels.

Lay Ministry—Sr. ANN E. MCDERMOTT, O.S.F., Dir. ADELE GONZALEZ, D.Min. (Cand.), M.A., Asst. Dir.; Sr. CLAUDIA STEGER, O.S.F., Prog. Coord. MARIA CANTON, Hispanic Ministry Outreach; MARY TERESA MORGAN, M.A., Educator; MARGARITA ROMAGOSA, M.A., Admin. Asst. MAYRA ROSSELL; MARILYN CANO, Staff.

Continuing Education for the Clergy—Rev. ARTHUR DENNISON, Dir., *9401 Biscayne Blvd., Miami, 33138.* Tel: 305-757-6241, Ext. 225.

Priests' Sabbaticals—Rev. ARTHUR DENNISON, Chm.

Retired Priests' Committee—Rev. SEAMUS DOYLE, Chm.; Rev. Msgr. GERARD T. LACERRA; Rev. Msgr. JOHN J. VAUGHAN; Rev. Msgr. BRYAN WALSH; Revs. MICHAEL HOYER; MARTIN CASSIDY; SEAMUS DOYLE; VINCENT KELLY; Very Rev. ANDREW ANDERSON; PATRICK FITZGERALD, (Legal).

Ministry to Professional Groups—

Catholic Educators' Guild—Rev. Msgr. WILLIAM MCKEEVER, Chap.

Catholic Funeral Directors' Guild—Very Rev. ANDREW ANDERSON, Chap.

Catholic Lawyers' Guild—Very Rev. ANDREW ANDERSON, Chap.

Catholic Physicians' and Dentists' Guild—Very Rev. TOMAS M. MARIN, Chap., DADE; Rev. WILLIAM MYLCHREEST, Chap., BROWARD.

Catholic Law Enforcement Ministry—Police Chaplains: Rev. PAUL EDWARDS, Coord. (Metro-Dade Police); Rev. Msgr. JOHN J. VAUGHAN, (Miami Beach Police); Rev. MICHAEL KISH, (City of Miami Police); Vacant, (Florida Highway Patrol, Troop K); Vacant, (FBI, Broward Co./City of Coral Springs).

Catholic Fire Service Ministry—Fire Chaplains: Revs. THOMAS ENGBERS, Coord. (City of Miami; Metro Dade); MICHAEL LYNCH, (City of Coral Gables/ Margate).

Special Apostolates

Amor En Accion—(Love in Action)—P.O. Box 141523, Coral Gables, 33114. ALICIA MARRILL. Tel: 305-266-9533. LOURDES ROVIRA. Tel: 305-448-1359.

Archbishop Hurley Scholarship Fund—Rev. VINCENT T. KELLY, Vicar, Christian Formation, *9401 Biscayne Blvd., Miami, 33138.* Tel: 305-757-6241.

Campaign for Human Development—Rev. THOMAS G. WENSKI, Acting Archdiocesan Dir., *9401 Biscayne Blvd., Miami Shores, 33138.* Tel: 305-754-2444.

Catholic Alumni Club of South Florida—Vacant.

Catholic Relief Services—Rev. THOMAS G. WENSKI, Archdiocesan Dir.

Downtown Senior Citizens' Community Center at Gesu Church—Sr. MAURA PHILLIPS, O.P., *118 N.E. 2nd St., Miami, 33132.* Tel: 305-374-6099.

Food for the Poor, Inc.—FERDINAND G. MAHFOOD, *550 S.W. 12 Ave., Deerfield Beach, 33442.* Tel: 305-427-2222 (Broward).

Holy Childhood Association—Rev. FREDERICK BRICE, Dir.

Pilgrimages—Rev. RICHARD SOULLIERE, Archdiocesan Dir., Natl. Shrine of the Immaculate Conception, Washington, DC.

Priests' Purgatorial Society—Rev. FREDERICK BRICE.

Serra Club—Mrs. IDALIA LASTRA, Pres., *2498 S.W. 3rd. Ave., Miami, 33129.* Tel: 305-856-7180. Chaplains—Dade County: Vacant; N. Broward Co.: Rev. Msgr. FRANCIS FAZZALARO; Rev. JOSEPH KOTTAYIL, Assoc.

The St. Vincent De Paul Society of Miami, Inc.—Revs. WILLIAM ELBERT, Dade Co. Chap.; FREDERICK BRICE, Broward County Chap.

CLERGY, PARISHES, MISSIONS AND PAROCHIAL SCHOOLS

CITY OF MIAMI
(Dade County)

1—ST. MARY'S CATHEDRAL (1930), Very Rev. Andrew Anderson, Rector. Assoc. Rectors: Revs. Jean Pierre; Carlos Vega. In res., Rev. Innocent Ajuonu (Nigeria).
Res., 7525 N.W. 2nd Ave., 33150. Tel: 305-759-4531; 4532; Fax: 305-757-7456.
School—Tel: 305-757-1993. Sr. Jane Stoecker, S.S.J., Prin.
Sisters of St. Joseph of St. Augustine 4; Lay Teachers 13; Students 317.
Catechesis/Religious Programs—Students 300.

2—CHRIST THE KING (1961), Revs. Leo Dionne, O.M.I.; Raymond Crowe, O.M.I. In res., Revs. Bernard Clancy, O.M.I.; Paul Frank, O.M.I.; Edwin Hayes, O.M.I.
Res., 16000 S.W. 112th Ave., 33157. Tel: 305-238-2485; Fax: 305-254-0330.
Catechesis/Religious Programs—Tel: 305-235-0293.
Students 207.

3—CORPUS CHRISTI (1941), Revs. Jose L. Menendez; Rolando J. Castillo. In res., Rev. Sergio Carrillo.
Res., 3220 N.W. 7th Ave., 33127. Tel: 305-635-1331; Fax: 305-635-2031.
School—Tel: 305-635-8571. Sr. Gina Geraci, S.T.J., Prin.
Sisters 2; Lay Teachers 11; Students 305.
Catechesis/Religious Programs—Sr. Carmen Alvarez, M.R.I. Tel: 305-633-5824.
Students 704.
Missions—Miami, San Francisco y Santa Clara, 2699 Biscayne Blvd., 33132.; Miami, San Juan Bautista, 3100 N.W. 2nd Ave., 33127.; Miami, Nuestra Senora de Altagracia, 1779 N.W. 28th St., 33142.; Miami, La Milagrosa, 1860 N.W. 18th Ter., 33125.

4—EPIPHANY (1951), Rev. Msgr. Jude O'Doherty; Rev. Francisco Hernandez.
Res., 8235 S.W. 57th Ave., 33143. Tel: 305-667-4911; Fax: 305-667-8067.
School—Tel: 305-667-5251. Sr. Mary Henrich, I.H.M., Prin.
Sisters Servants of the Immaculate Heart of Mary 3; Lay Teachers 55; Students 975.
Catechesis/Religious Programs—Tel: 305-665-0037.
Students 288.

5—GESU (1896), Revs. Thomas J. Madden, S.J.; Sergio Figueredo, S.J.; Fernando Lopez, S.J.; Thomas A. Griffin, S.J.; Michael J. Kossak, S.J.; William Kidwell, S.J.; Salvator J. San Marco, S.J.
Res., 118 N.E. 2nd St., 33132. Tel: 305-379-1424; Fax: 305-372-9544.

6—GOOD SHEPHERD (1977), Revs. Michael Greer; Miguel Gomez; Damian Flanagan.
Res., 6804 S.W. 139th Pl., 33183. Tel: 305-386-1580.
Church—14187 S.W. 72nd St., 33183. Tel: 305-385-4320; Fax: 305-386-2407.
Catechesis/Religious Programs—Tel: 305-388-9877. D.R.E.: Deacon Jorge Prieto; Maria Changsut.
Students 1,139.

7—HOLY REDEEMER (1951), Rev. Richard Sudlik, O.M.I.
Church—1301 N.W. 71st St., 33147. Tel: 305-691-1701; Fax: 305-691-7074.
Catechesis/Religious Programs—Students 55.

8—MOTHER OF CHRIST (1983), Revs. Raul Angulo; Anibal Morales.
Rectory: 2390 S.W. 139th Pl., 33175. Tel: 305-551-7046 (Office).
Church—14141 S.W. 26th St., 33175. Tel: 305-559-6111; Fax: 305-551-7047.
Catechesis/Religious Programs—Tel: 305-559-0163.
Students 700.

9—MOTHER OF OUR REDEEMER (1988), Rev. Fernando Compaired (Spain). In res., Rev. Federico Capdepon.
Res., 18928 N.W. 80th Ct., 33015. Tel: 305-558-4404; Fax: 305-558-4413.
Church—18295 N.W. 68th Ave., 33015.
Catechesis/Religious Programs—Students 355.

10—NOTRE DAME D'HAITI (1981), Revs. Thomas Wenski; Mary Kidney St. Jean.
Res., 110 N.E. 62nd St., 33138. Tel: 305-751-6289; Fax: 305-756-6470.
Catechesis/Religious Programs—Tel: 305-758-5560.
Students 1,050.
Missions—Fort Lauderdale, Broward Co., Divine Mercy, 1105 N.W. 6th Ave., Fort Lauderdale, 33311. Tel: 954-764-8519; Pompano Beach, Broward Co., St. Joseph, 1210 N.W. 6th Ave., Fort Lauderdale, 33302. Tel: 954-941-3095; Fax: 954-941-3115.

11—OUR LADY OF DIVINE PROVIDENCE (1973), Revs. Luis Rivera; Reynaldo Terrero (Cuba).
Church and Mailing Address—10205 W. Flagler St., 33172. Tel: 305-551-8113; 8114; Fax: 305-220-3164.
Res., 10420 S.W. 4th St., 33174. Tel: 305-226-7589.
Catechesis/Religious Programs—Tel: 305-225-0009.
Students 294.

12—OUR LADY OF THE HOLY ROSARY (1959), Revs. Sean Hyland; Michael Tabit (COL); Eduardo Jimenez.
Res., 9500 S.W. 184th St., 33157. Tel: 305-235-5135; Fax: 305-254-9045.
School—Tel: 305-235-5442. Carol Ann Ziecina, Prin.; Lyn Bimonte, Co-Prin.
Lay Teachers 26; Students 550.
Catechesis/Religious Programs—Students 270.

13—OUR LADY OF LOURDES (1985), Revs. Anthony Massi; Juan Luis Sanchez.
Res., 14202 S.W. 111 Ln., 33186. Tel: 305-386-4121; Fax: 305-386-6881.
Church—11291 S.W. 142 Ave., 33186.
Catechesis/Religious Programs—Tel: 305-386-4894.
Students 1,201.

14—PRINCE OF PEACE (1987), Rev. Francisco Diaz.
Res., 275 N.W. 130 Ave., 33182. Tel: 305-559-3171; Fax: 305-559-3172.
Catechesis/Religious Programs—Students 280.

15—ST. AGATHA (1971), Revs. Felipe Estevez; Chris Marino; Samuel Muodiaju, C.S.Sp. In res., Rev. Kris Bartos.
Res., 1111 S.W. 107th Ave., 33174. Tel: 305-222-1500; Fax: 305-222-1505.
School—Tel: 305-222-1510; Fax: 305-222-1517. Dr. Carlota Morales, Prin.
Sisters 1; Lay Teachers 42; Students 764.
Catechesis/Religious Programs—Tel: 305-222-1508. Mr. Efrain E. Sora, D.R.E.
Students 1,100.

16—ST. BRENDAN (1954), Revs. Jose P. Nickse; Raul Soutuyo; Francisco Calderon; Charles Peterman.
Res., 8725 S.W. 32 St., 33165. Tel: 305-221-0881; Fax: 305-226-6249.
School—Tel: 305-221-2722. Mrs. Emma A. Ventura.
Lay Teachers 33; Students 653.
Catechesis/Religious Programs—Tel: 305-226-2628; 221-2861. D.R.E.: Sr. Bertha Penabad; Rosmery Ortega.
Students 860.

17—ST. CATHERINE OF SIENA (1968), Revs. Juan J. Sosa; Francis Akwue, C.S.Sp.; Eliades Petit (Cuba).
In res., Rev. Daniel Kent.
Res., 9200 S.W. 107 Ave., 33176. Tel: 305-274-6333; Fax: 305-274-6337.
Catechesis/Religious Programs—Tel: 305-270-0830. Maria Mezquita, D.R.E.
Students 522.

18—ST. DOMINIC (1962), Revs. Jorge Presmanes, O.P.; Restituto Perez, O.P.; Christopher T. Eggleton, O.P. In res., Revs. Mark Wedig, O.P.; George Boudreau, O.P.; Henry Groover, O.P.; Emiliano Zapata, O.P.; Jose L. Vazquez.
Res., 5909 N.W. 7th St., 33126. Tel: 305-264-0181; Fax: 305-262-4685.
Catechesis/Religious Programs—Tel: 305-264-3372.
Students 496.

19—St. Francis Xavier (1927), Rev. John Raymond Lau, O.M.I.
Mailing Address: P.O. Box 01-1901, 33101-1901.
Res., 1698 N.W. 4th Ave., 33136. Tel: 305-576-2957; Fax: 305-576-3120.
School—Tel: 305-573-8532.
Lay Teachers 10; Students 152.
Catechesis/Religious Programs—Students 60.

20—St. James (1952), Revs. Gerard Darbouze; Ruy Montealegre.
Res., 540 N.W. 132nd St., 33168. Tel: 305-681-7428; Fax: 305-685-0631.
School—Tel: 305-681-3822.
Religious 1; Lay Teachers 14; Students 205.
Catechesis/Religious Programs—Tel: 305-681-2676.
Students 251.

21—St. Joachim (1972), Rev. Jesus Saldana.
Res., 11711 S.W. 193rd St., 33177. Tel: 305-233-1278; Fax: 305-233-2573.
Church—19150 S.W. 117th Ave., 33177.
Catechesis/Religious Programs—Students 465.

22—St. John Bosco (1962), Rev. Msgr. Emilio Vallina; Rev. Francisco Lemus, S.J. In res., Rev. Msgr. Angel Gaztelu (Cuba); Rev. Msgr. William F. McKeever.
Mailing Address: P.O. Box 993, 33125.
Res., 1301 W. Flagler St., 33135. Tel: 305-649-5464; 5465; Fax: 305-541-0988.
Catechesis/Religious Programs—Tel: 305-649-5466. Angela Esparraguera, D.R.E.
Students 667.

23—St. John Neumann (1982), Revs. David Russell; James McCreanor.
Res., 12125 S.W. 107th Ave., 33176. Tel: 305-255-6642; Fax: 305-233-3742.
School—Tel: 305-255-7315; 7316; Fax: 305-255-7316. Mrs. Maria M. Fernandez, Prin.
Lay Teachers 154; Students 335.
Catechesis/Religious Programs—Tel: 305-253-3081. Myrna E. Gallagher, D.R.E.
Students 1,315.

24—St. Kevin (1963), Revs. Alfred Cioffi; Jose Garcia (Cuba); Jose D. Lopez; Ignacio Blasco.
Res., 12525 S.W. 42 St., 33175. Tel: 305-223-0633; Fax: 305-554-9950.
School—4001 S.W. 127 Ave., 33175. Tel: 305-223-4015; Fax: 305-220-9048. Mrs. America Novas, Prin.; Mr. Kevin McGee, Vice Prin.
Lay Teachers 42; Students 661.
Catechesis/Religious Programs—Tel: 305-223-2469. Mrs. Maggie Enjamio, D.R.E.
Students 1001.

25—St. Kieran (1967), Revs. James B. Curran, S.D.B.; Donald Zarkoski, S.D.B.; Richard Purnam, S.D.B. In res., Revs. Vincent Villar, S.D.B.; Innocent Clementi, S.D.B.
Res., 3605 S. Miami Ave., 33133. Tel: 305-854-1521; Fax: 305-854-5986.
Mission—Miami, La Purisima. 901 SW 3rd Ave.,#6.

26—St. Louis (1963), Revs. James F. Fetscher; Michael A. Kish; Wallace A. McGowan; Jeffrey McCormick.
Res., 7270 S.W. 120 St., 33156. Tel: 305-238-7562; Fax: 305-238-6844.
Catechesis/Religious Programs—Tel: 305-238-7461. Peggy Santella, D.R.E.
Students 1,274.

27—St. Michael the Archangel (1947), Revs. Jose M. Paz; Eduardo Pastor; Armando Alonso. In res., Rev. Jordi Rivero.
Res., 2987 W. Flagler St., 33135. Tel: 305-649-1811; Fax: 305-642-6815.
School—300 N.W. 28 Ave., 33125. Tel: 305-642-6732. Sr. Florinda Bermudez, R.A., Prin.
Sisters 6; Lay Teachers 30; Students 600.
Catechesis/Religious Programs—Tel: 305-643-4661. George Briz, D.R.E.
Students 656.

28—SS. Peter and Paul (1938), Revs. Juan M. Lopez; Jose Luis Reyes. In res., Rev. Michael Keener.
Res., 900 S.W. 26th Rd., 33129. Tel: 305-858-2621; Fax: 305-858-8073.
School—Tel: 305-858-3722.
Sisters of St. Joseph of St. Augustine 3; Lay Teachers 33; Students 650.
Catechesis/Religious Programs—Students 360.

29—St. Raymond (1969), Revs. Armando Balado; Sergio Cabrera.
Res., 3475 S.W. 17 St., 33145. Tel: 305-446-2427; Fax: 305-445-0472.
Catechesis/Religious Programs—Tel: 305-446-5108.
Students 261.

30—St. Richard (1969), Revs. Ronald Pusak; Jorge A. Sardinas.
Res., 7500 S.W. 152 St., 33157. Tel: 305-233-8711; Fax: 305-254-2756.
Catechesis/Religious Programs—Tel: 305-233-8755.
Students 619.

31—St. Robert Bellarmine (1968), Rev. Omar A. Huesca.
Res., 3405 N.W. 27th Ave., 33142. Tel: 305-633-6009; Fax: 305-638-9480.
Catechesis/Religious Programs—Sr. Flor Maria Matamoros, O.P., D.R.E.
Students 335.

32—St. Thomas the Apostle (1959), Revs. Daniel I. Kubala; Fernando Heria.
Res., 7310 S.W. 62 St., 33143. Tel: 305-665-5600; Fax: 305-662-1450.
School—Tel: 305-661-8591; Fax: 305-661-7468. Sr. Madeleine Kreps, O.C.D., Prin.
Lay Teachers 30; Students 510.
Catechesis/Religious Programs—Students 260.

33—St. Timothy (1960), Rev. Msgr. Gerard T. LaCerra; Revs. Curtis Kiddy; Oscar Mendez, S.J.; Jesus Arias.
Office: 5300 S.W. 102 Ave., 33165. Tel: 305-274-8224; Fax: 305-598-1159.
School—Tel: 305-274-8229; Fax: 305-596-2952. Mrs. Jo-Ann Leskanic, Prin.
Sisters of St. Dominic of Newburgh 1; Claretian Sisters of Florida 1; Lay Teachers 34; Students 666.
Catechesis/Religious Programs—Tel: 305-274-8225. Sr. Mary Carolyn Meehan, O.P., D.R.E.
Students 1,038.

34—St. Vincent De Paul (1962), Revs. John V. Kennedy, C.M.; J. Terence Mooney, C.M.; Jose C. Sanchez, C.M.
Res., 2000 N.W. 103rd St., 33147. Tel: 305-691-0771; Fax: 305-691-3352.
Catechesis/Religious Programs—Students 220.

35—Visitation (1956), Rev. Joseph Angelini.
Res., 19100 N. Miami Ave., 33169. Tel: 305-652-3624; Fax: 305-652-5207.
Catechesis/Religious Programs—100 N.E. 191 St., 33169. Tel: 305-651-7044.
Students 190.

METROPOLITAN DADE COUNTY

Coconut Grove, St. Hugh (1959), Revs. George Garcia; Joaquin Rodriguez.
Res., 3460 Royal Rd., 33133. Tel: 305-444-8363; Fax: 305-444-4312.
School—Tel: 305-448-5602. Sr. Kathleen Donnelly, O.P., Prin.
Sisters 3; Lay Teachers 21; Students 329.
Catechesis/Religious Programs—Students 95.

Coral Gables, Little Flower (1926), Revs. Xavier Morras; Hernando Villegas; Anthony O'Brien; Arnaldo Bazan. In res., Rev. Sean O'Sullivan.
Office: 2711 Indian Mound Tr., 33134. Tel: 305-446-9950; Fax: 305-446-7624.
Res., 1270 Anastasia Ave., 33134. Tel: 305-446-9950.
School—2701 Indian Mound Tr., 33134. Tel: 305-446-1738; Fax: 305-446-2877.
Sisters 4; Lay Teachers 44; Students 946.
Catechesis/Religious Programs—Tel: 305-446-5540.
Students 401.

St. Augustine (1969), Revs. Terence Hogan; Pedro Corces.
Res., 1400 Miller Rd., 33146. Tel: 305-661-1648; Fax: 305-661-6392.
Catechesis/Religious Programs—Students 302.

Hialeah

1—Immaculate Conception (1954), Revs. Gustavo Miyares, V.F.; Jorge Noda (Cuba); Alberto Lahens; Enrique Boned; Ernest Biriruka.
Res., 4497 W. First Ave., 33012. Tel: 305-822-2011; Fax: 305-821-3481.
School—Tel: 305-822-6461. Sr. Theresita O'Sullivan, R.S.M., Prin.
Sisters of Mercy (Enniskillen, North Ireland) 1; Lay Teachers 46; Students 992.
Catechesis/Religious Programs—Tel: 305-823-9563. Nubia Stanley, D.R.E.
Students 814.

2—San Lazaro (1982), Revs. Pedro Luis Perez; Carlos Perez (Cuba). In res., Rev. Kenneth Schwanger.
Res., 4400 W. 18th Ave., 33012. Tel: 305-556-1717; Fax: 305-556-8918.
Catechesis/Religious Programs—Tel: 305-558-4078. Sr. Gloria Plasencia, D.R.E.
Students 800.

3—St. Benedict (1973), Revs. Jose L. Paniagua (Spain); John M. Paszko; Jose Bardino (Cuba).
Res., 650 W. 80th St., 33014. Tel: 305-558-2150; 556-3278; Fax: 305-558-3705.
Church—701 W. 77th St., 33014.
Catechesis/Religious Programs—Tel: 305-557-2511. Maria de la Fe, D.R.E.
Students 1,127.

4—St. Cecilia (1971), Revs. Emiliano Ordax; Isidro Perez.
Res., 1040 W. 29th St., P.O. Box 2931, 33012. Tel: 305-885-4614; 4615; Fax: 305-885-2327.
Catechesis/Religious Programs—Tel: 305-885-5504.
Students 323.

5—St. John the Apostle (1945), Revs. Emilio Martin; Brendan Shannon. In res., Revs. George Cardona, (Retired); Ignacio Morras, (Retired); Luis Casabon.
Res., 475 E. 4th St., 33010. Tel: 305-888-9769; Fax: 305-888-9341.
School—Tel: 305-888-6819; Fax: 305-887-1256. Ms. Elizabeth Furmanick, Prin.
Lay Teachers 27; Students 620.
Catechesis/Religious Programs—Students 602.

Hialeah Gardens, Santa Barbara (1987), Revs. Rafael Pedroso; Jorge Perales.
Res., 11960 N.W. 87 Ct., 33016. Tel: 305-556-4442; Fax: 305-558-7256.
Catechesis/Religious Programs—Students 473.

Homestead, Sacred Heart (1929), Revs. Jose Espino; Ronald Noguera.
Mailing Address: P.O. Box 1248, 33090.
Res., 106 S.E. 2 Rd., 33030. Tel: 305-247-4405; Fax: 305-245-3002.
Church—106 S.E. 1 Dr., 33030.
School—Tel: 305-245-2678. James Stiber, Prin.
Lay Teachers 10; Students 212.
Catechesis/Religious Programs—Tel: 305-247-0760.
Students 377.

Key Biscayne, St. Agnes (1954), Revs. Jose L. Hernando; Enrique Delgado.
Res., 100 Harbor Dr., 33149. Tel: 305-361-2351; 361-2451; Fax: 305-361-8514.
Catechesis/Religious Programs—Students 279.

Leisure City, St. Martin de Porres Church (1990), Rev. Rolando Garcia.
Res., 28514 S.W. 147 Pl., 33033. Tel: 305-248-5355; Fax: 305-245-3047.
Church—14881 S.W. 288 St., 33033.

Miami Beach

1—St. Francis de Sales (1964), Revs. Alvaro Guichard; Manuel Martin (Venezuela); Francis J. Dunleavy.
Res., 621 Alton Rd., 33139. Tel: 305-672-0093; Fax: 305-673-8559.
Catechesis/Religious Programs—Students 150.

2—St. Joseph (1942), Revs. Noel I. Bennett; Oscar Sarmiento.
Res., 8670 Byron Ave., 33141. Tel: 305-866-6567; Fax: 305-864-1069.
School—Tel: 305-866-1471; Fax: 305-866-3175. Mr. Richard S. Lynn, Prin.
Lay Teachers 17; Students 300.
Catechesis/Religious Programs—Students 350.

3—St. Mary Magdalen (1955), Rev. Laurence J. Conway. In res., Rev. Manuel Ortega.
Res., 17775 N. Bay Rd., 33160. Tel: 305-931-0600; Fax: 305-931-0601.

4—St. Patrick (1926), Rev. Msgr. John J. Vaughan; Rev. Julio Solano. In res., Rev. George Puthusseril.
Office: 3716 Garden Ave., 33140.
Res., 3700 Meridian Ave., 33140. Tel: 305-531-1124; 532-5996; Fax: 305-538-3203.
School—Tel: 503-534-4616. Mrs. Josephine Kenna, Prin.
Lay Teachers 17; Students 251.
Catechesis/Religious Programs—Students 251.

Miami Lakes, Our Lady of the Lakes (1967), Revs. James Murphy; T. Mannix Stack; Francisco Martin.
Res., 15801 N.W. 67 Ave., 33014. Tel: 305-558-2202; Fax: 305-558-2631.
School—6600 Miami Lakeway N., 33014. Tel: 305-362-5315. Virgil Rogers, Prin.
Lay Teachers 32; Students 596.
Catechesis/Religious Programs—Mary T. Tate, D.R.E.
Students 750.

Miami Shores, St. Martha (1970), Rev. Thomas J. Engbers. In res., Rev. Carl T. Morrison.
Res., 9301 Biscayne Blvd., 33138. Tel: 305-751-0005; Fax: 305-754-6930.
Catechesis/Religious Programs—Tel: 305-751-8759.
Students 106.

St. Rose of Lima (1946), Very Rev. Seamus Doyle; Rev. Pedro Lleo. In res., Revs. Ernesto Molano; Raymond E. Brown, S.S.
Res., 415 N.E. 105 St., 33138. Tel: 305-758-0539; Fax: 305-751-8398.
School—Tel: 305-751-4257. Sr. Rita Murphy, I.H.M., Prin.
Sisters 6; Lay Teachers 40; Students 715.

Miami Springs, Blessed Trinity (1952), Revs. Joseph T. Carney; Anthony Mercieca (Malta); Joaquin Paret (Cuba).
Res., 4020 Curtiss Pkwy., 33166. Tel: 305-871-5780; Fax: 305-871-5781.
School—Tel: 305-871-5766. Mr. Pio Tei, Prin.
Lay Teachers 19; Students 260.

Catechesis/Religious Programs—Students 200.
Naranja, St. Ann Mission (1960), Rev. Pedro Garcia.
Res., 13875 S.W. 264 St., P.O. Box 322205, 33032-1505. Tel: 305-258-3968; 258-9682; Fax: 305-258-3591.
Catechesis/Religious Programs—Students 410.
North Miami, Holy Family (1950), Revs. Bernard G. Kirlin; Ferry Brutus; Luis A. Perez. In res., Rev. Desmond Agbaka, C.S.Sp.
Res., 14500 N.E. 11 Ave., 33161. Tel: 305-947-5043; 947-1471; Fax: 305-949-5591.
School—Tel: 305-947-6535; Fax: 305-949-5591. Mrs. Kristen Hughes, Prin.
Sisters 1; Lay Teachers 19; Students 315.
Catechesis/Religious Programs—Students 447.
North Miami Beach, St. Lawrence (1956), Revs. Roger Holoubek; Sergio Garcia-Miro.
Res., 2200 N.E. 191 St., 33180. Tel: 305-932-3560; Fax: 305-936-8050.
School—Tel: 305-932-4192. Ms. Virginia Hutton, Prin.
Lay Teachers 14; Students 232.
Catechesis/Religious Programs—Tel: 305-931-6650.
Students 180.
Opa Locka, Our Lady of Perpetual Help Church (1954), Rev. Oscar Castaneda. In res., Rev. Gregory Njoku, C.S.Sp.
Church & Res.: 13401 N.W. 28 Ave., 33054. Tel: 305-688-9663;688-9664; Fax: 305-685-8031.
Catechesis/Religious Programs—Tel: 305-685-5354.
Students 210.
St. Monica (1959), Revs. Alejandro Roque; Leo LeBlanc, O.M.I.; Norman Parent, O.M.I.
Res., 3490 N.W. 191 St., 33056. Tel: 305-621-9846; Fax: 305-621-5608.
School—Tel: 305-621-2356.
Sisters 2; Lay Teachers 11; Students 163.
Catechesis/Religious Programs—Tel: 305-624-5132.
Students 243.
St. Philip (1953), Rev. John Madigan, O.M.I.
Res., 15700 N.W. 20 Ave. Rd., 33054. Tel: 305-624-6641.
Catechesis/Religious Programs—Students 84.

OUTSIDE METROPOLITAN DADE COUNTY

Big Pine Key, Monroe Co., St. Peter (1962), Rev. Thomas Mullane.
Res., U.S. 1, P.O. Box 430657, 33043. Tel: 305-872-2537; Fax: 305-872-0122.
Coconut Creek, Broward Co., St. Luke (1985), Rev. Stephen Hilley.
Res., 2370 Hammock Blvd., 33063. Tel: 954-977-0427; Fax: 954-978-1902.
Catechesis/Religious Programs—Tel: 954-974-1863.
Students 230.
Coral Springs, Broward Co., St. Andrew (1969), Revs. Arthur Dennison; Karunei Joseph; Gabriel Vigues; John Peloso.
Res., 9950 N.W. 29 St., 33065. Tel: 954-752-3950; Fax: 954-752-3986.
School—Tel: 954-753-1280; Fax: 954-753-1933. Mrs. Mary Louise Balog, Prin.
Lay Teachers 24; Students 426.
Catechesis/Religious Programs—Tel: 954-752-3988. D.R.E.: Deborah Andra; Mary Serra.
Students 996.
St. Elizabeth Ann Seton (1985), Rev. Edward M. Kelly.
Res., 1401 Coral Ridge Dr., 33071. Tel: 954-753-3330; Fax: 954-753-8442.
Catechesis/Religious Programs—Tel: 305-345-7071.
Students 1,550.
Dania, Broward Co., Church of the Resurrection (1958), Revs. Michael J. Hughes, O.S.A.; James G. Glennon, O.S.A.
Res., 441 N.E. Second St., 33004. Tel: 954-923-2806; Fax: 954-923-1018.
Davie, Broward Co., St. David (1974), Revs. Gabriel O'Reilly; Jan Malicki; Rev. Msgr. Michael Conway (PAT).
Res., 3900 S. University Dr., 33328. Tel: 954-475-8046; Fax: 954-370-0819.
School—Tel: 954-472-7086; Fax: 954-452-8243. Mrs. Mariann Kiar, Prin.
Lay Teachers 45; Students 710.
Catechesis/Religious Programs—Tel: 954-475-1521. Pam McMillan, D.R.E.
Students 800.
Deerfield Beach, Broward Co., Our Lady of Mercy (1974), Rev. Michael Sullivan.
Parish Center and Office: 5201 N. Military Trail, Pompano Beach, 33064. Tel: 954-421-3246; Fax: 954-421-1973.
St. Ambrose (1962), Revs. John Bryan Dalton; James Connaughton, Pastor Emeritus; Kenneth Whittaker; John L. McCullen (TOL).
Res., 353 S.E. 12 Ave., P.O. Box 999, 33441. Tel: 954-427-2225; Fax: 954-421-1638.
School—Tel: 954-427-2226. Ms. Anita Gentile, Prin.
Lay Teachers 16; Students 400.
Catechesis/Religious Programs—Students 185.
Fort Lauderdale, Broward Co.,
1—Blessed Sacrament, (1961), Rev. John P. McLaughlin.
Res., 1701 E. Oakland Park Blvd., 33334. Tel: 954-564-1010; Fax: 954-566-0301.
2—Our Lady Queen of Martyrs, (1956), Revs. Michael Hoyer; Armando Perez; Roman J. Schaefer (NU); Rev. Dr. William Muniz.
Res., 2731 S.W. 11 Ct., 33312. Tel: 954-583-8725; Fax: 954-583-9315.
School—Tel: 305-583-8112. Mrs. Althea Mossop, Prin.
Lay Teachers 21; Students 340.
Catechesis/Religious Programs—Students 225.
3—St. Anthony, (1923), Revs. Timothy G. Hannon; Patrick O'Shea.
Res., 901 N.E. 2nd St., 33301. Tel: 954-463-4614; Fax: 954-527-5411.
School—820 S.E. Third St., 33301. Tel: 954-467-7747. Mrs. Elaine L. Patterson, Prin.
Lay Teachers 23; Students 333.
Catechesis/Religious Programs—Tel: 954-467-7749.
Students 185.
4—St. Bonaventure, (1985), Rev. Edmond Prendergast.
Res., 1301 S.W. 136th Ave., Davie, 33325. Tel: 954-424-9504; 9505; Fax: 954-424-9505.
Catechesis/Religious Programs—Tel: 954-476-5204. Amy Mellinger, D.R.E.
Students 1,778.
5—St. Clement, (1954), Revs. Peter Lambert; Albert R. Cutie; Henry Mullin, C.S.Sp. In res., Rev. Dennis Rausch, S.V.D.
Res., 2975 N. Andrews Ave., 33311. Tel: 954-563-1183; Fax: 954-564-6628.
School—Tel: 954-563-5608. Ms. Mary Ellen McKinney, Prin.
Sisters of St. Casimir 3; Lay Teachers 16; Students 283.
Catechesis/Religious Programs—Tel: 954-561-4641.
Students 310.
6—St. George, (1964), Revs. Seamus O'Shaughnessy; Martin K. Adu.
Res., 3640 N.W. 8th St., 33311. Tel: 954-583-5892; Fax: 954-583-0725.
7—St. Helen, (1968), Rev. Msgr. William Dever; Rev. Msgr. William E. Powers (GR); Revs. Joseph Kalariparampil; Isidore Baky.
Res., 3033 N.W. 33rd Ave., 33311. Tel: 954-731-7314; Fax: 954-739-9632.
School—Tel: 954-739-7094; Fax: 954-739-0797. Sr. Marie Colette Gerry, Prin.
Lay Teachers 16; Students 252.
Catechesis/Religious Programs—Students 240.
8—St. Jerome, (1960), Revs. Joseph Cinesi; Francis X. McCarthy, (Retired).
Res., 2533 S.W. 9th Ave., 33315. Tel: 954-525-4133; Fax: 954-525-0964.
School—Tel: 954-524-1990; Fax: 954-524-7439. Sr. Vivian Gomez, R.F., Prin.
Sisters of St. Philip Neri 3; Lay Teachers 18; Students 332.
Catechesis/Religious Programs—2601 SW 9 Ave., Ft. Lauderdale, 33315.
Students 70.
9—St. John the Baptist, (1969), Revs. Vincent T. Kelly; James F. Daly, C.S.Sp.
Res., 4595 Bayview Dr., 33308. Tel: 954-771-8950; Fax: 954-771-4178.
Catechesis/Religious Programs—Students 160.
10—St. Mark, (1985), Revs. Edmond F. Whyte; Robert Tywoniak.
Res., 5601 S. Flamingo Rd., 33330. Tel: 954-434-3777; Fax: 954-434-3125.
Catechesis/Religious Programs—Tel: 954-252-9899. Shirley Sandusky, D.R.E.
Students 1,117.
11—St. Maurice, (1970), Rev. Sean C. Mulcahy.
Res., 2851 Stirling Rd., 33312. Tel: 954-961-7777; Fax: 954-961-4358.
Catechesis/Religious Programs—Tel: 954-961-4358.
Students 286.
12—St. Pius X, (1959), Revs. Patrick C. Slevin; James J. Hampton; Harry Ringenberger.
Res., 2500 N.E. 33rd Ave., 33305. Tel: 954-564-1763.
Church—2511 N. Ocean Blvd. (A1A), 33308. Fax: 954-568-2212.
13—St. Sebastian, (1959), Rev. Msgr. Patrick McDonnell, V.F.; Rev. William F. Mylchreest.
Res., 2518 Barbara Dr., 33316. Tel: 954-524-9344; Fax: 954-524-9347.
Hallandale, Broward Co., St. Charles Borromeo (1968), Rev. Gary R. Steibel. In res., Rev. Jan Fiedurek, S.Ch.
Res., 123 N.W. 6 Ave., 33009. Tel: 954-458-1914; Fax: 954-458-8770.
St. Matthew (1959), Revs. Leonard Puisis; Paul Deyo, SS.CC.
Res., 542 Blue Heron Dr., 33009. Tel: 954-458-1590; Fax: 954-458-0612.
Catechesis/Religious Programs—Students 72.
Hollywood, Broward Co., Little Flower (1926), Revs. Thomas O'Dwyer; Paul Kane; Thomas Hanly.
Res., 1805 Pierce St., 33020. Tel: 954-922-3517; Fax: 954-922-6634.
School—Tel: 954-922-1217; Fax: 954-927-8962. Deacon William A. Watkins, Prin.
Lay Teachers 18; Students 271.
Catechesis/Religious Programs—Students 170.
Nativity (1960), Very Rev. Patrick J. Murnane; Revs. Andres Coucelo; James Russel, S.M.; Joseph Pallivathuckal (India). In res., Rev. Michael Davis.
Res., 5220 Johnson St., 33021. Tel: 954-987-3300; Fax: 954-987-3044.
School—Tel: 954-983-4981. Mrs. Elena Ortiz, Prin.
Sisters Servants of Immaculate Heart of Mary 1; Lay Teachers 31; Students 763.
Catechesis/Religious Programs—Students 471.
St. Bernadette (1959), Rev. Brendan Dalton; Rev. Msgr. Robert Yates, (Retired); Rev. Sean O'Dea, (Retired).
Res., 7450 Stirling Rd., 33024. Tel: 954-432-5313; Fax: 954-432-5344.
School—Tel: 954-432-7022. Mrs. Lynn Vander Wyde, Prin.
Sisters 1; Lay Teachers 18; Students 343.
Catechesis/Religious Programs—Tel: 954-432-6300.
Students 375.
Key Largo, Monroe Co., St. Justin Martyr (1973), Rev. Edward Olszewski.
Res., 105500 Overseas Hwy., 33037. Tel: 305-451-1316; Fax: 305-451-4633.
Key West, Monroe Co., St. Mary, Star of the Sea (1846), Revs. Gerald F. McGrath; Roberto Garza.
Res., 1010 Windsor Ln., 33040. Tel: 305-294-1018; Fax: 305-292-8096.
School—Tel: 305-294-1031.
Sisters 2; Brothers 1; Deacons 1; Lay Teachers 13; Students 190.
Catechesis/Religious Programs—Tel: 305-295-9615.
Students 190.
Lighthouse Point, Broward Co., St. Paul the Apostle (1968), Revs. Frederick J. Brice; John Richard Soulliere; Sergio Dall'Agnese, C.S.
Res., 2700 N.E. 36 St., 33064. Tel: 305-943-9154; 9155; Fax: 305-943-9155.
Catechesis/Religious Programs—Students 147.
Marathon, Monroe Co., San Pablo (1958), Rev. Gerald R. Morris.
Res., 550 122 St., Ocean, 33050. Tel: 305-289-0636; Fax: 305-743-8192.
Margate, Broward Co., St. Vincent (1960), Revs. Neil Doherty; Michael Lynch.
Res., 6350 N.W. 18th St., 33063. Tel: 954-972-0434; Fax: 954-971-9411.
Catechesis/Religious Programs—Tel: 954-972-7708.
Students 205.
Miramar, Broward Co., St. Bartholomew (1962), Revs. Paul Vuturo; Franky Jean. In res., Rev. Edmund Ogbonna (Nigeria).
Res., 8005 Miramar Pkwy., 33025. Tel: 305-431-3600; Fax: 305-435-9591.
School—Tel: 305-431-5253. Maria Glass, Prin.
Lay Teachers 17; Students 305.
Catechesis/Religious Programs—Students 500.
St. Stephen (1956), Revs. James E. Taggart, O.M.I.; James Flavin, O.M.I.; Russell Nickerson, O.M.I.
Res., 6044 S.W. 19 St., 33023. Tel: 954-987-1100; Fax: 954-966-9881.
School—Tel: 954-983-2636; Fax: 954-986-8557.
Sisters of St. Joseph of St. Augustine 3; Lay Teachers 16; Students 273.
Catechesis/Religious Programs—Tel: 305-962-2112.
Students 851.
North Lauderdale, Broward Co., Our Lady Queen of Heaven (1974), Revs. Joseph Huck; Francis A. Lyons.
Res., 6771 Kimberly Blvd., 33068.
Church—1400 South St., Rd. 7, 33068. Tel: 954-971-5400; Fax: 954-972-4008.
Catechesis/Religious Programs—Tel: 954-973-3406.
Students 372.
Parkland, Mary Help of Christians Church (1989), Rev.

Thomas Wisniewski.
Church—5980 University Dr., 33067. Tel: 954-340-6462; Fax: 954-340-6838.
Catechesis/Religious Programs—Tel: 954-340-2872.
Students 500.

Pembroke Pines, Broward Co., St. Boniface (1971), Revs. Antonio R. Silio; Timothy Sperber.
Res., 8330 Johnson St., 33024. Tel: 305-432-2750; Fax: 305-432-2756.
Catechesis/Religious Programs—Students 238.

St. Edward, Rev. Michael Eivers.
Res., 1101 N.W. 184 Ter., 33029. Tel: 954-436-7944; Fax: 954-436-7506.

St. Maximilian Kolbe (1983), Revs. James Vitucci; Joseph Kottayil (India); Walter Mitchell.
Res., 11051 N.W. 16 St., 33026. Tel: 954-432-0206; Fax: 954-432-0775.
Church—701 N. Hiatus Rd., 33026. Tel: 954-432-0206.
Catechesis/Religious Programs—Tel: 954-435-3000.
Students 941.

Plantation, Broward Co., St. Gregory (1959), Rev. Msgr. Noel Fogarty, P.A.; Revs. Michael Grady; Abel Barajas.
Res., 200 N. University Dr., 33324. Tel: 954-473-6261; Fax: 954-473-4599.
School—Tel: 954-473-8169; Fax: 954-472-1638. Sr. Diane Bernback, O.S.F., Prin.; Mrs. Antoinette McNamara, Asst. Prin.
Sisters 2; Lay Teachers 33; Students 777.
Catechesis/Religious Programs—Tel: 954-473-8321.
Students 430.

Pompano Beach, Broward Co.,

1—Assumption, (1951), Revs. Martin J. Cassidy; Senan Murray, C.S.Sp.
Res., 2001 S. Ocean Blvd., 33062. Tel: 954-941-7647; Fax: 954-941-9620.

2—San Isidro, (1970), Revs. Ricardo C. Castellanos; Filiberto Melchor, F.M.M. (Guatemala); Gerardo Calderon, F.M.M. (Guatemala); Hyacinth Edokwe, C.S.Sp.
Res., 2310 Martin Luther King Blvd., 33069-1591. Tel: 954-971-8780.
Dade: Tel: 954-940-8719; Fax: 954-972-3607.
Catechesis/Religious Programs—Students 223.

3—St. Coleman, (1959), Revs. Thomas F. Foudy; Joseph Maroor (India); Juan Montoya.
Res., 1200 S. Federal Hwy., 33062. Tel: 954-942-3533; Fax: 954-942-7869.
School—Tel: 954-942-3500; Fax: 954-785-0603.
Sisters 3; Lay Teachers 26; Aides 5; Students 643.
Catechesis/Religious Programs—Tel: 954-782-1461.
Students 325.

4—St. Elizabeth of Hungary Catholic Church, (1959), Rev. Msgr. John W. Glorie; Rev. Fernando Isern.
Res., 3331 N.E. 10 Terrace, 33064-5298. Tel: 954-941-8117; Fax: 954-941-0999.
School—901 N.E. 33rd. St., 33064. Tel: 954-942-2161. Mrs. Rita A. O'Leary, Prin.
Sisters 1; Lay Teachers 24; Students 475.
Catechesis/Religious Programs—Tel: 954-943-6801.
Students 155.

5—St. Gabriel, (1967), Rev. Msgr. Francis J. Fazzalaro; Rev. James Parappally.
Res., 731 N. Ocean Blvd., P.O. Box 3044, 33062. Tel: 954-943-3684; Fax: 954-943-3656.

6—St. Henry, (1969), Revs. James B. Reynolds; George Duffy.
Res., 1500 S.W. 12th Ave., 33069. Tel: 954-785-2450; Fax: 954-785-6958.
Catechesis/Religious Programs—Students 60.

Sunrise, Broward Co., All Saints (1982), Rev. Anthony J. Mulderry. In res., Rev. Guy Fenger.
Office: 10900 W. Oakland Park Blvd., 33351. Tel: 954-742-2666; Fax: 954-741-7238.
Catechesis/Religious Programs—Tel: 954-742-7742.
Students 1,207.

St. Bernard (1971), Very Rev. Michael Hourigan, V.F.
Res., 8279 Sunset Strip, 33322. Tel: 954-741-7800; Fax: 954-742-4558.
Catechesis/Religious Programs—Tel: 954-741-0275.
Students 172.

Tamarac, Broward Co., St. Malachy (1973), Revs. Dominick O'Dwyer; Daniel Cernauskas (Nassau).
Res., 6200 John Horan Terr., 33321. Tel: 954-726-1237; Fax: 954-726-1288.
Catechesis/Religious Programs—Tel: 954-721-5337; Fax: 954-726-0822. Lucille Moran, D.R.E.
Students 233.

Tavernier, Monroe Co., San Pedro (1954), Rev. John D. McGrath.
Res., Overseas Hwy., Plantation Key, P.O. Box 456, 33070. Tel: 305-852-5372; Fax: 305-852-3315.
Catechesis/Religious Programs—Students 117.

West Hollywood, Broward Co., Annunciation (1959), Rev. Michael Quilligan.
Res., 3781 S.W. 39th St., 33023. Tel: 954-989-0606; Fax: 954-989-0660.
School—Tel: 954-989-8287. Sr. Josephine Sherry, R.S.M., Prin.
Sisters 1; Lay Teachers 17; Students 294.
Catechesis/Religious Programs—Students 180.

Chaplains of Public Institutions

Special Assignment:
Reverend Fathers—
Biain, Jose, O.F.M.
Clements, Charles, Baptist Hospital & South Miami Hospital, Miami
Dorrity, Daniel, Genesis, 3675 S. Miami Ave., Miami, FL 33133. Tel: 305-856-1043
Doyle, Dan F., S.M., 4921 Lincoln St., Hollywood, FL 33021. Tel: 954-964-1026
Fernandez, Nelson, Mount Sinai & Miami Heart Hospitals, Miami Beach
Fishwick, Joseph, Baptist Hospital & South Miami Hospital, Miami
O'Neill, Patrick H.
Smith, David, Jackson Memorial Hospital

On Duty Outside the Archdiocese:
Reverend Monsignors—
Navarro, Pablo A.
Reverend Fathers—
Carbajales, Ignacio, Spain
Gonzalez-Abreu, Hector, Fort Myers (Venice)
O'Hala, Stephen, Boynton Beach (St. Vincent de Paul Seminary) (West Palm Beach)
O'Leary, John, Peru
Scheiding, Philip, Mexico

Military Chaplains:
Reverend Fathers—
Gubbins, John
Melley, James

Higher Studies:
Reverend Fathers—
Estrada, Enrique, Rome, Italy
Rios, Juan Carlos, Rome, Italy
Souckar, Michael, Rome, Italy
Vallee, Robert, Belgium

Sabbatical:
Reverend Monsignors—
Delaney, John

Absent on Sick Leave:
Reverend Fathers—
Brantome, Oscar
Puerta, Jorge
Reiser, John

Absent on Leave:
Reverend Fathers—
Christman, Robert
Fernandez, Fausto
Grogan, Brendan
Hayes, Joseph
Kudlo, Frank
Miyares, Carlos
Piano, Timothy
Velie, Richard

Retired:
Most Rev.—
McCarthy, Edward A.
Reverend Monsignors—
Fernandez, Orlando
Walsh, Bryan O.
Reverend Fathers—
Cahill, Frank
Cardona, George
Cliff, Joseph
Connaughton, James
Dennehy, Thomas
Dunleavy, Francis
Fernandez, Miguel A.
Gunther, William
Hanly, Thomas
Hudak, Cyril
Ireland, Donald
Jackson, Charles
Lucking, Aloysius
Lyons, Lawrence
McKeever, William
Morras, Ignacio
Murray, Patrick
O'Sullivan, Sean
Perez, Maximiliano
Planas, Salvador
Punch, David
Quinlan, Eugene
Quinn, James E.
Scherer, Richard
Schlinkmann, John W.
Stadalnikas, Casimir J.
Valoret, Joseph
Vann, John C.

Permanent Deacons:
Abdallah, Mitchell C.
Aceto, Igino, Rockville Centre, NY
Aguayo, Orlando
Aguilu, Thomas
Alfonso, Manuel
Alonso, Jose P.
Asselin, Allen
Avery, John
Baez, Rodolfo, Santo Domingo, Dominican Republic
Ballota, Armando, On Duty Outside the Archdiocese
Bautista, Andres, Santo Domingo, Dominican Republic
Bechily, Antonio, Chicago
Benavides, Luis Pensacola
Binder, Robert
Blaha, Daniel C.
Blais, Robert, On Duty Outside the Archdiocese
Blanco, Eduardo
Bouker, Richard
Brizuela, Humberto
Buigas, Manual
Calvo, Pedro P.
Camacho, Vidal, New York, NY
Canovaca, Manuel
Carieri, Carl
Carroll, Dr. Norman
Carroll, Richard A.
Chavez, Diego
Chinelly, John, Sr.
Colastin, Max
Coniglio, Philip
Costea, Nicholas
Crawford, Jr. Frederick, On Duty Outside the Archdiocese
Cresswell, William H.
Cronin, Donald
Cuesta, Angel L.
Currier, Roger
D'Angelo, Anthony
DeCola, Joseph, Brooklyn, NY
DeLuca, Arnold J.
DeNunzio, Arthur
Diehl, William
Dietsch, Charles, III, On Duty Outside the Archdiocese
DiLeonardo, Ignatius, On Duty Outside the Archdiocese
Dinsmore, Robert B.
Draughon, Woodworth R.
Dugan, Richard
Eberling, Vincent, Jr.
Estrada, Francisco
Fallon, Martin, On Duty Outside the Archdiocese
Farinato, Vincent
Fathauer, Ronald, On Duty Outside the Archdiocese
Fernandez, Pablo A.
Fiore, Charles
Friel, John
Fuentes, Rafael
Galard, John, On Duty Outside the Archdiocese
Garcia, Jose M.
Gazitua, Ralph
Gervasi, Angelo
Gibson, George
Gonzalez, Blas
Gonzalez, Jorge G.
Gonzalez, Luis
Gonzalez, Miguel
Goulet, Guy
Gouthro, Ronald
Green, John F.
Guerra, Jose M.
Hanlon, Thomas F.
Hanlon, Willie
Hubbell, Carl
Hummel, John
Jordan, Dennis E.
Karrenberg, William H.
Knox, Terrence, On Duty Outside the Archdiocese
Kroll, John
Lam, Alex S.
Lang, Irving
Lannon, Billy, Jr.
Leon, Felipe de
Leon, Michael
Lezama, Jose V., On Duty Outside the Archdiocese
Livingstone, Donald
Llaneza, Oscar

Long, George H., Jr.
Lopez, Mario
Lopez, Pedro
Lopez, Victor
Loyola, Benito
Maceo, Antonio J.
Martinez, Jose
McClain, Kirby
McInerney, Vincent
Mickwee, George, On Duty Outside the Archdiocese
Mieyal, Denis
Mindel, Albert
Minetti, Bernard, On Duty Outside the Archdiocese
Moreno, Vicente
Moretti, Daniel
Munter, Paul H.
Murphy, Charles
Murray, Paul, On Duty Outside the Archdiocese
Musselman, Randall O.
Nerys, Jose A., San Juan, Puerto Rico
O'Malley, Robert F., Jr.
Ochoa, Roberto
Ortega, Ray
Padron, Rodolfo
Parlade, Miguel
Pearce, Joseph M.
Peremenis, John
Perez, Manuel
Perron, Charles
Pintado, Angel
Pita, Bernardo
Plummer, Joseph
Plummer, Michael
Polcari, Joseph A., On Duty Outside the Archdiocese
Prieto, Jorge
Raymond, Donald, On Duty Outside the Archdiocese
Renuart, Albert, On Duty Outside the Archdiocese
Reyes, Rafael de los
Rizo, Ornan, Jr.
Rodriguez, Diego, Boston, MA
Rodriguez, Jorge
Rodriguez, Jose L., San Juan, Puerto Rico
Rodriguez, Santos
Ruiz-Castaneda, Norman
Saavedra, Manuel
Scherrer, Thomas
Shaw, Roger M.
Sierra, Feliciano
Sierra, Luis
Smith, David
Solorzano, Jose
Sommovigo, Joseph
Soucy, Joseph O.
Starzinski, Louis
Sutcavage, George P.
Taylor, Ian
Taylor, Timm
Teolis, Matthew, Chicago
Thesing, John
Tola, Vincent
Tomonto, James R.
Tosco, Jesus
Velez, Gregorio, On Duty Outside the Archdiocese
Venezia, Richard
Vitale, Perry
Waldman, Gerald
Watkins, William A.
White, James, On Duty Outside the Archdiocese
Zayas, Julio
Zayas, Luis

INSTITUTIONS LOCATED IN THE ARCHDIOCESE

[A] SEMINARIES, ARCHDIOCESAN

MIAMI. *St. John Vianney College Seminary*, 2900 S.W. 87th Ave., 33165. Tel: 305-223-4561; 4562; Fax: 305-223-0650. Very Rev. John Noonan, Rector; Ms. Zoila Diaz, D.Min., Academic Dean; Maria Rodriguez, Librarian; Revs. Fernandez Gilberto, Spiritual Dir.; Joseph Waters, Vice-Rector, Dean of Students; Stephen Trzecieski, C.M., Dir. Pre-Theology Programs; Manuel Garcia Fidalgo; LaFrance Val, O.P. In res., Rev. Liam Quinn. Students 44.

[B] COLLEGES AND UNIVERSITIES

MIAMI. *Barry University*, 11300 N.E. 2nd Ave., 33161. Tel: 305-899-3000.
For a complete listing, refer to the Colleges and Universities section.

OPA LOCKA. *St. Thomas University*, 16400 N.W. 32nd Ave., 33054. Tel: 305-625-6000; Fax: 305-628-6511.
For a complete listing, refer to the Colleges and Universities section.

[C] HIGH SCHOOLS, ARCHDIOCESAN

MIAMI. *Archbishop Curley-Notre Dame High School*, 4949 N.E. 2nd Ave., 33137. Tel: 305-751-8367; Fax: 305-751-3517. Bro. Richard J. DeMaria, C.F.C., Prin.; Ms. Beatriz Rodriguez, Asst. Prin.; Rev. Michael Keener, Chap. Priests 1; Brothers 6; Lay Teachers 29; Students 460.

La Salle High School, 3601 S. Miami Ave., 33133. Tel: 305-854-2334. Sr. Shermane Delgado, F.M.A., Prin.; Mr. Paul Herring, Asst. Prin. for Student Affairs; Ms. Antonia Ruiberriz, Asst. Prin. for Curriculum; Sr. Maryann Schaeffen, F.M.A., Admin. Asst.; Rev. Richard Putnam, S.D.B., Coord. of Youth Ministry. Priests 2; Brothers 1; Sisters 5; Lay Teachers 30; Students 587.

Msgr. Edward Pace High School, 15600 Spartan Blvd., N.W. 32 Ave., 33054. Tel: 305-624-8534. Dr. Richard J. Perhla, Prin.; Revs. Gustavo Miyares, Supervising Prin.; Cyril J. Smith, O.S.A., Academic Dean; John Madigan, Chap.; Mrs. Candi Lacey, Asst. Prin. for Academics; Mr. Samuel Lilly, Dean of Students. Priests 3; Lay Teachers 48; Students 850.

Our Lady of Lourdes Academy, 5525 S.W. 84th St., 33143. Tel: 305-667-1623. Sr. Susan Marie Kuk, I.H.M., Prin.; Rev. William Kidwell, S.J., Chap. Servants of the Immaculate Heart of Mary 8; Lay Teachers 56; Students 812.

St. Brendan High School, 2950 S.W. 87 Ave., 33165. Tel: 305-223-5181; Fax: 305-220-7434. Rev. John Noonan, Supervising Prin.; Mr. Alan J. Powers, Prin.; Ms. Barbara Behnke, Dean of Students. Priests 2; Lay Teachers 66; Counselors 4; Students 1,255.

FORT LAUDERDALE. *Cardinal Gibbons High School*, 4601 Bayview Dr., 33308. Tel: 954-491-2900. Very Rev. Joseph J. Kershner, Sch.P., Prin.; Sr. Marie Schramko, O.S.F., Asst. Prin.; Revs. Francis Pala, Sch.P., Asst. Prin.; Oscar Alonso, Sch.P.; Charles Newburn, Sch.P.; John Callan; Bro. Grant R. Ferris, O.S.F.S. Priests 5; Brothers 1; Sisters of St. Francis 4; Lay Teachers 57; Students 1,100.

St. Thomas Aquinas High School, 2801 S.W. 12 St., 33312. Tel: 9541-2127; 581-0700. Revs. Vincent T. Kelly, Supervising Prin.; Michael Davis, Asst. Prin.; Mrs. Tina Jones-Atkins, Asst. Prin.; Mr. Willim M. Heller, Prin.; Sr. Peggy Manning, O.P., Campus Minister; Mr. Paul Gomulinski, Dean of Students; Revs. Michael Grady; Guy Fenger (OG). Priests 4; Sisters 4; Lay Teachers 81; Students 1,653.

[D] HIGH SCHOOLS, PRIVATE

MIAMI. *Belen Jesuit Preparatory School*, 500 S.W. 127 Ave., 33184. Tel: 305-223-8600. Very Rev. Benjamin Gonzalez-Buelta, Prov.; Revs. Marcelino Garcia, S.J., Pres, Prin., Contact; Pedro Cartaya, S.J.; Jorge Sardina, S.J.; Jose Maria Izquierdo; Jose R. Tey, S.J.; Juan Manuel Dorta, S.J.; Eduardo Alvarez, S.J.; Jorge Munguia, S.J.; Francisco J. Lemus, S.J.; Andres Benitez, S.J.; Francisco Perez-Lerena, S.J.; Victor M. Hernandez, S.J.; Bros. Pedro Estevez, S.J.; S. Willie Garcia-Tunon, S.J. Priests 12; Brothers 2; Lay Teachers 54; Students 972.

Carrollton School of the Sacred Heart, 3747 Main Hwy., 33133. Tel: 305-446-5673. Sr. Ann Taylor, R.S.C.J., Headmistress. Religious of the Sacred Heart 5; Lay Teachers 72; Students 596.

Christopher Columbus High School, 3000 S.W. 87 Ave., 33165. Tel: 305-223-5650; Fax: 305-559-4306. Revs. Chris Marino, Campus Minister; Liam Quinn; Bros. Angelo Palmieri, F.M.S., Prin.; Edmund Sheehan, F.M.S., Asst. Prin. (Scheduling); Kenneth Curtin, F.M.S.; Mrs. Patricia Call, Asst. Prin. (Grades & Academic Credit); Mr. Christopher McKeon, Asst. Prin. (Discipline). Priests 1; Marist Brothers 15; Lay Teachers 65; Students 1,330.

HOLLYWOOD. *Chaminade-Madonna College Preparatory*, 500 Chaminade Dr., 33021-5800. Tel: 305-989-5150. Bro. John Campbell, S.M., Pres.; Robert E. Minnaugh, Prin. Marianist Brothers 7; Lay Teachers 47; Students 780.

[E] ELEMENTARY SCHOOLS, PRIVATE

KEY WEST. *Mary Immaculate Star of the Sea*, 700 Truman Ave., 33040. Tel: 305-294-1031. Brothers 1; Sisters 2; Lay Teachers 14; Students 185.

[F] SHELTERS

MIAMI. *Camillus House, Inc.*, P.O. Box 1829, 33101-1829.
For a complete listing, refer to the Special Care Facilities section.

Gift of Hope, Missionaries of Charity, 724 N.W. 17 St., 33136. Tel: 305-326-0032.
For a complete listing, refer to the Special Care Facilities section.

[G] GENERAL HOSPITALS

MIAMI. *Mercy Hospital*, 3663 S. Miami Ave., 33133. Tel: 305-854-4400.
For a complete listing, refer to the Hospitals section.

FORT LAUDERDALE. *Holy Cross Hospital*, 4725 N. Federal Hwy., 33308. Tel: 954-771-8000; Fax: 954-492-5741.
For a complete listing, refer to the Hospitals section.

[H] MONASTERIES AND RESIDENCES OF PRIESTS AND BROTHERS

MIAMI. *Casa San Lorenzo*, 16400 N.W. 32 Ave., 33054. Tel: 305-624-0775. Augustinian Fathers. Revs. Cyril J. Smith, O.S.A.; James L. MacDougall, O.S.A., Prior, Contact; Raymond E. Geisser, O.S.A.; Gary N. McCloskey, O.S.A.; John J. Kelly, O.S.A.; Thomas R. Cook, O.S.A. Total in Res. 7.

Franciscan Fathers' Residence, 2044 S.W. 22nd Ter., 33145. Tel: 305-856-5257. Revs. Jose Biain, O.F.M.; Angel Villaronga, O.F.M.

Jesuit Fathers of the Province of the Antilles, Inc., 13339 S.W. 9 Ter., 33184. Tel: 305-559-9066. Revs. Eduardo Alvarez, S.J., Superior Contact; Florentino Azcoitia, S.J.; Marcelino Garcia, S.J.; Andres Benitez; Victor Hernandez; Tomas Macho, S.J.; Enrique Osle, S.J.; Francisco Perez-Lerena, S.J.; Jose R. Tey, S.J.; Jose Maria Izquierdo, S.J.; Jorge Sardina, S.J. Seminarians: Guillermo Garcia-Tunon, S.J.; Fulgencio Mayorga, S.J.; Bro. Pedro Estevez, S.J.

Marist Brothers Residences, 8230 S.W. 136th St., 33156. Bros. Charles Filiatraut, F.M.S., Contact; George McManus, F.M.S.; Lawrence Poirier, F.M.S.; Daniel Andrew, F.M.S.; Norbert Rodriguez, F.M.S.; Simeon Ouellet, F.M.S., 2790 S.W. 89 Ave., 33165. Bros. Bernard Nolan, F.M.S.; Thomas Edward, F.M.S.; Cornelius Russell, F.M.S.; Lucien Duguay, F.M.S.

Villa Arrieta, 2928 S.W. 10 St., 33135. Tel: 305-541-6221. Revs. Pedro A. Suarez, S.J., (Superior) Contact; Pedro Cartaya, S.J.; Juan Manuel Dorta, S.J.; Gerardo Freire, S.J.; Otto Martinez, S.J.; Jorge Munguia, S.J.

BAL HARBOUR. *Dominican Friars Residence*, The Plaza, No. 201, 10185 Collins Ave., 33154. Tel: 305-864-6593. Rev. Daniel P. Madden, O.P.

[I] CONVENTS AND RESIDENCES FOR SISTERS

MIAMI. *Congregation of the French-Cuban Dominican Sisters of Holy Rosary, Inc.*, 8900 S.W. 19th St., 33165. Tel: 305-221-0384. Sr. Olga Martinez, Contact; Sr. Mary Cecilia Alonso, Pres. & Treas. Houses of Religious Women 1; Total in Residence 6.

Daughters of Charity of St. Vincent de Paul. (Santurce, P.R.), Mision San Vicente de Paul. 500 N.W. 63rd Ave., 33126. Tel: 305-266-6485. Ermita Nuestra Senora de la Caridad, 3609 S. Miami Ave., P.O. Box 330555, 33133. Tel: 305-854-2404.
Asociacion Hijas de la Caridad de San Vicente de Paul del Estado de la Florida, Inc. Sr. Eva Perez-Puelles, Contact.

Daughters of St. Paul, 11117 S.W. 2nd St., 33174. Tel: 305-554-0175. Sr. Karen Joseph, F.S.P., Supr. Contact). Houses of Religious Women 1; Total in Residence 6.

Guadalupan Missionaries of the Holy Spirit, 2483 S.W. 4 St., 33135. Tel: 305-642-9544. U.S. Delegation Headquarters. Other Address: 869 S.W. Third St., Florida City, 33034-4605. Tel: 305-248-3735. Other Address: 1311 N.E. 105 St., Miami Shores, 33138. Legal Title: *Missionary Guadalupanas of the Holy Spirit, Inc.* Sr. Edith Lugo. House of Religious Women 2; Total in Residence 8; House of Studies 1; Total in Residence 6.

Handmaids of the Sacred Heart of Jesus A.C.J., 1615 N.E. 108 St., 33161. Tel: 305-891-9161. Sr. Kathleen Doherty, Contact. Sisters 5.

Missionaries of Charity, 727 N.W. 17th St., 33136. Tel: 305-545-5699. Sr. M. Ajaya, M.C., Supr. (Contact). Houses of Religious women 1; Total in Residence 6.

FORT LAUDERDALE. *Sisters of Mercy Ministry Corporation*, 4841 N.E. 20th Ave., 33308. Tel: 954-776-3290; Fax: 954-776-3014. Sr. Genevra Baer, R.S.M., Contact Person.

MIAMI SHORES. *Franciscan Sisters of Allegany*.
Addresses: 138 N.E. 111 St., 33161. Tel: 305-751-3093. Total in Residence 3. St. Francis Convent, 99 N.W. 115 St., Miami, 33168. Tel: 305-751-1544. Total in Residence 4.

[J] RETREAT HOUSES

MIAMI. *Dominican Retreat House, Mary Queen of Apostles*, 7275 S.W. 124 St., 33156. Tel: 305-238-2711. Dominican Sisters of St. Catherine de Ricci (Motherhouse-Elkins Park, PA). Sisters 4; Capacity for Overnight Retreat Programs 66; Retreat Center 1; Total in Residence 4; Staff 7.

John Paul II Retreat House, 720 N.E. 27th St., 33137-4697. Tel: 305-576-2748; 573-1418; Fax: 305-576-2748. Rev. Amando Llorente, S.J., Spiritual Dir., Contact.

[K] CENTERS

MIAMI. *Family Life Ministry*. 9401 Biscayne Blvd., Miami Shores, 33138. Tel: 305-757-6241, Ext. 333; Fax: 305-754-8422. Mrs. Carol A. Farrell, Dir.

Respect Life Office, 18340 N.W. 12 Ave., 33169. Tel: 305-653-2921; Fax: 305-653-1001. Rev. Jordi S. Rivero, Dir.; Ms. Joan Crown, Contact. Special Centers for Social Services 1; Total Assisted 8,702; Staff 7.

St. Paul Book and Media Center, 145 S.W. 107th Ave., 33174. Tel: 305-559-6715; 6716; Fax: 305-559-6717. Sr. Karen Joseph, F.S.P., Supr. Daughters of St. Paul 6; Houses of Religious Women 1; Total in Residence 6; St. Paul Book & Media Center 1; Staff 13.

Shrine of Our Lady of Charity, 3609 S. Miami Ave., P.O. Box 330555, 33133. Tel: 305-854-2404. Most Rev. Agustin Roman, V.G., Dir. Associate Directors: Revs. Romeo Rivas; Francisco Santana. Sisters 5; Houses of Religious Women 1; Total in Residence 5.

Southeast Pastoral Institute, 7700 S.W. 56th St., 33155. Tel: 305-279-2333; Fax: 305-279-0925. Rev. Mario B. Vizcaino, Sch.P., Dir.

Southeast Regional Office for Hispanic Ministry, Inc., 7700 S.W. 56th St., 33155. Tel: 305-279-2333; Fax: 305-279-0925. Rev. Mario B. Vizcaino, Sch.P., Reg. Dir.

[L] SECULAR INSTITUTES

MIAMI. *Teresian Institute, Inc. (Rome, Italy), Teresian Institute of Florida, Inc.*, 3400 S.W. 99th Ave., 33165. Tel: 305-553-8567; 226-3117.

[M] MISCELLANEOUS LISTINGS

MIAMI. *Alumni Association of the Apostolate of Cuba (in Exile), Inc.*, P.O. Box 650721, 33265-0721. Tel: 305-271-4151. Maria Antonia Pena, Treasurer (Contact.

Alumni of Apostolate Charity Foundation, Inc., P.O. Box 650721, 33265-0721. Maria Antonia Rodriguez, Pres. Tel: 305-226-8110; Maria Antonia D. Pena, Treas., Contact. Tel: 305-271-4151.

Claretian Missions, Inc., 7080 S.W. 99 Ave., 33173. Sr. Ondina Cortes, Superior (Contact). Sisters 5; Houses of Religous Women 3; Total in Residence 12.

Discalced Carmelite Friars of Miami, Inc. Our Lady of Mt. Carmel Spiritual Life Center. 18330 N.W. 12 Ave., 33169. Tel: 305-654-9760; Fax: 305-654-9345. Revs. Eusebio Gomez, O.C.D., Pres., Contact; Lucio del Burgo, O.C.D., Vice Pres.; Jose Francisco Rosario, O.C.D. Retreat Center 1; Total in Residence 3; Staff 6.

Dominican Fathers of Miami, Inc., 5909 N.W. 7th St., 33126-3199. Tel: 305-264-0181; Fax: 305-262-4685.

St. Dominic Priory. Houses of Religous Men 1; Total in Residence 9.

Southern Dominican Province Vocations Office, P.O. Box 431283, 33423.

Human Services Division/Pierre Toussaint Haitian Catholic Center, Inc. (A Florida Not-for-Profit Corporation), 110 N.E. 62 St., 33138. Tel: 305-758-2462; Fax: 305-758-8216. Special Centers for Socail Services & Assistance 1; Total Assisted 7,000; Total Staff 32.

St. Luke's Center, Inc., 7707 N.W. 2nd Ave., 33150. Tel: 305-795-0077; Fax: 305-795-0030. Patricia Carter, Interim Dir. (Contact).

SEPI Evangelization and Education Foundation, Inc., 7700 S.W. 56th St., 33155. Tel: 305-279-2333. Rev. Mario B. Vizcaino, Sch.P., Exec. Dir.

Teresian Institute, Inc. (Rome, Taly), Teresian Institute of Florida, Inc., 3400 S.W. 99 Ave., 33165. Tel: 305-553-8567; 226-3317. An International Association of the Faithful. Carmen Martin, (Contact).

CORAL GABLES. *Bahamas Mission of Florida, Inc.*, c/o J. Patrick Fitzgerald, Esq., 110 Merrick Way, Ste. 3-B, 33134. Tel: 305-443-9162; Fax: 305-443-6613.

Magnificat, Inc., 5031 Maggiore St., 33146. Board of Directors: Cristina Beato; Maria P. Vadia; Beatriz Harriman; Maria Horvath; Aida Lucas.

Peruvian Mission, Inc. (A Florida Not-for-Profit Corporation), 110 Merrick Way, Ste. 3-B, 33134. Tel: 305-443-9162; Fax: 305-443-6613.

FORT LAUDERDALE. *Schott Memorial Center Foundation, Inc.* (A Florida Not-for-Profit Corporation), 6591 S.W. 124th Ave., 33330. Tel: 305-434-3306; 434-7437; Fax: 305-434-3307. John R. Green, Exec. Dir., (Contact). Special Centers for Social Services & Assistance 1; Total Assisted 11,520; Total Staff 6.

HIALEAH. *Dominicas de la Inmaculada Concepcion*, 571 W. 33 Pl., 33012. Tel: 305-823-3282. Houses of Religous Women 1; Total in Residence 4.

KEY LARGO. *1-800-Mass-Times Trust*, 67 N. Bounty Lne, 33037. Tel: 305-852-4530. Robert A. Hummel, Chm.; Phyliss H. Hummel, Secretary. Governing Board: Jerry Early; Rev. Jose P. Nickse. Toll-free telephone listing of local Catholic Churches with Mass times to assist travelers in finding Mass schedules.

MIAMI SHORES. *DOM, Inc.*, 9401 Biscayne Blvd., 33138. Tel: 305-757-6241.

Francis Realty Corporation, 9401 Biscayne Blvd., 33138. Tel: 305-757-6241.

Marbella Condominium 207 Association, Inc., 9401 Biscayne Blvd., 33138. Tel: 305-757-6241.

P.O.M., Inc., 9401 Biscayne Blvd., 33138. Tel: 305-757-6241.

Pooled Income Trust Fund, 9401 Biscayne Blvd., 33138. Tel: 305-757-6241.

Provincial Realty Associates, Inc. (A Florida Not-for-Profit Corporation), 9401 Biscayne Blvd., 33138. Tel: 305-757-6241.

Land Holding Corporation.

ST. PETERSBURG. *Franciscan Sisters of Allegany, NY*, Region III Office, 631-11 St. North St., 33705. Tel: 813-824-0857. Sr. Gladys Sharkey, Reg. III Minister.

St. Francis Medical & Health Care Foundation, Inc.

St. Francis Medical & Health Care Services, Inc. Allegany Health System, 6200 Courtney Campbell Dr., Ste. 100, Tampa, 33067. Tel: 800-290-9093.

RELIGIOUS INSTITUTES OF MEN REPRESENTED IN THE ARCHDIOCESE

For further details refer to the corresponding bracketed number in the Religious Institutes of Men or Women section.

[0140]—*The Augustinians*. (St. Thomas of Villanova Prov.).—O.S.A.

[0200]—*Benedictine Monks*.—O.S.B.

[0810]—*Brothers of Mercy*.—M.M.

[0600]—*Brothers of the Congregation of Holy Cross*.—C.S.C.

[0580]—*Brothers of the Good Shepherd*.—B.G.S.

[1100]—*Brothers of the Sacred Heart*.—S.C.

[0470]—*Capuchin Friars*.—O.F.M.Cap.

[0270]—*Carmelite Fathers & Brothers*.—O.Carm.

[0310]—*Congregation of Christian Brothers*. (Eastern Prov.).—C.F.C.

[1330]—*Congregation of the Mission*.—C.M.

[]—*Congregation of the Resurrection*.—C.R.

[1140]—*Congregation of the Sacred Hearts of Jesus and Mary*.—SS.CC.

[0260]—*Discalced Carmelite Friars*.—O.C.D.

[0520]—*Franciscan Friars*. (Most Holy Name & San Sebastion Provs.).—O.F.M.

[0650]—*Holy Ghost Fathers*.—C.S.Sp.

[0690]—*Jesuit Fathers and Brothers*. (Antilles & New Orleans Provs.).—S.J.

[0770]—*The Marist Brothers*. (Esopus & Poughkeepsie Provs.).—F.M.S.

[0800]—*Maryknoll*.—M.M.

[0910]—*Oblates of Mary Immaculate*.—O.M.I.

[0920]—*Oblates of St. Francis de Sales*.—O.S.F.S.

[0950]—*Oratorians*.—C.O.

[0430]—*Order of Preachers (Dominican)*. (St. Joseph & Southern Provs.).—O.P.

[1040]—*Piarist Fathers*.—Sch.P.

[1070]—*Redemptorist Fathers*.—C.SS.R.

[1190]—*Salesians of John Bosco*.—S.D.B.

[0760]—*Society of Mary (Marianists)*.—S.M.

[0370]—*Society of St. Columban*.—S.S.C.

[1060]—*Society of the Precious Blood*.—C.PP.S.

[0560]—*Third Order Regular of St. Francis*.—T.O.R.

RELIGIOUS INSTITUTES OF WOMEN REPRESENTED IN THE ARCHDIOCESE

[0370]—*Carmelite Sisters of the Most Sacred Heart of Los Angeles*.—O.C.D.

[0685]—*Claretian Missionary Sisters*.—R.M.I.

[0270]—*Congregation of Bon Secours*.—C.B.S.

[3710]—*Congregation of the Sisters of St. Agnes*.—C.S.A.

[1710]—*Congregation of the Third Order of St. Francis of Mary Immaculate, Joliet, IL*.—O.S.F.

[0760]—*Daughters of Charity of St. Vincent de Paul*.—D.C.

[0790]—*Daughters of Divine Charity*.—F.D.C.

[0850]—*Daughters of Mary Help of Christians*.—F.M.A.

[]—*Daughters of Mary, Mother of Mercy (Nigeria)*.—D.M.M.M.

[1070-13]—*Dominican Sisters (Adrian)*.—O.P.

[]—*Dominican Sisters (Colombia)*.—O.P.

[1070-17]—*Dominican Sisters (Elkins Park)*.—O.P.

[1070-06]—*Dominican Sisters (Newburgh)*.—O.P.

[1070-03]—*Dominican Sisters (Sinsinawa)*.—O.P.

[]—*Dominican Sisters of Bethany Congregation*.—O.P.

[]—*Dominican Sisters of Our Lady of the Most Holy Rosary (Columbia)*.—O.P.

[]—*Dominicas de la Inmaculada Concepcion (Ecuador)*.

[1180]—*Franciscan Sisters of Allegany, New York*.—O.S.F.

[1845]—*Guadalupan Missionaries of the Holy Spirit*. (Mexico).—M.G.Sp.S.

[1870]—*Handmaids of the Sacred Heart of Jesus*.—A.C.J.

[2575]—*Institute of the Sisters of Mercy of the Americas*. (Pittsburgh, PA; Cedar Rapids, IA; Rochester, NY; Merion, PA; North Carolina; Clogher, Ireland; Newfoundland, Canada).—R.S.M.

[]—*Marianitas*.—R.M.

[2710]—*Missionaries of Charity*.—M.C.

[3040]—*Oblate Sisters of Providence*.—O.S.P.

Oblates of the Sacred Heart of Jesus (El Salvador).—O.C.J.

[3130]—*Our Lady of Victory Missionary Sisters*.—O.L.V.M.

[0950]—*Pious Society Daughters of St. Paul*.—F.S.P.

[3380]—*Religious of the Apostolate of the Sacred Heart*.—R.A.

[3390]—*Religious of the Assumption*.—R.A.

Santa Mariana de Jesus Insitute, Inc..—R.M.

[2970]—*School Sisters of Notre Dame*. (Baltimore, MD; Chicago, IL; Wilton, CT).—S.S.N.D.

[0430]—*Sisters of Charity of the Blessed Virgin Mary (Davenport, IA)*.—B.V.M.

[]—*Sisters of Charity of the Sacred Heart of Jesus (Spain)*.—S.C.S.H.J.

[2540]—*Sisters of Mercy*.—R.S.M.

[3000]—*Sisters of Notre Dame de Namur (Baltimore, MA; Cincinnati, OH)*.—S.N.D.deN.

[3350]—*Sisters of Providence*.—S.P.

[4080]—*Sisters of Social Service*.—S.S.S.

[3740]—*Sisters of St. Casimir*.—S.S.C.

[1620]—*Sisters of St. Francis of Millvale, Pennsylvania*.—O.S.F.

[1630]—*Sisters of St. Francis of Penance and Christian Charity*.—O.S.F.

[1650]—*Sisters of St. Francis of Philadelphia*.—O.S.F.

[3830-16]—*Sisters of St. Joseph (Baden, PA)*.—S.S.J.

[3830-09]—*Sisters of St. Joseph (Brentwood, NY)*.—C.S.J.

[3830-13]—*Sisters of St. Joseph (Erie, PA)*.—C.S.J.

[]—*Sisters of St. Joseph (Rutland, VT)*.—S.S.J.

[3830-05]—*Sisters of St. Joseph (Springfield, MA)*.—C.S.J.

[]—*Sisters of St. Joseph Benedict Cottolengo*.—S.S.J.C.

[3900]—*Sisters of St. Joseph of St. Augustine, Florida*.—S.S.J.

[]—*Sisters of St. Philip Neri Missionary Teachers*.—R.F.

[0260]—*Sisters of the Blessed Sacrament*.—S.B.S.

[1970]—*Sisters of the Holy Family of Nazareth*.—C.S.F.N.

[2070]—*Sisters of the Holy Union*.—S.U.S.C.

[2180]—*Sisters of the Immaculate Heart of Mary*.—I.H.M.

[2150]—*Sisters, Servants of the Immaculate Heart of Mary*.—I.H.M.

[2160]—*Sisters, Servants of the Immaculate Heart of Mary*.—I.H.M.

[2170]—*Sisters, Servants of the Immaculate Heart of Mary*.—I.H.M.

[2460]—*Society of Mary Reparatrix*.—S.M.R.

[4020]—*Society of St. Teresa of Jesus*.—S.T.J.

[4070]—*Society of the Sacred Heart*.—R.S.C.J.

[]—*Theatine Sisters of the Immaculate Conception (Religiosas Teatinas de la Inmaculada Concepcion)*.—R.T.

NECROLOGY

† Harris, Yates, (Retired). —Died Nov. 1, 1996.

† Martin, Jerome, Fort Lauderdale, FL, Blessed Sacrament Church. —Died May 12, 1996.

† Rastatter, Rev. Msgr. Rowan, (Retired). —Died Jan. 8, 1996.

† Saghy, Paul, (Retired). —Died Sept. 19, 1996.

Archdiocese for the Military Services, U.S.A.

Military Ordinariate

Most Reverend

JOSEPH T. RYAN, D.D.

Retired Ordinary of the Archdiocese for the Military Services, U.S.A.; ordained June 3, 1939; appointed First Archbishop of Anchorage February 7, 1966; consecrated March 25, 1966; appointed Titular Archbishop of Gabi and Coadjutor to the Military Vicar October 24, 1975; installed December 13, 1975; appointed Ordinary of the Archdiocese for the Military Services, U.S.A. March 16, 1985; installed March 25, 1985; retired May 13, 1991. *Res., 832 Varnum St., N.E., Washington, DC, 20017.*

Most Reverend

FRANCIS X. ROQUE, D.D.

Auxiliary Bishop; ordained September 19, 1953; appointed Titular Bishop of Bagai and Auxiliary Bishop to the Military Vicar March 29, 1983; consecrated May 10, 1983.

Most Reverend

JOHN G. NOLAN, D.D.

Auxiliary Bishop; ordained June 11, 1949; appointed Titular Bishop of Natchez and Auxiliary Bishop of the Archdiocese for the Military Services December 12, 1987; consecrated January 6, 1988.

Most Reverend

JOSEPH T. DIMINO, D.D.

Archbishop of the Archdiocese of the Military Services; ordained June 4, 1949; appointed Titular Bishop of Carini and Auxiliary Bishop to the Military Vicar March 29, 1983; consecrated May 10, 1983; appointed Ordinary to the Military Services May 13, 1991.

Chancery: P.O. Box 4469, Washington, DC, 20017-0469. Tel.: 301-853-0400; Fax: 301-853-2246.

Most Reverend

JOSEPH J. MADERA, M.SP.S., D.D.

Auxiliary Bishop; ordained June 15, 1957; appointed Coadjutor Bishop of Fresno with the right of succession December 18, 1979; consecrated March 4, 1980; succeeded to See July 1, 1980; appointed Titular Bishop of Orte and Auxiliary Bishop of the Archdiocese for the Military Services May 28, 1991.

Most Reverend

JOHN J. GLYNN, D.D.

Auxiliary Bishop; ordained April 11, 1951; appointed Titular Bishop of Monteverde and Auxiliary Bishop of the Archdiocese for the Military Services December 10, 1991; ordained Bishop January 6, 1992.

ESTABLISHED AS MILITARY VICARIATE OF THE UNITED STATES SEPTEMBER 8, 1957.

CREATED ARCHDIOCESE FOR THE MILITARY SERVICES, U.S.A. (ORDINARIATUS CASTRENSIS) MARCH 25, 1985.

Serving U.S. Catholics of the Army, Navy, Air Force, Marine Corps, Coast Guard, Department of Veterans Affairs and those in Government Service overseas.

STATISTICAL OVERVIEW

Personnel	
Archbishop	1
Retired Archbishops	1
Auxiliary Bishops	4
Priest chaplains are on loan from their diocese or religious community.	
Deacons who assist at chapels are volunteers from the local diocese.	
Educational	
Catechesis/Religious Education Programs:	
High School Students	21,500
Elementary Students	45,300

Total	66,800
Religious Education Teachers	5,150
Directors, Religious Education:	
Sisters	10
Lay Teachers	225
Total	235
Vital Statistics	
Receptions into the Church:	
Infant Baptism Totals	6,389
Adult Baptism Totals	1,118
Received into Full Communion	485
First Communions	3,362

Confirmations	2,896
Marriages:	
Catholic	788
Interfaith	633
Total Marriages	1,421
Catholics, Active Duty Military	380,200
(Family members)	533,000
Reserve/Guard Catholic personnel	204,000
Catholic residents, VA facilities	29,000
Civilian Catholics overseas	69,000
Total	1,215,200

Former Military Vicars—His Eminence PATRICK CARDINAL HAYES, cons. Titular Bishop of Tagaste, Oct. 28, 1914; appt. "Bishop Ordinary of U.S. Army and Navy Chaplains," Nov. 24, 1917; appt. Archbishop of New York, March 10, 1919; created Cardinal, March 24, 1924; died Sept. 4, 1938.—His Eminence FRANCIS CARDINAL SPELLMAN, cons. Auxiliary Bishop of Boston, Sept. 8, 1932; appt. Archbishop of New York, April 15, 1939; appt. "Military Vicar for the Armed Forces of U.S.," Dec. 11, 1939; created Cardinal, Feb. 18, 1946; died Dec. 2, 1967.—His Eminence TERENCE CARDINAL COOKE, cons. Auxiliary Bishop of New York, Dec. 13, 1965; appt. Archbishop of New York, March 2, 1968; appt. "Military Vicar of U.S. Armed Forces," April 4, 1968; created Cardinal, April 28, 1969; died Oct. 6, 1983.—Most Rev. JOSEPH T. RYAN, appt. first Archbishop of Anchorage, Feb. 7, 1966; cons. March 25, 1966; appt. Titular Archbishop of Gabi and Coadjutor Archbishop of the Military Vicar, Oct. 24, 1975; installed first Ordinary of the Archdiocese for the Military Services March, 25, 1985; retired May 13, 1991.

Vicar General—Vacant.

Regional Episcopal Vicars

Europe—Rev. RICHARD B. HIGGINS, Chap., *HQ USAFE/HCP Unit 3050, Box 50, APO AE, 09094-5050.* Rev. LOUIS L. SCHMIT, Chap., *HQ USAREUR & 7A CMR 420, Box 2977, APO AE, 09063.*

Japan—Rev. CAMPION LALLY, O.F.M., *St. Francis Friary, 14-20 Tsutsumi-Cho-3-Chome, Kiryu-Shi, Gumma-Ken, 376. Japan.*

Okinawa—Rev. CHARLES BANTLE, O.F.M.Cap., *Catholic Mission, 314 Asato, Naha, Okinawa, 902. Japan.*

Korea—Rev. PATRICK H. MANDOCK, *HHC 19th TAACOM, Unit 15015, Box 2023, APO AP, 96218-0171.*

Oceana—Most Rev. ANTHONY SABIAN APURON, O.F.M.Cap., Archbishop of Agana, *Chancery Office, P.O. Box 126, Cuesta San Ramon, 26, Agana, Guam, M.I.*

Archdiocese Offices

Chancery—3311 Toledo Ter., Ste. A 201, Hyattsville, MD, 20782-4135. Tel: 301-853-0400; Fax: 301-853-2246.

Moderator of the Curia / Chancellor—Rev. Msgr. ALOYSIUS R. CALLAGHAN, S.T.L, J.C.D.

Office of Chaplain Personnel—

Vicar for Chaplains and Seminarians—Most Rev. JOHN J. GLYNN, D.D.

Director—MARGARET SCUDERI.

Pastoral Support, and Vocations—Most Rev. JOSEPH MADERA, M.Sp.S., D.D.

Veterans Concerns—Most Rev. FRANCIS X. ROQUE, D.D.

Assistant to the Archbishop—PATRICIA L. THACKER.

Director of Administration—JOHN SMITH.

Director of Sacramental Records—FRANK CALANDRA.

Vicar for Development—Most Rev. JOHN G. NOLAN, D.D.

Director of Development—WILLIAM SHEPARD.

Tribunal—

Judicial Vicar—Rev. MICHAEL C. CONNOLLY, O.S.F.S., J.C.L.

Judges (Part-time)—Rev. Msgr. ALOYSIUS R. CALLAGHAN, J.C.D.; Revs. EDWARD C. PFNAUSCH, J.C.D.; JOSEPH J. MORRELL, J.C.L.; G. PAUL HERBERT, J.C.L.; MARK A. PLEWKA, J.C.L.; Mr. STEVEN J. CRIBARI, J.C.L., J.D.

Defenders of the Bond (Part-time)—Rev. Msgr. DAVID J. MORRISON, J.C.D.; Revs. DAVID F. O'CONNOR, S.T., J.C.D.; ALFRED A. SCHLERT, J.C.L.

Procurator-Advocates (Part-time)—Most Rev. JOHN J. GLYNN, D.D.; Rev. FRANCIS X. ROQUE, D.D.

Notary—MAY TOEPFER.

Presbyteral Council—Most Rev. JOSEPH T. DIMINO, D.D.; Rev. Msgr. ALOYSIUS R. CALLAGHAN, Exec. Sec.; Rev. Msgr. DONALD SHEA, (U.S.A.); Rev. Msgr. JOHN KAISING, (U.S.A.); Revs. JOSEPH W. ESTABROOK, (U.S.N.); CHARLES BOURKE, (U.S.N.); Rev. Msgr. ARTHUR S. THOMAS, (U.S.A.F.); Rev. Msgr. WILLIAM J. DENDINGER, (U.S.A.F.); Revs. RICHARD DUNNE, (V.A.); AIDAN WALSH, (V.A.).

Military Council of Catholic Women—Most Rev. FRANCIS X. ROQUE, Episcopal Moderator.

Areas of Service

Armed Forces, Active Duty

The Archdiocese for the Military Services is responsible for the pastoral care of the Catholic men and women who serve on active duty in the five branches of the U.S. Armed Forces. It is also responsible for the dependents of these persons. Included also are the cadets and resident personnel of the three military academies (West Point, the U.S. Air Force Academy at Colorado Springs, the U.S. Naval Academy at Annapolis) and the U.S. Coast Guard Academy at New London as well as the U.S. Merchant Marine Academy at Kings Point, NY. Pastoral care is provided by priest chaplains on loan from their dioceses or religious communities to serve as chaplains for the Military and Department of Veterans Affairs. The pastor at West Point is a civilian priest of the Archdiocese of New York. Members of the Marines and Coast Guard are served by Navy Chaplains.

Armed Forces, Reserves, National Guard

In addition to the personnel on active duty in the Armed Forces, there is a considerable reserve component. Some of these personnel serve a number of days each year on active duty with a branch of the service; some serve on extended tours of active duty; all are subject to recall to active duty in a national emergency. In addition to the reserve components of the Army, Air Force, Navy and Coast Guard, are the Army and Air Force National Guard units, which are organized on a state-by-state basis.

Department of Veterans Affairs

The Archdiocese for the Military Services is responsible for the spiritual care of Catholics at V.A. medical facilities. Chaplaincy services are provided by full- and part-time priests, many of whom are retired military chaplains.

U.S. Government Civilian Employees Abroad

U.S. citizens in government service abroad (and their family members living with them) are subjects of the Archdiocese for the Military Services.

Civil Air Patrol

The Civil Air Patrol, as an auxiliary of the Air Force, is under the jurisdiction of the Archdiocese for the Military Services. The jurisdiction applies to its chaplains and members only when participating in exercises on a military installation.

UNITED STATES ARMY CHAPLAINS

REGULAR ARMY CHAPLAINS

Reverends

Amezcua, Mario M., *l.c.*
Arnoldt, David L. (WIN)
Bengco, Jose C. (Philippines)
Blickhan, Donald (SFD)
Bluett, James K. (PT)
Bolton, Paul (PRO)
Bomba, Paul (WOR)
Breaker, Donald J. (CIN)
Briganti, Phillip (PAT)
Burns, Vincent deP. (PH)
Carey, William F. (BGP)
Chilen, Michael D. (CC)
Coindreau, James M., *l.c.*
D'Emma, Gregory J. (NEW)
Drozd, Henry (DAL)
D'Silva, Joseph R. (India)
Ehrhart, Charles (RVC)
Flaska, John A., Jr. (SFE)
Grace, James N. (CHI)
Gunti, Charles E., *o.f.m.*
Habarek, Jerome (PRO)
Himmelsbach, James R. (STP)
Imberi, Anthony M. (SFS)
Inghilterra, Vincent J. (TR)
Jones, James, *o.f.m.cap.*
Kaising, John J. (CIN)
Kenehan, David A., *o.s.f.s.*
Mandock, Patrick H. (GBG)
Marceaux, Sidney (BEA)
Mauricio, Clemente B., *m.s.c.*
Menz, Anthony, *o.c.s.o.*
Minch, Richard (SAV)
Morency, Raymond (PRT)
Mulvaney, Andrew (OG)
Niemeier, Dennis A. (CIN)
O'Keeffe, Joseph L., *s.j.*
Prendergast, John (PEO)
Rappl, Joseph (BUF)
Richter, Robert J. (MIL)
Rodriguez, Aloysius M. (BR)
Rutherford, Donald (ALB)
Sanner, James E. (E)
Santos, Elenito B. (Philippines)
Schmid, Wayne L. (WCH)
Schmit, Louis L., *c.pp.s.*
Schroeder, Kenneth J., *c.pp.s.*
Seifried, Kenneth A. (SC)
Shea, Donald W. (HEL)
Spiegel, Robert H. (DAV)
Sykes, Gregory (OG)
Teahan, Timothy (BRK)
Tellez, Jairo, *c.m.f.* (Colombia)
Travaglione, Michael (NY)
Whalen, Frank J. (CIN)
Willett, William (OWN)
Wydeven, John L. (OAK)

ARMY RESERVE ON ACTIVE DUTY

Reverends

Albertson, Eric (ARL)
Apura, Nilo S. (Philippines)
Augustyn, Boguslaw (Poland)
Bernans, Arvids (COL)
Betz, James (CAM)
Bleboo, Lawrence (Africa)
Borkowski, Frank J. (NY)
Borycz, Edmund S. (DET)
Bowman, James (RVC)
Castillo, Rolando C. (Philippines)
Cavanaugh, Kevin (HRT)
Cerrone, Michael J. (SAV)
Czech, Edward M. (CLV)
Deken, John C. (STL)
Denig, Philip (DEN)
Deponai, Joseph (NY)
DiGregorio, Joseph (PH)
Dormer, David J. (SCR)
Dory, Michael A. (GB)
Dynek, Wieslaw A. (Poland)
Fleury, Joseph, *s.m.*
Floch, W. Roy (SPK)
Fuller, Orlando (Philippines)
Glasgow, Robert (MAN)
Gott, Camillus H., *o.f.m.conv.*
Goudreau, Joseph L. (PRT)
Hannon, Joseph (SD)
Healy, Patrick, *s.s.j.*
Herrera, Jose (STV)
Herron, Jack B. (FAR)
Hightower, Oliver L. (HEL)
Hill, Philip W. (NY)
Honor, Michael (Philippines)
Jagielski, James J. (DET)
Jaramillo, Peter (AMA)
Kelley, Edward (PRO)
Kinast, Timothy, *s.o.l.t.*
Kirk, David R. (TOL)
Lagasse, Ronald (OAK)
Lanuevo, Victor (Philippines)
Mankowski, Marcin, *o.p.*
Menz, Anthony E., *o.c.s.o.*
Mintegui, Marc (CHR)
Mullen, Owen (WIL)
O'Grady, John F. (PAT)
Pamula, Robert (Poland)
Patton, Patrick G. (HEL)
Ratigan, Patrick (OG)
Reyes, Armando (Philippines)
Roetzel, Robert E., *c.s.c.*
Rzasowski, Jerzy (Poland)
Saltysiak, Paul (WDC)
Santry, Robert (HON)
Serban, Ronald (SR)
Sheil, James (CLV)
Spring, Mark (DAV)
Stahl, Allen M. (ORL)
Stevenson, R. Francis (SAC)
Sunberg, David (CIN)
Tadeo, Victor (Philippines)
Torm, Agustin (CHR)
Vakoc, Timothy (STP)
Wilk, Mitchell (SPC)

UNITED STATES AIR FORCE CHAPLAINS

REGULAR AIR FORCE

Reverends

Barlow, James P. (SA)
Barmann, Karl W. (NO)
Berthlette, Ernest (PRO)
Biewind, Michael, *c.j.*
Blair, Stephen (East Anglia)
Booth, Stephen, *m.m.*
Bruno, Robert, *o.f.m.*
Burnet, Donald T., *o.m.i.*
Burnett, James (DAV)
Collins, John M. (LA)
Cote, David P. (PRT)
Crowley, Edmund G. (MAN)
Cusack, John J. (PAT)
Dendinger, William J. (OM)
Diab, Thomas P. (SAN)
Dillon, James P. (BRK)
Diphe, Juan (HEL)
Di Renzo, Michael J. (STU)
Dixon, James R. (NO)
Dunn, Richard B. (SY)
Fey, Thomas (ALX)
Figel, Terence, *o.m.i.*
Flood, Peter J. (TR)
Gaeta, David (SLC)
Gallagher, Robert (STU)
Glatts, Joseph M. (PH)
Gosselin, Lawrence (NTN)
Grochowski, Bernard (WOR)
Guico, Manuel R. (Philippines)
Hall, Douglas (OM)
Hanley, Dennis (HRT)
Hanrahan, William P. (NEW)
Higginbotham, Robert (BLX)
Higgins, Francis E. (SC)
Highfill, H. Brian (NO)
Ippolitto, Robert, *m.s.*
Jeselnick, Stephen E. (E)
Kaczmarek, James A. (MAR)
Kinney, John (LAF)
Koser, Rudolph J. (GBG)
Kovalcin, John (STL)
Kuan, Joseph (Philippines)
Lambert, Peter S. (DUL)
Lamy, Raymond (MAN)
Leurck, Raymond J. (CIN)
Lim, Joseph (Philippines)
Ludwikoski, James E. (KCK)
McCahon, Joseph (SP)
Malinsky, Gregory J. (PIT)
Mikalofsky, Hilarion (MIL)
Montecalvo, Carlo F. (PRO)
Moran, Edward C. (RIC)
Mueller, Jerome, *o.f.m.*
Mulnix, Gabriel R., *c.p.*
Mulvaney, Andrew R. (OG)
Munsell, Richard (GF)
Newland, Ronald A. (NEW)
Nguyen, Phillip D. (GR)
Nolan, John J. (SFD)
Novotny, Richard (RC)
Olszyk, Thomas P. (MIL)
O'Neill, Michael F. (NO)
Otto, Peter B. (AMA)
Regan, Richard (SAN)
Revello, James P. (DEN)
Ryan, Patrick J., *m.m.*
Saluta, Froilan (Philippines)
Sandi, Thomas P. (NY)
Schiffer, James A., *c.p.*
Schnipke, Eugene *c.pp.s.*
Schueller, LaVerne L. (DUB)
Silva, Caesar (HT)
Srode, John S., *c.pp.s.*
Stewart, Paul (PT)
Supa, Joseph (Czechoslovakia)
Thomas, Arthur S. (NU)
Thomas, James (ALN)
Thompson, William D. (BGP)
Toledo, Nelson (Philippines)
Vella, Joseph C. (BRK)
Volmi, Dennis G. (WIL)
Wagner, Joseph (SFS)
Wallroth, Joseph R., *o.carm.*
White, Alan (NSH)
Zinzer, Walter W. (STL)
Zoshak, William H. (NY)

AIR FORCE RESERVE ON ACTIVE DUTY

Reverends

Abbott, Kerry, *o.f.m.cap.*
Adams, Walter (NY)
Angelo, Thomas (NOR)
Bailey, Lawrence (SEA)
Bartoul, William (SAM)
Beale, Kenneth (NEW)
Beck, R. Patrick (BEA)
Bell, Brian T. (TUC)
Benz, David H. (PH)
Bernadas, Rene (Philippines)
Blazek, Eugene E. (HON)
Breig, Gary (STL)
Brosk, Steven (NEW)
Butler, Timothy (BO)
Clegg, Timothy (LAF)
Cody, Kevin N. (MAN)
Connor, Kevin T. (MAN)
Coonan, James (PH)
Czartorynski, David F. (ALN)
DeAntonio, Michael R. (CHR)
Decker, James D. (MAN)
Deichert, Joseph (BIS)
Demers, Richard D. (OG)
Douglas, John, *c.p.*
Doyle, Lawrence J., *o.s.m.*
Doyle, Thomas, *o.p.*
Fitzgerald, R. Martin (R)
Fitz-Patrick, David (WDC)
Fleta, Heraclio (Philippines)
Fletcher, Patrick (PCE)
Gaeta, David (SLC)
Gonia, Raymond (SUP)
Hanley, Dennis P. (HRT)
Harbour, Linn (OM)
Hennessy, Joseph P. (PIT)
Higgins, Richard B. (SAC)
Hochreiter, Robert S. (SCR)
Humenay, Robert (E)
Ivey, David (Taiwan)
Kelly, Thomas (DEN)
Kelly, William (PT)
Kowalik, Jacek (VEN)
Krogman, David L. (SFS)
Lee, Roy (MIL)
Llanos, Philip (LA)
Lowe, Francis (SB)
McKenna, Timothy (SEA)
McManus, Gerald (PH)
Malloy, Francis (MIL)
Marrell, Dennis (LA)
Moreno, Antonio, *o.f.m.conv.*
Motsay, Joseph R. (SCR)
Myers, Christopher, *s.o.l.t.*
O'Brien, Leo P., *o.praem.*
Omana, Max B.T. (Philippines)
Papp, Christopher (WIL)
Pieczara, Stanislaw, *s.d.s.*
Plourde, John G. (SP)
Raux, Redmond (BO)
Reilly, David (CIN)
Roberts, Randall, *o.f.m.*
Sanchez, Raul N. (GAL)
Sirianni, Klaus W. J. (WDC)
Sizelove, Dennis (NO)
Starbuck, James (OAK)
Swetnam, R. William (STL)
Tran, Joseph (RIC)
Tran, Luan Quach (P)
Underwood, Gary (TUC)
Voelker, David (BEL)
Voyt, Stephen (PT)
Vu, Joseph Minh (TUL)
Weber, Michael J., *o.praem.*
Williams, Anthony (KCK)
Zeller, Leonard H. (BAL)

UNITED STATES NAVY CHAPLAINS

REGULAR NAVY CHAPLAINS

Reverends

Anderson, James, *m.ss.a.*
Banken, Robert (STL)
Barrett, Miles (SC)
Borger, Theodore (DAV)
Bourke, Charles E. (BO)
Brown, Michael (TOL)
Buchmiller, Ronald J. (SD)
Buenaventura, Cesar V. (Philippines)
Caiazzo, Gregory G., (RIC)
Carter, John T. (BAL)
Casimano, Santino A. (GLP)
Condon, Edwin D., Jr. (BO)
Coyle, Patrick, *ss.cc.*
Creider, Philip B. (OKL)
Danner, James L. (MEM)
Dansak, Thomas E. (PIT)
Diaz, Michael, *s.c.j.*
Dillon, William P., *s.a.*
Eis, Charles R. (SPK)
Elkin, Frederic F. (SY)
Estabrook, Joseph W. (ALB)
Fahey, James W. (FR)
Falkenthal, Thomas W. (CHI)
Ferraro, Joseph A., *o.ss.t.*
FitzGerald, John L. (BAL)
Friel, John F., *o.s.f.s.*
Fryer, Patrick L. (WH)
Gallagher, Michael F. (NY)
Gomulka, Eugene T. (ALT)
Guarnieri, Leo J., *c.s.c.*
Gubbins, John M. (MIA)
Gwudz, John S., Jr. (NOR)
Hall, Thomas P., *c.s.p.*
Hines, Joseph W. (WDC)
Holloway, David (KC)
Iasiello, Louis V., *o.f.m.*
Ignacio, Simon G. (Philippines)
Kaul, John L. (DET)
Keane, Robert L., *s.j.*
Kelly, Brian (SCR)
Kienzle, Jerome (MIL)
Klarer, Michael (MAD)
Krzywicki, Lance (PT)
Lamonde, Joseph (PIT)
Leibold, James C. (BRK)
Lesak, William (NEW)
McCord, Kent (MET)
McCormack, Patrick J. (ATL)
McGoery, Peter (NY)
McKenzie, John H., *o.s.b.*
McLaughlin, Paul (VEN)
Madden, John (SAV)
Malene, Robert (E)
Melley, James F. (MIA)
Mennis, James F. (SAC)
Murphy, Kenneth J. (IND)
Murphy, Thomas E. (WDC)
NGuyen, Joseph (Vietnam)
Nordhaus, Jeffrey J. (TOL)
Oddo, Peter A. (NEW)
Panec, Robert (NY)
Panes, Roy P. (Philippines)
Paris, Angel, *o.f.m.*
Pucciarelli, George W. (BO)
Remy, David P. (DUB)
Rocheford, Dennis J. (WOR)
Rodes, Kenneth, *s.d.b.*
Sodano, Ralph H. (PAT)
Soto, Charles, *o.f.m.*
Spatorico, Joseph (BUF)
Trapani, Anthony (RVC)
Valko, Robert A. (PIT)
Vanden Boogard, Steven, *o.praem.*
Walsh, Michael A. (PAT)
Wright, John M. (IND)
Yagesh, Richard C. (PIT)
Young, David (CI)
Zuffoletto, Michael (BUF)

NAVY RESERVE CHAPLAINS ON ACTIVE DUTY

Reverends

Aguilera, Salvador (ELP)
Anson, Cesar R. (Philippines)
Barrett, Miles (SC)
Berchmanz, Antony (NEW)
Biala, Romeo (Philippines)
Bjorklund, Brian (DET)
Boisvert, Marc, *o.m.i.*
Borzych, Alexander (GI)
Boucher, Roger R. (WOR)
Boyle, Dennis (PH)
Brown, Benedict (L)
Brown, Lewis (ROC)
Brown, Shaun S. (NTN)
Brzek, Jon (PIT)
Buchanan, Donald (IND)
Camarda, Ronald (STA)
Carlos, Joseph, *o.f.m.*
Clark, Robert J., *s.s.c.*
Colaco, Leslie A. (Pakistan)
Concha, Alfonso (PH)
Connolly, James (ALN)
Csete, Ivan (NY)
Cuddy, William (BO)
Cummings, Carl (BAL)
Cunningham, Gerard M. (WDC)
Cusick, Kevin (WDC)
D'Aurora, Joseph (RIC)
DeAngelis, Mark J. (BO)
Deeley, Kevin J. (BO)
Delis, Robert, *s.d.b.*
Devine, Joseph (HRT)
Devine, William (BO)
Dillon, Jerome V. (OM)
Dombrowski, Stanley J., *o.s.f.s.*
Domme, Edward, *o.m.v.*
D'Souza, Matthew (LUB)
Duesterhaus, Michael (ARL)
Dux, John H. (STA)
Egan, Brennan, *o.f.m.*
Erestain, Alfonso (Philippines)
Evers, Paul (HON)
Ferretti, Sam (SCR)
Finley, James F. (BRK)
Fix, Donald (PIT)
Foley, Francis P. (PH)
Fry, James Q. (ORG)
Gardocki, Patrick, *o.f.m.*
Garvey, Michael P. (Y)
Gay, James (BGP)
Gegotek, Tadeuxz (BEL)
Gergel, Stephen (ALT)
Gervacio, Adrian R. (HON)
Hall, Daniel, *c.s.v.*
Hicks, Stephen (SAN)
Hogan, Timothy (DET)
Holl, Kermit, *o.s.c.*
Hoog, Eric, *c.ss.r.*
Hughes, Robert W. (MAD)
Hummer, Lawrence (COL)
Hussey, Daniel C. (GAL)
Ingram, James A. (ORL)
Janning, Timothy (CIN)
Jennings, Tommie (SD)
Johnson, Lawrence P. (DUL)
Johnson, Patrick, *c.s.p.*
Joslyn, James (CHI)
Kanicki, Phillip (RIC)
Kennedy, William (BO)
Klepacki, Michael (CHL)
Kloak, David G. (CHI)
Koester, Timothy (BUF)
Kurilec, Robert E., *s.c.j.*
Kuss, Allen (BIS)
Labaro, Alfredo (Philippines)
Lamb, Gary (MEM)
Legarski, Anthony (ALT)
Leslie, Lawrence (COV)
Lindblad, Karl A. (NY)
Linehan, Stephen J. (BO)
Lopes, Richard, *o.f.m.cap*
Lott, Lawrence (MOB)
McClanahan, Robert (PT)
McLaughlin, Peter (CAM)
MacNew, James. J., *o.s.f.s.*
Madej, Paul (SY)
Madey, Louis (LAN)
Mandato, Kieran (NY)
Maxwell, Bruce, *o.s.c.*
Mensah, Gabriel (VIC)
Mikstay, Michael (Y)
Milewski, Robert F. (E)
Moran, James (BO)
Morris, John J. (NEW)
Moss, Donald (AUS)
Mudd, David (WDC)
Mueller, Michael (ORL)
Mulkerin, Terrence (BRK)
Nowak, Bernard U. (BUF)
Osendorf, James, *c.m.*
Panek, Robert M. (NY)
Parisi, Michael (PAT)
Petruska, William (SCR)
Pugliese, Frank (NY)
Quinn, John T. (SD)
Robinson, Jerome (MOB)
Rock, Stephen B. (BO)
Rodes, Kenneth, *s.d.b.*
Roma, Paul (MAN)
Russo, Lawrence J., Jr. (BO)
Schaller, Robert (LC)
Scordo, Joseph, *o.p.*
Shaughnessy, Paul J., *s.j.*
Shuley, Keith (CC)
Simpson, Brian L. (CHI)
Smith, Douglas, *c.s.c.*
Smith, Lawrence, *s.j.*
Soutiere, Ronald A. (BUR)
Spangenberg, George, *c.s.sp.*
Stake, Ronald P. (CHI)
Stavoy, Stephen J. (SCR)
Steed, Donald, *m.m.*
Targonski, Conrad, *o.f.m.*
Traczyk, Edward, *s.ch.*
Tran, Quang Minh (SAV)
Vidrine, Richard (LAF)
Wallace, Richard J. (P)
Walsh, Francis (SPR)
Welch, Bernard (PRT)
Wheatley, R. Carroll (OWN)
Williams, Gary (Ecuador)
Yossa, Kenneth (Canton)

AUXILIARY CHAPLAINS

Reverends
Ahern, John J. (CHI)
Amateis, Jacques (Saudi Arabia)
Ashkar, Dominic (SAM)
Balizan, Daniel M. (SFE)
Bauer, John J., *c.s.s.r.*
Bauer, Richard W. (SLC)
Betowski, E. Paul, *s.j.*
Boyle, Patrick J., *s.J.*
Bracken, John (BRK)
Brady, Jeremiah D. *s.s.j.*
Buckley, Charles, *o.s.b.*
Butler, Michael (COS)
Carlin, Bernard, *c.ss.r.*
Cavanaugh, Michael, (MIo.s.f.s.
Chai, John (Taipei)
Chong, Young-Ku (Korea)
Cleary, William J., *o.s.a.*
Coady, John E. (GF)
Connolly, Leo L. (COL)
Crandall, Thomas A. (PT)
Creary, James (MEM)
Cuneo, James J.
Dentinger, Roy E. (L)
Devine, Kevin (BO)
Diniz, Felicio (Saudi Arabia)
Doody, Patrick, *c.s.sp.*
Dorney, James J. (NY)
Dunn, Stephen (SD)
Early, Thomas (ALX)
Effing, Myron (Agana)
Evanstock, Philip, *c.s.sp.*
Farias, Joseph (PAT)
Ferrer, Gonzalo, *t.o.r.*
Fewell, Michael, *c.m.f.*
Flannery, Michael (NY)
Fosselman, David, *c.s.c.*
Frank, Lawrence J., *o.m.i.*
Freeman, James (TUC)
Gillespie, Paul G., *o.s.f.s.*
Gitzen, Blase, *o.f.m.cap.*
Graves, Joseph A. (PEO)
Graves, William, *c.s.sp.*
Gribbon, Joseph, *c.ss.r.*
Habenight, James F., *m.m.*
Hacker, Louis, *o.s.b.*
Hamilton, Thomas M. *s.m.*
Hartgen, William, *s.s.*
Healy, Patrick, *o.m.i.*
Heathcote, Howard (AUS)
Hickey, Dennis W., *c.s.p.*
Hillyard, Matthew J. *o.s.f.s*
Hoffman, Louis, *s.f.*
Kelley, Thomas W., *o.s.f.s.*
Kelley, William J., *s.v.d.*
Kelly, James C., *o.s.b.*
Kelly, John R. (NY)
Keutzer, Walter (STL)
Kiczuk, Casimir, *c.m.*
Kieffer, Thomas (MRY)
Kita, Edward, *m.s.*
Klinger, Nevin (ALN)
Kneip, Paschal, *o.s.b.*
Kobza, John, *m.i.c.*
Kohler, Joseph (STL)
Kroker, Wolfgang (Germany)
Kucera, Edward J., *o.s.b.*
Kuchar, Matthew, *o.s.b.*
Kyzysteczko, Gothard, *c.m.*
Labo, Timothy (ORL)
Leveille, Andre (Japan)
Listecki, Jerome E. (CHI)
Loftus, Conrad, *o.f.m.*
Loth, Alan J. (OKL)
McCormick, Thomas, *s.j.*
McGrath, John (BLX)
McHale, Damian, *c.p.*
McHugh, James *c.p.*
McLoughlin, Patrick (United Kingdom)
McNally, Stephen (RIC)
McNicholas, Edward (BRK)
McQuilan, Cornelius, *c.s.sp.*
McSwigan, William, *c.s.sp.*
Madden, Paul J., *o.praem.*
Mages, Mark, *o.s.b.*
Majerus, Daniel (SCL)
Marsh, John, *c.ss.r.*
Martin, Michael, *o.s.b.*
Martinez, Anthony L. (SFE)
Massoth, Charles, *o.s.b.*
Matson, Mark, *c.r.*
Merfeld, Vincent (DUB)
Messaro, Michael, *m.ss.cc.*
Metsy, Norman (PRO)
Metzbower, Francis X., *s.j.*
Middendorf, Cyril, *s.m.*
Mooney, Msgr. Robert M. (PRO)
Morley, John
Mulhern, Joseph P., *o.p.*
Murphy, Dennis F., *s.a.*
Murphy, Msgr. Terrence J. (STP)
Nguyen, Huong Xuan (NO)
Nusbaum, Daniel C. (ALB)
O'Donnell, Brian, *s.j.*
O'Keeffe, Msgr. Richard W. (TUC)
O'Loughlin, Michael, *s.s.c.*
O'Neill, Joseph, *m.m.*
O'Neill, Keith, *o.f.m.conv.*
Olson, Benedict, *o.p.*
Perumpilly, Marcel (Bahrain)
Phillips, Christopher (SA)
Phillips, Randall (DET)
Picard, Norman, *c.i.c.m.*
Piskura, Joseph (CLV)
Power, Bernard, *c.ss.r.*
Quinlivan, Francis L., *c.s.c.*
Regan, John J. (BO)
Richardson, Edward, *s.m.a.*
Rimmele, Leo, *o.s.b.*
Roberson, Ronald G., *c.p.*
St. Pierre, Romeo A. (PRT)
Sanders, Peter, *c.o.*
Saucci, Robert R., *m.m.*
Scheller, John (OKL)
Schmidt, Raymond (BRK)
Schreiber, Gerard, *c.ss.r.*
Sego, Msgr. Arthur (LFT)
Shay, Michael, *s.d.s.*
Shay, Robert M., *s.t.*
Sierra, Frank (SD)
Simonelli, Bruno, *o.f.m.cap.*
Slater, Dennis (SY)
Smith, Ignatius E., *o.f.m.*
Smith, Msgr. Thomas (HBG)
Sousa, Peter, *c.ss.r.*
Spiteri, Joseph (Panama)
Stadmueller, Roman, *s.d.s.*
Steffener, Gerard J., *s.d.s.*
Succi, Vincento, *o.f.m.cap.*
Sueper, Alban A., *s.s.c.*
Sullivan, Alan, *o.f.m.*
Thelen, Robert (BRK)
Thomas, Donald (HON)
Tomas, Francisco (Azores)
Valenti, Palmo, *s.j.*
Valentino, Francis P., *s.j.*
Vaz, Rock I., *s.j.*
Waite, Patrick (SC)
Ward, Thomas, *s.f.*
Wood, Michael (SA)
Woster, Michael B. (RC)

DEPARTMENT OF VETERANS AFFAIRS HOSPITALS AND CHAPLAINS

Revs.
Richard Dunne (BRK), Chap. Mgr., Region I
Patrick Diffley (BRK), Prog. Mgr. for Continuing Education

ALABAMA

Birmingham Vacant.

Montgomery Vacant.

Tuscaloosa Vacant.

Tuskegee Vacant.

ARIZONA

Phoenix
Revs.
Kenneth R. Kleiber (CHI)
Peter F. Morello (GLP)
Bernard L. Young (NO)

Prescott
Revs.
Gerald J. Caffrey, *c.m.f.*
Jack G. Hencier, *c.m.f.*

Tucson Vacant.

ARKANSAS

Fayetteville
Rev.
Dennis M. Wood (LR)

North Little Rock
Revs.
Victor E. Bertrand, C.S.V.
Stephen Binz (LR)

CALIFORNIA

Fresno
Revs.
Richard F. Bevenour (DAV)
David LaPierre, *o.f.m.cap.*

Loma Linda
Rev.
Adolph Chavez (SB)

Long Beach
Revs.
Anselm T. Deehr, *s.t.*
Leo Miller, *o.m.i.*

Palo Alto
Revs.
John Kenneth Coleman (SFR)
Augustine Koilparampil (India)
Rev. Msgr.
William M. Roche (ROC)

San Diego
Revs.
Alred L. Fiorino, *s.j.*
Theodore Gryga (SY)
Jerry Hamperzonian (PSC)

San Francisco
Rev.
L. David Mani (India)

Sepulveda
Rev.
Patrick J. O'Hagan, *ss.cc.*

West Los Angeles
Revs.
Harry C. Cronin, *c.s.c.*
Francis Kelly (LA)
Jonathan D. Lao (Philippines)

COLORADO

Denver
Rev.
Thomas J. Woerth (DEN)

Fort Lyon
Rev.
Philip J. Coury, *c.m.*

Grand Junction Vacant.

CONNECTICUT

Newington
Rev.
Francis Vella (OAK)

West Haven
Rev.
Daniel Scott, *m.s.*

DELAWARE

Wilmington
Revs.
Sean P. Connery, *o.s.f.s.*
William J. Dougherty, *o.s.f.s*

DISTRICT OF COLUMBIA

Revs.
John A. D'Antonio, *o.praem.*
John W. Kobza, *m.i.c.*
Luis Picazo, *s.f.*
John A. Welch, *m.s.*

FLORIDA

Bay Pines
Revs.
Daniel P. Greene (YAK)
Arthur D. Murray, *o.f.m.*
E. Matthew Turk, *s.j.*

Gainesville
Rev.
Francisco Revilla (STA)

Lake City
Rev.
Anthony Sebra (STA)

Miami
Revs.
J. Patrick Byrne (COL)
Gerardo Freire, *s.j.*
John W. Murray (CHI)

Tampa
Revs.
Jeldo J. Schiavone (LFT)
Robert Schindler (Mexico)

West Palm Beach
Rev.
Sebastian L. Muccilli (MET)

GEORGIA

Augusta
Rev.
P. James Costigan (SAV)

Decatur
Rev.
Thad B. Rudd (ATL)

Dublin Vacant.

IDAHO

Boise
Rev.
Donald J. Riffle (B)

ILLINOIS

Chicago—Lakeside
Revs.
Robert J. Borre (MAD)
Sebastian A. Ugochukwu (Nigeria)

Chicago—West Side
Rev.
John Carroll (CHI)

Danville
Rev.
John Schultz (LFT)

Hines
Revs.
John G. Birk (SPK)
Max E.M. Saldua (Philippines)

Marion
Rev.
Richard G. Mohr (BEL)

North Chicago
Revs.
Edward E. Lisowski (MIL)
Paul B. McDermott (PEO)
William Vander Heyden (GB)

INDIANA

Fort Wayne
Rev.
Daniel R. Leeuw (FTW)

Indianapolis
Revs.
Joseph Kiene, *o.f.m.conv.*
Gordon P. Wagoner (LFT)

Marion
Revs.
Joseph W. Grace (FTW)
Edward Narcowich (FTW)
August Reemmer (FTW)
James R. Rose (FTW)

IOWA

Des Moines
Rev.
Paul S. Holt (WDC)

Iowa City
Revs.
Andrew E. Kelly (DAV)
Louis J. Leonhart (DAV)

Knoxville
Rev.
Mark Swanson (DAV)

KANSAS

Leavenworth
Rev.
Ambrose Karels (KC)

Topeka
Rev.
James E. Moster, *o.f.m.cap.*

Wichita
Rev.
David W. Linnebur (WCH)

KENTUCKY

Lexington
Revs.
Wilton Henry Kenney, *s.j.*
George Maynard, *s.j.*

Louisville
Revs.
Simon Sauer, *o.f.m.conv.*
John L. Weyhing (L)

LOUISIANA

Alexandria
Revs.
Joseph S. Hasieber (ALX)
Wallace F. Przybylski, *o.f.m.*

New Orleans
Revs.
Lawrence A. DeMaria (NO)
Joseph Laboon (PIT)

Shreveport
Rev.
Philip Michiels (ALX)

MAINE

Togus
Rev.
Francis J. Kane (PRT)

MARYLAND

Baltimore
Revs.
Avelino R. Garcia (SP)
Casimir Pugevicius (BAL)

Fort Howard
Rev.
Conan H. Timoney, *c.p.*

Perry Point
Rev.
John J. Abrahams (BAL)

MASSACHUSETTS

Bedford
Revs.
Philip Cabasino, *c.ss.r.*
Ronald Lawson (Montreal)
Joseph P. Robinson (BO)
Aidan J. Walsh (BO)

Boston
Revs.
Philip Salois (FR)
Roger A. Sinclair (GBG)

Brockton
Revs.
Patrick McShane (CLV)
Austin Nagle, *ss.cc.*
Henry Nichols (BO)

Northampton
Rev.
Lionel E. Bonneville (SPR)

MICHIGAN

Ann Arbor
Rev.
Vincent VanDoan (LAN)

Battle Creek
Revs.
Juan Porras-Landeo (Peru)
Michael Stafford, *o.s.b.*

Detroit
Revs.
John P. Melepuram (India)
Joseph Duc Vu (Vietnam)

Iron Mountain
Rev.
Patrick E. Murphy (MAR)

Saginaw
Revs.
Richard E. Jozwiak (SAG)
Joseph A. Schabel (SAG)

MINNESOTA

Minneapolis
Revs.
Joseph N. Safraniec (STU)
Richard F. Skluzacek (STP)

St. Cloud
Revs.
Lloyd Haupt (SCL)
Alfred E. Stangl (SCL)

MISSISSIPPI

Biloxi
Rev. Msgr.
M. Francis Farrell (BLX)
Revs.
Joseph A. Dilettuso (BLX)
Denis Harlow (BLX)
Frank X. Popeleski, *m.ss.a.*

Jackson
Rev.
Daniel N. Gallagher (JKS)

MISSOURI

Columbia
Rev.
Eugene J. Robl (JC)

Kansas City
Revs.
Thomas J. Cronin (KC)
Ambrose Karels (KC)

Poplar Bluff
Rev.
Michael V. McDevitt (SPC)

St. Louis
Revs.
George P. Brennan (STL)
Raymond Joyce (WCH)
John H. Schneider (STL)

MONTANA

Fort Harrison Vacant.

Miles City Vacant.

NEBRASKA

Grand Island
Revs.
Donald O'Brien (GI)
Walter M. Phelan (GI)
David L. Rykwalder (GI)

Lincoln
Revs.
Thomas Holoman (LIN)
Edwin L. Stander (LIN)

Omaha
Rev.
Richard Wolbach (OM)

NEVADA

Las Vegas
Rev.
Gerard J. McNulty (LA)

Reno Vacant.

NEW HAMPSHIRE

Manchester
Rev.
Francis A. Talbot (MAN)

NEW JERSEY

East Orange
Revs.
Thomas J. Davis, *o.f.m.cap.*
James Sagala (PAT)

Lyons
Revs.
Joseph C. Chacko (India)
George F. Kelly, *c.ss.r.*
William Warman (BAL)

NEW MEXICO

Albuquerque
Revs.
Leonard L. Bayer (SFE)
Julian M. Rousseau, *s.s.s.*

NEW YORK

Albany
Revs.
Paul J. Antos (ALB)
Martin J. Fisher (ALB)
James R. McNerney (ALB)
John Minkler (ALB)
Charles S. San Fratello, *o.f.m.*
Paul P. Tartaglia (ALB)
Gregory S. Weider (ALB)

Batavia
Revs.
Donald W. Becker (BUF)
John P. Bernard (CAM)

Bath
Rev.
Ronald A. Marecki (CHL)

Bronx
Revs.
Roland P. LaFontant (France)
Gregory Lyttle (NY)
Rev. Msgr.
Joseph J. Zammit (NY)

Brooklyn
Revs.
Robert Chalany, *o.s.b.*
James Devine (BRK)
Joseph M. Gleeson (NY)
Luke M. Karpil (Philippines)
Thomas J. Mullin (NY)
Vito Tiboni (NEW)

Buffalo
Revs.
Francis Chmielewski (BUF)
Clatus E. Snyder (BUF)

Canandaigua
Revs.
Miecislaus Curzydlo, *s.a.c.*
George Maj, *s.a.c.*
Francis Vogt (ROC)

Castle Point
Revs.
John W. Borzuchowski (NY)
Robert J. Brennan (NY)
Uldarico De la Pena (Philippines)
Donald B. Licata (NY)
Raymond A. Pavlick (PAT)

Montrose
Revs.
Daniel Lynch, *o.carm.*
Robert D. Tracy, *o.carm.*

New York City
Revs.
Bernardine P. Laghezza, *ss.cc.*
Frederick McCaffrey, *o.carm.*
Francis Morgan, *ss.cc.*

Northport
Revs.
Eugene Jarcynski, *c.s.c.*
Augustine Sheehan (RVC)

Syracuse
Revs.
Wilfred F. Evans (SY)
David J. James (SY)
Gregory C. LeStrange (SY)

NORTH CAROLINA

Asheville
Rev.
Andrew J. Latsko (CHL)

Durham Vacant.

Fayetteville Vacant.

Salisbury
Rev.
Thomas P. Clements (CHL)

NORTH DAKOTA

Fargo Vacant.

OHIO

Chillicothe
Rev.
Richard F. Engle (COL)
Rev. Msgr.
A. Anthony Frecker (COL)

Cincinnati
Rev.
Warren Zeisler, *o.f.m.*

Cleveland
Revs.
John Bolan, *c.pp.s.*
Thomas J. Gallagher (CLV)

Dayton
Revs.
John J. Butler (HON)
J. Luis Fernandez (NO)

OKLAHOMA

Muskogee Vacant.

Oklahoma City Vacant.

OREGON

Portland
Rev.
William Wickham, *c.s.c.*

Roseburg
Rev.
Leroy Calkins, *o.s.m.*

White City
Revs.
Donald H. Salisbury, *o.p.*
Joseph Shirey, *s.j.*

PENNSYLVANIA

Altoona
Rev.
Edward Dabcosky (ALT)

Butler
Revs.
Henry Preneta (GBG)
William J. Ritzert (PIT)

Coatesville
Rev.
McKinley E. Williams (RIC)

Erie
Revs.
Robert G. Craig (E)
Thomas M. Fialkowski (E)

Lebanon
Revs.
D. Gilbert Sweeney, *s.j.*
Dennis M. Young (STA)

Philadelphia
Revs.
Edward V. Griffin, *o.s.a.*
Joseph Griffin, *o.s.f.s.*
James E. King (NTN)

Pittsburgh—Highland Drive
Revs.
Frank A. Mitolo (PIT)
Pascall J. Schaller, *o.f.m.cap.*
Emett J. Schuler, *o.f.m.cap.*

Pittsburgh—University Drive
Revs.
Mark W. Glasgow (PIT)
John M. Jendzura, *c.s.sp.*
Ralph Zehe, *o.f.m.cap.*

Wilkes-Barre
Revs.
Benjamin Foerch, *o.f.m.*
Valentine R. Plevyak (SCR)

RHODE ISLAND

Providence
Rev.
Francis J. Crowley (BO)

SOUTH CAROLINA

Charleston
Rev.
William C. Burn (CHR)

Columbia Vacant.

SOUTH DAKOTA

Fort Meade
Rev.
Paul Dahms (RC)

Hot Springs
Rev.
Thomas Tierney, *s.j.*

Sioux Falls
Rev.
Kenneth J. Koster (SFS)

TENNESSEE

Memphis
Rev.
John J. Behnke, *c.s.p.*

Mountain Home Vacant.

Murfreesboro
Rev.
R. Orville Briscoe (NSH)

Nashville
Rev.
James Norman Miller (NSH)

TEXAS

Amarillo
Rev.
Francis Crowe, *o.p.*

Big Spring
Rev.
Christopher Coleman, *m.s.c.*

Bonham
Rev.
Jerome Jayasuriya (DAL)

Dallas
Rev.
Timothy Gollob (DAL)

Houston
Revs.
Peter Girardin (BO)
Clarito Z. Rara (Philippines)

Kerrville
Rev.
Tony Vilano (SAT)

Marlin Vacant.

San Antonio
Revs.
Richard R. Benonis (PH)
Ralph Intranuovo, *s.c.j.*
Harry Martin (SAT)

Temple
Rev.
Harry Bilski (AUS)

Waco
Revs.
Richard J. Beyer (DAV)
Thomas Niemira (JKS)

UTAH

Salt Lake City
Rev.
Gebran Bou-Merhi (SAM)

VERMONT

White River Junction
Revs.
Adrien Pelletier, *s.m.*
Ronald Saunders, *s.m.*

VIRGINIA

Hampton
Revs.
Donald Cavey (RIC)
Lloyd F. Stephenson (RIC)

Richmond
Rev.
Benedict R. McDermott, *o.s.b.*

Salem
Rev.
Wayne L. Ball (RIC)

WASHINGTON

Seattle
Rev.
Thomas R. Park, *o.s.b.*

Spokane
Rev.
George H. McCabe (SPK)

Tacoma
Revs.
David Prebula, *o.s.b.*
Leo R. Rimmele, *o.s.b.*

Walla Walla
Rev.
Otto Koltzenburg (SPK)

WEST VIRGINIA

Beckley
Rev.
Frank A. O'Kruta (WH)

Clarksburg
Rev.
George J. Romage (WH)

Huntington Vacant.

Martinsburg
Revs.
William E. Coen, *s.t.*
William J. Nolte, Jr. (WH)
T. Matthew Rowgh (WH)
Bert W. Valdes (WH)
Rev. Msgr.
Stephen McCarren (GBG)

WISCONSIN

Madison
Rev.
Lawrence Heitke (MAD)

Milwaukee
Revs.
Lawrence W. Koncewicz, *c.m.*
James F. Kovarik, *o.s.cam.*
Norman Oswald (MIL)

Tomah
Rev.
Myles J. Kenny, *c.s.sp.*

WYOMING

Cheyenne Vacant.

Sheridan
Revs.
John B. Norton, *o.p.*
Eugene P. Sullivan (CHY)

PUERTO RICO

San Juan
Revs.
Hector Diaz (SJN)
Luis A. Lopez-Alvarado (CGS)
Jose F. Quintero (SJN)

RESERVE CHAPLAINS

Reverends

Abreu, Felix, *c.s.s.p.*
Acosta, Humberto (BWN)
Albrecht, Louis (BAK)
Almendras, Joel (MRY)
Ameling, Richard H. (GRY)
Amora, Edito (Philippines)
Anderson, Ronald C. (BWN)
Anderson, Terence R. (SF)
Arens, John F. (BO)
Arroyo, Brigido (Guam)
Austin, Walter (NO)
Baggetta, Joseph J. (BO)
Bailey, Douglas, *s.d.s.*
Bain, John K. (RNO)
Baratelli, David (NEW)
Barber, Michael, *s.j.*
Barnhill, Robert K. (LIN)
Barry, Robert L., *o.p.*
Becker, Donald W. (BUF)
Beers, Michael (ALN)
Belanger, Gerald R.
Berberich, Thomas E. (HRT)
Bergbower, Daniel J. (SPC)
Bill, Ronald C. (SY)
Blais, Robert L. (PRO)
Blascovich, Joseph D. (HBG)
Blessin, Thomas C., *s.j.*
Bolduc, Norman P., Jr. (MAN)
Bonnot, Bernard R. (Y)
Bowe, John F. (PH)
Bower, Alan (STA)
Bower, Lawrence (BAK)
Brando, Joseph (KNX)
Bratko, Kenneth R., *c.r.*
Breaux, Duane (BR)
Brennan, Brian C. (NY)
Brinkmann, Frederick C., *c.ss.r.*
Broussard, Andre (NO)
Brown, William (SF)
Bruckner, Ronald L. (SFE)
Bruno, Anthony J. (HRT)
Bryan, Allen K. (BUF)
Bucon, Raymond H. (DET)
Burns, Malcolm (GAL)
Butler, Michael (STL)
Butler, William L. (BO)
Cain, Robert (TLS)
Calderone, Joseph D., *o.s.a.*
Canez, Jorge A. (PHX)
Cannon, Richard (BO)
Cannon, Robert (VEN)
Caputo, Louis, *s.d.v.*
Carmody, James F. (WOR)
Caron, David (BO)
Carter, Eli K., Jr. (HON)
Casaleggio, David (RNO)
Charbonneau, William R. (HRT)
Chavez, Filimon (SFE)
Chavez, Johnny Lee (SFE)
Chimiak, Karl A. (WDC)
Clark, John S., *s.s.s.*
Clarke, Thomas J., *c.s.c.*
Coby, Thomas W. (RVC)
Collogan, Robert E. (JOL)
Condron, Patrick
Congro, Basil (CHR)
Connor, Kevin (MAN)
Coogan, Roch A., *o.f.m.*
Coulthard, Gregory
Cordery, Robert (BO)
Coyle, Robert J. (RVC)
Cregan, James A. (STA)
Crews, John S. (SR)
Criqui, Joseph (STL)
Crosby, Msgr. Charles E. (MAN)
Crotty, Desmond (NO)
Cuevas, Randy M. (BR)
Cunningham, Douglas (SY)
Curcio, Ralph V. (NY)
Curley, Thomas J. (NY)
Dare, Glenn O. (PRT)
Darling, William G. (ROC)
Dawson, John H. (LA)
Decker, Douglas A. (OG)
DePorter, Arnold (WDC)
Dermott, William R. (ALN)
DeSanctis, Peter A. (BRK)
DeSocia, John (ROC)
Diacetis, Anthony (ALB)
Diegel, Ronald (FRS)
Diesta, Arwyn N. (Philippines)
DiLella, Mario (ATL)
Dinello, John E. (PIT)
Dolbec, Jacques D. (CC)
Donahue, Brian G. (FAR)
Donahue, John G. (STP)
Donohoe, Richard (BIR)
Donohue, Michael T. (NOR)
Doran, John E. (WOR)
Dougherty, William J. (PH)
Dowds, James, *c.ss.r.*
Dowling, Joseph K. (NSH)
Doyle, Michael J. (BO)
Doyle, Vincent J. (NEW)
Durbin, Samuel E. (COL)
Duzza, Donald (ALT)
Dziedzic, Gerald H. (HRT)
Echevia, Les Suberi (Philippines)
Emechete, Innocent A. (SAC; Nigeria)
Engelbrecht, Henry (NO)
English, Robert L., *c.o.*
Erikson, Richard M. (BOS)
Esquibel, Msgr. John L. (SFE)
Esterka, Peter (STP)
Ethen, Jeffrey (SCL)
Everett, Willis E. (COL)
Faraci, Douglas F. (BUF)
Farana, Mario P. (SFR)
Fawcett, Msgr. Henry F. (SD)
Feltis, Jerome (FAR)
Fernandes, Stephen (FR)
Fialkowski, Thomas M. (E)
Fischer, Richard O. (BAK)
Fitzgibbons, Peter (CHL)
Fitz-Henry, Edward (MRY)
Fitzpatrick, Robert M. (OM)
Flanigan, Thomas P. (PH)
Fleta, Heraclio (Philippines)
Flores, Jose (ARE)
Follett, John E. (CAM)
Folsom, Paul (SCL)
Foote, John, *o.s.b.*
Foster, Raymond, *o.carm.*
Fredericks, Michael (SB)
Gaeta, Bernard N. (Y)
Gaglione, John R. (BUF)
Gale, Robert V. (BO)
Gallagher, John P. (DAV)
Gallagher, William (BUF)
Garcia, Millan J., *s.f.*
Gayton, John, *m.i.c.*
Gerber, Francis J. (DEN)
Gerres, Daniel (WIL)
Giese, Samuel (WDC)
Gills, Thomas (BAL)
Giordani, Mark J. (PAT)
Girardin, Peter T. (BO)
Glasgow, Thomas (NO)
Granadino, David F. (LA)
Greig, Harry D. (LAF)
Grice, Edward M. (NO)
Griffin, Thomas E., *o.s.a.*
Grizzelle-Reid, Paul, *s.c.j.*
Gross, Gary L. (LIN)
Guidry, Kevin James (ATL)
Hadnett, William D. (LA)
Hagearty, Charles (BGP)
Hamaday, Ronald A., *o.s.a.*
Hannigan, John (CHI)
Hargrove, Jerry E. (WDC)
Hart, John B. (SLC)
Hays, Michael D. (SEA)
Healy, Stephen M. (BOS)
Hebert, Donald J. (SY)
Hellwig, Lee (HRT)
Hendel, Lawrence M. (SJ)
Henke, James T. (SA)
Henson, Jerome M., *o.p.*
Herbert, G. Paul (WDC)
Herzog, Ronald P. (BLX)
Hewes, Robert (RVC)
Hill, Donald W. (BIS)
Hoffman, Christopher (ORL)
Hogan, Michael J. (CHI)
Holland, William (SAC)
Honan, Eugene D. (SPR)
Howard, James (ALP)
Howard, Mark S. (STP)
Hower, William (MAD)
Hubbs, Timothy (SCR)
Hudak, Thomas R. (SCR)
Hubmann, William, *c.pp.s.*
Hughes, Donald R. (BUF)
Hurley, Paul K. (BO)
Isopo, Dominic (ALB)
Jackson, James (WCH)
Jackson, Robert (CLV)
Jacques, Roger N. (BO)
Jaeger, James (ROC)
Jankowski, Daniel (CHI)
Jindra, Frank (OM)
Johannes, Nicholas A. (GB)
Johnson, James B. (SP)
Johnson, Lawrence (DUL)
Jones, Michael (WDC)
Judge, Timothy M. (PH)
Kadera, Thomas (CHY)
Kahlich, Daniel (SA)
Kane, Edward R. (BRK)
Kasprzyk, James (BUF)
Kaszcak, Ivan (STF)
Kayatta, Francis P. (PRO)
Keenan, Patrick J. (NY)
Kehoe, James P. (CHI)
Keller, Robert J. (DET)
Keller, Thomas W. (LR)
Kelly, C. Richard, Jr. (DET)
Kiene, Joseph L., *o.f.m.conv.*
Kinnane, James F. (HRT)
Kinney, Thomas E. (NO)
Kiselica, John J., *s.m.*
Ko Suk, Joon (Seoul)
Koster, Kenneth J. (SF)
Kozen, Bert S. (SCR)
Krische, James (BR)
Krough, Jack Lee (WIN)
Kuczborski, Joseph (PEO)
Kukucka, Joseph (PBL)
Kurzak, John F. (SC)
Labo, Timothy (ORL)
Ladniak, Lawrence J. (CHI)
Laible, Jeffrey (PEO)
LaMorte, Joseph P. (NY)
Lane, Frank (COL)
Lang, James P. (Y)
Langan, William J.P. (SCR)
Langston, Micheas, *o.s.b.*
Larche, James (OG)
Laroche, Christopher (PRT)
Lazarek, John D. (PSC)
Legaspi, Alex (SFR)
Leone, William B. (ROC)
Linsky, Gary S. (CHR)
Lioi, Phillip J. (ROC)
Listecki, Jerome E. (CHI)
Logan, Aidan, *o.c.s.o.*
Lomax, Mark (NO)
Lordemann, Francis W. (OM)
Lott, Lawrence M. (MOB)
Lyle, John W., *o.s.f.s.*
McCabe, Kenneth O., *ss.cc.*
McCarthy, James C. (HEL)
McConville, James P. (STP)
McDonald, G. Malcolm (PIT)
McGinnis, James J. (PH)
McGrade, Kevin (BO)
McGuill, Martin F. (ARL)
McGuine, Peter (SD)
McHugh, Brian (BO)
McInnis, Francis L. (GF)
McLaughlin, Richard P. (BO)
McNalis, John P. (CHI)
McNamara, Brian J. (RVC)
McNulty, Gerard J.
Macek, Joseph S., *s.s.j.*
Mack, John (BUF)
Madden, James J., *o.praem.*
Maguire, Stephen (NY)
Mahalic, Philip A. (LAF)
Maikowski, Thomas R. (GLP)
Manzo, Louis A., *c.s.c.*
Marcantonio, Robert (PRO)
Marcinano, Robert (PRO)
Martinez, Vidal (SFE)
Maskell, Anthony J. (BAL)
Mathis, Raymond P. (SY)
Matienzo, Ariel R. (Arecibo)
Maughan, Richard N. (NO)
Mazziotta, Richard, *c.s.c.*
Medairos, Anthony (BO)
Meier, Denis E. (SFS)
Merrell, Arthur (PIT)
Mescher, Michael (DUB)
Messier, Joseph H. (BUR)
Metzdorf, William C. (WDC)
Midura, Francis S. (RVC)
Miller, Robert A. (NEW)
Mink, John (WIL)
Mitolo, Frank A. (PIT)
Mizeur, Thomas R. (PEO)
Mockler, Patrick (BLX)
Molloy, Msgr. Thomas E. (RVC)
Mongale, Robert J. (BO)
Moore, William (STO)
Moran, Michael (MIL)
Morgan, Gerald (NY)
Morgan, Thomas T. (SP)
Moss, Robert D. (BUF)
Motta, Anthony (ALB)
Muhm, William J. (NY)
Mullin, Thomas (NY)
Murray, Gerald (NY)
Musni, Eduardo (Philippines)
Naughton, William M. (PAT)
Neitzke, Ron (JOL)
Nenneau, Thomas D. (LAN)

Neuman, Eugene C. (MIL)
Nguyen, Van T. (NO)
Nishigaya, Raymond J. (HON)
Nolan, Kevin L. (LA)
Noone, Charles J. (PH)
O'Brien, Sean (SY)
O'Carroll, Eugene R. (PHX)
O'Connor, John L. (ROC)
O'Donoghue, John J. (SA)
O'Grady, J. Frank (PAT)
O'Hara, Daniel (SY)
O'Hear, Daniel J. (SPR)
O'Leary, David M. (BO)
O'Malley, John J., *o.p.*
Oberts, David P. (SUP)
Ohm, Edward U. (PEO)
Oge, Raymond J. (STL)
Orlandi, Joseph (PAT)
Orzel, David (SY)
Ornelas, Angel, Jr. (CHY)
Padazinski, Michael (SFR)
Parenti, Thomas M. (SFR)
Parker, Paul R. (BO)
Parker, Thomas (SR)
Passamonti, Paul (WDC)
Pelletier, George C. (PRT)
Penkaul, Joseph H. (BUF)
Peoples, Joseph E. (HEL)
Perez, Gregory (AUS)
Pfeiffer, Carl A., *o.ss.t.*
Piekarczyk, Marian, *s.d.s.*.
Piontkowski, Richard (GI)
Pizza, Albert J. (CHI)
Plaushin, Mark F., *o.s.f.s.*
Pleiness, Gregg A. (LAN)
Polk, Thomas T. (BAL)
Posey, Thaddeus J., *o.f.m.cap.*
Prez, Daniel J. (E)
Prinz, Gerald (HT)
Quinn, James A. (MIA)
Randall, Kevn S. (NOR)
Rapp, James F., *o.s.f.s.*
Reamer, Mark, *o.f.m.*
Reeson, David G. (OM)
Renard, John F. (NEW)
Reyes, Marco (LA)
Rigdon, Vincent J. (WDC)
Rimassa, Paul (TR)
Rivera-Saez, Adalin (PCE)
Robbins, Thomas (COV)
Roberson, Henry (OKL)
Robert, Darin Thomass (LAN)
Robichaud, Paul G., *c.s.p.*
Rogers, Francis J. (WIL)
Rogers, Patrick W. (COL)
Rowan, Mark (RVC)
Rowe, William (SAC)
Russo, Richardo, *o.f.m.*
Ryan, Kenneth (NO)
Sable, Robert (DET)
Sacus, Samuel S. (WH)
St. Martin, Robert J. (HRT)
Saldua, Max (Philippines)
Scalone, Jonathan (FWT)
Schaff, Tyrone J. (SP)
Schaub, Gregory P., *o.s.b.*
Scheer, John R., *s.a.c.*
Schindler, Carl A., *c.ss.r.*
Schultz, Charles F. (SB)
Seminack, Richard S. (PH)
Sera, Enrique J. (ORG)
Sewell, Jack K. (ORG)
Shannon, Richard (CHI)
Shea, Michael J. (SFE)
Sheehan, Joseph P. (PH)
Shuppert, William (TUC)
Sickler, Robert, *m.ss.a.*
Siesle, John W., Jr. (STL)
Silva, Caesar (HT)
Silvestri, Anthony F., *o.s.f.s.*
Sippel, Bernard S. (MIL)
Sirianni, Richard D. (P)
Skufca, Ronald (MAR)
Slowinski, Thomas (DET)
Smith, Francis J. (ELP)
Smith, Gabriel (CHR)
Smith, Lawrence H. (BRK)
Sousa, Peter S., *c.ss.r.*
Spellman, John, *o.s.f.s.*
Spencer, F. Richard (BAL)
Spiegel, Thomas J. (DAV)
Stakem, Ward G., *o.f.m.cap.*
Staley, Robert (R)
Stang, William, *c.pp.s.*
Staszewski, Joseph P. (E)
Staszewski, Robert M. (PIT)
Stefula, Salvatore M., *t.o.r.*
Steiner, John W. (LC)
Stenson, Patrick J., *m.s.c.*
Stephenson, Alfonse (PAT)
Sticco, Peter, *s.a.c.*
Stites, John F. (TOL)
Strittmatter, Lawrence R. (CIN)
Studniewski, Gary (WDC)
Sturn, Michael L. (SB)
Suellentrop, Anthony (DOD)
Sullivan, Daniel James (HRT)
Sullivan, Robert J. (BIR)
Sutton, Stephen R. (BAL)
Szczesniak, Harry F. (BUF)
Tamalis, John J. (SCR)
Taylor, Samuel J. (NY)
Taylor, Thomas (LAN)
Tejada, Denis J. (LC)
Tero, Richard D. (ANC)
Tetreault, Raymond A. (PRO)
Theroux, Paul D. (PRO)
Thomas, Royce R. (LR)
Thompson, Richard B. (MAN)
Thorne, Thomas P. (BGP)
Toner, Patrick A. (COL)
Torsiello, Ralph C. (WDC)
Trabold, George R. (NEW)
Tracy, Robert D., *o.carm.*
Tran, Philip (NY)
Travers, Patrick (JUN)
Troutman, Richard E. (TUC)
Tuite, Thomas (RVC)
Tyrrell, Robert D. (BO)
Uhde, Peter M. (NEW)
Urnick, Charles B. (NEW)
Vakoc, Henry T. (STP)
Valdez, Paul (MRY)
Valenzano, Joseph A. (BRK)
Valko, George J. (ALT)
Vandeberg, Joseph (SCL)
Ventura, John J. (BIR)
Verbrugghe, Albert E. (TUC)
Vialpando, Kenneth L. (SLC)
Vigil, Michael (GLP)
Vigilanti, John A. (NY)
Vucinovich, Albert P. (SFR)
Wagner, William c. (CIN)
Waibel, Philip, *o.s.b.*
Weber, Joseph A. (STL)
Wedeking, Patrick (GLP)
Weisner, Mark (OAK)
Welton, Arthur T. (NY)
Wendel, Alfred W. (CHY)
Wielunski, Gregory C. (BRK)
Willette, Donald (DEN)
Williams, Ronald R. (DET)
Wilz, John C. (PH)
Wojtasczyk, John S. (CC)
Woods, Curtis W. (ALX)
Worster, John (B)
Wulinski, Stanley (BRK)
Zeck, George F. (DUL)
Ziemkiewicz, Frank, *o.s.b.*
Zientek, Benedict J. (SAN)
Zizka, Peter J. (HRT)
Zotter, Thomas (SF)
Zygadlo, Mitchell (ROC)

CIVIL AIR PATROL CHAPLAINS

Reverends
Albrecht, Louis H. (BAK)
Allen, Joseph P. (CHI)
Berean, Christopher H. (NY)
Birk, John G. (SPK)
Bolduc, Gerard, *o.m.i.*
Booth, Edward N. (STA)
Borkowski, Thomas (KC)
Breski, Martin A., *o.f.m.conv.*
Broderick, John F., *s.j.*
Brown, John T. (OWN)
Cameron, Albert S. (MAN)
Cantlow, Cronan (BAL)
Carney, John J. (BAL)
Caron, Eduardo J., *c.s.sp.*
Carpenter, Frank David, *s.m.m.*
Churchill, Raymond (HON)
Connolly, James M. (ALN)
Coogan, Roch A. (SAV)
Cosmen, Basilio, *o.p.*
Crowley, Francis J. (BO)
DeCrans, Joseph J. (CR)
Demeck, Norman, *c.p.*
DeMure, Salvatore Patrick (HRT)
Devorak, James W. (NU)
Diener, John E. (CIN)
Dignan, Thomas L. (BIS)
Dupuis, George H. (BUR)
Duran, Alphonsus M., *m.j.*
Ebner, Frank H. (SCL)
Elliott, Edward C. (MEM)
Emala, Walter (MEM)
Falsey, James F. (FBK)
Farland, David M. (SPR)
Feltz, John G. (BUR)
Fisette, Kevin R. (PRO)
Fitzgerald, John P. (PIT)
Friederick, John J. (DUB)
Gildea, Arthur P., *c.ss.r.*
Goeser, Peter J., *o.s.b.*
Greer, Michael G. (COV)
Guischard, John A. (BUR)
Hayden, Joseph M. (CAM)
Heinlein, John (RVC)
Hencier, Jack G., *c.m.f.*
Hennington, Bruce M. (MAD)
Hoffmaster, Harry E. (DET)
Hurley, Most Rev. Francis T. (ANC)
Jakobiak, Arthur (SFE)
Jenner, David C. (MAR)
Kaiser, Joseph W. (RCK)
Kaszczak, Ivan (STF)
Kelley, James F. (FR)
Kelly, George F., *c.ss.r.*
Kennelly, James J. (E)
Kiernan, R. Donald (ATL)
King, James E. (NTN)
Kost, Harold J. (SCL)
Kovarik, James, *o.s.cam.* (MIL)
Kremeier, James (GI)
Kukucka, Joseph G. (PBL)
LaBuda, David E., *m.m.*
Lamitie, Robert O. (OG)
LaPlante, Jean Paul (BUR)
McCarthy, William J., *m.ss.a.*
McClure, John A. (TOL)
McGuire, Richard J. (E)
Maag, Ronald (BAK)
Males, John A. (TLS)
Mallette, Lawrence E. (OG)
Maskell, Anthony J. (BAL)
Merrill, Arthur R. (PIT)
Michalski, Thaddeus (CLV)
Miller, Bruce (ALX)
Miller, James N. (NSH)
Mulhearn, James M., *c.m.*
Nevins, Albert J., *m.m.*
Nollette, Neal P. (GI)
O'Connell, Msgr. James E. (LR)
O'Grady, Frank (PAT)
Ondik, Michael J. (CLV)
Orlando, Vincent, *s.j.*
Parker, James (CHR)
Parsons, John F. (CHL)
Petrini, Aldo (WDC)
Phillips, George M. (OG)
Ratchford, Robert J., *s.j.*
Richard, Edward D. (MAN)
Roggenbaum, James G. (E)
Scanlan, Cornelius J. (JUN)
Scanlan, Francis G. (CHI)
Schaefer, Roman J. (MIA)
Sevigny, Robert, *o.m.i.*
Shamsher, Paul (HRT)
Shortt, David J. (PBR)
Smith, Hubert J., *c.ss.r.*
Smith, Lawrence C., *s.j.*
Sommer, Allan J. (MIL)
Strachota, Dennis J. (BAL)
Smith, Lawrence C., *s.j.*
Therrien, Shawn M. (MAN)
Vaughan, Richard F. (AMA)
Voity, Maurice J. (SAN)
Wallace, Robert F. (PIT)
Walters, James L. (LR)
Weber, Gabriel M., *o.s.m.*
Whitney, Peter (GAL)
Williams, John L. (HRT)
Winkels, Robert H., *m.m.*

PERMANENT DEACONS SERVING IN THE ARCHDIOCESE FOR THE MILITARY SERVICES

AMS Chancery
Deacon
Crowley, Ronald C.

Air Force
Deacons
Bonanno, Frederick R.
Ellis, Billy Joe
Jachimowicz, John J.
Kuntz, Edward E.
Leavitt, James P.
McAtee, Ralph H., Jr.
Moseley, Phil
Neville, Richard F.
Perry, Robert W.
Pfleger, James W.
Pinto, Richard A.
Prentiss, Richard C.
Richardson, Walter H.
Sarver, Richard H.
Scarbo, David
Sekinger, Eugene E.
Sheldon, Lawrence F.
Yarawsky, William S.

Air National Guard
Deacon
Sloan, Joseph S.

Army
Deacons
Adam, Klaus M.
Dew, Joseph M.
Foster, George H.
Holbritter, Milton A.
Horne, Wilfred
Jones, Frederick, Jr.
Miller, Larry L.
Plowman, Kent M.
Rienzi, Thomas M.
Rowland, Robert D.
Schoebel, James G.
Shuffer, George M.

National Guard
Deacon
Salchert, John J.

Navy
Deacons
Castellana, Alphonse J.
Cortezano, Alfredo M.
Enderle, Francis X.
Gubatan, Nemsy, Jr.
Henn, Thomas W.
Ladouceur, Gerald J.
McGlade, Henry D.
McMahon, Anthony
Nartowicz, Edward C.
Pellosie, John C.
Pepe, Joseph
Ryan, Richard

Marines
Deacons
Hernandez, Nieves J.
Meader, James A.
Schmitt, Giles V.

State Department
Deacon
Perez, Julio

Veterans Administration
Deacons
Abler, Donald J.
Hare, Martin
Luft, Dennis M.
Menke, Richard A.
Muccio, Anthony V.
Rinkus, Louis
Salchert, John J.
Watson, John W.

Civil Air Patrol
Deacon
Schaible, John A.

DIOCESES WITH PRIESTS SERVING IN THE ARCHDIOCESE FOR THE MILITARY SERVICES

Albany
Alexandria
Allentown
Altoona-Johnstown
Amarillo
Arlington
Atlanta
Austin
Baltimore
Baton Rouge
Beaumont
Belleville
Bridgeport
Bismarck
Biloxi
Boise
Boston
Brooklyn
Buffalo
Burlington
Caguas, Puerto Rico
Camden
Canton (Romanian Catholic Diocese of St. George)
Caroline Islands
Charleston
Charlotte
Cheyenne
Chicago
Cincinnati
Cleveland
Columbus
Corpus Christi
Covington
Dallas
Davenport
Denver
Detroit
Dodge City
Dubuque
Duluth
El Paso
Erie
Fall River
Fargo
Fort Wayne-South Bend
Gallup
Galveston-Houston
Grand Island
Grand Rapids
Great Falls-Billings
Green Bay
Greensburg
Hartford
Helena
Honolulu
Houma-Thibodaux
Indianapolis
Jackson
Jefferson City
Kansas City
Kansas City-St. Joseph
LaCrosse
Lafayette, IN
Lafayette, LA
Lansing
Lincoln
Little Rock
Los Angeles
Louisville
Lubbock
Madison
Manchester
Marquette
Memphis
Metuchen
Miami
Milwaukee
Mobile
Nashville
Newark
New Orleans
Newton (Melkite Rite)
New Ulm
New York
Norwich
Oakland
Ogdensburg
Oklahoma City
Omaha
Orange
Orlando
Owensboro
Passaic (Byzantine)
Paterson
Pensacola-Tallahassee
Peoria
Philadelphia
Pittsburgh
Ponce, Puerto Rico
Portland, ME
Portland, OR
Providence
Raleigh
Rapid City
Richmond
Rochester
Rockville Centre
Sacramento
Saginaw
St. Augustine
St. Cloud
St. Louis
St. Maron
St. Paul-Minneapolis
St. Petersburg
St. Thomas, Virgin Islands
Salt Lake City
San Angelo
San Antonio
San Bernardino
San Diego
San Francisco
San Jose
San Juan, Puerto Rico
Santa Fe
Santa Rosa
Savannah
Scranton
Seattle
Sioux City
Sioux Falls
Spokane
Springfield-Cape Girardeau
Springfield, IL
Springfield, MA
Steubenville
Superior
Syracuse
Toledo
Trenton
Tucson
Tulsa
Venice
Victoria
Washington, DC
Wheeling-Charleston
Wichita
Wilmington
Winona
Worcester
Yakima
Youngstown

COUNTRIES WITH PRIESTS SERVING IN THE ARCHDIOCESE FOR THE MILITARY SERVICES

Africa
Canada
Colombia
Czechoslovakia
Ecuador
France
Ghana
India
Mexico
Nigeria
Pakistan
Peru
Philippines
Poland
Spain
Taiwan
United Kingdom
Vietnam

RELIGIOUS INSTITUTES WITH PRIESTS SERVING IN THE ARCHDIOCESE FOR MILITARY SERVICES

C.J. Josephite Fathers
C.M. Vincentian Fathers
C.M.F. Claretian Missionaries
C.P. Congregation of the Passion
C.PP.S. Society of the Precious Blood
C.S.C. Congregation of the Holy Cross
C.S.P. Paulist Fathers
C.S.Sp. Holy Ghost Fathers
C.SS.R. Redemptorist Fathers
C.S.V. Viatorian Fathers
L.C. Legionaries of Christ
M.I.C. Congregation of Marians of the Immaculate Conception
M.M. Maryknoll Missioners
M.S. Missionaries of Our Lady of LaSalette

M.S.C. Missionaries of the Sacred Heart
M.Ss.A. Missionaries of the Holy Apostles
O. Carm. Carmelite Fathers
O.C.S.O. Cistercians of the Strict Observance
O.F.M. Franciscan Fathers
O.F.M.Cap. Capuchins
O.F.M.Conv. Conventual Franciscans
O.M.I. Oblates of Mary Immaculate
O.M.V. Oblates of the Virgin Mary
O.P. Order of Preachers
O.Praem. Premonstratensian Fathers
O.S.A. The Augustinians
O.S.B. Benedictine Fathers
O.S.C. Crozier Fathers
O.S.Cam. Order of St. Camillus
O.S.F.S. Oblates of St. Francis de Sales
O.S.M. Servite Fathers
O.SS.T. Trinitarian Fathers
S.A. Atonement Fathers
S.A.C. Society of the Catholic Apostolate
S.Ch. Society of Christ
S.C.J. Sacred Heart Fathers
S.D.B. Salesian Fathers
S.D.S. Society of Divine Savior
S.F. Sons of the Holy Family
S.J. Jesuit Fathers
S.M. Marist Fathers
S.O.L.T. Society of Our Lady of the Most Holy Trinity
SS.CC. Fathers of the Sacred Hearts
S.S.J. St. Joseph's Society of the Sacred Heart
S.S.S. Congregation of the Blessed Sacrament
S.T. Missionary Servants of the Most Holy Trinity

ASSOCIATIONS SUPPORTING THE MISSION OF THE ARCHDIOCESE

The Centurions
The Chaplains Aid Association

Archdiocese of Milwaukee

(Archidioecesis Milvauchiensis)

Most Reverend

REMBERT G. WEAKLAND, O.S.B., D.D.

Archbishop of Milwaukee; ordained June 24, 1951; appointed Archbishop of Milwaukee September 20, 1977; consecrated and installed as Ninth Archbishop November 8, 1977. *Res., 3303 S. Lake Dr., St. Francis, WI, 53235-3703. All official communications to the Most Rev. Archbishop should be addressed to: Archbishop Cousins Catholic Center, 3501 S. Lake Dr., P.O. Box 07912, Milwaukee, WI, 53207-0912.*

Most Reverend

RICHARD J. SKLBA, D.D.

Auxiliary Bishop of Milwaukee; ordained December 20, 1959; appointed Titular Bishop of Castro November 6, 1979; consecrated December 19, 1979. *Res., 2491 N. Murray Ave., Milwaukee, WI, 53211.* Tel.: 414-962-3941.

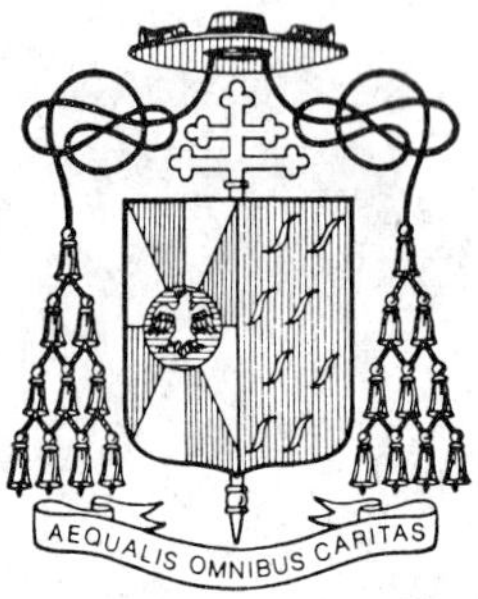

ESTABLISHED NOVEMBER 28, 1843; CREATED ARCHBISHOPRIC FEBRUARY 12, 1875.

Square Miles 4,758.

Corporate Title: *"Archdiocese of Milwaukee."*

Comprises the Counties of Dodge, Fond du Lac, Kenosha, Milwaukee, Ozaukee, Racine, Sheboygan, Walworth, Washington and Waukesha in the State of Wisconsin.

For legal titles of parishes and archdiocesan institutions, consult the Chancery Office.

Chancery Office: Archbishop Cousins Catholic Center, 3501 S. Lake Dr., P.O. Box 07912, Milwaukee, WI, 53207-0912. Tel.: 414-769-3340; Fax: 414-769-3408.

Web site address: http://www.archmil.org

E-mail address: archmil@execpc.com

STATISTICAL OVERVIEW

Personnel	
Archbishop	1
Auxiliary Bishops	1
Retired Bishops	1
Abbots	1
Retired Abbots	2
Priests: Diocesan Active in Diocese	303
Priests: Active Outside Diocese	20
Priests: Diocesan in Foreign Missions	6
Priests: Retired, Sick or Absent	161
Number of Diocesan Priests	490
Religious Priests in Diocese	345
Extern Priests in Diocese	24
Ordinations:	
Diocesan Priests	1
Religious Priests	7
Transitional Deacons	1
Permanent Deacons	7
Permanent Deacons in Diocese	154
Total Brothers	96
Total Sisters	2,233
Parishes	
Parishes	277
With Resident Pastor:	
Resident Diocesan Priests	209
Resident Religious Priests	23
Without Resident Pastor:	
Administered by Priests	34
Administered by Women Religious	4
Administered by Lay People	7
Pastoral Centers	21
Professional Ministry Personnel:	
Brothers	1
Sisters	64
Lay Ministers	325
Welfare	
Catholic Hospitals	11
Total Assisted	1,224,200
Health Care Centers	1
Total Assisted	14,000
Homes for the Aged	24
Total Assisted	4,119
Day Care and Extended Day Care Centers	7
Total Assisted	1,070
Specialized Homes	1
Total Assisted	16
Special Centers for Social Services	39
Total Assisted	231,396
Other Institutions	3
Total Assisted	810
Educational	
Seminaries, Diocesan	1
Students from This Diocese	21
Seminaries, Religious	1
Students Religious	12
Total Seminarians	33
Colleges and Universities	5
Total Students	21,395
High Schools, Diocesan and Parish	7
Total Students	4,517
High Schools, Private	6
Total Students	3,187
Elementary Schools, Diocesan and Parish	145
Total Students	28,381
Elementary Schools, Private	1
Total Students	46
Non-residential Schools for the Disabled	2
Total Students	17
Catechesis/Religious Education:	
High School Students	14,393
Elementary Students	38,638
Total Students Under Catholic Instruction	110,607
Teachers in the Diocese:	
Priests	76
Scholastics	16
Brothers	10
Sisters	245
Lay Teachers	3,639
Vital Statistics	
Receptions into the Church:	
Infant Baptism Totals	9,417
Adult Baptism Totals	555
Received into Full Communion	537
First Communions	9,291
Confirmations	5,905
Marriages:	
Catholic	2,507
Interfaith	1,197
Total Marriages	3,704
Deaths	6,060
Total Catholic Population	605,232
Total Population	2,080,883

Former Bishops—Most Rev. JOHN MARTIN HENNI, D.D., cons. March 19, 1844; created Archbishop, Feb. 11, 1875; died Sept. 7, 1881.—Most Rev. MICHAEL HEISS, D.D., cons. Bishop of La Crosse, Sept. 6, 1868; appt. Coadjutor of Milwaukee and Titular Archbishop of Adrianople, March 14, 1880; succeeded to Archbishop Henni in 1881; died March 26, 1890.—Most Rev. FREDERICK XAVIER KATZER, D.D., cons. Sept. 21, 1886; Bishop of Green Bay; transferred to Milwaukee and raised to the Archiepiscopal Dignity, Jan. 30, 1891; died July 20, 1903.—Most Rev. SEBASTIAN GEBHARD MESSMER, D.D., D.C.L., ord. July 23, 1871; cons. March 27, 1892; Bishop of Green Bay, Wis. transferred to Milwaukee and raised to the Archiepiscopal dignity December 10, 1903 made assistant at the Pontifical Throne, Nov. 16, 1906; died Aug. 4, 1930.—His Eminence SAMUEL ALPHONSUS STRITCH, D.D., ord. May 21, 1910; cons. Nov. 30, 1921; Bishop of Toledo, Ohio; transferred to Milwaukee and raised to the Archiepiscopal dignity, Aug. 26, 1930; transferred to Chicago, Dec. 27, 1939; created Cardinal, Feb. 18, 1946; died May 27, 1958.—Most Rev. MOSES E. KILEY, S.T.D., appt. Bishop of Trenton, Feb. 10, 1934; cons. March 17, 1934; appt. Archbishop of Milwaukee, Jan. 1, 1940; died April 15, 1953.—His Eminence ALBERT G. MEYER, S.T.D., S.S.L., ord. July 11, 1926; cons. Bishop of Superior, Wis., April 11. 1946; appt. Archbishop of Milwaukee, July 21, 1953; transferred to Chicago, Sept. 24, 1958; created Cardinal, Dec. 14, 1959; died Apr. 9, 1965.—Most Rev. WILLIAM E. COUSINS, D.D., ord. April 23, 1927; appt. Titular Bishop of Forma and Auxiliary Bishop of Chicago

Dec. 17, 1948; cons. March 7, 1949; appt. Bishop of Peoria, May 19, 1952; installed July 2, 1952; appt. Archbishop of Milwaukee, Dec. 18, 1958; installed Jan. 27, 1959; retired Sept. 20, 1977; died Sept. 14, 1988.

Chancery Office, Archbishop Cousins Catholic Center—3501 S. Lake Dr., P.O. Box 07912, Milwaukee, 53207-0912. Tel: 414-769-3340; Fax: 414-769-3408.

Vicars General—Most Rev. RICHARD J. SKLBA, D.D.; Very Rev. CARROL C. STRAUB.

Deans—Very Revs. KENNETH J. METZ, District 1; JOSEPH F. HORNACEK, District 2; DENNIS E. VAN BEEK, District 3; EDWARD R. WIELAND, District 4; ROBERT D. GOSMA, District 5; BERNARD S. SIPPEL, District 6; CHARLES H. WESTER, District 7; RICHARD J. ROBINSON, District 8; RICHARD J. CERPICH, District 9; Very Rev. Msgr. THOMAS J. GAJDOS, District 10; Very Revs. THOMAS F. KERSTEIN, District 11; DENNIS R. ACKERET, District 12; JOHN R. KERN, District 13; WILLIAM W. KEY, District 14; THOMAS P. EICHENBERGER, District 15; WILLIAM E. KOHLER, District 16.

Chancellor—BARBARA ANNE CUSACK, J.C.D.

Vice Chancellor—Rev. JAMES E. CONNELL, J.C.D.

Archivist—TIMOTHY D. CARY.

Secretary to Archbishop—Rev. LEONARD S. VAN VLAENDEREN, *Res., 3303 South Lake Dr., Milwaukee, 53207.* Tel: 414-769-7988.

Secretary to the Cabinet—Rev. DONALD H. THIMM.

Metropolitan Tribunal Archbishop Cousins Catholic Center—3501 S. Lake Dr., P.O. Box 07912, Milwaukee, 53207-0912. Tel: 414-769-3300. Please direct all Rogatory Commissions to: Rev. JOHN D. AIELLO, Defender of the Bond.

Judicial Vicar—Rev. THOMAS T. BRUNDAGE, M.Div., J.C.L.

Executive Secretary—MAURICE C. THOMPSON.

Judges for First Instance—Revs. THOMAS T. BRUNDAGE, M.Div., J.C.L.; DENNIS C. KLEMME, J.C.D.; JOSEPH N. PERRY, M.Div., J.C.L.; JAMES J. JARUMBO, J.C.L.; JACK HOPKA, J.C.L.

Judges for Second Instance—Revs. DENNIS C. KLEMME, J.C.D.; FRANK ARESTA, S.C.J., J.C.L.; THOMAS T. BRUNDAGE, J.C.L.; JAMES E. CONNELL, J.C.D.; BARBARA ANNE CUSACK, J.C.D.; Revs. CURT J. FREDERICK, J.C.L.; JACK HOPKA, J.C.L.; JAMES J. JARUMBO, J.C.L.; JOSEPH A. JANICKI, J.C.L.; MICHAEL T. NEWMAN, J.C.L.; JOSEPH N. PERRY, M.Div., J.C.L.; BERNARD S. SIPPEL, M.Div.; PHILIP D. REIFENBERG, J.C.L.

Defender of the Bond Second Instance—Rev. JOHN D. AIELLO, M.Div.

Procurator Advocates—THOMAS DARROW, M.A.; BONNIE JACHOWICZ, M.Div.; THOMAS R. BUDDE.

Promoters of Justice—Revs. ROBERT G. SAMPON, S.T.L., J.C.D.; PHILIP D. REIFENBERG, J.C.L.

Assessor/Due Process Coordinator—JOHN CARINI, J.D.

Notaries—Rev. JOHN D. AIELLO, M.Div.; MAURICE C. THOMPSON; MARY CHRIS ELLISON; NANCY DANIELS; JOYCE HRYNIEWICKI; ALICE PRIER.

Office for Marital Reconciliation-Separation—Rev. DENNIS C. KLEMME, J.C.D., Delegate.

Office for Conciliation—Rev. THOMAS T. BRUNDAGE, M.Div., J.C.L.

Archdiocesan Consultors—Most Rev. RICHARD J. SKLBA, D.D.; Very Rev. RICHARD J. CERPICH; Revs. ROLLAND T. GLASS; RALPH C. GROSS; JEFFREY R. HAINES; JOHN P. HANLEY; Very Rev. JOSEPH F. HORNACEK; Revs. DAVID H. REITH; DANIEL J. SANDERS.

Archdiocesan Council of Priests—Very Rev. RICHARD J. ROBINSON, Moderator, *3501 S. Lake Dr., P.O. Box 07912, Milwaukee, 53207-0912.* Tel: 414-769-3300.

Archdiocesan Pastoral Council—3501 S. Lake Dr., P.O. Box 07912, Milwaukee, 53207-0912. Tel: 414-769-3499.

Ministerial Formation - Saint Francis Seminary—— Very Rev. ANDREW L. NELSON, S.T.L., Ph.D., Rector, *3257 S. Lake Dr., St. Francis, 53235.* Tel: 414-747-6400.

Continuing Formation of Clergy—Rev. STEPHEN V. DELEERS, Dir. Tel: 414-747-6417.

Vocations Office—Rev. ROBERT X. STIEFVATER, Dir., *3257 S. Lake Dr., St. Francis, 53235.* Tel: 414-747-6437.

Department for Clergy Personnel—Archbishop Cousins Catholic Center, 3501 S. Lake Dr., P.O. Box 07912, Milwaukee, 53207-0912. Tel: 414-769-3484.

Vicar for Clergy Personnel—Very Rev. CARROL C. STRAUB.

Priests' Placement Board—Revs. LEONARD M. BARBIAN, Assoc. Vicar, Clergy; JAMES J. BRADY; JEROME P. MEYER; MICHAEL F. MORAN; ROBERT G. SAMPON; RICHARD J. STOFFEL; R. THOMAS VENNE. Tel: 414-769-3458.

St. Michael's Priest Fund—Rev. HERBERT B. SCHUBERT, Sec.

Priests' Pension Plan—Rev. GEORGE M. REBATZKI, Chm.

Deacon Services—Deacon KENNETH L. VERNON, Coord. Tel: 414-769-3409.

Archdiocesan Offices and Agencies

The following offices and agencies are located at the Archbishop Cousins Catholic Center unless otherwise indicated

Archbishop Cousins Catholic Center—3501 S. Lake Dr., P.O. Box 07912, Milwaukee, 53207-0912. Tel: 414-769-3300; Fax: 414-769-3408.

Department for Parishes

Archbishop's Delegate for Parishes—MAUREEN GALLAGHER, Ph.D. Tel: 414-769-3450.

Office for Multi-Cultural Services—Sr. SHAWNEE SYKES, S.S.N.D., Multi-Cultural Consultant/Dir., African-American Ministry. Tel: 414-769-3411. PEDRO MARTINEZ, Multi-Cultural Consultant/Dir., Hispanic Ministry. Tel: 414-769-3393. ROSINE L. SCHMITT, Dir. Multi-Cultural Consultant/Dir., Asian Ministry. Tel: 414-769-3376.

Parish Consultants—Districts 1, 2, 3: VALERIE KELLER-,Districts 4, 5, 7: NOREEN WELTE,Districts 6, 8, 9: PEG MUDROCH,Districts 10, 11, 12, 13: EVA J. DIAZ; CATHERINE O'NEILL,Districts 14, 15, 16: ROBERTO CORTES; MARK PETERS. Tel: 414-769-3539.

Parish Council Leadership Formation—DONALD LOZIER, Dir. Tel: 414-769-3378.

Office for Parish Human Concerns/Respect Life—PEG FLAHIVE, Dir. Tel: 414-769-3426.

Office for Parish Finances—Vacant. Tel: 414-769-3377.

Archdiocesan Building Commission—Vacant. Tel: 414-769-3377.

Office for Parish Planning & Collaboration—Sr. BARBARA DANNHAUSEN, O.P., Dir. Tel: 414-769-3379. ROBERT MELCHER, Assoc. Dir. Tel: 414-769-3381.

Office for Prayer and Worship—PETER GHILONI, Dir. Tel: 414-769-3350. MICHAEL NOVAK, Assoc. Dir. Tel: 414-769-3348.

Office for Adult and Family Ministry—THERESA JOHANEK, Dir. Tel: 414-769-3439.

Marriage and Family Ministry—RANDY NOHL, Assoc. Dir. Tel: 414-769-3440.

Singles, Separated, Divorced—Ms. PAT DOCKTOR, Assoc. Dir. Tel: 414-769-3445.

Bereavement Ministry—POLLY HORKY, Assoc. Dir. Tel: 414-769-3456.

Engaged Programs—MARIE GREVSMUEHL, Coord. Tel: 414-769-3441.

Campus Ministry—Milwaukee: CONSTANCE M. POPP; Rev. ROBERT J. LOTZ. Tel: 414-964-6640. Kenosha/Racine: EDITH PADGETT. Tel: 414-654-3630. Whitewater: Rev. JAMES M. GODIN. Tel: 414-473-5555.

Special Needs—THERESA JOHANEK. Tel: 414-769-3439.

Ministry to the Hearing Impaired—CYNTHIA DEEHR-KOOB, Assoc. Dir. Tel: 414-769-3455 (V/TTY).

Adult Formation—ROSALIE HARTMANN, Assoc. Dir. Tel: 414-769-3447.

Office for Schools and Child-Youth Ministries—JOHN T. NORRIS, Supt. Schools/Dir. Schools, Child & Youth Ministries. Tel: 414-769-3366.

Student Activities & Services—W. SCOTT WEYDA, Assoc. Dir. Tel: 414-769-3359.

Staff Development—CAMILLE MORTIMORE, Assoc. Dir. Tel: 414-769-3358.

Curriculum & Instruction—DAVID PROTHERO, Assoc. Dir. Tel: 414-769-3357.

Youth & Young Adult Ministry—DONALD SCHWORZHOFF, Assoc. Dir. Tel: 414-769-3361.

Catechetics to Children—JEAN MARIE WEBER, Assoc. Dir. Tel: 414-769-3373.

Early Adolescent Ministry—MARY VACCARO, Assoc. Dir. Tel: 414-769-3360.

Department for Community Services

Archbishop's Delegate for Community Services—Deacon WARREN D. BRAUN. Tel: 414-769-3389.

Ecumenical and Interfaith Concerns—JUDITH A. LONGDIN, Dir. Tel: 414-769-3483.

Office for Social Concerns—WARREN BRAUN, Dir. Tel: 414-769-3389. MARJORIE MORGAN, Assoc. Dir. Tel: 414-769-3402.

Campaign for Human Development—MARY GROPPI, Coord. Tel: 414-769-3424.

Office for World Mission—Sr. FRANCIS CUNNINGHAM, O.S.F., Dir. Tel: 414-769-3404.

"Catholic Herald"—Official Publication of Archdiocese of Milwaukee. ETHEL M. GINTOFT, Assoc. Publisher/Exec. Editor, *3501 S. Lake Dr., P.O. Box 07913, Milwaukee, 53207-0913.* Tel: 414-769-3500.

Catholic Charities—THOMAS R. SCHNEIDER, Exec. Dir. Tel: 414-769-3419. (Legal Title: *Catholic Charities of the Archdiocese of Milwaukee, Inc.).*

Residential Programs for Developmentally Disabled—RONALD J. SPITZ, Dir. Tel: 414-769-3401.

Ministry on Aging—WILLIAM LEON, Dir. Tel: 414-769-3412.

Sexual Abuse Response Coordinator—ELIZABETH C. PIASECKI, Psy.D. Tel: 414-769-3436.

Department for Archdiocesan Finance and Administration

Archbishop's Delegate for Archdiocesan Finance and Administration—WAYNE A. SCHNEIDER. Tel: 414-769-3319.

Consultant for Legal Counsel—WAYNE A. SCHNEIDER. Tel: 414-769-3319.

Office for Archdiocesan Finance and Administrative Services—WAYNE A. SCHNEIDER, Dir./Controller; JOHN W. BOEHM, Asst. Controller/Dir., Data Processing. Tel: 414-769-3530.

Office for Cemeteries and Mausoleums—GREGG F. APOSTOLOFF, Dir., *7301 W. Nash St., Milwaukee, 53216.* Tel: 414-438-4430.

Office for Building Services—DONNA RUGOLO, Dir. Tel: 414-769-3491.

Office for Printing Services—THOMAS WAL, Dir. Tel: 414-769-3487.

Department for Human Resources

Archbishop's Delegate for Human Resources and Secretary to the Cabinet—Rev. DONALD H. THIMM. Tel: 414-769-3336.

Office for Human Resources, Central Offices and Agencies—JUDITH A. MYERS, Dir. Tel: 414-769-3328.

Office for Parish and School Personnel—RICHARD J. TANK, Dir. Tel: 414-769-3370.

Archdiocesan Women's Commission—Vacant. Tel: 414-769-3434.

Office for Religious—Rev. ALAN D. VEIK, O.F.M.Cap., Dir. Tel: 414-769-3375.

Department for Communication and Development

Archbishop's Delegate for Communication and Development—M. DANIEL HENRY, Ph.D. Tel: 414-769-3322.

Annual Giving—BARBARA CAPLIN, Dir. Tel: 414-769-3538.

Donor Relations/Major & Planned Giving—DEBRA LETHLEAN, Dir. Tel: 414-769-3322.

Combined Collections—M. DANIEL HENRY, Ph.D. Tel: 414-769-3322.

Internal Communications—JEAN MULLOOLY, Dir. Tel: 414-769-3461. MARY CONARCHY, Coord. Publications. Tel: 414-769-3460.

External Relations—Tel: 414-769-3454. MARY SCHWEISBERGER, Assoc. Dir., Mktg. Tel: 414-769-3517.

CLERGY, PARISHES, MISSIONS AND PAROCHIAL SCHOOLS

CITY OF MILWAUKEE
(Milwaukee County)

1—ST. JOHN CATHEDRAL (1847), Very Rev. John H. Endejan. In res., Revs. James E. Connell; Carrol C. Straub.

Res., 802 N. Jackson St., 53202. Tel: 414-276-9814; Fax: 414-276-8285.

2—ST. ADALBERT (1908), Rev. John J. Wutscheck.

Res., 1923 W. Becher St., 53215-2611. Tel: 414-645-0413.

School—1913 W. Becher St., 53215-2688. Tel: 414-645-5450. Ms. Julia Hutchinson, Prin.

Lay Teachers 12; Students 154.

3—ST. AGNES. Closed. For sacramental records contact Archivist, Archdiocese of Milwaukee.

4—ST. ALBERT. Merged with Holy Redeemer and St. Nicholas to form Congregation of the Blessed Trinity. See listing for details.

5—ST. ALEXANDER'S (1926), Rev. Robert W. Nawrocki.

Res., 3373 S. 15th Pl., 53215. Tel: 414-645-9820.

School—3344 S. 16th St., 53215. Tel: 414-383-3453. Sr. Elmerine Acker, S.S.S.F., Prin.

Sisters 3; Lay Teachers 5; Students 212.

6—ST ANNE'S. Closed. For sacramental records contact Archivist, Archdiocese of Milwaukee.

7—ST. ANTHONY'S (1872), Revs. Lawrence V. Dulek; Edward Griesemer, S.C.J. In res., Revs. John B. Thanh Hung; Robert F. Mueller.

Res., 1711 S. 9th St., 53204. Tel: 414-645-1455; Fax: 414-645-1456.

School—1747 S. 9th St., 53204. Tel: 414-384-1730. Richard Mason, Prin.

Sisters 6; Lay Teachers 3; Students 267.

Catechesis/Religious Programs—Tel: 414-347-4465. Dennis Hondel, D.R.E.

Students 381.

8—ST. ANTHONY OF PADUA (1923), Rev. James M. Heisler, S.A.C.

Res., 7622 W. Stevenson St., 53213. Tel: 414-453-5344; Fax: 414-453-4225.
School—7632 W. Stevenson St., 53213. Tel: 414-258-4165. Sr. Janet Neureuther, Prin.
Sisters 1; Lay Teachers 9; Students 175.

9—ST. AUGUSTINE'S (1888) (German), Rev. Thomas F. Wittliff; Ms. Chiara Sainer, Pastoral Assoc.
Res., 2530 S. Howell Ave., 53207. Tel: 414-744-0808.
School—2523 S. Graham St., 53207. Tel: 414-481-5151. Mr. Gilbert Jaworski, Prin.
Sisters 2; Lay Teachers 12; Students 139.

10—ST. BARBARA'S, Rev. Richard H. Broach; Deacon Chester A. Moczydlowski.
Res., 2059 S. 33rd St., 53215. Tel: 414-645-9172; Fax: 414-645-4732.
School—Grades K-4; in collaboration with Holy Spirit Parish, Milwaukee. 2075 S. 32nd St., 53215. Tel: 414-643-6090. Kurt Lundgren, Prin.
Sisters 1; Lay Teachers 5; Students 105.

11—ST. BENEDICT THE MOOR (1908), Rev. Michael Sullivan, O.F.M.Cap.; Deacon John Champagne. In res., Rev. Michael Crosby, O.F.M.Cap.; Bros. Larry Ampe, O.F.M.Cap.; Kent Bauer, O.F.M.Cap.; Jerome Smith, O.F.M.Cap.; David Schwab, O.F.M.Cap.
Res., 1015 N. 9th St., 53233. Tel: 414-271-0135; Fax: 414-271-0637.

12—ST. BERNADETTE (1958), Rev. William H. Whalen; Deacon John A. Ebel.
Res., 8200 W. Denver Ave., 53223. Tel: 414-358-4600.
School—8202 W. Denver Ave., 53223. Tel: 414-358-4603. Mary Lorusso, Prin.
Lay Teachers 10; Students 234.

13—BLESSED SACRAMENT (1927) (Polish), Revs. Robert H. Katorski; Robert D. Turner; Sr. Sophie Banczak, S.S.J., Pastoral Assoc.
Res., 3100 S. 41st St., 53215. Tel: 414-649-4720; Fax: 414-649-4726.
Church—S. 41st St. and W. Oklahoma Ave., 53215.
School—3126 S. 41st St., 53215. Tel: 414-649-4730. Ms. Gloria Slottke, Prin.
School Sisters of St. Francis 1; Lay Teachers 16; Students 307.
Catechesis/Religious Programs—Tel: 414-649-4727.
Students 175.

14—CONGREGATION OF THE BLESSED TRINITY (1991), Rev. Jerome P. Meyer, Admin.; Sheila Day, Pastoral Assoc. & Lit. Coord.; Deacon Peter Gust.
Pastoral Offices—4717 N. 38th St., 53209. Tel: 414-463-6921; Fax: 414-463-0349.
School—5375 N. Green Bay Ave., 53209. Tel: 414-228-9030; Fax: 414-228-7516. Jane Uebelher, Prin.
Lay Teachers 16; Students 186.

15—ST. BONIFACE. Closed. For sacramental records contact Archivist, Archdiocese of Milwaukee.

16—ST. CASIMIR'S (1894) (Polish), Rev. James M. Flynt, Adm.
Mailing Address: 2618 N. Bremen St., 53212.
Res., 3055 N. Fratney St., 53212. Tel: 414-264-9814 (Res.); 414-263-8228 (Office); Fax: 414-263-8233.
School—All Saints Consolidated. See All Saints Catholic East School System, Inc., Listing in the Consolidated Elementary Schools section.

17—ST. CATHERINE (1922), Rev. Darryl Olszewski, Dir.; Deacon Ralph W. Kornburger, Jr. In res., Revs. Charles A. Kleefisch; M.A. Lourdusamy (India).
Res., 5101 W. Center St., 53210. Tel: 414-445-5115. [CEM]
School—2647 N. 51st St., 53210. Tel: 414-445-2846; Fax: 414-445-0448. Deborah Zabinski, Prin.
Lay Teachers 11; Students 185.

18—ST. CATHERINE (Granville) (1855), Rev. Jeffery A. Prasser.
Office:—Tel: 414-365-2020; Fax: 414-365-2021.
Res., 8661 N. 76th Pl., 53223. Tel: 414-365-2039. [CEM]
School—8660 N. 76th Pl., 53223. Tel: 414-365-2030. Mrs. Barbara Heil, Prin.
Lay Teachers 11; Students 215.
Catechesis/Religious Programs—Tel: 414-365-2025. Judith Jowalski, Ph.D., D.R.E.
Students 160.

19—ST. CHARLES BORROMEO (1960), Rev. Edward M. Safiejko.
Res., 5571 S. Marilyn Ave., 53221. Tel: 414-281-8115.
School—3100 W. Parnell Ave., 53221. Tel: 414-282-7010.
Lay Teachers 14; Students 268.
Catechesis/Religious Programs—Students 200.

20—CORPUS CHRISTI (1958), Rev. Michael D. Strachota; Deacon James L. Aschenbrener; Judith Adrian, Pastoral Assoc.
Parish Center: 8607 W. Villard Ave., 53225. Tel: 414-464-5033.
School—8545 W. Villard Ave., 53225. Tel: 414-464-5775; Fax: 414-464-5775. Mark Joerres, Prin.
Lay Teachers 12; Students 166.

21—SS. CYRIL AND METHODIUS (1893) (Polish), Rev. Paul L. Raczynski.
Office: 2427 S. 15th St., 53215. Tel: 414-383-3973; Fax: 414-383-3974.

22—ST. EMERIC'S (1919) (Hungarian), Rev. Bela Krigler, Sch.P.
Worship at Sacred Heart Church, Milwaukee. c/o 917 N. 49th St., 53208. Tel: 414-774-9418.

23—ST. ELIZABETH'S. Closed. For sacramental records contact Archivist, Archdiocese of Milwaukee.

24—ST. FLORIAN'S (1906) (German), Revs. Leonard R. Copeland, O.C.D.; Timothy McGough, O.C.D. In res., Revs. Dominic T. Scheerer, O.C.D.; William Healy, O.C.D.; Philip Thomas, O.C.D.; Bros. Ralph Elias-Haddix, O.C.D.; Bonaventure Potter, O.C.D.
Res., 1233 S. 45th St., 53214. Tel: 414-383-3565; Fax: 414-383-2708.
School—1215 S. 45th St., 53214. Tel: 414-383-4204.
Sisters 2; Lay Teachers 9; Students 123.

25—ST. FRANCIS OF ASSISI (1871), Revs. Niles Kauffman, O.F.M.Cap.; Robert Kose, O.F.M.Cap. In res., Revs. Ulric Buening, O.F.M.Cap.; Robert Wheelock, O.F.M.Cap.; Michael Sullivan, O.F.M.Cap.; Michael Zuelke, O.F.M.Cap.; Bro. Isidore Herriges, O.F.M.Cap.
Res., 327 W. Brown St., 53212. Tel: 414-374-5750; Fax: 414-374-5553.

26—ST. GABRIEL (1913) (Lithuanian), Rev. Paul L. Raczynski.
Res., 1575A S. 10th St., 53204. Tel: 414-645-5478; Fax: 414-383-3974.

27—ST. GALL. Closed. For sacramental records contact Archivist, Archdiocese of Milwaukee.

28—ST. GERARD'S (1925), Rev. Marvin I. Lazarski.
Res., 3027 S. 16th St., 53215. Tel: 414-645-8928.
Catechesis/Religious Programs—Students 186.

29—GESU PARISH (1893), Revs. George E. Winzenburg, S.J.; John D. Campbell, S.J.; Michael G. Lee, S.J.; Patrick E. Walsh, S.J.; James Warosh, S.J.; Kenneth J. Herian, S.J.
Res., 1210 W. Michigan St., P.O. Box 495, 53201-0495. Tel: 414-288-7101; Fax: 414-288-5339.

30—CONGREGATION OF THE GREAT SPIRIT (1989) (Native American), Rev. Edward J. Cook.
Mailing Address: 3126 W. Kilbourn Ave., 53208. Tel: 414-342-0370.

31—ST. GREGORY THE GREAT (1955), Rev. Russell J. Stommel.
Office: 3160 S. 63rd St., 53219. Tel: 414-543-8292; Fax: 414-328-3881.
Res., 3129 S. 63rd St., 53219. Tel: 414-541-9059.
School—3132 S. 63rd St., 53219. Tel: 414-321-1350.
Lay Teachers 22; Students 488.
Catechesis/Religious Programs—Tel: 414-541-3720.
Students 287.

32—ST. HEDWIG (1871) (Polish), Rev. James N. Jablonowski.
Res., 1716 N. Humboldt Ave., 53202. Tel: 414-271-2165; Fax: 414-271-7988.
School—All Saints Catholic Elementary. See All Saints Catholic East School System, Inc., Listing in the Consolidated Elementary Schools section. Tel: 414-372-5530 (All Saints); 414-964-1770 (Catholic East).

33—ST. HELEN'S (1925) (Polish), Sr. Helen Bronner, S.S.N.D., Pastoral Min.
Res., 3307 S. 10th St., 53215. Tel: 414-744-3695; 744-8292.
School—3329 S. 10th St., 53215. Tel: 414-744-7188. Sr. Jeanette Skornia, C.S.S.F., Prin.
Sisters 5; Lay Teachers 4; Students 137.
3249 S. 18th St., 53215. Tel: 414-384-2460.

34—HOLY ANGELS. Closed. For sacramental records contact Archivist, Archdiocese of Milwaukee.

35—HOLY CROSS (1879), Revs. Robert Albers, S.A.C.; Paul Coutinha, S.A.C. (India).
Res., 5424 W. Bluemound Rd., 53208. Tel: 414-774-4420.
School—5522 W. Bluemound Rd., 53208. Tel: 414-258-0687. Ms. Barbara Kozleuchar, Prin.
School Sisters of Notre Dame 2; Lay Teachers 11; Students 152.

36—HOLY REDEEMER. Merged with St. Albert and St. Nicholas to form Congregation of the Blessed Trinity. See listing for details.

37—HOLY ROSARY (1885) (Irish), Rev. Melvin P. Breit; Sr. Ellen Barrett, B.V.M., Admin. Assoc.; Deacon C. Edward Weber.
Res., 2003 N. Oakland Ave., 53202. Tel: 414-271-8605.
Church—E. Lafayette Pl. and N. Oakland Ave., 53202.
School—Catholic East Elementary. See All Saints Catholic East School System, Inc., Listing in the Consolidated Elementary Schools section. Tel: 414-964-1770.

38—HOLY SPIRIT (1902), Rev. Denis P. Weis; Deacons William A. Banach; David R. Pollak.
Res., 3132 W. Lincoln Ave., 53215-2497. Tel: 414-645-1742.
School—Holy Spirit School. Grades 5-8; in collaboration with St. Barbara Parish. 2251 S. 31st St., 53215. Tel: 414-645-1300.
Lay Teachers 8; Students 79.

39—HOLY TRINITY-OUR LADY OF GUADALUPE (1849) (Hispanic), Rev. Michael F. Michalski; Deacon Jose H. Gutierrez.
Res., 613 S. 4th St., 53204. Tel: 414-271-6181.
Catechesis/Religious Programs—Tel: 414-271-6543.
Students 189.

40—ST. HYACINTH'S (1883), Rev. Ronald E. Kotecki. In res., Rev. Bronislaw Slodowski.
Res., 1414 W. Becher St., 53215. Tel: 414-383-4010.

41—ST. IGNATIUS LOYOLA. Merged with St. Barbara Parish. For sacramental records see St. Barbara Parish, Milwaukee.

42—IMMACULATE CONCEPTION (1870), Rev. Dennis M. Witz; Deacon John Wargin.
Res., 1023 E. Russell Ave., 53207. Tel: 414-769-2480.
School—1051 E. Russell Ave., 53207. Tel: 414-769-2485.
Lay Teachers 10; Students 185.
Catechesis/Religious Programs—Tel: 414-769-2488.
Students 55.

43—ST. JOHN KANTY'S (1907) (Polish), Rev. Carl M. Kazmierczak.
Res., 966 W. Dakota St., 53215. Tel: 414-744-5885.
School—2834 S. 10th St., 53215. Tel: 414-483-8780; 744-1846. Lois Maczuzak, Prin.
School Sisters of Notre Dame 2; Lay Teachers 8; Students 161.

44—ST. JOHN DE NEPOMUC. Closed. For sacramental records contact Archivist, Archdiocese of Milwaukee.

45—BASILICA OF ST. JOSAPHAT (1886) (Polish), Revs. William P. Callahan, O.F.M.Conv.; Robert Joseph Switanowski, O.F.M.Conv.; Deacon John C. Welnicki. In res., Bro. James M. Jankowski, O.F.M.Conv.
Res., 2333 S. 6th St., 53215. Tel: 414-645-5623; Fax: 414-645-1174.
School—801 W. Lincoln Ave., 53215. Tel: 414-645-4378. Mrs. Carolyn Trawitzki, F.S.S.J., Prin.
Lay Teachers 12; Students 165; School Sisters of St. Francis 1.

46—ST. LAWRENCE (1888), Very Rev. William W. Key.
Res., 2604 W. Orchard St., 53204. Tel: 414-645-2088.
School—1418 S. Layton Blvd., 53215. Tel: 414-645-4922.
Sisters 4; Lay Teachers 5; Students 189.

47—ST. LEO'S. Closed. For sacramental records contact Archivist, Archdiocese of Milwaukee.

48—ST. MARGARET MARY (1955), Revs. Ralph C. Gross; Robert S. Kroeger; Deacon Michael R. Rooney.
Res., 3930 N. 92nd St., 53222-2588. Tel: 414-461-6073; Fax: 414-461-5590.
School—3950 N. 92nd St., 53222-2587. Tel: 414-463-8760; Fax: 414-463-2373. Susan Nelson, Prin.
Sisters of St. Agnes 1; Lay Teachers 24; Students 410.
Catechesis/Religious Programs—Tel: 414-462-9660.
Students 289.

49—OLD ST. MARY'S (1846) (Bavarian/German), Rev. George M. Rebatzki; Deacon Claude Kennedy.
Res., 836 N. Broadway, 53202. Tel: 414-271-6180; Fax: 414-271-7782.

50—ST. MARY OF CZESTOCHOWA (1907), Rev. James M. Flynt.
Res., 3055 N. Fratney St., 53212. Tel: 414-264-0049; Fax: 414-264-7177.
School—All Saints Catholic Elementary. See All Saints Catholic East School System, Inc., Listing in the Consolidated Elementary Schools section. Tel: 414-372-5530.

51—ST. MARY MAGDALEN (1925) (Polish), Rev. Frank J. Yaniak.
Res., 1854 W. Windlake Ave., 53215. Tel: 414-645-4773.

52—ST. MATTHEW'S (1892), Rev. James L. Dammeir; Sr. Leora Leon, S.S.S.F., Pastoral Assoc.; Michael P. Mernagh, Pastoral Assoc., Dir. of Lit.
Office: 1138 S. 25th St., 53204. Tel: 414-645-8786.
School—1114 S. 25th St., 53204. Tel: 414-383-2157. Sr. Marilyn Winkel, C.S.A., Prin.
Sisters of St. Agnes, Fond du Lac, WI 1; Lay Teachers 11; Students 106.

53—ST. MATTHIAS (1851), Revs. Carl A. Last; James T. Volkert; Brian G. Mason.

9306 W. Beloit Rd., 53227. Tel: 414-321-0893; Fax: 414-321-1330. [CEM]
School—Tel: 414-321-0894.
Sisters 3; Lay Teachers 21; Students 488.
Catechesis/Religious Programs—Tel: 414-321-8680.
Students 340.

54—St. Michael's (1883), Rev. Dennis J. Lewis, Admin. Pastoral Associates: Sr. Alice Thephouthay, Laotian Pastoral Ministry; Deacons Blong Yang, Hmong Pastoral Ministry; Juan Molina, Hispanic Pastoral Ministry.
Res., 1445 N. 24th St., 53205. Tel: 414-933-3143; Fax: 414-933-1956.
Catechesis/Religious Programs—Students 320.

55—Mother of Good Counsel (1925), Revs. Daniel T. Pekarske, S.D.S.; Fred Schmit, S.D.S.; Deacon Dean J. Collins. Pastoral Associates: Sr. Diane Goetzinger, S.D.S.; Sr. Anne Koszarek, S.S.J.-T.O.S.F.
Res., 6924 W. Lisbon Ave., 53210-1259. Tel: 414-442-7600; Fax: 414-444-0408.
School—3001 N. 68th St., 53210. Audrey Neu, Prin.
Sisters 1; Lay Teachers 23; Students 414.

56—Mother of Perpetual Help (1941), Rev. John H. Baumgartner; Deacon Thomas J. Schimmels.
Res., 5409 W. Villard Ave., 53218. Tel: 414-438-4780.
School—Tel: 414-438-4783; Fax: 414-438-4782. Thomas Hage, Prin.
Sisters 3; Lay Teachers 13; Students 216.

57—St. Nicholas. Merged with St. Albert and Holy Redeemer to form Congregation of the Blessed Trinity. See listing for details.

58—Our Lady of Good Hope (1952), Revs. Paul A. Stanosz; Joseph A. Wolf; Deacons Joseph H. Kastenholz; Robert M. Schieffer; Venton Barno, Bus. Mgr. In res., Rev. John R. Kolanko.
Office: 7152 N. 41st St., 53209. Tel: 414-352-1148; Fax: 414-352-3042.
School—7120 N. 41st St., 53209. Tel: 414-352-7980. Nancy Behr, Prin.
Lay Teachers 13; Students 163.
Catechesis/Religious Programs—Tel: 414-352-8140. Barbara Krieger, D.R.E.
Students 244.

59—Our Lady of Lourdes (1958), Revs. Thomas M. Suriano; Michael G. Savio; Mrs. Judith Bialk, Pastoral Assoc.
Office: 3722 S. 58th St., 53220. Tel: 414-545-4316; Fax: 414-541-2251.
Catechesis/Religious Programs—Tel: 414-541-9470.
Students 316.

60—Our Lady, Queen of Peace (1948), Rev. Gilbert G. Arciszewski.
Res., 3222 S. 29th St., 53215. Tel: 414-672-0313; Fax: 414-672-0441.
School—2733 W. Euclid Ave., 53215. Tel: 414-672-6660. Christopher Multhauf, Prin.
Sisters 1; Lay Teachers 10; Students 238.

61—Our Lady of Sorrows (1955), Rev. Gregory A. Chycinski.
Res., 4063 N. 64th St., 53216. Tel: 414-463-3180.
School—4059 N. 64th St., 53216. Tel: 414-463-3878. Miss Patricia Wilkum, Prin.
Lay Teachers 11; Students 166.

62—St. Martin de Porres (1994) (African American), Rev. Philip D. Reifenberg, Admin.
Office: 128 W. Burleigh St., 53212-2046. Tel: 414-372-3090; Fax: 414-372-0356.

63—All Saints (1994), Rev. Joseph N. Perry; Deacons Kenneth Vernon; Edward Blaze. In res., Rev. David Ihenacho (Nigeria).
Office: 4060 N. 26th St., 53209-6695. Tel: 414-444-5610; Fax: 414-444-5709.

64—St. Patrick's (1876), Revs. Richard P. Abert, S.J.; David M. Shields.
Res., 723 W. Washington St., 53204. Tel: 414-645-7624.
Catechesis/Religious Programs—Tel: 414-645-7624.
Students 185.

65—St. Paul (1920), Revs. James Winiarski, M.S.; Frank Kula, M.S.
Res., 1720 E. Norwich Ave., 53207. Tel: 414-482-3510.
School—3945 S. Kansas Ave., 53207. Tel: 414-482-4790.
Lay Teachers 9; Students 143.

66—SS. Peter and Paul (1889) (German), Very Rev. John R. Kern. Pastoral Assocs.: Rita Kuhnen; Monica Meagher; Thomas Koester. Tel: 414-962-8103. In res., Most Rev. Richard J. Sklba.
Res., 2491 N. Murray Ave., 53211. Tel: 414-962-2443.
School—Catholic East Elementary, Tel: 414-964-1770; Fax: 414-962-8183.
See All Saints Catholic East School System, Inc., Listing in the Consolidated Elementary Schools section.
Day Care Center—2480 N. Cramer St., 53211. Tel: 414-964-6638.
Children 100.
Catechesis/Religious Programs—East Side Child & Youth Ministry. Consolidated from the following parishes: SS. Peter & Paul, St. Casimir, St. Mary Czestochowa, St. Hedwig, Holy Rosary, Cathedral of St. John the Evangelist. 924 E. Clarke St., 53212. Tel: 414-263-8230.
Students 34.

67—St. Philip Neri (1956), Rev. John G. Yockey. In res., Rev. Roman S. Stikel.
Res., 5566 N. 69th St., 53218. Tel: 414-464-6721.
School—5501 N. 68th St., 53218. Tel: 414-466-0470. Sr. Suzanne Zinda, Prin.
Schoenstatt Sisters of Mary 1; Lay Teachers 8; Students 140.
Catechesis/Religious Programs—Tel: 414-466-4481. Mrs. Rita Leren, D.R.E.
Students 66.

68—St. Rita's (1936) (Italian), Rev. Melvin P. Breit; Sr. Marie Louise Balistrieri, S.C.S.J.A., Pastoral Assoc.
Res., 1603 N. Cass St., 53202. Tel: 414-276-1157.
School—Catholic East Elementary. See All Saints Catholic East School System, Inc., Listing in the Consolidated Elementary Schools section.

69—St. Robert's (1912), Revs. John J. Pulice; Roman S. Stikel.
Res., 4019 N. Farwell Ave., 53211. Tel: 414-332-0117; Fax: 414-332-2599.
School—2200 E. Capital Dr., 53211. Tel: 414-963-9540; Fax: 414-332-7355. Larry Patterson, Prin.; Sr. Ruth Brings, Pastoral Assoc.; Eileen Ambrose Steckbauer, Pastoral Min.
Sisters 1; Lay Teachers 25; Students 357.
Catechesis/Religious Programs—Tel: 414-332-2230.
Students 285.

70—St. Roman (1956) (Polish), Rev. Robert L. Betz; Deacon William J. Lukacevich.
Res., 1710 W. Bolivar Ave., 53221. Tel: 414-282-9063; Fax: 414-282-6464.
School—1810 W. Bolivar Ave., 53221. Tel: 414-282-7970.
Lay Teachers 20; Students 461.
Catechesis/Religious Programs—Students 200.

71—St. Rose (1888), Rev. Dennis J. Lewis; Deacon Juan Molina.
Res., 544 N. 31st St., 53208. Tel: 414-342-1778; Fax: 414-342-7510.
School—Confer Elementary Schools, Archdiocesan, Catholic Urban Academies. Tel: 414-933-6070; Fax: 414-933-6071.

72—Sacred Heart (1917) (Croatian), Rev. Stephen Bedenikovic, O.F.M. (Croatia).
Res., 917 N. 49th St., 53208. Tel: 414-774-9418; Fax: 414-774-7406.

73—St. Sebastian's (1911), Revs. Charles H. Schramm; Charles T. Hanel; Deacons James J. Peterson; Warren D. Braun.
Res., 5400 W. Washington Blvd., 53208. Tel: 414-453-1061; Fax: 414-453-9449.
School—1747 N. 54th St., 53208. Tel: 414-453-5830.
Sisters 1; Lay Teachers 20; Students 380.
Catechesis/Religious Programs—Tel: 414-453-7150.
Students 230.

74—St. Stanislaus (1866), Rev. LeRoy A. Petta.
Res., 524 W. Mitchell St., 53204. Tel: 414-645-8170.

75—St. Stephen (1847) (German). (Airport). Rev. Joseph A. Aufdermauer; Anita H. Kowalski, Pastoral Assoc.
Office: 5880 S. Howell Ave., 53207. Tel: 414-483-2685. [CEM 2]
Catechesis/Religious Programs—Tel: 414-483-2658.
Lay Teachers 9; Students 197.

76—St. Stephen, Martyr (1907) (Slovak), Rev. John H. Baumgartner.
Res., 4234 N. 50th St., 53216. Tel: 414-445-9640.
School—4200 N. 50th St., 53216. Tel: 414-462-3660; Fax: 414-462-8914. Sr. Judy Rivas, Prin.
Sisters 2; Lay Teachers 12; Students 202.

77—St. Therese (1954), Rev. Roger C. Heck.
Res., 9525 W. Bluemound Rd., 53226. Tel: 414-771-2500.
Catechesis/Religious Programs—Tel: 414-476-5580. D.R.E.: Ralph Robers; Barbara Searing.
Students 190.

78—St. Thomas Aquinas. Closed. For sacramental records contact Archivist, Archdiocese of Milwaukee.

79—St. Veronica's (1926), Revs. Joseph B. Frederick; Gary D. Nowicki; Deacons John R. Burns; John Dziennik.
Res., 4017 S. Whitnall Ave., 53207. Tel: 414-482-2920; Fax: 414-482-3025.
School—341 E. Norwich St., 53207. Tel: 414-744-1214. Sr. Marie Estelle Kuczynski, Prin.
Sisters 1; Lay Teachers 21; Students 421.
Catechesis/Religious Programs—Tel: 414-481-0777.
Students 232.

80—St. Vincent de Paul's (1888) (Polish), Rev. Stephen J. Lampe; Deacon John Martinez.
Res., 2114 W. Michell St., 53204. Tel: 414-645-3400; Fax: 414-645-3450.

81—St. Wenceslaus (1883) (Hispanic), Rev. Julio E. Miralbes-Drago.
Res., 1410 W. Scott St., 53204. Tel: 414-645-6497.

OUTSIDE THE CITY OF MILWAUKEE

Adell, Sheboygan Co., St. Patrick (1853) (Irish). Also serves St. Mary, Cascade; St. Nicholas, Dacada; St. Michael, Mitchell; & St. Mary, Random Lake. Very Rev. Richard J. Cerpich.
Mailing Address: St. Mary, 230 Butler St., Random Lake, 53075-9435. Tel: 414-994-4380; Fax: 414-994-2605. [CEM]
Church—W4960 S. Hwy. A, 53001.

Allenton, Washington Co., Sacred Heart (1917). Also serves St. Anthony, Allenton; & Ss. Peter & Paul, Nenno. Rev. Michael L. Wild.
Tri-Parish Office: 215 Main St., Box 96, 53002. Tel: 414-629-5240. [CEM]
Catechesis/Religious Programs—Tel: 414-629-1500.
Students 146.
Convent—632 Church St., P.O. Box 356, 53002. Tel: 414-629-5342. School Sisters of Notre Dame.

St. Anthony (1851). Also serves Sacred Heart, Allenton; & Ss. Peter & Paul, Nenno. Rev. Michael L. Wild.
Tri-Parish Office: P.O. Box 96, 53002-0096. Tel: 414-629-5240. [CEM]
Convent—632 Church St., 53002. Tel: 414-629-5342. School Sisters of Notre Dame

Armstrong, Fond du Lac Co., Our Lady of Angels (1856) (Irish). Also serve St. Michael, Dotyville. Very Rev. Richard J. Robinson.
Res., W762 Armstrong Rd., Campbellsport, 53010-1400. Tel: 414-477-3201. [CEM 2]
School—W771 Armstrong Rd., Campbellsport, 53010. Tel: 414-477-2081. Roselyn Baker, Prin.
Lay Teachers 3; Students 42. Also serves St. Michael, Dotyville.

Ashford, Fond du Lac Co., St. Martin's (1847). Also serves St. Kilian, St. Kilian. Rev. Wayne J. Barta, Admin.
1271 Minnie Ln., Campbellsport, 53010. Tel: 414-533-8644. [CEM]

Auburn, Fond du Lac Co., St. Matthias (1863) (German), Rev. Nicholas L. Goebel.
Res., Campbellsport, 53010. Tel: 414-533-8351. [CEM]

Beaver Dam, Dodge Co., St. Michael's (1893) (Polish), Rev. John J. Radetski; Deacon Randal S. Wells.
Res., 835 Madison St., 53916. Tel: 414-885-3885. [CEM]
Catechesis/Religious Programs—344 Rosendale St., 53916. Tel: 414-887-7082.
Students 190.

St. Patrick's (1860) (Irish), Rev. Charles A. Scheuerell; Deacon Robert A. Truttschel.
Res., 131 W. Maple Ave., 53916. Tel: 414-887-2082. [CEM]
School—Unified Catholic Parish Schools of Beaver Dam. See St. Peter. Tel: 414-885-5558.

St. Peter's (1855), Rev. John L. Simon.
Res., 101 E. South St., 53916-2599. Tel: 414-885-5525; Fax: 414-885-4999. [CEM]
School—Consolidated with St. Patrick and St. Michael to form Unified Catholic Parish Schools of Beaver Dam. 503 S. Spring St., 53916-2598. Tel: 414-885-5558; Fax: 414-885-5510.
Lay Teachers 23; Students 189.
Catechesis/Religious Programs—Christian Formation, 503 S. Spring St., 53196-2598. Tel: 414-885-6023.
Students 290.

Belgium, Ozaukee Co., St. Mary's (1848), Rev. Donald A. Schmidt.
Res., 6092 Lake Church Rd., 53004. Tel: 414-285-3040. [CEM]
School—Tel: 414-285-3532. Sr. Suzanne Dietz, Prin.
Sisters 1; Lay Teachers 4; Students 76.
Catechesis/Religious Programs—675 Hwy. D, 53004.
Students 166.

Big Bend, Waukesha Co., St. Joseph's (1920), Rev. Robert F. Surges.
Res., S89 W22650 Milwaukee Ave., 53103. Tel: 414-662-2832; Fax: 414-662-0783.
School—W227 S8930 St. Joseph Dr., 53103. Tel: 414-662-2737; Fax: 414-662-0783. Bill Bass, Prin.

Lay Teachers 14; Students 230.
Catechesis/Religious Programs—Tel: 414-662-3317. D.R.E.: Mary L. Kozlik; Barb Gawlik.
Students 345.

Brandon, Fond Du Lac Co., St. Brendan. Also serves St. Joseph, Waupun and St. Mary, Springvale. Revs. Benjamin Knopp, O.F.M.Conv.; Russan Cole, O.F.M.Conv.
Mailing Address: 118 W. Main St., Waupun, 53963. Tel: 414-324-5400.

Brighton, Kenosha Co., St. Francis Xavier (1839) (German), Rev. Lawrence Sepich.
Res., 1704 240th Ave., Kansasville, 53139. Tel: 414-878-2267. [CEM]
School—Consolidated with St. John the Baptist, 1481-172 N. Ave., Paris, Union Grove, WI 53182, Tel.: 414-859-2007. 1714 240th Ave., Kansasville, 53139. Tel: 414-878-2713.
Lay Teachers 10; Students 152.

Bristol, Kenosha Co., St. Scholastica (1945), Rev. Andrew V. Garber, O.S.B.
Res., 18700 116th St., 53104. Tel: 414-857-2068. [CEM]

Brookfield, Waukesha Co., St. Dominic (1886), Revs. Curt J. Frederick; Mark R. Jones; Deacons John Libecki; Larry LaFond; Diane Diederich, Pastoral Assoc.
Res., 18255 W. Capitol Dr., 53045. Tel: 414-781-3480; Fax: 414-781-3283. [CEM]
School—18105 W. Capitol Dr., 53045. Tel: 414-783-7565. Ms. Joyce Steffan, Prin.
Lay Teachers 22; Students 430.
Catechesis/Religious Programs—Tel: 414-783-4248. Kathie Beuscher, D.R.E.
Students 598.

St. John Vianney (1956), Revs. Dennis M. Andrews; William C. Burkett.
Office: 1755 N. Calhoun Rd., 53045-5036. Tel: 414-796-3940; Fax: 414-782-0372.
School—17500 W. Gebhardt Rd., 53045-5096. Tel: 414-796-3942. Colleen Terry, Prin.
Lay Teachers 25; Students 480.
Catechesis/Religious Programs—Tel: 414-796-3944.
Students 998.

St. Luke (1956), Rev. Harvey W. Brahm.
Res., 1300 San Lucas Dr., 53045. Tel: 414-782-0032; Fax: 414-782-6057.
School—Tel: 414-782-4892. Ronald Andryk, Prin.
Lay Teachers 14; Students 252.
Catechesis/Religious Programs—Tel: 414-782-0892. Sr. Virgena Clark, R.S.M., D.R.E.
Students 185.
Convent—1305 Davidson Rd., 53045. Tel: 414-782-8148.

Burlington, Racine Co., Immaculate Conception (1838), Revs. David H. Reith; Michael C. Petersen.
Res., 108 McHenry St., 53105. Tel: 414-763-1500; Fax: 414-763-1680. [CEM]
School—225 W. State St., 53105. Tel: 414-763-1515; Fax: 414-763-1508.
Priests 2; Lay Teachers 19; Students 419.
Catechesis/Religious Programs—Tel: 414-763-1505. Mary Spiegelhoff, D.R.E.
Students 218.
Chapel—Powers Lake, St. Theresa.

St. Charles (1910) (Irish), Rev. Michael C. Benham.
Res., 456 Kendall St., 53105. Tel: 414-763-2260. [CEM]
School—449 Conkey St., 53105. Tel: 414-763-2848; 763-4880 (Grade School); Fax: 414-763-3818. Kris M. Tibbetts, Prin.
Lay Teachers 14; Students 267.
Catechesis/Religious Programs—Tel: 414-763-1505.
Students 209.

Butler, Waukesha Co., St. Agnes (1915), Rev. Richard A. Liska; Deacon Donald P. Wenzel.
Office:—12801 W. Fairmount Ave., 53007. Tel: 414-781-9521.
School—Tel: 414-781-4996; Fax: 414-781-3512. Sr. Mary Alice Walters, C.S.A., Prin.
Sisters 1; Lay Teachers 12; Students 256.
Catechesis/Religious Programs—Tel: 414-781-6998. Robert Thibault, D.R.E.
Students 300.

Byron, Fond du Lac Co., St. John's (1847). Also serves St. James, Oakfield. Rev. Donald F. Zerkel.
Res., W5882 Church Rd., Fond du Lac, 54937. Tel: 414-922-1167. [CEM]
Catechesis/Religious Programs—Tel: 414-921-5807.
Students 198.

Caledonia, Racine Co., St. Louis (1846), Rev. Glen G. Graczyk.
Parish Office: 13207 Hwy. G, 53108. Tel: 414-835-4533; Fax: 414-835-0421. [CEM]
School—13125 Hwy. G, 53108. Tel: 414-835-2166. Sr. Virginia Kinsella, O.P., Prin.
Lay Teachers 8; Students 90.

Campbellsport, Fond du Lac Co., St. Matthew's (1864), Rev. Edwin M. Kornath; Deacon Robert Fazen.
Parish Center: P.O. Box 740, 419 Mill St., 53010. Tel: 414-533-4441; Fax: 414-533-4688. [CEM]
School—Tel: 414-533-4103. Mrs. Susan Nygaard, Prin.
Lay Teachers 13; Students 148.
Catechesis/Religious Programs—Students 351.

Cascade, Sheboygan Co., St. Mary's (1852). Also serves St. Mary, Random Lake; St. Patrick, Adell; St. Nicholas, Dacada; & St. Michael, Mitchell. Very Rev. Richard J. Cerpich.
Mailing Address: 230 Butler St., Random Lake, 53075. Tel: 414-994-4380; Fax: 414-994-2605. [CEM]

Cedarburg, Ozaukee Co., Divine Word Catholic Church (1970), Very Rev. Msgr. Thomas Gajdos.
Res., 1375 Covered Bridge Rd., 53012. Tel: 414-377-1070.
Catechesis/Religious Programs—Tel: 414-377-7371.
Students 264.

St. Francis Borgia (1844), Rev. Edward J. Wawrzyniakowski.
Res., N44 W6055 Hamilton Rd., 53012. Tel: 414-377-1968. [CEM]
School—N43 W6005 Hamilton Rd., 53012. Tel: 414-377-2050. Sue Brandley, Prin.
Lay Teachers 28; Students 396.
Catechesis/Religious Programs—Tel: 414-377-4891. D.R.E.: Janet Sprink; Helen Jackson; Chris Dunst.
Students 287.

Clyman, Dodge Co., St. John's (1900), Rev. Msgr. Guy J. Gurath.
Res., Box 190, 53016. Tel: 414-696-3430. [CEM 2][JC]

Cudahy, Milwaukee Co., St. Frederick's (1896), Rev. Jan M. Kieliszewski.
Res., 4611 S. Kirkwood Ave., 53110. Tel: 414-744-6622. [JC]
Catechesis/Religious Programs—Tel: 414-481-6880. Susan Kinane Kirch, D.R.E.
Students 215.

Holy Family (1900), Very Rev. Thomas P. Eichenberger; Deacon Gerald Ponec.
Res., 3767 E. Underwood Ave., 53110. Tel: 414-744-6892.
School—3776 E. Hammond Ave., 53110. Tel: 414-481-0930.
Sisters 3; Lay Teachers 10; Students 182.

St. Joseph's (1909) (Slovak and Moravian), Patricia B. Knuth, Parish Dir.
Res., 4970 S. Swift Ave., 53110. Tel: 414-744-7565.
Catechesis/Religious Programs—Tel: 414-483-8370.
Students 130.

Dacada, Sheboygan Co., St. Nicholas (1848) (Luxembourg), Very Rev. Richard J. Cerpich.
Mailing Address: Also serves St. Mary, Random Lake; St. Patrick, Adell; St. Mary, Cascade; & St. Michael, Mitchell. 230 Butler St., Random Lake, 53075-9435. Tel: 414-994-4380; Fax: 414-994-2605.
Church—W4270 Hwy. K, Random Lake, 53075. [CEM]

Delavan, Walworth Co., St. Andrew's (1848), Rev. Joseph E. Debski.
Res., 714 E. Walworth Ave., 53115. Tel: 414-728-5922. [CEM]
School—Tel: 414-728-6211. Julie Supernaw, Prin.
Lay Teachers 9; Students 206.
Catechesis/Religious Programs—Mrs. Kathy Zambito, D.R.E.
Students 249.

Dotyville, Fond du Lac Co., St. Michael (1853) (German), Very Rev. Richard J. Robinson.
Parish Address: N5730 County Rd. W., Mount Calvary, 53057-9620.
Res., Also serves Our Lady of Angels, Armstrong. W762 Armstrong Rd., Campbellsport, 53010-1400. Tel: 414-477-3201. [CEM]

Dousman, Waukesha Co., St. Bruno's (1850), Rev. John P. Schreiter; Deacon Thomas Filipiak.
Res., 266 W. Ottawa Ave., 53118. Tel: 414-965-2332; Fax: 414-965-4749. [CEM]
School—Tel: 414-965-2291. David Lesczynski, Prin.
Lay Teachers 9; Students 125.
Catechesis/Religious Programs—Tel: 414-965-4200.
Students 296.

Eagle, Waukesha Co., St. Theresa's (1852) (German), Rev. Mariangela Pledl, Parish Dir.
Res., 136 Waukesha Rd., 53119. Tel: 414-594-5200. [CEM]
Catechesis/Religious Programs—Tel: 414-594-5201.
Students 104.

East Troy, Walworth Co., St. Peter's (1854), Rev. Kenneth J. Derfus.
Res., 1975 Beulah Ave., 53120. Tel: 414-642-7225; Fax: 414-642-7228.
School—3001 Elm St., 53120. Tel: 414-642-5533. Ms. Linda Cooney, Prin.
Lay Teachers 10; Students 150.
Catechesis/Religious Programs—Tel: 414-642-3634.
Students 295.

Eden, Fond du Lac Co., St. Mary's (1888), Rev. Robert G. Braun.
Res., Box 128, 53019. Tel: 414-477-3741. [CEM][JC]
School—Tel: 414-477-3551.
Lay Teachers 5; Students 82.

Eldorado, Fond Du Lac Co., St. Mary. Also serves St. John the Baptist, Woodhull. Rev. Roger A. Savage.
Mailing Address: W8272 Forest Ave. Rd., 54932-8901. Tel: 414-922-2412.

Elba, Dodge Co., St. Columbkille. Also serves Holy Family, Reeseville. Rev. Edward J. Hussli.
Mailing Address: P.O. Box 277, Reeseville, 53579. Tel: 414-623-3989.

Elkhart Lake, Sheboygan Co., St. George's (1896). Also serves St. Fridolin, Glenbeulah. Rev. Daniel J. Lasecki.
Res., 94 N. Lincoln, 53020-0396. Tel: 414-876-2457. [CEM]
Catechesis/Religious Programs—Tel: 414-876-2360. Lori Nielsen, D.R.E.
Students 277.

Elkhorn, Walworth Co., St. Patrick's (1878), Rev. Terrance J. Huebner; Sr. Mary Lou Fischbach, Pastoral Assoc.
Res., 107 W. Walworth St., 53121. Tel: 414-723-5565. [CEM]
School—534 Sunset Dr., 53121. Tel: 414-734-4258. Mrs. Mary Steele, Prin.
Lay Teachers 14; Students 200.
Catechesis/Religious Programs—Students 217.

Elm Grove, Waukesha Co., St. Mary's (1848), Revs. Daniel J. Pakenham; Romanus Nwaru; Deacons Charles J. Kustner; Richard Piontek.
Res., 1260 Church St., 53122. Tel: 414-782-4575; Fax: 414-782-0677. [CEM]
School—Tel: 414-782-7057. Sr. Elizabeth Uchytil, S.S.N.D., Prin.
Sisters 2; Lay Teachers 18; Students 399.
Catechesis/Religious Programs—13000 Juneau Blvd., 53122. Tel: 414-782-9470.
Students 188.

Farmington, Washington Co., St. John of God. Also serves St. Michael's, St. Michael. Sr. Carol Ann Jaeger, S.S.S.F., Dir.
Mailing Address: 8877 Forestview Rd., Kewaskum, 53040. Tel: 414-334-5270.

Fond du Lac, Fond du Lac Co.,

1—St. Joseph's, (1871), Revs. Patrick E. Heppe; Thomas J. Walker.
Res., 83 E. Second St., 54935. Tel: 414-921-0454; Fax: 414-921-5494.
School—Consolidated into the F.A.C.E.S. School System St. Joseph Parishoners, (Grades K-8). Tel: 414-921-5300. Kenneth Bond, Prin.
Students 192.
Catechesis/Religious Programs—Tel: 414-922-8229. Ray Mrozinski, D.R.E.
Students 447.

2—St. Louis, (1847) (French), Rev. Jerome A. Wagner; Deacon Ricardo Munoz.
Rectory: 209 N. Macy St., 54935. Tel: 414-921-0580; Fax: 414-921-0580. [JC]
Catechesis/Religious Programs—Tel: 414-922-8868. Beverly Sabel, D.R.E.
Students 204.

3—St. Mary's, (1866) (German), Rev. Peter C. Drenzek.
Res., 93 Marquette St., 54935. Tel: 414-921-1311; Fax: 414-921-7576.
School—Fond du Lac Area Catholic Education System (FACES), (Grades 6-8) 63 E. Merrill St., 54935. Tel: 414-922-3364.
St. Mary Campus Middle School—Tel: 414-921-9610.
Catechesis/Religious Programs—Tel: 414-923-4353. Rick Voell, D.R.E.
Students 383.

4—St. Patrick's, (1855), Rev. Michael O. Sturm; Sr. Roberta Meis, C.S.A., Pastoral Assoc.
Res., 41 E. Follett St., 54935. Tel: 414-921-0347; Fax: 414-921-6708. [JC]
School—Fond du Lac Area Catholic Education System (FACES), (Grades K-5). Tel: 414-922-3364.
Catechesis/Religious Programs—Tel: 414-921-6214.
Students 305.

5—Sacred Heart, (1957) (German), Rev. Eugene C. Neuman.
Res., 232 S. Peters Ave., 54935. Tel: 414-921-8831; Fax: 414-921-8879. [JC]
School—Fond du Lac Area Catholic Education

System (FACES), Tel: 414-921-5873.
Catechesis/Religious Programs—Tel: 414-922-7690. Barbara Kratz, D.R.E.
Students 280.

Fontana, Walworth Co., St. Benedict (1912), Rev. Stephen J. Stradinger.
Res., Box 110, 53125. Tel: 414-275-2480; Fax: 414-275-6426.
Catechesis/Religious Programs—Tel: 414-275-2993. D.R.E.: Barbara Obligato; Linda Gullo.
Students 309.

Fox Lake, Dodge Co., Immaculate Conception - St. Mary (1850) (Irish), Rev. Donald B. Braun.
Res., Also serves St. Mary, Lost Lake; & St. Gabriel, Randolph. 305 W. Green St., P.O. Box 85, 53933-0085. Tel: 414-928-3513; Fax: 414-928-6334. [CEM]

Fox Point, Milwaukee Co., St. Eugene (1957), Rev. Kenneth P. Knippel; Mrs. Pat Quinn-Casper, Pastoral Assoc. In res., Rev. Francis J. O'Rourke.
Res., 7600 N. Port Washington Rd., 53217. Tel: 414-241-6002; Fax: 414-241-6022.
School—Tel: 414-241-6020. Mr. K. James Colle, Prin.
Lay Teachers 16; Students 195.
Catechesis/Religious Programs—Tel: 414-241-6030. D.R.E.: Miss Mary Joy Dick; Mrs. Rita Capriolo.
Students 350.

Franklin, Milwaukee Co., St. James (1857), Rev. Kenneth J. Augustine; Judy Brooks, Pastoral Assoc.
Office: 7219 S. 27th St., 53132. Tel: 414-761-0480; Fax: 414-761-2208. [CEM]
Catechesis/Religious Programs—Students 271.

Sacred Hearts of Jesus and Mary (1858). Also serves Holy Assumption, St. Martins. Revs. Charles Bisgrove, S.C.J.; Anthony Russo, S.C.J. In res., Rev. John Nitzki, S.C.J.
Res., 7963 S. 116th St., 53132. Tel: 414-425-1114; Fax: 414-425-2527. [CEM]
School—7933 S. 116th St., 53132. Tel: 414-425-9200. Deacon A. Ronald Colaianni, Prin.
Lay Teachers 8; Students 155.
Catechesis/Religious Programs—Students 495.

Fredonia, Ozaukee Co., St. Rose of Lima (1909). Also serves Mother of Sorrows, Little Kohler; & Holy Cross, Holy Cross. Rev. Neil G. Zinthefer; Deacon Gerald Malueg.
Res., 305 Fredonia Ave., P.O. Box 250, 53021. Tel: 414-692-9994.
School—Rosemary Catholic, 53021. Tel: 414-692-2141; Fax: 414-692-9994. Sr. Rosemary O'Brien, S.S.S.F., Prin.
Sisters 1; Lay Teachers 6; Students 66.
Catechesis/Religious Programs—Students 78.

Genesee Depot, Waukesha Co., St. Paul (1863), Very Rev. Robert D. Gosma; Deacon Larry Normann; Len Grassman, Pastoral Assoc.
Res., 53127. Tel: 414-968-3865; Fax: 414-968-3865. [CEM]
School—Tel: 414-968-3175. Ms. Jeanne Karl, Prin.
Lay Teachers 11; Students 187.
Catechesis/Religious Programs—Tel: 414-968-2276. D.R.E.: Bob Graf, (Grades K-12); Tom Stratman, (Adult).
Students 452.

Germantown, Washington Co., St. Boniface (1845), Very Rev. Bernard S. Sippel; Deacon Kenneth W. Wolf.
Res., W204 N11940 Goldendale Rd., 53022. Tel: 414-628-2040. [CEM]
School—W204 N11968 Goldendale Rd., 53022. Tel: 414-628-1955.
Lay Teachers 11; Students 145.
Catechesis/Religious Programs—William Farrell, D.R.E.
Students 277.

Glenbeulah, Sheboygan Co., St. Fridolin. Also serves St. George, Elkhart Lake. Rev. Daniel J. Lasecki.
Mailing Address: Box T, Elkhart Lake, 53020. Tel: 414-876-2437.

Grafton, Ozaukee Co., St. Joseph's (1849), Rev. Michael G. Barrett; Terri Schiller, Pastoral Assoc. & D.R.E.; Deacons Richard J. Govek; Donald F. Kabara.
Pastoral Center: 1619 Washington St., 53024. Tel: 414-375-6500; Fax: 414-375-6509. [CEM]
School—1206 16th Ave., 53024. Tel: 414-375-6505.
Lay Teachers 10; Students 210.
Catechesis/Religious Programs—Tel: 414-375-6510.
Students 494.

Greendale, Milwaukee Co., St. Alphonsus (1938), Revs. Richard J. Aiken, Admin.; Aurelio Perez; Deacon Theodore A. Gurzynski. In res., Rev. Hugh G. Birdsall, S.D.S., M.A., M.S.
Res., 5960 W. Loomis Rd., 53129. Tel: 414-421-2442; Fax: 414-421-8744.
School—6000 W. Loomis Rd., 53129. Tel: 414-421-1760. Margaret Roushar, Prin.
Sisters 1; Brothers 1; Lay Teachers 29; Students 514.
Catechesis/Religious Programs—Tel: 414-421-0690.
Students 706.

Greenfield, Milwaukee Co., St. John the Evangelist (1916), Revs. Richard J. Talaska; Richard R. Verberg.
Res., 8500 W. Cold Spring Rd., 53228. Tel: 414-321-1965.
School—53228. Tel: 414-321-8540. Sr. Francine Hribar, O.S.F., Prin.
Sisters of St. Francis of Christ the King 3; Lay Teachers 9; Students 255.
Catechesis/Religious Programs—Tel: 414-321-4450. D.R.E.: Debbie Melian; Therese Hoeser Tel: 414-321-8922.
Students 221.

Hales Corners, Milwaukee Co., St. Mary's (1842), Revs. Arthur G. Heinze; James J. Brady; Gregory J. Greiten; Mary Matestic, Pastoral Assoc.
Res., 9520 W. Forest Home Ave., 53130. Tel: 414-425-2174; Fax: 414-425-9432. [CEM]
School—9553 W. Edgerton Ave., 53130. Tel: 414-425-3100; Fax: 414-425-6270. Sr. Marie Rene Kuban, Prin.; Mary Kopp, Vice Prin.
Sisters 1; Lay Teachers 24; Students 456.
Catechesis/Religious Programs—Tel: 414-425-3101; Fax: 414-425-9432. Barbara Schwartz, D.R.E.
Students 841.

Hartford, Washington Co., St. Kilian (1863), Rev. Michael J. Petrie.
Res., 264 W. State St., 53027. Tel: 414-673-4831; Fax: 414-673-4872. [CEM 2]
School—245 High St., 53027. Tel: 414-673-3081. Mary Caspar, Prin.
Lay Teachers 16; Students 275.
Catechesis/Religious Programs—Tel: 414-673-3746.
Students 342.

Hartland, Waukesha Co., St. Charles (1906), Rev. Thomas P. Demse.
Office: 313 Circle Dr., 53029-1899. Tel: 414-367-0800.
Res., 521 Renson Rd., 53029. Tel: 414-367-6704; Fax: 414-367-6960. [CEM]
School—Tel: 414-367-2040. Sr. Rosemary Rombalski, Prin.
Lay Teachers 9; Students 234.
Catechesis/Religious Programs—Tel: 414-367-3277.
Students 723.

Holy Cross, Ozaukee Co., Holy Cross (1845) (Luxemburg), Rev. Neil G. Zinthefer.
Res., Also serves St. Rose of Lima, Fredonia; & Mother of Sorrows, Little Kohler. 5330 Hwy. B, Belgium, 53004. Tel: 414-285-3658. [CEM]

Holy Hill, Washington Co., St. Mary of the Hill (1860), Rev. Fred Alexander, O.C.D.
Res., P.O. Box 38, Hubertus, 53033. Tel: 414-628-3606; 673-7505. [CEM]
Catechesis/Religious Programs—Marilyn Zwick, D.R.E.
Students 179.

Horicon, Dodge Co., St. Malachy (1856), Rev. M. Eugene Kinney; Deacon Gerald Buyck Tel: 414-485-3100.
Parish Center: 113 Valley St., 53032. Tel: 414-485-2427.
Res., 109 Valley St., 53032. Tel: 414-485-2937. [CEM]
Catechesis/Religious Programs—Tel: 414-485-2708. David Froemming, D.R.E.
Students 173.

Hubertus, Washington Co., St. Hubert's (1846), Rev. John A. Furtmann.
Res., 3727 Hubertus Rd., 53033. Tel: 414-628-1141. [CEM]
School—3733 Hubertus Rd., 53033. Tel: 414-628-1711.
Lay Teachers 15; Students 152.
Catechesis/Religious Programs—Tel: 414-628-2840.
Students 216.

Johnsburg, Fond du Lac Co., St. John the Baptist (1840), Rev. Donald T. Musinski.
Res., N9288 County W, Fond du Lac, 54935. Tel: 414-795-4316. [CEM]
Schools—(Grades 4-6). Tel: 414-795-4222. Sharon Allen, Coord.; Consolidated Parochial Elementary School. See Holy Cross, Mount Calvary. Tel: 414-753-4811.

Juneau, Dodge Co., Immaculate Conception (1870), Rev. Guy G. Gurath.
Res., 319 N. Main St., 53039. Tel: 414-386-4964. [CEM]
Catechesis/Religious Programs—Tel: 414-386-4964. Teresa Anderson, D.R.E.
Students 180.

Kansasville, Racine Co., St. Mary's-Dover (1869), Rev. James B. Cera.
Mailing Address: P.O. Box 126, 53139.
Res., 23211 Church Rd., 53139. Tel: 414-878-1762. [CEM]

Kenosha, Kenosha Co.,

1—St. Anthony's, (1910) (Slovak), Rev. Ray W. Wawiorka.
Mailing Address: 2223 51st St., 53140. Tel: 414-652-1844. [JC]

2—St. Casimir's, (1901), Rev. Robert T. McDermott.
Res., 1009 Washington Rd., 53140. Tel: 414-657-6544; Fax: 414-657-9955. [CEM]
High School—St. Joseph Interparish Jr. High School, 2401 69th St., 53143. Tel: 414-654-8651. Mr. Richard Ruhl, Prin.
Lay Teachers 6; Students 130. Sponsored by St. Casimir, St. Mark, St. Therese and St. Thomas Aquinas, Kenosha.

3—St. George, (1851), Rev. Gerald P. Schmitz.
Res., 4804 7th Ave., 53140. Tel: 414-657-6875; Fax: 414-657-1495. [CEM]

4—St. James, (1845) (Irish), Rev. Frederick A. Heuser.
Res., 5804 Sheridan Rd., 53140. Tel: 414-658-8071; Fax: 414-658-2490. [CEM]

5—St. Mark's, (1924), Very Rev. Kenneth J. Metz; Rev. Pere Cane-Gombau; Karen Metallo, Pastoral Assoc.; Deacons Patrick H. Frye; Gregorio M. Lebron; Patricia L. Andrews, Bus. Mgr.
Res., 7117 14th Ave., 53143. Tel: 414-652-1972; Fax: 414-656-7375.
School—7202 14th Ave., 53143. Tel: 414-652-4022. Miss Shirley A. Boss, Prin.
School Sisters of St. Francis 1; Lay Teachers 14; Students 267.
Junior Academy—(Preschool).
Lay Teachers 15; Students 162.
Catechesis/Religious Programs—Tel: 414-652-3226. Colleen A. Reddy, D.R.E.
Students 416.
Latin American Center—1320 73rd St., 53143-5459. Tel: 414-657-7222. Rev. Gerald J. Hessel, Dir.

6—St. Mary's, (1929), Revs. Howard G. Haase; Mark J. Danczyk; Deacons Ronald F. Lesjak; James S. Francois; Wilson Shierk.
Res., 7307 40th Ave., 53142. Tel: 414-694-6018; Fax: 414-694-6048.
School—7400 39th Ave., 53142. Tel: 414-694-6650; Fax: 414-694-6740. Jerry Hubert, Prin.
Lay Teachers 24; Students 406.
Catechesis/Religious Programs—Tel: 414-694-5474. D.R.E.: Jane Delfield; Sandy Slivon.
Students 945.

7—Our Lady of Mount Carmel, (1904) (Italian), Rev. John J. Richetta.
Res., 1919 54th St., 53140. Tel: 414-652-7660; 652-7683; Fax: 414-652-2542.
School—5400 19th Ave., 53140. Tel: 414-652-7660. Paul Cera, Prin.
Lay Teachers 7; Students 135.
Catechesis/Religious Programs—Tel: 414-652-5057.
Students 190.

8—Our Lady of the Holy Rosary, (1904) (Italian), Revs. John J. Molnar, O.S.A.; Henry B. Maibusch, O.S.A.; Bros. Fred Kaiser, O.S.A.; Robert Schurman, O.S.A.; Deacon Philip Cook, O.S.A.
Res., 2224 45th St., 53140. Tel: 414-652-2771; Fax: 414-652-0183.
School—4400 22nd Ave., 53140. Tel: 414-652-5950. Sr. M. Bertina, F.S.S.J., Prin.
Franciscan Sisters of St. Joseph (Hamburg, NY) 6; Lay Teachers 13; Students 382.
Catechesis/Religious Programs—Bro. Fred Kaiser, O.S.A., D.R.E.
Students 265.

9—St. Peter's, (1903), Revs. Dan Cambra, M.I.C.; Pete Cibulskis, M.I.C.; Deacon Terrance A. Maack.
Res., 2224 30th Ave., 53144. Tel: 414-551-9004.
School—Tel: 414-551-8383. Mr. Sigmund Kolano, Prin.
Lay Teachers 6; Students 118.
Catechesis/Religious Programs—Tel: 414-897-2602.
Students 275.

10—St. Therese, (1953), Rev. Brian T. Holbus.
Res., 9005 22nd Ave., 53143-6699. Tel: 414-694-4695; Fax: 414-694-7284.
School—2020 91st St., 53143. Tel: 414-694-8080. Mrs. Jean Kuklenski, Prin.
Lay Teachers 10; Students 136.

11—St. Thomas Aquinas, (1911), Rev. Thomas A. LeMieux.
Res., 6202 25th Ave., 53143-4370. Tel: 414-658-8662.
School—St. Joseph Interparish Jr. High School, 2401 69th St., 53143. Tel: 414-654-8651. Rick Ruhl, Prin.

Lay Teachers 8; Students 146. Sponsored by St. Casimir, St. Mark, St. Therese, St. Thomas Aquinas, and Our Lady of Mt. Carmel, Kenosha.

Kewaskum, Washington Co., Holy Trinity (1861), Rev. John L. Brophy.
Res., 331 Main St., P.O. Box 461, 53040. Tel: 414-626-2860. [CEM 2]
School—305 Main St, 53040. Tel: 414-626-2603. Mrs. June Gauvin, Prin.
Sisters 1; Lay Teachers 12; Students 171.
Catechesis / Religious Programs—Tel: 414-334-4195. Sr. Eileen Curran, S.S.N.D., D.R.E.
Students 253.

Kohler, Sheboygan Co., St. John Evangelist (1927), Rev. Louis J. Wilimek.
Res., 600 Green Tree Rd., 53044. Tel: 414-452-9623; Fax: 414-452-9633.
Catechesis / Religious Programs—Tel: 414-458-9931.
Students 163.

Lake Five, Washington Co., St. Columba. Also serves St. John, Monches. Rev. Richard L. Grebasch.
Mailing Address: W302 N9583 O'Neil Rd., Hartford, 53029. Tel: 414-628-9089.

Lake Geneva, Walworth Co., St. Francis de Sales (1842), Revs. David J. Braun; Scott R. Leannah.
Res., 148 West Main St., 53147. Tel: 414-248-8524; Fax: 414-248-5302. [CEM]
School—130 Main St., 53147. Tel: 414-248-2778.
Lay Teachers 9; Students 222.
Catechesis / Religious Programs—Tel: 414-248-8526. Sr. Evelyn Trapp, S.S.S.F., D.R.E.
Students 251.

Le Roy, Dodge Co., St. Andrew's (1849), Rev. Robert J. Berghammer.
Res., W3081 County Trk Y, Lomira, 53048. Tel: 414-583-4125; 387-4321. [CEM]

Lima, Sheboygan Co., St. Rose. Also serves St. George, St. George. Rev. Eugene D. Winkler.
Mailing Address: N3589 County Rd., A.E., Sheboygan Falls, 53085. Tel: 414-467-4576.

Little Kohler, Ozaukee Co., Mother of Sorrows. Also serves St. Rose of Lima, Fredonia and Holy Cross, Holy Cross. Rev. Neil G. Zinthefer.
Mailing Address: 305 Fredonia Ave., P.O. Box 250, Fredonia, 53021. Tel: 414-692-9994.

Lomira, Dodge Co., St. Mary (1870), Rev. Vincent B. Holubowicz.
Res., 645 Milwaukee St., 53048. Tel: 414-269-4429. [CEM]
School—(Grades 1-8) 705 Milwaukee, 53048. Tel: 414-269-4326. Sr. Rosemary Herriges, O.S.F., Prin.
Sisters 1; Lay Teachers 8; Students 124. Consolidated with St. Theresa to form Consolidated Catholic School of Lomira-Theresa. Tel: 414-488-4543.
Catechesis / Religious Programs—Tel: 414-583-4286.
Students 180.

Lost Lake, Dodge Co., St. Mary's (1893). Also serves St. Gabriel, Randolph; & St. Mary, Fox Lake. Rev. Donald B. Braun.
Res., W11821 Concord Rd., Randolph, 53956. Tel: 414-326-3585. [CEM]

Lyons, Walworth N Co., St. Kilian. Also serves St. Joseph, Lyons. Mr. Daniel L. Hull, Dir.
Mailing Address: P.O. Box 60, 53148-0060. Tel: 414-763-2050.

St. Joseph's, Walworth Co., (1870). Also serves St. Kilian, Lyons. Rev. Daniel L. Hull, Parish Dir.
Res., 1540 Mill St., Box 60, 53148-0060. Tel: 414-763-2050. [CEM]

Mapleton, Waukesha Co., St. Catherine (1847) (Irish), Rev. David A. Verhasselt; Deacon Harry Gliniecki.
Res., W359 N8512 Brown St., Oconomowoc, 53066. Tel: 414-474-7000; Fax: 414-474-4661. [CEM]
Catechesis / Religious Programs—Students 151.

Marytown, Fond du Lac Co., St. Mary (1849), Rev. Joseph H. Coerber.
Res., N10232 Hwy. 149, New Holstein, 53061. Tel: 414-898-4040; Fax: 414-898-9002. [CEM]
School—See Holy Cross, Mt. Calvary for details. Tel: 414-753-4811.

Mayville, Dodge Co., St. Mary's (1856), Very Rev. Charles H. Wester.
Res., 112 S. German St., P.O. Box 22, 53050. Tel: 414-387-2470; 387-3130 (Parish Center). [CEM]
School—28 Naber St., 53050. Tel: 414-387-2920.
Lay Teachers 7; Students 140.
Catechesis / Religious Programs—Tel: 414-387-3130.
Students 265.

Menomonee Falls, Waukesha Co.,

1—St. Anthony's, (1846), Revs. Anthony G. Klink; Kevin J. Wester; Deacons David L. Zimprich; Robert Wodushek.
Res., N74 W13604 Appleton Ave., 53051. Tel: 414-251-5910; Fax: 414-251-6564. [CEM]
School—N74 W13646 Appleton Ave., 53051. Tel: 414-251-4390; Fax: 414-251-2412. Jacob J. Jilling, Prin.
Lay Teachers 10; Students 225.
Catechesis / Religious Programs—Tel: 414-251-8868. Mary A. DuQuaine, D.R.E.
Students 389.

2—Good Shepherd, (1957), Rev. Paul A. Daniels; Deacon Gene Christensen; Joseph Strazishar, Dir. of Admin. Svcs.
Church—N88 W17658 Christman Rd., 53051-2699. Tel: 414-255-2035; Fax: 414-255-2020.
Res., W177 N8916 St. Thomas Dr., 53051-2099. Tel: 414-255-1341.
Catechesis / Religious Programs—Tel: 414-255-2210. D.R.E.: Matthew Hakes; Jean Newman; Richard Harter.
Students 628.

3—St. James, (1847), Revs. Eugene J. Doda, Jr.; Joseph J. Juknialis.
Res., W 220-N 6588 Town Line Rd., 53051. Tel: 414-251-3944; Fax: ES1653. [CEM]
Catechesis / Religious Programs—Tel: 414-251-0891; Fax: 414-250-2679. D.R.E.: Margie Lang; Danine Smeaton.
Students 543.

4—St. Mary's, (1904), Rev. Joseph A. Janicki; Deacons Robert H. Buth; Thomas H. Wuchterl; Thomas Monday.
Res., N 89 W 16297 Cleveland Ave., 53051. Tel: 414-251-0220; Fax: 414-251-6948. [CEM]
School—N 89 W 16215 Cleveland Ave., 53051. Tel: 414-251-1050. Barbara C. Lee, Prin.
Lay Teachers 23; Students 428.
Catechesis / Religious Programs—Tel: 414-251-1154. D.R.E.: Margaret Geyer; Nancy Dubord, Pastoral Assoc.
Students 431.

Mequon, Ozaukee Co., St. James (1851) (German), Revs. Gregory M. Spitz; George Ssebadduka (Uganda) Tel: 414-242-3541. In res., Rev. William Wallaik Tel: 414-242-3750.
Res., 11300 N. St. James Ln., 28W, 53092. Tel: 414-242-7967; Fax: 414-242-7970. [CEM]
School—(Grades 4-8). Tel: 414-242-7960; Fax: 414-512-8986. Mr. Richard Goeden, Prin.
Lay Teachers 24; Students 485. Consolidated with St. Cecilia, Thiensville to form SS. Cecilia and James.
Catechesis / Religious Programs—Tel: 414-242-7963; Fax: 414-242-7970. Ms. Pat Roehrig, D.R.E.
Students 560.

Mitchell, Sheboygan Co., St. Michael. Also serves St. Mary, Random Lake; St. Patrick, Adell; St. Mary, Cascade; St. Nicholas, Dacada. Very Rev. Richard J. Cerpich.
Mailing Address: 230 Butler St., Random Lake, 53075. Tel: 414-994-4380; Fax: 414-994-2605.

Monches, Waukesha Co., St. John's (1843). Also serves St. Columba, Lake Five. Rev. Richard L. Grebasch.
Res., W302 N9583 O'Neil Rd., Hartland, 53029. Tel: 414-966-2777; Fax: 414-966-3731. [CEM]
Catechesis / Religious Programs—Tel: 414-628-3939. Mrs. Katy Twiford, D.R.E.
Students 215.

Mount Calvary, Fond du Lac Co., Holy Cross (1849), Rev. Peter P. Kutch, O.F.M.Cap.
Res., P.O. Box 176, 53057. Tel: 414-753-3311. [CEM]
School—(Grades 1-8) 100 Notre Dame St., 53057. Tel: 414-753-4811.
Lay Teachers 15; Students 79. Consolidated Parochial Elementary School of Mount Calvary (CPES): St. John the Baptist, Johnsburg; St. Mary, Marytown; Holy Cross, Mount Calvary; St. Cloud, St. Cloud.
Catechesis / Religious Programs—Tel: 414-753-3311.
Students 135.

Mukwonago, Waukesha Co., St. James (1896), Rev. Robert J. Drutowski.
Res., 830 Hwy. NN East, 53149. Tel: 414-363-7615; Fax: 414-363-2416.
School—Tel: 414-363-8152. Pamala Yerke, Prin.
Lay Teachers 8; Students 184.
Catechesis / Religious Programs—Tel: 414-363-5529.
Students 703.

Muskego, Waukesha Co., St. Leonard Congregation (1957), Revs. Jerome A. Rinzel; Loyola Amalraj; Deacon Ralph Wisniewski; Carlene S. Larson, Pastoral Assoc.
Res., W173 S7743 Westwood Dr., 53150. Tel: 414-679-1773; Fax: 414-679-4210.
School—Tel: 414-679-0451. Mr. Robert Radomski, Prin.
Lay Teachers 15; Students 264.
Catechesis / Religious Programs—Tel: 414-679-0880. Judee Weber, D.R.E.
Students 861.

Nabob, Washington Co., St. Matthias (1848), Rev. Alois R. Van Beek.
Mailing Address: 4886 Hwy. 175, Hartford, 53027. Tel: 414-644-5701. [CEM]

Nenno, Washington Co., SS. Peter and Paul (1848), Rev. Michael L. Wild.
Tri-Parish Office: Also serves St. Anthony, Allenton; & Sacred Heart, Allenton. 215 Main St., P.O. Box 96, Allenton, 53002-0096. Tel: 414-629-5240. [CEM]
Convent—632 Church St., P.O. Box 356, Allenton, 53002. Tel: 414-629-5342. School Sisters of Notre Dame

Neosho, Dodge Co., St. Matthew's (1857) (German). Also serves St. Mary, Woodland; & St. John, Rubicon. Rev. Laurin J. Wenig.
Res., 148 W. Lehman St., P.O. Box 45, 53059. Tel: 414-625-3144. [CEM]
Catechesis / Religious Programs—Tel: 414-625-3290.
Students 202.

New Berlin, Waukesha Co., Holy Apostles (1855), Very Rev. Edward R. Wieland; Revs. Timothy C. Bickel; William L. Ericksen; Deacon Edward J. Nowicki.
Res., 16000 W. National Ave., 53151. Tel: 414-786-7330; Fax: 414-786-0425. [CEM]
School—Tel: 414-786-7331. Brenda Sue White, Prin.
Sisters 2; Lay Teachers 19; Students 502.
Catechesis / Religious Programs—Tel: 414-786-2035.
Students 747.

St. Elizabeth Ann Seton (1981), Revs. Steven J. Amann; Michael Ignaszak.
Church & Office—12700 W. Howard Ave., 53151. Tel: 414-782-6760; Fax: 414-782-4763.
Catechesis / Religious Programs—Tel: 414-782-8982. Joanne Prei, D.R.E.
Students 497.

Newburg, Washington Co., Holy Trinity (1859), Rev. Robert G. Sampon.
Res., Box 1, 53060. Tel: 414-675-6256. [CEM 3]
Stations—Trenton, St. Augustine, (1857); Farmington, St. Peter, (1855).

New Munster, Kenosha Co., St. Alphonsus (1851) (German), Rev. Thomas E. Biersack.
Res., 6301 344th Ave., P.O. Box 767, 53152. Tel: 414-537-4370; Fax: 414-537-4370. [CEM]
School—Tel: 414-537-4379.
Lay Teachers 4; Students 68.

North Fond du Lac, Fond du Lac Co., Presentation of the Blessed Virgin (1902), Rev. John A. O'Brien, Ph.D.; Deacon Paul S. Monzel.
Res., 705 Michigan Ave., 54937. Tel: 414-921-9383. [JC]
Catechesis / Religious Programs—Tel: 414-921-5873. Sandy O'Loughlin, D.R.E.
Students 313.

North Lake, Waukesha Co., St. Clare's (1916), Rev. Anthony T. McCarthy.
Res., Box 68, 53064. Tel: 414-966-2191; Fax: 414-966-1829. [CEM]
Catechesis / Religious Programs—Tel: 414-966-7010.
Students 434.

Oak Creek, Milwaukee Co., St. Matthew's (1841), Rev. Joseph G. Sukup.
Res., 9303 S. Chicago Rd., 53154. Tel: 414-762-4200; Fax: 414-571-9973. [CEM]
School—9329 S. Chicago Rd., 53154. Tel: 414-762-6820.
Franciscan Sisters of Our Lady of Perpetual Help 1; Sisters of St. Francis of Assisi 1; Lay Teachers 9; Students 241.
Catechesis / Religious Programs—Tel: 414-762-6847.
Students 419.

Oakfield, Fond Du Lac Co., St. James. Also serves St. John, Bryon. Rev. Donald F. Zerkel.
Mailing Address: W5882 Church Rd., Fond Du Lac, 54937. Tel: 414-583-4376; Fax: 414-922-1167.
Res., 101 N. Main, 53065.

Oconomowoc, Waukesha Co., St. Jerome's (1860), Rev. Thomas A. Tearney.
Res., 211 S. Main St., 53066. Tel: 414-569-3020; Fax: 414-569-3022. [CEM]
School—110 Third St., 53066. Tel: 414-569-3030.
Franciscan Sisters of Perpetual Adoration 1; Lay Teachers 19; Students 313.
Catechesis / Religious Programs—Tel: 414-569-3025.
Students 422.

Okauchee, Waukesha Co., St. Joan of Arc (1923), Rev. James P. Loehr.
Res., N50 W34851 Wisconsin Ave., P.O. Box 116, 53069. Tel: 414-567-3466; Fax: 414-567-5786. [CEM]
School—N50 W34835 Wisconsin Ave., P.O. Box 116, 53069. Tel: 414-567-5775. Sr. Julie Wambach,

S.S.N.D., Prin.
School Sisters of Notre Dame 2; Lay Teachers 6; Students 82.
Catechesis/Religious Programs—Tel: 414-567-5775. Barbara Dunn, D.R.E.
Students 175.

Paris, Kenosha Co., St. John the Baptist (1859), Rev. Thomas G. Fait.
Parish Office: 1501 172nd Ave. Paris, Union Grove, 53182. Tel: 414-859-2484. [CEM]
School—Providence Catholic School. Consolidated with St. Francis Xavier, Brighton. 1481 172nd Ave., Paris, Union Grove, 53182. Tel: 414-859-2007; 414-878-2713. Sr. Kathryn Dean Strandell, O.S.F., Prin.
Lay Teachers 9; Students 162; Religious 2.
Catechesis/Religious Programs—Students 35.

Pell Lake, Walworth Co., St. Mary's (1928), Rev. Dennis D. Callahan; Deacon Anthony Martino; Marilyn Kingston, Pastoral Assoc.
Res., Box 34, 53157. Tel: 414-279-6295. [JC]

Pewaukee, Waukesha Co., St. Anthony's (1918), Rev. R. Thomas Venne; Deacon Dennis Anderson.
Res., W 280 N 2101 Hwy. SS., 53072. Tel: 414-691-2326; Fax: 414-691-7376.
School—Tel: 414-691-0460; 691-1173 (Parish Center).
Lay Teachers 10; Students 149.
Catechesis/Religious Programs—Kathleen Amidei, D.R.E.
Students 438.

St. Mary's (1858), Rev. Carl P. Alberte.
Res., 449 W. Wisconsin Ave., P.O. Box 64, 53072. Tel: 414-691-1535; Fax: 414-691-8606. [CEM]
School—Tel: 414-691-2120. Mrs. Kathleen Rempe, Prin.
Notre Dame Sisters 1; Lay Teachers 7; Students 135.
Catechesis/Religious Programs—Students 165.

SS. Peter and Paul (1848), Rev. R. Michael Grellinger.
Mailing Address: W225 N3131 Duplainville Rd., 53072. Tel: 414-691-3430.
Res., 3827 N. 66 St., Milwaukee, 53216. Tel: 414-527-2700. [CEM]
Church—W225 N3131 Duplainville Rd., 53072. Tel: 414-691-3430.
Catechesis/Religious Programs—Jackie Schulz, D.R.E.
Students 100.

Plymouth, Sheboygan Co., St. John the Baptist's (1861), Rev. Wayne W. Bittner.
Res., 215 W. Main St., 53073. Tel: 414-892-4006. [CEM]
School—116 Pleasant St., 53073. Tel: 414-893-5961. Mary Jo Sizonen, Prin.
Lay Teachers 18; Students 270.
Catechesis/Religious Programs—Tel: 414-892-6015.
Students 365.

Port Washington, Ozaukee Co., St. Mary's (1853), Rev. Allan J. Sommer.
Office: 430 N. Johnson St., 53074. Tel: 414-284-5771. [CEM]
School—Consolidated with St. Peter of Alcantara to form Port Washington Catholic School, Inc. 1802 N. Wisconsin St., 53074. Tel: 414-284-2441 (K-4); 284-2682 (5-8).
School Sisters of Notre Dame 1; Lay Teachers 20; Students 337.
Catechesis/Religious Programs—Tel: 414-284-6472. Patricia Gibes, D.R.E.
Students 329.

St. Peter of Alcantara (1966), Rev. Joseph H. Haas; Deacon Thomas J. Surges.
Res., 1800 N. Wisconsin St., 53074. Tel: 414-284-4266; Fax: 414-284-4216.
School—Port Washington Catholic School. See St. Mary for details. Tel: 414-284-2682.
Catechesis/Religious Programs—Tel: 414-284-6472. D.R.E.: Patricia Gibes, (Grades K-6); Kathleen Gordon, (Grades 7-12), Tel: 414-284-2102.
Students 222.

Racine, Racine Co.,

1—St. Casimir's, (1913) (Lithuanian), Rev. Russell G. Roetzer.
Res., 815 Park Ave., 53403. Tel: 414-634-2811. [JC]

2—Cristo Rey, (1980) (Hispanic), Rev. Robert J. McGlinn (CHI) Admin.
Res., 800 Wisconsin Ave., 53403. Tel: 414-632-3151.

3—Holy Name, (1884) (German), Rev. Edward A. Vogel.
Res., 1509 Grand Ave., 53403. Tel: 414-637-8374.
School—1510 Villa St., 53403. Tel: 414-637-7673. Susan Chenoweth, Prin.
Lay Teachers 13; Students 260.
Catechesis/Religious Programs—Students 170.

4—Holy Trinity, (1914) (Slovak). Also serves St. Stanislaus, Racine. Rev. Louis P. Luljak.
Res., 1754 Grand Ave., 53403-2693. Tel: 414-634-6926. [JC]

5—St. Edward's, (1919), Rev. Richard J. Molter.
Office: 1430 Grove Ave., 53405. Tel: 414-636-8040; Fax: 414-636-8052.
Res., 1401 Grove Ave., 53405. Tel: 414-636-8049.
School—1435 Grove Ave., 53405. Tel: 414-636-8044. Joseph Majowski, Prin.
Dominican Sisters (Racine) 1; Lay Teachers 22; Students 410.
Catechesis/Religious Programs—Tel: 414-636-8042.
Students 208.

6—St. John Nepomuk, (1896), Rev. Thomas F. Lijewski.
Res., 700 English St., 53402. Tel: 414-634-5647; Fax: 414-637-1436. [JC]
School—1923 Green St., 53402. Tel: 414-637-9349. School Sisters of St. Francis 2; Lay Teachers 10; Students 142.

7—St. Joseph's, (1875) (German), Rev. Richard J. Stoffel.
Office: 1532 N. Wisconsin St., 53402. Tel: 414-633-8284; Fax: 414-633-8285.
Res., 1712 Chatham St., 53402. Tel: 414-632-6487. [JC 4]
School—1525 Erie St., 53402. Tel: 414-633-2403. Charles T. Cooper, Prin.
Lay Teachers 14; Students 245.
Catechesis/Religious Programs—Tel: 414-633-9005. Susan Gehrig, D.R.E.
Students 214.

8—St. Lucy's, (1958), Rev. Jeffrey M. Thielen.
Res., 3059 Carpenter Ave., 53403. Tel: 414-554-1801; Fax: 414-554-2009.
School—3035 Drexel, 53403. Tel: 414-554-1091.
Lay Teachers 9; Students 273.
Catechesis/Religious Programs—Tel: 414-554-1801. Sandra Gottfredsen, D.R.E.
Students 360.

9—St. Mary's by the Lake, (1852), Rev. Leon J. Schneider, Admin.; Deacon James Devona.
Mailing Address: Box 1782, 53401-1782.
Res., 1440 Main, 53403. Tel: 414-633-2336. [JC]
Church—7605 Lakeshore Dr., 53402. Tel: 414-639-3616.

10—St. Patrick's, (1856), Sr. Carol Kottewitz, R.C., Parish Dir.; Deacons Russell A. Misurelli; Emilio Coca.
Res., 1100 Erie St., 53402. Tel: 414-632-8808. [JC 4]

11—St. Paul the Apostle, (1965), Rev. Paul M. Esser; Deacon Willard Widmar.
Res., 5700 Washington Ave., 53406-4082. Tel: 414-886-0530; Fax: 414-886-0737. [JC]
Catechesis/Religious Programs—Tel: 414-886-0531. D.R.E.: Christine H. Mueller; James Beuscher.
Students 240.

12—St. Rita's, (1925), Revs. Joseph G. Stobba, O.S.A.; John T. Shirley, O.S.A.
Res., 4339 Douglas Ave., 53402. Tel: 414-639-3223; Fax: 414-681-0628. [CEM]
School—Tel: 414-639-3333.
Lay Teachers 11; Students 275.
Catechesis/Religious Programs—Tel: 414-639-6280.
Students 256.

13—St. Rose, (1886), Rev. Russell G. Roetzer.
Res., 715 Eleventh St., 53403. Tel: 414-633-1796.

14—Sacred Heart, (1916), Very Rev. Joseph F. Hornacek; Deacon Joseph H. Hying.
Res., 2201 Northwestern Ave., 53404. Tel: 414-634-5526; Fax: 414-634-5767.
School—2023 Northwestern Ave., 53404. Tel: 414-637-2012. Mr. Robert Hesse, Prin.
Lay Teachers 10; Students 256.
Catechesis/Religious Programs—Tel: 414-634-3607. Alan Mc Cauley, D.R.E.
Students 215.

15—St. Stanislaus, (1904) (Polish). Also serves Holy Trinity, Racine. Rev. Louis P. Luljak.
Res., 1754 Grand Ave., 53403. Tel: 414-634-6926. [JC]

Randolph, Columbia C Co., St. Gabriel. Also serves St. Mary, Lost Lake and St. Mary, Fox Lake. Rev. Donald B. Braun.
Mailing Address: W11821 Concord Rd., 53956. Tel: 414-326-3585.

Random Lake, Sheboygan Co., St. Mary's (1855). Also serves St. Patrick, Adell; St. Mary, Cascade; St. Nicholas, Dacada; & St. Michael, Mitchell. Very Rev. Richard J. Cerpich.
Res., 230 Butler St., 53075. Tel: 414-994-4380; Fax: 414-994-2605. [CEM]
School—Also serves St. Nicholas, Dacada & St. Patrick, Adell. 306 Butler St., 53075. Tel: 414-994-9962.
Sisters 1; Lay Teachers 7; Students 175.
Catechesis/Religious Programs—Students 125.

Reeseville, Dodge Co., Holy Family (1901). Also serves St. Columbkille, Elba. Rev. Edward J. Hussli.
Res., 302 Prairie St., P.O. Box 277, 53579. Tel: 414-927-3102. [CEM 2]

Richfield, Washington Co., St. Mary (1854) (German), Rev. Walter J. Vogel.
Res., 2414 Hillside Rd., 53076. Tel: 414-628-3533; Fax: 414-628-3533. [CEM]

Ripon, Fond du Lac Co., St. Patrick (1858), Rev. John A. Schmitz.
Res., 218 Blossom St., 54971. Tel: 414-748-2345. [CEM]
School—222 Blossom St., 54971. Tel: 414-748-3760. Norita Barrett, Prin.
Lay Teachers 6; Students 66.
Catechesis/Religious Programs—Students 235.

St. Wenceslaus (1896) (Polish), Rev. William L. Toelle.
Res., 411 E. Fond du Lac St., 54971-1591. Tel: 414-748-2325.
Catechesis/Religious Programs—Tel: 414-748-3826.
Students 147.

Rubicon, Dodge Co., St. John's (1870) (German). Also serves St. Matthew, Neosho; & St. Mary, Woodland. Rev. Laurin J. Wenig.
Res., 148 W. Lehman, Neosho, 53059. Tel: 414-625-3144. [CEM][JC]
Church—W1170 Rome Rd., P.O. Box 17, 53078. Tel: 414-673-3380.
Catechesis/Religious Programs—Tel: 414-673-3380.
Students 224.

St. Cloud, Fond du Lac Co., St. Cloud (1870) (German), Rev. Peter P. Kutch, O.F.M.Cap.
Res., 924 Main St., P.O. Box 138, 53079. Tel: 414-999-2011. [CEM]
School—(Grades 6-8) 920 Main St., Box 89, 53079-0138. Tel: 414-999-2411. Mrs. Jeanette Jankowski, Bldg. Coord. Consolidated Parochial Elementary School. See Holy Cross, Mount Calvary.

St. Francis, Milwaukee Co., Sacred Heart of Jesus (1868), Alexandra Guliano, Parish Dir.
Office: 3635 S. Kinnickinnic Ave., 53235. Tel: 414-481-2330; Fax: 414-744-7222. [CEM]
School—Tel: 414-744-2483. Shirley Hubbard, Prin.
Sisters 1; Lay Teachers 15; Students 250.
Catechesis/Religious Programs—Tel: 414-486-3945.
Students 127.

St. George, Sheboygan Co., St. George (1860). Also serves St. Rose, Lima. Rev. Eugene D. Winkler; Deacon William T. Jens.
Res., N3589 County Rd. A E., Sheboygan Falls, 53085. Tel: 414-467-4576. [CEM]

St. Joe, Fond du Lac, Co., St. Joseph's (1858) (German), Rev. Peter P. Kutch, O.F.M.Cap.
Res., W620 County G, P.O. Box 138, St. Cloud, 53079-0138. Tel: 414-999-3131. [CEM]

St. Kilian, Fond du Lac Co., St. Kilian's (1848), Rev. Wayne J. Barta, Admin. In res., Rev. Victor A. Kemmer.
Res., N185 Hwy. W, Rte. 4, Campbellsport, 53010. Tel: 414-626-2636. [CEM]

St. Lawrence, Washington Co., St. Lawrence (1846) (German), Rev. Alois R. Van Beek.
Res., 4886 Hwy. 175, Hartford, 53027. Tel: 414-644-5701. [CEM]
Catechesis/Religious Programs—Tel: 414-644-0011.
Students 188. Also serves St. Matthias, Nabob.

St. Martins, Milwaukee Co., Holy Assumption. Also serves Sacred Hearts of Jesus and Mary, Franklin. Revs. Charles Bisgrove, S.C.J.; Anthony Russo, S.C.J.
Mailing Address: 7963 S. 116th St., Franklin, 53132. Tel: 414-529-1202; Fax: 414-425-1114.
Res., 1132 W. St. Martins Rd.

St. Michael, Washington Co., St. Michael's (1846) (German). Also serves St. John of God, Farmington. Sr. Carol Ann Jaeger, S.S.S.F., Parish Dir.; Deacon Ralph Horner.
Res., 8877 Forestview Rd., Kewaskum, 53040. Tel: 414-334-5270. [CEM]
Catechesis/Religious Programs—Tel: 414-334-4195. Sr. Eileen Curran, S.S.N.D., D.R.E.
Students 198.

St. Peter, Fond du Lac Co., St. Peter (1867) (German), Rev. William M. Heffron.
Res., N8079 Church Rd., Malone, 53049. Tel: 414-921-3583. [CEM]
Catechesis/Religious Programs—W. 3880 Evergreen Ct., Malone, 53049. Tel: 414-922-3914.
Students 198.

Saukville, Ozaukee Co., Immaculate Conception (1858),

Rev. Karl H. Acker.
Res., 145 W. Church St., 53080. Tel: 414-284-0276. [CEM]
School—341 S. Dries St., 53080. Tel: 414-284-0277. Sr. Jean Hassenberg, S.S.N.D., Prin.
Sisters 1; Lay Teachers 5; Students 60.
Catechesis/Religious Programs—Students 224.

Sharon, Walworth Co., St. Catherine, Thomas McKenna, Parish Dir.
Mailing Address: P.O.Box 502, 53585. Tel: 414-736-4615.
Res., Tel: 815-569-2530. [CEM]

Sheboygan, Sheboygan Co.,

1—St. Clement's, (1914), Rev. James Vojtik; Deacon Baleriano Gonzales.
Res., 522 New York Ave., 53081. Tel: 414-457-4629. [JC]

2—SS. Cyril and Methodius, (1910) (Slovenian), Rev. Richard J. Fleischman.
Res., 822 New Jersey Ave., 53081. Tel: 414-457-7110. [CEM]

3—St. Dominic, (1927), Rev. James J. Jarumbo.
Res., 2133 N. 22nd St., 53081. Tel: 414-458-8787; Fax: 414-458-3280. [JC]
School—2100 N. 21st St., 53081. Tel: 414-452-8747. Peggy Henseler, Prin.
Lay Teachers 11; Students 151.
Catechesis/Religious Programs—Tel: 414-458-5390. D.R.E.: Brian Reindl; Jean Puls; Sharon Pentek, (Preschool).
Students 585.

4—Holy Name, (1845) (German), Rev. Daniel J. Sanders; Deacon August Meyer.
Res., 807 Superior Ave., 53081. Tel: 414-458-7721; Fax: 414-459-9108. [CEM]
School—814 Superior Ave., 53081. Tel: 414-452-1571. Valerie Black, Prin.
Lay Teachers 21; Students 323.
Catechesis/Religious Programs—Tel: 414-452-0129. D.R.E.: Mary Ann Zoch; Sue Seymour.
Students 284.

5—Immaculate Conception, (1903) (Lithuanian), Rev. Glenn E. Powers.
Res., 2705 S. 14 St., 53081. Tel: 414-457-3967; Fax: 414-457-5885. [CEM]
School—Christ Child Academy. (Grades K-5): 1449 S. 12th St., 53081. Tel: 414-459-2663; (Grades 6-8): 2722 Henry St., 53081. Tel: 414-459-2660. Marilyn Burns, Prin.
Lay Teachers 17; Students 230.
Catechesis/Religious Programs—Tel: 414-459-2665. Donald Wright, D.R.E.
Students 194.

6—St. Peter Claver, (1888) (German), Revs. Brian J. Szyszko; Paul J. Fliss.
Res., 1444 S. Eleventh St., 53081. Tel: 414-457-9408; Fax: 414-457-5290. [CEM]
School—Christ Child Academy, (Grades PreK-5). See Immaculate Conception for Details. Tel: 414-459-2663.
Catechesis/Religious Programs—Tel: 414-452-2759. D.R.E.: Judy Stalter; Barbara Leonhardt.
Students 302.

Sheboygan Falls, Sheboygan Co., St. Mary's (1896) (German), Rev. Michael F. Moran.
Rectory: 327 Giddings Ave., 53085. Tel: 414-467-4616; Fax: 414-467-4290. [CEM]
School—Tel: 414-467-6291. Sr. Marcia Vogl, Prin.
Sisters 1; Lay Teachers 7; Students 173.
Catechesis/Religious Programs—Sally Schenk, D.R.E., Tel: 414-467-4616.
Students 265.

Slinger, Washington Co., St. Peter's (1856) (German), Rev. Robert J. Bales; Deacon Bernard J. Wendt.
Res., 202 E. Washington St., 53086. Tel: 414-644-8083. [CEM 2]
School—Tel: 414-644-8325. Virginia Miller, Prin.
Lay Teachers 12; Students 148.
Catechesis/Religious Programs—Tel: 414-644-7333. William Thimm, D.R.E.
Students 561.

South Milwaukee, Milwaukee Co.,

1—St. Adalbert's, (1898) (Polish), Rev. Herbert B. Schubert; Deacon Leon Zalewski, Pastoral Assoc.
Res., 1611 Manitoba Ave., 53172. Tel: 414-762-0291. [JC]
School—1800 16th Ave., 53172. Tel: 414-762-0064. Felician Sisters 2; Lay Teachers 8; Students 232.
Catechesis/Religious Programs—Students 195.
Convent—1610 Minnesota Ave., 53172. Tel: 414-762-2885.

2—St. John's, (1893) (Irish), Rev. Joseph G. Anderson; Deacon John P. Monday.
Res., 800 Marquette Ave., 53172. Tel: 414-762-2440. [JC]
School—Holy Cross. Consolidated with St. Mary. 805 Marquette Ave., 53172. Tel: 414-762-4670.
Lay Teachers 10; Students 170.
Catechesis/Religious Programs—Tel: 414-762-8600. Kristine Schell, D.R.E.
Students 250.

3—St. Mary's, (1893), Rev. Ronald G. Engel.
Res., 1304 Manitoba Ave., 53172. Tel: 414-762-6810. [JC]
School—Consolidated with St. John's, Holy Cross School. Tel: 414-762-4670.
Catechesis/Religious Programs—1310 Manitoba Ave., 53172. Tel: 414-764-3350.
Students 181.

4—St. Sylvester's, (1962), Rev. Thomas A. Trepanier; Deacon A. James Leggett.
Res., 675 College Ave., 53172. Tel: 414-762-6800.
School—695 College Ave., 53172. Tel: 414-764-4360; Fax: 414-764-7078.
Lay Teachers 12; Students 218.
Catechesis/Religious Programs—Tel: 414-764-5488. Patricia Walsh, D.R.E.
Students 214.

Springvale, St. Mary. Also serves St. Joseph, Waupun and St. Brendan, Brandon. Revs. Benjamin Knopp, O.F.M.Conv.; Russan Cole, O.F.M.Conv.
Mailing Address: 118 W. Main St., Waupun, 53963. Tel: 414-324-5400.

Sturtevant, Racine Co., St. Sebastian's (1906), Rev. James Kendzierski, O.F.M.; Deacon DeSales Wisniewski, O.F.M., Pastoral Assoc.
Res., 3126 95th St., 53177. Tel: 414-886-4398.
School—3030 95th St., 53177. Tel: 414-886-2806. Diane Davis, Prin.
Lay Teachers 10; Students 202.
Catechesis/Religious Programs—Tel: 414-886-4420.
Students 133.

Theresa, Dodge Co., St. Theresa's (1849) (German), Rev. Charles J. Verhalen, Admin.
Res., P.O. Box 330, 53091. Tel: 414-488-4382. [CEM]
School—(Grades 1-4). Consolidated with St. Mary, Lomira to form Consolidated Catholic School of Lomira-Theresa. 105 W. Rock River St., 53091. Tel: 414-488-4543. Sr. Rosemary Herriges, S.S.S.F., Prin.

Thiensville, Ozaukee Co., St. Cecilia's (1919), Rev. Gerald J. Dominiak; Deacon Joseph P. Wenzler.
Res., 101 Ellenbecker Rd., 53092. Tel: 414-512-8980; Fax: 414-242-7976.
School—(Grades K4-3). Consolidated with St. James, Mequon to form SS. Cecilia and James. 116 N. Orchard, 53092. Tel: 414-242-7965. Mr. Richard Goeden, Prin.
Lay Teachers 11; Students 272.
Catechesis/Religious Programs—Program consolidated with St. James, Mequon. Tel: 414-242-7979. Patricia Roehrig, D.R.E.
Students 560.

Thompson, Washington Co., St. Patrick's (Tn. Erin) (1855), Rev. Walter J. Vogel.
Res., 1908 Hwy. 83 S., Hartford, 53027. Tel: 414-673-2988. [CEM]

Twin Lakes, Kenosha Co., St. John's (1932), Rev. Ronald C. Kowalski.
Res., 701 N. Lake Ave., 53181. Tel: 414-877-2557; Fax: 414-877-2431. [CEM]
Catechesis/Religious Programs—Tel: 414-877-3033. Diane Baltazar, D.R.E.
Students 160.

Union Grove, Racine Co., St. Robert Bellarmine (1965), Rev. Charles E. Conley.
Res., 3320 S. Colony Ave., P.O. Box 107, 53182. Tel: 414-878-3476. [JC]
Catechesis/Religious Programs—Tel: 414-878-2009. Ms. Kris Seifert, D.R.E.
Students 293.

Waterford, Racine Co., St. Thomas Aquinas (1851), Very Rev. Dennis E. Van Beek.
Res., 305 First St., 53185. Tel: 414-534-2255; Fax: 414-534-2929. [CEM]
School—Tel: 414-534-2265.
Lay Teachers 9; Students 245.
Catechesis/Religious Programs—Students 340.

Waukesha, Waukesha Co.,

1—St. Joseph's, (1844), Revs. Ronald J. Gramza; John C. Lukaszewicz; Deacon Gene Kempka.
Res., 822 N. East Ave., 53186. Tel: 414-542-2589; Fax: 414-542-2570.
School—Waukesha Catholic School System, (Grades 6-8) 841 Martin St., 53186. Tel: 414-896-2930; Fax: 414-896-2930. Mrs. Pat Crane, Prin.
Franciscan Sisters of Christian Charity Sisters 3; Lay Teachers 17; Students 290.
Catechesis/Religious Programs—Tel: 414-542-9392; Fax: 414-542-2570. Ruth Weiss, D.R.E.
Students 639.

2—St. Mary, (1950), Revs. Michael T. Newman; Gordon A. Weber.
Res., 225 S. Hartwell Ave., 53186. Tel: 414-547-6555.
School—Tel: 414-896-2932. Sr. Kathleen Swain, Prin.
Sisters 4; Lay Teachers 11; Students 343.
Catechesis/Religious Programs—Tel: 414-547-6326. Nancy Metz, D.R.E.
Students 411.

3—St. John Neumann, (1981), Rev. Dennis G. Budka; Deacon Thomas McGuine.
Res., 2400 W. STH 59, P.O. Box 965, 53187. Tel: 414-549-0223; 549-0898; Fax: 414-549-0444.
School—Waukesha Catholic School System, (Grades PreK-8). Tel: 414-547-3020.
Students 111.
Catechesis/Religious Programs—D.R.E.: Sr. Dolores Pertzborn; Sr. Virginia Azweta; Shelly McGuine.
Students 758.

4—St. William, (1957), Rev. David C. Filut.
Res., 440 N. Moreland Blvd., 53188. Tel: 414-542-0456; Fax: 414-896-2925. [JC]
School—Waukesha Catholic School System, (Grades PreK-5) 444 N. Moreland Blvd., 53188. Tel: 414-896-2920. Sr. Toni Gradisnik, O.S.F., Campus Prin.
Students 200.
Catechesis/Religious Programs—Tel: 414-547-2763. Rosemary Strauss, D.R.E.
Students 750.

Waupun, Fond du Lac Co., St. Joseph's (1866). Also serves St. Brendan, Brandon; & St. Mary, Springvale. Revs. Benjamin Knopp, O.F.M.Conv.; Russan Cole, O.F.M.Conv.
Res., 118 W. Main St., 53963. Tel: 414-324-5400.
Catechesis/Religious Programs—Tel: 414-324-3891. D.R.E.: Bev Moriearty; Karen Schmidt.
Students 157.

Wauwatosa, Milwaukee Co.,

1—St. Bernard's, (1911) (Irish), Rev. Victor R. Capriolo. In res., Revs. Robert E. Massey; Donald F. Quartana.
Res., 1500 Wauwatosa Ave., 53213. Tel: 414-258-4320.
School—7440 Harwood Ave., 53213. Tel: 414-258-9977. Consuelo Roybal, Prin.
Religious 2; Lay Teachers 14; Students 236.
Catechesis/Religious Programs—Tel: 414-476-5968.
Students 220.

2—Christ King, (1939), Very Rev. Dennis R. Ackeret; Rev. Paul B. R. Hartmann; Deacon Arthur C. Dallman.
Res., 2604 Swan Blvd., 53226. Tel: 414-258-2604; Fax: 414-258-1993.
School—2646 N. Swan Blvd., 53226. Tel: 414-258-4160. Sr. Martha Meyer, S.S.N.D., Prin.
School Sisters of Notre Dame 1; Lay Teachers 24; Students 471.
Catechesis/Religious Programs—Tel: 414-258-0916. Barbara Schveidler, D.R.E.
Students 347.

3—St. Joseph Congregation, (1855), Revs. Jerome M. Hudziak; Robert Fictum, S.D.S.; Deacon Jose Gonzales.
Mailing Address: Office, 12130 W. Center St., 53222-4096. Tel: 414-771-4626; Fax: 414-771-4311.
Res., 12130 W. Hadley St., 53222-4097. Tel: 414-771-4627.
School—2750 N. 122nd St., 53222. Tel: 414-771-5577. Linda Harrigan, Prin.
Lay Teachers 18; Students 280.
Catechesis/Religious Programs—Tel: 212-771-6096. Ann Stadelhofer, D.R.E.
Students 569.

4—St. Jude the Apostle, (1928), Rev. Peter P. Carek; Sr. Mary La Von Lauer, O.S.F., Pastoral Assoc.; Deacon Donald Borkowski. In res., Rev. Emmanuel Udo (Nigeria).
Res., 734 Glenview Ave., 53213. Tel: 414-258-8821; Fax: 414-258-0165.
School—8042 St. Jude Ct., 53213. Tel: 414-771-1520. Roger Baehr, Prin.
Sisters 1; Lay Teachers 22; Students 459.
Catechesis/Religious Programs—Tel: 414-259-0950. D.R.E.: Gary Heun; Dave Baudry.
Students 149.

5—St. Pius X, (1952), Rev. Keith Brennan, S.D.S.
Res., 2506 Wauwatosa Ave., 53213. Tel: 414-453-3875; Fax: 414-453-7570.
School—2520 Wauwatosa Ave., 53213. Tel: 441-778-0880.
Lay Teachers 15; Students 162.
Catechesis/Religious Programs—Tel: 414-453-1153. Mary Jane Duffey, D.R.E.
Students 306.

Wayne, Washington Co., St. Bridget. Also serves Holy Trinity, Kewaskum. Rev. John L. Brophy.
Mailing Address: 331 Main St., P.O. Box 461, Kewaskum, 53040. Tel: 414-626-2603.

West Allis, Milwaukee Co.,

1—St. Aloysius, (1920), Revs. Mark J. Stangel; Daniel J. Massie; Deacon John A. Fricano.
Res., 1414 S. 93rd St., 53214. Tel: 414-476-3803.

School—1435 S. 92nd St., 53214. Tel: 414-476-0751. Richard Bagemihl, Prin.
Sisters 1; Lay Teachers 12; Students 246.
Catechesis/Religious Programs—Tel: 414-257-3088. Martha Van Duser, D.R.E.
Students 160.

2—ST. AUGUSTINE'S, (1928) (Croatian), Rev. Lawrence Frankovich, O.F.M.
Res., 6762 W. Rogers St., 53219. Tel: 414-541-5207.
School—6763 W. Rogers St., 53219. Tel: 414-545-2120.
Sisters 3; Lay Teachers 5; Students 163.

3—HOLY ASSUMPTION, (1902), Rev. David E. Cooper; Deacon George P. Sherman. In res., Rev. Henry W. Kiwanuka (Kampala).
Res., 1525 S. 71st St., 53214. Tel: 414-774-3010.
School—1532 S. 72nd St., 53214. Tel: 414-476-0508. Mary Kathleen Tate, Prin.
School Sisters of Notre Dame 2; Lay Teachers 9; Students 195.

4—IMMACULATE HEART OF MARY, (1948), Rev. Karl J. Schneider; Deacons Dennis E. Fietz; Walter Henry; Ray Kaczmarek.
Res., 1121 S. 116th St., 53214. Tel: 414-453-5192; Fax: 414-453-0137.
Catechesis/Religious Programs—Tel: 414-453-0300.
Students 139.

5—ST. JOSEPH'S, (1909) (Polish), Rev. Leonard E. Piechowski.
Res., 1642 S. 65th St., 53214. Tel: 414-543-8310.

6—MARY, QUEEN OF HEAVEN, (1958), Very Rev. William E. Kohler; Rev. Michael F. Merkt.
Office: 2322 S. 106th St., 53227. Tel: 414-328-5566; Fax: 414-328-5561.
School—2360 S. 106th St., 53227. Tel: 414-328-5577; Fax: 414-328-5573. Mrs. Marilyn Marzolf, Prin.
Lay Teachers 8; Students 165.
Catechesis/Religious Programs—Tel: 414-328-5570. Nicholas Balducci, D.R.E.
Students 245.

7—ST. MARY, HELP OF CHRISTIANS, (1907) (Slovenian), Rev. Joseph L. Cunningham.
Res., 1210 S. 61st St., 53214. Tel: 414-771-8313.

8—OUR LADY OF MT. CARMEL, (1938) (Italian), Rev. James B. Posanski, Admin.
Res., 6625 W. Beloit Rd., 53219. Tel: 414-543-9210; Fax: 414-543-6919.

9—ST. RITA'S, (1924), Revs. Richard E. Mirsberger; Kevin J. Kowalske; Deacons Sam Lupo; Richard Brown.
Res., 2318 S. 61st St., 53219. Tel: 414-541-7515; Fax: 414-541-7568.
School—6021 W. Lincoln Ave., 53219. Tel: 414-327-5020. Sr. Joyce Wagner, S.S.S.F., Prin.
School Sisters of St. Francis 4; Lay Teachers 15; Students 291.
Catechesis/Religious Programs—Tel: 414-541-7515. Sr. Mary Theiss, D.R.E.
Students 252.

West Bend, Washington Co., Holy Angels (1855), Revs. Gerald W. Brittain; Jerome V. Repenshek.
Res., 138 N. 8th Ave., 53095. Tel: 414-334-3038. [CEM]
School—230 N. 8th Ave., 53095. Tel: 414-338-1148; Fax: 414-334-1334. Mike Sternig, Prin.
Lay Teachers 21; Students 463.
Catechesis/Religious Programs—Tel: 414-334-9393. Nan Jacoby, D.R.E.
Students 524.

Immaculate Conception (1857), Rev. Patrick R. Wendt.
Res., 406 Jefferson St., 53095. Tel: 414-338-5600. [CEM]
School—Tel: 414-338-5602.
Lay Teachers 8; Students 202.
Catechesis/Religious Programs—Tel: 414-338-5605. D.R.E.: Dolores Ecker; Marge Schinker.
Students 372.

St. Frances Cabrini (1955), Revs. Jeffrey R. Haines; Kenneth A. Mich; Deacons Michael Koebel; Steven Przedpelski; Mike Sepersky, Dir. of Admin. Svcs.
Res., 1025 S. 7th Ave., 53095. Tel: 414-338-2366; Fax: 414-338-2348. [JC]
School—529 Hawthorn Dr., 53095. Tel: 414-334-7142; Fax: 414-334-8168. Janice Stauske, Prin.
Lay Teachers 30; Students 441.
Catechesis/Religious Programs—Tel: 414-334-9511. Judy Schroeder, D.R.E.
Students 625.

Whitefish Bay, Milwaukee Co., St. Monica's (1923), Rev. Alan F. Jurkus; Deacon Eugene Van Garsse. In res., Revs. John R. Paczesny; Richard C. Brietbach.
Res., 160 E. Silver Spring Dr., 53217. Tel: 414-332-1576; 332-1577; Fax: 414-332-2462.
School—Tel: 414-332-3660; Fax: 414-332-8649. Dr. Irwin T. Johnson, Prin.
School Sisters of St. Francis 2; Lay Teachers 29; Students 426.
Catechesis/Religious Programs—Tel: 414-964-8780. Sr. Fran Buschell, D.R.E.
Students 225.

Holy Family (1949), Very Rev. Thomas F. Kerstein; Rev. Timothy L. Kitzke; Deacon Daniel T. Zozakiewicz.
Office: 4825 N. Wildwood Ave., 53217. Tel: 414-332-9220; Fax: 414-961-7396.
School—4849 N. Wildwood Ave., 53217. Tel: 414-332-8175. Rebecca Jones, Prin.
Lay Teachers 16; Students 194.
Catechesis/Religious Programs—Tel: 414-332-8156. Barbara O'Neil, D.R.E.
Students 450.

Whitewater, Walworth Co., St. Patrick's (1853), Revs. Ronald O. Crewe; John W. Van Abel.
Office: 1225 W. Main St., 53190-1620.
Res., 126 S. Elizabeth St., 53190-1628. Tel: 414-473-3143; Fax: 414-473-7010. [CEM]
Catechesis/Religious Programs—Tel: 414-473-8834. Sr. Therese Rekowski, S.S.N.D., D.R.E.
Students 226.

Wilmot, Kenosha Co., Holy Name of Jesus (1856), Sr. Kathleen Hurley, O.S.F., Parish Dir.
Res., P.O. Box 188, 53192. Tel: 414-862-6466; Fax: 414-862-6466. [CEM]
Catechesis/Religious Programs—Tel: 414-862-2361.
Students 232.

Wind Lake, Racine Co., St. Clare (1965), Rev. John D. Hemsing; Deacon Richard E. Milbauer.
Mailing Address: Parish Office, 7616 Fritz St., 53185.
Res., 26714 Katherine St., 53185. Tel: 414-895-7820.
Catechesis/Religious Programs—Tel: 414-895-2729. Mrs. Millie Luhmann, D.R.E.
Students 226.

Woodhull, Fond du Lac Co., St. John the Baptist. Also serves St. Mary, Eldorado. Rev. Roger A. Savage.
Res., W8272 Forest Ave. Rd., Eldorado, 54932-9801. Tel: 414-922-2412. [CEM]
Catechesis/Religious Programs—Linda Greene, D.R.E.
Students 137.

Woodland, Dodge N Co., St. Mary. Also serves St. Matthew, Neosho; & St. John, Rubicon. Rev. Laurin J. Wenig.
Mailing Address: 148 W. Lehman St, P.O. Box 45, Neosho, 53059. Tel: 414-625-3144.

Chaplains of Public Institutions

MILWAUKEE. *Milwaukee County House of Correction.* Attended by St. James Parish, Franklin.
Milwaukee County Jail. Bro. Jerome Smith, O.F.M.Cap., Chap.
St. Luke's Medical Center, Box 21677, 53221. Rev. Donald E. Sass, Chap.

JUNEAU. *Dodge County Center.* Attended by Immaculate Conception Church.

KENOSHA. *Kenosha Hospital and Medical Center,* 6308 8th Ave., 53143-5082. Rev. Michael P. Dineen, Chap.

WALES. *Ethan Allen School for Boys,* P.O. Box 900, 53183. Tel: 414-646-3341. Rev. Mark L. Molling, Chap.

WAUWATOSA. *Froedtert Memorial Lutheran Hospital.* Chaplains: Revs. Bruce Schute, S.A.C.; Richard Lorenz, S.A.C., 5424 W. Bluemound Rd., Milwaukee, 53208. Tel: 414-258-0653.
Milwaukee Regional Medical Center. Chaplains: Revs. Jerome A. Hapka, S.A.C.; Richard Lorenz, S.A.C., 5424 W. Bluemound Rd., Milwaukee, 53208. Tel: 414-258-0653.

WEST ALLIS. *West Allis Memorial Hospital,* 8901 W. Lincoln Ave., 53227. Tel: 414-328-6000. Rev. Charles G. Zabler, Chap.

WOOD. *Veterans Administration Medical Center,* P.O., 53193. Tel: 414-385-2000. Chaplains: Revs. Lawrence W. Koncewicz, C.M.; Norman R. Oswald.

Special Assignment:
Reverend Fathers—
Aiello, John D., Metropolitan Tribunal, 3501 S. Lake Dr., P.O. Box 07912, Milwaukee, WI 53207-0912
Avella, Steven M., Marquette University Faculty, 442 E. Fremont Pl., Milwaukee, WI 53207
Bandle, Ronald J., Nursing Home Ministry, 5937 N. 35th St., #2, Milwaukee, WI 53209
Barbian, Leonard M., Assoc. Vicar of Clergy, Priests' Placement Bd., 3501 S. Lake Dr., P.O. Box 07912, Milwaukee, WI 53207-0912
Brundage, Thomas T., Judicial Vicar, Metropolitan Tribunal, 3501 S. Lake Dr., P.O. Box 07912, Milwaukee, WI 53207-0912
Connell, James E., Vice Chancellor, Archdiocese of Milwaukee, 3501 S. Lake Dr., P.O. Box 07912, Milwaukee, WI 53207-0912
Duffy, James H.
Hammer, Michael J., Coord. Catholic AIDS Ministry, 802 N. Jackson St., Milwaukee, WI 53202-3879
Janette, Paul D., Service for Senior Priests, 3501 S. Lake Dr., P.O. Box 07912, Milwaukee, WI 53207-0912. Tel: 414-769-3345
Massey, Robert E., Marquette Univ. Faculty, 1500 Wauwatosa Ave., Wauwatosa, WI 53213
O'Brien, Timothy J., Faculty, Marquette University, 8521 Kenyon Ave., Wauwatosa, WI 53226
Stiefvater, Robert X., Dir. Office of Vocations, 3257 S. Lake Dr., St. Francis, WI 53235. Tel: 414-747-6437
Stoll, Jerome L., Nursing Home Ministry, Archdiocese of Milwaukee, P.O. Box 207, Waterford, WI 53185-0207
Thimm, Donald H., Archbishop's Delegate for Human Resources, 3501 S. Lake Dr., P.O. Box 07912, Milwaukee, WI 53207-0912
Van Vlaenderen, Leonard S., Sec. to the Archbishop, 3501 S. Lake Dr., P.O. Box 07912, Milwaukee, WI 53207-0912
Wheatley, Charles J., Chap., Archdiocesan Cemetery System, 4463 S. Taylor Ave., Milwaukee, WI 53207
Very Rev.—
Straub, Carrol C., Vicar General, Vicar for Clergy Personnel, 3501 S. Lake Dr., P.O. Box 07912, Milwaukee, WI 53207-0912

On Duty Outside the Archdiocese:
Reverend Monsignors—
Harvey, James M., Villa Stritch, Via Della Nocetta, 63, Rome, 00164 Italy
Malloy, David J., Permanent Observer Mission of the Holy See to the United Nations, 20 E. 72nd St., New York, NY 10021-4196
Reverend Fathers—
Bryl, Thaddeus J., Cathedral of the Risen Christ, Box 6877, Lincoln, NE 68506
Clapp, Kenneth A., Holy Family Parish, Apartado 53, Azua, Dominican Republic
DeVries, Thomas D., NCCB Office for the Catechism, 3211 4th St., N.E., Washington, D.C. 20017-1194
Dolezal, Richard R., 5053 N. Ridgeway, Chicago, IL 60625
Gaberle, Jiri P., Farni Urad, 69102 Velke Bilovice, Czech Republic
Hying, Donald J., Holy Family Parish, Apartado 53, Azua, Dominican Republic
Kobida, Vincent F., Diocese of San Juan De La Maguana, D.R., c/o Lynx Air-SDQ, Box 407052, Fort Lauderdale, FL 33340
Konkel, Eugene J., S.S., Vatican II Institute, 320 Middlefield Rd., Menlo Park, CA 54025
Lamb, Matthew L., Faculty, Boston College, Horizon East 411, 125 Coolidge Ave., Watertown, MA 02172
Lisowski, Edward E., 2600 Sunset Ave., Waukegan, IL 60087
Marek, Dean V., Box 1332, Rochester, MN 55903
Palermo, Albert A., St. Albert the Great Parish, 1104 Huntridge Cir., Austin, TX 78758
Pocernich, Eugene S., Catholic Mission Assoc., 3029 Fourth St., N.E., Washington, D.C. 20017-1102
Shmauz, Donald A., 5570 Woodland Dr., Waunakee, WI 53597
Skeris, Robert A., Christendom College, 2101 Shenandoah Shores Rd., Front Royal, VA 22630
Stanfield, William L., Siraria Catholic Church, Box 13, Tarime, Tanzania
Thompson, Jerome F., 4 rue D'Alger, 1000 Tunis RP, Tunisia
Tino, Robert F., Western State Hospital, 9601 Steilacoom Blvd., S.W., Tacoma, WA 98498-7213

Military Chaplains:
Reverend Fathers—
Kienzle, Jerome C.
Lee, Roy A.
Malloy, Francis X.
Mikalofsky, Hilarion A.
Olszyk, Thomas P.
Richter, Robert J.

Graduate Studies:
Reverend Fathers—
Schuerman, James T., 3257 S. Lake Dr., St. Francis, WI 53235
Shecterle, Ross A., St. Mary's Seminary, 5400 Roland Ave., Baltimore, MD 21210-1994

On Leave:
Reverend Fathers—
Becker, Franklyn W.
Collova, S. Joseph
Holt, Thomas G.
Lanser, Jerome E.
Neuberger, Michael T.

Sosa, Carlos
Wagner, John C.

Sick Leave:
Reverend Fathers—
Walter, Charles W.

Awaiting Assignment:
Reverend Fathers—
Beno, Brian M.
Kimla, James E.
Meinholz, David J.
Slodowski, Bruno

Retired:
Reverend Monsignors—
Donovan, John T., 3501 S. Lake Dr., St. Francis, WI 53235
Emmenegger, Joseph E., 3501 S. Lake Dr., St. Francis, WI 53235
Gass, Sylvester F., 3501 S. Lake Dr., St. Francis, WI 53235
Kapalczynski, Eugene J., 3501 S. Lake Dr., St. Francis, WI 53235
Murphy, John F., 5510 N. Lake Dr., Oconomowoc, WI 53066
Prudell, Harold O., 2462 N. Prospect Ave., Milwaukee, WI 53211
Schmit, Ralph R., 3253 S. Lake Dr., St. Francis, WI 53235
Reverend Fathers—
Adamsky, Raymond J., 3253 S. Lake Dr., St. Francis, WI 53235
Amrhein, Peter T., 530 N. 103rd St., #22, Milwaukee, WI 53226
Andre, Leonard J., 11926 W. Mill Rd., #1, Milwaukee, WI 53225
Badem, Wendel J., 3253 S. Lake Dr., #206, St. Francis, WI 53253
Baran, Joseph L., 2022 N. 86th St., Wauwatosa, WI 53226
Baranowski, Stanley A., W782 Cty. Rd. A, Randolph, WI 53956
Beck, Richard P., 5606 Cynthia Ln., Sarasota, FL 34235
Beitzinger, George J., 4139 Los Altos Ct., Naples, FL 34109
Belda, Leo W., N64 W24470 Main St., No. 14, Sussex, WI 53089
Bier, Joseph V., 10100 W. Bluemound Rd., Wauwatosa, WI 53226
Bistricky, Frederick J., 5171 N. 64th St., Milwaukee, WI 53218
Braun, Edgar F., N6895 Lost Lake Rd., Pearson, WI 54462
Brey, Lawrence S., 5871 County Rd. 137, St. Cloud, MN 56301
Brielmaier, Leon J., 422 Fox Isle Pk., Waterford, WI 53185
Briske, Larry F., 12753 Caminito Cancion, Unit 128, San Diego, CA 92128
Budzynski, Daniel A., 3253 S. Lake Dr., #305, St. Francis, WI 53235
Callahan, Raymond J., 10101 W. Wisconsin Ave., Wauwatosa, WI 53226
Carroll, Edward E., 15000 W. Cleveland Ave., #226, New Berlin, WI 53151
Clark, Gerard J., 3508 5th Ave., South Milwaukee, WI 53172
Conley, Joseph J., 3501 S. Lake Dr., St. Francis, WI 53235
Cox, William E., 4816 Westway Ave., Racine, WI 53406
Darnieder, Donald A., 3253 S. Lake Dr., St. Francis, WI 53235
Dionne, Earl J., 3501 S. Lake Dr., St. Francis, WI 53235
Dougherty, Matthew C., 3540 S. 43rd St., Milwaukee, WI 53220
Dowd, Patrick A., 12686 Cijon St., San Diego, CA 92129
Dreher, Ernest O., 310 E. 11th St., Fond du Lac, WI 54935
Elverman, Donald A., 3501 S. Lake Dr., St. Francis, WI 53235
Enders, Robert F., 238 S. Hartwell Ave., Waukesha, WI 53186
Ernster, James M., 570 Highway D, Belgium, WI 53004
Eschweiler, Edward R., 3501 S. Lake Dr., St. Francis, WI 53235
Eschweiler, Francis L., 3501 S. Lake Dr., St. Francis, WI 53235
Etzel, George A., 348 Mill St., Campbellsport, WI 53010
Farrell, William J., 10100 W. Bluemound Rd., Wauwatosa, WI 53226
Fechhelm, Richard A., 302 N. Henninger St., Mayville, WI 53050
Fetterer, Raymond A., 930 N. 6th St., Sheboygan, WI 53081
Fischer, Joseph A., 686 Airport Rd., Campbellsport, WI 53010
Fleischmann, George R., 3501 S. Lake Dr., St. Francis, WI 53235
Garity, Linus J., Dammert Geriatrics, 9500 W. State, Rte. 15, Belleville, IL 62223
Gehl, Walter N., Rte. 2, Box 250, Hiles, WI 54511
Gibbons, George J., 3501 S. Lake Dr., St. Francis, WI 53235
Glass, Rolland T., 531 W. 11th St., Fond du Lac, WI 54935
Haen, Edmund H., 9301 N. 76th St. #371E, Milwaukee, WI 53223
Halmo, John F., 4216 21st Ave., Kenosha, WI 53142
Hanauska, Joseph F., 31068 Timber lane, Burlington, WI 53105
Hanley, John P., 3501 S. Lake Dr., St. Francis, WI 53235
Hauser, Gerald B., 3501 S. Lake Dr., St. Francis, WI 53235
Hentzner, John T., 3501 S. Lake Dr., St. Francis, WI 53235
Herkowski, Arthur M., 2576-5 Sunny Slope Dr., Sparks, NV 89434
Hess, James W., 1607A N. 8th St., Sheboygan, WI 53081
Hickey, Thomas D., 3253 S. Lake Dr., #303, St. Francis, WI 53235
Hmircik, Donald A., 104 St. Franciscus St., Mount Calvary, WI 53057
Hopf, George S., 80 W. Northwest Hwy., Palatine, IL 60067
Huber, George L., 3253 S. Lake Dr., St. Francis, WI 53235
Ide, Harold J., 3501 S. Lake Dr., St. Francis, WI 53235
Jautz, Martin L., 10100 W. Bluemound Rd., Wauwatosa, WI 53226
Johnson, Howard J., W6332 Lake Ellen Dr., Cascade, WI 53011
Jordan, Francis W., 2527 Ole Davidson Rd., Racine, WI 53405
Kaiser, Cletus H., 239 Terrace Dr., West Bend, WI 53095-4748
Kasten, Edward F., 203 W. Coventry Ct., Glendale, WI 53217
Kemmer, Victor A., 188 Hwy. W S., Rte. 4, Campbellsport, WI 53010
Klauck, Stanley B., 12621 E. Laurel Ln., Scottsdale, AZ 85259
Kleefisch, Charles A., 5101 W. Center St., Milwaukee, WI 53210
Knoernschild, William F., 10101 W. Wisconsin Ave., Wauwatosa, WI 53226
Knotek, John T., 5116 22nd Ave., Kenosha, WI 53140
Kolanda, George A., 10101 W. Wisconsin Ave., Wauwatosa, WI 53226
Kolanko, John R., 7164 N. 42nd St., #2, Milwaukee, WI 53209
Koren, Louis F., 10101 W. Wisconsin Ave., Wauwatosa, WI 53226
Kowalski, Leo S., 3441 S. 10th St., Milwaukee, WI 53215-5117
Kreuzer, Eugene T., 21618 Plank Rd., Kansasville, WI 53139
Kurkiewicz, Raymond J., 3501 S. Lake Dr., St. Francis, WI 53235
Labaj, Stephen V., 1439 Ohio St., Racine, WI 53405
Lambert, Leo M., 3501 S. Lake Dr., St. Francis, WI 53235
Leack, Lawrence J., 1845 N. 60th St., Milwaukee, WI 53208
Lippert, Paul R., Box 238, Plainfield, WI 54966-0238
Litzau, John B., 10100 W. Bluemound Rd., Wauwatosa, WI 53226
Loehr, Charles D., W1452 Hwy. T, Mount Calvary, WI 53057
Lyons, Mark J., 10100 W. Bluemound Rd., Wauwatosa, WI 53226
Mackin, William H., 3501 S. Lake Dr., St. Francis, WI 53235
Macoskie, Melvin H., 3501 S. Lake Dr., St. Francis, WI 53235
Maney, Robert L., 9431 W. Beloit Rd., #308, Milwaukee, WI 53227
Matt, Erwin H., 3253 S. Lake Dr., St. Francis, WI 53235
McCormick, Robert J., 11274 Pineapple Rd., Punta Gorda, FL 33955
McLaughlin, Owen F., 400 Sunnyslope Dr., Apt. 119, Hartland, WI 53029
Mogilka, Erwin E., 4321 Marine Dr., Burlington, WI 53105
Morgan, Walter N., 523 W. 11th St., Fond du Lac, WI 54935
Mueller, Joseph J., 10100 W. Bluemound Rd., Wauwatosa, WI 53226
Mueller, Robert F., 1711 S. 9th St., Milwaukee, WI 53204
Murphy, John M., 3501 S. Lake Dr., St. Francis, WI 53235
Murphy, Lawrence C., P.O. Box 50, Boulder Junction, WI 54512-0050
Murray, William F., 3253 S. Lake Dr., St. Francis, WI 53235
Myszel, George G., 26503 Angelica Rd., Punta Gorda, FL 33955
Nickolai, Arthur A., 6100 Hwy. 73N., Rte. 2, Marshall, WI 53559
Novotny, Robert J., 3253 S. Lake Dr., St. Francis, WI 53235
O'Brien, Eugene C., 1193 Masterpiece Dr., Oceanside, CA 92057
O'Rourke, Francis J., 7600 N. Port Washington Rd., Fox Point, WI 53217
Okopinski, Louis S., 3253 S. Lake Dr., St. Francis, WI 53235
Orzechowski, Walter B., N8180 Lakeview Rd., Fond du Lac, WI 54935
Parr, Raymond A., 4031 E. Van Norman Ave., Cudahy, WI 53110
Peters, Donald R., 3215 Baird Ave., P.O. Box 91245, Lakeland, FL 33804-1245
Podolak, William S., 3501 S. Lake Dr., St. Francis, WI 53235
Quartana, Donald F., 1500 Wauwatosa Ave., Wauwatosa, WI 53213
Rausch, John W., Box 475, Eagle, WI 53119
Rodriguez, Robert, 731 S. 25th St., Milwaukee, WI 53204
Roensch, Frederick J., P.O. Box 25578, Milwaukee, WI 53225
Roscioli, Dominic J., 5412 23rd Ave., Kenosha, WI 53140-3505
Rykowski, Valerian J., 3503 Silver Lake Dr., Traverse City, MI 49684
Sablica, Michael J., W6020 Stelling Rd., E., Tomahawk, WI 54487
Sanfelippo, Frank J., P.O. Box 1504, Milwaukee, WI 53201-1504
Schaefer, Verne B., 213 S. Jefferson, #2, Waterford, WI 53185
Schlaffer, James J., 9244 29th Ave., #206, Kenosha, WI 53143
Schmelzer, Linus L., 3501 S. Lake Dr., St. Francis, WI 53235
Schmidt, Frederick N., Rte. 3, Box 96, Pardeeville, WI 53954
Schmitt, Warren J., 9115 S. Cactus Ln., Sun Lakes, AZ 85248
Schmitz, Gerald T., Box 455, Campbellsport, WI 53010
Schneider, Robert W.
Schneider, Vincent N., 33108 80th St., Rte. 5, Burlington, WI 53105
Schuster, Valery P., 199 Vine St., Sun Prairie, WI 53590
Schwinn, Joseph F., 3253 S. Lake Dr., St. Francis, WI 53235
Seramur, Leo J., 3253 S. Lake Dr., St. Francis, WI 53235
Silvestri, Vincent A., 10100 W. Bluemound Rd., Wauwatosa, WI 53226
Simon, Martin M., 1401 Grove Ave., Racine, WI 53405
Sippel, Edward F., 519 W. 11th St., Fond du Lac, WI 54935
Smith, Fred A., 3916 S. Tara Hill Dr., Greenfield, WI 53220
Sowinski, Albin F., 20295C Independence Dr., Brookfield, WI 53045
Stier, Joseph S., 10101 W. Wisconsin Ave., Wauwatosa, WI 53226
Strenski, Joseph A., 3501 S. Lake Dr., St. Francis, WI 53235
Strupp, James A., 580 S. 18th Ave., West Bend, WI 53095
Sutschek, Francis C., 111 S. Maple Ave. #2, Slinger, WI 53086
Theisen, John J., 536 Lake Dr., Random Lake, WI 53075
Trenier, Anthony S., 1154 N. 45th St., Milwaukee, WI 53208-2733
Twomey, John E., 2885 Klovar Ln., #3, East Troy, WI 53120
Uhen, Cletus V., 1100 Fountain Dr. #208A, Racine, WI 53406
Urban, Matthew J., 3790 S. Town Rd., New Berlin, WI 53151
Valdez, Jose R., 3126 S. 21st St., Milwaukee, WI 53215
Van Beck, Alfred F., 2009 Elevada St., Oceanside, CA 92054
Wagner, Ralph J., 9802 Menomonee Park Ct. #2, Milwaukee, WI 53225
Wallaik, William H., 11300 N. St. James Ln., 28W, Mequon, WI 53092
Walter, John F., 10100 W. Bluemound Rd., Wauwatosa, WI 53226
Weber, Donald N., Brookfield Highlands #1006,

20950 George Hunt Cir., Waukesha, WI 53186
Weishar, Paul M., N110 W16973 Ashbury Cir., #6, Germantown, WI 53022
Wilbur, David F., 1013 McKinley, West Bend, WI 53095
Witkowski, Raymond A., 3939 S. 92nd St., Greenfield, WI 53228
Wittemann, Paul J., 104 St. Franciscus St., Mount Calvary, WI 53057
Wolf, Robert J., 32200 45th St., Lot 74A, Burlington, WI 53105
Wollet, George H., 630 W. Montclaire Ave., Milwaukee, WI 53217
Zeihen, Joseph N., 3501 S. Lake Dr., St. Francis, WI 53235
Zens, Roger A., 2620 S. 30th St., Milwaukee, WI 53215
Zwaska, Victor L., 1201 Hughitt Ave., Box 969, Superior, WI 54880

Permanent Deacons:
Acosta, Carlos R., Leave of Absence
Aird, Gordon R. (PHX), Divine Word, Cedarburg
Anderberg, Russell F. (CHI), St. Benedict, Fontana
Anderson, Dennis D., St. Anthony, Pewaukee
Aschenbrener, James L., Corpus Christi, Milwaukee
Banach, William A., Holy Spirit, Milwaukee
Beck, Lawrence E., (Retired)
Blaze, Edward, All Saints, Milwaukee
Borkowski, Donald A., St. Jude the Apostle, Wauwatosa
Brah, Eugene D., Out of Archdiocese
Braun, Warren D., St. Sebastian, Milwaukee
Brousseau, Gerald A., Leave of Absence
Brown, Richard J., St. Rita, West Allis
Burns, John R., St. Veronica, Milwaukee
Buth, Robert H., St. Mary's, Menomonee Falls
Buyck, Gerald W., St. Malachy, Horicon
Castaneda, Claudio C., Leave of Absence
Cebrzynski, Stanly J., (Retired)
Cesarec, Michael E., Unassigned
Champagne, John I., St. Benedict the Moor, Milwaukee
Christensen, Eugene M., Good Shepherd, Menomonee Falls
Coca, Emilio, St. Patrick, Racine
Colainni, Arthur R., St. Joseph, Lyons
Collins, Dean J., Mother of Good Counsel, Milwaukee
Corsten, Dale, Leave of Absence
Dahlen, Clarence J., (Retired)
Dallman, Arthur C., Christ King, Wauwatosa
Doerr, George J., Out of Archdiocese
Dziennik, John R., St. Veronica, Milwaukee
Ebel, John A., St. Bernadette, Milwaukee
Fazen, Robert J., St. Matthew, Campbellsport
Ference, Dennis H., Leave of Absence
Fietz, Dennis E., Immaculate Heart of Mary, West Allis
Filipiak, Thomas P., St. Bruno, Dousman
Flynn, Richard M., Leave of Absence
Francois, James S., St. Mary, Kenosha
Fricano, John A., St. Aloysius, West Allis
Frye, Patrick H., St. Mark, Kenosha
Gamez, Antonio U., Leave of Absence
Gliniecki, Harry F., St. Catherine, Mapleton
Gonzales, Jose U., St. Joseph, Wauwatosa
Gonzalez, Baleriano O., St. Clement, Sheboygan
Goodman, Robert E., Sacred Heart of Jesus, St. Francis
Govek, Richard J., St. Joseph, Grafton
Gramza, Richard G., (Retired)
Griffiths, Joseph J., Out of Archdiocese
Grimyser, Peter G., Leave of Absence
Gurzynski, Theodore A., St. Alphonsus, Greendale
Gust, Peter L., (Retired)
Guttierrez, Jose H., Holy Trinity-Guadalupe, Milwaukee
Guzman, Armindo, Out of Archdiocese
Hammond, Eugene R., (Retired)
Henry, Walter, Immaculate Heart of Mary, West Allis
Hiller, Richard D., (Retired)
Horner, Ralph E., St. Michael, St. Michael; St. John of God, Farmington
Hughes, Larry L., Unassigned
Hughes, Wayne W., Leave of Absence
Hying, Joseph H., Sacred Heart, Racine
Janasik, Ralph R., Personal Leave
Jens, William T., St. George, St. George; St. Rose of Lima, Lima
Kabara, Donald F., St. Joseph, Grafton
Kaczmarek, Raymond J., Sick Leave
Kastenholz, Joseph H., Our Lady of Good Hope, Milwaukee
Kehrer, Daniel F., St. George, Kenosha
Kempka, Eugene A., St. Joseph, Waukesha
Kennedy, Claude V., Old St. Mary's, Milwaukee
Kennedy, David L., Out of Archdiocese
Klinkhammer, Phillip H., (Retired)
Koebel, Michael S., St. Frances Cabrini, West Bend
Kornburger, Ralph W., Jr., St. Catherine, Milwaukee
Kuban, Donald J. (PHX), St. Peter, East Troy
Kustner, Charles J., St. Mary, Elm Grove
La Fond, M. Larry, Jr., St. Dominic, Brookfield
Lazaga, Alfred C., Out of Archdiocese
Lebron, Gregorio, Latin Amerian Center, Kenosha and St. Mark
Leggett, A. James, St. Sylvester, South Milwaukee
Lesjak, Ronald F., St. Mary, Kenosha
Libecki, John K., St. Dominic, Brookfield
Lo Coco, Peter L., Unassigned
Losiniecki, Thomas, Leave of Absence
Lukacevich, William J., St. Roman, Milwaukee
Lupo, Samuel J., St. Rita, West Allis
Lydolph, Donald J., Immaculate Conception, West Bend
Maack, Terrance A., St. Peter, Kenosha
Mahnke, Carl A., St. Thomas Aquinas, Waterford
Maier, Louis A., Jr., Out of Archdiocese
Majewski, Edward H., (Retired)
Malischke, Carl J., Leave of Absence
Malueg, Gerald D., St. Rose of Lima, Fredonia; St. Mary, Little Kohler
Mandujano, J. Eufemio, Leave of Absence
Martinez, John S., St. Vincent de Paul, Milwaukee
Martino, Anthony, St. Mary, Pell Lake
McGuine, Thomas W., St. John Neumann, Waukesha
Mensah, Anthony J., Awaiting Assignment
Merten, Arthur H., (Retired)
Meyer, August M., Holy Name, Sheboygan
Milbauer, Richard E., St. Clare, Wind Lake
Miller, Kenneth J., Sick Leave
Missureli, Russell A., St. Patrick, Racine
Moczydlowski, Chester A., St. Barbara, Milwaukee
Molina, Juan A., St. Rose of Lime, St. Michael, St. Francis of Assisi, Milwaukee
Monday, John P., St. John, South Milwaukee
Monday, Thomas C., St. Mary, Menomonee Falls
Monzel, Paul S., Presentation, North Fond du Lac
Moser, Arnet L., (Retired)
Mueller, Arthur W., Sick Leave
Munoz, Ricardo, St. Louis, Fond du Lac
Nawrocik, Zenon L., Out of Archdiocese
Nicholas, Keith P., Leave of Absence
Normann, Larry E., St. Paul, Genesee Depot
Nowicki, Edward J., Holy Apostles, New Berlin
Ode, LeRoy, Sacred Heart of Jesus, St. Francis
Oelke, Gordon R., Leave of Absence
Pemper, Frank, Out of Archdiocese
Peterson, James J., St. Sebastian, Milwaukee
Petre, Harvey A., (Retired)
Pettey, Lawrence C., (Retired)
Pollak, David R., Holy Spirit, Milwaukee
Ponec, Gerald R., Holy Family, Cudahy
Poulin, Edwin D., Leave of Absence
Przedpelski, Steven J., St. Francis Cabrini, West Bend
Regan, Sylvester R., (Retired)
Rick, Wayne W., Leave of Absence
Rodriguez, Virgilio, Out of Archdiocese
Rooney, Michael R., St. Margaret Mary, Milwaukee
Schieffer, Robert M., Our Lady of Good Hope, Milwaukee
Schimmels, Thomas J., Mother of Perpetual Help, Milwaukee
Schopper, Eugene E., Out of Archdiocese
Sherman, George, Holy Assumption, West Allis
Shierk, Wilson A., St. Mary, Kenosha
Sinden, Carroll J., Sick Leave
Spoke, Chester R., (Retired)
Surges, Thomas J., St. Peter of Alcantara, Port Washington
Thomas, Jean, (Retired)
Thoresen, Norman, Retired
Treichel, Robert B., Out of Archdiocese
Truttschel, Robert A., St. Patrick, Beaver Dam
Van Garsse, Eugene E., St. Monica, Whitefish Bay
Vernon, Kenneth L., All Saints, Milwaukee
Wargin, John R., Immaculate Conception, Milwaukee
Weber, C. Edward, Holy Rosary, Milwaukee
Wells, Randal S., St. Michael, Beaver Dam
Welnicki, John C., St. Josaphat Basilica, Milwaukee
Wendt, Bernard J., St. Peter, Slinger
Wenzel, Donald P., St. Agnes, Butler
Wenzler, Joseph P., St. Cecilia, Thiensville
Widmar, Willard M., St. Paul the Apostle, Racine
Wisniewski, Ralph, St. Leonard, Muskego
Wodushek, Robert A., St. Anthony, Menomonee Falls
Wolf, Kenneth W., St. Boniface, Germantown
Wuchterl, Thomas H., St. Mary, Menomonee Falls
Yang, Blong P., St. Michael (Hmong Community), Milwaukee
Zalewski, Leon J., St. Adalbert, South Milwaukee
Zimprich, David L., St. Anthony, Menomonee Falls
Zozakiewicz, Daniel T., Holy Family, Whitefish Bay

INSTITUTIONS LOCATED IN THE ARCHDIOCESE

[A] SEMINARIES, ARCHDIOCESAN

MILWAUKEE. *Saint Francis Seminary*, 3257 S. Lake Dr., 53235. Tel: 414-747-6400. Very Rev. Andrew L. Nelson, S.T.L., Ph.D., Rector; Rev. Bryan N. Massingale, M.Div., S.T.L., S.T.D., Vice Rector; Dr. David A. Stosur, Academic Dean; Rev. Kenneth E. Omernick, Th.M., S.T.L., Spiritual Dir.; Mr. Gary Pokorny, M.Div., Dir. Lay Formation; Dr. Nancy A. Sell, M.T.S., D.Min., Dir. Pastoral Formation; Rev. Michael G. Witczak, M.Div., S.L.L., S.L.D., Dir. Worship; Sr. Mary Jane Wagner, S.S.S.F., M.A., Assoc. Dir. Worship; Sr. Mary Ellen Collins, O.S.F., M.A., Assoc. Dir. Worship for Music; Ms. Mary Burgett, B.S., Dir. Salzmann Library; Ms. Meredith Curtis, M.L.I.S., Technical/Public Service Librarian; Mr. Timothy Charek, M.Div., Dir. Certificate Division; Ms. Barbara V. Schauer, M.T.S., Assoc. Dir. Certificate Division; Ms. Maria Borda-Wiesner, B.A., M.A.P.S., C.N.A., Coord., Spanish-Speaking Certificate Formation Programs; Ms. DeAnn Cortez, B.A., Coord., Pastoral Form. Certificate Programs; Mr. Paul A. Hudec, M.B.A., Treas./Business Dir.; Ms. Patricia Young, B.A., Advancement Dir.; Revs. Joseph J. Juknialis, B.A., M.A., Dir. Preaching Institute; Stephen V. DeLeers, B.A., M.Div., M.A.; Stephen J. Lampe, S.T.D., M.A., M.Div., S.S.L.; Melvin E. Michalski, M.Ph., Ph.L., D.Theo.; Dr. Dennis D. Sylva, Ph.D.; Dr. Barbara G. Turner, Ph.D. Administration & Faculty 23; Priests 8; Sisters 2; Lay Staff 13; Seminary Students 86.

College Formation Program, East Hall, 915 W. Wisconsin Ave., 53233. Tel: 414-288-7526. Revs. Dennis A. Dirkx, Dir.; Lawrence V. Dulek, Dir. Casa Program. Priests 2; Students 18.

[B] SEMINARIES, RELIGIOUS OR SCHOLASTICATES

FRANKLIN. *Xaverian Missionary Fathers College Seminary*, 6838 S. 51st St., 53132. Tel: 414-421-0831. Very Rev. Vasco J. Milani, S.X.; Revs. Alfredo Turco, S.X. (Italy); Ngo Anthony Chinh, S.X. (Vietnam); Dominic Caldognetto, S.X. (Italy). Priests 4.

HALES CORNERS. *Sacred Heart School of Theology*, 7335 S. Highway 100, P.O. Box 429, 53130-0429. Tel: 414-425-8300; Fax: 414-529-6999. Very Rev. James D. Brackin, S.C.J., M.Div., J.D., Pres.-Rector; Revs. Otto Bucher, O.F.M.Cap., S.T.L., S.S.L., Vice Rector, Dir. of Recruitment; Thomas L. Knoebel, Ph.D., Academic Dean & Dir. M.A. Programs, Dir. of Admissions; Robert Schiavone, M.A., Dir. Field Education; Peter Schuessler, S.D.S., M.A., Dir. Spiritual Formation; Ms. Margaret E. Boyles, M.E.P.D., Dir. Public Relations; Ms. Kathleen M. Harty, M.R., M.A.L.S., Dir. of Library; Mr. Richard Kirsch, M.S., Dir. Continuing Education; Ms. Sally Smits, M.B.A., Vice Pres. Finance/Personnel; Mr. Gary Talsky, Ph.B., Ph.L., Registrar & Asst. to Academic Dean; Revs. Matthias P. Cremer, S.C.J., S.T.L., Professor Emeritus; John T. O'Connor, S.C.J., J.C.L., S.T.D., Professor Emeritus; Joseph Gole, S.T.D. (Slovenia), Professor Emeritus; Sr. Martine Hundelt, S.S.S.F., Ph.D., Professor Emerita; Sr. Agnese Jasko, P.H.J.C., M.A.L.S., Professor Emerita.
Full-Time Faculty: Revs. Martin Barnum, M.A., M.Div.; Hugh Birdsall, S.D.S., M.A., M.S.; Vincent McNally, Ph.D. (Canada); Raul Gomez, S.D.S., M.Div., M.P.A.; Paul Grizzelle-Reid, S.C.J., M.S., M.Div.; Jerome Higgins, O.F.M.Cap., M.Ed., M.A.S.; Andre Papineau, S.D.S., M.A.; Richard Schlenker, Ph.D.; Sr. Mary C. Carroll, S.S.S.F., M.A.; Sr. Elizabeth M. Hoell, S.S.N.D., M.M., M.Chr.Sp.; Sr. Joan Koehler, S.S.S.F., M.Ed., M.A.; Sr. Christine Morkovsky, C.D.P., Ph.D.; Sr. Roseann Wagner, S.S.S.F., B.M., M.T.S.; Dr. John Gallam, Ph.D.; Dr. Richard Lux, Ph.D.; Dr. Bruce Malchow, Ph.D.; Mr. Mark Ginter, M.A., Ph.D. Candidate; Mr. C. Christian Rich, B.A., M.M.; Ms. Linda Gonzales, M.L.I.S.
Part-Time Faculty: Revs. Thomas Brundage, J.C.L.; Paul Kelly, S.C.J., M.Div., M.A.; Rev. Msgr. Roy M. Klister, J.C.L., Ph.D.; Revs. Joseph Perry, M.Div., J.C.L.; John Yockey, Ph.D.; Sr. Jane Elyse Russell, S.S.S.F., Ph.D.; Dr. Carol Elsholz, Ph.D.; Dr. Mark Kemmeter, M.T.S., D.Min.; Mr. Peter Ghiloni, B.A., M.A.; Ms. Glenna Gustin, B.A., M.F.A.; Ms. Maria M. Rivera, B.S. Priests 21; Sisters 8; Lay Staff 15; Non-Catholic Clergymen 1; Rabbis 1; Religious Candidates 8; Diocesan Candidates 85; M.A. Candidates 16; Students 135; Total Staff 41.

MOUNT CALVARY. *St. Felix Friary*, W1754 State Hwy. 149, 53057. Tel: 414-753-3111. Novitiate House of the Capuchin Province of St. Joseph and St. Mary.

Revs. Paul Koenig, O.F.M.Cap., Vocation Dir.; Michael Marigliano, O.F.M.Cap., Novitiate Team, Supr.; Kenneth R. Casper, O.F.M.Cap., Novice Dir. Priests 3; Novices 4.

St. Lawrence Seminary, 53057. Tel: 414-753-3911; Fax: 414-753-2907. High School Seminary and Ministry Program. Revs. Keith Clark, O.F.M.Cap., Pres.; Dennis Druggan, O.F.M.Cap., Rector; Edwin Dziedziejko, O.F.M.Cap., Supr.; Kenan Siegel, O.F.M.Cap., Dir. Devel.; Campion Baer, O.F.M.Cap.; Oliver Bambenek, O.F.M.Cap., Supr.; Gerald Kafer, O.F.M.Cap.; Gary Wegner, O.F.M.Cap.; Randall Knauf, O.F.M.Cap.; Elroy Pesch, O.F.M.Cap.; Bros. Douglas Bode, O.F.M.Cap.; John Freienstein, O.F.M.Cap.; Dismas Seward, O.F.M.Cap.; Neal Plale, O.F.M.Cap.; Carl Schaefer, O.F.M.Cap.; John Willger, O.F.M.Cap.; Larry Groeschel, O.F.M.Cap.; Jerome Campbell, O.F.M.Cap.; John Scherer, O.F.M.Cap.; Mr. Dennis Holm, Dean; Mr. Harlan Swift, Business Mgr.; Mr. Kenneth Holehouse, Guidance Dir. Priests 10; Brothers 9; Sisters 1; Lay Teachers 12; Students 221; Total Staff 32.

[C] COLLEGES AND UNIVERSITIES

MILWAUKEE. *Alverno College*, 3401 S. 39th St., P.O. Box 343922, 53234-3922. Tel: 414-382-6000; Fax: 414-362-6354.

For a complete listing, refer to the Colleges and Universities section.

Cardinal Stritch College, 6801 N. Yates Rd., 53217. Tel: 414-352-5400.

For a complete listing, refer to the Colleges and Universities section.

**Marquette University*, P.O. Box 1881, 53201-1881. Tel: 414-288-7250.

For a complete listing, refer to the Colleges and Universities section.

Mount Mary College, 2900 N. Menomonee River Pkwy., 53222-4545. Tel: 414-258-4810.

For a complete listing, refer to the Colleges and Universities section.

FOND DU LAC. *Marian College of Fond du Lac*, 45 S. National Ave., 54935. Tel: 414-923-7600.

For a complete listing, refer to the Colleges and Universities section.

[D] HIGH SCHOOLS, ARCHDIOCESAN AND PAROCHIAL

MILWAUKEE. *Pius XI High School*, 135 N. 76th St., 53213. Tel: 414-290-7000. Mr. John J. Halupka, Prin.; Revs. Robert V. Carney, S.A.C.; Richard J. Gunderman, S.A.C.; Anthony S. Zimmer, Chap. School Sisters of St. Francis 7; Sisters of Mercy 2; Lay Teachers 79; Students 1,606.

Thomas More High School, 2601 E. Morgan Ave., 53207. Tel: 414-481-8370; Fax: 414-481-3382. (Coed). Sr. Jean Ford, S.S.N.D., Prin. Sisters 3; Lay Teachers 34; Students 776; Total Staff 53.

BURLINGTON. *Catholic Central High School*, 148 McHenry St., 53105. Tel: 414-763-1510. Mr. Kenneth D. Kortens, M.Ed., Prin.; Rev. Lawrence J. Chapman, Chap. Priests 1; Lay Teachers 15; Students 231.

FOND DU LAC. *St. Mary's Springs High School*, 255 County Rd. K, 54935. Tel: 414-921-4870. Thomas J. Borek, Prin. Sisters 1; Lay Teachers 17; Students 333; Total Staff 18.

KENOSHA. *St. Joseph High School*, 2401 69th St., 53143. Tel: 414-654-8651. Mr. Rick J. Ruhl, Prin. Sisters 2; Lay Teachers 20; Students 426; Total Staff 22.

WAUKESHA. *Catholic Memorial High School*, 601 E. College Ave., 53186. Tel: 414-542-7101; Fax: 414-542-1633. Mr. Paul Stauffacher, Pres. & Prin.; Rev. Robert P. Wells, Chap. Franciscan Sisters of Christian Charity 6; Priests 1; Lay Teachers 59; Students 1,015; Total Staff 88.

[E] HIGH SCHOOLS, PRIVATE

MILWAUKEE. *Divine Savior Holy Angels High School*. (Girls). 4257 N. 100th St., 53222. Tel: 414-466-3706; Fax: 414-466-4778. Sponsored by the Sisters of the Divine Savior. Dr. Angela T. Pienkos, Chief Admin.; Rev. Jerome G. Herda. Priests 1; Sisters 3; Lay Teachers 37; Students 549; Total Staff 66.

Marquette University High School. (Boys). 3401 W. Wisconsin Ave., 53208. Tel: 414-933-7220.

(See separate listing for resident information). Revs. Douglas J. Leonhardt, S.J., Pres.; Terrence M. Brennan, S.J.; Michael R. Kolb, S.J.; John A. Schwantes, S.J.; Charles L. Stang, S.J.; Edward G. Witt, S.J. Priests 6; Scholastics 2; Lay Teachers 56; Students 926; Total Staff 64.

St. Joan Antida High School, Inc. (Girls). 1341 N. Cass St., 53202. Tel: 414-272-8423; Fax: 414-272-3135. Sr. Monica Fumo, S.C.S.J.A., Prin. Sisters of Charity of St. Joan Antida 6; Lay Teachers 24; Students 378; Total Staff 41.

RACINE. *St. Catherine's High School*, 1200 Park Ave., 53403. Tel: 414-632-2785; Fax: 414-632-5144. Ms. Marilyn J. McGoldrick, Prin.; Sr. Jane Weiss, Asst. Prin.; Rev. Russell G. Roetzer. Dominican Sisters (Racine) 4; Lay Teachers 39; Students 625.

WHITEFISH BAY. *Dominican High School*, 120 E. Silver Spring Dr., 53217. Tel: 414-332-1170. Paul M. McInerny, Ph.D., Pres.; Michael Maguire, Prin.; Judy Down, Assoc. Prin.; Sr. Margaret Ann Brennan, O.P., Chm. Religion Dept. Dominican Sisters of the Congregation of the Most Holy Rosary, Sinsinawa, WI 3; Lay Teachers 36; Students 480.

[F] ELEMENTARY SCHOOLS, ARCHDIOCESAN

MILWAUKEE. *St. Leo School, Inc.* St. Leo Catholic Urban Academy, 2458 W. Locust St., 53209. Tel: 414-442-1100. Sponsored and accredited by the Archdiocese of Milwaukee. Sisters 1; Lay Teachers 11; Students 210; Total Staff 13.

St. Rose Catholic Urban Academy, 514 N. 31st St., 53208. Tel: 414-933-6070. Sponsored and accredited by the Archdiocese of Milwaukee. Sisters 1; Lay Teachers 15; Students 240; Total Staff 20.

[G] ELEMENTARY SCHOOLS, PRIVATE

MILWAUKEE. *Nativity Jesuit Middle School, Inc.* (Boys). 1115 S. Seventh St., 53204. Tel: 414-645-1060. Wisconsin Province of the Society of Jesus. Rev. William T. Johnson, S.J., Pres.; Mr. Lawrence H. Siewert, Prin. Priests 1; Sisters 1; Seminarians 1; Lay Teachers 8; Students 46; Total Staff 11.

Notre Dame Middle School, Inc., 1420 W. Scott St., 53204. Tel: 414-671-3000. Sr. Ann Kilkelly, S.S.N.D., Admin.; Maria Tagliavia, Prin. Sponsored by: School Sisters of Notre Dame. Purpose: To educate at-risk girls for college preparatory high schools and for community service and leadership.

St. Coletta Day School of Milwaukee, 1740 N. 55th St., 53208. Tel: 414-453-1850. For Exceptional Children. William A. Koehn, Prin. & Admin. Lay Teachers 2; Students 12.

[H] CONSOLIDATED ELEMENTARY SCHOOLS

MILWAUKEE. *All Saints Catholic East School System, Inc.*, 1716 N. Humboldt Ave., 53202. Tel: 414-276-9814. Sponsored by the following Milwaukee parishes: Cathedral of St. John the Evangelist; St. Casimir; St. Hedwig; Holy Rosary; Old St. Mary's; St. Mary Czestochowa; Ss. Peter and Paul; St. Rita. Rev. John H. Endejan, Chm., Pastor Liaison.

All Saints Catholic Elementary. (Grades K-8), 3027 N. Fratney St., 53212. Tel: 414-372-5530. Ms. Mary Ann Rudella, Prin. Lay Teachers 8; Students 126.

Catholic East Elementary. (Grades K-8), 2461 N. Murray Ave., 53211. Tel: 414-964-1770. Mr. Christopher Montezon, Prin. Sisters 3; Lay Teachers 7; Students 153.

BEAVER DAM. *Unified Catholic Parish Schools of Beaver Dam*, 503 S. Spring St., 53916-2598. Tel: 414-885-5558; Fax: 414-885-5510. Barbara M. Haase, Prin. Lay Teachers 23; Students 357. Members: St. Michael, St. Patrick, St. Peter.

FOND DU LAC. *Fond du Lac Area Catholic Education System (FACES)*, 706 Minnesota Ave., 54937. Tel: 414-924-0993. Members: St. Joseph; St. Louis; St. Mary; St. Patrick; Sacred Heart; Presentation of the Blessed Virgin, North Fond du Lac. Mr. Steven Meyers, System Admin.

Faces-St. Joseph Campus & Faces Preschool, 95 E. Second St., 54935. Tel: 414-923-5300. Mr. Ken Bond, Prin. Lay Teachers 15; Students 241.

Faces-St. Mary Middle School Campus, 63 E. Merrill St., 54935. Tel: 414-921-9610. Mr. John Pavek, Site Base Coord. Lay Teachers 18; Students 217.

Faces-St. Patrick Campus, 37 E. Follett St., 54935. Tel: 414-921-6710. Mr. Ken Bond, Prin. Lay Teachers 11; Students 198.

LOMIRA. *Consolidated Catholic School*, 705 Milwaukee St., 53048. Tel: 414-269-4326. Sr. Rosemary Herriges, O.S.F., Prin. Sisters 1; Lay Teachers 8; Students 124. Members: St. Mary, Lomira; & St. Theresa, Theresa.

MEQUON. *Ss. Cecilia and James School*, 11300 N. St. James Ln., #28 W, 53092. Mr. Richard Goeden, Prin., St. Cecilia Campus: (Grades K-3), 116 W. Orchard St., Thiensville, 53092. Tel: 414-242-7965. St. James Campus: (Grades 4-8), 11300 N. St. James Ln., 53092. Tel: 414-242-7960. Lay Teachers 26; Students 479.

MOUNT CALVARY. *Consolidated Parochial Elementary School*, 101 Notre Dame St., 53057. Tel: 414-753-4811. Sr. Alicia Collins, Prin. Sisters 2; Lay Teachers 16; Students 230. Members: St. John the Baptist, Johnsburg; St. Mary, Marytown; Holy Cross, Mount Calvary; St. Cloud, St. Cloud.

SOUTH MILWAUKEE. *Holy Cross School*. (Catholic Centennial School System), 805 Marquette Ave., 53172. Tel: 414-762-4670. Carol J. Makholm, Prin. Lay Teachers 15; Students 170. Members: St. John, St. Mary.

WAUKESHA. *Waukesha Catholic School System, Inc.*, 440 N. Moreland Blvd., 53188. Rev. Thomas Demse, Pastor Liaison. Tel: 414-549-0223. Members: St. Joseph, St. Mary, St. John Neumann, St. William.

St. Joseph Campus, 822 N. East Ave., 53186. Tel: 414-896-2930. Patricia McGrane, Prin. Sisters 3; Lay Teachers 14; Students 254.

St. Mary Campus, 520 N. Newhall Ave., 53186. Tel: 414-896-2932. Sr. Kathleen Swain, O.S.F., Prin. Sisters 3; Lay Teachers 15; Students 351.

St. William Campus, 444 N. Moreland Blvd., 53188. Tel: 414-896-2920. Sr. Toni Gradisnik, O.S.F., Prin. Sisters 1; Lay Teachers 11; Students 195.

[I] SPECIAL SCHOOLS

WEST ALLIS. *Holy Assumption School for the Blind*, 1526 S. 72nd St., 53214. Tel: 414-774-8783. Sr. Melmarie Stoll, S.S.N.D., Dir. School Sisters of Notre Dame 1; Lay Teachers 1; Students 5.

[J] CHILD CARE CENTERS

MILWAUKEE. *Guardian Angel Nursery and Kindergarten, Inc.*, 1323 N. Cass St., 53202. Tel: 414-277-9474; Fax: 414-272-3135. Sisters of Charity of St. Joan Antida. Sr. Marie Louise Balistrieri, S.C-.S.J.A., Admin. Sisters of Charity of St. Joan Antida 3; Lay Teachers 22; Students 92. The center is licensed for ages 6 weeks to 6 years with a full academic 4K & 5K program.

Seton Children's School, Inc., 8677 N. Port Washington Rd., 53217. Tel: 414-352-6115. Operated by the Daughters of Charity of St. Vincent de Paul. A licensed center for comprehensive early childhood educational programs and day care. Children 189. Other Locations: 2220 E. North Ave., 53202. Tel: 414-291-9231. Children 52. 13133 N. Port Washington Rd., Mequon, 53097. Tel: 414-243-7318. Children 49.

South Day Care Center of St. Joseph, 3249 S. 18th St., 53215. Tel: 414-645-5337. Sr. M. Carolita Turzin, C.S.S.F., Admin. Felician Sisters 10; Lay Teachers 37; Children 590; Total Staff 47.

SOUTH MILWAUKEE. *Franciscan Villa Child Day Care Center*, 3601 S. Chicago Ave., 53172. Tel: 414-764-4100. Judy Greene, Supervisor. Children 22.

WAUWATOSA. *Carmelite Home, Inc.*, 1214 Kavanaugh Pl., 53213. Tel: 414-258-4791. Residential Treatment Center for Adolescent Boys. Sr. M. Regina, Admin.; James E. Lewis, Treatment Dir. Residents 40; Lay Teachers 4.

WEST ALLIS. *St. Joan Antida Day Care Center, Inc.*, 6640 W. Beloit Rd., 53219. Tel: 414-541-6575; 541-9840; Fax: 414-541-8040. Day Care for children ages 3-5. Sr. Maria Augustine Giannini, S.C.S.J.A., Admin. Sisters of Charity of St. Joan Antida 3; Lay Teachers 4; Children 76.

[K] GENERAL HOSPITALS

MILWAUKEE. *St. Francis Hospital*, 3237 S. 16th St., 53215. Tel: 414-647-5000.

For a complete listing, refer to the Hospitals section.

St. Joseph's Hospital of Franciscan Sisters, Milwaukee, Inc., 5000 W. Chambers St., 53210. Tel: 414-447-2000.

For a complete listing, refer to the Hospitals section.

St. Mary's Hospital of Milwaukee, 2323 N. Lake Dr., P.O. Box 503, 53201-0503. Tel: 414-291-1000; Fax: 414-291-1048.

For a complete listing, refer to the Hospitals section.

St. Michael Hospital of Franciscan Sisters of Milwaukee, Inc., 2400 W. Villard Ave., 53209. Tel: 414-527-8000.

For a complete listing, refer to the Hospitals section.

BROOKFIELD. *Elmbrook Memorial Hospital, Inc.*, 19333 W. North Ave., 53045. Tel: 414-785-2000.

For a complete listing, refer to the Hospitals section.

FOND DU LAC. *Genesys HealthCare of Fond du Lac, Inc.*, 430 E. Division St., 54935. Tel: 414-929-2300; Fax: 414-929-1866.

For a complete listing, refer to the Hospitals section.

KENOSHA. *St. Catherine's Hospital*, 3556 Seventh Ave., 53140. Tel: 414-656-3011.

For a complete listing, refer to the Hospitals section.

MEQUON. *St. Mary's Hospital Ozaukee, Inc.*, 13111 N. Port Washington Rd., 53097. Tel: 414-243-7300; 800-848-2844; Fax: 414-243-7416.

For a complete listing, refer to the Hospitals section.

RACINE. *St. Mary's Medical Center*, 3801 Spring St., 53405. Tel: 414-636-4011; Fax: 414-636-4540.

For a complete listing, refer to the Hospitals section.

SHEBOYGAN. *St. Nicholas Hospital*, 1601 N. Taylor Dr., 53081. Tel: 414-459-8300.

For a complete listing, refer to the Hospitals section.

WAUPUN. *Waupun Memorial Hospital*, 53963. Tel: 414-324-5581.

For a complete listing, refer to the Hospitals section.

[L] SPECIAL HOSPITALS AND SANATORIA

MILWAUKEE. *Sacred Heart Rehabilitation Institute, Inc.*, 2350 N. Lake Dr., 53211. Tel: 414-298-6700.

For a complete listing, refer to the Special Care Facilities section.

[M] PROTECTIVE INSTITUTIONS

MILWAUKEE. *Daystar, Inc.*, P.O. Box 11709, 53217. Tel: 414-228-8887.
For a complete listing, refer to the Special Care Facilities section.

Rosalie Manor, Inc., 4803 W. Burleigh St., 53210. Tel: 414-449-2868.
For a complete listing, refer to the Special Care Facilities section.

St. Charles Youth and Family Services, 151 S. 84th St., P.O. Box 14005, 53214. Tel: 414-476-3710.
For a complete listing, refer to the Special Care Facilities section.

MOUNT CALVARY. *Cristo Rey Ranch, Inc.*, N8102 Calvary St., 53057.
For a complete listing, refer to the Special Care Facilities section.

[N] HOMES FOR AGED AND NURSING HOMES

MILWAUKEE. *Alexian Village of Milwaukee, Inc.*, 7979 W. Glenbrook Rd., 53223. Tel: 414-355-9300.
For a complete listing, refer to the Special Care Facilities section.

Catholic Charities Senior Daycare Center, 4021 N. 90th St., 53222. Tel: 414-464-8004.
For a complete listing, refer to the Special Care Facilities section.

Marian Catholic Center, Inc., 3333 W. Highland Blvd., 53208. Tel: 414-344-8100.
For a complete listing, refer to the Special Care Facilities section.

Marian Franciscan Center, Inc., 9632 W. Appleton Ave., 53225. Tel: 414-461-8850.
For a complete listing, refer to the Special Care Facilities section.

**Milwaukee Catholic Home*, 2462 N. Prospect Ave., 53211-4462. Tel: 414-224-9700.
For a complete listing, refer to the Special Care Facilities section.

St. Ann Rest Home, 2020 S. Muskego Ave., 53204. Tel: 414-383-2630.
For a complete listing, refer to the Special Care Facilities section.

St. Anne's Home for the Elderly, 3800 N. 92nd St., 53222. Tel: 414-463-7570; Fax: 414-463-2311.
For a complete listing, refer to the Special Care Facilities section.

St. Mary's Nursing Home, 3516 W. Center St., 53210. Tel: 414-873-9250.
For a complete listing, refer to the Special Care Facilities section.

The Terrace at St. Francis, Inc., 3200 S. 20th St., 53215 Fax: 414-389-3300.
For a complete listing, refer to the Special Care Facilities section.

Villa St. Francis, Inc., 1910 W. Ohio Ave., 53215 Fax: 414-649-2880.
For a complete listing, refer to the Special Care Facilities section.

FOND DU LAC. *St. Francis Home for Aged*, 365 Gillett St., 54935. Tel: 414-923-7980; Fax: 414-923-7995.
For a complete listing, refer to the Special Care Facilities section.

GREENFIELD. *Clement Manor Health Center*, 3939 S. 92nd St., 53228. Tel: 414-321-1800.
For a complete listing, refer to the Special Care Facilities section.

Clement Manor Retirement Community, 9339-9405 W. Howard Ave., 53228. Tel: 414-546-7375.
For a complete listing, refer to the Special Care Facilities section.

KENOSHA. *St. Joseph's Adult Day Care Center, Inc.*, 9244 29th Ave., 53144. Tel: 414-694-6000.
For a complete listing, refer to the Special Care Facilities section.

St. Joseph's Home for the Aged, 9244 29th Ave., 53143. Tel: 414-694-0080.
For a complete listing, refer to the Special Care Facilities section.

LOMIRA. *Hope Nursing Home, Inc.*, 438 Ashford Ave., P.O. Box 280, 53048-0280. Tel: 414-269-4386; Fax: 414-269-4616.
For a complete listing, refer to the Special Care Facilities section.

MOUNT CALVARY. *Villa Loretto Nursing Home*, 53057. Tel: 414-753-3211.
For a complete listing, refer to the Special Care Facilities section.

RACINE. *Marian Housing Center, Inc*, 4105 Spring St., 53405. Tel: 414-633-5807.
For a complete listing, refer to the Special Care Facilities section.

St. Monica's Senior Citizens Home, Inc., 3920 N. Green Bay Rd., 53404. Tel: 414-639-5050.
For a complete listing, refer to the Special Care Facilities section.

ST. FRANCIS. *Canticle Court, Inc.*, 3201 S. Lake Dr., 53235. Tel: 414-744-9959; Fax: 414-744-7636.
For a complete listing, refer to the Special Care Facilities section.

Juniper Court, Inc., 3209 S. Lake Dr., 53235-3702. Tel: 414-744-5878; Fax: 414-744-7636.
For a complete listing, refer to the Special Care Facilities section.

St. Ann Adult Day Care, Inc., 3221 S. Lake Dr., 53235. Tel: 414-482-1340.
For a complete listing, refer to the Special Care Facilities section.

SOUTH MILWAUKEE. *Franciscan Villa*, 3601 S. Chicago Ave., 53172. Tel: 414-764-4100.
For a complete listing, refer to the Special Care Facilities section.

WAUWATOSA. *St. Camillus Health Center, Inc.*, 10101 W. Wisconsin Ave., 53226. Tel: 414-258-1814.
For a complete listing, refer to the Special Care Facilities section.

San Camillo, Inc., 10200 W. Bluemound Rd., 53226. Tel: 414-259-6300.
For a complete listing, refer to the Special Care Facilities section.

WEST ALLIS. *St. Joan Antida Home, Inc.*, 6700 W. Beloit Rd., 53219. Tel: 414-541-6575; 541-9840; Fax: 414-541-8040.
For a complete listing, refer to the Special Care Facilities section.

Villa Clement Health Center, 9047 W. Greenfield Ave., 53214. Tel: 414-453-9290.
For a complete listing, refer to the Special Care Facilities section.

[O] PERSONAL PRELATURES

BROOKFIELD. *Opus Dei-Prelature of the Holy Cross and Opus Dei.*, 12900 W. North Ave., 53005. Tel: 414-784-1523. Layton Study Center for men. Revs. Robert P. Bucciarelli; John C. Kubeck. Legal Title: *The Work of God, Inc.*

[P] MONASTERIES AND RESIDENCES FOR PRIESTS AND BROTHERS

MILWAUKEE. *Alexian Brothers Community*. Immaculate Conception Province, 7979 W. Glenbrook Rd., 53223. Tel: 414-355-9300. Bros. Anthony Ragucci, C.F.A., Dir.; Robert Petersen, C.F.A.; Theodore Loueks, C.F.A. Brothers 3.

Arrupe House Jesuit Community, 831 N. 13th St., 53233. Tel: 414-274-7460. Society of Jesus, Wisconsin Province. Revs. John L. Treloar, S.J., Supr.; Thomas N. Brennan, S.J.; Eugene M. Dutkiewicz, S.J.; Peter J. Etzel, S.J.; J. Robert Hilbert, S.J.; D. Thomas Hughson, S.J.; Lawrence D. Kelly, S.J.; Michael R. Kolb, S.J.; Philip J. Rossi, S.J.; Charles L. Stang, S.J. Priests 10.

Francis and Clare House, 1648 S. 37th St., 53215-1724. Tel: 414-383-7934. Revs. Eliot Bacia, O.F.M.; Stephen Malkiewicz, O.F.M.; Jerome Zawada, O.F.M.; Cantius J. Kobak, O.F.M.; Roch Niemier, O.F.M.; Hugh Zurat, O.F.M. Priests 6.

Jesuit Community at Marquette University, 1404 W. Wisconsin Ave., 53233. Tel: 414-288-5000. Marquette Jesuit Associates, Inc. Very Rev. Eugene F. Merz, S.J., Rector; Revs. Robert W. Leiweke, S.J., Asst. Rector; Thomas A. Caldwell, S.J., Min.; Richard P. Abert, S.J.; Richard H. Ahler, S.J.; Frank A. Arcuri, S.J.; Francis Xavier Baskara Tulus Wardaya, S.J. (Indonesia); Ronald R. Bieganowski, S.J.; Thaddeus J. Burch, S.J.; Patrick J. Burns, S.J.; Albert J. DiUlio, S.J.; John P. Donnelly, S.J.; William E. Dooley, S.J.; Patrick J. Dorsey, S.J.; Philip F. Dreckman, S.J.; James M. Ewens, S.J.; Edwin F. Falteisek, S.J.; James E. Fitzgerald, S.J.; Raymond T. Gawronski, S.J.; James E. Grummer, S.J.; Bro. Antony Irudayam, S.J. (Madurai); Revs. Robert J. Joda, S.J.; William T. Johnson, S.J.; William J. Kelly, S.J.; William J. Kidd, S.J.; James M. Kubicki, S.J.; Michael D. Kurimay, S.J.; William S. Kurz, S.J.; Robert W. Lambeck, S.J.; Wendell E. Langley, S.J.; John D. Laurance, S.J.; Jeffrey R. Loebl, S.J.; Michael W. Maher, S.J.; Frank A. Majka, S.J.; Albert William Manuel (Madurai); D. Edward Mathie, S.J.; Donald R. Matthys, S.J.; James E. Mauel, S.J.; Richard A. McGarrity, S.J.; T. Michael McNulty, S.J.; Charles J. Mehok, S.J.; Glenn A. Menezes, S.J. (Patna); William L. Mugan, S.J.; John E. Naus, S.J.; Francis Paul Prucha, S.J.; Robert F. Purcell, S.J.; Charles Isaac Puthota, S.J. (Andhra); Richard R. Roach, S.J.; Gregory A. Schissel, S.J.; Thomas N. Schloemer, S.J.; Richard F. Sherburne, S.J.; David M. Shields, S.J.; Walter J. Stohrer, S.J.; Roland J. Teske, S.J.; Andrew J. Thon, S.J.; George Sebastian Vallocheril (Kerala); William A. Van Roo, S.J.; Robert A. Wild, S.J.; Michael J. Zeps, S.J.; Francis G. Ziegler, S.J. Priests 59; Brothers 1; Scholastics 4.

Jesuit Provincial Office, Wisconsin Province, P.O. Box 08277, 53208-0277. Tel: 414-937-6949; Fax: 414-937-6950. Very Rev. D. Edward Mathie, S.J., Prov. and Coord. for Higher Education; Revs. James E. Grummer, S.J., Asst. Prov., Asst. Intl. Ministries & Coord. Province Planning & Communication; James M. Kubicki, S.J., Asst. for Formation; Eugene M. Dutkiewicz, S.J., Asst. for Finance; J. Robert Hilbert, S.J., Asst. for Pastoral and Retreat Min.; Warren J. Sazama, S.J., Dir. of Devel. Priests 6.

Corporate Title: Wisconsin Province of the Society of Jesus.

Priests of the Province Serving Abroad: Rev. Robert L. Faricy, S.J., Gregoriana University, Piazza della Pilotta 4, Rome, Italy, 00187. Revs. Frederick E. Brenk, S.J.; Donald F. Rauscher, S.J.; Robert G. North, S.J., Via della Pilotta 25., Rome, Italy, 00187. Rev. John P. Egan, S.J., Regis College, 15 St. Mary St., Toronto, Canada, M4Y 2R5. Rev. Eugene C. Kollasch, S.J., Sogang University Jesuit Residence, CPO Box 1142, Seoul, Korea, 100-611. Rev. Francis E. Hogan, S.J., (Yoro), Iglesia El Carmen, El Negrito, Honduras. Rev. Philip E. Pick, S.J., Casa Cural, Yoro, Honduras, 23101. Rev. Nicholas E. Schiel, S.J., AP 676, Tegucigalpa, Honduras. Rev. John R. Schak, S.J., Iglesia San Jose Obrero, J. Larrea 1161, Salta Ciudad, Argentina, 4440. Rev. Robert P. Raszkowski, S.J., St. John's College, Landivar, P.O. Box 548, Belize City, Belize. Rev. Francis J. Ring, S.J., Box 25, Punta Gorda, Belize. Revs. Anthony J. Wach, S.J.; William J. Callahan, S.J., P.O. Box 7300, Kampala, Uganda. Rev. Jonathan Haschka, S.J., P.O. Box 21399, Nairobi, Kenya. Rev. Robert W. Dundon, S.J., St. Albert's Church, P.O. Box 10380, Benin City, Nigeria. Rev. Charles C. Murphy, S.J., P.O. Box 21399, Nairobi, Kenya. Rev. Daniel J. Kenney, S.J., Holy Family Minor Basilica, P.O. Box 40891, Nairobi, Kenya.

Priests of the Province Not Otherwise Listed: Rev. Joseph A. Brown, S.J., 2500 Peniston St., New Orleans, LA, 70115. Rev. Thomas P. Sweetser, S.J., 4849 W. Hutchinson, Chicago, IL, 60641. Rev. James F. Hanley, S.J., 5110 S. 49th St., Apt. 609, Omaha, NE, 68117. Rev. Joseph F. Eagan, S.J., St. Patrick's Parish, 114 King St., Larkspur, CA, 94939. Rev. William R. Duffey, S.J., 9455 Watertown Plank Rd., 53226. Rev. Edwin F. Falteisek, S.J., Georgetown No. 48, 125 Kennedy Dr., S. Burlington, VT, 05403-6729. Rev. William M. Kegel, S.J., 30 Mandalay Rd., Oakland, CA, 94618. Rev. Edward J. McCarthy, S.J., 1320 Padre Dr., Salinas, CA, 93901. Rev. Joseph D. Scallon, S.J., P.O. Box 145, St. James on Beaver Island, MI, 49782. Rev. Gerald T. Regan, S.J., Spring Hill College, Mobile, AL, 36608. Rev. John E. Bernbrock, S.J., Our Lady of Perpetual Help, 7655 Main St., Scottsdale, AZ, 85252. Rev. Oscar L. Benzinger, S.J., Presentation Heights, 1500 N. Main, Aberdeen, SD, 57401. Rev. William J. Mehok, S.J., 5320 12th St. S., Apt. 218, Fargo, ND, 58104. Rev. George A. Maloney, S.J., St. Patrick Novitiate, 7820 Bolsa Ave., Midway City, CA, 92655. Rev. Joseph F. Gregory, S.J., St. Stanislaus, Rte. 1, Box 99, Minto, ND, 58261. Rev. William J. Brennan, S.J., St. Mary's Parish, P.O. Box 189, Spur, TX, 79370. Rev. Paul B. Steinmetz, S.J., St. Anthony of Padua Parish, 1000 Cambridge St., Novato, CA, 94947. Rev. Lawrence A. Jonas, S.J., St. Dominic's Parish, 800 E. Walnut, Canton, SD, 57013. Rev. Joseph D. Sheehan, S.J., St. Stephen's Parish, 423 N. Duluth, P.O. Box 5033, Sioux Falls, SD, 57117. Rev. Hubert G. Boschert, S.J., St. Joseph Church, 512 Elm St., Owatonna, MN, 55060. Rev. Benno G. Kornely, S.J., Manresa Jesuit Retreat House, 1390 Quarton Rd., Bloomfield Hills, MI, 48304-3554. Rev. Richard A. Tomasek, S.J., Pontifical College Josephinum, 7625 N. High St., Columbus, OH, 43225-1498. Rev. William J. Ellos, S.J., 7626 Callaghan, Apt. 2201, San Antonio, TX, 78229-2722. Rev. James L. Empereur, S.J., Cathedral of San Fernando, 115 Main Plaza, San Antonio, TX, 78205-2787. Rev. Theodore M. Kalamaja, S.J., Loyola University, 6363 St. Charles Ave., New Orleans, LA, 70118-6195. Rev. James T. Bretzke, S.J., 2535 LeConte Ave., Berkeley, CA, 94709-1133. Rev. Theodore F. Zuern, S.J., Leonard Neale House, 1726 New Hampshire Ave., NW, Washington, DC, 20009-2526. Rev. John L. McCarthy, S.J., Jesuit Hall, 3601 Lindell Blvd., St. Louis, MO, 63108-3393. Rev. Gregory F. Lucey, S.J., Leonard Neale House, 1726 New Hampshire Ave., Washington, D.C., 20009-2526. Rev. Richard C. Burbach, S.J., Leonard Neale House, 1726 New Hampshire Ave., N.W., Washington, DC, 20009-2526. Rev. Daniel C. McDonald, S.J., Leonard Neale House, 1726 New Hampshire Ave., Washington, DC, 20009-2526. Rev. James E. Hug, S.J., Center of Concern, 320 K. St., N.W., Washington, DC, 20002-3522. Rev. Eugene F. Shaw, S.J., Loyola Center, St. Joseph's University, 5600 City Ave., Philadelphia, PA, 19131-1395. Rev. John E. Blewett, S.J., Jesuit Hall, 3601 Lindell Blvd., St. Louis, MO, 63108-3393. Rev. Leon S. Rausch, S.J., P.O. Box 36, Gays Mills, 54631. Rev. James P. Scull, S.J., 120 Retreat Ave., Apt. A4, Hartford, CT,

06106-2539. Rev. John H. Rainaldo, S.J., Apostleship of Prayer, 3 Stephen Ave., New Hyde Park, NY, 11040. Rev. James J. O'Leary, S.J., 139 I Ave., Coronado, CA, 92118. Rev. Timothy J. Howard, S.J., 5808 N. Placita Esplendora, Tucson, AZ, 85718. Rev. James E. O'Hearn, S.J., 4530 58th Ave. N. Apt. 330, Brooklyn Center, MN, 55429. Rev. Charles J. Scherman, S.J., 412 S. Main St., Chippewa Falls, 54729. Rev. J. Roger Lucey, S.J., Santa Maria Parish, 20 Santa Maria Way, Orinda, CA, 94563-2677. Rev. Walter H. Halloran, S.J., San Rafael Parish, 17252 Bernardo Center, Rancho Bernardo, CA, 92128. Revs. George R. Sullivan, S.J.; Patrick J. Connolly, S.J., 5322 Franklin Ave., Los Angeles, CA, 90027. Rev. Philip C. Fischer, S.J., Jesuit Hall, 3601 Lindell Blvd., St. Louis, MO, 63108-3393. Rev. Nicholas F. Pope, S.J., Jesuit Hall, 3601 Lindell Blvd., St. Louis, MO, 63108-3393. Rev. Ned H. Cassem, S.J., Campion Center, 319 Concord Rd., Weston, MA, 02193-1310. Rev. Edward V. Vacek, S.J., Hopkins House, 40 Kirkland St., Cambridge, MA, 02138-2031.

Priests of the Province Engaged in Higher Studies: Rev. Michael W. Maher, S.J., Marquette University, 1404 W. Wisconsin Ave., 53233. Rev. George W. Drance, S.J., Notre Dame Parish, 405 W. 114th St., New York, NY, 10025. Rev. Thomas P. Sherman, S.J., University of Toronto, 94 Kendal Ave., Toronto, Ontario, Canada, M5R 1L9. Rev. James P. Flaherty, S.J., Xavier High School Jesuit Community, 30 W. 16th St., New York, NY, 10011-6302. Rev. Stephen R. Schloesser, S.J., Nobili Hall, Santa Clara University, Santa Clara, CA, 95053. Rev. Timothy R. Lannon, S.J., 6 Sumner Rd., Cambridge, MA, 02138-3015. Rev. John F. Montag, S.J., St. Edmund's College, Cambridge, United Kingdom, CB3 OBN. Rev. John M. Belmonte, S.J., Pedro Arrupe House, 6 Manassas Ave., Cambridge, MA, 02138-2014. Rev. Thomas J. Hansen, S.J., Jesuit Community, Creighton University, 2500 California Plaza, Omaha, NE, 68178-0522. Rev. Todd W. Harrison, S.J., Ferdinand Wheeler House, 3048 Guilford Ave., Baltimore, MD, 21218. Rev. Thomas D. Stegman, S.J., Immaculate Heart of Mary Rectory, 2855 Briarcliff Rd., N.E., Atlanta, GA, 30329.

La Salette Fathers. Missionaries of Our Lady of La Salette. 1607 E. Howard Ave., 53207. Tel: 414-769-7113. Revs. Frances Kula, M.S.; Anthony Dudek, M.S.; James Winiarski, M.S.; Carlos Hoffner, M.S.; Bro. Gerald Buraczewski, M.S. Priests 4; Brothers 1; Total in Residence 12.

Pallotti House, 5424 W. Bluemound Rd., 53208. Tel: 414-258-0653; 259-0688 (Provincial Offices). Residence of Fathers and Brothers and Offices of Mother of God Province of the Society of the Catholic Apostolate. Very Rev. Robert V. Carney, S.A.C., Prov. Supr.; Revs. Francis T. Hueller, S.A.C., Rector; Jerome A. Hapka, S.A.C.; Leon J. Martin, S.A.C.; William E. Lemanski, S.A.C.; Eugene H. Jarosch, S.A.C.; Richard J. Lorenz, S.A.C.; Richard F. Storch, S.A.C.; Bruce J. Schute, S.A.C.; Paul Coutinha, S.A.C.; Bro. Donald Wagner, S.A.C. Priests 10; Brothers 1.

Pere Marquette House Jesuit Community, 726 N. 34th. St., 53208-3301. Society of Jesus, Wisconsin Province. Revs. John A. Schwantes, S.J., Rector; Terrence M. Brennan, S.J.; Douglas J. Leonhardt, S.J.; Edward G. Witt, S.J.; Warren J. Sazama, S.J.; Bro. James E. Garvey, S.J. Priests 5; Scholastics 1; Brothers 1.

Provincial Offices - Discalced Carmelites, 1233 S. 45th St., 53214-3693. Tel: 414-672-7212; Fax: 414-672-3138. Very Rev. Phillip Thomas, O.C.D., Prov.; Sr. Beth Lyman, S.S.S.F., Prov. Sec.

Serving abroad: Revs. Thomas Martin, O.C.D., Philippines; Alan J. Rieger, O.C.D., Philippines; Ignacio Read, O.C.D., Philippines; Arnold Boehme, O.C.D., Philippines; Reginald Foster, O.C.D., Rome; John Sullivan, O.C.D., Rome; Lawrence Daniels, O.C.D. (Nairobi); Dennis Geng, O.C.D. (Nairobi); Daniel Chowning, O.C.D. (Rome); George Mangiaracina, O.C.D (Rome).

Priests of the Province not otherwise listed: Revs. Michael Ciullo, O.C.D.; Gabriel Gates, O.C.D.; Guy Lofy, O.C.D.; Daniel McCauley, O.C.D.; William McNamara, O.C.D.; James Meldrum, O.C.D.; Vincent Bowes, O.C.D. Total in Residence 23; Total Staff 8.

St. Conrad House, 3138 N. 2nd St., 53212. Tel: 414-372-3620. Capuchin Friars, Province of St. Joseph. Revs. Myron Kowalsky, O.F.M.Cap, Supr.; Otto N. Bucher, O.F.M.Cap.; Richard Hart, O.F.M.Cap.; Jerome Higgins, O.F.M.Cap.; Adrian Staehler, O.F.M.Cap.; Claude Pulvermacher, O.F.M.Cap.; Bros. Robert Smith, O.F.M.Cap.; Edward Hagman, O.F.M.Cap.; Michael Auman, O.F.M.Cap. Priests 6; Brothers 3; Total in Residence 9.

St. Joseph House of Formation, 937 N. 37th St., 53208. Tel: 414-344-0710. Priests of the Sacred Heart. Revs. Justin Gross, S.C.J.; Paul Kelly, S.C.J., Supr.; Jack Kurps, S.C.J.; Steve Wiese, S.C.J. Priests 4; Scholastics 1.

St. Vincent Community, 145 S. 76th St., 53214. Tel: 414-476-3211. Very Rev. Robert Carney, S.A.C., Rector; Revs. George Gawin, S.A.C.; Richard Gunderman, S.A.C.; Harold Liebl, S.A.C.

Salvatorian Formation Community, 1039 E. Russell Ave., 53207-1898. Tel: 414-482-1144. Society of the Divine Savior. Revs. Donald Loskot, S.D.S., Dir. Formation & Dir. Novices; Thomas Tureman, S.D.S., (In Transfer); Bros. Wayne Madala, S.D.S., Dir. Candidates; John Rice, S.D.S. Priests 2; Novices 1; Brothers 2; Scholastics 1.

Salvatorian Provincial Residence, 1735 Hi-Mount Blvd., 53208-1720. Tel: 414-258-1735; Fax: 414-258-1934. Society of the Divine Savior.

USA Provincial Team: Very Rev. Dennis D. Thiessen, S.D.S., Prov.; Revs. Michael Shay, S.D.S., Vicar & Dir. Finance; Jean Blais, S.D.S., Dir. Personnel; Joseph Rodrigues, S.D.S., Dir. Planning & Communications.

1735 Hi-Mount Blvd.: Revs. Joseph Henn, S.D.S.; Michael Hoffman, S.D.S., Dir. Vocations; Bruce Brentrup, S.D.S.; Joseph Lubrano, S.D.S.; C. Robert Nugent, S.D.S.; Chad Puthoff, S.D.S.; Joseph Turner, S.D.S.; Luke McArthur, S.D.S.; Roman Pikula, S.D.S.; Bros. Fidelis Rausch, S.D.S.; Arthur Studt, S.D.S.; Paul Sullivan, S.D.S.; Maurus Ellery, S.D.S.

Priests at Residences Not Listed Elsewhere: Revs. Raphael Birringer, S.D.S. Tel: 414-476-9261; Neil Durham, S.D.S. Tel: 414-453-6786; Bro. Van Todd, S.D.S. Tel: 414-258-6730, 7811 W. Center St., 53222-4920. Rev. Julian Guzman, S.D.S., Box 129, Ulster Park, NY, 12487-0129. Tel: 914-338-7357. Rev. Raymond Schrimpf, S.D.S., Box 142, Francis Creek, 54214-0142. Tel: 414-684-5384. Rev. Scott Wallenfelsz, S.D.S., 7100 W. Old Loomis Rd., Greendale, 53129-2761. Tel: 414-427-8117. Rev. Jude Weisenbeck, S.D.S., Archdiocese of Louisville, Ecumenism Office, 1935 Lewiston Pl., Louisville, KY, 40216-2569. Tel: 502-448-4359. Rev. Bruce Clanton, S.D.S., P.O. Box 574, Racine, 53401-0574. Tel: 414-633-4032. Rev. Leonard Walker, S.D.S., P.O. Box 90042, Phoenix, AZ, 85066-0042. Tel: 602-243-3213. Rev. Barry Griffin, S.D.S., 1703 Hoover St., New Holstein, 53061-1662. Tel: 414-898-5790. Rev. Peter Schuessler, S.D.S., Salvatorian House of Studies, 2400 Virginia St., Berkeley, CA, 94709-1206. Tel: 510-845-7701. Rev. Donald Skwor, S.D.S., 51 Washington St., Montclair, NJ, 07042-4544. Tel: 201-783-9002.

Priests of the USA Province Serving at the Generalate in Rome, Italy: Revs. Richard Driscoll, S.D.S.; Michael Henseler, S.D.S.; Thomas Novak, S.D.S.

Salvatorians - Jordan Hall, 3800 N. 92nd St., 53222-2589. Tel: 414-463-6733. Fathers & Brothers of the Society of the Divine Savior. Bro. John Hauenstein, S.D.S., Local Coord.; Revs. Edward DeBruin, S.D.S.; Paul Fierro, S.D.S.; Claude Klotz, S.D.S.; Gary McGinnis, S.D.S.; Eric Middlecamp, S.D.S.; Donald Verhagen, S.D.S.; Bros. Joseph Kreutzer, S.D.S.; Nilus Taddy, S.D.S.; Virgil Mertzlufft, S.D.S.; Ladislaus Markoski, S.D.S.; Julian Landolf, S.D.S.; Luke Manning, S.D.S.; Alex Peserik, S.D.S.; Camillus Becker, S.D.S.; Charles Kubat, S.D.S. Priests 6; Brothers 10.

St. Mary's Home for the Aged, 2005 Division St., Manitowoc, 54220-5699. Revs. Eugene Brochtrup; Robert Casper; Romuald Dibble; Reginald Schrimpf.

BENET LAKE. *St. Benedict's Abbey,* 12605 224th Ave., 53102. Tel: 414-396-4311. Rt. Revs. Leo M. Ryska, O.S.B., Abbot; Andrew V. Garber, O.S.B., Resigned Abbot; Very Rev. Edmund J. Boyce, O.S.B., Prior; Bro. Richard J. Aplington, O.S.B., Subprior; Revs. Henry V. Nurre, O.S.B.; Francis C. Reedy, O.S.B.; Quentin S. Koplinka, O.S.B.; Kevin J. Murphy, O.S.B.; Patrick J. O'Roake, O.S.B.; Leonard J. van Ackeren, O.S.B., St. Mary's Ringling Convent, 1208 Oak St., Baraboo, 53913. Rev. Basil J. Anderson, O.S.B., Holy Family Church, 612 S. Copper Ave., Deming, NM, 88030. Dependent Priory: San Benito Abad, Apdo. 296, 58000 Morelia, Michoacan, Mexico. Rev. Jaime Velasco Rivera, O.S.B.; Rt. Rev. Robert C. Schoofs, O.S.B., Prior; Rev. Miguel Zamorano Valdez, O.S.B. Priests 13; Brothers 16.

BURLINGTON. *Queen of Peace Friary,* 523 S. Brown's Lake Dr., P.O. Box 40, 53104-0040. Tel: 414-763-3241. Franciscan Friars of the Assumption B.V.M. Province. Retirement Home for Franciscan Friars. Revs. Robert Konkol, O.F.M., Guardian; Albin Miklaszewski, O.F.M.; Alexius Lukasik, O.F.M.; Basil Janasik, O.F.M.; Dacian Bluma, O.F.M.; Edmund Czech, O.F.M.; Herbert Silko, O.F.M.; Humphrey Tobias; James Verdick, O.F.M.; Joachim Studwell, O.F.M.; Mark Szych, O.F.M.; Reginald Maslinski, O.F.M.; Reynold Jarecki, O.F.M.; Sante De Angelis, O.F.M.; Sereno Baiardi, O.F.M. Priests 15; Brothers 9.

EAST TROY. *Divine Word Seminary,* Box 107, 53120. Tel: 414-642-3300; Fax: 414-642-7754. Society of the Divine Word. Revs. John F. Fincutter, S.V.D.; John Beemster, S.V.D.; Bernard Fisher; Sylvester Jaworski, S.V.D.; Thomas Lavin; Pablito Tagura, S.V.D.; Raymond Weisenberger, S.V.D.; Ralph Wiltgen, S.V.D.; Joseph Kallanchira, S.V.D.; Bros. Bernard Scherger, S.V.D.; Raymond Albers, S.V.D. Priests 9; Brothers 2; Total in Residence 11.

FRANKLIN. *Dehon House,* 10731 W. Rawson Ave., 53132. Tel: 414-425-3768. Priests of the Sacred Heart. Rev. Paul J. McGuire, S.C.J.

Priests of the Province Living Outside the Community: Rev. Edward Kilianski, S.C.J., P.O. Box 960, Occidental, CA, 95465. Rev. James Schroeder, S.C.J., 5375 Kenrick Parke Dr. N. #305, St. Louis, MO, 63119. Priests 3.

St. Francis Residence, 12001 W. Woods Rd., 53132. Tel: 414-529-0332. Provincial Residence, Priests of the Sacred Heart. Revs. John Czyzynski, S.C.J.; Howard Melzer, S.C.J.; Peter Miller, S.C.J.; Anthony P. Russo, S.C.J., Supr. Priests 4.

Villa Maria, 7330 S. Lovers Lane Rd., 53132. Tel: 414-425-5968; 425-5981. Revs. Jim Alexander, S.C.J.; Frank Aresta, S.C.J.; Donald Barnd, S.C.J.; Patrick M. Cremer, S.C.J.; John Dalbec, S.C.J.; Wm. Denis Devine; Bros. Raymond Kozuch, S.C.J.; Benedict Humpfer, S.C.J., Supr.; Steve Cyr, S.C.J.; Matthew Miles, S.C.J.; Frank Miller, S.C.J.; Conrad Thelen, S.C.J.; Deacon Marion Quagliariello, S.C.J.; Rev. Thomas Hunt, S.C.J., 3553 S. 41st St., Milwaukee, 53221. Priests 6; Brothers 6; Deacons 1.

HALES CORNERS. *Priests of the Sacred Heart,* 6871 S. Lovers Lane Rd., P.O. Box 289, 53130-0289. Tel: 414-425-6910; Fax: 414-425-2938. Rev. John Czyzynski, S.C.J., Prov. Supr.; Bro. Raymond Kozuch, S.C.J., Prov. Sec.; Revs. Jerome Schaad, S.C.J., Prov. Treas.; Frank Arresta, S.C.J., Dir. Foreign Missions; Robert Bossie, S.C.J., Dir. J&P; Michael Burke, S.C.J., Dir. Formation; Richard Johnston, S.C.J., Dir. Apostolates; Jack Kurps, S.C.J., Dir. Vocations.

Priests of the Province Serving Abroad: Most Rev. Evert Baaij, S.C.J., P.O. Box 2440, North End, 6056 Port Elizabeth, Rep. of S. Africa.

Provincialate Residence: Priests of the Sacred Heart, 12001 W. Woods Rd., 53132. Revs. John Czyzynski, S.C.J., Prov. Supr.; Howard Melzer, S.C.J.; Peter Miller, S.C.J.; Anthony P. Russo, S.C.J.

Attached to the Province but Living Elsewhere: Rev. Jerome Clifford, S.C.J., 300 S. Grand Blvd., #701, St. Louis, MO, 63103. Rev. Joseph Doscher, S.C.J., 6701 82nd Ave. N., Pinellas Park, FL, 33781. Rev. David Emerick, S.C.J., 211 Dominion Park Dr., #723, Houston, TX, 77090. Rev. Pat Gonsorcik, S.C.J., Ontario, 130 Springhurst, #203, Ottawa, Canada, K1S OE5. Rev. John Kasparek, S.C.J., 1200 E. 10th St., Stuart, FL, 34996. Rev. Terence Langley, S.C.J., St. Irene Rectory, 187 East St., Carlisle, MA, 01741. Rev. Robert Markunas, S.C.J., 412 Noya Ln., Apopka, FL, 32712. Bro. Thomas Bridges, S.C.J., 1403 N. St. Mary's St., San Antonio, TX, 78215. Bro. Steven Roy, 3723 Ross Ave., Schofield, 54476. Bro. Bernard Taube, S.C.J., 3833 Moland St., #3, Madison, 53704. Bro. Leonard Zaworski, S.C.J., 1925 Loop 431, Apt. 302, Eagle Pass, TX, 78852.

Sacred Heart Monastery. Priests of the Sacred Heart, 7335 S. Lovers Ln., P.O. Box 566, 53130. Tel: 414-425-5323. Revs. George Balderrama, S.C.J.; James Brackin, S.C.J.; Joseph Gole (Ljubljana); Justin Guiltnane, S.C.J., Supr.; Wayne Jenkins, S.C.J.; Kevin McInnis, S.C.J.; John T. O'Connor, S.C.J.; Paul Reid, S.C.J.; Jerome Schaad, S.C.J.

Attached to the Province but Living Elsewhere: Rev. Guy Blair, S.C.J., St. Joseph, 1905 Belt Line Hwy., Madison, 53713. Rev. Thomas Garvey, S.C.J., Kerela, EDA Cochin-682006, Cochin, India. Rev. Patrick Lloyd, S.C.J., 1724 Madison St., New Holstein, 53061-1326. Rev. Edward Griesemer, S.C.J., 1711 S. 9th St., Milwaukee, 53204. Rev. Richard Zelonis, S.C.J., 3920 N. Green Bay Rd., Racine, 53404. Total in Residence 9.

HOLY HILL. *Discalced Carmelite Monastery,* 1525 Carmel Rd., Hubertus, 53033. Tel: 414-628-1838; 673-3540; Fax: 414-628-4294. Revs. Jude Peters, O.C.D., Prior; Matthias Montgomery, O.C.D., Subprior & Dir. Novices; Paul Fohlin, O.C.D.; Daniel Chowning, O.C.D.; Francis Xavier Cotter, O.C.D.; Patrick J. Farrel, O.C.D.; Joseph-Mary Flanery, O.C.D.; Michael Griffin, O.C.D.; Cyril Guise, O.C.D., Shrine Dir.; Denis Read, O.C.D.; Ernest Unverdorben, O.C.D.; Redemptus Short, O.C.D.; Fred Alexander, O.C.D.; Bros. Martin Murphy, O.C.D.; Augustine Wharf, O.C.D. Professed: Deacon John Grennon, O.C.D. Priests 13; Brothers 2; Novices 2.

Holy Hill National Shrine of Mary Help of Christians, 1525 Carmel Rd., Hubertus, 53033.

MOUNT CALVARY. *St. Lawrence Friary,* 301 Church St., 53057. Tel: 414-753-3911. Revs. Edwin F. Dziedziejko, O.F.M.Cap.; Oliver Bambenek, O.F.M.Cap., Supr.; Gary Wegner, O.F.M.Cap.; Campion Baer,

O.F.M.Cap.; Keith Clark, O.F.M.Cap.; Jogues Constance; Dennis Druggan, O.F.M.Cap.; Ronald Jansch, O.F.M.Cap.; Gerald Kafer, O.F.M.Cap.; Randall Knauf, O.F.M.Cap.; Elroy Pesch, O.F.M.Cap.; Emil F. Schneweis, O.F.M.Cap.; Kenan Siegel, O.F.M.Cap.; Luis Sonntag, O.F.M.Cap.; Eugene Tuller, O.F.M.Cap.; Anthony Will, O.F.M.Cap.; Eugene Wolf, O.F.M.Cap.; Paul Yaroch, O.F.M.Cap.; Hilary Zach, O.F.M.Cap.; Roger Zach, O.F.M.Cap.; Bros. Douglas Bode, O.F.M.Cap.; Jerry Campbell, O.F.M.Cap.; John Freienstein, O.F.M.Cap.; Larry Groeschel, O.F.M.Cap.; Neal Plale, O.F.M.Cap.; Mark Rehlinger, O.F.M.Cap.; Arnold Sauter, O.F.M.Cap.; Carl Schaefer, O.F.M.Cap.; John Scherer, O.F.M.Cap., Vicar; Dismas Seward, O.F.M.Cap.; John Willger, O.F.M.Cap. Priests 20; Brothers 11.

OCONOMOWOC. *Austin Hall*, 954 Dousman Rd., 53066. Augustinians/Province of Our Mother of Good Counsel, Olympia Fields, IL. Rev. Michael J. O'Connor, O.S.A., Contact Person, St. Rita Monastery, 7740 S. Western, Chicago, IL, 60620-5867. Tel: 312-925-6600.

RACINE. *Augustinian Novitiate*, 4335 Douglas Ave., 53402-2956. Tel: 414-681-3221. Revs. Alvin P. Metzger, O.S.A., Prior, Treas.; James D. McBurney, O.S.A., Novice Dir. Priests 2; Novices 5.

ST. FRANCIS. *St. Camillus Formation Community*, 3661 S. Kinnickinnic Ave., 53235. Tel: 414-481-3696. Rev. Louis Lussier, O.S.Cam., Supr.; Bros. Nelson DeLoria, O.S.Cam.; Stephen E. Braddock, O.S.Cam.; Mario Crivello, O.S.Cam. Priests 1; Brothers 3.

TWIN LAKES. *La Salette Missionaries Shrine*, Box 777, 53181. Tel: 414-877-3111. Revs. Thaddeus Galuszka, M.S.; Terrence Niziolek, M.S., Supr.; John Gabriel, M.S.; Henry Wojtunik, M.S.; Bros. Adam Mateja, M.S.; Anthony Such, M.S., Oblate. Priests 5; Brothers 1; Oblate Brothers 1.

WAUWATOSA. *Jesuit Community at St. Camillus*, 10100 W. Bluemound Rd., 53226-4386. Tel: 414-259-3784 (Court East); 258-1814 (Skilled Care). Society of Jesus, Wisconsin Province. Revs. Luis Rodriguez, S.J., Supr.; Anthony L. Dagelen, S.J., Asst. Supr.; Robert R. Boyle, S.J.; Leo J. Burns, S.J.; James B. Corrigan, S.J.; M. Joseph Costelloe, S.J.; Norbert C. Eberhardt, S.J.; Robert J. Flahavan, S.J.; Robert M. Frommelt, S.J.; George J. Guenther, S.J.; Bro. Henry J. Guenther, S.J.; Revs. Cletus J. Healy, S.J.; Robert A. Johnston, S.J.; Bro. Gerald E McKeever, S.J.; Revs. John T. O'Brien, S.J.; Robert C. Ostertag, S.J.; Richard L. Porter, S.J.; Bro. Marion J. Reichmuth, S.J.; Revs. Perry J. Roets, S.J.; Jerome E. Rohrer, S.J.; Charles T. Shinners, S.J.; Paul G. Stockhausen, S.J. Priests 19; Brothers 3.

St. Camillus Community House, 600 N. 103rd St., 53226. Tel: 414-259-3789. Revs. James Kovarik, O.S.Cam., Supr.; Raoul Thibeault, O.S.Cam.; Vitaliano Turci, O.S.Cam.; Joseph Bisoffi, O.S.Cam.; Allen Bratkowski, O.S.Cam., (Exclaustration); Carlo Notaro, O.S.Cam.; Bros. Herman Moellenhoff, O.S-.Cam.; Roland Wild, O.S.Cam.; Michael Zingsheim, O.S.Cam. Priests 5; Brothers 3.

St. Camillus Provincialate, 10101 W. Wisconsin Ave., 53226. Tel: 414-259-4511. Provincial offices for the North American Province of the Order of the Servants of the Sick (Order of Saint Camillus). Very Rev. William F. Cronin, O.S.Cam., Prov. Prov. Counselors: Revs. Lou Lussier, O.S.Cam., First Counselor/Vicar; James Kovarik, O.S.Cam.; Bros. Nelson Deloria, O.S.Cam.; Thomas Farrell, O.S.Cam.

[Q] CONVENTS AND RESIDENCES FOR SISTERS

MILWAUKEE. *Ancilla Convent*. Inter-Community, hospitality for religious women. 3601 S. 41st St., 53221. Tel: 414-384-6535. Sr. Agnese Jasko, P.H.J.C., Dir.; Rev. Patrick M. Cremer, S.C.J., Chap. Sisters 31.

Marian Hall, 2925 W. Orchard St., 53215. Tel: 414-384-0995. Retired School Sisters of St. Francis. Sr. Cecilia Zachman, O.S.F., Admin. Sisters 53.

Mercedes Molina - Instituto Santa Mariana de Jesus, 1234 N. 24th Pl., 53205. Tel: 414-931-7163. Sr. Gloria Piedad Garzon, Supr. Sisters 4.
Corporate Title: Mercedes Molina, Inc.

Monastery of the Perpetual Rosary, 217 N. 68th St., 53213. Tel: 414-258-0579. Cloistered Dominican Sisters of the Perpetual Rosary. Mother Miriam Leonard, O.P., Prioress. Professed Sisters 12.

Sacred Heart Center, 1545 S. Layton Blvd., 53215. Tel: 414-383-4490. Home for retired and infirm School Sisters of St. Francis. S. Joann Riesterer, Coord. of Health and Housing Services; Sr. Patricia Bates, O.S.F., Coord. Sisters Living Group. Sisters 50.

St. Clare Convent, 3276 S. 16th St., 53215. Tel: 414-647-5812; 647-2437. Felician Sisters. Sr. M. Laurentine Zygmuntowicz, Local Min. Sisters 4.

St. Dominic Center, 1727 S. 9th St., 53204. Tel: 384-4873. Vietnamese Dominican Sisters. Sr. Clara Nguyen, O.P., Supr. Sisters 4; Postulants 23.

St. Felix Convent, 3159 S. 16th St., 53215. Tel: 414-389-9803. Felician Sisters. Sr. Lisa Marie Drover, C.S.S.F., Local Minister. Sisters 2.

St. Francis Convent, 3170 S. 17th St., 53215. Tel: 414-643-6387. Felician Sisters. Sr. M. Gemma Franczak, C.S.S.F., Local Minister. Sisters 5.

St. Joseph Convent, General Motherhouse of the School Sisters of St. Francis, 1501 S. Layton Blvd., 53215. Tel: 414-384-4105; Fax: 414-645-7198. Sr. Frances Brenner, O.S.F., Pres.; Sr. Phyllis Vater, 1st Vice Pres.; Sr. Raphaela Muench, Vice Pres.; Sr. Alida Lopez, Vice Pres.; Sr. Celestine Schall, Prov.; Rev. James Mauel, S.J., Chap. Sisters 68; Total in Congregation 1,638. Legal Titles: *Generalate-School Sisters of St. Francis, Inc.*; *School Sisters of St. Francis of St. Joseph's Convent, New Castle, Inc.*

Sisters of Charity of St. Joan Antida. St. Rita Convent, 1621 N. Cass St., 53202. Tel: 414-276-5153. Sr. Elizabeth Anne Weber, S.C.S.J.A. Sisters 5.

Sisters of Charity of St. Joan Antida Convent (Emmanuel), 1522 N. Astor St., 53202. Tel: 414-289-0774. Sr. Monica Fumo, S.C.S.J.A., Supr. Sisters 4.

Sisters of Charity of St. Joan Antida Convent (Maranatha), 3044 N. 25th St., 53206. Tel: 414-444-3994. Sr. Andrea Christine Peters, S.C.S.J.A. Sisters 3.

Sisters of Charity of St. Joan Antida Convent (Presentation), 1329 N. Cass St., 53202. Tel: 414-276-4173. Sr. Jennifer Louise Daul, S.C.S.J.A., Supr. Sisters 11.

Sisters of Charity of St. Joan Antida Regina Mundi Provincial House and Novitiate, 8560 N. 76th Pl., 53223. Tel: 414-354-9233; Fax: 414-355-6463. Sr. Mary Joachim Waskovich, S.C.S.J.A., Prov. Sisters 4; Total in Community 49.

Sisters of the Divine Savior, 4311 N. 100th St., 53222-1393. Tel: 414-466-0810; Fax: 414-466-4335. Provincial Administration. Prov. Team: Sr. Sheila Novak, S.D.S., Prov. Leader; Sr. Mary Lee Grady, S.D.S., Vicaress. Sisters 11.
Corporate Title: Sisters of the Divine Savior.

Salvatorian Heights Assisted Living Unit, 2720 N. 36th St., 53210. Tel: 414-445-8485. Sr. Rita Faust, S.D.S., Coord.; Patricia Smith, Health Care Coord. Sisters 21.

United States Province, 1515 S. Layton Blvd., 53215. Tel: 414-384-1515; Fax: 414-384-1950. School Sisters of St. Francis. Provincial Team: Sr. Celestine Schall, O.S.F.; Sr. Therese Thoenen, O.S.F.; Sr. Jane Elyse Russell, O.S.F. Total in U.S. Province 1,084.
Corporate title: The School Sisters of St. Francis of St. Joseph's Convent, Milwaukee, Wisconsin.
Corporate Title: Congregational Support Charitable Trust.

BENET LAKE. *Holy Family Priory*, 53102. Benedictine Sisters of Erie, PA. Mount St. Benedict Monastery, 6101 E. Lake Rd., Erie, PA, 16511.

BROWN DEER. *Sisters of the Sorrowful Mother-Generalate, Inc.*, 9056 N. Deerbrook Tr., 53223. Tel: 414-357-8940. Sr. M. Helen Malolepsy.

CAMPBELLSPORT. *St. Joseph Convent*, 526 Mill St., 53010. Tel: 414-533-8351; Fax: 414-533-5394. School Sisters of St. Francis. Retirement Home/Health Care Center. Sr. Phyllis Wirtz, S.S.S.F., Facility Dir.; Sr. Dorothy McKeague, S.S.S.F., Living Group Coord.; Sr. Theresa Marie Jarvis, S.S.S.F., R.N., Dir. Nursing; Sr. Cathy Wottreng, S.S.N.D., Dir. Pastoral Svcs.; Rev. Nicholas L. Goebel, Chap. Sisters 177.

CEDAR GROVE. *Sacred Heart of the Lake Chalet*, Box 46A, 53013. Tel: 414-285-3084. Recreation Home for Sisters of St. Mary's Home for Aged, Manitowoc, WI & Felician Sisters of the Mother of Good Counsel Province.

DELAVAN. *Villa Celine*, 3127 S. Shore Dr., 53115. Tel: 773-792-6363; Fax: 773-792-9590. Summer Rest Home for Sisters of the Resurrection. Sr. Virginia Ann Wanzek, C.R., Prov. Supr.

ELM GROVE. *Notre Dame of Elm Grove*, 13105 Watertown Plank Rd., 53122-2292. Tel: 414-782-1450; Fax: 414-782-2349.
S.S.N.D. Assisted Care, Independent Living. School Sisters of Notre Dame. Total in Residence 159; Total Staff 87.

School Sisters of Notre Dame, 13105 Watertown Plank Rd., 53122-2291. Tel: 414-782-1450; Fax: 414-782-2349. Sr. Laura Jean Spaeth, S.S.N.D., Prov. Leader. Total in Milwaukee Province 646; Total Staff 27; Total in Residence 208. Legal Titles: *School Sisters of Notre Dame at Milwaukee, Wisconsin, Inc.*; *School Sisters of Notre Dame at Milwaukee, Wisconsin, Inc. Charitable Trust.*

FOND DU LAC. *Convent of the Sisters of St. Agnes*. Motherhouse. 475 Gillett St., 54935. Tel: 414-923-2121. Legal Title: *Congregation of Sisters of St. Agnes of Fond du Lac, Wisconsin, Inc.* Sr. Mary Mollison, C.S.A., General Superior; Rev. Tony Will, O.F.M.Cap., Chap. Sisters 40; Total Religious in Community 429.

Nazareth Heights, Inc., 1755 E. Johnson St., 54935. Tel: 414-921-5826. Retirement Home sponsored by the Congregation of the Sisters of St. Agnes. Mary Hansen, Admin. Sisters 104.

KENOSHA. *Kenosha Dominicans*, P.O. Box 1288, 53141-1288. Tel: 414-694-2067; Fax: 414-694-6542. Congregation of the Dominican Sisters of St. Catherine of Siena of Kenosha. Sr. Susan Anne Snyder, O.P., Prioress. Total Religious in Community 37.

MANITOWOC. *Sisters of Saint Elizabeth, Inc.*, 2005 Division St., 53005. Tel: 414-684-7171 (St. Mary's Home). Sisters of St. Elizabeth. Mother Mary Rita Amrhein, S.S.E., Mother General. Sisters 6.

MEQUON. *Sisters of the Sorrowful Mother, Novitiate House*, 4823 Bonniwell Rd., 53092. Tel: 414-242-5770. Sisters 4.

MOUNT CALVARY. *Loretto Convent*, 53057. Tel: 414-753-3211. General Motherhouse of Sister-Servants of Christ the King. Sr. Mary Rose, Supr. Sisters 9.
Corporate Title: Congregation of Sister Servants of Christ the King, Inc.

Our Lady of Mt. Carmel Convent, 53057. Tel: 414-753-2131; 753-2036. Leadership Team: Sr. Muriel Glodosky, S.S.N.D.; Sr. Mary Dora Kipp, S.S.N.D. Home for Retired Sisters. School Sisters of Notre Dame 51.

OCONOMOWOC. *Villa St. Joseph Summer Day Camp*, 2653 Mill Rd., 53066. Tel: 414-646-2185. Sponsored by Felician Sisters. Sr. M. Carolita Turzin, C.S.S.F., Admin. Total Assisted 194; Total Staff 24.

PEWAUKEE. *Carmel of the Mother of God*, W267 N2517 Meadowbrook Rd., 53072. Tel: 414-691-0336. Discalced Carmelite Nuns. Sr. Mary Agnes Kramer, O.C.D., Prioress; Rev. Dennis C. Klemme, Chap. Professed Sisters 6; Novices 2.

RACINE. *Convent of St. Catherine of Siena*. Siena Center, 5635 Erie St., 53402. Tel: 414-639-4100. Motherhouse of the Sisters of St. Dominic (Congregation of St. Catherine of Siena). Sr. Evelyn Lins, O.P., Pres. Sisters 205; Total Religious in Community 275.
Corporate title: Sisters of St. Dominic.

ST. FRANCIS. *St. Francis Convent, Motherhouse of the Sisters of St. Francis of Assisi*, 3221 S. Lake Dr., 53235-3799. Tel: 414-744-1160; Fax: 414-744-7193. Sr. Marita Maschmann, O.S.F., Dir. of the Congregation. Assoc. Directors: Sr. Joanne Schatzlein, O.S.F.; Sr. Charlotte Roost, O.S.F. Total in Community 378.
Corporate title: The Sisters of St. Francis of Assisi, Milwaukee, Wis. Legal Titles: *The Sisters of St. Francis of Assisi*; *The Ongoing Community Support Fund of the Sisters of St. Francis of Assisi.*

SHEBOYGAN. *Hospital Sisters of the Third Order of St. Francis*, 1724 N. 29th St., 53081. Tel: 414-459-8785. Hospital Sisters of the Third Order of St. Francis 3.

SLINGER. *Franciscan Sisters of Christian Charity (O.S.F.)*. San Damiano Convent, 4270 Cedar Creek Rd., 53086-9795. Tel: 414-644-8916. Sr. Emy Beth Furrer, O.S.F., Supr. Sisters 28; Total Staff 2.

WAUWATOSA. *Provincial Motherhouse of the Carmelite Sisters of the Divine Heart of Jesus*, 1230 Kavanaugh Pl., 53213. Tel: 414-453-4040; Fax: 414-453-5603. Sr. M. Immaculata, Prov. Supr. Sisters 5; Total Religious in Province 28; Total Assisted 185; Total Staff 93.
Corporate title: Carmelite Sisters of the Divine Heart of Jesus, Milwaukee, Wisconsin.

WEST ALLIS. *Missionary Sisters of the Holy Family*. (Poland). 1665 S. 64th St., 53214. Tel: 414-327-4068. Sr. Maria Sarafin, M.S.F., Supr.; Sr. Danuta Kujalowicz, M.S.F., Supr. Asst. Sisters 6.

Sisters of Charity of St. Joan Antida Convent, 6640 W. Beloit Rd., 53219. Tel: 414-541-6575. Sr. Theresa Lucibello, S.C.S.J.A., Supr. Sisters 9.

[R] HERMITAGES

CAMPBELLSPORT. *Hermitage of the Trinity*, N3493 Chapel Heights Rd., 53010. Sr. Joseph Marie, Hermit of the Trinity (Solitary).

[S] RETREAT HOUSES

MILWAUKEE. *Archdiocesan Retreat Center at Archbishop Cousins Catholic Center*, 3501 S. Lake Dr., P.O. Box 07912, 53207-0912. Tel: 414-769-3491. Donna Rugolo, Dir. Bldg. Svcs. Total Staff 2.

Cardoner Retreat Center, 1501 S. Layton Blvd., 53215. Tel: 414-384-2120. Rev. James E. Mauel, S.J., Dir.

The Dwelling Place, 528 N. 31st St., 53208. Tel: 414-933-1100. Revs. Francis J. Dombrowski, O.F.M.Cap.; Jerome Schroeder, O.F.M.Cap.; Mary Klotz, Team Member. Priests 2; Total in Residence 3; Total Staff 3.

BURLINGTON. *Franciscan Retreat Center, Inc.*, 503 S. Browns Lake Dr., 53105. Tel: 414-763-3600. Mr. Frederick Stoltz, Pres.; Ms. Eloise Samano-Williamson, Admin. Total in Residence 4.

ELKHORN. *St. Vincent Pallotti Center*. Pallottine Fathers, N. 6409 Bowers Rd., 53121. Tel: 414-723-2108. Retreat and Christian formation Center. Revs. Gregory P. Serwa, S.A.C., Dir.; Robert J. Albers, S.A.C. Priests 2; Lay Staff 8.

OCONOMOWOC. *Perpetual Help Retreat Center*, 1800 N. Timber Trail Ln., 53066. Tel: 414-567-6900. Revs. Peter Connolly, C.Ss.R., Supr.; John A. Broker, C.Ss.R.; William Broker, C.Ss.R.; Bro. John Matthys, C.Ss.R.; Sr. Olga Neft, O.S.F. Priests 3; Total in Residence 5; Sisters 1; Brothers 1.

WAUKESHA. *Schoenstatt Retreat Center*, W284 N698 Cherry Ln., 53188-9402. Tel: 414-547-7733. Sr. M. Darlene Jankiewicz, Supr. Sisters 10; Total Staff 2.

[T] SECULAR INSTITUTES

MILWAUKEE. *Secular Institute of the Schoenstatt Sisters of Mary*, 5310 W. Wisconsin Ave., 53208. Tel: 414-774-0520. Sr. M. Michelle Mindham, Supr. Sisters 8.

WAUKESHA. *Secular Institute of Schoenstatt Fathers*. Schoenstatt Fathers, W284 N746 Cherry Ln., 53188. Tel: 414-548-9061; Fax: 414-548-9593. Revs. Dietrich A. Haas, Supr.; Charles Boskamp; Gerold M. Langsch; Jonathan J. Niehaus. Priests 7; Total in Residence 4.
Attached to the house but living elsewhere: Revs. Robert DeCock, C.C.; Antonio Rodriguez, C.C.; Hector R. Vega, C.C.

Secular Institute of the Schoenstatt Sisters of Mary, W284 N404 Cherry Ln., 53188-9416. Tel: 414-542-4384; 542-1544. Sr. M. Jacoba Kesselheim, Prov. Supr.; Sr. M. Jacinta Brunner, Supr. Sisters 30.

[U] ASSOCIATIONS OF THE FAITHFUL

MILWAUKEE. *The Christian Sisters*, 1927 S. 7th St., 53204. Tel: 414-643-1188. Sr. M. Corona Kroes, C.S., Pres. Sisters 5.

BELOIT. *Franciscan Sisters of Our Lady*, 2110 Bootmaker Dr., 53511. Tel: 608-365-7257. Sr. Mary Timothy Geenen, F.S.O.L., Supr. Sisters 4.

FRANKLIN. *Franciscan Sisters of Saint Clare, Inc.*, 7732 S. 51st St., 53132. Tel: 414-421-8257. Non-Cloistered Contemplative Community. Sr. Mary Celine Stein, F.S.S.C., Supr. Gen. Professed Sisters 3; Associate Sisters 2; Lay Affiliates 46.

KENOSHA. *Franciscans of the Sorrowful Mother*, 935 Washington Rd., 53140. Tel: 414-605-9480. Ana Maria Solis, Moderator. Members 3.

[V] MISSIONARY ACTIVITIES

MILWAUKEE. *Milwaukee Archdiocesan Office for World Mission.* (Formerly Latin American Office), 3501 S. Lake Dr., P.O. Box 07912, 53207-0912. Tel: 414-769-3406. Sr. Frances Cunningham, O.S.F., Dir. Sends priests and supports laity in overseas mission. Educates and raises funds for worldwide mission.

Missionary Association of Catholic Women, 3501 S. Lake Dr., 53235. Tel: 414-769-3406. Provides aid to home and foreign missions.

Our Blessed Lady of Victory Mission, Inc., 5430 W. Vliet St., 53208-2175. Tel: 414-774-3128. Rev. Lawrence J. Leack, Chap.; Agnes J. Ryan, Pres.

St. Boniface Mission League, Inc., 3501 S. Lake Dr., P.O. Box 07912, 53207-0912. Tel: 414-769-3406. Furnishes aid to home and foreign missions since 1913, with a special focus on the archdiocesan sister parish in the Dominican Republic.

Society for the Propagation of the Faith, Holy Childhood Association. (Pontifical Mission Aid Societies). 3501 S. Lake Dr., P.O. Box 07912, 53207-0912. Tel: 414-769-3406. Raises funds and educates for worldwide mission, under papal auspices.

ELM GROVE. *Family Unity International, Inc.*, 12750 Stephen Pl., 53122. Tel: 414-784-7448. Patricia J. Parks, Pres. Raises and distributes funds to the missions of the Working Boys' Center. Organization is under the supervision of the Director of the Milwaukee Archdiocesan Office for World Mission.

[W] SOCIETIES

MILWAUKEE. *Council of Catholic Women*, 3501 South Lake Dr., P.O. Box 07912, 53207-0912. Tel: 414-695-1406. Mrs. Dorothy Conrad, Pres.; Rev. Eugene D. Winkler, Moderator.

Cursillos in Christianity, P.O. Box 07033, 53207. Revs. Eugene C. Neuman, Spiritual Dir.; Denis Read, O.C.D., Dir. Spanish Speaking Cursillo; Sr. Anne Mary Rischar, O.S.F., Dir. English Speaking Secretariat. Total in Residence 4; Total Staff 6.

People's Eucharistic League, 4680 W. Bradley Rd., 53223. Tel: 414-355-3131. Sr. Mary Francis Nuss, S.S.N.D., Exec. Dir.; Rev. Robert G. Sampon, Chap.

Priests' Purgatorial Society, 3501 S. Lake Dr., P.O. Box 07912, 53207-0912. Tel: 414-769-3300. Barbara Anne Cusack, Sec.

St. Vincent de Paul Society, 9601 W. Silver Spring Dr., 53225. Tel: 414-462-7837; Fax: 414-462-5458. Mr. Gerald H. Felsecker, Exec. Dir., Milwaukee Archdiocesan Council, Council of Racine, 926 La-Salle St., Racine, 53404. Council of Kenosha, 6201 14th Ave., Kenosha, 53143. Council of Fond du Lac, 401 N. Hickory, Fond du Lac, 54935. Council of Sheboygan, 4215 Hwy. 42 N., Sheboygan, 53083. Council of Waukesha, 305 E. Main St., Waukesha, 53186. Council of Beaver Dam, 316 S. Spring St., Beaver Dam, 53916. Council of Washington County, 420 River Rd., West Bend, 53095. Council of Ozaukee County, P.O. Box 59, Port Washington, 53074. Total Assisted 30,000; Total Staff 5,200.

HORICON. *Legion of Mary*, 109 Valley St., 53032. Tel: 414-485-2937. Rev. M. Eugene Kinney, Spiritual Dir.; Mrs. Dorothy Conrad, Pres.

WAUWATOSA. *Apostolate of Suffering*. A Pious Union of the Sick. 7452 Harwood Ave., 53213. Tel: 414-771-7466.

Milwaukee Archdiocesan Holy Name Society, 2431 N. 63rd St., 53213. Mr. John Lando, Pres.; Deacon Bertrand C. Mulroy, Spiritual Dir.

[X] NEWMAN CENTERS

MILWAUKEE. *Marquette University Ministry*. Alumni Memorial Union 236, P.O. Box 1881, 53201. Tel: 414-288-6873; Fax: 414-288-1986. Dr. Mary Feeley, Dir.; Dr. Susan Mountin, Assoc. Dir.

Milwaukee Archdiocesan Campus Ministry, P.O. Box 07912, 53207-0912. Tel: 414-769-3439. Legal Title: *Campus Ministry of the Archdiocese of Milwaukee*.
University of Wisconsin - Milwaukee, Newman Center, 3001 N. Downer Ave., 53211. Tel: 414-964-6640. Constance M. Popp; Rev. Robert J. Lotz.
U.W. Parkside and Carthage College, 6203-54th. Ave., Kenosha, 53142. Tel: 414-654-3630. Edith Padgett.
Whitewater Campus Ministry (Whitewater), 344 N. Prairie St., Whitewater, 53190. Tel: 414-473-5555. Rev. James M. Godin.

[Y] MISCELLANEOUS

MILWAUKEE. *Agape Community Center of Milwaukee, Inc.*, 3400 W. Silver Spring Dr., 53209. Tel: 414-464-4440. A subsidiary corporation of the Sisters of the Sorrowful Mother-Ministry Corporation. Sr. Myra Smith, Exec. Dir.

Alternative Residential Arrangements, Inc., P.O. Box 07912, 53207-0912; Fax: 414-769-3428. Group Homes for Developmentally disabled adults.
Other Locations: 6609 N. 53rd St., 53223. 5255 S. 18th St., 53221. Sponsored by Catholic Charities of the Archdiocese of Milwaukee, Inc.

Apostleship of the Sea, 3501 S. Lake Dr., P.O. Box 07912, 53207-0912.

Archdiocesan Marian Shrine. 141 N. 68th St., 53213. Tel: 414-257-0155. Rev. Anthony S. Trenier, Dir.

Assisi Community Organization, Inc., 5325 W. Burleigh, 53210. Tel: 414-449-3960. Sponsored by Franciscan Sisters, Daughters of the Sacred Hearts of Jesus and Mary (Wheaton, Illinois). Robert J. Makowski, Pres. Total Staff 6.

Assisi Homes - Eldr Manor, Inc., 5325 W. Burleigh St., 53210. Tel: 630-462-9271. Robert J. Cisek, Pres.; Garth Seehawer, Contact Person. Franciscan Sisters, Daughters of the Sacred Heart of Jesus and Mary of Wheaton, Illinois.

Assisi Homes - Gateway, Inc., 5325 W. Burleigh St., 53210. Ms. Judy Leiterman, Pres. Tel: 630-462-9271; Garth Seehawer, Contact Person. Franciscan Sisters, Daughters of the Sacred Hearts of Jesus and Mary of Wheaton, IL. To acquire or develop and operate housing projects for low income families and elderly persons; and to provide for human and other charitable/benevolent services required by the residents.

Assisi Homes - Howard Woods, Inc., 5325 W. Burleigh St., 53210. Tel: 630-462-9271. Judith A. Leiterman, Pres.; Garth Seehawer, Contact Person. Franciscan Sisters, Daughters of the Scred Hearts of Jesus and Mary of Wheaton, Illinois. Purpose: To acquire, or develop, and operate housing projects for low income families and elderly persons; and to provide for human and other charitable/benevolent services required by the residents.

Assisi Homes - Jefferson Court, Inc., 415 E. Knapp St., 53202. Tel: 630-462-9271. Ms. Susan M. Dillberg, Pres. Franciscan Sisters, Daughters of the Sacred Hearts of Jesus and Mary of Wheaton, Illinois.

Assisi Homes - Kenosha, Inc., 5325 W. Burleigh St., 53210. Tel: 414-449-3960. Phil Schultz, Pres. Franciscan Sisters, Daughters of the Sacred Hearts of Jesus and Mary of Wheaton, IL. Independent Housing for Low Income Elderly.

Assisi Homes - Mabess Manor, Inc., 5325 W. Burleigh St., 53210. Tel: 630-462-9271. Robert Cisek, Pres.; Garth Seehawer, Contact Person. Franciscan Sisters, Daughters of the Sacred Hearts of Jesus and Mary of Wheaton, IL. Purpose: To acquire or develop, and operate housing projects for low income families and elderly persons.

Assisi Homes - Rock View, Inc., 5325 W. Burleigh St., 53210. Tel: 630-462-9271. Judy Leiterman, Pres.; Garth Seehawer, Contact Person. Franciscan Sisters, Daughters of the Sacred Hearts of Jesus and Mary of Wheaton, Illinois. Housing Projects for Low Income Families.

Assisi Homes - Saxony, Inc., 5325 W. Burleigh St., 53210. Tel: 630-462-9271. Steve Kuklin, Pres.; Garth Seehawer, Contact Person. Franciscan Sisters, Daughters of the Sacred Heart of Jesus and Mary of Wheaton, Illinois. Independent Housing for Low Income Elderly.

Assisi Homes of Milwaukee, Inc., 5325 W. Burleigh St., 53210. Tel: 630-462-9271. Susan M. Dillberg, Pres.; Garth Seehawer, Contact Person. Franciscan Sisters, Daughters of the Sacred Hearts of Jesus and Mary of Wheaton, Illinois. Purpose: To acquire, or develop and operate housing projects for low income families and elderly persons and to provide for human and other charitable services required by the residents.

Assisi Homes of Wisconsin, Inc., 5325 W. Burleigh St., 53210. Tel: 630-462-9271. Franciscan Sisters, Daughters of the Sacred Hearts of Jesus and Mary, Wheaton, IL. Susan M. Dillberg, Pres. Total in Residence 148; Total Staff 6.

Capuchin Franciscan Tertiary Province of St. Joseph of Wisconsin, Inc., 327 W. Brown St., 53212. Tel: 414-374-5750. Rev. Ulric Buening, O.F.M.Cap., Prov. Asst.

Capuchin Franciscan Volunteer Corps, Inc., 1015 N. 9th St., 53233-1468. Tel: 414-271-0135. Purpose: To serve as a religious organization which recruits, places, and supports Christian volunteers in service to people in need. Bro. David Schwab, O.F.M.Cap., Pres. Total Assisted 130,000; Total Staff 2.

The Catholic Charismatic Renewal Office of Southeastern Wisconsin, Inc., P.O. Box 07912, 53207-0912. Tel: 414-482-1727. Deacon Robert E. Goodman, Liaison; Mary Goodman, Admin.

Catholic Charities Child Care, Inc., 3501 S. Lake Dr., P.O. Box 07912, 53207-0912. Tel: 414-769-3400. Thomas R. Schneider, Pres.

Catholic Charities Foundation, Inc., 3501 S. Lake Dr., P.O. Box 07912, 53207-0912. Tel: 414-769-3400. Thomas R. Schneider, Registered Agent.

Catholic Charities of the Archdiocese of Milwaukee, Inc., 3501 S. Lake Dr., P.O. Box 07912, 53207-0912. Tel: 414-769-3400; Fax: 414-769-3428. Mr. Thomas R. Schneider, Exec. Dir.
Regional Offices: 2021 N. 60th St., 53208. Tel: 414-771-2881. 2711 19th St., Racine, 53403. Tel: 414-637-8888. 503 Wisconsin Ave., Sheboygan, 53081. Tel: 414-458-5726. 741 N. Grand Ave., Suite 210, Waukesha, 53186. Tel: 414-547-2463.
Area Offices: 5820 3rd Ave., Kenosha, 53140. Tel: 414-658-2088. 191 S. Main St., Fond du Lac, 54935. Tel: 414-923-2550.
Other Offices: Beaver Dam, Brookfield, Burlington, Germantown, Menomonee Falls, Milwaukee North, Milwaukee South, Milwaukee Southwest, Port Washington, West Bend. Total Assisted Annually 33,500.

Catholic Information Center, 633 W. Wisconsin Ave., Suite 1008, 53203. Tel: 414-272-8285. Rev. Charles J. Mehok, S.J., Dir.

Clare Towers II, Inc. dba Clare Woods, 3576 S. 43rd St., 53220. Tel: 414-643-6501. Sponsored by School Sisters of St. Francis. Housing Facility for physically disabled to live independently. Apartments 32.

Clare Towers, Inc., 1546 S. 29th St., 53215. Tel: 414-643-6501. Sponsored by School Sisters of St. Francis. Housing facility for physically disabled to live independently. Apartments 25.

Connective Ministries, 8769 Herbert St., 53225. Tel: 414-466-2648. Sr. Jacque Roller, C.S.A.

Convergence, Inc., 1501 S. Layton Blvd., 53215. Tel: 414-384-4105. Sr. Jeanne Schweickert, S.S.S.F., Pres. & Exec. Dir.; Sr. Anne Beitzinger, Vice Pres. Board Members: Sr. Charlita Foxhoven; Sr. Alphonsa Puls.

Covenant Community Foundation, Inc., 1126 S. 70th St., Ste. S306, P.O. Box 14970, 53214-0970. E. Thomas Sheahan, Pres. Sponsored by Franciscan Sisters, Daughters of the Sacred Hearts of Jesus and Mary, Wheaton, IL.

Covenant Healthcare System, Inc., 1126 S. 70th St., Ste. S306, P.O. Box 14970, 53214-0970. Tel: 414-456-2300; Fax: 414-456-2363. E. Thomas Sheahan, Pres. & CEO. Franciscan Sisters, Daughters of the Sacred Hearts of Jesus and Mary, Wheaton, IL. Congregation of the Sisters of St. Felix of Cantalice (Felician Sisters), Chicago, IL.

Covenant Home Health, Inc., 9688 W. Appleton Ave, Ste. A, 53225. Tel: 414-535-6900; Fax: 414-535-6902. Franciscan Sisters, Daughters of the Sacred Hearts of Jesus and Mary, Wheaton, IL.

Divine Savior Holy Angels High School Endowment Foundation, Inc., 4311 N. 100th St., 53222. Tel: 414-466-0810.

East Side Service for Senior Citizens, 2480 N. Cramer St., 53211. Tel: 414-961-0661. Jo Ann M. Schmidt, Dir.
Corporate Title: East Side Service for Senior Citizens, Inc. - an Interfaith Outreach Program. Sponsored by St. Hedwig, Holy Rosary, SS. Peter and Paul, St. Rita, Lake Park Lutheran Church in

Milwaukee and United Church of Christ, Plymouth, St. Casmir's and St. Mary Czestochoa. Total Assisted 475; Total Staff 2.

Foundation for Religious Retirement, Inc., 3195 S. Superior St., 53207-3000. Tel: 414-483-9128; Fax: 414-483-9130. Mary Frances Lewis, Exec. Dir. Raises funds to fulfill the needs of retired women religious in the Milwaukee Archdiocese.

Franciscan Pilgrimage Programs, Inc., 1648 S. 37th St., 53215-1724. Tel: 414-383-9870. Rev. Roch Niemier, O.F.M., Pres. Operate a Catholic Franciscan Pilgrimage Program for religious men and women, leaders in Franciscan based institutions, members of the Secular Franciscan Order and others who desire to deepen their Franciscan values and spirituality.

Franciscan Seniors, Kenosha, Inc., 5325 W. Burleigh St., 53210. Tel: 630-462-9271. Robert J. Cisek, Pres.; Garth Seehawer, Contact Person. Franciscan Sisters, Daughters of the Sacred Hearts of Jesus and Mary of Wheaton, IL.

House of Peace, 1702 W. Walnut St., 53205-1616. Tel: 414-933-1300. Revs. Al Veik, O.F.M.Cap., Co-Dir.; Matthew Gottschalk, O.F.M.Cap., Co-Dir.; Bro. Booker T. Ashe, O.F.M.Cap., Dir. Emeritus. In res., Rev. Martin Pable, O.F.M.Cap. Total Assisted 5,000; Total in Residence 4; Total Staff 4.

International Institute of the Heart of Jesus, 7236 Wellauer Dr., 53213-3666. Tel: 414-475-2694. Dennis J. Brand (USA), Exec. Vice Pres. & Treas.; Rev. Roger Vekemans, S.J. (Chile), Pres.; Rev. Msgr. Walter O. Kern (USA), Vice Pres. & Sec.

The Jesuit Partnership, 3400 W. Wisconsin Ave., 53208. Tel: 414-937-6955. Revs. E. M. Dutkiewicz, S.J., Treas.; Warren J. Sazama, S.J., Pres.

Korean Catholic Community, 1842 W. Windlake Ave., 53215. Tel: 414-672-6416. Rev. Augustine Park.

**LaFarge Lifelong Learning Institute, Inc.*, 1501 S. Layton Blvd., 53215. Tel: 414-383-2550. Continuing Education Program for older adults. Marion K. Hook, Exec. Dir.; Sr. Celia Schulte, Admin. Asst.

M.F.S.I., Inc., 3301 W. Highland Blvd., 53208. Wilfred F. Loebig, Jr., Pres. Sponsored by Franciscan Sisters, Daughters of the Sacred Hearts of Jesus and Mary, Wheaton, IL.

Milwaukee Achiever Program, Inc., 1506 W. Pierce St., 53204. Tel: 414-643-5108. Dennis J. Purtell, Esq., Legal Counsel. Sponsored by the School Sisters of St. Francis; Sisters of St. Francis of Assisi; School Sisters of Notre Dame.
Purpose: To provide adult literacy education to economically and educationally disadvantaged adults in the Greater Milwaukee area. Total Assisted 400; Total Staff 13.

Milwaukee Archdiocesan Council of Deacons. P.O. Box 07912, 53207-0912. Advisory/Governing Board of Deacons. Deacon Gerald R. Ponec, Pres.

Milwaukee Archdiocesan Elementary Principal's Association, 3501 S. Lake Dr., P.O. Box 07912, 53201-0912. Tel: 414-284-2682. Ms. Helen Gilles, Coord. & Contact Person.

National Association of Catholic Chaplains, 3501 S. Lake Dr., P.O. Box 07473, 53207-0473. Tel: 414-483-4898; Fax: 414-483-6712. Rev. Joseph J. Driscoll (BO), Exec. Dir.

National Office of Post-Abortion Reconciliation and Healing, Inc., 3501 S. Lake Dr., P.O. Box 07477, 53207-0477. Tel: 414-483-4141; Fax: 414-483-7376. Victoria M. Thorn, Pres. Total Assisted 2,400; Total Staff 3.

O.S.F. Services, Inc., 1126 S. 70th St., Ste. S306, P.O. Box 14970, 53214-0970. Tel: 414-456-2300. Mr. Wilfred F. Loebig, Jr., Pres. Sponsored by Franciscan Sisters, Daughters of the Sacred Hearts of Jesus and Mary, Wheaton, IL.

Pallottine Apostolic Associates, 5424 W. Bluemound Rd., 53208. Tel: 414-258-3633. Ms. Kristen Davis, Dir. Total in Residence 4; Total Staff 1.

Pallottine Fathers and Brothers, Inc., Disability Trust, 5424 W. Bluemound Rd., 53208. Very Rev. Robert V. Carney, S.A.C., Pres.; Rev. Harold J. Liebl, S.A.C., Treas.

Pallottine Fathers and Brothers, Inc., Educational and Apostolic Ministry Trust, 5424 W. Bluemound Rd., 53208. Tel: 414-259-0688. Very Rev. Robert V. Carney, S.A.C., Prov.; Rev. Harold J. Liebl, S.A.C., Sec. & Treas.

S.E.T. Ministry, Inc., 2977 N. 50th St., 53210. Tel: 414-449-2680. Sr. Lucina Halbur, C.S.A., Pres. & C.E.O. Wheaton Franciscan Services, Inc., Corporate Sponsor, Joint Sponsored by 17 Religious Congregations.

S.F.A. of Racine, Inc., 1126 S. 70th St., Ste. S306, 53214-0970. Mr. Wilfred F. Loebig, Jr., Pres. Sponsored by Franciscan Sisters, Daughters of the Sacred Hearts of Jesus and Mary, Wheaton, IL.

S.I.S. (Sisters Interacting with Seniors), 1720 S. 29th St., #420, 53215. Tel: 414-643-4529. Sr. Irene Kay, R.S.M., Coord. Total Assisted 1,700; Total Staff 3.

St. Benedict Community Meal. (Province of St. Joseph of the Capuchin Order, Inc.). 1015 North 9th St., 53233. Tel: 414-271-0135. Mr. Tom Plakut, Dir. Provides a free evening meal Sunday through Friday to those in need. Total Assisted 130,000 Meals Served; Total Staff 4.

St. Catherine Residence For Women, 1032 E. Knapp St., 53202. Tel: 414-272-8470. A residence supporting disadvantaged women in transition and students, with onsite programs advocating self-sufficiency. Includes a Right Start Program for first-time, single, pregnant women over the age of 18. Sr. Ruth Mutchler, R.S.M., Admin. Sisters 5; Residents 150. Legal Title: *St. Catherine Residence, Inc.*

St. Clare Management, Inc., 1545 S. Layton Blvd., 53215. Tel: 414-643-6501. Philip Aggen, Pres. & CEO. Sponsored by the School Sisters of St. Francis.

St. Francis Corporation, 3237 S. 16th St., 53215; Fax: 414-647-5565. Gregory A. Banaszynski. Total Staff 37.

St. Mary's Hospital, Milwaukee Foundation, Inc., 1101 N. Market St., Suite 125, 53202. Tel: 414-291-1425; Fax: 414-291-1427. Mr. Mark D. Langer, Chm.; Sr. Renee Rose, D.C., Pres. Sponsored by the Daughters of Charity of St. Vincent de Paul.

St. Michael Hospital Community Foundation, Inc., 2400 W. Villard Ave., 53209. Tel: 414-527-8205. John H. Kopmeier, Jr., Pres. Franciscan Sisters, Daughters of the Sacred Hearts of Jesus and Mary, Wheaton, IL.

St. Stephen's League. (of the Archdiocesan Council of Deacons). P.O. Box 07912, 53207-0912. Deacon Juan A. Molina, Pres.

St. Thomas More Lawyers Society, 4060 N. 26th St., 53209. Tel: 414-444-5610. Rev. Joseph N. Perry, Chap.

Santa Fe Communications, Inc., 1126 S. 70th. St., Ste. S216A, 53214. Tel: 414-475-4444. Dr. William Thorn, Pres.; Rev. Anthony Scannell, O.F.M.Cap., Treas. Total Staff 3.

The School Sisters of St. Francis of St. Joseph's Convent, Milwaukee WI, Inc. Congregational Support Charitable Trust. 1515 S. Layton Blvd., 53215. Tel: 414-384-1515. Sr. Helen Butzler, Trustee.

Seton Health Care Services, Inc., 4545 N. Port Washington Rd., 53212. Tel: 414-291-1300; Fax: 414-291-1319. Operated by the Daughters of Charity of St. Vincent de Paul.

Seton Health Corporation of Wisconsin, 2320 N. Lake Dr., 53211. Sr. Veronica Ann Brown, D.C., Chm. Operated by the Daughters of Charity of St. Vincent de Paul.

Shade Tree Family Resource Center, Inc., 2661 N. Teutonia Ave., 53206. Tel: 414-562-7934. Mary Tandberg, Pres.; Sherri Mays, Contact Person. Sponsored by: School Sisters of Notre Dame. Operation of a community-based family center committed to the preservation of families and the prevention of violence; conducts programs, education, support groups and self awareness. Total Assisted 1,027; Total Staff 11.

Shared Therapeutic Services, Inc., 2500 N. Mayfair Rd., 53226. Tel: 414-778-6688. Ms. Karen Lemanczyk, Dir. Subsidiary of Sacred Heart Rehabilitation Institute.

Sisters of the Sorrowful Mother-Ministry Corporation, 11925 W. Lake Park Dr., 53224. Tel: 414-359-1060. Sr. M. Lois Bush, S.S.M., Pres. & CEO.

**St. Francis Foundation of Milwaukee, Inc.*, 3237 S. 16th St., 53215. Tel: 414-647-5566. Sponsored by the Felician Sisters. Sr. Julie Weckwerth.

**St. Joan Antida High School Foundation, Ltd.*, 1341 N. Cass St., 53202. Tel: 414-354-9233. Sr. Marie Louise Balistrieri, Contact Person.

**St. Josaphat Basilica Foundation, Inc.*, 569 W. Lincoln Ave., 53207. Tel: 414-385-3263; Fax: 414-385-3270. Mr. Michael J. Murry, Chm.; Mr. Richard C. Thomas, Admin.

Telos, Inc. dba Clare Heights, Clare Meadows, Clare Lakes, Clare Court, Clare Place and Clare Central. 1545 S. Layton Blvd., 53215. Tel: 414-643-6501. Sponsored by the School Sisters of St. Francis. Housing for physically disabled to live independently. Sr. Regina Pacis, Pres. Apartments 107.

Villa St. Joseph, Inc., 8526 W. Mill Rd., 53225. Tel: 630-462-9271. Steve Kuklin, Pres.; Garth Seehawer, Contact Person. Franciscan Sisters, Daughters of the Sacred Hearts of Jesus and Mary of Wheaton, IL. To acquire or develop and operate housing projects for low income families and elderly persons.

Villa St. Theresa, Inc., 5325 W. Burleigh St., 53210. Tel: 630-462-9271. Judy Leiterman, Pres.; Garth Seehawer, Contact Person. Franciscan Sisters, Daughters of the Sacred Hearts of Jesus and Mary of Wheaton, IL. To acquire or develop and operate housing projects for low income families and elderly persons.

VISION Ministries, Inc., 1515 S. Layton Blvd., 53215. Tel: 414-384-1515. Sr. Regina Pacis Meservey, Exec. Dir. Sponsored by The School Sisters of St. Francis of St. Joseph's Convent, Milwaukee, WI, Inc.
Purpose: To manage, promote support and engage in related ministries.

BRISTOL. *Mercy Retreat Center*, 12009 221st Ave., 53104. Tel: 414-862-6648. Sisters of Mercy of the Americas, Regional Community of Chicago.

BROWN DEER. *Sisters of the Sorrowful Mother Charitable Trust*, 9056 N. Deerbrook Rd., 53223. Sr. M. Helen Malolepsy. Provides for the needs of the aged and infirm members of the Sisters of the Sorrowful Mother.

Sisters of the Sorrowful Mother International Finance, Inc., 9056 N. Deerbrook Terr., 53223. Tel: 414-357-8940. Sr. M. Helen Malolepsy.

FOND DU LAC. *Hazotte Ministries, Inc.*, 475 Gillett St., 54935. Tel: 414-923-2121. Sponsored by the Congregation of the Sisters of St. Agnes. Sr. Hertha Longo, C.S.A., Pres.

St. Francis Home Foundation Inc., 365 Gillett St., 54935. Mary Weber, Pres. Sponsored by the Congregation of the Sisters of St. Agnes.

FRANKLIN. *Congregation of the Priests of the Sacred Heart Support and Maintenance Trust*, 6871 S. Lovers Lane Rd., 53132. Trustees: Revs. Justin Guiltnane, S.C.J.; Edward Kilianski, S.C.J.; Bro. Benedict Humpfer, S.C.J.

Friends of Theophane, P.O. Box 32101, 53132. Mr. Ronald Zeilinger, Contact Person. To collect information and promote knowledge of the reputation for holiness of the late Frater Theophane Prenderville, S.C.J.

GREENDALE. *Volunteer Missionary Movement (VMM)*, 5980 W. Loomis Rd., 53129. Tel: 414-423-8660; Fax: 414-423-8964. Mary Jo Runnoe, Dir. Recruits, trains and sends Christian men and women to areas of need in the world.

HALES CORNERS. *Development Office*. Sacred Heart Monastery-Priests of the Sacred Heart-Reign of the Sacred Heart, Inc. 6889 S. Lovers Lane Rd., P.O. Box 900, 53130. Tel: 414-425-3383. Mr. Patrick R. Thompson, Pres. U.S. Province of the Priests of the Sacred Heart.

KENOSHA. *Dominican Fund of Kenosha, Inc.*, P.O. Box 1288, 53141-1288. Tel: 402-393-7661. James R. Kaskie, Contact Person. Sponsored by: Dominican Sisters of St. Catherine of Siena of Kenosha, Inc.

Dominican Health Care, Inc., 3560 7th Ave., 53140. Tel: 414-656-3011. Mr. Ryland P. Davis, Pres. & CEO. Sponsored by the Congregation of the Dominican Sisters of St. Catherine of Siena of Kenosha, WI.

St. Mark Latin American Center, 1320 73rd St., 53143-5459. Tel: 414-657-7222. Rev. Gerald J. Hessel, Dir. Total Assisted 1,075; Total Staff 2.

The Women's Health Center Foundation, Inc., 3556 Seventh Ave., 53140. Susan Dyke, Chpn.

MANITOWOC. *Sisters of St. Elizabeth, Inc., Congregational Support Charitable Trust*, 2005 Division St., 54220-5699. Tel: 414-684-7171, Ext. 291; 303. Mother M. Rita Amrhein, S.S.E., Trustee.

MEQUON. *St. Mary's Foundation Ozaukee, Inc.*, 13133 N. Port Washington Rd., Ste. G01, 53097. Tel: 414-243-7472; Fax: 414-243-7416. Ms. Jean Ansay, Chm. Sponsored by Daughters of Charity of St. Vincent DePaul.

NASHOTAH.

**Tyme Out Youth Ministry Center, Inc.*, W332 N6786 County Rd. C, 53058-9737. Tel: 414-966-1800. Sr. Kieran Sawyer, S.S.N.D., Dir. Total in Residence 2; Total Staff 17.

RACINE. *All Saints Healthcare Foundation, Inc.*, 3801 Spring St., 53405. Edward DeMeuLenaere, Pres. Franciscan Sisters, Daughters of the Sacred Hearts of Jesus and Mary, Wheaton, IL.

All Saints Healthcare System, Inc., 3801 Spring St., 53405. Tel: 414-636-4860; Fax: 414-636-4540. Edward DeMeulenaere, Pres. Franciscan Sisters, Daughters of the Sacred Hearts of Jesus and Mary, Wheaton, IL.

All Saints Visiting Nurse Association and Hospice of Racine, Inc., 4000 Spring St., P.O. Box 4045, 53404-0045. Tel: 414-635-7580. Debra A. Ostroski, Pres. Franciscan Sisters, Daughters of the Sacred Hearts of Jesus and Mary of Wheaton, IL.

Catherine Marian Housing, Inc., 5635 Erie St., 53402. Tel: 414-639-4100. Racine Dominican Ministries, Inc. and Franciscan Ministries, Inc.

Dominican College of Racine, Inc., 5635 Erie St., 53402. Tel: 414-639-4100. Sr. Evelyn Lins, O.P., Pres.

Marian Center of Racine, Inc., 3801 Spring St., 53405. Tel: 414-636-4011; Fax: 414-636-4540. Mr. Edward P. DeMeulenaere, Pres. Franciscan Sisters, Daughters of the Sacred Hearts of Jesus and Mary, Wheaton, IL.

Missionary Community of St. Paul the Apostle and Mary, Mother of the Church, Inc., 2512 Westwood Dr., 53404. Tel: 414-634-2666; Fax: 414-635-1910. Rev. Pere Cane, Pres. A private Association of Christian Faithful, comprised of clergy and laity, with missions in Africa and South America, while promoting mission awareness internationally.

Racine Dominican Ministries, Inc., 5635 Erie St., 53402. Tel: 414-639-4100. Sr. Evelyn Lins, O.P., Pres.

St. Catherine's High School Corporation, 1200 Park Ave., 53403. Tel: 414-632-2785; Fax: 414-632-5144. John Crimmings, Chpn.

St. Catherine's High School of Racine, Inc., 5635 Erie St, 53402. Tel: 414-639-4100. Sr. Evelyn Lins, O.P., Pres.

St. Catherine's Infirmary, Inc., 5635 Erie St., 53402. Tel: 414-639-4100. Sr. Evelyn Lins, O.P., Pres.

St. Francis Health Care Corporation of Racine, 3801 Spring St., 53405. Tel: 414-636-4011; Fax: 414-636-4540. Edward DeMeulenaere, Pres. Franciscan Sisters, Daughters of the Sacred Hearts of Jesus and Mary, Wheaton, IL.

Senior Companion Program. (Racine Dominican Ministries, Inc.). 5365 Erie St., 53402. Tel: 414-639-4100. Sr. Brenda Walsh, O.P., Dir.

Villa St. Anna, Inc., 5737 Erie St., 53402. Tel: 414-639-9757. Sponsored by Franciscan Sister, Daughters of the Sacred Hearts of Jesus and Mary of Wheaton, Illinois and the Sisters of St. Dominic of Racine, Wisconsin. To provide assisted living for the elderly of low and moderated income. Steve Kuklin, Pres. Residents 71.

SHEBOYGAN. *St. Thomas High School, Inc.*, 822 New Jersey Ave., 53081. Tel: 414-457-7110. Rev. Richard J. Fleischman, Sec. & Treas. A fund to provide youth and adult religious education programs within the county.

SHOREWOOD. *Association of Ladies of Charity of Milwaukee, Wisconsin*, 4117 N. Maryland Ave., 53211. Rev. Timothy L. Kitzke, Archdiocesan Spiritual Advisor; Ann K. Hurley, Contact Person.

TAYCHEEDAH. *St. Charles Cemetery*. See St. Patrick Parish. Fond du Lac, 54935. Tel: 414-921-0347.

WATERFORD. *General Secretariat of the Franciscan Missions, Inc.*, P.O. Box 130, 53185. Tel: 414-534-5470; Fax: 414-534-4342. Revs. Sereno Baiardi, O.F.M., Dir.; Sante De Angelis, O.F.M., Assoc. Dir. General Secretariat of the Franciscan Missions, Inc.

WAUWATOSA. *Franciscan Shared Laboratory, Inc.*, 11020 W. Plank Ct., Ste. 100, 53226. Sponsored by Franciscan Sisters, Daughters of the Sacred Hearts of Jesus and Mary, Wheaton, IL. James Fantus, Pres. Medical Laboratory Serving Healthcare Institutions.

Friends of Calvary Cemetery, Inc., 2554 N. 66th St., 53213. Tel: 414-778-1187. Mr. Keith Schultz, Pres. Purpose: To raise funds in connection with the restoration of Calvary Chapel located at Calvary Cemetery, 5503 West Bluemound Rd., Milwaukee, Wisconsin, and overseeing such restoration.

St. Camillus Communities, Inc., 10101 W. Wisconsin Ave., 53226. Tel: 414-259-4511. Very Rev. William F. Cronin, O.S.Cam., Pres. & Prov. Supr.

St. Camillus Institute, Inc., 10100 W. Bluemound Rd., 53226. Very Rev. William F. Cronin, O.S.Cam., Pres. & Prov. Supr.; Revs. Louis Lussier, O.S.Cam., Vice Pres.; James Kovarik, O.S.Cam., Vice Pres. & Treas. Management Corporation. Order of the Servants of the Sick (Order of St. Camillus).

St. Camillus Ministries, Inc., 10101 W. Wisconsin Ave., 53226. Tel: 414-259-4511; 259-4664; Fax: 414-259-7702. Very Rev. William F. Cronin, O.S.Cam., Pres. & Prov. Supr.; Bro. Stephen E. Braddock, O.S.Cam., Ph.D., Exec. Dir.

WEST ALLIS.

**Archdiocese of Milwaukee Supporting Fund, Inc.*, 1126 S. 70th St., Suite S-506, 53214-3151. Tel: 414-475-2673. Erica P. John, CEO.

**Region 6 Development Association*, 6753 W. Rogers, 53219. Tel: 414-545-2120. Sr. Mary Coffelt, F.D.C., Vice Pres.

Purpose: To build a community of educators with new resiliency in Catholic education, emphasize the critical importance of on-going professional development.

RELIGIOUS INSTITUTES OF MEN REPRESENTED IN THE ARCHDIOCESE

For further details refer to the corresponding bracketed number in the Religious Institutes of Men or Women section.

[0120]—*Alexian Brothers*. (Immaculate Conception Prov.).—C.F.A.
[0140]—*The Augustinians*. (Mother of Good Counsel Prov.).—O.S.A.
[0200]—*Benedictine Monks*.—O.S.B.
[0600]—*Brothers of the Congregation of Holy Cross*. (Midwest Prov.).—C.S.C.
[0470]—*The Capuchin Friars*. (Prov. of St. Joseph).—O.F.M.Cap.
[0740]—*Congregation of Marians of the Immaculate Conception*.—M.I.C.
[1130]—*Congregation of the Priests of the Sacred Heart*.—S.C.J.
[0480]—*Conventual Franciscans*. (St. Bonaventure, Prov. of Our Lady of Consolation).—O.F.M.Conv.
[0260]—*Discalced Carmelite Friars*. (Prov. of the Immaculate Heart of Mary).—O.C.D.
[0520]—*Franciscan Friars*.—O.F.M.
[0690]—*Jesuit Fathers and Brothers*.—S.J.
[0720]—*The Missionaries of Our Lady of La Salette*. (Prov. of Mary, Queen of Peace).—M.S.
[0240]—*Order of St. Camillus-Camillian Fathers*.—O.S.Cam.
[1070]—*Redemptorist Fathers*. (St. Louis Prov.).—C.SS.R.
[0990]—*Society of the Catholic Apostolate*. (Mater Dei Prov.).—S.A.C.
[1200]—*Society of the Divine Savior*. (American Prov.).—S.D.S.
[0420]—*Society of the Divine Word*. (Northern Prov.).—S.V.D.
[1360]—*Xaverian Missionary Fathers*.—S.X.

RELIGIOUS INSTITUTES OF WOMEN REPRESENTED IN THE ARCHDIOCESE

[0230]—*Benedictine Sisters of Pontifical Jurisdiction*. (Erie, PA).—O.S.B.
[0360]—*Carmelite Sisters of the Divine Heart of Jesus*.—Carmel.D.C.J.
[]—*The Christian Sisters (Pious Union)*.—C.S.
[]—*Congregation of Institutio Santa Mariana de Jesus*.
[3710]—*Congregation of the Sisters of Saint Agnes*.—C.S.A.
[1780]—*Congregation of the Sisters of the Third Order of St. Francis of Perpetual Adoration*. (Eastern Region).—F.S.P.A.
[0760]—*Daughters of Charity of St. Vincent De Paul*.—D.C.
[0790]—*Daughters of Divine Charity*.—F.D.C.
[0420]—*Discalced Carmelite Nuns*.—O.C.D.
[1060]—*Dominican Contemplative Sisters*.—O.P.
[1070-03]—*Dominican Sisters*.—O.P.
[1070-09]—*Dominican Sisters*.—O.P.
[1070-25]—*Dominican Sisters*.—O.P.
[1070-27]—*Dominican Sisters*.—O.P.
[]—*Dominican Sisters*. (Vietnam).
[1170]—*Felician Sisters*.—C.S.S.F.
[1230]—*Franciscan Sisters of Christian Charity*.—O.S.F.
[]—*Franciscan Sisters of Our Lady (Pious Union)*.—F.S.O.L.
[1430]—*Franciscan Sisters of Our Lady of Perpetual Help*.—O.S.F.
[]—*Franciscan Sisters of St. Clare (Pious Union)*.—F.S.S.C.
[1470]—*Franciscan Sisters of St. Joseph*.—F.S.S.J.
[1240]—*Franciscan Sisters, Daughters of the Sacred Hearts of Jesus and Mary*.—O.S.F.
[]—*Hermitage of the Trinity*.
[1820]—*Hospital Sisters of the Third Order of St. Francis*.—O.S.F.
[]—*Missionary Sisters of the Holy Family*.—M.S.F.
[3230]—*Poor Handmaids of Jesus Christ*.—P.H.J.C.
[2970]—*School Sisters of Notre Dame*.—S.S.N.D.
[1680]—*School Sisters of St. Francis*.—O.S.F.
[]—*Secular Institute of Schoenstatt Sisters of Mary*.—I.S.S.M.
[0600]—*Sisters of Charity of St. Joan Antida*.—S.C.S.J.A.
[0430]—*Sisters of Charity of the Blessed Virgin Mary*.—B.V.M.
[2575]—*Sisters of Mercy of the Americas*.—R.S.M.
[3800]—*Sisters of St. Elizabeth*.—S.S.E.
[1705]—*The Sisters of St. Francis of Assisi*.—O.S.F.
[1520]—*Sisters of St. Francis of Christ the King*.—O.S.F.
[3930]—*Sisters of St. Joseph of the Third Order of St. Francis*.—S.S.J.-T.O.S.F.
[4020]—*Sisters of St. Rita*.—O.S.A.
[1030]—*Sisters of the Divine Savior*.—S.D.S.
[4100]—*Sisters of the Sorrowful Mother (Third Order of St. Francis)*.—S.S.M.
[3510]—*Sisters Servants of Christ the King*.—S.S.C.K.

ARCHDIOCESAN CEMETERIES

MILWAUKEE. *Calvary*.
Holy Cross.
Holy Trinity.
Mount Olivet.
St. Adalbert.
FRANKLIN. *All Souls*.
KENOSHA. *All Saints*.
MEQUON. *Resurrection*.
WAUKESHA. *St. Joseph*.

NECROLOGY

† Darnieder, Leslie A., (Retired). —Died Dec. 23, 1995.
† Draeger, Robert R., Milwaukee, WI, St. Joseph Hospital. —Died March 20. 1996.
† Effinger, William J., (On Leave). —Died Dec. 4, 1996.
† Gawinek, Walter J., (Retired). —Died June 24, 1996.
† Grochowski, Edwin A., (Retired). —Died Sept. 4, 1996.
† Gunther, Carroll A., (Retired). —Died March 11, 1996.
† Kapellen, John A., (Retired). —Died Nov. 22, 1995.
† Lesniewski, Eldred B., (Retired). —Died Aug. 22, 1996.
† Nichols, Richard W., (Retired). —Died July 25, 1996.
† Oman, Richard B., (Retired). —Died May 27, 1996.
† Pfeil, Elmer F., (Retired). —Died Jan. 7, 1996.
† Rathke, Jerome J., (Retired). —Died Nov. 27, 1995.
† Winkler, Raymond J., (Retired). —Died July 19, 1996.

Archdiocese of Mobile

(Archidioecesis Mobiliensis)

Most Reverend

OSCAR H. LIPSCOMB, D.D., PH.D.

Archbishop of Mobile; ordained July 15, 1956; appointed July 29, 1980; consecrated November 16, 1980. *Res., 400 Government St., P.O. Box 1966, Mobile, AL, 36633.* Tel.: 334-434-1585.

Chancery Office: 400 Government St., P.O. Box 1966, Mobile, AL, 36633. Tel.: 334-434-1585; Fax: 334-434-1588.

ESTABLISHED AS VICARIATE-APOSTOLIC OF ALABAMA AND THE FLORIDAS, 1825; DIOCESE OF MOBILE, MAY 15, 1829; NAME CHANGED TO DIOCESE OF MOBILE-BIRMINGHAM, JULY 9, 1954; REDESIGNATED, JUNE 28, 1969. RAISED TO RANK OF ARCHDIOCESE NOVEMBER 16, 1980.

Square Miles 22,969.

Comprises the lower 28 Counties of the State of Alabama, namely: Choctaw, Clarke, Wilcox, Dallas, Autauga, Elmore, Lee, Russell, Macon, Montgomery, Lowndes, Barbour, Bullock, Pike, Crenshaw, Butler, Monroe, Conecuh, Escambia, Covington, Coffee, Geneva, Dale, Henry, Houston, Washington, Baldwin and Mobile.

For legal titles of parishes and archdiocesan institutions consult the Chancery Office.

STATISTICAL OVERVIEW

Personnel	
Archbishop	1
Retired Abbots	1
Priests: Diocesan Active in Diocese	76
Priests: Active Outside Diocese	4
Priests: Retired, Sick or Absent	27
Number of Diocesan Priests	107
Religious Priests in Diocese	44
Extern Priests in Diocese	7
Ordinations:	
Diocesan Priests	1
Religious Priests	1
Permanent Deacons in Diocese	41
Total Brothers	15
Total Sisters	223
Parishes	
Parishes	77
With Resident Pastor:	
Resident Diocesan Priests	53
Resident Religious Priests	24
Without Resident Pastor:	
Administered by Priests	1
Missions	15
Pastoral Centers	3
Professional Ministry Personnel:	
Brothers	3
Sisters	20
Lay Ministers	30
Welfare	
Catholic Hospitals	1
Total Assisted	153,924
Health Care Centers	4
Total Assisted	3,971
Homes for the Aged	3
Total Assisted	372
Residential Care of Children	1
Total Assisted	200
Day Care and Extended Day Care Centers	4
Total Assisted	232
Specialized Homes	2
Total Assisted	63
Special Centers for Social Services	9
Total Assisted	89,762
Residential Care of Disabled	3
Total Assisted	170
Other Institutions	3
Total Assisted	260
Educational	
Diocesan Students in Other Seminaries	15
Total Seminarians	15
Colleges and Universities	1
Total Students	946
High Schools, Diocesan and Parish	3
Total Students	1,618
Elementary Schools, Diocesan and Parish	21
Total Students	7,688
Catechesis/Religious Education:	
High School Students	832
Elementary Students	3,551
Total Students Under Catholic Instruction	14,650
Teachers in the Diocese:	
Brothers	1
Sisters	16
Lay Teachers	396
Vital Statistics	
Receptions into the Church:	
Infant Baptism Totals	1,218
Adult Baptism Totals	191
Received into Full Communion	359
First Communions	1,273
Confirmations	1,271
Marriages:	
Catholic	195
Interfaith	281
Total Marriages	476
Deaths	667
Total Catholic Population	67,205
Total Population	1,452,506

Former Prelates—Rt. Rev. MICHAEL PORTIER, D.D., First Bishop; cons. Nov. 5, 1826; died May 14, 1859.—Rt. Rev. JOHN QUINLAN, D.D., cons. Dec. 4, 1859; died March 9, 1883.—Rt. Rev. DOMINIC MANUCY, D.D., appt. Vicar Apostolic of Brownsville and cons. Bishop of Dulma Dec. 8, 1874; transferred to Mobile March 9, 1884, but resigned in the same year; died at Mobile, Dec. 4, 1885.—Rt. Rev. JEREMIAH O'SULLIVAN, D.D., cons. Sept. 20, 1885; died Aug. 10, 1896.—Rt. Rev. E. P. ALLEN, cons. May 16, 1897; died Oct. 21, 1926.—Most Rev. THOMAS J. TOOLEN, D.D., cons. May 4, 1927; appt. Archbishop "ad personam," May 27, 1954; resigned Oct. 8, 1969; died Dec. 4, 1976.—Most Rev. JOHN L. MAY, D.D., ord. May 3, 1947; appt. Titular Bishop of Tagarbala and Auxiliary Bishop of Chicago, June 21, 1967; cons. Aug. 24, 1967; transferred to Mobile, Oct. 8, 1969; installed Dec. 10, 1969; appt. to Saint Louis, January 29, 1980; died March 24, 1994.

Vicar General—Very Rev. JOHN AHERNE, V.G., *Holy Name of Jesus Church, P.O. Box 557, Semmes, 36575.* Tel: 334-694-4794.

Regional Episcopal Vicars—Rev. Msgr. KEVIN F. DUIGNAN, *St. Peter Church, 219 Adams Ave., P.O. Box 114, Montgomery, 36101.* Tel: 334-262-7304. Rt. Rev. HILARY DREAPER, O.S.B., *St. Joseph, 34290 U.S. Hwy 98, Lillian, 36549.* Tel: 334-962-2049. Rev. PATRICK GALLAGHER, *St. Columba Church, 2700 W. Main St., Dothan, 36301.*

Archivist—BERNADETTE MATHEWS.

Chancery Office—400 Government St., P.O. Box 1966, Mobile, 36633. Tel: 334-434-1571; Fax: 334-434-1588.

Chancellor—Very Rev. G. WARREN WALL, S.T.L., M.S.W.

Vice Chancellor—Rev. WILLIAM F. FIELDS, S.S.L.

Metropolitan Tribunal—14 S. Franklin St., P.O. Drawer D, Mobile, 36601. Tel: 334-432-4609. Please address all rogatory commissions and matrimonial matters to the Office of the Tribunal.

Judicial Vicar—Rev. Msgr. ANTHONY MCDEVITT, J.C.D., S.T.L.

Adjutant Judicial Vicar—Rev. Msgr. JOHN R. AMOS, J.C.D., M.Div.

Associate Judge—Rev. Msgr. KENNETH J. KLEPAC, J.C.L.

Defenders of the Bond—Rev. Msgr. JOHN R. AMOS; Sr. MARY ELIZABETH BUTLER, M.S.B.T.

Advocate—VICTOR WHELAN.

Court Clerk For 1st Instance—DANICE ENTREKIN.

Court Clerk For Appeal Court—JEAN MCGOWAN.

Notaries—DOROTHY BARRETT.

Archdiocesan Consultors—Rev. Msgr. OLIVER E. ADAMS; Very Rev. JOHN AHERNE, V.G.; Rev. Msgr. JOHN R. AMOS; Revs. PETER J. CUNNINGHAM; FRANCIS V. CUSACK; PATRICK MAHER; Rev. Msgr. PATRICK C. O'CONNOR; Rev. WILLIAM J. SKONEKI; Very Rev. G. WARREN WALL.

Vicars for Religious—Mobile District-Baldwin Escambia Deanery: Rev. ROBERT B. RIMES, S.J., *Spring Hill College, 4000 Dauphin St., Mobile, 36608.* Tel: 334-460-2175. Montgomery-Dothan Deaneries: Rev. Msgr. WILLIAM R. JAMES, *P.O. Drawer 1367, Robertsdale, 36567.* Tel: 334-947-5054.

Acting Vicar for Education—THOMAS L. DOYLE, Ph.D., *P.O. Box 129, Mobile, 36601.* Tel: 334-438-4611.

Vicar for Ministry to Persons with Disabilities and the Deaf—Rev. PATRICK J. MADDEN, *4350 Moffett Rd., Mobile, 36618.* Tel: 334-342-6449.

Vicar for Vietnamese Affairs—c/o Chancery, P.O. Box 1966, Mobile, 36633.

Archdiocesan Offices and Directors

Apostleship of Prayer—Rev. Msgr. J. EDWIN STUARDI, *Mercy Medical, P.O. Box 1090, Daphne, 36526.* Tel: 334-626-2694.

Apostleship of the Sea—Very Rev. G. WARREN WALL, Port Chap. JOSEPH V. CONNICK, III, Dir., *Catholic Maritime Club, 261 Dauphin St., Mobile, 36602.* Tel: 334-432-7339; Fax: 334-433-4618.

Apostolate for Aging—Rev. Msgr. GEORGE C. ROYER, *Sacred Heart Residence, P.O. Box 6805, Mobile, 36660.*

Archdiocese of Mobile Cursillo Center—Tel: 334-887-5540. Rev. JAMES DANE, Spiritual Dir., *1001 Hand Ave., Bay Minette, 36507.* Tel: 334-937-2026. ELLIE SHOOK, *4940 C. Vaughn Pointe Dr., Montgomery, 36116.*

Archdiocesan Council of Catholic Women (ACCW)—Mrs. PAT SHRAND, Pres. MARIE D. MARTIN, Pres., *Priests Burse Club, 400 Government St., Mobile, 36602.*

Boy Scouts—Rev. STEVEN WILLIAMS, *St. Mary Church, 1453 Old Shell Rd., Mobile, 36604.* Tel: 334-432-8678.

Campaign for Human Development—Rev. WILLIAM J.

SKONEKI, Dir. Funding Office for charitable and other works of Archdiocese, *356 Government St., P.O. Box 230, Mobile, 36601.* Tel: 334-438-9668; Fax: 334-434-1547.

Catholic Charities Appeal Office—Rev. WILLIAM J. SKONEKI, Dir. Funding Office for charitable and other works of Archdiocese, *356 Government St., P.O. Box 230, Mobile, 36601.* Tel: 334-438-9668; Fax: 334-434-1547.

Catholic Housing of Mobile, Inc.—Most Rev. OSCAR H. LIPSCOMB, Pres.; Very Rev. G. WARREN WALL, Vice Pres.; Rev. Msgr. JOHN R. AMOS, Sec./Treas. Non-profit Corp. of the State of Alabama, *Office: P.O. Box 1966, Mobile, 36633.* Tel: 334-434-1585.

Queen's Court I Apartments—W. Clark Ave., Prichard, 36610.

Catholic Housing Authority of Montgomery, Inc.—Rev. CHARLES TRONCALE, Pres.; BILL PEARSON, Vice Pres.

Catholic Publishing Co., Inc.—Publisher of the Archdiocesan Newspaper *"The Catholic Week"*; LARRY WAHL, Editor, *P.O. Box 349, Mobile, 36601.* Tel: 334-432-3529.

Catholic University, Friends of—Rev. RUSSELL BIVEN, *Our Savior Church, 1801 Cody Rd., Mobile, 36695.* Tel: 334-633-6762.

Catholic Youth Organization—PAUL CRANE, Exec. Dir., *P.O. Box 6955, Mobile, 36660.* Tel: 334-471-0062.

Catholic Youth Ministry—GREG S. THOMPSON, Dir., *2518 Forbes Rd., Montgomery, 36110.* Tel: 334-265-2722. WARREN DAZZIO, Assoc. Dir., *1413 Old Shell Rd., Seton Center, Mobile, 36604.* Tel: 334-433-4138.

Cemeteries—Very Rev. G. WARREN WALL, *P.O. Box 1966, Mobile, 36633.* Tel: 334-434-1585. Deacon ROBERT L. NOUWEN, Dir., *1700 Dr. Martin Luther King Jr. Ave., Mobile, 36617.* Tel: 334-479-5305.

Censor Librorum—Rev. J. ALEX SHERLOCK, S.T.M., M.A., *St. Pius X Church, 217 S. Sage Ave., Mobile, 36606.* Tel: 334-471-2449; Fax: 334-471-2441.

Charismatic Movement—Liaisons: Deacon EUGENE STAKER; Mrs. STAKER, *Our Lady Queen of Mercy Parish, 4421 Narrow Lane Rd., Montgomery, 36116.* Tel: 334-288-2850; Fax: 334-281-7884.

Charities—(Listing under Catholic Social Services).

Clergy Retirement Association—Very Rev. JOHN AHERNE, Chm., *Holy Name of Jesus Church, P.O. Box 557, Semmes, 36575.* Tel: 334-649-4794.

Archdiocesan Coordinator of Health Affairs—Sr. ELISE BOUDREAUX, D.C., Pres., *Providence Hospital, 6801 Airport Blvd., P.O. Box 850429, Mobile, 36685.* Tel: 334-633-1000.

Ecumenical Commission—Rev. W. BRY SHIELDS, Chm., *St. Ignatius Church, 3704 Spring Hill Ave., Mobile, 36608.* Tel: 334-342-9221.

Family Life Director—Vacant.

Handicapped, Apostolate to the—Rev. PATRICK MADDEN, Dir., *4350 Moffett Rd., Mobile, 36618.* Tel: 334-342-6449.

Hispanic Apostolate—Rev. CHRISTOPHER VISCARDI, S.J., Dir., *Spring Hill College, 4000 Dauphin St., Mobile, 36608.* Tel: 334-380-3085.

Holy Childhood Association—Rev. JOHN C. ROBINSON, Dir., *Holy Family Church, 1304 Garland St., Mobile, 36618.* Tel: 334-344-0271.

Holy Name Society—Vacant.

Liturgical Commission—Very Rev. G. WARREN WALL, Chm., *P.O. Box 1966, Mobile, 36633.*

McGill Institute, A Corporation—P.O. Box 1966, Mobile, 36633.

McGill-Toolen Foundation, The—BEVERLY FINKBOHNER, Dir., Devel., *1501 Old Shell Rd., Mobile, 36604.* Tel: 334-432-0788, Ext. 48.

Office of Ministry to the Deaf—4350 Moffett Rd., Mobile, 36618.

Mobile Provincial Conference of Bishops and Priests' Councils—P.O. Box 1966, Mobile, 36633. Tel: 334-434-1585.

Newspaper "The Catholic Week"—LARRY WAHL, Editor, *356 Government St., P.O. Box 349, Mobile, 36601.* Tel: 334-432-3529; 432-3520.

Pastoral Council—GEORGE VELLA, Chm., *6657 Hounds Run N., Mobile, 36608.* Tel: 334-344-9839.

Permanent Diaconate Program—Very Rev. JOHN AHERNE, Dir.; Deacon JOSEPH MCGONAGIE, Assoc. Dir., *Holy Name of Jesus Church, P.O. Box 557, Semmes, 36575.* Tel: 334-649-4794.

Planned Giving—Deacon WILLIAM R. DOLAN, Dir., *P.O. Box 230, Mobile, 36601.* Tel: 334-432-1369.

Priests' Council—Most Rev. OSCAR H. LIPSCOMB, Pres. Officers: Rev. Msgr. PATRICK O'CONNOR, Chm.; Very Rev. G. WARREN WALL, Vice Chm.; Rev. WILLIAM F. FIELDS, Treas.; Rev. MICHAEL KELLY, Record. Sec. DAVID CARUCCI, Corresponding Sec.

Ex-Officio Members—Rt. Rev. HILARY DRAPER, O.S.B., Baldwin Dean; Rev. Msgr. KEVIN DUIGNAN, Montgomery Dean; Very Rev. JOHN P. AHERNE, V.G. Consultors: OLIVER E. ADAMS; Rev. Msgr. JOHN R. AMOS; Very Rev. G. WARREN WALL; Rev. PATRICK MAHER; Rev. PETER CUNNINGHAM; Very Rev. JOHN AHERNE; Rev. FRANCIS CUSACK; Rev. Msgr. PATRICK O'CONNOR.

Appointed Members & Consultors—Rev. Msgr. JOHN R. AMOS; Very Rev. G. WARREN WALL.

Elected Members—Group I: Rev. Msgr. WILLIAM R. JAMES; Rev. Msgr. PATRICK C. O'CONNOR; Rev. FRANK CUSACK. Group II: Very Rev. JOHN AHERNE, V.G.; Rev. F. CHARLES TRONCALE; Rev. Msgr. TIMOTHY DEASY. Group III: Rev. ADRIAN L. COOK; Rev. Msgr. JOHN R. AMOS; Rev. MATTHEW O'CONNOR. Group IV: Rev. JOSEPH S. WADAS; Revs. WILLIAM F. FIELDS; WILLIAM SKONEKI.

Religious—Revs. ROBERT MCCOWN, S.J.; CHARLES MOFFATT, S.S.J.

Priests' Eucharistic League—Rev. Msgr. J. EDWIN STUARDI, *Mercy Medical, P.O. Box 1090, Daphne, 36526.* Tel: 334-626-2694.

Priests' Personnel Board—Rev. Msgr. OLIVER E. ADAMS, Chm., *St. Catherine of Siena Church, 2605 Springhill Ave., Mobile, 36607.* Tel: 334-473-1415.

Priests' Retirement Fund—Very Rev. JOHN AHERNE, Pres., *P.O. Box 1966, Mobile, 36633.* Tel: 334-434-1585.

Propagation of the Faith—Rev. JOHN C. ROBINSON, *Holy Family Church, 1304 Garland St., Mobile, 36618.* Tel: 334-344-0271.

Radio and Television Communications—c/o Chancery Office, P.O. Box 1966, Mobile, 36633. Tel: 334-434-1585.

School Education Department—GWEN BYRD, Supt., *P.O. Box 129, Mobile, 36601.* Tel: 334-438-4611.

Office of Religious Education—14 S. Franklin St., P.O. Drawer D, Mobile, 36601. Tel: 334-433-6991. Ms. LORIE CREPEAU, Dir., *533 S. Union St., Montgomery, 36104.* Tel: 334-269-2389. Sr. FRANCIS ASSISI PIELMEIER, C.S.A., Dir., *P.O. Box A, Ozark, 36360.* Tel: 334-774-3214. Sr. PENNY SMITH, O.P., Dir.

Serra Club of Mobile—GEORGE VELLA, Pres., *6657 Hounds Run N., Mobile, 36608.*

Seton Haven Management Corporation—Col. DALE SCOTT, Pres., *3721 Wares Ferry Rd., Montgomery, 36193.* Tel: 334-272-4000.

Toolen Institute for Parish Services (TIPS)—Dr. AIDAN LICARI, Dir., *Drawer D, Mobile, 36601.* Tel: 334-438-6121.

Vocations—Rev. MARK I. NESKE, Dir., *Little Flower Church, 2053 Government St., Mobile, 36606.* Tel: 334-478-3381. Rev. ARTHUR SCHRENGER, Assoc. Dir., *Holy Spirit Church, 1150 Vaughn Rd., Pike Rd., 36064.* Tel: 334-277-5631.

CLERGY, PARISHES, MISSIONS AND PAROCHIAL SCHOOLS

CITY OF MOBILE
(Mobile County)

1—CATHEDRAL OF THE IMMACULATE CONCEPTION (1704), Most Rev. Oscar H. Lipscomb, D.D., Ph.D.; Rev. Msgr. James W. Oberkirch, Rector; Rev. William F. Fields; Deacon William R. Dolan. In res., Rev. James F. Dorrill.
Cathedral & Rectory—400 Government St., P.O. Box 1966, 36633. Tel: 334-434-1565; Fax: 334-434-1588.

2—ST. CATHERINE OF SIENA (1913), Rev. Msgr. Oliver E. Adams; Rev. Antony Nirappel (India).
Res., 2605 Springhill Ave., 36607. Tel: 334-473-1415; 473-1427.
Convent—2609 Spring Hill Ave., 36607. Tel: 334-473-5130.

3—CORPUS CHRISTI (1958), Revs. James F. Zoghby; John S. Boudreaux (LAF); Deacon Arthur W. Robbins.
Res., 6300 McKenna Dr., 36608. Tel: 334-342-1852; Fax: 334-342-6313.
School—Tel: 334-342-5474. Mrs. Brenda C. Elsevier, Prin.
Lay Teachers 22; Students 461; Aides 9.
Catechesis/Religious Programs—Students 170.

4—ST. DOMINIC (1958), Revs. William J. Skoneki; Johnny S. Savoie; Deacon Edward Connick. In res., Rev. Msgr. Francis C. Murphy.
Res., 4156 Burma Rd., 36693. Tel: 334-661-5130; Fax: 334-661-0469.
School—4160 Burma Rd., 36693. Tel: 334-661-5226; Fax: 334-661-0469. Mrs. Ann Zimlich, Prin.
Sisters of Mercy 2; Lay Teachers 22; Students 555.
Catechesis/Religious Programs—Students 108.
Convent—Tel: 334-661-3229.

5—ST. FRANCIS XAVIER (1867), Revs. Paul Oberg, S.S.J., Admin.; Paul Kluthe, S.S.J.; Bro. Ricardo Gourrier, S.S.J., Pastoral Assoc.; Deacon Alexander Moore.
Res., 2034 St. Stephens Rd., 36617. Tel: 334-473-4975; Fax: 334-473-4940.

6—HOLY FAMILY (1959), Revs. John C. Robinson; Ernest R. Hyndman, Jr.; Deacon Patrick Kelly.
Res., 1304 Garland St., 36618. Tel: 334-344-0271; Fax: 334-344-0296.
School—Tel: 334-344-1781. Mrs. Teresa Schaefer, Prin.
Lay Teachers 15; Students 313.

7—ST. IGNATIUS (Spring Hill) (1949), Very Rev. G. Warren Wall; Revs. J. Frank Sofie, Jr.; W. Bry Shields; Deacons Joseph P. McGonagle; J. Carleton Wilkins; Charles J. Fontana; Marvin C. Johns; Abraham Lopez.
Res., 3704 Spring Hill Ave., 36608. Tel: 334-342-9221; Fax: 334-341-1481.
School—Tel: 334-342-5442. Miss Janet Murray, Prin.
Lay Teachers 35; Students 655.
Catechesis/Religious Programs—Tel: 334-342-0516; Fax: 334-341-1481.
Students 132.

8—ST. JOAN OF ARC (1920), Rev. William Folsom.
Res., 1260 Elmira St., 36604. Tel: 334-432-3505; Fax: 334-432-4422.

9—ST. JOSEPH (1857), Rev. E. J. Jacques, S.J.
Res., 808 Springhill Ave., 36602. Tel: 334-432-4218.

10—ST. JOSEPH (Maysville) (1944), Rev. Cornelius Sexton, S.S.J.
Res., 1703 Dublin St., 36605. Tel: 334-473-3761.
Convent—1701 Dublin St., 36605. Tel: 334-478-3292.

11—LITTLE FLOWER (1928), Rev. Mark I. Neske; Rev. Msgr. Maurice L. Shields, Pastor Emeritus; Rev. Vincent Phan; Deacons Wallace McKinney; Fenwick Walsh; Hank Pouliot. In res., Rev. Austin Conry.
Res., 2053 Government St., 36606. Tel: 334-478-3381.
School—2103 Government St., 36606. Tel: 334-479-5761. Sr. Mary Joyce Bringer, C.S.J., Prin.
Lay Teachers 14; Students 272; Aides 3.
Catechesis/Religious Programs—Students 45.
Convent—411 Little Flower Ave., 36606. Tel: 334-479-1198.

12—ST. MARY (1867), Rev. Msgr. Kenneth J. Klepac; Rev. Msgr. Cordell J. Lang; Rev. Paul G. Zoghby; Deacon Ernest J. Johnson, Jr. In res., Rev. Steven T. Williams; Sr. M. Magdalena Langlois, C.S.A., Pastoral Assoc.
Res., 1453 Old Shell Rd., 36604. Tel: 334-432-8678.
School—Tel: 344-433-9904. Miss Angela R. Ostmann, Prin.
Lay Teachers 12; Students 238.
Catechesis/Religious Programs—Students 251.

13—ST. MATTHEW (1904), Rev. Joseph M. Bolling, Admin.
Res., 906 Garrity St., 36605-4699. Tel: 334-432-4784.

14—ST. MONICA (1950), Rev. Cu Minh Duong; Deacon James C. Burns.
Res., 1131 Dauphin Island Pkwy., 36605. Tel: 334-479-7360.
Convent—1950 St. Monica Dr., 36605. Tel: 334-479-1239.

15—MOST PURE HEART OF MARY (1901), Rev. Charles P. Moffatt, S.S.J. In res., Rev. William McKenna, S.S.J.
Mailing Address: P.O. Box 994, 36601. Tel: 334-432-3344.
Res., 304 Sengstak St., 36601.
School—Most Pure Heart of Mary. Sr. Nancy Crossen, O.S.F., Prin.
Religious 6; Lay Teachers 9; Students 195.
Catechesis/Religious Programs—Students 40.
Convent—310 Sengstak St., 36603. Tel: 334-433-6519.

16—OUR LADY OF LOURDES, Rev. Peter J. Cunningham; Deacon Gordon Kenny.
Res., 1621 Boykin Blvd., 36605. Tel: 334-479-9885.
School—Tel: 334-479-4007; 479-2367. Mrs. Carol Dupree, Prin.
Lay Teachers 11; Students 193.
Catechesis/Religious Programs—Students 30.

17—OUR SAVIOR, Rev. Louis Russell Biven. In res., Rev. Msgr. Anthony McDevitt.
Office: 1801 Cody Rd., 36695. Tel: 334-633-6762; Fax: 334-633-7790.
Catechesis/Religious Programs—Students 168.

18—PRINCE OF PEACE (1970), Rev. Paul J. Oberg, S.S.J.
Res., 454 Charleston St., 36603. Tel: 334-432-2364.
Catechesis/Religious Programs—Students 90.

19—ST. PIUS X (1954), Revs. J. Alex Sherlock; James S. Kee; Charles J. McCabe; Deacons William L. Tew; Gerald F. Kingman.
Res., 217 S. Sage Ave., 36606. Tel: 334-471-2449; Fax: 334-471-2441.

School—Tel: 334-473-5004; Fax: 334-473-5008. Mrs. Alice S. Tibbetts, Prin.
Sisters 1; Lay Teachers 27; Students 530.
Catechesis/Religious Programs—Tel: 334-473-4381.
Students 33.

OUTSIDE THE CITY OF MOBILE

Andalusia, Covington Co., Christ the King, Rev. Robert W. Fulton.
Res., 504 Sanford Rd., P.O. Drawer 1546, 36420. Tel: 334-222-4808.

Atmore, Escambia Co., St. Robert Bellarmine (1943), Rev. Michael Sreboth.
Res., 600 S. Main St., 36502. Tel: 334-368-3615.

Auburn, Lee Co., St. Michael (1965), Revs. Stephen M. Staff, C.M.; James N. Dean, Campus Min.
Res., 302 E. Magnolia Ave., 36830. Tel: 334-887-5540; 887-5573; Fax: 334-887-5572.
Catechesis/Religious Programs—Students 250.
Joyland Child Development Center—Tel: 334-821-7624.
Chaplaincy—Auburn University, Auburn University Chapel, Catholic Student's Association.
Convent—Tel: 334-821-0588.

Bay Minette, Baldwin Co., St. Agatha Church, Rev. James E. Dane.
Church—1001 Hand Ave., 36507. Tel: 334-937-2026; 580-0503 (Res.).

Bayou LaBatre, Mobile Co., St. Margaret (1880), Revs. Patrick Madden; Trung John Nguyen.
Res., P.O. Box 365, 36509. Tel: 334-824-2415; Fax: 334-824-4114. [CEM]
Catechesis/Religious Programs—Students 120.

Belle Fontaine, Mobile Co., St. Philip Neri (1908), Rev. John R. La Brake, S.S.E.
Res., 9101 Dauphin Island Pkwy., 36582. Tel: 334-973-2096.

Brewton, Escambia Co., St. Maurice, Rev. Adrian L. Cook.
Res., 202 E. Jackson St., P.O. Box 206, 36427. Tel: 334-867-5189; Fax: 334-867-7993.

Butler, Choctaw Co., St. John (1958), Rev. Eamon Miley.
Res., 401 E. Pushmataha St., P.O. Box 456, 36904. Tel: 205-459-3129.
Mission—Chatom, Washington Co., St. Paul, Chatom, 36518.

Camden, Wilcox Co., St. Joseph, Rev. John Barbernitz.
Res., P.O. Box 248, Orrville, 36737. Tel: 205-996-8850.
Mission—Orrville, Dallas Co., Mission of Immaculate Conception, Orrville, 36767.

Chastang, Mobile Co., St. Peter the Apostle (1860), Revs. Henry E. Dickson, S.S.J., Admin.; Armand Manuel, S.S.J.
Mailing Address: P.O. Box 456, Mount Vernon, 36560. Tel: 334-829-6263.
Missions—West Mount Vernon, Mobile Co., St. Theresa; Fairford, Washington Co., Our Lady of Sorrows.

Chickasaw, Mobile Co., St. Thomas the Apostle, Rev. John Lynes; Sr. Anne Matisek, C.S.A., Pastoral Asst.
Res., 251 N. Craft Hwy., P.O. Box 11061, 36611. Tel: 334-456-7931; Fax: 334-452-9837.
Parish Center—253 N. Craft Hwy., 36611. Tel: 334-452-9837.

Citronelle, Mobile Co., St. Thomas (1919), Rev. John Coghlan.
Res., 8025 State St., P.O. Box 61, 36522. Tel: 334-866-7505.

Daphne, Baldwin Co., Christ the King (1896), Rev. Msgr. Timothy Deasy; Rev. Timothy Evans; Deacons Malcolm Zellner; Leo Ollinger; Sr. Joan O'Donovan, Pastoral Asst.
Res., 715 College Ave., P.O. Box 549, 36526. Tel: 334-626-2343; 626-3740; Fax: 334-626-3740. [CEM]
School—Tel: 334-626-1692; Fax: 334-626-9976. Sr. Maureen Nolan, Prin.
Presentation Sisters 3; Lay Teachers 24; Students 499.
Catechesis/Religious Programs—Tel: 334-626-5963.
Students 224.
Convent—713 College Ave., P.O. Box 901, 36526. Tel: 334-626-2431.
Presentation Sisters 3.

Shrine of the Holy Cross (1900), Rev. Robert M. McCown, S.J.
Res., P.O. Box 1497, 36526. Tel: 334-626-1447.
Mission—Bromley, St. John.

Dauphin Island, Mobile Co., St. Edmund-by-the-Sea, Rev. David I. McGuinness.
Res., P.O. Box 6, 36528. Tel: 334-861-2352. [CEM]
Church—Cadillac Ave.

Dothan, Houston Co., St. Columba, Rev. Patrick J. Gallagher; Deacon Ron Moore. In res., Rev. Jose Joffre Paillacho, Hispanic Min.; Deacon Harold Grant.
Res., 2700 W. Main St., 36301. Tel: 334-793-5802; Fax: 334-792-2816. [JC]
Mission—Columbia, Houston, Good Shepherd, Columbia, 36319.

Elberta, Baldwin Co., St. Bartholomew (1911) (German), Rev. Howard Moussier, O.S.B.
Res., P.O. Drawer A, 36530. Tel: 334-986-8142; Fax: 334-986-5253. [CEM]
School—Tel: 334-986-8143. Mrs. Claudia Adam, Prin.
Lay Teachers 12; Students 165; Aides 4.
Catechesis/Religious Programs—St. Benedict's School.
Students 175.

Enterprise, Coffee Co., St. John, Rev. Hugh Maguire; Deacon Gary Rasponi.
Church—123 Heath St. P.O. Box 100, 36331. Tel: 334-347-6751.
Res., 614 Alberta, 36331. Tel: 334-347-7345.
Catechesis/Religious Programs—Students 216.
Mission—Geneva, Geneva Co., St. Mary, Geneva, 36340.

Eufaula, Barbour Co., Holy Redeemer (1859), Rev. Joseph S. Wadas, Admin.
Res., 515 W. Broad St., 36027. Tel: 334-687-3716; Fax: 334-687-3766.
Missions—Union Springs, Bullock Co., St. Piux X, 308 Kennon St., Union Springs, 36089.; Union Springs, Bullock Co., Bullock County Correctional Facility, P.O. Box 5107, Union Springs, 36089. Tel: 334-738-5625; Clayton, Barbour Co., Ventress Correctional Facility, P.O. Box 769, Clayton, 36016. Tel: 334-775-3331.

Fairhope, Baldwin Co., St. Lawrence (1961), Revs. Gordon Milsted; Primitivo Maravilla (Phillipines); Deacon Henry O'Brien.
Res., 370 S. Section St., 36532. Tel: 334-928-5931.
Church—Sacred Heart, Battles Wharf, 36532.
Catechesis/Religious Programs—Students 275.
Chapel—Battles Wharf, Baldwin Co., Sacred Heart.

Foley, Baldwin Co., St. Margaret (1951), Rev. Charles Reiner, O.S.B.
Res., 601 Laurel St., 36535. Tel: 334-943-4009. [CEM]

Grand Bay, Mobile Co., St. John Baptist (1924), Rev. John J. Stryjewski.
Res., P.O. Box 417, 36541. Tel: 334-865-6902.

Greenville, Butler Co., St. Elizabeth (1894), Rev. Robert Fulton, Admin.
Res., 407 E. Walnut St., 36037. Tel: 334-382-6203.

Grove Hill, Clarke Co., Sacred Heart (1944), Rev. James Havens. In res., Rev. Francis Messing.
Res., Hwy. 43 N., P.O. Box 70, 36451. Tel: 334-275-3665.
Missions—Jackson, Clarke Co., Visitation, 135 W. Clinton St., Jackson, 36545.; Thomasville, Clarke Co., St. Joseph, W. Front St., Thomasville, 36784.

Gulf Shores, Baldwin Co., Our Lady of the Gulf (1952), Rev. Msgr. Patrick C. O'Connor; Rev. Lee O'Neil.
Res., 308 E. 22nd Ave., P.O. Box 515, 36547-0515. Tel: 334-968-7062.

Heron Bay, Mobile Co., St. Michael the Archangel (1880), Rev. William N. Gorman.
Mailing Address: 15872 Heron Bay Loop Rd. E., Coden, 36523. Tel: 334-873-4719.

Holy Trinity, Russell Co., St. Joseph, Rev. Thaddeus Searles, S.T. In res., Rev. Maurice Haiss; Bros. Pascal Haas, S.T.; Christopher Ilg, S.T.; Boris Farrah, S.T.; Rene Martin, S.T.; Matthew Rezmer, S.T.
Church—1444 Hwy. 165, 36859. Tel: 334-855-3148; Fax: 334-855-3256.
School—Tel: 334-855-4675. Mrs. Bonnie Curry, Prin.
Lay Teachers 7; Students 110.

Lillian, Baldwin Co., St. Joseph, Rt. Rev. Hilary Dreaper, O.S.B.
Res., 34290 U.S. Hwy. 98, 36549. Tel: 334-962-2049. [JC]

Magnolia Springs, Baldwin Co., St. John the Baptist (1881), Rev. Msgr. Guido Calleja.
Res., 10797 St. John's Ln., P.O. Box 206, 36555. Tel: 334-965-7719. [CEM]
Mission—Bon Secour, Our Lady of Bon Secour.

Millbrook, Elmore Co., St. Elizabeth Ann Seton (1978), Rev. Albert P. Kelly; Deacon A. B. King.
Church—4831 Hwy. 14, 36054-0585. Tel: 334-285-7000.
Res., 109 Crossgate Dr., Elmore, 36025.
Mission—Wetumpka, Elmore Co., St. Mark's, P.O. Box 765, Wetumpka, 36092.

Mon Luis Island, Mobile Co., St. Rose of Lima (1853), Rev. Msgr. John R. Amos.
Res., 2951 Durette Ave. (Mon Luis Island), Coden, 36523. Tel: 334-973-2592. [CEM]

Monroeville, Monroe Co., Annunciation, Rev. Sean Horgan, C.Ss.R.
Res., Whetstone St., P.O. Box 883, 36460. Tel: 334-575-2644.
Catechesis/Religious Programs—Students 55.
Missions—Uriah, Monroe Co., Our Lady of Mount Carmel, Hwy. 21 N., Uriah, 36480.; Vredenburgh, Monroe Co., St. Martin de Porres, Beech St., Vredenburgh, 36481. Tel: 334-337-4671.

Montgomery, Montgomery Co.,

1—St. Peter, (1834), Rev. Msgr. Kevin F. Duignan; Rev. Edwin Beachum.
Res., 219 Adams Ave., P.O. Box 114, 36101. Tel: 334-262-7304. [CEM]

2—Church of St. Andrew The Apostle, Rev. Wilbur Kissell.
Res., 433 Clayton St., P.O. Box 2052, 36103. Tel: 334-262-3241.

3—St. Bede, (1925), Revs. Patrick Maher; Michael Farmer; Fergus Prendergast; Deacons Eugene Wadas; John B. Hamilton; Charles Gulley.
Office: 3870 Atlanta Hwy., 36109. Tel: 334-272-3463; Fax: 334-272-3492.
School—3850 Atlanta Hwy., 36109. Tel: 334-272-3033; Fax: 334-272-9394. Mr. Gerald Shook, Prin.
Lay Teachers 23; Students 407.
Catechesis/Religious Programs—Students 125.
Children's Center—3840 Atlanta Hwy., 36109. Tel: 334-277-8551. Eleanor McCormack, Dir.

4—Church of the Holy Spirit, (1977), Rev. Arthur C. Schrenger.
Res., 8570 Vaughn Rd., Pike Road, 36064. Tel: 334-277-5631; Fax: 334-277-2895.
Catechesis/Religious Programs—Tel: 334-277-1989.
Students 223.

5—St. John the Baptist, (1908), Rev. David Carucci.
Res., 553 S. Union St., 36104. Tel: 334-264-6274; Fax: 334-262-3012.

6—St. Jude, (1934), Rev. Matthew A. Sindik. In res., Rev. James Holden.
Res., 2048 W. Fairview Ave., St. Jude, 36108. Tel: 334-265-1390.
School—Tel: 334-263-6121. Miss Mildred Lewis, Prin.
Sisters 2; Lay Teachers 15; Students 265.
High School—Tel: 334-264-5376; Fax: 334-264-6669. Mrs. Geraldine Perry, Prin.
Lay Teachers 13; Students 142.

7—Our Lady, Queen of Mercy, (1954), Rev. Michael D. Kelly; Deacons Gene Staker; James LaBadie.
Res., 4421 Narrow Lane Rd., 36116. Tel: 334-288-2850; Fax: 334-281-7884.
School—Tel: 334-288-5334; Fax: 334-288-5395. Mrs. Mary Kaye McCooey, Prin.
Lay Teachers 14; Students 177.
Catechesis/Religious Programs—Tel: 334-288-5342. Mary Lou Staker, D.R.E.
Students 29.
Child Development Center—Tel: 334-613-0340.

8—Resurrection Catholic Church, (1943), Rev. Manuel Williams, C.R. In res., Revs. Casimir J. Wilczynski, C.R.; Norman Choate, C.R.; John J. Krozser, C.M., Retired USAF Chap.
Res., 2815 Forbes Rd., 36110. Tel: 334-269-1770; Fax: 334-265-8081.
School—St. John/Resurrection School, Tel: 334-265-4615; Fax: 334-263-4999. Mrs. Dorothy Moore, Prin.
Religious 6; Lay Teachers 17; Students 200.
Mission—Montgomery, Montgomery Co., Resurrection Catholic Mission, 2815 Forbes Rd., 36110. Tel: 334-263-4221; 269-1770. Rev. Manuel Williams, C.R., Dir.

Mount Vernon, Mobile Co., St. Cecilia (1929), Rev. John Coghlan.
Res., 1305 Military Rd., P.O. Box 847, 36560. Tel: 334-829-9531. [CEM]

Opelika, Lee Co., St. Mary of the Mission (1910), Rev. William M. Allegretto, C.M.; Deacons Donald Canonica; John Taylor.
Res., 1000 4th Ave., 36801. Tel: 334-749-8359.
Catechesis/Religious Programs—Tel: 334-745-3432.
Students 61.

Orange Beach, Baldwin Co., St. Thomas by the Sea, Rev. Francis V. Cusack; Deacon Raymond Ba Soco.
Mailing Address: P.O. Box 1190, 36561. Tel: 334-981-8138; 981-8132.

Orrville, Dallas Co., Immaculate Conception, Rev. John Barbernitz.
Church—13663 Alabama Hwy. 22 W., 36767.
Res., P.O. Box 248, 36767. Tel: 334-996-8850.
Mission—Camden, Wilcox Co., St. Joseph, 300 Whiskey Run Rd., 36726.

Ozark, Dale Co., St. John (1963), Rev. Brendan J. Keller.
Res., 709 Camilla Ave., P.O. Box 1008, 36360. Tel:

334-774-6826; Fax: 334-774-3923. [JC]
Catechesis/Religious Programs—Students 89.

Phenix City, Russell Co., St. Patrick (1911), Rev. Eugene Sheridan, C.M.
Res., 1502 Broad St., P.O. Box 147, 36868-0147. Tel: 334-298-9025; Fax: 334-298-9025.
Catechesis/Religious Programs—Students 50.
Convent—St. Patrick's Missionary Cenacle, 2701 40th St., 36867. Tel: 334-298-0708.
Missionary Servants of the Most Blessed Trinity 6.

Mother Mary Parish (1941), Rev. James McKenna, S.D.S.
Res., 318 Seale Rd., 36869. Tel: 334-298-2343.
School—Tel: 334-298-6371. Sr. M. Cecelia Harrison, F.M.S., Prin.
Sisters 2; Lay Teachers 8; Students 166.
Catechesis/Religious Programs—Students 160.

Plateau, Mobile Co., Our Mother of Mercy (1926), Rev. Charles McNeice, S.S.E.
Mailing Address: P.O. Box 10306, Prichard, 36610.
Res., 805 East St., 36610. Tel: 334-456-3551.

Prattville, Autauga Co., St. Joseph Church (1963), Rev. F. Charles Troncale; Deacon Samuel Shippen.
Res., 511 N. Memorial Dr., 36067-2133. Tel: 334-365-8680.

Prichard, Mobile Co., Our Lady of Fatima (1949), Rev. Charles McNeice, S.S.E.
Mailing Address: P.O. Box 10306, 36610.
Res., 805 East St., Plateau, 36610. Tel: 205-456-3551.

St. James Major (1911), Rev. Henry E. Dickson, S.S.J.
Res., 714 S. College St., 36610. Tel: 334-456-6842; Fax: 334-456-6843.
School—Tel: 334-452-1883. Sr. Mary Stella Aquilina, D.C., Prin.
Daughters of Charity 3; Lay Teachers 8; Students 205.
Catechesis/Religious Programs—Students 65.
Convent—927 W. Prichard Ave., 36610. Tel: 334-457-9396.

Robertsdale, Baldwin Co., St. Patrick (1974), Rev. Msgr. William R. James.
Res., P.O. Box 1367, 36567. Tel: 334-947-5054; Fax: 334-947-7395.
School—(Grades K-8) P.O. Drawer 609, 36567. Tel: 334-947-7395. Sr. Margaret Harte, P.B.V.M., Prin.
Presentation Sisters 1; Lay Teachers 11; Students 180.
Convent—P.O. Box 609, 36567. Tel: 334-947-7396.

Selma, Dallas Co., Our Lady Queen of Peace, Rev. Carroll W. Plourde, S.S.E.
Office: 309 Washington St., 36701. Tel: 334-874-8931.
Res., 2511 Summer Field Rd., 36701. Tel: 334-874-8475.
Catechesis/Religious Programs—Students 87.

Semmes, Mobile Co., Holy Name of Jesus (1977), Very Rev. John Aherne, V.G.
Res., 2275 Snow Rd., P.O. Box 557, 36575. Tel: 334-649-4794.
Catechesis/Religious Programs—Students 75.

Tallassee, Elmore Co., St. Vincent De Paul (1955), Rev. Francis A. Lynch, C.M.
Res., 620 Gilmer Ave., P.O. Box 329, 36078. Tel: 334-283-2169.

Tillman's Corner, Mobile Co., St. Vincent de Paul (1971), Rev. Matthew O'Connor; Deacon Robert Nouwen.
Res., 5023 Camelot Dr., Mobile, 36619. Tel: 334-661-3908.
School—Kendall F. McKee, Prin. Lay Teachers 10; Students 187.
Catechesis/Religious Programs—Tel: 334-666-4066.
Students 117.

Troy, Pike Co., St. Martin, Rev. David J. Tokarz.
Res., Elba Hwy., P.O. Box 313, 36081. Tel: 334-566-2630; Fax: 334-566-9105.
Catechesis/Religious Programs—Students 55.
Station—Luverne.

Tuskegee Institute, Macon Co., St. Joseph (1940), Rev. William D. Hogan, S.S.J.
Res., 2007 Montgomery Rd., 36088. Tel: 334-727-2710.
School—(Grades K-8) 2009 Montgomery Rd., 36088. Tel: 334-727-0620; 727-0642. Miss Jacqueline Grant, Prin.
Sinsinawa Dominicans 1; Lay Teachers 8; Students 117.

Whistler, Mobile Co., St. Bridget (1864), Rev. Leo Blanchet.
Res., 3625 W. Main St., P.O. Box 13357, 36613. Tel: 334-452-3676.

Chaplains of Public Institutions

CLAYTON. *Ventress Correctional Institution*, 36016. Rev. Joseph S. Wadas.

UNION SPRINGS. *Bullock County Correctional Facility*, 36089. Rev. Joseph S. Wadas.

On Duty Outside the Archdiocese:
Reverend Fathers—
Becherer, David, Parroquia, Del Santisimo, Sacramento, Apartado #324, Piura, Peru
McKenna, Philip A., Casa Parroquial, Zorritos, Tumbes, Peru

On Leave from the Archdiocese:
Reverend Monsignors—
Cullen, Thomas J.
Reverend Fathers—
Dahmen, Vernon
Dalton, Peadar
Kinane, James G.
Lemming, Patrick W.
Lott, Lawrence
Nicholson, Patrick
Reskey, George
Robinson, Jerome
Smith, Edward E.
Stauter, Andrew
Trosch, David
Weise, Thomas

Retired:
Reverend Monsignors—
Aucoin, Charles
Jennings, Joseph
Madigan, James F.
McArdle, Joseph G.
McGuinness, Michael
Murphy, Francis
O'Connor, Francis
Royer, George C.
Stuardi, J. Edwin
Reverend Fathers—
Desmond, Barry
Gill, Cecil J.
Hay, Theodore H., S.T.L.
McDonnell, Vincent
Rogers, Furman

Permanent Deacons:
Ba Soco, Raymond
Burns, James C.
Canonica, Donald A.
Connick, Edward G.
Dolan, William R.
Fontana, Charles J.
Grant, Harold
Gulley, Charles
Hamilton, John B.
Hicks, George, (Retired)
Johns, Marvin C.
Johnson, Ernest
Kelly, Patrick
Kenny, Gordon
King, A. B.
Kingman, Gerald
LaBadie, James
Lopez, Abraham
May, Frank J.
McGonagle, Joseph P.
McKinney, Wallace R.
McMeans, Leo
Moore, Alexander
Nouwen, Robert
O'Brien, Henry F.
Ollinger, H. Leo, Jr.
Pouliot, Henry
Pry, Jackie T.
Rasponi, Gary A.
Robbins, Arthur
Sheldon, Paul
Shippen, Samuel
Staker, Gene
Taylor, John E.
Tew, William L., Jr.
Vrazel, Raymond
Wadas, Eugene
Walsh, Fenwick
Wilkins, J. Carleton
Zellner, Malcolm

INSTITUTIONS LOCATED IN THE ARCHDIOCESE

[A] SEMINARIES, RELIGIOUS OR SCHOLASTICATES

SELMA. *Edmundite House of Formation*, Ujima House, 1423 Broad St., 36701-4314. Tel: 334-875-6089; Fax: 334-872-3777. Revs. Richard M. Myhalyk, S.S.E., Dir., Novices and Post-Novitiate Formation; David G. Cray, S.S.E., Dir. of Vocations; Stephen W. Hornat, S.S.E., Dir., Edmundite Mission Corps; Bros. Francis J. Hagerty, S.S.E., Nurse Practitioner; Brian Dwyer, Non-Professed Postulant. Temporary Professed: Bros. Christopher Daignault, S.S.E., Seminarian, Weston School of Theology, Cambridge, MA.; Daniel Manzano, S.S.E., Collegian, St. Michael's College, Colchester, VT.; Kenneth D. White, S.S.E., Brother-in-Training, Bishop Perry Middle School, New Orleans, LA.

[B] COLLEGES AND UNIVERSITIES

MOBILE. *Spring Hill College*, (1830) 4000 Dauphin St., 36608. Tel: 334-380-3866; Fax: 334-460-2111.
For a complete listing, refer to the Colleges and Universities section.

[C] HIGH SCHOOLS, ARCHDIOCESAN

MOBILE. *McGill-Toolen High School*, 1501 Old Shell Rd., 36604. Tel: 334-432-0784. Revs. W. Bry Shields, Pres. & Prin.; Steven T. Williams. Priests 2; Brothers of the Sacred Heart 2; Sisters of Loretto 1; Lay Teachers 86; Students 1,196.

MONTGOMERY. *Montgomery Catholic High School*, 5350 Vaughn Rd., 36116. Tel: 334-272-7220. Mr. Faustin N. Weber, Prin. Sisters of Loretto 1; Lay Teachers 20; Students 265.

St. Jude High School, 2048 W. Fairview Ave., 36108. Tel: 334-264-5377. Mrs. Geraldine Perry, Prin. Lay Teachers 15; Students 149.

[D] CHILDREN'S HOMES

MOBILE. *St. Mary's Home*, 4350 Moffat Rd., 36618. Tel: 334-344-7733.
For a complete listing, refer to the Special Care Facilities section.

[E] GENERAL HOSPITALS

MOBILE. *Providence Foundation*, 6701 Airport Blvd., Ste. C-130, P.O. Box 850429, 36608. Tel: 334-639-2050.
For a complete listing, refer to the Hospitals section.

Providence Healthcare Services, 6801 Airport Blvd., P.O. Box 850429, 36685. Tel: 334-633-1000; Fax: 334-633-1679.
For a complete listing, refer to the Hospitals section.

Providence Hospital, 6801 Airport Blvd., P.O. Box 850429, 36608(36685). Tel: 334-633-1000; Fax: 334-633-1679.
For a complete listing, refer to the Hospitals section.

Seton Health Corp. of South Alabama, 6801 Airport Blvd., P.O. Box 850429, 36608(36685). Tel: 334-633-1660; Fax: 334-633-1679.
For a complete listing, refer to the Hospitals section.

Seton Medical Management, Inc., 6801 Airport Blvd., P.O. Box 850429, 36685. Tel: 334-633-1600.
For a complete listing, refer to the Hospitals section.

[F] SPECIAL HOSPITALS, SCHOOLS AND HOMES FOR THE AGED

MOBILE. *Allen Memorial Home Skilled Nursing Facility*, 735 S. Washington Ave., 36603. Tel: 334-433-2642.
For a complete listing, refer to the Special Care Facilities section.

Little Sisters of the Poor, Home For the Aged, Inc., Sacred Heart Residence, 1655 McGill Ave., 36604. Tel: 334-476-6335; Fax: 334-478-6519.
For a complete listing, refer to the Special Care Facilities section.

DAPHNE. *Mercy Medical*, P.O. Box 1090, 36526. Tel: 334-626-2694.
For a complete listing, refer to the Special Care Facilities section.

MARBURY. *Resurrection Catholic Nursing Home*, 165 County Rd. 20 E., P.O. Box 89, 36051-0089.
For a complete listing, refer to the Special Care Facilities section.

MONTGOMERY. *City of St. Jude, Inc., The*, 2048 W. Fairview Ave., 36108. Tel: 334-265-6791.
For a complete listing, refer to the Special Care Facilities section.

Father Purcell Memorial Exceptional Children Center, 2048 W. Fairview Ave., 36108. Tel: 334-834-5590; Fax: 334-834-5592.
For a complete listing, refer to the Special Care Facilities section.

Father Walter Memorial Center for Handicapped Children, 2815 Forbes Dr., 36199. Tel: 334-262-6421; Fax: 334-262-2265.
For a complete listing, refer to the Special Care Facilities section.

St. Bede's Children's Center, 3840 Atlanta Hwy., 36109.
For a complete listing, refer to the Special Care Facilities section.

St. John Resurrection Early Childhood Center, 2815 Forbes Dr., 36110.
For a complete listing, refer to the Special Care Facilities section.

[G] HOUSING FOR THE ELDERLY

MOBILE. *Cathedral Place*, 351 Conti St., 36602. Tel:

334-434-1590.
For a complete listing, refer to the Special Care Facilities section.

MONTGOMERY. *Laboure Complex Foundation*, P.O. Box 3074, 36109. Tel: 334-277-5213.
For a complete listing, refer to the Special Care Facilities section.
Seton Haven, 3721 Wares Ferry Rd., 36109. Tel: 334-272-4000.
For a complete listing, refer to the Special Care Facilities section.

PRICHARD. *Queen's Court I Apartments*, W. Clark Ave., 36610.
For a complete listing, refer to the Special Care Facilities section.

[H] MONASTERIES AND RESIDENCES OF PRIESTS AND BROTHERS

MOBILE. *Brothers of the Sacred Heart*, 60 N. Catherine St., 36604. Tel: 334-438-3812. Bros. Paul Mulligan, S.C., Dir.; Victor Bendillo, S.C., Sub.-Dir.; Flavian Udinsky, S.C.; Alcuin Kelly, S.C.; Celestine Algero, S.C.; John Moore, S.C. Brothers 6.

SELMA. *Edmundite Fathers*, Edmundite Missions House, 1401 Broad St., 36701. Tel: 334-872-6221. Legal Title: *Fathers of St. Edmund Southern Missions, Inc.* Revs. Roger J. LaCharite, S.S.E., Missions Dir.; David G. Cray, S.S.E., Programs Dir.; Stephen W. Hornat, S.S.E., Missions Corp. Dir.; Edward F. Conlin, S.S.E.; Francis A. Donnellan, S.S.E.; Carroll W. Plourde, S.S.E.; James F. Ryan, S.S.E.; Nelson B. Ziter, S.S.E.; Bros. Richard R. Gallerani, S.S.E.; Francis J. Hagerty, S.S.E. Priests 8; Brothers 2.

[I] CONVENTS AND RESIDENCES OF SISTERS

MOBILE. *Blessed Trinity Missionary Cenacle*, 604 Barksdale Dr. W., 36606. Tel: 334-476-4803. Missionary Servants 3.
Convent of the Sisters of Mercy of the Americas Baltimore Regional Community, 101 Wimbledon Dr., W., 36608. Tel: 334-344-1377. Sr. Carolyn Oberkirch, R.S.M., Admin.
Other Residences: 4301 Bit & Spur Rd., 36608. Tel: 334-344-1377. 606 Bay Bluff East, Daphne, 36526. Tel: 334-626-0130. 2902 Brierwood Dr., 36606. Tel: 334-476-4605. 172 N. Lafayette St., 36604. Tel: 334-432-3178. Portier Place, 4363 Old Shell Rd., 36608. Sr. Ruth Handren, Admin., Huntleigh Woods, Apt. N-205, 375 Hillcrest Rd., 36608. Tel: 334-344-9388. 3700 Whispering Pines, Apt. 47C, 36608-1149. Tel: 334-343-4435. Sisters 18.
Convent of the Sisters of St. Agnes, 1701 Dublin St., 36605. Tel: 334-478-3292. Sr. Charlotte O'Neill, C.S.A., Ph.D., Education. Sisters 6.
Monastery of Discalced Carmelite Nuns, 716 Dauphin Island Pkwy., 36606. Rev. Mother Agnes, O.C.D., Prioress. Solemnly Professed 7.
Sisters of Loretto, 1408 Old Shell Rd., 36604-2244. Tel: 334-431-6735. Sr. Sandra Ardoyno, S.L.
Sisters of Mercy of the Americas, St. Louis Regional Community, 4009 Old Shell Rd., Apt. C-23, 36608. Tel: 334-460-0478. Sr. Mary Giles Peresich, R.S.M.
Visitation Monastery and Retreat House, 2300 Spring Hill Ave., 36607. Tel: 334-473-2321. Mother Rose Marie Kinsella, Supr. Sisters 13.

ALBERTA. *Alberta Health Center*, P.O. Box 97, 36720. Tel: 334-573-2493.

AUBURN. *St. Louise Missionary Cenacle*, 302 E. Magnolia Ave., 36830. Tel: 334-821-0588. Missionary Servants of the Most Blessed Trinity 1.

CAMDEN. *Sisters of St. Joseph*, Rte. 2, Box 21-A, 36726. Tel: 334-682-4144. Sisters 2.
Sisters of St. Joseph of Philadelphia, 15 Cherokee Dr., 36726. Tel: 334-682-9874. Sr. Donna Jo Loeper, S.S.J.

DOTHAN. *Holy Spirit Missionary Cenacle*, 3205 Redmond Rd., 36303. Tel: 334-983-3116.

HAYNEVILLE. *Daughters of the Holy Spirit*, 1016 Hwy. 12, 36040. Tel: 334-563-7382. Sisters 3.

HOLY TRINITY. *Blessed Trinity Shrine Retreat and Cenacle*, 36859. Tel: 334-855-4474. Sr. Ann Maura O'Keefe, M.S.B.T., Dir. Missionary Servants of the Most Blessed Trinity 4; Lay Volunteers 2; Retreat House Capacity 40.

HURTSBORO. *Spirit of Peace Missionary Cenacle*, P.O. Box 117, 38660. Tel: 334-667-6536. Sr. Zelie Therese Pendergast, M.S.B.T.

MARBURY. *Dominican Monastery of St. Jude (St. Jude Monastery)*, P.O. Box 170, 36051. Mother Mary Aimee, O.P., Prioress. Cloistered Dominican Nuns of Perpetual Adoration and Rosary. Professed Sisters 9.

MONTGOMERY. *Daughters of Charity*, 577-579 Eastdale Rd., S., 36117. Tel: 334-272-3354. Sisters 5.
Mater Dei Missionary Cenacle, 784 Spring Valley Rd., 36116. Tel: 334-288-4544. Missionary Servants of the Most Blessed Trinity 3.
Sisters of Loretto, 2842 Marti Ln., 36116. Tel: 334-288-9421. Sr. Leo Marie Reynolds, S.L. Sisters 2.

OZARK. *Sinsinawa Dominican Sisters*, Rte. 3, Box 50, 36360. Tel: 334-299-6671. Sr. Penny Smith, O.P.

PHENIX CITY. *St. Patrick's Missionary Cenacle*, 2701 Fortieth St., 36867. Tel: 334-298-0708. Missionary Servants of the Most Blessed Trinity 6.

PINE APPLE. *Sisters of St. Joseph*, Rte. 2, P.O. Box 9-A, 36768. Tel: 334-746-2584. Sisters 4.

SELMA. *Sisters Residence*, 1423 Broad St., 36701. Tel: 334-874-6536. Sisters 3.

VREDENBURGH. *Emmanuel Community*, P.O. Box 365, 36481. Tel: 334-337-4484.

[J] ARCHDIOCESAN SOCIAL SERVICE

MOBILE. *Catholic Social Services, Archdiocese of Mobile*, Mailing Address: P.O. Box 759, 36601. Tel: 334-432-1603. 400 Government St., 36602. Tel: 334-438-1603; Fax: 334-434-1549. Sr. Francis Louise Sheridan, M.S.B.T., Archdiocesan Dir.; Sr. Mary Gerald Kiely, M.S.B.T., Dir., Branch Offices, P.O. Box 454, Montgomery, 36101. Tel: 334-269-2387. Sr. Patricia Louise Langan, M.S.B.T., Dir., P.O. Box 870, Robertsdale, 36567. Tel: 334-947-2293. Mrs. Michele Prockup, Dir., P.O. Box 1105, Chatom, 36518. Tel: 334-847-2708. Mrs. Joyce Yocum, Supvr., P.O. Box 6184, Dothan, 36302. Tel: 334-793-3601. Sr. Lucy Smoker, M.S.B.T., Supvr.
Service Center of Catholic Social Services, 555 Dauphin St., 36602. Tel: 334-434-1500. Sr. Judith Vander Grinten, C.S.A., M.S.W., Dir.

CHATOM. *Chatom Office of Catholic Social Services*, P.O. Box 1105, 36518. Tel: 334-847-2708. Joyce Yocum, Supvr.

DOTHAN. *Dothan Office of Catholic Social Services*, P.O. Box 6184, 36302. Tel: 334-793-3601.

MONTGOMERY. *Catholic Social Services of Montgomery*, 4455 Narrow Lane Rd., 36116. Tel: 334-288-8890; Fax: 334-288-9322. Sr. Patricia Langan, M.S.B.T., Dir.

ROBERTSDALE. *Robertsdale Office of Catholic Social Services*, P.O. Box 870, 36567. Tel: 334-947-2293. Mrs. Michele Procrup, Dir.

[K] NEWMAN CENTERS

MOBILE. *University of South Alabama Catholic Student Center*, 6051 Old Shell Rd., 36608. Tel: 334-343-3662. Rev. James F. Dorrill, Ph.D., Chap.; Sonia Moulard, Dir. & Asst. Campus Min.

AUBURN. *Auburn University Newman Center*, 302 E. Magnolia Ave., 36830. Tel: 334-887-5380. Rev. James N. Dean; Victoria Bolling, Asst. Campus Min.

BAY MINETTE. *Faulkner State Jr. College Newman Center*, 1001 Hand Ave., 36507. Tel: 334-937-2026; 580-0503 (Res.). Rev. James E. Dane.

DOTHAN. *Wallace Community College Newman Center*, 2700 W. Main St., 36301. Tel: 334-793-5802. Rev. Msgr. Patrick J. Gallagher.

MONROEVILLE. *Alabama Southern Community College Newman Center*, P.O. Box 883, 36460-0883. Tel: 334-275-3665. Rev. Sean Horgan, C.Ss.R.

MONTGOMERY. *Alabama State University Newman Center*, 553 S. Union St., 36104. Tel: 334-264-6274. Rev. David Carucci.
Faulkner University Newman Center, 433 Clayton St., P.O. Box 2052, 36103. Tel: 334-262-3241. Rev. Wilbur Kissell.
Huntington College Newman Center, 4421 Narrow Lane Rd., 36116. Tel: 334-288-2850. Rev. Michael Kelly.

SELMA. *Marion Institute Newman Center*, 309 Washington St., 36703. Tel: 334-874-8931. Rev. Carroll W. Plourde, S.S.E.

TROY. *Troy State University Newman Center*, P.O. Box 313, 36081. Tel: 334-566-2630. Rev. David Tokarz.

TUSKEGEE INSTITUTE. *Tuskegee University Newman Center*, 2007 Montgomery Rd., 36088. Tel: 334-727-2710. Rev. William D. Hogan, S.S.J., Chap.

[L] MISCELLANEOUS LISTINGS

MOBILE. *Catholic High Schools Alumni Association of Mobile*, 1501 Old Shell Rd., 36604. Tel: 334-432-0784. Eleanor Woolsey, Alumni Dir.
L'Arche, 151 S. Ann St., 36604. Tel: 334-438-2094. Christian non-profit organization-community where handicapped and non-handicapped people live. Marty O'Malley, Dir. Handicapped People 19; Assistants 14.
Ladies of Charity, 207 So. Florida St., 36606. Tel: 334-479-0089. Mrs. P. J. Cooney, Pres.
**Providence Building Corporation*, P.O. Box 850429, 36685. 6801 Airport Blvd., 36608. John R. Roeder, Pres.; Sr. Marilyn Moore, D.C., Chm.; Sr. Theresa Sullivan, D.C., Sec.
Society of St. Vincent de Paul, 411 S. Broad St., 36603. Tel: 334-432-5173. Wes Chiniche, Pres., 411 S. Broad St., 36603.

DAPHNE. *Apostleship of Prayer*, P.O. Box 1090, 36532. Tel: 334-626-2694. Rev. Msgr. J. Edwin Stuardi.

HAYNEVILLE. *Lowndes County Catholic Center*, 1016 Hwy. 12, 36040. Tel: 205-563-9139.

HURTSBORO. *John XXIII Center*, P.O. Box 117, 36860. Tel: 334-667-7770. Sr. Zelie Therese Pendergast, M.S.B.T., Admin.

MONTGOMERY. *The City of St. Jude, Inc.*, 2048 W. Fairview Ave., 36108. Tel: 334-265-6791. Mr. Thomas C. Logan, Exec. Dir.; Rev. Msgr. Matthew A. Sindik, Dir.
St. John's Soup Kitchen, Inc., 553 S. Union St., 36104. Tel: 334-264-6274. P.O. Box 230512, 36123-0512. Tel: 334-834-5794. Rev. David Carucci.
St. Margaret's Foundation, 818 S. Perry St., Ste. 2, 36104. Tel: 334-262-0785. Susan Meehan, Pres.; Paul Flagg, Chm.; Dr. Ray Furlong, Chm.; Haywood M. Sport, Vice Chm.; Mary Francis J. Moore, Sec. & Treas.
St. Margaret's Services, 818 S. Perry St., Ste. 2, 36104. Tel: 334-262-0784. Susan Meehan, Pres.; Sr. Mary Ann O'Brien, D.C., Chm.; Sr. Virginia Delaney, D.C., Vice Chm.; Harold Parrish, Sec. & Treas. Daughters of Charity of St. Vincent de Paul 3. Care for the poor, frail elderly and homebound disabled through Elderly Outreach and Interfaith Volunteer Caregivers.

PRICHARD. *Ladies of Charity*, 1013 N. College St., 36610. Tel: 334-456-1142. Mrs. Jean Lewis, Pres.

RELIGIOUS INSTITUTES OF MEN REPRESENTED IN THE ARCHDIOCESE

For further details refer to the corresponding bracketed number in the Religious Institute of Men or Women section.

[0200]—*Benedictine Monks.*—O.S.B.
[1100]—*Brothers of the Sacred Heart.* (New Orleans Prov.).—S.C.
[1330]—*Congregation of the Mission.* (Eastern Prov.).—C.M.
[1080]—*Congregation of the Resurrection.* (Chicago Prov.).—C.R.
[0690]—*Jesuit Fathers and Brothers.* (New Orleans Prov.).—S.J.
[0840]—*Missionary Servants of the Most Holy Trinity.*—S.T.
[1030]—*Paulist Fathers.*—C.S.P.
[0700]—*St. Joseph's Society of the Sacred Heart.* (Baltimore, MD).—S.S.J.
[0440]—*Society of Saint Edmund.* (Selma, AL).—S.S.E.

RELIGIOUS INSTITUTES OF WOMEN REPRESENTED IN THE ARCHDIOCESE

[0200]—*Benedictine Sisters of Pontifical Jurisdiction.* (Cullman, AL; Ferdinand, IN).—O.S.B.
[3710]—*Congregation of the Sisters of Saint Agnes.*—C.S.A.
[1780]—*Congregation of the Sisters of the Third Order of St. Francis of Perpetual Adoration.*—F.S.P.A.
[0760]—*Daughters of Charity of St. Vincent de Paul.*—D.C.
[0820]—*Daughters of the Holy Spirit.*—D.H.S.
[0420]—*Discalced Carmelite Nuns.*—O.C.D.
[1050]—*Dominican Contemplative Nuns.*—O.P.
[1070-03]—*Dominican Sisters.*—O.P.
[1070-13]—*Dominican Sisters.*—O.P.
[1070-18]—*Dominican Sisters.*—O.P.
[2575]—*Institute of the Sisters of Mercy of the Americas.*—R.S.M.
[2340]—*Little Sisters of the Poor.*—L.S.P.
[2790]—*Missionary Servants of the Most Blessed Trinity.*—M.S.B.T.
[0430]—*Sisters of Charity of the Blessed Virgin Mary.*—B.V.M.
[2360]—*Sisters of Loretto At the Foot of the Cross.*—S.L.
[2550]—*Sisters of Mercy.*—R.S.M.
[3360]—*Sisters of Providence of Saint Mary-of-the-Woods, Indiana.*—S.P.
[1650]—*Sisters of St. Francis of Philadelphia.*—O.S.F.
[3830-14]—*Sisters of St. Joseph.*—S.S.J.
[3830-15]—*Sisters of St. Joseph.*—C.S.J.
[3840]—*Sisters of St. Joseph of Carondelet.*—C.S.J.
[3850]—*Sisters of St. Joseph of Chambery.*—C.S.J.
[1970]—*Sisters of the Holy Family of Nazareth.*—C.S.F.N.
[2150]—*Sisters, Servants of the Immaculate Heart of Mary.*—I.H.M.
[3330]—*Union of the Sisters of the Presentation of the Blessed Virgin Mary.*
[4170]—*Vincentian Sisters of Charity.* (Perryville, PA).—V.S.C.
[4190]—*Visitation Nuns.*—V.H.M.

NECROLOGY

† Palumbo, Louis, (Retired). —Died Sept. 6, 1996.

Diocese of Monterey in California

(Montereyensis in California)

Most Reverend

SYLVESTER D. RYAN, D.D.

Bishop of Monterey; ordained May 3, 1957; appointed Auxiliary Bishop of Los Angeles and Titular Bishop of Remesiana February 17, 1990; ordained Bishop on May 31, 1990; appointed Bishop of Monterey January 28, 1992; installed March 19, 1992.

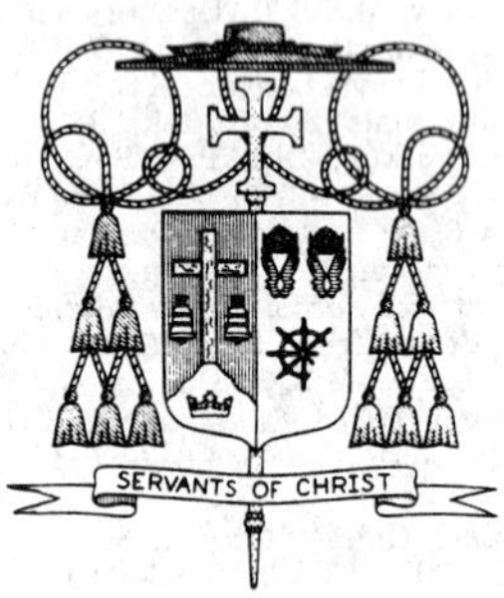

Pastoral Office: 580 Fremont St., P.O. Box 2048, Monterey, CA, 93942-2048. Tel.: 408-373-4345; Fax: 408-373-1175.

E-mail address: ammdom@aol.com

Most Reverend

HARRY ANSELM CLINCH, D.D.

Retired Bishop of Monterey; ordained June 6, 1936; appointed Titular Bishop of Badiae and Auxiliary to the Bishop of Monterey-Fresno December 5, 1956; consecrated February 27, 1957; installed as Third Bishop of Monterey in California December 14, 1967; retired January 19, 1982. *Res., 3400 Paul Sweet Rd., C-119, Santa Cruz, CA, 95065.* Tel.: 408-476-5847.

ESTABLISHED NOVEMBER 20, 1849. RE-ESTABLISHED DECEMBER 14, 1967. FORMERLY DIOCESE OF MONTEREY-FRESNO.

Square Miles 8,475.

Legal Titles:

Diocese of Monterey in California.

The Diocese of Monterey Education and Welfare Corporation.

The Roman Catholic Bishop of Monterey, California, a Corporation Sole.

The Bishop Harry A. Clinch Endowment Fund of the Diocese of Monterey.

Catholic Charities of the Diocese of Monterey (Corporation).

Villa Serra Corporation.

Comprises the Counties of Monterey, San Benito, San Luis Obispo and Santa Cruz in the State of California.

For legal titles of parishes and diocesan institutions, consult the Pastoral Office.

STATISTICAL OVERVIEW

Personnel	
Bishop	1
Retired Bishops	2
Priests: Diocesan Active in Diocese	56
Priests: Active Outside Diocese	1
Priests: Retired, Sick or Absent	27
Number of Diocesan Priests	84
Religious Priests in Diocese	22
Extern Priests in Diocese	5
Ordinations:	
Diocesan Priests	4
Permanent Deacons in Diocese	2
Total Brothers	29
Total Sisters	114
Parishes	
Parishes	46
With Resident Pastor:	
Resident Diocesan Priests	38
Resident Religious Priests	6
Without Resident Pastor:	
Administered by Priests	1
Administered by Women Religious	1
Missions	10
New Parishes Created	1
Welfare	
Catholic Hospitals	1
Total Assisted	166,586
Homes for the Aged	4
Total Assisted	444
Educational	
Diocesan Students in Other Seminaries	9
Students Religious	9
Total Seminarians	18
High Schools, Diocesan and Parish	2
Total Students	625
High Schools, Private	2
Total Students	750
Elementary Schools, Diocesan and Parish	12
Total Students	3,336
Elementary Schools, Private	3
Total Students	536
Catechesis/Religious Education:	
High School Students	1,658
Elementary Students	9,721
Total Students Under Catholic Instruction	16,644
Teachers in the Diocese:	
Brothers	8
Sisters	32
Lay Teachers	264
Vital Statistics	
Receptions into the Church:	
Infant Baptism Totals	5,532
Adult Baptism Totals	216
Received into Full Communion	750
First Communions	3,478
Confirmations	978
Marriages:	
Catholic	829
Interfaith	219
Total Marriages	1,048
Deaths	1,111
Total Catholic Population	170,321
Total Population	851,604

Former Prelates of the Diocese of Monterey—Rt. Rev. FRANCISCO GARCIA DIEGO Y MORENO, O.F.M., cons. Bishop of Both Californias, Oct. 1840; died April 30, 1846.—Most Rev. JOSEPH SADOC ALEMANY, O.P., cons. Bishop of Monterey, June 30, 1850; appt. first Archbishop of San Francisco, July 29, 1853; resigned and appointed Titular Archbishop of Pelusium, Dec. 28, 1884; died April 14, 1888.—Rt. Rev. THADDEUS AMAT, C.M., cons. Bishop of Monterey March 12, 1854 became Bishop of Monterey-Los Angeles, 1859; died May 12, 1878.—Rt. Rev. FRANCIS MORA, cons. Titular Bishop of Mosynopolis and Coadjutor to Bishop Amat, August 3, 1873 became Bishop of Monterey-Los Angeles, 1878; resigned May 6, 1896; named Titular Bishop Hierapolis; died August 3, 1905.—Rt. Rev. GEORGE MONTGOMERY, D.D., cons. April 8, 1894; Bishop of Tmul and Coadjutor-Bishop of Monterey-Los Angeles (cum jure successionis); succeeded to May 6, 1896; appt. Coadjutor-Archbishop of San Francisco, Titular Bishop of Auxum, January 1, 1903; died Jan. 10, 1907.—Rt. Rev. THOMAS JAMES CONATY, cons. Nov. 24, 1901; Titular Bishop of Samos; appt. Bishop of Monterey-Los Angeles, March 27, 1903; died Sept. 18, 1915.—Most Rev. JOHN J. CANTWELL, D.D., LL.D., appt. Bishop of Monterey-Los Angeles, September 21, 1917; cons. December 5, 1917 assumed the title Bishop of Los Angeles-San Diego June 1, 1922; appt. Assistant to the Pontifical Throne, Sept. 30, 1929; elevated to Archepiscopal Dignity, June 11, 1936; installed Dec. 3, 1936; died Oct. 30, 1947.—Most Rev. JOHN B. MACGINLEY, D.D., cons. May 10, 1910; Bishop of Nueva Caceres; transferred to Monterey-Fresno as first Bishop, March 24, 1924; resigned Sept. 30, 1932; named Titular Bishop of Croae; died Oct. 18, 1969.—Most Rev. PHILIP G. SCHER, D.D., ord. June 6, 1903; appt. April 28, 1933; cons. June 29, 1933; died Jan. 3, 1953.—Most Rev. ALOYSIUS J. WILLINGER, C.SS.R., ord. July 2, 1911; appt. Bishop of Ponce, March 8, 1919; cons. October 28, 1929; appt. Titular Bishop of Bida and Coadjutor of Monterey-Fresno (cum jure successionis), December 12, 1946; installed Bishop of Monterey-Fresno, Jan. 3, 1953; appt. Assistant to the Pontifical Throne, Nov. 13, 1953; resigned Oct. 25, 1967; died July 25, 1973.—Most Rev. HARRY ANSELM CLINCH, D.D., ord. June 6, 1936; appt. Titular Bishop of Badiae and Auxiliary to the Bishop of Monterey-Fresno, Dec. 5, 1956; cons. Feb. 27, 1957; installed as Third Bishop of Monterey in California, Dec. 14, 1967; retired Jan. 19, 1982.—Most Rev. THADDEUS SHUBSDA, D.D., Fourth Bishop of Monterey; ord. April 26, 1950; Titular Bishop of Trau and Auxiliary Bishop of Los Angeles; Episcopal Ordination; appt. Feb. 19, 1977; named Bishop of Monterey in California, June 1, 1982; installed as fourth Bishop of Monterey, July 1, 1982; died April 26, 1991.—Rev. CHARLES G. FATOOH, appt. Administrator of the Diocese of Monterey, Apr. 26, 1991 - March 19, 1992.

Moderator of the Curia / Chancellor—Rev. CHARLES G. FATOOH.

Vicar General—Rev. Msgr. D. DECLAN MURPHY.

Pastoral Office—580 Fremont St., P.O. Box 2048, Monterey, 93942-2048. Tel: 408-373-4345; Fax: 408-373-1175. DONA LOGEMAN ACUFF, Exec. Sec.

Pastoral Office, Ecclesiastical Notaries—DONA LOGEMAN ACUFF.

Deans—Monterey: Very Rev. JERRY MCCORMICK, V.U., Santa Cruz: Very Rev. JOHN GRIFFIN, V.F., Salinas: Very Rev. MANUAL CANAL, V.F., San Luis Obispo: Very Rev. JOSEPH R. HERCEK, V.F.

Diocesan Departments, Directors and Offices

Archivist—Bro. JOHN F. O'BRIEN, C.F.X., K.H.S., *580 Fremont St., P.O. Box 2048, Monterey, 93942-2048.* Tel: 408-373-4345; Fax: 408-373-1175.

Attorney—ALBERT S. HAM, ESQ., *470 Camino El Estero,*

Monterey, 93940. Tel: 408-649-3111; Fax: 408-649-3043.

Business Manager—THOMAS H. RIORDAN, *580 Fremont St., P.O. Box 2048, Monterey, 93942-2048.* Tel: 408-373-4345; Fax: 408-373-1175.

Communication—"The Observer"; Rev. EDWARD J. KAMINSKI, C.S.C., Dir.; Most Rev. SYLVESTER D. RYAN, Publisher, *500 Church St., P.O.Box 2079, Monterey, 93942-2079.* Tel: 408-373-2919; Fax: 408-373-4510.

Curator—Sir RICHARD MENN, K.C.S.G., K.H.S., K.M., *3080 Rio Rd., Carmel, 93923.* Tel: 408-624-3600; Fax: 408-624-0658.

Finance Office—WILLIAM J. COAKER, III, Controller; ANNE M. MCGUIRE, Business Outreach Coord., *580 Fremont St., P.O.Box 2048, Monterey, 93942-2048.* Tel: 408-373-4666; Fax: 408-373-1175.

Health Care Coordinator—Sr. JEANNE BURNS, O.P., *Dominican Santa Cruz Hospital, 1555 Soquel Dr., Santa Cruz, 95060.* Tel: 408-462-7670; Fax: 408-462-7555.

Human Resources—MOLLY A. MCDONALD, ESQ., *470 Camino El Estero, Monterey, 93940.* Tel: 408-649-3111; Fax: 408-649-3043.

Stewardship—Most Rev. SYLVESTER D. RYAN; DANIEL J. HEALY, Dir., Stewardship, *580 Fremont St., P.O.Box 2048, Monterey, 93942-2048.* Tel: 408-373-4345; Fax: 408-373-1175.

Campus Ministry Department—AGNES LEONARDICH, Diocesan Dir.; Sr. THERESA HARPIN, C.S.J., Dir., Campus Ministry San Luis Obispo; Rev. ROLAND BUNDA, S.M., Dir., Campus Ministry Santa Cruz, *500 Church St., P.O. Box 350, Monterey, 93942-0350.* Tel: 408-373-1608.

Catechetical Ministries Department—530 Ramona Ave., Monterey, 93940. Tel: 408-373-1607; Fax: 408-373-1601. Sr. DOLORES FENZEL, S.A., Dir.; LORRAINE BUONOCORE, Admin. Asst.; MARGARET COREY, Audio Visual Coord. Tel: 408-373-3506. SALLY EQUINOA, Consultant, San Luis Obispo Deanery, *221 Daly Ave., San Luis Obispo, 93405.* Tel: 805-541-1441.

Scouting—Rev. CARL M.D. FARIA, Chap., *303 Hillcrest Ave., Marina, 93933.* Tel: 408-384-5434; Fax: 408-384-7011.

Youth and Young Adult Ministry (English), Department of Catechetical Ministry—Sr. DOLORES FENZEL, S.A., Dir., *530 Ramona Ave., Monterey, 93940.* Tel: 408-373-1607; Fax: 408-373-1601.

Catholic Schools Department—500 Church St., P.O.Box 350, Monterey, 93942-0350. Tel: 408-373-1608; Fax: 408-373-0173. AGNES LEONARDICH, Supt. Assistant Superintendents: Sr. BARBARA MATASCI, S.N.D.; Bro. JAMES WISECAVER, S.M.; MONICA FAGAN; MIRIAM "MIMI" SCHWERTFEGER, Admin. Asst.

Cemeteries—CLANCY D'ANGELO, Dir.; VIRGINIA NOBIDA, Asst.; REX HILL, Operations Mgr., *Cemeteries Administrative Office, 792 Fremont St., Monterey, 93940.* Tel: 408-372-0327; Fax: 408-372-8726., *Mailing Address: P.O.Box 2048, Monterey, 93942-2048.*

Diocesan Tribunal—690 Figueroa St., P.O.Box 350, Monterey, 93942-0350. Tel: 408-373-1833; Fax: 408-373-6761.

Judicial Vicar—Rev. KENNETH J. LAVERONE, M.A.

Asministrator—FRAYLNE SAN FILIPPO.

Judges—Revs. KENNETH J. LAVERONE; DAVID SCHUYLER, S.M., J.C.D.

Defenders of the Bond—Sr. LILIANA BONELLO, I.M., J.C.L.; Revs. PATRICK DOOLING; THOMAS KIEFFER, Orat. PAUL R. VALDEZ.

Advocates—Revs. JOHN C. GRIFFIN; MICHAEL MARINI.

Promotor of Justice—Rev. THOMAS KIEFFER, Orat.

Notaries—DONA LOGEMAN ACUFF; FRAYLNE SAN FILIPPO.

Divine Worship Department—Sr. BARBARA ANN LONG, O.P., Dir. ANN KREYCHE, Admin. Asst., *126 High St., Santa Cruz, 95060.* Tel: 408-423-4797; Fax: 408-423-1043.

Hispanic Ministry Department—Sr. PATRICIA MURTAGH, I.M., Dir. JUANITA ZEPEDA, Exec. Sec. BEATRIZ MUNOZ, Sec., *22 Stone St., P.O. Box 1684, Salinas, 93902-1684.* Tel: 408-424-4076; Fax: 408-424-5221.

Migrant Ministry Coord.—MARINA O'CAMPO, *22 Stone St., P.O. Box 1684, Salinas, 93902-1684.* Tel: 408-424-4076; Fax: 408-424-5221.

Youth and Young Adult Ministry—22 Stone St., P.O. Box 1684, Salinas, 93902-1684. Tel: 408-424-4076.

Respect Life Department—DORA LEE RARAS, Dir., *231-C Green Valley Rd., Freedom, 95019.* Tel: 408-761-2636; Fax: 408-761-9629.

Certified Natural Family Planning Practitioner—SHEILA ST. JOHN, C.N.F.P.P., *1217 Tyler St., Salinas, 93906.* Tel: 408-433-3743.

Vicar for Clergy and Diocesan Director for RENEW—Rev. MICHAEL MILLER, *Madonna del Sasso Church, 320 E. Laurel Dr., Salinas, 93906.* Tel: 408-422-5323; Fax: 408-424-3359.

Vicars for Religious—Rev. THOMAS LONG, C.S.V., *Sacred Heart Church, P.O. Box 1040, Hollister, 95023.* Tel: 408-637-9212. Sr. ADRIENNE PIENNETTE, O.P., *St. Angela's Church, 146- 8th St., Pacific Grove, 93950.* Tel: 408-655-4162; Fax: 408-372-5026.

Vocations—Rev. ANTONIO SANCHEZ, Dir., *Our Lady of the Assumption Church, 100 Salinas Rd., Watsonville, 95076.* Tel: 408-722-1104; Fax: 408-722-1254. Rev. MICHAEL VOLK, Assoc. Dir., *St. Theodore's Church, P.O. Drawer B, Gonzales, 93926.* Tel: 408-675-8648; Fax: 408-675-8360.

Catholic Relief Services—DANIEL J. HEALY, Dir., *580 Fremont St., P.O. Box 2048, Monterey, 93942-2048.* Tel: 408-373-4345; Fax: 408-373-1175.

Campaign for Human Development—DANIEL J. HEALY, Dir., *580 Fremont St., P.O. Box 2048, Monterey, 93942-2048.* Tel: 408-373-4345; Fax: 408-373-1175.

Charismatics—Rev. GERONIMO CUEVAS, Diocesan Dir., *St. Mary of the Nativity Church, 1702 Second Ave., Salinas, 93905.* Tel: 408-758-1669; Fax: 408-758-4715.

Cursillo—Rev. PETER CRIVELLO, Spiritual Dir., *Holy Cross Church, 126 High St., Santa Cruz, 95060.* Tel: 408-423-4182; Fax: 408-423-1043. Rev. MICHAEL VOLK, Spiritual Dir., *St. Theodore's Church, Drawer B, Gonzales, 93926.* Tel: 408-675-3648; Fax: 408-675-8360.

Ecumenism—Rev. JOHN KEANE, S.A., Dir., *St. Francis Xavier Church, 1475 LaSalle Ave., P.O. Box 247, Seaside, 93955-0247.* Tel: 408-394-8546; Fax: 408-394-5414.

Holy Childhood Association—Rev. FELIX MIGLIAZZO, Dir., *P.O. Box 88, Monterey, 93942-0088.* Tel: 408-372-9120; Fax: 408-372-9120.

Propagation of the Faith—Rev. FELIX MIGLIAZZO, Dir., *P.O. Box 88, Monterey, 93942-0088.* Tel: 408-372-9120.

St. Vincent de Paul—Rev. RICHARD BONJEAN, Dir., *P.O. Box 350, Santa Margarita, 93453.* Tel: 805-438-5383.

Catholic Charities of the Diocese of Monterey—

Central Office—Vacant, *530 Ramona Ave., Monterey, 93940.* Tel: 408-375-1577; Fax: 408-373-3416.

Counseling Program—Tel: 408-375-3165.

Direct Material Aid—Tel: 408-375-1577.

Salinas Office—Buckley Hall, St.Mary of the Nativity Church, 1705 2nd Ave., Salinas, 93905. Tel: 408-422-0602.

Counseling—Tel: 408-422-0609.

Direct Material Aid—Tel: 408-375-1577.

Immigration—Tel: 408-422-0602.

Watsonville Office—406 Main St., #308, Watsonville, 95076. Tel: 408-722-2675.

Direct Material Aid—Tel: 408-722-2675.

Counseling—Tel: 408-772-2791.

Immigration—Tel: 408-722-2675.

Boards, Commissions, Committees and Councils

Administrative Committee Priest's Pension Plan—Revs. EUGENIO ARAMBURO; GARY BYRNE; PETER CRIVELLO; MICHAEL CROSS, Chm.; PAUL R. VALDEZ.

Annual Bishop's Appeal Advisory Board—Most Rev. SYLVESTER D. RYAN, D.D.; Revs. PATRICK DOOLING; CARL M.D. FARIA; CHARLES G. FATOOH; EDWARD FITZ-HENRY; Mr. CARL FIGENSHOW; CARL FRENCH; Rev. JOSEPH L. OCCHIUTO; MARIE PUCCINELLI; THOMAS H. RIORDAN; FRANK ST. DENIS; Rev. FRANK THOME; DANIEL J. HEALY, Exec. Dir.

Bishop Harry A. Clinch Endowment Fund, and Bishop Thaddeus Shubsda Memorial Seminary Endowment Burse—Most Rev. SYLVESTER D. RYAN; RAY AMRHEIN; CHARLES BRIGGS; Rev. CHARLES G. FATOOH; ELIZABETH HELFRICH; BOB HOUGARDY; MICHAEL MORRIS, Chm.; RONALD J. PASQUINELLI; LARRY SAGE; RICHARD UCCELLI; JOHN WECKER. Ex-Officios: DANIEL J. HEALY, Exec. Dir.; THOMAS H. RIORDAN, Diocesan Business Mgr.; DONA LOGEMAN ACUFF, Recording Sec.

Building Commission—Contact Persons: Rev. JOHN GRIFFIN, *Holy Eucharist, 527 Corralitos Rd., Corralitos, 95076.* Tel: 408-722-5490; Fax: 408-722-8157. TOM RIORDAN, *Diocese of Monterey, P.O. Box 2048, Monterey, 93942.* Tel: 408-373-4345; Fax: 408-373-1175.

Catholic Charities—ROBERT BANKS; Col. WILLIAM BOYCE, Vice Pres.; Lt. Gen. ROBERT COFFIN; Mrs. ROBIN L. COURTNEY; Rev. CHARLES G. FATOOH, Pres.; RUBEN GARCIA; PAUL C. JOHNSON; ANN KEYES; Rev. JERRY MCCORMICK; MARTINA S. O'SULLIVAN; Most Rev. SYLVESTER D. RYAN; LARRY SAGE, Treas.; WILLIAM SLEZAK; FRANK ST. DENIS. Consultants: DANIEL J. HEALY; THOMAS H. RIORDAN, Diocesan Business Mgr.; DONA LOGEMAN ACUFF, Recording Sec.

Ecumenical Commission—KAREN ALBERTUS; Rev. JOEL ALMENDRAS; RICHARD O. GORMAN; JACQUES J. HENRARD; Sr. MARY KELLY, S.A.; Rev. CORNELIUS (SCOTT) MCCARTHY; Rev. KIM NELSON; SUSAN PETERSON; Revs. RUDY RUIZ; BILL YOUNG; Bro. ANTHONY YOUNG, S.M.; Rev. JOHN J. KEANE, S.A., Dir.

Educational Board—AGNES LEONARDICH, Chm.; Sr. DOLORES FENZEL, S.A.; Sr. PATRICIA MURTAGH, I.M.; Rev. CHARLES G. FATOOH, Ex-Officio.

Emergency Preparedness Task Force—VIC COLLINS; Rev. CHARLES G. FATOOH; JAMES GARDINER; AGNES LEONARDICH; MOLLY MCDONALD; JACK MCGILVARY, Chm. TERRY MEDINA; THOMAS H. RIORDAN.

Finance Council—Revs. EUGENIO ARAMBURO; MICHAEL L. CROSS; CHARLES G. FATOOH; PEGGY HARRAY, Chm. MCKENZIE MOSS; Rev. Msgr. D. DECLAN MURPHY; RONALD PASQUINELLI; JOHN PETERSDOFF; Most Rev. SYLVESTER D. RYAN; Rev. PAUL R. VALDEZ. Consultants: THOMAS H. RIORDAN, Diocesan Business Mgr.; DONA LOGEMAN ACUFF, Recording Sec.

Historical Review Comission—Sir RICHARD MENN, K.C.S.G., K.H.S., K.M., Diocesan Curator; Bro. JOHN O'BRIEN, C.F.X., Diocesan Archivist; Rev. Msgr. FRANCIS J. WEBER, Archivist, Archdiocese of Los Angeles.

Insurance Committee—MARTI A. HAM, ESQ.; MICHAEL KELLY, Chm. JOHN MAHONEY, JR.; THOMAS H. RIORDAN; Rev. PAUL R. VALDEZ.

Lay Employees Non-Qualified Pension Committee—Revs. MICHAEL L. CROSS, Chm. CHARLES G. FATOOH; Rev. Msgr. D. DECLAN MURPHY, V.G.; THOMAS H. RIORDAN. Consultants: ALBERT S. HAM; TONY KARACHALE; NORMAN "NIC" NICOLAY.

Lay Employee Pension Plan Committee—Rev. MICHAEL L. CROSS, Chm.; Rev. CHARLES G. FATOOH; AGNES LEONARDICH; RONALD J. PASQUINELLI; THOMAS H. RIORDAN; TOD D. SANCHEZ. Consultants: ALBERT S. HAM; TONY KARACHALE; NORMAN "NIC" NICOLAY.

Presbyteral Council—Very Rev. MANUAL CANAL, V.F.; Revs. SIRO DAL DEGAN, V.F.; PATRICK DOOLING; CHARLES G. FATOOH; JAMES FRERKES; Very Revs. JOHN C. GRIFFIN; JOSEPH R. HERCEK, V.F.; Revs. LARRY KAMBITSCH; KENNETH J. LAVERONE; MICHAEL A. MARINI; Very Rev. JERRY MCCORMICK, V.R.; Rev. JERRY MAHER; Rev. Msgr. D. DECLAN MURPHY, V.G.; Most Rev. SYLVESTER D. RYAN; Rev. GREGORY L. SANDMAN; Rev. FRANK THOME; PATRICIA FITZPATRICK, Recording Sec.

Priestly Life and Ministry—Rev. KENNETH J. LAVERONE, Chm. ANDY ANDERSON; Rev. EUGENIO ARAMBURO; Sr. RITA EILEEN DEAN, O.P.; Sr. JOAN DOYLE, S.N.J.M.; ROSEMARY MATZERATH; Revs. CORNELIUS (SCOTT) MCCARTHY; JERRY MCCORMICK; RICHARD MCMANUS, O.F.M.; MATTHEW PENNINGTON; MICHAEL A. VOLK.

Personnel Board—Revs. MICHAEL L. CROSS; CHARLES G. FATOOH; JOHN GRIFFIN; MICHAEL A. MARINI; JERRY MCCORMICK; Most Rev. SYLVESTER D. RYAN; Rev. ANTONIO SANCHEZ.

Real Estate Committee—RICK KENNIFER; DAVID KENT, Chm. THOMAS H. RIORDAN; RICHARD SELDOW; SAM WRIGHT.

Stewardship Board—Most Rev. SYLVESTER D. RYAN; Mr. WILLIAM AGEE; Mrs. MARY AGEE; Mr. DON CHAPIN; Judge WILLIAM CLARK; Mrs. JOAN CLARK; Mr. PETER CONIGLIO; Sr. JULIE HYER, O.P.; Mr. JOHN KILMARTIN; Mr. JOSEPH KORDSMEIER; Mr. ALEX MADONNA; Mrs. PHYLLIS MADONNA; Mr. ROGER MAIROSE; Mrs. WENDY MAIROSE; Mr. CLEM RICHARDSON. Ex-Officios: Rev. CHARLES G. FATOOH; THOMAS H. RIORDAN; DANIEL J. HEALY, Exec. Dir.

Villa Serra Board—Rev. CHARLES G. FATOOH, Sec.; ROGER HITE; Sr. JULIE HYER, O.P., Pres.; MCKENZIE MOSS; JOHN PETERSDORF, Treas.; THOMAS H. RIORDAN, Vice Pres.

Vocation Board—Rev. ANTONIO SANCHEZ, Voc. Dir.; Rev. EUGENIO ARAMBURO; PATRICIA FITZPATRICK; Sr. PATRICIA MURTAGH, I.M.; Rev. MATTHEW PENNINGTON; Very Rev. GREGORY L. SANDMAN, V.F.; Rev. MICHAEL A. VOLK.

CLERGY, PARISHES, MISSIONS AND PAROCHIAL SCHOOLS

CITY OF MONTEREY
(Monterey County)

1—CATHEDRAL OF SAN CARLOS BORROMEO (1770), Revs. Joseph L. Occhiuto, Rector; Gerald John Maher (Ireland); Deacon Harold Miller, Pastoral Assoc. In res., Rev. John G. Murphy, (Retired).

Res. & Mailing Address: 550 Church St., 93940. Tel: 408-373-2628; Fax: 408-373-0518. [CEM]

Preschool—450 Church St., 93940. Tel: 408-375-1324; Fax: 408-375-9736. Sr. Mary Jane Clark, O.P., Prin.

Dominican Sisters (Adrian, MI) 2; Lay Teachers 25;

Students 300.
Catechesis/Religious Programs—500 Church St., 93940. Tel: 408-373-4101.
Students 218.

OUTSIDE THE CITY OF MONTEREY

Aptos, Santa Cruz Co., Resurrection (1968), Rev. Kenneth J. Laverone.
Res., 7600 Soquel Dr., P.O. Box 87, 95001. Tel: 408-688-4300; Fax: 408-688-6921.
School—Good Shepherd School (Inter-Parish), (Grades K-8). See Star of the Sea Parish, Santa Cruz.
Catechesis/Religious Programs—Tel: 408-688-4300; Fax: 408-688-6921.
Students 99.

Arroyo Grande, San Luis Obispo Co., St. Patrick (1886), Revs. James Henry, Pastor; Heibar Castaneda.
Res., 501 Fair Oaks Ave., P.O. Box 860, 93421. Tel: 805-489-2680; Fax: 805-489-1316.
School—(Grades K-8) 900 W. Branch St., 93420. Tel: 805-489-1210. Raymond Burnell, Prin.
Sisters of Mercy 5; Lay Teachers 7; Students 332.
Catechesis/Religious Programs—Tel: 805-481-2990.
Students 332.
Mission—Oceano, St. Francis of Assisi.
Shamrock Thrift Shop—924 Grand Ave., Grover City, 93433. Tel: 805-481-0612. Andy Tellez.

Atascadero, San Luis Obispo Co., St. William's (1948), Very Rev. Joseph R. Hercek, V.F.
Mailing Address: P.O. Box 2230, 93423. Tel: 805-466-0849; Fax: 805-461-0743.
Res., 6410 Santa Lucia Rd., 93422.
Catechesis/Religious Programs—Students 299.

Boulder Creek, Santa Cruz Co., St. Michael (1921), Rev. Martin McDonald.
Res., 13005 Pine St., 95006. Tel: 408-338-6112; Fax: 408-338-6112.
Catechesis/Religious Programs—Students 54.

Cambria, San Luis Obispo Co., Santa Rosa (1961), Rev. Derek Hughes.
Res., 1174 Main St., 93428. Tel: 805-927-4816; Fax: 805-927-2880. [CEM]
Catechesis/Religious Programs—Students 80.

Capitola, Santa Cruz Co., St. Joseph (1904), Revs. Patrick Dooling; Tom Foster, S.J.; Sr. Marie Wiedner, O.P., Pastoral Assoc.
Res., 435 Monterey Ave., 95010. Tel: 408-475-8211; Fax: 408-475-2601.
School—Good Shepherd School (Inter-Parish), (Grades K-8). See Star of the Sea Parish, Santa Cruz and Resurrection Church, Aptos. Tel: 408-476-4000; Fax: 408-476-0948.
Catechesis/Religious Programs—Tel: 408-475-8213; Fax: 408-475-2601.
Students 147.

Carmel, Monterey Co., San Carlos Borromeo Basilica (1771). (Carmel Mission). Rev. Msgr. D. Declan Murphy; Revs. Richard D. Clark; James L. Plastino.
Res., Rio Rd. and Lasuen Dr., P.O. Box 2235, 93921. Tel: 408-624-1271; Fax: 408-624-8050.
School—Junipero Serra School, (Grades K-8) 2992 Lasuen Dr., 93923. Tel: 408-624-8322; Fax: 408-624-8050. Mary V. Marchi, Prin.
Sisters 1; Lay Teachers 13; Students 250.
Catechesis/Religious Programs—Tel: 408-624-6846.
Students 135.
Mission—Big Sur, Monterey Co., St. Francis of the Redwoods, Hwy. 1, Big Sur, 93920.
Chapel—Blessed Sacrament.

Carmel Valley, Monterey Co., Our Lady of Mt. Carmel (1953), Rev. Cornelius McCarthy.
Res., 9 El Caminito, P.O. Box 195, 93924. Tel: 408-659-2224; Fax: 408-659-9186.
Catechesis/Religious Programs—Students 70.

Castroville, Monterey Co., Our Lady of Refuge (1869), Rev. Rudy Ruiz.
Res., 11140 Preston St., 95012. Tel: 408-633-4015; Fax: 408-633-4653.
Catechesis/Religious Programs—Tel: 408-633-4016; Fax: 408-633-4563.
Students 370.

Cayucos, San Luis Obispo Co., St. Joseph (1907), Revs. Cornelius Sweeney, Admin.; Anthony Gurnell.
Res., 360 Park Ave., P.O. Box 437, 93430. Tel: 805-995-3243; Fax: 805-995-2838.

Corralitos, Santa Cruz Co., Holy Eucharist (1969), Rev. John Cullen Griffin.
Res., 527 Corralitos Rd., 95076. Tel: 408-722-5490; Fax: 408-722-8157.
Catechesis/Religious Programs—Students 145.

Davenport, Santa Cruz Co., St. Vincent De Paul (1915), Rev. Siro Dal Degan, O.S.J.
Res., 544 W. Cliff Drive, Santa Cruz, 95060. Tel: 408-423-7658; 429-1426; Fax: 408-457-1317.

Felton, Santa Cruz Co., St. John (1952), Rev. Msgr. Michael L. Cross.
Res., Russell at Hwy. 9, P.O. Box M-1, 95018. Tel: 408-335-4657; Fax: 408-335-4648.
Catechesis/Religious Programs—Students 156.

Gonzales, Monterey Co., St. Theodore (1892), Rev. Michael Volk.
Res., 120 First St., P.O. Drawer B, 93926. Tel: 408-675-3648; Fax: 408-675-8360.
Catechesis/Religious Programs—Tel: 408-675-2100; Fax: 408-675-2974.
Students 670.

Greenfield, Monterey Co., Holy Trinity (1951), Rev. Eugenio Aramburo.
Res., 803 Elm Ave., Box 276, 93927. Tel: 408-674-5428; Fax: 408-674-5285.
Catechesis/Religious Programs—Tel: 408-674-3695. Gregoria Alvarez, D.R.E.
Students 470.

Hollister, San Benito Co., Sacred Heart (1877), Revs. Gary Byrne; Ronald Green; Fabian Vela. In res., Rev. Thomas Long, C.S.V.
Res., 540 College St., P.O. Box 1040, 95024. Tel: 408-637-9212; Fax: 408-637-7299. [CEM]
Pastoral Center—680 College St., P.O. Box 1040, 95023. Tel: 408-637-9212; Fax: 408-637-7299.
School—(Grades K-8) 670 College St., 95023. Tel: 408-637-4157; Fax: 408-637-4164. Mrs. Mary White, Prin.
Lay Teachers 14; Students 396.
Catechesis/Religious Programs—Tel: 408-637-8291. D.R.E.: Tish Scargill; Lety Perez; Eileen McCullough.
Students 595.

Jolon, Monterey Co., San Antonio Mission (1771), Revs. Salvador Parisi, O.F.M.; Bill Haney, O.F.M. In res., Rev. Bartholomew Welsh, O.F.M.; Bros. Joachim Grant, O.F.M.; Anthony F. Lavorin, O.F.M.
Res., Box 803, 93928. Tel: 408-385-4478; Fax: 408-386-9332.

King City, Monterey Co., St. John the Baptist (1891) (Hispanic), Rev. Lawrence J. Kambitsch.
Res., 504 N. Third St., 93930. Tel: 408-385-3377; Fax: 408-385-3317.
Catechesis/Religious Programs—Tel: 408-385-3464; Fax: 408-385-3317. D.R.E.: Cindy LaFont; Claudia Zuniga.
Students 420.
Mission—San Lucas, Monterey Co., St. Luke. Main St.

Los Gatos, Santa Cruz Co., Christ Child (1983), Rev. Marvin J. Steffes, C.PP.S.
Res., 23230 Summit Rd., 95030. Tel: 408-353-2210; Fax: 408-353-8680.

Los Osos, San Luis Obispo Co., St. Elizabeth Ann Seton (1984), Rev. Mark Stetz, Pastor.
Res., 2050 Palisades Ave., 93402. Tel: 805-528-5319; Fax: 805-528-8893.
Catechesis/Religious Programs—Students 150.

Marina, Monterey Co., St. Jude Parish Community (1963), Rev. Carl M.D. Faria.
Res., 303 Hillcrest Ave., 93933-3599. Tel: 408-384-5434; Fax: 408-384-7011.
Catechesis/Religious Programs—Tel: 408-384-8268; Fax: 408-384-7011.
Students 146.

Morro Bay, San Luis Obispo Co., St. Timothy (1950), Rev. Cornelius Sweeney.
Res., 962 Piney Way, 93442. Tel: 805-772-2840.
Catechesis/Religious Programs—951 Pacific, 93442. Tel: 805-772-3032; Fax: 805-772-3184. Elizabeth Olson, D.R.E.
Students 87.

Nipomo, San Luis Obispo Co., St. Joseph (1968), Revs. Jose Chavez; James J. Frerkes.
Res., 298 S. Thompson, 93444. Tel: 805-929-1922; Fax: 805-929-2662.

Pacific Grove, Monterey Co., St. Angela (1928), Revs. Anthony Phuc, C.SS.R., Assoc. Pastor; Jerry McCormick.
Res., 161 Ninth St., 93950. Tel: 408-655-4160; Fax: 408-372-5026.
Office: 146 Eighth St., 93950.
Preschool—136 Eighth St., 93950. Tel: 408-372-3555. Virginia Ziomek, Prin.
Catechesis/Religious Programs—Tel: 408-373-6311.
Students 300.

Paso Robles, San Luis Obispo Co., St. Rose (1922), Sr. Maris Stella O'Loughlen, Admin.
Office: 642 Trigo Ln., P.O. Box 790, 93447. Tel: 805-238-2218; Fax: 805-238-2762.
Res., 820 Creston Rd., P.O. Box 790, 93447. Tel: 805-238-2218; Fax: 805-238-2762. [CEM]
School—(Grades PreK-8) 900 Tucker Ave., 93447. Tel: 805-238-0304; Fax: 805-238-7393. James Brescia, Prin.
Lay Teachers 16; Students 315.
Catechesis/Religious Programs—Tel: 805-238-0194.
Students 225.

Pismo Beach, San Luis Obispo Co., St. Paul the Apostle (1930), Rev. Charles Kozanecki, O.F.M.Conv. In res., Revs. Alphonse Van Guilder, O.F.M.Conv.; Peter Parchem, O.F.M.Conv., Pastor Emeritus.
Res., 800 Bello St., 93449. Tel: 805-773-2219; Fax: 805-773-8617. [JC]

Salinas, Monterey Co.,

1—Christ the King, (1995), Rev. Manuel Canal.
Res., 240 Calle Cebu, 93901. Tel: 408-422-6543; Fax: 408-422-7218.
Religious Education Office: Tel: 408-422-6722.
Catechesis/Religious Programs—Students 500.

2—Sacred Heart, (1877), Revs. Paul R. Valdez; Dennis Gilbert; Antonio Cortes.
Res., 22 Stone St., 93901. Tel: 408-424-1959; Fax: 408-424-0788.
School—(Grades K-8) 123 W. Market St., 93901. Tel: 408-771-1310; Fax: 408-771-1314. Sr. Paulette Tiefenbrunn, S.S.N.D., Prin.
Sisters 2; Lay Teachers 9; Students 307.
Catechesis/Religious Programs—Tel: 408-772-8232. Sr. Cristina Bortolotti, I.M., D.R.E.
Students 600.

3—St. Mary of the Nativity, (1947). Rev. Geronimo Cuevas, Pastor; Sr. Patricia Reinhart, P.B.V.M., Pastoral Assoc.
Res., 1702 Second Ave., 93905. Tel: 408-758-1669; Fax: 408-758-4715.
Catechesis/Religious Programs—Tel: 408-422-9964. Mrs. Elizabeth Pulido, D.R.E.
Students 682.

4—Madonna Del Sasso, (1960), Revs. Ronald R. Shirley, Pastor; John Burns; Mrs. Gail Branner, Pastoral Assoc.; Rev. Michael Miller.
Res., 320 E. Laurel Dr., 93906. Tel: 408-422-5323; Fax: 408-422-0536.
School—(Grades K-8) 20 Santa Teresa Way, 93906. Tel: 408-424-7813; Fax: 408-424-3359.
Sisters of Notre Dame 1; Lay Teachers 7; Students 274.
Catechesis/Religious Programs—Tel: 408-422-1439.
Students 355.

San Juan Bautista, San Benito Co., San Juan Bautista (1797). (Old Mission). Rev. Edward Fitz-Henry.
Res., 2nd & Mariposa St., P.O. Box 400, 95045. Tel: 408-623-2127; Fax: 408-623-2433. [CEM]
Catechesis/Religious Programs—Tel: 408-623-4178.
Students 94.

San Luis Obispo, San Luis Obispo Co., San Luis Obispo (1772). (Old Mission). Revs. Francis E. Thome; John Arul; Vincent Walsh; Larry Betrozoff.
Res., 751 Palm St., 93401. Tel: 805-781-8220; Fax: 805-781-8214.
Preschool—221 Daly Ave., 93401. Tel: 805-549-8819. Jim Gentilucci, Prin.
School—(Grades 1-8) 761 Broad St., 93401. Tel: 805-543-6019; Fax: 805-543-6246. Jim Gentilucci, Prin.
Lay Teachers 13; Students 275.
Catechesis/Religious Programs—Students 168.
Nativity of Our Lady (1964), Rev. Michael Cicinato; Deacon David Leach.
Res., 221 Daly Ave., 93405-1099. Tel: 805-544-2357; Fax: 805-544-6756.
Catechesis/Religious Programs—Students 70.

San Miguel, San Luis Obispo Co., San Miguel (1797). (Old Mission). Revs. Salvador Parisi, O.F.M.; Bill Haney.
Res., 775 Mission St., P.O. Box 69, 93451. Tel: 805-467-3256; Fax: 805-467-2448. [CEM]
Catechesis/Religious Programs—Students 69.
Missions—San Ardo, Monterey Co., Our Lady of Ransom; Bradley, Monterey Co., Our Lady of Guadalupe.
Station—Heritage Ranch.

Santa Cruz, Santa Cruz Co., Holy Cross (1889), Revs. Michael A. Marini; Peter Crivello.
Res., 126 High St., 95060. Tel: 408-423-4182; Fax: 408-423-1043. [CEM]
School—(Grades K-8) 150 Emmet St., 95060. Tel: 408-423-4447; Fax: 408-423-0752. Marlene Canzano, Prin.
Lay Teachers 17; Students 245.
Catechesis/Religious Programs—Tel: 408-458-3041; Fax: 408-458-1043.
Students 210.
Star of the Sea (1947), Rev. Rene Iturbe, S.M.; Deacon Ken Johnson, S.M.
Res., 515 Frederick St., 95062. Tel: 408-429-1018; Fax: 408-429-5832.
Good Shepherd Preschool—(Inter-Parish) 2727 Mattison Ln., 95062. Tel: 408-476-4000; Fax: 408-476-0948. Sr. Geraldine McNamara, O.P., Prin.
Students 140.
Catechesis/Religious Programs—Students 324.
Chapel—Villa Maria del Mar, Tel: 408-475-1236;

Fax: 408-475-8867.

Santa Margarita, San Luis Obispo Co., Holy Angels (1934), Rev. Joseph Grech, Admin.
Res., 22515 H St., P.O. Box 350, 93453-0350. Tel: 805-438-5383; Fax: 805-438-4313.
Mission—Carrissa Plains, San Luis Obispo Co., St. James Mission.

Scotts Valley, Santa Cruz Co., San Agustin (1969), Rev. Matthew Pennington.
Res., 257 Glenwood Dr., 95066. Tel: 408-438-3633; Fax: 408-438-0973.
Catechesis/Religious Programs—Students 140.

Seaside, Monterey Co., St. Francis Xavier (1950), Revs. John J. Keane, S.A.; Henry Mair, S.A. In res., Revs. Michael Daniel, S.A.; Charles G. Fatooh.
Res., 1475 LaSalle Ave., P.O. Box 247, 93955. Tel: 408-394-8546; Fax: 408-394-5414.
Catechesis/Religious Programs—Tel: 408-394-8546; Fax: 408-394-5414.
Students 298.

Soledad, Monterey Co., Our Lady of Solitude (1933), Rev. Eleutherio Sanz.
Res., 235 Main St., 93960. Tel: 408-678-2731; Fax: 408-678-2731.
Catechesis/Religious Programs—Tel: 408-678-1277; 675-2975. Sr. Ros Angela Fillipini, D.R.E.
Students 700.
Mission—Soledad, Monterey Co., Nuestra Senora de la Soledad, Rte. 1, Box 72, 93960. Tel: 408-678-2586.

Spreckels, Monterey Co., St. Joseph (1969), Rev. Jim Nisbet.
Res., 1 Railroad Ave., P.O. Box 7158, 93962. Tel: 408-455-2249; Fax: 408-455-9357.
Catechesis/Religious Programs—Tel: 408-455-1337; Fax: 408-455-9357. Sr. Liliana Bonello, I.M., J.C.L., D.R.E.
Students 272.

Tres Pinos, San Benito Co., Immaculate Conception (1904), Revs. Gary Byrne; Ron Green; Fabian Vela.
Res., 7290 Airline Hwy., P.O. Box 247, 95075. Tel: 408-628-3216.
Catechesis/Religious Programs—Sr. Carol Pesce, S.H.F., D.R.E.
Students 70.

Watsonville, Santa Cruz Co., Our Lady Help of Christians (1854), Rev. Bernardo Soares.
Res., 2401 E. Lake Ave., 95076. Tel: 408-722-2665; Fax: 408-722-8305. [CEM]
Catechesis/Religious Programs—Students 52.

St. Patrick (1861), Revs. Gregory Sandman; Jesus Enrique Herrera; Ignacio Martinez.
Res., 721 Main St., 95076. Tel: 408-724-1317; Fax: 408-724-1627.
Catechesis/Religious Programs—Tel: 408-724-2141. D.R.E.: Sr. Inez Sherwood, S.N.J.M., (English, Grades 1-6); Mrs. Elvira Sanchez, (Spanish, Grades 1-6); Walter Washington, (Junior High & High School).
Students 736.

Assumption (1953) (Hispanic), Rev. Raul H. Carvajal, Pastor. In res., Rev. Antonio Sanchez, Admin.
Res., 100 Salinas Rd., 95076. Tel: 408-722-1104; Fax: 408-722-1254. [CEM]
Catechesis/Religious Programs—Tel: 408-722-9938. Sr. Rosa Dolores Rodriguez, D.C., D.R.E.
Students 628.

Shrines

Santa Cruz, Santa Cruz Co., Shrine of St. Joseph Guardian of the Redeemer,
Res., 544 W. Cliff Dr., 95060-6147. Tel: 408-471-0442; Fax: 408-457-1317. Rev. Larry Toschi, O.S.J., Rector.
Guardian of the Redeemer Bookstore—Tel: 408-471-1700; Fax: 408-457-1317.

Chaplains of Public Institutions

ATASCADERO. *Atascadero State Hospital*. Rev. Vincent Walsh.

BOULDER CREEK. *Ben Lomond Youth Authority Camp*. Rev. Martin McDonald.

PASO ROBLES. *El Paso de Robles School*. Dept. of the Youth Authority.Vacant.

SAN LUIS OBISPO. *California Men's Colony East*. Rev. Alphonse Van Guilder, O.F.M.Conv.
California Men's Colony West. Rev. Michael T. Bell.

SOLEDAD. *Correctional Training Facility*. Rev. Joel Almendras.

On Duty Outside the Diocese:
Reverend Fathers—
Adams, Michael T., Archdiocese of Samoa, APIA, Fetuolemoana, P.O. Box 532 APIA, Western Samoa. Tel: 685-20-400 20-401
Cadera, James R., 601-C Washington, Coalinga, CA 93210. Tel: 209-934-1450

Special Assignment:
Reverend Fathers—
Fatooh, Charles G., Chancellor/Moderator of the Curia, Diocese of Monterey, P.O. Box 2048, Monterey, CA 93940. Tel: 408-373-4345
Miller, Michael, Vicar for Clergy and Diocesan Dir. for RENEW, Madonna de Sasso, 320 E. Laurel Dr., Salinas, CA 93906. Tel: 408-422-5323
Sanchez, Antonio, Dir. of Vocations, Our Lady of the Assumption, 100 Salinas Rd., Watsonville, CA 95076. Tel: 408-722-1104; Fax: 408-722-1254

Absent on Sick Leave:
Reverend Fathers—
Enciso, Herman, Our Lady of Guadalupe, 39100 Orchard Ave., Cherry Valley, CA 92223-3797
Mai, Emmanuel K., P.O. Box 85, Mt. View, CA 94042

Retired:
Reverend Monsignors—
Kennedy, John, P.O. Box 4023, Felton, CA 95018. Tel: 408-335-3119
Lane, William, 3400 Paul Sweet Rd., C-130, Santa Cruz, CA 95065. Tel: 408-479-3775
MacMahon, Eamon, 24631 Guadalupe St., Carmel, CA 93923. Tel: 408-624-2275
Marron, James, 246 Ridge Rd., Pismo Beach, CA 93449. Tel: 805-773-3549
McGuinness, Brendan, P.O. Box 789, Monterey, CA 93942-0789. Tel: 408-375-7301
Morgan, Thomas, 1118 Victoria St., Hollister, CA 95023. Tel: 408-637-1084
Stieger, Joseph, c/o 161 Broad St., San Luis Obispo, CA 93405. Tel: 805-543-3284

Reverend Fathers—
Bonjean, Richard, 490 Elizabeth Ct., Templeton, CA 93465. Tel: 805-434-2449
Cowan, Vincent, P.O. Box 3186, Fremont, CA 94539-3186. Tel: 415-656-7175
Freiermuth, Harry, P.O. Box 6923, Salinas, CA 93912-6923. Tel: 408-757-6656
Hall, Henry, P.O. Box 462312, Escondido, CA 92046-2316. Tel: 619-737-9001
Keating, Douglas, P.O. Box 2284, Avila Beach, CA 93424. Tel: 805-595-9415
Kelly, James, c/o Valley Heights, 925 Freedom Blvd., A-114, Watsonville, CA 95076. Tel: 408-728-6565
Leonard, Joseph, 18430 Vista Granada Way, Los Gatos, CA 95030
Markey, Francis, 375 Coastview Dr., Santa Cruz, CA 95065. Tel: 408-475-7436
Matz, Leo, Mount Angel Towers, One Tower Ln., Mount Angel, OR 97362. Tel: 503-845-7568
McEvoy, John, 14 Herrmann Dr., Monterey, CA 93940. Tel: 408-375-3828
McSweeney, John, 1320 Padre Dr., Salinas, CA 93901. Tel: 408-422-4584
Migliazzo, Felix, 1249 Josselyn Canyon Rd., P.O. Box 88, Monterey, CA 93942. Tel: 408-373-9120
Murphy, John, San Carlos Cathedral, 550 Church St., Monterey, CA 93940. Tel: 408-373-2628
O'Halloran, Richard, 1335 Byron Dr., Salinas, CA 93901. Tel: 408-758-6285
O'Sullivan, Laurence, Craemers Ct., Belgooly, Cork, Ireland
O'Sullivan, Michael, 2247 Idylwild Pl., Arroyo Grande, CA 93420. Tel: 805-489-9160
Rodrigues, Antonio, 143 Swift St., Santa Cruz, CA 95060. Tel: 408-423-0650
Santamaria, Max, Cr. de Arizala 7, 31178 Abaruza, Navarra, Spain. Tel: 011-344-452-0021
Schwarz, Robert, Golden Oaks #4103, 30 Monte Vista Dr., Monterey, CA 93940. Tel: 408-372-8848
Sweeney, James, 194 Island St., Morro Bay, CA 93442. Tel: 805-773-4108
Toan, Francis, 2034 N. Main St., Salinas, CA 93906. Tel: 408-449-0449
Watt, Joseph, 2010 Pleasant Valley Rd., Aptos, CA 95001. Tel: 408-724-2829

Permanent Deacons:
Leach, David, Nativity of Our Lady, 221 Daly Ave., San Luis Obispo, CA 93401. Tel: 805-544-2357
Miller, Harold, 121 Robin Dr., Marina, CA 93933. Tel: 408-883-2601

INSTITUTIONS LOCATED IN THE DIOCESE

[A] SEMINARIES, RELIGIOUS OR SCHOLASTICATES

BIG SUR. *New Camaldoli*. (See Monasteries). Priests 4; Brothers 1; Seminary Students 7.

[B] HIGH SCHOOLS, PRIVATE

MONTEREY. *Santa Catalina Upper School*. (Girls), 1500 Mark Thomas Dr., 93940. Tel: 408-655-9372. Sr. Carlotta, Head of School. Lay Teachers 65; Total Enrollment (Grades PreK-12) 556.

SALINAS. *Christian Brothers Institute of California, Inc. dba Palma High School*. (Grades 7-12), 919 Iverson St., 93901-1898. Tel: 408-422-6391; Fax: 408-422-5065. Congregation of Christian Brothers. Bro. Patrick D. Dunne, C.F.C., Prin. Brothers 8; Lay Teachers 30; Boys (Jr. High) 182; Boys (Total) 627.
Congregation of Christian Brothers Residence, 935 Iverson St., 93901. Tel: 408-758-2127. Bro. Frank L. Dalton, C.F.C., Dir. Brothers 11.

[C] HIGH SCHOOLS, DIOCESAN

SALINAS. *Notre Dame High School*, 455 Palma Dr., 93901. Tel: 408-751-1850; Fax: 408-757-5749. Dr. Roger D. Richter, Prin. Sisters 1; Lay Teachers 36; Girls 430.

SAN LUIS OBISPO. *Mission College Preparatory Catholic High School*, 682 Palm St., 93401. Tel: 805-543-2131; Fax: 805-543-4359. Rev. Charles J. Tilley, S.J., Prin. Lay Teachers 18; Students 195.

[D] ELEMENTARY SCHOOLS, PRIVATE

MONTEREY. *Santa Catalina Lower School*. (Grades PreK-8). (Coed), 1500 Mark Thomas Dr., 93940. Tel: 408-655-9324. Dr. Nancy Diamonti, Dir.; Jane Stile, Sec. Lay Teachers 30; Students 226.

CORRALITOS. *Salesian Sisters' School: Mary Help of Christians Youth Center*. (Grades K-8), 605 Enos Ln., 95076. Tel: 408-728-4700; 728-5518; Fax: 408-728-5802. Sr. Phyllis Neves, F.M.A., Prin. Sisters 8; Lay Teachers 9; Students 204.

WATSONVILLE. *Moreland Notre Dame School*, 133 Brennan St., 95076. Tel: 408-728-2051; Fax: 408-728-2052. Sisters of Notre Dame de Namur. Sr. Teresa Ann Leahy, S.N.D., Prin. Lay Teachers 8; Students 320.
St. Francis Youth Center, 2400 E. Lake Ave., 95076. Tel: 408-763-4484. Conducted by the Salesians of St. John Bosco. Revs. Christian H. Woerz, S.D.B., Dir.; Jesse Montes, S.D.B.; Richard A. Voigt, S.D.B.; Bros. Abel Zanella, S.D.B.; William Regner, S.D.B.; Michael Herbers, S.D.B. Lay Staff 8; Total Enrollment 4,850.

[E] GENERAL HOSPITALS

SANTA CRUZ. *Dominican Santa Cruz Hospital*, 1555 Soquel Dr., 95065. Tel: 408-462-7700; Fax: 408-462-7555.
For a complete listing, refer to the Hospitals section.

[F] SPECIAL HOSPITALS AND SANATORIA ACUTE CARE HOSPITAL

MONTEREY. *Ave Maria Convalescent Hospital*, 1249 Josselyn Canyon Rd., P.O. Box 1977, 93940. Tel: 408-373-1216.
For a complete listing, refer to the Special Care Facilities section.

SANTA CRUZ. *Dominican Health Services*, 1555 Soquel Dr., 95065. Tel: 408-462-7700; Fax: 408-462-7555.
For a complete listing, refer to the Special Care Facilities section.

[G] MONASTERIES AND RESIDENCES OF PRIESTS AND BROTHERS

MONTEREY. *Oratorian Community-Congregation of the Oratory of Pontifical Right*, 302 High St., P.O. Box 1688, 93942. Tel: 408-373-0476. Very Rev. Peter C. Sanders, Orator, Provost. Tel: 408-375-9769; Revs. Michael P. Drury, Orator, Vicar. Tel: 408-646-8278; Lidio Limon, Orator, Assoc. Vocational Apostolate. Tel: 408-372-6094; Thomas A. Kieffer, Orator, Treasurer. Tel: 408-372-1325. Priests 4.

ARROYO GRANDE. *St. Joseph Cupertino Province, Provincial Center*, P.O. Box 820, 93421. Tel: 805-489-1012. Revs. Allen A. Ramirez, O.F.M.Conv., Minister Prov.; Stephen R. Gross, O.F.M.Conv., Vicar Prov.; Paul Fazio, O.F.M.Conv., Prov. Sec.
St. Joseph's Cupertino Novitiate, 1352 Dale Ave., P.O. Box 820, 93421. Tel: 805-473-2256. Bros. James M. Reiter, O.F.M.Conv., Dir. Novices & Guardian; Patrick Lytell, O.F.M.Conv., Prov. Sec.; Revs. Roch Bartman, O.F.M.Conv., (Retired); Richard Otto, O.F.M.Conv., Home Missioner, de familia; Norbert Rackensperger, O.F.M.Conv., Parish Ministry, de familia; Christopher Lucas, O.F.M.Conv., Asst. Dir. Novices & Vicar; Charles Shelton, O.F.M.Conv., Vocation Dir. Brothers 2; Priests 4; Novices 10.

BIG SUR. *New Camaldoli Hermitage*, 93920. Tel: 408-667-2456; Fax: 408-667-0480. Very Rev. Robert Hale, O.S.B.Cam., Prior; Revs. Bruno Barnhardt, O.S.B.Cam.; John Powell, O.S.B.Cam.; Joseph Diemer, O.S.B.Cam.; Bernard Massicotte, O.S.B.Cam.; Louis Coddaire, O.S.B.Cam.; Aelred Squire, O.S.B.Cam.;

Isaiah Teichert, O.S.B.Cam.; Raniero Hoffman, O.S-.B.Cam.
On Special Assignment: Rev. Andrew Colnaghi, O.S.B.Cam., Prior, Incarnation Priory, 2208 Cedar, 94709. Rev. Romuald Duscher, O.S.B.Cam., Prior, Epiphany Monastery, 96 Scobie Rd. Professed Monks (including 10 priests) 23; Brothers 13.

SALINAS. *Palma Community*, 935 Iverson St., 93901. Tel: 408-758-2127. Congregation of Christian Brothers. Bros. B. Sebastian Samp, C.F.C.; F. L. Dalton, C.F.C.; John D. Donnelly, C.F.C.; Patrick D. Dunne, C.F.C.; Anthony C. O'Grady, C.F.C.; Benjamin L. Favero, C.F.C.; John O'Brien, C.F.X.; Dennis J. Peterson, C.F.C.; Daniel L. Oehrle, C.F.C.; Charles J. Avendano, C.F.C.; Kevin J. Reilly, C.F.C. Brothers 11.

SAN LUIS OBISPO. *Monastery of the Risen Christ*, P.O. Box 3931, 93403. Tel: 805-544-1810. Men's Residence, 2308 O'Connor Way, 93405. Tel: 805-544-1810. Rt. Rev. David Geraets, O.S.B., Superior; Revs. Raymond V. Roh, O.S.B., Prior; Stephen Odenbrett, O.S.B.; Albert Meyer, O.S.B.; Raymond Greco, O.S.B., (Retired).

SAN MIGUEL. *Franciscan Friars, O.F.M.* (Province of St. Barbara, Old Mission), P.O. Box 69, 93451. Tel: 805-467-3256; Fax: 805-467-2248. Revs. John Vaughin, O.F.M., Guardian; Jerry Ahles, O.F.M.; Salvador Parisi, O.F.M.; Thomas Messner, O.F.M.; Bros. Bartholomew Mitchell, O.F.M.; Quentin Watson, O.F.M.; Marion Alfonso, O.F.M.; Victor Hunter, O.F.M.; Peter Boegl, O.F.M.

Novitiate House for the Franciscan Friars, O.F.M. (Province of St. Barabara), P.O. Box 69, 93451. Tel: 805-467-2801; Fax: 805-467-2448. Revs. John Vaughn, O.F.M., Master of Novices; Thomas Messner, O.F.M.; Bros. Marion Alfonso, O.F.M.; Peter Beogel, O.F.M. Novices 5.

SANTA CRUZ. *Oblates of St. Joseph Provincial House and Shrine*, 544 W. Cliff Dr., 95060.
Religious Community. Tel: 408-471-1702.
Provincial. Tel: 408-457-1868; Fax: 408-457-1317.
Shrine of St. Joseph. Tel: 408-471-0442. Revs. Siro Dal Degan, O.S.J. (Italy), Rector; Aldo Grasso, O.S.J. (Italy); Bronius Kaunas, O.S.J. (Lithuania); Larry Toschi, O.S.J., Prov. Supr.; Thomas Russo, O.S.J.; Bro. Duain O'Mara. Priests 5; Total in Residence 6.
Religious Community. Tel: 408-471-1702. Legal Title: *Oblates of St. Joseph, Provincial House and Shrine of St. Joseph, Guardian of the Redeemer*.

Society of Mary, Marianists, 285 Meder St., 95060. Tel: 408-423-9400; Fax: 408-423-8163. Rev. Roland Bunda, S.M., Dir.; Bros. Anthony Young, S.M.; Michael Vollmer, S.M. Total Staff 3; Total in Residence 3.

Society of Mary, Marists, Marist Community, 436 Effey St., 95062-2640. Tel: 408-425-5202; Fax: 408-429-5832. Revs. Rene Iturbe, S.M.; Dennis Steik, S.M.; George Fahey, S.M.; Deacon Ken Johnson, S.M.

[H] CONVENTS AND RESIDENCES FOR SISTERS

MONTEREY. *Ave Maria Convent*, 1249 Josselyn Canyon Rd., P.O. Box 1977, 93942-1977. Tel: 408-373-1216. Motherhouse of the Franciscan Sisters of the Immaculate Conception and St. Joseph for the Dying. Sr. Constance, Supr.; Rev. Filex Migliazzo, Chap. Sisters 7.

APTOS. *St. Joseph's Monastery of the Poor Clares (Colettines)*, 1671 Pleasant Valley Rd., P.O. Box 160, 95001-0160. Tel: 408-761-9659; 9481. Mother Mary Clare, P.C.C., Abbess. Professed Sisters (Cloistered) 10; Postulants 2; Extern 2; Novices 1.

CARMEL. *Carmelite Monastery of Our Lady and St. Therese*, 27601 Hwy. 1, 93923. Tel: 408-624-3043; Fax: 408-624-5495. Mother Therese of the Heart of Jesus, Prioress. Nuns 14.

CORRALITOS. *Daughters of Mary Help of Christians*, 605 Enos Ln., 95076. Tel: 408-728-4700; Fax: 408-728-5802. Sr. Phyllis Neves, F.M.A., Supr. Residents 13.

GONZALES. *Sisters of Charity of the Infant Mary Community of Formation*, 512 Fairview Dr., Box 178, 93926. Tel: 408-675-2975. Sr. Rosangela Filippini, I.M., Supr. Residents 5.

SALINAS. *Bethany*, 15785 Alto Way, 93907. Tel: 408-663-3675. Sisters of Charity of the Infant Mary. Sr. Gabriela Covi-Maffei, Supr. Residents 4.

Congregation of the Sisters of the Holy Cross, 1335 Byron Dr., 93901. Tel: 408-758-0931. Madonna Manor Convent. Sr. Sebastian Adza, C.S.C., Admin.; Rev. Richard O'Halloran, Chap. Sisters 5; Total in Residence 66.

Madonna Del Sasso Convent, 163 Rosarita Dr., 93906. Tel: 408-424-4370. Sisters of Notre Dame. Residents 3.

SAN JUAN BAUTISTA. *Franciscan Sisters of the Atonement*, P.O. Box 1094, 95045. Tel: 408-623-4267. Franciscan Sisters of Atonement 6.

SAN LUIS OBISPO. *Monastery of the Risen Christ*. (Women's Residence), P.O. Box 3931, 93403-3931. 2304 O'Connor Way, 93405. Tel: 805-544-7808. Sr. Marie DiSciullo, O.S.B., O.B.L.

Sisters of St Joseph of Carondelet, Casa Viriditas, 108 Los Cerros Dr., 93405. Tel: 805-544-9020. Sr. Theresa Harpin, C.S.J.; Sr. Miriam Therese Larkin, C.S.J.; Sr. Janet Husung, C.S.J.

SANTA CRUZ. *Adrian Dominican Sisters*, Pacific West Mission Chapter, P.O. Box 2235, 95063-2235. Tel: 408-457-7117; Fax: 408-457-7139. Sr. Molly Giller, O.P., Chapter Prioress.

Franciscan Hospitaller Sisters of the Immaculate Conception, 1522 W. Cliff Dr., 95060. Tel: 408-426-8413. Sr. Maria dos Anjos Francisco, Local Supr. Total Residents; 3.

Villa Maria del Mar, 2-1918 East Cliff Dr., 95062. Tel: 408-475-1236; Fax: 408-475-8867. Sr. Geraldine Will, S.N.J.M., Dir. Sisters of the Holy Names of Jesus and Mary 6.

SOQUEL. *St. Clare's Retreat*, 2381 Laurel Glen Rd., 95073. Tel: 408-423-8093. Sr. Mary Pauline Chang, O.S.F., Supr. Total Staff 10; Total Residents 10.

WATSONVILLE. *Moreland Notre Dame Convent*, 656 Main St., 95076. Tel: 408-724-7696; 724-3670. Sisters of Notre Dame de Namur. Sr. Denis Marie Harney, S.N.D., Coord. Residents 5.

[I] RETREAT HOUSES

APTOS. *Camp St. Francis*, 2320 Sumner Ave., 95003. Tel: 408-684-0300. Office: 2400 E. Lake Ave., Watsonville, 95076. Tel: 408-763-4486.
Conducted by Salesians of St. John Bosco. Summer Camp for Boys 8-14, Meeting Center for large groups, and Retreat Center for large groups of youth or adults.

BIG SUR. *New Camaldoli Hermitage*, 93920. Tel: 408-667-2456; Fax: 408-667-0480. Very Rev. Robert Hale, O.S.B.Cam., Prior. Camaldolese Hermitage and retreat house. Total in Residence 27.

SAN JUAN BAUTISTA. *St. Francis Retreat Center*, P.O. Box 970, 95045. Tel: 408-623-4234; Fax: 408-623-9046.
Conducted by Franciscan Friars. Province of St. Barbara. Revs. Godfrey D. McSweeney, O.F.M.; Richard McManus, O.F.M., Dir. and Local Guardian. Priests 2; Brothers 1; Total in Residence 8; Total Staff 18. Retreats for men, women, singles, married couples, A.A. and 12-step. Programs include Spiritual Growth, Ecumenical, Spanish.

SAN MIGUEL. *San Miguel Retreat House*, P.O. Box 69, 93451. Tel: 805-467-3256. Revs. John Vaughn, O.F.M., Supr.; Salvador Parisi, O.F.M.; Jerome Ahles, O.F.M.; Thomas Messner, O.F.M.

SANTA CRUZ. *Siena Retreat Center - A Small Part of the Holy Cross*, 108 High St., 95060. Tel: 408-423-7544; Fax: 408-423-1638. Michaela Terrio, Manager.

Villa Maria del Mar, 2-1918 E. Cliff Dr., 95062. Tel: 408-475-1236; Fax: 408-475-8867. Sr. Geraldine Will, S.N.J.M., Contact. Sisters of the Holy Names of Jesus and Mary 6.

SOQUEL. *St. Clare's Retreat House*, 2381 Laurel Glen Rd., 95073. Tel: 408-423-8093; Fax: 408-423-1541. Sr. Mary Francis Coleman, O.S.F., Retreat Dir.; Revs. Enda Heffernan, O.F.M.Cap., Retreat Master; Godfrey D. McSweeney, O.F.M., Asst. Retreat Master. Franciscan Missionary Sisters of Our Lady of Sorrows 10; Total Staff 18.

[J] NEWMAN CHAPLAINS AND CENTERS

MONTEREY. *Department of Campus Ministry*, P.O. Box 350, 93942. Tel: 408-373-1608. Agnes Leonardich, Dir.; Miriam "Mimi" Schwertfeger, Admin. Asst. Total Staff 16.

California State Polytechnic Institute/Cuesta College, Newman Catholic Center, 1472 Foothill Blvd., San Luis Obispo, 93405-1416. Sr. Theresa Harpin, C.S.J., Dir. Campus Ministry; Bonnie MacDonald, Assoc. Dir.; Nancy Sanchez, Admin. Asst.; Sr. Moira Lyons, I.H.M., Asst. Admin. Asst.; Sr. Jan Husung, C.S.J., Assoc. Dir. Student Assistants: Natalie Gibson; Victor Elia; Rev. Vincent Walsh, Chap.

Cabrillo College, Santa Cruz, 95064. Revs. Roland Bunda, S.M., Dir. Campus Ministry, Newman Catholic Community, (Marianist); Dennis Steik, S.M., Asst. Dir.; Bros. Anthony Young, S.M., Outreach & Ecumenical Min.; Michael Vollmer, S.M., Assoc. Dir., (Marianist).

University of California at Santa Cruz, 285 Meder St., Santa Cruz, 95060. Revs. Roland Bundal, S.M., Chap. & Dir. Campus Ministry, Newman Catholic Community, (Marianist); Dennis Steik, S.M., Asst. Dir.; Bros. Anthony Young, S.M., Outreach & Ecumenical Min.; Michael Vollmer, S.M., Assoc. Dir., (Marianist).

California State University of Monterey Bay, 303 Hillcrest Ave., Marina, 93933. Rev. Carl M.D. Faria, Chap., 1475 LaSalle Ave., Seaside, 93955. Rev. John Keane, S.A., Chap.

[K]SENIOR RESIDENCES

SALINAS, CA. *Madonna Manor Retirement Home*, 1335 Byron Dr., 93901. Tel: 408-758-0931. Owned and operated by Catholic Daughters of America Home, Inc. Administered and Managed by the Sisters of the Holy Cross. Sr. Sebastion Adza, C.S.C., Admin.; Rev. Richard O'Halloran, Chap.

Villa Serra Corporation, 1320 Padre Dr., 93901. Tel: 408-754-5532; Fax: 408-754-5609. Clyde Vaughn, Mgr. Sponsored by the Diocese of Monterey and Dominican Santa Cruz Hospital. Total in Residence 135; Total Staff 50.

SANTA CRUZ, CA. *Dominican Oaks Corporation*, 3400 Paul Sweet Rd., 95065. Tel: 408-462-6257; Fax: 408-462-6742. Jack Baskin, Pres.; Tom Newlove, Mgr. Sponsored by the Dominican Santa Cruz Hospital. Total Staff 60; Total Residents 220.

[L] MISCELLANEOUS

MONTEREY. *Newman Institute for Historical and Religious Studies*, Domus Patris Foundation, P.O. Box 748, 93942. Tel: 408-373-0477. Rev. Thomas A. Kieffer, O.R.A.T., Admin.

SALINAS. *Villa Serra Corporation*, 1320 Padre Dr., 93901. Tel: 408-754-5532. Total in Residence 135; Total Staff 50.

SAN LUIS OBISPO. *Catholic Schools of Mission*, 772 Palm St., 93401.

WATSONVILLE. *Magnificat the Monterey Bay Chapter*, 120 Enos Ln., 95076. Tel: 408-724-6933. Maureen Roach, Coord.

St. Thomas More Society, c/o 262 E. Lake Ave., 95076. Tel: 408-722-2456; Fax: 408-722-0414. Raymond A. AmRhein, Pres.

RELIGIOUS INSTITUTES OF MEN REPRESENTED IN THE DIOCESE

For further details refer to the corresponding bracketed number in the Religious Institutes of Men or Women section.

[1350]—*Brothers of St. Francis Xavier*.—C.F.X.
[]—*Camaldolesi Hermits*.—O.S.B.Cam.
[1320]—*Clerics of St. Viator*.—C.S.V.
[0310]—*Congregation of Christian Brothers*. (San Francisco Prov.; Western U.S.).—C.F.C.
[]—*Congregation of the Holy Cross*.—C.S.C.
[0480]—*Conventual Franciscans*.—O.F.M.Conv.
[]—*DeLaSalle Christian Brothers*.—F.S.C.
[0520]—*Franciscan Friars*. (Santa Barbara Prov.).—O.F.M.
[0530]—*Franciscan Friars of the Atonement*. (Graymoor, Garrison, NY).—S.A.
[0930]—*Oblates of St. Joseph*. (Asti, Italy).—O.S.J.
[0950]—*Oratorians*.—C.O.
[0200]—*Order of St. Benedict*. Monastery of the Risen Christ.—O.S.B.
[1070]—*Redemptorist Fathers*.—C.SS.R.
[1190]—*Salesians of Don Bosco (Truin, Italy)*.—S.D.B.
[0690]—*Society of Jesus*.—S.J.
[0760]—*Society of Mary, Marianists*.—S.M.
[]—*Society of Mary, Marist*.—S.M.
[1060]—*Society of the Precious Blood*.—C.PP.S.

RELIGIOUS INSTITUTES OF WOMEN REPRESENTED IN THE DIOCESE

[1070-13]—*Congregation of the Most Holy Rosary-Adrian Dominican Sisters*.—O.P.
[1920]—*Congregation of the Sisters of the Holy Cross*. (Western Region).—C.S.C.
[1780]—*Congregation of the Sisters of the Third Order of St. Francis of Perpetual Adoration*.—F.S.P.A.
[0760]—*Daughters of Charity of St. Vincent de Paul*.—D.C.
[0880]—*Daughters of Mary & Joseph*.—D.M.J.
[0850]—*Daughters of Mary of Help of Christians*.—F.M.A.
[0420]—*Discalced Carmelite Nuns*.—O.C.D.
[1270]—*Franciscan Hospitaller Sisters of the Immaculate Conception*.—F.H.I.C.
[1390]—*Franciscan Missionary Sisters of Our Lady of Sorrows*.—O.S.F.
[1190]—*Franciscan Sisters of the Atonement*.—S.A.
[1300]—*Franciscan Sisters of the Immaculate Conception and St. Joseph for the Dying*.—O.S.F.
[]—*Immaculate Heart of Mary*.—I.H.M.
[2575]—*Institute of the Sisters of Mercy of the Americas*.—R.S.M.
[]—*Maryknoll Missioners*.—M.M.
[3760]—*Order of St. Clare*.—P.C.C.
[2970]—*School Sisters of Notre Dame*.—S.S.N.D.
[1960]—*Sister of the Holy Family*.—S.H.F.
[]—*Sisters of Charity of the Infant Mary*.—I.M.
2990*Sisters of Notre Dame*.—S.N.D.

[3000]—*Sisters of Notre Dame de Namur.*—S.N.D.deN.

[]—*Sisters of St. Benedict.* Monastery of the Risen Christ.—O.S.B.

[3840]—*Sisters of St. Joseph of Carondolet.*—C.S.J.

[1990]—*Sisters of the Holy Name of Jesus and Mary.*—S.N.J.M.

DIOCESAN CEMETERIES

MONTEREY. *Diocesan Cemeteries Office,* 792 Fremont St., 93940. Tel: 408-372-0327. Mailing Address: P.O. Box 2048, 93942-2048. Mr. Clancy D'Angelo, Dir.
San Carlos. Tel: 408-372-0327.

CAMBRIA. *Old Santa Rosa.* Tel: 805-541-0584.

HOLLISTER. *Sacred Heart/Calvary.* Tel: 408-637-0131.

SALINAS. *Queen of Heaven.* Tel: 408-449-5890.

SAN LUIS OBISPO. *Old Mission.* Tel: 805-541-0584.

SANTA CRUZ. *Holy Cross.* Tel: 408-475-3222.

NECROLOGY

† Farrell, Victor, (Retired). —Died April 13, 1996.

† O'Connor, Colm, (Retired). —Died March 6, 1996.

Diocese of Nashville

(Dioecesis Nashvillensis)

Most Reverend

EDWARD U. KMIEC, D.D., S.T.L.

Bishop of Nashville; ordained December 20, 1961; appointed Titular Bishop of Simidicca and Auxiliary Bishop of Trenton August 26, 1982; consecrated November 3, 1982; appointed Bishop of Nashville October 13, 1992; installed December 3, 1992. *Office: The Catholic Center, 2400 21st Ave., S., Nashville, TN, 37212.* Tel.: 615-383-6393.

Most Reverend

JAMES D. NIEDERGESES, D.D.

Retired Bishop of Nashville; ordained May 20, 1944; appointed April 8, 1975; consecrated May 20, 1975; retired October 13, 1992. *Res., 239 Cana Cir., Nashville, TN, 37205.*

ESTABLISHED JULY 28, 1837.

Square Miles 16,302.

Comprises the Counties of Bedford, Cannon, Cheatham, Clay, Coffee, Davidson, DeKalb, Dickson, Franklin, Giles, Grundy, Hickman, Houston, Humphreys, Jackson, Lawrence, Lewis, Lincoln, Macon, Marshall, Maury, Montgomery, Moore, Overton, Perry, Putnam, Robertson, Rutherford, Smith, Stewart, Sumner, Trousdale, VanBuren, Warren, Wayne, White, Williamson and Wilson in the State of Tennessee.

For legal titles of parishes and diocesan institutions, consult the Chancery Office.

Chancery Office: 2400 21st Ave., S., Nashville, TN, 37212. Tel.: 615-383-6393; Fax: 615-292-8411.

E-mail address: nashdio@aol.com

STATISTICAL OVERVIEW

Personnel	
Bishop	1
Retired Bishops	1
Priests: Diocesan Active in Diocese	32
Priests: Active Outside Diocese	6
Priests: Retired, Sick or Absent	15
Number of Diocesan Priests	53
Religious Priests in Diocese	20
Extern Priests in Diocese	4
Ordinations:	
Permanent Deacons in Diocese	27
Total Brothers	2
Total Sisters	159
Parishes	
Parishes	50
With Resident Pastor:	
Resident Diocesan Priests	30
Resident Religious Priests	8
Without Resident Pastor:	
Administered by Priests	10
Administered by Women Religious	1
Administered by Lay People	1
Missions	3
Professional Ministry Personnel:	
Sisters	10
Lay Ministers	25
Welfare	
Catholic Hospitals	1
Total Assisted	144,084
Homes for the Aged	3
Total Assisted	451
Day Care and Extended Day Care Centers	3
Total Assisted	307
Specialized Homes	1
Total Assisted	280
Special Centers for Social Services	6
Total Assisted	37,790
Other Institutions	2
Total Assisted	760
Educational	
Diocesan Students in Other Seminaries	11
Total Seminarians	11
Colleges and Universities	1
Total Students	415
High Schools, Diocesan and Parish	1
Total Students	1,000
High Schools, Private	1
Total Students	190
Elementary Schools, Diocesan and Parish	13
Total Students	3,482
Elementary Schools, Private	2
Total Students	690
Catechesis/Religious Education:	
High School Students	1,520
Elementary Students	6,357
Total Students Under Catholic Instruction	13,665
Teachers in the Diocese:	
Priests	1
Sisters	49
Lay Teachers	404
Vital Statistics	
Receptions into the Church:	
Infant Baptism Totals	1,352
Adult Baptism Totals	229
Received into Full Communion	504
First Communions	1,436
Confirmations	1,116
Marriages:	
Catholic	182
Interfaith	240
Total Marriages	422
Deaths	394
Total Catholic Population	59,924
Total Population	1,782,729

Former Bishops—Rt. Rev. RICHARD PIUS MILES, O.P., D.D., cons. Sept. 16, 1838; died Feb. 21, 1860.—Rt. Rev. JAMES WHELAN, O.P., D.D., cons. May, 1859; resigned May, 1863; died Feb. 18, 1878.—Rt. Rev. P. A. FEEHAN, cons. Nov. 1, 1865; created first Archbishop of Chicago, Sept. 10, 1880; died July 12, 1902.—Rt. Rev. JOSEPH RADEMACHER, D.D., cons. June 24, 1883; transferred to Ft. Wayne, July 13, 1893; died Jan. 12, 1900.—Rt. Rev. THOMAS S. BYRNE, D.D., cons. July 25, 1894; died Sept. 4, 1923.—Most Rev. ALPHONSE J. SMITH, D.D., cons. March 25, 1924; died Dec. 16, 1935.—Most Rev. WILLIAM L. ADRIAN, D.D., cons. April 16, 1936; died Feb. 13, 1972.—Most Rev. JOSEPH A. DURICK, D.D., cons. March 24, 1955; retired April 8, 1975; died June 26, 1994.—Most Rev. JAMES D. NIEDERGESES, D.D., cons. May 20, 1975; retired Oct. 13, 1992.

Vicar General (Moderator of the Curia)—Rev. J. PATRICK CONNOR, *3019 Cayce Ln., Columbia, 38401.*

Vicar General—Rev. Msgr. GEORGE W. ROHLING, *237 Cana Cir., Nashville, 37205.*

Vicar General Emeritus—Rev. Msgr. CHARLES M. WILLIAMS, P.A., *100 James Blvd., Apt. 13, Signal Mountain, 37377.*

Deans—Central Deanery: Rev. W. BERNARD NIEDERGESES, Northeast Deanery: Rev. DAVID R. CHOBY, Northwest Deanery: Rev. CHARLEY GIACOSA, Southeast Deanery: Rev. JOHN L. KIRK, Southwest Deanery: Rev. RICHARD G. BUCHIGNANI.

Vicar for Education—Rev. J. PATRICK CONNOR, V.G.

Vicar for Catholic Charities—Rev. WILLIAM J. FLEMING.

Chancery Office—2400 21st Ave. S., Nashville, 37212. Tel: 615-383-6393; Fax: 615-292-8411. Office Hours: Mon.-Fri. 8:30-4:30 All Official business should be directed to this office.

Chancellor—ANN K. KRENSON.

Assistant Chancellors—BETTY L. SALZMAN; RAMONA F. STEJSKAL.

Stewardship Representative—WILLIAM J. DUNIGAN.

Accounting Systems—MICHAEL F. NOLAN, Chief Financial Officer; TERESA OSBORNE, Mgr., Central Accounting.

General Counsel—Rev. JAMES K. MALLETT.

Diocesan Tribunal—2400 21st Ave. S., Nashville, 37212. Tel: 615-383-6393; Fax: 615-292-8411.

Judicial Vicar—Rev. DEXTER S. BREWER, J.C.L.

Defenders of the Bond—Revs. JOHN C. HENRICK; JOSEPH A. SANCHES.

Advocates—Revs. EDWARD F. STEINER; ERIC FOWLKES; MARK R. FULLER; Mrs. PATRICIA BURNS; Mrs. JULIE CONNOLLY; Mrs. LINDA NELSON.

Judges—Revs. DEXTER S. BREWER; DAVID R. CHOBY; RICHARD G. BUCHIGNANI.

Assessors—Mrs. LINDA NELSON; Sr. MARY CARL WHITE, R.S.M.; Mrs. PATRICIA BURNS.

Formal Case Instructor—Mrs. JULIE CONNOLLY.

Documentary Case Instructor—Mrs. LINDA NELSON.

Auditors—All priests and deacons assigned in the Nashville and Knoxville dioceses.

Secretary-Notaries—Mrs. PATRICIA BURNS; Mrs. JULIE

CONNOLLY; Mrs. LINDA NELSON; Mrs. ANN H. KANENGIETER.

Presbyteral Council and College of Consultors—Most Rev. EDWARD U. KMIEC; Revs. MARK BECKMAN, Vice Chm. MICHAEL BIGLEY, S.D.S.; PHILIP M. BREEN; MATTHEW CHEERAMKUZHY, C.M.I.; DAVID R. CHOBY; J. PATRICK CONNOR, V.G.; MARK R. FULLER; WIATT A. FUNK; JOHN C. HENRICK, Chm.; PATRICK J. KIBBY; STEPHEN A. KLASEK.

The Diocesan Finance Board—Most Rev. EDWARD U. KMIEC; Mr. JOHN C. FOX, Chm.; Rev. Msgr. GEORGE W. ROHLING; Revs. J. PATRICK CONNOR; STEPHEN A. KLASEK; JAMES K. MALLETT; Mr. MICHAEL F. NOLAN; Mr. RICHARD D. TAYLOR; Mr. PAUL HEER; Mr. KEVIN MARCHETTI; Mr. STEVE FRIDRICH; Mr. WILLIAM J. DICKSON; Mr. L. GINO MARCHETTI; Mr. TOM CONNOR; Mr. J. TERRY HUNTER; Mr. RICHARD QUICK, Emeritus Member.

DIONASH—A Partnership acting as Nominee for marketable securities for the Diocese of Nashville.

Diocesan Offices and Directors

The following offices and agencies are located at the Chancery unless otherwise indicated

The Chancery—2400 21st Ave. S., Nashville, 37212. Tel: 615-383-6393; Fax: 615-292-8411.

Archives, Records and Catholic Center Management—ANN K. KRENSON.

Campaign for Human Development—Mr. WILLIAM P. SINCLAIR, Dir., *St. Mary Villa, 30 White Bridge Rd., Nashville, 37205.*

Campus Ministries—

Vanderbilt—Rev. JAMES F.X. PRATT, S.J., *Vanderbilt Catholic Community, Box 6311, Station B, Nashville, 37235.* Tel: 615-322-2457.

MTSU-Murfreesboro—Rev. WIATT A. FUNK, *St. Rose of Lima Church, 1601 N. Tennessee Blvd., Murfreesboro, 37130.* Tel: 615-893-1843.

Austin Peay-Clarksville—Rev. ERIC FOWLKES, *Immaculate Conception, 716 Franklin St., Clarksville, 37040.* Tel: 615-645-6275.

Tenn. Tech-Cookeville—Rev. MICHAEL BIGLEY, S.D.S., *St. Thomas Aquinas Church, 401 N. Washington Ave., Cookeville, 38501.* Tel: 615-565-2575.

Fisk-Meharry-Tennessee State University Campus Ministries—Rev. DERRAN COMBS, O.F.M., *St. Vincent de Paul Church, 1700 Heiman St., Nashville, 37208.* Tel: 615-320-0695.

Univ. of South-Sewanee—Rev. DEXTER S. BREWER, *Good Shepherd Church, 200 Tammy Dr., Decherd, 37324.* Tel: 615-967-0961.

Catholic Charismatic Renewal—Rev. JOHN KIRK, Bishop's Liaison; Mrs. TERESA SEIBERT, Assoc. Liaison.

Catholic Charities of Tennessee, Inc.—WILLIAM P. SINCLAIR, A.C.S.W., Dir., *St. Mary Villa, 30 White Bridge Rd., Nashville, 37205.* Tel: 615-352-3087; Fax: 615-352-8591.

Catholic Public Policy Commission of TN—JOSEPH SWEAT, Exec. Sec.

Catholic Social Services of Nashville—Ms. EILEEN BEEHAN, Dept. Dir., *St. Mary Villa, 30 White Bridge Rd., Nashville, 37205.* Tel: 615-352-3087.

Catholic Youth Office and Search Program—Rev. MARK BECKMAN, *2011 West End Ave., Nashville, 37203.* Tel: 615-327-0674.

Cemeteries—MICHAEL F. NOLAN, Dir.

Censor Librorum—Rev. JAMES K. MALLETT.

Clergy Benefit Foundation—Most Rev. EDWARD U. KMIEC, Pres.; Revs. CHARLEY GIACOSA; ERIC FOWLKES; JOHN SIMS BAKER; ALBERT SIENER; JAMES K. MALLETT; JOSEPH MCMAHON; EDWARD F. STEINER, Chm. J. PATRICK CONNOR; Mr. MICHAEL F. NOLAN.

Clergy Personnel Board—Most Rev. EDWARD U. KMIEC; Revs. WILLIAM J. FLEMING, Chm.; MICHAEL O. JOHNSTON; STEPHEN A. KLASEK; MARK BECKMAN.

Continuing Education of Clergy—Rev. MARK FULLER, Dir.

Cursillo—JAMES CORBY, Lay Dir.; Rev. MATTHEW CHEERAMKUZHY, C.M.I., Spiritual Advisor; Deacon MARTIN DESCHENES, Assoc. Spiritual Advisor.

Permanent Diaconate Office—Rev. MARK FULLER, Dir.

Diocesan Planning—Rev. STEPHEN A. KLASEK.

Ecumenical and Interreligious Relations—Deacon WILLIAM J. DICKSON.

Hispanic Ministry—Rev. RICHARD GAGNON, Dir., *30 White Bridge Rd., Nashville, 37205.* Tel: 615-356-2708.

Holy Childhood Association—Mr. STEPHEN J. HAMMOND, Dir.

Lay Retirement Administrative Board—ANN K. KRENSON; MICHAEL F. NOLAN; GLENN SEAGRAVES; JACK SMITHWICK, Chm. ROBERT TRUE.

Liturgical Life—Rev. PATRICK J. KIBBY, Dir.

Ministry Formation Services—Sr. ADRIAN MULLOY, R.S.M., Dir. Contact this office for the following concerns: Religious Education, Family Ministry, Youth Ministry, Pastoral Services, Liturgy, Parish Councils, Leadership Training, Lay Ministry, Rite of Christian Initiation of Adults, Pro-Life Education Evangelization, Peace & Justice.

Newspaper—*"The Tennessee Register"*, ANTHONY J. SPENCE, Editor.

Prison Ministry—TERRANCE HORGAN, Ph.D., Criminal Justice Advocacy.

Propagation of the Faith—ANN K. KRENSON, Dir.

Catholic Charities Refugee Resettlement Program—WILLIAM TOWLE, Dir., *10 S. 6th St., Nashville, 37206.* Tel: 615-259-3567; Fax: 615-259-2851.

Schools Office—STEPHEN J. HAMMOND, Supr.

Office of Stewardship and Development—ANDY GAERTNER, Dir.

Vocations—Rev. JOSEPH V. MCMAHON, Dir., *6401 Harding Rd., Nashville, 37205.* Tel: 615-352-2259.

CLERGY, PARISHES, MISSIONS AND PAROCHIAL SCHOOLS

CITY OF NASHVILLE
(Davidson County)

1—CATHEDRAL OF THE INCARNATION (1909), Revs. William J. Fleming; Patrick J. Kibby. In res., Most Rev. Edward U. Kmiec; Rev. James F.X. Pratt, S.J.
Res., 2001 West End Ave., 37203. Tel: 615-327-2330; Fax: 615-320-5650.
Catechesis/Religious Programs—Barbara Dodd, D.R.E.
Students 234.

2—ST. ANN (1921), Rev. Philip M. Breen.
Res., 5101 Charlotte Ave., 37209. Tel: 615-298-1782; Fax: 615-297-4326.
School—Tel: 615-269-0568. Betty Krogman, Prin.
Lay Teachers 14; Students 185.
Catechesis/Religious Programs—Martin Mulloy, D.R.E.
Students 55.

3—ASSUMPTION (1859). Attended by St. Pius X Church, Nashville. Rev. W. Bernard Niedergeses; Evelyn Kempson, Parish Coord.
Church—1227 Seventh Ave. N., 37208. Tel: 615-256-2729; Fax: 615-256-0987.

4—CHURCH OF CHRIST THE KING (1937), Rev. James K. Mallett.
Res., 3001 Belmont Blvd., 37212. Tel: 615-292-2884; Fax: 615-383-0026.
School—Tel: 615-292-9465. Mrs. Alice Valiquette, Prin.
Lay Teachers 17; Students 235.
Catechesis/Religious Programs—Christine Caron, D.R.E.
Students 66.

5—ST. EDWARD'S (1952), Rev. Joseph P. Breen.
Res., 188 Thompson Ln., 37211. Tel: 615-833-5520; Fax: 615-833-9739.
School—Tel: 615-833-5770. Therese S. Williams, Prin.
Lay Teachers 25; Students 455.
Catechesis/Religious Programs—Sr. Louise Shoulta, R.S.M., D.R.E.
Students 206.

6—ST. HENRY (1958), Revs. Michael O. Johnston; John Sims Baker; Deacons Jack Srouji; Martin Deschenes. In res., Rev. Joseph V. McMahon.
Res., 6401 Harding Rd., 37205. Tel: 615-352-2259; Fax: 615-356-6321.
School—Tel: 615-352-1328. Sr. John Mary Fleming, O.P., Prin.
Dominican Sisters of St. Cecilia Congregation 4; Lay Teachers 38; Students 645.
Catechesis/Religious Programs—Sr. Suzanne Stalm, R.S.M., D.R.E.
Students 264.

7—HOLY ROSARY (1954), Rev. Stephen A. Klasek; Deacons Jonathan P. Borgerding; Joseph Coen, Sr.; Gilbert P. Huhlein; Kenneth Steinbrecher.
Res., 190 Graylynn Dr., 37214. Tel: 615-889-4065; Fax: 615-885-5100.
School—Tel: 615-883-1108. Peggy Walker, Prin.
Lay Teachers 30; Students 564.
Catechesis/Religious Programs—Students 105.

8—ST. MARY VILLA PARISH COMMUNITY (1982), Rev. Msgr. George W. Rohling.
Church—30 White Bridge Rd., 37205.
Res., 237 Cana Cir., 37205. Tel: 615-352-3087.

9—ST. MARY'S OF THE SEVEN SORROWS (1838), Rev. James Norman Miller.
Mailing Address: P.O. Box 190606, 37219.
Res., 2823 Hazelwood Dr., #4, 37212.
Church—330 Fifth Ave. N., 37219. Tel: 615-256-1704; Fax: 615-256-7307.

10—CHURCH OF THE MOST HOLY NAME (1857), Rev. Joseph A. Sanches (ATL) Admin.
Res., 521 Woodland St., 37206. Tel: 615-254-8847; Fax: 615-254-1106.
Catechesis/Religious Programs—Mary Chabot, D.R.E.
Students 39.

11—ST. PATRICK'S (1891), Rev. Joseph A. Sanches (ATL) Admin.; Deacon William J. Dickson.
Res., 1219 2nd Ave. S., 37210. Tel: 615-256-6498.
Catechesis/Religious Programs—Gerald Farris, D.R.E.
Students 25.

12—ST. PIUS X (1958), Rev. W. Bernard Niedergeses.
Res., 2800 Tucker Rd., 37218. Tel: 615-244-4093; Fax: 615-256-0987.
School—Tel: 615-255-2049. Sr. Robert Ann Britton, O.P., Prin.
Dominican Sisters of St. Cecilia Congregation 5; Lay Teachers 11; Students 130.
Catechesis/Religious Programs—Allison Berhardt, D.R.E.
Students 10.

13—ST. VINCENT DE PAUL (1932), Revs. Fernand J. Cheri, O.F.M.; J. Derran Combs, O.F.M.
Res., 1700 Heiman St., 37208. Tel: 615-320-0695; Fax: 615-320-0698.
School—Tel: 615-320-1374. Dorothy A. Gupton, Prin.
Lay Teachers 17; Students 275.

OUTSIDE THE CITY OF NASHVILLE

Antioch, Davidson Co., St. Ignatius of Antioch (1976), Rev. John C. Henrick; Deacons Jack Nulty; P. J. Hoefler.
Res., 601 Bell Rd., 37013. Tel: 615-367-0085; Fax: 615-367-1712.
Catechesis/Religious Programs—Michael Baker, D.R.E.
Students 244.

Ashland City, Cheatham Co., St. Martha (1975), Rev. Peter Do Quang Chau.
Church—Bell St., P.O. Box 306, 37015. Tel: 615-792-4255.
Catechesis/Religious Programs—Carol Twork, D.R.E.
Students 60.

Brentwood, Williamson Co., Holy Family (1989), Rev. Edward T. Alberts.
Res., 9108 Demery Ct., 37027.
Church—9100 Crockett Rd., 37027. Tel: 615-373-4696; Fax: 615-377-3823.
Catechesis/Religious Programs—Patricia Gaines, D.R.E.
Students 907.

Centerville, Hickman Co., Christ the Redeemer (1983), Rev. John P. Baltz.
Mailing Address: Holy Trinity, 610 Kimmins St., Hohenwald, 38462.
Church—1515 Woodland Dr., 37033. Tel: 615-729-4669.

Clarksville, Montgomery Co., Immaculate Conception (1845), Revs. Eric L. Fowlkes; Wieslaw Burakowski (Poland).
Res., 716 Franklin St., 37040. Tel: 615-645-6275; Fax: 615-552-0331.
Catechesis/Religious Programs—Dominick Azzara, D.R.E.
Students 714.

Columbia, Maury Co., St. Catherine (1843), Rev. J. Patrick Connor.
Res., 5018 Hays Dr., 38401.
Church—3019 Cayce Ln., 38401. Tel: 615-388-3803; Fax: 615-381-8837.
Catechesis/Religious Programs—Candice Barton, D.R.E.
Students 377.

Cookeville, Putnam Co., St. Thomas Aquinas (1951), Revs. Peter Coffey, S.D.S.; Michael Bigley, S.D.S.
Res., 401 N. Washington Ave., 38501. Tel: 615-526-2575; Fax: 615-526-5869.
Catechesis/Religious Programs—Kay Herman, D.R.E.
Students 217.
Mission—Celina, Clay Co., Divine Savior.

Decherd, Franklin Co., Good Shepherd (1900), Rev. Dexter S. Brewer.
Res., 2021 Decherd Blvd., 37324. Tel: 615-967-0961; Fax: 615-967-3569.
School—2037 Dechard Blvd., Winchester, 37398. Tel: 615-967-5673. Michele Counts, Prin.
Lay Teachers 14; Students 156.
Catechesis/Religious Programs—Mary Jo Gallagher, D.R.E.
Students 90.
Mission—Alto, Franklin Co., St. Margaret Mary.

Dickson, Dickson Co., St. Christopher (1961), Rev. Charley Giacosa.
Res., 713 W. College St., 37055. Tel: 615-446-3927; Fax: 615-446-7339.
Catechesis/Religious Programs—Peggy Laws, D.R.E.

Students 175.

Dover, Stewart Co., St. Francis of Assisi (1982), Rev. Thomas Maurer, S.D.S.
Mailing Address: P.O. Box 307, 37058-0307.
Church—417 Spring St., Tel: 615-232-6982.
Catechesis/Religious Programs—Norma Smith, D.R.E.
Students 19.

Fayetteville, Lincoln Co., St. Anthony (1983), Rev. Thomas McElhinney, Glmy.
Res., 1900 Huntsville Hwy., 37334. Tel: 615-433-6525.
Catechesis/Religious Programs—Major Hamilton, D.R.E.
Students 68.

Franklin, Williamson Co., St. Matthew (1979), Rev. Luzerne A. Schnupp; Deacons Sam Francescon; Harold McBrayer; James Walsh; James Henry.
Res., 535 Sneed Rd., 37069. Tel: 615-646-0378; Fax: 615-646-5230.
Catechesis/Religious Programs—Sr. Thomasetta Mogan, R.S.M., D.R.E.
Students 227.

St. Philip (1843), Rev. Edward C. Arnold; Deacon Alphonse Toppeto (CHI).
Res., 113 2nd Ave. S., 37064. Tel: 615-794-4236.
Catechesis/Religious Programs—Kimberly Leisinger, D.R.E.
Students 804.

Gallatin, Sumner Co., St. John Vianney (1929), Rev. David R. Choby.
Res., 449 N. Water St., 37066. Tel: 615-452-2977; Fax: 615-452-0323.
Catechesis/Religious Programs—Students 115.

Hendersonville, Sumner Co., Our Lady of the Lake (1969), Rev. William S. Bevington; Sr. Maria Edwards, R.S.M., Pastoral Assoc.; Deacon Thomas E. Bomkamp.
Mailing Address: Box 279, 37077.
Church—New Shackle Island Rd., 37075. Tel: 615-824-3276; Fax: 615-824-7989.
Catechesis/Religious Programs—C. Edward Ryckeley, D.R.E.
Students 346.

Hohenwald, Lewis Co., Holy Trinity (1983), Rev. John P. Baltz.
Church—610 Kimmins St., 38462. Tel: 615-796-3738.
Catechesis/Religious Programs—Students 21.

Joelton, Davidson Co., St. Lawrence's (1885), Rev. Msgr. James R. Hitchcock.
Church—5655 Clarksville Hwy., 37080. Tel: 615-876-2127. [CEM]
Catechesis/Religious Programs—Students 41.

Lafayette, Macon Co., Holy Family (1982). Attended by St. Frances Cabrini, Lebanon. Rev. Mark Fuller.
Church—901 Vinson Rd., 37083. Tel: 615-666-6466.
Catechesis/Religious Programs—Students 14.

Lawrenceburg, Lawrence Co., Sacred Heart (1870), Rev. Richard G. Buchignani.
Res., 206 Berger St., P.O. Box 708, 38464. Tel: 615-762-3183; Fax: 615-762-5128. [CEM]
School—Tel: 615-762-6125. Sr. Mary Janice, R.S.M., Prin.
Catechesis/Religious Programs—Connie Hollman, D.R.E.
Students 41.
Convent—220 Berger St., Tel: 615-762-5207.
Sisters of Mercy 1; Lay Teachers 10; Students 134.

Lebanon, Wilson Co., St. Frances Cabrini (1953), Rev. Mark Fuller.
Res., 300 S. Tarver Ave., 37087. Tel: 615-444-0524; Fax: 615-444-3704.
Catechesis/Religious Programs—Dottie Climer, D.R.E.
Students 151.
Station—Smith & Trousdale counties.

Lewisburg, Marshall Co., St. John the Evangelist (1982). (Attended by St. William, Shelbyville). Rev. Zacharias Payikat, C.M.I.; Sr. Cathryn Kever, O.S.F., Pastoral Assoc.
Mailing Address: P.O. Box 1133, 37091.
Church—1031 S. Ellington, 37091. Tel: 615-359-5017.
Catechesis/Religious Programs—Lisa Jackson, D.R.E.
Students 79.

Loretto, Lawrence Co., Sacred Heart (1872), Rev. Matthew Cheeramkazhy, C.M.I.; Deacon Samuel Beckman.
Mailing Address: P.O. Box 86, 38469.
Res., 305 Church St., 38469. Tel: 615-853-4370; Fax: 615-853-4373. [CEM]
School—Tel: 615-853-4388. Mrs. Catherine N. Bradley, Prin.
Lay Teachers 6; Students 97.
Catechesis/Religious Programs—Students 32.

McEwen, Humphreys Co., St. Patrick (1855), Rev. Joseph Kevin Dowling.
Res., 123 St. Patrick St., 37101. Tel: 615-582-3417; Fax: 615-582-8851. [CEM]
School—Tel: 615-582-3493. Sr. Mary Aquinas, O.P., Prin.
Dominican Sisters of St. Cecilia Congregation 3; Lay Teachers 5; Students 76.
Station—Humphreys Co.

McMinnville, Warren Co., St. Catherine (1958), Rev. James J. Bretl, S.D.S.
Res., Faulkner Spring Rd., 37110. Tel: 615-473-4932; Fax: 615-473-0799.
Catechesis/Religious Programs—Judy Davis, D.R.E.
Students 86.
Station—Van Buren Co.

Madison, Davidson Co., St. Joseph's (1953), Revs. Edward F. Steiner, III; Mathai J. Thonikuzhiyil, C.M.I.
Res., 1225 Gallatin Rd. S., 37115. Tel: 615-865-1071; Fax: 615-868-4900.
School—Sr. Mary Charles, O.P., Prin. Dominican Sisters of St. Cecilia Congregation 4; Lay Teachers 25; Students 440.
Catechesis/Religious Programs—Rose M. Nicholson, D.R.E.
Students 150.

Murfreesboro, Rutherford Co., St. Rose of Lima (1929), Rev. Wiatt A. Funk.
Mailing Address: P.O. Box 4169, 37133-4169.
Res., 1601 N. Tennessee Blvd., 37130. Tel: 615-893-1843; Fax: 615-895-9787.
Catechesis/Religious Programs—Robert Carney, D.R.E.
Students 624.

Old Hickory, Wilson Co., St. Stephen (1952), Rev. David R. Perkin; Deacon James M. Batcheldor.
Res., 14544 Lebanon Rd., 37138. Tel: 615-758-2424; 754-4454; Fax: 615-754-0043.
Catechesis/Religious Programs—Donna Young, D.R.E.
Students 354.

Pulaski, Giles Co., Immaculate Conception (1941). Attended by St. Anthony, Fayetteville. Rev. Thomas McElhinney, Glmy. Parish Coordinators: Sr. Mary Gregory Berres, S.A.; Sr. Jean Tavin, S.A.
Mailing Address: Box 363, 38478.
Church—Elkton Hwy. South, Tel: 615-363-5776.
Catechesis/Religious Programs—Students 38.

Saint Joseph, Lawrence Co., St. Joseph (1872). Attended by Sacred Heart, Loretto. Rev. Matthew Cheeramkuzhy, C.M.I.
Mailing Address: P.O. Box 86, Loretto, 38469.
Church—American Rd., 38481.

Shelbyville, Bedford Co., St. William (1941), Rev. Zacharias Payikat, C.M.I.
Res., 731 N. Main St., 37160. Tel: 615-684-8745; Fax: 615-684-6154.
Catechesis/Religious Programs—Patricia Petty, D.R.E.
Students 75.

Smithville, DeKalb Co., St. Gregory (1982). Attended by St. Catherine, McMinnville. Rev. James J. Bretl, S.D.S.
Mailing Address: P.O. Box 712, 37166.
1024 Faulkner Spring Rd., McMinnville, 37110. Tel: 615-473-4932.
Catechesis/Religious Programs—Jan Trahan, D.R.E.
Students 24.

Smyrna, Rutherford Co., St. Luke (1982), Revs. Richard Gagnon, S.D.S.; Augustine Lucca, S.D.S. In res., Rev. Lorenzo Martinez (Mexico); Deacon Ken Levinson.
Res., 10682 Nashville Hwy., 37167. Tel: 615-459-9672; 459-3046; Fax: 615-459-3989.
Catechesis/Religious Programs—Denise M. Leaver, D.R.E.
Students 182.

Sparta, White Co., St. Andrew (1982). Attended by St. Thomas Aquinas, Cookeville. Revs. Peter Coffey, S.D.S.; Michael Bigley, S.D.S.
Mailing Address: 401 N. Washington Ave., Cookeville, 38501.
Church—Hwy. 111, 38583. Tel: 615-526-2575.
Catechesis/Religious Programs—Jim & Cindy Winton, D.R.E.
Students 21.

Springfield, Robertson Co., Our Lady of Lourdes (1946), Rev. Mark Beckman.
Res., 103 Golf Club Ln., 37172. Tel: 615-384-6200; Fax: 615-384-5837. [CEM]
Catechesis/Religious Programs—Jan Hennessy, D.R.E.
Students 110.
Mission—Cedar Hill, Robertson Co., St. Michael. [CEM]

Tennessee Ridge, Houston Co., St. Elizabeth Ann Seton (1982). Attended by St. Patrick, McEwen. Rev. Joseph Kevin Dowling. Pastoral Assocs: Sr. Marlene Huck, C.PP.S.; Sr. Darlene Huck, C.PP.S.
Res., Rte. 3, Box 161, Erin, 37061. Tel: 615-289-5401.
Mailing Address: P.O. Box 85, 37178.
Church—Hwy. 49.
Catechesis/Religious Programs—Students 20.

Tullahoma, Coffee Co., St. Paul the Apostle (1954), Rev. John L. Kirk.
Res., 304 W. Grizzard St., 37388. Tel: 615-455-3050; Fax: 615-455-8298.
School—Tel: 615-455-4221. Suzanne Miller, Prin.
Lay Teachers 11; Students 130.
Catechesis/Religious Programs—Lisa Anderson, D.R.E.
Students 120.
Station—Manchester, Coffee Co.

Waynesboro, Wayne Co., St. Cecilia (1982). Attended by Holy Trinity, Hohenwald. Rev. John P. Baltz.
Mailing Address: Holy Trinity Church, 610 Kimmins St., Hohenwald, 38462.
Church—526 Hwy. 64 E., 38485. Tel: 615-796-3738.
Catechesis/Religious Programs—Students 10.

Chaplains of Public Institutions

On Duty Outside the Diocese:
Reverend Fathers—
Campion, Owen F., Our Sunday Visitor, 200 Noll Plaza, Huntington, IN 46750
Flaherty, Jay M., Holy Cross Church, 144 Wears Valley Rd., Pigeon Forge, TN 37863
McMurry, John E., S.S., St. Mary's Spiritual Center, 600 N. Paca St., Baltimore, MD 21201-1995
McMurry, Vincent deP., S.S., St. Mary's Seminary, 5400 Roland Ave., Baltimore, MD 21210
Miller, Brendan, New Subiaco Abbey, Subiaco, AR 72865

Military Chaplains:
Reverend Fathers—
White, Alan, Chap., U.S.A.F.

Absent on Leave:
Reverend Fathers—
Ney, Charles N.
Stolowski, Stephen
Strobel, Charles
Wallace, Scott H.

Retired:
Reverend Monsignors—
Williams, Charles M., 100 James Blvd., Apt. 13, Signal Mountain, TN 37377
Reverend Fathers—
Ballentine, Edgar S., 702 Nichol St., Pulaski, TN 38478
Baltz, John P., Jr., 2146 Oakland St., Nashville, TN 37210
Briscoe, Orville, P.O. Box 3118, Murfreesboro, TN 37133
Cain, John N., 305 Davidson Rd., Nashville, TN 37205
Clements, Daniel A., 924 Rose Petal Ln., Knoxville, TN 37938
Julius, Joseph W., St. Francis of Assisi, 7715 River Rd., Townsend, TN 37882
Murray, James B., 25720 Hickory Blvd. S.W., Apt. 414-B, Bonita Springs, FL 33923
Nolan, William N, 6666 Brookmont Terr., Nashville, TN 37205
Rudisill, James A., 1500 Hampshire Pike, K-8, Columbia, TN 38401
Siener, Albert, 4505 Harding Rd., Condo No. 129, Nashville, TN 37205

Permanent Deacons:
Bainbridge, Frank, Prison Ministry, Nashville; St. Christopher, Dickson
Batcheldor, James M., Jr., St. Stephen, Old Hickory
Bauman, Frank, Unassigned
Beckman, Samuel C., Sacred Heart, Loretto
Bomkamp, Thomas E., Our Lady of the Lake, Hendersonville
Borgerding, Jonathan P., Holy Rosary, Nashville
Carroll, John B., (Retired)
Coen, Joseph, Sr., Holy Rosary, Nashville
Deschenes, Martin, St. Henry, Cursillo, Nashville
Dickson, William J., St. Patrick, Nashville; Diocesan Ecumenical Dir.
Francescon, Samuel A., St. Matthew, Franklin
Henry, James R., St. Matthew, Franklin
Hoefler, Paul J., St. Ignatius, Antioch
Hooper, Hugh C., (Retired)
Huhlein, Gilbert P., Holy Rosary, Nashville
Levinson, Ken, St. Luke, Smyrna
McBrayer, J. Harold, Jr., St. Matthew, Franklin
McBride, Gordon W., Sr., St. Joseph, Madison
McGinn, George P., Hospital Ministry, Nashville
Nulty, Jack, St. Ignatius, Antioch
Srouji, Jack, St. Henry, Nashville
Steinbrecher, Kenneth, Holy Rosary, Nashville

Steltemeier, William, Jr., Unassigned
Toppeto, Alphonse A. (CHI), St. Philip, Franklin
Von Mann, Milton, Prison Ministry, St. Edward, Nashville
Walsh, James F., Jr., St. Matthew, Franklin
Welsh, Theodore B., St. Joseph, Madison

INSTITUTIONS LOCATED IN THE DIOCESE

[A] COLLEGES

NASHVILLE. *Aquinas College*, 4210 Harding Rd., 37205. Tel: 615-297-7545.
For a complete listing, refer to the Colleges and Universities section.

[B] HIGH SCHOOLS, DIOCESAN

NASHVILLE. *Father Ryan Board of Trust*, Development & Alumni Office, 770 Norwood Dr., 37204. Tel: 615-269-7926.
Father Ryan High School (1925), 700 Norwood Dr., 37204. Tel: 615-383-4200; Fax: 615-383-9056. Corporate Title: Father Ryan High School, Inc. Mr. M. Edward Krenson, Prin.; Rev. Joseph McMahon, Assoc. Prin. Pastoral Affairs. Priests 1; Sisters 1; Lay Teachers 76; Students 1000.

[C] HIGH SCHOOLS, PRIVATE

NASHVILLE. *St. Cecilia Academy* (1860), Dominican Campus, 4210 Harding Rd., 37205. Tel: 615-298-4525; Fax: 615-297-9128. Legal Title: *St. Cecilia Academy*. Conducted by the St. Cecilia Congregation of Dominican Sisters. Sr. Mary Elizabeth, O.P., Prin. Sisters 8; Lay Teachers 20; Students 190.

[D] ELEMENTARY SCHOOLS, PRIVATE

NASHVILLE. *Overbrook School*, 4210 Harding Rd., 37205. Tel: 615-292-5134; Fax: 615-783-0560. The St. Cecilia Congregation of Dominican Sisters. Sr. Catherine Marie, O.P., Prin. Sisters 8; Lay Teachers 27; Students 360.
**St. Bernard Academy and After School Program*, 2020 24th Ave. S., 37212-4202. Tel: 615-385-0440; Fax: 615-783-0241. Legal Title: *Saint Bernard Academy Corporation*. Dr. Margaret Isabell, Dir. Sisters 5; Lay Teachers 21; Students 330.

[E] CHILD-CARING INSTITUTIONS

NASHVILLE. *St. Bernard After School Program*, 2020 24th Ave. S., 37212. Tel: 615-298-1298.
For a complete listing, refer to the Special Care Facilities section.
St. Mary Orphanage, Inc. dba St. Mary Villa, 30 White Bridge Rd., 37205.
For a complete listing, refer to the Special Care Facilities section.
St. Mary Villa Child Development Center, 30 White Bridge Rd., 37205. Tel: 615-356-6336.
For a complete listing, refer to the Special Care Facilities section.
**Villa Child Care, Inc.*, 30 White Bridge Rd., 37205. Tel: 615-356-6111.
For a complete listing, refer to the Special Care Facilities section.

[F] GENERAL HOSPITALS

NASHVILLE. *St. Thomas Hospital*, (1898) 4220 Harding Rd., 37205. Tel: 615-222-2111.
For a complete listing, refer to the Hospitals section.

[G] HOMES FOR THE AGED

NASHVILLE. *St. Mary Villa Retirement Community, Inc.*, 2400 21st Ave., 37212.
For a complete listing, refer to the Special Care Facilities section.
Villa Maria Manor, Inc. dba Villa Maria Manor, 32 White Bridge Rd., 37205. Tel: 615-352-3084.
For a complete listing, refer to the Special Care Facilities section.

[H] MONASTERIES AND RESIDENCES OF PRIESTS AND BROTHERS

NASHVILLE. *Dominican Friars*, 1608 Tynewood Dr., 37215. Tel: 615-665-0929. Revs. John I. Reardon, O.P.; Mark Geary, O.P.

[I] CONVENTS AND RESIDENCES FOR SISTERS

NASHVILLE. *Mercy Convent*, 2629 Pennington Bend Rd., 37214. Tel: 615-885-1863. Sr. Mary Judith Coode, R.S.M., Dir. Legal Title: *Sisters of Mercy of Nashville, TN, Inc.* Sisters 32.
St. Cecilia Convent, 801 Dominican Dr., 37228-1909. Tel: 615-256-5486. Motherhouse and Novitiate of St. Cecilia Congregation of Dominican Sisters. Mother Christine Born, O.P., Prioress Gen.; Sr. Anne Therese Moats, O.P., Prioress; Rev. Joseph Angers, O.P., Chap. Sisters in Residence 84; Novices 4; Postulants 9.

[J] CAMPS AND COMMUNITY CENTERS

FAIRVIEW. *Camp Marymount*, 1639 Fairview Blvd. E., 37062. Tel: 615-799-0410. Catholic summer camp for boys and girls. John Foreman, Dir.

[K] RENEWAL CENTERS

LIBERTY. *Carmelites of Mary Immaculate Center of Spirituality*, 610 Bluff Rd., 37095. Tel: 615-536-5177; Fax: 615-536-5499. P.O. Box 117, 37095. Rev. Matthew Cheeramkuzhy, C.M.I., Dir.

[L] MISCELLANEOUS

NASHVILLE. *Catholic Foundation of Tennessee, Inc.*, 2400 21st Ave. S., 37212.
**Catholic Media Productions*, 700 Harpeth Knoll Ct., 37221. James F. Walsh, Jr., Pres.
Diocesan Council of Catholic Women, 2400 21st Ave. S., 37212. Rev. Richard G. Buchignani, Dir.
Diocesan Properties, Inc. dba Marina Manor East Apartments, 2400 21st Ave. S., 37212. Tel: 615-383-6393. Michael F. Nolan, Sec./Treas.
**Dismas, Inc.*, 30 White Bridge Rd., 37205. Tel: 615-352-6807. John Deckop, Ph.D., Pres.; Terrence Horgan, Ph.D., Exec. Dir. Homes in which former prisoners and college students live.
Glenmary Department of Pastoral Services, 1312 5th Ave. N., 37208. Tel: 615-256-1900. A national center serving parishes and other ministries staffed by Glenmary Home Missioners. Rev. Dennis Leo Holly, Dir. Pastoral Svcs.; Bro. William D. Wright.
Glenmary Co-Missioners, 1312 5th Ave. N., 37208. Tel: 615-248-6325. A Lay Missionary Association working in the rural South among struggling communities. Muzaffar Fazaluddin, Coord.
Glenmary Personnel Office, 1312 5th Ave. N., 37208. Tel: 615-259-1235. Resource for Glenmary Member's Personnel. Rev. Robert Hare, Personnel Dir.
Establishing Mission Churches with Lay Leaders, 1312 5th Ave. N., 37208. Tel: 615-256-4384. A project for establishing new missions with lay persons. Rev. Frank Ruff, Dir.
Haitian Office, 2400 21st Ave. S., 37212. Mr. Harry Hosey, Diocesan Dir.
Holy Name Loaves and Fishes Community Meal, 521 Woodland St., 37206.
Ladies of Charity Center, Inc., 2216 State St., 37203. Tel: 615-327-3453; 327-3430. Affiliated with the Ladies of Charity of the United States of America, LCUSA, and the Association of International Charities, AIC.
Ladies of Charity Welfare Agency, Inc., 2212 State St., 37203. Tel: 615-327-3430. Mrs. Terri Puma, Exec. Dir.; Rev. Msgr. George W. Rohling, V.G., Moderator.
Mid-Tennessee Rural Outreach Association, 30 White Bridge Rd., 37205. Tel: 615-352-3087.
Catholic Social Services - Clarksville Branch, 709 Franklin St., 37040. Tel: 615-645-9793. Legal Title: *Mid-Tennessee Rural Outreach Association; Assumption-St. Vincent North Nashville Outreach Association.*
St. Patrick Ecumenical Shelter for the Homeless, 30 White Bridge Rd., 37205.
**St. Henry Property Development, Inc. dba The Cloister*, 30 White Bridge Rd., 37205.
HENDERSONVILLE. *Legion of Mary*, P.O. Box 279, 37077-0279. Rev. William S. Bevington, Dir.
Priests Eucharistic League, P.O. Box 279, 37077-0279. Rev. William S. Bevington, Dir.

RELIGIOUS INSTITUTES OF MEN REPRESENTED IN THE DIOCESE

For further details refer to the corresponding bracketed number in the Religious Institutes of Men or Women section.
[0275]—*Carmelites of Mary Immaculate*.—C.M.I.
[0520]—*Franciscan Friars*. (Prov. of Sacred Heart).—O.F.M.
[0570]—*Glenmary Home Missioners*.—Glmy.
[0690]—Jesuit Fathers and Brothers.—S.J.
[0430]—*Order of Preachers-Dominicans*. (Southern Prov.).—O.P.
[1200]—*Society of the Divine Savior*. (Milwaukee, WI).—S.D.S.

RELIGIOUS INSTITUTES OF WOMEN REPRESENTED IN THE DIOCESE

[0760]—*Daughters of Charity of St. Vincent de Paul*. (East Central Prov., Evansville, IN).—D.C.
[1070-03]—*Dominican Sisters*.—O.P.
[1070-07]—*Dominican Sisters*.—O.P.
[1070-09]—*Dominican Sisters*.—O.P.
[1070-13]—*Dominican Sisters*.—O.P.
[1190]—*Franciscan Sisters of the Atonement*.—S.A.
[2370]—*Institute of the Blessed Virgin Mary (Loretto Sisters)*.—I.B.V.M.
[2575]—*Institute of the Sisters of Mercy of the Americas*. (Baltimore, MD; Cincinnati, OH).—R.S.M.
[1680]—*School Sisters of St. Francis*.—S.S.S.F. - O.S.F.
[0440]—*Sisters of Charity of Cincinnati, Ohio*.—S.C.
[0570]—*Sisters of Charity of Seton Hill, Greensburg, Pennsylvania*.—S.C.
[0990]—*Sisters of Divine Providence*. (St. Louis Prov.).—C.D.P.
[3840]—*Sisters of St. Joseph of Carondolet*.—C.S.J.
[1970]—*Sisters of the Holy Family of Nazareth*.—C.S.F.N.
[3270]—*Sisters of the Most Precious Blood*.—C.PP.S.

DIOCESAN CEMETERIES

NASHVILLE. *Calvary Cemetery*, 1001 Lebanon Rd., 37210.

NECROLOGY

(No Deaths)

Archdiocese of Newark

(Archidioecesis Novarcensis)

Most Reverend

PETER LEO GERETY, D.D.

Archbishop Emeritus of Newark; ordained June 29, 1939; appointed Coadjutor Bishop of Portland March 4, 1966; Episcopal ordination June 1, 1966; appointed Apostolic Administrator February 18, 1967; succeeded to See September 15, 1969; appointed Archbishop of Newark April 2, 1974; installed June 28, 1974; Pallium conferred December 12, 1974; retired June 1, 1986. *Res., 60 Home Ave., Rutherford, NJ, 07070.* Tel.: 201-460-1369; Fax: 201-842-0724.

Most Reverend

ROBERT F. GARNER, D.D.

Retired Auxiliary Bishop of Newark; ordained June 15, 1946; appointed Titular Bishop of Blera and Auxiliary Bishop of Newark May 3, 1976; Episcopal ordination June 25, 1976; retired August 1, 1995. *Res., 311 Prospect St., Midland Park, NJ, 07432.* Tel.: 201-652-3240; Fax: 201-652-2669.

Most Reverend

JOSEPH A. FRANCIS, S.V.D., D.D.

Retired Auxiliary Bishop of Newark; ordained October 7, 1950; appointed Titular Bishop of Vallipostia and Auxiliary Bishop of Newark May 3, 1976; Episcopal ordination June 25, 1976; retired August 1, 1995. *Res., Claridge House II, 2 Claridge Dr., Apt. 1FW, Verona, NJ, 07044.* Tel.: 201-239-6851; Fax: 201-239-6751.

Most Reverend

NICHOLAS A. DiMARZIO, PH.D., D.D.

Auxiliary Bishop of Newark; ordained May 30, 1970; appointed Titular Bishop of Mauriana and Auxiliary Bishop of Newark September 10, 1996; Episcopal ordination October 31, 1996. *Res., Our Lady of Mt. Carmel Rectory, 259 Oliver St., Newark, NJ, 07105.* Tel.: 201-589-2090; Fax: 201-589-2662. *Mailing Address: 1160 Raymond Blvd., Newark, NJ, 07105.*

Most Reverend

THEODORE E. McCARRICK, PH.D., D.D.

Archbishop of Newark; ordained May 31, 1958; appointed Auxiliary Bishop of New York and Titular Bishop of Rusibisir May 24, 1977; Episcopal ordination June 29, 1977; appointed First Bishop of Metuchen November 19, 1981; installed January 31, 1982; appointed Archbishop of Newark May 30, 1986; Pallium conferred June 29, 1986; installed July 25, 1986. *Office: 171 Clifton Ave., P.O. Box 9500, Newark, NJ, 07104-9500.* Tel.: 201-497-4011; Fax: 201-497-4018 (Office); 482-4793 (Cathedral).

Archdiocesan Center: 171 Clifton Ave., P.O. Box 9500, Newark, NJ, 07104-9500. Tel.: 201-497-4000; Fax: 201-497-4033.

Most Reverend

DOMINIC A. MARCONI, D.D.

Auxiliary Bishop of Newark; ordained May 30, 1953; appointed Titular Bishop of Bure and Auxiliary Bishop of Newark May 3, 1976; Episcopal ordination June 25, 1976. *Res., 238 E. Blancke St., Linden, NJ, 07036.* Tel.: 908-486-1022; Fax: 908-486-7701.

Most Reverend

DAVID ARIAS, O.A.R., D.D.

Auxiliary Bishop of Newark; ordained May 31, 1952; appointed Titular Bishop of Badie and Auxiliary Bishop of Newark January 25, 1983; Episcopal ordination April 7, 1983. *Res., St. Joseph of the Palisades Rectory, 6401 Palisade Ave., West New York, NJ, 07093.* Tel.: 201-861-6644; Fax: 201-861-7799.

Most Reverend

CHARLES J. McDONNELL, D.D.

Auxiliary Bishop of Newark; ordained May 29, 1954; appointed Titular Bishop of Pocofelto and Auxiliary Bishop of Newark March 15, 1994; Episcopal ordination May 12, 1994. *Res., Our Lady of Sorrows Rectory, 217 Prospect St., South Orange, NJ, 07079.* Tel.: 201-763-5454; Fax: 201-763-9506.

DIOCESE ESTABLISHED, 1853; ERECTED AN ARCHDIOCESE, DECEMBER 10, 1937.

Square Miles 513.

Comprises Four Counties in the State of New Jersey, viz.: Bergen, Hudson, Essex and Union.

For legal titles of parishes and archdiocesan institutions, consult the Chancery Office.

STATISTICAL OVERVIEW

Personnel	
Archbishop	1
Retired Archbishops	1
Auxiliary Bishops	4
Retired Bishops	2
Abbots	1
Priests: Diocesan Active in Diocese	597
Priests: Active Outside Diocese	38
Priests: Retired, Sick or Absent	192
Number of Diocesan Priests	827
Religious Priests in Diocese	250
Extern Priests in Diocese	70
Ordinations:	
Diocesan Priests	15
Religious Priests	2
Transitional Deacons	14
Permanent Deacons in Diocese	225
Total Brothers	124
Total Sisters	1,757
Parishes	
Parishes	238
With Resident Pastor:	
Resident Diocesan Priests	205
Resident Religious Priests	33
Without Resident Pastor:	
Missions	2
Pastoral Centers	172
Professional Ministry Personnel:	
Brothers	15
Sisters	152
Lay Ministers	226
Welfare	
Catholic Hospitals	8
Total Assisted	876,107
Health Care Centers	86
Total Assisted	24,970
Homes for the Aged	7
Total Assisted	500
Day Care and Extended Day Care Centers	126
Total Assisted	3,000
Specialized Homes	4
Total Assisted	163
Special Centers for Social Services	235
Total Assisted	142,797
Residential Care of Disabled	2
Total Assisted	40
Other Institutions	7
Total Assisted	13,855
Educational	
Seminaries, Diocesan	3
Students from This Diocese	97
Students from Other Diocese	24
Diocesan Students in Other Seminaries	4
Seminaries, Religious	1
Students Religious	17
Total Seminarians	118
Colleges and Universities	4
Total Students	16,252
High Schools, Diocesan and Parish	18
Total Students	8,573
High Schools, Private	19
Total Students	7,371
Elementary Schools, Diocesan and Parish	142
Total Students	43,992
Elementary Schools, Private	6
Total Students	1,517
Non-residential Schools for the Disabled	4
Total Students	193
Catechesis/Religious Education:	
High School Students	4,984
Elementary Students	45,271
Total Students Under Catholic Instruction	128,271
Teachers in the Diocese:	
Priests	138
Brothers	49
Sisters	377
Lay Teachers	3,574
Vital Statistics	
Receptions into the Church:	
Infant Baptism Totals	17,656
Adult Baptism Totals	482
Received into Full Communion	753
First Communions	13,902
Confirmations	10,925
Marriages:	
Catholic	4,655
Interfaith	870
Total Marriages	5,525
Deaths	12,437
Total Catholic Population	1,346,185
Total Population	2,656,348

Former Bishops—Most Rev. JAMES ROOSEVELT BAYLEY, D.D., cons. Oct. 30, 1853; promoted to the Archiepiscopal See of Baltimore, July 30, 1872; died Oct. 3, 1877.—Most Rev. MICHAEL AUGUSTINE CORRIGAN, D.D., cons. May 4, 1873; promoted to the Archiepiscopal See of Petra, Oct. 1, 1880; succeeded to the Archiepiscopal See of New York, Oct. 10, 1885; died May 5, 1902.—Most Rev. WINAND MICHAEL WIGGER, D.D., cons. Oct. 18, 1881; died Jan. 5, 1901.—Most

Rev. JOHN JOSEPH O'CONNOR, D.D., ord. Dec. 22, 1877; cons. July 25, 1901; died May 20, 1927.—Most Rev. THOMAS J. WALSH, S.T.D., J.C.D., ord. Jan. 27, 1900; appt. Bishop of Trenton, May 10, 1918; cons. July 25, 1918 made Assistant at the Pontifical Throne March 13, 1922; transferred to the See of Newark, March 2, 1928; appt. Archbishop of Newark, Dec. 10, 1937 Pallium conferred, Dec. 18, 1937; installed April 27, 1938; died June 6, 1952.—Most Rev. THOMAS A. BOLAND, S.T.D., LL.D., ord. Dec. 23, 1922; appt. Titular Bishop of Hirina and Auxiliary to the Archbishop of Newark, May 21, 1940; cons. July 25, 1940; transferred to Paterson, June 21, 1947; appt. Archbishop of Newark, Nov. 15, 1952; installed Jan. 14, 1953 Assistant at the Pontifical Throne, May 6, 1965; retired April 2, 1974; died March 16, 1979.—Most Rev. PETER LEO GERETY, D.D., ord. June 29, 1939; appt. Coadjutor Bishop of Portland, March 4, 1966; cons. June 1, 1966; succeeded to See, Sept. 15, 1969; appt. Archbishop of Newark, April 2, 1974; installed June 28, 1974; retired June 1, 1986.

Chancery—Archdiocesan Center, 171 Clifton Ave., P.O. Box 9500, Newark, 07104-9500. Tel: 201-497-4000; Fax: 201-497-4033. Open Mon.-Fri. 8:45-4:45. (Dispensation Requests or Questions regarding Canonical Matters can be directed to: Rev. Msgr. Frank G. Del Prete, J.C.D., Judical Vicar, at P.O. Box 9500, Newark, NJ 07104-9500. Tel: 201-497-4145; Fax 201-497-4138.).

Vicar General and Moderator of Curia—Rev. Msgr. RONALD J. ROZNIAK, V.G. Tel: 201-497-4002; Fax: 201-497-4018.

Vicar General for the Apostolates—Rev. Msgr. JOSEPH T. SLINGER, Ph.D. V.G. Tel: 201-497-4318; Fax: 201-497-4249.

Chancellor/Delegate for Religious—Sr. THOMAS MARY SALERNO, S.C., M.A. Tel: 201-497-4010; Fax: 201-497-4018.

Vice Chancellor for Archdiocesan Archives—Rev. Msgr. FRANCIS R. SEYMOUR. Tel: 201-497-4012; Fax: 201-497-4018.

Secretaries to the Archbishop—Revs. ROBERT G. TEMPLETON; THOMAS P. NYDEGGER. Tel: 201-497-4005; 4006; Fax: 201-497-4018.

Secretrary to the Archbishop for Development—Rev. Msgr. GEORGE R. TRABOLD. Tel: 201-497-4134; Fax: 201-497-4031.

Judicial Vicar Archdiocesan Metropolitan Tribunal—Rev. Msgr. FRANK G. DELPRETE, J.C.D. Tel: 201-497-4145; Fax: 201-497-4138.

Judicial Vicar, Interdiocesan Tribunal of Second Instance, Provice of Newark—Rev. Msgr. VINCENT J. DOYLE, J.C.D. Tel: 201-497-4145; Fax: 201-497-4138.

Vicar for Priests—Rev. Msgr. PAUL G. BOOTKOSKI, *St. Gabriel the Archangel, 88 E. Saddle River Rd., Saddle River, 07458.* Tel: 201-327-5663; Fax: 201-327-7063.

Vicar for Permanent Deacons—Rev. Msgr. THOMAS M. O'LEARY, *700 Wyckoff Ave., Wyckoff, 07481.* Tel: 201-891-1122; Fax: 201-847-8518.

Director of Vocations—Rev. JAMES S. CHOMA. Tel: 201-497-4365; Fax: 201-497-4369.

Secretary for Education—Sr. DOMINICA ROCCHIO, S.C., Ed.D. Tel: 201-497-4250; Fax: 201-497-4249.

Vicar for Evangelization—Rev. Msgr. WILLIAM J. KOPLIK. Tel: 201-497-4360; Fax: 201-497-4033.

Vicar for Pastoral Life—Rev. Msgr. LOUIS F. FIMIANI. Tel: 201-497-4322; Fax: 201-497-4317.

Vicar for Human Services—Most Rev. NICHOLAS A. DIMARZIO, D.D. Tel: 201-596-4050; Fax: 201-596-3807.

Secretary for Temporal Admin.—Mr. JOSEPH C. NEHILA. Tel: 201-497-4051; Fax: 201-497-4033.

Regional Bishops—Most Rev. CHARLES J. MCDONNELL, D.D., Regional Bishop - Bergen Co.; Most Rev. NICHOLAS A. DIMARZIO, D.D., Regional Bishop - Essex Co.; Most Rev. DAVID ARIAS, O.A.R., D.D., Regional Bishop, Hudson Co./Vicar, Hispanic Affairs; Most Rev. DOMINIC A. MARCONI, D.D., Regional Bishop, Union Co.

Episcopal Vicars—

Bergen County—Northwest (Deaneries 1, 4): Rev. Msgr. THOMAS DONATO, V.E., *St. Paul, 200 Wyckoff Ave., Ramsey, 07446.* Tel: 201-327-0976. South Bergen (Deaneries 5, 7): Rev. Msgr. THOMAS G. MADDEN, V.E., *Queen of Peace, 10 Franklin Pl., N. Arlington, 07031.* Tel: 201-997-0700. East Bergen (Deaneries 2, 3, 6): Very Rev. JOSEPH O'BRIEN, O.Carm., V.E., *St. Cecilia, 55 Demarest Ave., Englewood, 07631.* Tel: 201-568-0364.

Hudson County—North Hudson (Deaneries 8, 9, 14): Rev. Msgr. MICHAEL J. DESMOND, V.E., *St. Stephen, 141 Washington Ave., Kearney, 07032.* Tel: 201-998-3314. South Hudson (Deaneries 10-13): Rev. Msgr. JAMES J. FINNERTY, V.E., *St. Mary, 219 Third St., Jersey City, 07302.* Tel: 201-653-2217.

Essex County—West Essex (Deaneries 15-18): Rev. Msgr. CHARLES W. GUSMER, V.E., *St. Catherine of Siena, 339 Pompton Ave., Cedar Grove, 07009.* Tel: 201-239-7960. City of Newark: Very Rev. LUKE EDELEN, O.S.B., V.E., *Newark Abbey, 528 Martin Luther King Blvd., Newark, 07102.* Tel: 201-643-4800.

Deans—

BERGEN COUNTY—Northwest Bergen Region Deanery 1: Rev. Msgr. OWEN J. HENDRY, V.F., *Blessed Sacrament Rectory, 787 Franklin Lake Rd., Franklin Lakes, 07417.* Tel: 201-891-4200. Northeast Bergen Region Deanery 2: Rev. Msgr. PHILIP D. MORRIS, V.F., *St. John the Baptist, 69 Valley St., P.O. Box 308, Hillsdale, 07642.* Tel: 201-664-3131. Central Bergen Region Deanery 3: Very Rev. DONALD P. SHEEHAN, V.F., *St. Mary Rectory, 280 Washington Ave., Dumont, 07628.* Tel: 201-384-0557. Southwest Bergen Region Deanery 4: Very Rev. PAUL L. BOCHICCHIO, V.F., *Our Lady of Mt. Virgin Rectory, 188 MacArthur Ave., Garfield, 07026.* Tel: 201-772-2295. South Central Bergen Deanery 5: Very Rev. JOSEPH C. DOYLE, V.F., *St. Francis Rectory, 114 Mt. Vernon St., Ridgefield Park, 07660.* Tel: 201-641-6464. Southeast Bergen Region Deanery 6: Very Rev. GERALD F. GREAVES, V.F., *Holy Rosary Rectory, 365 Undercliff Ave., Edgewater, 07020.* Tel: 201-945-0135. South Bergen Region Deanery 7: Very Rev. CHARLES J. MILLER, V.F., *Sacred Heart Rectory, 324 Ridge Rd., Lyndhurst, 07071.* Tel: 201-438-2200.

HUDSON COUNTY—North Hudson Deanery 8: Very Rev. ANTHONY G. ROBAK, V.F., *Sacred Heart, 246 Hudson Pl., Cliffside Park, 07010.* Tel: 201-943-0305. Central Hudson Region Deanery 9: Very Rev. ROBERT C. CHABAK, V.F., *Sts. Peter and Paul Rectory, 404 Hudson St., Hoboken, 07030.* Tel: 201-659-2276. Jersey City North Region Deanery 10: Very Rev. VICTOR P. KENNEDY, V.F., *St. Anne Rectory, 3545 Kennedy Blvd., Jersry City, 07037.* Tel: 201-656-2490. Jersey City Downtown Deanery 11: Very Rev. GREGORY J. STUDERUS, V.F., *St. Bridget Rectory, 372 Montgomery St., Jersey City, 07302.* Tel: 201-434-8500. Jersey City South Deanery 12: Very Rev. JOHN J. CRYAN, V.F., *Our Lady of Mercy Rectory, 40 Sullivan Dr., Jersey City, 07305.* Tel: 201-434-7500. Bayonne Deanery 13: Rev. Msgr. EDWARD J. HAJDUK, V.F., *St. Henry Rectory, 82 W. 29th St., Bayonne, 07002.* Tel: 201-436-0857. West Hudson Region Deanery 14: Very Rev. NORBERT T. LASKOWSKI, V.F., *St. Cecilia Rectory, 120 Kearny Ave., Kearny, 07032.* Tel: 201-991-1116.

ESSEX COUNTY—West Essex Deanery 15: Rev. Msgr. DONALD E. GUENTHER, V.F., *St. Joseph Rectory, 44 Benvenue Ave., West Orange, 07052.* Tel: 201-669-3221. North Essex Deanery 16: Very Rev. DENNIS COCOZZA, V.F., *St. Anthony Rectory, 750 N. 7th St., Newark, 07107.* Tel: 201-481-1991. Central Essex Deanery 17: Very Rev. THOMAS P. LIPNICKI, V.F., *Holy Spirit/Help of Christians, 17 N. Clinton St., E. Orange, 07017.* Tel: 201-673-1077. South Essex Deanery 18: Very Rev. RICHARD J. KELLY, V.F., *Our Lady of Sorrows Rectory, 217 Prospect St., South Orange, 07079.* Tel: 201-763-5454. North Newark Essex Deanery 19: Very Rev. ANTHONY J. LIONELLI, V.F., *Immaculate Conception Rectory, 390 Woodside Ave., Newark, 07104.* Tel: 201-482-0619. Central Newark Deanery 20: Very Rev. PAUL D. SCHETELICK, V.F., *Blessed Sacrament, 15 Van Ness Pl., Newark, 07108.* Tel: 201-824-6548. Ironbound Deanery 21: Very Rev. MATTHIAS T. CONVA, V.F., *St. Benedict Rectory, 65 Barbara St., Newark, 07105.* Tel: 201-589-7930.

UNION COUNTY—Union Northwest Deanery 22: Very Rev. ROBERT B. STAGG V.F., *St. James Rectory, 45 S. Springfield Ave., Springfield, 07081.* Tel: 201-376-3044. Union North Deanery 23: Very Rev. JOSPEH S. BEJGROWICZ, V.F., *St. Theresa Rectory, 541 Washington Ave., Kenilworth, 07033.* Tel: 908-272-4444. Union County Southeast Deanery 24: Rev. KARL J. ROESCH, O.S.B., *St. Elizabeth of Hungary, 179 Hussa St., Linden, 07036.* Tel: 908-486-2514. Elizabeth Deanery 25: Very Rev. ROBERT J. HARRINGTON, V.F., *St.Mary of the Assumption Rectory, 155 Washington St., Elizabeth, 07202.* Tel: 908-352-5154. Union County Southwest Deanery 26: Very Rev. JOHN F. KENNEDY, V.F., *Immaculate Heart of Mary Rectory, 1571 S. Martine Ave., Scotch Plains, 07076.* Tel: 908-889-2100.

Advisory Bodies

College of Consultors—Most Rev. THEODORE E. MCCARRICK, Pres.; Rev. Msgr. WILLIAM C. HATCHER, Sec.; Most Rev. DAVID ARIAS, O.A.R.; Most Rev. NICHOLAS A. DIMARZIO; Most Rev. DOMINIC A. MARCONI; Most Rev. CHARLES J. MCDONNELL; Rev. Msgr. EDWARD J. CIUBA; Rev. Msgr. RICHARD J. ARNHOLS; Rev. Msgr. PETER S. CHEPLIC; Rev. Msgr. EDWARD J. EILERT; Rev. Msgr. OWEN J. HENDRY; Rev. Msgr. JOHN GILCHRIST; Rev. Msgr. THOMAS P. IVORY.

Presbyteral Council—Most Rev. THEODORE E. MCCARRICK, Pres.; Rev. Msgr. EDWARD CIUBA, Exec. Sec. Members: Most Rev. DAVID ARIAS; Most Rev. DOMINIC A. MARCONI; Most Rev. CHARLES J. MCDONNELL; Most Rev. NICHOLAS A. DIMARZIO; Rev. Msgr. RICHARD J. ARNHOLS; Rev. Msgr. PETER S. CHEPLIC; Rev. Msgr. JOHN GILCHRIST; Rev. Msgr. OWEN J. HENDRY; Rev. Msgr. THOMAS IVORY; Rev. Msgr. EDWARD KAVIN; Rev. Msgr. PHILIP MORRIS; Rev. Msgr. RAYMOND POLLARD; Revs. ROBERT ANTCZAK; MIGUEL ARATA; LOUIS CAPUTO, S.D.V.; ROBERT CHABAK; GEORGE GILLEN; EUGENE KOCH; GERARD H. MCCARREN; MICHAEL MERLUCCI; ANTHONY RANDAZZO; WILLIAM C. REED; TIMOTHY SHUGRUE.

Priest Personnel Policy Board—Rev. Msgr. JAMES T. BOUFFARD; Rev. Msgr. THOMAS M. O'LEARY; Rev. Msgr. EDWARD G. PRICE; Revs. ROBERT B. STAGG; JOSEPH P. MASIELLO, Archbishop's Delegate; FRANK J. MCNULTY; MICHAEL A. HANLY.

Conference of Permanent Deacons—Deacons ROBERT V. THOMANN, Chm. CHARLES F. KILEY, Vice Chm. Tel: 201-497-4223.

Priestly Vocation Board—Most Rev. ROBERT F. GARNER; Rev. Msgr. ROBERT FUHRMAN; Rev. Msgr. THOMAS MADDEN; Rev. Msgr. MICHAEL DESMOND, V.E.; Revs. JOSEPH BEJGROWICZ; THOMAS M. CEMBOR; Rev. Msgr. THOMAS O'LEARY; Revs. JORGE CHACON; ROBERT EMERY; C. ANTHONY ZICCARDI; Rev. Msgr. WILLIAM DALY.

Women & Men Religious Council—

Chairman—Sr. THOMAS MARY SALERNO, S.C., Chancellor/Delegate for Religious. Members: Sr. ALMA BLUME, M.P.F.; Sr. ELIZABETH CAHILL, S.C.; Sr. MARY FEEHAN, O.S.B.; Rev. ASHLEY HARRINGTON, O. Carm.; Sr. ELAINE KEENAN, O.P.; Rev. EDWIN LEAHY, O.S.B.; Sr. MARILYN MINTER, C.S.F.; Bros. STEPHEN OKERT, F.S.C.; MICHAEL STECHMANN, O.A.R.

Archdiocesan Finance Council—RICHARD J. BOYLE; CHARLES C. CARELLA; LAWRENCE R. CODEY; JOHN W. CULLIGAN; DONALD M. DANIELS; ADRIAN M. FOLEY, JR.; ALBERT R. GAMPER, JR.; ANNE EVANS ESTABROOK; LESLIE A. HYNES; ARTHUR E. IMPERATORE; MILTON F. LEWIS; BRIAN D. MCAULEY; W. PETER MCBRIDE; JOSEPH L. MUSCARELLE, JR.; FRANK A. OLSON; ARTHUR RYAN; EDWARD F. RYAN; GARRY J. SCHEURING; ANTHONY P. TERRACCIANO; JOSEPH A. UNANUE.

Medical-Moral Committee—Rev. Msgr. HAROLD P. DARCY, S.T.L., J.C.D., Chm. Tel: 201-642-8859.

Archdiocesan Pastoral Council—KENNETH KELLY, Chm. MARY PAT BOGART, Vice Chm. CATHERINE JACKSON, Sec.; Sr. VIRGINIA STANTON, S.S.J., Staff. Tel: 201-497-4350.

Archdiocesan Commission for Christain Unity—Rev. Msgr. PHILIP D. MORRIS, S.T.D., Chm.; Rev. PHILIP F.A. LATRONICO, Exec. Sec., *69 Valley St., P.O. Box 308, Hillsdale, 07642.* Tel: 201-497-4338.

Archdiocesan Commission for Interreligious Affairs—Rev. Msgr. JOHN GILCHRIST, Chm.; Rev. PHILIP F.A. LATRONICO, Exec. Sec. Tel: 201-497-4338.

Metropolitan Tribunal of the Archdiocese of Newark

Archdiocesan Center, 171 Clifton Ave., Newark, 07104. Tel: 201-497-4145; Fax: 201-497-4138.

Judicial Vicar—Rev. Msgr. FRANK DEL PRETE, J.C.D.

Associate Judicial Vicar—Rev. Msgr. JAMES P. MCMENEMIE, S.T.L.

Archdiocesan Staff—Sr. CATHERINE MARY RAYMOND, J.C.L.; Bro. LEONARD VOEGTLE, J.C.D.; Rev. JOHN F. CONNOR, S.T.B.

Part-time Staff—Revs. BARTLEY BAKER, M.Div.; EVAN BANKS, O.F.M.; FERNANDO CARRANZA; Rev. Msgr. VINCENT P. COBURN, J.C.D.; Rev. Msgr. FRANCIS HOUGHTON; Rev. Msgr. VINCENT J. DOYLE, J.C.D.; Rev. Msgr. GEORGE R. TRABOLD, J.C.L.; Revs. WILLIAM A. MAHON; JEREMIES REBANAL, J.C.D.; GABRIEL B. COSTA, Ph.D.; JOHN J. CRYAN, M.Div.; EDWARD DONOHUE, O.F.M.; ROBERT E. EMERY, J.C.L.; RICHARD G. FRANCESCO, J.C.L.; Rev. Msgr. ROBERT HARRINGTON; Revs. NORBERT LASKOWSKI, B.A.; ROBERT G. MCBRIDE, J.C.L.; JEREMIAH MCGINLEY, O.F.M.; Deacon VINCENT E. MESSINA, M.Div.; Revs. BERNARD N. MOHAN, B.S.; JOHN S. OLSZEWSKI, S.T.L.; ROBERT S. MEYER, J.C.L.; Rev. Msgr. FRANCIS A. REINBOLD; Revs. VINCENT S. SOROKOSKI, M.Div.; MICHAEL M. WALTERS, J.C.L.

Promotor of Justice—Rev. Msgr. ROBERT F. COLEMAN, J.C.D.

Notaries—SANTA WOLFEE; MARGARET RUSSO; SANDRA PERRINI; BETSY TRUNZO; JOHN WALSH.

Interdiocesan Tribunal of Second Instance Province of Newark—Archdiocesan Center, 171 Clifton Ave., Newark, 07104. Tel: 201-497-4145; Fax: 201-497-4138.

Judicial Vicar—Rev. Msgr. VINCENT J. DOYLE, S.T.B., J.C.D.

Vicar General and Moderator of the Curia

Rev. Msgr. RONALD J. ROZNIAK, *Archdiocesan Center,*

171 Clifton Ave., Newark, 07104. Tel: 201-497-4002; Fax: 201-497-4018.

Office of Development—Rev. Msgr. GEORGE R. TRABOLD, Sec. to the Archbishop for Devel. Tel: 201-497-4135; Fax: 201-497-4031.

Archbishop's Annual Appeal—JOHN F. WALSH, Exec. Dir. Tel: 201-497-4125.

Special Events Office—JOHN NEVINS, Dir. Tel: 201-497-4130.

Planned Giving—BARBARA WARNER, Assoc Dir. Tel: 201-497-4125.

Office of Counsel—WILLIAM A. CAMBRIA, ESQ. Tel: 201-497-4302; Fax: 201-497-4310.

Office of Archdiocesan Internal Audit—ANDREW T. SUKALA, C.P.A., Dir. Tel: 201-497-4085; Fax: 201-497-4033.

Office of Communications and Public Relations—MICHAEL HURLEY, Dir. Tel: 201-497-4190; Fax: 201-497-4185.

Chancellor/Delegate for Religious—Sr. THOMAS MARY SALERNO, S.C., M.A. Tel: 201-497-4010; Fax: 201-497-4018.

Vice Chancellor for Archives—Rev. Msgr. FRANCIS R. SEYMOUR. Tel: 201-497-4012; Fax: 201-497-4018.

Office of Research and Planning—JOSEPH A. VANCIO, M.A., Dir. Tel: 201-497-4025; Fax: 201-497-4028.

Health Care Personnel—Sr. THOMAS MARY SALERNO, S.C., M.A. Tel: 201-497-4009; Fax: 201-497-4018.

Pastoral Associates—Sr. THOMAS MARY SALERNO, S.C., M.A. Tel: 201-497-4009; Fax: 201-497-4018.

St. John Vianney Priests' Residence—Rev. Msgr. EDWARD F. KAVIN, Dir.; Mrs. JOAN D'GEROLAMO, Admin., *60 Home Ave., Rutherford, 07070.* Tel: 201-933-5155.

Propagation of the Faith—Co.Dirs.: Rev. Msgr. ROBERT E. DUFFY; Rev. ROBERT J. FUHRMAN. Tel: 201-497-4375.

Women's Commission—Sr. THOMAS MARY SALERNO, S.C. Tel: 201-497-4010.

Office of Clergy Personnel—Rev. WILLIAM J. FADROWSKI, Exec. Dir., *171 Clifton Ave., P.O. Box 9500, Newark, 07104-9500.* Tel: 201-497-4222; Fax: 201-497-4219.

Diocesan Priest Personnel—Rev. WILLIAM J. FADROWSKI, Dir.; Ms. JOSEPHINE CHOKRAN, Admin. Asst. Tel: 201-497-4222; Fax: 201-497-4219.

Adjunct Clergy Personnel—Rev. WILLIAM J. FADROWSKI, Dir.; Ms. FRANCES DOWNING, Admin. Asst. Tel: 201-497-4222.

Ministry to Retired Priest—Rev. Msgr. EDWARD F. KAVIN, Dir. Tel: 201-497-4224.

Continuing Education of Priests—Rev. THOMAS A. MCCARTHY, Dir. Tel: 201-497-4221.

Continuing Formation of Priests—Rev. STEVEN FEEHAN, Dir. Tel: 201-497-4221.

Permanent Diaconate—Deacon MICHAEL E. MATTHEWS, Dir. Tel: 201-497-4223. Deacon DANIEL RAVELO, Assoc. Dir.- Hispanic Deacons; Rev. Msgr. RICARDO GONZALEZ, Spiritual Dir.- Hispanic Deacons.

Secretary For Temporal Administration—JOSEPH C. NEHILA, C.P.A., Sec. Tel: 201-497-4051; Fax: 201-497-4031.

Office of Business Administration—JOSEPH A. FRANK, Dir. Tel: 201-497-4040; Fax: 201-497-4031.

Accounting—GEORGE PERALTA, Dir. Tel: 201-497-4055; Fax: 201-497-4031.

Office of Banking and Investments—JOHN MALONEY, Dir. Tel: 201-497-4070; Fax: 201-497-4031.

Office of Plant Services—JOHN P. MINIERI, Dir. Tel: 201-497-4110; Fax: 201-497-4033.

Office of Catholic Cemeteries—Rev. Msgr. WILLIAM NAEDELE, Dir.; Rev. JAMES T. FAHEY, Exec. Dir., *340 Ridge Rd., N. Arlington, 07032.* Tel: 201-991-7404.

Office of Parish Services—ROBERT KENNA, Dir. Tel: 201-497-4080; Fax: 201-497-4033.

Office of Parish Internal Audit—JEROME JARECKI, Dir. Tel: 201-497-4074; Fax: 201-497-4031.

Office of Personnel and Benefits—WILLIAM E. MULLIS, III, Dir. Tel: 201-497-4104; Fax: 201-497-4103.

Cooperative Supply Services—STEPHEN MIHALIK, Dir., *171 Clifton Ave., Newark, 07104.* Tel: 201-497-4170; Fax: 201-497-4174. ERICA PHINN, Customer Svc. Rep. Tel: 201-497-4166.

Vicar General and Moderator of the Curia is the Archbishop's liaison to the following:

Archdiocesan Commission for Christian Unity—Rev. Msgr. PHILIP D. MORRIS, S.T.D., Chm.; Rev. PHILIP F.A. LATRONICO, Exec. Sec. Tel: 201-497-4338.

Archdiocesan Commission for Interreligious Affairs—Rev. Msgr. JOHN J. GILCHRIST, M.A., Chm.; Rev. PHILIP LATRONICO, Exec. Sec. Tel: 201-497-4338.

Archdiocesan Commission on Justice and Peace—Most Rev. JOSEPH A. FRANCIS, S.V.D., D.D., Chm. THOMAS MCCANN, Exec. Sec. Tel: 201-497-4341.

Archdiocesan Liturgical Commission—Sr. SANDRA DEMASI, S.S.J., Chm. Tel: 201-497-4347.

Archdiocesan Pro-Life Commission—DAN KRAFT, Chm., *1805 Penbrook Ter., Union, 07036.* Tel: 908-925-6442.

Vicar General for the Apostolates

Rev. Msgr. JOSEPH T. SLINGER, Ph.D., *Archdiocesan Center, 171 Clifton Ave., P.O. Box 9500, Newark, 07104-9500.* Tel: 201-497-4319; Fax: 201-497-4249.

"The Catholic Advocate," Archdiocesan Newspaper—Mr. ROBERT DYLAK, Publisher, *171 Clifton Ave., Newark, 07104-9500.* Tel: 201-497-4200; Fax: 201-497-4192.

Secretariat For Education—Sr. DOMINICA ROCCHIO, S.C., Ed.D., Sec. Tel: 201-497-4250; Fax: 201-497-4249.

Catechetical Office—Mr. RONALD L. PIHOKKER, M.A., Dir. Tel: 201-497-4285. Sr. ELIZABETH CAHILL, S.C., M.A., Catechist Certification. Tel: 201-497-4293. Sr. ALICIA CAVANAUGH, C.S.J.P., Ph.D., Union Co.-Catechetical Leaders. Tel: 201-497-4289. ANITA HERNANDEZ, M.A., Catechesis for Hispanics. Tel: 201-497-4290. CHRISTINE MAGGIO, Educational Technology. Tel: 201-497-4292. JOAN ROVERE, M.A., Bergen Co.-Adult Catechesis. Tel: 201-497-4295. Sr. FRANCES SCARFONE, S.C., M.Div., Hudson Co.-Catechist Formation. Tel: 201-497-4296. PATRICIA VAILLANCOURT, M.A., Catechesis with Families. Tel: 201-497-4297.

Scholarship Fund for Inner City Children—KEVIN P. MORIARTY, Dir. Tel: 201-497-4281; Fax: 201-497-4279.

Office of the Superintendent of Schools—Sr. DOMINICA ROCCHIO, S.C., Ed.D., Supt. Tel: 201-497-4260. Mr. JOHN O'NEIL, M.A., Deputy Supt.- Secondary Schools; Sr. PATRICIA BUTLER, S.C., Deputy Supt.- Elementary Schools; Sr. CATHERINE ROCHE, S.S.J., M.A., Admin. Asst.; Bro. JAMES A. FINNEGAN, C.F.C., M.A., Planning; Bro. RALPH DARMENTO, F.S.C., M.A., Secondary Schools; Sr. ELIZABETH SCULLY, C.N.D., M.A., Christian Formation; Sr. SUZANNE BELLENOIT, S.S.J., M.A., Govt. Programs; Bro. JAMES MCVEIGH, O.S.F., M.A.T., Asst. Supt. Essex Co.-Elementary; Sr. MARIE GAGLIANO, M.P.F., M.A., Asst. Supt. Hudson Co.-Elementary; Sr. JOAN AMELIA FERRUGGIARO, S.S.J., M.A., Asst. Supt. Union Co.-Elementary; Sr. MARIE LALANDE, C.S.J., M.S., Asst. Supt. Bergen Co.-Elementary; Rev. JOHN CONNOLLY, S.D.B., M.A., Dir.- Education Technology; Mrs. ESTELLE FRESE, M.A., Dir. Personnel; Mrs. GRACE PIETROPINTO, B.A., Dir. Finance; Deacon RONALD R. WICKS, B.S., LL.B., Dir. Marketing; GLORIA CASTUCCI, M.A., Dir. Early Childhood; Sr. LOUISE CABABE, O.P., M.A., Dir. Corriculum & Testing; MARVIN N. BROWN, B.S., Dir.- Data Systems Operator & Technician.

Vicar for Evangelization—Rev. Msgr. WILLIAM J. KOPLIK, *34 Maple Ave., Hackensack, 07601.* Tel: 201-343-5170.

Vicar for Pastoral Life—Rev. Msgr. LOUIS F. FIMIANI. Tel: 201-497-4322; Fax: 201-497-4317.

Hispanic Apostolate—Rev. JORGE E. CHACON, Dir. Tel: 201-497-4335.

Office of Black Catholic Affairs—Mrs. LUCILLE E. FOREMAN, Dir. Tel: 201-497-4340.

Black Catholic Coordinating Team—Tel: 201-497-4340.

Council for Multi-Cultural Concerns—Rev. Msgr. LOUIS F. FIMIANI, Chm., *171 N. Clifton St. - P.O. Box 9500, Newark, 07104-9500.* Tel: 201-497-4321.

Chinese Apostolate—Rev. JOSEPH FU, Coord., *188 MacArthur Ave., Garfield, 07026.* Tel: 201-772-2295.

Indian Apostolate—Rev. SABASTIAN KUNNATH, Coord. & Chap.- India Catholic Association (Syro-Malabar Rite), *Pollak Hospital, 100 Clifton Pl., Jersey City, 07304.* Tel: 201-432-1000.

Filipino Apostolate—Rev. JEREMIAS REBANAL, Coord., *800 Bergen Ave., Jersey City, 07306.* Tel: 201-433-6800.

Haitian Apostolate—Rev. JEAN-MARIE FRITZ LIGONDE, Coord., *492 Bramhall Ave., Jersey City, 07304.* Tel: 201-332-8600.

Liaison to the Irish Community—Rev. Msgr. MICHAEL E. KELLY, *120 Northfield Ave., W. Orange, 07052.* Tel: 201-325-6624.

Italian Apostolate—Rev. JOSEPH F. AMBROSIO, Coord., *St. Anthony's Rectory, 615 8th St., Union City, 07087.* Tel: 201-867-3818.

Korean Apostolate—Rev. AUGUSTIN PARK, Coord., *St. Andrew Kim Parish, 257 Central Ave., Orange, 07050.* Tel: 201-673-1366.

Polish Apostolate—Rev. FELIZ R. MARCINIAK, Coord., *St. Casimir, 164 Nichols St., Newark, 07105-2596.* Tel: 201-344-2743.

Portuguese Apostolate—Rev. Msgr. JOHN S. ANTAO, Coord., *403 Spring St., Elizabeth, 07201.* Tel: 908-355-3810.

Vietnamese Apostolate—Rev. JOSEPH TRI MINH NGUYEN, Coord., *2217 Kennedy Blvd., Jersey City, 07304.* Tel: 201-433-4152.

Department of Human Concerns—THOMAS MCCANN, Dir. Tel: 201-497-4341.

Department of Shared Responsibility—Sr. REGINA SUPLICK, S.C., Dir. Tel: 201-497-4353.

Ministerial Development Center—Sr. VIRGINIA STANTON, S.S.J., Dir. Tel: 201-497-4350.

Worship Office—Sr. SANDRA DE MASI, S.S.J., Dir. Tel: 201-497-4345; Fax: 201-497-4348. Rev. MICHAEL J. SHEEHAN, Dir.- RCIA; Rev. THOMAS B. IWANOWSKI, Assoc Dir.- Liturgical Formation; Rev. ROBERT G. LAFERRERA, Assoc Dir.- Parish Liturgical Services.

Respect Life Office—Rev. Msgr. RICHARD M. MCGUINNESS, S.T.L., Ph.D., *1805 Penbrook Ter., Linden, 07036.* Tel: 908-925-6442.

Campus Ministry—Mrs. NOEL WICKS, Dir., *Newman Center, 45 Bleeker St., Newark, 07112.* Tel: 201-642-1613; Fax: 201-642-1613.

Family Life Ministries—Ms. JUDITH MILLER, M.A., Dir. BARBARA KATULKA, Admin. Asst., *Archdiocesan Center, 171 Clifton Ave., P.O. Box 9500, Newark, 07104-9500.* Tel: 201-497-4325.

Family Life Center—256 Franklin Ave., Maplewood, 07040. Tel: 201-763-7659.

Pre-Cana Reservations—NANCY DELLISANTI. Tel: 201-497-4328.

Ministry with Separated, Divorced and Widowed Catholics—MARY GIBLIN, Assoc. Dir.; Revs. JOSEPH GIRONE, Chap., Separated and Divorced; THOMAS ARMINIO, Chap., Widows and Widowers. Tel: 201-497-4327.

Hispanic Family Life Ministries—REINA BASUALDO, Assoc. Dir. Tel: 201-497-4326.

Catholic One Parent Organization—Rev. JOSEPH M. DOYLE, Chap. Tel: 201-433-0950.

Engaged Encounter—Rev. PHILIP F. LATRONICO, Chap., *70 W. Passaic Ave., Rutherford, 07070.* Tel: 201-935-0344. Chaircouple: HARRY KUHLES; TERRY KUHLES.

Marriage Encounter Resources—Rev. RICHARD D. CARLSON, Chap., *411 Rutgers Ave., Hillside, 07205.* Tel: 908-686-0722. Chaircouple: TOM RONDINELLA; SHARON RONDINELLA, *17 Oxford Ter., W. Orange, 07052.* Tel: 201-325-7831.

Natural Family Planning—Rev. RICHARD CARRINGTON, Chap./Coord. Chaircouple: KAREN DOYLE; KEVIN DOYLE, *31 Hill St., Haworth, 07641.* Tel: 201-384-9458.

CYO Youth Ministries—Rev. WILLIAM J. DOWD, Exec. Dir., *499 Belgrove Dr., Kearny, 07032.* Tel: 201-998-0088; Fax: 201-998-9606. *Central Services:* Mr. JOHN CAMMARANO, Youth Center Dir. FRANK MAHENO, Finance Mgr. JUAN PAVLOWSKI, Acctg. Mgr. ROBERT GARRITY, Dir.- Food Services. Tel: 201-998-9607. JOHN HRONCICH, Dir.- Spirituality/Bergen Co. Dir. DELIA BAYONA, Hispanic Youth Ministry/Hudson Co. Dir. JOSEPH HAN, Korean Youth Ministry/Essex Co. Dir. JOANNE TRAINA, Sports Specialist; ALBERT FORSYTHE, Special Events/Union Co. Dir.; Rev. RONALD J. MARCZEWSKI, Dir.- Young Adult Ministry; SERGIO RODRIGUES, Asst. Dir.-Young Adult Ministry; GABRIEL D. FELTZ, Boy Scouts Coord. MAUREEN COLEMAN, Girl Scouts Coord.

Boy Scouts of America/Catholic Committee on Scouting—GABRIEL FELTZ, Coord.; Revs. RICHARD KWIATKOWSKI, Chap. MICHAEL M. WALTERS, Chap., Bergen Co., *84 Custer Ave., Newark, 07112.* Tel: 201-926-1607. GABRIEL FELTZ, Chm. Vice Chm.: RICHARD CONKLIN; ANTHONY DE STEFANO; MICHAEL C. MILDEN, JR. Tel: 201-432-3878; 656-3683. Bayonne Council: JOSEPH GABLE, *20 E. 29th St., Bayonne, 07002.* Tel: 201-339-5066. Bergen Council: EDWARD ROSE, *244 Ottawa Ave., Hasbrouck Heights, 07604.* Tel: 201-288-2355. MICHAEL M. WALTER, Chap.; Essex Council: RICHARD CONKLIN, *P.O. Box 167, Bloomfield, 07002.* Tel: 201-429-9008. CHARLES MCTAGUE, Chap.; Hudson Hamilton Council: GABRIEL FELTZ, *37 High St., Jersey City, 07306.* Tel: 201-656-3683. EUGENE KASPER, Chap.; Ridgewood-Glen Rock Council: THOMAS P. DURKIN, *179 Forest Rd., Glen Rock, 07452.* Tel: 201-444-0117. Watchung Council: SCOTT E. MCCUE, *617 Maple Ave., Elizabeth, 07202.* Tel: 908-351-4688. Rev. JOSEPH SAPETA, Chap.

Girl Scouts of America—MAUREEN COLEMAN, Archdiocesan Coord.; Rev. DONALD K. HUMMELL, Chap. Committee: ROSEMARIE BRODEUR; CAROL PISCZO; KATHY DONOHUE; JOANNE OZIEMBLO, *499 Belgrove Dr., Kearny, 07032.* Tel: 201-998-0088.

Archdiocesan Council of Catholic Women—MARY LOFTUS, Pres.; Rev. Msgr. WALTER GORSKI, Moderator, *171 Clifton Ave., Newark, 07104.* Tel: 201-497-4356. District Moderators: Bergen-Paramus: Rev. ROBERT DOYLE,Bergen-Hackensack: Rev. FRANCIS A. IGNACUINAS,North Hudson: Rev. KENNETH JONES,South Hudson: Rev. ROBERT PATTERSON,Essex-Suburban: Rev. GEORGE R. DENMAN,Union-Westfield: Vacant Union-Elizabeth: Vacant.

Charismatic Renewal—Rev. PHILIP J. ROTUNNO, Coord., *5808 Kennedy Blvd., W. New York, 07093.* Tel: 201-867-2642.

The Community of God's Love—70 W. Passaic Ave., Rutherford, 07070. Tel: 201-935-0344. PAUL J.

GRIFFO, Dir.; Rev. PHILIP LATRONICO, Chap.; Deacon TIMOTHY LAWLESS.

Cursillo Movement—Cursillo House, 119 Chestnut St., Kearny, 07032. Tel: 201-992-8218. Rev. JAMES F. REILLY, Archdiocesan Coord. Tel: 201-991-1116.

RENEW International, Office of—Rev. Msgr. THOMAS A. KLEISSLER, Dir., *1232 George St., Plainfield, 07062-1717.* Tel: 908-769-5400; Fax: 908-769-5660. Sr. CECILIA KING, C.S.J.P., Coord.-International RENEW; MARGO LEBERT, Coord.- RENEW 2000; Sr. KATHY WARREN, O.S.F., Coord.-American RENEW; Sr. MARY MCGUINNESS, O.P., Coord.- Small Christian Communities; Sr. MARIA LOUISE IGLESIAS, S.C., Coord.- Hispanic RENEW. International Service Team: BOB BURSLEY; Sr. PAT CROWLEY, O.P.; Sr. CHERYL ERB, R.S.M.; Rev. JACK FARLEY, S.V.D.; Sr. BARBARA GARLAND, S.C.; Sr. CARMEN OLIVERA, O.P.; MARY REDDY; Rev. NORMAN J. SIMMONS, C.SS.R.; CARLOS TORRADO; Sr. ALICE YOHE, S.S.J., Admin. Asst. JOHN LANDVATER, Fin. Asst. ROSANNE BARONE, Office Mgr.

Medical-Moral Committee—Rev. HAROLD P. DARCY, Chm., *Seton Hall University School of Law, 1111 Raymond Blvd., Newark, 07102.* Tel: 201-642-8859.

Sacred Heart Institute—585 Bloomfield Ave., Ste. 5C, Caldwell, 07006. Tel: 201-226-7077. Rev. GERALD P. RUANE, Dir.; Sr. RUTHANN WILLIAMS, O.P., Admin.

Vicariate for Human Services

Executive Office—1160 Raymond Blvd., Newark, 07102. Tel: 201-596-4050; Fax: 201-596-3807. All offices at this address unless otherwise indicated. Most Rev. NICHOLAS A. DIMARZIO, Ph.D., D.D., L.S.W., Vicar & Exec. Dir. Tel: 201-596-4050. THOMAS J. CATLAW, M.A., Chief Oper. Officer. Tel: 201-596-4054. CATHERINE L'INSALATA, M.S., Special Asst. for Vicariate Services. Tel: 201-596-4060.

Catholic Community Services—Affiliated Agencies: Associated Catholic Charities; Mount Carmel Guild; New Jersey Boystown; The Guild Social Service Center.

General and Administative Offices—BARBARA B. DESMOND, L.C.S.W., Dir.- Program Devel. Tel: 201-596-4038; Fax: 201-596-3819. CHRIS MARICS, M.S.A., Grant & New Program Specialist. Tel: 201-596-4058. ELAINE V. COHEN, Ph.D., Dir.- Evaluation & Planning. Tel: 201-596-4057. DANIEL DEAN, J.D., Dir.- Public Affairs. Tel: 201-596-4046. TIMOTHY SULLIVAN, M.A., Dir.- Communications. Tel: 201-596-4086. Finance Office:Tel: 201-596-3949. JOHN CARDILLO, Controller. Tel: 201-596-3945. Human Resources. Tel: 201-596-4071; Fax: 201-596-3822. ANTHONY BIUNNO, Dir.- General Services. Tel: 201-596-4092. DONALD GAROFALO, M.B.A., Dir.- Information Systems. Tel: 201-693-6637. DANIEL A. CORDASCO, Dir.- Special Events. Tel: 201-596-4063; Fax: 201-596-3819. Legal Services: JACQUELINE I. HEATH, General Counsel. Tel: 201-596-4120; Fax: 201-242-0791. Bro. BENEDICT LO BALBO, Dir.- Board Affairs. Tel: 201-596-4180; Fax: 201-596-3819.

Detailed list of services and staff—

Apostolate for the Developmentally Disabled—Sr. EILEEN BYRNE, O.P., M.A. Tel: 201-226-9402.

Apostolate for the Deaf—Sr. JOAN WALTERS, S.C. Ed.D. Tel: 201-348-0527; TTY: 596-3893.

Ministry to the Deaf—THOMAS SMITH, B.A., C.S.W. Tel: 201-596-3962; TTY: 596-3893.

New Day Community—VINCENT MCMAHON, M.A., Program Dir. Tel: 201-596-4060; TTY: 763-7949.

Emergency Food & Nutrition Network—SHARON REILLY-TOBIN, Program Dir. Tel: 201-596-4060; Fax: 201-596-3735.

Parish Access Center - Central Office—Sr. ROSE PHILIP, M.S.B.T., A.C.S.W. Tel: 1-800-CCS-7413.

HIV/AIDS—1160 Raymond Blvd., Newark, 07102. Mr. ROBERTHANSON, Program Dir. Tel: 201-596-3932.

Bergen County—W. 50 Midland Ave., Paramus, 07652. Tel: 201-967-4177; Fax:. Rev. JOHN MCCRONE, Coord.

Hudson County—Tel: 201-596-3932.

Essex County—212 Hunterdon St., Newark, 07103. Tel: 201-824-1652. Rev. JOHN P. NICKAS, Coord.

Union County—280 Parker Ave., Maplewood, 07040. Tel: 201-763-5019. Rev. DOMINIC G. FUCCILE, Coord.

Hispanic Community—3900 New York Ave., Union City, 07087. Tel: 201-863-5116. Rev. Msgr. THOMAS W. HECK, Coord.

AIDS Support Center—(See Catholic Community Services Essex).

Franciska House—(See Catholic Community Services Hudson).

Criminal Justice Ministry—75 Greenville Ave., Jersey City, 07305. Tel: 201-433-1124. THOMAS LYNCH.

Parish Service for the Prevention of Addictions—Rev. JOHN J. CRYAN, Dir., *1160 Raymond Blvd., Newark, 07102.* Tel: 201-596-4060.

Ministry to the People on the Move—

Apostleship of the Air—Rev. DAVID J. BARATELLI, Dir., *Newark International Airport Chaplaincy, 691 West Side Ave., Jersey City, 07304.* Tel: 201-200-1465.

Apostleship of the Sea—Rev. SALVATORE LOBALBO, *Newark International Seaport Chaplaincy - Stella Maris Chapel, 114 Corbin St., Newark, 07101.* Tel: 201-483-0356.

Office of the Consultant for Health Affairs—Bro. BENEDICT LO BALBO. Tel: 201-596-4180; Fax: 201-596-3819.

Campaign for Human Development—Sr. CATHERINE DALY, O.P., M.S. Tel: 201-596-3890; Fax: 201-596-3933.

Quest Essex Youth Services—St. Charles Center, 85 Custer St., Newark, 07102. Tel: 201-926-9895; Fax: 201-926-0448. Dr. REGINA ADESANYA, Div. Dir. JOYCE SMITH CARTER, Program Dir.

Archdiocesan Housing Office—CHRIS GARLIN, Dir. Tel: 201-639-6647. The Vicar for Human Services is the Archbishop's Liaison to the Archdiocesan Housing Commission and serves as General Secretary for this Commission.

BERGEN COUNTY Division—WILMA CASELLA, M.S.W., Div. Dir., *425 Paramus Rd., Paramus, 07652.* Tel: 201-444-3883. Tel: 201-444-3172. Programs: Catholic School Social Service Programs; Outreach/Case Management for HIV Hispanics; One Stop Case Management; Eldercare Consultation & Referral; Parish Access Center.

New Jersey Boystown—499 Belgrove Dr., Kearny, 07032. Tel: 201-991-3770. Tel: 201-991-7306. Programs: New Beginnings - Counseling, Adoption & Search Services; Project Rachel.

Mt. Carmel Guild Behavioral Healthcare System—LEONARD S. ALTAMURA, D.S.W., Div. Dir. Tel: 201-639-6597; Fax: 201-639-6663. Dr. AMBROSE MGBAKO, M.D., Medical Dir. Tel: 201-596-4043; Fax: 201-596-3701. PATRICIA J. SEAVER, L.C.S.W., Deputy Dir. Tel: 201-596-4109; Fax: 201-596-3809. ROSE MARIE PRATT, L.C.S.W., Asst. Dir. Tel: 201-596-3855.

Behavioral Healthcare - Essex County—JULIE WILLIS, L.C.S.W., Reg. Dir. Tel: 201-596-4099; Fax: 201-242-0563.

Behavioral Healthcare - Bergen County—425 Paramus Rd., Paramus, 07652. Tel: 201-444-3883; Fax: 201-444-3172.

Behavioral Healthcare - Union County—108 Alden St., Cranford, 07016. Tel: 908-272-8910; Fax: 908-272-9268. WILLIAM HODGDON, L.C.S.W., Reg. Dir.

Behavioral Healthcare - Hudson County—249 Virginia Ave., Jersey City, 07304. Tel: 201-332-4365.

ESSEX COUNTY Division—REGINA MARSHALL ADESANYA, Psy.D., Div. Dir. Tel: 201-596-4040; Fax: 201-596-4037.

AmeriCorps Volunteer Program—Tel: 201-596-4040.

Catholic School Social Service Program—Tel: 201-596-4147.

Parish Access Center—Tel: 201-639-6541.

Eric J. Feldman Child & Family Development Center—

Communication Disorders—Tel: 201-596-3965; Fax: 201-596-3869.

Child Development Center—(Includes Child Study Teams; Speech/Language Pathology; Therapeutic Nursey.

Industrial Audiology,—Tel: 201-596-3965.

AIDS/HIV Support Center—Tel: 201-491-0591; Fax: 201-491-5219.

St. Bridget's Residence—404 University Ave., Newark, 07102. Tel: 201-491-0591.

Special Education Schools—MARIAN KUGELMASS, M.Ed., Dir. Tel: 201-596-4065; Fax: 201-596-4037.

Mt. Carmel Guild School—60 Kingsland Ave., Kearny, 07032. Tel: 201-991-7733; Fax: 201-991-7776. KATHRYN KRUPER, Prin.

Mt. Carmel Guild Pre-school—10 Commerce Ct., Newark, 07102. Tel: 201-639-6622; Fax: 201-639-6626. KATHARINE THORNTON, Prin.

St. Anthony's School—25 N. 7th St., Belleville, 07109. Tel: 201-751-2550; Fax: 201-751-5725. Sr. ANNE ROSALIE, Prin.

St. Patrick's School—72 Central Ave., Newark, 07102. Tel: 201-643-6772; Fax: 201-643-7625.

The Guild Social Service Center—56 Freeman St., Newark, 07105. Tel: 201-344-0067; Fax: 201-344-6750. ROBERT ROBINSON, Dir.

Halfway House for Alcoholic Men—Tel: 201-344-0514.

Senior Day Care for the Frail and Elderly—

Visually Handicapped Socialization Program.—494 Broad St., Newark, 07102. Tel: 201-642-6367. PAULINE ZIOMEK, R.N., Dir.

St. Ann's Family Emergency Residence (SAFER) Youth Chance.—368 S. 7th St., Newark, 07103. Tel: 201-242-6646; Fax: 201-242-2864. DWAYNE KEELING, Dir.

St. Rocco's Family Residence (Women & Children)—355 S. 6th St., Newark, 07103. Tel: 201-242-7242; Fax: 201-242-4854. TREVA YOUNG, Dir.

Mt. Carmel Guild Children's Center—

St. Rocco's Children's Center—39 Bleeker St., Newark, 07102. Tel: 201-643-4956. KATHLEEN O'PRAY, M.A., Dir.

St. Rocco's Outreach Center (Men)—712 Springfield Ave., Newark, 07103. Tel: 201-371-5266; Fax: 201-371-5850. NOEL HICKS, B.A., Dir.

HUDSON COUNTY Division—249 Virginia Ave., Jersey City, 07304. Tel: 201-332-4365; Fax: 201-332-6585. MARGARET M. MURTHA, L.C.S.W., C.A.D.C., Div. Dir. LESLEY MOORE, L.C.S.W., Asst. Dir.

Parish Access Center—3201 Central Ave., Union City, 07087. Tel: 201-863-8085. Tel: 201-863-8320. CARMEL GALASSO, M.A., Dir.

Foster Grandparents—249 Virginia Ave., Jersey City, 07304. Tel: 201-332-2175. MELINDA ACEVEDO, Dir.

Edna McLaughlin Residence—162 Bidwell Ave., Jersey City, 07305. Tel: 201-413-1556. Sr. BRIDGET KAPIN, Dir.

Community Mental Health Center (Jersey City)—249 Virginia Ave., Jersey City, 07304. Tel: 201-332-4365; Fax: 201-322-6585. LESLEY MOORE, L.C.S.W., Dir. Programs: Catholic School Social Service Program; Project Home; Hispanic Outreach Program; Addictions Services; Day Treatment, Outpatient Department.

MICA Outreach (Mentally Ill Chemical Abuser)—308 Academy St., Jersey City, 07306. Tel: 201-217-9665; Fax: 201-219-1902. VALERIE ROSEN, M.S.W., Dir.

Mt. Carmel Guild Family Resource Centers—

Intensive Family Counseling Program—3040 Kennedy Blvd., Jersey City, 07306. Tel: 201-656-3557; Fax: 201-656-1707. ELIZABETH MCCLENDON, L.C.S.W.; ROSA JONES, M.A.; DIANE JORDAN, M.A.

Malta Providence Residence—114 Clifton Pl., Jersey City, 07365. Tel: 201-915-1212. Tel: 201-985-2343. THOMAS LYNCH, L.C.S.W.

Hudson County Correctional Program—75 Greenville Ave., Jersey City, 07305. Tel: 201-946-1007. Tel: 201-946-1202.

PRIDE Mentoring Program—VIRGINIA HART, L.C.S.W.

Family Crisis Intervention—114 Clifton Ave., Jersey City, 07304. Tel: 201-915-1202; Fax: 201-985-2343. DOLORES WESTBROOKS, M.A.

St. Lucy's Homeless Programs—619 Grove St., Jersey City, 07310. Tel: 201-656-7201; Fax: 201-656-0412. ROBERT MACK, M.A.,Programs: Counceling and Outreach; Single Residence (Men & Women); Neuville Family Residence.

Franciska House—615 Grove St., Jersey City, 07310. Tel: 201-653-5395. MICHAEL BACON, B.A.

Anthony House—246 2nd St., Jersey City, 07302. Tel: 201-420-1070. NANCY PINEDA.

UNION COUNTY Division—

Employee Assistance Program (CARE),—Tel: 908-709-2170. SHARON LINDSAY, Ph.D.

Catholic School Social Service Program,—Tel: 908-709-2118. MARY LOU SHERRY, M.S.W.

Senior Adult Services—Tel: 908-709-2150; Fax: 908-709-4583. SUSAN CRANK, L.C.S.W.

Adult Protective Services,—Tel: 908-709-2140.

Retired Senior Volunteer Program (RSVP),—Tel: 908-709-2152. JOANN CROTEAU,Programs: CARES Volunteers; MED ED SEZ; Telephone Reassurance Program; Senior Shopping Service; Senior Health Insurance Program; Volunteer Income Tax Assistance; Senior Handyman Program.

Hispanic Seniors Multi-Service Center,—Tel: 908-709-2163.

The Engel Center (Senior Day Care)—Tel: 908-709-2156.

Visually Impaired Seniors Program,—Tel: 908-709-2150.

Parish Access Center—215 Court St., Elizabeth, 07206. Tel: 908-289-8043. Sr. MARY STEWART, M.A.

Raphael House—231 Court St., Elizabeth, 07206. Tel: 908-354-4750. PATRICIA EADDY.

Special Services Division—494 Broad St., Newark, 07102. Tel: 201-242-1999; Fax: 201-242-3755. GEORGE PIEGARO, M.A., Div. Dir.

Educational Training Programs—PATRICIA PEDIADITIS, M.A.

Citizenship/Immigration Assistance—FEN LU.

Refugee Resettlement & Employment Services—GIZELLA MENDLOVICH.

Project Haven—BARBARA LONEGRO, L.C.S.W.

Office of Migration—972 Broad St., Newark, 07102. Tel: 201-733-3516; Fax: 201-733-9631. DANIEL VENDRELL.

Immigration Assistance—

Hispanic Women's Resource Center—533 35th St., Union City, 07087. Tel: 201-866-3208; Fax: 201-866-5854. MARTA SAN MARTIN, M.A.,Programs: Employment

& Training; Citizenship/Immigration Assistance; Refugee Resettlement; Drug/Alcohol Counceling and Education.

Italian Social Service Center—380 Monmouth St., Jersey City, 07302. Tel: 201-653-6515; Fax: 201-653-1301. NAM NGUYEN, M.A.,Programs: Employment & Training; Citizenship/Immigration Assistance; Refugee Resettlement.

Office of Migration—505 South Ave., East Cranford, 07016. Tel: 908-709-2108. PIERRE MOREAU, B.A.,Programs: Employment & Training; Citizenship/ Immigration Assistance; Refugee Resettlement.

Haitian Outreach Center—37 Evergreen Pl., East Orange, 07017. Tel: 201-672-6607. PIERRE MOREAU, B.A.,Programs: Employment & Training; Citizenship/Immigration Assistance; Refugee Resettlement.

Archbishop Boland Rehabilitation Skills Training Center—494 Broad St., Newark, 07102. Tel: 201-242-1999. Tel: 201-242-3755. MICHAEL MYERS, M.A. *Sheltered Workshop—101 Universtiy Ave., Newark, 07102.*

Miscellaneous

Affirmative Action Council—Most Rev. JOSEPH A. FRANCIS, S.V.D., Chm. WILLIAM A. CAMBRIA, Officer, *Archdiocesan Center, 171 Clifton Ave., Newark, 071042.* Tel: 201-497-4300.

Blue Army—Vacant; Natl. & Archdiocesan Dir. Tel: 201-497-4011.

Catholic Relief Services—171 Clifton Ave., Newark, 071042. Tel: 201-497-4000.

Censores Librorum—Rev. Msgr. EDWARD J. CIUBA, S.T.L., S.S.L.; Rev. Msgr. JOSEPH F. FLUSK, Music; Rev. Msgr. CARL D. HINRICHSEN, S.T.L., Ph.D.; Rev. Msgr. THOMAS P. IVORY, S.T.D.; Rev. Msgr. JOHN H. KOENIG, S.T.L.; Rev. Msgr. RICHARD M. LIDDY, S.T.D.; Revs. JAMES M. CAFONE, S.T.D.; FRANCIS A. DEDOMENICO, S.T.L.; CHARLES W. GUSMER, S.T.D.; GEORGE M. KEATING; FRANK MCNULTY, S.T.D.; JOHN RUSSELL, O.Carm.; ARTHUR J. SERRATELLI, S.T.D., S.S.L.; JAMES B. SULLIVAN, S.T.L., Ph.D.

Confraternity of the Blessed Sacrament—Rev. Msgr. WALTER J. JARVAIS, Dir., *60 Home Ave., Rutherford, 07111.* Tel: 201-933-8138.

Archdiocesan School Advisory Board—MARY D. BAIER; JOHN CRUITT; FRANCIS X. FALCICCHIO; DAVID KIENAST; BRENDA LEAHY; KATHLEEN MASKER; MICHAEL SCILINGO; Sr. LILLIAN SHARROCK, S.C.; Bro. MICHAEL STECHMANN, O.A.R.

Scholarship Fund for Inner-City Children—DAVID C. FARRAND, Pres., Board of Trustees; DIEGO R. VISCEGLIA, ESQ., Treas. JOHN C. WALCOTT, Sec. KEVIN P. MORIARTY, Exec. Dir., *Archdiocesan Center, 171 Clifton Ave., Newark, 07104.* Tel: 201-497-4279.

Federation of Home School Association—School Office Liaison: Sr. SUZANNE BELLENOIT, S.S.J. Tel: 201-497-4260.

Holy Name Federation—Rev. Msgr. RICHARD M. MCGUINNESS, Archdiocesan Dir. County Dirs.: Revs. JOHN LAFERRARA, Essex-West Hudson; RICHARD J. CARRINGTON, Hudson; MARTIN SILVER, Bergen; HAROLD T. HERMANS, Union, *1805 Penbrook Ter., Linden, 07036.* Tel: 908-486-6363.

Lawyers Guild—Rev. Msgr. HAROLD P. D'ARCY, Dir., *Seton Hall University, School of Law, 1111 Raymond Blvd., Newark, 07102.* Tel: 201-642-8859.

Legion of Mary—Newark Comitum: Vacant; Dir. Tel: 201-497-4011. Bergen Curia: Rev. Msgr. ROGER REYNOLDS, *29 Jefferson Ave., Emerson, 07630.* Tel: 201-262-1122. Hudson County Curia: Rev. JAMES W. MCFARLAND, Dir., *21 Skillman Ave., Jersey City, 07306.* Tel: 201-963-7640. Hudson Hispanic Curia: Rev. NAZARENO ORLANDI, *4206 Kennedy Blvd., Union City, 07107.* Tel: 201-863-1427. Essex and Union Hispanic Curia: Rev. MICHAEL A. FUINO, Dir., *243 Abington Ave., Newark, 07107.* Tel: 201-482-8410. Korean Curia: Rev. AUGUSTIN PARK, *257 Central Ave., Orange, 07050.* Tel: 201-673-1366.

New Jersey Catholic Historical Records Commission—JOSEPH F. MAHONEY, Dir., *Seton Hall University Archives, S. Orange, 07079.* Tel: 201-761-9476.

Our Lady of Fatima First Saturday Club—Rev. PAUL BOCHICCHIO, Chap., *188 MacArthur Ave., Garfield, 07026.* Tel: 201-772-2295.

Propagation of the Faith; Society of St. Peter the Apostle Missionary Union of Priests / Religious—Rev. Msgr. ROBERT E. DUFFY, Dir.; Rev. ROBERT J. FUHRMAN, Assoc. Dir., *Archdiocesan Center, 171 Clifton Ave., Newark, 07104.* Tel: 201-497-4375.

Priests' Eucharistic League—Rev. Msgr. WALTER G. JARVAIS, *60 Home Ave., Rutherford, 07070.* Tel: 201-939-8138.

Serra Clubs—Dr. AGNES M. MORSE, Governor-District 22, *137 Bergen Ct., Ridgewood, 07450.* Tel: 201-444-0710.

CLERGY, PARISHES, MISSIONS AND PAROCHIAL SCHOOLS

CITY OF NEWARK

1—CATHEDRAL OF THE SACRED HEART BASILICA (1889), Rev. Fernando Carranza; Rev. Msgr. Richard Groncki. In res., Most Rev. Theodore E. McCarrick; Rev. Msgr. Ronald J. Rozniak; Revs. Robert Coleman; Manuel Cruz; Thomas P. Nydegger; Robert E. Templeton.
Res., 89 Ridge St., 07104. Tel: 201-484-4600; Fax: 201-483-8253; 482-4793.

2—ST. PATRICK'S PRO-CATHEDRAL (1848), Rev. Neil J. Mahoney. In res., Rev. Msgr. Horton Raught; Rev. Paul A. Viale.
Res., 91 Washington St., 07102. Tel: 201-623-0497; Fax: 201-623-2030.

3—BLESSED SACRAMENT (1905) (African American), Very Rev. Paul D. Schetelick, V.F.; Rev. Joseph A. Barrow.
Res., 15 Van Ness Pl., 07108. Tel: 201-824-6548; Fax: 210-624-6030.
School—600 Clinton Ave., 07108. Tel: 201-824-5859.
Sisters of St. Joseph 2; Lay Teachers 14; Students 300.
Convent—Tel: 201-824-8475.

4—ST. ALOYSIUS (1877), Rev. Javier Losarcos, V.F. In res., Rev. Arthur B. Schute.
Res., 66 Fleming Ave., 07105. Tel: 201-344-4736.

5—ST. ANTONINUS (1875), Revs. Paul J. Lehman; Eustace Edomobi.
Res., 337 S. Orange Ave., 07103. Tel: 201-623-0258.

6—ST. ANN (1886), Rev. Msgr. Ronald Roznick.
Church Office: 60 Jay St.
Res., Tel: 201-642-4217; Fax: 818-766-7254.

7—ST. AUGUSTINE'S (1874) (German), Rev. Paul Viale, Admin.; Deacons Vicente Rodriquez; Daniel Mendez.
Church Office: 60 Jay St.
Res., Tel: 201-482-1817; Fax: 201-482-5475.
Convent—168 Sussex Ave., 07103. Tel: 201-483-0165. Sisters Missionaries of Charity
Women's Shelter Queen of Peace—170 Sussex Ave., 07103. Tel: 201-481-9056.

8—ST. BENEDICT'S (1854), Revs. Matthias T. Conva; Anthony DaSilva. Pastoral Associates: Sr. Philomena McCartney; Sr. Ann Jerome Kociolek.
Res., 65 Barbara St., 07105. Tel: 201-589-7930; Fax: 201-589-3665.
School—124 Niagara St., 07105. Tel: 201-589-7295. Mrs. Susan Wilson, Prin.
Lay Teachers 23; Students 380.
Catechesis / Religious Programs—Students 120.

9—ST. BRIDGET'S (1887). Merged with St. Patrick's Pro-Cathedral. Records located at St. Patrick's, Newark. Tel: 201-623-0497.

10—ST. CASIMIR'S (1908) (Polish), Revs. Felix R. Marciniak; Zbigniew Choromanski (Poland).
Res., 164 Nichols St., 07105-2596. Tel: 201-344-2743; Fax: 201-344-5629.
School—(1910), 366 E. Kinney St., 07105. Tel: 201-589-0108; Fax: 201-589-0239. Sr. Mary Lourdes, C.S.S.F., Prin.
Felician Sisters 3; Lay Teachers 13; Students 303.
Catechesis / Religious Programs—Tel: 201-596-4500, Ext. 3674.
Students 303.
Convent—Tel: 201-589-5737.

11—ST. CHARLES BORROMEO'S (1910), Rev. Edward J. Galvin, S.M.A.
Res., 84 Custer Ave., 07112. Tel: 201-923-6798.

12—ST. COLUMBA'S (1869) (Hispanic), Rev. Decimo Crevani, C.S.
Res., 25 Thomas St., 07114. Tel: 201-622-7712; Fax: 201-621-2021.
School—(1908), 25 Pennsylvania Ave., 07114. Tel: 201-623-8859.
Sisters of Charity 1; Lay Teachers 16; Students 340.
Convent—Tel: 201-622-7325.

13—EPIPHANY (1992) (Portuguese), Rev. Peter M. Uhde, Admin.
Res., Holy Trinity Rectory, 207 Adams St., 07105. Tel: 201-491-9761; Fax: 201-344-5641.

14—QUEEN OF ANGELS (1930) (African American), Rev. James J. McConnell, S.M.A.; Deacons Robert Botts, (Retired); Edward Botts, (Retired). In res., Rev. Chris Anyanwu (Nigeria).
Res., 44 Irvine Turner Blvd., 07103. Tel: 201-642-1610; Fax: 201-642-0755.
School—28 Irvine Turner Blvd., 07103. Tel: 201-642-1531. Bro. Stephen Schlitte, F.M.S., Prin.
Brothers 3; Lay Teachers 9; Students 250.
Catechesis / Religious Programs—Tel: 201-642-0857.
Students 18.

15—ST. FRANCIS XAVIER (1914), Revs. Arthur Frank Humphrey, S.T.M., M.A.; James Redstone; Frederick A. Pfeifer; Deacons Louis A. Acocella, Ed.D.; Paul R. Daniele, J.D. In res., Rev. Michael A. Fuino.
Res., 243 Abington Ave., 07107-2598. Tel: 201-482-8410; Fax: 201-482-9416.
School—(1924), 594 N. Seventh St., 07107. Tel: 201-482-9410.
Maestre Pie Filippini (Religious Teachers Filippini) 4; Lay Teachers 12; Students 350.
Catechesis / Religious Programs—Students 200.
Convent—Tel: 201-484-5200.

16—HOLY TRINITY (1901) (Lithuanian), Rev. Peter M. Uhde, Admin.
Res., 207 Adams St., 07105. Tel: 201-344-6847; Fax: 201-344-5641.

17—ST. JAMES (1854) (Brazilian-Portuguese), Revs. George Lutz; Angelo Amaral, Pastoral Assoc. In res., Rev. Charles H. McTague.
Res., 143 Madison St., 07105. Tel: 201-344-8322; Fax: 201-344-6158.
Catechesis / Religious Programs—Students 30.

18—ST. JOHN'S (1826), Rev. Msgr. John P. Hourihan.
Res., 22 Mulberry St., 07102. Tel: 201-623-0822; Fax: 201-623-6804.

19—ST. JOSEPH'S (1850). Closed. Records located at Seton Hall University Archives, South Orange, 07079. Tel: 201-761-9476; Fax: 201-761-9550.

20—IMMACULATE HEART OF MARY (1924) (Spanish), Revs. Antonio Terrassa, T.O.R. (Spain); John Riera, T.O.R. (Spain).
Res., 114 Prospect St., 07105. Tel: 201-589-8249; Fax: 201-589-1858.
Catechesis / Religious Programs—Tel: 201-589-5794.
Students 331.
Convent—121 Congress St., 07105. Tel: 201-589-5794.
Missionary Sisters of the Blessed Sacrament and Mary Immaculate 4.

21—IMMACULATE CONCEPTION (1925), Rev. Anthony J. Lionelli. In res., Rev. John F. O'Connor, S.T.B.
Res., 390 Woodside Ave., 07104. Tel: 201-482-0619.

22—ST. LUCY'S (1891) (Italian), Rev. Msgr. Joseph J. Granato; Revs. Joseph S. Nativo; Anthony Forte.
Res., 118 Seventh Ave., 07104. Tel: 201-482-6663; Fax: 201-483-7569.
School—(1904), 12 Amity Pl., 07104. Tel: 201-482-4756; Fax: 201-482-7363.
Sisters 5; Lay Teachers 8; Students 212.
Catechesis / Religious Programs—Students 228.
Convent—Tel: 201-482-5750.

23—ST. MARY'S, Essex Co., (1842). (Newark Abbey Church). Revs. Philip Waters, O.S.B.; Linus V. Edogwo (Nigeria); Sr. Linda Klaiss, S.S.J., Pastoral Assoc.
Res., 528 Martin Luther King, Jr. Blvd., 07102. Tel: 201-643-4800, Ext. 202; Fax: 201-643-6922.
School—(1842), Tel: 201-643-4800, Ext. 300.
Sisters of St. Joseph of Chestnut Hill 3; Lay Teachers 15; Students 260.
Convent—Tel: 201-824-8475.

24—ST. MARY MAGDALENE (1893). Closed. Records located at Seton Hall University Archives, South Orange, 07079. Tel: 201-761-9476; Fax: 201-761-9550.

25—ST. MICHAEL'S (1878), Revs. Louis Caputo, S.D.V., V.F.; Angelito Rosales, S.D.V.; John Bosco Lima; Giosue Scotto DiCesare, S.D.V.; Deacons Alberto Gomez; Daniel Ravelo; Restituto Quintana. In res., Rev. A. Felix Antonitti, S.D.V.
Res., 25 Crittenden St., 07104. Tel: 201-484-7100; Fax: 201-482-7209.
School—(1881), 27 Crittenden St., 07104. Tel: 201-482-7400; Fax: 201-482-1833.
Sisters of Charity 2; Sisters of Charity of Ottawa 3; Lay Teachers 20; Students 651.
Perpetual Help Day Nursery—170 Broad St., 07104. Tel: 201-484-3535.
Vocationist Sisters 6; Lay Teachers 8; Children 170.
Catechesis / Religious Programs—Students 453.
Convent—Tel: 201-484-5261.

26—OUR LADY OF FATIMA (1956) (Portuguese), Revs. Jose Manuel Fernandes, Admin.; Carlos C. Mamede; James A. Manos.
Res., 82 Congress St., 07105. Tel: 201-589-8433; Fax: 201-589-2611.
Day Nursery—79 Jefferson St., 07105. Tel: 201-589-1639.
Catechesis / Religious Programs—Students 1,080.

27—OUR LADY OF GOOD COUNSEL (1902), Revs. Robert Tooman; John E. Rodriguez Gamboa.
Res., 654 Summer Ave., 07104. Tel: 201-482-1274.
School—(1913), 239 Woodside Ave., 07104. Tel: 201-482-1241; Fax: 201-482-8257.
Sisters of St. Joseph, Chestnut Hill 4; Lay Teachers

24; Students 594.
High School—(1922), Tel: 201-482-1209.
Sisters of St. Joseph, Chestnut Hill 9; Marist Brothers 1; Lay Teachers 24; Students 411.
Catechesis/Religious Programs—Tel: 201-482-1274.
Students 150.
Convent—Tel: 201-483-4256.

28—OUR LADY OF MT. CARMEL (1889) (Italian), Most Rev. Nicholas A. DiMarzio. In res., Rev. Msgr. Eugene Fanelli; Rev. Joseph Ambrosio, Admin.
Res., 259 Oliver St., 07105. Tel: 201-589-2090; Fax: 201-589-2662.

29—OUR LADY OF THE ROSARY (1918) (Italian). Closed. For inquiries for parish records contact Our Lady of Mt. Carmel, Newark. Tel: 201-589-2090.

30—ST. PETER'S (1864). Closed. For inquiries for parish records contact Seton Hall University Archives, South Orange.

31—ST. PHILIP NERI (1887). Closed. For inquiries for parish records contact Seton Hall University Archives, South Orange.

32—ST. ROCCO'S (1899). (National Historic Landmark). Rev. John P. Nickas.
Res., 206 Hunterdon St., 07103. Tel: 201-824-1652.
School—21 Ashland St., 07103. Tel: 201-622-0428. Sr. Eileeny Jude West, S.S.J., Prin.
Lay Teachers 18; Students 453.
St. Rocco's Children Center—(Preschool-K) 212 Hunterdon St., 07103. Tel: 201-624-7890.
Children 45.

33—ST. ROSE OF LIMA (1888), Rev. Msgr. William J. Linder; Rev. Robert Cormier.
Res., 11 Gray St., 07107. Tel: 201-482-0682; Fax: 201-482-2137.
School—(1892), 540 Orange St., 07107. Tel: 201-481-5582. Arthur L. Wilson, Prin.
Sisters 2; Lay Teachers 12; Students 320.
Convent—Tel: 201-481-6566.

34—SACRED HEART (Vailsburg) (1892), Very Rev. Patrick W. Donohue, V.F.; Revs. Valentine Ugwuanya; G. Arokiasamy (India).
Res., 481 Sandford Ave., 07106. Tel: 201-373-9790.
School—24 Hazelwood Ave., 07106. Tel: 201-372-4441; Fax: 201-372-4157.
Lay Teachers 50; Students 800.
Convent—Tel: 201-374-2730; Fax: 210-374-4656.

35—ST. STANISLAUS (1889) (Polish), Rev. Bogumil Chrusciel.
Res., 146 Irvine Turner Blvd., 07103. Tel: 201-642-7961; Fax: 201-642-2295.

36—ST. STEPHEN'S (1902). Closed. For inquiries for parish records contact Seton Hall University Archives, South Orange.

37—ST. THOMAS AQUINAS (1957), Rev. Ray A. Francis; Mary C. Tighe, Pastoral Assoc.; Deacon Jose A. Rodriguez.
Res., 40 Ludlow St., 07114. Tel: 201-242-6703.

OUTSIDE THE CITY OF NEWARK

Allendale, Bergen Co., Guardian Angel (1954), Rev. Msgr. Cajetan P. Salemi.
Res., 320 Franklin Turnpike, 07401. Tel: 201-327-4359; Fax: 201-327-6478.
School—St. Thomas More Interparochial School. See Nativity Parish, Midland Park for details.
Catechesis/Religious Programs—Tel: 201-327-0352.
Students 347.

Bayonne, Hudson Co.,

1—ST. MARY STAR OF THE SEA, (1861), Revs. Lawrence J. Miller; Thomas P. Conheeney; Gerard T. Prindiville; Sr. Jane Veronica Walsh, S.S.J., Pastoral Assoc.
Res., 326 Avenue C, 07002. Tel: 201-437-4090.
School—(1879), 19 W. 13th St., 07002. Tel: 201-437-2888.
Sisters of St. Joseph 2; Lay Teachers 9; Students 215.
Catechesis/Religious Programs—Tel: 201-437-0010.
Students 260.
Convent—Tel: 201-436-0870.

2—ST. ANDREW'S, (1914), Rev. John R. Doherty; Rev. Msgr. Edward F. Wojtycha, Pastor Emeritus; Revs. Thomas J. Ciba; Eugene Joseph Field; Deacon Raymond Sanderson.
Res., 125 Broadway, 07002. Tel: 201-437-0833; Fax: 201-858-3477.
School—124 Broadway, 07002. Tel: 201-437-0139.
Sisters of St. Joseph 3; Lay Teachers 7; Students 205.
Catechesis/Religious Programs—Students 400.

3—ST. HENRY'S, (1889), Rev. Msgr. Edward J. Hajduk, S.T.L., M.S.S.; Revs. Thomas M. Foye; Albert J. Berner.
Res., 82 W. 29th St., 07002. Tel: 201-436-0857; Fax: 201-823-4611.
Catechesis/Religious Programs—Avenue C & 28 St., 07002. Tel: 201-339-0319. Sr. Beatrice Doria, M.P.F.
Students 390.

4—ST. JOSEPH'S, (1888) (Slovak), Rev. Msgr. Edward M. Matash.
Res., 317 Ave. E, 07002. Tel: 201-339-1122; Fax: 201-339-1009.

5—ST. VINCENT DE PAUL, (1894), Revs. Michael J. O'Grady; Victor Paloma (Philippines); Michael A. Patete; Joseph Murray. In res., Rev. Carl Arico.
Res., 979 Ave. C., 07002. Tel: 201-436-2222; Fax: 201-437-5235.
School—(1920), 80 W. 47th St., 07002. Tel: 201-339-4438.
Lay Teachers 12; Students 227.
Catechesis/Religious Programs—Tel: 201-823-0184.
Students 450.

6—MT. CARMEL, (1898) (Polish), Rev. Msgr. Joseph A. Marjanczyk, Pastor Emeritus; Revs. Anthony J. Kulig; Eugene Diurczak; Kazimierz Kuczynski; William G. Cook; Thaddeus L. Zaorski, Pastor Emeritus; Deacon Robert Zywicki.
Res., 39 E. Twenty-second St., 07002. Tel: 201-339-2070; Fax: 201-339-3676.
School—(1902), 19 E. Twenty-second St., 07002. Tel: 201-339-1839.
Felician Sisters 4; Lay Teachers 10; Students 251.
Catechesis/Religious Programs—Students 150.
Convent—Tel: 201-436-5820.

7—OUR LADY OF THE ASSUMPTION, (1902) (Italian), Revs. Donald Di Pasquale; Paul Pesenti, O.M.I.; Deacon William Giordano.
Res., 531 Ave. C, 07002. Tel: 201-436-8160.
Church—91 W. Twenty-third St., 07002.
School—101 W. Twenty-third St., 07002. Tel: 201-339-0249.
Religious Teachers Filippini 4; Lay Teachers 9; Students 154.
Catechesis/Religious Programs—Tel: 201-437-1867.
Students 263.
Convent—95 W. Twenty-third St., 07002. Tel: 201-858-0202.

8—ST. MICHAEL'S, (1907) (Lithuanian), Revs. Albert J. Matulis; James F. Tortora, Ph.D. In res., Rev. J. M. Patricius.
Res., 15 E. Twenty-third St., 07002. Tel: 201-436-1412.
Catechesis/Religious Programs—Students 165.

Belleville, Essex Co., St. Anthony's (1901) (Italian), Revs. Dennis Cocozza; Joseph J. Cestaro, Pastor Emeritus; Neil J. Collins; Eugene Bernas (Philippines). In res., Rev. Salvatore T. Malanga.
Res., 750 N. Seventh St., Newark, 07107. Tel: 201-481-1991; Fax: 201-481-1993.
Church—63 Franklin Ave., Newark, 07107.

St. Peter's (1837), Rev. Msgr. Joseph T. Slinger; Revs. Mark A. O'Connell; Robert E. Emery; Andres Reyes; Deacon William Valladares.
Res., 155 William St., 07109. Tel: 201-751-2002; Fax: 201-751-6201. [CEM]
School—(1854), 152 William St., 07109. Tel: 201-759-3143.
Sisters of Charity 4; Lay Teachers 12; Students 240.
Catechesis/Religious Programs—Tel: 201-759-4244.
Students 240.
Convent—Tel: 201-759-2432.

Bergenfield, Bergen Co., St. John the Evangelist (1909), Rev. Msgr. George R. Trabold; Rev. Msgr. Joseph J. Donovan, (Retired); Revs. Ernesto Tibay; Anthony Lipari; Raymond R. Filipski; Francesco Carraro; Deacon Patrick Miney.
Res., 29 N. Washington Ave., 07621. Tel: 201-384-0101; Fax: 201-384-2055.
School—(1921), 17 Bradley Ave., 07621. Tel: 201-384-3627.
Sisters 3; Lay Teachers 17; Students 298.
Catechesis/Religious Programs—35 N. William St., 07621. Tel: 201-384-3601.
Students 802.
Convent—Tel: 201-384-2675.

Berkeley Heights, Union Co., Church of the Little Flower (1955), Very Rev. John P. McGovern; Revs. David Milliken; Alfred Burke.
Res., 110 Roosevelt Ave., 07922. Tel: 908-464-1585; Fax: 908-464-6342.
Church—310 Plainfield Ave., 07922.
Catechesis/Religious Programs—Tel: 908-464-7444.
Students 545.

Bloomfield, Essex Co., Sacred Heart (1878), Revs. Richard P. Kwiatkowski; Peter West; Theodore Osbahr.
Res., 76 Broad St., 07003. Tel: 201-748-1800; Fax: 201-748-2028. [CEM]
School—(1879), 683 Bloomfield, 07003. Tel: 201-743-4015; Fax: 201-743-0723.
Sisters of Charity 3; Lay Teachers 17; Students 345.
Convent—Tel: 201-743-0838.
Catechesis/Religious Programs—Tel: 201-743-4061.
Students 234.

St. Valentine (1899) (Polish), Revs. Stanley J. Urbanik; Michael C. Santoro. In res., Rev. John J. Donohue.
Res., 125 N. Spring St., 07003. Tel: 201-743-0220; Fax: 201-743-2041.
Catechesis/Religious Programs—Mrs. Joyce Bowen, D.R.E.
Students 181.

Church of St. Thomas the Apostle (1939), Rev. Msgr. William C. Hatcher; Revs. John D. Gabriel; Peter K. Funesti; Rev. Msgr. Vincent P. Coburn, Pastor Emeritus. Pastoral Assocs.: Sr. Antoinette Munafo, S.S.J.; Sr. Anita Sibilia, M.P.F.; Sr. Patricia Michael, S.C. In res., Revs. Stephen S. Feehan; John Connolly, S.D.B.
Res., 60 Byrd Ave., 07003. Tel: 201-338-9190; Fax: 201-338-4224.
School—(1940), 50 Byrd Ave., 07003. Tel: 201-338-8505; Fax: 201-338-9565.
Sisters of Charity 5; Lay Teachers 24; Students 460.
Catechesis/Religious Programs—Tel: 201-338-7400.
Students 767.
Convent—Tel: 201-338-9118.

Bogota, Bergen Co., St. Joseph's (1929), Revs. Paul Schweizer, O.Carm.; Edward Ward, O.Carm.; Deacons Walter Lynn; Michael Fitzgerald. In res., Revs. Robert Wolfe, O.Carm.; John Lord, O. Carm.
Res., 115 E. Fort Lee Rd., 07603. Tel: 201-342-6300; Fax: 201-883-9392.
School—(1925), 131 E. Fort Lee Rd., 07603. Tel: 201-487-8641; Fax: 201-487-7405. Sr. Regina Miriam, F.S.P., Prin.
Franciscan Sisters of Peace 1; Lay Teachers 9; Students 240.
Catechesis/Religious Programs—Tel: 201-343-4316.
Students 554.
Convent—Tel: 201-342-4684.

Caldwell, Essex Co., St. Aloysius (1892), Revs. John J. Laferrera; Robert D. Jacunski; Mark Francis O'Malley. In res., Rev. Lester A. McGuinness.
Res., 219 Bloomfield Ave., 07006. Tel: 201-226-0221; Fax: 201-226-2204.
School—(1991). (Co-Sponsored) Trinity Academy 235 Bloomfield Ave., 07006. Tel: 201-226-3386; Fax: 201-226-6548.
Sisters 6; Lay Teachers 36; (PreK-8) 480.
Catechesis/Religious Programs—Tel: 201-226-0209.
Students 545.

Cedar Grove, Essex Co., St. Catherine of Siena (1949), Rev. Msgr. Charles W. Gusmer; Revs. Kevin J. Schott; John Chadwick; Deacon Leo Montini.
Res., 339 Pompton Ave., 07009. Tel: 201-239-7960; Fax: 201-857-5086.
School—(1958), 39 E. Bradford Ave., 07009. Tel: 201-239-6968; Fax: 201-239-1008.
Sisters of St. Dominic 1; Lay Teachers 19; Students 276; Franciscan Sister of Peace 1.
Catechesis/Religious Programs—Tel: 201-239-3332.
Students 400.
Convent—Tel: 201-239-3362.

Clark, Union Co., St. Agnes (1961), Revs. Eugene F. Marcone; Armand Mantia.
Res., 332 Madison Hill Rd., 07066. Tel: 908-388-7852; Fax: 908-388-7064.
School—(1963), 342 Madison Hill Rd., 07066. Tel: 908-381-0850.
Lay Teachers 12; Students 204.
Catechesis/Religious Programs—Students 370.

Cliffside Park, Bergen Co., Epiphany (1916), Revs. Thomas F. Olsen; Robert P. Cozzini; Joseph A. Scarangella.
Res., 247 Knox Ave., 07010. Tel: 201-943-7320; Fax: 201-943-1779.
School—(1930), 263 Lafayette Ave., 07010. Tel: 201-945-1194.
Lay Teachers 11; Students 279; Religious 6.
Catechesis/Religious Programs—Tel: 201-945-1164.
Students 281.
Convent—228 Knox Ave., 07010. Tel: 201-943-2660.

Closter, Bergen Co., St. Mary's (1912), Rev. James T. McKenna. In res., Rev. Gerald Bajek.
Res., 20 Legion Pl., 07624. Tel: 201-768-7565; Fax: 201-784-5814.
School—300 High St., 07624. Tel: 201-768-2627.
Sisters 1; Lay Teachers 9; Students 123.
Catechesis/Religious Programs—Tel: 201-767-8247.
Students 210.

Cranford, Union Co., St. Michael's (1872), Revs. Lawrence W. Cull; Krzysztof Maslowski; Noel J. Levantino; Deacon Daniel Wilverding.
Res., 40 Alden St., 07016. Tel: 908-276-0360; Fax: 908-272-0273.
School—(1929), Alden and Miln Sts., 07016. Tel: 908-276-9425.
Lay Teachers 26; Students 396.
Catechesis/Religious Programs—100 Alden St., 07016. Tel: 908-276-2050.
Students 793.

Cresskill, Bergen Co., St. Therese of Lisieux (1924), Rev. James J. Boyce, O.Carm.; Bro. Richard Supple; Rev. Brian H. Henden, O.Carm.; Sr. Rosalie O'Connor, O.S.F., Pastoral Assoc.
Res., 120 Monroe Ave., 07626. Tel: 201-567-2528; Fax: 201-567-6759.
School—220 Jefferson Ave., 07626. Tel: 201-568-4296.
Lay Teachers 15; Students 192.
Catechesis/Religious Programs—200 Jefferson Ave., 07627. Tel: 201-567-4781; Fax: 201-541-1269.
Students 520.

Demarest, Bergen Co., St. Joseph's (1931), Revs. William O'Malley, O.Carm.; Eugene Bettinger, O.Carm.
Res., 280 County Rd., 07627. Tel: 201-768-2371; Fax: 201-768-2466.
School—St. Joseph, Sacred Heart Interparochial School, 573 Piermont Rd., 07627. Tel: 201-768-5534.
Lay Teachers 11; Students 156.
Catechesis/Religious Programs—Tel: 201-768-6886.
Students 173.
Mission—Demarest, Bergen Co., St. Joseph Korean Catholic Community, 274 County Rd., 07627. Tel: 201-767-1854.

Dumont, Bergen Co., St. Mary's (1914), Revs. Donald P. Sheehan; Edward C, Thompson; Donald McLaughlin; Sr. Elizabeth Mullen, C.S.J., Pastoral Assoc. In res., Revs. Mathew Chandrankunnel (India); Theodore A. Szelest, (Retired).
Res., 280 Washington Ave., 07628. Tel: 201-384-0557; Fax: 201-384-4986.
School—(1951), 21-31 New Milford Ave., 07628. Tel: 201-384-0512.
Sisters 5; Lay Teachers 17; Students 304.
Catechesis/Religious Programs—Tel: 201-384-3062.
Students 619.

East Newark, Hudson Co., St. Anthony's (1901) (Italian), Rev. Anthony F. Granato. In res., Rev. Francis T. Maione.
Res., 409 N. Second St., 07029. Tel: 201-483-4680.

East Orange, Essex Co.,

1—Holy Name of Jesus, (1910), Revs. Robert J. Rischmann, Admin.; Eric L. Kowalski; Deacon Leo Woodruff. In res., Rev. Joseph L. Affanoso.
Parish Center—200 Midland Ave., P.O. Box 5244, 07017-1855. Tel: 201-675-4444; Fax: 201-674-1767.

2—Holy Spirit-Our Lady Help of Christians, (1882), Very Rev. Thomas Paul Lipnicki, V.F.; Rev. Nerva W. Dugue. In res., Rev. George Kelly, C.SS.R.
Res., 17 N. Clinton St., 07017. Tel: 201-673-1077.
School—(1883), 23 N. Clinton St., 07017. Tel: 201-677-1546.
Lay Teachers 17; Students 535.

3—St. Joseph's, (1916) (Italian), Rev. Bernard N. Mohen; Deacons Joseph Fiore, (Retired); Alonzo C. Jackson.
Res., 110 Telford St., 07018. Tel: 201-678-4030.
School—115 Telford St., 07018. Tel: 201-674-2326.
Religious Teachers Filippini 2; Lay Teachers 16; Students 417.
Catechesis/Religious Programs—Students 417.
Convent—Tel: 201-677-0812.

4—Our Lady of All Souls, (1914). Closed. For inquiries for parish records contact Seton Hall University Archives, South Orange. Tel: 201-761-9476; Fax: 201-761-9550.

5—Our Lady of the Most Blessed Sacrament, (1916). Closed. For inquiries for parish records contact Seton Hall University Archives, South Orange. Tel: 201-761-9476; Fax: 201-761-9550.

East Rutherford, Bergen Co., St. Joseph's (1872), Revs. Richard S. Husted, O.F.M.; Edward J. Donahue, O.F.M.; Brian Linehan, O.F.M.; Paul Sinnema, O.F.M.; Sr. Agnes Morrisseey, S.C., Pastoral Min., Tel: 201-507-8842. In res., Rev. Kieran Cassion, O.F.M.
Res., 120 Hoboken Rd., 07073. Tel: 201-939-0457; Fax: 201-939-4196. [CEM]
School—(1879), 20 Hackensack St., 07073. Tel: 201-939-3193; Fax: 201-939-1913. Mrs. Frances Alberta, Prin.
Lay Teachers 12; Students 264.
Catechesis/Religious Programs—Tel: 201-939-3441.
Students 522.
Convent—Tel: 201-460-4961.

Edgewater, Bergen Co., Holy Rosary (1906), Rev. Gerald F. Greaves; Deacon Robert E. Thomson. In res., Rev. Frank G. DelPrete.
Res., 365 Undercliff Ave., 07020. Tel: 201-945-6329 (Parish Center); Fax: 201-945-6599.

Elizabeth, Union Co.,

1—St. Mary of the Assumption, (1844), Rev. Msgr. Robert J. Harrington; Revs. Joseph D. Girone; William Crum; Manuel D. Rios. Pastoral Assocs.: Sr. Ruth Morgan, R.S.M.; Sr. Elaine Maguire, F.S.P.; Maria Castillo; Colleen Reynolds. In res., Revs. D. Joseph Fiorino; Robert Becerra.
Res., 155 Washington Ave., 07202. Tel: 908-352-5154; Fax: 908-352-0350. [CEM]
School—(1868), 237 S. Broad St., 07202. Tel: 908-352-0717.
Sisters 1; Lay Teachers 10; Students 211.
High School—Tel: 908-352-4350; Fax: 908-352-2359.
Sisters 3; Lay Teachers 26; Students 356.
Child Care Center—Tel: 908-355-8723.
Sisters 1; Students 69.
Catechesis/Religious Programs—Tel: 908-352-0296.
Students 390.
Convent—Tel: 908-352-1455.

2—St. Adalbert's, (1905) (Polish), Revs. Ronald J. Marczewski; Dariusz Ziebowicz; Marek Wysocki; Deacon Joseph J. Lubas.
Res., 250 E. Jersey St., 07206. Tel: 908-352-2791; Fax: 908-354-2828. [CEM]
School—(1905), Tel: 908-353-3160.
Felician Sisters 2; Lay Teachers 9; Students 167.

3—St. Anthony's, (1895) (Italian), Revs. Vincent Zuliani, S.D.B.; John P. Murphy, S.D.B.; Johon Masiello, S.D.B.; Xavier Aracil, S.D.B.; Paul Bedard, S.D.B. In res., Rev. Mario Balbi-Port; Bro. Charles Thenier, S.D.B.
Res., 853 Third Ave., 07202. Tel: 908-351-3300; Fax: 908-351-3609.
School—229 Centre St., 07202. Tel: 908-352-7419.
Sisters of Charity of Convent Station 4; Lay Teachers 12; Students 410.
Catechesis/Religious Programs—Students 310.
Convent—Tel: 908-354-0825.

4—Blessed Sacrament, (1922), Revs. Sean Raymond Cunneen; John Stanley Gomes.
Res., 1096 North Ave., 07201. Tel: 908-352-0338; Fax: 908-352-4553.
School—(1926), 1086 North Ave., 07201. Tel: 908-352-8629.
Sisters of St. Benedict 1; Lay Teachers 9; Students 215.
Convent—Tel: 908-352-6681.

5—Immaculate Conception, (1907), Revs. Alfred J. Kowalski; Fabio R. Brenes-Chavez.
Res., 425 Union Ave., 07208. Tel: 908-352-6662.
School—(1913), 417 Union Ave., 07208. Tel: 908-351-4242.
Sisters of St. John the Baptist 4; Lay Teachers 6; Students 234.
Convent—424 Westminister Ave., 07208. Tel: 908-353-8463.

6—St. Genevieve's, (1920), Rev. Msgr. Hugh A. O'Donnell; Rev. Msgr. Edward G. Price, Pastor Emeritus; Revs. Roy James DeLeo; John G. Netta.
Res., 200 Monmouth Rd., 07208. Tel: 908-351-4444; Fax: 908-351-5454.
School—(1929), 209 Princeton Rd., 07208. Tel: 908-355-3355.
Benedictine Sisters 4; Lay Teachers 23; Students 435.
Catechesis/Religious Programs—Tel: 908-355-1584.
Students 284.
Convent—Tel: 908-353-0736.

7—St. Hedwig's, (1926) (Polish), Rev. Bronislaw Wielgus. In res., Rev. Thomas J. Lewczak.
Res., 716 Clarkson Ave., 07202. Tel: 908-352-1448; Fax: 908-352-8389.
School—(1928), Clarkson Ave. and Myrtle St., 07202. Tel: 908-354-5653.
Little Servant Sisters of the Immaculate Conception 3; Lay Teachers 11; Students 248.
Catechesis/Religious Programs—Tel: 908-354-5650.
Students 278.
Convent—717 Polonia Ave., 07202. Tel: 908-355-8409.

8—St. Joseph's, (1911) (Slovak). Closed. Records at Holy Family, Linden. Tel: 908-862-1060.

9—Our Lady of Most Holy Rosary/St. Michael, (1886/1852), Revs. Jan Sasin; Jean F. Salomon. In res., Rev. William C. Reed.
Res., 52 Smith St., 07201. Tel: 908-354-2454; Fax: 908-354-3207. [JC]

10—St. Patrick's, (1858) (Hispanic), Rev. Msgr. Richard J. Arnhols; Revs. Jose Montes De Oca; Dennis Kaelin, Chap. In res., Rev. James G. Marr (STU).
Res., 215 Court St., 07206. Tel: 908-354-0023; Fax: 908-355-0926. [CEM]
School—(1863). See Elizabethport Catholic School. 227 Court St., 07206. Tel: 908-351-2188.
High School—(1863), 221 Court St., 07206. Tel: 908-353-5220; Fax: 908-629-1123.
Brothers 1; Sisters 1; Lay Teachers 15; Students 233.

11—Sacred Heart, (1871). Merged Records at Our Lady of Fatima Parish, Elizabeth. Tel: 908-355-3810.

12—Holy Rosary, (1886). Merged Records at Our Lady of Most Holy Rosary/St. Michael, Elizabeth. Tel: 908-354-2454; Fax: 908-354-3207.

13—SS. Peter and Paul's, (1895) (Lithuanian), Revs. Alfred Zemeikis; Peter M. Aquino; Deacon Henry Keturwitis.
Res., 211 Ripley Pl., 07206. Tel: 908-352-2271.
School—(1913), 220 Monsignor Kemezis Pl., 07206. Tel: 908-289-6843.
Sisters of St. Francis of the Providence of God 3; Lay Teachers 10; Students 168.
Convent—Tel: 908-352-9391.

14—Immaculate Heart of Mary, (1947) (Spanish), Revs. Francisco Dols, T.O.R. (Spain); Jorge Oliver, T.O.R.
Res., 205 E. Jersey St., 07206. Tel: 908-355-0807; Fax: 908-355-0526.
Convent—Tel: 908-354-8388.

15—Our Lady of Fatima, (1973) (Portuguese), Rev. Msgr. John S. Antao.
Res., 403 Spring St., 07201. Tel: 908-355-3810.
Catechesis/Religious Programs—Students 650.

Elmwood Park, Bergen Co., St. Leo's (1912), Revs. Brian P. Cullinane, O.F.M.; Roland A. Fregault, O.F.M.; Theodore F. Lehr, O.F.M.; Theodore Cavanaugh, O.F.M.; Robert J. Norton, O.F.M.
Res., 324 Market St., 07407. Tel: 201-796-3521; Fax: 201-703-8408.
School—(1912), 300 Market St., 07407. Tel: 201-796-5156.
Franciscan Sisters of Peace 3; Lay Teachers 15; Students 417.
Catechesis/Religious Programs—Students 230.
Convent—Tel: 201-797-6993.

Emerson, Bergen Co., Church of the Assumption (1947), Rev. Eugene J. Hazewski; Rev. Msgr. Caesar G. Orrico, Pastor Emeritus; Revs. Mathew Aymanathil (India); Bryan F.J. Adamcik.
Res., 29 Jefferson Ave., 07630. Tel: 201-262-1122; Fax: 201-262-7855.
School—35 Jefferson Ave., 07630. Tel: 201-262-0300; Fax: 201-262-5910.
Sisters 5; Lay Teachers 18; Students 315.
Catechesis/Religious Programs—Tel: 201-986-0970.
Students 320.

Englewood, Bergen Co., St. Cecilia's (1866), Very Rev. Joseph O'Brien, O.Carm., V.E., Pastor & Prior; Revs. Emil Agostino, O.Carm.; Victor Lopez, O.Carm. In res., Rev. Brendan Gilmore, O.Carm.; Very Rev. Timothy Moore, O.Carm.; Revs. Ellis Reinert, O.Carm.; Anthony Palo, O.Carm.
Res., 55 Demarest Ave., 07631. Tel: 201-568-0364; Fax: 201-568-0654.
School—St. Cecilia Interparochial School, (1874), 85 W. Demarest Ave., 07631. Tel: 201-568-2615.
Lay Teachers 10; Students 200.
Catechesis/Religious Programs—Students 88.

Fairfield, Essex Co., St. Thomas More (1962), Revs. Charles P. O'Connor; Santos Bertiz; George Ruane; Sr. Agnes Bernard, O.P., Pastoral Assoc.
Res., 210 Horseneck Rd., 07004. Tel: 201-227-0055; Fax: 201-227-2495.
Catechesis/Religious Programs—(Grades 1-8) 12 Hollywood Ave., 07004. Tel: 201-227-3607.
Students 395.

Fair Lawn, Bergen Co., St. Anne's (1909), Revs. James Nero, O.F.M.; Jack Kull, O.F.M.; Jeremiah V. McGinley, O.F.M.; John Alderson, O.F.M.; Evan Banks, O.F.M.; Deacons Joseph Marcom; Richard Titmas; Richard McGarry. In res., Revs. Brennan Connelly, O.F.M.; Felican Foy, O.F.M.
Res., 15-05 Saint Anne St., 07410. Tel: 201-791-1616; Fax: 201-791-1871.
School—(1950), 1-30 Summit Ave., 07410. Tel: 201-796-3353.
Sisters of St. Joseph of Peace 1; Lay Teachers 21; Students 352.
Catechesis/Religious Programs—Students 544.
Convent—Tel: 201-796-1899.

Fairview, Bergen Co., St. John the Baptist (1873), Revs. John J. Gibbons; James J. Carroll; Deacon Anton Tarabokija. In res., Revs. Giordano Belaxich (PAT); Gildardo Garcia.
Res., 239 Anderson Ave., 07022. Tel: 201-945-4865; Fax: 201-945-8171.

School—St. Elizabeth Seton Interparochial School, (1991). Co-Sponsored. Fourth & Walker, 07022. Tel: 201-945-2212.
Lay Teachers 9; Students 230.
Catechesis/Religious Programs—Tel: 201-945-2073.
Students 300.

Our Lady of Grace (1922) (Italian), Revs. Francis Gaetano, S.A.C.; Pompeo Luciani, S.A.C.
Res., 395 Delano Pl., 07022. Tel: 201-943-0904.
School—400 Kamena St., 07022. Tel: 201-945-8300.
Lay Teachers 15; Students 342.
Catechesis/Religious Programs—Tel: 201-945-1201.
Students 225.

Fort Lee, Bergen Co., Holy Trinity (1906), Revs. James B. Sullivan; Michael T. Mickelson.
Res., 2367 Lemoine Ave., 07024. Tel: 201-947-1216; Fax: 201-947-1217.
School—Christ the Teacher Interparochial School. Co-Sponsored. (See Madonna Parish, Fort Lee). Tel: 201-944-0421.
Catechesis/Religious Programs—Tel: 201-585-0381.
Students 172.
Convent—Tel: 201-944-2911.

Madonna (1858), Revs. John P. Ryan, Admin.; John L. Paprocki; Camilo L. Lopez. In res., Rev. Msgr. Eugene A. Fanelli.
Res., 340 Main St., 07024. Tel: 201-944-2727. [CEM]
School—(1991). Christ the Teacher Interparochial School 359 Whiteman St., 07024. Tel: 201-944-0421.
Sisters 1; Lay Teachers 19; Students 260.
Catechesis/Religious Programs—Madonna Religious Education Center.
Students 174.

Franklin Lakes, Bergen Co., Most Blessed Sacrament (1961), Rev. Msgr. Owen J. Hendry; Rev. Msgr. Carl D. Hinrichsen, Pastor Emeritus; Rev. Brian G. Plate.
Res., 787 Franklin Lake Rd., 07417. Tel: 201-891-4200; Fax: 201-891-1736.
School—(1963), 785 Franklin Lake Rd., 07417. Tel: 201-891-4250; Fax: 201-847-9227.
Sisters of St. Joseph of Chestnut Hill 2; Lay Teachers 20; Students 240.
Catechesis/Religious Programs—Tel: 201-891-8390.
Students 680.
Convent—Tel: 201-891-4292.

Garfield, Bergen Co.,

1—Our Lady of Mt. Virgin, (1901) (Italian), Revs. Paul L. Bochicchio; Joseph Fu (China); Miguel A. Arata (Chile); Deacon Dominic Riccio.
Res., 188 MacArthur Ave., 07026. Tel: 201-772-2295; Fax: 201-478-4389.
School—Garfield Catholic Academy, (1951) (Grades PreK-8). (Mt. Vernon Campus) 200 MacArthur Ave., 07026. Tel: 201-772-0416; Fax: 201-772-3301. Sr. Patricia Dunham, M.P.F., Prin.
Religious Teachers Filippini 2; Lay Teachers 10.
Catechesis/Religious Programs—Tel: 201-253-1399. Sr. Jo Ann Jankowski, M.P.F., D.R.E.
Students 175.
Convent—410 Maywood Ave., Maywood, 07607. Tel: 201-845-9568.

2—Holy Name, (1911), Rev. Benedict P. Militello.
Res., 99 Marsellus Pl., 07026. Tel: 201-340-0032; Fax: 201-340-1618.
School—Garfield Catholic Academy, (Grades PreK-8) 200 MacArthur Ave., 07026.

3—Church of Our Lady of Sorrows, (1917), Revs. John K. Gurski; Michael Guba.
Res., 69 Market St., 07026. Tel: 201-772-7889.
School—Garfield Catholic Academy, (Grades PreK-8) 200 MacArthur Ave., 07026.

4—St. Stanislaus Kostka, (1917) (Polish), Revs. Edward P. Szpiech; Marian Spanier; Bogdan Palka, S.D.S.; Eugene S. Kowalski, Pastor Emeritus.
Res., 184 Ray St., 07026. Tel: 201-772-7922; Fax: 201-772-4178.
School—Garfield Catholic Academy, (1919) (Grades K-8). (Kostka Campus) 210 Lanza Ave., 07026. Tel: 201-772-0345; Fax: 201-772-8393.
Felician Sisters 1; Lay Teachers 9; Students 171.
Catechesis/Religious Programs—Tel: 201-794-0620.
Students 250.
Convent—Tel: 201-772-4644.

Garwood, Union Co., Church of St. Anne (1925), Rev. Msgr. John Philip O'Connor; Revs. Michael J. Kreder; Joseph J. Derbyshire.
Res., 325 Second Ave., 07027. Tel: 908-789-0280; Fax: 908-789-3099.
Catechesis/Religious Programs—315 Second Ave., 07027. Tel: 908-789-1436.
Students 325.

Glen Rock, Bergen Co., St. Catharine (1953), Rev. Dennis Cohan; Rev. Msgr. Richard J. Holmes, Pastor Emeritus; Revs. Jose Agan; James J. Weiner. Pastoral Assocs.: Catherine Furlani; Roberta Maguire; Vicki Peluse; Deacons Leonard A. Minichino; Paul Schnieder; James Mueller. In res., Rev. John A. Merity.
Res., 905 S. Maple Ave., 07452. Tel: 201-445-3703; Fax: 201-670-7149.
School—St. Catharine Interparochial School, 180 Rodney St., 07452. Tel: 201-445-0622. Sr. Mary Elizabeth DeBoer, O.P., Prin.
Sisters 1; Lay Teachers 25; Students 435.
Catechesis/Religious Programs—Tel: 201-444-5690.
Students 755.
Convent—Tel: 201-447-4342.

Guttenberg, Hudson Co., St. John Nepomucene (1910) (Slovak), Rev. John F. Renard.
Res., 7007 Polk St., 07093. Tel: 201-869-6834; Fax: 201-869-2408.
School—7111 Polk St., North Bergen, 07047. Tel: 201-869-5404.
School Sisters of St. Francis 4; Lay Teachers 12; Students 281.
Convent—Tel: 201-869-2099.

Hackensack, Bergen Co.,

1—Holy Trinity, (1861), Rev. Msgr. William J. Koplik; Rev. Msgr. Robert M. Brennan; Revs. J. Orlando Rengifo; Alfonso DeCondorpusa; Deacon Vincent Messina; Sr. Emily Marie Walsh, Parish Min.
Res., 34 Maple Ave., 07601. Tel: 201-343-5170; Fax: 201-343-5067. [CEM]
School—(1869), 43 Maple Ave., 07601. Tel: 201-489-6870.
Sisters of Charity 5; Lay Teachers 8; Students 198.
Catechesis/Religious Programs—Mrs. Carol Thee, D.R.E.
Students 243.
Convent—Tel: 201-342-1996.

2—Immaculate Conception, (1891), Rev. Thomas F. Lynch.
Res., 49 Vreeland Ave., 07601. Tel: 201-440-2798.

3—St. Joseph's, (1909), Rev. Martin J. Silver.
Res., 460 Hudson St., 07601. Tel: 201-440-3224.

4—St. Francis, (1917) (Italian), Revs. Peter Nicosia, O.F.M.Cap.; Michael Ristori, O.F.M.Cap.; Deacon Arthur Causeglia.
Res., 50 Lodi St., 07601. Tel: 201-343-6243; Fax: 201-343-0854.
School—100 S. Main St., 07601. Tel: 201-488-8862.
Lay Teachers 11; Students 283.

Harrington Park, Bergen Co., Our Lady of Victories (1910), Rev. Edward V. Duffy. In res., Rev. Msgr. Roger A. Reynolds; Rev. Bernard L. Keitz, O.P.
Res., 81 Lynn St., 07640-1831. Tel: 201-768-1706; Fax: 201-768-3962.
School—Holy Family Interparochial School, Norwood. (See Immaculate Conception, Norwood. Tel: 201-768-1605). Tel: 201-768-1605.
Catechesis/Religious Programs—(Grades K-8) 155 The Parkway, 07640-1820. Tel: 201-768-1400. Miss Elizabeth Foer, D.R.E.
Students 309.
Convent—Tel: 201-768-1705; Fax: 201-768-8006.

Harrison, Hudson Co., Holy Cross (1865), Rev. Msgr. John J. Gilchrist; Rev. Antonio Bico. In res., Revs. Carlos A. Bracci; James J. Reilly; Sr. Doris DeLotto, S.S.C., Pastoral Assoc.
Res., 16 Church Sq., 07029. Tel: 201-484-5678; Fax: 201-484-0906.
School—(1871), 14 S. F.E. Rodgers Blvd., 07029. Tel: 201-485-0340.
Lay Teachers 15; Students 237.
Catechesis/Religious Programs—Students 272.
Convent—Tel: 201-485-2632. Holy Cross Convent

Our Lady of Czestochowa (1908) (Polish), Revs. Rudolf Zubik; Henry P. Marciniak; Piotr Michota.
Res., 115 S. Third St., 07029. Tel: 201-483-2255.

Hasbrouck Heights, Bergen Co., Corpus Christi (1897), Rev. Msgr. Francis A. DeDomenico; Revs. Raymond M. Holmes; Andrew Zmerlicki; Deacon Joseph Romano.
Res., 206 Washington Pl., 07604. Tel: 201-288-4844; Fax: 201-288-0237.
School—(1928), 215 Kipp Ave., 07604. Tel: 201-288-0614; Fax: 201-288-5956.
Sisters of Charity 1; Lay Teachers 24; Students 432.
Catechesis/Religious Programs—Tel: 201-288-5133.
Students 510.
Convent—Tel: 201-288-1075.

Haworth, Bergen Co., Sacred Heart (1914), Rev. Msgr. James F. Bouffard; Rev. Joseph W. Nealon, Pastor Emeritus.
Res., 123 Maple St., P.O. Box S, 07641. Tel: 201-387-0080; Fax: 201-439-1395.
School—St. Joseph's Interparochial School. (See St. Joseph, Demarest. Tel: 201-768-5534).
Catechesis/Religious Programs—400 St. Nicholas Ave., 07641. Tel: 201-384-6454.
Students 175.

Hillsdale, Bergen Co., St. John the Baptist (1925), Rev. Msgr. Philip D. Morris; Revs. Michael J. Moran; Kevin E. Carter. Pastoral Assocs.: Sr. Thomas Therese, S.S.J.; Catherine Wollyung.
Res., 69 Valley St., 07642. Tel: 201-664-3131; Fax: 201-664-0772.
School—St. John the Baptist Interparochial School, (1955), 460 Hillsdale Ave., 07642. Tel: 201-664-6364; Fax: 201-664-8096.
Sisters of St. Joseph, Chestnut Hill, PA 2; Lay Teachers 23; Students 360.
Catechesis/Religious Programs—The Duffy Center, Tel: 201-666-2707.
Students 476.
Convent—Tel: 201-664-3800.

Hillside, Union Co., St. Catherine of Siena (1912), Revs. Richard A. Villanova; Robert L. Daly, Pastor Emeritus. In res., Rev. Thomas R. McLaughlin.
Res., 19 King St., 07205. Tel: 908-351-1515; Fax: 908-351-2139.
School—(1920), 1003 N. Broad St., Elizabeth, 07205. Tel: 908-352-8029.
Lay Teachers 15; Students 240.
Catechesis/Religious Programs—Elizabeth, Tel: 908-352-8068.
Students 170.

Christ the King (1948), Revs. Richard D. Carlson; Jean Markelor Berthoumieux.
Res., 411 Rutgers Ave., 07205. Tel: 908-686-0722; Fax: 908-686-2504.
School—(1953), 397 Columbia Ave., 07205. Tel: 908-686-6740; Fax: 908-686-3819.
Sisters 2; Lay Teachers 17; Students 225.
Catechesis/Religious Programs—Tel: 908-686-0234.
Students 116.
Convent—Tel: 908-686-2560.

Hoboken, Hudson Co.,

1—Our Lady of Grace, (1851), Revs. Richard J. Carrington; Arcadio Munoz; Frederick M. Eid.
Res., 400 Willow Ave., 07030. Tel: 201-659-0369; Fax: 201-659-5833.
School—(1864), Fifth St. & Willow Ave., 07030. Tel: 201-659-3025.
Lay Teachers 14; Students 225.
Convent—Tel: 201-659-1216.
Catechesis/Religious Programs—Students 185.

2—St. Joseph's, (1871), Revs. Terence Pescatore, O.F.M.Conv., Admin.; Joseph Angelini, O.F.M.Conv.; Deacons Luis Montanez; Pedro Rivera. In res., Revs. John Bickle, O.F.M.Conv.; Otto Fouser, O.F.M.Conv.; Aquin Hankinson, O.F.M.Conv.; Andrew Sioleti, O.F.M.Conv.; Bro. Edward Handy, O.F.M.Conv.
Res., 61 Monroe St., 07030. Tel: 201-659-0221.
School—John Paul II Interparochial School. (See St. Ann, Hoboken).
Convent—Tel: 201-659-1514.

3—St. Francis, (1888) (Italian), Revs. Michael V. Guglielmelli, O.F.M.Conv.; Otto Fouser, O.F.M.Conv.
Res., 308 Jefferson St., 07030. Tel: 201-659-1772; Fax: 201-222-7975.
School—John Paul II Interparochial School. (See St. Ann, Hoboken. Tel: 201-963-9535).

4—SS. Peter and Paul's, (1889), Very Rev. Msgr. Robert M. Chabak, V.F.; Revs. George Faour; Charles W.A. Herr; Deacon Primitivo Cruz. In res., Rev. John J. Paladino.
Res., 404 Hudson St., 07030. Tel: 201-659-2276; Fax: 201-659-5062.
School—(1889), 410 Hudson St., 07030. Tel: 201-659-7158.
Caldwell Dominicans 3; Lay Teachers 8; Students 240.
Convent—Tel: 201-659-1784.

5—St. Ann's, (1900) (Italian), Revs. Andrew Jamieson, O.F.M.Cap.; Joseph Mezzanote, O.F.M.Cap.; Philip Volpe, O.F.M.Cap.
Res., 704 Jefferson St., 07030. Tel: 201-659-1114; Fax: 201-659-1416.
School—John Paul II Interparochial School, (1955), 555 Seventh St., 07030. Tel: 201-963-9535.
Sisters 3; Lay Teachers 11; Students 235.

Hohokus, Bergen Co., St. Luke's (1864), Rev. John E. Basil; Rev. Msgr. Joseph F. Flusk; Deacon Edwin J. Alsing. In res., Rev. Msgr. Richard J. Holmes, Pastor Emeritus.
Res., 340 N. Franklin Tpke., 07423. Tel: 201-444-0272; Fax: 201-652-7044. [CEM]
School—St. Thomas More Interparochial School. Serving the Parish Communities of St. Luke's, Nativity and Guardian Angel. (See Nativity Parish, Midland Park).
Catechesis/Religious Programs—Tel: 201-447-2779. Sr. Regina Chassar, S.S.J., D.R.E.
Students 527.

Irvington, Essex Co.,

1—ASSUMPTION OF THE BLESSED VIRGIN MARY, (1907) (Hungarian). Closed. For inquiries for parish records contact Seton Hall University Archives, South Orange. Tel: 201-596-9476.

2—ST. LEO'S, (1878), Revs. Thomas M. Cembor; Eugene E. Geiger; Frederick C. Koerner; Dennis McKenna, Pastor Emeritus; Deacon Victor Reyes.
Res., 103 Myrtle Ave., 07111. Tel: 201-372-1272; Fax: 201-416-8819.
School—(1892), 123 Myrtle Ave., 07111. Tel: 201-372-7555. Ms. Debra Brower, Prin.
Lay Teachers 16; Students 302.
Convent—Tel: 201-374-6397.

3—SACRED HEART OF JESUS, (1925) (Polish), Revs. Robert T. Ulak; Burnet Moise; Jordan Mysliwiec, S.D.S.
Res., 537 Grove St., 07111. Tel: 201-373-2232.
School—(1929), 15 Smalley Ter., 07111. Tel: 201-372-6372.
Felician Sisters 1; Lay Teachers 9; Students 190.
Convent—Tel: 201-372-6528.

4—ST. PAUL THE APOSTLE, (1948), Revs. William R. Smalley; Venantius M. Fernando.
Res., 954 Stuyvesant Ave., 07111. Tel: 201-375-8568; Fax: 201-375-7040.
School—(1950), 285 Nesbit Ter., 07111. Tel: 201-375-0659; Fax: 201-375-7040.
Sisters of St. Dominic 4; Lay Teachers 9; Students 250.
Convent—972 Stuyvesant Ave., 07111. Tel: 201-374-2277.
Catechesis/Religious Programs—Tel: 201-375-2688.
Students 225.

Jersey City, Hudson Co.,

1—ST. AEDAN'S, (1912), Revs. Jeremias R. Rebanal, J.C.D., Ph.D.; John Corbett; Edito Gamallo, S.T.B. In res., Rev. Thomas Kunnath.
Res., 800 Bergen Ave., 07306. Tel: 201-433-6800; Fax: 201-433-1222.
School—(1913), 41 Tuers Ave., 07306. Tel: 201-435-6528; Fax: 201-985-8975.
Sisters 5; Lay Teachers 18; Students 394.
Convent—Tel: 201-451-8109.

2—ST. ALOYSIUS, (1897), Rev. Msgr. Peter A. Cheplic; Rev. Msgr. Martin Kelly; Revs. Thomas Thottungal; Kenneth E. Jennings; Deacon Stephen Liptak. In res., Revs. David J. Baratelli; Joseph A. Petrillo; William Gyure.
Res., 691 West Side Ave., 07304. Tel: 201-433-6365; Fax: 201-451-6438.
Schools—(1897), 721 West Side Ave., 07306. Tel: 201-433-4270; Fax: 201-433-6916.
Sisters of Charity 3; Lay Teachers 27; Students 455; High School Sisters of Charity, Tel: 201-435-9240; Fax: 201-435-2115.
Sisters 3; Lay Teachers 18; Students 300.
Catechesis/Religious Programs—Students 209.
Convent—Tel: 201-433-5759.

3—ST. ANNE'S, (1903), Very Rev. Victor P. Kennedy, V.F.; Revs. Juan Perez De Mesa; Arnelo A. Galeon. In res., Revs. Gerard J. Sudol; Kevin P. Ashe.
Res., 3545 J.F. Kennedy Blvd., 07307. Tel: 201-656-2490; Fax: 201-795-3817.
School—(1904), 255 Congress St., 07307. Tel: 201-659-0450. Mrs. Marlene Bartram, Prin.
Lay Teachers 17; Students 346.
Catechesis/Religious Programs—Tel: 201-659-1794. Sr. Alberta Manzo, F.S.R., D.R.E.
Students 178.
Convent—Tel: 201-963-0998.

4—ST. ANN'S, (1910) (Lithuanian). Closed. For inquiries for parish records contact Seton Hall University Archives, South Orange. Tel: 201-761-9476, Fax: 201-761-9550.

5—ST. ANN'S, (1911) (Polish), Revs. Thaddeus Stasik; George Idzik.
Res., 291 St. Paul's Ave., 07306-5008. Tel: 201-656-4018; Fax: 201-222-9727.

6—ST. ANTHONY OF PADUA, (1884) (Polish), Revs. Michael E. Gubernat, Admin.; Stanley Kostrzomb.
Res., 330 Sixth St., 07302. Tel: 201-653-0343.

7—ASSUMPTION/ALL SAINTS, (1896), Revs. Eugene Squeo; Jean Marie Fritz Ligonde; Francis E. Shiller; Gabriel Vargas; Deacon Joseph Del Monte.
Res., 344 Pacific Ave., 07304. Tel: 201-333-1971.
School—301 Whiton St., 07304. Tel: 201-433-6087.
Sisters of Charity 5; Lay Teachers 7; Students 260.
Convent—Tel: 201-451-2765.

8—ST. BONIFACE'S, (1863), Rev. Msgr. Ricardo Gonzalez; Deacons Leopoldo Polanco; Pedro Gonzalez.
Office: 262 First St., 07302. Tel: 201-792-2504; Fax: 201-656-2638.
Catechesis/Religious Programs—Tel: 201-795-2761.
Students 150.

9—ST. BRIDGET'S, (1869), Rev. Gregory Studerus.
Res., 372 Montgomery St., 07302. Tel: 201-434-8500; Fax: 201-333-1816.
School—(1873), 370 Montgomery St., 07302. Tel: 201-432-3588.
Sisters of Charity 3; Lay Teachers 8; Students 270.
Catechesis/Religious Programs—Students 250.
Convent—Tel: 201-333-7592.

10—CHRIST, THE KING, (1930) (African American), Rev. John Edmunds, S.T.; Deacon Leon Johnson.
Res., 768 Ocean Ave., 07304. Tel: 201-333-4862; Fax: 201-433-6352.

11—HOLY ROSARY, (1885) (Italian), Revs. Robert G. Laferrera; Gerard M. Santora, Pastor Emeritus; Joseph A. Ferraro. In res., Rev. Robert M. Iaquinto.
Res., 344 Sixth St., 07302. Tel: 201-795-0120; Fax: 201-610-1389.
School—189 Brunswick St., 07302. Tel: 201-653-1699; Fax: 201-418-9019. Sr. Dolores Jensen, Prin.
Religious Teachers Filippini 2; Lay Teachers 12; Students 227.
Catechesis/Religious Programs—Tel: 201-792-7959; Fax: 201-610-1389.
Students 23.
Convent—Tel: 201-653-0697.

12—ST. JOHN THE BAPTIST, (1884), Rev. Msgr. Charles G. Stengel; Revs. Paul A. Cannariato; Varughese Kilichumala (India); Rev. Msgr. Joseph A. Beggans, Pastor Emeritus. In res., Rev. Edward S. Malkiewicz.
Res., 3026 John F. Kennedy Blvd., 07306. Tel: 201-653-8814; Fax: 201-653-3771.
School—(1886) (Grades PreK-8). Co-Sponsored. Saints John and Ann School. 3044 Kennedy Blvd., 07306. Tel: 201-653-4416; Fax: 201-653-7452.
Lay Teachers 17; Students 346.

13—ST. JOSEPH'S, (1856), Revs. James V. Pagnotta; John J. Spino.
Res., 511 Pavonia Ave., 07306. Tel: 201-653-0392.
Church—Baldwin Ave., 07306.
School—(1876), 509 Pavonia Ave., 07306. Tel: 201-653-0128; Fax: 201-222-5324.
Sisters of Charity 1; Lay Teachers 10; Students 200.
Convent—Tel: 201-963-1428.
Catechesis/Religious Programs—Tel: 201-659-5929.
Students 168.

14—ST. LUCY'S, (1884). Closed. For inquiries for parish records contact St. Michael's Parish. Tel: 201-653-2147.

15—ST. MARY'S, (1854) (Hispanic-Filipino), Rev. Msgr. James J. Finnerty; Revs. Robert A. Antczak; John B. Martin.
Res., 219 Third St., 07302. Tel: 201-653-2217; Fax: 201-653-1943.
School—(1868), 209 Third St., 07302. Tel: 201-653-3333; Fax: 201-653-4518. Sr. Eleanor Uhl, O.P., Prin.
Sisters of Charity 2; Lay Teachers 8; Students 265.
High School—Tel: 201-656-8008.
Sisters of Charity 3; Lay Teachers 25; Students 450.
Convent—Tel: 201-653-7495.

16—ST. MICHAEL'S, (1867), Rev. Hugh V. Fitzgerald; Deacon Jaime Ortiz; Sr. Jean Young, S.C., Pastoral Assoc.
Res., 252 Ninth St., 07302. Tel: 201-653-2147; 653-7328; Fax: 201-653-2247.
Shrine—Jersey City, Shrine of St. Jude. (Perpetual Novena). Tel: 201-653-2147.

17—MT. CARMEL, (1905) (Italian), Rev. Michael A. Merlucci. In res., Revs. Walter L. Genzlinger; Gabriel Vargas.
Res., 99 Broadway, 07306. Tel: 201-435-7080; Fax: 201-432-4476.
School—(1955), 95 Broadway, 07306. Tel: 201-435-0209; Fax: 201-435-0298.
Religious Teachers Filippini 1; Lay Teachers 11; Students 185.

18—ST. NICHOLAS, (1886) (German), Revs. Peter P. Galdon; Jose Saltarin; Rev. Msgr. Joseph C. Manz, Pastor Emeritus. In res., Rev. Msgr. Jose M. Alba; Rev. Mert Cordero (Philippines).
Res., 122 Ferry St., 07307. Tel: 201-659-5354; Fax: 201-798-6868.
School—(1884), 118 Ferry St., 07307. Tel: 201-659-5948.
Sisters of Christian Charity 4; Lay Teachers 14; Students 331.
Catechesis/Religious Programs—Tel: 201-653-5282.
Students 150.
Convent—Tel: 201-659-5644.

19—OUR LADY OF CZESTOCHOWA, (1911) (Polish), Revs. Thomas B. Iwanowski; Tadeusz Trela (Poland). In res., Rev. Alexander Santora.
Res., 120 Sussex St., 07302. Tel: 201-434-0798; Fax: 201-985-0918.
School—(1911), Marin Blvd. & York St., 07302. Tel: 201-434-2405.
Felician Sisters 1; Lay Teachers 10; Students 198.
Convent—Tel: 201-434-5579.

20—OUR LADY OF MERCY, (1963), Revs. John J. Cryan; Bartley P. Baker; Robert A. Doyle; Deacon Nicholas Fargo.
Res., 40 Sullivan Dr., 07305. Tel: 201-434-7500; Fax: 201-432-2885.
School—254 Bartholdi Ave., 07305. Tel: 201-434-4091; Fax: 201-434-8405.
Sisters of St. Joseph of Chestnut Hill (S.S.J.) 1; Lay Teachers 30; Students 638.
Convent—Tel: 201-451-4615.
Catechesis/Religious Programs—Students 156.

21—CHURCH OF OUR LADY OF SORROWS, (1914), Rev. James F. O'Brien; Sr. Alice McCoy, O.P., Pastoral Assoc.
Res., 93-95 Clerk St., 07305. Tel: 201-433-0626; Fax: 201-433-2928.

22—OUR LADY OF VICTORIES, (1917), Revs. Walter J. Swenson; Seamus Clements, C.S.Sp.; John Nadura.
Res., 2217 John F. Kennedy Memorial Blvd., 07304-1497. Tel: 201-433-4152.
School—(1930), Tel: 201-434-4040; Fax: 201-434-5356.
Lay Teachers 22; Students 570.

23—ST. PATRICK'S, (1869), Revs. Eugene P. Squeo, J.D.; Francis E. Schiller, J.D.; Edward J. Kearney; Jean-Marie F. Ligonde.
Res., 492 Bramhall Ave., 07304. Tel: 201-332-8600; Fax: 201-324-3919.
School—(1909), Tel: 201-433-4664.
Sisters of Charity of St. Elizabeth 4; Lay Teachers 32; Students 500.
Convent—345 Pacific Ave., 07304. Tel: 201-451-2765.

24—ST. PAUL OF THE CROSS, (1868), Revs. George A. Ligos; William Halbing; Guillermo Arias (Colombia). In res., Rev. Msgr. Robert E. Duffy.
Res., 156 Hancock Ave., 07307. Tel: 201-798-7900.
School—(1869), 211 Sherman Ave., 07307. Tel: 201-659-6919.
Sisters of Charity 4; Lay Teachers 10; Students 252.
Catechesis/Religious Programs—Students 315.
Convent—Tel: 201-659-1414.

25—ST. PAUL'S, (1861), Revs. Stephen F. Duffy; Jose Gamba; John F. Bauman.
Res., 14 Greenville Ave., 07305. Tel: 201-433-8500; Fax: 201-433-9886.
School—(1872), 193 Old Bergen Rd., 07305. Tel: 201-435-8204; Fax: 210-435-8205.
Sisters of St. Dominic 1; Lay Teachers 19; Students 313.
Catechesis/Religious Programs—Students 155.
Convent—Tel: 201-333-2443.

26—ST. PETER'S, (1831) (Hispanic), Rev. Vincent B. Sullivan, S.J. Pastoral Associates: Revs. Richard I. Caplice, S.J.; D. James French, S.J.; Sr. Grace Reape, S.C.; Deacon Louis N. Mauro, S.J.
Res., 144 Grand St., 07302. Tel: 201-547-6442; Fax: 201-547-6476.
School—(1864), 153 York St., 07302. Tel: 201-434-8145; Fax: 201-434-1613.
Sisters of Charity 3; Lay Teachers 15; Students 300.
Catechesis/Religious Programs—Students 29.
Convent—Tel: 201-434-5919.

27—SACRED HEART, (1905), Rev. Charles T. Quinn, O.P., Pastor; Sr. Elaine Keenan, O.P., Pastoral Assoc.
Res., 183 Bayview Ave., 07305. Tel: 201-332-6771 (Parish); 332-6773 (Priory); Fax: 201-332-8375.
School—(1913), 183 Bayview Ave., 07305. Tel: 201-332-7111; Fax: 201-332-7160. Sr. Maureen Killough, S.C., Prin.
Sisters of Charity 5; Sisters of St. Joseph 2; Lay Teachers 15; Students 411.
Sacred Heart Priory—Revs. Gerard Maley, O.P., Prior; Hugh D. Burns, O.P.; Daniel B. Crowley, O.P.; John Stephen Fitzhenry, O.P.; Val La France, O.P.; John Michael Pietrzyk, O.P.; Bro. John Jude Locchetto, O.P.

Kearny, Hudson Co., St. Cecilia's (1893), Rev. Norbert Laskowski; Rev. Msgr. Joseph A. Carroll, Pastor Emeritus; Revs. Eginor Cunha; Brendan H. Quinn. In res., Rev. Msgr. Francis R. Seymour; Rev. Patrick R.C. Wilhelm.
Res., 120 Kearny Ave., 07032. Tel: 201-991-1116.
School—(1896), 114 Chestnut St., 07032. Tel: 201-991-9142.
Lay Teachers 11; Students 220.
Catechesis/Religious Programs—Students 390.

Our Lady of Sorrows (1915) (Lithuanian), Rev. Msgr. Dominick A. Pocus; Rev. Michael J. O'Brien, Admin.; Deacon Leonard J. Mackesy.
Res., 136 Davis Ave., 07032. Tel: 201-998-4616; Fax: 201-997-8659.
Catechesis/Religious Programs—Students 130.
Convent—Tel: 201-991-7983.

St. Stephen's (1904), Very Rev. Msgr. Michael J.

Desmond, V.E.; Revs. Donald B. Ransom; Scott F. Attanasio.
Res., 141 Washington Ave., 07032. Tel: 201-998-3314.
School—(1904), 131 Midland Ave., 07032. Tel: 201-991-3217; Fax: 201-998-4924.
Sisters of Charity 2; Lay Teachers 15; Students 260.
Catechesis/Religious Programs—Tel: 201-991-0236. D.R.E.: Sr. Rita Kearney, S.S.J.; Dorothy Reid.
Students 560.
Convent—Tel: 201-991-1422.

Kenilworth, Union Co., St. Theresa's (1949), Revs. Joseph S. Bejgrowicz; Charles Kern; Dominick Lenoci; Louis Scarpa, Pastoral Assoc. In res., Rev. George M. Keating.
Res., 541 Washington Ave., 07033. Tel: 908-272-4444; Fax: 908-272-2252.
School—540 Washington Ave., 07033. Tel: 908-276-7220.
Salesian Sisters 3; Lay Teachers 14; Students 275.
Catechesis/Religious Programs—Tel: 908-276-4881.
Students 360.
Convent—Tel: 908-276-5028.

Leonia, Bergen Co., St. John the Evangelist's (1912), Revs. Robert Traudt, O.Carm.; Ronald Gray, O.Carm.; Gregory Houck, O.Carm.; Bro. Michael Telposky, O.Carm.
Res., 235 Harrison St., 07605. Tel: 201-947-4545.
School—260 Harrison St., 07605. Tel: 201-944-4361; Fax: 201-944-2195.
School Sisters of Notre Dame 1; Lay Teachers 9; Students 230.
Catechesis/Religious Programs—Tel: 201-944-4346.
Students 318.
Convent—Tel: 201-944-4362.

Linden, Union Co.,

1—St. Elizabeth's, (1909), Revs. Karl J. Roesch, O.S.B.; Donal R. Fox, O.S.B.; Patrick M. Hurley, O.S.B.; Wilfred Schulz, O.S.B.
Res., 179 Hussa St., 07036. Tel: 908-486-2514; Fax: 908-486-1757.
School—(1927), 170 Hussa St., 07036. Tel: 908-486-2507; Fax: 908-486-1757.
Dominican Sisters of Caldwell 6; Lay Teachers 20; Students 500.
Convent—Tel: 908-486-2737.
Catechesis/Religious Programs—170 Hussa St., Tel: 908-486-2509.
Students 392.

2—Holy Family, (Tremley Point) (1955) (Slovak), Rev. Pierce D. Byrne; Rev. Msgr. Michael Komar, Pastor Emeritus; Rev. Msgr. Sebastian Kunnath (India) Weekend Asst.
Res., 210 Monroe St., 07036. Tel: 908-862-1060.
Church—2709 Parkway Ave., 07036.

3—St. John the Apostle, (1948), Rev. Msgr. Richard M. McGuinness; Revs. Brian McFadden; Thomas J. Henry; Joseph A. Meagher; Deacons Guy Paredes, (Retired); George Ross.
Res., 1805 Penbrook Ter., 07036. Tel: 908-486-6363; Fax: 908-486-5345.
School—(1950), 1 Ridgeview Ter., Clark, 07066. Tel: 908-388-1360.
Sister of St. Dominic 2; Lay Teachers 20; Students 485.
Catechesis/Religious Programs—Tel: 908-388-1253. Sr. Cynthia Johnson, D.R.E.
Students 450.
Convent—Tel: 908-388-3768.

4—St. Theresa of the Child Jesus, (1925) (Polish), Revs. Eugene R. Koch; Marek Chachlowski (Poland); Jan Kwiecien (Poland); Sr. Mary Monica Drogon, C.S.S.F., Pastoral Assoc.; Deacon Alexander Czerepka.
Res., 122 Liberty St., 07036. Tel: 908-862-1116; Fax: 908-862-2930.
Church—131 E. Edgar Rd., 07036.
School—(1930), 705 Clinton St., 07036. Tel: 908-862-7551.
Lay Teachers 14; Students 202.
Catechesis/Religious Programs—Students 380.
Convent—18 Liberty Ave., 07036. Tel: 908-862-4820.

Little Ferry, Bergen Co., St. Margaret of Cortona (1941), Rev. James O. Sheerin.
Res., 31 Chamberlain Ave., 07643. Tel: 201-641-2988; Fax: 201-641-2989.
Catechesis/Religious Programs—Tel: 201-641-3937; Fax: 201-641-0664. Sr. Dorothy A. Donovan, S.S.J., D.R.E.
Students 350.

Livingston, Essex Co., St. Philomena (1927), Rev. Msgr. Edward J. Eilert; Rev. Msgr. William J. Daly, Pastor Emeritus; Rev. Robert A. O'Leary; Rev. Msgr. Robert T. Lennon; Rev. Lawrence J. Fama; Deacon Joseph Francione. Pastoral Assocs.: Sr. Marilyn Zaino, S.C.; Anita Foley.
Res., 386 S. Livingston Ave., 07039. Tel: 201-992-0994; Fax: 201-992-0970.
Schools—Aquinas Academy, (1952), 388 S. Livingston Ave., 07039. Tel: 201-992-1587; Fax: 201-992-1742. Sr. Patricia Tavis, Prin.
Dominican Sisters of Caldwell 2; Lay Teachers 29; Students 299; Early Childhood Center.
Lay Teachers 11; Students 115.
Catechesis/Religious Programs—Tel: 201-992-4466.
Students 385.
Convent—Tel: 201-992-1581.

St. Raphael (1961), Rev. Msgr. G. Thomas Burns; Revs. Andrew Prachar; Anthony Ciorra, Weekend Assoc. In res., Rev. John E. O'Brien.
Res., 346 E. Mt. Pleasant Ave., 07039. Tel: 201-992-9490; Fax: 201-740-0236.
Catechesis/Religious Programs—Students 550.

Lodi, Bergen Co., St. Francis de Sales (1854), Revs. Charles F. Theobald; Jesus A. Encisco. In res., Rev. John B. Baron.
Res., 125 Union St., 07644. Tel: 201-779-4330; Fax: 201-779-8842. [CEM]
School—Mother Cabrini Interparochial, (1991), 123 Union St., 07644. Tel: 201-777-4635.
Felician Sisters 2; Lay Teachers 12; Students 230.
Catechesis/Religious Programs—Tel: 201-779-3949.
Students 110.
Convent—Tel: 201-773-4366.

St. Joseph's (1913) (Italian), Revs. Hector DiNardo, C.R.M.; Americo Salvi, C.R.M., Pastoral Assoc. In res., Rev. Gabriel M. Lucarelli, C.R.M.
Res., 40 Spring St., 07644. Tel: 201-779-0643; Fax: 201-447-1442.
School—Mother Cabrini Interparochial School, (1991), 123 Union St., 07644. Tel: 201-777-4635.
Lay Teachers 12; Students 230.
Catechesis/Religious Programs—Tel: 201-779-8275.
Students 347.

Lyndhurst, Bergen Co., Sacred Heart (1905), Revs. Charles J. Miller; Steven Conner; Juancho De Leon. In res., Rev. William P. Sheridan.
Res., 324 Ridge Rd., 07071. Tel: 201-438-1147; Fax: 201-507-5861. [CEM]
School—620 Valley Brook Ave., 07071. Tel: 201-939-4277; Fax: 201-896-1016.
Sisters 1; Lay Teachers 28; Students 561.
Catechesis/Religious Programs—Tel: 201-935-3094.
Students 355.

Our Lady of Mount Carmel (1966) (Italian), Revs. Robert Marotta; Henry M. Naddeo.
Res., 197 Kingsland Ave., 07071. Tel: 201-935-1177; Fax: 201-935-5675.
Catechesis/Religious Programs—146 Copeland Ave., 07071. Tel: 201-935-5467.
Students 230.

St. Michael's (1912) (Polish), Revs. Richard S. Czachorowski; Joseph Szklarski; John Borowik; Deacon Vincent Serzan. In res., Rev. Msgr. James Mc Menemie.
Res., 624 Page Ave., 07071. Tel: 201-939-1161; Fax: 201-939-7571.
School—(1951), 622 Page Ave., 07071. Tel: 201-939-0350.
Felician Sisters 3; Lay Teachers 8; Students 149.
Convent—Tel: 201-438-0430.

Mahwah, Bergen Co., Immaculate Heart of Mary (1915) (Polish), Revs. Joseph Tyminski, S.D.B.; Alfred J. Sokol, S.D.B.; Joseph S. Bajorek, S.D.B.
Res., 47 Island Rd., 07430. Tel: 201-529-3517; Fax: 201-529-4401.
School—St. Paul's Interparochial School, (1991). (See St. Paul's, Ramsey. Tel: 201-327-1108; Fax: 201-327-6197).
Sisters of Charity 2; Lay Teachers 12; Students 255.

Immaculate Conception (1929), Rev. M. Christen Beirne; Sr. S. Geraldine Muller, S.S.J., Pastoral Assoc. In res., Rev. James R. White.
Res., 900 Darlington Ave., 07430. Tel: 201-327-1276; Fax: 201-327-0185.
School—St. Paul's Interparochial School, Tel: 201-327-1108; Fax: 201-327-6197.
Catechesis/Religious Programs—Tel: 201-825-0333; Fax: 201-327-0185. Mrs. Roberta Medalis, D.R.E.
Students 214.

Maplewood, Essex Co., Immaculate Heart of Mary (1955), Revs. Frank J. Rocchi; Dominic G. Fuccile.
Res., 280 Parker Ave., 07040. Tel: 201-763-5019; Fax: 201-763-3622.
School—(1957), 276 Parker Ave., 07040. Tel: 201-763-0031.
Lay Teachers 10; Students 212.

St. Joseph's (1914), Revs. Thomas Wisniewski; George Sharp; John T. Browne, O.S.B.
Res., 767 Prospect St., 07040. Tel: 201-761-5933; Fax: 201-761-5311.
School—(1930), 240 Franklin Ave., 07040. Tel: 201-761-4033.
Lay Teachers 17; Students 157.
Catechesis/Religious Programs—Students 246.

Maywood, Bergen Co., Our Lady Queen of Peace (1950), Revs. Joseph P. Pietropinto; Stephen J. Cinque; James A. Hamel; Deacon Anthony Balistieri; Sr. Louise DelCarpine, Pastoral Assoc. In res., Rev. Paul Nolan.
Res., 400 Maywood Ave., 07607. Tel: 201-845-9566; Fax: 201-845-3742.
Catechesis/Religious Programs—Tel: 201-845-9545.
Students 358.
Convent—Tel: 201-845-9568.

Midland Park, Bergen Co., Nativity (1955), Revs. John R. O'Connell; James P. Whelan. In res., Most Rev. Robert F. Garner, (Retired).
Res., 315 Prospect St., 07432. Tel: 201-444-6362; Fax: 201-444-5056.
School—St. Thomas More Interparochial School, 321 Prospect St., 07432. Tel: 201-447-3088; Fax: 201-447-4145.
Lay Teachers 12; Students 162.
Bishops Residence—311 Prospect St., 07432. Tel: 201-652-3240; Fax: 201-652-2669.
Catechesis/Religious Programs—Tel: 201-447-1776.
Students 415.

Montclair, Essex Co., Immaculate Conception (1864), Rev. Msgr. Timothy J. Shugrue; Revs. Francis J. Burla; Richard G. Francesco. Pastoral Assocs.: Sr. Margaret Tierney, S.C.; Sr. Cora Marie McGuire, M.S.B.T. In res., Rev. Louis Pambello.
Res., 30 N. Fullerton Ave., 07042. Tel: 201-744-5650; Fax: 201-744-7936. [CEM]
School—(1881), 17-19 Munn St., 07042. Tel: 201-744-6672; Fax: 201-744-7348.
Sisters 3; Lay Teachers 12; Students 110.
High School—(1919), 33 Cottage Pl., 07042. Tel: 201-744-7445; Fax: 201-744-3926.
Sisters 3; Lay Teachers 23; Students 240.
Catechesis/Religious Programs—Tel: 201-744-0338.
Students 239.

Our Lady of Mt. Carmel (1907) (Italian), Revs. Thomas J. Petrillo; Donald Cialene; Deacon Henry Haas.
Res., 94 Pine St., 07042. Tel: 201-744-1074.

St. Peter Claver (1932), Rev. John P. Nickas; Deacons John Coffey; Wilfred Leconte.
Res., 56 Elmwood Ave., 07042. Tel: 201-783-4852; Fax: 201-783-3261.

Moonachie, Bergen Co., St. Anthony (1931). Closed. For inquiries for parish records contact Seton Hall University Archives: South Orange. Tel.: 201-761-9476; Fax: 201-761-9550.

Mountainside, Union Co., Our Lady of Lourdes (1958), Revs. Patrick J. Leonard, Admin.; Paul J. Prevosto; Gerard J. McGarry, Pastor Emeritus.
Res., 300 Central Ave., 07092. Tel: 908-232-1162; Fax: 908-232-0776.
School—Holy Trinity Interparochial School, (1991). (See Holy Trinity, Westfield. Tel: 908-233-0484).
Lay Teachers 15; Students 312.
Catechesis/Religious Programs—Tel: 908-233-1777. Sr. Brenda E. Rowe, M.P.F., D.R.E.
Students 300.

New Milford, Bergen Co., Ascension (1953), Rev. Msgr. Thomas P. Ivory; Rev. Raymond Labranche; Deacon Harold Bates.
Res., 256 Azalea Dr., 07646. Tel: 201-836-8961; Fax: 201-836-5896.
School—1092 Carnation Dr., 07646. Tel: 201-836-7074.
Sisters of St. Dominic 2; Students 244.
Catechesis/Religious Programs—Tel: 201-836-3085.
Students 293.

New Providence, Union Co., Our Lady of Peace (1942), Rev. Msgr. Joseph P. Plunkett; Rev. Msgr. Paul J. Hayes, Pastor Emeritus; Rev. Robert Cio. In res., Rev. Thomas Hart.
Res., 111 South St., 07974. Tel: 908-464-7600.
School—99 South St., 07974. Tel: 908-464-8657.
Sisters of St. Dominic 2; Lay Teachers 10; Students 213.
Catechesis/Religious Programs—Tel: 908-464-8156.
Students 400.
Convent—Tel: 908-464-8223.

North Arlington, Bergen Co., Queen of Peace (1922), Rev. Msgr. Thomas G. Madden; Revs. Samuel Monaco; Peter Smutelovic; Stephen A. Kopacz; Deacons William R. Benedetto; William H. Myers. In res., Rev. William J. Fadrowski.
Res., 10 Franklin Pl., 07031. Tel: 201-997-0700; Fax: 201-997-6214.

School—(1925), 21 Church Pl., 07031. Tel: 201-998-8222.
Sisters of St. Joseph of Chestnut Hill 4; Lay Teachers 19; Students 475.
High School—(1930), 191 Rutherford Pl., 07031. Tel: 201-998-8227; Fax: 201-998-3040.
Brothers of the Christian School 6; Sisters 5; Lay Teachers 58; Students 875.
Catechesis/Religious Programs—Tel: 201-998-0901.
Students 465.
Convent—Tel: 201-997-2141.

North Bergen, Hudson Co., Sacred Heart (Hudson Heights Station) (1917) (Polish), Rev. Anthony G. Robak.
Mailing Address: Box 9007, 07047.
Res., 246 Hudson Pl., Cliffside Park, 07010. Tel: 201-943-0305; Fax: 201-943-2676.
School—St. Elizabeth Seton Interparochial School, (1991). Co-Sponsored. (See St. John's Parish, Fairview. Tel: 201-945-2212).

St. Brigid (1900), Rev. Jorge Chacon.
Res., 4501 Liberty Ave., 07047. Tel: 201-863-0160; Fax: 201-863-0173.

Our Lady of Fatima (1963), Rev. John J. Korbelak; Rev. Msgr. George O'Gorman, Pastor Emeritus.
Res., 8016 Kennedy Blvd., 07047. Tel: 201-869-7244; Fax: 201-869-0940.
Catechesis/Religious Programs—Tel: 201-869-0506.
Students 307.

North Caldwell, Essex Co., Notre Dame (1962), Rev. Msgr. Edward J. Ciuba; Rev. Anthony J. Randazzo; Sr. Carol Jarusewski, R.S.M., Pastoral Assoc.
Res., 358 Central Ave., 07006. Tel: 201-226-0979; Fax: 201-226-4118.
Catechesis/Religious Programs—Tel: 201-228-3338.
Students 490.

Northvale, Bergen Co., St. Anthony's (1890) (Italian), Revs. Gerard J. Graziano; Robert J. Halliwell. In res., Rev. Thomas Norton.
Res., 199 Walnut St., 07647. Tel: 201-768-1177.
School—Holy Family School. (See Immaculate Conception, Norwood).

Norwood, Bergen Co., Immaculate Conception (1921), Rev. Charles B. Urnick; Deacon James Puliatte.
Res., 211 Summit St., 07648. Tel: 201-768-1600; Fax: 201-768-8006.
School—Holy Family Interparochial School, (1991), 200 Summit St., 07648. Tel: 201-768-1605; Fax: 201-768-0796.
Sisters 3; Lay Teachers 17; Students 285.
Catechesis/Religious Programs—Tel: 201-768-1771; Fax: 201-768-8006. Sr. Susanne Reynolds, S.S.J.
Students 300.

Nutley, Essex Co., St. Mary's (1876), Revs. Leonard Dembow; Matthew Kunnath; Gerard Sogliuzzo.
Res., 17 Msgr. Owens Pl., 07110. Tel: 201-235-1100; Fax: 201-661-0233.
School—Good Shepherd Academy. (See Holy Family, Nutley. Tel: 201-667-2049).
Catechesis/Religious Programs—Tel: 201-667-8239; Fax: 201-661-0233.
Students 600.
Convent—Tel: 201-667-0611.

Holy Family (1909) (Italian), Rev. Msgr. Louis F. Fimiani; Revs. Francis A. Heinen; Albert Malgeri; Deacon Charles H. Bond.
Res., 28 Brookline Ave., 07110. Tel: 201-667-0026; Fax: 201-661-1714.
School—Good Shepherd Academy, (1992). Co-sponsored by 3 area churches. 24 Brookline Ave., 07110. Tel: 201-667-2049; Fax: 201-661-9259.
Religious Teachers Filippini 5; Lay Teachers 21; Students 450.
Catechesis/Religious Programs—Tel: 201-667-6018.
Students 951.
Convent—Tel: 201-667-2050.

Our Lady of Mount Carmel (1925) (Polish), Revs. Edward A. Haber; Richard Odoemela.
Res., 120 Prospect St., 07110. Tel: 201-667-2580; Fax: 201-667-0648.
School—Good Shepherd Academy. (See Holy Family, Nutley). Tel: 201-667-2049.
Catechesis/Religious Programs—Students 194.

Oakland, Bergen Co., Our Lady of Perpetual Help (1960), Rev. Robert A. Connors. In res., Rev. George Mader.
Res., 25 Purdue Ave., 07436. Tel: 201-337-7596; Fax: 201-337-7810.
Catechesis/Religious Programs—Tel: 201-337-7596, Ext. 21.
Students 499.
Convent—Tel: 201-337-5364.

Old Tappan, Bergen Co., St. Pius X (1954), Rev. Joseph H. Murphy; Deacon Richard G. Hodges.
Res., 5 Charles Pl., 07675. Tel: 201-664-0913; Fax: 201-664-1013.
School—Holy Family Interparochial School. (See Immaculate Conception, Norwood. Tel: 201-768-1605). Fax: 201-768-0796.
Catechesis/Religious Programs—Tel: 201-664-0927.
Students 325.

Oradell, Bergen Co., St. Joseph's (1903), Revs. George M. Reilly; Peter J. Palmisano; Rino Lavaroni; Joseph Coda, Weekend Asst.
Res., 105 Harrison St., New Milford, 07646. Tel: 201-261-0148; Fax: 201-261-0369.
School—(1939), 305 Elm St., 07649. Tel: 201-261-2388; Fax: 201-261-0830.
Sisters 9; Lay Teachers 23; Students 510.
Catechesis/Religious Programs—300 Elm St., 07649. Tel: 201-265-8880. Marie Sellers, D.R.E.
Students 725.
Convent—Tel: 201-265-0289.

Orange, Essex Co.,

1—St. John's, (1851) (Hispanic), Rev. Robert J. Patterson, S.T.B.; Rev. Msgr. John J. Fahy, Pastor Emeritus; Revs. Manuel Revuelto; Edward G. Bradley, Weekend Asst.
Res., 94 Ridge St., 07050. Tel: 201-674-0110. [CEM]
School—(1855), 455 White St., 07050. Tel: 201-674-8951; Fax: 201-674-6126.
Sisters of Charity 5; Lay Teachers 10; Students 354.
Convent—Tel: 201-673-1263.

2—Our Lady of the Valley, (1873), Revs. Floyd Rotunno; Dennis E. Reiff. In res., Rev. Dioscoro P. Bocod.
Res., 510 Valley St., 07050. Tel: 201-674-7500; Fax: 201-672-8341.
School—(1882), 518 Valley St., 07050. Tel: 201-672-1512; Fax: 201-672-1951.
Lay Teachers 8; Students 260.

3—St. Venantius, (1886). Merged For inquiries for parish records contact St. Andrew Kim Parish, Orange. Tel: 201-673-1366.

4—Mt. Carmel, (1896) (Italian), Revs. Achilles Cassiere, O.F.M.Cap.; Edward Henning, O.F.M.Cap. In res., Rev. Alexander Davis, O.F.M.Cap.
Res., 103 S. Center St., 07050. Tel: 201-674-2052; Fax: 201-675-1342.
School—(1939), 268 Capuchin Way, 07050. Tel: 201-673-5933; Fax: 201-677-2166. Sr. Margaret Mary Hanlon, M.P.F., Prin.
Religious Teachers Filippini 1; Lay Teachers 10; Students 235.
Convent—264 Capuchin Way, 07050. Tel: 201-678-7720.

5—Holy Spirit, (1931). Merged For inquiries for parish records contact Holy Spirit-Our Lady Help of Christians, East Orange. Tel: 201-673-1077.

6—St. Andrew Kim, (1972) (Korean), Rev. Augustin C. Park. In res., Revs. Michael Lim; Paul Kang.
Res., 257 Central Ave., 07050. Tel: 201-673-1366; 672-6650; Fax: 201-673-6720.
Catechesis/Religious Programs—Students 245.
Convent—Tel: 201-674-1618.

Palisades Park, Bergen Co., St. Michael's (1912), Revs. Vincent J. Quinn; David C. Hubba.
Res., 19 Central Blvd., E., 07650. Tel: 201-944-1061; Fax: 201-947-1798.
Schools—Notre Dame Interparochial, Elementary Division, (1991) (Grades 2-8) 312 First St., 07650. Tel: 201-947-5262.; Primary Division, (1991) (Grades PreK-1) 555 Prospect Ave., Ridgefield, 07657. Tel: 201-943-5757. Sr. Ellen McMahon, Prin.
Catechesis/Religious Programs—324 First St., 07650. Tel: 201-944-0070; Fax: 201-947-1798. Mary Fleischbein, D.R.E.
Students 205.

St. Nicholas (1923) (Italian), Revs. Antonio L. da Silva, S.D.V. (Brazil); Anthony Basso, S.D.V.
Res., 442 Brinkerhoff Ave., 07650. Tel: 201-944-1154; 944-1138; Fax: 201-944-9510.
School—Notre Dame Interparochial School, (1991). (See St. Matthew, Ridgefield for Primary Division. Tel: 201-943-5757) (See St. Michael Palisades Park for Elementary Division. Tel: 201-947-5262).

Paramus, Bergen Co., Our Lady of the Visitation (1952), Rev. Msgr. Francis R. Lo Bianco; Revs. Algonso Di Giovanni; Ulysses L. Ubalde. In res., Revs. Joseph S. Chiang; Donald K. Hummell.
Res., 234 Farview Ave., 07652. Tel: 201-261-6080; Fax: 201-261-2995.
School—Visitation Academy, (1991). Co-Sponsored. 222 Farview Ave., 07652. Tel: 201-262-6067; Fax: 201-261-4613. Sr. Louise Parisot, S.C., Prin.
Sisters 3; Lay Teachers 17; Students 346.
Catechesis/Religious Programs—Tel: 201-265-3812. Mrs. Barbara D'Arrigo, D.R.E.
Students 518.

Annunciation (1953), Revs. Michael J. Sheehan; Charles Pinyan; Deacons Joseph Niland; William D. Joyce; Sr. Rita Dermody, S.C., Pastoral Assoc. In res., Rev. John M. McCrone.
Res., 50 W. Midland Ave., 07652. Tel: 201-261-6322; Fax: 201-261-6227.
School—(1991). (See Visitation Academy, Our Lady of the Visitation Parish, Paramus).

Carmelite Chapel of St. Therese (1970), Revs. Brice E. Riordan, O.Carm., Dir.; Norman G. Werling, O.Carm.; Zachary Monet, O.Carm.; Daniel Smith, O.Carm.; Richard W. Bradley, O.Carm.
Res., 135 Gertrude St., 07652. Tel: 201-845-6392.
Church—Bergen Mall, 07652. Tel: 201-845-6115.

Park Ridge, Bergen Co., Our Lady of Mercy (1902), Revs. Charles P. Granstrand; Eugene P. Heyndricks; Rev. Msgr. James C. Turro, Weekend Asst. In res., Rev. Msgr. Carl D. Hinrichsen.
Res., 2 Fremont Ave., 07656. Tel: 201-391-5315; Fax: 201-391-5614.
School—Our Lady of Mercy Interparochial School, (1950), 25 Fremont Ave., 07656. Tel: 201-391-3838.
Lay Teachers 22; Students 393.
Catechesis/Religious Programs—50 Pascack Rd., 07656. Tel: 201-391-3590.
Students 750.
Convent—Tel: 201-391-7788.

Plainfield, Union Co., St. Mary (1851), Revs. Kenneth Jones; Francisco R. Ponce; Renzo L. Scaramella. In res., Revs. Aloysius S. Carney; Henry T. Kaminski.
Res., 516 W. Sixth St., 07060. Tel: 908-756-0085; Fax: 908-756-1658. [CEM]
Catechesis/Religious Programs—Tel: 908-561-7143.
Students 306.
Convents—524 W. Sixth St., 07060. Missionary Sisters of the Most Blessed Sacrament & Mary Immaculate
Sisters 3; 513 Liberty St., 07060. Tel: 908-754-1978.
Missionaries of Charity, (Contemplative)
Sisters 21.

St. Bernard's (1921), Revs. Joseph F. Barbone; Thomas C. Roberts.
Office: 368 Sumner Ave., P.O. Box 2844, 07062. Tel: 908-756-3393; Fax: 908-756-3059.
Rectory—1235 George St., 07062.

St. Stanislaus Kostka (1919), Rev. Henry T. Kaminski.
Res., St. Mary's Rectory, 516 W. Sixth St., 07060. Tel: 201-756-9178.
Church—1020 W. Seventh St., 07063. (For Churches in North and South Plainfield see Diocese of Metuchen).

Rahway, Union Co., St. Mary's (1854), Revs. Michael J. Feketie; Edward J. Myers; J. Rico Madrilejos; David S. McLaughlin; Deacons J. William Courtney; James O'Neill.
Res., 232 Central Ave., 07065. Tel: 908-388-0082. [CEM]
School—(1873), 244 Central Ave., 07065. Tel: 908-382-0011.
Lay Teachers 16; Students 253.
Catechesis/Religious Programs—Tel: 201-382-0004.
Students 306.

St. Mark's (1871) (German), Rev. Eugene J. Kasper.
Res., 287 Hamilton St., 07065. Tel: 908-499-9230.
Catechesis/Religious Programs—Tel: 908-388-7036.
Students 100.

Ramsey, Bergen Co., St. Paul (1904), Rev. Msgr. Thomas A. Donato; Revs. James R. O'Neill, Pastor Emeritus; Victor K. Lynch.
Res., 200 Wyckoff Ave., 07446. Tel: 201-327-0976; Fax: 201-327-6197.
School—St. Paul's Interparochial School, 187 Wyckoff Ave., 07446. Tel: 201-327-1108; Fax: 201-237-6197.
Sisters of Charity 1; Lay Teachers 20; Students 255.
Catechesis/Religious Programs—Tel: 201-327-8010.
Students 825.

Ridgefield, Bergen Co., St. Matthew's (1899), Revs. Timothy J. Horgan; Michael M. Walters; Deacon Gustave Grieder. In res., Rev. Msgr. James Johnson; Rev. John Komar.
Res., 555 Prospect Ave., 07657. Tel: 201-945-3500; Fax: 201-945-3796.
School—Notre Dame Interparochial Primary Division, (1991) (Grades PreK-1) Edgewater Ave., 07657. Tel: 201-943-5757; Fax: 201-943-4209; 947-8319.
Sisters 2; Lay Teachers 22; Students 519.
Catechesis/Religious Programs—Students 247.

Ridgefield Park, Bergen Co., St. Francis of Assisi (1890), Revs. Joseph C. Doyle; Christoph Lintz; Sr. Catherine Higgins, S.C., Pastoral Assoc.; Deacon Nicholas Simonelli; Brenda McWeeney, Pastoral Assoc.
Res., 114 Mt. Vernon St., 07660. Tel: 201-641-6464; Fax: 201-641-2282.
School—(1915), 110 Mt. Vernon St., 07660. Tel: 201-641-9159; Fax: 201-641-4091. Sr. Patricia

Meidhof, Prin.
Sisters 3; Lay Teachers 19; Students 320.
Catechesis/Religious Programs—Tel: 201-641-9467.
Students 330.

Ridgewood, Bergen Co., Our Lady of Mount Carmel (1889), Revs. Robert G Gibney; William S. O'Brien; Patrick M. Mulewski; Peter Baldacchino; Sr. Lucy Sullivan, S.C., Pastoral Assoc.; Deacon Robert V. Thomann. In res., Rev. Joseph A. Stulb.
Res., 1 Passaic St., 07450-4309. Tel: 201-444-2000; Fax: 201-444-2002.
School—St. Catharine's Interparochial School. (See St. Catharine, Glen Rock). Tel: 201-445-0622.
Catechesis/Religious Programs—Tel: 201-444-0211; Fax: 201-444-4421. Sr. Bernard Mary Herlihy, M.S.B.T., D.R.E.
Students 999.
Convent—Tel: 201-445-2077.

River Edge, Bergen Co., St. Peter the Apostle (1948), Revs. Robert H. Slipe; Michael J. German; Rev. Msgr. David J. Casazza, Pastor Emeritus; Rev. Michael A. Saporito; Deacon Edward Bowen.
Res., 445 Fifth Ave., 07661. Tel: 201-261-3366; Fax: 201-261-0117.
School—St. Peter Academy, (1952), 431 Fifth Ave., 07661. Tel: 201-261-3468.
Sisters 2; Lay Teachers 17; Students 280.
Catechesis/Religious Programs—Tel: 201-265-6019.
Students 450.
Convent—Tel: 201-845-9568.

Rochelle Park, Bergen Co., Sacred Heart (1917), Very Rev. Lewis V. Papera, V.F.; Rev. Rajmund Kopek. In res., Rev. John F. Gordon.
Res., 12 Terrace Ave., 07662. Tel: 201-843-1722; Fax: 201-843-3542.
School—(1991). Co-Sponsored. (See Visitation Academy, Our Lady of Visitation Parish, Paramus). Tel: 201-262-6067.
Catechesis/Religious Programs—Tel: 201-843-1077. Mary Ann Cassidy, D.R.E.
Students 251.

Roseland, Essex Co., Our Lady of the Blessed Sacrament (1955), Revs. Frank J. McNulty; Richard J. Chilmark; Edward R. Bognacki. Pastoral Assocs.: Sr. Rie Crowley, S.S.J., (Youth); Sr. Mary Ganly, S.S.J., (Sick & Shut-ins); Maurica Twaddell, (Sacramental Programs); Philip Mealey, (Liturgical Music).
Res., 28 Livingston Ave., 07068. Tel: 201-226-7288; Fax: 201-226-4893.
Catechesis/Religious Programs—Tel: 201-226-5251. Kathleen A. Detlet, Ph.D., D.R.E.
Students 500.

Roselle, Union Co., Church of St. Joseph the Carpenter (1895), Revs. George D. Gillen; Beaubrun Ardouin.
Res., 157 E. Fourth Ave., 07203. Tel: 908-241-1250; Fax: 908-241-6311.
School—(1913), 150 E. Third Ave., 07203. Tel: 908-245-6560.
Sisters 3; Lay Teachers 17; Students 475.
Convent—135 E. Fourth Ave., 07203. Tel: 908-245-1594. Sisters of St. Joseph, Chestnut Hill.

Roselle Park, Union Co., The Assumption (1907), Rev. Msgr. Joseph F. Loreti; Revs. Joseph M. Duykim Tran; Joseph Mukald. In res., Rev. Msgr. Edward G. Price, (Retired).
Res., 113 Chiego Pl., 07204. Tel: 908-245-1107.
Catechesis/Religious Programs—110 Chiego Pl., 07204. Tel: 908-245-6572.
Students 541.

Rutherford, Bergen Co., St. Mary's (1908), Revs. Peter J. Reilly; Joseph L. Cassidy; Robert H. Langdon; Stanley Lobo (India).
Res., 91 Home Ave., 07070. Tel: 201-438-2200; Fax: 201-438-1098.
School—(1916), 72 Chestnut St., 07070. Tel: 201-933-8410.
Lay Teachers 16; Students 315.
High School—(1928), 64 Chestnut St., 07070. Tel: 201-933-5220; Fax: 201-933-0834.
Lay Teachers 23; Students 342.
Catechesis/Religious Programs—Students 500.
Convent—Tel: 201-933-2910.

Saddle Brook, Bergen Co., St. Philip the Apostle (1953), Revs. Robert G. McBride; Matthew Fonseka; Richard J. Mroz; Deacons Paul Magarelli; Philip Salerno.
Res., 488 Saddle River Rd., 07663. Tel: 201-843-1888; Fax: 201-368-9161.
School—492 Saddle River Rd., 07663-4634. Tel: 201-843-2240; Fax: 201-843-3150.
Sisters 2; Lay Teachers 10; Students 242.
Catechesis/Religious Programs—Students 425.

Saddle River Borough, Bergen Co., St. Gabriel the Archangel (1952), Rev. Msgr. Paul G. Bootkoski; Revs. John J. O'Brien, S.J.; Timothy G. Graff.
Res., 3 W. Church Rd., 07458. Tel: 201-327-5663; Fax: 201-327-7063.
School—St. John's Academy. (See St. John's Parish, Hillsdale). Tel: 201-664-6364; Fax: 201-664-8096.
Catechesis/Religious Programs—Tel: 201-825-0275.
Students 235.

Scotch Plains, Union Co., St. Bartholomew (1948), Very Rev. Peter J. Zaccardo, V.F.; Rev. Msgr. Francis A. Reinbold, Pastor Emeritus; Revs. John J. Lester; Thomas A. Grogan. In res., Joy Alookaran (India).
Res., 2032 Westfield Ave., 07076. Tel: 908-322-5192; Fax: 908-322-2598.
School—St. Bartholomew Interparochial, (1950), Tel: 908-322-4265; Fax: 908-322-2598.
Religious Teachers Filippini 5; Lay Teachers 7; Students 240.
Catechesis/Religious Programs—Tel: 908-322-2359.
Students 235.
Convent—Tel: 908-322-5619.

Immaculate Heart of Mary (1964), Revs. John F. Kennedy; Ken Evans; William Mahon.
Res., 1571 S. Martine Ave., 07076. Tel: 908-889-2100; Fax: 908-889-9477.
Catechesis/Religious Programs—Tel: 908-889-6263.
Students 575.

Secaucus, Hudson Co., Immaculate Conception (1908), Revs. William M. Giblin; Raymond T. Lukenda; Richard Corbett.
Res., 1219 Paterson Plank Rd., 07094. Tel: 201-863-4840; Fax: 201-863-3537.
School—(1949), 760 Post Pl., 07094. Tel: 201-864-9346.
School Sisters of Notre Dame 4; Lay Teachers 7; Students 242.
Catechesis/Religious Programs—Tel: 201-863-4899.
Students 506.
Convent—Tel: 201-866-4752.

Short Hills, Essex Co., St. Rose of Lima (1852), Rev. Msgr. William P. Devine; Revs. Michael Charles Fugee; Kevin A. Gugliotta; Deacons Charles D. Behringer; Joseph M. Persinger; Daniel McCarren. In res., Rev. Msgr. Vincent P. Coburn.
Res., 50 Short Hills Ave., 07078. Tel: 201-379-3912; Fax: 201-379-6157. [CEM]
School—(1869), 52 Short Hills Ave., 07078. Tel: 201-379-3973; Fax: 201-379-3722.
Lay Teachers 18; Students 250; Sisters of St. Joseph 2.
Catechesis/Religious Programs—61 Short Hills Ave., 07078. Tel: 201-376-1960.
Students 450.

South Orange, Essex Co., Our Lady of Sorrows (1887), Most Rev. Charles J. McDonnell, D.D.; Revs. Peter Vinh Q. Nguyen; Richard J. Kelly; John A. Palasits.
Res., 217 Prospect St., 07079. Tel: 201-763-5454; Fax: 201-763-9506.
School—(1890), 172 Academy St., 07079. Tel: 201-763-5169.
Lay Teachers 25; Religious 1; Students 348.
Catechesis/Religious Programs—Students 353.

Springfield, Union Co., St. James (1923), Revs. Robert B. Stagg; Robert J. Piatkowski; Anthony J. Nardo; Deacons John M. Baltus; Jerry Bongiavanni; Roseann M. Treston, S.S.J., Pastoral Assoc.
Res., 45 S. Springfield Ave., 07081. Tel: 201-376-3044; Fax: 201-376-0560.
School—41 S. Springfield Ave., 07081. Tel: 201-376-5194. Sr. Mary Elizabeth Guyer, S.S.J., Prin.
Sisters of St. Joseph 2; Lay Teachers 10; Students 210.
Catechesis/Religious Programs—Tel: 201-376-2061. Lynne A. Haley, D.R.E.
Students 275.

Summit, Union Co., St. Teresa's (1863), Rev. Msgr. Robert E. Harahan; Rev. Msgr. Anthony F. Bogdziewicz, Pastor Emeritus; Rev. Thomas Blind; Deacons Joseph Wall; Frank Gisoldi. In res., Rev. Msgr. John H. Koenig.
Res., 306 Morris Ave., 07901. Tel: 908-277-3700; Fax: 908-273-5909. [CEM]
Catechesis/Religious Programs—Tel: 908-273-6975.
Students 765.

Teaneck, Bergen Co., St. Anastasia's (1908), Revs. Hilary Milton, O.Carm.; Gerald Heinen, O.Carm.; Deacon Roland Bianchi. In res., Rev. Emeric Carmody, O.Carm.
Res., 1095 Teaneck Rd., 07666. Tel: 201-837-3354.
School—St. Cecilia's Interparochial School. (See St. Cecilia, Englewood. Tel: 201-568-2615).
Catechesis/Religious Programs—Tel: 201-837-3356. Sr. Adrienne Bradley, S.S.J., D.R.E.
Students 230.
Convent—Tel: 201-837-3153.

Tenafly, Bergen Co., Our Lady of Mount Carmel (1873), Revs. Ashley Harrington, O.Carm.; Joseph Atcher, O.Carm.
Res., 10 County Rd., 07670. Tel: 201-568-0545; Fax: 201-568-3215.
School—(1879), Tel: 201-567-6491.
Franciscan Sisters 1; Lay Teachers 16; Students 261.
Catechesis/Religious Programs—Tel: 201-871-4662.
Students 330.

Union, Union Co., St. Michael's (1928), Revs. Kenneth Herbster; Charles B. McDermott; Anselm I. Nwaorgu.
Res., 1212 Kelly St., 07083. Tel: 908-688-1232; Fax: 908-810-1076.
School—(1931), 1211 Orange Ave., 07083. Tel: 908-688-1063; Fax: 908-687-7927. Sr. Margaret William, Prin.
Sisters of St. Dominic 3; Lay Teachers 18; Students 334.
Catechesis/Religious Programs—Tel: 908-964-0965; Fax: 908-810-1076. Sylvia McGeary, D.R.E.
Students 850.
Convent—Tel: 908-686-3839.

Holy Spirit (1963), Rev. Msgr. Vincent J. Doyle; Rev. Msgr. John H. Koenig, Pastor Emeritus; Revs. Edward G. Furrevig; John Ballweg, Weekend Asst.; Stanley E. Ortyl.
Res., 971 Suburban Rd., 07083. Tel: 908-687-3327; Fax: 908-687-1312.
School—Morris Ave. & Suburban Rd., 07083. Tel: 908-687-8415.
Lay Teachers 10; Students 216.
Catechesis/Religious Programs—984 Suburban Rd., 07083. Tel: 908-964-7533.
Students 600.

Union City, Hudson Co.,

1—HOLY FAMILY, (1857), Rev. Msgr. William J. Reilly, Admin.
Res., 530 35th St., 07087. Tel: 201-867-6535.
Catechesis/Religious Programs—Students 150.

2—ST. AUGUSTINE'S, (1886), Rev. Msgr. Thomas W. Heck; Revs. Pedro Navarro; Felipe Lopez; Deacon John McCarthy.
Res., 3900 New York Ave., 07087. Tel: 201-863-0233.
School—(1891), 3920 New York Ave., 07087. Tel: 201-865-5319.
Sisters of Charity 6; Lay Teachers 15; Students 460.
Catechesis/Religious Programs—Students 807.
Convent—312 39th St., Union, 07083. Tel: 201-348-0527.

3—SS. JOSEPH AND MICHAEL, (1887; 1851), Revs. James O'Shea; Kenneth Walsh, C.P.; Neil Tiedemann, C.P.
Res., 1314 Central Ave., 07087. Tel: 201-865-2325.
School—Mother Seton Grammar School, 1501 New York Ave., 07087. Tel: 201-863-8433.
Lay Teachers 14; Students 330.
Catechesis/Religious Programs—Tel: 201-863-8145.
Students 290.

4—ST. ANTHONY OF PADUA, (1899) (Italian), Revs. Ilario Crepaz (Italy); Randy A. Guillen; Leone Donini.
Res., 615 Eighth St., 07087. Tel: 201-867-3818; Fax: 201-867-8859.
School—700 Central Ave., 07087. Tel: 201-864-5605.
Religious Teachers Filippini 1; Lay Teachers 13; Students 260.
Catechesis/Religious Programs—Students 200.

5—ST. ROCCO'S, (1912) (Italian), Rev. Nazareno Orlandi.
Res., 4206 Kennedy Blvd., 07087. Tel: 201-863-1427.
Mission House—4214 Kennedy Blvd., 07087. Tel: 201-863-5727.
Religious Teachers Filippini 3.

Upper Montclair, Essex Co., St. Cassian (1896), Rev. Msgr. John E. Doran; Rev. Eugene G. Gniewyk; Deacon Thomas J. Nilan.
Res., 187 Bellevue Ave., 07043. Tel: 201-744-2850; Fax: 201-744-6187.
School—190 Lorraine Ave., 07043. Tel: 201-746-1636; Fax: 201-746-3271.
Lay Teachers 15; Students 231.
Catechesis/Religious Programs—Students 375.

Upper Saddle River, Bergen Co., Church of the Presentation (1961), Rev. Msgr. John F. McDermott; Rev. Gerald Hahn.
Office: 271 W. Saddle River Rd., 07458. Tel: 201-327-1313; Fax: 201-818-0722.
Res., 41 Riverview Ter., 07458.
School—St. Paul's Interparochial School, (1990). (See St. Paul, Ramsey). Tel: 201-327-1108.
Catechesis/Religious Programs—Tel: 201-327-3055.
Students 1,470.

Verona, Essex Co., Our Lady of the Lake (1923), Revs. Michael A. Hanly; Jerome S. Arthasseril; Joseph A. D'Amico; Deacons Pat Vuolo; David Garcia. In res., Rev. John D. Dennehy; Sr. Anne Marie Lennon, O.P., Pastoral Assoc.

Res., 32 Lakeside Ave., 07044. Tel: 201-239-5696; Fax: 201-239-7190.
School—(1924), 22 Lakeside Ave., 07044. Tel: 201-239-1160. Sr. Mary Agnes Sullivan, O.P., Prin.
Sisters 2; Lay Teachers 13; Students 278.
Catechesis/Religious Programs—Tel: 201-239-7643.
Students 600.

Wallington, Bergen Co., Most Sacred Heart of Jesus (1942) (Polish), Rev. Msgr. Walter J. Gorski; Revs. Jan Krzysztof Lebdowicz; Marek Bokota; Joseph Urban.
Res., 127 Paterson Ave., 07057. Tel: 201-778-7405; Fax: 201-778-7750.
School—(1943), 6 Bond St., 07057. Tel: 201-777-4817.
Sisters 2; Lay Teachers 12; Students 234.
Catechesis/Religious Programs—Students 406.

Washington Township, Bergen Co., Our Lady of Good Counsel (1959), Revs. Thomas A. McCarthy; Donald A. Cooper; Stephen J. Duffe. In res., Rev. John G. Judge.
Res., 668 Ridgewood Rd., Westwood P.O., 07675. Tel: 201-664-6624; Fax: 201-664-0095.
School—Our Lady of Mercy Interparochial School. (See Our Lady of Mercy, Park Ridge. Tel: 201-391-3838; Fax: 201-391-5614).
Catechesis/Religious Programs—Tel: 201-664-1679. Catherine Russo, D.R.E.
Students 469.
Youth Ministry Office—Tel: 201-664-2464. Sr. Joseph Miriam Blackwell, M.S.B.T., Pastoral Assoc.

Weehawken, Hudson Co., St. Lawrence's (1887), Rev. Charles F. Noble, Admin.
Res., 22 Hackensack Ave., 07087. Tel: 201-863-6464.
School—John Paul II Interparochial School. (See St. Francis, Hoboken).

Westfield, Union Co., St. Helen (1968), Rev. Msgr. James A. Burke; Revs. William T. Morris; Peter K. O'Brien.
Res., 1600 Rahway Ave., 07090. Tel: 908-232-1214; Fax: 908-232-1867.
School—Holy Trinity Interparochial School, (1991). Co-Sponsored. (See Holy Trinity Parish, Westfield). Tel: 908-233-0484; Fax: 908-233-6204.
Catechesis/Religious Programs—Tel: 908-233-8757.
Students 1,895.

Holy Trinity (1872), Revs. Joseph P. Masiello; Matthew D. Looney; Nicholas G. Figurelli; Sr. Catherine Looker, S.S.J., Pastoral Assoc.; Deacons Charles F. Kiley; Thomas A. Pluta.
Res., 315 First St., 07090. Tel: 908-232-8137; Fax: 908-654-8780.
School—(1991) (Grades PreK-8). Co-Sponsored, Holy Trinity Interparochial School. 336 First St., 07090. Tel: 908-233-0484; Fax: 908-233-6204.
Lay Teachers 18; Students 273.
Catechesis/Religious Programs—Tel: 908-233-7455. Sr. Kathleen J. Burton, S.S.J., D.R.E.
Students 370.

West New York, Hudson Co., St. Mary Help of Christians (1895), Rev. Carlo Fortunio, O.P., (Italy) Admin.; Deacon Martin Hemberger.
Res., 6502 Jackson St., 07093. Tel: 201-868-9444.
Catechesis/Religious Programs—Students 200.

St. Joseph of the Palisades (1875), Most Rev. David Arias, O.A.R., D.D (Spain); Revs. Frank Rose; Agustin Pedrosa, S.M. (Spain); Minh Hai Nguyen; Baltasar Dominguez (Colombia); Gioacchino Basile.
Res., 6401 Palisade Ave., 07093. Tel: 201-854-7006; Fax: 201-861-7799.
School—(1872), 6408 Palisade Ave., 07093. Tel: 201-861-3327.
Franciscan Missionary Sisters of the Sacred Heart 5; Lay Teachers 20; Students 492.
High School—5400 Broadway, 07093. Tel: 201-864-9700.
Priests 1; Sisters 5; Lay Teachers 13; Students 220.
Catechesis/Religious Programs—Students 905.
Chapels—North Bergen, Immaculate Heart of Mary.; Cor Jesu.
Convent—Tel: 201-861-3337.

Our Lady of Libera (1902) (Italian), Rev. Philip J. Rotunno.
Res., 5808 John F. Kennedy Memorial Blvd., 07093. Tel: 201-867-2642.
School—5800 John F. Kennedy Memorial Blvd., 07093. Tel: 201-864-5557.
Sisters 2; Lay Teachers 13; Students 425.
Convent—Tel: 201-868-6113. Religious Teachers Filippini

West Orange, Essex Co., Our Lady of Lourdes (1914), Revs. Gerald A. Marchand; Michael H. Hansen.
Res., 1 Eagle Rock Ave., 07052. Tel: 201-325-0110.
School—(1925), 100 Valley Way, 07052. Tel: 201-325-0555. Mary Cassels, Prin.
Sisters of Charity 1; Lay Teachers 12; Students 288.
Catechesis/Religious Programs—Tel: 201-325-0029. Sr. Ann Sweeney, O.P., D.R.E.
Students 228.
Convent—Tel: 201-325-0318.

St. Joseph's (1932), Rev. Msgr. Donald E. Guenther; Rev. John D. Sweeney; Deacon Joseph F.X. Cunningham. In res., Rev. Msgr. William J. Daly.
Res., 44 Benvenue Ave., 07052. Tel: 201-669-3221; Fax: 201-669-0385.
School—(1956), 8 St. Cloud Pl., 07052. Tel: 201-731-3503.
Lay Teachers 10; Students 238.
Catechesis/Religious Programs—Students 300.

Westwood, Bergen Co., St. Andrew's (1889), Revs. Ward P. Moore; Rocco F. Provinzano; Deacon Joseph J. Paulillo. Pastoral Assocs.: Joan M. Rovere, Parish Catechesis; Mary Jean Conroy, Child Catechesis; Alan Pitman, Teens.
Res., 124 Washington Ave., 07675. Tel: 201-666-1100; Fax: 201-722-1432. [CEM]
School—St. John's Academy. (See St. John the Baptist, Hillsdale. Tel: 201-664-6364; Fax: 201-664-8096).
Catechesis/Religious Programs—Tel: 201-664-6777.
Students 404.

Woodcliff Lake, Bergen Co., Our Lady Mother of the Church (1967), Rev. Thomas G. Arminio; Sr. Frances Schier, O.P., Pastoral Assoc. In res., Rev. Msgr. Joseph C. Manz; Rev. Edward Kearney.
Res., 130 Apple Ridge, 07675. Tel: 201-391-2826.
School—St. John the Baptist Interparochial School. (See St. John the Baptist, Hillsdale).

Wood-Ridge, Bergen Co., Our Lady of the Assumption (1926), Revs. James W. Czerwinski, O.F.M.; Richard Trezza, O.F.M.; Edwin Robinson, O.F.M.; Paul Sinnema, O.F.M.; Thomas Kelly, O.F.M.
Res., 143 First St., 07075. Tel: 201-438-5555; Fax: 201-438-6747.
School—151 First St., 07075. Tel: 201-933-0239.
Franciscan Sisters of Allegany 1; Lay Teachers 18; Students 250.
Catechesis/Religious Programs—Hayes Center, 151 Second St., Tel: 201-933-6118.
Students 362.
Convent—Tel: 201-939-4274.

Wyckoff, Bergen Co., St. Elizabeth (1902), Rev. Msgr. Thomas M. O'Leary, V.F.; Revs. Charles W. Hartling; Thomas A. Dente; Deacons Robert Kratchman; Joseph De Maria.
Res., 700 Wyckoff Ave., 07481. Tel: 201-891-1122; Fax: 201-847-8518.
School—Greenwood Ave., 07481. Tel: 201-891-1481. Sisters of St. Joseph of Peace; Lay Teachers 15; Students 290.
Catechesis/Religious Programs—Tel: 201-891-3262. Marlene Malenda, D.R.E.
Students 850.
Convent—Tel: 201-891-1495.

Chaplains of Public Institutions

Hospital Chaplaincy

NEWARK. *Office of Health Care Personnel,* 171 Clifton Ave., 07102. Tel: 201-497-4009. Sr. Thomas Mary Salerno, S.C., Chancellor.

Bergen County

ENGLEWOOD. *Englewood Hospital,* 350 Engle St., 07631. Tel: 201-894-3000. Chaplains: Revs. Mathew Chandrankunnel; John E. Komar.

HACKENSACK. *Hackensack Medical Center,* 22 Hospital Pl., 07601. Tel: 201-996-2000; 996-2345. Chaplains: Revs. William Yeo, Dir.; Bernard Fernando; Deacon Nicholas Simonelli.

PARAMUS. *Bergen Pines County Hospital,* E. Ridgewood Ave., 07652. Tel: 201-967-4177; Fax: 201-967-4277. Chaplains: Revs. John McCrone; Joseph P. Rice; Gerald Bojek; Deacons Michael Morend; Edward Moran.

RIDGEWOOD. *Valley Hospital,* Linwood Ave. & N. Van Dien Ave., 07451. Tel: 201-447-8160. Chaplains: Revs. John G. Judge; Joseph A. Stulb; Anne Devine, Dir.

TEANECK. *Holy Name Hospital,* 718 Teaneck Rd., 07666. Tel: 201-833-3000. Chaplains: Sr. Lois Jablonski, S.S.J., Dir.; Revs. Paterno Gorospe; James F. Reilly; Deacon Willy Malarcher.

WESTWOOD. *Pascack Valley Hospital,* Old Hook Rd., 07675. Tel: 201-358-3000. Chaplains: Revs. Thomas Norton; John G. Judge.

Essex County

NEWARK. *Beth Israel Hospital,* 201 Lyons Ave., 07112. Tel: 201-926-7000. Revs. Joseph Puthenparambil, Chap.; Thomas McLaughlin.
St. James Hospital, 155 Jefferson St., 07015. Tel: 201-489-1300. Chaplains: Mrs. Mary Hoffman; Sr. Josephine Cervi; Rev. Joseph Khai Vu.
St. Michael Medical Center, 306 Martin Luther King Blvd., 07102. Tel: 201-877-5467. Chaplains: Revs. Michael Scheip; Chris Anyanwu; Manuel Cruz; Joseph Khai Vu.
United Hospitals Of Newark, 15 S. Ninth St., 07107. Tel: 201-268-7000. Rev. Michael A. Fuino.
University of Medicine & Dentistry, 100 Bergen St., 07103. Tel: 201-982-5658. Rev. Eustace Edomobi, Chap.

BELLEVILLE. *Clara Maass Hospital,* I-A Franklin Ave., 07109. Tel: 201-450-2000. Rev. John Donahue, Chap.; Deacon Ralph Cordasco.

CEDAR GROVE. *Essex County Hospital Center,* 125 Fairview Ave., 07009. Tel: 201-456-4300. Rev. Ronald R. Regula, Chap.

EAST ORANGE. *East Orange Hospital,* 300 Central Ave., 07019. Tel: 201-672-8400. Rev. Deo Bocad, Chap.
Veterans Administration Hospital, Tremont Ave. & Center St., 07019. Tel: 201-676-1000. Revs. James F. Sagala; Alexander Davis, O.F.M.Cap.

LIVINGSTON. *St. Barnabas Medical Center,* 94 Old Short Hills Rd., 07039. Tel: 201-533-5015. Chaplains: Revs. Leo O. Farley; Gerard Lombardo; Sr. Adele Solari, S.S.J.

MONTCLAIR. *Mountainside Hospital,* Bay Ave. & Highland Ave., 07042. Tel: 201-429-6000. Chaplains: Revs. Joseph L. Affanoso; Louis Pambello.
St. Vincent Nursing Home, 45 Elm St., 07102. Tel: 201-746-4000. Sr. Anita William O'Neil, S.C., Chap.; Deacon Henry Stark.

ORANGE. *Hospital Center at Orange,* 188 S. Essex St., 07051. Tel: 201-266-2000. Rev. Deo Bocad, Chap.

Hudson County

BAYONNE. *Bayonne Hospital,* 29 E. 29th St., 07002. Tel: 201-858-5000. Rev. J. M. Patricius.

HOBOKEN. *St. Mary's Hospital,* 308 Willow Ave., 07030. Tel: 201-714-8900. Rev. Alan Guiglielmo.

JERSEY CITY. *B.S. Pollak Hospital,* 100 Clifton St., 07304. Tel: 201-434-5883. Rev. Sebastian Kunnath.
Christ Hospital, 176 Palisades Ave., 07304. Tel: 201-795-8200. Sr. Marie Tansey, S.C.; Sr. Margaret McCabe, S.C.; Rev. Mamerto Cordero.
Jersey City Medical Center, 50 Baldwin Ave., 07304. Tel: 201-915-2000. Rev. Edmundo A. Surban.
St. Francis Health Center, 25 McWilliams Pl., 07302. Tel: 201-792-8314. Rev. Gerald J. Sudol; Sr. Mary Meehan, S.S.N.D.; Rev. Thomas Kunnath.

KEARNY. *West Hudson Hospital,* 206 Bergen Ave., 07032. Tel: 201-955-7000. Rev. Patrick R.C. Wilhelm.

NORTH BERGEN. *Palisades General Hospital.* Vacant. 7600 River Rd., 07047. Tel: 201-854-5000.

Union County

BERKELEY HEIGHTS. *Runnells County Hospital,* 07922. Tel: 908-771-5700. Rev. William T. Hart.

ELIZABETH. *Elizabeth General Medical Center.* Chaplain's Office: 655 E. Jersey St., 07206. Tel: 908-351-9000. Revs. William C. Reed; Robert Becerra.
St. Elizabeth Hospital, 225 Williamson St., 07202. Tel: 908-527-5000. Revs. Joseph Fiorino; Virgilio P. Chagas.

PLAINFIELD. *Muhlenberg Medical Center,* Park Ave. & Randolph Rd., 07061. Tel: 908-668-2007. Rev. Aloysius S. Carney.

RAHWAY. *Rahway Hospital,* 865 Stone St., 07065. Tel: 908-381-4200. Deacons J. William Courtney; James O'Neill.

ROSELLE. *Center for Hope Hospice,* 219 E. Fourth Ave., 07203. Tel: 908-241-1132. Rev. Charles Hudson; Sr. Mary McGrath; Deacon Cyril Massar.

SUMMIT. *Overlook Hospital,* 99 Beauvoir Ave., 07902. Tel: 908-522-2000; 522-2108. Revs. John Quill; John P. Holian; Sr. Patricia Murphy, S.S.J., Dir.

UNION. *Union Hospital,* 1000 Galloping Hill Rd., 07083. Tel: 908-687-1900. Rev. George M. Keating.

Prison Chaplaincy

NEWARK. *Essex County Jail,* 60 Nelson Pl., 07102. Tel: 201-621-5163. Rev. Edward J. Galvin, S.M.A. Tel: 201-923-6798; Sr. Peg Ryan, S.S.N.D. Tel: 908-352-8068.
Northern State Prison, 168 Frontage Rd., 07101. Tel: 201-465-0068. Deacons Frederick G. Kopp; Samuel Ventula.

ELIZABETH. *Union County Jail,* 15 Elizabeth Town Plaza, 07201. Tel: 908-558-2600. Rev. John G. Netta Tel: 201-351-4444.

HACKENSACK. *Bergen County Sheriff Detention Center,* 160 S. River St., 07601. Tel: 201-488-1190. Rev. Joseph E. Buzzerio; Deacon Thomas F. Collins.

KEARNY. *Hudson County Correctional Center,* 35 Hackensack Ave., 07032. Tel: 201-491-5500. Revs. William Gyure; Timothy Tighe.

PARAMUS. *Bergen County Youth Detention Center,* 296 E. Ridgewood Ave., 07652. Tel: 201-599-6185. Rev. Joseph R. Buzzerio.

Special Assignment:
Reverend Fathers—
Ashe, Kevin P., Exec. Dir. Park Theatre Performing Arts Ctr., Inc.
DiGirolamo, Dante M., Dir. Eucharistic Shrine of the Adorable Face of Jesus

On Duty Outside the Archdiocese:
Reverend Monsignors—
Casale, Franklyn M., St. Thomas University, 16400 N.W. 32nd Ave., Miami, FL 33054
McDade, Thomas J., 4001 14th St. N.E., Washington, DC 20017
Radano, John A., Villa Stritch, Via Della Nocetta 63, Rome, 00164 Italy
Synan, Edward A., Pontifical Institute of Medieval Studies, 59 Queen Park Crescent Rd., Toronto, Ontario M5S23 Canada
Reverend Fathers—
Arvay, Alfred S., 5128 Mentmore Ave., Spring Hill, FL 34606
Batista, George L., Church of St. Luke, 2892 S. Congress Ave., Lake Worth, FL 33461
Ciccarino, Christopher M., North American College, Casa Santa Maria, Via d'Umilta, 30, Rome, 00187 Italy
Kenna, Thomas J., Church of St. William, P.O. Box 7188, Naples, FL 33941
Kirchner, James A., Our Divine Savior Church, 1205 Love ave., P.O. Box 212, Tifton, GA 31793
Krozser, John J., C.M., Church of the Resurrection, 2815 Forbes Dr., Montgomery, AL 36110
Kukura, Joseph W., 4455 Woodson Rd., St. Louis, MO 63134
Kunze, Robert W., St. Francis de Sales Church, 514 Camden Ave., Salisbury, MD 21801
Leahy, Robert T., St. Pius X Church, 203 W. Lacey Rd., Forked River, NJ 08731
Livolsi, Sylvester J., Sanctuary of Mary, R.R. 1, Box 106, Branchville, NJ 07826
Merdinger, Philip E., Brotherhood of Hope, 194 Summer Ave., Sumerville, MA 02143
Miller, Frederick L., St. Charles Borromeo Seminary, 1000 E. Wynnewood Rd., Overbrook, PA 19096
Moise, Burnet, c/o The Repemdorist Monastery, 13 Rue St., P.O. Box 550, Port-Au-Prince, Haiti
Mulvey, John J., M.Div., Church of St. Charles Borromeo, 21505 Augusta Ave., Port Charlotte, FL 33952
Papalia, Pasquale A., Sts. Peter & Paul, 285 Hamilton St., Somerset, NJ 08873
Perricone, John A., St. Agnes, 143 E. 43rd St., New York, NY 10017
Reinbold, Charles, Mt. St. Francis, 250 South St., Peekskill, NY 10566
Russo, Michael A., St. Mary College, Box 5166, Moraga, CA 94575
Sikora, James M., 1301 - 20th St. S., Great Falls, MT 59405
Smith, Paul H., 1717 Ala Wai Blvd., Apt. 1806, Honolulu, HI 96815
Sypko, Tadeusz Marek, St. Rose of Lima Parish, 311 Central Ave., Safford, AZ 85546
Tiboni, Vito, Veteran's Hospital, 800 Poly Pl., Apt. 15 W., Brooklyn, NY 11209
Vaccaro, Joseph V., Carmel Blessed Virgin Mary, 8251 De Montreville Tr. N., Lake Elmo, MN 55042
Wilson, William P., Nativity of Blessed Virgin Mary, 99 E. Tioga St., Tunkhannock, PA 18657

Military Chaplains:
Reverend Fathers—
Arminio, Alfonse M., Naval Support Activity, Code 011A, New Orleans, LA 70142
Beale, Kenneth R., Capt., 155 Alabama Ave., Columbus AFB, MS 39701
Berchmanz, Anthony, Vista Pacifica, Apt. 1405, 1066 Calle del Gerro, San Clemente, CA 92672
Brosk, Steven J., PSC 3, Box 1393, APO, AP 96266
D'Emma, Gregory J., 701 Little John Dr., Hinesville, GA 31313
Hanrahan, William P., Chap., 2411 Postal Service Center, Nellis AFB, NV 89191
Lesak, William P., US Sixth Fleet, Code 014, Unit 50148, FPO, AE 09501
Morris, John J., CHC USNR, 5424 Keystone Pl., Virgnia Beach, VA 23464
Newland, Ronald A., Chap. Lt. Col., HQ AETC.HC, P.O. Box 258, Randolph AFB, TX 78148
Oddo, Peter A., 421 Westminster Pl., Lodi, NJ 07644
Pinho, Antonio M., 417 BSB, Unit 26410, CMR 408-Box 125, APO, AE 09182
Rossi, John B., Capt., HHC7-227th AVNRGT, Unit 20197, Box 69, APO, AE 09165

Higher Studies:
Reverend Fathers—
Figueiredo, Anthony J., Casa Santa Maria, Via dell'Umilta, 30, Rome, 00187 Italy
Muller, Michael, St. Ann's Parish, 4001 Yuma St. N.W., Washington, D.C. 20010

Retired:
Reverend Monsignors—
Abramowicz, Sylvester, 893 Westfield Ave., Elizabeth, NJ 07208
Alba, Jose M., St. Nicholas, 122 Ferry st., Jersey City, NJ 07307
Beggans, Joseph A., St. John Vianney Residence, 60 Home Ave., Rutherford, NJ 07070
Bogdziewicz, Anthony, St. John Vianney Residence, 60 Home Ave., Rutherford, NJ 07070
Bonelli, Theodore V., Clearbrook Village, 120B Ironwood Plaza, Cranbury, NJ 08512
Capozzelli, Emmanuel, 632 Bayside Ave., Beachwood, NJ 08722
Carroll, Joseph A., St. Cecilia's, 120 Kearny Ave., Kearny, NJ 07032
Casazza, David J., 426 Jefferson Ave., Avon-by-the-Sea, NJ 07717
Coburn, Vincent P., 1802 Ravine Dr., Forked River, NJ 08731
Daly, William J., St. Joseph's Rectory, 44 Benvenue Ave., West Orange, NJ 07052
Donovan, Joseph J., 13 Cruiser Ct., Toms River, NJ 08753
Egan, Robert P., P.O. Box 476, Convent Station, NJ 07961
Fahy, John J., 60 Home Ave., Rutherford, NJ 07070
Fanelli, Eugene A., Our Lady of Mt. Carmel, 259 Oliver St., Newark, NJ 07105
Fleming, Edward J., Immaculate Conception Seminary, Seton Hall University, South Orange, NJ 07079
Hayes, Paul J., 197 Riverside Dr. N., Bricktown, NJ 08724
Hinrichsen, Carl D., Our Lady of Mercy Rectory, 2 Freemont Ave., Park Ridge, NJ 07656
Hogan, William F., St. John Vianney Res., 60 Home Ave., Rutherford, NJ 07070
Holmes, Richard J., St. Luke, 430 N. Franklin Tpke., Ho-Ho-Kus, NJ 07423
Houghton, Francis J., 2316 Blue Jay Tr., Point Pleasant, NJ 08742
Jarvais, Walter G., 60 Home Ave., Rutherford, NJ 07070
Johnson, James, 555 Prospect Ave., Ridgefield, NJ 07657
Koenig, John, St. Teresa of Avila, 306 Morris Ave., Summit, NJ 07901
Komar, Michael A., 5 Golden Ct., Whiting, NJ 08759
Manz, Joseph C., Our Lady Mother of the Church, 130 Apple Ridge, Woodcliff Lake, NJ 07675
Marjanczyk, Joseph A., P.O. Box 456, Point Pleasant, NJ 08742
Murray, Harold A., 50 Willow Way, Manasquan, NJ 08736
O'Brien, John F., c/o Mrs. M. Kenah, 31 Walnut Dr., Spring Lake Heights, NJ 07762
O'Gorman, George A., 60 Home Ave., Rutherford, NJ 07070
Ockay, Clement A., 60 Home Ave., Rutherford, NJ 07070
Orrico, Caeser G., 20 Locust Ave., Emerson, NJ 07630
Piazza, Benjamin A., 619 Waters Edge Dr., Toms River, NJ 08753
Pollard, Raymond J., 2316 Blue Jay Tr., Point Pleasant, NJ 08742
Price, Edward G., Church of the Assumption, 113 Chiego Pl., Roselle Park, NJ 07204
Reinbold, Francis A., 250 South St., Peekskill, NJ 10566
Reynolds, Roger A., Our Lady of Victories Rectory, 81 Lynn St., Harrington Park, NJ 07640
Sullivan, Edwin V., Seton Hall University, South Orange Ave., South Orange, NJ 07079
Turro, James C., Immaculate Conception Seminary, Seton Hall University, South Orange, NJ 07079
Walsh, Gerard W., 2940 Bowspirit Ln., St. James City, FL 33956
Welsh, Aloysius J., 60 Home Ave., Rutherford, NJ 07070
Wojtycha, Edward F., 1800 SE St. Lucie Blvd., Stuart, FL 34996
Reverend Fathers—
Adamczyk, Stanley J., St. John Vianney Res., 60 Home Ave., Rutherford, NJ 07070
Anta, Antonio, c/o Maria Rodriguez, 95 Prospect St., Newark, NJ 07105
Babulski, Robert E., 28 E. Stimpson Ave., Linden, NJ 07036
Bergeur, John X., St. John Vianney Res., 60 Home Ave., Rutherford, NJ 07070
Bukowski, Vincent J., 450 Island Rd., Apt. 87, Ramsey, NJ 07446
Byrne, W. Gordon, 37 Atlantic Ave., Ocean Grove, NJ 07756
Callahan, James, Post Chaplains Office, 1821 Dora Dr., Cardiff, CA 92007
Carey, Thomas, One Upper Mountain Ave., Montclair, NJ 07042
Cestaro, Joseph J., St. John Vianney Residence, 60 Home Ave., Rutherford, NJ 07070
Clyde, George A., 2121 Butternut Rd., Sea Girt, NJ 08750
Coda, Joseph F., 60 Home Ave., Rutherford, NJ 07070
Daly, Robert L., 387-0 Newport Way, Jamesburg, NJ 08831
Danik, Daniel A., 2046 Ingalls Ave., Linden, NJ 07036
Davis, Thomas E., 367 Stiles Ct., West Orange, NJ 07052
Debold, Walter A., Seton Hall University, S. Orange Ave., South Orange, NJ 07079
Derbyshire, Joseph V., St. Anne Rectory, 325 Second Ave., Garwood, NJ 07027
Di Peri, Joseph B., Leisure Ridge, 303 Devon St., Lakehurst, NJ 08733
Doherty, George E., 133 S. Second St., Harrison, NJ 07029
Dowling, John C., 585 Bloomfield Ave., Apt. 35, West Caldwell, NJ 07006
Dowling, Michael J., 4 Brookline Ct., Middletown, NJ 07748
Doyle, John F., 1724 Lockhart St. R.D. #3, Toms River, NJ 08757
Doyle, Joseph M., 145 Pearsall Ave., Jersey City, NJ 07305
Drexler, George D., Box 316, Sea Girt, NJ 08750
Driscoll, James J., P.O. Box 541, Spring Lake, NJ 07762
Egan, John J., 31 Fitzroy Dr., Charleston, SC 29414
Eid, Frederick M., 400 Willow Ave., Hoboken, NJ 07030
Fagan, Joseph P., P.O. Box 545, Spring Lake, NJ 07762
Ferrazoli, Henry R., 149 Orlando Blvd., Toms River, NJ 08757
Finn, Francis J., 26 Kent Dr., Bricktown, NJ 08723
Fitzpatrick, Patrick F.X., Allendale Nursing Home, 85 Harreton Ave., Allendale, NJ 07401
Foley, James F., St. mary's Life Care Center, 135 S. Center St., Orange, NJ 07050
Frank, Joseph A., 44 Saltspray Dr., Forked River, NJ 08731
French, Walter V., 26 Rogerene Way, Landing, NJ 07850
Galdon, Richard M., P.O. Box 10, Jemez Springs, NM 87025
Garoffolo, Vincent, 71 Market St., Garfield, NJ 07026. Tel: 201-340-9029
Gavin, Francis T., Seton Hall University, S. Orange Ave., South Orange, NJ 07079
Genzlinger, Walter L., Mt. Carmel, 99 Broadway, Jersey City, NJ 07306
Gillick, Thomas A., St. John Vianney Residence, 60 Home Ave., Rutherford, NJ 07070
Hanley, John G., Pope John Paul II Pavilion, 135 S. Center St., Orange, NJ 07050
Hayes, Edward J., St. Joseph's Home, 140 Sheperd Ln., Totowa, NJ 07512
Hearns, Joseph A., 44 Wilson St., Oakland, NJ 07436
Hermanns, Harold T., St. John Vianney Residence, 60 Home Ave., Rutherford, NJ 07070
Kenny, Thomas A., 24 Chesapeake St., Barnegat, NJ 08005
Kowalski, Eugene S., 15 E. Eighth St., Clifton, NJ 07011
Laudati, Joseph J., 36 Milton Ave., Nutley, NJ 07110
Loughlin, James F., 1943 Ship Ct., Toms River, NJ 08753
Ludlum, William, St. Francis Life Care Corp., 21 Pocono Rd., Denville, NJ 07834
Lynch, Charles M., St. Francis Life Care Corp., 21 Pocono Rd., Denville, NJ 07834
Macho, George S., 1825 Buttonwood Ave., Toms River, NJ 08755
Madden, John J., 60 Home Ave., Rutherford, NJ 07070
Mahoney, Daniel F., 7450 Dundee Way, Brooksville, FL 34613
Malkiewicz, Edward S., 3026 Kennedy Blvd., Jersey City, NJ 07306
McCloskey, James F., 85 Harreton Rd., Allendale, NJ 07401
McFarland, James W., 21 Skillman Ave., Jersey City, NJ 07306
McGuinness, Lester A., St. Aloysius, 219 Bloomfield Ave., Caldwell, NJ 07006

McKenna, Denis R., 149 Meisel Ave., Springfield, NJ 07081
McKeon, Raymond T., St. James Rectory, 143 Madison St., Newark, NJ 07105
McTague, Charles H., St. James Rectory, 143 Madison St., Newark, NJ 07105
Merity, John A., 905 S. Maple Ave., Glen Rock, NJ 07452
Merzena, Carl J., 60 Home Ave., Rutherford, NJ 07070
Miller, Ferdinand B., 309 Downer St., Mantoloking, NJ 08738
Mills, James Leo, 6131 Grand Ave., Apt. 7C, North Bergen, NJ 07047
Miodowski, Chester A., Richmond Rd., Lake Lackawanna, Stanhope, NJ 07874
Miodowski, Leonard A., St. John Vianney Res., 60 Home Ave., Rutherford, NJ 07070
Murphy, Daniel A., Seton Hall University, S. Orange Ave., South Orange, NJ 07079
Nealon, Joseph W., 3360 Canoe Creek Tr., Palm City, FL 34990
O'Brien, John E., 346 Mt. Pleasant Ave., Livingston, NJ 07039
O'Keefe, Maurice L., 60 Home Ave., Rutherford, NJ 07070
O'Neill, James R., St. Paul's, 200 Wyckoff Ave., Ramsey, NJ 07446
Olszewski, John S., St. Mark's Rectory, 287 Hamilton St., Rahway, NJ 07065
Osorio, RudolfoEdward B., 2438 Fruit Ave. S.E., Port Lucie, FL 34952
Prestera, Vincent J., 1015 Aoloa Pl. #450, Kailua, HI 96734
Quinlan, Joseph M., 18 Ellsworth Ct., Red Bank, NJ 07701
Rischmann, Edward, 146 Skyline Drive, Brick, NJ 08724
Rock, John J., 200 Springfield Ave., Apt. 5023, Springfield, NJ 07081
Rutkowski, Stephen C., 1730 NE 63rd Ct., Ft. Lauderdale, FL 33334
Santora, Gerard M., 60 Home Ave., Rutherford, NJ 07070
Sapeta, Joseph S., St. Hedwig, 1062 Dewey Pl., Elizabeth, NJ 07202
Scanlan, Charles V., 60 Home Ave., Rutherford, NJ 07070
Scherer, Donald R., P.O. Box 764, Robert, LA 70455
Schulte, William P., Brester's Guest House, 477 Mt. Prospect Ave., Newark, NJ 07104
Sheehan, Joseph G., St. John the Apostle, 1805 Penbrook Ter., Linden, NJ 07036
Shih, John M., 1509 Bergenline Ave., Union City, NJ 07087
Simko, Michael S., 380 Avenue E, Bayonne, NJ 07002
Swierzbinski, Edward, P.O. Box 342, Normandy Beach, NJ 08739
Szelest, Theodore A., Church of St. Mary, 280 Washington Ave., Dumont, NJ 07628
Tracy, John A., 17 Third Ave., Hawthorne, NJ 07506
Waldron, John R., Troy Towers, 40 Conger St., Apt.302A, Bloomfield, NJ 07003
Wightman, John H., 1215 Windlass Dr., Manahawkin, NJ 08050
Young, Carl A., 1738 Certainty Dr., Point Pleasant, NJ 08742
Zaorski, Thaddeus, St. Joseph's Home, One St. Joseph's Terr., Woodbridge, NJ 07095
Zuber, Thaddeus F., 60 Home Ave., Rutherford, NJ 07070

Permanent Deacons:
Acocella, Louis, St. Francis Xavier, Newark
Allgaier, John, On Duty Outside the Archdiocese
Alsing, Edwin J., St. Lukes, Ho-Ho-Kus
Alvarez, Juan, On Duty Outside the Archdiocese
Amaro, Claudino, On Duty Outside the Archdiocese
Anders, Joseph L., On Duty Outside the Archdiocese
Andrews, Marshall, Our Lady of the Valley, Orange
Antola, Aldo P., St. Thomas the Apostle, Bloomfield
Araya, Alfonso, On Duty Outside the Archdiocese
Balestrieri, Anthony A., Our Lady of Peace, Maywood
Baltus, John M., St. James, Springfield
Barrett, Thomas J., St. Joseph's and St. Michael's, Union City
Basch, Peter J.
Bates, Harold L., Ascension, New Milford
Behringer, Charles, (Retired)
Benedetto, William R., Queen of Peace, North Arlington
Berkise, John, On Duty Outside the Archdiocese
Besida, Dennis J., St. Thomas, Bloomfield
Bond, Charles H., (Retired)
Bongiovanni, Jerome C., St. James, Springfield
Bonilla, Benjamin, On Duty Outside the Archdiocese
Botts, Edward, Queen of Angels, Newark
Botts, Robert, Queen of Angels, Newark
Bowen, Edmund, (Retired)
Bowen, Edward J., St. Peter the Apostle, River Edge
Brennan, Vishno H., On Duty Outside the Archdiocese
Byrnes, Richard, Our Lady of Good Counsel, Washington Township
Caloza, Dionisio, M.D., On Duty Outside the Archdiocese
Campione, Frank J., St. Thomas More, Fairfield
Carr, Patrick V., Community Hospital, Montclair
Cata, David
Cauceglia, Arthur J., Our Lady of the Assumption, Wood Ridge
Cerrato, Gerard F., III, St. Rocco's, Union City
Charriez, Nestor, On Duty Outside the Archdiocese
Christie, William A., On Duty Outside the Archdiocese
Coffey, John J., St. Peter Claver, Montclair
Collins, Thomas F., Bergen Pines Hospital
Colon, German, On Duty Outside the Archdiocese
Colon, Hector, On Duty Outside the Archdiocese
Concepcion, Asuncion, On Duty Outside the Archdiocese
Cook, William R., On Duty Outside the Archdiocese
Cordasco, Ralph J., Clara Maass Medical Center, Belleville
Courtney, J. William, St. Mary's, Rahway
Coyle, Thomas J., St. Thomas, Bloomfield
Cruz, Primitivo, Sts. Peter & Paul, Hoboken
Cullinane, John, On Duty Outside the Archdiocese
Cunningham, Joseph, St. Joseph, West Orange
Czerepka, Alexander J., St. Theresa, Linden
Daniele, Paul, St. Francis Xavier, Newark
Davignon, Paul M., On Duty Outside the Archdiocese
DeBenedictus, Thomas, SS. Joseph and Michael, Union City
Degnon, Robert F., On Duty Outside the Archdiocese
Del Monte, Joseph J., Assumption-All Saints, Jersey City
Delgado, Carlos, On Duty Outside the Archdiocese
DeLucca, Nicholas J., Our Lady, Mother of the Church, Woodcliff Lake
DeMaria, Joseph, Jr., St. Elizabeth, Wyckoff
Dempsey, John J.
Diaz-Rojas, Andres, (Retired)
DiMeo, John J., St. Mary's, Rutherford
Dove, Winston, On Duty Outside the Archdiocese
Downey, John L., St. Cecilia's, Kearny
Fargo, Nicholas C., Our Lady of Mercy, Jersey City
Fernandez, Jose R., Inactive
Ferraiuola, Lex, Our Lady of Mt. Carmel, Tenafly
Fiore, Joseph, St. Joseph's, East Orange
Fischer, Robert, On Duty Outside the Archdiocese
Fitzgerald, Michael J., St. Joseph, Bogota
Francione, Joseph, St. Philomena, Livingston
Freeman, Gerald, St. Paul, Irvington
Fuentes, Julio, Leave of Absence
Garcia, David, Our Lady of the Lake, Verona
Gilheany, Thomas J., On Duty Outside the Archdiocese
Giordano, William J., Our Lady of Assumption, Bayonne
Gisoldi, Frank A., St. Teresa of Avila, Summit
Glogoza, Theodore J., Sacred Heart, Bloomfield
Gomez, Alberto, St. Michael's, Newark
Gonzalez, Faustino (NY), Leave of Absence
Gonzalez, Pedro
Gorini, Joseph, On Duty Outside the Archdiocese
Gowarty, Joseph, On Duty Outside the Archdiocese
Gray, Brandon, On Duty Outside the Archdiocese
Grieder, Gustave, St. Matthew, Ridgefield
Haas, Henry W., Our Lady of Mt. Carmel, Montclair
Hall, J. Bruce, On Duty Outside the Archdiocese
Heinrich, Joseph R., On Duty Outside the Archdiocese
Hemberger, Martin R., St. Mary's, West New York
Higgins, Leonard F., Our Lady of Mercy, Park Ridge
Hildebrandt, Edward J.
Hodges, Richard G., St. Pius X, Old Tappan
Hoefling, Edward J., On Duty Outside the Archdiocese
Hrdina, Joseph, (Retired)
Huff, Sidney E., Holy Spirit-Help of Christians, East Orange
Inguaggiato, John M., Our Lady of Sorrows, South Orange
Jackson, Alonzo, St. Joseph, East Orange
Johnson, Leon, Christ the King, Jersey City
Joyce, William, Annunciation, Paramus
Jurjevic, Svetko, On Duty Outside the Archdiocese
Kelly, Walter, On Duty Outside the Archdiocese
Keturwitis, Henry J., Sts. Peter & Paul, Elizabeth
Kiley, Charles F., Permanent Diaconate Preparation Program
King, Aidan P., St. Thomas More, Fairfield
Kirkham, Donald F., On Duty Outside the Archdiocese
Kramer, Richard D., On Duty Outside the Archdiocese
Kratchman, Robert M., St. Elizabeth, Wyckoff
Lawless, Timothy, (Outside Archdiocese)
Leary, Gerald, St. Mary, Closter
LeConte, Wilfrid, St. Peter Claver, Montclair
Liptak, Stephen J., St. Aloysius, Jersey City
Llanza, Oscar, On Duty Outside the Archdiocese
Loman, David B., Our Lady of Mt. Carmel, Tenafly
Lopez, George, On Duty Outside the Archdiocese
Lopez, Sixto, Immaculate Heart of Mary, Newark
Lubas, Joseph, St. Adalbert, Elizabeth
Lynn, Walter, St. Joseph, Bogota
Macaluso, Martin P., St. Mary, Plainfield
Mackesy, Leonard J., Our Lady of Sorrows, Kearny
Magarelli, Paul S., St. Philip the Apostle, Saddle Brook
Mainero, Frank A., On Duty Outside the Archdiocese
Malarcher, Willy J., Holy Name Hospital, Teaneck
Marcom, Joseph E., Permanent Diaconate Preparation Program
Maron, Edward
Martinez, Jose, St. Columba, Newark
Massar, Cyril J., Leave of Absence
Matos, William, Jr., St. Columba, Newark
Matthews, Michael, Permanent Diaconate Office
McAulay, John R., Leave of Absence
McCarren, Daniel G., Jr., St. Rose of Lima, Short Hills
McCarthy, John T., St. Augustine's, Union City
McComb, David, On Duty Outside the Archdiocese
McFadden, Edward, St. Michael's Hospital, Newark
McGarry, Richard M. (SA), St. Anne's, Fairlawn
McNulty, James, On Duty Outside the Archdiocese
Mendez, Daniel, St. Augustine's, Newark
Messina, Dominic S., St. Thomas More, Fairfield
Messina, Vincent, Holy Trinity, Hackensack
Meyers, Vincent J., (Retired)
Miney, Patrick F., St. John's, Bergenfield
Minichino, Leonard A., St. Catharine's, Glen Rock
Mistretta, Alfonso G., Leave of Absence
Montanez, Luis A., St. Joseph, Hoboken
Montemurro, Michael V., Little Flower, Berkeley Heights
Montini, Leo, St. Catherine, Cedar Grove
Moore, Brett O., Sacred Heart, Lyndhurst
Morend, Michel, On Duty Outside the Archdiocese
Morris, William, University Hospital, Newark
Mueller, James A., St. Catherine, Glen Rock
Myers, William, Queen of Peace, North Arlington
Nazzaro, Joseph J., On Duty Outside the Archdiocese
Negron, Victor, On Duty Outside the Archdiocese
Nilan, Thomas, St. Cassian's, Upper Montclair
Niland, Joseph, Annunciation, Paramus
Niles, Donald P., St. Elizabeth of Hungary, Linden
Noone, Thomas H., On Duty Outside the Archdiocese
O'Connell, Brian, On Duty Outside the Archdiocese
O'Neill, James, St. Mary's, Rahway
Ortega, Cesar, St. Ann, Newark
Ortiz, Jaime, St. Michael's, Jersey City
Osborne, Charles E., St. Rocco, Newark
Paredes, Guy, (Retired)
Paulillo, Joseph J., St. Andrew's, Westwood
Perez, Buenaventura, On Duty Outside the Archdiocese
Perez, Prudencio, On Duty Outside the Archdiocese
Persinger, Joseph M., St. Rose of Lima, Short Hills
Peterson, Victor, Bergen County Institutions
Pluta, Thomas A, Holy Trinity, Westfield
Polanco, Leopoldo, St. Boniface, Jersey City
Porter, Edward W., Jr., Cathedral of the Sacred Heart
Postadan, Romulo D., On Duty Outside the Archdiocese
Puglisi, Robert, On Duty Outside the Archdiocese
Puliatte, James, Immaculate Conception, Norwood
Quintana, Restituto, St. Michael's, Newark
Ravelo, Daniel, Office of the Permanent Diaconate
Raymundo, Ranulfo, Sacred Heart, Bloomfield
Restiro, Louis, On Duty Outside the Archdiocese
Reyes, Jose, On Duty Outside the Archdiocese
Reyes, Modesto, On Duty Outside the Archdiocese
Reyes, Victor, St. Leo, Irvington
Riccio, Dominick, O.L. of Mt. Virgin, Garfield
Rice, George F., Our Lady of Mercy, Park Ridge
Riche, Philip, St. Mary's, Nutley
Rivera, Pedro, St. Joseph's, Hoboken
Roccanova, Rocco
Rodack, Stephen
Rodriguez, Gustavo, (Outside Archdiocese)
Rodriguez, Jose A., St. Thomas Aquinas, Newark
Rodriguez, Justo, St. Rocco, Newark
Rodriguez, Vicente, St. Augustine's, Newark
Rolon, Cristobal, On Duty Outside the Archdiocese

Romano, Joseph R., Vocations Office and Corpus Christi, Hasbrouck Heights
Romero, Alberto, St. Joseph of the Palisades, West New York
Rosado, Jose F., Immaculate Conception, Elizabeth
Ross, George A., St. John the Apostle, Linden
Salerno, Philip, St. Philip, Saddle Brook
Sanderson, Raymond, St. Andrew's, Bayonne
Schneider, Paul, St. Catherine's, Glen Rock
Serzan, Vincent C., St. Michael's, Lyndhurst
Shea, Raymond, On Duty Outside the Archdiocese
Shelhamer, William, On Duty Outside the Archdiocese
Simonelli, Nicholas, St. Francis, Ridgefield Park
Somma, Alfred P., St. Joseph, Oradell
Soto, Anibal, Bergen County Jail
Sotolongo, Javier, Inactive
Stanecki, Walter J.
Stark, Henry A., (Retired)
Stoehr, George, On Duty Outside the Archdiocese
Stumbar, James P., Little Flower, Berkeley Heights
Suarez, Ibrahim, (Outside Archdiocese)
Suarez, Juan B., St. Cecilia, Kearny
Swider, Charles P., On Duty Outside the Archdiocese
Tarabokija, Anton, St. John's, Fairview
Taylor, Michael A., On Duty Outside the Archdiocese
Thomann, Robert V., Mt. Carmel, Ridgewood
Thomson, Robert E., Holy Rosary, Edgewater
Titmas, Richard C., St. Anne's, Fair Lawn
Tizzano, Albert H., St. Thomas, Bloomfield
Torres, Antonio, On Duty Outside the Archdiocese
Turner, Robert M., On Duty Outside the Archdiocese
Tynan, Charles, Sacred Heart, Lyndhurst
Valladares, Guillermo, St. Peter's, Belleville
Vargas, Rafael, St. Michael's Medical Center, Newark
Ventola, Samuel, Northern State Prison, Newark
Vitale, Incoronato M., On Duty Outside the Archdiocese
Vrindten, Joseph G., Ramapo College, Mahwah
Vuolo, Pasquale, Our Lady of the Lake, Verona
Walker, George, On Duty Outside the Archdiocese
Wall, Joseph J., St. Teresa, Summit
Wandell, Raymond A., St. Joseph's and St. Michael's, Union City
White, Thomas, On Duty Outside the Archdiocese
Wicks, Ronald, On Duty Outside the Archdiocese
Wilverding, Daniel J., St. Michael, Cranford
Woodruff, Leo A., Holy Name, East Orange
Yannazzone, Robert, Assumption, Roselle Park
Zywicki, Robert S., Mount Carmel, Bayonne

INSTITUTIONS LOCATED IN THE ARCHDIOCESE

[A] SEMINARIES, ARCHDIOCESAN

KEARNY. *Redemptoris Mater.* Archdiocesan Missionary Seminary, 672 Passaic Ave., 07032. Tel: 201-997-3220; Fax: 201-997-5552. Revs. Jose Matias Diaz, Pro-Rector; Luis P. Gonzalez, Asst. to the Rector; Renato Grasselli, Asst. to the Rector. Priests 3.

SOUTH ORANGE. *Immaculate Conception Seminary,* 400 S. Orange Ave., 07079. Tel: 201-761-9575. Officers of Admin.: Very Rev. Thomas Peterson, O.P., S.T.D., Ph.D., Chancellor; Rev. Msgr. Robert T. Sheeran, S.T.D., Pres.; Rev. Msgr. John W. Flesey, S.T.D., Rector/Dean; Rev. Msgr. Andrew T. Cusack, M.A., M.Div., Ph.D. (BGP), Dir. of Formation; Rev. Msgr. Robert F. Coleman, J.C.D., Vice Rector, Business Mgr.; Rev. Msgr. James C. Turro, S.T.L., S.S.L., M.A., Ph., Dir. Library Svcs.; Revs. Martin F. O'Brien, Dir. Field Education; John Russell, O.Carm., S.T.D., S.T.L., Spiritual Dir.; Dr. John Grondelski, Ph.D., Assoc. Dean; Mrs. Patricia Feoranz, Registrar.

The Darlington Fund. Development Agency for Immaculate Conception Seminary. Nick Mazza, Dir. of Devel. Full-Time Faculty: Rev. Msgr. Robert J. Wister, S.T.B., S.T.M., D.Eccl.Hi; Rev. Msgr. Robert J. Wister, S.T.B., S.T.M., D.Eccl.Hi; Revs. C. Anthony Ziccardi, S.S.L.; W. Jerome Bracken, C.P., Ph.D.; Thomas G. Guarino, S.T.D.; Boniface Ramsey, O.P., S.T.D.; Arthur J. Serratelli, S.T.D., S.S.L.; Lawrence B. Porter, S.T.B., S.T.L., Ph.D.; David R. Foster, Ph.D.; Zeni Fox, Ph.D.; William J. Toth, Ph.D.; Leonard Maluf, Ph.D. Priests 7; Lay Teachers 4.

Seton Hall University College Seminary, St. Andrew Hall, 07079. Tel: 201-761-9420. Rev. Thomas R. Peterson, O.P., Chancellor; Rev. Msgr. Robert T. Sheeran, Pres.; Rev. Msgr. Robert J. Fuhrman, M.Div., M.A., Rector; Rev. William Sheridan, Spiritual Dir. In res., Rev. Msgr. Walter G. Jarvais, P.A., Spiritual Dir. Emeritus. Priests 3.

[B] COLLEGES AND UNIVERSITIES

CALDWELL. *Caldwell College,* 9 Ryerson Ave., 07006. Tel: 201-228-4424.
For a complete listing, refer to the Colleges and Universities section.

JERSEY CITY. *Saint Peter's College,* 2641 Kennedy Blvd., 07306-5997. Tel: 201-915-9000; Fax: 201-451-0036.
For a complete listing, refer to the Colleges and Universities section.

LODI. *Felician College,* 262 S. Main St., 07644. Tel: 201-778-1190; Fax: 201-778-4111.
For a complete listing, refer to the Colleges and Universities section.

SOUTH ORANGE. *Seton Hall University,* (1856) 400 South Orange Ave., 07079. Tel: 201-761-9000; Fax: 201-275-2361.
For a complete listing, refer to the Colleges and Universities section.

[C] HIGH SCHOOLS, PRIVATE

NEWARK. *St. Benedict's Preparatory School.* (Grades 7-12), 520 Dr. Martin Luther King, Jr. Blvd., 07102. Tel: 201-643-4800. Rev. Edwin D. Leahy, O.S.B., Headmaster. Benedictine Monks of Newark Abbey 18; Priests 15; Brothers 3; Lay Teachers 40; Boys 545.

St. Vincent Academy. (Girls), 228 W. Market St., 07103. Tel: 201-622-1613. Sr. June Favata, Admin. Dir. Sisters of Charity of St. Elizabeth 6; Lay Teachers 24; Students 320.

BAYONNE. *Holy Family Academy,* 239 Ave. A, 07002. Tel: 201-339-7341; Fax: 201-339-9295. Sisters of St. Joseph of Chestnut Hill, Philadelphia, PA. Sr. Joan Immaculate O'Donnell, S.S.J., Prin. Sisters 9; Lay Teachers 20; Girls 305.

Marist High Schoool. (Coed), 1241 Kennedy Blvd., 07002. Tel: 201-437-4544; Fax: 201-823-2232. Marist Brothers. Bro. Kevin Handibode, F.M.S., Prin. Brothers 9; Sisters 2; Lay Teachers 24; Students 500.

CALDWELL. *Mount St. Dominic Academy.* (Girls), 3 Ryerson Ave., 07006-6196. Tel: 201-226-0660; Fax: 201-226-2693. Sisters of St. Dominic of Caldwell. Sr. Doris Ann Bowles, O.P., Prin. Sisters 11; Lay Teachers 23; Girls 268.

DEMAREST. *Academy of the Holy Angels.* (Girls), 315 Hillside Ave., 07627. Tel: 201-768-7822. Conducted by School Sisters of Notre Dame. Sr. Claire Bonneau, S.S.N.D., Pres. Sisters 12; Lay Teachers 40; Girls 537.

ELIZABETH. *Benedictine Academy,* 840 N. Broad St., 07208-2599. Tel: 908-352-0670. Benedictine Sisters of Elizabeth, NJ. Adele Kosinski, Prin. Sisters 2; Lay Teachers 19; Girls 191. College Preparatory High School (Girls).

HOBOKEN. *Academy of the Sacred Heart.* (Girls), 713 Washington St., 07030. Tel: 201-659-7139. Sisters of Charity of St. Elizabeth. Sr. Diane Collesano, S.C., Prin. Sisters 4; Lay Teachers 17; Girls 160.

JERSEY CITY. *Academy of St. Aloysius.* (Girls: Grades 8-12), 2495 John F. Kennedy Memorial Blvd., 07304. Tel: 201-433-8877; Fax: 201-433-8839. Sisters of Charity of St. Elizabeth. Marion A. Rozger, Exec. Dir. Sisters 6; Lay Teachers 16; Students 160.

St. Anthony High School, 175 Eighth St., 07302. Tel: 201-653-5143. Conducted by Felician Sisters. Sr. Mary Felicia, C.S.S.F., Prin. Sisters 5; Lay Teachers 23; Students 325.

St. Dominic Academy. (Girls), 2572 John F. Kennedy Memorial Blvd., 07304. Tel: 201-434-5938. Dominican Sisters of Caldwell. Sr. Bettyanne Schultz, O.P., Prin. Sisters 10; Lay Teachers 36; Students 521.

St. Peter's Preparatory School, 144 Grand St., 07302. Tel: 201-434-4400; Fax: 210-547-6421. Revs. D. James French, S.J., Rector; James F. Keenan, S.J., Pres.; Mr. John R. Raslowsky, Prin.; Mr. Patrick Reidy, Vice Prin.; Mr. James Horan, Vice Pres. External Affairs; Mr. James Collins, Dean of Students; Revs. Charles F.X. Dolan, S.J., Vice Pres. Alumni Affairs; Anthony J. Azzarto, S.J., Chap.; Raymond J. Balduf, S.J., College Admissions; Erwin G. Beck, S.J.; John E. Browning, S.J.; Bro. Ralph Cilia, S.J.; Revs. Robert G. Cregan, S.J.; Thomas Denny, S.J., Community Min.; James S. Foley, S.J.; Francis J. Hamill, S.J.; Bro. Paul J. Harrison, S.J.; Revs. Michael R. Hoag, S.J.; Thomas V. O'Connor, S.J.; Harold J. Oppido, S.J.; Enrico Raulli, S.J., Res., 220 W. 98th St., Apt. 4E, New York, NY, 10025. In res., Revs. Michael E. Browne, S.J.; John J. Rohr, S.J.; Bro. Frank Turnbull, S.J.; Jose Luis Salazar; Revs. Edward J. Snyder, S.J.; Joseph T. Watson, S.J.; Bro. Joseph J. Griffin, S.J. Priests 19; Brothers 4; Scholastics 1; Sisters 1; Lay Teachers 60; Students 795.

LODI. *Immaculate Conception High School,* 258 S. Main St., 07644. Tel: 201-773-2400. Sr. Anelle Velivis, Ph.D., Prin. Sisters 4; Lay Teachers 22; Girls 186.

ORADELL. *Bergen Catholic.* (Boys), 1040 Oradell Ave., 07649. Tel: 201-261-1844; Fax: 201-599-9507. Congregation of Christian Brothers. Rev. James R. White, Chap.; Bro. J.G. Sullo, C.F.C., Pres.; Mr. Joseph S. Fusco, Prin. Priests 1; Brothers 12; Lay Teachers 48; Boys 920.

RAMSEY. *Don Bosco Preparatory High School for Boys,* 492 N. Franklin Tpke., 07446. Tel: 201-327-8003. Salesians of St. John Bosco. Revs. John Grinsell, S.D.B., Dir./Prin.; Louis Molinelli, S.D.B., Coord. of Youth Ministry; Brendan K. Kilroy, S.P.S., Guidance Dir.; Peter Sella, S.D.B.; Jerzy Schneider, S.D.B.; Paul Chuong Nguyen, S.D.B.; Anthony Luongo, S.D.B.; Bros. Donald Caldwell, S.D.B.; Joseph Lody, S.D.B.; Mark Sulocaa, S.D.B.; Gerald Warner, S.D.B. Priests 8; Brothers 4; Sisters 1; Lay Teachers 51; Students 725.

SOUTH ORANGE. *Marylawn of the Oranges, High School for Girls,* 445 Scotland Rd., 07079. Tel: 201-762-9222. Sisters 10; Lay Teachers 15; Girls 160.

SUMMIT. *Oak Knoll School of the Holy Child Upper School.* (Grades 7-12). (Girls), 44 Blackburn Rd., 07901. Tel: 908-522-8100. Conducted by the Sisters of the Holy Child Jesus. Sr. Cynthia Vives, S.H.C.J., Ed.D., Headmistress; Mary Ellen Ryan, Prin. Sisters 1; Lay Teachers 36; Students 276.

UPPER MONTCLAIR. *Lacordaire Academy, Secondary Division,* 155 Lorraine Ave., 07043. Tel: 201-744-1156; Fax: 210-783-9521. Sisters of St. Dominic. Sr. Suzanne McCaffrey, O.P. Priests 1; Sisters 3; Lay Teachers 15; Girls 120.

WEST ORANGE. *Seton Hall Preparatory School,* 120 Northfield Ave., 07052. Tel: 201-325-6624; Fax: 201-325-6652. Rev. Msgr. Michael E. Kelly, M.A., Headmaster.
Resident Faculty: Revs. Edward G. Bradley, S.T.L., M.A.; Nicholas Figurelli, M.A.; Martin J. Foran, S.T.B., M.A.; Bruce G. Janiga, M.A.; Stephen M. Kilcarr, B.A.; William J. Melillo, M.A., M.Div.; Joseph R. Reilly, S.T.B., S.T.L., B.A.; Joseph F. Wortmann, M.A., S.T.L. Priests 9; Lay Instructors 65; Students 800.

[D] HIGH SCHOOLS, DIOCESAN

CLARK. *Mother Seton (Girls) Regional High School,* Valley Rd., 07066. Tel: 908-382-1952. Sisters of Charity of St. Elizabeth. Sr. Regina Martin, S.C., Prin.; Rev. Alex Pinto. Priests 1; Sisters 12; Lay Teachers 25; Girls 400.

EAST ORANGE. *Essex Catholic Boys High School,* 135 Glenwood Ave., 07017. Tel: 201-674-4200; Fax: 201-674-9121. Congregation of Christian Brothers. Bro. James A. DePiro, C.F.C. Priests 1; Sisters 1; Brothers 6; Lay Teachers 25; Boys 400.

JERSEY CITY. *Hudson Catholic High School,* 790 Bergen Ave., 07306. Tel: 201-332-5970. Brothers of Christian Schools. Bro. Charles Barbush, F.S.C., Prin. Brothers 7; Sisters 1; Lay Teachers 30; Boys 585.

MONTVALE. *St. Joseph Regional High School.* (Boys), 40 Chestnut Ridge Rd., 07645. Tel: 201-391-3300; Fax: 201-391-8073. Brothers of St. Francis Xavier. Bro. William Cushing, C.F.X., Prin.; Rev. John F. Gordon, Chap. Priests 1; Brothers 6; Sisters 2; Lay Teachers 24; Boys 430.

PARAMUS. *Paramus Catholic High School.* (Coed), 425 Paramus Rd., 07652. Tel: 201-445-6465; Fax: 201-445-6440. Sr. Maureen Sullivan, S.C., Pres.; Mrs. Barbara C. Griffin, Prin.; Rev. Donald Hummel, Chap. Sisters of Charity of St. Elizabeth. Priests 1; Sisters 8; Lay Teachers 56; Boys 390; Girls 510.

ROSELLE. *Roselle Catholic High School.* (Coed), Raritan Rd., 07203. Tel: 908-245-2350; Fax: 908-241-3869. Marist Brothers. Bro. Vincent Damian, F.M.S., Prin. Brothers 4; Lay Teachers 44; Students 785.

SCOTCH PLAINS. *Union Catholic Regional High School.* (Coed), 1600 Martine Ave., 07076. Tel: 908-889-1600; Fax: 908-889-7867. Sr. Percy Lee Hart, R.S.M., Prin.; Rev. Donald Blumenfeld, Chap. Priests 1; Sisters 6; Lay Teachers 34; Students 683.

SUMMIT. *The Oratory Catholic Preparatory School.* (Grades 7-12), 1 Beverly Rd., 07901. Tel: 908-273-1084. Revs. F. Kevin Murphy, Headmaster; Edmund G. Bernauer; John F. Johnston (BRK); Paul R. Manning, Res., 14 Bedford Rd. Tel: 908-273-7563. Priests 4; Lay Teachers 17; Students 209.

WASHINGTON TOWNSHIP. *Immaculate Heart Academy.* (Girls), 500 Van Emburgh Ave., 07675. Tel: 201-445-6800. Apostles of the Sacred Heart. Sr. Ellen Cronan, A.S.C.J., Prin. Sisters 7; Lay Teachers 42; Girls 740.

[E] ELEMENTARY SCHOOLS, PRIVATE

NEWARK. *Link Community School, Inc.,* 139 Livingston St., 07103. Tel: 201-642-0529; 642-8510. Dominican Sisters of Caldwell. Sr. Patricia McKearney, Prin. Sisters 4; Lay Teachers 10; Students 115.

St. Lucy Filippini Academy, 142 Jefferson St., 07105. Tel: 201-344-4806. Sr. Mary Valitzski, M.P.F., Prin. Sisters 2; Lay Teachers 23; Students 400.

ELIZABETH. *Bender Memorial Academy,* 416 Linden Ave., 07202. Tel: 908-352-4406. Sisters of St. Benedict. Sr. Marie Therese Hayes, O.S.B., Prin. Sisters

5; Lay Teachers 8; Students 200.

Elizabethport Catholic School. (3 Campuses), 214 Ripley Pl., 07206. Tel: 908-352-9391; Fax: 908-352-4794. Ms. Jo Ann Mathews, Dir.

SS. Peter and Paul Campus-Early Childhood Center. (Ages 3-5), 220 Msgr. Kemezis Pl., 07206. Tel: 908-289-6843. Students 60.

St. Adalbert Campus Lower School. (Grades 1-4), 261 Fulton St., 07206. Tel: 908-353-3160; Fax: 908-352-3878. Students 140.

St. Patrick Campus Upper School. (Grades 5-8), 227 Court St., 07206. Tel: 908-351-2188; Fax: 908-351-6086. Students 200.

JERSEY CITY. *St. Joseph's School for the Blind,* 253 Baldwin Ave., 07306. Tel: 201-653-0578; Fax: 201-653-4087. Mr. Herbert Miller, Admin.; Dr. Stuart Wittenstein, Prin. School for visually impaired, multi-disabled children; non-graded; Early Intervention Program, 5-day Residential Program, Outreach Services. Students 100.

KEARNY. *Sacred Heart School,* 22 Wilson Ave., 07032. Tel: 201-991-0628. Sisters of the Catholic Apostolate. Sr. M. Leonore Parlati, C.S.A.C., Prin. Sisters 9; Lay Teachers 17; Students 380.

Day Care Center. Mrs. Nora Munoz, Head Teacher. Lay Teachers 10; Students 103.

LODI. *The Felician School for Exceptional Children,* 260 S. Main St., P.O. Box 530, 07644. Tel: 201-777-5355; Fax: 201-777-0725. Sr. Mary Ramona, C.S.S.F., Dir.

Day Program. Capacity 140. Sisters 4; Lay Teachers 16; Children 140.

SUMMIT. *Oak Knoll School of The Holy Child, Lower School.* (Grades K-6). (Coed), 44 Blackburn Rd., 07901. Tel: 908-522-8120. Sr. Cynthia Vives, S.H.C.J., Headmistress; Mrs. Elizabeth Barclay, Prin.; Mrs. Susan Livera, Guidance Counselor. Lay Teachers 24; Students 230.

UNION CITY. *Holy Rosary Academy,* 501 15th St., 07087. Tel: 201-864-0332. Sr. M. Gertrude, C.S.A.C., Prin. Sisters of the Catholic Apostolate (Pallottine) 8; Lay Teachers 6; Students 230.

St. Francis Academy, 1601 Central Ave., 07087. Tel: 201-863-4112. Missionary Franciscan Sisters of the Immaculate Conception. Sr. Dora Sartino, O.S.F., Prin. Sisters 1; Lay Teachers 8; Students 238.

UPPER MONTCLAIR. *Lacordaire Academy-Elementary Division,* 155 Lorraine Ave., 07043. Tel: 201-746-2660. Dominican Sisters of Caldwell. Mrs. Mary Anne Ford, Prin. Lay Teachers 10; Students 100.

[F] CATHEDRAL HEALTHCARE SYSTEM OF ARCHDIOCESE OF NEWARK

NEWARK. *Cathedral Healthcare System, Inc.,* 219 Chestnut St., 07105. Tel: 201-690-3600; Fax: 201-690-3601. Mr. Frank L. Fumai, Pres. & CEO.

Cathedral Health Services, Inc.

St. Michael's Medical Center Division, Newark.

St. James Hospital Division, Newark.

St. Mary's Life Center Inc.-Pope John Paul II Pavilion.

[G] GENERAL HOSPITALS

NEWARK. *Catholic Community Services (C.C.S.) Mt. Carmel Guild Hospital,* 1160 Raymond Blvd., 07102. Tel: 201-596-4084.

For a complete listing, refer to the Hospitals section.

St. James Hospital, 155 Jefferson St., 07105. Tel: 201-589-1300.

For a complete listing, refer to the Hospitals section.

Saint Michael's Medical Center, 268 Dr. Martin Luther King. Jr. Blvd., 07102-9880. Tel: 201-877-5411; Fax: 201-877-2714.

For a complete listing, refer to the Hospitals section.

ELIZABETH. *St. Elizabeth Hospital,* 225 Williamson St., 07207. Tel: 908-527-5000; Fax: 908-820-0554.

For a complete listing, refer to the Hospitals section.

HOBOKEN. *St. Mary Hospital,* 308 Willow Ave., 07030. Tel: 201-418-1000; Fax: 201-418-1013.

For a complete listing, refer to the Hospitals section.

JERSEY CITY. *St. Francis Hospital,* 25 McWilliams Pl., 07302. Tel: 201-418-1000; Fax: 201-418-2011.

For a complete listing, refer to the Hospitals section.

ORANGE. *Saint Mary Life Center, Inc. - Pope John Paul II Pavillion,* 135 S. Center St., 07050. Tel: 201-266-3000.

For a complete listing, refer to the Hospitals section.

TEANECK. *Holy Name Hospital,* 718 Teaneck Rd., 07666. Tel: 201-833-3000; Fax: 201-833-3230.

For a complete listing, refer to the Hospitals section.

[H] HOMES FOR AGED

JERSEY CITY. *St. Ann's Home for the Aged,* 198 Old Bergen Rd., 07305. Tel: 201-433-0950.

For a complete listing, refer to the Special Care Facilities section.

MONTCLAIR. *Mother Seton Residence,* 51 Washington St., 07042. Tel: 201-783-1400.

For a complete listing, refer to the Special Care Facilities section.

St. Vincent's Nursing Home, 45 Elm St., 07042. Tel: 201-754-4800; Fax: 201-746-2362.

For a complete listing, refer to the Special Care Facilities section.

PARAMUS. *Mount St. Andrew Villa,* 55 W. Midland Ave., 07652. Tel: 201-261-5950.

For a complete listing, refer to the Special Care Facilities section.

SADDLE RIVER. *Villa Marie Claire,* 12 W. Saddle River Rd., 07458.

For a complete listing, refer to the Special Care Facilities section.

[I] HOMES FOR THE BLIND

JERSEY CITY. *St. Joseph's Home for the Blind,* 537 Pavonia Ave., 07306. Tel: 201-653-8300.

For a complete listing, refer to the Special Care Facilities section.

[J] DAY NURSERIES

NEWARK. *Our Lady of Perpetual Help Day Nursery,* 170 Broad St., 07104. Tel: 201-484-3535. Vocationist Sisters. Sisters 7; Lay Teachers 10; Children 170.

ELIZABETH. *Immaculate Heart of Mary Nursery, School & Kindergarten,* 205 E. Jersey St., 07206. Tel: 201-354-8388. Sr. Marianna Perrella, M.P.F., Prin. Religious Teachers Filippini 4; Children 111.

JERSEY CITY. *St. Elizabeth's Child Care Center,* 129 Garrison Ave., 07306. Tel: 201-795-1443; Fax: 201-795-4121. Franciscan Sisters of St. Elizabeth. Mother Rose Cosenza, Supr. Sisters 13; Total Staff 32; Children 270.

NUTLEY. *Holy Family Day Nursery and Convent,* 174 Franklin Ave., 07110. Tel: 201-235-1170. Franciscan Sisters of St. Elizabeth. Mother Romilda Chiga, F.S.S.E., Supr. Sisters 7; Children 80.

RAMSEY. *St. Joseph Pre-School,* 372 Wyckoff Ave., 07430. Tel: 201-825-8386. Franciscan Sisters of St. Elizabeth. Sr. Rosemary Di Lauro, Supr. Sisters 4; Children 25.

[K] PROTECTIVE INSTITUTIONS

NEWARK. *Queen of Peace,* 60 Jay St., 07103. Tel: 201-481-9056.

For a complete listing, refer to the Special Care Facilities section.

HOBOKEN. *Good Counsel, Inc. (St. Francis Home),* 303 Madison St., 07030. Tel: 201-798-9059; 795-0637; 800-723-8331 (Hotline); Fax: 201-795-0809.

For a complete listing, refer to the Special Care Facilities section.

JERSEY CITY. *St. Joseph's Home,* 81 York St., 07302. Tel: 201-413-9280.

For a complete listing, refer to the Special Care Facilities section.

KEARNY. *New Jersey Boystown,* 499 Belgrove Dr., 07032. Tel: 201-991-2850.

For a complete listing, refer to the Special Care Facilities section.

[L] HOMES FOR WOMEN

JERSEY CITY. *St. Mary's Residence for Business and Professional Women,* 240 Washington St., 07302. Tel: 201-432-6289.

For a complete listing, refer to the Special Care Facilities section.

[M] PERSONAL PRELATURES

SOUTH ORANGE. *Opus Dei.* (Prelature of the Holy Cross and Opus Dei), 170 Montrose Ave., 07079. Tel: 201-763-8397; Fax: 201-762-1794. Revs. James W. Albrecht; Thomas J. Lamb. Legal Title: *The Work of God, Inc.*

[N] MONASTERIES AND RESIDENCES OF PRIESTS AND BROTHERS

NEWARK. *Marist Brothers,* Queen of Angels Brothers' Residence, 28 Irvine Turner Blvd., 07103. Tel: 201-642-4820. Bros. Luke Reddington, Dir.; John Klein; Stephen Schlitte. Brothers 3.

Newark Abbey, 528 Dr. Martin Luther King, Jr. Blvd., 07102. Tel: 201-643-4800; Fax: 201-643-6922. Rt. Rev. Melvin J. Valvano, O.S.B., Abbot & Pres. American Cassinese Congregation, O.S.B.; Very Revs. Mark M. Payne, O.S.B., Prior; Boniface J. Treanor, O.S.B., Subprior; Revs. John T. Browne, O.S.B.; Declan J. Cunniff, O.S.B.; Augustine J. Curley, O.S.B.; Lucien R. Donnelly, O.S.B.; Luke A. Edelen, O.S.B.; Albert T. Holtz, O.S.B., Novice Master; Theodore J. Howarth, O.S.B.; Edwin D. Leahy, O.S.B.; Bro. Thomas R. Lee, O.S.B.; Revs. Malachy M. McPadden, O.S.B.; Emilian Muschette, O.S.B.; Maynard G. Nagengast, O.S.B.; Bro. Gereon J. Reuter, O.S.B.; Revs. Benedict E. Tyler, O.S.B.; Philip J. Waters, O.S.B.; Bro. Francis M. Woodruff, O.S.B.; Rev. Matthew S. Wotelko, O.S.B., St. Maur Priory, 4615 N. Michigan Rd., Indianapolis, IN, 46208. Very Rev. Charles W. Henry, O.S.B., Prior; Revs. Robert McElaney, O.S.B.; Bernardin J. Patterson, O.S.B.; Bros. Francis Dachs, O.S.B.; Mark Hayden, O.S.B.; Jerome Rice, O.S.B.; Anthony Streit, O.S.B. Priests 20; Non-Clerical Brothers 7.

BAYONNE. *Marist Brothers,* Champagnat Residence, 1241 Kennedy Blvd., 07002. Tel: 201-437-4115. Bro. Ralph Dinielli, F.M.S., Dir. Brothers 8.

CLIFFSIDE PARK. *St. Patrick's Missionary Society,* 70 Edgewater Rd., 07010. Tel: 201-943-6575. Revs. Brendan Kilroy, S.P.S.; Donald McDonagh, S.P.S.; Michael Moore, S.P.S.; James Barry. Total Staff 4; Total in Residence 4.

EAST ORANGE. *Congregation of Christian Brothers,* Essex Catholic Brothers' Residence, 135 Glenwood Ave., 07017. Tel: 201-676-3334. In res., Rev. Dennis Kaelin, Chap.; Bros. H. A. McKenzie, Local Leader; P. R. Duffy; D. F. McCulloch; S. J. Johnsen; J. A. DePiro; J. J. Fagan; J. P. Hamilton. Priests 1; Brothers 7.

HOBOKEN. *F.A.I.T.H. Services.,* 307 Willow Ave., 07030. Tel: 201-792-6161; (Brothers Residence) 420-1554. Brothers of the Poor of St. Francis (C.F.P.). Bro. Robert J. Reinke, C.F.P. Total Staff 22; Total Assisted 3,584.

HOHOKUS. *St. Anthony of Padua,* 67 Arbor Dr., P.O. Box 40, 07423. Tel: 201-612-9763; Fax: 201-612-9869. Revs. Daniel Lanahan, O.F.M., Guardian; Kevin Cronin, O.F.M.; John Kelleher, O.F.M.; Emmet Murphy, O.F.M.; Francis N. Smith, O.F.M.

JERSEY CITY. *Brothers of the Christian Schools.* Hudson Catholic Brothers' Residence, 790 Bergen Ave., 07306-4535. Tel: 201-332-0971. Bro. Raymond Murphy, F.S.C. Brothers 9.

Jesuits of Saint Peter's College, Inc., 50 Glenwood Ave., 07306-4606. Tel: 201-433-2527. Revs. John F. Wrynn, S.J., Rector; James F. Dolan, S.J., Minister; William M. Abbott, S.J.; Thomas C. Blessin, S.J.; Edward W. Brande, S.J.; John M. Buckley, S.J.; Claudio M. Burgaleta, S.J.; Laurence L. Cassidy, S.J.; Eugene K. Culhane, S.J.; James H. Dahlinger, S.J.; Mark T. DeStephano, S.J.; Eugene J. Devlin, S.J.; J. Juan Diaz Vilar, S.J. (Spain); Bro. Patrick T. Flanagan, S.J.; Revs. Charles A. Gallagher, S.J.; Edward B. Gillen, S.J.; Jerome H. Gruszczyk, S.J.; Edward J. Heavey, S.J.; Joseph A. Kelly, S.J. (Ireland); Robert E. Kennedy, S.J.; James N. Loughran, S.J.; Joseph W. Lux, S.J.; T. Patrick Lynch, S.J.; Donal T. MacVeigh, S.J.; Oscar Magnan, S.J.; William F.X. Maher, S.J.; Edmund W. Majewski, S.J.; Carsten P. Martensen, S.J.; Robert E. McCarty, S.J.; William A. McKenna, S.J.; Aidan C. McMullen, S.J.; John J. O'Brien, S.J.; John P. Ruane, S.J.; John P. St. George, S.J.; Thomas L. Sheridan, S.J.; David X. Stump, S.J. Total Staff 14; Total in Residence 34.

MONTCLAIR. *Comboni Missionaries of the Heart of Jesus (Verona Fathers),* 88 High St., P.O. Box 138, 07042-0138. Tel: 201-744-8080; Fax: 201-744-8919. Revs. Remus A. Catellani, M.C.C.J.; J.M. Carillo, M.C.C.J.; David P. Baltz, M.C.C.J., Supr. Total Staff 7; Total in Residence 3.

MONTVALE. *Xaverian Brothers,* Xaverian Brothers' Residence, 40 Chestnut Ridge Rd., 07645. Tel: 201-391-8071; Fax: 201-391-8073. Brothers 5.

NORTH ARLINGTON. *Brothers of the Christian Schools,* Christian Brothers' Residence, 200 Ridge Rd., 07031. Tel: 201-991-0235. Brothers 10.

ORADELL. *Congregation of Christian Brothers,* Bergen Catholic Brothers' Residence, 1040 Oradell Ave., 07649. Tel: 201-261-1816. Brothers 14.

ORANGE. *St. Veronica Giuliani Friary, Capuchin Franciscan Friars,* Province of St. Mary, 518-B Valley St., 07050-1231. Tel: 201-672-8080. Bro. John Shento, O.F.M.Cap., Guardian; Rev. John Gallagher, O.F.M.Cap., Vicar; Bros. Terrence Taffe, O.F.M.Cap.; John Conway, O.F.M.Cap.; Celestino Arias, O.F.M.Cap.; Maurice Moreau, O.F.M.Cap.; Larry Evans, O.F.M.Cap.; Luis Ramos, O.F.M.Cap.; Richard Crawley, O.F.M.Cap.; Oliver Anastacio, O.F.M.Cap.; Scott Leet, O.F.M.Cap.

ROSELLE. *Marist Brothers Residence,* Roselle Catholic High School, 1 Raritan Rd., 07203. Tel: 908-245-3574. Brothers 11.

RUTHERFORD. *St. John Vianney Residence for Priests,* 60 Home Ave., 07070. Tel: 201-933-5155; Fax: 201-933-4467. Mrs. Joan D'Gerolamo, Admin.; Rev. Msgr. Edward F. Kavin, Dir. In res., Most Rev. Peter L. Gerety, Archbishop Emeritus; Rev. Msgr. John J. Fahy; Rev. Msgr. Walter G. Jarvais, P.A.; Rev. Msgr. Anthony Bogdziewicz; Rev. Msgr. Joseph Beggans; Revs. Joseph Coda; Harold Hermanns; Thomas Gillick; Rev. Msgr. William F. Hogan; Rev. Carl Merzena; Rev. Msgr. George O'Gorman; Revs. Maurice O'Keefe; Gerard M. Santora; Rev. Msgr. Aloysius Welsh; Revs. Clarles V. Scanlan; John Bergeur; Leonard Midowski; John Madden; Thadius Zuber; Joseph Cestaro. Resident Priests 1; Total in Residence 22; Total Staff 14.

SOUTH ORANGE. *Don Bosco Residence,* 315 Self Pl., 07079. Tel: 201-761-0201; Fax: 201-761-1032. E-mail: sdbso@aol.com

Revs. Frank Klauder, Confessor; John Puntino, Dir. Tel: 201-761-0153; Timothy Zack; Bro. John Zito, Devel.; Deacon Joseph Dedalonis.

Maryknoll Fathers, 64 Fielding Ct., 07079. Tel: 201-761-5883. Rev. John C. Ganly, M.M., Dir. Total in Residence 1.

Salesian Residence, 9 Kingman Rd., 07079. Tel: 201-763-5350.
E-mail: salres@aol.com
Revs. William Ferruzzi, Vice Dir.; Frank Nugent.

TENAFLY. *Society of African Missions, Provincialate, S.M.A. Fathers*, 23 Bliss Ave., 07670. Tel: 201-567-0450; Fax: 201-567-7156. Very Rev. Douglas B. Gilbert, S.M.A., Prov. Supr. Tel: 201-567-9085 (Prov. Office); Revs. Ernest Magee, S.M.A., Prov. Treas.; Ulick Bourke, S.M.A., Local Supr.; Daniel Cullen, S.M.A.; Francis Gilfether, S.M.A.; Albert James, S.M.A.; George Landry, S.M.A.; John Francis Murray, S.M.A.; James O'Sullivan, S.M.A.; Kevin Scanlan, S.M.A.; James McConnell, S.M.A.; Edward Galvin, S.M.A.; John Feeney, S.M.A.

UNION CITY. *Capuchin Friars - Prov. Stigmata of St. Francis*, P.O. Box 809, 07087. Tel: 201-865-0611; Fax: 201-866-7035. Very Rev. Robert Grix, O.F.M.Cap., Vicar Prov.; Rev. Cyprian Rosen, O.F.M.Cap., Vicar Prov.; Bro. Kellen Mears, O.F.M.Cap., Councillor & Vocation Dir.; Revs. Vincent Fortunato, O.F.M.Cap., Councillor & Dir. Formation; Achilles Cassiere, O.F.M.Cap., Councillor; Francis Sariego, O.F.M.Cap., Prov. Sec. & Dir. Missionary Activity; Paul Daleo, O.F.M.Cap., Dir. Devel.; Thomas Crangle, O.F.M.Cap., Vocation Dir.

Congregation of the Passion (Passionists)-St. Michael's Residence, 526 Monastery Pl., 07087. Tel: 201-864-0018.

Center of Social Concerns. Rev. Kilian McGowan, C.P., Dir. Tel: 201-864-0018.

Passionist Missionaries, Inc. Tel: 201-867-6400; 867-6404. Revs. Sebastian Kolinovsky, C.P., Pass. Missionaries, Dir.; Morgan Hanlon, C.P., Prov. Archivist; Victor Hoagland, C.P., Dir. Passionist Press & Supr. Tel: 201-864-0018; Paul Zilonka, C.P.; James Fitzgerald, Lay Assoc.; Revs. Morgan P. Hanem, C.P., Prov. Archivist. Tel: 201-617-0110; Darrell J. Mell, Dir. Devel. Tel: 201-867-0235; Roger Gannon, C.P., Dir. Planned Giving. Tel: 201-867-0235.

VERONA. *The Salvatorian Fathers*. (Polish Mission House), 23 Crestmont Rd., 07044. Tel: 201-746-8770. Revs. Edward A. Toman, S.D.S., Supr. & Treas.; John L. Kozuch, S.D.S.; Wlodzimierz R. Las, S.D.S., Consultor; Andrzej Kielkowski, S.D.S.; Andrew J. Pitlok, S.D.S.; Andrzej Waszczenko, S.D.S.; Jan J. Mysliwiec, S.D.S.; Krzysztof Bugno, S.D.S., Vice Supr.; Grzegorz Szewczyk, S.D.S.; Strzadala Wieslaw, S.D.S.; Palka Bogdan, S.D.S.; Majcher Tadeusz, S.D.S., Consultor.

WEST ORANGE. *Augustinian Recollects*. Prov. Res., Monastery of St. Cloud, 29 Ridgeway Ave., 07052. Tel: 201-731-0616; Fax: 201-731-1033. Very Rev. Francis E. Peluso, O.A.R., Prior Prov.; Revs. Francis de la Vega, O.A.R.; Jose Arias, O.A.R. (Mexico); Placido Lanz, O.A.R. (Mexico); Jose Mendez, O.A.R. (Mexico); Galo Espinoza, O.A.R. (Mexico); Bros. Anthony Torretti, O.A.R.; Michael Stechmann, O.A.R. Priests 6; Brothers 2.

[O] CONVENTS AND RESIDENCES FOR SISTERS

NEWARK. Franciscan Sisters of the Immaculate Heart of Mary, F.I.H.M. Sr. Kulandai Therese Sowri, F.I.H.M.

Hermanas Missionaras del Corazon de Jesus. Parish Ministry. Sacred Heart Convent, 109 Park Ave., 07104. Tel: 201-484-1516. Sr. Innocentia, Supr. Sisters 4.

Missionary Sisters of the Most Blessed Sacrament and Mary Immaculate. Day Care Center. Immaculate Heart of Mary Convent, 121 Congress St., 07105. Tel: 201-589-5794. Sr. Guadalupe Grande, Supr. Sisters 4.

Monastery of St. Dominic, 375 13th Ave., 07103. Tel: 201-622-6622. Dominican Nuns of the Order of Preachers (Cloistered). Sisters 20.

St. Michael's Convent, 182 Broadway, 07104. Tel: 201-482-7400 (School). Confraternity School of Religion; Lay Apostolate; Home Visiting. Sisters 6.

Sisters of Our Lady of Mercy. Mercederian Missionaries from Barcelona (Spain), 16 Longfellow Ave., 07106. Tel: 201-399-7322. Sisters of Our Lady of Mercy.

Sisters of St. Joseph of Chestnut Hill, Thea House, 39 Bleeker St., 07102. Tel: 201-622-7056. Total in Residence 4.

Vocationist Sisters, 172 Broad St., 07104. (Our Lady of Perpetual Help Center). Perpetual Help Day Nursery. Sisters 7.

CALDWELL. *Motherhouse and Novitiate of Sisters of St. Dominic*, 1 Ryerson Ave., 07006. Tel: 201-403-3331; Fax: 201-228-9611. Sr. Joan Doyle, Prioress. Sisters in Community 234; Sisters in Diocese 205.

ELIZABETH. *Little Servant Sisters of the Immaculate Conception (L.S.I.C.)*, St. Hedwig's School, 717 Polonia Ave., 07201. Tel: 908-355-8409. Sisters 3.

St. Walburga Monastery, 851 N. Broad St., 07208. Tel: 908-352-4278. Benedictine Sisters of Elizabeth, NJ. Sr. Germaine Fritz, O.S.B., Prioress. In Archdiocese 56; Professed Sisters 73.

Servants of St. Joseph Convent, 49 Smith St., 07201. Tel: 201-351-5749. Sr. Fabiola Ospina, Supr. Sisters 4.

ENGLEWOOD CLIFFS. *St. Joseph Province Shalom Center*, 399 Hudson Terrace, 07632. Tel: 201-568-6348; Fax: 201-568-3764. Congregation of Sisters of St. Joseph of Peace. Sr. Ann Rutan, C.S.J.P., Prov.; Sr. Gail DeMaria, C.S.J.P., Vice Prov.; Sr. Theresette Hunting, C.S.J.P., Archivist. Sisters in Community 169. Provincial Office for St. Joseph's Province of the Sisters of St. Joseph of Peace.

St. Ann's Home for the Aged. Total Staff 166; Total in Residence 106.

St. Ann Day Care. Staff 6; Children 35.

St. Joseph Home for the Blind. Total Staff 95; Total in Residence 129.

St. Joseph School for the Blind. Total Staff 100; Total in Residence 47.

St. Joseph Home. Total Staff 13; Total in Residence 102.

St. Mary's Residence. Total Staff 7; Total in Residence 38.

Villa Marie Claire. Total Staff 8; Total in Residence 19.

Nurturing Place Day Care. Staff 15; Children 50.

St. Michael Villa, 399 Hudson Ter., 07632. Tel: 201-871-1620; Fax: 201-871-7313. Sisters of St. Joseph of Peace. Sr. Clare McNerney, C.S.J.P., Admin.; Rev. Walter Cron, Chap. Sisters 46; Total Staff 42. Senior Sisters Residence for St. Joseph Province.

IRVINGTON. *Immaculate Conception Convent*, 121 Myrtie Ave., 07111. Tel: 201-374-6397. Augustinian Recollect Sisters (Cloistered) 10.

JERSEY CITY. *Holy Rosary Convent*, 189 Brunswick St., 07302. Religious Teachers of St. Lucy Filippini 9.

Religious Institute of Our Lady of Mercy of Barcelona (Spain), 320 Whiton St., 07304. Tel: 201-451-0453. Sr. Maria Luz Palomino, R.M.M.

St. Nicholas Convent, 115 Ferry St., 07307. Tel: 201-659-5644. Sr. Mary Mark Smith, S.C.C., Supr.

Sisters of Charity of St. Elizabeth (Convent, NJ) Northern Provincial House, 41 Emory St., 07301. Tel: 201-435-0868; Fax: 201-435-3134. Sr. Mary Morley, S.C., Prov. Supr. Sisters 5.

Sisters of St. Joseph of Peace, 25 Reservoir Ave., 07307. Tel: 201-656-7928.

KEARNY. *Our Lady of Sorrows Convent*, 55 Ivy St., 07032. Tel: 201-991-7983. Sr. Mary Ann Reis, O.S.F. Total in Residence 4.

LODI. *Immaculate Conception Convent*, 260 S. Main St., 07644-2196. Tel: 201-473-7447. Sr. Mary Antonelle Chunka, C.S.S.F. Chaplains: Revs. Harold Niedzwiecki, O.F.M.; Sebastian Kus, O.F.M.; Damian Colicchio, O.F.M.Cap. Sisters in Community 248; Professed Sisters 247.
Provincial House, Novitiate and Infirmary of the Felician Sisters.

PLAINFIELD. *Contemplative Convent of the Missionaries of Charity*, 513 Liberty St., 07060. Tel: 908-754-1978. Total in Residence 18.

SCOTCH PLAINS. *Union Catholic Convent*, 1600 Martine Ave., 07076. Sisters of Mercy of New Jersey (R.S.M.). Total in Residence 7.

SOUTH ORANGE. *Marylawn of the Oranges Convent*, 425 Scotland Rd., 07079. Sisters 11.

SPRINGFIELD. *St. James Convent*, 35 S. Springfield Ave., 07081. Tel: 201-376-7596. Sisters of St. Joseph, Chestnut Hill, Philadelphia. Total in Residence 11.

SUMMIT. *Monastery of Our Lady of the Rosary*, Morris and Springfield Aves., 07901. Tel: 908-273-1228. Sr. Mary Martin de Porres of Jesus, O.P., Prioress; Rev. Mathew V. Reilly, O.P., Chap. Tel: 908-277-6472. Legal Title: *Monastery of Our Lady of the Rosary, Dominican Nuns of the Perpetual Adoration and Perpetual Rosary*. Professed Sisters 21; Novices 2.

TENAFLY. *Convent of Our Lady of the Angels*, 253 Knickerbocker Rd., 07670. Tel: 201-568-2171; Fax: 201-568-2352. Missionary Franciscan Sisters of the Immaculate Conception. Sr. Marion Morrissey, O.S.F., Supr. Sisters 68.
Attended by Carmelite Fathers from Tenafly.

UNION CITY. *Holy Rosary Villa*, 1509 Bergenline Ave., 07087. Tel: 201-867-1376. Sisters of the Catholic Apostolate (Pallotines). Sr. Carmel Favazzo, C.S.A. Sisters 16.

Monastery of the Dominican Nuns of the Perpetual Rosary. (Contemplative), 14th St. and West St., 07087-3199. Mother Mary Jordan, O.P., Prioress. Professed Sisters 9; Novices 1; Aspirants 2; Total Staff 2; Total in Residence 10.

WEST ORANGE. *Provincialate, Southern Province, Sisters of Charity of St. Elizabeth*, 139 Gregory Ave., 07052; Fax: 201-669-2844. Sisters in Provincial House 2; Sisters in Province 263.

[P] RETREAT HOUSES

MAHWAH. *Carmel Retreat House*, 1071 Ramapo Valley Rd., 07430. Tel: 201-327-7090; Fax: 201-327-9133. Carmelite Community and House of Prayer. Retreats (groups, directed, private), Days of prayer, recollection for priests, religious and laity. Revs. David Simpson, O.Carm., Dir.; Paul Kirchner, O.Carm., (Retired); Ivan Cormac Marsh, O.Carm., Prior; Kurt Holderied, O.Carm.; Bro. Bruce Baker, O.Carm. Priests 4; Sisters 1; Brothers 1; Total Staff 9; Total in Residence 5.

[Q] CAMPUS MINISTRY

NEWARK. *Archdiocesan Campus Ministry*, 45 Bleeker St., 07102. Tel: 201-642-1613. Mrs. Noel B. Wicks, Dir. Campus Ministry.

Essex County College, Rutgers University/Newark, NJIT, 45 Bleeker St., 07102. Tel: 201-642-1613. Mrs. Noel Wicks, Dir. Campus Ministers & Chaplains: Bro. Robert Clark, F.M.S.; Rev. John D. Dennehy. Legal Title: *Essex County College, Rutgers University/Newark Campus, New Jersey Institute of Technology*.

BLOOMFIELD. *Bloomfield College*, 12 Austin Pl., 07003. Tel: 201-748-9000, Ext. 250. Rev. James J. Reilly, Chap. & Campus Min.

CRANFORD. *Union County College*, 1033 Springfield Ave., 07016. Tel: 908-709-7092. Rev. James J. Reilly, Campus Min.

HOBOKEN. *Stevens Institute of Technology*, Castle Point on the Hudson, 07030. Tel: 201-963-4324. Rev. John J.F. Paladino, Campus Min. & Chap.

JERSEY CITY. *Jersey City State College*, 2039 Kennedy Blvd., 07305. Tel: 201-963-4324. Rev. John J. Paladino, Campus Min. & Chap.

MAHWAH. *Ramapo College*, 505 Ramapo Valley Rd., Room SC207, 07430. Tel: 201-825-9693. Rev. George Mader, Chap. & Campus Min.; Deacon Joseph Vrindten, Campus Min. Total Staff 2; Students 4,700.

TEANECK. *Fairleigh Dickinson Univ.-Teaneck Campus*, 1000 River Rd., 07666. Tel: 201-692-2406. Rev. John B. Baron, Campus Min. Total Staff 1.

UNION. *Kean College*, Catholic Student Community, Green Ln., 1000 Morris Ave., 07083-7131. Tel: 908-629-7106; Fax: 201-985-0918. Rev. Alexander M. Santora, Campus Min.

UPPER MONCLAIR. *Montclair State University*, Newman Catholic Center, 894 Valley Rd., 07043-2116. Tel: 201-746-2323; Fax: 201-783-3313. Rev. Albert J. Berner, B.A., S.T.D., M.A., Campus Min. & Chap.; Mrs. Mary Lou Vinges, Admin. Asst. Total Staff 2.

[R] SHRINES

KEARNY. *Eucharistic Shrine of the Adorable Face of Jesus*, 672 Passaic Ave., P.O. Box 455, 07032. Tel: 201-997-6173; Fax: 201-997-1270. Rev. Dante M. DiGirolamo, Dir.

[S] MISCELLANEOUS LISTINGS

NEWARK. *CatholiCare, Inc.*, 171 Clifton Ave., P.O. Box 9500, 07104-9500. Tel: 201-497-4007. Rev. Msgr. Ronald J. Rozniak, V.G., Dir.

Conference of Permanent Deacons, Archdiocesan Center, 171 Clifton Ave., P.O. Box 9500, 07104-9500. Tel: 201-497-4223. Deacon Michael Matthews.

Deacon St. Lawrence Welfare Fund, Office of Permanent Diaconate, 171 Clifton Ave., P.O. Box 9500, 07104-9500. Tel: 201-497-4223.

New Jersey Caritas Corporation, Inc., 171 Clifton Ave., P.O. Box 9500, 07104-9500. Tel: 201-497-4007. Rev. Msgr. Ronald J. Rozniak, V.G., Dir.

CCS Holding Corporation, Inc. Catholic Community Services (See Curia Section, Vicariate for Human Services).

Domus Corporation, Inc.

Sunrise House, 1160 Raymond Blvd., 07102. Tel: 201-596-4050. Most Rev. Nicholas A. DiMarzio, Ph.D., L.S.W., Dir.

Carmel House of Jersey City, Inc., 1160 Raymond Blvd., 07102. Tel: 201-596-4050. Most Rev. Nicholas A. DiMarzio, Ph.D., L.S.W., Dir.

BAYONNE. *Marist Brothers Support Trust*, 1241 Kennedy Blvd., 07002. Tel: 201-823-1115. Bros. Stephen Martin, F.M.S.; Benedict Lo Balbo, F.M.S. Congregation of the Marist Brothers, Province of Esopus.

CALDWELL. *Siena Senior Citizen Housing Corp.*, 7 Ashland St., 07006. Tel: 201-226-0730. Sr. Alice Matthews, O.P., Contact Person. To provide for senior citizen housing and health care services for low and moderate income senior citizens.

ELIZABETH. *Alexian Brothers of Elizabeth, Inc.*, 655 E. Jersey St., 07206. Tel: 201-351-9000. Congregation of Alexian Brothers, Immaculate Conception Province. Bruce Fisher, Pres. & CEO.

Alexian Brothers of New Jersey, Inc., 655 E. Jersey St., 07206. Parent Corporation of Alexian Brothers of Elizabeth, Inc.

St. Joseph's Social Service Center, 118 Division St., 07201. Tel: 201-352-2989; 352-2966. Sr. Jacinta Fernandes, O.S.B., Dir. Total Staff 5; Total Assisted 4,052.

HOBOKEN. *F.A.I.T.H. Services Inc.*, 307 Willow Ave., 07030. Tel: 201-792-6161. Bro. Robert J. Reinke, C.F.P., Admin.; Sr. Renee Zinciuk, C.S.W., L.C.S.W., Dir. Clinical Svcs. & Referrals for Svcs. Total Staff 22; Total Assisted 1,747. Extends the religious apostolate of charitable services of the Franciscan Sisters of the Poor, a religious congregation of the Roman Catholic Church by fulfilling the specific purposes set forth as follows: To provide community-based case management, education, counseling and other social support services for HIV/AIDS persons, their significant others and caregivers.

JERSEY CITY. *Franciscan Health System of New Jersey, Inc.*, One McWilliams Pl., 07332. Tel: 201-714-8900. Sr. Mary Meehan, S.S.N.D., Corp.Vice Pres. Mission.

KEARNY. *The Family of Nazareth, Inc.*, 672 Passaic Ave., 07032. Tel: 201-997-3220; Fax: 201-997-5552. Fred Canlas, Pres. A foundation to support the work of the Redemptoris Mater House of Formation and for new evangelization.

LODI.
**The Promise Outreach, Inc.*, 260 S. Main St., 07644.

MAHWAH. *Paulist Press*, 997 MacArthur Blvd., 07430. Tel: 201-825-7300. Revs. Kevin A. Lynch, C.S.P.; Lawrence Boadt, C.S.P.

PARK RIDGE. *A Search for Christian Maturity*, Box 131, 07656. Tel: 201-934-1605. John J. Corcoran, Board of Trustees Pres.

RUTHERFORD. *The Community of God's Love*, 70 W. Passaic Ave., 07070. Tel: 201-935-0344. Catholic Charismatic Community. Paul Griffo, Dir.; Rev. P. Latronico, Chap.

SCOTCH PLAINS. *Ministry Resource Center for Women Religious*, 1600 Martine Ave., 07076. Tel: 908-889-6425.
E-mail: ministrc@webspan.com
Sr. Bernadette Dougherty, S.S.J., Dir.

**The Mercy Conservatory of Music*, 1600 Martine Ave., 07076. Tel: 908-889-8356. Sr. Mary Sharon Gross, R.S.M., Dir.

SOUTH ORANGE. *The Pallottines of South Orange, Inc.*, 204 Raymond Ave., 07079-2305. Tel: 201-763-5591. Revs. James MacDonald, S.A.C.; Angelo Palermo, S.A.C.; Bro. Francis Meo, S.A.C., Supr.
Salesians of Don Bosco, S.D.B.
Consultation Services Center, 11 Kingman Rd., 07079. Tel: 201-763-0740; 763-1805; Fax: 201-763-1720. Rev. Clement Cardillo, Vice Prov.
Don Bosco Annex, 361 Irving Ave., 07079. Tel: 201-761-0345.
E-mail: joeydba@aol.com
Rev. Timothy Zak, Coord. of Community Activities. In Residence 6.
U.S. Catholic China Bureau, Presidents Hall, Seton Hall University, 07079. Tel: 201-761-9785; Fax: 201-275-2223. Laurence T. Murphy, M.M., Chm.; Janet Carroll, M.M., Exec. Dir.; John P. Daly, S.J., Assoc. Dir. Promotes understanding among Catholics in America about the reality of the Chinese Catholic Church and fosters mutually in relations between the Sister-Churches, publishes quarterly newsletter, sponsors National Catholic China Conference, religious study tours to China and other activities to sustain a shared commitment to mission in China. Total Staff 1.

TEANECK. *Holy Name Health Care Foundation*, 725 Teaneck Rd., 07666. Tel: 201-833-3187. Sisters of St. Joseph of Peace. Sr. Patricia A. Lynch, C.S.J.P., Pres.

UNION CITY. *Park Performing Arts, Inc.* (Home of the Passion Play, 560 32nd St., 07087. Tel: 201-865-6980; Fax: 201-865-5339. Rev. Kevin Ashe, Exec. Dir. Total Staff 7.

RELIGIOUS INSTITUTES OF MEN REPRESENTED IN THE ARCHDIOCESE

For further details refer to the corresponding bracketed number in the Religious Institutes of Men or Women section.

[0100]—*Adorno Fathers*.—C.R.M.
[0200]—*Benedictine Monks*. (Newark Abbey; St. Mary Abbey).—O.S.B.
[0330]—*Brothers of Christian Schools*. (Baltimore Prov.; New York Prov.).—F.S.C.
[1350]—*Brothers of St. Francis Xavier*.—C.F.X.
[0460]—*Brothers of the Poor of St. Francis*.—C.F.P.
[0470]—*The Capuchin Friars*. (Prov. of the Stigmata; Prov. of St. Mary).—O.F.M.Cap.
[0270]—*Carmelite Fathers & Brothers*. (American Prov.).—O.Carm.
[0380]—*Comboni Missionaries of the Heart of Jesus (Verona)*.—M.C.C.J.
[0310]—*Congregation of Christian Brothers*.—C.F.C.
[1000]—*Congregation of the Passion*. (Eastern Prov.).—C.P.
[0480]—*Conventual Franciscans*.—O.F.M.Conv.
[0520]—*Franciscan Friars*. (Prov. of Most Holy Name; Prov. of the Assumption).—O.F.M.
[0530]—*Franciscan Friars of the Atonement*.—S.A.
[0690]—*Jesuit Fathers and Brothers*. (Prov. of New York).—S.J.
[0770]—*The Marist Brothers*.—F.M.S.
[0800]—*Maryknoll*.—M.M.
[1210]—*Missionaries of St. Charles (Scalabrinians)*.—C.S.
[0840]—*Missionary Servants of the Most Holy Trinity*.—S.T.
[0430]—*Order of Preachers-Dominicans*. (Prov. of St. Joseph, Eastern Dominican Prov.).—O.P.
[0150]—*Order of the Augustinian Recollects*.—O.A.R.
[1030]—*Paulist Fathers*.—C.S.P.
[]—*Province of the Immaculate Conception*.
[1070]—*Redemptorist Fathers* (Byzantine Ukrainians).—C.Ss.R.
[1170]—*St. Patrick Missionary Society*.—S.P.S.
[1190]—*Salesians of Don Bosco*.—S.D.B.
[0110]—*Society of African Missions*.—S.M.A.
[0990]—*Society of the Catholic Apostolate*. (Prov. of the Immaculate Conception).—S.A.C.
[1200]—*Society of the Divine Savior*.—S.D.S.
[0560]—*Third Order Regular of Saint Francis*. (U.S.A. Commissarate of the Spanish Prov.).—T.O.R.
[]—*Union Lumen Dei*.—L.D.
[1340]—*Vocationist Fathers*.—S.D.V.

RELIGIOUS INSTITUTES OF WOMEN REPRESENTED IN THE ARCHDIOCESE

[0100]—*Adorers of the Blood of Christ*.—A.S.C.
[0130]—*Apostles of the Sacred Heart of Jesus*.—A.S.C.J.
[]—*Augustinian Recollect Sisters*.—O.A.R.
[0230]—*Benedictine Sisters of Pontifical Jurisdiction-Newark*. (Benedictine Sisters of Baltimore; Benedictine Sisters of Elizabeth).—O.S.B.
[0760]—*Daughters of Charity of St. Vincent de Paul*. (North East Prov.).—D.C.
[0790]—*Daughters of Divine Charity*.—F.D.C.
[0850]—*Daughters of Mary Help of Christians*.—F.M.A.
[]—*Daughters of Mary, Mothers of Mercy*. (Nigeria).—D.M.M.M.
[1050]—*Dominican Contemplative Nuns (Cloistered)*.—O.P.
[1070-11]—*Dominican Sisters*. (Sparkill, NY).—O.P.
[1070-15]—*Dominican Sisters*. (Blauvelt, NY).—O.P.
[1070-18]—*Dominican Sisters*. (Caldwell, NJ).—O.P.
[1070-06]—*Dominican Sisters of Hope*. (Newburgh, NY).—O.P.
[1070-09]—*Dominican Sisters of St. Catherine of Siena (Philippines)*.
[1170]—*Felician Sisters*.—C.S.S.F.
[1400]—*Franciscan Missionary Sister of the Sacred Heart*.—F.M.S.C.
[1180]—*Franciscan Sisters of Allegany, New York*.—O.S.F.
[1425]—*Franciscan Sisters of Peace*.—F.S.P.
[1420]—*Franciscan Sisters of Ringwood*.—F.S.R.
[1460]—*Franciscan Sisters of St. Elizabeth*.—F.S.S.E.
[]—*Franciscan Sisters of the Immaculate Heart of Mary (India)*.—F.I.H.M.
[1440]—*Franciscan Sisters of the Poor*.—S.F.P.
[1240]—*Grey Nuns of the Sacred Heart*.—G.N.S.H.
[]—*Hermanas Missionaras del Corazon de Jesus*. (Dominican Republic).—H.M.C.J.
[3790]—*Institute of the Sisters of St. Dorothy*.—S.S.D.
[2300]—*Little Servant Sisters of the Immaculate Conception*.—L.S.I.C.
[]—*Mercedarian Sisters (Missionary Sisters of Our Lady of Mercy)*.—R.M.M.
[2710]—*Missionaries of Charity*.—M.C.
[1360]—*Missionary Franciscan Sisters of the Immaculate Conception*.—M.F.I.C.
[2790]—*Missionary Servants of the Most Blessed Trinity*.—M.S.B.T.
[2760]—*Missionary Sisters of the Immaculate Conception of the Mother of God*.—S.M.I.C.
[2780]—*Missionary Sisters of the Most Blessed Sacrament and Mary Immaculate*.—M.SS.M.I.
[]—*Religious of the Virgin Mary (Philippines)*.—R.V.M.
[3430]—*Religious Teachers Filippini*.—M.P.F.
[2970]—*School Sisters of Notre Dame*.—S.S.N.D.
[1700]—*School Sisters of the Third Order of St. Francis*. (Bethlehem, PA).—O.S.F.
[0540]—*Sisters of Charity of Ottawa*.—S.C.O.
[0590]—*Sisters of Charity of Saint Elizabeth, Convent Station*.—S.C.
[0660]—*Sisters of Christian Charity*.—S.C.C.
[2575]—*Sisters of Mercy of the Americas*. (New Jersey).—R.S.M.
[]—*Sisters of Our Lady of Perpetual Help (Korea)*.—S.O.L.P.H.
[1620]—*Sisters of Saint Francis of Millvale, Pennsylvania*.—O.S.F.
[3893]—*Sisters of Saint Joseph of Chestnut Hill, Philadelphia*.—S.S.J.
[3730]—*Sisters of St. Basil the Great*.—O.S.B.M.
[1650]—*The Sisters of St. Francis of Philadelphia*.—O.S.F.
[1650]— *The Sisters of St. Francis of Philadelphia*.—O.S.F.
[3820]—*Sisters of St. John the Baptist*.—C.S.J.B.
[3890]—*Sisters of St. Joseph of Peace*.—C.S.J.P.
[3930]—*Sisters of St. Joseph of the Third Order of St. Francis*.—S.S.J.-T.O.S.F.
[3140]—*Sisters of the Catholic Apostolate (Pallottine)*.—C.S.A.C.
[2980]—*Sisters of the Congregation of Notre Dame*.—C.N.D.
[1490]—*Sisters of the Third Franciscan Order*.—O.S.F.
[3610]—*Sisters Servants of Mary Immaculate*.—S.S.M.I.
[3595]—*Sisters, Servants of St. Joseph*.—S.S.J.
[2160]—*Sisters, Servants of the Immaculate Heart of Mary (Scranton)*.—I.H.M.
[4060]—*Society of the Holy Child Jesus*.—S.H.C.J.
[]—*Union Lumen Dei*.—L.D.
[4210]—*Vocationist Sisters*.—S.D.V.

ARCHDIOCESAN CEMETERIES

COLONIA. *St. Gertrude*.
DARLINGTON. *Maryrest*.
EAST HANOVER. *Gate of Heaven*.
EAST ORANGE. *Holy Sepulchre*.
St. Mary.
FRANKLIN LAKES. *Christ the King*.
JERSEY CITY. *Holy Name*.
Saint Peter.
NORTH ARLINGTON. *Holy Cross*.

PAROCHIAL CEMETERIES

NEWARK. *Mount Olivet*.
BELLEVILLE. *St. Peter's*.
BLOOMFIELD. *Mount Olivet*.
CLARK. *St. Mary's*.
FORT LEE. *Madonna*.
HACKENSACK. *St. Joseph's*.
HO-HO-KUS. *St. Luke's*.
LINDEN. *Mount Calvary*.
LYNDHURST. *St. Joseph's*.
ORANGE. *St. John's*.
PLAINFIELD. *St. Mary's*.
RIVER VALE. *St. Andrew's*.
SHORT HILLS. *St. Rose of Lima*.
SUMMIT. *St. Teresa's*.
TENAFLY. *Mount Carmel*.
UPPER MONTCLAIR. *Immaculate Conception*.

NECROLOGY

† Carroll, Rev. Msgr. Joseph A., Kearny, NJ, St. Cecilia. —Died Dec. 29, 1996.
† Conway, John William, Montclair, NJ, Immaculate Conception. —Died Feb. 4, 1996.
† Fitzpatrick, Rev. Msgr. Michael J., (Retired). —Died May 6, 1996.
† Funk, Hubert J., South Orange, NJ, Seton Hall University. —Died Oct. 1, 1996.
† Hresko, George, (Retired). —Died May 16, 1996.
† Jordick, Leonard J., Newark, NJ, St. Antoninus. —Died July 24, 1996.
† Kelley, Rev. Msgr. James F., (Retired). —Died Sept. 11, 1996.
† Long, Jeremiah, Secaucus, NJ, Immaculate Conception. —Died Oct. 16, 1996.
† Mannion, John J., South Orange, NJ, Seton Hall University. —Died Nov. 20, 1996.
† Mark, Albert Andrew, Midland Park, NJ, Nativity. —Died April 4, 1996.
† McTernan, Frederick J., (Retired). —Died Sept. 2, 1996.
† Oates, John, Linden, NJ, St. Elizabeth. —Died June 2, 1996.
† Salazar, Mario Arias, (Retired). —Died July 21, 1996.
† Shea, Joseph Thomas, (Retired). —Died March 14, 1996.
† Sheridan, Stephen Edward, Jersey City, NJ, St. Aloysius. —Died April 10, 1996.
† Sorokowski, Vincent, Little Ferry, NJ, St. Margaret. —Died May 7, 1996.

Archdiocese of New Orleans

(Archidioecesis Novae Aureliae)

Most Reverend

FRANCIS B. SCHULTE, D.D.

Archbishop of New Orleans; ordained May 10, 1952; appointed Titular Bishop of Afufenia and Auxiliary Bishop of Philadelphia June 27, 1981; ordained to the episcopacy August 12, 1981; appointed Sixth Bishop of Wheeling-Charleston June 4, 1985; promoted to Metropolitan See of New Orleans December 13, 1988; installed February 14, 1989. *Office: 7887 Walmsley Ave., New Orleans, LA, 70125-3496.* Tel.: 504-861-9521.

Archdiocesan Administration Building: 7887 Walmsley Ave., New Orleans, LA, 70125-3496. Tel.: 504-861-9521; Fax: 504-866-2906.

Web site address: http://www.catholic.org/neworleans/archdiocese.html

Most Reverend

PHILIP M. HANNAN, D.D., J.C.D., S.T.L.

Former Archbishop of New Orleans; ordained December 8, 1939; appointed Titular Bishop of Hieropolis and Auxiliary Bishop of Washington June 16, 1956; consecrated August 28, 1956; promoted to Archbishop of New Orleans September 29, 1965; installed October 13, 1965; retired February 14, 1989. *Address correspondence to: 2929 S. Carrollton Ave., New Orleans, LA, 70118-4301.* Tel.: 504-866-7411.

Most Reverend

NICHOLAS D'ANTONIO, O.F.M., D.D.

Retired; ordained June 7, 1942; appointed Prelate Nullius, Ordinary of Olancho, Honduras, C.A. December 31, 1963; consecrated July 25, 1966; appointed Vicar for Spanish-Speaking, New Orleans August 22, 1977; retired July 10, 1991. *Res., 1221 Mandeville St., New Orleans, LA, 70117-8498.* Tel.: 504-943-5561.

Most Reverend

DOMINIC CARMON, S.V.D., D.D., V.G.

Auxiliary Bishop of New Orleans and Titular Bishop of Rusicade; ordained February 2, 1960; appointed December 16, 1992; consecrated February 11, 1993. *Office: 5500 Paris Ave., New Orleans, LA, 70122-2699.* Tel.: 504-288-4224.

Most Reverend

GREGORY M. AYMOND, D.D., V.G.

Auxiliary Bishop of New Orleans and Titular Bishop of Acolla; ordained May 10, 1975; appointed November 19, 1996; consecrated January 10, 1997. *Office: 2901 S. Carrollton Ave., New Orleans, LA, 70118-4391.* Tel.: 504-866-7426.

CREATED A DIOCESE APRIL 25, 1793; ARCHDIOCESE JULY 19, 1850.

Square Miles 4,208.

Comprises the following Parishes of Louisiana: Orleans, St. Bernard, Plaquemines, Jefferson, St. Charles, St. John the Baptist, St. Tammany and Washington.

For legal titles of parishes and archdiocesan institutions, consult the Chancery Office.

STATISTICAL OVERVIEW

Personnel	
Archbishop	1
Retired Archbishops	1
Auxiliary Bishops	2
Retired Bishops	1
Abbots	1
Priests: Diocesan Active in Diocese	181
Priests: Active Outside Diocese	10
Priests: Retired, Sick or Absent	40
Number of Diocesan Priests	231
Religious Priests in Diocese	227
Extern Priests in Diocese	29
Ordinations:	
Diocesan Priests	3
Religious Priests	2
Transitional Deacons	3
Permanent Deacons	25
Permanent Deacons in Diocese	198
Total Brothers	141
Total Sisters	873
Parishes	
Parishes	147
With Resident Pastor:	
Resident Diocesan Priests	108
Resident Religious Priests	35
Without Resident Pastor:	
Administered by Priests	4
Missions	8
Pastoral Centers	1
Welfare	
Health Care Centers	3
Total Assisted	1,059
Homes for the Aged	17
Total Assisted	2,936
Residential Care of Children	3
Total Assisted	318
Day Care and Extended Day Care Centers	18
Total Assisted	1,159
Specialized Homes	4
Total Assisted	3,660
Special Centers for Social Services	79
Total Assisted	447,133
Residential Care of Disabled	9
Total Assisted	95
Other Institutions	14
Total Assisted	2,167
Educational	
Seminaries, Diocesan	2
Students from This Diocese	19
Students from Other Diocese	135
Diocesan Students in Other Seminaries	1
Seminaries, Religious	4
Students Religious	22
Total Seminarians	42
Colleges and Universities	3
Total Students	10,296
High Schools, Diocesan and Parish	10
Total Students	6,580
High Schools, Private	13
Total Students	9,812
Elementary Schools, Diocesan and Parish	74
Total Students	33,127
Elementary Schools, Private	6
Total Students	1,325
Non-residential Schools for the Disabled	1
Total Students	194
Catechesis/Religious Education:	
High School Students	4,640
Elementary Students	18,855
Total Students Under Catholic Instruction	84,871
Teachers in the Diocese:	
Priests	91
Brothers	38
Sisters	174
Lay Teachers	3,307
Vital Statistics	
Receptions into the Church:	
Infant Baptism Totals	7,353
Adult Baptism Totals	406
Received into Full Communion	390
First Communions	6,709
Confirmations	5,572
Marriages:	
Catholic	2,007
Interfaith	602
Total Marriages	2,609
Deaths	4,620
Total Catholic Population	484,263
Total Population	1,330,855

Former Bishops and Archbishops—Rt. Rev. LUIS PENALVER Y CARDENAS, D.D., cons. in 1793; transferred to Guatemala, in 1801; resigned in 1806; retired to Havana, Cuba; died in Havana, July 17, 1810 Under the administration of the Archbishop of Baltimore from 1805-1815.—Rt. Rev. FRANCIS PORRO, Bishop-elect.—Rt. Rev. LOUIS WILLIAM DUBOURG, S.S., D.D., cons. Sept. 24, 1815; died Archbishop of Besancon, Dec. 1833.—Rt. Rev. JOSEPH ROSATI, D.D., C.M., cons. March 25, 1824; Bishop of Tanagre and coadjutor; transferred to St. Louis, March 20, 1827; died Sept. 25, 1843.—Rt. Rev. LEO DE NECKERE, C.M., D.D., cons. Aug. 4, 1829; died Sept. 4, 1833.—Most Rev. ANTOINE BLANC, first Archbishop; cons. Nov. 22, 1835; Archbishop, July 19, 1850; died June 20, 1860.—Most Rev. JEAN MARIE ODIN, C.M., D.D., cons. Bishop of Claudiopolis and Vicar-Apostolic of Texas, March 6, 1842; transferred to Galveston, 1847; promoted to New Orleans in 1861; died at Ambierle, France, May 25, 1870.—Most Rev. NAPOLEON J. PERCHE, cons. Bishop of Abdera and coadjutor, March 21, 1870; promoted to the See of New Orleans, May 25, 1870; died Dec. 1883.—Most Rev. F. X. LERAY, D.D., cons. Bishop of Natchitoches, April 22, 1877; appt. coadjutor of New Orleans, and Bishop of Janopolis, Oct. 23, 1879; promoted to the See of New Orleans, Dec., 1883; died at Chateaugiron, France, Sept. 23, 1887.—Most Rev. FRANCIS JANSSENS, D.D., cons. Bishop of Natchez, MS, May 1, 1881; promoted to the Archiepiscopal See of New Orleans, Aug. 7, 1888; died June 9, 1897.—Most Rev. PLACIDE LOUIS CHAPELLE, D.D., Apostolic Delegate Extraordinary for Cuba and Porto Rico; Archbishop of New Orleans; appt. Bishop of Arabissus and Coadjutor of Santa Fe *cum jure successionis,* Aug. 21, 1891; cons. Nov. 1, 1891; promoted to the Titular Archiepiscopal See of Sebaste May 10, 1893; Archbishop of Santa Fe, Jan. 9, 1894; appt. to New Orleans, Dec. 1, 1897; died Aug. 9, 1905.—Most

Rev. JAMES H. BLENK, S.M., D.D., appt. Bishop of Porto Rico, June 12, 1899; cons. July 2, 1899; promoted to the See of New Orleans, April 20, 1906; died April 20, 1917.—Most Rev. JOHN W. SHAW, D.D., appt. Coadjutor Bishop of San Antonio, Feb. 7, 1910; cons. Titular Bishop of Castabala, April 14, 1910; succeeded to the See of San Antonio, March 11, 1911 made assistant at the Pontifical Throne, Sept., 1916; promoted to the See of New Orleans, Jan. 25, 1918; died Nov. 2, 1934.—Most Rev. JOSEPH FRANCIS RUMMEL, D.D., ord. May 24, 1902; appt. Bishop of Omaha, March 30, 1928; cons. May 29, 1928; appt. Archbishop of New Orleans, Mar. 9, 1935; died Nov. 8, 1964.—His Eminence JOHN CARDINAL CODY, D.D., cons. July 2, 1947; promoted to Coadjutor *cum jure successionis* of New Orleans, Aug. 10, 1961; acceded See, Nov. 8, 1964; transferred to Chicago, June 16, 1965; created Cardinal, June 26, 1967; died April 25, 1982.—Most Rev. PHILIP M. HANNAN, D.D., Archbishop of New Orleans; ord. Dec. 8, 1939; appt. Titular Bishop of Hieropolis and Auxiliary Bishop of Washington, June 16, 1956; cons. Aug. 28, 1956; promoted to Archbishop of New Orleans, Sept. 29, 1965; retired Feb. 14, 1989.

Vicars General—Most Rev. DOMINIC CARMON, S.V.D., *5500 Paris Ave., New Orleans, 70122-2699.* Tel: 504-288-4224; Fax: 504-288-2152. Most Rev. GREGORY M. AYMOND, V.G., *2901 S. Carrollton Ave., New Orleans, 70118-4391.* Tel: 504-866-7426; Fax: 504-866-3119. Rev. Msgr. THOMAS J. RODI, V.G., *7887 Walmsley Ave., New Orleans, 70118-3496.* Tel: 504-861-6262; Fax: 504-866-2906.

Chancellor and Moderator of the Curia—Rev. Msgr. THOMAS J. RODI, V.G. Tel: 504-861-6262; 861-9521; Fax: 504-866-2906.

Controller—Mr. JOSEPH E. INGRAHAM.

Archdiocesan Administration Building—*7887 Walmsley Ave., New Orleans, 70125-3496.* Office Hours: Mon.-Fri. 9-5. Tel: 504-861-9521; Fax: 504-866-2906.

Metropolitan Tribunal—*7887 Walmsley Ave., New Orleans, 70125-3496.* All rogatorial commissions should be sent to this address: c/o; Very Rev. VIEN THE NGUYEN, J.C.L.

Judicial Vicar—Very Rev. VIEN THE NGUYEN, J.C.L.

Adjutant Judicial Vicars—Rev. Msgr. CLINTON J. DOSKEY, J.C.L.; Rev. JOSEPH P. MULLIN, S.M., S.T.L.

Judges—Rev. Msgr. THOMAS C. DOWLING, M.A.; Rev. Msgr. LOUIS P. LEBOURGEOIS; Rev. Msgr. THOMAS J. RODI, V.G.; Rev. Msgr. L. EARL GAUTHREAUX, J.C.L.; Revs. THOMAS E. KINNEY, J.C.L.; GERARD LAPORTE, C.SS.R., J.C.L.; PETER O'GRADY.

Associate Judges—Rev. ANDREW C. TAORMINA, J.D.; Mr. PETER E. DUFFY, J.D.; Mr. FRANS LABRANCHE, JR., J.D.; Mr. PAUL A. NALTY, J.D.; Mr. PETER C. RIZZO, J.D.

Defensores Vinculi—Very Rev. GERALD L. SEILER, JR., J.C.L.; Revs. WILLIAM J. O'DONNELL, J.C.L.; BENJAMIN PIOVAN, M.A.; LEE J. SALOY, M.Div.; Sr. WALDIA A. WARDEN, O.P., J.C.L.

Executive Secretary—Sr. WALDIA A. WARDEN, O.P., J.C.L.

Archdiocesan Consultors—Most Rev. DOMINIC CARMON, S.V.D., D.D., V.G.; Most Rev. GREGORY M. AYMOND, V.G.; Rev. Msgr. FRANCIS G. BOESHANS; Rev. Msgr. CLINTON J. DOSKEY; Rev. Msgr. RAY P. HEBERT; Rev. Msgr. CROSBY W. KERN; Rev. Msgr. JOHN P. REYNOLDS; Rev. Msgr. THOMAS J. RODI, V.G.

Deans—Cathedral Deanery I: Very Rev. FRANCIS M. HULL, S.S.J., V.F., City Park-Gentilly Deanery II: Rev. NEAL W. MCDERMOTT, O.P., V.F., Uptown Deanery III: Very Rev. HENRY H. ENGELBRECHT, V.F., Inner City Deanery IV: Very Rev. KENNETH BORGESEN, O.SS.T., V.F., East Jefferson Deanery V: Rev. Msgr. CROSBY W. KERN, V.F., St. John-St. Charles Deanery VI: Very Rev. RODNEY P. BOURG, V.F., West Bank Deanery VII: Very Rev. MICHAEL B. FRASER, V.F., Algiers-Plaquemines Deanery VIII: Rev. Msgr. ALLEN J. ROY, V.F., St. Bernard Deanery IX: Very Rev. ALAN R. WESEMAN, V.F., St. Tammany-Washington Deanery X: Rev. Msgr. FRANCIS G. BOESHANS, V.F.

Archdiocesan Administrative Council—Most Rev. FRANCIS B. SCHULTE, D.D., Chm.; Rev. Msgr. THOMAS J. RODI, V.G., Vice Chm.; Very Rev. GERALD L. SEILER, JR., Sec. Members of the Board: Most Rev. DOMINIC CARMON, S.V.D., V.G.; Most Rev. GREGORY M. AYMOND, V.G.; Sr. SUELLEN TENNYSON, M.S.C.; Rev. Msgr. RAY P. HEBERT; Mr. JOSEPH E. INGRAHAM; Rev. Msgr. ROGER P. MORIN; Rev. Msgr. ROBERT D. MASSETT.

Archdiocesan Pastoral Council—Dr. RALPH DAUTERIVE, Pres.

Priests Council—Most Rev. FRANCIS B. SCHULTE, D.D., Pres.; Very Rev. ALAN R. WESEMAN, V.F., Chm.

Archdiocesan Finance Council—Most Rev. FRANCIS B. SCHULTE, Chm.; Rev. Msgr. THOMAS J. RODI, V.G., Vice Chm.

Censores Librorum—Very Rev. GERALD L. SEILER, JR., Coord.

Louisiana Catholic Conference—Mr. KIRBY J. DUCOTE, Dir., *3423 Hundred Oaks Ave., Baton Rouge, 70808-1548.* Tel: 504-344-7120; Fax: 504-383-9591.

Office of the Vicar General and Moderator of the Curia; Rev. Msgr. THOMAS J. RODI, V.G., Vicar General, *7887 Walmsley Ave., New Orleans, 70125-3496.* Tel: 504-861-6262; Fax: 504-866-2906

Catholic Foundation for the Archdiocese of New Orleans, Inc.—Mr. JOSEPH L. LANGENDERFER, Exec. Dir., *1000 Howard Ave., Ste. 700, New Orleans, 70113-1903.* Tel: 504-596-3045; Fax: 504-596-3068.

Communications—Mr. THOMAS M. FINNEY, Dir., *7887 Walmsley Ave., New Orleans, 70125-3496.* Tel: 504-861-6239; 861-9521; Fax: 504-861-2906.

Development Office—Mr. JOSEPH L. LANGENDERFER, Exec. Dir., *1000 Howard Ave., New Orleans, 70113-1903.* Tel: 504-596-3045; Fax: 504-596-3068.

Legal Services—Rev. Msgr. THOMAS J. RODI, V.G., Dir. CHARLES I. DENECHAUD, JR.; THOMAS A. RAYER; CHARLES I. DENECHAUD, III; OTTO SCHOENFELD; EDWARD DENECHAUD; DON M. RICHARD, *1207 First NBC Bldg., New Orleans, 70112-4100.* Tel: 504-522-4756; Fax: 504-568-0783.

Newspaper—*"Clarion Herald",* Newspaper of the Archdiocese of New Orleans. Published by Clarion Herald Publishing Co., Inc., PETER P. FINNEY, JR., Gen. Mgr. & Exec. Editor, *1000 Howard Ave., Ste. 400, New Orleans, 70113-1903.* Tel: 504-596-3030; Fax: 504-596-3020.

Department of Christian Formation

Executive Director—Rev. Msgr. ROBERT D. MASSETT, *7887 Walmsley Ave., New Orleans, 70125-3496.* Tel: 504-861-6236; 861-9521; Fax: 504-866-2906.

Campus Ministry—Rev. Msgr. ROBERT D. MASSETT, *7887 Walmsley Ave., New Orleans, 70125-3496.* Tel: 504-861-6236; 861-9521; Fax: 504-866-2906.

Catholic Schools Office—Mr. HOWARD J. JENKINS, Supt. Assoc. Supts.: Mrs. JANE O'CONNELL BAKER; Mrs. SYLVIA A. GAFFNEY; Dr. MARIAN O'NEIL; Mr. JOSEPH R. ROSOLINO; Dr. MYLES SEGHERS. Asst. Supts.: Mr. THOMAS E. MCLAUGHLIN; Mr. JOSEPH PEYCHAUD; VINCENT SCOZZARI; Mr. RODNEY J. THOULION, Dir., Mktg. & Pub. Rels.; Dr. MILES M. SEGHERS, Coord., Personnel Svcs.; Sr. MARY HILARY SIMPSON, O.P., Dir., Instrumental Music; Sr. LILLIAN MCCORMACK, S.S.N.D., Dir., Special Education, *7887 Walmsley Ave., New Orleans, 70125-3496.* Tel: 504-861-6220; 861-9521; Fax: 504-866-2906.

Catholic Youth Organization and Catholic School Athletic League—MICHAEL PATIN, Dir.; Mr. EDWARD RUDIGER, Assoc. Dir., *3801 Monroe St., New Orleans, 70118-3499.* Tel: 504-486-6289; Fax: 504-486-4087.

Lay Retreats—Rev. H. WILLIAM REED, Coord., Adult Programs, *2545 Bayou Rd., New Orleans, 70119-2398.* Tel: 504-945-3591; Fax: 504-945-3216. Youth Retreats: Contact CYO-Youth Ministry Office, *3801 Monroe St., New Orleans, 70118-3499.* Tel: 504-486-6289; Fax: 504-486-4087.

Ministry of Evangelization & Spiritual Renewal—Rev. Msgr. ROBERT I. GUSTE, *3700 Jean Lafitte Pkwy., Chalmette, 70043-1199.* Tel: 504-271-3939; Fax: 504-279-8023.

Religious Education—Bro. EDWARD KIEFER, S.M., Dir., *7887 Walmsley Ave., New Orleans, 70125-3496.* Tel: 504-861-6270; 861-9521; Fax: 504-866-2906.

Department of Clergy

Executive Director—Rev. Msgr. RAY P. HEBERT, *4401 7th St., Marrero, 70072-2099.* Tel: 504-341-9516; Fax: 504-341-9517.

Continuing Formation for Priests—Rev. ROGER A. SWENSON, *2916 Paris Ave., New Orleans, 70119-1840.* Tel: 504-945-8754; Fax: 504-949-8899.

Jesus Caritas Fraternity of Priests—Rev. Msgr. ROBERT I. GUSTE, *3700 Jean Lafitte Pkwy., Chalmette, 70043-1199.* Tel: 504-271-3039; Fax: 504-279-8023.

Permanent Diaconate—Mr. JAMES W. SWILER, Dir., *7887 Walmsley Ave., New Orleans, 70125-3496.* Tel: 504-861-6265; 861-9521; Fax: 504-866-2906.

Priest Personnel Office—Rev. JOHN C. SAX, *7887 Walmsley Ave., New Orleans, 70125-3496.* Tel: 504-861-6269; 861-9521; Fax: 504-866-2906.

Priests for Life (Organization of Priests Dedicated to the Protection of All Human Life)—Rev. ROGER A. SWENSON, Coord., *2916 Paris Ave., New Orleans, 70119-1840.* Tel: 504-945-8754; Fax: 504-949-8899.

Retired Priests—Rev. W. WENDELL SONTHEIMER, Coord., *1029 N. Atlanta St., Metairie, 70003-5803.* Tel: 504-467-2193; Fax: 504-466-4858.

Vocation Office—Rev. HENRY J. BUGLER, Dir., *7887 Walmsley Ave., New Orleans, 70125-3496.* Tel: 504-861-6298; 861-9521; Fax: 504-866-2906.

Liaison with Conference of Major Superiors of Men and Retired Priests—

Department of Community Services

Executive Director—Rev. Msgr. ROGER P. MORIN, *1000 Howard Ave., New Orleans, 70113-1900.* Tel: 504-596-3090; Fax: 504-596-3098.

Archdiocesan Alcoholism Counseling Ministry—Rev. ANTHONY J. WHITE, Dir., *724 Camp St., New Orleans, 70130-3757.* Tel: 504-525-4413; Fax: 504-568-1324.

Apostleship of the Sea—Deacon GILBERT W. SMITH, JR., Port Chap. & Dir., *Stella Maris Maritime Center, 4219 Constance, New Orleans, 70115-1440.* Tel: 501-891-6677; Fax: 504-891-1237.

Archbishop's Community Appeal (Philmat, Inc.)—Sr. ADELE LAMBERT, C.S.J., Dir., *1000 Howard Ave., Ste. 800, New Orleans, 70113-1900.* Tel: 504-596-3083; Fax: 504-596-3098.

Campaign for Human Development—Sr. ADELE LAMBERT, C.S.J., *1000 Howard Ave., New Orleans, 70113-1900.* Tel: 504-596-3085; Fax: 504-596-3098.

Catholic Human Relations Commission—Rev. Msgr. ROGER P. MORIN, Dir., *1000 Howard Ave., Ste. 800, New Orleans, 70113-1900.* Tel: 504-596-3090; Fax: 504-596-3098.

Charities—*Catholic Charities Archdiocese of New Orleans*—Mr. ALVIN KENNEY, Pres., Board of Advisors; Sr. ANTHONY BARCZYKOWSKI, D.C., Chief Exec. Dir., *1000 Howard Ave., New Orleans, 70113-1916.* Tel: 504-523-3755; Fax: 504-523-2789. Mr. DAVID J. LOGSDON, Chief Financial Officer; Mr. ORVILLE DUGGAN, Chief Admin. Officer. Div. Dirs.: Ms. JANE BREWER; Dr. REBECCA LOMAX.

AIDS Housing / Shelter:—Ms. LOIS FALK.

Beyond Shelter—Ms. ANNE BYRNE.

Ciara Community Services—Ms. MONETTA CLARK, Ciara House, Ciara Independent Living Program.

Health Education Department—Ms. JANET DILEO.

Hope Haven Center—Mr. ROBERT GUASCO,Hope Haven-Madonna Manor; St. Elizabeth's; Independent Living Skills Program.

AIDS Transportation Service—Mr. KEVIN BLAKES.

Regional AIDS Interfaith Network (RAIN)—Ms. ANITA TIRCUIT.

Padua Community Services—Ms. JENNY VIEITO, Padua Adult Residential Program, Ocean Avenue Community Home, St. Catherine of Siena Supervised Apartment, St. Jude the Apostle, Sts. Mary and Elizabeth, St. Peter the Fisherman, St. Rosalie, Supervised Apartments.

Padua Adult Vocational Programs—Ms. BARBARA DICKERSON.

Padua Pediatric Residential Program—Ms. JENNY VIEITO.

Adult Day Health Care Centers—Ms. ELLEN SOMERS,Alpha House, Kenner, New Directions, Greenwalt Center for Alzheimer's Day Care & Research.

Big Brothers-Big Sisters of Southeast LA—Ms. DOLORES MEDINA-WHITFIELD.

Children's Day Care Centers—Ms. ELLEN SOMERS,Cabrini Head Start, El Yo Yo, Flint Goodridge, Florida Head Start, Leslie Center, Louise, St. Anthony Head Start, St. Jude Baby Village.

Maternity and Adoption Services—Ms. JANE BREWER, ACCESS Pregnancy/Referral Centers; Adoption Services; St. Vincent Maternity Clinic; Second Glance Resale Shoppe.

Immigration and Refugee Services—Ms. SUSAN WEISHAR, E.S.L. for Jobs; Immigration Legal Services; Refugee Health Screening; Refugee Resettlement Services; Refugee Social Services; Targeted Assistance for Refugees; Vietnamese Youth Services.

Social Adjustment—Ms. SHARON ALEXIS,Audubon Senior Center, Gert Town, Save Our Selves (S.O.S.); Outward Bound.

CARE Centers—Ms. CONNIE ANDRY,CARE Center, New Orleans; Jefferson Parish CARE Center.

Clinical Counseling Programs—Ms. JANE BREWER, Metairie & New Orleans Office, *433 Metairie Rd., Ste. 206, Metairie, 70005-4324.* Tel: 504-835-5007.

St. Tammany Parish Office—Ms. ANN LABAUVE, *1926 Corporate Sq., Suites D & E, Slidell, 70458-3165.* Tel: 504-641-8120.

St. Charles Parish Branch Office—Mr. PETER YUSLUM, *P.O. Box 60, Hahnville, 70057-6000.* Tel: 504-783-2906.

St. John The Baptist Parish Branch Office—Ms. DIANE LEONARD, *1706 Cannes Dr., LaPlace, 70068-2407.* Tel: 504-652-4330.

St. Bernard Parish Office—Ms. BARBARA LAUGHLIN, *2626 Charles Dr., Chalmette, 70043-3773.* Tel: 504-279-7636.

Westbank Office—*1101 Barataria Blvd., Marrero, 70072-3085.* Tel: 504-348-9302.

Crescent House—Ms. LYNN HOLLAND.

Deaf Action Center of Greater New Orleans—Ms. KATHY TREUBIG.

Information and Referral—Ms. PEGGY RAGAS-MATTHEWS.

Family Preservation—Ms. MAMIE HALL-LANDRY.

Job Search—Ms. NELLIE STOKES-PERRY.

Parish Social Ministry—Sr. JANINE BENIGER, C.S.J.; Mr. VINCENT LIBERTO.

Senior Citizens Groups—Mr. Raphael Foley.
Project S.A.V.E.—Ms. Jane Woodard-Robson.
Therapeutic Family Services—Ms. Arthea Larson.
Foster Grandparents—Ms. Doris Lala.

Christopher Homes, Inc.—Mr. Thomas P. Perkins, Exec. Dir., *1000 Howard Ave., Ste. 100, New Orleans, 70113-1903.* Tel: 504-596-3460; Fax: 504-596-3466.

Disaster Relief—Rev. Msgr. Roger P. Morin, Dir., *1000 Howard Ave., Ste. 800, New Orleans, 70113-1900.* Tel: 504-596-3090; Fax: 504-596-3098.

Social Apostolate Office (PHILMAT, Inc.)—Most Rev. Francis B. Schulte, Pres.; Sr. Adele Lambert, C.S.J., Dir. Gordon R. Wadge, Assoc. Dir., *1000 Howard Ave., Ste. 800, New Orleans, 70113-1900.* Tel: 504-596-3080; Fax: 504-596-3098.

Food for Families/Food for Seniors—Mr. Timothy Robertson, Dir., *8326 Apricot St., New Orleans, 70118-3198.* Tel: 504-861-3555; Fax: 504-861-1435.

Second Harvesters Food Bank of Greater New Orleans, Inc.—Mr. S. Brian Greene, Dir., *1201 Sams Ave., Harahan, 70123-2236.* Tel: 504-734-1322; 733-8336; Fax: 504-733-8336.

Summer Social Action Program (Witness)—*1000 Howard Ave., New Orleans, 70113-1903.* Tel: 504-596-3080; Fax: 504-596-3098.

Social Action Centers.

Incarnate Word Center—Mrs. Carolyn Potts, Dir., *8326 Apricot St., New Orleans, 70118-3198.* Tel: 504-866-8918; Fax: 504-861-1435.

Our Lady of Lourdes Center—Mrs. Janet M. Rousso, Dir., *2401 Jena St., New Orleans, 70115-5998.* Tel: 504-895-0216; Fax: 504-895-0629.

St. John the Baptist—Sr. Marion Brett, D.C., Dir., *1920 Clio St., New Orleans, 70113-1214.* Tel: 504-581-4987; Fax: 504-581-4991.

St. Louis Community Center—Mrs. Ellen McNair, *1022 Barracks St., New Orleans, 70116-2526.* Tel: 504-524-7023; Fax: 504-524-2881.

St. Mary of the Angels—Sr. Margaret Hoffman R.C.S.C.J., *2301 Gallier St., New Orleans, 70117-5833.* Tel: 504-949-1506; Fax: 504-945-9115.

St. Philip Social Service Center—Mrs. Dominique B. Wheeler, Dir., *3333 Clouet St., New Orleans, 70126-5700.* Tel: 504-944-8848; Fax: 504-944-8853.

Spur-Senior Advocacy Program—Mr. John Graham, Acting Dir., *7100 St. Charles Ave., New Orleans, 70118-3595.* Tel: 504-861-4951; Fax: 504-861-3395.

Department of Financial Services

Executive Director—Mr. Joseph E. Ingraham, *7887 Walmsley Ave., New Orleans, 70125-3496.* Tel: 504-861-6252; 861-9521; Fax: 504-866-2906.

Accounting Office—Ms. Judy Schott, Account Mgr., *7887 Walmsley Ave., New Orleans, 70125-3496.* Tel: 504-861-6201; 861-9521; Fax: 504-866-2906.

Assessment Committee—Mr. Joseph E. Ingraham, Coord., *7887 Walmsley Ave., New Orleans, 70125-3496.* Tel: 504-861-6252; 861-9521; Fax: 504-866-2906.

Building Office—Most Rev. Francis B. Schulte, Pres.; Mr. Joseph E. Ingraham, Exec. Dir.; Mr. August J. Barbier, Jr., Dir., *7887 Walmsley Ave., New Orleans, 70125-3496.* Tel: 504-861-6210; 861-9521; Fax: 504-866-2906.

Employee Benefits Committee—Mr. Joseph E. Ingraham, Chm., *7887 Walmsley Ave., New Orleans, 70125-3496.* Tel: 504-861-6252; 861-9521; Fax: 504-866-2906.

Financial Review Office—Mrs. Kim O. Ramsey, *7887 Walmsley Ave., New Orleans, 70125-3496.* Tel: 504-861-6253; 861-9521.

Insurance Office—Mr. Joseph E. Ingraham, Exec. Dir.; Mrs. Cheryl Harper, Claim Mgr., *7887 Walmsley Ave., New Orleans, 70125-3496.* Tel: 504-861-6259; 861-9521; Fax: 504-866-2906.

Missions Office—Society for the Propagation of the Faith, Holy Childhood Pontifical Assn., Missionaries of St. Therese—Most Rev. Gregory M. Aymond, V.G., Dir., *7887 Walmsley Ave., New Orleans, 70125-3496.* Tel: 504-866-7410; Fax: 504-866-3119.

New Orleans Archdiocesan Cemeteries and New Orleans Cemeteries Trust—Mr. Michael D. Boudreaux, Dir., *1000 Howard Ave., New Orleans, 70113-1903.* Tel: 504-596-3050; Fax: 504-596-3055.

Parish Sites & Boundaries Committee—Rev. Msgr. Martin Van Der Werff, Chm.; Rev. Msgr. Thomas J. Rodi, V.G., Coord., *7887 Walmsley Ave., New Orleans, 70125-3496.* Tel: 504-861-6262; 861-9521; Fax: 504-866-2906.

Personnel Office—Mr. Joseph E. Ingraham, Dir., *7887 Walmsley Ave., New Orleans, 70125-3496.* Tel: 504-861-6252; 861-9521; Fax: 504-866-2906.

Property Committee—Most Rev. Francis B. Schulte, D.D., Pres.; Rev. Msgr. Charles E. Duke, Chm., *4845 Meadowdale St., Metairie, 70006-4037.* Tel: 504-889-0850; Fax: 504-888-4934.

Purchasing Services—Mr. William Eden, Purchasing Agent, *7887 Walmsley Ave., New Orleans, 70125-3496.* Tel: 504-861-6207; 861-9521; Fax: 504-866-2906.

Retired Priests' Pension Commission—Mr. Joseph E. Ingraham, Coord., *7887 Walmsley Ave., New Orleans, 70125-3496.* Tel: 504-861-6252; 861-9521; Fax: 504-866-2906.

School Food Services—Rev. Msgr. John P. Reynolds, Supt.; Mr. George A. Sanderson, Jr., Dir., *1000 Howard Ave., Ste. 300, New Orleans, 70113-1919.* Tel: 504-596-3434; Fax: 504-596-3459.

Department of Pastoral Services

Executive Director—Very Rev. Gerald L. Seiler, Jr., *7887 Walmsley Ave., New Orleans, 70125-3496.* Tel: 504-861-6294; 861-9521; Fax: 504-866-2906.

Archbishop Antoine Blanc Memorial—Rev. Msgr. Alvin J. O'Reilly, Admin., *1100 Chartres St., New Orleans, 70116-2596.* Tel: 504-529-2001; Fax: 504-529-2001.

Archives (Archdiocesan)—Dr. Charles E. Nolan, *1100 Chartres St., New Orleans, 70116-2596.* Tel: 504-529-2651; Fax: 504-529-2001.

Black Catholics Office—Deacon Dan Vincent, *7887 Walmsley Ave., New Orleans, 70125-3496.* Tel: 504-861-6207; 861-9521; Fax: 504-866-2906.

Canonical Permissions and Dispensations—Very Rev. Gerald L. Seiler, Jr.; Rev. Joseph P. Mullin, S.M., *7887 Walmsley Ave., New Orleans, 70125-3496.* Tel: 504-861-6294; 861-9521; Fax: 504-866-2906.

Charismatic Renewal—Liaisons: Mr. Al Mansfield; Mrs. Al Mansfield, *3100 Division St., Ste. 200, Metairie, 70002-5812.* Tel: 504-455-1361; Fax: 504-885-2132.

Ecumenical Commission—Rev. Earl F. Niehaus, S.M., Chm., *1706 Jackson Ave., New Orleans, 70113-1593.* Tel: 504-524-5192.

Family Life Apostolate—Mrs. Paula D'Albor Stuckart, Dir., *7887 Walmsley Ave., New Orleans, 70125-3496.* Tel: 504-861-6243; 861-9521; Fax: 504-866-2906.

Commission for Persons with Disabilities—Mrs. Paula D'Albor Stuckart, *7887 Walmsley Ave., New Orleans, 70125-3496.* Tel: 504-861-6243; Fax: 504-866-2906.

Hispanic Ministries—Rev. Salvador Galvez, Coord., *2701 Lawrence St., New Orleans, 70114-3099.* Tel: 504-367-7730; Fax: 504-367-2603.

Hispanic Apostolate—Mrs. Dora Zuniga, Exec. Dir., *3368 Esplanade Ave., New Orleans, 70119-3132.* Tel: 504-486-1983; Fax: 504-486-3985.

Mensaje, Inc.—Rev. Pedro Nunez, *3368 Esplanade Ave., New Orleans, 70119-3132.* Tel: 504-482-8803; Fax: 504-943-9461.

Holy Name Societies—Mr. Ben Raphael, Exec. Dir., *7887 Walmsley Ave., New Orleans, 70125-3496.* Tel: 504-866-7320; Fax: 504-866-2906.

Pastoral Planning—Sr. Myra Banquer M.S.C., Coord., *7887 Walmsley Ave., New Orleans, 70125-3496.* Tel: 504-861-6222; Fax: 504-861-2906.

Prisons Apostolate—Deacon Louis Stall, Archdiocesan Dir., *P.O. Box 388, Gretna, 70054-0388.* Tel: 504-374-7700, Ext. 3109.

Renovacion Carismatica Catolica Hispana—Rev. Alberto Bermudez, Dir., *4401 7th St., Marrero, 70072-2099.* Tel: 504-341-9516; Fax: 504-341-9517.

Vietnamese Catholics Office—Rev. Msgr. Dominic Luong, Dir., *5069 Willow Brook Dr., New Orleans, 70129-0745.* Tel: 504-254-5660; Fax: 504-254-9250.

Worship Office—Rev. Kenneth J. Hedrick, Dir.; Deacon Ronald Guidry, Assoc. Dir., *7887 Walmsley Ave., New Orleans, 70125-3496.* Tel: 504-861-6300; 861-9521; Fax: 504-866-2906.

Liturgical Commission—Rev. Kenneth J. Hedrick, Coord., *7887 Walmsley Ave., New Orleans, 70125-3496.* Tel: 504-861-6300; 861-9521; Fax: 504-866-2906.

Master of Ceremonies—Rev. Kenneth J. Hedrick; Deacon Ronald Guidry, *7887 Walmsley Ave., New Orleans, 70125-3496.* Tel: 504-861-6300; 861-9521; Fax: 504-866-2906.

Department of Religious

Executive Director—Sr. Suellen Tennyson, M.S.C., *7887 Walmsley Ave., New Orleans, 70125-3496.* Tel: 504-861-6281; 861-9521; Fax: 504-866-2906.

Liaison with Leadership Conference of Women Religious, Religious Institutes of Brothers and Sisters and Secular Institutes—

Archdiocesan Offices and Corporations

ACC Development Corporation—Sr. Anthony Barczykowski, D.C., Registered Agent, *1000 Howard Ave., New Orleans, 70113-1916.* Tel: 504-523-3755.

Accuserv—Mr. David J. Logsdon, Pres., *1000 Howard St., New Orleans, 70113-1916.* Tel: 504-523-3755.

Archdiocesan Horizons Fund for the Aged, Inc.—Most Rev. Francis B. Schulte, Pres., *7887 Walmsley Ave., New Orleans, 70125-3496.* Tel: 504-861-9521.

Bernard A. Grehan Trust—*7887 Walmsley Ave., New Orleans, 70125-3496.* Tel: 504-861-9521.

Catholic Charities Children's Day Care Centers—Registered Office: *1000 Howard Ave., Ste. 1200, New Orleans, 70113-1916.*

Catholic Charities Children's Group Homes—Registered Office: *1000 Howard Ave., Ste. 1200, New Orleans, 70113-1916.*

Community Host Campaign—Most Rev. Francis B. Schulte, Pres., *7887 Walmsley Ave., New Orleans, 70125-3496.* Tel: 504-861-9521.

Mental Health Association Development Corporation—*7887 Walmsley Ave., New Orleans, 70125-3496.* Tel: 504-861-9521.

New Life, Inc.—Sr. Anthony Barczykowski, D.C., Sec. & Treas., *1000 Howard Ave., Ste. 1200, New Orleans, 70113-1916.* Tel: 504-523-3755.

St. Elizabeth's Home Registered Office—*1000 Howard Ave., Ste. 1200, New Orleans, 70113-1916.*

St. Gertrude's Retirement Center—Most Rev. Francis B. Schulte, D.D., Pres., *7887 Walmsley Ave., New Orleans, 70125-3496.*

St. Mary's Catholic Orphan Boy's Asylum Board—*1000 Howard Ave., Ste. 1200, New Orleans, 70113-1916.*

St. Vincent's Infant and Maternity Home Registered Office—*1000 Howard Ave., Ste. 1200, New Orleans, 70113-1916.*

Lay Organizations

Apostleship of Prayer—Rev. Joseph Reising, S.J., Dir., *500 S. Jefferson Davis Pkwy., New Orleans, 70119-7192.* Tel: 504-821-0334; Fax: 504-822-5322.

Archdiocesan Federation of Christian Life Communities—Rev. H. William Reed, Spiritual Dir., *2545 Bayou Rd., New Orleans, 70119-2398.* Tel: 504-945-3591; Fax: 504-945-3216.

Archconfraternity of St. Ann—Rev. Msgr. Joseph E. Bourgeois, Spiritual Dir., *4920 Loveland St., Metairie, 70006-4099.* Tel: 504-455-7071; Fax: 504-455-7076.

Blessed Brother Andre Acadians Prayer Group—Deacon Irving J. Daigle, Spiritual Moderator, *529 S. Telemachus, New Orleans, 70119-7043.* Tel: 504-486-7190.

Blue Army of Our Lady of Fatima—Rev. Denzil M. Perera, Spiritual Dir., *1342 Moss St., New Orleans, 70119-2998.* Tel: 504-488-2659; Fax: 504-488-6741.

Catholic Alumni Club—Miss Marie Spicuzza, Pres., *668 Spartan Ln., Kenner, 70065-2644.* Tel: 504-466-1552.

Catholic Charities Association Inc.—Mrs. Leon Cabes, Pres., *1000 Howard Ave., Ste. 1200, New Orleans, 70113-1916.* Tel: 504-581-BALL.

Catholic Knights of America—Rev. Benjamin Piovan, Spiritual Dir., *799 Fairway Dr., LaPlace, 70068-2007.* Tel: 504-652-2615; Fax: 504-652-7291.

Catholic Order of Foresters—Mr. Edwin Hadley, State Chief Ranger, *4701 Stephen Girard, New Orleans, 70126-4757.* Tel: 504-282-5432.

Catholic Physicians Guild of New Orleans—Rev. Msgr. Elmo L. Romagosa, Chap., *700 Maple St., Harvey, 70058-4008.* Tel: 504-368-1397; Fax: 504-368-0662.

Chateau de Notre Dame Guild—Rev. Joseph J. Lawlor, S.S.J., Spiritual Dir., *2832 Burdette St., New Orleans, 70125-2596.* Tel: 504-866-2741; Fax: 504-866-6769.

Closer Walk Ministries—Rev. Harold F. Cohen, S.J., Dir., *P.O. Box 50860, New Orleans, 70150-0860.* Tel: 504-834-4200; Fax: 504-834-4204.

Come, Lord Jesus Program of Prayer and Scripture—Ms. Marie Wojdac, Coord., *1728 Pine St., New Orleans, 70118-5322.* Tel: 504-861-4189.

Community of St. John the Evangelist—Mr. Dan Demers, Chm., *3342 Hyman Pl., New Orleans, 70131-7040.* Tel: 504-394-1795.

Confraternity of the Holy Face—Rev. Msgr. Lanaux J. Rareshide, Dir., *2327 S. Galvez St., New Orleans, 70125-3198.* Tel: 504-821-9500; Fax: 504-821-9500.

Council of Catholic Men—Mr. Ben Raphael, Dir., *7887 Walmsley Ave., New Orleans, 70125-3496.* Tel: 504-866-7320.

Council of Catholic School Cooperative Clubs—Rev. H. William Reed, Spiritual Moderator, *2545 Bayou Rd., New Orleans, 70119-2398.* Tel: 504-945-3591; Fax: 504-945-3216.

Council of Catholic Women—Rev. H. William Reed, Spiritual Dir., *2545 Bayou Rd., New Orleans, 70119-2398.* Tel: 504-945-3591. Mrs. Bernice Bonzant, Pres.

Courage (Catholic Ministry to Homosexual Persons)—*P.O. Box 8074, New Orleans, 70182-8074.* Tel: 504-288-6877.

Engaged Encounter—Gary Levy; Claudia Levy. Tel: 504-837-9121.

Eucharistic Adoration Society—Miss Lucille F. Corpora, Pres., *101 Harding St., Jefferson, 70121-3915.* Tel: 504-834-1984.

Knights of Columbus—Rev. FRANCIS J. CARABELLO, Archdiocesan Chap., *610 6th St., Gretna, 70053-6098.* Tel: 504-368-1313; Fax: 504-368-6841.

Knights of Peter Claver—Mr. W. CHARLES KEYES, JR., Exec. Sec., *1825 Orleans Ave., New Orleans, 70116-2894.* Tel: 504-821-4225; Fax: 504-821-4253.

Korean Catholic Community Center—140 27th St., Kenner, 70062-4906. Tel: 504-469-3956.

Ladies of Charity of the Archdiocese—Rev. HAROLD DICHARRY, Spiritual Dir., *1025 Napoleon Ave., New Orleans, 70115-2898.* Tel: 504-899-1378; Fax: 504-899-0480.

Ladies of Madonna—Mrs. E. J. DEVERGES, Pres., *2818 Palmer Ave., New Orleans, 70118-5620.* Tel: 504-866-5809.

Lay Carmelites of Our Lady of Mount Carmel—420 R.E. Lee Blvd., New Orleans, 70124-2596. Tel: 504-288-8553.

Legion of Mary—Rev. HAROLD DICHARRY, Spiritual Dir., New Orleans Comitium, *1025 Napoleon Ave., New Orleans, 70115-2898.* Tel: 504-899-1378; Fax: 504-899-0480.

Living Waters Program (Radio Ministry)—Rev. Msgr. ROBERT I. GUSTE, Dir., *3700 Jean Lafitte Pkwy., Chalmette, 70043-1199.* Tel: 504-271-3039; Fax: 504-279-8023.

Magnificat, Ministry to Catholic Women—Mrs. PETER QUIRK, Pres. Central Svc. Team, *1201 Beverly Gardens Dr., Metairie, 70002.* Tel: 504-834-0057.
Metairie Chapter—3617 Metairie Ct., Metairie, 70002.
New Orleans Chapter—2010 Franklin Ave., New Orleans, 70117.
Slidell Chapter—633 Dale Dr., Slidell, 70458.
West Bank Chapter—1232 Farrington Dr., Marrero, 70072.
West St. Tammany Chapter—207 Mako Nako Dr., Mandeville, 70471.

Marians of New Orleans—Mrs. HELEN W. DELAHOUSSAYE, Pres., *2716 Whitney Pl., #417, Metairie, 70002-6232.* Tel: 504-838-9145.

Marians of Metairie—Mrs. ANNA JOBES, Pres., *4520 Chateau Dr., Metairie, 70002-1510.* Tel: 504-885-3628.

Marriage Encounter—GARY DAIGLE; MARCIA DAIGLE. Tel: 504-649-0999. JOE GYAN; PAM GYAN. Tel: 504-738-5683.

Maryknoll Education Center (Promotions of Missionary Work)—Mr. MATT ROUSSO, Education Asst., *7214 St. Charles Ave., New Orleans, 70118.* Tel: 504-866-8516.

Mary's Children—Mrs. PRISCILLA ANDONIE, Pres., *3617 Lake Dr., Metairie, 70002-1533.* Tel: 504-888-6017.

Mary's Helpers (Medjugorje Information)—Mrs. MARGARET TROSCLAIR, Dir., *P.O. Box 1853, Marrero, 70072-1853.* Tel: 504-348-7729.

Medjugorje Star—Rev. CHARLES SELLARS, O.M.I., Spiritual Dir. Dirs.: HUBIE MULE; KAY MULE, *2627 David Dr., Metairie, 70003-4599.* Tel: 504-889-1708; Fax: 504-889-1714.

MIR Group (Medjugorje Information Center)—Ms. GERI FAIA, *400 Poydras St., Ste. 2650, New Orleans, 70130-3245.* Tel: 504-595-6921; Fax: 504-595-6923.

Missionaries of St. Theresa—Most Rev. GREGORY M. AYMOND, V.G., Spiritual Moderator, *2901 S. Carrollton Ave., New Orleans, 70118-4391.* Tel: 504-866-7410; Fax: 504-866-3119.

Naim Conference—Ms. GLORIA COMISKEY LACOUR, Pres., *905 Bragg St., New Orleans, 70124-3907.* Tel: 504-486-1255.

National Council of Catholic Men—Mr. BEN RAPHAEL, Dir., *7887 Walmsley Ave., New Orleans, 70125-3496.* Tel: 504-866-7320.

National Council of Catholic Women—Rev. H. WILLIAM REED, Spiritual Dir., *2545 Bayou Rd., New Orleans, 70119-2398.* Tel: 504-945-3591.

New Life, Inc.—4948 W. Esplanade Ave., Ste. B, Metairie, 70006-2670.

Pax Christi New Orleans—DON BOAGNI-DOW, Coord., *916 St. Andrew St., New Orleans, 70130-5020.* Tel: 504-522-3751; Fax: 504-525-0011.

St. Elizabeth's Guild—Mrs. JOHN D'ARCY BECKER, Pres., *1000 Howard Ave., Ste. 1200, New Orleans, 70113-1916.*

St. Margaret's Daughters—Mrs. AUGUSTINE MOLL, Pres., *926 Charbonnet St., New Orleans, 70117-2655.* Tel: 504-943-0706.

St. Thomas More Catholic Lawyers Association—Rev. JOSEPH S. PALERMO, JR., *160 Imperial Woods Dr., Harahan, 70123-4998.* Tel: 504-737-2915.

St. Vincent de Paul Society—Mrs. TOBY CHARBONNET, Pres.; Mr. ARMAND H. BERTIN, SR., Exec. Sec., *2601 Canal St., New Orleans, 70119-6498.* Tel: 504-822-9288; Fax: 504-822-1964.

Scouting—Deacon DANIEL FLYNN, Chap., Boy Scouts, *251 Halsey Dr., Harahan, 70123-4401.* Tel: 504-737-8370. Mrs. COLLEEN R. LAROCCA, Chm., Girl Scouts, *25 Brentwood Dr., Metairie, 70003-3831.* Tel: 504-734-8527.

Serra Clubs—Serra Club of New Orleans; Rev. HENRY J. BUGLER, Chap., *7887 Walmsley Ave., New Orleans, 70125-3496.* Tel: 504-861-6298; Fax: 504-866-2906. Serra Club of Downtown New Orleans; Rev. ANDREW C. TAORMINA, Chap., *448 Metairie Rd., Metairie, 70005-4371.* Tel: 504-834-0340. Serra Club of East Jefferson; Rev. JAMES LOHAN, Chap., *105 Bonnabel Blvd., Metairie, 70005-3798.* Tel: 504-835-9343. Serra Club of St. Bernard; Rev. WAYNE C. PAYSSE, Chap., *5500 Paris Ave., New Orleans, 70122-2699.* Tel: 504-288-4224.

The Theresians—Mrs. ELIZABETH RARESHIDE, Pres., *3840 Napoleon Ave., New Orleans, 70125-4444.* Tel: 504-861-8673.

Victorious Missionaries—Deacon ALBERT LEVY, III, Chap., *621 Lebeau St., Arabi, 70032.* Tel: 504-277-5053.

CLERGY, PARISHES, MISSIONS AND PAROCHIAL SCHOOLS

CITY OF NEW ORLEANS
(Orleans Civil Parish)

1—ST. LOUIS CATHEDRAL (1720). (A Minor Basilica). Revs. Kenneth J. Hedrick, Rector; Frank Montalbano, O.M.I.; John C. Sax, O.M.I.; Deacon Ron Guidry.
Res., 615 Pere Antoine Alley, 70116-3291. Tel: 504-525-9585; Fax: 504-525-9583.
School—820 Dauphine St., 70116-3089. Tel: 504-525-3860; Fax: 504-525-3193. Sr. Maria Luisa Aldape, Prin.
Sisters of the Society of St. Teresa of Jesus 4; Brother of the Sacred Heart 1; Lay Teachers 10; Students 203.
Mission—New Orleans, Orleans Civil Parish, Our Lady of Guadalupe, Tel: 504-525-1551; Fax: 504-525-1827.
Shrine—International Shrine of St. Jude. Revs. Ray J. Marek, O.M.I.; John Sokolski, O.M.I.; Mr. Michael W. Thomas, Pastoral Assoc.
Res., 411 N. Rampart St., 70112-3594. Tel: 504-525-1551; 525-1557; Fax: 504-525-1827.
St. Jude Community Center—400 N. Rampart St., 70112-3594. Tel: 504-522-8290; Fax: 504-522-8830.

2—ALL SAINTS (1919), Rev. Rawlin Enette, S.S.J.
Res., 1441 Teche St., 70114-5899. Tel: 504-361-8835; Fax: 504-361-9802.
School—1415 Teche St., 70114-5898.
Sisters of the Holy Family 4; Lay Teachers 12; Students 289.

3—ANNUNCIATION (1844), Most Rev. Nicholas D'Antonio, O.F.M., D.D. In res., Rev. Sebastian Bonavia, O.F.M.Cap. (Malta).
Res., 1221 Mandeville St., 70117-8498. Tel: 504-943-5561; Fax: 504-943-5562.

4—BLESSED SACRAMENT (1915) (African American), Very Rev. John O. Hallaran, S.S.J. In res., Revs. Howard W. Byrd, S.S.J.; Joseph E. Okoro, C.M.F. (Nigeria).
Res., 5018 Constance St., 70115-1798. Tel: 504-897-0955; Fax: 504-897-0950.

5—CORPUS CHRISTI (1916) (African American), Revs. John E. O'Hallaran, S.S.J.; Emmanuel Madu (Nigeria); Bro. Louis Tomasso, S.S.J.; Deacon Alfred D. White.
Res., 2022 St. Bernard Ave., 70116-1388. Tel: 504-945-8931; Fax: 504-947-5347.
School—Tel: 504-943-6131. Sr. Elizabeth Ann Holmes, S.S.F., Prin.
Sisters 7; Lay Teachers 41; Students 455.
Catechesis/Religious Programs—Students 125.

6—EPIPHANY (1948), Very Rev. Joseph J. McKinley, S.S.J.; Rev. Ashley J. Perry, S.S.J.
Res., 1949 Duels St., 70119-1198. Tel: 504-944-2646; Fax: 504-945-5251.

7—HOLY GHOST (1915) (African American), Revs. Alphonce Kimathy, C.S.Sp.; Michel Boutot, C.S.Sp. In res., Rev. O. Hugh Stout.
Res., 2015 Louisiana Ave., 70115-5294. Tel: 504-891-3172; Fax: 504-891-9284.
School—2035 Toledano St., 70115-5295. Tel: 504-899-6782. Sr. Angela Smith, S.S.F., Prin.
Sisters 4; Lay Teachers 6; Students 290.

8—HOLY NAME OF JESUS (1892), Revs. Daniel A. Creagan, S.J.; W. Peter Bayhi, S.J.; J. Donald Pearce, S.J.; Deacon Philip De Verges.
Res., 6220 LaSalle Pl., 70118-6236. Tel: 504-865-7430; Fax: 504-866-3391.
School—6325 Cromwell Pl., 70118-6299. Tel: 504-861-1466; Fax: 504-861-1480. Sr. Mary Nicholas Schiro, R.S.M., Prin.
Sisters of Mercy 6; Lay Teachers 40; Students 538.
Catechesis/Religious Programs—Tel: 504-572-2469.
Students 60.

9—HOLY NAME OF MARY (ALGIERS) (1848), Rev. Raymond Carr, S.M.
Res., 500 Eliza St., 70114-1098. Tel: 504-362-5511; Fax: 504-367-3504. [CEM 2]
School—502 Oliver St., 70114-1099. Tel: 504-361-4004. Sr. Doris Daigle, M.S.C., Prin.
Sisters 5; Lay Teachers 7; Students 224.

10—HOLY SPIRIT (1972), Rev. Msgr. Allen J. Roy, V.F.; Deacon Raphael Duplechan, Jr.
Res., 6201 Stratford Pl., 70131-7397. Tel: 504-394-5492; Fax: 504-398-0901.
Catechesis/Religious Programs—Tel: 504-392-0927; Fax: 504-398-0901. Beverly Baldwin, D.R.E.
Students 135.

11—IMMACULATE CONCEPTION (1851), Revs. Harry W. Tompson, S.J.; Paul W. Schott, S.J.
Res., 130 Baronne St., 70112-2304. Tel: 504-529-1477; 1478; Fax: 504-524-0155.

12—IMMACULATE HEART OF MARY (1954), Rev. Joseph M. de Water; Deacon Paul Mumme.
Res., 6300 Pines Blvd., 70126-2697. Tel: 504-242-6900; Fax: 507-243-6655.
School—6360 Pines Blvd., 70126-2699. Dr. Geralyn Dell, Prin.
Lay Teachers 4; Students 10.

13—INCARNATE WORD (1922), Rev. Msgr. Roger P. Morin; Rev. Francis Ferrie.
Res., 8316 Apricot St., 70118-3199. Tel: 504-866-3679; Fax: 504-866-0722.

14—MARY, QUEEN OF VIETNAM (1983) (Vietnamese), Rev. Msgr. Dominic Mai Thanh Luong; Revs. Peter Nam Van Tran; Peter Neuman, I.C.
Res., 5069 Willow Brook Dr., P.O. Box 29745, 70129-1047. Tel: 504-254-5560; Fax: 504-254-9250. [JC]
Catechesis/Religious Programs—Tel: 504-254-5247.
Students 953.
Mission—New Orleans, Orleans Civil Parish, Our Lady of La Vang, 6054 Vermillion Blvd., 70122-4296. Tel: 504-283-0559; Fax: 504-286-1937. Rev. Dominic Huyen Duc Nguyen.
Chapel—Vietnamese Martyrs, 14400 Peltier Dr., New Orleans East, 70129-1713. Tel: 504-254-5660; Fax: 504-254-9250.

15—MATER DOLOROSA (1848), Rev. Msgr. Jerome T. Mire; Deacons Donald Walsh; Walter Beyer. In res., Rev. David A. Boileau.
Res., 8128 Plum St., 70118-2012. Tel: 504-866-3669; Fax: 504-866-2349.
Catechesis/Religious Programs—Tel: 504-866-3660.
Students 120.

16—OUR LADY OF GOOD COUNSEL (1887), Revs. Kenneth Borgesen, O.SS.T.; Francis Whatley, O.SS.T.; Vincent Bechamps, O.SS.T.; Deacon Ray Richardson.
Res., 1307 Louisiana Ave., 70115-2494. Tel: 504-891-1906; Fax: 504-895-5871.

17—OUR LADY OF GUADALUPE /INTERNATIONAL SHRINE OF ST. JUDE. (Quasi Parish). Revs. John Sokolski, O.M.I.; Ray John Marck, O.M.I.; Mr. Michael W. Thomas, Pastoral Assoc.
Res., 411 N. Rampart St., 70112. Tel: 504-525-1551; Fax: 504-525-1827.

18—OUR LADY OF LOURDES (1905), Rev. Curtis R. Thomas; Deacon Everett Williams.
Res., 4423 La Salle St., 70115-5909. Tel: 504-891-4401; Fax: 504-891-4402.
School—2437 Jena St., 70115-5998. Tel: 504-897-0154; Fax: 504-897-0155.
Lay Teachers 10; Students 212.

19—OUR LADY OF THE ROSARY (1907), Rev. James A. Tarantino; Rev. Msgr. Edward L. Boudreaux, Pastor Emeritus; Rev. Denzil M. Perera; Deacons Ralph J. Schonacher; John David Hamm; Henry Nuss.
Res., 1342 Moss St., 70119-2998. Tel: 504-488-2659; Fax: 504-448-6741.

20—OUR LADY STAR OF THE SEA (1911), Rev. Eugene F. Jacques; Deacon Tony Peres.
Res., 1835 St. Roch Ave., 70117-8199. Tel: 504-944-0166; Fax: 504-948-9555.

21—THE RESURRECTION OF OUR LORD (1963), Revs. Cyprian Devold; Patrick Collum; Deacon William P. Curry, Jr.
Res., 9701 Hammond St., 70127-3519. Tel: 504-242-8669; Fax: 504-242-8767.
School—4861 Rosalia Dr., 70127-3598. Tel: 504-242-6222; Fax: 504-241-7363. Ms. Angela Francis, Prin.
Lay Teachers 26; Students 429.
Catechesis/Religious Programs—Students 97.

22—SACRED HEART OF JESUS (1879), Revs. C. Richard

Nowery, C.S.C.; Joseph M. Moyer, C.S.C.; Deacon Irving J. Daigle. In res., Rev. Thomas E. Chambers, C.S.C.; Bros. Shawn Priggel, C.S.C.; Richard Kelly, C.S.C.; Mr. James Ponce, C.S.C.
Res., 139 S. Lopez St., 70119-6284. Tel: 504-827-1481; Fax: 504-821-5109.

23—ST. ALPHONSUS (1847) (Irish), Revs. Charles R. Landry, C.SS.R.; Gerard B. LaPorte, C.SS.R.; Binh Thanh Ta, C.SS.R.; Luong Uong, C.SS.R.; Sr. Jane Briseno, R.S.M., Pastoral Assoc.; Bro. Andrew Lawson, C.SS.R.; Deacon Maurice J. Hartson, III.
Res., 2030 Constance St., 70130-5099. Tel: 504-522-6748; Fax: 504-523-3734.
School—2001 Constance St., 70130-5094. Tel: 504-523-6594. Sr. Monica Ellerbusch, R.S.M., Prin.
Sisters 3; Lay Teachers 16; Students 246.

24—ST. ANDREW THE APOSTLE (1952), Rev. Msgr. John A. Tomasovich; Revs. Joel P. Cantones; Raymond P. Martinez; Deacon Chris J. DiGrado.
Res., 3101 Eton St., 70131-5399. Tel: 504-393-2334; Fax: 504-392-0635.
School—Tel: 504-394-4171; Fax: 504-391-3627.
Sisters 3; Lay Teachers 43; Students 780.
Catechesis/Religious Programs—Tel: 504-394-4010.
Students 112.

25—ST. ANTHONY OF PADUA (1915), Very Revs. Donald T. Dvorak, O.P.; Thomas A. Clifford, O.P., Prior; Revs. Wayne Cavalier, O.P.; Carl Trutter, O.P.; John J. Boll, O.P.; Bryan Fontenot, O.P.; John N. Morgenthaler, O.P.; James S. McHatton, O.P.; Robert L. Every, O.P.; John A. Powers, O.P.; Very Rev. Alberto Rodriguez, O.P., Prov.; Revs. Michael O'Rourke, O.P.; Scott T. O'Brien, O.P.; Marcelo Solorzano, O.P.; Michael O'Rourke, O.P.; Bros. Timothy Wrinn, O.P.; Herman Johnson; Sr. M. Aimee Haulard, O.P., Pastoral Assoc.; Sr. Diane McOsker, O.P., Pastoral Assoc.
Res., 4640 Canal St., 70119-5892. Tel: 504-488-2651; Fax: 504-488-1842.
School—St. Anthony of Padua School for Technology, 4601 Cleveland Ave., 70119-5893. Tel: 504-488-4426; 482-3672; Fax: 504-488-5373. Sr. Ruth Angelette, O.P., Prin.
Sisters of St. Dominic 2; Lay Teachers 25; Students 420.
Catechesis/Religious Programs—Students 44.

26—ST. AUGUSTINE (1841), Rev. Jerome LeDoux, S.V.D.; Deacon Lloyd St. Clair Glapion.
Res., 1210 Gov. Nicholls St., 70116-2324. Tel: 504-525-5934; Fax: 504-523-2473.

27—ST. BRIGID (1977), Rev. Thomas G. Glasgow.
Res., 13435 Granville St., P.O. Box 29626, 70129-1210. Tel: 504-254-3538; Fax: 504-254-3520.
Catechesis/Religious Programs—Tel: 504-254-5115. Mary Kittles, D.R.E.
Students 80.

28—ST. CECILIA (1897), Rev. Ronald F. Whitlow. In res., Rev. Gerard P. Kinane.
Res., 1015 France St., 70117-5398. Tel: 504-945-1597; 945-6622; Fax: 504-945-0188.

29—ST. DAVID (1937), Very Rev. Francis M. Hull, S.S.J., V.F.; Deacon Irvin Williams.
Res., 5617 St. Claude Ave., 70117-2533. Tel: 504-947-2853; Fax: 504-948-7852.
School—Tel: 504-943-1523. Sr. Teresa Rooney, C.H.F., Prin.
Sisters 4; Lay Teachers 7; Students 230.
Catechesis/Religious Programs—Iris Labeaud, D.R.E.
Students 105.

30—ST. DOMINIC (1924), Revs. Neal McDermott, O.P.; Edward W. Conley, O.P., Prior; Victor Brown, O.P.; Richard Murphy, O.P., (Retired); William J. Brady, O.P., (Retired); Val A. McInnes, O.P., Dir. Devel.; Dominic J. Tamburello, O.P.; Bros. Roger Shondel, O.P.; Richard Bon Tempo, O.P.; Deacons Chris J. Weber; John Pippinger.
Res., 775 Harrison Ave., 70124-3192. Tel: 504-482-4156; Fax: 504-488-0906.
School—Tel: 504-482-4123; Fax: 504-486-3870.
Sisters 1; Lay Teachers 41; Students 654.
Catechesis/Religious Programs—Tel: 504-486-9731.
Students 151.

31—ST. FRANCES XAVIER CABRINI (1952), Most Rev. Dominic Carmon; Revs. Wayne C. Paysse; Joseph Thang Dinh Tran; Deacons John Paul Muhleisen; Norbert Gubert; Peter C. Rizzo.
Res., 5500 Paris Ave., 70122-2699. Tel: 504-288-4224; Fax: 504-288-2152.
School—1500 Prentiss Ave., 70122-2098. Tel: 504-288-4249; Fax: 504-283-8161.
Sisters 4; Lay Teachers 21; Students 304.

32—ST. FRANCIS OF ASSISI (1890), Rev. Desmond G. Crotty; Deacon Ames P. LeBlanc, Jr.
Res., 631 State St., 70118-5899. Tel: 504-891-4479; Fax: 504-891-4470.

33—ST. FRANCIS DE SALES (1870) (African American), Rev. Victor H. Cohea; Deacon Raymond Lewis.
Res., 2203 Second St., 70113-2545. Tel: 504-895-7749; Fax: 504-899-0434.
Catechesis/Religious Programs—Tel: 504-891-9544.
Students 60.

34—ST. GABRIEL THE ARCHANGEL (1954) (African American), Rev. Msgr. Douglas A. Doussan, Admin.; Rev. Bernard Schmaltz.
Office: 4700 Pineda St., 70126-3599. Tel: 504-282-0296; Fax: 504-288-8585.
Catechesis/Religious Programs—Tel: 504-288-7914. Dorothy Nelson, D.R.E.
Students 100.

35—ST. GERARD (1971), Rev. Pedro F. Nunez.
Res., 3037 Dauphine St., 70117-6724. Tel: 504-943-2456; Fax: 504-945-7200.

36—ST. HENRY (1856), Very Rev. Henry H. Engelbrecht, V.F.; Deacons Henry A. Garon; Raymond J. Guillot. In res., Rev. Wilfred F. Meridier.
Res., 812 General Pershing St., 70115-2797. Tel: 504-891-6359; Fax: 504-895-0486.

37—ST. JAMES MAJOR (1920), Rev. Leo A. Meyer. In res., Rev. Douglas C. Brougher.
Res., 3736 Gentilly Blvd., 70122-6199. Tel: 504-945-2165; Fax: 504-945-9899.
School—3774 Gentilly Blvd., 70122-6198. Tel: 504-945-1015; Fax: 504-945-1015.
Sisters 2; Lay Teachers 14; Students 281.

38—ST. JOAN OF ARC (1909) (African American), Rev. Peter C. Weiss, S.S.J. In res., Rev. Robert Allanach, O.M.I.; Deacon Irvin Stewart, Sr.
Res., 8321 Burthe St., 70118-1195. Tel: 504-866-7330; Fax: 504-866-1319.
School—Tel: 504-861-2887; Fax: 504-866-9588.
Sisters of Holy Family 4; Lay Teachers 11; Students 220.

39—ST. JOHN THE BAPTIST (1851), Rev. Matthias Moore, C.S.Sp.
Res., 1139 Oretha Castle Haley Blvd., 70113-1215. Tel: 504-525-1726; Fax: 504-522-0012.

40—ST. JOSEPH (1844). (Legal Title: St. Joseph Roman Catholic). Rev. Perry F. Henry, C.M.
Res., 1802 Tulane Ave., 70112-2246. Tel: 504-522-3186; Fax: 504-522-3171.

41—ST. JULIAN EYMARD (1952), Rev. Salvador Galvez; Deacon Harold Vincent.
Res., 2701 Lawrence St., 70114-3099. Tel: 504-367-7730; Fax: 504-367-2603.

42—ST. LEO THE GREAT (1920), Rev. Roger A. Swenson.
Res., 2916 Paris Ave., 70119-1840. Tel: 504-945-8750; Fax: 504-949-8899.
School—1501 Abundance St., 70119-2098. Tel: 504-943-1482; Fax: 504-944-5895.
Dominican Sisters (Cabra, Ireland) 2; Lay Teachers 21; Students 427.
Catechesis/Religious Programs—Tel: 504-945-8750; Fax: 504-949-8899.
Students 70.

43—ST. MARIA GORETTI (1965), Rev. Msgr. L. Earl Gauthreaux; Rev. Jaime G. Apolinares (Philippines); Deacons Peter E. Duffy; Ildefonso R. DeLeon.
Mailing Address: 7300 Crowder Blvd., 70127-1599. Tel: 504-242-7554; Fax: 504-242-0755.
School—(Nursery-PreK). Tel: 504-242-1313.
Lay Teachers 2; Students 14.
Catechesis/Religious Programs—Students 225.

44—ST. MARY OF THE ANGELS (1925), Rev. Bart Pax, O.F.M. In res., Rev. Andre McGrath, O.F.M.; Bros. Gordon Boykins, O.F.M.; Martin Humphreys, O.F.M., Pastoral Assoc.; Valerie Shields, Pastoral Assoc.
Res., 3501 N. Miro St., 70117-5899. Tel: 504-945-3186; Fax: 504-945-9115.
School—2225 Congress St., 70117-5898. Tel: 504-943-5687. Sr. Carmelita Mulry, S.H.Sp., Prin.
Lay Teachers 9; Students 214.

45—ST. MATTHIAS (1920) (African American), Revs. John Cisewski; James Schott. In res., Revs. Edmund Akordor (Ghana); John Asare-Dankwah; Deacon Jose A. Sierra.
Res., 4230 S. Broad St., 70125-3699. Tel: 504-822-3394; Fax: 504-822-3395.
Catechesis/Religious Programs—Students 89.

46—ST. MAURICE (1852), Rev. Urbano Gracias.
Res., 605 St. Maurice Ave., 70117-1598. Tel: 504-279-5231; Fax: 504-279-5232.

47—ST. MONICA (1924), Rev. Msgr. Lanaux J. Rareshide.
Res., 2327 S. Galvez St., 70125-3198. Tel: 504-821-9500; Fax: 504-821-9500.
School—2323 Galvez St., 70125-3199. Tel: 504-821-3321.
Sisters of the Blessed Sacrament 2; Religious 1; Lay Teachers 8; Students 185.
Catechesis/Religious Programs—Students 35.

48—ST. NICHOLAS OF MYRA (1971), Rev. Arthur J. Ginart.
Res., Rte. 6, Box 146-BE, 70129-9799. Tel: 504-662-5339; Fax: 504-662-5339.

49—ST. PATRICK (1833), Rev. Msgr. John P. Reynolds; Rev. Anthony J. White.
Res., 724 Camp St., 70130-3757. Tel: 504-525-4413; Fax: 504-568-1324.

50—ST. PAUL THE APOSTLE (1947) (African American), Rev. William Feldner, S.V.D.; Deacon Daniel P. Vincent.
Res., 6828 Chef Menteur Hwy., 70126-5297. Tel: 504-242-7934; Fax: 504-242-1777. [CEM]
School—Tel: 504-242-5962; Fax: 504-242-0584.
Lay Teachers 9; Students 205.
Catechesis/Religious Programs—Students 95.

51—ST. PETER CLAVER (1920) (African American), Rev. Michael P. Jacques, S.S.E.; Deacon Rudolph Rayfield. Pastoral Assocs.: Sr. Mary Anne Hebert, C.S.J.; Pearl Dupart; Bro. Peter Stanfield, S.S.E.; Rosie Papion.
Office: 1923 St. Philip St., 70116-2199. Tel: 504-822-8059; Fax: 504-822-9251.
School—1020 N. Prieur St., 70116-2194. Tel: 504-822-8191. Mr. Don Boucree, Prin.
Brothers 1; Lay Teachers 15; Students 285.
Catechesis/Religious Programs—Alena Boucree, D.R.E.
Students 230.

52—SS. PETER AND PAUL (1848), Rev. Michael Roberson; Rev. Msgr. Arthur W. Hauth, Pastor Emeritus.
Res., 2317 Burgundy St., 70117-8587. Tel: 504-945-1531; Fax: 504-945-1537.

53—ST. PHILIP THE APOSTLE (1949) (African American), Rev. Michael P. Jacques, S.S.E.; Deacon Raymond Rayfield, Sr.
Res., 3304 Metropolitan St., 70126-5799. Tel: 504-945-2122; Fax: 504-945-2128.
Catechesis/Religious Programs—Students 60.

54—ST. PIUS X (1953), Rev. Msgr. Clinton J. Doskey; Deacons Chris T. Weber; William A. Glennon.
Res., 6666 Spanish Fort Blvd., 70124-4398. Tel: 504-282-3332; Fax: 504-283-8984.
School—Tel: 504-282-2811.
Lay Teachers 30; Students 478.
Catechesis/Religious Programs—Students 100.

55—ST. RAPHAEL THE ARCHANGEL (1947), Rev. Horace L. Brignac, Jr.; Rev. Msgr. Vernon P. Aleman, Pastor Emeritus.
Res., 2212 Prentiss Ave., 70122-5399. Tel: 504-282-6494; Fax: 504-282-2955.
School—5601 Elysian Fields Ave., 70122-4286. Tel: 504-288-1474. Sr. Jean Held, S.C.C., Prin.
Sisters of Christian Charity 2; Lay Teachers 5; Students 168.

56—ST. RAYMOND (1927), Revs. Michael D. Wilson, S.S.J.; Henry J. Davis, S.S.J.; Deacons John B. Williams; Dwight Alexander.
Res., 3738 Paris Ave., 70122-2399. Tel: 504-288-1272; Fax: 504-283-3069.
School—Tel: 504-282-5563; Fax: 504-282-2344. Sr. Patricia Ann Williams, S.S.F., Prin.
Sisters of the Holy Family 4; Lay Teachers 12; Students 296.
Catechesis/Religious Programs—Students 90.

57—ST. RITA (1921), Revs. Henry J. Bugler; Rodney Anthony Ricard; Deacons Gerald K. Martinez; Wilbur A. Toups.
Res., 2729 Lowerline St., 70125-3599. Tel: 504-866-3621; Fax: 504-861-0338.
School—65 Fontainebleau Dr., 70125-3495. Tel: 504-866-1777; Fax: 504-861-8512.
Marianites of Holy Cross 7; Lay Teachers 5; Students 272.

58—ST. ROSE OF LIMA (1857), Rev. H. William Reed.
Res., 2545 Bayou Rd., 70119-2398. Tel: 504-945-3591; Fax: 504-945-3216.

59—ST. SIMON PETER (1986), Rev. Martin J. Smullen; Deacons Peter C. Rizzo; Daniel Haggerty, Jr.; Jesse A. Watley.
Office: 7600 Gannon Rd., 70128-1402. Tel: 504-243-9214; Fax: 504-243-9251.
Res., 14010 Kingswood Dr., 70128-2610. Tel: 504-242-3337.
School—Tel: 504-243-9241. Mrs. Camille Treaudo, Prin.

60—ST. STEPHEN (1849), Revs. James Garcia Ward, C.M.; Harold E. Dicharry, C.M.; Deacon Charles J. Smith, Jr. In res., Revs. Jerome Calcagno, C.M.; Gilbert R. Walker, C.M.; Perry Henry, C.M.; Bro. James Steinbach, C.M.
Res., 1025 Napoleon St., 70115-2898. Tel: 504-899-1378; Fax: 504-899-0480.
School—4310 Chestnut St., 70115-2790. Tel: 504-891-1927; Fax: 504-891-1928. Sr. Juanita Chenevert, D.C., Prin.
Daughters of Charity of St. Vincent de Paul 3; Lay Teachers 10; Students 279.

61—ST. THERESA OF AVILA (1848), Revs. Teodoro Agudo, O.F.M.Cap. (Spain); Eutiquiano Miguel, O.F.M.Cap.; Deacon Francis J. Fleischer.

Res., 1404 Erato St., 70130-4387. Tel: 504-525-4226; Fax: 504-525-6014.

62—ST. THERESA OF THE CHILD JESUS (1927), Rev. Quentin Moody; Deacon Herman Bastian.
Res., 3810 Leonidas St., 70118-4698. Tel: 504-482-1668; Fax: 504-486-8179.

63—ST. THOMAS THE APOSTLE. (University of New Orleans). Rev. Francis Berner; Deacon Eric Gamble.
Res., UNO Newman Center, 70148-0001. Tel: 504-288-6336; Fax: 504-288-6344.

64—ST. THOMAS MORE (1970). (The Community of St. Thomas More for Tulane Univ.). Revs. John J. Boll, O.P.; Marcelo Solorzano, O.P.; Deacon Joseph R. Rosato.
Res., 1037 Audubon St., 70118-5294. Tel: 504-866-0984; Fax: 504-865-1914.
Catechesis/Religious Programs—Students 105.

65—ST. VINCENT DE PAUL (1838), Rev. Pedro F. Nunez; Deacon Lawrence Keller.
Res., 3053 Dauphine St., 70117-6794. Tel: 504-943-5566; Fax: 504-943-5501.

OUTSIDE THE CITY OF NEW ORLEANS

Abita Springs, St. Tammany Parish, St. Jane de Chantal (1887), Rev. William J. MacCandless, O.S.B.; Deacons Frans Labranche, Jr.; Don Bourgeois.
Res., 22122 Main St., P.O. Box 187, 70420-0187. Tel: 504-892-1439; Fax: 504-871-9547. [JC]
Catechesis/Religious Programs—72049 Hickory St., 70420-3931. Tel: 504-893-3914.
Students 250.
Mission—Bush, St. Tammany Civil Parish, St. Michael the Archangel, Hwy. 41, Tel: 504-886-3868.

Ama, St. Charles Parish, St. Mark (1974), Rev. John M. Perino.
Res., P.O. Box 556, 70031-0556. Tel: 504-431-8505; Fax: 504-431-8506.
Catechesis/Religious Programs—Charlene Troxler, D.R.E.
Students 113.

Arabi, St. Bernard Parish, St. Louise De Marillac (1954), Rev. Edward M. Grice; Deacons Alvin C. Miester, Jr.; Alex J. Seruntine, Jr.
Res., 6800 Patricia St., 70032-1496. Tel: 504-271-4671; Fax: 504-271-7727.
School—Tel: 504-271-1677. Constance Thorn, Prin.
Congregation of the Most Holy Sacrament Sister 1; Lay Teachers 26; Students 464.

St. Robert Bellarmine (1964), Rev. Lich Van Nguyen; Deacon Curles P. Reeson.
Res., 408 Cougar Dr., 70032-2098. Tel: 504-279-8215; Fax: 504-277-7656.
School—815 Badger Dr., 70032-1996. Tel: 504-279-6466.
Lay Teachers 22; Students 514.
Catechesis/Religious Programs—Tel: 504-271-9112.
Students 75.

Avondale, Jefferson Parish, St. Bonaventure (1965), Rev. Dennis J. Hayes, III; Deacon J. Vernon Insley.
Res., 329 S. Jamie Blvd., 70094-2821. Tel: 504-436-1279; Fax: 504-436-1300.
Catechesis/Religious Programs—Tel: 504-436-0744. Trudy Cook, D.R.E.
Students 161.

Belle Chasse, Plaquemines Parish, Our Lady of Perpetual Help (1928), Revs. Michael J. Schneller; James Nguyen Bach; Deacon Charles P. Moore; Sr. Cynthia Sabathier, C.S.J.
Res., 8968 Hwy. 23, 70037-2296. Tel: 504-394-0314; Fax: 504-394-0376. [CEM]
School—Tel: 504-394-0757. Sr. Elizabeth Hebert, S.L.W., Prin.
Sisters 3; Lay Teachers 25; Students 276.
Catechesis/Religious Programs—Tel: 504-394-0314; Fax: 504-394-0314.
Students 260.

Bogalusa, Washington Parish, Annunciation B.V.M. (1907), Rev. Kevin Clark, O.S.B.; Deacon Charles Hartman.
Res., 517 Avenue B, 70427-3723. Tel: 504-732-4280; Fax: 504-735-1042.
School—511 Avenue C, 70427-3797. Tel: 504-735-6643; Fax: 504-735-6119.
Lay Teachers 15; Students 233.

Bridge City, Jefferson Parish, Holy Guardian Angels (1963), Rev. Msgr. J. Anthony Luminais.
Res., 1701 Bridge City Ave., P.O. Box 9069, 70094-9069. Tel: 504-436-4712; Fax: 504-436-4070.
Catechesis/Religious Programs—Students 162.

Buras, Plaquemines Parish, Our Lady of Good Harbor (1864), Rev. Msgr. Terry B. Becnel.
Mailing Address: 240 Buras River Rd., 70041-9188. Tel: 504-657-9873; Fax: 504-657-9878.
Catechesis/Religious Programs—Students 211.
Missions—Empire, Plaquemines Parish, St. Ann; Venice, Plaquemines Parish, St. Anthony. [CEM]

Chalmette, St. Bernard Parish, Our Lady of Prompt Succor (1951), Revs. Warren L. Cooper; Joseph Duc Dzien; Deacons Henry A. Cassou, Jr.; Julius Zimmer.
Res., 2320 Paris Rd., 70043-5098. Tel: 504-271-3441; Fax: 504-271-2927.
School—2305 Fenelon St., 70043-4951. Tel: 504-271-2953. Evelyn Kingston, Prin.
School Sisters of Notre Dame 2; Lay Teachers 37; Students 681.
Catechesis/Religious Programs—Tel: 504-271-1217. Brenda Tromatore, D.R.E.
Students 428.

Prince of Peace (1977), Revs. Walter J. Austin; Robert I. Guste; Deacon Frank W. Rhodes, Jr.
Res., 3700 Jean Lafitte Pkwy., 70043-1199. Tel: 504-271-1664; Fax: 504-279-8023.
Catechesis/Religious Programs—Tricia Hanzo, D.R.E.
Students 252.

St. Mark (1964), Very Rev. Alan R. Weseman, V.F.; Revs. Joseph Man Tran; Phillip G. Landry; Deacons Raymond Rivere; Albert A. Levy, III; Kenneth Madere.
Res., 3024 Charles Dr., 70043-3798. Tel: 504-279-6073; Fax: 504-279-9403.
School—Tel: 504-271-1694; Fax: 504-277-7195. Pam Truxillo, Prin.
Daughters of Divine Providence 2; Lay Teachers 28; Students 603.
Catechesis/Religious Programs—Tel: 504-277-2584. Sr. Pier Carla, F.D.P., D.R.E.
Students 561.
Convent—3100 Mumphrey Rd., 70043-3735. Tel: 504-279-4619; Fax: 504-279-4619. Daughters of Divine Providence

Covington, St. Tammany Parish, St. Peter (1843), Revs. William J. McGough; Patrick B. Wattigny; Deacons Carmelo Graffagnini; Charles Heine; Charles Read.
Res., 128 E. 19th St., 70433-3195. Tel: 504-892-2422; Fax: 504-898-1998.
School—Tel: 504-892-1831. Mrs. Sharon Coll, Prin.
Lay Teachers 30; Students 573.
Catechesis/Religious Programs—Tel: 504-893-2446.
Students 467.

Crown Point, Jefferson Parish, St. Pius X (1971), Rev. Terence Hayden.
Res., Rte. 1, Box 368, Marrero, 70072-9704. Tel: 504-689-2381; Fax: 504-689-7417.
Catechesis/Religious Programs—Students 89.

Des Allemands, St. Charles Parish, St. Gertrude (1955), Rev. Steven Leszczynski; Deacon Landry Matherne.
Res., P.O. Box 767, 70030-0767. Tel: 504-758-7542; Fax: 504-758-7591. [CEM]
Catechesis/Religious Programs—Tel: 504-758-1332. Sr. Bernadette Nguyen, D.R.E.
Students 157.

Destrehan, St. Charles Parish, St. Charles Borromeo (1723), Revs. John Phuc; Ray Hymel; Deacons Harry Schexnayder; Theodore Roussel.
Res., 13396 River Rd., P.O. Box 428, 70047-0428. Tel: 504-764-6383; Fax: 504-764-3948. [CEM]
School—Lay Teachers 31; Students 445.

Diamond, Plaquemines Parish, St. Jude (1981), Rev. John C. Hegarty, C.S.Sp.
Res., P.O. Box 36, Port Sulphur, 70083-0036. Tel: 504-564-2182; Fax: 504-564-2077.
School—Tel: 504-564-3773. Sr. Suzanne Clark, O.S.F., Prin.
Sisters of St. Francis of Perpetual Adoration 4; Lay Teachers 5; Students 160.

Edgard, St. John the Baptist Parish, St. John the Baptist (1770), Rev. Donald Duffy.
Res., 2361 Hwy. 18, 70049-9101. Tel: 504-497-3412; 497-8470; Fax: 504-497-3965. [CEM]
Catechesis/Religious Programs—Students 263.

Florissant, St. Bernard Parish, San Pedro Pescador (1966), Rev. John Patrick Grenham.
Church—P.O. Box 457, St. Bernard, 70085-0457. Tel: 504-676-3719; Fax: 504-676-9996.
Res., 205-B Florissant Hwy., St. Bernard, 70085-9703.
Catechesis/Religious Programs—Tel: 504-676-3565. D.R.E.: Mrs. Kristie Vollentine; Mrs. Carla Lee, (Youth).
Students 169.

Folsom, St. Tammany Parish, St. John the Baptist (1921), Rev. Jonathan DeFrange, O.S.B.; Deacon Clayton J. Guitterrez.
Res., 11345 St. John Church Rd., 70437-7155. Tel: 504-796-3806; Fax: 504-796-9554.
Catechesis/Religious Programs—Tel: 504-796-5507.
Students 141.

Franklinton, Washington Parish, Holy Family (1982), Rev. William H. Blank.
Res., 1213 14th Ave., P.O. Box 471, 70438-0471. Tel: 504-839-4040; Fax: 504-839-2429.

Garyville, St. John the Baptist Parish, St. Hubert, Rev. Charles J. Caluda; Deacon Joseph Mamou.
Res., P.O. Box K, 70051-0851. Tel: 504-535-2828; Fax: 504-535-1849.

Gretna, Jefferson Parish, St. Anthony (1920), Rev. Msgr. Gerard W. Poche; Rev. Louis A. Persac, (Retired). In res., Very Rev. Gerald L. Seiler, Jr.
Res., 924 Monroe St., 70053-2299. Tel: 504-368-6161; Fax: 504-362-7811.
School—Tel: 504-367-0689; Fax: 504-361-0054. Mrs. Marie K. Cannon, Prin.
Sisters of the Living Word 2; Lay Teachers 10; Students 283.
Catechesis/Religious Programs—Students 105.

St. Cletus (1965), Rev. Msgr. Martin van der Werff; Rev. Quang Nguyen; Sr. Mary Estelle Foucheaux, Pastoral Assoc.; Deacons Louis W. Stall; Peter B. Schlette; Elliott Arendt, Sr.
Res., 3600 Claire Ave., 70053-7699. Tel: 504-367-7951; Fax: 504-367-7928.
School—Tel: 504-366-3538. Mrs. Carolyn Morvant, Prin.
Lay Teachers 40; Students 598.
Catechesis/Religious Programs—Tel: 504-361-4805. Mrs. Ruth Susslin, D.R.E.
Students 230.

St. Joseph (1857), Revs. Francis J. Carabello; Ronald J. Braud.
Res., 610 Sixth St., 70053-6098. Tel: 504-368-1313; Fax: 504-368-6841.

Hahnville, St. Charles Parish, Our Lady of the Holy Rosary (1877), Rev. Bernard C. Francis.
Res., #1 Rectory Ln., 70057. Tel: 504-443-1793; Fax: 504-783-1974. [CEM]

Harahan, Jefferson Parish, St. Rita (1950), Revs. Frank J. Giroir; Joseph S. Palermo; Mr. Al Martin, Pastoral Assoc. & D.R.E.; Deacons Nolen J. LeBlanc; Nicholas L. Mistretta; Danny Flynn.
Res., 160 Imperial Woods Dr., 70123-4998. Tel: 504-737-2915; Fax: 504-737-2921.
School—194 Ravan Ave., 70123-4999. Tel: 504-737-0744. Mr. Thomas Becker, Prin.
Lay Teachers 24; Students 454.
Catechesis/Religious Programs—Students 150.

Harvey, Jefferson Parish,

1—INFANT JESUS OF PRAGUE, (1969), Rev. Msgr. Elmo L. Romagosa; Deacon Ferris Duet.
Res., 700 Maple St., 70058-4008. Tel: 504-368-1397; Fax: 504-368-0662.
Catechesis/Religious Programs—Students 98.

2—ST. JOHN BOSCO, (1983), Revs. Sidney Figlia, S.D.B.; Ernest Faggioni, S.D.B.
Res., 2114 Oakmere Dr., 70058-2275. Tel: 504-340-0444; Fax: 504-340-9521.
Catechesis/Religious Programs—Brenda C. Baker, D.R.E.
Students 160.

3—ST. MARTHA, (1973), Rev. William O'Riordan; Deacon Leslie D. Vincent.
Res., 2555 Apollo Dr., 70058-5813. Tel: 504-366-1604; Fax: 504-366-1100.

4—ST. ROSALIE, (1949), Revs. Thomas E. Ruekert, S.D.B.; Gregory Fishel, S.D.B. In res., Rev. Jonathan Parks, S.D.B.
Parish Offices:—600 2nd Ave., 70058-2728. Tel: 504-340-1962; Fax: 504-340-1546.
Res., 608 1st Ave., 70058-2799. Tel: 504-341-5656.
School—617 Second Ave., 70058-2798. Tel: 504-341-4342; Fax: 504-347-0271.
Middle School—2115 Oakmere Dr., 70058-2276. Tel: 504-348-9330; Fax: 504-348-9331.
Dominican Sisters (Cabra, Ireland) 3; Lay Teachers 50; Students 1,200.

Jefferson, Jefferson Parish, St. Agnes (1931), Revs. Peter O'Grady; Robustiano D. Morgia (Philippines); Deacons Piero Caserta; Nelvin Luke. In res., Rev. Msgr. Louis P. LeBourgeois.
Res., 3310 Jefferson Hwy., 70121-2699. Tel: 504-833-3366; Fax: 504-834-1532.
School—Lay Teachers 22; Students 409.

Kenner, Jefferson Parish,

1—NATIVITY OF OUR LORD, (1977) (Spanish), Rev. Danilo C. Digal; Deacons John LeDoux; Eddy Beckendorf; Roberto Mendieta.
Office: 3325 Loyola Dr., 70065-2567. Tel: 504-466-5016; Fax: 504-467-8575.
Catechesis/Religious Programs—Tel: 504-464-9664. Mrs. Donna Johnsen, D.R.E.
Students 230.

2—OUR LADY OF PERPETUAL HELP, (1869), Rev. Richard M. Miles.
Res., 1908 Short St., 70062-7599. Tel: 504-464-0361; Fax: 504-465-0930.
School—Tel: 504-464-0531; Fax: 504-464-0725. Ms. Christine Wick, Prin.
Sisters of Mercy 3; Lay Teachers 26; Students 447.

3—ST. ELIZABETH ANN SETON, (1981), Revs. Albert C. Ernst; Paul S. Hart; Deacons Andrea Capaci; Noel W. Martinsen; Garland Bourgeois.

Res., 4111 St. Blase Dr., P.O. Box 641000, 70065-1656. Tel: 504-468-1441; Fax: 504-468-3305.
School—Lay Teachers 13; Students 506.

4—St. Jerome, (1963), Revs. Robert C. Cavalier; Luis Emilio Henao; Deacons Daniel Cordes; Edgar Dragon; Luis Campuzano, Sr.; Ernesto Morales.
Res., 2400 33rd St., 70065-3899. Tel: 504-443-3174; Fax: 504-443-5499.
Catechesis/Religious Programs—Gail Bordelon, D.R.E.
Students 257.

Lacombe, St. Tammany Parish, Sacred Heart, Rev. Paul H. Desrosiers; Deacon James Biales.
Res., P.O. Box 1080, 70445-0338. Tel: 504-882-5229; Fax: 504-882-9034.

St. John of the Cross (1984), Rev. Msgr. Francis G. Boeshans; Deacon Joseph LeRose. In res., Rev. Kieran O'Hara, (Retired).
Res., 61051 Brier Lake Dr., 70445-2911. Tel: 504-882-3779; Fax: 504-882-9282.
Catechesis/Religious Programs—Students 142.

Lafitte, Jefferson Parish, St. Anthony (1936), Rev. John Ryan.
Res., Rte. 1, Box 499A, 70067-9714. Tel: 504-689-4101; Fax: 504-689-4102. [CEM]
Catechesis/Religious Programs—Tel: 504-689-2451. Esther Belsome, D.R.E.
Students 320.

La Place, St. John the Baptist Parish, Ascension of Our Lord (1979), Rev. Benjamin Piovan; Deacons Arthur Sandman, Sr.; Percy Vicknair; Paul H. Dupuy, Jr.
Res., 799 Fairway Dr., 70068-2007. Tel: 504-652-2615; Fax: 504-652-7291.
School—1809 Greenwood Dr., 70068-2098. Tel: 504-652-4532.
Lay Teachers 23; Students 420.
Catechesis/Religious Programs—Students 170.

St. Joan of Arc (1947), Revs. Robert G. Vincent; Michael N. Nguyen.
Res., P.O. Box 490, 70069-0490. Tel: 504-652-9100; Fax: 504-651-2920. [JC]
School—412 Fir St., 70068-4310. Tel: 504-652-6310. Sr. Mary Germaine, O.P., Prin.
Sisters of St. Dominic 2; Lay Teachers 43; Students 794.
Catechesis/Religious Programs—Tel: 504-651-0894. Mrs. Connie Cambre, D.R.E.
Students 411.

Luling, St. Charles Parish, Holy Family (1980), Rev. John P. Finn; Deacon Coy Landry.
Res., 155 Holy Family Ln., 70070-6103. Tel: 504-785-8585; Fax: 504-785-1167.
Catechesis/Religious Programs—D.R.E.: Harriet Williamson, (High School); Anita Hymel, (Grade School).
Students 584.

St. Anthony of Padua (1961), Rev. Patrick Gannon; Deacon Paul J. Donnaud. In res., Rev. Patrick J. R. Kennedy.
Res., 234 Angus Dr., 70070-9513. Tel: 504-785-8885; Fax: 504-785-8882.
Catechesis/Religious Programs—Tel: 504-785-0050.
Students 181.

Madisonville, St. Tammany Parish, St. Anselm (1962), Rev. Randy P. Roux; Deacon John Glover.
Res., P.O. Box 40, 70447-0040. Tel: 504-845-7342; Fax: 504-845-3076.
Catechesis/Religious Programs—Celie Clark, D.R.E.
Students 335.

Mandeville, St. Tammany Parish, Mary Queen of Peace (1988), Rev. Ronald L. Calkins; Deacons Anthony J. Ferretti; Dwight J. Johnson.
Res., 1501 W. Causeway Approach, 70471-3047. Tel: 504-626-6977; Fax: 504-626-6971.
School—Tel: 504-674-2466. Mrs. Rhonda Parenton, Prin.
Students 32.
Catechesis/Religious Programs—Students 520.

Our Lady of the Lake (1850), Rev. Msgr. Joseph L. Chotin; Rev. Dean Robins; Deacons Joseph Lazo; Harry C. Schmidt, Jr.; Louis N. Mire; Forrest Wallace.
Res., 2115 Jefferson St., 70448-5820. Tel: 504-626-5671; Fax: 504-626-5422.
School—Tel: 504-626-5678; Fax: 504-626-4337. Joseph Miller, Prin.
Lay Teachers 40; Students 751.
Catechesis/Religious Programs—Tel: 504-626-7901. Richard Beben, D.R.E.
Students 1000.

Marrero, Jefferson Parish,

1—Immaculate Conception, (1924), Rev. Msgr. Ray P. Hebert; Revs. Nicholas Pericone; Alberto Bermudez; Deacons Wilfred Robichaux, Jr.; Rodolfo Martinez. In res., Rev. Denver B. Pentecost.
Res., 4401 7th St., 70072-2099. Tel: 504-341-9516; Fax: 504-341-9517.
School—601 Avenue C, 70072-2098. Tel: 504-347-4409; Fax: 504-341-2766. Sr. Fernanda Rossi, F.M.A., Prin.
Salesian Sisters 3; Lay Teachers 44; Students 936.
High School—Immaculata, 537 Avenue D, 70072-2027. Tel: 504-341-6217; Fax: 504-341-6229. Sr. Rosann Ruiz, F.M.A., Prin.
Sisters 2; Lay Teachers 40; Students 536.
Catechesis/Religious Programs—Tel: 504-347-8449.
Students 185.

2—St. Agnes Le Thi Thanh (1995) (Vietnamese). Unassigned. (Personal Parish for Southeast Asians).
Res., 1000 Westwood Dr., 70072-2415. Tel: 504-347-4725; Fax: 504-340-2476.
Church—6851 8th St., 70072-2556. Rev. John Baptist Vu Han.
Missions—Avondale, Jefferson Civil Parish, Assumption of Mary, 172 Noel Dr., Avondale, 70094-2900. Rev. Andrew Tran Cao Tuong, Admin.; New Orleans, Jefferson Civil Parish, St. Joseph, 6450 Kathy Ct., New Orleans, 70131-7515. Rev. Joseph Pham Van Tue, Admin.
Catechesis/Religious Programs—1216 Ave. G, 70072-3750. Tel: 504-348-8206.
Students 940.

3—St. Joachim, (1985), Rev. Burnick J. Terrebonne; Deacon Charles Duhe.
Res., 5505 Barataria Blvd., 70072-6660. Tel: 504-341-9226; Fax: 504-340-8829.
Catechesis/Religious Programs—Tel: 504-347-6829. Mrs. Peggy Toyne, D.R.E.
Students 223.

4—St. Joseph the Worker, (1955) (African American), Rev. Paul G. McQuillen, S.S.E.; Deacon Herman J. Williams.
Res., 455 Ames Blvd., 70072-1599. Tel: 504-347-8438; Fax: 504-340-9538.
School—Tel: 504-347-3704; Fax: 504-347-0852. Dr. Theoclaire Ducksworth, Prin.
Lay Teachers 13; Students 265.
Catechesis/Religious Programs—Students 265.

5—The Visitation of Our Lady, (1963), Very Rev. Michael B. Fraser, V.F.; Rev. John Nhan Van Tran; Deacons Larry Murphy; Francis Minor.
Res., 3500 Ames Blvd., 70072-5699. Tel: 504-347-2203; Fax: 504-347-2223.
School—3520 Ames Blvd., 70072-5698. Tel: 504-347-3377; Fax: 504-341-5378. Mary Kitterman, Prin.
Lay Teachers 39; Students 842.
Catechesis/Religious Programs—Tel: 504-341-4499. Cheryl Tourelle, D.R.E.
Students 265.

Metairie, Jefferson Parish,

1—Our Lady of Divine Providence, (1965), Revs. Milton L. Reisch; Lance J. Campo; Deacons Fred C. Memleb, Jr.; Clarence Foret, Jr.; Barry Campeaux. In res., Rev. W. Wendell Sontheimer.
Res., 1000 N. Starrett Rd., 70003-5899. Tel: 504-466-4511; Fax: 504-466-4858.
School—917 N. Atlanta St., 70003-5898. Tel: 504-466-0591; Fax: 504-466-0671. Mrs. Shirley Bertucci, Prin.
Lay Teachers 35; Students 585.
Catechesis/Religious Programs—Mrs. Mary Le Bourgeois, D.R.E.
Students 270.

2—St. Angela Merici, (1964), Rev. Msgr. Crosby W. Kern, V.F.; Rev. Patrick B. Sanders; Deacons Gilbert R. Schmidt; Charles Attaway; Nicholas Chetta.
Res., 901 Beverly Gardens Dr., 70002-5085. Tel: 504-835-0324; Fax: 504-834-9709.
School—835 Melody Dr., 70002-5095. Tel: 504-835-8491; Fax: 504-835-4463. Jim Campbell, Prin.
Lay Teachers 26; Students 616.
Catechesis/Religious Programs—Tel: 504-837-9347.
Students 80.

3—St. Ann Church and Shrine, (1971), Rev. Msgr. Joseph E. Bourgeois; Rev. Jose Roel G. Lungay (Philippines); Deacon Phillip E. Doolen.
Res., 4920 Loveland St., 70006-4099. Tel: 504-455-7071; Fax: 504-455-7076.
School—4921 Meadowdale St., 70006-4098.
Lay Teachers 70; Students 1200.

4—St. Benilde, (1964), Revs. Carroll E. Heffner; Joseph Dau Van Nguyen; Deacons Biaggio DiGiovanni; Clifford S. Wright; Richard Brady.
Res., 1901 Division St., 70001-2798. Tel: 504-834-4980; Fax: 504-831-5810.
School—1801 Division St., 70001-2799. Tel: 504-833-9894; Fax: 504-834-4380. Mrs. Cheryl Orillion, Prin.
Lay Teachers 40; Students 662.
Catechesis/Religious Programs—Students 95.

5—St. Catherine of Siena, (1921), Revs. James Lohan; James J. Jeanfreau, Jr.; Deacons Michael Coney; Jere Crago; Sr. Rose Mary Wessel, M.S.C., Pastoral Assoc.
Res., 105 Bonnabel Blvd., 70005-3798. Tel: 504-835-9343; 835-5491; Fax: 504-835-1525.
School—400 Codifer Blvd., 70005-3797. Tel: 504-831-1166; Fax: 504-833-8982. Sr. Imelda Moriarty, Prin.
Sisters of Charity of the Incarnate Word 4; Lay Teachers 63; Students 1,160.
Catechesis/Religious Programs—Tel: 504-835-9343; Fax: 504-835-1525.
Students 41.

6—St. Christopher the Martyr, (1947), Revs. H. J. Adams, Jr.; Kenneth Harney; Charles L. Mueller; Deacons Charles Duke; S. J. Calamia.
Res., 309 Manson Ave., 70001-4898. Tel: 504-837-8214; Fax: 504-837-8303.
School—(Grades PreK-8) 3900 Derbigny St., 70001-4999. Tel: 504-837-6871; Fax: 504-834-0522. Ruth Meche, Prin.
Lay Teachers 35; Students 867.
Catechesis/Religious Programs—Tel: 504-831-7691. Doris Marse, D.R.E.
Students 93.

7—St. Clement of Rome, (1965), Rev. Msgr. Ralph E. Carroll; Rev. David Dufour; Deacons Kenneth Boe; Ed Dorvin; Jerry Harrison; Jeff Fariss.
Res., 4317 Richland Ave., 70002-3097. Tel: 504-887-7821; Fax: 504-454-3906.
School—3978 W. Esplanade Ave., 70002-3099. Tel: 504-888-0386; Fax: 504-885-8273. Glenn Gennaro, Prin.
Lay Teachers 28; Students 576.
Catechesis/Religious Programs—Students 160.

8—St. Edward the Confessor, (1964), Revs. Gilmer J. Martin; Amaldoss; Vien The Nguyen; Deacons A. David Warriner, Jr.; Gerard J. Fasullo, Sr.; August Mendel. Parish Office: 4921 W. Metairie Ave., 70001-4466. Tel: 504-888-0703; Fax: 504-455-5443.
School—Tel: 504-888-6353. Sr. Mary de Lourdes, S.L.W., Prin. & D.R.E.
Sisters of the Living Word 2; Lay Teachers 26; Students 601.
Catechesis/Religious Programs—Students 79.

9—St. Francis Xavier, (1924), Revs. Andrew C. Taormina; Thomas Kinney; Deacons Paul Nalty; Charles E. Coudrain, Jr.
Res., 448 Metairie Rd., 70005-4371. Tel: 504-834-0340; 837-4733; Fax: 504-837-8735.
School—215 Betz Ave., 70005-4167. Tel: 504-833-1471; Fax: 504-833-1498. Steve Labranche, Prin.
Lay Teachers 25; Students 460.
Catechesis/Religious Programs—444 Metairie Rd., 70005-4307. Tel: 504-834-0348.
Students 120.

10—St. Lawrence the Martyr, (1958), Rev. Richard N. Maughan; Deacons Randall L. Engel; Sterling Ohlmeyer; Alfred Zeringue.
Res., 2525 Maine Ave., 70003-5446. Tel: 504-466-6236; Fax: 504-467-4945.
School—2505 Maine Ave., 70003-5498. Tel: 504-469-5262; Fax: 504-469-5293. Louise A. Olsen, Ed.D., Prin.
Lay Teachers 11; Students 223.
Catechesis/Religious Programs—Tel: 504-466-8344.
Students 108.

11—St. Louis King of France, (1947), Rev. Msgr. Joseph O. Lorio; Rev. Gerard Stapleton; Deacon Wilbur Martinez. In res., Rev. Lawrence A. deMaria.
Res., 1609 Carrollton Ave., 70005-1498. Tel: 504-834-9977; Fax: 504-834-9979.
School—1600 Lake Ave., 70005-1499. Tel: 504-833-8224; Fax: 504-838-9938.
Lay Teachers 31; Students 537.

12—St. Mary Magdalen, (1955), Rev. Msgr. Robert D. Massett; Rev. Nghiem Vinh Nguyen; Deacons Charles Nunez; Angeles Robin.
Res., 6425 W. Metairie Ave., 70003-4395. Tel: 504-733-0922; Fax: 504-733-0869.
School—6421 W. Metairie Ave., 70003-4395. Tel: 504-733-1433. Sr. Amelia Ibarra, Prin.
Teresians Sisters 2; Lay Teachers 28; Students 655.
Catechesis/Religious Programs—Students 275.

13—St. Philip Neri, (1960), Revs. Lee John Saloy; James Richard Day; Deacons Christopher S. Bertucci, Jr.; Thomas E. Caffery, Jr.; Edward R. Cannon; Paul A. Cimino.
Res., 6500 Kawanee Ave., 70003-3298. Tel: 504-887-5535; Fax: 504-885-6259.
School—6600 Kawanee Ave., 70003-3199. Tel: 504-887-5600; Fax: 504-456-6857.
Lay Teachers 35; Students 629.
Catechesis/Religious Programs—Tel: 504-889-0089.
Students 142.

Norco, St. Charles Parish, Sacred Heart of Jesus (1959), Rev. John J. Marse.
Res., 401 Spruce St., P.O. Box 515, 70079-2197. Tel: 504-764-6503; Fax: 504-725-0512.
School—Tel: 504-764-9958; Fax: 504-764-0041. Colleen S. Remont, Prin.

Lay Teachers 13; Students 240.
Catechesis/Religious Programs—Tel: 504-764-6503; Fax: 504-725-0512.
Students 201.

Paradis, St. Charles Parish, St. John the Baptist (1971), Rev. Msgr. James C. Moragne.
Res., P.O. Box 1498, 70080-1498. Tel: 504-758-2668; Fax: 504-758-2901.
Catechesis/Religious Programs—Students 194.

Pearl River, St. Tammany Parish, SS. Peter and Paul (1970), Rev. Bac-Hai Viet Tran; Deacon John F. Howard.
Res., 66009 St. Mary Dr., 70452-5705. Tel: 504-863-7935; Fax: 504-863-5431.
Catechesis/Religious Programs—Students 162.

Pointe a la Hache, Plaquemines Parish, St. Thomas (1844) (African American), Rev. Thomas J. Miller, C.S.Sp.
Res., P.O. Box 98, 70082-0098. Tel: 504-333-4465; Fax: 504-333-9933.
Mission—Braithwaite, Plaquemines Parish, Assumption of the Blessed Virgin, 6951 Hwy. 39, Braithwaite, 70040-0063. Tel: 504-682-5607. [CEM]

Port Sulphur, Plaquemines Parish, St. Patrick (1956), Rev. John T. Hinton.
Res., 28698 Hwy. 23, 70083-9623. Tel: 504-564-3284; Fax: 504-564-3108. [CEM]
Catechesis/Religious Programs—Tel: 504-564-2803.
Students 126.
Mission—Potash, Plaquemines Parish, St. Joseph.

Reserve, St. John the Baptist Parish, Our Lady of Grace (1937), Rev. George W. Burden, S.S.J.; Bro. Peter J. McLaughlin, S.S.J.
Res., 778 Hwy. 44, 70084-0464. Tel: 504-536-2613; Fax: 504-536-1819.
School—Ms. Wilhelmina Armour, Admin.; Ms. Olivia French. Lay Teachers 9; Students 163.
Catechesis/Religious Programs—Myrtle Ann Lucas, D.R.E.
Students 139.

St. Peter (1864), Very Rev. Rodney P. Bourg, V.F.; Rev. Herbert J. Kiff, Jr.; Deacon David W. Farinelli.
Res., 1550 Hwy. 44, P.O. Box 435, 70084-0435. Tel: 504-536-2887; Fax: 504-536-7078. [CEM]
School—Tel: 504-536-4296. Helena Cupit, Prin.
Lay Teachers 10; Students 169.
Catechesis/Religious Programs—Students 215.

River Ridge, Jefferson Parish, St. Matthew the Apostle (1959), Rev. Brendan Morgan; Deacons Russell LeBlanc; Dan Dorsey; Roland Bienvenu.
Res., 10021 Jefferson Hwy., 70123-2498. Tel: 504-737-4537; Fax: 504-737-4033.
School—Tel: 504-737-4604; Fax: 504-738-7985.
Lay Teachers 31; Students 629.
Catechesis/Religious Programs—Students 107.

St. Benedict, St. Tammany Parish, St. Benedict (1970), Rev. Marian E. Larmann, O.S.B.
Res., Smith-Stafford Rd., 70457-9999. Tel: 504-892-1216; Fax: 504-892-4211.
Catechesis/Religious Programs—Tel: 504-892-0784.
Students 175.

St. Bernard, St. Bernard Parish, St. Bernard (1787), Rev. Donald M. Byrnes.
Res., 2805 Bayou Rd., P.O. Box 70085-0220, 70085-9748. Tel: 504-682-5493; 682-3709; Fax: 504-682-8915. [CEM]

Slidell, St. Tammany Parish,

1—Our Lady of Lourdes, (1890), Rev. Msgr. Howard H. Hotard; Deacon Charles B. Faler, Jr.
Res., 3924 Berkley Ave., 70458-5198. Tel: 504-643-4137; Fax: 504-643-1675.
School—345 Westchester Pl., 70458-5299. Tel: 504-643-3230; Fax: 504-645-0648. Mr. Robert V. Kiefer, Jr., Prin.
Sisters 1; Lay Teachers 24; Students 539.
Catechesis/Religious Programs—Tel: 504-643-1742. Mrs. Patricia S. Andrews, D.R.E.
Students 425.

2—St. Genevieve, (1968), Rev. Mark Lomax; Deacon George Menges.
Res. and Mailing Address: 58203 Hwy. 433, 70460-3121. Tel: 504-643-3832; Fax: 504-649-5294.
Catechesis/Religious Programs—Tel: 504-641-5220. Claire Campbell, D.R.E.
Students 314.

3—St. Luke the Evangelist, (1982), Revs. Adrian B. Hall; Rhenne A. Cervantes (Philippines); Deacons Harold J. Burke; Robert Trainor.
Office: 910 Cross Gates Blvd., 70461-8414. Tel: 504-641-6429; Fax: 504-847-0742.
Catechesis/Religious Programs—Tel: 504-641-2570.
Students 800.

4—St. Margaret Mary, (1965), Rev. Msgr. Richard L. Carroll; Revs. Joseph Benson; Thomas Gallagher, S.P.S.; Deacons Clarence Vicroy; John C. Weber; Robert Binney.
Res., 1050 Robert Blvd., 70458-2098. Tel: 504-643-6124; Fax: 504-643-6126.
School—Tel: 504-643-4612. Mr. Bobby Ohler, Prin.
Sisters 2; Lay Teachers 32; Students 758.
Catechesis/Religious Programs—Tel: 504-649-3055.
Students 720.

Terrytown, Jefferson Parish, Christ the King (1963), Revs. Lawrence A. Mecker; Jose Ladra; Deacons Cornelius Armshaw; James Swiler; Robert G. Beaumont, Sr.
Res., 535 Deerfield Rd., 70056-2899. Tel: 504-361-1500; Fax: 504-361-0632.
School—Tel: 504-367-3601; Fax: 504-367-3679.
Lay Teachers 24; Students 536.
Catechesis/Religious Programs—Students 234.

Violet, St. Bernard Parish, Our Lady of Lourdes (1916), Revs. Frank J. Lipps; Mauro Raul Venust Lobo (India); Sr. Jeanne Moore, O.P., Pastoral Assoc.; Deacon William Chiappetta.
Res., 6305 E. St. Bernard Hwy., 70092-9506. Tel: 504-682-3046; Fax: 504-682-4470.
Catechesis/Religious Programs—6413 E. St. Bernard Hwy., 70092-9508. Tel: 504-682-0919.
Students 403.

Waggaman, Jefferson Parish, Our Lady of the Angels (1978), Rev. Paul Nguyen Van Tung; Deacon Gilbert Smith.
Res., 139 Herman St., 70094-2404. Tel: 504-436-4459; Fax: 504-436-4459.
Catechesis/Religious Programs—D.R.E.: Mrs. Rhetta Hebert; Mr. Augustus Alby.
Students 162.

Westwego, Jefferson Parish, Our Lady of Prompt Succor (1920), Rev. Anthony M. Serio; Deacon Ernest F. Elfer, Jr.
Res., 146 Fourth St., 70094-4297. Tel: 504-341-9522; Fax: 504-341-5957. [CEM]
School—531 Avenue A, 70094-4294. Tel: 504-341-9505; Fax: 504-341-9508. Sr. Rose Zanella, F.M.A., Superior; Sr. Dolores Riojas, F.M.A., Prin.
Sisters 3; Lay Teachers 19; Students 405.
Catechesis/Religious Programs—Students 348.

Non-Parochial Churches & Chapels

New Orleans, Orleans Parish,

1—Holy Trinity Church, (1847). (Chapel of Ease). Rev. Pedro F. Nunez.
Church—721 St. Ferdinand St., 70117-7395. Tel: 504-943-5566; Fax: 504-943-5501.

2—Our Lady of Prompt Succor National Shrine Church, Deacon Charles E. Coudrain, Jr.
Church—2635 State St., 70118-6339. Tel: 504-866-1472.

3—St. Mary Church, (1845). (Shrine of St. Lazarus of Jerusalem). Rev. Msgr. Alvin J. O'Reilly, Rector.
Church—1116 Chartres St., 70116-2596. Tel: 504-529-3040; Fax: 504-529-2001.

4—St. Mary's Assumption, (1858), Rev. Charles R. Landry, C.SS.R.
Church—2030 Constance St., 70130-5099. Tel: 504-522-6748; Fax: 504-523-3734.

5—Chapel of the Vietnamese Martyrs, (1978) (Vietnamese), Rev. Msgr. Dominic Mai Thanh Luong.
Church—14400 Peltier Dr., 70129-1713. Tel: 504-254-5660; Fax: 504-254-9250.

Pilgrimage Shrines

New Orleans, Orleans Parish, Our Lady of Prompt Succor National Shrine, Deacon Charles E. Coudrain, Jr.
Res., 2635 State St., 70118-6339. Tel: 504-866-1472.

St. Roch's Chapel in St. Roch's Cemetery,
Res., 1725 St. Roch Ave., 70117-8223. Tel: 504-596-3050; Fax: 504-596-3055.

Shrine of St. Lazarus of Jerusalem, Rev. Msgr. Alvin J. O'Reilly, Rector.
Church—1116 Chartres St., 70116-2596. Tel: 504-529-2651; Fax: 504-529-2001.

Metairie, Orleans Parish, St. Ann Shrine, Rev. Joseph E. Bourgeois.
Church—4920 Loveland, 70002-4099. Tel: 504-455-7071; Fax: 504-455-7076.

Non-Parochial Community

New Orleans, Orleans Parish, Byzantine Catholic Mission (1978). Ruthenian Rite Jurisdiction. Rev. Ellis L. DePriest, S.M., Admin.
Res
Church—3801 Monroe St., 70118-3490. Tel: 504-524-5192.

Chaplains of Public Institutions

Hospitals

New Orleans. *Charity Hospital,* 1532 Tulane Ave., 70140-1015. Tel: 504-568-3262. Rev. Eutiquiano Miguel, O.F.M.Cap., Chap.

Children's Hospital, 200 Henry Clay Ave., 70118-5799. Tel: 504-899-9511; Fax: 504-896-9707. Chaplains: Deacons Roland Bienvenu Tel: 504-737-8166; Charles J. Smith, Jr. Tel: 504-271-5124.

F. Edward Herbert Hospital. Vacant. No. 1 Sanctuary Dr., 70114-1500. Tel: 504-363-2200.

Jo Ellen Smith Convalescent Center, 4502 General Meyer Ave., 70114-3531. Tel: 504-361-7923. Deacon Robert G. Beaumont, S.R.

Memorial Medical Center. Mid-City Campus, 301 N. Jefferson Davis Pkwy., 70119-5397. Tel: 504-483-5000. Revs. Clement Monroe, C.SS.R., Chap.; Nicholas F. Husain.

Memorial Medical Center. Uptown Campus, 2700 Napoleon Ave., 70115-6996. Tel: 504-899-9311. Revs. Nicholas F. Husain, Chap., Tel: 504-891-8369; Jeffrie S. Reynolds.

Methodist Hospital, 5620 Read Rd., 70127-0103. Tel: 504-244-5100. Deacon John P. Muhleisen, Chap., Tel: 504-282-5114.

Touro Infirmary, 1401 Foucher St., 70115-3593. Tel: 504-897-7011. Rev. Douglas C. Brougher, Chap., Tel: 504-897-7011; 945-5878; Deacon Charles E. Coudrain, Jr., Assoc. Chap., Tel: 504-833-0221.

Transitional Hospital Corporation Facility, 3601 Coliseum St., 70115-3687. Tel: 504-899-1555; Fax: 504-899-1509. Chaplains: Deacons Richard E. Deichmann; William A. Glennon.

United Medical Center. Attended from St. Vincent de Paul Parish. 3419 St. Claude Ave., 70117-6198. Tel: 504-948-8200.

University Hospital, 2021 Perdido St., 70112-1396. Tel: 504-588-3000. Rev. Vincent Bechamps, O.SS.T., Chap., Tel: 504-588-3175.

Veterans Affairs Medical Center, 1601 Perdido St., 70146-2000. Tel: 504-568-0811. Chaplains: Revs. Joseph D. Laboon; Lawrence DeMaria.

Chalmette. *Chalmette Medical Centers,* 9001 Patricia St., 70043-1799. Tel: 504-277-8011. 801 Virtue St., 70043-1298. Tel: 504-277-7711. Deacon Raymond H. Rivere, Chap.

Covington. *Lakeview Regional Medical Center,* 95 E. Fairway Dr., 70433. Tel: 504-867-3800. Chaplains: Deacons Harry C. Schmidt, Jr.; Louis N. Mire.

Gretna. *Meadowcrest Hospital,* 2500 Belle Chasse Hwy., 70056-7127. Tel: 504-392-3131. Deacon Leslie D. Vincent, Dir. Pastoral Care.

Jefferson. *Elmwood Medical Center,* 1221 S. Clearview Pkwy., 70121-1029. Tel: 504-734-1900; Fax: 504-736-4901. Rev. Lawrence Pandolfo, O.P., Chap.

Ochsner Foundation Hospital, 1516 S. Clearview Pkwy., 70121-2484. Tel: 504-842-3000. Rev. Wilfred F. Meridier, Chap., Tel: 504-899-4660.

Mandeville. *Southeast Louisiana Hospital,* P.O. Box 3850, 70470-3850. Tel: 504-626-6317; Fax: 504-626-6658. Rev. Msgr. Marion Schutten, Chap., Tel: 504-892-9493; Deacon Robert Binney, Assoc.

Marrero. *West Jefferson General Hospital,* 4500 11th St., 70072-3191. Tel: 504-347-5511. Rev. Denver B. Pentecost, Chap.

Wynhoven Health Care Center, 1050 Medical Center Blvd., 70072-3170. Tel: 504-347-0777. Rev. Denver B. Pentecost, Chap.

Metairie. *Columbia Lakeside Hospital,* 4700 S. I-10 Service Rd., 70001. Tel: 504-885-3342. Deacon August B. Mendel, Chap.

Doctors Hospital of Jefferson, 4320 Houma Blvd., 70002-2973. Tel: 504-456-5555. Deacon Charles Duke, Chap.

East Jefferson General Hospital, 4200 Houma Blvd., 70002-2970. Tel: 504-454-4000. Rev. Charles L. Mueller, Chap.; Deacon Raymond E. Heap, Assoc. Chap.

Slidell. *Greenbriar Nursing & Convalescent Home,* 505 Robert Rd., 70458-1699. Tel: 504-643-6900. Chaplains: Rev. Msgr. Richard L. Carroll Tel: 504-643-6124; Revs. Joseph A. Benson; Thomas Gallagher, S.P.S.

Greenery Neurologic Rehabilitation Center at Slidell, 1400 W. Lindberg Dr., 70458-3193. Tel: 504-641-4985. Chaplains: Rev. Msgr. Richard L. Carroll Tel: 504-643-6124; Revs. Joseph A. Benson; Thomas Gallagher, S.P.S.

Guest House of Slidell Nursing Home, 1051 Robert Rd., 70458-2011. Tel: 504-643-5630. Chaplains: Rev. Msgr. Richard L. Carroll Tel: 504-643-6124; Revs. Joseph A. Benson; Thomas Gallagher, S.P.S.

North Shore Living Center, 106 Medical Center Dr., 70461-7833. Tel: 504-643-0307. Rev. Adrian B. Hall, Chap.

North Shore Regional Medical Center, 100 Medical Center Dr., 70461-7833. Tel: 504-649-7070. Rev. Adrian B. Hall, Chap.

Slidell Memorial Hospital. Attended from Slidell/Lacombe area. 1001 Gause Blvd., 70458-2987. Tel: 504-643-2200.

Colleges and Universities

NEW ORLEANS. *Delgado College,* 615 City Park Ave., 70119. Tel: 504-288-6336. Rev. Francis Berner, Chap.; Deacon Eric Gamble, Assoc. Chap.

Delgado Community College, School of Nursing, 4133 Banks St., 70119-6883. Tel: 504-486-6631. Rev. Louis E. Meyers, S.J., Chap.

Louisiana State University Medical Center, 4133 Banks St., 70119-6883. Tel: 504-486-6631. Rev. Louis E. Meyers, S.J., Chap.

Southern University in New Orleans, UNO Newman Center, 70148-0001. Tel: 504-288-6336. Rev. Francis Berner, Chap.; Bro. Thomas Ward, F.S.C., Assoc. Chap.

Tulane-Newcomb, 1037 Audubon St., 70118-5294. Tel: 504-866-0984. Revs. John J. Boll, O.P.; Marcelo Solorzano, O.P.

University of New Orleans, UNO Newman Center, 70148-0001. Tel: 504-288-6336. Rev. Francis Berner, Chap.

Prisons

NEW ORLEANS. *Orleans Parish Correctional Center,* 521 S. Broad St., 70119-7490. Tel: 504-822-8000. Chaplains: Rev. Theodore M. Kalamaja, S.J.; Deacons Joseph Mamon; Randolph J. Crochet, Jr.; Jeffrey Fariss; Jose A. Sierra.

Orleans Parish House of Detention, 2735 Perdido St., 70119-7390. Tel: 504-822-8000. Rev. Thomas Mulcrone, S.J., Chap., Pastoral Ministers: Sr. Lilianne Flavin, O.P.; Sr. Victor Allain, R.S.M.

ANGIE. *Washington Correctional Institute,* 27268 Hwy. 21, 70426-3030. Tel: 504-848-5232. Deacon Charles Hartman, Chap.

CHALMETTE. *St. Bernard Parish Prison,* St. Bernard Courthouse, 70043-4793. Tel: 504-279-8823. Deacon Alex J. Seruntine, Jr., Chap.

GRETNA. *Jefferson Parish Correctional Center,* P.O. Box 388, 70054-0388. Tel: 504-368-5360, Ext. 109. Chaplains: Rev. Robert J. Ratchford, S.J.; Deacons Louis Stall; Ralph Fray.

HARVEY. *Rivarde Juvenile Detention Home,* 1525 Manhattan Blvd., 70058-3405. Tel: 504-392-2097. Deacon Ralph Fray, Chap.

MANDEVILLE. *St. Tammany Parish Prison.* c/o St. Joseph Abbey, St. Benedict, 70457-9999. Tel: 504-892-1800. Chaplains: Rev. Daniel Cobb, O.S.B.; Deacon Charles Read, Jr. Tel: 504-892-8324.

On Duty Outside the Archdiocese:
Reverend Fathers—
Calkins, Arthur B., Villa Stritch, Via della Nocetta, 63, 00164, Rome, Italy
Fernandez, Luis J., VA Medical Center, 4165 D Indian Runn Dr., Dayton, OH 45415
Grennan, Thomas J., Incarnate Word Convent, 1101 N.E. Water St., Victoria, TX 77901
Mongeon, Peter M., 1410 West St., Wrentham, MA 02093
Nguyen, Michael Joseph Vinh Ngoc, Rome, Italy
Picado, Rodrigo, 50 Vs, E. Cortel, Curridabat, San Jose, Costa Rica
Planea, John (Philippines)

Military Chaplains:
Reverend Fathers—
Dixon, James R., U.S.A.F., 380 Winchester Pl., Fairview Heights, IL 62208
Highfill, H. Brian, U.S.A.F., PSC 80, Box 12349, APO AP, 96367-2349
O'Neill, Michael F., U.S.A.F., SMC/HC, 325 Challenger Way, Ste. 1090, Los Angeles AFB, CA 90245-4677
Sizelove, Dennis M., PSC 94, Box 93, APO-AE, 09824
Young, Bernard L., VA Medical Center, 6205 N. 21st Dr., Phoenix, AZ 85015

Unassigned:
Reverend Monsignors—
Rodi, Thomas J., Vicar General
Reverend Fathers—
Duffy, Stephen
Gilbride, Thomas
O'Donnell, William J., Metropolitan Tribunal

Absent on Leave:
Reverend Fathers—
Calamari, Paul
Keane, Patrick
Manko, Rodney A.
Schmaltz, Bernard W., (Administrative Leave)

Retired:
Reverend Monsignors—
Aleman, Vernon P., Chateau de Notre Dame, 2832 Burdette St., New Orleans, LA 70125
Bane, Raymond T., P.O. Box 1550, Paradis, LA 70080-1550
Boudreaux, Edward L., 1342 Moss St., New Orleans, LA 70119
Dowling, Thomas C., 303 Jeff Davis, Waveland, MS 39576
Duke, Charles J., 4845 Meadowdale St., Metairie, LA 70006
Hauth, Arthur W., Wynhoven Health Care Center, Marrero, LA 70072
Iverson, Stanley J., 5501 Tullis Dr., Bldg. 13-108, New Orleans, LA 70131
Landry, Michael, 36405 Old Bayou Liberty Rd., Slidell, LA 70460
Martin, Harrison A., 349 Bonnabel Blvd., Metairie, LA 70005
O'Reilly, Alvin, 1116 Chartres St., New Orleans, LA 70116
Reid, Marion M., 4665 Lafaye St., New Orleans, LA 70122
Roeten, Winus, 9512 Kuepferle Ct., River Ridge, LA 70123
Woods, Earl C., 1438 Verna St., New Orleans, LA 70119
Reverend Fathers—
Arbizu, Juventino, 41 Calle, 12-29 Villasol, Zona 12, Guatemala City, Guatemala
Barattini, John H., Casella Postale 79, 16043, Chiavari, Italy
Bruns, J. Edgar, Notre Dame Seminary, 2901 S. Carrollton Ave., New Orleans, LA 70118
Dabria, Jerry J., 401 S. Gatehouse Dr., Apt. G, Metairie, LA 70001-2039
De La Pinera, Fernando, Casa Sacerdotal, Plaza Bendicho, 9, Almeria, 14001 Spain
Gonzales, Gabriel, 4011 Gen. Pershing St., New Orleans, LA 70125
Grennan, Thomas J., 431 First St., Refugio, TX 78377
Hajtas, Francis, Karlsruherstrasse 9, Heidelberg, Germany
Kennedy, Patrick J.R., 234 Angus Dr., Luling, LA 70070
Lamendola, Francis S., 2820 Burdette St., New Orleans, LA 70125
Mele, Rudolph, 2832 Burdette St., New Orleans, LA 70125
Mitchell, Royce, 1512 Gardena Dr., New Orleans, LA 70122
Monzillo, Oneil, 532 Indian Bluff, Las Vegas, NV 89128
Ngo, Joseph Linh Duy, 2711 Barrington St., Arlington, TX 76014-2101
Perera, Denzil, 1342 Moss St., New Orleans, LA 70119-2998
Perkovic, Anton, 446 Adair St., Mandeville, LA 70448
Persac, Louis A., 924 Monroe St., Gretna, LA 70053
Pieris, Timothy, 6779 Canal Blvd., New Orleans, LA 70124
Pijoan, L. Adrian M. Figuerola, St. Augustine Home, 2345 W. 86th St., Indianapolis, IN 46260
Qui, Vincent, 421 Pat Dr., Avondale, LA 70094
Sontheimer, W. Wendell, 1029 N. Atlanta St., Metairie, LA 70003
Texada, David Ker, 1923 Salem St., Alexandria, LA 71301-3840
Tranchina, Joseph, 2832 Burdette St., New Orleans, LA 70125
Trinchard, Paul, 446 Crystal St., New Orleans, LA 70124
Vitte, Jules, 38 Grande Rue, 25300, Les Fourges, France
Walsh, Laurence, 8035 S. Quebec St., Englewood, CO 80112

Permanent Deacons:
Alexander, Dwight, St. Raymond (Orleans Parish Prison), New Orleans
Arendt, Elliott, Sr., St. Cletus, Gretna
Armshaw, Cornelius, Christ the King, Terrytown
Attaway, Charles, St. Angela Merici, Metairie
Baham, Philip C., (On Leave)
Balderas, Robert, Sr., National Dir., U.S. Apostleship of the Sea, Washington DC
Bastian, Herman, St. Theresa of the Child Jesus, New Orleans
Beaumont, Robert G., Christ the King, Terrytown
Beckendorf, Edward, Nativity of Our Lord, Kenner
Bertucci, Chris, St. Philip Neri, Metairie; Orleans Parish Correctional Ctr., New Orleans
Beyer, Walter L., Mater Dolorosa, DePaul Hospital, New Orleans
Bialas, James, Sacred Heart, Lacombe; Lazarus House, New Orleans
Bienvenu, Roland, St. Matthew the Apostle, River Ridge; Children's Hospital, New Orleans
Binney, Robert, St. Margaret Mary, Slidell; Southeast LA Hospital, Mandeville
Blanchard, John, (On Leave)
Boe, Kenneth, St. Clement of Rome, Metairie
Bourgeois, Don, St. Jane de Chantal, Abita Springs
Bourgeois, Garland, St. Elizabeth Ann Seton, Kenner
Brady, Richard, St. Benilde, Metairie; Orleans Parish Correctional Center, New Orleans
Burke, Harold J., St. Luke the Evangelist, Slidell
Caffery, Thomas E., Jr., Assoc. Dir. Archdiocesan Spirituality Ctr., St. Philip Neri, Metairie
Calamia, S.J., St. Christopher the Martyr, Metairie
Campeaux, Barry G., Our Lady of Divine Providence, Metairie
Campuzano, Luis A., St. Jerome, Kenner
Cannon, Edward, St. Philip Neri, Metairie
Capaci, Andrea, St. Elizabeth Ann Seton, Kenner; Assoc. Dir., Family Life Apostolate
Caserta, Piero, St. Agnes, Jefferson; Covenant House, New Orleans
Cassou, Henry A., Jr., Our Lady of Prompt Succor, Chalmette
Chetta, Nick, St. Angela Merici, Metairie
Chiappetta, William, Our Lady of Lourdes, Violet
Cimino, Paul, St. Philip Neri, Metairie; Ozanam Inn, New Orleans
Cleveland, Carl, (On Leave)
Coney, Michael, St. Catherine of Siena, Metairie
Cordes, Daniel J., St. Jerome, Kenner
Coudrain, Charles E., Jr., Touro Infirmary & Our Lady of Prompt Succor Shrine, New Orleans; St. Francis Xavier, Metairie
Crago, Jere, St. Catherine of Siena, Metairie
Crochet, Randolph J., Orleans Parish Correctional Ctr. and Ozanam Inn, New Orleans
Curry, William P., Jr., Resurrection of Our Lord, New Orleans
Daigle, Irving J., Sacred Heart of Jesus, New Orleans
Daly, Edward, (Retired), Unassigned
Deichmann, Richard, Transitional Hospital, New Orleans
DeLeon, Ildefonso R., St. Maria Goretti, New Orleans
DeVerges, Philip, Holy Name of Jesus, New Orleans
DiGiovanni, Biaggio, St. Benilde, Metairie
DiGrado, Chris, St. Andrew the Apostle, New Orleans
DiMaggio, John, On Leave
Donnaud, Paul J., St. Anthony of Padua, Luling
Doolen, Philip E., St. Ann, Metairie
Dorsey, Dan, St. Matthew the Apostle, River Ridge
Dorvin, Edwin, St. Clement of Rome, Metairie
Dragon, Edgar P., St. Jerome, Kenner
Duet, Ferris J., Jr., Infant Jesus of Prague, Harvey
Duffy, Peter E., St. Maria Goretti, New Orleans
Duhe, Charles J., St. Joachim, Marrero
Duke, Charles, St. Christopher the Martyr, Metairie
Duplechain, Raphael, Jr., Holy Spirit, New Orleans
Dupuy, Paul H., Jr., Ascension of Our Lord, La Place
Durbin, Oscar A., Jefferson Parish Sheriff's Office
Elfer, Ernest C., Jr., Stella Maris Maritime Center, New Orleans; Our Lady of Prompt Succor, Westwego
Engel, Randall L., St. Lawrence the Martyr, Metairie
Faler, Charles Pete, Our Lady of Lourdes, Slidell
Fandal, Wendolen, Jr., (Retired)
Farinelli, David W., St. Peter, Reserve; Assoc. Dir., Family Life Apostolate
Fariss, Jeffrey, St. Clement of Rome, Metairie; Chap. of Orleans Parish Correctional Center
Fasullo, Gerard, Sr., St. Edward the Confessor, Metairie
Ferretti, Anthony J., Mary Queen of Peace, Mandeville
Fleischer, Francis J., St. Theresa of Avila, New Orleans
Flynn, Dan, St. Rita, Harahan, Catholic Committee on Scouting
Foret, Clarence, Jr., Our Lady of Divine Providence, Metairie
Fray, Ralph, Jefferson Parish Correctional Ctr., Gretna; Rivarde Juvenile Detention Home, Harvey
Gaiennie, Richard M., Our Lady of the Rosary, New Orleans
Gamble, Eric, St. Thomas the Apostle, UNO, and Covenant House, New Orleans; St. Clement of Rome, Metairie
Garon, Henry A., St. Henry & Ozanam Inn, New Orleans
Genna, Al, On Duty Outside the Diocese
Glapion, Lloyd St. Clair, St. Augustine, New Orleans
Glennon, William A., Jr., St. Pius X, Transitional Hospital Corporation Facility, New Orleans
Glover, John A., St. Anselm, Madisonville
Graffagnini, Carmelo, St. Peter, Covington
Gubert, Norbert, St. Frances Xavier Cabrini, New Orleans
Guidry, Ronald, Assoc. Dir., Office of Worship, St. Louis Cathedral, New Orleans
Guillot, Raymond J., Stella Maris Maritime Ctr.;

St. Henry, New Orleans
Guitterrez, Clayton J., St. John the Baptist, Folsom
Haggerty, Daniel, Jr., St. Simon Peter, New Orleans; Chap., Slidell Police Dept.
Hamm, John David, Our Lady of the Rosary, New Orleans
Harrison, Jerry, St. Clement of Rome, Metairie
Hartman, Charles, Annunciation, Bogalusa; Washington Correctional Institute, Angie
Hartson, Maurice, III, St. Alphonsus & Project Lazarus, New Orleans
Heap, Raymond E., East Jefferson Hospital, Metairie
Heine, Charles, St. Peter, Covington
Hooper, Edward B., (Retired)
Howard, John, Sts. Peter & Paul, Pearl River
Insley, J. Vernon, St. Bonaventure, Avondale
Jeansonne, Bennie, (Retired)
Johnson, Allen P., (Retired)
Johnson, Dwight J., Mary Queen of Peace & Our Lady of the Lake, Mandeville
Jones, Melvin C., Sr., On Leave
Keller, Lawrence, St. Vincent de Paul, New Orleans
Labranche, Frans, Jr., St. Jane de Chantal, Abita Springs
Landry, Coy, Holy Family, Luling
Lazo, Joseph, Our Lady of the Lake (Northshore Hospice Prog.), Mandeville
LeBlanc, Ames P., Jr., Sacred Heart, Norco
LeBlanc, Nolen J., St. Rita, Harahan
LeBlanc, Russell T., (Retired), St. Matthew the Apostle, River Ridge
LeDoux, John, Nativity of Our Lord, Kenner
LeRose, Joseph R., St. John of the Cross, Lacombe
Levy, Albert A., III, St. Mark, Chalmette
Lewis, Raymond, St. Francis de Sales, New Orleans
Luke, Nelvin, St. Agnes, Jefferson
Madere, Kenneth P., St. Mark, Chalmette; Chap., Covenant House, New Orleans
Mallerich, Walton J., On Leave
Mamou, Joseph, St. Hubert, Garyville; Chap., Orleans Parish Correctional Center
Martinez, Gerald J., St. Rita, New Orleans
Martinez, Rodolfo J., Immaculate Conception, Marrero
Martinez, Wilbur, St. Louis King of France, Metairie
Martinsen, Noel W., St. Elizabeth Ann Seton, Kenner
Matherne, Landry, St. Gertrude, Des Allemands
Mathews, Michael Schmid, (On Duty Outside the Diocese)
Memleb, Fred C., Jr., Our Lady of Divine Providence, Metairie
Mendel, August B., St. Edward the Confessor; Chap., Columbia Lakeside Hospital, Metairie
Mendieta, Roberto, Nativity of Our Lord, Kenner
Menges, George, St. Genevieve, Slidell
Miester, Alvin C., Jr., St. Louise de Marillac, Arabi
Minor, Francis M., Visitation of Our Lady, Marrero; Chap., Ozanam Inn
Mire, Louis N., Our Lady of the Lake, Mandeville; St. Tammany Parish & Highland Park Hospitals, Covington
Mistretta, Nicholas L., St. Rita, Harahan
Moore, Charles R., Our Lady of Perpetual Help, Belle Chasse
Moragas, Lucien, STET
Morales, G. Ernesto, St. Jerome, Kenner
Muhleisen, John P., St. Frances Xavier Cabrini, New Orleans
Mumme, Paul, Sr., Immaculate Heart of Mary, New Orleans
Murphy, Larry, Visitation of Our Lady, Marrero
Nalty, Paul A., St. Francis Xavier, Metairie; Chap, Malta Park Assisted Living Residence, New Orleans
Nestor, Mike, On Duty Outside the Archdiocese
Nunez, Charles R., Sr., St. Mary Magdalen, Metairie
Nuss, Henry, Our Lady of the Rosary, New Orleans
O'Connor, Gerard R., Center of Jesus the Lord, New Orleans
O'Regan, William D., (Retired), St. Francis Xavier, Metairie
Ohlmeyer, Sterling, St. Lawrence the Martyr, Metairie
Peres, Anthony W., Our Lady Star of the Sea, New Orleans
Pham, Hup, Mary Queen of Vietnam
Pippenger, John, St. Dominic, New Orleans
Rayfield, Rudolph J., Sr., St. Peter Claver & St. Philip the Apostle, New Orleans
Read, Charles, Jr., St. Peter, Covington; St. Tammany Prison, Mandeville
Reeson, Curles P., Jr., St. Robert Bellarmine, Arabi; Chap., Ozanam Inn
Rhodes, Frank W., Jr., Prince of Peace, Chalmette
Richard, Don Michael, Administrative Leave
Richardson, Ray, Our Lady of Good Counsel, New Orleans
Rivere, Raymond H., St. Mark, Chalmette; Chap., Chalmette Medical Facility
Rizzo, Peter C., St. Frances Xavier Cabrini & St. Simon Peter, New Orleans
Robichaux, Wilfred, Jr., Immaculate Conception, Marrero
Robicheaux, Dalferes F., Jr., (Retired)
Robin, Angelas, St. Mary Magdalen, New Orleans
Rosato, Joseph R., St. Thomas More & Children's Hospital, New Orleans
Rougelot, Sidney, (Retired)
Roussel, Theodore, St. Charles Borromeo, Destrehan
Sandman, Arthur, Sr., Ascension of Our Lord, La Place
Schaubhut, Anthony L., On Leave
Schexnayder, Harry, St. Charles Borromeo, Destrehan
Schlette, Peter B., St. Cletus, Gretna; Chap., Ozanam Inn
Schmidt, Gilbert R., St. Angela Merici, Metairie
Schmidt, Harry C., Jr., Our Lady of the Lake, Mandeville; St. Tammany Parish & Highland Park Hospitals
Schonacher, Ralph, Our Lady of the Rosary, New Orleans
Seruntine, Alex J., Jr., St. Louise de Marillac, Arabi
Shelly, Ceaser, (On Leave)
Sherman, Lynn, (On Duty Outside the Diocese)
Sierra, Jose A., St. Matthias, New Orleans; Chap., Orleans Parish Correctional Center
Smith, Charles J., Children's Hospital and St. Stephen, New Orleans
Smith, Gilbert, Our Lady of Angels, Waggaman; Port Chap., Stella Maris Ctr., New Orleans
Sorensen, George A., Jr., On Duty Outside the Archdiocese
Stall, Louis W., St. Cletus, Prisons Apostolate, Dir. Jefferson Parish Correctional Ctr., Gretna
Stewart, Irvin, Sr., St. Joan of Arc, New Orleans
Strahan, Douglas H., St. Bernard, St. Bernard
Swiler, James W., Dir. Office of Permanent Diaconate, Christ the King, Terrytown
Theard, Malgy D., Sr., (Retired)
Toups, Wilbur A., St. Rita, New Orleans
Trainor, Robert, St. Luke the Evangelist, Slidell
Vicknair, Percy, Ascension of Our Lord, La Place
Vicroy, Clarence, (Retired), St. Margaret Mary, Slidell
Vincent, Dan, St. Paul the Apostle, Dir. Black Catholics Office, New Orleans
Vincent, Harold, St. Julian Eymard, New Orleans
Vincent, Leslie D., St. Martha, Harvey; Chap., Meadowcrest Hospital, Gretna
Wallace, Forrest, Our Lady of the Lake, Mandeville
Walsh, Donald, Mater Dolorosa, Ozanam Inn, New Orleans
Warriner, David, St. Edward the Confessor, Metairie
Watley, Jesse A., St. Simon Peter, New Orleans
Weber, Chris J., St. Dominic & St. Pius X, New Orleans
Weber, John C., St. Margaret Mary, Slidell
White, Alfred, Corpus Christi, New Orleans
Williams, Everett, Our Lady of Lourdes, New Orleans
Williams, Herman, St. Joseph the Worker, Marrero
Williams, Irvin, St. David, New Orleans
Williams, John B., St. Raymond, New Orleans
Wilson, Earl McMahon, Jr., On Leave
Wong, Peter, On Duty Outside the Archdiocese
Wright, Clifford S., St. Benilde, Metairie
Zeringue, Alfred, St. Lawrence the Martyr, Metairie
Zimmer, Julius T., Our Lady of Prompt Succor, Chalmette
Zornman, Raymond L., On Leave

INSTITUTIONS LOCATED IN THE ARCHDIOCESE

[A] SEMINARIES, ARCHDIOCESAN

NEW ORLEANS. *Notre Dame Seminary Graduate School of Theology* (1923), 2901 S. Carrollton Ave., 70118-4391. Tel: 504-866-7426; Fax: 504-866-3119. Administration: Most Rev. Gregory M. Aymond, M.Div., V.G., Pres. & Rector; Revs. Clarence C. Menard, O.M.I., H.E.L., H.E.D., Academic Dean; Geoffrey Graystone, S.M., S.T.D., S.S.D., Asst. Dean; Bonaventure Sauer, O.C.D., M.Div., M.A., Spiritual Dir.; Carl J. Davidson, M.Mu., Dir. Spiritual Formation; Jose I. Lavastida, M.A., S.T.L., S.T.D., Asst. Dir of Spiritual Formation; Stanley J. Klores, M.A. M.Div. S.T.L. S.T.D., Dir. Student Guidance & Welfare; Sr. Barbara Dupuis, M.S.C., M.S.L.S., Dir. Library; Sr. Joycelin Staempfli, M.S.C., M.A., Dir. Finances; Rev. Msgr. Ignatius M. Roppolo, M.Div., Dir. Field Education; Rev. Patrick J. Williams, M.Div., M.S., Assis. Dir. of Spiritual Formation; Mrs. Margaret Ann Breaux, Registrar; Mr. John A. Brun, Ph.D., Psychological Counselor. Faculty: Revs. J. Edgar Bruns, S.T.D.; Glenn D. LeCompte, M.Div., S.T.L.; Rev. Msgr. Franz Graef, M.A., S.T.L., S.T.D.; Revs. Terry T. Tekippe, M.A., S.T.L., Ph.D.; Vien T. Nguyen,., M.Div., J.C.L.; J. Emile Pfister, S.J., S.T.L., S.T.D., Dir. Special Projects & Alumni; Gerald L. Seiler, M.Div., J.C.L.; David L. Rabe, M.Div., S.T.D. (Cand.); Frank Montalbano, O.M.I., S.T.L., S.S.L.; Dennis J. Hayes, M.Div., S.T.L.; Dau Nguyen, M.Div., S.T.L.; Ellis L. Depriest, S.M., M.A.; Sr. Elizabeth Willems, S.S.N.D., M.A., Ph.D.; Sr. Elizabeth Fitzpatrick, O.Carm., M.A.; Dr. Gregory Vall, M.A., Ph.D.; Sr. Janet Bodin, M.S.C., M.A., Ph.D.; Dr. Charles Nolan, H.E.D., M.Ed.; Bro. Philip Murphy, F.S.C.; Sr. Noel Toomey, O.P., M.A.; Revs. Roger Swenson, M.A.Ed., M.Ed., M.A.; David Boileau, Ph.D.; Mrs. Paula D'Albor-Stuckart, M.R.E. Priests 14; Laymen 1; Women Religious 3; Students 132.

ST. BENEDICT. *St. Joseph's Seminary College* (1890), 70457-9999. Tel: 504-892-1800; Fax: 504-867-2270. Benedictine Monks. Conducted by Provinces of New Orleans and Mobile and Monks of St. Joseph's Abbey. Very Rev. Scott J. Underwood, O.S.B., M.Ed., M.T.S., Rector-Pres.; Rev. Matthew R. Clark, O.S.B., M.A., Vice Rector & Dean of Students; Sr. Jeanne d'Arc Kernion, O.S.B., M.A., Dir. of Admin.; Bro. Brian Harrington, O.S.B., Asst. Dean of Students; Revs. Sean B. Duggan, O.S.B., M.F.A., M.A., Dir. Spiritual Formation; Aelred M. Kavanagh, O.S.B., S.S.L., S.T.D., Academic Dean; Ms. Suzanne Koerner, Dir. Devel.; Mr. Thomas A. Siegrist, M.Ed., Ed.S., Registrar & Dir. Admissions. Faculty: Revs. Lawrence J. Phelps, O.S.B., M.Ed.; William J. MacCandless, O.S.B., S.S.L.; Dominic R. Braud, O.S.B., M.Mus.; Gregory M. Boquet, O.S.B., M.A.; Timothy J. Burnett, O.S.B., M.S.L.S., M.A.Th.; Peter E. Hammett, O.S.B., Th.M., M.T.S., M.A.Th.; Adam Begnaud, M.S.; Albert Terrillion, O.S.B., M.A., M.Div.; Marian E. Larmann, O.S.B., M.A.; Jonathan M. DeFrange, O.S.B., Ph.D.; Augustine E. Foley, O.S.B., M.A., M.A.Th.; William F. Maestri, M.A.; Thomas E. Perrier, O.S.B., M.A.; Rt. Rev. Patrick J. Regan, O.S.B., S.T.D.; Rev. Ambrose G. Wathen, O.S.B., S.T.D., Ph.D.; John E. Hebert, Ph.D.; Ann K. Nauman, Ph.D.; Sarah D. Spence, Ph.D.; Peter M. Emerson, Ph.D.; Aileen Mootoo, M.A.; Ms. Jan M. Fluitt-Dupuy, M.A.; Ms. Clara V. Muller, M.A.; Dr. Edward J. Dupuy, M.A., Ph.D.; Herbert Roussel, Jr., M.A., Ph.D.; Mr. Michael Greene; Dr. J. E. Trowbridge, Jr., M.A., Ph.D.; Russell Pottle, Ph.D. Priests 19; Brothers 1; Sisters 2; Lay Teachers 11; Seminarians 64.

[B] SEMINARIES, RELIGIOUS OR SCHOLASTICATES

NEW ORLEANS. *Divine Word Missionaries, Augustine Tolton House of Studies*, 2236 D'Abadie St., 70119-2639. Tel: 504-943-4917. Rev. Alvin Dixon, Dir.

Josephite House of Studies, 2000 St. Bernard Ave., 70116-1390. Tel: 504-945-1359; Fax: 504-948-3049. Very Rev. Thomas R. Frank, S.S.J., Rector. Priest Candidates 3.

St. John of the Cross, Discalced Carmelite House of Studies, 2925 S. Carrollton Ave., 70118-4301. Tel: 504-861-9102; Fax: 504-865-1751. Rev. Jerome Earley, O.C.D. Priests 1; Brothers 2.

METAIRIE. *Congregation of the Mother Coredemptrix Formation House*, 112 Lilac St., 70005-1817. Tel: 504-835-9746. Rev. Luke M. Do Binh Dinh, C.M.C., Dir. Priests 1; Brothers 10.

[C] COLLEGES AND UNIVERSITIES

NEW ORLEANS. *Loyola University*, (1912) 6363 St. Charles Ave., 70118-6195. Tel: 504-865-2011; Fax: 504-865-3851.

For a complete listing, refer to the Colleges and Universities section.

Our Lady of Holy Cross College, 4123 Woodland Dr., 70131-7399. Tel: 504-394-7744; Fax: 504-391-2421.

For a complete listing, refer to the Colleges and Universities section.

Xavier University of Louisiana, Palmetto and Pine Sts., 70125-1098. Tel: 504-486-7411; Fax: 504-482-2801.

For a complete listing, refer to the Colleges and Universities section.

[D] HIGH SCHOOLS, ARCHDIOCESAN

NEW ORLEANS. *Redeemer-Seton High School*, 1453 Crescent St., 70122-2099. Tel: 504-288-1494; Fax: 504-288-1499. Mr. Arthur L. Schmitt, Pres.; Joan G. Johnson, Prin. School Sisters of Notre Dame 1; Daughters of Charity 1; Lay Teachers 36; Students 465.

COVINGTON. *St. Scholastica Academy*, P.O. Box 1210, 70434-1210. Tel: 504-892-2540; Fax: 504-893-5256. Mrs. Marguerite S. Celestin, Prin. Priests 1; Lay Teachers 39; Girls 464.

GRETNA. *Archbishop Blenk High School*, 17 Gretna Blvd., 70053-4989. Tel: 504-367-2626; Fax: 504-367-7128. Mr. David Pooley, Prin. Priests 1; Lay Teachers 42; Girls 567.

LA PLACE. *St. Charles Catholic High School*, 100 Dominican Dr., 70068-3499. Tel: 504-652-3809; Fax: 504-652-2609. Mr. Andrew C. Cupit, Prin. Lay Teachers 29; Students 448.

MARRERO. *Archbishop Shaw High School*, 1000 Salesian Ln., 70072-2950. Tel: 504-340-6727; Fax: 504-347-9883. Salesians of St. John Bosco. Rev. Steve Dumais, S.D.B., Dir. & Prin.; Mr. John Corb, Financial Admin.; Revs. George L. Atok, S.D.B.; Michael Conway, S.D.B., Coord. Youth Ministry; Mark Devlin, S.D.B.; Joseph Vien Hoang, S.D.B.; Eric T. Wyckoff, S.D.B. Priests 5; Brothers 2; Lay Teachers 50; Boys 459.

MERAUX. *Archbishop Hannan High School*, 2501 Archbishop Philip M. Hannan Blvd., 70075-2630. Tel: 504-279-1921; Fax: 504-279-0200. Mr. John Serio, Prin. Priests 1; Brothers 1; Sisters 1; Lay Teachers 43; Students 530.

METAIRIE. *Archbishop Chapelle High School*, 8800 Veterans Blvd., 70003-5235. Tel: 504-467-3105; Fax: 504-466-3191. Miss Beth Johnson, Prin. Priests 1; Sisters 2; Lay Teachers 83; Girls 1,200.

Archbishop Rummel High School, P.O. Box 663, 70004-0663. Tel: 504-834-5592; Fax: 504-832-4016. 1901 Severn Ave., 70001-2893. Mr. David J. Hardin, Prin. Brothers 2; Lay Teachers 86; Boys 1,350.

Rummel Alumni Association, Inc.

SLIDELL. *Pope John Paul II High School*, 1901 Jaguar Dr., 70461-9098. Tel: 504-649-0914; Fax: 504-649-5494. Ms. Carmen Schexnaildre, Prin. Sisters 1; Lay Teachers 25; Students 420.

[E] HIGH SCHOOLS, PAROCHIAL

MARRERO. *Immaculata High School*, 537 Avenue D, 70072-2027. Tel: 504-341-6217; Fax: 504-341-6229. Sr. Rosann Ruiz, F.M.A., Prin. Sisters 3; Lay Teachers 37; Girls 537.

[F] HIGH SCHOOLS, PRIVATE

NEW ORLEANS. *Academy of the Sacred Heart "The Rosary"* (1887), 4521 St. Charles Ave., 70115-9990. Tel: 504-891-1943; Fax: 504-891-9939. Sr. Shirley Miller, Headmistress. Religious of the Sacred Heart 3; Lay Teachers 26; Girls 243.

Brother Martin High School (1869), 4401 Elysian Fields Ave., 70122-3898. Tel: 504-283-1561; Fax: 504-286-8462. Bro. Ivy LeBlanc, S.C., Pres.; Mr. John J. Devlin, III, Prin. Sisters 3; Brothers of the Sacred Heart 13; Lay Teachers 80; Boys 1,480.

Cabrini High School, 1400 Moss St., 70119-2997. Tel: 504-482-1193; Fax: 504-483-8671. Mrs. Frances Dee Tarantino, Pres./Prin. Missionary Sisters of the Sacred Heart 4; Lay Teachers 33; Girls 420.

Cabrini High School, Inc.

De La Salle Senior High School (1949). (Grades 10-12), 5300 St. Charles Ave., 70115-4999. Tel: 504-895-5717; Fax: 504-895-1300. (Coed). Mrs. Yvonne Gelpi, Pres.; Bro. Jeffrey Calligan, F.S.C., Prin. Brothers of the Christian Schools 4; Sisters 2; Lay Teachers 68; Students 820.

Holy Cross School (1879), 4950 Dauphine St., 70117-4399. Tel: 504-942-3100; Fax: 504-943-7676. Bro. Stephen Walsh, C.S.C., Headmaster. Brothers of the Congregation of Holy Cross, Southwest Province 6; Lay Teachers 36; Boys 526.

Jesuit High School (1847), 4133 Banks St., 70119-6883. Tel: 504-486-6631; Fax: 504-483-3816. (Boys). Revs. Edward P. Buvens, S.J., Rector; Anthony F. McGinn, S.J., Pres.; Mr. Barry J. Neuberger, Prin.; Revs. Claude P. Boudreaux, S.J.; Peter Callery, S.J.; John J. Capelle, S.J.; Raymond R. Fitzgerald, S.J.; Thomas W. Hoffman, S.J.; Donald A. Hawkins, S.J.; Martin V. Jarreau, S.J.; Norman B. O'Neal, S.J.; Nicholas T. Schiro, S.J.; Joseph H. Reising. Priests 12; Brothers 1; Lay Teachers 76; Boys 1,145.

Mount Carmel Academy, 7027 Milne Blvd., 70124-2395. Tel: 504-288-7626; Fax: 504-288-7629. Congregation of Our Lady of Mount Carmel. Sr. Camille Anne Campbell, O.Carm., Pres./Prin. Sisters 8; Lay Teachers 80; Girls 1,037.

St. Augustine High School (1951), 2600 A.P. Tureaud Ave., 70119-1299. Tel: 504-944-2424; Fax: 504-947-7712. Josephite Community. Rev. Joseph M. Doyle, S.S.J., Pres.; Mr. Carl A. Blouin, Sr., Prin. (See Separate Listing for Residence.). Priests 8; Brothers 2; Lay Teachers 32; Boys 616.

St. Mary's Academy of the Holy Family, 6905 Chef Menteur Hwy., 70126-5291. Tel: 504-245-0200; Fax: 504-245-8732. Sr. Mary Leona Bruner, S.S.F., Prin. Sisters of the Holy Family 21; Lay Teachers 20; Girls 687.

St. Mary's Dominican High School, 7701 Walmsley Ave., 70125-3494. Tel: 504-865-9401; Fax: 504-866-5958. Sr. Mary Dominic Savio Estorge, O.P., Pres.; Ms. Cynthia A. Thomas, Prin. Sisters 4; Brothers 1; Lay Teachers 65; Students 987.

Ursuline Academy, 2635 State St., 70118-6399. Tel: 504-866-2725; Fax: 504-861-7392. Secondary Dept. Day School College Prep. Sr. Ann Barrett, O.S.U., Prin. Sisters 3; Lay Teachers 38; Girls 378.

Xavier Prep School, 5116 Magazine St., 70115-1899. Tel: 504-899-6061; Fax: 504-891-0347. Mrs. Ann Zanders, Pres.; Mr. Alvarez A. Peychaud, Prin. Priests 1; Sisters 7; Lay Teachers 31; Girls 507.

COVINGTON. *The St. Paul's School* (1911). (Grades 8-12), P.O. Box 928, 70434-0928. Tel: 504-892-3200; Fax: 504-892-4048. Bro. Raymond Bulliard, F.S.C., Prin.; Rev. Peter Blanchard, S.M., Chap. Boarding and Day School for Young Men. Brothers of the Christian Schools of the New Orleans-Santa Fe Province 5; Lay Teachers 45; Boys 600.

[G] ELEMENTARY SCHOOLS, ARCHDIOCESAN

NEW ORLEANS. *Marian Central Catholic Middle School*, 2221 Mendez St., 70122-5267. Tel: 504-288-1411; Fax: 504-286-0209. Sr. Maeve McMahon, O.P., Pres.; Sr. Jennie Jones, S.S.F., Prin. Sisters 5; Lay Teachers 19; Students 400.

Redeemer-Seton Junior High School. (Grades 8-9), 1453 Crescent St., 70122-2099. Tel: 504-288-1494; Fax: 504-288-1499. Mr. Al Armbruster, Prin. Sisters 1; Lay Teachers 8; Students 172.

MARRERO. *Archbishop Shaw Junior High School*. (Grades 8-9), 1000 Salesian Ln., 70072-2950. Tel: 504-340-6727; Fax: 504-347-9883. Mr. Dennis R. Coulon, Prin.; Rev. Steven Dumais, S.D.B., Dir. Priests 5; Brothers 2; Lay Teachers 42; Students 227.

METAIRIE. *Archbishop Rummel Junior High School*. (Grades 8-9), 1901 Severn Ave., 70001-2893. Tel: 504-834-5592; Fax: 504-832-4016. Ms. Ellen Windstein, Prin. Brothers 2; Lay Teachers 48; Boys 500.

[H] ELEMENTARY SCHOOLS, PRIVATE

NEW ORLEANS. *Academy of the Sacred Heart*. (Grades Nursery-8), 4521 St. Charles Ave., 70115-9990. Tel: 504-891-1943; Fax: 504-891-9939. Sr. Shirley Miller, R.S.C.J., Headmistress. Religious of the Sacred Heart 3; Lay Teachers 46; Girls 516.

Brother Martin High School. (Grade 8), 4401 Elysian Fields Ave., 70122-3898. Tel: 504-283-1561; Fax: 504-286-8462. Mr. John J. Devlin, III, Prin. Brothers of the Sacred Heart 5; Lay Teachers 22; Boys 224.

Cabrini High School. (Grades 8-12), 1400 Moss St., 70119-2997. Tel: 504-482-1193; Fax: 504-483-8671. Mrs. Frances Dee Tarantino, Pres./Prin.

Christian Brothers School. (Grades 5-7), City Park, #8 Frederichs Ave., 70124-4602. Tel: 504-486-6770; Fax: 504-486-1053. Bro. Andre P. Lacoste, F.S.C., Prin. Brothers 7; Lay Teachers 8; Boys 245.

De La Salle Junior High School. (Grades 8-9), 5300 St. Charles Ave., 70115-4999. Tel: 504-895-5717; Fax: 504-895-1300. (Coed). Mrs. Yvonne Gelpi, Pres.; Ms. Gina F. Hall, Prin. Lay Teachers 29; Students 274.

Holy Cross School. (Grades 5-8), 4950 Dauphine St., 70117-4399. Tel: 504-942-3100; Fax: 504-943-7676. Bro. Stephen Walsh, C.S.C., Headmaster. Brothers of the Congregation of Holy Cross 6; Lay Teachers 27; Boys 248.

Jesuit High School. (Grade 8), 4133 Banks St., 70119-6883. Tel: 504-486-6631; Fax: 504-483-3816. Rev. Anthony F. McGinn, S.J., Pres.; Mr. Barry J. Neuberger, Prin. Priests 3; Lay Teachers 17; Boys 240.

St. Augustine High School. (Grade 8), 2600 A.P. Tureaud Ave., 70119-1299. Tel: 504-944-2424; Fax: 504-947-7712. Rev. Joseph M. Doyle, S.S.J., Pres. Priests 3; Lay Teachers 6; Boys 46.

St. Mary's Academy. (Grades 7-8), 6905 Chef Menteur Hwy., 70126-5291. Tel: 504-245-0200; Fax: 504-245-8732. Sr. M. Leona Bruner, S.S.F., Prin. Priests 1; Sisters of the Holy Family 10; Lay Teachers 18; Girls 713.

St. Mary's Dominican High School, 7701 Walmsley Ave., 70125-3494. Tel: 504-865-9401; Fax: 504-866-5958. Sr. M. Dominic Savio Estorge, O.P., Pres.; Ms. Cynthia A. Thomas, Prin. Brothers 1; Sisters 4; Lay Teachers 65; Girls 987.

Ursuline Academy. (Grades Toddler-8), 2635 State St., 70118-6399. Tel: 504-866-5260; Fax: 504-861-7392. Mrs. Elizabeth LaForge, Prin. Sisters 3; Lay Teachers 32; Students 317.

COVINGTON. *The St. Paul's School*. (Grades 8-12), P.O. Box 928, 70434-0928. Tel: 504-892-3200; Fax: 504-892-4048. Brothers of the Christian Schools. Bro. Raymond Bulliard, F.S.C., Prin.; John Morvant, Asst. Prin. Brothers 5; Lay Teachers 45; Boys 600. (See St. Paul's School Under High Schools, Private).

[I] SPECIAL EDUCATION

NEW ORLEANS. *Archdiocesan Department of Special Education*. St. Michael Special School, 1522 Chippewa St., 70130-4513. Tel: 504-524-7285; Fax: 504-524-5883. Sr. M. Lillian McCormack, S.S.N.D., Dir. Religious 4; Lay Teachers 21; Students 193.

Bishop Perry Middle School. (Grades 5-8), 1941 Dauphine St., 70116-1697. Tel: 504-943-3734. (Boys). Rev. David Theroux, S.S.E., Pres.; Dr. Rudolph Detiege, Prin. Society of St. Edmund Fathers 2; Lay Teachers 4; Boys 41.

Holy Rosary Academy, 1342 Moss St., 70119-2998. Tel: 504-482-7173; Fax: 504-482-7229. Mrs. Rose Howrilla, Prin. Sisters 3; Lay Teachers 3; Students 40.

House of the Holy Family School. (Grades 1-3), 7100 Chef Menteur Hwy., 70126-5220. Tel: 504-242-1810. Sr. Mary Louisette DeSalle, S.S.F., Admin. Children 56.

St. Gerard Majella Alternative School, 8131 Plum St., 70118-2011. Tel: 504-861-7571; Fax: 504-861-7571. Mrs. Dolores Perrien, Prin.

MARRERO. *Hope Haven Center*, 1101 Barataria Blvd., 70072-3085. Tel: 504-347-5581; Fax: 504-340-2075. Mrs. Barbara Garland, M.Ed., Prin. Lay Teachers 16; Students 92.

[J] DAY CARE CENTERS AND PRESCHOOLS

NEW ORLEANS. *Cabrini Head Start*, 817 St. Philip St., 70116-2419. Tel: 504-523-4020; Fax: 504-943-6813. Sr. Irma Williams, M.S., Prog. Dir. Total Staff 10; Total Assisted 42.

El Yo Yo Bilingual Day Care Center, 735 Gen. Pershing St., 70115-1448. Tel: 504-899-6165; Fax: 504-895-3129. Ms. Gaynell Anderson, Prog. Dir. Total Assisted 100; Total Staff 14.

Flint-Goodridge Day Care Center, 3306 Freret St., 70115-6029. Tel: 504-895-3488; Fax: 504-895-3129. Susie Foucher, Prog. Dir.

Florida Head Start, 2631 Alvar St., 70117-3364. Tel: 504-945-8115; Fax: 504-943-6813. Mrs. Liz Bailey, Prog. Dir. Total Assisted 66; Total Staff 11.

Incarnate Word Preschool Program, 8326 Apricot St., 70118-3198. Tel: 504-866-2309; Fax: 504-861-1435. Ms. Carolyn Potts, Dir. Lay Staff 14; Children 70.

Lafon Child Development Center, 7024 Chef Menteur Hwy., 70126-5295. Tel: 504-242-2431. Sr. Sienna Marie Braxton, S.S.F., Admin. Sisters 2; Children (Daily Average) 130.

Leslie Day Care Center, 2126 Constance St., 70130-5044. Tel: 504-522-2725. Ms. Ellen Somers, Admin. Total Staff 5.

Louise Day Care Center, 1205 Louisiana Ave., 70115-2488. Tel: 504-891-2871; Fax: 504-895-3129. Ms. Irma Cavalier, Prog. Dir. Total Assisted 85; Total Staff 17.

Mary Queen of Peace Child Development Center, 5075 Willow Brook Dr., 70129-1047. P.O. Box 29073, 70189-9073. Tel: 504-254-1528; Fax: 504-254-9250. Sr. Mary Francis Dang, F.M.S.R., Dir. Staff 12; Children (Daily Average) 55.

St. Anthony Head Start, 5407 Dauphine St., 70117-3023. Tel: 504-943-6952; Fax: 504-943-6813. Ms. Melba Hart, Program Dir.

St. John Berchmans Child Development Center, 2710 Gentilly Blvd., 70122-3098. Tel: 504-943-5060. P.O. Box 8623, 70182-8623. Sr. Mary Laurita Oliver, S.S.F., Admin. Sisters 2; Lay Staff 13; Children 130.

St. John the Baptist Pre-School Program, 1920 Clio St., 70113-1214. Tel: 504-529-2557; Fax: 504-581-4991. Lay Staff 10; Children 57.

St. Joseph Alpha Montessori Preschool, 1200 Mirabeau Ave., 70122-1997. Tel: 504-283-7533. Sr. Mary Smith, C.S.J., Dir. Total Staff 3; Children 40.

St. Jude Baby Village (1972), 1723 S. White St., 70125-2937. Tel: 504-821-4686; Fax: 504-895-3129. Mrs. Esperanza L. Martinez, Prog. Dir. Total Assisted 42; Total Staff 8.

St. Philip Preschool, 3333 Clouet St., 70126-5700. Tel: 504-944-2640; Fax: 504-944-8853. Mrs. Betty Lavigne, Supvr. Staff 10; Children (Daily Average) 40.

CHALMETTE. *Our Lady of Prompt Succor Child Care Center*, 2217 Fenelon St., 70043-4991. Tel: 504-271-3491. Mrs. Cynthia Dazet, Dir.

METAIRIE. *St. Lawrence the Martyr Child Care Center*, 2525 Maine Ave., 70003-5446. Tel: 504-469-3988. Ms. LaDonna Delaune, Dir. Staff 8; Children (Daily Average) 40.

St. Mary Magdalen Early Childhood Development Center, 1005 Airline Park Blvd., 70003-4395. Tel: 504-736-0863. Ms. Dina L. Castille, M.Ed., Dir. Staff 16; Children (Daily Average) 55.

[K] HOMES FOR CHILDREN AND YOUTH

NEW ORLEANS. *Boys Hope*, 4128 Baudin St., 70119-6815. Tel: 504-486-6030.

For a complete listing, refer to the Special Care Facilities section.

**Covenant House*, 622 N. Rampart St., 70112-3540. Tel: 504-584-1111; 800-999-9999 (Hotline); Fax: 504-584-1171.

For a complete listing, refer to the Special Care Facilities section.

BELLE CHASSE. *Padua Community Services Pediatric Residential Program,* 200 Beta St., 70037-1499. Tel: 504-392-0502; Fax: 504-392-5411.
For a complete listing, refer to the Special Care Facilities section.

MARRERO. *Hope Haven Center,* (1925) 1101 Barataria Blvd., 70072-3085. Tel: 504-347-5581; Fax: 504-340-2075.
For a complete listing, refer to the Special Care Facilities section.
St. Elizabeth's at Hope Haven, 1101 Barataria Blvd., 70072-3085. Tel: 504-347-5581; Fax: 504-340-2075.
For a complete listing, refer to the Special Care Facilities section.

[L] RESIDENCES, ADULT

NEW ORLEANS. *CARE CENTER,* 4222 S. Broad St., 70125-3660. Tel: 504-822-3751; Fax: 504-822-3761. Mrs. Connie Andry, Admin. Temporary Residence for Homeless Women and their Children.
Ciara House, 1131 St. Andrew St., 70130-5124. Tel: 504-524-8394; Fax: 504-524-0224. Ms. Monetta Clark, Admin.
Crescent House. Office, 1000 Howard Ave., 70113-1928. Tel: 504-523-3755; Fax: 504-523-0007. Temporary residence for abused women and their children. Ms. Lynn Holland, Prog. Dir.
Marie's Family Home, 2118 Martin Luther King Blvd., 70113-2315. Tel: 504-523-3716. Sponsored by St. Vincent de Paul Society. Shelter for Women and Children. Ms. Lolita Rochon, Admin.
Ozanam Inn, 843 Camp St., 70130-3751. Tel: 504-523-1184; Fax: 504-523-1187. Sponsored by Society of St. Vincent de Paul. Shelter for Homeless Men. Roy R. Allain, Admin. Sisters 1; Lay Staff 12.
Project Lazarus, P.O. Box 3906, 70177-3906. Tel: 504-949-3609; Fax: 504-944-7944. Residential Program for Persons with AIDS. Ms. Susan Banks, Exec. Dir.

GRETNA. *Ocean Avenue Community Home,* 361 Ocean Ave., 70053-4726. Tel: 504-361-0674; Fax: 504-367-6952. Residential Facility for Developmentally Disabled Adults. Total Assisted 6; Total Staff 7.
St. Jude the Apostle, 1430 Claire Ave., 70053-7436. Tel: 504-361-8457; Fax: 504-367-6952. Residential Facility for Developmentally Disabled Adults.
St. Rosalie, 119 Kass St., 70056-3852. Tel: 504-361-8320; Fax: 504-367-6952. Padua Adult Residential Program for Developmentally Disabled Adults.
Supervised Apartments, 1430 Claire Ave., 70053-7436. Tel: 504-367-1465; Fax: 504-367-6952. Supervised Apartments for Developmentally Disabled Adults.

HARVEY. *St. Catherine of Siena Supervised Apartment,* 3021 Sienna Dr., 70058-2180. Tel: 504-347-6069; Fax: 504-367-6952. Residential Program for Developmentally Disabled Adults.

MARRERO. *Jefferson Care Center,* 1108 Barataria Blvd., 70072-3085. Tel: 504-347-0772. Ms. Earline Perique, Prog. Dir. Temporary Residence for Homeless Families.

METAIRIE. *Sts. Mary & Elizabeth,* 720 N. Elm St., 70003-6022. Tel: 504-738-6959; Fax: 504-367-6952. Residential Facility for Developmentally Disabled Adults. Total Assisted 6; Total Staff 11.

SLIDELL. *St. Peter the Fisherman,* 62269 Airport Rd., 70460-5242. Tel: 504-641-4914; Fax: 504-367-6952. Residential Facility for Developmentally Disabled Adults.

[M] DAY CARE CENTERS (ADULT)

NEW ORLEANS. *Carmel in the Business District.* (Ministry to Women and Day Care Center), 246 Loyola Ave., 70112-2002. Tel: 504-529-8856; Fax: 504-529-8861. Sr. Gwen Grillot, O.Carm., Exec. Dir.; Sr. Brenda Lege, O.Carm., Prog. Dir. Total Assisted 80; Total Staff 10.
New Directions Adult Day Health Care Center, 1523 N. Dorgenois St., 70119-2419. Tel: 504-943-9418; Fax: 504-948-3633. Ms. Bertha Harris, Prog. Dir. Total Assisted 43; Total Staff 10.
People Program, 1200 Mirabeau Ave., 70122-1886. Tel: 504-288-3171; Fax: 504-288-3503. Ms. Mary Catherine Lombard, Prog. Dir.; Ms. Barbara McCurdy, Devel. Dir.

COVINGTON. *Alpha House Adult Day Health Care Center,* 324 E. Boston St., 70434-2802. Tel: 504-892-7074; Fax: 504-893-1962. Ms. Steve Ryan, Prog. Dir.

KENNER. *The Greenwalt Center for Alzheimer's Day Care and Research,* 1926 18th St., 70062-6208. Tel: 504-461-5889; Fax: 504-461-5795. Ms. Linda Greenwalt, Asst. Admin.
Kenner Adult Day Health Care Center, 1001 Moisant St., 70062-6715. Tel: 504-469-9492; Fax: 504-465-0632. Ms. Julie Allen-Nelson, Prog. Dir. Total Assisted 35; Total Staff 6.

NORCO. *Norco Adult Day Care,* 425 Spruce St., 70079-2355. Tel: 504-764-9084; Fax: 504-764-0041. Ms. Kathleen Landry, R.N., Dir.

[N] HOMES AND RESIDENCES FOR FAMILIES AND SENIOR CITIZENS

NEW ORLEANS. *The 1540 House,* 1540 N. Johnson St., 70116-1721. Tel: 504-945-0253.
For a complete listing, refer to the Special Care Facilities section.
Annunciation Inn, 1220 Spain St., 70117-8369. Tel: 504-944-0512; Fax: 504-944-0514.
For a complete listing, refer to the Special Care Facilities section.
Carriage House Apartments, Pontchartrain Housing Corp. I, 10151 Curran Blvd., 70127-1390.
For a complete listing, refer to the Special Care Facilities section.
Chateau de Notre Dame, 2832 Burdette St., 70125-2596. Tel: 504-866-2741; Fax: 504-866-6769.
For a complete listing, refer to the Special Care Facilities section.
Christopher Inn Apts., 2110 Royal St., 70116-1693. Tel: 504-949-0312; Fax: 504-945-2634.
For a complete listing, refer to the Special Care Facilities section.
DeLille Inn, 6924 Chef Menteur Hwy., 70126-5260. Tel: 504-241-4877; Fax: 504-241-1828.
For a complete listing, refer to the Special Care Facilities section.
Haydel Heights Apartments, 4402 Reynes St., 70126. Tel: 504-242-4438; Fax: 504-242-4061.
For a complete listing, refer to the Special Care Facilities section.
Josephine Apartments, 1410 St. Andrew St., Apt. #6, 70130-5344. Tel: 504-522-5425; Fax: 504-522-5446.
For a complete listing, refer to the Special Care Facilities section.
Lafon Nursing Home of the Holy Family, 6900 Chef Menteur Hwy., 70126-5296. Tel: 504-246-1100; Fax: 504-241-6672.
For a complete listing, refer to the Special Care Facilities section.
Mary-Joseph Residence for the Elderly, (1868) 4201 Woodland Dr., 70131-7398. Tel: 504-394-2200; Fax: 504-391-3347.
For a complete listing, refer to the Special Care Facilities section.
Nazareth II, 9640 Hayne Blvd., 70127-4725. Tel: 504-246-9640; Fax: 504-241-9631.
For a complete listing, refer to the Special Care Facilities section.
Nazareth Inn, 9630 Hayne Blvd., 70127-1260. Tel: 504-241-9630; Fax: 504-241-9631.
For a complete listing, refer to the Special Care Facilities section.
St. John Berchmans Manor, 3400 St. Anthony St., 70122-3098. Tel: 504-943-9343; Fax: 504-947-6090.
For a complete listing, refer to the Special Care Facilities section.
St. Margaret's Daughters' Home for Aged Women, 6220 Chartres St., 70117-1595. Tel: 504-279-6414; Fax: 504-277-1834.
For a complete listing, refer to the Special Care Facilities section.
St. Martin Manor, 1501 N. Johnson St., 70116-1720. Tel: 504-945-7728; Fax: 504-945-1645.
For a complete listing, refer to the Special Care Facilities section.
Timber Ridge Apartments Pontchartrain Housing Corp. III, 6364 Woodland Hwy., 70131-7474. Tel: 504-391-9841; Fax: 504-391-9996.
For a complete listing, refer to the Special Care Facilities section.
Villa St. Maurice, 500 St. Maurice Ave., 70117-1568. Tel: 504-277-8477; Fax: 504-277-8493.
For a complete listing, refer to the Special Care Facilities section.
Villa St. Maurice II (Villa Additions), 6101 Douglas St., 70117-2100. Tel: 504-277-8731; Fax: 504-277-8493.
For a complete listing, refer to the Special Care Facilities section.

LA PLACE. *Place Dubourg, Inc.,* 201 Rue Dubourg, 70068-2433. Tel: 504-652-1981; Fax: 504-651-6147.
For a complete listing, refer to the Special Care Facilities section.

MANDEVILLE. *Rouquette Lodge,* 4300 Hwy. 22, 70448-2824. Tel: 504-626-5217; Fax: 504-626-9226.
For a complete listing, refer to the Special Care Facilities section.

MARRERO. *Villa D'Ames Apartments,* 6305 Fourth St., 70072-1513. Tel: 504-347-0474; Fax: 504-347-0476.
For a complete listing, refer to the Special Care Facilities section.
Wynhoven Apartments and Wynhoven II, 4600-10th St., 70072-3048. Tel: 504-347-8443; Fax: 504-340-6076.
For a complete listing, refer to the Special Care Facilities section.
Wynhoven Health Care Center, 1050 Medical Center Blvd., 70072-3170. Tel: 504-347-0777; 347-3443 (Convent); Fax: 504-341-7240.
For a complete listing, refer to the Special Care Facilities section.

MERAUX. *St. Bernard Manor, St. Bernard II, and St. Bernard III,* 2400 Archbishop Hannan Blvd., 70075-2640. Tel: 504-277-2441; Fax: 504-277-6300.
For a complete listing, refer to the Special Care Facilities section.

METAIRIE. *Cascades Apartments, Walmsley Housing Corp.,* 2212 N. Arnoult Rd., 70001-1807. Tel: 504-835-2998; Fax: 504-835-3647.
For a complete listing, refer to the Special Care Facilities section.
Metairie Manor, Metairie II, and Metairie III, 4929 York St., 70001-1013. Tel: 504-456-1467; Fax: 504-887-3718.
For a complete listing, refer to the Special Care Facilities section.
Rock Creek Apartments, Walmsley Housing Corp., 4817 York St., 70001-1168. Tel: 504-455-3886; Fax: 504-455-3888.
For a complete listing, refer to the Special Care Facilities section.

ST. ROSE. *River Road Apartments, Pontchartrain Housing Corp. II,* 100 A East Club Dr., 70087-9411. Tel: 504-464-0326; Fax: 504-466-1987.
For a complete listing, refer to the Special Care Facilities section.

[O] CATHOLIC HEALTH SERVICES

NEW ORLEANS. *Daughters of Charity Services of New Orleans,* 3900 S. Carrollton Ave., 70118-4712. Tel: 504-482-2080; Fax: 504-483-6016.
For a complete listing, refer to the Hospitals section.
St. John's Place of New Orleans, Inc. dba Mercy Family Center, 3816 Bienville St., 70119-5206. Tel: 504-482-6600.
For a complete listing, refer to the Hospitals section.

[P] MONASTERIES AND RESIDENCES OF PRIESTS AND BROTHERS

NEW ORLEANS. *Brothers of the Sacred Heart.* Provincial Office, New Orleans Province, 4540 Elysian Fields Ave., 70122-3826. Tel: 504-282-5693; Fax: 504-288-9920. Bro. Ray Hebert, S.C., Vocation Dir. Tel: 504-282-2228, Hospitality Center/Pre-Novitiate, 4600 Elysian Fields Ave., 70122-3938. Tel: 504-282-5631. Bro. Jean Sobert, S.C., Dir., 4601 Elysian Fields Ave., 70122-3937. Tel: 504-288-8301. Bro. Warren Laudumiey, S.C., Dir., 2150 Brutus St., 70122-3958. Tel: 504-282-1995. Bro. Neal Golden, S.C., Dir., Novitiate House, 1156 City Park Ave., 70119-3736. Tel: 504-488-1353. Bro. Dwight Kenney, S.C., Dir., 4671 Painters St., 70122-5001. Tel: 504-283-6448. Bro. Louis Couvillon, S.C., Dir. Total Brothers 28. Ordained Brothers: Bro. Ray Hebert, S.C., 4671 Painters St., 70122. Bro. Louis Couvillon, S.C., 4671 Painters St., 70122. Bro. Carl Evans, S.C., 209 S. Hollywood Rd., Houma, 70360. Bro. Albert Guarino, S.C., 4601 Elysian Fields Ave., 70122-3937. Bro. Farrel Lorio, S.C., 175 St. Joseph St., Thibodaux, 70301. Bro. William McCue, S.C., 855 Hearthstone Dr., Baton Rouge, 70806. Bro. Vincent Bono, S.C., 1236 N. Rampart St., 70116-2497.
Dominican Fathers & Brothers, Southern Dominican Province. Provincial Headquarters, 1421 N. Causeway Blvd., Ste. 200, Metairie, 70001-4144. Tel: 504-837-2129; Fax: 504-837-6604. Very Revs. Alberto Rodriguez, O.P., Prov.; Carl B. Trutter, O.P., Socius & Vicar Prov.; Wayne Cavalier, O.P., Promoter of Permanent Formation and for Community Life; Rev. Henry B. Groover, O.P. (MIA), Promoter of Vocations. Priests in the Archdiocese 24; Brothers in the Archdiocese 4.
Assigned but working elsewhere: Revs. Albert J. Coburn, O.P.; John E. Keefer, O.P.; Alfred Q. Lister, O.P.; Gerald Fath, O.P., On Leave; Paul D. Watkins, O.P., On Leave; Richard Paul MacLeay, O.P.; Scott I. O'Brien, O.P.; Bruce B. Schultz, O.P.; Bro. Francis Dinet (SB).
Working Abroad: Rev. Emanuel M. Camilleri, O.P., Home for the Clergy, Fleur de Lys, Malta, BRK 09. Rev. James Linus Dolan, O.P., Provincia Dominicana de San Juan Bautista del Peru, Apartado 4169, Lima, Peru. Deacon Juan Carlos Duran, O.P., Casa de San Martin de Porres, Apartado 337, David, Chiriqui, Panama. Rev. Raymond C. Finn, O.P., Curia Generalizia Domenicani, Convento Santa Sabina, Piazza Pietro d'Illiria, 1 (Aventino), Rome, Italy, 00153. Rev. Jesus de Vianney Guerra, O.P., Parroquia de Santiago Apostol, Av. Varsovia Malta-California Sur, Apdo. 76176, Caracas, Venezuela, 1070. Rev. Carmen Mele, O.P., Casa de Santo Tomas de Aquino, Apartado 96-2400, Desamparados, San Jose, Costa Rica. Rev. Brian J. Pierce, O.P., Dominicos, Apartado 2608, San Pedro Sula, Honduras. Rev. Alfred W. Wilder, O.P., Universita San Tommaso, Largo Angelicum 1, Rome, Italy, 00184.
Dominican Vocation Sponsors, 1421 N. Causeway

Blvd., Ste. 200, Metairie, 70001-4144. Rev. Bryan J. Fontenot, O.P., Dir.
Southern Dominican Foundation, 1421 N. Causeway Blvd., Ste. 200, Metairie, 70001-4144. Revs. Alberto Rodriguez, O.P., Pres.; Carl B. Trutter, O.P., Vice Pres./Sec.; Val A. McInnes, O.P., Promoter of Devel.; Nora P. Fine, Dir. of Devel.
Southern Dominican Global Missions, 1421 N. Causeway Blvd., Ste. 200, Metairie, 70001-4144. Rev. James A. McDonough, O.P. (AUS), Dir., Shrine of St. Martin de Porres, 1421 N. Causeway Blvd., Ste. 200, Metairie, 70001-4144.
Franciscan Fraternity. Tau House, 1029 Gov. Nicholls St., 70116-2432. Tel: 504-529-3569; Fax: 504-558-0429. Revs. Ralph R. Parthie, O.F.M.; Michael J. Jennrich, O.F.M.; Bro. Edward-Marc Arambasich, O.F.M. Center for the Spiritual Empowerment of those infected with or affected by the HIV/AIDS.
Ignatius Residence, 6321 Stratford Pl., 70131-7325. Tel: 504-394-2411. Revs. Clair M. Cazayoux, S.J., Supr.; Emmett M. Bienvenu, S.J.; Joseph E. Browning, S.J.; Harold L. Cooper, S.J.; James M. Deshotels, S.J.; Bro. C. Robert Doherty, S.J.; Revs. Russell L. Dornier, S.J.; John P. Driscoll, S.J.; Lawrence J. Luettgen, S.J.; Warren S. Martin, S.J.; John Q. Minvielle, S.J.; Laurence M. O'Neill, S.J.; Herve P. Racivitch, S.J.; S. Joseph Rivoire, S.J.; Roy W. Vollenweider, S.J.; Bros. Lloyd A. Barry, S.J.; H. Francis Hinze, S.J.; Dennis P. Lonergan, S.J.; Alfred M. Nowak, S.J.; Hilliard F. Stiegler, S.J. Brothers 6.
Jesuit Provincial Office. (New Orleans Prov.), 500 S. Jefferson Davis Pkwy., 70119-7192. Tel: 504-821-0334; Fax: 504-822-5322. Legal Title: *Catholic Society of Religious and Literary Education*. Very Rev. James P. Bradley, S.J., Prov.; Revs. John F. Armstrong, S.J., Socius & Prov. Asst. Education; Donald J. Martin, S.J., Prov. Asst. Parishes & Retreat Ministry; Robert J. Ratchford, S.J., Staff Asst.; Joseph H. Reising, S.J., Prov. Asst. Formation; Bro. Lawrence J. Lundin, S.J., Treas. Priests 5; Brothers 1.
Priests of the Province Abroad: Rev. Charles B. Thibodeaux, S.J., Casa Parroquial, Santa Rosa (Misiones), Paraguay. Rev. John F. Schroder, S.J., P.O. Box 34, Corozal Town, Belize. Rev. Edward J. Dougherty, S.J., Ave. Rio de Janiero 327, Campinas, SP, Brazil, 13031-340. Rev. Edward G. Benya, S.J., CP 521, Teresina, Brazil, 64010. Rev. A. Gerard Fineran, S.J., R. Ricardo Tim, 183, Campinas, Brazil, 13041-460. Rev. Carlos E. de la Cruz, S.J., Casa Parroquial, Santa Rosa (Misiones), Paraguay. Rev. David C. Borbridge, S.J., Rua Marques de S. Vicente, 293, Rio de Janiero, RJ, Brazil, 22451. Rev. David H. Romero, S.J., Cx. P. 2452, Manaus-AM, Brazil, 69001-970. Rev. Mark Lewis, S.J., Casa deg. Scrittori, Via del Penitenzieri 20, Rome, Italy, 00193. Rev. Patrick S. Madigan, S.J., P Bag A6109, Avondale, Harare, Zimbabwe. Rev. Stephen C. Rowntree, S.J., P Bag A6109, Avondale, Harare, Zimbabwe. Rev. John R. Stacer, S.J., P Bag A6109, Avondale, Harare, Zimbabwe. Rev. Earl C. Muller, S.J., Pontifical Univ. Gregoriana, Piazza della Pilotta, 4, Rome, Italy, 00187. Rev. Joseph A. Tetlow, S.J., Curia, Society of Jesus, CP 6139, Rome, Italy, 00195. Rev. Reynaldo Garcia, S.J., Cx. P. 2452, Manaus-AM, Brazil, 69001-970. Rev. Thomas H. Stahel, S.J., Jesuit Novitiate, P.O. Box 854, Benin City, Nigeria. Rev. Leo V. Leise, S.J., Casa Parroquial, Iturbe 870, San Ignacio (Misiones), Paraguay. Rev. O. Kenneth Johnson, S.J., P.O. Box 660195, Monze, Zambia. Rev. Roland J. Lesseps, S.J., P.O. Box 30652, Lusaka, Zambia.
Jesuit Health Trust. Rev. Eugene M. Dutkiewicz, S.J., Chm.; Bro. Lawrence J. Lundin, S.J., Sec.
Josephite Fathers and Brothers. St. Augustine High School Faculty House, 1911 Law St., 70119-1397. Tel: 504-943-6593; Fax: 504-947-7712. Very Rev. Nelson A. Moreira, S.S.J., Rector; Rev. Robert P. Pavlak, S.S.J., Vice Rector; Bro. Laurence E. Price, S.S.J.; Revs. Robert Bowen, S.S.J.; Wilbur J. Atwood, S.S.J.; Vincent Keenan, S.S.J.; Joseph M. Doyle, S.S.J.
(See Separate Listing for School).
Vincentian Fathers. DePaul Residence, 812 Constantinople St., 70115-2726. Tel: 504-897-3976; Fax: 504-899-7603. Very Rev. Robert E. Lamy, C.M., Supr.; Revs. Anthony D. Fassbender, C.M.; Ignatius L. Foley, C.M.; Lee B. Zimmerman, C.M.; P. Francis Zimmermann, C.M.; Bernard P. Degan, C.M.

LACOMBE. *Redemptorist Fathers and Brothers - Holy Redeemer Mission Center*, Hwy. 434, P.O. Box 218, 70445. Tel: 504-882-5147. Rev. Joseph R. Armshaw, C.Ss.R., Supr.

ST. BENEDICT. *St. Joseph Abbey* (1890), 70457-9999. Tel: 504-892-1800; Fax: 504-892-3723. Rt. Rev. Patrick J. Regan, O.S.B., Abbot; Revs. Raphael Barousse, O.S.B.; Hugh Baumann, O.S.B.; Adam Begnaud, O.S.B.; Gregory Boquet, O.S.B.; Dominic Braud, O.S.B.; Justin Brown, O.S.B.; Timothy Burnett, O.S.B.; Kevin Clark, O.S.B.; Matthew Clark, O.S.B.; Daniel Cobb, O.S.B.; Jonathan M. DeFrange, O.S.B.; Sean Duggan, O.S.B.; Augustine Foley, O.S.B.; Ignatius Fossier, O.S.B.; Peter Hammett, O.S.B.; Gerald Hindman, O.S.B.; Adrian Hovey, O.S.B.; Michael Jung, O.S.B.; Aelred Kavanaugh, O.S.B.; Jerome Land, O.S.B.; Marian Larmann, O.S.B.; William MacCandless, O.S.B.; Paul Miranne, O.S.B.; Stan Moseley, O.S.B.; Thomas Perrier, O.S.B.; Lawrence Phelps, O.S.B.; Francis Sander, O.S.B.; Albert Terrillion, O.S.B.; Scott Underwood, O.S.B.; Ambrose Wathen, O.S.B. Priests 31; Brothers 17; Novices 5.

[Q] CONVENTS AND RESIDENCES FOR SISTERS

NEW ORLEANS. *Congregation of Divine Providence, C.D.P.*, 504 Fern, 70118-3830. Tel: 504-861-0284. Total Sisters in Archdiocese 2.
Congregation of the Sisters of the Holy Faith, C.H.F., 2741 St. Anthony St., 70119-1298. Tel: 504-945-7743. Total Sisters in Archdiocese 4.
Daughters of Charity of St. Vincent de Paul, D.C. Sisters' Residence, 1040 Calhoun St., Helis #2, 70118-5999. Tel: 504-899-8228. Sr. Catherine Chernick, D.C., Supr. Total Sisters in Archdiocese 31.
Daughters of Our Lady of the Holy Rosary Provincial House, F.M.S.R., 1492 Moss St., 70119-2904. Tel: 504-486-0039. Sr. John Bosco Dinh Thi Kim Thanh, F.M.S.R., Prov. Supr. Total Sisters in Archdiocese 41.
Dominican Sisters (Cabra, Ireland) O.P., 1930 Robert E. Lee Blvd., 70122-3518. Tel: 504-288-1593. Sr. Elizabeth Ferguson, O.P., Reg. Supr. Total Sisters in Archdiocese 10.
Eucharistic Missionaries of St. Dominic, O.P., 3801 Canal St., Ste. 400, 70119-6049. Tel: 504-486-1133; Fax: 504-486-6547. Total Sisters in Archdiocese 21.
Regina Coeli Retreat Center, 17225 Regina Coeli Rd., Covington, 70435-9156. Tel: 504-892-4110.
Generalate of the Dominican Sisters, O.P., Congregation of St. Mary, 580 Broadway, 70118-3593. Tel: 504-861-8183; Fax: 504-861-8184. Sr. Therese Leckert, O.P., Prioress. Generalate Staff Sisters 5; Total Sisters in Archdiocese 67.
Little Sisters of the Poor, L.S.P., 4201 Woodland Dr., 70131-7398. Tel: 504-394-2200. Sisters 12.
Marianites of Holy Cross, M.S.C. (1848), 1011 Gallier St., 70117-6111. Tel: 504-945-1620; Fax: 504-944-0756. Sr. Mary Kay Kinberger, Congregational Leader. Total Sisters in Archdiocese 97.
Missionary Sisters of the Sacred Heart (Cabrini) M.S.C., 3400 Esplanade Ave., 70119-2993. Tel: 504-488-4174; Fax: 504-483-4180. Total Sisters in Archdiocese 4.
Presentation Sisters of the Blessed Virgin Mary, Union of, P.B.V.M. (United States Province), 1920 Robert E. Lee Blvd., 70122-3512. Tel: 504-283-3352. Total Sisters in Archdiocese 4.
Religious of the Good Shepherd, R.G.S., 2914 Napoleon Ave., 70115-6918; Fax: 504-899-2052. Total Sisters in Archdiocese 8.
Religious of the Sacred Heart, R.S.C.J., 1837 Milan St., 70115-9990. Tel: 504-899-3037. Sisters 5. 4600 Carondelet St., 70115-4822. Tel: 504-891-0412. Sisters 4. 1719 Napoleon Ave., 70115-4809. Tel: 504-899-6027; Fax: 504-899-6210. Sr. Margaret Hoffman, R.S.C.J., Dir. Sisters 5. Total Sisters in Archdiocese 14.
St. Clare's Monastery of the Blessed Sacrament, O.S.C. (1885), 720 Henry Clay Ave., 70118-5891. Tel: 504-895-2019. Nuns of the Order of St. Clare. Sr. Elizabeth Mortell, O.S.C., Abbess. Solemn Professed Nuns 11.
School Sisters of Notre Dame (Dallas, TX), S.S.N.D., Redeemer Convent, 7010 Milne Blvd., 70124-2343. Tel: 504-288-5002. Total Sisters in Archdiocese 21.
Sisters of Mercy of the Americas, R.S.M. (St. Louis Regional Community), 6000 Charlotte Dr., 70122-2732. Tel: 504-282-4651; Fax: 504-482-6125. Mercy Family Center, 3816 Bienville St., 70119. Tel: 504-482-6600.
Mercy Hospital Convent, 301 N. Jefferson Davis Pkwy., 70119-5397. Tel: 504-483-5000. Total Sisters in Archdiocese 53.
Sisters of St. Joseph of Medaille, New Orleans, C.S.J., 1200 Mirabeau Ave., 70122-1997. Tel: 504-283-9493; Fax: 504-288-4044. Sr. Anne Meridier, C.S.J., Coord. of Complex. Total Sisters in Archdiocese 62.
People Program, Inc., 1200 Mirabeau Ave., 70122-1997. Tel: 504-288-3171; Fax: 504-288-3503. Sr. Carolyn Brady, C.S.J., Pres.; Mrs. Mary Catherine Lombard, Dir.
Sisters of the Blessed Sacrament, S.B.S., 947 S. Cortez St., 70125-1105. Tel: 504-488-5325. 947 S. Cortiz St., 70125. Tel: 504-486-4257. 5116 Magazine St., 70115. Tel: 504-897-0235. 4936 Dixon St., 70125. Tel: 504-486-7426. 5014 Howard Ave., New Oleans, 70125. Tel: 504-486-0917. 3812 Pine St., 70125. Tel: 504-482-0917. 2323 S. Galvez St., 70125. Tel: 504-821-1134. Total Sisters in Archdiocese 36.
Sisters of the Holy Family Motherhouse and Novitiate, S.S.F. (1842), 6901 Chef Menteur Hwy., 70126-5290. Tel: 504-242-8315; 504-241-5400; Fax: 504-241-3957. Mother M. de Chantal St. Julien, S.S.F., Supr. Gen. Total Sisters in Archdiocese 138.
Sisters of the Holy Family Development Office, 2710 Gentilly Blvd., 70122-3098. Tel: 504-949-4572; Fax: 504-241-3957.
Sisters, Servants of Mary, S.M., 5001 Perlita St., 70122-1999. Tel: 504-282-5549. Sr. Auxilio Corrales, S.M., Supr. Total Home Nursing Sisters in Archdiocese 21.
Ursuline Sisters of Crystal City, MO, O.S.U. (1727), 2734 Nashville Ave., 70115-7008. Tel: 504-866-1472. Sr. Susan Kienzler, O.S.U., Prioress. Total Sisters in Archdiocese 19.

CHALMETTE. *Daughters of Divine Providence, F.D.P.*, 3100 Mumphrey Rd., 70043-3735. Tel: 504-279-4617. Total Sisters in Archdiocese 2.

COVINGTON. *Carmelite Nuns, Discalced, O.C.D., Monastery of St. Joseph and St. Theresa* (1877), 73530 River Rd., 70435-2206. Tel: 504-898-0923; Fax: 504-871-9060. Professed Nuns 9.
Teresian Sisters (Society of St. Teresa of Jesus), S.T.J., Provincial House, 18080 St. Joseph's Way, 70435-5623. Tel: 504-893-1470; Fax: 504-893-2476. Sr. Carmen Gloria Plasencia, S.T.J., Prov. Sisters 20.
Formation House, 18158 St. Joseph's Way, 70435-5624. Tel: 504-893-1557. Sr. Marina Aranzabal, S.T.J., Dir. Novices.

GRETNA. *Sisters of the Living Word, S.L.W.*, 901 Hancock St., 70053-2227. Tel: 504-366-5358. Sisters 2; Total Sisters in Archdiocese 11.

HARVEY. *Sinsinawa Dominican Congregation of the Most Holy Rosary, O.P.*, 2824 Keith Way Dr., 70058-1921. Tel: 504-340-6822. Sr. Carol Artery, O.P.; Sr. Priscilla Wood, O.P. Sisters 2.

LACOMBE. *Congregation of Our Lady of Mount Carmel, O.Carm.* (1833), Generalate P.O. Box 476, 70445-0476. Tel: 504-882-7577; 524-2398; Fax: 504-524-5011. Sr. Rose Marie Penouilh, O.Carm., Pres. Sisters 61. Mount Carmel Development Office, P.O. Box 1160, 70445-1160. Tel: 504-882-7577; 524-2398; Fax: 504-524-5011. Sr. Andree Marie Bindewald, O.Carm., Dir.

MANDEVILLE. *St. Gertrude's Convent, Benedictine Sisters*, c/o Prieto & Prieto, Attorneys, 2900 E. Causeway Approach, Ste. D, 70448-3597.

MARRERO. *Lovers of the Holy Cross, L.H.C.*, 1216 Avenue G, 70072-3750. Tel: 504-348-8206. Sr. Martha Ann Nguyen, L.H.C., Supr. Total Sisters in Archdiocese 5.
Salesian Sisters (Daughters of Mary Help of Christians) F.M.A., Immaculate Conception Convent, 612 Avenue B, 70072-2016. Tel: 504-347-8449; Fax: 504-341-6229. Sisters in Archdiocese 9.
Sisters of the Holy Cross, C.S.C., 1050 Medical Center Blvd., 70072-3170. Tel: 504-347-3443. Sisters 3.

METAIRIE. *Daughters of St. Paul Convent, F.S.P.*, St. Paul Book & Media Center, 4403 Veterans Memorial Blvd., 70006-5321. Tel: 504-887-7631; Fax: 504-888-4745. Total Sisters in Archdiocese 4.
Incarnate Word Sisters, C.C.V.I., 2904 Houma Blvd., Apt. D, 70006-1422. Tel: 504-888-1410. Total Sisters in Archdiocese 6.
Religious of Our Lady of the Retreat in the Cenacle, R.C., The Cenacle Retreat House, 5500 St. Mary St., P.O. Box 8115, 70011-8115. Tel: 504-887-1420; Fax: 504-887-6624. Sr. JoAnn Viviano, R.C., Supr. Sisters 7.
Sisters of the Most Holy Sacrament, M.H.S., 420 Bonnabel Blvd., 70005-3240. Tel: 504-831-5786. Total Sisters in Archdiocese 7.

PORT SULPHUR. *Sisters of St. Francis of Perpetual Adoration, O.S.F.*, St. Jude Convent, P.O. Box 36, 70083-0036. Tel: 504-564-3234. Sr. M. Louise Pfeifer, Supr. Sisters 4.

SLIDELL. *Dominican Sisters (Adrian), O.P.*, 952 Asheville Dr., 70458-2145. Tel: 504-643-7007. Total Sisters in Archdiocese 4.

[R] RETREAT HOUSES

NEW ORLEANS. *Archdiocesan Spirituality Center*, 2901 S. Carrollton Ave., 70118-4391. Tel: 504-861-3254. Sr. Noel Toomey, O.P., Dir.
Center of Jesus the Lord, 1236 N. Rampart St., 70116-2497. Tel: 504-529-1636; Fax: 504-529-5003. Rev. Vincent Bono, S.C., Dir.
Dominican Conference Center, 540 Broadway, 70118-3593. Tel: 504-861-8711; Fax: 504-861-8718. Sr. Mary Ann Culotta, O.P., Dir.
Sophie Barat House, 1719 Napoleon Ave., 70115-4809. Tel: 504-899-6027; Fax: 504-899-6210. Sr. Margaret Hoffman, R.S.C.J.; Sr. Jane McKinlay, R.S.C.J.; Sr. Anne Sturges, R.S.C.J. Total Staff 3; Total in Residence 5.

COVINGTON. *Regina Coeli Retreat Center*, 17225 Regina Coeli Rd., 70435-9156. Tel: 504-892-4110. Managers: Earl Magner; June Magner.

LACOMBE. *Blessing Place*, P.O. Box 130, 70445-0130.

Tel: 504-882-7579; Fax: 504-524-5011. Sr. Barbara Breaud, O.Carm., Dir. Personal growth and development community for women and men religious and clergy.

MARRERO. *Ave Maria Retreat House*, HC 62, Box 368 AB, 70072-9704. Tel: 504-689-3837; Fax: 504-689-2785. Rev. Gerald J. Fogarty, O.M.I., Dir.; Bro. Danna J. Gauthreaux, O.M.I., Assoc. Dir. Total Staff 7; Total in Residence 2.

METAIRIE. *Cenacle Retreat House*, 5500 St. Mary St., P.O. Box 8115, 70011-8115. Tel: 504-887-1420; Fax: 504-887-6624. Sr. JoAnn Viviano, R.C., Retreat House Admin.; Sr. Mary C. Daniel, O.P., Ministry Coord.; Rev. John L. Hein, S.J., Chap. Religious 8; Total Staff 32.

PONCHATOULA. *Magnificat Center of the Holy Spirit*, 23629 Faith Rd., 70454. Tel: 504-362-4356; 800-531-9710. Rev. Vincent Bono, S.C., Dir.

ST. BENEDICT. *Abbey Christian Life Center*, St. Joseph Abbey, 70457-9999. Tel: 504-892-3473; 892-1800. Conducted by Benedictine Monks. Rev. Thomas Perrier, O.S.B., Dir.

[S] MISCELLANEOUS

NEW ORLEANS. *Christian Brothers Foundation*, #8 Friederichs Ave., 70124-4602. Tel: 504-482-3349.

Equestrian Order of the Holy Sepulchre. (of Jerusalem, Southeastern Lieutenancy of the U.S.), 5614 Marcia Ave., 70124-1006. Lt. George H. Toye, K.G.C.H.S.

**Focus Syndicate, Inc.*, 2929 S. Carrollton Ave., 70118.

Foundation for Christian Education, S.T.J., 1611 Mirabeau Ave., 70112-2511. Tel: 504-288-1289; Fax: 504-288-9946. Sr. Carmen Gloria Plasencia, S.T.J., Pres.

Jesuit Program for Living and Learning of New Orleans, Inc., 4128 Baudin St., 70119-6815. Rev. Robert Allanach, O.M.I., Ph.D., Exec. Dir.

Jesuit Seminary and Mission Bureau, 500 S. Jefferson Davis Pkwy., 70119-7192. Tel: 504-827-4043; Fax: 504-827-9931. Revs. Thomas H. Clancy, S.J., Dir.; Martin V. Jarreau, S.J., Assoc. Dir.

MCA Foundation, 420 Robert E. Lee Blvd., 70124-2596. Tel: 504-524-2398. Sr. Rose Marie Penouilh, O.Carm., Dir.

The Patrons of the Vatican Museums in the South, Inc., 775 Harrison Ave., 70124-3192. Very Rev. Val A. McInnes, O.P., Founder & Pres. Emeritus; Mr. Paul A. Nalty, Pres.

Pierre Toussaint Foundation of New Orleans, Inc., 2600 A.P. Tereaud Ave., 70119-1299. Tel: 504-949-3113. Rev. Joseph M. Doyle, S.S.J., Pres.

Stella Roman Foundation, Inc., 1207 First NBC Bldg., 70112-2385. Rev. Msgr. John P. Reynolds, Pres.

**WLAE-TV, Educational Broadcasting Foundation, Inc.*, 2929 S. Carrollton Ave., 70118-4301. Tel: 504-866-7411; Fax: 504-861-5186. Most Rev. Philip M. Hannan, Pres., Bd. of Trustees.

MANDEVILLE. *Mary Queen of Peace School*, 1501 W. Causeway Approach, 70471.

METAIRIE. *Southern Dominican Foundation*, 1421 N. Causeway Blvd., Ste. 200, 70001-4144. Tel: 504-837-2129; Fax: 504-837-6604. Revs. Alberto Rodriguez, O.P., Pres.; Carl B. Trutter, O.P., Vice Pres./Sec.; Val A. McInnes, O.P., Promoter of Development; Nora P. Fine, Dir. of Development.

Southern Dominican Global Missions, 1421 N. Causeway Blvd., Ste. 200, 70001-4144. Rev. James A. McDonough, O.P. (AUS), Dir.

SLIDELL.

**S.A.V.E., Inc.*, P.O. Box 1594, 70459. Tel: 504-847-0133. Ms. Linda Jefferson, Pres.

SECULAR INSTITUTES

NEW ORLEANS. *Society of Our Lady of the Way*, 6044 Louis XIV St., 70124-2919. Tel: 504-486-2506.

ABITA SPRINGS. *Caritas*, Administration Center, P.O. Box 308, 70420-0308. Tel: 504-892-4345.

Daraja House, 810 N. Madison St., Covington, 70433-2130. Tel: 504-893-2261.

RELIGIOUS INSTITUTES OF MEN REPRESENTED IN THE ARCHDIOCESE

For further details refer to the corresponding bracketed number in the Religious Institutes of Men or Women section.

[0200]—*Benedictine Monks*.—O.S.B.
[1350]—*Brothers of St. Francis Xavier*.—C.F.X.
[0330]—*Brothers of the Christian Schools*. (New Orleans Prov.).—F.S.C.
[0600]—*Brothers of the Congregation of Holy Cross*. (Midwest; Southwest Provs.).—C.S.C.
[0470]—*The Capuchin Friars*.—O.F.M.Cap.
[0270]—*Carmelite Fathers*.—O.Carm.
[0360]—*Claretian Missionaries*.—C.M.F.
[0220]—*Congregation of the Blessed Sacrament*.—S.S.S.
[1330]—*Congregation of the Mission Fathers & Brothers*. (Southern Prov.).—C.M.
[]—*Congregation of the Mother Coredemptrix*.—C.M.C.
[0260]—*Discalced Carmelite Friars*.—O.C.D.
[0520]—*Franciscan Friars*.—O.F.M.
[0650]—*Holy Ghost Fathers*. (Western Vice Prov.; Ireland).—C.S.Sp.
[]—*Incarnational Consecration*.—I.C.
[0690]—*Jesuit Fathers and Brothers*. (New Orleans).—S.J.
[0780]—*Marist Fathers and Brothers*. (Washington Prov.).—S.M.
[0840]—*Missionary Servants of the Most Holy Trinity*.—S.T.
[0910]—*Oblates of Mary Immaculate*. (Southern American Prov.).—O.M.I.
[0430]—*Order of Preacher-Dominicans*. (Southern Prov.).—O.P.
[1310]—*Order of the Most Holy Trinity*.—O.SS.T.
[1100]—*Priests and Brothers of the Sacred Heart*. (Metuchen, NJ).—S.C.
[0610]—*Priests of the Congregation of Holy Cross*. (Southern Prov.).—C.S.C.
[1070]—*Redemptorist Fathers and Brothers*. (New Orleans).—C.SS.R.
[0700]—*St. Joseph's Society of the Sacred Heart*. (Baltimore, MD).—S.S.J.
[1170]—*St. Patrick Missionary Society*.—S.P.S.
[1190]—*Salesians of Don Bosco*.—S.D.B.
[0760]—*Society of Mary*. St. Louis Province.—S.M.
[0440]—*Society of St. Edmund*.—S.S.E.
[0420]—*Society of the Divine Word*. (St. Augustine Prov.).—S.V.D.

RELIGIOUS INSTITUTES OF WOMEN REPRESENTED IN THE ARCHDIOCESE

[0230]—*Benedictine Sisters of Pontifical Jurisdiction*. (Cullman, AL; Colorado; Atchison, KS).—O.S.B.
[0400]—*Congregation of Our Lady of Mount Carmel*.—O.Carm.
[3110]—*Congregation of Our Lady of the Retreat in the Cenacle*.—R.C.
[1940]—*Congregation of Sisters of the Holy Faith*.—C.H.F.
[2410]—*Congregation of the Marianites of Holy Cross*.—M.S.C.
[0460]—*Congregation of the Sisters of Charity of the Incarnate Word*.—C.C.V.I.
[1920]—*Congregation of the Sisters of the Holy Cross*.—C.S.C.
[1950]—*Congregation of the Sisters of the Holy Family*.—S.S.F.
[0800]—*Daughters of Divine Providence*.—F.D.P.
[0850]—*Daughters of Mary Help of Christians*.—F.M.A.
[]—*Daughters of Our Lady of the Holy Rosary*.—F.M.S.R.
[0760]—*Daughters of St. Vincent de Paul*.—D.C.
[0420]—*Discalced Carmelite Nuns*.—O.C.D.
[1110]—*Dominican Sisters of Our Lady of the Rosary and of Saint Catherine of Siena, Cabra, Ireland*.—O.P.
[1070-08]—*Dominican Sisters, Congregation of St. Mary*.—O.P.
[1070-02]—*Dominican Sisters, Congregation of St. Mary of the Springs*.—O.P.
[1070-13]—*Dominican Sisters, Congregation of the Most Holy Rosary*.—O.P.
[1070-03]—*Dominican Sisters, Sinsinawa Dominican Congregation of the Most Holy Rosary*.—O.P.
[1140]—*Eucharistic Missionaries of St. Dominic*.—O.P.
[1430]—*Franciscan Sisters of Our Lady of Perpetual Help*.—O.S.F.
[]—*Handmaids of the Holy Child of Jesus*.—H.H.C.J.
[2340]—*Little Sisters of the Poor*.—L.S.P.
[2390]—*Lovers of the Holy Cross Sisters*.—L.H.C.
[2490]—*Medical Mission Sisters*.—M.M.S.
[2790]—*Missionary Sisters of the Most Blessed Trinity*.—M.S.B.T.
[2860]—*Missionary Sisters of the Sacred Heart*.—M.S.C.
[0950]—*Pious Society Daughters of St. Paul*.—F.S.P.
[3760]—*Poor Clare Nuns, Order of St. Clare*.—O.S.C.
[2970]—*School Sisters of Notre Dame*. (Dallas & Mankato, South Central Prov.).—S.S.N.D.
[]—*Sisters for Christian Community*.—S.F.C.C.
[0660]—*Sisters of Christian Charity*. (Wilmette, IL).—S.C.C.
[1010]—*Sisters of Divine Providence of San Antonio, Texas*.—C.D.P.
[2575]—*Sisters of Mercy of the Americas*. (Brooklyn; St. Louis).—R.S.M.
[2630]—*Sisters of Mercy of the Holy Cross*.—S.C.S.C.
[]—*Sisters of St. Francis*. (Glen Riddle, PA).—O.S.F.
[1640]—*Sisters of St. Francis of Perpetual Adoration*.—O.S.F.
[1670]—*Sisters of St. Francis of Savannah*.—O.S.F.
[1530]—*Sisters of St. Francis of the Congregation of Our Lady of Lourdes, Sylvania, Ohio*.—O.S.F.
[3840]—*Sisters of St. Joseph of Carondelet*.—C.S.J.
[3880]—*Sisters of St. Joseph of Medaille*.—C.S.J.
[3830-11]—*Sisters of St. Joseph, Kalamazoo*.—S.S.J.
[0260]—*Sisters of the Blessed Sacrament for Indians and Colored People*.—S.B.S.
[1830]—*Sisters of the Good Shepherd*.—R.G.S.
[2050]—*Sisters of the Holy Spirit and Mary Immaculate*.—S.H.Sp.
[2120]—*Sisters of the Immaculate Conception*.—C.I.C.
[2350]—*Sisters of the Living Word*.—S.L.W.
[2940]—*Sisters of the Most Holy Sacrament*.—M.H.S.
[3320]—*Sisters of the Presentation of the B.V.M.* (Aberdeen, SD; Newburgh, NY; Ireland).—P.B.V.M.
[3600]—*Sisters Servants of Mary*.—S.M.
[4020]—*Society of St. Teresa of Jesus*.—S.T.J.
[4060]—*Society of the Holy Child Jesus*.—S.H.C.J.
[4070]—*Society of the Sacred Heart*.—R.S.C.J.
[4110]—*Ursuline Nuns*.—O.S.U.
[4120]—*Ursuline Nuns, of the Congregation of Paris*. (Paola, KS).—O.S.U.
[]—*West Indian Franciscans*.—W.I.F.

NECROLOGY

(No Deaths)

Diocese of New Ulm

(Dioecesis Novae Ulmae)

Most Reverend

RAYMOND A. LUCKER, S.T.D.

Bishop of New Ulm; ordained June 7, 1952; appointed Titular Bishop of Meta July 12, 1971; consecrated September 8, 1971; appointed to New Ulm December 23, 1975; installed February 19, 1976. *Res., Catholic Pastoral Center, 1400 6th St., N., New Ulm, MN, 56073-2099.* Tel.: 507-359-2966; Fax: 507-354-3667.

ESTABLISHED NOVEMBER 18, 1957.

Square Miles 9,863.

Comprises the Counties of Big Stone, Brown, Chippewa, Kandiyohi, Lac Qui Parle, Lincoln, Lyon, McLeod, Meeker, Nicollet, Redwood, Renville, Sibley, Swift and Yellow Medicine in the State of Minnesota.

For legal titles of parishes and diocesan institutions, consult the Catholic Pastoral Center.

Catholic Pastoral Center: 1400 6th St., N., New Ulm, MN, 56073-2099. Tel.: 507-359-2966; Fax: 507-354-3667.

E-mail address: dnucomm@ic.new-ulm.mn.us

STATISTICAL OVERVIEW

Personnel	
Bishop	1
Priests: Diocesan Active in Diocese	55
Priests: Active Outside Diocese	8
Priests: Diocesan in Foreign Missions	3
Priests: Retired, Sick or Absent	29
Number of Diocesan Priests	95
Extern Priests in Diocese	3
Ordinations:	
Permanent Deacons in Diocese	3
Total Sisters	99
Parishes	
Parishes	81
With Resident Pastor:	
Resident Diocesan Priests	47
Without Resident Pastor:	
Administered by Priests	14
Administered by Women Religious	17
Administered by Lay People	3
Missions	2
Professional Ministry Personnel:	
Sisters	1
Lay Ministers	50
Welfare	
Catholic Hospitals	1
Total Assisted	7,314
Health Care Centers	2
Total Assisted	7,985
Homes for the Aged	6
Total Assisted	452
Other Institutions	1
Total Assisted	1,172
Educational	
Diocesan Students in Other Seminaries	5
Total Seminarians	5
High Schools, Diocesan and Parish	3
Total Students	669
Elementary Schools, Diocesan and Parish	19
Total Students	3,498
Catechesis/Religious Education:	
High School Students	4,070
Elementary Students	8,687
Total Students Under Catholic Instruction	16,929
Teachers in the Diocese:	
Sisters	12
Lay Teachers	247
Vital Statistics	
Receptions into the Church:	
Infant Baptism Totals	1,025
Adult Baptism Totals	60
Received into Full Communion	112
First Communions	1,426
Confirmations	1,320
Marriages:	
Catholic	253
Interfaith	229
Total Marriages	482
Deaths	759
Total Catholic Population	71,272
Total Population	282,768

Former Bishop—Most Rev. ALPHONSE J. SCHLADWEILER, D.D., ord. June 9, 1929; appt. Nov. 28, 1957; cons. Jan. 29, 1958; retired Dec. 23, 1975; died April 3, 1996.

Diocesan Officials

Catholic Pastoral Center—Most Rev. RAYMOND A. LUCKER, S.T.D., *1400 6th St. N., New Ulm, 56073-2099.* Tel: 507-359-2966; Fax: 507-354-3667.

Vicar General—Rev. DENNIS C. LABAT, *Catholic Pastoral Center, 1400 6th St. N., New Ulm, 56073-2099.* Tel: 507-359-2966.

Chancellor—EUGENE E. BURKE, *Catholic Pastoral Center, 1400 6th St. N., New Ulm, 56073-2099.* Tel: 507-233-5322; 359-2966.

Vice-Chancellor—Rev. JOHN G. BERGER, *Church of St. Willibrord, 1032 Ash Ave., Gibbon, 55335-9998.* Tel: 507-834-6461.

Diocesan Tribunal—

Officialis—Rev. JOHN G. BERGER, *Church of St. Willibrord, 1032 Ash Ave., Gibbon, 55335-9998.* Tel: 507-834-6461.

Associate Judges—Revs. EUGENE L. LOZINSKI; GERALD S. MEIDL; JAMES E. MORAN; JEROME E. PAULSON; GERMAIN P. RADEMACHER; PAUL L. WOLF; DOUGLAS L. GRAMS.

Defenders of the Bond—Rev. JAMES E. MORAN; EUGENE L. LOZINSKI.

Auditor—EUGENE E. BURKE.

Advocates—Rev. MICHAEL L. SUMMERFIELD; EUGENE E. BURKE.

Notaries—ROSEMARY SCHUELLER; JANELLE DREXLER; SHERI JOHNSON.

Diocesan Boards and Councils

Building Committee—Revs. PAUL L. WOLF, Chm., *Church of St. Anne, 950 North St., P.O. Box 239, Wabasso, 56293-0239.* Tel: 507-342-5190; 342-5155. EUGENE C. HACKERT; ROBERT J. MRAZ; STEVEN J. VERHELST; RAY MCCLELLAN; RICHARD GREENE; LUCILLE O'DONNELL; JANE BERNARD; GREG WALSH; JOE EIKMEIER.

College of Consultors—Revs. GEORGE V. SCHMIT; PATRICK L. CASEY; RICHARD C. GROSS; BRIAN L. MANDEL; WILLIAM A. SPRIGLER; DENNIS C. LABAT; PAUL L. WOLF.

Committee on Parishes—Most Rev. RAYMOND A. LUCKER; EUGENE E. BURKE. Staff: Revs. ANTHONY J. STUBEDA; DENNIS C. LABAT; GERALD S. MEIDL; MICHAEL L. SUMMERFIELD; Sr. KATHYRN SCHOOLMEESTERS, S.S.N.D.; JOSEPH EIKMEIER; JUDI WEBER; ROBERT ALCORN; DONALD A. CLASEMANN; ROSE JONCAS; WILLIAM HENDRICKSON.

Corporate Board—Most Rev. RAYMOND A. LUCKER; Rev. DENNIS C. LABAT; Mr. EUGENE E. BURKE; Mr. WILLIAM T. O'CONNOR; Mr. PAUL ZINS.

Diocesan Pastoral Council—WAYNE KRAMER, Chm., *Box 353, Arlington, 55307.* Tel: 612-237-5165(Office); 964-2830(Home). EUGENE E. BURKE, Staff. Members: MARY ANN BLANCHETTE; JOSE CENICEROS; SHERRY DREITZ; SUE FLEEGEL; GREG GOBLIRSCH; DONNA HANLON; Sr. JEANETTE HOMAN, O.S.F.; KEVIN KALKOFF; EVONNE KREMER; KEN KREMER; LEO MCTIGHE; AGNES MEIUM; JULIE MOORHEAD; DONALD PALS; CAROL KRAMER; MARION MONNENS; CLIFF SCHLOSSER; ANDREW RHODE; RAYMOND TRAEN; WALLY MAUS; MARY ANN KRAMER; Revs. RICHARD C. GROSS; PAUL L. WOLF.

Finance Council—Revs. GERMAIN P. RADEMACHER; BERNARD J. STEINER; ANTHONY J. STUBEDA; GERI BURESH; DANIEL BERANEK; RAY MCCLELLAN; NANCY O'LEARY; THOMAS SENDEN; SANDY REDDING.

Priests' Council—Rev. PAUL L. WOLF, Chm., *Church of St. Anne, 950 North St., P.O. Box 239, Wabasso, 56293-0239.* Tel: 507-342-5190; 342-5155. Rev. WILLIAM A. SPRIGLER, Vice Chm. PATRICK L. CASEY, Treas.; Revs. GEORGE V. SCHMIT; DENNIS C. LABAT; RICHARD C. GROSS; BRIAN L. MANDEL.

Sisters' Council—Sr. JANET MALLAK, S.S.N.D., Chm., *Center for Spiritual Development, 211 S. 10th St., P.O. Box 538, Bird Island, 55310-0538.* Tel: 320-365-3644. Sr. BETTY LARSON, O.S.B., Vice Chm.; Sr. GLADYS MEINDL, O.S.F., Treas./Sec.; Sr. BETTY LARSON, O.S.B., Staff Liaison.

Catholic Pastoral Center

Coordinator of Diocesan Staff—EUGENE E. BURKE, *Catholic Pastoral Center, 1400 6th St. N., New Ulm, 56073-2099.* Tel: 507-359-2966; 233-5322.

Office of Finance—Mr. RAY MCCLELLAN, Dir., *Catholic Pastoral Center, 1400 6th St. N., New Ulm, 56073-2099.* Tel: 507-359-2966.

Office of Development—Rev. ANTHONY J. STUBEDA, Dir., *Catholic Pastoral Center, 1400 6th St. N., New Ulm, 56073-2099.* Tel: 507-359-2966; 233-5327.

Evangelization and Catechesis—

Religious Education/Adult Religious Education—JOANN BORCHERT, Dir., *Catholic Pastoral Center, 1400 6th St. N., New Ulm, 56073-2099.* Tel: 507-359-2966.

Catholic Schools Ministry Formation—Sr. BETTY LARSON, O.S.B., Dir., Schools, *Catholic Pastoral Center, 1400 6th St. N., New Ulm, 56073-2099.* Tel: 507-359-2966.

Youth & Young Adult Ministry—BILL CASEY, Dir., *Catholic Pastoral Center, 1400 6th St. N., New Ulm, 56073-2099.* Tel: 507-359-2966.

A-TEC (Adult/Teens Encounter Christ)—Rev. DENNIS C. LABAT, Coord., *Catholic Pastoral Center, 1400*

6th St. N., New Ulm, 56073-2099. Tel: 507-359-2966.

Communications—PAULA MARTI, Dir., *Catholic Pastoral Center, 1400 6th St. N., New Ulm, 56073-2099.* Tel: 507-359-2966; Fax: 507-354-3667.

"Prairie Catholic"—PAULA MARTI, Editor, *Catholic Pastoral Center, 1400 6th St. N., New Ulm, 56073-2099.* Tel: 507-359-2966.

Committee for Evangelization & Catechesis—JERRY NEUBAUER; Chm. Revs. PATRICK L. CASEY; PHILIP M. SCHOTZKO; ANNA MARIE REITER; Sr. MARY BUTZER, S.S.N.D.; ARLISS STENGER; Sr. MARY BUTZER, S.S.N.D.; KIM SMITH; MARIANNE PAFFEL; SUE FLEEGEL; JUDITH SCHINDLER.

Office of Worship and Spiritual Life—JANE BERNARD, Dir., *1400 6th St. N., New Ulm, 56073-2099.* Tel: 507-359-2966.

Worship Committee—JANE BERNARD, Staff, *1400 6th St. N., New Ulm, 56073-2099.* Tel: 507-359-2966. Members: Rev. JEFFREY P. HOREJSI, Chm.; Revs. GERALD S. MEIDL; RONALD V. HUBERTY; Sr. MONICA WAGNER, S.S.N.D.; Sr. BETTY LARSON, O.S.B.; JOANN BORCHERT; MARY BETH HAUSER; KATIE HENRICH; TOM JOHNSON; KAY OSBORNE; JOANNE WINDSCHITL; TERESA GUILLEMETTE; MARY BOLEK; GEORGE BLACKNEY.

RCIA Network—JANE BERNARD, *1400 6th St. N., New Ulm, 56073-2099.* Tel: 507-359-2966.

Charismatic Renewal—JAN CROWE, Diocesan Liaison, *21907 705th Ave., Dassel, 55325.* Tel: 320-275-2424.

Retreat Team—JAN CROWE, Coord., *21907 705th Ave., Dassel, 55325.* Tel: 320-275-2424.

Center for Spiritual Development—Co-Dirs.: Sr. JANET MALLAK, S.S.N.D.; Sr. MARJORIE KLEIN, S.S.N.D., *211 10th St., P.O. Box 538, Bird Island, 55310-0538.* Tel: 320-365-3644.

Ecumenical Director—Rev. HARRY P. BEHAN, *Church of St. Peter, 524 W. Myrtle St., P.O. Box 522, St. Peter, 56082-0522.* Tel: 507-931-1628.

Members—Sr. CAROLYN PUCCIO, C.S.J.; TOM CROWE; JAN CROWE; JUDITH SCHINDLER; TOM CHRISTOFFER.

Office of Social Concerns and Family Life—CHRISTOPHER A. LOETSCHER, Dir., *1400 6th St. N., New Ulm, 56073-2099.* Tel: 507-359-2966.

Social Concerns Committee—CHRISTOPHER A. LOETSCHER; Rev. JOHN A. NORDICK; ARNOLD NIMPS; JOAN NIMPS; CLIFF SCHLOSSER.

Family Life—CHRISTOPHER A. LOETSCHER, Dir., *1400 6th St. N., New Ulm, 56073-2099.* Tel: 507-359-2966. Marriage Preparation, Natural Family Planning, Resources & Referral for Marriage & Family Concerns, Divorced/Separated.

Retrouvaille—BOB PLAETZ; JULIE PLAETZ, *P.O. Box 52, Lucan, 56255.* Tel: 507-747-2345.

AIDS Ministry—Rev. PAUL A. SCHUMACHER, *Church of St. Brendan, P.O. Box 85, Green Isle, 55338-0085.* Tel: 507-326-5111.

Caritas Family Services: Pregnancy Counselor & Pro-Life Activities—BARBARA DIETZ, *1400 6th St. N., New Ulm, 56073-2099.* Tel: 507-359-2966.

Propagation of the Faith/Holy Childhood Association—Rev. WILLIAM H. BOWLES, *1400 6th St. N., New Ulm, 56073-2099.* Tel: 507-359-2966. San Lucas Mission Office; Rev. Msgr. GREGORY T. SCHAFFER; KATHY HUEBERT, *1400 6th St. N., New Ulm, 56073-2099.* Tel: 507-359-2966.

Hispanic Ministry—Rev. ANTHONY J. STUBEDA, Dir., *1400 6th St. N., New Ulm, 56073-2099.* Tel: 507-359-2966.

Office of Personnel—

Priest Personnel—Rev. DENNIS C. LABAT, Dir., *1400 6th St. N., New Ulm, 56073-2099.* Tel: 507-359-2966.

Priest Personnel Board—Revs. DENNIS C. LABAT, Dir. ROBERT J. MRAZ; GERMAIN P. RADEMACHER; JOSEPH A. STEINBEISSER; CELESTINE C. PISTULKA; FREDERICK T. FINK; BRIAN W. OESTREICH.

Pastoral Administrators—Rev. DENNIS C. LABAT; Supvr., *1400 6th St. N., New Ulm, 56073-2099.* Tel: 507-359-2966.

Bishop's Delegate in Matters Pertaining to Sexual Misconduct—EUGENE E. BURKE, *Catholic Pastoral Center, 1400 6th St. N., New Ulm, 56073-2099.* Tel: 507-359-2966; 233-5322.

New Ulm Diocesan Review Board on Sexual Misconduct—LILA SCHMIDT, Chm. STEVE SCHNEIDER; Vice Chm. EUGENE E. BURKE; MARY BOHLMANN; Rev. PAUL A. SCHUMACHER; WILLIAM F. WAGNER Ph.D.; MARY LINDSTROM.

Conciliation—EUGENE E. BURKE, Interim Dir., *1400 6th St. N., New Ulm, 56073-2099.* Tel: 507-359-2966; 233-5322.

Vocations—Rev. JOSEPH A. STEINBEISSER, Co-Dir., *1400 6th St. N., New Ulm, 56073-2099.* Tel: 507-359-2966., *Church of St. Mary, 713 12th St. S.W., Willmar, 56201-3099.* Tel: 320-235-0118; Fax: 320-235-0153. Rev. BRIAN W. OESTREICH, Co-Dir., *Cathedral of the Holy Trinity, 605 N. State St., New Ulm, 56073-1898.* Tel: 507-354-4158; Fax: 507-354-2563. Sr. SUE TORGERSEN C.S.J., Assoc. Dir., *1400 6th St. N., New Ulm, 56073-2099.* Tel: 507-359-2966; 359-5328.

Continuing Education of Clergy—Sr. SUE TORGERSEN C.S.J., Dir., *1400 6th St. N., New Ulm, 56073-2099.* Tel: 507-359-2966.

Committee for Continuing Education of Clergy—Rev. Msgr. ANTONY J. LEIFELD; Revs. GERMAIN P. RADEMACHER; EUGENE C. HACKERT; RONALD V. HUBERTY; MICHAEL M. DOYLE; ANDREW J. MICHELS; Sr. CATHERINE FIEGEN, P.B.V.M.; Sr. SUE TORGERSEN, C.S.J.; Rev. DENNIS C. LABAT; Sr. VIVIAN PETERSEN, O.S.B.

Board of Trustees for Pension Plan for Priests—Revs. DENNIS C. LABAT; JOHN H. BRUNNER; FREDERICK T. FINK; WILLIAM A. SPRIGLER; DONALD GUGGEMOS; MICHAEL G. REYNOLDS; KENNETH W. KUEHNER; RAY MCCLELLAN.

Vicar for Retired Priests—Rev. Msgr. ANTONY J. LEIFELD, *717 6th St. N., New Ulm, 56073-1853.* Tel: 507-359-9848.

Organizations in the Diocese of New Ulm

Diocesan Council of Catholic Women—JUNE BRUST, Pres., *Box 208, 203 Maye St., Tyler, 56178.* Tel: 507-247-5862. Rev. EUGENE L. LOZINSKI, Spiritual Dir.

Girl Scouts—Mrs. MARJORIE NELSON, *720 Bonham Blvd., Willmar, 56201-2953.* Tel: 320-235-1566.

Boy Scouts—Rev. ANDREW J. MICHELS, *Church of St. John, 421 Madison Ave., P.O. Box 205, Ortonville, 56278-0205.* Tel: 320-839-2772.

Marriage Encounter—DWAYNE WITTE; MARY LOU WITTE, *714 6th Ave. N.E., Sleepy Eye, 56085.* Tel: 507-794-7848.

Minnesota Pax Christi—Most Rev. RAYMOND A. LUCKER, Pres., *1400 6th St. N., New Ulm, 56073-2099.* Tel: 507-359-2966.

CLERGY, PARISHES, MISSIONS AND PAROCHIAL SCHOOLS

CITY OF NEW ULM
(Brown County)

1—CATHEDRAL OF THE HOLY TRINITY (1856). Clustered with Searles. Revs. George V. Schmit, Jr.; Ronald V. Huberty; Brian W. Oestreich; Rev. Msgr. Antony J. Leifeld, (Retired).
Res., 605 N. State St., 56073-1898. Tel: 507-354-4158; Fax: 507-354-2563. [CEM][JC]
School—New Ulm Area Catholic Schools. See separate listing under the Institutions for further explanation and statistics. Tel: 507-354-2719; Fax: 507-354-5711.
Catechesis/Religious Programs—Students 339.

2—ST. MARY (1911), Revs. Michael L. Summerfield; Eugene M. Brown.
Res., 404 S. German St., 56073-2113. Tel: 507-354-4043. [JC]
School—New Ulm Area Catholic Schools. See separate listing under the Institutions for further explanation and statistics.
Catechesis/Religious Programs—Tel: 507-354-6497.
Students 458.

OUTSIDE THE CITY OF NEW ULM

Appleton, Swift Co., St. John (1880) (Norwegian-Polish), Rev. Paul J. Hadusek.
Mailing Address: 450 S. Gaulke St., 56208-1516. Tel: 320-289-1211. [CEM 2]
Church—350 S. Edquist St., 56208. Tel: 320-289-1146.
Catechesis/Religious Programs—Tel: 320-289-1146.
Students 97.

Arlington, Sibley Co., St. Mary (1864). Clustered with Faxon Township, Green Isle, Henderson & Jessenland. Rev. James D. Barry.
Res., 504 7th Ave., N.W., P.O. Box 392, 55307-0392. Tel: 507-964-5413. [CEM]
Catechesis/Religious Programs—Students 169.

Barry, Big Stone Co., St. Barnabas. Closed. For sacramental records contact Holy Rosary, Graceville.

Beardsley, Big Stone Co., St. Mary (1884). Clustered with Graceville. Rev. John A. Nordick, (Graceville), Tel: 320-748-7313; Sr. Kathleen Henneberry, C.H.M., Pastoral Admin.
Res., 101 Church St., P.O. Box 299, 56211-0299. Tel: 320-265-6916 (Church); 265-6113 (Rectory). [CEM]
Catechesis/Religious Programs—Students 69.

Bechyn, Renville Co., St. Mary. Closed. For sacramental records contact St. Aloysius, Olivia.

Belgrade, Nicollet Co., St. Michael. Closed. For sacramental records contact St. Paul, Nicollet.

Benson, Swift Co., St. Francis (1881). Clustered with Clontarf, Danvers, De Graff & Murdock. Rev. Steven J. Verhelst Tel: 320-843-2342. Area Pastoral Leaders: Rev. Ronald V. Huberty, (Murdock), Tel: 320-875-2451; Sr. Clara M. Stang, O.S.F., Pastoral Admin. (Danvers), Tel: 320-567-2278; Sr. Darlene Gutenkauf, P.B.V.M., Pastoral Admin. (De Graff), Tel: 320-843-3883; Sr. Dorothy Jorgenson, C.S.J., Pastoral Minister (Clontarf), Tel: 320-843-2026.
Area Office—Tel: 320-842-4271; Fax: 320-843-2264.
Church—508 13th St., N., 56215-1228. [CEM]
Catechesis/Religious Programs—Students 239.

Birch Coolie, Renville Co., St. Patrick. Closed. For sacramental records contact Sacred Heart, Franklin.

Bird Island, Renville Co., St. Mary (1879). Clustered with Hector. Rev. Philip M. Schotzko.
Res., 220 S. 10th St., P.O. Box 500, 55310-0500. Tel: 320-365-3593; Fax: 320-365-3142. [CEM]
School—(Grades K-8). Tel: 320-365-3693. Sr. Patricia McCusker, S.S.N.D., Prin.
Sisters 1; Lay Teachers 12; Students 193.
Catechesis/Religious Programs—Students 88.

Canby, Yellow Medicine Co., St. Peter (1897). Clustered with St. Leo. Rev. Paul H. van de Crommert.
Res., 307 W. 4th St., 56220-1211. Tel: 507-223-7304. [CEM]
School—(Grades K-6). Tel: 507-223-7729. Mary Kontz, Prin.
Sisters 1; Lay Teachers 6; Students 102.
Catechesis/Religious Programs—(Grades PreK-10). Tel: 507-223-7304.
Students 186.

Clara City, Chippewa Co., St. Clara (1890). Clustered with Granite Falls. Sr. Catherine Fiegen, P.B.V.M., Pastoral Admin.; Rev. William A. Sprigler, (Granite Falls), Tel: 320-564-2335.
414 N. Main St., P.O. Box 310, 56222-0310. Tel: 320-847-2256. [CEM 2]
Catechesis/Religious Programs—Tel: 320-847-2445.
Students 163.

Clarkfield, Yellow Medicine Co., St. Isidore. Closed. For sacramental records contact St. Joseph, Montevideo.

Clements, Redwood Co., St. Joseph (1902). Clustered with Morgan. Rev. Eugene C. Hackert, (Morgan), Tel: 507-249-3643; Sr. Kathryn Schoolmeesters, S.S.N.D., Pastoral Admin.
120 Ash St., P.O. Box 56, 56224-0056. Tel: 507-692-2181. [CEM]

Clontarf, Swift Co., St. Malachy (1878). Clustered with Benson, Danvers, De Graff & Murdock. Rev. Steven J. Verhelst, (Benson), Tel: 320-843-2342. Area Pastoral Leaders: Rev. Ronald V. Huberty, (Murdock), Tel: 320-875-2451; Sr. Clara M. Stang, O.S.F., Pastoral Admin. (Danvers), Tel: 320-567-2278; Sr. Darlene Gutenkauf, P.B.V.M., Pastoral Admin. (De Graff), Tel: 320-843-3883; Sr. Dorothy Jorgenson, C.S.J., Pastoral Minister (Clontarf), Tel: 320-843-2026.
Area Office—Tel: 320-842-4271.
Church—P.O. Box 218, 56226-0218. Tel: 320-843-2026; 843-2514 (Parish Hall); Fax: 320-843-2264. [CEM]
Catechesis/Religious Programs—Students 76.

Comfrey, Brown Co., St. Paul (1900). Clustered with Leavenworth. Thomas R. Christoffer, Pastoral Admin.; Rev. Mark S. Mallak, (Leavenworth), Tel: 507-794-6974.
Res., 209 N. Field St., P.O. Box 277, 56019-0277. Tel: 507-877-2361. [CEM]
Catechesis/Religious Programs—Students 93.

Cottonwood, Lyon Co., St. Mary (1902). Clustered with Green Valley. Rev. John A. Pearson.
Res., 225 W. 4th St., R.R. 1 Box 17A, 56229-9702. Tel: 507-423-5220. [CEM]
Catechesis/Religious Programs—Lori Bednarek, D.R.E.
Students 162.

Danvers, Swift Co., Church of the Visitation (1885). Clustered with Benson, Clontarf, De Graff & Murdock. Sr. Clara M. Stang, O.S.F., Pastoral Admin., Tel: 320-567-2278; Revs. Ronald V. Huberty, (Murdock), Tel: 320-875-2451; Steven J. Verhelst, (Benson), Tel: 320-843-2342. Area Pastoral Leaders: Sr. Darlene Gutenhauf, P.B.V.M., Pastoral Admin. (De Graff), Tel: 320-843-3883; Sr. Dorothy Jorgenson, C.S.J., Pastoral Admin. (Clontarf), Tel: 320-843-2026.
Church—P.O. Box 18, 56231-0018. Tel: 320-842-4271 (Area Office); Fax: 320-843-2264. [CEM]

Darwin, Meeker Co., St. John (1861) (Irish). Clustered with Forest City. Rev. Frederick T. Fink.
Res., 106 N. 4th St., 55324-9998. Tel: 320-693-6878; 275-2915. [CEM]
Catechesis/Religious Programs—Tel: 320-286-2800.
Students 220.

Dawson, Lac Qui Parle Co., St. James (1898). Clustered with Madison. Sr. Vivian Petersen, O.S.B., Pastoral Admin.; Rev. Robert P. Goblirsch, (Madison), Tel: 320-598-3690.
Res., 10th & Locust, P.O. Box 270, 56232-0270. Tel: 320-769-4465. [CEM]
Catechesis/Religious Programs—Students 106.

De Graff, Swift Co., St. Bridget (1876) (Irish). Clustered with Benson, Clontarf, Danvers & Murdock. Rev. Merle W. Monnens, (Clontarf), Tel: 612-843-2026; Sr. Darlene Gutenkauf, P.B.V.M., Pastoral Admin. (De Graff), Tel: 612-843-3883; 612-842-4271 (Area Office). Area Pastoral Leaders: Revs. Ronald V. Huberty, (Murdock), Tel: 320-875-2451; Steven J. Verhelst, (Benson), Tel: 320-843-2342; Sr. Clara M. Stang, O.S.F., Pastoral Admin. (Danvers), Tel: 320-567-2278; Sr. Darlene Gotenkauf, P.B.V.M., Pastoral Admin.; Sr. Dorothy Jorgenson, C.S.J., Pastoral Minister (Clontarf), Tel: 320-843-2026.
Church—501 3rd St. S., 56271. Tel: 320-843-3883. [CEM]
Catechesis/Religious Programs—St. Bridget Activity Center, 405 5th St. S., DeGraff, 56233. Tel: 320-843-2005.
Students 28.

Eden Valley, Meeker Co., St. Peter (1903). Clustered with Eden Valley - St. Cloud Diocese. Rev. Virgil R. Braun (SCL).
Church—349 State St. S., P.O. Box 9, 55329-0009. Tel: 320-453-2788. [CEM]
Catechesis/Religious Programs—Tel: 320-453-5765.
Students 77.

Fairfax, Renville Co., St. Andrew (1871) (German). Clustered with Franklin. Rev. John H. Brunner.
Res., 15 S.E. First St., P.O. Box C, 55332-0903. Tel: 507-426-7125. [CEM]
School—(Grades 1-6). Tel: 507-426-7739.
Lay Teachers 4; Students 37.
Catechesis/Religious Programs—Students 117.

Faxon Township, Sibley Co., St. John-Assumption (1859). Clustered with Arlington, Green Isle, Henderson & Jessenland. Sr. Marian Kemper, O.S.B., Pastoral Admin., Tel: 612-873-4390; Rev. Paul A. Schumacher Tel: 507-326-5111.
Res., R.R. 2, Box 183, Belle Plaine, 56011-9302. Tel: 320-873-4390. [CEM 2]
Catechesis/Religious Programs—Students 56.

Forest City, Meeker Co., St. Gertrude (1857). Clustered with Darwin. Rev. Frederick T. Fink, (Darwin), Tel: 320-693-6878; Thomas E. Johnson, Pastoral Admin.
Res., 31626 650th Ave., Litchfield, 55355-9998. Tel: 320-693-7801. [CEM]
Catechesis/Religious Programs—Students 83.

Franklin, Renville Co., Sacred Heart (1898). Clustered with Fairfax. Rev. John H. Brunner, (Fairfax).
Res., 15 S.E. First St., P.O. Box C, Fairfax, 55332-0903. Tel: 507-426-7125. [CEM 2]
Church—P.O. Box 175, 55333-0175.
Catechesis/Religious Programs—Students 55.

Gaylord, Sibley Co., St. Michael (1882). Clustered with St. Francis de Sales, Winthrop. Rev. Richard G. Bonin.
Res., 361 4th St., P.O. Box 357, 55334-0357. Tel: 507-237-2851.
Catechesis/Religious Programs—Tel: 320-237-2693. Betsy Shea, D.R.E.
Students 130.

Ghent, Lyon Co., St. Eloi (1883). Clustered with Minneota & Taunton. Rev. Gerald A. Hillesheim, (Minneota), Tel: 507-872-6346; Sr. Carol Quinn, P.B.V.M., Pastoral Admin.
Church—306 W. McQuestion, 56239. Tel: 507-428-3285.
Res., 409 N. Adams St., R.R. 1, Box 431, Minneota, 56264-9801. Tel: 507-872-6346. [CEM]
Catechesis/Religious Programs—Students 68.

Gibbon, Sibley Co., St. Willibrord (1886), Rev. John G. Berger.
Res., 1032 Ash Ave., 55335-9998. Tel: 507-834-6461. [CEM]
Catechesis/Religious Programs—Students 116.

Glencoe, McLeod Co., St. George. Closed. For sacramental records contact St. Pius X, Glencoe.
Ss. Peter and Paul. Closed. For sacramental records contact St. Pius X, Glencoe.
St. Pius X (1983), Rev. Eugene L. Lozinski.
Res., 1014 Knight Ave., 55336-2300. Tel: 320-864-5162; 864-2963 (Rectory). [CEM]
School—(Grades PreK-4). Tel: 320-864-3214. Teresa Kuester, Prin.
Lay Teachers 6; Students 101.
Catechesis/Religious Programs—Students 211.

Graceville, Big Stone Co., Holy Rosary (1878). Clustered with Beardsley. Rev. John A. Nordick; Deacon Art D. Abel Tel: 320-748-7573.
Res., 511 Studdart Ave., P.O. Box 7, 56240-0007. Tel: 320-748-7313.
Catechesis/Religious Programs—517 Studdart Ave., 56240. Tel: 320-748-7501.
Students 198.

Granite Falls, Yellow Medicine Co., St. Andrew (1885). Clustered with Clara City. Rev. William A. Sprigler.
Res., 1094 Granite St., 56241-1355. Tel: 320-564-2335; Fax: 320-564-2335. [CEM]
Catechesis/Religious Programs—1056 Fourth St., 56241. Tel: 320-564-2336.
Students 189.

Green Isle, Sibley Co., St. Brendan (1857) (Irish). Clustered with Arlington, Faxon Township, Henderson & Jessenland. Rev. Paul A. Schumacher.
Res., P.O. Box 85, 55338-0085. Tel: 507-326-5111. [CEM]
Catechesis/Religious Programs—Students 60.

Green Valley, Lyon Co., St. Clotilde (1912) (Belgian). Clustered with Cottonwood. Rev. John A. Pearson, (Cottonwood).
Church—R.R. 3, Marshall, 56258-9803. Tel: 507-532-2841. [CEM]
Res., P.O. Box 17A, Cottonwood, 56229. Tel: 507-423-5220.
Catechesis/Religious Programs—Students 75.

Greenleaf, Meeker Co., St. Columban. Closed. For sacramental records contact St. Philip, Litchfield.

Hector, Renville Co., Church of St. John (1878). Clustered with Bird Island. Sr. Sharon Nohner, O.S.B., Pastoral Admin.; Rev. Philip M. Schotzko, (Bird Island), Tel: 320-365-3593.
Church—301 Cedar Ave., E., P.O. Box 295, 55342-0295. Tel: 320-848-6437. [CEM]
Catechesis/Religious Programs—Students 78.

Hegbert, Swift Co., St. Agnes. Closed. For sacramental records contact St. John, Appleton.

Henderson, Sibley Co., St. Joseph (1859). Clustered with Arlington, Faxon Township, Green Isle & Jessenland. Rev. James D. Barry, (Arlington), Tel: 507-964-5413; Sr. Jovann Irrgang, S.S.N.D., Pastoral Admin.
Res., 213 S. 6th St., P.O. Box 427, 56044-0427. Tel: 507-248-3550. [CEM]
Catechesis/Religious Programs—Students 77.

Holloway, Swift Co., St. Joseph. Closed. For sacramental records contact St. John, Appleton.

Hutchinson, McLeod Co., Church of St. Anastasia (1866). Clustered with Stewart. Revs. Dennis E. Becker; James W. Devorak.
Res., 460 Lake St., S.W., 55350-2349. Tel: 320-587-6507; Fax: 320-234-6756. [CEM]
School—(Grades PreK-6). Tel: 320-587-2490. Sr. Joyce Willenbring, O.S.B., Prin.
Sisters 1; Lay Teachers 14; Students 258.
Catechesis/Religious Programs—Students 527.

Ivanhoe, Lincoln Co., SS. Peter & Paul (1900). Clustered with Wilmo. Rev. David L. Breu.
Res., 111 N. Sherwood, P.O. Box 49, 56142-0049. Tel: 507-694-1402; Fax: 507-694-1437. [CEM]
Catechesis/Religious Programs—Rte. 1, Box 59, 56142. Tel: 507-694-1225; Fax: 507-694-1548. Sr. M. Ellen Hoemberg, I.S.S.M.
Students 121.

Jessenland, Sibley Co., St. Thomas (Mission) (1856). Clustered with Arlington, Faxon Township, Green Isle, & Henderson. Rev. James D. Barry, (Arlington), Tel: 507-964-5413; Sr. Jovann Irrgang, S.S.N.D., Pastoral Admin.
Res., 213 S. Sixth St., P.O. Box 427, Henderson, 56044-0427. Tel: 507-248-3550. [CEM]

Kandiyohi, Kandiyohi Co., St. Patrick (1868). Clustered with Lake Lillian. Rev. Robert P. Clark; Mr. Doug Moudry, Pastoral Minister.
Res., 245 3rd St. E., P.O. Box 164, 56251-0164. Tel: 320-382-6424. [CEM]
Catechesis/Religious Programs—Students 237.

Lafayette, Nicollet Co., St. Gregory the Great (1942) (German). Clustered with West Newton Township. Rev. James E. Moran.
Res., 440 6th St., P.O. Box 5, 56054-0005. Tel: 507-228-8298. [CEM]
Catechesis/Religious Programs—Students 85.

Lake Benton, Lincoln Co., St. Genevieve (1897). Clustered with Tyler. Rev. Michael M. Doyle, (Tyler), Tel: 507-247-3464.
Mailing Address: 119 S. Sherman St., P.O. Box 348, 56149-0348. Tel: 507-368-4232. [CEM]
Res., 513 E. Hughes St., P.O. Box 310, Tyler, 56178-0310. Tel: 507-247-5167.
Catechesis/Religious Programs—Tel: 507-368-4232.
Students 85.

Lake Lillian, Kandiyohi Co., St. Thomas More (1934). Clustered with Kandiyohi. Rev. Robert P. Clark, (Kandiyohi), Tel: 320-382-6424; Mr. Doug Moudry, Pastoral Min.
Church—840 Second St. E., P.O. Box 57, 56253-0057. Tel: 320-664-4810.
Res., 245 3rd St. E., P.O. Box 164, Kandiyohi, 56251-0164.
Catechesis/Religious Programs—Students 43.

Lamberton, Redwood Co., St. Joseph (1895). Clustered with Sanborn and Wanda. Sr. Pauline Micke, O.S.B., Pastoral Admin.; Rev. Bernard J. Steiner, Sacramental Min. (Wanda), Tel: 507-752-7523; 342-5451.
Res., 400 W. 2nd Ave., P.O. Box 458, 56152-0458. Tel: 507-752-7269. [CEM]
Catechesis/Religious Programs—Students 89.

Leavenworth, Brown Co., Japanese Martyrs (1867) (German). Clustered with Comfrey. Rev. Mark S. Mallak.
Res., R.R. 2, Box 93, Sleepy Eye, 56085-9624. Tel: 507-794-6974. [CEM]
Catechesis/Religious Programs—Tel: 507-794-6460.
Students 63.

Lester Prairie, McLeod Co., St. Conrad. Closed. Incorporated but never organized. No sacramental records.

Litchfield, Meeker Co., St. Philip (1859), Rev. Peter C. Nosbush.
Res., 306 N. Holcombe Ave., 55355-2223. Tel: 320-693-3313. [CEM]
School—(Grades K-5). Tel: 320-693-6283. Teresa Hanks, Prin.
Lay Teachers 7; Students 85.
Catechesis/Religious Programs—225 E. Third St., 55355.
Students 332.

Lucan, Redwood Co., Our Lady of Victory (1889). Clustered with Milroy. Rev. Merle W. Monnens.
Res., P.O. Box 96, 56255-0096. Tel: 507-747-2231. [CEM]
School—(Grades (1-6)) 301 3rd St, 56255-0096. Tel: 507-747-2233. Mrs. Richard Kramer, Prin.
Lay Teachers 3; Students 19.
Church of the Holy Name (Vesta). Closed. For sacramental records, contact St. Catherine, Redwood Falls.

Madison, Lac Qui Parle Co., St. Michael (1884) (German-Norwegian). Clustered with Dawson. Rev. Robert P. Goblirsch.
Res., 412 3rd St., 56256-1494. Tel: 320-598-3690. [CEM]
Catechesis/Religious Programs—Tel: 320-598-3690.
Students 154.

Manannah, Meeker Co., Church of Our Lady (1876), Rev. Francis J. Garvey.
Res., 57382 CSAH 3, Grove City, 56243-9786. Tel: 320-231-5100. [CEM]
Catechesis/Religious Programs—Students 49.

Marshall, Lyon Co., Holy Redeemer (1883), Revs. Gerald S. Meidl; Celestine C. Pistulka; Brian L. Mandel.
Res., 503 W. Lyon St., 56258-1390. Tel: 507-532-5711; Fax: 507-532-5712. [CEM]
School—(Grades K-8). Tel: 507-532-6642.
Lay Teachers 22; Students 380.
Catechesis/Religious Programs—503 S. Whitney St., 56258. Tel: 507-532-3602. D.R.E.: Patti Watkins, (Grades K-6); Mary Beth Johnson, (Grades 7-12).
Students 657.

Middle Lake, Nicollet Co., St. Nicholas. Closed. For sacramental records contact St. Paul's, Nicollet.

Milroy, Redwood Co., St. Michael (1904) (German-Irish-Belgian). Clustered with Lucan. Rev. Merle W. Monnens, (Lucan), Tel: 507-747-2231; Sr. Justin Wirth, S.S.N.D., Pastoral Admin.
Res., P.O. Box 117, 56263-0117. Tel: 507-336-2505. [CEM]
Catechesis/Religious Programs—Students 119.

Minneota, Lyon Co., St. Edward (1880). Clustered with Ghent & Taunton. Rev. Gerald A. Hillesheim.
Res., R.R. 1, Box 431, 56264-9801. Tel: 507-872-6346; Fax: 507-872-5263. [CEM]
Church—409 N. Adams St., 56264-9801.
School—(Grades 1-8). Tel: 507-872-6391. Mrs. Carol J. DeSmet, Prin.
Lay Teachers 9; Students 131.
Catechesis/Religious Programs—Students 196.

Montevideo, Chippewa Co., St. Joseph (1882), Rev. Jerome E. Paulson.
Res., 521 Eureka Ave., 56265-1899. Tel: 320-269-8623. [CEM]
Church—512 Black Oak Ave., 56265-1874. Tel: 320-269-5954.
Catechesis/Religious Programs—Students 239.

Morgan, Redwood Co., St. Michael (1887). Clustered with Clements. Rev. Eugene C. Hackert.
Res., 514 W. 3rd St., P.O. Box 443, 56266-0443. Tel: 507-249-3643. [CEM]
School—(Grades 1-6) 612 W. 3rd St., P.O. Box 443, 56266-0443. Tel: 507-249-3192. Sr. Gladys Meindl, O.S.F., Prin.
Sisters 2; Lay Teachers 6; Students 72.
Catechesis/Religious Programs—Tel: 507-692-2181.

Students 108.

Morton, Renville Co., St. John (1873). Clustered with Redwood Falls. Rev. Germain P. Rademacher, (Redwood Falls), Tel: 507-637-8114; Sr. Jo Anne Backes, O.S.B., Pastoral Admin.
Res., 341 W. 3rd St, P.O. Box 88, 56270-0088. Tel: 507-697-6120. [CEM]
Catechesis/Religious Programs—Students 47.

Murdock, Swift Co., Church of the Sacred Heart (1879). Clustered with Benson, Clontarf, Danvers & De Graff. Rev. Ronald V. Huberty, (Murdock). Area Pastoral Leaders: Rev. Steven J. Verhelst, (Benson), Tel: 320-843-2342; Sr. Clara M. Stang, O.S.F., (Danvers), Tel: 320-567-2278; Sr. Darlene Gutenkauf, P.B.V.M., (De Graff), Tel: 320-843-3883; Sr. Dorothy Jorgenson, C.S.J., (Clontarf), Tel: 320-843-2026.
Res., 201 Orleans, P.O. Box 9, 56271-0009. Tel: 320-875-2451; 842-4271 (Area Office); Fax: 320-843-2264. [CEM]
Catechesis/Religious Programs—Students 121.

Nassau, Lac Qui Parle Co., St. James (1902) (German). Clustered with Ortonville and Rosen. Rev. Andrew J. Michels, (Ortonville).
Res., P.O. Box 205, 421 Madison Ave., Ortonville, 56278-0205. Tel: 320-839-2772. [CEM]

Nicollet, Nicollet Co., St. Paul (1907), Rev. William H. Bowles.
Res., 411 5th St., P.O. Box 248, 56074-0248. Tel: 507-225-3857. [CEM 4]
Catechesis/Religious Programs—Students 143.
The Church of the Visitation. Closed. For sacramental records contact St. Paul, Nicollet.

North Mankato, Nicollet Co., Holy Rosary (1924), Rev. Edward J. Ardolf.
Res., 525 Grant Ave., 56003-2939. Tel: 507-387-6501.
School—546 Grant Ave., 56003-0698. Tel: 507-345-6765. Sr. Mary Donald, Prin.
School is part of Mankato Area Catholic Schools, Diocese of Winona. Numbers are reported by Winona Diocese.
Catechesis/Religious Programs—Students 450.

Olivia, Renville Co., St. Aloysius (1888). Clustered with Renville.
Res., 302 S. 10th St., 56277-1288. Tel: 320-523-2030. [CEM 2] Rev. Patrick L. Casey.
Catechesis/Religious Programs—Tel: 320-523-2030.
Students 303.

Ortonville, Big Stone Co., St. John (1879). Clustered with Nassau & Rosen. Rev. Andrew J. Michels.
Res., P.O. Box 205, 421 Madison Ave., 56278-0205. Tel: 320-839-2772.
Catechesis/Religious Programs—Tel: 320-839-2873.
Students 150.

Raymond, Kandiyohi Co., Sacred Heart. Closed. For sacramental records contact St. Clara, Clara City.

Redwood Falls, Redwood Co., St. Catherine (1870). Clustered with Marton. Rev. Germain P. Rademacher.
Church—900 E. Flynn St., P.O. Box 383, 56283-0383. Tel: 507-637-2278. [CEM]
Res., 904 E. Flynn St., P.O. Box 383, 56283-0383. Tel: 507-637-8114.
Catechesis/Religious Programs—Students 371.

Regal, Kandiyohi Co., St. Anthony (Mission) (1933). Clustered with Spicer. Rev. Felix J. Fasching, (Spicer).
Res., 13722 Hwy. 23 N.E., Spicer, 56288-9659. Tel: 320-796-5664. [CEM]
Catechesis/Religious Programs—Students 34.

Renville, Renville Co., Holy Redeemer (1891). Clustered with Olivia. Donald A. Clasemann, Pastoral Admin.; Rev. Patrick L. Casey, (Olivia), Tel: 320-523-2030.
Church—106 S.E. 3rd St., P.O. Box 401, 56284-0401. Tel: 320-329-3884. [CEM]
Catechesis/Religious Programs—Tel: 320-329-8219.
Students 161.

Rosen, Lac Qui Parle Co., St. Joseph (1885) (German). Clustered with Nassau & Ortonville. Rev. Andrew J. Michels, (Ortonville).
Res., P.O. Box 205, 421 Madison Ave., Ortonville, 56278-0205. Tel: 320-839-2772. [CEM]
Catechesis/Religious Programs—Tel: 320-568-2428.
Students 62.

St. Leo, Yellow Medicine Co., St. Leo (1881). Clustered with Canby. Rev. Paul H. van de Crommert, (Canby), Tel: 507-223-7304.
Church—202 W. Church St., 56286-0114. Tel: 507-224-2289. [CEM]

St. Peter, Nicollet Co., St. Peter (1856), Rev. Harry P. Behan; Deacon Sylvester J. Sauer Tel: 507-931-4519.
Res., 524 W. Myrtle St., P.O. Box 522, 56082-0522. Tel: 507-931-1628; Fax: 507-931-2977. [CEM]
School—John Ireland School, (Grades K-6) 618 S. 5th, 56082-1412. Tel: 507-931-2810. Mr. James Engels, Prin.
Lay Teachers 10; Students 132.
Catechesis/Religious Programs—Tel: 507-931-3662.
Students 403.
Immaculate Conception. Closed. For sacramental records contact St. Peter's, St. Peter.

Sanborn, Redwood Co., St. Thomas (1902). Clustered with Lamberton & Wanda. Rev. Bernard J. Steiner, (Wanda), Tel: 507-752-7523; 342-5451; Sr. Jeanette Homan, O.S.F., Pastoral Admin.
Res., 310 Winona St., P.O. Box 176, 56083-0176. Tel: 507-648-3754.
Catechesis/Religious Programs—Students 69.

Seaforth, Redwood Co., St. Mary (1880). Clustered with Wabasso. Rev. Paul L. Wolf, (Wabasso).
Res., P.O. Box 239, Wabasso, 56293-0239. Tel: 507-342-5190; 984-5411 (Church); 342-5155 (Rectory). [CEM 2]

Searles, Brown Co., St. John the Baptist (1905) (German). Clustered with Cathedral, New Ulm. Sr. Monica Wagner, S.S.N.D., Pastoral Admin.; Rev. George V. Schmit, (New Ulm, Cathedral), Tel: 507-354-4158.
113 1st Ave. S., P.O. Box 113, 56084-0113. Tel: 507-359-4244. [CEM]
School—New Ulm Area Catholic Schools. See separate listing for details. Tel: 507-354-2719; Fax: 507-354-5711.
Catechesis/Religious Programs—Fax: 507-354-2563.
Students 29.

Silver Lake, McLeod Co., St. Adalbert. Closed. For sacramental records contact Holy Family, Silver Lake.
St. Joseph. Closed. For sacramental records contact Holy Family, Silver Lake.
Church of the Holy Family (1993), Rev. Robert J. Mraz.
Res., 720 W. Main St., P.O. Box 326, 55381-0326. Tel: 320-327-2261; Fax: 320-327-2261. [CEM 4]
School—Silver Lake Catholic School, (Grades 1-6) 700 Main St., P.O. Box 346, 55381-0346. Tel: 320-327-2356.
Lay Teachers 7; Students 85.
Catechesis/Religious Programs—Tel: 320-327-2931; 327-2930.
Students 180.

Sleepy Eye, Brown Co., St. Mary (1876), Rev. John A. Richter.
Res., 636 1st Ave. N., 56085-1004. Tel: 507-794-4171; Fax: 507-794-4841. [CEM]
School—(Grades PreK-8). Tel: 507-794-4121. Mr. Wayne Pelzel, Prin.
Sisters 1; Lay Teachers 21; Students 480; Preschool 60.
High School—Tel: 507-794-4121. Mr. Jerry Neubauer, Prin.
Sisters 1; Lay Teachers 20; Students 281.
Catechesis/Religious Programs—Students 184.

Spicer, Kandiyohi Co., Our Lady of the Lakes (1962). Clustered with Regal. Rev. Felix J. Fasching.
Res., 13722 Hwy. 23 N.E., 56288-9659. Tel: 320-796-5664. [CEM]
Catechesis/Religious Programs—Tel: 320-796-5968.
Students 338.

Springfield, Brown Co., St. Raphael (1874) (German & Irish), Rev. Darold R. Lehman.
Res., 112 W. Van Dusen St., 56087-1396. Tel: 507-723-4727. [CEM]
School—(Grades K-6). Tel: 507-723-4291. Sr. Thomasin Sergot, S.S.N.D., Prin.
Sisters 2; Lay Teachers 7; Students 91.
Catechesis/Religious Programs—Tel: 507-723-4292.
Students 237.

Stewart, McLeod Co., Church of St. Boniface (1877). Clustered with Hutchinson. Sr. Idamarie Primus, O.S.B., Pastoral Admin.; Rev. James W. Devorak, (Hutchinson), Tel: 320-587-6507.
Res., 551 Main St., P.O. Box 202, 55385-0202. Tel: 320-562-2344. [CEM]
Catechesis/Religious Programs—Students 90.

Swan Lake, Nicollet Co., Visitation. Closed. For sacramental records contact St. Paul, Nicollet.

Taunton, Lyon Co., SS. Cyril and Methodius (1895) (Polish-Belgian-German). Clustered with Ghent & Minneota. Sr. Roselle Zollar, S.S.N.D., Pastoral Admin.; Rev. Gerald A. Hillesheim, (Minneota), Tel: 507-872-6346.
Res., Lincoln St., P.O. Box 368, 56291-0368. Tel: 507-872-5150. [CEM 2][JC 2]
Catechesis/Religious Programs—Students 44.

Tracy, Lyon Co., St. Mary (1880). Clustered with Walnut Grove. Rev. Douglas L. Grams.
Res., 249 6th St., 56175-1114. Tel: 507-629-3227. [CEM]
Church—285 6th St., 56175.
School—(Grades K-6). Tel: 507-629-3270. Rev. Douglas L. Grams, Prin.
Lay Teachers 7; Students 73.
Catechesis/Religious Programs—Tel: 507-629-3667.
Students 118.

Tyler, Lincoln Co., St. Dionysius (1880). Clustered with Lake Benton. Rev. Michael M. Doyle.
Res., 513 E. Hughes St., P.O. Box 310, 56178-0310. Tel: 507-247-5167; 247-3464 (Office). [CEM]
Church—213 Linwood St., 56178. Tel: 507-247-5807.
Catechesis/Religious Programs—Tel: 507-247-5807; 368-4232.
Students 144.

Vesta, Redwood Co., Holy Name. Closed. For sacramental records contact the Chancery.

Wabasso, Redwood Co., St. Anne (1900). Clustered with Seaforth. Rev. Paul L. Wolf.
Res., P.O. Box 239, 1021 Cedar St., 56293-0239. Tel: 507-342-5155; 342-5190 (Office). [CEM]
School—(Grades K-6). Tel: 507-345-5389. Patricia McCauley, Prin.
Lay Teachers 8; Students 140.
Catechesis/Religious Programs—Tel: 507-342-5190.
Students 125.

Walnut Grove, Redwood Co., St. Paul (1902) (German). Clustered with Tracy. Rev. Douglas L. Grams, (Tracy), Tel: 507-629-3227.
Res., 600 3rd St., P.O. Box 236, 56180-0236. Tel: 507-859-2164. [CEM]

Wanda, Redwood Co., St. Mathias (1871). Clustered with Lamberton & Sanborn. Rev. Bernard J. Steiner.
Res., 308 St. Mathias Blvd., P.O. Box 308, 56294-0308. Tel: 507-342-5451; 752-7523. [CEM]
Catechesis/Religious Programs—Students 61.

Watkins, Meeker Co., Church of St. Anthony (1889) (German), Rev. Richard C. Gross.
Res., 151 Central Ave. S., P.O. Box 439, 55389-0439. Tel: 320-764-2755. [CEM]
Catechesis/Religious Programs—Tel: 320-764-5722.
Students 194.

West Newton Township, Nicollet Co., St. George (1857) (German). Clustered with Lafayette. Rev. James E. Moran, (Lafayette).
Church—Tel: 507-228-8298.
Res., P.O. Box 5, 440 6th St., Lafayette, 56054-0005. Tel: 507-228-8298; 359-9013. [CEM]
Catechesis/Religious Programs—Students 51.

Willmar, Kandiyohi Co., St. Mary (1871), Revs. Joseph A. Steinbeissen; Jeffrey P. Horejsi; Deacon Jack Herzog Tel: 612-235-5535.
Church—713 12th St., S.W., 56201-3099. Tel: 320-235-0118; Fax: 320-235-0153. [CEM]
Res., 716 11th St. S.W., 56201-3025. Tel: 320-235-6365.
Catechesis/Religious Programs—Tel: 320-235-3982.
Students 851.

Wilno, Lincoln Co., St. John Cantius (1883) (Polish). Clustered with Ivanhoe. Rev. David L. Breu, (Ivanhoe).
Res., R.R. 1, Box 59, Ivanhoe, 56142. Tel: 507-694-1225; 694-1402; Fax: 507-694-1548. [CEM]
Catechesis/Religious Programs—Sr. Ellen M. Hoemberg, I.S.S.M.
Students 159.

Winsted, McLeod Co., Holy Trinity (1869) (German), Rev. Robert J. Wyffels.
Res., 111 Winsted Ave., W., P.O. Box 9, 55395-0009. Tel: 320-485-4421; Fax: 320-485-4283. [CEM 2]
School—(Grades PreK-6). Tel: 320-485-2314. Mrs. Ann Brown, Prin.
Lay Teachers 12; Students 292.
High School—(Grades 9-12). Tel: 320-485-2186. Rev. Robert J. Wyffels, Supt.; Mr. John Dokken, Prin.
Lay Teachers 13; Students 163.
Catechesis/Religious Programs—Students 155.

Winthrop, Sibley Co., St. Francis de Sales (1906). Clustered with St. Michael's, Gaylord. Rev. Richard G. Bonin.
Res., 361 4th St., P.O. Box 357, Gaylord, 55334-0357. Tel: 507-237-2851.
Church—P.O. Box 447, 55396-0447. Tel: 507-647-5334.
Catechesis/Religious Programs—P.O. Box 262, Gaylord, 55334-0357. Tel: 507-237-2693.
Students 74.

Chaplains of Public Institutions

IVANHOE. *Divine Providence Hospital & Home*. Rev. Marion G. Casey, Chap.

WILLMAR. *Regional Treatment Center*. Rev. Francis J. Garvey, Chap.

WINSTED. *St. Mary's Care Center*. Rev. Martin Rath, O.S.B., Chap.

Special or Diocesan Assignment:
Reverend Fathers—
Labat, Dennis C.
Stubeda, Anthony J.

On Duty Outside the Diocese:
Reverend Monsignors—
Schaffer, Gregory T., Parroquia San Lucas Toliman, Depto. Solola 07013, Guatemala. Tel: 011-502-722-0112; Fax: 011-502-722-0112
Reverend Fathers—
Brandes, John F. (STP), Parroquia San Lucas Toliman, Depto. Solola, 07013 Guatemala. Tel: 011-502-722-0112; Fax: 011-502-722-0112
Goggin, John T., Parroquia San Lucas Toliman, Depto. Solola, 07013 Guatemala. Tel: 011-502-722-0112; Fax: 011-502-722-0112
Hansen, Lawrence H., Mercy Catholic Medical Center, Lansdowne Ave. & Baily Rd., Darby, PA 19023. Tel: 215-237-4000
Martinka, Stanley V., San Alfonso Mission, 1218 Lonewood, El Paso, TX 79925. Tel: 915-598-0900
Mead, Leland C., R.R. 1, Box 47, Madison Lake, MN 56063-9706. Tel: 507-243-3868
Plathe, Anthony H., 9501 McIntosh Dr., El Paso, TX 79925. Tel: 915-591-0939

Military Chaplains:
Reverend Monsignors—
Thomas, Arthur S., Chap. Maj. Gen. & Chief of Air Force Chap. Svc., HQ USAF/HC Bldg. 5683, Washington, DC 20332-5000. Tel: 202-767-4577
Reverend Fathers—
Wagener, John M., Lt. Col. (Retired), 117 E. Summit Ave., San Antonio, TX 78212

Absent on Leave:
Reverend Fathers—
Berg, John Leonard, 308 Center St., Apt. 2, Decorah, IA 52101-1222. Tel: 319-382-8325
Pryor, Patrick W., 3151 Chowen Ave. S., Apt. 137, Minneapolis, MN 55416. Tel: 612-927-0153

Retired:
Reverend Monsignors—
Berg, Arnold J., 107 W. Lincoln, Springfield, MN 56087-1302. Tel: 507-723-6316
Leifeld, Antony J., 717 6th St. N., New Ulm, MN 56073-1853. Tel: 507-359-9848
Ward, John C., Leo C. Byrne Residence, 60 S. Mississippi Blvd, Apt. 225, St. Paul, MN 55105-1052. Tel: 612-698-8175
Reverend Fathers—
Adrian, Stephen J., 10410 E. Twilight Dr., Sun Lakes, AZ 85248. Tel: 602-895-0465
Casey, Marion G., Divine Providence Health Center, 312 E. George, Box G, Ivanhoe, MN 56142-0136. Tel: 507-694-1414
Cepress, Adalbert J., Woodbury Health Care Center, 7012 Lake Rd., Woodbury, MN 55125-2499. Tel: 612-735-6000
Exley, Thomas G., 1128 Iowa Ave. W., St. Paul, MN 55108-2242. Tel: 612-489-3562
Fleming, John R., Gallery Towers Apt. 801, 26 W. 10th St., St. Paul, MN 55102-1038. Tel: 612-228-1717
Gleason, John L., 43601 Florida Ave., Apt. 13, Hemet, CA 92544-5259. Tel: 909-927-2729
Gorman, Paul J., P.O. Box 983, Winnebago, MN 56098-0983. Tel: 507-854-3103
Guetter, Michael A., R.R. 2, Box 2A4B, Wabasso, MN 56293-9998. Tel: 507-342-5201
Guillemette, Arthur T., Oak Terrace Senior Apartments, Apt. 112, 640 Third St., P.O. Box 386, Gaylord, MN 55334-0386. Tel: 507-237-5586
Hayden, Ralph W., R.R.3, Box 110, Le Sueur, MN 56058-9428. Tel: 507-665-4143
Hesse, Harold W., Madison Ave. Apartments, Apt. 110, 700 N. Madison Ave., Minneota, MN 56264-9373. Tel: 507-872-5333
Irrgang, Kenneth E., 740 14th St. S, Apt. 13, St. Cloud, MN 56301-5518. Tel: 320-654-1008
Jenniges, Leonard J. (STP), R.R. 2 Box 142, Sanborn, MN 56083. Tel: 507-342-5134
Karels, Agdus S. (STP), 513 4th St. N.W., Ortonville, MN 56278-1305. Tel: 320-839-3766
Kasel, Joseph M., 701 Madison St., Apt. A-1, Minneota, MN 56264-9801. Tel: 507-872-6289
Krystosek, Robert H. (GI), P.O. Box 425, Clara City, MN 56222-0425. Tel: 320-847-2615
McGowan, Myles P., Leo C. Byrne Residence, 60 S. Mississippi River Blvd., Apt. 223, St. Paul, MN 55105. Tel: 612-690-9002
Merth, Robert J., 19414 Cedar Island Ct., Richmond, MN 56368-8300. Tel: 320-597-3788
Murphy, John M., 390 Cottage Ave. W., Apt. 33, St. Paul, MN 55117-4251. Tel: 612-487-9821
O'Connor, Michael F., Church of St. Joseph, 23945 Nicolai Ave. E., Hastings, MN 55033-9650. Tel: 612-437-3526
O'Connor, Richard T., 2001 Stanford Ave., St. Paul, MN 55105-1657. Tel: 612-699-1966
Penzimas, Joseph A., 3746 3rd St. N.E., Columbia Hts., MN 55421-3736. Tel: 612-781-6499
Roney, David A., Parroquia San Lucas Toliman, Depto. Solola 07013, Guatemala. Tel: 011-502-722-0112; Fax: 011-502-722-0112
Schaefer, Roman J., Church of Our Lady Queen of Martyrs, 2731 SW 11th Ct., Ft. Lauderdale, FL 33312. Tel: 305-583-8725
Schreiner, Bernard P., Watkins Retirement Center, 341 4th St. N, Apt.1, Watkins, MN 55389-0246. Tel: 320-764-2894
Schwinn, Alexander L., Leo C. Byrne Residence, 60 S. Mississippi River Blvd., Apt. 319, St. Paul, MN 55105-1000. Tel: 612-690-4111
Siebenand, Ambrose F., Benedict Village, 2000 15th Ave., S.E., Apt. 314, St. Cloud, MN 56304-2423. Tel: 320-253-2655
Siebenand, John N., Benedict Village, 2000 15th Ave., S.E., Apt. 313, St. Cloud, MN 56304-2423. Tel: 612-253-2655
Wojtowicz, Edward L., Leo C. Byrne Residence, 60 S. Mississippi River Blvd., Apt. 226, St. Paul, MN 55105. Tel: 612-698-6926
Zwicky, Richard C., Leo C. Byrne Residence, 60 S. Mississippi River Blvd., Apt. 310, St. Paul, MN 55105-1000. Tel: 612-690-3544

INSTITUTIONS LOCATED IN THE DIOCESE

[A] NEW ULM AREA CATHOLIC SCHOOLS

NEW ULM. *New Ulm Area Catholic Schools*, 515 N. State St., 56073-1897. Tel: 507-354-2719. David Schieffert, Supt. Consolidated: The five schools consolidated under the above title are as follows:
Edu Care Pre-School and Daycare, 527 S. Minnesota, 56073. Tel: 507-359-7331. Jean Nielsen, Dir.
St. John's Elementary School, Searles, 56084. Tel: 507-359-4511. Kris Hodapp, Head Teacher.
St. Mary's Elementary School, 519 S. Minnesota St., 56073-2199. Tel: 507-354-2928. Paul Schieffert, Head Teacher.
Holy Trinity Middle School, 515 N. State St., 56073-1897. Tel: 507-354-4311. Sr. Sharon Waldoch, S.S.N.D., Elementary Prin.
Cathedral High School, 600 N. Washington St., 56073-1897. Tel: 507-354-4511. Paul Klinkhammer, Prin.
High School: Sisters 1; Lay Teachers 16; Students 225.
Elementary: Sisters 1; Lay Teachers 41; Students 567.

[B] GENERAL HOSPITALS

GRACEVILLE. *Graceville Health Center dba Holy Trinity Hospital and Grace Home*, 115 W. 2nd St., 56240-0157. Tel: 320-748-7223.
For a complete listing, refer to the Hospitals section.

IVANHOE. *Divine Providence Health Center*, 312 E. George St., P.O. Box G, 56142-0136.
For a complete listing, refer to the Hospitals section.

WINSTED. *St. Mary's Care Center*, 551 4th St. N., P.O. Box 750, 55395-0750. Tel: 612-485-2151; Fax: 612-485-4241.
For a complete listing, refer to the Hospitals section.

[C] HOMES FOR AGED

SLEEPY EYE. *Divine Providence Community Home & Lake Villa Maria Senior Apts.*, 700 3rd Ave. N.W., 56085-1099. Tel: 507-794-3011;794-5333.
For a complete listing, refer to the Special Care Facilities section.

[D] RETREAT HOUSES

BIRD ISLAND. *Center for Spiritual Development*, P.O. Box 538, 211 S. 10th St., 55310-0538. Tel: 320-365-3644; Fax: 320-365-4042. Co-Directors: Sr. Marjorie Klein, S.S.N.D.; Sr. Janet Mallak, S.S.N.D. Total in Residence 5; Total Staff 6.

SLEEPY EYE. *Schoenstatt Sisters of Mary*, R.R. 4, Box 157, 56085-9428. Tel: 507-794-7727; 507-794-5622. Sr. Marie Day, I.S.S.M., Dir.; Sr. Rita Marie Otto, I.S.S.M., Supr.; Sr. M. Alice Kunz, I.S.S.M., Librarian; Sr. M. Danielle Peters, I.S.S.M., Coord.; Sr. M. Isabel Bracero, Hispanic Ministry; Sr. M. Donna Knmarzick, Maintenance.

[E] YOUTH CENTERS

NEW ULM. *Center for Youth Ministry*, c/o Catholic Pastoral Center, 1400 6th St. N., 56073-2099. Tel: 507-359-2966. Bill Casey, Dir. Youth Ministry.

[F] MISCELLANEOUS

GRACEVILLE. *Graceville Missionary Benedictine Sisters, Inc.*, 116 W. 3rd St., P.O. Box 276, 56240-0276. Sisters 4.

WILLMAR. *Willmar Regional Treatment Center*, 1550 Hwy. 71 N.E., 56201-1128. Tel: 612-231-5100; Fax: 612-231-5329. Rev. Francis J. Garvey, Chap.

[G] HEALTH CARE CENTERS

ST. PETER. *St. Peter Regional Treatment Center*, 100 Freeman Dr., 56082-1599. Tel: 507-931-7114.
For a complete listing, refer to the Hospitals section.

RELIGIOUS INSTITUTES OF MEN REPRESENTED IN THE DIOCESE

For further details refer to the corresponding bracketed number in the Religious Institutes of Men or Women Section.

[0200]—*Benedictine Monks*. (Collegeville, MN).—O.S.B.

RELIGIOUS INSTITUTES OF WOMEN REPRESENTED IN THE DIOCESE

[]—*Benedictine Monks (Sisters)*. (Collegeville, MN).—O.S.B.

[0230]—*Benedictine Sisters of Pontifical Jurisdiction*. (St. Joseph, MN; Federation of St. Benedict, Duluth, MN; Crookston, MN).—O.S.B.

[2100]—*Congregation of the Humility of Mary*. (Davenport, IA).—C.H.M.

[0940]—*Daughters of St. Mary of Providence*. (Chicago, IL).—D.S.M.P.

[1310]—*Francisan Sisters of Little Falls, Minnesota*. (Little Falls, MN).—O.S.F.

[0210]—*Missionary Benedictine Sisters*. (Norfolk, NE).—O.S.B.

[]—*Schoenstatt Sisters of Mary*. (Waukesha, WI).

[2970]—*School Sisters of Notre Dame*. (Mankato, MN).—S.S.N.D.

[1680]—*School Sisters of St. Francis*. (Milwaukee, WI).—O.S.F.

[1070-03]—*Sinsinawa Dominicans*. (Sinsinawa, WI).—O.P.

[1570]—*Sisters of St. Francis of the Holy Family*. (Dubuque, IA).—O.S.F.

[3840]—*Sisters of St. Joseph of Carondelet*. (St. Paul, MN).—C.S.J.

[]—*Sisters of St. Joseph of La Grange*. (La Grange Park, IL).—C.S.J.

[3320]—*Sisters of the Presentation of the B.V.M.* (Aberdeen, SD).—P.B.V.M.

[1720]—*Sisters of the Third Order Regular of St. Francis of the Congregation of Our Lady of Lourdes*. (Rochester, MN).—O.S.F.

[]—*Sisters of St. Francis of Assisi*. (Milwaukee, WI).—O.S.F.

NECROLOGY

✠ Schladweiler, Most Rev. Alphonse J., (Retired). —Died April 3, 1996.

Archdiocese of New York

(Archidioecesis Neo-Eboracensis)

His Eminence

JOHN CARDINAL O'CONNOR, D.D., PH.D.

Archbishop of New York; ordained December 15, 1945; appointed Titular Bishop of Curzola and Auxiliary Bishop to the Military Vicar April 24, 1979; consecrated May 27, 1979; appointed Bishop of Scranton May 10, 1983; installed June 29, 1983; appointed Archbishop of New York January 31, 1984; installed March 19, 1984. Created Cardinal Priest May 25, 1985. *Res., 452 Madison Ave., New York, NY, 10022.*

Chancery: 1011 First Ave., New York, NY, 10022. Tel.: 212-371-1000; Fax: 212-826-6020.

Most Reverend

PATRICK V. AHERN, D.D.

Auxiliary Bishop of New York; Titular Bishop of Najiera; ordained January 27, 1945; appointed February 3, 1970; consecrated March 19, 1970. *Res., St. Thomas More, 65 E. 89th St., New York, NY, 10128.*

Most Reverend

JAMES P. MAHONEY, D.D.

Auxiliary Bishop of New York; Titular Bishop of Ipagro; ordained May 19, 1951; appointed July 25, 1972; consecrated September 15, 1972. *Res., St. Mary, 19 Clinton St., Wappingers Falls, NY, 12590.*

Most Reverend

ANTHONY F. MESTICE, D.D.

Auxiliary Bishop of New York; Titular Bishop of Villanova; ordained June 4, 1949; appointed March 5, 1973; consecrated April 27, 1973. *Res., Resurrection, 910 Post Rd., Rye, NY, 10580.*

Most Reverend

FRANCISCO GARMENDIA, D.D.

Auxiliary Bishop of New York; Titular Bishop of Limisa; ordained June 28, 1947; appointed May 24, 1977; consecrated June 29, 1977. *Res., St. Thomas Aquinas, 1900 Crotona Pkwy., Bronx, NY, 10460.*

Most Reverend

AUSTIN B. VAUGHAN, D.D.

Auxiliary Bishop of New York; Titular Bishop of Cluain Iraird; ordained December 8, 1951; appointed May 24, 1977; consecrated June 29, 1977. *Res., Our Lady of Consolation, 3103 Arlington Ave., Bronx, NY, 10463.*

Most Reverend

WILLIAM J. McCORMACK, D.D.

Auxiliary Bishop of New York, Titular Bishop of Nicives; ordained February 21, 1959; appointed December 23, 1986; consecrated January 6, 1987. *Res., 142 E. 29th St., New York, NY, 10016.*

Most Reverend

PATRICK J. SHERIDAN, D.D.

Auxiliary Bishop of New York; Titular Bishop of Curzola; ordained March 1, 1947; appointed October 30, 1990; consecrated December 12, 1990. *Res., 452 Madison Ave., New York, NY, 10022.*

Most Reverend

EDWIN F. O'BRIEN, D.D.

Auxiliary Bishop of New York; Titular Bishop of Tizica; ordained May 26, 1965; appointed February 6, 1996; consecrated March 25, 1996. *Res., St. Joseph's Seminary, Yonkers, NY, 10704.*

SEE ERECTED APRIL 8, 1808.

CREATED AN ARCHDIOCESE JULY 19, 1850.

Square Miles 4,683.

(Legal title: Archdiocese of New York).

Comprises the Boroughs of Manhattan, Bronx, and Richmond of the City of New York, and the Counties of Dutchess, Orange, Putnam, Rockland, Sullivan, Ulster and Westchester in the State of New York.

STATISTICAL OVERVIEW

Personnel	
Cardinal	1
Auxiliary Bishops	7
Retired Bishops	1
Priests: Diocesan Active in Diocese	611
Priests: Active Outside Diocese	52
Priests: Retired, Sick or Absent	248
Number of Diocesan Priests	911
Religious Priests in Diocese	1,120
Extern Priests in Diocese	220
Ordinations:	
Diocesan Priests	11
Transitional Deacons	7
Permanent Deacons	12
Permanent Deacons in Diocese	307
Total Brothers	445
Total Sisters	4,020
Parishes	
Parishes	413
With Resident Pastor:	
Resident Diocesan Priests	314
Resident Religious Priests	78
Without Resident Pastor:	
Administered by Priests	22
Welfare	
Catholic Hospitals	17
Total Assisted	1,893,420
Health Care Centers	3
Total Assisted	151,260
Homes for the Aged	17
Total Assisted	20,000
Residential Care of Children	14
Total Assisted	38,900
Day Care and Extended Day Care Centers	15
Total Assisted	1,677
Specialized Homes	5
Total Assisted	600
Special Centers for Social Services	148
Total Assisted	635,000
Educational	
Seminaries, Diocesan	2
Students from This Diocese	67
Students from Other Diocese	17
Diocesan Students in Other Seminaries	2
Seminaries, Religious	2
Students Religious	3
Total Seminarians	72
Colleges and Universities	12
Total Students	60,500
High Schools, Diocesan and Parish	25
Total Students	13,685
High Schools, Private	30
Total Students	14,419
Elementary Schools, Diocesan and Parish	223
Total Students	75,172
Elementary Schools, Private	15
Total Students	3,680
Non-residential Schools for the Disabled	4
Total Students	195
Catechesis/Religious Education:	
High School Students	13,050
Elementary Students	98,300
Total Students Under Catholic Instruction	279,073
Teachers in the Diocese:	
Priests	50
Brothers	49
Sisters	269
Lay Teachers	4,177
Vital Statistics	
Receptions into the Church:	
Infant Baptism Totals	35,522
Adult Baptism Totals	898
Received into Full Communion	546
First Communions	25,492
Confirmations	18,345
Marriages:	
Catholic	6,842
Interfaith	1,613
Total Marriages	8,455
Deaths	16,956
Total Catholic Population	2,327,300
Total Population	5,351,854

Succession of Prelates—Rev. R. LUKE CONCANEN, O.P., D.D., first Bishop; cons. April 24, 1808; died June 19, 1810.—Rt. Rev. JOHN CONNOLLY, O.P., D.D., second Bishop; cons. Nov. 6, 1814; died Feb. 6, 1825.—Rt. Rev. JOHN DUBOIS, S.S., D.D., third Bishop; cons. Oct. 29, 1826; died Dec. 20, 1842.—Most Rev. JOHN HUGHES, D.D., cons. Titular Bishop of Basileopolis and coadjutor to the Bishop of New York, Jan. 7, 1838; succeeded to the See of New York, Dec. 20, 1842; created first Archbishop, July 19, 1850; died Jan. 3, 1864.—His Eminence JOHN CARDINAL MCCLOSKEY, second Archbishop; cons. Titular Bishop of Axiere, and coadjutor to the Bishop of New York, March 10, 1844 translated to the See of Albany, May 21, 1847; promoted to New York, May 6, 1864; created Cardinal Priest of the Holy Roman Church, March 15, 1875 under the title of Sancta Maria Supra Minervam; died Oct. 10, 1885.—

Most Rev. MICHAEL AUGUSTINE CORRIGAN, D.D., third Archbishop; cons. Bishop of Newark, NJ May 4, 1873; promoted to the Archiepiscopal See of Petra and made coadjutor to His Eminence CARDINAL McCLOSKEY, Archbishop of New York, with the right of succession, Oct. 1, 1880; succeeded to the See of New York, Oct. 10, 1885 made Assistant at the Pontifical Throne, April 19, 1887; died May 5, 1902.—His Eminence JOHN CARDINAL FARLEY, fourth Archbishop of New York; ord. June 11, 1870; cons. Titular Bishop of Zeugma and Auxiliary to the Archbishop of New York, Dec. 21, 1895; promoted to this See, Sept. 15, 1902; preconized June 22, 1903 made Assistant at the Pontifical Throne, Dec. 4, 1904; created Cardinal Priest of the Holy Roman Church under the Title of Sancta Maria Supra Minervam, Nov. 27, 1911; died Sept. 17, 1918.—His Eminence PATRICK CARDINAL HAYES, fifth Archbishop of New York; ord. Sept. 8, 1892; appt. Auxiliary to the Archbishop of New York, July 3, 1914; cons. Titular Bishop of Tagaste, Oct. 28, 1914; appt. Bishop Ordinary of U.S. Army and Navy Chaplains by the Holy See, Nov. 24, 1917; promoted to the See of New York, March 10, 1919; created Cardinal Priest of the Holy Roman Church under the title of Sancta Maria in Via, March 24, 1924; died Sept. 4, 1938.—His Eminence FRANCIS CARDINAL SPELLMAN, sixth Archbishop of New York; ord. May 14, 1916; appt. Auxiliary Bishop of Boston, July 30, 1932; cons. Sept. 8, 1932; appt. to the See of New York, April 15, 1939; appt. Military Vicar for the Armed Forces of the United States, Dec. 11, 1939; created and proclaimed Cardinal under the title of SS. John and Paul in the Consistory, Feb. 18, 1946; died Dec. 2, 1967.—His Eminence TERENCE CARDINAL COOKE, seventh Archbishop of New York; ord. Dec. 1, 1945; appt. Auxiliary Bishop of New York, Sept. 15, 1965; cons. Dec. 13, 1965; appt. to the See of New York, March 8, 1968; installed and appt. Military Vicar of the United States Armed Forces, April 4, 1968; created and proclaimed Cardinal under the title of SS. John and Paul in the Consistory, April 28, 1969; died Oct. 6, 1983.

Vicar General—Most Rev. PATRICK J. SHERIDAN, D.D., V.G.

Episcopal Vicars of the Archdiocese—

Manhattan (West)—Rev. Msgr. THOMAS P. LEONARD, *Holy Trinity, 213 W. 82nd St., New York, 10024.* Tel: 212-787-0634.

Manhattan (North)—Rev. Msgr. JOACHIM B. BEAUMONT, *St. Elizabeth, 268 Wadsworth Ave., New York, 10033.* Tel: 212-568-8803.

Manhattan (South)—Rev. Msgr. KEVIN P. O'BRIEN, *Immaculate Conception, 414 E. 14th St., New York, 10009.* Tel: 212-254-0200.

Manhattan (East)—Rev. Msgr. JOHN G. WOOLSEY, *St. John the Martyr, 259 E. 71st St., New York, 10021.* Tel: 212-744-4880. Rev. Msgr. THOMAS A. MODUGNO, *St. Monica, 413 E. 79th St., New York, 10021.* Tel: 212-288-6250.

Bronx (Northwest)—Rev. Msgr. PATRICK J. BOYLE, *St. Brendan's, 333 E. 260th St., Bronx, 10467.* Tel: 718-547-6655.

Bronx (Northeast)—Rev. Msgr. FRANCIS X. TONER, *St. Barnabas, 409 E. 241st St., Bronx, 10470.* Tel: 718-324-1478.

Bronx (East)—Vacant.

Bronx (South)—Most Rev. FRANCISCO GARMENDIA, *St. Thomas Aquinas, 1900 Crotona Pkwy., Bronx, 10460.* Tel: 718-589-5235.

Richmond—Rev. Msgr. JOSEPH C. ANSALDI, *St. Joseph-by-the-Sea High School, 5150 Hylan Blvd., Huguenot, Staten Island, 10312.* Tel: 718-984-6500.

Westchester (Central)—Most Rev. ANTHONY F. MESTICE, D.D., *Resurrection, 910 Post Rd., Rye, 10580.* Tel: 914-967-0142.

Westchester (Yonkers)—Rev. Msgr. HUGH CORRIGAN, *Immaculate Conception, 103 S. Broadway, Yonkers, 10701.* Tel: 914-963-0156.

Westchester (South Shore)—Rev. Msgr. A. FRANCIS BURNS, *St. Ursula's, 214 E. Lincoln Ave., Mt. Vernon, 10552.* Tel: 914-668-0085.

Westchester (North) and Putnam—Rev. Msgr. DERMOT R. BRENNAN, *St. Patrick, 137 Moseman Rd., Yorktown Hts., 10598.* Tel: 914-962-5050.

Dutchess—Most Rev. JAMES P. MAHONEY, D.D., *Catholic Center, 242 Church St., Poughkeepsie, 12601.* Tel: 914-452-1400.

Orange—Most Rev. AUSTIN B. VAUGHAN, D.D., *Res., Our Lady of Consolation Residence, 3103 Arlington Ave., Bronx, 10463.* Rev. Msgr. GEORGE J. VALASTRO, *St. Joseph, 149 Cottage St., Middletown, 10940.* Tel: 914-343-6013.

Rockland—Rev. Msgr. WILLIAM J. BELFORD, *St. Catharine, 523 Western Hwy., Blauvelt, 10913.* Tel: 914-359-0542.

Ulster—Rev. Msgr. WILLIAM E. WILLIAMS, *St. Joseph, 242 Wall St., Kingston, 12401.* Tel: 914-338-1554.

Sullivan—Rev. EDWARD GREENE, O.F.M., *St. George's, Jeffersonville, 12748.* Tel: 914-482-4640.

Archbishopric of New York—1011 First Ave., New York, 10022. (Cable Address: Curia New York). Tel: 212-371-1000.

Chancery—1011 First Ave., New York, 10022. Tel: 212-371-1000; Fax: 212-826-6020.

Chancellor—Rev. Msgr. ROBERT A. BRUCATO; VINCENT T. EUK, Admin. Asst. to the Chancellor.

Vice-Chancellors—Rev. Msgr. EDWARD O'DONNELL; Rev. Msgr. GEORGE THOMPSON; Revs. JOHN D. FLANAGAN; DOGLAS MATHERS, J.D., J.C.L.; Miss DOLORES BERNADETTE GRIER, M.A.

Secretary to the Archbishop—Rev. Msgr. GERALD T. WALSH; Rev. THOMAS F. PETRILLO.

Metropolitan Tribunal—1011 First Ave., New York, 10022. Tel: 212-371-1000.

Judicial Vicar—Rev. Msgr. DESMOND J. VELLA, J.C.D., S.T.L.

Vice Judicial Vicars—Revs. JOHN DELANEY, J.D.; JOSEPH CAMPO, S.T.L., J.C.L; JOHN VIGILANTI, J.C.L., Ph.D.

Judges—Rev. FRANCIS J. MULLER, O.F.M., J.C.D.; Rev. Msgr. JOSEPH G. GOODWINE, J.C.D.; Revs. VINCENT GROGAN, O.F.M., J.C.D.; ALBERT DELUCA, M.S.; WILLIAM S. ELDER, J.C.D.; WALTER F. KENNY, S.T.D.; KENNETH SMITH, M.A., S.T.B.; Rev. Msgr. FRANCIS X. TONER, M.A.; Sr. AMADEUS McKEVITT, O.S.U., J.C.L.

Defenders of the Bond—Revs. GABRIEL LA PAZ, J.C.L.; ROBERT J. HOSPODAR, J.C.L.; CHRISTIAN HOWE, O.Carm., J.C.L.; PETER THUMMA, J.C.D.; MAREK SUCHOCK, J.C.L.; Sr. AMADEUS McKEVITT, O.S.U., J.C.L.

Promoter of Justice—Rev. DOUGLAS MATHERS, J.C.L.

Canonical Consultants—Sr. AILEEN KELLY, S.C., M.S.; Sr. DORIS HEINLEIN, S.C., M.S.; Mrs. ROSEMARY P. DOHERTY; Revs. KENNETH SMITH, M.A., S.T.B.; RAFAEL CORNIEL.

Mt. Kisco Office—Rev. JOHN VIGILANTI, J.C.L., Ph.D., *12 Green St., Mt. Kisco, 10549.* Tel: 914-666-2583.

Poughkeepsie Office—Revs. JOSEPH CAMPO, J.C.L.; GERARD J. COLACICCO, J.C.L., *240 Church St., Poughkeepsie, 12601.* Tel: 914-452-1400.

Interdiocesan Tribunal of New York State—1011 First Ave., New York, 10022. Tel: 212-371-1000.

Judicial Vicar—Rev. Msgr. DESMOND J. VELLA, J.C.D., S.T.L.; Rev. Msgr. WALTER F. KENNY, S.T.D.

Vicar for the Religious—Rev. BARTHOLOMEW DALY, M.H.M., *1011 First Ave., New York, 10022.* Tel: 212-371-1000, Ext. 2575. Sr. CATHERINE QUINN, 212-371-1000, Ext. 2576.

Archdiocesan Offices and Directors

Catholic Health Care Network in the Archdiocese of New York—MARY HEALEY-SEDUTTO, Ph.D., Exec. Dir., *1011 First Ave., New York, 10022.* Tel: 212-371-1000.

Apostleship of Prayer—Rev. Msgr. JAMES G. WILDERS, Archdiocesan Dir. Tel: 212-628-2800.

Apostleship of the Sea—Rev. KEVIN J. NELAN, Dir., *Stella Maris Maritime Center for Seamen, Pier 52, New York, 10019.* Tel: 212-265-5020.

Archdiocesan Consultors—Rev. Msgr. EDWARD CONNORS; Rev. Msgr. JOSEPH MURPHY; Most Rev. PATRICK SHERIDAN; Most Rev. EDWIN F. O'BRIEN; Rev. Msgr. LAWRENCE CONNAUGHTON; Rev. Msgr. THOMAS J. BERGIN; Rev. Msgr. ROBERT A. BRUCATO, *1011 First Ave., New York, 10022.* Tel: 212-371-1000.

Archives—Sr. MARGUERITA SMITH, Archivist, *St. Joseph's Seminary, 201 Seminary Ave., Yonkers, 10704.* Tel: 914-476-6333.

Bishops' Resettlement Committee for Refugees—Mr. PAUL MARTIN, Dir., *1011 First Ave., New York, 10022.* Tel: 212-371-1000.

Black Ministry, Office of—Bro. TYRONE DAVIS, C.F.C., Dir., *1011 First Ave., New York, 10022.* Tel: 212-371-1000.

Building Commission—St. Joseph's Seminary, Yonkers, 10704. Tel: 914-476-1058.

Director—WILLIAM J. O'CONNOR.

Business Manager—STEVEN BELLOISE.

Consultants—ANDREW J. CRYAN; HOWARD R. EVANS; DANIEL M. HARRIGAN; Deacon JOHN LARKIN; JOHN J. MASTRONARDI; LAURENCE J. RICE; PHILIP J. WHALEN.

Cardinal's Archdiocesan Appeal—CAROLINE HENNESSY, Dir., *1011 First Ave., New York, 10022.* Tel: 212-371-1000.

Cardinal's Committee of the Laity—Mr. JACK DUNNE, Dir., *1011 First Ave., New York, 10022.* Tel: 212-371-1000.

Catechumenate, Office of—Srs. ROSE VERMETTE, R.C.D.; ONELLYS VILLEGAS, M.H.S.H. Tel: 212-371-1000, Ext. 2690.

Catholic High School Association—1011 First Ave., New York, 10022.

Center for Catholic Lay Leadership Formation—RUDY VARGAS, IV, Exec. Dir., *1345 Grand Concourse, Bronx, 10452.* Tel: 718-588-4100.

Catholic New York—(See Ecclesiastical Communications Corp.), ANNE BUCKLEY, Editor; ARTHUR L. McKENNA, Gen. Mgr., *1011 First Ave., New York, 10022.* Tel: 212-688-2399.

Cemeteries—(The Trustees of St. Patrick's Cathedral in the City of New York, Inc.); Mr. ANTHONY V. ROINA, Exec. Dir., *1011 First Ave., New York, 10022.* Tel: 212-753-4883.

Censors—Board of Diocesan Censors of Books, Rev. Msgr. DANIEL V. FLYNN, J.C.D., Chm., *215 Halsted Ave., Harrison, 10528.*

Center for Spiritual Development—ANN MARIE WALLACE, Ph.D., Dir.; Sr. MARY FRANCES MILLS, O.S.F., Assoc. Dir., *96 Milton Rd., Rye, 10580.* Tel: 914-967-7328.

Central Services—Archdiocese of New York, 1011 First Ave., New York, 10022. Tel: 212-371-1000.

Catholic Charities—Rev. Msgr. JAMES J. MURRAY; Rev. Msgr. WILLIAM J. TOOHY, *1011 First Ave., New York, 10022.* Tel: 212-371-1000. (Consult separate listing.).

Chinese Apostolate—Rev. PETER MA, *1011 First Ave., New York, 10022.* Tel: 212-371-1000.

Commission on Church Music—Mr. JOHN MICHAEL CAPRIO, Dir., *1011 First Ave., New York, 10022.* Tel: 212-371-1000, Ext. 2290.

Committee on Housing—Mr. ROBERT PAUL, Coord., *1011 First Ave., New York, 10022.* Tel: 212-371-1000, Ext. 2536-2537.

Communications Office (Bureau of Information for the Media)—Mr. JOSEPH ZWILLING, Dir.; Mrs. HOLLY M. GONZALEZ, Asst. Dir.; Rev. PAUL KEENAN, Asst. Dir., Radio Min.; Mrs. TANIA RIOS, Asst. Dir. Spanish Communications, *1011 First Ave., New York, 10022.* Tel: 212-371-1000, Ext. 2990.

Conciliation and Arbitration, Office of—Rev. DOUGLAS J. MATHERS, Dir., *1011 First Ave., New York, 10022.* Tel: 212-371-1000.

Coordinating Committee of Catholic Lay Organizations—Rev. Msgr. WILLIAM J. TOOHY, Moderator, *1011 First Ave., New York, 10022.* Tel: 212-371-1000.

Criminal Justice, Office of—Mr. KENNETH HOFFARTH, Dir., *1011 First Ave., New York, 10022.* Tel: 212-371-1000, Ext. 3166.

The Data Systems Center—Mr. ANDREW J. DONNELLY, Dir., *1011 First Ave., New York, 10022.* Tel: 212-371-1000. Mr. JAMES F. MAHER, D.P. Oper. Mgr.; Mr. BRENDAN J. RYAN, Programming & Systems Mgr., *201 Seminary Ave., Yonkers, 10704.* Tel: 914-968-2303.

Telecommunications Office—ANDREW J. DONNELLY, Dir.; Telecommunications Dir. Vacant.

Deaf, Catholic Center for—Rev. Msgr. PATRICK P. McCAHILL, Dir., *1011 First Ave., New York, 10022.* Tel: 212-988-8563.

Development, Archdiocesan Office of—Rev. Msgr. CHARLES M. KAVANAGH, Vicar; HELEN T. LOWE, Exec. Dir., *1011 First Ave., New York, 10022.* Tel: 212-371-1000.

Ecclesiastical Assistance Corporation—1011 First Ave., New York, 10022. Tel: 212-371-1000.

Ecclesiastical Communications Corp.—1011 First Ave., New York, 10022. Tel: 212-371-1000.

Ecclesiastical Maintenance Services, Inc.—Mr. EDWARD WOODS, Gen. Mgr. Area Supvrs.: Mr. STEVEN MILISITS; Mr. FRANK ORTIZ; Mr. ROBERT SCULLY, *1011 First Ave., New York, 10022.* Tel: 212-371-1000.

Ecclesiastical Properties Corporation—1011 First Ave., New York, 10022.

Ecumenical and Interreligious Affairs, Commission on—Rev. Msgr. EDWARD D. O'DONNELL, Chm.; Rev. Msgr. FERDINANDO D. BERARDI, M.A., S.T.L., Vice Chm.; Rev. JAMES LOUGHRAN, S.A., Dir., *1011 First Ave., New York, 10022.*

Educational Services of the Archdiocese of New York, Inc.—1011 First Ave., New York, 10022.

Education, Dept. of, Archdiocese of New York—1011 First Ave., New York, 10022. Tel: 212-371-1000. (Consult separate listing.).

Education, Vicar for—Rev. Msgr. THOMAS J. BERGIN, Vicar; Sr. EILEEN CLIFFORD, O.P., Assoc. Vicar, *1011 First Ave., New York, 10022.* (Consult separate listing.).

Ethnic Affairs, Office of—Rev. DOUGLAS MATHERS, J.C.L., Dir., *1011 First Ave., New York, 10022.* Tel: 212-371-1000.

Evangelization, Office of—Rev. Msgr. FRANCIS OLIVERIO, Coord., *1011 First Ave., New York, 10022.* Tel: 212-371-1000.

Family Consultation Service—Rev. GEORGE E. REINHEIMER, Ph.D., Dir. FRANK CATALANO, Ph.D., Supervising Psychologist, *1011 First Ave., New York, 10022.* Tel: 212-371-1000.

Family Life/Respect Life Office—Rev. JOHN BONNICI S.T.D., Dir., *1011 First Ave., New York, 10022.* Tel: 212-371-1000. (Consult separate listing.).

Hispanic Affairs, Vicar—(Vicario, Asuntos Hispanos), Rev. Msgr. NEIL GRAHAM, *1011 First Ave., New York, 10022.* Tel: 212-371-1000, Ext. 2982.

Catholic Charismatic Center—(Centro Carismatico

Catolico); Rev. Josu Iriondo, C.R.L., Center Dir., *826 E. 166th St., Bronx, 10460.* Tel: 212-378-1734.

Hispanic Institute of Pastoral Formation—(Instituto Hispano de Formacion Pastoral); Deacon Guillermo Romagosa, Dir.; Sr. Maria Transito Sanchez, Exec. Sec. Tel: 212-371-1000, Ext. 8270.

Permanent Diaconate Formation Program—(Programa de Formacion para Diaconos); Deacon Anthony Cassaneto, Dir., *St. Joseph's Seminary, Dunwoodie, 10704.* Tel: 914-968-6200, Ext. 8269.

Intercultural Institute—Rev. Msgr. Neil Graham, Dir. Angela Martinez, Sec. Tel: 212-371-1000, Ext. 2982.

Intercultural Council—Most Rev. Patrick Sheridan, Chm.; Dr. Ruth Doyle, Facilitator. Tel: 212-371-1000, Ext. 3250.

Language Institute—Class Schedule: Wed. 4-7 pm Cardinal Hayes High School. Edward Crespo, Supvr., *1011 First Ave., New York, 10022.* Tel: 212-371-1000, Ext. 2982.

Light and Life Evangelization Program—(Luz y Vida), *St. Joseph's Cursillo Center, 523 W. 142nd St., New York, 10031.* Tel: 212-926-7433.

St. Joseph's Cursillo Center—Rev. Frank Peluso, O.A.R., Dir., *275 West 230th St., Bronx, 10463.* Tel: 718-796-4340.

Palante-Con-Cristo Evangelization and Prayer Movement—Rev. John Oldfield, O.A.R., Spiritual Dir.; Deacon Luis Fontanez, Asst. Spiritual Dir., *Tagaste Monastery, Suffern, 10901.* Tel: 914-357-0067. Deacon Edmundo Ramos. Tel: 718-204-0816.

Mary Help of Christians Ev. Community—(Auxiliadora); Rev. Kenneth Smith, Spiritual Dir.; Deacon Luis Fontanez, Asst. Dir., *328 W. 14th St., New York, 10014.*

Holy Childhood, Pontifical Association—Rev. Msgr. Ferdinando D. Berardi, Dir.; Sr. Pauline Churchirillo, P.B.V.M., Mission Education Dir., *1011 First Ave., New York, 10022.* Tel: 212-371-1000.

Holy Name Society Archdiocesan Union of New York—Rev. James P. Connolly, Dir.; Mr. Anthony J. Merolla, Exec. Sec., *1011 First Ave., New York, 10022.* Tel: 212-931-9239.

Hospital Apostolate—Rev. Msgr. Marc J. Filacchione, *1011 First Ave., New York, 10022.* Tel: 212-371-1000.

Information, Bureau of and Radio-T.V. Communications—See Communications.

Inner City Scholarship Fund, Inc.—William Goodloe, Dir., *1011 First Ave., New York, 10022.* Tel: 212-371-1000.

Institutional Commodity Services Corporation—Mr. Richard Costello, Dir.; Mr. Vincent Heintz, Gen. Mgr. Dept. Mgrs.: Richard Hession; Robert McGrath; Phyllis Palumbo; Robert Schiavi; Nanette Melera, Food Serv. Dir., *1011 First Ave., New York, 10022.* Tel: 212-371-1000.

Instructional T.V. Communications Center—Mr. Michael Lavery, Dir., *St. Joseph's Seminary, 201 Seminary Ave., Yonkers, 10704.* Tel: 914-968-7800.

Insurance Division—Vacant; Dir., *1011 First Ave., New York, 10022.* Tel: 212-371-1000, Ext. 3024.

Inter-Parish Financing, Commission for—Rev. Dennis P. Keane, Chm.; Rev. Msgr. George F. Bardes, Exec. Sec., *1011 First Ave., New York, 10022.* Tel: 212-371-1000.

Italian Apostolate—Rev. Msgr. George J. Cascelli, Dir., *1011 First Ave., New York, 10022.* Tel: 212-371-1000.

Justice and Peace, Archdiocesan Office of—*1011 First Ave., New York, 10022.* Tel: 212-371-1000.

Legion of Mary—Rev. Lawrence M. Paolicelli, Dir., *1011 First Ave., New York, 10022.*

Liturgical Commission, Archdiocesan—Sr. Janet Baxendale, S.C., Exec. Sec., *Liturgical Resource Center, 1011 First Ave., New York, 10022.* Tel: 212-371-1000, Ext. 2692; 2685.

Parish Councils, Archdiocesan Office for—Rev. Robert J. Aufieri, Dir.; Sr. Rosalie Kaley, S.C., Assoc. Dir., *1011 First Ave., New York, 10022.* Tel: 212-371-1000.

Parish Mission Team—Rev. Thomas Devery, Dir., *38 Montebello Rd., Suffern, 10901.* Tel: 914-357-1300.

Pastoral Council, Archdiocesan—Madeleine Morrissey, Chm.; Rev. Robert J. Aufieri, Exec. Sec.

Pastoral Life Conference—*1011 First Ave., New York, 10022.* Tel: 212-371-1000.

Pastoral Research and Planning Office—Dr. Ruth T. Doyle, Dir., *1011 First Ave., New York, 10022.* Tel: 212-371-1000.

Pastoral Services, Archdiocese of New York—*1011 First Ave., New York, 10022.* Tel: 212-371-1000.

Pension Office, Archdiocesan—Mr. William J. Daly, Exec. Sec., *1011 First Ave., New York, 10022.* Tel: 212-371-1000.

Personnel Board, Archdiocesan—Rev. Msgr. Edward D. O'Donnell, Dir.; Rev. Msgr. George Thompson, Vice-Chancellor, Priest Personnel. Members of the Board: Rev. Msgr. Francis Boyle; Rev. Robert Verrigni; Rev. Msgr. Daniel Peake; Rev. Msgr. Richard Guastella; Rev. Anthony Sorgie, *1011 First Ave., New York, 10022.* Tel: 212-371-1000.

Preaching and Liturgy, Institute for—Vacant.

Priests Council of the Archdiocese of New York—His Eminence John J. O'Connor, Pres.; Rev. Msgr. Wallace A. Harris, Chm.; Rev. Msgr. Daniel V. Flynn, Vice Chm.; Rev. Anthony Sorgie, Sec./Treas., *1011 First Ave., New York, 10022.* Tel: 212-371-1000.

Prison Apostolate—Rev. Msgr. Leslie J. Ivers, Dir., *1011 First Ave., New York, 10022.* Tel: 212-371-1000.

Propagation of the Faith—Archdiocesan Office, Rev. Msgr. Ferdinand O. Berardi, Archdiocesan Dir.; Sr. Pauline Churchirillo, P.B.V.M., Mission Education Coord., *1011 First Ave., New York, 10022.* Tel: 212-371-1000.

Propagation of the Faith—National Office, Most Rev. William J. McCormack, Natl. Dir., *366 Fifth Ave., New York, 10001.* Tel: 212-563-8700.

Real Estate Division—Mr. David Brown, Dir., *1011 First Ave., New York, 10022.* Tel: 212-371-1000.

Retirement Plan for Priests—Rev. Msgr. Robert A. Ford, Chm., *1011 First Ave., New York, 10022.* Tel: 212-371-1000, Ext. 2935.

Schools, Superintendent of—Dr. Catherine Hickey, Supt., *1011 First Ave., New York, 10022.* Tel: 212-371-1000. (Consult separate listing.).

Sodalities, Federation—*1011 First Ave., New York, 10022.* Tel: 212-371-1000.

Spiritual Development, Office of—Rev. Eugene J. Fulton, Dir., *One Pryer Manor Rd., Larchmont, 10538.* Tel: 914-235-6839.

Trustees of St. Patrick's Cathedral in the City of New York, Inc.—Rev. Msgr. James K. Vaughey, Exec. Dir., Cemeteries; Mr. Anthony V. Roina, Asst. Exec. Dir., Cemeteries.

University Apostolate—Rev. Michael Crimmins, Coord., *1011 First Ave., New York, 10022.* Tel: 212-371-1000.

Vocations—Rev. Robert McKeon, Special Asst. to the Archbishop, *St. Joseph's Seminary, Yonkers, 10704.* Tel: 914-968-1340. Sr. Deanna Sabetta, Dir., Women's Vocations, *1011 First Ave., New York, 10022.* Tel: 212-371-1000.

Women Religious, Archdiocesan Council of—Sr. Margaret Kelly, S.C., Pres.; Sr. Rosalie Kaley, S.C., Exec. Sec., *1011 First Ave., New York, 10022.* Tel: 212-371-1000.

CLERGY, PARISHES, MISSIONS AND PAROCHIAL SCHOOLS

NEW YORK CITY
BOROUGH OF MANHATTAN

1—Cathedral of St. Patrick (Old, 1809; New, 1879), Rev. Msgr. Anthony Dalla Villa, Rector; Revs. Thomas A. Nielson; Brian C. Brennan; Eugene G. Connolly; William Scafidi, M.Ss.A.; Marion Cascino.
Rectory: 460 Madison Ave., 10022. Tel: 212-753-2261; Fax: 212-755-4128.
Res., 452 Madison Ave., 10022. Most Revs. Patrick J. Sheridan; Henry Mansell; Rev. Gregory Mustaciuolo; Rev. Msgr. James McCarthy.
Chapel—New York, Sts. Faith, Hope and Charity. Records at St. Patrick Cathedral.

2—St. Agnes (1873), Rev. Msgr. Eugene V. Clark; Revs. William M. Shelley; Matthew Farrelly, C.S.Sp.; Venant LeLonde, O.F.M.; Kasimierz A. Kowalski. In res., Rev. Msgr. Florence Cohalan; Rev. Msgr. Carl J. Marucci (CAM); Revs. John A. Perricone; Thomas Donlan, O.P.; James M. Reinert (LIN); George W. Rutler.
Res., 143 E. 43rd St., 10017. Tel: 212-682-5722; Fax: 212-370-5791.
High School—High School for Boys, 555 West End Ave., 10024. Tel: 212-873-9100. Bro. Thomas Potenza, F.M.S., Prin.
Brothers 6; Lay Teachers 16; Students 300.

3—St. Albert (1916). Closed. Parochial records at Sacred Heart.

4—All Saints (1879) (African American), Rev. Theodore K. Parker, O.S.C.; Bro. Timothy T. Tomczak, O.S.C., Pastoral Assoc.; Deacon Joseph Price. In res., Revs. William C. Graham (DUL); Francis Kelly Scheets, O.S.C.; Timothy Conlon, O.S.C.
Res., 47 E. 129th St., 10035. Tel: 212-534-3535; Fax: 212-987-1930.
School—(1900), 52 E. 130th St., 10037. Tel: 212-534-0558; Fax: 212-831-6343. Sr. Marguerite Lewis, S.B.S., Prin.
Sisters of the Blessed Sacrament 6; Lay Teachers 11; Students 235.
Convent—14 E. 129 St., 10035. Tel: 212-410-3197.
Chapels—St. Benedict's Day Nursery, 34 W. 134th St., 10035. Tel: 212-283-3350; Rice High School Christian Brothers, 124 St. & Lenox Ave., 10035. Tel: 212-369-4100; Fax: 212-348-4631; Franciscan Handmaids of Mary Convent, 15 W. 124th St., 10035. Tel: 212-289-5655; Fax: 212-987-5447.
Catechesis/Religious Programs—Students 225.

5—St. Aloysius (1899), Revs. Thomas P. Green, S.J.; Edward J. Durkin, S.J. In res., Rev. Joseph F. Burke, S.J.
Res., 219 W. 132nd St., 10027. Tel: 212-234-2848; Fax: 212-234-4198.
School—(1940), 223 W. 132nd St., 10027. Tel: 212-283-0921. Ms. Laurel D. Senger, Prin.
Priests 2; Lay Teachers 15; Students 270.

6—St. Alphonsus (1847). Closed. Records at St. Anthony of Padua.

7—St. Ambrose (Chapel Centro Maria) (1897). Closed. Records at Sacred Heart Church.

8—St. Andrew (1842). Blessed Sacrament Fathers and Brothers. Revs. Roger Pageot, S.S.S.; James Hayes, S.S.S.; Lionel Lavigne, S.S.S.; Thomas Waldie, S.S.S., Chap.; Thomas McKeon, S.S.S., New York Infirmary Beekman Downtown Hospital; James P. Hayes, Pace University. In res., Bros. Stanley Kolwaski, S.S.S.; Thomas Morrissey, S.S.S.; Thomas Mella, S.S.S.
Res., 20 Cardinal Hayes Pl., 10007. Tel: 212-962-3972; 3973.
Stations—New York Infirmary Beekman Downtown Hospital, 170 William St., 10007; St. Margaret's House, 49 Fulton St., 10007; Pace University, Pace Plaza, 10007.

9—St. Ann's Armenian Catholic Church (1852) (Armenian), Most Rev. Hovhannes Tertzakian.
Res., 110 E. 12th St., 10003. Tel: 212-477-2030; Fax: 212-477-2185.

10—St. Ann's Roman Catholic Church (1852), Rev. Msgr. Kevin P. O'Brien, Admin.
Res., 110 E. 12th St., 10003. Tel: 212-475-2590.

11—St. Ann (1911) (Spanish), Revs. Victor Muzzin, F.D.P. (Italy); Pasquale Ruggieri, F.D.P. (Italy).
Res., 312 E. 110th St., 10029. Tel: 212-534-3856.
School—(1926), 314-318 E. 110th St., 10029. Tel: 212-722-1295. Sr. Josephine Cioffi, Prin.
Priests 1; Sisters, Servants of the Immaculate Heart of Mary 4; Lay Teachers 12; Students 320.
Chapel—St. Ann's Convent, 319 E. 109 St., 10029. Tel: 212-534-8321.

12—Annunciation (1853), Revs. Felix Jimenez (Spain); Jose M. Clavero, Sch.P. (Spain); Aroldo Guerra, Sch.P. (Cuba); Felix Ganuza (Spain).
Res., 88 Convent Ave., 10027. Tel: 212-234-1919; Fax: 212-281-7205.
School—(1858), 461 W. 131st St., 10027. Tel: 212-281-7174. Oscar Aviles, Prin.
Lay Teachers 16; Students 411.
Catechesis/Religious Programs—Students 500.

13—St. Anthony of Padua (Org. 1859; Re-org. 1866), Revs. Daniel Morey, O.F.M.; Dennis Baum, O.F.M.; Bro. Vincent Ciaravino.
Res. & Chapel—154 Sullivan St., 10012. Tel: 212-777-2755; Fax: 212-673-6684.
School—(1874), 60 MacDougal St., 10012. Tel: 212-477-1297.
Franciscan Sisters of Allegany 1; Lay Teachers 10; Students 210.
Catechesis/Religious Programs—Tel: 212-477-5792. Sr. Agenesine M.H.S.H., D.R.E.
Students 20.

14—Ascension (1895), Revs. John P. Duffell; Sixto Quezada (Dominican Republic); Philip Kelly; Deacon Constancio Soto.
Res., 221 W. 107th St., 10025. Tel: 212-222-0666; Fax: 212-961-1086.
School—(1912), 220 W. 108th St., 10025. Tel: 212-222-5161.
Lay Teachers 11; Students 202.
Catechesis/Religious Programs—Tel: 212-749-5938.
Students 285.
Chapels—C.Y.O. Grace Ministry, 218 W. 108th St., 10025. Tel: 212-666-6598; Convent, 302 W. 106th St., 10025. Tel: 212-663-9354; Riverside Study Center. (Opus Dei) 330 Riverside Dr., 10025. Tel: 212-222-3285; Fax: 212-316-3629.

15—Assumption (1858). Closed. Records at Sacred Heart Church.

16—St. Benedict the Moor (1883) (Spanish). Attended by Sacred Heart of Jesus, 212-265-5020, 457 W. 51st St, New York, NY 10019. Rev. Kevin J. Nelan.
Res., 457 W. 51st St., 10019. Tel: 212-265-5020.

17—ST. BERNARD (1868), Rev. Kenneth J. Smith; Rev. Msgr. Joseph T.V. Snee, Pastor Emeritus. In res., Revs. Celsus Tria, C.M.; Cesar Ching Espineda, S.V.D.
Res., 328 W. 14th St., 10014. Tel: 212-243-0265.
School—(1916), 327 W. 13th St., 10014. Tel: 212-243-6368; Fax: 212-99-7363. Ms. Imelda David, Prin.
Sisters of Charity of St. Vincent de Paul 1; Lay Teachers 9; Students 220.
Chapel—Sisters of Charity Convent, 326 W. 14th St., 10014. Tel: 212-255-5431.

18—BLESSED SACRAMENT (1887), Revs. Robert B. O'Connor; Kevin V. Madigan; Alfredo Balinong, S.J. (Philippines); Alexis Bastides (Venezuela). In res., Rev. Msgr. William J. Toohy.
Res., 152 W. 71st St., 10023. Tel: 212-877-3111; Fax: 212-799-6233.
School—(1902), 147-152 W. 70th St., 10023. Tel: 212-724-7561. Janice Desmond, Prin.
Sisters 1; Lay Teachers 9; Students 248.
Chapels—Convent of Blessed Sacrament, 133 W. 70th St., 10023. Tel: 212-877-8076; St. Agnes' Home, 237 W. 74th St., 10023. Tel: 212-874-9203; Archdiocese Teachers Residence, 22 W. 70th St., 10023.

19—ST. BONIFACE (1858). Closed. Records at Holy Family Church.

20—ST. BRIGID (1848; 1955), Revs. Michael J. Conway, O.SS.T., Admin.; Joseph C. Gidaro, O.SS.T. In res., Rev. Aaron M. Dowdell, O.SS.T.
Res., 119 Avenue B, 10009. Tel: 212-228-5400.
School—185 E. Seventh St., 10009. Tel: 212-677-5210; Fax: 212-260-2262.
Lay Teachers 9; Students 100.

21—ST. CATHERINE OF GENOA (1887), Rev. Robert T. Ritchie.
Res., 506 W. 153rd St., 10031. Tel: 212-862-6130; Fax: 212-491-6272.
School—(1910), 508-510 W. 153rd St., 10031. Tel: 212-926-0252.
Lay Teachers 10; Students 330.
Catechesis/Religious Programs—Students 240.

22—ST. CATHERINE OF SIENA (1897), Very Rev. Christopher Johnson, O.P., Prior; Revs. Vincent F. McHenry, O.P., Sub-Prior; George L. Concordia, O.P.; John J. Conroy, O.P.; Paul B. Fu, O.P.; Patrick F. Connolly, O.P.; Gregory Maturi, O.P.; Robert P. Fitzsimmons, O.P.; Athanasius Sulavik, O.P.; John Thaddeus Murphy, O.P.
Res., 411 E. 68th St., 10021. Tel: 212-988-8300; Fax: 212-988-6918.

23—ST. CECILIA (1873), Revs. James P. Brennan, C.SS.R.; Daniel Francis, C.SS.R.; Thomas Maceda, C.SS.R.; William Jacob, C.SS.R.; Rev. Msgr. John K. Graham, C.SS.R.; Rev. Bruce Lewandowski, C.SS.R.; Bros. Francis Alfone, C.SS.R.; Christopher Colarossi, C.SS.R.
Res., 125 E. 105th St., 10029. Tel: 212-534-1350; Fax: 212-410-6177.
Day Nursery—118 E. 106 St., 10029. Tel: 212-534-8423. Sisters of the Atonement.

24—ST. CHARLES BORROMEO (1888), Rev. Msgr. Wallace A. Harris.
Res., 211 W. 141st St., 10030. Tel: 212-281-2100; Fax: 212-862-1881.
School—(1904), 214 W. 142 St., 10030. Tel: 212-368-6666. Sr. Marianne Poole, Prin.
Sisters of the Blessed Sacrament 7; Lay Teachers 17; Students 520.

25—ST. CLARE (1903). Closed. Records at St. Raphael's Church.

26—ST. CLEMENS MARY (1909). Closed. Records at Holy Cross Church, Manhattan.

27—ST. COLUMBA (1845), Rev. Msgr. Edward M. O'Brien; Rev. Frank Scanlon, Admin. In res., Rev. Joseph Hien.
Res., 343 W. 25th St., 10001. Tel: 212-807-8876.
School—(1847), 331-333 W. 25th St., 10001.
Sisters of Congregation of Notre Dame 2; Lay Teachers 9; Students 243.
Chapel—Sisters of Congregation of Notre Dame, 329 W. 25 St., 10001.

28—CORPUS CHRISTI (1906), Rev. Msgr. Patrick J. Carney; Rev. Roberto J. Ricci, S.J. (Argentina); Rev. Msgr. Myles M. Bourke, Pastor Emeritus. In res., Rev. Linus Inwanyanwu (Nigeria).
Res., 529 W. 121st St., 10027. Tel: 212-666-9350.
School—(1907), 535 W. 121st St., 10027. Tel: 212-662-9344; Fax: 212-662-2725. Ms. Niki Montalro, Prin.
Lay Teachers 11; Students 271.
Catechesis/Religious Programs—Students 271.

29—SS. CYRIL AND METHODIUS - ST. RAPHAEL (1913; 1886) (Croatian), Revs. Marko Puljic, O.F.M.; Stephen Raich, O.F.M.; Valentin Vukoja, O.F.M.
Res., 502 W. 41st St., 10036. Tel: 212-563-3395; Fax: 212-868-1203.

30—ST. CYRIL (1916) (Slovenian). Unassigned.
Res., 62 St. Mark's Pl., 10003. Tel: 212-674-3442; Fax: 212-674-3442.

31—ST. ELIZABETH (1869), Rev. Msgr. Joachim B. Beaumont; Revs. Rudolph F. Gonzalez; Jose Serrano; Carlos Perez (Puerto Rico); Deacon Odalis R. Rosado.
Res., 268 Wadsworth Ave., 10033. Tel: 212-568-8803; Fax: 212-781-2754.
School—(1936), 612 W. 187th St., 10033. Tel: 212-568-7291; Fax: 212-928-2515.
Sisters 2; Lay Teachers 19; Students 696.
Catechesis/Religious Programs—Tel: 212-923-4900.
Students 600.
Chapels—Sisters Residence, 612 W. 187th St., 10033; Cabrini Chapel, 701 Ft. Washington Ave., 10040.
Isabella Geriatric Center—515 Audubon Ave., 10040.

32—ST. ELIZABETH OF HUNGARY (1891) (Slovak), Rev. Msgr. Patrick P. McCahill. In res., Rev. Francis X. Elsinghorst, S.J.
Res., 211 E. 83rd St., 10028-2854. Tel: 212-734-5747; 988-1903 (TTY); Fax: 212-988-1903.
Catechesis/Religious Programs—Students 30.

33—ST. EMERIC (1949), Revs. Peter K. Meehan; Luis M. Dolan, C.P. (Argentina).
Res., 185 Avenue D, 10009. Tel: 212-228-4494.
Catechesis/Religious Programs—Students 205.

34—EPIPHANY (1868) (Irish), Rev. Msgr. Walter J. Niebrzydowski; Revs. James A. Collignon, M.M.; Erno B. Diaz (Archdiocese of Manila); Sr. Doris Sayhonne, R.C.D., Pastoral Assoc.; Sr. Christine Gates, R.G.S., Social Worker. In res., Revs. Edmond J. Nixon, C.SS.R. (Australia); John Bonnici.
Res., 239 E. 21st St., 10010. Tel: 212-475-1966; Fax: 212-477-0537.
School—(1869), 234 E. 22nd St., 10010. Tel: 212-473-4128; Fax: 212-473-4392.
141 E. 28th St., 10016. Tel: 212-473-4496; Fax: 212-473-4537.
Sisters 1; Lay Teachers 35; Students 510.
Catechesis/Religious Programs—Students 150.

35—ST. FRANCIS OF ASSISI (1844) (Franciscan), Revs. Ronald P. Stark, O.F.M., Guardian & Pastor; Thomas J. Walters, O.F.M., Vicar; Peter Brophy, O.F.M.; Christian F. Camadella, O.F.M.; Eric Carpine, O.F.M.; Gerald F. Carr, O.F.M.; Brian Carroll, O.F.M.; Bros. Denis Gordon Clark, O.F.M.; F. Edward Coughlin, O.F.M.; Revs. Alcuin Coyle, O.F.M.; Marshall Della Penna, O.F.M.; Anthony Fedell, O.F.M.; John M. Felice, O.F.M.; Brennan Fitzgerald, O.F.M.; Robert A. Gavin, O.F.M.; Bro. Charles Gilmartin, O.F.M.; Revs. Vincent B. Grogan, O.F.M.; Joseph M. Hertel, O.F.M.; Michael Judge, O.F.M.; Joseph Juracek, O.F.M.; Francis de Paul Kealy, O.F.M.; Francis Kim, O.F.M.; Vincent A. Laviano, O.F.M.; Miguel A. Loredo, O.F.M.; Bro. William Mann, O.F.M.; Revs. Francis Matthews, O.F.M.; Vincent McCann, O.F.M.; Marcellus A. McCartney, O.F.M.; Michael McDonnell, O.F.M.; John W. McDowell, O.F.M.; Felix P. McGrath, O.F.M.; Cassian Miles, O.F.M.; Bro. Timothy Miskowski, O.F.M.; Revs. John J. McVean, O.F.M.; Francis J. Muller, O.F.M.; Bro. Nathanael Necaster, O.F.M.; Revs. Robert Nee, O.F.M.; Quintin A. Neyland, O.F.M.; James R. O'Connell, O.F.M.; Miguel A. Sepulveda, O.F.M.; Timothy J. Shreenan, O.F.M.; Bro. Sebastian Tobin, O.F.M.; Revs. Kevin Tortorelli, O.F.M.; Lambert F. Valentine, O.F.M.; Allan G. Von Kobs, O.F.M.; Thomas J. Walters, O.F.M.; Rayner Williams, O.F.M.; Dennis Wilson, O.F.M. (For priests and brothers not listed here see St. Francis Monastery under Monasteries and Residences of Priests and Brothers.).
Res., 135 W. 31 St., 10001. Tel: 212-736-8500; Fax: 212-736-8545.

36—ST. FRANCIS DE SALES (1894), Rev. Robert V. Lott, S.T.M.; Rev. Msgr. Oscar Aquino, J.C.D.; Joseph M. McLafferty, Pastoral Assoc.
Res., 135 A E. 96th St., 10128. Tel: 212-289-0425; Fax: 212-996-2028.
School—St. Francis de Sales & St. Lucy Academy, (1993), 116-120 E. 97th St. & 340 E. 104th St., 10029. Tel: 212-289-0680; 534-4021; Fax: 212-534-4130. Bro. Paul Beaudin, C.F.C., Prin.
Congregation of Christian Brothers 4; Lay Teachers 18; Students 600.

37—ST. FRANCIS XAVIER (1847), Revs. Louis S. Sogliuzzo, S.J.; John P. Bucki, S.J. Pastoral Assocs.: Mr. Thomas Sanger; Ms. Kathleen Duffy; Sr. Honora Nicholson, R.S.M.
Office: 55 W. 15th St., 10011. Tel: 212-627-2100; Fax: 212-675-6997.

38—ST. FRANCES XAVIER CABRINI (1973), Rev. Joseph P. Gorman.
Res., 555 Main St., Roosevelt Island, 10044. Tel: 212-832-6778.

39—THE CHURCH OF ST. GABRIEL (1867). Closed. Records at Church of Sacred Hearts of Jesus and Mary.

40—ST. GREGORY (1907), Revs. Raymond M. Rafferty; Arturo Motolinia, O.S.A. (Mexico). In res., Rev. Kevin L. Sullivan.
Res., 144 W. 90th St., 10024. Tel: 212-724-9766; 9767.
School—(1913), 138 W. 90th St., 10024. Ms. Deborah Hurd, Prin.
Lay Teachers 9; Students 210.

41—GOOD SHEPHERD (1912), Revs. Patrick Traynor, C.S.P.; Lionel A. de Silva, C.S.P.; Kevin A. Devine, C.S.P.; Gerard Tully, C.S.P.; Sr. Acela Rodriguez, H.C.C.S.; Deacon Rafael Then. In res., Revs. Lawrence E. Boadt, C.S.P.; Steven Harris, C.S.P.; Marcos Zamora, C.S.P.
Res., 608 Isham St., 10034. Tel: 212-567-1300; Fax: 212-567-1476.
School—(1925), Cooper and Isham Sts., 10034. Tel: 212-567-5800; Fax: 212-567-5839.
Sisters of Mercy of the Union 3; Lay Teachers 29; Students 600.
Catechesis/Religious Programs—Mrs. Jacqueline Martin, D.R.E., Pastoral Assoc.
Students 275.
Chapel—Convent of Sisters of Mercy. (Private) 630 Isham St., 10034. Tel: 212-567-1600.

42—GUARDIAN ANGEL (1888), Rev. Msgr. Edward M. O'Brien; Revs. Philip Phan; John Martin, C.S.S.R.
Res., 193 Tenth Ave., 10011. Tel: 212-929-5966.
School—(1911). Maureen McElduff, Prin.
Sisters of St. Dominic 2; Lay Teachers 8; Students 247.
Chapel—Sisters of St. Dominic & Franciscan Sisters, 407 W. 21st St., 10011. Tel: 212-243-2266.

43—ST. HEDWIG (1934). Closed. Parochial records at St. Stanislaus Church.

44—HOLY AGONY (1930) (Spanish), Revs. Jesus M. Oses, C.M.; Candido Arrizurieta, C.M.; Santiago Lluch, C.M.
Res., 1834 Third Ave., 10029. Tel: 212-289-5589.

45—HOLY CROSS (1852), Rev. Peter M. Colapietro; Deacon Lawrence C. McNeill.
Res., 329 W. 42nd St., 10036. Tel: 212-246-4732; Fax: 212-307-5033.
School—(1864), 332 W. 43rd St., 10036. Tel: 212-246-0923. Sr. Mary Theresa Dixon, O.P., Prin.
Sisters of St. Dominic of Blauvelt 1; Lay Teachers 13; Students 328.
Chapels—Dominican Convent, 460 W. 44th St., 10036. Tel: 212-246-9768; St. Joseph's Home, 425 W. 44th St., 10036. Tel: 212-246-5363; Covenant House, 692 Eighth Ave., 10036. Tel: 212-613-0300.

46—HOLY FAMILY (1924), Revs. Robert J. Robbins; Robert E. O'Brien, S.J. In res., Rev. John J. McAuley, M.M.
Res., 315 E. 47th St., 10017-2318. Tel: 212-753-3401; Fax: 212-753-3428.

47—HOLY INNOCENTS (1866), Rev. Msgr. Donald Sakano; Rev. William J. Delaney.
Res., 128 W. 37th St., 10018. Tel: 212-279-5861; Fax: 212-714-9313.

48—HOLY NAME OF JESUS (1868), Revs. James F. Hynes, O.F.M.; Charles Miller, O.F.M.; Richard Trezza, O.F.M.; Robert J. Kennedy, O.F.M.; Paul Lostrittu, O.F.M.; Bro. Bill Herbst, O.F.M.
Res., 207 W. 96th St., 10025. Tel: 212-749-0276; Fax: 212-749-2045.
School—(1905), Amsterdam Ave. & 97th St., 10025. Tel: 212-749-1240; Fax: 212-663-1939. Bro. Richard Grieco, F.S.C., Prin.
Brothers 2; Lay Teachers 20; Students 655.
Catechesis/Religious Programs—Tel: 212-655-1888. Jayne Porcelli, D.R.E.
Students 240.

49—HOLY ROSARY (1884) (Augustinian), Revs. Angel Dulanto, O.S.A.; Abel Alvarez, O.S.A.; Juan Manuel Chaguaceda, O.S.A.
Res., 444 E. 119th St., 10035. Tel: 212-534-0740; Fax: 212-534-7572.
School—(1949), 371 Pleasant Ave., 10035. Tel: 212-876-7555; Fax: 212-876-0152.
Sisters 1; Lay Teachers 9; Students 180.
Catechesis/Religious Programs—Students 180.

50—HOLY TRINITY (1898), Rev. Msgr. Thomas P. Leonard; Rev. Gerardo Bengochea, S.J. In res., Rev. Michael Lanning, O.F.M.; Rev. Msgr. Neil J. Graham.
Res., 213 W. 82 St., 10024. Tel: 212-787-0634; Fax: 212-787-4917.
Chapel—Chinese Catholic Information Center, 86 Riverside Dr., 10024. Tel: 212-787-6969; Fax: 212-787-0351.

51—ST. IGNATIUS LOYOLA (1851), Revs. Walter F. Modrys, S.J.; William J. Bergen, S.J.; Damian A. O'Connell, S.J.; Mark C. Hallinan, S.J.; Thomas D. McCall, S.J.; Deacon Charles J. O'Byrne, S.J.; Ms. Mary Christine O'Connor, M.Div., Pastoral Assoc.
Res., 980 Park Ave., 10028. Tel: 212-288-3588; Fax: 212-734-3671.
School—(1854), 50 E. 84th St., 10028. Tel: 212-861-3820; Fax: 212-879-8248.

Sisters of Charity of St. Vincent de Paul 4; Lay Teachers 21; Students 507.
Day Nursery—240 E. 84th St., 10028. Tel: 212-734-6427; Fax: 212-734-6972.
Lay Assistants 15; Capacity 107.
Catechesis/Religious Programs—Tel: 212-861-4764. Ms. Joanne Cunneen M.A., D.R.E. Students 535.
Chapels—St. Ignatius Loyola Convent, Tel: 212-288-5544; Regis High School, 55 E. 84th St., 10028. Tel: 212-288-1100; Fax: 212-794-1221; Loyola School, Tel: 212-288-3522; Fax: 212-861-1021; Marymount School, 1028 Fifth Ave., 10028. Tel: 212-744-4486; Fax: 212-744-0163.

52—IMMACULATE CONCEPTION (1855), Rev. Msgr. Kevin P. O'Brien; Revs. Francis X. Buu; John P. Moore; Richard J. Neuhaus; Misael Bacleon. In res., Rev. Msgr. Desmond J. Vella; Revs. Edwin J. Conlin; John J. Delaney; John Gibson.
Res., 414 E. 14th St., 10009. Tel: 212-254-0200; Fax: 212-505-7610.
School—(1864), 419 E. 13th St., 10009. Tel: 212-475-2590; Fax: 212-475-7413.
Sisters 1; Lay Teachers 14; Students 390.

53—INCARNATION (1908), Rev. Msgr. Gerald T. Walsh; Revs. John N. Paddack; Gabriel LaPaz; Robert M. Dunn.
Res., 1290 St. Nicholas Ave., 10033. Tel: 212-927-7474.
School—(1910), 568-570 W. 175th St., 10033.
Lay Teachers 22; Students 596.

54—ST. JAMES (1827), Revs. Robert J. Poveromo; Jesus P. Enojo; Joseph Chao.
Res., 23 Oliver St., 10038. Tel: 212-233-0161.
School—(1854), 37 St. James Place, 10038. Tel: 212-267-9289. Sr. Josefa Marie Curcio, C.S.J.B., Prin.
Sisters of St. John the Baptist 4; Lay Teachers 8; Students 210.
Chapel—St. James Convent, 21 Oliver St., 10038. Tel: 212-962-0840.

55—ST. JEAN BAPTISTE (1882), Revs. John Kamas, S.S.S.; Bernard J. Camire, S.S.S.; Edmund Slattery, S.S.S.; Donald Brouillard, S.S.S. In res., Revs. William O'Halloran, S.S.S.; Eugene LaVerdiere, S.S.S.; Williams Dahms, S.S.S.; Nicholas Zolnerowich, S.S.S.
Res., 184 E. 76th St., 10021. Tel: 212-288-5082.
School—St. Jean Baptiste High School, 173 E. 75th St., 10021. Tel: 212-288-1645; Fax: 212-288-6540.
Sisters of the Congregation of Notre Dame 8; Religious 2; Lay Teachers 32; Students 495.
Chapel—Sisters' Convent, Tel: 212-472-1230 (Apt. A); 472-8821 (Apt. B).

56—ST. JOACHIM (1888) (Italian). Closed. Parochial records are at Church of St. Joseph.

57—ST. JOHN THE BAPTIST (1840) (Capuchin-Franciscan Friars), Revs. Francis Gasparik, O.F.M.Cap., Guardian & Pastor; Joseph Mullen, O.F.M.Cap.; Gerard Mulvey, O.F.M.Cap.; Philip Romano, O.F.M.Cap.; Justin Joos, O.F.M.Cap., (Retired). In res., Revs. Armand Dasseville, O.F.M.Cap., Spiritual Asst. of Secular Order of St. Francis; John Clermont, O.F.M.Cap.; Peter Kaseta, O.F.M.Cap., Dir. of Devel./Capuchin Mission Assn.; John Conner, O.F.M.Cap.; Thomas Faiola, O.F.M.Cap.; Thomas Houle, O.F.M.Cap., Chap.; Leonard Glavin, O.F.M.Cap., (Retired); Ramon Frias, O.F.M.Cap., Chap.; Bros. Luke Benbrook, O.F.M.Cap., Pastoral Assoc.; George McCloskey, O.F.M.Cap., Dir. Communications.
Res., 210 W. 31st St., 10001-2876. Tel: 212-564-9070; Fax: 212-564-3964.

58—ST. JOHN THE EVANGELIST (1840), Rev. Msgr. Michael J. Wrenn; Rev. James P. Connolly; Rev. Msgr. George A. Kelly; Rev. Msgr. Thomas J. Bergin.
Res., 348 E. 55th St., 10022. Tel: 212-753-8418; Fax: 212-826-1848.

59—ST. JOHN NEPOMUCENE (1895) (Slovak), Revs. Robert J. Tomlian; Marian Kacir (Slovakia). In res., Rev. Msgr. George J. Cascelli.
Res., 411 E. 66th St., 10021. Tel: 212-734-4613; 734-4370.
Chapel—Sisters' Convent, 320 E. 66th St., 10021. Tel: 212-734-6640.

60—ST. JOHN THE MARTYR (1903), Rev. Msgr. John G. Woolsey; Rev. Joseph W. Baker; Rev. Msgr. George P. Thompson.
Res., 259 E. 71st St., 10021-4596. Tel: 212-744-4880; 4881; Fax: 212-628-6662.

61—ST. JOSEPH (1829), Revs. Aldo J. Tos; William A. White; Michael K. Holleran; Sr. Anne Tahaney, O.P., Pastoral Assoc.; Deacon Thomas Johnson; Carol M. Reina, Parish Mgr.
Res., 371 Sixth Ave., 10014. Tel: 212-741-1274; Fax: 212-741-2147.
School—111 Washington Pl., 10014. Tel: 212-929-5134; Fax: 212-929-5105.
Lay Teachers 10; Students 222.

62—ST. JOSEPH (1873) (German), Rev. Msgr. Lawrence M. Connaughton; Revs. Charles T. Murr; Gary G. Seibert, S.J. In res., Rev. William S. Elder.
Res., 404 E. 87th St., 10128. Tel: 212-289-6030; Fax: 212-831-4043.
School—(1880), 420 E. 87th St., 10128. Tel: 212-289-3057; Fax: 212-289-7239.
Sisters 2; Lay Teachers 9; Students 240.

63—ST. JOSEPH OF THE HOLY FAMILY (1860), Rev. Msgr. Howard W. Calkins; Revs. Isaac Agambi (Nigeria); Henry Mills; Peter Okoli (Nigeria); Deacon Domingo Lopez.
Res., 405 W. 125th St., 10027. Tel: 212-662-9125.
School—(1862), 168 Morningside Ave., 10027. Tel: 212-662-1736; Fax: 212-662-1490.
Daughters of Charity of St. Vincent de Paul 4; Lay Teachers 7; Students 250.
Catechesis/Religious Programs—Students 170.
Convent—400 W. 126th St., 10027. Tel: 212-678-0585.

64—ST. JOSEPH (1924), Revs. Andrew Brizzolara, C.S.; Peter Tsoi, (Chinese Apostolate).
Res., 5 Monroe St., 10002. Tel: 212-267-8376; Fax: 212-267-8379.
School—(1926), 1 Monroe St., 10002. Tel: 212-233-5152; Fax: 212-267-8379.
Apostles of the Sacred Heart of Jesus 4; Lay Teachers 8; Students 220.
Convent—83 Madison St., 10002. Tel: 212-233-5670.
Apostles of the Sacred Heart of Jesus 4.

65—ST. JUDE (1949), Revs. Elias Isla, Sch.P.; Jose M. Aguilar; Ricardo Fajardo; Deacon Porfirio Rodriguez.
Res., 431 W. 204th St., 10034. Tel: 212-569-3000.
School—(1953), 433 W. 204th St., 10034.
Lay Teachers 17; Students 588.
Chapel—New York, St. Jude Convent.

66—ST. LEO (1880). Closed. Parochial records at St. Stephen's Church.

67—ST. LUCY (1900) (Hispanic), Revs. Esviardo Palomino; Jose Herrero, O.S.A.
Res., 344 E. 104th St., 10029. Tel: 212-534-1470.
School—(1942). Consolidated with St. Francis de Sales School to form St. Francis de Sales-St. Lucy Academy (1993). 340 E. 104th St., 10029. Tel: 212-534-4021; Fax: 212-354-4130. Bro. Paul Beaudin, C.F.C., Prin.

68—ST. MALACHY'S (1902). (The Actors' Chapel). Revs. Michael C. Crimmins; Joseph A. Kelly, S.J.; Sr. Maureen Gibbons, O.P.
Res., 239 W. 49th St., 10019. Tel: 212-489-1340; Fax: 212-262-6224.
Encore Community Services—Fax: 212-757-0244. Sr. Elizabeth Hasselt, O.P., Exec. Dir., Tel: 212-489-1341; Sr. Bernadette Gayor, S.H.C.J., Finance Dir., Tel: 212-489-1943.
Encore Community Center & Programs—Tel: 212-581-2910. Sr. Lillian McNamara, O.P., Dir.
Encore 49 Residence—Tel: 212-246-0880; 581-3490. Mrs. Mary Noone, R.N., Housing Dir.

69—ST. MARK THE EVANGELIST (1907), Revs. Leonard Tuozzolo, C.S.Sp.; Daniel McCarthy, C.S.Sp.
Res., 65 W. 138th St., 10037. Tel: 212-281-4931; Fax: 212-491-6803.
School—(1912), 55 W. 138th St., 10037. Tel: 212-283-4848; Fax: 212-926-0419. Sr. Catherin Hagan, D.C., Prin.
Daughters of Charity of St. Vincent de Paul 5; Lay Teachers 10; Students 251.
Chapel—St. Mark's Convent, Tel: 212-283-4966.

70—ST. MARY (1826), Rev. Msgr. Neil A. Connolly; Rev. Msgr. Thomas J. Keogh, Pastor Emeritus; Revs. Peter Ma, (Chinese Apostolate); Andrew O'Connor.
Res., 28 Attorney St., 10002. Tel: 212-674-3266.

71—ST. MARY MAGDALEN (1873) (German). Closed. Parochial records at Immaculate Conception Church.

72—MARY HELP OF CHRISTIANS (1908) (Spanish), Revs. Thomas Brennan, S.D.B.; Jose Berrueta, S.D.B.; Denis Kelleher, S.D.B.; Bro. Adelard La Bonte, S.D.B.
Res., 440 E. 12th St., 10009. Tel: 212-254-0058; Fax: 212-505-3769.
School—435-437 E. 11th St., 10009. Tel: 212-254-3596.
Daughters of Mary Help of Christians 4; Lay Teachers 8; Students 230.
Catechesis/Religious Programs—Students 230.
Convent—429 E. 12 St., 10009.

73—ST. MATTHEW (1902). Closed. Parochial records at Blessed Sacrament Church.

74—ST. MICHAEL (1857), Rev. Msgr. Marc A. Filacchione; Rev. John Mattimore, S.J. In res., Rev. John F. Harvey, O.S.F.S.
Res., 424 W. 34th St., 10001. Tel: 212-563-2575.
High School—(1866-1874), 425 W. 33 St., 10001. Tel: 212-563-2547. Sr. Kathleen Cusak, P.B.V.M., Prin.
Sisters of the Presentation 7; Lay Teachers 28; Girls 435.
Chapel—Sacred Heart, 419 W. 33rd St., 10001.

75—ST. MICHAEL CHAPEL (1936) (Russian), Rev. John Soles; Deacon Christopher LiGreci.
Res., 266 Mulberry St., 10012. Tel: 212-226-2644.

76—ST. MONICA (1879), Rev. Msgr. Thomas A. Modugno; Revs. Lazarus Sequeira (India); William M. Leydon. In res., Rev. George E. Baker; Rev. Msgr. Ferdinando Berardi.
Res., 413 E. 79th St., 10021. Tel: 212-288-6250; Fax: 212-570-1562.
Chapel—St. Monica Convent, 404 E. 80th St., 10021. Tel: 212-288-5016.

77—MOST HOLY CRUCIFIX (1925) (Italian), Rev. Christopher Hartley, Admin.
Res., 378 Broome St., 10013. Tel: 212-226-2556.

78—MOST HOLY REDEEMER (1844), Revs. Joseph Tizio, C.SS.R.; Jerome Holland, C.SS.R. In res., Rev. Terrance Moran, C.SS.R.
Res., 173 E. Third St., 10009. Tel: 212-673-4224; Fax: 212-472-4097.
Catechesis/Religious Programs—Tel: 212-673-4224; Fax: 212-477-4097.
Students 162.

79—MOST PRECIOUS BLOOD (1891) (Italian), Revs. Fabian Grifone, O.F.M.; Louis Troiano, O.F.M.
Res., 109 Mulberry St., 10013. Tel: 212-226-6427.

80—NATIVITY (1842) (Jesuit), Revs. D. Michael Flynn, S.J.; Donald C. Gannon, S.J.; Joseph J. Kavanagh, S.J.; Michael J. Sala, S.J.; George M. Anderson, S.J.; James F. Joyce, S.J.; Anthony S. Aracich, S.J.
Res., 44 Second Ave., 10003. Tel: 212-674-8590; 8591; Fax: 212-674-8789.
Nativity Mission Center—204 Forsyth St., 10002. Tel: 212-477-2472. Rev. John J. Podsiadlo, S.J., Dir. & Supr.

81—ST. NICHOLAS (1833) (German). Closed. Parochial records at Most Holy Redeemer Church.

82—NOTRE DAME (1910), Rev. Msgr. Christopher Maloney; Rev. Rees Doughty. In res., Revs. Timothy Valentine, S.J.; Ngozi Osuji (Nigeria); George Drance, S.J.; Richard Roach, S.J.
Res., 405 W. 114th St., 10025. Tel: 212-866-1500; Fax: 212-222-5704.
Station—New York, St. Luke's Hospital Amsterdam House.

83—OUR LADY QUEEN OF ANGELS (1886) (German), Revs. Philip F. Bohan, O.F.M.Cap.; Martin Curtin, O.F.M.Cap., Guardian & Pastoral Assoc.; Bros. Pius Blandino, O.F.M.Cap.; Christopher Varley, O.F.M.Cap.; George Tucker, O.F.M.Cap.; Deacon Luis Martinez.
Res., 226 E. 113th St., 10029. Tel: 212-534-6218; Fax: 212-534-6285.
School—(1886 and 1955), 229-231 E. 112th St., 10029. Tel: 212-722-9277. Bro. Louis J. Esposito, O.F.M.Cap., Prin. & Vicar.
Priests 1; Brothers 1; Sisters 1; Lay Teachers 18; Students 546.
Chapel—Convent of Sisters of St. Agnes, 232 E. 113th St., 10029. Tel: 212-369-5291.

84—OUR LADY OF ESPERANZA (1912) (Spanish), Rev. Msgr. Peter C. O'Donnell.
Res., 624 W. 156th St., 10032. Tel: 212-283-4340.
Catechesis/Religious Programs—Students 300.

85—OUR LADY OF GOOD COUNSEL (1886), Revs. Dennis P. Keane, Ph.D.; Arthur Leone; Richard Terga.
Res., 230 E. 90th St., 10128. Tel: 212-289-1742; Fax: 212-427-5643.
School—(1904), 323-329 E. 91st St., 10128. Tel: 212-289-6730. Mr. Donald Kramer, Prin.
Lay Teachers 10; Students 200.

86—OUR LADY OF GRACE (1907). Closed. Parochial records at Church of the Nativity.

87—OUR LADY OF GUADALUPE (1902) (Spanish), Revs. Peter R. Precourt, A.A.; Philip Bonvouloir, A.A.; Deacons Rafael Bello; Henry Bernal; Rene Garcia. In res., Revs. Bernard L. Guillet, A.A.; Albert E. Brochu, A.A.
Res., Priests of the Assumption, Inc., 229 W. 14th St., 10011. Tel: 212-243-5317; Fax: 212-675-0637.
Chapel—251 W. 14th St., 10011. Tel: 212-243-9414.

88—OUR LADY OF LORETO (1891) (Sicilian), Rev. Msgr. John B. Ahern; Rev. Patrick J. Carroll; Rev. Msgr. Philip J. Murnion.
Res., 309 Elizabeth St., 10012. Tel: 212-431-9840.
Holy Name Centre for Homeless Men—Tel: 212-226-5848.

89—OUR LADY OF LOURDES (1901), Revs. Thomas B. Fenlon; Fabio E. Jaramillo (Quibdo). In res., Revs. Lawrence E. Lucas; Alphonsus Anumudu (Orlu).
Res., 472 W. 142nd St., 10031. Tel: 212-862-4380; Fax: 212-862-4126.
School—(1903), 462-468 W. 143rd St., 10031. Tel: 212-926-5820. Mr. Warren Switzler, Prin.
Lay Teachers 22; Students 640.
Catechesis/Religious Programs—Students 695.

Chapel—Convent of Our Lady of Lourdes, 463 W. 142nd St., 10031. Tel: 212-926-1150; Fax: 212-862-4126.

90—OUR LADY OF THE MIRACULOUS MEDAL (1926). Closed. Records at Holy Agony.

91—OUR LADY OF MT. CARMEL (1884) (Italian), Revs. Peter J. Rofrano, S.A.C.; Severino Dominicis, S.A.C.; Anthony Kelly, S.A.C.; Girolamo D'Ambrosi, S.A.C.
Res., 448 E. 116th St., 10029-0614. Tel: 212-534-0681; Fax: 212-534-0629.
School—Mt. Carmel-Holy Rosary, 371 Pleasant Ave., 10035. Tel: 212-876-7555. Desiree Edwards, Prin.
Sisters 3; Lay Teachers 8; Students 175.
Convent—456 E. 116th St., 10029-0614. Tel: 212-427-2381.
Sisters of Charity 10.

92—OUR LADY OF PERPETUAL HELP (1887), Revs. Frank J. Freel, C.SS.R.; James May, C.SS.R.; William Heanue, C.SS.R. In res., Revs. Thomas O'Connell, C.SS.R.; Joseph Noll, C.SS.R.; Thomas McPartland, C.SS.R.; Raymond McCarthy, C.SS.R.; James Ferris, C.SS.R.
Church—328 E. 62nd St., 10021. Tel: 212-832-9087.
High School—Commercial High School. Sr. Anthony Mary, S.S.N.D., Prin.
Sisters of Notre Dame 1; Lay Teachers 8; Girls 170.
Chapel—New York, National Shrine of the Infant of Prague.

93—OUR LADY OF PEACE (1918) (Italian), Rev. Bartholomew Daly, M.H.M., Admin. In res., Rev. Paul A. Keenan.
Res., 237 E. 62nd St., 10021. Tel: 212-838-3189; Fax: 212-308-4819.

94—OUR LADY OF POMPEII (1892) (Italian), Revs. Ralph A. Bove, C.S.; Bernabe Sison; Bro. Michael La Mantia, C.S. In res., Rev. Giulivo Tessarolo, C.S.
Res., 25 Carmine St., 10014. Tel: 212-989-6805; Fax: 212-727-3139.
School—(1930), 240 Bleecker St., 10014. Tel: 212-242-4147; Fax: 212-691-2361.
Apostles of the Sacred Heart of Jesus 3; Lay Teachers 9; Students 240.

95—OUR LADY QUEEN OF MARTYRS (1927), Revs. Daniel S. Kearney; Lorenzo Ato, S.M. (Peru); Deacon Narciso Hernandez. In res., Rev. Donald Johnston, Chap., Columbia Presbyterian Hospital.
Res., 91 Arden St., 10040. Tel: 212-567-2637; Fax: 212-567-1305.
School—(1932), 71 Arden St., 10040. Tel: 212-567-3190; Fax: 212-304-8587. Andrew Woods, Prin.
Lay Teachers 18; Students 520.
Catechesis/Religious Programs—Students 795.

96—OUR LADY OF THE ROSARY (1883). Shrine of St. Elizabeth Ann Seton. Rev. Msgr. Timothy S. Collins; Rev. Msgr. James G. Wilders, Pastor Emeritus; Revs. William J. Sweeney; Martin Betances Torres. In res., Rev. John D. Flanagan.
Res., 7 State St., 10004. Tel: 212-269-6865.

97—OUR LADY OF THE SCAPULAR/ST. STEPHEN (1889; 1848) (Spanish), Revs. Kenneth Murphy, O.Carm.; Francis Amodio, O.Carm.; John Canning, O.Carm. In res., Most Rev. William J. McCormack; Rev. Msgr. Andrew P. Landi (BRK).
Res., 142 E. 29th St., 10016. Tel: 212-683-1675; 532-2232; Fax: 212-683-7921.
Catechesis/Religious Programs—Students 163.
Chapels—Bellevue Hospital, Chapel of Our Lady Helper of the Sick, Tel: 212-561-4440. Revs. John Logan, O.Carm.; Robert Greco, O.Carm.; Philip Marani, O.Carm.; Veterans Administration Hospital, Tel: 212-686-7500. Rev. Edmund McCaffrey, O.Carm.

98—OUR LADY OF SORROWS (1867) (English-Spanish), Rev. Gavin Reilly, O.F.M.Cap., Guardian; Bro. Robert Gerdin, O.F.M.Cap. In res., Revs. Myles Parsons, O.F.M.Cap.; John Mellitt, O.F.M.Cap; Bro. James Wieland, O.F.M.Cap.
Res., 213 Stanton St., 10002-1898. Tel: 212-673-0900; Fax: 212-982-0166.
Church—103 Pitt St., 10002.
School—(1867), 219 Stanton St., 10002. Tel: 212-473-0320; Fax: 212-420-0285.
Lay Teachers 13; Students 288.
Catechesis/Religious Programs—Students 262.

99—OUR LADY OF VICTORY (1944), Rev. Msgr. Edward J. Mitty; Revs. Emil L. Bettley; Jan Deptula (Poland); Arulanandam Devasagayam (India); Sebastian Ousepparampil (India). In res., Rev. John E. Fanning.
Res., 60 William St., 10005. Tel: 212-422-5535; Fax: 212-509-5336.

100—OUR LADY OF VILNA (1905) (Lithuanian), Rev. Dr. Eugene A. Sawicki, R.N., J.C.L., Admin.
Res., 32 Dominick St., 10013. Tel: 212-255-2648; Fax: 212-924-6210.
Church—570 Broome St., 10013.

101—OUR SAVIOUR (1955), Rev. Msgr. Thomas F. Heneghan; Revs. Richard J. Neilson; Edward Dougherty, M.M.; Rennyson Howell, (St. Vincent's).
Res., 59 Park Ave., 10016. Tel: 212-679-8166; Fax: 212-213-0352.

102—ST. PATRICK OLD CATHEDRAL (1809), Rev. Msgr. Guy S. Vinci; Revs. Andrew Thi; Carlos A. Mullins; Rev. Msgr. Nicholas Marinacci, Pastor Emeritus.
Res., 263 Mulberry St., 10012. Tel: 212-226-8075.
School—Boys and Girls Departments, (1817), 233-239 Mott St., 10012.
32-38 Prince St., 10012.
Sisters of Charity of St. Vincent de Paul 7; Lay Teachers 17; Students 832.
Chapels—Immaculate Conception, 32 Prince St., 10012; St. Michael, 266 Mulberry St., 10012.

103—ST. PAUL (1834), Revs. Rafael G. Corniel, Temp. Admin.; Jose Otero (Argentina).
Res., 113 E. 117th St., 10035. Tel: 212-534-4422.
School—(1870), 114-122 E. 118th St., 10035.
Sisters of Charity of St. Vincent de Paul 5; Lay Teachers 9; Students 204.
Convent—149 E. 117th St., 10035.

104—ST. PAUL THE APOSTLE (1858), Revs. Charles Kullmann, C.S.P.; Rudolph T. Vorisek, C.S.P., Hospital Chap.; James B. Lloyd, C.S.P.; Joseph F. Mahon, C.S.P., Dir. of Missions; John C. Reynolds, C.S.P.; Richard J. Walsh, C.S.P.; Joseph P. Flynn, C.S.P.; Francis X. Diskin, C.S.P.; John E. Collins, C.S.P.; Donal F. Forrester, C.S.P.; Kevin A. Lynch, C.S.P.; John D. Mitchell, C.S.P.; Charles S. White, C.S.P.; Lawrence V. McDonnell, C.S.P.; Donald C. Campbell, C.S.P., Supr.; Joseph F. Troy, C.S.P.; James F. McQuade, C.S.P., Hospital Chap.; Robert A. O'Donnell, C.S.P.; John B. Ardis, C.S.P., Dir. of Vocations; Steven J. Connor, C.S.P. Pastoral Assocs.: Revs. Marcos Zamora, C.S.P.; Eric Andrews, C.S.P.
Mailing Address: 415 W. 59th, 10019. Tel: 212-265-3495; Fax: 212-262-9239.
Chapel—Oblates of Jesus the Priest.

105—ST. PETER (1785), Rev. Msgr. Robert M. O'Connell, Admin.; Revs. Michael B. Dibble; Donald T. Fussner; James J. Halligan.
Res., 16 Barclay St., 10007. Tel: 212-233-8355.
Chapel—St. Joseph's Chapel, 385 South End Ave., 10280. In res., Rev. Msgr. Joseph J. Zammit, Chap., N.Y.C. Police Dept.

106—ST. RAPHAEL (1886). See Sts. Cyril and Methodius.

107—RESURRECTION (1907) (African American-Hispanic). Unassigned.
Res., 276 W. 151st St., 10039. Tel: 212-690-7555; Fax: 212-690-6590.
School—(1910), 282 W. 151 St., 10039. Tel: 212-690-7524.
Lay Teachers 7; Students 160.

108—ST. ROSE (1868). Closed. Parochial records at St. Mary Church.

109—ST. ROSE OF LIMA (1901), Revs. Manuel Machado; Richard T. Adams; Ralph V. Curcio.
Res., 510 W. 165th St., 10032. Tel: 212-568-0091.
School—(1924), 517 W. 164th St., 10032.
Dominican Nuns (Sparkill, NY) 2; Lay Teachers 16; Students 483.
Chapel—St. Rose of Lima Convent, 509 W. 164th St., 10032. Medical Centre.

110—SACRED HEART OF JESUS (1876), Rev. Kevin J. Nelan; Sr. Ana Ospina, Pastoral Assoc.; Rev. Tomas DelValle. In res., Rev. Msgr. Edward D. O'Donnell.
Res., 457 W. 51st, 10019. Tel: 212-265-5020; Fax: 212-977-4116.
School—(1892), 456 52nd St., 10019. Tel: 212-246-3264.
Congregation of Christian Brothers 3; Lay Teachers 9; Students 260.
Chapels—Centro Maria, 539 W. 54th St., 10019; Convent of Sacred Heart, 450 W. 51st St., 10019.
Catechesis/Religious Programs—Students 210.

111—SACRED HEARTS OF JESUS AND MARY (1914), Rev. Albert J. DeLuca; Rev. Msgr. William J. Rinschler, Pastor Emeritus.
Res., 307 E. 33rd St., 10016. Tel: 212-889-2133; Fax: 212-889-2133.
Chapel—Convent of the Sacred Heart of Jesus and Mary, 325 E. 33rd St., 10016. Tel: 212-889-3886.
Station—N.Y.U. Rehabilitation Hospital, Tel: 212-889-3886.

112—ST. SEBASTIAN (1915). Closed. Parochial records at Epiphany Church.

113—ST. STANISLAUS (1872) (Polish), Revs. Christopher Wieliczko, O.S.P.; Bogdan Kolmaga, O.S.P.
Res., 101 E. Seventh St., 10009. Tel: 212-475-4576.

114—ST. STEPHEN (1848). Consolidated in 1990. See Our Lady of Scapular/St. Stephen for details.

115—ST. STEPHEN OF HUNGARY (1902), Revs. Neil J. O'Connell, O.F.M., Guardian Franciscan Community; Dominic Csorba, O.F.M. (Hungary); Vianney M. Devlin, O.F.M.; Gregory V. Gebbia, O.F.M.; Bro. Joseph C. Botelho, O.F.M. In res., Revs. Leo Clifford, O.F.M. (Ireland); Reginald A. Redlon, O.F.M.; Dennis M. Wilson, O.F.M.
Res., 414 E. 82nd St., 10028. Tel: 212-861-8500; Fax: 212-535-9221.
School—(1918), 408 E. 82nd St., 10028. Carol O'Connor, Prin.
Sisters 1; Lay Teachers 7; Students 150.

116—ST. TERESA (1863), Revs. Dennis J. Sullivan; John B. Chiang (China); Alfredo Monteiro (India).
Res., 141 Henry St., 10002. Tel: 212-233-0233.
Church—16 & 18 Rutgers St., 10002.
Catechesis/Religious Programs—Students 207.

117—ST. THOMAS THE APOSTLE (1889), Revs. Paul Grauls, S.D.B.; George Hanna, S.D.B.; Vincent Paczkowski, S.D.B.; Bro. Anthony Ambrogio, S.D.B.
Res., 262 W. 118th St., 10026. Tel: 212-662-2693. [CEM]
Don Bosco Harlem Association, Inc.—262 W. 118th St., 10026. Tel: 212-662-9228.

118—ST. THOMAS MORE (1950), Revs. John A. Boehning; John E. Halborg; Stanley Moseley. In res., Most Rev. Patrick V. Ahern; Rev. Thomas Shelley.
Res., 65 E. 89th St., 10128. Tel: 212-876-7718; Fax: 212-836-5756.
Catechesis/Religious Programs—Narnia Clubs, 20 Sutton Pl. S., 10022. Tel: 212-593-4879.
Students 191.
Chapel—Convent of Sacred Heart and Academy, 1 E. 91st St., 10022. Tel: 212-722-4745.

119—TRANSFIGURATION (1827) (Chinese-English), Rev. Raymond J. Nobiletti, M.M.
Res., 29 Mott St., 10013. Tel: 212-962-5157; Fax: 212-962-5217.
School—(1853), Tel: 212-962-5265; Fax: 212-964-8965. Suzanne O'Reilly, Prin.
Lay Teachers 8; Students 278.

120—ST. VERONICA (1887), Rev. Kenneth J. Smith, Admin.
Res., 328 W. 14th St., 10014. Tel: 212-243-0265.
Church—149-155 Christopher St., 10014. Tel: 212-924-5628.
Mission—New York, New York Co., Gift of Love, 657 Washington St., 10014. Tel: 212-645-0587.

121—ST. VINCENT FERRER (1867), Very Rev. James Boniface Ramsey, O.P., Prior; Revs. Alfred A. Gately, O.P.; John P. Gerhard, O.P., Subprior; Frederick D. Hoesli, O.P., Subprior; Bros. Christopher McCabe, O.P.; Damian McCarthy, O.P.
Res., 869 Lexington Ave., 10021-6680. Tel: 212-744-2080.
High School—151 E. 65th St., 10021. Tel: 212-535-4680; Fax: 212-988-3455. Sr. Gilmary McCabe, O.P., Prin.
Sisters of St. Dominic, Columbus, OH 4; Lay Teachers 22; Girls 440.
Chapels—Sisters of St. Dominic, 152 E. 66th St., 10021. Tel: 212-744-2375; Dominican Academy, 44 E. 68th St., 10021. Tel: 212-744-0195; Grace Institute, 1233 Second Ave., 10021. Tel: 212-832-7605.

122—ST. VINCENT DE PAUL (1840) (French), Revs. Maurice E. Carroll; Harry Tiercelin (France); Bartholomew Peron (Haiti).
Res., 116 W. 24th St., 10011. Tel: 212-243-4727.
Church—123 W. 23rd St., 10011.
Chapel—Jeanne d'Arc Home, 253 W. 24th St., 10011.

BOROUGH OF BRONX

123—ST. ADALBERT (1898) (Polish). Closed. For inquiries for parish records contact the Chancery.

124—ST. ANGELA MERICI (1899), Revs. Carlos Mullins; Michael O'Kere.
Res., 917 Morris Ave., 10451. Tel: 718-293-0984; Fax: 718-293-6617.
Church—E. 163rd St., 10451.
School—(1917), Morris Ave. & 163rd St., 10451. Tel: 718-293-3365. Patrick Kelly, Prin.
Lay Teachers 19; Students 586.

125—ST. ANN (1927), Rev. Msgr. Robert M. Trainor; Rev. Michael Lipareli. In res., Rev. Varghese Chethipuzha (India).
Res., 3519 Bainbridge Ave., 10467. Tel: 718-547-9350.
School—(1928), Bainbridge Ave. and Gun Hill Rd., 10467. Tel: 718-655-3449; Fax: 718-547-4020. Miss L. DiJusto, Prin.
Students 275.
Catechesis/Religious Programs—Students 150.

126—ST. ANSELM (1892), Revs. Blas Montenegro, O.A.R.; Jose Luis Duenas, O.A.R.; Dionisio Gutierrez, O.A.R.
Res., 685 Tinton Ave., 10455. Tel: 718-585-8666.
School—(1908), Tel: 718-993-9464. Sr. Peter Brigid Smith, O.P., Prin.
Sisters of St. Dominic of Blauvelt 2; Lay Teachers 22; Students 680.

127—ST. ANTHONY (1908) (Hispanic), Revs. Joseph J. Kelly; John Tran. In res., Rev. Michael J. Allessandro.

Res., 1496 Commonwealth Ave., 10460. Tel: 718-931-4040; 4041; Fax: 718-792-4622.
School—(1931), St. Lawrence Ave. and Mansion St., 10460. Tel: 718-892-1244; Fax: 718-863-0202.
Sisters of Charity of St. Vincent de Paul of NY 1; Lay Teachers 9; Students 230.
Catechesis/Religious Programs—Students 229.
Chapel—Sisters of Charity, 1492 Commonwealth Ave., 10460.

128—ST. ANTHONY (1919) (Italian), Rev. Nicholas F. Milazzo.
Res., 4505 Richardson Ave., 10470. Tel: 718-324-8787; Fax: 718-324-6354.
School—(1953), 4520 Matilda Ave., 10470. Mrs. Roma Barone, Prin.
Lay Teachers 13; Students 189.
Convent—4500 Matilda Ave., 10470.

129—ST. ANTHONY OF PADUA (1903) (African American & Hispanic), Rev. Josu Iriondo, C.R.L., Admin.
Res., 832 E. 166th St., 10459. Tel: 718-542-7293.

130—ST. ATHANASIUS (1907), Rev. Msgr. William J. Smith; Rev. Pompilio Alvarez (Spain); Deacon Alejandro Rosado. In res., Rev. Louis R. Gigante.
Res., 878 Tiffany St., 10459. Tel: 718-328-2558.
School—(1913), 830 Southern Blvd., 10459. Tel: 718-542-5161. Marianne Kraft, Prin.
Sisters 2; Lay Teachers 12; Students 370.
Catechesis/Religious Programs—Tel: 718-328-3121.
Students 310.

131—ST. AUGUSTINE (1849), Revs. Alexander Iheonunekwu (Nigeria); S. Keith Outlaw, Admin. In res., Revs. Ruben Cammayo (PH); Gregory Lyttle.
Res., 1183 Franklin Ave., 10456. Tel: 718-893-0072; Fax: 718-542-7871.
Church—E. 167th St., 10456.
School—(1887), 1176 Franklin Ave., 10456. Tel: 718-542-3633. J. Kent Horton, Prin.
Lay Teachers 15; Students 400.

132—ST. BARNABAS (1910), Rev. Msgr. Francis X. Toner; Revs. Brian P. McCarthy; Michael P. Morris; Deacons John Hennessy; Vincent Laurato; Cornelius Manning. In res., Rev. Cyprian I. Onyeihe (Nigeria); Rev. Msgr. John J. Considine, Pastor Emeritus.
Res., 409 E. 241st St., 10470. Tel: 718-324-1478; Fax: 718-324-1479.
School—(1912), 415 E. 241st St., 10470. Tel: 718-324-1088.
Sisters 1; Lay Teachers 22; Students 622.
High School—High School for Girls, (1924), 425 E. 240th St., 10470. Tel: 718-325-8800.
Sisters 12; Lay Teachers 20; Students 335.
Catechesis/Religious Programs—Tel: 718-324-0865.
Students 225.
Chapel—Annunciation, 1033 McLean Ave., Yonkers, 10704.

133—ST. BENEDICT (1923), Revs. Kenneth L. Marks; David K. Clifford; Deacon John Simpson. In res., Rev. Millard Cook, O.S.B (GBG).
Res., 2969 Otis Ave., 10465-2198. Tel: 718-828-3403; Fax: 718-829-1304.
School—(1923), 1016 Edison Ave., 10465. Tel: 718-829-9557.
Sisters 2; Lay Teachers 21; Students 500.
Catechesis/Religious Programs—Tel: 718-829-1200.
Students 358.
Chapel—St. John, 1082 Edison Ave., 10465.

134—BLESSED SACRAMENT (1927), Revs. Thomas Farrelly; Carlos M. Rodriguez; Deacon Epi Portalatin.
Res., 1170 Beach Ave., 10472. Tel: 718-892-3214; Fax: 718-892-3907.
School—(1929), 1160 Beach Ave. and 1141 Taylor Ave., 10472. Tel: 718-892-0433. Mary Fallon, Prin.
Lay Teachers 19; Students 506.
Catechesis/Religious Programs—Tel: 718-863-4620.
Students 210.

135—ST. BRENDAN (1908), Rev. Msgr. Patrick J. Boyle; Rev. Msgr. William B. O'Brien; Revs. Michael J. Morrow; David F. Nolan.
Res., 333 E. 206th St., 10467. Tel: 718-547-6655; Fax: 718-547-6579.
School—(1912), 268 E. 207th St., 10467. Tel: 718-653-2293. Mrs. Patricia Gatti, Prin.
Sisters of St. Dominic (Sparkill, NY) 2; Lay Teachers 18; Students 639.
Catechesis/Religious Programs—Students 310.
Chapel—Dominican Sisters, 260 E. 207th St., 10467. Tel: 718-798-2460.

136—ST. CLARE OF ASSISI (1929) (Italian), Revs. Richard Guarnieri; Thomas DeLucci.
Res., 1918 Paulding Ave., 10462. Tel: 718-863-8974; Fax: 718-863-8975.
Church—1027 Rhinelander Ave., 10462.
School—(1951), 1911 Hone Ave., 10461. Tel: 718-892-4080. Sr. Josephine Stabile, Prin.
Sisters 5; Lay Teachers 17; Students 615.
Catechesis/Religious Programs—Tel: 718-829-9624.
Students 180.
Chapel—Bronx, Morningside House Chapel.

137—CHRIST THE KING (1926), Revs. Patrick Hennessy; Guillermo Velez Lopez.
Res., 141 Marcy Pl., 10452. Tel: 718-538-5546; Fax: 718-538-3081.
School—Tel: 718-538-5959.
Lay Teachers 13; Students 535.
Catechesis/Religious Programs—Students 689.

138—ST. DOMINIC (1924) (Italian), Revs. Thomas K. Dicks; S. Anthony Samy (India). In res., Rev. Emanuele Augustine (India).
Res., 1739 Unionport Rd., 10462. Tel: 718-828-2424; Fax: 718-823-4450.
School—(1953), 1684 White Plains Rd., 10462. Tel: 718-829-4837; Fax: 718-792-6912. Sr. Josefa Curcio, C.S.J.B., Prin.
Sisters of St. John Baptist 7; Lay Teachers 19; Students 525.
Convent—1710 Unionport Rd., 10462. Tel: 718-824-2580.
Sisters 10.

139—ST. FRANCIS OF ASSISI (1928), Rev. Carlos Lopez Acosta.
Mailing Address: P.O. Box 520013, 10452.
Res., 1544 Shakespeare Ave., 10452. Tel: 718-731-6840; 6841.

140—ST. FRANCIS OF ASSISI (Baychester Ave.). See Mt. Vernon for details.

141—ST. FRANCES DE CHANTAL (1927), Rev. Msgr. Daniel J. Keehan; Rev. Msgr. Joseph M. Devlin, Pastor Emeritus; Rev. Donald C. Baker.
Res., 190 Hollywood Ave., 10465. Tel: 718-792-5500; Fax: 718-792-1824.
School—(1930), 2962 Harding Ave., 10465. Tel: 718-892-5359. Marie McCarrick, Prin.
Lay Teachers 31; Students 806.
Catechesis/Religious Programs—Students 415.
Convent—198 Hollywood Ave., 10465. Tel: 718-863-2264. Convent of Sisters of Life
Chapels—Monastery of the Poor Clares, 142 Hollywood Ave., 10465. Tel: 718-822-7271; House of the Holy Family, 2780 Schurz Ave., 10465. Tel: 718-863-9134.

142—ST. FRANCES OF ROME (1898), Revs. Karl A. Bauer; Sebastian Buccellato, O.F.M.; Austin E. Titus. In res., Rev. Bernard Iheoha.
Res., 4307 Barnes Ave., 10466. Tel: 718-324-5340; 5341; Fax: 718-324-5373.
Church—Moore Plaza & E. 236 St., 10466.
School—(1926), 4321 Barnes Ave., 10466. Tel: 718-324-7360; Fax: 718-994-3694. Dina Monti, Prin.
Sisters of the Presentation 2; Lay Teachers 14; Students 265.

143—ST. FRANCIS XAVIER (1928), Revs. Joseph W. Hickey; Kenneth A. Jesselli; Robert Holick; Sancho E. Garrote (Philippines).
Res., 1703 Lurting Ave., 10461. Tel: 718-892-3330; Fax: 718-931-6890.
School—(1930), 1711 Haight Ave., 10461. Tel: 718-863-0531. Robert Heckmann, Prin.
Lay Teachers 25; Students 530.
Chapel—St. Francis Xavier Convent, 1661 Haight Ave., 10461. Tel: 718-892-9466.

144—ST. GABRIEL (1939), Rev. Thomas R. Kelly; Rev. Msgr. Charles McManus, Senior Priest; Rev. Myles P. Murphy; Rev. Msgr. John T. Doherty, Pastor Emeritus; Deacon Eugene Burke.
Res., 3250 Arlington Ave., 10463. Tel: 718-548-4470; Fax: 718-548-6451.
Church—235th & Netherland Ave., 10463.
School—590 W. 235th St., 10463. Tel: 718-548-0444. Sr. Claire Dandeneau, R.J.M., Prin.
Lay Teachers 9; Students 265.
Catechesis/Religious Programs—Tel: 718-548-6585. Mr. Glenn A. McCarthy, D.R.E.
Students 125.

145—ST. HELENA (1940), Rev. Msgr. Philip Mulcahy; Revs. Joseph J. O'Shea; John J. Haggerty; Thomas B. Derivan; Edmundo Gomez; Albert P. Bartlett, S.J.
Res., 1315 Olmstead Ave., 10462. Tel: 718-892-3232.
School—(1941), 2050 Benedict Ave., 10462. Tel: 718-892-3234. Angela Deegan, Prin.
Sisters of St. Dominic (Sparkill, NY) 2; Lay Teachers 19; Students 465.
High School—Msgr. Scanlan High School, (1949). (Coed) 915 Hutchinson River Pkwy., 10465. Tel: 718-430-0100.
Sisters of St. Dominic (Sparkill, NY) 12; Lay Teachers 32; Students 700.
School—Commercial School, St. Helen's, (1957). (Coed) 955 Hutchinson River Pkwy., 10465. Tel: 718-792-1395.
Sisters of St. Dominic (Sparkill, NY) 6; Lay Teachers 10; Students 250.

146—HOLY CROSS (1921), Revs. Aubrey McNeil, O.F.M.; Joseph G. Rozansky, O.F.M., Guardian & Dir. of Franciscan Formation; Peter Alheim, O.F.M.; Maurice J. Brick, O.F.M.; Kenneth R. Himes, O.F.M.; Joachim A. Mahler, O.F.M.; Matthew A. Pravetz, O.F.M.; Anthony Schneider, O.F.M.; Thadeus M. Sapio, O.F.M.; Deacons Luis Fontanez; Juan Rodriguez.
Res., 600 Soundview Ave., 10473. Tel: 718-893-5550; Fax: 718-893-9267.
School—(1923 and 1955), Randall & Thieriot Aves., 10473. Tel: 718-842-4492.
Franciscan Sisters of Allegany, NY 6; Lay Teachers 15; Students 554.
Chapel—Franciscan Sisters of Allegany, Thieriot Ave., 10473. Tel: 718-842-2615.

147—HOLY FAMILY (1896), Revs. James D. Flanagan; Joseph P. McAndrew; Deacon Dhoel Canals.
Res., 2158 Watson Ave., 10472. Tel: 718-863-9156; Fax: 718-597-5560.
School—(1913), 2169 Blackrock Ave., 10472. Tel: 718-863-7280; Fax: 718-931-8690.
Sisters of St. Agnes 1; Lay Teachers 32; Students 740.
Catechesis/Religious Programs—2169 Black Rock Ave., 10472. Tel: 718-822-8030.
Students 170.
Chapel—Sisters of St. Agnes, 2155 Blackrock Ave., 10472. Tel: 718-828-4488.

148—HOLY ROSARY (1925), Revs. Lamont R. Hamilton; John J. Higgins; Deacons Joseph D'Aiello; Joseph Solanto. In res., Rev. Msgr. Leslie J. Ivers.
Res., 1510 Adee Ave., 10469. Tel: 718-379-4432; 379-4654; Fax: 718-379-9028.
School—(1927; 1955), 1500 Arnow Ave., 10469. Tel: 718-652-1838. Edward Beglane, Prin.
Sisters of the Presentation 2; Lay Teachers 21; Students 650.
Chapel—Holy Rosary Convent, 2755 Woodhull Ave., 10469. Tel: 718-798-6435.

149—HOLY SPIRIT (1901), Rev. Pascual Cervera, Admin.; Deacon Felix Morillo.
Res., 1940 University Ave., 10453. Tel: 718-583-0120; Fax: 718-583-1444.
School—(1913), 1960 University Ave., 10453. Tel: 718-583-1570.
Lay Teachers 14; Students 357.
Catechesis/Religious Programs—Students 287.

150—IMMACULATE CONCEPTION (1853) (German), Very Rev. Francis Skelly, C.Ss.R.; Revs. John McTighe, C.Ss.R.; Dennis Walsh, C.Ss.R.; William Gaffney, C.S.s.R.; Yoshi Akano, C.S.s.R.; Daniel Francis, C.S.s.R.; Bro. Stephen Lendvay, C.Ss.R.; Deacon Cristobal Rodriguez.
Res., 389 E. 150th St., 10455. Tel: 718-292-6970; Fax: 718-292-4603.
Perpetual Help Center—294 E. 150th St., 10455. Tel: 718-585-3678; Fax: 718-993-5870.
School—(1854), 378 E. 151st St., 10455. Tel: 718-585-4843; Fax: 718-585-6846.
Sisters of Christian Charity 9; Lay Teachers 18; Students 712.
Catechesis/Religious Programs—Oscar Cruz, D.R.E. Students 210.
Chapel—Sisters of Christian Charity, 371 E. 150th St., 10455. Tel: 718-585-8981.

151—IMMACULATE CONCEPTION (1903), Revs. Michael Ristori, O.F.M.Cap.; Paschal Caccavalle, O.F.M.Cap.; Robert Calabrese, O.F.M.Cap.; Camillus Protomastro, O.F.M.Cap.; Francis Sariego; Bro. Matthew DeFamio, O.F.M.Cap.; Deacon Carlos Mercado.
Res., Capuchin Friary, 754 Gun Hill Rd., 10467. Tel: 718-653-2200.
School—Tel: 718-547-3346.
Priests 5; Brothers 2; Lay Teachers 13; Students 601.
Chapel—Immaculate Conception Convent, 3305 Wallace Ave., 10467.

152—ST. JEROME'S (1869), Revs. John Grange; Carmelo Amantegui, S.J.
Res., 230 Alexander Ave., 10454. Tel: 718-665-5533.
School—(1871), 222 Alexander Ave., 10454.
Lay Teachers 10; Students 267.
Catechesis/Religious Programs—Students 150. D.R.E.: Dina Monti; Sr. Josephin Stabile.

153—ST. JOAN OF ARC (1949), Revs. Edward Bader; Julius Mwau; Deacon Ismael Camacho.
Res., 1372 Stratford Ave., 10472. Tel: 718-842-2233.
Catechesis/Religious Programs—Students 353.

154—ST. JOHN'S (1886), Revs. Edward J. Fagan, O.A.R.; Gerard Cosgayon, O.A.R.; Fernando Olivera, O.A.R.; Deacons Andrew Rivera; Donald Quigley. In res., Very Rev. Francis Peluso, O.A.R.; Revs. Jose Luis Domaica, O.A.R.; Domingos Machado, O.A.R.; Bro. Mario Alvarez, O.A.R.
Res., 3021 Kingsbridge Ave., 10463. Tel: 718-548-1221; Fax: 718-548-7774.
School—(1903), 3143 Kingsbridge Ave., 10463. Tel: 718-548-0255; Fax: 718-548-0864. Sr. Patricia Brito, R.J.M., Prin.
Sisters 2; Lay Teachers 11; Students 348.

Catechesis/Religious Programs—Tel: 718-884-2627.
Students 348.
Convent—3029 Godwin Ter., 10463. Tel: 718-548-4902; 543-2454. Religious of Jesus and Mary.

155—ST. JOHN CHRYSOSTOM'S (1899), Revs. Joseph P. O'Meara; John P. Sheehan; Deacon Victor Pino.
Res., 985 E. 167th St., 10459. Tel: 718-542-6164.
School—(1914), 1144 Hoe Ave., 10459. Tel: 718-328-7226; Fax: 718-378-5368. Sr. Mary Elizabeth Mooney, O.P., Prin.
Sisters of St. Dominic (Sparkill, NY) 13; Lay Teachers 18; Students 649.
Catechesis/Religious Programs—Tel: 718-328-3580.
Students 367.

156—ST JOHN NAM (1989) (Korean), Rev. Simon Nam.
Res., 3663 White Plains Rd., 10467. Tel: 718-231-2414; Fax: 718-405-0053.

157—ST. JOHN VIANNEY, CURE OF ARS (1960), Revs. Antonio Lasheras, O.A.R.; Jesus Sobejano, O.A.R.; Blas Montenegro, O.A.R.; Deacons Rafael Martinez; Al Leasiolagi; Rafael A. Ramos; Ismael Camacho.
Res., 715 Castle Hill Ave., 10473. Tel: 212-863-4411.
School—2141 Seward Ave., 10473. Tel: 718-892-4400.
Lay Teachers 9; Students 270.

158—ST. JOSEPH (1873), Rev. Rufino Lecumberri.
Res., 1949 Bathgate Ave., 10457. Tel: 718-731-2504.
School—(1905), 1946 Bathgate Ave., 10457. Tel: 718-583-9432; Fax: 718-299-0780. Janine A. Duffy, Prin.
Lay Teachers 13; Students 280.

159—ST. LUCY (1927), Revs. Herbert F. D'Argenio; Paul M. Waddell; Clifford C. Ekwueme (Nigeria); Deacons Wilfredo Miranda; William Bebert. In res., Rev. Frederick J. Becker.
Church—833 Mace Ave., 10467. Tel: 718-882-0710.
School—(1955), 830 Mace Ave., 10467. Tel: 718-882-2203; Fax: 718-547-8351. Sr. Marah Sabell, R.S.M., Prin.
Lay Teachers 24; Students 567.
Catechesis/Religious Programs—Tel: 718-655-4922.
Students 318.

160—ST. LUKE (1897) (Hispanic-African American), Rev. Msgr. Gerald J. Ryan; Rev. William G. Harder. Pastoral Assocs.: Mary Kay Louchart; Sharon Joslyn.
Res., 623 E. 138th St., 10454. Tel: 718-665-6677; Fax: 718-665-0898.
School—(1910), 604-616 E. 139th St., 10454. Tel: 718-585-0380.
Sisters of St. Dominic (Blauvelt) 2; Lay Teachers 15; Students 350.
Catechesis/Religious Programs—Tel: 718-665-8956.
Students 350.
Chapel—St. Luke Convent, 621 E. 138th St., 10454. Tel: 718-292-3016.

161—ST. MARGARET OF CORTONA (1887), Revs. William E. Warren; Robert A. Quarato; Thomas Murphy, S.J. In res., Rev. Robert J. Aufieri.
Res., 6000 Riverdale Ave., 10471. Tel: 718-549-8053; Fax: 718-543-3432.
School—(1926), 452 W. 260th St., 10471. Tel: 718-549-8580. Sr. Nancy McNamara, Prin.
Sisters 3; Lay Teachers 12; Students 373.
Catechesis/Religious Programs—Tel: 718-884-9777.
Students 160.
Chapel—Bronx, Our Lady of Grace.

162—ST. MARGARET MARY (1923), Revs. Robert P. Arce; John C. Albino. In res., Revs. Robert A. Jeffers; Hyacinth Njoku (Nigeria).
Res., 1914 Morris Ave., 10453. Tel: 718-299-4233; Fax: 718-583-3726.
School—(1923), 121 E. 177th St., 10453. Tel: 718-731-5905; Fax: 718-731-8924.
Sisters of Mercy of the Americas 4; Lay Teachers 11; Students 350.
Catechesis/Religious Programs—Students 365.

163—ST. MARTIN OF TOURS (1897), Revs. John C. Flynn; Vicente Florido; Sr. Peggy Gannon, O.P., Pastoral Min.; Deacons Frankie Vazques; Reynaldo Rosado.
Res., 664 Grote St., 10457. Tel: 718-295-0913.
School—(1926), E. 182nd St. & Crotona Ave., 10457. Tel: 718-733-0347. Sr. M. Cecilia, Prin.
Dominican Sisters (Sparkill, NY) 2; Lay Teachers 16; Students 288.
Catechesis/Religious Programs—Students 350.
Chapel—Dominican Convent, 695 E. 182nd St., 10457.

164—ST. MARY (1866), Rev. John B. Sullivan. In res., Rev. James Cunningham.
Res., 650 E. 226th St., 10466. Tel: 718-547-8000; Fax: 718-547-8001.
Church—White Plains Rd., 10466.
School—(1950), 3956 Carpenter Ave., 10466. Tel: 718-547-0500; Fax: 718-547-0530.
Lay Teachers 13; Students 292.
Chapel—Convent, 3961 Carpenter Ave., 10466. Tel: 718-652-2873. School chapel, E. 224th St., 10466.

165—ST. MARY STAR OF THE SEA (1887), Revs. Robert J. Moore; Donald F. Partridge; Thomas Myladil, O.C.D. (India); Deacon William J. Mueller.
Res., 595 Minneford Ave., 10464-1118. Tel: 718-885-1440.
Church—600 City Island Ave., 10464.
School—(1931), 580 Minneford Ave., 10464. Tel: 718-885-1527.
Dominican Sisters of Blauvelt 2; Lay Teachers 9; Students 270.
Chapel—Dominican Sisters, 176 Kilroe St., 10464. Tel: 718-885-0849.

166—ST. MICHAEL (1969), Revs. William J. Luciano; Edward F.X. Kennedy, S.J.
Res., 765 Co-Op City Boulevard, 10475-1601. Tel: 718-671-8050; Fax: 718-320-3776.

167—NATIVITY OF OUR BLESSED LADY (1924), Rev. Jaime H. Duenas.
Res., Rectory, 1531 E. 233rd St., 10466. Tel: 718-324-3531; Fax: 718-324-3531.
School—(1953), 3893 Dyre Ave., 10466. Tel: 718-324-2188; Fax: 718-324-3531.
Lay Teachers 20; Students 326.
Convent—1534 E. 233rd St., 10466.

168—ST. NICHOLAS OF TOLENTINE (1906), Revs. John F. Dello Russo, O.S.A.; Francis Barr, O.S.A.; Sr. Susan McCarthy, R.D.C., Pastoral Assoc.; Revs. Thomas Wilhelm, O.S.A.; Joseph Tran. In res., Revs. Robert Grodnicki, O.S.A.; William J. Wallace, O.S.A.; Bro. Michael Duffy, O.S.A.
Res., 2345 University Ave., 10468. Tel: 718-295-6800; Fax: 718-367-7411.
School—(1907), 2336 Andrews Ave., 10468. Tel: 718-364-5110; Fax: 718-364-0309.
Sisters of St. Dominic of Blauvelt 1; Lay Teachers 12; Students 384.
Catechesis/Religious Programs—Tel: 718-295-6770.
Students 542.
Chapels—Convent of St. Nicholas of Tolentine, 2341 University Ave., 10468. Tel: 718-367-3102; St. Nicholas of Tolentine School Chapel, Tel: 718-364-5110.

169—OUR LADY OF ANGELS (1924), Revs. David P. Casella; Antonio Aldana (Mexico); Kevin O'Reilly; Deacon Luis Delgado.
Res., 2860 Webb Ave., 10468. Tel: 718-548-3005; Fax: 718-884-2450.
Church—2860 Sedgwick Ave., 10468.
School—(1928), 2865 Claflin Ave., 10468. Tel: 718-549-3503. Sr. Mary Ann Cleary, Prin.
Sisters of Charity of St. Vincent de Paul 3; Lay Teachers 18; Students 470.
Catechesis/Religious Programs—Students 310.

170—OUR LADY OF THE ASSUMPTION (1923), Rev. Donald M. Dwyer; Rev. Msgr. Michael F. O'Donnell, Pastor Emeritus; Revs. Dennis P. Williams; Jarlath Quinn; Deacons Francis Kelly; Howard Banker.
Res., 1634 Mahan Ave., 10461. Tel: 718-824-5454; Fax: 718-824-5456.
School—(1928), 1617 Parkview Ave., 10461. Tel: 718-829-1706.
Sisters 1; Lay Teachers 18; Students 480.
Catechesis/Religious Programs—Tel: 718-904-8464.
Students 450.
Chapel—Convent, 1639 Parkview Ave., 10461. Tel: 718-829-7980.

171—OUR LADY OF GOOD COUNSEL (1969) (Albanian), Revs. Peter Popovich, Admin.; Andrew Nargaj, O.F.M.
Res., Albanian Roman Catholic Center, 4221 Park Ave., 10457. Tel: 718-294-6981. [CEM]

172—OUR LADY OF GRACE (1924), Revs. Walter A. Birkle; Philip J. Caruso; Felix J. Gonzalez (Venezuela).
Res., 3985 Bronxwood Ave., 10466. Tel: 718-652-4817.
School—Denise Rigano, Prin. Lay Teachers 1; Students 410.

173—OUR LADY OF MERCY (Fordham) (1852-1892), Revs. Lawrence J. Quinn; John Rueda (Colombia); Pablo Rentino (Philippines).
Res., 2496 Marion Ave., 10458. Tel: 718-933-4400.
School—(1907), 2512 Marion Ave., 10458. Tel: 718-367-0237.
Sisters 5; Lay Teachers 14; Students 530.
Catechesis/Religious Programs—Students 210.
Chapel—Convent, 2473 Valentine Ave., 10458. Tel: 718-367-5558.

174—OUR LADY OF MT. CARMEL (1906) (Italian), Rev. Msgr. John A. Ruvo; Rev. Richard Veras. In res., Revs. Nicholas F. Basile; Anthony D'Antonio; Anthony Giampietro, C.S.B.
Res., 627 E. 187th St., 10458. Tel: 718-295-3770.
School—(1925), 189th St. & Bathgate Ave., 10458. Tel: 718-295-6080. James E. Irwin, Prin.
Brothers of the Congregation of Holy Cross 1; Lay Teachers 11; Students 281.
Catechesis/Religious Programs—Students 150.
Convent—2410 Hughes Ave., 10458. Tel: 718-329-0390. Suore Missionarie del Catechismo.
Sisters 4.
Chapel—Brothers of Holy Cross, Tel: 718-733-8036.

175—OUR LADY OF PITY (1908) (Italian and Hispanic), Rev. Peter Damian Nuzzo, O.F.M., Guardian & Pastor; Deacon James Francis.
Res., 276 E. 151st St., 10451. Tel: 718-665-3880.

176—OUR LADY OF REFUGE (1923), Rev. Msgr. John J. Jenik.
Res., 290 E. 196th St., 10458. Tel: 718-367-4690; Fax: 718-365-7644.
School—(1923), 2708 Briggs Ave., 10458. Tel: 718-367-3081; Fax: 718-365-7644.
Lay Teachers 10; Students 285.
Catechesis/Religious Programs—Tel: 718-367-3384.
Students 450.

177—OUR LADY OF SOLACE (1902), Revs. John M. Knapp; Francisco Imperial; Thomas Seraphin Parambi, C.S.T.
Res., 731 Morris Park Ave., 10462. Tel: 718-863-3282; Fax: 718-792-4950.
School—(1916), 1804 Holland Ave., 10462. Tel: 718-792-9947.
Religious of the Presentation 2; Lay Teachers 8; Students 321.

178—OUR LADY OF VICTORY (1909), Rev. Peter Gavigan.
Res., 1512 Webster Ave., 10457. Tel: 718-583-4044; Fax: 718-583-4044.

179—OUR SAVIOUR (1912) (Hispanic), Revs. Serafin Pineda, O.A.R.; Francisco Oviedo, O.A.R.
Res., 2317 Washington Ave., 10458. Tel: 718-295-9600; Fax: 718-295-9601.

180—SANTA MARIA (1926) (Italian), Revs. Fernando Real, M.ID., Admin.; Robert Badillo, M.ID.; Antimo Fiorillo, Pastor Emeritus; Eduardo Rodriguez, M.ID.
Res., 2352 St. Raymond Ave., 10462. Tel: 718-828-2380.
School—(1951), 1510 Zerega Ave., 10462. Sr. Christian Price, Prin.
Sisters Apostles of the Sacred Heart 4; Lay Teachers 9; Students 238.
Chapel—Santa Maria Convent, 1460 Zerega Ave., 10462.

181—ST. PETER AND ST. PAUL (1897), Rev. Vincent A. Resta.
Res., 833 St. Ann's Ave., 10456. Tel: 718-665-3924.
School—(1911), 838 Brook Ave., 10456. Tel: 718-665-2056.
Sisters 5; Lay Teachers 14; Students 485.
Chapel—Sisters of Charity, 839 St. Ann's Ave., 10456. Tel: 718-292-7057.

182—SS. PHILIP AND JAMES (1949), Rev. Thomas E. McNamara; Sr. Sharon Donohue, R.S.M., Pastoral Assoc.; Deacons Albert V. Welhous; Robert Santana. In res., Revs. Bededict Paul; Nicholas Iwuagwu.
Res., 1160 E. 213th St., 10469. Tel: 718-547-2203; Fax: 718-231-8160.
School—(1953), 1160 E. 213th St., 10469. Tel: 718-882-4576.
Sisters of St. Dominic (Blauvelt) 1; Lay Teachers 9; Students 300.
Chapel—Dominican Sisters Convent, 1180 E. 214th St., 10469.

183—ST. PHILIP NERI (1898), Rev. Msgr. Kevin J. Colleran; Revs. Sean Horrigan, C.S.Sp. (Ireland); Stephen Ryan; Deacon Hector Rodriguez. In res., Revs. Paul Miki Gyamfi; Martin Onyebuchi (Nigeria).
Res., 3025 Grand Concourse, 10468. Tel: 718-733-3200.
School—(1913), 3031 Grand Concourse, 10468. Tel: 718-365-8806. Bro. Brian Johnston.
Irish Franciscan Brothers 1; Ursuline Sisters 1; Lay Teachers 24; Students 690.
Catechesis/Religious Programs—Students 240.
Chapels—Convent of Mount St. Ursula, Marion Ave. & 200th St., 10468. Tel: 718-365-7410; Kolping Residence, Kolping Society, 2916 Grand Concourse, 10468. Tel: 718-733-6119; Ursuline Residence, 2850 Marion Ave., 10468. Tel: 718-295-6094; Irish Franciscan Brothers, 260 E. 201 St., 10468. Tel: 718-365-5694; St. Mary's Hall. (Ursuline) 323 E. 198th St., 10468. Tel: 718-933-9894.

184—ST. PIUS V (1907), Revs. Paul J. LeBlanc; Adolfo Romero-Rios (Argentina); Deacons Raul Padron; Luis Torres.
Res., 420 E. 145th St., 10454. Tel: 718-665-6642.
School—(1913), 413 E. 144th St., 10454. Tel: 718-665-5075; Fax: 718-665-2987.

Lay Teachers 9; Students 230.
High School—500 Courtlandt Ave., 10454. Tel: 718-292-3636; Fax: 718-402-1704.
Lay Teachers 13; Students 210.
Catechesis/Religious Programs—Students 160.

185—ST. RAYMOND (1842), Rev. Msgr. Charles M. Kavanagh; Rev. Msgr. Henry J. Vier, Pastor Emeritus; Rev. Msgr. George A. Cocuzzi (ROC); Revs. Edward M. Conroy; Joseph Tyrrell; Anthony P. Settle; Deacons Aldo Preti; Roberto Fernandez.
Res., 1759 Castle Hill Ave., 10462. Tel: 718-792-4044; Fax: 718-863-8509. [CEM 2]
School—(1909), 2380 E. Tremont Ave., 10462. Tel: 718-597-3232. Victor J. Presto, Prin.
Sisters 1; Lay Teachers 20; Students 630.
High Schools—(Boys) 2151 St. Raymond Ave., 10462. Tel: 718-824-5050. Bro. Frank Byrne, F.S.C., Prin.
Sisters 1; Brothers of the Christian Schools 8; Lay Teachers 42; Students 770; (Girls). Tel: 718-824-4220. Sr. Marian Jude, S.C., Prin.
Sisters of Charity 10; Sisters 1; Lay Teachers 14; Students 300.
Catechesis/Religious Programs—Mrs. Ann O'Keefe, D.R.E.
Students 406.
Family Outreach Program—1720 Metropolitan Ave., 10462. Tel: 718-792-2087. Bro. Raymond Meagher, F.S.C., Dir.
Chapel—Brothers Residence, 1754 Castle Hill Ave., 10462.
Brothers of the Christian Schools 10.

186—ST. RITA OF CASCIA SHRINE CHURCH (1900), Rev. Jesus Perez Recio, O.A.R.
Res., 448 College Ave., 10451. Tel: 718-585-5900.

187—ST. ROCH (1899) (Spanish), Rev. Francisco Oviedo, O.A.R., Admin.
Res., 525 Wales Ave., 10455. Tel: 718-292-3834.

188—SACRED HEART (1875), Rev. Mark T. Cregan, C.S.C. Pastoral Assocs.: Sr. Josefina Monales, S.S.N.D.; Ms. Charo Jimenez. In res., Rev. William Pensia, C.S.C.
Res., 1253 Shakespeare Ave., 10452. Tel: 718-293-2766; Fax: 718-293-1581.
Schools—Primary Division, (1950), 95 W. 168th St., 10452. Tel: 718-293-4288; Fax: 718-293-4886. Joanne Walsh, Prin.
Lay Teachers 15; Students 452; Middle School, (1926), 1248 Nelson Ave., 10452. Tel: 718-293-6040. Bro. Stephen Milan, F.M.S., Prin.
Lay Teachers 16; Students 442.
Catechesis/Religious Programs—Sr. Christina Dougherty, P.B.V.M., D.R.E.
Students 340.
Chapel—St. Eugene, 979 Ogden Ave., 10452. Tel: 718-681-2222.

189—ST. SIMON STOCK (1919), Revs. Michael Kissane, O.Carm.; Ruben Rodriguez, O.Carm.
Res., 2191 Valentine Ave., 10457. Tel: 718-367-1251.
Church—East 182nd St. & Ryer Ave., 10457.
School—182nd St. & Valentine Ave., 10457.
Lay Teachers 20; Students 700.

190—ST. THERESA OF THE INFANT JESUS (1927) (Italian), Revs. Robert F. Grippo; Robert F. Ashman; Rev. Msgr. John L. Guido, Pastor Emeritus; Deacon Anthony P. Cassaneto; Christopher A. Buonocore, Parish Mgr. In res., Rev. Msgr. John G. Woolsey.
Res., 2855 St. Theresa Ave., 10461. Tel: 718-892-1900.
School—(1954), 2872 St. Theresa Ave., 10461. Tel: 718-792-3688; Fax: 718-892-9441. Mr. Malachy Cleary, Prin.
Lay Teachers 19; Students 387.

191—ST. THOMAS AQUINAS (1890), Most Rev. Francisco Garmendia, D.D.; Revs. Peter J. Byrne, Admin.; Fernando A. Hernandez. In res., Rev. Paul Adogamhe (Nigeria).
Res., 1900 Crotona Pkwy., 10460. Tel: 718-589-5235.
School—(1907), 1909 Daly Ave., 10460. Tel: 718-893-7600.
Lay Teachers 21; Students 510.
Convent—1899 Daly Ave., 10460.

192—ST. VALENTINE (1891) (Polish), Rev. Msgr. Stanislaus Jablonski.
Res., 810 E. 221st St., 10467. Tel: 718-652-3197.

193—VISITATION (1928), Rev. Msgr. Robert W. Larkin; Revs. Arthur T. Welton; Noel Clarke (Ireland); Deacon George McGowan. In res., Rev. Francis P. O'Malley.
Res., 160 Van Cortlandt Park S., 10463. Tel: 718-548-1455.
School—(1932), Putnam Ave. & W. 239th St., 10463. Tel: 718-543-2250; Fax: 718-543-3665.
Priests 3; Sisters 6; Lay Teachers 4; Students 269.

BOROUGH OF RICHMOND
STATEN ISLAND

194—ST. ADALBERT (Elm Park) (1901) (Polish), Revs. John J. Hynes; Joseph T. Chirayil; Rev. Msgr. Edmund J. Fabisinski, (Retired); Deacon Joseph J. Rentkowski.
Res., 30 St. Adalbert Pl., Elm Park, 10303. Tel: 718-442-8476.
School—(1905), 355 Morningstar Rd., Elm Park, 10303. Tel: 718-442-2020; Fax: 718-447-2012.
Priests 2; Lay Teachers 9; Students 316.
Catechesis/Religious Programs—Tel: 718-442-5446.
Students 316.

195—ST. ANN (1914), Rev. Lawrence T. Quinn; Rev. Msgr. Vincent F. Clyne, Pastor Emeritus; Revs. Sylvester P. McGinn; Matthew Iraly (India); Thomas Basquel, C.S.Sp. In res., Rev. Edmund P. Connors.
Res., 101 Cromwell Ave., 10304. Tel: 718-351-0270; Fax: 718-980-4731.
School—(1955), 125 Cromwell Ave., 10304. Tel: 718-351-4343.
Presentation Nuns 1; Lay Teachers 12; Students 329.
Catechesis/Religious Programs—Michael Mazella, D.R.E.
Students 485.

196—ST. ANTHONY (1908), Rev. Msgr. Raphael F. Pakulniewicz.
Res., 24 Shelly Ave., 10314. Tel: 718-761-6660.
Church—Victory Blvd., 10314.

197—ASSUMPTION (1922) (Italian), Rev. John A. Pinterbone.
Res., 15 Webster Ave., 10301. Tel: 718-727-4594.

198—ST. BENEDICTA (1925). Closed. For inquiries for parish records contact Our Lady of Mount Carmel.

199—BLESSED SACRAMENT (1910), Rev. Msgr. Francis V. Boyle; Revs. Arthur A. Golino; Joseph Victor Arenas (Philippines). In res., Rev. Francis A. Naccarato; Rev. Msgr. Daniel L. Sullivan.
Res., 30 Manor Rd., 10310. Tel: 718-442-1581; Fax: 718-442-1398.
Church—Manor Rd. & Forest Ave., 10310.
School—(1917), 830 Delafield Ave., 10310. Tel: 718-442-3090; Fax: 718-442-9654. Sr. Ann McLaughlin, I.H.M., Prin.
Sisters, Servants of the Immaculate Heart of Mary 6; Lay Teachers 15; Students 694.
Catechesis/Religious Programs—Tel: 718-448-0378.
Students 312.

200—ST. CHARLES (1960), Rev. Msgr. Thomas J. Gaffney; Rev. Msgr. Robert J. Kelly, Pastor Emeritus; Rev. Mark G. Vaillancourt; Deacons Vincent Brigande; Michael Calafiore.
Res., 644 Clawson St., 10306. Tel: 718-987-2670; Fax: 718-987-7950.
School—Tel: 718-987-0200.
Sisters of St. Dominic (Blauvelt) 1; Lay Teachers 21; Students 817.
Catechesis/Religious Programs—Tel: 718-979-6800.
Students 525.

201—ST. CHRISTOPHER (1926) (Italian-Irish), Rev. Msgr. Kenneth A. Gerathy; Revs. George Mikolajczyk, M.M.; Michael A. Arputham.
Res., 130 Midland Ave., 10306. Tel: 718-351-2452.
School—(1930), 15 Lisbon Pl., 10306. Tel: 718-351-0902. Catherine Mizzi-Gili, Prin.
Lay Teachers 11; Students 335.
Catechesis/Religious Programs—Students 200.

202—ST. CLARE (1921), Rev. Msgr. Joseph P. Murphy; Rev. Michael W. Cichon; Deacon Richard Mitchell.
Res., 110 Nelson Ave., 10308. Tel: 718-984-7873; Fax: 718-966-8420.
School—151 Lindenwood Rd., 10308. Tel: 718-984-7091. Sr. Rosemary Ward, Prin.
Sisters Religious of the Presentation 3; Lay Teachers 18; Students 694.
Catechesis/Religious Programs—Tel: 718-948-4829.
Students 1,800.

203—ST. CLEMENT (1910), Rev. Msgr. Nicholas J. Soares; Revs. Manuel I. Rojas (Peru); Longinus Y. Nazareth (India).
Res., 207 Harbor Rd., 10303. Tel: 718-442-1688; Fax: 718-442-4689.
Church—126 Van Pelt Ave., 10303.
Catechesis/Religious Programs—Tel: 718-727-6442.
Students 238.

204—HOLY CHILD (1966), Rev. Msgr. John D. Burke; Revs. Morgan J. Kuhl; Emmanuel Nwogwugwu; Renato B. Cruz; Rev. Msgr. Francis M. Brennan, Pastor Emeritus.
Res., 4747 Amboy Rd., 10312. Tel: 718-356-5890; Fax: 718-356-5995.
Preschool Office—4747 Amboy Rd., 10312. Tel: 718-356-5159; Fax: 718-356-1933.
School—School of Religion, Tel: 718-356-5277; Fax: 718-227-0898.
Lay Teachers 116; Students 1,200.

205—HOLY FAMILY (1966), Rev. Msgr. Thomas A. Marinak; Rev. Msgr. Francis J. Glynn, Pastor Emeritus; Revs. Henry S. Gentile, C.S.; Michael P. Reilly.
Res., 366 Watchogue Rd., 10314. Tel: 718-761-6663.
School—School of Religion. (Elementary & High School) (1967) 330 Watchogue Rd., 10314. Tel: 718-761-1598.
Sisters 1; Lay Teachers 54; Students 540.
Convent—85 Delmore St., 10314. Tel: 718-698-3118.

206—HOLY ROSARY (1927), Rev. Msgr. Richard J. Guastella; Revs. Joy Mampilly, C.M.I. (India); Stephen G. Challman; Deacon Rosario Tirella. In res., Rev. Simon Raj, Chap.
Res., 80 Jerome Ave., 10305. Tel: 718-727-3360; Fax: 718-448-6819.
School—(1955), 100 Jerome Ave., 10305. Tel: 718-447-1195. Florence M. Bricker, Prin.
Lay Teachers 19; Students 557.
Catechesis/Religious Programs—Tel: 718-273-6695. Sr. Catherine Shanahan, D.R.E.
Students 406.

207—IMMACULATE CONCEPTION (1887), Rev. Peter J. Byrne.
Res., 128 Targee St., 10304. Tel: 718-447-2165.
School—(1908), 104 Gordon St., 10304. Tel: 718-447-7018; Fax: 718-447-7018. Sr. Mary Timothy, Prin.
Sisters 2; Lay Staff 8; Students 201.
Catechesis/Religious Programs—Students 65.
Chapel—Bayley Seton Hospital, Bay St., 10304. Tel: 718-390-6000. Rev. Edward Datty, S.A.

208—ST. JOHN THE BAPTIST DE LA SALLE (1900), Rev. Peter J. Byrne, Admin.
Res., 128 Targee St., 10304. Tel: 718-447-2165.
Church—76 Jackson St., 10304.

209—ST. JOHN NEUMANN (1982), Revs. James Malley; Julius Rodulfa.
Res., 1380 Arthur Kill Rd., 10312. Tel: 718-984-8535; Fax: 718-984-8840.
Catechesis/Religious Programs—Tel: 718-966-7327.
Students 562.

210—ST. JOSEPH (1902) (Italian), Rev. Msgr. John T. Servodidio.
Parish Office: 463 Tompkins Ave., 10305. Tel: 718-816-0047; Fax: 718-816-4529.
Res., 171 St. Mary's Ave., 10305.
Church—466 Tompkins Ave., 10305.
School—139 St. Mary's Ave., 10305. Tel: 718-447-7686. Linda Bilotti, Prin.
Lay Teachers 12; Students 332.

211—ST. JOSEPH, ST. THOMAS (1848), Rev. Msgr. Peter G. Finn; Revs. Peter R. Pilsner; Evangelio R. Suaybagio (Philippines); Francisco H. Lanzaderas (Philippines).
Res., 6135 Amboy Rd., 10309. Tel: 718-984-4572. [CEM]
School—Tel: 718-356-3344. Theresa Simmonds, Prin.
Lay Teachers 10; Students 385.
Catechesis/Religious Programs—Tel: 718-984-1156.
Students 750.

212—ST. MARGARET MARY (1926), Rev. Robert J. Navins; Deacon Joseph Graf. In res., Rev. Msgr. John Gordan.
Res., 560 Lincoln Ave., 10306. Tel: 718-351-2612.
School—(1925), 556 Lincoln Ave., 10306. Tel: 718-351-4778. Sr. Kathryn Anderson, Prin.
Sisters, Religious of the Presentation 2; Lay Teachers 7; Students 191.
Catechesis/Religious Programs—Students 190.

213—ST. MARY (1852), Revs. Victor J. Buebendorf; Brendan A. Ross.
Res., 1101 Bay St., 10305. Tel: 718-727-0671. [CEM]
School—(1853), 1124 Bay St., 10305. Tel: 718-447-1842. Virginia Savarese, Prin.
Lay Teachers 10; Students 275.

214—ST. MARY OF THE ASSUMPTION (1853), Rev. William Harder, Admin.
Res., 2230 Richmond Ter., 10302. Tel: 718-442-6372; Fax: 718-442-3299. [CEM]
Mission—New York, Richmond Co., Christ the King, 182 Park Ave., 10302.

215—ST. MICHAEL (1922), Rev. Msgr. Nicholas J. Soares; Revs. Manuel I. Rojas (Peru); Longinus V. Nazareth (India).
Res., 207 Harbor Rd., 10303. Tel: 718-442-1688; Fax: 718-442-4689.
Church—211-213 Harbor Rd., 10303.
Catechesis/Religious Programs—Tel: 718-727-6442.
Students 288.

216—OUR LADY OF GOOD COUNSEL (1898), Revs. Joseph S. Mostardi, O.S.A., Pastor/Prior; Robert T. Drummond, O.S.A.; Augustus C. Sandmann, O.S.A.; Luis A. Vera, O.S.A.; Deacons Arthur W. Eccleston;

Walter Sweeney; Alfred Thompson.
Res., 10 Austin Pl., 10304. Tel: 718-447-1503; Fax: 718-447-7361.
School—(1923), 42 Austin Pl., 10304. Tel: 718-447-7260. Mrs. Frances Santangelo, Prin.
Lay Teachers 10; Students 265.
Catechesis/Religious Programs—Students 265.

217—OUR LADY HELP OF CHRISTIANS (1898), Revs. Jeremiah P. O'Neill; Abraham B. Dominic (Sri Lanka); Deacons Edward J. Wetherall; John Singler.
Res., 7396 Amboy Rd., 10307. Tel: 718-317-9772.
School—(1910 and 1955), 23 Summit St., 10307. Tel: 718-984-1360; Fax: 718-966-9356. Mrs. Nancy Lucas, Prin.
Lay Teachers 10; Students 260.
Catechesis/Religious Programs—Tel: 718-356-3888.
Students 600.

218—OUR LADY OF MT. CARMEL-ST. BENEDICTA (1913), Revs. Philip Cordisco, O.SS.T.; Carl A. Pfeiffer, O.SS.T. In res., Rev. Joseph F. Lupo, O.SS.T.
Res., 1265 Castleton Ave., 10310. Tel: 718-442-3411; Fax: 718-442-3997.
School—285 Clove Rd., 10310. Tel: 718-981-5131.
Catechesis/Religious Programs—Students 275.

219—OUR LADY, QUEEN OF PEACE (1922), Revs. Robert I. Gannon; John A. DeBellis; John J. Sheehan; Deacon Ross Calimano. In res., Rev. James Garisto.
Res., 90 Third St., 10306. Tel: 718-351-1093.
School—(1924), 22 Steele Ave., 10306. Tel: 718-351-0370. Sr. Mary Regina Gibbons, Prin.
Sisters of the Presentation 1; Lay Teachers 17; Students 600.
Catechesis/Religious Programs—Tel: 718-979-0989.
Students 570.
Mission—New Dorp Beach, Richmond Co., Our Lady of Lourdes, Cedar Grove Ave., 10306.
Chapel—St. Therese of the Child Jesus, 62 Cloister Pl., 10306. Tel: 718-351-0209.

220—OUR LADY OF PITY (1923) (Italian), Rev. Msgr. Philip J. Franceschini; Rev. Msgr. Robert R. Mazziotta, Pastor Emeritus; Rev. John E. Mercer.
Res., 1616 Richmond Ave., 10314. Tel: 718-761-5421; Fax: 718-983-6225.
Catechesis/Religious Programs—Tel: 718-761-5463.
Students 706.

221—OUR LADY STAR OF THE SEA (1935), Rev. Msgr. Jeffrey Conway; Revs. Robert Porpora; Angelo Palermo, S.A.C.; John Francis Antony, Hospital Chap.; Dr. Patrick Del Zoppo, Pastoral Assoc.
Res., 5371 Amboy Rd., Huguenot Park, 10312. Tel: 718-984-0593; Fax: 718-984-5203.
School—(1958), 5411 Amboy Rd., 10312. Tel: 718-984-5750.
Brothers 1; Sisters 1; Lay Teachers 20; Students 690.
Catechesis/Religious Programs—5411 Amboy Rd., 10312. Tel: 718-984-1885.
Students 1,200.

222—ST. PATRICK (1862), Rev. Msgr. John M. McCarthy; Revs. John G. Pedulla; James P. McCauley, S.J.
Res., 53 St. Patrick's Pl., 10306. Tel: 718-351-0044.
School—(1919), 3560 Richmond Rd., 10306. Tel: 718-979-8815; 979-4227 (Parish). Sr. Mary Ferro, S.S.D., Prin.
Sisters 3; Lay Teachers 21; Students 583.
Catechesis/Religious Programs—Tel: 718-979-1272.
Students 410.

223—ST. PAUL (1924), Rev. Vincent Bartley; Sr. Jean Conaty, I.H.M.
Res., 148 Cassidy Pl., 10301. Tel: 718-447-6362.
School—(1954), 129 Clinton Ave., 10301. Tel: 718-447-5774; Fax: 718-447-5881. Ms. Fran Jorin, Prin.
Lay Teachers 9; Students 200.
Chapel—St. Paul Convent, 145 Clinton Ave., 10301. Tel: 718-720-1013.

224—ST. PETER (1839), Rev. Msgr. James J. Dorney; Revs. John T. Thenen; Matthias Ndulaka (Nigeria).
Res., 53 St. Mark's Pl., 10301. Tel: 718-727-2672; Fax: 718-720-9269. [CEM]
School—300-310 Richmond Ter., 10301. Tel: 718-447-1796; Fax: 718-447-4240.
Lay Teachers 12; Students 303.
High Schools—Boys High School, 200 Clinton Ave., 10301. Tel: 718-447-1676; Fax: 718-447-4027. Mr. John Fodera, Prin.; Bro. James Kelly, F.S.C., Pres. Brothers of the Christian Schools 6; Lay Teachers 29; Students 679; Girls High School, Tel: 718-447-0304. Dr. Susan Siefert, Prin.
Lay Teachers 9; Students 137.
Chapel—Sacred Heart Convent of Sisters of Charity, 280 Richmond Ter., 10301. St. Joseph, Brothers' House, Tel: 718-447-2815.

225—ST. RITA (1921), Rev. John F. Reardon.
Res., 281 Bradley Ave., 10314. Tel: 718-698-3746; Fax: 718-698-3791.
School—(1922), 30 Wellbrook Ave., 10314. Tel: 718-961-2504.
Dominican Sisters 1; Lay Teachers 16; Students 585.
Catechesis/Religious Programs—Students 415.
Chapel—Dominican Sisters. (Roman Congregation of St. Dominic) 61 Wellbrook Ave., 10314. Tel: 718-761-1171.

226—ST. ROCH (1922), Revs. Alfred J. Pucci; John Boyle. In res., Rev. G. David Sears (SY).
Res., 602 Richmond Ave., 10302. Tel: 718-442-4755; 448-2424. [CEM]
School—465 Villa Ave., 10302. Sr. Mary Patricia, Prin.
Sisters of St. John the Baptist 3; Lay Teachers 8; Students 290.
Catechesis/Religious Programs—Tel: 718-981-4455.
Students 130.

227—SACRED HEART (1875), Rev. James E. Burke; Rev. Msgr. Andrew F. Quinn, Pastor Emeritus; Revs. Selvaraj Manickam (India); John J. Wroblewski.
Res., 981 Castleton Ave., 10310. Tel: 718-442-0058; Fax: 718-816-8006.
School—(1875), 301 N. Burgher Ave., 10310. Tel: 718-442-0347. Mrs. Zoilita M. Herrera, Prin.
Lay Teachers 20; Students 558.
Catechesis/Religious Programs—Tel: 718-448-1536.
Students 301.

228—ST. STANISLAUS KOSTKA (1923) (Polish), Revs. John A. Pinterbone, M.Th., M.A., Admin.; Marek Suchocki, J.C.L., M.Th. (Poland).
Res., 109 York Ave., 10301. Tel: 718-447-3937.

229—ST. SYLVESTER (1921), Revs. Eugene V. Mangan; Sebastian Thozhuthumparambil, C.M. (India); Rev. Msgr. Anthony O. Erhueh (Nigeria); Rev. Msgr. Daniel L. Sullivan, Pastor Emeritus.
Res., 854 Targee St., 10304. Tel: 718-727-4639.
School—(1930), 884 Targee St., 10304. Tel: 718-442-4938; Fax: 718-442-8177. Nancy Bushman, Prin.
Lay Teachers 10; Students 275.

230—ST. TERESA (1926), Rev. William J. Boldt.
Res., 1634 Victory Blvd., 10314. Tel: 718-442-5412.
School—(1955), 1632 Victory Blvd., 10314.
Sisters of the Presentation 4; Lay Teachers 17; Students 600.
Chapel—St. Nicholas, La Bau Ave. & Northern Blvd., 10314.

OUTSIDE THE CITY OF NEW YORK

Amenia, Dutchess Co., Immaculate Conception (1868), Rev. John L. Durkin; Deacon David Weinstein.
Res., 4 Lavelle Rd., 12501. Tel: 914-373-8193. [CEM]
Catechesis/Religious Programs—Students 207.
Mission—Millerton, Dutchess Co., St. Patrick, Church St., Millerton, 12546. [CEM]

Ardsley, Westchester Co., Our Lady of Perpetual Help (1929), Revs. Robert J. Duane; Emeka Godfrey Amanchukwu.
Res., 1 Cross Rd., 10502. Tel: 914-693-0030; Fax: 914-674-9020.
Catechesis/Religious Programs—Tel: 914-693-3831.
Students 320.

Armonk, Westchester Co., St. Patrick (1966), Revs. John F. Quinn; Daniel J. Brady; Rev. Msgr. Walter L. Schroeder, Pastor Emeritus.
Res., 29 Cox Ave., P.O. Box 6, 10504. Tel: 914-273-9724.
Catechesis/Religious Programs—Tel: 914-273-8226. Mrs. Ann O'Sullivan, D.R.E.
Students 375.

Bangall, Dutchess Co., Immaculate Conception (1919), Rev. Msgr. John G. Shevlin, Pastor Emeritus; Rev. Richard O'Gorman.
Res., Hunns Lake Rd., 12506. Tel: 914-868-1923. [CEM]
Mission—Clinton Corners, Dutchess Co., St. Joseph, (1883) Clinton Corners, 12514.

Barrytown, Dutchess Co., Sacred Heart. Closed. Parochial records at St. Christopher, Red Hook.

Beacon, Dutchess Co., St. Joachim (1853), Revs. Donald J. Poulin; Ronald P. Altrui. In res., Rev. Donald B. Licata.
Res., 61 Leonard St., 12508. Tel: 914-831-0377; Fax: 914-831-9504. [CEM]
Church—57 Leonard St., 12508.
School—(1861). School is now consolidated with St. John the Evangelist School. All school reports emanate from the school office there. 60 Liberty St., 12508.
St. John Evangelist (1887), Revs. Joseph J. Bisignano; Matthew M. Jelenek; Nimal Mendis.
Res., 35 Willow St., 12508. Tel: 914-831-0422; Fax: 914-831-1009.
School—St. Joachim - St. John School, (1908) (Grades PreK-3) 31 Willow St., 12508. Tel: 914-831-1358.
Lay Teachers 10; Students 225.
Catechesis/Religious Programs—Tel: 914-831-3638; Fax: 914-831-1009.
Students 211.

Bedford, Westchester Co., St. Patrick (1928), Rev. Msgr. Thomas A. Gartland; Rev. John B. Kauta (Uganda).
Res., State Rd., 10506. Tel: 914-234-3668.
School—(1956), State Rd., 10506. Tel: 914-234-7914. Mrs. Catherine Mendrzycki, Prin.
Lay Teachers 9; Students 195.
Catechesis/Religious Programs—Tel: 914-234-3775.
Students 358.

Blauvelt, Rockland Co., St. Catharine (1868), Rev. Msgr. William J. Belford; Revs. Dennis Dinan; Abraham Orapankal; Deacon John C. Kelleher.
Res., 523 Western Hwy., 10913. Tel: 914-359-0542; Fax: 914-365-2387. [CEM]
School—(1957), 517 Western Hwy., 10913. Tel: 914-359-4330. Sr. Alice Kirk, O.P., Prin.
Sisters of St. Dominic of Blauvelt 2; Lay Teachers 10; Students 225.
Catechesis/Religious Programs—Tel: 914-359-4014. Sr. Marie Murphy, O.P., D.R.E.
Students 505.

Brewster, Putnam Co., St. Lawrence O'Toole (1878), Revs. Robert J. DeJulio; John A. Bida; Deacons Benjamin Wallace; Mark Shkreh.
Res., 31 Prospect St., 10509. Tel: 914-279-2021; Fax: 914-279-7441. [CEM]
School—(1928), Eastview Ave., 10509. Tel: 914-279-5164; Fax: 914-279-8165. Mrs. Sharyn O'Leary, Prin.
Lay Teachers 13; Students 340.
Catechesis/Religious Programs—Tel: 914-279-6098. Sr. Catherine Murphy, S.H.C.J., D.R.E.
Students 585.

Briarcliff Manor, Westchester Co., St. Theresa (1926), Rev. Msgr. James K. Vaughey; Rev. Thomas P. Kiely.
Res., 1394 Pleasantville Rd., 10510. Tel: 914-941-1646; Fax: 914-944-9503.
School—Tel: 914-762-1050.
Sisters 2; Lay Teachers 8; Students 170.
Catechesis/Religious Programs—Tel: 914-923-3286.
Students 435.
Mission—Millwood, Westchester Co., Our Lady of the Wayside.

Bronxville, Westchester Co., St. Joseph (1906), Rev. Msgr. James M. Connolly; Revs. Francis J. Stinner; Carmine J. Rita. In res., Revs. Dawson Ambosta; Paul Vezhaparambil, C.M.I.
Res., 15 Cedar St., 10708. Tel: 914-337-1660; Fax: 914-337-1342.
School—(1951), 30 Meadow Ave., 10708. Tel: 914-337-0261; Fax: 914-395-1192. Mauro Durso, Prin.
Lay Teachers 18; Students 270.
Catechesis/Religious Programs—28 Meadow Ave., 10708. Tel: 914-337-6383.
Students 478.

Buchanan, Westchester Co., St. Christopher (1929), Rev. Msgr. Donald W. Hendricks; Rev. Leonard J. DiNola; Deacon Ronald J. Schlitt.
Res., 94 Albany Post Rd., 10511. Tel: 914-737-1046.

Callicoon, Sullivan Co., Holy Cross (1870), Rev. Ignatius E. Smith, O.F.M.
Res., 12723. Tel: 914-887-5450. [CEM]
Mission—Long Eddy, Sullivan Co., St. Patrick, Long Eddy, 12760.
Chapel—Callicoon, Holy Cross Rectory.

Carmel, Putnam Co., St. James the Apostle (1913), Revs. Joseph J. Faraone; Andrew J. Walsh; Americo Savoca; Deacons James Attridge; Charles T. Borsavage; Tony Gruerio. In res., Rev. Samuel Asantey.
Res., 14 Gleneida Ave., 10512. Tel: 914-225-2079; Fax: 914-225-5566.
School—(1954), Tel: 914-225-9365.
Lay Teachers 14; Students 280.
Catechesis/Religious Programs—Tel: 914-225-6504.
Students 1,060.
Mission—Lake Carmel, Putnam Co., Our Lady of the Lake, Noonan Dr., 10512.

Centerville, Ulster Co., St. John the Evangelist (1886), Rev. Msgr. William E. Williams; Deacon Edwin R. Topple. In res., Rev. James W. Derrenbacher.
Res., 915 Rte. 212, Saugerties, 12477. Tel: 914-246-9581; Fax: 914-246-9582.
Office: Tel: 914-246-9581.
Catechesis/Religious Programs—Students 250.

Chappaqua, Westchester Co., St. John and St. Mary (1922), Rev. Msgr. Timothy A. McDonnell; Rev. Kenneth O'Toole, Senior Priest. In res., Rev. John A. Vigilanti.
Res., 15 St. John's Pl., 10514. Tel: 914-238-3260; Fax: 914-238-3354.
Catechesis/Religious Programs—30 Poillon R

10514. Tel: 914-238-3696. Deacon Thomas Morrette, D.R.E.
Students 406.

Chester, Orange Co., St. Columba (1875), Rev. Thomas J. Curley; Sr. Anna Roche, S.C., Sacramental Min.; Deacon Frank Carlino.
Res., 27 High St., 10918. Tel: 914-469-2108; Fax: 914-469-2109. [CEM]
Catechesis/Religious Programs—Tel: 914-469-9503.
Students 320.
Station—Greycourt, Camp La Guardia. (NYC Homeless Shelter). Tel: 914-469-6200.

Cold Spring-on-Hudson, Putnam Co., Our Lady of Loretto (1834), Rev. Frederick Sullivan; Deacon John O'Reilly.
Res., 24 Fair St., Cold Spring, 10516. Tel: 914-265-3718; Fax: 914-265-4309.
Catechesis/Religious Programs—Tel: 914-265-2594. Sr. Ann Teresa Nagy, S.A., D.R.E.
Students 280.
Mission—Garrison, Putnam Co., St. Joseph, Garrison, 10524.

Congers, Rockland Co., St. Paul (1896), Rev. Msgr. Thomas E. Gilleece; Rev. William A. Kelleher; Deacons Dominic Buonocore; John W. McSherry.
Res., 82 Lake Rd. W., 10920. Tel: 914-268-4464; Fax: 914-268-6790. [CEM]
School—365 Kings Hwy., Valley Cottage, 10989. Tel: 914-268-6506; Fax: 914-268-1809. Sr. Stephen Gerard, O.P., Prin.
Sisters 2; Lay Teachers 13; Students 347.
Catechesis/Religious Programs—Tel: 914-268-5442.
Students 736.
Chapel—Congers, Sisters' Convent and School.

Cornwall-on-Hudson, Orange Co., St. Thomas of Canterbury (1870), Revs. John F.X. Smith; Bernard P. Heter.
Res., 10 Second St., 12520. Tel: 914-534-2547. [CEM]
School—(1913), Hudson St., 12520. Tel: 914-534-2019. Sr. Ann Cecilia Regan, O.P., Prin.
Sisters 2; Lay Teachers 8; Students 253.
Catechesis/Religious Programs—Tel: 914-534-9393.
Students 520.
Chapel—St. Thomas' Convent, 336 Hudson St., 12520. Tel: 914-534-4215.

Cortlandt Manor, Westchester Co., St. Columbanus (Van Cortlandtville) (1950), Rev. Msgr. Patrick J. Keenan; Rev. Joseph A. Blenkle; Deacon John J. Coppola. In res., Rev. Augustine Ansu Damoah (Ghana).
Res., 122 Oregon Rd., 10566. Tel: 914-737-4705; Fax: 914-736-7476.
School—122 Oregon Rd., 10566. Tel: 914-739-1200.
Sisters 3; Lay Teachers 8; Students 235.
Catechesis/Religious Programs—Tel: 914-739-2441.
Students 825.
Mission—Lake Peekskill, Putnam Co., North American Martyrs, 55 Oscawana Lake Rd., Putnam Valley, 10579. Tel: 914-528-6433.

Holy Spirit (1966), Rev. Msgr. James P. Cassidy, Ph.D.; Rev. Msgr. William J. McMahon, Ph.D.; Rev. Anthony Afful-Broni; Deacon Raymond Parchen.
Res., 1969 Crompond Rd., 10566-4113. Tel: 914-737-2316; Fax: 914-737-6882.
Catechesis/Religious Programs—Tel: 914-734-9243.
Students 536.
Chapel—Cortlandt Manor.

Crestwood, Westchester Co., Church of the Annunciation (1931), Rev. Msgr. James R. Moore; Revs. Eugene J. Carrella; Salvatore Riccardi, C.P.; Deacon Albert Conner.
Res., 470 Westchester Ave., 10707. Tel: 914-779-7345; 779-7542; Fax: 914-337-8878.
School—(1943), 465 Westchester Ave., 10707. Tel: 914-337-8760. Mr. Louis J. Capozi, Prin.
Sisters 7; Lay Teachers 17; Students 430.

Croton Falls, Westchester Co., St. Joseph (1845), Revs. James E. Borstelmann; John Voglio.
Res., 10 Croton Falls Rd., 10519. Tel: 914-277-3765; 277-3877; Fax: 914-277-1823.
School—(1949), Tel: 914-277-3783.
Lay Teachers 9; Students 165.
Catechesis/Religious Programs—14 Croton Falls Rd., 10519. Tel: 914-276-1067.
Students 825.
Missions—Goldens Bridge, Westchester Co., St. Michael, 10 Croton Falls Rd., Goldens Bridge, 10526; North Salem, Westchester Co., St. John, North Salem, 10560. [CEM]

Croton-on-Hudson, Westchester Co., Holy Name of Mary (1874), Revs. Gennaro L. Gentile; Matthew Yatkauskas; Deacons Richard Santana; Albert Mazza.
Res., 110 Grand St., 10520. Tel: 914-271-4797; Fax: 914-271-6841.
Catechesis/Religious Programs—114 Grand St., 10520. Tel: 914-271-4254.
Students 361.
Mission—Harmon, Westchester Co., Church of the Good Shepherd, 10520.

Dobbs Ferry, Westchester Co., Sacred Heart (1862), Rev. Terry Attridge; Sr. Connie Koch, O.P., Pastoral Assoc.; Deacons Patrick D. Troy; John J. Kollar.
Res., 18 Bellewood Ave., 10522. Tel: 914-693-0119; Fax: 914-693-3408.
Church—Broadway and Ashford Ave., 10522.
Catechesis/Religious Programs—Students 245.

Our Lady of Pompeii (1922) (Italian), Rev. Carmelo Glavina, Admin.; Deacon N. Anthony Barbieri.
Res., 95 Palisade St., 10522. Tel: 914-693-1839.

Dover Plains, Dutchess Co., St. Charles Borromeo (1859), Rev. Edward Barry.
Res., P.O. Box 56, 12522. Tel: 914-877-9934; Fax: 914-877-9936. [CEM]
Catechesis/Religious Programs—Tel: 914-877-9010.
Students 337.
Mission—Wingdale, Dutchess Co., Our Lady of Solace Mission, P.O. Box 329, Wingdale, 12594. Tel: 914-832-6989.

East Kingston, Ulster Co., St. Colman (1904), Rev. John C. McGuire, Admin.
Res., 18 Brigham St., Kingston, 12401. Tel: 914-336-8237.

Ellenville, Ulster Co., St. Mary and St. Andrew (1850), Rev. Msgr. Robert P. Hickey; Rev. Robert J. Ginel.
Res., 137 S. Main St., 12428. Tel: 914-647-6080.
Mission—Kerhonkson, Ulster Co., Our Lady of Lourdes, Kerhonkson, 12446.

Elmsford, Westchester Co., Our Lady of Mt. Carmel (1904), Rev. Vincent A. Lancellotti; Deacon Peter E. Reynolds.
Res., 59 E. Main St., 10523. Tel: 914-592-6789; Fax: 914-592-7526.
School—(1929), E. Main St., 10523. Tel: 914-592-7575; Fax: 914-592-7526.
Sisters of Divine Compassion 4; Lay Teachers 7; Students 237.

Fishkill, Dutchess Co., Church of St. Mary, Mother of the Church (1953), Rev. Msgr. Joseph A. Martin; Revs. Kent Wilson; Rick De La Pena; Deacon Martin Kazimir.
Res., 103 Jackson St., P.O. Box L, 12524-0499. Tel: 914-896-6400; Fax: 914-896-4575.
School—(1955), Tel: 914-896-9561. Mrs. Elizabeth Carufe.
Lay Teachers 9; Students 260.
Catechesis/Religious Programs—Tel: 914-896-6430.
Students 950.

Florida, Orange Co., St. Joseph (1895) (Polish), Rev. William M. Turowski, Admin.
Res., 14 Glenmere Ave., 10921. Tel: 914-651-7792. [CEM]
School—(1915), 21 Glenmere Ave., 10921. Tel: 914-651-7873.
Sisters 1; Lay Teachers 8; Students 100.
Catechesis/Religious Programs—Students 160.
Mission—Pellets Island (New Hampton), Orange Co., St. Andrew Bobola, Maple Ave., Pellets Island, 10958.
Chapel—St. Joseph Convent, 19 Glenmere Ave., 10921. Tel: 914-651-4213.

Forestburgh, Sullivan Co., St. Thomas Aquinas (1900), Rev. Msgr. Robert J. McCabe; Deacon Paul A. Rausch.
Res., 5 Forestburgh Rd., 12777. Tel: 914-791-7400. [CEM]

Gardiner, Ulster Co., St. Charles Borromeo (1883), Rev. John L. Quinn; Rev. Msgr. Robert E. Moore, Pastor Emeritus; Deacon Harold N. Carroll.
Res., 12525. Tel: 914-255-1374; Fax: 914-256-9050. [CEM]
Catechesis/Religious Programs—Students 246.

Garnerville, Rockland Co., St. Gregory Barbarigo (1961), Revs. John J. Backes; Herbert P. De Garis; Deacon Augustine A. Pappalardo.
Res., 21 Cinder Rd., 10923. Tel: 914-947-1873.
School—Tel: 914-947-1330; Fax: 914-947-4392. Sr. Kathleen Gorres, O.P., Prin.
Sisters of St. Dominic (Sparkill) 2; Lay Teachers 10; Students 270.
Catechesis/Religious Programs—Tel: 914-429-2775. Marie Kiely, D.R.E.
Students 830.

Glasco, Ulster Co., St. Joseph (1921) (Italian-Irish), Rev. Charles F. Zanotti.
Res., Glasco Turnpike, Box 208, 12432. Tel: 914-246-5453.
A-Villa St. Dominic—Rest House for Ladies. Dominican Sisters (Sparkill). Also Known as Corazon Center. Tel: 914-246-8941.
Catechesis/Religious Programs—Tel: 914-246-6644.
Students 150.

Goshen, Orange Co., St. John the Evangelist (1837), Revs. Richard T. Adams; Robert G. Hilfiker.
Res., 71 Murray Ave., 10924. Tel: 914-294-5328. [CEM]
School—77 Murray Ave., 10924. Tel: 914-294-6434. Sr. M. Paracleta, O.P., Prin.
Sisters 2; Lay Teachers 7; Students 264.
Catechesis/Religious Programs—Tel: 914-294-6847.
Students 425.
Chapels—Immaculate Conception Convent, 73 Murray Ave., 10924.; Presentation Sisters Convent, Fletcher St., 10924; John S. Burke H. S. Chapel; Our Lady of the Blessed Sacrament, Broadlea, 10924. Tel: 914-294-5481.
Stations—Orange County Home and Infirmary, Tel: 914-294-7971; Orange County Jail, Tel: 914-294-6166; Campbell Hall Nursing Facility, Tel: 914-294-8154; Arden Hill Life-Care Center, Tel: 914-294-9797.

Greenburgh, Westchester Co., Church of Our Lady of Shkodra, Rev. Peter Popovich.
Res., 361 W. Hartsdale Ave., Hartsdale, 10530.

Greenwood Lake, Orange Co., Holy Rosary (1954), Revs. Robert J. Sweeney; Joseph F. Fitzpatrick, S.J.; Deacon Ralph Longo.
Res., 41 Windemere Ave., 10925-9875. Tel: 914-477-8378; Fax: 914-477-0984.
Catechesis/Religious Programs—Tel: 918-477-0906.
Students 293.

Harriman, Orange Co., St. Anastasia (1899), Rev. Joseph F. Reynolds; Deacon Eugene E. Bormann. In res., Rev. Lawrence X. McCaffrey, S.J.
Res., 21 N. Main St., 10926. Tel: 914-783-3571. [CEM]
Catechesis/Religious Programs—Tel: 914-782-5099.
Students 380.

Harrison, Westchester Co., St. Gregory the Great (1900), Rev. Msgr. Daniel V. Flynn, J.C.D.; Rev. Msgr. Guy Vinci; Rev. Msgr. Joseph J. Raimondo, Senior Priest; Rev. Philip J. Gagliano.
Res., 215 Halstead Ave., 10528. Tel: 914-835-0677; Fax: 914-835-0796.
School—(1953), 94 Broadway, 10528. Tel: 914-835-1278; Fax: 914-835-2070. Debra A. Trignani, Prin.
Lay Teachers 10; Students 170.
Catechesis/Religious Programs—189 Fremont St., 10528. Tel: 914-835-4291.
Students 604.

Hartsdale, Westchester Co., Sacred Heart (1926), Rev. Msgr. John V. Wilkinson; Rev. Richard Seagraves; Deacon Benjamin D'Arconte.
Res., 10 Lawton Ave., 10530. Tel: 914-949-0028.
School—(1953), 59 Wilson St., 10530. Tel: 914-946-7242. Sr. Margaret Smith, S.C., Prin.
Sisters 4; Lay Teachers 16; Students 235.
Catechesis/Religious Programs—Tel: 914-428-5043.
Students 179.
Convent—11 Lawton Ave., 10530. Tel: 914-946-2581.

Hastings-on-Hudson, Westchester Co., St. Matthew (1892), Rev. Msgr. Edward J. McCorry; Rev. James Smyth.
Res., 616 Warburton Ave., 10706. Tel: 914-478-2822; Fax: 914-478-3681.
School—(1911), Tel: 914-478-3343. Sr. Margaret Patricia, O.P., Prin.
Sisters 2; Lay Teachers 8; Students 166.
Catechesis/Religious Programs—Students 235.

St. Stanislaus Kostka (1912) (Polish), Rev. Msgr. Edward J. McCorry.
Res., 616 Warburton Ave., 10706. Tel: 914-478-2822; Fax: 914-478-3681.
Church—52 Main St., 10706.

Haverstraw, Rockland Co., St. Peter (1848), Revs. Charles S. Kelly; Nimal B. Mendis; George Kalapurra.
Res., 115 Broadway, 10927. Tel: 914-429-2196. [CEM]
School—(1884), Ridge St., 10927. Tel: 914-429-5311. Miss Cathleen Dunn, Prin.
Lay Teachers 10; Students 230.
Stations—West Haverstraw, Helen Hayes Hospital; Walnut Hill, Senior Citizen Apts.; Haverstraw, Green Hills Home; Haverstraw, Riverdale Nursing Home.

St. Mary (1899) (Slovak), Rev. Mario Zicarelli.
Res., 46 Conklin Ave., 10927. Tel: 914-429-2245.

Hawthorne, Westchester Co., Holy Rosary (1901), Revs. Daniel T. Davies, O.P.; James A. Nicolicchia, O.P.; James B. Muller, O.P.
Res., 170 Bradhurst, 10532. Tel: 914-769-0030; Fax: 914-769-3326.
School—(1955), 180 Bradhurst Ave., 10532. Tel: 914-769-4549; Fax: 914-769-2768.
Lay Teachers 10; Students 246.

Catechesis/Religious Programs—Tel: 914-769-3338. Sr. June Quinian, O.P., D.R.E.
Students 586.

Highland, Ulster Co., St. Augustine (1899), Revs. Eugene Keane; Thomas Lutz.
Res., 55 Main St., 12528. Tel: 914-691-7673.
School—(1958), Phillips Ave. and Elting Pl., 12528. Tel: 914-691-2338. Mr. John George, Prin.
Lay Teachers 10; Students 226.
Catechesis/Religious Programs—Students 296.

Highland Falls, Orange Co., Sacred Heart of Jesus (1870). Unassigned.
Res., 353 Main St., 10928. Tel: 914-446-4609; Fax: 914-446-2343. [CEM]
School—(1930), 7 Cozzens Ave., 10928. Tel: 914-446-2674.
Lay Teachers 8; Students 180.
Catechesis/Religious Programs—Maryann Brigham, D.R.E.
Students 219.
Chapel—Fort Montgomery, Blessed Sacrament. Rev. Michael P. McLoughlin.

Highland Mills, Orange Co., St. Patrick (1957), Revs. Gerard P. Travers; Sebastian Pandarathikudiyil, V.C. (India); Deacon Paul Weireter.
Res., 18 Hunter St., 10930. Tel: 914-928-6027.
Catechesis/Religious Programs—Tel: 914-928-6688.
Students 600.

Hopewell Junction, Dutchess Co., St. Columba (1992), Rev. Msgr. Dominick J. Lagonegro; Rev. Martin J. Mahoney; Deacons William Alvarado; John Reilly; George Stewart; Warren Testa.
Res., 601 Rte. 82, P.O. Box 428, 12533. Tel: 914-227-8380; Fax: 914-227-8390.
School—St. Denis-St. Columba, Tel: 914-227-7777. Sr. Ann Daniels, Prin.
Sisters 2; Lay Teachers 15; Students 503.
Catechesis/Religious Programs—P.O. Box 368, Hopewell Jct., 12533. Tel: 914-221-4900. Rev. Bruce O. Bowes, D.R.E.
Students 1,629.

St. Denis (1899), Rev. William B. Cosgrove; Deacons Walter Dauerer; Stanley Aviles.
Res. & Office: 325 Beekman Rd., P.O. Box 10, 12533. Tel: 914-227-8382; Fax: 914-227-3951. [CEM]
School—St. Denis-St. Columba. See St. Columba for details. Tel: 914-227-7777; Fax: 914-227-8390.
Catechesis/Religious Programs—P.O. Box 368, 12533. Tel: 914-221-4900.
Students 771.

Hyde Park, Dutchess Co., Regina Coeli (1863), Rev. Peter J. Vianney; Deacons William E. Biskup; John C. Kuhn; Frank J. Gohl; George R. Stewart. In res., Rev. James J. LeBar; Rev. Msgr. Harold E. Hicks.
Res., 2 Harvey St., 12538. Tel: 914-229-2134.
School—(1955), Albany Post Rd., 12538.
Lay Teachers 14; Students 269.
Mission—Staatsburg, Dutchess Co., St. Paul, (1851) Staatsburg, 12580.

Irvington-on-the-Hudson, Westchester Co., Immaculate Conception (1873), Revs. Raymond J. Byrne; Timothy J. Scannell; Abraham Vettiyankal, C.M.I.
Res., 16 N. Broadway, 10533. Tel: 914-591-7480; Fax: 914-591-7806.
School—(1908), Tel: 914-591-9330.
Lay Teachers 16; Students 222.
Catechesis/Religious Programs—Tel: 914-591-7740.
Students 275.

Jeffersonville, Sullivan Co., St. George, Rev. Edward Greene, O.F.M.
Res., 12748. Tel: 914-482-4640.

Katonah, Westchester Co., St. Mary of the Assumption (1908), Revs. William P. Dalton; Adrian C. Piotrowski, O.S.C.
Res., 117 Valley Rd., 10536. Tel: 914-232-3356.
Catechesis/Religious Programs—99 Valley Rd., 10536. Tel: 914-232-4648.
Students 553.
Missions—Bedford Hills, Westchester Co., St. Matthias, (1909) Babbitt Rd., Bedford Hills, 10507; South Salem, Westchester Co., S. Salem Presbyterian Church, Spring St., South Salem, 10590.

Kingston, Ulster Co.,

1—Holy Name of Jesus, (1884), Rev. Edmund M. Burke; Deacon Robert B. Sheeley. In res., Deacon John Sullivan.
Res., 11 Fitch St., 12401. Tel: 914-331-1606.

2—Immaculate Conception, (1896) (Polish), Rev. John W. Borzuchowski (Poland).
Res., 467 Delaware Ave., 12401. Tel: 914-331-0846; Fax: 914-331-7647. [CEM]

3—St. Joseph, (1868), Rev. Msgr. Charles McDonagh; Revs. Frank J. Damis; Alfred Glancy; Deacons Donald Droulette; Richard Frohmiller; Robert Winrow; John Peters; Joseph Doherty. In res., Rev. Msgr. James V. Keating.
Res., 242 Wall St., 12401. Tel: 914-338-1554.
School—(1869), Wall and Pearl Sts., 12401. Tel: 914-339-4390.
Sisters, Society of St. Ursula 1; Lay Teachers 13; Students 149.
Chapel—St. Joseph Mission, Zandhoeck Rd., Hurley, 12443.

4—St. Mary, (1842), Rev. Edmund M. Burke; Deacon John Sullivan. In res., Rev. Cornelius C. Woulfe, C.S.Sp., Chaplain Kingston Hosp.
Res., 160 Broadway, 12401. Tel: 914-331-0301. [CEM]
School—Kingston Catholic School, (1867), 159 Broadway, 12401. Tel: 914-331-9318. Sr. Esther Fazione, S.C.C., Prin.
Sisters of Christian Charity 3; Lay Teachers 8; Students 216.
Catechesis/Religious Programs—Students 180.

5—St. Peter, (1858) (German), Rev. Msgr. William J. Collins.
Res., 93 Wurts St., 12401. Tel: 914-331-0436. [CEM]
Chapel—Kingston, Sisters of Christian Charity Convent, Tel: 914-338-7319.

Lake Katrine, Ulster Co., St. Catherine Laboure (1957), Rev. John T. Kearney.
Res., Tuytenbridge Rd., P.O. Box 271, 12449. Tel: 914-382-1133.

Larchmont, Westchester Co., St. Augustine (1892), Rev. Msgr. Walter F. Kenny. In res., Rev. Joseph A. DeSanto.
Res., 18 Cherry Ave., 10538. Tel: 914-834-1220.
Catechesis/Religious Programs—Tel: 914-834-9523.
Students 340.

SS. John and Paul (1949), Revs. Joseph Boyd; Robert J. Verrigni; Deacon James Brown.
Res., 280 Weaver St., 10538. Tel: 914-834-5458; Fax: 914-833-5081.
School—(1952), Tel: 914-834-6332. Anne A. Menno, Prin.
Lay Teachers 12; Students 240.
Catechesis/Religious Programs—Tel: 914-834-4597.
Students 407.

Liberty, Sullivan Co., St. Peter (1894), Rev. Edward F. Straub; Deacon John Riley.
Res., 264 N. Main St., 12754. Tel: 914-292-4525. [CEM]
Catechesis/Religious Programs—Students 200.

Livingston Manor, Sullivan Co., St. Aloysius (1899), Rev. Alfred M. Croke.
Res., Church St., Box 206, 12758. Tel: 914-439-5625. [CEM]
Missions—De Bruce, Sullivan Co., Sacred Heart, 12758; Roscoe, Sullivan Co., Gate of Heaven, Highland Ave., Roscoe, 12776.
Catechesis/Religious Programs—Students 180.

Mahopac, Putnam Co., St. John the Evangelist (1889), Rev. Msgr. Raymond T. Powers, S.T.D.; Revs. Andrew P. Carrozza; William F. Woodruff; Deacons John Armo; Robert Esposito.
Res., 235 Msgr. O'Brien Blvd., 10541. Tel: 914-628-2006; Fax: 914-628-5970.
School—(1955), Tel: 914-628-6464.
Religious of the Divine Compassion 2; Lay Teachers 8; Students 200.
Catechesis/Religious Programs—Tel: 914-628-5222.
Students 1,712.
Chapel—Convent of Religious of the Divine Compassion, Tel: 914-628-6497.

Mamaroneck, Westchester Co., Holy Trinity (1874), Revs. Joseph F. Irwin; William A. Rooney; Michael J. O'Brien, (Retired); Gabriel Muteru (Kenya).
Res., 320 E. Post Rd., 10543. Tel: 914-698-5944; Fax: 914-698-5274.

St. Vito (1911) (Italian), Revs. James F. Healy; Peter Tran Van Phat (Vietnam).
Res., 816 Underhill Ave., 10543. Tel: 914-698-2648.

Marlboro, Ulster Co., St. Mary (1900), Rev. Alfred R. Pizzuto; Rev. Msgr. Edward T. Dugan, Pastor Emeritus. Pastoral Team: Tel: 914-236-4340. Sr. Norma Carney, P.B.V.M.; Sr. Elena O'Neill P.B.V.M.; Sr. Mary O'Neill, P.B.V.M.; Deacons John T. Repke; Thomas Cornell.
Res., Bloom St., 12542. Tel: 914-236-4340. [CEM]
Catechesis/Religious Programs—Students 450.
Mission—Roseton, Orange Co., Our Lady of Mercy, River Rd., 12550.

Massapequa Park, Nassau Co., Our Lady of Lourdes (1955), Revs. Robert Mason; Thomas Reynolds; Anthony Heinlein; Deacons Dominick Valdaro; Steve Delligatti.
Res., 855 Carmans Rd., 11762. Fax: 516-797-9851.
Catechesis/Religious Programs—379 Linden St., 11762. Tel: 516-541-3270; Fax: 516-797-9851.
Students 715.

Maybrook, Orange Co., Assumption (1907), Rev. Andrew T. Magee; Deacon Edward M. Grosso.
Res., 211 Homestead Ave., 12543. Tel: 914-427-2046.
Catechesis/Religious Programs—Tel: 914-427-5318.
Students 243.

Middletown, Orange Co., St. Joseph (1865), Rev. Msgr. George J. Valastro; Revs. Joseph P. Fallon; Ludovico Angella (Italy); Gerald Blom (Sri Lanka) Hospital Chaplain; Deacon Richard Trapani.
Res., 149 Cottage St., 10940. Tel: 914-343-6013; Fax: 914-344-4735. [CEM]
School—(1889), 113 Cottage St., 10940. Tel: 914-343-3139. Deborah Scofield, Prin.
Lay Teachers 14; Students 259.
Catechesis/Religious Programs—Tel: 914-343-4415.
Students 630.

Our Lady of Mt. Carmel (1912), Rev. Lucian W. Beltzner, O.Carm. Pastoral Assocs.: Revs. Edward Duffy, O.Carm.; Raymond Bagdonis, O.Carm.; Sean Harlow, O.Carm.; David Kearns, O.Carm.; Patrick McGuigan, O.Carm.; Deacons Edward Woods; John Frohbose. In res., Very Rev. Mario Esposito, O. Carm.
Res., 90 Euclid Ave., 10940. Tel: 914-343-4121; Fax: 914-343-4433.
School—205 Wawayanda Ave., 10940. Tel: 914-343-8836.
Lay Teachers 10; Students 289.
Catechesis/Religious Programs—Tel: 914-342-1510.
Students 380.
Missions—Bloomingburgh, Sullivan Co., Our Lady of the Assumption, P.O. Box 216, Bloomingburgh, 12721. Tel: 914-733-1477; Fax: 914-733-6691; Bullville, Orange Co., St. Paul, Rte. 17K, Bullville, 10915. Tel: 914-361-3107; Fax: 914-361-4201; South Centerville, Orange Co., Holy Cross, 626 County Rte. 22, South Centerville, 10973. Tel: 914-355-4439; Unionville, Orange Co., Our Lady of the Scapular, 125 Main St., Unionville, 10988. Tel: 914-726-3222.

Millbrook, Dutchess Co., St. Joseph (1890), Revs. James T. O'Connor; Alphonse Prabhu.
Res., North Ave., 12545. Tel: 914-677-3422; Fax: 914-679-3423. [CEM]
School—(1957), Tel: 914-677-3670.
Lay Teachers 9; Students 246.
Catechesis/Religious Programs—Tel: 914-677-3273.
Students 330.
Chapel—Millbrook, Cardinal Hayes Home for Children.
Stations—Millbrook, County Infirmary.; Millbrook, Green Briar Home.

Milton, Ulster Co., St. James (1874) (Italian), Rev. Fred Kempfirl. In res., Rev. Eugene Daniels.
Res., State Rd., 12547. Tel: 914-795-2255.

Monroe, Orange Co., Sacred Heart (1957), Revs. Carl D. Johnson; Vernon Wickrematunge (India); Thomas L. Kreiser; Deacons Peter Brockmann; James Burns.
Res., 26 Still Rd., 10950. Tel: 914-782-8510; Fax: 914-782-3593.
School—(1965), Tel: 914-783-0365. Winifred M. Sartoris, Prin.
Sisters 1; Lay Teachers 11; Students 255.
Catechesis/Religious Programs—(Grades PreK-8). Tel: 914-782-7420. Sr. Rose O'Rourke, D.R.E.
Students 1,109.
Convent—Still Rd., 10950.
Chapel—Stage Rd., 10950.

Montgomery, Orange Co., Holy Name of Mary (1868), Rev. Joseph D. Sullivan.
Res., 89 Union St., 12549. Tel: 914-457-5276.
Catechesis/Religious Programs—Tel: 914-457-1738. Sr. Grace Mary McGuire, D.R.E.
Students 330.

Monticello, Sullivan Co., St. Peter (1874),
Res., 10 Liberty St., 12701. Tel: 914-794-5577. [CEM]
Catechesis/Religious Programs—Tel: 914-791-7172.
Students 406.
Missions—Monticello, Sullivan Co., St. Joseph, 12701; Monticello, Sullivan Co., St. Anne, 12701.

Mt. Kisco, Westchester Co., St. Francis of Assisi (1871), Rev. Ralph A. Villani. In res., Rev. Michael M. Burke (CC).
Res., 2 Green St., 10549. Tel: 914-666-5986; Fax: 914-666-3859. [CEM]
Catechesis/Religious Programs—Tel: 914-666-3161; Fax: 914-666-5474.
Students 350.

Mt. Vernon, Westchester Co.,

1—Sacred Heart, (1872), Rev. Owen J. Lafferty.
Res., 115 S. Fifth Ave., 10550. Tel: 914-668-7440.
School—(1895), Second St. & S. Fifth Ave., 10550
Lay Teachers 8; Students 243.

Chapel—Sacred Heart Convent, 67 S. Fifth Ave., 10550.

2—ST. FRANCIS OF ASSISI, (1949), Revs. Anthony J. Giuliano; Thomas D'Angelo; James P. Clark.
Res., 4343 Baychester Ave., Bronx, 10466. Tel: 718-994-8736.
Church—S. 10th Ave. & W. Seventh St., 10550.
School—4300 Baychester Ave., Bronx, 10466. Tel: 718-994-4650; Fax: 718-994-6990. Dr. Patrick Taharally, Prin.
Sisters 1; Lay Teachers 11; Students 281.
Chapel—

3—OUR LADY OF VICTORY, (1871), Rev. Msgr. Thomas F. Scanlon; Rev. Vincent O. Ajayi (Nigeria).
Res., 28 W. Sidney Ave., 10550. Tel: 914-668-5861; Fax: 914-668-0161.
School—(1898), 38 N. Fifth Ave., 10550. Tel: 914-667-4063. Margaret Balfe, Prin.
Lay Teachers 11; Students 254.
Chapel—Dominican Convent, Tel: 914-667-2564.

4—ST. MARY, (1894), Rev. John T. Meehan.
Res., 23 S. High St., 10550. Tel: 914-664-5855.

5—OUR LADY OF MOUNT CARMEL, (1897) (Italian), Revs. Octavio Jose Salinas, O.F.M.; James Villa, O.F.M.; Benedict D'Alessandro, O.F.M.; Bro. Dominic Poirier, O.F.M.; Deacon Vincent T. Piro.
Res., 10550. Tel: 914-668-3540; Fax: 914-668-4393.

6—SS. PETER AND PAUL, (1929) (Italian), Rev. Msgr. Patrick J. Barry; Revs. Leonard Da Custa; Augustine Matthew, C.M.I.
Res., 129 Birch St., 10552. Tel: 914-668-9815.
School—Tel: 914-664-1321.
Sisters 1; Lay Teachers 12; Students 240.
Catechesis/Religious Programs—Tel: 914-668-9880.
Students 170.

7—ST. URSULA, (1908), Rev. Msgr. A. Francis Burns; Rev. Sabbas J. Kilian, O.F.M.; Deacons Thomas J. Abbamont; Pasquale Giglio; Carl Degenhardt.
Res., 214 E. Lincoln Ave., 10552. Tel: 914-668-0085; Fax: 914-668-4228.
Saint Ursula's Learning Center For the Learning Disabled—183 Rich Ave., 10552. Tel: 914-664-6656; Fax: 914-668-0592.
Catechesis/Religious Programs—Tel: 914-699-7964. Sr. Roberta Smith, O.S.F., D.R.E.
Students 225.
Convent—29 Clinton Pl., 10552. Tel: 914-668-4031.

Nanuet, Rockland Co., St. Anthony (1897), Revs. William V. Reynolds; Peter Tran Van Phat; Robert Saccoman; Deacon John Maloney. In res., Rev. Joseph Anyimaduwireko.
Res., 36 West Nyack Rd., 10954. Tel: 914-623-2138; Fax: 914-623-5556. [CEM]
School—(1953), 32-34 West Nyack Rd., 10954. Tel: 914-623-2311. Barbara Casey, Prin.
Sisters 8; Lay Teachers 13; Students 501.
Catechesis/Religious Programs—Tel: 914-624-2230. Ms. Ann Malloy, D.R.E.
Students 825.

Narrowsburg, Sullivan Co., St. Francis Xavier (1862), Rev. Thomas Jones, O.F.M.
Res., 151 Bridge St., 12764. Tel: 914-252-6681; Fax: 914-252-6519. [CEM]
Mission—Lake Huntington, Sullivan Co., Our Lady of the Lake, Lake Huntington, 12752. Tel: 914-252-6681.

Newburgh, Orange Co.,

1—ST. PATRICK, (1836), Rev. Msgr. John J. Budwick; Revs. Louis Van Thanh; Alfonso Henao (Colombia); Deacons Fred Steup; Frank Russell; William Glover. Spanish Apostolates: Sr. Yliana Hernandez; Sr. Paula Cormier.
Res., 55 Grand St., 12550. Tel: 914-561-0885. [CEM]
Catechesis/Religious Programs—Tel: 914-561-6470. Sr. Francis Morley, D.R.E.
Students 550.
Mission—Orange Lake, Orange Co., Our Lady of the Lake.

2—ST. FRANCIS OF ASSISI, (1909) (Polish), Rev. John J. Vondras, Admin.; Deacons Jack Seymour; John Buckley.
Res., 145 Benkard Ave., 12550. Tel: 914-561-1317; Fax: 914-561-1337. [CEM]
School—Now Sacred Heart-St. Francis of Assisi School. Merged in Sept. 1992. 24 S. Robinson Ave., 12550. Tel: 914-561-1433.
Catechesis/Religious Programs—Tel: 914-561-6697. Louise Pisano, D.R.E.
Students 390.
Chapel—St. Francis Convent, (1955), 153 Benkard Ave., 12550. Tel: 914-561-5914; Fax: 914-561-1123.

3—ST. MARY, (1875), Rev. Msgr. James E. White. In res., Most Rev. Austin B. Vaughan, D.D.
Res., 180 South St., 12550. Tel: 914-562-0862.

4—SACRED HEART, (1912) (Italian), Revs. George C. Lodi; John M. Lagiovane; Deacons Dominick Casadone; Peter Haight; Arthur Manzione. In res., Rev. Donald Timone.
Res., 301 Ann St., 12550. Tel: 914-561-2264.
School—(1951), 24 S. Robinson Ave., 12550. Tel: 914-561-1433.
Lay Teachers 15; Students 285.
Catechesis/Religious Programs—Tel: 914-561-2589.
Students 598.

New City, Rockland Co., St. Augustine (1957), Rev. Msgr. William J. Foley; Revs. James B. Hynes; George T. Vadakel (India); Deacons Michael G. McCabe; Lawrence O'Toole.
Res., 140 Maple Ave., 10956. Tel: 914-634-3641; Fax: 914-639-6118.
School—Tel: 914-634-7060; Fax: 914-634-8725. Sr. Helen Doychak, O.P., Prin.
Sisters 1; Lay Teachers 13; Students 289.
Catechesis/Religious Programs—Tel: 914-634-8462.
Students 882.

New Paltz, Ulster Co., St. Joseph (1894), Revs. Michael Banks, O.F.M.Cap.; Paul Steffan, O.F.M.Cap.; Knute Kenlon, O.F.M.Cap., Chap.; Bro. Timothy Jones, O.F.M.Cap., Univ. Chap.
Res., 34 S. Chestnut St., 12561. Tel: 914-255-5635; Fax: 914-255-5679.
Catechesis/Religious Programs—Tel: 914-255-0237; Fax: 914-256-0687.
Students 430.
Station—Lake Mohonk.

New Rochelle, Westchester Co.,

1—BLESSED SACRAMENT, (1848), Rev. Msgr. William J. Bradley; Revs. Charles Imokhai (Nigeria); Patrick Puthotta (India); Samuel Savio (India); Deacons Charles Rizzo; Frank Orlando; Charles Wendelken. In res., Rev. Msgr. Eugene F. Richard.
Res., 15 Shea Pl., 10801. Tel: 914-632-2300; Fax: 914-632-0732. [CEM]
School—New Rochelle Catholic Elementary, (1866), 24 Maple Ave., 10801. Tel: 914-632-0511. Joan Woods, Prin.
Lay Teachers 16; Students 197.
High School—(Coed) 24 Shea Pl., 10801. Tel: 914-632-2595; Fax: 914-632-3321. Bro. Brendan Ramos, C.F.C., Prin.
Congregation of Christian Brothers 4; Sisters 4; Lay Teachers 18; Students 250.
Catechesis/Religious Programs—Tel: 914-235-7311. Sr. Margaret Breslin, O.P., D.R.E.
Students 600.

2—ST. GABRIEL, (1893), Revs. Patrick V. McNamara; Jude Paulraj (India); John Muscat, Chap.
Res., 120 Division St., 10801. Tel: 914-632-0211.
Chapel—Sisters of Charity of St. Vincent de Paul, 13 Washington Ave., 10801.

3—ST. JOSEPH, (1901) (Italian), Revs. Cosimo Fazio; Cajetan Uchendu; Jess Eric Solier.
Res., 280 Washington Ave., 10801. Tel: 914-632-0675; Fax: 914-633-4264.
Catechesis/Religious Programs—Students 170.

4—HOLY FAMILY, (1913), Rev. Msgr. John Mescall; Rev. James B. Teague. In res., Rev. Augustine T. Badgely.
Res., 83 Clove Rd., 10801. Tel: 914-632-0673; Fax: 914-576-8556.
Church—Mayflower Ave. & Mt. Joy Pl., 10801.
School—(1921), Mayflower Ave., 10801. Tel: 914-632-3810.
Lay Teachers 12; Students 195.
Catechesis/Religious Programs—Tel: 914-636-6758.
Students 330.
Chapels—Ursuline Sisters, 1352 N. Ave., 10804. Tel: 914-636-3456; Iona Grammar and Preparatory Schools, 173 Stratton Rd., 10804. Tel: 914-633-7744; 632-2727; Fax: 914-235-6338; Iona College, 715 N. Ave., 10801. Tel: 914-633-2000; New Rochelle, St. Patrick Prov., 30 Montgomery Circle, 10801. Tel: 914-633-6851; New Rochelle, St. Joseph Chapel; Edmond Rice Hall, 33 Pryer Ter., 10804. Tel: 914-636-6194; Crosier Fathers, 125 Paine Ave., 10804. Tel: 914-636-3614; Opus Dei, 99 Overlook Cir., 10804. Tel: 914-235-1201; Holy Cross Brothers Provincialate, 85 Overlook Cir., 10804. Tel: 914-632-1951; Fax: 914-632-2490.

5—HOLY NAME OF JESUS, (1929), Revs. Martin J. Biglin; John P. DeLora; Deacons Carmine DeMarco; Robert Gontcharuk.
Res., 75 Lispenard Ave., 10801. Tel: 914-636-4856.
Church—Petersville Rd. and Halligan St., 10801.
School—(1954), 70 Petersville Rd., 10801. Tel: 914-576-6672. Mr. Albert D'Angelo, Prin.
Sisters 2; Lay Teachers 10; Students 243.
Catechesis/Religious Programs—Tel: 914-576-6038.
Students 182.
Chapel—Sisters of Charity Convent, 78 Petersville Rd., 10801. Tel: 914-636-4354.

New Windsor, Orange Co., St. Joseph (1962), Rev. Laurence H. Gibney; Deacons Joseph Lieby; Anthony Ferraiuolo.
Res., 4 St. Joseph Pl., 12553. Tel: 914-561-8467.
School—148 Windsor Hwy., 12553. Tel: 914-565-5110.
Sisters 1; Lay Teachers 12; Students 208.
Catechesis/Religious Programs—Tel: 914-561-8475.
Students 374.

North Tarrytown, Westchester Co., St. Teresa of Avila (1853), Rev. Francis P. Gorman; Rev. Msgr. Robert E. Moore; Rev. John J. McDonagh.
Res., 130 Beekman Ave., 10591. Tel: 914-631-0720.
Catechesis/Religious Programs—Tel: 914-631-1831.
Students 227.
Holy Cross (1921) (Slovak-Polish), Rev. Francis P. Gorman; Rev. Msgr. Cyril J. Potocek.
Res., 118 Beekman Ave., 10591. Tel: 914-631-1493.
Immaculate Conception (1917) (Italian), Revs. Louis J. Mazza; Salvatore Fiore, S.J., (Italy) (Retired).
Res., 199 N. Broadway, 10591. Tel: 914-631-0446.

Nyack, Rockland Co., St. Ann (1869), Rev. Msgr. Edmund Netter, Pastor Emeritus; Revs. Robert P. Henry, Admin.; Peter J. Kihm; Frederick Leo (Sri Lanka).
Res., 16 Jefferson St., 10960. Tel: 914-358-4707; Fax: 914-358-3246.
School—(1892), Tel: 914-358-0125; Fax: 914-358-7911. Sr. Angelene Matero, F.M.S.C., Prin.
Lay Teachers 5; Students 70.
Catechesis/Religious Programs—19 Jefferson St., Nyak, 10960. Tel: 914-358-3758.
Students 184.
Chapel—Convent, 150 Third Ave., 10960. Tel: 914-358-2697.

Obernburg, Sullivan Co., St. Mary (1854) (German), Rev. Fabian A. Flynn, O.F.M.; Deacon Lawrence Knack.
Res., 12767. Tel: 914-482-5541. [CEM]

Ossining, Westchester Co., St. Augustine (1853), Rev. Msgr. Hilary Franco; Rev. Msgr. Robert F. McCormick, Pastor Emeritus; Rev. Robert G. Hilfiker.
Res., Eagle Park Rte. 9, 10562. Tel: 914-941-0067. [CEM]
School—(1893), Tel: 914-941-3849. Sr. Mary Elizabeth Donoghue, Prin.
Priests 2; Sisters of St. Dominic (Columbus) 1; Lay Teachers 25; Students 46.
St. Ann (1927), Rev. Edward G. Byrne; Sr. Eileen Finnerty, Pastoral Assoc.; Deacon Jose DeJesus. In res., Rev. Cyril Owambo (Kenya).
Res., 25 Eastern Ave., 10562. Tel: 914-941-2556; Fax: 914-923-9239.
School—16 Elizabeth St., 10562. Tel: 914-941-0312. Mrs. Dorethea Muccigrosso, Prin.
Sisters 1; Lay Teachers 12; Students 387.
Catechesis/Religious Programs—Tel: 914-941-2420.
Students 360.
Convent—10 Elizabeth St., 10562.

Otisville, Orange Co., Holy Name (1969), Rev. Gerard J. Di Senso.
Res., P.O. Box 597, 10963. Tel: 914-386-1320. [CEM]
Catechesis/Religious Programs—Tel: 914-386-2327. Mrs. Nancy Doran, D.R.E.
Students 210.

Patterson, Putnam Co., Sacred Heart (1957), Revs. James P. Flynn; Richard C. Joyce, Pastor Emeritus.
Res., 414 Haviland Dr., 12563. Tel: 914-279-4832.
Catechesis/Religious Programs—Students 435.

Pawling, Dutchess Co., St. John the Evangelist (1848), Revs. John J. Duff; James J. Moriarty, Pastor Emeritus.
Res., 39 E. Main St., 12564. Tel: 914-855-5488. [CEM]
Catechesis/Religious Programs—Tel: 914-855-9408.
Students 350.

Pearl River, Rockland Co., St. Margaret (1923), Rev. Msgr. James Doyle; Rev. George Stewart; Sr. Eileen Reilly, O.P., Pastoral Assoc.; Deacon William Tobin.
Res., 115 W. Central Ave., 10965. Tel: 914-735-4746.
School—(1953), N. Magnolia St., 10965. Tel: 914-735-2855. Mrs. Nancy Langehennig, Prin.
Lay Teachers 13; Students 275.
Catechesis/Religious Programs—Tel: 914-735-5489. Sr. Maryann Lawlor, O.P., D.R.E.
Students 550.
St. Aedan (1966), Rev. Msgr. Joseph P. Penna; Rev. Msgr. Edward J. Quirk, Pastor Emeritus; Rev. John M. Lagiouane.
Res., 23 Reld Dr., 10965. Tel: 914-735-7405; Fax: 914-735-4125.
Catechesis/Religious Programs—Tel: 914-735-2531.
Students 550.

Peekskill, Westchester Co., Assumption (1859) (Indian & Hispanic), Rev. Msgr. Francis J. Ansbro; Revs.

Arthur R. Leo; Steven E. Clark; Deacon James F. Roberts.
Res., 131 Union Ave., 10566. Tel: 914-737-2071; Fax: 914-737-1633. [CEM]
School—(1907), S. Division & First St., 10566. Tel: 914-737-0680.
Sisters 4; Lay Teachers 9; Students 230.
Catechesis/Religious Programs—Students 160.
Chapel—St. Joseph Home, Tel: 914-737-3373; Fax: 914-73-9614.

Pelham, Westchester Co., St. Catharine (1896), Rev. Peter F. Bannan.
Res., 25 Second Ave., 10803. Tel: 914-738-1491.
Catechesis/Religious Programs—Tel: 914-738-1332.
Students 270.

Pelham Manor, Westchester Co., Our Lady of Perpetual Help (1954), Rev. Msgr. Hugh D. Curran; Deacon Guy Pellegrini.
Res., 559 Pelham Manor Rd., 10803. Tel: 914-738-1449; Fax: 914-738-9454.
School—(1957), 575 Fowler Ave., 10803. Tel: 914-738-5158. Sr. Marie Morris, S.C., Prin.
Sisters 2; Lay Teachers 11; Students 225.
Catechesis/Religious Programs—Tel: 914-738-0670.
Students 485.

Phoenicia, Ulster Co., St. Francis de Sales (1902), Revs. Aloysius M. McPartland, M.S.; Hector O. LaChapelle, M.S.
Res., Main St., P.O. Box 25, 12464. Tel: 914-688-5617; Fax: 914-688-5630. [CEM]
Missions—Allaben, Ulster Co., Our Lady of Lourdes, Rte. 28, Allaben, 12480; Boiceville, Ulster Co., Our Lady of La Salette, Boiceville, 12412.

Piermont, Rockland Co., St. John (1852), Rev. John T. Dwyer.
Res., 895 Piermont Ave., 10968. Tel: 914-359-0078.

Pine Bush, Orange Co., The Infant Saviour (1951), Rev. Msgr. James S. Conlan; Rev. Martin Suitan.
Res., Holland Ave., P.O. Box 81, 12566. Tel: 914-744-2391.
Catechesis/Religious Programs—Tel: 914-744-9944.
Students 470.
Mission—Walker Valley, Ulster Co., Our Lady of the Valley, Walker Valley, 12588.

Pine Island, Orange Co., St. Stanislaus (1912) (Polish), Rev. Joaquim J. Olendzki.
Res., Pulaski Hwy., 10969. Tel: 914-258-4426. [CEM]

Pine Plains, Dutchess Co., St. Anthony (1958), Rev. John P. Gallant; Deacon Salvatore P. Patricola.
Res., 68 Poplar Ave., 12567. Tel: 518-398-7115.
Catechesis/Religious Programs—Students 170.

Plattekill, Ulster Co., Our Lady of Fatima, Revs. John Jaume, C.R.; Anthony Homar, C.R.
Res., P.O. Box 77, 12568. Tel: 914-564-4972.
Catechesis/Religious Programs—Students 185.

Pleasant Valley, Dutchess Co., St. Stanislaus Kostka (1903), Revs. Charles P. Quinn; Cyril Kuragama.
Res., Main St., P.O. Box 558, 12569. Tel: 914-635-1700; Fax: 914-635-8675.
Catechesis/Religious Programs—Tel: 914-635-8611.
Students 501.

Pleasantville, Westchester Co., Holy Innocents (1894), Revs. Raymond Daley, O.P.; James B. Sheridan, O.P.; John P. Sullivan, O.P.; Sean J. McConway, O.P.; Harry T. Donoghue, O.P. In res., Rev. Joseph Payne, O.P.
Res., 431 Bedford Rd., 10570. Tel: 914-769-0025; Fax: 914-747-2476. [CEM]
Catechesis/Religious Programs—Tel: 914-769-3297. Linda DeMarkey, D.R.E.
Students 495.
Mission—Pleasantville Park, Westchester Co., Our Lady of Pompeii.

Pocantico Hills, Westchester Co., The Magdalene (1894), Rev. Msgr. Donald J. Pryor; Rev. Msgr. Stephen J. Fitzgerald, Pastor Emeritus.
Res., 525 Bedford Rd., North Tarrytown, 10591. Tel: 914-631-0529.

Port Chester, Westchester Co.,

1—Our Lady of Mercy, (1854), Rev. Ralph V. Curcio; Rev. Msgr. Cornelius M. O'Brien, Pastor Emeritus; Revs. Rudolph F. Gonzalez; Thomas D. Mestriparampil (India); Joe Braganza (India); Sr. Lorraine Dougherty, P.B.V.M., Parish Min. In res., Rev. James T. Gorman.
Res., 260 Westchester Ave., 10573. Tel: 914-939-0612; Fax: 914-939-2807. [CEM]
Catechesis/Religious Programs—Tel: 914-937-5288.
Students 232.
Chapel—Sister of Charity, 18 Spring St., 10573. Tel: 914-937-2440.

2—Corpus Christi, (1925) (Italian), Revs. James A. McKenna, S.D.B.; Peter Granzotto, S.D.B.; John Blanco, S.D.B.; Jaroslaw Zaniewski, S.D.B.; Armand Quinto, S.D.B.; Deacons John B. Munnick, Jr.; Dan Ciccone.
Res., 136 S. Regent St., 10573. Tel: 914-939-3169; Fax: 914-939-7249.
School—135 S. Regent St., 10573. Tel: 914-937-4407; Fax: 914-937-6904.
Sisters, Daughters of Mary Help of Christians 4; Lay Teachers 15; Students 368.
Catechesis/Religious Programs—Students 275.

3—Our Lady of the Rosary, (1904) (Italian), Revs. Joseph Berruete, S.D.B.; Bill Burk, S.D.B.; Emiliano Chiriboga, S.D.B.
Church—22 Don Bosco Pl., 10573. Tel: 914-939-0547.
Res., 23 Nicola Pl., 10573. Tel: 914-937-5532.
School—(1945), Central Ave., 10573. Tel: 914-939-1021. Ms. Colleen Fitzgerald, Prin.
Lay Teachers 17; Students 210.
Chapel—Port Chester, Eucharistic Adoration.

4—Sacred Heart of Jesus, (1917), Rev. Henry G. d'Anjou.
Res., 229 Willett Ave., 10573. Tel: 914-939-1497.

Port Ewen, Ulster Co., Presentation of the Virgin Mary (1856), Rev. Paul A. Miller, C.SS.R.
Res., Fr. Kelley Dr., 12466. Tel: 914-331-0053.
Catechesis/Religious Programs—Students 200.
Mission—Esopus, Ulster Co., Sacred Heart, P.O. Box 219, Esopus, 12429. Tel: 914-384-6828. Rev. Eugene J. Grohe, C.SS.R.

Port Jervis, Orange Co., Immaculate Conception (1851), Revs. John J. Murray; John E. Rooney, Pastor Emeritus; Thomas J. Melican, Pastor Emeritus; Deacon Philip Bouwmans.
Res., 46 Ball St., Box 712, 12771. Tel: 914-856-8212; Fax: 914-858-8375. [CEM]
Catechesis/Religious Programs—Students 350.
Most Sacred Heart (1899), Rev. David A. De Simonc.
Res., 12 McAllister St., 12771. Tel: 914-856-1331; Fax: 914-858-0687.

Poughkeepsie, Dutchess Co.,

1—St. Peter, (1837), Rev. Leo R. Prince; Deacons James R. Hayes; George F. Cacchione; Albert J. Klein.
Res., 424 Violet Ave., 12601. Tel: 914-452-8580.
School—(1853), Tel: 914-471-6600.
Sisters of Charity of St. Vincent de Paul 3; Lay Teachers 15; Students 230.
Catechesis/Religious Programs—Students 250.
Chapels—Poughkeepsie, Convent of St. Peter; Poughkeepsie, Hudson River Psychiatric Center, Our Lady of the Holy Rosary, Tel: 914-471-2537.
Catechesis/Religious Programs—Students 250.

2—St. Mary, (1873), Revs. John J. Brinn, M.A.; John J. Hunter, M.S.; Deacon Richard Dingee. In res., Rev. Anthony Marian, Ph.D (India) Chap. Vassar Brothers Hospital.
Res., 269 Church St., 12601-4201. Tel: 914-452-8250; Fax: 914-452-8266.
Catechesis/Religious Programs—Tel: 914-471-4747.
Students 182.

3—Holy Trinity, (1921), Revs. Joseph P. LaMorte; James Cerbone. In res., Rev. Gamini E. Fernando (Sri Lanka) Chap., Green Haven Correctional Facility.
Res., 775 Main St., 12603. Tel: 914-452-1863; Fax: 914-452-1867.
School—(1952), 20 Springside Ave., 12603. Tel: 914-471-0520. Mrs. Mary Ann McGivney, Prin.
Sister Servants of the Immaculate Heart of Mary 3; Lay Teachers 9; Students 289.
Catechesis/Religious Programs—Tel: 914-471-5838. Sr. Maureen Davey, S.U., D.R.E.
Students 490.
Chapel—Holy Trinity Convent, 769 Main St., 12603. Tel: 914-454-2160.

4—St. John the Baptist, (1923), Rev. Richard A. La Monte, Admin.
Res., 1 Grand St., 12601. Tel: 914-452-4943.

5—St. Joseph, (1901) (Polish), Rev. Jan Jacmierski.
Res., 9 Lafayette Pl., 12601. Tel: 914-452-2333.
Chapels—Poughkeepsie, Rectory.; Cemetery Chapel, Evergreen Ave., 12601.

6—St. Martin de Porres, (1962), Revs. Brian E. McWeeney, D.Min.; Philip Tran. Pastoral Assoc.: Deacons Robert Jarmick; Victor Salamone; Patrick Hogan.
Res., 40 Cedar Valley Rd., 12603. Tel: 914-473-4222; Fax: 914-473-4223. [CEM]
School—38 Cedar Valley Rd., 12603. Tel: 914-452-4428. Mrs. Mary Jane Daley, Prin.
Lay Teachers 11; Students 281.
Catechesis/Religious Programs—Tel: 914-471-8728. Eileen Andros, D.R.E.
Students 735.

7—Our Lady of Mt. Carmel, (1910), Rev. Richard A. LaMorte.
Res., 11 Mt. Carmel Pl., 12601. Tel: 914-454-0340; Fax: 914-454-0393.
School—Tel: 914-471-2460. Mr. Gabriel F. Ponte, Prin.
Lay Teachers 15; Students 276.

Red Hook, Dutchess Co., St. Christopher (1875), Revs. Charles P. Coen; Peter Kulandai.
Res., 58 S. Broadway, 12571. Tel: 914-758-3732; Fax: 914-758-1214. [CEM]
Catechesis/Religious Programs—Tel: 914-758-5506.
Students 356.

Rhinebeck, Dutchess Co., The Good Shepherd (1901), Revs. George J. Kuhn; Ramon Madrid.
Res., 3 Mulberry St., 12572. Tel: 914-876-4583; Fax: 914-876-3912. [CEM]
Catechesis/Religious Programs—Tel: 914-876-7298.
Students 340.
Mission—Rhinecliff, Dutchess Co., St. Joseph, Rhinecliff, 12574.
Chapels—Astor Home for Children, Tel: 914-876-4081; Fax: 914-876-2020; Rhinebeck, Ferncliff Nursing Home, Tel: 914-876-2011; Fax: 914-876-4810; Rhinecliff, Holy Cross Campus of Pius XII School, Tel: 914-876-4084; Fax: 914-876-4199; Rhinebeck, Sisters of St. Ursula, Linwood Retreat House, Tel: 914-876-4178; Fax: 914-876-6544.

Rosendale, Ulster Co., St. Peter (1855), Revs. Paul Dmoch; Raphael Nwachukwu (Nigeria); Deacons John J. Larkin; John J. Liggan.
Res., 12472. Tel: 914-658-3117; Fax: 914-658-3540. [CEM]
School—(Old: 1890; New: 1965), Tel: 914-658-9209; Fax: 914-658-9827. Gerianne O'Rourke, Prin.
School Sisters of St. Francis (Milwaukee, WI) 1; Lay Teachers 10; Students 120.
Catechesis/Religious Programs—Tel: 914-658-8911.
Students 345.
Mission—High Falls, Ulster Co., Our Lady Help of Christians, J.F.K. Ln., High Falls, 12440.

Rye, Westchester Co., Resurrection (1880), Most Rev. Anthony F. Mestice, D.D.; Rev. Msgr. Daniel A. Peake; Revs. Jack Arlotta; Zacharias Nadackal, C.M.I. (India); Rev. Msgr. Thomas McMahon, Pastor Emeritus.
Res., 910 Boston Post Rd., 10580. Tel: 914-967-0142; 967-0254; Fax: 914-967-6494.
School—(1906), 116 Milton Rd., 10580. Tel: 914-967-1218; Fax: 914-967-0295.
Sisters 1; Lay Teachers 14; Students 277.
Catechesis/Religious Programs—Tel: 914-967-1270.
Students 752.
Chapel—Seton Hall Convent of the Sisters of Charity, Tel: 914-967-7085.

Saugerties, Ulster Co., St. Mary of the Snow (1833), Revs. Hugh R. Grace; Christopher H. Berean; Deacons Perry Bunyar; Donald Trees; Karl Pietkiewicz; Arnie Hyland.
Res., 36 Cedar St., 12477. Tel: 914-246-4913; Fax: 914-246-4996. [CEM]
School—(1881), 25 Cedar St., 12477. Tel: 914-246-6381. Miss Christine M. Molinelli, Prin.
Lay Teachers 9; Students 158.
Chapel—Saugerties, Parish Center.
Catechesis/Religious Programs—Tel: 914-246-7534.
Students 201.

Scarsdale, Westchester Co., Immaculate Heart of Mary (1912), Rev. Msgr. John J. Scanlon; Revs. Thomas J. Tolentino; Joseph S. Dietz; Deacons Ernest F. Salomone; Robert di Targiani.
Res., 8 Carman Rd., 10583. Tel: 914-723-0276; Fax: 914-722-0628.
School—(1928), 201 Boulevard., 10583. Tel: 914-723-5608; Fax: 914-723-8004. Robert W. Billings, Prin.
Lay Teachers 19; Students 260.
Catechesis/Religious Programs—Tel: 914-723-7593; Fax: 914-723-7209.
Students 850.
Our Lady of Fatima (1948), Rev. Msgr. Hugh F. McManus; Rev. Thomas J. McCaffrey; Deacons Francis Griffin; Michael J. Fox. In res., Rev. Gerard F. Rafferty; Irene Ingham Kollar, Pastoral Assoc.
Res., 5 Strathmore Rd., 10583. Tel: 914-723-7421; Fax: 914-723-7229.
School—(1950), Tel: 914-723-0460. Mrs. Barbara Stofko, Prin.
Lay Teachers 10; Students 202.
St. Pius X (1954), Rev. Msgr. Francis J. Melican; Rev. Francis J. Fajella, M.Ss.A.; Deacons Theodore A. Gaskin; William J. Hill.
Res., 91 Secor Rd., 10583. Tel: 914-725-2755; Fax: 914-725-2782.
School—(1957), 85 Palmer Ave., 10583. Tel: 914-725-0541; Fax: 914-725-2782.
Sisters 1; Lay Teachers 9; Students 151.

Shrub Oak, Westchester Co., Saint Elizabeth Ann

Seton (1963), Rev. Msgr. Edmund F. Fogarty; Revs. Peter A. Gelsomino; S. Kulandairajan.
Res., Main St., 10588. Tel: 914-528-3547.
School—Sr. Gabriel Miriam, S.C., Prin. Sisters 2; Lay Teachers 23; Students 550.
Catechesis/Religious Programs—Sr. Maureen Fitzpatrick, F.S.P., Prin.
Students 830.

Sloatsburg, Rockland Co., St. Joan of Arc (1966), Rev. John J. McKenna.
Res., 32 Eagle Valley Rd., 10974. Tel: 914-753-5239.
Catechesis/Religious Programs—Students 229.

Spring Valley, Rockland Co., St. Joseph (1894), Revs. Rudolph J. Eisler; Carl Sansaricq; Armand Iavarone, O.SS.T.
Res., 333 Sneden Pl. W., 10977. Tel: 914-356-0311; Fax: 914-352-8126.
School—(1927), 245 N. Main St., 10977. Tel: 914-356-0054. Mrs. Dorothy Kelly, Prin.
Lay Teachers 11; Students 215.
Catechesis/Religious Programs—Tel: 914-352-5686.
Students 400.

Stony Point, Rockland Co., Immaculate Conception (1889), Revs. Robert J. Staar; Michael Challinor; Deacon Philip Marino.
Res., 26 John St., 10980. Tel: 914-786-2742; Fax: 914-942-2614.
School—(1902), Main St., 10980. Tel: 914-786-5245.
Lay Teachers 10; Students 304.
Catechesis/Religious Programs—Tel: 914-786-5298.
Students 350.

Suffern, Rockland Co., Sacred Heart (1868), Rev. Msgr. Joseph P. Meehan; Rev. Ronald M. Vierling; Deacons John Baterbury; Robert J. Johnson; Joseph R. Verboys; Joseph A. Witt.
Res., 125 Lafayette, 10901. Tel: 914-357-0035.
School—(1909), 60 Washington Ave., 10901. Tel: 914-357-1684; Fax: 914-357-0318. Sr. Rose Andrew, Prin.
Sisters 3; Lay Teachers 19; Students 416.
Catechesis/Religious Programs—Tel: 914-357-6044.
Students 820.
Chapels—Dominican Sisters Convent, Tel: 914-357-1544; Good Samaritan Hospital, Tel: 914-368-5000; Tagaste Monastery, Tel: 914-357-0067.

Tappan, Rockland Co., Our Lady of the Sacred Heart (1952), Rev. John F. Dwyer.
Res., 120 King's Hwy., 10983. Tel: 914-359-1230; 359-1410.
Catechesis/Religious Programs—Tel: 914-359-1410.
Students 205.

Tarrytown, Westchester Co., Transfiguration (1896), Revs. Alfred J. Isacsson, O.Carm.; Leo Broniszewski, O.Carm. In res., Rev. Robert P. Tracy, O.Carm.
Res., 268 S. Broadway, 10591. Tel: 914-631-1672; Fax: 914-524-9352.
School—(1949), Prospect Ave., 10591. Tel: 914-631-3737; Fax: 914-631-6640. Mary Margaret Henshaw, Prin.
Sisters 1; Lay Teachers 14; Students 217.
Catechesis/Religious Programs—Tel: 914-631-2380.
Students 219.

Tivoli, Dutchess Co., St. Sylvia (1890), Rev. H. Theriault, M.Div.
Res., 104 Broadway, P.O. Box 95, 12583-0095. Tel: 914-757-2442. [CEM]

Tuckahoe, Westchester Co., Immaculate Conception (1853), Rev. Msgr. Anthony Maltese; Revs. Patrick A. Walsh, S.M.A.; Robert S. Ashman.
Res., 53 Winter Hill Rd., 10707. Tel: 914-961-3643; Fax: 914-961-0283. [CEM]
School—(1913), Tel: 914-961-3785; Fax: 914-961-6054. Dr. Elaine Farrell, Prin.; Dr. James Morgan, Asst. Prin.
Sisters 2; Lay Teachers 22; Students 483.
Catechesis/Religious Programs—Tel: 914-961-1076. Lynn Callahan, D.R.E.
Students 754.
Chapel—Sisters Convent, Tel: 914-961-3970.
Assumption (1911) (Italian), Rev. Msgr. Anthony Maltese.
Res., 53 Winter Hill Rd., 10707. Tel: 914-961-3643.
Church—100 Pleasant Ave., 10707. Tel: 914-961-0283.

Tuxedo, Orange Co., Our Lady of Mt. Carmel (1895), Rev. John F.X. Smith.
Res., Rte. 17, P.O. Box 697, 10987. Tel: 914-351-5284.

Valhalla, Westchester Co., Holy Name of Jesus (1896), Revs. Salvatore Matarazzo, O.P.; Leo Pelkington, O.P.; William Ryan, O.P.; Patrick P. Walsh, O.P.
Res., Two Broadway, 10595. Tel: 914-949-2323; Fax: 914-949-2367.
School—Tel: 914-948-1744. Judith Foster, Prin.
Lay Teachers 10; Students 110.
Catechesis/Religious Programs—Tel: 914-949-1422.
Students 486.

Verplanck, Westchester Co., St. Patrick (1843), Revs. Francis M. Newman, Pastor Emeritus; Andrew E. Kurzyna.
Res., 240 11th St., 10596. Tel: 914-737-0635. [CEM]
Catechesis/Religious Programs—Students 180.
Chapel—Convent, Seventh St., 10596. Tel: 914-737-1373.

Walden, Orange Co., Most Precious Blood (1894), Rev. Kenneth M. Loughman.
Res., 42 Walnut St., 12586. Tel: 914-778-5719.
School—Tel: 914-778-3028.
Sisters of St. Dominic (Sparkill) 2; Lay Teachers 8; Students 186; PreK 16.
Catechesis/Religious Programs—Tel: 914-778-7081.
Students 405.
Mission—Wallkill, Ulster Co., St. Benedict, Wallkill, 12589.

Wappingers Falls, Dutchess Co., St. Mary (1850), Rev. Msgr. Francis P. Bellew; Rev. Simon Panyadimai (India). In res., Most Rev. James P. Mahoney, D.D., Vicar of Dutchess County.
Res., 19 Clinton St., 12590. Tel: 914-297-6261; 6262; Fax: 914-297-3227. [CEM]
School—(1890 and 1955), Convent Ave., 12590. Tel: 914-297-7500. Sr. Miriam Gregory, Prin.
Sisters 2; Lay Teachers 12; Students 203.
Catechesis/Religious Programs—Tel: 914-297-7586. Patricia Manuli, D.R.E.
Students 637.
Chapel—Mt. Carmel, St. Mary Convent.

Warwick, Orange Co., St. Stephen (1865), Rev. Msgr. Bernard Corrigan; Rev. Peter J. Madori.
Res., 75 Sanfordville Rd., 10990. Tel: 914-986-4028. [CEM]
School—Tel: 914-986-3533.
Lay Teachers 16; Students 210.
Catechesis/Religious Programs—Tel: 914-986-2231.
Students 932.
Mission—Florida, Orange Co., St. Edward, (1881) Florida, 10921.

Washingtonville, Orange Co., St. Mary (1902), Rev. Msgr. James F. Cox.
Res., 2 Fr. Tierney Cir., 10992. Tel: 914-496-3730; Fax: 914-496-3159. [CEM]
Catechesis/Religious Programs—Tel: 914-496-4101.
Students 1,500.

Wesley Hills, Rockland Co., St. Boniface (1966), Rev. John Keaveney.
Res., 5 Willow Tree Rd., 10952. Tel: 914-354-7307.
Catechesis/Religious Programs—Students 437.

West Hurley-Woodstock, Ulster Co., St. John (Woodstock) (1860), Rev. George W. Hommel.
Res., 12 Holly Hills Dr., Woodstock, 12498. Tel: 914-679-7696; Fax: 914-679-8393.
Catechesis/Religious Programs—Students 320.
Mission—West Shokan, Ulster Co., St. Augustine, Watson Hollow Rd., West Shokan, 12494.

West Nyack, Rockland Co., St. Francis of Assisi (1964), Rev. Edward J. Weber; Deacon Donald O'Brien. In res., Rev. John Breen.
Res., 128 Parrott Rd., 10994. Tel: 914-634-4957; Fax: 914-639-6629.
Catechesis/Religious Programs—Tel: 914-638-4215.
Students 511.

West Point, Orange Co., Catholic Chapel of the Most Holy Trinity (1899), Revs. Edson J. Wood, O.S.A.; Owen J. Mullen; John T. McLoughlin.
Res., United States Military Academy, 699 Washington Rd., 10996. Tel: 914-446-5575; Fax: 914-446-6851.
Catechesis/Religious Programs—Tel: 914-446-2656.
Students 254.

White Plains, Westchester Co.,

1—St. Anthony, (1952) (Italian), Revs. Lawrence C. Inzeo; Peter C. Scaramuzzo; Deacon Arthur Manzione.
Res., 85 Harrison St., West Harrison, 10604. Tel: 914-948-1480; Fax: 914-948-0488.
School—(1957), Gainsborg Ave., West Harrison, 10604. Tel: 914-949-6986.
Sisters of Divine Compassion 5; Students 177.
Catechesis/Religious Programs—Tel: 914-949-0212.
Students 375.

2—St. John the Evangelist, (1868), Rev. Msgr. James M. McDermott; Rev. Msgr. William B. Delaney, Pastor Emeritus; Revs. Christopher H. Daly; Thomas J. Joyce; Donald V. O'Brien, S.J.; Thomas Kalarickal, C.M.I. (India).
Res., 148 Hamilton Ave., 10601. Tel: 914-949-0439; Fax: 914-949-0462. [CEM]
School—(1890), 146 Hamilton Ave., 10601. Tel: 914-949-4374.
Lay Teachers 9.
Catechesis/Religious Programs—Students 270.

3—St. Bernard, (1926), Revs. Edward M. Roos; Jose Vilaplana, S.J. (Spain); George Spiteri (Malta); Benedict J. Kuolt, Chap.
Res., 51 Prospect St., 10606. Tel: 914-949-2111; Fax: 914-949-6044.
Catechesis/Religious Programs—Students 511.

4—Our Lady of Mt. Carmel, (1902), Revs. Samuel J. Fayad, C.S.S.; Lodovico Nicolodi, C.S.S. In res., Rev. Leonard DellaBadia, C.S.S.
Res., 92 S. Lexington Ave., 10606. Tel: 914-948-5909.

5—Our Lady of Sorrows, (1929), Revs. Patrick J. Dunne; Ignatius Vu; Rev. Msgr. John K. Daly, Pastor Emeritus.
Res., 920 Mamaroneck Ave., 10605. Tel: 914-949-9819; Fax: 914-949-4148.
School—(1957), Tel: 914-761-0124; Fax: 914-761-0176. Sr. Mary Cecile, Prin.
Lay Teachers 13; Students 219.
Catechesis/Religious Programs—Tel: 914-761-5257.
Students 290.

Woodbourne, Sullivan Co., Immaculate Conception (1957), Rev. John J. Lynch.
Res., P.O. Box 66, 12788. Tel: 914-434-7643.
Catechesis/Religious Programs—Tel: 914-436-7370.
Students 215.

Wurtsboro, Sullivan Co., St. Joseph (1880), Rev. Hugh A. Dardis.
Res., Sullivan St., P.O. Box 277, 12790. Tel: 914-888-4522. [CEM]

Yonkers, Westchester Co.,

1—St. Anthony, (Nepera Park) (1923), Rev. Msgr. Harold J. Robertson; Revs. Philip J. Gagliano; John F. Fraser.
Res., 10 Squire Ave., 10703. Tel: 914-965-2733; Fax: 914-963-2285.
Church—1405 Nepperhan Ave., 10703.
School—Tel: 914-476-8489. Sr. Constance Christie, Prin.
Sisters 1; Lay Teachers 10; Students 205.

2—St. Anthony, (Willow St.). Closed. For inquiries for parish records contact Our Lady of Mt. Carmel, Yonkers.

3—St. Ann, (1947), Revs. Anthony M. Napolitano; John Carson; Lazar Sundararaj (India).
Res., 854 Midland Ave., 10704. Tel: 914-965-1555; 965-5584; Fax: 914-965-0678.
School—40 Brewster Ave., 10704. Tel: 914-965-4333. Sr. Joanne Shortall, Prin.
Lay Teachers 11; Students 287.
Catechesis/Religious Programs—Students 156.

4—St. Bartholomew, (1911), Rev. Msgr. Vincent T. Case; Rev. Msgr. Charles J. McManus, Pastor Emeritus; Rev. John Coppinger, S.A., Pastoral Assoc.; Deacon Robert A. Clemens.
Res., 15 Palmer Rd., 10701. Tel: 914-965-0566.
School—(1958), 278 Saw Mill River Rd., 10701. Tel: 914-476-7949. Sr. Ann Marie McMahon, P.B.V.M., Prin.
Sisters 2; Lay Teachers 13; Students 320.

5—St. Casimir, (1899) (Polish), Rev. Eugene A. Kosnik; Deacon John Radzilowicz.
Res., 239 Nepperhan Ave., 10701. Tel: 914-963-1254.
School—(1906), 259 Nepperhan Ave., 10701-3461. Tel: 914-965-2730. Sr. Roberta, C.R., Prin.
Sisters 3; Lay Teachers 8; Students 120.
Chapel—Convent of the Sisters of the Resurrection, Tel: 914-965-9332.

6—Christ the King, (1927), Revs. William F. DiRaffaele; John J. Foley; William Damroth.
Res., 740 N. Broadway, 10701. Tel: 914-963-7474; 963-7564; Fax: 914-963-7548.
School—(1955), 750 N. Broadway, 10701. Tel: 914-476-1711. Bernadette Dunne, Prin.
Sisters 3; Lay Teachers 12; Students 370.

7—St. Denis, (1910), Revs. Edward O'Halloran; Varghese Maliakal (India); Rev. Msgr. David B. Welsh, Pastor Emeritus.
Res., 470 Van Cortlandt Park Ave., 10705. Tel: 914-963-8468.
School—(1928), McLean Ave. & Lawrence St., 10705. Tel: 914-963-3438. Sr. John Maria Reeves, Prin.
Sisters 1; Lay Teachers 9; Students 252.
Catechesis/Religious Programs—Tel: 914-476-8077. Deacon Joseph Mulryan, D.R.E.
Students 110.

8—St. Eugene, (1949), Revs. James P. Griffin; Leonard F. Villa.

Res., 32 Massitoa Rd., 10710. Tel: 914-779-5460.
School—(1951), 707 Tuckahoe Rd., 10710. Tel: 914-779-2956.
Sisters 3; Lay Teachers 20; Students 500.
Catechesis/Religious Programs—Tel: 914-793-2158.
Students 165.
Chapel—Yonkers, Franciscan Sisters Convent.

9—IMMACULATE CONCEPTION, (1848) (Spanish-Arabic), Rev. Msgr. Hugh J. Corrigan; Revs. Sami Totah (Jordan); Virgilio Compentente (Philippines).
Res., 103 S. Broadway, 10701. Tel: 914-963-0156; Fax: 914-963-1803. [CEM]
School—(1860), 15 St. Mary's St., 10701. Tel: 914-965-7048; Fax: 914-423-2826. Bro. Robert Falcone, Prin.
Sisters 3; Lay Teachers 7; Students 238.
Chapel—Sisters of Charity, St. Mary Convent, 4 St. Mary's St., 10701. Tel: 914-963-1449.
Good Shepherd Arabic Community of St. Mary—Rev. Sami Totah (Jordan) Dir.

10—ST. JOSEPH, (1871), Revs. Patrick M. Carroll; Paul V. Sullivan; Canice Osuji (Nigeria); Deacon Abraham Santiago.
Res., 141 Ashburton Ave., 10701. Tel: 914-963-0730; 963-0780. [CEM]
Convent—Tel: 914-965-1351. Sisters of Charity Sisters 7.

11—ST. JOHN THE BAPTIST, (1903) (Italian-Irish), Revs. John W. Lennon; Peter A. Migueli; Peter McKeown; Deacon Martin J. Olivieri.
Res., 670 Yonkers Ave., 10704. Tel: 914-963-1486; Fax: 914-963-1503.
School—(1954), Tel: 914-965-2356.
Sisters 3; Lay Teachers 8; Students 360.
Catechesis/Religious Programs—Marian Caputo, D.R.E.
Students 175.
Chapel—Convent, 176 Sweetfield Circle, 10704. Tel: 914-965-1837.

12—ST. MARGARET OF HUNGARY, (1928), Rev. Gabriel Kiss, S.J., (Hungary) Admin.; Deacon Louis Juhasz.
Res., 76 Locust Hill Ave., 10701. Tel: 914-423-2211.

13—OUR LADY OF MT. CARMEL, (1913) (Italian), Revs. Terzo Vinci, S.A.C.; Barry Bossa, S.A.C.; Deacons Alfred R. Impallomeni; Nick A. Mazzei, Jr.
Res., 70 Park Hill Ave., 10701. Tel: 914-963-4766; Fax: 914-375-1069.
School—Mt. Carmel-St. Anthony, 85 Linden St., 10701. Tel: 914-476-8888; Fax: 914-375-1069. Mrs. Kathleen Conley, Prin.
Lay Teachers 10; Students 260.
Catechesis/Religious Programs—Tel: 914-423-8848.
Students 305.

14—OUR LADY OF THE ROSARY, (1907) (Portuguese), Revs. George Ribeiro, S.A.; Daniel O'Shea, S.A.; Bro. Nicholas De Gruccio, S.A. In res., Rev. Carmen Giuliano, S.A.
Res., 226 Warburton Ave., 10701. Tel: 914-963-0806; Fax: 914-963-3958.

15—ST. PAUL THE APOSTLE, (1923), Rev. Msgr. John A. Gallagher; Deacon James Hamilton; Sr. Eileen Treanor, Parish Ministry.
Res., 602 McLean Ave., 10705. Tel: 914-963-7330.
Church—Lincoln Pl., 10705.
School—(1949), 77 Lee Ave., 10705. Tel: 914-965-2165. Grace Mallardi, Prin.
Lay Teachers 10; Students 312.

16—ST. PETER, (1894), Rev. Edward J. Keehan; Rev. Msgr. John Carlin; Deacons Pedro Irizarry; Randy Velez. In res., Rev. Brendan McCabe.
Res., 91 Ludlow St., 10705. Tel: 914-963-0822; Fax: 914-968-9305.
School—(1894 and 1955), 204 Hawthorne Ave., 10705. Tel: 914-963-2314; Fax: 914-966-8822.
Sisters 2; Lay Teachers 10; Students 278.
Catechesis/Religious Programs—Tel: 914-476-7946.
Students 463.

17—SACRED HEART, (1891), Revs. Bernard M. Maloney, O.F.M.Cap., Guardian; Christopher Dietrich, O.F.M.Cap.; Thomas Murphy, O.F.M.Cap.; Peter McCall, O.F.M.Cap.; John B. Riordan, O.F.M.Cap., Community Vicar; Bros. Roger Deguire, O.F.M.Cap.; Richard Therrien, O.F.M.Cap.
Res., 110 Shonnard Pl., 10703. Tel: 914-963-4205; Fax: 914-476-4960.
School—(1893), 108 Shonnard Pl., 10703. Tel: 914-963-5318. Ms. Mary Teresa Singer, Prin.
Sisters 1; Lay Teachers 9; Students 269.
High School—34 Convent Ave., 10703. Tel: 914-965-3114; Fax: 914-965-4510. Mrs. Bernadette Dunne, Prin.
Sisters 1; Lay Teachers 21; Students 358.
Convent—27 Convent Ave., 10703.

18—MOST HOLY TRINITY, (1894) (Slovak), Rev. Anthony J. Pleho. In res., Rev. Anthony Pucci.
Res., 18 Trinity Pl., 10701. Tel: 914-963-0720.
Chapel—Franciscan Friars of the Renewal, 15 Trinity Pl., 10701. Tel: 914-476-7279. Rev. Andrew Apostoli, C.F.R.

19—OUR LADY OF FATIMA, (1977) (Portuguese), Revs. Francisco Jorge; Aderbal T. De Paula.
Res., Portuguese R.C. Center, 355 S. Broadway, P.O. Box 283, 10705. Tel: 914-423-9688; Fax: 914-476-9434.

Yorktown Heights, Westchester Co., St. Patrick (1898), Rev. Msgr. Dermot R. Brennan; Revs. Alan F. Travers; Louis Jerome; Deacon Paul V. Vorel.
Res., 137 Moseman Rd., 10598. Tel: 914-962-5050; 5051; Fax: 914-962-0595.
School—(1953), 117 Moseman Rd., 10598. Tel: 914-962-2211.
Sisters 2; Lay Teachers 22; Students 343.
Catechesis/Religious Programs—Tel: 914-962-5586; Fax: 914-962-3207.
Students 1,660.

Youngsville, Sullivan Co., St. Francis of Assisi, Rev. Edward Greene, O.F.M.
Res., 12791. Tel: 914-482-4640.

Yulan, Sullivan Co., St. Anthony of Padua (1907), Rev. Evan J. Greco, O.F.M.
Res., 12792. Tel: 914-557-8512; Fax: 914-557-3527. [CEM]
Mission—Pond Eddy, Sullivan Co., Sacred Heart, Pond Eddy, 12770.

Chaplains of Public Institutions

Military Installations

NEW YORK. *National Catholic Community Service.* (Cardinal Spellman Servicemen's Club), 487 Park Ave., 10022. Rev. Msgr. Richard Cahill, Dir.
New York City Veterans Administration Hospital, 406 First Ave., 10022. Rev. Edmund McCaffrey, O.Carm.

BRONX. *Veterans Administration Hospital,* 130 W. Kingsbridge Rd., 10460. Rev. Edward A. Kozlowski; Rev. Msgr. Charles P. Boccio.

MONTROSE. *Franklin D. Roosevelt Hospital.* Revs. Daniel F. Lynch, O.Carm.; Albert Daly, O.Carm.; William J. O'Donnell.

WEST POINT. *Stewart Field.* Rev. Nash P. Geany.
West Point. U.S. Military Academy, 10966.

Societies

NEW YORK. *Marine and Aviation Department.* Rev. Robert J. Brennan.
New York Fire Department. Rev. Msgr. Guy S. Vinci.
New York Police Department. Rev. Msgr. Joseph J. Zammit.
New York Postal Service. Rev. Jerome J. Murphy.
New York Sanitation Department. Rev. Msgr. John L. Guido.

YONKERS. *Yonkers Fire Department.* Rev. Msgr. Francis J. Melican.
Yonkers Police Department. Rev. John J. Foley.

Prisons

CITY. *Adolescent Remand & Detention Center.* Sr. Margaret McCabe; Rev. John Wilkinson, 11-11 Hazen St., East Elmhurst, 11370. Tel: 718-546-7223.
Anna M. Kross Center. Revs. George Dash, O.F.M.Cap.; Thomas Houle, O.F.M.Cap., 18-18 Hazen St., East Elmhurst, 11370. Tel: 718-546-3623.
Bronx House of Detention. Revs. Vincent P. McNamara; George J. Kuhn, 653 River Ave., Bronx, 10451. Tel: 718-579-4371.
Correctional Institution for Men. Sr. Mary O'Connor; Rev. Frank Passenant, 10-10 Hazen St., East Elmhurst, 11370. Tel: 718-546-5796.
George M. Motchan Detention Center. Rev. Joseph P. Kane, S.J., 15-15 Hazen St., East Elmhurst, 11370. Tel: 718-956-2611.
George Viero Center. Rev. Joseph Kane; Sr. Marie Hermann, 09-09 Hazen St., East Elmhurst, 11370. Tel: 718-204-5079, Ext. 2254.
James A. Thomas Center. Sr. Simone Ponnet; Rev. Thomas Houle, O.F.M.Cap., 14-14 Hazen St., East Elmhurst, 11370. Tel: 718-546-5425.
Manhattan Detention Center. Rev. Robert Spencer; Deacon Kenneth Radcliff, 125 White St., New York, 10013. Tel: 212-618-9538.
MTF. Rev. Reginald John, 1 Halleck St., Bronx, 10474. Tel: 718-579-8300.
North Infirmary Command. Rev. Lawrence E. Lucas; Sr. Amy Henry, 15-00 Hazen St., East Elmhurst, 11370. Tel: 718-546-1256.
Otis Bantum Correctional Center. Rev. Lawrence Lucas; Sr. Constance Kennedy, 16-00 Hazen St., East Elmhurst, 11370. Tel: 718-546-6617.
Rose M. Singer Center. Jane Leggett; Rev. Joseph Kane. Tel: 718-546-7498; Sr. Marion DeFeis, 19-19 Hazen St., East Elmhurst, 11370.
Spofford Juvenile Center. Rev. Joseph Pasciutto, 1221 Spofford Ave., Bronx, 10474. Tel: 718-579-0100. 19-19 Hazen St. E., Elmhurst, 11370.
West Facility. Rev. Frank Passenant, 16-06 Hazen St., East Elmhurst, 11370. Tel: 718-546-4495.

COUNTY. *Dutchess County Jail.* Rev. Ernest D'Onofrio, O.F.M., Tel: 914-297-5706.
Orange County Jail. Attended from St. John, Goshen. Tel: 914-294-5328.
Putnam County Jail. Attended by St. James, Carmel. Tel: 914-225-2079.
Rockland County Jail. Attended by St. Augustine, New City. Tel: 914-634-3641.
Sullivan County Jail. Attended by St. Peter, Monticello. Tel: 914-794-5577.
Ulster County Jail. Attended by Church of St. Joseph, Kingston. Tel: 914-338-1554.
Westchester County Jail. Revs. Brendan McCabe; Michael O'Shea, Box 389, Valhalla, 10595. Tel: 914-347-6132.

FEDERAL. *Federal Correctional Institution.* Rev. Michael O'Hara, O.M.I., Otisville, 10963. Tel: 914-386-5855.
Metropolitan Correctional Center. Rev. Juan Soles, 150 Park Row, New York, 10007-1779. Tel: 212-791-9130.

STATE. *Arthur Kill Correctional Facility.* Rev. Frank Naccarato, 2911 Arthur Kill Rd., Staten Island, 10309-1197. Tel: 718-356-7333.
Bayview Correctional Facility. Rev. George J. Dash, O.F.M.Cap., 550 W. 20th St., New York, 10011-2878. Tel: 212-255-7590.
Beacon Correctional Facility. Rev. Michael O'Hara; Deacon John O'Reilly, Box 780, Beacon, 12508-0780. Tel: 914-831-4200.
Bedford Hills Correctional Facility. Rev. Msgr. James T. Gorman, 247 Harris Rd., Bedford Hills, 10507-2499. Tel: 914-241-3100.
Downstate Correction Facility. Rev. Donald Licata; Deacon Anthony Gruerio, Box 445, Fishkill, 12524-0445. Tel: 914-831-6600.
Eastern Correctional Facility. Rev. Ramon Madrid; Deacon Franklyn Russell, Napanoch, 12458-0338. Tel: 914-647-7400.
Edgecombe Correctional Facility. Deacon Nicholas Mazzei, 611 Edgecombe Ave., New York, 10032-4398. Tel: 212-923-2575.
Fishkill Correctional Facility. Rev. Donald Licata, Box 307, Beacon, 12508. Tel: 914-831-4800.
Fulton Correctional Facility. Deacon Nicholas Mazzei, 1511 Fulton Ave., Bronx, 10457-8398. Tel: 718-583-8000.
Green Haven Correctional Facility. Rev. Msgr. Edward J. Donovan; Rev. Gamini Fernando, Stormville, 12582. Tel: 914-221-2711.
Lincoln Correctional Facility. Deacon Nicholas Mazzei, 31-33 W. 110 St., New York, 10026-4398. Tel: 212-860-9400.
Mid-Orange Correctional Facility. Deacon Ricardo Rosado; Rev. Augustine Graap, Warwick, 10990-0990. Tel: 914-986-2291.
Otisville Correctional Facility. Rev. Augustine Graap; Deacon Eugene Bormann, Box 8, Otisville, 10963-0008. Tel: 914-386-1490.
Parkside Correctional Facility. Deacon Nicholas Mazzei, 10 Mt. Morris Park W., New York, 10027-6395. Tel: 212-860-6835.
St. Clare's Secure Unit. Deacon Thomas Johnson; Rev. George Dash, O.F.M.Cap., 415 W. 51st St., New York, 10019. Tel: 212-459-8227.
Shawangunk Correctional Facility. Rev. Joseph Kenlon, O.F.M.Cap., Box 750, Wallkill, 12589-0750. Tel: 914-895-2081.
Sing Sing Correctional Facility. Rev. Ronald Lemmert; Sr. Antonia Maguire, 354 Hunter St., Ossining, 10562-5442. Tel: 914-941-0108.
Sullivan Correctional Facility. Rev. Stanislaus Ogbonna, P.O. Box AG, Fallsburg, 12733-0116. Tel: 914-434-2080.
Taconic Correctional Facility. Sr. Antonia Maguire; Rev. George Dash, O.F.M.Cap., 250 Harris Rd., Bedford Hills, 10507-2498. Tel: 914-241-3010.
Ulster Correctional Facility. Deacon Richard D. Dingee, Berme Rd., P.O. Box 800, Napanoch, 12458. Tel: 914-647-1670.
Wallkill Correctional Facility. Rev. Joseph Kenlon, O.F.M.Cap., Box G, Wallkill, 12589-0286. Tel: 914-895-2021.
Woodbourne Correctional Facility. Rev. Marcelo Blazquez Rodrigo, Pouch 1, Woodbourne, 12788. Tel: 914-434-7730.

Hospitals

BEACON. *Craig House Hospital.* Serviced by St. Joachim, Beacon. Tel: 914-831-1200.

BRONX. *Bronx Municipal Hospital Center, Abraham Jacobi Hospital, Nathan B. VanEtten Hospital.* Revs. Sancho Garrote; Robert Holick, M.H.M. Tel: 212-430-8771.
Bronx Psychiatric Center. Tel: 212-931-0600. Rev. James J. Cunningham.
Bronx-Lebanon Hospital Center. Tel: 212-590-1800; 518-5059. Revs. Robert Jeffers; Ruben Cammayo; Sr. Catherine Mary Doran, L.S.A.; Deacon Alfonso Ramos.
Calvary Hospital. Tel: 212-518-2114. Rev. Michael

Alessandro, Chap.; Sr. Mary Teresa O'Neill, R.S.H.M., Asst. Admin. Pastoral Ministries.
Lincoln Medical and Mental Health Center. Tel: 212-579-5000; 579-5059. Sr. Eileen Finnerty, O.S.U.; Rev. Abel Alvarez, O.S.U.
Montefiore Medical Center. Tel: 212-920-4997. Rev. Brendan McCabe, Dir. Pastoral Care.
North Central Bronx Hospital. Rev. Varghese Chethipuzha, Tel: 212-519-5000.
Our Lady of Mercy Medical Center. Revs. Frederick J. Becker, Vice Pres. Pastoral Svcs.; Thomas D'Angelo; Bernard Iheoha; Sr. Cathanne McVicar, S.M.; Sr. Joan Marie O'Leary, O.P.; Bro. Henry Owens, F.S.C.,
Pelham Bay Division, Sr. Kathleen Doyle, F.S.P., Tel: 212-920-9086; 920-9000.
St. Barnabas Hospital. Tel: 212-960-9000. Revs. Thomas McGarry; Godfrey Anyaka; Sr. Miriam Hanratty, O.P.; Deacon Victor Pino.
U.S.V.A. Medical Center. Revs. John F. Dwyer; Bernardine Saglimbeni; Gregory Little, Tel: 212-584-9000, Ext. 1878.
Union Hospital. Serviced by St. Barnabas Hospital. Tel: 212-200-2020.
Westchester Square Hospital. Serviced by Santa Maria Parish. Tel: 718-828-2380.

BRONXVILLE. *Lawrence Hospital.* Tel: 914-337-7300. Rev. Paul Vezhaparambil, C.M.I.; Sr. Agnes Regina Hughes, S.C.

CALLICOON. *Community General Hospital.* Tel: 914-887-5530. Rev. Edward Burke, O.F.M.

CARMEL. *Putnam Hospital Center.* Serviced by St. James the Apostle, Carmel. Tel: 914-279-5711.

CASTLE POINT. *Veterans Administration Medical Center.* Tel: 914-831-2000, Ext. 5453. Revs. Raymond Pavlick; John W. Borzuchowski; Robert Brennan; Donald Licata; Richard De La Pena.

COLD SPRING. *Julia L. Butterfield Memorial Hospital.* Serviced by Our Lady of Loretto, Cold Spring. Tel: 914-265-3642.

CORNWALL. *The Cornwall Hospital.* Serviced by St. Thomas of Canterbury, Cornwall-on-Hudson. Tel: 914-534-2547.

DOBBS FERRY. *Community Hospital of Dobbs Ferry.* Serviced by Sacred Heart, Dobbs Ferry. Tel: 914-693-0700.
St. Cabrini Nursing Home. Tel: 914-693-6800. Sr. Suzanne Poulin, C.N.D.; Rev. Patrick Boyle, O.F.M.

ELLENVILLE. *Ellenville Community Hospital.* Serviced by the Church of St. Mary & St. Andrew, Ellenville. Tel: 914-647-6080.

GOSHEN. *Arden Hill Hospital.* Serviced by St. John, Goshen. Tel: 914-294-5441.

HARRIS. *Community General Hospital of Sullivan County.* Serviced by St. Peter, Monticello, NY. Tel: 914-292-4525.

HARRISON. *St. Vincent Hospital and Medical Center of New York.* Rev. Joseph F. Cavoto, S.A., Dir. Pastoral Care, Tel: 914-967-6500.

HAWTHORNE. *Rosary Hill Home.* Tel: 914-769-0114. Rev. John Proppe, O.F.M.Cap.

KINGSTON. *Benedictine Hospital.* Tel: 914-338-2500. Sr. Kathleen Sharkey, O.S.B., Dir. Pastoral Care.; Revs. Martin Svitan; Lionel Trudel, M.M.
Kingston City Hospital. Tel: 914-331-3131. Rev. Cornelius C. Woulfe, C.S.Sp.

MANHATTAN. *Beekman Downtown - New York Infirmary.* Tel: 212-312-5000; 233-5300. Revs. Thomas McKeon, S.S.S.; Peter Ma.
Bellevue Hospital. Revs. John Logan, O.Carm.; Robert Greco, O.Carm.; Philip Marani, O.Carm.; Sr. Mary Elizabeth Steffens, R.G.S.
Beth Israel Medical Center. Tel: 212-420-2000. Rev. Edwin Conlin.
Bird S. Coler Memorial Hospital and Home. Tel: 212-838-8155. Revs. Harold F.X. O'Donnell, S.J.; Joseph N. Pershe, S.J.
Cabrini Medical Center. Tel: 212-995-6056. Rev. Andrew Sioleti, O.F.M., Coord. Patient/Chaplaincy Svcs., Chaplains: Revs. Raymond Pierini, M.M.; John Dias, C.S.C.; Sr. Jean Cook, I.C.M.; Sr. Sofia Unneta Wood, R.S.C.J.; Sr. Stephanie Kabacinksi, M.S.C.; Sr. Consolata Demma, M.S.C.
Columbia Presbyterian Medical Center. Revs. Ralph La Belle; Donald Johnson,
Allen Pavilion, Rev. Linus Iwuanyanwu; Deacon Miguel Granda.
Doctor's Hospital. Serviced by St. Joseph. Tel: 212-870-9000.
Goldwater Memorial Hospital. Tel: 212-750-6800; 750-6674. Chaplains: Rev. Timothy A. Healey, S.J.; Mrs. Margaret Karwoski; Mrs. Roselaine Simonis, Assoc. Chap.
Gouverneur Hospital. Tel: 212-374-4000. Rev. Dennis J. Sullivan; Sr. Clare Roche, P.B.V.M.
Gracie Square. Serviced by St. Jean Baptiste. Tel: 212-988-4400.
Harlem Hospital. Serviced by St. Mark. Tel: 212-491-8061.
Hospital for Special Surgery. Tel: 212-606-1000. Rev. Gregory Maturi, O.P.
Lenox Hill Hospital. Tel: 212-439-2547. Rev. Edmund Slattery, S.S.S.; Bro. Michael Perez, S.S.S.; Sr. Denise Lafferriere, C.N.D.
Manhattan Eye, Ear & Throat Hospital. Serviced by St. Vincent Ferrer. Tel: 212-838-9200.
Manhattan Psychiatric Center. Tel: 212-369-0500, Ext. 2530. Rev. Andrew Cuu Nguyen.
Medical Arts Center Hospital. Serviced by St. Patrick Cathedral. Tel: 212-755-0200.
Memorial Sloan Kettering Cancer Center. Tel: 212-639-5982. Revs. William Gannon, O.P.; Jerome Conroy, O.P.
Metropolitan Hospital. Tel: 212-230-6262. Rev. Michael J. Sala, S.J.
Mount Sinai Medical Center. Revs. George Baker; Matthew Eraly; Sr. Mary Damian Glenane, S.A.
New York Eye & Ear Infirmary. Tel: 212-673-3480.
New York Hospital. Tel: 212-746-4690. Revs. Vincent F. McHenry, O.P.; Paul B. Fu, O.P.; Robert P. Fitzsimmons, O.P.; Athanasius Sullivan, O.P.; Sr. Margaret T. Oettinger, O.P.
New York University Medical Center. Tel: 212-263-7300. Revs. Francisco Abaya; Albert J. DeLuca; John Gibson,
Hospital for Joint Disease, Serviced by Mary Help of Christians, 212-254-0058.
North General Hospital. Serviced by All Saints. Rev. Lawrence E. Lucas, Tel: 212-650-4511.
Rockefeller University. Tel: 212-570-8000. Rev. John T. Murphy, O.P.
St. Clare's Hospital & Health Center. Tel: 212-586-1500. Rev. John J. Donahue, C.S.C.; Sr. Pascal Conforti, O.S.U.
St. Luke's-Roosevelt Hospital Center. Tel: 212-523-2016.
Roosevelt Site, Rev. James McQuade, C.S.P.
St. Vincent Hospital. Tel: 212-790-7000. Revs. John Bickle, O.F.M., Dir. Pastoral Care; Praxid DeSilva; Sr. Eileen Lambert, O.S.F.; Sr. Bernadette Baer, S.C.; Rev. Jefferson Hammer.
Terence Cardinal Cooke Health Care Center. Tel: 212-360-1000. Revs. Keith Fennessy; Ronald Green; Sr. Joan Gannon, R.S.C.J.
U.S.V.A. Medical Center. Tel: 212-686-7500. Revs. Charles Lovato, S.F.; Edmund McCaffrey, O.Carm.; Francis C. Morgan, SS.CC.

MIDDLETOWN. *Horton Memorial Hospital.* Serviced by St. Joseph, Middletown. Tel: 914-343-2424.
Middletown Psychiatric Center Tel: 914-342-5511.

MONTROSE. *FDR DVA Hospital.* Revs. Daniel F. Lynch, O.Carm.; William J. O'Donnell.

MOUNT KISCO. *Northern Westchester Hospital.* Serviced by St. Francis, Mt. Kisco. Tel: 914-666-1200.

MOUNT VERNON. *Mount Vernon Hospital.* Rev. Isaac Agambi, Tel: 914-664-8000.

NEW HAMPTON. *MID Hudson Psychiatric Center.* Rev. John Haggerty, O.Carm., Senior Chap., Tel: 914-374-3171, Ext. 3601.

NEW ROCHELLE. *New Rochelle Hospital Medical Center.* Rev. John Muscat, Tel: 914-632-5000.

NEWBURGH. *St. Luke Hospital.* Serviced by St. Patrick. Tel: 914-561-4400.

NORTH TARRYTOWN. *Phelps Memorial Hospital.* Rev. Msgr. Robert Moore, Tel: 914-631-0720.

NYACK. *Nyack Hospital.* Serviced By St. Ann, Nyack. Shirley Blair, Dir. Pastoral Care, Tel: 914-358-6200.

ORANGEBURG. *Rockland Psychiatric Center.* Revs. Donald T. Driscoll; John Sullivan, O.P., Tel: 914-359-1000, Ext. 3589.

OSSINING. *Stony Lodge Hospital.* Serviced by St. Augustine, Ossining. Tel: 914-941-7400.

PEEKSKILL. *The Community Hospital.* Rev. Joseph G. Sexton, Tel: 914-737-9000.

POMONA. *Dr. Robert L. Yeager Health Center.* Susan Osborne, Pastoral Care, Tel: 914-354-0200, Ext. 2889.

PORT CHESTER. *United Hospital.* Serviced by Our Lady of Mercy, Portchester, NY. Tel: 914-939-0612.

PORT JERVIS. *Mercy Community Hospital.* Tel: 914-856-5351. Sr. Margaret Costa, R.S.M., Dir. Pastoral Care; Rev. Bernard McDonald; Sr. M. Audrey Hallahan, R.S.M.; Deacon John Nash.

POUGHKEEPSIE. *Hudson River Psychiatric Center.* Tel: 914-452-8000, Ext. 378. Rev. James J. LeBar; Deacon George Cacchone, Assoc. Chap.
St. Francis Hospital. Tel: 914-471-2000. Rev. Thomas McDonald, M.S., Dir. Pastoral Care, Pastoral Care Assocs.: Sr. Alice M. Howley, O.S.F.; Sr. Mary Rosaire, O.S.F.; Sr. Marie Colette, O.S.F.
Vassar Brothers Hospital. Tel: 914-454-8500. Rev. Anthony S. Marian.

RHINEBECK. *Northern Dutchess Hospital.* Serviced by Good Shepherd, Rhinebeck. Tel: 914-876-4583.

RYE. *Rye Psychiatric Hospital Center.* Serviced by Church of the Resurrection, Rye. Tel: 914-967-4567.

STATEN ISLAND. *Bayley Seton Hospital.* Tel: 718-390-6000. Rev. Edward J. Datty, S.A., Dir. Pastoral Care, Chaplains: Sr. Claire Marian Barton, S.C.; Bro. Kieran Cullen, S.A.
Doctor's Hospital of Staten Island. Serviced by St. Sylvester. Tel: 718-727-4639.
St. Vincent's Medical Center of Richmond. Tel: 718-876-1234. Sr. Therese Monaghan, O.P., Dir. Pastoral Care, Chaplains: Rev. Ralph Dawis; Bro. Vincent Basile, C.P.; Sr. Therese Monaghan, O.P.
Seaview Hospital and Home. Tel: 718-371-3000, Ext. 3284. Rev. Blase Kardos, O.F.M.Conv.
Staten Island University Hospital North. Rev. Simon Savarimuthu; Deacon Rosario J. Tirella.
Staten Island University Hospital South. Tel: 718-260-2000. Rev. John Francis Anthony.

SUFFERN. *Good Samaritan Hospital.* Tel: 914-357-3300. Sr. Sheila Mullins, O.P., Dir. Pastoral Care; Rev. Gerardo DeFillippes; Sr. Marie Tansey, S.C.; Sr. Anne Tonne, S.C.; Revs. George Mattioni, O.A.R.; Frank Cregon, O.A.R.

THIELLS. *Letchworth Village.* Tel: 914-947-2050. Rev. Joseph J. Smolinski; Sr. Mary Peter Farrelly.

TUXEDO PARK. *Tuxedo Memorial Health Care Center.* Tel: 914-351-4751.

VALHALLA. *Blythdale Children's Hospital.* Serviced by Holy Name of Jesus. Tel: 914-592-7555.
Westchester County Medical Center. Tel: 914-347-7000. Revs. Michael Connolly, O.F.M.Cap.; James Stewart, O.F.M.Cap.; Paul Tolve, O.F.M.Cap.

WARWICK. *St. Anthony Community Hospital.* Tel: 914-986-2276. Rev. Edward Sullivan, O.F.M.

WASSAIC. *Wassaic Development Center.* Revs. Sylvan J. Conover, O.F.M.Cap.; John Longweld, O.F.M.Cap.

WEST HAVERSTRAW. *Helen Hayes Hospital.* Rev. Anthony Luzzi, S.D.B.

WHITE PLAINS. *Burke Rehabilitation Center.* Tel: 914-948-0050. Revs. Patrick J. Dunne, Pastor; John Quinn; Sr. Laura Morgan, F.M.S.C.
New York Hospital - Cornell Medical Center. Rev. Richard Liew, Dir. Pastoral Care & Education.
St. Agnes Hospital. Tel: 914-681-4500. Sr. Mary Virginia Brady, R.D.C., Dir. Pastoral Care; Sr. Mary Vogl, Pastoral Assoc.; Revs. John Soraci; James Larkin; Sr. Mary Lusk, P.B.V.M.
White Plains Hospital. Tel: 914-681-0600. Rev. Benedict J. Kuolt.

WINGDALE. *Harlem Valley Psychiatric Center.* Tel: 914-832-6611, Ext. 1152. Rev. Anthony Donahue, O.F.M.Cap.

YONKERS. *St. John Hospital.* (Night Call-Christ the King, Yonkers, 914-963-7474). Tel: 914-964-4444. Rev. Neal Kerrigan, O.F.M.Cap.
St. Joseph Hospital. Tel: 914-378-7000. Sr. Mary Spano, S.C., Dir. Pastoral Care; Sr. Dolores Doyle, P.B.V.M., Pastoral Care Assoc.; Rev. Thomas Murphy, O.F.M.Cap.; Sr. Carolyn Posker, R.S.M.
Yonkers General Hospital. See Archdiocesan Directory for Parishes that Service Nursing Homes and Homes for the Aged. Tel: 914-964-7399. Rev. Anthony A. Pucci.

On Duty Outside the Archdiocese:
Most Rev.—
McCormack, William J., Society for the Propagation of the Faith
Reverend Monsignors—
Balvo, Charles D., Apostolic Nunciatura, Prague, Czech Republic Ecuador
Meier, John P., Catholic University of America, Washington, DC
O'Brien, William B., Daytop Village, 54 W. 40th St., New York, NY 10018
Reverend Fathers—
Brown, Charles, Congregation Pro, Doctrina Fidei
Carson, David L., O.F.M., Dept. of Veterans Affairs, Bath, NY
Chiang, John B., Oblates of Hong Kong
Dillon, Richard J., Fordham University, Fordham Rd., Bronx, NY 10458
Haggerty, Donald, Mt. St. Mary's Seminary, Emmitsburg, MD
Hartmann, Edward, Archdiocese of Fairbanks
Imbelli, Robert, Boston College
Irwin, Kevin W., Catholic University, Washington, DC
Kang, Paul, St. Andrew Kim, Orange, NJ
Kennedy, Robert T., Catholic University of America, Washington, DC
Komonchak, Joseph A., Catholic University of America, Washington, DC
Lonek, Stephen, Diocese of Wilmington
Malcolm, Dennis E.
Marino, Umberto J.
McDonald, Thomas M., Fordham University, Lincoln Center, NY
Murnion, Philip, National Pastoral Life Conference
O'Donnell, William J., V.A. Hospital, Montrose, NY
Pavone, Frank A., Priests for Life
Rafferty, Raymond, Netherlands
Rutler, George W., Legatus Apostolate
Serra, Dominic, St. Pauls Seminary, St. Paul, MN
Smarsh, Charles F., University of Maryland

Tou, John, Holy Family, Singapore
White, William, St, Vincent de Paul Seminary, Boynton Beach, FL
Whitson, Robley E., United Institute, Bethelem, CT
Young, William, Archdiocese of Santa Fe, St. Anthony's Church, P.O. Box 200, Questa, NM 87556

Military Chaplains:
Reverend Fathers—
Adams, Walter C., U.S.A.F.
Borkowski, Francis, U.S.A.
Csete, Ivan, U.S.N.
Deponai, Joseph J., U.S.A.
Gallagher, Michael F., U.S.N.
Hill, Philip, U.S.A.
Keeley, Patrick P., (Retired), U.S.A.F.
Kelly, John R., U.S.A.
Lindblad, Karl-Albert, U.S.N.
Mandato, Kieran, U.S.N.
McGeory, Peter, U.S.N.
O'Reilly, Edward M., U.S.A.
Panek, Robert M., U.S.N.
Pugliese, Francis A.
Sandi, Thomas P., U.S.A.F.
Zoshak, William H., U.S.A.F.

On Special or Other (Arch)Diocesan Assignment:
Reverend Monsignors—
Barrett, Harry C., New York Medical College, Valhalla, NY 10595
Vaughey, James K., Exec. Dir., Cemeteries, The Trustees of St. Patrick's Cathedral in the City of New York, Inc.
Reverend Fathers—
O'Malley, Francis P., M.S. in Education, St. Vincent Hospital and Medical Center of New York, NY 10014

Graduate Studies:
Reverend Fathers—
Baker, Richard
Donnoonny, George
Hull, Michael
King, Andrew
Lynch, Thomas
Murray, Gerald
Mustacuiolo, Gregory

Absent on Sick leave:
Most Rev.—
Vaughan, Austin
Reverend Fathers—
Coleman, John
Conlan, James
Conte, James W.
Coyne, James F.
Jordan, Patrick J.
McKay, Frank
Mulloy, Matthew F.
O'Connor, Maurice
Sandstrom, Philip J.
Slattery, Maurice

Absent on Leave:
Reverend Fathers—
Antony, Charles
Barjacoba, Peter
Brogan, William
Calabrese, Daniel
Calhoun, C. John
Carden, Robert J.
Cassiero, Daniel
Ciaravolo, Ronald
Clark, Andrew
Dalton, Howard
Doherty, John B.
Donahue, Joseph
Dumpson, Roland
Elmo, Francis E.
Eremito, Anthony
Geraghty, James
Gollinge, Donald
Hoeshmann, George
Hoffay, Thomas
Holhmann, George
Horst, Kenneth
Kovach, Raymond J.
LeBlanc, Paul
Malone, Donald
McGill, Joseph F.
McLucas, James
Mulloy, William
Mulvanerty, Thomas
Pane, Andrew
Peluso, Michael J.
Pipala, Edward A.
Plo, John
Quigley, Patrick
Quinn, James
Surace, Robert J.

Retired:
Most Rev.—
Ahern, Patrick, St. Thomas More, 65 E. 89th St., New York, NY 10128
Reverend Monsignors—
Arpie, Robert A., 5 Lyon Ct., Hampton Bays, NY 11946
Bardes, George F., Stephinac H.S., 950 Mamaroneck Ave., White Plains, NY 10605
Bourke, Myles M., Portsmouth Abbey School, Portsmouth, RI
Brady, Daniel J., St. Patrick's, 29 Cox Ave., Armonk, NY 10504
Brennan, Francis P., Terrence Cardinal Nursing Home, 1249 5th Ave., New York, NY 10029
Brennan, Francis M., 6 Beech Rd., Suffern, NY 10901
Brooks, John N., Box 26, Rifton, NY 12471
Byrne, Harry J., 222 E. 93rd St., Apt. 39E, New York, NY 10128
Carlin, John A., 5635 Netherland Ave., Bronx, NY 10471
Clyne, Vincent F., 376 Baden Pl., Staten Island, NY 10306
Cohalan, Florence, St. Agnes, 143 E. 43rd St., New York, NY 10017
Connors, Edward M., Stepinac High School, 950 Mamaroneck Ave., White Plains, NY 10605
Considine, John J., Cardinal Spellman High School, 1991 Needham Ave., Bronx, NY 10466
Costello, Francis M., 30 Inlets Blvd., Nokomis, FL 34275
Curtin, Richard B., Lucas Ave., Cottekill, NY 12419
Daly, John, 14309 A Canalview Dr., Delray Beach, FL 33484
Delaney, William B., 43 W. Orland Rd., Milford, CT 06460
Devlin, Joseph M., 190 Hollywood Ave., Bronx, NY 10465
DiBlasi, Augustine J., Stepinac High School, 950 Mamaroneck, White Plains, NY 10605
Doherty, John T., Stepinac High School, 950 Mamaroneck Ave., White Plains, NY 10605
Duffy, Francis X., 1083 Washington Green, New Windsor, NY 12553
Dugan, Edward T., St. Mary's, Main St., Marlboro, NY 12542
Dunne, Joseph A., 10777 Sample Rd., Coral Springs, FL 33065
Dwyer, Michael F., 3121 Ninth Ave. N., St. Petersburg, FL 33713
Finnerty, Edward G., 105 Wood St., Mahopac, NY 10541
Fitzgerald, Stephen J., 525 Bedford Rd., Pocantico Hills, NY 10591
Forrester, Henry W., 210 Sand Ln., Staten Island, NY 10306
Fowler, Eugene A., 19 Saddle Ridge Dr., Hopewell Junction, NY 12533
Gallagher, Thomas V., Our Lady of Consolation, 3103 Arlington Ave., Bronx, NY 10463
Geissler, Robert, 196 Azalea Cir., Jackson, NY 08527
Gillen, John J., St. John Newmann Residence, 5655 Arlington Ave., Bronx, NY 10471
Glynn, Francis J., Holy Family, 366 Watchogue Rd., Staten Island, NY 10314
Goodwine, John J., St. Patrick's Home, 66 Van Cortlandt Park, Bronx, NY 10463
Goodwine, Joseph G., 960 Palm View Rd., Naples, FL 33942
Gordon, John, St. Margaret Mary, 560 Lincoln Ave., Staten Island, NY 10306
Green, Gerard A., 66 Van Cortlandt Park, Bronx, NY 10463
Guido, William F., 121 Egbert Ave., Staten Island, NY
Hammer, Edmond, Bethel Nursing Home, Ossining, NY 10562
Hanlon, James J., 150 Riverside Dr., New York, NY 10024
Harrington, John M., Immaculate Conception, Stony Point, NY 10980
Heide, Herman L., Stepinac High School, 950 Mamaroneck Ave., White Plains, NY 10605
Higgins, William, Our Lady of Consolation, 3103 Arlington Ave., Bronx, NY 10463
Jablonski, Stanislaus, St. Valentine, 810 E. 221 St., Bronx, NY
Jeffers, Vincent W., Stepinac High School, 950 Mamaroneck Ave., White Plains, NY 10605
Keating, James V., St. Joseph, 242 Wall St., Kingston, NY 12401
Kelleher, Stephen, Kateri Nursing Home, 150 Riverside Dr., New York, NY 10024
Kelly, George A., 107-10 Shore Front Pkwy., Rockaway Beach, NY 11694
Kelly, Robert J., 644 Clawson St., Staten Island, NY 10306
Keogh, John, 4 Dogwood Rd., Hampton Bays, NY 11946
Keogh, Thomas J., NY 11946
King, William, St. Michael's Church, 424 W. 34th St., New York, 10001
Leonard, Francis, Mt. Alverno Center, 20 Grand St., Warwick, NY 10990
Loftus, Robert, Kateri Nursing Home, 150 Riverside Dr., New York, NY 10024
Mahoney, Francis, 141 Port Royal Dr., Toms River, NJ 08757
Marbach, Joseph, 3410 Amalfi Dr., W. Palm Beach, FL 33417
Marinacci, Nicholas, St. Patrick's Old Cathedral, 263 Mulberry St., New York, NY 10012
Mazziotta, Robert R., P.O. Box 705, Philmont, NY 12565
McCormack, Robert, 150 Theodore Fremd Ave., Rye, NY
McDonnell, James T., New Horizens, 400 Hemenway St., Marlbourgh, MA 01752
McEnaney, Owen J., Kateri Nursing Home, 150 Riverside Dr., New York, NY 10024
McMahon, Thomas, Stepinac High School, 950 Mamaroneck Ave., White Plains, NY 10605
McMahon, William J., Holy Spirit, 1969 Crompond Rd., Cortland Manor, NY 10566
McManus, Charles J., St. Gabriel, 3250 Arlington Ave., Bronx, NY 10461
Montano, Edward J., 4 Fiero Rd., P.O. Box 152, Malden-on-Hudson, NY 12453
Moore, Robert E., 130 Beekman Ave., North Tarrytown, NY 10591
Narkun, Peter P., Cardinal Hayes High School, 650 Grand Concourse, Bronx, NY 10451
Netter, Edmund W., c/o Joseph Robertson, 275 Amberfield Dr., NJ 08054
O'Brien, Cornelius M., Stepinac High School, 950 Mamaroneck Ave., White Plains, NY 10605
O'Connor, James, St. Francis Gardens, 904 Las Lomas Rd., Albuquerque, NM 87102
Pavis, Victor S., Cardinal Hayes High School, 650 Grand Concourse, Bronx, NY 10451
Potocek, Cyril J., Holy Cross, 118 Beekman Ave., N., Tarrytown, NY 10591
Quinn, Andrew, Sacred Heart, 981 Castleton Ave., Staten Island, NY 10310
Quinn, John J., St. Joseph's Seminary, Yonkers, NY 10704
Quinn, Joseph J., John Paul II Residence, 603 First Ave., New York, NY 10016
Raimondo, Joseph, St. Gregory the Great, 215 Halstead Ave., Harrison, NY 10528
Reisig, William E., 1230 Lafayette Ave., Bronx, NY 10474
Reynolds, Edward, John Paul II Residence, 603 First Ave., New York, NY 10016
Richard, Eugene, Blessed Sacrament, 15 Shea Pl., New Rochelle, NY 10805
Rigney, James, 40 Dick Finn Rd., P.O. Box 8192, New Fairfield, CT 06812
Rigney, Raymond P., Stepinac High School, 950 Mamaroneck Ave., White Plains, NY 10605
Rinschler, William, 445 21st St., New York, NY 10011
Rooney, Hugh J., Our Lady of Consolation Residence, 3103 Arlington Ave., Bronx, NY 10463
Rossbach, George F., 45-315 Lilipuna Rd., B202, Kaneoke, HI 96744
Rosselli, Charles, 9765 B Tabebuia Tree Dr., Boynton Beach, FL 33436
Ryan, Gerald J., St. Luke's, Bronx, NY
Santulin, Joseph M., John Paul II Residence, 603 First Ave., New York, NY 10016
Schroeder, Walter L., 525 Bedford Rd., North Tarrytown, NY 10591
Shevlin, John G., Immaculate Conception, Bangal, NY
Snee, Joseph T.V., St. Bernard, 328 W. 14th St., New York, NY 10014
Sullivan, Daniel L., Blessed Sacrament, 30 Manor Rd., Staten Island, NY 10310
Vier, Henry J., St. Raymond, 1759 Castle Hill Ave., Bronx, NY 10462
Walsh, James J., 950 Mamaroneck Ave., White Plains, NY 10605
Welsh, David B., 470 Van Cortlandt Park Ave., Yonkers, NY 10705
Wilders, James G., Mary Manning Walsh Home, 1339 York Ave., New York, NY 10021
Reverend Fathers—
Adamo, Joseph, Our Lady of Consolation, 3103 Arlington Ave., Bronx, NY 10463
Alessandro, Michael J., 1496 Commonwealth Ave., Bronx, NY 10460
Basile, Nicholas F., Our Lady of Mt. Carmel, 627 E. 187 St., Bronx, NY 10458
Breen, John F., St. Francis of Assisi Rectory, 128 Parrott Ave., W. Nyack, NY 10994
Brennan, Robert J., Chelsea Ridge Apartments, 4B Winthrop Ct., Wappingers Falls, NY 12590

Brogan, Edward P., Our Lady of Consolation, 3103 Arlington Ave., Bronx, NY
Buttinelli, Anthony, Via Valle della Storta 75, Rome, 00123
Cavanaugh, John L., Stepinac High School, 950 Mamaroneck Ave., White Plains, NY 10605
Cholette, John B., 6606 Fairpines Rd., Chesterfield, VA 23832
Connolly, Martin J., John Paul II Residence, 603 First Ave., New York, NY 10016
Conti, John P., 537 Third St., Brooklyn, NY 11215
Crotty, John M., 660 Americana Dr., Annapolis, MD 21403
Cusma, Joseph S., 22584 Vistawood Way, Boca Raton, FL 33428
D'Anjou, Henry G., Stepinac High School, 950 Mamaroneck Ave., White Plains, NY 10605
D'Antonio, Anthony, Our Lady of Mt. Carmel, 627 E. 187 St., Bronx, NY 10458
D'Auriol, Vincent, Sts. Peter & Paul Parish, 833 St. Ann Ave., Bronx, NY 10456
Dale, James E., Cabrini Nursing Home
Darby, Thomas J., John Paul II Residence, 603 First Ave., New York, NY 10016
Derrenbacher, James W., St. John Evangelist, 915 Rte. 212, Woodstock Rd., Saugerties, NY 12477
Doersam, Carl G., Ferncliff Nursing Home
Donachie, Joseph J., 900 Intervale St., Bronx, NY 10459
Doyle, Philip R., Box 1088, Carmel, NY 10512
Duffy, Edwin, c/o Corroon, 612 Purchase, Rye, NY 10580
Dunn, Robert T., 854 Hudis St., Rohnert Park, CA 94928
Fagnani, Anthony G., 357 Yankee Lake Rd., Wurtsboro, NY 12790
Fiorillo, Antimo, 2352 St. Raymond's Ave., Bronx, NY 10462
Flannery, Michael, 8200 Shore Front Pkwy., Rockaway Beach, NY 11693
Fleming, John F., 1083 Washington Green, New Windsor, NY 12553
Flynn, John J., 21 Catlin Ave., Staten Island, NY 10304
Fogarty, Daniel, 13222 Salmon River Rd., San Diego, CA 92129
Gallagher, Eugene P., 40 W. Point Hwy., Highland Falls, NY 10928
Giammarino, George, 1789 Seminole Ave., Bronx, NY 10461
Grace, John, Mary Manning Walsh Home, 1339 York Ave., New York, NY 10021
Gussoni, Lino, Via Rodini Tedeschi 19, Piacenza, 29100 Italy
Halpin, Leo F., 5 Tanglewylde Ave., Apt. 6H, Bronxville, NY 10708
Holihan, John W., c/o Alandy, 18 DeKarla Dr., Middletown, NJ 07748
Jacolino, Dominic, John Paul II Residence, 603 First Ave., New York, NY 10016
Jenko, Aloysius, New York, NY 10016
Joyce, Richard C., St. Theresa Home, 120 Highland Ave., Middletown, NY 10940
Kelly, William E., Our Lady of Consolation, 3103 Arlington Ave., Bronx, NY 10463
Kennedy, William J., John Paul II Residence, 603 First Ave., New York, NY 10016
Larkin, John P., John Paul II Residence, 603 First Ave., New York, NY 10016
Laurenzano, Roch M., 8753 Como Lake Dr., Jacksonville, FL 32216
Magee, Andrew T., John Paul II Residence, 603 First Ave., New York, NY 10016
Maher, John J., 43 Hearth Dr., New Windsor, NY 10704
McGann, Joseph F., P.O. Box 2593, Montauk, NY 11954
McHall, Charles P., 266 Near Rd., Red Hook, NY 12571
McPeak, William J., Our Lady of Consolation, 3103 Arlington Ave., Bronx, NY 10463
McShane, Vincent, Stepinac High School, 950 Mamorneck Ave., White Plains, NY 10605
Meade, John F., 65 Wright Ave., Malverne, NY 11565
Miller, Frederick J., 56 Sprague Ave., Staten Island, NY 10307
Minielli, Anthony, Via Colombo 9, 70028 Sannicandro, Bari
Molony, Francis, Our Lady of Consolation Residence, 3103 Arlington Ave., Bronx, NY 10463
Moran, Thomas J., Ferncliff Nursing Home, 52 River Rd., Rhinebeck, NY 12572
Moriarty, James J., St. John the Evangelist, Pawling, NY
Murphy, Jerome J., Ferncliff Nursing Home, 52 River Rd., Rhinebeck, NY 12572
Newman, Francis M., 174 Westchester Ave., Buchanan, NY
O'Brien, Michael, c/o Kathleen O'Brien, 108 New Canaan, Norwalk, CT 06850
O'Hara, Eugene R., Our Lady of Consolation Residence, 3103 Arlington Ave., Bronx, NY 10463
O'Keefe, Thomas E., Stepinac High School, 950 Mamaroneck Ave., White Plains, NY 10605
O'Shea, Joseph J., St. Helena, 1315 Olmstead Ave., Bronx, NY 10462
O'Toole, Kenneth E., 15 St. John's Pl., Chappaqua, NY 10514
Pacacha, Joseph E., 1820 Smith Dr., N., Titesville, FL 32780
Parsons, Harold J., 227 Sunset Ave., Island Park, NY 11558
Phillips, Thomas, 292 Noxon Rd., Poughkeepsie, NY 12603
Pisanelli, Humbert, Our Lady of Consolation, 3103 Arlington Ave., Bronx, NY 10463
Quirk, Edward J., c/o Jeanne Quirk, 7 Normandy Village, Nanuet, NY 10954
Sheridan, Eugene, HC 1, Box 34, Greenfield Park, NY 12435
Sullivan, Paul V., St. Joseph, 141 Ashburton Ave., Yonkers, NY 10701
Szarama, Roman J., 32 Massitoa Blvd., Yonkers, NY 10710
Tobin, James B., Stepinac High School, 950 Mamaroneck Ave., White Plains, NY 10605
Tubridy, James J., 1214 Springdale Rd., Croton-on-Hudson, NY 10520
Vala, John B., John Paul II Residence, 605 First Ave., New York, NY 10016

Permanent Deacons:
Abbamont, Thomas J., St. Ursula, Mount Vernon
Almanzar, Andres A., St. John Vianney, Bronx
Alvarado, William, St. Columba, Hopewell Junction
Anderson, John J., Plant City, FL
Armo, John, St. John Evangelist, Mahopac
Attridge, James C., St. James the Apostle, Carmel
Aviles, Stanley, St. Denis, Hopewell Junction, NY
Banker, Howard A., Our Lady of Assumption, Bronx
Barbieri, Nicola A., Our Lady of Pompeii, Dobbs Ferry
Baterbury, John J., Sacred Heart of Jesus, Suffern
Battersby, William L., St. Mary, Mount Vernon
Bellacicco, John A., St. Augustine, Highland
Bello, Rafael J., Our Lady of Guadalupe, South Manhattan
Bernal, Enrique, Our Lady of Guadalupe, South Manhattan
Biasotti, John C.
Biskup, William E., Regina Coeli, Hyde Park
Blake, George W., Block Island, RI
Bonanno, Joseph M., Regina Coeli, Hyde Park
Bormann, Eugene, St. Anastasia, Harriman
Borsavage, Charles T., St. James The Apostle, Carmel
Bouwmans, Philip R., Immaculate Conception, Port Jervis
Brigande, Vincent G., St. Charles, Staten Island
Brockmann, Peter, Sacred Heart, Monroe
Brown, James A., SS. John & Paul, Larchmont
Bruno, Gaspare F., St. Elizabeth Ann Seton, Shrub Oak
Buckley, John J., St. Francis of Assisi, Newburgh
Bunyar, Perry A., St. Mary of the Snow, Saugerties
Buonocore, Dominc A., St. Paul, Congers
Burke, Eugene F., St. Gabriel, Bronx
Burnett, Robert V., Antigua, West Indies
Burns, James T., Sacred Heart, Monroe
Cacchione, George F., St. Peter, Poughkeepsie
Calafiore, Michael R., St. Charles, Staten Island
Calimano, Ross J., Our Lady Queen of Peace, Staten Island
Camacho, Ismael, Joan of Arc, Bronx, NY
Camacho, Vidal J., St. Elizabeth of Hungary, FL
Canals, Dhoel M., Holy Family, Bronx
Carlino, Frank R., St. Columba, Chester
Carroll, Harold N., St. Charles Borromeo, Gardiner
Casadone, Dominic G., Sacred Heart, Newburgh
Cassaneto, Anthony P., St. Theresa of the Child Jesus, Bronx
Castellanos, Luis, Miami Beach, FL
Charlesworth, Myles J., Our Lady of Lourdes Parish, Raleigh, NC
Check, Raymond P., Richmond, VA
Ciccone, Daniel J., Corpus Christi, Port Chester
Clemens, Robert A., St. Bartholomew, Yonkers
Collins, George J., St. Thomas More, Boynton Beach, FL
Conner, Albert C., Annunciation, Crestwood
Coppola, John J., St. Columbanus, Peekskill
Cosme, Felix, Georgia
Cotto, Angel L., Caguas, PR
D'Aiello, Joseph, Holy Rosary, Bronx
D'Arconte, Benjamin, Sacred Heart, Hartsdale
Darlestin, Leones J., Holy Name of Jesus, Manhattan
Dauerer, Walter P., St. Denis, Hopewell Junction
Daur, Raymond, Our Lady of Mercy, Port Chester
De Jesus, Jose L., St. Ann, Ossining
De Los Santos, German, Incarnation, North Manhattan
De Maio, Donald J., Naples, FL
De Marco, Carmine J., Holy Name of Jesus, New Rochelle
De Meis, John, Italo-Greek Albanian Community
Degenhardt, Carl, St. Ursula, Mount Vernon
Del Campo, Francis, Our Lady Rosary, Port Chester
Delgado, Luis, Our Lady of Angels, Bronx
Deschler, Bernard M., Breezy Point, NY
di Targiani, Robert, Immaculate Heart of Mary, Scarsdale
Dingee, Richard D., Ulster Correctional Facility, Napanoch
Doherty, Joseph, St. Joseph, Kingston
Dringus, William L., East Greenbush, NY
Droulette, Donald L., St. Joseph, Kingston
Eccleston, Arthur W., Our Lady of Good Counsel, Staten Island
Edgerton, John M., St. Patrick's Parish, Tarpon Springs, FL
Esposito, Robert A., St. John the Evangelist, Mahopac
Estela, Jorge, Our Lady of Mercy, Bronx
Feliciano, Ulises, Tagaste Monastery, Suffern, NY
Fernandez, Roberto, St. Raymond, Bronx
Ferraiuolo, Anthony P., St. Joseph, New Windsor
Ferreira, Emetrio
Fien, Robert A., Our Lady of Mercy, Port Chester
Fontanez, Luis, Holy Cross, Bronx
Fox, Michael J., Our Lady of Fatima, Scarsdale
Francis, James, Our Lady of Pity, Bronx
Frohbose, John M., Our Lady of Mt. Carmel, Middletown
Frohmiller, Richard J., St. Joseph, Kingston
Gallagher, Daniel J., Palm Beach, FL
Garcia, Rene, Our Lady of Guadalupe, NY
Gaskin, Theodore A., St. Pius X, Scarsdale
Giglio, Pasquale, St. Ursula, Mount Vernon
Glover, William, St. Patrick, Newburgh
Gohl, Frank, Regina Coeli, Hyde Park
Gontcharuk, Robert, Holy Name of Jesus, New Rochelle
Gonzalez, Faustino, Santiago de Compostella, Spain
Gonzalez, Ismael, Cayey, PR
Gorzka, Stephen S.
Graf, Joseph J., St. Margaret Mary, Staten Island
Granda, Miguel E., St. Paul, Manhattan
Griffin, Francis J., Our Lady of Fatima, Scarsdale
Grosso, Edward, Assumption, Maybrook
Gruerio, Anthony G., St. James, Carmel
Hafemann, Joseph R., St. Joachim, Beacon
Haight, Peter R., Sacred Heart, Newburgh
Hamilton, Eugene R., St. Peter, Haverstraw
Hamilton, James J., St. Paul the Apostle, Yonkers
Hanson, Lee, Sun City West, AZ
Haughey, Patrick, J., St. Patrick's Cathedral, Manhattan
Hayes, James R., St. Peter, Poughkeepsie
Hennessy, John L., St. Barnabas, Bronx
Hernandez, Narcisco, Our Lady Queen of Martyrs, Manhattan
Hill, William J., St. Pius X, Scarsdale
Hodges, Raymond, Our Savior, Pine Bush
Hogan, Patrick J., St. Martin de Porres, Poughkeepsie
Hooghuis, Joseph, St. Patrick, Staten Island
Hopkins, Farrell J., Key West, FL
Horvath, Robert J., St. Thomas More Parish, Sarasota, FL
Howley, Herbert, Greenwich, NY
Hudson, Alan A.
Impallomeni, Alfred R., Our Lady of Mount Carmel, Yonkers
Ippolito, Steve J.
Irizarry, Pedro, St. Peter, Yonkers
Jarmick, Robert E., St. Martin de Porres, Poughkeepsie
Jean-Gilles, Gabriel
Johnson, Robert, Sacred Heart, Suffern
Johnson, Thomas R., St. Joseph, Greenwich Village
Juhasz, Lajos, St. Margaret of Hungary, Yonkers
Kawula, Lawrence, Sacred Heart, Newburgh, NY
Kazimir, Martin, St. Mary, Fishkill
Kelleher, John C., St. Catharine, Blauvelt
Klein, Albert J., St. Peter, Poughkeepsie
Klein, John P., St. Mary
Knack, Lawrence F.
Knight, Charles C., Marysville, OH
Koch, George J., Sun City West, AZ
Kollar, John J.
Kowalik, Raymond J., (On Leave)
Lagotta, Anthony A., Our Lady of Mt. Carmel, St. Benedicta, Staten Island
Larkin, John J., St. Peter, Rosendale
Laurato, Vincent I., St. Barnabas, Bronx
Le Blanc, Vincent F.
Leasiolagi, Taulafoga, St. John Vianney, Bronx

Li Greci, Christopher, St. Michael Chapel, Manhattan
Lieby, Joseph, St. Joseph, New Windsor
Liggan, John J., St. Peter, Rosendale
Longo, Ralph D., Holy Rosary, Greenwood Lake
Lopez, Domingo, St. Joseph of the Holy Family, Harlem
Lugo, Alejandro, St. Cecilia, Manhattan
Maher, James, St. Aedans, Pearl River, NY
Maldonado, Eusebio
Maloney, John R., St. Anthony, Nanuet
Manning, Cornelius J., St. Barnabas, Bronx
Manzione, Arthur, St. Anthony of Padua, W. Harrison, NY
Marino, Philip A., Immaculate Conception, Stony Point
Maroon, Phillip J., St. Rita, Staten Island
Martinez, Luis A., Our Lady Queen Angels, Manhattan
Martinez, Rafael, Caguas, PR
Mazza, Albert, Holy Name of Mary, Croton-on-Hudson, NY
Mazzei, Nicholas A., Our Lady of Mt. Carmel, Yonkers
McCabe, Michael G., St. Augustine, New City
McCarthy, Richard, Sacred Heart, Monroe
McCormick, Daniel F., Virginia Beach, VA
McGowan, George J., Visitation B.V.M., Bronx
McIvor, Brian F.
McKenna, Francis J., Toms River, NJ
McNeill, Lawrence C., Holy Cross, Manhattan
McSherry, John W., St. Paul, Congers
Meier, Anthony C., Raleigh, NC
Mercado, Carlos V., Immaculate Conception, Bronx
Mirando, Wilfredo, St. Lucy, Bronx
Mitchell, Richard F., St. Clare, Staten Island
Monegro, Juan, Incarnation, Manhattan
Morillo, Felix M., Holy Spirit, Bronx
Morrette, Thomas, SS. John & Mary, Chappaqua
Mueller, William J., St. Mary Star of the Sea, Bronx
Mulryan, W. Joseph, St. Denis, Yonkers
Munnick, John B., Corpus Christi, Port Chester
Munoz, Jose A., Prison Chap., Scranton, PA
Murphy, John G., St. Frances de Chantal, Bronx
Nash, John J., Mercy Hospital, Port Jervis
Nielsen, William, St. Thomas of Canterbury, Cornwall-on-Hudson, NY
Nolasco, Ronald, Our Lady of Mercy, Bronx, NY
Nunez, Acadio, Puerto Rico
O'Brien, Donald, St. Francis of Assisi, West Nyack
O'Brien, Henry F., Spanish Fort, AL
O'Connor, Gerard R., Center of Jesus the Lord, New Orleans, LA
O'Reilly, John F.
O'Toole, Lawrence, St. Augustine, New York, NY
Ocasio, Roberto, Kissimmee, FL
Olivieri, Martin J., St. John the Baptist, Yonkers
Orlando, Francis B., Blessed Sacrament, New Rochelle
Ortiz, Louis, Ponce, PR
Ortiz, Pablo, St. Thomas Aquinas, Bronx
Ottaviano, Frank S., St. Augustine, Highland
Pacheco, Angel, St. Isaac Jogues Parish, Orlando, FL
Padron, Jose R., St. Pius V, Bronx
Palladino, Joseph, St. Joseph, New Paltz
Pappalardo, Augustine A., St. Gregory Barbarigo, Garnerville
Parchen, Raymond, Holy Spirit, Peekskill
Patricola, Salvatore P., St. Anthony's, Pine Plains
Pelella, John V., St. Thomas of Canterbury, Cornwall-on-Hudson
Pellegrini, Guy A., Our Lady Perpetual Help, Pelham
Peters, John, St. Joseph, Kingston, NY
Pietkiewicz, Karl J., St. Mary of the Snow, Saugerties
Pino, Victor M., St. John Chrysostom, Bronx
Pipher, Jesse E., Sarasota, FL
Piro, Vincent T., Our Lady of Mt. Carmel, Mt. Vernon
Pollick, Donald F., Westchester Medical Center Hospital, Valhalla
Porcel, Carlos M.
Portalatin, Epimegnio, Blessed Sacrament, Bronx
Preti, Aldo, St. Raymond, Bronx
Price, Joseph E.
Quigley, Donald M., St. John, Kingsbridge Ave., Bronx
Quinn, Thomas J., Holy Child, Staten Island
Radcliffe, Kenneth L., Resurrection, Central Harlem
Radzilowicz, John, St. Casimir, Yonkers
Ramos, Alfonso, Sacred Heart, Bronx
Ramos, Edmundo A., Tagaste Monastery, Suffern
Ramos, Epifanio, Orlando, FL
Ramos, Rafael, St. John Vianney, Bronx
Rausch, Paul A., St. Thomas Aquinas, Forestburg
Reilly, John P., St. Columba, Hopewell Junction
Rentkowski, Joseph, St. Adalbert, Staten Island
Repke, John W., St. Mary, Malboro
Rescildo, Ralph J., St. Augustine, New City
Rettino, P. Robert, St. Joseph, Spring Valley
Reynolds, Peter E., Our Lady of Mt. Carmel, Elmsford
Riley, John M., St. Peter, Liberty
Rivera, Andrew A., St. John, Kingsbridge Ave., Bronx
Rivera, Jose A., Aquas Buenas, PR
Rizzo, Charles A., Blessed Sacrament, New Rochelle
Roberts, James F., Our Lady of the Assumption, Peekskill
Rodriguez, Arnaldo, Nativity, Manhattan
Rodriguez, Cristobal, Immaculate Conception, Bronx
Rodriguez, Hector, St. Philip Neri, Bronx
Rodriguez, Jacinto, St. Anthony, Bronx, NY
Rodriguez, Jesus
Rodriguez, Juan J., Holy Cross, Bronx
Rodriguez, Porfirio, St. Jude, Manhattan
Romagosa, Guillermo P., Manhattan College, Bronx
Rosado, Alejandro, St. Athanasius, Bronx
Rosado, Odalis R., St. Elizabeth, New York
Rosado, Reynaldo, St. Martin of Tours, Bronx
Rosado, Ricardo, Mid-Orange Correctional Facility, Warwick
Rush, James J., Charleston, SC
Russell, Franklyn R., St. Patrick, Newburgh
Russo, Richard J., St. Jean Baptist, Manhattan
Salamone, Victor A., St. Martin de Porres, Poughkeepsie
Salomone, Ernest F., Immaculate Heart of Mary, Scarsdale
Sanchez, Oscar, Puerto Rico
Santana, Richard, Holy Name of Mary, Croton-on-Hudson
Santana, Robert, SS. Philip & James, Bronx
Santiago, Abraham, St. Joseph, Yonkers
Schlitt, Ronald, St. Christopher, Buchanan
Sepulveda, Miguel A., Ponce, PR
Serrano, Jose I.
Seymour, John L., St. Francis of Assisi, Newburgh
Sheeley, Robert B., Holy Name of Jesus, Kingston
Shiel, Thomas P., Incarnation, Tampa, FL
Shkreli, Marash, St. Lawrence O'Toole, Brewster
Simpson, John J., St. Benedict, Bronx
Sin-Garciga, Felipe, St. Paul Apostle, Manhattan
Singler, John A., Our Lady Help of Christians, Staten Island
Smith, John A., Delaware
Solanto, Joseph P., Holy Rosary, Bronx
Soto, Constancio, Ascension, Manhattan
Stahlnecker, James J., St. Mary of the Assumption, Staten Island
Steup, Fredrick C., St. Patrick, Newburgh
Stewart, George, St. Columba, Hopewell Junction
Suarez, Israel, Guaynaiso, PR
Sullivan, John D., Holy Trinity, West Harwich, MA
Sullivan, John M., St. Mary, Kingston
Sweeney, Walter F., Our Lady of Good Counsel, Staten Island
Tayco, Renato
Testa, Warren
Then, Rafael, Good Shepherd, Manhattan
Thompson, Albert, Our Lady of Good Counsel, Staten Island, NY
Tirado, Alberto, St. Ann's, Bronx
Tirella, Rosario J., Holy Rosary, Staten Island
Tobin, William D., St. Margaret, Pearl River
Tola, Vincente, Sunrise, FL
Topple, Edwin R., St. John the Evangelist, Centerville
Torres, Gilberto, Deltona, FL
Torres, Luis, Mayaguez, PR
Torres, Luis A., St. Pius V., Bronx
Toymil, Richard, Our Lady of Grace, Bronx
Trapani, Richard, St. Joseph, Middletown
Trees, Donald F., St. Mary of the Snow, Saugerties
Treiling, John F., St. Joseph Home & Hospital, Yonkers
Troy, Patrick D., Sacred Heart, Dobbs Ferry
Vaccaro, William N., Our Lady of the Rosary, Port Chester
Vargas, Thomas A., Holy Trinity, Mamaroneck
Vazquez, Juan F., St. Martin of Tours, Bronx
Velez, Randy, St. Peter, Yonkers
Venezia, Ignatius, St. Boniface, Wesley Hills
Verboys, Joseph, Sacred Heart, Suffern
Vorel, Vladislav P., St. Patrick, Yorktown Heights
Wallace, Benjamin S., St. Lawrence O'Toole, Brewster
Weinstein, David, Immaculate Conception, Amenia
Weir, John E., Bridgeport, CT
Weireter, Paul J., St. Patrick, Highland Mills
Weiss, Robert W., St. Augustine, Highland
Welhous, Albert V., SS. Philip & James, Bronx
Wendelken, Charles L., Blessed Sacrament, New Rochelle
Wetherall, Edward J., Our Lady Help of Christians, Staten Island
Winrow, Robert P., St. Joseph, Kingston
Witt, Joseph A., Sacred Heart, Suffern
Woods, Edward J., Our Lady of Mt. Carmel, Middletown
Wyka, Stanley A., St. Casimir, Yonkers
Zatarga, Michael, N. Palm Beach, FL

INSTITUTIONS LOCATED IN THE ARCHDIOCESE

[A] SEMINARIES, ARCHDIOCESAN

NEW YORK. *Cathedral Preparatory Seminary*. Archdiocesan Preparatory Seminary, 946 Boston Post Rd., Rye, 10580. Tel: 914-921-3994. Revs. Desmond O'Connor, Headmaster; Arthur Mastrolia, Spiritual Dir.; Frank Dias, Dean of Students; Mr. William J. Poli, Academic Dean. Priests 3; Sisters 1; Lay Teachers 12; Students 53.

Bishop Ford Residence, St. Joseph's Seminary, Dunwoodie, Yonkers, 10704. Tel: 914-968-2916. In res., Revs. Desmond O'Connor; Arthur Mastrolia. Students 37.

YONKERS. *St. Joseph's Seminary*, Archdiocesan Major Seminary, 201 Seminary Ave., 10704-1852. Tel: 914-968-6200; Fax: 914-968-7912. Most Rev. Edwin F. O'Brien, S.T.D., Rector; Rev. Msgr. William B. Smith, S.T.D.; Rev. Msgr. John J. Farley, M.Ed.; Revs. John Coughlin, J.C.D., Spiritual Dir.; Joseph P. Tierney, M.Div., Dean of Students & Dir. Pastoral Formation; Rev. Msgr. Francis J. McAree, S.T.D., Vice Rector; Revs. Peter J. Cameron, O.P., M.F.A.; Edmund J. Whalen, S.T.D.; Anthony D. Sorgie, Ed.D., Academic Dean & Dir. of Music; Edward L. Warnken, M.Div., Dean of Spirituality Year-Northampton; Rev. Msgr. John J. Quinn, M.A.; Rev. Joseph R. Giandurco, J.C.D., Faculty Sec. & Dean of Admissions.

Non-Resident Faculty: Rev. Kevin McMorrow, S.A., S.T.D.; Dr. Mary Ellen Hubbard, Ph.D., Dean of Institute of Religious Studies; Revs. Thomas J. Shelly, Ph.D.; Andrew D. Apostoli, C.F.R., M.S.; Dr. Francisco M. Alvarez, Ph.D.; Mrs. Frances Broderick, M.A.; Dr. Philip Cristantiello, Ph.D.; Dr. Paul L. Moglia, Ph.D.; Sr. Janet Baxendale, S.C., M.A.; Sr. M. Timothea Elliott, R.S.M., S.S.D.; Sr. Marie Pappas, C.R., M.A.; Rev. Paul Zilonka, C.P., S.S.L.; Mr. Christopher M. Bellitto, Ph.D.; Revs. Donald J. Keefe, S.J., S.T.D.; Frederick L. Miller, S.T.D.; Rev. Msgr. George Cascelli, M.S.; Revs. Gerard F. Rafferty, S.S.L.; Richard J. Neuhaus, M.Div.; Benedict J. Groeschel, C.F.R., Ed.D.; Robert G. Kelly, S.J., M.A.T.; James B. Lloyd, C.S.P., Ph.D.; Robert McKeon, Vocation Dir.; Avery Dulles, S.J., S.T.D., Visiting Scholar; Sr. Regina Anne Melican, O.P., M.S.L.S., Dir. of Library; Mrs. Isabel Cartolano, Registrar. Priests 26; Sisters 4; Lay Teachers 3; Students 73 (of Archdiocese 42); North American College 9.

Mark Seven - DePaul House of Studies, c/o St. Joseph's Seminary, 201 Seminary Ave., 10704-1852. Tel: 914-375-3466.

[B] SEMINARIES, RELIGIOUS OR SCHOLASTICATES

NEW YORK. *St. Francis Novitiate*, 500 Todt Hill Rd., 10304. Tel: 718-981-3131; 981-3212. Revs. Justin A. Biase, O.F.M.Conv., Guardian & Novice Dir.; Blase Kardos, O.F.M.Conv., Chap.; Shawn Nolan, O.F.M.Conv., Retreat Dir.; Bros. Joseph Freitag, O.F.M.Conv., Hospice Chap.; Thomas Purcell, O.F.M.Conv., Advanced Studies.

Friars Minor Conventual Immaculate Conception Province Charitable Trust.

Society of St. Paul, 2187 Victory Blvd., 10314. Tel: 718-761-0047; Fax: 718-761-0057. Rev. Ignatius Staniszewski, S.S.P., Supr. & Dir. Alba House Publications; Bro. Peter C. Lyne, S.S.P., Vocations Dir. Book Stores Coordinators: Bros. Kevin J. Cahill, S.S.P.; Augustine Condon, S.S.P.; Lawrence H. Schubert, S.S.P., Bursar; Revs. Edmund C. Lane, S.S.P.; Victor L. Viberti, S.S.P.; Clarence A. Warren, S.S.P. Priests 4; Brothers 15.

BEACON. *St. Lawrence of Brindisi Friary*, Province of the Stigmata of St. Francis, 182 Sargent Ave., 12508-3993. Tel: 914-831-0394; 831-0451; 838-0759 (Infirmary); Fax: 914-831-0918. (Friary and Infirmary). Bros. Hilary Rodgers, O.F.M.Cap., Guardian; Efrain Sosa, O.F.M.Cap., Vicar & Dir. of Infirmary; Revs. Innocent Amore, O.F.M.Cap.; Seraphin Tirone, O.F.M.Cap.; Bros. John Boehm, O.F.M.Cap.; Lawrence Emmert, O.F.M.Cap.; Revs. John Frega, O.F.M.Cap.; Gerard De Leonardis, O.F.M.Cap.; Henry D'Angelis, O.F.M.Cap.; Sylvester Catallo, O.F.M.Cap.; Cosmas Niedhammer, O.F.M.Cap. Priests 7; Brothers 4; Lay Staff 11.

MARYKNOLL. *Center for Mission Research and Study at*

Maryknoll, P.O. Box 305, 10545-0305. Tel: 914-941-7590; Fax: 914-941-5753. Rev. William D. McCarthy, M.M., Exec. Dir.; Anne Reissner, Dir. of Study; Jean Paul Weist, Dir. of Research; Mary Ann Cejka, Assoc. Researcher; Catherine McDonald, Coord., Society History.
Purpose: To investigate the contexts, trends and challenges of Christian Mission among Christians and peoples of other living faiths, and to foster reflection on the practical implications of these investigations. Priests 1; Lay Persons 4.

SUFFERN. *Tagaste Monastery*, 220 Lafayette Ave., 10901. Tel: 914-357-0067. Major Seminary of the Province of St. Augustine of the Augustinian Recollect Fathers & Brothers. Revs. John J. Oldfield, Prior; George Mattioni, O.A.R., Sub-prior, Prefect of the Professed; Francis Moriones, O.A.R. (Spain); Francis A. Cregan, O.A.R.; Deacon Ulises Feliciano, O.A.R.; Bros. Paul Rodriguez, O.A.R.; Joseph Joly, O.A.R.; Gerardo DeFillippo, O.A.R. Priests 4; Brothers 3; Permanent Deacons 1; Simple Professed 3; Solemn Professed Clerics 3.

[C] COLLEGES AND UNIVERSITIES

NEW YORK. *College of Mount Saint Vincent*, 6301 Riverdale Ave., 10471-1093. Tel: 718-405-3200; Fax: 718-549-2603.
For a complete listing, refer to the Colleges and Universities section.
Marymount Manhattan College, 221 E. 71st St., 10021. Tel: 212-517-0400.
For a complete listing, refer to the Colleges and Universities section.

*BRONX. *Fordham University*, (1841) Fordham Rd., 10458 Fax: 718-817-4925.
For a complete listing, refer to the Colleges and Universities section.
Manhattan College, Manhattan College Pkwy., 10471. Tel: 718-862-7200; 800-MC2-XCEL.
For a complete listing, refer to the Colleges and Universities section.

DOBBS FERRY. *Mercy College in Dobbs Ferry*, 541 Broadway, 10522. Tel: 914-693-4500.
For a complete listing, refer to the Colleges and Universities section.

*NEW ROCHELLE. *College of New Rochelle*, 29 Castle Pl., 10805. Tel: 914-654-5000; Fax: 914-654-5290.
For a complete listing, refer to the Colleges and Universities section.
Iona College, 715 North Ave., 10801. Tel: 914-633-2000.
For a complete listing, refer to the Colleges and Universities section.

NEWBURGH. *Mt. St. Mary College*, 1954, 12550. Tel: 914-561-0800.
For a complete listing, refer to the Colleges and Universities section.

ORANGEBURG. *Dominican College of Blauvelt*, 10962. Tel: 914-359-7800.
For a complete listing, refer to the Colleges and Universities section.

POUGHKEEPSIE. *Marist College*, 12601-1328. Tel: 914-575-3000.
For a complete listing, refer to the Colleges and Universities section.

SPARKILL. *St. Thomas Aquinas College*, 10976. Tel: 914-398-4000; Fax: 914-359-8136.
For a complete listing, refer to the Colleges and Universities section.

STATEN ISLAND. *St. John's University Staten Island Campus*, 300 Howard Ave., 10301. Tel: 718-390-4545; Fax: 718-816-4520.
For a complete listing, refer to the Colleges and Universities section.

TARRYTOWN. *Marymount College*, 10591. Tel: 914-631-3200.
For a complete listing, refer to the Colleges and Universities section.

[D] DEPARTMENT OF EDUCATION

NEW YORK. *Department of Education*, 1011 First Ave., 10022. Tel: 212-371-1000. Rev. Msgr. Thomas J. Bergin, Vicar for Education; Sr. Eileen Clifford, O.P., Assoc. Vicar for Education; Rev. Michael C. Crimmins, Assoc. Vicar for Higher Education; Sr. Lois Darold, C.S.J.B., Consultant.
Office of Finance. Mr. John D. Poling, Dir. Finance; Mr. Gerald Judge, Controller; Mr. John Coyne, Asst. Controller.
Office of Seminary Education. St. Joseph's Seminary, Seminary Ave., Yonkers, 10704. Tel: 914-968-6200. Neumann Residence, 5655 Arlington Ave., 10471. Tel: 718-549-4511. Most Rev. Patrick Sheridan, D.D., Chancellor of the Seminary System; Rev. Msgr. James White, Dir.; Rev. Msgr. Edwin F. O'Brien, Rector, Cathedral Prep. Seminary, 946 Boston Post Rd., 10580. Tel: 914-921-3994. Deacon Anthony Cassaneto, M.A., M.S. in Education, Permanent Diaconate, St. Joseph's Seminary, Institute for Religious Studies, Yonkers, 10704. Tel: 914-476-1172; 476-1185. Mary Ellen Hubbard, Ph.D., Dean, Vocations Office, 1011 First Ave., 10022. Tel: 212-371-1000. Rev. Robert McLeon, Asst. to the Archbishop for St. Joseph's Seminary. Tel: 914-968-1340; Sr. Deanna Sabetta, C.N.D., Dir. Vocations for Women, Division of Elementary and Secondary Education, 1011 First Ave., 10022. Tel: 212-371-1000. Dr. Catherine Hickey, Supt. of Schools; Mr. Paul Ward, Deputy Supt. Assoc. Supts.: Sr. Dorothy Flanagan, Religious Education; Mrs. Mary Jane Krebbs, Curriculum; Mr. James Mahoney, Publicly Assisted Programs; Bro. Thomas Schady, Secondary Education; Mr. James Simone, Special Education; Sr. Kathleen Sullivan, S.C., Teacher Recruitment. Asst. Supts.: Jeanette Galvin, Admin.; Sr. Winifred Lyons, Pro-Life Coord., Parent Volunteer Program & Teachers Institute; Mrs. Nora Murphy, Communications Mktg. Directors: Sr. Breda Galavan, R.S.H.M., Writing to Read; Sr. Angela Palermo, R.C.D., Catechist Formation; Ann Maschin, Admin. Asst.; Sr. Lucy Sabatini, O.S.F., Early Childhood, 215 W. 15th St., 10011. Tel: 212-243-1881. District Supts.: Sr. Patricia Anastasio, P.B.V.M., Bronx; Sr. Kathleen FitzSimons, C.N.D., Staten Island; Deacon Arthur Manzione, Westchester & Putnam; Sr. Marilyn O'Brien, P.B.V.M., Rockland, Archdiocesan Drug Abuse Prevention Program, 2789 Schurz Ave., Bronx, 10465. Tel: 718-904-1333. Mrs. Frances Maturo, Dir., Cooke Foundation for Special Education, 456 W. 52nd St., 10019. Tel: 212-245-3376. Dr. Gay Culverhouse, Dir., Seton Foundation for Learning, 104 Gordon St., Staten Island, 10303. Tel: 718-447-1750. Ms. Diane D. Cunningham, Dir., Bronx Alternative Special Education, 1725 Castle Hill Ave., Bronx, 10462. Tel: 718-792-9669. James A. Simone, Assoc. Supt.; Mrs. Mary Carman, Admin. Asst., St. Ursula Learning Center, 183 Rich Ave., Mt. Vernon, 10550. Tel: 914-664-6656. Mrs. Barbara Stefaniki, Ed. Dir.

Joan Ann Kennedy Memorial Preschool, 26 Sharpe Ave., Staten Island, 10302. Tel: 718-876-0939. Ms. Kathryn Meyer, Dir., Family Life/Respect Life Office, 1011 First Ave., 10022. Tel: 212-371-1000. Rev. John S. Bonnici, Asst. Dir.; Mr. Patrick Del Zoppo, Ph.D., CAS., Asst. Dir. & Coord. of Bereavement Ministry & Project Rachael Ministry; Mr. Edward Mechmann, Asst. Dir. & Coord. of Marriage Preparation Programs; Dr. Charles Potter, Assoc. Dir., Natural Family Planning Program; Mr. Jose Pedrozo, Coord., Hispanic Activities; Susan L. Zappo, Coord., Divorced & Separated Min.; Dana Larson, Coord., Wedding Anniversary Awards Ceremony; Kate Griffin, Coord. of 'At Peace With Your Unborn'; Mrs. Eileen Murphy, Assoc. Dir. of Ed. for Parenting, Hudson River East, 103 Jackson St., Box L, Fishkill, 12524. Tel: 914-896-0728. Mrs. Virginia Brown, Assoc. Dir., Ed. for Parenting, Hudson River West, 149 Cottage St., Middletown, 10940. Tel: 914-342-0908. Jim & Joanne Martin, Coord. Couple, Engaged Encounter. Tel: 914-228-1002; Jim & Nancy Rizzi, Coord. Couple, Marriage Encounter. Tel: 718-966-0990; 317-5881, Respect Life Programs, 2885 St. Theresa Ave., 10461. Tel: 718-892-8100. Rev. Kevin S.D. Connelly, Coord., Pro-Life Activities; Mrs. Nancy Rizzi, Asst. Coord. of Pro-Life Activities, Archdiocesan Catechetical Office, 1011 First Ave., 10022. Tel: 212-371-1000. Sr. Joan Curtin, C.N.D., Archdiocesan Dir.; Ms. Anne Coghlan, Dir. Spec. Religious Education; Sr. Mary Elizabeth Kelleher, O.P., Dir. Catechist Formation; Bro. Dennis Cronin, F.S.C., Dir. Adolescent Catechesis; Sr. Teresita Morse, R.J.M., Dir. Formation of Directors/Coordinators; Sr. Marie Elena Dio, S.C.H., Dir. Multi-Cultural Catechesis; Mrs. Frances De Frange, Chm., Catechetical Congress. Catechetical Regional Offices: South, Northwest & Northeast Bronx, 323 E. 198th St., Bronx, 10458. Tel: 718-367-0420; Fax: 718-367-0420. Sr. Katherine Naughton, O.S.U., Dir., North and West Manhattan, Harlem & East Bronx, c/o Mother Cabrini High School, 701 Fort Washington Ave., 10040. Tel: 212-923-0950. Sr. Catherine Ryan, F.S.P., Dir., Staten Island, 203 Sand Ln., Staten Island, 10305. Tel: 718-273-3833; Fax: 718-273-3833. Mrs. Frances De Frange, Regional Dir., Dutchess & Ulster Counties, Dutchess Office: 26 S. Hamilton Ave., Poughkeepsie, 12601-2599. Tel: 914-471-5427. Ulster Office, 157 Broadway, Kingston, 12401. Tel: 914-338-3222. Sr. Miriam Eugene Fenton, S.C., Dir., Southern & Central Westchester, 50 Washington Ave., New Rochelle, 10801. Tel: 914-633-3631. Sr. Kathleen Harrington, P.V.B.M., Regional Dir., Orange & Rockland Counties, Orange Office: John S. Burke Catholic H.S., Fletcher St., P.O. Box 114, Goshen, 10924. Tel: 914-294-6428. Rockland Office: 798 Rte. 304 & Germonds Rd., P.O. Box 9162, Bardonia, 10954-1694. Tel: 914-627-1236. Sr. Anne Connelly, O.P., Regional Dir., Northern Westchester and Putnam Counties, 1011 First Ave., Room 1879, 10022. Tel: 212-371-1000, Ext. 2864. Bro. Dennis Cronin, F.S.C., Regional Dir., Sullivan County, Blessed Kateri Tekakwitha Center, P.O. Box 1011, Liberty, 12754. Tel: 914-292-9100. Sr. Kevin John Shields, O.P., Regional Dir., Commission on Church Music, 1011 First Ave., 10022. Tel: 212-371-1000. Mr. John Michael Caprio, Exec. Dir., Center for Spiritual Development, 96 Milton Rd., Rye, 10580. Tel: 914-967-7328. Anne Marie Wallace, Ph.D., Dir., Office of Spiritual Development, 1 Pryor Manor Rd., Larchmont, 10538. Tel: 914-235-6839. Rev. Benedict J. Groeschel, C.F.R., Dir., Trinity Retreat House, 1 Pryor Manor Rd., Larchmont, 10538. Tel: 914-235-6839. Rev. Eugene Fulton, Dir., Instructional Television, 215 Seminary Ave., Yonkers, 10704. Mr. Michael Lavery, Administrative Dir. Elementary School; Sisters 168; Brothers 8; Order Priests 3; Lay Teachers 2,689. High School; Sisters 100; Brothers 41; Order Priests 23; Diocesan Priests 24; Lay Teachers 1,472.

Catechetical Regional Offices. Sr. Joan Curtin, C.N.D., Dir.; Sr. Mary Elizabeth Kelleher, O.P., Dir., Catechist Formation; Sr. Teresita Morse, R.J.M., D.R.E.; Miss Anne Coughlan, Dir., Special Religious Education; Bro. Dennis Cronin, F.S.C., Dir., Adolescent Catechesis; Mrs. Frances DeFrange, Chair, Catechetical Congress.
Northeast, Northwest, & South Bronx, 323 E. 199th St., 10458. Tel: 718-367-0420. Sr. Katherine Naughton, O.S.U., Regl. Dir.
North & West Manhattan, Harlem, East Bronx, c/o Mother Cabrini High School, 701 Fort Washington Ave., Bronx, 10040. Tel: 212-923-0950. Sr. Catherine Ryan, F.S.P., Regl. Dir.
East & South Manhattan, c/o St. Stephen of Hungary, 414 E. 82nd St., 10028. Tel: 212-879-6798. Sr. Marie Elena Dio, S.C.H., Regl. Dir. & Dir., Multi-Cultural Catechesis.
Staten Island, 203 Sand Ln., 10305. Tel: 718-273-3833. Mrs. Frances DeFrange, Regl. Dir.
Dutchess, 26 S. Hamilton Ave., Poughkeepsie, 12601-2599. Tel: 914-471-5427. Sr. Miriam Eugene Fenton, S.C., Regl. Dir.
Ulster, 157 Broadway, Kingston, 12401. Tel: 914-338-3222. Sr. Miriam Eugene Fenton, S.C., Regl. Dir.
Orange, John S. Burke Catholic High School, Fletcher St., P.O. Box 114, Goshen, 10924. Tel: 914-294-6428. Sr. Anne Connelly, O.P., Regl. Dir.
Rockland, 798 Rte. 304 & Germonds Rd., P.O. Box 9162, Bardonia, 10954-1694. Tel: 914-627-1236. Sr. Anne Connelly, O.P., Regl. Dir.
Central & Southern Westchester & Yonkers, 50 Washington Ave., 10801. Tel: 914-633-3631. Sr. Kathleen Harrington, P.B.V.M., Regl. Dir.
Putnam & Northern Westchester, 1011 First Ave., Room 1879, 10022. Tel: 212-371-1000. Bro. Dennis Cronin, F.S.C., Regl. Dir.
Sullivan County, Blessed Kateri Tekakwitha Center, P.O. Box 1011, Liberty, 12754. Tel: 914-292-9100. Sr. Kevin John Shields, O.P., Regl. Dir. Total Enrollment 28,121.
The Little Angels Head Start Program of the Archdiocese of New York, 2340 Andrews Ave., 10468. Tel: 212-371-1000, Ext. 2831. Nora Feury, Contact Person.

[E] HIGH SCHOOLS, ARCHDIOCESAN

NEW YORK. *Cardinal Hayes High School*, 650 Grand Concourse, 10451. Tel: 718-292-6100; Fax: 718-292-5607. (Boys). Rev. Msgr. John K. Graham, Prin.; Mr. James G. Clarkin, Dean of Studies; Revs. Harry Burke; James T. Byrnes; Alfred D'Incecco; Matthew Fernan; Jeffrey Galens; Robert Harrison; John T. Mulligan; John N. Paddack; Rev. Msgr. Victor C. Pavis. In res., Rev. Msgr. Peter P. Narkun. Priests 10; Brothers 3; Sisters 1; Lay Teachers 52; Students 1,060.
Cardinal Spellman High School. One Cardinal Spellman Pl., Bronx, 10466. Tel: 718-881-8000; Fax: 718-515-6615. Rev. Msgr. Jeremiah P. Monahan, Prin.; Revs. James J. Corrigan; Francis J. Corry; Richard F. Gorman; John R. Kraljic; John F. Lauri; John T. Monaghan; James J. O'Shaughnessy; Lawrence M. Paolicelli; Francis J. Principe. In res., Rev. Msgr. John J. Considine; Revs. Thomas P. D'Angelo; Vincent T. Euk. Priests 10; Sisters 4; Lay Teachers 80; Students 1,600.
Cathedral High School, 350 E. 56th St., 10022. Tel: 212-688-1545. (Girls). Rev. Msgr. Thomas Bergin, Pres.; Sr. Mary Kilmartin, S.C., Prin.; Sr. Elizabeth Graham, O.P., Dean of Studies; Rev. Msgr. George J. Cascelli, Spiritual Dir. Priests 3; Sisters 14; Lay Teachers 33; Students 735.
Monsignor Farrell High School, 2900 Amboy Rd., 10306. Tel: 718-987-2900; Fax: 718-987-4241. Revs. Emmet R. Nevin, Prin.; John P. Comiskey; Robert G. Macchietto. Priests 3; Brothers 4; Sisters 3; Lay Teachers 66; Students 1,097.
Moore Catholic High School, 100 Merrill Ave., 10314. Tel: 212-761-9200. Revs. Robert Gannon; Edmund P. Connors. Priests 2; Sisters of the Presentation 1; Lay Teachers 32; Students 772.

GOSHEN. *John S. Burke Catholic High School*, Fletcher St., 10924. Tel: 914-294-5481. Sr. Josephine Ortner,

P.B.V.M., Prin.; Rev. Trevor Nicholls. Priests 1; Sisters 3; Lay Teachers 34; Students 534.

HARTSDALE. *Maria Regina High School*, 500 W. Hartsdale Ave., 10530. Tel: 914-761-3300. Sisters of the Resurrection. Sr. Eustelle Kozakiewicz, C.R., Supr.; Sr. Danielle M. Baran, C.R., Prin. Sisters 9; Lay Teachers 24; Students 450.

HURLEY. *John A. Coleman Catholic High School*, 430 Hurley Ave., 12443. Tel: 914-338-2750; Fax: 914-388-0250. Bro. James F. McKnight, F.M.S., Prin. Brothers 3; Sisters 2; Lay Teachers 19; Students 240.

POUGHKEEPSIE. *Our Lady of Lourdes High School*, 131 Boardman Rd., 12603. Tel: 914-471-0400. Bros. Donnell Neary, F.M.S., Pres.; Larry Lavallee, F.M.S., Prin.; Larry Gordon, F.M.S., Dean of Studies; Larry Hanshumacher, F.M.S.; Vincent Moriarty, F.M.S.; George DiCarluccio, F.M.S.; Henry Sawicki, F.M.S.; Gregory DelaNoy, F.M.S.; James Stevens, F.M.S.; Mr. William Dahncke, Dean of Men; Mrs. Judith Maher, Dean of Women; Sr. Lois Dee, O.P., Admin. Asst. Priests 1; Brothers 9; Lay Teachers 32; Students 674.

SOMERS. *John F. Kennedy High School*, Rte. 138, 10589. Tel: 914-232-5061; Fax: 914-232-3416. Sisters of Divine Compassion. Revs. Anthony D. Marchitelli, Prin.; Mark J. Connell; Brian McSweeney; Sr. Barbara Heil, Treas.; Mr. Thomas Dolan, Dean of Students; Sr. M. Christopher, R.D.C., Dir. of Alumni Affairs. Priests 3; Sisters 8; Lay Teachers 36; Students 620.

WHITE PLAINS. *Archbishop Stepinac High School*, 950 Mamaroneck Ave., 10605. Tel: 914-946-4800; Fax: 914-686-3615. Rev. Msgr. John J. O'Keefe, Pres.; Mr. Ronald Tedesco, Headmaster; Mr. Ralph Nicoletti, Admin. Asst. & Dean of Students; Rev. Eric P. Raaser, Assoc. Dean of Students. Staff of School: Revs. Patrick M. Carroll; Thomas E. Collins; Philip J. Quealy. In res., Rev. Msgr. George F. Bardes; Rev. John L. Cavanaugh; Rev. Msgr. Edward Connors; Rev. Henry G. d'Anjou; Rev. Msgr. Augustine J. DiBlasi; Rev. Msgr. John T. Doherty; Rev. Msgr. Robert A. Ford; Rev. Msgr. Herman L. Heide; Rev. Msgr. Vincent W. Jeffers; Rev. Msgr. Thomas V. McMahon; Rev. Vincent J. McShane; Rev. Msgr. Cornelius O'Brien; Rev. Thomas E. O'Keefe; Rev. Msgr. Raymond P. Rigney; Rev. James B. Tobin; Rev. Msgr. James J. Walsh. Priests 5; Sisters 2; Lay Teachers 38; Students 599.

[F] HIGH SCHOOLS, PRIVATE

NEW YORK. *Academy of Mount St. Ursula*, 330 Bedford Park Blvd., 10458. Tel: 718-364-5353; Fax: 718-584-1507. (Girls). Ursuline Nuns. Sr. Mary Beth Read, O.S.U., Prin. Priests 1; Sisters 7; Lay Teachers 35; Students 520.

All Hallows Institute. (also known as all Hallows High School). 111 E. 164th St., 10452. Tel: 212-293-4545. (Boys). Mr. Gerald E. Grimmeyer, Prin.; Rev. Peter Lekwot. Congregation of Christian Brothers 12; Lay Teachers 17; Students 450.

Aquinas High School. 685 E. 182nd St., Bronx, 10457. Tel: 718-367-2113; Fax: 718-295-5864. Sisters 21; Lay Teachers 36; Students 814. (Girls). Sr. Margaret Ryan, O.P., Prin.

Convent of the Sacred Heart, One E. 91st St., 10128-0654. Tel: 212-722-4745. (Girls). Religious of the Sacred Heart. Sr. N. Salisbury, R.S.C.J., Headmistress. Sisters 8; Lay Teachers 63; Students 518.

Dominican Academy, 44 E. 68th St., 10021. Tel: 212-744-0195; Fax: 212-744-0375. (Girls). Sr. Martha Kunesh, O.P., Prin. Sisters 7; Lay Teachers 23; Students 223.

Fordham Preparatory School, E. Fordham Rd., 10458. Tel: 718-367-7500; Fax: 718-367-7598. (Boys). Mr. Kevin R. Hackett, Chm. Bd.; Rev. Joseph P. Parkes, S.J., Pres.; Mr. Robert J. Gomprecht, Headmaster; Rev. John J. Mattimore, S.J., Asst. Headmaster; Mr. Bruce G. Bott, Dean of Students; Rev. Mallick J. Fitzpatrick, S.J., Dir. Guidance; Bro. Sebastian A. Boccabella, S.J.; Revs. Pierce A. Brennan, S.J.; Matthew C. Flood, S.J.; John J. Leonard, S.J.; Stanley J. O'Konsky, S.J.; William J. O'Malley, S.J.; Joseph S. Rooney, S.J.; Charles D. Sullivan, S.J.; Raymond M. Sweitzer, S.J. Priests 11; Lay Teachers 73; Students 970.

La Salle Academy, 44-50 E. Second St., 10003. Tel: 212-475-8940; Fax: 212-529-3598. (Boys). Brothers of The Christian Schools. Bros. Carl Malacalza, F.S.C., Pres.; Michael Farrell, F.S.C., Prin. Brothers 6; Sisters 2; Lay Teachers 28; Students 505.

Loyola School, 980 Park Ave., 10028. Tel: 212-288-3522. (Coed). Society of Jesus. Mr. James A. Beha, Chm. Bd.; Revs. Joseph J. Papaj, S.J., Pres. and Headmaster; John L. Farrand, S.J.; James J. Curry, S.J.; Eugene J. Prior, S.J.; Thomas S. Prout, S.J.; Michael Sehler, S.J. Priests 6; Lay Teachers 20; Students 197.

Mother Cabrini High School, 701 Ft. Washington Ave., 10040. Tel: 212-923-3540. (Girls) (Grades 9-12 & ESL program). Brian Donahue, Prin. Sisters 3; Lay Teachers 29; Students 389.

Notre Dame Academy High School, 134 Howard Ave., 10301. Tel: 718-447-8878. Congregation of Notre Dame. Mrs. Angela T. Ferrando, Prin. Sisters 2; Lay Teachers 30; Girls 365.

Notre Dame School of Manhattan, 104 St. Mark Pl., 10009. Tel: 212-982-0740. (Girls). Mr. John Joven, Prin. Brothers 1; Sisters 4; Lay Teachers 14; Students 175.

Preston High School, 2780 Schurz Ave., 10465. Tel: 718-863-9134. (Girls). Sr. Lucille Coldrick, R.D.C., Prin. Asst. Prins.: Linda Youngren; Sr. Laura Donovan, R.D.C. Sisters of the Divine Compassion 10; Lay Teachers 35; Students 452.

Regis High School, 55 E. 84th St., 10028. Tel: 212-288-1100; Fax: 212-794-1221. (Boys). Society of Jesus. Revs. J. Thomas McClain, S.J., Pres.; Thomas H. Feely, S.J., Headmaster; Mr. Francis J. Walsh, Asst. Headmaster; Mr. William E. O'Brien, Registrar; Mr. Daniel T. Dougherty, Dean of Students; Revs. Arthur C. Bender, S.J.; Vincent L. Biagi, S.J.; James R. Carney, S.J.; James J. DiGiacomo, S.J.; Joseph A. Dorgan, S.J.; Stephen V. Duffy, S.J.; Philip G. Judge, S.J.; Charles F. Gilley, S.J. Priests 10; Lay Teachers 46; Students 514. Res., 53 E. 83rd St., 10028.

Rice High School, 74 W. 124th St., 10027. Tel: 212-369-4100. (Boys). Congregation of Christian Brothers. Bro. John M. Walderman, C.F.C., Pres. Brothers 6; Lay Teachers 23; Students 370.

St. Catharine Academy, 2250 Williamsbridge Rd., 10469. Tel: 718-882-2882; Fax: 718-231-9099. (Girls). Francine Scioli, Prin. Sisters 9; Lay Teachers 52; Students 971.

St. John Villa Academy High School, 26 Landis Ave., 10305. Sr. Ann Dolores VanWagenen, C.S.J.B., Prin. Sisters 12; Lay Teachers 39; Girls 579.

St. Joseph by the Sea, High School, 5150 Hylan Blvd., 10312. Tel: 718-984-6500. (Coed). Rev. Msgr. Joseph C. Ansaldi, Prin.; Rev. James Garisto; Rev. Msgr. James Bolger; Rev. Michael Reilly. Priests 4; Sisters 9; Lay Teachers 57; Students 1,300.

Xavier High School, 30 W. 16th St., 10011. Tel: 212-924-7900. (Boys). Society of Jesus. Revs. Kenneth J. Boller, S.J., Pres.; Terrence A. Baum, S.J., Headmaster; Mr. Franklin N. Caesar, Asst. Headmaster; Mr. Franklin D. Gregory, Dean of Students; Mr. Christopher C. Casey, S.J.; Revs. Vincent E. Butler, S.J.; Michael Corcoran, S.J.; John F. Garvey, S.J.; Daniel J. Gatti, S.J.; William J. McGowan, S.J.; Robert V. O'Hare, S.J.; Marc J. Roselli, S.J.; Russell J. Sloun, S.J.; Vincent A. Taylor, S.J.; Joseph J. Walter, S.J.; David F. White, S.J.
(See listing for Xavier Jesuit Community for additional names of priests and brothers.). Priests 7; Scholastics 1; Lay Teachers 50; Students 875.

BARDONIA. *Albertus Magnus*, 798 Rte. 304, 10954. Tel: 914-623-8842. Sisters of St. Dominic (Sparkill) 7; Lay Teachers 29; Students 382.

BRONX. *Mount St. Michael Academy*, 4300 Murdock Ave., 10466. Tel: 718-515-6400; Fax: 718-994-7729. (Boys). Bros. Anthony M. Iazzetti, F.M.S., Pres.; James Kearney, F.M.S., Prin. Sisters 2; Brothers 14; Lay Teachers 60; Students 1,001.

Junior High School. Mrs. Lillian Dippolito, F.M.S., Prin. Lay Teachers 5; Students 124.

DOBBS FERRY. *Our Lady of Victory Academy High School*, 565 N. Broadway, 10522. Tel: 914-693-1633. (Girls). Sisters of Mercy. Sr. Patricia Vetrano, R.S.M., Prin. Sisters 10; Lay Teachers 22; Students 372.

NEW ROCHELLE. *Iona Preparatory School*, Wilmot Rd., 10804. Tel: 914-632-0714; Fax: 914-632-9760. (Boys). Congregation of Christian Brothers. Bro. William M. Stoldt, C.F.C., Pres.; Mr. Edward O'Neill, Headmaster; Mr. John Fogler, Asst. Headmaster; Mr. Dan Poccia, Asst. Headmaster for Student Life; Bros. Anthony K. Cavat, C.F.C., Supr.; Gerard M. Gaffney, C.F.C., Dean of Faculty; Mr. Martin Keefe, Business Mgr. Brothers 9; Lay Teachers 49; Students 760.

Salesian High School, 148 Main St., 10801. Tel: 914-632-0248; Fax: 914-632-1362. Rev. John J. Serio, S.D.B., Dir. & Pres.; Mr. John P. Flaherty, Prin.; Sr. Barbara Wright, O.P., Asst. Prin.; Mr. Arthur Schoenherr, Dean of Students; Bro. Thomas Sweeney, S.D.B., Coord. of Youth Ministry; Sr. Marie-Celine Miranda, O.S.U., Business Mgr.; Revs. Donald M. Delaney, S.D.B.; Richard Rosin, S.D.B., Guidance Dir. & Vicar; Hector Poulin, S.D.B., Admin.; Bros. Kevin Connolly, S.D.B.; Roger Ochoa, S.D.B.; Thomas Provenzano, S.D.B. Priests 4; Brothers 2; Scholastics 2; Sisters 2; Lay Teachers 27; Students 415.

Ursuline School. (Grades 6-12), 1354 North Ave., 10804. Tel: 914-636-3950; Fax: 914-636-3949. (Girls). Sr. Jean Baptiste Nicholson, O.S.U., Prin. Priests 1; Sisters 11; Lay Teachers 48; Students 685.

RYE. *School of the Holy Child*. (Grades 5-12), Westchester Ave., 10580. Tel: 914-967-5622; Fax: 914-967-6476. (Girls). Sr. Jean Marie O'Meara, S.H.C.J., Head. Society of the Holy Child Jesus 2; Lay Teachers 28; Students 206.

STATEN ISLAND. *St. Joseph Hill Academy*, 850 Hylan Blvd., 10305-2095. Tel: 718-447-1374. (Girls). Daughters of Divine Charity. Sr. M. Charlotte, Prin. Sisters 3; Lay Teachers 24; Students 369.

WHITE PLAINS. *Academy of Our Lady of Good Counsel*, 52 N. Broadway, 10603. Tel: 914-949-0178; Fax: 914-949-5169. (Girls). Ms. Joan Close, Prin. Sisters of the Divine Compassion 9; Lay Teachers 30; Students 430.

[G] SPECIAL SCHOOLS

NEW YORK. *Grace Institute*, 1233 Second Ave., 10021. Tel: 212-832-7605. Sisters of Charity, Mt. St. Vincent. Sr. Mary Ellen O'Boyle, Admin. Sisters 6; Lay Teachers 6; Students 800.

Mount St. Ursula Speech Center. 200th St. and Marion Ave., Bronx, 10458. Tel: 718-584-7679. Ursuline Nuns. Sr. M. Winifred Danwitz, Ph.D., Admin. Sisters 1; Lay Clinicians 8; Support Staff 6; Total Enrollment 150.

Seton Foundation for Learning, Inc. 104 Gordon St., Staten Island, 10304. Tel: 718-447-1750. Rev. Msgr. Joseph C. Ansaldi, Chm.; Mr. John Haugen, Pres.; Diane Cunningham, Exec. Dir. Lay Teachers 4; Assistants 5; Enrollment 40.

MILLBROOK. *Cardinal Hayes School for Special Children*, North Ave., P.O. Box CHHC, 12545. Tel: 914-677-6363; Fax: 914-677-6691. Fred Apers, Exec. Dir.

Hayes Nursery School and Day Care Center. Capacity 75. Educational programs for multi-handicapped children. Lay Teachers 5; Capacity 35; Enrollment 30.

NEW ROCHELLE. *Angela House, Inc*., 39 Willow Dr., 10805.

[H] ELEMENTARY SCHOOLS, PRIVATE

NEW YORK. *Academy of St. Dorothy*, 1305 Hylan Blvd., 10305. Tel: 718-351-0939. Sr. Sharon A. McCarthy, S.S.D., Prin. Sisters of St. Dorothy 3; Lay Teachers 7; Students 309.

Convent of the Sacred Heart, 1 E. 91st St., 10128. Tel: 212-722-4745. (Girls). Sr. N. Salisbury, R.S.C.J., Headmistress. Sisters 7; Lay Teachers 65; Students 572.

Marymount School. (Grades Nursery-12), 1026 Fifth Ave., 10028. Tel: 212-744-4486; Fax: 212-744-0163. Religious of the Sacred Heart of Mary. Sr. Kathleen Fagan, R.S.H.M., Headmistress. Sisters 6; Lay Teachers 49; Students 360.

Notre Dame Academy-Elementary School, 78 Howard Ave., 10301. Tel: 718-273-9096. Congregation of Notre Dame. Sr. Rose Mary Galligan, C.N.D., Prin. Lay Teachers 13; Students 340.

Sacred Heart Private Elementary School, Inc., 1651 Zerega Ave., 10462. Tel: 718-863-5047. Apostles of the Sacred Heart of Jesus. Sr. Carole Anne Stackpole, A.S.C.J., Prin. Sisters 6; Lay Teachers 7; Students 182.

St. John Villa Academy Elementary School, Mailing Address: 57 Cleveland Pl., 10305. Sr. Rita Marie Carey, C.S.J.B., Prin. Sisters 9; Lay Teachers 10; Students 418.

St. Joseph Hill Academy Elementary, 850 Hylan Blvd., 10305. Sr. M. Mercedes, F.D.C., Prin. Sisters 3; Lay Teachers 30; Students 561.

Villa Maria Academy, 3335 Country Club Rd., 10465. Tel: 212-824-3260. Congregation of Notre Dame. Sr. Marie A. Martin, C.N.D., Prin. Sisters 3; Lay Teachers 26; Students 570.

BRONX. *St. Joseph's School for the Deaf*, 1000 Hutchinson River Pkwy., 10465. Tel: 718-828-9000; 828-1671 (TDD); Fax: 718-792-6631. (Birth-14 yrs). Directed by Daughters of the Heart of Mary. Ms. Patricia Martin, Exec. Dir. Capacity 200; Enrollment 140.

NEW ROCHELLE. *Iona Grammar School*. (Grades PreK-8), 173 Stratton Rd., 10804; Fax: 914-235-6338. (Boys). Bro. John D. Dugan, C.F.C., Pres. & Headmaster. Brothers 4; Lay Teachers 18; Students 240.

NEWBURGH. *Bishop Dunn Memorial School*, 50 Gidney Ave., 12550. Sisters of St. Dominic. Mrs. Kathleen Mellon, Prin. Sisters 2; Lay Teachers 11; Students 153.

PORT JERVIS. *Trinity Catholic School*, 44 Ball St., 12771. Herman Seidel, Pres.; Carol Doll, Prin. Sisters 2; Lay Teachers 6; Enrollment 115.

WHITE PLAINS. *Academy of Our Lady of Good Counsel*. (Elementary Dept.), 52 N. Broadway, 10603. Tel: 914-949-8186. Sr. Clare Arenholz, R.D.C. Sisters 2; Lay Teachers 12; Students 172.

[I] THE CATHOLIC CHARITIES OF THE ARCHDIOCESE OF NEW YORK

NEW YORK. *The Catholic Charities of the Archdiocese of New York*, 1011 First Ave., 10022. Tel: 212-371-1000. Rev. Msgr. James J. Murray, Exec. Dir.; Rev. Msgr. William J. Toohy, Assoc. Exec. Dir.; Rev. Kevin L. Sullivan, Chief Oper. Officer; Mr. Kenneth Dempsey, Chief Financial Officer; Rev. Michael F.

Gannon, Coord. Upstate Counties, 240 Church St., Poughkeepsie, 12601. Tel: 914-452-1400.
Administrative Departments: Rev. Msgr. William J. Toohy, Dir., Social Research; Sr. Una McCormack, O.P., Dir. Child Care; Mr. John J. Hughes, Dir., Family & Children's Svcs.; Mary Healy-Sedutto, Ph.D., Dir. Health & Hospitals; Mr. George B. Horton, Dir., Social Devel.; Ms. Joanne Abruzzese, Dir. Personnel; Mr. Joseph Panepinto, Acting Dir.

Service Units-Dept. of Family & Children's Services: Harlem: John Paul II Apartments, 211 W. 141 St., 10030. Tel: 212-281-2100. Sr. Ann Shea, D.C., Inwood, Washington Heights: 652 W. 187 St., 10033. Tel: 212-795-6860. Ms. Carmela Cantoni, Lower Manhattan: 530 Grand St., 10002. Tel: 212-777-3111. Sr. Mary Matthew Labunski, M.S.B.T., Central Manhattan: 1011 First Ave., 10022. Tel: 212-371-1000. Mr. John Stanolevich, Bronx County: 2380 Belmont Ave., Bronx, 10458. Tel: 718-364-7700. Marjorie Stuckle, Ph.D., Staten Island: 120 Anderson Ave., Staten Island, 10302. Tel: 718-447-6330. Mr. James Ryan, Dutchess County: 240 Church St., Poughkeepsie, 12601. Tel: 914-452-1400. Orange County: 185 Liberty Ave., Newburgh, 12550. Tel: 914-561-3452. Mrs. Maria McTiernan, Rockland County: 333 Sneden Pl. W., Spring Valley, 10977. Tel: 914-426-3441. Ms. Kathleen Rigney, Westchester/Putnam Counties: 1045 Park St., Peekskill, 10566. Tel: 914-737-7338. Ms. Mary Galgano, 4 St. Mary's St., Yonkers, 10701. Tel: 914-476-2700. Ms. Polly Kerrigan, Sullivan County: North St. & Liberty St., P.O. Box 395, Monticello, 12701. Tel: 914-791-6023. Ms. Patricia Brennan, Ulster County: 275 Fair St., Kingston, 12401. Tel: 914-339-8817. Dr. Emil Pin.

Parish Social Ministry, 1011 First Ave., 10022. Tel: 212-371-1000, Ext. 2032. Mrs. Dorothy Meehan.

Special Services. Offices of the Disabled:

Catholic Guild for the Blind, 1011 First Ave., 10022. Tel: 212-371-1000, Ext. 2020. Miss Ann T. Snyder, Dir.

New York Catholic Deaf Center, 1011 First Ave., 10022. Tel: 212-371-1000, Ext. 2506. Rev. Msgr. Patrick P. McCahill, Supvr.

Services to Parishes for Older Adults, 1011 First Ave., 10022. Tel: 212-371-1000, Ext. 2003. Mrs. Eleanor M. Ramos.

Upstate Offices, 240 Church St., Poughkeepsie, 12601. Tel: 914-452-1400, Ext. 4214. Sr. Jean Canora, O.S.F.

Department of Social Development. Mr. George B. Horton, Dir.; Mr. Kenneth Hoffarth, Admin. Supvr. Criminal Justice Ministries; Mr. Carlos Bajo, Dir. Immigrant and Refugee Svcs.; Ms. Patricia O'Callaghan, Coord. Irish Outreach; Mr. Paul Martin, Dir. Refugee Resettlement; Sr. Ann Murray, Dir. Office for the Homeless and Hungry.

New York Institute for Human Development.

Department of Neighborhood Housing. Mr. Jean Vernet, Dir.; Mr. Robert Paul, Dir. Housing & Urban Renewal Office.

The Ladies of Charity of the Catholic Charities of the Archdiocese of New York. Ms. Susan Grady, Exec. Dir.; Miss Christina M. Krupka, Pres. Spiritual Directors: Rev. Msgr. William J. Toohy; Rev. Msgr. Peter Finn.

Catholic Charities Counselling Service, Archdiocese of New York, 1011 First Ave., 10022. Rev. Msgr. William J. Toohy.

Roman Catholic Fund for Children and Other Purposes, 1011 First Ave., 10022. Rev. Msgr. James J. Murray.

Holy Name Centre for Homeless Men, Inc., 18 Bleecker St., 10012. Tel: 212-226-5848. Rev. Msgr. John B. Ahern, Dir.

**Providence Health Services*, 1249 Fifth Ave., 10029. Mary Healey-Sedutto, Ph.D., Pres.

[J] SOCIAL DEVELOPMENT

NEW YORK. *Catholic Charities Department of Social Development*, 1011 First Ave., 10022. Tel: 212-371-1000, Ext. 2480. Mr. George B. Horton, Dir.

Department of Neighborhood Housing, 1011 First Ave., 10022. Tel: 212-371-1000.

Immigrant and Refugee Services, 1011 First Ave., 10022. Tel: 212-371-1000; Fax: 212-826-6254. Mr. Carlos Bajo, Dir. Immigrant Svcs.; Miss Patricia O'Callaghan, Coord. Project Irish Outreach; Mr. Paul J. Martin, Dir. Refugee Settlement.

New York Institute for Human Development, Inc., 1011 First Ave., 10022. Tel: 212-371-1000, Ext. 2495. Mr. Jean Vernet, Dir.

Office for Justice and Peace, 1011 First Ave., 10022. Tel: 212-371-1000, Ext. 2480.

Office for the Homeless and Hungry, 1011 First Ave., 10022. Tel: 212-371-1000. Sr. Ann Murray, S.H.C.J., Dir.

Office of Criminal Justice, 1011 First Ave., 10022. Tel: 212-371-1000, Ext. 3166. Mr. Kenneth Hoffarth, Dir.

[K] FAMILY AND CHILDREN'S SERVICES

NEW YORK. *Family and Children's Services*, 1011 First Ave., 10022. Tel: 212-371-1000.
Mental Health Service Centers:

Bronx Center, 2380 Belmont Ave., Bronx, 10458. Tel: 212-364-7700. Marjorie Stuckle, Ph.D., Admin. Supvr.

Inwood (Washington Heights) Center, 652 W. 187th St., 10033. Tel: 212-795-6860. Ms. Carmela Cantone, Admin. Supvr.

Peekskill Center, 1045 Park St., Peekskill, 10566. Tel: 914-737-7338. Mrs. Mary Galgano, Admin. Supvr.

Yonkers Center, 4 St. Mary's St., Yonkers, 10701. Tel: 914-473-2700. Ms. Mary Kerrigan, Admin. Supvr.

Mental Health & Community Residences:

NEW YORK. *Beacon of Hope House*, Central Administrative Office, 116 E. 16th St., 5th Fl., 10003-2112. Tel: 212-982-3560; Fax: 212-982-2869. Alan H. Bernstein, Exec. Dir.; Joy Jasper, Dir. Personnel; Ravi Ramaswam, C.P.A., Controller.

Supervised Units, 1400 Waters Pl., Bronx, 10461. Tel: 212-892-3494; Fax: 212-892-5507. Christine Lawry, Admin. Asst.; Robert Franco, Prog. Mgr., Beacon I: Vadim Moldovan, Program Supvr. Tel: 718-931-0600 Ext. 3376, Beacon II: Kimberly Jones, Program Supvr. Tel: 718-931-0600 Ext. 2637, Beacon III: Susana Vasquez, Program Supvr. Tel: 718-931-0600 Ext. 3289.

Terence Cardinal Cooke Residence, 2467 Bathgate Ave., Bronx, 10458. Tel: 718-367-6990; Fax: 718-365-2544. Karen Oser, Program Mgr.

Supervised Units, 777 Seaview Ave., Bldg. D, 2nd Fl., Staten Island, 10305. Tel: 718-980-1072; Fax: 718-980-1077. Dennis Scimone, Regional Dir., Brooklyn & Staten Island Svcs.; Sharon Quattrachi, Admin. Sec., Beacon I: Program Supvr. Tel: 718-980-0041, Beacon II: Pam Reichenberg, Program Supvr. Tel: 718-980-1072.

Staten Island Apartment Programs. Laurence Baker, Program Mgr., 90-92 Hancock St., Staten Island, 10305. Tel: 718-979-6241.

Highbridge Neighborhood Supported Housing Program, 1435 Ogden Ave., Bronx, 10452. Tel: 718-293-1009; Fax: 718-293-0939. Rick Downes, Prog. Supv.

Kingsborough Intensive Supported Apartment Program, 647 Vanderbilt Ave., Brooklyn, 11238. Tel: 718-398-4556; Fax: 718-398-4807. Veronica Rose, Prog. Supv.

Services to the St. Anthony's Residence, 410 E. 156th St., Bronx, 10455. Tel: 718-993-5060. Margo Gill, Program. Mgr.

BARRYVILLE. *New Hope Manor*, 35 Hillside Rd., 12719; Fax: 914-557-6603. Nicholas A. Roes, Dir.
See Miscellaneous listing for further details. Board of Directors: Revs. Dan Egan; Arte Johnson; Sr. Rita Shea; Sr. Madeline Murphy; Sr. Cecilia La Pietra. Staff: Rev. Aquinas Thomas, S.A., Dir., In-Service Training; Sr. Maureen Conway, O.P., Dir. of Education; Sr. Patricia Conway, O.P., Counselor & Teacher; Sr. Rose Respol, O.P., Dir., Religious Ed.

SPRING VALLEY. *Good Counsel / The Cardinal Cooke Residence*, 22 Linden Ave., 10977. Tel: 914-356-0517; Fax: 914-356-4175. Christopher Bell, Exec. Dir.; Michele Dominguez, House Mgr. A program of Good Counsel in Hoboken, NJ, helping pregnant and single mothers with children.

Good Counsel / The Paraclete Foundation, 1157 Fulton Ave., Bronx, 10456. Tel: 718-328-8620. Christopher Bell, Exec. Dir.; Ms. Sandra Jones, House Mgr.

Good Counsel, 38 N. Clinton St., Poughkeepsie, 12601. Tel: 914-452-2944. Christopher Bell, Exec. Dir.; Sr. Mona O'Connell, S.N.D., House Mgr.

Good Counsel, 38 Wiman Pl., Staten Island, 10305. Tel: 718-727-8266. Christopher Bell, Exec. Dir.; Ann Jarosz, House Mgr. Total Assisted 336; Total Staff 32.

STATEN ISLAND. *Good Counsel*, 38 Wiman Pl., 10305. Tel: 718-727-8266. Christopher Bell, Exec. Dir.; Rev. Benedict J. Groeschel, C.F.R., Chm.

[L] YOUTH SERVICES

NEW YORK. *Catholic Youth Organization of the Archdiocese of New York Inc.*, Executive Office, 1011 First Ave., 10022-4187. Tel: 212-371-1000; Fax: 212-371-1000, Ext. 3465. Mr. J. Peter Grace, Pres.; Mr. Henry Humphreys, Chm.; Rev. Msgr. James F. Bolger, Exec. Dir.; Mr. Joseph E. Panepinto, Deputy Exec. Dir.

Archdiocesan Committee on Scouting: Rev. Anthony D. Marchitelli, Archdiocesan Boy Scout Chap.; Sr. Kathleen Finnerty, O.S.U., Archdiocesan Girl Scout Chap.; Rev. Lawrence J. Quinn, Sea Cadet Chap.; Deacon Larry Battersby, Dir. of Parish-Based Youth Ministry; Ms. Arlene Karolewicz, Acting Dir., Fund Raising and Public Relations; Sr. Judy Frasinetti, S.M.R., Dir. Blair Lodge and Young Adult Ministry; Ms. Antoinette Levin, Dir. Outdoor Ministry.

CYO Manhattan County: Mr. Anthony D'Angelo, 242 Bathgate Ave., Bronx, 10458. Tel: 718-367-7659.

Grace Youth Ministry Center: Mr. Jorge Gonzalez, Dir., 218 W. 108th St., 10025. Tel: 212-666-6598.

Cardinal Spellman Center: Mr. Thomas Rosati, 137 E. Second St., 10009. Tel: 212-677-6600.

Lt. Joseph P. Kennedy, Jr., Memorial Center: 34 W. 134th St., 10037. Tel: 212-882-6401. Ms. Gloria Burke.

CYO Staten Island Office: Judith Trancucci.
120 Anderson Ave., Staten Island, 10302. Tel: 718-448-4950.

Staten Island Center, 120 Anderson Ave., 10302. Tel: 718-448-4949. Fran Mitilieri, Dir.

CYO Westchester Office: Co-Directors: Frank Magaletta; Ms. Antoinette Levin, 9 Brookview Blvd., Chestnut Ridge, 10977. Tel: 914-624-0889; 225-4651.

CYO Orange Office: Mr. Robert Lopez, 425 Sarasino Dr., Maybrook, 12543. Tel: 914-427-5315.

CYO Rockland Office: Thomas F. Collins, 34 Granecy Ct., Pearl River, 10965. Tel: 914-735-8419.

CYO Dutchess Office: Co-Directors: John Van Voorhis; Bro. Dominick Pujia, F.M.S., 33 Meadow Dr., Wappinger Falls, 12590. Tel: 914-297-7721.

CYO Ulster Office: Thomas Brinkmann, 157 Broadway, Kingston, 12401. Tel: 914-338-1510. Sr. Kevin John Shields, Sullivan Co. Coord., Box 1011, Liberty, 12750. Tel: 914-292-9100.

[M] SOCIETY OF ST. VINCENT DE PAUL

NEW YORK. *Society of St. Vincent De Paul, Archdiocesan Central Council of New York*, 1011 First Ave., 10022. Tel: 212-755-8615. Legal Title: *The Society of St. Vincent de Paul of the Archdiocese of New York, Inc.* Territory: Archdiocese of New York. Mr. Ramon Vidal, Pres.; Rev. Robert T. Ritchie, Spiritual Advisor.

District Council of Manhattan, 1011 First Ave., Ste. 607, 10022. Tel: 212-755-8615. Legal Title: *The Society of St. Vincent de Paul in the City of New York*. Territory: Manhattan. Mr. Edmund Keane, Pres.; Rev. Msgr. Wallace A. Harris, Spiritual Advisor; Mr. Vincent D. Reilly, Exec. Sec.

District Council of the Bronx, 402 E. 152nd St., Bronx, 10455. Tel: 718-292-9090. Virginia Mulligan, Pres.

District Council of Staten Island, 28 Bryson Ave., Staten Island, 10302. Carmen Malandro, Pres.

Council of Rockland County, 37 E. Mayer Dr., Suffern, 10901. Deacon Joseph Verboys, Pres.

BRONX. *District Council of the Bronx*, 402 E. 152nd St., 10455. Tel: 718-292-9090. Legal Title: *The Society of St. Vincent de Paul, District Council of the Bronx, Inc.* Territory: Borough of The Bronx & Lower Westchester. Rev. Walter A. Birkle, Spiritual Dir.; Virginia M. Mulligan, Pres.

STATEN ISLAND. *Particular Council of Staten Island*. Carmen Malandro, Pres.; Deacon Joseph Graf, Spiritual Dir.

[N] INSTITUTIONS FOR DEPENDENT CHILDREN

NEW YORK. *Covenant House Under 21*, 460 W. 41st St., 10036.
For a complete listing, refer to the Special Care Facilities section.

Pius XII Youth and Family Services, Office of the Pres., 866 Third Ave., 30th Floor, 10022. Tel: 212-702-9850.
For a complete listing, refer to the Special Care Facilities section.

BLAUVELT. *St. Dominic Home*, 10913. Tel: 914-359-3400; Fax: 914-359-4253.
For a complete listing, refer to the Special Care Facilities section.

BRONX. *Saint Dominic's Home - Prevention Program (ASTAAN)*, 2345 University Ave., 10468. Tel: 718-584-4407.
For a complete listing, refer to the Special Care Facilities section.

NANUET. *St. Agatha Home of the New York Foundling Hospital*, 135 Convent Rd., 10954. Tel: 914-623-3461.
For a complete listing, refer to the Special Care Facilities section.

WEST PARK. *St. Cabrini Home*, 12493. Tel: 914-384-6500; Fax: 914-384-6001.
For a complete listing, refer to the Special Care Facilities section.

WHITE PLAINS. *Cardinal McCloskey Services*, Two Holland Ave., 10603. Tel: 914-997-8000.
For a complete listing, refer to the Special Care Facilities section.

[O] SPECIALIZED CHILD CARING HOMES

NEW YORK. *Good Shepherd Services*, 305 7th Ave., 9th Floor, 10001. Tel: 212-475-4245.
For a complete listing, refer to the Special Care Facilities section.

Kennedy Child Study Center, 151 E. 67th St., 10021. Tel: 212-988-9500.
For a complete listing, refer to the Special Care Facilities section.
Lavelle School for the Blind, 221st St. and Paulding Ave., 10469. Tel: 718-882-1212.
For a complete listing, refer to the Special Care Facilities section.
Mission of the Immaculate Virgin. Mount Loretto Staten Island, 10309. Tel: 718-317-2600.
For a complete listing, refer to the Special Care Facilities section.
New York Foundling Charitable Corp., 590 Avenue of the Americas, 10011. Tel: 212-633-9300.
For a complete listing, refer to the Special Care Facilities section.
New York Foundling Hospital for Pediatric, Medical and Rehabilitative Care, Inc., The, 590 Avenue of the Americas, 10011. Tel: 212-633-9300.
For a complete listing, refer to the Special Care Facilities section.
New York Foundling Hospital, The, 590 Avenue of the Americas, 10011. Tel: 212-633-9300.
For a complete listing, refer to the Special Care Facilities section.

MILLBROOK. *Cardinal Hayes Home for Children*, North Ave., P.O. Box CHHC, 12545. Tel: 914-677-6363; Fax: 914-677-6691.
For a complete listing, refer to the Special Care Facilities section.

RHINEBECK. *Astor Home for Children, The*, 36 Mill St., P.O. Box 5005, 12572-5005. Tel: 914-876-4081; Fax: 914-876-2020.
For a complete listing, refer to the Special Care Facilities section.
Astor Learning Center, The, 36 Mill St., P.O. Box 5005, 12572-5005. Tel: 914-876-4081; Fax: 914-876-2020.
For a complete listing, refer to the Special Care Facilities section.

[P] CHILDREN'S AGENCIES & PROTECTIVE INSTITUTIONS

NEW YORK. *Catholic Guardian Society*, 1011 First Ave., 10022. Tel: 212-371-1000.
For a complete listing, refer to the Special Care Facilities section.
Catholic Home Bureau, 1011 First Ave., 10022. Tel: 212-371-1000.
For a complete listing, refer to the Special Care Facilities section.
Guild of the Infant Savior, 1011 First Ave., Room 1116, 10022. Tel: 212-371-1000, Ext. 2440.
For a complete listing, refer to the Special Care Facilities section.
Pelletier School & Services, 147 W. 70th St., 10023.
For a complete listing, refer to the Special Care Facilities section.

LINCOLNDALE. *Lincoln Hall*, P.O. Box 600, 10540. Tel: 914-248-7474; Fax: 914-248-5173.
For a complete listing, refer to the Special Care Facilities section.

[Q] CATHOLIC CHARITIES - CHILD CARING AGENCIES

OSSINING. *The Cardinal McCloskey Emergency Residential School*, 155 N. Highland Ave., 10562.
For a complete listing, refer to the Special Care Facilities section.

[R] DAY NURSERIES

NEW YORK. *Featherbed Lane Day Care Center*. 98108 Featherbed Ln., Bronx, 10452. Tel: 212-583-8970. Mrs. Joyce Thompson, Dir. Group Day Care Children 33; Family Day Care Children 76.
Nazareth Nursery, 214-216 W. 15th St., 10011-6501. Tel: 212-243-1881. Montessori Day Care. Sr. Lucy Sabatini, O.S.F., Dir. & Admin. Sisters of St. Francis of the Mission of the Immaculate Virgin 2; Capacity 55 Children; Total Staff 14.
Providence Rest Child Day Care Center, Inc., 3310 Campbell Dr., 10465. Tel: 718-823-3588. Total Assisted 20/Day; Total Staff 6.
St. Benedict's Day Nursery, Day Care Center, 34 W. 134th St., 10037. Tel: 212-283-3350. Sr. Miriam Cecilia, Dir., Day Nursery. Handmaids of the Most Pure Heart of Mary 4; Children 82.
St. Cecilia's Day Nursery, 118 E. 106th St., 10029. Tel: 212-534-8423. Sr. Frances Arduini, S.A., Dir. Franciscan Sisters of the Atonement 3; Capacity 30; Total Served 30.
San Jose Day Nursery, 432 W. 20th St., 10011. Tel: 212-929-0839. Sr. Guadalupe Sordo, Supr.; Josefina Jimenez, Dir. Mothers of the Helpless 7; Children 57.
Sr. Elizabeth Boyle Child Learning Center, Inc. Bay St. and Vanderbilt Ave., Staten Island, 10304. Tel: 718-390-5655. Total Assisted 75; Total Staff 12.

YONKERS. *Queen's Daughters Day Care Center, Inc.*, 73 Buena Vista Ave., 10701. Tel: 914-969-4491. Barbara Berrios, Dir. Children 175; Total Staff 20.

[S] GENERAL HOSPITALS

NEW YORK. *Bayley Seton Hospital*. 75 Vanderbilt Ave. Staten Island, 10304. Tel: 718-390-6000.
For a complete listing, refer to the Hospitals section.
Cabrini Medical Center (Cabrini Development Council, Inc.), 227 E. 19th St., 10003. Tel: 212-995-6000.
For a complete listing, refer to the Hospitals section.
Our Lady of Mercy Medical Center. 233rd St. Division, 600 E. 233 St. Bronx, 10466. Tel: 718-920-9000.
For a complete listing, refer to the Hospitals section.
St. Clare's Hospital and Health Center, 415 W. 51st St., 10019. Tel: 212-586-1500.
For a complete listing, refer to the Hospitals section.
St. Vincent's Hospital and Medical Center of New York, 153 W. 11th St., 10011. Tel: 212-604-7000.
For a complete listing, refer to the Hospitals section.
Saint Vincent's Medical Center of Richmond. 355 Bard Ave. Staten Island, 10310. Tel: 718-876-1234.
For a complete listing, refer to the Hospitals section.

BEACON. *St. Francis Hospital*, Delavan Ave., 12508. Tel: 914-831-3500.
For a complete listing, refer to the Hospitals section.

KINGSTON. *Benedictine Hospital*, 105 Mary's Ave., 12401. Tel: 914-338-2500.
For a complete listing, refer to the Hospitals section.

PORT JERVIS. *Mercy Community Hospital*, 160 E. Main St., 12771. Tel: 914-856-5351; Fax: 914-856-5659.
For a complete listing, refer to the Hospitals section.

POUGHKEEPSIE. *St. Francis Hospital*, North Rd., 12601. Tel: 914-471-2000.
For a complete listing, refer to the Hospitals section.

SUFFERN. *Good Samaritan Hospital of Suffern*, 10901. Tel: 914-368-5000.
For a complete listing, refer to the Hospitals section.

WARWICK. *St. Anthony Community Hospital, Inc.*, 15-19 Maple Ave., 10990. Tel: 914-986-2276.
For a complete listing, refer to the Hospitals section.

WHITE PLAINS. *St. Agnes Hospital and Children's Rehabilitation Center*, 305 North St., 10605. Tel: 914-681-4500; Fax: 914-681-4974.
For a complete listing, refer to the Hospitals section.

YONKERS. *St. Joseph's Medical Center*, 127 S. Broadway, 10701. Tel: 914-378-7000; Fax: 914-965-4838.
For a complete listing, refer to the Hospitals section.

[T] SPECIAL HOSPITALS AND SANATORIA FOR INVALIDS

NEW YORK. *Calvary Hospital*. 1740 Eastchester Rd. Bronx, 10461. Tel: 718-863-6900.
For a complete listing, refer to the Special Care Facilities section.
St. Rose's Home, 71 Jackson St., 10002. Tel: 212-677-8132.
For a complete listing, refer to the Special Care Facilities section.
Terence Cardinal Cooke Health Care Center, 1249 Fifth Ave., 10029. Tel: 212-360-1000.
For a complete listing, refer to the Special Care Facilities section.

HARRISON. *St. Vincent's Hospital and Medical Center of New York, Westchester Branch*, 275 North St., 10528. Tel: 914-967-6500; Fax: 914-967-1633.
For a complete listing, refer to the Special Care Facilities section.

HAWTHORNE. *Rosary Hill Home*, 10532. Tel: 914-769-0114.
For a complete listing, refer to the Special Care Facilities section.

YONKERS. *St. Eleanora's Home for Convalescents*, 127 S. Broadway, 10701. Tel: 914-378-7000.
For a complete listing, refer to the Special Care Facilities section.

[U] ORDERS OF NURSING SISTERS

NEW YORK. *Convent of the Little Sisters of the Assumption*, 2604 Davidson Ave., 10468. Sr. Jean McCormack, Prov. Coord.; Sr. Mary Joseph, Local Coord. Sisters 6.
Family Health Service, Inc.; Little Sisters of the Assumption, 426 E. 119th St., 10035. Tel: 212-987-4422; Fax: 212-987-4430. Sr. Judith Garson, Exec. Dir.

BRONX. *Convent of the Sisters Servants of Mary S.M.*, 3305 Country Club Rd., 10465-1296. Tel: 718-829-0428. Mother Angeles Aizpurua. Mission: Private nursing in the homes. Sisters 20.

OSSINING. *Dominican Sisters Family Health Services, Inc.*, 299 N. Highland Ave., 10562. Tel: 914-941-1710. A community-based certified voluntary Home Health Agency. Sr. Virginia Hanrahan, O.P., R.N., B.S.N., M.S., Ph.D., Exec. Dir.
Bronx Office, 279 Alexander Ave., Bronx, 10454. Tel: 718-665-6557. Margaret Sweeney, R.N., B.S.N., M.A., Admin.
Westchester Offices, 299 N. Highland Ave., 10562. Tel: 914-941-1654. Evelyn Bobb, R.N., B.S.N., Admin.
Suffolk County Office, 103-6 W. Montauk Hwy., Box 209, Hampton Bays, 11946. Tel: 516-728-0181. Box 866, Amagansett, 11930. Tel: 516-267-1090. Joanna O'Connell, R.N., B.S.N., Admin. Total Assisted 5,800.

STATEN ISLAND. *Pax Christi Hospice*, 355 Bard Ave., 10310. Hospice and Home Care Services for the terminally ill. Sisters of Charity Health Care System.

[V] NURSING HOMES

NEW YORK. *Kateri Residence*, 150 Riverside Dr., 10024. Tel: 212-769-0744; Fax: 212-873-0658.
For a complete listing, refer to the Special Care Facilities section.
Mary Manning Walsh Home, 1339 York Ave., 10021. Tel: 212-628-2800.
For a complete listing, refer to the Special Care Facilities section.
St. Vincent dePaul Residence, 900 Intervale Ave., 10459. Tel: 718-589-6965.
For a complete listing, refer to the Special Care Facilities section.
Terence Cardinal Cooke Health Care Center, 1249 Fifth Ave., 10029. Tel: 212-360-1000; Fax: 212-289-2739.
For a complete listing, refer to the Special Care Facilities section.

BRONX. *Franciscan Health System of New York, Inc.*, 2975 Independence Ave., 10463-4699. Tel: 718-548-1700; Fax: 718-601-3384.
For a complete listing, refer to the Special Care Facilities section.
Jeanne Jugan Residence, 3200 Baychester Ave., 10475 Fax: 718-671-0305.
For a complete listing, refer to the Special Care Facilities section.
Medical Missionaries of Mary, 563 Minneford Ave., 10464-1118. Tel: 718-885-0945; Fax: 718-885-0010.
For a complete listing, refer to the Special Care Facilities section.
Providence Rest, 3304 Waterbury Ave., 10465. Tel: 718-931-3000.
For a complete listing, refer to the Special Care Facilities section.
St. Patrick's Home for the Aged and Infirm, 66 Van Cortlandt Park S., 10463. Tel: 718-519-2800.
For a complete listing, refer to the Special Care Facilities section.

DOBBS FERRY. *St. Cabrini Nursing Home*, 115 Broadway, 10522. Tel: 914-693-6800.
For a complete listing, refer to the Special Care Facilities section.

MIDDLETOWN. *St. Teresa's Nursing Home*, 120 Highland Ave., 10940. Tel: 914-342-1033; Fax: 914-344-5631.
For a complete listing, refer to the Special Care Facilities section.

RHINEBECK. *Ferncliff Nursing Home*, 52 River Rd., 12572. Tel: 914-876-2011; Fax: 914-876-2019.
For a complete listing, refer to the Special Care Facilities section.

STATEN ISLAND. *Carmel Richmond Nursing Home, Inc.*, 88 Old Town Rd., 10304-4299. Tel: 718-979-5000.
For a complete listing, refer to the Special Care Facilities section.

WARWICK. *Villa Frances at the Knolls*, 20 Grand St., 10990. Tel: 914-986-2267.
For a complete listing, refer to the Special Care Facilities section.

[W] ADULT RESIDENCES

NEW YORK. *Cor Mariae*, 251 W. 14th St., 10011. Tel: 212-929-9837.
For a complete listing, refer to the Special Care Facilities section.
The Dwelling Place, 409 W. 40th St., 10018. Tel: 212-564-7887.
For a complete listing, refer to the Special Care Facilities section.
El Carmelo Residence, 249 W. 14th St., 10011. Tel: 212-242-8224.
For a complete listing, refer to the Special Care Facilities section.
The Jeanne d'Arc Residence, 253 W. 24th St., 10011. Tel: 212-989-5952.
For a complete listing, refer to the Special Care Facilities section.
Kolping Society of New York Men's Residence (Catholic Kolping Society New York, Inc.), 165 E. 88th St., 10128. Tel: 212-369-6647.
For a complete listing, refer to the Special Care Facilities section.
Kolping-on-Concourse. 2916 Grand Concourse Bronx, 10458. Tel: 212-733-6119.
For a complete listing, refer to the Special Care Facilities section.
Leo House, 332 W. 23rd St., 10011. Tel: 212-929-1010.
For a complete listing, refer to the Special Care Facilities section.
Padre Pio Shelter for Homeless Men. 419 E. 155th St. Bronx, 10455. Tel: 718-292-3713.

For a complete listing, refer to the Special Care Facilities section.

Sacred Heart Residence, 432 W. 20th St., 10011. Tel: 212-929-5790.

For a complete listing, refer to the Special Care Facilities section.

St. Agnes' Residence, 237 W. 74th St., 10023. Tel: 212-874-1361.

For a complete listing, refer to the Special Care Facilities section.

St. Joseph's Immigrant Home, 425 W. 44th St., 10036. Tel: 212-246-5363.

For a complete listing, refer to the Special Care Facilities section.

St. Mary's Residence, 225 E. 72nd St., 10021. Tel: 212-249-6850.

For a complete listing, refer to the Special Care Facilities section.

St. Zita's Home for Adults, 143 W. 14th St., 10011. Tel: 212-243-7200.

For a complete listing, refer to the Special Care Facilities section.

Thorpe Family Residence, Inc., 2252 Crotona Ave., 10457.

For a complete listing, refer to the Special Care Facilities section.

GARRISON. *St. Christopher's Inn*, P.O. Box 150, 10524-0150. Tel: 914-424-3616.

For a complete listing, refer to the Special Care Facilities section.

MONTROSE. *Kolping-on-Hudson*, 95 Montrose Point Rd., 10548. Tel: 914-737-9547.

For a complete listing, refer to the Special Care Facilities section.

TUXEDO. *Samaritan Manor at Tuxedo, Inc.*, Meyers Rd., 10987.

For a complete listing, refer to the Special Care Facilities section.

WASHINGTON, DC. *Centro Maria, Inc.*, 650 Jackson St., NE, 20017. Tel: 202-635-1697.

For a complete listing, refer to the Special Care Facilities section.

[X] CATHOLIC CAMPS

NEW YORK. *The Catholic Camp Association Inc.*, 1011 First Ave., 10022. Tel: 212-371-1000.

John V. Mara CYO Camps, Putnam Valley.

Hill Camp. Capacity 120.

Valley Camp. Capacity 120. Total Assisted 147; Total in Residence 271; Total Staff 48.

[Y] COMMUNITY CENTERS

NEW YORK. *Cardinal Spellman Center, Inc.*, 137 E. Second St., 10009. Tel: 212-677-6600; Fax: 212-995-8537. Mr. Thomas Rosati, Dir. All Centers are engaged in full time recreational and educational activities. Serves Lower East Side parishes and includes Cardinal Spellman Headstart. Total Staff 35; Total Assisted 1,550.

Casita Maria Inc. 928 Simpson St., Bronx, 10459; Fax: 718-842-4622. Cristina Toosie, Exec. Dir.; Mrs. Jacqueline Weld, Chm. Serves the Bronx and East Harlem. Casita Maria serves over 5,500 individuals each year through after school recreation, social services, senior citizens centers, and homeless seniors.

Casita Maria-Carver Community Center, 55 E. 102nd St., 10029. Cristina Toosie, Exec. Dir.; Orlando Tomas Martinez, Dir. Serves Carver Houses and adjacent areas of E. Harlem.

Drew-Hamilton CYO Center, 220 W. 143rd St., 10030. Serves Central Harlem.

Lieut. Joseph P. Kennedy, Jr. Memorial Community Center, 34 W. 134th St., 10037. Mrs. Gloria Burke, Exec. Dir. Serves Central Harlem. Serves 200 youth in afternoon and afterschool programs and 500 teenagers in evening programs.

Life Experience and Faith Sharing Association, 149 E. 117th St., 10035. Tel: 212-996-7303. Team: Sr. Dorothy Gallant, S.C.; Sr. Teresa H. Skehan, R.S.M.; Mr. Darryl Gillis; Mr. Arthur Addison; Sr. Mary Spratt, R.C.; Stephanie Veluz; Sr. Cecilia Palange, S.C.I.M.; Godfrey Xaba. Total Assisted 2,500; Total Team 8.

Staten Island CYO Center. 120 Anderson Ave., Port Richmond, Staten Island, 10302. Tel: 718-448-4949; Fax: 718-273-8361. Frances M. Mitilieri, Dir. Serves residents of Port Richmond and surrounding areas.

[Z] MONASTERIES AND RESIDENCES OF PRIESTS AND BROTHERS

NEW YORK. *"America;" Residence and publication office of the America Press*, 106 W. 56th St., 10019. Tel: 212-581-4640; Fax: 212-399-3596. Revs. George W. Hunt, S.J., Editor-in-Chief; Robert C. Collins, S.J.; James J. DiGiacomo, S.J.; John W. Donohue, S.J.; Vincent T. O'Keefe, S.J., Supr.; George M. Anderson, S.J.; Eugene J. O'Brien, S.J.; Patrick H. Samway, S.J.; Charles M. Whelan, S.J.; Walter J. Smith, S.J.; Edward J. Mattimoe, S.J.; Vincent J. Duminuco, S.J.; Frederick J. O'Brien, S.J.; Dennis Linehan, S.J.; Deacon Charles J. O'Byrne, S.J. Priests 12; Deacons 1.

Apostolic Society of the Crusade of the Holy Spirit. c/o St. John's Rectory, 35 Willow St., Beacon, 12508. Tel: 914-831-0422; Fax: 914-831-1009. Revs. Ignatius Peries, C.Sp. (Argentina), Dir. Gen., Argentina; Bernard Kelly, C.Sp. (U.K.), Vicar Gen., U.K.; Nimal Mendis, C.Sp. (U.S.A.), Asst. Gen., Sec. Gen. & Treas. Gen., U.S.A.

Atonement Friars, 138 Waverly Pl., 10014-3845. Tel: 212-243-4692. Rev. Elias D. Mallon, S.A., Dir. Graymoor Ecumenical & Interreligious Institute; Bro. William Martyn, S.A., Exec. Sec. Commission on Ecumenical & Interreligious Affairs, Archdiocese of NY; Rev. Joseph F. Cavoto, S.A., Vocation Dir., Tel: 212-675-6389. Rev. James J. Gardiner, S.A., Natl. Pastoral Life Center, Tel: 212-255-6731. Rev. Charles Sharon, S.A., Admin.

Augustinian Recollects Provincial Residence, Province of St. Nicholas of Tolentine, 2800 Schurz Ave., 10465. Tel: 212-823-0460. Legal Title: *The Province of St. Nicholas of Tolentine of the Augustinian Recollect Fathers*. Revs. Jose Luis Duenas Navarro, O.A.R.; Carmelo Arroyo Gonzalez, O.A.R.

Brothers of the Christian Schools of Manhattan College, Inc. 4415 Post Rd., Bronx, 10471. Tel: 212-884-0613. Bros. Kenneth Fitzgerald, F.S.C., Dir.; Luke Salm, F.S.C., Sub-Dir.; Thomas Scanlan, F.S.C., Pres. In res., Revs. Reynold Borzaga, F.S.C.A.; Anthony L. Rubsys, F.S.C.A.; Caesar Russo, M.A., J.C.L., 5050 Fieldston Rd., Riverdale, Bronx, 10471. Tel: 718-549-2384. Total Staff 9; Total in Residence 38.

Calasanzian Fathers (Piarists), 88 Convent Ave., 10027. Tel: 212-234-1919. Revs. Felix Jimenez, Sch.P.; Jose M. Clavero, Sch.P.; Aroldo Guerra, Sch.P.; Felix Ganuza, Sch.P.

Franciscan Friars, Order of Friars Manor, Holy Name Province Provincialate, 126 W. 32nd St., 10001-3202. Tel: 212-721-1600; Fax: 212-721-1605. Revs. John M. Felice, O.F.M., Prov. Minister; Charles J. Miller, O.F.M., Prov. Vicar.

Priests of the Province in Residences not listed elsewhere: Rev. Justin J. Bailey, O.F.M., St. Bonaventure Friary, 56 Spadina Rd., Toronto, Ontario, M5R 2T3, Canada. Rev. Raymond A. Beane, O.F.M., Mailing Address: Box 590, Big Pine Key, FL, 33043-0590. Rev. David M. Bossman, O.F.M., Seton Hall University, South Orange, NJ, 07079-2696. Rev. Patrick C. Callaghan, O.F.M., Rte. 1, Saint Regis Falls, 12980-9712. Rev. W. Russell Carroll, O.F.M., St. Francis Gardens, 904 Las Lomas Rd., NE, Albuquerque, NM, 87102-2691. Rev. Owen Colligan, O.F.M., Staff Chap., Fort Bayard Medical Center, P.O. Box 219, Fort Bayard, NM, 88036-0219. Rev. Joseph Ganssle, O.F.M., 4165 Eaton St., Denver, CO, 80212-7306. Rev. Depaul A. Genska, O.F.M., Catholic Theological Union, 5401 S. Cornell Ave., Chicago, IL, 60615-5608. Rev. John Coughlin, O.F.M., St. Joseph's Seminary, Dunwoodie, Yonkers, 10704-1852. Rev. J. Patrick Kelly, O.F.M., FrancisCare, Elmwood Park Plaza, 475 Market St., Elmwood Park, NJ, 07407-3104. Rev. Venant Lalonde, O.F.M., St. Agnes Rectory, 143 E. 43 St., 10017-4065. Rev. Guy Morgan, O.F.M., 1408 Yount St., Fort Collins, CO, 80524. Rev. J. Patrick Kelly, O.F.M., FrancisCare, Elmwood Park Plaza 07407-3104, 475 Market St., Elmwood Park. Rev. Venant Lalonde, O.F.M., St. Agnes Rectory, 143 E. 43 St., 10017-4065. Rev. Andrew Nargaj, O.F.M., Our Lady of Shkodra Church, 361 W. Hartsdale Ave., Hartsdale, 10530-0704. Rev. Demetrius O'Friel, O.F.M., 1375 Prince of Wales Dr., Box 1609, Ottawa, Ont., K2C 3L5, Canada. Rev. Rene F. Phillips, O.F.M., 850 Thomas Ln., Angola, 14006-9572. Rev. Lawrence Schulmeister, O.F.M., 612 Warner St., Baltimore, MD, 21230. Rev. Xavier Seubert, O.F.M., 1420 Locust St., Philadelphia, PA, 19102-4209. Rev. Benedict M. Taylor, O.F.M., Create Inc., 73 Lenox Ave., 10026. Rev. Gerard Lee, O.F.M., 341 Manning Blvd., Albany, 12206-1815. Rev. Gerald M. Dolan, O.F.M., 609 S. Convent Rd., Aston, PA, 19014. Rev. Edward C. Metzger, O.F.M., St. John the Baptist Rectory, 1085 Englewood Ave., Buffalo, 14223. Rev. James Vacco, O.F.M., Fredonia Newman Center, 222 Temple St., Fredonia, 14063. Rev. Peter S. Chepaitis, Bethany Ministries, Box 420, Middleburgh, 12122-0420. Rev. Douglas R. Glassman, O.F.M., 221 Windward St., Venice, CA, 90291-3764. Rev. Alfonso D. Guzman, O.F.M., Centro Vocacional Franciscano, Apartado 173, Sabana Seca, PR, 00952.

Military Chaplains: Rev. Louis V. Iasiello, O.F.M., Commander Naval Surface Force, US Atlantic Fleet, 1430 Mitscher Ave., Norfolk, VA, 23551-2494. Rev. Alan Sullivan, O.F.M., 3310 First Ave., San Diego, CA, 92103. Rev. Conrad W. Loftus, O.F.M., Fitzsimons Medical Center, Dept. of Ministry & Pastoral Care, Aurora, CO, 80045-5000.

Priests Abroad: Rev. Edward J. Dillon, O.F.M., Gethsemane, P.O. Box 186, 91001 Jerusalem, Israel. Rev. Howard O'Shea, Presbytere, 34, Place des Martyrs de la Resistance, Aix-en-Province, France, 13100. For Information Regarding Vocations to the Brotherhood & Priesthood, write Franciscan Vocation Office, St. Francis Friary, 134 W. 31st St., New York, NY 10001-3439. For information regarding the Franciscan Family Circle Pilgrimage Tours, contact: Rev. Cassian Miles, O.F.M., at the Franciscan Pilgrimage Office, at St. Francis Friary, 135 W. 31st St., New York, NY 10001-3439. Solemnly Professed Priests (including 4 Bishops) 413; Brothers 77; Temporary Vows: Brothers 77; Clerics 15; Novices 8; Perpetual Tertiaries 1; Permanant Deacons 3; Affiliates 10.

Franciscan Province of the Immaculate Conception, 147 Thompson St., 10012. Tel: 212-674-4388; 674-5490. Franciscan Province of the Immaculate Conception of New York City. Legal Title: *Friars Minor of the Order of St. Francis, Incorporated, New York, 1871*. Revs. Robert M. Campagna, O.F.M., Minister Prov.; Steven M. Sysol, O.F.M., Vicar Prov.; Simeon Distefano, O.F.M., Prov. Sec.; Alban Montella, O.F.M., Prov. Promoter of Missions.

Franciscan Mission Associates, 274-280 W. Lincoln Ave., Mt. Vernon, 10550. Ms. Madeline Bonnici, Exec. Dir.; Rev. Claude Scrima, O.F.M., Dir. of Secular Franciscans, St. Christopher Friary, P.O. Box 230, Boston, MA, 02113. Pious League of Saint Anthony, 151 Thompson St., P.O. Box 489, 10013-0489.

Priests of the Province Abroad: Rev. Giles Barreda, O.F.M., Franciscan Chapel Center, 2-37 Roppong; 4-Chome; Minatu-Ku 106, Tokyo, Japan.

Military Chaplains: Rev. Charles Soto, O.F.M., Command Chap., Comregsuppgru, P.O. Box 280057, Mayport, FL, 32228-0057. Rev. Michael Travaglione, O.F.M., 5445 Jadwin Loop, Fort Belvoir, VA, 22060.

Retired Military Chaplains: Rev. Edwin Bobrek, O.F.M., 1427 Ave. de las Adelsas, Encinatas, CA, 92024. Revs. Brennan Egan, O.F.M., (Awaiting Assignment); Jack Hoak, O.F.M., Serra Friary, 200 Hershey Sr., McKeesport, PA, 15132.

Priests of the Province Residing Elsewhere: Rev. Sigmund Brambilla, O.F.M. 15A Park Ave., Northampton, MA, 01060. Rev. Sebastian Buccellato, O.F.M. St. Francis of Rome Church, 4307 Barnes Ave., Bronx, 10466. Rev. Felician Napoli, O.F.M., Incarnation Church, 5124 Gateway Dr., Tampa, FL, 33615. Rev. Bartholomew De Simone, O.F.M., St. Gregory Church, 200 N. University Dr., Plantation, FL, 33324. Rev. Thaddeus Palmieri, O.F.M., Mary Help of the Christians Church, 6281 N.W. 66th Way, Parkland, FL, 33067. Rev. Clement Procopio, O.F.M., Our Lady of Joy Church, Cave Creek & Pima Rd., P.O. Box 1359, Carefree, AZ, 85377. Rev. Boniface Rezza, O.F.M., 8 Garden Pl., Bay Shore, 11706. Rev. Victor Cesario, O.F.M., 2467 Finlandia Ln. #73, Clearwater, FL, 34623. Rev. John Bucchino, O.F.M., 14 Stuyvesant Oval #5D, 10009. Rev. Louis De Tommaso, O.F.M., St. Ignatius Rectory, P.O. Box 1306, Tarpon Springs, FL, 34688-1306. Rev. Ralph Di Pasquale, O.F.M., 2008 Crowberry Dr., Port St. Lucie, FL, 34983. Rev. Adolph Giorda, O.F.M., St. Patrick's Rectory, 460 Madison Ave., 10022. Rev. Francis Hanudel, O.F.M., 50 Luisser St., Clifton, NJ, 07012. Rev. Mark Leone, O.F.M., 4 Winslow St., Apt. 1310, Arlington, MA, 02174. On Sick Leave: Rev. Xavier Carnicelli, O.F.M., St. Cabrini Nursing Home, 115 Broadway, Dobbs Ferry, 10552. Rev. Vincent Mele, O.F.M., Kateri Residence, 150 Riverside Dr., 10024. Rev. Cyril Morisco, O.F.M., St. Joseph Manor Nursing Care Facility, 1133 Washington Ave., Portland, ME, 04103.

Residing in Canada: Immaculate Conception Friary, 2 Richardson Ave., Toronto, Ont., M6M 3R4. Revs. Amadeo Nardone, O.F.M.; Marcellinus Borg, O.F.M.; Benedict Goveas, O.F.M., St. Charles Borromeo Friary, 811 Lawrence Ave., Toronto, Ont., M6A 1C3. Revs. Antonio Nardoianni, O.F.M.; Salvatore DeBenedictis, O.F.M.; Michael D'Cruz, O.F.M., St. Francis Friary, 72 Mansfield Ave., Toronto, Ont., M6J 2B2. Revs. Gregory Botte, O.F.M.; Isidoro di Miglio, O.F.M.; Frederick Mazzarella, O.F.M.; James Wells, O.F.M., St. Lawrence Friary, 2210 Lawrence Ave. E., Scarborough, Ont., M1P 2P9. Rev. Ralph Paonessa, O.F.M., St. Bonaventure, 56 Spadina Rd., Toronto, Ont., M5R 2T3. Rev. Celestine Pennisi, O.F.M., St. Jane Francis Friary, 2747 Jane St., Downsview, Ont., M3L 2E8. Revs. Claudio Moser, O.F.M.; Brennan Egan, O.F.M., (Awaiting Military Assignment); Augustin Donini, O.F.M., St. Jude Friary, 3265 Weston Rd., Weston, Ont., M9M 2T9. Revs. Celestino Canzio, O.F.M.; Frank Jannetta, O.F.M.; Blaise Tranchida, O.F.M. Priests 154; Brothers 29; Permanent Deacons 3; Bishops 3.

The Franciscan Vocation Ministry of Holy Name Province, 135 W. 31st St., 10001-3439. Tel: 212-629-5868; 800-677-7788. Rev. Peter V. Brophy, O.F.M., Dir., HNP Vocation Ministry; Bro. Nathanael Necaster, O.F.M., Admin. Asst.

Immaculate Conception Friary, 754 E. Gun Hill Rd., 10467. Tel: 212-653-2200. Capuchin Friars of the Province of the Stigmata of St. Francis. Revs. Robert Grix, O.F.M.Cap.; Pius Caccavalle, O.F.M.Cap.; Robert Yurgel, O.F.M.Cap.; Eric Hall, O.F.M.Cap. Total Assisted 190; Total Staff 20; Priests 4; Brothers 2.

Jesuit Community at Fordham University, 441 E. Fordham Rd., 10458. Tel: 212-817-5322. Priests 91; Scholastics 2; Brothers 3; Total in Residence 96; Total Staff 37. Loyola Hall, Jesuit Community. Very Rev. Joseph A. Novak, S.J., Rector; Revs. David J. Casey, S.J., Min.; Joseph V. Dolan, S.J., Sub Min.; John D. Alexander, S.J.; Joseph Atanga, S.J. (West Africa); Albert P. Bartlett, S.J.; Thomas V. Bermingham, S.J.; John D. Boyd, S.J.; William E. Boyle, S.J.; Francis P. Canavan, S.J.; Edward F. Clark, S.J.; W. Norris Clarke, S.J.; T. Gerard Connolly, S.J.; Daniel A. Degnan, S.J.; Frederick J. Dillemuth, S.J.; G. Richard Dimler, S.J.; Robert R. Dobbins, S.J.; Edward T. Dowling, S.J.; George F. Driscoll; Gerard F. Fagan, S.J.; Daniel J. Fitzpatrick, S.J.; Joseph R. Frese, S.J.; C. Homer Giblin, S.J.; L. Augustine Grady, S.J.; Thomas C. Hennessy, S.J.; George B. Hoch, S.J.; William T. Hogan, S.J.; Bro. Frank W. Jensen, S.J.; Revs. J. Raymond Johnson; Robert G. Kelly, S.J.; John J. King, S.J.; Albert J. Loomie, S.J.; Edward F. Maloney; John J. McCarthy, S.J.; George C. McCauley, S.J.; Gerald A. McCool, S.J.; Joseph Mitros, S.J. (Poland); Vincent M. Novak, S.J.; Ladislas Orsy, S.J.; John W. Ortner, S.J.; Louis B. Pascoe, S.J.; James H. Reid, S.J.; Herbert W. Rogers, S.J.; Robert J. Roth, S.J.; James A. Sadowsky, S.J.; Robert J. Sealy, S.J.; J. Francis Stroud, S.J.; Daniel J. Sullivan, S.J.; Patrick J. Sullivan, S.J.; Edward J. Sweeney, S.J.; Eamon G. Taylor, S.J., Jesuit Community, Kohlmann Hall. Tel: 718-584-1638. Rev. John J. Scully, S.J., Min.; Bro. Sebastian A. Boccabella, S.J.; Revs. Pierce A. Brennan, S.J.; Mallick J. Fitzpatrick, S.J.; Matthew C. Flood, S.J.; John J. Leonard, S.J.; John J. Mattimore, S.J.; Stanley J. O'Konsky, S.J.; William J. O'Malley, S.J.; Joseph P. Parkes, S.J.; Joseph S. Rooney, S.J.; Michael E. Sehler, S.J.; Charles D. Sullivan, S.J., Cardinal Spellman Hall, Jesuit Community. Tel: 718-817-5330. Very Revs. Joseph A. Novak, S.J., Rector; Joseph A. O'Hare, S.J., Pres.; Rev. Daniel J. O'Brien, S.J., Min.; Bro. Donald J. Kavanagh, S.J., Sub Min.; Revs. Michael J. Agliardo, S.J.; Jeffrey P. Baerwald, S.J.; Robert D. Cloney, S.J.; John J. Conley, S.J.; Brian Davies, O.P. (England); Avery Dulles, S.J.; William V. Dych, S.J.; John T. Dzieglewicz, S.J.; Rev. Msgr. Charles J. Fahey (SY); Revs. Garrett J. Fitzgerald, S.J.; Robert R. Grimes, S.J.; Martin A. Hegyi, S.J. (Hungary); Alfred T. Hennelly, S.J.; Joseph W. Koterski, S.J.; Miguel Lambino, S.J.; Joseph T. Lienhard, S.J.; Nicholas D. Lombardi, S.J.; Mark S. Massa, S.J.; Donald C. Matthews, S.J.; George J. McMahon, S.J.; Joseph M. McShane, S.J.; Michael D. Moga, S.J.; John A. Mullin, S.J.; Jung-Woo Park (Korea); Richard J. Regan, S.J.; Patrick J. Ryan, S.J.; Deacon Charles G. Wrightington, S.J., Jesuit Scholastic.

Jesuit Provincial's Office, 39 E. 83rd St., 10028. Tel: 212-774-5500; Fax: 212-774-5510. Very Rev. Kenneth J. Gavin, S.J., Prov.; Revs. Thomas E. Smith, S.J., Exec. Asst. to Prov.; Frederick J. O'Brien, S.J., Asst. for Secondary Education; James F. Joyce, S.J., Asst. Social & Pastoral Ministries; Bro. Gilbert J. Scott, S.J., Asst. to Prov.; Revs. J. Raymond Johnson, S.J., Prov. Treas. & Auditor & American Rep. of the Missions of the Society of Jesus, Vatican City; William T. Wood, S.J., Asst. to the Prov. for the Intl. Apostolate; Thomas P. Gaunt, S.J., Asst. for Formation for Maryland & New York Provinces; Joseph S. Constantino, S.J., Vocation Dir. for Maryland & New York Provinces.

Military Chaplains: Rev. L. Joseph O'Keeffe, S.J., Ft. L.J. McNair, Attn: ANMC-CH, Washington, DC, 20319.

Priests of the Province Abroad: Rev. Vincent F. Blehl, S.J., Rabenkopfstr. 2, Apt. 229, Freiburg, Germany, 79102. Rev. Vincent J. Duminuco, S.J., America House, 106 W. 56th St., 10019. Revs. John M. McDermott, S.J.; Michael P. Hilbert, S.J.; Paul W. McNellis, S.J., Pontificia Universita Gregoriana, Piazza della Pilotta 4, 00187 Rome, Italy. Revs. Juan C. Villegas, S.J.; Arthur A. Clarke, S.J.; Francis P. Golden, S.J., Colegio San Ignacio, 1940 Calle Sauco, Rio Piedras, San Juan, PR, 00927. Rev. Lawrence P. Searles, S.J., Parroquia San Ignacio, 1904 Calle Narciso, San Juan, Puerto Rico, 00927. Rev. John F. Long, S.J., Mt. St. Mary's Seminary, 5400 Roland Ave., Baltimore, MD, 21210. Rev. Henry J. Bertels, S.J., Pontifical Biblical Institute, via della Pilotta 25, 00187 Rome, Italy. Rev. Keith F. Pecklers, S.J., Coll Bellarmino, Via del Seminario 120, 00186 Rome, Italy. Rev. John J. Halligan, S.J., Apdo. 17-01-3112, Quito, Ecuador. Rev. Michael F. Suarez, S.J., Campion Hall, Oxford, England, 0X1 1QS. Rev. Dennis M. Leder, S.J., Parroquia La Merced, 5a Calle 11-67, Zona 1, 01001. Rev. Charles J. Beirne, S.J., Universidad Rafael Landivar, Apartado 39C, Zona 16, Guatemala, C.A., 01016. Rev. J. Dean Brackley, S.J., UCA-Centro Mons Romero, Apdo. 01-168, San Salvador, El Salvador. Rev. Charles H. Lohr, S.J., Raimundus-Lullus Institute der Universitat, Werthmann Platz, 3, D-79085 Freiburg i Br., Germany. Rev. Richard R. Galligan, S.J., Cansius Jesuit Community, 2001 Main St., Buffalo, 14208. Rev. Donald C. Maldari, S.J., Residence Ignace De Loyola, CP 1710, Port-au-Prince, Haiti.

Priests of the Province in Residences not listed elsewhere: Rev. Theodore V. Francois, S.J., 507 Macon St., Brooklyn, 11233. Rev. Robert A. McGuire, S.J., House of Prayer, 300 Washington Ave., Plainview, 11803. Rev. Gerard H. Ettlinger, S.J., 162-31 9th Ave., Apt. 5A, Whitestone, 11357. Rev. Brian E. Daley, S.J., 16203 Candlewycke St., Granger, IN, 46530. Rev. John F. Walters, S.J., IAM Counseling Center, Tesserville Farm, R.D. 1, Box 75, New Albany, PA, 18833. Rev. Edward J. Mally, S.J., 1S 150 Spring Rd., Apt. 2E, Oakbrook Terrace, IL, 60181. Rev. Alfred L. Fiorino, S.J., 12385 Santiago Rd. E., San Diego, CA, 92128. Rev. John J. Gerhard, S.J., 850 Hylan Blvd., Staten Island, 10305. Rev. Louis A. Padovano, S.J., 169 E. 78 St., Apt 7-C, 10021. Rev. Joseph P. Kane, S.J., 2674 Valentine Ave., Apt., 1A, Bronx, 10458. Rev. Harry A. Reese, S.J., 16 Spindrift Ct., #4, Williamsville, 14221. Rev. Gerard P. Bell, S.J., 8611 Cedar St., Silver Spring, MD, 20910. Revs. Rene Dousdebes, S.J. (Ecuador); John H. Rainaldo, S.J., 3 Stephan Ave., New Hyde Park, 11040. Rev. Martin Doyle, S.J., Xavier High School, P.O. Box 220, Chuuk, FM, 96942. Rev. Thomas D. McCall, S.J., St. Ignatius Residence, 53 E. 83 St., 10028. Rev. George H. Belgarde, S.J., St. Regis Mission, P.O. Box 429, Hogansburg, 13655.

Awaiting Assignment: Revs. Henry W. Traub, S.J.; James E. Shields; Richard P. Gorgon, Mt. Manresa, 239 Fingerboard Rd., Staten Island, 10305.

Other Jesuit Residences: 126 West 17th St., 10011. Tel: 212-620-0537. Revs. John P. Bucki, S.J.; William P. Cain, S.J.; Thomas E. Clarke, S.J.; Michael E. Donahue, S.J.

Jesuit Residence, 30 W. 16th St., 10011. Revs. Donald C. Gannon; Hermann Breulmann; Francisco Bustamante; James H. Dahlinger, S.J.; Alfred E. Caruana, S.J.; Joseph G. Musselman, S.J.; James P. Jurich, S.J.; Edward J. McMahon, S.J.; George W. Drance; Harold F. O'Donnell, S.J.; Leo P. Prengaman, S.J.; Francis J. Tierney, S.J.; Joseph J. Walter, S.J.; James J. Yannarell, S.J.; James P. Flaherty; David P. Marcotte; James L. Pierce; Joseph S. Rossi; Michael V. Tueth.

Ciszek Hall, 2502 Belmont Ave., Bronx, 10458. Tel: 718-365-8752. Revs. Gerald J. Chojnacki, S.J.; Raymond M. Sweitzer, S.J.; Charles L. Moutenot, S.J.

Jesuit Community, 860 Manida St., Bronx, 10474. Tel: 718-542-2283. Connected with Nativity Rectory. 44 Second Ave., 10003. In res., Rev. Joseph C. Towle, S.J.

Jesuit Seminary and Mission Bureau, Inc. (Jesuit Deferred Funds), 39 E. 83rd St., 10028. Tel: 212-734-1144. Revs. John G. Marzolf, S.J., Dir.; Gerard E. Braun, S.J.; Bro. John J. Campbell, S.J.; Revs. Anthony F. LaBau, S.J.; James F. O'Brien, S.J.; William J. Scanlon, S.J.

Little Brothers of the Gospel, 58 E. Fourth St., 5th Fl., #14, 10003. Bro. Paziente Tiraboschi. Brothers 4.

Marist Brothers Residence. Our Lady of Grace Residence, 850 E. 226th St., Bronx, 10466. Tel: 212-652-1848. Bros. Francis Kelly, F.M.S.; John Malich, F.M.S.; Michael E. Flanigan, F.M.S.

Marist Brothers Champagnat Hall Community, 4300 Murdock Ave., Bronx, 10466. Tel: 718-994-4227. Bros. John Bantz, Dir.; Joseph Cerin Balet; Valerian Doiron; Peter Leonard; Simeon Gerald; Dennis Buckley; Francis Hughes; Godfrey Robertson; John Colbert; Kenneth Marino; James Gaffney; Robert Leclerc; Denis Caverley; Vincent Xavier; George L. Mathews; Christopher Shannon; Thomas Simmons; Frederick Sambor; Eugene Birmingham.

Marist Residence, 156 E. 38th St., 10016. Tel: 212-889-1176. Bros. James Devine, Dir.; Matthew Snowden; Patrick Tyrrell; James Kearney.

Marist Residence, 143 W. 87th St., 10024. Tel: 212-362-4039. Bros. Donnell Neary, Dir.; Anthony Iazzetti; Gerald Doherty; Thomas Schady.

Marist Provincial House, 26 First Ave., Pelham, 10803. Tel: 914-738-1218. Bros. Patrick McNamara, Prov.; Dermot Healy, Asst. Prov.; Thomas Long; Vincent B. Moriarty.

Marist Brothers, 40 S. Hamilton St., Poughkeepsie, 12601. Tel: 914-471-4077. Bros. George DiCarluccio, Dir.; James Stevens; Lawrence Gordon; Lawrence Lavallee.

Marist Brothers, 2 Eden Ter., Poughkeepsie, 12601-4803. Tel: 914-471-8354. Bros. John Nash, Dir.; Michael Williams.

Maryknoll House, 121 E. 39th St., 10016. Tel: 212-697-4470. Catholic Foreign Mission Society. Bros. Donald Miriani, M.M.; Brendan Corkery, M.M.

Murray-Weigel Hall, 515 E. Fordham Rd., 10458-5004. Tel: 718-430-4900; Fax: 718-365-8650. Revs. Gerald J. McMahon, S.J., Supr.; Edward C. Lynch, S.J., Min.; Joseph C. McKenna, S.J., Sub Min.; Robert O. Brennan, S.J., Sub Min.; Bro. Gerard W. Schade, S.J., Infirmary; Revs. Thomas E. Ambrose, S.J.; Edward J. Berbusse, S.J.; Andrew J. Brady, S.J.; James F. Coleman, S.J.; John F.X. Condon, S.J.; Theodore J. Cunnion, S.J.; Paul J. Curtin, S.J.; S. Oley Cutler, S.J.; James A. Daly, S.J.; Roy A. Drake, S.J.; Richard P. English, S.J.; John K. Fahey, S.J.; William J. Farrell, S.J.; William J. Farricker, S.J.; James J. Fedigan, S.J.; James J. Finley, S.J.; William J. Gleason, S.J.; Robert J. Haskins, S.J.; Edwin C. Haungs, S.J.; Lawrence B. Hill, S.J.; John F. Hoek, S.J.; Cornelius P. Hurley, S.J.; Joseph V. Landy, S.J.; J. Quentin Lauer, S.J.; William G. Lawlor, S.J.; Howard A. McCaffrey, S.J.; John McConnell, S.J.; Thomas F. McGann, S.J.; Stephen J. Meany, S.J.; John A. Morrison, S.J.; Robert H. Neubeck, S.J.; John A. Nicholson, S.J.; Raymond A. Nolan, S.J.; Robert Jerome O'Connell, S.J.; Robert John O'Connell, S.J.; Richard J. Pendergast, S.J.; Eugene J. Quigley, S.J.; Francis V. Rooney, S.J.; Peter J. Roslovich, S.J.; Joseph D. Ryan, S.J.; Joseph B. Schuyler, S.J.; Gary W. Schwartzkopf, S.J.; David E. Sippel, S.J.; Louis E. Soloman, S.J.; Francis J. Tierney, S.J.; Richard F. Timone, S.J.; James J. Wheeler, S.J.; Bros. Stephen J. Andrews, S.J.; Gerald F. Boyle, S.J.; Ignatius J. Fitzroy, S.J.; Edward A. Moran, S.J.; Sidney C. Saucier, S.J.; Carl J. Seitz, S.J.; Albert A. Wozniak, S.J. Priests 51; Brothers 8.

Our Lady of Consolation Residence. 3103 Arlington Ave., Corner of W. 231st St., Bronx, 10463. Tel: 718-548-0888. In res., Rev. Stanislaus K. Treu, O.S.A.

Our Lady of Consolation Residence. 3103 Arlington Ave., Corner of W. 231st St., Bronx, 10463. Tel: 718-548-0889. Rev. Charles R. Klein, Dir.; Most Rev. Austin B. Vaughan; Rev. Msgr. Edward P. Brogan; Rev. Msgr. Thomas V. Gallagher; Rev. Msgr. William Higgins; Rev. Msgr. Hugh J. Rooney; Revs. Joseph P. Adamo; William E. Kelly; William J. McPeak; Francis J. Molony; Eugene P. O'Hara; Maurice C. Slattery; Humbert D. Pisanelli. In res., Rev. Stanislaus K. Treu, O.S.A.

Padua Friary, 151 Thompson St., 10012. Tel: 212-254-9553. Revs. Francis X. D'Alessandro, O.F.M., Guardian, Prov. Treas.; John-Marie Cassese, O.F.M., Vicar, Prov. Archivist & Chronicler; Bro. Luke Storino, O.F.M., Prov. Bookkeeper; Revs. Marino Cascino, O.F.M., FMU Prom.; Emmanuel Faraone, O.F.M.; Albin Fusco, O.F.M.; George Mazzocchia, O.F.M.; Peter Walsh, O.F.M.

Pallottine Fathers, Society of the Catholic Apostolate, 448 E. 116th St., 10029. Revs. Peter J. Rofrano, S.A.C.; Severino Dominicis, S.A.C., Mt. Carmel Society & Catholic Apostolate Assoc.; Girolamo D'Ambrosi, S.A.C.; Tony Kelly, S.A.C., Spanish Apostolate. Total Assisted 300; Total Staff 15.

Passionist Spiritual Center. 5801 Palisade Ave., Riverdale, 10471. Very Rev. John Powers, C.P., Rector; Revs. Benedict Berlo, C.P.; Richard Scheiner, C.P.; Donald Ware, C.P., Retreat Dir.; Bros. Damian Carroll, C.P.; Terence Skorka, C.P.

Pope John Paul II Residence, 603 First Ave., 10016. Tel: 212-686-3483. Rev. James S. Pfeiffer, Dir.; Rev. Msgr. Joseph J. Quinn; Revs. Martin Connolly; Dominic Jacolino; John B. Vala; Thomas J. Darby; William J. Kennedy; Harry Tiercelin; Andrew Magee; Rev. Msgr. Edward J. Reynolds; Rev. Msgr. Joseph M. Santulin; Rev. Msgr. John P. Larkin.

Pope Paul VI Residence.

Frances Schervier Long Term Home Health Care. 2975 Independence Ave., Bronx, 10463. Rev. Albert Pellicane, C.P.

St. Catherine of Siena Priory, 411 E. 68th St., 10021. Tel: 212-988-8300; Fax: 212-988-6918. Very Rev. Cristopher Johnson, O.P., Prior; Revs. Vincent Ferrer McHenry, O.P., Subprior; John Jerome Conroy, O.P.; Patrick Francis Connolly, O.P.; John Thaddeus Murphy, O.P.; Robert Philip Fitzsimmons, O.P.; Bartholomew Paul Fu, O.P.; George Lawrence Concordia, O.P.; Brian Martin Mulcahy, O.P.; Athanasius Sulavik, O.P.

Priests assigned but serving elsewhere: Revs. John Alphonsus Madigan, O.P.; Michael Joseph McCormack, O.P.; John Alexander Gregory Maturi, O.P.

St. Clare Friary, 440 W. 36th St., 10018. Revs. James

E. Goode, O.F.M., Ph.D., Dir. of Solid Ground, A Franciscan Ministry with African American Families; Stephen Caforio, O.F.M.; Sebastian Buccellato, O.F.M. Total in Residence 3; Total Staff 2.

St. Crispin Friary. Franciscan Friars of the Renewal, 420 E. 156th St., Bronx, 10455. Tel: 212-665-2441. Revs. Benedict J. Groeschel, C.F.R.; Robert Lombardo, C.F.R.; Stanley Fortuna, C.F.R., Local Servant; Terry Messer, C.F.R., Vicar. Priests 3; Brothers 4.

St. Ignatius Loyola Residence, 53 E. 83rd St., 10028. Tel: 212-288-6200. Revs. Arthur C. Bender, S.J., Rector; James F. O'Brien, S.J., Minister; William J. Bergen, S.J.; Vincent L. Biagi, S.J.; Gerard E. Braun, S.J.; Edwin J. Brooks, S.J.; Bro. John J. Campbell, S.J.; Revs. James R. Carney, S.J.; Francis J. Cosgrove, S.J.; Joseph S. Costantino; James J. Curry, S.J.; Joseph A. Dorgan, S.J.; Francis K. Drolet, S.J.; Stephen V. Duffy, S.J.; John L. Farrand, S.J.; William J. Farrell, S.J.; Thomas H. Feely, S.J.; Kenneth J. Gavin, S.J.; Charles Gilley, S.J.; Mark Hallinan, S.J.; Timothy A. Healey, S.J.; Philip G. Judge, S.J.; Anthony F. LaBau, S.J.; Joseph A. Latella, S.J.; Thomas D. McCall, S.J.; J. Thomas McClain, S.J. (Detroit); Walter F. Modrys, S.J.; Damian A. O'Connell, S.J.; Daniel G. O'Hare, S.J.; Joseph J. Papaj, S.J.; Eugene J. Prior, S.J.; Thomas S. Prout, S.J.; William J. Scanlon, S.J.; Bros. Gilbert J. Scott, S.J.; Edward P. Sheehy, S.J.; Revs. Thomas E. Smith, S.J.; Paul J. Tabor, S.J. (Boston); William T. Wood, S.J.

St. John Neumann Residence. 5655 Arlington Ave., Bronx, 10471. Tel: 718-549-4511; Fax: 718-549-4513. Rev. Msgr. James E. White, Rector; Revs. Thomas F. Madden, M.S., Spiritual Dir.; John P. O'Brien, Procurator & Dean of Students; Pat Rossi, Ph.D., Academic Dean. In res., Rev. Msgr. John J. Gillen; Revs. Richard D. Baker; Robert McKeon.

St. Joseph's Friary, 523 W. 142nd St., 10031. Tel: 212-234-9089. House of Formation Friars: Bro. Michael Kmiotek, C.F.R., Local Servant; Revs. Herald Brock, C.F.R., Vicar; Conrad Osterhout, C.F.R., Dir. of Postulants. Postulants 16.

St. Vincent dePaul Residence, 900 Intervale Ave., 10459. Total Assisted 3,120; Total Staff 8.

St. Vincent Ferrer Priory, 869 Lexington Ave., 10021. Tel: 212-744-2080; Fax: 212-327-3011. Dominican Friars Provincial House (Province of St. Joseph). Very Revs. Walter Urban Voll, O.P., Prov.; Robert Alan Morris, O.P., Vicar Prov. & Socius; Joseph Fox, O.P., Vicar Prov.; James Boniface Ramsey, O.P., Prior; Revs. Edward T. Myers, O.P., Prov. Treas.; John Peter Gerhard, O.P., Subprior; John James Sullivan, O.P.; Nicholas Francis Halligan, O.P.; William Robert Gannon, O.P.; Raymond Ferrer Halligan, O.P.; Frederick Damien Hoesli, O.P.; Deacon Edward Thomas Aquinas Dolan, O.P.; Bros. Bernard Christopher McCabe, O.P.; John Damian McCarthy, O.P.

Priests assigned but serving elsewhere: Revs. John Aedan McKeon, O.P.; Alan Augustine Evans, O.P.; James Moneta Moyna, O.P.; Robert William Vaughn, O.P.; Ronald Henery, O.P.; Peter John Cameron, O.P.; Joseph Hugh Mulhern, O.P.; Robert Urban Sharkey, O.P.; John Aquinas Farren, O.P.; John Patrick Burchill, O.P.

Vincentian Fathers, 1834 Third Ave., 10029. Tel: 212-289-6156; Fax: 212-289-8321. Legal Title: *Padres Paules Community (Vincentians) Inc.* Revs. Jesus M. Oses, C.M., Supr.; Candido Arrizurieta, C.M.; Santiago Lluch, C.M.

West Side Jesuit Community, 220 West 98th St., 10025. Tel: 212-866-6156. Revs. Daniel J. Berrigan, S.J.; W. Alan Briceland, S.J.; Robert E. Carter, S.J.; Owen W. Daley, S.J.; James F. Fox, S.J.; Theodore V. Francois, S.J.; Gerald T. Huyett, S.J.; Robert J. Keck, S.J.; Benedict Kim, S.J.; Daniel Madigan, S.J.; Jose Magadia, S.J.; Bro. Edward L. McCarthy, S.J.; Revs. John G. McSherry, S.J.; Donald J. Moore, S.J., Supr.; Edward J. Murphy, S.J.; Peter Murray, S.J.; Frederic M. O'Connor, S.J.; Angelo Paiano, S.J.; Joseph N. Pershe, S.J.; Enrico Raulli, S.J.; Gary G. Seibert, S.J.; Robert Springer, S.J.; David S. Toolan, S.J.; Alex Soesilo Wijoyo, S.J.; Edward G. Zogby, S.J.

Xavier Jesuit Community, 30 West 16th St., 10011. Tel: 212-924-7900; Fax: 212-337-7545. Revs. Donald C. Gannon, S.J., Rector; Henry A. Hoffen, S.J.; Alfred E. Caruana, S.J.; Gregory J. O'Meara, S.J., Scholastic Dominican; James L. Pierce, S.J.; Bro. Daniel M. Hoey, S.J.; Revs. James P. Jurich, S.J.; Joseph G. Musselman, S.J.; Michael V. Tueth, S.J.; Harold F. O'Donnell, S.J.; Leo P. Prengaman, S.J.; Joseph J. Walter, S.J.; James J. Yannarell, S.J.; Joseph S. Rossi, S.J.; James P. Flaherty, S.J.; David P. Marcotte, S.J.; Edward J. McMahon, S.J.; Louis P. Sogliuzzo, S.J.; Henry J. Zenorini, S.J.; James A. Catalano, S.J.

Jesuit Residence. 126 W. 17th St., 10011. Tel: 212-620-0537. Revs. William P. Cain, S.J.; Thomas E. Clarke, S.J.; John P. Bucki, S.J., Supr.; Michael E. Donahue, S.J.; Bro. Michael E. Breault, S.J. (For list of faculty see the high school listing for Xavier High School).

BRONX. *Idente Missionaries of Santa Maria Residence*, 2352 St. Raymond, 10462. Tel: 718-828-2380. Revs. Fernando Real, M.ID., Prov. Supr.; Robert Badillo, M.ID., Formation Dir.; Eduardo Rodriguez, M.ID., Residence Rector.

CHELSEA. *Word of the Cross Passionist Community*, Chelsea Rd., 12512. Revs. Bennet Kelley, C.P., Co-ord.; Owen Lally, C.P.

CORNWALL. *Jogues Retreat*, Mailing Address: P.O. Box F, 12518. Tel: 914-534-7570; Fax: 914-534-3276. Revs. Herbert T. Kane, S.J., Supr. & Guest Master; Edward H. McGlinchy, S.J., Treas.

ESOPUS. *Marist Brothers F.M.S. (Province of St. Joseph)*, Mailing Address: P.O. Box 197, 12429. Bros. Henry J. Sawicki, F.M.S., Dir.; Donald Nugent, F.M.S., Retreat Dir. Brothers 6.

Redemptorist Priests and Brothers C.Ss.R. (Province of Baltimore), Mount Saint Alphonsus, Rte. 9W, P.O. Box 219, 12429. Tel: 914-384-6550. Very Rev. John G. Kingsbury, C.Ss.R., Rector; Bro. Robert Skinner, C.Ss.R.; Revs. Francis J. Gargani, C.Ss.R.; Dennis Kelleher, C.Ss.R.; Raymond Weithman, C.Ss.R., Parish Missionary. In res., Revs. Eugene J. Grohe, C.Ss.R.; John Kennington, C.Ss.R.; Paul A. Miller, C.Ss.R.; W. Richard, Bonner, C.Ss.R. Priests 8; Brothers 1.

GARRISON. *Franciscan Friars of the Atonement*, Graymoor, P.O. Box 300, 10524-0300. Tel: 914-424-3671; 3672; 3673; Fax: 914-424-3635. Revs. Fred Alvarez, S.A.; Norman Boyd, S.A.; Bros. Joseph Buettner, S.A.; John Joseph Bursis, S.A.; Revs. Xavier Butler, S.A.; Daniel Callahan, S.A.; Bros. Raphael Colaciello, S.A.; Jeremiah Dalton, S.A.; Revs. Daniel Egan, S.A.; Joseph Egan, S.A.; Gregory Figueroa, S.A.; Bros. Francis Gutman, S.A.; Stephen Hanley, S.A.; Revs. Simeon Heine, S.A.; Alphonsus Hoban, S.A.; Alexander Kelliher, S.A.; Bonaventure Koelzer, S.A.; Thomas Orians, S.A.; Bros. Chrysostom Lane, S.A.; Pius MacIsaac, S.A.; Joseph O'Gara, S.A.; Gregory Lucrezia, S.A.; Rev. Januarius Martinelli, S.A.; Bros. Dominic McDonnell, S.A.; James McHugh, S.A.; Revs. Kevin McMorrow, S.A.; Cuthbert Micali, S.A.; Charles Murphy, S.A.; William Murphy, S.A., Guardian, Senior Community; Bro. Theodore Novak, S.A.; Rev. Mark O'Connor, S.A.; Bro. Rocco Pace, S.A.; Rev. Normand Prevost, S.A.; Bro. Edward Rankey, S.A.; Revs. George Ribeiro, S.A.; Bosco Schmidt, S.A.; Bros. Denis Sennett, S.A.; Edmund Sheridan, S.A.; Richard Skolinski, S.A.; Robert Taylor, S.A.; Revs. Peter Taran, S.A.; Patrick Walsh, S.A.; Bros. Liam Young, S.A.; Joseph Marie Zakia, S.A.

St. Francis of Assisi Novitiate, Graymoor, P.O. Box 300, 10524-0300. Revs. Henry Marchese, S.A., Novice Dir.; Owen Murphy, S.A.; Bros. John Baptist Hildreth, S.A.; Raymond Saville, S.A.; William Weeks, S.A. Novices 3.

St. Christopher's Inn, Graymoor, P.O. Box 150, 10524-0150. Rev. Bernard Palka, S.A., Dir.; Bros. Thomas Banacki, S.A.; George Clay, S.A.; Donald Perry, S.A.; Benedict Terasawa, S.A.; Revs. Robert Warren, S.A.; Charles Angell, S.A.

Graymoor Ecumenical and Interreligious Institute, 475 Riverside Dr., Room 1960, New York, 10115-1999. Tel: 212-870-2342; 870-2330; Fax: 212-870-2001. Rev. Elias Mallon, S.A., Dir.

Generalate of the Franciscan Friars of the Atonement-St. James Friary, Mailing Address: P.O. Box 5, 10524-0005. Tel: 914-424-3539; Fax: 914-424-3978. Very Rev. Emil F. Tomaskovic, S.A., Minister Gen.; Rev. Thomas Gumprecht, S.A., Vicar General; Bros. Peter Gannon, S.A.; Raymond Saville, S.A., Sec. Gen.; Revs. Bernard Palka, S.A., Treas. Gen.; Elias Mallon, S.A., 2nd General Councillor; Henry Marchese, S.A., 3rd General Councillor; Dennis Polanco, S.A., 4th General Councillor; Bro. William Martyn, S.A., Procurator General to the Holy See.

Friar-Priests serving in Japan, Diocese of Yokohama: Revs. Pacificus Von Essen, S.A.; Peter Katsuno, S.A.; Fidelis Fujihara, S.A. (Japan); Cyril Colton, S.A.; Charles Brozat, S.A.; Joseph Hiramatsu, S.A. (Japan), Regional Minister; Gabriel Shiraki, S.A. (Japan); Damian Sato, S.A.; Eric Tampe, S.A.

Friars on assignments or studies: Revs. Malcolm Martin, S.A., Holy Rosary Parish, Yonkers, NY; William Linakis, S.A.; Noel McSweeney, S.A.; Dennis Murphy, S.A., Chap., Walter Reed Med. Center, Washington, DC; David Poirier, S.A.; Joseph Scerbo, S.A.; Aquinas Thomas, S.A.

Friars stationed in England: Revs. Robert Mercer, S.A. (England); Michael Seed, S.A. (England); Emmanuel Sullivan, S.A.; Bro. Gerard Hand, S.A.

Friars stationed in Canada, Archdiocese of Vancouver: Bros. Savio McNeice, S.A.; Daniel Houde, S.A.; Timothy MacDonald, S.A.

Diocese of London, Ontario, Canada: Revs. Damian MacPherson, S.A. (Canada); Walter Gagne, S.A.; Michael Graham, S.A.; Paschal Breau, S.A. (Canada).

Archdiocese of Toronto, Canada: Revs. John Kiesling, S.A., Holy Cross Parish, Toronto; Peter Tomaino, S.A.; Timothy MacDonald, S.A.; Bede MacEachen, S.A. (Canada); Bros. Guy Gartland, S.A.; Brian Terry, S.A.; Denis Burgelin, S.A.; Philip Buckley, S.A.; Daniel Sylvain, S.A.

Archdiocese of Halifax, N.S. Canada: Rev. Arthur Gouthro, S.A. (Canada).

Friars in Military Service: Rev. William Dillon, S.A.

Friars residing in Italy: Revs. David Fitzgerald, S.A.; James Puglisi, S.A.

St. Joseph's Rehabilitation Center, Inc., Saranac Lake. Legal Titles: *Friars of the Atonement, Inc.*; *St. Christopher's Inn, Inc.*; *Union That Nothing Be Lost, Inc.*; *St. Joseph's Rehabilitation Center, Inc.*; *Paul Wattson Human Resources Fund, Inc.* St. Christopher's Inn: Total Assisted 2,500; Total Staff 30; Other institutions: Total in Residence 162; Total Staff 101.

St. Christopher's Friary, Mailing Address: Box 150, 10524-0150. Tel: 914-424-3541. Revs. Charles Angell, S.A., Guardian; Robert Warren, S.A.; Bros. George Clay, S.A.; Donald Perry, S.A.; Benedict Terasawa, S.A.; Thomas Banacki, S.A.; Charles Kenny, S.A.

St. Francis Friary (Glenclyffe).

Capuchin Franciscan Province of St. Mary, New York, New England. Mailing Address: Box 191, Garrison (Glenclyffe), 10524. Tel: 914-424-3488. Revs. Gabriel Massaro, O.F.M.Cap., Guardian, Preaching Ministry; Paul Engel, O.F.M.Cap., Downeyside Inc.; Roderick Brennan, O.F.M.Cap., Hispanic Preaching Ministry; John E. Mahoney, O.F.M.Cap., Business Officer; James P. Gavin, O.F.M.Cap., Preaching Ministry; David Couturier, O.F.M.Cap., Center of Structural Conversion; Anthony Vetrano, O.F.M.Cap., Youth & Family Ministries; Robert Abbatiello, O.F.M.Cap., Vicar & Vocation Ministry; Bros. Francis Liermann, O.F.M.Cap.; Lawrence Emmert, O.F.M.Cap.; Antonine Lizama, O.F.M.Cap.; Walter Puhal, O.F.M.Cap.

HARTSDALE. *Mill Hill Fathers Residence*, 222 W. Hartsdale Ave., 10530-1667. Tel: 914-682-0645; Fax: 914-682-0862. Very Rev. Terence J. Lee, M.H.M., Regl. Rep.; Revs. Thomas A. Halpin, M.H.M.; Cornelius M. Snoeren, M.H.M.; Emile Frische, M.H.M.; Bro. Theodore Tolboom, M.H.M.

MARYKNOLL. *M.M.A.F. Charitable Trust*, Treasury Office, P.O. Box 306, 10545-0306. Tel: 914-941-7590; Fax: 914-941-2411. Rev. Richard B. Callahan, M.M., Contact Person.

Maryknoll Fathers and Brothers, 10545-0305. Tel: 914-941-7590; Fax: 914-762-0316. General Council: Revs. Raymond J. Finch, M.M., Supr. Gen.; Jeremiah R. Burr, M.M., Vicar Gen.; Thomas P. Henehan, M.M., Asst. Gen.; Michael J. Snyder, M.M., Asst. Gen.; Bro. Wayne J. Fitzpatrick, M.M., Asst. Gen.; Revs. Richard B. Callahan, M.M., Treas. Gen.; Norbert J. Rans, M.M., Asst. Treas.; Joseph P. LaMar, M.M., Asst. Treas.; Edward J. Manning, M.M., Asst. Treas.; Jose A. Aramburu, M.M.; Joseph B. Arsenault, M.M.; Brian Barrons, M.M.; Richard A. Bell, M.M.; Joseph E. Brannigan, M.M.; John T. Brinkman, M.M.; Robert J. Carleton, M.M.; Peter L. Chabot, M.M.; John E. Conway, M.M.; William S. Donnelly, M.M.; Edward V. Davis, M.M.; Wayman P. Deasy, M.M.; Stephen T. DeMott, M.M.; Thomas F. Donnelly, M.M.; Edward M. Dougherty, M.M.; Michael A. Duggan, M.M.; Emile E. Dumas, M.M.; George A. Egan, M.M.; Joseph Fedora, M.M.; William B. Frazier, M.M.; William J. Galvin, M.M.; Charles F. Girnius, M.M.; Fidelis C. Goodman, M.M.; Ronald L. Green, M.M.; J. Gerard Greene, M.M.; John K. Halbert, M.M.; Scott T. Harris, M.M.; Edward A. Hayes, M.M.; Charles T. Huegelmeyer, M.M.; James H. Kroeger, M.M.; Daniel P. Jensen, M.M.; David J. Jones, M.M.; Stephen P. Judd, M.M.; John M. Kaserow, M.M.; Thomas H. Keefe, M.M.; Joseph P. LaMar, M.M.; Carmen G. La Mazza, M.M.; Peter M. Le Jacq, M.M.; Francis J. Leong, M.M.; Lawrence J. Lewis, M.M.; Robert J. Lloyd, M.M.; Martin J. Lowery, M.M.; John J. McAuley, M.M.; Leo F. McCarthy, M.M.; William D. McCarthy, M.M.; William T. Madden, M.M.; John P. Martin, M.M.; John J. Mihelko, M.M.; William F. Mullan, M.M.; Edward J. Manning, M.M.; George F. Painter, M.M.; John A. Rich, M.M.; Alan J. Ryan, M.M.; James M. Scanlon, M.M.; Steven Scherrer, M.M.; Leo B. Shea, M.M.; Michael A. Simone, M.M.; Leo J. Sommer, M.M.; John H. Spain, M.M.; Raymond F. Sullivan, M.M.; Joseph L. Thaler, M.M.; Eugene A. Thalman, M.M.; Kenneth F. Thesing, M.M.; Kevin T. Thomas, M.M.; William J. Tokus, M.M.; Joseph W. Towle, M.M.; John C. Tynan, M.M.; Joseph R. Veneroso, M.M.; Edward F. Walck, M.M.; David I. Walsh, M.M.; John J. Walsh, M.M.; Michael P. Walsh; Edward M. Wroblewski, M.M.

Maryknoll Fathers and Brothers. 728 Kitchawan Rd., Ossining, 10562. Rev. Brian Barrons, M.M.,

Mailing Address:, 10545-0305. Tel: 914-923-3711.

Maryknoll St. Teresa's Residence, 10545-0321. Tel: 914-941-4240; 941-4247. Staff: Revs. Thomas B. Kirchmyer, M.M., Dir.; James P. Nieckarz, M.M., Asst. Dir.; John P. Hudert, M.M. In res., Revs. Donald W. Aubry; Joseph E. Avery, M.M.; John E. Bergwall, M.M.; Donat W. Chatigny, M.M.; William J. Coleman, M.M.; William J. Eggleston, M.M.; Albert V. Fedders, M.M.; Gregory J. Gilmartin, M.M.; Thomas C. Higgins, M.M.; Gregory J. Keegan, M.M.; August R. Kircher, M.M.; Most Rev. William F. Kupfer, M.M.; Revs. Theodore M. Kuechmann, M.M.; J. Edmund McClear, M.M.; Thomas F. McDermott, M.M.; Edwin R. McDevitt, M.M.; Michael J. McKillop, M.M.; Robert J. Reiley, M.M.; Bernard F. Wieland, M.M.; Most Rev. John W. Comber, M.M.; Revs. Gervis J. Coxen, M.M.; Allan J. Dennis, M.M.; Christopher W. Gibbons, M.M.; Most Rev. Richard J. Ham, M.M.; Revs. Eugene F. Higgins, M.M.; Raymond C. Hohlfeld, M.M.; Robert E. Lee, M.M.; Arthur C. Kiernan, M.M.; Most Rev. William F. Kupfer, M.M.; Revs. John F. Fay, M.M.; Joseph P. Meaney, M.M.; Francis S. Meccia, M.M.; William R. McCarthy, M.M.; James E. McLaughlin, M.M.; George McPeak, M.M.; John J. O'Brien, M.M.; Thomas P. O'Rourke, M.M.; Dennis J. Slattery, M.M.; James F. Smith, M.M.; Paul J. Sommer, M.M.; Joseph E. VanDenBogaard, M.M.; John Kelly Walsh, M.M.; Bernard F. Wieland, M.M.; Robert H. Winkels, M.M.

Special Assignments: Revs. Edward R. Arnold, M.M.; Patrick A. Bergin, M.M.; Ronald J. Boccieri, M.M.; Stephen R. Booth, M.M.; Roy L. Bourgeois, M.M.; Joseph E. Brannigan, M.M.; John T. Brinkman, M.M.; Curtis R. Cadorette, M.M.; James A. Collignon, M.M.; George G. Cotter, M.M.; Joseph F. Croghan, M.M.; Donald J. Doherty, M.M.; Paul J. Duffy, M.M.; Joseph Fedora, M.M.; Francis J. Flynn, M.M.; Bartholomew J. Galvin, M.M.; Most Rev. Hugo M. Gerbermann, M.M.; Revs. David J. Jones, M.M.; Richard S. Kardian, M.M.; John E. Keegan, M.M.; Edward R. Killackey, M.M.; John R. King, M.M.; Joseph R. Lang, M.M.; Daniel A. Lanza, M.M.; Robert L. Mackesy, M.M.; Thomas J. Maney, M.M.; John L. Martin, M.M.; William E. McCarthy, M.M.; Thomas P. McDonnell, M.M.; John J. Meaney, M.M.; George M. Mikolajczyk, M.M.; William H. Moeschler, M.M.; Peter P. Mullen, M.M.; Laurence T. Murphy, M.M.; James B. Nagle, M.M.; Albert J. Nevins, M.M.; Raymond J. Nobiletti, M.M.; Richard E. Paulissen, M.M.; Raymond G. Pierini, M.M.; Joseph S. Pulaski, M.M.; Albert I. Reymann, M.M.; Patrick J. Ryan, M.M.; J. Daniel Schneider, M.M.; Edward R. Schoellmann, M.M.; Daniel J. Sherman, M.M.; Joseph S. Smith, M.M.; Donald R. Steed, M.M.; Lionel G. Trudel, M.M.; Wayne T. Weinlader, M.M.; Walter W. Winrich, M.M.; C. Thomas Wilcox, M.M.; John F. Wymes, M.M.

The Maryknoll Fathers & Brothers Charitable Trust, 10545. Trustees: Revs. Richard B. Callahan, M.M.; Edward V. Davis, M.M.; Wayman P. Deasy, M.M.; Thomas H. Keefe, M.M.; Thomas B. Kirchmyer; William F. Mullan, M.M.; Bro. Adrian Mazuchowski, M.M.

Maryknoll Fathers and Brothers. 586 McLean Ave., 10705. Tel: 914-963-0270. Revs. Alan J. Ryan, M.M.; John C. Tynan, M.M.; Carmen G. La Mazza, M.M.

MIDDLETOWN. *Brandsma Priory*, Carmelite Interprovincial Novitiate, Carmelite Dr., P.O. Box 2127, 10940. Tel: 914-343-2959. Carmelite Friars (North American Prov. of St. Elias and Most Pure Heart of Mary Province). Revs. Sean Harlow, O.Carm.; David McEvoy, O.Carm., Novice Dir.; Paul Denault, O.Carm., Prior and Novice Dir. Novices 4.

St. Albert's Priory, Mailing Address: P.O. Box 868, Carmelite Dr., 10940. Tel: 914-344-2220. Carmelite Friars (North American Prov. of St. Elias). Very Rev. Mario Esposito, O.Carm., Prior Provincial, Tel: 914-344-2223; Fax: 914-344-2210. Very Rev. Matthias DesLauriers, O.Carm., Dir., Natl. Shrine of Our Lady of Mt. Carmel & Prior, St. Albert's Community, Tel: 914-344-0876; Fax: 914-344-0093. Revs. Albert Daly, O.Carm.; Sean Reid, O.Carm.; Very Rev. Richard Nagle, O.Carm.; Revs. Brendan Hourihan, O.Carm.; Daniel F. Lynch, O.Carm.; Norbert P. Hansen, O.Carm.; Very Rev. Charles J. Haggerty, O.Carm.; Revs. Augustine Graap, O.Carm.; Patrick McGuigan, O.Carm.; Bro. James Andrews.

Provincial Offices: Carmelite Dr., P.O. Box 3079, 10940-3079. Very Rev. Mario Esposito, O.Carm., Prior Prov. Tel: 914-344-2223; Revs. Paul Denault, O.Carm., Prov. Procurator. Tel: 914-344-2224; Michael Kissane, O.Carm., Vocation Dir. Tel: 914-344-2225; Very Rev. Matthias DesLauriers, O.Carm., Dir., Devel. Office & Dir., National Shrine, Carmelite Dr., P.O. Box 868, 10940-0868. Tel: 914-344-0876; Fax: 914-344-0093.

MOUNT VERNON. *Kolbe Friary*, 274-280 W. Lincoln Ave., 10550. Franciscan Friars, Province of the Immaculate Conception. Bro. Angelo Monti, O.F.M., Guardian.

St. Bernardine of Siena Friary, 25 Laurel Ave., 10552. Tel: 914-699-1221. Franciscan Friars, Province of Immaculate Conception. In res., Revs. Patrick D. Boyle, O.F.M., Guardian; Alban V. Montella, O.F.M., Vicar; Anthony P. Abate, O.F.M.; Frank M. Geneive, O.F.M.; Roger A. Imperiale, O.F.M.; John R. Scarangello, O.F.M. Priests 6.

NEW PALTZ. *St. Joseph Friary*, 34 S. Chestnut St., 12561. Tel: 914-255-5635; Fax: 914-255-5677. Capuchin Friars, Province of St. Mary. Revs. Michael Banks, O.F.M.Cap., Supr.; Paul Steffan, O.F.M.Cap.; Knute Kenlon, O.F.M.Cap., Chap., Wallkill Correctional Facility; Bro. Timothy Jones, O.F.M.Cap., Chap., State University at New Paltz.

NEW ROCHELLE. *Brothers of Holy Cross of the Eastern Province of the United States of America, Inc.*, 85 Overlook Cir., 10804. Tel: 914-632-4468; 632-4469; Fax: 914-632-2490. Bros. John Gleason, C.S.C., Prov.; John E. McGovern, C.S.C., Asst. Prov. & Councilor Schools; Peter Martin, C.S.C., Councilor for Financial Svcs. Councilors: Bros. Mark Knightly, C.S.C.; Stephen La Mendola, C.S.C.; John Thornton, C.S.C.; Paul Bednarczyk, C.S.C. In res., Bros. George Schmitz, C.S.C.; William Farrell, C.S.C.; John Nicpon, C.S.C.; Jack Replogle, S.J. Professed Brothers 7.

Crosier (Canons Regular of the Order of the Holy Cross), Holy Cross Priory, 125 Paine Ave., 10804. Tel: 914-636-3614. Very Rev. James E. Hentges, O.S.C., Prior; Revs. Roger Vaughn, O.S.C.; Theodore K. Parker, O.S.C.; Adrian C. Piotrowski, O.S.C.; Timothy C. Conlon, O.S.C.; Francis K. Sheets, O.S.C.

Holy Cross Brothers, Eastern Province, Charitable Trust, 85 Overlook Cir., 10804. Trustees: Bros. Peter Martin, C.S.C., Treas.; Renatus Foldenauer, C.S.C.; Richard Kiniry, C.S.C.; Stephen LaMendola, C.S.C.; George Schmitz, C.S.C.

Saint Joseph's Residence, Inc., 30 Montgomery Cir., 10804-4413. Tel: 914-633-6851; Fax: 914-633-5579. Congregation of Christian Brothers. Bros. James B. Moffett, C.F.C., Pres.; Robert J. Roepke, C.F.C., Vice Pres. Admin.; Thomas C. Higgins, Sec.; Thomas F. Feerick, Vice Pres. Finance. A facility of limited care for male religious. Total in Residence 18; Total Staff 4.

St. Patrick's Provincial House (Congregation of Christian Brothers), 21 Pryer Terr., 10804. Tel: 914-636-6194; Fax: 914-636-0021. Bros. James B. Moffett, C.F.C., Prov.; Brian M. Walsh, C.F.C., Deputy Prov. Consultors: Bros. Lawrence A. Killelea, C.F.C.; V. Gregory McNally, C.F.C.; J. Edward Roepke, C.F.C.; Vincent J. Dougherty, Prov. Treas.; R. Kenneth. Grondin, C.F.C., Dir. Vocations; H. Michael Delaney, C.F.C., Dir. Devel.; Charles F. Miller, C.F.C., Dir. Mission Education; A. Eugenio DeLorenzo, C.F.C., Dir. Archives; John J. McCarthy, C.F.C., Dir. Assocs.; S. Anthony Ferro, C.F.C., Dir. Communications; Thomas R. Leto, Dir. Education; Kevin Griffith, C.F.C., Dir. Formation, St. Joseph Care Center, 30 Montgomery Cir., 10804. Tel: 914-633-6851. Limited facility for male religious. Brothers Living in Community 6; Limited Care Center Total in Residence 15; Total Staff 7.

Salesian Cooperators of St. John Bosco, 148 Main St., 10802. Denis Cahill, Prov. Coord.; Rev. Timothy Zak, S.D.B., Prov. Delegate, Mailing Address: 315 Self Pl., South Orange, NJ, 07079. Tel: 201-761-0201.

Salesian Provincial House, 148 Main St., P.O. Box 639, 10802-0639. Tel: 914-636-4225; Fax: 914-636-0159. Very Rev. Timothy C. Ploch, S.D.B., Prov.; Revs. Paul Aronica, S.D.B.; Edward Cappelletti, S.D.B., Mission Procurator; James Chiosso, S.D.B.; Dennis Donovan, S.D.B., Vicar, Devel. Dir.; Edward Frizzell, S.D.B.; David Gonder, S.D.B., Prov. Treas.; Joseph Maffei, S.D.B.; Michael Mendl, S.D.B., Supr.; David Moreno, S.D.B., Supr.; Philip Pascucci, S.D.B.; Joseph Ros, S.D.B. (Antilles); Robert Savage, S.D.B.; Anthony Spano, S.D.B., Financial Admin.; Waclav Swierzbiolek, S.D.B.; Louis Vyoral, S.D.B.; Bros. Andrew Lacombe, S.D.B.; Charles Mayer, S.D.B.; Gerald Meegan, S.D.B., Prov. Councilor; Aldo Roman, S.D.B.; David Tierney, S.D.B. Priests 16; Brothers 5.

PELHAM MANOR. *St. Vincent's Residence*, 190 Mt. Tom Rd., 10803-3309. Tel: 914-738-6138. The Passionists. Revs. Leo J. Gorman, C.P., Supr.; Stephen Haslach, C.P.; Paschal Smith, C.P.; Vincent Youngberg, C.P.

RYE. *Legionaries of Christ*, 815 Boston Post Rd., 10580. Tel: 914-967-7403. Revs. Peter Hopkins, L.C., Supr.; William Slattery, L.C.; Bros. Thomas Rudkins, L.C.; Paul Clarke, L.C.

SCARBOROUGH. *Carmelite Fathers, NY Prov. of St. Elias*, Carmelite Priory, 3 Woodlea Ln., 10510. Tel: 914-762-3719. Revs. Timothy C. Donohue, O.Carm.; Joachim J. Snyder, O.Carm.

SCARSDALE. *Paulist Fathers Generalate*, 86 Dromore Rd., 10583. Tel: 914-472-4800. Very Rev. Francis P. DeSiano, C.S.P., Pres.; Revs. Robert J. O'Donnell, C.S.P.; Thomas W. Jones, C.S.P.; Edward D. Whitley, C.S.P.

Paulist Priests at Paulist Foundations outside the U.S.: Via Venti Settembre 14, Rome, Italy, 00187. Revs. Paul G. Robichand, C.S.P.; Dennis W. Hickey, C.S.P., 659 Markham St., Toronto, Ontario, Canada, M6G 2M1. Revs. Michael P. Kerrigan, C.S.P.; Ronald A. Franco, C.S.P.; Thomas R. Marshall, C.S.P.; Thomas P. Murphy, C.S.P.; Robert E. Moran, C.S.P.; Deacon Richard J. Boudreau, C.S.P.

Military Chaplains: Revs. Gregory G. Caiazzo, C.S.P.; Thomas P. Hall, C.S.P.; Patrick D. Johnson, C.S.P.

On Special Assignment in the U.S. and Abroad: Revs. Edward R. Donovan, C.S.P.; Justin J. McCormick, C.S.P.; Mark-David Janus, C.S.P.; Thomas A. Kane, C.S.P.; Joachim Lally, C.S.P.; Norman J. O'Connor, C.S.P.; Martin J. O'Looney, C.S.P.; Thomas F. Stransky, C.S.P.

Retired: Revs. Charles W. Albright, C.S.P.; Walter Anthony, C.S.P.; Robert W. Baer, C.S.P.; Wilfred Brimley, C.S.P.; William J. Cantwell, C.S.P.; Ralph T. Carpenter, C.S.P.; John A. Carr, C.S.P.; Thomas E. Comber, C.S.P.; Leo E. Conlin, C.S.P.; James B. Corbett, C.S.P.; Phillip J. Cunningham, C.S.P.; Robert P. Curtis, C.S.P.; Wilfred F. Dewan, C.S.P.; Francis X. Diskin, C.S.P.; John P. Donahue, C.S.P.; Charles A. Donovan, C.S.P.; Harry J. Dooley, C.S.P.; J. Aloysius Farrell, C.S.P.; James F. Fisher, C.S.P.; Joseph P. Flynn, C.S.P.; Donal F. Forrester, C.S.P.; Harold J. Foye, C.S.P.; Joseph T. Griffin, C.S.P.; Joseph M. Hanly, C.S.P.; George F. Helmich, C.S.P.; Donald E. Howard, C.S.P.; James E. Joyce, C.S.P.; William J. Kenney, C.S.P.; James B. Lloyd, C.S.P.; Edward J. Lyons, C.S.P.; Stanley F. MacNevin, C.S.P.; Edward A. Maher, C.S.P.; William F. Manning, C.S.P.; Thomas J. Marley, C.S.P.; Harold J. Masterson, C.S.P.; Edward J. McDonald, C.S.P.; Neil J. McEleney, C.S.P.; Kenneth H. McGuire, C.S.P.; Louis F. McKernan, C.S.P.; James F. McLean, C.S.P.; James D. McNulty, C.S.P.; Robert P. Michele, C.S.P.; John Dennis Mitchell, C.S.P.; Ernest C. Mort, C.S.P.; John W. Mulhall, C.S.P.; Thomas P. Murphy, C.S.P.; Robert A. O'Donnell, C.S.P.; Edward P. O'Hern, C.S.P.; Harold J. Powers, C.S.P.; Robert F. Quinn, C.S.P.; John C. Reynolds, C.S.P.; Vincent J. Sampietro, C.S.P.; Warren H. Seedorf, C.S.P.; Arthur J. Spear, C.S.P.; Robert J. Stulting, C.S.P.; Walter J. Sullivan, C.S.P.; Joseph F. Troy, C.S.P.; Rudolph T. Vorisek, C.S.P.; James G. Walsh, C.S.P.; Richard J. Walsh, C.S.P.; Charles S. White, C.S.P.; Clarence E. Wilson, C.S.P.; Edward D. Wroblewski, C.S.P.

On Leave: Revs. Gregory G. Caiazzo, C.S.P.; Philip W. Hart, C.S.P.; Albert K.H. Kim, C.S.P.; James Kolb, C.S.P.; Kevin F. Novack, C.S.P.; Gregory A. Romanski, C.S.P.; Leslie M. Sieg, C.S.P.; Robert A. Sirico, C.S.P.; Joseph F.X. Smith, C.S.P.; Timothy F. Sullivan, C.S.P.; Thomas M. Tureman, C.S.P.; James M. Utendorf, C.S.P.; Nathan Wilburn, C.S.P.; Christopher P. Witt, C.S.P.

STATEN ISLAND. *Scalabrinian Missionaries*, 209 Flagg Pl., 10304. Tel: 718-351-0232. Scalabrinian Mission Center, The Center for Migration Studies; St. Charles Residence. Revs. Dominic Rodighiero, C.S., Supr. & Dir. Devel. Office; Lydio Tomasi, C.S., Dir. Center for Migration Studies. In res., Revs. James Viero, C.S.; Henry Gentile, C.S.; Bro. Louis Calisto, C.S.

SUFFERN. *Parish Mission Team Res.*, 38 Montebello Rd., 10901. Sr. Bethann Herrmann, O.S.F.; Rev. Thomas P. Devery; Jaime Rickert; Scott Krug; Nicole Smith. In res., Rev. Msgr. James S. Conlan; Sr. Maureen Colleary, F.S.P.; Jose Antonio Suarez; Katie Feeney.

TAPPAN. *St. Eliseus Priory*. (Carmelite Pre-novitiate), P.O. Box 27, 10983-0027. Tel: 914-359-5299; Fax: 914-359-0856. Rev. Michael Kissane, O.Carm., Dir. Students 4.

Office of Lay Carmelites. (Carmelite Third Order). Tel: 914-359-0535. Rev. Brocard Connors, O.Carm., Dir.

WASSAIC. *Guardian Angel Chapel*, Mailing Address: Box 443, 12592. Tel: 914-877-6821, Ext. 3350. Rev. John Langweld, O.F.M.Cap.

WEST PARK. *Congregation of Christian Brothers*, Santa Maria-on-Hudson, 12493. Tel: 914-384-6750. Bros. D. D. Crimmins, Supr.; W. S. Barry; J. L. Heathwood; P. C. Leavy; John F. Farrel, F.S.C. Total in Residence 5.

WHITE PLAINS. *St. Conrad Friary*, 30 Gedney Park Dr., 10605. Tel: 914-761-3008; Fax: 914-948-6429. Legal Titles: *The Province of St. Mary of the Capuchin Order*; *Capuchin Friars International, Inc.* (For Finance). Provincial Headquarters of the Province of St. Mary of the Capuchin Order. Development Office: 210 W. 31st St., New York, 10001. Very Rev. Bernard Smith, O.F.M.Cap., Min. Prov.; Revs. Regis Armstrong, O.F.M.Cap., Vicar Prov.; Jerome

McHugh, O.F.M.Cap., Sec.-Treas.; Paul Tolve, O.F.M.Cap., Chap.; James Stewart, O.F.M.Cap., Chap.; Bro. Joseph Yakimovich, O.F.M.Cap., Asst. Sec.-Treas. Priests 5; Brothers 1. (Nature of Apostolate: Provincial Administration, Hospital, Prison, Preaching, Recruitment). Subject to the Provincial, Revs. Jose McCarthy, O.F.M.Cap., Puerto Rico; Gregory Reisert, O.F.M.Cap., Washington, DC; Allan O'Brien, O.F.M.Cap., Warwick, NY; Michael Connolly, O.F.M.Cap., West Harrison, NY; Joseph Anthony Egan, O.F.M.Cap., Burlington, VT; John Rathschmidt, O.F.M.Cap., Ossining, NY; Anthony Ciorra, O.F.M.Cap., Summit, NJ.

Serving in the Military: Rev. James Jones, O.F.M.Cap., Chap., U.S.A. Total in Residence 67; Total Staff 10.

YONKERS. *St. Clare Friary*, 34 Convent Ave., P.O. Box 243, 10703-0243. Tel: 914-423-2392. Capuchin Franciscan Friars, Province of St. Mary. Residence for senior friars. Revs. Senan Taylor, O.F.M.Cap., Supr.; Darius Devito, O.F.M.Cap., Vicar; Neal Kerrigan, O.F.M.Cap.; Donatus Goetz, O.F.M.Cap.; Noel Scanlon; Celsus Repole; Sylvan Conover; Charles Repole; Bros. Bernard Frey, O.F.M.Cap.; Paul Murray, O.F.M.Cap.; Patrick Nolan; Peter Reilley. Total in Residence 15; Total Staff 3.

Saint Felix Friary. (House of Formation), 15 Trinity Plaza, 10701. Revs. Andrew D. Apostoli, C.F.R., Gen. Community Servant; Robert Stanion, C.F.R., Vicar; Bros. Richard Roemer, C.F.R.; Bernard Murphy, C.F.R.; Angelus Marie Houle, C.F.R.; Thomas Cacciola, C.F.R.

St. Joseph's Friary. (House of Formation), 523 W. 142nd St., New York, 10031. Tel: 212-234-9089. Friars: Bro. Michael Kmiotek, C.F.R., Local Servant; Revs. Herald Brock, C.F.R., Vicar; Conrad Osterhout, C.F.R., Dir. of Postulants. Postulants 16. Professed Friars 6.

[AA] CONVENTS AND RESIDENCES OF SISTERS

NEW YORK. *Academy of St. Dorothy*. 1305 Hylan Blvd., Staten Island, 10305. Tel: 718-987-0677. Sisters of St. Dorothy. Sr. Sharon A. McCarthy, S.S.D., Coord. Sisters 9.

Blessed Trinity Missionary Cenacle, 414 E. 14th St., 10009. Tel: 212-475-1450. Missionary Social Work and Parish Ministry. Family Division of Catholic Charities of New York, Campus Ministry N.Y.U. Missionary Servants of the Most Blessed Trinity 10; Total Assisted 3,873; Total Staff 6. Catholic Charities Family and Children's Services, 530 Grand St., 10002.

Carmelite Sisters Teresas of St. Joseph, Inc., 249 W. 14th St., 10011. Sr. Angela Perez, Supr.

Convent of Our Lady of the Presentation, 419 Woodrow Rd., 10312. Tel: 718-356-2121. Motherhouse and Novitiate of the Sisters of the Presentation. Sr. Mary O'Keefe, P.B.V.M. Sisters 37.

Convent of Sisters of the Congregation de Notre Dame, 76 Howard Ave., 10301. Tel: 718-447-0291. Sisters 12.

Corpus Christi Monastery, 1230 Lafayette Ave., 10474. Tel: 718-328-6996. Sr. Lee, Prioress. Solemnly Professed 15; Perpetually Professed 2; Novices 5.

Dalton Center for Mission and Peace, Sisters of the Holy Child Jesus, 325 E. 33rd St., 10016. Tel: 212-689-3548; 889-3886; Fax: 212-545-7804. Total in Residence 5; Total Staff 3.

Daughters of Mary Immaculate, 15 Stori Rd., 12550. Sr. Putorti, Admin. Total Assisted 240; Total Staff 3.

The Dwelling Place of New York, Inc., 409 W. 40th St., 10018. Tel: 212-564-7887. Sr. Nancy Chiarello, Admin. Sisters 4.

Franciscan Handmaids of Mary Convent, 15 W. 124th St., 10027. Generalate of the Franciscan Handmaids of Mary. Sr. Loretta Theresa Richards, F.H.M., Supr. Sisters 24; Total Assisted 150; Total Staff 15. Other Convents: Camp St. Edward, 445 Woodvale Ave., Staten Island, 10309. St. Benedict Convent, 34 W. 134th St., 10037.

Handmaids of Mary Novitiate, 444 Woodvale Ave., Staten Island, 10309. Tel: 718-984-1625. Novitiate of the Franciscan Handmaids of the Most Pure Heart of Mary. Sr. Maria Goretti, Dir., Formation. Sisters 3; Associates 2.

Franciscan Missionaries of Mary. Provincialate, 3305 Wallace Ave., Bronx, 10467-6599. Tel: 718-547-4604; Fax: 718-547-4607. Holy Name Convent, 204 W. 97th St., 10025-5620. Tel: 212-678-6901; Fax: 212-678-6865. Cardinal Hayes Home Convent, Box K, Millbrook, 12545. Tel: 914-677-9520.

Franciscan Sisters of Little Falls, Minn., 20 Walden Ave., 10306. Sisters 2.

Franciscan Sisters of the Poor Foundation, Inc., 708 Third Ave., Ste. 200, 10017. Tel: 212-818-1987; Fax: 212-808-0096.

Franciscan Sisters of the Poor Health System, Inc., 708 Third Ave., Ste. 200, 10017. Tel: 212-818-1987; Fax: 212-808-0096.

Little Sisters of the Assumption, 214 E. 30 St., 10016. Tel: 212-889-4310; Fax: 212-889-7358. Sr. Jean McCormack, Prov. Coord. Sisters 26; Sisters in Province 48; Total Assisted 3,000; Total Staff 35.

Other residences in New York: 218 E. 105th St., 10029. Tel: 212-534-4932. 475 E. 115th St., 10029. Tel: 212-369-2097. 310 E. 120th St., 10035. 410 Grand St., Apt. 26H, 10002. Tel: 212-533-6496. 2604 Davidson Ave., Bronx, 10468. Tel: 212-933-0377. 98 Gladstone Ave, Walden, 12586. Tel: 914-778-7252. 159-A Johnston St., Newburgh, 12550. Tel: 914-562-0700.

Missionaries of Charity, Inc., 335 E. 145th St., 10451. Tel: 718-292-0019. Sr. M. Sabita, M.C., Reg. Supr.; Sr. M. Dominga, M.C., Supr., 406 W. 127th St., 10027. Tel: 212-222-7229. Sr. M. Fredina, M.C., Supr., 657 Washington St., 10014. Tel: 212-645-0587. Sr. M. Rochelle, M.C., Supr. Total Assisted 1,200; Total Staff (shared apostolates) 24.

Missionary Sisters of the Immaculate Heart of Mary, 238 E. 15th St., 10003. I.C.M. Missionary Sisters. Sr. Gisela Braekmans, I.C.M. Sisters 6.

Monastery of St. Clare, 142 Hollywood Ave., 10465. Tel: 718-822-7271. Sr. Mary Bernadette Quinn, O.S.C., Abbess. Sisters 14.

Oblate Sisters of the Most Holy Redeemer, 1027 Grand Concourse, 10452. Tel: 293-9180. Sr. Ligia M. Latorre, Supr.

Oblates of the Mother of Orphans, 20 E. 72nd St., 10021. Sr. Maria Emanuele, Supr.

Parish Visitors of Mary Immaculate. 2151 Watson Ave., Bronx, 10472. Tel: 718-823-0350. Sr. Rose Aimee Trembloy, P.V.M.I., Supr. Sisters 5.

Sacred Heart Catechetical Center, 248 E. 62nd St., 10021. Tel: 212-838-0033. Mission Helpers of the Sacred Heart. Sisters 7.

St. Benedict's Convent, 34 W. 134th St., 10037. Tel: 212-234-6870. Franciscan Handmaids of the Most Pure Heart of Mary. Mother Miram Cecilia, Supr. Sisters 3.

St. Joseph Provincialate, 205 Major Ave., 10305. Tel: 718-720-4377. Provincialate of the Daughters of Divine Charity. Sisters 2; In Province 72.

Schoenstatt Sisters of Mary, Secular Institute, 337 Cary Ave., 10310. Tel: 718-727-8005. Sisters 7; Total Staff 4.

Shalom Convent, 714 W. 231st St., 10463. Franciscan Sisters of the Poor 4.

Sisters of Charity Center, Mount Saint Vincent, 6301 Riverdale Ave., 10471-9930; Fax: 718-884-3013. Sr. Elizabeth A. Vermaelen, Pres. Legal Titles: *The Sisters of Charity of Saint Vincent de Paul of New York; Sisters of Charity Center; Mount Saint Vincent on Hudson; The Sisters of Charity of Saint Vincent de Paul of New York Pension Trust*. Total in Congregation 587; In Archdiocese 543.

The Elizabeth Seton Federation, Inc., Sisters of Charity Center, 6301 Riverdale Ave., Bronx, 10471. Sr. Mary McCormick, S.C., Pres.

Sisters of the Good Shepherd, 337 E. 17th St., 10003-3804. Tel: 212-475-4245. Legal Title: *Sisters of the Good Shepherd-New York City*. Sr. M. Victoria Andreoli, R.G.S., Supr. Sisters 10.

Society of Helpers. 385 W. 263rd St., Bronx, 10471. Tel: 718-884-3100. Sr. Geraldine Finan, Supr. Sisters 8.

Society of the Sacred Heart, R.S.C.J., 363 W. 51st St., 10019. Tel: 212-581-4698; 581-5746.

Other Residences: 436 W. 49th St., 10019. Tel: 212-581-3894. 222 E. 93rd St., 10128. Tel: 212-876-2276. 406 E. 80st. St., 10021. Tel: 212-288-1986; 288-5116. 515 E. 118th St., 10035. Tel: 212-876-2895. 236 E. 15th St., 10003. Tel: 212-529-3447. 519 E. 118th St., 10035. Tel: 212-410-3465. Total Assisted 111; Total Staff 5.

173 E. 111th St., #7, 10029. Tel: 212-410-4315.

Ursuline Bedford Park Convent, 2885 Marion Ave., 10458. Tel: 212-364-1289; 220-3387. Sr. Marie Jerome Murray, O.S.U., Supr. Sisters 41.

Ursuline Provincialate. 323 E. 198th St., Bronx, 10458. Tel: 718-365-7410. Provincialate of the Ursulines of the Roman Union, Eastern Province. Sr. Madeline Welch, O.S.U., Prov. Sisters in Province 206.

Ursuline Sisters of Andrews Avenue, Inc., 323 E. 198th St., Bronx, 10458. Sr. Madeline Welch, O.S.U., Pres.

BEACON. *Carmelite Monastery*, 139 De Puyster Ave., 12508-3540. Sr. Marjorie Robinson, Prioress. Professed Nuns 10.

BLAUVELT. *Congregation of St. Dominic General Motherhouse of the Sisters of St. Dominic of Blauvelt*, 496 Western Hwy., 10913. Tel: 914-359-5600; Fax: 914-359-5773. Sr. Barbara Werner, O.P., Pres.; Sr. Julia O'Brien, O.P., Asst. to the Pres.; Revs. John L. Sullivan, O.P., Chap.; John P. Farrell, O.P., Chap., Emeritus. Sisters 243. Legal Title: *Congregation of Saint Dominic General Motherhouse of the Sisters of St. Dominic of Blauvelt*.

BRONX. *Sisters of St. John the Baptist*, 10465. Tel: 718-518-7820; Fax: 718-518-8930. Provincial Residence. Sr. Mary Cecile Swanton, C.S.J.B., Prov. Supr.

Mt. St. John Convent, Purchase, 10577. Sr. Frederick Mary DePew, C.S.J.B., Supr. Sisters 28; In Province 126; In Archdiocese 105; Total Assisted 45; Total Staff 9.

Immaculate Heart Novitiate, 150 Anderson Hill Rd., Purchase, 10577. Sr. Loretta Marie Florio, Dir. Formation.

ESOPUS. *Mother of Perpetual Help Monastery*, 12429. Redemptoristine Nuns. Sr. Paula Schmidt, O.SS.R., Prioress. Sisters 10.

GRAYMOOR. *Mother Lurana House*. Old W. Point Rd., Rte. 1, Box 186, Garrison, 10524. Franciscan Sisters of the Atonement. Adult Social Day Care. Sr. Barbara Ohl, S.A., Directress.

Motherhouse and Novitiate of the Franciscan Sisters of the Atonement, St. Francis Convent, R1, Box 163B, 10524-9717. Legal Title: *Franciscan Sisters of the Atonement, Inc.* Sr. Diane Bernier, S.A., Congregation Minister. Local Coord.: Sr. Consiline Flynn, S.A.; Sr. Eilish Sweeney, S.A. Sisters 74.

Our Lady's Guest and Retreat House, Graymoor, R.I. Box 163B, 10524-9717. Tel: 914-424-3300. Franciscan Sisters of the Atonement. Sr. Ita Flynn, S.A., Directress. Sisters 3.

HARRIMAN. *St. Patrick's Villa*, 10926. Provincial Retirement Home and Provincialate of the Sisters of the Catholic Apostolate (Pallottine). Sr. M. Nataline, Supr.; Sr. M. Kathleen Thompson, Prov.; Rev. Lawrence X. McCaffrey, S.J., Chap. Sisters 36.

HARTSDALE. *Institute of the Sisters of Mercy of the Americas, Regional Community of New York*, 150 Ridge Rd., 10530-2205. Tel: 914-328-3200; Fax: 914-328-3761. Sisters of Mercy. Sr. Patricia Wolf, R.S.M., Reg. Pres. Sisters of Mercy of the Americas 214.

HASTINGS-ON-HUDSON. *Sisters of St. Francis*, 49 Jackson Ave., 10706-3217; Fax: 914-478-5470. Sisters of St. Francis, Hastings-on-Hudson. Motherhouse and Novitiate. Sr. M. Bernadette Wyman, O.S.F., Gen. Minister; Rev. Robert Cheesman, C.Ss.R., Chap. Sisters 89.

HAVERSTRAW. *Sisters of St. Francis of Peace*, Congregation Center, 20 Ridge St., 10927. Sr. Margaret Gaffikin, Congregation Min.

HAWTHORNE. *Motherhouse & Novitiate of the Sisters of St. Dominic, Congregation of St. Rose of Li*, 10532. Mother Anne Marie, O.P., Mother Gen.; Rev. John Proppe, O.F.M.Cap., Chap. Legal Title: *Motherhouse and Novitiate of the Sisters of St. Dominic, Congregation of St. Rose of Lima*. Professed Sisters 28; Sisters in Community 80; In Archdiocese 40.

HIGHLAND MILLS. *Religious of Jesus and Mary*, 10930. Sr. Christine Carrigg, R.J.M., Supr.; Rev. Thomas E. Clarke, S.J. Sisters 14; Total Staff 4.

HOPEWELL JUNCTION. *St. Aloysius Novitiate*, Beekman Rd., P.O. Box 98, 12533. Oblates to the Blessed Trinity. Mother Gloria Castro, Supr. Gen. Sisters 11; Novices 2; Postulants 2; Total in Residence 41; Total Staff 31.

LIBERTY. *Blessed Kateri Tekakwitha Religious Education Center*, Mailing Address: Box 1011, 12754. Tel: 914-292-9100. Dominican Sisters.

LIVINGSTON MANOR. *Monastic Sisters of Bethlehem and of the Assumption of the Virgin*, Grooville Rd., 12758. Sr. Amena Figeat, M.S.B.A.V., Supr. Total in Residence 12.

MARYKNOLL. *Maryknoll Residential Care*, Maryknoll Sisters Center, 10545-0311. Tel: 914-941-9230; Fax: 914-941-0213. Skilled Nursing home for the Maryknoll sisters only. Sr. Mary T. Connell, M.M., Admin. Beds 58; Sisters 54.

Maryknoll Sisters Charitable Trust, Treasury Office, P.O. Box 306, 10545-0306. Rev. Richard B. Callahan, M.M., Contact Person.

Maryknoll Sisters Cloister, Mailing Address: P.O. Box 311, 10545-0311. Contemplative Community of the Maryknoll Sisters of St. Dominic. Sr. Theresa Baldini, M.M., Coord. Sisters 14.

Maryknoll Sisters of St. Dominic Inc., P.O. Box 311, 10545-0311. Tel: 914-941-7575; Fax: 914-923-0733. Sr. Rosemary Healy, Center Coord. Professed Sisters 266; Total in Residence 270.

MILLBROOK. *Franciscan Missionaries of Mary*, Mailing Address: Box K, 12545. Sr. Anne Turbini, F.M.M., Local Coord. Sisters 6.

MONROE. *Parish Visitors of Mary Immaculate (P.V.M.I.)*, Mailing Address: Generalate Juniorate, Novitiate, Box 658, 10950. Tel: 914-783-2251. Sr. Carole Marie Troskowski, Gen. Supr. Professed Sisters 65; Novices 8.

St. Joseph's Convent-Day Care Center, Harriman Heights Rd., R.R. 3, Box 165, 10950; Fax: 914-782-5645. Sr. M. Olivia, Coord. Sisters of the Catholic Apostolate (Pallottine) 6; Total Assisted 45; Total Staff 4.

MONSEY. *St. Zita's Villa*, 10952. Motherhouse and Novitiate of Sisters of Reparation of the Congregation of Mary. Sr. Maureen Francis, Supr. Sisters 14.

MONTICELLO. *St. Thomas Villa*, 12701. Sr. Rita Epilone, C.S.J., Admin. Summer residence for Sisters of St. Joseph, Brentwood.

NANUET. *St. Patrick Villa*, 2 Duryea Ln., 10954. Tel: 914-623-3371. Sisters of Charity of St. Vincent de Paul. Sr. Eileen A. Grubert, Admin. Sisters 29.

NEW ROCHELLE. *Ursuline Convent of St. Teresa*, 39 Willow Dr., 10805. Tel: 914-632-1199; Fax: 914-633-5281. Legal Title: *Ursuline Convent of St. Teresa's, New York*. Sr. Phyllis Hinchcliffe, O.S.U., Supr. Sisters 58.

Ursuline Residence, Inc., 1338 North Ave., 10804. Tel: 914-636-3456; Fax: 914-576-2620. Sr. Jeanne Giebelhouse, O.S.U., Supr. Sisters 30.

NEW WINDSOR. *Mt. St. Joseph*, 880 Jackson Ave., 12553. Tel: 914-564-6620. Motherhouse of the Sisters of the Presentation of the Blessed Virgin Mary of Newburgh. Sr. Carla Lorenz, Pres.; Sr. Laura Follmer, Community Archivist. Ministry in the field of academic education in parochial and high schools; pastoral services; health care; social services. Sisters 123.

NEWBURGH. *Center of Hope Sisters' Residence*, 320 Powell Ave., 12550. Dominican Sisters of Hope. Sr. Maura Schefter, O.P., Admin.

Daughters of Mary Immaculate, 15 Stori Rd., 12550. Italian Apostolate in Sacred Heart Church.

OSSINING. *Dominican Sisters of Hope*, 299 N. Highland Ave., 10562. Tel: 914-941-4420. Sr. Catherine Walsh, O.P., Prioress.

PEEKSKILL. *Mt. St. Francis, Motherhouse & Infirm of Franciscan Missionary Sisters of Sacred Heart*, 250 South St., 10566. Tel: 914-737-5409. Sr. M. Raphael Conlon, Prov. Supr.; Sr. M. Bernadette Zaleski, F.M.S.C., Supr. Legal Title: *Missionary Sisters of the Third Order of St. Francis*. Sisters of the Good Shepherd 3; Total Staff 3.
Canonical Name: Franciscan Missionary Sisters of the Sacred Heart.

Mt. St. Francis Infirmary, 250 South St., 10566. Sr. Bonaventure Bellarmino, F.M.S.C., Supr.

Novitiate. Sr. Petra Zanghi, F.M.S.C., Directress of Formation.

Sisters of the Good Shepherd, 250 South St., 10566. Tel: 914-737-0019. Sisters of the Good Shepherd 4.

PURCHASE. *Society of the Sacred Heart*, Manhattanville College, 10577. Tel: 914-694-2200.

RHINEBECK. *Linwood Spiritual Center*, 139 S. Mill Rd., 12572. Sisters of St. Ursula. Sr. M Isaac Jogues, S.U., Reg. Supr.; Maureen Steeley, S.U., Dir. Spiritual Center. Sisters 9.

RYE. *Convent of the Holy Child*, 25 Convent Ln., 10580. Tel: 914-967-5544. H.C. Carriage House, 9 Convent Ln. Tel: 914-967-9440. Sisters 23.

SLOATSBURG. *St. Mary's Villa, Spiritual & Educational Center*, 150 Sisters Servants Ln., P.O. Box 6, 10974-0006. Tel: 914-753-5100. Sisters Servants of Mary Immaculate.

SPARKILL. *Dominican Convent of Our Lady of the Rosary*, 175 Rte. 340, 10976-1047. Motherhouse and General Novitiate of Dominican Sisters of Congregation of Our Lady of the Rosary. Sr. Kathleen Kane, O.P., Pres.; Rev. Emmanuel Bertrand, O.P., Chap. Sisters 139 in Residence in Dominican Convent; Sisters 475 in Congregation.

STATEN ISLAND. *Daughters of St. Paul, Pious Society*, 78 Fort Pl., 10301. Tel: 718-447-5071. Missionary Sisters of the Communications Media. Sr. Deborah James Timmis, F.S.P., Supr. Sisters 9.

Pious Disciples of the Divine Master, Regional and Formation House, 60 Sunset Ave., 10314. Tel: 718-761-2323; 494-8597; Fax: 718-494-8521. Sr. M. Lucille Van Hoogmoed, Regional Supr. Sisters 9.

SUFFERN. *Sisters of Our Lady of Christian Doctrine aka Institute of Christian Doctrine*, Marydell Center, 23 Haskell Ave., 10901. Tel: 914-357-0046. Sr. Virginia Johnson, R.C.D., Pres. Sisters 39; Total in Residence 2; Total Staff 4.

TARRYTOWN. *Provincial Center, Religious Sacred Heart of Mary*, 50 Wilson Park Dr., 10591. Tel: 914-655-3440; 631-8872; Fax: 914-631-7803. Sr. Martina Crowley, Supr. Prov. Councillors: Sr. Letizia Pappalardo; Sr. Edna O'Connor; Sr. Frances Lane, Sec.; Sr. Marion Therese Shanahan, Treas.; Sr. Monica Walsh, Dir. Formation; Sr. Joanne Safian, Dir. Communications. Total in Residence 66; Total Staff 32.

WALDEN. *Convent of Most Precious Blood*, 100 Ulster Ave., 12586. Sisters 2.

Little Sisters of the Assumption, 98 Gladstone Ave., 12586. Sr. Jean McCormack, Provincial; Sr. Kathleen Gorham, Local Coord. Sisters 7.

WARWICK. *Franciscan Sisters of Poor Mt Alverno Center, Inc. Franciscan Health Systems of Warwick, Inc.*, 20 Grand St., 10990. Tel: 914-986-2267. Ms. Jeanne Lee, CEO; Miss Jean Wetstine, Admin.; Sr. Mary Veronica Donohue, S.F.P., Community Minister; Rev. Edward Sullivan, O.F.M., Chap. Legal Title: *Franciscan Sisters of the Poor Mt. Alverno Center, Inc. Franciscan Health System of Warwick, Inc.*

WHITE PLAINS. *Convent of Our Lady of Good Counsel*, 52 N. Broadway, 10603; Fax: 914-949-5169. Motherhouse of the Sisters of the Divine Compassion. Sr. Helen Coldrick, R.D.C., Pres.

RDC Center for Counseling and Human Development, Inc., 52 N. Broadway, 10603. Sr. Patricia Sheridan, R.D.C. To provide counseling services for laity, religious and clergy. Individual and group counseling are offered as well as marital and family therapy. Sisters 51.

YONKERS. *Blessed Sacrament Monastery*. 235 Bellvale Lakes Rd., Warwick, 10990-3403. Tel: 914-988-5424. Sisters 16. Sacramentine Nuns. Sr. Veronica, Prioress.

[BB] RETREAT HOUSES

NEW YORK. *Cardinal Spellman Retreat House*, Passionist Spiritual Center, 5801 Palisade Ave., 10471. Tel: 718-549-6500. Revs. Donald Ware, C.P., Dir.; William J. Gilberg, Admin. Ministry Staff: Rev. Benedict Berlo, C.P.; Bro. Damian Carroll, C.P.; Maureen Corrigan. Retreats for adults and youths and hosted non-profit groups.

Sisters of Mary Reparatrix, 225 E. 234th St., 10470. Tel: 212-324-2252. Sr. Margaret Hoey, S.M.R., Prov. Supr. Sisters 5; Total in Residence 34.

BEDFORD VILLAGE. *Cenacle Retreat House*, Rte. 22, P.O. Box 467, 10506. Tel: 914-234-3344. Directors: Sr. Thelma Hall, r.c.; Sr. Kathleen O'Brien, r.c. Directed retreats, Spiritual Direction, Days of prayer for individuals or small groups (religious or lay). Total in Residence 2; Total Staff 2.

BRONX. *St. Joseph's Center*. (Spanish Cursillo Center), 275 W. 230th St., 10463. Tel: 718-796-4340. Revs. Francis E. Peluso, O.A.R., Dir.; Gregario Arista, O.A.R. (Mexico); Domingos Machado, O.A.R. (Portugal); Bro. Mario Alvarez, O.A.R., Admin. Total in Residence 1; Total Staff 4.

ESOPUS. *Marist Brothers of Ulster County*, Mailing Address: P.O. Box 197, 12429. Tel: 914-384-6106; 384-6620. Bro. Donald Nugent, F.M.S., Dir. Total in Residence 15; Total Staff 4.

Mount St. Alphonsus Redemptorist Retreat Center, 12429. Tel: 914-384-6550. Redemptorist Fathers and Brothers. Very Rev. John G. Kingsbury, C.Ss.R., Rector; Bro. Robert Skinnner, C.Ss.R.; Revs. Francis J. Gargani, C.Ss.R.; Dennis Kelleher, C.Ss.R. Groups and individual retreats, conferences, workshops, and days of prayer. Available for Religious Chapters. Capacity 105 Rooms.

HIGHLAND MILLS. *Bethany Retreat House*, County Rd. 105, P.O. Box 1003, 10930. Tel: 914-928-2213. Religious of Jesus and Mary. Sr. Catherine Kenny, R.J.M., Dir. In res., Rev. Thomas E. Clarke. Total in Residence 16; Total Staff 7.

LARCHMONT. *Trinity Retreat*, 1 Pryer Manor Rd., 10538. Tel: 914-235-6839. Revs. Eugene Fulton, Dir.; Benedict J. Groeschel, C.F.R., Assoc. Dir.

MIDDLETOWN. *National Shrine of Our Lady of Mount Carmel*, Carmelite Dr., P.O. Box 868, 10940-0868. Tel: 914-344-0876; Fax: 914-344-0093. Very Rev. Matthias DesLauriers, O.Carm., Dir. Total Staff 8.

NEWBURGH. *Our Lady of Hope Center*, 434 River Rd., 12550. Conducted by the Oblates of Mary Immaculate of the Eastern Province. Revs. Gordon Orsino, O.M.I., Supr.; Patrick Brady, O.M.I.; Gerard McCormick, O.M.I.; Richard Kulwiec, O.M.I.; George M. White, O.M.I.; Charles Beausoleil, O.M.I.; Bros. Charles E. Quinn, O.M.I.; Charles Timothy Fuqua, O.M.I.

SLOATSBURG. *St. Mary's Villa*, 150 Sisters Servants Ln., P.O. Box 6, 10974-0006. Tel: 914-753-5100. Spiritual and Educational Center. (Retreats). Sisters Servants of Mary Immaculate. Total in Residence 7; Total Staff 9.

STATEN ISLAND. *Mount Manresa Jesuit Retreat House*, 239 Fingerboard Rd., 10305. Tel: 718-727-3844. Jesuits. Revs. John T. Ryan, S.J., Dir.; Joseph T. Browne, S.J., Supr.; William B. Cogan, S.J.; Robert E. Groenewold, S.J.; John J. King, S.J.; Deacon Michael R. Marsh, S.J.; Revs. Joseph E. Moltesz, S.J.; Thomas J. Quinn, S.J. Total in Residence 8; Total Staff 8.

WALDEN. *St. Andrew's Retreat House*, 257 St. Andrew's Rd., 12586. Tel: 914-778-5941. Sr. Deana Kohlman, Supr. Gen.; Sr. Ellen Patrick Stapleton, Business Mgr. North American Union Sisters of Our Lady of Charity.

WAPPINGERS FALLS. *Mt. Alvernia Retreat House*, 12590. Revs. Thomas More Nicastro, O.F.M.; Ernest D'Onofrio, O.F.M.; Armand Padula, O.F.M.; Andre Cirino, O.F.M.; Roch Ciandella, O.F.M.; Bros. Joseph Messina, O.F.M.; Giles Kelly, O.F.M.

WARWICK. *Mount Alverno Center and Convent*, 20 Grand St., 10990. Tel: 914-986-2267. Franciscan Sisters of the Poor. Miss Jean Wetstine, Exec. Dir.; Sr. Mary Veronica Donohue, S.F.P., Local Community Min.; Rev. Edward Sullivan, O.F.M., Chap.

WEST HAVERSTRAW. *Don Bosco Retreat Center and Marian Shrine*, Filors Ln., Box 9000, 10993. Tel: 914-947-2200; Fax: 914-947-2203. Founded 1947. Bro. Mario Audero, S.D.B.; Rev. Jay Horan, S.D.B., Vice Dir., Youth Retreat Coord.; Bros. Richard Pasiak, S.D.B.; John Cauda, S.D.B.; Jerome Cincotta, S.D.B.; Thomas J. Higgs, S.D.B.; Emil Dube, S.D.B., Vocations; Bernard Zdanowicz, S.D.B.; Alfred Flatoff, S.D.B.; Joseph Botto, S.D.B.; Mario Audero, S.D.B.; Revs. Peter Lappin, S.D.B.; Richard Crager, S.D.B., Finances; Gennaro Sesto, S.D.B., Shrine Coord.; Chester Szemborski, S.D.B.; Roy J. Shelly, S.D.B., Dir.; Stephen Schenck, S.D.B.; Anthony Luzzi, S.D.B.; John Divizia, S.D.B.; August Kita, S.D.B.; Eugene Walter, S.D.B.; Domenic DiGuardo, S.D.B.; Daniel O'Donovan, S.D.B. Total in Residence 22; Total Staff 30.

Marian Shrine, Filors Ln., P.O. Box 9000, 10993. Tel: 914-947-2200; Fax: 914-947-2203. Revs. Roy J. Shelly, S.D.B., Dir.; John Divizia, S.D.B.; Gennaro Sesto, S.D.B., Shrine Coord.; Jay Horan, S.D.B., Vice Dir., Coord. Youth Ministry; Peter Lappin, S.D.B.; Richard Crager, S.D.B., Finances; Daniel O'Donovan, S.D.B.; Domenic DiGuardo, S.D.B.; August Kita, S.D.B.; Stephen Schenck, S.D.B.; Chester Szemborski, S.D.B.; Anthony Luzzi, S.D.B.; Eugene Walter, S.D.B.; Bros. Mario Audero, S.D.B.; John Cauda, S.D.B.; Jerome Cincotta, S.D.B.; Thomas Higgs, S.D.B.; Emile Dube, S.D.B., Vocations; Richard Pasaik, S.D.B.; Alfred Flatoff, S.D.B.; Joseph Botto, S.D.B.; Bernard Zdanowicz, S.D.B. Total in Residence 22; Total Staff 30.

[CC] UNIVERSITY APOSTOLATES

NEW YORK. *University Apostolate*, 1011 First Ave., 10022. Tel: 212-371-1000, Ext. 2805. Rev. Michael C. Crimmins, Coord.

Bronx Community College, 2352 St. Raymond Ave., Bronx, 10462. Tel: 718-828-2380. Rev. Eduardo Rodriguez.

City College of New York, 469 W. 142nd St., 10031. Tel: 212-368-9555. Mr. Gregory Pope.

Columbia University, 110 Earl Hall, 10027. Tel: 212-854-5110; 866-1500 (Notre Dame Rectory). Rev. Msgr. Christopher Maloney; Rev. Rees Doughty.

Dominican College, 470 Western Hwy., Orangeburg, 10962. Tel: 914-359-7800, Ext. 255. Sr. Barbara McEneany, O.P.

Fordham University at Lincoln Center, 113 W. 60th St., Room 217, 10023. Tel: 212-636-6267. Rev. James Pierce, S.J.; Ms. Judith Bruder.

Fordham University at Rosemill, Bronx, 10458. Tel: 718-817-4500 (C.M. Office); 817-1000 (Info.); Fax: 718-817-4505. Revs. James Hentges, O.S.C.; Michael Agliardo, S.J.; Frank Stoud, S.J.; Sr. Ann Walsh, R.S.H.M.; Rev. John Mullin, S.J.; Mr. Robert Minotti; Ms. Grace Holcomb.

Herbert H. Lehman College, Student Life Bldg.(202E), Bedford Park Blvd. W., Bronx, 10468. Tel: 718-960-4979. Sr. Madeleine Smith, S.H.C.J.; Mrs. Kathryn Mastriaco.

Hostos Community College, 500 Grand Concourse, Room C371, Bronx, 10451. Tel: 718-518-4313. Ms. Lidia Fernandez.

Hunter/Baruch College, 695 Park Ave., Room 1206 E. Bldg., 10021. Tel: 212-772-4752. Sr. Barbara Ann Mueller, O.P.

Iona College, New Rochelle, 10801. Tel: 914-633-2340; 633-2632. Rev. Louis Phillips, F.A.C.; Mr. Michael Hovey; Mr. Carl Procario-Foley; Bro. Robert Fitzsimmons, C.F.C.; Ms. Barbara Hetzel.

Manhattan College, Bronx, 10471. Tel: 718-920-0972. Rev. Cesar Russo; Bros. Dennis Lee, F.S.C.; James Loxham, F.S.C.

Manhattanville College, 125 Purchase St., Purchase, 10577. Tel: 914-323-5150. Rev. J. Joseph Flynn, O.F.M.Cap.

Marist College, Poughkeepsie, 12601. Tel: 914-575-3000, Ext. 2130; Fax: 914-471-6213. Rev. Luke McCann, Ph.D., Chap. Tel: 914-452-7330; Bros. Frank Kelly, F.M.S.; Michael Williams, F.M.S.

Marymount College, Tarrytown, 10591. Tel: 914-332-8248. Sr. Victoria Busch, R.S.H.M.

Marymount Manhattan College, 221 E. 71st St., 10021. Tel: 212-517-0597. Sr. Rosaleen O'Haloran.

Mt. St. Mary College, Campus Ministry Office, Newburg, 12550. Tel: 914-569-3154. Rev. James Gilhooly.

College of Mt. St. Vincent, Riverdale, 10471. Tel: 718-405-3200. Rev. John A. Vigilanti; Mrs. Henrietta Carew; Mr. Terence McCorry.

College of New Rochelle, 29 Castle Pl., New Rochelle, 10805. Tel: 914-654-5339. Sr. Joan Garvey, O.P.

New York Maritime College, Fort Schyler, Bronx, 10465. Tel: 718-409-7200. Rev. Michael Moynihan.

New York University, Catholic Center at NYU, 58 Washington Square South, 10012. Tel: 212-674-7236. Revs. John McGuire, O.P.; Gregory Keeler, O.P.; Sr. Thomasmari Gore, M.S.B.T.

Pace University, 20 Cardinal Hayes Pl., 10007. Tel: 212-962-3972. Rev. Paul Bernier, S.S.S.

Pace University-Westchester, Suny, Purchase, 72 Carman Rd., Scarsdale, 10583. Tel: 914-723-0972. Mrs. Dorothy Lambert.

Rockland Community College, 145 College Rd., Suffern, 10901. Tel: 914-574-4531; Fax: 914-574-4425. Mr. Michael Ver'Schneider.

St. John's University, 300 Howard Ave., Staten Island, 10301. Tel: 718-390-4973; Fax: 718-390-4497. Rev. Michael J. Cummins, C.M.; Sr. Patty Ann O'Brien, D.C.

St. Thomas Aquinas, 175 Rte. 340, Sparkill, 10976. Tel: 914-398-4062; Fax: 914-398-4061. Sr. Catherine Patrice Morgan, O.P.; Rev. Bernard Keitz, O.P.

Suny/New Paltz, St. Joseph's Church, 34 S. Chestnut, New Paltz, 12561. Tel: 914-257-3024. Bro. Tim Jones, O.F.M.Cap.

United States Military Academy, Most Holy Trinity, West Point, 10996. Tel: 914-445-5575. Rev. John T. McLoughlin.

Wagner & Staten Island College, 143-48 84th Dr., Briarwood, 11435-2232. Tel: 718-526-3595. Sr. Elaine R. Schenk.

Vassar College, University Apostolate, Vassar College Box 381, Poughkeepsie, 12601-6198. Tel: 914-437-5847. Rev. Marc Oliver; Mrs. Valerie Oliver. Tel: 914-437-5548.

[DD] MISCELLANEOUS

NEW YORK. *Alfred E. Smith Memorial Foundation, Inc., The*, 1011 First Ave., 10022-4134. Tel: 212-371-1000, Ext. 3315. Rev. Msgr. Charles M. Kavanagh, Exec. Vice Pres.

America Press, Inc., The, Business & Editorial Offices,106 W. 56th St., 10019. Tel: 212-581-4640. Revs. George W. Hunt, S.J., Pres.; Charles M. Whelan, S.J., Vice. Pres.; Robert C. Collins, S.J., Sec. & Treas.

American Committee on Italian Immigration, Inc., 352 W. 44th St., 10036. Tel: 212-247-7373. Rev. Giulio Poggi, C.S., Sec. Total Staff 3. To insure fair immigration policy favoring reunion of families and cultural integration of Italian Americans.

American St. Boniface Society, Incorporated, Mailing Address: P.O. Box D, 10466-0604. Tel: 718-994-0989; Fax: 718-994-6119. Rev. Joachim Von Kerssenbrock, S.J., Prov.; Germainiae Septentrionalis, Exec. Dir.

Apostolate for Family Consecration, Inc., Canonical Global Center, 350 Fifth Ave., Ste. 3304, 10118-0069. Tel: 212-971-1370. Jerome Coniker, Pres.

Archdiocesan Council of Catholic Nurses. (Includes Manhattan), 1011 First Ave., 10022. Tel: 212-371-1000.

Brooklyn Prep Alumni Association, Loyola Hall, Fordham Univ., 10458. Tel: 718-817-5447; Fax: 718-733-4456. Rev. John D. Alexander, S.J., Moderator. Membership 4,616.

Calvary Fund, Inc. 1740 Eastchester Rd., Bronx, 10461. Tel: 718-518-2077; Fax: 718-518-2477. Frank A. Calamari, Pres.; Dennis E. Berberich, Chm.

Camp Wethersfield, 1011 First Ave., 10022.

Cardinal Cooke Guild, 1011 First Ave., 10022. Tel: 212-371-1000. Official organization for information on the cause of canonization of Cardinal Terence J. Cooke. Sr. M. Aloysius McBride, O.Carm., Coord.

Cardinal Cooke Memorial Foundation, 1011 First Ave., Room 1940, 10022.

Cardinal's Fund for Children, 1011 First Ave., Room 1940, 10022.

Carmel Housing Development Fund Co., Inc., 1011 First Ave., 10022. Tel: 212-371-1000. Rev. Kevin Sullivan, Pres.

Catholic Actors Guild of America, Inc., The, 1501 Broadway, Ste. 518, 10036; Fax: 212-398-1868. William O'Mally, Pres.; Rev. Thomas Donlan, Chap.

Catholic Alumni Club of the Archdiocese of New York, 83 Christopher St., 10014. Tel: 212-243-6513; 243-0901. Evie Pullis, Pres.

Catholic Big Brothers of New York, Inc., 45 E. 20th St., 10003. Tel: 212-477-2250; Fax: 212-477-2739. Total Assisted 275; Total Staff 14.

The Catholic Big Sisters, Archdiocese of New York-Manhattan Family Court, 60 Lafayette St., 10013. Tel: 212-349-4400; Fax: 212-349-4403. Total Families Assisted 180; Total Staff 6.

Catholic Daughters of the Americas and Its Courts, 10 W. 71st St., 10023. Tel: 212-877-3041; Fax: 212-724-5923. Mrs. Grace M. Rinaldi, National Regent; Mrs. Margaret O'Brien, Contact Person.

Catholic Foundation for the Dominican Republic, 1011 First Ave., 10022. Rev. Msgr. James P. Cassidy, Ph.D., Pres.; Oscar de la Renta, Chm.; Gerald Cunningham, Treas.; Richard Concannon, Sec.

Catholic Health Care Network, 1011 First Ave., Ste. 1150, 10022. Tel: 212-371-1000. Mary Healy Sedutto, Ph.D., Dir.

Catholic High School Association of New York, 1011 First Ave., Room 1856, 10022. Tel: 212-371-1000.

Catholic High Schools' Athletic Association of the Archdiocese of New York, 650 Grand Concourse, 10451. Tel: 718-585-5556. 4300 Murdock Ave., Bronx, 10466. Tel: 718-325-6423. Mr. Richard Tricario, Pres.

Catholic Interracial Council of N.Y., The, 899 10th Ave., 10019. Tel: 212-237-8255. Herbert A. Johnson, Exec. Dir.

Catholic Medical Mission Board, Inc., National Headquarters, 10 W. 17th St., 10011. Tel: 212-242-7757; Fax: 212-807-9161. His Eminence John Cardinal O'Connor; Rev. Vincent M. Cooke, S.J.; Rev. Msgr. Ferdinando D. Berardi; John A. Donnelly; Rev. Robert J. Fuhrman; Theodore J. Dubuque, Jr., M.D.; Thomas F. Murphy; Thomas P. Melady, Ambassador; Rev. William T. Wood, S.J.; Floyd J. Donahue, M.D.; Sr. Marilyn Fischer, S.F.P.; Terry Kirch, Pres./CEO; Thomas V. Whelan.

Catholic Near East Welfare Association, 1011 First Ave., 10022. His Eminence John Cardinal O'Connor, Pres. & Treas.; His Eminence William H. Keeler, Vice Pres.; Rev. Msgr. Robert L. Stern, Sec. Gen.

Catholic Social Policy Coalition of the Archdiocese of New York, The, 1011 First Ave., Room 1116, 10022. Agnes Kearns, Pres.

Catholic Women's Union. c/o Eunice Vasile, 15-25 Utopia Pkwy., Queens, 11357. Eunice Vasile, Pres.; Anna K. Weisz, Vice Pres.; Hilda McGlew, Treas.; Mary Sophie Ruedi, Sec.

**Catholics United for Spiritual Action, Inc.*, 63 Wall St., 10005. Mrs. Joan Donnelly, Pres.

The Center for Spirituality and Justice. 323 E. 198th St., Bronx, 10458. Rev. Thomas F. Madden; Bro. Charles A. Reutemann, F.S.C., Vice Pres.; Sr. Miriam Cleary, O.S.U., Sec. Total Assisted 15; Total Staff 3.

Centro Carismatico Catolico Hispano De La Arquidiocesis De Nueva York. 826 E. 166th St., Bronx, 10459. Tel: 718-378-1734; Fax: 718-378-1819. Rev. Josu Iriondo, C.R.L., Dir.

Chinese Catholic Information Center, 86 Riverside Dr., 10024. Tel: 212-787-6969. Rev. Paul Chan (Taiwan), Dir. Total in Residence 3; Total Staff 3.

Chinese Clergy & Religious Association in North America, 29 Mott St., 10013. Tel: 212-962-5157; 732-8558. Rev. Joseph S. Chiang, Coord.

Christ House, Inc. 432 E. 142nd St., Bronx, 10454. Tel: 718-665-8740. Shared Residence for Religious and Young Men lacking Family Support. Bros. Thomas P. Draney, C.F.C., Dir.; James V. Hanney, C.F.C., Asst. Dir.

The Christophers, 12 E. 48th St., 10017. Tel: 212-759-4050; Fax: 212-838-5073. Rev. Thomas J. McSweeney, Dir. A multi-media organization reaching millions with the Gospel message. Total Staff 44.

Courage, St. Michael Rectory, 424 W. 34th St., 10001. Tel: 212-421-0426; Fax: 212-268-7150. Rev. John F. Harvey, O.S.F.S., Dir. Total Staff 9.

Dominican Friars' Guild, 141 E. 65th St., 10021.

St. Jude Dominican Missions, 141 E. 65th St., 10021. Tel: 212-734-4784. Rev. Edward L. Martin, O.P., Dir.

Dominican Rosary Apostolate, 141 E. 65th St., 10021. Tel: 212-744-2410.

Deserving Poor Boys Priesthood Association, 141 E. 65th St., 10021. Tel: 212-744-2410; Fax: 212-737-3875.

St. Martin de Porres Guild, 141 E. 65th St., 10021. Tel: 212-744-2410.

Dominican Shrine of St. Jude, Inc., St. Catherine of Siena Priory, 411 E. 68th St., 10021. Tel: 212-249-6067; 988-8300. Very Rev. Christopher Johnson, O.P.; Rev. George L. Concordia, O.P., Admin. Dir.

**Don Bosco Harlem Association, Inc.*, 147-159 St. Nicholas Ave., 10026. Tel: 212-662-2693. Rev. George Hanna, S.D.B., Contact Person.

Felix Varela Foundation, Inc., The, 1011 First Ave., 10022. Rev. Msgr. Octavio Cisneros, Pres.

Focolare Movement, Mailing Address: Box 496, 10021.

Focolare Movement, Men's Branch, Mariapolis Luminosa, 196 Cardinal Rd., Hyde Park, 12538. Mr. Julian Ciabattini, Dir.

Focolare Movement, Women's Branch, Mariapolis Luminosa, 204 Cardinal Rd., Hyde Park, 12538. Miss Sharry Silvi, Dir. Focolare also known as Work of Mary. Founded in Trent, Italy in 1943. International Headquarters are in Rome, Italy.

Franciscan Missionary Union, Province of the Most Holy Name. Headquarters, St. Francis Friary, 135 W. 31st St., 10001-3439. Tel: 212-736-8500. Bro. Denis Clark, O.F.M., Prov. Promoter.

Three schools in Brazil.

Franciscans of the Holy Name Province Sick, Aged and Retired Trust, 126 W. 32nd St., 10001-3202.

Franciscans of the Holy Name Province Education and Formation Trust.

Friends of American Art in Religion, Inc., 143 E. 43rd St., 10017. Tel: 212-661-3290. His Eminence John Cardinal O'Connor, Pres.; Rev. Msgr. Eugene V. Clark, Sec. & Treas.

Friends of RADIO MARIA, Inc., 352 W. 44th St., 10036. Tel: 212-246-9620. Rev. Walter Tonelotto, C.S., Sec.

Gregorian University Foundation, The, 106 W. 56th St., 10019. Tel: 212-582-5433. Rev. Eugene J. O'Brien, S.J., Pres.

Guild of Catholic Lawyers, The. Mailing Address: 6 MacDonald Pl., Scarsdale, 10583. Tel: 914-723-3211. 1011 First Ave., 10022. Tel: 212-371-1000, Ext. 2950. Rev. George W. Rutler, Spiritual Dir.; Gregory de Sousa, Pres., Emeritus, Exec. Dir.

Healing Through God Word Ministries, Inc., P.O. Box 080525, 10308-0007. Jean Marie Timko, Pres. Legal Title: *Healing Through God Word Ministries, Inc./Apostolate of Intercession Healing & Teaching the Word of God.* An evangelistic ministry of teaching the scriptures, intercession, and healing. Involves missions, retreats, days of renewal, healing services, and Bible studies.

Hispanic Catholic Charismatic Center of the Archdiocese of New York. 826 E. 166th St., Bronx, 10459. Tel: 718-378-1734; Fax: 718-378-1819. Rev. Josu Iriondo, C.R.L., Dir.

House of Peace, Inc. 1291 Allerton Ave., P.O. Box 696, Bronx, 10469-0696. Tel: 718-547-3230. Rev. Peter McCall, O.F.M.Cap.; Maryanne Lacy. Healing Prayer Center for the Peace of Christ Prayer Ministry.

The Housing Fund of the Archdiocese of New York, 1011 First Ave., 10022. Rev. Msgr. James J. Murray, Pres.; Rev. Kevin Sullivan, Vice. Pres.; Rev. Msgr. Donald Sakano, Sec. & Treas.

Hungarian Catholic League of America, Inc., 30 E. 30th St., 10016. Tel: 212-684-3623. Rev. Dominic L. Csorba, O.F.M., Pres.; Rev. Msgr. William I. Varsany, P.A., Chm. Bd.; Mr. Adam Tarnoczy, Exec. Sec.

Incarnation Children's Center Fund, Inc., 1290 St. Nicholas Ave., 10033. Capacity 18.

Institute of the Helpers. 385 W. 263rd St., Bronx, 10471. Sr. Teresa Cole, Pres.

Intercommunity Center for Justice & Peace, 20 Washington Square N., 10011. Tel: 212-475-6677. Sr. Marie Danaher, O.P., Exec. Dir. Peace and Justice Center is Sponsored by 37 religious congregations. The congregation assists its members in implementing values of peace and justice according to social teachings of the church. Total Staff 6.

International Catholic Child Bureau/North America, Inc., 866 United Nations Plaza, Ste. 529, 10017. Tel: 212-355-3992; Fax: 212-754-4674. Rev. David J. Sauer, Vice Pres., Admin. Services, The Catholic Health Association. An international convening agency for child care professionals interested in developing pilot projects, training seminars, research and advocacy for the physical, psychological, social, spiritual and religious well being of all children worldwide.

Italian Seamen's Club, The, 352 W. 44th St., 10036. Tel: 212-246-9620. Directed by the Missionaries of St. Charles/Scalabrinians (NY Prov.). Rev. Walter Tonelotto, C.S., Dir.

Jesuit Seminary and Mission Bureau, Inc., 39 E. 83rd St., 10028. Tel: 212-734-1144. Revs. William J. Scanlon, S.J.; Gerard E. Braun, S.J.; Bro. John J. Campbell, S.J.; Revs. Anthony F. LaBau, S.J.; James F. O'Brien, S.J.

John LaFarge Institute, The, c/o America Press, Inc., 106 W. 56th St., 10019. Tel: 212-581-4640. Rev. Vincent T. O'Keefe, S.J., Dir.

La Casa Sollievo Della Sofferenza Opera Di Padre Pio, 1154 First Ave., 10021. The United States and Canada National Office of La Casa Sollievo Della Sofferenza Opera Di Padre Pio and The Padre Pio Prayer Groups. Mr. Mario Bruschi, Dir. & Coord. Total in Residence, Total Staff 1.

LAMP Ministries, Inc. 2704 Schurz Ave., Bronx, 10465. Tel: 718-409-5062; Fax: 718-904-0048. Co-Directors: Tom Scheuring, Ph.D.; Lyn Scheuring, Ph.D. Assoc. Directors: Marybeth Greene; Ed Greene.

LaSalle New York City, Inc., 44 E. 2nd St., 10003; Fax: 212-529-3598. Bros. Michael Corry, F.S.C., Chm.; Carl Malacalza, F.S.C., Vice Chm. Total Assisted 500; Total Staff 46.

Legion of Mary, Office, 1011 First Ave., 10022. Tel: 212-752-7966. Rev. Lawrence Paolicelli, Spiritual Dir.

Lower East Side Catholic Area Conference-Pastoral Center, 23 Oliver St., 10038. Tel: 212-962-1850; Fax: 212-571-4126.

Lumen Dei, 340 W. 53rd St., 10019. Tel: 212-586-4447; Fax: 212-586-1640. Rev. Wilberto Reyes Garced, Spiritual Dir. Priests of Lumen Dei 1; Sisters of Lumen Dei 8.

Manhattan North Community Services, Inc., 91 Arden St., 10040. Niki Montaluo, Pres.

Maria Droste Services, 386 Park Ave. S., Ste. 903, 10016-8804. Tel: 212-889-4042. Legal Title: *St. Germaine's Services.*

**Monsignor Robert Fox Memorial Shelter Housing Development, Inc.*, Fox House, 111 E. 117th St., 10035. Sr. Florence Speth, Exec. Dir. Total Assisted 151; Total Staff 17.

Narnia Catechetical & Cultural Centre, Inc., 20 Sutton Pl. S., 10022. Mrs. Charles Teetor, Pres.; Mr. George Sim Johnston, Sec.-Treas.

National Catholic Resettlement Council, 1011 First Ave., 10022. Tel: 212-371-1000. Vacant. Contact the Chancery for details.

National Federation for Life, 1011 First Ave., 10022.

National Italian Apostolate Conference, 1011 First Ave., 10022. Tel: 212-371-1000. Rev. Msgr. William A. Varvaro, S.T.L., J.C.D., Exec. Dir.

Nativity Mission Center, Inc., 204 Forsyth St., 10002. Rev. John J. Podsiadlo, S.J., Dir. Students 57; Total Staff 15.

**Nazareth Housing, Inc.*, 519 E. 11th St., 10009.

New York Catholic Forum, c/o St. Thomas More Church, 65 E. 89th St., 10128. George Sim Johnston, Chm.

New York Foundling Charitable Corp., 590 Ave. of the Americas, 10011. Sr. Carol Barnes, Pres.

Nocturnal Adoration Society of the United States, 184 E. 76th St., 10021. Tel: 212-288-5082. Congregation of the Blessed Sacrament. Rev. Bernard J. Camire, S.S.S., Natl. Dir.

North American College of Rome, Alumni Assoc. of, Mailing Address: 1011 First Ave., Ste. 1957, 10022. Rev. Warren Wall, P.O. Box 1966, Mobile, AL, 36633. Rev. Edmund J. Whalen, S.T.D., St. Joseph's Seminary, 201 Seminary Ave., Yonkers, 10704.

North East Hispanic Catholic Center, Inc., 1011 First Ave., 10022. Tel: 212-751-7045. Mr. Mario J. Paredes, Exec. Dir.

Northeast Hispanic Catholic Center, 1011 First Ave., 10022. Tel: 212-751-7045. His Eminence John Cardinal O'Connor, Pres.; Mario J. Paredes, Exec. Dir.

Partnership for Quality Education, Inc., 1011 First Ave., 10022. Rev. Msgr. Charles M. Kavanaugh, Vicar Devel. Partnership for quality educaton, assisting 16 inner-city schools.

Passionist Residence. 5801 Palisade Ave., Bronx, 10471. Tel: 718-548-1182; Fax: 718-548-2945. Revs. Paul Fagan, C.P., Contact Person; Edward Beck, C.P.; Paul Wieeichs, C.P.; Bros. Gordon Mathieu, C.P.; Michael Moran, C.P. Total in Residence 5.

Patrons of the Arts in the Vatican Museums, 143 E. 43rd St., 10017. His Eminence John Cardinal O'Connor, Chm. of the Board; Rev. Msgr. Eugene V. Clark, Pres. Total Staff 2.

Pauline Books And Media. 78 Fort Pl., Staten Island, 10301. Tel: 718-447-5071; 447-5086; Fax: 718-816-1332. Legal Title: *Pauline Books & Media*. Other location: 150 E. 52nd St., 10022. Tel: 212-754-1110; Fax: 212-754-2268. Total in Residence 9; Total Staff 6.

Pax Christi Metro New York, 135 W. Fourth St., 10012. Tel: 212-420-0250; Fax: 212-673-0826. Rachel Keeler, Dir. We are a regional chapter of Pax Christi USA, the national Catholic movement for peace.

Perpetual Help Center. Redemptorist Fathers of New York. 294 E. 150th St., Bronx, 10451. Tel: 718-585-3678. Bro. Stephen Lendvay, C.SS.R.

Pius XII Foundation, Inc., 866 Third Ave., 10022. Tel: 212-319-0464. Bro. Robert Fontaine, C.S.C., Pres.

Polish Knights of Malta, Inc., 15 E. 65th St., 10021. Mr. Witoli Sulimirski, Pres.

Regina Coeli Society, Mailing Address: P.O. Box 939, 10272-0604. Tel: 212-374-5060. First Friday Club for the Catholic Women of New York City Police Dept. Jacquelyn Fleming, Pres.

S.H.A.R.E. - New York, Inc. 1601 Bronxdale Ave., Bronx, 10462. Tel: 718-518-1513. Ms. Lee Stuart, Pres.

St. Ansgar Scandinavian Catholic League, 40 W. 13th St., 10011. Tel: 212-675-0400. Rev. Philip Sandstrom, Spiritual Dir.; Dr. Astrid M. O'Brien, Pres.; Revs. Thomas A. Nielson, Chap.; John E. Halborg, Dir. Programs, Editor of the Bulletin; Karl-Albert Lindblad, Asst. Chap.; Mr. Viggo F.E. Rambusch, Honorary Pres.; Mr. Nicholas Falco, Vice Pres. Membership.

St. Anthony Welfare Center, c/o Chancery Office, Room #1940, 1011 First Ave., 10022. Rev. Msgr. William J. McMahon, Dir.

St. Benedict the Moor Center, 283 St. Ann's Ave., 10454. Tel: 212-665-9693. James Roundtree, Pres.

St. Joseph's Union of Staten Island, New York Inc. 108 Bedell St., Staten Island, 10309. Tel: 718-984-9296. Sr. Una McCormack, O.P., Treas.

St. Paul's Guild, Inc., 1011 First Ave., Room 1940, 10022. Rev. Msgr. Francis X. Duffy, Exec. Sec.

St. Rose's Settlement, 1011 First Ave., Room 1940, 10022. Tel: 212-371-1000.

St. Thomas Aquinas Foundation, National Headquarters (St. Joseph Province), 141 E. 65th St., 10021. Tel: 212-737-5757. Very Rev. Urban Voll, O.P., Pres. Legal Title: *St. Thomas Aquinas Foundation of the Dominican Fathers of the United States (STAF)*.

Shrine of St. Jude, Inc., St. Stephen of Hungary Church, 414 E. 82nd St., 10028. Revs. John M. Felice, O.F.M., Pres.; Neil J. O'Connell, O.F.M., Spiritual Dir.

Sisters of Charity Health Care System Corp. 75 Vanderbilt Ave., Staten Island, 10304. Tel: 718-390-5080.

Sisters of Charity of New York Charitable Trust. Sisters of Charity Center, 6301 Riverdale Ave., Bronx, 10471-9930; Fax: 718-884-3013. Trustees: Sr. Elizabeth A. Vermaelen; Sr. Mary Ellen Brosnan; Sr. Mary Ellen Butler; Sr. Kathleen Hanrahan; Sr. Helen Mary Marks.

Sisters of the Holy Child Jesus-African Province Office, 325 E. 33rd St., 10016-9401. Tel: 212-696-5503; Fax: 212-545-7804. Sr. Margaret Rogers, S.H.C.J., Interim Dir. Legal Title: *Sisters of the Holy Child Jesus - African Province Office for the African Apostolates*.

Society for the Renewal of Christian Art, The, 217 E. 66th St., 10021. Tel: 212-288-8186. Rt. Rev. Alban W. Boultwood, O.S.B., Chm. of the Bd.; Albert J. Bouchard, Pres. Purpose: To work for the renaissance of Christian Art in our time and to foster a Christian dimension in the New York art world.

Contemporary Christian Art, Inc., 217 E. 66th St., 10021. Tel: 212-288-8186.
(Affiliated with the Society for the Renewal of Christian Art.). Emily Bouchard, Dir. Purpose: To work with artists in designing and producing Christian Art, art used in worship, presented in a contemporary manner. To bring the creators of Christian art and their works into contact with those who seek good art.

Society of Helpers. 385 W. 263rd St., Bronx, 10471. Tel: 718-884-3100. Sr. Geraldine Finan, Supr. Sisters 8.

**The Catholic League for Religious and Civil Rights*, 1011 First Ave., 10022. Tel: 212-371-3191. Dr. William A. Donohue, Pres. Total Staff 9.

**The Elizabeth Seton Housing Development Fund Corporation*, 1991 Lexington Ave., 10035. Sr. Elizabeth Vermaelon, Pres. Total Assisted 400; Total Staff 3.

Thorpe Family Residence, Inc 2252 Crotona Ave., Bronx, 10457. Total Assisted 64; Total Staff 12.

Tri-State Coalition for Responsible Investment, 20 Washington Sq. N., 10011. Tel: 212-475-6677; Fax: 212-475-6969. Sr. Patricia Daly, O.P., Exec. Dir.

United States Catholic Historical Society, The, 1011 First Ave., 10022. Tel: 800-225-7999. Dr. Brian Butler, Pres. & Chm. of the Bd.; Mr. Charles J. James, Exec. Dir.

Vatican Museums, Information Office of the, 143 E. 43rd St., 10017. Tel: 212-661-3290; Fax: 212-370-5791. Rev. Msgr. Eugene V. Clark, Dir.

Xavier Society for the Blind, 154 E. 23rd St., 10010. Tel: 212-473-7800; Fax: 212-473-7801. Revs. Alfred E. Caruana, S.J., Exec. Dir.; James Jurich, S.J.

BARRYVILLE. *New Hope Manor*, 35 Hillside Rd., 12719. Tel: 914-557-8353. Nicholas A. Roes, Exec. Dir.; Barbara Skidmore, Program Dir.; Sr. Maureen Conway, Dir. Education; Rev. Aquinas Thomas, S.A., Dir. Inservice Training. Members of the Board: Revs. Daniel Egan, S.A.; Arte Johnson, S.A.; Sr. Cecelia LaPietra, O.P.; Sr. Rita Shea, O.P. Sparkill Dominican Sisters. A live-in therapeutic community for the substance abuse rehabilitation of women 13-40 years old.

BRONX. *Abraham House, Inc.*, 342 Willis Ave., 10452. Rev. Msgr. Howard Calkins, Pres. Total Assisted 10,000; Total Staff 4.

Foundation of Christ the Redeemer & Institute Id, Misioneros y Misioneras Identes, 2352 St. Raymond Ave., 10462.

St. Joseph's Center, 275 W. 230th St., 10463. Rev. Francis E. Peluso, O.A.R., Contact Person. For the development of Lay Leaders, Cursillo Center, Marriage Encounter. (Spanish). Total in Residence 1; Total Staff 4; Capacity 45.

St. Joseph's School for the Deaf Development, Inc., 1000 Hutchinson River Pkwy., 10465. St. Joseph's School for the Deaf assists the students and faculty in their study, work, living, and extracurricular activities.

Saint Jutta Foundation, Inc., c/o Rev. John Adam, S.J., Fordham University, Loyola Hall, 10458. Rev. John Adam, S.J., Contact Person.

**The Resource Center for Community Development, Inc.*, 1900 Crotona Pkwy., 10460. Tel: 718-893-0778. Most Rev. Francisco Garmedia, Pres. Total Assisted 5,000; Total Staff 35.

**Tolentine-Zeiser Community Life Center, Inc.*, 2345 University Ave., 10468; Fax: 718-733-1653. Total Assisted 172; Total Staff 19.

Ursuline Social Outreach, Inc., 323 E. 198th St., 10458. Sr. Eileen Fane, O.S.U., Pres.

CHELSEA. *The Fellowship of the Beloved Disciple*, Mailing Address: Box 38, 12512. Tel: 914-831-7791. The Word of the Cross Community. Co-Directors: Rev. Owen Lally, C.P.; Yvonne Zeller.

ESOPUS. *Holy Shroud Guild*. Mailing Address: P.O. Box 993, Canandaigua, 14424. Tel: 716-394-2606. Material Distribution Center, 294 E. 150th St., Bronx, 10451. Tel: 212-585-3678. Executive Council: Rev. Adam J. Otterbein, C.SS.R., Pres.; Very Rev. Frederick C. Brinkmann, Pres., Protem.; Revs. John V. McGuire, C.SS.R., Sec.-Treas.; Hilary Conti, O.S.B.; John Kennington, C.Ss.R.; Frederick Brinkmann, C.SS.R.

GARRISON. *House of Nazareth Life Institute Ltd. (Nazareth Life Center)*, Philipse Brook Rd., Box 242, 10524. Tel: 914-424-3116. Sr. Marita Paul, F.S.P., Dir. Total in Residence 8; Total Staff 2.

HARTSDALE. *Contemplative Outreach, Ltd.*, 200 N. Central Ave., Ste. 100, 10530; Fax: 201-492-5795. Rt. Rev. Thomas Keating, O.C.S.O., Pres.; Gail Fitzpatrick-Hopler, Exec. Dir. Total Staff 5.

HIGHLAND FALLS. *Ladycliff College Alumnae Association, Inc.*, P.O. Box 104, 10928. Tel: 914-446-2973.

HIGHLAND MILLS. *Thevenet Montessori School*, Country Road 105, 10930. Religious of Jesus and Mary. PreK-1 Enrollment 124.

LIVINGSTON MANOR. *The Monastic Family of Bethlehem*, Grooville Rd., 12758.

MARYKNOLL. *Friends of St. Maria Goretti, U.S.A., Inc.*, P.O. Box 0043, 10545-0043. Tel: 914-941-6372; Fax: 914-945-0715. Bro. Goretti Zilli, Pres.; Rev. William T. Madden, M.M., Treas.; Mrs. Marie Finn, Sec.

Maryknoll Mission Association of the Faithful, P.O. Box 307, 10545-0307. Tel: 914-762-6364; Fax: 914-762-7031.
E-mail: bethany@igc.apc.org. Center Coordinating Team: Sheila Matthews; Thomas J. Rowan; Victoria Armour-Hileman. Leadership Team: Revs. Charles Dittmeier; William Vos; Barbara Fraser; Mary Mallahan Hicken; Sheila Matthews; Kathryn Vargas. Sponsored by the Maryknoll Society and the Maryknoll Congregation. Purpose: promoting and further developing a Catholic global mission effort which is open to Catholic lay, clerical, and religious mission vocations. The Association recruits and trains Catholic lay women, lay men, Priests, Brothers, and Sisters to conduct mission work. The Association sponsors Catholic lay men, lay women, Priests, Brothers, and Sisters in the performance of mission work and provides them with financial and other necessary support in the performance of mission work and provides them with financial and other necessary support in the performance of such work. Active in Bolivia, Brazil, Cambodia, Chile, China, El Salvador, Hong Kong, Japan, Kenya, Mexico, Peru, Sudan, Tanzania, Thailand, United States, Venezuela, and Vietnam.

Maryknoll Mission Association of the Faithful, Inc., Philadelphia, PA.

Maryknoll Mission Association of the Faithful, Inc., Takoma Park, MD.

Maryknoll Mission Association of the Faithful, Inc., El Paso, TX.

Maryknoll Mission Association of the Faithful, Inc., Castro Valley, CA.

MOUNT VERNON. *Franciscan Mission Associates*, 274-280 W. Lincoln Ave., P.O. Box 598, 10550. Tel: 914-664-5604; Fax: 914-664-3017. Province of the Immaculate Conception. Very Rev. Robert Campagna, O.F.M., Prov.; Madeline Bonnici, Exec. Dir.

St. Dymphna Devotion, 274-280 W. Lincoln Ave., P.O. Box 598, 10550. Tel: 914-664-5604; Fax: 914-664-3017. Province of the Immaculate Conception. Very Rev. Robert Campagna, O.F.M., Prov.; Madeline Bonnici, Exec. Dir.

NEW ROCHELLE. *Songcatchers, Inc.*, 4 Hemlock Pl., 10805. Tel: 914-576-6774. Sr. Beth Dowd, O.S.U., Dir.

Ursuline Companions in Mission, Inc., College of New Rochelle, College Center - Room 155, 10805. Tel: 914-654-5270; Fax: 914-654-5554.

NEWBURGH.

**Newburgh Ministry*, 9 Johnston St., 12550. Tel: 914-561-0070. Sr. Jean McCormack, L.S.A., Chairperson, Bd. of Dir.

Our Lady of Comfort Women's Center, 91 Ann St., 12550. Tel: 914-561-6267; Fax: 914-565-0572. Nina Faulkner, Treas. Shelter for Women & Children.

Providence House, 135-137 Washington St., 12550. Tel: 914-561-6306; 561-6267; Fax: 914-565-0572. Men's shelter.

Province House for Homeless Men, 135-37 Washington St., 12550; Fax: 914-565-0572.

NORTH TARRYTOWN. *RSHM Life Center, Inc.*, 32-34 Beekman Ave., N., 10591. Sacred Heart of Mary. Total Assisted 165; Adults 150; Children 115; Total Staff 143.

OSSINING. *Dominican Sisters of Hope Ministry Trust*, 299 N. Highland Ave., 10562.

PEEKSKILL. *My Father's House, Inc.*, 143 Lafayette Pl., 10566. Rev. Ronald J. Lemmert, Pres.

PELHAM. *Passionist Communications, Inc.*, Mailing Address: P.O. Box 440, 10803-0440.
E-mail: sundaymass@aol.com
Rev. Leo J. Gorman, C.P., Exec. Producer. Assoc. Producers: Revs. Paschal Smith, C.P.; Stephen Haslach, C.P.

Passionist Communications Center, 19 Second Ave., 10803. Tel: 914-738-3344; Fax: 914-738-7652.

RIVERDALE. *Holy Innocents Foundation*, 5272 Post Rd., 10471. Kevin T. O'Reilly, Pres.

RYE. *Alpha Omega Family Center, Inc.*, 815 Boston Post Rd., 10580. Total Assisted (annually) 1,500; Total Staff 3.

Center for Spiritual Development, 96 Milton Rd., 10580. Tel: 914-967-7328; Fax: 914-967-7387. Ann Marie Wallace, Ph.D., Dir.; Sr. Mary Frances Mills, O.S.F., Assoc. Dir.

Legion of Christ, Incorporated, 815 Boston Post Rd., 10580. Bro. Juan Sabadell, L.C., Contact Person.

SCARSDALE. *Catholic Charismatic Renewal Office*, 194 Gaylor Rd., 10583. Tel: 914-725-1773; Fax: 914-725-5227. Co-Liaisons: Sr. Pauline Cinquini, S.C.; Rev. William B. Cosgrove, Tel: 914-227-8382; Fax: 914-227-3951.

The United States Catholic Widows and Widowers Association, Inc., c/o William B. Oakes, Jr., P.O. Box 40 H, 10583. Tel: 914-769-4386. Total Staff 1.

SPARKILL. *Hallel Institute*, 175 Rte. 340, 10976-1047. Tel: 914-365-2277. Rev. George J. Torok, Pres. Total in Residence 37; Total Staff 9.

SUFFERN. *Covenant Corporation of Suffern, NY*, c/o Good Samaritan Hospital, Rte. 59, 10901. Sr. Barbara Conroy, Pres.

Good Samaritan Foundation for Better Health, Inc., 255 Lafayette Ave., 10901-4869. Sr. M. Angelica Doris, Pres.; Michael A. Divers, Exec. Dir. Fundraising arm of Good Samaritan Hospital, Suffern, NY.

TARRYTOWN. *Ladycliff College Alumnae Association*, 88 Wilson Park Dr.

Religious of the Sacred Heart of Mary Charitable Trust, 50 Wilson Park Dr., 10591. Tel: 914-631-2979. Sr. Bernadette Kenny, Contact Person.

THORNWOOD. *Montessori Community, Inc.*, 118 Whittier Dr., 10594. Mary McElroy, Vice. Pres.

WHITE PLAINS. *Company of St. Paul*, 52 Davis Ave., 10605. Rev. Stuart Sandberg, Pres.

Religious of Divine Compassion Charitable Trust, 52 N. Broadway, 10603.

YONKERS. *Leviticus 25:23 Alternative Fund, Inc.*, 928 McLean Ave., 10704-4103. Tel: 914-237-3306; Fax: 914-237-3916. Bro. George C. Schmitz, C.S.C., Exec. Dir.; Sr. Agnes O'Grady, Loan Servicing Officer; Sr. Patricia Walsh, S.C., Admin. Asst.

[EE] PERSONAL PRELATURES

NEW ROCHELLE. *Opus Dei (Prelature of the Holy Cross and Opus Dei)*, 99 Overlook Cir., 10804. Tel: 914-235-0198. Rev. Msgr. James A. Kelly, Ph.D., Reg. Vicar; Revs. Robert A. Brisson; Edward Maristany. Other priests residing in New York: Revs. Bradley K. Arturi, J.C.D.; Orestes Gonzales, 117 Overlook Cir., 10804. Tel: 914-235-6128. Revs. Martin J. Miller; Robert A. Connor, 330 Riverside Dr., New York, 10025. Tel: 212-222-3285.

RELIGIOUS INSTITUTES OF MEN REPRESENTED IN THE ARCHDIOCESE

For further details refer to the corresponding bracketed number in the Religious Institutes of Men or Women section.

[0130]—*Assumptionists.*—A.A.
[0140]—*The Augustinians.* (Prov. of St. Joseph).—O.S.A.
[0330]—*Brothers of the Christian Schools.* (New York Prov.).—F.S.C.
[0600]—*Brothers of the Congregation of Holy Cross.*—C.S.C.
[0400]—*Canons Regular of the Order of the Holy Cross.* (Prov. of St. Odilia, Minneapolis, MN).—O.S.C.
[0470]—*The Capuchin Friars.* (St. Mary Prov.).—O.F.M.Cap.
[0270]—*Carmelite Fathers & Brothers.* (St. Elias Prov.).—O.Carm.
[0310]—*Congregation of Christian Brothers.* (Eastern U.S.).—C.F.C.
[0220]—*Congregation of the Blessed Sacrament.*—S.S.S.
[1330]—*Congregation of the Mission.*—C.M.
[1210]—*Congregation of the Missionaries of St. Charles.*—C.S.
[1000]—*Congregation of the Passion.* (St. Paul,Prov.).—C.P.
[0480]—*Conventual Franciscans.* (Immaculate Conception Prov.).—O.F.M.Conv.
[0520]—*Franciscan Friars.* (Provs. of Most Holy Name of Jesus, Immaculate Conception; Commissariats of Holy Cross, Holy Family).—O.F.M.
[0530]—*Franciscan Friars of the Atonement.*—S.A.
[0650]—*Holy Ghost Fathers.* (Eastern Prov.).—C.S.Sp.
[0690]—*Jesuit Fathers and Brothers.* (New York Prov.).—S.J.
[0730]—*Legionaries of Christ.*—L.C.
[]—*Little Brothers of the Gospel.*
[0770]—*The Marist Brothers.*—F.M.S.
[0780]—*Marist Fathers.* (Northeastern Prov.).—S.M.
[0800]—*Maryknoll.*—M.M.
[0830]—*Mill Hill Missionaries.*—M.H.M.
[0720]—*The Missionaries of Our Lady of La Salette.*—M.S.
[0910]—*Oblates of Mary Immaculate.* (Eastern Prov.).—O.M.I.
[0430]—*Order of Preachers-Dominicans.* (St. Joseph Prov.).—O.P.
[0150]—*Order of the Augustinian Recollects.*—O.A.R.
[1020]—*Pauline Fathers and Brother.*—S.S.P.
[1030]—*Paulist Fathers.*—C.S.P.
[1040]—*Piarist Fathers.*—Sch.P.
[1070]—*Redemptorist Fathers.* (Baltimore Prov.).—C.SS.R.
[1190]—*Salesians of Don Bosco.* (St. Philip Prov.).—S.D.B.
[0990]—*Society of the Catholic Apostolate.*—S.A.C.
[1280]—*Stigmatine Fathers and Brothers.*—C.S.S.
[1300]—*Theatine Fathers.*—C.R.
[0560]—*Third Order Regular of Saint Francis.*—T.O.R.

RELIGIOUS INSTITUTES OF WOMEN REPRESENTED IN THE ARCHDIOCESE

[0130]—*Apostles of the Sacred Heart of Jesus.*—A.S.C.J.
[0230]—*Benedictine Sisters of Pontifical Jurisdiction.*—O.S.B.
[0330]—*Carmelite Sisters for the Aged and Infirm.*—O.Carm.
[3110]—*Congregation of Our Lady of the Retreat in the Cenacle.*—R.C.
[2410]—*Congregation of the Marianites of Holy Cross.*—M.S.C.
[3710]—*Congregation of the Sisters of Saint Agnes.*—C.S.A.
[1920]—*Congregation of the Sisters of the Holy Cross.*—C.S.C.
[1710]—*Congregation of the Third Order of St. Francis of Mary Immaculate.*—O.S.F.
[0760]—*Daughters of Charity of St. Vincent de Paul.*—D.C.
[0790]—*Daughters of Divine Charity.* (St. Joseph Prov.).—F.D.C.
[0850]—*Daughters of Mary Help of Christians.*—F.M.A.
[0860]—*Daughters of Mary of the Immaculate Conception.*—D.M.
[0950]—*Daughters of St. Paul.*—F.S.P.
[0810]—*Daughters of the Heart of Mary.*—D.H.M.
[0420]—*Discalced Carmelite Nuns.*—O.C.D.
[1050]—*Dominican Contemplative Nuns.*—O.P.
[1070-02]—*Dominican Sisters.*—O.P.
[1070-03]—*Dominican Sisters.*—O.P.
[1070-05]—*Dominican Sisters.*—O.P.
[1070-06]—*Dominican Sisters.*—O.P.
[1070-11]—*Dominican Sisters.*—O.P.
[1070-13]—*Dominican Sisters.*—O.P.
[1070-15]—*Dominican Sisters.*—O.P.
[1070-16]—*Dominican Sisters.*—O.P.
[1070-23]—*Dominican Sisters.*—O.P.
[1120]—*Dominican Sisters of the Roman Congregation.*—O.P.
[1170]—*Felician Sisters.*—C.S.S.F.
[1260]—*Franciscan Handmaids of the Most Pure Heart of Mary.*—F.H.M.
[1370]—*Franciscan Missionaries of Mary.*—F.M.M.
[1400]—*Franciscan Missionary Sisters of the Sacred Heart.* (Peekskill, NY).—F.M.S.C.
[1180]—*Franciscan Sisters of Allegany, New York.*—O.S.F.
[1310]—*Franciscan Sisters of Little Falls, Minnesota.*—O.S.F.
[1425]—*Franciscan Sisters of Peace.*—F.S.P.
[1190]—*Franciscan Sisters of the Atonement.*—S.A.
[1440]—*Franciscan Sisters of the Poor.*—S.F.P.
[3790]—*Institute of the Sisters of St. Dorothy.*—S.S.D.
[2310]—*Little Sisters of the Assumption.*—L.S.A.
[2340]—*Little Sisters of the Poor.*—L.S.P.
[2470]—*Maryknoll Sisters of St. Dominic.*—M.M.
[2480]—*Medical Missionaries of Mary.*—M.M.M.
[2680]—*Misericordia Sisters.*—S.M.
[2720]—*Mission Helpers of the Sacred Heart.*—M.H.S.H.
[2710]—*Missionaries of Charity.*—M.C.
[1360]—*Missionary Franciscan Sisters of the Immaculate Conception.*—O.S.F.
[2790]—*Missionary Servants of the Most Blessed Trinity.*—M.S.B.T.
[2900]—*Missionary Sisters of St. Charles Borromeo.*—M.S.S.C.B.
[2750]—*Missionary Sisters of the Immaculate Heart of Mary.*—I.C.M.
[2860]—*Missionary Sisters of the Sacred Heart.*—M.S.C.
[2920]—*Mothers of the Helpless.*—M.D.
[3030]—*Oblates of the Most Holy Redeemer.*—O.SS.R.
[3035]—*Oblates of the Mother of Orphans.*—O.M.O.
[3760]—*Order of St. Clare.*—O.S.C.
[2010]—*Order of the Most Holy Redeemer.*—O.SS.R.
[3160]—*Parish Visitors of Mary Immaculate.*—P.V.M.I.
[3450]—*Religious of Jesus-Mary.*—R.J.M.
[3460]—*Religious of Mary Immaculate.*—R.M.I.
[2070]—*Religious of the Holy Union of the Sacred Hearts.*—S.U.S.C.
[3465]—*Religious of the Sacred Heart of Mary.* (Eastern North American Prov.).—R.S.H.M.
[2519]—*Religious Sisters of Mercy, Alma MI.*—R.S.M.
[3490]—*Sacramentine Nuns.*—O.S.S.
[2970]—*School Sisters of Notre Dame.*—S.S.N.D.
[1680]—*School Sisters of St. Francis.*—O.S.F.
[0980]—*Sister Disciples of the Divine Master.*—P.D.D.M.
[1830]—*Sister of the Good Shepherd.*—R.G.S.
[3020]—*Sisters Oblates of the Blessed Trinity.*—O.B.T.
[0590]—*Sisters of Charity of Saint Elizabeth, Convent Station.*—S.C.
[0650]—*Sisters of Charity of St. Vincent de Paul, New York.*—S.C.
[0660]—*Sisters of Christian Charity.*—S.C.C.
[2360]—*Sisters of Loretto.*—S.L.
[2575]—*Sisters of Mercy of the Americas.*—R.S.M.
[3000]—*Sisters of Notre Dame de Namur.*—S.N.D.deN.
[3080]—*Sisters of Our Lady of Christian Doctrine.*—R.C.D.
[3740]—*Sisters of St. Casimir.*—S.S.C.
[1510]—*Sisters of St. Francis of the Mission of the Immaculate Virgin.*—O.S.F.
[3820]—*Sisters of St. John the Baptist.*—C.S.J.B.
[3830-05]—*Sisters of St. Joseph.*—C.S.J.
[3890]—*Sisters of St. Joseph of Peace.*—C.S.J.P.
[0260]—*Sisters of the Blessed Sacrament for Indians and Colored People.*—S.B.S.
[3140]—*Sisters of the Catholic Apostolate (Pallottine).*—C.S.A.C.
[2980]—*Sisters of the Congregation de Notre Dame.*—C.N.D.
[0970]—*Sisters of the Divine Compassion.*—R.D.C.
[1000]—*Sisters of the Divine Providence of Kentucky.*—C.D.P.
[1990]—*Sisters of the Holy Names of Jesus & Mary.*—S.N.J.M.
[3320]—*Sisters of the Presentation of the B.V.M.* (Newburgh; Staten Island).—P.B.V.M.
[3320]—*Sisters of the Presentation of the B.V.M.* (Aberdeen, SD).—P.B.V.M.
[3470]—*Sisters of the Reparation of the Congregation of Mary.*—S.R.C.M.
[3480]—*Sisters of the Resurrection.*—C.R.
[1490]—*Sisters of the Third Franciscan Order (Syracuse).*
[3600]—*Sisters, Servants of Mary.*—S.M.
[2160]—*Sisters, Servants of the Immaculate Heart Of Mary.*—I.H.M.
[1890]—*Society of Helpers.*—H.H.S.
[2460]—*Society of Mary Repartrix.*—S.M.R.
[4040]—*Society of St. Ursula.*—S.U.
[4060]—*Society of the Holy Child Jesus.*—S.H.C.J.
[4070]—*Society of the Sacred Heart.*—R.S.C.J.
[4110]—*Ursuline Nuns.*—O.S.U.
[4130]—*Ursuline Sisters (Tildonk).*—O.S.U.
[4230]—*Xaverian Missionary Sisters.*—X.M.M.

ARCHDIOCESAN CEMETERIES

HAWTHORNE. *Cemetery of the Gate of Heaven.*
LONG ISLAND CITY. *Calvary.*
MONSEY. *Cemetery of the Ascension.*
STATEN ISLAND. *Cemetery of the Resurrection.*

NECROLOGY

† Aumann, Peter A., New Rochelle, NY, Blessed Sacrament. —Died Jan. 12, 1996.
† Barrett, Brian P., Yonkers, NY, St. Joseph's Seminary. —Died July 13, 1996.
† Caldarola, Rev. Msgr. John B., (Retired). —Died Aug. 26, 1996.
† Campbell, Rev. Msgr. Arthur A., Nyack, NY, St. Ann. —Died Sept. 10, 1996.
† Cockerill, Rev. Msgr. James, Manchester, NY, St. Veronica. —Died Oct. 18, 1996.
† Cusack, Joseph P., (Retired). —Died Sept. 11, 1996.
† D'Argenio, Herbert F., Bronx, NY, St. Lucy. —Died March 9, 1996.
† Donachie, Joseph, Bronx, NY, St. Vincent de Paul Residence. —Died May 6, 1996.
† Dunn, Robert T., (Retired). —Died March 31, 1996.
† Fabisinski, Rev. Msgr. Edmund J., Hastings-on-Hudson, NY, St. Stanislaus. —Died July 19, 1996.
† Fleming, Rev. Msgr. John M., (Retired). —Died Oct. 17, 1996.
† Fogarty, Rev. Msgr. Edmund F., Shrub Oak, NY, St. Elizabeth Ann Seton. —Died Aug. 2, 1996.
† Grace, John A., (Retired). —Died Dec. 3, 1996.
† Guido, Rev. Msgr. John L., New York, NY, Our Lady of Consolation Residence. —Died May 22, 1996.

† Hearn, Robert J., (Retired). —Died May 16, 1996.

† Hicks, Rev. Msgr. Harold E., Hyde Park, NY, Regina Coeli. —Died April 9, 1996.

† Marinak, Rev. Msgr. Thomas A., Staten Island, NY, Holy Family. —Died Aug. 14, 1996.

† Markowski, Rev. Msgr. Alexander F., Newburgh, NY, St. Francis of Assisi. —Died March 16, 1996.

† McCool, Francis, New York, NY, Murray-Weigal Hall. —Died April 20, 1996.

† Melican, Thomas J., Sloatsburg, NY, St. Joseph's Home. —Died Feb. 14, 1996.

† Mulcahy, Rev. Msgr. Philip M., Bronx, NY, St. Helena. —Died April 3, 1996.

† Murphy, James D., Staten Island, NY, St. Joseph-St. Thomas. —Died July 17, 1996.

† O'Brien, Michael J., Mamaroneck, NY, Holy Trinity. —Died Dec. 3, 1996.

† O'Donnell, Rev. Msgr. Michael F., Bronx, NY, Our Lady of Assumption. —Died Sept. 26, 1996.

† Pietrzyk, Rev. Msgr. Stanley, (Retired), Poughkeepie, NY, St. Joseph's. —Died Oct. 31, 1996.

† Poulin, Donald J., Beacon, NY, St. Joachim. —Died Sept. 27, 1996.

† Rooney, John E., Port Jervis, NY, Immaculate Conception. —Died June 23,1996.

Diocese of Norwich

(Dioecesis Norvicensis)

Most Reverend

DANIEL A. HART, D.D.

Bishop of Norwich; ordained February 2, 1953; consecrated Auxiliary Bishop of Boston October 18, 1976; appointed September 12, 1995; installed as Bishop of Norwich November 1, 1995. *Res., 274 Broadway, Norwich, CT, 06360.*

ESTABLISHED AUGUST 6, 1953.

Square Miles 1,978.

CORPORATE TITLE: *The Norwich Roman Catholic Diocesan Corporation.*

Comprises the Counties of Middlesex, New London, Tolland and Windham in the State of Connecticut and Fishers Island, a portion of Suffolk County in the State of New York.

For legal titles of parishes and diocesan institutions, consult the Chancery Office.

Chancery: 201 Broadway, P.O. Box 587, Norwich, CT, 06360. Tel.: 860-887-9294; Fax: 860-886-1670.

STATISTICAL OVERVIEW

Personnel	
Bishop	1
Priests: Diocesan Active in Diocese	101
Priests: Active Outside Diocese	3
Priests: Retired, Sick or Absent	38
Number of Diocesan Priests	142
Religious Priests in Diocese	83
Extern Priests in Diocese	7
Ordinations:	
Diocesan Priests	1
Transitional Deacons	2
Permanent Deacons in Diocese	50
Total Brothers	33
Total Sisters	326
Parishes	
Parishes	78
With Resident Pastor:	
Resident Diocesan Priests	66
Resident Religious Priests	11
Without Resident Pastor:	
Administered by Priests	1
Missions	10
Pastoral Centers	23
Professional Ministry Personnel:	
Brothers	1
Sisters	35
Lay Ministers	14
Welfare	
Homes for the Aged	3
Total Assisted	249
Special Centers for Social Services	1
Total Assisted	130
Educational	
Diocesan Students in Other Seminaries	9
Seminaries, Religious	1
Students Religious	5
Total Seminarians	14
High Schools, Diocesan and Parish	3
Total Students	1,713
High Schools, Private	2
Total Students	307
Elementary Schools, Diocesan and Parish	22
Total Students	4,646
Catechesis/Religious Education:	
High School Students	4,204
Elementary Students	15,559
Total Students Under Catholic Instruction	26,443
Teachers in the Diocese:	
Priests	1
Brothers	1
Sisters	15
Lay Teachers	23
Vital Statistics	
Receptions into the Church:	
Infant Baptism Totals	3,391
Adult Baptism Totals	144
Received into Full Communion	336
First Communions	2,932
Confirmations	2,065
Marriages:	
Catholic	736
Interfaith	258
Total Marriages	994
Deaths	2,009
Total Catholic Population	221,599
Total Population	625,450

Former Bishops—Most Rev. BERNARD J. FLANAGAN, D.D., J.C.D., cons. Nov. 30, 1953; installed Dec. 9, 1953; transferred to See of Worcester, Aug. 12, 1959.—Most Rev. VINCENT J. HINES, D.D., J.C.D., cons. March 17, 1960; retired June 17, 1975; died April 23, 1990.—Most Rev. DANIEL P. REILLY, D.D., cons. Aug. 6, 1975; transferred to See of Worcester, Dec. 8, 1994.

The Chancery

Chancery—201 Broadway, P.O. Box 587, Norwich, 06360. Tel: 860-887-9294; Fax: 860-886-1670.

Vicar General—Rev. Msgr. THOMAS R. BRIDE, P.A., V.G.

Chancellor—Rev. Msgr. ROBERT L. BROWN.

Asst. Chancellor—SALVATORE A. MAZZOTTA, ESQ., K.S.G.

Diocesan Advisor on Canonical Matters—Rev. Msgr. HENRY J. DZIADOSZ, J.C.D.

Diocesan Archivist Consultant and Historian—Rev. J. RALPH KELLEY, (Retired).

Diocesan Attorney—MICHAEL E. DRISCOLL, Esq., *22 Courthouse Sq., Norwich, 06360.* Tel: 860-889-3321.

Diocesan Attorney Emeritus—JAMES J. DUTTON, JR., Esq., K.S.G., *22 Courthouse Sq., Norwich, 06360.* Tel: 860-889-3321.

Diocesan Computer Center—Rev. ANTHONY P. GRUBER, Computer Consultant & System Admin.

Diocesan Finance Office—Mr. WILLIAM J. CONNELL, Chief Financial Officer; Mr. KEVIN KEEGAN, Asst. Controller; Mr. VICTOR WELTIG, Internal Auditor; MARY ANN JACOBS, Bookkeeper, Lay Pension; Ms. ROBIN HOLTSCLAW, Risk Mgr. (CMRS); Miss JANET WEST, Accounts Receivable.

College of Consultors—Rev. Msgr. THOMAS R. BRIDE, P.A., V.G.; Rev. Msgr. HENRY N. ARCHAMBAULT, P.A.; Rev. Msgr. ROBERT L. BROWN; Rev. Msgr. ANTHONY ROSAFORTE; Revs. RUSSELL BOISVERT; LAURENCE LAPOINTE; MARK O'DONNELL; MICHAEL O'HARA; JOHN W. MCWEENEY, M.S.

Presbyteral Council—Most Rev. DANIEL A. HART, D.D., Pres.; Revs. ROBERT CRONIN, Chm.; RUSSELL BOISVERT, Vice Chm.; LAURENCE LAPOINTE, Sec. Members: Rev. Msgr. THOMAS R. BRIDE, P.A., V.G.; Rev. Msgr. HENRY ARCHAMBAULT; Rev. Msgr. ROBERT L. BROWN; Rev. Msgr. HENRY DZIADOSZ; Rev. Msgr. RICHARD P. LAROCQUE; Rev. Msgr. ANTHONY S. ROSAFORTE; Revs. ROBERT BARNES; ANTHONY GRUBER; CHARLES MCGRAIL; JOHN MCWEENEY, M.S.; MARK O'DONNELL; MICHAEL O'HARA; MICHAEL SMITH; JOHN WHITE.

Conciliation and Arbitration, Boards of—These due process boards each consist of five individuals. The Bishop of Norwich appoints the Executive Coordinator to process any grievance, submitted in writing, in accord with procedures available from the Executive Director: Rev. Msgr. RICHARD P. LAROCQUE, *The Chancery, 201 Broadway, Norwich, 06360.* Tel: 860-887-9294.

Deans—Rev. FRANCIS J. O'KEEFE, Putnam; Rev. Msgr. M. DAVITT FOX, Middletown; Revs. LAURENCE LAPOINTE, Willimantic; JOHN J. WHITE, Vernon; Rev. Msgr. HENRY N. ARCHAMBAULT, P.A., Norwich; Revs. WILLIAM SCHNEIDER, New London; THOMAS W. AHERN, Old Saybrook.

Secretary to the Bishop—Rev. MICHAEL L. PHILLIPPINO.

Diocesan Pastoral Council—Rev. Msgr. HENRY ARCHAMBAULT, P.A.; Ms. DIANE BAKER; Rev. ROBERT BARNES; Ms. SARAH BECKER; Rev. Msgr. THOMAS BRIDE, P.A., V.G.; Rev. Msgr. ROBERT BROWN; Mrs. CAROL CONKLIN; Sr. PATRICIA COOK, R.S.M.; Mr. AL FECTEAU; Rev. Msgr. M. DAVITT FOX; Mrs. NOREEN GRAVEL, R.N.; Bro. J. ROBERT HOULIHAN, C.F.X.; Mrs. AGNES KELLY; Dr. ROBERT MILLER; Dr. PETER MOORE, Ph.D.; Mrs. JUDITH PAPPAGALLO; Mrs. SUSAN ROURKE; Mrs. NANCY RUDEK; Mr. ALEXANDER SAUNDERS; Mrs. FRANCES SCHOEN; Mr. JAMES SMART; Rev. Msgr. WILLIS WEST.

The Tribunal

Diocesan Tribunal—17 Otis St., P.O. Box 587, Norwich, 06360. Tel: 860-887-9294.

Judicial Vicar—Rev. Msgr. HENRY N. ARCHAMBAULT, P.A., J.C.D.

Associate Judicial Vicar—Rev. JOHN W. MCWEENEY, M.S.

Judges—Revs. THOMAS W. AHERN; J. CLIFFORD CURTIN; JOHN J. WHITE; FRANCIS J. O'KEEFE; JOSEPH CASTALDI, J.C.L.; WILLIAM FLYNN; LESZEK JANIK, J.C.L.; JOSEPH MORRISSETTE; J. LAWRENCE OUIMET; MICHAEL O'HARA; Sr. SALLY TOLLES, D.H.S., J.D., J.C.L.

Defender of the Bond—Rev. ROGER J. LAMOUREUX, O.M.I.

Advocates—Revs. RUSSELL L. BOISVERT; MICHAEL T. DONOHUE; WILLIAM T. FLYNN; PAUL J. GAUMOND; PAUL L. HEBERT; RUSSELL F. KENNEDY; FRANCIS A. LISZEWSKI; LEO S. SUTULA; STANLEY J. SZCZAPA; ROBERT WASHABAUGH; Sr. BEATRICE THEROUX, D.H.S.

Secretary of the Tribunal—Mrs. MARY J. SHEA.

Notaries—Rev. Msgr. THOMAS R. BRIDE, P.A., V.G.; Rev. Msgr. ROBERT L. BROWN; Mrs. MARY J. SHEA.

Vicar for Clergy—Rev. Msgr. RICHARD P. LAROCQUE, Sec.; Mrs. SUSAN GARDINER.

Diocesan Offices, Ministries, Societies

Annual Bishop's Appeal (ABA)—See Development, Diocesan Office.

Bishop's Delegate to Hispanic Permanent Deacons—Mr. JESUS A.DIEZ CANSECO, *110 Pruett Pl., Oakdale, 06370.*

Diocesan Finance Council—Most Rev. DANIEL A. HART,

D.D., Chm.; Rev. Msgr. THOMAS R. BRIDE, P.A., V.G.; Revs. THOMAS SMITH; KENNETH FLINT; JAMES CRONIN; FRED PERKINS, C.P.A.; PETER LAMALFA; JOYCE PAGE; BERNARD PHANEUF; WILLIAM MCGURK; DIANE KELLY; TERRENCE CAHILL; KENNETH PARZYCH; THOMAS GALLIVAN; VINCENT ROEMMELE.

Diocesan Pastoral Council—See Chancery listing.

Bishop's Liaison with the Retired Clergy—Rev. Msgr. RICHARD P. LAROCQUE, *The Chancery, 201 Broadway, Norwich, 06360.* Tel: 860-887-9294.

Board of Education—See School Office.

Building Commission—Rev. Msgr. M. DAVITT FOX, Chm.; Rev. Msgr. WILLIS W. WEST; Revs. JOHN J. WHITE; MICHAEL DONOHUE.

Campaigns—

Campaign for Human Development—Rev. MICHAEL T. DONOHUE, *St. Matthias Rectory, Boston Post Rd., P.O. Box 25, East Lyme, 06333.* Tel: 860-739-5208.

Catholic Relief Services—Rev. Msgr. ROBERT L. BROWN, Dir.; Mrs. SUE SULLIVAN; Sec., *P.O. Box 587, Norwich, 06360.* Tel: 860-887-9294.

Campus Ministry—Rev. LAURENCE A.M. LAPOINTE, Diocesan Dir., *Newman Hall, 290 Prospect St., Willimantic, 06226.* Tel: 860-423-0856. (See separate category under Institutions for details).

Catechetical Ministry, Office of Director—See Faith Formation, Office for.

Catholic Charities-Catholic Family Services—Mr. JOHN SMEY, Diocesan Dir., *11 Bath St., Norwich, 06360.* Tel: 860-889-8346; Fax: 860-889-2658. Counsellors: Sr. SUZANNE GEBRIAN, M.H.S.H.; Mr. MICHAEL PETRIDES; Ms. SANDRA COULLARD, M.S.W.

District Offices—New London: *10 Pearl St., New London, 06320.* Tel: 860-443-5328. Mrs. KATHLEEN W. MCGUIRE, District Sec.; Windham: *61 Club Rd., Windham, 06280.* Tel: 860-423-7065.

Catholic Mental Health Clinic—Rev. BERTIN GLENNON, S.T., Dir., *11 Bath St., Norwich, 06360.* Tel: 860-889-8346.

Catholic Mutual Relief Society—Diocesan Insurance, Ms. ROBIN HOLTSCLAW, Risk Mgr., *467 Bloomfield Ave., Bloomfield, 06002.* Tel: 1-800-331-2561. National Office, *4223 Center St., Omaha, NE, 68105.* Tel: 1-800-228-6108.

Catholic Youth Organization (CYO)—See Faith Formation, Office for.

CCD—See Faith Formation, Office for.

Cemetery Corporation and Subsidiaries, Diocesan—Norwich Diocesan Cemetery Corp., 815 Boswell Ave., Norwich, 06360. Rev. Msgr. WILLIS W. WEST, Dir., *St. Joseph Rectory, 99 Jackson St., Willimantic, 06226.* Tel: 860-423-8439. NICHOLAS W. MIGNONE, Mgr., Office: *815 Boswell Ave., Norwich, 06360.* Tel: 860-887-1019; Fax: 860-889-4804.

Subsidiary Diocesan Cemeteries—Norwich: *St. Mary & St. Joseph Cemetery, 815 Boswell Ave., Norwich, 06360.* Tel: 860-887-1019. New London: *St. Mary Cemetery of New London, 600 Jefferson Ave., New London, 06320.* Tel: 860-443-3465. Taftville: *Harland Rd., Taftville, 06320.* Tel: 860-887-1019., *Office: 815 Boswell Ave., Taftville, 06360.* Tel: 860-887-1019. Westbrook: *Resurrection Cemetery, Rte. 145, Westbrook, 06498.* Tel: 860-339-6503.

Commission on Women—Mrs. V. JANE LEGER, Diocesan Dir., *323 Main St., Norwich, 06360.* Tel: 860-889-7374 (Office); 449-9584 (Home); Mrs. PAULINE CLOUTIER; Mrs. CAROL FREEDMAN; Mrs. JANET GRIFFIN; Ms. RUTH KULMACZ; Mrs. SUSAN WOOD; Ms. MARTHA KOWAC; Mrs. JANE LEGER; Miss JOSEPHINE RISICA; Mrs. JOHANNA REILLY; Ms. JANE ENGELKE; Ms. LINNEA LINDSTROM; Ms. BEATRICE MACKENZIE; Mrs. JUDY PAPPAGALLO; Ms. JEANNE SKIBA; Sr. ARLENE VANNIE, R.S.M.; Ms. IRENE BOULEY; Ms. CYNTHIA DELUCIA.

Communications, Office of—Miss JACQUELINE M. KELLER, Dir. LOUISE DUMAINE, Sec., *The Bishop Flanagan Ministry Center, 1595 Norwich-New London Tpke., Uncasville, 06382.* Tel: 860-848-2237.

Community Ministries—Mrs. BARBARA BELLONE, Diocesan Dir., *323 Main St., Norwich, 06360.* Tel: 860-889-7374 (Office). MARDIE FISHER, Asst. Admin., *323 Main St., Norwich, 06360.*

The Hope Shop—*327 Main St., Norwich, 06360.*

Saint Vincent de Paul Place—Norwich: *323 Main St., Norwich, 06360.* Tel: 860-889-7374. Middletown: *617 Main St., P.O. Box 398, Middletown, 06457.* Tel: 860-344-0097; Fax: 860-343-0023. Mr. PETER HARDING, Dir.; Sr. CAROL BEAUDOIN, R.S.M., Soup Kitchen Coord. Tel: 860-265-6999.

Connecticut Catholic Conference—Dr. MARIE HILLIARD, Exec. Dir., *134 Farmington Ave., Hartford, 06105.* Tel: 860-524-7882.

Continuing Education and Formation Commission—Rev. MARK O'DONNELL, Chm.

Council of Catholic Nurses—Rev. THOMAS SMITH, Diocesan Moderator, *St. Mary Rectory, 10 Huntington St., New London, 06320.* Tel: 860-437-1889.

Council of Catholic Women—Tel: 860-889-8346. Rev. EDWARD KONOPKA, Moderator, *St. Peter Rectory, 30 St. Peter Ln., P.O. Box 707, Higganum, 06441.* Tel: 860-345-8018. District Moderators: Revs. JAMES SUCHOLET, Middletown Deanery; JOSEPH F. DECOSTA, New London Deanery; EUGENE PILATOWSKI, Norwich Deanery; CHARLES LEBLANC, Putnam Deanery; Rev. Msgr. WILLIS W. WEST, Willimantic Deanery; Rev. PAUL MURDOCK, Rockville Deanery.

The Deaf, Ministry to—Sr. M. ESTHER COCKBURN, M.H.S.H., Dir., *God's Gift House, 325 Main St., P.O. Box 813, Norwich, 06360.* Tel: 860-886-1281 (Voice & TTY).

Development, Diocesan Office of (DOD)—Mr. RICHARD COSTELLO, Exec. Dir., *31 Perkins Ave., Norwich, 06360.* Tel: 860-886-1928.

Annual Bishop's Appeal—Mr. RICHARD COSTELLO, Dir., *31 Perkins Ave., Norwich, 06360.* Tel: 860-886-1928.

Planned Giving Office—Mr. RICHARD COSTELLO, Dir., *31 Perkins Ave., Norwich, 06360.* Tel: 860-886-1928.

Disabilities-People with—See His Able People, Ministry of.

Ecumenism—

Diocesan Commission for Ecumenical and Interreligious Affairs—Sr. MARYANNE GUERTIN, S.S.J., Chm.; Mrs. CAROL HANSEN; Mr. MARK KRISTOFF; Revs. MARK D. O'DONNELL; RICHARD K. GROSS, S.J.; Ms. PAULINE COTNOIR; Mrs. ANITA POWERS; Mrs. GEORGIA TRACEY; Mr. MICHAEL TURCIO; Bro. THOMAS BERUBE, S.S.E.

Ecumenical & Interreligious Affairs, Office of—Sr. MARYANNE GUERTIN, S.S.J., Dir., *Bishop Flanagan Ministry Center, 1595 Norwich-New London Tpke., Uncasville, 06382-1319.* Tel: 860-848-2237.

Evangelization & Catechumenate (RCIA), Office of—Sr. CLAIRE PELLETIER, D.H.S., Dir. SUSAN MYSHRALL, Admin. Asst. R.C.I.A. Team: ERNEST GOLNIK; Sr. KATHERINE MCKENNA, P.B.V.M.; GAYLE MADDEN; THOMAS MADDEN; MILDRED STEARNS; Rev. STANLEY J. SZCZAPA; SUSAN MYSHRALL, *The Bishop Flanagan Ministry Center, 1595 Norwich-New London Tpke., Uncasville, 06382-1319.* Tel: 860-848-2237.

Faith Formation, Office for—Bishop Flanagan Ministry Center, 1595 Norwich-New London Tpke., Uncasville, 06382-1319. Tel: 860-848-2237. Sr. ELEANOR PERFETTO, Dir.; Rev. KEVIN RANDALL, Scout Chaplain. Assoc. Dirs.: Ms. PAULINE COTNOIR; Mrs. DONNA GILLILAND; Sr. BETTY PAUL, S.P., Assoc. Dir., Diocesan Media Center; Mrs. EILEEN PASSERO.

Family Life, Office of—Rev. BERTIN GLENNON, S.T., Dir., *The Bishop Flanagan Ministry Center, 1595 Norwich-New London Tpke., Uncasville, 06382-1319.* Tel: 860-848-2237.

"Four County Catholic"—See Newspaper.

God's Gift House—See Community Ministries.

Haitian Ministries—Mr. MICHAEL BOYLE, Dir., *Bishop Flanagan Ministry Center, 1595 Norwich-New London Tpke., Uncasville, 06382-1319.* Tel: 860-848-2237. EMILY SMACK, Chm. Members: Mr. ANDREW HOFFMAN; Ms. LOUISE LABBE; Mrs. MARY WEHRLE; Sr. MARILYN CANNING, R.S.M.; Mrs. EVELYN KIRBY; Rev. PAUL BOUDREAU; Mrs. THEO HAMELL; Ms. JANET MINELLA-DIDIER; Mr. FRANCIS TRAINOR; Rev. MICHAEL SMITH; DONALD BERGIN; BERNYCE RUIZ.

His Able People, Ministry of—Deacon EDUARDO DOGUE, Dir., *P.O. Box 242, Wauregan, 06387.* Tel: 860-779-0362.

Hispanic Ministry—Sr. MARY JUDE LAZARUS, S.C.M.C., Interim Dir., *61 Club Rd., Windham, 06280.* Tel: 860-423-8617.

New London—Rev. RUSSELL KENNEDY, Priest Dir., New London Area, *St. Mary Rectory, 70 Central Ave., Norwich, 06360.* Tel: 860-887-2565. Deacon MARIANO RAMOS; Sr. IRMA GARCIA, R.O.D.A.; Sr. MARIELOS BALLESTEROS, Pastoral Assoc.

Windham—Rev. PAUL MURDOCK, Dir.; Deacon FELIPE SILVA; Sr. MARY JUDE, S.C.M.C., Pastoral Assoc., *La Iglesia del Sagrado Corazon de Jesus Office, 61 Club Rd., 06280.* Tel: 860-423-8617.

Middletown—Revs. JOSEPH ASHE, Pastor; RUSSELL KENNEDY, Priest Dir., *St. John, 19 St. John Sq., Middletown, 06457.* Tel: 860-343-0466.

Norwich—Rev. RUSSELL KENNEDY, Priest Dir.; Sr. BERTA NAJERA, R.O.D.A., Pastoral Assoc., *St. Mary Church, 70 Central Ave., Norwich, 06320.* Tel: 860-887-2565.

Rockville—Rev. PAUL MURDOCK, Priest Dir.; Deacon MICHAEL BERSTENE, *St. Bernard, 25 St. Bernard's Terr., Rockville, 06066.*

Holy Childhood—See Pontifical Association of the Holy Childhood.

Holy Name Societies—Holy Name Societies, c/o Msgr. Thomas Bride, P.A., V.G., 201 Broadway, P.O. Box 587, Norwich, 06360. Tel: 860-887-9294.

Insurance—See Catholic Mutual Relief Society (C.M.R.S.).

Justice & Peace, Office of—Mr. RAY MASTRONUNZIO, Dir., *The Bishop Flanagan Ministry Center, 1595 Norwich-New London Tpke., Uncasville, 06382.* Tel: 860-848-2237.

Lawyers, Guild of Catholic—Mailing Address: *The Chancery, 201 Broadway, Norwich, 06360.* Tel: 860-887-9294. Atty. MICHAEL E. DRISCOLL, Pres.; Atty. SALVATORE MAZZOTTA, Exec. Dir.; Rev. Msgr. HENRY ARCHAMBAULT, P.A., Chap.

Legion of Mary—Rev. ROBERT B. LYNCH, Diocesan Spiritual Dir., *St. Mary Rectory, 70 Central Ave., Norwich, 06360.* Tel: 860-887-2565.

Liturgy, Office of—Sr. PATRICIA CUSHING, C.S.J., Dir., Bishop Flanagan Ministry Center. Tel: 860-848-2237.

Marriage Encounter—The Bishop Flanagan Ministry Center, 1595 Norwich-New London Tpke., Uncasville, 06382. Tel: 860-848-2237.

Medical Ethics Committee—Most Rev. DANIEL A. HART, D.D.; MARCIA S. BELL; Rev. THEODORE KLEIN, Ph.D.; JOHN MONTALBANO; CELINE BAKKALA; Dr. JOHN CAREY, M.D.; Dr. DAVID LAULER, M.D.; FRANCIS T. LONDREGAN; SUSAN WOOD, R.N.; C. FRANCIS DRISCOLL.

Mercy Xavier Development Corporation—Mr. JAMES JOYCE, Pres., *181 Randolph Rd., Middletown, 06457.* Tel: 860-347-2343; 346-7735.

Ministry Formation and Permanent Diaconate, Office of—Sr. PATRICIA COOK, R.S.M., Dir.; Sr. ANN KANE, C.S.J., Assoc. Dir.; Deacon ROLAND J. LACASSE, Asst. Delegate, *The Bishop Flanagan Ministry Center, 1595 Norwich-New London Tpke., Uncasville, 06382.* Tel: 860-848-2237.

Newspaper—Official monthly newspaper of Diocese of Norwich-*"Four County Catholic"*; Mr. PETER L. GILL, Editor; Mr. BRUCE AVERY, Advertising Mgr., *Office of Communications, Bishop Flanagan Ministry Center, 1595 Norwich-New London Tpke., Uncasville, 06382.* Tel: 860-889-0202; Fax: 860-848-2816.

Nurses—See Council of Catholic Nurses.

Pastoral Planning, Office of—Sr. MARY ALICE KLINE, R.S.M., Coord., *Bishop Flanagan Ministry Center, 1595 Norwich-New London Tpke., Uncasville, 06382.* Tel: 860-848-2237.

People with Disability—See His Able People, Ministry of.

Permanent Deacon, Office of—Rev. Msgr. RICHARD P. LAROCQUE, Vicar for Clergy, *The Chancery, 201 Broadway, Norwich, 06360.* Tel: 860-887-9294.

Planned Giving Office—See Development, Diocesan Office of.

Pontifical Association of the Holy Childhood—Rev. Msgr. THOMAS R. BRIDE, P.A., V.G., Dir., *201 Broadway, P.O. Box 587, Norwich, 06360.* Tel: 860-887-9294.

Pontifical Society for the Propagation of the Faith—Rev. Msgr. THOMAS R. BRIDE, P.A., V.G., Dir.; Mrs. ANN DEPTA, Sec., *201 Broadway, P.O. Box 587, Norwich, 06360.* Tel: 860-887-9294.

Priests on Duty Outside Diocese—Revs. THOMAS M. ANGELO; JOHN GWUDZ; GERARD KIRBY.

Prison Ministry for Diocese of Norwich—Ms. MEG BRODHEAD, Dir.; Deacon DENNIS F. DOLAN, *Bishop Flanagan Ministry Center, 1595 Norwich-New London Tpke., Uncasville, 06382.* Tel: 860-848-2237.

Pro-Life Activities—Mr. JOSEPH P. COLLISON, Dir., *201 Broadway, P.O. Box 587, Norwich, 06360.* Tel: 860-887-9294.

Project Northeast—A program of Evangelization for the unchurched poor. Rev. RICHARD L. ARCHAMBAULT, Dir., *81 Church St., Putnam, 06260.* Tel: 860-928-4078. Sr. ELEANOR BALDONI, D.H.S., Assoc. Dir., *67 Railroad Ave., Putnam, 06260.* Tel: 860-928-5965.

RCIA—See Catechumenate, Office of.

Religious—See Vicar for Religious.

Retired Clergy—Rev. Msgr. BRONISLAW GADAROWSKI; Rev. Msgr. THADDEUS F. MALANOWSKI; Rev. Msgr. EDWARD MCKENNA; Rev. Msgr. JAMES J. O'BRIEN; Rev. Msgr. PAUL ST. ONGE; Revs. LEO ALMENDRA; HENRY BIALOWSKI; ROBERT W. CRONIN; J. CLIFFORD CURTIN; EDWARD J. DAVIS; KENNETH FLINT; ALBERT GIAQUINTO; JOSEPH HORAN; J. RALPH KELLEY; JOHN KOZON; ANTHONY P. KUZDAL; ALFRED R. LANDRY; JOHN MARCINIAK; DANIEL F. MCGRATH; ROBERT E. MCNULTY; HUGH J. MURPHY; JOSEPH E. NICHOLS; EDWARD J. POULIN; ADAM PUPSYS; PAUL F. RAMEN; JOSEPH M. RICARD; JOHN J. SULLIVAN; EDWARD J. WISNESKI; ROBERT J. WOOD.

Retirement—See Priests' Retirement Commission.

School Office, Diocesan—Dr. HOWARD BENNETT, Supt.; Mr. FRANK FARINA, Assoc. Supt.; Sr. MARIE TREANOR, S.N.D., Assoc. Supt.; Sr. RACHEL ANDERSON, C.S.C., Sec., *43 Perkins Ave., Norwich, 06360.* Tel: 860-887-4086; 887-9371.

Board of Education—Mrs. GAY MULLEN; Sr. MARIE TREANOR, S.N.D., Chm.; Mrs. ANDREA BULLARD; Mrs. MARGARET LANGER, Chm.; Dr. HOWARD BENNETT; ELMO GIANANTONI; Rev. Msgr. ANTHONY S. ROSAFORTE, Pastor with a school. Ex-Officios: Rev. Msgr. THOMAS R. BRIDE P.A., V.G.; Mrs. PATRICIA

AUSTIN; MR. FRANK FARINA; MR. JOHN CIRILLO, Vice-Chm.; Revs. ROBERT W. BARNES; WILLIAM F. O'NEIL, JR., K.S.G.

Scouting—See Faith Formation, Office for.

Sick, Ministry to the—Sr. RITA JOHNSON, S.S.N.D., Dir., *W.W. Backus Hospital, 326 Washington St., Norwich, 06360.* Tel: 860-889-8331.

Soup Kitchen—See Community Ministries, Saint Vincent de Paul Place.

Spanish Speaking Apostolate—See Hispanic Ministry.

The Spiritual Renewal Services of the Diocese of Norwich—Rev. RAYMOND D. INTROVIGNE, Diocesan Dir.; Mrs. JUDITH HUGHES, Assoc. Dir., *God's Gift House, 325 Main St., P.O. Box 6, Norwich, 06360.* Tel: 860-887-0702. Dial-A-Prayer. Tel: 860-887-7767.

Vicar for Religious—Rev. JOHN W. MCWEENEY, M.S., J.C.L.; Sr. SALLY J. TOLLES, D.H.S., J.D., J.C.L., Assoc. Vicar, *The Tribunal, Otis St., P.O. Box 587, Norwich, 06360.* Tel: 860-887-9294.

Vocation Review Committe, Diocesan—Rev. Msgr. THOMAS R. BRIDE, P.A., V.G.; Rev. Msgr. RICHARD P. LAROCQUE; Rev. Msgr. WILLIS W. WEST; Revs. R. THOMAS MCCONAGHY; MARK O'DONNELL; MICHAEL PHILLIPPINO; Bro. WILLIAM CIGANEK, C.F.X.

Vocations—Rev. Msgr. THOMAS R. BRIDE, P.A., V.G., Diocesan Dir.; Revs. MICHAEL PHILLIPPINO, Asst. Dir. Vocations; MARK O'DONNELL, Diocesan Dir. for Promotion & Devel.; Mrs. ANN DEPTA, Sec., *201 Broadway, P.O. Box 587, Norwich, 06360.* Tel: 860-887-9294.

Youth Ministry—See Faith Formation, Office of.

Youth Retreat Centers—*Alpha House East,* Griswold. *Alpha House West,* Higganum. For details, contact; Sr. BETTY PAUL, S.P., *Bishop Flanagan Ministry Center, 1595 Norwich-New London Tpke., Uncasville, 06382.* Tel: 860-848-2237.

Women, Commission on—See Commission on Women.

CLERGY, PARISHES, MISSIONS AND PAROCHIAL SCHOOLS

CITY OF NORWICH
(New London County)

1—ST. PATRICK CATHEDRAL (1879), Rev. Msgr. Anthony S. Rosaforte; Rev. George J. Richards; Deacon Al R. Fecteau.
Res., 213 Broadway, 06360. Tel: 203-889-8441.
School—211 Broadway, 06360. Tel: 860-889-4174. Sr. Mary Bernard Rivest, S.C.M.C., Prin.
Sisters of Charity of Our Lady Mother of the Church 3; Lay Teachers 7; Students 220.
Catechesis/Religious Programs—Tel: 860-886-1060.
Students 349.

2—SACRED HEART (Norwichtown) (1902), Rev. J. Lawrence Ouimet; Deacon Robert P. Hayes. In res., Rev. Michael L. Phillippino.
Res., 52 W. Town St., Norwichtown, 06360. Tel: 860-887-1030; Fax: 860-887-6550.
Catechesis/Religious Programs—Tel: 860-887-1715.
Students 129.
Mission—Fitchville, New London Co., St. John, 190 Fitchville Rd., Bozrah, 06334.

3—ST. JOSEPH, New London Co., (1904) (Polish), Rev. Eugene Pilatowski.
Res., 120 Cliff St., 06360. Tel: 860-887-1565.
Catechesis/Religious Programs—Tel: 860-887-4565.
Students 216.

4—ST. MARY (1845), Rev. Robert B. Lynch; Deacon Dennis Doyle. In res., Revs. Joseph G. Finnerty; Russell F. Kennedy.
Res., 70 Central Ave., 06360. Tel: 860-887-2565.
Catechesis/Religious Programs—Tel: 860-889-8347.
Students 75.

5—SS. PETER AND PAUL (1938), Revs. Barry C. Meehan, S.J.; Edward Howard, S.J.
Res., 181 Elizabeth St., 06360. Tel: 860-887-9857; Fax: 860-886-4728.
Catechesis/Religious Programs—Tel: 860-887-5294.
Students 149.

OUTSIDE THE CITY OF NORWICH

Ballouville, Windham Co., St. Anne (1882), Rev. Sylva P. LeCours.
Res., 06233. Tel: 860-774-6164.
Catechesis/Religious Programs—Students 93.

Baltic, New London Co., St. Mary of the Immaculate Conception (1886), Rev. Joseph Tito, Admin.
Res., 06330. Tel: 860-822-6378. [CEM]
School—St. Joseph, Tel: 860-822-6141; Fax: 860-822-6141.
Sisters of Charity of Our Lady Mother of the Church 5; Lay Teachers 6; Students 126.
Catechesis/Religious Programs—Students 160.

Bolton, Tolland Co., St. Maurice (1954), Rev. William J. Olesik.
Res., 32 Hebron Rd., 06043. Tel: 860-643-4466.
Catechesis/Religious Programs—Tel: 860-643-8374.
Students 251.

Brooklyn, Windham Co., Our Lady of La Salette (1968), Rev. Gerard J. Boulanger, M.S. In res., Rev. John W. McWeeney, M.S.
Res., 06234. Tel: 860-774-6275.
Catechesis/Religious Programs—Students 309.
Mission—Hampton, Windham Co., Our Lady of Lourdes, Brooklyn 06234.

Canterbury, Windham Co., St. Augustine (1978), Rev. Gonzalo E. Regalado; Deacon Paul R. Baillargeon.
Res., 144 Westminister Rd., 06331. Tel: 860-546-6074.

Chester, Middlesex Co., St. Joseph (1885), Rev. Thomas W. Ahern; Deacon W. Ridgely O'Sullivan.
Res., 48 Middlesex Ave., 06412. Tel: 860-526-5495. [CEM]
Catechesis/Religious Programs—Students 206.

Clinton, Middlesex Co., St. Mary of the Visitation (1934), Rev. Michael Sequeira (India); Deacon Paul Weber.
Res., 54 Grove St., 06413-1999. Tel: 860-669-8512; Fax: 860-669-9052. [CEM]
Catechesis/Religious Programs—Tel: 860-669-7375.
Students 473.

Colchester, New London Co., St. Andrew (1860), Revs. Michael C. Giannitelli, Parochial Admin.; Frank W. McKenna; Deacons Robert Barlow; Dennis Dolan.
Res., 128 Norwich Ave., P.O. Box 135, 06415. Tel: 860-537-2355; Fax: 860-537-2356. [CEM]
Catechesis/Religious Programs—Tel: 860-537-5415.
Students 643.

Columbia, Tolland Co., St. Columba (1960), Rev. Daniel C. Cronin.
Res., Rte. 66 at Rte. 87, P.O. Box 146, 06237. Tel: 203-228-3735.
Catechesis/Religious Programs—Tel: 860-228-3727.
Students 223.

Coventry, Tolland Co., St. Mary (1877), Rev. Paul Boudreau.
Res., 1600 Main St., P.O. Box 250, 06238. Tel: 860-742-0681. [CEM]
Catechesis/Religious Programs—Students 352.
Mission—Eagleville, Tolland Co., St. Joseph.

Cromwell, Middlesex Co., St. John (1882), Revs. Raymond Borkowski, O.F.M.Conv.; Hilary Brzostowski, O.F.M.Conv.; Sr. Dominic Joseph Valla, A.S.C.J., Pastoral Assoc.
Res., 5 St. John Ct., 06416. Tel: 860-635-5590; Fax: 860-635-5591.
Catechesis/Religious Programs—Tel: 860-635-5156.
Students 592.

Danielson, Windham Co., St. James (1869), Revs. John J. O'Neill, M.S.; Brian D. Schloth, M.S.; Joseph F. Whalen, M.S.
Res., 12 Franklin St., 06239. Tel: 860-774-3900; Fax: 860-774-4205. [CEM]
School—Tel: 860-774-3281; Fax: 860-779-2137. Ms. Marguerite Ovellette, Prin.
Lay Teachers 11; Students 250.
Catechesis/Religious Programs—Tel: 203-774-8459.
Students 270.
Mission—East Killingly, Windham Co., Our Lady of Peace, 06239.

Dayville, Windham Co., St. Joseph (1874), Rev. William J. McNulty.
Res., 350 Hartford Pike, Box 487, 06241. Tel: 860-774-8656. [CEM]
Catechesis/Religious Programs—Tel: 860-774-2451. D.R.E.: Alyce Chartier; Norma Pokoski.
Students 104.
Convent—21 Williamsville Rd., Box 158, Rogers, 06263. Tel: 203-774-8154. Parish House Daughters of the Holy Spirit

Durham, Middlesex Co., Notre Dame (1953), Rev. Augustine Naduvilekoot.
Res., 272 Main St., 06422. Tel: 860-349-3058.
Catechesis/Religious Programs—Tel: 860-349-3059. Mr. Charles Colella, D.R.E.
Students 279.

East Hampton, Middlesex Co., St. Patrick (1879), Rev. Thomas G. Twomey; Deacon Warren J.F. Cyr.
Res., 47 W. High St., 06424-1077. Tel: 860-267-6644. [CEM]
Catechesis/Religious Programs—Students 396.

East Lyme, New London Co., St. Matthias (Flanders) (1939), Rev. Michael T. Donohue.
Res., 159 Boston Post Rd., P.O. Box 25, 06333. Tel: 860-739-5208; Fax: 860-739-0524.
Catechesis/Religious Programs—Students 240.

Ellington, Tolland Co., St. Luke (1961), Rev. Louis M. Galluppi; Deacon Richard A. Boucher.
Res., 141 Maple St., P.O. Box 246, 06029. Tel: 203-875-8552; Fax: 860-872-6548.
Catechesis/Religious Programs—Tel: 203-875-0497.
Students 550.

Essex, Middlesex Co., Our Lady of Sorrows (1926), Revs. Francis W. Murphy; Bradley Pierce, S.M.M.A.
Res., 14 Prospect St., 06426. Tel: 203-767-1284.
Catechesis/Religious Programs—Students 243.

Fishers Island, Suffolk Co., Our Lady of Grace, Rev. Zenon A. Smilga Tel: 516-788-7353.
Res., Alpine Ave., Box 425, 06390. Tel: 516-788-7353.

Gales Ferry, New London Co., Our Lady of Lourdes (1960), Revs. William F. Schneider; Kevin S. Randall; Justinian B. Rweyemamu; Sr. Muriel Audette, S.S.A., Pastoral Assoc.; Deacon Steve Reed.
Res., 1650 Rte. 12, P.O. Box 278, 06335. Tel: 860-464-7251; Fax: 860-464-7252.
Catechesis/Religious Programs—Tel: 860-464-6676.
Students 577.

Groton, New London Co., Sacred Heart (1905), Revs. John J. Meagher, S.S.E.; Francis X. McMahon, S.S.E.
Res., 56 Sacred Heart Dr., 06340. Tel: 860-445-2905; 445-6648.
School—(Grades PreK-8). Tel: 460-445-0611. Sr. Linda Corona, A.S.C.J., Prin.
Lay Teachers 18; Aides 4; Students 383.
Catechesis/Religious Programs—Students 190.

St. Mary (1964), Rev. Theodore J. Klein; Sr. Jacquelyn Donohue, I.H.M., Pastoral Assoc.
Res., 69 Groton Long Point Rd., 06340. Tel: 860-445-1446; Fax: 860-448-0529.
Catechesis/Religious Programs—Students 324.

Hebron, Tolland Co., The Church of the Holy Family (1987), Rev. Roland C. Cloutier.
Mailing Address: P.O. Box 146, 06248. Tel: 860-228-0096; Fax: 860-228-1629.
Catechesis/Religious Programs—Mark L. McCann, D.R.E.
Students 480.

Higganum, Middlesex Co., St. Peter (1958), Rev. Edward M. Konopka.
Res., 30 St. Peter Ln., P.O. Box 707, 06441. Tel: 860-345-8018.
Catechesis/Religious Programs—Tel: 860-345-4726.
Students 206.

Jewett City, New London Co., St. Mary (1870), Co-Pastors: Revs. John E. Welch, M.S.; Rene L. Parent, M.S.; Deacon Francis Bachand.
Res., 34 N. Main St., 06351. Tel: 860-376-2044. [CEM 2]
School—54 N. Main St., 06351. Tel: 860-376-0446. Fred Cale, Prin.
Lay Teachers 10; Students 157.
Catechesis/Religious Programs—Students 363.

Killingworth, Middlesex Co., St. Lawrence (1978), Rev. Michael J. O'Hara; Deacon Raymond Gosselin.
Res., 19 Hemlock Dr., 06419. Tel: 860-663-2576; Fax: 860-663-2576.
Catechesis/Religious Programs—Tel: 860-663-1828.
Students 207.

Lebanon, New London Co., St. Francis of Assisi (1980), Rev. Peter B. Liszewski.
Res., W. Town St., P.O. Box 172, 06249. Tel: 860-642-6711.
Catechesis/Religious Programs—Students 188.

Middlefield, Middlesex Co., St. Colman (1890), Rev. Lester G. Morris.
Res., 145 Hubbard St., P.O. Box 457, 06455. Tel: 860-349-3868.
Catechesis/Religious Programs—Tel: 860-349-8074.
Students 182.

Middletown, Middlesex Co.,

1—ST. FRANCIS, (1903), Rev. Msgr. Michael D. Fox; Rev. Richard T. Buongirno.
Res., 10 Elm St., 06457. Tel: 860-347-4684; Fax: 860-347-7669.
Catechesis/Religious Programs—Tel: 860-344-1098.
Students 118.

2—ST. JOHN, (1843), Rev. Joseph C. Ashe; Sr. Ann Mack, R.S.M., Pastoral Assoc.
Res., 19 John's Sq., 06457. Tel: 860-347-5626.

[CEM]
School—Tel: 860-347-3202.
Lay Teachers 14; Students 245.
Catechesis/Religious Programs—Students 72.

3—St. Mary of Czestochowa, (1903) (Polish), Revs. Aloysius J. Kisluk; Clement Jarnot, O.F.M.Conv.; James J. Sucholet. In res., Rev. John J. Sullivan.
Res., 79 S. Main St., 06457. Tel: 860-347-2365; Fax: 860-347-2110. [CEM]
School—87 S. Main St., 06457. Tel: 860-347-2978. Mrs. Kathleen Dutil, Prin.
Lay Teachers 10; Students 270.
Catechesis/Religious Programs—Students 160.

4—St. Pius X, (1957), Revs. Frederick Nickle, O.F.M.Cap.; Terrence O'Toole, O.F.M.Cap.; James Hammer, O.F.M.Cap. In res., Revs. Colman Boylan, O.F.M.Cap.; Cyprian Murray, O.F.M.Cap.; Richard Donaldson, O.F.M.Cap.; John Tokaz, O.F.M.Cap.; Bro. Eugene Sheehan, O.F.M.Cap.
Res., 310 Westfield St., 06457-2047. Tel: 860-347-4441; 4442; Fax: 203-347-3001.
Catechesis/Religious Programs—Tel: 860-346-9100.
Students 508.

5—St. Sebastian, (1930) (Italian), Revs. Joseph D. Sibilano, O.S.J.; Daniel L. Schwebs, O.S.J.; Deacons John P. Catalano; Nicholas J. Cannata.
Res., 155 Washington St., 06457. Tel: 860-347-2638; Fax: 860-347-6736. [CEM]
School—61 Durant Ter., 06457. Tel: 860-347-3438. Sr. Patricia Dora, C.S.J., Prin.
Lay Teachers 10; Students 153.
Catechesis/Religious Programs—Students 216.

Montville, New London Co., St. John (1881), Rev. Russel L. Boisvert Tel: 203-848-1257; Deacon Melvin Nygaard. In res., Rev. Msgr. Robert L. Brown, Chancellor, Tel: 860-848-3771; Rev. Mark D. O'Donnell, Chap. St. Bernard High School, Tel: 860-848-1271.
Res., 22 Maple Ave., Uncasville, 06382. Tel: 860-848-9335. [CEM]
Catechesis/Religious Programs—Tel: 203-848-1409.
Students 199.

Moodus, Middlesex Co., St. Bridget (1914), Rev. Msgr. Henry J. Dziadosz.
Res., 75 Moodus-Leesville Rd., P.O. Box 422, 06469-0422. Tel: 860-873-8623. [CEM]
Catechesis/Religious Programs—Students 270.

Moosup, Windham Co., All-Hallows (1859), Revs. Anthony Gruber; Gregorz P. Brozonowicz, Parochial Vicar.
Res., 130 Prospect St., 06354. Tel: 860-564-2668; Fax: 860-564-3941. [CEM]
School—Plainfield Catholic, Tel: 860-564-3476.
Lay Teachers 13; Students 243.
Catechesis/Religious Programs—Tel: 860-564-5409.
Students 308.
Mission—Sterling, Windham Co., St. Joseph.

Mystic, New London Co., St. Patrick (1870), Rev. Charles A. McGrail.
Res., 32 E. Main St., P.O. Box 236, 06355. Tel: 860-536-1800; Fax: 860-536-9635. [CEM]
Catechesis/Religious Programs—Tel: 860-536-6808.
Students 189.

New London, New London Co., St. Joseph (1907) (Italian), Revs. Joseph Castaldi; Joseph F. DeCosta; Rev. Msgr. Paul St. Onge, (Retired); Deacon Gerard Gaynor.
Res., 17 Squire St., 06320. Tel: 860-443-5393.
School—Tel: 860-442-1720.
Lay Teachers 10; Students 226.
Catechesis/Religious Programs—Students 240.

St. Mary, Star of the Sea (1870), Rev. Thomas J. Smith; Rev. Msgr. Thomas R. Bride, P.A.; Revs. Dennis M. Perkins; Russell P. Kennedy, Dir. of Hispanic Min.; Deacons Mariano Ramos; Jesus A. Diez-Canseco; Sr. Brta Najela, R.O.D.A., Hispanic Min. Pastoral Assocs.: Sr. Giuseppina Frontini, S.C.I.C.; Sr. Gemma Mancini, S.C.I.C.
Res., 10 Huntington St., 06320-6198. Tel: 860-447-1431; Fax: 860-437-1889.
School—Tel: 860-443-7758. Sr. Angese Quarta, S.C.I.C., Prin.
Priests 2; Sisters 4; Lay Teachers 14; Students 268.
Catechesis/Religious Programs—Tel: 860-443-5870. Sr. Immacolata DeCossio, S.C.I.C., D.R.E.
Students 425.
Convent—28 Huntington St., 06320. Sr. Giuseppina Frontini, S.C.I.C., Supr. The Sisters of Charity of the Immaculate Conception of Ivrea.
Convent—197 Broadway, Norwich, 06360. Tel: 860-886-6092. Sr. Brta Najela, R.O.D.A., Supr. The Oblate Sisters of Divine Love.
Hispanic Ministry—60 Jay St., 06320. Tel: 860-437-1285. Rev. Russell P. Kennedy, Dir. The Oblate Sisters of Divine Love.

Niantic, New London Co., St. Agnes (1922), Rev. Arthur A. Archer; Deacons Roland J. LaCasse; Maurice J. Walsh.
Res., 22 Haigh Ave., 06357. Tel: 860-739-9722.
Catechesis/Religious Programs—Tel: 860-739-9992.
Students 259.
Chapel—Crescent Beach, St. Francis Chapel (Summer).

North Grosvenordale, Windham Co., St. Joseph (1872), Revs. Gregoire J. Fluet; George Parker.
Res., Main St., 06255. Tel: 860-923-2361. [CEM]
School—Tel: 860-923-2090. Sr. Priscilla S.C.M.C., Prin.
Sisters of Charity of Our Lady Mother of the Church 3; Lay Teachers 7; Students 150.
Catechesis/Religious Programs—Students 308.
Mission—West Thompson, Windham Co., Sacred Heart, P.O. Box 897, N. Grosvenordale 06255.

North Stonington, New London Co., St. Thomas More (1977), Rev. John C. Nash; Deacon Donald Donahue.
Res., 87 Mystic Rd., 06359. Tel: 860-535-1601.
Catechesis/Religious Programs—Tel: 860-535-3229.
Students 198.

Oakdale, New London Co., Our Lady of the Lakes (1966), Rev. Michael J. Gill.
Res., 752 Norwich, Salem Tpke., 06370. Tel: 860-859-1575.
Catechesis/Religious Programs—Students 275.

Occum, New London Co., St. Joseph (1887), Rev. Robert W. Barnes.
Res., 11 Baltic Rd., Box 256, Versailles-Occum, 06383. Tel: 860-822-8020.
Catechesis/Religious Programs—Tel: 860-822-6963. Mrs. Monica Bernier, D.R.E.
Students 174.
Saint Society Church—(Corporate Title: St. Joseph Church Society of Occum, CT, Inc.).

Old Lyme, New London Co., Christ the King (1934), Rev. Msgr. Richard P. LaRocque; Rev. Leszek T. Janik; Sr. Katherine M. McKenna, P.B.V.M., Pastoral Assoc.
Office: 20 Lyme St., P.O. Box 443, 06371. Tel: 860-434-1669; Fax: 860-434-7140.
Res., 30 Lyme St., P.O. Box 443, 06371. Tel: 860-434-1660.
Catechesis/Religious Programs—Tel: 860-434-9873.
Students 307.
Chapel—Our Lady of Good Counsel at Sound View. (Summer Chapel) Shore Rd., 06371.

Old Saybrook, Middlesex Co., St. John (1884), Revs. Joseph H. Hanks; Marek Masnicki.
Res., 161 Main St., 06475. Tel: 860-388-3787; Fax: 860-388-6008. [CEM]
Catechesis/Religious Programs—42 Maynard Rd., 06475. Tel: 203-388-6288.
Students 310.

Pawcatuck, New London Co., St. Michael (1860), Revs. R. Thomas McConaghy; Dariusz K. Dudzik; Deacon James R. McMahon.
Res., 60 Liberty St., 06379. Tel: 860-599-5580; Fax: 860-599-8079. [CEM]
School—Tel: 860-599-1084. Sr. Guytina Campisi, M.P.F., Prin.
Sisters 2; Lay Teachers 8; Students 239.
Catechesis/Religious Programs—Tel: 860-599-0040. Mrs. Susan Berggren, D.R.E.
Students 311.

Plainfield, Windham Co., St. John the Apostle (1907), Rev. Charles R. LeBlanc.
Res., 10 Railroad Ave., 06374. Tel: 860-564-3313. [CEM]
Catechesis/Religious Programs—12 Railroad Ave., 06374. Tel: 860-564-8380.
Students 206.

Pomfret, Windham Co., Most Holy Trinity (1886), Rev. Paul L. Hebert.
Res., 568 Pomfret St., P.O. Box 235, 06258-0235. Tel: 860-928-5830.
Catechesis/Religious Programs—Tel: 860-928-5830.
Students 262.

Portland, Middlesex Co., St. Mary (1872), Rev. John F. Ashe; Sr. Mary Ida Dolan, R.S.M., Pastoral Assoc.
Res., 51 Freestone Ave., P.O. Box 307, 06480. Tel: 203-342-2328. [CEM]

Preston, New London Co., St. Catherine of Siena (1975), Rev. V. Anthony J. Alaharasan; Sr. Cathleen Ryan, O.P., Pastoral Assoc.
Res., 243 Rte. 164, 06365-8726. Tel: 860-887-9966; Fax: 860-889-7640.
Catechesis/Religious Programs—Students 130.

Putnam, Windham Co., St. Mary (1866), Revs. Francis J. O'Keefe; Thomas Plathottam; Deacons Pierre M. Desilets; Bernard A. Phaneuf.
Res., 218 Providence St., 06260. Tel: 860-928-6535; Fax: 860-928-7246. [CEM]
School—23 Marshall St., 06260. Tel: 860-928-7046; 928-1104; Fax: 860-928-9379. Ms. Phyllis Hickey, Prin.
Catechesis/Religious Programs—15 Marshall St., 06260. Tel: 860-928-4507; 860-2032.
Students 157.

Quaker Hill, New London Co., Our Lady of Perpetual Help (1904) (Polish), Rev. Leo S. Sutula; Deacon Ronald S. Kitlinski.
Res., 63 Old Norwich Rd., P.O. Box 329, 06375. Tel: 860-443-1875.
Catechesis/Religious Programs—Students 107.
Convent—59 Old Norwich Rd., 06375. Tel: 860-447-3550. Sisters of St. Joseph of Third Order of St. Francis

Quinebaug, Windham Co., St. Stephen (1955), Rev. William J. O'Rourke.
Res., Junction Rtes. 131 & 197, 06262. Tel: 860-935-5205; Fax: 860-935-5205.

Rockville, Tolland Co., St. Bernard (1854), Rev. John J. White. In res., Rev. Roger M. Comtois.
Res., 25 St. Bernard's Terr., 06066. Tel: 860-875-0753. [CEM]
School—20 School St., 06066. Tel: 860-875-0475; Fax: 860-872-2444. Sr. Mary Gerald, R.S.M., Prin.
Sisters 2; Lay Teachers 8; Students 175.
Catechesis/Religious Programs—22 School St., 06066. Tel: 860-872-3828.
Students 165.
Convent—32 School St., 06066. Tel: 860-875-4016. Sisters of Mercy
Cemetery Office:—Tel: 203-872-6601.

St. Joseph (1905) (Polish), Rev. Joseph M. Olczak.
Res., 33 West St., 06066. Tel: 860-871-1970.
School—41 West St., 06066. Tel: 860-875-4943. Sr. Janice Marie Gaudette, Prin.
Felician Sisters 5; Lay Teachers 7; Students 149.
Catechesis/Religious Programs—Students 143.

Rogers, Windham Co., St. Ignatius (1939), Rev. William J. McNutty.
Res., 350 Hartford Pike, Box 487, Dayville, 06241. Tel: 860-774-8656.
Church—21 Williamsville Rd., Box 158, 06263.
Convent—17 Williamsville Rd., Box 158, 06263. Tel: 860-774-8154. St. Ignatius Parish House Daughters of the Holy Spirit

Somersville, Tolland Co., All Saints (1915), Revs. Thomas W. Murphy; Timothy C. Valliere; Deacons James J. Burgess; Lawrence W. Deraleau; John J. Abdalla, D.R.E.
Res., 25 School St., P.O. Box M, 06072. Tel: 860-749-8625.
Catechesis/Religious Programs—Tel: 860-763-0348.
Students 396.

Stafford Springs, Tolland Co., St. Edward (1869), Revs. Francis J. Lombardo, O.F.M.Conv.; Richard-Jacob Forcier, O.F.M.Conv.; Bro. Dennis Sokolowski, O.F.M.Conv.
Mailing Address: 6 Benton St., 06076. Tel: 860-684-2705; Fax: 860-684-0757.
Res., 55 High St., 06076. [CEM]
School—(Grades Pre K-8). Tel: 860-684-2600.
Lay Teachers 10; Students 250.
Catechesis/Religious Programs—Students 224.
Mission—Staffordville, Tolland Co., St. Joseph, 6 Benton St., Stafford Springs 06076.

Stonington, New London Co., St. Mary (1850), Rev. Philip J. Geogan; Deacon Henry E. O'Reilly.
Res., 95 Main St., 06378-1219. Tel: 860-535-1700. [CEM]
Catechesis/Religious Programs—Tel: 860-535-4252. Mrs. Mary Maranell, D.R.E.
Students 170.

Storrs, Tolland Co., St. Thomas Aquinas (1947), Revs. Richard Gross, S.J.; Paul Holland, S.J.; Martin MacDonnell, S.J.; Sr. Alberta Surowiec, F.S.S.J.
Res., 46 N. Eagleville Rd., 06268. Tel: 203-429-6436; Fax: 860-429-6437.
Catechesis/Religious Programs—Tel: 203-429-6436.
Students 184.

Taftville, New London Co., Sacred Heart (1883), Rev. Msgr. Henry N. Archambault, P.A.; Rev. Brian J. Converse. In res., Rev. Raymond D. Introvigne, Diocesan Dir. Spiritual Renewal Svcs.
Res., 156 Providence St., P.O. Box 208, 06380. Tel: 860-887-3072; Fax: 203-887-3072.
School—15 Hunters Ave., 06380. Tel: 860-887-1757. Sr. Mary David, Prin.
Sisters of Charity of Our Lady Mother of the Church 5; Lay Teachers 5; Students 150.
Catechesis/Religious Programs—Students 217.

Tolland, Tolland Co., St. Matthew (1964), Rev. James P. Carini; Deacon Ronald Freedman.
Mailing Address: P.O. Box 100, 06084. Tel: 860-872-0200; Fax: 860-875-4413.
Catechesis/Religious Programs—Tel: 860-875-8663. D.R.E.: Peter R. Chabot, (Grades 7-12); Mrs. Nancy Rudek, (Pre K-6).
Students 671.

Vernon, Tolland Co., Sacred Heart (1958), Rev. Stanley J. Szczapa; Deacon Charles B. White.
Church—550 Hartford Tpke., 06066-5000. Tel: 860-875-4563; Fax: 860-872-2535.
Catechesis/Religious Programs—Students 265.

Voluntown, New London Co., St. Thomas Apostle (1892), Rev. Eslyn Joseph Drummond.
Res., 61 Preston City St., P.O. Box 99, 06384. Tel: 860-376-2293. [CEM]
Mission—Glasgo, New London Co., St. Ann, Rte. 201, 06384.

Warrenville, Windham Co., St. Philip (1937). Unassigned. Rev. Joseph P. Murphy.
Res., 64 Pompey Hollow Rd., Ashford, 06278-1540. Tel: 860-429-2860; Fax: 860-487-5730. [CEM 2]
Catechesis/Religious Programs—Tel: 860-429-1921.
Students 170.

Waterford, New London Co., St. Paul (1960), Rev. Richard F. Roughan; Deacon Richard K. Walker.
Res., 170 Rope Ferry Rd., 06385. Tel: 860-443-5587.
Catechesis/Religious Programs—Tel: 860-443-3375.
Students 310.

Wauregan, Windham Co., Sacred Heart (1889) (French), Revs. Paul J. Gaumond; Theodore Berube, Pastor Emeritus.
Res., W. Main St., P.O. Box 468, 06387. Tel: 860-774-6892. [CEM]

West Willington, Tolland Co., St. Jude (1981), Rev. Thomas W. Sennik.
Res., 25 Old Farms Rd., P.O. Box 240, Willington, 06279. Tel: 860-429-9655.
Catechesis/Religious Programs—Tel: 860-429-8604.
Students 120.

Westbrook, Middlesex Co., St. Mark (1961), Rev. Richard Albamonti.
Res., 222 McVeagh Rd., P.O. Box 551, 06498. Tel: 860-399-9207.
Catechesis/Religious Programs—Students 189.

Windham, Windham Co., Sagrado Corazon de Jesus (1991) (Hispanic), Rev. Paul J. Murdock; Sr. Mary Jude Lazarus, S.C.M.C., Pastoral Assoc.; Deacon Felipe Silva.
Mailing Address: 61 Club Rd., 06280. Tel: 860-423-8617.
Catechesis/Religious Programs—Students 143.

Willimantic, Windham Co., St. Joseph (1859), Rev. Msgr. Willis W. West; Revs. Luke A. Walaszek, O.P.; Deus-Dedit Byabato; Gregory P. Galvin. In res., Rev. Edward F. Frigault.
Res., 99 Jackson St., 06226. Tel: 860-423-8439; Fax: 860-423-6825. [CEM]
School—St. Mary-St. Joseph, 35 Valley St., 06226. Tel: 860-423-8479. Mother Marie Dominica, S.C.M.C., Prin.
Catechesis/Religious Programs—Students 249.
Convent—88 Jackson St., 06226. Tel: 203-423-5122.
Mission—Scotland, Windham Co., St. Margaret, Tel: 203-423-1791.

St. Mary (1903) (French), Revs. Roger J. Lamoureux, O.M.I.; Martin W. Jones.
Res., 80 Maple Ave., 06226. Tel: 860-423-5835; Fax: 860-423-9933.
School—St. Mary-St. Joseph, 35 Valley St., 06226. Tel: 860-423-8479. Mother Marie Dominica, S.C.M.C., Prin.
Sisters 5; Lay Teachers 10; Students 304.
Catechesis/Religious Programs—Students 150.
Convent—88 Jackson St., 06226. Sisters of Charity of Our Lady
Faith Formulation—Tel: 203-423-9700. Mrs. Tina Popeleski, Dir.

Chaplains of Public Institutions

NORWICH. *William W. Backus Hospital,* 06360. Tel: 860-889-8331. Sr. Rita Johnson, S.S.N.D., Chaplaincy Svcs.

MIDDLETOWN. *Connecticut Valley Hospital,* Eastern Dr., P.O. Box 351, 06457. Tel: 860-344-2546; 344-2666. Rev. Jose Rizal Dimapilis, O.P., Prin. Chap.
Long Lane School. Mailing Address: P.O. Box 882, 06457. Tel: 860-344-2820. Rev. Noel G. Ahrems, O.Carm.
Middlesex Memorial Hospital, 28 Crescent St., 06457-0822. Tel: 860-347-9471, Ext. 6725. Rev. Richard Dolandson, O.F.M.Cap.

NEW LONDON. *Lawrence and Memorial Hospitals,* Montauk Ave., 06320. Tel: 860-442-0711, Ext. 2609. Bro. Robert Vozzo, C.S.C., Chap.; Deacons Ron Kitlinski; Roland J. LaCasse.

NIANTIC. *State Farm for Women.* Vacant.

On Special or Other (Arch)Diocesan Assignment:
Reverend Monsignors—
Bride, Thomas R., P.A., Vicar Gen., The Chancery
Brown, Robert L., Chancellor, The Chancery

On Duty Outside the Diocese:
Reverend Fathers—
Caiazzo, Nicholas
Giaquinto, Albert G., Theological College, 401 Michigan Ave., N.E., Washington, DC 20002
Kirby, Gerald S., Diocesan Mission House, c/o Lynx Air, P.O. Box 407139, Ft. Lauderdale, FL 33340

Military Chaplains:
Reverend Fathers—
Angelo, Thomas M., Ch., Capt., 23 Wg/MC, Pope AFB, NC 28308
Gwudz, John S., Office of Chap., U.S.S. Independence, CV 62, FPO, AP 96618-2760

Absent on Leave:
Reverend Fathers—
Bolieau, Henry G.
Dempsey, Edward M.
Gaulin, Roger
Jean, Raymond J.
Liszewski, Francis A.
Surprenant, John L.

Retired:
Reverend Monsignors—
Gadarowski, Bronislaw A., Winter, 357 Pineview Dr., Venice, FL 34293
Malanowski, Thaddeus F., 100 Bluffview Dr., Apt. 615 A, Belleair Bluffs, FL 33540
McKenna, Edward J., 90 McKinley Ave., New Haven, CT 06515. Tel: 860-387-3126
O'Brien, James J., St. Mary Home, 2021 Albany Ave., West Hartford, CT 06117
St. Onge, Paul J., 45 Squire St., New London, CT 06320
Reverend Fathers—
Almendra, Leoncio T., Real St. Abuyog, Leyte, Philippines
Berube, Theodore E., Sacred Heart Rectory, W. Main St., P.O. Box 468, Wauregan, CT 06387. Tel: 860-774-6892
Bialkowski, Henry A., 162 Eddy Glover Blvd., New Britain, CT 06053. Tel: 203-223-4242
Curtin, Clifford J., 799 Prospect Ave. B-6, West Hartford, CT 06105. Tel: 860-236-2493
Davis, Edward J., 179 Train St., Dorchester, MA 02122. Tel: 617-282-0479
Flint, Kenneth, Box 4, Charlestown, RI 02813. Tel: 401-364-1071
Giaquinto, Albert C., Theological College, 401 Michigan Ave., N.E., Washington, D.C. 20064
Horan, Joseph, P.O. Box 1043, Cowpens, SC 29330
Kelley, J. Ralph, Heritage Commons, 38 Boston Rd., Middletown, CT 06457. Tel: 860-343-0164
Kozon, John A., 7060 Snyder Rd., Memphis, TN 38125
Kuzdal, Anthony P., 1714 Beach Pkwy., A-2, Cape Coral, FL 33904. Tel: 813-542-9261
Landry, Alfred R., St. Joseph Living Center, 14 Club Rd., Windham, CT 06280. Tel: 860-456-1107
Liszewski, Francis, 8 Hillcrest Dr., Tolland, CT 06084
Marciniak, John, 70 W. 18th Rd., Broad Channel, NY 11693
McGrath, Daniel F., 2433 Main St., Rocky Hill, CT 06067
McNulty, Robert E., 5 Holmes St., E-14, Mystic, CT 06355. Tel: 860-536-1758
Morrissette, Joseph H., 30 School Hill Rd., Baltic, CT 06330
Murphy, Hugh J., P.O. Box 261, Pomfret, CT 06258
Nichols, Joseph E., 810 Walnut St., Lebanon, PA 17042
Poulin, Edward C., 13 Blissville Rd., Lisbon, CT 06351. Tel: 860-887-3689
Pupsys, Adam, P.O. Box 2163, Westerly, RI 02891
Ramen, Paul F., 350 Pond Hill Rd., Moosup, CT 06354. Tel: 860-887-2565
Ricard, Joseph M., 233 Spanish Moss Rd., Davenport, FL 33837
Sullivan, John J., St. Mary Rectory, 79 S. Main St., Middletown, CT 06457
Wisneski, Edward, S.T.D., Ph.D., 78 E. Ridge Rd., Middletown, CT 06457
Wood, Robert J., P.O. Box 1896, Statesboro, GA 30458

Permanent Deacons:
Abdalla, John, All Saints, Somerville
Bachand, Francis J., St. Mary Church, Jewett City
Baillargeon, Paul R., St. Augustine Church, Canterbury
Barlow, Robert C., St. Andrew, Colchester
Berstene, Michael C., St. Bernard, Rockville
Boucher, Richard A., St. Luke Church, Ellington
Burgess, James J., All Saints & Office of Evangelization, Somersville
Cannata, Nicholas J., St. Sebastian Church, Middletown
Cartier, L. Roger
Catalano, John P., St. Sebastian Church, Middletown
Cote, Albert J., St. Francis, Lebanon
Cyr, Warren, St. Patrick, East Hampton
Danesi, Peter H., III, St. Mary, Groton
Deraleau, Lawrence W., All Saints Church, Somersville
Desilets, Pierre M., Project Northeast & St. Mary, Putnam
Diez Conseco, Jesus A., St. Mary, Hispanic Apostolate New London & Bishop's Delegate to Hispanic Permanent Deacons
Dogue, Eduardo, Ministry to Handicapped, Wauregan
Dolan, Dennis F., Prison Ministry
Donahue, Donald J., St. Thomas More Church, N. Stonington
Doyle, Dennis A., III, St. Mary, Norwich
Fecteau, Al R., Cathedral of St. Patrick, Norwich
Freedman, Ronald, St. Matthew Church, Tolland
Gaynor, Gerard J., Saint Joseph Church, New London
Goodwin, Lawrence, St. Margaret Mission Church, Scotland
Gosselin, Raymond P., St. Lawrence, Killingworth
Grospitch, Harry J., St. Bernard, Rockville
Hayes, Robert P., St. John, Fitchville
Jolin
Kitlinski, Ronald S., Our Lady Perpetual Help, Quaker Hill
LaCasse, Roland J., Chap. Asst., Lawrence & Memorial Hospitals, Asst., St. Agnes
LaPlante, Joseph A., Manset, ME
McMahon, James R., Sr., St. Michael Church, Pawcatuck
Melendez, Carlos
Nygaard, Melvin G., St. John Church, Uncasville
O'Reilly, Henry E., St. Mary, Stonington
O'Sullivan, W. Ridgely, Bishop's Delegate for Permanent Deacons, St. Joseph Church, Chester
Osuba, Jose, Columbia
Phaneuf, Bernard A., St. Mary, Putnam
Ramos, Mariano, Hispanic Ministry, St. Mary, New London
Reed, Steven W., Our Lady of Lourdes, Gales Ferry
Saunders, Alexander, St. Bernard Church, Rockville
Silva, Felipe, St. Joseph Church, Willimantic
Walker, Richard K., St. Paul Church, Waterford
Walsh, Maurice, St. Agnes, Niantic
Weber, F. Paul, St. Mary of the Visitation Church, Clinton
White, Charles B., St. Luke Church, Ellington

INSTITUTIONS LOCATED IN THE DIOCESE

[A] SEMINARIES, RELIGIOUS OR SCHOLASTICATES

CROMWELL. *Holy Apostles College and Seminary,* 33 Prospect Hill Rd., 06416. Tel: 860-632-3000; 632-3030 (Admissions); Fax: 860-632-0176. Revs. Douglas L. Mosey, C.S.B., Ph.D., Pres. & Rector; Maurice Sheehan, O.F.M.Cap.; Pasquale Taliercio, M.Ss.A., Dean of Men; Michael A. Gauthier, Business Mgr.; Revs. Raymond Halliwell, M.Ss.A., Dir. of Admissions & Vice Rector; Addison Hallock, M.Ss.A., Spiritual Dir.; Bradley Pierce, M.Ss.A., Dir. Field Education; Ronan P. Callahan, C.P.; Philip Kiley, S.J.; Benedict Klucinec, M.Ss.A., Priestly Formation; Joseph C. Henchey, C.S.C.; David Q. Liptak; John Marcoux, M.Ss.A.; John McHugh; Robert McQueeney, M.Ss.A.; Michael Motta; Robert Murphy, M.Ss.A.; Ronald H. Mikasauskas, M.Ss.A.; Brian Mullady, O.P.; James O'Connor, S.T.D.; Joseph Olczak; Martin Rooney, M.Ss.A.; Robert Sickler, M.Ss.A.; Richard Skarbek, M.Ss.A. Priests 25; Brothers 6; Sisters 6; Lay Teachers 6; Seminarians 75; Seminary Division Lay Students 50; Total 160.

ENDERS ISLAND. *St. Edmund's Novitiate,* P.O. Box 399, 06355. Tel: 860-572-9538; Fax: 203-572-7655. Society of St. Edmund. Revs. Stanely M. Deresienski, S.S.E., Supr.; Thomas F.X. Hoar, S.S.E.; Paul Pinard, S.S.E.; Bros. Martin Slattery, S.S.E.; Thomas Berube, S.S.E.; Sr. Jeanette Serra, S.S.C.

MYSTIC. *Edmundite Seminary Guild.* Society of St. Edmund of Connecticut, Inc., 06355. Tel: 860-536-4949; Fax: 203-536-7540. Revs. Roger J. LaCharite, S.S.E., Exec. Dir.; Joseph L. Hart, S.S.E., Dir.; Thomas F.X. Hoar, S.S.E., Treas.

[B] HIGH SCHOOLS, DIOCESAN

MIDDLETOWN. *Mercy High School*, 1740 Randolph Rd., 06457. Tel: 860-346-6659; Fax: 860-344-9887. Sisters of Mercy. Sr. Mary A. McCarthy, R.S.M., Prin.; Sr. Jean Dwyer, C.N.D., Vice Prin.; Mr. Steven Brickey, Dean of Students; Sr. Margaret O'Neill, R.S.M., Admin. Asst.; Miss Ann Derbacher, Campus Min.; Rev. Michael S. Smith, Chap. Sisters 11; Lay Teachers 39; Students 550.

Xavier High School, 181 Randolph Rd., 06457. Tel: 860-346-7735; Fax: 860-346-6859. Brothers of St. Francis Xavier. Bro. Lawrence Harvey, C.F.X., Prin.; Rev. Michael S. Smith, Chap. Brothers 7; Lay Teachers 47; Students 770.

UNCASVILLE. *St. Bernard High School*, 1593 Norwich-New London Tpke., 06382. Tel: 860-848-1271; Fax: 860-848-1274. Rev. Joseph Nguyen, Chap.; Sr. Mary Patrick, S.C.M.C., Prin.; Mother Mary Luke, S.C.M.C., Headmistress. Priests 2; Lay Teachers 35; Students 410.

[C] HIGH SCHOOLS, PRIVATE

BALTIC. *Academy and Boarding-School of the Holy Family*, W. Main St., 06330. Tel: 203-822-8241. Sisters of Charity of Our Lady Mother of the Church. Sr. Mary Patrick, Prin.; Rev. Michael A. Massaro, C.S.C. Sisters 7; Lay Teachers 6; Students 96.

THOMPSON. *Marianapolis Preparatory School*, 06277. Tel: 860-923-9565. Marian Fathers. Revs. Timothy Roth, M.I.C., Supr. & Headmaster; Donald Finney, M.I.C., Asst. Headmaster; Albin Gurklis, M.I.C.; Bros. Donald Schaefer, M.I.C., Treas., Registrar & Dir. Devel.; Brian Manian, M.I.C.; Victor Incardona, M.I.C.; Joseph Keil. Brothers 4; Lay Teachers 20; Students 172.

[D] PROTECTIVE INSTITUTIONS

DEEP RIVER. *Mount St. John*, 135 Kirtland St., 06417. Tel: 203-526-5391; Fax: 203-526-3846.
For a complete listing, refer to the Special Care Facilities section.

[E] HOMES FOR AGED

WILLIMANTIC. *Holy Family Home and Shelter, Inc.*, 88 Jackson St., P.O. Box 884, 06226. Tel: 860-423-7719.
For a complete listing, refer to the Special Care Facilities section.

WINDHAM. *St. Joseph Living Center*, 14 Club Rd., 06280. Tel: 860-456-1107.
For a complete listing, refer to the Special Care Facilities section.

[F] MONASTERIES AND RESIDENCES OF PRIESTS AND BROTHERS

BALTIC. *Marian Friary of Our Lady of Guadalupe*, 22 School Hill Rd., 06330. Tel: 860-822-8606. Bros. Angelo Mary of the Incarnation & Cross, F.F.I., Father Vicar; Maximilian Mary of the Immaculate Conception, F.F.I.; Pio Maria Gabriele of the Crucified, F.F.I. Priests 2; Professed 3.

CROMWELL. *Missionaries of the Holy Apostles*, 33 Prospect Hill Rd., 06416. Tel: 860-632-3039; 623-3000; Fax: 860-632-3035. Society of the Missionaries of the Holy Apostles. Revs. Benedict Klucinec, M.Ss.A., Provincial Animator; Martin D. Rooney, M.Ss.A., Dir. Vocations, Dir. Mission Office, & Sec. to the Provincial; Robert McQueeney, M.Ss.A.; Pasquale Taliercio, M.Ss.A.; John Marcoux, M.Ss.A.; Raymond Halliwell, M.Ss.A.; Ronald Mikasauskas, M.Ss.A.; Robert Murphy, M.Ss.A.; Bradley Pierce, M.Ss.A.; Richard Skarbek, M.Ss.A.; Addison Hallock, M.Ss.A.
Working Outside the Diocese: Revs. David Zercie; George Realmuto; J. Patrick Boyhan.

HAMPTON. *Brothers of St. Francis Xavier*, P.O. Box 177, 06247. Tel: 860-774-3340.

MIDDLETOWN. *Congregation of the Brothers of St. Francis Xavier*, 181 Randolph Rd., 06457-5606. Tel: 860-346-8585; Fax: 860-346-6859. Bros. William Ciganek, C.F.X., Dir.; D. Paschal Alford, C.F.C.; Eugene Behenna, C.F.X.; Lawrence Harvey, C.F.X.; J. Robert Houlihan, C.F.X.; John J. McDonald, C.F.X.; K. Paul McGlade, C.F.C.; H. Lawrence Nyhan, C.F.X.; Harold Pray, C.F.X.; Thomas Ryan, C.F.X.; Andre Shine, C.F.X.; James Boyle, C.F.X. Total in Residence 13.

MYSTIC. *Society of St. Edmund*, P.O. Box 399, 06355. Tel: 860-572-9538; Fax: 860-572-7655. Revs. Stanley M. Deresienski, S.S.E., Supr.; Thomas F.X. Hoar, S.S.E.; Paul Pinard, S.S.E.; Bros. Martin Slattery, S.S.E.; Thomas Berube, S.S.E.; Sr. Jeanette Serra, S.S.C., Dir. of the Apostolate Ctr. Total in Residence 6.

THOMPSON. *Marian Fathers*, Marianapolis Prep School, 06277. Tel: 860-923-9798. Revs. Timothy Roth, M.I.C., Supr. & Headmaster; Donald Finney, M.I.C., Asst. Headmaster & Second Councillor; Peter Barauskas, M.I.C.; Albin Gurkis, M.I.C.; Albin Sheputa, M.I.C.; Bros. Donald Schaefer, M.I.C., Treas. & First Councillor; Brian Manian, M.I.C.; Victor Incardona, M.I.C.; Joseph Keil, M.I.C. Total in Residence 9.

WILLIMANTIC. *Oblates of Mary Immaculate*, 289 Windham Rd., P.O. Box 55, 06226. Tel: 203-423-8484. Rev. Robert G. Levesque, O.M.I., Dir.
Retreat Masters: Revs. Olivier Renaud, O.M.I.; Raymond LaCasse, O.M.I., Dir.; Daniel Nassaney, O.M.I.; Henri A. DeLisle, O.M.I., Treas.; Joseph Horton, O.M.I., Clinical Psychologist.

[G] CONVENTS AND RESIDENCES FOR SISTERS

NORWICH. *School Sisters Notre Dame*, 7 Otis St., 06360. Tel: 860-886-6948.

ASHFORD. *Benedictine Monastery*, Seckar Rd., 06278. Tel: 860-429-7457.
Community of Our Lady of Mount Caritas Monastery, O.S.B.; Sisters of the Order of St. Benedict. Comtemplative. R.M. Mary Peter, O.S.B., Supr. Professed 2; Lay Oblates 6; Novices 1.

BALTIC. *Holy Family Motherhouse*, 06330. Tel: 860-822-8241. Sisters of Charity of Our Lady, Mother of the Church. Mother M. Theresita, Supr. Gen.; Rev. M.R.P. Sevastian, Chap. Professed 81; Junior Professed 9; Novices 5; Postulants 1; Total Assisted 210; Total Staff 7.

Sisters of the Holy Cross, 133 Main St., Box 199, 06330. Tel: 203-822-6794.

HIGGANUM. *Apostles of the Sacred Heart of Jesus*, Sacred Heart on the Lake, 529 Brainard Hill Rd., 06441. Tel: 860-345-4653.

MIDDLETOWN. *Mill Hill Sisters*, 6 Bluebird Rd., 06457. Total in Residence 3.

Sisters of Mercy, 1740 Randolph Rd., 06457. Tel: 860-347-4636.
Other Locations: 419 High St., 06457. Tel: 860-344-8569. 203 East St., Hebron, 06248. Tel: 860-228-0849. 56 Beaver Brook Rd., R.D. 3, Lyme, 06371-3201. Tel: 860-434-0724. 103 Golden St., #3, Norwich, 06360. Tel: 860-886-9196. 159 Otrobando Ave., Norwich, 06360. Tel: 860-887-5168. 32 School St., P.O. Box 177, Rockville, 06066. Tel: 860-875-4016. 28 Liberty St., Pawcatuck, 06379. Tel: 860-599-4816. 43 W. High St., East Hampton, 06424. Tel: 860-267-6112. 4 S. View Cir., Old Saybrook, 06475. Tel: 860-395-0913.

Sisters of Our Lady of the Garden, 67 Round Hill Rd., 06457. Tel: 203-346-5765. Convent and Nursery School. Sr. Mary Eugene Sanita, O.L.G., Supr. Total Assisted 82; Total Staff 8.

Sisters of St. Joseph, T.O.S.F., 9 Woodman St., 06457. Tel: 860-347-8936.

MOODUS. *Sisters of St. Joseph of Chambery*. Mailing Address: P.O. Box 22, 06469. Tel: 203-873-1581.

MYSTIC. *Society of the Sisters for the Church*. Sr. Jeanette Serra, S.S.C., Edmundite Apostolate Center, P.O. Box 399, 06355. Tel: 860-572-9787.

PUTNAM. *Holy Spirit Provincial House*, 72 Church St., 06260. Tel: 860-928-0891. Daughters of the Holy Spirit. Sr. Bonnie Morrow, Prov.; Sr. Anita Paul, Coord.; Mrs. Annemarie Shiroka, Admin.; Rev. Richard L. Archambault, Chap. Sisters 63.
Other Locations: Madonna Community, 207 Sabin St., Apt. 42, 06260. Tel: 860-928-2466. Ker Joa Community, 31 Ravine St., 06260. Tel: 860-928-6197. Notre Dame Community, 4 Ravine St., 06260. Tel: 860-928-6163; 928-9129. Our Lady of Peace Community, 26 Church St., 06260. Tel: 860-928-6869. 67 Railroad St., 06260. Tel: 860-928-5965. 357 Church St., 06260. Tel: 860-928-7806. 117 Norwood Ave., New London, 06320. Tel: 860-443-8577. St. Ignatius Parish House Community, 17 Williamsville Rd., Rogers, 06263. Tel: 860-774-8154. Provincialate Community, 124 Rte. 169, Woodstock, 06281. Tel: 860-928-7072. St. Mary Convent, 40 N. Main St., Jewett City, 06351. Tel: 860-376-4020. All Hallows Convent, 152 Prospect St., Moosup, 06354. Tel: 860-564-5409. 815B Boswell Ave., Norwich, 06360. Tel: 860-885-0419. 124 Rte. 169, Woodstock, 06281. Tel: 860-928-9649. 33 Pinecrest Ridge, Apt. E, Woodstock, 06281. Tel: 860-928-2099. DHS, 12 St. Regis Dr., Danielson, 06239. Tel: 860-779-0790. 14 Windsor Ave., E-20, Plainfield, 06374. Tel: 860-564-0617. 31 Lincoln Park Rd., B-4, Preston, 06365. Tel: 860-886-2993.

Immaculate Conception Convent, Spiritual Renewal Center and Novitiate, 600 Liberty Hwy., 06260-2503. Tel: 860-928-7955; Fax: 860-928-1930. Sr. M. Paul Savickas, Prov. Sisters of the Immaculate Conception of the Blessed Virgin Mary 10; Total in Residence 11; Total Staff 7.

Matulaitis Nursing Home Inc., 10 Thurber Rd., 06260. Tel: 860-928-7976; Fax: 860-963-1920. Sisters of the Immaculate Conception of the Blessed Virgin Mary. Jane Logan, Admin.; Rev. Rapolas Krasauskas, Chap. Sisters 10; Residents 119.

UNCASVILLE. *Emmaus Community*, 24 Maple Ave., 06382. Tel: 860-848-3379. Total in Residence 3; Total Staff 3.

WILLIMANTIC. *Sisters of Charity of Our Lady, Mother of the Church*, St. Joseph Convent, 88 Jackson St., 06226. Total in Residence 8; Total Staff 8.

WINDHAM. *Carmelite Sisters of the Eucharist*, 1 Stanley Rd., 06280. Tel: 203-423-0067. Other Location, 26 Deborah Ln., Colchester, 06415. Tel: 860-267-1149. Sr. Mary Grace.

WOODSTOCK. *Provincialate Community of the Daughters of the Holy Spirit*, 124 Rte. 169, 06281; Fax: 860-928-6496. Sr. Bonnie Morrow, D.H.S., Prov. Tel: 860-928-7072; Sr. Linda Babineau, D.H.S., Prov. Councillor. Tel: 860-928-3882.

[H] PRIVATE ASSOCIATIONS OF THE FAITHFUL

ASHFORD, CT. *Benedictine Monastery*. Community of Our Lady of Mount Caritas Monastery, O.S.B.; Sisters of the Order of St. Benedict. Contemplative. Seckar Rd., 06278. Tel: 860-429-7457. Rev. Mother Mary Peter, O.S.B., Supr. Professed 2; Lay Oblates 7; Novices 1.

WINDHAM, CT. *Carmelite Sisters of the Eucharist*, One Stanley Rd., 06280. Tel: 860-423-0067. 26 Deborah Ln., Colchester, 06415. Tel: 860-267-1149. Sr. Mary Grace.

[I] RETREAT HOUSES

ENDERS ISLAND. *Edmundite Apostolate Center*, P.O. Box 399, 06355-0399. Tel: 860-536-0565; Fax: 860-572-7655. Rev. Thomas F.X. Hoar, S.S.E., Dir. of Devel.; Sr. Jeanette Serra, S.S.C., Dir. of the Ctr.; Bro. Martin Slattery, S.S.E.; Rev. Stanley M. Deresienski, S.S.E., Coord. of Pastoral Counseling & Spiritual Direction; Mrs. Claire St. Clair, Business Mgr. Total in Residence 6; Total Staff 5.

HAMPTON. *Community of the Way*. Mailing Address: P.O. Box 177, 06247. Tel: 860-774-3340. Bro. John M. Collins, C.F.X., Dir. Total in Residence 2; Total Staff 2.

MOODUS. *My Father's House*, Box 22, 39 N. Moodus Rd., 06469. Co-Directors: Rev. William McCarthy, M.Ss.A.; Sr. Bernadette Sheldon, C.S.J. A Christian renewal and retreat center.

WAUREGAN. *Ministry of His Able People*. Mailing Address: P.O. Box 242, 06387. Tel: 860-779-0362. Deacon Eduardo Dogue, Dir.

Ave Maria Place. Rev. Patrick Martin. Tel: 203-774-0278.

WILLIMANTIC. *Immaculata Retreat House*, 06226. Tel: 860-423-8484. Oblate Fathers of Mary Immaculate: Province of St. John the Baptist. Revs. Raymond Lacasse, O.M.I., Supr. & Dir.; Henri A. Delisle, O.M.I., Treas.
Retreat Masters: Revs. Oliver Renaud, O.M.I.; Daniel Nassaney, O.M.I.

[J] RENEWAL CENTERS

PORTLAND. *Affirmation Counseling Center*, 553 Portland Cobalt Rd., 06480. Tel: 860-342-0760; Fax: 860-342-4226. Sr. Arlene Vannie, R.S.M., M.A., Dir. Total Assisted 940; Total Staff 8.

UNCASVILLE. *Emmaus-Diocesan Spiritual Life Center*, 24 Maple Ave., 06382. Tel: 860-848-3427. Sr. Mary Barbara Hobbs, P.B.V.M., Admin.
Staff: Sr. Julia Grey, O.P.; Sr. Jane Higgins, R.S.M.; Rev. Joseph G. Finnerty, St. Mary Rectory, 70 Central Ave., 06360. Tel: 860-889-6657; 848-0555. Sisters 3; Total in Residence 3; Total Staff 4.

[K] CAMPUS MINISTRY

WILLIMANTIC. *Campus Ministry*. Eastern Connecticut State University, Newman Hall. 290 Prospect St., 06226. Tel: 860-423-0856. Rev. Laurence A.M. LaPointe, Diocesan Dir. Campus Ministry.
Wesleyan University-The University Ministry (Middletown), 171 Church St., Middletown, 06457. Tel: 860-685-2277. Rev. Gerald P. Cohen, C.S.C., Chap.
Connecticut College (New London), New London, 06320. Tel: 860-439-2452. Rev. Laurence A.M. LaPointe, Catholic Chap.
University of Connecticut (Storrs), St. Thomas Aquinas Chapel, 46 N. Eagleville Rd., Storrs, 06268. Tel: 860-429-6436. Chaplains: Revs. Richard K. Gross, S.J.; Paul Holland, S.J.; Martin MacDonnell, S.J.

[L] SECULAR INSTITUTES

CROMWELL. *Little Franciscan Family*. A secular institute for women. 319 Main St., 06416. Julie Curley, Contact Person. Tel: 860-635-6384.

[M] MISCELLANEOUS

MIDDLETOWN. *Mercy Alumnae & Development Office*, 1740 Randolph Rd., 06457. Tel: 860-347-8957; Fax: 860-344-9887. Karen Wall, Dir.

Mercy-Xavier Fund Corporation, 181 Randolph Rd., 06457.

Xavier Alumni & Development Office, 181 Randolph Rd., 06457. Tel: 203-347-6079.

PUTNAM. *The Daughters of the Holy Spirit Charitable Trust*, 72 Church St., 06260. Tel: 860-928-0891. Sr. Paulette Gariepy, D.H.S., Prov. Supr. & Contact Person.

The Holy Spirit Health Care Center, Inc., 72 Church St., 06260. Tel: 860-928-0891. Sr. Paulette Gariepy, D.H.S., Prov. Supr. & Contact Person.

WILLIMANTIC. *St. Joseph's Home for the Aged.* Mailing Address: c/o Msgr. Willis W. West, 99 Jackson St., 06226. 88 Jackson St., 06226.

WINDHAM. *Sagrado Corazon de Jesus, Inc. of Windham*, 61 Club Rd., 06280.

RELIGIOUS INSTITUTES OF MEN REPRESENTED IN THE DIOCESE

For further details refer to the corresponding bracketed number in the Religious Institutes of Men or Women section.

[0200]—*Benedictine Monks.*—O.S.B.

[1350]—*Brothers of St. Francis Xavier.* (St. Joseph Prov.).—C.F.X.

[0610]—*Brothers of the Congregation of Holy Cross.*—C.S.C.

[0470]—*The Capuchin Friars.* (Prov. of St. Mary).—O.F.M. Cap.

[0270]—*Carmelite Fathers and Brothers.*—O.Carm.

[0480]—*Conventual Franciscans.*—O.F.M.Conv.

[0533]—*Franciscan Friars of the Immaculate.*—F.F.I.

[0690]—*Jesuit Fathers and Brothers.*—S.J.

[0740]—*Marian Fathers.*—M.I.C.

[0720]—*The Missionaries of Our Lady of La Salette.* (American Prov.).—M.S.

[0910]—*Oblates of Mary Immaculate.* (St. John the Baptist Prov.).—O.M.I.

[0930]—*Oblates of St. Joseph.* (Eastern Prov.).—O.S.J.

[0430]—*Order of Preachers (Dominicans).*—O.P.

[0440]—*Society of St. Edmund.*—S.S.E.

[0590]—*Society of the Missionaries of the Holy Apostles.*—M.Ss.A.

[1280]—*Stigmatine Fathers and Brothers.*—C.S.S.

RELIGIOUS INSTITUTES OF WOMEN REPRESENTED IN THE DIOCESE

[0130]—*Apostoles of the Sacred Heart of Jesus.*—A.S.C.J.

[1920]—*Congregation of Sisters of Holy Cross.*—C.S.C.

[0820]—*Daughters of the Holy Spirit.*—D.H.S.

[1070]—*Dominican Sisters.*—O.P.

[1170]—*Felician Sisters.*—C.S.S.F.

[]—*Franciscan Apostolic Sisters.*—F.A.S.

[2575]—*Institute of the Sisters of Mercy of the Americas.*—R.S.M.

[1410]—*Mill Hill Sisters.*—F.M.S.J.

[2720]—*Mission Helpers of the Sacred Heart.*—M.H.S.H.

[3465]—*Religious of the Sacred Heart of Mary.*—R.S.H.M.

[3430]—*Religious Teachers Filippini.*—M.P.F.

[]—*Roncalli Sisters.*

[2970]—*School Sisters of Notre Dame.*—S.S.N.D. Servants of Immaculate Heart of Mary.—I.H.M.

[]—*Sisters Oblates to Divine Love.*—R.O.D.A.

[]—*Sisters of Charity of Immaculate Conception of Irrea, Italy.*—S.C.I.C.

[0530]—*Sisters of Charity of Our Lady, Mother of the Church.*—S.C.M.C. Sisters of Holy Cross.—C.S.C.

[3000]—*Sisters of Notre Dame de Namur.* (Connecticut Prov.).—S.N.D.deN.

[]—*Sisters of Our Lady of the Garden.*—O.L.G.

[3360]—*Sisters of Providence of Saint Mary-of-the-Woods, Indiana.*—S.P.

[3720]—*Sisters of Saint Anne.*—S.S.A.

[3830]—*Sisters of St. Joseph.*—S.S.J.

[3930]—*Sisters of St. Joseph of the Third Order of St. Francis.*—S.S.J.-T.O.S.F.

[3180]—*Sisters of the Cross of Passion.*—C.P.

[1970]—*Sisters of the Holy Family of Nazareth.* (Immaculate Heart of Mary Prov.).—C.S.F.N.

[2140]—*Sisters of the Immaculate Conception of the Blessed Virgin Mary (Lithuanian).*

[3320]—*Sisters of the Presentation of the B.V.M.*—P.B.V.M.

[]—*Society of the Sisters for the Church.*—S.S.C.

NECROLOGY

† Cukuras, Valdemar, Putnam, CT, Immaculate Conception Convent. —Died July 17, 1996.

† Pronovost, Raoul, Moosup, CT, All Hallows Church. —Died Nov. 2, 1996.

Diocese of Oakland

(Dioecesis Quercopolitana)

Most Reverend

JOHN S. CUMMINS, D.D.

Bishop of Oakland; ordained January 24, 1953; appointed Titular Bishop of Lambesi and Auxiliary Bishop of Sacramento February 26, 1974; consecrated May 16, 1974; appointed Bishop of Oakland May 3, 1977; installed June 30, 1977. *Res., 634 21st St., Oakland, CA, 94612.*

Chancery Office: 2900 Lakeshore Ave., Oakland, CA, 94610. Tel.: 510-893-4711; Fax: 510-893-0945.

ESTABLISHED JANUARY 13, 1962.

Square Miles 1,467.

Comprises two Counties in the State of California—viz., Alameda and Contra Costa.

Legal Title: The Roman Catholic Bishop of Oakland, a Corporation Sole.

For legal titles of parishes and diocesan institutions, consult the Chancery Office.

STATISTICAL OVERVIEW

Personnel	
Bishop	1
Priests: Diocesan Active in Diocese	173
Priests: Active Outside Diocese	11
Priests: Retired, Sick or Absent	44
Number of Diocesan Priests	228
Religious Priests in Diocese	78
Extern Priests in Diocese	12
Ordinations:	
Diocesan Priests	1
Permanent Deacons in Diocese	80
Total Brothers	16
Total Sisters	330
Parishes	
Parishes	86
With Resident Pastor:	
Resident Diocesan Priests	59
Resident Religious Priests	16
Without Resident Pastor:	
Administered by Priests	14
Administered by Lay People	1
Completely Vacant	2
Missions	3
Pastoral Centers	11
Professional Ministry Personnel:	
Brothers	1
Sisters	35
Lay Ministers	319
Welfare	
Catholic Hospitals	1
Total Assisted	29,000
Health Care Centers	1
Total Assisted	6
Homes for the Aged	3
Total Assisted	1,219
Day Care and Extended Day Care Centers	5
Total Assisted	1,400
Specialized Homes	4
Total Assisted	16,000
Special Centers for Social Services	5
Total Assisted	25,017
Residential Care of Disabled	2
Total Assisted	736
Other Institutions	4
Total Assisted	19,038
Educational	
Diocesan Students in Other Seminaries	22
Students Religious	71
Total Seminarians	93
Colleges and Universities	3
Total Students	4,500
High Schools, Diocesan and Parish	3
Total Students	1,922
High Schools, Private	6
Total Students	4,090
Elementary Schools, Diocesan and Parish	51
Total Students	14,419
Catechesis/Religious Education:	
High School Students	1,700
Elementary Students	8,000
Total Students Under Catholic Instruction	34,724
Teachers in the Diocese:	
Brothers	16
Sisters	20
Lay Teachers	850
Vital Statistics	
Receptions into the Church:	
Infant Baptism Totals	9,265
Adult Baptism Totals	463
Received into Full Communion	768
First Communions	6,864
Confirmations	2,444
Marriages:	
Catholic	1,198
Interfaith	436
Total Marriages	1,634
Deaths	3,110
Total Catholic Population	431,272
Total Population	2,195,411

Former Bishops—Most Rev. FLOYD L. BEGIN, S.T.D., cons. May 1, 1947; appt. Bishop of Oakland on Feb. 21, 1962; died April 26, 1977.

Chancery Office—2900 Lakeshore Ave., Oakland, 94610-3697. Tel: 510-893-4711; Fax: 510-893-0945. Office Hours: 8:30-4:45.

Vicar General/Director of Pastoral Life—Rev. PAUL ROSS VASSAR, V.G.

Chancellor/Office of the Bishop—Sr. BARBARA FLANNERY, C.S.J.

Director of Financial Services—Rev. ALBANO G. OLIVEIRA.

Associate Director of Financial Services—Rev. DAVID STAAL.

Director of Services and Resources—KENNETH J. REGGIO.

Judicial Vicar/Director of Canonical Services—Vacant.

Adjutant Judicial Vicar & Canonical Consultant to the Bishop—Rev. ROBERT MCCANN, J.C.L.

Director of Planning & Communication Services—CHARLES SIEBENAND.

Director of School Services—Dr. ANN MEYERS MANCHESTER.

Director of Ethnic & Cultural Services—Sr. FELICIA SARATI, C.S.J.

Canon Law Department—

Judicial Vicar—Rev. DAVID MCCARTHY, J.C.L.

Adjutant Judicial Vicars and Canonical Consultants to the Bishop—Revs. ROBERT MCCANN, J.C.L.; GARY M. LUIZ, C.PP.S., J.C.L.; DONALD R. HUDSON, J.C.L.

Defenders of the Bond—Revs. DAVID T. MCCARTHY, J.C.L.; ANTHONY PHAN LAM, J.C.D.

Pro Synodal Judges—Revs. ANTHONY PHAN LAM, J.C.D.; ROBERT MCCANN, J.C.L.; GARY LUIZ, C.PP.S., J.C.L.; DONALD R. HUDSON, J.C.L.; DAVID T. MCCARTHY, J.C.L.

Notaries of the Tribunal—Sr. MAUREEN MCCALL, S.N.J.M.; ALICE VIZCAINO; MARY O'SULLIVAN; MELISSA MATSUOKA; CAROL GAISER.

Promoter of Justice—Vacant.

Auditors of the Tribunal—MERCEDES C. CORRAL; CAROL GAISER; ED KENT; THERESA KOBAK; JOANNE MORGRET.

Consultors—Revs. DANIEL CARDELLI; FERNANDO CORTEZ; VINCENT COTTER; DANIEL DANIELSON; QUANG DONG; JAYSON LANDEZA; JOHN MAXWELL; GERARD MORAN; FRED RICCIO; LARRY SILVA; PAUL VASSAR.

Presbyteral Council—Revs. FRED RICCIO, Pres.; VINCENT COTTER, Vice Pres.; JAYSON LANDEZA, Sec.; DANIEL CARDELLI; FERNANDO CORTEZ; DANIEL DANIELSON; QUANG DONG; ROBERT KUBISIAK; JOHN MAXWELL; GERARD MORAN; LARRY SILVA; PAUL VASSAR.

Deans—#1: Rev. DANIEL DANIELSON; #2: Rev. FRED RICCIO; #3: Rev. JOHN MALLON, #4: Vacant; #5: Rev. BRIAN JOYCE; #6: Rev. FRANCISCO VICENTE, O.P.; #7: Vacant; #8: Rev. WILLIAM MACCHI; #9: Rev. JERROLD F. KENNEDY; #10: Rev. SEAMUS GENOVESE; #11: Rev. IGNATIUS DEGROOT, O.F.M.; #12: Rev. JAMES MATTHEWS; #13: Rev. LARRY SILVA; #14: Rev. Msgr. MANUEL SILVA; #15: Rev. RAMON GOMEZ; #16: Rev. GERARD MORAN; #17: Rev. RAY ZIELEZIENSKI; #18: Rev. JOHN CRUMLISH; #19: Rev. ALEXANDER CRUMLISH; #20: Rev. GEORGE CRESPIN, O.P.; #21: Rev. ANTONIO VALDIVIA; #22: Rev. JOHN MAXWELL; #23: Rev. MELVIN HARY.

Pastoral Leadership Placement Board (PBPB)—Most Rev. JOHN S. CUMMINS; Ms. CATHY BROWN; Sr. CYNTHIA CANNING, S.N.J.M.; Rev. VINCENT COTTER; Sr. BARBARA FLANNERY, C.S.J.; Revs. MICHAEL JOYCE; WILLIAM MACCHI; Ms. JOANN MASS; Rev. MICHAEL NORKETT; Mr. MICHAEL RAMOS; Sr. FELICIA SARATI; Revs. TIMOTHY STIER; PAUL VASSAR; Mr. BERNIE SUTTLE; Rev. Msgr. MARTIN WALSH.

Ethnic Pastoral Centers—Sr. FELICIA SARATI, C.S.J., Dir. Ethnic and Cultural Svcs. Div., *3014 Lakeshore Ave., Oakland, 94610.* Tel: 510-763-0301.

African American Catholic—Mr. THOMAS MCGOWAN, *3014 Lakeshore Ave., Oakland, 94610.* Tel: 510-763-0301.

Chinese Catholic—Rev. THOMAS NG, Dir., *176 Ridgeway Ave., Oakland, 94611.*

Ethnic Youth Director—ARIEL SAN PEDRO, *521 Boden Way, Oakland, 94610.* Tel: 510-763-0301.

Director of Spanish Youth—JOSE MORAN, *521 Boden Way, Oakland, 94610.* Tel: 510-763-0301.

Filipino Catholic—STANLEY LEE, Dir., *3014 Lakeshore Ave., Oakland, 94610.* Tel: 510-893-4711.

Ge'ez Community—Rev. TEKLE YOHANIS, Bay Area Reg. Dir., *600 Parker St., San Francisco, 94118.* Tel: 415-666-6420.

Hispanic Pastoral Center—MICHAEL RAMOS, Dir., *3014 Lakeshore Ave., Oakland, 94610.* Tel: 510-763-0301.

Khmmu/Laotian Catholic Community—Rev. DON MACKINNON, C.SS.R., *Holy Redeemer Center, 8945*

Golf Links Rd., P.O. Box 5007, Oakland, 94605. Tel: 510-653-6341.

Korean Catholic—Rev. JAMES SOONG, Dir., *St. Andrew Kim Catholic Pastoral Center, 6226 Camden St., Oakland, 94605.* Tel: 510-562-3843.

Polish Center—Rev. LESZEK BARTOSZEWSKI, Dir., *1631-A Monument, Concord, 94520.* Tel: 510-825-7646.

Portuguese Pastoral Center—Rev. ANTONIO DOS REIS, Dir., *997 Sueirro Dr., Hayward, 94541.* Tel: 510-887-2912.

St. Joseph's Center for Deaf and Hard of Hearing—ARDITH A. LYNCH, Dir., *3880 Smith St., Union City, 94587.* Tel: 510-489-9784 (Voice). Tel: 510-489-9786 (TTY).

Tongan Community—Sr. SOFIA LANGE, Bay Area Reg. Dir., *1515 Dolan Ave., San Mateo, 94401.* Tel: 415-342-2470.

Vietnamese Catholic—Vacant, *3014 Lakeshore Ave., Oakland, 94610.* Tel: 510-763-0311.

Bishop's Representative for Eastern Rite Catholics—Rev. DAVID LINK.

Bishop's Representative for Permanent Deacons—Deacon DAVID REZENDES.

Bishop's Representative for Catholic Charismatics—CHARLES PEISSNER.

Bishop's Representative for Italian Speaking Faithful—Rev. DANIEL E. CARDELLI.

The Roman Catholic Welfare Corporation of Oakland—*2900 Lakeshore Ave., Oakland, 94610.*

Diocesan Offices and Directors

Apostleship of the Sea—Vacant; Port Chaplain, *4001 7th St., Berth 40, Oakland, 94607.* Tel: 510-444-7885.

Archivist/Records Management—MARY C. BATIZA, *3014 Lakeshore Ave., Oakland, 94610.*

Design Review Board—Revs. GERARD MORAN, Chm. PATRICK GOODWIN; ROBERT LOUGHERY, C.S.C.; RON SCHMIDT; DAVID STAAL; LAWRENCE YOUNG; Ms. LAURA HELD; WILLIAM GILLIS, A.I.A.; DAVID MESSINGER, S.E.

Facilities & Planning Services—C. J. FINNEY, Dir. ALEX HERNANDEZ, Assoc. Dir. J. H. MCCANN, Property Mgr.

Campaign for Human Development—PAUL WOOLEY, Dir., *433 Jefferson St., Oakland, 94607.*

Catholic Charities—Mrs. BARBARA TERRAZAS, Dir., *433 Jefferson St., Oakland, 94607.* Legal Title: *Catholic Charities of the Diocese of Oakland.*

Catholic Relief Services—PAUL WOOLLEY, Dir., *433 Jefferson St., Oakland, 94607.*

Cemeteries—ANTHONY SILVA, Dir., *1965 Reliez Valley Rd., P.O. Box 488, Lafayette, 94549.*

Censor—Rev. ROBERT MCCANN.

Clergy Personnel, Office of—Rev. PAUL SCHMIDT, *3014 Lakeshore Ave., Oakland, 94610.* Tel: 510-763-0301.

Cursillo Movement—Rev. FERNANDO CORTEZ, Spiritual Dir., *5562 Clayton Rd., Concord, 94521.* Tel: 510-672-5800.

Diocesan Pastoral Council—Vacant, *2900 Lakeshore Ave., Oakland, 94610.*

Ecumenical Affairs, Office of—THOMAS R. MCGOWAN, Dir., *3014 Lakeshore Ave., Oakland, 94610.* Tel: 510-763-0301.

Special Religious Education Department (SPRED)—Sr. AURORA PEREZ, Dir., *4025 Martin Luther King, Jr. Way at 40th St., Oakland, 94609.* Tel: 510-654-2869.

Education—Mrs. ANN MEYERS MANCHESTER, Ed.D., Supt. of Schools; Ms. PENNY PENDOLA, Assoc. Supt. of Schools: Curriculum and Personnel Svcs.; Sr. BARBARA BRAY, S.N.J.M., Asst. Supt.

FACE (Family Aid Catholic Education)—A division of The Roman Catholic Welfare Corporation of Oakland, ANNE RYNDERS, Exec. Dir., *2900 Lakeshore Ave., Oakland, 94610.*

Family Life Center and Divorced & Separated Catholics—Mrs. RITA BILLECI, Dir. Family Life; JUAN AMBRIZ, Assoc. Dir. SUE MEDINA, Coord. Divorced & Separated Catholics; Respect Life, Women's Pregnancy Service and Bioethics; MONIKA RODMAN, *2350 Pacheco St., Concord, 94520.* Tel: 510-680-8510.

Hospital Ministries—Rev. JOHN RANALLO, Dir., *3014 Lakeshore Ave., Oakland, 94610.* Tel: 510-763-0301.

Legion of Mary—*2900 Lakeshore Ave., Oakland, 94610.*

Newspaper: "The Catholic Voice"—MONICA CLARK, Editor, *3014 Lakeshore Ave., Oakland, 94610.* Tel: 510-893-5339.

Department of Human Resources—Mr. WILLIAM COY, Dir., *3014 Lakeshore Ave., Oakland, 94610.* Tel: 510-763-0301.

Office for Episcopal Liturgies—Mrs. CARMEN VINELLA, Dir., *521 Boden Way, Oakland, 94610.* Tel: 510-834-7311.

Vicar for Religious—Sr. BARBARA FLANNERY, C.S.J.

Liturgical Commission—Rev. PAUL VASSAR, Contact, *2900 Lakeshore Ave., Oakland, 94610.*

Christian Initiation—MARK GONZALEZ.

Environment and Art—Revs. JOHN KASPER, Co-Chm. RON SCHMIT, Co-Chm.

Music—Vacant.

Department for Faith and Ministerial Formation (Diocesan Institute for Ministerial Leadership; Permanent Diaconate Formation Program)

Director—Rev. Msgr. THEODORE W. KRAUS, Ph.D., *521 Boden Way, Oakland, 94610.* Tel: 510-834-7311.

Associate Director for In-Service Programming—Sr. PAT CHOONG.

Associate Director for Spanish Programming—CARLOS RIVAS.

Administrative Associate for Faith Services—Mr. LUIS RIVILLA, M.Div.

Department for Youth and Young Adults

Director—Mr. WILLIAM FORD, *521 Boden Way, Oakland, 94610.* Tel: 510-893-7311.

Associate Director of CYO Athletics and Catholic Scouting—Mr. WILLIAM FORD.

Associate Director of Youth Ministry—Ms. EVELYN GONZALEZ.

Associate Director of Spanish Youth Ministry—Mr. JOSE MORAN.

Associate Director of Ethnic Youth Ministry—ARIEL SAN PEDRO.

Office of the Bishop's Representative to Deacons

Bishop's Representative—Deacon DAVID REZENDES, *521 Boden Way, Oaklands, 94610.* Tel: 510-834-7311.

Diocesan Division for Parish Life

Director—Rev. PAUL R. VASSAR, V.G., *2900 Lakeshore Ave., Oakland, 94610.* Tel: 510-983-4711.

Resource Specialists—Parish Catechetics: Mr. MARC GONZALEZ, Latino Catechetics; Ms. ALICIA RESTREPO. Renewal: Ms. NORA PETERSEN, (Parish); Mr. HECTOR MEDINA, (Latino); LINDA KREHMEIER, Liturgical Resource.

Pontifical Association of the Holy Childhood—Rev. GARY B. TOLLNER, Dir.; Sr. MARIE STAFFORD, S.H.F., Assoc. Dir., *3014 Lakeshore Ave., Oakland, 94610.*

Propagation of the Faith—Rev. GARY B. TOLLNER, Dir., *3014 Lakeshore Ave., Oakland, 94610.* Legal Title: Oakland Society for the Propagation of the Faith.

Development/Stewardship—Ms. KATHERINE KING, *2900 Lakeshore Ave., Oakland, 94610.*

St. Peter the Apostle Society—Rev. GARY B. TOLLNER, *3014 Lakeshore Ave., Oakland, 94610.*

St. Vincent de Paul Society—VAUGHN DONOHUE, Alameda County Dir., *9235 San Leandro St., Oakland, 94603.* Tel: 510-638-7600. CHAREE LORD, Contra Costa County Dir., *2210 Gladstone Dr., Pittsburg, 94565.* Tel: 510-439-5060.

Vocations, Priestly and Religious—Rev. FERNANDO CORTEZ, Dir. & Dir. for Seminarians.

Diocesan Admissions Committee for Seminarians—In process of reformation.

Women, Diocesan Council of Catholic—SHIRLEY MANNETTE.

CLERGY, PARISHES, MISSIONS AND PAROCHIAL SCHOOLS

CITY OF OAKLAND
(Alameda County)

1—CATHEDRAL OF ST. FRANCIS DE SALES (1886). Merged with St. Mary, Immaculate Conception to form St. Mary, Immaculate Conception-St. Francis de Sales.

2—ST. ANDREW-ST. JOSEPH (1965) (Latino-African American), Revs. Larry Silva; Thomas Edwards; Deacons Morris Soublet; Leo Edgerly; Eugene Stelly. In res., Rev. Ernest Brainard.
Res., 925 Brockhurst St., 94608. Tel: 510-653-7411; Fax: 510-652-5839.
Schools—St. Martin De Porres School (Deanery School).; St. Patrick Campus, (Grades 6-8). Tel: 510-832-1757.; Sacred Heart Campus, (Grades K-5). Tel: 510-652-2220; St. Columba Campus, (Grades PreK-K). (future site), Tel: 510-652-2956.

3—ST. ANTHONY'S (1871), Rev. Thuong Hoai Nguyen; Deacon Arcadio Torres. In res., Revs. Prisco Cajes; Jeff Acebo; Fernando Cortez.
Res., 1535 16th Ave., 94606. Tel: 510-534-2117; Fax: 510-534-2119.
School—Tel: 510-534-3334.
Lay Teachers 9; Students 203.
Catechesis/Religious Programs—Tel: 510-534-4420.
Students 203.

4—ST. AUGUSTINE'S (1907), William Johnson, Admin.
Res., 400 Alcatraz Ave., 94609. Tel: 510-653-8631; Fax: 510-652-4219.
School—410 Alcatraz Ave., 94609. Tel: 510-652-6727.
Sisters 2; Lay Teachers 10; Students 273.

5—ST. BENEDICT (1930), Rev. James Matthews; Deacon John Gilbert. In res., Rev. Cuthbert Aronyu (Uganda).
Res., 2245 82nd Ave., 94605. Tel: 510-632-1847; Fax: 510-633-2092.
School—Tel: 510-562-7015.
Lay Teachers 6; Students 183.

6—ST. BERNARD'S (1912) (Hispanic-African American), Rev. Joseph Scott, S.V.D.; Deacon Javier Fuentes. In res., Rev. Stephen Ernest, S.V.D.
Res., 1620-62nd Ave., 94621. Tel: 510-632-3013; Fax: 510-633-1714.
School—1630-62nd Ave., 94621. Tel: 510-632-6323.
Lay Teachers 8; Students 192.
Catechesis/Religious Programs—Students 240.

7—ST. COLUMBA'S (1898), Rev. Mario L. Borges, Admin.
Res., 6401 San Pablo Ave., 94608. Tel: 510-654-7600; Fax: 510-654-7615.
School—Tel: 510-652-2956.
Lay Teachers 12; Students 300.

8—ST. CYRIL (1926) (Korean-Vietnamese), Rev. John Fernandes, Parochial Admin. In res., Revs. Javier F. Kutsche; James Song (Korea) Korean Pastoral Center; Anthony Phan Lam; Robert Ponciroli.
Res., 6226 Camden St., 94605. Tel: 510-638-1447; Fax: 510-638-5244.
School—3200 Second Ave., 94605. Tel: 510-638-9445; Fax: 510-638-0744.
Lay Teachers 10; Students 182.

9—ST. ELIZABETH'S (1892), Revs. Ignatius DeGroot, O.F.M.; Pedro Umana, O.F.M.; Peter Krieg, O.F.M.; Deacons Arcadio Torres; Noe Gonzalez. In res., Rev. Gordon Urbine, O.F.M.
Res., 1500 34th Ave., 94601. Tel: 510-536-1266; Fax: 510-536-8560.
School—Tel: 510-532-7392; Fax: 510-532-0321.
Sisters 2; Lay Teachers 16; Students 484.
Catechesis/Religious Programs—Tel: 510-532-3766.
Students 713.
Mission—Oakland, Alameda Co., Mary Help of Christians, 2611 E. 9th St., 94601. Tel: 510-534-3501; Fax: 510-436-5157.

10—ST. JARLATH'S (1910), Revs. Raymond G. Breton; Denis A. Des Rosiers. In res., Rev. Robert A. Mathews.
Res., 2620 Pleasant St., 94602. Tel: 510-532-2068; Fax: 510-532-3745.
School—2634 Pleasant St., 94602. Tel: 510-532-4387.
Lay Teachers 9; Students 275.

11—ST. LAWRENCE O'TOOLE (1916), Rev. Robert W. Charm. In res., Rev. Robert E. Freitas.
Res., 3725 High St., 94619. Tel: 510-530-0761; Fax: 510-530-0974.
School—Tel: 510-530-0266; Fax: 510-530-7568.
Lay Teachers 14; Students 279; Extended care: Director 1; Assistants 6.

12—ST. LEO'S (1911), Rev. Timothy K. Johnson. In res., Rev. Thomas Ng.
Res., 176 Ridgeway Ave., 94611-5122. Tel: 510-654-6177; Fax: 510-654-4203.
School—Tel: 510-654-7828; Fax: 510-654-4057.
Lay Teachers 10; Students 251.

13—ST. LOUIS BERTRAND (1908) (Hispanic-African American), Rev. Edgar Haasl.
Res., 1410-100th Ave., 94603. Tel: 510-568-1080; Fax: 510-635-8618.
School—1445-101st Ave., 94603. Tel: 510-568-1067.
Lay Teachers 9; Students 275.
Catechesis/Religious Programs—Students 870.

14—ST. MARGARET MARY (1922), Revs. George D. Sullivan (STO) Admin.; Paul J. Schmidt.
Res., 1219 Excelsior Ave., 94610. Tel: 510-482-0596.

15—MARY HELP OF CHRISTIANS MISSION (1915), Sr. Cecilia Calva, Pastoral Admin.
Res., 2611 E. Ninth St., 94601. Tel: 510-534-3501; Fax: 510-436-5157.

16—ST. MARY, IMMACULATE CONCEPTION. Merged with St. Francis de Sales to form St. Mary, Immaculate Conception-St. Francis de Sales.

17—ST. MARY, IMMACULATE CONCEPTION-ST. FRANCIS DE SALES (1993), Revs. James T. Keeley; Peter McGrath, S.J. In res., Rev. Joseph Carroll, S.J.
Res. & Office: St. Francis de Sales Rectory: 634 21st St., 94612. Tel: 510-832-5057; Fax: 510-832-0212.
Catechesis/Religious Programs—Students 150.

18—OUR LADY OF LOURDES (1921), Rev. Seamus D.

Genovese; Sr. Mary Gallagher, S.H.J.M.
Res., 2808 Lakeshore Ave., 94610. Tel: 510-451-1790; Fax: 510-832-3776. [CEM]

19—ST. PASCHAL BAYLON (1955), Rev. Robert K. Rien.
Res., 3700 Dorisa Ave., 94605. Tel: 510-636-0335; Fax: 510-636-0287.
School—Tel: 510-635-7922; Fax: 510-635-4219.
Lay Teachers 10; Students 170.

20—ST. PATRICK'S (1879) (African American-Hispanic), Rev. Charles D. Burns, S.V.D.; Deacons James Barnes, Sr.; Gaston Duhe.
Res., 1023 Peralta St., 94607. Tel: 510-444-1081; Fax: 510-444-1113.
School—St. Martin De Porres, 1630 Tenth St., 94607. Tel: 510-832-1757; Fax: 510-832-6481. Mr. Rhuepell Stroud, Jr., Prin.; Robert Ratto, Co-Prin.
Lay Teachers 4; Students 75.

21—SACRED HEART (1876), Rev. Jose R. Arong, O.M.I.
Res., 4025 Martin Luther King Way, 94609. Tel: 510-655-9209; Fax: 510-652-1958.
School—St. Martin De Porres, 664 41st St., 94609. Tel: 510-652-2220. Mr. Robert Ratto, Prin.
Lay Teachers 7; Students 197.
Catechesis/Religious Programs—Special Religious Education Department. (SPRED). Tel: 510-654-2869; Fax: 510-654-3067. Sr. Aurora Perez, S.H.F., D.R.E.
Students 16.

22—ST. THERESA OF THE INFANT JESUS (THE LITTLE FLOWER) (1925), Rev. Msgr. Bernard J. Moran; Rev. William Kegel, S.J.
Res., 30 Mandalay Rd., 94618. Tel: 510-547-2777; Fax: 510-653-3575.
School—Tel: 510-547-3146; Fax: 510-547-3253.
Lay Teachers 14; Students 278.
Catechesis/Religious Programs—Students 135.

OUTSIDE THE CITY OF OAKLAND

Alameda, Alameda Co.,

1—ST. ALBERT, (1976). Unassigned.
Res., 1022 Holly St., 94502. Tel: 510-522-2185; Fax: 510-522-1055.

2—ST. BARNABAS, (1925), Rev. Jeffrey R. Keyes, C.PP.S.; Deacon Timothy Erwin. In res.,
Res., 1427 Sixth St., 94501. Tel: 510-522-8933; Fax: 510-522-8380.
School—Tel: 510-521-0595; Fax: 510-521-3560.
Lay Teachers 11; Students 199.

3—ST. JOSEPH BASILICA, (1885), Revs. Jeremiah Holland, SS.CC.; Francis Doherty, SS.CC.; Patrick J. Crowley, SS.CC.
Res., 1109 Chestnut St., 94501. Tel: 510-522-0181; Fax: 510-522-2864.
School—St. Joseph Elementary School, Tel: 510-522-4457; Fax: 510-522-2890.
Sisters 1; Lay Teachers 15; Students 309.
High School—See separate category under High Schools, Parochial. Tel: 510-523-1526; Fax: 510-523-2181.
Catechesis/Religious Programs—Tel: 510-522-0445. D.R.E.: Charles Sevin; Steve Mullin.
Students 823.

4—ST. PHILIP NERI, (1925), Revs. Jerrold F. Kennedy; Michael Lacey, M.S.C.
Res., 3108 Van Buren St., 94501. Tel: 510-522-2299; Fax: 510-522-1625.
School—1335 High St., 94501. Tel: 510-521-0787; Fax: 510-521-2418.
Lay Teachers 16; Students 286.

Antioch, Contra Costa Co., Holy Rosary (1874), Revs. Francisco Vicente; Mark C. Padrez, O.P.; Bro. Joseph Sergott, O.P.; Mrs. Jackie Hooke, Pastoral Assoc.
Res., 1313 A St., 94509. Tel: 510-757-4020; Fax: 510-757-6828. [CEM][JC]
School—Tel: 510-757-1270; Fax: 510-757-9309.
Lay Teachers 24; Students 457.
Catechesis/Religious Programs—21 E. 15th St., 94059. Tel: 510-757-9515.
Students 700.

St. Ignatius (1979), Revs. Vince Cotter; Leo Edgerly, Jr.; Deacon Al Fleischer.
Res., 209 Tanganyika Ct., 94509. Tel: 510-778-0768; Fax: 510-778-0845. [CEM]
Catechesis/Religious Programs—3351 Contra Loma Blvd., 94509. Tel: 510-778-1314.
Students 365.

Berkeley, Alameda Co.,

1—ST. AMBROSE, (1909), Rev. Thomas J. Ryan.
Res., 1145 Gilman St., 94706. Tel: 510-525-2620; Fax: 510-525-5399.

2—HOLY SPIRIT PARISH, (1967). (U.C. Newman Hall). Revs. Michael B. McGarry, C.S.P.; Frank Sabatte, C.S.P.; Albert Moser, C.S.P.
Res., 2700 Dwight Way, 94704-3113. Tel: 510-848-7812; Fax: 510-848-0179. [CEM]
Catechesis/Religious Programs—Students 156.

3—ST. JOSEPH THE WORKER, (1879), Revs. William J. O'Donnell; George E. Crespin. In res., Revs. Thomas Martin (Australia); Thomas J. McElligott (SFR).
Res., 1640 Addison St., 94703. Tel: 510-843-2244; Fax: 510-843-2730.
School—2125 Jefferson St., 94703. Tel: 510-845-6266.
Sisters 1; Lay Teachers 9; Students 193.

4—ST. MARY MAGDALEN, (1923), Rev. George Matanic, O.P. In res., Revs. Victor Cavalli, O.P.; Bruno Gibson, O.P.; David O'Rourke, O.P.
Res., 2005 Berryman St., 94709. Tel: 510-526-4811; Fax: 510-525-3638.
School—School of the Madeleine, 1225 Milvia St., 94709. Tel: 510-526-4744; Fax: 510-526-5152.
Lay Teachers 21; Students 315.

Brentwood, Contra Costa Co., Immaculate Heart of Mary (1949), Rev. John G. Garcia; Deacon Frank Bustos.
Res., 813 First St., 94513. Tel: 510-634-4154; Fax: 510-516-9340.
Catechesis/Religious Programs—Students 265.

Byron, Contra Costa Co., St. Anne (1917), Rev. Ronald G. Schmit.
Res., 5604 Schooner Loop, Discovery Bay, 54514. Tel: 510-634-6625; Fax: 510-634-4194.

Castro Valley, Alameda Co., Our Lady of Grace (1947), Revs. Robert W. Gavotto, O.S.A.; Thomas W. Behan, O.S.A.; Paul Quante, O.S.A.; Deacon Robert Dowling.
Res., 3433 Somerset Ave., 94546-3398. Tel: 510-537-0806; Fax: 510-537-6281.
School—19950 Anita Ave., 94546-3398. Tel: 510-581-3155; Fax: 510-581-1059.
Lay Teachers 15; Students 304.
Catechesis/Religious Programs—Tel: 510-538-3464; 582-9266; 889-7017; Fax: 510-537-6281.
Students 374.

Transfiguration (1961), Rev. John C. Crumlish; Deacons Timothy L. Moore; Burt Rigley. In res., Rev. John E. Ranallo.
Res., 4000 E. Castro Valley Blvd., 94552. Tel: 510-538-7941; Fax: 510-538-7983.
Catechesis/Religious Programs—Tel: 510-537-1502.
Students 370.

Concord, Contra Costa Co.,

1—ST. AGNES, (1964), Revs. George E. Mockel; Donald Crosby, S.J.
Res., 3966 Chestnut Ave., 94519. Tel: 510-689-0838; Fax: 510-689-7899.
School—3886 Chestnut Ave., 94519. Tel: 510-689-3990; Fax: 510-689-3455.
Lay Teachers 15; Students 342.
Catechesis/Religious Programs—Tel: 510-689-3757.
Students 384.

2—ST. BONAVENTURE, (1957), Revs. Richard A. Mangini; Walter Borkowski.
Res., 5562 Clayton Rd., 94521. Tel: 510-672-5800; Fax: 510-672-4606.
Catechesis/Religious Programs—Tel: 510-672-5500.
Students 652.

3—ST. FRANCIS OF ASSISI, (1984). (Formerly Most Precious Blood, 1955). Revs. William V. Macchi; (Eugene) Thomas P. Bonacci; Deacons William E. Bothe; Charles Palomares. In res., Rev. Msgr. Edward T. Varni, Pastor Emeritus.
Res., 860 Oak Grove Rd., 94518. Tel: 510-682-5447; Fax: 510-682-5491.
School—866 Oak Grove Rd., 94518. Tel: 510-682-5414; Fax: 510-682-5480.
Sisters 2; Lay Teachers 17; Students 338.
Catechesis/Religious Programs—Tel: 510-682-5422.
Students 248.

4—QUEEN OF ALL SAINTS, (1923), Revs. Michael Cunningham; Joseph Welch. Pastoral Assocs.: EllenDianne L. Midgley; Deacons George Peters; Robert Karp.
Res., 2390 Grant St., 94520. Tel: 510-825-0350; Fax: 510-825-6975. [CEM]
School—2391 Grant St., 94520. Tel: 510-685-8700; Fax: 510-685-2034.
Lay Teachers 13; Students 267.
Catechesis/Religious Programs—Tel: 510-685-5852.
Students 220.

Crockett, Contra Costa Co., St. Rose of Lima (1912), Rev. Ciarian Dillon, O.M.I.
Res., 555 Third Ave., 94525. Tel: 510-787-2052; Fax: 510-787-2163.
Mission—Port Costa, Contra Costa Co., St. Patrick, c/o St. Rose, Port Costa, 94569.

Danville, Contra Costa Co., St. Isidore's (1910), Revs. Daniel E. Cardelli; Terry Tompkins. In res., Revs. James E. Driscoll, (Retired); Frank L. Colacicco (SAN).
Res., 445 LaGonda Way, 94526-2522. Tel: 510-837-2122; Fax: 510-837-3954.
School—Tel: 510-837-2977; Fax: 510-837-2407.
Lay Teachers 19; Students 444.
Catechesis/Religious Programs—Tel: 510-837-1306.
Students 625.

Dublin, Alameda Co., St. Raymond (1961), Revs. Patrick A. Goodwin; Joseph Duong Phan; John Blaker.
Res., 11555 Shannon Ave., 94568. Tel: 510-828-2460.
School—Tel: 510-828-4064.
Sisters 2; Lay Teachers 14; Students 288.

El Cerrito, Contra Costa Co., St. Jerome's (1941), Rev. E. Donald Osuna.
Res., 308 Carmel Ave., 94530. Tel: 510-525-0876; Fax: 510-526-2721.
School—310 San Carlos, 94530. Tel: 510-525-9484; Fax: 510-525-5227.
Sisters of the Sacred Hearts of Jesus and Mary 1; Lay Teachers 15; Students 325.

St. John the Baptist (1925), Revs. John Maxwell; Leo Asuncion; Raymond Ogbemure; Deacons Thomas McGowan; Thomas McGowan.
Res., 11150 San Pablo Ave., 94530. Tel: 510-232-5659; Fax: 510-236-0960.
School—Tel: 510-234-2244.
Sisters of Mercy (Ireland) 2; Lay Teachers 9; Students 314.
Catechesis/Religious Programs—Students 144.

El Sobrante, Contra Costa Co., St. Callistus (1952), Rev. Richard Gagliardi.
Res., 3580 San Pablo Dam Rd., 94803. Tel: 510-223-1153; Fax: 510-223-1137.
Catechesis/Religious Programs—Tel: 510-222-0432.
Students 100.

Fremont, Alameda Co.,

1—CORPUS CHRISTI, (1914), Rev. Timothy Stier; Deacons Charles Marchese; Luis Trucios.
Res., 37891 Second St., 94536. Tel: 510-790-3207; Fax: 510-790-3227. [CEM]
Catechesis/Religious Programs—Tel: 510-790-3226.
Students 350.

2—HOLY SPIRIT, (1886), Revs. Gerard K. Moran; Declan Deane; Helmut Richter; Deacons Rudolph Brazil; William Drobick; Richard Yee.
Res., 37588 Fremont Blvd., 94536. Tel: 510-797-1660; Fax: 510-797-7080. [CEM]
School—Tel: 510-793-3553.
Lay Teachers 12; Students 330.
Catechesis/Religious Programs—Tel: 510-797-5395.
Students 785.

3—ST. JAMES THE APOSTLE, (1972), Revs. Paul E. Cleu, Admin.; John W. Morgan, Pastor Emeritus.
Res., P.O. Box 7084, 94537. Tel: 510-792-1962.

4—ST. JOSEPH MISSION CHURCH, (1797), Rev. Msgr. Manuel C. Simas; Rev. Jayson J. Landeza.
Res., P.O. Box 3276, Mission San Jose, 94539. Tel: 510-656-2364; Fax: 510-656-2438. [CEM]
School—43222 Mission Blvd., 94539. Tel: 510-656-6525; Fax: 510-656-3608.
Dominican Sisters of San Jose 3; Lay Teachers 10; Students 279.
Catechesis/Religious Programs—Tel: 510-657-0905; Fax: 510-657-4165.
Students 455.

5—ST. LEONARD, (1959), Rev. Joseph Cantillon. In res., Rev. Gerard Beigel.
Res., 3600 St. Leonard's Way, 94538. Tel: 510-656-4921; Fax: 510-226-0714.
School—3635 St. Leonard's Way, 94538. Tel: 510-657-1674; Fax: 510-657-3659.
Sisters 2; Lay Teachers 8; Students 270.
Catechesis/Religious Programs—Tel: 510-651-4966.
Students 275.

6—SANTA PAULA, (1965), Rev. James Cummings; Deacons Ovide Guesnon; Bill Martinez.
Res., 4358 Bora Bora Ave., 94538. Tel: 510-657-4043; 657-4040; Fax: 510-657-4055.
Catechesis/Religious Programs—Tel: 510-657-3777.
Students 228.

Hayward, Alameda Co.,

1—ALL SAINTS, (1898), Revs. Robert J. McCann; Mark Wiesner; Emmanuel H. Gardon, C.P.; Deacon Nelson Gonsalves. In res., Rev. Peter Conaty, C.S.Sp. (Ireland).
Church—22824 Second St., 94541. Tel: 510-581-2570; Fax: 510-581-9538. [CEM]
School—Tel: 510-582-1910; Fax: 510-582-0866.
Lay Teachers 14; Students 307.
Catechesis/Religious Programs—Tel: 510-538-2711.
Students 330.

2—St. Bede, (1955), Revs. Seamus J. Farrell; Marciano Santiago, II (Philippines); Jose de Jesus Nieto-Ruiz; Rev. Msgr. George J. Francis, Pastor Emeritus; Sr. GuadaLupe Jurado, O.P., Pastoral Assoc.
Res., 26950 Patrick Ave., 94544. Tel: 510-782-2171; Fax: 510-782-9712.
School—26910 Patrick Ave., 94544. Tel: 510-782-3444.
Lay Teachers 19; Students 309.
Catechesis/Religious Programs—Tel: 510-782-4292.
Students 500.

3—St. Clement, (1951), Revs. James C. Buckley, C.S.C.; Thomas McNally, C.S.C.; Deacon Paul Frumkin. In res., Rev. Robert Loughery, C.S.C.
Res., 738 Calhoun St., 94544. Tel: 510-582-7282; 582-7240; Fax: 510-582-1875.
School—790 Calhoun St., 94544. Tel: 510-538-5885; Fax: 510-538-1693. Mrs. Joan Burman, Prin.
Lay Teachers 9; Students 309.
Catechesis/Religious Programs—Students 345.

4—St. Joachim, (1951), Revs. Ray Zielezienski; Sergio Mora.
Res., 21250 Hesperian Blvd., 94541. Tel: 510-783-2766; Fax: 510-783-2760.
School—Tel: 510-783-3177; Fax: 510-783-2161.
Lay Teachers 13; Students 311.
Catechesis/Religious Programs—Tel: 510-785-1818.
Students 311.

Lafayette, Contra Costa Co., St. Perpetua (1952), Rev. Harry B. Morrison, Admin. In res., Rev. Francis J. Houdek, S.J.
Res., 3454 Hamlin Rd., 94549. Tel: 510-283-0272; Fax: 510-283-6534.
School—Tel: 510-284-1640; Fax: 510-284-5676.
Lay Teachers 14; Students 260.
Catechesis/Religious Programs—Students 302.

Livermore, Alameda Co., St. Charles Borromeo (1964), Rev. Richard McCafferty, S.J.
Res., 1315 Lomitas Ave., 94550. Tel: 510-447-4549; Fax: 510-373-7088. [JC]
Catechesis/Religious Programs—Tel: 510-449-0133.
Students 310.

St. Michael's (1878), Revs. Michael Joyce; Stephan Kappler; David E. Staal; Deacons David Rezendez; Ross Hoblitzell; Bill Archer. In res., Revs. Augustine Koilparampil (India); Walter W. Mayer.
Res., 458 Maple St., 94550. Tel: 510-447-1585; Fax: 510-447-0520. [CEM]
School—Tel: 510-447-1888; Fax: 510-447-6720.
Sisters 1; Lay Teachers 14; Students 342.
Catechesis/Religious Programs—Tel: 510-447-8814.
Students 394.

Martinez, Contra Costa Co., St. Catherine of Siena (1873), Revs. Vincent R. Brylka; Carl H. Seewald, S.V.D.
Res., 1100 Estudillo St., 94553. Tel: 510-228-2230; Fax: 510-228-1318. [CEM]
School—Tel: 510-228-4140; Fax: 510-228-0697. Mr. Mark DeMarco, Prin.
Lay Teachers 10; Students 258.
Catechesis/Religious Programs—1125 Ferry St., 94553. Tel: 510-228-5087.
Students 210.

Moraga, Contra Costa Co., St. Monica (1965), Mrs. Cath McGhee, Admin.; Deacon Jack Jordan. In res., Rev. Thomas M. Mulvanerty (NY).
Res., 1001 Camino Pablo, P.O. Box 128, 94556. Tel: 510-376-6900; Fax: 510-376-9796.
Catechesis/Religious Programs—Tel: 510-376-0500.
Students 622.

Newark, Alameda Co., St. Edward's (1920), Revs. Ronald P. Wiecek, C.PP.S.; Jeff Finley, C.PP.S.; Gene Wilson, C.PP.S.; Deacons Ernest Perez; Nick Bruckner; Roger Wedl; Antonio Barreto.
Res., 5788 Thornton Ave., 94560. Tel: 510-797-0241; Fax: 510-797-4557.
School—P.O. Box 245, 94560. Tel: 510-793-7242.
Sisters 2; Lay Teachers 10; Students 312.
Catechesis/Religious Programs—Tel: 510-797-5588.
Students 1,265.

Oakley, Contra Costa Co., St. Anthony (1925), Rev. Bernardino Andrade; Deacons Joseph Tovar; Alan Layden.
Res., 971 O'Hara Ave., 94561. Tel: 510-625-2048; Fax: 510-625-4433. [JC]
Catechesis/Religious Programs—Tel: 510-625-2077.
Students 314.

Orinda, Contra Costa Co., Santa Maria (1947), Revs. J. Roger Lucey, S.J.; Paul B. Steinmetz, S.J. In res., Rev. Msgr. William J. Mullen, (Retired).
Res., 20 Santa Maria Way, 94563. Tel: 510-254-2426; Fax: 510-254-2468.
Catechesis/Religious Programs—Tel: 510-254-0554. D.R.E.: Dorothy Harrington, (Children); Dianna Rees, (Youth-CLW).
Students 258.

Piedmont, Alameda Co., Corpus Christi (1929), Revs. Albano Oliveira; John Kasper, O.S.F.S. In res., Rev. Basil DePinto.
Res., 322 St. James Dr., 94611. Tel: 510-530-4343; Fax: 510-530-6824.
School—1 Estates Dr., 94611. Tel: 510-530-4056; Fax: 510-530-5926.
Lay Teachers 14; Students 285.
Catechesis/Religious Programs—Students 214.

Pinole, Contra Costa Co., St. Joseph's (1947), Revs. P. Michael Galvan; Quang Minh Dong; Ramiro Flores; Deacon Benjamin P. Agustin. In res., Rev. Thomas Kalapurackal, S.D.B. (India).
Parish Center/Office/Mailing Address: 2100 Pear St., 94564.
Church—837 Tennent Ave., 94564. Tel: 510-741-4900; Fax: 510-724-9185.
School—Tel: 510-724-0242.
Lay Teachers 20; Students 315.
Catechesis/Religious Programs—Tel: 510-741-4912; 4913.
Students 658.

Pittsburg, Contra Costa Co., Good Shepherd (1965), Revs. Larry Young; Louis Dabovich, Pastor Emeritus; Deacon Ferris J. Anthony.
Res., 3200 Harbor St., 94565. Tel: 510-432-6404; Fax: 510-432-6748.
Catechesis/Religious Programs—Tel: 510-439-1091.
Students 600.

Our Lady Queen of the World (1962), Revs. Theo Palis, Pastor Emeritus; Richard Culver, Admin.; Thomas Duong Binh Minh.
Res., 3155 Winterbrook Dr., 94565. Tel: 510-458-4718; Fax: 510-458-3161.
Catechesis/Religious Programs—Tel: 510-458-4574.
Students 310.

St. Peter Martyr of Verona (1914), Rev. Dana Michaels.
Res., 740 Black Diamond St., 94565. Tel: 510-432-4771; Fax: 510-432-3389.
School—Tel: 510-439-1014; Fax: 510-439-1506.
Lay Teachers 10; Students 274.
Catechesis/Religious Programs—Tel: 510-432-7200.
Students 364.

Pleasant Hill, Contra Costa Co., Christ the King (1951), Rev. Msgr. James J. Wade, Pastor Emeritus; Revs. Brian T. Joyce; Robert P. Kubisiak; Jim McGee, S.S.; Margo Schorno, Pastoral Assoc.
Res., 199 Brandon Rd., 94523. Tel: 510-682-2486; Fax: 510-682-5021.
School—Tel: 510-685-1109. Sr. Timothy Anne Daly, C.S.J., Prin.
Sisters of St. Joseph of Carondelet 4; Lay Teachers 13; Students 335.
Catechesis/Religious Programs—Tel: 510-686-1017.
Students 551.

Pleasanton, Alameda Co., St. Augustine (1901), Revs. Daniel E. Danielson; James Pickett; Paul D. Minnihan; Deacons Richard Martin; Thomas Perry; James Campbell; Ernest Freeman; Edward Quigley. In res., Rev. Anthony W. Herrera.
Res., 3999 Bernal Ave., P.O. Box 817, 94566. Tel: 510-846-4489; Fax: 510-426-0586. [CEM]
Catechesis/Religious Programs—Tel: 510-846-3531.
Students 1,511.
Mission—Pleasanton, Alameda Co., St. Elizabeth Seton, (1991) 4001 Stoneridge Dr., 94566. Tel: 510-484-5020.

Point Richmond, Contra Costa Co., Our Lady of Mercy (1902), Rev. James C. Clift.
Res., 301 W. Richmond Ave., 94801. Tel: 510-232-1843; Fax: 510-232-1805.

Richmond, Contra Costa Co., St. Cornelius (1952), Revs. Antonio A. Valdivia; Pascual Remirez; Deacon Juan Beltran.
Res., 225-28th St., 94804. Tel: 510-233-5215; Fax: 510-233-7342. [CEM]
School—201-28th St., 94805. Tel: 510-232-3326; Fax: 510-232-4071.
Lay Teachers 11; Students 235.
Catechesis/Religious Programs—Students 220.

St. David of Wales (1952), Rev. Ronald E. Atwood.
Res., 5641 Esmond Ave., 94805. Tel: 510-237-1531.
School—871 Sonoma St., 94805. Tel: 510-232-2283; Fax: 510-231-0484. Mrs. Barbara Kringle, Prin.
Lay Teachers 15; Students 336.
Catechesis/Religious Programs—5418 Esmond Ave., 94805. Tel: 510-236-6690.
Students 336.

St. Mark's (1912), Rev. Antonio A. Valdivia, Admin.
Res., 159 Harbour Way, 94801. Tel: 510-234-5886; Fax: 510-236-5711.

Rodeo, Contra Costa Co., St. Patrick's (1923), Revs. Melvin J. Hary; Thomas Kalapurackal.
Res., 825 Seventh St., 94572. Tel: 510-799-4406; Fax: 510-799-5681.
School—907 Seventh St., 94572. Tel: 510-799-2506; Fax: 510-799-6781.
Sisters of the Immaculate Heart of Mary 2; Lay Teachers 12; Students 285.

San Leandro, Alameda Co.,

1—Assumption of the Blessed Virgin Mary, (1951), Rev. Msgr. Michael Lucid; Rev. Joseph Duong Phan. In res., Rev. Michael Norkett.
Res., 1100 Fulton Ave., 94577. Tel: 510-352-1537; Fax: 510-352-9155.
School—Tel: 510-357-8772; Fax: 510-357-7018.
Lay Teachers 13; Students 296.

2—St. Alphonsus Liguori, (1955), Rev. Joseph A. Ferreira.
Res., 2085 Miramar Ave., 94578. Tel: 510-276-3907.

3—St. Felicitas, (1952), Rev. Wayne Campbell; Deacon Jose Prado. In res., Revs. Tran Thuc Dinh (Vietnam) (Retired); Leszek Bartoszewski (Poland).
Res., 1604 Manor Blvd., 94579. Tel: 510-351-5244; Fax: 510-351-5730.
School—1650 Manor Blvd., 94579. Tel: 510-357-2530; Fax: 510-357-5358.
Sisters of St. Joseph of Wichita 1; Lay Teachers 10; Students 300.
Catechesis/Religious Programs—Tel: 510-483-4880.
Students 235.

4—St. Leander, (1864), Revs. John Prochaska; Thomas Lester; Deacons Dennis Davis; Victor Silveira; Antonio Baptista; Frank Beville. In res., Revs. Matthew R.D. Regan; Antonio Reis.
Office: 474 W. Estudillo Ave., 94577. Tel: 510-895-5631; Fax: 510-352-3578.
School—Tel: 510-351-4144; Fax: 510-483-6060.
Sisters 1; Lay Teachers 9; Students 291.
Catechesis/Religious Programs—Students 288.

5—Our Lady of Good Counsel, (1966), Rev. Alexander N. Snyder.
Res., 14112 Azores Pl., 94577. Tel: 510-483-6731; Fax: 510-483-7705.

San Lorenzo, Alameda Co., St. John the Baptist (1925), Revs. William J. Dunn; David Link; Deacon Leonard J. Bettencourt; Rev. Patrick J. Bishop, S.M.
Res., 264 E. Lewelling Blvd., 94580. Tel: 510-351-5050; Fax: 510-481-1128.
School—Tel: 510-276-6632; Fax: 510-276-5645. Sr. Joan Mulvihill, P.B.V.M., Prin.
Sisters 2; Lay Teachers 10; Students 304.
Catechesis/Religious Programs—Tel: 510-278-5080.
Students 226.

San Pablo, St. Paul (1864), Revs. Juniper Schneider, O.F.M.Conv.; Ignatius Hinkle, O.F.M.Conv.; Paul Fazio, O.F.M.Conv.; Deacons Ysidro Madrigal; Isidoro R. Flores; Donaciano Perez.
Res., 1845 Church Ln., 94806. Tel: 510-232-5931; Fax: 510-232-1846.
School—Tel: 510-233-3080; Fax: 510-231-8777.
Lay Teachers 12; Students 308.
Catechesis/Religious Programs—1825 Church Ln., 94806.
Students 500.

San Ramon, Contra Costa Co., St. Joan of Arc (1979), Revs. Fred A. Riccio; Herman M. Leong.
Res., 2601 San Ramon Valley Blvd., 94583. Tel: 510-830-0600; Fax: 510-830-5059.
Catechesis/Religious Programs—Tel: 510-830-4710.
Students 1,350.

Union City, Alameda Co., Our Lady of the Rosary (1951), Rev. Jose M. Leon; Deacons Federico Ceja, (Retired); Richard L. Folger; Gustaaf Roemers. In res., Rev. Roy Eco (Philippines).
Res., 703 C St., 94587. Tel: 510-471-2609; Fax: 510-471-4601.
School—Tel: 510-471-3765.
Lay Teachers 7; Students 159.
Catechesis/Religious Programs—Tel: 510-471-7419.
Students 390.

St. Anne (1973), Revs. Ramon J. Gomez; Louis Shen, S.J.
Res., 32223 Cabello St., P.O. Box 292, 94587. Tel: 510-471-7766; Fax: 510-487-6540.
Catechesis/Religious Programs—Tel: 510-489-2080.
Students 865.

Walnut Creek, Contra Costa Co.,

1—St. Anne, (1965), Rev. Msgr. John T. McCracken; Sr. Ruth Anne Saunders, C.S.J., Pastoral Assoc.; Rev. Anthony S. Hannick (YAK).
Res., 1600 Rossmoor Pkwy., 94595-2507. Tel: 510-932-2324; Fax: 510-932-4628.

2—St. John Vianney, (1965), Revs. Vincent J. Scott; Christopher Berbena.
Res., 1650 Ygnacio Valley Rd., 94598. Tel: 510-939-7911; Fax: 510-939-0450.

Catechesis/Religious Programs—Tel: 510-939-9544.
Students 339.

3—ST. MARY'S, (1941), Revs. John J. Mallon; John R. Kenny; George Alengadan; George Palamattathil. In res., Rev. Peter Charankat (India).
Res., 1201 Alpine Rd., 94596. Tel: 510-934-2544; Fax: 510-934-1358.
School—Tel: 510-935-5054; Fax: 510-935-5063. Mrs. Barbara McCallough, Prin.
Lay Teachers 13; Students 282.
Catechesis/Religious Programs—2039 Mt. Diablo Blvd., 94596. Tel: 510-937-2414; Fax: 510-937-6487.
Students 225.

4—ST. STEPHEN, (1966), Revs. Brian Timoney; Harry B. Morrison.
Res., 525 Madonna Ln., 94596. Tel: 510-939-3826; Fax: 510-988-0417.

Chaplains of Public Institutions

Hospitals

OAKLAND. *Children's Hospital.* Sr. Bernice Gotelli, P.B.V.M. Tel: 510-428-3325; 428-3000.
Highland Hospital. Sr. Maura O'Connor, S.N.J.M. Tel: 510-437-4800.
Kaiser-Permanente Medical Center. Tel: 510-428-5000. Rev. Basil DePinto; Mrs. Jodi Henrekin Tel: 510-596-1000.
Summit Medical Center, Pastoral Care. Attended by Sacred Heart Parish. Tel: 510-835-4500.

ANTIOCH. *Delta Memorial Hospital.* Attended by Holy Rosary Parish.

BERKELEY. *Alta Bates Hospital.* Sr. Kathleen Corbett, C.S.J. Tel: 510-204-4444.
Alta Bates-Herrick Hospital. Attended by St. Joseph the Worker Parish, Berkeley.

CASTRO VALLEY. *Eden Hospital.* Rev. John Ranallo, O.S.A. Tel: 510-537-1234.

CONCORD. *Mount Diablo Hospital, Pastoral Care.* Attended by Queen of All Saints Church. Tel: 510-682-8200.

FREMONT. *Washington Hospital.* Rev. Richard Peiris Tel: 510-505-0599; 797-1111; Sr. Jeanne Sullivan, S.N.D. Tel: 510-797-1111; Rev. Jeffrey Finley, C.PP.S. Tel: 510-797-1111.

HAYWARD. *Kaiser-Permanente Medical Center.* Attended by St. Bede Parish.

LIVERMORE. *Veterans Administration Hospital.* Rev. Augustine Koilparampil. Tel: 510-447-2560; 447-1585.

MARTINEZ. *Contra Costa Hospital.* Attended by St. Catherine of Siena Parish.
Kaiser-Permanente Medical Center. Sr. Moira MacPherson. Tel: 510-372-1000.

PINOLE. *Doctor's Hospital.* Attended by St. Joseph Parish, Pinole.

PITTSBURG. *Los Medanos Hospital.* Attended by Good Shepherd Parish.

RICHMOND. *East Bay Hospital.* Attended by St. Cornelius Parish & St. Mark Parish.
Kaiser-Permanente. Attended by St. Mark Parish.

SAN LEANDRO. *Fairmont Hospital, Redemptorists.* Tel: 510-667-3251. Bro. Rick Fischer.
Humana Hospital. Attended by St. Leander Parish.
Physicians Community Hospital. Attended by Assumption Parish.

SAN PABLO. *Brookside-Hospital.* Attended by St. Paul Parish. Tel: 510-235-7000.

SAN RAMON. *San Ramon Regional Medical Center.* Attended by St. Joan of Arc Parish. Tel: 510-275-9200 (Hospital).

WALNUT CREEK. *John Muir Memorial Hospital, Pastoral Care.* Attended by St. John Vianney Parish. Tel: 510-939-3000 (Hospital).
Kaiser-Permanente Medical Center. Rev. Peter Charankat. Tel: 510-372-1000.
Walnut Creek Hospital. Attended by St. John Vianney Parish.

Prisons and Jails

OAKLAND. *North County Jail.* Deacon Eugene Stelley. Tel: 510-652-5453.
Victim Offender Reconciliation Program. (VORP). Rick Mockler, Dir., Tel: 510-834-5656.

MARTINEZ. *Contra Costa County Jails.* Pat Conroy. Tel: 510-672-7822.
Contra Costa County Juvenile Institution. Deacon Frank Beville. Tel: 510-834-5656.

PLEASANTON. *Alameda County Jail-Santa Rita Rehabilitation Center.* Deacon Frank Beville. Tel: 510-834-5656; 828-5400, Ext. 261.
Federal Correctional Institution. Sr. Joan Campbell, P.B.V.M.; Rev. Efrin Casio. Tel: 510-829-3522.

SAN LEANDRO. *Alameda County Juvenile Institutions.* Deacon Frank Beville, Coord., Tel: 510-834-5656.

On Special Assignment:
Reverend Fathers—
Vella, Francis, Chap., V.A. Medical Center, Alexandria, LA

Military Chaplains:
Reverend Monsignors—
Walsh, Martin E., Army Reserves
Reverend Fathers—
Brennan, Bernard F., Oakland Army Base, Oakland
Buenaventura, Cesar, Lt., C.H.C., U.S. Naval Reserves
Hannick, Anthony S., Veterans Admin. Hospital, Martinez
Koilparampil, Augustine, U.S. Veterans Hospital, Livermore
Lagasse, Ronald J., Lt. Col., U.S. Army Reserves, Schofield Army Base, Hawaii
Pokladowski, Gregory F., Cmdr., C.H.C., U.S. Navy, Oak Knoll Naval Hospital, Oakland
Starbuck, James
Wydeven, John

Graduate Studies:
Reverend Fathers—
Macias, Salvadore

Retired:
Reverend Monsignors—
Adams, Robert
Clogher, John J.
Francis, George J.
McGinty, Michael J.
Mullen, William J.
Varni, Edward J.
Wade, James J.
Walsh, Martin
Zitko, Aloysius
Reverend Fathers—
Brainard, Ernest B.
Broderson, Donald
Cabral, Kenneth J.
Daly, George
Dollard, John J.
Driscoll, James
Eggerling, Milton
Gallagher, Thomas
Harcar, Anthony
Hayburn, Edmund
Keane, James
Kozina, Vladimir
Lu, Matthias
Manning, John
Marshall, William
McLeod, Daniel
Mifsud, Carmelo
Morgan, John
Murray, Adrian
Ribero, Arthur
Ruffing, Norman
Russell, Kenneth
Schwab, Joseph

Permanent Deacons:
Agustin, Benjamin, St. Joseph, Pinole
Anthony, Ferris J., Good Shepherd, Pittsburg
Archer, William, St. Michael, Livermore
Baptista, Antonio, St. Leander, San Leandro
Barnes, Frank, Christ the King, Pleasant Hill
Barnes, James, St. Patrick, Oakland
Barreto, Antonio, St. Edward, Newark
Beltran, Juan, Unassigned
Bettencourt, Leonard, St. John the Baptist Church, San Lorenzo
Beville, Frank, St. Leander, San Leandro
Bothe, William, St. Francis of Assisi, Concord
Brazil, Rudolph, Holy Spirit, Fremont
Bruckner, Nick, St. Edward, Newark
Bustos, Frank, Immaculate Heart of Mary, Brentwood
Cain, Jerry, Leave of Absence
Calub, Benigno, St. Ann, Union City
Campbell, James, St. Augustine, Pleasanton
Ceja, Federico, Our Lady of the Rosary, Union City
Davis, Dennis, St. Leander, San Leandro
Dowling, Robert, Our Lady of Grace, Castro Valley
Drobick, William, Holy Spirit, Fremont
Duhe, Gaston J., St. Patrick, West Oakland
Edgerly, Leo, Sr., St. Andrew-St. Joseph, Oakland
Fihn, Norbert, St. Mary's College
Fleischer, Alfred, St. Ignatius, Antioch
Flores, Isidore, St. Paul, San Pablo
Flores, Jose, Most Holy Rosary, Antioch
Folger, Richard, Our Lady of the Rosary, Union City
Freeman, Ernest, St. Augustine, Pleasanton
Frumkin, Paul, St. Clement, Hayward
Fuentes, Javier, St. Bernard, Oakland
Gall, William, St. Bonaventure, Concord
Gilbert, John, St. Benedict, Oakland
Gomez, Ruben, St. Joan of Arc, San Ramon
Gonsalves, Nelson, All Saints, Hayward
Gonzalez, Noe, St. Elizabeth, Oakland
Grigg, Jerry, Most Holy Rosary, Antioch
Guesnon, Ovide, Santa Paula, Fremont
Hagenbach, Robert, On Duty Outside the Diocese
Hernandez, Gabriel, St. Bede, Hayward
Hoblitzell, Ross, St. Michael, Livermore
Horan, Ronald, Unassigned
Jordan, Jack, St. Monica, Moraga
Layden, Alan, St. Anthony, Oakley
Lee, Stanley, The Filipino Pastoral Center
Lewandowski, Daniel, On Duty Outside the Diocese
Madrigal, Ysidro, St. Paul, San Pablo
Marchese, Charles, Jr., Corpus Christi, Fremont
Martin, Richard, St. Augustine, Pleasanton
Martinez, Bill, (Retired)
McGowan, Thomas, St. John, El Cerrito
Moll, Herbert, On Duty Outside the Diocese
Moore, Timothy, Transfiguration, Castro Valley
Palomares, Charles, St. Francis of Assisi, Concord
Perez, Donaciano, St. Paul, San Pablo
Perez, Ernest, St. Edward, Newark
Perry, Thomas, St. Augustine, Pleasanton
Peters, George, Queen of All Saints, Concord
Prado, Jose, St. Felicitas, San Leandro
Quigley, Edward, St. Augustine, Pleasanton
Rabuy, Carlos, St. Ann, Union City
Rezendes, David, St. Michael, Livermore
Rigley, Burton, Transfiguration, Castro Valley
Rivilla, Luis, Faith and Ministerial Formation
Romers, Gustaaf, St. Ann, Union City
Ryken, Dennis, St. Bede, Hayward
Silva, Richard, On Duty Outside the Diocese
Silveira, Victor, St. Leander, San Leandro
Smith, Leo, (Retired)
Soublet, Morris, St. Andrew-St. Joseph, Oakland
Stelly, Eugene, St. Andrew-St. Joseph, Oakland
Torres, Arcadio, (Retired)
Tovar, Joseph, St. Anthony, Oakley
Turcios, Luis, Corpus Christi, Fremont
Victoria, Hector, St. Raymond, Dublin
Warren, William, Jr., On Duty Outside the Diocese
Wedl, Roger, St. Edward, Newark
Yee, Richard, Holy Spirit, Fremont

INSTITUTIONS LOCATED IN THE DIOCESE

[A] SEMINARIES, RELIGIOUS OR SCHOLASTICATES

OAKLAND. *Graduate School of Theology, School of Applied Theology*, 5890 Birch Ct., 94618. Tel: 510-652-1651. Apostolate of the California Province of the Society of Jesus. Graduate School of Sabbaticals and Christian Leadership. An Affiliate of the Graduate Theological Union. Dr. Frank B. Nieman, Ph.D., Pres. & Dean; Sr. Therese McGroddy, R.S.H.M., Dir. Admissions.
Trustees: Mr. William J. Boyle, C.P.A.; Claude Welch, Ph.D.; Dr. Glenn Bucher; Sr. Rosemary Chinnici; Mr. James Jackson; Rev. Francis J. Houdek, S.J.; Ms. Jennie Magid; Mr. James Penna, J.D.; Revs. Eugene R. Zimmers, S.J.; Francis Buckley, S.J. Sisters 2; Lay Teachers 1; Students 54.

BERKELEY. *Dominican School of Philosophy and Theology*, 2401 Ridge Rd., 94709. Tel: 510-849-2030. (Dominican House of Studies at the Graduate Theological Union). Revs. Gregory Rocca, O.P., Pres. & Faculty (Regular); Edward Krasevac, O.P., Dean & Faculty; Ms. Cheryl A. Trainor, Registrar; Mrs. Pam Thomas, Dean of Students; Mrs. Eleanor Westbrooke, Sec.
Faculty (Regular): Rev. Luke Buckles, O.P.; Mr. Mark Delp; Revs. Stephen Ernest, S.V.D.; Michael Dodds, O.P.; Sr. Barbara Green, O.P.; Revs. Edward Krasevac, O.P.; Eugene M. Ludwig, O.F.M.Cap.; John Hilary Martin, O.P.; Michael T. Morris, O.P., Emeritus; Samuel Parsons, O.P.; Gregory Rocca, O.P.; Richard Schenk, O.P.
Faculty (Adjunct): Revs. Joseph Boenzi, S.D.B.; Owen Carroll; Dr. Marilyn Anne Coffy; Revs. Charles Hess, O.P.; Arthur Lenti, S.D.B.; John McDonough, S.D.B.; Michael Ribotta, S.D.B.; Mr. Carl Ploss. Priests 9; Sisters 1; Lay Teachers 1; Students 105.
Franciscan School of Theology, 1712 Euclid Ave., 94709. Tel: 510-848-5232; Fax: 510-549-9466. Rev. William M. Cieslak, O.F.M.Cap., Pres.; Bro. William J. Short, O.F.M., Academic Dean; Sr. Paschal Hocum, O.S.F., Registrar; Mr. Dale Gilson, Coord. of Student Svcs.
Faculty: Revs. Michael D. Guinan, O.F.M.; William M. Cieslak, O.F.M.Cap.; Rigoberto Caloca-Rivas,

O.F.M.; Richard Gula, S.S.; Kenan B. Osborne, O.F.M.; Xavier J. Harris, O.F.M.; Joseph P. Chinnici, O.F.M.; Thomas West, O.F.M.; Sr. Mary McGann, R.S.C.J.; Sr. Eva Lumas, S.S.S.; Bro. William J. Short, O.F.M. Total Enrollment 100.

Franciscan School of Theology Student Residence, 1920-7th St., 94710. Tel: 510-841-4102. Revs. Ben Innes, O.F.M., Supr.; Giles Valcovich, O.F.M.; Bros. Jeremiah Grimaud, O.F.M.; Jorge Hernandez, O.F.M.; David Cobian, O.F.M.; Dan Barica, O.F.M.; Charles Talley, O.F.M.; Carlos Hernandez, O.F.M.; Garrett Galvin, O.F.M.

The Jesuit School of Theology at Berkeley, 1735 LeRoy Ave., 94709. Tel: 510-841-8804. A Pontifical Faculty of Theology. One of two theological centers of the U.S. Jesuit Conference, Society of Jesus. A Member of the Graduate Theological Union (GTU), Berkeley. Revs. George E. Griener, S.J., Acting Academic Dean; T. Howland Sanks, S.J., Pres.; George Murphy, S.J., Vice Pres. & Dean of Students; Ms. Rita Dollard-O'Malley, Asst. Dean of Students; Sr. Michaeline O'Dwyer, R.S.H.M., Vice Pres. for Devel. & Pub. Rels.; Mr. Robert Lassalle-Klein, Dir. of Field Education; Rev. Donald Arel, O.M.I., Co-Dir., Institute for Spirituality & Worship; Ms. Lorna Wallace McKeown, Asst. Academic Dean & In-House Registrar; Mrs. Karen Ripsom, Asst. Treas.; Ms. Alice Ducey, Dir. of Admissions; Mr. Steven Argyris, Vice Pres. for Finance & Admin.

Faculty (Emeriti): Revs. Harry T. Corcoran, S.J.; John E. Huesman, S.J.; John H. Wright, S.J.; Richard A. Hill, S.J.

Faculty: Rev. John F. Baldovin, S.J.; Sr. Anne Brotherton, S.F.C.C.; Revs. James Bretzke, S.J.; John A. Coleman, S.J.; John Donahue, S.J.; Sr. Mary Ann Donovan, S.C.; Rev. John C. Endres, S.J.; Dr. Alejandro Garcia-Rivera; Revs. Donald L. Gelpi, S.J.; George E. Griener, S.J.; Dr. Gina Hens-Piazza; Rev. Francis J. Houdek, S.J.; Mr. Robert Lassalle-Klein; Revs. William R. O'Neill, S.J.; T. Howland Sanks, S.J.; Sr. Sandra M. Schneiders, I.H.M.; Rev. David J. Stagaman, S.J.; Dr. Seung Ai Yang. Full-time faculty 22; Students 178. (See listing for The Jesuit Community at The Jesuit School of Theology at Berkeley).

MORAGA. *St. Mary's College, Assumption Hall Vocation Office*. Conference Center & Retreat Center, Mailing Address: P.O. Box 4687, 94575. Tel: 510-631-4186. Bro. J. Gary Hough, F.S.C., Admin.

[B] COLLEGES AND UNIVERSITIES

OAKLAND. *Holy Names College*, (1868) 3500 Mountain Blvd., 94619. Tel: 510-436-1000.
For a complete listing, refer to the Colleges and Universities section.

FREMONT. *Queen of the Holy Rosary College*. Mailing Address: P.O. Box 3908 Mission San Jose, 94539. Tel: 510-657-2468; Fax: 510-657-1734.
For a complete listing, refer to the Colleges and Universities section.

MORAGA. *Saint Mary's College*, 94575. Tel: 510-631-4000.
For a complete listing, refer to the Colleges and Universities section.

[C] HIGH SCHOOLS, DIOCESAN

OAKLAND. *Bishop O'Dowd High School*, 9500 Stearns Ave., 94605. Tel: 510-577-9100; Fax: 510-638-3259. Basilian Fathers (Congregation of St. Basil). Revs. John Huber, C.S.B.; Richard A. Ranalletti, C.S.B., Prin.; John B. Malo, C.S.B., Supr.; Robert H. Glass, C.S.B.; Robert Moslosky, C.S.B.; Benjamin Owens, C.SS.R.; Les F. Schaefer, C.S.B. Priests 7; Lay Teachers 69; Students 1,050.

St. Elizabeth High School, 1530-34th Ave., 94601. Tel: 510-532-8947. Dr. Matilda Ignacio, Prin. Sisters 3; Lay Teachers 23; Students 330.

[D] HIGH SCHOOLS, PAROCHIAL

ALAMEDA. *Saint Joseph Notre Dame High School*, 1011 Chestnut St., 94501. Tel: 510-523-1526; Fax: 510-523-2181. Mr. Anthony V. Aiello, Prin. Priests 1; Lay Teachers 50; Students 540.

[E] HIGH SCHOOLS, PRIVATE

OAKLAND. *Holy Name High School*, 4660 Harbord Dr., 94618. Tel: 510-450-1110. Sisters of the Holy Names of Jesus and Mary. Sr. Adele Hancock, P.B.V.M., Prin. Sisters 9; Lay Teachers 21; Students 271.

BERKELEY. *Saint Mary's College High School of Berkeley, Inc.*, 94706. Tel: 510-526-9242; Fax: 510-559-6298. Brothers of the Christian Schools. Dr. John T. Collins, Prin. Brothers 4; Lay Instructors 33; Students 556.

CONCORD. *Carondelet High School*, 1133 Winton Dr., 94518-3598. Tel: 510-686-5353; Fax: 510-671-9429. Sisters of St Joseph of Carondelet. Sr. Kathleen Lang, C.S.J., Prin. Sisters 6; Lay Teachers 48; Students 814.

De La Salle High School of Concord, Inc. dba De La Salle High School. (Boys), 1130 Winton Dr., 94518. Tel: 510-686-3310; Fax: 510-686-3474. Brothers of the Christian Schools (De La Salle Christian Brothers). Mr. James Tschann, Pres.; Bros. Robert J. Wickman, F.S.C., Prin.; Tom Westberg, F.S.C., Asst. Prin. & Brothers' Community Dir.; Mr. Robert Jordan, Dir. of Campus Min. Brothers 12; Lay Teachers 56; Students 900.

HAYWARD. *Moreau Catholic High School*, 27170 Mission Blvd., 94544. Tel: 510-881-4300; Fax: 510-582-8405. Brothers of Holy Cross. Patricia Geister, Prin.; Joseph Connell, Ph.D., Pres.; Margaret J. Walsh, Corp. Treas. Lay Teachers 62; Students 1,260.

RICHMOND. *Salesian High School*, 2851 Salesian Ave., 94804. Tel: 510-234-4433; Fax: 510-236-4636. Salesians of St. John Bosco. Rev. John Itzaina, S.D.B., Dir. & Prin.; Bro. Patrick Maloney, S.D.B., Business Mgr.; Revs. Arthur Brainard, S.D.B., (Retired); Laurence Byrne, S.D.B., (Retired); Mel Trindad, S.D.B., D.R.E.; Angel Baldonado, S.D.B.; Bro. Jerry Weirich, S.D.B., Dean of Discipline. Priests 5; Brothers 2; Lay Teachers 30; Students 460.

[F] EARLY CHILDHOOD EDUCATION CENTERS

MISSION SAN JOSE. *Dominican Kindergarten*, 43326 Mission Blvd., P.O. Box 3908, 94539; Fax: 510-657-1734. Sr. Judith Mary Reagan, O.P., Prin. Sisters 1; Students 36.

[G] SUMMER SCHOOLS

OAKLAND. *Holy Names College*, 3500 Mountain Blvd., 94619. Tel: 510-436-1000. Sisters of the Holy Names of Jesus and Mary. Resident and Non-Resident Students.

MISSION SAN JOSE. *Queen of the Holy Rosary College*, 43326 Mission Blvd., P.O. Box 3908, 94539. Tel: 510-657-2468; Fax: 510-657-1734. Sisters of the Third Order of St. Dominic of the Congregation of the Queen of the Holy Rosary.

MORAGA. *St. Mary's College*, 94575. Brothers of the Christian Schools, District of San Francisco. Priests 1; Brothers 13; Lay Teachers 109.

[H] CATHOLIC CHARITIES OF THE DIOCESE OF OAKLAND

OAKLAND. *Catholic Charities of the Diocese of Oakland, Inc.*, 433 Jefferson St., 94607. Tel: 510-834-5656. Legal Title: *Catholic Charities of the Diocese of Oakland, Inc., A Non-Profit Corporation*. Barbara S. Terrazas, Exec. Dir.; Gregory R. Kepferle, Assoc. Exec. Dir.; Marilyn Kihara, Controller; Marilyn Lovelace, Human Resources Dir.; Esme Marconi, CFRE, Dir., Fund Dev./Public Affairs.

COMMUNITY AND PARISH SERVICES: Bro. Richard Kearney, M.S.W., Dir.

Counseling Services:

Alameda County Area Supervisor, Marguerite Dean, 433 Jefferson St., 94607. Tel: 510-834-5656.

Chancery Annex, 3014 Lakeshore Ave., 94610. Tel: 510-763-0301. Regional Offices.

Alameda, 1109 Chestnut St., Alameda, 94501. Tel: 510-569-9307.

Antioch, 21 E. 15th St., Antioch, 94509. Tel: 510-778-7929.

Berkley, 2700 Dwight Way, Berkley. Tel: 510-834-5657, Ext. 4022.

East Oakland, 6226 Camden St., 94605. Tel: 510-569-9307.

Fremont Offices, 3767 Decoto Rd., Fremont, 94536. Tel: 510-792-2444. Fremont-Mission San Jose, 43148 Mission Blvd., Fremont, 94539. Tel: 510-490-5452.

Hayward, 22824 Second St., Hayward, 94541. Tel: 510-886-1331.

Hayward, 21250 Hesperian Blvd., Hayward, 94541. Tel: 510-886-1462.

Livermore, 458 Maple St., Livermore, 94550. Tel: 510-828-1462.

Concord, 2350 Pacheco St., Concord, 94521. Tel: 510-825-3099. Pat Spohn, Contra Costa County Area Supervisor.

Pinole, 2150 Pear Ave., Pinole, 94564. Tel: 510-724-6263.

Pittsburg, 455 W. Fourth St., Pittsburg, 94565. Tel: 510-432-7363.

Richmond, 225 Civic Center St., Richmond, 94804. Tel: 510-232-1377.

San Ramon, 2601 San Ramon Valley Blvd., San Ramon, 94583. Tel: 510-828-1462.

Services to Parish Schools, 433 Jefferson St., 94607. Tel: 510-834-5656. Marguerite Dean.

Department of Aging, 433 Jefferson St., 94607. Tel: 510-834-5656. Heidi Cartan, Dir.

HIV/AIDS Services, 433 Jefferson St., 94607. Tel: 510-834-5656. Randy Marcotte, Dir.

Services to Gays & Lesbians & Their Families, 433 Jefferson St., 94607. Tel: 510-834-5656. Rev. James Schexnayder, Dir.

Victim Offender Reconciliation Program, 433 Jefferson St., 94607. Tel: 510-834-5656. Lou Ann Aaberg, Dir.

Detention Ministry, 433 Jefferson St., 94607. Tel: 510-834-5656. Frank Beville, Coord.

Social Justice Resource Center, 1232-33rd Ave., 94601. Tel: 510-532-3518. Paul Woolley, Dir.

COMMUNITY SERVICES:

433 Jefferson St., 94607. Tel: 510-834-5656. Sr. Elisabeth Lang, O.P., Dir.

Business Education Center, 1600 San Pablo Ave., 94612. Tel: 510-834-5461. Stan Varn, Dir.

Emergency Services, 433 Jefferson St., 94607. Tel: 510-834-5656. Angelina Toscano, Dir.

English Action Center, 2369 Barrett Ave., Richmond, 94804. Tel: 510-234-5110. Barbara Racek, Dir.

English Action Center-Verde School, 2000 Giaramita, Room 17 & 18, Richmond, 94808. Tel: 510-234-5305.

English Action Center, 3200 Barrett Ave., Richmond, 94804. Tel: 510-234-2416.

HIV Prison Project, 433 Jefferson Ave., 94607. Tel: 510-834-5656. Judy Greenspan, Dir.

Housing Services, 433 Jefferson Ave., 94607. Tel: 510-834-5656. Kenneth Richardson, Dir.

Refugee and Immigrant Services, 1232-33rd Ave., 94601. Tel: 510-261-1538. Raquel Aguirre, Dir.

Refugee Employment Assistance Center, 100 Hacienda Ave., P.O. Box 247, San Lorenzo, 94580. Tel: 510-481-0131. Vu Pham, Dir.

Refugee Employment Assistance Center, 707 Jefferson St., 94607. Tel: 510-465-0642.

Refugee Employment Assistance Center, 4700 Calaveras Ave., Fremont, 94538. Tel: 510-745-8731.

SPECIAL PROGRAMS:

Campaign for Human Development (CHD), 433 Jefferson St., 94607. Tel: 510-834-5656. Paul Woolley, Diocesan Dir.

Catholic Relief Services (CRS), 433 Jefferson St., 94607. Tel: 510-834-5656. Paul Woolley, Dir.

[I] SOCIETY OF ST. VINCENT DE PAUL

OAKLAND. *Society of St. Vincent de Paul of Alameda County*, 9235 San Leandro St., 94603. Tel: 510-638-7600; Fax: 510-638-8354. Donald Gerigk, Pres.

Society of St. Vincent de Paul of Alameda County. Free Dinning Room, 675 23rd St., 94612. Tel: 510-451-7676. Total Assisted; 23,335; Total Staff 130.

[J] DAY NURSERIES

OAKLAND. *Saint Vincent's Day Home*, 1086 Eighth St., 94607-2697. Tel: 510-832-8324. Legal Title: *Saint Vincent's Day Home, A Corporation*. Corinne M. Mohrmann, CEO. Religious 1; Lay Staff 36; Capacity 199; Total Assisted 300; Total Staff 37.

[K] GENERAL HOSPITALS

HAYWARD. *St. Rose Hospital*, 27200 Calaroga Ave., 94545. Tel: 510-782-6200.
For a complete listing, refer to the Hospitals section.

[L] ORGANIZATIONS FOR DEAF AND HARD OF HEARING

UNION CITY. *St. Joseph's Center for Deaf and Hard of Hearing*, 3880 Smith St., 94587. Tel: 510-489-9784 (Voice); 489-9786 (TDD). Legal Title: *St. Joseph's Center for the Deaf and Hard of Hearing, A Corporation*. Ardith A. Lynch, Diocesan Dir.

[M] RETIREMENT AND CARE FACILITIES

OAKLAND. *Bishop Begin Villa*, 3418 E. 18th St., 94601.
For a complete listing, refer to the Special Care Facilities section.

Mercy Retirement and Care Center, 3431 Foothill Blvd., 94601. Tel: 510-534-8540; Fax: 510-261-7551.
For a complete listing, refer to the Special Care Facilities section.

[N] MONASTERIES AND RESIDENCES OF PRIESTS AND BROTHERS

OAKLAND. *Dominican Order (Western Province), St. Albert's Priory*, Dominican House of Formation, 5890 Birch Ct., 94618. Tel: 510-596-1800. Very Rev. Denis Daniel Reilly, O.P., Prior; Revs. Vincent Serpa, O.P., Novice Master; Michael Dodds, O.P., Master of Students; Finbarr Hayes, O.P.; Charles Hess, O.P.; Fabian Parmisano, O.P.; Sergius Propst, O.P.; Antoninus Wall, O.P.; Janko Zagar, O.P.; Luke Buckles, O.P.; Martin Walsh, O.P.; Bros. Robert Lavigne, O.P.; Pasquale Manalio, O.P.; Jose Romero, O.P. In res., Revs. Basil Cole, O.P.; Gerard Ehler, O.P.; Richard Schenk, O.P.; Bros. Chris Renz, O.P.; Roberto Bravo, O.P.; Alejandro Crosthwaite-Martinez, O.P.; Steven Maekawa, O.P.; Carl Schlicte, O.P.; Jordan Vajda, O.P.; Bartholomew Hutcherson, O.P. Total in Residence 24.

Dominican Order, Siena House, 5730 Presley Way, 94618. Tel: 510-654-8735. Revs. Mark G. O'Leary, O.P., Supr.; Anthony G. Cordeiro, O.P., Prov. Treas.;

Leo D. Tubbs, O.P.; Michael Kelly (SR); Emmerich Vogt, O.P., Mission Band; Gregory Rocca, O.P., Pres., D.S.P.T. Priests 3.

Franciscan Friars, St. Elizabeth Friary, 1500 34th Ave., 94601. Tel: 510-536-1287. Revs. Ignatius De-Groot, O.F.M.; Kenny Scott, O.F.M., Vicar; Peter Krieg, O.F.M.; Tom West, O.F.M.; Gordon Urbine, O.F.M.; Rigoberto Caloca-Rivas, O.F.M.; Pedro Nmana, O.F.M.; Bros. John Gutierrez, O.F.M., Guardian; Antonio Herrera, O.F.M.; Michael Bearce, O.F.M.; Jose Alberto Barrera, O.F.M.; David Gaa, O.F.M.; Juan Urias, O.F.M.; Edgar Magana, O.F.M.; Raul Alejos, O.F.M.; Balbino Rodriguez, O.F.M.; James Locksman, O.F.M.; Alberto Villafan, O.F.M.; Hoang Trinh, O.F.M.; Gustavo Castillanos, O.F.M.; Keith Warner, O.F.M.; Cesar Montelongo, O.F.M.; Ramiro Munoz, O.F.M.

Franciscan Friars Provincial Office, Province of St. Barbara, 1500-34th Ave., 94601. Tel: 510-536-3722; Fax: 510-536-3970. Revs. Joseph P. Chinnici, O.F.M., Prov.; Finian McGinn, O.F.M., Vicar Prov.; Melvin A. Jurisich, O.F.M., Sec.; Ms. Guadalupe Aceves, Treas.; Rev. John Hardin, O.F.M., Assoc. Treas.; Bro. Angelo Cardinalli, O.F.M., Vocation; Rev. Miguel Obregon, O.F.M., Vocations. Priests 5; Total Staff 16.

On Duty Outside the Province: Revs. Angus Cooper, O.F.M., General Curia, Rome, Italy; Christopher F. Tomatis, O.F.M., The Antonanium Rome, Italy; Marcos A. Figueroa, O.F.M., The Pontifical University, Mexico.

Franciscan Friars, 1508 Arch St., Berkeley, 94708. Tel: 510-845-1124. Revs. Michael Doherty, O.F.M., Guardian; Joseph P. Chinnici, O.F.M.; Melvin A. Jurisich, O.F.M.; John S. Hardin, O.F.M.; William Cieslak, O.F.M.Cap.

Murray Residence Community, 171 Santa Rosa Ave., 94610-1316. Tel: 510-655-8334. Revs. John A. Baumann, S.J., Supr.; Bernard M.C. Chu, S.J.; Thomas C. Weston, S.J.; John A. Coleman, S.J.

Oblate Provincial House & Procure, 290 Lenox Ave., 94610. Tel: 510-452-1550; Fax: 510-452-3421. Provincial Headquarters of the Oblates of Mary Immaculate, Western Prov. Very Rev. David Ullrich, O.M.I., Prov.; Revs. Leo Dummer, O.M.I., Prov. Treas.; Richard Haslam, O.M.I., 4th Asst./Sec.; Paul Waldie, O.M.I., 3rd Asst.; William Antone, O.M.I., 2nd Asst.; Thomas Rush, O.M.I., 1st Asst. In res., Revs. James P. McSorley, O.M.I.; Ruben Martinez, O.M.I.; John Kelly, O.M.I. Legal Title: *Oblate Fathers Western Province Inc.; Western Oblates Support Trust Fund*. Total in Residence 5; Total Staff 2.

Order of Preachers (Southern Province). De Porres House of Studies. 2215 Rose St., Berkeley, 94709. Tel: 510-644-8247; Fax: 510-644-8249. Revs. Jude Siciliano, O.P., Supr. & Prof., DSPT. Tel: 510-644-8247; John Markey, O.P., Assoc. Dir. Formation.

Redemptorists, 8945 Golf Links Rd., 94605. Tel: 510-562-9740; Fax: 510-562-1406. Very Rev. Stephen Meyer, C.Ss.R., Supr.; Revs. Fred Arpin, C.Ss.R.; Carlyle Blake, C.Ss.R.; Robert Kirkpatrick, C.Ss.R.; James Farrell; Patrick Leehan, C.Ss.R.; Francis McMahon, C.Ss.R.; John Shaughnessy, C.Ss.R.; Donald Mackinnon, C.Ss.R.; Bros. Denis Schroeder, C.Ss.R.; Martin Temple, C.Ss.R.; Richard Fischer, C.Ss.R.; Damian Bronson, C.Ss.R. Legal Title: *Redemptorist Society of California*.

Holy Redeemer Retreat and Conference Center, P.O. Box 5427, 94605. Tel: 510-635-6341.

Western Dominican Province, 5877 Birch Ct., 94618-1626. Tel: 510-658-8722; Fax: 510-658-1061. Province of the Holy Name, Inc., A California Corporation. Very Revs. Daniel Syverstad, O.P., Prior Prov. & Corp. Pres.; Reginald E. Martin, O.P., Socius-Vicar Prov., Corp. Vice Pres. & Dir. Devel.; Revs. Anthony G. Cordeiro, O.P., Prov., Corp. Treas. & Dir, St. Dominic's Cemetery; Luke D. Buckles, O.P., Regent of Studies & Corporate Sec.; George M. Matanic, O.P., Promoter of Dominican Laity; Basil B. Cole, O.P., Western Reg. Dir. Holy Name Society; Martin Walsh, O.P., Dir. Vocations; Vincent A. Serpa, O.P., Master of Novices; Michael J. Dodds, O.P., Master of Students; Donald J. Bramble, O.P., Dir., Mission Foundation; Thomas J. Hayes, O.P., Dir., Shrine of St. Jude. Directors, Western Dominican Preaching: Revs. Sergius R. Propst, O.P.; Reginald E. Martin, O.P.

U.S. Religious Serving in Latin America: Revs. David Bello, O.P.; Robert V. Foerstler, O.P.; Thomas D. Kraft, O.P.; Michael Rolland, O.P.; Bro. Raymond C. Bertheaux, O.P.

U.S. Religious Serving in Africa: Rev. Kieran J. Healy, O.P. Total in Residence 155.

BERKELEY. *Capuchin Franciscan Order, House of Studies*, 1534 Arch St., 94708. Tel: 510-841-2229. Saint Conrad Friary. Revs. Robert A. Barbato, O.F.M.Cap., Guardian & Formation Dir.; James Johnson, O.F.M.Cap., Vicar, Formation Team; Bros. Francis Driscoll, O.F.M.Cap., Formation Team; Peter Ciolino, O.F.M.Cap., Formation Team. Friars in residence 16; Friars in formation 10; Total Staff 4.

Carmelite (Discalced) House of Studies, 2542 Hilgard Ave., 94709. Tel: 510-549-3918. Revs. David Centner, O.C.D.; John Melka, O.C.D. Total in Residence 6; Total Staff 2.

Holy Cross Fathers-Holy Cross Center, 2597 Virginia St., 94709. Tel: 510-548-8515; Fax: 510-548-7903. Revs. Donald G. Fetters, C.S.C., Religious Supr.; Daniel G. Groody, C.S.C.; William J. Dohar, C.S.C.; Terence H. Linton, C.S.C.; Bro. Ronald Whelan, C.S.C.

Jesuit Community at Jesuit School of Theology at Berkeley, 2621 Ridge Rd., 94709-1098. Tel: 510-841-2487; Fax: 510-549-1114. Rev. Charles L. Moutenot, S.J., Rector; Bro. Joseph M. Ritzman, S.J., Asst. Rector, Minister, & Treas.; Revs. Jose A. Aguilar, S.J. (Columbia); John F. Baldovin, S.J. (New York); Kevin M. Bradt, S.J. (New York); James T. Bretzke, S.J. (Wisconsin); Thomas J. Buckley, S.J. (California); Hartono Budi, S.J. (Indonesia); James J. Burshek, S.J. (Missouri); Andrew Cameron-Mowat, S.J. (Spain); Joseph P. Carroll, S.J. (California); John A. Coleman, S.J. (California); Harry T. Corcoran, S.J. (California); Donald F. Crosby, S.J. (California); Declan Deane, S.J. (Ireland); John R. Donahue, S.J. (Maryland); John C. Endres, S.J. (Oregon); Robert J. Fabing, S.J. (California); Donald L. Gelpi, S.J. (New Orleans); George E. Griener, S.J. (New Orleans); Simon J. Hendry, S.J. (New Orleans); Fred M. Henley, S.J. (Detroit); Francis J. Houdek, S.J. (Detroit); John E. Huesman, S.J. (California); William M. Kegel, S.J. (Wisconsin); Mathew Jayanth Kodekkanel, S.J. (India); Stephen T. Krupa, S.J. (Detroit); David L. Lawrence, S.J. (New Orleans); Lester E. Love, S.J. (Chicago); J. Roger Lucey, S.J. (Wisconsin); Francis X. McAloon, S.J. (Maryland); Peter R. McGrath, S.J. (New England); George R. Murphy, S.J. (New England); Robert J. Ochs, S.J. (Chicago); William R. O'Neill, S.J. (California); Joseph M. Palacios, S.J. (California); Joseph M. Powers, S.J. (California); Thierry-Jean Robouam, S.J. (Japan); T. Howland Sanks, S.J. (Maryland); David J. Stagaman, S.J. (Chicago); Osamu Takeuchi, S.J. (Japan); Aquilene Tarimo, S.J. (Africa); John H. Wright, S.J. (Oregon).

(See also listing for The Jesuit School of Theology at Berkeley).

Marist Fathers and Brothers, 2335 Warring St., 94704. Tel: 510-486-1232; 486-1276; Fax: 510-848-7204. Rev. Thomas M. Hamilton, S.M., Supr. & Formation Dir.; Bro. Peter DiFrancescantonio, S.M., Formation Staff. Legal Title: *Marist Society of California*.

Seminary Name: St. Peter Chanel Seminary - Marist Theologate. In res., Rev. Michael Galinada, S.M.

St. Thomas Aquinas House, 2401 Ridge Rd., 94709. Tel: 510-849-0842. Revs. Edward Krasevac, O.P.; John Hilary Martin, O.P.; Alain Durocher.

Salesian Community, Don Bosco Hall, 1831 Arch St., 94709. Tel: 510-204-0800; Fax: 510-843-4335. Revs. Arthur Lenti, S.D.B.; Ralph J. Murphy, S.D.B., Treas.; Michael Ribotta, S.D.B.; Thomas Prendiville, S.D.B., Dir.; Joseph Boenzi, S.D.B.; Anthony Fernandes, S.D.B. (Kenya); Eric Freed, S.D.B. (Japan); Thomas Grzegorzewski, S.D.B. (Kenya); William Keane, S.D.B. (Paterson); Am Nguyen, S.D.B. (Vietnam); Joseph Nguyen Phuoc, S.D.B. (Vietnam); Denis Kong, S.D.B (Hong Kong); Henry Woo, S.D.B. (Korea); Raphael Lobo, S.D.B. (India); Lucas Mendonca, S.D.B. (India); Sagayaraj Philominathan, S.D.B. (India); Niphon Sarachit, S.D.B. (Thailand). Total in Residence 27; Total Staff 2.

Servite Community, Sarpi Priory. (Western Province), 2400 Virginia St., 94709-1206. Tel: 510-849-2472. Revs. Bruce J. Klikunas, O.S.M.; Patrick Donovan, O.S.M., Prior.

Society of the Precious Blood, 2800 Milvia, 94703. Tel: 510-845-2777; 848-3076. Sonnino Mission House. Revs. Ronald P. Wiecek, C.PP.S., Dir.; Gary M. Luiz, C.PP.S., Dir.; James Sloan, C.PP.S.

Candidates: Agustin Ramirez, C.PP.S.; Arturo Neri, C.PP.S.; Luis Motta; Gerardo Rivas; Javier Soto. Total in Residence 7.

MORAGA. *Dominican Community*, Siena Hall, St. Mary's College, P.O. Box 5185, 94575-5185. Tel: 510-631-4315; Fax: 510-631-4315. Dominican Order. Revs. John McDonough, O.P., Supr.; Michael Carey, O.P.; Michael T. Morris, O.P. Priests 3.

SAN LEANDRO. *Society of the Precious Blood*, 2337 W. Ave. 134th, 94577-4132. Tel: 510-357-4982. Province of the Pacific, Provincial Headquarters, Provincial Center. Very Rev. James E. Franck, C.PP.S., Prov. Dir.; Deacon Joseph L. Brown, C.PP.S., Treas.; Rev. John R. Klopke, C.PP.S., Sec. Total in Residence 3; Total Staff 4.

SAN PABLO. *Franciscans, Conventual of California*, St. Francis of Assisi Friary, House of Studies, 1850 Church Ln., 94806-3706. Tel: 510-235-9119; Fax: 510-235-2045. Rev. Paul Fazio, O.F.M.Conv., Guardian and Dir. of Candidates. Total in Residence 10; Total Staff 1.

[O] CONVENTS AND RESIDENCES FOR SISTERS

OAKLAND. *Dominican Sisters of Mission San Jose*, St. Elizabeth Convent, 1555-34th Ave., 94601. Tel: 510-532-8344. Sisters 16.

Dominican Sisters of Oakford, Bethany House, 919 Aileen St., 94608. Tel: 510-652-0986. Sisters 2.

Dominican Sisters of San Rafael, House of Hope, 4264 Howe St., 94611. Tel: 510-654-8334. 1927 Haste, Berkeley, 94704. Tel: 510-631-4316.

Franciscan Missionaries of Mary, 570 Boden Way, Apt. 2, 94610. Tel: 510-444-8265. Sisters 3.

Franciscan Sisters of St. Francis of Penance and Christian Charity, 1815-33rd Ave., 94601. Tel: 510-534-4330. Sisters 5.

Novitiate House. Novices 1; Professed 4. House of Hope, 2027 Nina Ct., Hayward, 94541. Tel: 510-357-1026.

Holy Names Sisters. Mailing Address: Provincial Administration, P.O. Box 907, Los Gatos, 95031. Tel: 408-395-5150; Fax: 408-354-8305. Holy Names College Convent, 3500 Mountain Blvd., 94619. Tel: 510-436-6635. Holy Names High School Convent, 4660 Harbord Dr., 94618. Tel: 510-547-1468; Fax: 510-547-3111. Sisters 15. St. Mary's Residence, 621-18th St., 94612. Tel: 510-465-9996. Sisters 2. St. Theresa Convent, 4850 Clarewood Dr., 94618. Tel: 510-547-1354. Sisters 4. Assumption Convent, 1851 136th Ave., San Leandro, 94578. Tel: 510-352-0383. Sisters 3. St. Bede Convent, 26900 Patrick Ave., Hayward, 94544. Tel: 510-782-6700. Sisters 6. Sisters 14.

Presentation Sisters, 11 Warren St., No. 7, 94611. 1725 Oxford St., #308, Berkeley, 94709. 1725 Oxford St., #104, Berkeley, 94709. 1055 47th St., #C, Emeryville, 94608. 1515 Lincoln St., Berkeley, 94703.

Providence Sisters, Summit South, 3100 Summit St., P.O. Box 23020, 94623-9966. Tel: 510-835-4500. Sisters 4.

St. Lawrence O'Toole Convent, 3693 High St., 94619-2105. Tel: 510-530-2621. Adrian Dominican Sisters. Total in Residence 4.

Sisters of Charity of Cincinnati, 809-42nd St., 94608. Tel: 510-658-7990. 529-41st St., No. 9, 94609. Tel: 510-654-7328.

Sisters of Mercy, Burlingame, Mercy Retirement and Care Center, 3431 Foothill Blvd., 94601. Tel: 510-534-8540. Sisters 4.

Sisters of the Holy Family. St. Vincent's Day Home, 1086 Eighth St., 94607. Tel: 510-832-8324. 7797 Hansom Dr., 94605. Tel: 510-635-3050.

Child Day Care Center(s): Sisters 4; Total Assisted 188; Total Staff 36.

Social Service Sisters, 4000 Waterhouse, 94602. 851 Trestle Glen Rd., 94610. Sisters 6.

ALAMEDA. *Sisters of Notre Dame de Namur*, St. Joseph Convent, 1834 San Antonio Ave., 94501. Tel: 510-865-0800. Sr. Agnes Anzoli, S.N.D.

BERKELEY, 1725 Oxford St. No. 204, 94709. Tel: 510-841-6237. Sr. Therese McGroddy, R.S.H.M.

Dominican Sisters of Mission San Jose, St. Mary Magdalen Community, 2004 Eunice St., 94709. Tel: 510-527-4817. Sisters 7.

Dominican Sisters of San Rafael, Benincase House of Formation, 2901 Channing Way, 94704. Tel: 510-540-6658. Sisters 5.

Franciscan Sisters of Little Falls, MN, 1418 A Fifth St., 94710.

Sisters of Charity, B.V.M., 1746 Addison St., 94703. Tel: 510-841-8791. 1708 Euclid Ave., No. 11, 94709. Tel: 510-843-0684. Sisters 2.

Sisters of Notre Dame de Namur, 1717 Oxford St., No. 101, 94709. Tel: 510-845-2113. 1717 Oxford St., No. 202, 94709. Tel: 510-540-6896. 1725 Oxford St., No. 210, 94709. Tel: 510-848-7439.

Sisters of St. Joseph of Carondelet, 2025 Durant Ave. #110, 94704. Tel: 510-540-0796; 486-8061. Sisters 3.

CASTRO VALLEY. *Sisters of St. Joseph in the Third Order of St. Francis*, 22120 Center St., No. 523, 94546. Tel: 510-886-1170. 2063 Boniface St., Concord, 94520. Tel: 510-680-7396. 6626 Pioneer Ln., Dublin, 94568. Tel: 510-829-5139. 5427 Valley View Rd., El Sobrante, 94803. Tel: 510-222-0492.

Sisters of the Holy Family, Holy Family Convent, 19697 Redwood Rd., 94546. Tel: 510-582-7314. Sr. M. John Bosco Crivello, Local Coord. Total in community 12.

CONCORD. *Sisters of St. Joseph of Carondelet*, 1133 Winton Dr., 94518. St. Francis of Assisi Community, 866 Oak Grove Rd., 94518. Tel: 510-682-5418. Sisters 3. Bay Area Crisis Nursery, Inc., 1506 Mendocino Dr., 94521. Tel: 510-685-8052; 510-685-9740. Concord Residential Club, 2141 California St., 94520. Tel: 510-689-4939. Kwanza House Community, 529 Jean St., Oakland, 94610. Tel: 510-655-2382. Sisters 2. Christ the King Community, 528 Monti Cir., Pleasant Hill, 94523. Tel: 510-682-0533. Sisters 3. St. Anthony Community, 1520 E. 15th St., Oakland, 94606. Tel: 510-532-9455. Sisters 4.

St. Catherine of Siena Community, 1125 Ferry St., Martinez, 94553. Tel: 510-228-9051. Sisters 5.

Sisters of St. Joseph of the Third Order of St. Francis, 2301 Mt. Diablo St., 94520. Tel: 510-680-7396; 825-2091.

DUBLIN. *Sisters of St. Joseph of the Third Order of St. Francis*, St. Raymond Convent, 6626 Pioneer Ln., 94568. Tel: 510-829-5139. Sisters 2.

EL CERRITO. *Franciscan Sisters of Perpetual Adoration (FSPA)*, 1317 Liberty St., No. 17, 94530. Tel: 510-233-9797. 2629 34th Ave., Oakland, 94601. Tel: 510-536-1266.

Mercy Sisters, Ireland, St. John the Baptist Convent, 11154 San Pablo Ave., 94530. Tel: 510-233-6769. Sisters 4.

Sisters of Sacred Hearts of Jesus and Mary, California Regional House, 8644 Don Carol Dr., 94530. Tel: 510-528-6542; 527-3328. St. Jerome Convent, 310 San Carlos Ave., 94530. Tel: 510-525-6554. Sisters 5. Sisters 4.

EL SOBRANTE. *Sisters of St. Joseph of the Third Order of St. Francis, S.S.J.-T.O.S.F.*, 5427 Valley View Rd., 94803. Tel: 510-222-0492. 22120 Center St., #523, Castro Valley, 94546. Tel: 510-886-1170. 2063 Bonifacio St., Concord, 94520. Tel: 510-680-7396. 6626 Pioneer Ln., Dublin, 94568. Tel: 510-829-5139. Sisters 2.

FREMONT. *Sisters of the Holy Family*, Callison Day Home, Inc., 159 Washington Blvd., 94539. Tel: 510-624-4598. Legal Title: *Callison Day Hone. Sisters of the Holy Family, Corp.* Sr. Teresa Marie Stiegler, Pres. Sisters 51.

HAYWARD. *Dominican Sisters of Adrian, MI*, 23910 Second St. #36, 94541. Tel: 510-582-2568.

Holy Names Sisters, St. Bede Convent, 26900 Patrick Ave., 94544. Tel: 510-782-6700. Sisters 6.

Sisters of St. Joseph of Wichita, KS. (Member of the CSJ Health System, Inc., of Wichita.). Mr. Michael P. Mahoney, Pres.; Revs. David F. Pace, Chap.; Roy V. Eco, Chap., St. Rose Hospital, 27200 Calaroga Ave., 94545. Tel: 510-264-4000. Religious 5; Beds 175; Patients assisted annually 78,153. St. Rose Medical Office Bldg., 27200 Calaroga, 94545. St. Rose Hospital Foundation, 27200 Calaroga, 94545.

KENSINGTON. *Discalced Carmelite Nuns*, 68 Rincon Rd., 94707. Tel: 510-526-5050. Solemn Professed 6.

Holy Names Sisters, 224 Lake Dr., 94708. Tel: 510-524-2231.

LAFAYETTE. *Sisters of St. Joseph of Carondelet*, St. Perpetua Convent, 3446 Hamlin Rd., 94549. Tel: 510-283-0888. Sisters 3; Homeless Center: Total Assisted 1,800/month.

LIVERMORE. *Dominican Sisters of San Rafael*, St. Michael Convent, 375 Maple St., 94550. Tel: 510-443-1666; Fax: 510-447-6720. Sisters 4.

MARTINEZ. *Sisters of St. Joseph of Carondelet*, St. Catherine of Siena Convent, 1125 Ferry St., 94553. Tel: 510-228-9051. Sisters 5.

MISSION SAN JOSE. *Dominican Sisters of Mission San Jose*, 43326 Mission Blvd., P.O. Box 3908, 94539. Tel: 510-657-2468; Fax: 510-657-1734. Generalate Motherhouse and Novitiate of the Dominican Sisters of Mission San Jose, Congregation of The Queen of the Holy Rosary. Sr. Rose Marie Hennessy, Prioress Gen. Sisters 129.

Queen of Peace Community. Sr. Rebecca Shinas, O.P., Supr.

St. Joseph Priory. Sr. Mary LaSalette Fuselier, O.P., Prioress; Sr. Evelyn Casper, O.P., Supr.

St. Martin Infirmary.

San Domenico Community. Sr. Rose Marie Hennessy, O.P., Supr./Prioress Gen.

Siena House. Sr. Phyllis Marie Bridenbecker, O.P., Supr.

St. Edward Convent, 37088 Arden St., Newark, 94560-3702. Tel: 510-793-9447. Sr. Mary Paul Mehegan, O.P., Supr.

St. Elizabeth Convent, 1555-34th Ave., P.O. Box 7465, Oakland, 94601-0465. Tel: 510-532-8344. Sr. Kathleen Marie Ramirez, O.P., Supr.

St. Mary Magdelen Convent, 2004 Eunice St., Berkeley, 94709-1926. Tel: 510-527-4817. Sr. Ingrid Clemmensen, O.P., Supr.

Our Lady of Guadalupe Convent, 631 Aztec Ct., Fremont, 94539-7164. Tel: 510-490-6902. Sr. Andre Marie Fujier, O.P., Supr.

NEWARK. *Dominican Sisters of Mission San Jose*, St. Edward Convent, 37088 Arden St., 94560. Tel: 510-793-9447. Sisters 4.

PLEASANT HILL. *Holy Family Sisters*, Holy Family Center, 2059 Pleasant Hill Rd., 94523. Tel: 510-935-6151. Sisters 4; Total in Residence 4; Total Staff 2.

Sisters of St. Joseph of Carondelet, Christ the King Convent, 528 Monte Cir., 94523. Tel: 510-682-0533. Sisters 3; Total Assisted 65; Total Staff 4.

RODEO. *Sisters of Immaculate Heart of Mary*, St. Patrick Convent, 815 Seventh St., 94572. Tel: 510-799-6683. Sisters 3.

SAN LEANDRO. *Dominican Sisters of Oakford*, Our Lady of Guadalupe House of Formation, 327 Woodland Park, 94577. Tel: 510-569-9189. Total in Residence 4; Total Staff 1. Sisters 4.

Holy Names Sisters, Assumption Convent, 1851-136th Ave., 94578. Tel: 510-352-0383. Sisters 2.

Sisters of St. Joseph of Wichita, St. Felicitas Convent, 1662 Manor Blvd., 94579. Tel: 510-351-5244. Sisters 2.

SAN LORENZO. *Presentation Sisters, Kildare, Ireland*, St. John the Baptist Convent, 16642 Ashland Ave., 94580. Tel: 510-278-7128. Sisters 6.

UNION CITY. *Sisters of Charity of the Blessed Virgin Mary*, Union City House, 2500 Medallion Dr., No. 172, 94587. Tel: 510-489-0163. Sisters 2.

[P] PASTORAL CENTERS

BERKELEY. *Jesuit Volunteer Corps Southwest*. Non-Profit Corporation. Mailing Address: P.O. Box 3266, 94703. Tel: 510-653-8564; Fax: 510-653-5145. E-mail:jvcswl@aol.com
Kevin O'Neill, Exec. Dir. Volunteers 110.

DANVILLE. *San Damiano Retreat*, Franciscan Retreat House, Mailing Address: Box 767, 94526. Tel: 510-837-9141; Fax: 510-837-0522. Retreat House for men, women and married couples. Revs. Paul F. Warren, O.F.M., Dir.; Brian Flynn, O.F.M., Guardian; Raymond J. Boucher, O.F.M., Dir. Total in Residence 7; Total Staff 35.

LAFAYETTE. *Diocesan Youth Retreat Center*, 1977 Reliez Valley Rd., 94549. Tel: 510-934-5802; Fax: 510-934-5802. Total in Residence 4; Total Staff 3.

PLEASANT HILL. *Holy Family Center*, 2059 Pleasant Hill Rd., 94523. Tel: 510-935-6151. Ministries: Personal Growth Programs, Counseling, Spiritual, Direction, Adult Faith Formation.

[Q] NEWMAN CENTERS

OAKLAND. *Holy Names College Campus Ministry*, 3500 Mountain Blvd., 94619. Sr. Sharon Casey, O.P., Dir. Campus Min.; Sr. Nora Schaefer, O.P., Assoc. Campus Min.

Mills College Newman Center, 5000 MacArthur Blvd., 94605. Rev. Donald C. Pologruto, C.S.P., Chap.

BERKELEY. *Holy Spirit Parish, University of California, Newman Hall*, 2700 Dwight Way, 94704. Tel: 510-848-7812; Fax: 510-848-0179. Ms. Mary Doyle, Admin.; Ms. Colleen Lenord; Revs. Albert Moser, C.S.P.; Michael B. McGarry, C.S.P.; Frank Sabatte, C.S.P.

HAYWARD. *California State University/Campus Ministry Center*, 25580 Campus Dr., 94542-1199. Tel: 510-581-1970; Fax: 510-581-1026. Rev. Robert J. Loughery, C.S.C., Dir. Total Staff 1.

MORAGA. *St. Mary's College Campus Ministry*, Box 4777, 94575-4777. Tel: 510-631-4366; Fax: 510-631-4332. Scott Connolly, Music Min.; Revs. John McDonough, O.P.; Salvatore Ragusa, S.D.S.; David Deibel; Michael Carey, O.P.; Sr. Ingrid Clemmensen, O.P.

[R] MISCELLANEOUS LISTINGS

OAKLAND. *Adventus*, 2900 Lakeshore Ave., 94610. Tel: 510-893-4711; Fax: 510-893-0945. Rev. David E. Staal. Purpose: To support the mission of the Roman Catholic Diocese of Oakland.

The Benilde Religious & Charitable Trust, c/o Plageman & Assoc., 1999 Harrison St., Ste. 2700, 94612. Mr. William Plageman, Jr., Contact Person. Charitable trust fund to benefit the educational activities of the Brothers of the Christian Schools of San Francisco.

Casa Vincentia, 3210 62nd Ave., 94605. Tel: 510-729-0316. Home for single pregnant women, 18-25 yrs. Sr. Bernardine Dominick, S.S.J.-T.O.S.F., Dir.

Catholic Ladies' Aid Society, Grand Chaplain, 3014 Lake Shore Ave., 94610. Tel: 510-893-4711; Fax: 510-273-4946. Rev. Gary B. Tollner.

Catholic Parent Teacher Groups, 2900 Lake Shore Ave., 94610. Sr. Rose Marie Hennessy, O.P., Moderator.

The Center for AIDS Services, 5720 Shattuck Ave., 94609. Tel: 510-655-3435. Providing practical supportive services and counseling to persons with Acquired Immune Deficiency Syndrome (AIDS), HIV disease and their caregivers. Pastoral counseling and spiritual services available along with a day center, hot lunch meals, transportation, massage, childcare, and other activities. Total Assisted 1,200; Total Staff 14.

Dominican Community Support Charitable Trust, 5877 Birch Ct., 94618. Tel: 510-658-8722. Anthony J. Cordeiro, O.P., Contact Person. Tel: 510-658-8722.

A Friendly Manor/A Friendly Place, 2298 San Pablo Ave., 94612. Tel: 510-451-8923. Sr. Maureen Lyons, C.S.J. Purpose: Daytime hospitality center for homeless women.

Hesed Community, Benedictine Urban Community of Christian Meditation, 3745 Elston Ave., 94602. Tel: 510-482-5573. Sr. Barbara Hazzard, O.S.B.

Institute of Lay Theology, 5890 Birch Ct., 94618. Revs. Eugene R. Zimmers, S.J., Pres.; Michael Zimmers, S.J., Vice. Pres.; Frank B. Nieman, Ph.D., Sec.; John A. Privett, S.J.; Robert L. St. Clair, S.J. A Study Center and Promoter of Evangelization.

Italian Catholic Federation, 2900 Lake Shore Ave., 94610. Rev. Daniel E. Cardelli.

Missionaries of the Kingship of Christ, 1500-34th Ave., 94601. Tel: 510-536-1266. A Franciscan Secular Institute for Women, Men, Priests. Rev. Geoffrey Bridges, O.F.M., Contact Person. Tel: 510-647-2704.

Next Step Learning Center, 2222 Curtis St., 94607. Sr. Cynthia Canning, S.N.J.M., Contact Person.

Pacific Institute for Community Organization, 171 Santa Rosa Ave., 94610. Tel: 510-655-2801; Fax: 510-655-4816. Rev. John A. Baumann, S.J., Exec. Dir.; Dr. Carlos Prietto, Chm.; Rev. Msgr. Norman Rotert, Vice Chm.

St. Mary's Center, 635-22nd St., 94612. Tel: 510-893-4723. Sr. Marilyn Medan, Dir. Food for all Ages Prog.; Susan Werner, Dir. Homeless Prog.; Corinne Lund, Dir. Pre-School Prog.; Rev. Eleanor Shepardson, Exec. Dir.

**The Gamelin-California Association*, Providence House, 540-23rd St., 94612-1718. Tel: 510-444-0839. Apartment building designed for disabled persons and persons with AIDS. Timothy Zaricznyj, Dir. Units 40.

BERKELEY. *Academy of American Franciscan History*, 1712 Euclid Ave., 94709. Tel: 510-848-5232; 548-1755 (Library).

Incarnation Monastery, Camaldolese Benedictines, 1369 La Loma Ave., 94708. Tel: 510-845-0601; Fax: 510-548-6439. Rev. Andrew Colnaghi, Prior. In res., Bros. Cassian Hardie, O.S.B.Cam.; Randy Sweringen.

Inter-Friendship House Association, Friendship Center, 1646 Addison St., 94703. Tel: 510-843-7675. Rev. Bernard M.C. Chu, S.J. (China), Dir. Total Staff 1.

BERKLEY. *Multicultural Institute*, 1712 Euclid Ave., 94709. Tel: 510-848-4075; Fax: 510-848-4095. Board of Directors: Revs. Joseph Baur, O.F.M.; George E. Crespin; Bernie V. Elissagaray; Jose Joel Garcia, Ph.D., J.D.; Revs. Finian McGinn, O.F.M., Ph.D.; Kenan B. Osborne, O.F.M., Ph.D.; Alfredo Terrazas, J.D.; Barbara Terrazas, M.P.H.

CONCORD. *East Bay Services to the Developmentally Disabled*, 1485 Enea Cir., Ste. 1470, 94520. Tel: 510-825-2091; Fax: 510-825-2439. Nonresidence Serves 1,600; Residence 65; Staff 60.

EMERYVILLE. *Lasallain Educational Opportunities, Inc.*, 1266-61st St., 94608. Tel: 510-450-0555. Bro. Christopher Bassen, F.S.C., Prog. Dir. Total Assisted 107; Total Staff 4.

LAFAYETTE. *La Casa de la Luz/The Institute for Spiritual Direction*, 936 Dewing Ave., Ste. I, 94549. Tel: 510-284-5714. Spiritual Direction and Personal Growth of Men and Women. Pamela Prime Sullivan, Dir. Total Staff 4.

MENLO PARK. *The Roman Catholic Communications Corporation of the Bay Area*, 324 Middlefield Rd., 94025. Tel: 510-326-7850; Fax: 510-415-4605. Most Revs. John S. Cummins, Chm.; Pierre DuMaine, Vice Chm. Legal Title: *The Roman Catholic Communications Corporation of the Bay Area. The Catholic Television Network of the Bay Area.*

MISSION SAN JOSE. *Dominican Sisters of Mission San Jose Foundation (A Non-Profit Corp.)*, Mailing Address: P.O. Box 3908, 94539. Tel: 510-657-2468; Fax: 510-657-1734. Sr. Charlotte Shea, O.P., Exec. Vice Pres.; Hugh Campbell, Pres.; Catherine Lyons, Secy. & Treas.

SAN LEANDRO. *Venerable Merlini Foundation*, 2337 W. Ave. 134th, 94577-4132. Tel: 510-357-4982. Marvin J. Steffes, Pres.; Joseph L. Brown, Treas.

RELIGIOUS INSTITUTES OF MEN REPRESENTED IN THE DIOCESE

For further details refer to the corresponding bracketed number in the Religious Institutes of Men or Women section.

[[0140]]—*The Augustinians*.—O.S.A.
[0170]—*Basilian Fathers*.—C.S.B.
[0330]—*Brothers of the Christian Schools*. (Prov. of San Francisco).—F.S.C.
[0600]—*Brothers of the Congregation of Holy Cross*. (Southwest Prov.).—C.S.C.
[0200]—*Camaldolese Benedictines*.—O.S.B.Cam.
[0470]—*The Capuchin Friars*.—O.F.M.Cap.
[0480]—*Conventual Franciscans*.—O.F.M.Conv.
[0260]—*Discalced Carmelite Friars*.—O.C.D.
[1140]—*Fathers of the Sacred Hearts*.—SS.CC.
[0520]—*Franciscan Friars*. (Santa Barbara Prov.).—O.F.M.
[0530]—*Franciscan Friars of the Atonement*.—S.A.
[0690]—*Jesuit Fathers and Brothers*.—S.J.
[0770]—*The Marist Brothers*.—F.M.S.
[0910]—*Oblates of Mary Immaculate*. (Western Prov.).—O.M.I.
[0920]—*Oblates of St. Francis De Sales*.—O.S.F.S.

[0430]—*Order of Preachers-Dominicans*. (Prov. of Holy Name of Jesus).—O.P.

[1030]—*Paulist Fathers*.—C.S.P.

[0610]—*Priests of the Congregation of Holy Cross*.—C.S.C.

[1070]—*Redemptorist Fathers*. (Oakland Prov.).—C.SS.R.

[1190]—*Salesians of Don Bosco*. (Turin, Italy).—S.D.B.

[1240]—*Servites*. (Western Prov.).—O.S.M.

[0760]—*Society of Mary*.—S.M.

[0420]—*Society of the Divine Word*. (Techny, IL).—S.V.D.

[1060]—*Society of the Precious Blòod*. (Prov. of the Pacific).—C.PP.S.

RELIGIOUS INSTITUTES OF WOMEN REPRESENTED IN THE DIOCESE

[0340]—*Carmelite Sisters of Charity*.—C.a.Ch.

[1780]—*Congregation of the Sisters of the Third Order of St. Francis of Perpetual Adoration*. (Spokane, WA).—F.S.P.A.

[0420]—*Discalced Carmelite Nuns*.—O.C.D.

[1070-03]—*Dominican Sisters*.—O.P.

[1070-04]—*Dominican Sisters*.—O.P.

[1070-12]—*Dominican Sisters*.—O.P.

[1070-13]—*Dominican Sisters*.—O.P.

[1070-30]—*Dominican Sisters*.—O.P.

[2470]—*Maryknoll Sisters of St. Dominic*.—M.M.

[]—*Sisters for Christian Community*.—S.F.C.C.

[0430]—*Sisters of Charity of the Blessed Virgin Mary*. (Mt. Carmel, Dubuque, IA).—B.V.M.

[2360]—*Sisters of Loretto At the Foot of the Cross*. (Nerink, KY).—S.L.

[2516]—*Sisters of Mercy*.—S.M.

[2570]—*Sisters of Mercy*. (Burlingame, CA).—S.M.

[3000]—*Sisters of Notre Dame de Namur*. (Prov. of California).—S.N.D.deN.

[3350]—*Sisters of Providence*. (Sacred Heart Prov.).—S.P.

[4080]—*Sisters of Social Service of Los Angeles, Inc.*.—S.S.S.

[1630]—*Sisters of St. Francis of Penance and Christian Charity*.—O.S.F.

[1650]—*Sisters of St. Francis of Philadelphia*.—O.S.F.

[3840]—*Sisters of St. Joseph of Carondelet*. (Los Angeles Prov.).—C.S.J.

[3830-03]—*Sisters of St. Joseph of Orange*.—C.S.J.

[3930]—*Sisters of St. Joseph of the Third Order of St. Francis*. (Prov. of Our Lady of Czestochowa).—S.S.J.-T.O.S.F.

[3830-18]—*Sisters of St. Joseph of Wichita*.—C.S.J.

[1960]—*Sisters of the Holy Family*.—S.H.F.

[1990]—*Sisters of the Holy Names of Jesus and Mary*. (Prov. of Calif.).—S.N.J.M.

[3320]—*Sisters of the Presentation of the B.V.M.* (San Francisco, CA).—P.B.V.M.

[3680]—*Sisters of the Sacred Heart of Jesus and Mary*.—S.H.J.M.

[2150]—*Sisters, Servants of the Immaculate Heart of Mary*.—I.H.M.

[3330]—*Union of the Sisters of the Presentation of the Blessed Virgin Mary*.

DIOCESAN CEMETERIES AND MAUSOLEUMS

OAKLAND. *The Roman Catholic Cemeteries of the Diocese of Oakland*, 2900 Lakeshore Ave., 94610. Tel: 510-893-4711; Fax: 510-893-0945. Directors: Most Rev. John S. Cummins; Revs. Albano Oliveira; David E. Staal; Sr. Barbara Flannery, C.S.J.
St. Mary's.

ANTIOCH. *Holy Cross*.

HAYWARD. *Holy Sepulchre Cemetery and Mausoleum*.

LAFAYETTE. *Queen of Heaven*.

PLEASANTON. *Christ the King*.

SAN PABLO. *St. Joseph's Cemetery and Mausoleum*.

NECROLOGY

† Cabral, Kenneth, (Retired). —Died March 3, 1996.

† Gracias, Edward, Alameda, CA, St. Albert. —Died Sept. 7, 1996.

† McGinty, Michael J., (Retired). —Died March 3, 1996.

† O'Connor, James, (Retired). —Died May 24, 1996.

Diocese of Ogdensburg

(Dioecesis Ogdensburgensis)

Most Reverend

PAUL S. LOVERDE, D.D., S.T.L., J.C.L.

Bishop of Ogdensburg; ordained December 18, 1965; appointed Titular Bishop of Ottabia and Auxiliary Bishop of Hartford February 3, 1988; consecrated April 12, 1988; transferred to Ogdensburg November 11, 1993; installed January 17, 1994. *Res., 624 Washington St., Ogdensburg, NY, 13669.*

Chancery Office: 622 Washington St., P.O. Box 369, Ogdensburg, NY, 13669. Tel.: 315-393-2920; Fax: 315-394-7401.

Most Reverend

STANISLAUS J. BRZANA, S.T.D., LL.D.

Retired Bishop of Ogdensburg; ordained June 7, 1941; appointed Titular Bishop of Cufruta and Auxiliary of Buffalo May 24, 1964; consecrated June 29, 1964; transferred to Ogdensburg October 22, 1968; retired November 11, 1993. *Res., 12 Pine Park, Cheektowaga, NY, 14225.* Tel.: 716-894-9461.

ERECTED BY HIS HOLINESS PIUS IX, FEBRUARY 16, 1872.

Square Miles 12,036.

Incorporated by a special act of the Legislature of the State of New York, April 10, 1945, with the title: The Roman Catholic Diocese of Ogdensburg, New York.

Comprises that part of Herkimer and Hamilton Counties north of the northern line of the townships of Ohio and Russia as existing in 1872 with the entire Counties of Lewis, Jefferson, St. Lawrence, Franklin, Clinton and Essex in the State of New York.

For legal titles of parishes and diocesan institutions, consult the Chancery Office.

STATISTICAL OVERVIEW

Personnel	
Bishop	1
Retired Bishops	1
Priests: Diocesan Active in Diocese	120
Priests: Active Outside Diocese	11
Priests: Diocesan in Foreign Missions	2
Priests: Retired, Sick or Absent	45
Number of Diocesan Priests	178
Religious Priests in Diocese	20
Ordinations:	
Diocesan Priests	1
Religious Priests	1
Transitional Deacons	2
Permanent Deacons	8
Permanent Deacons in Diocese	58
Total Brothers	11
Total Sisters	193
Parishes	
Parishes	121
With Resident Pastor:	
Resident Diocesan Priests	89
Resident Religious Priests	5
Without Resident Pastor:	
Administered by Priests	25
Administered by Women Religious	2
Missions	28
Pastoral Centers	9
New Parishes Created	1
Closed Parishes	1
Professional Ministry Personnel:	
Brothers	1
Sisters	29
Welfare	
Health Care Centers	2
Total Assisted	48,122
Homes for the Aged	3
Total Assisted	880
Day Care and Extended Day Care Centers	1
Total Assisted	26
Special Centers for Social Services	8
Total Assisted	15,407
Educational	
Seminaries, Diocesan	1
Students from This Diocese	6
Students from Other Diocese	17
Diocesan Students in Other Seminaries	9
Total Seminarians	15
Colleges and Universities	1
Total Students	335
High Schools, Diocesan and Parish	2
Total Students	649
Elementary Schools, Diocesan and Parish	24
Total Students	4,476
Catechesis/Religious Education:	
High School Students	3,100
Elementary Students	10,109
Total Students Under Catholic Instruction	18,684
Teachers in the Diocese:	
Priests	2
Brothers	1
Sisters	31
Lay Teachers	306
Vital Statistics	
Receptions into the Church:	
Infant Baptism Totals	1,950
Adult Baptism Totals	167
Received into Full Communion	94
First Communions	1,890
Confirmations	1,473
Marriages:	
Catholic	475
Interfaith	282
Total Marriages	757
Deaths	1,698
Total Catholic Population	138,865
Total Population	420,111

Former Bishops—Rt. Rev. EDGAR P. WADHAMS, D.D., cons. May 5, 1872; died Dec. 5, 1891.—Rt. Rev. HENRY GABRIELS, D.D., cons. May 5, 1892; died April 23, 1921.—Most Rev. JOSEPH H. CONROY, D.D., LL.D., cons. May 1, 1912; succeeded to the See, Nov. 21, 1921; died March 20, 1939.—Most Rev. FRANCIS J. MONAGHAN, S.T.D., LL.D., cons. June 29, 1936; succeeded to the See, March 20, 1939; died Nov. 13, 1942.—Most Rev. BRYAN J. MCENTEGART, D.D., LL.D., cons. Aug. 3, 1943; transferred to Titular See of Aradi, Aug. 19, 1953; appt. June 26, 1953 to Rectorship of Catholic University of America, Washington, D.C., appt. Bishop of Brooklyn, April 16, 1957; installed June 13, 1957; appt. Archbishop, April 15, 1966; retired and appt. Titular Archbishop of Gabii, July 17, 1968; died Sept. 30, 1968.—Most Rev. WALTER P. KELLENBERG, D.D., cons. Oct. 5, 1953; appt. to Ogdensburg, Jan. 19, 1954; transferred to See of Rockville Centre, April 16, 1957; installed May 27, 1957; died Jan. 11, 1986.—Most Rev. JAMES J. NAVAGH, D.D., cons. Sept. 24, 1952; appt. to Ogdensburg, May 8, 1957; transferred to Paterson, Feb. 12, 1963; died in Rome, Oct. 2, 1965.—Most Rev. LEO R. SMITH, D.D., appt. Auxiliary Bishop of Buffalo, July 9, 1952; cons. Sept. 24, 1952; appt. Bishop of Ogdensburg, Feb. 12, 1963; died in Rome Oct. 9, 1963.—Most Rev. THOMAS A. DONNELLAN, D.D., appt. March 4, 1964; cons. April 9, 1964; appt. to Atlanta, May 29, 1968; transferred to Archdiocese of Atlanta, July 16, 1968; died in Atlanta, Oct. 15, 1987.—Most Rev. STANISLAUS J. BRZANA, S.T.D., LL.D, ord. June 7, 1941; appt. Titular Bishop of Cufruta and Auxiliary of Buffalo, May 24, 1964; cons. June 29, 1964; transferred to Ogdensburg, Oct. 22, 1968; retired Nov. 11, 1993.

Chancery Office—622 Washington St., P.O. Box 369, Ogdensburg, 13669. Tel: 315-393-2920; Fax: 315-394-7401. Office Hours: Mon.-Fri. 8:15-4:30 (Sept.-June); Summer hours: 8:45-4.

Secretary to the Bishop—Bro. DAVID EDDY C.F.X., *P.O. Box 369, Ogdensburg, 13669.* Tel: 315-393-2920.

Vicar General—Rev. Msgr. ROBERT L. LAWLER, P.A., V.G., *St. Mary's Rectory, P.O. Box 187, Waddington, 13694.* Tel: 315-388-4466; Fax: 315-388-4722.

Moderator of the Curia and Episcopal Vicar for Pastoral Services—Rev. Msgr. JOHN R. MURPHY, S.T.L., M.A.

Chancellor and Episcopal Vicar for Diocesan Services—Rev. TERRY R. LAVALLEY, J.C.L.

Fiscal Officer—Mr. JOHN J. GRAY, JR., C.P.A., M.B.A.

Diocesan Archivist—Rev. LAWRENCE E. COTTER, S.T.L., *622 Washington St., P.O. Box 369, Ogdensburg, 13669.* Tel: 315-393-2920.

Judicial Vicar—Rev. Msgr. HARRY K. SNOW, M.A., J.C.L.

Secretary to the Tribunal—Sr. MARY PATRICK MURPHY, S.S.J., M.S.; Rev. DOUGLAS J. LUCIA, Assoc. Sec.

Adjutant Judicial Vicars—Revs. PHILIP T. ALLEN; L. WILLIAM GORDON, S.T.L., M.Ed.; TERRY R. LAVALLEY, J.C.L.

Promoter of Justice—Rev. Msgr. PETER R. RIANI, S.T.D., M.Ed.

Defenders of the Bond—Rev. Msgr. JOHN F. PENDERGAST; Rev. Msgr. PAUL E. WHITMORE; Revs. LAWRENCE E. COTTER; JAMES A. DELBEL; RAYMOND J. MOREAU; JOSEPH MORGAN; KEVIN O'BRIEN; ALAN D. SHNOB; J. LEE SNOW; JOHN R. YONKOVIG.

Pro-Synodal Judges—Rev. Msgr. ROBERT H. AUCOIN; Rev. Msgr. BERNARD E. CHRISTMAN; Rev. Msgr. CLARENCE M. DEVAN; Rev. Msgr. HERBERT J. HANNAN; Rev. Msgr. ANTHONY A. MILIA; Rev. Msgr. FRANCIS A. WHITE; Revs. FLOYD J. BLEAUX; ROBERT L. COTTER; JOSEPH W. ELLIOTT; DANIEL T. KEEFE; CLYDE A. LEWIS; GILBERT B. MENARD; EARL W. NICHOLS; F. JAMES SHURTLEFF.

Notary—Mrs. DIANNA SHAVER.

Advocates—Sr. MARY PATRICK MURPHY, S.S.J., M.S.; Rev. Msgr. DENNIS J. DUPREY; Rev. Msgr. JOHN R. MURPHY, S.T.L., M.A.; Revs. FAY W. AGER; DOUGLAS A. DECKER; GARVIN J. DEMARAIS; GARRY B. GIROUX; ALBERT J. HAUSER; ALAN J. LAMICA; WILLIAM G. REAMER; DERK M. SCHUDDE.

Diocesan Consultors—Rev. Msgr. ROBERT L. LAWLER, P.A., V.G.; Rev. Msgr. BERNARD E. CHRISTMAN; Rev. Msgr. CLARENCE M. DEVAN; Rev. Msgr. LEEWARD J. POISSANT; Revs. F. JAMES SHURTLEFF; JAMES T. SPENARD; JAMES M. FLATTERY.

Deans—Adirondack: Rev. TIMOTHY J. SOUCY, V.F., Clinton: Rev. Msgr. C. JOHN MCAVOY, V.F., Essex: Rev. Msgr. FRANCIS A. WHITE, V.F., Franklin: Rev. ARTHUR J. LABAFF, V.F., Hamilton and Herkimer: Rev. LAWRENCE E. MARULLO, V.F., Jefferson: Rev. Msgr. ANTHONY A. MILIA, V.F., Lewis: Rev. LEO A. WILEY, V.F., St. Lawrence: Rev. ANDREW J. AMYOT, V.F.

Council of Priests—Most Rev. PAUL S. LOVERDE, Chm.; Rev. Msgr. BERNARD E. CHRISTMAN, Vice Chm.; Rev. Msgr. ROBERT L. LAWLER, P.A., V.G.; Rev. Msgr. CLARENCE M. DEVAN; Rev. Msgr. GERALD H. SERVICE; Revs. RICHARD S. STURTZ; JAMES T. SPENARD, O.S.A.; JOHN R. YONKOVIG; THOMAS E. KORNMEYER; WILLIAM G. MUENCH; VINCENT T. FREEH, M.S.C.; LEO A. WILEY, V.F.; EUCLID A. MARIER; F. JAMES SHURTLEFF.

Co-Vicars for Religious—Rev. Msgr. DENNIS J. DUPREY; Sr. CATHERINE LIVERS, S.P., *Chancery Office, 622 Washington St., P.O. Box 369, Ogdensburg, 13669-0369.*

Diocesan Offices and Directors

Apostleship of Prayer—Rev. ALBERT J. HAUSER, Dir.

Bishop's Fund Office—Rev. Msgr. GERALD H. SERVICE, Dir. & Chm. of the Committee; Mrs. JANICE SHOEN, Co-Dir., *622 Washington St., P.O. Box 369, Ogdensburg, 13669.* Tel: 315-393-2920.

Building Commission—Most Rev. PAUL S. LOVERDE, Chm. Members: Rev. TERRY R. LAVALLEY, J.C.L.; Rev. Msgr. ROBERT J. GIROUX; Rev.Msgr. JOHN R. MURPHY, S.T.L., M.A.

Catholic Charities of the Diocese of Ogdensburg—Ogdensburg Office—Sr. DONNA FRANKLIN, D.C., Diocesan Dir., *P.O. Box 296, Ogdensburg, 13669.* Tel: 315-393-2255; Fax: 315-393-9362. Mr. PATRICK LYONS, Dir., *P.O. Box 296, Ogdensburg, 13669.* Tel: 315-393-2660. Watertown Office—Mrs. ANNE BOULTER-DAVIS, Dir., *812 State St., Watertown, 13601.* Tel: 315-788-4330; Fax: 315-786-0539. Plattsburgh Office—PAMELA WILSON, M.S., Dir., *4914 S. Catherine St., Plattsburgh, 12901.* Tel: 518-561-0470; Fax: 518-561-0472. Malone Office— *63 E. Main St., P.O. Box 896, Malone, 12953.* Tel: 518-483-1460; Fax: 518-483-1460. Lowville Office— *7514 S. State St., Lowville, 13367.* Tel: 315-376-4141. Port Henry Office— *14 Park Pl., Port Henry, 12974.* Tel: 518-546-3565. Tupper Lake Office— *60 Park St., P.O. Box 701, Tupper Lake, 12986.* Tel: 518-359-7688.

Catholic Relief Services—Sr. DONNA FRANKLIN, D.C., *716 Caroline St., P.O. Box 296, Ogdensburg, 13669.* Tel: 315-393-2660.

Cemeteries—Rev. Msgr. ROBERT J. GIROUX, Dir., *622 Washington St., P.O. Box 369, Ogdensburg, 13669.*

Censor Librorum—Rev. LAWRENCE E. COTTER, B.S., S.T.L., M.S., *St. Patrick's Rectory, P.O. Box 315, Colton, 13625.*

Charismatic Renewal—Rev. FRANCIS CORYER, Liaison, *St. Henry's Church, P.O. Box 301, Dekalb Junction, 13630.*

Clergy and Pastoral Personnel—Rev. Msgr. DENNIS J. DUPREY, Dir., *P.O. Box 369, Ogdensburg, 13669.* Tel: 315-393-2920.

Continuing Education of Priests—Rev. J. ROGER MCGUINNESS, Chm.

Ecumenical Commission—Rev. Msgr. JOSEPH G. BAILEY, Chm., *RD 2, P.O. Box 551, Hammond, 13646.*

Education—Sr. KATHLEEN MURPHY, O.S.F., Supt., Schools; Sr. THERESA LABRAKE, G.N.S.H., Asst. Supt., *622 Washington St., P.O. Box 369, Ogdensburg, 13669.* Tel: 315-393-2920.

Employee Benefits—Mrs. DEBRA L. MOUSAW, *P.O. Box 369, Ogdensburg, 13669.*

Family Life and Pre-Cana—Dr. JOHN MIDDLETON; Mrs. JOHN MIDDLETON, *P.O. Box 519, Chazy, 12921.*

Holy Childhood—Rev. GEORGE MAROUN, Dir., *604 Washington St., P.O. Box 369, Ogdensburg, 13669.*

Information, Bureau of—Rev. TERRY R. LAVALLEY, J.C.L., Dir., *P.O. Box 369, Ogdensburg, 13669.* Tel: 315-393-2920.

Legion of Mary—Rev. Msgr. EDMUND H. DUMAS, *St. Alphonsus Church, P.O. Box 166, Tupper Lake, 12986.*

Natural Family Planning Services—Mr. ANGELO PIETROPAOLI, Pres.; Mrs. ANGELO PIETROPAOLI, Pres., *36 1st St., Malone, 12953.*

Newman Centers—Rev. HARRY E. GIROUX, Diocesan Dir.; Deacon WILLIAM S. RAVEN; Revs. BRUCE T. FAVREAU; J. ROGER MCGUINNESS; FRANCIS J. FLYNN.

Newspaper—"North Country Catholic"; Mrs. MARY LOU KILIAN, Editor; Mr. SCOTT WILSON, Circulation/ Advertising. Tel: 315-393-2540. All communications should be addressed to: *North Country Catholic, P.O. Box 326, Ogdensburg, 13669.*

Ogdensburg Peruvian Apostolate—Revs. JAY SEYMOUR; PATRICK MUNDY, *San Martin de Porres, Casilla 105, Mollendo, Peru, S.A.*

Pastoral Council—Most Rev. PAUL S. LOVERDE, Chm.; Sr. MARY PATRICK MURPHY, S.S.J., Sec., *Mater Dei College, Riverside Dr., Ogdensburg, 13669.*

Pastoral Planning—Rev. Msgr. ROBERT J. GIROUX, Dir.; Rev. TERRY R. LAVALLEY, J.C.L.; Rev. Msgr. DENNIS J. DUPREY, *P.O. Box 369, Ogdensburg, 13669.* Tel: 315-393-2920.

Permanent Diaconate—Revs. HOWARD J. VENETTE, Formation Dir. DONALD J. MANFRED, Continuing Education, *P.O. Box 369, Ogdensburg, 13669.* Tel: 315-393-2920.

Personnel Board—Rev. Msgr. DENNIS J. DUPREY, Dir., Clergy Personnel; Rev. Msgr. JOHN F. PENDERGAST; Revs. J. MICHAEL GAFFNEY; L. WILLIAM GORDON; RAYMOND J. MOREAU; DONALD A. ROBINSON.

Priests' Eucharistic League—Rev. ALBERT J. HAUSER, Dir.

Propagation of the Faith—Rev. GEORGE MAROUN, Dir., *604 Washington St., P.O. Box 369, Ogdensburg, 13669.* Tel: 315-393-0368.

Radio and Television—LINDA KELLEY, Dir., *1900 State Hwy. 11B, Potsdam, 13676.* Tel: 315-265-0261; Fax: 315-268-7104.

Religious Education—(Department of Christian Formation), Mr. MICHAEL WAGNER, Diocesan Dir., *866 Arsenal St., Watertown, 13601.* Tel: 315-782-3620; Fax: 315-782-2009. Ogdensburg Regional Center, *604 Washington St., Ogdensburg, 13669.* Tel: 315-393-0368. Sr. MOLLY SMITH, D.C., Ogdensburg Reg. Dir. Plattsburgh Regional Center, *114A Cornelia St., Plattsburgh, 12901.* Tel: 518-563-2022; Fax: 518-563-2138. Sr. IMELDA KIRKEY, O.S.M, Plattsburgh Dir. Watertown Regional Center, *866 Arsenal St., Watertown, 13601.* Tel: 315-782-3620. Mr. MICHAEL WAGNER, Watertown Reg. Dir.

St. Vincent de Paul Society—Sr. DONNA FRANKLIN, D.C., *716 Caroline St., P.O. Box 296, Odgensburg, 13669.* Tel: 315-393-2660.

Scouts—Sr. MARY RITA KEMPNEY, S.S.J., Diocesan Liaison, *866 Arsenal St., Watertown, 13601.* Tel: 315-782-3620.

Council of Religious—ANN BROUSSEAU, D.H.M., Pres.; Sr. RITA MARY MORISSETTE, O.S.M., Vice Pres.; Sr. RUTH SEGUIN, R.S.M., Sec.; Sr. PATRICIA MURTAGH, R.S.M., Treas.

Vocations—Revs. DONALD A. ROBINSON, Dir. Vocations & Dir. Seminarians Assoc. Vocations Directors; Revs. TIMOTHY CANAAN; CHRISTOPHER CARRARA, *Wadhams Hall, 6866 State Hwy. 37, Ogdensburg, 13669.* Tel: 315-393-4231.

Worship—ALBERT J. HAUSER, Dir.; Sr. ALICE MORAN, O.S.U., Assoc. Dir., *P.O. Box 369, Ogdensburg, 13669.* Tel: 315-393-0368.

Youth Ministry—Mrs. GAYLE FRANK, Dir., *P.O. Box 369, Ogdensburg, 13669.* Tel: 315-393-0368.

CLERGY, PARISHES, MISSIONS AND PAROCHIAL SCHOOLS

CITY OF OGDENSBURG
(St. Lawrence County)

1—ST. MARY'S CATHEDRAL, Rev. Msgr. Leeward J. Poissant, Rector; Rev. Kris C. Lauzon; Rev. Msgr. William J. Argy; Rev. Douglas J. Lucia; Deacons D. Thomas Sharrow; William M. Taylor; Richard E. Winter; Sr. Cecilia Carey, O.P., Pastoral Assoc. In res., Revs. Thomas G. Votraw; Euclid A. Marier; Rev. Msgr. David W. Stinebrickner.
Res., 415 Hamilton St., 13669. Tel: 315-393-3930; Fax: 315-393-6680. [CEM]
Catechesis/Religious Programs—Tel: 315-393-1820. Mrs. Diane Quintal, D.R.E.
Students 257.

2—NOTRE DAME (1859), Revs. John M. Hunt; John M. Demo; Roland G. Gonyo; Deacons Victor Demers; Thomas Kilian; Sr. Ann Marie Conway, O.P., Pastoral Assoc. In res., Rev. Msgr. Dennis Duprey; Rev. Msgr. Robert J. Giroux.
Res., 125 Ford Ave., P.O. Box 149, 13669. Tel: 315-393-5050; Fax: 315-393-5962. [CEM]
School—Ogdensburg Catholic Central School, (Grades K-5) 315 Gates St., 13699. Tel: 315-393-0165. Ms. Nancy LaRue, Prin.
Lay Teachers 9; Students 127.
Catechesis/Religious Programs—Bishop Conroy Christian Formation Program, 214 Morris St., 13669. Tel: 315-393-1820.
Students 175.

OUTSIDE CITY OF OGDENSBURG

Adams, Jefferson Co., St. Cecilia (1870), Rev. Paul J. Kelly.
Res., 23 Grove St., 13605. Tel: 315-232-2392. [CEM]
Catechesis/Religious Programs—Students 196.

Alexandria Bay, Jefferson Co., St. Cyril of Alexandria (1000 Islands) (1885), Rev. Thomas F. Driscoll; Deacon Francis Bradley.
Res., Box 477, 13607. Tel: 315-482-2670. [CEM]
Catechesis/Religious Programs—Students 108.

Altona, Clinton Co., Holy Angels (1865), Rev. Gilbert O. Boisvert.
Res., P.O. Box 113, 12910. Tel: 518-236-5848. [CEM]
Oratory—Jericho, St. Alexis.
Catechesis/Religious Programs—Rebecca Boyea, D.R.E.
Students 142.

Antwerp, Jefferson Co., St. Michael (1849), Rev. Liam O'Doherty.
Res., 30 Maple St., P.O. Box 70, 13608. Tel: 315-659-8372. [CEM]
Mission—Philadelphia, Jefferson Co., St. Joseph, 13608.

Au Sable Forks, Clinton Co., Holy Name (1848), Rev. Donald F. Kramberg; Deacon Joseph H. Gilbert, II.
Res., 10 Church St., P.O. Box 719, 12912. Tel: 518-647-8225. [CEM]
School—(Grades PreK-6) Pleasant St., 12912. Tel: 518-647-8444. Sr. Annunciata Collins, S.S.J., Prin.
Sisters of St. Joseph 1; Lay Teachers 8; Students 114.
Catechesis/Religious Programs—Students 134.

Black Brook, Clinton Co., St. Matthew (1848), Rev. Donald F. Kramberg; Deacon Joseph H. Gilbert, II.
Res., 10 Church St., P.O. Box 719, Au Sable Forks, 12912. Tel: 518-647-8225. [CEM]

Black River, Jefferson Co., St. Paul (1901), Rev. Theodore M. Gillette.
Res., 208 LeRay St., P.O. Box 275, 13612. Tel: 315-773-5672.
Church—210 LeRay St., 13612.
Catechesis/Religious Programs—Students 79.

Bloomingdale, Essex Co., St. Paul (1897), Rev. Joseph P. Trombley.
Res., 50 Saranac Ave., P.O. Box 356, 12913. Tel: 518-891-0144; Fax: 518-891-5259. [CEM 2]
Mission—Gabriels, Franklin Co., Assumption of the B.V.M., Rte. 86, Gabriels, 12939.
Catechesis/Religious Programs—Tel: 518-891-3576. Thelma Niederbuhl, D.R.E.
Students 105.

Bombay, Franklin Co., St. Joseph, Rev. Martin Farrell, O.S.D.
Res., P.O. Box 499, Fort Covington, 12937. Tel: 518-358-4471.

Brasher Falls, St. Lawrence Co., St. Patrick (1830), Rev. Clark S. White; Deacons Floyd J. Barton; Francis Horan. In res., Rev. Msgr. Herbert J. Hannan.
Res., P.O. Box 208, 13613. Tel: 315-389-5401.
Parish Center: Tel: 315-389-5191. [CEM]
Catechesis/Religious Programs—Tel: 315-387-5191. Helen Brown, D.R.E.
Students 199.

Brownville, Jefferson Co., Immaculate Conception of the B.V.M. (1874), Rev. Joseph W. Elliott; Sr. Norah Phelan C.S.C., Pastoral Assoc. & D.R.E.
Res., 119 W. Main St., P.O. Box 99, 13615. Tel: 315-782-1143.
Catechesis/Religious Programs—Tel: 315-788-7240.
Students 306.
Mission—Dexter, St. Elizabeth Seton, 13615. Tel: 315-639-3888.

Brushton, Franklin Co., St. Mary (1870), Revs. Albert G. Salmon; Edward E. Papp. In res., Rev. Michael S. Jarecki.

Res., 12916. Tel: 518-529-7433; Fax: 518-529-6720. [CEM]
Catechesis/Religious Programs—Marian Roscoe, D.R.E.
Students 340.

Burke, Franklin Co., St. George (1874), Rev. Bill Edwards.
Res., P.O. Box 105, Main St., 12917. Tel: 518-483-5687. [CEM]

Cadyville, Clinton Co., St. James Minor (1854), Rev. George W. Tobin.
Res., P.O. Box 117, 12918-0117. Tel: 518-293-7026. [CEM]
Catechesis/Religious Programs—Students 164.

Canton, St. Lawrence Co., St. Mary (1874), Rev. Msgr. Gerald H. Service.
Res., 66 Court St., P.O. Box 308, 13617. Tel: 315-386-2543. [CEM]
School—(Grades PreK-6) 2 Powers St., 13617. Tel: 315-386-3572. Sr. Rita Frances Brady, G.N.S.H., Prin.
Sisters 1; Lay Teachers 8; Students 106.
Catechesis/Religious Programs—D.R.E.: Mrs. Michele Meyers; Angela Klimaszewski.
Students 159.

St. Thomas More (1959). (Campus Parish). Rev. Harry E. Giroux.
Res., 39 Court St., P.O. Box 424, 13617. Tel: 315-386-8425; Fax: 315-386-8425.

Cape Vincent, Jefferson Co., St. Vincent of Paul, Rev. Timothy M. Ladden.
Res., Box 288, 13618. Tel: 315-654-2662. [CEM]

Carthage, Jefferson Co., St. James Minor (1818), Revs. James T. Spenard, O.S.A.; Eugene A. DelConte, O.S.A., Prior; James P. Beinlich, O.S.A.; Sr. M. Victorine Brenon, S.S.J., Pastoral Assoc.; Deacon Richard J. Staab.
Res., 327 West St., 13619. Tel: 315-493-3224; Fax: 315-493-3280. [CEM]
School—Augustinian Academy, (Grades PreK-8) 317 West St., 13619. Tel: 315-493-1301. Sr. John Mary Brockway, S.S.J., Prin.; Sr. M. Victorine Brenon, S.S.J., Supr.
Sisters of St. Joseph 1; Lay Teachers 12; Students 233.
Catechesis/Religious Programs—Students 181.
Convent—Tel: 315-493-1672.
Mission—Natural Bridge, St. Henry.

Champlain, Clinton Co., St. Mary (1861), Rev. Joseph Morgan; Deacon Leonard Patrie.
Res., 86 Church St., P.O. Box 368, 12919. Tel: 518-298-8244. [CEM 2]
School—(Grades K-6). Tel: 518-298-3372. Sr. Marie Cordata, S.S.J., Prin.
Daughters of Charity of the Sacred Heart of Jesus 1; Lay Teachers 8; Students 145.
Catechesis/Religious Programs—Students 195.

Chasm Falls, Franklin Co., St. Helen (1881), Rev. Arthur J. LaBaff; Sr. Sheila Moran, S.S.J., Admin.
Res., P.O. Box 266, Malone, 12953. [CEM]
Church Office: R.F.D. No. 1, Box 311, Malone, 12953. Tel: 518-483-1515.
Catechesis/Religious Programs—Students 63.
Missions—Lake Titus, Franklin Co., St. Mary, 12953.; Owl's Head, Franklin Co., St. Joseph, 12953.

Chateaugay, Franklin Co., St. Patrick (1848), Rev. Fay W. Ager; Sr. Mary Hallahan, O.S.U., Pastoral Assoc.
Res., 11 W. Main St., P.O. Box 908, 12920. Tel: 518-497-6673. [CEM]
Catechesis/Religious Programs—Tel: 518-497-6165.
Students 295.
Mission—Brainardsville, Franklin Co., St. Jude, 12920.

Chaumont, Jefferson Co., All Saints (1922), Rev. John J. Cosmic.
Res., P.O. Box 100, 13622. Tel: 315-649-2717. [CEM]

Chazy, Clinton Co., Sacred Heart, Rev. Louis C. Gardner; Deacon Robert J. LeClair.
Res., P.O. Box 459, 12921. Tel: 518-846-7650. [CEM]

Churubusco, Clinton Co., Immaculate Heart of Mary (1880), Rev. Howard McCasland, Admin.
Res., Rte. 189, 12923. Tel: 518-497-9956. [CEM]
Catechesis/Religious Programs—St. Edmund's Center, Ellenburg, Tel: 518-594-3907.
Students 77.

Clayton, Jefferson Co., St. Mary of Clayton (1838), Rev. Daniel L. Chapin; Deacon Gary A. Frank.
Res., 521 James St., 13624. Tel: 315-686-3398. [CEM 2][JC]
Catechesis/Religious Programs—515 Mary St., 13624. Tel: 315-686-2638.
Students 110.

Colton, St. Lawrence Co., St. Patrick (1864), Rev. Lawrence E. Cotter.
Res., P.O. Box 315, 13625. Tel: 315-262-2871; 262-2188. [CEM]
Catechesis/Religious Programs—Students 85.
Missions—South Colton, St. Lawrence Co., St. Paul, 13625.; Parishville, St. Lawrence Co., St. Michael, 13625.

Constable, Franklin Co., St. Francis of Assisi (1872), Rev. Garry B. Giroux; Deacon Garry N. Burnell.
Res., Maple St., P.O. Box 86, 12926. Tel: 518-483-2775; 483-0486 (Office). [CEM]
Catechesis/Religious Programs—Students 320.
Mission—Westville, Franklin Co., Our Lady of Fatima, 12926.

Constableville, Lewis Co., St. Mary (1820), Rev. Paschal Rys, O.F.M.Conv.
Res., P.O. Box 382, 13325. Tel: 315-397-2556. [CEM][JC 2]
Catechesis/Religious Programs—Students 108.

Coopersville, Clinton Co., St. Joseph (1790), Rev. Normand C. Cote.
Res., 74 Mason Rd., Champlain, 12919-9763. Tel: 518-298-8619. [CEM]
Catechesis/Religious Programs—Students 90.

Copenhagen, Lewis Co., St. Mary (1901), Rev. Charles E. Chase.
Res., High St., P.O. Box 12, 13626. Tel: 315-688-2683. [CEM]
Mission—New Boston, Lewis Co., SS. Peter and Paul. [CEM]

Croghan, Lewis Co., St. Stephen (1869), Rev. Leo A. Wiley.
Res., Main St., P.O. Box 38, 13327. Tel: 315-346-6958. [CEM]
Catechesis/Religious Programs—Tel: 315-346-6963. Thomas Schneeberger, D.R.E.
Students 267.
Oratories—Belfort, St. Vincent de Paul; New Bremen, St. Peter. [CEM]

Crown Point, Essex Co., Sacred Heart Church (1874), Revs. William G. Muench; William G. Reamer; Sr. Leila Spaulding, S.A., Pastoral Assoc.; Deacon Elliott A. Shaw.
Church—12928. Tel: 518-597-3924. [CEM]

Dannemora, Clinton Co., St. Joseph (1853), Rev. John J. Looby; Deacon Edward Mazuchowski. In res., Rev. Peter M. Berg.
Res., 179 Smith St., Box 418, 12929-0418. Tel: 518-492-7118; Fax: 518-492-7742. [CEM 2]
Catechesis/Religious Programs—Tel: 518-492-2524. Lynn Lynch, D.R.E.
Students 195.

Deferiet, Jefferson Co., St. Rita (1900), Revs. James T. Spenard, O.S.A.; Eugene A. DelConte, O.S.A., Prior; James P. Beinlich, O.S.A.
Res., 327 West St., Carthage, 13619. Tel: 315-493-3224.

De Kalb Junction, St. Lawrence Co., St. Henry (1893), Rev. Francis J. Coryer.
Res., 3 Josephine St., P.O. Box 301, 13630. Tel: 315-347-3540; Fax: 315-347-4925. [CEM]
Catechesis/Religious Programs—Students 8.
Mission—Russell, St. Lawrence Co., St. Rene Goupil, 13630.

Edwards, St. Lawrence Co., Sacred Heart (1894), Rev. Francis J. Coryer; Deacon Peter J. Lawless.
Res., P.O. Box 301, De Kalb Junction, 13630. Tel: 315-347-3540; Fax: 315-347-4925. [CEM]
Catechesis/Religious Programs—Students 15.

Elizabethtown, Essex Co., St. Elizabeth (1881), Rev. Msgr. Francis A. White, V.F.
Res., P.O. Box 368, 12932. Tel: 518-873-6760. [CEM]
Catechesis/Religious Programs—Students 108.

Ellenburg, Clinton Co., St. Edmund, Rev. Gilbert B. Menard; Deacon Larry Debiec.
Res., 12933. Tel: 518-594-3907. [CEM]
Catechesis/Religious Programs—D.R.E.: Marie Trombley; Betty Bulriss.
Students 281.

Essex, Essex Co., St. Joseph, Rev. Eugene J. Beaudet.
Res., P.O. Box 607, Willsboro, 12996. Tel: 518-963-4524.

Evans Mills, Jefferson Co., St. Mary (1847), Rev. Pierre Aubin, M.S.C.
Res., 8408 S. Main St., P.O. Box 179, 13637. Tel: 315-629-4425; Fax: 315-629-4581. [CEM]
Mission—Theresa, Jefferson Co., St. Theresa of Avila, 318 Main St., Theresa, 13691.

Fort Covington, Franklin Co., St. Mary, Rev. Martin Farrell, O.S.D.
Res., P.O. Box 499, 12937. Tel: 518-358-4471. [CEM]

Glenfield, Lewis Co., St. Mary (1919), Revs. David Wisniewski; Bernard Jacubco, M.S.C.
Res., 5441 Shady Ave., Lowville, 13367. Tel: 315-376-6662; Fax: 315-376-6663. [CEM]
Mission—Greig, Lewis Co., St. Thomas, (1876). [CEM]

Gouverneur, St. Lawrence Co., St. James (1875), Rev. Vincente Jazmines.
Res., 164 E. Main St., 13642. Tel: 315-287-0114. [CEM 2]
School—(Grades PreK-6) S. Gordon St., 13642. Tel: 315-287-0130. Sr. Ronald Marie Hax, S.S.J., Prin.
Sisters 2; Lay Teachers 7; Students 154.
Catechesis/Religious Programs—Elizabeth Bradford, D.R.E.
Students 181.

Hammond, St. Lawrence Co., St. Peter (1905), Rev. Msgr. Lawrence M. Deno.
Res., P.O. Box 218, 13646. Tel: 315-324-5718; Fax: 315-324-6338.
Mission—Rossie, St. Lawrence Co., St. Patrick, 13646. [CEM]

Harrisville, Lewis Co., St. Francis Solanus (1879), Rev. Howard J. Venette; Deacon Philip Looby.
Res., P.O. Box 208, 13648. Tel: 315-543-2421; Fax: 315-543-7637. [CEM]
Oratory—Lake Bonaparte, St. Rita.

Heuvelton, St. Lawrence Co., St. Raphael's (1880), Rev. Rolland A. Hart.
Res., 5 Clinton St., P.O. Box 377, 13654. Tel: 315-344-2383.

Hogansburg, Franklin Co., St. Patrick (1834), Rev. Msgr. Clarence M. Devan, Admin.
Res., Church St., P.O. Box 427, 13655. Tel: 518-358-2557. [CEM][JC]

Hopkinton, St. Lawrence Co., Church of the Holy Cross, Rev. James A. Delbel.
Res., P.O. Box 288, St. Regis Falls, 12980. Tel: 518-856-9456. [CEM]

Houseville, Lewis Co., St. Hedwig (1922), Revs. David Wisniewski; Bernard Jakubco.
Res., St. Peter's Church, 5541 Shady Ave., Lowville, 13367-1615. Tel: 315-376-6662; Fax: 315-376-6663.

Indian Lake, Hamilton Co., St. Mary's (1958), Rev. Victor E. Lamore.
Res., Rte. No. 28, P.O. Box 332, 12842. Tel: 518-648-5422. [CEM]
Catechesis/Religious Programs—Students 52.
Mission—Blue Mountain Lake, Hamilton Co., St. Paul, 12842.

Inlet, Hamilton Co., St. Anthony of Padua (1897), Rev. Lawrence Marullo, V.F.; Deacon Ronald Ste.-Marie.
Mailing Address: P.O. Box 236, Old Forge, 13420. Tel: 315-369-3554.

Keene, Essex Co., St. Brendan (1868), Rev. Alan J. Lamica.
Res., P.O. Box 130, 12942. Tel: 518-576-4434.
Mission—Wilmington, Essex Co., St. Margaret.

Keeseville, Clinton and Essex Cos., Church of the Immaculate Conception, Rev. Msgr. Joseph Aubin.
Res., 1804 Main St., 12944-1039. Tel: 518-834-7100. [CEM]
Oratory—Clintonville, St. Catherine of Sienna. (Closed).

St. John the Baptist, Rev. Msgr. Joseph Aubin.
Res., 1804 Main St., 12944-1039. Tel: 518-834-7100. [CEM]
Catechesis/Religious Programs—1806 Main St., 12944-1039. Tel: 518-834-6002.
Students 193.

Lafargeville, Jefferson Co., St. John the Evangelist (1898), Rev. Daniel L. Chapin.
Res., 521 James St., Clayton, 13624. Tel: 315-686-3398.
Church—35923 Rte.180, P.O. Box 157, 13656. Tel: 315-658-2295 (Parish Center). [CEM]

Lake Clear, Franklin Co., St. John in the Wilderness (1887), Rev. Bruce T. Favreau.
Res., P.O. Box 260, 12945. Tel: 518-891-2286. [CEM][JC]
Catechesis/Religious Programs—Pius X Inter-Parish Religious Education Center, 23 River St., Saranac Lake, 12983. Tel: 518-891-3111.
Students 45.
Mission—Paul Smiths, Franklin Co., St. Gabriel, Pickett Hall #106, Paul Smiths, 12970. Tel: 518-327-6225.
Summer Station—Fish Creek, State Campsite.

Lake Placid, Essex, Co., St. Agnes (1896), Rev. J. Michael Gaffney.
Res., 6 Hillcrest Ave., 12946. Tel: 518-523-2200. [CEM]
School—(Grades PreK-6) 4 Hillcrest Ave., 12946. Tel: 518-523-3771. Gregory F. Camelo, Prin.
Lay Teachers 10; Students 160.
Catechesis/Religious Programs—Tel: 518-523-3998. Mrs. Margaret Malone, D.R.E.
Students 125.

Lake Pleasant, Hamilton Co., St. James, Major, Rev. Robert Jollet, M.S.C.
Res., P.O. Box 214, Speculator, 12164. Tel: 518-548-6275.

Lisbon, St. Lawrence Co., SS. Philip and James (1870), Rev. Msgr. William J. Argy; Sr. Joan Marie Casey,

R.S.M., Admin. Lay Ministers: Elaine Craig; David Sandburg.
Mailing Address: P.O. Box 175, 13658. Tel: 315-393-3796.
Catechesis/Religious Programs—Students 56.

Long Lake, Hamilton Co., St. Henry (1908), Rev. Robert Decker.
Res., 5 Adams Ln., Newcomb, 12852. Tel: 518-624-2541. [JC]

Louisville, St. Lawrence Co., St. Lawrence (1930), Rev. Thomas A. Moody; Sr. Mary Stephen Durant, O.S.M., Pastoral Assoc.
Res., 30 Willard Rd., Massena, 13662. Tel: 315-769-3120. [CEM]
Catechesis/Religious Programs—Tel: 515-764-0488.
Students 95.

Lowville, Lewis Co., St. Peter (1870), Revs. David Wisniewski; Bernard Jakubco, M.S.C.; Sr. Mary William Argy, S.S.J, Pastoral Assoc.
Res., 5441 Shady Ave., 13367. Tel: 315-376-6662; Fax: 315-376-6663.
School—(Grades PreK-6) 5445 Shady Ave., 13367. Tel: 315-376-2424; Fax: 315-376-2568.
Sisters of St. Joseph 1; Lay Teachers 8.

Lyon Mountain, Clinton Co., St. Bernard (1875), Rev. Msgr. Bernard E. Christman; Deacons Reginald Merrill; Francis Siskavich.
Res., 10 Church Pond Rd., P.O. Box 23, 12952. Tel: 518-735-4357. [CEM]
Catechesis/Religious Programs—Students 99.
Mission—Standish, Clinton Co., St. Michael. [CEM]

Madrid, St. Lawrence Co., St. John the Baptist (1869), Rev. Thomas A. Moody.
Res., 30 Willard Rd., Massena, 13662. Tel: 315-769-3120. [CEM]
Catechesis/Religious Programs—Students 133.

Malone, Franklin Co., Notre Dame (1868), Rev. Arthur J. LaBaff; Rev. Msgr. F. Gordon Coseo, Pastor Emeritus; Revs. Thomas E. Kornmeyer; Gerard Lupa; Sr. Maureen Welch, O.S.U., Pastoral Assoc.
Res., 11 Church Pl., P.O. Box 547, 12953. Tel: 518-483-4074; Fax: 518-483-4185. [CEM]
School—Holy Family, (Grades PreK-8). (Multi-Parish). Tel: 518-483-4443. Sr. Jeraldine Fritz, D.C., Prin.
Sisters 6; Lay Teachers 14; Students 278.
Catechesis/Religious Programs—Tel: 518-483-7380. D.R.E.: Carol Higgins, (Grades K-6); Diane Grant, (Grades 6-8).
Students 271.

St. John Bosco (1935), Rev. Roland V. Menard.
Res., 57 Rennie St., 12953. Tel: 518-483-3642. [CEM]
Catechesis/Religious Programs—Students 131.

St. Joseph's (1837), Rev. F. James Shurtleff; Deacon Richard D. Hart, Pastoral Assoc.
Res., 132 W. Main St., 12953. Tel: 518-483-1300. [CEM 2]
Catechesis/Religious Programs—Valerie Sherwin, D.R.E.
Students 241.

Massena, St. Lawrence Co., Sacred Heart (1874), Rev. Msgr. John F. Pendergast; Revs. James M. Larche; Kevin J. O'Brien; Sr. Juliana Fitzpatrick, O.S.M., Pastoral Assoc.; Deacon James J. Hotte.
Res., 212 Main St., P.O. Box 329, 13662. Tel: 315-769-2469; Fax: 315-769-6973. [CEM]
Catechesis/Religious Programs—Students 327.

St. Joseph, Rev. John L. Downs.
Res., 72 Malby Ave., 13662. Tel: 315-769-3972; Fax: 315-764-5409. [JC]

St. Mary (1913), Rev. Alan D. Shnob.
Res., 105 Cornell Ave., P.O. Box 609, 13662. Tel: 315-764-0239; Fax: 315-769-5526. [JC]
School—Trinity Catholic School, (Grades PreK-6) 188 Main St., 13662. Tel: 315-769-5911. Sr. Mary Eamon Lyng, S.S.J., Prin.
Sisters of Saint Joseph and Servants of Mary 4; Lay Teachers 14; Students 352.
Catechesis/Religious Programs—D.R.E.: Anne Borsellino, (Grades K-6); Henry Deshaies, (Grades 7-12).
Students 211.

Mineville, Essex Co., The Church of All Saints (1872), Rev. Michael A. Toth.
Mailing Address: P.O. Box C, 12956.
Res., 66 Pleasant St., P.O. Box M, Westport, 12993. Tel: 518-942-5953; 962-8610. [CEM]

Mooers, Clinton Co., St. Joseph, Rev. Gerald A. Cerank. In res., Rev. W. Cyril Rapin.
Res., 83 Maple St., 12958. Tel: 518-236-7142. [CEM]
Mailing Address: P.O. Box 98, Mooers Forks, 12959. Tel: 518-236-5632.
Catechesis/Religious Programs—Students 105.

Mooers Forks, Clinton Co., St. Ann (1860), Rev. Gerald Cerank; Deacon Tyrone A. Rabideau.
Res., 3062 Rte. 11, P.O. Box 98, 12959. Tel: 518-236-5632. [CEM]
Catechesis/Religious Programs—Students 128.

Morrisonville, Clinton Co., St. Alexander (1897), Revs. Stephen H. Gratto; James P. Loughren.
Res., 5 Church St., P.O. Box 159, 12962. Tel: 518-561-5039. [CEM][JC]
School—(Grades PreK-8). Tel: 518-563-5615. Sr. Jeanette Roy, F.C.S.C.J., Prin.
Daughters of Charity of the Sacred Heart of Jesus 2; Lay Teachers 10; Students 122.
Catechesis/Religious Programs—Tel: 518-563-7855. Pamela Ballantine, D.R.E.
Students 276.

Morristown, St. Lawrence Co., St. John the Evangelist (1941), Rev. Harry K. Snow.
Res., P.O. Box 216, 13664. Tel: 315-375-6571.
Catechesis/Religious Programs—Students 115.
Mission—Brier Hill, Our Lady of Grace, 13664.

Newcomb, Essex Co., St. Therese (1902), Rev. Robert L. Decker.
Res., 5 Adams Ln., 12852. Tel: 518-582-3671. [CEM]

Norfolk, St. Lawrence Co., Visitation of the B.V.M. (1880), Rev. Andrew J. Amyot.
Res., 3 Morris St., P.O. Box 637, 13667. Tel: 315-384-4242. Rev. Msgr. Thomas J. Robillard.; Res., 11 Hepburn St., P.O. Box 505, 13667. Tel: 315-384-3847. [CEM]
Catechesis/Religious Programs—Students 106.

North Bangor, Franklin Co., St. Augustine (1887), Rev. Raymond J. Moreau; Deacon John C. Dwyer.
Res., P.O. Box 327, 12966. Tel: 518-483-6674. [CEM]
Catechesis/Religious Programs—Jean Jacques, D.R.E.
Students 200.
Mission—West Bangor, Franklin Co., St. Edward, 12966.

North Lawrence, St. Lawrence Co., St. Lawrence (1875), Rev. Clark S. White.
Res., P.O. Box 127, 12967. Tel: 315-389-4594. [CEM]

Norwood, St. Lawrence Co., St. Andrew (1876), Rev. Paul F. Worczak.
Res., 2 Park Ave., 13668. Tel: 315-353-7303. [CEM]
Catechesis/Religious Programs—Tel: 315-353-2824.
Students 121.

Old Forge, Herkimer Co., St. Bartholomew (1897), Rev. Lawrence Marullo, V.F.
Res., P.O. Box 236, 13420. Tel: 315-369-3554.

Olmstedville, Essex Co., St. Joseph (1871), Rev. Richard S. Sturtz.
Mailing Address: Box 368, Schroon Lake, 12870. Tel: 518-251-2565; 532-7100; Fax: 518-532-7461. [CEM]

Peru, Clinton Co., St. Augustine (1883), Revs. Peter R. Riani; John Silver.
Res., 3035 Main St., P.O. Box 569, 12972. Tel: 518-643-2435; Fax: 518-643-0960.
School—Tel: 518-643-9505. Sr. Mary Helen Herman, S.S.J., Prin.
Sisters 2; Lay Teachers 7; Students 185.
Catechesis/Religious Programs—Tel: 518-643-0089.
Students 370.
Mission—West Peru, Clinton Co., St. Patrick, 12972. [CEM 2]

Plattsburgh, Clinton Co.,

1—Our Lady of Victory, (1907), Rev. Floyd J. Bleaux, Jr. In res., Rev. Joseph A. Conti.
Res., 4919 S. Catherine St., 12901. Tel: 518-561-1842; Fax: 518-561-2269. [CEM]
School—Our Lady of Victory Academy, 4917 S. Catherine St., 12901. Tel: 518-563-4262. Lorraine Laframboise, Prin.
Sisters 1; Lay Teachers 7; Students 146.
Convent—4907 S. Catherine St., 12901. Tel: 518-563-7479. Our Lady of Victory Sr. Bernadette Ducharme, S.C.S.L., Regional Supr.

2—St. John the Baptist, (1837), Rev. Msgr. C. J. McAvoy; Revs. Timothy Canaan; Victor G. Pore. Pastoral Assocs.: Sr. Mary Felicitas Wells, R.S.M.; Sr. Elizabeth Sayah, R.S.M. In res., Rev. John M. Crable.
Res., 7 Margaret St., 12901. Tel: 518-563-0730; Fax: 518-563-0754. [CEM]
School—(Grades PreK-8) 59 Broad St., 12901. Tel: 518-563-2260; Fax: 518-563-4553. John Fairchild, Prin.
Priests 1; Sisters 1; Lay Teachers 26; Students 310.
Catechesis/Religious Programs—Tel: 518-561-6694.
Students 129.

3—St. Joseph, (Treadwells Mill) (1935), Revs. Stephen H. Gratto; James Loughren.
Mailing Address: 1349 Military Tpke., 12901. Tel: 518-563-6301.
Res., 5 Church St., P.O. Box 159, Morrisonville, 12962.

4—St. Mary of the Lake, (Cumberland Head) (1965), Rev. Danel T. Keefe.
Res., P.O. Box 704, 12901. Tel: 518-561-2488; Fax: 518-561-3732. [CEM]
Catechesis/Religious Programs—Eunice Trombly, D.R.E.
Students 91.

5—St. Peter, (1853), Revs. John R. Yonkovig; Joseph Wheelock; Deacons Robert King; Robert Diehl, Spiritual Life Dir. In res., Rev. Msgr. Morris L. Dwyer.
Res., 114 Cornelia St., 12901. Tel: 518-563-1692. [CEM]
School—(Grades N-8) St. Charles St., 12904. Tel: 518-561-7132. Mrs. Jean Mockry, Prin.
Sisters 2; Lay Teachers 19; Students 290.
Catechesis/Religious Programs—Tel: 518-563-3278. Sr. Ellen Donahue, S.A., D.R.E.
Students 198.

6—Newman Parish, John XXIII College Community, (1970), Rev. J. Roger McGuinness. Pastoral Assocs.: Mrs. Teri Hart; Sr. Bernadette Ducharme, S.C.S.L.
Res., 90 Broad St., 12901. Tel: 518-563-6852; 561-7545 (Office); Fax: 518-561-1004.

Port Henry, Essex Co., St. Patrick (1854), Rev. L. William Gordon.
Res., 17 St. Patrick's Pl., 12974. Tel: 518-546-7254; Fax: 518-546-3439. [CEM]
Catechesis/Religious Programs—Tel: 518-546-3374.
Students 155.

Port Leyden, Lewis Co., St. Martin (1879), Rev. Msgr. Paul E. Whitmore.
Res., P.O. Box 431, 13433. Tel: 315-348-6104. [CEM]
Catechesis/Religious Programs—Students 92.
Mission—Lyons Falls, Lewis Co., St. John.

Potsdam, St. Lawrence Co., St. Mary (1841), Revs. John P. Kennehan; Douglas Decker; Deacon Frederick A. Brousseau. In res., Rev. Francis Flynn.
Res., 17 Lawrence Ave., 13676. Tel: 315-265-9680; Fax: 315-268-1443. [CEM]
School—(Grades PreK-6). Tel: 315-265-3511.
Lay Teachers 7; Students 117.
Catechesis/Religious Programs—Tel: 315-265-6220.
Students 230.

St. Francis of Assisi Campus Parish (Newman Center) (1969), Rev. Francis J. Flynn.
Office: 39-41 Main St., 13676-2004. Tel: 315-265-9520.
Catechesis/Religious Programs—Students 90.

Raquette Lake, Hamilton Co., St. William, Rev. Lawrence Marullo, V.F.
Mailing Address: P.O. Box 326, Old Forge, 13360. Tel: 315-369-3551.

Raymondville, St. Lawrence Co., St. Raymond (1920), Rev. J. Everett Denesha.
Res., P.O. Box 178, 13678-0178. Tel: 315-384-3191.

Redford, Clinton Co., Assumption of the B.V.M. (1869), Rev. Philip T. Allen.
Res., 78 Clinton St., 12978. Tel: 518-293-6259. [CEM]
School—(Grades K-6). Tel: 518-293-6231. Mrs. Beth Newell, Prin.
Lay Teachers 6; Students 57.

Redwood, Jefferson Co., St. Francis Xavier (1848), Rev. Thomas F. Driscoll. In res., Rev. James L. Meehan, (Retired).
Mailing Address: P.O. Box 477, Alexandria Bay, 13607.
Res., P.O. Box 903, 13679. Tel: 315-482-6359. [CEM]

Rosiere, Jefferson Co., St. Vincent de Paul, Rev. Timothy Ladden. In res., Rev. Eugene A. Kelly.
Res., 31385 County Rte. 4, Cape Vincent, 13618. Tel: 315-654-2576. [CEM]

Rouses Point, Clinton Co., St. Patrick, Rev. Wilfred DeRoche; Deacon Noel A. Hinerth.
Res., 138 Lake St., P.O. Box 217, 12979. Tel: 518-297-7361. [CEM]
Catechesis/Religious Programs—Tel: 518-297-6945; 6387. Patricia Canning, D.R.E.
Students 301.

Sackets Harbor, Jefferson Co., St. Andrew (1886), Rev. Douglas G. Comstock; Deacon Norman Hunneyman.
Res., 110 E. Main St., Box 530, 13685. Tel: 315-646-3341.
Catechesis/Religious Programs—Students 64.
Mission—Henderson, Jefferson Co., Queen of Heaven, 13685.

Saint Regis Falls, Franklin Co., St. Ann, Rev. James A. Delbel.

Res., P.O. Box 288, 12980. Tel: 518-856-9456. [CEM]
Oratory—Santa Clara, St. Peter, Santa Clara.

Saranac Lake, Franklin Co., St. Bernard (1888), Revs. Timothy J. Soucy; Christopher Carrara; Sr. Rita Mary Morrissette, O.S.M., Pastoral Assoc.; Deacons Frederick R. Oberst; Joseph Szweb.
Res., 19 St. Bernard St., 12983. Tel: 518-891-4616; Fax: 518-891-4619. [CEM]
School—Tel: 518-891-2830. Rebecca P. Marlowe, Prin.
Lay Teachers 7; Students 165.
Catechesis/Religious Programs—Pius X Center, 32 River St., 12983. Tel: 518-891-3111. Mrs. Kathy Gonyea, D.R.E.
Students 230.

Schroon Lake, Essex Co., Our Lady of Lourdes (1883), Rev. Richard S. Sturtz.
Res., P.O. Box 368, 12870. Tel: 518-532-7100; Fax: 518-532-7461. [CEM]

Sciota, Clinton Co., St. Louis (1899), Rev. Gilbert O. Boisvert.
Res., P.O. Box 113, Altona, 12910. Tel: 518-236-5848. [CEM]

Star Lake, St. Lawrence Co., St. Hubert (1893), Rev. Robert L. Cotter, Admin.
Res., Oswegatchie Tr., Box 9, 13690. Tel: 315-848-3612. [CEM]
Missions—Newton Falls, St. Lawrence Co., St. Anthony of Padua; Fine, St. Lawrence Co., St. Michael, Fine, 13635. [CEM]

Ticonderoga, Essex Co., St. Mary (1852), Revs. William G. Muench; William G. Reamer; Sr. Leila Spaulding, S.A., Pastoral Assoc.; Deacon Elliott A. Shaw.
Res., 12 Father Jogues Pl., 12883. Tel: 518-585-7144; Fax: 518-585-3632. [CEM]
School—(Grades K-8) 301 Amherst Ave., 12883. Tel: 518-585-7433; Fax: 518-585-3632. Sr. Sharon Anne Dalton, S.S.J., Prin.; Sr. M. Juliana Raymond, S.S.J., Supr.
Sisters 2; Lay Teachers 7; Students 213.
Catechesis/Religious Programs—Students 150.
Convent—307 Lake George Ave., 12883. Tel: 518-585-6547.

Trout River, Franklin Co., St. Bridget (1865), Rev. Garry Giroux; Deacon Garry Burnell.
Res., St. Francis Rectory, P.O. Box 86, Constable, 12926. Tel: 518-483-2775. [CEM]

Tupper Lake, Franklin Co., Holy Name of Jesus (Faust) (1904), Rev. Robert M. Shurtleff.
Res., 114 Main St., 12986. Tel: 518-359-9194. [CEM]
Catechesis/Religious Programs—Tel: 518-359-8089. Mrs. Claire Maroun, D.R.E.
Students 330.

St. Alphonsus, Rev. Donald J. Manfred; Rev. Msgr. Edmund H. Dumas, Pastor Emeritus; Deacons James T. Ellis; James R. Keough; Gerald H. Savage; Sr. Barbara R. McCarthy, O.P., Pastoral Assoc.
Res., 48 Wawbeek Ave., P.O. Box 1166, 12986. Tel: 518-359-3405. [CEM]
School—(Grades PreK-6). Tel: 518-359-2203.
Lay Teachers 7; Students 122.

Waddington, St. Lawrence Co., St. Mary (1826), Rev. Msgr. Robert L. Lawler, P.A., V.G.
Res., P.O. Box 187, 13694. Tel: 315-388-4466; Fax: 315-388-4722. [CEM 3]
Catechesis/Religious Programs—Msgr. Arquett Parish Center, Tel: 315-388-4423.
Students 83.

Watertown, Jefferson Co.,

1—Holy Family, (1895), Revs. Clyde A. Lewis; Albert R. Plante; Scott D. Fobare; Deacons Edward R. Miller; Douglas J. Marlow; Andrew Yarchuk; David F. Moltz; Richard Gaebel.
Res., 129 Winthrop St., 13601. Tel: 315-782-2468; Fax: 315-782-4684.
School—(Grades N-8). Tel: 315-788-7011. Sr. Ellen Rose Coughlin, S.S.J., Prin.
Sisters of St. Joseph 3; Lay Teachers 16; Students 330.
Catechesis/Religious Programs—Holy Family Religious Education Office, Sterling Pl., 13601. Tel: 315-782-6750.
Students 236.

2—Our Lady of the Sacred Heart, Missionaries of the Sacred Heart, (1922), Revs. Vincent T. Freeh, M.S.C.; Benoit C. Dostie, M.S.C.; Richard Huber, M.S.C.; William Connor, M.S.C.; Paul E. Labrosse, M.S.C.; Mark A. Zacker, M.S.C.; Deacon David N. Henningan.
Parish Office: 664 Thompson St., 13601. Tel: 315-782-1474; Fax: 315-782-0473.
Res., 668 Thompson St., 13601. Tel: 315-782-3480; Fax: 315-782-0473. [JC]
School—(Grades K-8) 320 W. Lynde St., Tel: 315-782-3060. Sr. Bernadette Marie Collins, S.S.J., Prin.
Sisters 2; Lay Teachers 14; Students 200.
Preschool and Day Care—Tel: 315-782-3060.
Catechesis/Religious Programs—Beverly A. Hennigan, D.R.E.
Students 110.

3—St. Anthony, (1913), Rev. Msgr. Anthony A. Milia, V.F.; Deacons Vincent J. Frattali; Richard C. Warner, Sr. In res., Rev. Steven M. Murray.
Res., 850 Arsenal St., 13601. Tel: 315-782-1190. [JC]
School—(Grades PreK-8). Tel: 315-788-1461. Mrs. Annette M. Connolly, Prin.
Lay Teachers 10; Students 206.

4—St. Patrick, (1854), Rev. Ivan G. Boyea; Deacon William G. Schmidt.
Res., 724 Ives St., 13601. Tel: 315-782-6086; Fax: 315-782-2909. [CEM]
School—(Grades K-8) 733 S. Massey St., 13601. Tel: 315-788-3935; Fax: 315-788-4447. Sr. Mary Gregory Munger, S.S.J., Prin.
Sisters of St. Joseph 1; Lay Teachers 10; Students 177.
Catechesis/Religious Programs—Students 111.

Wells, Hamilton Co., St. Anne, Rev. Robert Jollet, M.S.C.
Mailing Address: Rt. 8, P.O. Box 214, Speculator, 12164. Tel: 518-548-6275. [CEM]
Catechesis/Religious Programs—Students 10.

West Chazy, Clinton Co., St. Joseph (1884), Rev. Garvin J. Demarais; Deacons Gerald Defayette; Victor Fisher.
Res., P.O. Box 224, 12992. Tel: 518-493-4521. [CEM]
Catechesis/Religious Programs—12992. Tel: 518-493-5222.
Students 140.

West Leyden, Lewis Co., St. Mary's Nativity, Rev. Alfred H. Fish.
Res., P.O. Box 305, 13489. Tel: 315-942-2595. [CEM]
Mission—Fish Creek, SS. Peter & Paul. [CEM]

Westport, Essex Co., St. Philip Neri (1879), Rev. Michael A. Toth.
Res., 66 Pleasant St., Box M, 12993. Tel: 518-962-8610. [CEM]

Willsboro, Essex Co., St. Philip of Jesus, Rev. Eugene J. Beaudet.
Res., P.O. Box 7, 12996. Tel: 518-963-4524. [CEM]

Witherbee, Essex Co., St. Michael (1911). Closed. For inquiries for parish records contact the Chancery.

Chaplains of Public Institutions

Military and Medical

Ogdensburg. *St. Lawrence Psychiatric Center,* St. Vincent's Chapel, 13669. Tel: 315-393-3000. Sr. Kathryn Healey, G.N.S.H., Chap.

Plattsburgh. *Champlain Valley Physicians Hospital Medical Center,* 12901. Rev. John M. Crable, Chap.

Tupper Lake, (Sunmount). *Sunmount Developmental Center for Mentally Handicapped,* 12986. Deacon Joseph Szweb, Chap.

Watertown. *Samaritan Medical Center,* 830 Washington St., 13601. Tel: 315-785-4000. Jean Clark, Chap. and Coord.
U.S. Army Headquarters Fort Drum. Revs. Lito B. Santos; Joseph Hannon; James J. Madden.

Prisons

Ogdensburg. *Ogdensburg Correctional Facility,* One Correction Way, 13669. Tel: 315-393-0281. Deacon D. Thomas Sharrow; Rev. Euclid A. Marier.
Riverview Correctional Facility, Box 158, 13669. Tel: 315-393-8400. Deacon D. Thomas Sharrow; Rev. Dennis J. Duprey.

Altona. *Altona Correctional Facility,* P.O. Box 125, 12910. Tel: 518-236-7841; Fax: 518-236-6235. Deacon Victor J. Fisher; Rev. Bill Edwards.

Cape Vincent. *Cape Vincent Correctional Facility,* 13618. Tel: 315-654-4100, Ext. 548. Deacon Andrew Yarchuk; Rev. William Connor, M.S.C.

Dannemora. *Clinton Correctional Facility,* P.O. Box 798, 12929-0798. Tel: 518-492-2511, Ext. 301. Deacon Eliseo Melendez; Rev. Peter M. Berg Tel: 518-492-7118.

Gabriels. *Gabriel's Correctional Facility,* P.O. Box 100, 12939. Tel: 518-327-3111, Ext. 258. Rev. Joseph Trombley, Chap.

Gouverneur. *Gouverneur Correctional Facility,* Scotch Settlement Rd., P.O. Box 370, 13642. Tel: 315-287-7351; Fax: 315-287-2533. Deacon Vincent E. Irvin, Jr.; Rev. Roland A. Hart.

Lyon Mountain. *Lyon Mountain Correctional Facility,* P.O. Box 23, 12952. Tel: 518-735-4540. Rev. Msgr. Bernard Christman.

Malone. *Barehill Correctional Facility,* Cady Rd., 12953. Tel: 518-483-8411, Ext. 409. Deacon John Trombly; Rev. Robert O. Lamitie.
Franklin Correctional Facility, P.O. Box 10, 12953-9720. Tel: 518-483-6040, Ext. 2402. Mailing Address: 132 W. Main St., 12953. Deacon John Trombly; Rev. James F. Lamitie.

Moriah. *Moriah Shock Incarceration Correctional Facility.* Fisher Hill Rd., P.O. Box 999, Mineville, 12956-0999. Tel: 518-942-7561. Rev. Alan J. Lamica, Home Address, P.O. Box 130, Keene, 12942. Tel: 518-576-4434.

Ray Brook. *Adirondack Correctional Facility,* Box 110, 12977-0110. Tel: 518-891-1343. Rev. Peter Mullen, M.M., Res., Star Rte., Box 152, Saranac Lake, 12983. Tel: 518-891-6540, 891-1343.
Federal Correctional Institution, P.O. Box 300, 12977. Tel: 518-891-5400. Deacon Fred Mader; Rev. Peter Mullen, M.M.

Watertown. *Watertown Correctional Facility,* 13601. Tel: 315-782-7490, Ext. 445. Rev. William Connor, M.S.C., Chap., Res., Missionaries of the Sacred Heart, 666 Thompson St., 13601. Tel: 315-782-3480.

Special Assignment:
Reverend Fathers—
Wertman, Raymond, Credo Foundation, 138 Winthrop St., Watertown, NY 13601

On Duty Outside the Diocese:
Reverend Fathers—
Ledermann, Paul F., Veterans Home, P.O. Box 7, Yountville, CA 94599
Leehy, Stephen G., 4483 Hopewell Rd., Wentzville, MO 63385
Mundy, Patrick W., San Martin De Porres, Casilla 105, Mollendo, Peru S.A.
O'Neil, Maurice L., 505 N. La Canada Dr., Green Valley, AZ 85614
Pease, Anthony F., Cumbermere, Ontario, KOJ ILO Canada
Sestito, Joseph N., 114 Stanwood Ln., Manlius, NY 13104
Seymour, James W., San Martin De Porres, Casilla 105, Mollendo, Peru, S.A.

Military Chaplains:
Reverend Fathers—
Demers, Richard D., U.S. Air Force, 31 Sharon Dr., Edwards AFB, CA 03523
Mulvaney, Andrew R., Chap., U.S. Army, CMR 430, Box 1301, 221 BSB, APO AE, 09096
Ratigan, Patrick A., Chap. U.S. Army, 3450 E. Henderson Way, Clarksville, TN 37042
Sykes, Gregory, Chap., U.S. Army, 709 Bittersweet Ct., Lansing, KS 66043

Absent on Leave:
Reverend Fathers—
Andrews, Lawrence W.
Donoghue, Kelly C.
McHenry, Joel T.
Monica, Ted J.

Absent on Sick Leave:
Reverend Fathers—
Fallon, John, The Towers, 401b, 5400 Montgomery, Albuquerque, NM 87109
Franklin, Edward L., 7821 Linda Vista Rd., Apt. 25, San Diego, CA 92111
Votraw, Thomas G., St. Mary's Cathedral, 415 Hamilton St., Ogdensburg, NY 13669

Retired:
Reverend Monsignors—
Argy, William, St. Mary's Cathedral Rectory, Ogdensburg, NY 13669. Tel: 315-393-3930
Bailey, Joseph G., R.D. 2, P.O. Box 551, Hammond, NY 13646
Berube, Louis D., 613 Green St., Ogdensburg, NY 13669
Coseo, F. Gordon, St. Joseph's Nursing Home, 420 Lafayette St., Ogdensburg, NY 13669
Devan, Clarence M., St. Patrick's Church, P.O. Box 307, Hogansburg, NY 13655
Dumas, Edmund H., 48 Wawbeek Ave., Tupper Lake, NY 12986
Dwyer, Morris L., St. Peter's Rectory, Plattsburgh, NY
Gefell, Gerard, 2332 Humphrey Rd., Cape Vincent, NY 13618. Tel: 315-654-3504
Gefell, Joseph, 2332 Humphrey Rd., Cape Vincent, NY 13618. Tel: 315-654-3504
Giroux, Robert J., Notre Dame Rectory, 125 Ford Ave., P.O. Box 149, Ogdensburg, NY 13669. Tel: 315-393-5050
Hannan, Herbert J., St. Patrick's Church, Brasher Falls, NY 13613
McCarthy, Robert J., 324 Pratt St., Watertown, NY 13601

Phillips, George M., P.O. Box 10, Jemez Springs, NM 87026
Robillard, Thomas J., 11 Hepburn St., Norfolk, NY 13667
Stinebrickner, David W., St. Mary's Cathedral, 415 Hamilton St., Ogdensburg, NY 13669

Reverend Fathers—
Beyette, Paul V., HC Box 218, Loon Lake, N.Y. 12989
Branche, John S., P.O. Box 2176, Amherst, MA 01004. Tel: 413-665-3949
Canning, John W., P.O. Box 712, Parishville, NY 13672
Coffey, William H., 109 Ten Eyck St., Watertown, NY 13601. Tel: 315-788-1394
Cotter, Charles B., 4139 Center St., P.O. Box 554, Lyons Falls, NY 13368
Igo, James P., 10 Daniels St., Arlington, MA 02174
Jarecki, Michael S., St. Mary's Church, Brushton, NY 12916
Kelly, Eugene A., St. Vincent De Paul Rosiere, 31385 County Route 4, Cape Vincent, NY 13618
LaLonde, Emile G., 40 Tangerine Ct., LeHigh Acres, FL 33936
Lyddy, Daniel F., 31 Sydney St., Lowell, MA 01852. Tel: 508-459-9448
Marier, Euclid, 415 Hamilton St., Ogdensburg, NY 13669
Martin, Roger, P.O. Box 273, Baltic, CT 06330
McCasland, Howard, Immaculate Heart of Mary, Rt. 189, Churubusco, NY 12923
Meehan, James L., St. Francis Xavier, Redwood
Menard, Francis A., 6862 E. Main St. Rd., Rte. #1, Box 35, Malone, NY 12953
Nichols, Earl W., 32 Church St., Apt. 15, Brasher Falls, NY 13613
Patterson, Terrence R., Mailing Address: Box 288, Potsdam, NY 13676. Tel: 315-265-2986
Poirier, Raoul J., Mill St., RFD 1, North Bangor, NY 12966
Poupore, Norman E., P.O. Box 824, Pierrepont Manor, NY 13674
Rapin, Cyril, St. Joseph's Church, P.O. Box 288, Mooers, NY 12958-0288
Richard, Charles J., Mater Dei College, 5428 State Hwy. 37, Ogdensburg, NY 13669
Snow, J. Lee, 1631 Palmland Dr., Boynton Beach, FL 33436

Permanent Deacons:
Barton, Floyd, St. Patrick, Brasher Falls
Bradley, Francis, St. Cyril, Alexandria Bay
Brousseau, Frederick A., St. Mary, Potsdam
Burnell, Garry N., St. Francis of Assisi, Constable
Debiec, Larry, St. Edmund, Ellenburg
Defayette, Gerald R., St. Joseph, West Chazy
Demers, Victor, Notre Dame, Ogdensburg
Diehl, Robert, St. Peter, Plattsburgh
Dwyer, John C., St. Augustine, N. Bangor
Ellis, James T., St. Alphonsus, Tupper Lake
Fisher, Victor J., St. Joseph, West Chazy
Frank, Gary A., St. Mary, Clayton
Fratali, Vincent J., St. Anthony, Watertown
Gaebel, Richard M., Holy Family, Watertown
Gilbert, Joseph H., Holy Name, Ausable Forks
Gilner, Gerard, St. Mary, Indian Lake
Hart, Richard D., St. Joseph, Malone
Hennigan, David N., Our Lady of the Sacred Heart, Watertown
Hinerth, Noel A., St. Patrick, Rouses Point
Horan, Francis W., St. Patrick, Brasher Falls
Hotte, James J., Sacred Heart, Massena
Hunneyman, Norman L., St. Andrew, Sackets Harbor
Irvin, Vincent E., Jr., Ogdensburg Correctional Facility, Ogdensburg
Keough, James R., St. Alphonsus, Tupper Lake
Kilian, Thomas F., Notre Dame, Ogdensburg
King, Robert A., St. Peter, Plattsburgh
Lawless, Peter J., Sacred Heart, Edwards
LeClair, Robert J., Sacred Heart, Chazy
Looby, Phillip M., St. Francis, Solanus, Harrisville
Mader, Frederick J., St. Paul, Bloomingdale
Marlow, Douglas, Holy Family, Watertown
Mazuchowski, Edward, St. Joseph, Dannemora
Melendez, Eliseo, Clinton Correctional Facility
Merrill, Reginald F., St. Bernard, Lyon Mountain
Miller, Edward R., Holy Family, Watertown
Moltz, David, Holy Family, Watertown
Oberst, Frederick R., St. Bernard, Saranac Lake
Patrie, Leonard L., St. Mary, Champlain
Rabideau, Tyrone, St. Ann, Mooers Forks
Raven, William S., St. Paul, Black River
Savage, Gerald H., St. Alphonsus, Tupper Lake
Schmidt, William G., St. Patrick, Watertown
Sharrow, Thomas, St. Mary's Cathedral, Ogdensburg
Shaw, Elliott A., St. Mary's, Ticonderoga
Siskavich, Francis, St. Bernard, Lyon Mountain
Staab, Richard J., St. James, Carthage
Ste. - Marie, Ronald, St. Anthony, Inlet
Szwed, Joseph, St. Bernard, Saranac Lake
Taylor, William M., St. Mary's Cathedral, Ogdensburg
Trombly, John J., Franklin Correctional Facility, Malone
Warner, Richard C., Sr., St. Anthony, Watertown
Winter, Richard E., St. Mary's Cathedral, Ogdensburg
Yarchuk, Andrew, Holy Family, Watertown

INSTITUTIONS LOCATED IN THE DIOCESE

[A] SEMINARIES, DIOCESAN

OGDENSBURG. *Wadhams Hall*, 6866 State Hwy. 37, 13669-9308. Tel: 315-393-4231; 393-9824 (Student); Fax: 315-393-4249. Open to candidates for the Diocesan and religious priesthood (and Christian Leadership Program). Four years College and two-year Pre-Theology Program. Rev. Msgr. Robert H. Aucoin, S.T.L., M.Ed., Pres., Chm. & Asst. Prof. Languages; Rev. Donald Robinson, M.A., Vice Pres., Chm. & Prof. Social Science, Dir. Health, Dir. of Admissions, Asst., Prof. of History; Rev. Msgr. Joseph G. Bailey, M.A., Prof. Religious Studies; Rev. Msgr. Leeward J. Poissant, Ph.D., Prof. Philosophy; Revs. Albert J. Hauser, S.T.L., M.A., Asst. Prof. Latin, Religious Studies; George F. Maroun, B.A., Dir. Spiritual Formation, Instructor Religious Studies, Dir. Social Justice; Edward J. Sheedy, M.A., M.S., Asst. Prof. Religious Studies; Stephen R. Rocker, Ph.D., Chm. & Prof. Philosophy, Dean of Students; Kevin J. O'Brien, M.A., J.D., Lecturer of Philosophy; Bro. Guy Roddy, F.I.C., B.A., M.A., M.S., D.Min., Chm. of Religious Studies, Dir. Special Prog., Assoc. Prof. of Social Sciences; Sr. Helen T. Martin, M.S.L.S., Dir. Library; Sr. Mary Christine Taylor, Ph.D., Academic Dean & Prof. Social Sciences; Mr. James D. Crowley, B.A., Lecturer Computer Science; Mr. Donald K. Fellows, M.M., Chair Fine Arts, Asst. Professor Music, Dir. Liturgical Music; Mrs. Rebecca Glover, Ph.D., Visiting Professor of Biology; Mrs. Diana C. Krisciunas, M.A., Chair. & Asst. Prof. English; Mr. Joseph M. Keenan, M.A., M.L.S., Library Asst., Asst. Prof. English; Mrs. Nancy C. Orologio, B.S., Dir. Finance; Mrs. M. Jennifer Palumbo, M.Ed., Instructor Spanish; Mrs. Beth O. Reynolds, M.S., Visiting Prof. Mathematics; Mrs. Rosalie Travison, M.M., Lecturer Fine Arts & Music. Priests 10; Brothers 1; Sisters 2; Lay Teachers 10; Total Staff 23. Students 27.

[B] COLLEGES AND UNIVERSITIES

OGDENSBURG. *Mater Dei College*, 5428 State Hwy. 37, 13669. Tel: 315-393-5930.
For a complete listing, refer to the Colleges and Universities section.

[C] HIGH SCHOOLS, INTERPAROCHIAL

PLATTSBURGH. *Seton Catholic Central*, 5135 N. Catherine St., 12901. Tel: 518-561-4031; Fax: 518-563-1193. Dr. Philip R. Fusco, Ed.D., Prin.; Rev. Joseph A. Conti, Chap. Priests 1; Sisters 2; Brothers 3; Lay Teachers 25; Students 344.

WATERTOWN. *Immaculate Heart Central High School*, 1316 Ives St., 13601. Tel: 315-788-4670. Mr. Pat A. Fontana, Prin.; Rev. Steven Murray, Spiritual Dir. Priests 1; Sisters 7; Lay Teachers 16; Students 335.

[D] RELIGIOUS EDUCATION

OGDENSBURG. *Bishop Conroy School of Religion*, 214 Morris St., 13669-1714.

SARANAC LAKE. *Pius X Center*, 32 River St., 12983.

WATERTOWN. *Watertown Catechetical Office*, Sterling Pl., 13601. Tel: 315-782-0030.

[E] SPECIAL HOSPITALS AND HOMES FOR INVALIDS AND AGED

OGDENSBURG. *St. Joseph's Home*, 420 Lafayette St., 13669. Tel: 315-393-3780; Fax: 315-393-3847.
For a complete listing, refer to the Special Care Facilities section.

LAKE PLACID. *St. Margaret Convent*, 420 Old Military Rd., 12946. Tel: 518-523-2929.
For a complete listing, refer to the Special Care Facilities section.
Uihlein Mercy Center, 420 Old Military Rd., 12946. Tel: 518-523-2464; Fax: 518-523-1401.
For a complete listing, refer to the Special Care Facilities section.

SARANAC LAKE. *St. Joseph's Rehabilitation Center, Inc.*, 99 Glenwood Estates, P.O. Box 470, 12983. Tel: 518-891-3950; 891-4135 (Admissions); Fax: 518-891-3986.
For a complete listing, refer to the Special Care Facilities section.

TUPPER LAKE. *Mercy Healthcare Center, Inc.*, 114 Wawbeek Ave., 12986. Tel: 518-359-3355.
For a complete listing, refer to the Special Care Facilities section.

[F] MONASTERIES AND RESIDENCES OF PRIESTS AND BROTHERS

SARANAC LAKE. *Atonement Friars*, 69 Franklin Ave., 12983. Tel: 518-891-2395. Revs. Timothy Sullivan, S.A.; Arthur M. Johnson, S.A. Total in Residence 2.
St. Joseph's Friary, P.O. Box 470, 12983. Tel: 518-891-3494. Rev. Mark Traenkle, S.A.; Bros. Alan Lemay, S.A.; Paschal Steen, T.S.A. Total in Residence 3.

[G] CONVENTS AND RESIDENCES FOR SISTERS

OGDENSBURG. *D'Youville House, Grey Nuns of the Sacred Heart*, 125 New York Ave., 13669. Tel: 315-393-7422. Sr. Agatha Doe, G.N.S.H., Coord.
Mater Dei College, Sisters of St. Joseph, 5428 State Hwy. 37, 13669. Tel: 315-393-5930. Sr. Mary Patrick Murphy, S.S.J., Supr.
St. Joseph's Convent, Grey Nuns of the Sacred Heart, 709 Franklin St., 13669. Tel: 315-393-1763. Sr. Joan McElwain, G.N.S.H., Supr.
Ursuline Community, P.O. Box 1744, 13669. Tel: 315-393-5423. Ursuline Nuns 3.

CARTHAGE. *St. James Convent, Sisters of St. Joseph*, 317 West St., 13619. Tel: 315-493-1672. Sr. Victorine Brenon, S.S.J., Supr. Total Staff 3; Total in Residence 3.

CHAMPLAIN. *St. Mary's Convent*, 1060 Rte. 9, 12919. Tel: 518-298-3141.

CHASM FALLS. *St. Helen's, Sisters of St. Joseph*, R.D. 1, P.O. Box 311, 12953. Tel: 518-483-1515.

CLAYTON. *Sisters of Holy Cross*, 38289 Rte. 12 E., 13624. Tel: 315-686-3640. Sr. Margaret Fleming, C.S.C. Sisters 2.

ELIZABETHTOWN. *Mercy Center, Sisters of Mercy of Brooklyn*, Water St., P.O. Box 796, 12932. Tel: 518-876-6509.

ELLENBURG CENTER. *Our Lady of the Adirondack's Inc. House of Prayer, Franciscan Sisters of the Atonement*, 7270 Star Rd., Rte. 190, 12934-9708. Tel: 518-594-3253. Sr. Jean T. Beyette, S.A., Dir.; Sr. Antonia Barbary, S.A. Our Lady of Adirondacks Community. Rita S. Parrott, O.L.A.; Theresa M. Lindsey, O.L.A.; Rev. Joseph P. Trombley, Spiritual Dir.

GOUVERNEUR. *St. James' Convent, Sisters of St. Joseph*, 28 S. Gordon St., 13642. Tel: 315-287-0658. Sr. Jane Frances Cutting, S.S.J., Supr. Total Staff 3; Total in Residence 3.

KEESEVILLE. *St. Stanislaus Convent*, 1808 Main St., Rte. 22, 12944. Tel: 518-834-9312. Sisters of Mercy of the Americas, Regional Community of Vermont.

LOWVILLE. *St. Peter's Convent, Sisters of St. Joseph*, 5445 Shady Ave., 13367. Tel: 315-376-6362. Total Staff 2; Total in Residence 2.

MALONE. *St. Joseph's Ursuline Convent, Ursuline Nuns*, 90 Elm St., 12953. Tel: 518-483-2880; Fax: 518-483-7091. Sr. Ann Peterson, O.S.U., Supr. Sisters 13.
Sisters Residence for Holy Family School, 27 Webster St., 12953. Tel: 518-483-1203. Sr. Maureen Sweeney, S.S.J.; Sr. Jeraldine Fritz, D.C.
Ursuline Community, Ursuline Nuns, 104 Park St., 12953. Tel: 518-483-5356. Sr. Maureen Welch, O.S.U., Coord.

MASSENA. *Sacred Heart Convent, Servants of Mary of Omaha, NE*, 188 Main St., P.O. Box 91, 13662. Tel: 315-769-6238. Total in Residence 4.
St. Joseph's Convent, Sisters of St. Joseph, 36 Alden St., 13662. Tel: 315-764-0379. Sr. Mary Eamon Lyng, S.S.J.; Sr. Mary Christine Taylor, S.S.J. Total in Residence 2.

PERU. *St. Augustine's Convent, Sisters of St. Joseph*, 3012 Rte. 22 (Main St.), 12972. Tel: 518-643-6768. Total in Residence 2.

PLATTSBURGH. *Franciscan Sisters of the Atonement*, 61 N. Catherine St., 12901. Tel: 518-563-8893.
Regina Maria Retreat House, Daughters of the Heart of Mary, 77 Brinkerhoff St., 12901. Tel: 518-561-3421. Mary Curran, D.H.M.
Sacred Heart Convent, Daughters of the Charity of the Sacred Heart of Jesus, 1349 Military Tpke., 12901. Tel: 518-561-2631. Sr. Jeannette Roy, F.C-.S.C.J., Supr.
St. John's Convent, 62 Court St., 12901. Tel: 518-561-9689. Sisters of Mercy 2.
St. Louis Community, Sisters of Charity of St. Louis, 4907 S. Catherine St., 12901. Tel: 518-563-7410.
St. Peter's Convent, Dominican Sisters of Hope, 5240 N. Catherine, 12901. Tel: 518-563-4451. Sr. Mary Stephanie Frenette, O.P., Contact Person. Total in Residence 2.

POTSDAM. *St. Mary's Convent, Grey Nuns of the Sacred Heart*, 45 Lawrence Ave., 13676. Tel: 315-265-6840.

ROUSES POINT. *St. Patrick's Convent, Sisters of Charity of St. Louis*, 12 Clinton St., 12979. Tel: 518-297-6712. Sr. Mary Edmund Boutin, S.C.S.L., Supr.

SARANAC LAKE. *St. Bernard's Convent, Servants of Mary-Omaha*, 30 River St., 12983. Tel: 518-891-4363.

St. Joseph's Carmelite Monastery, Discalced Carmelite Nuns, 68 Franklin Ave., 12983. Tel: 518-891-0655. Sr. Marie Gertrude Haughney, O.C.D., Prioress.

Sisters of Mercy of the Americas, Rte. 1, Box 351, 12983. Tel: 518-891-3234.

TICONDEROGA. *St. Mary's Convent, Sisters of St. Joseph*, 307 Lake George Ave., 12883. Tel: 518-585-6547. Sr. Sharon Anne Dalton, S.S.J., Co-Supr.; Sr. M. Juliana Raymond, S.S.J., Co-Supr. Total Staff 2; Total in Residence 2.

TUPPER LAKE. *Dominican Sisters of Hope, Ossining*, 37 Lake St., 12986. Tel: 518-359-9632. Total in Residence 2.

Holy Spirit Convent, 48 High St., 12986. Tel: 518-359-3838. Daughters of the Holy Spirit 2.

WATERTOWN. *Grey Nuns of the Sacred Heart*, 502 Dimmick St., Rear Apt., 13601-3911. Tel: 315-788-2548. Sr. Kathleen E. Hannan, G.N.S.H., Psychotherapy.

Precious Blood Monastery, Sister Adorers of the Prescious Blood, 400 Pratt St., 13601. Tel: 315-788-1669. Sr. Mary Grace Ayotte, A.P.B., Supr. Total Staff 9; Total in Residence 9.

Sisters of Mercy, Watertown, NY, 251 Stone St., 13601-3252. Tel: 315-788-2232. Sr. Rose Curtin, R.S.M., Coord., Additional Address: Villa Catherine, Chaumont. Sisters 4.

Sisters of St. Joseph Motherhouse, 1425 Washington St., 13601. Tel: 315-782-3460. Sr. M. Damien Quenville, S.S.J., Supr.; Sr. Jennifer Votraw, S.S.J., Major Supr. Total Staff 15; Total in Residence 41.

[H] RETREAT HOUSES

PLATTSBURGH. *Regina Maria Retreat House*, 77 Brinkerhoff St., 12901. Tel: 518-561-3421. Miss Louise Brushnefski, Admin. Daughters of the Heart of Mary 3.

[I] INCORPORATED CEMETERIES

BRASHER FALLS. *St. Patrick's Cemetery Association of Brasher Falls, N.Y.*, 13613.

CARTHAGE. *St. James Cemetery Corporation*, 13619.

CROGHAN. *St. Stephen's Cemetery Association, Inc.*, 13327.

MALONE. *Notre Dame Cemetery of Malone, N.Y., Inc.*, 12953.

St. Joseph's Cemetery of Malone, N.Y., Inc., 12953.

PLATTSBURGH. *Mount Carmel Cemetery*, St. John the Baptist Church, 7 Margaret St., 12901.

WATERTOWN. *Calvary Cemetery Association of Watertown, N.Y.*, Sacred Heart Church, 664 Thompson, 13601.

[J] MISCELLANEOUS LISTINGS

OGDENSBURG. *St. Joseph's Foundation, Inc.*, 420 Lafayette St., 13669.

HOGANSBURG (AKWESASNE). *St. Regis Mission*, Box 429, 13655. Tel: 613-575-2066. Reservation and parish on both sides of U.S.-Canadian border. Rev. George H. Belgarde, Admin. Priests 1; Brothers 1.

Roman Catholic Community Center, Inc. (Kateri Tekakwitha Center). Miss Debra Wilcox, Religious Education Coord. Tel: 518-358-2931.

PLATTSBURGH. *Christ Child Day Nursery*, 5115 N. Catherine, 12901. Tel: 518-561-6451. Mrs. Nancy Fournier, Dir. Total Staff 5; Total Assisted 26.

SARANAC LAKE. *Guggenheim Center for Religious Programs*, P.O. Box 664, 12983. Tel: 518-891-0809; 891-3323. Mr. Ralph Bennett, Dir., Res., 15 Leona St., 12983. Tel: 518-891-2844.

WATERTOWN. *Mission Project Service*, 662 Thompson St., 13601. Tel: 315-782-2382. Beverly Hennigan, Exec. Dir.; Rev. Pierre Aubin, M.S.C., Dir.

Sacred Heart Foundation, 668 Thompson St., 13601. Tel: 315-782-3480. Rev. Pierre Aubin, M.S.C., Dir.

Watertown Catholic Schools Development Council, P.O. Box 6800, 13601-6800.

RELIGIOUS INSTITUTES OF MEN REPRESENTED IN THE DIOCESE

For further details refer to the corresponding bracketed number in the Religious Institutes of Men or Women section.

[0140]—*The Augustinians*. (Villanova, PA).—O.S.A.

[0320]—*Brothers of Christian Instruction*. (Alfred, ME).—F.I.C.

[1350]—*Brothers of St. Francis Xavier*.—C.F.X.

[0530]—*Franciscan Friars of the Atonement*.—S.A.

[0690]—*Jesuit Fathers and Brothers*. (French Canadian Prov. of Montreal).—S.J.

[1110]—*Missionaries of the Sacred Heart*.—M.S.C.

[0850]—*Society of Missionaries of Africa*.—M.Afr.

RELIGIOUS INSTITUTES OF WOMEN REPRESENTED IN THE DIOCESE

[0760]—*Daughters of Charity of St. Vincent de Paul*.—D.C.

[0750]—*Daughters of the Charity of the Sacred Heart of Jesus*.—F.C.S.C.J.

[0810]—*Daughters of the Heart of Mary*.—D.H.M.

[0820]—*Daughters of the Holy Spirit*.—S.H.S.

[0420]—*Discalced Carmelite Nuns*.—O.C.D.

[1070-03]—*Dominican Sisters*.—O.P.

[1070-22]—*Dominican Sisters*.—O.P.

[1190]—*Franciscan Sisters of the Atonement*.—S.A.

[1840]—*Grey Nuns of the Sacred Heart*.—G.N.S.H.

[2575]—*Institute of the Sisters of Mercy of the Americas*. (Burlington, VT; Providence, RI; New York, NY).—R.S.M.

[3160]—*Parish Visitors of Mary Immaculate*.—P.V.M.I.

[3590]—*Servants of Mary*. (Servite Sisters).—O.S.M.

[3340]—*Sister of Providence*.—S.P.

[0110]—*Sisters Adorers of the Precious Blood*.—A.P.B.

[0620]—*Sisters of Charity of St. Louis*.—S.C.S.L.

[3840]—*Sisters of St. Joseph of Carondelet*.—C.S.J.

[3830-12]—*Sisters of St. Joseph of Watertown*.—S.S.J.

[4110]—*Ursuline Nuns*.—O.S.U.

NECROLOGY

† Chevalier, Alfred J., (Retired). —Died April 15, 1996.

† Waterhouse, Rev. Msgr. John M., (Retired). —Died Dec. 28, 1995.

Archdiocese of Oklahoma City

(Archidioecesis Oklahomapolitana)

Most Reverend

EUSEBIUS J. BELTRAN, D.D.

Archbishop of Oklahoma City; ordained May 14, 1960; appointed Bishop of Tulsa February 28, 1978; installed April 20, 1978; appointed Archbishop of Oklahoma City November 24, 1992; installed January 22, 1993. *Res., P.O. Box 32180, Oklahoma City, OK, 73123.*

Most Reverend

CHARLES A. SALATKA, D.D.

Retired Archbishop of Oklahoma City; ordained February 24, 1945; appointed Titular Bishop of Cariana and Auxiliary of Grand Rapids December 9, 1961; consecrated March 6, 1962; appointed Bishop of Marquette January 10, 1968; installed March 25, 1968; appointed Archbishop of Oklahoma City September 27, 1977; installed December 15, 1977; retired November 24, 1992. *Res., P.O. Box 32180, Oklahoma City, OK, 73123.*

ESTABLISHED FEBRUARY 6, 1973.

ERECTED INTO A VICARIATE APOSTOLIC BY BRIEF OF MAY 29, 1891. ERECTED INTO THE DIOCESE OF OKLAHOMA WITH THE SEE IN OKLAHOMA CITY BY A BRIEF OF POPE PIUS X, AUGUST 17, 1905. NAME CHANGED TO DIOCESE OF OKLAHOMA CITY AND TULSA BY BULL OF POPE PIUS XI, NOVEMBER 14, 1930. ERECTED INTO ARCHDIOCESE OF OKLAHOMA CITY BY A BULL OF POPE PAUL VI, DECEMBER 13, 1972. THE PROVINCE INCLUDES THE DIOCESES OF TULSA AND LITTLE ROCK.

Comprises the following 46 Counties: Alfalfa, Beaver, Beckham, Blaine, Caddo, Canadian, Carter, Cimarron, Cleveland, Comanche, Cotton, Custer, Dewey, Ellis, Garfield, Garvin, Grady, Grant, Greer, Harmon, Harper, Jackson, Jefferson, Johnston, Kay, Kingfisher, Kiowa, Lincoln, Logan, Love, McClain, Major, Marshall, Murray, Noble, Oklahoma, Pontotoc, Pottawatomie, Roger Mills, Seminole, Stephens, Texas, Tillman, Washita, Woods and Woodward.

Square Miles 42,470.

For legal titles of parishes and archdiocesan institutions, consult the Pastoral Office.

Pastoral Office: 7501 Northwest Expy., P.O. Box 32180, Oklahoma City, OK, 73123. Tel.: 405-721-5651; Fax: 405-721-5210.

STATISTICAL OVERVIEW

Personnel	
Archbishop	1
Retired Archbishops	1
Retired Abbots	3
Priests: Diocesan Active in Diocese	81
Priests: Active Outside Diocese	3
Priests: Retired, Sick or Absent	2
Number of Diocesan Priests	86
Religious Priests in Diocese	30
Extern Priests in Diocese	11
Ordinations:	
Diocesan Priests	1
Permanent Deacons in Diocese	52
Total Brothers	11
Total Sisters	151
Parishes	
Parishes	73
With Resident Pastor:	
Resident Diocesan Priests	61
Resident Religious Priests	8
Without Resident Pastor:	
Administered by Priests	3
Administered by Permanent Deacons	1
Missions	45
Pastoral Centers	1
Professional Ministry Personnel:	
Brothers	1
Sisters	12
Lay Ministers	59
Welfare	
Catholic Hospitals	5
Total Assisted	468,767
Homes for the Aged	3
Total Assisted	229
Day Care and Extended Day Care Centers	2
Total Assisted	385
Residential Care of Disabled	1
Total Assisted	25
Educational	
Diocesan Students in Other Seminaries	12
Seminaries, Religious	1
Total Seminarians	12
Colleges and Universities	1
Total Students	335
High Schools, Diocesan and Parish	1
Total Students	648
High Schools, Private	1
Total Students	255
Elementary Schools, Diocesan and Parish	17
Total Students	3,311
Elementary Schools, Private	1
Total Students	4,214
Catechesis/Religious Education:	
High School Students	2,700
Elementary Students	7,814
Total Students Under Catholic Instruction	19,289
Teachers in the Diocese:	
Priests	2
Sisters	14
Lay Teachers	228
Vital Statistics	
Receptions into the Church:	
Infant Baptism Totals	1,602
Adult Baptism Totals	294
Received into Full Communion	411
First Communions	1,712
Confirmations	1,430
Marriages:	
Catholic	353
Interfaith	361
Total Marriages	714
Deaths	708
Total Catholic Population	92,080
Total Population	2,003,512

Former Bishops—Rt. Rev. THEOPHILE MEERSCHAERT, D.D., ord. Dec. 23, 1871; appt. first Vicar-Apostolic of Indian Territory and Titular Bishop of Sidyma by Bulls of June 2, 1891; cons. in Natchez, Sept. 8, 1891; appt. first Bishop of Oklahoma, Aug. 23, 1905 made assistant at the pontifical throne, Nov. 30, 1916; died Feb. 21, 1924.—Most Rev. FRANCIS C. KELLEY, D.D., LL.D., Ph.D., Litt.D., Bishop of Oklahoma City & Tulsa; ord. Aug. 24, 1893; appt. Bishop of Oklahoma, June 25, 1924; cons. Holy Name Cathedral, Chicago, IL, Oct. 2, 1924; died Feb. 1, 1948.—Most Rev. EUGENE J. MCGUINNESS, D.D., Bishop of Oklahoma City & Tulsa; ord. May 22, 1915; cons. Bishop of Raleigh, Dec. 21, 1937; appt. Coadjutor, Oklahoma City and Tulsa *"cum jure successionis,"* Nov. 11, 1944; installed Jan. 10, 1945; succeeded to the See, Feb. 1, 1948; died Dec. 27, 1957.—Most Rev. VICTOR J. REED, D.D., Bishop of Oklahoma City & Tulsa; ord. Dec. 21, 1929; cons. March 5, 1958; died Sept. 8, 1971.—Most Rev. JOHN R. QUINN, D.D., ord. July 19, 1953; appt. Auxiliary Bishop of San Diego and Titular Bishop of Thisiduo, Oct. 21, 1967 Episcopal ordination, Dec. 12, 1967; translated to Oklahoma City and Tulsa, Nov. 18, 1971; appt. as Archbishop of the Archdiocese of Oklahoma City, Dec. 13, 1972; installed as Archbishop of Oklahoma City, Feb. 6, 1973; transferred to Archbishop of San Francisco, April 26, 1977.

First Prefect-Apostolic—Rt. Rev. ISIDORE ROBOT, O.S.B., died Feb. 15, 1887.

Second Prefect-Apostolic—Rt. Rev. IGNATIUS JEAN, O.S.B., resigned April, 1890; died Aug. 28, 1916.

Regional Vicars Region I—Rev. GERARD A. MACAULAY, *3901 S.W. 29th. St., Oklahoma City, 73119. Region II*, Rev. LOWELL STIEFERMAN, *7336 W. Britton Rd., Oklahoma City, 73132. Region III*, Rev. JOHN VRANA, *125 E St. S.W., Ardmore, 73401. Region IV*, Rev. JAMES D.M. STAFFORD, *P.O. Box 2546, Lawton, 73502. Region V*, Rev. STEPHEN CUDE, *P.O. Box 864, Elk City, 73648. Region VI*, Rev. EDWARD MENASCO, *P.O. Box 708, Woodward, 73802. Region VII*, Rev. JAMES J. MICKUS, *P.O. Box 117, Bison, 73720. Region VIII*, Rev. JOHN MICHALICKA, *P.O. Box 1330, Ponca City, 74602. Region IX*, Rev. PHILIP DONOHOE, *208 S. Evans, El Reno, 73036.*

Pastoral Office—7501 Northwest Expy., P.O. Box 32180, Oklahoma City, 73123. Tel: 405-721-5651; Fax: 405-721-5210. Office Hours: Mon.-Fri. 8:30-4:30.

Chancellor—Rev. JOHN A. STEICHEN.

Vice Chancellor—Rev. EDWARD J. WEISENBURGER, V.G.

Vicar for Ministries—Rev. ANTHONY B. TAYLOR.

Spiritual Direction for Priests—Rev. FRANKLIN WRIGLEY, Coord.

Archdiocesan Tribunal—7501 Northwest Expy., P.O. Box 32180, Oklahoma City, 73123. Tel: 405-721-5651.

Judicial Vicar—Rev. CHARLES H. SCHETTLER, S.T.L., J.C.D.

Assistant Judicial Vicar—Rev. EDWARD WEISENBURGER, V.G., M.A., J.C.L.

Pro-Synodal Judge—Revs. JOHN A. PETUSKEY, M.A.; EDWARD WEISENBURGER, V.G., M.A., J.C.L.; Mr. GEORGE RIGAZZI, J.C.L.

Defenders of the Bond—Revs. LOWELL STIEFERMAN; ALAN J. LOTH; JOHN W. FEEHILY.

Advocates—Rev. EDWARD MENASCO; Mrs. MONA CROSS; Mrs. WANDA J. LANE; Mrs. SUSAN LINDLEY.

Notaries—Mrs. MONA CROSS; Mrs. HELEN L. SELLERS; Mrs. TONI NICHOLLS.

Interdiocesan Tribunal of Second Instance for the Province of Oklahoma City—P.O. Box 32180, Oklahoma

City, 73123. Tel: 405-721-5651.

Judicial Vicar—Rev. ROBERTO QUANT, J.C.L.

Judges—Revs. JAMES A. KASTNER, V.G.; GERARD A. MACAULAY.

Defenders of the Bond—Revs. PHILIP M. DONOHOE; ELMER C. SCHWARZ.

Consultors Archdiocesan—Revs. THOMAS BOYER; JAMES A. KASTNER, V.G.; BRUCE NATSUHARA; JOSEPH R. ROSS; JOHN A. STEICHEN; EDWARD J. WEISENBURGER.

Council of Priests Archdiocesan—Rev. JOSEPH R. ROSS, Chm., *100 E. Stinson, Norman, 73072.* Revs. THOMAS J. BOYER; THOMAS DOWDELL; LARRY GATLIN; JAMES A. KASTNER, V.G.; MARTIN LUGO, O.S.B.; TIMOTHY LUSCHEN; BRUCE NATSUHARA; WILLIAM B. ROSS; JOHN A. STEICHEN; ANTHONY B. TAYLOR; EDWARD J. WEISENBURGER.

Health Panel, Archdiocesan—Rev. WILLIAM B. ROSS, Chm., *P.O. Box 1280, Purcell, 73080.* Tel: 405-527-3077.

Personnel Committee—Revs. RAY ACKERMAN; JAMES A. KASTNER, V.G.; WILLIAM B. ROSS; LOWELL STIEFERMAN.

Archdiocesan Offices and Directors

Office of Stewardship and Development—Mr. JAMES A. WEINMANN, Dir., *P.O. Box 32180, Oklahoma City, 73123.* Tel: 405-721-5651.

Archdiocesan Development Fund—formerly *Diocesan Development Fund;* also formerly known as *Diocesan Fund, Bishop's Fund for Diocesan Development; Mr.* JAMES A. WEINMANN, Dir., *7501 N.W. Expy., P.O. Box 32180, Oklahoma City, 73123.* Tel: 405-721-5651.

Planning Commission Archdiocesan—P.O. Box 32180, Oklahoma City, 73123.

Archdiocese of Oklahoma City Educational Trust Fund—Sr. CATHERINE POWERS, C.N.D., Dir., *7501 N.W. Expy., P.O. Box 32180, Oklahoma City, 73123.*

Associated Catholic Charities—Mr. TIMOTHY O'CONNOR, Dir., *1501 N. Classen Blvd., Oklahoma City, 73106.* Tel: 405-523-3000; Fax: 405-523-3030.

Archdiocesan Finance Council—Most Rev. EUSEBIUS J. BELTRAN, D.D.; Revs. JOHN A. STEICHEN; RICHARD STANSBERRY; THOMAS O'TOOLE; ANTHONY B. TAYLOR; Deacon DALE NEIKIRK; WILLIAM BEAVERS; Mr. ANTHONY KNAPSTEIN; Mrs. SUSAN LOOSEN; Mr. MICHAEL MILLIGAN; Mrs. JENNIFER HOANG PHAM; Mr. HUGH D. RICE; Mr. MICHAEL R. STERKEL; Mr. RICHARD D. VOSS, Business Mgr., *Business Office: P.O. Box 32180, Oklahoma City, 73123.* Tel: 405-721-5651.

Building Committee—Mr. RICHARD D. VOSS, *P.O. Box 32180, Oklahoma City, 73123.* Tel: 405-721-5651.

Catholic Foundation of Oklahoma, Inc.—Mr. RICHARD D. VOSS, Sec./Treas.; Mr. JAMES A. WEINMANN, Dir., Devel., *7501 Northwest Expy., P.O. Box 32180, Oklahoma City, 73123.* Tel: 405-721-5651.

Catholic Lawyers Guild—Rev. RAYMOND K. ACKERMAN, Spiritual Moderator, *2801 South Shartel, Oklahoma City, 73108.* Tel: 405-631-8865.

Catholic Social Services—1501 N. Classen Blvd., Oklahoma City, 73106. Tel: 405-523-3000; Fax: 405-523-3030.

Charismatic Renewal—Rev. MARVIN F. LEVEN, Episcopal Moderator, *P.O. Box 7948, Lawton, 73506.* Tel: 405-536-6351.

Communications, Archdiocesan Department of—Mr. JOHN MALLON, Dir., *P.O. Box 32180, Oklahoma City, 73123.* Tel: 405-721-1810; 721-5651.

Correction Related Ministry—Rev. MARK MASON, *1005 NE 15, Oklahoma City, 73117.* Tel: 405-236-4301.

Council of Catholic Women, Archdiocesan—Rev. JOSEPH C. KOLB; Mrs. LEONARD KOOS, *1313 S. Midwest Blvd., Midwest City, 73110.*

Cursillo Movement—Rev. DON WOLF, Archdiocesan Moderator, *2706 S. Shartel, Oklahoma City, 73109.* Tel: 405-634-2458.

Ecumenical and Interreligious Affairs, Office for Archdiocesan Dir.—Rev. JOHN A. PETUSKEY, *P.O. Box 510, Edmond, 73083.* Tel: 405-340-0691.

Education—Sr. CATHERINE POWERS, C.N.D., Archdiocesan Dir., *P.O. Box 32180, Oklahoma City, 73123.* Tel: 405-721-4202; 721-5651.

Catholic Schools, Office of—Sr. CATHERINE POWERS, C.N.D., Supt.; Sr. MARITA ROTHER, A.S.C., Assoc. Supt., *P.O. Box 32180, Oklahoma City, 73123.* Tel: 405-721-4202; 721-5651.

Religious Education, Office of—Mrs. D'ESTA VERDICCHIO, Dir. MARCO OCANA, Assoc. Dir., Hispanic Religious Education, *P.O. Box 32180, Oklahoma City, 73123.* Tel: 405-721-1415; 721-5651.

Pastoral Ministry Office—Mrs. SHEILA MUELLER, Dir., *P.O. Box 32180, Oklahoma City, 73123.* Tel: 405-721-1415; 721-5651. Affiliated with Kansas Newman College, Wichita, KS, and Aquinas Institute, St. Louis, MO.

Campus Ministry, Department of—Rev. C. JOSEPH MEINHART, *100 E. Stinson, Norman, 73072.* Tel: 405-321-0990.

Clergy Education, Department of—Rev. JAMES A. KASTNER, V.G., Dir., *P.O. Box 32180, Oklahoma City, 73123.* Tel: 405-721-5651.

Evangelization, Office of—Miss JOAN DARK, Dir., *P.O. Box 32180, Okla. City, 73123.* Tel: 405-728-3561; 721-5651, Ext. 150.

Family Life Department—Mr. NICK BAGILEO, *P.O. Box 32180, Oklahoma City, 73123.* Tel: 405-721-8943; 721-5651.

Health Affairs, Archdiocesan Coordinator of and Medical-Moral Consultant—Rev. STEPHEN D. CUDE, *St. Matthew Church, P.O. Box 864, Elk City, 73567.* Tel: 405-225-0066 & 0000.

Hispanic Affairs, Commission For—Rev. DON WOLF, Vicar, *P.O. Box 32180, Oklahoma City, 73123.* Tel: 405-721-5651.

Indian Ministries, Inc.—(Oklahoma), Rev. MICHAEL WHEELAHAN, Liaison, *P.O. Box 628, Anadarko, 73005.* Tel: 405-247-5255.

Infirm Priests Fund (Legal Title)—Rev. JOHN A. STEICHEN, *Pastoral Office, P.O. Box 32180, Oklahoma City, 73123.* Tel: 405-721-5651.

Justice and Human Development, Commission for—Deacon LOU HUFF, *1501 N. Classen Blvd., Oklahoma City, 73106.* Tel: 405-532-3000.

Legal Counsel—Mr. JACK R. LAWRENCE, *3030 Northwest Expy., Oklahoma City, 73112.* Tel: 405-948-6000.

Master of Ceremonies—Revs. ROBERT WOOD; TIMOTHY FULLER, Asst.

Millennium Committee—Rev. PAUL GALLATIN, *5024 North Grove, Oklahoma City, 73122.* Tel: 405-789-2595.

Ministry to Priests Program—Rev. ANTHONY B. TAYLOR, Dir., *P.O. Box 32180, Oklahoma City, 73123.* Tel: 405-721-5651.

Newspaper—"The Sooner Catholic"; Mr. JOHN MALLON, Editor, *P.O. Box 32180, Oklahoma City, 73123.* Tel: 405-721-1810; 721-5651.

Permanent Diaconate—Rev. C. JOSEPH MEINHART, Dir., *P.O. Box 32180, Oklahoma City, 73123.* Tel: 405-721-5651. Deacon JAMES YOUNG, Asst. to the Dir.

Priests' Retirement Board—Most Rev. EUSEBIUS J. BELTRAN, D.D.; Revs. A.G. MACAULAY; JOHN A. STEICHEN, *Pastoral Office, P.O. Box 32180, Oklahoma City, 73123.* Tel: 405-721-5651.

Propagation of the Faith, Holy Childhood Assoc., Missionary Cooperation Plan—Rev. JOHN A. STEICHEN, *P.O. Box 32180, Oklahoma City, 73123.* Tel: 405-721-5651.

Rural Life—Rev. JAMES GREINER, Dir., *1100 N. Sara Road, Musting, 73064.* Tel: 405-376-9435.

Scouting—Rev. MICHAEL WHEELAHAN, *P.O. Box 628, Anadarko, 73005.* Tel: 405-247-5255.

S.P.R.E.A.D.—(Santiago's Physical, Religious Educational, Advancement, Development), Archdiocesan mission of Santiago Atitlan Guatemala, Rev. JOHN A. STEICHEN, Archdiocesan Coord., *P.O. Box 32180, Oklahoma City, 73123.* Tel: 405-721-5651.

St. Ann's Retirement Village—JOY ECKER, Dir. Admin., *9400 St. Ann Dr., Oklahoma City, 73162.* Tel: 405-728-7888.

St. Francis de Sales Seminary (Legal Title)—Most Rev. EUSEBIUS J. BELTRAN, D.D., Pres. Vacant; Vice Pres.; Rev. JOHN A. STEICHEN, Sec. Trustees: Rev. DAVID F. MONAHAN; Mr. RICHARD D. VOSS, Treas., *P.O. Box 32180, Oklahoma City, 73123.*

St. Vincent dePaul, Society of Oklahoma City District Council—Rev. JOHN A. PETUSKEY, Spiritual Moderator, *P.O. Box 510, Edmond, 73083.* Tel: 405-340-0691.

Vocations and Seminarians—Rev. JOHN METZINGER, Dir., *Archdiocesan Pastoral Center, P.O. Box 32180, Oklahoma City, 73123.* Tel: 405-721-9351; 721-5651.

Worship and Spiritual Life, Office of—Rev. STEPHEN BIRD, Dir.; Sr. JOANNE YANKAUSKIS, O.S.B., Co-Dir., *P.O. Box 32180, Oklahoma City, 73123.* Tel: 405-721-5651.

Youth and Young Adult Ministry, Office of—Mrs. NANCY HOUSH, Dir., *P.O. Box 32180, Oklahoma City, 73123.* Tel: 405-721-9220; 721-5651.

CLERGY, PARISHES, MISSIONS AND PAROCHIAL SCHOOLS

OKLAHOMA CITY
(Oklahoma County)

1—CATHEDRAL OF OUR LADY OF PERPETUAL HELP, Revs. Thomas J. Boyer, Rector; Hoa Nguyen. In res., Ray Ackerman.
Res., 3214 N. Lake Ave., 73118. Tel: 405-525-2349; Fax: 405-525-3628. [JC]
School—Bishop John Carroll, 1100 N.W. 32, 73118. Tel: 405-525-0956; Fax: 405-523-3053.
Lay Teachers 13; Students 180.

2—ST. ANDREW DUNG-LAC (Vietnamese), Rev. Peter Nguyen; Deacon San Nguyen.
Church—2337 N.W. 19th St., 73107. Tel: 405-528-3260.
Mailing Address: P.O. Box 75875, 73107.

3—ST. CHARLES BORROMEO, Revs. Paul H. Gallatin; Richard Stansberry, Jr.; Deacons John Pitt; Marc LeWand; Walter Cullinan.
Res., 5024 N. Grove St., 73122. Tel: 405-789-2595; Fax: 405-789-4394. [JC]
School—5000 N. Grove St., 73122. Tel: 405-789-0224; Fax: 405-789-6292.
Lay Teachers 19; Students 265.

4—CHRIST THE KING, Revs. Joseph R. Ross; James A. Kastner; Deacon David Best.
Res., 8005 Dorset Dr., P.O. Box 20508, 73156. Tel: 405-842-1481; Fax: 405-842-1482. [JC]
School—Tel: 405-843-3909; Fax: 504-843-6519. Leslie Bloomer, Prin.
Lay Teachers 17; Students 258.

5—CORPUS CHRISTI, Revs. Mark Mason; Larok Obwano Martin (Uganda); Deacon James Barton.
Res., 1005 N.E. 15th St., 73117. Tel: 405-236-4301. [JC]
School—Tel: 405-232-4811.
Lay Teachers 7; Students 88.

6—CHURCH OF THE EPIPHANY OF THE LORD, Revs. Lowell L. Stieferman; Paul Mollan; Deacon Dale Neikirk.
Res., 7336 W. Britton Rd., 73132. Tel: 405-722-2110; Fax: 405-722-6719.

7—ST. EUGENE'S, Revs. Bill Pruett; Timothy M. Fuller; Deacon Patrick Reynolds.
Res., 2400 W. Hefner Rd., P.O. Box 20930, 73156. Tel: 405-751-7115; Fax: 405-751-8722. [JC]
School—Tel: 405-751-0067.
Lay Teachers 20; Students 305.

8—ST. FRANCIS OF ASSISI, Rev. William M. Eichhoff; Deacon Roland Benoit. In res., Rev. Charles H. Schettler.
Res., 1901 N.W. 18th St., P.O. Box 60569, 73146. Tel: 405-528-0485; Fax: 405-524-1260. [JC]
School—Rosary, 1910 N.W. 19th St., 73106. Tel: 405-525-9272. Mrs. Beverly Warden, Prin.
Sisters 1; Lay Teachers 14; Students 249.

9—ST. PAUL, APOSTLE, Rev. Kenneth E. Kulinski; Deacon Philip LePage; Rev. Mary Joseph Choo, (Korean Chap.).
Res., 3901 S. Sunnylane Rd., Del. City, 73115. Tel: 405-677-4873. [JC]

10—HOLY ANGELS (1924), Rev. Roberto Quant; Deacon Lucio Nieto.
Res., 317 N. Blackwelder St., 73106. Tel: 405-232-6572; Fax: 405-235-8334. [JC]
Convent—1522 N.W. Third St., 73106. Tel: 405-236-3407. Carmelite Missionaries of St. Teresa.

11—IMMACULATE CONCEPTION, Rev. A. Gerard MacAulay; Deacon Agustin Hernandez.
Res., 3901 S.W. 29th St., 73119. Tel: 405-685-4224. [CEM]

12—ST. JAMES, Revs. Larry B. Gatlin; Edward Moras (India); Deacons Otis Davis; Marti Gulikers.
Res., 4308 S. Blackwelder St., 73119. Tel: 405-636-6800; Fax: 405-636-6838.
School—1224 S.W. 41st St., 73109. Tel: 405-636-6810; Fax: 405-636-6839.
Sisters 2; Lay Teachers 17; Students 242.
Convent—4212 S. Blackwelder, 73119. Tel: 405-636-6830. Sisters of Charity of Leavenworth.

13—ST. JOSEPH'S. (Old Cathedral). Rev. Louis J. Lamb.
Church—301 N W 4th St., 73102.
Res., 333 N.W. 5th, #2101, 73102. Tel: 405-235-4565. [JC]
Church—301 N.W. 4th St., 73102.

14—OUR LADY OF MOUNT CARMEL AND ST. THERESE LITTLE FLOWER, Revs. Jenaro De La Cruz, O.C.D.; Marion Joseph Bui, O.C.D.
Res., 1125 S. Walker Ave., Box 26127, 73126. Tel: 405-235-2037. [JC]
Mission—Packing Town, Oklahoma Co., Our Lady of Guadalupe, 2123 S.W. 11th St., Packing Town, 73108.

15—ST. PATRICK'S, In res., Revs. Stephen J. Bird; Don C. Moore.
Res., 2121 N. Portland, P.O. Box 75835, 73147. Tel: 405-947-2275; 946-4441; Fax: 405-942-4894.

16—ST. PHILIP NERI, Rev. John W. Feehily; Deacons Matthew Browne; James G. Young.
Res., 301 Wilson Dr., Midwest City, 73110. Tel: 405-737-4476; Fax: 405-737-3462. [JC]
Catechesis / Religious Programs—Bro. Dominic M. O'Brien, F.M.S., D.R.E.
School—1121 Felix Pl., Oklahoma City, 73110. Tel: 405-737-4496; Fax: 045-741-0531.
Lay Teachers 18; Students 286.

17—SACRED HEART, Revs. Don Wolf; Thomas W. Darnall; Deacons George Leal; Michael Rockey.
Res., 2706 S. Shartel Ave., 73109. Tel: 405-634-2458. [JC]
School—2700 S. Shartel Ave., 73109. Mrs. Rosemary Kerber, Prin.
Sisters of Mercy of the Americas 1; Lay Teachers 11; Students 198.

OUTSIDE OKLAHOMA CITY

Ada, Pontotoc Co., St. Joseph, Rev. Robert T. Wood; Deacon Michael Radosevich.
Res., 1300 E. Beverly St., P.O. Box 1585, 74821. Tel: 405-332-4811.

Altus, Jackson Co., Prince of Peace, Rev. Timothy D. Luschen.
Res., 1500 Falcon Rd., P.O. Box 894, 73522. Tel: 405-482-3363.
Mission—Hollis, Harmon Co., Our Lady of Guadalupe.

Alva, Woods Co., Sacred Heart, Rev. David B. Imming.
Res., 627 12th St., 73717. Tel: 405-327-0339.
Mission—Waynoka, Woods Co., Our Mother of Mercy. 210 South Main St.

Anadarko, Caddo Co., St. Patrick's, Rev. Michael Wheelahan.
Res., 1115 W. Petree Rd., Box 628, 73005. Tel: 405-247-5255.
Missions—Binger, Binger Co., Our Lady of the Most Holy Rosary, Hwy. 152, Binger, 73009.; Carnegie, Caddo Co., St. Richard, Hwy. 9, Carnegie, 73015.

Ardmore, Carter Co., St. Mary, Rev. John P. Vrana.
Res., 125 E St. S.W., 73401. Tel: 405-223-0231; Fax: 405-226-2129. [CEM]
Missions—Healdton, Carter Co., St. Cecilia, 300 E. Lincoln Ave., Healdton, 73438.; Marietta, Love Co., Good Shepherd, Broadway and N. 7th, Marietta, 73448.

Bison, Garfield Co., St. Joseph's, Rev. Alan J. Loth.
Res., Box 117, 73720. Tel: 405-758-3558. [CEM]
Mission—Fairview, Major Co., St. Ann, 6th & Locust, Fairview, 73737. Tel: 405-229-2270.

Blackwell, Kay Co., St. Joseph's, Rev. Joseph W. Burger.
Res., 315 W. Blackwell Ave., P.O. Box 578, 74631. Tel: 405-363-2096.

Calumet, Canadian Co., Immaculate Heart of Mary, Rev. Gerald L. Ucker.
Church—239 Freehoma, 73014.
Res., 811 N.W. 13th, Oklahoma City, 73106. Tel: 405-232-8327.

Chandler, Lincoln Co., Our Lady of Sorrows, Rev. Dominic Hung Hoang; Deacon Robert Foster.
Res., 409 Price Ave., P.O. Box 543, 74834. Tel: 405-258-1239. [CEM]
Mission—Stroud, Lincoln Co., St.Louis, 99th & Eighth Ave., Meeker, 74079.

Cherokee, Alfalfa Co., St. Cornelius, Rev. David B. Imming; Deacon Gary Means.
Res., 404 S. Massachusetts, P.O. Box 197, 73728. Tel: 405-596-3228. [CEM]

Chickasha, Grady Co., Holy Name, Rev. Elmer C. Schwarz.
Res., 210 S. Seventh St., Box 748, 73023. Tel: 405-224-7513. [CEM]

Clinton, Custer Co., St. Mary's, Rev. Michael R. Vaught.
Res., 714 S. 12th St., 73601. Tel: 405-323-0309; 323-0345.
Mission—Cordell, Washita Co., St. Anne, 522 E. Third, Cordell, 73632.

Duncan, Stephens Co., Assumption, Revs. James F. Rapp, O.S.F.S.; Marc J. Clifford, O.S.F.S.; Charles A. LaPenta, O.S.F.S.; Deacon Bernard T. O'Loughlin.
Res., 711 Hickory Ave., 73533. Tel: 405-255-0590; Fax: 405-252-3583. [CEM]
Missions—Marlow, Stephens Co., Immaculate Conception, Fourth & Comanche, Marlow, 73055; Rush Springs, Grady Co., St. Francis of Assisi, Fifth & Choctaw, Rush Springs, 73082; Ryan, Jefferson Co., San Jose, 1117 Lincoln Ave., Ryan, 73565. Tel: 405-757-2830.

Edmond, Oklahoma Co., St. John the Baptist, Revs. John A. Petuskey; Shoury Ponnapati (India); Kevin J. Ratterman; Deacons Bill Coyle; Bill Bawden.
Res., 900 S. Littler St., P.O. Box 510, 73083. Tel: 405-340-0691; Fax: 405-340-5715.
School—St. Elizabeth Ann Seton School, 925 South Blvd., 73083. Tel: 405-348-5364.
Lay Teachers 20; Students 401.

St. Monica, Revs. Anthony B. Taylor; Carlos Castillo (Costa Rica); Deacon Conrad Reisinger.
Mailing Address: 2001 North Western, 73003. Tel: 405-359-2700; Fax: 405-341-0023.
Res., 1121 N.W. 199th St., 73003. Tel: 405-330-2699. [CEM]

Elk City, Beckham Co., St. Matthew's, Rev. Stephen D. Cude.
Mailing Address: 3001 E. Hwy. 6, P.O. Box 864, 73648. Tel: 405-225-0066;225-0000; Fax: 405-225-3522.
Res., 121 Merritt Rd., 73648. [CEM]
Mission—Sayre, Beckham Co., Queen of All Saints, 914 N. 5th St., Sayre, 73662. Tel: 405-928-5124.

El Reno, Canadian Co., Sacred Heart, Rev. Philip M. Donohoe.
Res., 208 S. Evans St., 73036. Tel: 405-262-1405. [CEM]
School—Sacred Heart School, 210 S. Evans, 73036. Tel: 405-262-2284. Ms. Lois Jeffrey, Prin.
Teachers 4students50.

Enid, Garfield Co., St. Francis Xavier, Rev. James J. Mickus; Deacon Anthony Crispo.
Res., 110 N. Madison, Box 3527, 73702. Tel: 405-237-0812; Fax: 405-237-0909. [JC]

St. Gregory the Great, Rev. Thomas R. Dowdell.
Church—1924 W. Willow, 73703. Tel: 405-233-4589; Fax: 405-233-4590.
Res., 2045 Lantern Ln., 73703. Tel: 405-233-1845.
Mission—Goltry, Alfalfa Co., St. Michael, Main St., Goltry, 73739. [CEM]

Frederick, Tillman Co., St. Helen, Rev. Peter G. Ashurst.
Res., 507 E. Highview Ave., Rte. No. 2, 73542. Tel: 405-335-3298; Fax: 405-335-3953.
Mission—Tipton, Tillman Co., Sacred Heart, 300 Frederick St., Tipton, 73570.

Guthrie, Logan Co., St. Mary's, Rev. Denis G. Hanrahan; Deacons Ray Ellison; Richard Washko.
Res., 411 N. Elm St., 73044. Tel: 405-282-4239. [CEM]
School—Lay Teachers 6; Students 59.
Mission—Crescent, Logan Co., St. Margaret Mary, P.O. Box 632, Crescent, 73028. Tel: 405-969-2351.

Guymon, Texas Co., St. Peter's, Revs. Charles R. Murphy; Joseph A. Jacobi; Deacons Joe Cruz; Belvin Dollins; Simon Guerra.
Res., 1220 N. Quinn St., P.O. Box 731, 73942. Tel: 405-338-7212. [CEM]
Missions—Hooker, Texas Co., Sacred Heart, 106 N. Albright, Hooker, 73945; Boise City, Cimarron Co., Good Shepherd, S. Ellis at Second, Boise City, 73933.

Harrah, Oklahoma Co., St. Teresa of Avila, Rev. James Murphy, O.S.B.
Res., 1576 Tim Holt Dr., Box 418, 73045. Tel: 405-454-2819. [CEM]

Hennessey, Kingfisher Co., St. Joseph's, Rev. Joseph C. Kolb.
Res., 211 N. Cherokee St., 73742. Tel: 405-853-4425. [CEM]
Mission—Marshall, Logan Co., St. Camillus, Main St., Marshall, 73056.

Jones, Oklahoma Co., St. Robert Bellarmine, Rev. Gary W. Kayler, Admin.
Mailing Address: P.O. Box 60793, Oklahoma City, 73146. Tel: 405-947-1024.
Res., First at Atlanta, 73049.
Mission—Luther, Oklahoma Co., Saint Theresa of the Infant Jesus, Ash & Third, Luther, 73054.

Kingfisher, Kingfisher Co., SS. Peter and Paul, Rev. James H. Ross.
Res., 309 S. Main St., 73750. Tel: 405-375-4581. [CEM]
School—Tel: 405-375-4616.
Carmelite Sisters 1; Lay Teachers 6; Students 73.

Konawa, Pottawatomie Co., Sacred Heart. Attended by St. Gregory Abbey, Shawnee. Deacon Bro. Justin Jones, O.S.B., Admin.
Res., Rte. 1, Box 101, 74849. Tel: 405-925-2145. [CEM]
Mission—Wanette, Pottawatomie Co., St. Mary.

Lawton, Comanche Co., Blessed Sacrament, Rev. James D.M. Stafford; Deacon Bill Adamson.
Res., 12 S.W. Seventh St., Box 2546, 73502. Tel: 405-355-2054; Fax: 405-355-2055.
School—St. Mary's, 611 A Ave., 73501. Tel: 405-355-5888; Fax: 405-355-2055.
Sisters of Divine Providence 5; Lay Teachers 17; Students 190.

Holy Family. (Formerly St. Barbara). Revs. Marvin F. Leven; James A. Goins; Deacons Herman Lawrence; Leo Martinez, Jr.
Res., 1010 N.W. 82nd St., P.O. Box 7948, 73506. Tel: 405-536-6351; Fax: 405-536-6352.

Mangum, Greer Co., Sacred Heart, Rev. David Monahan; Deacon Pedro Maldonado.
Res., 501 N. Byers, P.O. Box 310, 73554. Tel: 405-782-2657.
Mission—Hobart, Kiowa Co., Sts. Peter & Paul, 324 S. Randlett, P.O. Box 371, Hobart, 73651. Tel: 405-726-3925. [CEM]

McLoud, Pottowatomie Co., St. Vincent de Paul, Rev. Eugene Marshall, O.S.B.
Res., 122 S. 10th St., P.O. Box 585, 74851. Tel: 405-964-5606 (Res.); 878-5452;.

Medford, Grant Co., St. Mary's, Rev. Michael Hughes.
Res., 214 W. Cherokee, Box 360, 73759. Tel: 405-395-2148. [CEM]
Missions—Wakita, Grant Co., St. Mary's Assumption, Main & Birch, Wakita, 73771; Pond Creek, Grant Co., St. Joseph's, S. Hwy. 81, Pond Creek, 73766.

Moore, Cleveland Co., St. Andrew's, Rev. George J. Pupius; Deacons Angus Watford; James L. Keene.
Res., 800 N.W. Fifth, Box 6261, 73153. Tel: 405-799-3334; Fax: 405-799-4951.

Mustang, Canadian Co., Church of the Holy Spirit, Rev. James A. Greiner.
Church—1100 N. Sara Rd., 73064. Tel: 405-376-9435; 376-5218.

Newkirk, Kay Co., St. Francis of Assisi, Rev. Richard J. Beckman.
Res., 610 W. Ninth St., P.O. Box 11, 74647. Tel: 405-362-3320.

Nicoma Park, Oklahoma Co., Our Lady of Fatima, Rev. Wilbur E. Moore.
Res., 2255 W. Meyer Cir., Box 368, 73066. Tel: 405-769-2490.

Norman, Cleveland Co., St. Joseph's, Revs. Ernest A. Flusche; Matthew Price Oswalt; Deacon Larry Sousa.
Res., 425 E. Tonhawa, 73071. Tel: 405-321-8080; Fax: 405-321-4360. [CEM]

Church of St. Mark the Evangelist, Rev. John Metzinger; Deacon James Knight.
Mailing Address: P.O. Box 722217, 73070. Tel: 405-366-7676.
Res., 3701 Castlerock Rd., 73072. Tel: 405-447-3085; Fax: 405-447-0480.
Church—3939 W. Tecumseh Rd., 73070.

St. Thomas More University Parish, Revs. C. Joseph Meinhart; Pudhota J. Bosco, Jr (India); Deacon John Warren.
Church—100 E. Stinson, 73072. Tel: 405-321-0990; Fax: 405-321-0964.
Res., 1617 Homeland, 73072. Tel: 405-329-5319.

Okarche, Kingfisher Co., Holy Trinity, Rev. Edward J. Weisenburger.
Res., 211 W. Missouri, Box 185, 73762. Tel: 405-263-7930; Fax: 405-263-7721. [CEM]
School—Box 485, 73762. Tel: 405-263-4422; Fax: 405-263-7475. Mrs. Teresa Loudermilk, Prin.
Lay Teachers 8; Students 120.

Okeene, Blaine Co., St. Anthony's, Rev. Bruce K. Natsuhara.
Res., 211 S. Fifth St., Box 767, 73763. Tel: 405-822-3511; 822-3544. [CEM]
Mission—Seiling, Dewey Co., St. Thomas, 105 W. McAlister, Seiling, 73663.

Pauls Valley, Garvin Co., St. Catherine of Siena, Rev. Lawrence T. Kowalski.
Res., 205 W. Bert St., 73075. Tel: 405-238-3741; Fax: 405-238-5325.
Mission—Lindsay, Garvin Co., St. Peter's, E. Second & Quapah, Lindsay, 73052.

Perry, Noble Co., St. Rose of Lima, Rev. Kevin Devlin.
Res., 421 Ninth St., 73077. Tel: 405-336-9300. [CEM]
Mission—Billings, Noble Co., Sacred Heart, Broadway & Lowe, Billings, 74630.

Ponca City, Kay Co., Church of St. Mary, Revs. John J. Michalicka; Scott Adams.
Res., 707 E. Ponca St., Box 1330, 74602. Tel: 405-765-6031; Fax: 405-765-1327. [CEM]
Schools—St. Mary, 415 S. 7th, 74601. Tel: 405-765-4387.; Sisters of St. Joseph of Wichita, 311 Fairview St., 74601. Tel: 405-765-0482; Fax: 405-765-0562. Sally Caughlin, Prin.
Sisters 2; Lay Teachers 15; Students 243.

Prague, Lincoln Co., St. Wenceslaus, National Shrine of the Infant Jesus of Prague, Rev. Adrian Vorderlandwehr, O.S.B.
Res., Fourth & Broadway St., Box 488, 74864. Tel: 405-567-3404. [CEM]
Mission—Meeker, Lincoln Co., St.Michael, Hwy. 62, Meeker, 74855.

Purcell, McClain Co., Our Lady of Victory, Rev. William B. Ross.
Res., 316 W. Jefferson St., Box 1280, 73080. Tel: 405-527-3077.
Mission—Lexington, Cleveland Co., St. John the Baptist, 309 S.E. 3rd St., Lexington, 73051. [CEM]

Seminole, Seminole Co., Immaculate Conception, Rev. Thomas Rabideau, O.S.B.; Deacon E. Charles Collier.
Res., Hwy. 9 W., Box 164, 74868. Tel: 405-382-3602.
Mission—Maud, Seminole Co., St. Cecelia, Main St., Maud, 74854.

Shawnee, Pottawatomie Co., St. Benedict, Revs. Charles Massoth, O.S.B.; Basil Keenan, O.S.B.
Res., 632 N. Kickapoo, 74801. Tel: 405-275-0001. [CEM]

Sterling, Comanche Co., Our Lady of Perpetual Help,

Rev. Thomas L. O'Toole.
Res., P.O. Box 188, 73567. Tel: 405-365-4368. [CEM]
Missions—Elgin, Comanche Co., St. Ann, 910 Eighth St., Elgin, 73538. Tel: 405-492-5914; Apache, Caddo Co., Mother of Sorrows, 521 E. Wallace, Apache, 73006. [CEM]

Sulphur, Murray Co., St. Francis Xavier, Rev. David H. True.
Res., 1313 E. Seventh, 73086. Tel: 405-622-3070.
Church—700 E. Oklahoma Ave., 73086. Tel: 405-622-3780.
Missions—Madill, Marshall Co., Holy Cross, 14 W. Francis, Madill, 73446. Tel: 405-795-3721; Tishomingo, Johnston Co., St. Anthony, 305 E. Wilson, Tishomingo, 73460.

Tonkawa, Kay Co., St. Joseph's, Rev. Joseph W. Burger.
Res., 320 W. North St., P.O. Box 525, 74653. Tel: 405-628-2416. [CEM]

Union City, Canadian Co., St. Joseph's, Rev. John A. Steichen.
Res., 404 N. Kate Boevers Ave., Box 100, 73090. Tel: 405-483-5329. [CEM]

Walters, Cotton Co., St. Patrick, Rev. Vincent Traynor, O.S.B.
Mailing Address: P.O. Box 305, 73572. Tel: 405-875-3855.
Res., 209 E. Iowa, 73572.
Missions—Grandfield, Tillman Co., Our Lady of Perpetual Help, S. Main & 8th St., Grandfield, 73546; Waurika, Jefferson Co., St. Thomas Aquinas, 400 Block E, D St., Waurika, 73573.

Watonga, Blaine Co., St. Rose of Lima, Rev. Carl W. Janocha.
Res., 900 N. Clarence Nash, Box 58, 73772. Tel: 405-623-7740.
Missions—Hitchcock, Blaine Co., Sacred Heart, Hitchcock, 73744; Loyal, Kingfisher Co., St. Joseph, Loyal, 73756. [CEM]

Weatherford, Custer Co., St. Eugene's, Rev. Michael L. Chapman; Deacon Joseph Dubey.
Res., 704 N. Bryan, Box 407, 73096. Tel: 405-772-3209; Fax: 405-772-3541. [CEM 3]
Missions—Thomas, Custer Co., Blessed Sacrament, 520 N. Oklahoma, Thomas, 73669; Hinton, Caddo Co., Sacred Heart, 204 N. Clark Ave., Hinton, 73047. Deacon Joseph Dubey.

Wewoka, Seminole Co., St. Joseph. (Mission of St. Stephen). Rev. Matthew J. Brown, O.S.B.
Res., P.O. Box 935, Holdenville, 74848. Tel: 405-379-2512.

Woodward, Woodward Co., St. Peter's, Revs. Edward Menasco; Alphonse Gollapalli (India).
Res., 2020 Oklahoma Ave., Box 708, 73802. Tel: 405-256-5305.
Missions—Mooreland, Woodward Co., Sacred Heart, 301 N. Main, Mooreland, 73852; Shattuck, Ellis Co., Holy Name, 600 S. Main, Shattuck, 73858; Beaver, Beaver Co., St. Frances Cabrini, 101 Ave. C, Beaver, 73932; Buffalo, Harper Co., St. Joseph, 325 S.W. 2nd, Buffalo, 73834.

Yukon, Canadian Co., St. John Nepomuk, Rev. Ben Zoeller; Deacon Hi Joseph Roberts.
Mailing Address: P.O. Box 850249, 73085.
Church—600 S. 11th St., 73099. Tel: 405-354-2743; Fax: 405-354-2770.
School—Tel: 405-354-2509. Sr. Laurentia Koehler, A.S.C., Prin.
Sisters 1; Lay Teachers 11; Students 104.

INDIAN MISSIONS

Canton, Blaine Co., Las Casas Dominican Ministry Among the Cheyenne and Arapaho,
Res., 524 West Pine, OK 73724/9703. Tel: 405-886-3413.
THE WHITE EARTH CENTER—.

Chaplains of Public Institutions

Special Assignment:
Reverend Fathers—
Ackerman, Raymond K., President Mt. St. Mary High School, 2801 S. Shartel, Oklahoma City, OK 73109. Tel: 405-842-6639
Bash, Cletus, Chap. Mercy Health Center, 4300 W. Memorial Rd., Oklahoma City, OK 73120
Bird, Stephen J., Director, Office of Worship & Spiritual Life, P.O. Box 32180, Oklahoma City, OK 73123. Tel: 405-721-5651
Mason, Mark, Co-Chap. Oklahoma Health Center, 1005 N.E. 15th St., Oklahoma City, OK 73117
McSherry, Thomas, Micatokla, Santiago-Atitlan, Departmento Solola, Guatemala
Meinhart, Joseph C., Dir. Permanent Diaconate, P.O. Box 32180, Oklahoma City, OK 73123
Metzinger, John R., Director, Seminarians & Vocations, P.O. Box 32180, Oklahoma City, OK 73123
Mollan, Paul F., Chap. Dioconess and Baptist Hospitals, 7336 W. Britton Rd., Oklahoma City, OK 73132
Moore, Donald C., St. Ann's Home, 9400 St. Ann's Dr., Oklahoma City, OK 73162
Roberson, Henry, Chap., St. Mary Mercy Hospital, P.O. Box 467, Enid, OK 73702. Tel: 405-233-1345
Seeton, Philip, Chap., McGuinness High School, 901 N.W. 50th, Oklahoma City, OK 73118
Taylor, Anthony, Vicar for Ministries, P.O. Box 32180, Oklahoma City, OK 73123. Tel: 405-721-5651
Vas, Joseph S., Chap. St. Anthony Hospital, 1000 N. Lee St., P.O. Box 205, Oklahoma City, OK 73101. Tel: 405-272-6263
Wrigley, Franklin, Coord. Spiritual Direction for Priest, 700 N.E. 19th St., Oklahoma City, OK 73105. Tel: 405-524-1118

On Duty Outside the Archdiocese:
Reverend Fathers—
Cowden, David, 432 E. Fireweed Ave., Palmer, AK 99645
Parker, Rick, 26245 Ocean View Ave., Carmel, CA 93923

Graduate Studies:
Reverend Fathers—
Lafferty, David, Chicago Theological Union, 5420 S. Cornell, Apt. 204, Chicago, IL 60615. Tel: 312-752-4655

Military Chaplains:
Reverend Fathers—
Creider, Philip B., Office of the Chaplan, 810 Avenger Ave., Lemore, CA 209-998-4618

Absent on Leave:
Reverend Fathers—
Aultz, Gary C.
Siebs, Robert L.

Absent on Sick Leave:
Reverend Fathers—
Grimes, Price D., Jr., P.O. Box 32180, Oklahoma City, OK 73123. Tel: 405-720-9871
Prather, Edward W., 260 E. Chestnut St., Chicago, IL 60611
Schiff, John S.

Prison Ministry:
Reverend Fathers—
McMenamin, John, P.O. Box 32180, Oklahoma City, OK 73123. Tel: 405-720-7258

Retired:
Reverend Fathers—
Anthony, Howard A., P.O. Box 32180, Oklahoma City, OK 73123
Darnall, Thomas W., 2706 S. Shartel, Oklahoma City, OK 73109
Dockers, Anthony, 53 Amandusstr, Oudenaarde, Belgium B9700
Hardesty, Leo, 9400 St. Ann's Dr., Oklahoma City, OK 73162
McLaughlin, Joseph, 110 Rudy Dr., Apt. 15, Gallup, NM 87301. Tel: 505-973-2398
Scheller, John, P.O. Box 32180, Oklahoma City, OK 73123. Tel: 405-722-1902
Schwarz, Bernard F., Rte. 3, Box 203, Marlow, OK 73055
Talloen, Jerome G., 9243 N. MacArthur, Apt. D., Oklahoma City, OK 73132
Ucker, Gerald, 811 N.W. 13th, Oklahoma City, OK 73106. Tel: 405-232-8327
VandeWalle, Victor, P.O. Box 32180, Oklahoma City, OK 73123
Walch, John, P.O. Box 32180, Oklahoma City, OK 73123
White, Charles G., 2716 S. Cincinnati, Tulsa, OK 74114. Tel: 918-745-9317
Wilkiemeyer, Philip, St. Ann's Retirement Village, 9400 St. Ann's Dr., Oklahoma City, OK 73162
Zagar, John T., 19000 N. County Line Rd, Piedmont, OK 73078. Tel: 405-341-1048

Permanent Deacons:
Adamson, Bill, Blessed Sacrament, Lawton
Amend, Carl, On Duty Outside the Archdiocese
Avila, Tomas, On Duty Outside the Archdiocese
Barton, James D., Corpus Christi, Oklahoma City
Bawden, Bill, St. John the Baptist Church, Edmond
Benoit, Roland, St. Francis of Assisi Church, Oklahoma City
Best, David, Christ the King Church
Browne, Matt, St. Philip Neri, Midwest City
Christophe, Norman, Retired
Collier, E. Charles, Immaculate Conception, Seminole
Coyle, Bill, Jr., St. John the Baptist, Edmond
Crispo, Anthony, St. Francis Xavier, Enid
Cruz, Joe M., St. Peter, Guymon
Cullinan, Walter, St. Charles Borromeo Church, Oklahoma City
Davis, Otis L., St. James, Oklahoma City
Descher, Duane, Oklahoma Medical Complex, Oklahoma City
Dollins, Belvin G., St. Peter, Guymon
Dubey, Joe, St. Eugene, Weatherford
Ellison, Roy, St. Mary's, Guthrie
Forgue, Joseph, Chap., Federal Penitentiary, El Reno
Foster, Robert, Our Lady of Sorrows, Chandler
Guerra, Simon, St. Peter, Guymon
Gulikers, Marti, St. James, Oklahoma City
Hernandez, Agustin, Immaculate Conception, Oklahoma City
Huff, Louis, St. Robert Bellarmine Church, Jones
Jones, Bro. Justin, O.S.B., Sacred Heart Church, Konawa
Keene, James, St. Andrew Church, Moore
Knight, James, Asst. to Dir. of Diaconate, St. Mark the Evangelist Church, Norman
Knipp, Stanley, Medical Leave
Lawrence, Herman, Holy Family, Lawton
Leal, George, Sacred Heart Church, Oklahoma City
LePage, Philip, St. Paul Apostle, Del City
LeWand, Marc, St. Charles, Oklahoma City
Maldonado, Pedro, St. Peter and Paul, Hobart
Marchessault, Arthur, On Leave
Martinez, Leopoldo, Holy Family Church, Lawton
McLauchlin, Robert, Medical Leave
Means, Gary, St. Cornelius, Cherokee
Neikirk, Dale, Church of the Epiphany, Oklahoma City
Nguyen, San, St. Andrew Dung-Lac Church, Oklahoma City
Nieto, Lucio, Holy Angels, Oklahoma City
O'Loughlin, Bernard, Assumption Church, Duncan
Pitt, John, St. Charles Borromeo, Oklahoma City
Radosevich, Michael, St. Joseph, Ada
Reisinger, Conrad C., St. Monica Catholic Church, Edmond
Reynolds, Patrick, St. Eugene, Oklahoma City
Roberts, Hi Joseph, St. Nepomuk, Yukon
Robinson, Richard, St. Mary, Ponca City
Rockey, Michael, Sacred Heart Church, Oklahoma City
Sousa, Larry, St. Joseph, Norman
Thelin, Carl, On Leave
Tindall, Bill
Warren, John, St. Thomas More, Norman
Watford, Angus, St. Andrew, Moore
Young, James G., St. Philip Neri, Midwest City

INSTITUTIONS LOCATED IN THE ARCHDIOCESE

[A] COLLEGES AND UNIVERSITIES

SHAWNEE. *St. Gregory's College*, 74801. Tel: 405-878-5100; Fax: 405-878-5198.
For a complete listing, refer to the Colleges and Universities section.

[B] HIGH SCHOOLS, ARCHDIOCESAN

OKLAHOMA CITY. *Bishop McGuinness High School*. (Coed), 801 N.W. 50th St., 73118. Tel: 405-842-6638. Mr. Stephen Parsons, Pres.; Rev. Philip Seeton. Priests 1; Sisters 1; Lay Teachers 52; Students 648.

[C] HIGH SCHOOLS, PRIVATE

OKLAHOMA CITY. *Mount St. Mary High School*. (Coed), 2801 S. Shartel Ave., 73109. Tel: 405-631-8865; 8866. Sisters of Mercy of the Americas. Rev. Raymond K. Ackerman, Chap., Pres.; Mrs. Mary Jane Wittrock; Mrs. Joanne Forgue, Chm., Rel. Studies Dept. Priests 1; Sisters 2; Lay Teachers 21; Students 255.

[D] ELEMENTARY SCHOOLS, PRIVATE

OKLAHOMA CITY. *Villa Teresa*. (Grades N-4), 1216-1300 Classen Dr., 73103. Tel: 405-232-4286. Carmelite Sisters of St. Therese of the Infant Jesus. Mrs. Pamela Graham, Prin. Sisters 7; Lay Teachers 30; Students 285.

Villa Teresa Moore. (Grades N-K), 13501 S. Western Ave., 73170. Tel: 405-691-7737. Carmelite Sisters of St. Therese of the Infant Jesus. Mrs. Pamela Graham, Prin.; Sr. Sylvia Negrete, Dir. Sisters 1; Lay Teachers 10; Students 98.

NORMAN. *All Saints Catholic School*, 451 E. Tonhawa, 73071-5842. Tel: 405-447-4600. Ms. Glenda Peters, Prin. Lay Teachers 12; Grades: Pre-K 4; Students 160.

[E] GENERAL HOSPITALS

OKLAHOMA CITY. *Hillcrest Health Center, Inc.*, 2129 S.W. 59th St., 73119. Tel: 405-685-6671; Fax: 405-680-2817.
For a complete listing, refer to the Hospitals section.
Mercy Health Center, 4300 W. Memorial Rd., 73120. Tel: 405-755-1515.
For a complete listing, refer to the Hospitals section.
St. Anthony Hospital, 1000 N. Lee St., P.O. Box 205, 73101. Tel: 405-272-7000; Fax: 405-272-7075.
For a complete listing, refer to the Hospitals section.

ENID. *St. Mary Mercy Hospital*, 305 S. 5th St., Box 232, 73701. Tel: 405-233-6100.
For a complete listing, refer to the Hospitals section.

PONCA CITY. *St. Joseph Regional Medical Center*, 14th and Hartford, 74602. Tel: 405-765-3321; Fax: 405-765-0379.
For a complete listing, refer to the Hospitals section.

[F] SPECIAL CARE FACILITIES

OKLAHOMA CITY. *Villa Isenbart, Inc.*, c/o Associated Catholic Charities, 1501 Classen Blvd., 73106.
For a complete listing, refer to the Special Care Facilities section.

[G] ECUMENICAL CENTERS

OKLAHOMA CITY. *Archdiocesan Pastoral Center*, 7501 Northwest Expwy., P.O. Box 32180, 73123. Tel: 405-721-5651; Fax: 405-721-5210. Mr. James Weinmann, Dir.; Mrs. Jeanine McFall, Events Coord. Used for Archdiocesan Chancery; ecumenical activities; retreat-meeting center for ecumenical and non-profit organizations; and retired priests' residence.

[H] HOMES FOR THE AGED

OKLAHOMA CITY. *St. Ann's Home, Inc.*, 9400 St. Ann's Dr., 73162. Tel: 405-728-7888; Fax: 405-728-1302.
For a complete listing, refer to the Special Care Facilities section.

PONCA CITY. *St. Mary's Housing Foundation*, 408 S. 8th St., 74601.
For a complete listing, refer to the Special Care Facilities section.
Westminster Village, Inc., 1601 Academy Rd., 74604. Tel: 405-762-6641.
For a complete listing, refer to the Special Care Facilities section.

[I] MONASTERIES AND RESIDENCES OF PRIESTS AND BROTHERS

OKLAHOMA CITY. *House of Prayer for Priests*, 700 N.E. 19th, 73105. Tel: 405-524-1118. Rev. Franklin Wrigley, Coord. Spiritual Direction.
Monastery of Our Lady of Mount Carmel and Little Flower, 1125 S. Walker Ave., Box 26127, 73126. Tel: 405-235-2037. Order of Discalced Carmelites (Oklahoma Province).
Little Flower Clinic: Free medical service for the Poor. Assisted annually 1,500.

SHAWNEE. *St. Gregory's Abbey*, 1900 W. MacArthur Dr., 74801. Tel: 405-878-5490; Fax: 405-878-5198. Legal Title: *Benedictine Fathers of Sacred Heart Mission, Inc.* Order of St. Benedict, including Junior College, Novitiate, and Mabee-Gerrer Museum of Art. Very Rev. Martin Lugo, O.S.B., Admin.; Revs. Patrick McCool, O.S.B., Prior; Joachim Spexarth, O.S.B., Subprior. Retired Abbots: Rt. Revs. Philip A. Berning, O.S.B.; Charles Massoth, O.S.B.; Adrian R. Vorderlandwehr, O.S.B.; Revs. Matthew J. Brown, O.S.B.; Charles Buckley, O.S.B., Dir.; Augustine S. Horn, O.S.B.; Maurus Jaeb, O.S.B.; Basil Keenan, O.S.B.; Eugene C. Marshall, O.S.B.; James D. Murphy, O.S.B.; Thomas R. Rabideau, O.S.B.; Victor W. Roberts, O.S.B.; Theodore T. Seneschal, O.S.B.; Lawrence R. Stasyszen, O.S.B.; Daniel M. Suellentrop, O.S.B.; Vincent dePaul Traynor, O.S.B.; Paul J. Zahler, O.S.B. Priests 24; Brothers 10; Deacons 1.

[J] CONVENTS AND RESIDENCES FOR SISTERS

OKLAHOMA CITY. *Alverno Community*, 3108 Northwest Expwy., #101, 73112. Tel: 405-942-2947. Franciscan Sisters of Mary. Sisters 2. Bethlehem Community, 600 N.W. 4th, #320, 73102. Tel: 405-235-4670. Sisters 2. Infant of Prague Community, 600 N.W. 4th, #317, 73102. Tel: 405-239-6773. Sisters 2.
Carmelite Sisters of St. Therese of the Infant Jesus Motherhouse, Villa Teresa, 1300 Classen Dr., 73103. Tel: 405-232-7926. Sr. Immaculata Commet, C.S.T., Supr. Sisters in Community 28; Resident Sisters 21; Postulants 2.
Sisters of Mercy of the Americas, Mercy Health Center Convent, 4300 W. Memorial Rd., 73120. Tel: 405-755-1515. Retirement Center for Sisters of Mercy of Oklahoma. Sr. M. Ada Watson, R.S.M., Coord. Sisters 11.
Sisters of Mercy of the Americas, Mount St. Mary Convent, 2801 S. Shartel Ave., 73109. Tel: 405-634-1968. Sr. Carolyn Stoutz, Supr. Sisters 6.

PIEDMONT. *Carmel of St. Joseph*, 20,000 N. County Line Rd., 73078. Tel: 405-348-3947. Discalced Carmelite Nuns (Cloistered). Sr. Therese Ranallo, O.C.D., Prioress. Professed Sisters 11.
Sisters of Benedict Red Plains Monastery, 728 Richland Rd., SW, 73078-9324. Tel: 405-528-7965; 528-2715. Sr. Marie Ballmann, O.S.B., Prioress. Sisters in Community 12; Novices 1.

PONCA CITY. *Sisters of St. Joseph of Wichita*, 311 Fairview St., 74601. Tel: 405-765-0482. Sisters 6.

[K] CAMPUS MINISTRY & NEWMAN CENTERS

NORMAN. *Campus Ministry for the Archdiocese of Oklahoma City*, 100 East Stinson, 73072. Rev. C. Joseph Meinhart, Dir.
University of Oklahoma, 100 E. Stinson, 73072. Tel: 405-321-0990. Revs. C. Joseph Meinhart; Pudhota J. Bosco (India).
Oklahoma City University, P.O. Box 60569, Oklahoma City, 73146. Tel: 405-528-0485. Rev. William M. Eichhoff.
East Central State University, P.O. Box 1585, Ada, 74820. Tel: 405-332-4811. Rev. Robert Wood.
Northwestern Oklahoma State College, 627 12th St., Alva, 73717. Tel: 405-327-0339. Rev. David B. Imming.
University of Science & Arts of Oklahoma, P.O. Box 748, Chickasha, 73023. Tel: 405-224-7513. Rev. Elmer C. Schwarz.
University of Central Oklahoma, 321 E. Clegern, Edmond, 73034. Tel: 405-340-6300. Rev. Kevin J. Ratterman.
Oklahoma Panhandle State University, P.O. Box 277, Goodwell, 73942. Tel: 405-338-7212. Revs. Charles R. Murphy; Joseph A. Jacobi.
Cameron University, P.O. Box 7948, Lawton, 73506. Tel: 405-536-6351. Revs. Marvin F. Leven; James Goins.
Northern Oklahoma College, P.O. Box 525, Tonkawa, 74653. Tel: 405-628-2416. Rev. Joseph W. Burger.
Southwestern Oklahoma State University, P.O. Box 407, Weatherford, 73096. Tel: 405-772-3209. Rev. Michael Chapman; Deacon Joe Dubey.

[L] MISCELLANEOUS

OKLAHOMA CITY. *Trinity Place Apartments*. (Project under construction), c/o Mr. Timothy O'Connor, Associated Catholic Charities, 1501 N. Classen, 73106. 58 low income apartments for senior citizens.

DEL CITY, KS. *Korean Roman Catholic Community*, 3405 South Wofford, 73115.

PIEDMONT. *Benedictine Spirituality Center*. Location at Red Plains Monastery, 728 Richlard Rd., SW, 73078-9324.

SHAWNEE. *Oklahoma Benedictine Institute on Mental Retardation, Inc.*, 1900 W. MacArthur, 74801. Tel: 405-878-5288; Fax: 405-878-5114. Rev. Paul Zahler, O.S.B., Ph.D, Dir.
Oklahoma Benedictine Institute on Mental Retardation.
Harold C. and Connie Brand Early Child Development Center.
Home Start Program.
Lyle H. Boren Child Development Center.
Home Integration Program.
Community Integration Program.
Employment Integration Program.
St. Michael Foundation.
Ostrich Outreach Program.
Oklahoma Benedictine Institute TV Network for Success.
"The Greatest of These is Love" Fund.
International Institute on Mental Retardation.

RELIGIOUS INSTITUTES OF MEN REPRESENTED IN THE ARCHDIOCESE

For further details refer to the corresponding bracketed number in the Religious Institutes of Men or Women section.

[0200]—*Benedictine Monks*.—O.S.B.

[0260]—*Discalced Carmelite Friars*. (Oklahoma Prov.).—O.C.D.

[0920]—*Oblates of St. Francis De Sales*.—O.S.F.S.

RELIGIOUS INSTITUTES OF WOMEN REPRESENTED IN THE ARCHDIOCESE

[0100]—*Adorers of the Blood of Christ*.—A.S.C.

[0230]—*Benedictine Sisters of Pontifical Jurisdiction*.—O.S.B.

[0380]—*Carmelite Sisters of St. Therese of the Infant Jesus*.—C.S.T.

[0390]—*Congregation of Missionary Carmelites of St. Therese*. (Houston, TX).—C.M.S.T.

[0420]—*Discalced Carmelite Nuns*.—O.C.D.

[1070-13]—*Dominican Sisters*. (Adrian, MI).—O.P.

[1070-06]—*Dominican Sisters*. (Newburgh, NY).—O.P.

[1900]—*Eucharistic Missionaries of St. Theresa*. (Mexico).—M.E.S.T.

[1415]—*Franciscan Sisters of Mary*.—F.S.M.

[]—*Hermanas Catequistas Guadalupanas*.—H.C.G.

[1680]—*School Sisters of St. Francis*.—S.S.S.F.

[0480]—*Sisters of Charity of Leavenworth*.—S.C.L.

[2980]—*Sisters of Congregation de Notre Dame*.—C.N.D.

[1010]—*Sisters of Divine Providence of San Antonio, Texas*.—C.D.P.

[2575]—*Sisters of Mercy of the Americas*.—R.S.M.

[3840]—*Sisters of St. Joseph of Carondelet*.—C.S.J.

[2150]—*Sisters, Servants of the Immaculate Heart of Mary*.—I.H.M.

CEMETERIES

OKLAHOMA CITY. *Resurrection Memorial*, P.O. Box 32865, 73123. Tel: 405-721-4191.

NECROLOGY

† Bryce, Philip, Yukon, OK, St. John Nepomuk. —Died May 6, 1996.

† Mayfield, Gerald K., Mustang, OK, Holy Spirit Church. —Died Jan. 10, 1996.

† O'Nolan, Gerald M., (Retired). —Died Dec. 20, 1996.

† Wagner, George H., (Retired). —Died Jan. 7, 1996.

Archdiocese of Omaha

(Archidioecesis Omahensis)

Most Reverend

ELDEN FRANCIS CURTISS

Archbishop of Omaha; ordained May 24, 1958; appointed Bishop of Helena March 4, 1976; consecrated April 28, 1976; appointed Archbishop of Omaha May 4, 1993; installed June 25, 1993. *Chancery Office: 100 N. 62nd St., Omaha, NE, 68132-2795.*

Most Reverend

DANIEL E. SHEEHAN, D.D., J.C.D.

Retired Archbishop of Omaha; ordained May 23, 1942; appointed Titular Bishop of Capsu and Auxiliary January 4, 1964; consecrated March 19, 1964; succeeded to See June 11, 1969; retired . *Chancery Office: 100 N. 62nd St., Omaha, NE, 68132-2795.*

Chancery Office: 100 N. 62 St., Omaha, NE, 68132-2795. Tel.: 402-558-3100; Fax: 402-551-4212.

ESTABLISHED AS A VICARIATE-APOSTOLIC JANUARY 6, 1857.

ERECTED A DIOCESE OCTOBER 2, 1885; ARCHDIOCESE AUGUST 7, 1945.

Square Miles 14,051.

Comprises the Counties of Boyd, Holt, Merrick, Nance, Boone, Antelope, Knox, Pierce, Madison, Platte, Colfax, Stanton, Wayne, Cedar, Dixon, Dakota, Thurston, Cuming, Dodge, Burt, Washington, Douglas and Sarpy in the State of Nebraska.

For legal titles of parishes and archdiocesan institutions, consult the Chancery Office.

STATISTICAL OVERVIEW

Personnel	
Archbishop	1
Retired Archbishops	1
Retired Bishops	1
Abbots	1
Retired Abbots	1
Priests: Diocesan Active in Diocese	160
Priests: Active Outside Diocese	17
Priests: Diocesan in Foreign Missions	1
Priests: Retired, Sick or Absent	52
Number of Diocesan Priests	230
Religious Priests in Diocese	127
Extern Priests in Diocese	19
Ordinations:	
Diocesan Priests	9
Religious Priests	1
Transitional Deacons	7
Permanent Deacons	5
Permanent Deacons in Diocese	123
Total Brothers	25
Total Sisters	376
Parishes	
Parishes	165
With Resident Pastor:	
Resident Diocesan Priests	118
Resident Religious Priests	5
Without Resident Pastor:	
Administered by Priests	31
Administered by Permanent Deacons	1
New Parishes Created	1
Professional Ministry Personnel:	
Sisters	19
Lay Ministers	198
Welfare	
Catholic Hospitals	5
Total Assisted	217,101
Homes for the Aged	4
Total Assisted	594
Day Care and Extended Day Care Centers	5
Total Assisted	3,128
Specialized Homes	5
Special Centers for Social Services	6
Total Assisted	50,000
Other Institutions	2
Total Assisted	32,562
Educational	
Diocesan Students in Other Seminaries	39
Total Seminarians	39
Colleges and Universities	2
Total Students	7,227
High Schools, Diocesan and Parish	12
Total Students	2,826
High Schools, Private	5
Total Students	2,216
Elementary Schools, Diocesan and Parish	61
Total Students	15,898
Elementary Schools, Private	1
Total Students	17
Non-residential Schools for the Disabled	1
Total Students	48
Catechesis/Religious Education:	
High School Students	3,502
Elementary Students	15,874
Total Students Under Catholic Instruction	47,647
Teachers in the Diocese:	
Priests	13
Brothers	3
Sisters	32
Lay Teachers	1,150
Vital Statistics	
Receptions into the Church:	
Infant Baptism Totals	4,500
Adult Baptism Totals	179
Received into Full Communion	427
First Communions	4,393
Confirmations	3,891
Marriages:	
Catholic	947
Interfaith	563
Total Marriages	1,510
Deaths	1,885
Total Catholic Population	212,137
Total Population	808,076

Former Bishops—Rt. Rev. JAMES O'GORMAN, O.C.S.O., D.D., Vicar-Apostolic and Titular Bishop of Raphanea; cons. May 8, 1859; died July 4, 1874.—Rt. Rev. JAMES O'CONNOR, D.D., Vicar-Apostolic and Titular Bishop of Dibona; cons. Aug. 20, 1876; appt. first Bishop of Omaha, Oct. 2, 1885; died May 27, 1890.—Rt. Rev. RICHARD SCANNELL, D.D., cons. Bishop of Concordia, Nov. 30, 1887; transferred to Omaha, Jan. 30, 1891; died Jan. 8, 1916.—Most Rev. JEREMIAH J. HARTY, D.D., ord. April 28, 1878; cons. Archbishop of Manila, P.I., Aug. 15, 1903; transferred to Omaha, May 16, 1916; died Oct. 29, 1927.—Most Rev. FRANCIS J. BECKMAN, D.D., Bishop of Lincoln and Apostolic Administrator of Omaha from June 1, 1926 to July 4, 1928.—Most Rev. JOSEPH FRANCIS RUMMEL, D.D., Bishop of Omaha; appt. March 30, 1928; cons. May 29, 1928; installed July 4, 1928; transferred to the Archdiocese of New Orleans, March 9, 1935.—Most Rev. JAMES H. RYAN, D.D., appt. Titular Bishop of Modra, Aug. 15, 1933; cons. Oct. 25, 1933; transferred to See of Omaha, Aug. 3, 1935; installed Nov. 21, 1935 elected to Archiepiscopal dignity, Aug. 7, 1945; died Nov. 23, 1947.—Most Rev. GERALD T. BERGAN, D.D., ord. Oct. 28, 1915; appt. Bishop of Des Moines, March 24, 1934; cons. June 13, 1934; promoted to Omaha, Feb. 7, 1948; retired June 18, 1969 made Titular Archbishop of Tacarata; died July 12, 1972.—Most Rev. DANIEL E. SHEEHAN, D.D., J.C.D., ord. May 23, 1942; appt. Titular Bishop of Capsu and Auxiliary, Jan. 4, 1964; cons. March 19, 1964; succeeded to See, June 11, 1969; retired.

Vicar General—Most Rev. DANIEL E. SHEEHAN, D.D., J.C.D.

Vicar for Religious—Very Rev. JAMES R. CAIN, J.C.D.

Chancery Office—100 N. 62nd St., Omaha, 68132-2795. Tel: 402-558-3100; Fax: 402-551-4212. Office Hours: Mon.-Fri. 9-5.

Chancellor—Rev. MICHAEL F. GUTGSELL, J.C.L.

Moderator of the Curia—Rev. R. MICHAEL FITZPATRICK, J.C.L., S.T.L.

Finance Director (canonical)—Rev. R. MICHAEL FITZPATRICK, J.C.L., S.T.L.

Business and Finance Director—HERBERT L. KARRER.

Archdiocesan Tribunal—100 N. 62nd St., Omaha, 68132.

Judicial Vicar—Rev. R. MICHAEL FITZPATRICK, J.C.L., S.T.L.

Associate Judicial Vicar—Rev. MICHAEL F. GUTGSELL, J.C.L.

Judges—Rev. Msgr. ANTHONY B. MICKELLS, J.C.D.; Rev. JAMES R. CAIN, J.C.D.

Promoter of Justice—Rev. ELDON J. MCKAMY, J.C.L.

Defenders of the Bond—Revs. ELDON J. MCKAMY, J.C.L.; Rev. VALENTINE J. PETER, S.T.D., J.C.D.

Advocates—Revs. PATRICK C. HARRISON; GERALD P. MELCHIOR.

Attorneys—Appointed for each matrimonial case.

Appeal Court—The Tribunal of the Diocese of Lincoln, NE is the Appeal Court for Omaha.

Consultors—Most Rev. DANIEL E. SHEEHAN, D.D., J.C.D.; Revs. NORMAN F. HUNKE; MICHAEL B. MALLOY; ELDON J. MCKAMY, J.C.L.; MELVIN J. MERWALD; FRANK A. PARTUSCH; ROLAND A. PESCHEL; MICHAEL G. PRINTY; RICHARD J. REISER; JAMES P. SCHOLZ; DANIEL F. SOLTYS; STEVEN J. STILLMUNKS.

Deans—U.S.C.: Rev. FRANK A. PARTUSCH, U.S.E.: Rev. JOHN O. MCCASLIN, U.N.E.: Rev. NORMAN F. HUNKE, U.N.W.: Rev. ROLAND A. PESCHEL, U.W.: Rev. STEVEN J. STILLMUNKS, R.S.W.: Rev. RICHARD WHITEING, R.N.C.: Rev. KEITH D. REZAC, R.S.E.: Rev. FRANK LORDEMANN, R.C.: Rev. OWEN W. KORTE, R.N.W.: Rev. RICHARD REISER, R.N.E.: DAVID W. LAPLANTE.

Finance Council—Most Rev. ELDEN FRANCIS CURTISS; Most Rev. DANIEL E. SHEEHAN, D.D., J.C.D.; Revs. R. MICHAEL FITZPATRICK, J.C.L., S.T.L.; GERALD E. GONDERINGER; FRANK LORDEMANN; ELDON J. MCKAMY, J.C.L.; Mr. HERBERT L. KARRER; Mr. ROMAN UHING; Mr. HERMAN D. WEIST.

Archdiocesan Offices and Directors

Boy Scouts—Rev. DANIEL L. WITTROCK, Chap.

Building Commission—Rev. R. MICHAEL FITZPATRICK, J.C.L., S.T.L.; Mr. LEE KARRER, Contact Person; Rev. JAMES R. CAIN, J.C.D.; Mr. THOMAS L. FINLEY; Rev. ROBERT J. SMITH; Mr. DANIEL WITT; Bro. WILLIAM WOEGER, F.S.C.

Catholic University, Friends of—Rev. R. MICHAEL FITZPATRICK, J.C.L., S.T.L., Dir.

Cemeteries—Rev. ROBERT J. GASS, Dir.

Censor Librorum—Rev. VAL J. PETER, J.C.D., S.T.D.

Charities—SCOT L. ADAMS, Dir., *3300 N. 60th St., Omaha, 68104.*

Omaha Priests Retirement Plan and Trust, The—Revs. FRANCIS E. KUBART; ELDON J. MCKAMY, J.C.L.; Mr. JAMES KINEEN; Mr. DONALD E. RUTH; Mr. DAVID DUREN; Mr. HERBERT L. KARRER.

Commission for Ecumenical Affairs—Rev. GERALD P. MELCHIOR.

Commission on Divine Worship—Bro. WILLIAM WOEGER, F.S.C., Coord., Environment & Art; Rev. RONALD NOECKER, Coord., Music.

Conciliation Process—Rev. CARL A. SALANITRO, Conciliator. Alternate Conciliators: Mr. BERNARD BURBACH; Revs. FRANKLIN A. DVORAK; JOSEPH A. MIKSCH.

Council of Catholic Women, Archdiocesan—Rev. EDGAR J. WORTMANN, Archdiocesan Moderator, *3020 Curtis, Omaha, 68111.*

Deaf—Rev. JAMES VANCE, C.SS.R.

Diaconate Program—Revs. THOMAS J. ADAMS, Urban Dir. Tel: 402-455-4966. PAUL ORTMEIER, Rural Dir. Tel: 402-373-2233.

Catholic School Office—Sr. PATRICIA MULCAHEY, O.P., Supt., Schools, *3212 N. 60th St., Omaha, 68104.* Tel: 402-554-8493.

Religious Formation, Office of—*3212 N. 60th St., P.O. Box 4130, Omaha, 68104.* Mr. JAMES CORR, Dir.; Ms. LORI SPANBAUER, Asst. Dir., Young Adult; Ms. RITA RAMOS, Asst. Dir., Youth; Ms. MARY ALICE O'REILLY, Asst. Dir., Elementary Formation; Ms. NANCY KOLEY, Asst. Dir., Catechist Cert. & Media Resources. Tel: 402-554-8493; Fax: 402-554-8402.

Family Life—Sr. BARBARA MARKEY, N.D., Dir., *3214 N. 60th St., Omaha, 68104.* Tel: 402-551-9003.

Hispanic Ministry—Sr. DULCE FLORES, S.M.B.S., Dir., *3218 N. 60th St., Omaha, 68104.* Tel: 402-551-2255.

Holy Name Society—Rev. JOHN S. MICHALAK, Dir.

Hospitals—Rev. JAMES QUINN, S.J.

Legion of Mary—Rev. PETER F. DUNNE, Dir.

Natural Family Planning—Sr. BARBARA MARKEY, N.D., Dir., Family Life Office: *3214 N. 60th St., Omaha, 68104.* Tel: 402-551-9003.

Newspaper—Mr. STEPHEN M. KENT, Editor, *"The Catholic Voice", 6060 N.W. Radial Hwy., Omaha, 68104.* Tel: 402-558-6611; Fax: 402-558-6614.

Nocturnal Adoration Society—Vacant.

Pastoral Planning Office—Sr. RITA PARKS, R.S.M., Dir. Tel: 402-551-2255.

Priests' Eucharistic League—Rev. WILLIAM WHELAN.

Propagation of the Faith, Pontifical Association of Holy Childhood and Catholic Students Mission Crusade—Rev. R. MICHAEL FITZPATRICK, J.C.L., S.T.L., Dir., *100 N. 62nd St., Omaha, 68132.*

Retreats, Laymen—Rev. DENIS BARTLEY, S.S.C., Dir.

Rural Life Conference—Rev. FRANK J. BAUMERT.

St. Vincent de Paul Society—Rev. JOHN L. PIETRAMALE, Spiritual Dir.; Mr. PATRICK MCCARTHY, Pres., *2101 Leavenworth St., Omaha, 68102.*

St. Vincent de Paul Store, Inc.—2101 Leavenworth St., Omaha, 68102.

Priests' Council—

Officers—Revs. STEVEN STILLMUNKS, Pres.; OWEN KORTE, Vice Pres.; ROLAND PESCHEL, Sec.; KEITH D. REZAC, Treas.

Age Groups—Revs. ROBERT GASS; THOMAS FANGMAN; DAMIEN ZUERLEIN; JAMES GILG; FRANCIS KUBART; ROBERT SMITH; JAMES R. CAIN, J.C.D.; JOHN L. PIETRAMALE.

Religious Orders—Revs. ROBERT TILLMAN, S.J.; GERMAR NEUBERT, O.S.B.; ROBERT DELERICH, C.S.S.R.

Deans—Revs. FRANK A. PARTUSCH, (USC); JOHN O. MCCASLIN, (USE); MICHAEL GREWE, (US); NORMAN HUNKE, (UNE); ROLAND A. PESCHEL, (UNW); STEVEN STILLMUNKS, (UW); RICHARD WHITEING, (RSW); KEITH REZAC, (RNC); RICHARD REISER, (RNW); FRANK LORDEMANN, (RSE); DAVID W. LAPLANTE, (RNE); OWEN W. KORTE, (RC).

Archbishop's Appointees—Revs. R. MICHAEL FITZPATRICK, J.C.L., S.T.L.; ELDON J. MCKAMY, J.C.L.

Ex Officio—Most Rev. DANIEL E. SHEEHAN, D.D., J.C.D.; Revs. MEL MERWALD, Consultor; MICHAEL MALLOY; MICHAEL PRINTY; DANIEL SOLTYS.

Social Ministry Commission—Sr. MARY HOGAN, O.S.M., Coord.

Sodalities—Rev. THOMAS A. HALLEY, S.J.

Catholic Charities, Inc.—SCOT L. ADAMS, Exec. Dir., *3300 N. 60th St., Omaha, 68104.* Tel: 402-554-0520.

Catholic Charities, Inc. Satellite Offices and Services—

The Shelter—Care for battered women, children, therapy for spouse abusers. KATHY SCHINKER, Contact Person, *P.O. Box 4346, Omaha, 68104.* Tel: 402-558-5700.

St. Martin de Porres Center—Social Justice education, counseling, food pantry, refugee program. A'JAMAL BYNDON, Emergency Svcs. JUNITA ELLIOTT, Vision of H.O.P.E., *2417 Burdette St., Omaha, 68111.* Tel: 402-341-4004.

St. Gabriel's Center—Detoxification, inpatient treatment and extended care for low-income and indigent alcoholics. JAN VAN DOREN, Contact Person, *3483 Larimore Ave., Omaha, 68111.* Tel: 401-451-4264.

UCSS Counseling Services—JACK WRIGHT, *Sheehan Center, 3300 N. 60th St., Omaha, 68104.* Tel: 402-554-0520. RAY WILSON, Substance Abuse, *3300 N. 60th St., Omaha, 68104.* Tel: 402-554-0520.

Catholic Family Services—GORDON GREEN, Contact Person, *1761 26th Ave., P.O. Box 573, Columbus, 68602-0573.* Tel: 402-563-3833.

Catholic Family Services—1255 4th St., Ste. 220, Norfolk, 68701. Tel: 402-371-3555.

Vocations—Rev. MARK D. FILIPS, Dir.

Youth-Young Adult Ministry—Ms. RITA RAMOS, *3216 N. 60th St., Omaha, 68104.* Tel: 402-551-5070.

CLERGY, PARISHES, MISSIONS AND PAROCHIAL SCHOOLS

CITY OF OMAHA
(Douglas County)

1—ST. CECILIA'S CATHEDRAL, Revs. Norman F. Hunke; Joseph M. Wray; Donald Stortz. In res., Rev. R. Michael Fitzpatrick.
Res., 701 N. 40 St., 68131. Tel: 402-551-2313; Fax: 402-551-2306.
School—Tel: 402-556-6655.
Congregation of the Most Holy Rosary, Sinsinawa, WI 3; Lay Teachers 22; Students 464.
Catechesis/Religious Programs—Bonnie Pryor, D.R.E.
Students 464.

2—ST. ADALBERT, Rev. Frank A. Partusch. In res., Rev. John A. Flynn.
Res., 2617 S. 31 St., 68105. Tel: 402-345-1621.
Catechesis/Religious Programs—2124 S. 32 Ave., 68105. Tel: 402-341-5604.
Students 4.

3—ST. AGNES, Rev. William C. Kleffman.
Res., 2215 Q St., 68107. Tel: 402-731-0100.
School—Lay Teachers 10; Students 114.

4—ST. ANN, Rev. John C. Rizzo. In res., Rev. Nguyen Loi.
Res., 2247 Poppleton Ave., 68108. Tel: 402-341-6613.
School—All Saints Catholic School. See Elementary Schools, Interparochial Under Institutions Located in the Archdiocese.
Catechesis/Religious Programs—Students 14.

5—ST. ANTHONY, Rev. Carl F. Sodoro.
Res., 5401 S. 33 St., 68107. Tel: 402-733-2423.

6—ASSUMPTION, B.V.M., Rev. Rodney V. Kneifl; Deacon George Buglewicz.
Res., 5434 S. 22 St., 68107. Tel: 402-734-4500; Fax: 402-734-4502.
School—Tel: 402-734-4504.
Lay Teachers 12; Students 205.

7—ST. BENEDICT THE MOOR, Rev. Walter Boehme, S.J.
Res., 2423 Grant St., 68111. Tel: 402-348-0631.

8—ST. BERNADETTE, Revs. Robert F. Preisinger; John J. Whalen; Deacons Ron Casart; Pete Digilio; Duane Thome; Sebastian Enzolera. In res., Rev. Msgr. Albert L. Krejci.
Res., 7600 S. 42 St., Omaha, 68147. Tel: 402-731-4694; Fax: 402-731-8735.
School—Tel: 402-731-3033. Sr. Mary Ann Miller, O.P., Prin.
Sisters 2; Lay Teachers 23; Students 470.
Catechesis/Religious Programs—Tel: 402-731-9421. Sr. Maureen Heegan, C.S.J., D.R.E.
Students 108.

9—ST. BERNARD, Rev. Roland Peschel; Deacons Donald Kemp; Skip Baughman; Carl Miller; Edward Osterhaus. In res., Rev. Gerald P. Melchior.
Res., 3601 N. 65 St., 68104. Tel: 402-551-0269.
School—Tel: 402-553-4993; Fax: 402-556-7653. David Peters, Prin.
Lay Teachers 22; Students 347.
Catechesis/Religious Programs—Joanne Raleigh, D.R.E.
Students 144.

10—BLESSED SACRAMENT, Rev. Edgar J. Wortmann.
Res., 3020 Curtis Ave., 68111. Tel: 402-455-5200.
School—Tel: 402-455-4030.
Lay Teachers 12; Students 134.

11—ST. BRIDGET, Rev. James L. Weeke. In res., Rev. Paul Begley.
Res., 4112 S. 26 St., 68107. Tel: 402-733-8811.
Catechesis/Religious Programs—Students 22.

12—CHRIST THE KING, Revs. Robert J. Gass; John L. Pietramale; Deacon Glenn Tylutki.
Res., 654 S. 86 St., 68114. Tel: 402-391-3606; Fax: 402-391-1498.
School—Tel: 402-391-0977; Fax: 402-391-2418. Mrs. Mary Duffy, Prin.
Lay Teachers 27; Students 305.
Catechesis/Religious Programs—Tel: 402-391-3624. Colleen Leise, D.R.E.
Students 89.

13—ST. ELIZABETH ANN, Revs. Joseph G. Hanefeldt; William Safranek; Deacons Jack Finney; Richard Nelson; Ernie Gencarelli; Martin Crowley.
Res., 11212 Grande Ave., 68164. Tel: 402-493-2186; Fax: 402-493-0630.
School—St. James-Seton School. See Elementary Schools, Interparochial Under Institutions Located in the Archdiocese.
Catechesis/Religious Programs—Tel: 402-572-0369; Fax: 402-572-0368. Mrs. Doris Grillo, D.R.E.
Students 365.

14—ST. FRANCES CABRINI, Rev. Roger Kalscheuer, S.J., Admin.; Deacon Anthony Filipcic.
Res., 1334 S. Ninth St., 68108. Tel: 402-342-2464; Fax: 402-342-2470.
School—All Saints Catholic School. See Elementary Schools, Interparochial Under Institutions Located in the Archdiocese.

15—ST. FRANCIS ASSISI, Revs. John S. Michalak; John Buckson, Hispanic Ministry; Deacon Paul L. Matukewicz.
Res., 4513 S. 32nd St., 68107-1499. Tel: 402-731-2699.
School—Sisters 1; Lay Teachers 3; Students 60.

16—HOLY CROSS, Revs. Charles F. Swanson; Mark Bridgman. In res., Rev. Msgr. Edward C. O'Donnell, V.G.; Deacon George Elster.
Res., 4803 William St., 68106. Tel: 402-553-7500; Fax: 402-553-7735.
School—Tel: 402-551-3773.
Lay Teachers 22; Students 392.
Catechesis/Religious Programs—Students 102.

17—HOLY FAMILY, Deacon Ralph L. Hueser, Admin.
Res., 1715 Izard St., 68102. Tel: 402-345-1062.

18—HOLY GHOST, Revs. Ralph J. Steffensmeier; Gregory Benkowski; Deacons Tom Schulte; Paul Eubanks.
Res., 5219 S. 53rd St., 68117. Tel: 402-731-3176; Fax: 402-738-1409.
School—Tel: 402-731-5161; Fax: 402-738-1409. Jane Barreuther, Prin.
Lay Teachers 11; Students 215.
Catechesis/Religious Programs—Tel: 402-731-4574. Mary Fenton, D.R.E.
Students 80.

19—HOLY NAME, Revs. Brian Johnson, C.SS.R.; Robert Oelerich, C.SS.R.; Stephen Benden, C.SS.R.; James Vance, C.SS.R.; Michael Quinn, C.SS.R.; Bros. Charles Bergevin, C.SS.R.; William Cloughley, C.SS.R.
Res., 3014 N. 45th St., 68104. Tel: 402-451-6622; Fax: 402-457-6901.
School—(Grades K-8). Tel: 402-451-5403. Sofia Kock, Prin.
Lay Teachers 12; Students 243.
Catechesis/Religious Programs—Tel: 402-453-0873. Catherine Snyder, D.R.E.
Students 70.

20—IMMACULATE CONCEPTION, B.V.M., Rev. John O. McCaslin.
Res., 2708 S. 24th St., 68108. Tel: 402-342-1074; Fax: 402-342-1074.

School—All Saints Catholic School. See Elementary Schools, Interparochial Under Institutions Located in the Archdiocese.
Catechesis/Religious Programs—Students 10.

21—ST. JAMES, Rev. Michael W. Grewe; Rt. Rev. Raphael Walsh, O.S.B.; Deacons Ralph Brisson; Jerry Gau; Larry Heck; Joe Kessler; Stan Kurtz; Pat Lenz; Wayne Young. In res., Rev. James V. Brown, O.A.R.
Res., 9025 Larimore Ave., 68134. Tel: 402-572-0499; Fax: 402-572-0368.
School—St. James-Seton School. See Elementary Schools, Interparochial Under Institutions Located in the Archdiocese.
Catechesis/Religious Programs—Tel: 402-572-0369; Fax: 402-572-0368. Mrs. Doris Grillo, D.R.E. Students 198.

22—ST. JOAN OF ARC, Revs. Emmett F. Meyer; Joseph Broudou.
Res., 3122 S. 74 St., 68124. Tel: 402-393-2005.
School—Tel: 402-393-2314.
Sisters of Mercy 2; Lay Teachers 22; Students 360.
Catechesis/Religious Programs—Tel: 402-391-1906. Marilyn Opitz, D.R.E.
Students 180.

23—ST. JOHN, Revs. John J. Lynch, S.J.; Thomas A. Halley, S.J.; Philip Amidon, S.J.; Deacon Ken Kalkowski.
Office: 2500 California Plz., 68178. Tel: 402-280-3030; Fax: 402-280-2465.

24—ST. JOHN VIANNEY, Revs. Paul J. Schwaab; Thomas D. Furlong; Deacons Pete DesRosiers; Frank Telich. In res., Rev. James M. Sullivan (HEL).
Res., 5801 Oak Hills Dr., 68137. Tel: 402-895-0808; Fax: 402-895-0896.
Catechesis/Religious Programs—Anne Waldron, D.R.E.
Students 579.

25—ST. JOSEPH, Rev. John O. McCaslin. In res., Rev. Walter G. Wancewicz.
Res., 1730 S. 16th St., 68108. Tel: 402-342-1618.
School—All Saints Catholic School. See Elementary Schools, Interparochial Under Institutions Located in the Archdiocese.
Catechesis/Religious Programs—Students 64.

26—ST. LEO, Revs. R. Patrick McCaslin; Jeffrey L. Zyla.
Res., 1920 N. 102nd St., 68114. Tel: 402-397-0407; Fax: 402-397-2887.
School—St. Pius X-St. Leo School. See Elementary Schools, Interparochial Under Institutions Located in the Archdiocese.
Catechesis/Religious Programs—Students 435.

27—ST. MARGARET MARY, Revs. Melvin Merwald; Randall Donner.
Res., 6116 Dodge St., 68132. Tel: 402-558-2255; Fax: 402-551-5631.
School—Tel: 402-551-6663.
Lay Teachers 21; Students 505.
Catechesis/Religious Programs—Students 171.

28—ST. MARY, Revs. Carl F. Sodoro; Daniel F. Brick.
Res., 3529 Q St., 68107. Tel: 402-731-0204.
School—Lay Teachers 11; Students 145.

29—ST. MARY MAGDALENE, Revs. William L. Kelligar; Fernando C. Benliro.
Res., P.O. Box 3285, 68103. Tel: 402-342-4807.
School—All Saints Catholic School. See Elementary Schools, Interparochial Under Institutions Located in the Archdiocese.

30—MARY OUR QUEEN, Revs. Carl A. Salanitro; Ross C. Burkhalter; Deacon Paul Rooney.
Res., 3535 S. 119 St., 68144. Tel: 402-333-8662; Fax: 402-333-4504.
School—3405 S. 119 St., 68144. Tel: 402-333-8663; Fax: 402-334-6944.
Lay Teachers 28; Students 582.
Catechesis/Religious Programs—Tel: 402-333-8231. Barb Eastridge, D.R.E.
Students 418.

31—MOTHER OF PERPETUAL HELP. (Church of the Deaf). Rev. James Vance, C.SS.R.
Res., 5215 Seward St., 68104. Tel: 402-558-4214.

32—OUR LADY OF GUADALUPE, Revs. Damian J. Zuerlein; John R. Buckson; Gustavo Barrientos; Deacons Joe Ramirez; Duane Bronk.
Res., 2310 O St., 68107. Tel: 402-731-2196; Fax: 402-731-2196.
Catechesis/Religious Programs—Sr. Marcianne Trujillo, D.R.E.
Students 391.

33—OUR LADY OF LOURDES, Revs. Frank A. Partusch; Stanley T. Schmit; Deacons Frank Hilt; Michael Reynolds.
Res., 2110 S. 32nd Ave., 68105. Tel: 402-346-0900; Fax: 402-346-0901.
School—2124 S. 32nd Ave., 68105. Tel: 402-341-5604. Mr. Kenneth Hajek, Prin.
Sisters 1; Lay Teachers 20; Students 366.
Catechesis/Religious Programs—Students 45.

34—ST. PATRICK, Revs. Lucian S. Astuto; Paul Petko, F.SS.P.
Res., 1404 Castelar St., 68108. Tel: 402-341-1305; Fax: 402-342-5510.
School—All Saints Catholic School. See Elementary Schools, Interparochial Under Institutions Located in the Archdiocese.
Catechesis/Religious Programs—Students 31.

35—ST. PETER, Rev. John C. Rizzo.
Res., 709 S. 28th St., 68105. Tel: 402-341-4560.

36—SS. PETER AND PAUL, Revs. Donald W. Shane; Norman B. Parr.
Res., 5912 S. 36th St., 68107. Tel: 402-731-4578.
School—Tel: 402-731-4713. Joan Miller, Prin.
Lay Teachers 18; Students 332.
Catechesis/Religious Programs—Tel: 402-733-3344. Julie Bizal, D.R.E.
Students 228.

37—ST. PHILIP NERI, Revs. Eldon J. McKamy; LuVerne W. Steffes; Deacons Fred Sommer; Dick Edgerton; Fred Hendrick.
Res., 8200 N. 30th St., 68112. Tel: 402-455-1289; Fax: 402-455-8398.
School—Tel: 402-455-8666. Barbara Marchese, Prin.
Lay Teachers 13; Students 227.
Catechesis/Religious Programs—Tel: 402-455-2190. Joanne Raleigh.
Students 132.

38—ST. PIUS X, Revs. Lloyd A. Gnirk; Jay L. Kruse.
Res., 6905 Blondo St., 68104. Tel: 402-558-8446; Fax: 402-558-4986.
School—St. Pius X-St. Leo School. See Elementary Schools, Interparochial Under Institutions Located in the Archdiocese.
Catechesis/Religious Programs—Tel: 402-558-1898. Susie Naatz, D.R.E.
Students 235.

39—ST. RICHARD, Revs. Daniel P. Herek; Theodore L. Richling.
Res., 4320 Fort St., 68111. Tel: 402-455-2865.
School—Tel: 402-451-0692. Ms. Sue McCaslin, Prin.
Sisters 3; Lay Teachers 11; Students 197.

40—ST. ROBERT BELLARMINE, Revs. Eugene H. Kerwin; Dennis De Guzman; Deacons Fred Alexander; William Fell; John Kronschnabel. In res., Rev. Michael F. Gutgsell.
Res., 11802 Pacific St., 68154. Tel: 402-333-8989; Fax: 402-333-5489.
School—Tel: 402-334-1929; Fax: 402-333-7188. Craig V. Estee, Prin.
Lay Teachers 28; Students 570.
Catechesis/Religious Programs—Tel: 402-333-1959. Wilma D. Smith, D.R.E.
Students 228.

41—ST. ROSE, Rev. James L. Weeke. In res., Rev. Mark D. Filips.
Res., 4102 S. 13th St., 68107. Tel: 402-733-9327; Fax: 402-731-9937.

42—SACRED HEART, Rev. James P. Scholz; Deacons Charles Weskirchen; James Chambers.
Res., 2218 Binney St., 68110. Tel: 402-451-5755; Fax: 402-451-1731.
School—Tel: 402-451-5858.
Lay Teachers 12; Students 150.

43—ST. STANISLAUS, Rev. Richard L. Swolek.
Res., 4002 J St., 68107. Tel: 402-731-4152; Fax: 402-731-4389.
School—Tel: 402-731-0484.
Poor Sisters of St. Francis Seraph of Perpetual Adoration 1; Lay Teachers 8; Students 185.
Catechesis/Religious Programs—Students 256.

44—ST. STEPHEN THE MARTYR, Revs. Gerald E. Gonderinger; Thomas S. Gall.
Res., 17053 M St., 68135. Tel: 402-896-9682.
Church—16701 S St., 68135. Tel: 402-896-9675; Fax: 402-896-1990.
School—Tel: 402-896-0754. Mr. John Smith Prin.
Students 380.
Catechesis/Religious Programs—Students 1,335.

45—ST. THERESE OF THE CHILD JESUS, Rev. Thomas J. Adams.
Res., 5316 N. 14th Ave., 68110. Tel: 402-455-4966.

46—ST. THOMAS MORE, Revs. John E. Vernon; Craig J. Loecker. In res., Rev. Stanislaus Golik.
Res., 4804 Grover St., 68106. Tel: 402-556-1456.
School—Lay Teachers 22; Students 391.

47—ST. VINCENT DE PAUL, Sarpy Co., Revs. Dennis A. Hanneman; Thomas F. O'Brien; Deacon Donald K. Clausen.
Res., 14330 Eagle Run Dr., 68164. Tel: 402-496-7988 (Pastoral Center); 498-8425 (Rectory); Fax: 402-496-9933.
School—Tel: 402-492-2111. Dr. Vicky Grandy, Prin.
Students 544.
Catechesis/Religious Programs—Tel: 402-493-1642.
Students 610.

48—ST. WENCESLAUS, Revs. Franklin A. Dvorak; Leo Rigatuso; Deacons John Cerveny; Elvon Anderson; Donald Cowles. In res., Rev. James E. Gilg.
Res., 15353 Pacific St., Omaha, 68154. Tel: 402-330-0304; Fax: 402-330-1476.
School—(Grades K-8). Tel: 402-330-4356. Mary McGuire, Prin.
Students 752.
Catechesis/Religious Programs—Tel: 402-330-1889. Nancy Foral, D.R.E.
Students 903.

OUTSIDE THE CITY OF OMAHA

Albion, Boone Co., St. Michael, Rev. Wilfred J. Spenner.
Res., 524 W. Church St., 68620. Tel: 402-395-2393.
School—Tel: 402-395-2926.
Priests 1; Religious 1; Lay Teachers 8; Students 96.
Catechesis/Religious Programs—Students 235.

Aloys, Cuming Co., St. Aloysius, Rev. Stephen J. Gutgsell.
Res., 700 Hwy. 32, West Point, 68788. Tel: 402-372-2789. [CEM]

Atkinson, Holt Co., St. Joseph, Rev. Frank E. Jindra; Deacons Gerald Gonderinger; Art Villemure.
Res., 317 W. State St., P.O. Box 220, 68713. Tel: 402-925-2122; Fax: 402-925-5320. [CEM]
School—Tel: 402-925-2104.
Lay Teachers 10; Students 96.
Catechesis/Religious Programs—Tel: 402-925-5854. D.R.E.: Dennis Ryan; Patti Skrola.
Students 110.

Bancroft, Cuming Co., Holy Cross, Rev. David LaPlante.
Res., P.O. Box 524, Lyons, 68038. Tel: 412-846-5550.

Battle Creek, Madison Co., St. Patrick's, Rev. Steven E. Boes; Deacon Stephen Kuchar.
Res., 107 N. Third St., P.O. Box 40, 68715. Tel: 402-675-2485.
Catechesis/Religious Programs—Christine Brandl, D.R.E.
Students 118.
Mission—Schoolcraft, Madison Co., St. Francis de Sales.

Beemer, Cuming Co., Holy Cross, Rev. Ronald J. Noecker.
Res., 517 Fraisier St. N., P.O. Box 212, 68716. Tel: 402-528-3475. [CEM]

Bellevue, Sarpy Co., St. Mary, Revs. Thomas R. Ward; Daniel L. Wittrock; Deacons Ralph Hueser; Duane Iwanski; Chuck L'Archevesque; Andy Foray.
Res., 811 W. 23rd Ave., 68005. Tel: 402-291-1350; Fax: 402-291-1375.
School—(Grades PreK-8). Tel: 402-291-1666. Sr. Regina Wagner, Prin.
Lay Teachers 18; Students 297.
Catechesis/Religious Programs—Tel: 402-291-3964. Nina Tisinger, D.R.E.
Students 437.

Blair, Washington Co., St. Francis Borgia, Rev. Hugh F. Schwartz.
Res., P.O. Box 548, 68008. Tel: 402-426-3823. [CEM]
Catechesis/Religious Programs—402-426-5145 David Kaslon, D.R.E.
Students 400.

Bellevue, Sarpy Co., St. Matthew The Evangelist Church of Bellevue, Rev. Dennis R. Stolinksi.
Res., 3605 Looking Glass Dr., 68123. Tel: 402-292-7418.

Bloomfield, Knox Co., St. Andrew, Rev. Paul Ortmeier.
Res., 304 S. McNamara St., P.O. Box 416, 68718. Tel: 402-373-2233. [CEM]
Catechesis/Religious Programs—Tel: 402-373-2696. Barb Jackson, D.R.E.
Students 438.

Bow Valley, Cedar Co., SS. Peter and Paul, Rev. Michael B. Malloy.
Res., 106 W. 889th Rd. (Bow Valley), Hartington, 68739. Tel: 402-254-3311. [CEM]
School—East Catholic Elementary School. See Elementary Schools, Interparochial Under Institutions Located in the Archdiocese.
Catechesis/Religious Programs—Students 128.

Boys Town, Douglas Co., Immaculate Conception B.V.M., Rev. Val J. Peter. In res., Rev. Msgr. Peter F. Dunne; Rev. Eugene McReynolds, O.S.B.
Res., 68010. Tel: 402-498-1111.
Catechesis/Religious Programs—Students 567.

Butte, Boyd Co, SS. Peter and Paul, Rev. Lydell T Lape.
Res., P.O. Box 8, 68722. Tel: 402-775-2452. [CEM]
Mission—Naper, Boyd Co., Sacred Heart. [CEM]

Cedar Rapids, Boone Co., St. Anthony, Rev. John C. Starostka.
Res., P.O. Box 56, 68627. Tel: 308-358-0773. [CEM]
Catechesis/Religious Programs—Tel: 308-358-0773.
Students 123.
Mission—Primrose, Boone Co., St. Mary, 68627.

Tel: 308-358-0773. [CEM]

Central City, Merrick Co., St. Michael, Rev. Nelson A. Newman; Deacon Robert Flesch.
Res., 2402 20th Ave., 68826. Tel: 308-946-2855; Fax: 308-946-2982.
Catechesis/Religious Programs—D.R.E.: Teresa Hartwig; Marie Nicholas.
Students 114.

Clarks, Merrick Co., St. Peter, Rev. Kenneth P. Vavrina.
Res., P.O. Box 185, 68628. Tel: 308-773-2282. [CEM]
Catechesis/Religious Programs—Tel: 308-548-2573. Linda Vrboski, D.R.E.
Students 40.

Clarkson, Colfax Co., SS. Cyril and Methodius, Rev. Ronald Battiato.
Res., 120 Cherry St., P.O. Box 457, 68629. Tel: 402-892-3464.
School—St. John Neumann, Tel: 402-892-3474.
Lay Teachers 6; Students 70.
Catechesis/Religious Programs—Students 120.

Coleridge, Cedar Co., St. Michael, Rev. Keith D. Rezac.
Res., 315 S. Madison, R.R. 1, P.O. Box 123, 68727. Tel: 402-283-4614.
Catechesis/Religious Programs—Students 96.

Columbus, Platte Co., St. Anthony, Rev. Joseph A. Miksch; Deacons Michael Placzek; Robert Obershaw; Michael McGuire. In res., Rev. Wayne S Pavela Tel: 402-564-3473.
Res., 562 17th Ave., 68601. Tel: 402-564-3313; Fax: 402-563-1005.
School—Tel: 402-564-4767; Fax: 402-563-1005. Mary Jane Noble, Prin.
Lay Teachers 7; Students 127.
Catechesis/Religious Programs—Lori Olson, D.R.E.
Students 187.

St. Bonaventure, Revs. Daniel E. Keller; Anthony Espinosa; Deacons Arthur Spenner; Lawrence Mielak. In res., Rev. Edward J. Schad.
Res., 1565 18th Ave., 68601. Tel: 402-564-7151; Fax: 402-562-6025. [CEM]
School—Tel: 402-564-7153.
Sisters 2; Lay Teachers 13; Students 236.
Catechesis/Religious Programs—Rose V. Arp, D.R.E.
Students 299.

St. Isidore, Revs. Floyd A. Wessling; Michael D Schmitz.
Res., 3921 20th St., 68601. Tel: 402-564-8993; Fax: 402-564-8955.
School—Tel: 402-564-2604.
Missionary Benedictine Sisters 5; Lay Teachers 12; Students 248.
Catechesis/Religious Programs—Students 274.

Constance, Knox Co., St. Joseph. (Mission of Crofton). Rev. Ronald S Wasikowski.
Mailing Address: Box 335, Crofton, 68730. Tel: 402-388-4814. [CEM]
School—West Catholic Elementary. See Elementary Schools, Interparochial Under Institutions Located in the Archdiocese.

Creighton, Knox Co., St. Ludger, Rev. Jerome I. Spenner.
Res., 908 Lake St., R.R. 2, Box 25, 68729-9509. Tel: 402-358-3596.
School—410 Bryant Ave., 68729. Tel: 402-358-3501.
Sisters 2; Lay Teachers 5; Students 70.
Catechesis/Religious Programs—Tel: 402-358-3501. D.R.E.: Sr. Margaret Sibbel, S.S.S.F.; Helen Borgman; Jill Boelter.
Students 93.

Crofton, Knox Co., St. Rose of Lima, Rev. Ronald S. Wasikowski.
Res., 1316 W. Fifth St., P.O. Box 335, 68730. Tel: 402-388-4814. [CEM]
School—Tel: 402-357-3507.
Lay Teachers 8; Students 147.
Catechesis/Religious Programs—Arlene Steffen, D.R.E.
Students 129.

Dodge, Dodge Co., St. Wenceslaus, Rev. Melvern A. Wiese.
Res., 731 Second St., R.R. 2, P.O. Box 274, 68633. Tel: 402-693-2235. [CEM]
School—Tel: 402-693-2819. Sr. Rosalima Wilkinson, R.S.M., Prin.
Lay Teachers 5; Students 71.
Catechesis/Religious Programs—Tel: 402-693-2347. Joan Ruskamp, D.R.E.
Students 113.

Duncan, Platte Co., St. Stanislaus, Rev. James F. McCluskey.
Res., P.O. Box 192, 68634. Tel: 402-897-2625. [CEM]
Catechesis/Religious Programs—Students 115.

Elgin, Antelope Co., St. Boniface, Rev. Owen W. Korte; Deacon Dennis Wiehn.
Res., 301 S. Second St., 68636. Tel: 402-843-5460; Fax: 402-843-2253. [CEM]
School—Tel: 402-843-5460.
Sisters 2; Lay Teachers 8; Students 114.
Catechesis/Religious Programs—Students 221.

Elkhorn, Douglas Co., St. Patrick, Rev. Robert P. Irwin.
Res., 20500 W. Maple Rd., 68022. Tel: 402-289-4289; Fax: 402-289-4288. [CEM]
Catechesis/Religious Programs—Tel: 402-289-4947.
Students 170.

Emerson, Dakota Co., Sacred Heart, Rev. James V. Kramper.
Res., Sixth St. & Main St., P.O. Box 250, 68733. Tel: 402-695-2342. [CEM]
School—Tel: 402-695-2513.
Sisters 1; Lay Teachers 3; Students 52.

Ewing, Holt Co., St. Peter de Alcantara, Rev. Gerald A. Leise.
Res., P.O. Box 37, 68735. Tel: 402-626-7605.
Catechesis/Religious Programs—Helen Larson, D.R.E.
Students 104.

Fordyce, Cedar Co., St. John the Baptist, Rev. Christopher J. Grimmond.
Res., P.O. Box 170, 68736. Tel: 402-357-3506; Fax: 402-357-3506. [CEM]
School—West Catholic Elementary. See Elementary Schools, Interparochial Under Institutions Located in the Archdiocese.
Catechesis/Religious Programs—Kathy Magorian, D.R.E.
Students 67.

Fort Calhoun, Washington Co., St. John the Baptist, Rev. James F. Schwertley.
Res., 608 N. 13th St., Box 163, 68023. Tel: 402-468-5348.

Fremont, Dodge Co., St. Patrick, Revs. Francis W. Lordemann; David M. Korth; Michael P. Eckley; Deacons Robert Chapman; Edward Gentrup; Justin Lauer; Hugh Robinson; LeRoy Spieker.
Res., 422 E. Fourth St., 68025. Tel: 402-721-6611; Fax: 402-727-8167. [CEM]
High School—Archbishop Bergan, (Grades 7-12). Tel: 402-721-9683; Fax: 402-721-5366. Timothy George, Prin.
Lay Teachers 21; Students 274.
Catechesis/Religious Programs—Tel: 402-721-9710; Fax: 402-721-5366. Helen Kuiper, D.R.E.
Students 600.

Fullerton, Nance Co., St. Peter, Rev. Richard J. Whiteing.
Res., 315 N. Esther, P.O. Box 368, 68638. Tel: 308-536-2574. [CEM]
Catechesis/Religious Programs—Tel: 308-536-2574.
Students 201.

Genoa, Nance Co., St. Rose of Lima, Rev. Robert H. Nienaber.
Res., 116 N. Elm St., P.O. Box 490, 68640-0490. Tel: 402-993-2323.
Catechesis/Religious Programs—Tel: 402-993-2323.
Students 175.

Gretna, Sarpy Co., St. Patrick, Rev. Daniel F. Soltys.
Res., 508 Angus, P.O. Box 480, 68028. Tel: 402-332-4444. [CEM]
Catechesis/Religious Programs—Tel: 402-332-3242. Judy Huber, D.R.E.
Students 325.

Hartington, Cedar Co., Holy Trinity, Rev. William E. Sanderson.
Res., 404 S. Broadway Ave., P.O. Box 278, 68739. Tel: 402-254-6559. [CEM]
School—Tel: 402-254-6496.
Lay Teachers 13; Students 229.
Catechesis/Religious Programs—Students 158.

Heun, Colfax Co., Holy Trinity, Rev. Ray O. Bonham.
Res., P.O. Clarkson Rte. 1, Box 49, 68629. Tel: 402-986-1627. [CEM]
School—See Elementary Schools, Interparochial Under Institutions Located in the Archdiocese.
Catechesis/Religious Programs—Students 63.
Mission—Tabor, Colfax Co., St. Mary. [CEM]

Hooper, Dodge Co., St. Rose of Lima, Rev. William D. L'Heureux.
Res., 405 Elk St., P.O. Box 443, 68031. Tel: 402-654-3449. [CEM]
Catechesis/Religious Programs—Students 43.
Mission—Scribner, Dodge Co., St. Lawrence, 405 Elk St. Box 443, 68031. Tel: 402-654-3449. [CEM]
Catechesis/Religious Programs—Students 43.

Howells, Colfax Co., SS. Peter and Paul, Rev. Thomas J. Sellentin.
Res., 614 Center St., P.O. Box 40, 68641. Tel: 402-986-1653.
School—Howells Community Catholic School. See Elementary Schools, Interparochial Under Institutions Located in the Archdiocese.
Catechesis/Religious Programs—Students 65.

St. John Nepomucene, Rev. Thomas J. Sellentin.
Res., 614 Center St., P.O. Box 40, 68641. Tel: 402-986-1653. [CEM]
School—Howells Community Catholic School. See Elementary Schools, Interparochial Under Institutions Located in the Archdiocese.

Humphrey, Platte Co., St. Francis, Revs. J. Brian Beilman; Douglas P. Scheinost.
Res., P.O. Box 116, 68642. Tel: 402-923-0913; Fax: 402-923-1590. [CEM]
School—(Grades K-6). Tel: 402-923-0611; Fax: 402-923-1590.
Sisters 1; Lay Teachers 8; Students 186.
High School—Tel: 402-923-0818.
Lay Teachers 14; Students 140.
Catechesis/Religious Programs—Students 79.

Jackson, Dakota Co., St. Patrick, Rev. Michael G. Printy.
Res., 203 E. Elk St., P.O. Box 87, 68743. Tel: 402-632-4292.
Catechesis/Religious Programs—Claudette Albenesius, D.R.E.
Students 116.
Mission—Hubbard, Dakota Co., St. Mary, P.O. Box 126, Hubbard, 68741. Tel: 402-632-4283. [CEM 2]

Krakow, Nance Co., SS. Peter and Paul, Rev. Robert H. Nienaber, Admin.
Res., P.O. Genoa, R.R. 2, P.O. Box 18, 68640. Tel: 402-993-6600.

Laurel, Cedar Co., St. Mary, Rev. Alfred J. Salanitro; Deacon LeRoy Creamer.
Res., 406 Elm St., P.O. Box 828, 68745. Tel: 402-256-3303.
Catechesis/Religious Programs—Marietta Freeman, D.R.E.
Students 90.
Mission—Dixon, Dixon Co., St. Anne.

Leigh, Colfax Co., St. Mary, Rev. Francis E. Kubart.
Res., 220 W. Third St., P.O. Box 385, 68643. Tel: 402-487-2666. [CEM]
Catechesis/Religious Programs—Agnes Thalken, D.R.E.
Students 101.

Lindsay, Platte Co., Holy Family, Rev. James F. Novotny.
Res., P.O. Box 68, 68644. Tel: 402-428-2455. [CEM]
School—(Grades 1-6). Tel: 402-428-3455; Fax: 402-428-3231.
Lay Teachers 7; Students 111.
High School—(Grades 7-12). Tel: 402-428-3215; Fax: 402-428-3231.
Lay Teachers 13; Students 114.
Catechesis/Religious Programs—Students 58.

Lynch, Boyd Co., Assumption B.V.M., Rev. Donald M. Kros.
Res., P.O. Box 167, 68746. Tel: 402-569-2421. [CEM]

Lyons, Burt Co., St. Joseph, Rev. David W. LaPlante.
Res., 430 Lincoln St., P.O. Box 524, 68038. Tel: 402-687-2102.
Catechesis/Religious Programs—Students 94.

Madison, Madison Co., St. Leonard, Rev. William F. Weidner.
Res., 504 S. Nebr. St., P.O. Box 368, 68748. Tel: 402-454-3529. [CEM]
School—Tel: 402-454-3525.
Lay Teachers 4; Students 67.
Catechesis/Religious Programs—Students 190.

Menominee, Cedar Co., St. Boniface, Rev. Christopher J. Grimmond; Deacon Clarence Jansen.
Res., P.O. 170, Fordyce, 68736. Tel: 402-357-3506. [CEM]
School—West Catholic Elementary. See Elementary Schools, Interparochial Under Institutions Located in the Archdiocese.

Monterey, Cuming Co., St. Boniface, Rev. Stephen J. Gutgsell.
Res., 450 12th Rd., West Point, 68788. Tel: 402-372-3681. [CEM]

Neligh, Antelope Co., St. Francis, Rev. Frank J. Baumert; Deacons Bernard Burbach; Leonard Obershaw.
Res., 702 W. 11th St., P.O. Box 259, 68756. Tel: 402-887-4521.
Catechesis/Religious Programs—Students 202.
Mission—Neligh, Antelope Co., St. Theresa, 702 West 11th, 68756.

Newcastle, Dixon Co., St. Peter, Rev. James J. Bartak.
Mailing Address: P.O.Box 898, Ponca, 68770-0898.
Res., P.O. Box 127, 405 Annie St., 68757. Tel: 402-355-2620;402-755-2773 (office).
Catechesis/Religious Programs—Tel: 402-692-3232. Barb Wieseler, D.R.E.
Students 100.

Norfolk, Madison Co., Sacred Heart, Revs. Harold J. Buse; Thomas M. Faneman; Stanley L. Kasun; Deacons Jim Doolittle; Richard Mueting.
Res., 202 S. Fifth St., 68701. Tel: 402-371-2621; Fax: 402-371-0403.

School—(Grades K-12). Tel: 402-371-4584; 371-2784; Fax: 402-371-0403. Principals: Ron Brewer, (Grades K-6); Jeff Bellar, (Grades 7-12).
Priests 4; Lay Teachers 48; Students 744.
Catechesis/Religious Programs—Tel: 402-371-8658. Mary Throener, D.R.E. (Grades K-12).
Students 704.

North Bend, Dodge Co., St. Charles Borromeo, Rev. Daniel E. Galas.
Res., P.O. Box 457, 68649. Tel: 402-652-8484.
Catechesis/Religious Programs—Betty Marxsen, D.R.E.
Students 214.

Olean, Colfax Co., Sacred Heart, Rev. Kenneth Carl.
Res., R.R. 2, P.O. Box 612, Dodge, 68633. Tel: 402-693-2487. [CEM]
School—Howells Community Catholic School. See Elementary Schools, Interparochial Under Institutions Located in the Archdiocese.

O'Neill, Holt Co., St. Patrick, Revs. Richard J. Reiser; Mark K. Merkel; Deacon Robert Shoemaker; Lisa Lueninghoener, Liturgist.
Res., 301 E. Adams, 68763. Tel: 402-336-1602. [CEM]
School—Tel: 402-336-2664.
Sisters 1; Lay Teachers 11; Students 132.
High School—Tel: 402-336-4455.
Sisters 1; Lay Teachers 15; Students 119.
Catechesis/Religious Programs—Tel: 402-336-1602. Linda Lieswald, D.R.E.
Students 225.
Mission—Amelia, Holt Co., St. Joseph, Tel: 402-482-5283.

Osmond, Pierce Co., St. Mary of the Seven Dolors, Rev. Kenneth M. Potts.
Res., 509 Hill St., P.O. Box 397, 68765. Tel: 402-748-3340. [CEM]
School—Tel: 402-748-3433.
Lay Teachers 4; Students 63.
Catechesis/Religious Programs—Students 65.

Papillion, Sarpy Co., St. Columbkille, Revs. Steven J. Stillmunks; Mark A. Tomasiewicz; Deacons Ralph Tharp; Frank Mascarello; Jerry Overkamp; Eldon Lauber.
Res., 200 E. Sixth St., 68046. Tel: 402-339-3285; Fax: 402-592-4753.
School—Tel: 402-339-8706; Fax: 402-592-4147.
Lay Teachers 22; Students 541.
Catechesis/Religious Programs—Tel: 402-339-0990. Marge Koenigsman, D.R.E.
Students 822.

Pender, Thurston Co., St. John, Rev. James V. Kramper.
Res., 108 N. Fifth St., P.O. Box 96, 68047. Tel: 402-385-3258.
Catechesis/Religious Programs—Students 100.

Petersburg, Boone Co., St. John the Baptist, Rev. Gerald A. Connealy.
Res., Fourth & Norman Sts., P.O. Box 8, 68652. Tel: 402-386-5580. [CEM]
School—Tel: 402-386-5472.
Sisters 2; Lay Teachers 3; Students 45.
Catechesis/Religious Programs—Students 62.
Mission—Raeville, Boone Co., St. Bonaventure, P.O.Box 8, 68652.

Pierce, Pierce Co., St. Joseph, Rev. Thomas DeBacker.
Res., 116 W. Willow St., 68767. Tel: 402-329-4200. [CEM]
Catechesis/Religious Programs—Tel: 402-329-6655.
Students 202.

Plainview, Pierce Co., St. Paul, Rev. James M. Buckley.
Res., P.O. Box 387, 68769. Tel: 402-582-4413. [CEM]
Mission—Brunswick, Antelope Co., St. Ignatius.

Platte Center, Platte Co., St. Joseph, Rev. James C. Ryberg.
Res., P.O. Box 155, 68653-0155. Tel: 402-246-2255. [CEM]
Catechesis/Religious Programs—Tel: 402-246-5700. Angela Dolezal, D.R.E.
Students 117.

Ponca, Dixon Co., St. Joseph, Rev. James J. Bartak; Deacon Paul Poulosky.
Res., P.O. Box 127, Newcastle, 68757. Tel: 402-355-2620;402-755-2773 (office). [CEM]
Catechesis/Religious Programs—Kari Richards, D.R.E.
Students 120.

Raeville, Boone Co., St. Bonaventure, Rev. Gerald A. Connealy.
Res., Petersburg, 68652. Tel: 402-386-5580. [CEM]

Ralston, Douglas Co., St. Gerald, Revs. Lawrence J. Dorsey; Thomas Weisbecker.
Res., 7859 Lakeview St., 68127. Tel: 402-331-1955; Fax: 402-331-1961.
School—Tel: 402-331-4223; Fax: 402-331-1961. David Garland, Prin.
Lay Teachers 17; Students 456.
Catechesis/Religious Programs—Tel: 402-331-4523.
Students 425.

Randolph, Cedar Co., St. Frances de Chantal, Rev. Wayne W. Schlautman; Deacon Vincent Schmit.
Res., P.O. Box B, 68771. Tel: 402-337-0644. [CEM]
Catechesis/Religious Programs—Tel: 402-337-0341. La Donna Leiting, D.R.E.
Students 239.

St. Charles, Cuming Co., St. Anthony, Rev. Stephen J. Gutgsell.
Res., 445 15th Rd., West Point, 68788. Tel: 402-372-3681. [CEM]

St. Edward, Boone Co., St. Edward, Rev. Edward B. Gill.
Res., 805 Washington St., P.O. Box A, 68660-0136. Tel: 402-678-2642. [CEM]
Catechesis/Religious Programs—Sr. Agatha Marie Sadler, D.R.E.
Students 101.

St. Helena, Cedar Co., Immaculate Conception, Rev. Michael B. Malloy.
Res., Sts. Peter & Paul Church (Bow Valley), R.R. 3, 106 W. 889th Rd., Hartington, 68739. Tel: 402-357-2465. [CEM]
School—East Catholic Elementary. See Elementary Schools, Interparochial Under Institutions Located in the Archdiocese.
Catechesis/Religious Programs—Students 51.

St. James, Cedar Co., SS. Philip and James, Rev. Paul C. Zaccone.
Res., P.O. Box 65, Wynot, 68792. Tel: 402-357-2146. [CEM]
School—East Catholic Elementary. See Elementary Schools, Interparochial Under Institutions Located in the Archdiocese.

St. John, Holt Co., St. John, Rev. Gerald A. Leise, Jr.
Res., R.R. 1, P.O. Box 150, Clearwater, 68726. Tel: 402-485-2430.
Catechesis/Religious Programs—Beth Schueth, D.R.E.
Students 56.

Schuyler, Colfax Co., St. Augustine, Rev. William S. Whelan; Deacon Marvin Capoun.
Res., 619 Banner St., 68661. Tel: 402-352-3521. [CEM]
Catechesis/Religious Programs—320 W. 10 St., 68661. Tel: 402-352-2149.
Students 168.

St. Mary, Rev. Ralph A. Lammers; Deacon Evan Drozda.
Res., 308 W. 10 St., 68661. Tel: 402-352-3540; Fax: 402-352-2149.
Catechesis/Religious Programs—Tel: 402-352-2149. Leona Kracl, D.R.E.
Students 216.

Silver Creek, Merrick Co., St. Lawrence, Rev. Kenneth D Vavrina.
Res., P.O. Box 332, 68663. Tel: 308-773-2282. [CEM]
Catechesis/Religious Programs—Tel: 402-897-2510. Christine Starostka, D.R.E.
Students 62.

Snyder, Dodge Co., St. Leo, Rev. Daniel E Galas.
Res., P.O. Box 188, 68664. Tel: 402-568-2520. [CEM]
Catechesis/Religious Programs—Tel: 402-568-2586. Joyce Kreikemeier, D.R.E.
Students 54.

South Sioux City, Dakota Co., St. Michael, Revs. David F. Liewer; Charles R. Uhlik.
Res., 1405 First Ave., 68776. Tel: 402-494-5423; Fax: 402-494-2344.
School—Tel: 402-494-1526.
Lay Teachers 13; Students 205.
Catechesis/Religious Programs—1414 Third Ave., 68776. Tel: 402-494-2827; Fax: 402-494-2344.
Students 300.
Mission—Homer, Dakota Co., St. Cornelius.

Spencer, Boyd Co., St. Mary, Rev. Robert K. English.
Res., South & Harmon Sts., P.O. Box 149, 68777. Tel: 402-589-0067.
Catechesis/Religious Programs—D.R.E.: Mary Kirpatrick, (Grades 1-6), Tel: 402-589-1266; Bill Engelhaupt, (Grades 7-12), Tel: 402-589-9016.
Students 86.

Springfield, Sarpy Co., St. Joseph, Rev. James R. Cain.
Res., 102 S. Ninth St., P.O. Box 345, 68059. Tel: 402-253-2889.
Catechesis/Religious Programs—Tel: 402-253-2949. Linda Keller, D.R.E.
Students 139.

Stanton, Stanton Co., St. Peter, Rev. Timothy J. Lange.
Res., P.O. Box 557, 68779. Tel: 402-439-2147.
Catechesis/Religious Programs—D.R.E.: Valerie Morfeld Tel: 402-396-3207; Karen Petersen Tel: 402-439-2331.
Students 140.

Stuart, Holt Co., St. Boniface, Rev. Frank E. Jindra.
Res., 106 E. Fourth, P.O. Box 190, 68780. Tel: 402-924-3262; Fax: 402-924-3494. [CEM]
School—Tel: 402-924-3803.
Lay Teachers 5; Students 63.
Catechesis/Religious Programs—Students 113.

Tarnov, Platte Co., St. Michael, Rev. Leonard C. Ficenec, Admin.
Res., R.R. 1, P.O. Box 202, Humphrey, 68642. Tel: 402-246-4821. [CEM]

Tekamah, Burt Co., St. Patrick, Rev. Martin P. Conley.
Res., 1323 R St., 68061-1542. Tel: 402-374-1692.
Catechesis/Religious Programs—Tom Olson, D.R.E.
Students 79.
Mission—Decatur, Burt Co., Holy Family.

Tilden, Madison Co., Our Lady of Mt. Carmel, Rev. Robert A. Schmitz.
Res., P.O. Box 458, 68781. Tel: 402-368-7710.
Catechesis/Religious Programs—Tel: 402-368-5919. Corine Frey, D.R.E.
Students 102.

Valley, Douglas Co., St. John, Rev. Robert J. Smith; Deacon Gary Hennessey.
Res., 209 E. Sunset, 68064. Tel: 402-359-5783.
Catechesis/Religious Programs—Vonnie Abbott, D.R.E.
Students 201.

Verdigre, Knox Co., St. Wenceslaus, Rev. Gregory P. Baxter.
Res., 409 S. Third St., P.O. Box 9, 68783-009. Tel: 402-668-2331. [CEM]
Mission—Verdigre, Knox Co., St. William, P.O. Box 9, 68783-0009.

Walthill, Thurston Co., St. Joseph, Rev. Thomas E. Bauwens.
Res., P.O. Box GG, Winnebago, 68071. Tel: 402-846-5550; Fax: 402-878-2760.

Wayne, Wayne Co., St. Mary, Rev. Donald M. Cleary.
Res., 412 E. 8th St., 68787. Tel: 402-375-2000. [CEM]
School—Tel: 402-375-2337.
Lay Teachers 7; Students 58.
Catechesis/Religious Programs—Students 207.

West Point, Cumming Co., Assumption B.V.M., Revs. Gary L. Ostrander; Steven Emanuel; Deacon Vincent Maly.
Res., 343 N. Monitor St., 68788. Tel: 402-372-2188; Fax: 402-372-3563. [CEM]
School—Guardian Angel, Tel: 402-372-5328. Sr. Rochelle Kerkhof, Prin.
Priests 2; Sisters 3; Lay Teachers 19; Students 356.
Catechesis/Religious Programs—Carol Praest, D.R.E.
Students 104.

Winnebago, Thurston Co., St. Augustine's. (Indian Mission). Rev. Thomas E. Bauwens.
Res., P.O. Box GG, 68071. Tel: 402-878-2402; Fax: 402-878-2760.
School—Missionary Benedictine Sisters 3; Lay Teachers 6; Students 78.
Mission—Macy, Thurston Co., Our Lady of Fatima.

Wisner, Cuming Co., St. Joseph, Rev. David D. Belt.
Res., 1318 G Ave. W., P.O. Box 623, 68791. Tel: 402-529-3242. [CEM]
Catechesis/Religious Programs—Tel: 402-529-3891. Anne McManigal, D.R.E.
Students 124.

Wynot, Cedar Co., Sacred Heart, Rev. Paul C. Zaccone.
Res., P.O. Box 65, 68792. Tel: 402-357-2400. [CEM]
Catechesis/Religious Programs—Deanna Klug, D.R.E.
Students 59.

On Duty Outside the Archdiocese:
Reverend Monsignors—
Cupich, Blase J., Pres. & Rector, Pontifical College, Josephinum
Reverend Fathers—
Andrews, John, Theological Studies, Rome, Italy
Greisen, Thomas A., Conception Seminary, Conception, MO
Harrison, Patrick, Canon Law Studies, Rome, Italy
Kampschneider, Daniel J., Theological Studies, Rome, Italy

Military Chaplains:
Reverend Fathers—
Dendinger, William J., Chap., U.S.A.F.
Dillon, Jerome V., Chap., U.S.N.R.
Hall, Douglas C., U.S.A.F.
Harbour, Linn S., U.S.A.F.
Reeson, David G., U.S.A.F.

Absent on Leave:
Reverend Fathers—
Fiala, John M.
Gaughan, James M.
Henry, Patrick J.
Mainelli, Vincent P.
Matt, Thomas S.

McNeil, Joel
Rowe, Douglas L.
Rush, Gerald V.
Stevens, Clifford J.

Absent on Sick Leave:
Reverend Fathers—
Finch, Joseph E.

Retired:
Reverend Monsignors—
Ariano, Joseph W.
Hulsman, Francis J., 1515 St. John Court S., Beech Grove, IN 46107
Hupp, Robert P., 7508 Walnut St., Omaha, NE 68124
Kenny, Francis P., 7323 Shirley St., Omaha, NE 68124
Krejci, Albert L., 7600 S. 42 St., Omaha, NE 68147
Michaels, Anthony B., 2405 S. 48th Ave., Omaha, NE 68106
O'Donnell, Edward C., 4803 William St., Omaha, NE 68106
Werner, Cyril J., P.O. Box 562, Hartington, NE 68739
Reverend Fathers—
Bartek, James F., 900 N. 90th St., Omaha, NE 68114
Bartek, William C., 7323 Shirley Ct., Omaha, NE 68124
Beacom, John F., 757 E. Decatur, West Point, NE 68788
Begley, Paul, 4112 S. 26th St., Omaha, NE 68107
Brodersen, Charles F., 9230 Burt St. #223, Omaha, NE 68114
Carroll, Patrick A., 4752 N. 14th Ave., Omaha, NE 68110
Ciurej, Richard S., 4107 S. 38 St., Omaha, NE 68107
Dickes, Jerome H., 500 E. 8th St., Yankton, SD 57078
Duffy, Robert P., 7323 Shirley Ct., Omaha, NE 68124
Dunne, Peter F., Boys Town Center, Boys Town, NE 68010
Fangman, Paul J., Rte. 1, Box 139, Humphrey, NE 68642
Ficenec, Leonard C., R.R. 1, Box 202, Tarnov, NE 68642
Fitzgerald, William F.
Flisiak, Stefan, R.R. 2, Box 18, Genoa, NE 68640
Foster, William A., 4925 S. 99th St., Omaha, NE 68127
Golik, Stanislaus, 4804 Grover St., Omaha, NE 68106
Hebert, John M., 2325 Fifth Ave., Marshalltown, IA 50158
Hunkeler, Edward J., 5605 No. 105th Plaza-3, Omaha, NE 68134
Kelly, Michael J., 900 N. 90th St., Omaha, NE 68114
Kenny, James E., 7232 Shirley Ct., Omaha, NE 68124
Koros, John J., 120 Citrus Rd. N.E., Lake Placid, FL 33852
Kovar, Vaclav, General Delivery, Dodge, NE 68633
Krajicek, Robert P.
Kreikemeier, Leo A., Rt. 1, P.O. Box 25E, Cedar Bluffs, NE 68015
LaRocque, Benedict J., Saint Benedict Abbey, Atchison, KS 66002
Meiergerd, Godfrey A., Rt. 1, Box 250, Cedar Bluffs, NE 68124
Meister, Andrew H., P.O. Box 25D, Cedar Bluffs, NE 68015
Micek, Joseph S., 1655 E. Sahara, Apt. 1056, Las Vegas, NV 89104
Mitera, Stanislaus C., 1938 S. 38 Ave., Apt. 116, Omaha, NE 68105
Moreci, Francis A., 2642 N. Newland Ave., Chicago, IL 60635
Musteikis, Leonard, 420 Preston Circle, Sunny Hills, FL 32428
Peter, Paul F., 7323 Shirley Ct., Omaha, NE 68107
Petrasic, Martin J., 2603 S. 50 St., Omaha, NE 68106
Petrusic, Anthony A., 322 Virginia St., Hollywood, FL 33019
Price, Francis R., 401 N. 18th St., Norfolk, NE 68701
Schad, Edward J., 1565 18th Ave., Columbus, NE 68601
Tresnak, Anthony J., 900 N. 90th St., Omaha, NE 68114
Tuma, Anthony F., 1870 S. 75th St., Omaha, NE 68124
Wilwerding, Anthony P., #8 Madonna Dr., Hardy, AR 72542
Wolbach, Richard A., 4001 S. 36th St., Omaha, NE 68107

Permanent Deacons:
Alexander, Fred
Anderson, Andy
Archibald, Joseph
Barbour, Frank
Bartman, Frank
Batenhorst, Kenneth F.
Baughman, Charles
Brich, James
Brisson, Ralph
Bronk, Duane
Buglewicz, George
Capoun, Marvin
Casart, Ronald
Cerveny, John
Chambers, James
Chapman, Robert
Clausen, Donald
Creamer, LeRoy
Crowley, Martin
Cuva, Fred
Davis, Dennis
DeBlawn, James L.
DesRosiers, Peter
Dethlefs, Dennis
Digilio, Peter
Dineen, Lonnie
Doolittle, James
Dreifuerst, Lester
Drozda, Evan
Dunn, Donald
Edgerton, Richard
Elster, George
Enzolera, Sebastian
Eubanks, Paul
Fell, William
Filipcic, Anthony
Finney, Jack
Fitzgerald, Thomas
Flesch, Robert
French, Gary
Friend, Joseph
Gau, Jerome
Gencarelli, Ernest
Gentrup, Edward
Gonderinger, Gerald
Gurney, David
Heck, Lawrence
Hendricks, Fred
Hennessey, Gary
Hills, Lyle
Hilt, Frank
Horner, Ron
Huck, John
Hueser, Ralph
Iwanski, Duane
Jansen, Clarence
Janssen, Daniel
Johnson, Donald
Kaiser, Roland G.
Kalkowski, Kenneth
Kedrowski, Kirk
Kemp, Donald
Kessler, Joseph
Knockenhauer, George F.
Kronschnabel, John
Kube, Norman
Kurtz, Stanley
L'Archevesque, Charles
Lauber, Eldon
Lauer, Justin
Lenz, Patrick
Livingston, Tom
Maly, Vince
Mascarello, Frank
Mascarello, John
Matukewicz, Paul
McGuire, Michael
Mendick, Daniel
Mielak, Lawrence
Miles, Patrick
Miller, Carl
Moore, Fred
Mueting, Richard
Murphy, Thomas
Narducci, Warren
Nelson, Richard
Obershaw, Leonard
Obershaw, Robert
Overkamp, Jerry
Placzek, Michael
Poulosky, Paul
Purnell, Thomas
Ramirez, Joseph
Reynolds, Michael
Ridder, Frederick
Robinson, Hugh
Rooney, Paul
Sanders, Thomas
Schimonitz, Eugene
Schmmidt, Vincent
Schulte, Thomas
Schumacher, Allan
Shoemaker, Robert
Sommer, Fred
Spenner, Arthur
Spicer, Ernest
Spieker, LeRoy
St. Arnold, Irving
Staroski, Jim
Steenson, Gerald
Steffen, Andrew
Telich, Frank
Tharp, Bud
Thoene, Sylvan
Thome, Duane
Tylutki, Glenn
Villemure, Arthur
Werthmann, Ralph
Weskirchen, Charles
Wiehn, Dennis
Young, Wayne

INSTITUTIONS LOCATED IN THE ARCHDIOCESE

[A] COLLEGES AND UNIVERSITIES

OMAHA. *College of St. Mary*, 1901 S. 72 St., 68124. Tel: 402-399-2400.
For a complete listing, refer to the Colleges and Universities section.

**Creighton University*, 2500 California Plaza, 68178. Tel: 402-280-2700.
For a complete listing, refer to the Colleges and Universities section.

[B] HIGH SCHOOLS, DIOCESAN

OMAHA. *Daniel J. Gross Catholic High School of Omaha*, 7700 S. 43rd St., 68147. Tel: 402-734-2000; Fax: 402-734-4270. William Ford, Pres. & Contact. Assistant Principals: Dorothy Ostrowski; Rebecca Cleveland; Michelle Pohlman, Campus Ministry; Rev. Walter Wancewicz. Lay Teachers 45; Students 702.

Father Flanagan High School, 2606 Hamilton St., 68131. Tel: 402-498-3000. Dr. Pat McGinnis, Acting Prin. & Contact. Lay Teachers 26; Students 198.

Roncalli Catholic High School of Omaha, 6401 Sorensen Pkwy., 68152. Tel: 402-571-7670. Dr. Duane Gross, Pres. & Contact; Dr. Duane Gross, Prin. Sisters 1; Lay Teachers 25; Students 345.

V.J. & Angela Skutt Catholic High School of Omaha, 3131 S. 156 St., 68130. Tel: 402-333-0818. Rev. James E. Gilg, Pres. & Contact; Dr. W. Patrick Durow, Prin.; Mrs. Debora Masker, Asst. Prin.; Mr. David Miller, Activities Dir.; Mr. Clayton Freeman, Campus Minister; Rev. Jay Kruse, Chap. Priests 1; Lay Teachers 38; Students 484.

COLUMBUS. *Scotus Central Catholic High School.* (Grades 7-12), 1554 18th Ave., 68601. Tel: 402-564-7165. Mr. Daniel J. Schartz, Supt.; Mr. Thomas Walding, Prin. & Contact; Rev. Wayne S. Pavela, Campus Min. Priests 1; Lay Teachers 32; Students 465.

ELGIN. *Pope John XXIII Central Catholic High School at Elgin*, P.O. Box 179, 68636. Tel: 402-843-5325. Dennis Cannon, Prin. Priests 4; School Sisters of St. Francis 2; Lay Teachers 13; Students 107.

HARTINGTON. *Cedar Catholic High School*, 401 S. Broadway, 68739. Tel: 402-254-3906. Gary Dunn, Admin. & Contact; Rev. Keith Rezac, Spiritual Dir. Lay Teachers 16; Students 174.

NORFOLK. *Norfolk Catholic High School*, 2300 Madison Ave., 68701. Tel: 402-371-2784. Mr. Richard Bancke, Prin.; Mr. Jeff Beller, Prin. & Contact. Priests 3; Lay Teachers 27; Students 300.

WEST POINT. *Central Catholic High School*, 68788. Tel: 402-372-5326. Mr. John James, Prin. & Contact. Franciscan Sisters of Christian Charity 2; Lay Teachers 13; Students 140.

[C] HIGH SCHOOLS, PRIVATE

OMAHA. *Creighton Preparatory School*, 7400 Western Ave., 68114. Tel: 402-393-1190. Revs. Robert V. Hotz, S.J., Pres. & Contact; Robert J. Tillman, S.J., Supr.; Mr. John Naatz, Prin.; Revs. Burnell B. Bisbee, S.J.; Floyd A. Brey, S.J.; Robert E. Brodzeller, S.J.; Thomas C. Donohoe, S.J.; William J. Doran, S.J.; Philip J. Dougherty, S.J.; Willard J. Dressel, S.J.; Harry Eglsaer, S.J.; Michael L. Hindelang, S.J.; Eugene Jakubek, S.J.; Edward A. Larkin, S.J.; Paul A. Mahowald, S.J.; Michael J. Marco, S.J.; Charles F. Mullen, S.J.; Mark E. Niemann, S.J.; William F. O'Leary, S.J.; James M. Radde, S.J.; Thomas C. Richmond; James A. Sinnerud, S.J.; Bros. Paul J. Kemper, S.J.; Gerald E. Peltz, S.J.; James R. Zuercher, S.J. Priests 21;

Brothers 3; Scholastics 2; Lay Teachers 59; Students 964.

Duchesne Academy of the Sacred Heart, 36th & Burt Sts., 68131. Tel: 402-558-3800. Mrs. Sheila K. Haggas, Head of School & Contact. Society of the Sacred Heart 4; Lay Teachers 21; Girls 187.

Marian High School, 74th and Military Ave., 68134. Tel: 402-571-2618. Servants of Mary. Elizabeth Kish, Head of School & Contact. Sisters 4; Lay Teachers 44; Girls 586.

Mercy High School, 1501 S. 48th St., 68106. Tel: 402-553-9424. Sr. Johanna Burnell, R.S.M., Pres. & Contact; Carolyn Jaworski, Prin. Sisters of Mercy of the Americas 5; Lay Teachers 27; Girls 312.

BOYS TOWN. *Father Flanagan's Boys' Home*, 68010. Rev. Val Peter, Contact.
See Protective Institutions.

ELKHORN. *Mount Michael High School*, 22520 Mt. Michael Rd., 68022-3400. Tel: 402-289-2544; Fax: 442-289-4539. Rt. Rev. Theodore Wolff, O.S.B., Abbot & Contact; Revs. Robert Halter, O.S.B.; Charles Zach, O.S.B., Pres.; Richard Thell, O.S.B.; John Hagemann, O.S.B.; Michael Liebl, O.S.B.; Daniel Lenz, O.S.B.; Louis Sojka, O.S.B.; Stephen Plank, O.S.B. Priests 7; Sisters 2; Professed Brothers 4; Lay Teachers 9; Students 145.

[D] ELEMENTARY SCHOOLS, INTER-PAROCHIAL

OMAHA. *All Saints Catholic School*, 1335 S. 10th St., 68108. Tel: 402-346-5757. Diane Cronin, Prin. & Contact. Serving parishes of St. Ann, St. Frances Cabrini, St. Joseph, St. Mary Magdalene Immaculate Conception, St. Patrick. Lay Teachers 15; Students 222.

St. James-Seton School, 9212 Tomahawk Blvd., 68134. Tel: 402-572-0339. Kirk Estee, Prin. & Contact. Servants of Mary 2; Lay Teachers 32; Students 733.

St. Pius X-St. Leo School, 6905 Blondo St., 68104. Tel: 402-551-6667. Mrs. Joyce Gubbels, Prin. & Contact. Servants of Mary 2; Lay Teachers 44; Students 885.

FORDYCE. *West Catholic Elementary*, 303 Omaha St., Box 167, 68736-0167. Tel: 402-357-3507. Serving parishes in Constance, Fordyce & Menominee. Mrs. Marilyn Wiebelhaus, Prin. & Contact. Lay Teachers 3; Students 67.

HARTINGTON. *East Catholic Elementary*, 108 W. 889 Rd., 68739-6079. Tel: 402-357-2146. Marilyn Wiebelhaus, Prin. Serving parishes in Bow Valley, St. Helena & St. James. Lay Teachers 3; Students 51.

HOWELLS. *Howells Community Catholic School*, Box 70, 68641. Tel: 402-986-1689. Serving parishes in Howells, Olean, Heun, Aloys & Tabor. Mrs. Mary Ann Spicka, Prin. (Grades 1-6) & Contact. Lay Teachers 7; Students 118.

[E] ELEMENTARY SCHOOLS, PRIVATE

BOYS TOWN. *Father Flanagan's Boys' Home*. Rev. Val Peter, Contact. See Protective Institutions below.

[F] SPECIAL EDUCATION

OMAHA. *Cardinal Spellman Catholic Education Association Foundation*, 12210 S. 36 St., 68123. Patricia A. Buttell, Contact.

Christian Urban Education Service Foundation, 2218 Binney, 68110. Rev. James P. Scholz, Contact. Sisters 1; Lay Teachers 10; Students 150.

The Jesuit Middle School of Omaha, 2311 N. 22nd St., 68110. Tel: 402-346-4464. Rev. James L. Michalski, S.J., Contact Person. Students 17.

Madonna School for Exceptional Children, 2537 N. 62nd, 68104. Tel: 402-556-1883. John Palladina, Prin. Lay Teachers 9; Students 50.

Madonna Shop, 2014 N. 66, 68104. Tel: 402-551-5441. Jackie O'Brien, Mgr.

[G] GENERAL HOSPITALS

OMAHA. *Alegent Health*, 1018 N. 96th St., Ste. 200, 68114. Tel: 402-343-4430; Fax: 402-343-4337.
For a complete listing, refer to the Hospitals section.

**Alegent Health - Bergan Mercy Health System dba Algent Health - Bergan Mercy Medical Center*, 7500 Mercy Rd., 68124. Tel: 402-398-6060.
For a complete listing, refer to the Hospitals section.

Boys Town National Research Hospital, 555 N. 30 St., 68131. Tel: 402-498-6511; Fax: 402-498-6357.
For a complete listing, refer to the Hospitals section.

Catholic Health Corp., 920 S. 107 Ave., 68114. Tel: 402-393-7661.
For a complete listing, refer to the Hospitals section.

NORFOLK. *Our Lady of Lourdes Hospital*, 1500 Koenigstein Ave., 68701. Tel: 402-371-3402; Fax: 402-644-7468.
For a complete listing, refer to the Hospitals section.

O'NEILL. *St. Anthony's Hospital*, 68763. Tel: 402-336-2611; Fax: 402-336-2815.
For a complete listing, refer to the Hospitals section.

WAYNE. *Providence Medical Center*, 1200 Providence Rd., 68787.
For a complete listing, refer to the Hospitals section.

WEST POINT. *Franciscan Care Services, Inc., dba St. Francis Memorial Hospital*, 430 N. Monitor St., 68788-1595. Tel: 402-372-2404; Fax: 402-372-2360.
For a complete listing, refer to the Hospitals section.

[H] NURSING AND CONVALESCENT HOMES

*OMAHA. *Alegent Health - Bergan Mercy Health System dba Alegent Health - Mercy Care Center*, 1870 S. 75 St., 68124. Tel: 402-398-6800.
For a complete listing, refer to the Special Care Facilities section.

Mercy Villa, 1845 S. 72 St., 68124.
For a complete listing, refer to the Special Care Facilities section.

New Cassel Retirement Center, 900 N. 90 St., 68114. Tel: 402-393-2277.
For a complete listing, refer to the Special Care Facilities section.

NORFOLK. *St. Joseph Nursing Home*, 401 N. 18th St., 68701. Tel: 402-371-9404.
For a complete listing, refer to the Special Care Facilities section.

WEST POINT. *Franciscan Care Services, Inc., (d.b.a. St. Joseph Retirement Community)*, 320 E. Decatur, 68788. Tel: 402-372-3477.
For a complete listing, refer to the Special Care Facilities section.

[I] PROTECTIVE INSTITUTIONS

*BOYS TOWN. *Father Flanagan's Boys' Home*, 68010. Tel: 402-498-1111.
For a complete listing, refer to the Special Care Facilities section.

[J] FAMILY SERVICE CENTERS

OMAHA. *Catholic Charities*, Daniel E. Sheehan Center, 3300 N. 60th St., 68104. Tel: 402-554-0520; Fax: 402-554-0365. Scot L. Adams, Contact.

COLUMBUS. *Catholic Charities*, 1761 26th Ave., P.O. Box 573, 68602-0573. Tel: 402-563-3833. Gordon Green, Dir. & Contact.

NORFOLK. *Catholic Charities*, 1109 So. 13th St., Ste. 302, 68701. Tel: 402-371-3555. Gordon Green, Dir. & Contact.

[K] MONASTERIES AND RESIDENCES OF PRIESTS AND BROTHERS

OMAHA. *Campion House*, 518 N. 19th St., 68102. Tel: 402-341-2408. Revs. David G. Schultenover, S.J.; Lawrence E. Gillick, S.J.; G. Thomas Krettek, S.J.; John P. Fitzgibbons, S.J. Scholastics 10.

Jesuit Community At Creighton University, 2500 California St., 68178. Tel: 402-280-2700. Revs. Thomas J. Shanahan, S.J., Rector; Philip R. Amidon, S.J., Min. & Contact; Andrew Alexander, S.J.; Thomas E. Bannantine, S.J.; Walter E. Boehme; Sr. Gail G. Bohr, S.J.; Revs. Robert O. Burns, S.J.; Neil Cahill, S.J.; Rev. James F., Clifton; Revs. M. Joseph Costelloe, S.J.; Ervin J. Czarnecki, S.J.; Donald A. Doll, S.J.; Eugene L. Donahue, S.J.; Donald D. Driscoll, S.J.; James A. Egan, S.J.; Lawrence W. Flanagan, S.J.; Michael J. Flecky, S.J.; James J. Gladstone, S.J.; Bro. Morris M. Gondreau, S.J.; Revs. Thomas A. Halley, S.J.; M. Dennis Hamm, S.J.; Thomas J. Hansen, S.J.; Robert P. Hart, S.J.; Richard J. Hauser, S.J.; Bro. James Heidrick, S.J.; Revs. Lawrence C. Helmueller, S.J.; Robert E. Hoene, S.J.; Thomas A. Hoffman, S.J.; John G. Holbrook, S.J.; John P. Jelinek, S.J.; Howard E. Kalb, S.J.; William F. Kelley, S.J.; Charles T. Kestermeier, S.J.; William T. Kolarec, S.J.; James P. Kramper, S.J.; Norbert J. Lemke, S.J.; Leland E. Lubbers, S.J.; John J. Lynch, S.J.; Thomas Manahan, S.J.; David G. Matzko, S.J.; Robert F. McEniry, S.J.; Richard D. McGloin, S.J.; Dennis P. McNeilly, S.J.; Thomas S. McShane, S.J.; James L. Michalski, S.J.; Michael G. Morrison, S.J.; Robert I. Pihale, S.J.; Bernard J. Portz, S.J.; Francis A. Prokes, S.J.; Michael Proterra, S.J. (Baltimore); James J. Quinn, S.J.; Virgil J. Roach, S.J.; Perry L. Robinson, S.J.; John M. Scott, S.J.; Robert J. Shanahan, S.J.; Thomas J. Shanahan, S.J.; Edward A. Sharp, S.J.; Bros. Robert E. Smith, S.J.; Edmund W. Stetzen, S.J.; Revs. Gerald L. Stockhausen, S.J.; Ernesto Travieso, S.J.; Martin O. Vaske, S.J.; George E. Von Kaenel, S.J.; Clarence M. Wagener, S.J.; Joseph E. Weiss, S.J.; Bro. Michael R. Wilmet, S.J.; Revs. M. John Wymelenberg, S.J.; John D. Zuercher, S.J. Priests 62; Brothers 4. Legal Title: *Jesuit Community at Creighton University*.

ELKHORN. *Mount Michael Abbey*, 22520 Mount Michael Rd., 68022-3400. Tel: 402-289-2541; Fax: 402-289-4539. Benedictine Fathers. Rt. Rev. Theodore J. Wolff, O.S.B., Abbot & Contact; Very Rev. Robert Halter, O.S.B., Prior; Bro. Jerome Kmiecikn, O.S.B., Sub-Prior; Rt. Rev. Raphael Walsh, O.S.B.; Revs. Frederick Schindler, O.S.B.; Benedict Dohle, O.S.B.; Albert Massmann, O.S.B.; Adrian Liable, O.S.B.; Nathanael Foshage, O.S.B.; Eugene McReynolds, O.S.B.; Bernard Sheehan, O.S.B.; Charles Zach, O.S.B.; Richard Thell, O.S.B.; John Hagemann, O.S.B.; Michael Liebl, O.S.B.; Daniel Lenz, O.S.B.; Louis L. Sojka, O.S.B.; Stephen J. Plank, O.S.B. Priests 17; Professed Brothers 9.

ST. COLUMBANS. *St. Columban's Foreign Mission Society*. (Corporate Title: St. Columban's Foreign Mission Society), 68056. Tel: 402-291-1920. Regional Headquarters and Administration Offices of the Columban Fathers in the United States. Very Rev. Brendan O'Sullivan, S.S.C., Dir. & Contact; Revs. James J. Hastings, S.S.C., Vice Dir.; Richard Steinhilber, S.S.C., Editor "Columban Mission"; Paul E. Casey, S.S.C.; J. Donald Devine, S.S.C.; Edward Dolan, S.S.C.; P. Gerard Dunne, S.S.C.; Otto Imholte, S.S.C.; Oliver Kennedy, S.S.C.; Donal O'Farrell, S.S.C.; Colm Stanley, S.S.C.; Alban Sueper, S.S.C.; William Sweeney, S.S.C. Priests 14.
Other Assignments: Revs. W. Aedan McGrath, S.S.C., Legion of Mary; Thomas Normanly, S.S.C., Buffalo, NY; Raymond Karier, S.S.C., Lake City, FL; Robert Clark, S.S.C., U.S. Navy; Robert Lamby, S.S.C., Pending; Arturo Aguilar, S.S.C., Studies; George Da Roza, S.S.C., Studies; Thomas Vaughan, S.S.C., Pending; Gerard Markey, S.S.C., Pending; Michael Donnelly, S.S.C., Pending; George Herrgott, S.S.C., Studies; Sean McGrath, S.S.C., Pending; David Richers, S.S.C., St. Petersburg; John Wanaurny, Pending.

SCHUYLER. *Benedictine Mission House*, Christ the King Priory, 68661. Tel: 402-352-2177; Fax: 402-352-2176. Revs. Germar Neubert, Prior; Herman Kornbrust, O.S.B., Contact; Adam Patras, O.S.B.; Volker Futter, O.S.B. Brothers 7.

[L] CONVENTS AND RESIDENCES FOR SISTERS

OMAHA. *Contemplative Sisters of the Good Shepherd*, 3321 Fontenelle Blvd., 68104-3633. Sr. Clare Filipowicz, Supr. & Contact. Sisters 14. Attended by Jesuit Fathers.

Monastery of St. Clare, 3626 N. 65th Ave., 68104. Tel: 402-558-4916. Poor Clares (Second Order of St. Francis). Sr. Veronia Luebbert, Contact. Sisters 9. Attended by Jesuit Fathers.

Motherhouse of the Servants of Mary, Convent of Our Lady of Sorrows, 7400 Military Ave., 68134. Tel: 402-571-2547. Sr. Teresa Lux, O.S.M., Prov. & Contact; Sr. Zita Marie Sharrow, O.S.M., Asst. Prov. Professed 124; Sisters in Motherhouse 45.

Provincial Motherhouse and Novitiate of the Notre Dame Sisters, 3501 State St., 68112. Tel: 402-455-2994. Sr. Mary Ann Zimmer, N.D., Prov. Pres. & Contact. Professed 73; Sisters living at Motherhouse 43.

Regional Office of the Sisters of Mercy of the Americas (Regional Community of Omaha), 1801 S. 72nd St., 68124. Tel: 402-393-8225. Sr. Patricia McDermott, R.S.M., Pres.; Sandy Elsasser, Contact. Perpetually Professed 279.

School Sisters of St. Francis, Regional Office, 2117 S. 33rd St., 68105-3117. Tel: 402-342-5570; Fax: 402-342-5680. Sr. Nedine Ferris, Contact.

Sisters of the Annunciation of the Archdiocese of Omaha, 654 S. 86th St., 68114. Tel: 402-391-3606. Revs. Robert J. Gass; Matthew J. Gutowski; Carl F. Sodoro.

Sisters of the Good Shepherd (R.G.S.), 1106 N. 36th St., 68131. Tel: 402-551-2966. Sr. Eileen Schiltz. Sisters 4.

NORFOLK. *Immaculata Convent*, 300 N. 18th St., 68701-3687. Tel: 402-371-3438; Fax: 402-379-2877. Sr. Agnes Salber, O.S.B., Prioress & Contact. Legal Title: *Immaculata Convent, Priory Motherhouse and Novitiate of the Missionary Benedictine Sisters*. Sisters 43; Postulants 3; Novices 3.

O'NEILL. *St. Anthony's Convent*, 210 E. Adams St., 68763. Tel: 402-336-3576. Sr. Agnesmarie Slaight, Contact. Sisters of St. Francis of Pennance and Christian Charity 4.

[M] SECULAR INSTITUTES

OMAHA. *Apostolic Oblates*, 11002 N. 204th St., 68002. Tel: 402-289-2670. Secular Institute for women dedicated to promoting spiritual growth among the laity. Teresa Monaghen, Local Moderator, 6762 Western Ave., 68002. Tel: 402-553-4418. Franco Salvo, National Moderator; Palmira Tafani, Contact.

Institute of the Apostolic Oblates, 6762 Western Ave., 68132. Tel: 402-553-4418. Franca Salvo, National Moderator. A secular institute for women with the aim of promoting the universal call to holiness, through working apostolate of the Pro Sanctity Movement.

Apostolic Sodales - Secular Institute for Priests, Boys Town Center, 68010. Tel: 402-498-1469. Rev. Peter Dunne; Palmira Tafani, Contact.

ELKHORN. *Pro Sanctity Movement*, 11002 N. 204th St., 68022. Tel: 402-289-2670; Fax: 402-289-1938. Teresa Monaghen, National Dir. Tel: 402-289-2670;

Leonard Gabriel, Dir. Tel: 402-496-6210; Teresa Monaghen, Contact. Ecclesial organization: Promotes apostolates of holiness; teaches, supports and guides people seeking to deepen their spiritual life.

[N] EDUCATIONAL FOUNDATIONS AND TRUST FUNDS

OMAHA. *The Omaha Archdiocesan Educational Foundation, Inc.*, Department of Education, 3212 N. 60th St., 68104. Tel: 402-554-8493; Fax: 402-554-8402.

St. Michael Church of Albion, NE, Educational Endowment Trust, Albion.
St. Michael Church of Albion, NE, Parish Endowment Trust, Albion.
St. Joseph Church Educational Endowment Trust, Atkinson.
St. Mary Church Educational Endowment Trust, Bellevue.
SS. Peter and Paul Parish Endowments, Bow Valley.
East Catholic Elementary School Endowment, Bow Valley/St. Helena.
St. Anthony Church Endowment Trust, Cedar Rapids.
Parish Endowment Trust Fund of St. Michael Catholic Church, Central City.
St. Peter Parish Endowment Trust, Clarks.
Church of St. Theresa of Avila Educational Endowment, Clearwater.
Church of St. Theresa of Avila Parish Endowment, Clearwater.
St. Bonaventure Church Endowment Trust, Columbus.
St. Isidore Church Endowment Trust, Columbus.
St. Isidore Elementary School Endowment Trust, Columbus.
Scotus Central Catholic High School Endowment, Columbus.
St. Ludger Parish Endowment Trust, Creighton.
St. Rose of Lima Parish Endowment, Crofton.
St. Wenceslaus Educational Endowment, Dodge.
St. Stanislaus Church Educational Endowment Trust, Duncan.
St. Boniface School Endowment Trust, Elgin.
St. Boniface Parish Endowment Trust, Elgin.
Mt. Michael Foundation, Inc., Elkhorn.
St. Patrick School Tuition Assistance Endowment Trust, Elkhorn.
St. Patrick School Endowment Trust, Elkhorn.
St. Patrick Parish Endowment Trust, Elkhorn.
Sacred Heart Parish Educational Endowment Trust, Emerson.
West Catholic Educational Endowment, Fordyce/Menominee.
St. John the Baptist Church Educational Endowment Trust, Fort Calhoun.
St. Patrick Catholic Church Endowment Trust, Fremont.
St. Patrick Parish Educational Endowment (Lauer), Fremont.
St. Peter Catholic Church Endowment Trust, Fullerton.
Holy Trinity Parish Endowment, Hartington.
SS. Peter and Paul Catholic Church Endowment Trust for Howells Community Catholic School, Howells.
St. Patrick Parish Endowment Trust, Jackson.
St. Leonard Parish Endowment Trust, Madison.
Church of St. Boniface of Menominee, Menominee.
St. Boniface Parish Endowment, Menominee.
Church of St. Francis of Assisi Parish Educational Endowment, Neligh.
Church of St. Francis of Assisi Parish Endowment Fund, Neligh.
Sacred Heart Parish Endowment Fund, Norfolk.
Archbishop Sheehan Adult Education Fund.
All Saints Catholic School Endowment.
Black Students Educational Endowment.
Blessed Sacrament Parish Educational Endowment.
Christ the King Educational Endowment Trust.
Church of the Assumption Scholarship Educational Endowment.
Robert G. Cunningham Endowment Trusts.
John Flynn Family Endowment Trust.
Fr. James E. Fitzgerald Educational Memorial.
Holy Cross School/Clete and Claire Haney Memorial.
Holy Ghost Educational Endowment.
Marian High School, Inc. Scholarship Endowment Trust.
Marian High School, Inc. Endowment Trust.
Mary Our Queen Educational Endowment Trust.
McAuley Fund.
Music in Catholic Schools.
OAEF, Inc.- C.J. Miller Trust.
Our Lady of Lourdes Educational Endowment Trust.
Religious Education Department-St. Andrew Evangelization Fund.
Roncalli High School Endowment Funds.
St. Adalbert Church Educational Endowment Fund.
St. Bernard Memorial Endowment Fund.
St. Bernard Religious Educational Endowment Fund.
St. Cecilia Cathedral Endowment Trust.
St. Francis of Assisi Church of South Omaha Educational Endowment Fund.
St. James/Seton School Endowment Fund.
St. Joan of Arc Parish Educational Endowment Fund.
St. Joan of Arc Parish Endowment.
St. John Vianney Church of Millard Parish Endowment Trust.
St. Joseph High School Endowment Trust.
St. Margaret Mary Church Educational Endowment Trust.
St. Patrick Church Educational Endowment Trust.
St. Philip Neri Church of Omaha Endowment Trust.
St. Robert Bellarmine Church Educational Endowment Trust.
St. Robert Bellarmine Parish Endowment Trust.
St. Rose Parish Endowment.
St. Stanislaus Parish Endowment Trust.
St. Stanislaus School and Educational Endowment Trust.
St. Thomas More School Endowment Trust.
St. Wenceslaus Church of Omaha Educational Endowment Trust.
Skutt Catholic High School Endowment Trust.
St. Vincent dePaul School Educational Endowment.
St. Vincent dePaul Parish Endowment Trust.
Dolores Vipond Memorial Endowment.
St. Patrick Parish/St. Mary School Endowment, O'Neill.
St. Patrick Foundation, O'Neill.
St. Columbkille Educational Endowment Trust, Papillion.
Immaculate Conception School Endowment-Heine Memorial, St. Helena.
Cedar Catholic High School Endowment (Halemba), St. Helena.
SS. Philip & James Parish Educational Endowment, St. James.
St. Michael Educational Endowment, South Sioux City.
St. Mary Catholic Church Endowment, Spencer.
St. Boniface Elementary School Endowment Fund, Stuart.
St. Wenceslaus Church Parish Endowment Trust, Verdigre.
St. Mary Educational Endowment Fund, Wayne.
Church of the Assumption of the B.V.M. Parish Endowment Trust, West Point.
Guardian Angels Grade School Educational Endowment Trust, West Point.
West Point Central Catholic High School Educational Endowment Trust, West Point.
St. Augustine Indian Mission Endowment, Winnebago.

ST. COLUMBANS. *Columban Fathers Regional Administration*, P.O. Box 10, 68056-0010. Tel: 402-291-1920; Fax: 402-291-8693.

Priests Health and Retirement Plan Trust.
Educational Trust.
Regional Trust.
D-M-P Trust.
Columban Medical and Retirement Trust, St. Columban.
Gift Annuity Trust, St. Columban.
Bourse Estate Trust, St. Columban.

[O] MISCELLANEOUS

OMAHA. *Archdiocesan Consultation Service*, 3300 N. 60th St., 68104. Tel: 402-551-1135; Fax: 402-554-0365. Sr. Marie Micheletto, R.S.M., Dir. & Contact.

Archdiocesan Hispanic Ministry Office, 3216 N. 60th St., 68104. Tel: 402-558-3134. Sr. Dulce Maria Flores, S.M.B.S., Dir.

Beginning Experience, 3214 N. 60th St., 68104. Tel: 402-551-9003; Fax: 402-551-3050. Sr. Barbara Markey, Contact.

**Bergan Mercy Foundation, Inc.* (Provides support to the mission of Bergen Mercy Health System dba Alegent Health), 7500 Mercy Rd., 68124. Tel: 402-343-4430. Sr. Norita Cooney, R.S.M., Contact Person.

Cathedral Arts Project, Inc., 100 N. 62nd St., 68132. Tel: 402-558-3100. Bro. William J. Woeger, F.S.C., Exec. Dir. & Contact.

**Catholic Charities Foundation*, 3300 N. 60th St., 68104. Tel: 402-554-0520; Fax: 402-551-8797. Scot L. Adams, Ph.D., Pres. & Contact.

Catholic County Jail Ministry, 2710 S. 24th St., 68108-1342. Tel: 402-342-7142. Sr. Carol Kowalski, O.S.M., Dir. & Contact.

Catholic Education Association, 12210 S. 36th St., 68123. Tel: 402-291-2030. Mrs. Patty Buttell, Prin. & Contact.

Christ Child Society of Omaha, 1248 S. 10th St., 68108. Tel: 402-342-4566. C. Timothy Connor, Exec. Dir. & Contact.

Christian Family Movement (CFM), 3514 N. 63rd St., 68104. Tel: 402-558-1710. Contacts: Edwin & Sheila Osterhaus.

Christian Urban Education Service, 2218 Binney St., 68110. Rev. James P. Scholz.

Christians Encounter Christ, 1938 S. 149th Cir., 68144. Tel: 402-334-2497. Jan Ekstrom, Contact Person. Purpose: To promote the transferring of environments through Christian leaders who are willing to live and share their principles of being Christian. Through the ongoing development of their Christian Personality, strengthened by their 4th Day, these leaders strive to instill the spirit and sense of gospel to all environments in which they are actively involved.

Francis House. Men's Sheltering. 1702 Nicholas St., P.O. Box 217, 68102. Tel: 402-341-1821. Paul A. Koch, Dir. & Contact.

Harrington Homes Program, 7262 Mercy Rd., Ste. 102, 68124-2348. Tel: 402-398-6614; Fax: 402-398-6370. Sr. Carolyn Coffey, R.S.M., Contact Person.

Health System of Mercy, 7262 Mercy Rd., 68124. Tel: 402-393-8225. Sr. Joan Martin, R.S.M., Contact Person.

Heart of Mary Publishing Company, Incorporated dba Heart of Mary Ministry, 1613 Vinton St., #4, 68108-1430. Tel: 402-342-9265. Sr. Mary Lucy Astuto, Contact.

Holy Name Housing Corp., 3014 N. 45th St., 68104. Tel: 402-453-6100; Fax: 402-451-7187. Sr. Marilyn Ross, R.S.M., Exec. Dir. & Contact.

The Insitute for Priestly Formation, 320 North 20th St., 68178. Tel: 402-449-6384. Richard J. Gabuzda, Contact Person. Purpose: To offer program and support for the integration of theological study, spiritual growth and direction, and retreat experiences for seminarians.

Marriage Encounter, 100 N. 62nd St., 68132. Rev. Otto Imholte, S.S.C., Exec. Team Dir. & Contact.

McAuley Bergan Center, 3552 Farnam St., 68131. Tel: 402-342-1688. 3534 S. 108th St., 68144. Tel: 402-393-2696. Paul Maginn, Dir. & Contact.

McDermott Place, 7262 Mercy Rd., Ste. 102, 68124. Tel: 402-398-6614; Fax: 402-398-6370. Sr. Carolyn Coffey, R.S.M., Contact.

Mercy Housing dba Mercy House, 7262 Mercy Rd., 68124. Tel: 402-398-6614; Fax: 402-398-6032. Sr. Carolyn Coffey, R.S.M., Contact Person.

**Mercy Housing Midwest.*

Mercy Northglen.

Mercy Western Manor.

Mercy Crestview Village.

Mercy Twin Cities - Mercy Oakwood Gardens, 7262 Mercy Rd., Ste. 102, 68124. Tel: 402-398-6614; Fax: 402-398-6370. Sr. Carolyn Coffey, R.S.M., Contact Person. Purpose: To provide affordable housing to the economically poor.

New Covenant Center: Education for Justice and Peace, 2712 S. 24th St., 68108-1342. Tel: 402-345-5111. Sr. Maureen Connolly, S.S.S.F., Prog. Coord.

Notre Dame Housing, Inc., 3501 State St., 68112-1709. Tel: 402-455-2994; Fax: 402-455-3974. Sr. Mary Ann Zimmer, N.D., Contact Person.

Purpose: To provide housing for elderly and persons of low-income or otherwise unable to afford market rate housing.

Notre Dame Living Center, Inc., 3501 State St., 68112-1709. Tel: 402-455-2994. Sr. Mary Ann Zimmer, N.D., Contact Person & Pres. Purpose: Provides affordable housing to the elderly, particularly those of low-income status.

The Omaha Archdiocesan Community Foundation and Donor Directed Depository, P.O. Box 4130, 68104-0130. Tel: 402-554-8493. Rev. Msgr. John A. Flynn. This foundation receives asset gifts and distributes earnings at the direction of the donor participants for the support of Catholic ministries in the archdiocese.

Omaha Archdiocesan Educational Foundation, Inc., P.O. Box 4130, 68104. Mrs. Rosemary Daly, Pres.; Rev. John A. Flynn, Dir. Devel. & Contact.

Omaha Catholic Jail Ministry, 2500 California St., 68178. Tel: 402-280-2700.

Douglas County Correction Center, 710 S. 17th St., 68102. Tel: 402-444-7400. Bro. Morris Gondreau, S.J., Coord., Chap. & Contact.

Pope Paul VI Institute for the Study of Human Reproduction, 6901 Mercy Rd., 68106. Tel: 402-390-6600; Fax: 402-390-9851. Thomas W. Hilgers, M.D., Dir.

St. James Manor, Inc., 3118 N. 60th St., 68104. Tel: 402-551-4243. Joseph V. Rysavy, Pres. & Contact.

Siena - Francis House, Inc., P.O. Box 217, D.T.S., 68101. Tel: 402-341-1821; Fax: 402-341-5270. Paul A. Koch, Dir. & Contact.

Siena House. (Women's Sheltering), 1702 Nicholas St., P.O. Box 217, 68102. Tel: 402-341-1821; Fax: 402-341-5270. Paul A. Koch, Dir. & Contact.

TEC, Box 4130, 68104. Tel: 402-554-8493. Rita Ramos, Archdiocesan Liaison.

Widowed and Divorced Catholics of Omaha, 3214 N. 60th St., 68104. Tel: 402-551-9003. Kathy Goodman, Contact.

The Young Adult Beginning Experience, 3214 N. 60th St., 68104. Tel: 402-551-9003. Sr. Barbara Markey, Contact.

LYNCH. *Niobrara Valley House of Renewal*, P.O. Box 117, 68746. Rev. Donald M. Kros, Contact.

WINNEBAGO. *St. Augustine's Indian Mission*, P.O. Box GG, 68071. Rev. Thomas E. Bauwens, Dir.

RELIGIOUS INSTITUTES OF MEN REPRESENTED IN THE ARCHDIOCESE

For further details refer to the corresponding bracketed number in the Religious Institutes of Men or Women section.

[0200]—*Benedictine Monks*.—O.S.B.

[0330]—*Brothers of the Christian Schools*. (St. Louis, MO).—F.S.C.

[0690]—*Jesuit Fathers and Brother*. (Wisconsin Prov.).—S.J.

[0150]—*Order of the Augustinian Recollects*. (St. Augustine Prov.).—O.A.R.

[1070]—*Redemptorist Fathers*. (St. Louis Prov.).—C.SS.R.

[0370]—*Society of St. Columban*.—S.S.C.

RELIGIOUS INSTITUTES OF WOMEN REPRESENTED IN THE ARCHDIOCESE

[0230]—*Benedictine Sisters of Pontifical Jurisdiction*.—O.S.B.

[1070-03]—*Dominican Sisters*.—O.P.

[1230]—*Franciscan Sisters of Christian Charity*.—O.S.F.

[1430]—*Franciscan Sisters of Our Lady of Perpetual Help*.—O.S.F.

[2575]—*Institute of the Sisters of Mercy of the Americas*.—R.S.M.

[0210]—*Missionary Benedictine Sisters*.—O.S.B.

[2960]—*Notre Dame Sisters*.—N.D.

[3760]—*Order of St. Clare*.—O.S.C.

[1680]—*School Sisters of St. Francis*. (Our Lady of Angels Prov.).—O.S.F.

[3580]—*Servants of Mary*.—O.S.M.

[1630]—*Sisters of St. Francis of Peace and Christian Charity*. (Denver Prov.).—O.S.F.

[1640]—*Sisters of St. Francis of Perpetual Adoration*. (Colorado Springs, CO).—O.S.F.

[1830]—*Sisters of the Good Shepherd*.—R.G.S.

[3270]—*Sisters of the Most Precious Blood* . (O'Fallon, MO).—C.PP.S.

[3320]—*Sisters of the Presentation of the B.V.M.*—P.B.V.M.

[4070]—*Society of the Sacred Heart*.—R.S.C.J.

[4120]—*Ursuline Nuns, of the Congregation of Paris*.—O.S.U.

ARCHDIOCESAN CEMETERIES

OMAHA. *Calvary*.
Holy Sepulchre.
Resurrection.
St. Mary.
St. Mary Magdalene.

NECROLOGY

† Downey, John P., (Retired). —Died Aug. 8, 1996.

† Eimers, Robert J., Atkinson, NE, St. Joseph Church. —Died April 24, 1996.

† O'Donnell, Ralph M., (Retired). —Died Nov. 14, 1996.

† Oborny, Francis J., (Retired). —Died Nov. 12, 1995.

† Pluhacek, Anthony, (Retired). —Died June 6, 1996.

Diocese of Orange in California

(Arausicanae in California)

Most Reverend

NORMAN F. McFARLAND, D.D., J.C.D.

Bishop of Orange; ordained June 15, 1946; appointed Titular Bishop of Bida and Auxiliary of San Francisco June 5, 1970; consecrated September 8, 1970; appointed Apostolic Administrator December 6, 1974; appointed Bishop of Reno-Las Vegas February 10, 1976; installed March 31, 1976; appointed Bishop of Orange December 29, 1986; installed February 24, 1987. *Res., 200 W. La Veta Ave., Orange, CA, 92866. Office: Marywood Center, 2811 E. Villa Real Dr., Orange, CA, 92867.*

Most Reverend

MICHAEL P. DRISCOLL, M.S.W., D.D.

Auxiliary Bishop and Vicar General; ordained May 1, 1965; appointed Titular Bishop of Massita and Auxiliary December 19, 1989; consecrated March 6, 1990. *Res., 200 W. La Veta Ave., Orange, CA, 92866.*

ESTABLISHED JUNE 18, 1976.

Square Miles 782.

Comprises the County of Orange in the State of California.

DIOCESAN PATRON: Our Lady of Guadalupe.

Legal Titles: *(Prot. No. CD 528-76)*

The Roman Catholic Bishop of Orange, a Corporation Sole.

Diocese of Orange Education and Welfare Corporation.

Catholic Charities of Orange.

For legal titles of parishes and diocesan institutions, consult the Diocesan Pastoral Service Office.

Chancellor's Office: 2811 E. Villa Real Dr., P.O. Box 14195, Orange, CA, 92863-1595. Tel.: 714-282-3000; Fax: 714-282-3029.

STATISTICAL OVERVIEW

Personnel	
Bishop	1
Auxiliary Bishops	1
Abbots	1
Retired Abbots	1
Priests: Diocesan Active in Diocese	112
Priests: Active Outside Diocese	3
Priests: Diocesan in Foreign Missions	1
Priests: Retired, Sick or Absent	49
Number of Diocesan Priests	165
Religious Priests in Diocese	94
Extern Priests in Diocese	18
Ordinations:	
Diocesan Priests	2
Religious Priests	3
Transitional Deacons	2
Permanent Deacons in Diocese	50
Total Brothers	9
Total Sisters	407
Parishes	
Parishes	54
With Resident Pastor:	
Resident Diocesan Priests	46
Resident Religious Priests	8
Without Resident Pastor:	
Missions	5
Pastoral Centers	4
New Parishes Created	1
Professional Ministry Personnel:	
Brothers	4
Sisters	49
Lay Ministers	165
Welfare	
Catholic Hospitals	1
Total Assisted	47,546
Health Care Centers	2
Total Assisted	247,005
Homes for the Aged	1
Total Assisted	65
Day Care and Extended Day Care Centers	1
Total Assisted	100
Specialized Homes	5
Total Assisted	15,742
Special Centers for Social Services	3
Total Assisted	336,292
Residential Care of Disabled	2
Total Assisted	51
Other Institutions	1
Total Assisted	100
Educational	
Diocesan Students in Other Seminaries	45
Seminaries, Religious	2
Students Religious	13
Total Seminarians	58
Colleges and Universities	1
Total Students	100
High Schools, Diocesan and Parish	3
Total Students	4,605
High Schools, Private	3
Total Students	1,030
Elementary Schools, Diocesan and Parish	35
Total Students	13,030
Elementary Schools, Private	2
Total Students	706
Catechesis/Religious Education:	
High School Students	6,669
Elementary Students	29,611
Total Students Under Catholic Instruction	55,809
Teachers in the Diocese:	
Priests	8
Brothers	4
Sisters	55
Lay Teachers	889
Vital Statistics	
Receptions into the Church:	
Infant Baptism Totals	17,833
Adult Baptism Totals	885
Received into Full Communion	803
First Communions	9,825
Confirmations	3,990
Marriages:	
Catholic	2,850
Interfaith	743
Total Marriages	3,593
Deaths	2,510
Total Catholic Population	603,589
Total Population	2,624,300

Former Bishops—Most Rev. WILLIAM R. JOHNSON, appt. Titular Bishop of Biera and Auxiliary Bishop of Los Angeles, Feb. 9, 1971; cons. March 25, 1971; installed as first Bishop of Orange, June 18, 1976; died July 28, 1986.

Vicar General—Most Rev. MICHAEL P. DRISCOLL, D.D., Office: *Marywood Center, 2811 E. Villa Real Dr., Orange, 92867.* Tel: 714-282-3000.

Chancellor/Moderator of the Curia—Rev. Msgr. JOHN URELL, *Res., 24252 El Toro Rd., Laguna Hills, 92867.*, Office: *2811 E. Villa Real Dr., Orange, 92867.* Tel: 714-282-3000.

Secretary to the Bishop—Rev. Msgr. JOHN URELL.

Vicar for Religious Communities—Most Rev. MICHAEL P. DRISCOLL, D.D., *2811 E. Villa Real Dr., Orange, 92867.* Tel: 714-282-3000.

Vicar for Hispanic Communities—Rev. Msgr. JAIME SOTO, Office: *2811 E. Villa Real Dr., Orange, 92867.* Tel: 714-282-3000.

Vicar for Priests—Rev. EAMON O'GORMAN. Tel: 714-282-3000.

Vicar for Religious Education—Rev. CHRISTOPHER SMITH, Office: *2811 E. Villa Real Dr., Orange, 92867.* Tel: 714-282-3000.

Vicar for Pastoral and Community Affairs—Rev. Msgr. JOHN F. SAMMON, P.A., *Res., 200 W. La Veta Ave., Orange, 92866.*, Office: *2811 E. Villa Real Dr., Orange, 92867.* Tel: 714-282-3000.

Diocesan Pastoral Service Office—2811 E. Villa Real Dr., Orange, 92867. Tel: 714-282-3000. Office Hours: Mon-Fri. 9-5, *P.O. Box 14195, Orange, 92863-1484;* Fax: 714-282-3029.

Diocesan Tribunal—2811 E. Villa Real Dr., Orange, 92867. Tel: 714-282-3080.

Judicial Vicar—Rev. Msgr. DANIEL H. BRENNAN.

Adjutant Judicial Vicars—Rev. Msgr. DANIEL J. MURRAY, J.C.L.; Revs. JACK SEWELL, J.C.L.; WILLIAM J. VOHSING, J.C.L.

Secretary to the Tribunal—Rev. WILLIAM J. VOHSING, J.C.L.

Promotor of Justice—Rev. Msgr. HUGH O'CONNOR.

Judges—Rev. Msgr. JOHN G. CAMPBELL; Rev. Msgr. PAUL MARTIN; Rev. Msgr. JOHN URELL; Rev. Msgr. DANIEL J. MURRAY, J.C.L.; Revs. JAMES HARTNETT;

ARTHUR A. HOLQUIN; THOMAS HA; DANIEL R. HOPCUS; JOHN R. KELLER; JOSEPH NETTEKOVEN; TED OLSON; KENNETH SCHMIT; JACK SEWELL, J.C.L.; WILLIAM VOHSING, J.C.L.; JOHN CORONAN, O.Praem., J.C.L.

Defenders of the Bond—Revs. TIMOTHY RAMAEKERS; JOHN A. BRADLEY; TUAN PHAM, J.C.L.; DOUGLAS COOK, J.C.L.

Notaries—SANDRA K. DALTON; LINDA BRAUN; LAURIE MARMOLEJO.

National Organization for Decent Literature—Rev. Msgr. JOHN F. SAMMON, Dir., *2811 E. Villa Real Dr., Orange, 92867.* Tel: 714-282-3000.

Newman Apostolate—Rev. PATRICK PHILBIN, S.M., Dir., *P.O. Box 6030, Irvine, 92616.* Tel: 714-856-0211.

Parish Councils and Parish Development—Rev. Msgr. JOHN F. SAMMON, Dir., *2811 E. Villa Real Dr., Orange, 92867.* Tel: 714-282-3000.

Diaconate—Sr. JOANN TABOR, C.S.J., Dir. JACK BRENNAN, Asst. Dir., *2811 E. Villa Real Dr., Orange, 92867.* Tel: 714-282-3000.

Clergy Personnel Board—Rev. Msgr. WILLIAM MCLAUGHLIN, Chm.; Rev. Msgr. DANIEL MURRAY; Rev. Msgr. JOHN URELL, Auditor; Revs. CIRILO FLORES; KERRY BEAULIEU; JEROME KARCHER, *2811 E. Villa Real Dr., Orange, 92867.* Tel: 714-282-3000.

Communications Office—Rev. Msgr. LAWRENCE J. BAIRD, Dir., *2811 E. Villa Real Dr., Orange, 92867.* Tel: 714-282-3000.

Conciliation & Arbitration Office—Ms. DOLORES CHURCHILL, L.C.S.W., *2811 E. Villa Real Dr., Orange, 92867.* Tel: 714-282-3000.

Diocesan Council of Catholic Women—Rev. JOSEPH ROBILLARD, Moderator; DORIS CANTLAY, Pres., *2811 E. Villa Real Dr., Orange, 92867.* Tel: 714-282-3000.

Priests' Relief—Rev. EAMON O'GORMAN, *2811 E. Villa Real Dr., Orange, 92867.* Tel: 714-282-3000.

Council of Priests—Most Rev. MICHAEL DRISCOLL; Rev. Msgr. JOHN SAMMON; Rev. Msgr. DANIEL BRENNAN; Rev. Msgr. JAIME SOTO; Rev. Msgr. JOHN URELL; Rev. Msgr. PETER TIEN; Rev. Msgr. ANTONIO SUDARIO; Revs. RICHARD DELAHUNTY; PATRICK RUDOLPH; KENNETH KRAUSE; J. MICHAEL MCKIERNAN; KEVIN SWEENEY; STEVE SALLOT; JOE JUSTICE; DON ROMITO; MICHAEL HEHER; JEROME KARCHER; BRUCE LAVERY; BRENDAN SMITH, S.T.; VINCE GILMORE, O.Praem.; JOHN LENIHAN; JUSTIN MACCARTHY, *2811 E. Villa Real Dr., Orange, 92867.* Tel: 714-282-3000.

Consultors—Most Rev. MICHAEL DRISCOLL, D.D.; Rev. Msgr. DANIEL BRENNAN; Rev. Msgr. JOHN SAMMON; Rev. Msgr. JAIME SOTO; Rev. Msgr. PETER TIEN; Rev. Msgr. JOHN URELL; Revs. JOHN LENIHAN; JUSTIN MACCARTHY.

Propagation of the Faith—Rev. Msgr. JOHN F. SAMMON, Dir., *2811 E. Villa Real Dr., Orange, 92867.* Tel: 714-282-3000.

Religious Institute of Orange Executive Board—Sr. JOANN TABOR, C.S.J.; Sr. EYMARD FLOOD, O.S.C.; Sr. VICKY BRADY, R.S.M.; Sr. MAURA FITZSIMMON, P.B.V.M.; Sr. HELEN LOUISE LACEY, C.S.J.

Society of St. Vincent de Paul of Orange County—Mr. JAMES D. KAY; Rev. PEREGRINE GRAFFIUS, O.S.M., Spiritual Dir., *180 S. Cypress, Orange, 92866.* Tel: 714-633-9194.

Schools Office—Bro. WILLIAM CARRIERE, F.S.C., Supt.; Sr. MARY CATHERINE EVANS, O.P., Assoc. Supt., *2811 E. Villa Real Dr., Orange, 92867.* Tel: 714-282-3000.

Schools Advisory Board of Education—*2811 E. Villa Real Dr., Orange, 92867.* Tel: 714-282-3000.

Vocations Office—Rev. Msgr. DANIEL J. MURRAY, Dir., *2811 E. Villa Real Dr., Orange, 92867.* Tel: 714-282-3000.

Campaign for Human Development—Rev. Msgr. JOHN URELL, Dir.

Board of Directors—Most Rev. MICHAEL P. DRISCOLL, D.D.; DOLORES CHURCHILL; FRANK CHAVEZ; WALTER DALY; DIETER MYERS GONZALES; EDWARD EGAN; WILLIAM ERICKSON; VIRGINIA FAULKNER; Sr. REBECCA RODRIGUEZ, C.S.J.; FRED VEGA, *2811 E. Villa Real Dr., Orange, 92867.* Tel: 714-282-3000.

Diocesan Offices and Directors

Apostleship of Prayer—Rev. Msgr. HUGH O'CONNOR, *2050 W. Ball Rd., Anaheim, 92804.* Tel: 714-774-2595.

Archivist—Rev. WILLIAM KREKELBERG, Office: *990 Temple Ter., Laguna Beach, 92651.* Tel: 714-494-9701.

Boy Scouts—Rev. Msgr. JOHN F. SAMMON, *2811 E. Villa Real Dr., Orange, 92867.* Tel: 714-282-3000.

Liturgical Environment-Art Committee—Rev. ROD STEPHENS, Chm.; Very Rev. ARHTUR HOLQUIN; Revs. KERRY BEAULIEU; PAUL LEVESQUE, *2811 E. Villa Real Dr., Orange, 92867.* Tel: 714-282-3000.

Land Advisory Board—Most Rev. NORMAN F. MCFARLAND, Pres.; Most Rev. MICHAEL P. DRISCOLL, D.D., Admin.; Mr. ARTHUR BIRTCHER; Mr. TERENCE K. BARRY; Mr. JOSEPH HENNESSEY; Mr. DANIEL HOLDEN; Mr. R. RAND SPERRY; Rev. Msgr. JOHN URELL; KENNETH TAIT. Staff:: Mr. PHIL REIS; Mr. DON CROUGH.

Diocesan Construction Board—Mr. LLOYD ROSS; Mr. TERRANCE BARRY, Chm.; Mr. RON GAGNON; Mr. FRANK REYNOLDS; Mr. ARTHUR BIRTCHER; Mr. RICHARD HUNSAKER; Most Rev. MICHAEL P. DRISCOLL. Staff: Mr. PHIL RIES; Mr. DON CROUGH, Construction Mgr.

Diocesan Finance Council—Most Rev. MICHAEL DRISCOLL; Mr. JACK DERLOSHON, Chm.; Mr. TOM KLEINBAUER; Mr. GORDON LEE; Rev. Msgr. JOHN URELL; Mr. LEE MEYER; Mr. WILLIAM CRAWFORD; GUY WILSON; PAUL SCHLOEMER. Staff: Mr. PHIL RIES, Dir.; Mr. CARLOS VASQUEZ.

Director of Finance—Mr. PHIL RIES, Dir.; Mr. CARLOS VASQUEZ, Controller, *2811 E. Villa Real Dr., Orange, 92867.* Tel: 714-282-3000.

Catholic Charities of Orange—Most Rev. MICHAEL P. DRISCOLL, D.D., Vicar, Charities; KRISTAN SCHLICHTE, Exec. Dir., Office: *1506 Brookhollow, Ste. 112, Santa Ana, 92705.* Tel: 714-662-7500.

Cemeteries—Mr. THOMAS FLYNN, Dir., *2811 E. Villa Real Dr., Orange, 92867.* Tel: 714-282-3000.

Cemeteries Board—Rev. Msgr. JOHN F. SAMMON, Chm.; Most Rev. MICHAEL P. DRISCOLL, D.D.; Rev. Msgr. SINON F. FALVEY.

Ministry to Priests—Rev. EAMON O'GORMAN, Vicar, Priests; Rev. Msgr. BILL MCLAUGHLIN; Rev. Msgr. DANIEL BRENNAN; Rev. Msgr. HUGH O'CONNOR; Most Rev. MICHAEL P. DRISCOLL, D.D.; Revs. MICHAEL HOAN; RUDOLPH PRECIADO; LAURANCE DOLAN; AL BACA; RICHARD DELAHUNTY; KEN SCHMIT; JOHN MCANDREW; GORDON MORELAND, S.J.; JOSEPH JUSTICE; MICHEL PECHARICH; STEVE SALLOT, *2811 E. Villa Real Dr., Orange, 92867.* Tel: 714-282-3000.

Cursillo Movement—Revs. RAYMOND SKONEZNY, Exec. Spiritual Dir. DAVID VUELVAS-ARIAS, Spiritual Dir., Hispanic Cursillo; PETER VU DINH TRAC, Spiritual Dir., Vietnamese Cursillo, *2811 E. Villa Real Dr., Orange, 92867.* Tel: 714-538-2096.

Office for Deaf Ministry—CONNIE WILD, Dir.

Office for Religious Education—Rev. CHRISTOPHER H. SMITH, Vicar; RUTH BRADLEY, Dir. NURIA CHEKOURAS, Coord./Consultant, Hispanic Adult, Family and Child Religious Education; MARY BROSSEAU, Consultant, Special Religious Education. Assoc. Dirs., Youth & Young Adult Ministries: JAVIER CASTILLO; LINDA KRALL.

Library / Media Center—DIANE MURRAY, Dir.

Catechetical Institute—JOAN KULIK, Dir., Studies, *2811 E. Villa Real Dr., Orange, 92867.* Tel: 714-282-3000.

Religious Education Board—VIRGINIA CURLEY; RUTH BRADLEY; Bro. WILLIAM CARRIERE, F.S.C.; Sr. JENNIFER NGUYEN, L.H.C.; SHERRIE OLDHAM; STEVE ELLAIR; SUE LINKHORN; EUGENE O'TOOLE; MITZI PONGINETTI; Rev. CHRISTOPHER H. SMITH, *2811 E. Villa Real Dr., Orange, 92867.* Tel: 714-282-3000.

Ecumenical and Interreligious Affairs—Rev. Msgr. LAWRENCE J. BAIRD, Chm.; Sr. MARYANNE HUEPPER, C.S.J.; Rev. JOHN MONESTERO; Dr. CHARLES FRAZEE; Mrs. CECIL PIANTADOSI; Mrs. SUE MONTANO FENWICK; Dr. GEORGE E. SAINT-LAURENT; Rev. PAUL LEVESQUE; Mrs. JOSEPHINE BALL, *2811 E. Villa Real Dr., Orange, 92867.* Tel: 714-282-3000.

Family Life—Dir. Vacant, *2811 E. Villa Real Dr., Orange, 92867.* Tel: 714-282-3045. Commission Members: PHIL ANDERSEN; PHYLLIS ANDERSEN; RODOLFO GOMEZ; LALI GOMEZ; BOB DAUSCH; MARY DAUSCH; RICH JENISON; MARY JENISON.

Office of Hispanic Ministry—Rev. Msgr. JAIME SOTO, Dir.; Mrs. JUANA MARIA AMEZQUITA, Admin., *2811 E. Villa Real Dr., Orange, 92867.* Tel: 714-282-3000.

Holy Childhood—Rev. Msgr. JOHN F. SAMMON, Dir., *2811 E. Villa Real Dr., Orange, 92867.* Tel: 714-282-3000.

Holy Name Society—Rev. Msgr. JOHN F. SAMMON, Dir., *2811 E. Villa Real Dr., Orange, 92867.* Tel: 714-282-3000.

Insurance—Mr. THOMAS FLYNN, Dir., *2811 E. Villa Real Dr., Orange, 92867.* Tel: 714-282-3000.

Legion of Mary—Rev. Msgr. PEDRO YRIGAN, Dir., *Res., 922 N. Newhope St., Santa Ana, 92703.* Tel: 714-554-3437. Rev. Msgr. HUGH O'CONNOR, *Res., 2050 W. Ball Rd., Anaheim, 92804.* Tel: 714-774-2595.

Liturgy, Music, Evangelization & Adult Education—Rev. ROD STEPHENS, Dir., *2811 E. Villa Real Dr., Orange, 92867.* Tel: 714-282-3000.

Marriage Encounter—GREG ABRAMSON; LISA ABRAMSON, *2811 E. Villa Real Dr., Orange, 92867.* Tel: 714-282-3000.

Respect Life Program NCCB—Rev. Msgr. JOHN F. SAMMON, Dir., *2811 E. Villa Real Dr., Orange, 92867.* Tel: 714-282-3000.

Catecumenate—Rev. ROD STEPHENS, Dir., *2811 E. Villa Real Dr., Orange, 92867.* Tel: 714-282-3000.

Stewardship Office—BARBARA NELSON, Dir., *2811 E. Villa Real Dr., Orange, 92867.* Tel: 714-282-3000.

Planned Giving Office—Rev. Msgr. LAWRENCE BAIRD, *2811 E. Villa Real Dr., Orange, 92867.* Tel: 714-282-3000.

Perpetual Adoration Programs—Rev. Msgr. JOHN SAMMON, Dir., *2811 E. Villa Real Dr., Orange, 92867.* Tel: 714-282-3000.

CLERGY, PARISHES, MISSIONS AND PAROCHIAL SCHOOLS

CITY OF ORANGE

1—CATHEDRAL OF THE HOLY FAMILY (1921), Very Rev. Arthur Holquin, Rector; Rev. Msgr. Lawrence J. Baird; Rev. Malcolm Smith, M.Afr. In res., Revs. Timothy L. Ramaekers; Patrick N. Rudolph.
Res., 566 S. Glassell St., 92666. Tel: 714-639-2900; Fax: 714-639-8022.
School—530 S. Glassell St., 92666. Tel: 714-538-6012; Fax: 714-633-5892.
Lay Teachers 24; Students 610.
Catechesis / Religious Programs—Tel: 714-538-2800.
Students 720.

2—LA PURISIMA (1964), Revs. Valentin Ramon, C.M.F.; Richard Wozniak, C.M.F.; William Paiz, C.M.F.; Peter Vu Dinh Trac; Deacon Dr. Anthony Bube.
Res., 11712 N. Hewes, 92869. Tel: 714-633-5800; Fax: 714-633-8364.
School—Tel: 714-633-5411. Sr. Cecilia Duran, O.D.N., Prin.
Sisters of the Company of Mary 1; Lay Teachers 15; Students 331.
Catechesis / Religious Programs—Tel: 714-633-5344; Fax: 714-633-1588.
Students 783.

3—ST. NORBERT (1963), Revs. John M. Joyce; John-Paul Hopping. In res., Rev. Msgr. Peter Esterka; Rev. Jude Lucier, O. Praem; Deacons Timothy Carver; Jay Milam.
Res., 300 E. Taft Ave., 92865. Tel: 714-637-4360; Fax: 714-637-0201.
School—Tel: 714-637-6822; Fax: 714-637-3682.
Union of the Sisters of the Presentation of the Blessed Virgin Mary 2; Lay Teachers 11; Students 319.
Catechesis / Religious Programs—Tel: 714-998-1070. D.R.E.: Sr. Eveleen Conlon, P.B.V.M.; Sr. Marie Clare Fox, P.B.V.M.
Students 900.

ORANGE COUNTY OUTSIDE THE CITY

Anaheim

1—ST. ANTHONY CLARET (1955), Rev. Marito F. Rebamontan; Rev. Msgr. James F. Nash, Pastor Emeritus; Revs. Paul Levesque; Carlos Martinez.
Res., 1450 E. La Palma Ave., 92805. Tel: 714-776-0270; Fax: 714-776-6022.
School—Tel: 714-535-3284; Fax: 714-535-8558.
Lay Teachers 10; Students 264.
Catechesis / Religious Programs—Tel: 714-778-0580.
Students 777. D.R.E.: Maria Holper; Leonard Beckman.

2—ST. BONIFACE (1860), Rev. Msgr. Wilbur Davis; Revs. David Vuelvas-Arias; Craig Butters; Quang Vinh Chu.
Res., 120 N. Janss St., 92805. Tel: 714-956-3110; Fax: 714-956-3034.
School—500 W. Chartres St., 92805. Tel: 714-772-3060.
Dominican Sisters (Mission San Jose) O.P. 1; Lay Teachers 15; Students 286.
Catechesis / Religious Programs—Tel: 714-776-6473.
Students 1,150.

3—ST. JUSTIN MARTYR (1958), Rev. Joseph Nettekoven; Rev. Msgr. Hugh O'Connor, Pastor Emeritus; Revs. J. Douglas Dale; Antonio Zapata. In res., Rev. John Monestero.
Res., 2050 W. Ball Rd., 92804. Tel: 714-774-2595; Fax: 714-774-9849.
Church—Ball Rd. and Empire, 92804.
School—2030 W. Ball Rd., 92804. Tel: 714-772-4902; Fax: 714-772-2092.
Lay Teachers 13; Students 281.
Catechesis / Religious Programs—Tel: 714-535-6111.
Students 309.
Mission—Independencia, Orange Co., Sacred Heart, 10852 Harcourt, Independencia, 92804. Tel: 714-821-3133.

4—SAN ANTONIO (1977), Rev. Seamus A. Glynn. In res., Rev. William J. Vohsing; Deacons Doug Cook; Thomas Klos.

Res., 5800 E. Santa Ana Canyon Rd., 92807. Tel: 714-974-1416; Fax: 714-974-9630.
Catechesis/Religious Programs—Tel: 714-974-2053. Carolyn Buehler, D.R.E.
Students 645.

Brea, St. Angela Merici (1962), Rev. Theodore Olson; Rev. Msgr. Emmett McCarthy, Pastor Emeritus; Revs. John McAndrew; Fabian Richards; Deacons Fred von Voigt; Carlos Navarro. In res., Rev. Jose Morales, (Retired).
Res., 585 Walnut St., 92821. Tel: 714-529-1821; Fax: 714-529-0569.
Church—Walnut and Fir, 92821.
School—575 S. Walnut Ave., 92821. Tel: 714-529-6372; Fax: 714-529-.
Lay Teachers 11; Religious 1; Students 263.
Catechesis/Religious Programs—Tel: 714-529-2311.
Students 758.

Buena Park, St. Pius V (1948), Revs. Leo O'Sullivan, O.S.A.; Patrick Crilly, O.S.A.; Thomas Tevington, O.S.A.; Patrick A. Brennan, O.S.A.; Michael Brennock, O.S.A.; Declan (Finbarr) Fogarty, O.S.A.
Res., 7691 Orangethorpe Ave., 90621. Tel: 714-522-2193; Fax: 714-522-1730.
School—Tel: 714-522-5313; Fax: 714-522-1767.
Lay Teachers 19; Students 603.
Catechesis/Religious Programs—Tel: 714-522-3971.
Students 600.

Capistrano Beach, San Felipe de Jesus (1950) (Spanish), Rev. John A. Bradley; Rev. Msgr. John V. Coffield; Deacon Victor Samano.
Res., 27045-B Camino de Estrella, 92624. Tel: 714-661-7500; Fax: 714-661-7500.
Church—Domingo St. & Sepulveda, 92624.
Catechesis/Religious Programs—27045-B Camino de Estrella, 92624.
Students 135.

Costa Mesa, St. Joachim (1947), Revs. Kenneth J. Krause; Cirilo Flores; Douglas Cook.
Res., 1964 Orange Ave., 92627. Tel: 714-574-7400; Fax: 714-574-7407.
School—Tel: 714-574-7411.
Sisters of the Company of Mary 3; Lay Teachers 18; Students 285.
Catechesis/Religious Programs—Tel: 714-574-7416.
Students 870.

St. John the Baptist (1960), Revs. Jerome M. Henson; Tran Phuc Long; Bruce A. Patterson. In res., Rev. Msgr. Daniel H. Brennan.
Res., 1015 Baker St., 92626. Tel: 714-540-2214; Fax: 714-540-5902.
School—Tel: 714-557-5060.
Sisters of Mercy 1; Lay Teachers 20; Students 640.
Catechesis/Religious Programs—Tel: 714-546-4102.
Students 300.

Cypress, St. Irenaeus (1961), Rev. Michael Heher; Rev. Msgr. Antonio Sudario; Rev. Roy Kim; Deacon James Thompson.
Res., 5201 Evergreen Ave., 90630. Tel: 714-826-0760; Fax: 714-826-1608.
School—9201 Grindlay St., 90630. Tel: 714-827-4500; Fax: 714-827-2930.
Sisters 2; Lay Teachers 18; Students 598.
Catechesis/Religious Programs—9211 Grindlay St., 90630. Tel: 714-826-1140.
Students 690.

Dana Point, St. Edward (1969), Revs. John P. Lenihan; John W. Procter; Denis Lyons; Deacon John McQuade. In res., Rev. George Gonzales.
Res., 33926 Calle La Primavera, 92629. Tel: 714-496-1307; Fax: 714-496-1557.
School—33866 Calle LaPrimavera, 92629. Tel: 714-496-1241.
Lay Teachers 11; Students 318.
Catechesis/Religious Programs—Tel: 714-496-6011.
Students 700.

El Toro, Santiago de Compostela (1979), Revs. Kenneth A. Schmit; George P. Blais.
Res., 21682 Lake Forest Dr., Lake Forest, 92630. Tel: 714-951-8599; Fax: 714-951-2687.
Catechesis/Religious Programs—Tel: 714-951-0792.
Students 857.

Fountain Valley, Holy Spirit (1972), Revs. Joseph Knerr; Benjamin Fama; Tuan Pham.
Res., 17270 Ward St., 92708. Tel: 714-963-1811; Fax: 714-968-1775.
Catechesis/Religious Programs—Tel: 714-963-7871. Sr. Regina Stewart, D.R.E.
Students 574.

Fullerton, St. Juliana Falconieri (1965), Revs. Jude M. Herlihy, O.S.M.; Donald M. Duplessis, O.S.M.; Joseph P. Cheah, O.S.M., Chap. (California State Univ. - Newman Club); Deacons William Schlater; Jay L. Milam. In res., Rev. David M. Kondik, O.S.M.
Office: 1319 N. Acacia Ave., 92831. Tel: 714-879-1965; Fax: 714-526-6673.
Res., 1316 N. Acacia Ave., 92831. Tel: 714-879-1965.
School—1320 N. Acacia Ave., 92831. Tel: 714-871-2829.
Lay Teachers 9; Students 325.
Catechesis/Religious Programs—Students 309.

St. Mary's (1912), Revs. Joseph J. Gallardo, O.A.R.; Ramon de Jesus Pons, O.A.R.; Frank T. Wilder, O.A.R.; Deacons Carlos Gonzalez; Manuel Chavira.
Res., 400 W. Commonwealth Ave., 92632. Tel: 714-525-2500; Fax: 714-525-8944.
School—Tel: 714-525-9689.
Sisters of St. Joseph of Carondolet 1; Lay Teachers 10; Students 216.
Catechesis/Religious Programs—Tel: 714-992-5070.
Students 416.

St. Philip Benizi (1958), Revs. Peregrine M. Graffius, O.S.M.; Ignatius M. Kissel, O.S.M.; Gabriel Weber, O.S.M.; Manuel Maya, O.S.M.; Patrick Donovan, O.S.M.; Deacons Jack Brennan; Richard Glaudini.
Res., 235 S. Pine Dr., 92833-3294. Tel: 714-871-3610; Fax: 714-871-5827.
School—215 S. Pine Dr., 92833-3293. Tel: 714-871-6121; Fax: 714-992-4167. Neil Donat, Prin.
Lay Teachers 15; Students 320.
Catechesis/Religious Programs—Tel: 714-870-0561. Carol Meglio, D.R.E.
Students 440.

Garden Grove, St. Callistus (1961), Revs. Rudolph J. Preciado; Joseph Tuan Pham; Gerardo J. Tanilong; Paul Chu Van Chi. In res., Rev. Msgr. Daniel J. Murray.
Res., 12921 Lewis St., 92840. Tel: 714-971-2141; Fax: 714-971-9112.
Church—Garden Grove Blvd. and Lewis St., 92840.
School—12901 Lewis St., 92840. Tel: 714-971-2023; Fax: 714-971-2031.
Dominican Sisters 3; Lay Teachers 11; Students 287.
Catechesis/Religious Programs—Tel: 714-971-2091. Maureen Ross, D.R.E.
Students 518.

St. Columban (1953), Revs. Donald Romito; J. Michael McKiernan; Raphael Ho Xuan Nguyen; Dominic Hoa Nguyen; Deacon Robert Kelleher.
Res., 10801 Stanford Ave., 92640. Tel: 714-534-1174; Fax: 714-534-1937.
School—10855 Stanford Ave., 92640. Tel: 714-534-3947.
Religious Sisters of Charity 2; Lay Teachers 10; Students 322.

Huntington Beach

1—St. Bonaventure, Revs. Kerry Beaulieu; John R. Keller; Michael Hanifin; Joseph Luan Nguyen.
Res., 16400 Springdale St., 92649. Tel: 714-846-3350; 846-3359; Fax: 714-840-0480.
School—Union of the Sisters of the Presentation of the Blessed Virgin Mary 5; Lay Teachers 26; Students 627.
Catechesis/Religious Programs—16377 Bradbury Lane, 92647. Tel: 714-846-2472. Virginia Curley, D.R.E.
Students 950.

2—St. Mary's by the Sea (1977), Revs. Daniel Johnson; Eamon Mackin, C.H.S.
Res., 321 10th St., 92648. Tel: 714-536-6913; Fax: 714-536-2464.
Catechesis/Religious Programs—Students 150.

3—SS. Simon and Jude (1912), Revs. Laurence P. Dolan, O.F.M.; Christian Mondor, O.F.M.; Gustave R. Krumm, O.F.M. In res., Revs. Felipe Baldonado, O.F.M.; Ronald Colloty, O.F.M.; Emery Tang, O.F.M.
Res., 20444 Magnolia St., 92646. Tel: 714-962-3333; Fax: 714-965-6456.
School—Tel: 714-962-4451; Fax: 714-968-1329.
Benedictine Sisters 1; Lay Teachers 30; Students 634.
Catechesis/Religious Programs—Tel: 714-963-0014. Sherrie Oldham, D.R.E.
Students 870.

4—St. Vincent de Paul (1977), Revs. Jerome Karcher; Sy Uy Nguyen.
Res., 8345 Talbert Ave., 92646. Tel: 714-842-3000; Fax: 714-842-6780.
Catechesis/Religious Programs—Students 520.

Irvine, St. Elizabeth Ann Seton, Revs. Thomas Pado; Alex K. Kim.
Res., 9 Hillgate, 92612. Tel: 714-854-1000; Fax: 714-854-0079.
Catechesis/Religious Programs—Students 499.

St. John Neumann (1978), Revs. Colm Conlon; John E. Shetler; Ray Skonezny.
Res., 5101 Alton Pkwy., 92604-5499. Tel: 714-559-4006; Fax: 714-857-4788.
Catechesis/Religious Programs—Tel: 714-786-6105; Fax: 714-786-6102. Edith Marik, D.R.E.
Students 977.

St. Thomas More (1996), Rev. John E. Janze.
Res., 4112 Escudero Dr., 92620-3212. Tel: 714-551-8601; Fax: 714-551-5879.
Catechesis/Religious Programs—Students 90.

Laguna Beach, St. Catherine of Siena (1923), Revs. William Krekelberg; Stephen Duffin.
Res., 990 Temple Ter., 92651. Tel: 714-494-9701; Fax: 714-497-2610.
School—3090 S. Coast Hwy., 92651. Tel: 714-494-7339.
Lay Teachers 9; Students 295.
Catechesis/Religious Programs—Tel: 714-499-5876.
Students 197.

Laguna Hills, St. Nicholas (1965), Revs. Juan Caboboy; Pat Fee; Joseph Son Nguyen; Deacon Ray Havert. In res., Rev. Msgr. John Urell.
Res., 24252 El Toro Rd., 92653. Tel: 714-837-1090; Fax: 714-837-9510.
Catechesis/Religious Programs—Tel: 714-837-7676.
Students 400.

Laguna Niguel, St. Timothy (1980), Revs. Bruce Lavery; David Gruver; Donald Kolda, S.J.; Deacon Ed Salgado.
Res., 29102 Crown Valley Pkwy., 92677. Tel: 714-249-4091; Fax: 714-249-4094.
Catechesis/Religious Programs—Tel: 714-495-4126.
Students 403.

La Habra, Our Lady of Guadalupe (1947), Revs. Justin H. MacCarthy; James Croal; Cesar Salazar. In res., Rev. Eamon O'Gorman.
Res., 900 W. La Habra Blvd., 90631. Tel: 310-691-0533; Fax: 310-694-8328.
School—Tel: 310-697-9726; Fax: 310-905-0095.
Sisters of St. Joseph of Orange 2; Lay Teachers 21; Students 509.
Catechesis/Religious Programs—Tel: 310-691-2104.
Students 438.

Los Alamitos, St. Hedwig (1960), Revs. Daniel R. Hopcus; Alexander H. Ha; Rafael Luevano.
Res., 11482 Los Alamitos Blvd., 90720. Tel: 310-430-0509; Fax: 310-431-9989.
School—Tel: 310-431-5001; Fax: 310-799-1791.
Irish Sisters of Charity 2; Lay Teachers 21; Students 612.
Catechesis/Religious Programs—Tel: 310-493-2521.
Students 490.

Mission Viejo, St. Kilian (1970), Rev. James P. Dunning.
Res., 26872 Estanciero Dr., 92691. Tel: 714-586-4440; Fax: 714-454-1043.
Catechesis/Religious Programs—Tel: 714-586-4550. Marcia Burns, D.R.E.
Students 1,000.

Newport Beach, Our Lady of Mount Carmel (1923) (Irish), Rev. Patrick A. Doherty; Deacons John Barry; Glenn Erwin.
Res., 1441 W. Balboa Blvd., 92663. Tel: 714-673-3775; Fax: 714-673-3137.
Catechesis/Religious Programs—Tel: 714-673-2719.
Students 105.

Our Lady Queen of Angels (1953), Rev. Msgr. William McLaughlin; Rev. Msgr. William R. Harvey, Pastor Emeritus; Revs. Benjamin Benedicto; Robert W.P. Puhlman.
Res., 2046 Mar Vista Dr., 92660. Tel: 714-644-0200; Fax: 714-644-1349.
School—750 Domingo Dr., 92660. Tel: 714-644-1166; Fax: 714-644-6213.
Lay Teachers 21; Students 347.
Catechesis/Religious Programs—Tel: 714-640-1272.
Students 400.
Convent—2108 Aralia St., 92660. Tel: 714-644-0660.
Chapel—St. John Vianney, Tel: 714-675-2221. Rev. Msgr. Joseph F. Sharpe (LA).

Placentia, St. Joseph (1953), Revs. Fergus Clarke; Ricardo Garcia; James C. Ries; Deacons Chuck Gagnon; Ed Faulk. In res., Rev. Rod Stephens.
Res., 717 N. Bradford Ave., 92870-4599. Tel: 714-528-1487; Fax: 714-528-1569.
School—801 N. Bradford Ave., 92870-4599. Tel: 714-528-1794; Fax: 714-528-0668.
Lay Teachers 16; Students 300.
Catechesis/Religious Programs—Tel: 714-993-0830. D.R.E.: Pat Hobbs; Eloisa Ramirez, (Spanish).
Students 638.
Mission—Atwood, Orange Co., St. Therese, 636 Van Buren Ave., Atwood, 92811.

Rancho Santa Margarita, San Francisco Solano Church (1989), Revs. Michael Pecharich; Kevin Sweeney; Sr. Barbara Reder, S.P., Pastoral Assoc.

Res., 22082 Antonio Pkwy., 92688. Tel: 714-589-7767; Fax: 714-589-7768.
Catechesis/Religious Programs—Tel: 714-589-1709.
Students 1,455.

San Clemente, Our Lady of Fatima (1947), Revs. Frank Moran; Timothy Freyer; Rev. Msgr. Anthony McGowan, Pastor Emeritus.
Res., 105 La Esperanza, 92672. Tel: 714-492-4101; Fax: 714-492-4826. [CEM]
School—Lay Teachers 13; Students 313.
Catechesis/Religious Programs—Students 825.

San Juan Capistrano, (Old Mission) (1776) (Spanish), Rev. Msgr. Paul M. Martin; Rev. Msgr. John Campbell; Rev. Joseph Droessler; Deacons Joseph Halka; David Sire; Viviano Mireles. In res., Rev. Hal Fumo.
Res., P.O. Box 697, 92693. Tel: 714-248-2000; Fax: 714-248-2008 (parish office).
School—Tel: 714-248-2050; Fax: 714-240-8091.
Lay Teachers 19; Students 432.
Catechesis/Religious Programs—Tel: 714-248-2010. Linda Berkshire, D.R.E.
Students 723.

Santa Ana

1—Immaculate Heart of Mary (1960), Rev. Enrique Sera; Rev. Msgr. John Keenan; Revs. Ignatius Lau; Ismael Silva; Deacons Gerardo de Santos; Manual Alvarado.
Res., 1100 S. Center St., 92704. Tel: 714-751-5335.
School—Tel: 714-545-8185.
Sisters 3; Lay Teachers 7; Students 153.
Catechesis/Religious Programs—Tel: 714-546-5186.
Students 1,100.

2—Our Lady of Guadalupe (1927), Rev. Alonso Caceres. In res., Rev. Msgr. Jaime Soto.
Res., 541 E. Central Ave., 92707. Tel: 714-540-0902; Fax: 714-540-3053.
Catechesis/Religious Programs—Tel: 714-540-9231. Rosa Castro, D.R.E.
Students 1,148.

3—Our Lady of Guadalupe (1938) (Spanish), Revs. Anthony Palos, O.A.R.; Etelvino Iglesias, O.A.R.
Res., 1322 E. Third St., 92701. Tel: 714-836-4142; Fax: 714-836-7417.
Catechesis/Religious Programs—Tel: 714-835-8933. Margarita Garza, D.R.E.
Students 750.

4—Our Lady of Lourdes (1985) (Mexican), Rev. William Barman.
Res., 5021 W. 16th St., 92703. Tel: 714-636-3260; Fax: 714-539-0783.
Catechesis/Religious Programs—Students 300.

5—Our Lady of the Pillar (1965) (Hispanic), Revs. Gabino Perez, O.A.R.; Robert Huse, O.A.R.; Joachim Goni, O.A.R.; Euben Capacillo, O.A.R.
Res., 1622 W. 6th St., 92703. Tel: 714-543-1700; Fax: 714-543-9640.
School—601 N. Western Ave., 92703.
190125.
Catechesis/Religious Programs—Tel: 714-542-4684.
Students 1,450.

6—St. Anne's (1923) (Hispanic), Revs. Joseph C. Justice; Joseph Robillard; Salvador Landa; Leonicio Segura; Deacon Carlos Evyoque.
Res., 109 Borchard Ave., P.O. Box 2425, 92707. Tel: 714-835-7434; Fax: 714-835-4506.
School—Tel: 714-542-9328.
Sisters 3; Lay Teachers 13; Students 295.
Catechesis/Religious Programs—Tel: 714-542-1213.
Students 795.

7—St. Barbara's (1962), Revs. Richard C. Kennedy; Mhilivetr F. Rodriguez-Utia; Kiem Van Tran; Tuyen Van Nguyen.
Res., 730 S. Euclid St., 92704. Tel: 714-775-7733; Fax: 714-775-9467.
School—Tel.: 714-775-9477.
Lay Teachers 20; Students 456.
Catechesis/Religious Programs—Tel: 714-775-9475.
Students 1,355.

8—St. Joseph's (1887), Revs. Christopher H. Smith; Alfred S. Baca. In res., Rev. Steven Sallot.
Res., 727 Minter St., 92701. Tel: 714-542-4411; Fax: 714-542-9770.
School—Sisters 2; Lay Teachers 8; Students 180.
Catechesis/Religious Programs—Students 210.

Seal Beach, St. Anne's (1921), Rev. Robert S. Vidal; Rev. Msgr. Michael Collins, Pastor Emeritus.
Res., 340 Tenth St., 90740. Tel: 310-431-0721; Fax: 310-431-3050.
Catechesis/Religious Programs—Students 60.

Holy Family (1969), Rev. Msgr. Brian Coghlan; Rev. Msgr. James J. Pierse, Pastor Emeritus.
Res., 13900 Church Pl., 90740. Tel: 310-430-8170; Fax: 310-493-4643.

Stanton, St. Polycarp (1961), Revs. Edward Poettgen; John Shimotsu; John P. Graven; Thanh Van Nguyen; Thomas Ha.
Res., 8100 Chapman Ave., 90680. Tel: 714-893-2766; Fax: 714-898-6675.
School—8182 Chapman Ave., 90680. Tel: 714-893-8882.
Lay Teachers 8; Students 245.
Catechesis/Religious Programs—Tel: 714-892-3158.
Students 890.

Tustin, St. Cecilia (1957), Revs. Timothy MacCarthy; Christopher Heath; Deacons Lee Meyer; Jerry Miller; Jon Schlemmer.
Res., 1301 S.E. Sycamore, 92680. Tel: 714-544-3250; Fax: 714-838-1996.
School—Tel: 714-544-1533; Fax: 714-544-0643.
Lay Teachers 15; Students 355.
Catechesis/Religious Programs—Tel: 714-838-4466.
Students 1,150.

Westminster, Blessed Sacrament (1947), Revs. James Hartnett; Agustin Escobar; Michael Hoan; Tuan Nguyen. In res., Rev. Jack Sewell.
Res., 14072 S. Olive St., 92683. Tel: 714-892-4489; Fax: 714-892-5560.
School—14146 S. Olive St., 92683. Tel: 714-893-7701. Roisin McAree, Prin.
Lay Teachers 12; Students 330.
Catechesis/Religious Programs—14144 S. Olive St., 92683. Tel: 714-897-2142. D.R.E.: Madeline Mirarchi; Muriel Quick.
Students 600.

Yorba Linda, St. Martin (1970), Revs. Richard A. Delahunty; John T. Hiltz; Fred K. Bailey.
Res., 19767 Yorba Linda Blvd., 92886. Tel: 714-970-2771; Fax: 714-970-5654.
Catechesis/Religious Programs—Tel: 714-970-2521. Pam Bender, D.R.E.
Students 1,033.

Chaplains Of Public Institutions

Orange. *Juvenile Hall*, 331 The City Dr., 92868. Tel: 714-634-7611. Rev. Brendan Smith, S.T., 422 Almond, 92866. Tel: 714-633-6527.
Orange County Medical Center, 101 The City Dr. S., 92868. Tel: 714-634-5678. Served by St. Callistus Parish. 12921 Lewis St., Garden Grove, 92840. Tel: 714-971-2141.
Theo Lacy Minimum Security Facility. (Branch Jail), 501 The City Dr., 92862. Tel: 714-834-3090. Rev. Brendan Smith, S.T., Chap., 422 Almond, 92866. Tel: 714-633-6527.

Costa Mesa. *Fairview Developmental Center*, 2501 Harbor, 92626. Tel: 714-545-9331. Rev. Joseph McEneany, SS.CC.

El Toro. *El Toro Marine Base*. Revs. Marc Boisvert; Chin Van Dang; Thomas P. Hall, C.S.P., Station Chapel: U.S.M.C.A.S., 92709. Tel: 714-726-3824.

Garden Grove. *Palm Harbor General Hospital*, 12601 Garden Grove Blvd., 92804. Tel: 714-537-5160. Served by St. Callistus Parish. 12921 Lewis St., 92804. Tel: 714-971- 2141.

Tustin. *Marine Corps Air Station*. Rev. Tim Janning, M.C.A.S. (H), 92701. Tel: 714-726-7311.

Special Assignment:
Reverend Monsignors—
Duc Tien, Peter, Dir., Vietnamese Center, 1538 N. Century Blvd., Santa Ana, CA 92703. Tel: 714-554-4211
Sammon, John F., P.A., Vicar for Pastoral and Community Affairs
Reverend Fathers—
Brazil, Sean, S.S.C., Dir., Korean Center, 7655 Trask Ave., Westminster, CA 92683
Cho, Laurentius, St. Thomas Korean Catholic Center, Anaheim, CA 92801-6710
Karp, Joseph A., Dir., Polish Center, Yorba Linda
Kim, Benedict, St. Thomas Korean Catholic Center, Anaheim, CA 92801-6710
Moreland, Gordon, S.J., Dir., House of Prayer for Priests, 7734 Santiago Canyon Rd., Orange, CA 92869

On Duty Outside the Diocese:
Reverend Fathers—
Buckman, Franklin J., Our Lady of Mt. Carmel Church, 503 W. Chocktoot, P.O. Box 396, Chiloquin, OR 79624
Daley, Wallace
Hung, Joseph K., Gethsemane Abbey, KY

Military Chaplains:
Reverend Fathers—
Fry, James Q.

Absent on Sick Leave:
Reverend Fathers—
Croal, Thomas
DiStefano, Joseph
Fumo, Harold
Gonzales, George
Kinzer, Gary
Kolberg, Lawrence R.
Luongo, John
Monestero, John
Tu, Joachim Vu

Inactive Leave:
Reverend Monsignors—
Harris, Michael
Reverend Fathers—
Colleran, Desmond
Coughlin, Richard
Coulombe, Dale
Farris, James M.
Frost, Stephen
Geraughty, Michael
German, Timothy J.
Gibbons, Francis X.
Harvey, James
Jagosz, Mitchell
Melito, Joseph
Nguyen, Joseph Chuan
O'Callaghan, John
Perez, Henry
Ramos, Eleuterio
Ruhl, John
Ryder, Matthais
Schmidt, Nicholas
Theis, Jeffrey
Tressler, Robert
Widera, Siegfried

Retired:
Reverend Monsignors—
Coffield, John
Collins, Michael
Doyle, Timothy
Falvey, Sinon
Harvey, William R.
Hughes, Michael
McCarthy, Emmett
McGowan, Anthony
Nash, James F.
O'Brien, Terrence
O'Connor, Hugh
Pierse, James
Scannell, Peter
Yrigan, Pedro
Reverend Fathers—
Chinh, Peter
Ho, Mathias
Morales, Jose
Powers, Joseph
Sheahan, John A.

Permanent Deacons:
Alvarado, Manuel, Immaculate Heart of Mary, Santa Ana
Antunez, Jay, St. Polycarp, Stanton
Barry, Jack, Our Lady of Mt. Carmel, Newport Beach
Brenes-Rios, Anthony, Our Lady of Guadalupe, La Habra
Brennan, John, St. Philip Benizi, Fullerton
Bube, Tony, La Purisima, Orange
Carver, Tim, St. Norbert, Orange
Chavez, Frank, St. Martin de Porres, Yorba Linda
Chavira, Manuel, St. Mary, Fullerton
Cook, Doug, San Antonio de Padua, Anaheim Hills
Coughlin, Chuck, Blessed Sacrament, Westminster
De Santos, Gerry, Immaculate Heart of Mary, Santa Ana
Duthoy, Ray, St. Justin Martyr, Anaheim
Erwin, Glenn, Our Lady of Mt. Carmel, Newport Beach
Euyoque, Carlos, St. Anne, Santa Ana
Faulk, Ed, St. Joseph, Placentia
Gagnon, Chuck, St. Joseph, Placentia
Garza, Domingo, Our Lady of Guadalupe, Santa Ana
Glaudini, Richard, St. Philip Benizi, Buena Park
Gonzales, Carlos, St. Mary, Fullerton
Halka, Joseph, Mission San Juan Capistrano
Havert, Ray, St. Nicholas, Laguna Hills
Jones, Wesley, St. Boniface, Anaheim
Kelleher, Robert, St. Columban, Garden Grove
Klos, Tom, San Antonio de Padua, Anaheim
Larkin, Jim, St. Polycarp, Stanton
Luna, Frank, Catholic Deaf Center, Orange
McQuade, John, St. Edward, Dana Point
Merandi, Lou, Holy Cross Greek Melkite
Meyer, Lee, St. Cecilia, Tustin

Michel, Jesse, St. Philip Benizi, Fullerton
Milam, Jay, St. Juliana Falconieri, Fullerton
Miller, Gerald, St. Cecilia, Tustin
Mireles, Viviano, Mission San Juan Capistrano, Mission Viejo
Nalbach, George, (Retired)
Navarro, Carlos, St. Angela Merici, Brea
Pyne, Jerry, Our Lady of Guadalupe, La Habra
Reynoso, Jose Luis, St. Boniface, Anaheim
Richeson, Jim, Our Lady Queen of Angels, Newport Beach
Romero, Rafael, Our Lady of Lourdes, Santa Ana
Salgado, Eddie, St. Timothy, Laguna Niguel
Samano, Vic, San Felipe de Jesus, Capistrano Beach
Schlater, Bill, St. Juliana Falconieri, Fullerton
Schlemmer, Jon, St. Cecilia, Tustin
Sire, Dave, Mission, San Juan Capistrano
Stripling, Joe, Blessed Sacrament, Westminister
Sullivan, Neill, Our Lady Queen of Angels, Newport Beach
Swift, Bernard, (Retired)
Thompson, James, St. Irenaeus, Cypress
vonVoigt, Fred, St. Angela Merici, Brea

INSTITUTIONS LOCATED IN THE DIOCESE

[A] SEMINARIES AND SCHOLASTICATES FOR RELIGIOUS

MIDWAY CITY. *St. Patrick's Novitiate and Scholasticate*, 7820 Bolsa Ave., 92655. Tel: 714-897-8181; Fax: 714-898-9020. Conducted by the Brothers of St. Patrick. Brothers 4.

SANTA ANA. *Trinity Missions House of Studies*, 730 N. Garfield, P.O. Box 1933, 92702. Tel: 714-543-7292; Fax: 714-973-2348. Rev. Stan Bosch, S.T., Dir. Students & Vocations. In res., Revs. Brendan Smith, S.T.; Rudy Breunig, S.T.

SILVERADO. *St. Michael's Norbertine Postulancy, Novitiate and Juniorate*, 19292 El Toro Rd., 92676. Tel: 714-858-0222. Conducted by the Norbertine Fathers. Rt. Rev. Eugene J. Hayes, O.Praem., Abbot; Rev. Thomas W. Nelson, O.Praem., Dir. Formation & Novice Master; Very Rev. Hugh C. Barbour, O.Praem, Ph.D., Asst. Dir. Formation & Prof. Philosophy; Revs. John E. Caronan, O.Praem., Prof. Latin; Gregory M. Dick, O.Praem, Prof. Scripture. For listing of other Norbertine priests working in the Diocese, refer to St. Michael College Prep High School.

[B] COLLEGES AND UNIVERSITIES

ORANGE. *St. Joseph College, Orange*, 480 S. Batavia St., 92868. Tel: 714-633-8121; Fax: 714-744-3165.
For a complete listing, refer to the Colleges and Universities section.

[C] HIGH SCHOOLS, DIOCESAN

FULLERTON. *Rosary High School.* (Girls), 1340 N. Acacia Ave., 92831. Tel: 714-879-6302; Fax: 714-879-0853. Mrs. Trudy Mazzarella, Prin. Lay Teachers 40; Students 683.

RANCHO SANTA MARGARITA. *Santa Margarita Catholic High School*, 22062 Antonio Pkwy., 92688. Tel: 714-858-3350; Fax: 714-858-4399. Merritt V. Hemenway, Prin. Priests 1; Sisters 3; Lay Teachers 103; Students 1,820.

SANTA ANA. *Mater Dei High School.* (Coed), 1202 W. Edinger, 92707-2191. Tel: 714-754-7711; Fax: 714-754-1880. Norbertine Fathers; Franciscan Fathers; Brothers of St. Patrick; Sisters of St. Joseph of Orange; Religious Sisters of Charity; Sisters de l'Union Chretienne de St. Chaumond; Sisters of St. Louis; Sisters of the Company of Mary. Mr. Patrick Murphy, Prin.; Revs. Steven Sallot, Rector/Chaplain; Eugene David Burnett, O.F.M.; Robert S. Hodges, O.Praem.; Joseph Horn, O.Praem. Priests 4; Brothers 1; Sisters 7; Lay Teachers 123; Students 2,101.

[D] HIGH SCHOOLS, PRIVATE

ANAHEIM. *Cornelia Connelly School of the Holy Child.* (Girls), 2323 W. Broadway, 92804. Tel: 714-776-1717; Fax: 714-776-2534. Sisters of the Holy Child Jesus. Sr. Francine Gunther, S.H.C.J., Head of School.
Cornelia Connelly School Development Fund.
Cornelia Connelly School Scholarship Fund. Sisters 2; Lay Teachers 18; Students 215.
Servite High School; Servite High School Development Fund, 1952 W. La Palma, 92801. Tel: 714-774-7575; Fax: 714-774-1404. Servite Friars. Rev. Gerald M. Horan, O.S.M., Pres.; Mr. Raymond Dunne, Prin.; Revs. Paul Gins, O.S.M.; Edward M. Penonzek, O.S.M.; Michael P. Pontarelli, O.S.M.; Eugene M. Smith, O.S.M.; Bros. Bonfilius McGovern, O.S.M.; Philip M. Eikmeyer, O.S.M. Priests 5; Sisters 1; Brothers 2; Lay Teachers 47; Students 775.

SIVERADO. *St. Michael's College Preparatory High School.* (Grades 8-12). (Boarding school for boys), 19292 El Toro Rd., 92676-9710. Tel: 714-858-0222; Fax: 714-858-7365. Revs. Hubert S. Szanto, O.Praem., Ph.D., Prin.; Gabriel D. Stack, O.Praem., Asst. Prin.; Stephen M. Boyle, O.Praem.; Vincent M. Gilmore, O.Praem., Spiritual Dir.; Jerome M. Molokie, O.Praem.; Charles W. Willingham, O.Praem.; Adrian J. Connor, O.Praem.; Justin S. Ramos, O.Praem.; Nicholas M. Tacito, O.Praem; Jordan S. Anderson, O.Praem. Lay Teachers 9; Brothers 2; Priests 10; Students 60.

[E] ELEMENTARY SCHOOLS AND DAY NURSERIES, PRIVATE

ANAHEIM. *St. Catherine's Military School*, 215 N. Harbor Blvd., 92805. Tel: 714-772-1363. Legal Title: *St. Catherine's Military School, a Corp.* Sr. Carolyn MarieLiam Monahan, Admin. & Prin. Dominican Sisters of Mission San Jose 19; Sisters 9; Lay Teachers 14; Students 198.

RANCHO SANTA MARGARITA. *Serra Catholic Elementary School*, 23652 Antonio Pkwy., 92688-1993. Tel: 714-888-1990. Mrs. Audrey Tellers, Prin. Students 500.

SANTA ANA. *Santa Clara Day Nursery and Kindergarten*, 1021 N. Newhope, 92703. Tel: 714-554-8850; Fax: 714-554-58-86. Poor Clare Missionary Sisters (M.C.). Children 100.

TUSTIN. *Saint Jeanne de Lestonnac School*, 16791 E. Main, 92870. Tel: 714-542-4271. Sr. Mary of Jesus Rodriguez, O.D.N., Prin. Sisters of the Company of Mary 6; Lay Teachers 28; Students 546.

[F] GENERAL HOSPITALS

ORANGE. *St. Joseph Health System*, 440 S. Batavia St., 92868.
For a complete listing, refer to the Hospitals section.
St. Joseph Health System, A Sisters of St. Joseph of Orange Corporation, 440 S. Batavia St., 92868. Tel: 714-997-7690.
For a complete listing, refer to the Hospitals section.
St. Joseph Hospital of Orange, 1100 W. Stewart Dr., P.O. Box 5600, 92867. Tel: 714-633-9111.
For a complete listing, refer to the Hospitals section.
SRM Alliance Hospital Services, St. Joseph Health System, 440 S. Batavia St., 92668-3995.
For a complete listing, refer to the Hospitals section.

FULLERTON. *St. Jude Medical Center*, 101 E. Valencia Mesa Dr., 92834. Tel: 714-871-3280.
For a complete listing, refer to the Hospitals section.
St. Jude Memorial Foundation, P.O. Box 4138, 92834 Fax: 714-992-3033.
For a complete listing, refer to the Hospitals section.

MISSION VIEJO. *Mission Hospital Regional Medical Center*, 27700 Medical Center Rd., 92691. Tel: 714-364-1400.
For a complete listing, refer to the Hospitals section.

[G] SPECIAL SERVICES

ORANGE. *St. Vincent de Paul Society*, 180 S. Cypress, 92866. Tel: 714-633-9195; Fax: 714-771-2748. Mr. Dan Harney, Pres.; Mr. Joseph D. Kay, Exec. Dir.; Rev. Peregrine Graffius, O.S.M., Spiritual Dir.
Special Works of the St. Vincent de Paul Society:
Food Distribution Center. Serving Orange County. 426-A W. Almond, 92866. Tel: 714-771-1343. Mr. Ron Blake, Dir.
Mary's Home, Transitional Housing, La Habra, 180 S. Cypress, 92866. Tel: 714-547-5566.
St. Vincent de Paul Center for Community Reconciliation, 777 S. Main St., Ste. 200, 92868. Tel: 714-836-8585. Programs include: Catholic Detention Ministry, Friends Outside and Victim-Offender Reconciliation.
Stores and Workshops, 180 Cypress, 92866. Tel: 714-633-9194.
Search of Orange County, Inc., P.O. Box 4191, 92867. Tel: 714-753-3533.

ANAHEIM. *St. Thomas Korean Catholic Center*, 412 N. Crescent Way, 92801. Tel: 714-772-3993; Fax: 714-772-3636. Revs. Benedict Kim, Dir.; Laurentius Cho.

SANTA ANA. *Holy Family Services, Adoption and Foster Care*, 1403 S. Main St., 92707. Tel: 714-835-5551; Fax: 714-973-4971. David Ballard, Exec Dir.
St. Francis Home, 1718 W. 6th St., 92703. Tel: 714-542-0381. Franciscan Sisters of the Immaculate Conception, Inc. Sr. Leticia Rodriguez, O.S.F., Admin. Sisters 22.
Vietnamese Catholic Center, 1538 N. Century Blvd., 92703. Tel: 714-554-4211; 554-5565. Rev. Msgr. Peter Nguyen Duc Tien, Dir. In res., Rev. Joachim Vu Tu.

SILVERADO. *St. Michael's Summer Camp*, St. Michael's abbey, 19292 El Toro Rd., 92676-9801. Tel: 714-858-0444. Boys aged 6-12 years. Capacity 120.

WESTMINSTER. *Korean Catholic Ministry*, 7655 Trask Ave., 92683. Tel: 714-897-6510. Revs. Sean Brazil, S.S.C., Dir. Korean Martyrs Center; Martin Bourke, S.S.C. Tel: 714-891-6961.

YORBA LINDA. *Polish Center*, 3999 Rose Dr., 92886. Tel: 714-996-8161. Rev. Joseph A. Karp, Dir.

[H] MONASTERIES AND RESIDENCES OF PRIESTS AND BROTHERS

ORANGE. *Brothers of the Christian Schools*, Marywood Center, P.O. Box 14195, 92863-1595. Tel: 714-282-3000. Bro. William Carriere, F.S.C., Ph.D.
Claretian Missionaries, La Purisima,11712 N. Hewes, 92869. Tel: 714-633-5800.
Jesuits, House of Prayer, 7734 Santiago Canyon Rd., 92869. Tel: 714-639-9740. Rev. Gordon Moreland, S.J.
Marianists, House of Prayer, 7734 Santiago Canyon Rd., 92869. Tel: 714-633-2698. Rev. Patrick Philbin, S.M.
Missionaries of Africa, 566 S. Glassell St., 92866-3017. Tel: 714-639-2900.
Servite Fathers and Brothers, Sisters of St. Joseph of Orange, Regina Residence, 430 S. Batavia, 92868. Tel: 714-744-3153. Rev. Gerard M. Calkins, O.S.M.
Theatine Fathers, St. Joseph Hospital, 1100 W. Stewart Dr., 92692. Tel: 714-771-8137. Rev. David Maes, C.R.

ANAHEIM. *Servite Fathers and Brothers.* Servite Friars, Servite Priory, 1922 W. La Palma Ave., 92801-3595. Tel: 714-774-7575. Revs. Eugene M. Smith, O.S.M., Prior; Mel M. Corcoran, O.S.M.; Paul Gins, O.S.M.; Gerald M. Horan, O.S.M.; Edward M. Penonzek, O.S.M.; Michael M. Pontarelli, O.S.M.; Bros. Bonfilius M. McGovern, O.S.M.; Philip M. Eikmeyer, O.S.M., Servite High School, 1952 W. La Palma Ave., 92801-3595. Tel: 714-774-7575.

BUENA PARK. *Augustinian Fathers*, St. Pius V, 7691 Orangethorpe Ave., 90621. Tel: 714-522-2193.
Servite Fathers And Brothers, Servite Provincial Center, 5210 Somerset St., 90621-1498. Tel: 714-523-5810. Revs. Ignatius M. Kissel, O.S.M., Prov.; Peregrine M. Graffius, O.S.M., Asst. Prov.; Eugene M. Smith, O.S.M., Councillor; Justin M. Pisclotta, O.S.M., Councillor; Michael P. Pontarelli, O.S.M., Treas.; Gerald M. Horan, O.S.M., Archivist / Councillor; Donald M. Siple, O.S.M., Voc. Dir.
Personnel assigned outside the Province and Country: Rev. John M. Dowd, O.S.M., Curia Generalizia di Servi di Maria, Piazza San Marcello al Corso, 5, Rome, Italy, 00187. Rev. Robert M. Anderson, O.S.M., Monte Berico Novitiate, P.O. Box 1457, Nigel, Republic of South Af, 1490. Revs. Leo M. Spicer, O.S.M., Vicar Provincial of Western Australia; Robert M. Zivkovic, O.S.M.; Frank Christi, O.S.M.; Carlo M. Marchetti, O.S.M.; Patrick Boyle, O.S.M.; Christopher Ross, O.S.M.; Liam Mackle, O.S.M.; Myles Lynch, O.S.M.; Bros. Stephen Barker, O.S.M.; Robert M. Lee, O.S.M.

COSTA MESA. *Sacred Heart Fathers*, Fairview Developmental Center, 2501 Harbor Blvd., 92626. Tel: 714-957-5242. Rev. Joseph McEneany, SS.CC.

FULLERTON. *Augustinian Recollects*, St. Mary, 400 W. Commonwealth Ave., 92832-1713. Tel: 714-525-2500.
Servite Fathers and Brothers, St. Juliana Falconieri, 1316 N. Acacia, 92831. Tel: 714-879-1971. St. Philip Benizi, 235 S. Pine Dr., 92833-3294. Tel: 714-871-3613.

HUNTINGTON BEACH. *Franciscan Fathers*, SS. Simon and Jude, 20444 Magnolis St., 92646. Tel: 715-962-3333.

LAGUNA NIGUEL. *Jesuits*, St. Timothy, 29102 Crown Valley Pkwy., 92677. Tel: 714-249-4091. Rev. Donald Kolda, S.J.

MIDWAY CITY. *Brothers of St. Patrick, St. Patrick's Novitiate and Scholasticate*, 7820 Bolsa Ave., 92655. Tel: 714-897-8181. Bros. Livinus Bellew, F.S.P.; Aquinas Cassin, F.S.P.; Edwin Guidera, F.S.P.; Matthew Regan, F.S.P.

SANTA ANA. *Augustinian Recollects*, Our Lady of Guadalupe, 1322 E. 3rd St., 92701-5104. Tel: 714-836-4142. Our Lady of the Pillar, 1622 6th St., 92703. Tel: 714-543-1700.
Divine Word, 13962 Gimbert Ln., 92705. Tel: 714-544-1165. Rev. Henry Marusa, S.V.D.
Franciscan Fathers, Mater Dei High School, 1202 W. Edinger St., 92707. Tel: 714-754-7711. Rev. Eugene Burnett, O.F.M.
Trinitarian Missionaries/Missionary Servants of the Most Holy Trinity, Trinitarian House of Studies, P.O. Box 1933, 92702. Tel: 714-541-4840. Revs. Brendan Smith, S.T.; Stanley Bosch, S.T.; Rudy Breunig, S.T.

SILVERADO. *Norbertine Fathers*, 19292 El Toro Rd., 92676-9710. Tel: 714-858-0222. Rt. Revs. Eugene J. Hayes, O.Praem., Abbot; Ladislas K. Parker, O.Praem., Abbot Emeritus; Very Rev. Hugh Barbour, O.Praem., Prior; Revs. Vincent M. Gilmore, O.Praem., Subprior; Hubert S. Szanto, O.Praem.,

Prin. of School; Clement A. Rudnay, O.Praem.; Gerlac A. Horvath, O.Praem., Insurance Sec.; Leo J. Celano, O.Praem., Prison Chap.; Raymond L. Perez, O.Praem.; Michael U. Perea, O.Praem., Parish Apostolate; Herman-Joseph Rettig, O.Praem.; Gilbert O'Brien, O.Praem., Military Chap.; Stephen M. Boyle, O.Praem.; Francis M. Gloudeman, O.Praem.; Paul L. Gelencser, O.Praem.; Peter D. Muller, O.Praem.; Luke Laslavich, O.Praem.; Lawrence Johnson, O.Praem., Educ. Leave; Kolbe Moreno, O.Praem., Hospital Chap.; John Caronan, O.Praem., Treas.; Adrian Connor, O.Praem.; Benedict Horvath, O.Praem.; Jerome Molokie, O.Praem.; Thomas Nelson, O.Praem., Dir. Formation; Justin Ramos, O.Praem., Educ. Leave; Werenfried van Straaten, O.Praem.; Philip Smith, O.Praem.; Robert Hodges, O.Praem.; Joseph K. Horn, O.Praem.; Jordan Anderson, O.Praem.; Gregory Dick, O.Praem.; Nicholas Tacito, O.Praem.; Charles Willingham, O.Praem.; Gabriel Stack, O.Praem., Vice-Prin.; James Smith, O.Praem.

Teaching Ministry in Hungary: Revs. Martin Benzoni, O.Praem.; Theodore Smith, O.Praem.

Teaching Ministry in San Pedro: Revs. Patrick Foutts, O.Praem.; Bernard Johnson, O.Praem.; Norbert Wood, O.Praem.; Anthony Mary Kopp, O.Praem.; Pascal Nguyen, O.Praem. Priests 42; Clerics 10; Deacons 1; Postulants 4; Novices 3.

WESTMINSTER. *Columban Fathers*, Korean Martyrs Catholic Center, 7655 Trask Ave., 92683. Tel: 714-897-6510. Revs. Sean Brazil, S.S.C.; Martin Bourke, S.S.C.

[I] CONVENTS AND RESIDENCES FOR SISTERS

ORANGE. *Adrian Dominicans*, Marywood Center, 2811 E. Villa Real Dr., 92867. Tel: 714-282-3000.

Daughters of Mary and Joseph, 1129 W. Palmyra Ave. #C, 92868. Tel: 714-744-3726.

Servants of Mary, St. Joseph Motherhouse, 480 S. Batavia St., 92668. Tel: 714-633-8121.

Sisters of Charity of Leavenworth, 2427 Northumberland, 92865. Tel: 714-974-8518.

Sisters of Providence, Marywood Center, 2811 E. Villa Real Dr., 92867. Tel: 714-282-3000.

Sisters of St. Joseph of Carondelet, Sisters of St. Joseph of Cluny, Center for Spiritual Development, 434 S. Batavia, 92868. Tel: 714-744-3175. Sisters 2.

Sisters of St. Joseph of Orange Motherhouse Community, 480 S. Batavia, 92868. Tel: 714-633-8121, Ext. 735. Sr. Michelle Tochtrop, C.S.J., Gen. Sec. & Contact. Sisters 33. Regina Residence Community, 430 S. Batavia St., 92868. Tel: 714-744-3109. Sisters 71. Palmyra Community, 940 W. Palmyra, 92868. Tel: 714-744-3150. Sisters 6. Casa Magnolia Community, 954 W. Palmyra, 92868. Tel: 714-639-1030. Sisters 3. St. Joseph Hospital Community, P.O. Box 5600, 92868. Tel: 714-771-8040. Sisters 9. Greengrove Community, 2075 Greengrove St., 92665. Tel: 714-974-9079. Sisters 4.

Sisters of the Company of Mary, La Purisima Convent, 11712 N. Hewes, 92867. Tel: 714-538-0811. Sisters 4.

Sisters of the Holy Cross, St. Joseph Motherhouse, 480 S. Batavia St., 92868. Tel: 714-771-1738.

Sisters of the Presentation of the Blessed Virgin Mary, St. Norbert Convent, 343 E. Chestnut, 92867. Tel: 714-637-7390. Sisters 4.

ANAHEIM. *Cornelia Connelly Convent*, 2323 W. Broadway, 92804. Tel: 714-538-6228. Sisters of the Holy Child. Sisters 4. 9351 Greenwich, 92804. Tel: 714-776-9444. Sisters 2. Corporate Title: Society of the Holy Child Jesus, Inc.

Dominicans, Mission San Jose, St. Catherine Military School, 215 N. Harbor Blvd., 92803-3070. Tel: 714-772-1363. Sisters 18.

Religious Sisters of Mercy of the Americas, St. Boniface Parish, 120 N. Janss St., 92805. Tel: 714-956-3110. St. Justin Martyr, 2050 W. Ball Rd., 92804. Tel: 714-774-2407.

BREA. *Sisters of St. Clare*, St. Clare's Garden, 449 S. Pine Ave., 9281-6644. Tel: 714-257-1113. Sisters 4.

BUENA PARK. *Sisters of Our Lady of Perpetual Help*, 6751 Western Ave., 90621. Tel: 714-521-1345. Sisters 2.

COSTA MESA. *Sisters of Mercy of Ireland*, St. John the Baptist Convent, 2960 Mendoza Dr., 92626. Tel: 714-545-2116. Sisters 2.

Sisters of the Company of Mary, St. Joachim Convent, 1943 Orange Ave., 92727. Tel: 714-574-7408. Sisters 4.

CYPRESS. *Congregation of Holy Faith*, St. Irenaeus Convent, 5201 Evergreen Ave., 90630. Tel: 714-826-0760. Sisters 2.

Sisters of Charity of the Blessed Virgin Mary, 11267 Roanoke Ct., 90630.

Sisters of the Blessed Virgin Mary, St. Irenaeus Convent, 5201 Evergreen Ave., 90630. Tel: 714-527-4844.

DANA POINT. *Religious Sisters of Mercy*, 33941 Amber Lantern, 92629.

Sisters of Social Service, St. Edward, 33926 Calle La Primavera, 92629-2018. Tel: 714-496-1307.

Sisters of St. Joseph of Orange, Mission Hospital Community, 33392 Via Lenita, 92629. Tel: 714-488-0433. Sr. Michelle Tochtrop, C.S.J., Gen. Sec. & Contact. Tel: 714-633-8121 Ext. 735. Sisters 4.

FOUNTAIN VALLEY. *Sisters of Social Service*, 9076 La Colonia, 92708. Tel: 714-847-8981.

FULLERTON. *Sisters of St. Joseph of Orange*, Rosary Community, 1601 E. Alto Ln., 9281. Tel: 714-526-3141. Sr. Michelle Tochtrop, C.S.J., Gen. Sec. & Contact. Tel: 714-633-8121 Ext. 735. Sisters 6. St. Jude Hospital Community, P.O. Box 4138, 92834. Tel: 714-992-3000. Sisters 9. St. Mary Convent, 920 N. Grandview, 92832. Tel: 714-526-7349. Sisters 4.

GARDEN GROVE. *Eucharistic Missionaries of the Most Holy Trinity*, 11892 E. Lampson Ave., 92840. Tel: 714-530-5727. Sisters 4.

Religious Sisters of Charity, St. Columban Convent, 12555 Westlake St., 92650. Tel: 714-534-1003. Sisters 4.

Sisters of the Presentation of the Blessed Virgin Mary, St. Columban Residence, 10871 Stanford Ave., #18, 92840-5118. Tel: 714-537-2015.

HUNTINGTON BEACH. *Benedictines, Grand Terrace*, SS. Simon & Jude Convent, 20512 Tobermory Cir., 92646. Tel: 714-968-2237.

Sisters of Charity of the Blessed Virgin Mary, SS. Simon & Jude Convent, 20512 Tobermory Cir., 92646. Tel: 714-968-2237.

Sisters of the Presentation of the Blessed Virgin Mary, St. Bonaventure Convent, 16441 Bradbury Ln., 92647. Tel: 714-846-6212. Sisters 5.

LA HABRA. *Sisters of St. Joseph of Carondelet*, Villa Maria House of Prayer, 1252 N. Citrus Dr., 90631. Tel: 310-691-5838. Sisters 4.

Sisters of St. Joseph of Orange, Our Lady of Guadalupe Community, 920 W. La Habra Blvd., 90631. Tel: 310-691-9612. Sr. Michelle Tochtrop, C.S.J., Gen. Sec. & Contact. Sisters 3.

LAGUNA BEACH. *Benedictines, Grand Terrace and Rapid City*, St. Catherine of Siena Convent, 3090 S. Coast Hwy., 92651. Tel: 714-494-7339.

LAGUNA HILLS. *Sisters of Little Company of Mary*, St. Nicholas Convent, 24652 La Cienega, 92653. Tel: 714-643-8688. Sisters 2.

LAKE FOREST. *School Sisters of St. Francis*, 24001 Muirlands Blvd. #146, 92630. Tel: 714-951-8681. 24531 Raymond Way, Apt. B, 92630. Tel: 714-458-2747.

LONG BEACH. *Religious Sisters of Charity*, 2718 Knoxville Ave., 90815. Tel: 310-421-7943. Sisters 2.

MISSION VIEJO. *Franciscans, Syracuse*, 23581 Ribalta, 92692. Tel: 714-380-7302.

School Sisters of St. Francis, 23581 Ribalta, 92692. Tel: 714-380-7302.

NEWPORT BEACH. *Community of the Holy Spirit*, Our Lady Queen of Angels Convent, 2108 Aralia St., 92660. Tel: 714-644-0660.

Sisters of St. Joseph of Carondelet, Our Lady Queen of Angels Convent, 2108 Aralia St., 92660. Tel: 714-644-0660. Sisters 3.

RANCHO SANTA MARGARITA. *Sisters of Providence*, 243 Via Serena, 92688. Tel: 714-589-3322.

Sisters of the Holy Cross, 7 Via Amistosa, Apt. B, 92688.

SAN CLEMENTE. *Our Lady of Fatima Convent*, 300 Presidio Ave., 92672. Tel: 714-492-5608. Sisters 2.

SANTA ANA. *Dominicans, Mission San Jose*, St. Callistus Convent, 2541 N. Forest Ave., 92706. Tel: 714-953-4322. Sisters 4.

Franciscan Missionary Sisters of the Immaculate Conception, St. Francis Home for the Aged, 1718 W. 6th St., 92703. Tel: 714-542-0381. Sisters 22.

Franciscans, Rochester, Immaculate Heart of Mary Convent, 2202 McFadden, 92704. Tel: 714-545-7916. Sisters 5.

Lovers of the Holy Cross, 1401 S. Sycamore St., 92707. Tel: 714-973-1951. Sisters 8.

Poor Clare Missionary Sisters of the Blessed Sacrament, 1019 N. Newhope St., 92703. Tel: 714-554-8850. Sisters 13.

Sisters of Mercy of the Americas, 16350 Harbor Blvd., #2602, 92704-3836. Tel: 714-839-7893.

Sisters of St. Joseph of Carondelet, Hogar de San Jose, 507 N. Linwood Ave., 92701. Tel: 714-541-6480. St. Joseph, 727 Minter St., 92701. Tel: 714-550-8096.

Sisters of St. Joseph of Orange, Casa Guadalupe Community, 414 S. Broadway, 92701. Tel: 714-834-9381. Sr. Michelle Tochtrop, C.S.J., Gen. Sec. & Contact. Tel: 714-633-8121 Ext. 735. Sisters 5. Fifth Street Community, 519 E. 5th St., 92701. Tel: 714-543-6661. Sisters 4.

Sisters of the Company of Mary, St. Anne's Convent, 1339 S. Broadway, 92707. Tel: 714-558-1340. Sisters 3.

Society Devoted to the Sacred Heart, Heart of Jesus Retreat Center, 2927 S. Greenville St., 92704. Tel: 714-557-4538. Sisters 7. Sacred Heart Convent, 2911 S. Greenville St., 92704. Tel: 714-751-6335. Sisters 6.

SEAL BEACH. *Franciscans, Syracuse*, St. Anne Convent, 328 1/2 10th St., 90740. Tel: 310-493-4630.

SILVERADO. *Rosarian Dominicans*, St. Michael's Convent, 19292 El Toro Rd., 92676. Tel: 714-858-0487. Sisters 8.

TRABUCO CANYON. *Sisters of St. Joseph of Carondelet, Albany Province*, Boys Hope Residence, 92. Tel: 714-589-5783.

TUSTIN. *Adrian Dominicans*, St. Jeanne de Lestonnac Convent, 16791 E. Main St., 92780. Tel: 714-541-3125.

Sisters de L'Union-Chretienne de Chaumond, 14391 Clarissa Ln., 92780. Tel: 714-730-1475. Sisters 3.

Sisters of Charity of the Blessed Virgin Mary, 131 Hall Cir., #33, 92680.

Sisters of Providence, 14692 Charloma Dr., 92780. Tel: 714-544-9021. Sisters 3.

Sisters of St. Louis, 131 Hall Cir., #59, 92780.

Sisters of the Company of Mary, Provincial House, 16791 E. Main St., 92780. Tel: 714-541-3125. Sisters 17.

WESTMINSTER. *Sisters of our Lady of Perpetual Help*, Korean Sisters Residence, 7679 Trask Ave., #A, 92683. Tel: 714-373-2555. Sisters 2.

YORBA LINDA. *Sisters of Providence Residence*, Providence House, 4580 Casa Oro Dr., 92886. Tel: 714-996-5027. Sr. Jan Craven, S.P.; Sr. Paula Damiano, S.P. Sisters 2.

[J] CATHOLIC CHARITIES

SANTA ANA. *Catholic Charities of Orange County, Inc.*, 1506 Brookhollow Dr., Ste. 112, 92705. Tel: 714-662-7500; Fax: 714-662-1861. Kristan Schlichte, M.S., Exec. Dir.; Most Rev. Michael P. Driscoll, M.S.W., Vicar for Charities.

Counseling Services. Patricia Burgoyne, M.S.W., L.C.S.W., Program Dir.

Family Resource Center. Raoul Aroz, Admin.

Columbian House, Anaheim Hills. Frank Bartosik, Facility Mgr.

Columbian House, Garden Grove. Ann, Wohlgenant, Faculty Mgr. Residential care for children with developmental disabilities.

Family Support Center. Gilbert Rivera, Admin.

Employment Services. Mr. Hoang Tieu, Program Dir.

Family Service Center. Kathy Lenny, Admin.

Resettlement, Immigration & Citizenship Services. Thu Tran, Program Dir.

[K] RETREAT HOUSES

ORANGE. *Center for Spiritual Development*, 434 S. Batavia St., 92868-3907. Tel: 714-744-3175. Sr. Jane Delisle, C.S.J., Exec. Dir.

House of Prayer for Priests, 7734 Santiago Canyon Rd., 92869. Tel: 714-639-9740. Rev. J. Gordon Moreland, S.J., Dir. In res., Rev. Patrick B. Philbin, S.M.

Marywood Retreat Center, 2811 E. Villa Real Dr., 92867. Tel: 714-282-3099 (Evenings & Weekends). Mrs. Eileen Pfaff, Facilities Coord., Tel: 714-282-3098 (Days Mon.-Fri.). Sr. Joseph Patrice Shea, S.P., Res. Dir. Retreats for youth, men, women & married couple groups. Capacity 120.

FULLERTON. *Pro Sanctity Spirituality Center, Retreat House*, 205 S. Pine Dr., 92833. Tel: 714-956-1020. Agnes Rus, Dir. Capacity: 27-40 for day use.

Pro Sanctity Movement. Mr. Marko Botich, Dir.

LA HABRA. *Villa Maria House of Prayer*, 1252 N. Citrus Dr., 90631. Tel: 310-691-5838. Sisters of St. Joseph of Carondelet.

SANTA ANA. *Heart of Jesus Retreat Center*, 2927 S. Greenville St., 92704. Tel: 714-557-4538; Fax: 714-668-9780. Society Devoted to the Sacred Heart. Sisters 7.

[L] NEWMAN CENTERS

FULLERTON. *California State University Fullerton, Newman Center*, St. Juliana Falconieri, 1316 N. Acacia Ave., 92831. Tel: 714-526-7189.
E-mail: csufnewman@newman.org
Rev. Joseph P. Cheah, O.S.M.

IRVINE. *Campus Ministry-Diocese of Orange*, U.C.I. Interfaith Center, P.O. Box 6030, 92616-6030. Tel: 714-856-0211; 753-3373, Ext. 3. Rev. Patrick Philbin, S.M., Diocesan Dir. Campus Ministry.

University of California, Irvine, U.C.I. Interfaith Center, P.O. Box 6030, 92616-6030. Tel: 714-856-0211; 753-3373, Ext. 3. Rev. Patrick Philbin, S.M., Diocesan Dir. Campus Ministry.

[M] MISCELLANEOUS LISTINGS

ORANGE. *Sisters of St. Joseph Healthcare Foundation*, 480 S. Batavia St., 92868. Tel: 714-633-8121; Fax: 714-744-3165. Sr. Diane Hejna, C.S.J., Exec. Dir.

ANAHEIM. *Catholic Alumni Club of Orange County*, P.O. Box 4541, 92803. Tel: 714-502-8086.

EL TORO. *Aid to the Church In Need, Inc.*, P.O. Box 1000, 92630. Tel: 714-858-0222. Mr. David Budinger, Jr., Pres.; Revs. Hubert S. Szanto, O.Praem., Board Member; Gabriel D. Stack, O.Praem.; Mr. Robert Lully, Office Mgr.

FULLERTON. *Apostolic Oblates*, 2125 W. Walnut Ave., 92833. Tel: 714-871-5768. House of Formation for Professed Apostolic Oblates. Secular Institute of the Apostolic Oblates, Inc. Agnes Rus, Local Moderator.

RELIGIOUS INSTITUTES OF MEN REPRESENTED IN THE DIOCESE

For further details refer to the corresponding bracketed number in the Religious Institutes of Men or Women section.

[0140]—*Augustinian Fathers.*—O.S.A.
[0150]—*Augustinian Recollects.*—O.A.R.
[1160]—*Brothers of St. Patrick.*—F.S.P.
[0330]—*Brothers of the Christian Schools.*—F.S.C.
[0360]—*Claretian Missionaries.*—C.M.F.
[0370]—*Columban Fathers.*—S.S.C.
[0520]—*Franciscan Fathers.*—O.F.M.
[0690]—*Jesuit Fathers and Brothers.*—S.J.
[0780]—*Marist Fathers.*—S.M.
[0850]—*Missionaries of Africa.*—M.Afr.
[0900]—*Norbertine Fathers.*—O.Praem.
[1140]—*Sacred Heart Fathers.*—SS.CC.
[1240]—*Servite Fathers and Brothers.*—O.S.M.
[0420]—*Society of the Divine Word.*—S.V.D.
[1300]—*Theatine Fathers.*—C.R.
[0840]—*Trinity Missionaries.*—S.T.

RELIGIOUS INSTITUTES OF WOMEN REPRESENTED IN THE DIOCESE

[]—*Benedictine Sisters.* (Grand Terrace).—O.S.B.
[]—*Benedictine Sisters.* (Rapid City, SD).—O.S.B.
[2020]—*Community of the Holy Spirit.*—C.H.S.
[1920]—*Congregation of Sisters of the Holy Cross.*—C.S.C.
[0880]—*Daughters of Mary and Joseph.*—D.M.J.
[1070-13]—*Dominican Sisters.* (Adrian, MI).—O.P.
[]—*Dominican Sisters.* (Mission San Jose).—O.P.
[]—*Eucharistic Missionaries of the Most Holy Trinity.*—M.E.S.S.T.
[1350]—*Franciscan Missionary Sisters of the Immaculate Conception.*—O.S.F.
[]—*Franciscan Sisters.*
[]—*Franciscan Sisters.* (Syracuse, NY).—O.S.F.
[1650]—*Franciscan Sisters, Philadelphia Foundation.*—O.S.F.
[2390]—*Lovers of the Holy Cross Sisters.*—L.H.C.
[2840]—*Poor Clare Missionaries of Blessed Sacrament.*—M.C.
[3280]—*Presentation Sisters of Blessed Virgin Mary.*—P.B.V.M.
[3400]—*Religious Sisters of Charity.*—R.S.C.
[]—*Rosarian Dominican Sisters.*—O.P.
[1680]—*School Sisters of St. Francis.*—S.S.S.F.
[3580]—*Servants of Mary.*—O.S.M.
[]—*Sisters of Charity of Leavenworth.* (KS).—S.C.L.
[]—*Sisters of Charity of Poitiers.*—S.C.P.
[0430]—*Sisters of Charity of the Blessed Virgin Mary.*—B.V.M.
[1940]—*Sisters of Holy Faith.*—C.H.F.
[]—*Sisters of Mercy of Ireland.*—S.M.
[2575]—*Sisters of Mercy of the Americas.*—R.S.M.
[]—*Sisters of Our Lady of Perpetual Help.*—S.O.L.P.H.
[]—*Sisters of Providence.*—S.P.
[4090]—*Sisters of Social Service.*—S.S.S.
[3770]—*Sisters of St. Clare.*—O.S.C.
[3830-03]—*Sisters of St. Joseph.* (Orange).—C.S.J.
[3840]—*Sisters of St. Joseph of Carondelet.*—C.S.J.
[3840]—*Sisters of St. Joseph of Carondelet.* (Albany Prov.).—C.S.J.
[3860]—*Sisters of St. Joseph of Cluny.*—S.J.C.
[3935]—*Sisters of St. Louis.*—S.S.L.
[0700]—*Sisters of the Company of Mary.*—O.D.N.
[1990]—*Sisters of the Holy Names of Jesus and Mary.*—S.N.J.M.
[2270]—*Sisters of the Little Company of Mary.*—L.C.M.
[4050]—*Sisters of the Society Devoted to the Sacred Heart.*—S.D.S.H.
[4060]—*Society of the Holy Child Jesus.*—S.H.C.J.

DIOCESAN CEMETERIES

ORANGE. *Holy Sepulcher*, 7845 Santiago Canyon Rd., 92869. Steve Haupert, Supt.

ANAHEIM. *Holy Cross.*

EL TORO. *Ascension.* 24754 Trabuco Rd., Lake Forest. John D. Callahan, Jr., Supt.

HUNTINGTON BEACH. *Good Shepherd Cemetery and Mausoleum*, 8301 Talbert Ave., 92646. Joe Hernandez, Supt.

NECROLOGY

† O'Donnell, Thomas, Newport Beach, CA, Our Lady of Mt. Carmel. —Died Aug. 3, 1996.

Diocese of Orlando

(Dioecesis Orlandensis)

Most Reverend

NORBERT M. DORSEY, C.P., D.D., S.T.D.

Bishop of Orlando; ordained April 28, 1956; appointed Auxiliary Bishop of Miami January 10, 1986; ordained Titular Bishop of Mactaris and Auxiliary Bishop of the Archdiocese of Miami March 19, 1986; appointed Bishop of Orlando March 20, 1990; installed as Third Bishop of Orlando May 25, 1990. *Office: 421 E. Robinson, P.O. Box 1800, Orlando, FL, 32802.*

Most Reverend

THOMAS J. GRADY, D.D.

Retired Bishop of Orlando; ordained April 23, 1938; appointed Auxiliary Bishop of Chicago June 21, 1967; ordained Titular Bishop of Vamalla August 24, 1967; appointed Bishop of Orlando November 9, 1974; installed as Second Bishop of Orlando December 16, 1974; retired May 25, 1990. *Mailing Address: 421 E. Robinson, P.O. Box 1800, Orlando, FL, 32802.*

ESTABLISHED JUNE 18, 1968.

Square Miles 10,776.

Comprises the Counties of Brevard, Lake, Marion, Orange, Osceola, Polk, Seminole, Sumter and Volusia in the State of Florida.

For legal titles of parishes and diocesan institutions, consult the Chancery.

Chancery: 421 E. Robinson, P.O. Box 1800, Orlando, FL, 32802-1800. Tel.: 407-246-4800; Fax: 407-246-4942.

STATISTICAL OVERVIEW

Personnel	
Bishop	1
Retired Bishops	1
Priests: Diocesan Active in Diocese	100
Priests: Active Outside Diocese	7
Priests: Retired, Sick or Absent	16
Number of Diocesan Priests	123
Religious Priests in Diocese	54
Extern Priests in Diocese	17
Ordinations:	
Diocesan Priests	5
Transitional Deacons	1
Permanent Deacons	5
Permanent Deacons in Diocese	109
Total Brothers	10
Total Sisters	142
Parishes	
Parishes	70
With Resident Pastor:	
Resident Diocesan Priests	60
Resident Religious Priests	10
Without Resident Pastor:	
Missions	9
Professional Ministry Personnel:	
Brothers	5
Sisters	48
Lay Ministers	153
Welfare	
Day Care and Extended Day Care Centers	12
Total Assisted	900
Special Centers for Social Services	6
Total Assisted	21,000
Other Institutions	8
Total Assisted	834
Educational	
Diocesan Students in Other Seminaries	21
Total Seminarians	21
High Schools, Diocesan and Parish	4
Total Students	2,387
Elementary Schools, Diocesan and Parish	32
Total Students	11,531
Non-residential Schools for the Disabled	1
Total Students	65
Catechesis/Religious Education:	
High School Students	4,058
Elementary Students	20,538
Total Students Under Catholic Instruction	38,600
Teachers in the Diocese:	
Priests	4
Sisters	38
Lay Teachers	741
Vital Statistics	
Receptions into the Church:	
Infant Baptism Totals	5,482
Adult Baptism Totals	454
Received into Full Communion	779
First Communions	5,456
Confirmations	3,317
Marriages:	
Catholic	1,032
Interfaith	662
Total Marriages	1,694
Deaths	3,356
Total Catholic Population	301,958
Total Population	2,955,200

Former Bishops—Most Rev. WILLIAM D. BORDERS, D.D., ord. May 18, 1940; appt. Bishop of Orlando, May 2, 1968; cons. June 14, 1968; transferred to Baltimore, March 25, 1974 as Archbishop.—Most Rev. THOMAS J. GRADY, D.D., ord. April 23, 1938; appt. Second Bishop of Orlando, Nov. 9, 1974; installed Dec. 16, 1974; retired May 25, 1990.

Chancery—421 E. Robinson, P.O. Box 1800, Orlando, 32802-1800. Tel: 407-246-4800; Fax: 407-246-4942.

Vicar General—Rev. PATRICK J. CAVERLY, V.G., *P.O. Box 1800, Orlando, 32802.* Tel: 407-246-4800.

Archivist—JANE QUINN.

Chancellor—Sr. LUCY VAZQUEZ, O.P., J.C.D., *P.O. Box 1800, Orlando, 32802.* Tel: 407-246-4800.

Tribunal—421 E. Robinson, P.O. Box 1800, Orlando, 32802. Tel: 407-246-4850.

Officialis—Rev. MATTHEW J. CONNOLLY.

Adjutant Judicial Vicar—Rev. PAIGE BLAKELY, J.C.L.

Director of Tribunal—Sr. LUCY VAZQUEZ, O.P., J.C.D.

Promoter of Justice—Sr. LUCY VAZQUEZ, O.P., J.C.D.

Defenders of the Bond—Revs. PAIGE BLAKELY, J.C.L.; MATTHEW J. CONNOLLY; FERNANDO GIL, J.C.L., J.D.; Sr. LUCY VAZQUEZ, O.P., J.C.D.

Judges—Revs. PAIGE BLAKELY, J.C.L.; NICHOLAS KING; Sr. LUCY VAZQUEZ, O.P., J.C.D.; Revs. MATTHEW CONNOLLY; JOHN GIEL, J.C.L.

Comptroller—JOHN T. WETTACH.

Deans—Northern Deanery: Rev. ROBERT FUCHECK, Central Deanery South: Rev. SEAN HESLIN, Central Deanery North: Rev. CHARLES I. MITCHELL, Eastern Deanery: Rev. PAUL KAMIDE, Western Deanery: Rev. ANTHONY BLUETT, Southern Deanery: Rev. DAVID P. PAGE.

Priests' Council—Executive Committee: Most Rev. NORBERT M. DORSEY, C.P., Pres.; Revs. THOMAS MCMACKIN, Chm.; ROBERT KURBER, Vice Chm.; JOHN GIEL, Sec.; PATRICK J. CAVERLY, V.G., Ex-Officio; EMILE GENTILE, T.O.R., Ex-Officio. Members: Revs. FELIX BANOS; CARLOS BEDOYA; ANTHONY BLUETT; WILLIAM ENNIS; MANUEL FERNANDEZ; ROBERT FUCHECK; SEAN HESLIN; PAUL KAMIDE; CHARLES MITCHELL; JOSEPH NOLIN; DAVID P. PAGE; PETER UNIOWSKI; RICHARD WALSH.

Consultors—Revs. PATRICK J. CAVERLY, V.G.; SEAN HESLIN; ANTHONY BLUETT; PAUL KAMIDE; CHARLES I. MITCHELL; DAVID P. PAGE; ROBERT FUCHECK.

Bishop's Executive Staff—Most Rev. NORBERT M. DORSEY; Revs. PATRICK J. CAVERLY, V.G.; JOHN FLYNN, O.S.A.; EMILE GENTILE, T.O.R.; ROBERT WEBSTER; Sr. LUCY VAZQUEZ, O.P., J.C.D.; THOMAS AGLIO; JOHN WETTACH.

Vicar for Religious—Sr. LUCY VAZQUEZ, O.P., J.C.D., *P.O. Box 1800, Orlando, 32802.*

Vicar for Clergy—Rev. EMILE GENTILE, T.O.R.

Diocesan Offices and Organizations

B.A.S.E.—VITO NAPOLETANO, Dir.; Rev. PATRICK J. CAVERLY, V.G., *P.O. Box 1800, Orlando, 32802.* Tel: 407-246-4842.

Black & Haitian Ministry—Rev. RUDOLPH CLEARE, Dir., *P.O. Box 1800, Orlando, 32802.* Tel: 407-246-4925.

Building Commission—WILLIAM G. KRAMER, A.I.A., Co-ord., *P.O. Box 1800, Orlando, 32802.* Tel: 407-246-4870.

Campus Ministry—Rev. EMILE GENTILE, T.O.R., Dir., *P.O. Box 1800, Orlando, 32802.* Tel: 407-246-4875.

Catholic Social Services—THOMAS AGLIO, Dir., *1771 N. Semoran Blvd., Orlando, 32807.* Tel: 407-658-1818; Fax: 407-282-2891.

Cemeteries—Rev. THOMAS BARRETT, Dir., *P.O. Box 1800, Orlando, 32802.* Tel: 407-246-4870.

Censor of Books—Sr. LUCY VAZQUEZ, O.P., J.C.D., *Chancery Office, P.O. Box 1800, Orlando, 32802.*

Cursillos de Cristiandad—Rev. CON SHINE, Dir., *Immaculate Heart of Mary, P.O. Box 310, Candler, 32111.* Tel: 352-687-4031.

Prison & Jail Ministry—THOMAS GILLAN, *1771 N. Semoran Blvd., Orlando, 32807.* Tel: 407-658-1818.

Diocesan Pastoral Council—VITO NAPOLETANO, Bishop's Rep., *P.O. Box 1800, Orlando, 32802.* Tel: 407-246-4840.

Ecumenical Office—Rev. LARRY LOSSING, *P.O. Box 1800, Orlando, 32802.*

Education, Board of—Major CHUCK MORANT, Chm.

Education, Department of—MAUREEN HUNTINGTON, Ed.S., Supt., *P.O. Box 1800, Orlando, 32802.* Tel: 407-246-4900; Fax: 407-246-4940.

Family Life—ELAINE HENRIS, Dir., *P.O. Box 1800, Orlando, 32802.* Tel: 407-246-4865.

Farmworker Ministry, Office for—Rev. ROBERT MARKUNAS, Dir.; Sr. CATHERINE M. GORMAN, S.N.D.deN., Coord., *815 S. Park Ave., Apopka, 32703.* Tel: 407-886-5151; Fax: 407-884-6644.

Finance Committee—GERALD F. HILBRICH, *KPMG Peat Marwick, LTD., P.O. Box 3031, Orlando, 32802.*

Fiscal Management—JOHN WETTACH.

Hispanic Ministry Office—Rev. ROBERT MARKUNAS, Dir., *P.O. Box 1800, Orlando, 32802.* Tel: 407-246-4930; Fax: 407-246-4942.

Immigration Services—RICHARD LOGUE, Dir., *1771 N. Semoran Blvd., Orlando, 32807.* Tel: 407-658-0113; Fax: 407-249-5699.

Insurance Committee—ART HARRIS, Chm.

Lay Ministry Development—Dr. LINDA PERRONE ROONEY, Dir., *P.O. Box 1800, Orlando, 32802.* Tel: 407-246-4880; Fax: 407-246-4884.

Liturgical Commission—Rev. ROBERT WEBSTER, Dir., *P.O. Box 1800, Orlando, 32802.* Tel: 407-246-4860.

Newspaper—*"The Florida Catholic"*, HENRY LIBERSAT, Editor-Mgr., *P.O. Box 609512, Orlando, 32860-9512.* Tel: 407-660-9141.

Permanent Diaconate—Rev. EMILE GENTILE, T.O.R., Dir.; Deacon BOB KINSEY, Co-Dir., *P.O. Box 1800, Orlando, 32802.* Tel: 407-246-4875; Fax: 407-246-4942.

Priests' Continuing Education—Rev. RICHARD WALSH.

Priests Personnel—Rev. EMILE GENTILE, T.O.R., *P.O. Box 1800, Orlando, 32802.* Tel: 407-246-4875.

Propagation of the Faith—Rev. JOHN MCCORMICK, Dir., *Holy Redeemer, 1603 N. Thacker Ave., Kissimmee, 34741.* Tel: 407-846-3700.

Real Estate Committee—Rev. NICHOLAS KING, Chm., *P.O. Box 1800, Orlando, 32802.* Tel: 407-246-4800.

Refugee Resettlement—RICHARD LOGUE, Dir., *1771 N. Semoran Blvd., Orlando, 32807.* Tel: 407-658-0110; Fax: 407-249-5699.

Religious Education—Sr. LINDA L. GAUPIN, C.D.P., Ph.D., Dir., *P.O. Box 1800, Orlando, 32802.* Tel: 407-246-4910; Fax: 407-246-4940.

Media Center—DEBBIE O'MALLEY, Dir., *329 Broadway, Orlando, 32803.* Tel: 407-246-4895; Fax: 407-246-4942.

Respect Life Office—DEBORAH SHEARER, Dir., *1771 N. Semoran Blvd., Orlando, 32807.* Tel: 407-277-7266; Fax: 407-282-2891.

Scouting—*Office of Youth Ministry, P.O. Box 1800, Orlando, 32802.* Tel: 407-246-4910.

Sister Diocese-Mission Office—Sr. BERNADETTE MACKAY, O.S.U., Dir., *P.O. Box 1800, Orlando, 32802.* Tel: 407-246-4890; Fax: 407-246-4942.

Sister's Council—Sr. CLARICE MOYLE.

Society of St. Vincent de Paul—*P.O. Box 1800, Orlando, 32802.*

Spiritual Development—Rev. CARL VACEK, T.O.R., *2400 Dike Rd., Winter Park.* Tel: 407-671-6322.

Vietnamese Ministry—Rev. DUNG VAN "JOSEPH" BUI, *4001 Edgewater Dr., Orlando, 32804.* Tel: 407-293-9556.

Vocations—Rev. RICHARD TROUT, Dir., *P.O. Box 1800, Orlando, 32802.* Tel: 407-246-4875; Fax: 407-246-4942.

Youth Ministry—JULIE BUTSON MICKLER, M.A., *P.O. Box 1800, Orlando, 32802.* Tel: 407-246-4911; Fax: 407-246-4940.

CLERGY, PARISHES, MISSIONS AND PAROCHIAL SCHOOLS

CITY OF ORLANDO
(Orange County)

1—ST. JAMES CATHEDRAL (1881), Revs. Sean Heslin; J.P. Morgan; Rafael Villegas; Deacons Sam Ryan; Bruce Simpson.
Church—215 N. Orange Ave., 32801. Tel: 407-422-2005; Fax: 407-422-2009.
School—Tel: 407-841-4432; Fax: 407-648-4603.
Sisters 1; Lay Teachers 15; Students 377.
Catechesis/Religious Programs—Tel: 407-422-8624; Fax: 407-422-2009.
Students 381.
Mission—Orlando, Orange Co., St. Ignatius Kim Korean Mission, 1504 Muriel St., 32806. Tel: 407-897-6587. Rev. John Park.

2—BLESSED TRINITY (1965), Revs. James Henault, M.S.; Camillo Avitabile, M.S.; Rafael Villegas; Peter McKeown, M.S. In res., Revs. Matthew J. Connolly; William Kinney, M.S.
Res., 4545 E. Anderson Rd., 32812. Tel: 407-277-1702; Fax: 407-277-1973.
Catechesis/Religious Programs—Students 395.

3—GOOD SHEPHERD (1956), Revs. Eugene Barrette, M.S.; Joseph Kettner, M.S., Vicar; Jeffrey M. L'Arche, M.S.; Stephen J. Krisanda, M.S.
Mailing Address: 5900 Oleander Dr., 32807. Tel: 407-277-3938; Fax: 407-273-5148.
Res., 567 Hewitt Dr., 32807. Tel: 407-277-3938.
School—Tel: 407-277-3973; Fax: 407-277-2605.
Sisters 2; Lay Teachers 26; Students 550.
Pre-School—Tel: 407-277-1857.
Sisters 1; Lay Teachers 11; Students 101.
Catechesis/Religious Programs—Tel: 407-277-4200.
Students 622.

4—HOLY CROSS (1992), Rev. Robert Kurber.
Res., 12600 Marsfield Rd., 32837. Tel: 407-438-0990; Fax: 407-438-4090.
Catechesis/Religious Programs—Students 490.

5—HOLY FAMILY (1975), Revs. William Ennis; John O'Holohan, S.J.; Michael E. Giglio.
Res., 5125 S. Apopka-Vineland Rd., 32819. Tel: 407-876-2211; Fax: 407-876-1167. [JC]
School—5129 S. Apopka-Vineland Rd., 32819. Tel: 407-876-9344; Fax: 407-876-8775. Sr. Dorothy Sayers, M.P.F., Prin.; Sr. Angela Bulla, M.P.F., Asst. Prin.
Sisters 3; Lay Teachers 20; Students 590.
Catechesis/Religious Programs—Tel: 407-876-6331; Fax: 407-876-8775.
Students 1,000.

6—ST. ANDREW (1957), Revs. Ben Berinti, C.PP.S.; Rick Friebel, C.PP.S.; Tito Rojas; Deacons James M. Flynn; Heriberto Santana; Rafael Hernandez.
Res., 801 Hastings, 32808. Tel: 407-293-0730; Fax: 407-293-0739.
School—Tel: 407-295-4230.
Lay Teachers 24; Students 629.
Catechesis/Religious Programs—Students 333.

7—ST. CHARLES BORROMEO (1954), Revs. Donald G. Mainardi; Frank Cerio; Joseph Dung Van Bui; Deacon Richard Rupp. In res., Rev. Thomas Barrett.
Res., 4001 Edgewater Dr., 32804. Tel: 407-293-9556; Fax: 407-293-9213.
School—Tel: 407-293-7691.
Sisters of St. Joseph of St. Augustine 4; Lay Teachers 26; Students 595.
Preschool—Tel: 407-295-7041.
Lay Teachers 5; Students 58.
Catechesis/Religious Programs—Tel: 407-297-0284.
Students 84.

8—ST. ISAAC JOGUES (1987), Revs. Robert Hoeffner; Hernan Afanador; Deacons Robert Kloznick; Gerard W. White; Donald Warner; Angel Pacheco.
Mailing Address: P.O. Box 720009, 32872. Tel: 407-249-0906; Fax: 407-273-3236.
Catechesis/Religious Programs—Students 622.

9—ST. JOHN VIANNEY (1959), Revs. Paul J. Henry; Timothy Daly; Vidal Arboleda, (Retired); Carlos Bedoya; Deacon Miguel Beltran.
Res., 6200 S. Orange Blossom Tr., 32809. Tel: 407-855-5391; Fax: 407-859-3631.
School—Tel: 407-855-4660; Fax: 407-857-2760. Sr. Elizabeth Murphy, Prin.
Sisters of St. Francis of Philadelphia 5; Lay Teachers 25; Students 683.
Catechesis/Religious Programs—Tel: 407-859-1158. Tom Tagye, D.R.E.
Students 505.

10—ST. JOSEPH (1962) (Polish), Revs. Robert W. Brown; Larry Lossing; Joseph Piatek.
Res., 1501 N. Alafaya Tr., 32828. Tel: 407-275-0841.
Catechesis/Religious Programs—Tel: 407-282-7784.
Students 350.

OUTSIDE THE CITY OF ORLANDO

Altamonte Springs, Seminole Co., St. Mary Magdalen (1959), Revs. Charles I. Mitchell; Edward J. Thompson; Jose F. Munoz; Thomas Smith; Deacons Henry Libersat; Norm Kazyk; Jerry Kelly.
Res., 861 Maitland Ave., 32701. Tel: 407-831-1212; Fax: 407-831-1560.
School—Tel: 407-339-7301; Fax: 407-339-9556.
Sisters 3; Lay Teachers 31; Students 570.
Catechesis/Religious Programs—Tel: 407-834-2211.
Students 423.

Annunciation (1982), Revs. Patrick J. Caverly; Michael J. Cannon (Ireland); Christopher P. Caracci; Charles J. Deeney, O.M.I.
Mailing Address: P.O. Box 3846, Longwood, 32779. Tel: 407-869-9472; Fax: 407-869-4661.
Res., 1020 Montgomery Rd., 32714.
School—Annunciation Catholic Academy, (Grades K-8). Tel: 407-869-9404.
Lay Teachers 20; Students 450.
Catechesis/Religious Programs—Tel: 407-869-0934.
Students 1,450.

Apopka, Orange Co., St. Francis of Assisi (1966), Revs. Clyde A. Bonar; Tito Rojas; Deacons Julio Morales; Laurence Herbert.
Res., 834 S. Orange Blossom Trail, 32703. Tel: 407-886-4602; Fax: 407-886-9758.
Catechesis/Religious Programs—Students 525.

Barefoot Bay, Brevard Co., St. Luke (1986), Rev. Patrick J. Carroll.
Res., P.O. Box 779-114, 32976. Tel: 561-664-9310; Fax: 561-664-3374. [JC]

Bartow, Polk Co., St. Thomas Aquinas (1956), Rev. Domingo Gonzalez.
Res., 1305 E. Mann Rd., 33830. Tel: 941-533-4514.
Missions—Fort Meade, Polk Co., St. Elizabeth Ann Seton, 101 Edgewood, Fort Meade, 33841. Tel: 941-285-7390; Wahneta, Polk Co., Our Lady of Guadalupe, 2150 State Rd. 559, Wahneta, 33880. Tel: 941-299-3854. Rev. Norman Farland.
Catechesis/Religious Programs—Tel: 941-533-4514.
Students 107.

Belleview, Marion Co., St. Theresa (1951), Rev. James MacLoughlin.
Res., 11526 S.E. U.S. Hwy. 301, 34420. Tel: 904-245-2458; Fax: 904-245-1521.
Catechesis/Religious Programs—Tel: 904-245-5300.
Students 175.

Bushnell, Sumter Co., St. Lawrence (1959), Rev. F.X. Zammit.
Res., 223 E. Vermont Ave., Tel: 352-793-4636.
Church—320 E. Dade Ave., 33513. Tel: 352-793-7788.
Catechesis/Religious Programs—Students 85.
Mission—Wildwood, Sumter Co., St. Vincent de Paul Mission, 5195 E. CR 462, Wildwood, 34785. Tel: 904-330-0220.

Casselberry, Seminole Co., St. Augustine (1969), Revs. Joseph A. Genito, O.S.A.; John R. Flynn, O.S.A.; Kevin C. Mullins, O.S.A.
Res., 375 Sunset Dr., 32707. Tel: 407-695-3262; Fax: 407-699-8998.
Catechesis/Religious Programs—Students 342.

Clermont, Lake Co., Blessed Sacrament (1961), Rev. Andrew Wawrzycki.
Res., 720 12th St., 34711. Tel: 904-394-3562.
Catechesis/Religious Programs—Students 271.

Cocoa, Brevard Co., Blessed Sacrament (1967), Rev. Edmund S. Czarnecki; Deacon Richard J. Basso.
Mailing Address: P.O. Box 40, Sharpes, 32959.
Office: 5135 U.S. No. 1 N., 32927. Tel: 407-632-6333; Fax: 407-631-2560.
Catechesis/Religious Programs—Students 262.

Cocoa Beach, Brevard Co., Church of Our Saviour (1956), Rev. Eamon Tobin.
Res., 5301 N. Atlantic Ave., 32931. Tel: 407-783-4554; Fax: 407-868-6743.
School—Tel: 407-783-2330; Fax: 407-784-6330.
Lay Teachers 15; Students 224.
Catechesis/Religious Programs—Students 285.

Daytona Beach, Volusia Co., St. Paul's (1881), Revs. Robert E. Webster; Diego Londono; Peter A. Sagorski; Deacon Robert Landers.
Res., 317 Mullally St., P.O. Box 646, 32115. Tel: 904-252-5422; Fax: 904-252-1936.
School—Tel: 904-252-7915; Fax: 904-238-7903.
Lay Teachers 15; Students 297.
Catechesis/Religious Programs—Students 115.

Our Lady of Lourdes (1953), Rev. Philip J. Egitto. In res., Rev. Thomas J. Connery, S.D.B.
Res., 201 University Blvd., 32118. Tel: 904-255-0433; Fax: 904-238-1175.
School—Tel: 904-252-0391.
Lay Teachers 15; Students 240.
Catechesis/Religious Programs—Students 82.

DeBary, Volusia Co., St. Ann's (1959), Rev. Paige A. Blakely; Deacon William Cavins.
Res., 26 Dogwood Tr., P.O. Box 218, 32713-0218. Tel: 407-668-8270; Fax: 407-668-8471.
Catechesis/Religious Programs—Students 320.

De Land, Volusia Co., St. Peter's (1883), Rev. Msgr. Thomas Cannon, S.J.; Rev. William Gohring; Deacons Chester DeMarsh; Michael Alverez; Robert LaPlante; Joseph Costa; Robert Kinsey; Edward

Rinderle; Jack Lahart; Wilfred Steinmetz; Ronald Keehner.
Mailing Address: P.O. Box 3700, 32723. Tel: 904-822-6000.
Res., 359 W. New York Ave., 32720.
School—Tel: 904-822-6010; Fax: 904-822-6014. Mrs. Joan Kinsey, Prin.
Lay Teachers 16; Students 315.
Catechesis/Religious Programs—Ms. Colette Martineau, D.R.E.
Students 375.
Mission—Barberville, Volusia Co., San Jose Mission, 165 Emporia Rd., Barberville, 32005. Tel: 904-749-9372.

Deltona, Volusia Co., Our Lady of the Lakes (1970), Revs. Michael Hanrahan; Harry C. Wallace (SY); Oscar Salazar; Deacons Hervey Mondor; Ray Doyle; Bruno Wiencek; Dan Feinbaum; Gilberto Perez; Ricardo Gonzalez.
Res., 1310 Maximilian St., 32725. Tel: 407-574-2131; Fax: 407-860-0074.
Catechesis/Religious Programs—Tel: 407-574-4620.
Students 725.

St. Clare (1989), Rev. Christopher A. Hoffmann; Deacons Joseph Robert; Gilberto Torres; Charles Bernard.
Res., 2961 Day Rd., 32738. Tel: 904-789-9990; Fax: 904-789-2430.
Catechesis/Religious Programs—Students 207.

Dunnellon, Marion Co., St. John the Baptist (1976), Rev. Emilio G. Garcia; Deacon Fred Crawford, Jr.
Res., U.S. 41 N., P.O. Box 310, 34430. Tel: 352-489-3166; Fax: 352-489-3166.
Catechesis/Religious Programs—Students 106.

Eustis, Lake Co., St. Mary of the Lakes (1912), Revs. Manuel Fernandez; Richard Oser, S.J.; Deacon Louis Klein.
Res., 234 E. Badger Ave., 32726. Tel: 352-483-3500; Fax: 352-483-1370.
Catechesis/Religious Programs—Tel: 904-483-3458.
Students 372.

Goldenrod, Seminole Co., Saints Peter and Paul (1967), Revs. Sean K. Cooney; Pedro C. Puntal (Philippines); Deacons Al Castellana; James Campbell.
Mailing Address: P.O. Box 187, 32733. Tel: 407-657-6114; Fax: 407-657-9375.
Res., 5300 Howell Branch Rd., Winter Park, 32792.
Catechesis/Religious Programs—Fax: 407-657-9530.
Students 850.

Haines City, Polk Co., St. Ann (1969). (Formerly Transfiguration). Revs. Antonio Pons; Reinel Castro.
Res., 1311 E. Robinson Dr., P.O. Box 1285, 33845. Tel: 941-422-4370; Fax: 941-421-2522.
Catechesis/Religious Programs—Students 262.

Indialantic, Brevard Co., Holy Name of Jesus (1959), Revs. David Page; C. Stephen Lambour, C.S.C.; David Scotchie; Deacons Charles Foy; Joseph Richiuso.
Res., 3050 Hwy. A1A, 32903. Tel: 407-773-2783; Fax: 407-777-0929.
School—Tel: 407-773-1630; Fax: 407-773-7148.
Sisters 1; Lay Teachers 22; Students 384.
Catechesis/Religious Programs—Tel: 407-773-3905.
Students 629.

Kissimmee, Osceola Co., Holy Redeemer (1917) (Spanish), Revs. John McCormick; Luiz Bastos; Sante Reale, C.PP.S.
Res., 1603 N. Thacker Ave., 34741. Tel: 407-847-2500; 846-3700; Fax: 407-847-9687.
Catechesis/Religious Programs—Tel: 407-870-9055; Fax: 407-870-2214. Bro. James Needham, D.R.E.
Students 758.
Mission—Kissimmee, Osceola Co., St. Catherine of Siena, 430 Otter Creek Dr., P.O. Box 450698, 34745-0698. Tel: 407-344-9607; Fax: 407-344-9160. Rev. Vidal Martinez, O.S.M.

Lady Lake, Lake Co., St. Timothy (1985), Revs. Robert Fucheck; Louis J. Gonter.
1351 Paige Pl., 32159. Tel: 352-753-0989; Fax: 352-753-9602.

Lakeland, Polk Co.,

1—CHURCH OF THE RESURRECTION, (1963), Revs. Val J. Sheedy; Andrew Mallick; Deacon Joseph Wortman.
Res., 3720 Old Hwy. 37, 33813. Tel: 941-646-3556; Fax: 941-644-8697.
Catechesis/Religious Programs—Tel: 941-644-0585.
Students 376.

2—ST. ANTHONY'S, (1982), Revs. Vianney Cunningham, T.O.R.; Joseph M. Hayden; Richard Tucker; Roderick Soha, T.O.R. In res., Rev. Donald Frinsko.
Res., 820 Marcum Rd., P.O. Box 90164, 33804-0164. Tel: 941-858-8047; Fax: 941-859-1036.
School—(Grades PreK-3) 820 Marcum Rd., 33809. Tel: 941-858-0671. Sr. Michael Patrick Koegel, O.S.F.
Lay Teachers 11; Students 130.
Catechesis/Religious Programs—Tel: 941-858-8611.
Students 235.

3—ST. JOHN NEUMANN, (1988), Rev. Peter Uniowski.
Res., P.O. Box 1064, Mulberry, 33860-1064. Tel: 941-644-7201; Fax: 941-647-3691.
Church—501 E. Carter Rd., 33813. Tel: 941-647-3400.
Catechesis/Religious Programs—Tel: 941-647-3404.
Students 210.

4—ST. JOSEPH'S, (1898), Revs. John Caulfield; Franklin G. Buck; Reynord Araya-Morales; Deacons Marvin Busing; Joseph McCabe; James Coughlin; Antonio Martinez.
Res., 210 W. Lemon St., P.O. Box 30, 33802. Tel: 941-682-0555; Fax: 941-686-9546.
School—Tel: 941-686-6415.
Lay Teachers 18; Students 267.
Catechesis/Religious Programs—Tel: 941-687-8873.
Students 224.

Lake Wales, Polk Co., Holy Spirit (1927), Revs. Felix Banos; Leo Dobo, (Retired); Joseph R. Gurdak, O.F.M.Cap; Deacon Donald E. Raymond.
Res., 644 S. 9th St., P.O. Box 232, 33853. Tel: 941-676-1556; Fax: 941-676-2962.
Catechesis/Religious Programs—Tel: 813-678-1083.
Students 290.
Station—Nalcrest, Tel: 941-692-1057.

Leesburg, Lake Co., St. Paul's (1954), Revs. John C. Giel; Nicholas J. O'Brien; Deacon Lawrence Holder.
Res., 1330 Sunshine Ave., 34748. Tel: 352-787-6354; Fax: 352-787-5971.
School—Tel: 352-787-4657.
Lay Teachers 13; Students 130.
Catechesis/Religious Programs—Tel: 352-365-4252.
Students 180.

Longwood, Seminole Co., Church of the Nativity (1960), Revs. Kenneth R. Schnipke, C.PP.S.; Henry L. Frantz, C.PP.S.; Deacon Constantino Ferriola. In res., Rev. Norbert Adelman.
Res., 3255 N. County Rd. 427, 32750. Tel: 407-322-3961; Fax: 407-322-3981.
Catechesis/Religious Programs—Students 1,018.

Melbourne, Brevard Co., Our Lady of Lourdes (1931) (Spanish), Revs. William Nanley; Jose Bautista. In res., Rev. Matthew Mello; Deacons Howard Green; Dennis Jones; Sergio Colon.
Res., 1626 Oak St., 32902. Tel: 407-723-3636; Fax: 407-951-8029.
School—420 E. Fee Ave., 32901. Tel: 407-723-3631.
Lay Teachers 19; Students 269.
Catechesis/Religious Programs—Tel: 407-723-1224.
Students 175.

Ascension (1959), Revs. Francis X.J. Smith; Anthony Quinlivan, C.SS.R.; Deacons Richard Storum; Michael McElwee.
Mailing Address: 2950 N. Harbor City Blvd., 32935. Tel: 407-254-1595; Fax: 407-255-3490.
School—Tel: 407-254-5495; Fax: 407-259-0993.
Sisters of Mercy (Ardee, Ireland) 2; Lay Teachers 23; Students 541.
Catechesis/Religious Programs—Tel: 407-259-6693.
Students 711.

Melbourne Beach, Brevard Co., Immaculate Conception (1978), Rev. Joseph A. Nolan; Deacon Howard Pettengill, Jr.
Res., 3780 S. Hwy. A1A, 32951. Tel: 407-725-0552; Fax: 407-727-8218.
Catechesis/Religious Programs—Students 100.

Merritt Island, Brevard Co., Divine Mercy (1964), Revs. Edward McCarthy; Colin Kidd, O.F.M.; Kent A. Walker.
Res., 1940 N. Courtenay Pkwy., 32953. Tel: 407-452-5955; Fax: 407-455-2268.
School—Tel: 407-452-0263; Fax: 407-453-7573.
Sisters of Mercy (Galway) 2; Lay Teachers 16; Students 295.
Catechesis/Religious Programs—Tel: 407-459-2819; Fax: 407-455-2268.
Students 272.
Convent—1930 N. Courtenay Pkwy., 32953. Tel: 407-452-1279.
Sisters 2.

Mims, Brevard Co., Holy Spirit (1967), Rev. Bill Zamborsky.
Office: 2399 Holder Rd., 32754-2103. Fax: 407-269-2252.
Res., 2309 Holder Rd., 32754-2103. Tel: 407-269-2282; Fax: 407-269-2252. [JC]
Catechesis/Religious Programs—Tel: 407-269-7785.
Students 222.

Mount Dora, Orange Co., St. Patrick's (1973) (Hispanic), Revs. Emile Gentile, T.O.R.; Blase Romano, T.O.R.; Fred Thomas; Alfredo Ortiz; Deacon William Fisher.
Res., 6801 Old Hwy. 441 S., P.O. Box 211, 32757. Tel: 904-383-8556; Fax: 904-383-8443. [CEM]

New Smyrna Beach, Volusia Co., Sacred Heart (1926), Revs. Eugene Daigle, C.SS.R.; William Biffar, C.SS.R.; John Cavanaugh, C.SS.R.; Anthony Morris, C.SS.R.; Deacon George McMahon.
Res., 998 Father Donlan Dr., Box 729, 32170. Tel: 904-428-6426; Fax: 904-423-4088.
School—Tel: 904-428-4732; Fax: 904-428-4087.
Lay Teachers 18; Students 245.
Catechesis/Religious Programs—Blake Buruazos, D.R.E.
Students 209.
Mission—Edgewater, Volusia Co., 650 Roberts Rd., Edgewater, 32141. [CEM]

Our Lady Star of the Sea (1973), Rev. Thomas J. Bergin; Rev. Msgr. Francis Campagnone (BGP) (Retired); Deacon Paul Rock.
Res., 3837 Sandstone Ct., 32169. Tel: 904-427-4530; Fax: 904-423-6245.
Catechesis/Religious Programs—Tel: 904-427-4530; Fax: 904-423-6245.
Students 100.

Ocala, Marion Co.,

1—BLESSED TRINITY, (1922), Revs. Patrick J. Sheedy; Hugo Londono; Steven Phillips; Deacons James Boerstler; Vernon Krajeski; Harold Timmis.
Res., 5 S.E. 17th St., 34471. Tel: 904-629-8092; Fax: 904-351-8872.
School—Tel: 904-622-5808; Fax: 904-622-1660.
Lay Teachers 46; Students 601.
Catechesis/Religious Programs—Students 360.
Mission—Citra, Marion Co., Christ the King, 14047 N. U.S. Hwy. 301, Citra, 32112. Tel: 904-595-5605.

2—OUR LADY OF THE SPRINGS, (1982), Rev. William J. Neumann; Deacon John G. Collier, III.
Office—4047 N.E. 21st St., 34470. Tel: 352-236-2230; Fax: 352-236-1475.
Catechesis/Religious Programs—Fran Lopez, D.R.E. (Grades K-8).
Students 200.
Missions—Ocala National Forest, Marion Co., St. Joseph of the Forest, 17301 E. Hwy. 40, Silver Springs, 34488. Tel: 352-625-4222; Astor, Lake Co., St. Hubert of the Forest, P.O. Box 715, Astor, 32102. Tel: 352-236-2230.

3—QUEEN OF PEACE, (1987), Rev. Patrick J. O'Doherty; Deacon Richard Lacina.
Res., 6455 S.W. State Rd. 200, 34476. Tel: 904-854-2181; Fax: 904-854-7840. [JC]
Catechesis/Religious Programs—Students 96.

4—ST. JUDE'S, (1983), Rev. Anthony Palmese; Deacon Santos Santiago.
Res., 453 Marion Oaks Dr., 34473. Tel: 352-347-0154; Fax: 352-347-5211.
Catechesis/Religious Programs—Students 60.

Ormond Beach, Volusia Co., St. Brendan (1960), Revs. John J. Ryan; Steve Baumann.
Res., 136 Banyan Dr., 32176. Tel: 904-441-1505; Fax: 904-441-0774.
School—Tel: 904-441-1331.
Sisters 1; Lay Teachers 21; Students 308.
Catechesis/Religious Programs—Students 170.

Prince of Peace (1966), Revs. Thomas P. McMackin; Leo Hodges.
Res., 600 S. Nova Rd., 32174. Tel: 904-672-5272; Fax: 904-677-3224.
Catechesis/Religious Programs—Students 480.

Palm Bay, Brevard Co., Our Lady of Grace (1989), Revs. James Dore, O.S.M.; John Martin, O.S.M.; Deacons Richard C. Shaw; Francis Falatico.
Res., 115 Battersea S.E., 32909. Tel: 407-725-8742.
Church—300 Malabar Rd. S.E., 32907. Tel: 407-725-3066; Fax: 407-725-9534.
Catechesis/Religious Programs—Students 434.

St. Joseph (1914), Revs. Michael A. Farrell; Edward A. Hamilton; Chau Nguyen.
Res., 5330 Babcock St. N.E., P.O. Box 060507, 32906. Tel: 407-727-1565; Fax: 407-676-2579. [CEM]
School—Tel: 407-723-8866; Fax: 407-727-1181.
Sisters 2; Lay Teachers 15; Students 344.
Catechesis/Religious Programs—Tel: 407-725-5362.
Students 327.

Poinciana, Kissemmee Co., St. Rose of Lima (1994), Rev. Fernando Gil.
Res., 140 Pompei Dr., 34758. Tel: 407-932-5004; Fax: 407-932-0407.
Catechesis/Religious Programs—Students 170.

Port Orange, Volusia Co., Epiphany (1962), Rev. Paul T. Kamide. In res., Rev. Peter Mitchell.

Res., 201 Lafayette St., 32127. Tel: 904-767-6111; Fax: 904-767-0017.
Catechesis/Religious Programs—Students 285.
Our Lady of Hope (1981), Rev. Raymond J. O'Leary.
Res., P.O. Box 290216, 32129. Tel: 904-788-6144; Fax: 904-761-8840.
Catechesis/Religious Programs—Tel: 904-788-6747.
Students 350.

Rockledge, Brevard Co., St. Mary's (1917), Rev. Nicholas King; Rev. Msgr. Terence J. Farrelly, Pastor Emeritus; Rev. Patrick Grogan, (Retired).
Mailing Address: 75 Barton Ave., 32955. Tel: 407-636-6834; Fax: 407-632-4301. [JC]
School—Tel: 407-636-4208; Fax: 407-636-0591.
Sisters of Mercy (Limerick) 4; Lay Teachers 24; Students 572.
Catechesis/Religious Programs—Tel: 407-633-9985.
Students 330.

St. Cloud, Osceola Co., St. Thomas Aquinas (1968), Revs. Fabian G. Gimeno; Felicito S. Baybay.
Res., 701 Brown Chapel Rd., P.O. Box 700368, 34770-0368. Tel: 407-957-4495.
Church—900 Brown Chapel Rd., 34769.
School—800 Brown Chapel Rd., 34769. Tel: 407-957-1772.
Sisters 2; Lay Teachers 24; Students 486.
Catechesis/Religious Programs—Tel: 407-957-4057.
Students 325.

Sanford, Seminole Co., All Souls (1911), Revs. Richard W. Trout; Esau N. Garcia, C.P. (Columbia).
Res., 800 S. Oak Ave., 32771. Tel: 407-322-3795; Fax: 407-321-7255. [CEM]
School—Tel: 407-322-7090.
Sisters 1; Lay Teachers 13; Students 315.
Catechesis/Religious Programs—Students 344.

Silver Springs Shores, Marion Co., Immaculate Heart of Mary (1983), Revs. Sean Shine; Con Shine; Deacon Lou Bonneau.
Mailing Address: P.O. Box 310, Candler, 32111. Tel: 904-687-4031; Fax: 904-687-1811.
Catechesis/Religious Programs—Tel: 904-687-8818.
Students 46.

Titusville, Brevard Co., St. Teresa (1958), Revs. John S. Murray; Charles Viviano; Deacons Donald Boland; Charles I. Robichaud.
Res., Ojibway St., P.O. Box 1598, 32781. Tel: 407-268-3441; Fax: 407-268-3270.
School—Tel: 407-267-1643; Fax: 407-268-5124.
Sisters of Mercy (Gort, Ireland) 3; Lay Teachers 12; Students 307.
Catechesis/Religious Programs—Tel: 407-268-0440.
Students 288.
Convent—3380 Muirfield Dr., 32780. Tel: 407-267-1610.
Sisters 2.

Winter Garden, Orange Co., Resurrection (1967), Rev. Andrew O'Reilly, C.PP.S.
Church and Res.: P.O. Box 771257, 34777. Tel: 407-656-3113; Fax: 407-656-3113.
Catechesis/Religious Programs—Students 350.

Winter Haven, Polk Co., St. Joseph's (1923), Revs. Anthony Bluett; Joseph Pinchock; Deacon Nuoc Van Dang.
Res., 532 Ave. M N.W., 33881. Tel: 941-294-3144; Fax: 941-299-9709.
School—Tel: 941-293-3311.
Sisters of Notre Dame, Chardon, Ohio Province 3; Lay Teachers 21; Students 414.
Catechesis/Religious Programs—Students 296.
St. Matthew (1973), Rev. Fred R. Ruse.
Res., 365 Pasco Ct., 33884. Tel: 813-324-0357; Fax: 813-324-9181.
Catechesis/Religious Programs—Tel: 813-324-3559.
Students 200.

Winter Park, Orange Co., St. Margaret Mary (1947), Revs. Richard Walsh; Robert Wiseman, C.S.C.; Kurt Ewen.
Res., 526 N. Park Ave., 32789. Tel: 407-647-3392; Fax: 407-647-4492.
School—Tel: 407-644-7537.
Lay Teachers 28; Students 511.
Catechesis/Religious Programs—Tel: 407-647-5171.
Students 450.

Winter Springs, Seminole Co., St. Stephen (1985), Rev. John J. Bluett.
Res., 575 Tuscawilla Rd., 32708. Tel: 407-699-5683; Fax: 407-699-8408.
Catechesis/Religious Programs—Students 1,600.

Shrines

1—MARY QUEEN OF THE UNIVERSE SHRINE (1986), Revs. F. Joseph Harte; Barry Dowd; Fortune Frenoy, S.M.; William M. Boyle.
Res., 8300 Vineland Ave., 32821. Tel: 407-239-6600; Fax: 407-239-1362.

Special Assignment:
Reverend Fathers—
Barrett, Thomas, Office of Cemeteries
Blakely, Paige, Tribunal
Cleare, Rudi, Black/Haitian Ministry
Connolly, Matthew J., Officialis
Gentile, Emile A., T.O.R., Vicar for Clergy
Lossing, Larry, Office of Ecumenism
Markunas, Robert, Hispanic & Farmworker Ministry
Trout, Richard, Vocations
Walsh, Richard, Priests' Continuing Education
Webster, Robert, Office of Liturgy
Zammit, Francis X.

On Duty Outside the Diocese:
Reverend Fathers—
Gallagher, William
Henry, Peter, Switzerland
Ingram, James, U.S. Military
Kandel, Timothy, Miami
Mueller, Michael, U.S. Military
Stahl, Allen, U.S. Military
Traupman, Robert, Maryland

Sabbatical:
Reverend Fathers—
Bendixen, Arthur
Collins, Michael
Coyle, James, Inactive
Danen, Lyle
Finley, William
Granahan, Gerard, Inactive
Olds, Steve, Study in Rome
Uhran, Vernon

Retired:
Reverend Monsignors—
Bartok, Charles, P.O. Box 7261, Indian Lake Estates, FL 33855
Campagnone, Francis, 215 Cherry Wood Ln., Edgewater, FL 32132. Tel: 904-423-7360
Denehy, John, 460 Grant Ave., Satellite Beach, FL 32937
Farrelly, Terence J., 56 Barton Ave., Rockledge, FL 32955. Tel: 407-636-9099
Farris, Semaan, 604 Tupelo Dr., Melbourne, FL 32935. Tel: 407-255-2505
Gremillion, John E., 1190 Enterprise Rd., Enterprise, FL 32725
Reverend Fathers—
Angles, Sebastian, 2601 Muscatello St., Orlando, FL 32837. Tel: 407-851-1934
Arboleda, Vidal, St. John Vianney, 6200 S. Orange Blossom Tr., Orlando, FL 32809. Tel: 407-855-5391
Benitez, Eduardo, P.O. Box 1524, Davenport, FL 33837
Buzek, Joseph J., 1858 Maywood Rd., Winter Park, FL 32792. Tel: 407-671-1264
Cosgrove, J. Kelly, 4182 Mount Vernon Ave., Titusville, FL 32780. Tel: 407-267-8601
Dobo, Leo, P.O. Box 7245, Indian Lake Estates, FL 33855. Tel: 941-692-1057
Donnelly, Brendan, Little Mills House, Knockbridge Rd., Dundalk, County Louth, Ireland
Donohue, Peter, C.S.C., Christopher Lodge, 323 Arthur Ave., Cocoa Beach, FL 32931. Tel: 407-799-8383
Edwards, James F., P.O. Box 2188, Ormond Beach, FL 32175. Tel: 904-258-5293
Fanning, Leo, 14 Polar Bear Pk., Ormond Beach, FL 32174. Tel: 904-672-1725
Foley, William A., S.M., 31 Fillmore Ct., Satellite Beach, FL 32937. Tel: 407-773-7631
Franczek, Walter, 5062 S.E. 115th St., Belleview, FL 32620. Tel: 904-245-0658
Garvy, John, Blue Ridge Apartments, 108 N. Blue Ridge Rd., Black Mountain, NC 28711
Gonter, Louis J., 9980 S.E. 161st. Pl., Summerfield, FL 32691. Tel: 904-347-7289
Goodman, Frank, 350 S. Carolina Ave., Lake Alfred, FL 33850-2902
Grasso, Richard E., 88 Marvin Rd., Ormond Beach, FL 32176. Tel: 904-677-0188
Grogan, Patrick, St. Mary, 75 Barton Ave., Rockledge, FL 32955-2939. Tel: 407-636-6834
Hamilton, Edward, 1540 Waldorf Circle, N.E., Palm Bay, FL 32905. Tel: 407-768-6299
Hannon, Michael, 3581 Indigo Pond, Palm Harbor, FL 34685. Tel: 813-785-3900
Hayden, Joseph Mark, 4747 Road 33 N., #354, Lakeland, FL 33805. Tel: 941-686-8046
Hennes, Paul, 102 Wild Cherry Ave., Leesburg, FL 34748. Tel: 904-728-4716
Jennings, Francis, C.SS.R., St. Alphonsus Villa, P.O. Box 548, New Smyrna Beach, FL 32170
Jordan, Patrick, 880 Lancaster Rd., Deland, FL 32720. Tel: 904-740-1123
Karwacki, Marion T., 236 Lake Ira Dr. W., Winter Haven, FL 33884. Tel: 941-324-1385
Kidd, Colin, O.F.M., Divine Mercy, 1940 N. Courtenay Pkwy., Merritt Island, FL 32953. Tel: 407-452-5955
Knoll, Mark, C.SS.R., P.O. Box 1529, New Smyrna Beach, FL 32170-1529. Tel: 904-427-3094
Letourneau, F. E., The Veranda Nursing & Rehabilitation Center, 830 W. 29th St., Orlando, FL 32805
Lloyd, Vincent A., 713 Egret Ct., Edgewater, FL 32141. Tel: 904-423-8432
Lochner, Robert, C.S.C., Christopher Lodge, 323 Arthur Ave., Cocoa Beach, FL 32931. Tel: 407-799-8383
McNicholas, Stephen, 220-8 Moree Loop, Winter Springs, FL 32708
Mena, Jose, 501 N. Ocean St., Apt. 1703, Jacksonville, FL 32202
Mitzi, John J., P.O. Box 195878, Winter Springs, FL 32708
Moreau, George, (Jan.-June), P.O. Box 07267, Fort Myers, FL 33919
Moser, Charles J., S.M.A., 165 Bonita St., Titusville, FL 32780. Tel: 407-267-6863
Murphy, James, 1742 Colleen, Orlando, FL 32809. Tel: 407-851-1742
Nacca, John J., St. John the Baptist, P.O. Box 310, Dunnellon, FL 32630. Tel: 904-489-3166
Nolin, Joseph A., 219 Essex Dr., Ormond Beach, FL 32176. Tel: 904-441-2055
O'Farrell, William J., 320 Fleming Ave., Port Orange, FL 32019. Tel: 904-767-6114
O'Reilly, P. J., 2891 Nokomis Ave., Palm Bay, FL 32905. Tel: 407-724-6702
Pawlak, Edwin F., 2465 S. Washington Ave., Unit A106, Titusville, FL 32780. Tel: 407-269-6089
Power, Virgil, Sandy Oaks Park, 6760 N. Lecanto Hwy., Beverly Hills, FL 32665
Quinn, Peter, P.O. Box 7022, Daytona Beach, FL 32116
Rabideau, Richard, 1680 Sunny Brook Ln., Palm Bay, FL 32906. Tel: 407-725-9469
Redmond, Lawrence, P.O. Box 4159, St. Augustine, FL 32085
Rimshaw, Joseph J., S.S.J., 411 E. Lincoln Ave., Melbourne, FL 32901-4536. Tel: 407-723-1708
Ross, Kenneth, 604 White Plains Rd., East Chester, NY 10709
Serraino, Frederick, C.S.C., Christopher Lodge, 325 Arthur Ave., Cocoa Beach, FL 32931. Tel: 407-783-6312
Slafkosky, Andrew L., 610 Pine Rd., Silver Springs Shores, FL 34472. Tel: 904-687-8677
Thomas, Fred J., 11 Hawaiian Way, Leesburg, FL 34788. Tel: 904-742-1085
Tucker, Richard, 375 Brannen Rd., #229, Lakeland, FL 33813. Tel: 941-646-8744
VanNufflen, Albert, C.I.C.M., Aliki Condominium, 2828 N. Atlantic Ave., #202, Daytona Beach, FL 32118. Tel: 904-672-9098
Whipple, Donald, C.S.C., Christopher Lodge, 323 Arthur Ave., Cocoa Beach, FL 32931. Tel: 407-799-8383

Permanent Deacons:
Agers, Allen, (Retired), Holy Spirit, Mims
Almodovar, Ismael, Resurrection, Winter Garden
Alvarez, Jose M., St. Peter, DeLand
Barbieri, Robert, Inactive
Basso, Richard, Blessed Sacrament, Sharpes
Beltran, Miguel, St. John Vianney, Orlando
Bernard, Charles, St. Clare, Deltona
Boerstler, James, Blessed Trinity, Ocala
Boland, Donald, St. Teresa, Titusville
Bonneau, Louis, Immaculate Heart of Mary, Silver Springs Shores
Busing, Marvin, St. Joseph, Lakeland
Caloza, Dionisio, St. John Vianney, Orlando
Campbell, James, Sts. Peter & Paul, Goldenrod
Casares, Gabriel, St. Rose of Lima, Poinciana
Castellana, Al, Sts. Peter & Paul, Goldenrod
Cavins, William, St. Ann, DeBary
Collier, John, Our Lady of the Springs, Ocala
Colon, Sergio, Our Lady of Lourdes, Melbourne
Costa, Joseph, St. Peter, DeLand
Coughlin, James, St. Joseph, Lakeland
Crawford, Fred J., Jr., St. John the Baptist, Dunnellon
Crotty, John, St. Joseph, Orlando
Dang, Nuoc Van, St. Joseph, Winter Haven
de la Torre, Alfredo, Inactive
Decatrel, Leon, St. Joseph, Orlando
Del Papa, Richard, St. Timothy, Lady Lake
DeMarsh, Chet, Prince of Peace, Ormond Beach
Desjardins, Roland, On Duty Outside the Diocese
Deutsch, Nicholas, St. Timothy, Lady Lake
Diaz, Celso, Holy Cross, Orlando

Doyle, Raymond, (Retired), Our Lady of the Lakes, Deltona
Dwyer, Bruce, St. Mary, Rockledge
Falatico, Francis E., Our Lady of Grace, Palm Bay
Feinbaum, Daniel, Our Lady of the Lakes, Deltona
Ferriola, Constantino J., Nativity, Longwood
Fisher, William, Jr., St. Patrick, Mount Dora
Flynn, James, St. Andrew, Orlando
Foy, Les, Holy Name of Jesus, Indialantic
Gonzalez, Julio, Resurrection, Winter Garden
Gonzalez, Raphael, Resurrection, Winter Garden
Gonzalez, Ricardo, Our Lady of the Lakes, Deltona
Green, Howard, Our Lady of Lourdes, Melbourne
Gubatan, Nemsy, St. Margaret Mary, Winter Park
Henry, Vernon, Our Saviour, Cocoa Beach
Herbert, Larry, St. Francis of Assisi, Apopka
Hernandez, Rafael, St. Andrew, Orlando
Hindes, John T., St. Joseph of the Forest Mission, Silver Springs
Holder, Lawrence, St. Paul, Leesburg
Jones, Dennis, Our Lady of Lourdes, Melbourne
Kazyk, Norm, St. Mary Magdalen, Altamonte Springs
Keehner, Ron, St. Peter, DeLand
Kelly, Gerard, St. Mary Magdalen, Altamonte Springs
Kinsey, Robert, St. Peter, DeLand
Klein, Louis, (Retired), St. Mary of the Lakes, Eustis
Kloznick, Robert, St. Isaac Jogues, Orlando
Krajeski, Vernon, Blessed Trinity, Ocala
Lacina, Richard, Queen of Peace, Ocala
Lahart, John, St. Peter, DeLand
Lammers, Jack, St. Joseph of the Forest Mission, Silver Springs
Landers, Robert, St. Paul, Daytona Beach
LaPlante, Robert, St. Peter, DeLand
Libersat, Henry, St. Mary Magdalen, Altamonte Springs
Linford, Ronald, (Retired), On Duty Outside the Diocese
Maddex, Edward, Inactive
Maldonado, Eliezer, St. Catherine of Siena Mission, Kissimmee
Martin, Jack, Holy Cross, Orlando
Martin, Leonard, Holy Name of Jesus, Indialantic
Martinez, Antonio, St. Joseph, Lakeland
McCabe, Joseph, St. Joseph, Lakeland
McElwee, Michael, Ascension, Melbourne
McMahon, George, Sacred Heart, New Smyrna Beach
Messinger, George
Monat, Noe, St. Ann, Haines City
Mondor, Hervey, Our Lady of the Lakes, Deltona
Morales, Julio, St. Francis of Assisi, Apopka
Morales, Ramon, Holy Cross, Orlando
Murello, Andy, St. Mary, Rockledge
Ocasio, Roberto, St. Catherine of Siena Mission, Kissimmee
Olivo, Agapito, Centro Guadalupano Mission, Wahneta
Otradovec, Byron, St. Lawrence, Bushnell
Pacheco, Angel, St. Isaac Jogues, Orlando
Pellosie, John, Sts. Peter & Paul, Goldenrod
Perez, Gilberto, Our Lady of the Lakes, Deltona
Pettengill, Howard, Jr., Immaculate Conception, Melbourne Beach
Ramos, Epifanio, Inactive
Raymond, Donald, Holy Spirit, Lake Wales
Richiuso, Joseph, Holy Name of Jesus, Indialantic
Rinderle, Edward, St. Peter, DeLand
Rivera, Jose, St. Rose of Lima, Poinciana
Robert, Joseph, St. Clare, Deltona
Robichaud, Charles, St. Teresa, Titusville
Rock, Paul J., Our Lady Star of the Sea, New Smyrna Beach
Rodriguez, Alfonso, St. Joseph, Palm Bay
Roy, Reginald, On Duty Outside the Diocese
Rupp, Richard T., St. Charles Borromeo, Orlando
Ryan, Sam, St. James, Orlando
Sanborn, Philip, St. Theresa, Belleview
Santana, Heriberto, St. Andrew, Orlando
Santiago, Santos, St. Jude, Ocala
Shaw, Richard, Our Lady of Grace, Palm Bay
Simpson, Bruce, St. James, Orlando
Sowinski, James, On Duty Outside the Diocese
Steinmetz, Wilfred, St. Peter, DeLand
Storum, Richard, Ascension, Melbourne
Swart, Homer, Epiphany, Port Orange
Tagye, Thomas, Holy Spirit, Mims
Timmes, John, St. Margaret Mary, Winter Park
Timmis, Harold, Christ the King Mission, Ocala
Torres, Gilberto, St. Clare, Deltona
Warner, Donald, St. Isaac Jogues, Orlando
Wendel, David, St. John Neumann, Lakeland
White, Gerard, St. Isaac Jogues, Orlando
Wiencek, Bruno, Our Lady of the Lakes, Deltona
Wortman, Joseph, Resurrection, Lakeland

INSTITUTIONS LOCATED IN THE DIOCESE

[A] HIGH SCHOOLS, DIOCESAN AND PAROCHIAL

ORLANDO. *Bishop Moore High School*, 3901 Edgewater Dr., 32804. Tel: 407-293-7561. Rev. Tom Barrett. Priests 1; Lay Teachers 57; Students 1,025.

DAYTONA BEACH. *Father Lopez High School*, 960 Madison Ave., 32114. Tel: 904-253-5213. Mr. David Gonsalves, Prin.; Rev. Thomas Connery, Chap. Priests 1; Lay Teachers 27; Students 333.

LAKELAND. *Santa Fe Catholic High School*. (Grades 7-12), 3110 Highway 92 E., 33801. Tel: 941-665-4188; Fax: 941-665-4151. Ms. Mary Ellen Smith, Prin.; Rev. Vianney Cunningham, T.O.R., School Pastor. Priests 2; Sisters 1; Lay Teachers 24; Students 365.

MELBOURNE. *Central Catholic High School*, 100 E. Florida Ave., 32901. Tel: 407-727-0793; Fax: 407-727-1134. Mr. Joe Mancini, Prin.; Rev. Matthew Mello, School Pastor. Lay Teachers 48; Students 657.

[B] SPECIAL SCHOOLS

ORLANDO. *Morning Star School*, 954 Leigh Ave., 32804-2299. Tel: 407-295-3077. Sr. Elizabeth Marie Stoup, S.S.J., Prin. School for Exceptional Children. Sisters of St. Joseph of St. Augustine 2; Lay Teachers 7; Students 65.

[C] HOUSING ACCOMMODATIONS FOR THE ELDERLY

ORLANDO. *Monsignor Bishop Manor Apts., Inc.*, 824 Borders Cir., 32808. Tel: 407-293-3339; Fax: 407-295-3214.
For a complete listing, refer to the Special Care Facilities section.

DAYTONA BEACH. *Casa San Pablo*, 401 N. Ridgewood Ave., 32114. Tel: 904-253-2828.
For a complete listing, refer to the Special Care Facilities section.

MELBOURNE. *Ascension Manor*, 2960 Pineapple Ave., 32935. Tel: 407-757-9828.
For a complete listing, refer to the Special Care Facilities section.

OCALA. *Trinity Villas I, Inc.*, 3728 N.E. 8th Pl., 34470-1093. Tel: 904-694-5507; Fax: 904-694-7434.
For a complete listing, refer to the Special Care Facilities section.
Trinity Villas II, Inc., 3728 N.E. 8th Pl., 34470-1093. Tel: 904-694-5507; Fax: 904-694-7434.
For a complete listing, refer to the Special Care Facilities section.

ORMOND BEACH. *Prince of Peace Villas, Inc.*, 664 S. Nova Rd., 32174. Tel: 904-673-5080; Fax: 904-673-2008.
For a complete listing, refer to the Special Care Facilities section.

PORT ORANGE. *Epiphany Manor*, 4792 S. Ridgewood Ave., 32127.
For a complete listing, refer to the Special Care Facilities section.

WINTER HAVEN. *Episcopal Catholic Apartments*, 500 Ave. L N.W., 33881. Tel: 941-299-4481.
For a complete listing, refer to the Special Care Facilities section.

[D] RETREAT CENTERS

WINTER PARK. *San Pedro Spiritual Development Center*, 2400 Dike Rd., 32792. Tel: 407-671-6322; Fax: 407-671-3992. Revs. Carl Vacek, T.O.R., Dir.; Seraphin Conley, T.O.R.; Bros. Terence Thielen, T.O.R., Admin.; David Liedl, T.O.R. In res., Rev. Robert D'Aversa, T.O.R. Total Staff 4; Total in Residence 5.

[E] NEWMAN CENTERS OF CENTRAL FLORIDA

ORLANDO. *University of Central Florida Newman Center*, P.O. Box 26000, 32816. Tel: 407-823-5337. Rev. Charles Fiandaca, T.O.R.

DAYTONA BEACH. *Embry-Riddle Aeronautical University*, Office of the Chaplain, 600 S. Clyde Morris Blvd., 32114-3900. Tel: 904-226-6580. Rev. Leo Hodges, University Chap. & Dir. Campus Ministry.

DE LAND. *Stetson University Catholic Campus Ministry*, Newman House, 523 N. Amelia Ave., 32724. Tel: 904-822-8156. Rev. Chris Hoffmann; Deacon Edward Rinderle, Co-Dir. Total Staff 1.

LAKELAND. *Florida Southern College Newman Center*, c/o St. Anthony, P.O. Box 90164, 33804-0164. Tel: 941-858-8047. Rev. Vianney Cunningham, T.O.R. Total Staff 1; Total in Residence 1.

MELBOURNE. *Florida Institute of Technology Campus Ministry*, 150 W. University Blvd., 32901-6988. Tel: 407-768-8000, Ext. 8045. Rev. Douglas Bailey, S.D.S. Total Staff 2.

WINTER PARK. *Rollins College Campus Ministry*, c/o St. Margaret Mary, 526 Park Ave., N., 32789. Tel: 407-647-3392. Rev. Robert A. Wiseman, C.S.C.

[F] MONASTERIES AND RESIDENCES OF PRIESTS AND BROTHERS

ORLANDO. *Bethany House of Beutel*, 1600 Lakeside Dr., 32803. Tel: 407-894-8175. Revs. Jordan K. Grimes, C.P., Supr.; Conleth Overman, C.P.; Bro. Philip Frank, C.P. Prayer Center for Passionist Priests and Brothers.

COCOA BEACH. *Holy Cross Fathers, Eastern Priests Province*, 325 Arthur Ave., 32931-4065. Tel: 407-799-8383; Fax: 407-783-6312. Revs. Robert J. Brennan, C.S.C., Supr.; Robert McDonnell, C.S.C.; Robert J. Lochner, C.S.C.; Peter Donohue, C.S.C.; Cajetan Holland, C.S.C.; Philip C.M. Kelly, C.S.C.; Donald W. Whipple, C.S.C.; Bros. John Dolan, C.S.C.; Jerome Healey, C.S.C. Total Staff 2; Total in Residence 9.

NEW SMYRNA BEACH. *Redemptorist Fathers of the Vice Province of Richmond*, 313 Hillman St., P.O. Box 1529, 32170. Tel: 904-427-3094; 428-6481; Fax: 904-423-1270. Very Rev. Edward J. Gray, C.SS.R.; Revs. Mark Knoll, C.SS.R., Vice Prov. Procurator; Jack J. Fiske, C.SS.R., Leave of Absence; Joseph C. Rowan, C.SS.R.; Robert M. Pagliari, C.SS.R.; George Kelly, C.SS.R. Total Staff 6; Total in Residence 53.
St. Alphonsus Villa-Redemptorist Fathers and Brothers, 318 N. Riverside Dr., P.O. Box 548, 32170-0548. Tel: 904-428-6481. Revs. George Dorn, C.SS.R., Supr.; Walter Bueche, C.SS.R.; Mark Knoll, C.SS.R.; Lawrence Dolan, C.SS.R.; Paul T. Gillen, C.SS.R.; John Salamon, C.SS.R.; Leonard Cordier, C.SS.R.; Joseph Ellison, C.SS.R.; Donald Bolton, C.SS.R.; Joseph Rowan, C.SS.R.; Francis Donlan, C.SS.R.; Henry O'Toole, C.SS.R.; Leo Lanigan, C.SS.R.; James O'Malley, C.SS.R.; Bros. Thomas Kuhn, C.SS.R.; Louis Hoerner, C.SS.R. Total Staff 8; Total in Residence 16.

WINTER PARK. *Franciscan Friars, T.O.R., Provincial Residence, San Pedro Friary*, 2400 Dike Rd., 32792-8118. Tel: 407-671-6322; Fax: 407-671-3992.
Friars in Residence: Revs. Robert D'Aversa, T.O.R.; Seraphin Conley, T.O.R.; Carl Vacek, T.O.R.; Bros. Terence Thielen, T.O.R.; David Liedl, T.O.R. Total Staff 4; Total in Residence 5.
San Pedro Center, Third Order Regular of St. Francis, 2400 Dike Rd., 32792. Tel: 407-671-6322; Fax: 407-671-3992. Revs. Carl Vacek, T.O.R., Dir.; Seraphin Conley, T.O.R.; Bros. Terence Thielen, T.O.R., Admin.; David Liedl, T.O.R. In res., Rev. Robert J. D'Aversa, T.O.R. Total Staff 4; Total in Residence 5.

[G] MISCELLANEOUS

ORLANDO. *Good Shepherd Corporation of Orlando, Inc.*, 597-9 Bablonica Dr., 32807. Tel: 407-658-2909; Fax: 407-658-0005. Sr. Mary Brigid Lawlor, Pres. Total Assisted 30; Total Staff 2.

GOLDENROD.
**Catholic Volunteers in Florida, Inc.*, P.O. Box 702, 32733-0702. Tel: 407-331-6444; Fax: 407-331-6446. National recruitment for statewide (FL) placement of full-time volunteers in one-year service assignments. Co-sponsored by Florida's bishops, the Episcopal Advisor, is Most Reverend John J. Snyder. Ms. Gina C. Cawley, Volunteer Coord.; Mr. John R. Geiger, Dir. Staff 2; Lay Volunteers 10.

MELBOURNE. *Ascension Housing, Inc.*, 2950 N. Harbor City Blvd., 32935. Tel: 407-254-1595. Rev. Francis X.J. Smith, Contact Person.

WINTER GARDEN. *Sisters of St. Joseph's Architectural Stained Glass*, 930 Carter Rd., Ste. 212, 34787. Tel: 407-877-3220.

RELIGIOUS INSTITUTES OF MEN REPRESENTED IN THE DIOCESE

For further details refer to the corresponding bracketed number in the Religious Institutes of Men or Women section.

[0140]—*Augustinians.*—O.S.A.
[0470]—*Capuchin Friars.*—O.F.M.Cap.
[0610]—*Congregation of the Holy Cross (Southern Province).*—C.S.C.
[1000]—*Congregation of the Passion.*—C.P.
[0520]—*Franciscan Fathers.*—O.F.M.
[0690]—*Jesuit Fathers & Brothers.*—S.J.
[0760]—*Marist Fathers Society of Mary.*—S.M.
[7220]—*Missionaries of Our Lady of LaSalette.*—M.S.
[0910]—*Oblates of Mary Immaculate.*—O.M.I.
[0430]—*Order of Preachers (Dominican).*—O.P.
[1050]—*Pontifical Institute for Foreign Missions.*—P.I.M.E.
[1070]—*Redemptorist Fathers (Baltimore Province).*—C.SS.R.
[1190]—*Salesians of Don Bosco.*—S.D.B.
[1240]—*Servants of Mary (Servites).*—O.S.M.
[0110]—*Society of African Missions.*—S.M.A.

[1200]—*Society of the Divine Savior.*—S.D.S.
[1060]—*Society of the Precious Blood (Cincinnati Province).*—C.PP.S.
[0560]—*Third Order Regular of Saint Francis (Province of the Immaculate Conception).*—T.O.R.

RELIGIOUS INSTITUTES OF WOMEN REPRESENTED IN THE DIOCESE

[0230]—*Benedictine Sisters of Pontifical Jurisdiction.* (St. Petersburg).—O.S.B.
[3710]—*Congregation of the Sisters of St. Agnes.*—C.S.A.
[1070]—*Dominican Sisters.*—O.P.
[1180]—*Franciscan Sisters of Allegany, New York.*—O.S.F.
[2720]—*Mission Helpers of the Sacred Heart.*—M.H.S.H.
[2750]—*Missionary Sisters of the Immaculate Heart of Mary.*—I.C.M.
[3770]—*Order of St. Clare.*—O.S.C.
[3130]—*Our Lady of Victory Missionary Sisters.*—O.L.V.M.
[3320]—*Presentation Sisters of the Blessed Virgin Mary.*—P.B.V.M.
[2070]—*Religious of the Holy Union of the Sacred Hearts.*—S.U.S.C.
[3430]—*Religious Teachers Filippini.*—M.P.F.
[2970]—*School Sisters of Notre Dame.*—S.S.N.D.
[3590]—*Servants of Mary (Servite Sisters).*—O.S.M.
[]—*Sisters for Christian Community.*—S.F.C.C.
[0440]—*Sisters of Charity of Cincinnati, Ohio.*—S.C.
[0430]—*Sisters of Charity of the Blessed Virgin Mary.*—B.V.M.
[0990]—*Sisters of Divine Providence.*—C.D.P.
[2360]—*Sisters of Loretto at the Foot of the Cross.*—S.L.
[2640]—*Sisters of Mercy from Ireland.* (Meath Community).—R.S.M.
[2535]—*Sisters of Mercy from Ireland.* (Galway).—R.S.M.
[2523]—*Sisters of Mercy from Ireland.* (Longford).—R.S.M.
[2530]—*Sisters of Mercy from Ireland.* (Ardee-Dundalk).—R.S.M.
[2560]—*Sisters of Mercy from Ireland.* (Ennis).—R.S.M.
[2550]—*Sisters of Mercy from Ireland.* (Limerick).—R.S.M.
[2575]—*Sisters of Mercy of the Americas.*—R.S.M.
[2990]—*Sisters of Notre Dame.* (Chardon, OH).—S.N.D.
[3000]—*Sisters of Notre Dame de Namur.*—S.N.D.deN.
[3080]—*Sisters of Our Lady of Christian Doctrine.*—R.C.D.
[1570]—*Sisters of St. Francis of the Holy Family.*—O.S.F.
[1630]—*Sisters of St. Francis of Penance & Christian Charity.*—O.S.F.
[1650]—*Sisters of St. Francis of Philadelphia.*—O.S.F.
[3840]—*Sisters of St. Joseph of Carondelet.* (St. Louis, MO).—C.S.J.
[3850]—*Sisters of St. Joseph of Chambery.*—C.S.J.
[3900]—*Sisters of St. Joseph of St. Augustine, Florida.*—S.S.J.
[1830]—*Sisters of the Good Shepherd.*—R.G.S.
[1990]—*Sisters of the Holy Names of Jesus and Mary.*—S.N.J.M.
[2160]—*Sisters, Servants of the Immaculate Heart of Mary.* (Scranton, PA).—I.H.M.
[4110]—*Ursuline Nuns.*—O.S.U.

NECROLOGY

† Fahey, Cieran James, (Retired). —Died Nov. 15, 1995.

Diocese of Owensboro

(Dioecesis Owensburgensis)

Most Reverend

JOHN J. McRAITH, D.D.

Bishop of Owensboro; ordained February 21, 1960; appointed October 23, 1982; consecrated December 15, 1982. *Res., 501 W. Fifth St., Owensboro, KY, 42301. Address correspondence to: 600 Locust St., Owensboro, KY, 42301; Fax: 502-683-6883.*

CREATED DECEMBER 9, 1937.

ERECTED FEBRUARY 23, 1938.

Square Miles 12,502.

Comprises the following thirty-two Counties in the western part of the State of Kentucky: Allen, Ballard, Breckinridge, Butler, Caldwell, Calloway, Carlisle, Christian, Crittenden, Daviess, Edmonson, Fulton, Graves, Grayson, Hancock, Henderson, Hickman, Hopkins, Livingston, Logan, Lyon, McCracken, McLean, Marshall, Muhlenberg, Ohio, Simpson, Todd, Trigg, Union, Warren and Webster.

For legal titles of parishes and diocesan institutions, consult the Catholic Pastoral Center.

Catholic Pastoral Center: 600 Locust St., Owensboro, KY, 42301. Tel.: 502-683-1545; Fax: 502-683-6883.

STATISTICAL OVERVIEW

Personnel	
Bishop	1
Priests: Diocesan Active in Diocese	63
Priests: Active Outside Diocese	4
Priests: Retired, Sick or Absent	15
Number of Diocesan Priests	82
Religious Priests in Diocese	10
Extern Priests in Diocese	2
Ordinations:	
Diocesan Priests	1
Total Brothers	1
Total Sisters	242
Parishes	
Parishes	79
With Resident Pastor:	
Resident Diocesan Priests	48
Resident Religious Priests	4
Without Resident Pastor:	
Administered by Priests	24
Administered by Women Religious	2
Pastoral Centers	2
New Parishes Created	1
Professional Ministry Personnel:	
Sisters	39
Lay Ministers	34
Welfare	
Catholic Hospitals	1
Total Assisted	85,000
Health Care Centers	2
Total Assisted	8,000
Homes for the Aged	2
Total Assisted	176
Day Care and Extended Day Care Centers	3
Total Assisted	136
Special Centers for Social Services	2
Total Assisted	16,000
Educational	
Diocesan Students in Other Seminaries	17
Total Seminarians	17
Colleges and Universities	1
Total Students	760
High Schools, Diocesan and Parish	3
Total Students	1,034
Elementary Schools, Diocesan and Parish	19
Total Students	4,415
Catechesis/Religious Education:	
High School Students	1,326
Elementary Students	3,703
Total Students Under Catholic Instruction	11,255
Teachers in the Diocese:	
Priests	1
Brothers	1
Sisters	12
Lay Teachers	273
Vital Statistics	
Receptions into the Church:	
Infant Baptism Totals	976
Adult Baptism Totals	203
Received into Full Communion	233
First Communions	1,086
Confirmations	1,143
Marriages:	
Catholic	248
Interfaith	261
Total Marriages	509
Deaths	523
Total Catholic Population	51,339
Total Population	778,235

Former Bishops—Most Rev. FRANCIS R. COTTON, D.D., First Bishop of Owensboro; ord. June 17, 1920; appt. Dec. 16, 1937; cons. Feb. 24, 1938; died Sept. 25, 1960.—Most Rev. HENRY J. SOENNEKER, D.D., Second Bishop of Owensboro; ord. May 26, 1934; appt. March 10, 1961; cons. April 26, 1961; installed May 9, 1961; retired June 17, 1982; died Sept. 24, 1987.

Catholic Pastoral Center—600 Locust St., Owensboro, 42301. Tel: 502-683-1545; Fax: 502-683-6883. Refer all official business to this address.

Vicar General—Rev. JOSEPH M. MILLS, J.C.L., *Res., 5856 Ky. 81, Owensboro, 42301.* Tel: 502-685-0339.

Chancellor—Sr. JOSEPH ANGELA BOONE, O.S.U.

Archivist—Sr. EMMA CECILIA BUSAM, O.S.U.

Diocesan Tribunal—

Judicial Vicar—Rev. J. PATRICK REYNOLDS, J.C.L.

Adjutant Judicial Vicar—Vacant.

Defender of the Bond—Rev. KEVIN KARL.

Judges—Revs. LEONARD ALVEY; J. PATRICK REYNOLDS, J.C.L.; JOHN VAUGHAN, J.C.D.

Advocates—Priests and pastoral ministers of the diocese.

Case Promoters—Sr. VIVIAN MARIE BOWLES, O.S.U.

Administrative Assistants—Mrs. MARY ANN KURZ; Mrs. KAY M. RHODES.

Diocesan Boards and Councils

Diocesan Pastoral Council—Mr. MIKE THOMPSON; Ms. ANN MULLIGAN; Ms. FAY HIGDON; Sr. MAGGIE COOPER, S.C.N.; Mr. JIM TIDWELL; Ms. PAT MCGRUDER; Sr. EVA BOONE, O.S.U.; Mr. TOM HAYDEN; Sr. EULA JOHNSON, S.C.N.; Mr. DRURY HOWARD; Rev. HENRY WIEDER; Ms. SUE GRAY; Rev. RAY CLARK; Ms. JUDY MCCELLAN; Ms. HELEN WILLETT; Ms. BARBARA PENNER; Mr. LARRY HIGDON; Ms. JANE HOBBS; Mr. RAY GIARDINELLA; Mr. JIM SCOTT; Mr. PAUL BACHI; Mr. ZACK HODGES.

Consultors—Revs. KEVIN KARL; RAY CLARK; GREGORY TRAWICK; LEONARD ALVEY; Rev. Msgr. GEORGE HANCOCK.

Deans—Bowling Green: Rev. GERALD CALHOUN, Central: Rev. HENRY WIEDER, Eastern: Rev. BRAD WHISTLE, Fancy Farm: Rev. DELMA CLEMONS, Hopkinsville: Rev. JERRY BAKER, The Lakes: Rev. MAURICE TIELL, Owensboro: Rev. JOHN VAUGHAN, Paducah: Rev. JERRY RINEY.

Priests' Council—Revs. JOSEPH M. MILLS; MAURICE TIELL; GERALD CALHOUN; LEONARD ALVEY; KEVIN KARL; RAY CLARK; BRAD WHISTLE; GREG TRAWICK; Rev. Msgr. GEORGE HANCOCK; Revs. HENRY WIEDER; DELMA CLEMONS; JERRY BAKER; JOHN VAUGHAN; JERRY RINEY.

Council of Religious—Sr. EVA BOONE, O.S.U.; Sr. ELAINE BURKE, O.S.U.; Sr. CHARLES MARY BURNS, S.C.N.; Sr. EULA JOHNSON, S.C.N.; Sr. JOLINDA NAAS, O.S.B.; Sr. MARY LYNNE WROCKLAGE, G.H.M.S.; Sr. NANCY MURPHY, O.S.U.; Sr. ROSEMARY ESTERKAMP, G.H.M.S.

Pastoral Office for Administration—Sr. JOSEPH ANGELA BOONE, O.S.U., Dir.

Pastoral Office for Stewardship—Mr. TOM LILLY, Dir.

Committee for Administration—Mr. HOMER BARTON; Ms. JANET BERRY; Ms. BECKY LUCKETT; Sr. JOANN MARK, A.S.C.; Mr. CHARLES KAMUF; Mr. JOSEPH HANCOCK; Mr. LOUIS HAAS; Revs. BRAD WHISTLE; JOE MILLS; MARTY HAYES; Mr. MIKE THOMPSON.

Pastoral Office for Education—

Superintendent of Schools—Mr. JOSEPH O'BRYAN.

Director of Religious Education—Sr. KATHY GALLO, O.S.U.

Committee for Education—Mr. DEL HAYDEN; Rev. LEONARD ALVEY; Ms. JUDY MCCLELLAN; Sr. JOLINDA NAAS, O.S.B.; Rev. BOB WILLETT; Dr. DAN STUMPF; Ms. VICKIE CASH; Mr. PHIL HAIRE; Mr. STEVE SHOULTA; Ms. BARBARA KOONCE; Sr. ROSEANNE SPALDING, O.S.U.; Ms. BONNIE MARKS; Ms. JANET MURPHY; Ms. ANGEL PAYNE; Ms. CAROL HIGDON; Mr. KEVIN LAURENT.

Director of Ecumenism—Rev. JOSEPH O'DONNELL, Glmy., *P.O. Box 106, Beaver Dam, 42320.* Tel: 502-274-3414.

Director of Youth Ministry—Rev. HENRY WIEDER.

Director of Communications and Editor of the Diocesan Newspaper "Western Kentucky Catholic"—Mr. MEL HOWARD.

Pastoral Office for Worship—Rev. LARRY MCBRIDE, Dir. MARTHA HAGAN, Assoc. Dir.; Ms. PATTY BROWN, Dir. Diocesan Office for Music.

Diocesan Liturgical Committee—Revs. THOMAS CLARK; LARRY MCBRIDE, Chm.; Sr. LARRAINE LAUTER, O.S.U., Chm.; Rev. DARRELL VENTERS; Mr. MIKE CONLEY; Ms. SUE ECKMANS; Mr. NORMAN HOWARD; Sr. ANNALITA LANCASTER, O.S.U.; Rev. JOHN THOMAS; Ms. CLEO HIGDON; Sr. ALICIA COOMES, O.S.U.

Pastoral Office for Spiritual Life—Sr. DARLENE DENTON, O.S.U., *Mount St. Joseph, Maple Mount, 42356.* Tel: 502-229-4103.

Cursillo—Rev. TERRY DEVINE, Dir., *1317 Main St., Sturgis, 42459.* Tel: 502-333-4645.

Pastoral Office for Adult Formation—Sr. JULIA HEAD, O.S.U.

Pastoral Office for Outreach and Lay Ministry—Sr. PATRICIA FRONING, O.S.F., Dir.

Pastoral Office for Social Concerns—LEETA SHUECRAFT, Dir.

Diocesan Social Concerns Committee—LIZ FRANCIS; Sr. MAGGIE COOPER, S.C.N.; Sr. ROSE JEAN POWERS; Mr. JACK ALLARD; Ms. BARBARA HERTEL; Mr.

DAN ROBINSON; Ms. GLORIA ADAMS.
Catholic Relief Service Director—Ms. LEETA SHUECRAFT.
Campaign for Human Development—Ms. LEETA SHUECRAFT.
Respect Life Office—Ms. LEETA SHUECRAFT.
Rural Life Office—Ms. LEETA SHUECRAFT.
Mission Office—Rev. JOSEPH M. MILLS.
Pastoral Ministry with Refugees—Sr. THERESA MARIE WILKERSON, O.S.U.
Pastoral Office for Family Life—EDWINA HYLAND, Dir.
Diocesan Family Life Committee—JUDY KAPELSOHN; TOM HEILERS; KAREN HEILERS; MARTHA CRABTREE; ED PRUNTY; MELINDA PRUNTY; TOM HAYDEN; JOYCE HAYDEN; Rev. ED BRADLEY; GERALD GILLIAM; CASSIE GILLIAM; GAIL CRITCHELOW; DAVE FUSTING; CAROLYN FUSTING; CAROL YANIK.
Natural Family Planning—EDWINA HYLAND.
Pastoral Office for Personnel—
Priest Personnel Committee—Revs. GERALD CALHOUN; BRUCE FOGLE; PAUL POWELL; JERRY RINEY; JOHN THOMAS; DARRELL VENTERS.
Vocations Office—Rev. BRAD WHISTLE, *St. Romuald Parish, Hardinsburg, 40143.* Tel: 502-756-2356.
Continuing Education for Priests—Rev. RICHARD MEREDITH, *St. Joseph Parish, 434 Church St., Bowling Green, 42101.* Tel: 502-842-2525.
**Roman Catholic Diocese of Owensboro Charitable Trust Fund, Inc.*—Most Rev. JOHN J. MCRAITH; Revs. JOE MILLS; KEVIN KARL.
Hispanic Ministries—Sr. FRAN WILHELM, O.S.U., *91 Church St., O'boro, 42301.* Tel: 502-764-1484.

Organizations

St. Vincent de Paul Society—DAVID OSBORNE, *3507 Dove Loop N., Owensboro, 42301.*
Scouting Activities—Rev. HENRY WIEDER; Rev. STEVE ULRICH, Chap., *600 Locust St., Owensboro, 42301.* Tel: 502-683-1545.
Holy Childhood Association—Rev. JOSEPH M. MILLS.
Teens Encounter Christ—Rev. HENRY WIEDER, *600 Locust St., Owensboro, 42301.* Tel: 502-683-1545.
Legion of Mary—Vacant.

CLERGY, PARISHES, MISSIONS AND PAROCHIAL SCHOOLS

CITY OF OWENSBORO (Daviess County)

1—ST. STEPHEN CATHEDRAL, Revs. John R. Vaughan; Andy Ausenbaugh. Pastoral Assocs.: Sr. Ann McGrew; Mr. Larry Lyon.
Res., 614 Locust St., 42301. Tel: 502-683-6525; Fax: 502-683-3621.
Chapel—Blessed Sacrament Chapel, 602 Sycamore St., 42301. Tel: 502-926-4741. [CEM]
Rev. William Allard; Gloria Adams, Admin.

2—BLESSED MOTHER, Revs. C. Phil Riney; Carl McCarthy; Jan Storm, Admin. Asst.; Sr. Mary Henning, Music Coord.; Patricia Blair, Pastoral Assoc.
Office: 515 E. 22nd St., 42303.
Res., 601 E. 23rd St., 42303. Tel: 502-683-8444. [CEM]

3—THE IMMACULATE, Rev. Timothy Sweeney, O.S.B.; Sr. Geneva Stumler, O.S.B., Pastoral Assoc.
Parish Office: 2516 Christie Pl., 42301. Tel: 502-683-0689; Fax: 502-926-9016.
Res., 2601 Christie Pl., 42301. [CEM]

4—OUR LADY OF LOURDES, Rev. John Meredith.
Res., 4029 Frederica St., 42301. Tel: 502-684-5369; Fax: 502-683-8008. [CEM]

5—PRECIOUS BLOOD, Rev. Darrell Venters; Sr. Larraine Lauter, O.S.U., Pastoral Assoc.
Res., 3306 Fenmore St., 42301. Tel: 502-684-6888. [CEM]

6—ST. PIUS TENTH, Rev. Larry McBride.
Res., 3512 E. Sixth St., 42303. Tel: 502-684-5517. [CEM]

7—SS. JOSEPH AND PAUL, Rev. Kevin Karl. Pastoral Ministers: Martha Crabtree; Martha McCarty.
Res., 609 E. 4th St., 42303. Tel: 502-683-5641; Fax: 502-685-4766. [CEM]

OUTSIDE THE CITY OF OWENSBORO

Aurora, Marshall Co., St. Henry, Rev. Msgr. Richard L. Cash.
Res., 16097 U.S. Hwy. 68 E., Hardin, 42048. Tel: 502-474-8058. [CEM]

Axtel, Breckinridge Co., St. Anthony, Rev. Bruce Fogle.
Res., R.R. 3, Hardinsburg, 40143. Tel: 502-257-2132. [CEM]

Bardwell, Carlisle Co., St. Charles, Rev. Anthony Stevenson.
Res., R.R. 2, Box 317, 42023. Tel: 502-642-2586; Fax: 502-642-2586. [CEM]

Beaver Dam, Ohio Co., Holy Redeemer, Rev. Joseph O'Donnell, Glmy.; Sr. Luisa Bickett, O.S.U., Pastoral Assoc.
Office: P.O. Box 106, 42320. Tel: 502-274-3414.; 768 Horse Branch Loop, Horse Branch, 42349. Tel: 502-274-4285.

Big Clifty, Grayson Co., St. Mary. Closed. Records kept at St. Joseph's Church, Leitchfield.

Bowling Green, Warren Co., St. Joseph's, Rev. Richard Meredith.
Res., 434 Church St., 42101. Tel: 502-842-2525; Fax: 502-842-2525. [CEM]
Holy Spirit, Revs. Gerald Calhoun; Stan Puryear; Ms. Anita Willoughby, Pastoral Assoc.
Res., 2232 Smallhouse Rd., 42104-4141. Tel: 502-842-7777; Fax: 502-842-6174. [CEM]

Brown's Valley, Daviess Co., St. Anthony, Rev. Tony Jones.
Church—261 St. Anthony Rd., Utica, 42376. Tel: 502-733-4341. [CEM]

Cadiz, Trigg Co., St. Stephen, Rev. Leonard Arcilesi.
Res., 1698 Canton Rd., 42211. Tel: 502-522-3801.

Calhoun, McLean Co., St. Sebastian, Rev. Frank Roof.
Res., 180 State Rte. 136 W., 42327-9521. Tel: 502-273-3185.

Calvert City, Marshall Co., St. Pius Tenth, Rev. Aloysius Powers, Admin. Pastoral Assocs.: Sr. Lisa Marie Cecil, O.S.U.; Sr. Mary Edgar Warren, O.S.U.
Res., P.O. Box 495, 42029. Tel: 502-395-4727.

Central City, Muhlenberg Co., St. Joseph, Rev. Francis Mastrovito, T.O.R.; Sr. Rose Karen Johnson, O.S.U., Pastoral Assoc.
Res., 113 S. Third St., 42330. Tel: 502-754-1164.

Clarkson, Grayson Co., St. Elizabeth of Hungary, Rev. Charles G. Fischer.
Res., 1821 St. Paul Rd., Leitchfield, 42754. Tel: 502-242-7436. [CEM]

Clinton, Hickman Co., St. Jude, Rev. Steven Ulrich; Sr. Diane M. Payne, O.S.U., Pastoral Assoc.
Res., 42031. Tel: 502-653-6869.

Cloverport, Breckinridge Co., St. Rose, Rev. Tom Clark.
Res., 118 Chestnut St., 40111. Tel: 502-788-6422. [CEM]

Curdsville, Daviess Co., St. Elizabeth, Rev. Robert Drury.
Mailing Address: P.O. Box 9-A, 42334. Tel: 502-229-4134.

Dawson Springs, Hopkins Co., Resurrection, Rev. Martin Mattingly.
Res., 530 Industrial Park Rd., 42408. Tel: 502-383-4743; Fax: 502-383-5819.
Church—Tel: 502-797-8665.

Earlington, Hopkins Co., Immaculate Conception, Rev. Martin Mattingly.
Res., 125 S. Day St., 42410. Tel: 502-383-4743; Fax: 502-383-5819.

Eddyville, Lyon Co., St. Mark Church, Rev. Maurice J. Tiell.
Res., 302 Peachtree Ln., P.O. Box 1205, 42038-1205. Tel: 502-388-2133.
Stations—Kentucky State Penitentiary, Tel: 502-388-2133; Western Kentucky Correctional Complex, Tel: 502-388-2133.

Elkton, Todd Co., St. Susan, Rev. Thomas S. Charters. Pastoral Assocs.: Sr. Bernadette Hengstebek, G.H.M.S.; Sr. Catherine Schoenborn, G.H.M.S.
Res., P.O. Box 788, 42220. Tel: 502-265-5263.

Fancy Farm, Hickman Co., St. Denis, Rev. Anthony Stevenson.
Res., St. Charles Church, R.R. 2, Box 317, Bardwell, 42023. Tel: 502-642-2586; Fax: 502-642-2586. [CEM]
St. Jerome, Graves Co., Rev. Delma Clemons.
Res., P.O. Box 38, 42039. Tel: 502-623-8181; Fax: 502-623-6341. [CEM]
Catechesis/Religious Programs—Tel: 502-623-8181; Fax: 502-623-6341. Sr. Anastasia Lamb, D.R.E.
Students 279.

Fordsville, Ohio Co., St. John the Baptist, Rev. Joseph O'Donnell, Glmy.; Sr. Eva Marie Boone, O.S.U., Pastoral Assoc.
Res., P.O. Box 127, 42343. Tel: 502-276-3619.

Franklin, Simpson Co., St. Mary of the Woods, Rev. Frank Ruff, Glmy., Sacramental Min.; Sr. Lene Rubly, O.S.F., Pastoral Coord.; Sr. Davida Loosbrock, O.S.F., Pastoral Assoc.
Res., Box 388, 42135. Tel: 502-586-4515. [CEM]

Fulton, Fulton Co., St. Edward, Rev. Stephen W. Ulrich.
Res., 504 Eddings St., 42041. Tel: 502-472-2742; Fax: 502-472-2742.

Grand Rivers, Livingston Co., St. Anthony of Padua. (Grand Rivers Catholic Church). Rev. Msgr. George H. Hancock; Sr. Rosemary Esterkamp, G.H.M.S.
Res., 1518 J.H. O'Bryan Ave., P.O. Box 447, 42045. Tel: 502-362-0408.

Grayson Springs, Grayson Co., St. Augustine, Rev. Gary Hayes.
Res. & Mailing Address: c/o St. Anthony Church, 1256 St. Anthony Church Rd., Clarkson, 42726. Tel: 502-242-4791; Fax: 502-242-2601. [CEM]

Guthrie, Todd Co., Sts. Mary & James, Rev. Thomas S. Charters, G.H.M.S. Pastoral Ministers: Sr. Bernadette Hengstebeck, G.H.M.S.; Sr. Catherine Schoenborn, G.H.M.S.
Res., P.O. Box 325, 42234. Tel: 502-483-2571.

Hardinsburg, Breckinridge Co., St. Romuald, Revs. J. Brad Whistle; Pete Hughes; Sr. Martha Keller, O.S.U., Pastoral Assoc.
Res., 40143. Tel: 502-756-2356; Fax: 502-756-2099. [CEM]

Hawesville, Hancock Co., Immaculate Conception, Rev. Tony Bickett. Pastoral Assocs.: Sr. Karla Marie Kaelin, O.S.U.; Sr. Rita Lechner, S.P.
Res., 42348. Tel: 502-927-8419. [CEM]

Henderson, Henderson Co., Holy Name of Jesus, Revs. J. Edward Bradley; John M. Thomas. Pastoral Assocs.: Sr. Pauletta Kane, S.C.N.; Sr. Sharon Bittner, O.S.B.
Res., 511 Second St., 42420. Tel: 502-826-2096; Fax: 502-827-1494. [CEM]
School—618 Second St., 42420. Tel: 502-827-3425; Fax: 502-827-3432.
Sisters of Charity of Nazareth 1; Lay Teachers 32; Students 597.

Henshaw, Union Co., St. Ambrose, Rev. Terry Devine; Sr. Markan Freking, O.S.U., Pastoral Assoc.
Res., c/o St. Francis Borgia, 1308 N. Adams St., Sturgis, 42459. Tel: 502-333-4645. [CEM]

Hickman, Fulton Co., Sacred Heart, Rev. Steve Ulrich; Sr. Mary Agnes VonderHaar, O.S.U., Pastoral Assoc.
Res., 411 Moulton St., 42050-1327. Tel: 502-236-2071.

Hopkinsville, Christian Co., SS. Peter and Paul, Rev. Gerald H. Baker.
Res., 902 E. Ninth St., 42240. Tel: 502-885-8522; Fax: 502-885-5296.
School—Tel: 502-886-0172.
Lay Teachers 9; Students 209.

Irvington, Breckinridge Co., Holy Guardian Angels, Rev. Brad Whistle; Pete Hughes, Pastoral Assoc.
Res., 40146. Tel: 502-547-2132; 547-7314 (Rectory).

Knottsville, Daviess Co., St. William, Rev. Martin Hayes.
Res., 9515 Kentucky 144, Philpot, 42366. Tel: 502-281-4802; Fax: 502-281-9556. [CEM]
School—Mary Carrico Memorial School, Tel: 502-281-5546.
Ursuline Sisters 2; Lay Teachers 9; Students 128.

LaCenter, Ballard Co., St. Mary, Revs. Wm. Jerry Riney; Brian Roby; Sr. Alicia Coomes, Pastoral Assoc.
Church—P.O. Box 514, 42056. Tel: 502-665-5551 (Office); 665-5654 (Res.). [CEM]

Leitchfield, Grayson Co., St. Joseph's, Rev. Dave Johnson; Sr. Ruth Mattingly, O.S.U., Pastoral Min.
Res., 109 W. Walnut St., 42754. Tel: 502-259-3028.

Lewisport, Hancock Co., St. Columba, Rev. Tony Bickett. Pastoral Assocs.: Sr. Rita Lechner, S.P.; Sr. Karla Marie Kaelin, O.S.U.
Res., 815 Pell St., P.O. Box 358, 42351. Tel: 502-295-3682. [CEM]

Livermore, McLean Co., St. Charles, Rev. Francis M. Roof.
Res., St. Sebastian Church, 180 State Rte. 136 W., Calhoun, 42327-9521. Tel: 502-685-2559.
Church—506 Hill Ave., 42352.

McQuady, Breckinridge Co., St. Mary-of-the-Woods, Rev. Bruce Fogle.
Res., R.R. 3, Hardinsburg, 40143. Tel: 502-756-2093. [CEM]

Madisonville, Hopkins Co., Christ the King, Rev. Gregory Trawick.
Res., 1600 Kingsway Dr., 42431. Tel: 502-821-5494; Fax: 502-825-8612.
School—Tel: 502-821-8271; Fax: 502-825-9394.
Sisters 3; Lay Teachers 11; Students 154.
Preschool—Tel: 502-821-3954.
Students 50.

Marion, Crittenden Co., St. William, Rev. Terry Devine; Sr. Mary Louise Alvey, O.S.U., Pastoral Assoc.
Res., 860 S. Main St., 42064. Tel: 502-965-2477. [CEM]

Mayfield, Graves Co., St. Joseph, Rev. Ray Clark.
Res., 702 W. Broadway St., 42066. Tel: 502-247-2843; Fax: 502-247-6835. [CEM]
School—Tel: 502-247-4420; Fax: 502-247-6835.
Lay Teachers 7; Students 140.

Morganfield, Union Co., St. Ann's, Rev. Patrick M. Bittel; Ms. Patricia Claussen, Pastoral Min.
Res., 304 Church St., 42437. Tel: 502-389-2287; Fax: 502-389-0219. [CEM]

Morgantown, Butler Co., Holy Trinity, Rev. Joseph A. O'Donnell, Glmy.; Sr. Mary Lynne Wrocklage, G.H.M.S., Pastoral Assoc.
Res., 766 Logansport Rd., P.O. Box 222, 42261. Tel: 502-526-3723.

Murray, Calloway Co., St. Leo, Rev. Ray Goetz; Sr. Mary Matthias Ward, O.S.U., Pastoral Assoc.
Res., 401 N. 12th St., 42071. Tel: 502-753-3876; 759-1621 (Office).

Oak Grove, Christian Co., St. Michael the Archangel. Unassigned.
Res., Am Vet Bldg., 42262.

Paducah, McCracken Co.,

1—St. Francis de Sales, Revs. Robert Willett; Michael Clark; Adam Rewa, Pastoral Assoc.
Res., 116 S. Sixth St., 42001. Tel: 502-442-1923; Fax: 502-443-4616.

2—Rosary Chapel, Revs. Robert Willett; Michael Clark.
Res., 711 Ohio St., 42001. Tel: 502-444-6383.

3—St. John the Evangelist, Rev. Benjamin F. Luther.
Res., 6705 Old U.S. Hwy. 45, 42003. Tel: 502-554-3810; Fax: 502-554-3810.
School—7450 St. John Church Dr., 42003.
Lay Teachers 6; Students 91.

4—St. Thomas More, Revs. Jerry Riney; Brian Roby, Pastoral Assoc.; Sr. Marie Goretti Browing, O.S.U.
Office: 209 Wallace La., 42001. Tel: 502-444-7404; Fax: 502-444-9064.
Res., 5645 Blandville Rd., 42001. Tel: 502-444-7404; Fax: 502-444-9064.

Peonia, Grayson Co., St. Anthony's, Rev. Gary Hayes.
Res., 1256 St. Anthony Church Rd., Clarkson, 42726. Tel: 502-242-4791. [CEM]

Philpot, Daviess Co., St. Lawrence, Rev. Martin E. Hayes.
Res., 9515 Kentucky 144, Knottsville, 42366. Tel: 502-281-4802; Fax: 502-281-9556. [CEM]

Princeton, Caldwell Co., St. Paul, Rev. Richard T. Danhauer.
Res., 813 S. Jefferson, 42445. Tel: 502-365-6786.

Providence, Webster Co., Holy Cross, Rev. Carl J. Glahn.
Mailing Address: c/o St. Michael Church, P.O. Box 705, Sebree, 42455. Tel: 502-835-2584.

Reed, Henderson Co., St. Augustine, Rev. Msgr. Bernard Powers.
Res., 16777 Hwy. 60 E., 42451. Tel: 502-764-5599. [CEM]

Rome, Daviess Co., St. Martin, Rev. Joseph M. Mills; Rose Ann Payne, Pastoral Assoc.
Res., 5856 Kentucky 81, Owensboro, 42301. Tel: 502-685-0339. [CEM][JC]

Russellville, Logan Co., Sacred Heart, Rev. Lucian P. Hayden.
Res., 296 W. 6th St., 42276. Tel: 502-726-6963.

Scottsville, Allen Co., Christ the King, Rev. Frank Ruff, Glmy., Sacramental Min.; Sr. Lene Rubly, O.S.F., Pastoral Coord.; Sr. Davida Loosbrock, O.S.F., Pastoral Assoc.
Res., P.O. Box 463, 42164. Tel: 502-586-4515; 237-4404.
Station—Barren River, St. Peter the Fisherman. (Summer). Tel: 502-237-4404.

Sebree, Webster Co., St. Michael, Rev. Carl J. Glahn.
Res., P.O. Box 705, Church St., 42455. Tel: 502-835-2584.

St. Joseph, Daviess Co., St. Alphonsus, Rev. Robert Drury.
Res., 7950 Cummings Rd., Owensboro, 42301. Tel: 502-229-4566. [CEM]

St. Paul, Grayson Co., St. Paul, Rev. Charles G. Fischer.
Res., 1821 St. Paul Rd., Leitchfield, 42754. Tel: 502-242-7436. [CEM]
School—Tel: 502-242-7483.
Lay Teachers 5; Students 43.

Sorgho, Daviess Co., St. Mary Magdalene, Rev. J. Patrick Reynolds.
Res., 7232 Kentucky 56, Owensboro, 42301. Tel: 502-771-4436. [JC]

Stanley, Daviess Co., St. Peter of Alcantara, Rev. Paul P. Powell.
Res., 81 Church St., Owensboro, 42301. Tel: 502-764-1983. [CEM]

Sturgis, Union Co., St. Francis Borgia, Rev. Terry Devine; Sr. Marcan Freking, O.S.F., Pastoral Assoc.
Res., 1308 N. Adams St., 42459. Tel: 502-333-4645.

Sunfish, Edmondson Co., St. John the Evangelist, Rev. Dave Johnson. Pastoral Assocs.: Sr. Dolorita Robinson, O.S.U.; Sr. Rosaria Ray, O.S.U.
Church—430 St. John Church Rd., 42284. Tel: 502-286-4366. [CEM]

Uniontown, Union Co., St. Agnes, Rev. Henry Wieder; Sr. Jolinda Naas, O.S.B., Pastoral Assoc.
Res., P.O. Box 607, 42461. Tel: 502-822-4416; Fax: 502-822-4416. [CEM]

Waverly, Union Co., Sacred Heart, Rev. Anthony Ziegler.
Res., 201 E. Market St., 42462. Tel: 502-389-4224; Fax: 502-389-4224. [CEM]
St. Peter, Rev. Anthony Ziegler.
Res., 201 E. Market St., 42462. Tel: 502-389-4224; Fax: 502-389-4224. [CEM]

Wax, Grayson Co., St. Benedict, Rev. Gary Hayes.
Res., St. Anthony Church, 1256 St. Anthony Church Rd., Clarkson, 42726. Tel: 502-242-4791. [CEM]

Whitesville, Daviess Co., St. Mary of the Woods, Revs. Richard M. Powers; Maury Riney; Sr. Clarita Browning, O.S.U., Pastoral Assoc.
Res., 10534 Main Cross, P.O. Box 1, 42378. Tel: 502-233-4196. [CEM]
School—St. Mary's Grade School, Tel: 502-233-5253; Fax: 502-233-9360.
Lay Teachers 16; Students 260.

Non-Parochial Assignments:
Reverend Fathers—
Alvey, Leonard J., Brescia College, 717 Frederica St., Owensboro, KY 42301
Piskula, Louis, Chap., St. Joseph Monastery, 8564 Crisp Rd., Whitesville, KY 42378
Reisz, Leonard, 617 E. 23rd St., Owensboro, KY 42301
Shonis, Anthony, Chap., Mount St. Joseph, Maple Mount, KY 42356

On Duty Outside the Diocese:
Reverend Fathers—
Byrd, Freddie, St. Meinrad, IN, St. Meinrad Seminary

Studying Outside the Diocese:
Reverend Fathers—
Hostetter, Laurence, Casa Santa Maria, Via dell' Umilta 30, 00187, Rome, Italy. Tel: 001-39-6-69001; (Fax)001-39-6-679-1448

Absent on Leave:
Reverend Fathers—
Dunn, Stephen
McCarty, Bruce
Odom-Green, William
Payne, Gary

Military Chaplains:
Reverend Fathers—
Wheatley, Carroll, 954 Wrens Roost #3, Memphis, TN 38119
Willett, William D., CMR 416, Box 1228, HHC 11th Avn. Regt., APO, AE 09140

Retired:
Reverend Fathers—
Clements, Richard
DeNardi, Charles A., Ambassador Shores, 1705 St. Paul Rd., Leitchfield, KY 42754
Hagman, William J., Bishop Cotton Apts., 2501 Old Hartford Rd., Owensboro, KY 42303
Hancock, Walter, 102 Houston St., Cloverport, KY 40111
Hite, James C., Bishop Cotton Apts., 2501 Old Hartford Rd., Owensboro, KY 42303
Miller, Joseph C., Box 319, Nevis, MN 56467
O'Bryan, Henry, P.O. Box 114, Owensboro, KY 42302-0114
Rhodes, Joseph, Bishop Cotton Apts., 2501 Old Hartford Rd., Owensboro, KY 42303
Willett, Henry L., 6143 St. Lawrence Rd., Philpot, KY 42366. Tel: 502-281-9691
Wolford, Charles, Nazareth Village, I Apt. 318, P.O. Box 210, Nazareth, KY 40048

INSTITUTIONS LOCATED IN THE DIOCESE

[A] COLLEGES AND UNIVERSITIES

Owensboro. *Brescia College*, 717 Frederica St., 42301. Tel: 502-685-3131.
For a complete listing, refer to the Colleges and Universities section.

[B] HIGH SCHOOLS, INTER-PAROCHIAL

Owensboro. *Owensboro Catholic High School*, 1524 W. Parrish Ave., 42301. Tel: 502-684-3215; Fax: 502-684-7050. Mr. Harold Staples, Prin.; Rev. Tony Jones, Chm. Religion Dept.; Mr. Michael Goetz, Devel. Dir. Priests 1; Lay Teachers 45; Students 667.

Paducah. *St. Mary High School*, 1243 Elmdale Rd., 42003. Tel: 502-442-1681; Fax: 502-442-7920. Mr. Michael J. Collins, Prin. Sisters 1; Lay Teachers 18; Students 202.

Whitesville. *Trinity High School*, 42378. Tel: 502-233-5533. Mr. Steve Winkler, Prin. Priests 1; Lay Teachers 11; Students 163.

[C] ELEMENTARY SCHOOLS, INTER-PAROCHIAL

Owensboro. *Catherine Spalding School*. (Grades K-6), 4017 Frederica St., 42301. Tel: 502-684-7583. Mrs. Sandy Fleming, Prin. Lay Teachers 18; Students 354.
Francis R. Cotton School. (Grades K-6), 3418 U.S. Hwy. 60 E., 42303. Tel: 502-683-2268. Mrs. Joyce Hoffman, Prin. Ursuline Sisters 1; Lay Teachers 13; Students 226.
Henry J. Soenneker School. (Grades K-6), 3400 Fenmore St., 42301. Tel: 502-684-6487. Mr. Phil Spurlock, Prin. Lay Teachers 6; Students 116.
Holy Angels Elementary, P.O. Box 7244, Kentucky Hwy. 56, 42301. Tel: 502-771-4773. Ms. Mary Kennedy, Prin. Lay Teachers 10; Students 194.
Holy Family (Middle) School. (Grades 7-8). (Owensboro Catholic Middle School), 2540 Christie Pl., 42301. Tel: 502-683-0480; Fax: 502-683-0495. Mr. James T. Duffy, Prin. Lay Teachers 21; Students 338.
St. Angela Merici School. (Grades K-6), 525 E. 23rd St., 42303. Tel: 502-683-6989. P. J. Hayden, Prin. Ursuline Sisters 2; Lay Teachers 18; Students 383.

Bowling Green. *St. Joseph School*, 416 Church St., 42101-1887. Tel: 502-842-1235. Ms. Joanne Powell, Prin. Lay Teachers 18; Students 276.

Hardinsburg. *St. Romuald School*, N. Main St., 40143. Tel: 502-756-5504. Ms. Doris Waldeck, Prin. Sisters 2; Lay Teachers 10; Students 181.

Morganfield. *St. Ann Interparochial School*, 320 Church St., 42437. Tel: 502-389-1898. Sr. Pat Howell, O.S.U., Prin. Ursuline Sisters 1; Lay Teachers 14; Students 215.

Paducah. *St. Mary Elementary*, 377 Highland Blvd., 42003. Mrs. Nancy S. Collins, Prin. Lay Teachers 19; Students 371.
St. Mary Middle School. (Grades 6-8), 1243 Elmdale Rd., 42003. Ms. Rosann M. Whiting, Prin. Sisters 1; Lay Teachers 8; Students 167.

[D] GENERAL HOSPITALS

Paducah. *Lourdes Hospital*, 1530 Lone Oak Rd., P.O. Box 7100, 42002-7100. Tel: 502-444-2444.
For a complete listing, refer to the Hospitals section.

[E] HOMES FOR AGED

Owensboro. *Carmel Home*, 2501 Old Hartford Rd., 42303. Tel: 502-683-0227.
For a complete listing, refer to the Special Care Facilities section.

Knottsville. *Bishop Soenneker Home*. 9545 Kentucky 144 Philpot, 42366. Tel: 502-281-4881.
For a complete listing, refer to the Special Care Facilities section.

[F] MONASTERIES AND RESIDENCES OF PRIESTS AND BROTHERS

Hartford. *Glenmary House*, 300 Peach Alley, 42347. Tel: 502-298-9886. The Home Missioners of America. Directors: Bros. Dennis Craig; Larry Johnson.

South Union. *Fathers of Mercy*, 42283. Tel: 502-542-4146. Very Rev. John O'Brien, C.P.M., Supr. Gen.; Revs. John Molloy, C.P.M., Mission Dir.; Joseph H. Burgdorf, C.P.M., Novice Master; William Casey, C.P.M.; David Wilton, C.P.M.

[G] CONVENTS AND RESIDENCES FOR SISTERS

Owensboro. *The Glenmary Center*, P.O. Box 22264, 42304-2264. Tel: 502-686-8401. Glenmary Home Mission Sisters of America. Sr. Christine Beckett, Pres.
Special Centers for Social Services & Assistance. Total Assisted 3,500; Total Staff 5. Professed Sisters in Community 14.

Livermore. *The Glenmary Center for Mission Training*. Formation Program. 220 E. 7th St., P.O. Box 520, 42352-0520. Tel: 502-278-5239. Sr. Mae Koenig, Dir.; Sr. Martha Schuler, Assoc. Dir.

Maple Mount. *Mount St. Joseph*, 42356. Tel: 502-229-4103. Motherhouse and Convent of the Ursuline Nuns of the Congregation of Paris. Sr. Rose Marita O'Bryan, O.S.U., Supr.; Rev. Anthony J. Shonis,

Chap.; Sr. Emma Cecilia Busam, O.S.U., Archivist. Professed Sisters in Community 225.

WHITESVILLE. *St. Joseph's Monastery*, 8564 Crisp Rd., 42378. Tel: 502-233-4571; Fax: 502-233-4356. Religious of the Passion of Jesus Christ, (Passionist Nuns, Cloistered Contemplative). Sr. Mary Agnes Higgs, C.P., Supr.; Rev. Louis Piskula, Chap. Professed Sisters 18.

[H] RETREAT CENTERS

MAPLE MOUNT. *Mt. St. Joseph Retreat Center*, 42356. Tel: 502-229-4103. Sr. Darlene Denton, O.S.U., Dir. Assoc. Directors: Rev. Msgr. Bernard Powers; Sr. Elaine Burke, O.S.U.

[I] NEWMAN CENTERS

BOWLING GREEN. *Western Kentucky University Newman Center*, St. Thomas Aquinas Chapel, 1403 College St., P.O. Box 10170, 42102-4770. Tel: 502-843-3638. Rev. John Little, Dir.; Damian Oliver, Pastoral Min. Students 1,100.

MURRAY. *Murray State University Newman House*, 220 N. 13th St., 42071. Tel: 502-753-1391. Sr. Mary Matthias Ward, O.S.U.; Rev. J. Raymond Goetz. Students 500.

[J] MISCELLANEOUS LISTINGS

OWENSBORO. *Cathedral Preschool*, 600 Locust St., 42301. Tel: 502-926-1652. Students 206.

The Catholic Foundation of Western Kentucky, 600 Locust St., 42301.

**Daniel Pitino Shelter, Inc.*, 501 Walnut St., 42301. Tel: 502-688-9000. Provides soup kitchen seven days a week, shelter for 36 homeless, education facilities, food bank, legal aid and medical services for those unable to pay. Total Assisted 30,000; Employees 3; Volunteers 150.

Interparish Deposit Loan Fund Corp., 600 Locust St., 42301-2130. Sr. Joseph Angela Boone, Contact Person.

Owensboro Catholic Consolidated School System, 1524 W. Parrish Ave., 42301. Daryl Hagan, Dir.

**The Roman Catholic Diocese of Owensboro Kentucky Charitable Trust Fund, Inc.*, 600 Locust St., 42301. Tel: 502-683-1545; Fax: 502-683-6883. Sr. Joseph Angela Boone, O.S.U.

BOWLING GREEN. *Diocesan Shrine of Mary Mother of the Church and Model of all Christians*, St. Joseph, 434 Church St., 42101. Tel: 502-842-2525.

PADUCAH. *Our Lady of the Pines Prayer House, Inc.*, 717 S. 6th St., 42001. Tel: 502-443-3650.

St. Mary High School Benefit Fund, 1243 Elmdale Rd., 42003.

RELIGIOUS INSTITUTES OF MEN REPRESENTED IN THE DIOCESE

For further details refer to the corresponding bracketed number in the Religious Institutes of Men or Women section.

[0200]—*Benedictine Monks.*—O.S.B.

[0820]—*Congregation of the Fathers of Mercy.*—C.P.M.

[0570]—*Glenmary Home Missioners*. (Glendale OH).—Glmy.

[0560]—*Third Order Regular of Saint Francis.*—T.O.R.

RELIGIOUS INSTITUTES OF WOMEN REPRESENTED IN THE DIOCESE

[0100]—*Adorers of the Blood of Christ.*—A.S.C.

[0230]—*Benedictine Sisters of the Pontifical Jurisdiction.* (Ferdinand, IN).—O.S.B.

[0360]—*Carmelite Sisters of the Divine Heart of Jesus.*—Carmel. D.C.J.

[2080]—*Home Mission Sisters of America.*—G.H.M.S.

[2575]—*Institute of the Sisters of Mercy of the Americas.* (Cincinnati, OH; Detroit, MI).—R.S.M.

[3170]—*Religious of the Passion of Jesus Christ.*—C.P.

[0500]—*Sisters of Charity of Nazareth.*—S.C.N.

[3360]—*Sisters of Providence of Saint Mary-of-the-Woods, Indiana.*—S.P.

[2260]—*Sisters of the Lamb of God.*—A.D.

[1760]—*Sisters of the Third Order of St. Francis of Penance and Charity.* (Tiffin, OH).—O.S.F.

[1720]—*Sisters of the Third Order Regular of St. Francis of the Congregation of Our Lady of Lourdes.* Rochester, MN.—O.S.F.

[4120]—*Ursuline Nuns, of the Congregation of Paris.*—O.S.U.

[1570]—*Sisters of St.Francis of the Holy Family.* (Dubuque, IA).—O.S.F.

INTERPAROCHIAL CEMETERIES

OWENSBORO. *Mater Dolorosa*, 1860 W. 9th St., 42301.

Resurrection, 5404 Leitchfield Rd., 42303. Mr. Art Hodde, Dir.

NECROLOGY

† Boehmicke, George, (Retired). —Died Nov. 6, 1996.

Diocese of Palm Beach

Most Reverend

J. KEITH SYMONS, D.D.

Bishop of Palm Beach; ordained May 18, 1958; appointed Titular Bishop of Siguritanus and Auxiliary of St. Petersburg January 16, 1981; consecrated March 19, 1981; appointed Second Bishop of Pensacola-Tallahassee September 29, 1983; installed November 8, 1983; appointed Second Bishop of Palm Beach June 2, 1990; installed July 31, 1990. Fax: 561-775-7035.

The Pastoral Center: Mailing Address: P.O. Box 109650, Palm Beach Gardens, FL, 33410-9650. Location: 9995 N. Military Tr., Palm Beach Gardens, FL, 33410. Tel.: 561-775-9500; Fax: 561-775-9556.

ESTABLISHED OCTOBER 24, 1984.

Square Miles 5,115.

Comprises the Counties of Palm Beach, Martin, Indian River, Okeechobee and St. Lucie in the State of Florida.

Legal Corporate Title: *The Diocese of Palm Beach.*

For legal titles of parishes and diocesan institutions, consult the Chancery.

STATISTICAL OVERVIEW

Personnel	
Bishop	1
Priests: Diocesan Active in Diocese	74
Priests: Active Outside Diocese	3
Priests: Retired, Sick or Absent	16
Number of Diocesan Priests	93
Religious Priests in Diocese	41
Extern Priests in Diocese	11
Ordinations:	
Diocesan Priests	2
Transitional Deacons	2
Permanent Deacons in Diocese	37
Total Brothers	5
Total Sisters	178
Parishes	
Parishes	46
With Resident Pastor:	
Resident Diocesan Priests	41
Resident Religious Priests	5
Without Resident Pastor:	
Missions	5
Professional Ministry Personnel:	
Brothers	3
Sisters	29
Lay Ministers	47

Welfare	
Catholic Hospitals	1
Total Assisted	640,000
Homes for the Aged	1
Total Assisted	120
Day Care and Extended Day Care Centers	2
Total Assisted	101
Specialized Homes	1
Total Assisted	19
Special Centers for Social Services	23
Total Assisted	19,268
Residential Care of Disabled	1
Total Assisted	6
Educational	
Seminaries, Diocesan	1
Students from This Diocese	14
Students from Other Diocese	53
Diocesan Students in Other Seminaries	13
Total Seminarians	27
High Schools, Diocesan and Parish	3
Total Students	1,897
Elementary Schools, Diocesan and Parish	14
Total Students	5,176

Elementary Schools, Private	2
Total Students	570
Catechesis/Religious Education:	
High School Students	2,574
Elementary Students	14,360
Total Students Under Catholic Instruction	24,604
Teachers in the Diocese:	
Priests	9
Brothers	2
Sisters	26
Lay Teachers	394
Vital Statistics	
Receptions into the Church:	
Infant Baptism Totals	4,450
Adult Baptism Totals	338
Received into Full Communion	377
First Communions	3,681
Confirmations	1,966
Marriages:	
Catholic	961
Interfaith	359
Total Marriages	1,320
Deaths	2,380
Total Catholic Population	215,907
Total Population	1,415,520

Former Bishop—Most Rev. THOMAS V. DAILY, D.D., ord. Jan. 10, 1952; appt. Titular Bishop of Bladia and Auxiliary Bishop of Boston, Dec. 31, 1974; cons. Feb. 11, 1975; appt. first Bishop of Palm Beach, July 17, 1984; installed Oct. 24, 1984; transferred to Bishop of Brooklyn, Feb. 20, 1990.

The Pastoral Center—Mailing Address: P.O. Box 109650, Palm Beach Gardens, 33410-9650. Tel: 561-775-9500; Fax: 561-775-9556. *9995 N. Military Trail, Palm Beach Gardens, 33410-9650.*

Vicars General—Rev. Msgr. IRVINE J. NUGENT; Very Rev. CHARLES E. HAWKINS, V.G.

Episcopal Vicars—Rev. Msgr. JOHN R. MCMAHON; Revs. FRANCIS J. LECHIARA; TIMOTHY J. LYNCH; RICHARD MURPHY; ARTHUR J. VENEZIA.

Moderator of Curia—Rev. Msgr. IRVINE J. NUGENT, V.G.

Administrative Assistant to Bishop—Sr. MARIE CONSILIA MANTELLO, A.S.C.J.

Executive Secretary to Bishop—Miss ANNE LAPORTE.

Masters of Ceremonies—Revs. MICHAEL EDWARDS; NESTOR L. RODRIGUEZ.

Matrimonial Tribunal—

Judicial Vicar—Rev. Msgr. THOMAS J. KLINZING, J.C.L.

Adjutant Judicial Vicar—Rev. TIMOTHY J. LYNCH, J.C.L.

Judges—Rev. Msgr. RAYMOND BLAIR, J.C.D.; Revs. WILLIAM MARTIN, O.M.I., J.U.D.; GERALD HUGHES, J.C.D.; DAMIAN TOWEY, C.P., J.C.D.

Defender of the Bond—Rev. Msgr. JOSEPH MARBACH, J.C.D.

Assessors—Rev. MICHAEL P. ALLISON; Very Rev. CHARLES E. HAWKINS, V.G.; Mrs. LORRAINE SABATELLA.

Promotor of Justice—Rev. DAMIAN TOWEY, C.P., J.C.D.

Director of the Tribunal—Mrs. LORRAINE SABATELLA, B.A.

Notaries—Very Rev. CHARLES E. HAWKINS, V.G.; Ms. MARY LOU HUGHES; Mrs. LORRAINE SABATELLA.

Secretaries—Mrs. GEMA FERNANDEZ; Mrs. SANDRA DUBEAU; Mrs. PATRICIA COLLINS.

Advocates—Revs. MICHAEL P. ALLISON; GLEN J. POTHIER; Rev. Msgr. JAMES BURKE; Sr. MARIE JAMES MCCALLEN, R.S.M.; Mr. BERNARD CONKO; Mrs. KATHLEEN CONTE; Mrs. ELAINE WELLING; Mr. JOHN MCGREEVY; Ms. SYLVIA RAFTERY.

Chancellor—Very Rev. CHARLES E. HAWKINS, V.G. Tel: 561-775-9506.

Administrative Assistant to Vicar General / Chancellor—Ms. MARY LOU HUGHES.

Archives—Ms. MARY LOU HUGHES.

Archives Committee—Very Rev. CHARLES E. HAWKINS, V.G., Chm.

Vicariate for Christ's Faithful

Episcopal Vicar—Rev. ARTHUR J. VENEZIA.

Office for Seminarians—Rev. ARTHUR J. VENEZIA, Dir.

Office for Vocations—Rev. LOUIS GUERIN, Dir.

Diocesan Vocations Admissions Committee—Rev. FRANK FLYNN, Chm.

Vicar for Permanent Deacons—Rev. MICHAEL WOODCOCK; Deacon JACK PIERCE, Assoc. Vicar.

Vicar for Religious—Rev. MARK A. SZANYI, O.F.M.Conv.

Dir. for Religious Vocations—Sr. JOHN KEVIN MCNULTY, O.S.F., Assoc. Vicar.

Diocesan Commission of Religious—Sr. JEANNE DREA, O.P., Chm.

Laity—

Office for Black Catholic Ministry—Mrs. LORRAINE LYLES, Dir.

Office for Haitian Ministry—Deacon EMILE AMBROISE, Diocesan Coord. Haitian Centers: Belle Glade, Delray Beach, Fort Pierce, Lake Worth, and West Palm Beach.

Office for Hispanic Ministry—Sr. REGINA TUTZO, R.M.I.

Office for Hispanic Ministry in Indian River and St. Lucie Counties—Rev. DON REDDEN.

Rural Life Migrant Ministry—P.O. Box 1203, Stuart, 34995. Mrs. MARIA CHRISTINA MARQUEZ, Coord.

Holy Childhood Association—643 N.E. Fourth Ave., Boynton Beach, 33435. Rev. JOHN G. BLOCK, V.F., Dir.

Legion of Mary—Deacon ROBERT JACOBI, Assoc. Spiritual Moderator.

Vicariate for Catholic Charities

Vicar—Rev. Msgr. JOHN R. MCMAHON.

Catholic Charities—Mr. MARCEL O. CHARPENTIER, A.C.S.W., Exec. Dir.; Ms. MADELEINE SCHUTZ, L.C.S.W., Assoc. Dir.

Belle Glade Office—Sr. AMADEE MAXWELL, S.B.S.

Birthline Crisis Pregnancy Center—Mrs. ARLENE CONKLIN.

Campaign for Human Development & Catholic Relief Services—Mrs. BARBARA ROTH.

Elder Affairs Case Management & Guardianship—Sr. MARYROSE CROWLEY, S.S.N.D.

Emmaus Residence for Persons Living with AIDS—Rev. JOHN EDWARDS, S.J.

Lifeline Crisis Pregnancy Center—Mrs. ARLENE CONKLIN.

Martin County Offices (Hope Sound, Indiantown, East Stuart, Stuart)—Ms. PAMELA BLACK.
Maurawood Community Outreach for Pregnancy/ Parenting—Ms. PAIGE STUHR.
Nazareth Homes-Adult Group Homes for People with Developmental Disabilties—Alhambra House: Sr. RITA BAUM, S.S.J. Bethlehem House: Sr. RITA BAUM, S.S.J.
Office of Housing Management & Development—Ms. ROBIN TOLAR.
Okeechobee Outreach Center/After School Program—Ms. BARBARA ISAMAN.
Family First Family Program—Ms. CAROL KNIGHT.
Refugee Resettlement & Immigration Services—Mr. DEXTER ORANGE.
Saint Lucie County Office—Ms. CARMEN SIBRUN.
Samaritan Center for Homeless Families—Ms. KRIS ALTMAN; Mrs. JOYCE WILD.
Villa Assumpta Housing for the Elderly—Ms. LINDA MATZ.
Villa Franciscan Housing for the Elderly—Ms. MARIE HURLSTON.

Vicariate for Education

Vicar—Rev. FRANCIS J. LECHIARA.
Office of Catechesis and Leadership Development—Sr. MARIE THERESE EVRARD, S.S.J., Dir.; Ms. PATRICIA BOOTH, Assoc. Dir.
Missionary Cooperative Plan—Rev. JOHN G. BLOCK, V.F., *643 N.E. Forth Ave., Boynton Beach, 33435.*
Propagation of the Faith—Rev. JOHN G. BLOCK, V.F., *643 N.E. Fourth Ave., Boynton Beach, 33435.*
Office of Communications—Rev. MICHAEL EDWARDS, Dir.
Office of "The Florida Catholic"—Mr. THOMAS TRACY, Editor.
Office of the Catholic Schools—Sr. JOAN DAWSON, O.S.F., Supt.; Mrs. PATRICIA CANTIERI, Asst. Supt.
Office of Special Education - C.O.M.E.—Mrs. PATRICIA CANTIERI, Dir.

Vicariate for Marriage and the Family

Vicar—Rev. TIMOTHY J. LYNCH.
Family Life—
Office of Family Life Ministry—Dirs.: WALTER ATWELL; GERALDINE ATWELL.
Office of Youth Ministry and Young Adult Ministry—Rev. AIDAN LACY, Spiritual Moderator; Sr. JUDE RUGGERI, A.S.C.J., Dir.
Cursillo Movement—10970 State Rd. 703, N. Palm Beach, 33408. Rev. MICHAEL TSCHUDI, Spiritual Dir.
Cursillo Movement for Hispanics—9600 W. Atlantic Ave., Delray Beach, 33446. Rev. MATTHEW DIDONE, C.S.
Office of Ministry with People with Disabilities—Sr. RITA BAUM, S.S.J., Dir.
Office of Prison Ministry—Vacant; Chap.; Sr. BETTY FRASCINO, O.S.F., Dir.
Office of Ecumenical and Inter-Faith Activities—Revs. EDMUND SZPIEG, Dir. MICHAEL TSCHUDI, Assoc. Dir.
Office for Liturgy—Rev. MICHAEL DRISCOLL, O.Carm., Dir.
Office for Campus Ministry—Rev. MARTIN DEVEREAUX, Dir.
Chaplain for Catholic Scouting—THOMAS EUTENEUER, Chap.
Liaison to Charismatic Movement—Rev. WALTER DOCKERILL.
World Wide Marriage Encounter—Rev. FRANK B. GUINAN, Spiritual Moderator. Exec. Couple: LARRY BALIK; HERMIE BALIK, *220 Colony Way W., Jupiter, 33458.*
Office for Respect Life—Mr. DONALD KAZIMIR, Dir.

Vicariate for Pastoral Services

Vicar—Rev. RICHARD MURPHY.
Diocesan Financial Administrator—Mr. BASIL ZALOOM.
Financial Advisory Board—Rev. RICHARD MURPHY, Chm.
Office for Building and Renovations—Mr. PATRICK MOLAMPHY, Dir.
Commission for Building—Rev. RICHARD MURPHY, Chm.
Office of Cemeteries—Rev. THOMAS VENGAYIL, Dir.; Mrs. MARIAN HARRIS, Admin.
Office of Data Processing—Rev. RICHARD MURPHY.
Office of Resource Development—Vacant.
Pastoral Center Personnel—Mr. BASIL ZALOOM.
Committee for Parish Boundaries—Revs. JOHN G. BLOCK, Chm.
Legal Affairs—Mr. J. PATRICK FITZGERALD, ESQ., *110 Merrick Way, Ste. 3-B, Coral Gables, 33134.* Tel: 561-659-6438; Fax: 305-443-6613.

Consultative Bodies

College of Consultors—Rev. Msgr. IRVINE J. NUGENT, V.G.; Very Rev. CHARLES E. HAWKINS, V.G.; Rev. Msgr. JOHN R. MCMAHON; Revs. JOHN G. BLOCK; FRANCIS J. LECHIARA; TIMOTHY J. LYNCH; RICHARD MURPHY; JAMES MURTAGH; ARTHUR J. VENEZIA.
Presbyteral Council—Rev. Msgr. IRVINE J. NUGENT, V.G.; Rev. Msgr. JOHN R. MCMAHON; Rev. Msgr. THOMAS KLINZING; Very Rev. CHARLES E. HAWKINS, V.G.; Revs. CHRISTOPHER ALLEN; EDWARD MALONEY; JAMES MURTAGH; LOUIS GUERIN; JAMES SHEEHAN; JULIAN HARRIS; MATTHEW FITZGERALD; FRANCIS FINNIGAN, C.P.; FRANCIS J. LECHIARA; TIMOTHY J. LYNCH; RICHARD MURPHY; JOHN EDWARDS, S.J.; FRANCIS REARDON; ARTHUR J. VENEZIA; THOMAS VENGAYIL.

CLERGY, PARISHES, MISSIONS AND PAROCHIAL SCHOOLS

CITY OF PALM BEACH GARDENS (Palm Beach County)

1—CATHEDRAL OF ST. IGNATIUS LOYOLA (1984), Rev. Msgr. Thomas Klinzing, Rector; Revs. Glen K. Pothier; Nestor L. Rodriquez.
Res., 9999 N. Military Tr., Palm Beach Gardens, 33410. Tel: 561-622-2565; Fax: 561-624-9489.
Catechesis/Religious Programs—Students 1,078.

OUTSIDE THE CITY OF PALM BEACH GARDENS

Belle Glade, Palm Beach Co., St. Philip Benizi, Rev. Luis Aineto, S.D.B.; Bro. Michael Brinkman; Revs. Jeremiah Reen, S.D.B.; Attilio Klinger, S.D.B; James Morabito, S.D.B.; Bro. Lino Seneci, S.D.B.
Res., 710 S. Main St., 33430. Tel: 561-996-3870; Fax: 561-996-3899.
Catechesis/Religious Programs—Students 324.

Boca Raton, Palm Beach Co.,

1—ASCENSION, Revs. Matthew A. Morgan; Donald R. Munro.
Res., 7250 N. Federal Hwy., 33487. Tel: 561-997-5486; Fax: 561-997-5862.

2—OUR LADY OF LOURDES, Rev. Martin B. Mulqueen; Rev. Msgr. Joseph H. O'Shea, Pastor Emeritus; Revs. Richard E. George; Joseph M. Kuczborski (PEO).
Res., 20094 S.W. 57th Ave., 33428. Tel: 561-483-2440; Fax: 561-482-0626.
Catechesis/Religious Programs—Students 1,150.

3—ST. JOAN OF ARC, Rev. Msgr. John McMahon; Revs. Thomas J. Skindeleski (PH); John Sutton (PAT).
Res., 370 S.W. 3rd St., 33432. Tel: 561-392-0007; Fax: 561-392-0074.
School—Sisters of Mercy, Skibbereen. Sr. Ellen Murphy R.S.M., Prin.
Sisters 3; Lay Teachers 27; Students 630.
Catechesis/Religious Programs—Students 899.

4—ST. JOHN THE EVANGELIST, Rev. Ronald Schulz, Admin.
Res., 19785 Hampton Dr., Ste. #4, 33434. Tel: 561-488-1373.

5—ST. JUDE, Revs. Michael Driscoll, O.Carm.; Timothy Johnson, O.Carm.; Aquinas E. Stack, O.Carm. In res., Rev. Eugene Foley, O.Carm.
Res., 21693 Club Villa Terrace, 33433.
Church—21689 Toledo Rd., 33433. Tel: 561-392-8172; Fax: 561-362-0845.
School—Tel: 561-392-9160. Mr. Thomas Ducote, Prin.
Sisters 1; Lay Teachers 16; Students 340.
Catechesis/Religious Programs—Students 600.

Boynton Beach, Palm Beach Co., St. Mark, Rev. John G. Block.
Res., 643 N.E. 4th Ave., 33435. Tel: 561-734-9330; Fax: 561-735-3463.
School—Sisters of Charity of St. Elizabeth. Sr. M. Paula Blue, Prin.
Sisters 2; Lay Teachers 18; Students 315.
St. Thomas More, Rev. Frank O'Loughlin. In res., Rev. Al Victor, (Retired).
Res., 10935 S. Military Tr., 33436. Tel: 561-737-3095; Fax: 561-737-8697.

Delray Beach, Palm Beach Co.,

1—EMMANUEL, Rev. Raymond Hubert.
Res., 15700 S. Military Tr., 33484. Tel: 561-496-2480.

2—OUR LADY OF PERPETUAL HELP MISSION, Revs. Roland Desormeaux, C.S.; Danis Ridore (Canada).
Residence and Church—510 S.W. Eighth Ave., 33444. Tel: 561-276-4880; Fax: 561-276-7036.

3—OUR LADY QUEEN OF PEACE, Rev. Matthew DiDone, C.S., Admin.
Res., 9600 W. Atlantic Ave., 33446. Tel: 561-499-6234; Fax: 561-499-5513.
Claritian Missionaries 4.

4—ST. VINCENT FERRER, Revs. John A. Skehan; John Barrow; Aidan Lacy.
Res., 840 George Bush Blvd., 33483. Tel: 561-276-6892; Fax: 561-276-8068.
School—715 N.E. 8th Ave., 33483.
Sisters of Mercy (Kinsale, Ireland) 4; Lay Teachers 15; Students 322.

Fellsmere, Indian River Co., Our Lady of Guadalupe Mission, Rev. Don Redden.
Mailing Address: P.O. Box 9, 32948.
Res., 2410 Florida Ave., Fort Pierce, 34950. Tel: 561-464-2285.
Mission—Fellsmere, Indian River Co., Rte. 512, P.O. Box 9, 32948.

Fort Pierce, St. Lucie Co., Notre Dame Mission, Rev. Antoine Richert, S.M.M.
Res., 217 N. U.S. Hwy. #1, 34950. Tel: 561-466-9617.
St. Anastasia, Revs. Mark Christopher; Francis H. Reardon.
Res., 407 S. 33rd St., P.O. Box 430, 34954-0430. Tel: 561-461-2233.
School—Mrs. Vickie Guettler, Prin. Sisters 1; Lay Teachers 24; Students 601.
St. Mark, Revs. Richard Murphy; Edward Morley, O.C.S.O.
Res., 1924 Zephyr Ave., 34982. Tel: 561-461-8150.
Mailing Address: P.O. Box 2020, 34954.

Highland Beach, Palm Beach Co., St. Lucy, Revs. Gerald Grace, Pastor; Anthony J. Chepanis, Pastor Emeritus; Louis T. Guerin.
Res., 3510 S. Ocean Blvd., 33487. Tel: 561-278-1280; Fax: 561-278-8509.

Hobe Sound, Martin Co., St. Christopher, Revs. Leslie Cann; A. Christopher Allen; Aidan Hynes.
Res., 12001 S.E. Federal Hwy., 33455. Tel: 561-546-5150; Fax: 561-546-8820.
Mailing Address: P.O. Box 607, 33475.

Indiantown, Martin Co., Holy Cross, Revs. Juan de la Calle, Pastor Emeritus; Thomas Euteneur, Admin.
Res., 15927 S.W. 150 St., 34956. Tel: 561-597-2798.
Mailing Address: P.O. Box 999, 34956.

Jensen Beach, Martin Co., St. Martin de Porres, Revs. Thomas J. Rynne; Robert L. Magee.
Res., 2555 N.E. Savanna Rd., 34958. Tel: 561-334-4214; Fax: 561-334-8627.
Mailing Address: P.O. Box 1087, 34958.

Juno Beach, Palm Beach Co., St. Patrick, Rev. Frank Guinan.
Res., 2549 Hope Ln., W., Palm Beach Gardens, 33410. Tel: 561-626-8626; Fax: 561-622-6471.

Jupiter, Palm Beach Co., St. Peter, Rev. Charles Notabartolo. In res., Rev. Charles Hawkins.
Res., 1701 Indian Creek Pkwy., 33458. Tel: 561-575-0837; Fax: 561-793-4082.
Catechesis/Religious Programs—Students 950.

Lake Worth, Palm Beach Co., Sacred Heart, Revs. Francis Flynn; Francis X. Fenech, Pastor Emeritus; Peter VanNguyen; Andrew Riley, P.I.M.E.
Res., 425 N. M St., 33460. Tel: 561-582-4736; Fax: 561-588-5238.
Mailing Address: P.O. Box 551, 33460.
School—410 N. M St., 33460. Sr. Breeden Connolly, S.S.J., Prin.
Sisters 4; Lay Teachers 13; Students 283.
St. Luke, Revs. Daniel V. Cronin; Larkin Connolly, Pastor Emeritus; George L. Batista (NEW).
Res., 2892 S. Congress Ave., 33461. Tel: 561-965-8980; Fax: 561-965-1384.
School—Sr. Janet Finely, O.S.F., Prin.; Lay Teachers 11; Students 284.
St. Matthew, Rev. Clemens Hammerschmitt, Admin.
Res., 5417 Fearnley Rd., 33467-5654. Tel: 561-966-8878.

Lantana, Palm Beach Co., Holy Spirit, Revs. William L. O'Dea; Kevin MacGabhann; James Fiore.
Residence and Mailing—1000 Lantana Rd.,P.O. Box 2978, 33465. Tel: 561-585-5970.

North Palm Beach, Palm Beach Co., St. Clare, Revs. William D. O'Shea; Thomas P. O'Flanagan.
Res., 821 Prosperity Farms Rd., 33408. Tel: 561-622-7477.
School—Mr. Andrew J. Houvouras, Prin. Lay Teachers 25; Students 547.
St. Paul of the Cross, Revs. Arthur Venezia; Michael Tschudi. In res., Rev. Peter Duvelsdorf, S.D.B (RVC).
Res., 10970 State Rd. 703, 33408. Tel: 561-626-1873; Fax: 561-622-7307.

Okeechobee, Okeechobee Co., Sacred Heart, Rev. Hugh Duffy.
Mailing Address: P.O. Box 716, 34973.
Res., 701 S.W. Sixth St., 34973. Tel: 941-763-3727; Fax: 941-763-9334.

Pahokee, Palm Beach Co., St. Mary, Rev. John J. Mericantante.
Res., 1200 E. Main St., 33476. Tel: 561-924-7305; Fax: 561-924-9394.

Palm Beach, Palm Beach Co., St. Edward, Rev. Francis

J. Lechiara; Rev. Msgr. Bernard J. McGrenehan, Pastor Emeritus. In res., Rev. Msgr. James Burke.
Res., 144 N. County Rd., 33480. Tel: 561-832-0400; Fax: 561-833-3359.

Palm City, Martin Co., Holy Redeemer, Rev. Bernard F. Powell.
Mailing Address: P.O. Box 916, 34990.
Res., 1964 Capri St., 34990. Tel: 561-286-4590.

Port St. Lucie, St. Lucie Co., St. Lucie, Revs. Peter C. Dolan, Pastor Emeritus; Jacob Aymanamkuzhy; Rodney Q. Titus.
Res., 446 S.W. Irving St., 34983. Tel: 561-878-1215; Fax: 561-879-1684.
Catechesis/Religious Programs—Students 550.

St. Elizabeth Ann Seton, Revs. Clarence Podgorski; Francis E. Maloney.
Church—930 S.W. Tunis Ave., 34953. Tel: 561-336-0282; Fax: 561-336-1494.

Holy Family, Rev. Thomas F. Cauley.
Mailing Address: P.O. Box 8447, 34985. Tel: 561-335-2385; Fax: 561-335-2517.
Res., 2330 Mariposa Ave., 34953.

Riviera Beach, Palm Beach Co., St. Francis of Assisi, Revs. William M. McSweeney, O.M.I.; Rolland Bennett, O.M.I. In res., Rev. Robert Colfer, O.M.I.
Res., 200 W. 20th St., 33404. Tel: 561-842-2482; Fax: 561-863-2985.
School—Mrs. Judith Edelman, Prin. Lay Teachers 10; Students 160.

Royal Palm Beach, Palm Beach Co., Our Lady Queen of the Apostles, Revs. Edmund L. Szpieg; Michael Woodcock, Pastor.
Res., 172 Kings Way, 33411. Tel: 561-798-5661; Fax: 561-798-5663.
Mailing Address: 100 Crestwood Blvd., S., 33411.

Sebastian, Indian River Co., St. Sebastian, Revs. Timothy Sockol; Tomasz Makowski.
Mailing Address: P.O. Box 78-1212, 32978-1212.
Res., 13075 U.S. Hwy. 1, 32958. Tel: 561-589-5790; Fax: 561-388-0084.

Stuart, Martin Co., St. Joseph, Revs. Richard Murphy; John Morrissey; John Kasparek.
Res., 1200 E. 10th St., 34996. Tel: 561-287-2727; Fax: 561-278-4998.
School—Mrs. Marie Privuznak, Prin. Lay Teachers 21; Students 367.
Mission—Stuart, Martin Co., St. Andrew.

Tequesta, Palm Beach Co., St. Jude, Revs. Thomas Vengayil, Pastor; John J. McAtavey, Pastor Emeritus; Thomas Vengayil, Admin.; Rt. Rev. Edward Campbell, O.S.B.
Mailing Address: P.O. Box 3726, 33469.
Res., 204 U.S. Hwy. 1, 33469. Tel: 561-746-7974; Fax: 561-743-6127.

Vero Beach, Indian River Co., St. Helen, Rev. Msgr. Irvine Nugent, V.G.; Revs. John F. Flynn, S.M.A.; Ramon J. Echeverria.
Res., 2085 Tallahassee Ave., P.O. Box 2927, 32961. Tel: 561-567-5129; Fax: 561-567-4823.
School—2050 Vero Beach Ave., 32960.
Lay Teachers 9; Students 265.

Holy Cross, Rev. John B. O'Hare. In res., Rev. Donal J. O'Hare (WCH).
Mailing Address: P.O. Box 3758, 32964.
Res., 500 Iris Ln., 32964. Tel: 561-231-0671; Fax: 561-234-5653.

St. John of the Cross, Rev. John A. Crowley.
Res., 950 82nd Ave., 32966. Tel: 561-563-0057; Fax: 561-563-0057.

Wellington, Palm Beach Co., St. Rita, Revs. Walter J. Dockerill; Julian Harris; Maciej Piotrowicz.
Res., 13645 Paddock Dr., 33414. Tel: 561-793-8544; Fax: 561-793-4082.

West Palm Beach, Palm Beach Co.,

1—Holy Name of Jesus, Revs. James Murtagh; Lawrence E. Fenton (GI); John Cunningham; Alberto Rodrigues, O.S.S.T.
Res., 345 S. Military Tr., 33415. Tel: 407-683-3555; Fax: 407-683-1051.
School—Sr. Ruth Butler, Prin. Sisters 1; Lay Teachers 13; Students 300.

2—Mary Immaculate, Rev. Timothy J. Lynch.
Res., 390 Sequoia Dr., 33409. Tel: 561-686-8128; Fax: 561-686-8406.

3—St. Ann, Revs. William J. Mayer, S.J.; Wayne Herpin, S.J. In res., Revs. John Edwards, S.J.; Eugene Bannin, S.J.
Res., 310 N. Olive Ave., 33410. Tel: 561-832-3757; Fax: 561-659-1465.
School—Sisters 6; Lay Teachers 12; Students 200.

4—St. John Fisher, Revs. William Martin, O.M.I., Pastor; John Vereb, Pastor Emeritus; Joseph Milford, O.M.I. In res., Revs. Frank Curley, O.M.I.; Joseph Pucci, O.M.I.
Res., 4001 North Shore Dr., 33407. Tel: 561-842-1224.

5—St. Juliana, Revs. Michael O'Flaherty; Michael Edwards; Adrian Torres.
Res., 4500 S. Dixie Hwy., 33405. Tel: 561-833-9745.
School—Mrs. Mary Beth Quick, Prin. Sisters of St. Joseph 4; Lay Teachers 15; Students 261.

Special Assignment:
Reverend Fathers—
Armbrust, Leo F., P.O. Box 4746, Boynton Beach, FL 33424-4746
Devereaux, Martin C., Chap., Lynn University, 3601 N. Military Trail, Boca Raton, FL 33431. Tel: 561-994-0770

On Duty Outside the Diocese:
Reverend Fathers—
Hernandez, Alfredo, Casa Santa Maria, Via dell'Umilta 30, 00187 Rome Italy
McNally, Michael, St. Charles Borromeo Seminary, 1000 E. Wynnewood Rd., Overbrook, PA 19096
Ryan, Patrick, 58 B UPR Dorset St., Apt. 8, Dublin, Ireland

Retired:
Reverend Monsignors—
McGrenehan, Bernard J.
O'Shea, Joseph H.
Reverend Fathers—
Calle, Juan de la
Chepanis, Anthony
Connolly, Larkin
Dolan, Peter C.
Fenech, Francis
McAtavey, John J.
O'Donnell, Richard
Profeta, Salvatore
Sheehan, James
Stack, Christopher
Vereb, John
Victor, Al

Permanent Deacons:
Allgaier, John (NEW)
Ambroise, Emile
Castellanos, Luis, (Retired)
Clifford, Frank
Collins, George (NY)
DiLeonardo, Ignatius (MIA)
DiMauro, Joseph
Galard, John (MIA)
Gallagher, Daniel (NY)
Gluhosky, Frank (HRT)
Jacobi, Robert
Johnson, Louis
Kucera, John (BGP)
Lopez, Jesus
Melendez, Carlos
Mieses, Luis J. (Santo Domingo)
Pagliara, Daniel
Pfeiffer, Robert
Pierce, Jack
Raisch, Jack
Ramos, Geraldo (BGP)
Sawney, Ira (Grenada)
Seppanen, Henry (CAM)
Shellheimer, Bill (NEW)
Toussaint, Henk
Venezia, Richard
Wesley, Albert (FTW)
White, James E. (MIA)

INSTITUTIONS LOCATED IN THE DIOCESE

[A] SEMINARIES, RELIGIOUS OR SCHOLASTICATES

Boynton Beach. *St. Vincent de Paul Regional Seminary*, 10701 S. Military Tr., 33436. Tel: 561-732-4424; Fax: 561-737-2205. Rev. Msgr. Pablo A. Navarro, S.T.L. (MIA), Rector / Pres.; Revs. Stephen Bosso, S.S.L. (PEN), Academic Dean & Vice Rector; Mark Heuberger, M.A. (VEN), Treas.; Robert Stone, S.T.L., Spiritual Dir.; Mark Heuberger, Dir.; Sr. Janet Sullivan, O.S.F., Continuing Education Dir.; Dr. Sixto Garcia, Ph.D.; Dr. Antonio Lopez, Ph.D.; Mr. Art Quinn, L.S., Librarian; Rev. Msgr. William White, M.A. (NY); Revs. Steven O'Hala, S.T.D. (MIA); Peter Plourde, S.S.L. (SP); Juan Quijano, S.T.L. (MIA); Sr. Margarita Gomez, R.M.IK, S.T.L.

[B] HIGH SCHOOLS, DIOCESAN AND PAROCHIAL

Boca Raton. *Pope John Paul II High School*, 4001 N. Military Tr., 33431. Tel: 561-994-8998. Revs. John F. Horan, O.Carm., Pres.; Guy Fiano, O.Carm.; Thomas Zalewski, O.Carm.; Bros. Raymond Maher, O.Carm.; Roberto Perez, O.Carm.; Sr. Eileen Sullivan, O.P., Prin. Sisters 2; Lay Teachers 41; Students 686.

Fort Pierce. *John Carroll High School*, 3402 Delaware Ave., 34947-6116. Tel: 561-464-5200; Fax: 561-464-5233. Rev. Mark A. Szanyi, O.F.M.Conv., Rector; Mr. Clyde L. Russell, Prin.; Revs. Michael Sajda, O.F.M.Conv.; Joseph Dorniak, O.F.M.Conv. Sisters 3; Lay Teachers 27; Students 445.

West Palm Beach. *Cardinal Newman High School*, 512 Spencer Dr., 33409. Tel: 561-683-6266; Fax: 561-683-7307. Revs. David Carr, Pres.; Michael Allison, Chap.; Thomas Barrett. Lay Teachers 52; Students 765.

[C] SCHOOLS, PRIVATE

Indiantown. *Hope Rural School.* (Grades K-6), 15929 S.W. 150th St., 34956. Tel: 561-597-2203. Sr. Marie Celeste Gatti, O.P., Dir.; Sr. Marion Hangsterfer, O.P., Prin. Sisters 3; Lay Teachers 7; Students 148.

West Palm Beach.
**Rosarian Academy.* (Grades PreK-8), 807 N. Flagler Dr., 33401. Tel: 561-832-5131. Sisters of St. Dominic (Adrian, MI). Rev. William Martin, O.M.I., Chap.; Sr. Jean Aufderheide, O.P., Prin. Sisters 6; Lay Teachers 26; Students 317.

[D] GENERAL HOSPITALS

West Palm Beach. *St. Mary's Hospital, Inc.*, 901 45th St., 33407-2495. Tel: 561-881-2865; Fax: 561-881-2864.
For a complete listing, refer to the Hospitals section.

[E] HOMES FOR AGED

West Palm Beach. *Noreen McKeen Residence for Geriatric Care*, 315 Flagler Dr., S., 33401. Tel: 561-655-8544.
For a complete listing, refer to the Special Care Facilities section.

[F] PERSONAL PRELATURES

Delray Beach. *Opus Dei.* (Prelature of the Holy Cross and Opus Dei), 4409 Frances Dr., 33445. Tel: 561-498-1249. Legal Title: *The Work of God, Inc.* Revs. Jay Alvarez; Christopher Schmitt.

[G] MONASTERIES AND RESIDENCES OF PRIESTS AND BROTHERS

Boca Raton. *St. Elias Priory-Order of Carmelites, NY*, 4944 Rabbit Hollow, 33487. Tel: 561-995-6762; 997-2089. Revs. Thomas Zalewski, O.Carm.; Guy Fiano, O.Carm., Prior; John Horan, O.Carm.

North Palm Beach. *Our Lady of Florida Spiritual Center*, 1300 U.S. Hwy. No. 1, 33408. Tel: 561-626-1300; Fax: 561-627-3956. Revs. Francis Finnigan, C.P., Dir. Retreats; Damian Towey, C.P.; Isaias Powers, C.P.; Raphael Amrhein, C.P.; Bros. Raymond Maher, O.Carm.; Roberto Perez, O.Carm.; Sr. Breda Eustace, C.P. Priests 4.

Tequesta. *P.I.M.E. Missionaries*, 1550 Beach Rd., 33469. Tel: 561-746-7767. Revs. Nicholas Maestrini, P.I.M.E., Rector; Pasquale Persico, P.I.M.E.

Vero Beach. *Paulist Fathers Retirement Home*, 1225 20th Ave., 32960. Tel: 561-562-0500. Revs. James E. Joyce, C.S.P.; Thomas J. Marley, C.S.P.; Edward J. Lyons, C.S.P.; William J. Cantwell, C.S.P.; George Helmich, C.S.P.

[H] CONVENTS AND RESIDENCES FOR SISTERS

Delray Beach. *Christ the King Monastery of St. Clare.* (Solemn Vows, Papal Enclosure), 3900 Sherwood Blvd., 33445-5699. Tel: 561-498-3294. Mother Mary Veronica Butler, O.S.C., Abbess. Cloistered Sisters 9; Extern Sisters 3; Novices 1.

Claretian Missionary, Sisters of Florida, Inc., 9600 W. Atlantic Ave., 33446. Tel: 561-498-9239.

West Palm Beach. *Adrian Dominican Sisters, Florida Mission Chapter*, 810 N. Olive Ave., 33401. Tel: 561-832-6521; Fax: 561-820-8750. Sr. Marie Carleen Maly, O.P., Chapter Prioress.

[I] RETREAT HOUSES

Lantana. *The Cenacle, Spiritual Life Center*, 1400 S. Dixie Hwy., 33462-5492. Tel: 561-582-2534; Fax: 561-582-8070. Spiritual Life Center for laity, and religious. Sisters 7.

North Palm Beach. *Our Lady of Florida Spiritual Center*, 1300 U.S. Hwy. No. 1, 33408. Tel: 561-626-1300; Fax: 561-627-3956.

[J] MISCELLANEOUS LISTINGS

Palm Beach Gardens. *Christ Child Society of Boca Raton*, P.O. Box 109650, 33410-9650.

Con El, Inc., 33410-9650. Mailing Address: P.O. Box 109650, 33410-9650. 9995 N. Military Tr., 33410-9650.

Diocesan Council of Catholic Women, 33410-9650. Mailing Address: P.O. Box 109650, 33410-9650. 9995 N. Military Tr., 33410-9650. Rev. Msgr. Irvine Nugent, V.G., Diocesan Moderator; Mrs. Margaret Gray, Pres.

Diocesan Health Plan Trust, 33410-9650. Mailing Address: P.O. Box 109650, 33410-9650. 9995 N. Military Tr., 33410-9650. Most Rev. J. Keith Symons; Rev. Francis Lechiara, Chm.

Diocesan Pension Plan Trust, 33410-9650. Mailing Address: P.O. Box 109650, 33410-9650. 9995 N. Military Tr., 33410-9650.

Members: Most Rev. J. Keith Symons; Rev. Francis Lechiara.

Diocesan Property & Liability Insurance Committee, 34410-9650. Mailing Address: P.O. Box 109650, 33410-9650. 9995 N. Military Tr., 34410-9650. Rev. Richard Murphy, Chm.

Diocese of Palm Beach Endowment Trust, 33410-9650. Mailing Address: P.O. Box 109650, 33410-9650. 9995 N. Military Tr., 33410-9650.

The Florida Catholic of Palm Beach, Inc., 33410-9650. Mailing Address: P.O. Box 109650, 33410-9650. 9995 N. Military Tr., 33410-9650.

BOYNTON BEACH. *St. Vincent de Paul Regional Seminary Endowment Trust*, 10701 S. Military Tr., 33436.

JENSEN BEACH. *Villa Assumpta, Inc.*, 2539 N.E. Mission Dr., 9-8, 34957. Tel: 561-334-0009. Ms. Linda Matz, Res. Mgr.

NORTH PALM BEACH. *Christ Child Society of Palm Beach*, P.O. Box 14441, 33408. Tel: 561-626-4695. Marie Emsweiler, Contact Person.

PALM CITY. *St. Raphael Family Life Center*, P.O. Box 887, 34991. Tel: 561-287-9088.

RIVIERA BEACH. *Society of St. Vincent de Paul, District Council*, 2567 Old Dixie Hwy., 33404. Tel: 561-845-0562. Mr. Joseph Kaht, Contact Person.

Villa Franciscan, Inc., 2101 Avenue F, 33404. Tel: 561-840-0444; Fax: 561-840-9444.

VERO BEACH. *Society of St. Vincent de Paul, St. Sebastian Conference*, 5480 85th St. (Wabasso), 32967. Tel: 561-589-3338. Mr. Paul Wolff, Contact Person.

WEST PALM BEACH. *Catholic Charities of the Diocese of Palm Beach, Inc.*, 34410-9650. Mailing Address: P.O. Box 109650, 34410-9650. 9995 N. Military Tr., 34410-9650.

Emmaus Residence, P.O. Box 247, 33402-8999. Tel: 561-863-9227; Fax: 561-863-1680. Rev. John Edwards, S.J., Dir.

RELIGIOUS INSTITUTES OF MEN REPRESENTED IN THE DIOCESE

For further details refer to the corresponding bracketed number in the Religious Institutes of Men or Women section.

[0200]—*Benedictine Monks*.—O.S.B.
[0350]—*Cistercian Order*.—O.C.S.O.
[1330]—*Congregation of Mission*.—C.M.
[1030]—*Congregation of St. Paul*.—C.S.P.
[1000]—*Congregation of the Passionists*.—C.P.
[0480]—*Conventual Franciscans*.—O.F.M.Conv.
[0520]—*Franciscan Friars*. (Holy Name Prov.).—O.F.M.
[0520]—*Franciscan Friars*. (Immaculate Conception Prov.).—O.F.M.
[1210]—*Missionaries of St. Charles - Scalabrinians*.—C.S.
[0870]—*Monfort Missionaries*.—S.M.M.
[0270]—*Order of Carmelites*.—O.Carm.
[0910]—*Order of Mary Immaculate*.—O.M.I.
[1310]—*Order of the Most Holy Trinity*.—O.S.S.T.
[1050]—*Pontifical Institute for Foreign Missions*.—P.I.M.E.
[1190]—*Salesians of Don Bosco*.—S.D.B.
[0110]—*Society of African Missions*.—S.M.A.
[0690]—*Society of Jesus*.—S.J.
[0370]—*Society of St. Columban*.—S.S.C.

RELIGIOUS INSTITUTIONS OF WOMEN REPRESENTED IN THE DIOCESE

[0130]—*Apostles of the Sacred Heart of Jesus*.—A.S.C.J.
[0330]—*Carmelite Sisters for the Aged and Infirm*.—O.Carm.
[0685]—*Claretian Missionary Sisters*.—R.M.I.
[]—*Congregation of Sisters of the Passion*.—C.P.
[1070-03]—*Dominican Sisters*. (Sinsinawa, WI).—O.P.
[1070-13]—*Dominican Sisters*
[1070-06]—*Dominican Sisters*. (Newburgh, NY).—O.P.
[1070-16]—*Dominican Sisters*. (Ossining, NY).—O.P.
[1070-22]—*Dominican Sisters*. (Fall River, MA).—O.P.
[]—*Dominican Sisters of St. Catherine de Ricci*.—O.P.
[1140]—*Eucharistic Missionaries of St. Dominic*.—O.P.
[]—*Franciscan Sisters*. (Milwaukee, WI).—O.S.F.
[1180]—*Franciscan Sisters of Allegany, NY*.—O.S.F.
[1310]—*Franciscan Sisters of Little Falls*.—O.S.F.
[1845]—*Guadalupana Missionaries of the Holy Spirit*.—M.G.Sp.S.
[]—*Hermitage of Diocese of Palm Beach*.
[2575]—*Institute of Sisters of Mercy of the Americas*.—R.S.M.
[3760]—*Order of St. Clare*.—O.S.C.
[3460]—*Religious of Mary Immaculate*.—R.M.I.
[3110]—*Religious of Our Lady of the Cenacle*.—R.C.
[3465]—*Religious of the Sacred Heart of Mary*.—R.S.H.M.
[2970]—*School Sisters of Notre Dame*.—S.S.N.D.
[1680]—*School Sisters of St. Francis*.—S.S.S.F.
[0440]—*Sisters of Charity of Cincinnati, OH*.—S.C.
[0500]—*Sisters of Charity of Nazareth*.—S.C.N.
[0430]—*Sisters of Charity of the Blessed Virgin Mary*.—B.V.M.
[2110]—*Sisters of Humility of Mary*.—H.M.
[2560]—*Sisters of Mary Reparatrix*.—S.M.R.
[3000]—*Sisters of Notre Dame de Namur*.—S.N.D.deN.
[3340]—*Sisters of Providence*.—S.P.
[0590]—*Sisters of St. Elizabeth, Convent Station*.—S.C.
[1800]—*Sisters of St. Francis of the Third Order Regular*. (Williamsville, NY).—O.S.F.
[3840]—*Sisters of St. Joseph of Carondelet*.—C.S.J.
[]—*Sisters of St. Joseph of St. Augustine*.—S.S.J.
[0260]—*Sisters of the Blessed Sacrament*.—S.B.S.
[1990]—*Sisters of the Holy Names of Jesus and Mary*.—S.N.J.M.
[]—*Sisters of the Most Holy Soul of Jesus*.
[2150]—*Sisters, Servants of the Immaculate Heart of Mary*.—I.H.M.
[2490]—*Society of Catholic Medical Missionaries*.—S.C.M.M.

DIOCESAN CEMETERIES

WEST PALM BEACH. *Our Lady Queen of Peace Catholic Cemetery, Inc.*, 10941 Southern Blvd., 33406. Tel: 561-793-0711.

Board of Directors: Rev. Thomas Vengayil, Chm. & Dir.; Mrs. Marian Harris, Admin.; Mr. Joseph Altobello; Revs. Walter Dockerill; Michael Edwards; Mr. Albert Brooks; Mr. Earl Quattlebaum; Mr. Brad Zahn; Miss Diana Lewis.

NECROLOGY

† Watterson, Peter F., Palm Beach Gardens, FL, Prison Ministry. —Died Sep. 12, 1996.

Diocese of Paterson

(Dioecesis Patersonensis)

Most Reverend

FRANK J. RODIMER, D.D., J.C.D.

Bishop of Paterson; ordained May 19, 1951; appointed Bishop of Paterson December 13, 1977; ordained and installed February 28, 1978. *Res., 178 Derrom Ave., Paterson, NJ, 07504.*

ESTABLISHED DECEMBER 9, 1937.

Square Miles 1,214.

Comprises the Counties of Passaic, Morris and Sussex in the State of New Jersey.

For legal titles of parishes and diocesan institutions, consult the Chancery Office.

Diocesan Center: 777 Valley Rd., Clifton, NJ, 07013. Tel.: 201-777-8818; Fax: 201-777-8976.

STATISTICAL OVERVIEW

Personnel	
Bishop	1
Abbots	2
Retired Abbots	4
Priests: Diocesan Active in Diocese	193
Priests: Active Outside Diocese	23
Priests: Retired, Sick or Absent	57
Number of Diocesan Priests	273
Religious Priests in Diocese	201
Extern Priests in Diocese	16
Ordinations:	
Diocesan Priests	2
Permanent Deacons in Diocese	138
Total Brothers	42
Total Sisters	960
Parishes	
Parishes	111
With Resident Pastor:	
Resident Diocesan Priests	98
Resident Religious Priests	12
Without Resident Pastor:	
Administered by Priests	1
Pastoral Centers	5
Professional Ministry Personnel:	
Brothers	3
Sisters	57
Lay Ministers	108
Welfare	
Catholic Hospitals	3
Total Assisted	698,290
Homes for the Aged	9
Total Assisted	471
Residential Care of Children	2
Total Assisted	56
Day Care and Extended Day Care Centers	20
Total Assisted	900
Specialized Homes	2
Total Assisted	16,000
Special Centers for Social Services	13
Total Assisted	36,000
Residential Care of Disabled	8
Total Assisted	60
Educational	
Diocesan Students in Other Seminaries	8
Seminaries, Religious	4
Students Religious	11
Total Seminarians	19
Colleges and Universities	2
Total Students	1,614
High Schools, Diocesan and Parish	5
Total Students	2,411
High Schools, Private	5
Total Students	1,576
Elementary Schools, Diocesan and Parish	58
Total Students	16,156
Elementary Schools, Private	3
Total Students	572
Catechesis/Religious Education:	
High School Students	8,892
Elementary Students	31,530
Total Students Under Catholic Instruction	62,770
Teachers in the Diocese:	
Priests	45
Brothers	20
Sisters	193
Lay Teachers	1,111
Vital Statistics	
Receptions into the Church:	
Infant Baptism Totals	8,887
Adult Baptism Totals	184
Received into Full Communion	372
First Communions	7,152
Confirmations	3,936
Marriages:	
Catholic	1,638
Interfaith	577
Total Marriages	2,215
Deaths	3,756
Total Catholic Population	377,650
Total Population	1,048,018

Former Bishops—Most Rev. THOMAS H. MCLAUGHLIN, S.T.D., LL.D., cons. July 25, 1935; transferred to Paterson, Dec. 16, 1937; died March 17, 1947.—Most Rev. THOMAS A. BOLAND, S.T.D., cons. July 25, 1940; transferred to Paterson, June 21, 1947; transferred to Newark as Archbishop, Nov. 15, 1952; died March 16, 1979.—Most Rev. JAMES A. MCNULTY, D.D., appt. Auxiliary Bishop of Newark, Aug. 2, 1947; cons. Oct. 7, 1947; appt. Bishop of Paterson, April 9, 1953; transferred to Diocese of Buffalo, Feb. 12, 1963; died Sept. 4, 1972.—Most Rev. JAMES J. NAVAGH, D.D., cons. Sept. 24, 1952; appt. Bishop of Ogdensburg, May 8, 1957; transferred to Bishop of Paterson, Feb. 12, 1963; died Oct. 2, 1965.—Most Rev. LAWRENCE B. CASEY, D.D., appt. Auxiliary Bishop of Rochester, Feb. 10, 1953; cons. May 5, 1953; appt. Bishop of Paterson, March 9, 1966; died June 15, 1977.

Vicar General—Rev. Msgr. JOSEPH R. BRESTEL.

Vicar for Administration, Moderator of the Curia—Rev. Msgr. HERBERT K. TILLYER.

Vicar for Planning and Priorities—Rev. Msgr. JAMES T. MAHONEY.

Vicar for Retired Priests—Rev. RAYMOND LOPATESKY.

Vicar for Religious—Sr. JOAN KERWIN LAWLER, C.S.J.P.

Vicar for Deacons—Rev. ROBERT DIACHEK.

Deans—Paterson: Rev. Msgr. THOMAS J. COLETTA, Clifton: Rev. VICTOR J. MAZZA, Passaic: Rev. Msgr. JOHN PODGORNY, Mid Passaic County: Rev. Msgr. EUGENE BOLAND, Northern Passaic County: Rev. Msgr. PATRICK G. PANOS, Southwestern Morris County: Rev. WILLIAM NAUGHTON, Southeastern Morris County: Rev. Msgr. RONALD AMANDOLARE, Eastern Morris County: Rev. MARTIN MCDONNELL, Northeastern Morris County: Rev. Msgr. JOHN J. CARROLL, Northern Morris County: Rev. JOSEPH J. GOODE, Western Morris County: Rev. Msgr. JOHN FITZPATRICK, Sussex County: Rev. WILLIAM P. STOBER.

Diocesan Center—*777 Valley Rd., Clifton, 07013.* Tel: 201-777-8818; Fax: 201-777-8976. Office Hours: Mon.-Fri. 9-4:30 All mail should be addressed to this office.

Chancellor—Rev. Msgr. HERBERT K. TILLYER.

Vice Chancellors—Rev. T. MARK CONDON; Sr. JOAN KERWIN LAWLER, C.S.J.P.

Archivist—Rev. RAYMOND J. KUPKE.

Secretary to the Bishop—Rev. T. MARK CONDON.

Admin. Asst. to the Bishop—Mrs. KIT SPRINGER.

Admin. Asst. to the Chancellor—Mrs. GRACE MAZZA.

Secretary to the Vice Chancellor—Mrs. MARY PORTELLI.

Diocesan Counsel—Mr. JAMES EVERS.

Diocesan Tribunal—

Judicial Vicar—Rev. EDWARD J. KURTYKA, J.C.D.

Adjutant Judicial Vicars—Revs. JOSEPH T. ANGINOLI, J.C.L.; JOHN E. HART, J.C.L.

Advocates—Revs. JOHN T. CONNOLLY, M.Div.; MARK A. MANCINI, M.Div.

Auditors—Deacon PHILIP F. HEALY; Miss ANN SMITH HUGHES.

Defenders of the Bond—Rev. T. MARK CONDON, J.C.L.; Rev. Msgr. KENNETH E. LASCH, J.C.D.

Pro-Synodal Judges—Rev. Msgr. JOHN J. CARROLL, Ed.D.; Rev. JOHN T. CATOIR, J.C.D.; Rev. Msgr. JOHN J. DEMKOVICH; Rev. Msgr. JOHN H. DERICKS; Rev. EDWARD J. HINDS, J.C.L.; Rev. Msgr. HERBERT K. TILLYER, M.Ch.A.; Rev. Msgr. THOMAS J. TRAPASSO, S.T.L.; Rev. REGIS P. WALLACE, O.S.B.

Administrative Assistants and Notaries—Mrs. JULIE BARAM; Mrs. PATRICIA CZERNIEWSKI; Mrs. ROSE LUCIGNANI.

Consulting Psychologist—EDMUND J. RUBIN, Ph.D.; JAMES A. SAVAGE, Psy.D.

Presbyteral Council—Rev. Msgr. JOSEPH R. BRESTEL; Rev. Msgr. JOHN J. CARROLL; Rev. Msgr. HERBERT K. TILLYER; Revs. ALEX B. CYMERMAN, O.F.M.Conv.; HERNAN ARIAS; MICHAEL J. DRURY; Rev. Msgr. JAMES L. FALLON; Revs. GEORGE F. HUNDT; PAUL S. MANNING; JOHN J. KLEIN; PAUL DALY; MARTIN G. GLYNN; RICHARD RENTO; ROBERT WISNIEFSKI.

College of Consultors—Rev. Msgr. JOSEPH R. BRESTEL; Rev. Msgr. HERBERT K. TILLYER; Revs. HERNAN ARIAS; MICHAEL J. DRURY; Rev. Msgr. JAMES L. FALLON; Revs. PAUL S. MANNING; GEORGE F. HUNDT; PAUL DALY; MARTIN G. GLYNN; RICHARD RENTO; JOHN J. KLEIN; ROBERT WISNIEFSKI.

Diocesan Secretariats

Communications Secretariat—Mr. VICTOR F. WINKLER, *869 Broadway, Paterson, 07514.* Tel: 201-278-3491; Fax: 201-278-3202.

"The Beacon"—Diocesan Newspaper, Mr. VICTOR F.

WINKLER, Editor-in-Chief; Mr. RICHARD A. SOKERKA, Gen. Mgr.; Mr. JOSEPH TINTLE, News Editor, *597 Valley Rd., P.O. Box 1887, Clifton, 07015.* Tel: 201-279-8845.

Office of Evangelization / Communications—Rev. JOHN T. CATOIR, Dir., *63 Monroe St., Passaic, 07055.* Tel: 201-777-0303; Fax: 201-742-5033.

Communications Office—MARIANNA THOMPSON, Dir., *597 Valley Rd., P.O. Box 1887, Clifton, 07015.* Tel: 201-278-3202; Fax: 201-279-2265.

Secretariat For Parish Life—Mr. PHILIP A. RUSSO, Exec. Sec., *777 Valley Rd., Clifton, 07013.* Tel: 201-777-8818.

Office of Family/Respect Life—Mrs. MARY LYNN TOWNSLEY, Consultant.

Engaged Encounter—Rev. ROBERT J. MITCHELL, Spiritual Dir. Tel: 201-347-3190. Chair Couple: LORETTA CALDO; ROBERT CALDO. Tel: 201-697-2279.

Natural Family Planning—Rev. PAUL DUGGAN, Spiritual Dir. Chair Couple: FRANK TRACEY; DIANA TRACEY. Tel: 201-398-6246. Registration Couple: ANTHONY HOFFMAN; SHARON HOFFMAN. Tel: 201-785-4372.

Office of Parish Catechetics—Mr. THOMAS BROWN, Consultant.

Catechetical Leaders Association—Ms. LIZ TOMLINSON. Tel: 201-548-6028.

Office of Ministry Among Hispanics—Sr. MARY KATHLEEN FLANNERY, S.S.J., Consultant; Ms. IVANNIA VEGA, Consultant for Hispanic Youth & Family Ministry.

Commission for Hispanic Catholic Ministry—Rev. HERNAN ARIAS, Chm. Tel: 201-345-4070.

Office of Worship and Spirituality—Vacant.

Liturgical Commission—Rev. ELIAS LORENZO, O.S.B., Chm. Tel: 201-538-3231.

Environment and Architecture—Vacant.

Office of Youth Ministry—Mr. PHILIP RUSSO, Consultant.

Catholic Scouting—Rev. WAYNE VARGA. Tel: 201-539-2141.

Office for Campus Ministry—Rev. LOUIS J. SCURTI, Coord., Catholic Campus Ministers. Tel: 201-595-6184.

Ecumenical Officer—Rev. CHARLES J. PARR.

Media Resourcing—Mrs. GINGER MOLL.

Related Organizations—

Catholic Deaf Society—Rev. JOSEPH J. GOODE, Moderator. Tel: 201-627-0422. Rev. Msgr. THOMAS J. TRAPASSO, Asst. Moderator.

Charismatic Renewal—Rev. BRENDAN J. MURRAY, Liaison. Tel: 201-627-0313.

English Cursillos—Ms. MARY ANN ROGERS, Lay Dir. Spiritual Advisors: Rev. JOHN A. CONNELL; Deacon JOSEPH PARLAPIANO. Tel: 908-637-6174.

Spanish Cursillos—Mr. JOSE TRINIDAD, Lay Dir. Tel: 201-595-9327. Revs. PETER NAPOLI, O.F.M.Cap. Tel: 201-742-2142. JOSEPH SANTABIBIANA, S.D.B. Tel: 201-742-9695.

Pastoral Administration

Division of Clergy and Personnel—

Clergy Personnel Office—Rev. Msgr. THOMAS ZAZZELLA, Dir.; Mrs. ROSEMARY J. DONNELLY, Admin. Asst., *737 Valley Rd., Clifton, 07013.* Tel: 201-777-2955.

Deacon Internship Program—Rev. FRANCIS J. DUFFY, Dir., *6 Sussex Ave., Morristown, 07960.* Tel: 201-538-4851.

Ministry for Priestly Formation and Education—Rev. CHARLES J. PARR, Dir., *737 Valley Rd., Clifton, 07013.* Tel: 201-777-5651.

Mission Office—Rev. Msgr. JOHN J. DEMKOVICH, Dir.; Mrs. ELEANOR MATAS, Office Mgr., *24 DeGrasse St., Paterson, 07505.* Tel: 201-278-3491.

Office of Health Care Ministry—Rev. ROBERT M. DIACHEK, Dir., *74 Kahdena Rd., Morristown, 07960.* Tel: 201-538-3500.

Office of the Permanent Diaconate—Rev. ROBERT M. DIACHEK, Vicar; Sr. MARY CATHERINE WALTON, S.S.J., Dir., Formation, *74 Kahdena Rd., Morristown, 07960.* Tel: 201-538-6849.

Vicar for Religious Communities—Sr. JOAN KERWIN LAWLER, C.S.J.P., Vicar. Tel: 201-777-8818.

Vocations Office—Rev. PAUL S. MANNING, Dir., *737 Valley Rd., Clifton, 07013.* Tel: 201-472-2812.

Division of Finance and Budget—

Business Office—Mr. WILLIAM H. HINKES, Finance Officer; Mr. WAYNE G. LONG, Business Mgr.; Mr. JOSEPH LIPARI, Controller; Miss. DEBORAH MINNICH, Bookkeeper; Mrs. JOYCE LARSEN, Sec., *777 Valley Rd., Clifton, 07013.*

Diocesan Facilities Manager—Mr. JAMES FIERRO.

Insurance Office—Mrs. JAYNE CICCARELLI, Employee Benefits; Mrs. JOSEPHINE SWAN; Miss ZULMA TORRES, Property-Liability-Auto Claims; Mr. LEONARD ZEMECKIS, Claims Adjuster, *777 Valley Rd., Clifton, 07013.* Tel: 201-777-8818.

Buildings and Sites Commission—Rev. Msgr. GEORGE DUDAK, Chm., *Rte. 24, Schooleys Mountain, 07870.* Tel: 908-876-4395.

Diocesan Cemetery Office—Rev. Msgr. HERBERT K. TILLYER, Dir.; Mr. JOHN M. CAVANAUGH, Asst. Dir., *58 McLean Blvd., Paterson, 07513.* Tel: 201-279-2900.

School Division—Mr. FRANK PETRUCELLI, Supt.; Sr. MARY LOU LAFFERTY, O.S.F., Asst. Supt., Elementary Education; Sr. DOROTHY BANASHAK, S.S.C., Asst. Supt., Secondary Education and Governmental Programs; Sr. URSULA BUTLER, O.S.B., Asst. Supt., Elementary Education; Sr. NANCY GRASSIA, O.S.F., Asst. Supt., Planning and Research; Ms. GAIL STRONG, Asst. Supt., Elementary Education; Mr. PATRICK PEACE, Dir., School Finance; Mr. EDWIN PETERSON, Education Council Pres.; Ms. KAREN FASANELLA, Elementary Principals' Assoc. Pres., *777 Valley Rd., Clifton, 07013.* Tel: 201-777-8818.

Social Ministries—Mr. MICHAEL J. MAIELLO, Exec. Sec., *476 17th Ave., Paterson, 07504.* Tel: 201-523-7361.

Catholic Family and Community Services—Mr. MICHAEL J. MAIELLO, Exec. Dir.; Ms. PAT MATSON, Admin. Asst.; Ms. VIRGINIA GROSSI, Staff Attorney; Mr. ROBERT JACOBS, Controller, *24 De Grasse St., Paterson, 07501.* Tel: 201-279-7100.

Aging Services—Ms. PATRICIA REIDY, Dir., *24 DeGrasse St., Paterson, 07501.* Tel: 201-279-7100.

Family Services—Rev. THOMAS MCGRATH, Dir., *476 17th Ave., Paterson, 07504.* Tel: 201-523-9595.

Friendship Corner—Ms. JANET TERRY, Dir., *Alabama Ave., Paterson, 07509.* Tel: 201-684-3742.

Parish Social Ministries—Sr. CATHERINE FRANCIS LAMB, M.S.B.T., Dir., *476 17th Ave., Paterson, 07504.* Tel: 201-527-7361.

Hispanic Information Center—Mr. LORENZO HERNANDEZ, Dir., *270 Passaic St., Passaic, 07055.* Tel: 201-779-7022.

Immigration and Refugee Services—Ms. MAI LIEU, Dir., *24 DeGrasse St., Paterson, 07501.* Tel: 201-279-7100.

Italian Catholic Center—Miss PHILOMENA DESOPO, Dir., *24 DeGrasse St., Paterson, 07501.* Tel: 201-278-4955.

Mt. St. Joseph's Children Center—Sr. DOROTHY SHEAHAN, S.C., *124 Shepherd Ln., Totowa, 07512.* Tel: 201-595-5720.

Multi-Lingual Center—Ms. ROSE KARDASHIAN, Dir., *24 DeGrasse St., Paterson, 07501.* Tel: 201-279-7100.

The Palloti Center—Mr. SALVATORE TOLLIS, Dir., *44 Ward St., Paterson, 07051.* Tel: 201-523-5144.

Partnership for Social Services—Sr. THOMASINA GEBHARD, S.S.M., Dir., *48 Wyker Rd., Franklin, 07416.* Tel: 201-827-4702.

Father English Multi-Purpose Community Center—Deacon ROBERT VESOTA, Exec. Dir., *435 Main St., Paterson, 07501.* Tel: 201-881-0280.

Pre School Day Care Center Programs—A Child's World-El Mundo del Nino; EUNICE RAMIREZ, Dir. A Child's Time-El Tiempo del Nino; LILA BANKS, Dir., *433 Main St., Paterson, 07501.* Tel: 201-278-3110. El Mundo de Colores; LAURA ZARIFE, Dir., *44 Ward St., Paterson, 07505.* Tel: 201-523-0919.

Youth Haven—Shelter-Crisis Intervention, Ms. JESUSA ORGANISTA, Dir., *212 Slater St., Paterson, 07501.* Tel: 201-881-1611.

Catholic Social Services of Morris County, Inc. (Hope House)—Mrs. DIANNE KWIATKOWSKI, Exec. Dir.; Ms. CHRISTINE SCHUETTE, Dir., Community and Agency Resources; Mrs. CAROL STOLZ, Coord., Fix-It Program; Mr. NELSON ROBINSON, Coord., Alcoholism Programs; Mr. MICHAEL DAVID-WILSON, Dir., Aids Center; Ms. MARTHA OSTER, Asst. Dir., Aids Center; Mrs. MARY MURDTER, Coord., Home Sharing Program; GAIL CASSESE, Dir., Substance Abuse Program; Ms. JEANINE DAKIN, Dir., Finance and Admin.; Ms. FRANCES CHIODO, Coord., Chore Program; Mrs. DULCE B. HALEY, Clinical Supvr.; Ms. SHARON MATUSA, Coord., AIDS Pastoral Care, *19-21 Belmont Ave., Dover, 07801.* Tel: 201-361-5555.

Department for Persons with Disabilities—Mr. THOMAS A. BARRETT, Exec. Dir.; Ms. JULIE FEEHAN, Assoc. Dir. Quality Improvement Specialists: Ms. JENNIFER MURPHY; Ms. BARBARA OCKER; Mr. SCOTT MILLIKEN, Staff Trainer; Sr. JOAN KATHLEEN GERCKE, S.S.J., Dir., Human Resources; Mr. ROCCO ZAPPILE, Comptroller, *1049 Weldon Rd., Oak Ridge, 07438.* Tel: 201-697-4394.

Group Homes—

Murray House—Ms. DEBBIE LICHTER, Dir., *86 Allwood Pl., Clifton, 07015.* Tel: 201-470-5694.

Wayne Marathon House—Mrs. JOANN VALLES, Dir., *648 Black Oak Ridge Rd., Wayne, 07470.* Tel: 201-628-9074.

Finnegan House—Ms. BETTY PORMAN, Dir., *1049 Weldon Rd., Oak Ridge, 07438.* Tel: 201-697-1246.

Alexander House—Ms. ARLENE GROSENBECK, Dir., *1049 Weldon Rd., Oak Ridge, 07438.* Tel: 201-697-1812.

Columbus House—Ms. CHERYL COURTRIGHT, Dir., *1049 Weldon Rd., Oak Ridge, 07438.* Tel: 201-697-1644.

Wehrlen House—Ms. MARGARET DOYLE, Dir., *18 Bisset Dr., West Milford, 07480.* Tel: 201-208-1883.

Gruenert Adult Training Center—Mrs. KATHY ROSKO, Dir., *Belmont Ave., Dover, 07801.* Tel: 201-328-7479.

Basile Apartment—Mrs. GRISELDA MANJARRES, Dir., *Kings Arms Apts., Byrne Ct., Wayne, 07470.* Tel: 201-633-1809.

Keleher Apartments—Ms. PAMELA VAN ACK, Dir., *67B Pike Dr., Wayne, 07470.* Tel: 201-697-4394.

Straight and Narrow, Inc.—Rev. NORMAN O'CONNOR, C.S.P., Exec. Dir. LORNA PANGARA, Exec. Asst.; Dr. RICHARD GUILD, Dir., Adult Residential Treatment; Mrs. KAREN BAILEY, Dir., Alpha Program; JUDY HIRSCHLOG, Dir., Meadowview Program; Secaucus, NJ: Ms. PHYLLIS ANDERSON, R.N., Supt., Nurses; Dr. RICHARD GUILD, Dir., Cedar Out-Patient Clinic; Bro. KENNETH HARDING, O.F.M., Dir., Juvenile Treatment Unit; Revs. MICHAEL MOORE, (YAK) Dir. Pastoral Care Unit; GREG DROGON, Counselor, *296 Straight St., Paterson, 07501.* Tel: 201-345-6000.

McNulty Half-Way House—Mr. ANGELO ZECCA, Dir., *101 Cedar St., Paterson, 07501.* Tel: 201-279-7003.

Medical Day Care Center—HENRIETTA LEMON, R.N., Dir., *180 E. 19th St., Paterson.*

Methadone Maintenance Centers—DENIS MANSMANN, Dir., *Bergen Pines Hospital, E. Ridgewood Ave., Paramus, Bergen Pines Hospital, 75 E. Broadway, Hackensack.*

Affiliated Organizations—

Apostleship of Prayer—Rev. CHRISTOPHER DILELLA, Dir., *26 Green Village Rd., Madison, 07040.* Tel: 201-377-4000.

Diocesan Council of Catholic Women—Rev. Msgr. JOSEPH A. CIAMPAGLIO, Dir., *152 Mt. Pleasant Ave., Dover, 07801.* Tel: 201-366-7095. Mrs. KATHLEEN LEVENDUSKY, *126 Day St., Clifton, 07011.* Tel: 201-772-5918.

Justice and Peace Commission—Rev. PATRICK RICE.

Diocesan Holy Name Federation—Mr. FRANK STEINER, Pres.

Legion of Mary—Rev. Msgr. JOHN J. DEMKOVICH, Spiritual Dir. GEORGE A. PATINO, Pres., *63 Monroe St., Passaic, 07055.* Tel: 201-779-0427.

Priests Eucharistic League—Rev. CHRISTOPHER DILELLA, Dir., *26 Green Village Rd., Madison, 07040.* Tel: 201-377-4000.

Commission for Black Catholic Ministries—Mr. BRUCE B. LAWSON, Pres. Tel: 201-898-9260.

Commission for Hispanic Catholic Ministries—Rev. HERNAN ARIAS, Chm.

CLERGY, PARISHES, MISSIONS AND PAROCHIAL SCHOOLS

CITY OF PATERSON
(Passaic County)

1—CATHEDRAL OF ST. JOHN THE BAPTIST (1820), Rev. Msgr. Mark J. Giordani; Revs. Gilberto Gutierrez (Colombia); Luis A. Rendon (Colombia). In res., Deacon Manuel Santiago.
Res., 381 Grand St., 07505. Tel: 201-345-4070; Fax: 201-345-7831. [CEM]
School—Pope John Paul II School. See Elementary Schools, Diocesan under Institutions Located in the Diocese for details.

2—ST. AGNES (1883), Revs. Luciano Cruz; Juan Carlos Ruiz; Sr. Patricia Clossey, C.H.C., Pastoral Assoc.
Res., 681 Main St., 07503. Tel: 201-279-0250.

3—ST. ANTHONY'S (1909) (Italian), Revs. Joseph Santa-Bibiana, S.D.B.; Kenneth Shaw, S.D.B.; Vincent Duffy, S.D.B.; Bruce Craig, S.D.B.
Res., 138 Beech St., 07501. Tel: 201-742-9695; Fax: 201-881-0522.
School—(1921), 144 Beech St., 07501. Tel: 201-279-3510; Fax: 201-523-1757.
Salesian Sisters, Daughters of Mary Help of Christians 5; Lay Teachers 10; Students 318.

4—BLESSED SACRAMENT (1911) (Italian), Rev. Richard A. Rusconi.
Res., 224 E. 18th St., 07524. Tel: 201-523-5002; Fax: 201-523-3766.
School—(1953), 2896-Sixth Ave., 07524. Tel: 201-278-8787; Fax: 201-278-6436.
Maestre Pie Filippini (Religious Teachers Filippini) 2; Lay Teachers 12; Students 185.

5—ST. BONAVENTURE (1877), Revs. Alvin V. Faddish, O.F.M.; John T. Piccione, O.F.M.; Deacon Joseph Balough. In res., Rev. Angelus P. Gambatese, O.F.M.
Res., 174 Ramsey St., 07501. Tel: 201-279-1016; Fax: 201-279-2507.

6—ST. CASIMIR'S (1911) (Lithuanian), Rev. Msgr. Anthony Bertasius, Admin.

Res., 147 Montgomery St., 07501. Tel: 201-279-1922.

7—ST. GEORGE (1897), Revs. Nicholas G. Bozza; Jose Javier Nieves; Deacon William Hussey.
Res., 408 Getty Ave., 07503. Tel: 201-742-0350; Fax: 201-754-0657.
School—(1897), 30 Michigan Ave., 07503. Tel: 201-684-6754; Fax: 201-684-1988.
Lay Teachers 12; Students 380.

8—ST. GERARD MAJELLA (1962), Revs. George F. Hundt; Philip Le Beau; Deacons Robert McMullen; Joseph Sisco.
Res., 501 W. Broadway, 07522. Tel: 201-595-8446.
School—(1965).
Salesian Sisters of St. John Bosco 4; Lay Teachers 7; Students 340.

9—ST. JOSEPH'S (1867), Revs. Robert W. Wisniefski; Gregory Colucci.
Res., 399 Market St., 07501. Tel: 201-278-0030.
School—Pope John Paul II School. See Elementary Schools, Diocesan under Institutions Located in the Diocese for details.

10—ST. MARY'S (1873). (Auxilium Christianorum). Revs. Joseph G. Buffardi; Jorge Rodriguez, O.F.M.Conv.
Res., 410 Union Ave., 07502. Tel: 201-790-8651.
School—(1874), 196 Wayne Ave., 07502.
Salesian Sisters of St. John Bosco 5; Lay Teachers 11; Students 370.

11—ST. MICHAEL THE ARCHANGEL (1903) (Italian), Rev. Joseph J. Orlandi. In res., Rev. Greg Drogon.
Res., 70 Cianci St., 07501. Tel: 201-523-8413; Fax: 201-253-4279.

12—OUR LADY OF LOURDES (1882), Revs. Peter Napoli, O.F.M.Cap.; Paschal Caccavalle, O.F.M.Cap. In res., Bro. Remo Di Salvatore, O.F.M.Cap.
Res., 440 River St., 07524. Tel: 201-742-2142.
School—(1883), Tel: 201-278-0164; Fax: 201-278-3030.
Lay Teachers 9; Students 235.

13—OUR LADY OF POMPEI (1916) (Italian), Rev. Sal J. Panagia; Deacon Henry Gallo.
Res., 70 Murray Ave., 07501. Tel: 201-742-1969.

14—OUR LADY OF VICTORIES (1882), Rev. Msgr. Thomas J. Coletta; Rev. John F. Heusser; Deacon Leo Gardner.
Res., 100 Fair St., 07501. Tel: 201-279-0487.

15—ST. STEPHEN'S (1903) (Polish), Revs. John T. Connolly; James Donnelly. In res., Rev. Francis Maliszewski.
Res., 86 Martin St., 07501. Tel: 201-742-2822.

16—ST. THERESE (1926), Rev. Msgr. Charles J. Russo; Rev. Elias Tamayo.
Res., 80-13th Ave., 07504. Tel: 201-881-0400.
School—(1953), 765 14th Ave., 07504. Tel: 201-278-4135. Deacon Nicholas Varsalona, Prin.
Lay Teachers 11; Students 395.

OUTSIDE THE CITY OF PATERSON

Andover, Sussex Co., Good Shepherd (1976), Rev. Richard A. Steiger; Deacons John S. Larkin; Joseph Hilber.
Office: Rte. 517 (Tranquility Rd.), P.O. Box 464, 07821. Tel: 201-786-6631; 786-5520 (Res.).

Boonton, Morris Co., Our Lady of Mount Carmel (1847), Rev. Edward J. Hinds; Deacon Barry Costello.
Res., 910 Birch St., 07005. Tel: 201-334-1017; Fax: 201-335-1833. [CEM]
School—(1868), 205 Oak St., 07005. Tel: 201-334-2777.
Franciscan Sisters of Sacred Heart 1; Lay Teachers 8; Students 110.

SS. Cyril and Methodius (1907) (Slovak), Revs. James J. Termyna; Zozislaw Nawrocki, S.Ch., (Morris Co. Polish Apostolate).
Res., 215 Hill St., 07005. Tel: 201-334-0139; Fax: 201-402-9512. [CEM]

Branchville, Sussex Co., Our Lady Queen of Peace (1951), Rev. William P. Stober.
Res., 209 Rte. 206, 07826. Tel: 201-948-3185; Fax: 201-948-4799.

Budd Lake, Morris Co., St. Jude (1946), Revs. Joseph A. Cassidy; George Kuzhippallil; Deacon Anthony C. Siino.
Res., Mt. Olive Rd., 07828. Tel: 201-691-1561.

Butler, Morris Co., St. Anthony (1878), Revs. Frank McHugh, O.F.M.; John J. Doyle, O.F.M.; Sr. Cecilia Burns, S.C., Pastoral Assoc.
Res., 65 Bartholdi Ave., 07405. Tel: 201-838-0031; Fax: 201-838-0649. [CEM]
School—(1882), Tel: 201-838-0854; Fax: 201-838-1460.
Brothers 1; Lay Teachers 9; Students 201.
Parish House—71 Bartholdi Ave., 07405. Tel: 201-838-8585.

Cedar Knolls, Morris Co., Notre Dame of Mt. Carmel (1917), Revs. Regis P. Wallace, O.S.B.; Hillary O'Leary, O.S.B.
Res., 13 Halko Dr., 07927. Tel: 201-538-1358; Fax: 201-538-7403.

Chatham, Morris Co., St. Patrick's (1874), Rev. Msgr. Ronald A. Amandolare; Rev. Owen Moran; Deacons Joseph A. Wisneski; Francis P. McQuade.
Res., 85 Washington Ave., 07928. Tel: 201-635-0625; Fax: 201-635-0119.
School—(1872), 45 Chatham St., 07928. Tel: 201-635-4623; Fax: 201-635-2311.
Sisters of Christian Charity 2; Lay Teachers 16; Students 322.

Chatham Township, Morris Co., Corpus Christi (1966), Rev. Msgr. James Mahoney; Rev. Paul Gorrell.
Res., 234 Southern Blvd., Chatham, 07928. Tel: 201-635-0070; Fax: 201-675-5518.

Chester, Morris Co., St. Lawrence the Martyr (1950), Rev. Msgr. P. Kevin Flanagan; Rev. Lancelot Reis; Deacon Frank Owens.
Res., Main St., P.O. Box 730, 07930. Tel: 908-879-5371.

Clifton, Passaic Co.,

1—SACRED HEART, (1897) (Italian), Rev. Msgr. Julian B. Varettoni; Revs. Andrew T. Perretta; Michael D. Joly.
Res., 145 Randolph Ave., 07011. Tel: 201-546-6012; Fax: 201-546-1814.
School—(1953), 43 Clifton Ave., 07011. Tel: 201-546-4695; Fax: 201-546-8774.
Lay Teachers 15; Students 295.

2—ST. ANDREW THE APOSTLE, (Allwood) (1938), Rev. Msgr. Peter A. McBride; Rev. Msgr. Peter J. McHugh, Admin.; Rev. Patrick Cullen, S.P.S.; Deacon Robert J. Ayers.
Res., 400 Mt. Prospect Ave., 07012. Tel: 201-779-6873; Fax: 201-779-0573.
School—(1953), 410 Mt. Prospect Ave., 07012. Tel: 201-473-3711; Fax: 201-473-6611.
Sisters of the Presentation 2; Lay Teachers 10; Students 241.

3—ST. BRENDAN, (1945), Revs. Richard G. Rento; Robert J. Mitchell; Frank W. Weber. In res., Revs. Alan F. Savitt; Francis Matarazzo.
Res., 154 E. First St., 07011. Tel: 201-772-1115; Fax: 201-772-0497.
School—(1946), 155 E. First St., 07011. Tel: 201-772-1149.
Lay Teachers 12; Students 279.

4—ST. CLARE'S, (1913), Rev. Msgr. Brendan P. Madden; Rev. Thomas J. Fitzgerald.
Res., 69 Allwood Rd., 07014. Tel: 201-777-7588.
School—(1959), Tel: 201-777-7582; Fax: 201-473-0127.
Lay Teachers 17; Students 255.

5—SS. CYRIL AND METHODIUS, (1913) (Slovak), Rev. Msgr. Thomas J. Zazella; Deacon John Teresinski. In res., Rev. T. Mark Condon.
Res., 218 Ackerman Ave., 07011. Tel: 201-546-4390.

6—ST. JOHN KANTY, (1930) (Polish), Revs. Alex B. Cymerman, O.F.M.Conv.; Waclaw Sokolowski, O.F.M.Conv.; Joseph Lotz, O.F.M.Conv.; Deacon Robert Atilio.
Res., 49 Speer Ave., 07013. Tel: 201-779-4102; Fax: 201-779-2104.
School—(1958), 61 Wesley St., 07013. Tel: 201-471-9407.
Felician Sisters 2; Lay Teachers 12; Students 257.

7—ST. PAUL, (1914), Revs. Victor J. Mazza; Brian Flanagan; Deacon Joseph Puskas. In res., Rev. Robert K. Hooper.
Res., 124 Union Ave., 07011. Tel: 201-546-2746; Fax: 201-340-2083.
School—(1916), Tel: 201-546-2161; Fax: 201-546-0057.
Sisters of Charity 3; Lay Teachers 10; Students 200.

8—ST. PHILIP THE APOSTLE, (1943), Revs. Peter J. Doody; Robert J. Gordon; Raymond E. Conlin; Deacon Gregory DeLorenzo.
Res., 797 Valley Rd., 07013. Tel: 201-779-6200; Fax: 201-779-2959.
School—(1954), Tel: 201-779-4700.
Franciscan Sisters of Peace 3; Lay Teachers 29; Students 611.

Convent Station, Morris Co., St. Thomas More (1966), Rev. Msgr. J. Francis Feenan. In res., Rev. Zbigniew Kluba.
Res., Madison Ave., Box 286-C, 07961. Tel: 201-267-5330.

Denville, Morris Co., St. Mary's (1926), Rev. Msgr. James H. Murray; Rev. Richard V. Tartaglia; Deacons David McCaffrey; Al Klose; Charles Burrows.
Res., 15 Myers Ave., 07834. Tel: 201-627-0269.
School—(1954), Tel: 201-627-2606; Fax: 201-627-9316.
Sisters of St. Joseph 1; Lay Teachers 10; Students 230.

Dover, Morris Co., St. Mary's (1845), Revs. Richard H. Oliveri; Kenneth R. Hewitt; John J. Klein.
Res., 425 W. Blackwell St., 07801. Tel: 201-366-0184; Fax: 201-366-5377. [CEM]
School—(1878), S. Main St., 07801. Tel: 201-366-0309; Fax: 201-366-6252.
Sisters of Christian Charity Wharton, NJ 2; Lay Teachers 15; Students 213.

Our Lady Queen of the Most Holy Rosary (1959) (Hispanic), Rev. Msgr. Felipe N. Carvajal.
Res., 77 Richards Ave., 07801. Tel: 201-361-2725; Fax: 201-266-0814.

Sacred Heart (1904), Rev. Ronald J. Tully; Deacons Eugene P. Dolan; Brian Drury; Henry Hyle; Edward Whelan; Richard Zeich. In res., Rev. Msgr. Charles F. Powers.
Res., 4 Richards Ave., 07801. Tel: 201-366-0060.
School—(1923), 30 N. Essex St., 07801. Tel: 201-366-2068; Fax: 201-366-9428.
Sisters of Sorrowful Mother 1; Lay Teachers 11; Students 253.

East Hanover, Morris Co., St. Rose of Lima (1957), Rev. Msgr. William McCarthy; Rev. Charles J. Waller; Deacons Robert A. Lang; Alfredo Fanelli; Frank Puglia. Pastoral Assocs.: Sr. Dolores Alfone, F.S.R.; Sr. Concepta D'Amato, F.S.R.
Res., 312 Ridgedale Ave., 07936. Tel: 201-887-5572; Fax: 201-884-0476.
School—(1961), Tel: 201-887-6990.
Lay Teachers 12; Students 206.

Flanders, Morris Co., St. Elizabeth Ann Seton (1985), Rev. Msgr. John B. Wehrlen; Deacon James McGrory. In res., Rev. Vincent McCluskey.
Res., 61 Main St., 07836. Tel: 201-927-1629.

Florham Park, Morris Co., Holy Family (1950), Revs. Raymond J. Kupke; William J. Mooney. Pastoral Assocs.: Mrs. Barbara Froetscher; Mrs. Patricia Danishek; Mrs. Virginia Akhoury; Deacons William F. Ward; Mark McCabe.
Res., Lloyd Ave., 07932. Tel: 201-377-1817.
School—(1954), Tel: 201-377-4181; Fax: 201-377-0273.
Sisters of Christian Charity 3; Lay Teachers 18; Students 230.

Franklin, Sussex Co., Immaculate Conception (1867), Rev. Martin G. Glynn.
Res., 75 Church St., 07416. Tel: 201-827-9575; Fax: 201-827-7375. [CEM]

Green Pond, Morris Co., St. Simon the Apostle (Rockaway Twp.) (1942), Rev. Joseph T. Anginoli.
Res., 1010 Green Pond Rd., 07435. Tel: 201-697-4699.

Hainesville, Sussex Co., St. Thomas the Apostle (1941), Rev. Thomas G. Rainforth.
Mailing Address: P.O. Box 187, Layton, 07851. Tel: 201-948-2296; Fax: 201-293-8933.

Hamburg, Sussex Co., St. Jude the Apostle (1966), Rev. William B. Collins.
Res., Beaver Run Rd., P.O. Box 1, 07419. Tel: 201-827-8030.

Haskell, Passaic Co., St. Francis of Assisi (1905), Rev. Msgr. Remigio G. Rocco; Rev. Vincent M. Klim.
Res., 868 Ringwood Ave., 07420. Tel: 201-835-0480; Fax: 201-835-3277.
School—(1912), Tel: 201-835-3268; Fax: 201-616-7644.
Lay Teachers 11; Students 188.

Hawthorne, Passaic Co., St. Anthony's (1908), Rev. Msgr. Elso C. Introini; Rev. Eugene R. Sylva; Deacons Richard J. Brudzynski; Anthony E. Bernardine; George W. Forshay. In res., Rev. Msgr. Joseph R. Brestel, P.A., V.G.
Res., 276 Diamond Bridge Ave., 07506. Tel: 201-427-1478; Fax: 201-427-4826.
School—(1912), 268 Diamond Bridge Ave., 07506. Tel: 201-423-1818; Fax: 201-423-6065.
Sisters 1; Lay Teachers 12; Students 273.

Hewitt, Passaic Co., Our Lady Queen of Peace (1921), Rev. William Scully, O.F.M.; Deacon Charles Roche.
Res., Friary, 1911 Union Valley Rd., 07421. Tel: 201-728-8162; Fax: 201-728-0258.
School—(1960), Tel: 201-728-9339.
Franciscan Sisters 1; Lay Teachers 8; Students 153.

Highland Lakes, Sussex Co., Our Lady of Fatima (1954), Rev. Msgr. Aloysius J. Busch.
Mailing Address: P.O. Box 242, 07422. Tel: 201-764-4457.

Hopatcong, Sussex Co., St. Jude's (1931), Revs. George J. Gothie; John J. McGuigan; Deacon Vincent F. Hanwacker.
Res., 40 Maxim Dr., 07843. Tel: 201-398-6377.

Kinnelon, Morris Co., Our Lady of the Magnificat (1961), Rev. Msgr. John J. Carroll; Rev. Timothy Dowling; Deacon Joseph Richardson. In res., Rev. David L. Coppola.
Res., 2 Miller Rd., 07405. Tel: 201-838-6838; Fax: 201-838-0710. [CEM]
School—(1964), Tel: 201-838-6222; Fax: 201-838-0409. Ms. Karen Fasanella, Prin.

Lay Teachers 11; Students 250.

Lake Hopatcong, Morris Co., Our Lady Star of the Sea (Jefferson Twp.) (1910), Rev. P. Christopher Muldoon.
Res., Espanong Rd., P.O. Box 337, 07849. Tel: 201-663-0211; Fax: 201-663-4302.

Lincoln Park, Morris Co., St. Joseph's (1922), Rev. Dennis J. Hogan; Sr. Eileen Halloran, F.S.P., Pastoral Assoc.; Deacon Stephen Marabeti.
Res., 216 Comly Rd., 07035. Tel: 201-696-4411.

Little Falls, Passaic Co., Our Lady of the Holy Angels (1883), Revs. Thomas M. Gallagher, O.F.M.; Flavian Walsh, O.F.M.; John Leonard, O.F.M.; Deacon Frank Muoio. In res., Revs. Kenneh Paulli, O.F.M.; Paul D. Sansone, O.F.M.
Res., 07424. Tel: 201-256-5200; Fax: 201-256-0185.
School—(1903), 465 Main St., 07424. Tel: 201-256-1132.
Franciscan Missionary Sisters of the Sacred Heart 1; Lay Teachers 8; Students 195.

Long Valley, Morris Co., St. Luke (1982), Rev. Michael J. Drury.
Res., 3 Carl Ln., P.O. Box 416, 07853. Tel: 908-876-3515.
Church—265 W. Mill Rd., 07853.
St. Mark the Evangelist (1986), Rev. Allen F. Stepien.
Res., 59 Lane Rd., 07853. Tel: 908-850-0652.

Madison, Morris Co., St. Vincent Martyr (1805), Rev. Christopher C. DiLella. In res., Rev. James O'Kielty.
Res., 26 Green Village Rd., 07940. Tel: 201-377-4000; Fax: 201-377-8242. [CEM]
School—(1848), Tel: 201-377-1104; Fax: 201-377-8242.
Lay Teachers 15; Students 329.

McAfee, Sussex Co., St. Francis de Sales (1963), Rev. Msgr. John V. Boland; Rev. Patrick J. Rice.
Mailing Address: P.O. Box 785, 07428. Tel: 201-827-3248.

Mendham, Morris Co., St. Joseph's (1853), Rev. Msgr. Kenneth E. Lasch; Rev. John P. Hanley; Deacon Robert F. Santos.
6 New St., 07945. Tel: 201-543-5950; Fax: 201-543-2562. [CEM]
School—(1963), Tel: 201-543-7474.
Sisters of Christian Charity 1; Lay Teachers 11; Students 260.

Montague, Sussex Co., St. James the Greater (1943), Rev. Thomas G. Rainforth.
Res., 75 River Rd., 07827. Tel: 201-293-3379; Fax: 201-293-8933.

Montville, Morris Co., St. Pius X (1959), Revs. Joseph J. Garbarino; John A. Tarantino; Deacon Andrew L. Cavaliere.
Res., 18 Changebridge Rd., 07045. Tel: 201-334-4506; 334-4510; Fax: 201-331-1706.
School—(1963), Tel: 201-335-1253; Fax: 201-335-2392.
Franciscan Sisters of St. Elizabeth 3; Lay Teachers 8; Students 130.

Morris Plains, Morris Co., St. Virgilius (1881), Revs. John Andrew Connell; Ronald Sordillo; Sr. Mary Larkin, Pastoral Assoc.; Deacons Sylvester Mazzoccoli; Daniel Scrone; Merle Sisler. In res., Rev. Msgr. James L. Fallon, Pastor Emeritus.
Res., 18 W. Hanover Ave., 07950. Tel: 201-538-1418; Fax: 201-538-2992.
School—(1910), 11 W. Hanover Ave., 07950. Tel: 201-539-7267.
Sisters of St. Dominic 2; Lay Teachers 15; Students 250.

Morristown, Morris Co., Assumption of the Blessed Virgin Mary (1848), Rev. Msgr. Martin F. Rauscher; Rev. William L. Winston; Deacons P. Michael Hanly; Gabriel Lasch; William Harty; Tony DiLorenzo; Frank Para. In res., Revs. William P. Glennon; Joseph M. Casey.
Res., 91 Maple Ave., 07960. Tel: 201-539-2141; Fax: 201-984-0632. [CEM]
School—(1850), 63 MacCulloch Ave., 07960. Tel: 201-538-0590; Fax: 201-984-3632.
Sisters of Charity 4; Lay Teachers 34; Students 585.
St. Margaret's (1930), Revs. Francis J. Duffy; Andrew Velez. In res., Rev. Msgr. Christian D. Haag, P.A.; Bro. Hugh McGrath, O.S.F.
Res., 6 Sussex Ave., 07960. Tel: 201-538-0874; Fax: 201-538-4581.

Mountain Lakes, Morris Co., St. Catherine of Siena (1956), Rev. Msgr. David L. Mahon; Rev. A. Richard Carton; Deacon Joseph Parlapiano.
Res., 10 N. Pocono Rd., 07046. Tel: 201-334-7131.

Mount Arlington, Morris Co., Our Lady of the Lake (1888), Revs. Joseph Ryan; Desmond O'Connor, S.P.S.; Deacon Stanley Sisson.
Res., One Park Ave., 07856. Tel: 201-398-0240.

Mount Hope, Morris Co., St. Bernard's (1855), Rev. Joseph G. Farias.
Res., 446 Mt. Hope Rd., Wharton, 07885-2814. Tel: 201-627-0066; Fax: 201-625-627-3631.

Netcong, Morris Co., St. Michael's (1873), Rev. Msgr. Thomas J. Trapasso; Rev. Robert G. Hoffmann; Deacons Alex Buckholtz; Philip Pawlows; Joseph Keenan; Stuart Murphy. In res., Rev. Msgr. James J. Doyle, Pastor Emeritus.
Res., 4 Church St., 07857. Tel: 201-347-0032; Fax: 201-347-1560. [CEM]
School—(1922), Tel: 201-347-0039; Fax: 201-347-0054.
Sisters of Christian Charity 2; Lay Teachers 15; Students 406.

Newton, Sussex Co., St. Joseph's (1854), Rev. Edward M. Davey; Deacons Arthur Van Vleet; John Grimes; Raymond Biersbach. In res., Rev. Angelus Croce.
Res., 17 Elm St., 07860. Tel: 201-383-1985; Fax: 201-383-8164. [CEM]

New Vernon, Morris Co., Christ the King (1956), Revs. Patrick G. O'Donovan; Paul Duggan.
Res., Blue Mill Rd., 07976. Tel: 201-539-4955; Fax: 201-267-7070.

Oak Ridge, Morris Co., St. Thomas, the Apostle (1949), Rev. Msgr. John E. Fitzpatrick.
Res., 5635 Berkshire Valley Rd., 07438. Tel: 201-208-0090; Fax: 201-208-0092. [CEM]

Ogdensburg, Sussex Co., St. Thomas of Aquin (1881), Rev. Stanley C. Barron.
Res., 53 Kennedy Ave., 07439. Tel: 201-827-3190; Fax: 201-827-9738. [CEM]

Parsippany, Morris Co., St. Christopher (1944), Rev. Msgr. Frank B. Ferraioli; Rev. Sean McDonnell (Ireland); Deacons John J. Kelly; Michael Pirylis; John Bernero; Edward Lally.
Res., 1050 Littleton Rd., 07054. Tel: 201-539-7050; Fax: 201-539-3601.
School—(1962), Tel: 201-539-7053.
Sisters of St. Dominic 4; Lay Teachers 15; Students 413.
St. Ann (1982), Rev. Martin McDonnell; Deacons Donald O'Leary; Alfred Frank; Sr. Frances Sanzo, S.S.C., Pastoral Assoc.
Res., 781 Smith Rd., 07054. Tel: 201-884-1986; Fax: 201-884-0940.
St. Peter the Apostle (1938), Rev. Msgr. Herbert K. Tillyer; Revs. Peter Filipkowski; Ashiono Anthony Mabango; Sr. Sylvia Berzinski, S.S.C., Pastoral Assoc.; Sr. Regina McTiernan, C.S.J.B.; Deacons David Collins; George Dimler; Daniel Ferry.
Res., 179 Baldwin Rd., 07054. Tel: 201-334-2090; Fax: 201-334-5397.
School—(1958), Tel: 201-334-4704; Fax: 201-334-0622.
Sisters 4; Lay Teachers 12; Students 250.

Passaic, Passaic Co.,

1—St. Nicholas, (1868), Rev. Msgr. Robert B. Carroll; Rev. Daniel A. Kelly; Sr. Francis Cordis Bernardo, S.C., Pastoral Assoc.; Deacon Edward Ramirez.
Res., 153 Washington Pl., 07055. Tel: 201-779-7867; Fax: 201-815-1893.
School—(1874), 123 Jefferson St., 07055. Tel: 201-779-1987.
Sisters of Charity 2; Lay Teachers 11; Students 264.

2—St. Anthony of Padua, (1917) (Italian), Rev. Herman Arias.
Res., 95 Myrtle Ave., 07055. Tel: 201-777-4793; Fax: 201-779-6864.
School—(1960), 40 Tulip St., 07055. Tel: 201-773-0970.
Sisters 4; Lay Teachers 9; Students 245.

3—Assumption of the Blessed Virgin Mary, (1891) (Slovak), Rev. Msgr. John J. Demkovich. In res., Rev. John T. Catoir.
Res., 63 Monroe St., 07055. Tel: 201-779-0427; Fax: 201-472-5033.

4—Holy Rosary, (1918) (Polish), Rev. Msgr. John Podgorny; Revs. Stanley Lesniowski; Stefan Las.
Res., 6 Wall St., 07055. Tel: 201-473-1578.

5—Holy Trinity, (1900) (German), Rev. Msgr. John E. Morris; Revs. Walter M. Pruschowitz; Wayne F. Varga.
Res., 226 Harrison St., 07055. Tel: 201-778-9763.
School—(1906), 228 Hope Ave., 07055. Tel: 201-473-1043.
Sisters of St. Dominic 4; Lay Teachers 7; Students 141.

6—St. Joseph's, (1892) (Polish), Revs. Joseph Czerkies; Stanislaw Drzal, S.Ch.
Res., 7 Parker Ave., 07055. Tel: 201-473-0921.

7—Mt. Carmel, (1902) (Italian), Rev. Sam Frapaul, O.F.M.Cap.
Res., 10 St. Francis Way, 07055. Tel: 201-473-0246.
School—(1954).
Franciscan Sisters 3; Lay Teachers 12; Students 280.

8—Our Lady of Fatima, (1954) (Hispanic), Rev. Msgr. Raul Guzman; Revs. Hector Melendez; Nelson Betancur; Deacons Jesus Cortes; Juan Ortiz.
Res., 32 Exchange Pl., 07055. Tel: 201-472-0815; Fax: 201-472-0250.

9—St. Stephen's, (1902) (Magyar), Rev. Stephen N. Mustos, Sch.P.
Res., 223 Third St., 07055. Tel: 201-779-0332; Fax: 201-778-4263.

Pequannock, Morris Co., Holy Spirit (1949), Revs. Alfred J. Lampron; Edward A. Collins; Deacons Gil Leifer; Thomas Kimak.
Res., 318 Tpke., 07440. Tel: 201-696-1234.
School—(1956), Tel: 201-835-5680.
Maestre Pie Filippini (Religious Teachers Filippini) 2; Lay Teachers 15; Students 350.
Convent—Tel: 201-694-2111.
Our Lady of Fatima Chapel (Tridentine) (1994), Revs. William F. Ashley, F.S.S.P.; Joseph P. Terra, F.S.S.P. In res., Rev. Kenneth Baker, S.J.
Res., 32 West Franklin Ave., 07440. Tel: 201-694-6727; Fax: 201-694-7629.
School—St. Maximilian Kolbe School, 18 First St., 07440. Tel: 201-694-1034. Mrs. Mary Lou Bednar, Prin.
Lay Teachers 4; Students 40.

Pompton Lakes, Passaic Co., Our Lady of the Assumption (1906), Revs. John Carnevale, O.F.M.; Kevin Downey, O.F.M.; Sr. Arlene Kollar, S.S.C., Pastoral Assoc.; Bro. Richard McFeeley, O.F.M.; Deacons Paul A. Liotard; Edward Higgins; Steven Madreperla. In res., Rev. Thomas Hartle, O.F.M.
Res., St. Mary's Friary, 52 Lenox Ave., 07442. Tel: 201-839-1975; Fax: 201-835-8432.
School—(1951), Tel: 201-835-2010; Fax: 201-835-7529. Ms. Kathleen Berlino, Prin.
Lay Teachers 16; Students 262.

Pompton Plains, Morris Co., Our Lady of Good Counsel (1962), Rev. Patrick J. Scott; Deacons Don X. Bancroft; Ronald Ochner; Edward Jaroszewski; Charles Mallory. In res., Rev. Michael J. Lombardo.
Res., 155 W. Pkwy., P.O. Box 218, 07444. Tel: 201-839-2447; Fax: 201-839-9492.

Prospect Park, Passaic Co., St. Paul's (1924), Revs. Edward J. Kurtyka; Steven G. Shadwell; Thomas P. Valerio.
Res., 286 Haledon Ave., Paterson, 07508. Tel: 201-790-8169.
School—(1955), 13 Wagaraw Blvd., 07508. Tel: 201-942-9428.
Lay Teachers 10; Students 200.

Randolph, Morris Co., Resurrection (1978), Revs. William M. Naughton; Brendan McLoughlin; Mark Olenowski; Deacons Keith S. Farber; Robert M. Flavin; Gerard Hand.
Res., 651 Millbrook Ave., 07869. Tel: 201-895-4224; Fax: 201-895-3224.
St. Matthew the Apostle (1988), Rev. David McDonnell; Deacon William Peters.
Res., 267 Dover-Chester Rd., 07869. Tel: 201-584-1101.

Ringwood, Passaic Co., St. Catherine of Bologna (1917), Rev. Msgr. Patrick G. Panos; Rev. Gerald B. Kanzic; Deacons James Elliott; Richard Michalski.
Res., 112 Erskine Rd., 07456. Tel: 201-962-7032.
School—(1948), Tel: 201-962-7131; Fax: 201-962-0585.
Franciscan Sisters of Ringwood 2; Lay Teachers 14; Students 313.

Rockaway, Morris Co., St. Cecilia's (1869), Rev. Msgr. John E. Hart; Revs. Brendan J. Murray; J. Patrick Ryan (ALB). In res., Rev. Paul S. Manning.
Res., 70 Church St., 07866. Tel: 201-627-0313; 627-0316. [CEM]
School—(1958), Halsey Ave., 07866. Tel: 201-252-0760.
Sisters of Christian Charity 2; Lay Teachers 11; Students 280.
Sacred Heart (1923) (Slovak), Rev. Joseph J. Goode.
Res., 63 E. Main St., 07866. Tel: 201-627-0422; Fax: 201-627-6249.
School—(1965). Sisters of the Sorrowful Mother. Tel: 201-627-7689.
Lay Teachers 9; Students 271.

Rockaway Township, Morris Co., St. Clement, Pope and Martyr (1964), Rev. Msgr. Joseph A. Ciampaglio; Deacon Harry Dachisen.
Res., 154 Mt. Pleasant Ave., Dover, 07801. Tel: 201-366-7095; Fax: 201-366-7095.

Schooley's Mountain, Morris Co., Our Lady of the Mountain (1954), Rev. Msgr. George A. Dudak.
Res., Rte. 24, 07870. Tel: 908-876-4395. [CEM]

Sparta, Sussex Co., Our Lady of the Lake (1935), Rev. Msgr. Paul F. Knauer; Revs. James Moss; Gerald F. Lewis. In res., Rev. Chukwuol Obiajunwa (Nigeria).
Res., 294 Sparta Ave., 07871. Tel: 201-729-6107; Fax: 201-729-7203.
School—(1954), Tel: 201-729-9174; Fax: 201-729-0318. Ms. Barbara Campione, Prin.
Lay Teachers 25; Students 490.
Blessed Kateri Tekakwitha (1988), Revs. Daniel W. Murphy; Gregory A. White; Sr. Barbara Moore,

O.P., Pastoral Assoc.; Deacons Frank Padden; Andrew Calandriello.
Res., 427 Stanhope Rd., 07871. Tel: 201-729-1682; Fax: 201-729-0702.

Stirling, Morris Co., St. Vincent de Paul (1886), Revs. Patrick E. Brown; Arthur J. Colaiacovo; Albert Nix; Deacon James P. Morris.
Res., Bebout Ave., 07980. Tel: 908-647-0118; Fax: 908-647-5992. [CEM]
School—(1955), Tel: 908-647-0421.
Lay Teachers 12; Students 232.

Stockholm, Sussex Co., St. John Vianney (1958), Rev. Matthew J. Twiggs; Deacon Edmund Galinski.
Res., 07460. Tel: 201-697-6550; Fax: 201-697-6882.

Succasunna, Morris Co., St. Therese (1957), Revs. Joseph P. Davis; Marc Mancini; James A.D. Smith; Deacon Anthony Signorelli.
Res., 7 Hunter St., 07876. Tel: 201-584-8271; Fax: 201-584-0684.
School—(1963), Tel: 201-584-0812; Fax: 201-584-2029.
Sisters 2; Lay Teachers 8; Students 187.

Sussex, Sussex Co., St. Monica (1881), Rev. Charles A. Perricone; Deacon Jerome Schenker.
Res., 33 Unionville Ave., 07461. Tel: 201-875-4521; Fax: 201-875-7538.

Swartswood, Sussex Co., Our Lady of Mt. Carmel (1951), Rev. John J. Quinlan; Deacons Ellis F. Schweitzer; Robert T. Davis; Edward J. Muller.
Mailing Address: P.O. Box 124, 07877. Tel: 201-383-3566.

Totowa Borough, Passaic Co., St. James of the Marches (1926), Rev. Msgr. Eugene M. Boland; Revs. Paul Iovino; Joseph Murphy.
Res., 32 St. James Pl., Totowa, 07512. Tel: 201-790-0288; Fax: 201-790-7064.
School—(1956), Tel: 201-956-8824. Sr. Mary Ann Grimes, Prin.
Sisters 1; Lay Teachers 11; Students 220.

Wayne, Passaic Co.,

1—Annunciation, (1963), Rev. Msgr. Stanislaus E. Schinski; Rev. Absalom Coutinho; Deacons Charles Tenga; Andrew Kostic.
Res., 45 Urban Club Rd., 07470. Tel: 201-694-5700; Fax: 201-694-5706.

2—Holy Cross, (1925), Rev. John M. Heekin.
Res., 17 Van Duyne Ave., 07470. Tel: 201-696-1065.

3—Immaculate Heart of Mary, (1956), Rev. Msgr. Louis J. Bihr; Rev. George T. Shema; Deacons John Gaffney; Jaime Llanso; Philip Healy. In res., Rev. Roger Hebert.
Res., 580 Ratzer Rd., 07470. Tel: 201-694-3400; Fax: 201-694-3459.
School—(1958), Tel: 201-694-1225; Fax: 201-872-9043.
Lay Teachers 13; Students 210.

4—Our Lady of Consolation, (1963), Revs. James R. Hertel, J.C.D.; Zbieniew Tyburski; Deacon Robert Pringle.
Res., 1799 Hamburg Tpke., 07470. Tel: 201-839-3444; Fax: 201-839-9695.
School—(1967), Tel: 201-839-2323; Fax: 201-839-2428.
Sisters 3; Lay Teachers 12; Students 210.

5—Our Lady of the Valley, (1960), Rev. Msgr. James H. O'Rorke; Rev. Dennis Crowley; Deacons Michael Wallace; Raymond Kucinski.
Res., 614 Valley Rd., 07470. Tel: 201-694-4585.
School—(1962), Tel: 201-696-2212.
Sisters of St. Joseph 1; Lay Teachers 20; Students 331.

West Milford Township, Passaic Co., St. Joseph (1765), Revs. Boniface F. Hanley, O.F.M.; Bernard J. Splawski, O.F.M.; Deacon Milton Smilek.
Res., 454 Germantown Rd., West Milford, 07480. Tel: 201-697-6100; Fax: 201-697-3716.
School—(1956), Tel: 201-697-6896.
Lay Teachers 11; Students 220.

Whippany, Morris Co., Our Lady of Mercy (1854), Revs. John DeMattia; John P. Pilipie; Sr. Eileen Side, S.S.J., Pastoral Assoc.; Deacon Tim Manning; Sr. Ann McKeon, G.N.S.H., Youth Min.
Res., 9 Parsippany Rd., 07981. Tel: 201-887-0050; Fax: 201-887-0991. [CEM]
School—Tel: 201-887-2611. Sr. Catherine Duignan, C.S.J.P., Prin.
Lay Teachers 9; Students 201.

Chaplains of Public Institutions

Hospitals

Paterson. *Preakness Hospital*. Vacant. P.O. Box V, 07509. Tel: 201-278-6800.
St. Joseph Hospital, 703 Main St., 07503. Tel: 201-754-2000; 754-2060 (Office). Sr. Jane Frances Brady, Pres. & CEO; Revs. William N. Cramer, Dir. Pastoral Care; Francis Hanudel, O.F.M.; Felician Foy, O.F.M.; Rev. Msgr. James Rugel; Rev. Joseph Hearns; Sr. Bernice Romanick, F.S.P.; Sr. Marie Josetta Wethington, S.C.

Denville. *St. Clare Hospital*, Pocono Rd., 07834. Tel: 201-627-3000. Chaplains: Revs. Thomas Heffernan; Joseph C. McNamara, O.S.F.S.; Carmine Fazio, O.F.M.Cap.

Dover. *Dover General Hospital*, Jardine St., 07801. Tel: 201-939-3000. Rev. Jeffrie S. Reynolds (BIR).

Morris Plains. *Greystone Park Psychiatric Hospital*, 07950. Tel: 201-538-1800. Rev. Robert M. Diachek.

Morristown. *Morristown Memorial Hospital*, 100 Madison Ave., 07960. Tel: 201-540-5307. Revs. Zbigniew Kluba; Joseph M. Casey.

Newton. *Newton Memorial Hospital*, 175 High St., 07860. Tel: 201-383-2121. Rev. John J. Quinlan.

Passaic. *Passiac General Hospital*, 350 Blvd., 07055. Tel: 201-345-4300. Rev. Francis Matarazzo.
St. Mary Hospital, 211 Pennington Ave., 07055. Tel: 201-473-1000. Revs. Luke Guastella, O.F.M.Cap.; Vincent Liuzzo, O.F.M.Cap.

Pompton Plains. *Chilton Memorial Hospital*, 07444. Tel: 201-831-5000. Rev. Michael J. Lombardo.

Totowa. *North Jersey Developmental Center*. Rev. Louis J. Scurti.

Wayne. *Wayne General Hospital*, Hamburg Tpke., 07470. Tel: 201-942-6900. Rev. Michael Lombardo.

Correctional Facilities

Paterson. *Passaic County Jail*. Rev. Msgr. Mark J. Giordani; Rev. Hernan Arias.

Morris Plains. *Morris County Youth Center*. Rev. Robert G. Hoffmann.

Morristown. *Morris County Jail*. Rev. Patrick E. Brown.

Newton. *Sussex County Jail*. Rev. Robert G. Hoffmann.

Special Assignment:
Reverend Monsignors—
Puma, Vincent E., 970 Black Oak Ridge Rd., Wayne, NJ 07470
Reverend Fathers—
McGrath, Thomas M., 476 17th Ave., Paterson, NJ 07504. Tel: 201-523-9595

On Duty Outside the Diocese:
Reverend Monsignors—
Conway, Michael, Orlando, FL
Reverend Fathers—
Belanich, Giordano, Fairview, NJ
Brown, Patrick, Larchmont, NY
DiCristina, Frank A., Redlands, CA
Grasso, Richard, Daytona Beach, FL
Holterhoff, Edward G., Monterey, CA
Mastroeni, Anthony, Gaming, Austria
McLeod, David, Manahawkin, NJ
Pavlick, Raymond A., Walden, NY
Reading, Edward, Trenton, NJ
Stephenson, Alphonse J., Point Pleasant, NJ
Sullivan, John A., Brick, NJ
Vitillo, Robert J., Washington, DC
Weis, John H., Midland, MI

Military Chaplains:
Reverend Fathers—
Briganti, Philip J., USA
Cusack, John J., USAF
O'Grady, Frank, USA
Parisi, Michael, USN
Sodano, Ralph H., USN
Walsh, Michael A., USN

Sabbatical:
Reverend Monsignors—
Longua, Paul
O'Riordan, Jeremiah
Olenowski, Mark

Absent on Leave:
Reverend Monsignors—
Alonso, Jose A.
Reverend Fathers—
Bradley, Charles
Dauenhauer, John
Gorrell, Paul
Holliday, David D.
Lojewicz, John
Mockos, William J.
Northridge, Keith C.
O'Brien, John
O'Connor, John H.
Pisarcik, John G.
Wells, Peter V.B.

Unassigned:
Reverend Fathers—
Burke, Michael J.
Erwin, Patrick O.
Lambro, Edward
Peretta, Andrew J.
Scolamiero, Dominic A.

Retired:
Reverend Monsignors—
Biesiada, Louis W., 2001 N.E. 38th St., Lighthouse Point, FL 33064
Bischoff, Francis J., 140 Shepherd Ln., Totowa, NJ 07512
Carey, Leo P., Nazareth Village, Main St., Box 635, Chester, NJ 07930
Cassidy, Charles C., 516 Oak Hill Ct., Lanoka Harbor, NJ 08734
Corr, John F., 83 Primose Tr., Morristown, NJ 07960
Dericks, John H., 288 Lackawanna Dr., Andover, NJ 07821
Doyle, James J., 4 Church St., Netcong, NJ 07857
Fallon, James L., 10 W. Hanover Ave., Morris Plains, NJ 07950
Ferrito, Joseph L., 516 Oak Hill Ct., Lanoka Harbor, NJ 08734
Flek, Ladis Laus J., 140 Shepherd Ln., Totowa, NJ 07512
Gallo, Joseph J., 55 Quartz Ln., Paterson, NJ 07510
Gallo, Louis J., Nazareth Village, Main St., Box 635, Chester, NJ 07930
Haag, Christian D., 6 Sussex Ave., Morristown, NJ 07960
Hayes, Denis A., 140 Shepherd Ln., Totowa, NJ 07512
Lee, Thaddeus, P.O. Box 2044, Beach Haven, NJ 08008
McQuaid, Eugene, P.O. Box 628, Dingmans Ferry, PA 18328
Meyer, Joseph J., 140 Shepherd Ln., Totowa, NJ 07512
Murphy, Francis H., 4 Richards St., Dover, NJ 07801
Rugel, James J., 12 Grove Rd., Oak Ridge, NJ 07438
Ryan, John R., Nazareth Village, Main St. Box 635, Chester, NJ 07930
Ryan, Leo P., Nazareth Village, Main St. Box 635, Chester, NJ 07930
Wolsin, Carl J., Nazareth Village, Main St., Box 635, Chester, NJ 07930
Reverend Fathers—
Connolly, Martin C., Nazareth Village, Main St., Box 635, Chester, NJ 07930
Costigan, George, St. Francis Convent, Windemere Ave., Mt. Arlington, NJ 07856
Fanning, Leo M., 14 Polar Bear Path, Ormond Beach, FL 32174
Feeney, Bernard, R.R. 6, Box 399, Branchville, NJ 07826
Grieco, Charles, Nazareth Village, Main St., Box 635, Chester, NJ 07930
Hanley, James T.
Hebert, Roger, 580 Ratzer Rd., Wayne, NJ 07470
Jacobs, Richard A., 7 Middlesex Rd., E. Greenbush, NY 12061
Jasaitis, Raymond J., 61 Main St., Flanders, NJ 07836
Krajewski, Paul A., 10 Prime Rose Ln., Mount Arlington, NJ 07856
LoGatto, Joseph J., 424 Third St., Carlstadt, NJ 07072
Lugo, Joseph W., 78 Chestnut St., Bridgewater, NJ 08807
Maliszewski, Francis, 86 Martin St., Paterson, NJ 07501
McHugh, Dennis, Our Lady's Shrine, Knock, County Mayo, Ireland
Morris, Robert J., Nazareth Village, Main St., Box 635, Chester, NJ 07930
Mullan, Patrick, Nazareth Village, Main St., Box 635, Chester, NJ 07930
Mushinsky, John E., 22 Boston Rd., Neptune, NJ 07753
Ruddy, Edward J., 21 Marian Crescent, Dublin, Ballina County, Ireland

---

Permanent Deacons:
Acevedo, Pedro
Altilio, Robert M., St. John Kanty, Clifton
Ayers, Robert, St. Andrew the Apostle, Clifton
Balough, Joseph, St. Bonaventure, Paterson
Bancroft, Don X., Our Lady of Good Counsel, Pompton Plains
Bernardine, Anthony E., St. Anthony, Hawthorne
Bernero, John, St. Christopher, Parsippany
Bianchi, Roland, Archdiocese of Newark, NJ
Biersbach, Raymond, St. Joseph, Newton
Bitecola, Daniel
Brudzynski, Richard, St. Anthony, Hawthorne
Buckholtz, Alexander E., St. Michael Church, Netcong
Burrows, Charles, St. Mary, Denville
Cassidy, Joseph, Retired
Cavaliere, Andrew L., St. Pius X, Montville

Ciampa, Alfred
Colandriello, Andrew, Blessed Kateri Tekakwitha, Sparta
Collins, David, St. Peter the Apostle, Parsippany
Cortes, Jesus, Our Lady of Fatima, Passaic
Costello, Barry, Mt. Carmel Church, Boonton
Dachisen, Harry, St. Clement Pope and Martyr, Rockaway Township
Damato, Larry, Archdiocese of St. Louis, MO
Davis, Robert T., Our Lady of Mount Carmel, Swartswood
DeLorenzo, Gregory, St. Philip Church, Clifton
DiLorenzo, Anthony, Assumption, Morristown
Dimler, George, St. Peter Church, Parsippany
Dolan, Eugene P., Sacred Heart, Dover
Drury, Brian, Sacred Heart, Dover
Ehrlich, Jacob B., Our Lady Queen of Peace, Hewitt
Elliott, James, St. Catherine of Bologna, Ringwood
Fanelli, Alfredo, St. Rose of Lima, East Hanover
Farber, Keith, Resurrection, Randolph
Ferry, Daniel F., St. Peter the Apostle, Parsippany
Flavin, Robert
Fohn, Kurt, Diocese of Charlotte, NC
Forshay, George W., St. Anthony, Hawthorne
Frank, Alfred E., St. Ann, Parsippany
Gaffney, John F., Immaculate Heart of Mary Church, Wayne
Galinski, Edmund V., St. John Vianney, Stockholm
Gallo, Henry, Our Lady of Pompei, Paterson
Gardner, Leo, Our Lady of Victories, Paterson
Grimes, John, St. Joseph, Newton
Hand, Gerard, Resurrection, Randolph
Hanly, P. Michael, Assumption, Morristown
Hanwacker, Vincent F., St. Jude Church, Hopatcong
Harty, William, Assumption, Morristown
Healy, Philip, Our Lady of the Valley Church, Wayne
Healy, Thomas F., Jr., St. Luke, Long Valley
Higgins, Edward J., St. Mary, Pompton Lakes
Hilber, Joseph, Good Shepherd, Andover
Hussey, William E., St. George Church, Paterson
Hyle, Henry, Sacred Heart, Dover
Jaroszewski, Edward, Our Lady of Good Counsel Church, Pompton Plains
Jones, Frederick B., Jr., APO Germany
Keenan, Joseph, St. Michael, Netcong
Kelly, John, St. Christopher, Parsippany
Kimak, Thomas J., Holy Spirit, Pequannock
Klose, Albert P., St. Mary, Denville
Kostic, Andrew, Annunciation, Wayne
Kronyak, Robert, Diocese of Charleston, SC
Kruk, Leonard, Diocese of Trenton, NJ
Kucinski, Raymond, Our Lady of the Valley Church, Wayne
Lally, Edward J., St. Christopher, Parsippany
Lang, Robert A., St. Rose of Lima, East Hanover
Larkin, John S., Good Shepherd, Andover
Lasch, Gabriel L., Assumption BVM Church, Morristown
Lebron, Florencio G., St. Mary, Paterson
Leifer, Gil, Holy Spirit, Pequannock
Liotard, Paul A., St. Mary, Pompton Lakes
Llanso, Jamie, Father English Center, Paterson
Llibre, John, Unassigned
Madreperla, Steven A., St. Mary Church, Pompton Lakes
Mallory, Charles, Our Lady of Good Counsel Church, Pompton Plains
Manning, Tim, Our Lady of Mercy Church, Whippany
Marabeti, Stephen J., St. Joseph Church, Lincoln Park
Mathias, Charles T., Bl. Kateri Tekakwitha, Sparta
Mazzaccoli, Sylvester A., St. Virgil Church, Morris Plains
McCabe, Mark, Holy Family, Florham Park
McCaffrey, David, St. Mary, Denville
McGrory, James G., St. Elizabeth Ann Seton, Flanders
McMullin, Robert, St. Gerard Church, Paterson
McNally, Peter J., St. Patrick, Chatham
McQuaid, Francis P., St. Patrick, Chatam
Meyer, John, Diocese of Charleston, SC
Michalski, Richard, St. Catherine of Bologna, Ringwood
Minicozzi, John
Morris, James
Muller, Edward J., Our Lady of Mount Carmel, Swartswood
Munoz, Mario, Our Lady of Victories, Paterson
Muoio, Frank, Holy Angels Church, Little Falls
Murphy, Stuart, St. Michael, Netcong
O'Leary, Donald, St. Ann, Parsippany
Ochner, Ronald, Our Lady of Good Counsel Church, Pompton Plains
Ortiz, Juan, Our Lady of Fatima Church, Passaic
Owens, Frank, St. Lawrence the Martyr, Chester
Padden, Frank J., Blessed Kateri Tekawitha, Sparta
Para, Frank, Assumption, Morristown
Parlapiano, Joseph J., St. Catherine of Siena, Mountain Lakes
Pawlows, Philip T., St. Michael, Netcong
Peters, William L., St. Matthew, Randolph
Pirylis, Michael, St. Christopher, Parsippany
Pomales, Jose, St. John Cathedral, Paterson
Pringle, Robert H., Our Lady of Consolation Church, Wayne
Puglia, Frank, St. Rose of Lima, East Hanover
Puleo, Paul A., Blessed Kateri Tekakwitha, Sparta
Puskas, Joseph, St. Paul, Clifton
Quinn, Joseph, Morristown Memorial Hospital
Ramirez, Edward, St. Nicholas, Passaic
Raymond, Thomas, Archdiocese of Boston, MA
Reading, Edward J., Blessed Kateri Tekakwitha, Sparta
Reed, Daniel, St. Brendan, Clifton
Richardson, Joseph, Our Lady of Magnificat, Kinnelon
Roche, Charles, Our Lady Queen of Peace, Hewitt
Rodriguez, Angel, Our Lady of Lourdes Church, Paterson
Santana, Heriberto, Diocese of Orlando, FL
Santiago, Manuel, St. John the Baptist Cathedral, Paterson
Santos, Robert F., St. Joseph, Mendham
Schenker, Jerome, St. Monica, Sussex
Schwietzer, Ellis F., Our Lady of Mount Carmel, Swartswood
Scrone, Daniel, St. Virgil, Morris Plains
Shoemaker, William, Diocese of Austin, TX
Signorelli, Anthony, St. Therese, Succasunna
Siino, Anthony C., St. Jude, Budd Lake
Silva, Percy, St. Agnes, Paterson
Simeone, Enio, Passaic General Hospital
Sisco, Joseph, St. Gerard Majella, Paterson
Sisler, Merle F., St. Virgil, Morris Plains
Sisson, Stanley
Smilek, Milton, St. Joseph, West Milford
Tenga, Charles, Annunciation, Wayne
Teresinski, John S., SS. Cyril & Methodius Church, Clifton
Turner, John
Van Vleet, Arthur H., St. Joseph, Newton
Varsalona, Nicholas, St. Therese Church, Paterson
Vesota, Robert, Father English Center, Paterson
Walker, John
Wallace, Michael J., Our Lady of the Valley, Wayne
Walsh, Frank, Diocese of Phoenix, AZ
Ward, William, Holy Family, Florham Park
Whaley, Bruce, Archdiocese of Philadelphia, PA
Whelan, Edward, Sacred Heart, Dover
Wisneski, Joseph A., St. Patrick, Chatham
Zeich, Richard, Sacred Heart, Dover

INSTITUTIONS LOCATED IN THE DIOCESE

[A] SEMINARIES, RELIGIOUS OR SCHOLASTICATES

OAK RIDGE. *Paulist Novitiate*, 243 Mt. Paul Rd., 07438. Tel: 201-697-6341. Missionary Society of St. Paul the Apostle (Paulist Fathers). Revs. James R. Mc Cauley, C.S.P., Dir.; Thomas J. Connellan, C.S.P., Asst. Priests 2; Novices 4.

[B] COLLEGES AND UNIVERSITIES

HALEDON. *Salesian College*, 655 Belmont Ave., 07508.
For a complete listing, refer to the Colleges and Universities section.

MENDHAM. *Assumption College for Sisters*, 07945 Fax: 201-543-9459.
For a complete listing, refer to the Colleges and Universities section.

MORRISTOWN. *College of Saint Elizabeth*, 2 Convent Rd., 07961. Tel: 201-292-6300.
For a complete listing, refer to the Colleges and Universities section.

[C] HIGH SCHOOLS, DIOCESAN

PATERSON. *Paterson Catholic Regional High School*, 764-11th Ave., 07514. Tel: 201-278-1024. Sr. Gloria Perez, P.B.V.M., Prin.; Bro. Vincent Casamento, O.F.M., Asst. Prin.; Michele R. Fierro, Asst. Prin. Priests 1; Sisters 2; Brothers 3; Lay Teachers 27; Students 455.

DENVILLE. *Morris Catholic High School*, 07834. Tel: 201-627-6674. Bro. Hugh McGrath, O.S.F., Prin.; Sr. Jonathan Moyles, S.C.C., Asst. Prin.; Rev. Paul S. Manning, Chap. Priests 2; Sisters 11; Lay Teachers 25; Students 445.

MADISON. *Bayley-Ellard High School*, 07940. Tel: 201-377-2486. Mr. Frank O. Mattiace, Exec. Dir. & Prin.; Rev. Edward J. Dillon. Priests 3; Sisters 6; Lay Teachers 17; Students 164.

SPARTA. *Pope John XXIII High School*, 07871. Tel: 201-729-6125. Revs. Kieran A. McHugh, Prin.; M. Paul Daly. Lay Teachers 45; Students 672.

WAYNE. *De Paul High School*, 1512 Alps Rd., 07470. Tel: 201-694-3702; Fax: 201-633-5381. Sr. Patricia Flarity, Prin.; Rev. David L. Coppola. Sisters 2; Brothers 1; Lay Teachers 46; Students 675.

[D] HIGH SCHOOLS, PRIVATE

PATERSON. *Don Bosco Technical High School*, 202 Union Ave., 07502. Tel: 201-595-8800. Revs. Patrick Angelucci, S.D.B., Dir.; A. J. Louis, S.D.B.; Paul P. Avallone, S.D.B.; Patrick Diver, S.D.B.; Thomas McGahee, S.D.B.; Stephen Ryan, S.D.B.; Bros. Bruno Busatta, S.D.B.; John Andres, S.D.B.; Thomas Dion, S.D.B.; Louis Konopeski, S.D.B.; Henry VanDer-Velden, S.D.B.; Andrew Bertello, S.D.B. Priests 6; Brothers 6; Sisters 2; Lay Teachers 20; Students 325.

Don Bosco Volunteers, Inc. Rev. Paul P. Avallone, S.D.B., Contact Person.

CONVENT STATION. *Academy of St. Elizabeth*, 07961. Tel: 201-292-6414. Sisters of Charity. Sr. Patricia Mary McMullen, S.C., Prin. Sisters 10; Lay Teachers 22; Students 230.

MORRISTOWN. *Delbarton School*, 07960. Tel: 201-538-3231. Day School for Boys. (Grades 7-12). Rev. Giles P. Hayes, O.S.B., Headmaster. Asst. Headmasters: Mr. John Kowalik; Mr. Edward Kim; Revs. Luke Travers, O.S.B., Dir. of Admissions; Edward Seton Fittin, O.S.B., Dir. Campus Min. Monks 22; Laymen 70; Students 515.

Villa Walsh Academy, 07960. Tel: 201-538-3680. College Preparatory for girls (Grades 7-12). Conducted by Religious Teachers Filippini. Sr. Patricia Pompa, M.P.F., Prin. Sisters 18; Lay Teachers 16; Students 207.

NORTH HALEDON. *Mary Help of Christians Academy*, 659-723 Belmont Ave., 07508. Tel: 201-790-6200. Daughters of Mary Help of Christians (Salesian Sisters). Sr. Antoinette Cedrone, F.M.A., Supr.; Sr. Karen Dunn, F.M.A., Prin.; Rev. Ken Shaw, S.D.B., Chap. Sisters 24; Lay Teachers 14; Students 299.

[E] ELEMENTARY SCHOOLS, DIOCESAN

CLIFTON. *Pope John Paul II School*. Serving St. John the Baptist Cathedral and St. Joseph, Paterson, 775 Valley Rd., 07013. Tel: 201-458-9282. Sr. Judith Suprys, F.M.A., Prin.; Ms. Kathleen Fields, Asst. Prin. Sisters 5; Lay Teachers 27; Students 773.

[F] REGIONAL ELEMENTARY SCHOOLS

FRANKLIN. *Immaculate Conception Regional School*, 65 Church St., 07416. Mrs. Sheila O'Leary, Prin. Serves Immaculate Conception, Franklin; Our Lady of Fatima, Highland Lakes; St. John Vianney, Stockholm; St. Monica, Sussex; St. Thomas of Aquin, Ogdensburg; St. Francis De Sales, McAfee; St. Jude, Hamburg. Sisters 3; Lay Teachers 10; Students 287.

NEWTON. *St. Joseph Regional School*, Jefferson St., 07860. Sr. Betty Ann Martinez, F.M.A., Prin. Serves St. Joseph, Newton; Our Lady Queen of Peace, Branchville; Our Lady of Mount Carmel, Swartswood. Sisters 2; Lay Teachers 9; Students 200.

PASSAIC. *Passaic Catholic Regional School*, 212 Market St., 07055. Sr. Joselle Ratka, C.S.S.F., Prin. Serves Holy Rosary, St. Joseph, St. Stephen, St. Mary, Our Lady of Fatima, in Passaic. Sisters 1; Lay Teachers 10; Students 216.

[G] PRIVATE PRESCHOOL

FLORHAM PARK. *Magic Kingdom Day Care Nursery School*, 88 Brookline Rd., 07932. Tel: 201-966-9762. Vocationist Sisters. Sr. Romilda A. Borges, S.D.V., Prin. Sisters 8; Lay Teachers 3; Students 85.

NEWTON. *Camp Auxilium Center*, 14 Old Swartswood Rd., 07860. Tel: 201-383-2621. Salesian Sisters. Sr. Lou Ann Fantauzza, F.M.A., Prin. Sisters 2; Lay Teachers 13; Students 300.

PARSIPPANY. *St. Elizabeth's Nursery and Montessori School, Inc.*, 499 Park Rd., 07054. Tel: 201-540-0721. Sr. Rosa Maria Miranda, F.S.S.E., Contact Person. Students 187.

[H] CHILDREN'S CENTERS

PATERSON. *Mt. St. Joseph Children's Center* (Totowa), 124 Shepherd Ln., 07512. Tel: 201-595-5720. Residential Treatment Center for Emotionally Disturbed Boys. Under the direction of Catholic Family and Community Services. Sr. Dorothy Sheahan, S.C., Dir. Residents 32; Day Students 8.

DENVILLE. *St. Peter's Village*, 170 Diamond Spring Rd., 07834. Tel: 201-627-0212; Fax: 201-627-3338. Staffed by School Sisters of Notre Dame. Sr. Katherine M. Kinnally, S.S.N.D., Dir. Sisters 1; Residents 16.

[I] RETREAT HOUSES & HOUSES OF PRAYER

BRANCHVILLE. *Sanctuary of Mary-Our Lady of the Holy Spirit*, 252 Wantage Ave., 07826. Tel: 201-875-7625.

Rev. Silvester J. Livolsi (NEW).

CHESTER. *Hermits of Bethlehem of the Heart of Jesus*, Pleasant Hill Rd., 07930. Rev. Eugene L. Romano, Desert Father. Priests 1; Brother Candidates 1; Sisters 4.

CONVENT STATION. *Xavier Center*, 07961. Tel: 201-605-3600; Fax: 201-605-3663. A retreat & conference center. Sr. Carol Heller, S.C., Admin.

FLORHAM PARK. *Vocationist Fathers Retreat Center*, 90 Brooklake Rd., 07932. Tel: 201-966-6262. Rev. Edgar Da Cunha, S.D.V., Dir.

MENDHAM. *Villa Pauline*, 07945. Retreat House for Men & Women. Sisters of Christian Charity 5.

MORRISTOWN. *Good Shepherd Retreat Center*, 74 Kahdena Rd., 07960. Tel: 201-538-4233. Legal Title: *Sisters of the Good Shepherd of New Jersey*. Sr. Marie Barbara, R.G.S., Supr. Sisters 3.

Loyola House of Retreats, 161 James St., 07960. Tel: 201-539-0740. Society of Jesus. Revs. William P. Walsh, S.J., Supr. & Dir.; Richard J. Anable, S.J.; Donald G. Devine, S.J.; John J. McDonald, S.J.; William J. McLoughlin, S.J.; Edmund W. Nagle, S.J.; Emmet J. Norton, S.J.; William R. O'Leary, S.J., Admin.; Thomas F. Walsh, S.J.; Sr. Barbara Connell, S.C.; Sr. Irene M. Garvey, O.P. Priests 9; Sisters 2.

St. Mary's Abbey Retreat Center, 230 Mendham Rd., 07960. Tel: 201-538-5231, Ext. 2100. Rev. Beatus T. Lucey, O.S.B., Dir.

MOUNT ARLINGTON. *Felician Retreat House*, 35 Windemere Ave., 07856. Tel: 201-398-9806. Sr. Mary Gilbert Szaroleta, C.S.S.F., Dir.

NEWTON. *Queen of Peace Retreat House*, St. Paul's Abbey, P.O. Box 7, 07860. Tel: 201-383-2470; 393-0660. Rt. Rev. Justin Dzikowicz, O.S.B.; Deacon John S. Larkin.

Sacred Heart Retreat Center, 20 Old Swartswood Rd., 07860. Tel: 201-383-2620. Daughters of Mary Help of Christians. Sr. Carmen Pena, F.M.A., Supr. Sisters 6.

RINGWOOD. *Mt. St. Francis Retreat Center*, 474 Sloatsburg Rd., 07456. Tel: 201-962-9778. Sr. Clare Agnes Conforti, F.S.R., Admin.

[J] GENERAL HOSPITALS

PATERSON. *St. Joseph's Hospital and Medical Center*, 703 Main St., 07503. Tel: 201-754-2000.
For a complete listing, refer to the Hospitals section.

DENVILLE. *Sisters of the Sorrowful Mother Health Care Ministry Corp.*, 22 Bloomfield Ave., 07834. Tel: 201-586-1961.
For a complete listing, refer to the Hospitals section.

PASSAIC. *St. Mary's Hospital*, 211 Pennington Ave., 07055. Tel: 201-470-3000.
For a complete listing, refer to the Hospitals section.

[K] HOMES FOR AGED

PATERSON. *St. Joseph Rest Home for Aged Women*, 46 Preakness Ave., 07522.
For a complete listing, refer to the Special Care Facilities section.

DENVILLE. *Franciscan Oaks Independent Living Units & Health Center*, 21 Pocono Rd., 07834.
For a complete listing, refer to the Special Care Facilities section.

St. Francis Health Resort, 07834 Fax: 201-625-9245.
For a complete listing, refer to the Special Care Facilities section.

TOTOWA. *St. Joseph's Home for the Elderly*, 140 Shepherd Ln., 07512. Tel: 201-942-0300.
For a complete listing, refer to the Special Care Facilities section.

[L] RESIDENCES FOR WOMEN

PATERSON. *St. Frances Residence*, 25 Jackson St., 07501. Sr. Joyce Vincent, S.C., Admin. Sisters of Charity of St. Elizabeth, NJ 3; Residents 35.

MORRISTOWN. *Dericks Residence*, 70 MacCulloch Ave., 07960. Tel: 201-292-9517. Mr. James Stauner, Dir. Residents 25.

POMPTON LAKES. *Eugene Kennedy Residence*, 31 Pompton Ave., 07442. Tel: 201-835-1476. Sr. M. Beatrice Kereszi, F.S.P., Admin. Residents 13.

WAYNE. *Bethany Residence*, 738 Rte. 23, 07470. Tel: 201-628-8109. Sr. Joseph Loretto, M.S.B.T., Admin. Residents 12.

Kilroy Residence, 584 Ratzer Rd., 07470. Tel: 201-694-3594. Sr. Roseanna Seifert, F.S.P., Dir.; Sr. Maria Francis Shebellock, F.S.P., Asst. Dir. Residents 12.

WEST PATERSON. *Holy Family Residence*, 44 Rifle Camp Rd., P.O. Box 536, 07424. Conducted by the Missionary Sisters of the Immaculate Conception of the Mother of God. M. Catherine Dulio, Admin. Residents 66.

[M] MONASTERIES AND RESIDENCES OF PRIESTS AND BROTHERS

PATERSON. *St. Benedict the Moor Friary*, 146 Danforth Ave., 07501. Tel: 201-523-0808. Rev. Claude Lenehan, O.F.M.; Bros. Vincent Casamento, O.F.M.; Robert Frazzetta, O.F.M.; Edward Higgins, O.F.M.; Paul Santoro, O.F.M.

BUTLER. *St. Anthony Friary*, 07405. Tel: 201-838-4080. Order of Friars Minor. Revs. Richard P. Biasiotto, O.F.M., Guardian; John S. Ahearn, O.F.M.; Emmett A. Barrett, O.F.M.; Giulio F. Basetti-Sani, O.F.M.; Patrick M. Brown, O.F.M.; Flavian Colligan, O.F.M.; Bernard R. Creighton, O.F.M.; Emmanuel Duffy, O.F.M.; Cary Kean, O.F.M.; Matthew L. Gaskin, O.F.M.; Charles V. Hayes, O.F.M.; Cordius P. Kazanchy, O.F.M.; Leonard A. Kelly, O.F.M.; Basil F. Lobby, O.F.M.; Gerald R. McDonald, O.F.M.; Anthony McGuire, O.F.M.; Edward A. McGuire, O.F.M.; Frederick McKeever, O.F.M.; Theodore A. McNally, O.F.M.; Alexus J. Mulrenan, O.F.M.; LaSalle O'Friel, O.F.M.; Michael V. Perry, O.F.M.; John J. Pierce, O.F.M.; J. Felton Robertson, O.F.M.; Jude Smith, O.F.M.; Florian A. Walczyk, O.F.M.; Bros. Peter R. Butler, O.F.M.; Fintan Duffy, O.F.M.; Rosario Vieira, O.F.M.; William J. Heaney, O.F.M.; Daniel F. Murray, O.F.M. Priests 26; Brothers 5.

CLIFTON. *Holy Face of Jesus Monastery*, 1697 State Hwy. 3, P.O. Box 691, 07012. Sylvestrine Benedictine Monks. Revs. Hilary Conti, O.S.B.; Bruno Daniel, O.S.B.; Thomas Toomey, O.S.B.; Joseph Kulathinal, O.S.B. Priests 4.

FLORHAM PARK. *Father Justin Vocationary*, 90 Brooklake Rd., 07932. Tel: 201-966-6262. Revs. Mario Muccitelli, S.D.V., Delegate; Edgar da Cunha, S.D.V., Supr.; Ugo Fraraccio, S.D.V.; Robert Vass, S.D.V.

LAFAYETTE. *St. Francis Center*, 07848. Tel: 201-383-6465. Capuchin Friars. Bro. Julius Tkaczyk, O.F.M.Cap., Vicar; Rev. Brian Tomlinson, O.F.M.Cap., Local Minister. Priests 1; Brothers 1.

MORRISTOWN. *St. Mary's Abbey*, Delbarton, Mendham Rd., 07960. Tel: 201-538-3231. Rt. Revs. Gerald P. Lair, O.S.B., Abbot; Brian H. Clark, O.S.B., Abbot Emeritus; Leonard G. Cassell, O.S.B., Abbot Emeritus; Martin J. Burne, O.S.B., Abbot Emeritus; Very Rev. Elias R. Lorenzo, O.S.B., Prior; Revs. Jerome Borski, O.S.B.; Kevin M. Bray, O.S.B.; Thomas J. Confroy, O.S.B.; Benet W. Caffrey, O.S.B.; Christian J. Casper, O.S.B.; Gabriel M. Coless, O.S.B.; Michael J. Collins, O.S.B.; Mark W. Confroy, O.S.B.; Conall R. Coughlin, O.S.B.; Richard J. Cronin, O.S.B.; Edward Seton J. Fittin, O.S.B.; Jerome B. Fitzpatrick, O.S.B.; Germain L. Fritz, O.S.B.; Simon P. Gallagher, O.S.B.; Giles P. Hayes, O.S.B.; John E. Hesketh, O.S.B.; Joel J. Leikhim, O.S.B.; Beatus T. Lucey, O.S.B.; Adrian T. McLaughlin, O.S.B.; Arthur Mayer, O.S.B.; Kenneth H. Mayer, O.S.B.; Peter J. Meaney, O.S.B.; James O'Donnell, O.S.B.; Rembert F. Reilly, O.S.B.; Jude S. Salus, O.S.B.; Joachim B. Schweitzer, O.S.B.; Andrew T. Smith, O.S.B.; Luke L. Travers, O.S.B. Total Priests 42; Serving Out of Diocese 10; Brothers 9. Bros. Damian B. Breen, O.S.B.; Tarcisius Hoang-Hoa, O.S.B.; Jonathan M. Hunt, O.S.B.; Ambrose J. Kelly, O.S.B.; James J. Konchalski, O.S.B.; Christopher K. Rosa, O.S.B.; Kiernan M. Shiek, O.S.B.; Brendan A. Tumalty, O.S.B.
Resident Outside the Abbey: Revs. Timothy J. Brennan, O.S.B.; Donal R. Fox, O.S.B.; Patrick M. Hurley, O.S.B.; Karl J. Roesch, O.S.B.; Wilfred G. Schulz, O.S.B.; Bruno A. Ugliano, O.S.B.; Regis P. Wallace, O.S.B.; Benedict M. Worry, O.S.B.; Justino Capato, O.S.B.; Hilary O'Leary, O.S.B. Total Priests 44; Serving Out of Diocese 9; Brothers 11.

NEWTON. *St. Paul's Abbey*, 07860. Tel: 201-383-2470; Fax: 201-383-5782. (Formerly the Little Flower Monastery). Order of St. Benedict, Congregation of St. Ottilien. Rt. Revs. Justin E. Dzikowicz, O.S.B., Resigned; Augustine J. Hinches, O.S.B., (Resigned); Charles V. Coriston, O.S.B., (Resigned); Very Revs. Bede E. Classick, O.S.B., Prior; Joel P. Macl, O.S.B., Administrator; Revs. Boniface D. Cronin, O.S.B.; Andrew C. O'Sullivan, O.S.B.; Jude C. Bradley, O.S.B.; Patrick J. Bonner, O.S.B.; Basil J. Wallace, O.S.B.
Priests Residing Outside the Monastery: St. Alban D-86911. Rev. Alfred A. Humm, O.S.B., VA Hospital, Brooklyn, NY, 11209. Rev. Robert J. Chalany, O.S.B., Mailing Address: P.O. Box 213, Lushoto, Tanzania. Rev. Damian J. Milliken, O.S.B., Inkamana Abbey, P/Bag X9333, Vayheid 3100, South Africa. Rev. Peter W. Blue, O.S.B., Prince of Peace Priory, P.O. Box 900, Limuru, Kenya. Rev. Joel P. Macul, O.S.B. Priests 14; Lay Monks 3.

OAK RIDGE-MILTON. *St. Stanislaus B. M. Friary*, Manor Dr., 07438. Tel: 201-697-7757. Capuchin Fathers. Revs. Hyacinth M. Dabrowski, O.F.M.Cap.; Henry T. Krajewski, O.F.M.Cap., Superior; Francis Mucharski, O.F.M.Cap.; Francis J. Salwowski, O.F.M.Cap.; Sigmund M. Klimowicz, O.F.M.Cap.; Peter Gacki, O.F.M.Cap.; Francis Majewski, O.F.M.Cap., Vicar; George J. Korytkowski, O.F.M.Cap.; Joseph Kubiak, O.F.M.Cap.; Stephen Laliberte, O.F.M.Cap.; Ivot Miszkel, O.F.M.Cap. Priests 9.

RINGWOOD. *Holy Name Friary*, 2 Morris Rd., 07456. Tel: 201-962-7200. Revs. A. Francis Soucy, O.F.M., Guardian and Dir.; Bonaventure Brown, O.F.M.; Arthur Butler, O.F.M.; Marshall Della Penna, O.F.M.; Justin Eeles, O.F.M.; Robert Gabel, O.F.M.; Roch Knopke, O.F.M.; Gerard Lewis, O.F.M.; Carmel Lluria, O.F.M.; Cosmas Girard, O.F.M.; Edward J. Holleran, O.F.M.; Richard Leo Heppler, O.F.M.; Valentine Long, O.F.M.; Raphael McDonald, O.F.M.; Kieran F. McMahon, O.F.M.; Gregory A. O'Donnell, O.F.M.; Owen J. Ormsby, O.F.M.; Salvator J. Philips, O.F.M.; Lawrence F. Pafchik, O.F.M.; Vincent Shea, O.F.M.; Eric Shoppe, O.F.M.; Hilary Scott, O.F.M.; Gregory Toomey, O.F.M.; Bros. Hormisdas Marcotte, O.F.M.; Gilbert McEvoy, O.F.M.; Joseph P. Trunk, O.F.M.; Agapitus Rothmann, O.F.M.

STIRLING. *Holy Spirit Missionary Cenacle*, 1050 Long Hill Rd., 07980. Tel: 908-647-0208. Missionary Servants of the Most Holy Trinity. Revs. Peter Krebs, S.T., Custodian; Vincent Fitzpatrick, S.T.; Kenan Ryan, S.T.; Cajetan McDyre, S.T.; Ralph Frisch, S.T.; Campion Murphy, S.T.; Stephen Quinn, S.T.; Bro. Martin Pacholek, S.T. Priests 7; Brothers 1.

Serenity Retreat League, 1292 Long Hill Rd., Box 10, 07980. Tel: 908-647-1539. Sr. Mary T. Lynch, S.F.C.C., Dir.

Shrine of St. Joseph, 1050 Long Hill Rd., 07980. Tel: 908-647-0208. Rev. Peter Krebs, S.T., Custodian. Priests 8; Brothers 1; Sisters 5.

WAYNE. *P.I.M.E. Missionaries Residence*, 34 Grandview Dr., 07470. Tel: 201-694-1790. Revs. Luigi Acerbi, P.I.M.E.; Claudio Corti, P.I.M.E.

Xaverian Missionary Fathers, Provincal House, 12 Helene Court, 07470. Tel: 201-942-2975. Revs. Francis Signorelli, S.X., Prov.; Mark Marangone, S.X.; Dario Maso, S.X.; Frank Grappolli, S.X.; Herondi Fernandes, S.X.
Mission Assignments: Makeni, Sierra Leone: Revs. Gerard Furlan, S.X.; Victor Mosele, S.X.; Luciano Peterlini, S.X.
Belem, Brazil: Revs. Francis Gugliotta, S.X.; Danilo Lago, S.X.; Mario Pezzotti, S.X.
Cameroon: Rev. Rene Lovat, S.X.
Uvira, Zaire: Rev. Noel Tomasi, S.X.
Sao Paulo, Brazil: Revs. Gino Nasini, S.X.; Roberto Fransolin, S.X.
Padang, Indonesia: Revs. Bruno Orru, S.X.; Frank Qualizza, S.X.
Buenaventura, Columbia: Rev. Mark Marangone, S.X.
Torreon, Mexico: Revs. Danilo Boschetto, S.X.; Adolph Menendez, S.X.
Bujumbura, Burundi: Rev. Joseph Tavera, S.X.
Taiwan: Revs. Julian Perozzi, S.X.; Martino Roia, S.X.; Joseph Matteucig, S.X.

[N] CONVENTS AND RESIDENCES FOR SISTERS

PATERSON. *Daughters of Charity of the Most Precious Blood*, 46 Preakness Ave., 07522. Sr. Maria Goretti Chaloux, D.C.P.B., Supr. Sisters 11.

Daughters of Mary Help of Christians. Sr. Carmen Pena, F.M.A., Supr.

Missionary Sisters of the Immaculate Conception of the Mother of God, 779 Broadway, 07514. Mailing Address: P.O. Box 3026, 07509-3026. Sr. Saundra McKeta, S.M.I.C., Prov. Coord.

Missionary Sisters of the Immaculate Conception of the Mother of God, 396 E. 38th St., 07504. Sisters 4.

Missionary Sisters of the Immaculate of the Mother of God, 374-18th Ave., 07504. Sisters 6.

CHESTER. *Carmel of the Immaculate Heart of Mary*. Hermits of Our Lady of Mt. Carmel, 80 Pleasant Hill Rd., 07930-2135. Tel: 908-879-4990. Sr. Mary of Jesus and St. Joseph, H.O.Carm., Desert Mother. Sisters 6.

CLIFTON. *The Society of the Sisters for the Church*, 62 Ruth Ave., 07013. Professed Sisters 2.

CONVENT STATION. *Motherhouse of the Sisters of Charity*. Mailing Address: P.O. Box 476, 07961. Tel: 201-292-6545. Sr. Barbara Conroy, S.C., General Supr. Professed Sisters 105.

St. Anne Villa. Mailing Address: P.O. Box 476, 07961. Tel: 201-292-6555. Sisters of Charity of St. Elizabeth. Home for retired and infirm Sisters. Sr. Rosanne Caiazzo, S.C., Admin.; Rev. Mark W. Confroy, O.S.B., Chap. Bed Capacity 115.

DENVILLE. *Our Lady of Sorrows Convent, Sisters of Sorrowful Mother*, 9 Pocono Rd., 07834.
Residences: 4 Pocono Rd., 07834. 45 N. Shore Dr., 07834. 21 Cooper Rd., Boonton, 07005. 40 E. Main St., Rockaway, 07866. R.R. 1, Box 390, Hamburg, 07419. Sisters 39.

FLORHAM PARK. *Sister Joanna House of Formation*, 88 Brooklake Rd., 07932. Tel: 201-966-9762. Sr. Anna Maria Mancino, S.D.V., Delegate & Superior; Sr. Romilda A. Borges, S.D.V., Prin. Sisters 8.

GLADSTONE. *Mt. St. John Convent*, 07934. Tel: 908-234-1074; 234-0640. Sisters of St. John the Baptist. Sr. Angelita Vazzano, C.S.J.B., Admin.

HALEDON. *Institute of the Daughters of Mary Help of Christians*, 655 Belmont Ave., 07508. Tel: 201-790-7964. Provincialate of Daughters of Mary Help of Christians. Mother Theresa Kelly, F.M.A., Prov.; Sr. Grace Ruiz, F.M.A., Supr.; Rev. Innocent Clementi, S.D.B., Chap. Daughters of Mary Help of Christians (Salesian Sisters) 46.

HEWITT. *St. Joseph's Convent*, Long House Dr., 07421. Sisters of Mercy, Daughters of Charity of St. Vincent de Paul of Hungary. Rev. Vincent S. McCluskey, Chap. Sisters 6.

MENDHAM. *Mallinckrodt Convent-Motherhouse and Novitiate of the Sisters of Christian Charity*, 07945. Tel: 201-543-6528. Daughters of the Blessed Virgin Mary of the Immaculate Conception. Sr. Maria Assumpta Shurer, S.C.C., Prov. Supr. Sisters 56; Novices 3; Postulants 4.

MORRISTOWN. Monastery Discalced Carmelite Nuns of the Most Blessed Virgin Mary of Mt. Carmel, 189 Madison Ave., 07960. Mother Mary Michael, O.C.D., Prioress. Professed Nuns 7; Extern Sisters 1; Postulants 2.

St. Lucy Provincialate of the Religious Teachers Filippini, Novitiate, Villa Walsh Academy, 455 Western Ave., 07960-4928. Tel: 201-538-2886. Legal Title: *Pontifical Institute of the Religious Teachers Filippini*. Sr. Frances Lauretti, M.P.F., Prov.; Sr. Ascenza Tizzano, M.P.F., Supr.; Sr. Dolores Potkay, M.P.F., Dir. Formation. Sisters 85; Novices 1; Junior Professed 2.

MOUNT ARLINGTON. *Felician Sisters of St. Francis of Assisi Convent*, 37 Windemere Ave., 07856. Sr. Mary Josita, C.S.S.F., Local Supr. Professed Sisters 7.

OAK RIDGE. *Society of the Sisters of the Church*, 15 Heritage Ct., 07438. Tel: 201-208-1456. Sr. Sylvia Berzinski, S.S.C., Coord. Sisters 11.

PARSIPPANY. *St. Francis of Assisi Novitiate-Franciscan Sisters of St. Elizabeth*, 499 Park Rd., 07054. Tel: 201-539-3797. Mother Gina Maria Amico, F.S.S.E., Delegate General; Rev. Philip W. Nielsen, O.F.M., Chap., Tel: 201-605-8729; Fax: 201-539-3347. Perpetually Professed Sisters 17; Temp. Professed Sisters 15; Novices 7; Postulants 1.

PASSAIC. *Missionary Sisters of Divine Providence*, 302 Madison Ave., 07542. Tel: 201-278-1030. Sr. Faustina Paulino, M.S.D.P., Supr. Sisters 3; Associates 3.

Our Lady of Mt. Carmel Convent, Franciscan Sisters of Ringwood, 47 Reid Ave., 07055. Tel: 201-471-6352. Sr. M. Berard, F.S.R., Supr. Sisters 5.

St. Joseph Convent, 9 Quincy St., 07055. Sr. Krystyna Kwasniak, D.P.H.M., Supr.

RINGWOOD. *Mt. St. Francis*, 07456. Tel: 201-962-7411. General Motherhouse and Novitiate of the Franciscan Sisters. Sr. Francis Clare Verderosa, F.S.R., Gen. Coord.; Rev. Lawrence Burke, O.F.M. Professed Sisters 34.

STIRLING. *Blessed Trinity Missionary Cenacle*, 1190 Long Hill Rd., 07980. Tel: 908-647-1165. Missionary Servants of the Most Blessed Trinity 3.

Holy Trinity Convent, 1026 Long Hill Rd., 07980. Tel: 908-647-6584. Sr. Zofia Kedziora, Supr. Servants of Jesus 5.

WEST PATERSON. *Missionary Sisters of the Immaculate Conception of the Mother of God*, Generalate, 48 Garden Ave., 07424. Sr. Luci Fontenele, S.M.I.C., Coord. Gen. Sisters 4.

Missionary Sisters of the Immaculate Conception, Convent of the Immaculate Conception, 44 Rifle Camp Rd., 07424. Tel: 201-279-2621. Sr. Mary Jude Nicholson, S.M.I.C., Coord.; Rev. Donald Sella, Chap.

Missionary Sisters of the Immaculate Conception, Peace Community, 54 Garden Ave., 07424. Tel: 201-278-2693. Sisters 5.

The Society of Sisters for the Church, 396 Rifle Camp Rd., 07424. Sr. Anne Marie McNicholl, S.S.C., Pres. Sisters 22; Companions 3; Observers 3.

[O] NEWMAN CENTERS

CONVENT STATION. *College of St. Elizabeth Newman Center*, 07960. Tel: 201-292-6510; 292-6323. Rev. Anthony J. Ciorra.

HALEDON. *William Paterson College Catholic Campus Ministry Center*, 219 Pompton Rd., 07508. Rev. Louis J. Scurti.

MADISON. *Drew University Catholic Campus Ministry*. Chaplain's Office, President's House Annex, 07940. Tel: 201-408-3027. Rev. Joseph G. Farias. Tel: 201-627-0066.

Fairleigh Dickinson University and Drew University. Catholic Campus Ministry, Fairleigh Dickinson University, 285 Madison Ave., 07940. Tel: 201-593-8651. Rev. Joseph G. Farias, Res: 446 Mt. Hope Rd., Wharton, 07885-2814. Tel: 201-627-0066.

[P] MISCELLANEOUS LISTINGS

PATERSON. *Martin de Porres Village Corporation*, Green St., 07501. Tel: 201-881-8022. Rev. Msgr. Herbert K. Tillyer, Pres. Sponsoring Martin De Porres, Vill.

Riese Corporation, Twentieth Ave., 07501. Tel: 201-279-2262. Rev. Msgr. Joseph R. Brestel, Pres. Sponsoring Governor Paterson Towers, Maurice Brick Residence, Brestel Residence, William F. Hinchcliffe Manor.

St. Anthony's Guild, 07509. Tel: 201-777-3737. Membership organization supports the work of The Franciscan Friars of Holy Name Province. Revs. Joseph M. Hertel, O.F.M., Dir.; Cassian A. Miles, O.F.M.; Felician A. Foy, O.F.M.; Rayner F. Williams, O.F.M.

CHESTER. *Nazareth Village*, Main St., Box 635, 07930. Retirement residence for diocesan priests. Rev. Raymond M. Lopatesky, Dir. In res., Revs. Martin Connolly; Charles Grieco; Robert J. Morris; Patrick Mullan; Raymond J. Jasaitis; Rev. Msgr. Carl J. Wolsin; Rev. Msgr. Joseph J. Gallo; Rev. Msgr. Louis J. Gallo; Rev. Msgr. John R. Ryan; Rev. Msgr. Leo P. Ryan; Rev. Msgr. Leo P. Carey.

CONVENT STATION. *Seton Health Care, Inc.*, Convent of Saint Elizabeth, P.O. Box 476, 07961. Tel: 201-292-6545. Sr. Mary Canavan, S.C., Pres.

MORRISTOWN. *Priests Residence*, 74 Kahdena Rd., 07960. Revs. Robert M. Diachek; Hugh P. Murphy.

PASSAIC. *St. Jude Media Ministries*, 63 Monroe St., 07055. Tel: 201-777-0303; Fax: 201-472-5033. Rev. John T. Catoir, Dir.

PEQUANNOCK. School. *St. Maximilian Kolbe*, 18 First St., 07440. Tel: 201-694-1034. Mrs. Mary Lou Bednar, Prin. Lay Teachers 4; Students 40.

STIRLING. *Father Judge Apostolic Center*, 1292 Long Hill Rd., 07980. Tel: 908-647-7112; 647-2422 (Res.); Fax: 908-647-6045. Rev. Dennis Berry, S.T., Dir.; Bro. William Coombs, S.T., Asst. Dir.; Michael St. Pierre, Missionary Volunteer.

WAYNE. *Siena Village*, 458 Valley Rd., 07470. Tel: 201-226-0730. Sr. Aliuce Matthews, O.P., Dir.

RELIGIOUS INSTITUTES OF MEN REPRESENTED IN THE DIOCESE

For further details refer to the corresponding bracketed number in the Religious Institutes of Men or Women section.

[0200]—*Benedictine Monks*. (St. Mary, St. Paul Abbeys; Holy Face of Jesus Residence).—O.S.B.

[0470]—*The Capuchin Friars*(Italian, Polish).—O.F.M.Cap.

[0480]—*Conventual Franciscans*(Polish).—O.F.M.Conv.

[0520]—*Franciscan Friars*. (Holy Name Prov.).—O.F.M.

[0690]—*Jesuit Fathers and Brothers*. (New York Prov.).—S.J.

[0840]—*Missionary Servants of the Most Holy Trinity*. (Silver Spring, MD).—S.T.

[1030]—*Paulist Fathers*. (New York).—C.S.P.

[1190]—*Salesians of Don Bosco*. (Turin, Italy).—S.D.B.

[1340]—*Vocationist Fathers*.—S.D.V.

[1360]—*Xaverian Missionary Fathers*. (Wayne).—S.X.

RELIGIOUS INSTITUTES OF WOMEN REPRESENTED IN THE DIOCESE

[0230]—*Benedictine Sisters of Pontifical Jurisdiction*.—O.S.B.

[0740]—*Daughters of Charity of the Most Precious Blood*.—D.C.P.B.

[0850]—*Daughters of Mary Help of Christians*.—F.M.A.

[]—*Daughters of the Most Pure Heart of the Most Holy Virgin Mary*. (Passaic).

[0420]—*Discalced Carmelite Nuns*.—O.C.D.

[1070-06]—*Dominican Sisters*.—O.P.

[1070-18]—*Dominican Sisters*.—O.P.

[1170]—*Felician Sisters*.—C.S.S.F.

[1400]—*Franciscan Missionary Sisters of the Sacred Heart*. (Peekskill).—F.M.S.C.

[1420]—*Franciscan Sisters of Ringwood*.—F.S.R.

[1460]—*Franciscan Sisters of St. Elizabeth*.—F.S.S.E.

[]—*Hermits of Our Lady of Mt. Carmel*.—H.O.Carm.

[2340]—*Little Sisters of the Poor*.—L.S.P.

[2790]—*Missionary Servants of the Most Blessed Trinity*.—M.S.B.T.

[2760]—*Missionary Sisters of the Immaculate Conception of the Mother of God*.—S.M.I.C.

[3430]—*Religious Teachers Filippini*.—M.P.F.

[2970]—*School Sisters of Notre Dame*.—S.S.N.D.

[1700]—*School Sisters of the Third Order of St. Francis*.—O.S.F.

[3560]—*Servants of Jesus*. (Sterling).—S.J.

[3580]—*Servants of Mary*.—O.S.M.

[0590]—*Sisters of Charity of Saint Elizabeth, Convent Station*.—S.C.

[0660]—*Sisters of Christian Charity*.—S.C.C.

[3820]—*Sisters of St. John the Baptist*.—C.S.J.B.

[3830]—*Sisters of St. Joseph*. (Chestnut Hill, PA).—C.S.J.

[3890]—*Sisters of St. Joseph of Peace*.—C.S.J.P.

[1830]—*Sisters of the Good Shepherd*.—R.G.S.

[3320]—*Sisters of the Presentation of the B.V.M.*—P.B.V.M.

[4100]—*Sisters of the Sorrowful Mother (Third Order of St. Francis)*.—S.S.M.

[]—*The Society of the Sisters of the Church*. (Passaic).

[4210]—*Vocationist Sisters*.—S.D.V.

NECROLOGY

† D'Auria, Martin J., Paterson, NJ, Our Lady of Pompei. —Died Sept. 18, 1996.

† Gacquin, Rev. Msgr. James, Montague, NJ, St. James the Greater. —Died March 31, 1996.

† Hernandez, Manuel, Morristown, NJ, Morristown Memorial Hospital. —Died Sept. 27, 1996.

† Murphy, Rev. Msgr. Francis H., Clifton, NJ, St. Philip the Apostle. —Died May 9, 1996.

† Pulvirenti, Paul F., Paterson, NJ, St. John the Baptist Cathedral. —Died March 3, 1996.

† Zawistowski, Stanley J., Prospect Park, NJ, St. Paul. —Died Jan. 13, 1996.

Diocese of Pensacola-Tallahassee

(Dioecesis Pensacolensis-Tallaseiensis)

Most Reverend

JOHN H. RICARD, S.S.J., D.D., PH.D., V.G.

Bishop of Pensacola-Tallahassee; ordained May 25, 1968; ordained Auxiliary Bishop of Baltimore July 2, 1984; appointed Bishop of Pensacola-Tallahassee January 21, 1997.

ESTABLISHED NOVEMBER 6, 1975.

Square Miles 14,044.

Comprises the following Counties: Bay, Calhoun, Escambia, Franklin, Gadsden, Gulf, Holmes, Jackson, Jefferson, Leon, Liberty, Madison, Okaloosa, Santa Rosa, Taylor, Wakulla, Walton and Washington Counties.

For legal titles of parishes and diocesan institutions, consult the Pastoral Center.

Pastoral Center: P.O. Drawer 17329, Pensacola, FL, 32522. Tel.: 904-432-1515; Fax: 904-436-6424.

STATISTICAL OVERVIEW

Personnel	
Bishop	1
Priests: Diocesan Active in Diocese	52
Priests: Active Outside Diocese	10
Priests: Retired, Sick or Absent	12
Number of Diocesan Priests	74
Religious Priests in Diocese	10
Extern Priests in Diocese	13
Ordinations:	
Diocesan Priests	2
Transitional Deacons	1
Permanent Deacons in Diocese	53
Total Brothers	7
Total Sisters	61
Parishes	
Parishes	49
With Resident Pastor:	
Resident Diocesan Priests	41
Resident Religious Priests	6
Without Resident Pastor:	
Administered by Priests	2
Missions	9
Welfare	
Catholic Hospitals	1
Total Assisted	106,560
Homes for the Aged	3
Total Assisted	247
Special Centers for Social Services	7
Total Assisted	50,362
Other Institutions	3
Total Assisted	150
Educational	
Diocesan Students in Other Seminaries	9
Total Seminarians	9
High Schools, Diocesan and Parish	1
Total Students	570
Elementary Schools, Diocesan and Parish	8
Total Students	2,610
Non-residential Schools for the Disabled	1
Total Students	16
Catechesis/Religious Education:	
High School Students	1,307
Elementary Students	5,051
Total Students Under Catholic Instruction	9,563
Teachers in the Diocese:	
Sisters	10
Lay Teachers	195
Vital Statistics	
Receptions into the Church:	
Infant Baptism Totals	1,068
Adult Baptism Totals	164
Received into Full Communion	295
First Communions	1,201
Confirmations	824
Marriages:	
Catholic	147
Interfaith	189
Total Marriages	336
Deaths	458
Total Catholic Population	62,735
Total Population	1,256,474

Former Bishops—Most Rev. RENE H. GRACIDA, D.D., ord. May 23, 1959; appt. Titular Bishop of Masuccaba and Auxiliary of Miami, Dec. 6, 1971; cons. Jan. 25, 1972; appt. first Bishop of Pensacola-Tallahassee, Oct. 1, 1975; installed Nov. 6, 1975; transferred to Bishop of Corpus Christi, May 19, 1983.—Most Rev. J. KEITH SYMONS, D.D., Bishop of Pensacola-Tallahassee; ord. May 18, 1958; Titular Bishop of Siguritanus and Auxiliary of St. Petersburg; appt. Jan. 16, 1981; cons. March 19, 1981; Bishop of Pensacola-Tallahassee; appt. Sept. 29, 1983; installed Nov. 8, 1983; transferred to Bishop of Palm Beach, June 2, 1990.—Most Rev. JOHN M. SMITH, J.C.D., D.D., Bishop of Pensacola-Tallahassee; ord. May 27, 1961; Titular Bishop of Tre Taverne and Auxiliary of Newark; appt. Dec. 1, 1987; cons. Jan. 25, 1988; Bishop of Pensacola-Tallahassee; appt. June 25, 1991; installed July 31, 1991; transferred to Coadjutor of Trenton, Nov. 21, 1995.

Pastoral Center—11 N. "B" St., Pensacola, 32501. Tel: 904-432-1515; Fax: 904-436-6424., *Mailing Address: P.O. Drawer 17329, Pensacola, 32522.*

Chancellor—Rev. Msgr. JAMES AMOS, J.C.L.

Vicars for Priests—Revs. JOHN CASSIDY; MICHAEL FOLEY.

Vicar for Permanent Deacons—Deacon JOHN MORGAN.

Vicar for Religious—Rev. Msgr. JAMES AMOS, J.C.L.

Vice Chancellor & Notary—Rev. MICHAEL REED.

Vicars Forane—Cathedral Vicariate Forane: Very Rev. RICHARD J. BOWLES, V.F., Northwest Vicariate Forane: Very Rev. MICHAEL MOONEY, V.F., Southwest Vicariate Forane: Very Rev. STEVEN O'CONNOR, V.F., North Central Vicariate Forane: Very Rev. FRANCIS SZCZYKUTOWICZ, V.F., West Central Vicariate Forane: Rev. Msgr. RAYMOND MULLINS, East Central Vicariate Forane: Rev. Msgr. WILLIAM A. CROWE, V.F., Eastern Vicariate Forane: Very Rev. JOHN V. O'SULLIVAN, V.F.

Diocesan Tribunal—1000 W. Garden St., Pensacola, 32501., Mailing Address: P.O. Drawer 17329, Pensacola, 32522. Tel: 904-436-6454.

Judicial Vicar—Very Rev. JAMES J. FLAHERTY, J.C.L.

Associate Judicial Vicar—Rev. Msgr. JAMES AMOS, J.C.L.

Judges—Very Rev. JAMES J. FLAHERTY, J.C.L.; Revs. WILLIAM P. BROWN, J.C.L.; TODD O. HEVIA, J.C.D.

Promoter of Justice—Rev. TODD O. HEVIA, J.C.D.

Auditors—Revs. THOMAS BONANTI; JOSEPH CALLIPARE; EUGENE D. CASSERLY; MICHAEL REED.

Defender of the Bond—Rev. Msgr. JAMES AMOS, J.C.L.

Notaries—Revs. JOSEPH CALLIPARE; MICHAEL REED; Deacons GERARD WILLIAMSON; RAMON BONANNO; MS. BARBARA STOLLENWERK.

College of Consultors—Rev. Msgr. JAMES AMOS, J.C.L.; Rev. Msgr. RAYMOND MULLINS, V.F.; Very Rev. JAMES J. FLAHERTY; Revs. MICHAEL MOONEY; RICHARD CASTILLO; DANIEL BUTLER.

Administrative Council—Rev. Msgr. JAMES AMOS, J.C.L.; Very Revs. MICHAEL CHERUP; JAMES J. FLAHERTY; MICHAEL MOONEY; Rev. MICHAEL REED, Sec.; Sr. ELLEN KIERAN, M.S.B.T.; Mr. J. PATRICK REMICH.

Council of Permanent Deacons—Deacons JOHN MORGAN, Vicar for Deacons; HENRY BURRELL; THOMAS FRAITES; DALE JOHNSON; NELSON MADERA; BRADLEY SEABROOK.

Council of Sisters—Sr. MARGARET KUNTZ, A.S.C.J., Chm.; Sr. MARILYN DOUCETTE, C.N.D., Vice Chm.; Sr. MARGUERITE GIBBS, I.H.M., Sec. & Treas.; Sr. BARBARA MURRAY, R.S.M., Recording Sec.

Diocesan Commissions, Departments, And Offices

Apostleship of the Sea, Office of the—Very Rev. RICHARD J. BOWLES, V.F., Chap., *P.O. Drawer 17329, Pensacola, 32522.* Tel: 904-432-1515.

Archivist—Bro. STEPHEN QUENSE, *P.O. Drawer 17329, Pensacola, 32522.* Tel: 904-432-1515.

Black Catholics, Office of—Deacon BRADLEY SEABROOK, Dir., *P.O. Drawer 17329, Pensacola, 32522.* Tel: 904-432-1515.

Building & Renovation, Diocesan Commission for—Rev. Msgr. GEORGE E. SINDIK, Chm.; Rev. Msgr. JAMES AMOS, J.C.L.; Rev. Msgr. LUKE HUNT; Mr. B. J. NICKELSEN; Mr. THEODORE J. RUCKSTUHL; Mr. J. PATRICK REMICH; Bro. STEPHEN QUENSE, *P.O. Drawer 17329, Pensacola, 32522.* Tel: 904-432-1515.

Building & Renovation, Office of—Mr. B. J. NICKELSEN, Dir., *P.O. Drawer 17329, Pensacola, 32522.* Tel: 904-432-1515.

Campaign for Human Development, Office of—Rev. MICHAEL REED, Dir., *P.O. Drawer 17329, Pensacola, 32522.* Tel: 904-432-1515.

Campus Ministry—P.O. Drawer 17329, Pensacola, 32522. Tel: 904-432-1515. Pensacola-University of West Florida: Rev. MICHAEL FLYNN, Dir., *9945 Hillview Dr., Pensacola, 32514.* Tel: 904-477-3221. Tallahassee-Florida Agricultural & Mechanical University, St. Eugene Chapel: Rev. JOHN BOATENG-MENSAH, Dir., *701 Gamble St., Tallahassee, 32310.* Tel: 904-222-6482. Florida State University: Rev. TOM COLLINS, Dir., *P.O. Box 2395, Tallahassee, 32316.* Tel: 904-222-9630.

Catholic Daughters of the Americas—Rev. ROBERT F. MORRIS, Court Chap.; Mrs. JOYCE PFEIFFER, Regent, *304 N. Sunset Blvd., Gulf Breeze, 32507.*

Catholic Women, Diocesan Council of—Very Rev. RICHARD J. BOWLES, V.F., Spiritual Dir.; Mrs. JEANNETTE SCHAAL, Pres., *P.O. Drawer 17329, Pensacola, 32522.* Tel: 904-432-1515.

Catholic Social Services, Department of—Sr. ELLEN KIERAN, M.S.B.T., Dir. Offices—Pensacola: *222 E. Government St., Pensacola, 32501.* Tel: 904-436-6410. Fort Walton Beach: Mrs. MARTI DEADRICK, Supvr., *40 Beal Pkwy. S.W., Fort Walton Beach,*

32548. Tel: 904-244-2825. Panama City: Mrs. Millie Dickens, Supvr., *3218 E. 11th St., Panama City, 32401.* Tel: 904-763-0475. Tallahassee: Ms. Wendy J. Blair, Supvr., *P.O. Box 20165, Tallahassee, 32316.* Tel: 904-222-2180.

Cemetery Office—Deacon Jean White, Dir., *P.O. Drawer 17329, Pensacola, 32522.* Tel: 904-432-1515. *Holy Cross Cemetery, 1300 E. Hayes St., Pensacola, 32503.* Tel: 904-432-0878. Mr. Tom Moyer, Dir., *Calvary Cemetery, 834 Sunny Hills Blvd., Sunny Hills, 32428.* Tel: 904-773-2165. Mr. Fred McEvoy, Dir.

Charismatic Renewal, Diocesan Commission for—Rev. Eugene Pathe, Moderator; Dr. Yolanda Ramos, Chm., *P.O. Drawer 17329, Pensacola, 32522.* Tel: 904-432-1515.

Christian Formation, Office of—Sr. Christine Wiltrakis, M.S.B.T., Dir.; Sr. Rebecca Betz, M.S.B.T., Assoc. Dir.; Mrs. Rita Tolbert, Resource Center Coord., *P.O. Drawer 17329, Pensacola, 32522.* Tel: 904-436-6455.

Communications, Office of—Rev. Michael Mooney, Dir., *P.O. Drawer 17329, Pensacola, 32522.* Tel: 904-432-1515.

"The Florida Catholic"—Ms. Brenda Lawrence, Reporter for the Diocese of Pensacola-Tallahassee Edition of *"The Florida Catholic", P.O. Drawer 17329, Pensacola, 32522.* Tel: 904-432-5215.

Cursillo Movement—Rev. Michael Foley, Spiritual Dir.; Mr. William E. Schaal, Diocesan Lay Dir., *P.O. Drawer 17329, Pensacola, 32522.* Tel: 904-432-1515.

Ecumenical & Interreligious Affairs, Office of—Very Rev. Richard J. Bowles, V.F., Dir., *P.O. Box 12423, Pensacola, 32582.* Tel: 904-438-4985.

Education, Department of—*P.O. Drawer 17329, Pensacola, 32522.* Tel: 904-432-1515.

Schools, Diocesan Commission for—Mrs. Carolyn Ketchel, Chm.; Rev. Martin Holley; Mr. John Doherty; Mr. Robin Dickson; Mrs. Cynthia Lacour; Sr. Mary Caplice, C.N.D., Admin. Officer; Mrs. Roslyn Guyette; Mrs. Angela Heard; Mr. Richard Lurton; Mrs. Francine Neal; Dr. Catherine O'Malley; Dr. Nancy Roberts; Dr. Marion Williams, *P.O. Drawer 17329, Pensacola, 32522.* Tel: 904-432-1515.

Superintendent of Schools, Office of the—Sr. Mary Caplice, C.N.D., Supt., *P.O. Drawer 17329, Pensacola, 32522.* Tel: 904-432-1515.

Marriage & Family Life Ministries, Department of—Mrs. Louise Ritz, Dir., *P.O. Drawer 17329, Pensacola, 32522.* Tel: 904-432-1515. Ministries: Engaged Encounter, Leadership Development for Family, Marriage Encounter and Natural Family Planning (NFP).

Respect Life, Office of—Very Rev. James J. Flaherty, Dir.

Finance, Diocesan Commission for—Mr. Robert Emmanuel, Chm.; Mr. J. Patrick Remich; Rev. Msgr. Luke Hunt, Sec.; Rev. Msgr. James Amos, J.C.L.; Mr. Robert Hamel; Mr. Eric Nickelsen; Mr. Vince Whibbs, Jr.; Mr. Albert Williams, Jr., *P.O. Drawer 17329, Pensacola, 32522.* Tel: 904-432-1515.

Finance, Department of—Mr. J. Patrick Remich, Dir., *P.O. Drawer 17329, Pensacola, 32522.* Tel: 904-432-1515.

Hispanic Ministry, Office of—Rev. Richard Castillo, Dir., *P.O. Drawer 17329, Pensacola, 32522.* Tel: 904-432-1515.

Holy Childhood Association—Sr. Mary Caplice, C.N.D., Dir., *P.O. Drawer 17329, Pensacola, 32522.* Tel: 904-432-1515.

Holy Name Society—*P.O. Drawer 17329, Pensacola, 32522.* Tel: 904-432-1515.

Justice and Peace, Office of—Vacant, *P.O. Drawer 17329, Pensacola, 32522.* Tel: 904-432-1515.

Knights of Columbus—Rev. Msgr. Luke Hunt, Diocesan Chap., *P.O. Drawer 17329, Pensacola, 32522.* Tel: 904-432-1515.

Legion of Mary—Rev. Slade Crawford, Diocesan Spiritual Dir., *P.O. Drawer 17329, Pensacola, 32522.* Tel: 904-432-1515.

Liturgy, Office of—Rev. J. Craig Williams, Dir., *P.O. Drawer 17329, Pensacola, 32522.* Tel: 904-436-6455.

Permanent Diaconate Formation Board—Rev. Msgr. James Amos, J.C.L.; Rev. C. Slade Crawford; Very Rev. James J. Flaherty; Deacons Henry Burrell; Thomas Kennell; Mack Shook; Mrs. Louise Ritz; Mrs. Juanita Sanks, *P.O. Drawer 17329, Pensacola, 32522.* Tel: 904-432-1515.

Permanent Diaconate, Office of—Deacon John Morgan, Vicar for Deacons, *P.O. Drawer 17329, Pensacola, 32522.* Tel: 904-432-1515.

Priestly Life and Ministry, Office of—Very Rev. Robert Morris, Dir., *P.O. Drawer 17329, Pensacola, 32522.* Tel: 904-432-1515.

Priests' Pension Plan, Board for—Rev. Msgr. William A. Crowe, V.F.; Rev. Msgr. Luke Hunt; Rev. Msgr. Raymond Mullins, V.E.; Revs. Eugene Casserly; John Cassidy; Michael Foley. Consultants: Mr. John A. Panyko, Esq.; Mr. J. Patrick Remich.

Priests' Personnel Board—Rev. Msgr. George E. Sindik; Rev. Msgr. James Amos, J.C.L.; Very Rev. John V. O'Sullivan; Revs. Michael Foley; Kevin T. Johnson, *P.O. Drawer 17329, Pensacola, 32522.* Tel: 904-432-1515.

Propagation of the Faith, Office of—Rev. Francis Szczykutowicz, Dir., *P.O. Drawer 17329, Pensacola, 32522.* Tel: 904-432-1515.

Real Estate, Diocesan Commission for—Rev. Msgr. Luke Hunt, Chm.; Rev. Msgr. William A. Crowe, V.F.; Very Revs. Richard J. Bowles, V.F.; John V. O'Sullivan, V.F.; Rev. Francis Szczykutowicz, V.F.; Mr. Robert Emmanuel; Mr. J. Patrick Remich; Mr. John Donovan; Mr. John Morgan, Sec., *P.O. Drawer 17329, Pensacola, 32522.* Tel: 904-432-1515.

Real Estate, Office of—Mr. John Morgan, Dir., *P.O. Drawer 17329, Pensacola, 32522.* Tel: 904-432-1515.

St. Vincent de Paul Society—Pensacola Particular Council, Rev. Oliver Barrett, C.S.Sp., Spiritual Dir.; Mr. Al Godwin, Pres., *2200 W. Desoto St., Pensacola, 32505.* Tel: 904-434-6615. Tallahassee Chapter, Very Rev. Michael W. Tugwell, Spiritual Dir.; Mr. Albert A. Relation, Pres., *P.O. Box 2395, Tallahassee, 32316.* Tel: 904-576-6099.

Seminarian Candidate Review Board—Very Rev. Michael W. Tugwell, Chm.; Rev. Msgr. James Amos, J.C.L.; Rev. Joseph Callipare; Mr. William Nadicksbernd; Sr. Ellen Kieran, M.S.B.T.; Mrs. Rosemary Mason, *P.O. Drawer 17329, Pensacola, 32522.* Tel: 904-432-1515.

Seminarians, Office of—Rev. Michael W. Tugwell, Dir., *P.O. Drawer 17329, Pensacola, 32522.* Tel: 904-432-1515.

Vocations, Office of—Rev. Joseph Callipare, Dir., *Drawer 17329, Pensacola, 32522.* Tel: 904-432-1515.

Serra Club—Pensacola: Very Rev. James J. Flaherty, Spiritual Dir.; Mr. Joseph Pastucha, Pres.; Tallahassee: Rev. Richard S. Castillo, Spiritual Dir.; Mr. Stanley Kupiszewski, Pres.; Fort Walton Beach-Niceville: Rev. Edmond Perjak, Spiritual Dir.; Mr. Richard Hickenbotham, Pres., *P.O. Drawer 17329, Pensacola, 32522.* Tel: 904-432-1515.

Youth Ministry, Office of—Rev. Michael A. Cherup, Dir.; Mrs. Felecia Sonnier, Assoc. Dir., *P.O. Drawer 17329, Pensacola, 32522.* Tel: 904-432-1515.

CLERGY, PARISHES, MISSIONS AND PAROCHIAL SCHOOLS

GREATER PENSACOLA
(Escambia County)

1—Cathedral of the Sacred Heart (1905), Revs. Michael A. Cherup, Rector; Michael B. Shaw; Michael Reed; Deacons Henry Burrell; Jean White.
Res., 1101 E. Mallory St., P.O. Box 2248, 32503. Tel: 904-438-3131; Fax: 904-436-6444.
School—Sacred Heart Cathedral School, 1603 N. 12th Ave., 32503. Tel: 904-436-6440. Apostles of the Sacred Heart. Sr. Elizabeth Knight, A.S.C.J., Prin.
Catechesis/Religious Programs—Students 87.
Convent—1700 Conway Dr., 32503. Tel: 904-438-0560.

2—Little Flower (Myrtle Grove) (1945), Revs. C. Slade Crawford; Viet Huynh. In res., Rev. Ernest Patrick.
Res., 920 N. 65th Ave., P.O. Box 3009, Myrtle Grove, 32516. Tel: 904-455-5641.
School—Congregation of Notre Dame Sisters, Tel: 904-455-4851. Sr. Mary Caplice, C.N.D., Prin.
Sisters 1; Lay Teachers 9; Students 231.
Catechesis/Religious Programs—Students 150.

3—Holy Spirit (Warrington) (1968), Rev. Msgr. James Amos, V.G.; Rev. Msgr. James Gallagher, Pastor Emeritus; Deacons Eugene Geri; Clayton L. Overton.
Res., 10650 Gulf Beach Hwy., 32507. Tel: 904-492-0837 (Office).
Catechesis/Religious Programs—Students 109.

4—Nativity of Our Lord (1969), Revs. Michael P. Mooney; Michael J. Flynn; Deacons Randall Comeau; Dennis Dobransky.
Res., 9945 Hillview Rd., 32514. Tel: 904-477-3221; Fax: 904-494-1503.
Catechesis/Religious Programs—Tel: 904-478-5584, Ext. 20.
Students 356.

5—Our Lady Queen of Martyrs, Mission (1977), Rev. Augustine Nguyen Thanh Hue (Vietnam).
Res., 3295 S. Barrancas Ave., 32507. Tel: 904-455-2712.

6—St. Anne (Bellview) (1964), Rev. John F. Gray, Admin.; Deacon John C. McLellan.
Res., 5200 Saufley Field Rd., 32526-1626. Tel: 904-456-5966; Fax: 904-453-3138.
Preschool—Tel: 904-453-2119. Mrs. Anne M. Clapsadl, Dir.
Students 40.

7—St. Anne (Brownsville) (1953), Rev. D. Oliver Barrett, C.S.Sp.
Res., 2910 W. Gadsden St., 32505. Tel: 904-433-5467.

8—St. Anthony of Padua (1941) (African American), Rev. Thomas A. Bonanti.
Res., 1804 N. Davis St., 32503. Tel: 904-436-6422.

9—St. John the Evangelist (1859), Revs. Richard L. Altenbaugh; Joseph G. Going, O.P.; Deacons Gerard Williamson; Stanley Barrows.
Res., 303 S. Navy Blvd., 32507. Tel: 904-455-0356.
School—Sisters of Mercy, Tel: 904-456-5218; Fax: 904-456-5956. Sr. Patricia Ann Pepitone, R.S.M., Prin.
Sisters 3; Lay Teachers 15; Students 209.
Convent—325 S. Navy Blvd., 32507. Tel: 904-455-0355.

10—St. Joseph (1891) (African American), Rev. Thomas A. Bonanti; Sr. Maureen Joseph Kirwan, S.C., Pastoral Assoc.
Mailing Address: P.O. Box 13566, 32591. Tel: 904-436-6461.
Res., 141 W. Intendencia St., 32501.
Catechesis/Religious Programs—Students 89.

11—St. Mary (1941), Revs. Eugene D. Casserly; Eugene W. Pathe (England); Sr. Marilyn Doucette, C.N.D., Pastoral Outreach.
Mailing Address: P.O. Box 6117, 32503.
Res., 401 Van Pelt Ln., 32505. Tel: 904-478-2797.
Catechesis/Religious Programs—Tel: 904-478-1635.
Students 135.

12—St. Michael (1559), Very Rev. Richard J. Bowles, V.F.
Res., 19 N. Palafox St., P.O. Box 12423, 32582. Tel: 904-438-4985.

13—St. Paul (1963), Rev. Msgr. George E. Sindik, V.E.; Revs. Joseph Callipare; Martin Holley; Deacons John P. Morgan; Russell C. Packard.
Res., 3131 Hyde Park Rd., 32503. Tel: 904-434-2551; Fax: 904-436-6449.
School—Apostles of the Sacred Heart (Hamden, CT), Tel: 904-436-6435; Fax: 904-436-6437. Sr. M. Lizabeth Doty, A.S.C.J., Prin.
Sisters 2; Lay Teachers 18; Students 302.
Catechesis/Religious Programs—Tel: 904-436-6446.
Students 367.
Convent—1700 Conway Dr., 32503. Tel: 904-438-0560.
Mission—Pensacola, Escambia Co., Church of Our Savior, 6700 Old Spanish Tr., 32504.

14—St. Stephen (1922), Rev. Hector R.G. Perez, S.T.D.
Res., 900 W. Garden St., 32501. Tel: 904-432-9362.

15—St. Thomas More (1954), Rev. John T. Cassidy.
Mailing Address: 510 Bayshore Dr., 32507. Tel: 904-456-2543.

CITY OF TALLAHASSEE
(Leon County)

1—Co-Cathedral of St. Thomas More (1968), Revs. Michael W. Tugwell, Rector; Thomas S. Collins; Dennis O'Brien.
Res., 832 W. Tennessee St., P.O. Box 2395, 32316. Tel: 904-222-7371; 222-9630 (Office).
Catechesis/Religious Programs—Students 120.
Chapel—St. Eugene, Florida A&M University, 701 W. Gamble St., 32310. Tel: 904-222-6482. [JC]
Rev. John Boateng-Mensah, Chap.

2—Blessed Sacrament, Very Rev. John V. O'Sullivan, V.F.; Revs. Kevin Johnson; James Cregan.
Res., 624 Miccosukee Rd., 32308. Tel: 904-222-1321; Fax: 904-222-9772.
School—Trinity Catholic, Tel: 904-222-0444; Fax: 904-224-5067. Sr. Aileen McClain, O.P., Prin.
Sisters 2; Lay Teachers 34; Students 563.

3—Good Shepherd (1973), Revs. Michael Foley; Thomas Guido; Deacons Andrew Radigan; Robert Vossler.
Office: 4665 Thomasville Rd., 32308. Tel: 904-893-1837; 893-2381.
Catechesis/Religious Programs—Bette Scaringe, D.R.E.
Students 695.

4—St. Louis (1979), Rev. David McCreanor, Ph.D.; Deacons Nelson Madera, Ph.D.; Mack Shook.
Res., 4151 Miraflores Ln., 32303. Tel: 904-562-5140.
Catechesis/Religious Programs—Students 96.

OUTSIDE THE CITIES OF PENSACOLA AND TALLAHASSEE

Apalachicola, Franklin Co., St. Patrick (1851), Rev. Roger Latosynski.
Res., 27 Sixth St., P.O. Box 550, 32320. Tel: 904-653-9453. [JC]

Bayou George, Bay Co., Our Lady of the Rosary, Rev. W. P. Brown.
Res., 5622 Julie Dr., Panama City, 32404. Tel: 904-769-5067.
Catechesis/Religious Programs—Students 30.
Mission—Fountain, Bay Co., Our Lady Queen of Peace.

Blountstown, Calhoun Co., St. Francis of Assisi, Rev. John P. Selleck, Admin.
Res., 334 Gaskin St., 32424. Tel: 904-674-4482.
Mission—Wewahitchka, Gulf Co., St. Lawrence, Box 651, Wewahitchka, 32465. Tel: 904-639-5787.

Bonifay, Holmes Co., Blessed Trinity (1979), Rev. John F. Kelly.
Res., Rte. 4, Box 643, 32425. Tel: 904-547-3735.

Cantonment, Escambia Co., St. Jude Thaddeus (1966), Rev. Richard E. Dawson; Deacons John Bartoszewicz; Bradley Seabrook; Tom Simard.
Res., 303 Rocky Ave., 32533. Tel: 904-968-6189. [CEM]
Mission—Barrineau Park, Escambia Co., St. Elizabeth of Hungary, 303 Rocky Ave., 32533. Tel: 904-587-2550.
Catechesis/Religious Programs—Students 68.

Chattahoochee, Gadsden Co., Holy Cross Parish (1972), Rev. Sebastian C. Naslund, Admin.
Res., R.R. 1, Box 1562, 32324. Tel: 904-663-4610.

Chipley, Washington Co., St. Joseph the Worker, Rev. John F. Kelly.
Res., P.O. Box 266, 32428. Tel: 904-638-7654.
Catechesis/Religious Programs—Students 43.

Crestview, Okaloosa Co., Our Lady of Victory (1954), Rev. Brian G. Ryan, Admin.
Res., 143 Jeff Dr., 32536. Tel: 904-682-4622; Fax: 904-689-0335.
Catechesis/Religious Programs—Students 209.

De Funiak Springs, Walton Co., St. Margaret (1931), Very Rev. James J. Flaherty.
Res., Hwy. 331 N., Box 590, 32433. Tel: 904-892-9247.
Catechesis/Religious Programs—Students 51.
Mission—Freeport, Walton Co., Christ the King, Hwy. 331 S., 32439.

Destin, Okaloosa Co., Corpus Christi (1977), Rev. Robert F. Morris; Deacons Joseph Rose; Anthony Restivo.
Res., 307 Beach Dr., P.O. Box 635, 32540. Tel: 904-654-5422.
Catechesis/Religious Programs—Students 68.
Church of the Resurrection, Walton Co., Rev. Roy C. Marien.
Res., 259 Miramar Beach Dr., 32541. Tel: 904-837-0357; Fax: 904-837-2062.

Fort Walton Beach, Okaloosa Co., St. Mary (1914), Rev. Msgr. Raymond Mullins, V.F.; Revs. Jacob M. Pallivathukkall (India); Sean Garrett (SAT); Deacons Robert J. Saxer; Charles Wolf; Charles Shettle; John Howell.
Res., 110 St. Mary Ave., S.W., 32548-6645. Tel: 904-243-3742.
School—Tel: 904-243-8913. Mrs. Joy Webb, Prin.
Lay Teachers 20; Students 405.
Catechesis/Religious Programs—Tel: 904-244-1833.
Students 344.

Fountain, Bay Co., Our Lady Queen of Peace Mission, Rev. William P. Brown.
Mailing Address: P.O. Box 213, 32438. Tel: 904-769-5067.
Church—18005 Lazy Ln., 32438.

Freeport, Walton Co., Christ the King Mission (1984), Very Rev. James J. Flaherty; Deacon Grant Boughton.
Hwy. 331 N., P.O. Box 590, De Funiak Springs, 32422. Tel: 904-892-9247. See St. Margaret Parish, De Funiak Springs.

Gulf Breeze, Santa Rosa Co., St. Ann (1948), Rev. Msgr. Luke Hunt, V.E.; Rev. William Condren; Deacons Robert Kostic; Patrick O'Connell.
Res., 100 Daniel Dr., P.O. Drawer 1057, 32562. Tel: 904-932-2859; Fax: 904-934-2804.
St. Ann Discovery School—(Extended Care & Preschool). Tel: 904-932-9330. Directors: Mrs. Betty Watson; Mrs. Carol Lyvers.
Teachers 25; Students 235.
Catechesis/Religious Programs—Students 400.
Mission—Gulf Breeze, Santa Rosa Co., Our Lady of the Assumption, 920 Via de Luna, P.O. Box 1057, Pensacola Beach, 32561. Tel: 904-934-0222.

Lanark Village, Franklin Co., Sacred Heart of Jesus (1960), Rev. James F. Cregan.
Res., 109 Newman Dr., P.O. Box 729, 32323. Tel: 904-697-3445.

Madison, Madison Co., St. Vincent de Paul (1907), Rev. Joseph C. Schwab, O.M.I.
Res., 402 N.W. Sumter St., P.O. Box 730, 32341. Tel: 904-973-2428.

Marianna, Jackson Co., St. Anne (1947), Rev. Hugh Dolan.
Res., 3009 Fifth St., P.O. Box 1547, 32446. Tel: 904-482-3734. [JC]

Mary Esther, Okaloosa Co., St. Peter (1975), Rev. Edward A. Kirby; Deacon David P. Robinson.
Res., 100 Francis St., 32569. Tel: 904-581-2556.
Catechesis/Religious Programs—Students 70.

Medart, Wakulla Co., St. Elizabeth Ann Seton (1975), Rev. James B. MacGee, O.M.I.
Mailing Address: 3609 Coastal Hwy., Crawfordville, 32327. Tel: 904-926-1797. [CEM]
Catechesis/Religious Programs—Students 36.
Mission—Woodville, Leon Co., St. Stephen the Protomartyr, Natural Bridge Rd., P.O.Box 1142, Woodville, 32362. Tel: 904-421-9094.

Mexico Beach, Bay Co., Our Lady of Guadalupe Mission. See St. Dominic, Panama City.

Milton, Santa Rosa Co., St. Rose of Lima (1957), Revs. Todd O. Hevia; Thomas Lorigan; Deacons David Davey; Thomas Kennell.
Res., 515 Park Ave., S.W., 32570. Tel: 904-623-3600. [JC]
Catechesis/Religious Programs—Students 230.

Monticello, Jefferson Co., St. Margaret (1917), Rev. Joseph C. Schwab, O.M.I.
Res., P.O. Box 730, Madison, 32341. Tel: 904-973-2428.
Church—U.S. Hwy. 90 E., 32334. Tel: 904-997-3622.

Niceville, Okaloosa Co., Christ Our Redeemer (1989), Rev. J. Craig Williams; Deacons Michael Carucci; Joaquin Trevino.
Res., 1028 White Point Rd., 32578. Tel: 904-897-7797; Fax: 904-897-2422.
Catechesis/Religious Programs—Tel: 904-897-2974.
Students 275.
Holy Name of Jesus (1964), Revs. Daniel J. Butler; Dominic Phan Sa; Deacons David Casey; Thomas Fraites; Louis Marini; Willie O'Neal.
Res., 1200 Valparaiso Blvd., P.O. Box 576, 32588. Tel: 904-678-7813; Fax: 904-678-5775.
Catechesis/Religious Programs—Students 260.

Panama City, Bay Co., St. Dominic (1917), Rev. Msgr. William A. Crowe, V.F.; Revs. Joseph P. Caffrey; James J. Lambert; John B. Cayer; Deacon James Gardner.
Res., 3308 E. 15th St., 32405-7414. Tel: 904-785-4574; Fax: 904-872-0800.
Catechesis/Religious Programs—Tel: 904-763-7393.
Students 347.
Mission—Mexico Beach, Bay Co., Our Lady of Guadalupe, 1500 N. 15th St., Mexico Beach, 32410. Tel: 904-648-3006.
St. John the Evangelist (1945), Revs. Donald Suberlak, C.R.; Martin Bratek, C.R., Vicar; Deacons Dale Johnson; Earl C. Mirus; John Kreppein.
Res., 1807 W. 11th St., P.O. Box 978, 32401. Tel: 904-763-1821.
School—Tel: 904-763-1775. Sr. Mary Therese Yokiel, C.R., Prin.
Sisters of the Resurrection 3; Lay Teachers 17; Students 267.
Catechesis/Religious Programs—Students 132.
Convent—1008 Fortune Ave., 32401. Tel: 904-763-5783.
SS. Peter & Paul Mission (1981) (Vietnam), Rev. Andrew Nguyen Minh Tu (Vietnam) Admin.
Res., 3129 Fifth St., P.O. Box 3087, 32401. Tel: 904-785-6191. [JC]
Catechesis/Religious Programs—Students 79.

Panama City Beach, Bay Co., St. Bernadette (1956), Rev. David T. O Shea.
Res., 1214 Moylan Rd., 32407. Tel: 904-234-3490; Fax: 904-234-3266.
Catechesis/Religious Programs—Students 120.

Pensacola Beach, Escambia Co., Our Lady of the Assumption Mission (1979),
Mailing Address: P.O. Box 1057, Gulf Breeze, 32561. Tel: 904-932-2859; Fax: 904-934-2804.
920 Via de Luna, 32561. Tel: 904-934-0222. See St. Ann, Gulf Breeze.

Perry, Taylor Co., Immaculate Conception (1918), Rev. Edward Hauf, O.M.I. In res., Rev. Francis Bagan, O.M.I.
Res., 2750 S. Byron Butler Pkwy., 32347. Tel: 904-584-3169.
Center—Tel: 904-584-8853.

Port St. Joe, Gulf Co., St. Joseph (1925), Rev. Thom A. Crandall.
Res., 2006 Monument Ave., P.O. Box 820, 32456. Tel: 904-227-1417.
Church—20th & Monument Sts., 32456. Tel: 904-229-8637.
Mission—Port St. Joe, Gulf Co., San Blas Catholic Mission.

Quincy, Gadsden Co., St. Thomas the Apostle (1957), Rev. Richard S. Castillo; Sr. Maria Lauren Donohue, M.S.B.T., Pastoral Assoc. & Hispanic Ministry Contact; Deacons William Strange; Luis Benavides.
Res., Hwy. 90, Box 451, 32353. Tel: 904-627-2350.
Catechesis/Religious Programs—Tel: 904-627-8807. Sr. Maria Rincon, M.S.B.T., D.R.E.
Students 180.
Hispanic Ministry Office of St. Thomas—Religious Education Office.
Mission Juan Diego—Outreach Center for the Hispanic Migrants/Farmworkers, Greensboro, Tel: 904-442-9023. Mrs. Mary Matthews, Contact.
Mission—Greensboro, Gadsden Co., Casa Guadalupana, Catholic Center for Evangelization, P.O. Box 59, Greensboro, 32330. Tel: 904-442-4337.

Santa Rosa Beach, Walton Co., St. Rita (1982),
Mailing Address: 20 St. Rita Ln., P.O. Box 1223, 32459. Tel: 904-267-2761.

Sunny Hills, Washington Co., St. Theresa, Rev. Francis S. Szczykutowicz; Deacon Joseph Dealy.
Res., 384 Sunny Hills Blvd., 32428. Tel: 904-773-3406; Fax: 904-773-7008.

Tiger Point, Santa Rosa Co., St. Sylvester (1979), Very Rev. Steven J. O'Connor; Deacon Frank Wines.
Res., 3507 Gulf Breeze Pkwy., Gulf Breeze, 32561. Tel: 904-932-6807.
Catechesis/Religious Programs—Students 160.

Wewahitchka, Gulf Co., St. Lawrence Mission,
c/o 334 Gaskin St., Blountstown, 32424. See St. Francis of Assisi, Blountstown.

Woodville, Leon Co., St. Stephen the Protomartyr (1979),
Mailing Address: 3609 Coastal Hwy., Crawfordville, 32327.
P.O. Box 1142, 32362. Tel: 904-421-9094. See St. Elizabeth Ann Seton, Medart.

Chaplains of Public Institutions

PENSACOLA. *Escambia County Jail*. Deacon Stanley Barrows.

TALLAHASSEE. *Federal Correctional Institution*. Rev. Richard S. Castillo.

CHATTAHOOCHEE. *Florida State Hospital*. Rev. Sebastian Naslund, Chap.
River Junction Correctional Institution. Vacant.

EGLIN. *Eglin Federal Prison Camp Eglin Air Force Base*. Deacon Joaquin Trevino, Chap.

MARIANNA. *Dozier School for Boys Sunland Training Center, Jackson Vocation Center*. Vacant.
Florida Correctional Institutions. Sr. Ann Marie Raftery, O.S.F.

SNEADS. *Apalachee Correctional Institution*. Deacon Robert Moore.

On Duty Outside the Diocese:
Reverend Monsignors—
Kerr, William A., La Roche College, 9000 Babcock Blvd., Pittsburgh, PA 15237
Reverend Fathers—
Bosso, Stephen C., St. Vincent de Paul Regional Seminary, 10701 E. Military Tr., Boynton Beach, FL 33436
O'Brien, Dennis
Roland, Charles, St. Joseph Church, 2011 Darling Ave., Waycross, GA 31501
Sarmiento, Oscar, St. Isidro Parish, 2310 Martin Luther King Blvd., Pompano Beach, FL 33609-1591

Military Chaplains:
Reverend Fathers—
Bluett, James K.
Krzywicki, Lance P., Chap., PSC 810, Box 14, FPO, AE 09169
McClanahan, Robert P., NAS, Patuxent River, MD 20670
Stewart, Paul, Headquarters Keesler AFB, MS 39534
Voyt, Stephen A., Maj., Wright Patterson AFB, OH 45424

On Leave of Absence:
Rev.—
Jorden, James A., P.O. Box 447, Barlow, KY 42024
Wood, Peter N.

Retired:
Reverend Monsignors—
Cunningham, Patrick
Gallagher, James
Reverend Fathers—
Dzienkiewicz, Edwin
Halstead, Philip

Hogarty, Paul
Joseph, William
Kiem, Anthony
Lorigan, Thomas
Patrick, Ernest E.
Watters, Joseph

Permanent Deacons:
Barrows, Stanley, St. John the Evangelist, Warrington
Bartoszewicz, John M., St. Jude Thaddeus, Cantonment
Bodish, William, St. Mary, Fort Walton Beach
Bonanno, Frederick R., St. Mary, Fort Walton Beach
Boughton, Grant, St. Margaret, De Funiak Springs; Christ the King, Freeport
Burrell, Henry N., Cathedral of the Sacred Heart, Pensacola
Carucci, Michael J., Christ Our Redeemer, Niceville
Casey, David R., Holy Name of Jesus, Niceville
Cloud, Millard F., Inactive
Comeau, Randall O., Nativity of Our Lord, Pensacola
Davey, David, St. Rose of Lima, Milton
Dealy, Michael J., St. Theresa, Sunny Hills
Dobransky, Dennis, Nativity, Pensacola
Fraites, Thomas J., Holy Name of Jesus, Niceville
Gaines, William G., Leave of Absence
Gardner, James L., St. Dominic, Panama City
Geri, Eugene A., Holy Spirit, Pensacola
Greskovich, Frank J., Leave of Absence
Howell, John, St. Mary, Fort Walton Beach
Hromadka, Joseph J., (Retired)
Johnson, Dale R., St. John the Evangelist, Panama City
Kennell, Thomas H., St. Rose of Lima, Milton
Kostic, Robert B., St. Ann, Gulf Breeze
Kreppein, John, St. John the Evangelist, Panama City
Madera, Nelson I., St. Louis, Tallahassee
Marini, Louis, Holy Name of Jesus, Niceville
McLellan, John, St. Anne, Bellview
Mirus, Earl C., St. John the Evangelist, Panama City
Morgan, John P., St. Paul, Pensacola
O'Connell, Patrick F., (Retired)
O'Neal, Willie, Holy Name of Jesus, Niceville
Packard, Russell C., St. Paul, Pensacola
Radigan, Terence A., Good Shepherd, Tallahassee
Restivo, Anthony, Corpus Christi, Destin
Richardson, Walter H., St. Mary, Fort Walton
Robinson, David P., St. Peter, Mary Esther
Rose, Joseph, Corpus Christi, Destin
Saxer, Robert J., St. Mary, Fort Walton Beach
Seabrook, Bradley M., St. Jude, Cantonment
Shettle, Charles G., St. Louis, Tallahassee
Shook, Mack D., St. Louis, Tallahassee
Simard, Thomas, St. Jude, Cantonment
Trevino, Joaquin D., Christ Our Redeemer, Niceville
Vossler, Robert J., Good Shepherd, Tallahassee
Vota, Joseph L., (Retired)
White, Jean F., Cathedral of the Sacred Heart, Pensacola
Williamson, Gerard, St. John the Evangelist, Warrington
Wolf, Charles R., St. Mary, Fort Walton Beach

INSTITUTIONS LOCATED IN THE DIOCESE

[A] HIGH SCHOOLS, DIOCESAN

PENSACOLA. *Pensacola Catholic High School*, 3043 W. Scott St., 32505. Tel: 904-436-6400; Fax: 904-436-6405. Sr. Kierstin Martin, A.S.C.J., Prin. Sisters 2; Lay Teachers 50; Students 570.

[B] ELEMENTARY SCHOOLS, DIOCESAN

PENSACOLA. *St. Michael*, 601 N. Palafox St., 32501. Tel: 904-438-4059. Sisters of St. Joseph (Buffalo). Sr. Robert Anne, S.S.J., Prin. Sisters 2; Lay Teachers 13; Students 263.

[C] GENERAL HOSPITALS

PENSACOLA. *The Mother Seton Guild of Sacred Heart Hospital, Inc.*, 32504.
For a complete listing, refer to the Hospitals section.
Sacred Heart Foundation, Inc., 5225 Carmel Heights Dr., 32504.
For a complete listing, refer to the Hospitals section.
Sacred Heart Hospital of Pensacola, 5151 N. Ninth Ave., 32513. Tel: 904-416-7000.
For a complete listing, refer to the Hospitals section.

[D] HOMES FOR AGED

PENSACOLA. *Haven of Our Lady of Peace*, 5203 N. Ninth Ave., 32504. Tel: 904-477-0531; Fax: 904-477-6782. *For a complete listing, refer to the Special Care Facilities section.*

[E] APARTMENTS FOR THE ELDERLY AND HANDICAPPED

TALLAHASSEE. *Casa Calderon, Inc.*, 800 W. Virginia St., 32304. Tel: 904-222-4026.
For a complete listing, refer to the Special Care Facilities section.

[F] CONVENT AND RESIDENCES FOR SISTERS

PENSACOLA. *Blessed Trinity Missionary Cenacle*, 412 Bayshore Dr., 32507. Tel: 904-456-4141. Sisters 6.
Notre Dame Convent, Sisters of the Congregation of Notre Dame, 1001 Deason St., 32505. Tel: 904-438-5906. Sisters 6.
Sacred Heart Hospital Convent, 5151 N. Ninth Ave., 32504. Tel: 904-474-7920.
St. Michael Convent, 18 W. Jackson St., 32501-3956. Tel: 904-436-6460. Sisters of Mercy of the Americas; Sisters of St. Joseph (Buffalo); Sisters of Charity of St. Elizabeth of New Jersey. Sisters 3.

APALACHICOLA. *Martin House*, 149 10th St., 32320. Tel: 904-653-8774. Sinsinawa Dominicans Congregation of the Most Holy Rosary 3. Total Assisted 2,052.

MARIANNA. *Mission Helpers of the Sacred Heart Convent*, 3007 Fifth St., 32446. Tel: 904-526-3291. Sisters 2.

SUNNY HILLS. *Vestiarki Sisters of Jesus (Poland)*, 3919 Vistula Dr., 32428. Tel: 904-773-3302. Sisters 4; Total Assisted 6.

[G] HOMELESS SHELTERS

TALLAHASSEE. *Holy Family Home*. Catholic Social Services-Tallahassee. Rte. #7, Box 725, 32308. Tel: 904-877-6736.

PANAMA CITY. *Naomi House*, 2941 11th St., 32401. Tel: 904-769-5756.
St. Barnabas House, 2943 11th St., 32401. Tel: 904-769-0314. Coordinators: Dan Coleman, M.C.V.; Sheila Coleman, M.C.V. Total in Residence 77; Total Staff 5.

[H] RETREAT HOUSES

TALLAHASSEE. *The Saint John Neumann Spiritual Renewal Center*, 685 Miccosukee Rd., 32308. Tel: 904-224-2971. Sr. Christine Kelly, S.S.J., Dir. Sisters 3.

NAVARRE. *Casa Stella Maris*, 7650 Clark St., 32566. Tel: 904-932-6807. Very Rev. Steven J. O'Connor, Dir. Total Staff 1.

[I] MISCELLANEOUS

PENSACOLA. *Diocese of Pensacola-Tallahassee Education Foundation, Inc.*, P.O. Drawer 17329, 32522. Tel: 904-432-1515.
St. Michael Cemetery Foundation, Inc., P.O. Drawer 17329, 32522. Tel: 904-432-1515.

RELIGIOUS INSTITUTES OF MEN REPRESENTED IN THE DIOCESE

For further details refer to the corresponding bracketed number in the Religious Institutes of Men or Women section.

[0340]—*Cistercian Fathers*.—O.Cist.
[1080]—*Congregation of the Resurrection*. (Chicago Prov.).—C.R.
[0650]—*Holy Ghost Fathers*.—C.S.Sp.
[0590]—*Missionaries of the Holy Apostles*.—M.Ss.A.
[0910]—*Oblates of Mary Immaculate*. (Eastern American Prov.).—O.M.I.
[0430]—*Order of Preachers-Dominicans*. (Southern Prov.).—O.P.

RELIGIOUS INSTITUTES OF WOMEN REPRESENTED IN THE DIOCESE

[0130]—*Apostles of the Sacred Heart of Jesus*.—A.S.C.J.
[0760]—*Daughters of Charity of St. Vincent de Paul*. (Eastern Prov.).—D.C.
[1070-03]—*Dominican Sisters*.—O.P.
[1070-13]—*Dominican Sisters*.—O.P.
[1070-14]—*Dominican Sisters*.—O.P.
[2720]—*Mission Helpers of the Sacred Heart*.—M.H.S.H.
[2790]—*Missionary Servants of the Most Blessed Trinity*.—M.S.B.T.
[0430]—*Sisters of Charity of Blessed Virgin Mary*.—B.V.M.
[0590]—*Sisters of Charity of Saint Elizabeth, Convent Station*.—S.C.
[0990]—*Sisters of Divine Providence*.—C.D.P.
[2575]—*Sisters of Mercy of the Americas*. (Baltimore, MD).—R.S.M.
[1660]—*Sisters of Saint Francis of the Providence of God*.—O.S.F.
[3900]—*Sisters of St. Joseph of St. Augustine, Florida*.—S.S.J.
[2980]—*Sisters of the Congregation de Notre Dame*. (Blessed Sacrament Prov.).—C.N.D.
[3480]—*Sisters of the Resurrection*.—C.R.
[2150]—*Sisters, Servants of the Immaculate Heart of Mary*.—I.H.M.
[]—*Vestiarski Sisters of Jesus*. (Poland).—V.S.

NECROLOGY

† Licari, John, (Retired). —Died May 4, 1996.

Diocese of Peoria

(Dioecesis Peoriensis)

Most Reverend

JOHN J. MYERS, D.D., J.C.D.

Bishop of Peoria; ordained December 17, 1966; appointed July 14, 1987; consecrated September 3, 1987; acceded to See of Peoria January 23, 1990. *Res., 607 N.E. Madison Ave., Peoria, IL, 61603.* Tel.: 309-671-1550; Fax: 309-671-5079.

Chancery: 607 N.E. Madison Ave., P.O. Box 1406, Peoria, IL, 61655. Tel.: 309-671-1550; Fax: 309-671-5079.

Most Reverend

EDWARD W. O'ROURKE, D.D.

Retired Bishop of Peoria; ordained May 28, 1944; appointed May 24, 1971; consecrated July 15, 1971; installed July 15, 1971; retired January 23, 1990. *Res., St. Augustine Manor, 1301 N.E. Glendale, Peoria, IL, 61603.* Tel.: 309-673-0446.

ESTABLISHED 1877.

Square Miles 16,933.

A cross-section of Illinois, bounded on the north by the Counties of Whiteside, Lee, De Kalb, Grundy and Iroquois, and on the east by Kendall, Grundy, Kankakee and Ford, and on the south by Adams, Brown, Cass, Menard, Sangamon, Macon, Moultrie, Douglas and Edgar; comprising the Counties of Bureau, Champaign, Dewitt, Fulton, Hancock, Henderson, Henry, Knox, La Salle, Livingston, Logan, Marshall, Mason, McDonough, McLean, Mercer, Peoria, Piatt, Putnam, Rock Island, Schuyler, Stark, Tazewell, Vermilion, Warren and Woodford.

For legal titles of parishes and diocesan institutions, consult the Chancery.

STATISTICAL OVERVIEW

Personnel	
Bishop	1
Retired Bishops	1
Abbots	1
Retired Abbots	1
Priests: Diocesan Active in Diocese	174
Priests: Active Outside Diocese	12
Priests: Retired, Sick or Absent	60
Number of Diocesan Priests	246
Religious Priests in Diocese	57
Extern Priests in Diocese	1
Ordinations:	
Diocesan Priests	12
Transitional Deacons	8
Permanent Deacons in Diocese	83
Total Brothers	10
Total Sisters	303
Parishes	
Parishes	165
With Resident Pastor:	
Resident Diocesan Priests	144
Resident Religious Priests	21
Without Resident Pastor:	
Administered by Priests	4
Missions	39
Pastoral Centers	5
New Parishes Created	1
Professional Ministry Personnel:	
Sisters	41
Lay Ministers	44
Welfare	
Catholic Hospitals	8
Total Assisted	898,592
Homes for the Aged	2
Total Assisted	205
Residential Care of Children	1
Total Assisted	58
Day Care and Extended Day Care Centers	3
Total Assisted	315
Specialized Homes	2
Total Assisted	99
Special Centers for Social Services	1
Total Assisted	18,761
Residential Care of Disabled	1
Total Assisted	4
Other Institutions	5
Total Assisted	1,779
Educational	
Diocesan Students in Other Seminaries	36
Total Seminarians	36
Colleges and Universities	1
Total Students	152
High Schools, Diocesan and Parish	6
Total Students	2,604
High Schools, Private	1
Total Students	70
Elementary Schools, Diocesan and Parish	48
Total Students	12,517
Catechesis/Religious Education:	
High School Students	3,697
Elementary Students	13,319
Total Students Under Catholic Instruction	32,395
Teachers in the Diocese:	
Priests	6
Sisters	51
Lay Teachers	875
Vital Statistics	
Receptions into the Church:	
Infant Baptism Totals	3,124
Adult Baptism Totals	510
Received into Full Communion	596
First Communions	3,233
Confirmations	3,492
Marriages:	
Catholic	684
Interfaith	657
Total Marriages	1,341
Deaths	2,324
Total Catholic Population	234,298
Total Population	1,436,088

Former Bishops—Most Rev. JOHN LANCASTER SPALDING, D.D., cons. May 1, 1877; resigned Sept. 11, 1908; Titular Archbishop of Scitopolis; appt. Oct. 14, 1908; died Aug. 25, 1916.—Most Rev. EDMUND M. DUNNE, D.D., ord. June 24, 1887; cons. Sept. 1, 1909; died Oct. 17, 1929.—Most Rev. JOSEPH H. SCHLARMAN, D.D., Ph.D., J.C.D., ord. June 29, 1904; cons. June 17, 1930; named Assistant at Papal Throne, Nov. 16, 1950; Archbishop *ad personam; appt. June 27, 1951; died Nov. 10, 1951.—Most Rev.* WILLIAM E. COUSINS, D.D., ord. April 23, 1927; Titular Bishop of Forma and Auxiliary Bishop of Chicago; appt. Dec. 17, 1948; cons. March 7, 1949; Bishop of Peoria; appt. May 19, 1952; Archbishop of Milwaukee; appt. Dec. 17, 1958.—Most Rev. JOHN B. FRANZ, D.D., ord. June 13, 1920; Bishop of Dodge City; appt. May 29, 1951; cons. Aug. 29, 1951; transferred Peoria, Aug. 8, 1959; retired June 1, 1971; died July 3,1992.—Most Rev. EDWARD W. O'ROURKE, D.D., ord. May 28, 1944; Bishop of Peoria; appt. May 24, 1971; cons. July 15, 1971; retired Jan. 23, 1990.

Chancery—607 N.E. Madison Ave., P.O. Box 1406, Peoria, 61655. Tel: 309-671-1550. Please direct all calls for all departments to this number; Fax: 309-671-5079. Office Hours: Mon.-Fri. 8:30-4:30.

Vicar General—Rev. Msgr. JAMES F. CAMPBELL, Vicar General/Chancellor, *Sheen Pastoral Center, 412 N.E. Madison Ave., Peoria, 61603.* Tel: 309-671-1550; Fax: 309-671-1558.

Chancellor—Rev. Msgr. JAMES F. CAMPBELL, Vicar General/Chancellor, *Sheen Pastoral Center, 412 N.E. Madison Ave., Peoria, 61603.* Tel: 309-671-1550; Fax: 309-671-1558.

Vice Chancellors—Rev. Msgr. STEVEN P. ROHLFS; Rev. JOSEPH P. DONTON, *607 N.E. Madison Ave., Peoria, 61603.* Tel: 309-671-1550; Fax: 309-671-5079.

Director of Development—Mr. EDWARD N. LAUGHLIN, *Sheen Pastoral Center, 412 N.E. Madison Ave., Peoria, 61603.* Tel: 309-671-1550; Fax: 309-671-1595.

Director of Finance—Mr. ALLYN G. SCHMID, *Sheen Pastoral Center, 412 N.E. Madison Ave., Peoria, 61603.* Tel: 309-671-1550; Fax: 309-671-1595.

Diocesan Tribunal—Sheen Pastoral Center, 412 N.E. Madison Ave., Peoria, 61603. Tel: 309-671-1550; Fax: 309-671-1595.

Judicial Vicar—Rev. Msgr. RICK J. OBERCH, J.C.L.

Defenders of the Bond—Rev. JEROME JUNG, J.C.D.; Rev. Msgr. RICK J. OBERCH, J.C.L.; Rev. J. BRIAN REJSEK.

Adjutant Judicial Vicars—Revs. RICHARD SOSEMAN, J.C.L.; J. BRIAN REJSEK; Rev. Msgr. JOSEPH A. ZUBE.

Auditor—Sr. MARIANNA BURKHARD, O.S.B.

Associate Judges—Rev. Msgr. RICHARD G. FITZSIMMONS; Rev. DALE R. MALOY; Rev. Msgr. CLARENCE J. HETTINGER, J.C.L.; Sr. MARIANNA BURKHARD, O.S.B.

Advocates—Rev. J. BRIAN REJSEK; Rev. Msgr. RICK J. OBERCH; Mrs. CHERYL CRISS.

Notaries—Mrs. DEBRA WILLIAMS; Mrs. JANICE VICARY; Mrs. CAROLYN LAWLESS.

Diocesan College of Consultors—Most Rev. JOHN J. MYERS, D.D., J.C.D.; Rev. Msgr. JAMES F. CAMPBELL, V.G.; Rev. Msgr. RICHARD FITZSIMMONS; Rev. Msgr. STEVEN P. ROHLFS; Revs. THOMAS E. MACK;

TERRANCE O'BRIEN; GEORGE F. REMM; PAUL E. SHOWALTER; GERALD J. VERDUN; DALE L. WELLMAN; JOHN MARK WILLIAMS, *Sheen Pastoral Center, 412 N.E. Madison Ave., Peoria, 61603.* Tel: 309-671-1550; Fax: 309-671-1595.

Vicariates and Vicars—Bloomington: Rev. THOMAS W. MALONEY, Champaign: Rev. TERRANCE P. O'BRIEN, Danville: Rev. THADDEUS PRACZ, Henry: Rev. PATRICK K. O'NEAL, Kewanee: Rev. DUANE C. JACK, La Salle: Rev. Msgr. RICHARD FITZSIMMONS, Lincoln: Rev. Msgr. NORMAN D. GOODMAN, Macomb: Rev. RICHARD PRICCO, Monmouth: Rev. ERNEST PIZZAMIGLIO, Ottawa: Rev. Msgr. ALBERT W. HALLIN, Pekin: Rev. JAMES J. SWANER, Peoria, N.W.: Rev. Msgr. S. P. ROHLFS, Peoria, S.E.: Rev. J. MARK WILLIAMS, Pontiac: Rev. E. E. HIGGINS, Rock Island: Rev. PAUL E. SHOWALTER.

Diocesan Offices and Directors

Finance Council (Canon 492)—Most Rev. JOHN J. MYERS, D.D., J.C.D., Pres.; Rev. Msgr. JAMES F. CAMPBELL, V.G.; Sr. DIANE MARIE MCGREW, O.S.F.; Rev. ROBERT E. LEE; Rev. WILLIAM WATSON; Mr. GERALD T. WOMBACHER; Mr. DAVID DEJAEGHER; Mr. ALLYN G. SCHMID; Mrs. DORIS BERMINGHAM; Mr. DANIEL REYNOLDS; Mr. TOBY GUALANDRI; Mr. ALLYN G. SCHMID; Mr. ED LAUGHLIN, *Sheen Pastoral Center, 412 N.E. Madison Ave., Peoria, 61603.* Tel: 309-671-1550; Fax: 309-671-1595.

Art and Architecture Commission—Rev. TERRANCE P. O'BRIEN, *1303 Lincolnshire Dr., Champaign, 61821.* Tel: 217-359-4224; Fax: 217-359-9846.

Catholic Cemeteries—Rev. JOHN ANDERSON, *Sheen Pastoral Center, 412 N.E. Madison Ave., Peoria, 61603.* Tel: 309-671-1550; Fax: 309-671-1595.

Catholic Education Office—Dr. MELVIN KUHBANDER, Ph.D., Supt., Catholic Schools; Mrs. PATRICIA KAWCZYNSKI, Assoc. Supt.; Mr. WILLIAM A. JANICKI, Dir., Religious Education Dept.; Ms. BARBARA MCATEE, Assoc. Dir.; Mr. ERIC HENDRY, Assoc. Dir., *Sheen Pastoral Center, 412 N.E. Madison Ave., Peoria, 61603.* Tel: 309-671-1550; Fax: 309-671-1595.

Catholic Men, Council of—Rev. DONALD R. SCHLADEN, Moderator, *Box 26, Marseilles, 61341.* Tel: 815-795-2240.

Catholic Relief Services—Rev. JOHN C. ANDERSON, *412 N.E. Madison Ave., Peoria, 61603.* Tel: 309-671-1550; Fax: 309-671-1595.

Catholic Women, Council of—Rev. Msgr. DALE WELLMAN, Moderator, *312 W. 1st St., Milan, 61264.* Tel: 309-787-4593.

Censor Librorum—Rev. Msgr. STEVEN P. ROHLFS, *3300 N. Twelve Oaks Dr., Peoria, 61604.* Tel: 309-682-8642; Fax: 309-682-8955.

Clergymen's Aid Society—Most Rev. JOHN J. MYERS, D.D., J.C.D., Chm./Ex-officio; Revs. M. DUANE LECLERCQ, Pres. THOMAS E. MACK, Vice Pres.; Rev. Msgr. JAMES F. CAMPBELL, Exec. Sec./ Treas.; Rev. Msgr. ALBERT W. HALLIN, Sec.; Revs. THOMAS MALONEY; DAVID C. HEINZ; Rev. Msgr. NORMAN D. GOODMAN; Rev. MARK J. MERDIAN, *412 N.E. Madison Ave., Peoria, 61603.* Tel: 309-671-1550; Fax: 309-671-1595.

Commission for Ecumenism—Rev. Msgr. ALBERT W. HALLIN, *122 W. Washington St., Ottawa, 61350.* Tel: 815-433-0700.

Communications, Office of—STEPHEN MAMANELLA, Dir., *Sheen Pastoral Center, 412 N.E. Madison Ave., Peoria, 61603.* Tel: 309-671-1550; Fax: 309-671-1595.

Council of Conciliation and Arbitration—Rev. Msgr. JAMES F. CAMPBELL, Chm., *Sheen Pastoral Center, 412 N.E. Madison Ave., Peoria, 61603-2720.* Tel: 309-671-1550; Fax: 309-671-1558.

Cursillo Program—Rev. TIMOTHY NOLAN, Spiritual Dir.; Sr. JANICE KEENAN, O.S.F., Assoc. Dir., *Spalding Renewal Center, 401 N.E. Madison Ave., Peoria, 61603.* Tel: 309-676-4001.

Diocesan Office of Developement—Mr. EDWARD N. LAUGHLIN, Dir.; Mr. JOHN HOWARD, Planned Giving Dir., Development Office: *Sheen Pastoral Center, 412 N.E. Madison Ave., Peoria, 61603.* Tel: 309-671-1500; Fax: 309-671-1595.

Diocesan Education Commission—*Sheen Pastoral Center, 412 N.E. Madison Ave., Peoria, 61603.* Tel: 309-671-1550; Fax: 309-671-1595.

Diocesan Office of Finance—Mr. ALLYN G. SCHMID, Dir.; Mr. TOBY GUALANDRI, Auditor, Development Office: *Sheen Pastoral Center, 412 N.E. Madison Ave., Peoria, 61603.* Tel: 309-671-1500; Fax: 309-671-1595.

Diocesan Pastoral Council—Rev. Msgr. JAMES CAMPBELL, V.G., *Sheen Pastoral Center, 412 N.E Madison Ave., Peoria, 61603.* Tel: 309-671-1550; Fax: 309-671-1558.

Diocesan Personnel Board—Rev. Msgr. JAMES F. CAMPBELL, V.G., Dir., *Sheen Pastoral Center, 412 N.E. Madison Ave., Peoria, 61603.* Tel: 309-671-1550; Fax: 309-671-1558.

Divine Worship, Office of—Mrs. BARBARA A. LOGAN, Dir., *Sheen Pastoral Center, 412 N.E. Madison Ave., Peoria, 61603.* Tel: 309-671-1550; Fax: 309-671-1595.

Evangelization—Rev. JOHN MARK WILLIAMS, Dir., *Sheen Pastoral Center, 412 N.E. Madison Ave., Peoria, 61603.* Tel: 309-671-1550; Fax: 309-671-1595.

Family Life, Office of—Ms. MAUREEN MCNAMARA, Dir. Assoc. Dirs.: Ms. JEANNE WHALEN; Mr. PATRICK DIVETRI, *Sheen Pastoral Center, 412 N.E. Madison Ave., Peoria, 61603.* Tel: 309-671-1550; Fax: 309-671-1595.

Holy Childhood Association—Rev. JOHN C. ANDERSON, Dir., *412 N.E. Madison Ave., Peoria, 61603.* Tel: 309-671-1550; Fax: 309-671-1595.

Newspaper—"The Catholic Post"—Most Rev. JOHN J. MYERS, Publisher; Mr. THOMAS DERMODY, Editor-in-Chief, *409 N.E. Monroe Ave., Peoria, 61603.* Tel: 309-673-3603; Fax: 309-673-0334.

Nurses, Council of—Vacant.

Peoria Diocesan Marriage Enrichment—Mr. PATRICK DIVIETRI, Moderator, *Sheen Pastoral Center, 412 N.E. Madison Ave., Peoria, 61603.* Tel: 309-671-1550; Fax: 309-671-1595.

Permanent Diaconate, Office of—Rev. Msgr. CHARLES J. BEEBE, Episcopal Vicar/Dir., *1508 W. Wilhelm Rd., Dunlap, 61525.* Tel: 309-243-7811; Fax: 309-243-7810.

Marriage Preparation—Mr. PATRICK DIVIETRI, Moderator, *Sheen Pastoral Center, 412 N.E. Madison Ave., Peoria, 61603.* Tel: 309-671-1550; Fax: 309-671-1595.

Priests' Eucharistic League—Rev. Msgr. JOSEPH A. ZUBE, J.C.L., *Sheen Pastoral Center, 412 N.E. Madison Ave., Peoria, 61603.* Tel: 309-671-1550; Fax: 309-671-1595.

Propagation of the Faith—Rev. JOHN C. ANDERSON, Dir., *412 N.E. Madison Ave., Peoria, 61655.* Tel: 309-671-1550; Fax: 309-671-1595.

Purgatorial Society—Rev. Msgr. JAMES F. CAMPBELL, Dir., *Sheen Pastoral Center, 412 N.E. Madison Ave., Peoria, 61603.* Tel: 309-671-1550; Fax: 309-671-1558.

Rural Life Conference—Rev. GREGORY K. KETCHAM, Dir., *Church of the Immaculate Conception, 218 W. Broadway, Monmouth, 61462.* Tel: 309-634-7533.

Presbyteral Council—Rev. THOMAS E. MACK, Pres.; Rev. PHILIP D. HALFACRE, Sec./Treas.; Rev. Msgr. NORMAND D. GOODMAN, Vice Pres., *Sheen Pastoral Center, 412 N.E. Madison, Peoria, 61603.* Tel: 309-671-1550; Fax: 309-671-1595.

Social Service—Miss PEGGY A. ARIZZI, Diocesan Dir.; Mr. JEFF TURNBULL, Assoc. Dir., *2900 W. Heading Ave., P.O. Box 817, Peoria, 61652.* Tel: 309-671-5700., Rock Island Office: *816 20th St., Rock Island, 61201.* Tel: 309-788-9581., Bloomington Office: *106 W. Chestnut, Bloomington, 61701.* Tel: 309-788-9581., Champaign Office: *610 1-2 E. Park St., Champaign, 61820.* Tel: 217-352-5279., LaSalle Office: *535 3rd St., LaSalle, 61301.* Tel: 815-223-4007., Galesburg Office: *2401 N. Broad St., Galesburg, 61401.*, Macomb Office: *105 S. Johnson St., Macomb, 61455.* Tel: 309-833-1791.

TEC—Sr. JANICE KEENAN, Assoc. Dir.; Rev. TIMOTHY NOLAN, *Spalding Renewal Center, 401 N.E. Madison Ave., Peoria, 61603.* Tel: 309-676-4001.

Vocations—Rev. DAVID KIPFER, Dir., *607 N.E. Madison Ave., P.O. Box 1406, Peoria, 61655.* Tel: 309-671-1568; Fax: 309-671-5079.

CLERGY, PARISHES, MISSIONS AND PAROCHIAL SCHOOLS

CITY OF PEORIA
(Peoria County)

1—ST. MARY'S CATHEDRAL (1846), Most Rev. John J. Myers, S.T.L., J.C.D., Bishop of Peoria; Rev. David M. Kipfer.
Res., 607-A N.E. Madison Ave., 61603. Tel: 309-671-1568; Fax: 309-671-5079.

2—HOLY FAMILY (1956), Revs. James Ciaramitaro, O.F.M.Conv.; Steve McKinley, O.F.M.Conv.; Deacon James Maubach.
Res., 3720 N. Sterling, 61615. Tel: 309-688-3427; Fax: 309-688-2174.
School—2329 W. Reservoir, 61615. Tel: 309-688-2931; Fax: 309-681-5687. Gary Parmelee, Prin.
Lay Teachers 21; Students 420.

3—SACRED HEART (1879) (German), Revs. Marne Breckensiek, O.F.M.; Casimir Kolesar, O.F.M.; Fabian Gerstle, O.F.M.; Deacon Michael Reid.
Res., 504 Fulton St., 61602. Tel: 309-673-6316; 6317.

4—ST. ANN (1994), Rev. Richard E. Horvath; Deacons Richard Jones; Joseph Koeppel.
Mailing Address: 1010 S. Louisa St., 61605. Tel: 309-674-5072; Fax: 309-655-1566.

5—ST. BERNARD'S, Rev. David C. Heinz.
Res., 509 E. Kansas Ave., 61603. Tel: 309-682-1221; Fax: 309-6823462.
School—Tel: 309-682-5823.
Sisters 2; Lay Teachers 12; Students 180.

6—ST. BONIFACE'S (1881) (German). Merged with St. John's Parish July 1, 1994, to form St. Ann's Parish at 1010 S. Louisa St., 61605.
School—Consolidated with St. John and St. Martin de Porres, Tel: 309-674-0531.
Sisters 1; Lay Teachers 8; Students 103.
Convent—1009 S. Louisa St., 61605. Tel: 309-674-0225. Sisters of St. Benedict

7—ST. CECILIA'S. Closed. For Sacramental records write St. Philomena, 3300 N. Twelve Oaks Dr., Peoria, IL 61604.

8—ST. JOHN'S (1890) (Irish). Merged with St. Boniface July 1, 1994, to form St. Ann's Parish at 1010 S. Louisa St., 61605.
School—Consolidated with St. Ann and St. Martin de Porres, 1406 W. Antoinette St., 61605.
Sisters 1; Lay Teachers 8; Students 103.

9—ST. JUDE'S (1975), Rev. Msgr. Charles J. Beebe; Deacons Thomas Rapach; Kenneth Brinker.
Res., 1406 Wilhelm Rd., Dunlap, 61525. Tel: 309-243-7811; Fax: 309-243-7810. [CEM]
Catechesis/Religious Programs—Tel: 309-243-7324.
Students 320.

10—ST. MARK'S (1891), Revs. Robert G. Schladen; Jeffrey I. Windy; Deacons Bernard Filzen; Charles Tuerk.
Res., 1113 W. Bradley Ave., 61606. Tel: 309-673-1263.
School—Lay Teachers 16; Students 291.
Catechesis/Religious Programs—Tel: 309-673-2212.
Students 381.

11—ST. MARTIN DE PORRES (1976), Rev. Ben M. Rodriguez.
Res., 103 S. Sheridan, 61605. Tel: 309-676-0726.
Southside Catholic Child Care Center—1010 W. Johnson, 61605. Tel: 309-674-7340.

12—ST. PETER'S (1897), Rev. John Mark Williams; Deacon Richard Zimmerman. In res., Rev. Joseph P. Donton.
Res., 2719 N.E. Madison Ave., 61603. Tel: 309-685-3861; Fax: 309-688-1502.

13—ST. PHILOMENA'S (1945), Rev. Msgr. Steven P. Rohlfs; Rev. Jeffrey D. Stirniman; Deacons Robert England; Richard Hammel; Harry Ohl; David Reising. In res., Rev. Timothy Nolan.
Res., 3300 N. Twelve Oaks Dr., 61604-1464. Tel: 309-682-8642; Fax: 309-682-8955. [JC]
School—Sisters of St. Francis, Tel: 309-685-1208. Sr. Mary Joseph Bickett, O.S.F., Prin.
Sisters 5; Lay Teachers 19; Students 474.
St. Philomena Endowment Trust—.

14—ST. THOMAS (1937), Revs. William A. Watson; Thomas F. Gibson; Sr. Rachel Bergschneider, O.S.B., Pastoral Assoc. & D.R.E.; Deacons Donald Efinger; Robert Waldschmidt; Robert Stevenor.
Res., 904 E. Lake Ave., Peoria Heights, 61614. Tel: 309-688-3446; Fax: 309-688-3467.
School—4229 N. Monroe, Peoria Heights, 61614. Tel: 309-685-2533.
Lay Teachers 26; Students 480.
Catechesis/Religious Programs—Students 140.

15—ST. VINCENT DE PAUL (1962), Revs. Thomas R. Miller; John M. Verrier; Deacon Robert W. Myers, Sr. In res., Rev. Msgr. Clarence J. Hettinger.
Res., 6001 N. University St., 61614. Tel: 309-691-3602; Fax: 309-691-3687.
School—6003 N. University St., 61614. Tel: 309-691-5012.
Lay Teachers 22; Students 400.
Catechesis/Religious Programs—Tel: 309-691-6513.
Students 78.

OUTSIDE THE CITY OF PEORIA

Abingdon, Knox Co., Sacred Heart (1924), Rev. Francis M. Oman, I.C.
Res., 506 N. Main St., 61410. Tel: 309-462-3421.

Aledo, Mercer Co., St. Catherine's Church (1914), Rev. Gregory J. Plunkett.
Res., 106 N.E. Fourth, 61231. Tel: 309-582-7500. [CEM]
Catechesis/Religious Programs—Students 122.
Missions—Keithsburg, Mercer Co., St. Mary's, 602 S. 10th St., Keithsburg, 61442. Tel: 309-374-2420; New Boston, Mercer Co., St. Theresa of the Little Flower, 109 Washington, New Boston, 61272.

Alexis, Warren Co., St. Theresa's (1877) (Swedish), Rev. William C. Keebler, Jr.
Res., 131 Main St., 61412. Tel: 309-482-3935.

[CEM]
Mission—Wataga, Knoxville Co., St. Aloysius, N. Depot St., Wataga, 61488. Tel: 309-375-6835.

Andalusia, Rock Island Co., St. Patrick's (1974), Rev. James G. Pallardy.
Mailing Address: Box 211, 61232.
Res., 9616 140th St. W., Taylor Ridge, 61284. Tel: 309-798-2098.
Catechesis/Religious Programs—Tel: 309-798-2630.
Students 32.

Annawan, Henry Co., Sacred Heart (1893), Rev. John Paul Cox.
Res., 305 W. South Ave., 61234. Tel: 309-935-6911. [CEM]

Arlington, Bureau Co., St. Patrick's (1864), Rev. Kevin Gorman, O.S.B.
Res., 61312. Tel: 815-638-2323. [CEM]

Atkinson, Henry Co., St. Anthony's (1870), Rev. Donnelly J. Fitzpatrick.
Res., 204 W. Main St., P.O. Box 210, 61235-0210. Tel: 309-936-7900; Fax: 309-936-7900. [CEM]

Bartonville, Peoria Co., St. Anthony (1969), Rev. Thomas F. Kelly; Sr. Eleanor Hoffmann, O.P., Pastoral Assoc. & D.R.E.; Deacons Richard Hammond; Louis Tomlianovich.
Res., 2525 Skyway Rd., P.O. Box 4152, 61607. Tel: 309-697-0645; Fax: 309-697-2188.
Catechesis/Religious Programs—Students 228.

Bement, Piatt Co., St. Michael, Rev. Vien Van Do.
Res., 332 S. Macon, 61813. Tel: 217-762-2566.

Benson, Woodford Co., St. John (1873), Rev. Neri Greskoviak, O.F.M.
Res., 506 W. Randolph, Roanoke, 61561. Tel: 309-394-2615. [CEM]

Blackstone, Livingston Co., St. Bernard. Closed. For sacramental records contact, Immaculate Conception, Streater.

Bloomington, McLean Co.,

1—Holy Trinity, (1853), Revs. John J. Dietzen; Stephen A. Willard; Deacons Edward Ulbrich; Lewis Roesch.
Res., 704 N. Main St., 61701. Tel: 309-829-2197; Fax: 309-829-2243. [CEM]
School—705 N. Roosevelt, 61701. Tel: 309-828-7151; Fax: 309-827-8131.
1909 E. Lincoln St., 61701. Tel: 309-662-3712; Fax: 309-663-9115.
Sisters 2; Lay Teachers 26; Students 575.
Catechesis/Religious Programs—Tel: 309-828-8242. Mrs. Sharon Priester, D.R.E.
Students 295.

2—St. Mary's, (1867) (German), Revs. Ric Schneider, O.F.M.; Damian Cesanek, O.F.M.; Deacon Darrel Petri.
Res., 527 W. Jackson St., 61701. Tel: 309-827-8526; Fax: 309-829-3061. [CEM]
School—603 W. Jackson St., 61701. Tel: 309-828-5954.
Lay Teachers 10; Students 130.
Catechesis/Religious Programs—Students 211.

3—St. Patrick's, (1892), Revs. Glenn H. Harris, Admin.; Vincent E. Dietzen, Pastor Emeritus.
Res., 1209 W. Locust St., 61701. Tel: 309-829-1355. [JC]

4—St. Patrick Church of Merna, (1890), Revs. Gerald T. Ward; Lawrence A. Morlan.
Church—R.R. 1, Box 38, 61704. Tel: 309-662-7361; Fax: 309-664-6167. [CEM]
Catechesis/Religious Programs—Sr. Mary Therese Dolan, O.P., D.R.E.
Students 750.

Bradford, Stark Co., St. John the Baptist (1876), Rev. Thomas E. Taylor.
Res., 218 First St., Box 310, 61421. Tel: 309-897-4081. [CEM]

Brimfield, Peoria Co., St. Joseph's (1852), Rev. Joseph J. Kelly.
Res., 314 W. Clay St., 61517. Tel: 309-446-3275. [CEM]
Mission—Williamsfield, Knox Co., St. James, Williamsfield, 61489. Tel: 309-446-3275.

Budd, Livingston Co., St. Bernard's. Closed. For parish records contact Church of the Immaculate Conception, Streator.

Bushnell, McDonough Co., St. Bernard (1877), Rev. David L. Kurt.
Res., 376 W. Hail St., 61422. Tel: 309-772-2333.

Camp Grove, Marshall Co., St. Patrick (1866) (Irish). Unassigned. Rev. Michael J. Driscoll.
Res., 115 W. Camp St., 61424. Tel: 309-493-5261. [CEM]

Campus, Livingston Co., Sacred Heart (Irish), Rev. James Rickey, Admin.
Res., P.O. Box 70, Dwight, 60420. Tel: 815-584-3522; Fax: 815-584-1148. [CEM]

Canton, Fulton Co., St. Mary's (1862), Rev. Arthur D. Meyer; Deacon Victor Kovachevich.
Res., 229 N. 3rd Ave., 61520. Tel: 309-647-1473. [CEM 2]
Catechesis/Religious Programs—Tel: 309-647-0261.
Students 231.

Carthage, Hancock Co., Immaculate Conception (1860), Rev. Glenn J. Fontana.
Res., 125 N. Fayette, 62321. Tel: 217-357-3087. [CEM]
Mission—West Point, Hancock Co., St. Mary.

Champaign, Champaign Co.,

1—Holy Cross, (1912), Revs. Richard L. Mullen; Robert D. Spilman; Deacons Henry Hart; John Lalande.
Res., 405 W. Clark St., 61820. Tel: 217-352-8748.
School—410 W. White St., 61820. Tel: 217-356-9521; Fax: 217-356-1745.
Lay Teachers 17; Students 429.
Catechesis/Religious Programs—Sr. Joan Kaucher, C.S.J., D.R.E.
Students 147.

2—St. John's Catholic Chapel, (1918). (For Catholic Students at the University of Illinois). Rev. Msgr. Edward J. Duncan, Chap.; Revs. Gregory Jozefiak; Robert Barry, O.P.; Joseph T. Hogan.
Res., Newman Hall, 604 E. Armory Ave., 61820. Tel: 217-344-1184; Fax: 217-344-4957.

3—St. Mary's, (1857), Rev. Thomas J. Royer.
Res., 612 E. Park Ave., 61820. Tel: 217-352-8364; Fax: 217-352-6859. [CEM]

4—St. Matthew, Revs. Terrance P. O'Brien; Mark J. Merdian; John-Peter Phan.
Res., 1303 Lincolnshire Dr., 61821. Tel: 217-359-4224; Fax: 217-359-9846.
School—1307 Linconshire Dr., 61821. Tel: 217-359-4114; Fax: 217-359-7507.
Lay Teachers 19; Students 472.
Catechesis/Religious Programs—Tel: 217-359-8761.
Students 260.

Chatsworth, Livingston Co., SS. Peter and Paul (1877) (French), Rev. Richard W. Brunskill.
Res., 406 N. Fifth St., P.O. Box 546, 60921. Tel: 815-635-3127. [CEM]

Chenoa, McLean Co., St. Joseph's (1859), Rev. Terry Cassidy.
Res., 225 W. Owsley, 61726. Tel: 815-945-2561; Fax: 815-945-7634. [CEM]
Catechesis/Religious Programs—Tel: 815-945-2561.
Students 171.
Mission—Lexington, McLean Co., St. Mary, Tel: 815-945-7987.

Cherry, Bureau Co., Holy Trinity (1904), Rev. Kevin Gorman, O.S.B.
Res., P.O. Box 159, 212 S. Main, 61317. Tel: 815-894-2006; Fax: 815-894-2090. [CEM]

Chillicothe, Peoria Co., St. Edward's (1900), Rev. Anthony M. Ego; Deacons Gregory Serangeli; Richard Kauth.
Res., 1216 N. 6th St., 61523. Tel: 309-274-3809. [CEM]
School—Tel: 309-274-2994; Fax: 309-274-4150.
Lay Teachers 13; Students 231.

Clinton, De Witt Co., St. John the Baptist's, Rev. Robert H. Hoffmann; Sr. Patricia Rinn, O.P., Pastoral Assoc.
Res., 502 N. Monroe St., 61727. Tel: 217-935-3727.
Catechesis/Religious Programs—Tel: 217-935-3727.
Students 163.

Coal Valley, Rock Island Co., St. Maria Goretti, Rev. Richard F. Bresnahan; Deacons Charles Breeden; Robert Zimmerman.
Res., P.O. Box 159, 210 E. 22nd Ave., 61240. Tel: 309-799-3414.
Catechesis/Religious Programs—Tel: 309-799-7283.
Students 102.

Colfax, McLean Co., St. Joseph's (1850), Rev. Jeffrey G. Laible.
Res., P.O. Box 169, 107 W. North, 61728. Tel: 309-723-6229; Fax: 309-723-6229.
Mission—Strawn, Livingston Co., St. Rose.

Colona, Henry Co., St. Patrick's (1941), Rev. Edward E. Bush.
Res., P.O. Box C, 61241. Tel: 309-792-3854. [JC]
Catechesis/Religious Programs—Jean Sottos, D.R.E.
Students 337.

Creve Coeur, Tazewell Co., Sacre Coeur (1954), Rev. James E. King.
Res., 301 Roosevelt St., 61610. Tel: 309-699-8223.
Church—601 Rusche Ln., 61610. Tel: 309-699-8511.

Cullom, Livingston Co., St. John's (1881), Rev. Richard W. Brunskill.
Res., 113 Van Alstyne, P.O. Box 376, 60929. Tel: 815-689-2367.

Dalzell, Bureau Co., St. Thomas More (1934) (Italian), Rev. Placid W. Hatfield, O.S.B.; Deacon Robert Beltramini.
Res., 302 Chestnut, 61320. Tel: 815-663-6201.

Danville, Vermilion Co., Holy Family (1978), Rev. Ted Pracz; Deacons Herman Bott; Richard Smith.
Church—444 E. Main St., 61832. Tel: 217-431-5100; Fax: 217-431-5103. [CEM]
School—Tel: 217-431-5108.
Lay Teachers 12; Students 220.
St. Paul's (1915), Revs. Douglas J. Hennessy; R. Anthony Lee; Sr. Charles Allen, Pastoral Assoc.
Res., 1303 N. Walnut St., 61832. Tel: 217-442-5313; Fax: 217-442-5356. [JC]
School—1307 N. Walnut St., 61832. Tel: 217-442-8095.
Lay Teachers 26; Students 384.
Catechesis/Religious Programs—Students 144.

Delavan, Tazewell Co., St. Mary's (1859), Rev. Edward S. Kopec.
Res., Box 769, 61734. Tel: 309-244-8516. [CEM]
Mission—Hopedale, Tazewell Co., St. Joseph's.

Depue, Bureau Co., St. Mary's (1908), Rev. Thomas Badovsky.
Res., 312 Park St., Box 19, 61322. Tel: 815-447-2552. [CEM]

Downs, McLean Co., St. Mary's (1910), Rev. Gerald T. Ward, Admin.
Church—101 N. Lincoln, P.O. Box 66, 61736. Tel: 309-378-4679; Fax: 309-378-4080.
Catechesis/Religious Programs—Students 153.

Dunlap, Peoria Co., St. Clement's. Attended by St. Jude's, Peoria, 1508 Wilhelm Rd., 61525. [CEM].

Dwight, Livingston Co., St. Patrick's (1862), Rev. James E. Rickey.
Res., 126 W. Mazon Ave., P.O. Box 70, 60420. Tel: 815-584-3522. [CEM]
Catechesis/Religious Programs—Tel: 815-584-3110. Dolores Krischel, D.R.E.
Students 292.

Eagle Township, La Salle Co., Annunciation of Blessed Virgin Mary (1869) (Irish), Rev. Charles A. McCarthy, C.S.Sp.
Church—Rte. 3, Eagle Township, Streator, 61364. Tel: 815-672-6500.
Res., Rte 1, 957 N. 17th Rd., Tonica, 61370. Tel: 815-856-2502. [CEM]

Earlville, La Salle Co., St. Theresa's (1904), Rev. William D. Virtue.
Res., 221 Union St., Box 90, 60518. Tel: 815-246-4321. [CEM 2]

East Moline, Rock Island Co., St. Anne (1919), Rev. Robert D. O'Connor; Sr. Mary O'Connor, B.V.M, Pastoral Assoc.
Res., 555 18th Ave., 61244. Tel: 309-755-5071.
School—Tel: 309-755-9771.
Sisters of Charity of the B.V.M. 4; Lay Teachers 11; Students 254.
St. Mary's (1907), Rev. Donald L. Levitt.
Res., 1908 13th St., 61244. Tel: 309-755-4111. [JC]
School—Tel: 309-755-4352.
Lay Teachers 16; Students 190.
Catechesis/Religious Programs—1925 13th St., 61244.
Students 136.

East Peoria, Tazewell Co., St. Monica's (1898), Rev. Kenneth L. Marchulones; Sr. Marjorie Meismer, O.S.F., Pastoral Assoc.; Deacons William Fry; Ronald Rager; William Sloman.
Res., 303 Campanile Dr., 61611. Tel: 309-694-2061.
Catechesis/Religious Programs—Tel: 309-699-8458. Mrs. Cheryl Riddell, D.R.E.
Students 148.

Elkhart, Logan Co., St. Patrick (1856), Rev. Mubarak Anwar Amar.
Res., 213 S. Bogardus, P.O. Box 19, 62634. Tel: 217-947-2714.
Missions—Mount Pulaski, Logan Co., St. Thomas Aquinas, St. Patrick's, 62634; Middletown, Logan Co., St. John the Baptist, St. Patrick's, 62634.

Elmwood, Peoria Co., St. Patrick's (1870) (Irish), Rev. Thomas E. Seibert, I.C.; Deacon Deane Keefer.
Res., P.O. Box 440, 61529. Tel: 309-742-4921. [CEM]

El Paso, Woodford Co., St. Mary's (1863), Rev. Lawrence P. Morrissey.
Res., 79 W. Third, P.O. Box 197, 61738. Tel: 309-527-4555. [CEM 2]
Catechesis/Religious Programs—Tel: 309-527-3198. Mrs. Kevin Kearney, D.R.E.
Students 105.

Eureka, Woodford Co., St. Luke's (1982), Rev. James E. Purcell.
Res., 301 E. Pearson St., 61530. Tel: 309-467-4855. [JC]
Church—904 E. Regan Dr., P.O. Box 226, 61530.

Fairbury, Livingston Co., St. John the Baptist (1857),

Rev. Scott Archer.
Res., 110 E. Ash, 61739. Tel: 815-692-2555. [CEM]
Catechesis/Religious Programs—Students 127.
Mission—Forrest, Livingston Co., St. James, 322 S. William, Forrest, 61741.

Farmer City, De Witt Co., Sacred Heart (1899), Rev. Gerald J. Benbenek.
Res., 612 N. Plum St., 61842. Tel: 309-928-3855. [CEM]
Mission—Bellflower, Mclean Co., St. John.

Farmington, Fulton Co., St. Matthew's (1904), Rev. Thomas E. Seibert, I.C.; Deacon John Burton.
Res., 156 E. Vernon St., 61531. Tel: 309-245-4351.

Galesburg, Knox Co., Corpus Christi (1885), Rev. James P. McAteer, I.C.
Res., 273 S. Prairie St., 61401. Tel: 309-343-8256; Fax: 309-343-4793. [CEM]
School—Costa Catholic School. Operates with Immaculate Heart and St. Patrick. 2726 Costa Dr., 61401. Tel: 309-344-3151.
Sisters 1; Lay Teachers 23; Students 322.
Catechesis/Religious Programs—Students 189.

Immaculate Heart of Mary (1956), Revs. Ernest E. Pizzamiglio; John Thieryoung.
Mailing Address: P.O. Box 550, 61402. Tel: 309-344-3108; Fax: 309-344-1205.
Res., 2401 N. Broad St., 61401.
School—See Corpus Christi Parish.
Catechesis/Religious Programs—Students 432.

St. Patrick's (1863), Rev. Frederick Bruce King, I.C.; Deacon Jesse M. Ramirez.
Mailing Address: P.O. Box 589, 61402-0589. Tel: 309-343-9874; Fax: 309-343-9944.
Res., 858 S. Academy St., 61401. [JC]
School—See Corpus Christi Parish.

Galva, Henry Co., St. John's (1882) (Swedish), Rev. Bruce D. Lopez.
Res., 212 N.E. 1st St., 61434. Tel: 309-932-2409. [CEM]

Geneseo, Henry Co., St. Malachy's (1866), Revs. Michael G. Pakula; John A. Mahoney, Pastor Emeritus; Deacons Harley Chaffee; Walter Verbeck; Harley Harris; Thomas Wachtel.
Res., 595 E. Ogden Ave., 61254. Tel: 309-944-5393; Fax: 309-944-5319.
School—Tel: 309-944-3230.
Lay Teachers 8; Students 170.
Catechesis/Religious Programs—Tel: 309-944-3518.
Students 362.

Georgetown, Vermilion Co., St. Isaac Jogues (1942), Rev. John Paninski, M.S.
Res., 109 W. Seventh St., 61846. Tel: 217-662-6708.

Granville, Putnam Co., Sacred Heart Of Jesus (1908) (Italian), Rev. Patrick K. O'Neal.
Res., P.O. Box 217, 61323. Tel: 815-339-2138. [CEM]
Catechesis/Religious Programs—Students 132.
Mission—Bureau, Bureau Co., St. Francis Xavier, P.O. Box 217, 61323.

Havana, Mason Co., St. Patrick's, Rev. Eugene A. Radosevich.
Res., P.O. Box 345, 423 S. Orange, 62644. Tel: 309-543-3571. [CEM]
Mission—Manito, Mason Co., Immaculate Conception, 505 S. Adams, P.O. Box 242, Manito, 61546. Tel: 309-968-6826. Deacon William Meyer.

Hennepin, Putnam Co., St. Patrick's (1865), Rev. John A. Kwak.
Res., 10 St., P.O. Box 200, 61327. Tel: 815-925-7066; 925-7500. [CEM]
Mission—Mount Palatine, Putnam Co., Immaculate Conception, P.O. Lostant, Lostant, 61335. Tel: 815-882-2337. [CEM]

Henry, Marshall Co., St. Joseph's (1878), Rev. Walter A. Breuning.
Res., 401 South St., Box 75, 61537. Tel: 309-364-2224. [CEM 2]

St. Mary's (1851), Rev. Walter A. Breuning.
Res., Box 75, 61537. Tel: 309-364-2224. [CEM 2]
Catechesis/Religious Programs—Tel: 309-364-2011. Sr. Anita D.R.E.
Students 209.

Hoopeston, Vermilion Co., St. Anthony's (1877), Rev. Jerome R. Pilon; Deacon William C. Ringler.
Church—423 S. Third St., P.O. Box 414, 60942. Tel: 217-283-6211; Fax: 217-283-6252.

Hooppole, Henry Co., St. Mary's. Attended by Annawan.

Ivesdale, Champaign Co., St. Joseph's (1863) (Irish), Rev. Thomas J. Royer.
Mailing Address: Box 175, 61851. Tel: 217-621-8364; Fax: 217-352-6859.
Res., 612 E. Park, Champaign, 61820. Tel: 217-352-8364. [CEM]

Kewanee, Henry Co., St. Francis of Assisi (1906) (Polish), Rev. John Burns.
Res., 1009 N. Burr, 61443. Tel: 309-852-2761.
Mission—Cambridge, Henry Co., St. John Vianney, 313 S. West St., Cambridge, 61238. Tel: 309-937-3304.

St. Mary's Catholic Church, Rev. Duane C. Jack; Deacons Martin Van Meltebeck; John T. Mock; Raymond Van Wassenhove.
Res., Parish Center, 406 W. Central Blvd., 61443-2010. Tel: 309-852-4549; Fax: 309-853-4106. [CEM]
School—Visitation, 107 S. Lexington, 61443. Tel: 309-856-7451.
Lay Teachers 13; Students 186.
Catechesis/Religious Programs—Tel: 309-856-5451. Mrs. Phyllis Elliott, D.R.E.
Students 152.

Kickapoo, (Edwards) Peoria Co., St. Mary's of Kickapoo (1837), Rev. Harry A. Pierjok. In res., Rev. Msgr. Robert C. Livingston.
Res., 9910 W. Knox St., Kickapoo (Edwards), 61528. Tel: 309-691-2030 (Church). [CEM]
School—Tel: 309-691-3015.
Lay Teachers 6; Students 59.

Lacon, Marshall Co., Immaculate Conception (1853), Rev. Ronald E. Enderlin; Deacon J. Robert Murphy.
Res., 418 N. Center St., 61540. Tel: 309-246-5145. [CEM]

Ladd, Bureau Co., St. Benedict's (1893), Rev. Harold Datzman, O.S.B.
Res., 314 Bureau St., 61329. Tel: 815-894-2319; Fax: 815-894-2265.
Mission—Seatonville, Bureau Co., St. Gertrude, 711 Railroad Ave., Seatonville, 61359.

La Salle, La Salle Co.,

1—Queen of the Holy Rosary, (1925) (Italian), Rev. Dale R. Maloy.
Res., 529 Fourth St., 61301. Tel: 815-223-7129. [JC]

2—St. Hyacinth's, (1875), Rev. Joseph W. Anderson; Deacon Charles Burgess.
Res., 927 10th St., 61301. Tel: 815-223-0934. [CEM]
School—LaSalle Catholic, Tel: 815-223-5088. Sr. Mary Kathleen Stafford, D.C., Prin.
Sisters 1; Lay Teachers 16; Students 169.

3—Resurrection, (1979), Rev. John M. Onderko; Sr. Mary Jane Wallace, O.S.B., Pastoral Assoc.
Res., 913 Fifth St., 61301. Tel: 815-223-1459.
School—LaSalle Catholic School, Tel: 815-223-5088.
Sisters 1; Lay Teachers 9; Students 169.
Mission—Dimmick Township, Sacred Heart.

4—St. Patrick's, (1838) (Irish), Rev. M. Duane Leclercq.
Res., 725-Fourth St., 61301. Tel: 815-223-0641; Fax: 815-223-0523. [CEM]
School—Daughters of Charity of St. Vincent de Paul, Tel: 815-223-1166.
Sisters 2; Lay Teachers 10; Students 215.

Leonore, La Salle Co., SS. Peter and Paul's (1860) (German), Rev. Charles A. McCarthy, C.S.Sp.
Res., Rte. 1, Tonica, 61370. Tel: 815-856-2502. [CEM]

Lewistown, Fulton Co., St. Mary's (1865), Rev. Robert W. O'Connor.
Res., 705 N. Broadway St., P.O. Box 106, 61542. Tel: 309-547-3226; Fax: 309-547-3226. [CEM]
Mission—St. David, Fulton Co., St. Michael.

Lincoln, Logan Co., Holy Family (1857), Rev. Msgr. Norman D. Goodman. Pastoral Assocs: Revs. Daniel Wilder; Patrick DeMeulemeester.
Res., 316 S. Logan St., 62656. Tel: 217-732-4019; Fax: 217-732-8842. [CEM 2]
School—Carroll Catholic School, Tel: 217-732-7518.
Lay Teachers 13; Students 232.
Catechesis/Religious Programs—Holy Family Religious Education Center, 103 Fourth St., 62656. Tel: 217-735-3520. Mrs. Linda Buttell, D.R.E.
Students 530.
Missions—Atlanta, Logan Co., St. Mary, Atlanta, 61723; Mason City, Mason Co., St. Columba, Mason City, 62664.

Loretto, Livingston Co., St. Mary's (1873) (German). Closed. For inquiries for parish records contact the Chancery. Closed for inquiries contact St. Patrick, Dwight.

Lostant, La Salle Co., St. John the Baptist's (1883), Rev. William M. Gardner.
Res., P.O. Box 486, Wenona, 61377. Tel: 815-853-4558.
Church—301 N. Sheridan, 61334. Tel: 815-368-3339. [CEM]

Macomb, McDonough Co., St. Paul's (1854), Rev. Richard A. Pricco.
Res., 309 W. Jackson, 61455. Tel: 309-833-2496; Fax: 309-833-1560. [CEM]
School—Tel: 309-833-2470.
Lay Teachers 8; Students 143.
Catechesis/Religious Programs—Tel: 309-837-1024.
Students 211.
Mission—Tennessee, McDonough Co., Sacred Heart.

Mahomet, Champaign Co., Our Lady of the Lake (1981), Rev. John C. Horton; Deacon Robert Baxley.
Res., 501 W. State St., P.O. Box 109, 61853. Tel: 217-586-5153.
Catechesis/Religious Programs—Tel: 217-586-5141. Sr. Constance Heidewald, R.S.M., D.R.E.
Students 412.

Marseilles, La Salle Co., St. Joseph's (1902), Rev. Donald R. Schladen.
Res., 200 Broadway St., P.O. Box 26, 61341. Tel: 815-795-2240.

Matherville, Mercer Co., St. Anthony's Church (1916), Rev. Richard Slavish.
Office: P.O. Box 208, 61263. Tel: 309-754-8711. [CEM 2]
Mission—Viola, Mercer Co., St. John, Viola, 61486. Tel: 309-596-2950.

Mendota, La Salle Co., Holy Cross (1863), Rev. Msgr. Richard G. Fitzsimmons; Rev. Joseph Dondanville; Deacon Vincent Slomian.
Res., 1010 Jefferson St., 61342. Tel: 815-538-6151; Fax: 815-539-5014. [CEM]
School—1000 Jefferson St., 61342. Tel: 815-538-6016.
Sisters of the Third Order of St. Dominic (Springfield) 3; Lay Teachers 11; Students 267.
Catechesis/Religious Programs—Tel: 815-539-6050. Karen Zolper, D.R.E.
Students 180.

Metamora, Woodford Co., St. Mary's (1864) (German), Revs. Dacian Batt, O.F.M.; Benno Heidlage, O.F.M.; Charles B. Miller, O.F.M., (Retired).
Res., 415 W. Chatham St., 61548. Tel: 309-367-4407; Fax: 309-367-4114. [CEM]
School—Tel: 309-367-2528; Fax: 309-367-4114.
Sisters of St. Francis of the Immaculate Conception 1; Lay Teachers 11; Students 170.
Catechesis/Religious Programs—Tel: 309-367-2507. Sr. Betty Jean Haverback, O.S.F., D.R.E.
Students 114.

St. Mary of Lourdes, Rev. Robert Weakley, O.F.M.; Deacon Jack Gaetz.
Res., Rte. 2, 61548. Tel: 309-383-4460.

Milan, Rock Island Co., St. Ambrose (1924), Rev. Msgr. Dale L. Wellman; Sr. Charlotte Sonneville, O.S.B., Pastoral Assoc.; Deacon Frank Randazzo.
Res., 312 W. First St., 61264. Tel: 309-787-4593; Fax: 309-787-6403.
School—Operates as part of Jordan Catholic School of Rock Island, Tel: 309-793-7363.
Students 59.
Catechesis/Religious Programs—Tel: 309-787-6240. Diane Hansen, D.R.E.
Students 147.

Minonk, Woodford Co., St. Patrick's (1878), Rev. Robert F. Gilles.
Res., 420 E. Sixth St., Box 107, 61760-0107. Tel: 309-432-2700; Fax: 309-432-2700. [CEM]
Mission—Flanagan, Livingston Co., St. Joseph, 313 S. Main St., Flanagan, 61740. Tel: 815-796-4226.
Catechesis/Religious Programs—Students 128.

Moline, Rock Island Co., Christ the King (1967), Rev. Richard Barclift.
Parish Center: 3205 60th St., 61265. Tel: 309-762-4634; Fax: 309-762-7848.
Catechesis/Religious Programs—Tel: 309-797-5202. D.R.E.: Janet Myers, (PreK-6); Paula Anderson, (Jr. High School).
Students 255.

Sacred Heart (1906) (Belgian), Revs. Robert E. Lee; Brian K. Brownsey; Stanley L. Deptula; Deacon John Landry. Pastoral Assocs.: Sr. Kathleen Mullin; Sr. Susan Messer.
Lee Parish Center—1608 13th St., 61265. Tel: 309-762-2362; Fax: 309-757-5502.
School—Seton Catholic School, (Grades PreK-8). Tel: 309-757-5500.
Sisters 3; Lay Teachers 18; Students 462.
Catechesis/Religious Programs—Rita Luebbers, D.R.E.
Students 243.

St. Mary's (1876) (Hispanic), Rev. Deo Gratias R. Mutefunya.
Res., 412 10th St., 61265. Tel: 309-764-1562. [CEM]
School—Seton Catholic School, (Grades 6-8). Tel: 309-764-5418.
Sisters 2; Lay Teachers 7; Students 95.
Catechesis/Religious Programs—Tel: 309-762-6575. Mrs. Claire Sally Van Oteghem, D.R.E.
Students 183.

Monmouth, Warren Co., Immaculate Conception, Revs. Thomas E. Mack; Gregory K. Ketcham; Sr. Paula Helenthal, O.S.B., Pastoral Assoc.; Deacon William Clark.
Church—218 W. Broadway, 61462. Tel: 309-734-7533. [CEM]

School—Tel: 309-734-6037.
Sisters of St. Benedict 1; Lay Teachers 7; Students 119.
Convent—116 North A, 61462. Tel: 309-734-6327.
Mission—Oquawka, Henderson Co., St. Andrew.

Monticello, Piatt Co., St. Philomena, Rev. Vien Van Do.
Res., 1301 N. Market St., 61856. Tel: 217-762-2566. [CEM]

Morton, Tazewell Co., Blessed Sacrament (1957), Rev. Eugene L. Finnell; Deacon Thomas Moran.
Res., 261 E. Greenwood St., 61550. Tel: 309-266-9721; Fax: 309-266-9201.
School—Tel: 309-263-8442.
Lay Teachers 13; Students 212.
Catechesis/Religious Programs—Tel: 309-266-6791. Judy Krumholz, D.R.E.
Students 352.

Nauvoo, Hancock Co., SS. Peter and Paul's (1848) (German), Rev. Dwight P. Campbell.
Res., 150 N. Wells St., 62354. Tel: 217-453-2428. [CEM]
School—Lay Teachers 4; Students 56.
Catechesis/Religious Programs—Students 87.
Mission—Dallas City, Hancock Co., Sacred Heart, Dallas City, 62330.

Normal, McLean Co., Epiphany (1966), Rev. Tom Maloney; Deacon Richard Grimler.
Res., 1006 E. College Ave., 61761. Tel: 309-452-2585; 452-3223; Fax: 309-452-4851.
School—Tel: 309-452-3268.
Lay Teachers 13; Students 304.
Catechesis/Religious Programs—Mary Jean Kraft, D.R.E.
Students 465.

Odell, Livingston Co., St. Paul's (1901) (Irish), Rev. Francis J. Ryan.
Res., 313 W. Hamilton, 60460. Tel: 815-998-2197. [CEM]
School—Tel: 815-998-2194.
Lay Teachers 5; Students 152.

Oglesby, La Salle Co., Holy Family (1953), Rev. Anthony J. Trosley.
Res., 311 Woodland Ave., 61348. Tel: 815-883-8233.
School—Tel: 815-883-8916.
Lay Teachers 12; Students 172.

Ohio, Bureau Co., Immaculate Conception Church (1875) (Irish), Rev. Binh K. Tran.
Res., c/o St. John's, 204 N. Main St., Walnut, 61376-0370. Tel: 815-379-2602. [CEM]

Orion, Henry Co., Mary, Our Lady of Peace (1962), Rev. R. Michael Schaab.
Res., 1402 10th St., P.O.Box 175, 61273-0175. Tel: 309-526-8106. [CEM]
Catechesis/Religious Programs—Students 174.

Ottawa, La Salle Co.,

1—St. Columba, (1844) (Irish), Rev. Msgr. Albert W. Hallin; Rev. Gerald J. Meyer; Deacon Estal C. Daron.
Res., 122 W. Washington St., 61350. Tel: 815-433-0700; Fax: 815-433-0305. [CEM]
School—1110 LaSalle St., 61350. Tel: 815-433-1199.
Lay Teachers 16; Students 330.
Catechesis/Religious Programs—Students 165.

2—St. Francis of Assisi, (1858), Rev. Leo H. Gildner.
Res., 820 Sanger St., P.O. Box 2333, 61350-2333. Tel: 815-434-0969; Fax: 815-434-1073. [CEM]

3—St. Mary's, (1927), Rev. Harold F. Schmitt.
Res., 2005 Center St., Ottawa (Naplate), 61350. Tel: 815-433-2404; Fax: 815-433-9458.

4—St. Patrick's, (1893) (Irish), Rev. Robert J. Creager.
Res., 726 W. Jefferson St., 61350. Tel: 815-434-0768; Fax: 815-434-0768.
School—801 W. Jefferson St., 61350. Tel: 815-433-2889.
Dominican Sisters (Sinsinawa, WI) 3; Lay Teachers 10; Students 159.
Catechesis/Religious Programs—Tel: 815-433-3752. Mrs. Mary Jean Weihman, D.R.E.
Students 170.
Convent—727 W. Jefferson, 61350. Tel: 815-433-2637.

Pekin, Tazewell Co., St. Joseph's (1863), Revs. Gerald J. Verdun; James Kruse; Vandennis Nguyen; Deacons Charles Murray; Martin Pogioli.
Res., 303 S. Seventh St., 61554. Tel: 309-347-6108; Fax: 309-347-6959. [CEM]
School—Tel: 309-347-7194. Joan Moore, Prin.
Lay Teachers 16; Students 330 (including Preschool).
Catechesis/Religious Programs—Martha Novak, D.R.E.
Students 305.

Penfield, Champaign Co., St. Lawrence's (1898), Rev. Howard C. Barch.
Res., P.O. Box 49, 61862. Tel: 217-595-5560. [CEM]
Mission—Rankin, Vermilion Co., Holy Trinity, 200 S. Main, Rankin, 60960. Tel: 217-397-2967.

Peru, La Salle Co., St. Joseph's (1854), Revs. Henry Fritz, O.S.B.; Joseph Heyd, O.S.B.
Res., P.O. Box 608, 61354. Tel: 815-223-0718. [CEM]
School—Peru Catholic School System, (Grades PreK-8). Operated jointly by the Peru parishes. 2003 Fifth St., 61354. Tel: 815-224-1914.
Sisters 4; Lay Teachers 11; Students 316.
Catechesis/Religious Programs—Sandra Weger, D.R.E.
Students 165.

St. Mary's (1867) (Irish), Rev. Richard Kolczaski; Deacon Fred Sims.
Res., 1319 Sixth St., 61354. Tel: 815-223-2672.
School—Peru Catholic School System. See St. Joseph's for details. Tel: 815-224-1914.

St. Valentine's (1891) (Polish), Rev. Edward J. Bawiec.
Res., 1109 Pulaski St., 61354. Tel: 815-223-0315. [CEM]
School—Peru Catholic School System. See St. Joseph's for details. Tel: 815-224-1914.
Catechesis/Religious Programs—Students 192.

Pesotum, Champaign Co., St. Mary (1875) (German), Rev. Joseph M. Mai Chi Thanh.
Res., P.O. Box 169, 61863. Tel: 217-867-2434. [CEM]

St. Joseph (1904) (German), Rev. Joseph M. Mai Chi Thanh.
Res., P.O. Box 619, 61863. Tel: 217-867-2434. [CEM]

Peterstown, La Salle Co., SS. Peter and Paul (1872), Rev. Richard Fitzsimmons.
Res., 1010 Jefferson St., Mendota, 61342. Tel: 815-538-6151; Fax: 815-539-5014. [CEM]

Philo, Champaign Co., St. Thomas (1869), Rev. Dominic Vitaliano.
Res., 310 E. Madison, P.O. Box 266, 61864. Tel: 217-684-2571; Fax: 217-684-2309. [CEM]
School—Tel: 217-684-2309.
Sisters of the Third Order of St. Dominic (Springfield) 2; Lay Teachers 9; Students 153.
Mission—Bongard, Champaign Co., Immaculate Conception, 61864. [CEM]

Pontiac, Livingston Co., St. Mary's (1877), Revs. E. E. Higgins; Edward J. Roberts.
Res., 119 E. Howard St., P.O. Box 374, 61764. Tel: 815-844-7683; Fax: 815-844-6987. [CEM]
School—414 N. Main St., 61764. Tel: 815-844-6585.
Lay Teachers 10; Students 250.
Catechesis/Religious Programs—Students 153.

Princeton, Bureau Co., St. Louis (1865), Rev. Edward O. Harkrader.
Res., 616 S. Gosse Blvd., 61356. Tel: 815-879-0181.
School—Tel: 815-872-8521.
Sisters 2; Lay Teachers 11; Students 142.
Catechesis/Religious Programs—Tel: 815-872-1033.
Students 191.

Princeville, Peoria Co., St. Mary of the Woods (1867), Rev. J. Brian Rejsek.
Res., 407 S. Walnut, 61559. Tel: 309-385-4370. [CEM]

Ransom, La Salle Co., St. Patrick's (1883), Rev. William Arthur Ryan.
Res., 110 Wallace, P.O. Box 127, 60470. Tel: 815-586-4266. [CEM]
Mission—Grand Ridge, LaSalle Co., St. Mary, R.R. 1, Grand Ridge, 61325. Tel: 815-249-6871.

Rantoul, Champaign Co., St. Malachy's (1888), Revs. Stanley J. Malinowski; Jeffrey Lawrence; Deacon William Shipp Tel: 217-893-0741.
Office: Tel: 217-892-2023; Fax: 217-892-2378.
Res., 311 E. Grove Ave., 61866. Tel: 217-892-2044. [CEM]
School—340 E. Belle Ave., 61866. Tel: 217-892-2011.
Sisters 3; Lay Teachers 10; Students 180.
Convent—304 E. Belle Ave., 61866. Tel: 217-892-2870. Sisters of the Third Order of St. Dominic (Springfield)

Rapids City, Rock Island Co., St. John the Baptist (1857), Rev. James P. DeBisschop.
Res., 1416 Third Ave., P.O. Box 258, 61278. Tel: 309-496-2414. [CEM]
Catechesis/Religious Programs—Students 139.
Mission—Hampton, Rock Island Co., St. Mary, 708 State Ave., Rte. 84, Hampton, 61256. Tel: 309-755-5033. Deacon James Quinn.

Raritan, Henderson Co., Church of St. Patrick, Revs. Thomas Mack; Gregory Ketcham.
Res., P.O. Box 24, 61471. Tel: 309-734-7533.

Roanoke, Woodford Co., St. Joseph (1874), Rev. Neri Greskoviak, O.F.M.
Res., 506 W. Randolph, 61561. Tel: 309-923-3031.

Raritan, Henderson Co., St. Patrick's,
Res., P.O.Box 24, NJ 61471. Tel: 309-746-6223.

Rock Island, Rock Island Co.,

1—St. Mary, (1851). (Formerly Immaculate Conception). Revs. James K. Kramer; George Schroeder, Pastor Emeritus (Retired).
16 Waverly Dr., 61201. Tel: 309-793-1897.
Rectory—2208 Fourth Ave., 61201-8904. Tel: 309-788-3322.

2—Sacred Heart, (1900), Rev. Ambrose Cunningham; Sr. Mary Veronica Grennan, Pastoral Assoc.; Deacon Jack Kettering.
Res., 2810 Fifth Ave., 61201. Tel: 309-794-0660.
School—Jordan Catholic School of Rock Island, Tel: 309-793-7350.
Sisters 4; Lay Teachers 30; Students 605.

3—St. Joseph's, (1876), Rev. J. M. Logan, Admin.; Sr. Germaine Cupp, O.S.B., Pastoral Assoc.
Res., 1316 Second Ave., 61201. Tel: 309-794-9793.
School—Operates as part of Jordan Catholic School of Rock Island.

4—St. Pius X, (1955), Rev. Msgr. Paul E. Showalter; Rev. Francis M. Gallagher; Deacons Timothy Granet; Paul Martin. In res., Rev. Timothy Sauppe.
Res., 2502 29th Ave., 61201. Tel: 309-793-7373.
School—Operates as part of Jordan Catholic School of Rock Island. Tel: 309-793-7350.
Sisters 2; Lay Teachers 35; Students 248.
Catechesis/Religious Programs—Students 168.

Rushville, Schuyler Co., St. Rose (1870), Rev. Robert E. Reynolds.
Res., 319 N. Franklin St., P.O. Box 194, 62681-0292. Tel: 217-322-3424. [JC]

Rutland, La Salle Co., Sacred Heart (1895) (Irish), Rev. James C. Kretz.
Res., c/o 311 W. Santa Fe Ave., P.O. Box 165, Toluca, 61369. Tel: 815-452-2043. [CEM]

St. Augustine, Knox Co., St. Augustine (1863), Rev. Francis M. Oman, I.C.
Mailing Address: 506 N. Main St., Abingdon, 61410. Tel: 301-462-3421. [CEM]

Seneca, La Salle Co., St. Patrick's (1853), Rev. Msgr. Raymond J. Boyle.
Parish Center: 183 W. Union, 61360. Tel: 815-357-8509; Fax: 815-357-6239. [CEM]
Res., 115 S. Market, 61360. Tel: 815-357-6239; Fax: 414-785-9567.
Catechesis/Religious Programs—Fax: 815-357-8509.
Students 140.

Seymour, Champaign Co., St. Boniface (1878), Rev. George E. Wuellner, Pastor Emeritus.
Res., 416 County Rd., 1100 N., 61875. Tel: 217-863-2190. [CEM]

Sheffield, Bureau Co., St. Patrick's (1885), Rev. Paul J. Meismer.
Res., 231 W. Atkinson St., 61361. Tel: 815-454-2251. [CEM]
Mission—Wyanet, Bureau Co., St. Margaret Mary.

Silvis, Rock Island Co., Our Lady of Guadalupe (1963), Rev. Patrick M. Riordan; Deacon Henry Sandoval.
Res., 800 17th St., 61282. Tel: 309-792-3867.
Catechesis/Religious Programs—Students 168.

Spring Valley, Bureau Co.,

1—Immaculate Conception, (1884), Rev. Charles H. Kelly.
Res., 202 N. Greenwood St., 61362. Tel: 815-663-5351. [CEM]

2—St. Anne's. Closed. For sacramental records contact SS. Peter and Paul's, Spring Valley.

3—St. Anthony's, (1904) (Italian), Rev. Donald R. Henderson.
Res., P.O. Box 150, 510 Richard A. Mautino Dr., 61362-0150. Tel: 815-663-3731.
Catechesis/Religious Programs—Charles Palia, D.R.E.
Students 185.

4—SS. Peter and Paul's, (1891) (Polish), Rev. Donald Henderson. In res., Rev. Valentine Liss.
Res., 220 N. Terry St., P.O.Box 209, 61362. Tel: 815-663-3041. [CEM]

Streator, La Salle Co.,

1—Immaculate Conception, (1868) (Irish), Rev. Msgr. James L. Morrissey.
Res., 404 N. Park St., 61364. Tel: 815-672-2034. [CEM]
School—St. Mary's, Tel: 815-672-3811. Mrs. Janice M. Corrigan, Prin.
Lay Teachers 10; Students 120.

2—St. Anthony of Padua, (1881), Revs. Jerome Ham; Gregory Mikula.
Res., 407 S. Park St., 61364. Tel: 815-672-4523. [CEM]
School—410 S. Park St., 61364. Tel: 815-672-3847.
Sisters 1; Lay Teachers 9; Students 218.
Catechesis/Religious Programs—Students 125.

3—St. Casimir, (1916) (Polish), Rev. Gregory Mikula, Admin.
Res., 405 Illinois St., 61364. Tel: 815-672-2206. [CEM]
Catechesis/Religious Programs—Children attend

St. Anthony of Padua Parish Religious Education Classes.

4—ST. STEPHEN'S, (1884) (Slovak), Rev. Msgr. Peter E. Bolerasky; Revs. Jeffery Small; Edward U. Dhm.
Res., 711 Lundy St., 61364. Tel: 815-672-2474. [CEM 2]
School—807 E. Lundy St., 61364. Tel: 815-672-3265.
Sisters 3; Lay Teachers 7; Students 232.

Thomasboro, Champaign Co., St. Elizabeth's (1893), Rev. Charles P. Robards.
Res., 100 Church St., Box 367, 61878. Tel: 217-643-3395; Fax: 217-643-3395. [CEM]
Mission—Ludlow, Champaign Co., Sacred Heart, Ludlow, 60949.

Tiskilwa, Bureau Co., St. Mary's (1881), Rev. Michael Driscoll; Deacon John P. Murphy.
Res., P.O. Box 179, 61368. Tel: 815-646-4451; Fax: 815-646-4376. [CEM]
Mission—Bureau, Bureau Co., St. Francis Xavier. St. Francis Xavier Mission merged with Sacred Heart of Jesus Parish, Granville.

Tolono, Champaign Co., St. Patrick's (1859), Rev. Dennis H. O'Riley.
Res., 212 E. Washington St., P.O. Box K, 61880. Tel: 217-485-5194. [CEM]
Mission—Homer, Champaign Co., St. Charles Borromeo, 110 S. East, Homer, 61849.

Toluca, Marshall Co., St. Ann's (1895) (Italian), Rev. James C. Kretz.
Res., 311 W. Santa Fe Ave., Box 165, 61369. Tel: 815-452-2043. [CEM]

Urbana, Champaign Co., St. Patrick's (1901), Rev. George F. Remm; Sr. Charlene Cesario, S.S.C.M., Pastoral Assoc.; Deacon William McClellan.
Res., 708 W. Main St., 61801. Tel: 217-367-2665; Fax: 217-383-1002.
Catechesis/Religious Programs—Carolyn McElrath, D.R.E.
Students 450.

Utica, La Salle Co., St. Mary Church (1858), Rev. Philip D. Halfacre.
Res., 303 Division St., 61373. Tel: 815-667-4677; Fax: 815-667-4097. [CEM]

Walnut, Bureau Co., St. John's (1912), Rev. John R. Burns.
Res., P.O. Box 370, 204 N. Main St., 61376-0370. Tel: 815-379-2602.

Wapella, De Witt Co., St. Patrick's, Rev. Robert H. Hoffmann.
Res., 308 S. Locust St., 61777. Tel: 217-935-9242. [CEM]

Warsaw, Hancock Co., Sacred Heart (1874) (German), Rev. Raymond M. Lukoskie.
Res., 245 S. 9th St., 62379. Tel: 217-256-3284. [CEM]
Catechesis/Religious Programs—Students 162.
Mission—Hamilton, Hancock Co., St. Mary. Deacons William Gray; Eugene Heintz.

Washburn, Woodford Co., St. Elizabeth, Revs. Dacian Batt, O.F.M.; Benno Heidlage, O.F.M.
Res., 411 E. Parkside Dr., 61570. Tel: 309-248-7151; 367-4407 (St. Mary's Metamora). [CEM]

Washington, Tazewell Co., St. Patrick's (1941), Rev. James J. Swaner; Deacons Earl E. Hietter; Paul Neakrase.
Res., 705 E. Jefferson, 61571. Tel: 309-444-3524.
School—Tel: 309-444-4345; Fax: 309-444-7100.
Sisters of St. Mary of the Presentation 3; Lay Teachers 9; Students 198.
Catechesis/Religious Programs—Michelle Cooper, D.R.E.
Students 268.

Wedron, La Salle Co., St. Joseph's (1947), Rev. John G. Waugh.
Res., Box 60, 60557. Tel: 815-433-2962.

Wenona, Marshall Co., St. Mary's (1867), Rev. William M. Gardner. In res., Rev. William V. Carey, (Retired).
Res., P.O. Box 486, 61377. Tel: 815-853-4558. [CEM]

Westville, Vermilion Co., St. Mary's (1903), Rev. Dean M. Huyguet.
Res., 231 N. State St., 61883. Tel: 217-267-3334; Fax: 217-267-3335. [CEM]
School—225 N. State St., 61883. Tel: 217-267-7730; Fax: 217-267-3327.
Lay Teachers 14; Students 156.

SS. Peter and Paul. Closed. For inquiries for parish records contact St. Mary's, Westville.

Woodhull, Henry Co., St. John's (1889) (Swedish), Rev. Bruce Lopez.
Res., 390 E. Highway Ave., P.O. Box 248, 61490. Tel: 309-334-2180. [CEM 2]

Wyoming, Stark Co., St. Dominic's (1881), Rev. Thomas R. Brajkovich.
Res., 303 Galena Ave., 61491. Tel: 309-695-4031. [CEM]

Mission—Toulon, Stark Co., St. John, Toulon, 61483.

Chaplains of Public Institutions

DANVILLE. *Veterans' Administration Hospital.* Tel: 217-442-8000. Rev. John Schultz, Military Chap.

DWIGHT. *Dwight Correctional Center.* Attended from St. Patrick's, Dwight. Tel: 815-584-3522. Rev. James E. Rickey.

LINCOLN. *Lincoln State School.* Tel: 217-735-2361. Rev. Eugene Prendeville, O.M.I., Chap.
Logan Correctional Center. Vacant. Tel: 217-947-2714; 309-244-8516.

PONTIAC. *Illinois State Penitentiary.* Rev. Jonas Callanan, I.C., Chap., Res., 811 Hill St., 61704. Tel: 815-842-1150.

SHERIDAN. *Illinois Industrial School for Boys.* Rev. John G. Waugh, Chap.

Special Residence:
Reverend Fathers—
Carney, Edward
Zube, Joseph

Special Assignment:
Reverend Monsignors—
Hettinger, Clarence J., Diocesan Tribunal
Reverend Fathers—
Anderson, John C., Propagation of the Faith, Holy Childhood Assn., Catholic Relief Society

---

On Duty Outside the Diocese:
Reverend Fathers—
Baer, M. Stuart, 25 Pocono Rd., Denville, NJ 07834-2995
Guthrie, Raymond P., Diocese of Joliet
Henseler, J. Thomas, Diocese of Springfield, IL
Jacobowski, Raymond G., 10862 Macouba Pl., San Diego, CA 92124-2043
Kuczborski, Joseph M., St. Joan of Arc, 370 W. Third St., Boca Raton, FL 33432
Myers, James E., 32 Middlefield Rd., Menlo Park, CA 94025
Pillon, Gordon, Diocese of Charolette
Powell, Eric S., Congregation for Oriental Churches, Rome
Prendergast, John J., Chap., U.S. Air Force
Przybyla, Kenneth, Diocese of Colorado Springs
Sepich, Lawrence, Archdiocese of Milwaukee

Graduate Studies:
Reverend Fathers—
Swetland, Stuart W., Pope John Paul II Institute, Washington, D.C.

Absent on Leave:
Reverend Fathers—
Collins, Patrick W.
Engels, Francis C., P.O. Box 272, Kewanee, IL 61443-0272
Harbert, William S., 550 E. Carl Sandberg, Apt. 142, Galesburg, IL 61401
Hoghstatter, Theodore, 3747 E. 4th Rd., Mendota, IL 61342
McDermott, Paul B., 1500 Wadsworth, Wadsworth, IL 60083
Ryan, John J., 5500 South Shore Dr., Chicago, IL 60637
Shea, Thomas, Rte. 1, Secor, IL 61771

Retired:
Ciesielski, Heinc, 1553 Sobieski, LaSalle, IL 61301
Culleton, James P., 320 George St., Apt. W.2, Morris, IL 60450
Divan, Anthony L.
Hiland, George, 374 Benchopst, Sebastian, FL 32958
Reverend Monsignors—
Carton, George A., 2223 W. Heading Ave., Peoria, IL 61604
Haas, Murray V., 48 Riverview Dr., East Peoria, IL 61611
Hettinger, Clarence J., 6001 N. University, Peoria, IA 61614
Livingston, Robert C., St. Mary's Rectory, 8819 W. Knox St., Kickapoo, IL 61525
Motsett, C. Bourke, 1806 Washington, Danville, IL 61832
O'Dea, Joseph J., R.R. 3, Box 102AA, Pontiac, IL 61764
Render, Bernard A., 1301 N.E. Glendale Ave., Peoria, IL 61603
Reverend Fathers—
Aldrich, Ralph, 1817 Dale St., San Diego, CA 92102
Blough, E. C., St. Augustine Manor, 1301 N.E. Glendale, Peoria, IL 61603
Colgan, Marvin, St. Joseph's, 401 9th St., Lacon, IL 61540
Condon, Louis M., P.O. Box 10319, 3538 70th St., Moline, IL 61265
Crawford, Richard E., 1414 S. Monroe, Streator, IL 61364
Dietzen, Vincent, 436 South St., Danville, IL 61832
Gaughran, John, 312 N. State St., Westville, IL 61883
Gould, Eugene, 2551 19th Ave., Rock Island, IL 61201. Tel: 309-788-8510
Graves, Joseph A., 5335 Red Sky Dr., Colorado Springs, CO 80915
Hettinger, Paul W., R.R. 2, 3888 E. 1st Rd., Mendota, IL 61342
Hughes, Robert T., 1103 Peppertree Ln., Eureka, IL 61530
Isermann, William D., Livingston Manor, Pontiac, IL 61764
Jagodzinski, Chester C., 905 - 10th St., LaSalle, IL 61301
Jesiolowski, Sylvester E., 315 E. Second Ave., Box 21, Oglesby, IL 61348
Kane, Eugene, 1831 County Rd. 2500 N., Thomasboro, IL 61878
Karl, Charles, 3633 Richwoods Blvd., Peoria, IL 61604
King, John, P.O. Box 79, Starrucla, PA 18462
Krewer, Edward M., 1177 N. Gooding St., La Salle, IL 61301-1581
Lassuy, Raymond J., 7036 E. Orange Blossom Ln., Scottsdale, AZ 85253
Liss, Valentine, 220 Terry, Spring Valley, IL 61362
Mahoney, John A., 620 E. Ogden, Geneseo, IL 61254-1145
Mooney, Harold T., 712 W. Green, Champaign, IL 61820
Morrissey, Jerome V., St. Augustine Manor, 1301 N.E. Glendale Ave., Peoria, IL 61603
Morrissey, Lawrence M., St. Augustine Manor, 1301 N.E. Glendale, Peoria, IL 61603
Niemeyer, John, 132 Mobile-Land Ct., Bloomington, IL 61701
O'Connor, John F., 407 N. Franklin, River Forest, IL 60305
O'Toole, John J., R.R. 2, P.O. Box 85-A, Lexington, IL 61753
Prendergast, Robert E., P.O. Box 548, Kewanee, IL 61443
Raney, Richard E., 685 Mantanzas Ct., Fort Myers Beach, FL 33931
Reynolds, Robert E., 319 N. Franklin, Rushville, IL 62681-0292
Russo, Nicodemus A., 613 Fenwick, San Antonio, TX 78239
Schroeder, George J., 16 Waverly Dr., Rock Island, IL 61201
Shaughnessy, James D., St. Margaret's Living Center, 610 E. First, Spring Valley, IL 61362
Skirkus, Joseph K., Stark Co. Nursing Home, R.R. 1, Box 14, Toulon, IL 61483
Sors, Vladimir, 308 S. Monroe St., Streator, IL 61364
Sprague, George R., St. Augustine Manor, 1301 N.E. Glendale, Peoria, IL 61603
Thompson, George M., 3026 55th St., Moline, IL 61265
Van Raes, Michael, 1301 N.E. Glendale Ave., Peoria, IL 61603
Verhoye, Gerard A., 202 N. State, Box 603, Atkinson, IL 61235
Weishar, John A., St. Francis Continuing Care, 210 S. Fifth St., Burlington, IA 52601
Wuellner, George E., St. Boniface Church, 416 County Rd. 1110 N., Seymour, IL 61875
Very Rev. Canon—
Flattery, John J., Canon in Perpetuum, 20967 Walnut Hill, Danville, IL 61834. Tel: 217-442-2603

Permanent Deacons:
Adams, J. Rodger, Leave of Absence
Baxley, Robert, Our Lady of the Lake, Mahomet
Beltramini, Robert, St. Thomas More, Dalzell
Bott, Herman J., St. Joseph's, Danville
Breeden, Charles, St. Maria Goretti, Coal Valley
Brinker, Kenneth, St. Jude, Dunlap
Burgess, Charles E., St. Hyacinth's, LaSalle
Burton, John, St. Matthew, Farmington
Chaffee, Harley, St. Malachy, Genesco
Clark, William H., Immaculate Conception, Monmouth
Daron, Estal, St. Columba, Ottawa
Dimas, Claudio, Leave of Absence
Efinger, Donald, St. Thomas, Peoria
England, Robert, (Retired), St. Philomena, Peoria
Fahey, Dennis, St. Martin de Porres, Peoria
Filzen, Bernard R., St. Mark's Church, Peoria
Fry, William E., St. Monica's Church, East Peoria
Gaetz, Dale, St. Mary, Lourdes
Granet, Timothy, St. Pius X, Rock Island
Gratkowski, Daniel, Epiphany, Normal
Gray, William, St. Mary Mission, Hamilton

Grimler, Richard, Epiphany, Normal
Hammel, Richard F., St. Philomena's Church, Peoria
Hammond, Richard G., St. Anthony's Church, Bartonville
Harris, Harley, St. Malachy, Geneseo
Hart, Henry, Holy Cross, Champaign
Heintz, Eugene, St. Mary Mission, Hamilton
Hietter, Earl E., St. Patrick's, Washington
Jones, Richard W., St. Ann's, Peoria
Kauth, Richard, St. Edward, Chillicothe
Keefer, Wesley, Leave of Absence
Kettering, Jack M., Sacred Heart, Rock Island
Koeppel, Joseph, St. Ann's, Peoria
Kovachevich, Victor, St. Mary, Canton
Lalande, John, Holy Cross, Champaign
Landry, John, Sacred Heart, Moline
Mancuso, Terry, Leave of Absence
Martin, Paul, St. Pius X, Rock Island
Maubach, James, Holy Family, Peoria
McClellan, William, St. Patrick, Urbana
Meyer, William, Immaculate Conception, Manito
Moch, John, St. Mary, Kewanee
Moran, Thomas, Blessed Sacrament, Morton
Murphy, John, St. Mary, Tiskilwa
Murphy, John, Immaculate Conception, Lacon
Murphy, Robert, Leave of Absence
Murray, Charles, St. Joseph, Pekin
Myers, Robert, St. Martin de Porres, Peoria
Neakrase, Paul, St. Patrick, Washington
Nevinger, Ronald, Leave of Absence
Oenning, Frank W., Leave of Absence
Ohl, Harry, St. Philomena, Peoria
Petri, Darrel, St. Mary, Bloomington
Pogioli, Martin, St. Joseph, Pekin
Quinn, James, St. Mary Mission, Hampton
Rager, Ronald L., St. Monica's Church, East Peoria
Ramirez, Jesse, St. Patrick's, Galesburg
Randazzo, Frank G., St. Maria Goretti, Cont Valley
Rapach, Thomas, St. Jude's, Dunlap
Reid, Michael, Sacred Heart, Peoria
Reising, David, St. Philomena, Peoria
Ringler, William, St. Anthony's, Hoopeston
Roesch, Lewis, Holy Trinity, Bloomington
Sandoval, Henry, Our Lady of Guadalupe, Silvis
Serangeli, Gregory, St. Edward's, Chillicothe
Shipp, William, St. Malachy's, Rantoul
Sims, Fred, St. Mary, Peru
Sloman, William, St. Monica, East Peoria
Slomian, Vincent, Holy Cross, Mendota
Smith, Frank, St. John, Viola
Smith, Richard, Holy Family, Danville
Stevenor, Robert, St. Thomas the Apostle, Peoria Heights
Tomlianovich, Louis A., St. Anthony's, Bartonville
Tuerk, Charles W., St. Mark's Church, Peoria
Van Meltebeck, Martin, St. Mary, Kewanee
Verbeck, Walter, St. Malachy, Geneseo
Wachtel, Thomas, St. Malachy, Geneseo
Waldschmidt, Robert, St. Thomas, Peoria
Zimmerman, Richard, St. Peter, Peoria
Zimmerman, Robert, St. Maria Goretti, Coal Valley

INSTITUTIONS LOCATED IN THE DIOCESE

[A] SEMINARIES, RELIGIOUS OR SCHOLASTICATES

PEORIA. *Rosminian Novitiate*, 2327 W. Heading Ave., 61604. Tel: 309-676-6341. Revs. James Nugent, I.C., Asst./Vocation Dir.; William T. Miller, I.C., Novice Master. In res., Priests 2; Laymen 3; Total Staff 5.

PERU. *St. Bede Abbey and Academy*, 61354. Tel: 815-223-3140; Fax: 815-223-3140, Ext. 292. The Benedictine Society of St. Bede. Rt. Revs. Roger F. Corpus, O.S.B., Abbot; Marion E. Balsavich, O.S.B., (Resigned); Very Rev. Philip D. Davey, O.S.B., Prior; Bro. Nathaniel Grossman, O.S.B., Subprior, Novice Master, Junior Master; Revs. Raymond A. Matulenas, O.S.B.; Stephen J. Souse, O.S.B.; Eugene A. Lauer, O.S.B.; William J. Kirk, O.S.B.; John F. Fitzgerald, O.S.B.; Sebastian C. Lewis, O.S.B.; Kevin D. Gorman, O.S.B.; Alfred J. Scheidler, O.S.B.; Henry H. Fritz, O.S.B.; Bernard A. Horzen, O.S.B.; Claude J. Peifer, O.S.B.; Dunstan R. Morrissey, O.S.B.; Joseph J. Heyd, O.S.B.; Arthur G. Schmit, O.S.B.; Allen J. Mattingly, O.S.B.; Ambrose B. Hessling, O.S.B.; Placid W. Hatfield, O.S.B.; Matthew C. Mazzuchelli, O.S.B.; Benedict B. McKean, O.S.B.; Gabriel G. Bullock, O.S.B.; Harold L. Datzman, O.S.B.; Philip D. Davey, O.S.B.; Ronald L. Margherio, O.S.B.; Samuel D. Pusateri, O.S.B.; Patrick A. Fennell, O.S.B.; Dominic M. Garramone, O.S.B.; James M. Murray, O.S.B.; Bros. George Matsouka, O.S.B.; Bede D. Schuda, O.S.B.; Mark F. Strassburger, O.S.B.; Luke E. McLachlan, O.S.B.; Michael M. Calhoun, O.S.B. Priests 29; Brothers 6.

[B] HIGH SCHOOLS, DIOCESAN AND INTER-PAROCHIAL

PEORIA. *Notre Dame High School*, 5105 N. Sheridan, 61614. Tel: 309-691-8741; Fax: 309-691-0875. Mrs. Jane Hense, Dir. Devel.; Revs. Thomas Seibert, I.C., Asst. Chap.; Gary Caster, Asst. Chap. Priests 2; Sisters 4; Students 987.

BLOOMINGTON. *Central Catholic High School*, 712 N. Center St., 61701. Tel: 309-827-5373; Fax: 309-827-0173. Mrs. Joy Allen, Prin.; Rev. Jeffrey Laible. Priests 1; Lay Teachers 25; Students 297.

DANVILLE. *Schlarman High School*, 61832. Tel: 217-442-2725; Fax: 217-442-0293. James L. Monfredini, Prin.; Rev. R. Anthony Lee. Lay Teachers 14; Students 168.

OTTAWA. *Marquette High School*, 61350. Tel: 815-433-0125; Fax: 815-433-2632. James Messaglia, Prin.; Rev. Philip Halfacre, Chap. Lay Teachers 19; Students 270.

ROCK ISLAND. *Alleman High School*, 1103 40th St., 61201. Tel: 309-786-7793; Fax: 309-786-7834. Colin Letendre, Prin.; Revs. Daniel J. Mirabelli, C.S.V., Dir. of Devel.; Timothy Sauppe, Chap. Priests 2; Sisters 3; Lay Teachers 29; Students 589.

[C] HIGH SCHOOLS, PRIVATE

NAUVOO. *St. Mary's Academy*, 62354. Tel: 217-453-6619; Fax: 217-453-2316. Sr. Phyllis McMurray, O.S.B., Head of School. Sisters of St. Benedict 4; Lay Teachers 13; Students 72.

PERU. *St. Bede Academy*, 61354. Tel: 815-223-3140. Benedictine Fathers and Brothers. Rev. Ronald L. Margherio, O.S.B., Supt.; Mr. Joseph R. Benning, Prin.; Revs. Stephen J. Souse, O.S.B., Registrar; Dominic Garramone, O.S.B., Chap.; Bro. Bede Schuda, O.S.B., CFO; Mr. Bernie Moore, Dean of Students; Mr. Robert Leclercq, Dir. Guidance; Mr. Thomas McGunnigal, Business Mgr. Benedictine Priests 8; Brothers 3; Lay Teachers 14; Students 288.

[D] ELEMENTARY SCHOOLS, PRIVATE

PEORIA. *Father Sweeney School*, 403 N.E. Madison Ave., 61603. Tel: 309-637-6305; Fax: 309-637-6347. (Grades 4-8). The Father John Sweeney Memorial Program for the Academically Gifted. Mrs. Anne Carigen, Prin. Lay Teachers 11; Students 129.

[E] ELEMENTARY SCHOOLS INTER-PAROCHIAL

PEORIA. *Immaculate Conception Pre-Kindergarten*, 2408 W. Heading Ave., 61604. Tel: 309-674-6168. Sr. M. Elaine Haertjens, O.S.F., Dir. Sponsored by the Sisters of St. Francis of the Immaculate Conception. Students 20.

LA SALLE. *La Salle Catholic School*, 1055 Sixth St., 61301. Tel: 815-223-5088. Sr. Kathleen Stafford, Prin. Sisters 1; Lay Teachers 10; Students 169.

MOLINE. *Seton Catholic School*, 1611-14th St., 61265. Tel: 309-757-5500. Sr. Paula Vasquez, O.S.F., Admin. Sisters 2; Lay Teachers 30; Students 654.

ROCK ISLAND. *Jordan Catholic School of Rock Island, Inc.* Facilities at St. Ambrose, St. Pius, and Sacred Heart. 2901-24th St., P.O. Box 3490, 61204-3490. Tel: 309-793-7350. Daniel Lievens, Admin.
Directs the Elementary School System for the Rock Island-Milan area, operating facilities at Sacred Heart, St. Pius X. Parishes in Rock Island and St. Ambrose in Milan. Sisters 2; Lay Teachers 31; Students 584.
Commission on Education for Jordan Catholic School, P.O. Box 3490, 61204-3490. Tel: 309-793-7350. Sisters 2; Lay Teachers 31; Students 584.

[F] RELIGIOUS EDUCATION CENTERS, PRIVATE

PERU. *Sisters of St. Benedict*, Mounted Rte. 6, 61354. Tel: 815-223-6741. Sr. Mary Jane Wallace, O.S.B., Pastoral Assoc., Resurrection Church, La Salle, IL; Sr. Margaret Suerth, O.S.B., IVCC College; Sr. Catherine Maloney, O.S.B., Hospice Care, Illinois Valley Community Hospital, Peru, IL.

[G] CATHOLIC SOCIAL SERVICE OF PEORIA

WEST PEORIA. *Catholic Social Service of Peoria*, 2900 W. Heading Ave., 61604. Tel: 309-671-5730; Fax: 309-674-1664. Ms. Peggy A. Arizzi, Exec Dir.; Mr. Jeff Turnbull, Assoc. Dir.
Catholic Social Service West, 2900 W. Heading Ave., 61604. Tel: 309-671-5700. Foster Home Programs. Tel: 309-671-5750.
Catholic Social Service Institutions, 2900 W. Heading Ave., 61604. Guardian Angel Home. Tel: 309-671-5760. St. Anne Hall. Tel: 309-671-5755. Cabrini Hall Maternity Home. Tel: 309-671-5743. Jesu Children's Enrichment Center. Tel: 309-671-5660.
Peoria Community Area Project / LaCasa Center, 100 Walnut, Suite 404, Peoria, 61602. Tel: 309-637-6327. Family Counseling, Adoption Services, Senior Citizens In-Home Counseling, Women's Counseling & Support Services.
Catholic Social Service Counseling, 413 N.E. Monroe, Peoria, 61603. Tel: 309-672-2707.
Catholic Social Service Branch Offices: 603 N. Center St., Bloomington, 61701. Tel: 309-829-6307. 2714 McGraw Dr., Bloomington, 61704. Tel: 309-662-3840. 416 W. Locust St., Canton, 61520. Tel: 309-647-5014. 1315A Curt Dr., Champaign, 61820. Tel: 217-352-5179. 600 Sager Ave., Danville, 61832. Tel: 217-443-1772; 443-9111. 292 N. Chambers, Galesburg, 61401. Tel: 309-342-1136. 542 Crosat, LaSalle, 61301. Tel: 815-223-4007. 310 S. Logan, Lincoln, 62656. Tel: 217-732-3771. 103 S. 5th St., Lincoln, 62656. Tel: 217-732-9714. 527 Grant St., P.O. Box 355, Macomb, 61455-0355. Tel: 309-833-1791. 15 S. Capital, Ste. 215, Pekin, 61554. Tel: 309-353-9500. 816 20th St., Rock Island, 61201. Tel: 309-794-2200. 823 20th St., Rock Island, 61201. Tel: 309-786-0770. Fort Armstrong, 1900 3rd Ave., Rock Island, 61201. Tel: 309-788-9581.
Catholic Social Service Outreach Offices: Dwight Outreach Office, 126 Mazon Ave., Dwight, 60420. Tel: 815-584-3110. Geneseo Outreach Office, 217 N. Russell, Geneseo, 61254. Tel: 309-944-3518. Kewanee Outreach Office, 223 W. Central Blvd., Kewanee, 61443. Tel: 309-852-2564. Pontiac Outreach Office, 501 N. Chicago, Pontiac, 61764. Tel: 815-844-3629. Streator Outreach Office, 111 E. Spring St., Streator, 61364. Tel: 815-673-2311. Total Institutional Staff 153; Other Staff 525.

[H] CHILDREN'S HOMES

PEORIA. *Catholic Social Service Foster Care Placement*, 2900 W. Heading Ave., 61604. Tel: 309-671-5750; Fax: 309-671-1046.
For a complete listing, refer to the Special Care Facilities section.
Guardian Angel Home.
For a complete listing, refer to the Special Care Facilities section.
St. Anne Residential Treatment Center, 2900 W. Heading Ave., 61604. Tel: 309-671-5755.
For a complete listing, refer to the Special Care Facilities section.

[I] DAY CARE CENTERS

PEORIA. *Jesu Children's Enrichment Center, III*, 2900 W. Heading Ave., 61604. Tel: 309-671-5660. Jesu Childrens' Enrichment Center, I, 2903 W. Heading Ave., West Peoria, 61604. Tel: 309-671-5660. Jesu Childrens' Enrichment Centers, II, 2901 W. Heading Ave., West Peoria, 61604. Tel: 309-671-5660. Staff 41; Capacity 185; Served 225.
South Side Catholic Child Care Center, 1010 W. Johnson St., 61605. Tel: 309-674-7340; Fax: 309-682-2065. Ollie Bracket, Dir. Children 103; Total Staff 15.

[J] GENERAL HOSPITALS

PEORIA. *OSF Healthcare System*, 800 N.E. Glen Oak Ave., 61603.
For a complete listing, refer to the Hospitals section.
St. Francis' Medical Center, 530 N.E. Glen Oak Ave., 61637. Tel: 309-655-2000; Fax: 309-655-2347.
For a complete listing, refer to the Hospitals section.

BLOOMINGTON. *St. Joseph Medical Center*, 2200 E. Washington, 61701. Tel: 309-662-3311; Fax: 309-662-7143.
For a complete listing, refer to the Hospitals section.

DANVILLE. *United Samaritans Medical Center*, 812 N. Logan, 61832. Tel: 217-443-5000; Fax: 217-443-1965.
For a complete listing, refer to the Hospitals section.

GALESBURG. *St. Mary Medical Center*, 3333 N. Seminary St., 61401-1299. Tel: 309-344-3161; Fax: 309-344-9494.
For a complete listing, refer to the Hospitals section.

PONTIAC. *Saint James Hospital*, 610 E. Water, 61764. Tel: 815-842-2828; Fax: 815-842-4912.
For a complete listing, refer to the Hospitals section.

SPRING VALLEY. *St. Margaret's Hospital*, 600 E. First St., 61362. Tel: 815-664-5311; Fax: 815-664-1335.
For a complete listing, refer to the Hospitals section.

STREATOR. *St. Mary's Hospital*, 111 E. Spring St., 61364. Tel: 815-673-2311; Fax: 815-673-4541.
For a complete listing, refer to the Hospitals section.

URBANA. *Covenant Medical Center of Champaign / Urbana*, 1400 W. Park Ave., 61801. Tel: 217-337-2000; Fax: 217-337-4541.
For a complete listing, refer to the Hospitals section.

[K] SPECIAL HOSPITALS AND SANATORIA

PEORIA. *Cabrini Hall Maternity Home*, 2900 W. Heading Ave., 61604. Tel: 309-671-5743.
For a complete listing, refer to the Special Care Facilities section.

LACON. *St. Joseph's Nursing Home*, 61540. Tel: 309-246-2175.
For a complete listing, refer to the Special Care Facilities section.

ROCK ISLAND. *St. Anthony's Continuing Care Center*, 767 30th St., 61201. Tel: 309-788-7631.
For a complete listing, refer to the Special Care Facilities section.

[L] HOMES FOR AGED

PEORIA. *St. Augustine Manor*, 1301 N.E. Glendale Ave., 61603. Tel: 309-674-7069.
For a complete listing, refer to the Special Care Facilities section.
St. Joseph's Home of Peoria, 2223 W. Heading Ave., 61604. Tel: 309-673-7425.
For a complete listing, refer to the Special Care Facilities section.

[M] RETREAT HOUSES

GEORGETOWN. *LaSalette Missionaries*, 5065 Olivet Rd. (Olivet), 61846. Tel: 217-662-6671. Revs. John Paninski, c/o St. Issac Jognes Parish, Georgetown; Thaddeus Plawny, M.S.; Bro. Anthony Sepanik, M.S. Priests 2; Brothers 1; Total Staff 4.

HENRY. *King's House of Retreats - Diocese of Peoria*, 61537. Tel: 309-364-3084. Rev. John C. Anderson, Admin.; Deacon Frederick J. Kruse, Dir. Priests 1; Total in Residence 2; Total Staff 3.

[N] CONVENTS AND RESIDENCES FOR SISTERS

PEORIA. *Immaculate Conception Convent*. 2408 W. Heading Ave., West Peoria, 61604-5096. Tel: 309-674-6168. Motherhouse of the Sisters of St. Francis of the Immaculate Conception. Sr. M. Barbara Buckley, O.S.F., Pres.; Rev. James F. Campbell, Chap. Sisters 17; Professed Sisters 62.
Missionaries of Charity Convent, 506 Hancock St., 61603. Tel: 309-674-7160. Sr. M. Davis, M.C., Supr. Sisters 4; Total Assisted 96; Total Staff 2.
The Poor Clares. Our Lady of the Angels Convent, 3432 W. Baskin Ridge, 61604. Tel: 309-682-3182. Sisters 4.
St. Francis Medical Center Hospital - Convent, 740 N. Glen Oak Ave., 61603. Tel: 309-655-4014. Sr. M. Ildefonsa Richter, O.S.F., Supr., Tel: 309-655-2083; 655-2044. The Sisters of the Third Order of St. Francis 11.
St. Martin de Porres Convent, 709 W. Hurlburt, 61605. Tel: 309-673-4103. Franciscan Apostolic Sisters. Sisters 2; Total Assisted 103; Total Staff 10.

ALTON. *Mary, Queen of the Universe Convent*, 2120 Central Ave., Box 9020, 62002. Sr. M. Ingeborg Rohner, O.S.F.
St. Anselm Convent, 2120 Central Ave., Box 9020, 62002. Sr. M. Ingeborg Rohner, O.S.F.; Sr. Mary Claudia; Sr. Mary Colette; Sr. Mary Johanna; Sr. Mary Luka; Sr. Mary Timothea.

EAST PEORIA. *Motherhouse, The Sisters of the Third Order of St. Francis*, St. Francis Ln., 61611. Tel: 309-699-7215. Sr. Mary Ellen Flannery, O.S.F., Major Supr. Sisters in Residence 33; Total Sisters in Community 75.
Mt. Alverno Novitiate, St. Francis Ln., 61611. Tel: 309-699-9313. Rev. Msgr. Rick J. Oberch, Chap. Novitiate of The Sisters of the Third Order of St. Francis. Sisters 2; Novices 3; Postulants 1.

LACON. *St. Joseph Motherhouse and Novitiate*, 61540. Tel: 309-246-2175. Daughters of St. Francis of Assisi. Sr. M. Vaclava Ballon, Prov. Supr. Sisters 17; Sisters in Community (Professed) 31.

NAUVOO. *St. Mary Monastery, Motherhouse and Novitiate*, 62354. Tel: 217-453-2227. Sr. Ruth Ksyckl, O.S.B., Prioress. Benedictine Sisters of Pontifical Jurisdiction. Sisters in Community 76.

OTTAWA. *Sisters of Mercy of the Americas*, 906 Canal St., Apt. 516, 61350. Tel: 815-433-1357. Sisters 1; Total Asssisted 2; Total Staff 3.

ROCK ISLAND. *St. Mary of the Angels Convent*, 1000-30th St., 61201. Tel: 309-786-3733. Sr. Mary Dolores, O.S.F., Supr.; Rev. Raphael Fabish, Chap. Sisters in Residence 7.

STREATOR. *Franciscan Sisters*, 1509 E. Hickory St., 61364. Tel: 815-673-1259. Sr. Jean-Marie Schwarz, O.S.F., Coord.; Sr. Eleanora Marie Maurer, O.S.F.; Sr. Catherine Wiseen; Sr. Elvon Huser. Sisters 4.

WEST PEORIA. *Mother of Peace Home*, 2223 W. Heading Ave., 61604.

[O] NEWMAN CENTERS

PEORIA. *Newman Foundation at Bradley University & Illinois Central College*, 1116 W. College Ave., 61606-1728. Tel: 309-497-3759; 674-0208 (Office); Fax: 309-497-3759. Gina McKenna, Office Mgr. Congregation of St. John. Revs. Dominique Faure; Antoine Thomas; Bros. Louis Mary; Joseph Mary.

CHAMPAIGN. *St. John's Catholic Student Chapel and Newman Foundation, University of Illinois*, 604 E. Armory Ave., 61820. Tel: 217-344-1184; Fax: 217-344-4957. Rev. Msgr. Edward J. Duncan, S.T.D., Chap.; Revs. Gregory Jozefiak; Robert Barry, O.P.; Joseph T. Hogan. Total in Residence 4; Total Staff 4.

MACOMB. *St. Francis of Assisi Newman Center*, 1401 University Dr., 61455. Tel: 309-837-3988. Rev. Mark DeSutter, Chap.

NORMAL. *St. Robert Bellarmine Newman Center, Illinois State University*, 501 S. Main St., 61761-2996. Tel: 309-452-5046; 452-3983. Rev. Ronald L. Palmer, Chap. Total Staff 3.

ROCK ISLAND. *Augustana College Newman Center*, 61201. Tel: 309-794-7272. Sr. Marilyn Ring, O.S.B.

[P] MISCELLANEOUS

PEORIA. *Ephphetha - Be Opened*, 6514 Parkview, 60614. A musical organization sponsored by the Roman Catholic Diocese of Peoria.
Northside Office of Christian Response, 1825 N.E. Adams St., 61603. Tel: 309-637-0322. Mr. John Truitt, Dir. Total Assisted 186; Total Staff 1.
St. Augustine Community, 1301 N.E. Glendale, 61603. Tel: 309-674-7069. Rev. Mario Shaw, Chap.
Highwood Learning Center, 1301 N.E. Glendale Ave., 61603. Dick Langjahr, Admin. Total Assisted 112; Total Staff 17.
St. Vincent De Paul Society, 3612 N.E. Monroe St., 61603. Diocesan Council and Particular Council of Peoria. John and Mary Truitt, Co-Presidents. Total Assisted 800 Families.
SHARE Food Program of Central Illinois, Inc., 1825 N.E. Adams St., 61603. Tel: 309-637-0282. Total Staff 5.
Society for Religious Vocations, P.O. Box 0911, 61653-0911. Tel: 708-424-4550. Mr. William D. Fairman, Coord. Total in Residence 2; Total Staff 1.

BLOOMINGTON. *Homes of Hope, Inc.* Homes of Hope, 1570 Hunt Dr., Normal, 61761.

MOLINE. *The Order of the Legion of Little Souls of the Merciful Heart of Jesus*, 428 39th St., 61265-1641. Tel: 309-797-8491. Teresa I. Huyten, Moderator; Rev. Richard Soseman, Diocesen Chap.

ROCK ISLAND. *Sacred Heart House of Prayer*, 2810 Fifth Ave., 61201. Tel: 309-786-6785. Sr. Audrey Cleary, O.S.B., Assoc. Dir.; Sr. Marcia Baumert, F.S.P.A., Assoc. Dir. Total Staff 2.

RELIGIOUS INSTITUTES OF MEN REPRESENTED IN THE DIOCESE

For further details refer to the corresponding bracketed number in the Religious Institutes of Men or Women section.

[0200]—*Benedictine Monks*. (St. Bede Abbey).—O.S.B.
[]—*Congregation of St. John*.—F.J.
[1320]—*Clerics of St. Viator*.—C.S.V.
[0480]—*Conventual Franciscans*.—O.F.M.Conv.
[0520]—*Franciscan Friars*. (Prov. of St. John the Baptist).—O.F.M.
[0300]—*Institute of Charity*. (Rome, Italy).—I.C.
[0690]—*Jesuit Fathers and Brothers*. (Chicago Prov.).—S.J.
[0720]—*The Missionaries of Our Lady of La Salette*.—M.S.
[0910]—*Oblates of Mary Immaculate*. (Central Prov.).—O.M.I.
[0430]—*Order of Preachers (Dominicans)*. (Prov. of St. Albert the Great).—O.P.

RELIGIOUS INSTITUTES OF WOMEN REPRESENTED IN THE DIOCESE

[0230]—*Benedictine Sisters of Pontifical Jurisdiction*.—O.S.B.
[2100]—*Congregation of the Humility of Mary*.—C.H.M.
[1920]—*Congregation of the Sisters of the Holy Cross*.—C.S.C.
[1730]—*Congregation of the Sisters of the Third Order of St. Francis, Oldenburg, IN*.—O.S.F.
[1710]—*Congregation of the Third Order of St. Francis of Mary Immaculate, Joliet, IL*.—O.S.F.
[0760]—*Daughters of Charity of St. Vincent de Paul*.—D.C.
[0920]—*Daughters of St. Francis of Assisi*.—D.S.F.
[1070-03]—*Dominican Sisters*.—O.P.
[1070-10]—*Dominican Sisters*.—O.P.
[1450]—*Franciscan Sisters of the Sacred Heart*.—O.S.F.
[1820]—*Hospital Sisters of the Third Order of St. Francis*.—O.S.F.
[2575]—*Institute of the Sisters of Mercy of the Americas*.—R.S.M.
[2710]—*Missionaries of Charity*.—M.C.
[3230]—*Poor Handmaids of Jesus Christ*.—P.H.J.C.
[2970]—*School Sisters of Notre Dame*.—S.S.N.D.
[1680]—*School Sisters of St. Francis*.—O.S.F.
[3520]—*Servants of the Holy Heart of Mary*.—S.S.C.M.
[0430]—*Sisters of Charity of the Blessed Virgin Mary*.—B.V.M.
[0660]—*Sisters of Christian Charity*.—S.C.C.
[2450]—*Sisters of Mary of the Presentation*.—S.M.P.
[3360]—*Sisters of Providence of Saint Mary-of-the-Woods, Indiana*.—S.P.
[1540]—*Sisters of Saint Francis, Clinton, Iowa*.—O.S.F.
[1705]—*The Sisters of St. Francis of Assisi*.—O.S.F.
[1580]—*Sisters of St. Francis of the Immaculate Conception*.—O.S.F.
[3840]—*Sisters of St. Joseph of Corondelet*.—C.S.J.
[1820]—*Sisters of the Third Order of St. Francis (East Peoria, Illinois)*.—O.S.F.

DIOCESAN CEMETERIES

PEORIA. *Catholic Cemetery Association of Peoria, IL*. Tel: 309-674-2760. Operates St. Mary's Cemetery, St. Joseph's Cemetery and Resurrection Cemetery in Peoria.

BLOOMINGTON. *Holy Cross Cemetery Association of Bloomington, IL*. Tel: 309-829-2197.

DANVILLE. *Resurrection Catholic Cemetery Association of Danville, IL*. Tel: 217-431-5100.

FARMER CITY. *St. Joseph Cemetery Association of Farmer City, IL*. Tel: 309-928-3855.

GALESBURG. *St. Joseph's Cemetery Association of Galesburg, IL*. Tel: 309-342-1913.

PEKIN. *Catholic Cemetery Association of Pekin, IL*. Tel: 309-347-6109.

ROCK ISLAND. *Calvary Cemetery Association of Rock Island, IL*. Tel: 309-788-6197; 764-1928.

NECROLOGY

† Carey, William V., Wenona, IL, St. Mary's. —Died Nov. 3, 1996.
† DeWitte, Charles F., (Retired). —Died May 18, 1996.
† Hollerich, Cornelius J., Orion, IL, Mary, Our Lady of Peace. —Died Jan. 25, 1996.
† Peters, Rev. Msgr. Robert, (Retired). —Died Sept. 7, 1996.
† Phelan, Edward J., (Retired). —Died June 25, 1996.

Archdiocese of Philadelphia

(Archidioecesis Philadelphiensis)

His Eminence

ANTHONY CARDINAL BEVILACQUA, D.D., M.A., J.C.D., J.D.

Archbishop of Philadelphia; ordained June 11, 1949; appointed Titular Bishop of Aquaealba and Auxiliary Bishop of Brooklyn October 7, 1980; consecrated November 24, 1980; appointed Bishop of Pittsburgh October 7, 1983; installed December 12, 1983; installed Archbishop of Philadelphia February 11, 1988; Created Cardinal Priest June 28, 1991. *Office: 222 N. 17th St., Philadelphia, PA, 19103-1299. All official correspondence should be sent to this office.*

The Chancery: 222 N. 17th St., Philadelphia, PA, 19103-1299. Tel.: 215-587-4538; Fax: 215-587-3907.

Web site address: http://www.archdiocese-phl.org

Most Reverend

JOHN J. GRAHAM, D.D., V.G.

Retired Auxiliary Bishop of Philadelphia and Titular Bishop of Sabrata; ordained February 26, 1938; appointed Auxiliary Bishop of Philadelphia and Titular Bishop of Sabrata November 25, 1963; consecrated January 7, 1964; retired November 8, 1988. *Res., St. Joseph the Worker Church, 9172 New Falls Rd., Fallsington, PA, 19054.*

Most Reverend

MARTIN N. LOHMULLER, D.D., V.G.

Retired Auxiliary Bishop of Philadelphia and Titular Bishop of Ramsbury; ordained June 3, 1944; appointed Auxiliary Bishop of Philadelphia and Titular Bishop of Ramsbury February 11, 1970; consecrated April 2, 1970; retired October 11, 1994. *Res., Villa Maria House of Studies, King Rd., Immaculata, PA, 19345.*

Most Reverend

LOUIS A. DE SIMONE, D.D., V.G.

Auxiliary Bishop of Philadelphia and Titular Bishop of Cillio; ordained May 10, 1952; appointed Auxiliary Bishop of Philadelphia and Titular Bishop of Cillio June 27, 1981; consecrated August 12, 1981. *Res., St. Monica Church, 2422 S. 17th St., Philadelphia, PA, 19145.*

Most Reverend

EDWARD P. CULLEN, D.D., V.G.

Auxiliary Bishop of Philadelphia and Titular Bishop of Paria in Preconsilare; ordained May 19, 1962; consecrated April 14, 1994. *Res., St. Edmond's Home for Crippled Children, 320 South Roberts Rd., Rosemont, PA, 19010-1298.* Tel.: 610-525-8800.

Most Reverend

ROBERT P. MAGINNIS, D.D., V.G.

Auxiliary Bishop of Philadelphia and Titular Bishop of Siminina; ordained May 13, 1961; consecrated March 11, 1996. *Res., St. Coleman Rectory, 11 Simpson Rd., Ardmore, PA, 19003-2812.* Tel.: 610-642-0545.

Most Reverend

JOSEPH F. MARTINO, D.D., V.G.

Auxiliary Bishop of Philadelphia and Titular Bishop of Celle Di Mauritania; ordained December 18, 1970; consecrated March 11, 1996. *Res., St. Charles Borromeo Seminary, Overbrook, 100 E. Wynnewood Rd., Wynnewood, PA, 19096.* Tel.: 610-667-3394.

DIOCESE ESTABLISHED APRIL 8, 1808.

ERECTED AN ARCHDIOCESE FEBRUARY 12, 1875.

Square Miles 2183.28.

Comprises all the City and County of Philadelphia, and the Counties of Bucks, Chester, Delaware and Montgomery in the State of Pennsylvania.

PATRONS OF THE DIOCESE: I. Immaculate Conception B.V.M., December 8; II. Saints Peter and Paul, Apostles, June 29. This Archdiocese was solemnly consecrated to the Sacred Heart of Jesus on the Feast of Saint Teresa of Avila, October 15, 1873. On May 23, 1952, the Archdiocese of Philadelphia was solemnly consecrated to the Immaculate Heart of Mary at the Shrine of Our Lady of Fatima, Portugal.

For legal titles of parishes and archdiocesan institutions, consult The Chancery.

STATISTICAL OVERVIEW

Personnel	
Cardinal	1
Auxiliary Bishops	4
Retired Bishops	2
Abbots	2
Priests: Diocesan Active in Diocese	604
Priests: Active Outside Diocese	33
Priests: Diocesan in Foreign Missions	4
Priests: Retired, Sick or Absent	187
Number of Diocesan Priests	828
Religious Priests in Diocese	407
Extern Priests in Diocese	28
Ordinations:	
Diocesan Priests	10
Religious Priests	4
Transitional Deacons	7
Permanent Deacons	7
Permanent Deacons in Diocese	142
Total Brothers	141
Total Sisters	3,996
Parishes	
Parishes	287
With Resident Pastor:	
Resident Diocesan Priests	261
Resident Religious Priests	21
Without Resident Pastor:	
Administered by Priests	5
Missions	7
Pastoral Centers	17
Welfare	
Catholic Hospitals	7
Total Assisted	895,666
Health Care Centers	9
Homes for the Aged	19
Total Assisted	6,044
Residential Care of Children	5
Total Assisted	1,078
Day Care and Extended Day Care Centers	1
Total Assisted	91
Specialized Homes	3
Total Assisted	1,564
Special Centers for Social Services	14
Total Assisted	101,596
Residential Care of Disabled	4
Total Assisted	324
Other Institutions	143
Total Assisted	14,308
Educational	
Seminaries, Diocesan	1
Students from This Diocese	86
Students from Other Diocese	126
Seminaries, Religious	1
Students Religious	13
Total Seminarians	99
Colleges and Universities	11
Total Students	31,662
High Schools, Diocesan and Parish	25
Total Students	22,955
High Schools, Private	15
Total Students	6,705
Elementary Schools, Diocesan and Parish	221
Total Students	86,515
Elementary Schools, Private	21
Total Students	5,116
Non-residential Schools for the Disabled	5
Total Students	372
Catechesis/Religious Education:	
High School Students	6,908
Elementary Students	46,107
Total Students Under Catholic Instruction	206,439
Teachers in the Diocese:	
Priests	172
Scholastics	1
Brothers	46
Sisters	995
Lay Teachers	8,491
Vital Statistics	
Receptions into the Church:	
Infant Baptism Totals	17,559
Adult Baptism Totals	1,172
Received into Full Communion	714
First Communions	14,174
Confirmations	15,277
Marriages:	
Catholic	5,293
Interfaith	2,306
Total Marriages	7,599
Deaths	13,085
Total Catholic Population	1,404,268
Total Population	3,737,583

Former Bishops—Most Rev. MICHAEL FRANCIS EGAN, O.F.M., D.D., cons. Oct. 28, 1810; died July 22, 1814.—Most Rev. HENRY CONWELL, D.D., cons. Sept. 24, 1820; died April 22, 1842.—Most Rev. FRANCIS PATRICK KENRICK, D.D., cons. June 6, 1830; transferred to Baltimore in 1851; died July 8, 1863.—Saint JOHN NEPOMUCENE NEUMANN, C.SS.R., D.D., cons. March 28, 1852; died Jan. 5, 1860 Canonized June 19, 1977.—Most Rev. JAMES FREDERIC WOOD, D.D., cons. coadjutor, *cum jure successionis,* April 26, 1857; Bishop of Philadelphia, Jan. 5, 1860; appt. Archbishop Feb. 12, 1875; Sacred Pallium, June 17, 1875; died June 20, 1883.—Most Rev. PATRICK JOHN RYAN, D.D., cons. April 14, 1872 Bishop of Tricomia and Coadjutor with right of succession to the Archbishop of St. Louis; appt. Titular Archbishop of Salamis, Jan. 6, 1884 Archbishop of Philadelphia, June 8, 1884; died Feb. 11, 1911.—Most Rev. EDMOND FRANCIS PRENDERGAST, D.D., cons. Feb. 24, 1897, Titular Bishop of Scillio; Auxiliary Bishop of Philadelphia; Archbishop of Philadelphia, May 27, 1911; died Feb. 26, 1918.—His Eminence DENNIS CARDINAL DOUGHERTY, appt. Bishop of Nueva Segovia, P.I., April 7, 1903; cons. June 14, 1903; transferred to Jaro, P.I., April 19, 1908; transferred to Buffalo Nov. 30, 1915; transferred to Philadelphia April 30, 1918; installed as Archbishop of Philadelphia July 10, 1918 Pallium conferred May 6, 1919; created Cardinal Priest, March 7, 1921; died May 31, 1951.—His Eminence JOHN CARDINAL O'HARA, C.S.C., appt. Military Delegate of Armed Forces and Titular Bishop of Mylasa Dec. 11, 1939; cons. Jan. 15, 1940; transferred to Buffalo Mar. 10, 1945; transferred to Philadelphia Nov. 28, 1951; installed as Archbishop of Philadelphia Jan. 9, 1952 Pallium conferred Jan. 12, 1953; created Cardinal Priest Dec. 15, 1958; died Aug. 28, 1960.—His Eminence JOHN CARDINAL KROL, D.D., J.C.D., ord. Feb. 20, 1937; appt. Titular Bishop of Cadi and Auxiliary Bishop of Cleveland July 11, 1953; cons. Sept. 2, 1953; appt. Archbishop of Philadelphia Feb. 11, 1961; created Cardinal Priest June 26, 1967; retired Feb. 11, 1988; died March 3, 1996.

Vicars General—Most Rev. LOUIS A. DESIMONE, D.D., V.G. Tel: 215-334-4170. Most Rev. EDWARD P. CULLEN, D.D., V.G. Tel: 215-587-4507. Most Rev. ROBERT P. MAGINNIS, D.D., V.G. Tel: 610-642-0545. Most Rev. JOSEPH F. MARTINO, D.D., V.G. Tel: 610-667-3394.

Office of the Cardinal Archbishop—His Eminence ANTHONY CARDINAL BEVILACQUA, D.D., M.A., J.C.D., J.D., Archbishop of Philadelphia; Rev. MICHAEL F. BURBIDGE, Admin. Sec. to the Cardinal Archbishop, *222 N. 17th St., Philadelphia, 19103-1299.* Tel: 215-587-3800.

Office of the Vicar for Administration—Most Rev. EDWARD P. CULLEN, D.D., V.G., Vicar General. Tel: 215-587-4507; Fax: 215-587-4545. Revs. JOSEPH P. DUNCAN, Vicar Admin. JOSEPH R. CISTONE, Asst. Vicar Admin. Tel: 215-587-4549. Assocs. to the Vicar Admin.: Bro. JOSEPH WILLARD, F.S.C.; Mr. JAMES J. BOCK, JR.; Sr. LINDA M. SARIEGO, O.S.F., *222 N. 17th St., Philadelphia, 19103-1299.*

Regional Vicars—Rev. Msgr. JOHN V. BARTOS, Vicar for Bucks County, *685 York Rd., Warminster, 18974.* Tel: 215-957-1525. Rev. Msgr. JAMES T. MCDONOUGH, A.C.S.W., Vicar for Chester County, *2 Forrest Lane, Strafford, 19087-2504.* Tel: 610-995-9450. Rev. Msgr. FRANCIS A. MENNA, Vicar for Delaware County, *14th St. & Lansdowne Ave., Darby, 19023.* Tel: 610-461-0220. Rev. JOHN C. MARINE, Vicar for Montgomery County, *354 Conshohocken State Rd., Gladwyne, 19035.* Tel: 610-896-0567. Rev. Msgr. CHARLES V. DEVLIN, Vicar for Philadelphia-North, *632 W. Erie Ave., Philadelphia, 19140.* Tel: 215-228-1960. Rev. JOHN T. CONWAY, Vicar for Philadelphia-South, *525 Cobbs Pkwy., Philadelphia, 19143.* Tel: 215-476-7484. The Vicar for Philadelphia-South Supervises The St. Peter Claver Evangelization Center. *502 S. 12th St., Philadelphia, 19147.* Tel: 215-735-3164. The Vicar for Philadelphia-North Supervises The Catholic Institute for Evangelization. *4404 N. 5th St., Philadelphia, 19104.* Tel: 215-324-8291.

Office of the Vicar for Religious—

Vicar for Religious—Rev. ALEXANDER J. PALMIERI, J.C.L.

Coordinator for Vocations to Religious Life—Sr. KATHLEEN LEARY, S.S.J., Office: *222 N. 17th St., Philadelphia, 19103-1299.* Tel: 215-587-3795; Fax: 215-587-3790.

The Chancery—Rev. ALEXANDER J. PALMIERI, J.C.L., Chancellor, *222 North 17th St., Philadelphia, 19103-1299.* Tel: 215-587-4538; Fax: 215-587-3907.

Archivist—JOSEPH J. CASINO, M.A., M.S.L.S., Office: *St. Charles Borromeo Seminary, 100 E. Wynnewood Rd., Wynnewood, 19096-3001.* Tel: 610-667-2125.

Metropolitan Tribunal—*222 N. 17th St., Philadelphia, 19103-1299.* Tel: 215-587-3750; Fax: 215-587-0508. Communications should be sent to the above address.

Judicial Vicar—Rev. Msgr. JAMES J. GRAHAM, J.C.D.

Assistant Judicial Vicars—Revs. JOSEPH C. DIECKHAUS, J.C.L.; PAUL A. DIGIROLAMO, J.C.D.; EDUARDO G. MONTERO, J.C.L.

Archdiocesan Judges—Revs. MICHAEL J. FITZGERALD, J.D., J.C.D.; STEVEN J. HARRIS, J.C.D.; ALEXANDER J. PALMIERI, J.C.L.; Rev. Msgr. SAMUEL E. SHOEMAKER, J.C.D.; Rev. Msgr. VINCENT M. WALSH, J.C.D.

Promoter of Justice—Rev. THOMAS A. KANE, J.C.D.

Defenders of the Bond—Revs. JAMES D. BEISEL, M.Div.; JOHN P. BOLAND, M.A.; MICHAEL C. DIIORIO, M.Div.; THOMAS A. KANE, J.C.D.; ROBERT J. POWELL, D.M.A.; JOHN D. REARDON, M.Div.

Approved Advocates—Revs. EDWARD H. BELL, M.Div.; JOSEPH W. BONGARD, M.Div.; MARK J. HUNT, S.T.L.; W. FRED KINDON, M.A.; KENNETH P. MCATEER, M.Div.; GERARD C. MESURE, M.A.; JOSEPH J. NICOLO, M.Div.; JAMES M. OLIVER, M.Div.; Rev. Msgr. RICHARD T. POWERS; Revs. DANIEL J. SULLIVAN, M.Div.; VINCENT F. WELSH, M.Div., M.A.; THOMAS J. WISNIEWSKI, M.Div.; KARL A. ZEUNER, S.T.L.

Secretary—Rev. W. FRED KINDON, M.A.

Notaries—JOAN MCDOWELL; WINIFRED CANNON; MARY KAY DEVLIN.

Management Information Services—Mr. BRUCE JENSEN, Dir. Tel: 215-587-3567.

Office for Audit Services—Mr. PHILIP H. GALLAGHER, JR., C.P.A., Dir. Tel: 215-587-2474; Fax: 215-587-0512.

Office for General Services—Rev. Msgr. LOUIS A. D'ADDEZIO, Dir. Tel: 215-587-3633.

Office for Renewal of Pastoral Life—Most Rev. JOSEPH F. MARTINO, D.D., S.T.L., H.E.D., Dir. Tel: 215-587-0500.

Office for Research and Planning—Mr. ROBERT J. MILLER, Ed.D., Dir. Tel: 215-587-3545; Fax: 215-587-3817.

Secretariat for Catholic Education

All addresses are: *222 N. 17th St., Philadelphia, 19103* unless otherwise indicated.

Secretary for Catholic Education—Rev. Msgr. PHILIP J. CRIBBEN, M.A. Tel: 215-587-3700; Fax: 215-587-5644.

Office of Catholic Education—Rev. Msgr. PHILIP J. CRIBBEN, M.A., Sec. for Catholic Education; RICHARD V. MCCARRON, JR., Supt. of Schools; Rev. DANIEL J. KUTYS, Archdiocesan Dir. of Religious Education. Asst. Supts.: THOMAS ROONEY, Secondary Schools; Sr. MARGARET GRADL, I.H.M., Elementary Schools; Mrs. ELIZABETH O'DONNELL, Special Education.

Office for Youth and Young Adults—Rev. THOMAS M. HIGGINS, Dir.; Mr. LEONARD J. DIPAUL, Asst. Dir., *105 Argyle Rd., Ardmore, 19003.* Tel: 610-649-9476.

Parish Youth Ministry—Mr. LEONARD J. DIPAUL, Dir. Tel: 610-649-9410.

Archdiocesan Boy Scout—Rev. JOHN B. WENDRYCHOWICZ, Chap. Tel: 610-649-9476.

Camp Neumann Conference Center—STEPHEN TAYLOR, Dir. Tel: 215-343-6552.

Agape Camp Fire Program—SUSAN WRIGHT, Dir. Tel: 215-567-4284.

Community Service Corps—DAVID MCKENZIE, Dir. Tel: 215-567-4280.

Secretariat For Catholic Human Services

All addresses are: *222 N. 17th St., Philadelphia, 19103.* Tel: 215-587-3900 unless otherwise indicated.

Secretary for Catholic Human Services—Rev. Msgr. JOSEPH P. GARVIN, L.S.W. Tel: 215-587-3903.

Deputy Secretary—Rev. TIMOTHY C. SENIOR, L.S.W., M.B.A. Tel: 215-587-3908.

Chief Financial Officer—Mr. EDWARD T. CAHILL. Tel: 215-587-3889.

Catholic Social Services (300)—

Catholic Charities of the Archdiocese of Philadelphia—Rev. Msgr. JOSEPH P. GARVIN, L.S.W., Exec. Dir. Tel: 215-587-3903. Rev. TIMOTHY C. SENIOR, L.S.W., M.B.A., Deputy Exec. Dir. Tel: 215-587-3908. Mr. EDWARD T. CAHILL, Chief Financial Officer. Tel: 215-587-3889. Sr. MAUREEN ERDLEN, S.S.J., L.S.W., Dir. Professional Svcs. Tel: 215-587-3557. Mr. JAMES AMATO, L.S.W., Asst. Dir. Tel: 215-587-0529. Ms. ANNE MARIE BUCK, M.S., Asst. Dir. Tel: 215-587-3590. Mr. JOHN C. SMITH, L.S.W., Dir. Children's & Residential Services. Tel: 215-587-3754.

Family Service Centers—

Philadelphia Family Service Department—*227 N. 18th St., Philadelphia, 19103.* Tel: 215-854-7030. Ms. KAREN BECKER, L.S.W., Admin.-Senior Adult Services.

North Philadelphia Service Center—*Casa del Carmen, Reese & Blavis Sts., Philadelphia, 19140.* Tel: 215-329-5660. W. GIOVANNI MORANTE, M.A., Admin.

Northeast Philadelphia Service Center—*7340 Jackson St., Philadelphia, 19136.* Tel: 215-624-5920. Ms. AMY STONER, L.S.W., Site Supvr.

Bucks County Service Center—*100 Levittown Pkwy., Levittown, 19054.* Tel: 215-945-2550. MARGUERITE POWERS, L.S.W., Admin.

Chester County Service Center—*37 S. Pennsylvania Ave. - P.O. Box 119, Avondale, 19311.* Tel: 610-268-3510. Mr. WILLIAM KEFER, L.S.W., Site Supvr.

Delaware County Service Center—*130 E. 7th St., Chester City, 19013.* Tel: 610-876-9183. Mr. JAMES MCMASTER, Admin.

Montgomery County Service Center—*353 E. Johnson Hwy., Norristown, 19401.* Tel: 610-279-7372. Sr. PATRICIA KELLY, M.S.B.T., M.S.W., Site Supvr.

Specialized Services—

Adoption Services Department—*227 N. 18th St., Philadelphia, 19103.* Tel: 215-854-7050. MARY MERMAN, L.S.W., Admin.

Child Care Department—*222 N. 17th St., Philadelphia, 19103.* Tel: 215-587-3575. TERESA THOMPSON, L.S.W., Admin.

Housing/Homeless Services—*227 N. 18th St., Philadelphia, 19103.* Tel: 215-854-7060. JOHN M. WAGNER, Admin.

Support Services—LORRAINE KNIGHT, Admin.-Development. Tel: 215-587-3906. DAVID MOORE, Mgr. Tel: 215-587-2424.

Office for Human Relations—LORRAINE KNIGHT, Admin. Tel: 215-587-3906. Sr. MARION DILLON, M.S.B.T., Dir. Tel: 215-587-5655.

Research & Managememt Information Systems—*227 N. 18th St., Philadelphia, 19103.* Tel: 215-854-7065. LOUISE MAIA, Mgr.

Volunteer Coordinator—*227 N. 18th St., Philadelphia, 19103.* Tel: 215-854-7058. WILLIAM TANGRADI, L.S.W.

Nutritional Development Services—PATRICK F.E. TEMPLE-WEST, Dir., *111 S. 38th St., Philadelphia, 19104.* Tel: 215-895-3470.

Secretariat For Catholic Life and Evangelization

All addresses are: *222 N. 17th St., Philadelphia, 19103;* Fax: 215-587-5631 unless otherwise indicated.

Secretary for Catholic Life and Evangelization—BERNADETTE A. O'CONNELL, M.S., L.S.W. Tel: 215-587-5629.

Deputy Secretary for Catholic Life and Evangelization—THOMAS WAVRO. Tel: 215-587-5667.

Office for Black Catholics—Mrs. LINDA B. LOVE, Dir. Tel: 215-587-3634.

Office for Ecumenical and Interreligious Affairs—Rev. ANDREW J. GOLIAS, S.T.D., Dir. Tel: 215-587-3624.

Office for Evangelization—Sr. KATHLEEN M. COLL, S.S.J., Dir. Tel: 215-587-5630.

Parish Pastoral Councils—MARY GINDHART, Prog. Coord. Tel: 215-587-3694.

Family Life Office—Rev. JOSEPH T. MARINO, M.A., M.Div., Dir., *St. Charles Borromeo Seminary, 1000 E. Wynnewood Rd., Wynnewood, 19096-3069.* Tel: 610-660-9002.

Office for Hispanic Catholics—ANNA C. VEGA, Dir. Tel: 215-587-3786.

Office for Laity—FRANCIS P. COUGHLIN, Dir. Tel: 215-587-3552.

Office for Pastoral Care of Migrants and Refugees—Rev. THOMAS BETZ, O.F.M.Cap., Dir. Tel: 215-587-3540.

Apostleship of the Sea—Bro. HUGH MAGUIRE, F.S.C., Coord., *Seamen's Church Institute, 249 Arch St., Philadelphia, 19106.* Tel: 215-922-2562.

Cambodian Apostolate—Sr. MARY THERESA NGUYEN, A.C.J., Contact, *St. Thomas Aquinas Rectory, 1719 Morris St., Philadelphia, 19145.* Tel: 215-334-2312.

Chinese Apostolates—During regular school hours call 215-922-0999; other times call St. John the Evangelist Rectory. Tel: 215-563-4145.

Filipino Apostolate—Sr. LORETTO MAPA, R.A., Coord. Tel: 215-334-2312.

Haitian Apostolate—Rev. JAMES J. MCGINNIS, Coord., *Office: St. Martin de Porres Rectory, 2340 W. Lehigh Ave., Philadelphia, 19132.* Tel: 215-228-8330.

Hungarian Apostolate—Contact: Office for Pastoral Care for Migrants & Refugees. Tel: 215-587-3540.

Indian Apostolate, Syro Malabar Rite—Rev. JOHN KALLOOR, Coord. Tel: 215-334-4242.

Indian Apostolate, Syro Malankara Rite—Rev. ALEXANDER PANAMKUNNIL, Coord. Tel: 215-329-2320.

Irish Apostolate—Revs. MICHAEL J. KELLY, Contact, *St. Charles Borromeo Seminary, 100 E. Wynnewood Rd., Wynnewood, 19096-3099.* Tel: 610-667-3394, Ext. 268. JOSEPH C. MCLOONE, Contact, *St. Martin of Tours Rectory, 5450 Roosevelt Blvd., Philadelphia, 19124.* Tel: 215-535-2962. MICHAEL J. MCCLEANE, Contact, *Cathedral Basilica of Sts. Peter and Paul, 1723 Race St., Philadelphia, 19103.* Tel: 215-561-1313.

Korean Apostolate—Rev. PAUL HAK MOON CHO, Coord. Tel: 215-548-5535.

Laotian Apostolate—Contact: Office for Pastoral Care for Migrants & Refugees. Tel: 215-587-3540.

Portuguese Apostolate—Rev. JOSE NUNES, Coord., *Office: Incarnation of Our Lord Rectory, 5105 N. 5th St., Philadelphia, 19120.* Tel: 215-329-2320.

Vietnamese Apostolate—Rev. PETER N. QUINN, Coord. Tel: 215-727-0205.

Respect Life Office—Mrs. HELEN P. KELLEHER, Dir. Tel: 215-587-3530.

Department for AIDS Ministry—Rev. JOHN T. MAHER, C.M., Admin. Tel: 215-587-3839.

Department for Pastoral Care for Persons with Disabilities—Mrs. HELEN P. KELLEHER, Admin. Tel: 215-587-3530 (Voice); 0510 (TDD).

Apostolate to Deaf Persons—Rev. ANTHONY RUSSO, C.SS.R., Coord., *St. Boniface Church, 174 Diamond St., Philadelphia, 19122.* Tel: 215-423-9547 (Voice/TDD).

Department for Pro-Life Activities—Mrs. PATRICIA BARCLIFF, Admin. Tel: 215-587-3703. Rev. PAUL S. QUINTER, S.T.D., M.S., Delegate of the Cardinal to Pro-Life Organizations. Tel: 215-587-3703.

Pontifical Society for the Propagation of the Faith—Rev. JAMES FITZPATRICK, Dir. Tel: 215-587-3944.

Pontifical Society of St. Peter Apostle—Rev. JAMES FITZPATRICK, Dir. Tel: 215-587-3944.

Pontifical Missionary Society of the Holy Childhood (Holy Childhood Assn.)—Rev. JAMES FITZPATRICK, Dir. Tel: 215-587-3944.

Pontifical Missionary Union—Rev. JAMES FITZPATRICK, Dir. Tel: 215-587-3944.

Office for Worship—Rev. DANIEL E. MACKLE, Dir. Tel: 215-587-3537.

Secretariat For Clergy

All addresses are: *222 N. 17th St., Philadelphia, 19103* unless otherwise indicated.

Secretary for Clergy—Rev. WILLIAM J. LYNN. Tel: 215-587-4532.

Office for Clergy—

Department Priest Personnel—Revs. WILLIAM J. LYNN, Dir. MICHAEL T. MCCULKEN, Asst. Dir. Tel: 215-587-4532.

Priests' Personnel Board—Most Rev. LOUIS A. DESIMONE, D.D., V.G.; Most Rev. EDWARD P. CULLEN, D.D., V.G.; Rev. Msgr. JOHN V. BARTOS; Revs. MICHAEL F. BURBIDGE; JOHN T. CONWAY; THOMAS J. DEMPSEY; Rev. Msgr. CHARLES V. DEVLIN; Revs. J. MICHAEL FLOOD; WILLIAM J. LYNN; JOHN C. MARINE; MICHAEL J. MCLEANE; Most Rev. ROBERT P. MAGINNIS; Most Rev. JOSEPH F. MARTINO; Rev. Msgr. JAMES T. MCDONOUGH, A.C.S.W.; Rev. Msgr. FRANCIS A. MENNA; Revs. BARTHOLOMEW J. O'BRIEN; CHARLES L. SANGERMANO.

Department of Chaplaincies—Vacant.

Department of Continuing Formation for Diocesan Priests—Rev. THOMAS M. MULLIN, Dir.

Department Retired Clergy—Vacant.

Department Permanent Deacons—Rev. ANDREW J. GOLIAS, S.T.D., Admin.; Sr. VERONICA GROSS, R.S.M., Asst. Admin., *St. Charles Borromeo Seminary, 100 E. Wynnewood Rd., Wynnewood, 19096.* Tel: 610-664-2213.

St. Charles Borromeo Seminary—Rev. Msgr. JAMES E. MOLLOY, M.Div., M.A., Rector, *100 E. Wynnewood Rd., Wynnewood, 19096.* Tel: 610-667-3394.

Vocations Office for Diocesan Priesthood—Rev. GREGORY J. PARLANTE, Dir., *St. Charles Borromeo Seminary, 100 E. Wynnewood Rd., Wynnewood, 19096.* Tel: 610-667-5778.

Secretariat For Temporal Services

All addresses are: *222 N. 17th St., Philadelphia, 19103* unless otherwise indicated.

Secretary for Temporal Services and Chief Financial Officer—Mr. GLENN J. MASAKOWSKI, M.MGT. Tel: 215-587-3959; Fax: 215-598-0599.

Secretariat Coordinator—Ms. MAUREEN VAN THUYNE. Tel: 215-587-3958; Fax: 215-587-0599.

Secretariat Coordinator/Dir.-Parish Financial Services—Mr. EDWARD M. MERENDA, M.B.A., C.P.A. Tel: 215-587-2435; Fax: 215-587-3939.

Office for Capital Projects—DONALD RAUB, M.MGT., Dir. Tel: 215-587-3560; Fax: 215-587-0599.

Catholic Cemeteries Office—MARIE R. RYAN, Dir., *111 S. 38th St., Philadelphia, 19104.* Tel: 215-895-3450; Fax: 215-587-3458.

Human Resources Office—JOHN M. NOLAN, JR., Dir. Tel: 215-587-3910; Fax: 215-587-3572.

Office for Insurance Services—CHARLES J. DEBEVEC, C.P.C.U., Dir. Tel: 215-587-3644; Fax: 215-587-2498.

Office for Legal Services—Rev. MICHAEL J. FITZGERALD, J.D., J.C.D., Dir. Tel: 215-587-0511; Fax: 215-587-0512.

Real Estate Office—EUGENE F. BRAZIL, ESQ., Dir. Tel: 215-587-2453; Fax: 215-598-0512.

Office for Accounting Services—LAURA MONTGOMERY, Dir. Tel: 215-587-3943; Fax: 215-587-3939.

Office for Treasury Services—Tel: 215-587-3630; Fax: 215-587-3939.

Educational Financial Services—Mr. DAVID J. MAGEE, M.B.A., Dir. Tel: 215-587-3755; Fax: 215-587-3525.

Secretariat for External Affairs

All addresses are: *222 N. 17th St., Philadelphia, 19103* unless otherwise indicated.

Secretary for External Affairs—Mr. STAN H. RETIF. Tel: 215-587-3507; Fax: 215-587-3647.

Office for Public Affairs—Mr. GUY L. CIARROCCHI, Dir. Tel: 215-587-3509; Fax: 215-587-0515.

Office for Communications—Ms. SUSAN GIBBS, Dir. Tel: 215-587-3747; Fax: 215-587-3871.

Newspaper - "Catholic Standard and Times"—Rev. PAUL S. QUINTER, S.T.D., M.S., Editor. Tel: 215-587-3660; Fax: 215-587-3979.

Office for Development—STAN H. RETIF, Dir. Tel: 215-587-5650; Fax: 215-587-3647.

Business Leadership Organized for Catholic Schools (BLOCS)—ANNE HILEMAN, Admin., *311 N. 19th St., Philadelphia, 19103-1198.* Tel: 215-557-7868; Fax: 215-587-9059.

Archdiocesan Offices, Boards, Commissions and Committees

All addresses are: *222 N. 17th St., Philadelphia, 19103-1299* unless otherwise indicated.

Blind, Guild for all the—Rev. JOHN J. SHELLEM, Moderator. Tel: 215-587-3592.

Board of Trustees of Lay Employees Retirement Plan—His Eminence ANTHONY CARDINAL BEVILACQUA, D.D., M.A., J.C.D., J.D., Chm.; Mr. GLENN J. MASAKOWSKI, Vice Chm.

Diocesan Priests' Compensation and Benefits Committee—Rev. WILLIAM J. LYNN, Chm.; Most Rev. ROBERT P. MCGINNIS, D.D., V.G.; Rev. Msgr. JOHN E. BRESLIN; Revs. CHARLES E. GORMLEY; FRANCIS P. GROARKE; GEORGE P. HILLER; Mr. GLENN MASAKOWSKI; Mr. ROBERT SIMS; Revs. DANIEL J. SULLIVAN, M.Div.; SAMUEL A. VERRUNI; ROBERT C. VOGAN.

Building Committee—Rev. Msgr. RICHARD J. SKELLY, Chm. (Drawings of building plans are reviewed by this committee).

Cardinal's Committee for Christian Home and Family—Rev. JOSEPH T. MARINO, M.A., Dir., *St. Charles Borromeo Seminary, 100 E. Wynnewood Rd., Wynnewood, 19096.* Tel: 610-660-9002.

Catholic Health Association of the United States, The—Rev. TIMOTHY C. SENIOR, M.S.W., M.B.A., Moderator.

Catholic Relief Services—Rev. Msgr. WILLIAM J. PAUL, Dir., *St. John the Evangelist Church, 752 Big Oak Rd., Morrisville, 19067.* Tel: 215-295-4102.

Censores Librorum—Rev. Msgr. JAMES MCGRATH, J.C.D.; Revs. JOSEPH J. ANDERLONIS, S.T.D.; FRANCIS A. BARSZCZEWSKI, S.T.L., M.S.L.S.; ANDREW J. GOLIAS, S.T.D.

Charismatic Prayer Groups, Delegate of the Cardinal for—Rev. Msgr. D. JAMES MCGETTIGAN, *St. Charles Borromeo Seminary, 100 E. Wynnewood Rd., Wynnewood, 19096.* Tel: 610-668-HOPE.

Charismatic Publication Office - Key of David Publications—Rev. Msgr. VINCENT M. WALSH, J.C.D., *Presentation B.V.M. Church, 204 Haverford Rd., Wynnewood, 19096.* Tel: 610-642-8341.

Church Ministry Training Program—Rev. ANDREW J. GOLIAS, S.T.D., Coord.; Sr. VERONICA GROSS, R.S.M., Asst. Coord., *St. Charles Borromeo Seminary, 100 E. Wynnewood Rd., Wynnewood, 19096.* Tel: 610-664-2213.

College of Consultors—Rev. Msgr. PHILIP J. CRIBBEN, M.A.; Most Rev. EDWARD P. CULLEN, D.D., V.G.; Rev. THOMAS J. DEMPSEY; Most Rev. LOUIS A. DESIMONE, D.D, V.G.; Revs. WILLIAM J. LYNN; Most Rev. ROBERT P. MAGINNIS, D.D., V.G.; Most Rev. JOSEPH F. MARTINO, D.D., V.G.; JAMES P. MATTEO; Rev. Msgr. ROBERT T. MCMANUS; Rev. Msgr. ALBERT V. NORRELL; Revs. BARTHOLOMEW J. O'BRIEN; ALEXANDER J. PALMIERI, J.C.L.

Council of Managers for Development—Most Rev. EDWARD P. CULLEN, D.D., V.G., Chm.; Most Rev. LOUIS A. DESIMONE, D.D., V.G., Vice Chm. Tel: 215-587-4507.

Council of Priests—Revs. EDWARD H. BELL; MICHAEL J. BURKE; ROBERT J. CARROLL; Rev. Msgr. PAUL F. CURRAN; Most Rev. EDWARD P. CULLEN, D.D., V.G.; Most Rev. LOUIS A. DESIMONE, D.D, V.G.; Revs. WILLIAM J. DONNELLY, O.S.A.; THOMAS P. FLANIGAN; JAMES J. FOLEY; RICHARD C. GREEN; JOHN M. HALLORAN; WILLIAM J. LYNN; Most Rev. ROBERT P. MAGINNIS, D.D., V.G.; Most Rev. JOSEPH F. MARTINO, D.D., V.G.; Revs. JAMES P. MATTEO; MICHAEL P. MCCORMAC; HARRY E. MCCREEDY; JOSEPH P. MCGEOWN; Rev. Msgr. JAMES E. MALLOY; Rev. Msgr. ALBERT V. NORRELL; Rev. ALEXANDER J. PALMIERI, J.C.L.; Rev. Msgr. BERNARD J. TRINITY.

Educational Fund—Office for Financial Services. Tel: 215-587-3635.

Holy Name Society—Rev. JOSEPH D. DOUGHERTY, Spiritual Dir., *St. John Bosco Rectory, 235 E. County Line Rd., Hatboro, 19040.* Tel: 215-672-7280.

Information Line, Archdiocesan—Tel: 215-587-3600.

Interparochial Cooperation, Commission for—Rev. ARTHUR E. RODGERS, *St. Matthias Rectory, 128 Bryn Mawr Ave., Bala Cynwyd, 19004.* Tel: 610-664-0207.

Legion of Mary—Rev. Msgr. THOMAS B. FALLS, D.D., *5109 N. Broad St., Philadelphia, 19141.* Tel: 215-457-6343.

Moderator of Priests Conferences—Rev. WILLIAM J. LYNN, Sec. for Clergy. Tel: 215-587-4532.

Parish Sites and Boundaries, Commission for—Rev. Msgr. JAMES E. MORTIMER, Chm.

Pastors Review Board—Revs. THOMAS P. FLANIGAN; JOSEPH T. KANE; Rev. Msgr. ROBERT T. MCMANUS; Rev. Msgr. ALBERT V. NORRELL; Rev. MICHAEL C. PICARD.

Pennsylvania Catholic Conference—(Harrisburg); His Eminence ANTHONY CARDINAL BEVILACQUA, D.D., M.A., J.C.D., J.D., Board of Governors; Rev. JOSEPH R. CRISTONE; Mr. HERBERT G. KEENE, JR., Esq., Administrative Board; Rev. Msgr. PHILIP J. CRIBBEN, M.A.; Mr. RICHARD V. MCCARRON, JR., Education Dept.; Ms. MARGUERITE POWERS; Rev. TIMOTHY C. SENIOR, M.A., M.S.W., M.B.A., Social Welfare Dept.; Sr. MARION DILLON, M.S.B.T.; Mr. STAN H. RETIF, Justice and Rights Dept.

Priests Eucharistic League—Rev. Msgr. JOHN E. GILLESPIE, Dir., *Our Lady of Calvary Church, 11024 Knights Rd., Philadelphia, 19154.* Tel: 215-637-7515.

The Papal Foundation—Rev. Msgr. THOMAS J. BENESTAD, Exec. Dir. Tel: 215-587-4501., *222 N. 17th St., Philadelphia, 19103-1299.*

CLERGY, PARISHES, MISSIONS AND PAROCHIAL SCHOOLS

CITY OF PHILADELPHIA

(Philadelphia County)

1—CATHEDRAL BASILICA OF SS. PETER AND PAUL (1846), Rev. Msgr. James J. Howard; Revs. Michael J. McCleane; William S. Murphy. In res., Rev. Daniel E. Mackle; Deacon Epifano DeJesus.
Res., 1723 Race St., 19103. Tel: 215-561-1313; 1314.
Catechesis/Religious Programs—Students 62.
Chapel—Our Lady of the Miraculous Medal.

2—ST. ADALBERT (Polish), Rev. Msgr. Anthony E. Jaworowski; Revs. Jerome H. Pohl; Ronald M. Jakows; Edward J. Jablonski. In res., Revs. Joseph C. Stec; Marcel Kolakowski, O.F.M.
Res., 2645 E. Allegheny Ave., 19134. Tel: 215-739-3500.
School—3236 Edgemont St., 19134.
Sisters of the Holy Family of Nazareth 3; Lay Teachers 14; Students 362.

3—ST. AGATHA-ST. JAMES. Consolidated 1976. Rev. Karl A. Zeuner. Pastoral Assocs.: Revs. Charles J. Brinkman; George Strausser; Charles Pfeffer; Rayford E. Emmons.
Res., 3728 Chestnut St., 19104. Tel: 215-386-9732; 9733; Fax: 215-386-9734.

4—ST. AGNES-ST. JOHN NEPOMUCENE (1907) (Slovak). Consolidated January 1, 1980. Rev. Francis G. Lendacky.
Res., 319 Brown St., 19123. Tel: 215-627-0340.

5—ALL SAINTS (Bridesburg) (1860), Rev. Edward P. Burke. In res., Rev. James P. Olson.
Res., 2651 Buckius St., 19137. Tel: 215-535-4411; Fax: 215-744-6533. [CEM]
School—4623 E. Thompson St., 19137. Tel: 215-743-0715; 535-3699.
Sisters of St. Francis of Philadelphia 2; Lay Teachers 7; Students 170.

6—ALL SAINTS CHAPEL. Located at Philadelphia General Hospital. Spiritual records transferred to St. Agatha-St. James Church.

7—ST. ALOYSIUS (1894), Rev. John J. Bradley.
Res., 2600 Tasker St., 19145. Tel: 215-468-1088.
School—1624 S. 26th St., 19145. Tel: 215-334-0339.
Bro. Aloysius Hammond, F.C., Prin.
Lay Teachers 9; Students 150.

8—ST. ALPHONSUS. Closed. Located at 1400 S. Fourth St. from 1852 to 1972. Spiritual records are kept at Sacred Heart of Jesus Church.

9—ST. AMBROSE (1923), Revs. James N. Catagnus; Herbert J. Sperger; Raphael Kannanaickal, C.M.I.
Res., 363 E. Roosevelt Blvd., 19120. Tel: 215-329-7900; 7901; Fax: 215-328-9206.
Church—C St. & Roosevelt Blvd., 19120.
School—405 E. Roosevelt Blvd., 19120. Tel: 215-457-3083.
Sisters of St. Joseph 4; Lay Teachers 13; Students 445.

10—ST. ANDREW (1924) (Lithuanian), Revs. Peter M. Burkauskas, Admin.; George D. Degutis, Pastor Emeritus.
Res., 1913 Wallace St., 19130. Tel: 215-765-2322.

11—ST. ANNE, Revs. Thomas J. Kelley; Joseph T. Trinh; Anthony J. Costa. In res., Revs. Joseph R. Cistone; Thomas W. Wassel; Sr. Joan Maguire, S.S.J., Pastoral Min.
Res., 2328 E. Lehigh Ave., 19125. Tel: 215-739-4590.
School—2343 E. Tucker St., 19125.
Sisters of St. Joseph 5; Lay Teachers 19; Students 641.

12—ANNUNCIATION B.V.M., Revs. Paquale R. Catullo, Admin.; William S. Lange.
Res., 1511 S. 10th St., 19147. Tel: 215-334-0159.
School—12th & Wharton Sts., 19147.
Sisters, Servants of the Immaculate Heart of Mary 3; Lay Teachers 7; Students 250.

13—ST. ANSELM (1962), Revs. James J. Shields; Joseph F. Okonski; James A. Lyons. In res., Rev. Msgr. William A. Doolin; Deacon Gerald J. Whartenby.
Res., 12669 Dunks Ferry Rd., 19154. Tel: 215-637-3525; Fax: 215-637-4915.
School—12670 Dunks Ferry Rd., 19154. Tel: 215-632-1133. Sr. Seraphine I.H.M., Prin.; Sr. Rosemary I.H.M., Vice Prin.
Sisters of the Immaculate Heart of Mary 11; Lay Teachers 29; Students 1,031.

14—ST. ANTHONY OF PADUA (1886), Rev. David C. Sicoli.
Res., 2321 Fitzwater St., 19146. Tel: 215-545-6232; Fax: 215-546-3635.

15—ASCENSION OF OUR LORD (1899), Revs. William C. Kaufman; Michael S. Olivere; Deacon Leo Gladnick.
Res., 725 E. Westmoreland St., 19134. Tel: 215-739-1670; Fax: 215-739-1455.
School—735 E. Westmoreland St., 19134. Tel: 215-739-6226.
Sisters of St. Joseph 2; Lay Teachers 9; Students 270.

16—ASSUMPTION B.V.M. (1848). Closed. For inquiries for parish records contact St. John the Evangelist.

17—ST. ATHANASIUS (1928), Rev. Herbert A. Bevard; Deacon Sidney M. Harper.
Res., 2050 Walnut Ln., 19138. Tel: 215-548-2700; Fax: 215-927-6615.
School—7101 Limekiln Pike, 19138. Tel: 215-424-5045.
Sisters 4; Lay Teachers 8; Students 261.

18—ST. AUGUSTINE (1796) (Filipino). First foundation of Augustinian Order in U.S.A. Revs. Walter J. Quinn, O.S.A.; Pascal A. DeCicco, O.S.A., Pastoral Assoc. In res., Rev. William J. Krupa, O.S.A.
Res., 243 N. Lawrence S., 19106-1195. Tel: 215-627-1838; Fax: 215-627-3911.
School—St. Mary's Interparochial School, Fifth & Locust Sts., 19106. Tel: 215-923-7522.

19—ST. BARBARA (1921) (African American), Revs. John T. Lyons; Thomas F. Loughrey, Pastor Emeritus. In res., Rev. Joseph F. Gleason.
Res., 5359 Lebanon Ave., 19131. Tel: 215-473-1044.
School—5336 Diamond St., 19131. Tel: 215-477-3456.
Catechesis/Religious Programs—Students 163.

20—ST. BARNABAS (1919), Revs. Bernard J. Herron; John F. Babowitch; John J. Van Stone; James J. McLaughlin; Deacon Leonard J. Wolkowicz.
Res., 6300 Buist Ave., 19142. Tel: 215-726-1119; 1120; Fax: 215-726-1180.
School—64th St. & Buist Ave., 19142. Tel: 215-729-3603.
Sisters of Immaculate Heart of Mary 6; Lay Teachers 21; Students 601.
Convent—6328 Buist Ave., 19142. Tel: 215-729-1572.

21—ST. BARTHOLOMEW (1919), Revs. Joseph P. Denny; Carl F. Janicki; James J. Anziano. In res., Revs. Ildebrando E. Schifalacqua; John C. Dougherty; Deacon John J. Bean.
Res., 5600 Jackson St., 19124. Tel: 215-831-1224; 1225; Fax: 215-831-0467.
School—Jackson & Sanger St., 19124. Tel: 215-744-6393.
Lay Teachers 26; Students 714.
Catechesis/Religious Programs—Students 200.

22—ST. BENEDICT (1922), Rev. George B. Moore; Deacons Stephen Hopkins; James T. Walker; Calvin C. Smith.
Res., 1940 E. Chelten Ave., 19138. Tel: 215-924-4401.
School—1935 Medary Ave., 19138. Tel: 215-424-8073.
Lay Teachers 9; Students 200.
Convent—1942 E. Chelten Ave., 19138. Tel: 215-924-2876.

23—ST. BERNARD (1927), Revs. Charles J. Sullivan; Thomas J. Dunleavy; David Machain; Rev. Msgr. John B. Fee, Pastor Emeritus. In res., Rev. Paul A. DiGirolamo.
Res., 7341 Cottage St., 19136. Tel: 215-333-0446; Fax: 215-333-3215.
School—7340 Jackson St., 19136. Tel: 215-624-5204; Fax: 215-624-8806.
Lay Teachers 29; Students 805.

24—ST. BONAVENTURE (1889-1993). Closed. Spiritual records are kept at St. Veronica Church.

25—ST. BONIFACE (1865), Revs. Sean J. McGillicuddy, C.Ss.R.; Wenceslaus J. Smutny, C.SS.R.; Richard S. Bennett, C.Ss.R.; Bro. Mauel Martinez, C.SS.R.; Deacon Mario Lozada. In res., Revs. Anthony T. Russo, C.SS.R., Deaf Apostolate; Norman Simmons, C.SS.R.; Gerard Brinkmann, C.SS.R.; Alexander F. Ortiz, C.S.s.R.; Kevin R. Murray, C.SS.R.; Bro. Edgardo Lugo, C.Ss.R.
Res., 174 W. Diamond St., 19122. Tel: 215-739-6376; Fax: 215-739-5102.
School—142 W. Diamond St., 19122. Tel: 215-634-6588.
Religious 1; Lay Teachers 10.
Catechesis/Religious Programs—Students 230.

26—ST. BRENDAN (1925-1934). Closed. Spiritual records are kept at St. Francis of Assisi Church.

27—ST. BRIDGET (1853), Rev. Richard R. York.
Res., 3667 Midvale Ave., 19129. Tel: 215-844-4126; Fax: 215-842-2536.
School—3636 Stanton St., 19129. Tel: 215-843-2828. Sr. Christine Konopelski, S.S.J., Prin.
Sisters of St. Joseph 4; Lay Teachers 7; Students 241.
Convent—3665 Midvale Ave., 19129. Tel: 215-844-5663.

28—ST. CALLISTUS (1921), Revs. John F. Hummell, Admin.; Carmen F. Taraborelli.
Res., 700 N. 67th St., 19151-3614. Tel: 215-473-4417; Fax: 215-473-6728.
Convent—6714 Lansdowne Ave., 19151. Tel: 215-473-8153. Religious Sisters of Mercy

29—ST. CARTHAGE (1915) (African American), Rev. Msgr. Albert V. Norrell. In res., Rev. John T. Conway.
Res., 525 Cobbs Creek Pkwy., 19143. Tel: 215-747-3250; Fax: 215-476-9974.
School—6225 Cedar Ave., 19143. Tel: 215-748-4450. Lawrence C. Schoppet, IV, Prin.
Sisters of St. Joseph 1; Lay Teachers 9; Students 285.

30—ST. CASIMIR (1803) (Lithuanian), Rev. Eugene A. Wassel.
Res., 324 Wharton St., 19147. Tel: 215-468-2052.
School—Tel: 215-334-8407. Mrs. Ann O'Connor, Prin.
Lay Teachers 8; Students 149.

31—ST. CATHERINE OF SIENA (1910-1972). Closed. For inquiries for parish records contact the Chancery.

32—ST. CECILIA (1911), Rev. Msgr. Francis X. Dreger; Revs. Stephen F. Katziner; Marcel Knotek; Scott D. Brockson; Deacon Louis Malfara. In res., Rev. Daniel J. Kearns.
Res., 535 Rhawn St., 19111. Tel: 215-725-1240; Fax: 215-725-2130.
School—525 Rhawn St., 19111. Tel: 215-725-8588.
Sisters of the Immaculate Heart of Mary 9; Lay Teachers 32; Students 1,042.
Catechesis/Religious Programs—Tel: 215-725-2580.
Students 200.

33—ST. CHARLES BORROMEO (1868) (African American), Rev. George A. Mayoros.
Res., 902 S. 20th St., 19146. Tel: 215-735-0600.
Church—20th & Christian Sts., 19146.
School—2019 Montrose St., 19146. Tel: 215-735-6879. Sr. Denise Ware, S.F.C.C., Prin.
Lay Teachers 14; Students 384.
St. Charles Preschool—1941 Christian St., 19146. Tel: 215-735-1475.
Lay Teachers 3; Students 78.
Catechesis/Religious Programs—Tel: 215-735-6898.
Students 55.

34—CHRIST THE KING (1963), Revs. Henry G. Birkhead; Gregory J. Fairbanks; James T. Henry; Deacon Walter C. Fulmer.
Res., 3252 Chesterfield Rd., 19114. Tel: 215-632-1144; Fax: 215-632-4933.
School—3205 Chesterfield Rd., 19114. Tel: 215-632-1375; 637-3838.
Sisters of St. Joseph 6; Lay Teachers 19; Students 521.

35—ST. CHRISTOPHER (1950), Rev. Msgr. John E. Breslin; Revs. Vincent F. Welsh; Robert Marczewski; Joseph F. Smith, Pastor Emeritus.
Res., 13301 Proctor Rd., 19116. Tel: 215-673-5177; Fax: 215-698-0585.
School—13307 Proctor Rd., 19116. Tel: 215-673-5787; Fax: 215-673-8511.
Sisters of Mercy 3; Lay Teachers 34; Students 930.
Catechesis/Religious Programs—Students 180.

36—ST. CLEMENT (1865), Revs. John J. Cox; James P. Gorman; Deacon Walter Lance. In res., Rev. Joseph W. McCloskey.
Res., 2210 S. 71st St., 19142-1108. Tel: 215-729-0500.
School—SS. Clement-Irenaeus Consolidated School, 72nd St. & Paschall Ave., 19142-1108. Tel: 215-729-8368.
Sisters, Servants of the Immaculate Heart of Mary 7; Lay Teachers 19; Students 509.

37—ST. COLUMBA (1895-1993). Closed. Spiritual records are kept at St. Martin De Porres Church.

38—CORPUS CHRISTI (1921-1987). Closed. Spiritual records are kept at St. Martin De Porres Church.

39—ST. DOMINIC (1849), Revs. Joseph J. Sweeney; Bernard J. Benischeck; Winson Parekkat, C.M.I.; Thomas J. Rooney. Pastors Emeriti: Rev. Msgr. Joseph G. Sikora; Rev. Joseph A. McCloskey.
Res., 8504 Frankford Ave., 19136. Tel: 215-624-5502; 5503; Fax: 215-333-1750. [CEM]
School—8512 Frankford Ave., 19136. Tel: 215-333-6703.
Sisters, Servants of the Immaculate Heart of Mary 14; Lay Teachers 25; Students 725.
Convent—8510 Frankford Ave., 19136. Tel: 215-333-0144.

40—ST. DONATO (1910) (Italian), Revs. Ferdinand Buccafurni; Peter J. Talocci.
Res., 403 N. 65th St., 19151. Tel: 215-747-4131.
School—405 N. 65th St., 19151. Tel: 215-748-2994.
Sisters 1; Lay Teachers 10; Students 216.

41—ST. EDMOND (1912), Rev. Francis P. Groarke.
Res., 2130 S. 21st St., 19145. Tel: 215-334-3755; Fax: 215-334-2081.
School—23rd and Mifflin Sts., 19145. Tel: 215-334-0398.
Sisters, Servants of the Immaculate Heart of Mary 3; Lay Teachers 9; Students 185.

42—ST. EDWARD THE CONFESSOR (1865-1993). Closed. Spiritual records are kept at Visitation Church.

43—ST. ELIZABETH (1872-1993). Closed. Spiritual records are kept at St. Martin De Porres Church.

44—EPIPHANY OF OUR LORD (1889), Revs. Dominic M. Chiaravalle; John E. Calabro; Peter C. Funk; Kuriakose Mampuzhakal (India); Paul F. Maurer, Pastor Emeritus.
Res., 1121 Jackson St., 19148. Tel: 215-334-1035; Fax: 215-334-7885.
School—13th & Jackson Sts., 19148. Tel: 215-467-5385.
Lay Teachers 18; Students 500.

45—ST. FRANCIS OF ASSISI (1899), Rev. William S. Harrison; Deacon Allen Stevens.
Res., 45 W. Logan St., 19144. Tel: 215-842-1287.
School—St. Martin De Porres School, 44 W. Logan St., 19144. Tel: 215-842-1266. Miss Denise Winterberger, Prin.
Sisters of St. Joseph 1; Lay Teachers 7; Students 242.

46—ST. FRANCIS DE SALES (1890), Rev. Anthony W. Janton. In res., Rev. Herman Behrens, S.C.J.
Res., 4625 Springfield Ave., 19143. Tel: 215-222-5819; Fax: 215-222-5821.
School—912 S. 47th St., 19143. Tel: 215-387-1749; 727-3929.
Sisters, Servants of the Immaculate Heart of Mary 5; Lay Teachers 14; Students 535.
Catechesis/Religious Programs—Students 36.

47—ST. FRANCIS XAVIER, Revs. Paul C. Convery; Aloysius H. Vath, Pastor Emeritus. In res., Rev. George G. Thiers.
Res., 2319 Green St., 19130. Tel: 215-765-4568.
Oratory—2321 Green St., 19130. Tel: 215-765-4049.
School—24th & Wallace Sts., 19130. Tel: 215-763-6564.
Sisters, Servants of the Immaculate Heart of Mary 5; Lay Teachers 7; Students 269.
Convent—2324 Green St., 19130. Tel: 215-665-1340.

48—ST. GABRIEL (1895), Revs. Francis X. Cortese, O.Praem.; John J. Novielli, O.Praem.; Edward J. Kimpel, O.Praem., (Retired).
Res., 2917 Dickinson St., 19146. Tel: 215-463-4060; Fax: 215-755-2680.
School—30th & Dickinson Sts., 19146. Tel: 215-468-7230.
Sisters, Servants of the Immaculate Heart of Mary 3; Lay Teachers 12; Students 320.

49—ST. GEORGE (1902) (Lithuanian), Rev. Joseph J. Anderlonis; Rev. Msgr. Vito J. Martusevich, Pastor Emeritus.

Res., 3580 Salmon St., 19134. Tel: 215-739-3102; Fax: 215-739-7217.
School—2700 E. Venango St., 19134. Tel: 215-634-8803.
Lay Teachers 9; Students 204.
Convent—3570 Salmon St., 19134. Tel: 215-739-0472.
Sisters 4.

50—GESU (1868-1993). Closed. Spiritual records are kept at St. Malachy Church.

51—GOOD SHEPHERD (1925), Revs. Thomas J. Smith; Peter N. Quinn; Joseph P. Gausch, Pastor Emeritus.
Res., 6667 Chester Ave., 19142. Tel: 215-727-8300; Fax: 215-727-5932.
School—66th St. & Chester Ave., 19142. Tel: 215-729-8766.
Convent—Tel: 215-729-4043.
Sisters, Servants of the Immaculate Heart of Mary 3; Lay Teachers 8; Students 273.

52—ST. GREGORY. Closed. Located at 52nd and Warren Sts. from 1895 to 1981. Spiritual records kept at St. Rose of Lima Church.

53—ST. HEDWIG (1907) (Polish), Rev. Joseph C. Stec. In res., Rev. Edward J. Kennedy.
Res., 802 N. 24th St., 19130. Tel: 215-765-8550.

54—ST. HELENA (1924), Rev. Craig F. Brugger; Most Rev. John J. Graham, Pastor Emeritus; Revs. Albert C. DiGiacobbe; John M. Donohie.
Res., 6161 N. Fifth St., 19120-1497. Tel: 215-424-1300.
School—6101 N. Fifth St., 19120. Tel: 215-549-2947.
Sisters of St. Joseph 5; Lay Teachers 15; Students 437.

55—ST. HENRY (1916-1993) (German). Closed. Spiritual records are kept at Incarnation Church.

56—HOLY ANGELS (1906) (Korean), Revs. Paul H. Cho, Admin.; Luke J. Won; Edward J. Chwieroth.
Res., 70th Ave. & Old York Rd., 19126. Tel: 215-548-5535; Fax: 215-224-6615.
Catechesis / Religious Programs—Students 200.

57—HOLY CHILD (1909-1993). Closed. Spiritual records are kept at Our Lady of Hope Church.

58—HOLY CROSS (1890), Rev. H. James Hutchins; Deacon Richard Coyne. In res., Rev. Ronald Jakows.
Res., 154 E. Mt. Airy Ave., 19119. Tel: 215-247-0661.
School—144 E. Mt. Airy Ave., 19119. Tel: 215-242-0414.
Sisters of St. Joseph 6; Lay Teachers 8; Students 235.
Convent—148 E. Mt. Airy Ave., 19119. Tel: 215-247-0262.
Catechesis / Religious Programs—Tel: 215-247-3405. Mr. James Nelson, D.R.E.
Students 25.

59—HOLY FAMILY (1885), Revs. Francis X. McKee; James J. Martin; John W. Gsell, Pastor Emeritus. In res., Rev. Thomas F. Gibbons, M.M.; Deacon Eugene R. Leahy.
Res., 234 Hermitage St., 19127. Tel: 215-482-0450; 482-8608; Fax: 215-482-7531.
School—242 Hermitage St., 19127. Tel: 215-487-2796; 483-0903; Fax: 215-487-9134.
Sisters of the Immaculate Heart of Mary 4; Lay Teachers 14; Students 300.

60—HOLY INNOCENTS (1927), Revs. Michael J. Burke; Vincent The Tung Pham; Timothy F. O'Sullivan; Paul A. Castellani.
Res., 1337 E. Hunting Park Ave., 19124. Tel: 215-743-2600; Fax: 215-743-8041.
School—1312 E. Bristol St., 19124. Tel: 215-743-5909.
Sisters, Servants of the Immaculate Heart of Mary 10; Lay Teachers 23; Students 837.

61—HOLY NAME OF JESUS (Kensington) (1904), Very Rev. Stephen F. Carmody, O.P. Pastoral Associates: Revs. Nicholas R. Reid, O.P.; Ralph V. Townsend, O.P. In res., Rev. Michael Novacki, O.P.
Res., 701 E. Gaul St., P.O. Box 3605, 19125-2896. Tel: 215-739-3960; Fax: 215-739-7597.
School—E. Berks & Gaul Streets, 19125. Tel: 215-423-3334.
Sisters, Servants of the Immaculate Heart of Mary 6; Lay Teachers 18; Students 241.
Preschool:—Kensington, Tel: 215-423-3041. Sr. Christine Lamb, I.H.M., Prin.

62—HOLY REDEEMER (1941) (Chinese). Unassigned. (Mission Chapel of the Church of St. John the Evangelist).
School—915 Vine St., 19107. Tel: 215-922-0999; Fax: 215-922-6674.
Lay Teachers 9; Students 241.
Parish House:—916 Wood St., 19107. Tel: 215-627-5293; Fax: 215-563-9980.

63—HOLY SPIRIT (1964), Revs. John E. Mulgrew; Walter Thelappilly, C.M.I. (India).
Res., 1900 Geary St., 19145. Tel: 215-334-4242.
School—1845 Hartranft St., 19145. Tel: 215-389-0715; Fax: 215-336-7719.
Poor Servants of the Mother of God 3; Lay Teachers 7; Students 180.
Catechesis / Religious Programs—Students 220.

64—HOLY TRINITY (1789) (German). Attended by Old St. Mary's Church, Sixth and Spruce Streets.
252 South Fourth St., 19106. Tel: 215-923-7930. [CEM]

65—ST. HUBERT (1924). Located at Torresdale and Cottman Aves. from 1924-1940. Spiritual records transferred to St. Bernard Rectory.
7341 Cottage St., 19136. Tel: 215-333-0446.; Records prior to 1923: St. Leo Rectory: 6658 Keystone St., 19135. Tel: 215-333-0340.

66—ST. HUGH OF CLUNY (1922), Rev. Dennis M. Mooney; Deacon Jose L. Lozada-Figueroa. In res., Rev. Nelson J. Perez.
Res., 145 W. Tioga St., 19140. Tel: 215-634-1800.
School—3533 N. Mascher St., 19140. Tel: 215-634-3060; 634-3183.
Sisters of St. Joseph 2; Lay Teachers 8; Students 251.
Catechesis / Religious Programs—Students 195.

67—ST. IGNATIUS OF LOYOLA (1893) (African American), Rev. Federico A. Britto.
Res., 636 N. 43rd St., 19104. Tel: 215-386-5065; 386-1058; Fax: 215-386-2832.
School—644 N. 43rd St., 19104. Tel: 215-386-0302. Sr. Christine Smith, S.B.S., Prin.
Sisters of the Blessed Sacrament 5; Lay Teachers 7; Students 267.
Chaplaincy—St. Ignatius Nursing Home, Tel: 215-349-8800.

68—IMMACULATE CONCEPTION (1869), Revs. William A. Dombrow; Edmund C. Wesolowski.
Res., 1020 N. Front St., 19123. Tel: 215-627-2702; Fax: 215-627-7344.

69—IMMACULATE CONCEPTION (1902), Revs. Stephen F. Cantwell, C.M.; Richard J. Rock, C.M. In res., Revs. William J. O'Brien, C.M.; Charles T. Plock, C.M.; John W. Gouldrick, C.M.; Egbert J. Browne.
Res., 1020 E. Price St., 19138. Tel: 215-843-9468; Fax: 215-843-6570.

70—IMMACULATE HEART OF MARY (1952), Revs. Bartholomew J. O'Brien; Edward C. Kelly; Matthew J. Kornacki. In res., Rev. Francis W. Beach.
Res., 819 Cathedral Rd., 19128. Tel: 215-483-1000; Fax: 215-483-1732.
School—823 Cathedral Rd., 19128. Tel: 215-482-2029.
Lay Teachers 25; Students 521.

71—INCARNATION OF OUR LORD (1900), Rev. Msgr. Richard T. Powers; Revs. Geraldo J. Pinero; John Kallor. In res., Rev. Jose Nunes, (Portuguese Apostolate).
Res., 5105 N. Fifth St., 19120. Tel: 215-329-2320; Fax: 215-329-6149.
School—Tel: 215-457-2779. Sr. Patricia A. Walsh, I.H.M., Prin.
Sisters, Servants of the Immaculate Heart of Mary 4; Lay Teachers 15; Students 585.
Convent—401 W. Lindley Ave., 19120. Tel: 215-329-0672.

72—SAINT IRENAEUS (1966), Revs. Gavin W. Muir; A. James Chapman, Pastor Emeritus.
Res., 2728 South 73rd St., 19153. Tel: 215-727-2888; Fax: 215-329-6149.
School—Ss. Clement-Irenaeus Consolidated School, Tel: 215-729-8368.

73—ST. JAMES (1850-1976). Consolidated with St. Agatha to form St. Agatha-St. James. See separate listing for details.

74—ST. JEROME (1955), Revs. Joseph B. Graham; William J. Bispels; Martin F. O'Hara, Pastor Emeritus; Joseph P. Grailey; Deacons Frank Clark; Charles Pavonarius. In res., Rev. Edward V. Avery.
Res., 8100 Colfax St., 19136. Tel: 215-333-4461; Fax: 215-333-6791.
School—3031 Stamford St., 19136. Tel: 215-624-0637; Fax: 215-624-5711. William McDowell, Prin.
Sisters of St. Joseph 3; Lay Teachers 30; Students 914.

75—ST. JOACHIM (1845), Revs. Eugene J. McBride, O.S.F.S.; George W. Martin, O.S.F.S. In res., Rev. Charles J. Norman, O.S.F.S.; Bro. Robert Drelich, O.S.F.S.
Res., 1527 Church St., 19124. Tel: 215-535-0580; Fax: 215-831-1788. [CEM]
School—Penn & Church Sts., 19124. Tel: 215-288-9501.
Sisters, Servants of the Immaculate Heart of Mary 10; Lay Teachers 11; Students 315.
Catechesis / Religious Programs—Students 170.
Convent—1509 Church St., Tel: 215-535-6177.

76—ST. JOAN OF ARC (1919), Revs. James P. Matteo; Michael J. Heim. In res., Rev. Msgr. Philip J. Cribben.
Res., 2025 E. Atlantic St., 19134. Tel: 215-535-4641; 535-5138; Fax: 215-535-7477.
School—3556 Frankford Ave., 19134. Tel: 215-533-3210.
Sisters, Servants of the Immaculate Heart of Mary 6; Lay Teachers 9; Students 272.
Convent—3550 Frankford Ave., 19134. Tel: 215-533-0959.

77—ST. JOHN THE BAPTIST (1831), Revs. Frederick J. Riegler; Robert T. Feeney. In res., Rev. Thomas J. Grumm.
Res., 146 Rector St., 19127. Tel: 215-482-4600. [CEM]
School—4211 Cresson St., 19127. Tel: 215-483-0903.
Sisters, Servants of the Immaculate Heart of Mary 6; Lay Teachers 15; Students 530.

78—ST. JOHN CANTIUS (1892) (Polish), Rev. Msgr. Bernard E. Witkowski; Rev. Msgr. Adam J. Bydlon, Pastor Emeritus; Revs. Andrew D. McCormick; Dennis J. Witalec.
Res., 4415 Almond St., 19137. Tel: 215-535-6667.
School—4435 Almond St., 19137. Tel: 215-535-3446.
Sisters of the Holy Family of Nazareth 4; Lay Teachers 18; Students 369; Kindergarten 20.

79—ST. JOHN THE EVANGELIST (1830), Revs. Frederick Krause, O.F.M.Cap.; Roman M. Kozacheson, O.F.M.Cap.; Anselm Martin, O.F.M.Cap.; Dennis Klemash, O.F.M.Cap.; Bro. James Gavin, O.F.M.Cap. In res., Rev. Thomas Betz, O.F.M.Cap.
Res., 21 S. 13th St., 19107. Tel: 215-563-4145; Fax: 215-563-1770. [CEM]
Mission—Philadelphia, Philadelphia Co., Holy Redeemer Chinese Church, 915 Vine St., 19107. Tel: 215-922-0999; Fax: 215-922-6674.

80—ST. JOHN NEPOMUCENE (Slovak). Consolidated with St. John Nepomucene and St. Agnes January 1, 1980. Spiritual records transferred to St. Agnes.

81—ST. JOSAPHAT (1898) (Polish), Revs. Leonard A. Furmanski; Joseph Piesiur.
Res., 124 Cotton St., 19127. Tel: 215-483-4470; Fax: 215-483-4037.
School—137 Grape St., 19127. Tel: 215-482-0285; Fax: 215-483-4053.
Bernardine Sisters of St. Francis 2; Lay Teachers 9; Students 230.

82—OLD ST. JOSEPH'S (1733), Revs. William C. Rickle, S.J.; Leo A. Murray, S.J.; Robert Yankevitch, S.J. In res., Revs. Edward A. Jarvis, S.J.; William I. Nuttall, S.J.
Res., 321 Willings Alley, 19106. Tel: 215-923-1733; 1734; Fax: 215-574-8529.

83—ST. KATHERINE OF SIENA (1922), Rev. Msgr. James P. McBride; Revs. Marshall J. Kloda; John P. O'Connor; William F. Drobel, Pastor Emeritus; Joseph L. Coffey.
Res., 9700 Frankford Ave., 19114. Tel: 215-637-7548.
School—9720 Frankford Ave., 19114. Tel: 215-637-2181. Sr. M. John, C.S.F.N., Prin.
Sisters of the Holy Family of Nazareth 3; Lay Teachers 29; Students 750.
Catechesis / Religious Programs—Tel: 215-637-5119. Cookie Maratea, D.R.E.
Students 725.

84—KING OF PEACE (1926) (Italian), Rev. Ralph J. Chieffo. In res., Rev. Michael J. Blaine.
Res., 2530 Wharton St., 19146. Tel: 215-468-4107; Fax: 215-468-2882.
School—26th & Reed Sts., 19146. Tel: 215-468-7400. Sr. Janet Roddy, F.S.I.C., Prin.
Missionary Franciscan Sisters of the Immaculate Conception 5; Lay Teachers 9; Students 201.
Convent—1309 S. 26th St., 19146. Tel: 215-389-5414.

85—ST. LADISLAUS (1906) (Polish), Rev. George Ostaszewski.
Res., 1650 W. Hunting Park Ave., 19140. Tel: 215-225-8148.

86—ST. LAURENTIUS (1882) (Polish), Revs. Francis A. Gwiazda; Anthony F. Ziemba, Pastor Emeritus.
Res., 1608 E. Berks St., 19125. Tel: 215-739-1776.
School—1612 E. Berks St., 19125. Tel: 215-423-8834.
Felician Sisters of St. Francis 3; Lay Teachers 9; Students 272.
Catechesis / Religious Programs—Students 359.
Convent—1648 E. Berks St., 19125. Tel: 215-739-4447.

87—ST. LEO (1884), Revs. John J. Farry; Joseph E. O'Brien; James J. Coonan.
Res., 6658 Keystone St., 19135. Tel: 215-333-0340; Fax: 215-333-7590.
School—6649 Tulip St., 19135. Tel: 215-624-8669.
Sisters of St. Joseph 5; Lay Teachers 18; Students 409.
Catechesis / Religious Programs—Students 611.
Convent—4900 Unruh St., 19135. Tel: 215-624-1253.

88—ST. LUCY (Italian), Rev. Francis J. Sabatini. Pastors Emeritii: Revs. Albert J. Burruano; Francis J. Rauseo.
Res., 4503 Smick St., 19127. Tel: 215-483-0554.
School—146 Green Ln., 19127. Tel: 215-482-6578.
Lay Teachers 10; Students 225.

89—ST. LUDWIG (1891-1975) (German). Closed. Spiritual records transferred to St. Francis Xavier Church.

90—ST. MADELEINE SOPHIE (1925), Rev. Donald G. Birch. In res., Rev. John S. Heim.
Res., 6440 Greene St., 19119. Tel: 215-438-9464; Fax: 215-848-7953.
School—St. Martin De Porres School, 49 W. Logan St., 19144. Tel: 215-842-1266.

91—ST. MALACHY (1850), Rev. John P. McNamee. In res., Rev. Robert A. McLaughlin.
Res., 1429 N. 11th St., 19122. Tel: 215-763-1305.
School—1419 N. 11th St., 19122. Tel: 215-232-0696.
Lay Teachers 10; Students 223.
Convent—1415 N. 11th St., 19122. Tel: 215-763-5366.

92—SAINT MARTHA, Revs. Gerard H. Scherf; Richard Olszewski, O.F.M.
Res., 11001 Calera Rd., 19154. Tel: 215-632-3720.
School—11301 Academy Rd., 19154. Tel: 215-632-0320.
Lay Teachers 26; Students 649.

93—ST. MARTIN DE PORRES (1993) (African American), Revs. Daniel J. Sullivan; James McGinnis; Deacons William Stewart; Edward J. Andrews; Thomas A. Shields.
Res., 2340 W. Lehigh Ave., 19132. Tel: 215-228-8330; Fax: 215-221-6516.
School—23rd St. & Lehigh Ave., 19132. Tel: 215-223-6872.
Sisters of St. Joseph 5; Lay Teachers 14; Students 480.

94—ST. MARTIN OF TOURS (1923), Revs. Thomas A. Murray; George B. Cadwallader; Charles D. Smith; Joseph C. McLoone; Charles J. Zlock; Rev. Msgr. Michael F. Marley, Pastor Emeritus.
Res., 5450 Roosevelt Blvd., 19124. Tel: 215-535-2962; Fax: 215-535-3091.
School—Loretto Ave. & Sanger St., 19124. Tel: 215-533-3050.
Sisters of the Immaculate Heart of Mary 20; Lay Teachers 45; Students 1,628.
Catechesis/Religious Programs—Tel: 215-535-3090. Sr. Phyllis Direnzo, I.H.M., D.R.E.
Students 279.

95—OLD ST. MARY'S (1763), Rev. Msgr. John A. Sharkey.
Res., 252 S. Fourth St., 19106. Tel: 215-923-7930. [CEM]
School—Interparochial School. Children attending from following parishes: St. Augustine, Holy Trinity, St. John the Evangelist, Old St. Joseph's, Old St. Mary's, St. Patrick, St. Mary Magdalen De Pazzi. Fifth & Locust Sts., 19106. Tel: 215-923-7522.
Lay Teachers 9; Students 242.

96—ST. MARY OF THE ASSUMPTION (1849) (German), Revs. Thomas P. Horner; Emil C. Oestreich, Pastor Emeritus; Deacon Joseph Sexton.
Res., 176 Conarroe St., 19127. Tel: 215-482-4264; Fax: 215-482-7568. [CEM]
School—167 Canarroe St., 19127. Tel: 215-482-1611.
Sisters 2; Lay Teachers 10; Students 323.

97—ST. MARY OF CZESTOCHOWA (1927) (Polish), Revs. Bernard J. Herron, Admin.; John S. Klapp, Pastor Emeritus.
Res., 59th St. & Elmwood Ave., 19143. Tel: 215-729-2292.

98—ST. MARY OF THE ETERNAL (Italian). Closed. Spiritual records are kept at St. Martin De Porres Church.

99—ST. MARY MAGDALEN DE PAZZI (1852) (Italian), Revs. Donato P. Silveri; Alfred M. Natali, O.S.A., (Retired).
Res., 712 Montrose St., 19147. Tel: 215-922-3695.

100—MATER DOLOROSA (1911) (Italian), Revs. Joseph L. Logrip; Albert B. Palombo, Pastor Emeritus.
Res., 1676 Ruan St., 19124. Tel: 215-535-4036; 743-4718; Fax: 215-535-1267.
School—Paul & Ruan Sts., 19124. Tel: 215-743-4753. Miss Grace McGuirl, Prin.
Lay Teachers 12; Students 197.
Catechesis/Religious Programs—Students 273.

101—MATERNITY B.V.M. (1870), Rev. Msgr. Anthony W. McGuire; Revs. Ross J. Macartney; Francis E. Fox; Thomas M. Sodano; Deacons Victor Bonilla; Phillip Heaney; John C. Hynes.
Res., 9220 Bustleton Ave., 19115. Tel: 215-673-8127; 676-5144; Fax: 215-673-6597.
School—9322 Bustleton Ave., 19115. Tel: 215-673-0235. Sr. Bonita Smith, R.S.M., Prin.
Convent—Tel: 215-673-8118.
Sisters of Mercy 2; Lay Teachers 30; Students 899.

102—ST. MATTHEW (1927), Rev. Msgr. Charles E. McGroarty; Revs. Gerard C. Chapman; Anthony G. Flynn; Thomas D. Graham; Richard E. Rudy. In res., Rev. Msgr. Francis J. Gaughan, Pastor Emeritus; Rev. James F. Gough.
Res., 3000 Cottman Ave., 19149. Tel: 215-333-0585.
School—3040 Cottman Ave., 19149. Tel: 215-333-3142.
Sisters, Servants of the Immaculate Heart of Mary 7; Lay Teachers 36; Students 1,409.

103—ST. MICHAEL (1831), Rev. John M. Harkins; Deacon Zoilo Martes. In res., Rev. Francis Piro.
Res., 1445 N. Second St., 19122. Tel: 215-739-2358. [CEM]
School—1429 N. Second St., 19122. Tel: 215-426-5424.
Sisters of St. Joseph 3; Lay Teachers 7; Students 195.
Convent—1434 N. Second St., 19122. Tel: 215-739-3677.

104—ST. MICHAEL MISSION. (Formerly located in Torresdale.) Spiritual records transferred to Our Lady of Calvary Church.

105—ST. MICHAEL OF THE SAINTS. Closed. Located at 4811 Germantown Ave. from 1924 to 1982. Spiritual records kept at St. Francis of Assisi Church.

106—ST. MONICA (1895), Most Rev. Louis A. De Simone; Revs. Charles L. Sangermano; Christopher J. Papa. In res., Rev. Clement Kurowski, O.F.M.; Deacons John C. Orlando; Leonard D. DeMasi.
Res., 2422 S. 17th St., 19145. Tel: 215-334-4170.
School—1714 Ritner St., 19145. Tel: 215-467-5338; 334-3777.
Sisters, Servants of the Immaculate Heart of Mary 8; Lay Teachers 23; Students 810.
Catechesis/Religious Programs—Students 154.

107—MOST BLESSED SACRAMENT (1901) (African American), Rev. Roland D. Slobogin. In res., Rev. Joseph M. Corley.
Res., 5628 Chester Ave., 19143. Tel: 215-729-0694; Fax: 215-729-0712.
School—5601 Kingsessing Ave., 19143. Tel: 215-727-1863.
Sisters, Servants of Immaculate Heart of Mary 3; Lay Teachers 7; Students 220.

108—MOST PRECIOUS BLOOD (1907-1993). Closed. Spiritual records are kept at St. Martin De Porres Church.

109—MOTHER OF DIVINE GRACE (1926) (Italian), Rev. George J. Mazzotta; Deacon Joseph A. Micucci. In res., Rev. John B. Wendrychowicz.
Res., 2918 E. Thompson St., 19134. Tel: 215-739-0353; Fax: 215-739-9910.
School—2612 E. Monmouth St., 19134. Tel: 215-426-7325.
Lay Teachers 9; Students 209.
Catechesis/Religious Programs—Students 255.
Mission—Philadelphia, Philadelphia Co., St. Roch Chapel, E. Ontario, 19134.

110—NATIVITY OF THE BLESSED VIRGIN MARY (1882), Revs. Richard J. McAndrews; Daniel J. Moriarity; Angelo R. Citino.
Res., 2535 E. Allegheny Ave., 19134. Tel: 215-739-2735; Fax: 215-739-2748.
School—3255 Belgrade St., 19134. Tel: 215-739-8761.
Sisters of Christian Charity 1; School Sisters of Notre Dame 2; Lay Teachers 19; Students 450.
Catechesis/Religious Programs—Tel: 215-739-4667. Mrs. Susan Campbell, D.R.E.
Students 106.
Convent—3224 Belgrade St., 19134. Tel: 215-427-3261; Fax: 215-427-3263. Novitiate-Sisters of Our Lady of Mercy

111—ST. NICHOLAS OF TOLENTINE (1912) (Italian), Revs. Nicholas Martorano, O.S.A.; Peter J. Toscani, O.S.A.; Edward Doran, O.S.A. In res., Revs. Eugene M. Zega, O.S.A., (Retired); Anthony Gasparro, O.S.A., (Retired); Bro. John Holt, O.S.A.; Deacon Raymond Jacobucci.
Res., 910 Watkins St., 19148. Tel: 215-463-1326; Fax: 215-463-0888.
Church—Ninth St. below Morris St., 19148.
School—913 Pierce St., 19148. Tel: 215-468-0353; Fax: 215-334-9661.
Religious Sisters Filippini 3; Lay Teachers 21; Students 521.

112—OUR LADY OF ANGELS (1907) (Italian), Rev. Ferdinand Buccafurni, Admin.
Res., St. Donato Church, 403 N. 65th St., 19151. Tel: 215-747-4131.
Church—4970 Master St., 19131.

113—OUR LADY OF THE BLESSED SACRAMENT (1910-1972). Closed. Spiritual records transferred to Cathedral Basilica of SS. Peter and Paul.

114—OUR LADY OF CALVARY (1958), Rev. Msgr. John E. Gillespie; Revs. John P. Hutter; Sylwester Wiejata.
Res., 11024 Knights Rd., 19154. Tel: 215-637-7515; Fax: 215-637-7517.
School—11027 Kipling Ln., 19154. Tel: 215-637-1648; Fax: 215-632-3810.
Sisters of the Holy Family of Nazareth 4; Lay Teachers 31; Students 1,070.
Catechesis/Religious Programs—Tel: 215-632-1342.
Students 156.

115—OUR LADY OF CONSOLATION (1917) (Italian), Rev. Louis P. Ciaudelli. In res., Rev. Joseph C. Reino, Ph.D.
Res., 7056 Tulip St., 19135. Tel: 215-333-0442; 333-5774.
School—Princeton & Edmund Sts., 19135. Tel: 215-624-0505. Miss Patricia Quinter, Prin.
Sisters of St. Francis of Philadelphia 1; Lay Teachers 9; Students 338.
Convent—7052 Tulip St., 19135. Tel: 215-332-4426.

116—OUR LADY OF GOOD COUNSEL (1898-1932). Closed. Spiritual records are kept at St. Paul Church.

117—OUR LADY HELP OF CHRISTIANS (1885) (German), Rev. Leo J. McGee. In res., Rev. Gregory J. Hickey.
Res., 3160 Gaul St., 19134. Tel: 215-739-2211.
School—2424 E. Allegheny Ave., 19134. Tel: 215-427-3499.
Sisters of Christian Charity 3; Lay Teachers 9; Students 280.
Catechesis/Religious Programs—Students 342.
Convent—Tel: 215-739-7890.

118—OUR LADY OF THE HOLY SOULS (1909-1993). Closed. Spiritual records are kept at Our Lady of Hope Church.

119—OUR LADY OF HOPE (1993), Revs. Kenneth P. McAteer; Edward J. Hallinan; Thomas P. Kletzel; Deacons Israel Rosario; William Champagne.
Res., 5200 N. Broad St., 19141-1628. Tel: 215-329-8100; 329-8164; Fax: 215-324-4660.
School—5218 N. Broad St., 19141-1626. Tel: 215-324-4211.
Lay Teachers 12; Students 307.

120—OUR LADY OF LORETO (1932) (Italian), Rev. Vito J. Carbone.
Res., 6214 Grays Ave., 19142-2903. Tel: 215-726-5221; Fax: 215-726-8602.
School—2412 S. 62nd St., 19142. Tel: 215-727-1551; Fax: 215-727-2828.
Lay Teachers 10; Students 248.

121—OUR LADY OF LOURDES (1894), Revs. James C. Sherlock; Patrick E. Sweeney; George W. Crowe.
Res., 6315 Lancaster Ave., 19151. Tel: 215-473-1669; 473-1670.
School—1940 N. 63rd St., 19151. Tel: 215-877-2727.
Sisters of Mercy 2; Lay Teachers 11; Students 215.

122—OUR LADY OF MERCY (1889-1984). Closed. Records transferred to St. Malachy.

123—CHAPEL OF OUR LADY OF THE MIRACULOUS MEDAL (1912) (Spanish). Attended by Cathedral Basilica of SS. Peter and Paul, 1723 Race St., Philadelphia, PA 19103. Tel: 215-561-1313;1314. Rev. William S. Murphy.
Church—1903 Spring Garden St., 19130. Tel: 215-972-8116.

124—OUR LADY OF MT. CARMEL, Revs. Gerald D. Canavan; Thomas J. Duane; Edward H. Bell; Thomas W. Wassel, Pastor Emeritus; Mrs. Lucille Hillerman, Parish Minister.
Res., 2319 S. Third St., 19148. Tel: 215-334-7766.
School—2339 S. Third St., 19148. Tel: 215-334-0584.
Sisters of Mercy 3; Lay Teachers 18; Students 496.
Convent—251 Ritner St., 19148. Tel: 215-334-6800.

125—OUR LADY OF POMPEII (1914-1993) (Italian). Closed. Spiritual records are kept at St. Veronica Church.

126—OUR LADY OF RANSOM (1955), Revs. William F. McGeown; Laurence J. Gleason. In res., Rev. Msgr. Joseph J. McGlinn.
Res., 6701 Calvert St., 19149. Tel: 215-332-6166; Fax: 215-332-6811.
School—6740 Roosevelt Blvd., 19149. Tel: 215-332-4352.
Sisters, Servants of the Immaculate Heart of Mary 4; Lay Teachers 14; Students 526.
Convent—Tel: 215-624-1954.

127—OUR LADY OF THE ROSARY (1886), Rev. Joseph J. Nicolo.
Res., 345 N. 63rd St., 19139. Tel: 215-476-6511; 476-2050.
School—344 N. Felton St., 19139. Tel: 215-474-4011. Mrs. Margeuritte Henry, Prin.
Lay Teachers 10; Students 214.

128—OUR LADY OF THE ROSARY (Germantown) (1928-1977) (Italian). Closed. Spiritual records transferred to Immaculate Conception Church, Germantown.

129—OUR LADY OF VICTORY (1899), Rev. Henry J.

McKee; Deacon Richard G. Nightingale. In res., Rev. Thomas M. Higgins.
Res., 5412 Vine St., 19139. Tel: 215-747-7567; 747-6731.
School—54th & Summer Sts., 19139. Tel: 215-747-8004. Sr. Catherine Lengle, S.S.J., Prin.
Sisters of St. Joseph 6; Lay Teachers 9; Students 239.
Convent—5330 Vine St., 19139. Tel: 215-747-7040.

130—OUR MOTHER OF CONSOLATION (1855), Revs. Francis A. Sirolli, O.S.A.; Thomas J. Dillon, O.S.A., Hospital Chap.; Robert J. Guessetto, O.S.A., Pastoral Assoc.; Bro. William C. Harkin, O.S.A.; Deacons Clifford W. Brown; James M. Tormey.
Res., 9 E. Chestnut Hill Ave., 19118. Tel: 215-247-0430; Fax: 215-247-2506.
School—17 E. Chestnut Hill Ave., 19118. Tel: 215-247-1060. Sr. Lorraine Muglie, S.S.J., Prin.
Sisters of St. Joseph 5; Lay Teachers 7; Students 242.
Convent—23 E. Chestnut Hill Ave., 19118. Tel: 215-247-0552.

131—OUR MOTHER OF MERCY PRISON CHAPLAINCY, Rev. John M. Bonavitacola, Chap.
Res., 1350 Vernon Rd., 19150. Tel: 215-549-3760; Fax: 215-549-1271. Ministry to Philadelphia County Prisons; House of Correction; Detention Center; Curran-Fromhold Correctional Facility; Philadelphia Industrial Correctional Center, Special Detention Facilities, Tel: 215-685-8385. Fax: 215-685-8938.

132—OUR MOTHER OF SORROWS, Revs. Alexander Masluk; James P. Daly, Pastor Emeritus.
Res., 1030 N. 48th St., 19131. Tel: 215-878-0875; Fax: 215-878-7420.
School—1020 N. 48th St., 19131. Tel: 215-473-5828.
Sisters of St. Joseph 2; Lay Teachers 9; Students 265.
Convent—St. Carthage, Tel: 215-747-0122.

133—ST. PATRICK (1839), Rev. Msgr. Philip J. Dowling; Rev. Msgr. Peter A. Fitzpatrick, Pastor Emeritus. In res., Rev. Francis A. McDermott.
Res., 242 S. 20th St., 19103. Tel: 215-735-9900; Fax: 215-732-0998.
School—St. Mary Interparochial School, Tel: 215-923-7522.

134—ST. PAUL (1843), Rev. Michael J. Gambone. In res., Rev. Thomas J. Rossi, O.Praem.
Res., 808 S. Hutchinson St., 19147. Tel: 215-923-0355.
School—910 Christian St., 19147. Tel: 215-922-3049.
Lay Teachers 8; Students 175.

135—ST. PETER THE APOSTLE (1842) (Hispanic), Revs. John McGowan, C.SS.R.; Paul Oslovich, C.SS.R., Pastoral Assoc.; Deacon Miguel Betancourt. In res., Rev. Msgr. George Tomichek; Revs. Charles G. Fehrenbach, C.SS.R.; Joseph F. Berton, C.SS.R.; Edward J. Donahue, C.SS.R.; Bro. Hilary Basel, C.SS.R.
St. John Neumann Apostolate—Tel: 215-627-3080; Fax: 215-627-2366. Revs. Michael Barrett; James King, C.SS.R.; Joseph Oppitz; Seamus M. Quinn, C.SS.R.; Paul Bryan, C.SS.R.
Mission Band—Revs. William C. Maggs, C.SS.R.; Donald C. Miniscalco, C.SS.R.; William Gaffney, C.SS.R.
Res., 1019 N. Fifth St., 19123. Tel: 215-627-2386; Fax: 215-627-2366. [CEM]
School—1005 N. Fifth St., 19123. Tel: 215-627-3954; 922-5958.
School Sisters of Notre Dame 8; Lay Teachers 9; Students 294.

136—ST. PETER CLAVER (1889-1985). Closed. Spiritual records transferred to St. John the Evangelist Church.

137—ST. PHILIP NERI (1840), Rev. W. Fred Kindon. In res., Rev. Msgr. Louis A. D'Addezio.
Res., 218 Queen St., 19147. Tel: 215-468-1922; Fax: 215-465-3147.

138—ST. RAPHAEL (1904-1989). Closed. Spiritual records are kept at St. Irenaeus.

139—ST. RAYMOND OF PENAFORT (1941), Rev. John F. O'Brien. In res., Revs. Emil C. Oestreich; John M. Bonavitacola.
Res., 1350 Vernon Rd., 19150. Tel: 215-549-3760; Fax: 215-549-1271.
School—7940 Williams Ave., 19150. Tel: 215-548-1919.
Sisters of Mercy 1; Lay Teachers 10; Students 245.

140—RESURRECTION OF OUR LORD (1928), Rev. Msgr. Thomas J. Scanlon; Revs. Robert L. Brennan; Michael J. Ryan; Nicholas J. Martino.
Res., 2000 Shelmire Ave., 19152. Tel: 215-745-3211; Fax: 215-745-0587.
School—2020 Shelmire Ave., 19152. Tel: 215-742-1127; Fax: 215-742-0947. Ms. Elizabeth M. Keating, Prin.
Sisters of Notre Dame de Namur 1; Lay Teachers 30; Students 983.
Catechesis/Religious Programs—Students 300.

141—ST. RICHARD, Revs. Joseph J. Gallagher; John J. Morley, Pastor Emeritus.
Res., 3010 S. 18th St., 19145. Tel: 215-468-4777.
School—19th & Pollock Sts., 19145. Tel: 215-467-5430.
Servants of the Immaculate Heart of Mary 3; Lay Teachers 8; Students 220.
Convent—1827 Pollock St., 19145. Tel: 215-467-1878.

142—ST. RITA OF CASCIA (1907), Revs. Michael F. Di Gregorio, O.S.A.; John F. O'Rourke, O.S.A.; Deacon Leroy F. O'Kedas. In res., Rev. Edward J. Griffin, O.S.A.
Res., 1166 S. Broad St., 19146. Tel: 215-546-8333; Fax: 215-732-3510.

143—ST. ROSE OF LIMA (1921), Rev. Msgr. Wilfred J. Pashley.
Res., 1535 N. 59th St., 19151. Tel: 215-877-2991; Fax: 215-877-8255.
School—1522 N. Wanamaker St., 19131. Tel: 215-473-6030; Fax: 215-473-2338.
Sisters, Servants of the Immaculate Heart of Mary 3; Lay Teachers 7; Students 288.

144—SACRED HEART OF JESUS (1871), Revs. Michael J. Sheehan; William E. Dean. In res., Rev. Kevin C. Lawrence.
Res., 1404 S. Third St., 19147-6099. Tel: 215-465-4050; 4051.
School—1329 Moyamensing Ave., 19147. Tel: 215-462-4129; Fax: 215-462-9429. Sr. Janet Walters, I.H.M., Prin.
Sisters of the Immaculate Heart of Mary 5; Lay Teachers 7; Students 215.
Convent—1420 S. Third St., 19147. Tel: 215-463-8719.

145—SACRED HEART (1913-1977) (Hungarian). Closed. For inquiries for parish records contact St. Michael Church.

146—ST. STANISLAUS (Polish), Rev. Joseph B. Jarosz.
Res., 242 Fitzwater St., 19147. Tel: 215-925-2631.

147—STELLA MARIS (1954), Rev. Msgr. James F. Connelly, S.T.L., H.E.D.; Revs. John J. LaRosa; Anthony F. Orth.
Res., 2901 S. 10th St., 19148. Tel: 215-465-2336; 2337.
School—814 Bigler St., 19148. Tel: 215-467-6262.
Sisters of St. Joseph 6; Lay Teachers 14; Students 371.
Convent—2929 S. 10th St., 19148. Tel: 215-462-1111.

148—ST. STEPHEN (1843-1993). Closed. Spiritual records are kept at Our Lady of Hope Church. Tel: 215-329-8100.

149—ST. TERESA OF AVILA (1853-1972). Closed. Spiritual records are kept at St. Rita Church. Tel: 215-546-8333.

150—ST. THERESE OF THE CHILD JESUS (1925), Rev. Steven J. Harris; Sr. Sheila C. Holly, S.S.J., Dir. of Parish Services; Deacon Edward M. Purnell.
Res., 6611 Ardleigh St., 19119. Tel: 215-438-5279; Fax: 215-438-8031.
School—Anderson & Upsal Sts., 19119. Tel: 215-844-5654. Mrs. Camille Brown, Prin.
Lay Teachers 14; Students 270.

151—ST. THOMAS AQUINAS (1885), Revs. Arthur I. Taraborelli; Joseph Dinh C. Huynh. In res., Rev. Michael J. Fitzgerald; Deacon Salvatore J. Lucente.
Res., 1719 Morris St., 19145. Tel: 215-334-2312; Fax: 215-755-9369.
School—18th & Morris Sts., 19145. Tel: 215-334-0878.
Lay Teachers 15; Students 475.

152—ST. TIMOTHY (1928), Revs. Anthony W. Dieckhaus; Francis X. Morrison; John J. LaRosa; Francis P. Rogers; Joseph W. Callahan.
Res., 3001 Levick St., 19149. Tel: 215-624-6188; Fax: 215-624-1316.
School—Hawthorne & Levick Sts., 19149. Tel: 215-338-9797. Sr. Marie Notwick, S.S.J., Prin.
Sisters of St. Joseph 5; Lay Teachers 46; Students 1,190.
Catechesis/Religious Programs—Students 1,546.
Convent—3033 Levick St., 19149. Tel: 215-624-8333.

153—TRANSFIGURATION OF OUR LORD (1905), Rev. James A. Callahan.
Res., 5533 Cedar Ave., 19143. Tel: 215-476-1207.
School—5501 Cedar Ave., 19143. Tel: 215-474-7611.
Sisters, Servants of the Immaculate Heart of Mary 5; Lay Teachers 14; Students 420; Daycare 45.
Convent—Tel: 215-472-2936.

154—ST. VERONICA (1872), Revs. Michael A. Chapman; Angelo J. Hernandez, Parochial Vicar. In res., Deacons Rafael Maldonado; Alfonzo Fernandez.
Res., 533 W. Tioga St., 19140. Tel: 215-228-4878; 225-5677.
School—Sixth & Tioga St., 19140. Tel: 215-225-1575; Fax: 215-225-2595. Sr. Virginia Paschall, I.H.M., Prin.
Sisters, Servants of the Immaculate Heart of Mary 3; Lay Teachers 6; Students 251.
Catechesis/Religious Programs—Tel: 215-228-4878. Sr. Kathleen Brown, I.H.M., D.R.E.
Students 160.
Convent—3521 N. Sixth St., 19140. Tel: 215-223-9107.

155—ST. VINCENT DE PAUL (1851), Revs. Gregory P. Cozzubbo, C.M.; Aidan R. Rooney, C.M.; John Maher, C.M.
Res., 109 E. Price St., 19144. Tel: 215-438-2925; Fax: 215-438-4856.
School—St. Martin De Porres School, 49 W. Logan St., 19144. Tel: 215-842-1266.

156—VISITATION B.V.M. (1874), Rev. Msgr. Edward M. Deliman; Revs. Joseph T. Trinh; Rafael Mendez.
Res., 2625 B St., 19125. Tel: 215-634-1133; Fax: 215-634-1133.
School—Lehigh Ave. & B St., 19125. Tel: 215-634-7280.
Sisters of St. Joseph 4; Lay Teachers 15; Students 370.
Catechesis/Religious Programs—Students 170.

157—ST. WILLIAM (1920), Rev. Msgr. James E. Mortimer; Revs. Thomas J. McManus, S.T.L.; George C. Plasserry, C.M.I.; Michael J. Saban. In res., Rev. Msgr. Walter J. Conway, J.C.D., (Retired).
Res., 6200 Rising Sun Ave., 19111. Tel: 215-745-1389; Fax: 215-745-2650.
Primary School—6200 Palmetto St., 19111. Tel: 215-342-3369.
Intermediate School—Rising Sun and Robbins Aves., 19111. Tel: 215-342-4488.
Middle School—Rising Sun and Devereaux Aves., 19111. Tel: 215-725-2574.
Sisters, Servants of the Immaculate Heart of Mary 12; Lay Teachers 40; Students 1,231.
Day Care Center—514 Devereaux Ave., 19111. Tel: 215-745-7708.
Convent—6226 Rising Sun Ave., 19111. Tel: 215-745-3513.
Pastoral Care Ministry: Tel: 215-742-9992.

OUTSIDE THE CITY OF PHILADELPHIA

Abington, Montgomery Co., Our Lady Help of Christians (1953), Revs. Joseph D. Bowen; Thomas A. Nasta; Rev. Msgr. J. Clement Bennington, Pastor Emeritus; Deacon Joseph T. Rooney. In res., Rev. Albert J. Santorsola.
Res., 1500 Marian Rd., 19001. Tel: 215-886-3456; Fax: 215-886-7312.
School—Elkins & Crater Rds., 19001. Tel: 215-887-3067.
Lay Teachers 10; Students 204.
Catechesis/Religious Programs—Tel: 215-887-3466.
Students 200.

Ambler, Montgomery Co., St. Anthony of Padua (1886), Revs. Stephen P. McHenry; Thomas B. Troy; Deacon David E. Jones.
Res., 259 Forest Ave., 19002-5999. Tel: 215-646-4742; Fax: 215-646-4864. [CEM]
School—Ambler Catholic Elementary School. (Consolidation of St. Anthony and St. Joseph Schools, Ambler). Tel: 215-646-6150; Fax: 215-646-7435.
Sisters of St. Joseph 6; Lay Teachers 14; Students 283.
Catechesis/Religious Programs—Tel: 215-646-0586.
Students 294.
Convent—251 Forrest Ave., 19002. Tel: 215-646-0426.

St. Joseph (1920), Rev. John G. Fala.
Res., 16 S. Spring Garden St., 19002-4797. Tel: 215-646-0494.
School—Ambler Catholic Elementary School. (Consolidation of St. Anthony and St. Joseph Schools, Ambler). Tel: 215-646-2007.
Catechesis/Religious Programs—Tel: 215-646-0586.
Students 355.

Ardmore, Montgomery Co., St. Colman (1907), Most Rev. Robert P. Maginnis; Rev. Joseph M. Arnholt; Rev. Msgr. Francis J. Statkus, Pastor Emeritus; Rev. Joseph A. St. Clair, Pastor Emeritus. In res., Rev. Richard J. Wright.
Res., 11 Simpson Rd., 19003. Tel: 610-642-0545.
School—SS. Colman and John Neumann Consolidated School, Bryn Mawr, 19010. Tel: 610-525-3266.

Ardsley, Montgomery Co., Queen of Peace (1954), Rev. Msgr. Thomas J. Hilferty; Rev. John C. Moloney; Rev. Msgr. Joseph E. Lynaugh, Pastor Emeritus. In res., Rev. William J. Lynn.
Res., 820 North Hills Ave., 19038. Tel: 215-887-1838; Fax: 215-887-8328.

School—835 North Hills Ave., Tel: 215-886-4782; Fax: 215-886-2142.
Sisters of the Holy Family of Nazareth 1; Lay Teachers 11; Students 262.
Catechesis/Religious Programs—Students 215.
Convent—825 North Hills Ave., Tel: 215-887-4785.

Aston, Delaware Co., St. Joseph (1947), Revs. Robert C. Vogan; James M. Iannarella.
Res., 256 Concord Rd., 19014. Tel: 610-497-3340; Fax: 610-497-3383.
School—Tel: 610-494-0147. Ms. Anne Cook, Prin. Lay Teachers 19; Students 510.
Catechesis/Religious Programs—Ms. Patricia McGeever, D.R.E.
Students 290.

Bala-Cynwyd, Montgomery Co., St. Matthias (1906), Rev. Arthur E. Rodgers; Rev. Msgr. James J. Vizzard; Revs. Charles E. Gormley; Thomas A. Kane, Pastor Emeritus, (Retired); Deacon Gerald Kelly.
Res., 128 Bryn Mawr Ave., 19004-3099. Tel: 610-664-0207; Fax: 610-664-3559.
School—122 Bryn Mawr Ave., 19004. Tel: 610-664-1942.
Sisters of Mercy 2; Lay Teachers 15; Students 190.
Convent—108 Highland Ave., 19004. Tel: 610-667-1399.

Bensalem, Bucks Co.,

1—St. Charles Borromeo, (1903), Revs. Francis A. Carbine; Michael F. Hennelly. In res., Rev. Thomas M. Kohler.
Res., 1731 Hulmeville Rd., 19020. Tel: 215-638-3625.
School—1704 Bristol Pike, Tel: 215-639-3456.
Sisters, Servants of the Immaculate Heart of Mary 8; Lay Teachers 12; Students 550.
Catechesis/Religious Programs—Students 150.
Convent—1080 Kings Ave., Tel: 215-639-0113.

2—St. Elizabeth Ann Seton, (1976), Revs. William T. Joseph; John J. Duffy, Pastor Emeritus; Deacons Francis C. Klauder; Joseph W. Niland. In res., Rev. Joseph P. Kerrigan.
Res., 1200 Park Ave. East, 19020. Tel: 215-245-6122; Fax: 215-245-4211.
Catechesis/Religious Programs—Tel: 215-245-9756.
Students 178.

3—Saint Ephrem, (1966), Rev. James E. McGuire; Rev. Msgr. Edward S. Musial, Pastor Emeritus; Revs. Joseph E. Howarth; Anthony F. Orth.
Res., 5400 Hulmeville Rd., 19020. Tel: 215-245-1698; Fax: 215-245-4787. [CEM]
School—5340 Hulmeville Rd., 19020. Tel: 215-639-9488; Fax: 215-639-0206.
Sisters, Servants of the Immaculate Heart of Mary 8; Lay Teachers 24; Students 764.
Catechesis/Religious Programs—Students 435.
Convent—5300 Hulmeville Rd., 19020. Tel: 215-638-1024.

4—Our Lady of Fatima, (1954), Revs. Thomas D. Homa; John A. Griffin, Pastor Emeritus. In res., Rev. Richard J. Griffin.
Res., Fatima Acres, 19020. Tel: 215-639-4254.
School—Tel: 215-638-3256.
Sisters, Servants of the Immaculate Heart of Mary 6; Lay Teachers 6; Students 284.
Convent—2915 Street Rd., 19020. Tel: 215-639-1916. Fatima Acres

Berwyn, Chester Co., St. Monica (1897), Rev. George G. Hagenbach.
Res., 635 First Ave., 19312. Tel: 610-644-0110; Fax: 610-695-0850. [CEM]
School—First and Woodside Aves., Tel: 610-644-8848. Mrs. Mary Dunwoody, Prin.
Lay Teachers 14; Students 234.
Catechesis/Religious Programs—Tel: 610-647-4757.
Students 260.

Boothwyn, Delaware Co., St. John Fisher (1971), Rev. Sidney C. Burgoyne.
Res., 4225 Chichester Ave., 19061. Tel: 610-485-0441; Fax: 610-859-2109.
Catechesis/Religious Programs—Tel: 610-485-0581.
Students 175.

Bridgeport, Montgomery Co., St. Augustine (1892), Rev. Msgr. Francis X. Schmidt; Rev. Francis H. Gallen, Pastor Emeritus. In res., Rev. Charles J. Kennedy.
Res., 464 Ford St., 19405. Tel: 610-272-4088; Fax: 610-272-6396. [CEM]
Consolidated School—St. Augustine-Our Lady of Mt. Carmel, Tel: 610-275-8676.
Sisters, Servants of the Immaculate Heart of Mary 4; Lay Teachers 9; Students 207.
Convent—512 Bush St., 19405. Tel: 610-275-3348.
Catechesis/Religious Programs—Students 60.

Our Lady of Mt. Carmel (1924) (Italian), Rev. Salvatore J. Pronesti.
Res., 502 Ford St., 19405. Tel: 610-272-3479; Fax: 610-272-5449.
School—St. Augustine-Our Lady of Mt. Carmel, (Grades K-4). Consolidated. 504 Ford St., 19405. Tel: 610-279-4630.

Our Mother of Sorrows (1926) (Slovak), Revs. John Paul, Admin.; John M. Matsko, Pastor Emeritus.
Res., 504 Holstein St., 19405. Tel: 610-275-3170.

Bristol, Bucks Co., St. Ann (1906) (Italian), Revs. James R. Day, O.SS.T.; John DiMatteo, O.SS.T., Pastor Emeritus; Daniel Houde, O.S.S.T.
Res., 357 Dorrance St., P.O. Box 1175, 19007. Tel: 215-788-2128; Fax: 215-781-9782.
School—418 Jefferson Ave., 19007. Tel: 215-788-2030.
Sisters of the Most Holy Trinity 3; Lay Teachers 7; Students 215.
Convent—430 Jefferson Ave., 19907. Tel: 215-788-2531.
Mission—Tullytown, Bucks Co., Sacred Heart of Jesus, Main St., 19007.

St. Mark (1845), Revs. Albert T. Kostelnick; John J. McIntyre; Deacon Jose Antonio Morales.
Res., 1025 Radcliffe St., 19007. Tel: 215-788-2319. [CEM]
School—1024 Radcliffe St., 19007. Tel: 215-785-0973.
Lay Teachers 12; Students 256.
Catechesis/Religious Programs—Students 151.
Convent—921 Radcliffe St., 19007. Tel: 215-788-2031.

Brookhaven, Delaware Co., Our Lady of Charity (1952), Revs. Andrew J. Hanlon; James J. Kelly; John D. Schiele; Edmond J. Speitel.
Res., 231 Upland Rd., 19015. Tel: 610-872-6192; Fax: 610-872-1120.
School—249 Upland Rd., 19015. Tel: 610-874-0410.
Sisters, Servants of the Immaculate Heart of Mary 9; Lay Teachers 17; Students 420.
Catechesis/Religious Programs—Students 208.
Convent—245 Upland Rd., 19015. Tel: 610-874-8101.

Brookline, Delaware Co., Annunciation B.V.M. (1927), Revs. Ignatius L. Murray; Timothy J. Buckley. In res., Rev. Michael T. McCulken.
Res., 410 Sagamore Rd., Havertown, 19083. Tel: 610-449-1613; Fax: 610-449-7041.
School—411 Brookline Blvd., Havertown, 19083. Tel: 610-446-8430.
Sisters of Mercy 1; Lay Teachers 18; Students 298.
Catechesis/Religious Programs—Students 246.
Convent—421 Brookline Blvd., Havertown, 19083.

Broomall, Delaware Co., St. Pius X (1955), Revs. James J. Kelly; James T. McCabe; William T. Small. In res., Deacon Joseph E. Iannucci.
Res., 220 Lawrence Rd., 19008. Tel: 610-353-4880; Fax: 610-356-1084.
School—204 Lawrence Rd., 19008. Tel: 610-356-7222.
Sisters, Servants of the Immaculate Heart of Mary 5; Lay Teachers 25; Students 500.
Catechesis/Religious Programs—Tel: 610-353-6950.
Students 500.

Bryn Mawr, Delaware Co., St. John Neumann (1964), Rev. Msgr. James H. Meehan; Sr. Carol Kelly, S.S.J., Pastoral Min. In res., Rev. Msgr. David E. Walls; Rev. Michael J. Matz.
Res., 380 Highland Ln., 19010. Tel: 610-525-3100; Fax: 610-525-6363.
Consolidated School—SS. Colman & John Neumann, 372 Highland Ln., 19010. Tel: 610-525-3266. Mrs. Mary Ann DeAngelo, Prin.
Sisters 2; Lay Teachers 10; Students 248.
Catechesis/Religious Programs—Students 150.
Convent—340 Highland Ln., 19010. Tel: 610-527-1220; 3115.

Our Mother of Good Counsel, Montgomery Co., (1885), Revs. James E. Martinez, O.S.A.; Adrian Gilligan, O.S.A., Prior. In res., Revs. Anthony P. Burrascano, O.S.A.; Harry A. Cassel, O.S.A., (Retired).
Res., 31 Pennswood Rd., 19010. Tel: 610-525-0147; Fax: 610-525-0157.
Consolidated School—St. Thomas/Good Counsel School, 575 Lancaster Ave., 19010. Tel: 610-525-1407; Fax: 610-525-0471.
Sisters of Mercy 1; Lay Teachers 10; Students 181.
Catechesis/Religious Programs—Fax: 610-525-1507.
Students 131.

Center Square, Montgomery Co., St. Helena (1919), Revs. Joseph A. Vadino; John T. Coates, Pastor Emeritus. In res., Revs. David E. Diamond; Pasquale R. Catullo.
Res., P.O. Box 5085, 19422-0809. Tel: 610-275-7711.
School—Tel: 610-279-3345.
Sisters of Mercy 1; Lay Teachers 15; Students 350.
Catechesis/Religious Programs—Students 241.
Convent—Tel: 610-272-1383.

Chadds Ford, Delaware Co., St. Cornelius (1963), Rev. James E. Locke.
Res., 110 Ridge Rd., 19317. Tel: 610-459-2502.
Catechesis/Religious Programs—Students 292.

Chalfont, Bucks Co., St. Jude (1962), Rev. Msgr. James P. McCoy; Rev. Michael J. Gerlach; Deacons Vincent G. Ceneviva; John T. Riordan. In res., Rev. Msgr. James J. Reilly (FWT) (Retired).
Res., 321 W. Butler Ave., 18914-2329. Tel: 215-822-0179; Fax: 215-822-0638.
School—323 W. Butler Ave., 18914. Tel: 215-822-9225. Sr. Marie Melanie, R.S.M., Prin.
Sisters 2; Lay Teachers 18; Students 394.
Catechesis/Religious Programs—Tel: 215-822-7553. Ms. Margaret F. McMenamin, Prin.
Students 461.

Cheltenham, Montgomery Co., St. Joseph (1953), Rev. Joseph J. Qunidlen. In res., Rev. Edward J. Chwieroth.
Res., 120 Hilldale Rd., 19012. Tel: 215-635-5533; Fax: 215-635-4578.
School—Boncouer & Water Rds., Tel: 215-635-0102; Fax: 215-635-4881.
Daughters of Our Lady of the Sacred Heart 3; Lay Teachers 8; Students 201.
Convent—7633 Waters Rd., Tel: 215-224-2159.

Presentation of Blessed Virgin Mary (1890), Revs. John J. Shelley; John R. McFadden; Sr. Joan Anne Melley, S.S.J., Parish Service Dir. In res., Rev. Joseph A. Tracey.
Res., 100 Old Soldiers Rd., 19012. Tel: 215-379-1364; 379-1599; Fax: 215-379-1456.
School—Hasbrook Ave. & Old Soldiers Rd., 19012. Tel: 215-379-3798.
Lay Teachers 18; Students 494.
Catechesis/Religious Programs—Students 160.
Convent—107 Old Soldiers Rd., 19012. Tel: 215-379-8343.

Chester, Delaware Co.,

1—St. Anthony of Padua, (1908-1993) (Italian). Closed. Spiritual records are kept at Blessed Katharine Drexel Church. Tel: 610-872-3731.

2—Blessed Katharine Drexel, (1993), Revs. Russell Donnelly; Clemens J. Gerdelman.
1920 Providence Ave., 19013. Tel: 610-872-3731; Fax: 610-872-0545.
School—Tel: 610-872-7358.
Convent—1902 Providence Ave., 19013. Tel: 610-876-4916.
Mission—Chester, Delaware Co., Blessed Katharine Drexel Center for Evangelization, 2nd & Norris St., 19013.

3—St. Hedwig, (1902-1993) (Polish). Closed. Spiritual records are kept at Blessed Katharine Drexel Church. Tel: 610-872-3731.

4—Immaculate Heart of Mary, (1873-1993). Closed. Spiritual records are kept at Blessed Katharine Drexel Church. Tel: 610-872-3731.

5—St. Michael, (1842-1993). Closed. Spiritual records are kept at Blessed Katharine Drexel Church. Tel: 610-872-3731.

6—Our Lady of Vilna, (1924-1972) (Lithuanian). Closed. Sacramental records are kept at Blessed Katharine Drexel Church. Tel: 215-872-3731.

7—Resurrection of Our Lord, (1911-1993). Closed. Spiritual records are kept at Blessed Katharine Drexel Church. Tel: 610-872-3731.

8—St. Robert, (1922-1993). Closed. Spiritual records are kept at Blessed Katharine Drexel Church. Tel: 610-872-3731.

Chester Heights, Delaware Co., St. Thomas the Apostle (1729), Revs. Richard C. Williams; Anthony G. Flynn; Deacon Charles Devine.
Res., 430 Valley Brook Rd., Glen Mills, 19342. Tel: 610-459-2224; Fax: 610-459-2677. [CEM]
School—Tel: 610-459-8134; Fax: 610-459-8120.
Lay Teachers 14; Students 295.
Catechesis/Religious Programs—Tel: 610-459-3477.
Students 381.
Chaplaincies—Glen Mills Schools; Delaware County Prison; Brinton Manor; Rosehill.

Clifton Heights, Delaware Co., Sacred Heart (1910) (Polish), Rev. Francis A. Barszczewski, S.T.L.; Rev. Msgr. Francis J. Urbanowicz, Pastor Emeritus; Rev. Jan Palkowski; Deacon Boleslaw S. Wojewodka.
Res., 316 E. Broadway, 19018. Tel: 610-623-0409; Fax: 610-623-2926.
Kindergarten & Preschool—301 E. Berkley Ave., 19018. Tel: 610-623-4861.
Convent—300 E. Berkley Ave., 19018. Tel: 610-623-8804.
Mission—Chester, Delaware Co., St. Hedwig Chapel, 4th & Hayes Sts., Chester, 19013.

Coatesville, Chester Co.,

1—St. Cecilia, (1870), Revs. Francis J. Schlett; Francis C. Lewis.
Res., Sixth & Chestnut Sts., 19320. Tel: 610-384-0422; Fax: 610-384-4415. [CEM]

School—Coatesville Area Catholic Elementary School, 605 E. Lincoln Hwy., 19320. Tel: 610-384-5961.
Sisters, Servants of the Immaculate Heart of Mary 4; Lay Teachers 19; Students 530.
Convent—603 E. Lincoln Hwy., Tel: 610-384-0733; Fax: 610-384-5730.

2—OUR LADY OF THE ROSARY, (1917) (Italian), Rev. Harry A. Romano; Deacon Richard Stoughton.
Res., 80 S. 17th Ave., 19320. Tel: 610-384-1415.
Catechesis/Religious Programs—Students 305.

3—ST. JOSEPH, (1924) (Slovak), Rev. Cyril S. Ponisciak.
Res., 404 Charles St., 19320. Tel: 610-384-0360.

4—ST. STANISLAUS KOSTKA, (1907) (Polish), Rev. John V. Oulds.
Res., 209 W. Lincoln Hwy., 19320. Tel: 610-384-1172. [CEM]
School—Coatesville Area Catholic Elementary School, Church & Diamond Sts., 19320. Tel: 610-384-7999; Fax: 610-384-5730.

Collegeville, Montgomery Co., St. Eleanor (1911), Revs. John A. Franey; James P. McKelvey; Deacons Gerald McGrath; James Burns; Michael Woodal. In res., Revs. Philip J. Lowe; Francis P. Lennon, Pastor Emeritus.
Res., 647 Locust St., 19426. Tel: 610-489-1647; Fax: 610-489-7469.
School—Tel: 610-489-9434.
Lay Teachers 25; Students 495.
Catechesis/Religious Programs—Tel: 610-489-4677.
Students 492.
Convent—111 Sixth Ave., 19426. Tel: 610-489-1573.

Collingdale, Delaware Co., St. Joseph (1916), Revs. Donald E. Leighton; Michael J. Lonergan; William G. Donovan.
Res., 500 Woodlawn Ave., 19023. Tel: 610-583-4530; Fax: 610-583-7730.
School—Bartram & Woodlawn Aves., Tel: 610-586-0356. Sr. Rosemary Dougherty, I.H.M., Prin.
Sisters, Servants of the Immaculate Heart of Mary 11; Lay Teachers 19; Students 668.

Conshohocken, Montgomery Co., SS. Cosmas and Damian (1912) (Italian), Revs. Gasper A. Genuardi; Nicholas A. Lazzaro, Pastor Emeritus. In res., Rev. Alexander J. Palmieri, M.A., J.C.L.; Deacon Armand J. Maresca.
Res., 209 W. Fifth Ave., 19428. Tel: 610-828-0101; Fax: 610-828-5294.
School—Ss. Cosmos & Damian Primary Campus, 610-828-0101; St. Matthew Elementary Campus, 610-828-2007. Conshohocken Catholic School, 19428. Tel: 610-828-0755.
Religious 2; Lay Teachers 15; Students 324.

St. Mary (1905) (Polish), Rev. Msgr. Robert J. Grudowski.
Res., 140 W. Hector St., 19428. Tel: 610-828-0260; Fax: 610-828-9665. [CEM]

St. Matthew (1851), Rev. James W. Donlon. In res., Rev. John J. Ames.
Res., 219 Fayette St., 19428. Tel: 610-828-0424; Fax: 610-825-5168. [CEM]
School—School has merged to create Conshohocken Catholic School.
Catechesis/Religious Programs—Students 190.
Convent—Third Ave. & Harry St., Tel: 610-828-0174.

Croydon, Bucks Co., St. Thomas Aquinas (1922), Revs. Francis M. Gallagher, M.A.; John Tharayil, C.M.I.; Deacon Lawrence J. Gibson.
Res., 601 Bristol Pike, 19021-5496. Tel: 215-788-2989; 788-5813; Fax: 215-788-7626.
School—Walnut Ave. & Bristol Pike, Tel: 215-785-1130.
Lay Teachers 16; Students 364.

Darby, Delaware Co., Blessed Virgin Mary (1913), Rev. Peter J. Foley.
Res., 1101 Main St., 19023. Tel: 610-583-2128; Fax: 610-583-9829.
School—47 MacDade Blvd., 19023. Tel: 610-586-0638.
Sisters, Servants of the Immaculate Heart of Mary 3; Lay Teachers 11; Students 335.
Catechesis/Religious Programs—Tel: 610-586-2490.
Students 159.

Delphi, Montgomery Co., St. Mary (1926), Rev. Charles J. McElroy. In res., Rev. Joseph F. Rymdeika.
Res., 40 Spring Mount Rd., Schwenksville, 19473. Tel: 610-287-8156; Fax: 610-287-4226.
School—Tel: 610-287-7757.
Lay Teachers 11; Students 263.
Catechesis/Religious Programs—Tel: 610-287-0102.
Students 375.

Downingtown, Chester Co., St. Joseph (1851), Rev. Msgr. Robert T. McManus; Revs. Thomas P. Gillin; Walter J. Benn; Joseph A. Toth; William J. Smith, Pastor Emeritus.
Res., 338 Manor Ave., 19335. Tel: 610-269-8294; Fax: 610-269-2487. [CEM]
School—340 Manor Ave., 19335. Tel: 610-269-8999.
Sisters, Servants of the Immaculate Heart of Mary 3; Lay Teachers 19; Students 624.
Catechesis/Religious Programs—Tel: 610-873-8798.
Students 1,185.
Convent—336 Manor Ave., 19335. Tel: 610-363-6559.

Doylestown, Bucks Co., Our Lady of Mount Carmel (1850), Rev. Msgr. Raymond J. Teller; Revs. John J. Davids; William J. Dougherty; Daniel J. Gallagher; Rev. Msgr. Martin J. McDonough, Pastor Emeritus; Deacons George Corwell; Walter Kelly.
Res., 235 E. State St., 18901. Tel: 215-348-4190; Fax: 215-348-3104. [CEM]
School—E. Ashland St., 18901. Tel: 215-348-5907; Fax: 215-348-5671.
Sisters of St. Francis of Philadelphia 5; Lay Teachers 23; Students 523.
Catechesis/Religious Programs—Tel: 215-345-7089. Sr. Christa DeBacher, D.R.E.
Students 1,242.
Convent—209 E. State St., 18901. Tel: 215-348-4663.

Drexel Hill, Delaware Co.,

1—ST. ANDREW, (1916), Rev. Msgr. Vincent L. Burns; Revs. James E. McVeigh; Girard J. Cusatis; Deacon Daniel N. DeLucca. In res., Rev. James J. Bradley.
Res., 3500 School Ln., 19026. Tel: 610-259-1169.
School—529 Mason Ave., 19026. Tel: 610-259-5145. Mrs. Eileen Wilson, Prin.
Sisters of St. Joseph 3; Lay Teachers 22; Students 545.
Catechesis/Religious Programs—Students 405.
Convent—535 Mason Ave., 19026. Tel: 610-259-6130.

2—ST. BERNADETTE, (1947), Revs. William A. Wright; John H. Roebuck. In res., Rev. Daniel J. Kutys.
Res., 1035 Turner Ave., 19026. Tel: 610-789-7676; Fax: 610-789-9539.
School—1015 Turner Ave., 19026. Tel: 610-449-6126; Fax: 610-789-0890.
Oblate Sisters of St. Francis de Sales 3; Lay Teachers 24; Students 454.
Catechesis/Religious Programs—Tel: 610-853-1740. John Blisard, D.R.E.
Students 407.
Convent—Tel: 610-789-2325.

3—ST. CHARLES BORROMEO, (1849), Rev. Msgr. Daniel A. Murray, S.T.L., S.S.L.; Revs. John J. Bradley; Francis J. Cauterucci; Peter F. Cronin, (Retired); Deacons Francis Fabrizio; Peter Calabrese.
Res., 3422 Dennison Ave., 19026. Tel: 610-623-3800. [CEM]
School—3400 Dennison Ave., 19026. Tel: 610-626-4687.
Sisters, Servants of the Immaculate Heart of Mary 4; Lay Teachers 15; Students 440.
Catechesis/Religious Programs—Tel: 610-256-4389.
Students 270.
Convent—3407 Dennison Ave., 19026. Tel: 610-623-0965.

4—ST. DOROTHY, (1947), Rev. Msgr. Frederick J. Helduser; Rev. Michael D. Murphy; Deacon John J. Davaro.
Res., 4910 Township Line, 19026. Tel: 610-789-7788; 789-7338; Fax: 610-789-6936.
School—Tel: 610-789-4100.
Sisters, Servants of the Immaculate Heart of Mary 5; Lay Teachers 22; Students 460.
Catechesis/Religious Programs—Tel: 610-853-1499.
Students 350.
Convent—1201 Burmont Rd., 19026. Tel: 610-789-4112.

East Goshen, Chester Co., SS. Peter and Paul (1967), Revs. Joseph W. Dragon; Louis D. Kovacs, Pastor Emeritus; James J. Foley; Deacons Arthur G. Harrison; Thomas J. Horan; Robert J. Kefer.
Res., 1325 Boot Rd., West Chester, 19380. Tel: 610-692-2216; Fax: 610-692-7103.
Catechesis/Religious Programs—Tel: 610-692-5886.
Students 636.

East Greenville, Montgomery Co., St. Philip Neri (1919), Revs. John J. Scarcia; Edmond J. Speitel, Pastor Emeritus; Francis J. Bartos.
Res., 1325 Klinerd Rd., Pennsburg, 18073. Tel: 215-679-9275; 679-9330; Fax: 215-679-0386. [CEM]
School—Sixth & Washington Sts., 18041. Tel: 215-679-7481; Fax: 215-679-8370.
Students 144.
Catechesis/Religious Programs—Students 253.

East Lansdowne, Delaware Co., St. Cyril of Alexandria (1928), Revs. Peter D. Burke; Donald J. Farrell, Pastor Emeritus; J. Thomas Heron.
Res., 153 Penn Blvd., 19050-2698. Tel: 610-623-5160; Fax: 610-622-2479.
School—716 Emerson Ave., 19050. Tel: 610-623-1113.
Sisters, Servants of the Immaculate Heart of Mary 3; Lay Teachers 12; Students 344.
Catechesis/Religious Programs—19050. Tel: 610-623-1406.
Students 225.
Convent—171 Penn Blvd., 19050. Tel: 610-623-6590.

Eddystone, Delaware Co., St. Rose of Lima, Revs. William M. Fahey; Charles P. McMullen, Pastor Emeritus.
Res., 1901 Chester Pike, 19013. Tel: 610-876-6170.

Elkins Park, Montgomery Co., St. James (1923), Rev. Raymond J. Himsworth.
Res., 8320 Brookside Rd., 19027. Tel: 215-635-6210.
School—8304 Brookside Rd., 19027. Tel: 215-635-4673; Fax: 215-635-3521.
Lay Teachers 11; Students 225.

Essington, Delaware Co., St. Margaret Mary Alacoque (1921), Revs. John J. Nevins; Francis J. Cornely, Pastor Emeritus.
Res., 500 Wanamaker Ave., 19029. Tel: 610-521-9177.

Exton, Chester Co., SS. Philip and James (1959), Rev. Msgr. John J. Caulfield; Revs. John D. Silcox, Jr.; Quan Tran; Deacon Frank M. Bizal. In res., Rev. Samuel A. Verruni, Chap.
Res., 701 E. Lincoln Hwy., 19341. Tel: 610-363-6536; Fax: 610-524-7359.
School—Lincoln Hwy. & Ship Rd., 19341. Tel: 610-363-6530. Sr. Marita Shaun, I.H.M., Prin.
Sisters, Servants of the Immaculate Heart of Mary 5; Lay Teachers 20; Students 642.
Catechesis/Religious Programs—Tel: 610-363-1307. Sr. Eunice Marie, I.H.M., D.R.E.
Students 458.
Convent—705 E. Lincoln Hwy., 19341. Tel: 610-363-7068.

Fairless Hills, Bucks Co., St. Frances Cabrini (1952), Rev. Msgr. John J. Miller; Rev. Leo P. Oswald.
Res., 325 S. Oxford Valley Rd., 19030. Tel: 215-946-4040; 943-1116.
School—10 Goble Ct., 19030. Tel: 215-946-6334.
Sisters, Servants of the Immaculate Heart of Mary 2; Lay Teachers 19; Students 446.
Catechesis/Religious Programs—Tel: 215-946-1115.
Students 325.

Fallsington, Bucks Co., St. Joseph the Worker (1956), Rev. John J. Foster. In res., Most Rev. John J. Graham, (Retired).
Res., 9172 New Falls Rd., 19054. Tel: 215-945-4486; Fax: 215-945-3292.
School—9160 New Falls Rd., 19054. Tel: 215-945-4312.
Lay Teachers 14; Students 212.
Catechesis/Religious Programs—Tel: 215-945-4680.
Students 212.

Feasterville, Bucks Co., Assumption B.V.M. (1950), Revs. Daniel P. Devine; Robert H. Roedel; Craig B. Fisher. Pastoral Assocs.: Sr. Diane Wolf, S.S.J.; Sr. Madeline Dolores, I.H.M.
Res., 1900 Meadowbrook Rd., 19053. Tel: 215-357-1221; Fax: 215-357-2283.
School—Tel: 215-357-5499.
Sisters, Servants of the Immaculate Heart of Mary 2; Lay Teachers 17; Students 503.
Catechesis/Religious Programs—Tel: 215-357-3445. Sr. Kathryn Benham, I.H.M., D.R.E.
Students 403.
Convent—55 Bristol Rd., 19053. Tel: 215-355-3898.

Flourtown, Montgomery Co., St. Genevieve (1953), Revs. Joseph A. Duffey, O.S.A.; William A. Recchuti, O.S.A. In res., Rev. John P. Hennessy, O.S.A.; Deacons Kenneth A. Belanger; Joseph Manson.
Res., 1225 Bethlehem Pike, 19031. Tel: 215-836-2828; Fax: 215-836-7218.
School—1237 Bethlehem Pike, 19031. Tel: 215-836-5644; Fax: 215-836-0159.
Sisters of St. Joseph 4; Lay Teachers 16; Students 233.
Convent—1301 Bethlehem Pk., 19031. Tel: 215-233-4392.

Gladwyne, Montgomery Co., St. John Baptist Vianney (1927), Rev. John P. Gallagher. Pastors Emeriti: Revs. Ignatius C. Reynolds; Martin J. O'Halloran; Deacon Paul Kern. In res., Rev. Joseph T. Marino.
Res., 1110 Vaughans Ln., 19035. Tel: 610-642-0938.

Glenolden, Delaware Co., St. George (1923), Revs. William T. Joseph; Joseph F. Devlin.
Res., 22 E. Cooke Ave., 19036-1497. Tel: 610-237-1633; Fax: 610-237-9626.
School—Glen & Lamont Aves., 19036-1497. Tel: 610-583-0419.
Sisters 1; Lay Teachers 8; Students 225.

Catechesis/Religious Programs—Tel: 610-583-2460.
Students 277.
Convent—11 E. Lamont Ave., 19036-1497. Tel: 610-583-5160.

Glenside, Montgomery Co., St. Luke the Evangelist (1905), Revs. J. Michael Flood; Joseph T. Murphy; Dennis G. Van Thuyne. In res., Rev. James J. Mulligan.
Res., 2316 Fairhill Ave., 19038. Tel: 215-572-0128; Fax: 215-572-0482.
School—2336 Fairhill Ave., 19038. Tel: 215-884-0843. Sr. Helen Frederick, S.S.J., Prin.
Sisters of St. Joseph 2; Lay Teachers 21; Students 460.
Catechesis/Religious Programs—Tel: 215-884-2080. Mary Jane Dean, D.R.E.
Students 230.
Convent—2324 Fairhill Ave., 19038. Tel: 215-884-0225.

Hatboro, Montgomery Co., St. John Bosco (1953), Revs. Joseph D. Dougherty; Louis J. Kolenkiewicz.
Res., 235 E. County Line Rd., 19040. Tel: 215-672-7280.
School—215 E. County Line Rd., 19040. Tel: 215-675-1484.
Sisters, Servants of the Immaculate Heart of Mary 4; Lay Teachers 7; Students 227.
Catechesis/Religious Programs—Students 310.
Convent—189 E. County Line Rd., 19040. Tel: 215-675-2301.

Hatfield, Montgomery Co., St. Maria Goretti (1953), Revs. Thomas C. Hagan; Edward A. Windhaus.
Res., 1601 Derstine Rd., 19440. Tel: 215-721-0199.
School—Hatfield Valley Rd., 19440. Tel: 215-721-9098.
Sisters, Servants of the Immaculate Heart of Mary 4; Lay Teachers 10; Students 305.
Catechesis/Religious Programs—Tel: 215-368-0669.
Students 608.
Convent—Cowpath Rd., 19440. Tel: 215-368-1190.

Havertown, Delaware Co., St. Denis (1825), Revs. William J. Donnelly, O.S.A.; Robert Andrews, O.S.A., Pastoral Assoc.; Deacons John F. Schlegel; David B. Schaffer. In res., Revs. Edwin T. Grimes, O.S.A.; Joseph Loya, O.S.A.; James J. McCartney, O.S.A.; Bro. Richard C. Ekmann, O.S.A.
Res., 2401 St. Denis Ln., 19083. Tel: 610-446-0200; Fax: 610-446-4638. [CEM]
School—300 E. Eagle Rd., 19083. Tel: 610-446-4608.
Sisters of Mercy 2; Lay Teachers 30; Students 550.
Catechesis/Religious Programs—Tel: 610-449-7892.
Students 314.
Convent—Tel: 610-446-1263.

Highland Park, Delaware Co., St. Laurence (1917), Rev. Msgr. Thomas J. Herron; Revs. William S. Lange; Dominic Tran Minh Duc. In res., Rev. Msgr. Joseph P. Garvin.
Res., 30 St. Laurence Rd., Upper Darby, 19082. Tel: 610-449-0600; 0601; Fax: 610-449-4299.
School—8245 W. Chester Pike, 19082. Tel: 610-789-2670.
Sisters, Servants of the Immaculate Heart of Mary 3; Lay Teachers 20; Students 538.
Convent—Tel: 610-449-7042.

Hilltown, Bucks Co., Our Lady of the Sacred Heart (1919), Rev. John F. McBride. In res., Rev. Edward E. Brady.
Res., Rte. 152 & Broad St., 18927. Tel: 215-822-9224; Fax: 215-822-9102. [CEM]
School—St. Agnes-Sacred Heart School. Consolidated. Tel: 215-822-9174; Fax: 215-822-7942.
Catechesis/Religious Programs—Tel: 215-822-9020.
Students 385.

Holland, Bucks Co., St. Bede the Venerable (1966), Revs. Eugene G. Cusick; Gary Pacitti; Thomas J. Furey.
Res., 1054 Holland Rd., 18966. Tel: 215-357-5720; Fax: 215-396-0704.
School—1053 Holland Rd., 18966. Tel: 215-357-4720.
Sisters of St. Casimir 3; Lay Teachers 17; Students 400.
Catechesis/Religious Programs—Tel: 215-357-2130.
Students 800.
Convent—1071 Holland Rd., 18966. Tel: 215-355-2132.

Honey Brook, Chester Co., St. Peter (1963), Rev. William J. Cox.
Res., 1080 N. Manor Rd., 19344-9608. Tel: 610-942-2112.
Catechesis/Religious Programs—Tel: 610-942-4518.
Students 503.

Horsham, Montgomery Co., St. Catherine of Siena (1963), Revs. Henry J. Smyth; James E. Goerner; Deacons Timothy Urbanski; Richard Haddon.
Res., 321 Witmer Rd., 19044. Tel: 215-672-2881; 674-1025.
School—317 Witmer Rd., 19044. Tel: 215-674-1904.
Sisters of Mercy 1; Lay Teachers 21; Students 356.
Catechesis/Religious Programs—Tel: 215-674-8549.
Students 536.
Convent—319 Witmer Rd., 19044. Tel: 215-672-7221.

Huntingdon Valley, Montgomery Co., St. Albert the Great (1962), Rev. Msgr. Paul F. Curran; Rev. John J. Kelly; Sr. Maria D'Angelo, R.S.M., Parish Services Dir.
Res., 212 Welsh Rd., 19006. Tel: 215-947-3500; Fax: 215-938-9071.
School—216 Welsh Rd., 19006. Tel: 215-947-2332. Mary Randles, Prin.
Lay Teachers 21; Students 549.
Catechesis/Religious Programs—Students 215.

Jamison, Bucks Co., St. Cyril of Jerusalem (1965), Rev. Robert J. Powell, D.M.A., M.A., M.Div.; Deacon Joseph Windish. In res., Rev. Robert Povish, M.A.
Res., 1410 Almshouse Rd., 18929. Tel: 215-343-1288; Fax: 215-343-4996.
Catechesis/Religious Programs—Tel: 215-343-3139.
Students 490.

Jenkintown, Montgomery Co., Immaculate Conception (1866), Revs. John J. Conahan; Francis J. Gallagher.
Res., 604 West Ave., 19046. Tel: 215-884-4022; 887-0181; Fax: 215-887-4163.
School—606 West Ave., 19046. Tel: 215-887-1312.
Lay Teachers 15; Students 200.
Catechesis/Religious Programs—Tel: 215-885-5586.
Students 285.

Kennett Square, Chester Co., St. Patrick (1869), Revs. Victor F. Sharrett; Daniel J. Dougherty; Deacon James K. Madonna.
Res., 218 S. Meredith St., 19348. Tel: 610-444-2128; Fax: 610-444-4941. [CEM]
Parish Office: 212 Meredith St., 19348. Tel: 610-444-4364.
School—210 Meredith St., 19348. Tel: 610-444-3104.
Lay Teachers 10; Students 193.
Catechesis/Religious Programs—Tel: 610-444-2214. Mrs. Patricia Lohr, D.R.E.
Students 305.

Kimberton, Chester Co., St. Basil the Great (1965), Rev. Msgr. Joseph A. Shields. In res., Rev. William E. Grogan.
Res., Kimberton Rd. off Rte. 113, Box 637, 19442-0637. Tel: 610-933-2110; 933-4730.
School—Tel: 610-933-2453.
Lay Teachers 14; Students 288.
Catechesis/Religious Programs—Tel: 610-935-1261.
Students 236.
Convent—Tel: 610-933-2345. Sisters of St. Francis Residence

King of Prussia, Montgomery Co., Mother of Divine Providence (1954), Revs. Thomas P. Gaynard; Michael C. DiIorio.
Res., 333 Allendale Rd., 19406. Tel: 610-265-4178; Fax: 610-265-1653.
School—405 Allendale Rd., 19406. Tel: 610-265-2323.
Grey Nuns of the Sacred Heart 2; Lay Teachers 15; Students 287.
Catechesis/Religious Programs—Tel: 610-337-2173.
Students 347.
Convent—385 Allendale Rd., 19406. Tel: 610-265-2134.

Lafayette Hill, Montgomery Co., St. Philip Neri (1945), Rev. Msgr. Richard T. LaHart; Rev. Edward J. Kelly.
Res., 437 Ridge Pike, 19444. Tel: 610-828-5717; 834-1975; Fax: 610-834-0392.
School—3015 Chestnut St., 19444. Tel: 610-828-3082.
Sisters of St. Joseph 6; Lay Teachers 19; Students 455.
Catechesis/Religious Programs—Students 156.
Convent—Tel: 610-828-2866.

Lansdale, Montgomery Co., St. Stanislaus (1876), Rev. Msgr. Joseph W. Murray; Revs. Joseph F. Sabadish; Stephen A. Moerman; Kenneth W. Sharp; Rev. Msgr. Paul J. Cahill, Pastor Emeritus; Deacon Mathieu Tielemans.
Res., 51 Lansdale Ave., 19446. Tel: 215-855-3133; Fax: 215-855-5478. [CEM]
School—493 E. Main St., 19446. Tel: 215-368-0995; Fax: 215-393-4869. Diane McCaughan, Prin.; Mrs. Barbara Kelly, Asst. Prin.
Lay Teachers 33; Students 768.
Catechesis/Religious Programs—Tel: 215-855-9893.
Students 398.

Lansdowne, Delaware Co., St. Philomena (1898), Revs. Robert J. Chapman; Thomas J. Dempsey, Pastor Emeritus; John F. Meyers.
Res., 41 E. Baltimore Ave., 19050. Tel: 610-622-2420.
School—21 N. Highland Ave., 19050. Tel: 610-259-6817. Mrs. Mary Calderone, Prin.
Lay Teachers 9; Students 248.

Lenni, Delaware Co., St. Francis de Sales, Revs. Charles P. Vance; Joseph E. Walsh, Pastor Emeritus.
Res., P.O. Box 97, New Rd., 19052. Tel: 610-459-2203. [CEM]
School—Tel: 610-459-0799.
Sisters of St. Francis of Philadelphia 2; Lay Teachers 9; Students 188.
Convent—28 New Rd., Aston, 19014. Tel: 610-459-2501.
Stations—Delaware County Home.; Fair Acres Farm.; Sleighton School.

Levittown, Bucks Co., Immaculate Conception B.V.M. (1954), Revs. James J. Bones; John Mulholland.
Res., 5201 Emilie Rd., 19057-2505. Tel: 215-946-1638; 1639.
School—3810 Oxford Valley Rd., 19057. Tel: 215-949-2848.
Sisters, Servants of the Immaculate Heart of Mary 3; Lay Teachers 15; Students 396.
Catechesis/Religious Programs—Tel: 215-945-0826.
Students 225.
Convent—Tel: 215-945-4664.

St. Michael the Archangel (1953), Rev. Msgr. Richard T. Powers; Revs. Luke L. Chow; Francis X. Trauger; Joseph N. Accardi.
Res., 66 Levittown Pkwy., 19054. Tel: 215-945-1166; Fax: 215-945-6988.
School—130 Levittown Pkwy., 19054. Tel: 215-943-0222.
Lay Teachers 33; Students 776.
Catechesis/Religious Programs—Tel: 215-547-2518.
Students 409.
Convent—88 Levittown Pkwy., 19054. Tel: 215-943-8232.

Queen of the Universe (1955), Revs. Paul A. Wiedmann; Thomas A. McCann; Rev. Msgr. James A. Coyle, Pastor Emeritus; Deacon Joseph Upcavage. In res., Rev. Henry E. Dougherty.
Res., 2443 Trenton Rd., 19056. Tel: 215-945-8750; Fax: 215-945-0413.
School—Tel: 215-945-1866.
Sisters of St. Joseph 3; Lay Teachers 18; Students 340.
Catechesis/Religious Programs—Tel: 215-945-2704.
Students 480.
Convent—Tel: 215-945-6116.

Linfield, Montgomery Co., St. Clare (1963), Rev. Thomas J. Duffy.
Res., 228 Main St., 19468-1020. Tel: 610-495-7263.

Linwood, Delaware Co., Holy Saviour (1915), Rev. Thomas P. McKelvey.
Res., 108 E. Ridge Rd., 19061. Tel: 610-485-2520; 2521.
School—116 E. Ridge Rd., 19061. Tel: 610-485-0363. Judith Ann Devine, B.A., M.A., Prin.
Lay Teachers 16; Students 353.
Catechesis/Religious Programs—Students 136.
Convent—122 E. Ridge Rd., 19061. Tel: 610-485-7320.

Lower Makefield, Bucks Co., St. John the Evangelist (1964), Rev. Msgr. William J. Paul; Rev. Michael W. Swierzy.
Res., 752 Big Oak Rd., Morrisville, 19067. Tel: 215-295-4102; Fax: 215-295-3128.
School—728 Big Oak Rd., Morrisville, 19067. Tel: 215-295-0629.
Bernardine Sisters of St. Francis 1; Lay Teachers 14; Students 291.
Catechesis/Religious Programs—Tel: 215-295-9239.
Students 627.
Convent—Tel: 215-295-8201.

Malvern, Chester Co., St. Patrick (1915), Revs. James J. Ambrogi; Joseph G. Watson; Francis N. McDevitt, Pastor Emeritus; Deacon Lawrence P. Froio.
Res., 104 Channing Ave., 19355. Tel: 610-647-2345; Fax: 610-647-4997.
School—115 Channing Ave., 19355. Tel: 610-644-5797.
Catechesis/Religious Programs—Tel: 610-296-8899.
Students 280.

Manoa, Delaware Co., Sacred Heart (1927), Revs. George J. Boyle; James J. Whelan; Deacons John J. Suplee; Thomas J. Woods. Pastor Emeriti: Rev.

Msgr. James McGrath; Rev. Msgr. Thomas B. Falls. In res., Rev. Joseph Duncan.
Res., 105 Wilson Ave., Havertown, 19083. Tel: 610-449-3000; Fax: 610-449-2364.
School—Tel: 610-446-9198.
Sisters, Servants of the Immaculate Heart of Mary 3; Lay Teachers 12; Students 300.
Catechesis/Religious Programs—Tel: 610-446-7597. Eileen V. Lynch, D.R.E.
Students 315.
Convent—108 Shelbourne Rd., 19083. Tel: 610-446-3694.

Maple Glen, Montgomery Co., St. Alphonsus (1963), Revs. Wilfred F. Maloney; J. Jerome Wild; Thomas J. Kelly, Pastor Emeritus.
Res., 33 Conwell Dr., 19002. Tel: 215-646-4600; Fax: 215-646-0180.
School—29 Conwell Dr., 19002. Tel: 215-646-0150.
Lay Teachers 22; Students 357.
Catechesis/Religious Programs—Tel: 215-643-7938.
Students 251.
Convent—1563 Temple Dr., 19002. Tel: 215-646-6644.

Marcus Hook, Delaware Co., Immaculate Conception (1917) (Italian), Rev. Joseph A. Amalfitano.
Res., 21 W. Eighth St., P.O. Box 355, 19061. Tel: 610-485-1026.

Media, Delaware Co., St. Mary Magdalen (1963), Rev. James F. Hughes; Deacon E. Peter Zurbach. In res., Revs. John A. Freeman; Michael P. O'Malley.
Res., 2400 N. Providence Rd., 19063. Tel: 610-566-8821; Fax: 610-566-1005.
School—2430 N. Providence Rd., 19063. Tel: 610-565-1822; Fax: 610-627-9670.
Lay Teachers 20; Students 383.
Catechesis/Religious Programs—Tel: 610-565-5782; Fax: 610-566-1005.
Students 155.

Nativity of the Blessed Virgin Mary (1868), Revs. Francis A. Giliberti; Peter J. DiMaria; James F. Bradley, Pastor Emeritus. In res., Rev. Joseph Kennedy, Pastor Emeritus.
Res., 30 E. Franklin St., 19063. Tel: 610-566-0185. [CEM]
School—Gayley St., 19063. Tel: 610-566-6881.
Servants of the Most Sacred Heart of Jesus 5; Lay Teachers 7; Students 210.
Catechesis/Religious Programs—Students 330.
Convent—Tel: 610-565-8399.

Milmont Park, Delaware Co., Our Lady of Peace (1922), Revs. Charles M. O'Rourke; David W. Givey; George J. Ruhl, Pastor Emeritus.
Res., 501 Belmont Ave., 19033. Tel: 610-532-8081; 8082.
School—200 Milmont Ave., 19033. Tel: 610-534-0689. Sr. Denise Clifford, S.S.J., Prin.
Sisters of St. Joseph 4; Lay Teachers 11; Students 272.
Catechesis/Religious Programs—Students 272.
Convent—Tel: 610-532-4699.

Morrisville, Bucks Co., Holy Trinity, Revs. Thomas J. Calpin; Eugene M. Tully.
Res., 201 N. Pennsylvania Ave., 19067. Tel: 215-295-3045. [CEM]
School—227 N. Pennsylvania Ave., 19067. Tel: 215-295-6900. Mrs. Barbara Nuzzolo, Prin.
Lay Teachers 10; Students 275.

Morton, Delaware Co., Our Lady of Perpetual Help (1907), Rev. Msgr. Richard J. Skelly; Revs. Kevin P. Murray; John J. Kilgarriff, Pastor Emeritus. In res., Rev. Msgr. Joseph P. McFadden.
Res., O.L.P.H. Ct., 2130 Franklin Ave., 19070. Tel: 610-543-1046; Fax: 610-543-6150.
School—#5 O.L.P.H. Ct., 2130 Franklin Ave., 19070. Tel: 610-543-8350.
Sisters of St. Francis of Philadelphia 2; Lay Teachers 15; Students 402.
Catechesis/Religious Programs—Tel: 610-543-5448.
Students 390.
Convent—#3 O.L.P.H. Ct., 2130 Franklin Ave., 19070. Tel: 610-543-0186.

Narberth, Montgomery Co., St. Margaret (1900), Rev. Msgr. James J. Flood; Rev. John E. Fitzgerald. In res., Rev. Stephen J. Dougherty.
Res., 208 N. Narberth Ave., 19072. Tel: 610-664-3770.
School—227 N. Narberth Ave., 19072. Tel: 610-664-2640; Fax: 610-664-4677.
Sisters of Mercy 1; Lay Teachers 14; Students 241.
Catechesis/Religious Programs—Tel: 610-664-5715. Ms. Mary Katherine Roach, D.R.E.
Students 150.
Convent—301 Windsor Ave., 19072. Tel: 610-664-2748.

New Garden Township, Chester Co., St. Gabriel of the Sorrowful Mother (1988), Rev. Richard J. Maisano. Mailing Address: P.O. Box 709, Avondale, 19311. Tel: 610-268-0296; Fax: 610-268-5022.
Catechesis/Religious Programs—Students 168.

New Hope, Bucks Co., St. Martin of Tours (1885), Revs. John P. Schmeer; Paul J. Carey, Pastor Emeritus.
Res., 111 New St., 18938. Tel: 215-862-5472; Fax: 215-862-1829. [CEM]
Catechesis/Religious Programs—Students 159.

Newtown, Bucks Co., St. Andrew (1880), Revs. Michael C. Picard; J. Brian Bransfield; Edward T. Kearns. In res., Rev. John J. Pidgeon.
Res., 81 Swamp Rd., 18940. Tel: 215-968-2262; Fax: 215-579-9344. [CEM]
School—51 Wrights Rd., 18940. Tel: 215-968-2685; Fax: 215-968-4795.
Preschool—138 S. Sycamore St., 18940. Tel: 215-968-3464; Fax: 215-968-8606.
Sisters, Servants of the Immaculate Heart of Mary 6; Lay Teachers 35; Students 830.
Catechesis/Religious Programs—Tel: 215-968-6929.
Students 1,010.
Convent—Tel: 215-968-6568.

Newtown Square, Delaware Co., St. Anastasia (1912), Revs. John J. Shellem; Michael A. Colagreco; Leonard N. Peterson; Dennis L. Sullivan, T.O.R.; Rev. Msgr. Richard J. Simons, Pastor Emeritus.
Res., 3301 W. Chester Pike, 19073. Tel: 610-356-1613; Fax: 610-356-8332.
School—Tel: 610-356-6225.
Sisters of St. Joseph 3; Lay Teachers 29; Students 620.
Catechesis/Religious Programs—Tel: 610-356-5069.
Students 361.
Convent—3305 W. Chester Pike, 19073. Tel: 610-356-0273.

Norristown, Montgomery Co.,

1—Epiphany of Our Lord, (1957), Revs. James F. Baldrick; Patrick G. McCormick; Deacons William R. Radetzky; Kenneth P. Clancy; Joel M. Ziff; Alfred C. Lazaga. In res., Rev. Joseph P. Gentili.
Res., 3050 Walton Rd., 19401. Tel: 610-828-8634; Fax: 610-828-1802.
School—3040 Walton Rd., 19401. Tel: 610-825-0160.
Lay Teachers 12; Students 231.
Catechesis/Religious Programs—Tel: 610-825-6790. Mrs. Julia Noble, D.R.E.
Students 318.

2—St. Francis of Assisi, (1923), Rev. Msgr. Jerry Duraczynski; Revs. George P. Ettorre; Kevin C. Trautner; Lee Makowski, O.S.A.; Sr. Mary Jane Dunleavy, S.S.J., Pastoral Assoc. In res., Rev. Dominick F. Finn, O.S.F.S.
Res., 600 Hamilton St., 19401. Tel: 610-272-0402; Fax: 610-272-1794.
School—Oak & Buttonwood Sts., 19401. Tel: 610-272-0501; Fax: 610-272-8011.
Sisters of St. Joseph 2; Lay Teachers 14; Students 360.
Catechesis/Religious Programs—Tel: 610-272-9492.
Students 165.
Convent—Tel: 610-272-3686.

3—Holy Saviour, (1903) (Italian), Rev. Msgr. Arthur J. Centrella; Revs. Louis P. Bellopede; Anthony J. Cossavella; Rev. Msgr. John J. Busco, Pastor Emeritus; Deacons John Parker; Donald Kretsch.
Res., 407 E. Main St., 19401. Tel: 610-275-0958; Fax: 610-275-8464.
School—Airy & Walnut Sts., 19401. Tel: 610-272-8864.
Sisters, Servants of the Immaculate Heart of Mary 5; Lay Teachers 10; Students 249.
Catechesis/Religious Programs—Tel: 610-272-4445.
Students 296.
Convent—Tel: 610-272-4445.
Mission—Black Horse, Montgomery Co., Our Lady of Mount Carmel, 460 Fairfield Rd., 19401. Tel: 610-277-7739. [CEM]

4—St. Patrick, (1835), Rev. Joseph M. Derrig; Deacon Ismael Fuentes Cintron. In res., Rev. James T. McGuinn.
Res., 714 DeKalb St., 19401. Tel: 610-272-1408. [CEM]
Religious Education Building: Chestnut & Green Sts., 19401. Tel: 610-272-4500.
Convent—630 DeKalb St., 19401. Tel: 610-277-5962. Missionaries of Charity

5—St. Paul, (1963), Revs. Harry E. McCreedy; Walter Duraczynski. In res., Rev. Henry B. Degnan; Deacon Michael Dayoc (SFS) (Retired).
Res., 2007 New Hope St., 19401. Tel: 610-279-6725; Fax: 610-279-6749.
School—351 E. Johnson Hwy., 19401. Tel: 610-275-2990.
Lay Teachers 12; Students 224.

6—St. Titus, (1962), Revs. Robert E. Brennan; Martin E. Miller. In res., Rev. Joseph W. Bongard.
Res., 3006 Keenwood Rd., 19403. Tel: 610-279-4990; Fax: 610-279-8640.
School—Keenwood Rd. & Norriton Dr., 19403. Tel: 610-279-6043.
Bernardine Sisters of St. Francis of Philadelphia 2; Lay Teachers 13; Students 363.
Convent—Tel: 610-279-3111.

North Wales, Montgomery Co., Mary, Mother of the Redeemer (1987), Revs. Philip C. Ricci; Harry G. Richards.
Res., 1325 Upper State Rd., 19454. Tel: 215-362-7400; 362-8966; Fax: 215-362-4127.
Catechesis/Religious Programs—Students 705.

St. Rose of Lima (1919), Rev. John P. Boland. In res., Rev. Msgr. James J. Graham; Rev. Gerald S. Smith; Deacon Edward A. Konarski.
Res., 428 S. Main St., 19454-3224. Tel: 215-699-4617; Fax: 215-699-4452.
School—425 W. Pennsylvania Ave., 19454. Tel: 215-699-8831.
Lay Teachers 14; Students 231.
Catechesis/Religious Programs—Students 335.

Norwood, Delaware Co., St. Gabriel (1891), Revs. Daniel M. Dooley; John J. Large; Gerardo M. Caruso; Joseph J. Blanchfield, Pastor Emeritus.
Res., 233 Mohawk Ave., 19074. Tel: 610-586-1225.
School—Cleveland Ave., Tel: 610-532-3234.
Lay Teachers 18; Students 440.
Catechesis/Religious Programs—Tel: 610-534-7709.
Students 580.

Oreland, Montgomery Co., Holy Martyrs (1949), Rev. Ross J. Macartney. In res., Revs. Raymond F. Tribuiani; Ignatius J. Szal, Pastor Emeritus.
Res., 120 Allison Rd., 19075. Tel: 215-884-8575; Fax: 215-884-5924.
School—121 Allison Rd., 19075. Tel: 215-887-2044; Fax: 215-887-5907. Catherine C. McGough, Prin.
Lay Teachers 12; Students 167.
Preschool—207 Ulmer Ave., 19075. Tel: 215-572-8605.
Catechesis/Religious Programs—Students 192.

Ottsville, Bucks Co., St. John the Baptist (1743), Rev. Joseph Tobias, M.S.C.; Deacons Ernest D'Angelo; John O'Brien.
Res., 4050 Durham Rd., 18942. Tel: 610-847-5521. [CEM]
School—Tel: 610-847-5523.
Lay Teachers 13; Students 235.
Catechesis/Religious Programs—Tel: 610-847-5522.
Students 185.
Mission—Upper Black Eddy, Bucks Co., St. Joseph, Marienstein Rd., Upper Black Eddy, 18972.

Oxford, Chester Co., Sacred Heart (1914), Rev. William B. Dooner; Deacon Francis Murphy.
Res., 101 Church Rd., 19363. Tel: 610-932-5040.
Catechesis/Religious Programs—Students 438.

Paoli, Chester Co., St. Norbert (1956), Revs. Walter J. Burke, O.Praem.; Paul R. Fisher, O.Praem.
Res., 78 Leopard Rd., 19301. Tel: 610-644-1655; Fax: 610-644-0201.
School—Greenlawn & Leopard Rds., 19301. Tel: 610-644-1670.
Grey Nuns of the Sacred Heart 3; Lay Teachers 14; Students 253.
Catechesis/Religious Programs—Tel: 610-664-1342.
Students 183.
Convent—Tel: 610-644-1576.

Parkesburg, Chester Co., Our Lady of Consolation (1853), Revs. Victor J. Eschbach; George P. Schneider, Pastor Emeritus.
Res., 603 Second Ave., 19365. Tel: 610-857-3510; Fax: 610-857-2353. [CEM]
Catechesis/Religious Programs—10 Cemetery Rd., 19365. Tel: 610-857-1003.
Students 450.
Mission—Doe Run, Chester Co., St. Malachy. [CEM]

Penndel, Bucks Co., Our Lady of Grace (1908), Revs. Robert J. Conner; Robert A. Roncase; William J. Teverzczuk.
Res., 225 Bellevue Ave., 19047. Tel: 215-757-7700; 757-7786; Fax: 215-757-5377. [CEM]
School—300 Hulmeville Ave., 19047. Tel: 215-757-5287.
Sisters, Servants of the Immaculate Heart of Mary 3; Lay Teachers 21; Students 590.
Catechesis/Religious Programs—Tel: 215-757-5530.
Students 580.
Convent—338 Hulmeville Ave., 19047. Tel: 215-757-2272.

Penn Valley, Montgomery Co., St. Justin Martyr (1964), Rev. John B. De Mayo. In res., Revs. Christopher Redcay; Thomas J. Wisniewski.
Res., 1222 Hagysford Rd., Narberth, 19072. Tel: 610-664-0165; Fax: 610-664-5612.

Phoenixville, Chester Co.,

1—ST. ANN, (1907), Revs. John J. Newns; Michael G. Murtha.
Res., 502 Main St., 19460. Tel: 610-933-3732. [CEM]
School—Holy Family School, Third & Buttonwood Sts., 19460. Tel: 610-933-7562.
Lay Teachers 15; Students 340.
Catechesis/Religious Programs—Tel: 610-933-9350; Fax: 610-935-7958.
Students 212.
Parish Center—602 S. Main St., 19460.

2—HOLY TRINITY, (Polish), Rev. Joseph A. Daniel.
Res., 219 Dayton St., 19460. Tel: 610-933-3023. [CEM]
School—Holy Family School, Third & Buttonwood Sts., Tel: 610-933-7562.
Convent—221 Dayton St., 19460. Tel: 610-983-9446. Bernardine Sisters of the Third Order of St. Francis

3—ST. MARY OF THE ASSUMPTION, (1840), Rev. John C. Wilz.
Res., 212 Dayton St., 19460. Tel: 610-933-2526; Fax: 610-935-1706. [CEM 2]
School—Holy Family School, Third & Buttonwood Sts., 19460. Tel: 610-933-7562.

4—SACRED HEART, (1900) (Slovak), Rev. Msgr. John M. Galyo.
Res., 148 Church St., 19460. Tel: 610-933-3830. [CEM]

Pottstown, Montgomery Co., St. Aloysius (1856), Revs. John F. McCole; Francis G. Marszalek; Jason V. Kulczynski; Deacon Francis G. Duquesne.
Res., 214 N. Hanover St., 19464. Tel: 610-326-5877; Fax: 610-326-0901. [CEM 2]
School—Third & Hanover Sts., 19464. Tel: 610-326-6167.
Sisters of St. Francis of Philadelphia 2; Lay Teachers 20; Students 462.
Catechesis/Religious Programs—Students 402.
Convent—223 Beech St., 19464. Tel: 610-326-1498.

Holy Trinity (1899) (Slovak), Rev. Msgr. John M. Galyo, Admin.; Rev. Andrew L. Slafkosky, Pastor Emeritus.
Res., 370 South St., 19464. Tel: 610-326-2432. [CEM]

St. Peter (1924), Rev. Edward P. Kuczynski.
Res., 1128 South St., 19464. Tel: 610-326-5023.
School—1126 South St., 19464. Tel: 215-323-6730.
Bernardine Sisters of St. Francis 3; Lay Teachers 8; Students 209.
Convent—1124 South St., 19464. Tel: 610-323-9378.

Primos, Delaware Co., St. Eugene (1955), Rev. Joseph J. Meehan. In res., Rev. Joseph C. Bordonaro.
Res., 200 Oak Ave., 19018. Tel: 610-626-2866; Fax: 610-626-1904.
School—110 Oak Ave., 19018. Tel: 610-622-2909.
Lay Teachers 9; Students 245.
Catechesis/Religious Programs—Students 180.

Quakertown, Bucks Co., St. Isidore, Revs. Henry C. Graf; Thomas P. Kletzel.
Res., 531 W. Broad St., 18951. Tel: 215-536-4389. [CEM]
School—603 W. Broad St., Tel: 215-536-6052.
Lay Teachers 12; Students 274.

Richboro, Bucks Co., St. Vincent de Paul (1968), Revs. Joseph J. McLaughlin; John D. Gabin; William T. McBride, Pastor Emeritus.
Res., 654 Hatboro Rd., 18954-1039. Tel: 215-357-5905; Fax: 215-953-8190.
Catechesis/Religious Programs—Tel: 215-322-1932.
Students 596.

Ridley Park, Delaware Co., St. Madeline, Revs. Daniel J. Cavanaugh; Gavin W. Muir; Anthony C. Rodo.
Res., 110 Park St., 19078. Tel: 610-532-6880; Fax: 610-532-6653.
School—Tome & DuPont Sts., Tel: 610-583-3662.
Lay Teachers 16; Students 370.
Catechesis/Religious Programs—Students 256.

Riegelsville, Bucks Co., St. Lawrence (1974), Revs. Robert H. Breen; Joseph A. Henry, J.C.D., Pastor Emeritus.
Res., 345 Elmwood Ln., P.O. Box 126, 18077. Tel: 610-749-2684. [JC]

Roslyn, Montgomery Co., St. John of the Cross (1953), Revs. Thomas J. Duane; John J. Kilgallon; Paul C. Brandt.
Res., 2741 Woodland Rd., 19001. Tel: 215-659-4460.
School—2805 Woodland Rd., Tel: 215-659-1365. Sr. Patricia Maureen Mount, I.H.M., Prin.
Sisters, Servants of the Immaculate Heart of Mary 5; Lay Teachers 13; Students 300.
Catechesis/Religious Programs—Tel: 215-659-1451.
Students 212.
Convent—2803 Woodland Rd., Tel: 215-659-4483.

Royersford, Montgomery Co., Sacred Heart (1973), Rev. Thomas F. Doyle. In res., Rev. Vincent R. Morabito.
Res., 838 Walnut St., P.O. Box 64, 19468. Tel: 610-948-5915; 948-4087.
School—Area Catholic Elementary School of the Sacred Heart, Lewis Rd. & Washington St., 19468. Tel: 610-948-7206.
Lay Teachers 14; Students 180.
Catechesis/Religious Programs—Tel: 610-792-2997.
Students 337.

Rydal, Montgomery Co., St. Hilary of Poitiers (1962), Rev. Msgr. Michael J. Carroll. In res., Rev. Paul M. Kennedy, M.A.
Res., 820 Susquehanna Rd., 19046. Tel: 215-884-3252.
School—920 Susquehanna Rd., 19046. Tel: 215-887-4520; Fax: 215-887-6337.
Students 248.

Secane, Delaware Co., Our Lady of Fatima (1952), Revs. Engelbert G. Michel; William S. Kirk. In res., Rev. Thomas R. Urian.
Res., 1 Fatima Dr., 19018. Tel: 610-532-5800.
School—10 Fatima Dr., 19018. Tel: 610-586-7539.
Sisters, Servants of the Immaculate Heart of Mary 3; Lay Teachers 14; Students 454.
Catechesis/Religious Programs—Tel: 610-532-7430.
Students 190.
Convent—5 Fatima Dr., 19018. Tel: 610-532-1190.

Sellersville, Bucks Co., St. Agnes (1919), Rev. Msgr. Michael J. Long; Rev. John F. Bowe; Deacon Harry Tucker.
Res., 445 N. Main St., 18960. Tel: 215-257-2128. [CEM]
School—St. Agnes-Sacred Heart School. Consolidated. 393 N. Main St., 18960. Tel: 215-257-3571.
Lay Teachers 18; Students 515.
Catechesis/Religious Programs—Tel: 215-257-1811.
Students 393.

Sharon Hill, Delaware Co., Holy Spirit (1892), Revs. Martin E. Woodeshick; John A. Fitzgibbons; Daniel J. Kehoe, Pastor Emeritus; Deacons Albert Rayner; Thomas Butcavage.
Res., 1028 School St., 19079. Tel: 610-583-2220; Fax: 610-583-5130.
School—1036 School St., 19079. Tel: 610-532-7557.
Lay Teachers 9; Students 240.
Catechesis/Religious Programs—Students 103.

Southampton, Bucks Co., Our Lady of Good Counsel (1923), Rev. Msgr. Bernard J. Trinity; Revs. Gerald Dennis Gill; Mark J. Haynes.
Res., 611 Knowles Ave., 18966. Tel: 215-357-1300, Ext. 100; Fax: 215-357-4452.
School—Second St. Pike, 18966. Tel: 215-357-1300, Ext. 101. Mr. Frank Mokriski, Prin.
Lay Teachers 26; Students 649.
Catechesis/Religious Programs—Tel: 215-357-1300, Ext. 126.
Students 476.

South Coventry, Chester Co., St. Thomas More (1968), Rev. Hugh J. Dougherty; Deacon George W. Leonhardt, Jr. In res., Rev. Robert H. Mulligan.
Res., 2101 Pottstown Pike, Pottstown, 19465. Tel: 610-469-9304.
Catechesis/Religious Programs—Students 416.

Spring City, Chester Co., St. Joseph, Rev. John J. Dinda. In res., Revs. Michael W. Rzonca; Robert I. Riedy.
Res., 3640 Schuylkill Rd., 19475. Tel: 610-948-7760.

Springfield, Delaware Co., St. Francis of Assisi (1923), Revs. Salvatore M. Riccio; Louis C. Bier; Deacon James D. Kane, Sr.
Res., 136 Saxer Ave., 19064. Tel: 610-543-0848; Fax: 610-604-0283.
School—110 Saxer Ave., Tel: 610-543-0546.
Lay Teachers 17; Students 370.
Catechesis/Religious Programs—Students 395.

Holy Cross (1948), Revs. Edward B. Cahill; Mark G. Swope. In res., Rev. Joseph B. Curran, Pastor Emeritus; Deacon Robert Frankenberger.
Res., 651 E. Springfield Rd., 19064. Tel: 610-626-3321; Fax: 610-622-2920.
School—Bishop & Springfield Rds., 19064. Tel: 610-626-1709.
Sisters of Mercy 3; Lay Teachers 16; Students 340.
Catechesis/Religious Programs—Tel: 610-543-4892.
Students 245.
Convent—Tel: 610-626-2492.

St. Kevin, Revs. John J. Kane; Philip A. Scully, Pastor Emeritus. In res., Rev. Salvatore J. Pronesti.
Res., 200 W. Sproul Rd., 19064. Tel: 610-544-8777; 8778.
School—Tel: 610-544-4455.
Sisters of St. Joseph 2; Lay Teachers 10; Students 150.
Convent—Tel: 610-544-4535.

Stowe, Montgomery Co., St. Gabriel (1929), Revs. James W. Gormley; Patrick A. Duddy, Pastor Emeritus. In res., Rev. James A. Murphy, (Retired).
Parish Center: 127 E. Howard St., 19464. Tel: 610-326-5127.
Res., 421 Jefferson St., 19464. Tel: 610-327-2248.

Strafford, Chester Co., Our Lady of the Assumption (1908) (Italian), Revs. Eugene J. Carbo; Daniel J. Hoy. In res., Rev. Msgr. James T. McDonough.
Res., 35 Old Eagle School Rd., 19087. Tel: 610-688-1178; 688-6147; Fax: 610-293-9680. [CEM]
Preschool—135 Fairfield Ln., 19087. Tel: 610-688-5277.

Swarthmore, Delaware Co., Notre Dame de Lourdes (1959), Rev. William J. Benonis; Deacons Michael McAndrews; James Basilio. In res., Rev. Joseph L. Maloney.
Res., 950 Michigan Ave., 19081. Tel: 610-544-1270; Fax: 610-544-1271.
School—990 Fairview Rd., 19081. Tel: 610-328-9330.
Lay Teachers 13; Students 325.

Swedesburg, Montgomery Co., Sacred Heart (1907) (Polish), Rev. Joseph P. J. Zingaro; Rev. Msgr. Anthony E. Jaworowski, (Retired).
Res., 120 Jefferson St., 19405. Tel: 610-275-1750.
School—631 E. Fourth St., 19405. Tel: 610-277-4133.
Lay Teachers 12; Students 204.
Parish Center—635 E. Fourth St., 19405.

Trooper, Montgomery Co., Visitation B.V.M. (1954), Rev. Msgr. Francis J. Clemins; Revs. Francis X. Herron; Francis J. Mulranen; Zachary W. Navit. In res., Revs. Henry C. Schuyler; Joseph F. Smith, Pastor Emeritus.
Res., 196 N. Trooper Rd., Norristown, 19403. Tel: 610-539-5572.
School—N. Trooper Rd., R.D. 1, Norristown, 19403. Tel: 610-539-6080.
Sisters of the Holy Family of Nazareth 4; Lay Teachers 28; Students 771.
Catechesis/Religious Programs—Tel: 610-539-6211. Mary Beth Curran, D.R.E.
Students 600.
Convent—Tel: 610-539-5558.

Upper Darby, Delaware Co., St. Alice (Stonehurst) (1922), Revs. William P. Donnelly; Joseph Tran Kim Thien, Pastoral Assoc.; Rev. Msgr. William A. Doolin, Pastor Emeritus. In res., Revs. John P. Collins; David F. Brackenridge; Matthew Michael; Deacon Joseph F. Coyle.
Res., 150 Hampden Rd., 19082. Tel: 610-352-1431.
School—135 Copley Rd., 19082. Tel: 610-352-0725.
Sisters, Servants of the Immaculate Heart of Mary 4; Lay Teachers 12; Students 315.

Upper Gwynedd, Montgomery Co., Corpus Christi (1964), Revs. Thomas P. Flanagan, Ed.D.; Joseph L. Farrell; Francis J. Loughran, Pastor Emeritus. In res., Rev. Martin T. Cioppi.
Res., 1622 Supplee Rd., Lansdale, 19446. Tel: 215-855-1311.
School—920 Sumneytown Pike, Lansdale, 19466. Tel: 215-368-0582; Fax: 215-361-5927.
Sisters of St. Joseph 7; Lay Teachers 18; Students 575.
Catechesis/Religious Programs—Tel: 215-362-2292.
Students 835.
Convent—900 Sumneytown Pike, Lansdale, 19446. Tel: 215-368-0737.

Valley Forge, Montgomery Co., St. Teresa of Avila (1918), Revs. Francis E. Kelly; Thomas F. Walsh, Pastor Emeritus. In res., Rev. Msgr. James A. Coyle.
Mailing Address: Box 248, 19481.
Res., 1260 S. Trooper Rd., Norristown, 19403. Tel: 610-666-5820.
School—2550 S. Parkview Dr., Norristown, 19403. Tel: 610-666-6069.
Lay Teachers 8; Students 232.
Catechesis/Religious Programs—Tel: 610-666-0644.
Students 183.

Villanova, Delaware Co., St. Thomas of Villanova Parish Community (1848), Revs. Dennis J. Harten, O.S.A.; Michael Bielecki, O.S.A.; Deacon Albert T. Derivan.
Res., 1242 Montrose Ave., Rosemont, 19010. Tel: 610-525-4801; Fax: 610-525-6041.
School—St. Thomas of Villanova/Our Mother of Good Counsel. Consolidated. Pennswood Rd., Bryn Mawr, 19010. Tel: 610-525-1407; Fax: 610-525-0157.
St. Thomas of Villanova/Our Mother of Good Counsel Preschool—1236 Montrose Ave., Rosemont, 19010. Tel: 610-525-7554.

Wallingford, Delaware Co., St. John Chrysostom (1952, Revs. Joseph P. McGeown; Efren V. Esmilla; Rev. Msgr. Frederick J. Stevenson, Pastor Emeritus; Deacon Raymond Vadino.

Res., 617 S. Providence Rd., 19086. Tel: 610-874-3418; 876-3519; Fax: 610-872-1741.
School—607 Providence Rd., 19086. Tel: 610-876-7110.
Sisters of St. Joseph 4; Lay Teachers 20; Students 249.
Catechesis/Religious Programs—605 S. Providence Rd., 19086. Tel: 610-872-4673.
Students 639.
Convent—Tel: 610-872-7194.

Warminster, Bucks Co., Nativity of Our Lord (1956), Revs. William J. O'Donnell; Paul V. Dougherty; Kenneth G. Putz. In res., Rev. Msgr. John V. Bartos; Rev. James F. Endres.
Res., 625 W. Street Rd., 18974. Tel: 215-675-1925.
School—585 W. Street Rd., 18974. Tel: 215-675-2820.
Sisters of St. Joseph 1; Lay Teachers 25; Students 637.
Catechesis/Religious Programs—Tel: 212-672-5316.
Students 325.
Convent—615 W. Street Rd., 18974. Tel: 215-672-0147.

Warrington, Bucks Co., St. Joseph (1922), Revs. James A. Grant; Robert G. Suskey; Rev. Msgr. Leon J. Peck, Pastor Emeritus.
Res., 1795 Columbia Ave., 18976. Tel: 215-672-3020; Fax: 215-672-3114.
School—SS. Joseph & Robert Bellarmine. Consolidated. 1701 Columbia Ave., 18976. Tel: 215-672-0724.
Sisters, Servants of the Immaculate Heart of Mary 3; Lay Teachers 18; Students 504.
Catechesis/Religious Programs—Tel: 215-672-9990.
Students 255.
Station—Willow Grove Naval Air Station, Tel: 215-443-6002.

St. Robert Bellarmine (1968), Revs. Joseph T. Kane; Joseph M. McDermott.
Res., 856 Euclid Ave., 18976. Tel: 215-343-0315; Fax: 215-343-8592.
School—SS. Joseph & Robert Bellarmine. Consolidated. 1701 Columbia Ave., 18976. Tel: 215-672-0724.
Catechesis/Religious Programs—Euclid Ave. & Carriage Way, 18976. Tel: 215-343-9433.
Students 525.
Convent—189 E. County Line Rd., Hatboro, 19040. Tel: 215-675-2301.

Wayne, Chester Co., St. Isaac Jogues (1970), Rev. Msgr. Joseph C. Cunningham. In res., Rev. Boniface A.A. Osuji, Ph.D.
Res., 50 W. Walker Rd., 19087. Tel: 610-687-3366; Fax: 610-293-9529.
Catechesis/Religious Programs—Tel: 610-687-2481. Kathy Aaronson, D.R.E.
Students 208.

St. Katharine of Siena (1893), Rev. Msgr. John J. Jagodzinski; Rev. Msgr. Joseph P. Cooney, Pastor Emeritus; Sr. Elizabeth O'Hara, S.S.J., Pastoral Assoc.; Deacon George Bolter. In res., Rev. Pascal A. Monteleone.
Res., 104 S. Aberdeen Ave., 19087. Tel: 610-688-4584; Fax: 610-688-7951.
School—229 Windemere Ave., 19087. Tel: 610-688-5451. Sr. William Therese, I.H.M., Prin.
Sisters, Servants of the Immaculate Heart of Mary 4; Lay Teachers 16; Students 273.
Catechesis/Religious Programs—Tel: 610-688-7890. Mr. James Orega, D.R.E.
Students 240.

West Chester, Chester Co., St. Agnes (1793), Rev. Msgr. Thomas P. Craven; Revs. Robert B. McDermott; Joseph P. Gallagher; Lawrence F. Crehan; Deacon Victor Gonzalez. In res., Rev. Joseph D. Brandt; Rev. Msgr. Laurence F. Kelly, Pastor Emeritus.
Res., 233 W. Gay St., 19380. Tel: 610-692-2990; Fax: 610-692-9623. [CEM]
School—211 W. Gay St., 19380. Tel: 610-696-1260.
Sisters, Servants of the Immaculate Heart of Mary 4; Lay Teachers 23; Students 508.
Catechesis/Religious Programs—209 W. Gay St., 19380. Tel: 610-436-4640.
Students 536.
Convent—205 W. Gay St., 19380.

SS. Simon and Jude (1961), Revs. Francis X. Meehan; Michael Davis; Deacons James Lyon; Ben Stam. In res., Rev. James J. Melle.
Res., 8 Cavanaugh Ct., 19382. Tel: 610-696-3624; Fax: 610-696-3971.
School—6 Cavanaugh Ct., Tel: 610-692-5249; Fax: 610-696-4682.
Sisters, Servants of the Immaculate Heart of Mary 5; Lay Teachers 18; Students 580.
Catechesis/Religious Programs—Tel: 610-692-3118.
Students 518.
Convent—Tel: 610-692-4394.

West Conshohocken, Montgomery Co., St. Gertrude (1888), Rev. James J. McKeaney.
Res., 209 Merion Ave., 19428. Tel: 610-828-0268.
PreK-Kindergarten—150 Cedar Ave., 19428. Tel: 610-828-2161.

West Grove, Chester Co., Assumption B.V.M. (1873), Rev. John W. Graf. In res., Rev. Francis J. Depman.
Res., 107 Evergreen St., 19390. Tel: 610-869-2722. [CEM]
School—E. State Rd., 19390. Tel: 610-869-9576. Sr. Mary Sue Carwile, I.H.M., Prin.
Sisters, Servants of the Immaculate Heart 3; Lay Teachers 12; Students 265.
Catechesis/Religious Programs—Tel: 610-869-8575.
Students 425.
Convent—105 Evergreen St., 19390. Tel: 610-869-9832.
Mission—West Grove, Chester Co., Santa Maria, Madra de Dios, P.O. Box 1019, Avondale, 19311. Tel: 610-268-3365; Fax: 610-869-9395.

Westtown, St. Maximilian Kolbe (1986), Revs. Hugh P. Campbell; William A. Trader; Deacon Lawrence Brandon.
Res., 15 E. Pleasant Grove Rd., West Chester, 19382. Tel: 610-399-6936; 399-9642; Fax: 610-399-4828.
Catechesis/Religious Programs—Students 600.

Willow Grove, Montgomery Co., St. David (1919), Revs. Richard T. Bolger; Francis V. Bielski. In res., Rev. Joseph P. Devlin.
Res., 316 N. Easton Rd., 19090. Tel: 215-657-0252; Fax: 215-659-6516.
School—401 N. Easton Rd., 19090. Tel: 215-659-6393.
Sisters, Servants of the Immaculate Heart of Mary 7; Lay Teachers 13; Students 300.
Catechesis/Religious Programs—Tel: 215-659-4059.
Students 392.
Convent—400 N. Easton Rd., 19090. Tel: 215-659-0445.

Wyndmoor, Montgomery Co., Seven Dolors (1916), Revs. William J. Stanton, M.A.; John F. Cullen, M.A., Pastor Emeritus. In res., Rev. John D. Reardon, M.Div.
Res., 1200 E. Willow Grove Ave., 19038-7614. Tel: 215-233-2552; Fax: 215-233-2553.

Wynnewood, Montgomery Co., Presentation B.V.M. (1954), Rev. Msgr. Vincent M. Walsh, J.C.D.; Rev. Msgr. John C. Kavanagh, Pastor Emeritus; Sr. Alice Price, R.S.M., Pastoral Assoc.
Res., 204 Haverford Rd., 19096. Tel: 610-642-8341; Fax: 610-896-1970.
School—230 Haverford Rd., 19096. Tel: 610-642-8040. Mary Boyle, Prin.
Lay Teachers 13; Students 198.
Convent—240 Haverford Rd., 19096. Tel: 610-642-3803.
Sisters 2.

Yardley, Bucks Co., St. Ignatius of Antioch (1920), Rev. Msgr. Samuel E. Shoemaker, J.C.D.; Rev. James D. Tortorici, M.A. In res., Rev. Mark J. Hunt, S.T.L.
Res., 999 Reading Ave., 19067. Tel: 215-493-3377; Fax: 215-493-0450. [CEM][JC]
School—Tel: 215-493-3867.
Lay Staff 20; Students 302.
Catechesis/Religious Programs—Tel: 215-493-5204.
Students 662.

Yeadon, Delaware Co., St. Louis (1928), Rev. Charles E. Bonner.
Res., 821 W. Cobbs Creek Pkwy., 19050. Tel: 610-623-0553.

Chaplains of Public Institutions

PHILADELPHIA. *Philadelphia Prison System,* 8001 State Rd., 19136. Tel: 215-276-2288. Rev. John M. Bonavitacola, Chap.
Veterans Administration Medical Center, University & Woodland Aves., 19104. Tel: 215-823-5800, Ext. 2776. Rev. James E. King, O.S.F.S., Chap.

COATESVILLE. *Veterans Administration Medical Center.* Vacant. 19320. Tel: 215-384-7711, Ext. 190.

GRATERFORD. *Graterford State Correctional Institution,* 19426. Tel: 215-489-4151. Rev. Michael W. Rzonca, Chap.

NORRISTOWN. *Norristown State Hospital,* 19401. Tel: 215-270-1104. Rev. Dominick Finn, O.S.F.S., Chap.

On Duty Outside the Archdiocese:
Reverend Monsignors—
Bransfield, Michael J., National Shrine of the Immaculate Conception, Fourth St. & Michigan Ave., N.E., Washington, DC 20017
Green, James P., Apostolic Nunciature, Carnegielaan, 5, 2517 KH Den Haag, Netherlands
Pepe, Joseph A., Tribunal, Archdiocese of Santa Fe, 4000 Saint Joseph Pl., N.W., Albuquerque, NM 87120
Thomas, Daniel E., Pontifical North American College, Vatican City State, 00120 Europe
Reverend Fathers—
Benonis, Richard R., 7207 Southern Ridge Dr., Converse, TX 78109
Donofrio, Michael J., Parroquia San Pedro, Apartado 13, Andanuaylas, Apurimac, Peru
Garzarelli, Santo R., Velankanni Church, Society Rd., Irla, Bombay 40005-6 India
Grous, Albin J., SS. Cyril and Methodius Seminary, 3535 Indian Tr., Orchard Lake, MI 48324-0515
Hagan, Charles H., U.S. Catholic Conference, Dept. of Ed., 3211 Fourth St., N.E., Washington, DC 20017
McNamara, Donald P., Misioneros De Maryknoll, Apartado Postal 20.273, San Martin, Caracas 1020-A Venezuela, S.A.
Menei, Francis T., Trinity Spiritual Center, 3609 Simpson Ferry Rd., Shiremanstown, PA 17011
Perzan, Stephen B., Saint Francis of Assisi Church, P.O. Box 68, Lumberton, NM 87547
Ragan, Gerald P., Immaculate Conception Church, 204 N. Church St., Dublin, GA 31021
Shields, Hugh J., Society of Saint James the Apostle, 24 Clark St., Boston, MA 02109
Skindeleski, Thomas J., Saint Joan of Arc Church, 370 S.W. Third St., Boca Raton, FL 33432
Walsh, Edward J., Our Lady of Perpetual Help Church, 210 S. Wellwood Ave., Lindenhurst, NY 11757
Weber, Francis N., Holy Name of Jesus Church, 602 E. Kimberly Ave., Kimberly, WI 54136-1599

Military Chaplains:
Reverend Fathers—
Benz, David H.
Boyle, Dennis P.
Burns, Vincent P.
Concha, Alfonso J.
DiGregorio, Joseph L.
Foley, Francis P.
Glatts, Joseph M.
McManus, Gerald D.
Sullivan, James F.

Graduate Studies:
Reverend Fathers—
Gentili, Joseph P., Casa Santa Maria, Via dell'Umilta 30, Rome, 00187 Italy
Hunt, Mark J., St. Ignatius Rectory, 999 Reading Ave., Yardley, PA 19067
Magee, Michael K., Casa Santa Maria, Via dell'Umilta 30, Rome, 00187 Italy
Mahoney, Shaun L., Casa Santa Maria, Via dell'Umilta, Rome, 00187 Italy
Mesure, Gerard C., Oblates of St. Francis de Sales, 721 Lawrence St., N.E., Washington, DC 20017
O'Driscoll, John C., Casa Santa Maria, Via dell'Umilta 30, Rome, 00187 Italy
Oliver, James M., Casa Santa Maria, Via dell'Umilta 30, Rome, 00187 Italy
Pesarchick, Robert A., Casa Santa Maria, Via dell'Umilta 30, Rome, 00187 Italy
Prior, Joseph G., Casa Santa Maria, Via dell'Umilta 30, Rome, 00187 Italy
Tracy, Joseph A., Casa Santa Maria, Via dell'Umilta 30, Rome, 00187 Italy

---

Absent on Sick Leave:
Reverend Monsignors—
Nace, Arthur J.
Reverend Fathers—
Bloh, Stephen R.
Connors, Richard P.
Dougherty, William J.
Durney, Charles W.
Fala, John G.
Farley, Bernard C.
Gallagher, Joseph P.
Gana, Stanley M.
Kohler, Thomas M.
McCarthy, Michael J.
Roedel, Robert H.
Satchell, Martin J.
Smart, Raymond W.
Sweeney, Joseph J.
Wesolowski, Edmund C.
White, Stephen C.

Absent on Leave:
Reverend Monsignors—
Walls, David E.
Reverend Fathers—
Brennan, James J.
DiPaul, Lawrence M.
Egan, Francis M.
Galanaugh, Joseph T.
Genz, William J.
Jungers, Christopher J.
McLoughlin, Richard J.
Noone, Charles J.

O'Brien, Mark J.
Pelczar, Edward A.
Stewart, Kenneth K.J.
Waters, Samuel M.

Retired:
Reverend Monsignors—
Bennington, J. Clement, 3508 Bay Ave., Ocean City, NJ 08226
Busco, J. John, Holy Savior Rectory, 407 E. Main St., Norristown, PA 19041-5119
Bydlon, Adam J., Villa Saint Joseph, 1436 Lansdowne Ave., Darby, PA 19023-1298
Cahill, Paul J., Saint Stanislaus Rectory, 51 Lansdale Ave., Lansdale, PA 19446
Conway, Walter J., Saint William Rectory, 6200 Rising Sun Ave., Philadelphia, PA 19111
Cooney, Joseph P., Villa Saint Joseph, 1436 Lansdowne Ave., Darby, PA 19023-1298
Coyle, James A., Saint Teresa of Avila Rectory, P.O. Box 248, Valley Forge, PA 19481
Doolin, William A., Saint Anselm Rectory, 12669 Dunks Ferry Rd., Philadelphia, PA 19154
Falls, Thomas B., Villa Saint Joseph, 1436 Lansdowne Ave., Darby, PA 19023-1298
Fee, John B., Villa Saint Joseph, 1436 Lansdowne Ave., Darby, PA 19023-1298
Fitzmaurice, Francis J., Villa Saint Joseph, 1436 Lansdowne Ave., Darby, PA 19023
Gaughan, Francis J., Saint Matthew Rectory, 3000 Cottman Ave., Philadelphia, PA 19149
Jaworowski, Anthony E., Sacred Heart Rectory, 120 Jefferson St., Swedesburg, PA 19405
Kavanaugh, John C., Presentation B.V.M. Rectory, 204 Haverford Rd., Wynnewood, PA 19096
Kelly, Laurence F., Saint Agnes Rectory, 233 W. Gay St., West Chester, PA 19380
Keul, Francis X., Regina Coeli Residence for Priests, 685 York Rd., Warminster, PA 18974
Koenig, William A., Motherhouse, Sisters of Holy Redeemer, 521 Moredon Rd., Huntingdon Valley, PA 19006
Lynaugh, Joseph E., Villa Saint Joseph, 1436 Lansdowne Ave., Darby, PA 19023-1298
Marley, Michael F., Villa Saint Joseph, 1436 Lansdowne Ave., Darby, PA 19023-1298
Martusevich, Vito J., Saint George Rectory, 3580 Salmon St., Philadelphia, PA 19134
McDonough, Martin J., Villa Saint Joseph, 1436 Lansdowne Ave., Darby, PA 19023-1298
McGlinn, Joseph J., Our Lady of Ransom Rectory, 6701 Calvert St., Philadelphia, PA 19149
McGrath, James, 6101 34th St. W., 10 E, Bradenton, FL 34210-3701
Monaghan, Charles J., Villa Saint Joseph, 1436 Lansdowne Ave., Darby, PA 19023-1298
Musial, Edward S., Saint Mary Rectory, 140 W. Hector St., Conshohocken, PA 19428
Mynaugh, Charles B., Regina Coeli Residence for Priests, 685 York Rd., Warminster, PA 18974
Nugent, Arthur W., 1341 Osbourne Ave., Roslyn, PA 19001
Peck, Leon J., Regina Coeli Residence for Priests, 685 York Rd., Warminster, PA 18974
Pryor, Thomas P., Villa Saint Joseph, 1436 Lansdowne Ave., Darby, PA 19023
Schaeflein, Charles J., Mount Nazareth, 2775 Holme Ave., Philadelphia, PA 19152
Sikora, Joseph G., Saint Francis Country House, 1412 Lansdowne Ave., Darby, PA 19023-1298
Simons, Richard J., Villa Saint Joseph, 1436 Lansdowne Ave., Darby, PA 19023-1298
Statkus, Francis J., 208 E. Trenton Ave., Wildwood Crest, NJ 08260
Stevenson, Frederick J., Saint John Chrysostom Rectory, 605 S. Providence Rd., Wallingford, PA 19086-6998
Urbanowicz, Francis J., Sacred Heart Rectory, 316 E. Broadway Ave., Clifton Heights, PA 19018-1723
Vizzard, James J., Saint Matthias Rectory, 128 Bryn Mawr Ave., Bala Cynwyd, PA 19004
Reverend Fathers—
Barnes, Gerard J., Villa Saint Joseph, 1436 Lansdowne Ave., Darby, PA 19023-1298
Barr, Philip R., 1511 Grant Rd., West Chester, PA 19382
Blanchfield, Joseph J., St. Gabriel Rectory, 233 Mohawk Ave., Norwood, PA 19074-4019
Boland, Edward G., Villa Saint Joseph, 1436 Lansdowne Ave., Darby, PA 19023-1298
Bradley, James F., Saint Andrew Rectory, 3500 School Ln., Drexel Hill, PA 19026
Bradley, John J., Saint Charles Borromeo Rectory, 3422 Dennison Ave., Drexel Hill, PA 19026
Carey, Paul J., 1165 Beverly Rd., Rydal, PA 19046
Catullo, Pasquale R., St. Helena Rectory, P.O. Box 5085, Center Square, PA 19422
Cellucci, Carl D., 902 Surf Ave., North Wildwood, NJ 08260
Chapman, A. James, Villa Saint Joseph, 1436 Lansdowne Ave., Darby, PA 19023-1298
Coates, John T., Regina Coeli Residence for Priests, 685 York Rd., Warminster, PA 18974
Cornely, Francis J., Saint Margaret Mary Alacoque Rectory, 500 Wanamaker Ave., Essington, PA 19029
Cudemo, Nicholas V., 1310 Grovania Ave., Abington, PA 19001
Cullen, John F., Seven Dolors Church, 1200 E. Willow Grove Rd., Wyndmoor, PA 19118
Curran, Joseph B., Holy Cross Rectory, 651 E. Springfield Rd., Springfield, PA 19064
Czarnota, Reynold A., Villa Saint Joseph, 1436 Lansdowne Ave., Darby, PA 19023
Daly, James P., Villa Saint Joseph, 1436 Lansdowne Ave., Darby, PA 19023-1298
Daly, John J., Villa Saint Joseph, 1436 Lansdowne Ave., Darby, PA 19023-1298
Degnan, Henry B., St. Paul Rectory, 2007 New Hope St., Norristown, PA 19401
Degutis, George D., 8815 Calvert St., Philadelphia, PA 19152-1305
Dempsey, Thomas J., Villa Saint Joseph, 1436 Lansdowne Ave., Darby, PA 19023-1298
Devlin, Joseph F., St. George Rectory, 22 E. Cooke Ave., Glenolden, PA 19036
Dougherty, Henry E., Queen of the Universe Rectory, 2443 Trenton Rd., Levittown, PA 19056
Dougherty, John C., Saint Bartholomew Rectory, 5600 Jackson St., Philadelphia, PA 19124
Drobel, William F., Villa Saint Joseph, 1436 Lansdowne Ave., Darby, PA 19023-1298
Duddy, Patrick A., Villa Saint Joseph, 1436 Lansdowne Ave., Darby, PA 19023-1298
Duffy, John J., Five Whalerman Cove, Brigantine, NJ 08203
Dunne, Peter J., 815 Haycock Run Rd., Kintnersville, PA 18930
Dux, James M., Villa Saint Joseph, 1436 Lansdowne Ave., Darby, PA 19023-1298
Dziadosz, Edward T., 438 W. Mahanoy Ave., Mahanoy City, PA 17948-0095
Farrell, Donald J., Saint Cyril of Alexandria Rectory, 153 Penn Blvd., East Lansdowne, PA 19050
Feeney, Thomas M., 1341 Osbourne Ave., Roslyn, PA 19001
Fitzpatrick, Peter A., St. Patrick Rectory, 242 S. 20th St., Philadelphia, PA 19103
Gallen, Francis H., Hershey Mill, 118 Chandler Dr., West Chester, PA 19380
Gausch, Joseph P., 1240 Ohio Ave., Cape May, NJ 08240
Gibas, John J., 8018 Large St., Philadelphia, PA 19152
Glynn, John P., 137 105th St., Stone Harbor, NJ 08247
Gough, James F., St. Matthew Rectory, 3000 Cottman Ave., Philadelphia, PA 19149
Griffin, John A., Our Lady of Fatima Rectory, 2933 Street Rd., Fatima Acres, Bensalem, PA 19020
Griffin, Richard J., Our Lady of Fatima Rectory, 2933 Street Rd., Fatima Acres, Bensalem, PA 19020
Gsell, John W., Villa Saint Joseph, 1436 Landsdowne Ave., Darby, PA 19023-1298
Hartnett, Walter J., 3080 Lake Osborne Dr., Lake Worth, FL 33461
Henry, Joseph A., 1815 Carwithen St., Philadelphia, PA 19152
Jaworowski, Leon E., Villa Saint Joseph, 1436 Lansdowne Ave., Darby, PA 19023-1298
Kane, Aloysius T., Villa Saint Joseph, 1436 Lansdowne Ave., Darby, PA 19023-1298
Kane, Thomas A., St. Matthias Rectory, 128 Bryn Mawr Ave., Bala Cynwyd, PA 19004
Kehoe, Daniel J., Holy Spirit Rectory, 1028 School St., Sharon Hill, PA 19079
Kelly, James J., Villa Saint Joseph, 1436 Lansdowne Ave., Darby, PA 19023-1298
Kelly, Thomas J., Saint Francis Country House, 1412 Lansdowne Ave., Darby, PA 19023-1298
Kennedy, Joseph J., Nativity B.V.M. Rectory, 30 E. Franklin St., Media, PA 19096
Kerrigan, Joseph P., Saint Elizabeth Ann Seton Rectory, 1200 Park Ave. E., Bensalem, PA 19020
Kerwick, Robert J., Villa Saint Joseph, 1436 Lansdowne Ave., Darby, PA 19023-1298
Kilgarriff, John J., Saint Francis Country House, 1412 Lansdowne Ave., Darby, PA 19023-1218
Klapp, John S., 5630 N. Arbor St., Philadelphia, PA 19120
Klitsch, Anthony L., Villa Saint Joseph, 1436 Lansdowne Ave., Darby, PA 19023-1298
Koob, Edward H., 6612 Pleasure Ave., Sea Isle City, NJ 08243-1450
Kovacs, Louis D., Villa Saint Joseph, 1436 Lansdowne Ave., Darby, PA 19023-1298
Krick, Howard K., 8610 Windway Dr., San Antonio, TX 78239
Lazzaro, Nicholas A., Villa Saint Joseph, 1436 Lansdowne Ave., Darby, PA 19023
Leary, James V., Sacred Heart Rectory, 148 Church St., Phoenixville, PA 19460
Lennon, Francis P., St. Eleanor Rectory, 647 Locust St., Collegeville, PA 19426-2541
Lepleiter, Robert P., Regina Coeli Residence for Priests, 685 York Rd., Warminster, PA 18974
Loughran, Francis J., Villa Saint Joseph, 1436 Lansdowne Ave., Darby, PA 19023-1298
Loughrey, Thomas F., 651 W. Pine Ave., West Wildwood, NJ 08260
Maguire, Connell J., 2800 N. Ocean Dr., Apt. B15a, Riviera Beach, FL 33404
Mangan, John J., Villa Saint Joseph, 1436 Lansdowne Ave., Darby, PA 19023-1298
Matsko, John M., St. Francis Country House, 1412 Lansdowne Ave., Darby, PA 19023-1218
Maurer, Paul F., Epiphany of Our Lord Church, 1121 Jackson St., Philadelphia, PA 19148
McBride, William T., Regina Coeli Residence for Priests, 685 York Rd., Warminster, PA 18974
McCaffrey, Gerard D., Regina Coeli Residence for Priests, 685 York Rd., Warminster, PA 18974
McCloskey, Joseph A., St. Francis Country House, 1412 Lansdowne Ave., Darby, PA 19023-1218
McDermott, Francis A., St. Patrick Rectory, 242 S. 20th St., Philadelphia, PA 19103
McDevitt, Francis N., Villa Saint Joseph, 1436 Lansdowne Ave., Darby, PA 19023-1298
McMullen, Charles P., Saint Francis Country House, 1412 Lansdowne Ave., Darby, PA 19023-1218
Morley, John J., Villa Saint Joseph, 1436 Lansdowne Ave., Darby, PA 19023-1298
Murphy, James A., St. Gabriel Rectory, 127 E. Howard St., Stowe, PA 19464
Murphy, James J., 227 Brazilian Ave., Palm Beach, FL 33480
Murphy, James F., Saint Francis Country House, 1412 Lansdowne Ave., Darby, PA 19023-1218
Murphy, Joseph T., 812 Rowland Ave., Cheltenham, PA 19012
Murphy, Lawrence J., Villa Saint Joseph, 1436 Lansdowne Ave., Darby, PA 19023-1298
Murray, John J., Villa Saint Joseph, 1436 Lansdowne Ave., Darby, PA 19023-1298
O'Halloran, Martin J., Regina Coeli Residence for Priests, 685 York Rd., Warminster, PA 18974
O'Hara, Martin F., St. Jerome Rectory, 8100 Colfax St., Philadelphia, PA 19136-1801
Oestreich, Emil C., St. Raymond of Penafort Rectory, 1350 Vernon Rd., Philadelphia, PA 19150-2123
Palombo, Albert B., 14211 Alto Cedro Dr., Del Ray Beach, FL 33484-2550
Reynolds, Ignatius C., Villa Saint Joseph, 1436 Lansdowne Ave., Darby, PA 19023-1298
Riedy, Robert I., Saint Francis Country House, 1412 Lansdowne Ave., Darby, PA 19023-1218
Rilley, John F., Villa St. Joseph, 1436 Lansdowne Ave., Darby, PA 19023
Rogers, Francis P., St. Timothy Rectory, 3001 Levick St., Philadelphia, PA 19149
Rossi, Anthony M., Villa Saint Joseph, 1436 Lansdowne Ave., Darby, PA 19023-1298
Ruhl, George J., Saint Francis Country House, 1412 Lansdowne Ave., Darby, PA 19023-1218
Ryan, Robert F., St. Gabriel's Hall, P.O. Box 13, Audubon, PA 19407
Scherf, Gerard H., Saint Martha Rectory, 11301 Academy Rd., Philadelphia, PA 19154
Schifalacqua, Ildebrando E., St. Bartholomew Rectory, 5600 Jackson St., Philadephia, PA 19124
Schneider, George P., 109 Chestnut St., Parkesburg, PA 19365
Schuyler, Henry C., Visitation B.V.M. Rectory, 196 N. Trooper Rd., Norristown, PA 19403-2665
Scully, Philip A., Villa Saint Joseph, 1436 Lansdowne Ave., Darby, PA 19023-1298
Senske, Joseph A., Gillet Convent, Immaculata College, P.O. Box 731, Immaculata, PA 19345
Shea, Thomas F., Villa Saint Joseph, 1436 Lansdowne Ave., Darby, PA 19023-1298
Sheridan, James B., Villa Saint Joseph, 1436 Lansdowne Ave., Darby, PA 19023-1298
Shimkus, Bernard A., Villa Saint Joseph, 1436 Lansdowne Ave., Darby, PA 19023-1298
Slafkosky, Andrew L., 610 Pine Rd., Silver Spring Shores, Ocala, FL 34472-6167
Smith, Joseph F., Visitation B.V.M. Rectory, 196 N. Trooper Rd., Norristown, PA 19403-2665
Smith, Martin G., 111 Walnut Ave., Villas, NJ 08251
Smith, William J., 4051 Asbury Ave., Ocean City, NJ 08226
Soreth, James F., Saint Francis Country House, 1412 Lansdowne Ave., Darby, PA 19023-1218
Spaits, George S., Regina Coeli Resisdence for Priests, 685 York Rd., Warminster, PA 18974
Spicijaric, Anthony, Villa Saint Joseph, 1436 Lansdowne Ave., Darby, PA 19023-1298
St. Clair, Joseph A., Villa Saint Joseph, 1436 Lansdowne Ave., Darby, PA 19023-1298

Szal, Ignatius J., 460 Sunbury St., Minersville, PA 17954
Thomas, Joseph W., Villa Saint Joseph, 1436 Lansdowne Ave., Darby, PA 19023
Walker, Norbert J., 401 W. Brigantine Ave., Brigantine, NJ 08203
Walsh, George J., Villa Saint Joseph, 1436 Lansdowne Ave., Darby, PA 19023
Walsh, John M., Villa Saint Joseph, 1436 Lansdowne Ave., Darby, PA 19023-1298
Walsh, Joseph E., Saint Francis de Sales Rectory, 35 New Rd., P.O. Box 97, Lenni, PA 19052
Walsh, Thomas F., 730 Salem Ct., Yardley, PA 19067
Wassel, Eugene A., Saint Casimir Rectory, 324 Wharton St., Philadelphia, PA 19147
Wright, Richard J., Saint Colman Rectory, 11 Simpson Rd., Ardmore, PA 19003
York, James E., Villa Saint Joseph, 1436 Lansdowne Ave., Darby, PA 19023-1298
Ziemba, Anthony F., Saint Laurentius Rectory, 1608 E. Berks St., Philadelphia, PA 19125

Permanent Deacons:
All locations are Philadelphia unless otherwise indicated.
Andrews, Edward J., St. Martin De Porres Church
Basilio, James A., Notre Dame De Lourdes Church, Swarthmore
Bean, John J., St. Bartholomew Church
Belanger, A. Kenneth, St. Helena Church, Center Square
Bentancourt, Miguel, St. Peter the Apostle Church
Bizal, Francis M., SS. Philip and James Church, Exton
Bolter, George A., St. Katharine of Siena Church, Wayne
Bonilla, Victor M., Maternity B.V.M. Church
Brandon, Lawrence G., St. Maximilian Kolbe Church, West Chester
Brown, Clifford W., Our Mother of Consolidation Church
Burns, James H., St. Eleanor Church, Collegeville
Butcavage, Thomas E., Holy Spirit Church, Sharon Hill
Calabrese, Peter J., St. Charles Borromeo Church, Drexel Hill
Ceneviva, Vincent G., St. Jude Church, Chalfont
Champagne, William E., Our Lady of Hope Church
Clancy, Kenneth P., Epiphany of Our Lord Church, Norristown
Clark, Francis T., St. Jerome Church
Collazo, Apolonio, Visitation B.V.M. Church
Collazo, Ezequiel, Mission Santa Maria, West Grove
Conroy, Michael F., Sacred Heart Church, Royersford
Corwell, George V., Our Lady of Mt. Carmel Church, Doylestown
Coyle, Joseph P., St. Alice Church, Upper Darby
Coyne, Richard C., Holy Cross Church
Cruz, Felipe, Incarnation of Our Lord Church
D'Angelo, Ernest, St. John the Baptist Church, Ottsville
Davaro, John J., St. Dorothy Church, Drexel Hill
Dayoc, Michael J., St. Paul Church, Norristown
DeJesus, Epifanio, Cathedral Basilica of SS. Peter & Paul
Del Valle, Maximino, Incarnation of Our Lord Church
DeLucca, Daniel N., St. Andrew Church, Drexel Hill
DeMasi, Leonard, St. Monica Church
Derivan, Albert T., St. Thomas of Villanova Church, Rosemont
Devine, Charles F., St. Thomas the Apostle Church, Chester Heights
Dymek, Edward J., St. Ephrem Church, Bensalem
Eliason, William F., St. David Church, Willow Grove
Fabrizio, Francis S., St. Charles Borromeo Church, Drexel Hill
Favinger, M. Eugene, Our Lady of Consolation Church, Parkesburg
Fernandez, Alfonzo, St. Veronica Church
Fontanez, Jose, Incarnation of Our Lord Church
Frankenberger, Robert J., Holy Cross Church, Springfield
Froio, Lawrence P., St. Patrick Church, Malvern
Fuentes, Ismael, St. Patrick Church, Norristown
Fulmer, Walter C., Christ the King Church
Gibson, Lawrence J., St. Thomas Aquinas Church, Croyden
Gladnick, Leo T., Ascension of Our Lord Church
Gonzalez, Victor M., St. Agnes Church, West Chester
Gravlin, John J., St. Matthew Church
Guinane, William J., St. Madeline Church, Ridley Park
Haddon, Richard S., St. Catherine of Siena Church, Horsham
Hannum, Stephen W., Fitzgerald Mercy Hospital, Darby
Harkin, William C., Our Mother of Consolation Church
Harper, Sidney M., St. Athanasius Church
Harrison, A. Gerald, SS. Peter and Paul Church, West Chester
Hartmann, James E., St. John the Evangelist Church, Morrisville
Hartmann, Karl J., St. Joseph Church, Warrington
Heaney, Philip E., Maternity B.V.M. Church
Hernandez, Jose, Incarnation of Our Lord Church
Hopkins, Stephen, St. Benedict Church
Horan, Thomas J., SS. Peter & Paul Church, West Chester
Hynes, John, Maternity B.V.M. Church
Iannucci, Joseph E., St. Pius X Church, Broomall
Jacobucci, Raymond, St. Nicholas of Tolentine Church
Jones, David E., St. Anthony of Padua Church, Ambler
Kane, James D., Sr., St. Francis of Assisi Church, Springfield
Kefer, Robert J., SS. Peter & Paul Church, West Chester
Kelly, Gerald F., St. Matthias Church, Bala Cynwyd
Kelly, Walter E., Our Lady of Mount Carmel Church, Doylestown
Kern, Paul R., St. John Baptist Vianney Church, Gladwyne
Klauder, Francis, St. Elizabeth Ann Seton Church, Bensalem
Konarski, Edward A., St. Rose of Lima Church, North Wales
Kretsch, Donald J., Holy Savior Church, Norristown
Lance, Walter C., St. Clement Church
Lazaga, Alfred, Epiphany of Our Lord Church, Norristown
Leahy, Eugene R., Holy Family Church
Leonhardt, George W., St. Thomas More Church, South Coventry
Lozada, Jose Luis, St. Hugh of Cluny Church
Lozada, Mario, St. Boniface Church
Lyon, James E., SS. Simon & Jude Church, West Chester
Madonna, James K., St. Patrick Church, Kennett Square
Maldonado, Rafael, St. Veronica Church
Malfara, Louis S., St. Cecilia Church
Manson, Joseph J., St. Genevieve Church, Flourtown
Manzano, Edwin R., Visitation B.V.M. Church
Maresca, Armand J., SS. Cosmas & Damian Church, Conshohocken
Martes, Zoilo, St. Michael Church
McAndrews, Michael J., Notre Dame DeLourdes Church, Swarthmore
McGovern, Clement J., St. Cornelius Church, Chadds Ford
McGrath, Gerard P., St. Eleanor Church, Collegeville
Mendez, Jose M., St. Ambrose Church
Micucci, Joseph A., Mother of Divine Grace Church
Morales, Jose A., St. Mark Church, Bristol
Morris, George E., St. Robert Bellarmine Church, Warrington
Murphy, Francis X., Sacred Heart Church, Oxford
Nightingale, Richard G., Our Lady of Victory Church
Niland, Joseph W., St. Elizabeth Ann Seton Church, Bensalem
O'Brien, Gregory R., St. Madeline Church, Ridley Park
O'Kedas, Leroy F., St. Rita of Cascia Church
Orlando, John C., St. Monica Church
Parker, John, Holy Saviour Church, Norristown
Pavonarius, Charles A., St. Jerome Church
Purnell, Edward M., St. Theresa of the Child Jesus Church
Radetsky, William R., Epiphany of Our Lord Church, Norristown
Rayner, Albert E., Holy Spirit Church, Sharon Hill
Rebuck, Charles H., St. Gabriel Church, Stowe
Riordan, John T., St. Jude Church, Chalfont
Rooney, Joseph T., Our Lady Help of Christians Church, Abington
Rosario, Israel, Our Lady of Hope Church
Rouse, Daniel J., St. John Bosco Church, Hatboro
Ruiz, Luis, St. Ambrose Church
Schaffer, David B., St. Denis Friary, Havertown
Schlegel, John F., St. Denis Friary, Havertown
Seda, Victor, St. Veronica Church
Sexton, Joseph F., St. Mary of the Assumption Church
Shields, Thomas A., St. Martin De Porres Church
Singleton, Albert J., c/o Society of African Missions, Takoma Park, MD
Skawinski, Robert J., St. Ignatius Church, Yardley
Smith, Calvin C., St. Benedict Church
Stam, Bernardus C., SS. Simon & Jude Church, West Chester
Stevens, Allen T., St. Francis of Assisi Church
Stewart, Robert J., St. Ignatius Church, Yardley
Stewart, William H., St. Martin De Porres Church
Stoughton, Richard L., Our Lady of the Rosary Church, Coatesville
Suplee, John J., Sacred Heart Church, Havertown
Thomas, William C., Old St. Joseph's Church
Thompson, Vincent J., St. Francis Xavier Church
Tielemans, Mathieu M., St. Stanislaus Church, Lansdale
Tormey, James M., Our Mother of Consolation Church
Tucker, Henry E., St. Agnes Church, Sellersville
Urbanski, Timothy E., St. Catherine of Siena Church, Horsham
Vadino, Raymond M., St. John Chrysostom Church, Wallingford
Verna, Louis, Blessed Virgin Mary Church, Darby
Walker, James T., St. Benedict Church
Whartenby, Gerald J., St. Anselm Church
Windish, Joseph F., St. Cyril of Jersulem Church, Jamison
Wirth, Richard D., St. Cornelius Church, Chadds Ford
Wojewodka, Boleslaw S., Sacred Heart Church, Clifton Heights
Wolkowicz, Leonard J., St. Barnabas Church
Woodall, Michael V., St. Eleanor Church, Collegeville
Woods, Thomas J., Sacred Heart Church, Havertown
Ziff, Joel M., Epiphany of Our Lord Church, Norristown
Zurbach, E. Peter, St. Mary Magdalen Church, Media

INSTITUTIONS LOCATED IN THE ARCHDIOCESE

[A] SEMINARIES, ARCHDIOCESAN

WYNNEWOOD. *Theological Seminary of St. Charles Borromeo, Overbrook*, Administration: 1000 E. Wynnewood Rd., 19096-3099. Tel: 610-667-3394; Fax: 610-664-7913. Rev. Msgr. James E. Molloy, M.Div., M.A., Rector; Rev. John P. Murray, C.M., S.T.L., S.S.L., LL.D., Vice Rector; Charles H. Kerrigan, M.B.A., CFO; Elaine K. Rice, M.B.A., Coord. for Financial Svcs.; Mary C. Barker, B.A., Coord. for Campus Svcs.; Rev. Msgr. Thomas J. Herron, S.S.L., S.T.D., Academic Dean, Theology Division; Revs. John J. DelliCarpini, Ph.D., Academic Dean, College Division; John C. Marine, M.Div., Dean of Formation, Theology Division; Michael J. Kelly, M.A., M.Div., Dean of Formation, College Division; Robert J. Carroll, M.Div., M.A., Dir. Spiritual Formation, Theology Division; James R. Bajorek, M.Div., M.A., Dir. Spiritual Formation, College Division; Thomas J. Owens, M.Div., Dir., Pastoral and Apostolic Formation; Thomas M. Mullin, M.Div., M.A., S.S.L., Academic Dean, Religious Studies Division; Sr. Cor Immaculatum Connors, I.H.M., M.A., Asst. Academic Dean, Religious Studies Division; Lorena F. Boylan, M.L.S., M.A., Dir. of Library Svcs.; Sr. Joan Freney, R.S.M., M.A., Registrar; Revs. John M. Savinski, M.Div., M.A., Dir., Spiritual Year Prog.; Peter J. Welsh, Ph.D., Coord. of Spiritual Formation, Spiritual Year Prog.

Full Time Institutional Faculty: Mark E. Bradford, M.Mus.; Rev. Augustine M. Esposito, O.S.A., M.Div., Ph.D.; Mr. John M. Haas, S.T.L., Ph.D.; Janet Haggerty, Ph.D.; Mr. Atherton C. Lowry, Ph.D.; Rev. Msgr. Richard Malone, J.C.L., S.T.D.; Mr. Gerald H. Malsbary, Ph.D.; Revs. Kevin T. McMahon, S.T.D. (WIL); Michael J. McNally, Ph.D. (PMB); Frederick L. Miller, S.T.D. (NEW); Elizabeth M. Nagel, S.S.D.; Revs. Gabriel B. O'Donnell, O.P., M.A., S.T.D.; Gregory R. Salamone, O.P., S.T.B.; Christopher J. Schreck, Ph.D., S.T.D. (SAV); Mr. John Saward, M.A., M.Litt.; John D. Thornbrugh, Ph.D.

Adjunct Faculty: Mr. J. Brian Benestad, Ph.D.; Zoltan Domotor, Ph.D.; Rev. Stephen J. Dougherty, M.Div., M.A.; Mary Ellen Fattori, M.A.; Rev. Msgr. Ronald W. Gainer, J.C.L. (ALN); Rev. Msgr. James J. Graham, J.C.D.; Barbara Guiliano, M.A.; Paul T. Klucsarits, M.A.; John J. Kokolus; Sr. Mary Elizabeth Kratzinger, S.S.J., M.A.; Elizabeth Mintzer, M.A.; Joseph Mintzer, M.A.; Shawn Weldon, M.A.; Revs. Joseph T. Marino, M.A.; Stephen P. McHenry, Ph.D.; Paul S. Quinter, M.S., S.T.D.; Alexander J. Palmieri, M.A., J.C.L.; Joseph C. Stec, M.A.

Additional Formation Personnel: Revs. J. Thomas Heron, M.A.; Dennis J. Carbonaro, M.A.; Curtis L.

Clark, S.T.D. (cand.) (ARL); Stephen J. Marinucci, M.Div. In res., Rev. Msgr. Thomas J. Benestad, M.Div. (ALN); Rev. Andrew J. Golias, S.T.D.; Rev. Msgr. Joseph F. Martino, S.T.L., H.E.D.; Revs. Gregory J. Parlanti, M.Div., M.A.; Paul S. Quinter, M.S., S.T.D. Priests 20; Sisters 2; Lay Staff 12; College and Theology Division Students 209; Religious Studies Division Students 297; Seminarians from Archdiocese 90; Seminarians from other Dioceses 119.

[B] SEMINARIES, RELIGIOUS OR SCHOLASTICATES

PHILADELPHIA. *Brothers of the Christian Schools Scholasticate*, Jeremy House, 6633 Ardleigh St., 19119-3898. Tel: 215-843-1884. Bro. Dennis Malloy, F.S.C., Dir. Professed Brothers 5.

DePaul Novitiate, 5710 Magnolia St., 19144. Tel: 215-843-1581. Revs. Thomas J. Butler, C.M., Asst. Dir.; Charles M. Shanley, C.M., Asst. Dir. In res., Revs. Joseph L. Levesque, C.M.; Thomas F. McKenna, C.M.; Peter A. Campbell, C.M. National Novitiate for the Congregation of the Mission (Vincentians).

St. Vincent's Seminary, 500 E. Chelten Ave., 19144-1296. Tel: 215-848-1985. Very Rev. Joseph L. Levesque, C.M., Prov.; Revs. Thomas F. McKenna, C.M., Asst. Prov.; Robert Brandenberger, C.M., Supr.; Richard J. Kehoe, C.M., Dir. Missions; John W. Gouldrick, C.M., Treasurer; William J. O'Brien, C.M., Dir., Miraculous Medal Asst. Central House of the Eastern Province of the Congregation of the Mission, (Vincentians).

PAOLI. *Daylesford Abbey*, 220 S. Valley Rd., 19301-1900. Tel: 610-647-2530; Fax: 610-651-0219. Legal Title: *Norbertine Fathers of PA, Inc.* Rt. Rev. Jerome G. Tremel, O.Praem., Admin.; Very Rev. Robert F. Kelly, O.Praem., Prior; Rt. Rev. John E. Neitzel, O.Praem., Abbot Emeritus; Revs. Theodore J. Antry, O.Praem., Vocation Dir.; Edward J. Smith, O.Praem., Treas. Priests 14; Brothers 2.

SPRINGFIELD. *Don Guanella House of Formation*, 1795 S. Sproul Rd., 19064. Tel: 610-328-3406. Congregation of the Servants of Charity. Rev. Silvio De Nard, S.C. Priests 1.

VILLANOVA. *St. Augustine Friary*, 214 Ashwood Rd., 19085. Tel: 610-527-0325. Bro. John J. DelCasale, O.S.A., Prior. In res., Rev. Allan D. Fitzgerald, O.S.A.; Bro. John Konwerski, O.S.A.; Revs. Daniel E. Doyle, O.S.A.; John F. McAtee, O.S.A.

[C] COLLEGES AND UNIVERSITIES

PHILADELPHIA. *Chestnut Hill College*, 19118. Tel: 215-248-7000; Fax: 215-248-7155.
For a complete listing, refer to the Colleges and Universities section.

Holy Family College, (1954) Grant and Frankford Aves., 19114. Tel: 215-637-7700; Fax: 215-637-3787.
For a complete listing, refer to the Colleges and Universities section.

LaSalle University, 1900 W. Olney Ave., 19141. Tel: 215-951-1000; Fax: 215-951-1783.
For a complete listing, refer to the Colleges and Universities section.

St. Joseph's University, 5600 City Ave., 19131. Tel: 610-660-1000; Fax: 610-660-1201.
For a complete listing, refer to the Colleges and Universities section.

ASTON. *Neumann College*, One Neumann Dr., 19014-1298. Tel: 610-459-0905.
For a complete listing, refer to the Colleges and Universities section.

GWYNEDD VALLEY. *Gwynedd-Mercy College*, 19437. Tel: 215-646-7300; Fax: 215-641-5509.
For a complete listing, refer to the Colleges and Universities section.

IMMACULATA. *Immaculata College*, 19345. Tel: 610-647-4400.
For a complete listing, refer to the Colleges and Universities section.

RADNOR. *Cabrini College*, (1957) 610 King of Prussia Rd., 19087. Tel: 610-902-8100.
For a complete listing, refer to the Colleges and Universities section.

ROSEMONT. *Rosemont College of the Holy Child Jesus*, 19010-1699. Tel: 610-526-2984; Fax: 610-527-0341.
For a complete listing, refer to the Colleges and Universities section.

VILLANOVA. *Villanova University*, 19085. Tel: 610-519-4500; Fax: 610-519-4514.
For a complete listing, refer to the Colleges and Universities section.

[D] HIGH SCHOOLS, ARCHDIOCESAN

PHILADELPHIA. *Archbishop Ryan High School*, 11201 Academy Rd., 19154-3397. Tel: 215-637-1800. Opened September 7, 1966. Franciscan Friars, Order of Friars Minor. Revs. Charles Newman, O.F.M., Prin.; Rene Barczak, O.F.M.; Roderick Drag, O.F.M.; Carl Graczyk, O.F.M.; Francis Kelly, O.F.M.; Gabriel A. Rosetti, O.F.M.; Louis Stislow, O.F.M., Chap.; Michael Surufka, O.F.M. Priests 8; Brothers 9

Cardinal Dougherty High School, 6301 N. 2nd St., 19120. Tel: 215-276-2300; Fax: 215-276-2306. (Coed) Opened September 1956.
E-mail:cdhs@libertynet.org
Rev. Paul M. Kennedy, M.A., M.Div., Pres.; Mrs. Joanne H. Walls, M.S., Prin.; Rev. John B. Wendrychowicz, School Minister. Priests 6; Sisters 18; Lay Teachers 39; Students 1,060.

Father Judge High School for Boys, 3301 Solly Ave., 19136. Tel: 215-338-9494; Fax: 215-338-0250. Opened September 1954. Oblates of St. Francis de Sales. Revs. Thomas J. Erbrick, O.S.F.S., Supr.; Joseph A. DiMauro, O.S.F.S., Prin.; Charles F. Engelhardt, O.S.F.S.; Joseph A. Dougherty, O.S.F.S.; Thomas P. Gallagher, O.S.F.S.; Charles C. Garst, O.S.F.S.; Eugene L. Kelly, O.S.F.S.; Dennis W. Killion, O.S.F.S.; Gerard J. Mahoney, O.S.F.S.; David M. Merchant, O.S.F.S.; Edward L. Rauch, O.S.F.S., Pres.; Edward J. Roszko, O.S.F.S.; William O. Seelaus, O.S.F.S.; Al Smith; John Nees; Frank Greene; John Dennis; Stanley Dobkiewicz; Gerald Dunne; Bro. Thomas Brophy. Priests 19; Brothers 1; Lay Teachers 57; Students 1,400.

John W. Hallahan Catholic Girls High School, 311 N. 19th St., 19103-1198. Tel: 215-563-8930; Fax: 215-563-3809. Opened September 18, 1901. Sr. Marita Carmel, I.H.M.; Mrs. Lorraine S. Rice, Pres.; Rev. Joseph M. Corley, School Minister. Priests 1; Sisters 14; Lay Teachers 25; Students 760.

Little Flower Catholic High School for Girls, 10th and Lycoming Sts., 19140. Tel: 215-455-6900. Opened September 1, 1939. Sr. Kathleen Klarich, R.S.M., Prin.; Sr. Joan Rychalsky, I.H.M., Pres.; Rev. Joseph J. Kelley, School Minister. Sisters 21; Lay Teachers 34; Students 832.

Northeast Catholic High School for Boys, Kensington and Torresdale Aves., 19124. Tel: 215-831-1234. Opened September 7, 1926. Oblates of St. Francis de Sales. Res., 1840 E. Torresdale Ave., 19124-4418. Revs. Thomas B. Curran, O.S.F.S, Pres.; Michael S. Murray, O.S.F.S., Prin.; Very Rev. William E. Davis, O.S.F.S., Supr.; Rev. William T. McCandless, O.S.F.S., School Min. Priests 13; Brothers 3; Lay Faculty 47; Students 985.

Roman Catholic High School for Boys, 301 N. Broad St., 19107. Tel: 215-627-1270; 627-1570. Opened September 8, 1890. Revs. Francis W. Beach, M.A., Pres. & Rector; Gerard J. Hoffman, Prin.; Joseph F. Gleason, School Minister; Ronald Jakows, Teacher. Priests 4; Sisters 2; Lay Teachers 37; Students 836.

St. Hubert's Catholic High School for Girls, 7320 Torresdale Ave., 19136. Tel: 215-624-6840. Opened September 1941. Sr. Alma Rose Schlosser, S.S.J., Pres.; Rev. James P. Olson, Dir. School Ministry. Priests 1; Sisters 17; Lay Teachers 59; Students 1,507.

St. John Neumann High School. (Formerly Southeast Catholic High School), 2600 Moore St., 19145-1798. Tel: 215-389-4900; Fax: 215-462-3577. (Boys) Opened September 1, 1934. Canons Regular of Premontre Diocesan Priests forming Faculty. Revs. Michael J. Lee, O.Praem., Pres.; Ronald J. Rossi, O.Praem., Prin.; Steven J. Albero, O.Praem.; Hubert N. Beaudoin, O.Praem., School Ministry; John Zagarella, O.Praem; John M. Cagney, O.Praem., (Retired); James C. Rodia, O.Praem.; Bros. Joseph W. Mulholland, O.Praem.; John Michael Zychowski, O.deM.; Blase G. Corso, O.Praem.; John B. Ginder, O.Praem. Priests 7; Sisters 1; Brothers 4; Lay Teachers 37; Students 753.

St. Maria Goretti High School, 1736 S. 10th St., 19148. Tel: 215-465-8437. (Girls) Opened September 1955. Sr. M. Sheila Foy, I.H.M., Pres.; Candida Antonelli, Prin.; Rev. Michael Blaine, School Minister. Sisters 11; Lay Teachers 36; Students 870.

West Philadelphia Catholic High School, 4501 Chestnut St., 19139. Tel: 215-386-2244. Opened September 6, 1989. Bro. John McDonnell, F.S.C.; Rev. William J. Chiriaco, Dir. School Ministry. Priests 1; Religious 23; Lay Teachers 29; Students 820.

DREXEL HILL. *Archbishop Prendergast High School*, 401 N. Lansdowne Ave., 19026. Tel: 610-259-0265. Open September 1956. Sr. Catherine Robinson, S.S.J., Pres.; Mrs. Carol Ann Blair, Prin.; Rev. Michael J. Fitzpatrick, Dir. School Ministry. Priests 1; Sisters 19; Lay Teachers 37; Girls 937.

Monsignor Bonner High School, 403 N. Lansdowne Ave., 19026-1196. Tel: 610-259-0280; Fax: 610-259-1630. (Boys) Opened September 1953 as Archbishop Prendergast High School for Boys. New name adopted September 1956. Revs. John T. Denny, O.S.A., Prin.; William E. Atkinson, O.S.A.; Francis X. Devlin, O.S.A.; Augustine M. Esposito, O.S.A., Prior; John J. Ferrence, O.S.A.; George P. Magee, O.S.A.; Daniel McLaughlin, O.S.A.; Robert J. Murray, O.S.A. Priests 8; Sisters 4; Lay Teachers 43; Students 984.

FAIRLESS HILLS. *Conwell-Egan Catholic High School*, 611 Wistar Rd., 19030. Tel: 215-945-6200. Formerly Bishop Egan High School, Fairless Hills, and Bishop Conwell High School, Levittown. Mr. William L. Galante, Pres.; Miss Helen T. Chaykowsky, Prin.; Bro. Francis Haworth, T.O.R., School Min.; Revs. Fidelis F. Weber, T.O.R., Guidance Dir.; Gabriel Zeis, T.O.R. Sisters 9; Brothers 5; Deacons 1; Lay Teachers 60; Students 1,390.

NORRISTOWN. *Kennedy-Kenrick Catholic High School*, 250 E. Johnson Hwy., 19401. Tel: 610-275-2846. Formerly Bishop Kenrick High School, Norristown, and Archbishop Kennedy High School, Conshohocken. Rev. Gregory J. Hickey, Prin.; Harry R. Neenhold, Pres.; Revs. Joseph W. Bongard; James McQuinn; John P. Paul. Sisters 16; Lay Teachers 27; Students 641.

POTTSTOWN. *St. Pius X High School*, 844 N. Keim St., 19464. Tel: 610-326-8990. Opened 1954. Rev. Philip J. Lowe, Ed.D., Prin.; Mr. Salvatore DiNenna, Pres. Priests 4; Sisters 1; Lay Teachers 30; Students 553.

RADNOR. *Archbishop John Carroll High School*, 211 Matson Ford Rd., 19087. Tel: 610-688-7610; Fax: 610-688-8326. Opened September 1967. Rev. T. Christopher Redcay, Dir. of School Ministry. Priests 3; Sisters 6; Lay Teachers 43; Students 961.

SPRINGFIELD. *Cardinal O'Hara High School*, 1701 S. Sproul Rd., 19064. Tel: 610-544-3800; Fax: 610-544-1189. (Coed) Opened September, 1963. Rev. Msgr. Joseph P. McFadden, Pres.; Revs. John J. Ames; John P. Collins; Joseph Maloney; Joseph C. Bordonaro; Pascal A. Monteleone; Thomas R. Urian. Priests 7; Sisters 9; Lay Teachers 62; Students 1,602.

WARMINSTER. *Archbishop Wood Catholic High School*, 655 York Rd., 18974. Tel: 215-672-5050. Opened September 1964. Revs. James D. Beisel, Pres.; Robert W. Povish, Chap.; James F. Endres; Joseph P. Devlin; John J. Pidgeon. Priests 5; Sisters 12; Brothers 1; Lay Teachers 51; Students 1,187.

WEST CHESTER. *Bishop Shanahan High School*, 103 N. Everhart Sts., 19380. Tel: 610-696-7604. (Coed) Formerly St. Agnes High School opened in 1909; became diocesan high school September 1957. Sr. Helen Rapine, I.H.M., Pres.; Sr. Nancy McFadden, I.H.M., Prin.; Revs. James J. Melle; Joseph D. Brandt. Sisters, Servants of the Immaculate Heart of Mary 12; Priests 3; Lay Teachers 32; Students 775.

WYNCOTE. *Bishop McDevitt High School*, 125 Royal Ave., 19095-1198. Tel: 215-887-5575. Opened September 1958. Frederick J. Ciao, Ph.D., Pres.; Revs. Paul C. Brandt; James R. Jugenheimer; James J. Mulligan, S.T.L. Priests 3; Sisters 8; Lay Teachers 41; Students 880.

[E] VOCATIONAL HIGH SCHOOLS

PHILADELPHIA. *Mercy Vocational High School*, 2900 W. Hunting Park Ave., 19129. Tel: 215-226-1225. Sr. Patricia Flynn, R.S.M., Prin.; Mr. William J. Donahue, Vice Prin. Sisters of Mercy 7; Lay Teachers 29; Students 370.

[F] HIGH SCHOOLS, PAROCHIAL

LANSDALE. *Lansdale Catholic High School*, 700 Lansdale Ave., 19446-2995. Tel: 215-362-6160; 242-6160 (Philadelphia). Opened 1949 as a school of St. Stanislaus Parish. Mr. Slavatore J. DiNenna, Prin.; Rev. Martin T. Cioppi. Religious Sisters of Mercy 2; Sisters of Notre Dame 1; Priests 3; Lay Teachers 39; Students 901.

[G] HIGH SCHOOLS, PRIVATE

PHILADELPHIA. *Nazareth Academy High School*, 4001 Grant Ave., 19114-2999. Tel: 215-637-7676; Fax: 215-637-8523. Sr. Rosemarie Griffin, C.S.F.N., Prin. Sisters 17; Lay Teachers 43; Girls 431.

St. Joseph's Preparatory School, Office of the President, 1733 W. Girard Ave., 19130. Tel: 215-978-1950; Fax: 215-765-1710. Revs. David A. Sauter, S.J., Pres.; Herbert B. Keller, S.J., Prin.; Mr. Bernard E. Kueny, Jr., Admin. Vice Pres.; Mr. Charles J. Johnson, Treas.; Ms. Sara M. Adkins, Registrar; Mr. Kevin J. Kelly, Dean of Students; Revs. Peter P. D'Alessandro, S.J.; Stephen A. Garber, S.J.; F. Joseph Michini, S.J.; Francis E. Skechus, S.J.; J. Vincent Taggart, S.J. Priests 7; Sisters 2; Lay Teachers 50; Students 875.

BENSALEM. *Holy Ghost Preparatory School*, 2429 Bristol Pike, 19020. Tel: 215-639-2102; Fax: 215-639-4225. Rev. James P. McCloskey, C.S.Sp., Headmaster. Holy Ghost Fathers 4; Lay Teachers 37; Boys 455.

BRYN MAWR. *Country Day School of the Sacred Heart*, 480 Bryn Mawr Ave., 19010. Tel: 610-527-3915; Fax: 610-527-0942. Sr. Matthew Anita MacDonald, S.S.J., Head of School; Rev. Thomas P. Gillin. Sisters 1; Lay Teachers 35; Students 225.

DEVON. *Devon Preparatory School*, 19333. Tel: 610-688-7337; Fax: 610-688-2409. Piarist Fathers. Revs. James P. Shea, Sch.P., Rector & Headmaster; Richard S. Wyzykiewicz, Sch.P., Asst. Headmaster; Ladislaus Magyar, Sch.P.; Ferdinand Negrillos, Sch.P.;

Louis Mesko, Sch.P.; Geza Pazmany, Sch.P. Priests 3; Lay Teachers 21; Students 187.

FLOURTOWN. *Mt. St. Joseph Academy*, 120 W. Wissahickon Ave., 19031. Tel: 215-233-3177. Sr. Mary Dacey, S.S.J., Pres.; Sr. Karen Dietrich, S.S.J., Prin. Sisters of St. Joseph 19; Lay Teachers 32; Students 526.

GWYNEDD VALLEY. *Gwynedd-Mercy Academy*, 1345 Sumneytown Pike, 19437-0902. Tel: 215-646-8815. Sr. Mary Alice, R.S.M., Prin. Sisters 13; Lay Teachers 25; Girls 393.

HOLLAND. *Villa Joseph Marie High School for Girls*, 18966. Tel: 215-357-8810. Sr. M. Elaine, S.S.C., Prin.; Rev. John A. Cannon, Chap. Sisters of St. Casimir 5; Lay Teachers 20; Students 300.

MALVERN. *Malvern Preparatory School for Boys*, 19355. Tel: 610-644-5454. Revs. David J. Duffy, O.S.A., Pres.; Harry J. Erdlen, O.S.A., Prior; Richard J. Cochrane, O.S.A.; James R. Flynn, O.S.A.; Ronald A. Hamaday, O.S.A.; John H. Melton, O.S.A.; John R. Liggio, O.S.A. Priests 7; Lay Teachers 51; Students 527.

Villa Maria Academy High School, 370 Old Lincoln Hwy., 19355. Tel: 610-644-2551. Sr. Mary Kelly, I.H.M., Prin. Sisters, Servants of the Immaculate Heart of Mary 15; Lay Teachers 30; Girls 400.

MERION. *Merion Mercy Academy*, 19066. Tel: 610-664-6655; Fax: 610-664-6322. Day School for Girls. Sr. Teresa Mary, Prin. Sisters of Mercy 16; Lay Teachers 29; Students 383.

VILLANOVA. *Academy of Notre Dame de Namur*, 560 Sproul Rd., 19085. Tel: 610-687-0650; Fax: 610-687-1912. Sr. Regina Finnegan, Prin. Sisters 11; Lay Teachers 54; Girls 460.

WYNDMOOR. *LaSalle College High School*, 8605 Cheltenham Ave., 19038. Tel: 215-233-2911; Fax: 215-233-1418. Bro. Rene Sterner, F.S.C., Pres.; Mr. David T. Diehl, Prin.; Bro. Timothy Ahern, F.S.C., Religious Supr. Brothers of the Christian Schools 17; Lay Teachers 59; Students 948.

[H] ELEMENTARY SCHOOLS, PRIVATE

PHILADELPHIA. *Cecilian Academy*, 100-144 W. Carpenter Ln., 19119. Tel: 215-849-3252. (PreK-8 and Learning Disabilities Program). Sr. Margaret Lisowski, Prin. Convent, 6818 Chesheim Rd., 19119. Sisters of St. Joseph 9; Lay Teachers 12; Students 192.

The Gesu School, 18th & Thompson Sts., 19121. Tel: 215-762-3660; 763-9077(Development); Fax: 215-763-9844. Rev. George Bur, S.J., Pres.; Sr. Ellen Convey, I.H.M., Prin.; Rev. Neil Ver-Schneider, S.J.; Sr. Patricia McGrenra, I.H.M.; Sr. Carmela Anne Dauerbach, I.H.M. Priests, Society of Jesus 2; Sisters, Servants of the Immaculate Heart of Mary 4; Lay Teachers 19; Students 430.

Nazareth Academy Grade School, 4701 Grant Ave., 19114. Tel: 215-637-7777. Sr. M. Martin, C.S.F.N., Prin. Sisters of the Holy Family of Nazareth 3; Lay Teachers 14; Students 228.

Norwood-Fontbonne Academy for Boys and Girls, 8891 Germantown Ave., 19118. Tel: 215-247-3811. Sr. Monica Osaben, S.S.J., Dir. Sisters of St. Joseph 8; Lay Teachers 33; Students 479.

BRYN MAWR. *St. Aloysius Academy*. (Grades PreK-8), 401 S. Bryn Mawr Ave., 19010. Tel: 610-527-0506; 525-1670. Sr. Carolyn M. Dimick, I.H.M., Prin. Sisters, Servants of the Immaculate Heart of Mary 7; Lay Teachers 18; Students 274.

DREXEL HILL. *School of the Holy Child Jesus*. (Grades PreK-8), 450 Penn Ave., 19026. Tel: 610-259-2712. Sr. Barbara Foy, S.H.C.J., Prin. Sisters of the Holy Child Jesus 3; Lay Teachers 37; Students 227.

IMMACULATA. *Villa Maria Academy*, 19345. Tel: 610-644-4864. Sr. John Magdalen, I.H.M., Prin. Sisters, Servants of the Immaculate Heart of Mary 8; Lay Teachers 24; Girls 356.

MERION. *Waldron Mercy Academy*, 513 Montgomery Ave., 19066. Tel: 610-664-9847. Sr. Patricia Smith, R.S.M., Prin.; Mr. Stephen Stritch, Vice Prin. Sisters of Mercy 7; Lay Teachers 36; Students 555.

RADNOR. *Armenian Sisters Academy*, 440 Upper Gulph Rd., 19087. Tel: 610-687-4100. Montessori for ages 3-6. Ungraded Elementary for ages 7-14. Sr. Louisa Kassarjian, Prin. Sisters 3; Lay Teachers 24; Students 212.

ROSEMONT. *Rosemont School of the Holy Child*, 1344 Montgomery Ave., 19010. Tel: 610-525-1876; Fax: 610-525-7128. Sr. Mary Broderick, S.H.C.J., Prin. Sisters of the Holy Child Jesus 2; Lay Teachers 24; Students 270.

SPRING HOUSE. *Gwynedd-Mercy Academy*. (Grades K-8), Elementary Division, Norristown Rd., P.O. Box 241, 19477. Tel: 215-646-4916; 646-2406 (Business Office); Fax: 215-628-8441. Sr. Anne Crampsie, R.S.M., Prin. Sisters of Mercy 3; Lay Teachers 39; Students 450.

WYNCOTE. *Ancillae-Assumpta Academy*. (Grades PreK-8). (Coed), 2025 Church Rd., 19095. Tel: 215-885-1636. Sr. Elizabeth McCoy, A.C.J., Dir.; Sr. Maureen Gillespie, A.C.J., Prin. Handmaids of the Sacred Heart of Jesus 8; Lay Teachers 54; Students 557.

YARDLEY. *Grey Nun Academy*, 1750 Quarry Rd., 19067. Tel: 215-968-4151. (Coed Day School). Sr. Dolores Beatty, G.N.S.H., Prin. Grey Nuns of the Sacred Heart 4; Lay Teachers 25; Students 245.

[I] SPECIAL EDUCATION

PHILADELPHIA. *Our Lady of Confidence Day School*, 10th and Lycoming Sts., 19140. Tel: 215-329-2697; Fax: 215-324-7440. Mentally Handicapped. Sr. Francis Christi, S.S.J., Prin. Sisters of St. Joseph 1; Lay Teachers 10; Students 135.

LEVITTOWN. *Queen of the Universe Day Center*, 2443 Trenton Rd., 19056. Tel: 215-945-6090. Mrs. Sallie LaMorgia, Prin. Mentally Retarded and Brain-Damaged Students. Lay Teachers 4; Students 40.

NORWOOD. *Archbishop Ryan School for Children with Hearing Impairment*, 233 Mohawk Ave., 19074. Tel: 215-387-1711; Fax: 215-387-8999. Sr. Mary T. Toole, S.S.J., Prin.; Mrs. Judith Sexton, M.A., C.E.D. Convent. Tel: 215-386-1678. Sisters of St. Joseph 4; Lay Teachers 8; Students 49.

UPPER DARBY. *St. Lucy Day School for Children with Visual Impairments*, 130 Hampden Rd., 19082. Tel: 610-352-4550; 352-4555. Sr. M. Margaret Fleming, I.H.M., Prin. Sisters, Servants of the Immaculate Heart of Mary 4; Lay Teachers 4; Students 31.

WYNNEWOOD. *St. Katherine Day School*, 930 Bowman Ave., 19096. Tel: 610-667-3958; Fax: 610-667-3625. Children with Developmental Delay/Mental Retardation. Miss Lisa M. Cetroni, Prin. Lay Teachers 12; Students 135.

[J] THE CATHOLIC SOCIAL SERVICES OF THE ARCHDIOCESE OF PHILADELPHIA

PHILADELPHIA. *The Catholic Social Services of the Archdiocese of Philadelphia*, 222 N. 17th St., 19103. Tel: 215-587-3900; Fax: 215-587-2479. All addresses unless otherwise indicated. Rev. Msgr. Joseph P. Garvin, L.S.W., Exec. Dir.; Rev. Timothy C. Senior, L.S.W., M.B.A., Deputy Exec. Dir.; Edward T. Cahill, Chief Financial Officer; Sr. Maureen Erdlen, S.S.J., L.S.W., Dir. Professional Svcs.; John C. Smith, L.S.W., Dir. Children's & Residential Svcs.; John Amato, L.S.W., Asst. Dir.; Anne Marie Buck, M.S., Asst. Dir.; Teresa Thompson, L.S.W., Admin. Child Care Dept.; Lorraine Knight, Admin.; David Moore, Mgr.

Office for Human Relations. Tel: 215-587-5655. Sr. Marion Dillon, M.S.B.T., L.S.W., Dir.

Service Centers:

Philadelphia:

Northeast Philadelphia, 7340 Jackson St., 19136. Tel: 215-624-5920. Amy Stoner, L.S.W., Site Supvr.

North Philadelphia, Casa del Carmen, Reese St. & Blavis St., 19140. Tel: 215-329-5660. W. Giovanni Morante, M.A., Admin.

Bucks County:

Levittown, 100 Levittown Pkwy., Levittown, 19054. Tel: 215-945-2550. Marguerite Powers, L.S.W., Admin.

Middle Bucks County:

Southampton, 611 Knowles Ave., Southampton, 18966. Tel: 215-355-1960. Marguerite Powers, L.S.W., Admin.

Chester County:

Avondale, 37 S. Pennsylvania Ave., P.O. Box 119, Avondale, 19311. Tel: 610-268-3510. William Kefer, L.S.W., Site Supvr.

Downingtown:

Downingtown, 141 E. Lancaster Ave., Downingtown, 19335. Tel: 610-269-4060. William Kefer, L.S.W., Site Supvr.

Delaware County:

Chester, 130 E. 7th St., Chester, 19013. Tel: 610-876-9183. James McMaster, M.B.A., Admin.

Springfield:

Springfield, 1797 S. Sproul Rd., Springfield, 19064. Tel: 610-328-7090. James McMaster, M.B.A., Admin.

Montgomery County:

Norristown, 353 E. Johnson Hwy., Norristown, 19401. Tel: 215-279-7372. Sr. Patricia Kelly, M.S.B.T., L.S.W., Site Supvr. Total Assisted 162,206.

Holy Family Center, 227 N. 18th St., 19103.

Volunteer Coordinator, 227 N. 18th St., 19103.

Migration and Refugee Resettlement Dept., 227 N. 18th St., 19103.

Development, 222 N. 17th St., 19103. Karen Becker, L.S.W., Admin. Family Services Dept.; M. Louise Maia, Mgr., Research & Mgmt. Information Systems; Mary Merman, L.S.W., Admin. Adoption Svcs. Dept.; Marilyn Mock, Admin. Senior Adult Svcs.; John M. Wagner, Admin., Housing/Homeless Svcs.; William Tangradi, L.S.W., Volunteer Coord. Total Assisted 101,681; Total Staff 220.

[K] INSTITUTIONS FOR DEPENDENT CHILDREN

PHILADELPHIA. *Catholic Home for Girls*, 5238 N. Broad St., 19141. Tel: 215-324-2610.
For a complete listing, refer to the Special Care Facilities section.

St. Joseph's House for Boys, 4010-4012 Ashburner St., 19136-2801. Tel: 215-332-3490.
For a complete listing, refer to the Special Care Facilities section.

St. Vincent's Orphanage Tacony, 7201 Milnor St., 19135. Tel: 215-624-5601.
For a complete listing, refer to the Special Care Facilities section.

AMBLER. *St. Mary's Villa for Children*, 701 Bethlehem Pike, P.O. Box 388, 19002-0388. Tel: 215-242-0376; 643-7676.
For a complete listing, refer to the Special Care Facilities section.

BENSALEM. *St. Francis Homes for Boys*, 857 Langstroth Ln., 19020-5735. Tel: 215-638-9310.
For a complete listing, refer to the Special Care Facilities section.

[L] RESIDENTIAL SCHOOLS FOR MENTALLY HANDICAPPED CHILDREN AND ADULTS

SPRINGFIELD. *Cardinal Krol Center*, 1799 S. Sproul Rd., 19064. Tel: 610-543-3380. Rev. Romano DiRuscio, S.C., M.A., Admin. A residential facility for 131 mentally retarded male adults which provides an environment, both day and residential, that contributes to the individuals own growth and development by fulfilling their potential in the physical, mental, emotional, social, psychological, and spiritual areas of their lives. Priests 3; Residential Capacity 131; Day Program 20.

Divine Providence Village, 686 Old Marple Rd., 19064. Tel: 610-328-7730. Sr. Patricia Mc Cafferty, D.S.M.P., M.A., Admin.; Rev. James J. Brennan, Chap. Care & specialized training for developmentally disabled females. Sisters 6; Capacity 96.

Don Guanella School for Retarded Boys, 1797 S. Sproul Rd., 19064-1195. Tel: 610-543-1418. Rev. Romano DiRuscio, S.C., M.A., Admin. Provides specialized care and treatment program for mentally retarded boys ages 6-21. Capacity: Residents 40; Day Students 30.

[M] RESIDENTIAL HOMES FOR PHYSICALLY HANDICAPPED CHILDREN

ROSEMONT. *St. Edmond's Home for Children*, 320 S. Roberts Rd., 19010. Tel: 610-525-8800.
For a complete listing, refer to the Special Care Facilities section.

[N] PROTECTIVE INSTITUTIONS

PHILADELPHIA. *St. Gabriel's System*, Administrative Offices, 117 S. 17th St., Ste. 1701, 19103. Tel: 215-665-8777; Fax: 215-665-8821.
For a complete listing, refer to the Special Care Facilities section.

AUDUBON. *St. Gabriel's Hall*, Box 7280, 19407-7280. Tel: 215-247-2776 (Philadelphia); 610-666-7970 (Audubon).
For a complete listing, refer to the Special Care Facilities section.

[O] DAY TREATMENT CENTERS

PHILADELPHIA. *De La Salle-In-Towne Day Treatment Center*, 25 S. Van Pelt St., 19103. Tel: 215-567-5500; Fax: 215-567-6922. Bro. Robert J. Kinzler, F.S.C., M.S.W., Exec. Dir.; Charles E. Gaus, Dir. A community based day treatment program for court-committed delinquent boys, ages 14-17. Capacity 110; Total Staff 35; Total Assisted 275.

BENSALEM. *De La Salle Vocational Day Treatment Center*, Box 344, 19020. Tel: 215-464-0344. Bros. Robert Kinzler, F.S.C., M.S.W., Exec. Dir.; Dennis Malloy, F.S.C., A.C.S.W., M.A., Dir. A community based day treatment program for court-committed delinquent boys, ages 15-18. Capacity 125; Total Staff 40.

[P] RESIDENCES FOR UNMARRIED MOTHERS

HAVERTOWN. *St. Vincent's Maternity Residence*, 104 E. Township Line Rd., 19083. Tel: 610-446-0105. Sr. Louise Kane, S.S.J., L.S.W., Admin. Capacity 12. Information and Referrals. Tel: 215-324-2610. Total Assisted 100; Total Staff 12.

[Q] SENIOR CITIZEN CENTERS

PHILADELPHIA. *Norris Square Senior Citizens Center*, 2121 N. Howard St., 19133. Tel: 215-423-7241. Carmen Aponte, Coord.

St. Anne's Center, 2607 E. Cumberland St., 19125. Tel: 215-423-2772. Barbara Jo Gibson, Center Coord. Total Staff 6; Total Assisted 11,288.

St. Bernard's Senior Adult Program, 7340 Jackson St., 19136. Tel: 215-624-5920. Ms. Claire Mansfield, Prog. Dir.

St. Rita's Senior Citizen Center, 1150-1154 S. Broad St., 19146. Tel: 215-735-4300. Daryl Kezell, L.S.W.,

Coord. Total Staff 6; Total Assisted 400.
Star Harbor Center, 4700 Springfield Ave., 19143. Tel: 215-726-7468; Fax: 215-726-7496. Maryrose Smith, Coord.

[R] OUTREACH CENTERS

PHILADELPHIA. *Casa del Carmen*, 4400 N. Reese St., 19140. Tel: 215-329-5660. W. Giovanni Morante, M.A. Offers emergency crisis social services to the Spanish speaking community in Philadelphia and surrounding areas.
Catholic Center for the Deaf and Hard of Hearing, St. Boniface Rectory, 174 W. Diamond St., 19122. Tel: 215-423-9547. Rev. Anthony Russo, C.SS.R., Dir.
Mass and Homily in Sign Language: Resurrection Church, Castor Ave. & Vista St., 19152. St. Mary's Manor, 701 Lansdale Ave., Lansdale, 19446. Tel: 215-368-0900. St. Stanislaus Church, Main St. and Lansdale Ave., Lansdale, 19446. Tel: 215-855-3133. St. Charles Borromeo Church, Burmont Rd and Dennison Ave., Drexel Hill, 19026. Tel: 215-623-3800. Rev. Paul V. Dougherty, M.A.
Mass with Sign Language Interpreter: St. Francis of Assisi Church, Marshall and Buttonwood Sts., Norristown, 19401. Tel: 215-272-0402. S.S. Peter and Paul, Boot Rd. & Rte. 202, West Chester, 19380. Tel: 610-692-2216. St. Francis of Assisi, Marshall St. & Buttonwood St., Norristown, 19401. Tel: 610-272-0402. St. Joseph's Church, Bartram and Woodlawn Ave., Collingdale, 19023. Tel: 610-583-4530. St. Thomas Aquinas Church, Bristol Pike and Walnut Ave., Croydon, 19021.
Drueding Center, 413 W. Master St., 19122. Tel: 215-769-1830; 769-1931; Fax: 215-787-0999. Subsidiary of Holy Redeemer Health System, Inc. Sponsor: Sisters of the Holy Redeemer, C.S.R. Communications Department, c/o 1648 Huntingdon Pike, Meadowbrook, 19046. Provides transitional housing and support services for homeless women with children; daycare is provided for the children.
Mercy Hospice, 334 S. 13th St., 19107. Tel: 215-545-5153. Maureen Howe, Dir. Provides temporary and extended shelter care, hot meals, clothing, casework and referral services to homeless and transient women and women with children. Total Staff 33; Total Assisted 2,700.
St. John Hospice for Men, 1221 Race St., 19107. Tel: 215-563-7763. Staffed by Little Brothers of the Good Shepherd. Bro. Stanley MacNeil, D.G.S., Admin.
Women of Hope, 1210 Lombard St., 19147. Tel: 215-732-1341. Una Edwards, Dir. Residential Facility for chronically mentally ill homeless women. Capacity 24.
Women of Hope, 251 N. Lawrence St., 19106. Tel: 215-592-9116. Sr. Maureen Crissy, R.S.M., Prog. Dir. Residential facility for chronically mentally ill homeless women. Capacity 22; Total Staff 16; Total Assisted 22.
CHESTER. *Bernardine Center*, 2625 Ninth St., 19013. Tel: 215-497-3225. Sr. Rose MacDermott, O.S.F., Dir. Emergency food cupboard, motivation, education toward self-sufficiency, advocacy and social spirituality education. Sisters 4.

[S] DAY CARE CENTERS

PHILADELPHIA. *Bambino Gesu Child Development Center*, 5210 N. Broad St., 19141. Tel: 215-457-4330; Fax: 215-457-4216. Sr. Mary Julia Apolonio, O.S.P., Admin. Oblate Sisters of Providence 4; Total Staff 11.
St. Monica Day Care Center, 1441 Porter St., 19145. Tel: 215-334-6001. Sister, Servants of the Immaculate Heart of Mary. Sr. Maria Clemens, I.H.M., Admin. Total Staff 12; Total Assisted 110.
St. Vincent's Day Care Center, 7201 Milnor St., 19135. Tel: 215-624-5600; Fax: 215-624-8355. Rev. Msgr. William A. Koenig, Pres., Bd. of Mgrs.; Agnes Healey, Dir. Day Care.

[T] GENERAL HOSPITALS

PHILADELPHIA. *Mercy Catholic Medical Center*, Misericordia Hospital, 54th St. and Cedar Ave., 19143. Tel: 215-748-9000.
For a complete listing, refer to the Hospitals section.
Nazareth Hospital, 2601 Holme Ave., 19152. Tel: 215-335-6000.
For a complete listing, refer to the Hospitals section.
St. Agnes Medical Center, 1900 S. Broad St., 19145. Tel: 215-339-4100.
For a complete listing, refer to the Hospitals section.
DARBY. *Mercy Catholic Medical Center*, Fitzgerald Mercy Hospital, Lansdowne Ave. and Baily Rd., 19023. Tel: 215-237-4000.
For a complete listing, refer to the Hospitals section.
HAVERFORD. *Mercy Haverford Hospital*, 2000 Old West Chester Pike, 19083. Tel: 215-645-3600.
For a complete listing, refer to the Hospitals section.
HUNTINGDON VALLEY. *Holy Redeemer Foundation*, 521 Moredon Rd., 19006. Tel: 215-938-0505; Fax: 215-938-8717.
For a complete listing, refer to the Hospitals section.
HRH Management Corporation, 727 Welsh Rd., 19006. Tel: 215-938-0180; Fax: 215-938-1237.
For a complete listing, refer to the Hospitals section.
LANGHORNE. *St. Mary Medical Center*. Langhorne-Newton Rd., 19047. Tel: 215-750-2000.
For a complete listing, refer to the Hospitals section.
MEADOWBROOK. *Holy Redeemer Hospital and Medical Center*, 1648 Huntingdon Pike, 19046. Tel: 215-947-3000.
For a complete listing, refer to the Hospitals section.
NORRISTOWN. *Sacred Heart Hospital and Rehabilitation Center*, 1430 DeKalb St., 19401. Tel: 215-278-8200.
For a complete listing, refer to the Hospitals section.

[U] SPECIAL HOSPITALS AND SANATORIA

PHILADELPHIA. *Mount Nazareth*, 2755 Holme Ave., 19152. Tel: 215-338-8992.
For a complete listing, refer to the Special Care Facilities section.
ASTON. *Assisi House*, 600 Red Hill Rd., 19014. Tel: 215-459-8990.
For a complete listing, refer to the Special Care Facilities section.
DARBY. *Villa Saint Joseph*, 14th St. and Lansdowne Ave., 19023. Tel: 215-586-8535.
For a complete listing, refer to the Special Care Facilities section.
DOWNINGTOWN. *St. John Vianney Hospital*, 151 Woodbine Rd., 19335. Tel: 610-269-2600.
For a complete listing, refer to the Special Care Facilities section.
FLOURTOWN. *St. Joseph Villa*, 110 W. Wissahickon Ave., 19031-1898. Tel: 215-836-4179.
For a complete listing, refer to the Special Care Facilities section.
IMMACULATA. *Camilla Hall Nursing Home*, P.O. Box 100, 19345-0100. Tel: 610-644-1152.
For a complete listing, refer to the Special Care Facilities section.
MERION STATION. *McAuley Convent*, 517 Montgomery Ave., 19066. Tel: 610-667-2775.
For a complete listing, refer to the Special Care Facilities section.
VENTNOR. *Villa St. Joseph by the Sea*, 114 S. Princeton Ave., 08406. Tel: 609-822-7184.
For a complete listing, refer to the Special Care Facilities section.
WARMINSTER. *Regina Coeli Residence for Priests*, 685 York Rd., 18974. Tel: 215-441-4642.
For a complete listing, refer to the Special Care Facilities section.

[V] AFFILIATED SERVICES

PHILADELPHIA.
**Holy Redeemer, Nazareth & St. Mary Home Health Services*, 12265 Townsend Rd., Ste. 400, 19154. Tel: 215-671-9200; Fax: 215-671-1950. Subsidiary of Holy Redeemer Health System, Inc. Sponsor: Sisters of the Holy Redeemer. Jerald Cohen, Pres., Communications Department, c/o 1648 Huntingdon Pike, Meadowbrook, 19046. Medicare certified home health agency serving patients in their own homes; Medicare certified hospice program serving terminally ill patients and their families.
**Holy Redeemer Support Services.*
St. Benedict Thrift Shop, 437 W. Girard Ave., 19122. Tel: 215-235-1848. Karen Pushaw, Contact Person. A clothing and furniture thrift store operated by Franciscans.
St. Francis Inn, 2441 Kensington Ave., 19125. Tel: 215-423-5845. Rev. Michael A. Duffy, O.F.M., Contact Person. A hot meal and shelter service for the poor. Brothers 4.
Thea Women's Center, 2858 Kensington Ave., 19134. Sr. Marti Zeitz, O.S.F., Contact Person. Women's Day Center.
LANGHORNE. *St. Mary's Child Development Center*, c/o St. Mary's Hospital, Langhorne-Newton Rd., 19047. Tel: 215-750-5720. Ms. Judy McGovern.
PHOENIXVILLE. *St. Mary's Franciscan Shelter*, 209 Emmett St., 19460. Tel: 610-933-3097. Sr. Emma Mary Steckel, O.S.F., Dir.; Sr. Mary Teresa Coll, O.S.F., Housekeeping; Sr. Regina Carmel McMonagle, O.S.F., Coord. Volunteer and Food Prog.; Sr. Christine Kranichfeld, Maintenance Coord.; Rose Dougherty, Case Mgr. Total Staff 5; Families Assisted 26.

[W] NURSING AND CONVALESCENT HOMES

PHILADELPHIA. *Sacred Heart Free Home for Incurable Cancer*, 1315 W. Hunting Park Ave., 19140. Tel: 215-329-3222.
For a complete listing, refer to the Special Care Facilities section.
St. Ignatius Nursing Home, 4401 Haverford Ave., 19104. Tel: 215-349-8800; Fax: 215-222-3078.
For a complete listing, refer to the Special Care Facilities section.
St. John Neumann Nursing Home, 10400 Roosevelt Blvd., 19116. Tel: 215-698-5600.
For a complete listing, refer to the Special Care Facilities section.
DARBY. *St. Francis Country House*, 1412 Lansdowne Ave., 19023-1218. Tel: 610-461-6510; Fax: 610-237-6558.
For a complete listing, refer to the Special Care Facilities section.
DOWNINGTOWN. *St. Martha Manor*, 470 Manor Ave., 19335. Tel: 610-873-8490.
For a complete listing, refer to the Special Care Facilities section.
FLOURTOWN. *Sisters of St. Joseph of Philadelphia, St. Joseph Villa Staff*, 110 W. Wissahickon Ave., 19031-1898.
For a complete listing, refer to the Special Care Facilities section.

[X] BOARDING HOMES FOR THE AGED

PHILADELPHIA. *Holy Family Home*, 5300 Chester Ave., 19143-4993. Tel: 215-729-5153.
For a complete listing, refer to the Special Care Facilities section.
Immaculate Mary Home, 2990 Holme Ave., 19136-1829. Tel: 215-335-2100; Fax: 215-331-1016.
For a complete listing, refer to the Special Care Facilities section.
Sacred Heart Manor, 6445 Germantown Ave., 19119. Tel: 215-438-5268.
For a complete listing, refer to the Special Care Facilities section.
St. Joseph Housing Corporation.
For a complete listing, refer to the Special Care Facilities section.
DARBY. *Little Flower Manor*, 1201 Springfield Rd., 19023. Tel: 610-534-6000; Fax: 610-534-6039.
For a complete listing, refer to the Special Care Facilities section.
Villa St. Teresa, 1215 Springfield Rd., 19023. Tel: 610-583-0700.
For a complete listing, refer to the Special Care Facilities section.
ELVERSON. *St. Mary of Providence Center*, 227 Isabella Rd., 19520. Tel: 610-942-4166.
For a complete listing, refer to the Special Care Facilities section.
FLOURTOWN. *Bethlehem Retirement Village*, 100 W. Wissahickon Ave., 19031. Tel: 215-233-0998.
For a complete listing, refer to the Special Care Facilities section.
HOLLAND. *St. Joseph Home for the Aged*, 1182 Holland Rd., 18966. Tel: 215-357-5511; Fax: 215-357-1701.
For a complete listing, refer to the Special Care Facilities section.
HUNTINGDON VALLEY. *Redeemer Long Term Care & Elder Services*, 727 Welsh Rd., 19006. Tel: 215-938-0180; Fax: 215-938-1237.
For a complete listing, refer to the Special Care Facilities section.
Redeemer Village, 1551 Huntingdon Pike, 19006. Tel: 215-947-8168.
For a complete listing, refer to the Special Care Facilities section.
LANSDALE. *St. Mary Manor*, 701 Lansdale Ave., 19446. Tel: 215-368-0900; Fax: 215-362-2891.
For a complete listing, refer to the Special Care Facilities section.
YARDLEY. *D'Youville Manor*, 1750 Quarry Rd., 19067. Tel: 215-579-1750.
For a complete listing, refer to the Special Care Facilities section.

[Y] RESIDENCES FOR WOMEN

PHILADELPHIA. *Blessed Katharine Drexel Residence*, 7919 Forrest Ave., 19150. Tel: 215-549-5765. Sr. M. Kathleen Scannell, R.S.M., Dir.
Lucy Eaton Smith, The, 1929 Sansom St., 19103. Tel: 215-564-0561. Dominican Sisters of the Congregation of St. Catherine de Ricci. Total Staff 7; Residents 150.
St. Mary's Convent: Residence for Women, 5th and Locust Sts., 19106. Tel: 215-627-8655. Religious Sisters of Mercy. Sr. Catherine Rawley, R.S.M., Admin. Residents 31.

[Z] MONASTERIES AND RESIDENCES OF PRIESTS AND BROTHERS

PHILADELPHIA. *Archdiocesan Oratory of St. Philip Neri (C.O.)*, 2321 Green St., 19130-3196. Tel: 215-765-4568. Revs. Georges G. Thiers, Provost; Paul C. Convery.
Augustinian Community (O.S.A.), 910 Watkins St., 19148. Tel: 215-463-1326. Rev. Peter J. Toscani, O.S.A., Contact Person.
Brothers of Charity, St. Aloysius Residence, 2026 S. 28th St., 19145. Tel: 215-468-0251. Bro. Jerome Benway, F.C.

Brothers of Charity (F.C.), 6522 Belmar St., 19142. Tel: 215-729-4417. Bro. William Riley, F.C.

Brothers of the Christian Schools, West Catholic Community, 1919 S. 23rd St., 19145. Tel: 215-551-4191. Bro. Richard Buccina, F.S.C.

Brothers of the Christian Schools, St. Mary's Hall, 7018 Boyer St., 19119-1801. Tel: 215-248-2434; Fax: 215-248-4327. Bro. Edward Davis, F.S.C., Dir. Total in Residence 5.

Congregation of the Mission, St. Vincent's Seminary, 500 E. Chelten Ave., 19144-1203. Tel: 215-848-1985; Fax: 215-844-2085. Central House of the Congregation of the Mission (Vincentian Community), Eastern Province. Novitiate, Central Shrine of the Miraculous Medal in the United States, The Central Association of the Miraculous Medal and St. Catherine's Infirmary.

Provincial Administration: Very Rev. Joseph L. Levesque, C.M., Prov.; Revs. Thomas F. McKenna, C.M., Asst. Prov.; John W. Gouldrick, C.M., Prov. Treas.; Joseph L. Boegel, C.M., Assoc. Prov. Treas.; Bro. Peter A. Campbell, C.M., Prov. Planner.

House Administration: Revs. Robert J. Brandenberger, C.M., Supr.; Aloysius P. Grass, C.M., Asst. Supr.; Gerald E. Deitzer, C.M., Treas. In res., Revs. Robert J. Brandenberger, C.M.; Joseph L. Boegel, C.M.; George E. Browne, C.M.; John W. Caine, C.M.; John W. Carven, C.M., Prov. Archivist; William J. Casey, C.M.; Gerard D. Conroy; John J. Cusack, C.M.; Gerard E. Deitzer, C.M.; Walter F. Dirig, C.M.; Thomas M. Finley, C.M.; William P. Finn; Patrick J. Fleming, C.M.; Frederick J. Gaulin, C.M.; Fredric P. Gehring, C.M.; Aloysius P. Grass, C.M.; John J. Hodnett, C.M.; John D. Hummel, C.M.; Thomas R. Kennedy, C.M.; John F. King, C.M.; Daniel J. Kramer, C.M.; Richard A. Loeffler, C.M.; Edward C. Mannion, C.M.; Paul M. Murphy, C.M.; Bartholomew J. O'Malley, C.M.; Charles J. O'Connor, C.M.; John S. Pearce, C.M.; David L. Symes, C.M.; Joseph J. Symes, C.M.

De Paul Novitiate, 5710 Magnolia St., 19144. Revs. Thomas F. McKenna, C.M.; Thomas J. Butler, C.M., Dir.; Joseph L. Levesque, C.M.; Charles M. Shanley, C.M.; Bro. Peter A. Campbell, C.M.

St. Catherine Infirmary. Revs. John J. Conway, C.M.; Joseph P. McCaffrey, C.M.; John A. Murray, C.M.; Vincent J. Nugent, C.M.; Vincent E. Trunk, C.M.

Vincentian Fathers of the Eastern Province of the Congregation of the Mission serving on special assignments other than the Motherhouse: Revs. John J. Buckley, C.M., Ethiopia; Robert P. Crawford, C.M., Vietnamese Refugee Center, Box 100, Puerto Princesa Palawan. Revs. William J. Gormley, C.M.; Lester T. DeMott, C.M.; Robert P. Galchus, C.M.; Edward F. McQuillan, C.M.

St. Vincent Medical Center, 1800 Barrs St., Jacksonville, FL, 32203. Catholic Campus Parish, 26 Baycrest Ave., Box 301, East Quogue, NY, 11942. Revs. Patrick J. Griffin, C.M., Rome, Italy; John J. Lawlor, C.M.; Francis X. Maguire, C.M.; Thomas J. Hynes, C.M., Solomon Islands; Bruce J. Krause, C.M., Opelika, AL; Jose A. Medina, C.M., Cuba; John P. Murray, C.M., St. Charles Borromeo Seminary, 1000 E. Wynnewood Rd., Wynnewood, 19096.

Providence Hospital, 1150 Varnum St., N.E., Washington, DC, 20017. Revs. James E. Power, C.M.; Brian J. O'Connell, C.M., Notre Dame.

St. Lazare Retreat House, P.O. Box 462, Spring Lake, MI, 49456-0462. Revs. Carl L. Pieber, C.M.; Alfred R. Pehrsson, C.M.; Michael J. Shea, C.M., Wheeling Jesuit University, Wheeling, WV, 26003-0759. Rev. Francis W. Sacks, C.M., Wedowee, AL.

The Vincentian Mission of East Central Alabama, P.O. Box 654, Roanoke, AL, 36274-0645. Rev. Stephen P. Trzecieski, C.M.

St. Vincent de Paul Regional Seminary, 1701 S. Military Trail, Boynton Beach, FL, 33436-4899. Rev. Robert J. Stone, C.M., St. John Vianney College Seminary, 2900 S.W. 87th Ave., Miami, FL, 33165. Rev. Thomas A. Sendlein, C.M., Taiwan. Total in Residence 52.

Father Judge Faculty House, 3301 Solly Ave., 19136. Tel: 215-624-1604. Revs. Joseph G. Campellone, O.S.F.S.; James E. Dalton, O.S.F.S.; John J. Dennis, O.S.F.S.; Joseph A. Dougherty, O.S.F.S.; Gerald M. Dunne, O.S.F.S.; Charles F. Engelhardt, O.S.F.S.; Thomas P. Gallagher, O.S.F.S.; Francis J. Green, O.S.F.S.; Eugene L. Kelly, O.S.F.S.; James D. Keenan, O.S.F.S.; Dennis W. Killion, O.S.F.S.; Gerard J. Mahoney, O.S.F.S.; David M. Merchant, O.S.F.S.; Robert G. Mulligan, O.S.F.S.; Edward L. Rauch, O.S.F.S.; Richard T. Reece; Edward J. Roszko, O.S.F.S.; William O. Seelaus, O.S.F.S.; Albert J. Smith, O.S.F.S.; Bro. Thomas Brophy, O.S.F.S. Total Staff 20; Total in Residence 20.

Gesu School Jesuit Community and Outreach Center(S.J.), 1236 N. 18th St., 19121. Tel: 215-235-1662. Rev. George Bur, S.J., Contact Person.

Holy Ghost Fathers, 8101 Cresco Ave., 19136. Tel: 215-331-1039. Rev. Francis R. Duffy, C.S.Sp., Ph.D. Total in Residence 1.

Holy Name Priory, Dominican Friars. Province of St. Joseph. 701 E. Gaul St., 19125-2896. Tel: 215-739-3960; Fax: 215-739-7597. Revs. Stephen F. Carmody, O.P., Prior; Nicholas R. Reid, O.P., Admin. Councillors: Revs. Michael Leo Novacki, O.P.; Ralph V. Townsend, O.P.

Holy Spirit Missonary Cenacle, 1301 Oak Ln., 19126. Tel: 215-924-2257; Fax: 215-224-6808. Missionary Servants of the Most Holy Trinity. Bro. Paul Michalenko, S.T.

Inner City House, 1904 N. 22nd St., 19121. Tel: 215-765-1904. Rev. David I. Hagan, O.S.F.S., Dir. Total in Residence 1.

Jesuit Community at St. Joseph's University, 5600 City Ave., 19131. Tel: 610-660-1400.

Loyola Center: Revs. Charles L. Currie, S.J., Rector; Francis H. McGauley, S.J., Dir. Infirmary; Nicholas J. Rashford, S.J., Pres.; H. Cornell Bradley, S.J., Father Min.; Joseph A. Arroyo, S.J. (Spain); Michael L. Barber, S.J.; John E. Bennett, S.J.; Bruce M. Bidinger, S.J.; Michael J. Blee, S.J.; James A. Borbely, S.J.; Edward C. Bradley, S.J.; Francis F. Burch, S.J.; Peter A. Clark, S.J.; Donald G. Clifford, S.J.; Richard J. Colgan, S.J.; Jerome B. Coll, S.J.; John M. Comey, S.J.; Mark J. Connelly; W. A. Cunningham, S.J.; Joseph A. Diamond, S.J.; Thomas J. Doyle, S.J.; Joseph A. Duke, S.J.; Edward J. Farren, S.J.; Gerald F. Finnegan, S.J.; Stephen A. Garber, S.J.; Edward A. Geary, S.J.; Vincent J. Genovesi, S.J.; Paul J. Gilvary, S.J.; Howard J. Heim, S.J.; Frederick A. Homann, S.J.; Albert H. Jenemann, S.J.; C. Frederick Koehler, S.J.; Joseph L. Lombardi, S.J.; Bernard J. McConnell; John K. McCormack; John W. McDaniel, S.J.; Eric McDermott, S.J.; Michael A. McElwee, S.J.; Dennis E. McNally, S.J.; James W. Moore, S.J.; Patrick F. Murray, S.J.; William J. Ruppenthal, S.J.; William A. Ryan, S.J.; Charles A. Schnorr, S.J.; Patrick R. Shaules, S.J.; Eugene F. Shaw, S.J.; Francis E. Skechus, S.J.; Herbert F. Smith, S.J.; Robert A. Thoman; Martin R. Tripole, S.J.; Bro. Robert J. Fitzgerald, S.J. Priests 50; Brothers 1; Scholastics 2. Scholastics: Mr. Ryan J. Maher; Mr. Robert J. McTeigue.

St. Alphonsus House. Tel: 215-477-9220. Revs. Anthony J. Berret, S.J.; Joseph J. Feeney, S.J.; Joseph J. Godfrey, S.J.; Joseph M. Kakalec, S.J.; Bro. John J. McLane, S.J. Priests 4; Brothers 1.

Little Brothers of the Good Shepherd, B.G.S., St. John's Hospice, 1221 Race St., 19107. Tel: 215-563-7763. Bro. John Scully, B.G.S., Contact Person.

Maryknoll House, 6367 Overbrook Ave., 19151. Tel: 215-477-5892. Maryknoll Fathers and Brothers (Catholic Foreign Mission Society of America, Inc.). Rev. Joseph J. McGahren, M.M. In res., Bro. John J. Blazo, M.M., Dir.

Monastery of Our Lady of Mercy, 6398 Drexel Rd., 19151-2596. Tel: 215-877-4858; Fax: 215-877-7208. Order of the B.V.M. of Mercy (Mercedarian Friars). Post Novitiate formation house for the Order. Rev. Steven M. Rosczewski, O.de.M., Local Supr. Total in Residence 8.

Oblates of St. Francis De Sales, Northeast Catholic High School Faculty House, 1840 E. Torresdale Ave., 19124-4418. Tel: 215-535-9080. Oblates of St. Francis De Sales. Very Rev. W. E. Davis, O.S.F.S., Supr.; Revs. Robert D. Ashenbrenner, O.S.F.S.; Leon V. Bonikowski, O.S.F.S.; William J. Cleary, O.S.F.S.; Joseph A. DiMauro, O.S.F.S.; John V. DiFilippo, O.S.F.S.; Thomas M. Gillespie, O.S.F.S.; Joseph J. Griffin, O.S.F.S.; Robert P. Hanlon, O.S.F.S.; James P. Harvey, O.S.F.S.; William T. McCandless; Michael S. Murray, O.S.F.S.; Francis J. Pileggi, O.S.F.S.; Mark F. Plaushin, O.S.F.S.; William G. Scholl, O.S.F.S.; Edward J. Simons, O.S.F.S.; John J. Sullivan, O.S.F.S.; Cornelius F. Kilty, O.S.F.S.; Thomas B. Curran, O.S.F.S.; Bros. Harry G. Schneider, O.S.F.S.; Gerald M. Sweeney, O.S.F.S.; James F. Williams, O.S.F.S.; Daniel Wisniewski, O.S.F.S.; Mr. Serge Vasilevsky, Scholastics. Total in Residence 24.

Order of Friars Minor, Holy Name Province, St. Francis Inn, 1802 E. Hagert St., 19125. Tel: 215-423-2859. Revs. Michael A. Duffy, O.F.M.; Charles V. Finnegan, O.F.M.; Francis Pompei, O.F.M.; Bros. Xavier de la Huerta, O.F.M.; Thomas Ennis, O.F.M.

St. Alphonsus House, 5800 Overbrook Ave., 19131. Tel: 215-477-9220. Jesuit Fathers. Revs. Anthony J. Berret, S.J.; Joseph J. Feeney, S.J.; Joseph J. Godfrey, S.J.; Joseph M. Kakalec, S.J.; Bro. John J. McLane, S.J. Priests 4; Brothers 1.

St. Joseph's Preparatory School Jesuit Community, Arrupe House, 1226 N. 18th St., 19121. Tel: 215-765-1875. Residence of Jesuit Fathers. Revs. Herbert B. Keller, S.J., Rector; Peter P. D'Alessandro, S.J.; F. Joseph Michini, S.J.; David A. Sauter, S.J.; J. Vincent Taggart, S.J.

St. Michael's Passionist Residence, 6300 N. Seventh St., 19126. Tel: 215-549-1761. Revs. Alexis Paul, C.P., Dir.; Columkille Regan, C.P.; Fidelis Connolly, C.P. Total Staff 3; Total in Residence 6; Students 3.

St. Norbert Priory, 1815 S. 27th St., 19145. Tel: 215-389-5575. Canons Regular of Premontre Faculty residence for Norbertine Fathers who teach at St. John Neumann High School. Revs. Steven J. Albero, O.Praem.; Richard J. Antonucci, O.Praem., Supr.; Hubert N. Beaudoin, O.Praem.; John M. Cagney, O.Praem.; Michael J. Lee, O.Praem.; Ronald J. Rossi, O.Praem.; James C. Rodia, O.Praem.; John C. Zagarella, O.Praem.; Bros. Joseph Mulholland, O.Praem.; Blase Corso, O.Praem.; John B. Ginder, O.Praem.

St. Pius X Friary, 11051 Academy Rd., 19154. Tel: 215-632-1300. Order of Friars Minor, Assumption B.V.M. Province. Faculty Residence for Archbishop Ryan High School. Revs. Louis Stislow, O.F.M., Guardian; Rene Barczak, O.F.M.; Roderick Drag, O.F.M.; James Gannon, O.F.M.; Carl Graczyk, O.F.M.; Francis X. Kelly, O.F.M.; Linus E. Kopczewski, O.F.M.; Charles Newman, O.F.M.; Warren Rector, O.F.M.; Gabriel A. Rosetti, O.F.M.; Michael Surufka, O.F.M.; Joel Szydlowski, O.F.M.; Rudolph Wieszczek, O.F.M.

Society of the Brothers of the Holy Spirit (B.H.S.), Providence House, 3531 N. 19th St., 19140. Tel: 215-225-7231. Bro. Darryl-Joseph Branch, B.H.S., Contact Person. Total in Residence 2.

AUDUBON. *Christian Brothers (F.S.C.)*, St. Gabriel Hall Community, Pawlings Rd., P.O. Box 7280, 19407-7280. Tel: 215-247-2776: 610-666-7970.

BENSALEM. *Congregation of the Holy Ghost Fathers and Brothers*, Spiritan Hall, 2401 Bristol Pike, 19020. Tel: 215-638-0232; 0233. Faculty Residence for Priests & Brothers Teaching at Holy Ghost Preparatory School; Also Residence for Retired Priests and Brothers.

School Community: Revs. James P. McCloskey, C.S.Sp., Supr.; Robert Roach, C.S.Sp.; John A. Sawicki, C.S.Sp.; Christopher H. McDermott, C.S.Sp., Bursar; Denis P. Robinson, C.S.Sp.

Retirement Community: Revs. Robert N. Roach, C.S.Sp., Supr.; Jeremiah A. Falvey, C.S.Sp., Bursar; Anthony S. Kliche, C.S.Sp.; John R. Muka, C.S.Sp.; Vincent J. Niederberger, C.S.Sp.; Albert M. Seichepine, C.S.Sp.; Stephen A. Zamborsky, C.S.Sp.; Bro. Dominic Reardon, C.S.Sp.

BRYN MAWR. *Augustinians Brothers (O.S.A.)*, Our Mother of Good Counsel Community, 31 Pennswood Rd., 19010-3475. Tel: 610-525-0147. Rev. Adrian Gilligan, O.S.A., Contact Person.

DEVON. *Piarist Fathers (Order of the Pious Schools)*, 363 Valley Forge Rd., 19333. Tel: 610-688-6807.

Priests who teach at Devon Preparatory School: Revs. James J. Shea, Sch.P., Headmaster; Richard S. Wyzykiewicz, Sch.P., Prov.; Ladislaus Magyar, Sch.P.; Louis G. Mesko, Sch.P.; Ferdinand Negrillos, Sch.P.; Geza Pazmany, Sch.P.

Piarist Fathers Latin Mission. Revs. Richard Wyzykiewicz, Sch.P.; Mario Vizcaino, Sch.P. Total Staff 3; Total in Residence 18.

DOYLESTOWN. *Pauline Fathers Monastery, Shrine of Our Lady of Czestochowa*, 654 Ferry Rd., P.O. Box 2049, 18901. Tel: 215-345-0607; Fax: 214-348-2148. Office. Tel: 215-345-0600; 0601. Revs. Lucius Tyrasinski, O.S.P.P.E., Prov.; George J. Maj, O.S.P.P.E., Prior; Jan Kolmaga, O.S.P.P.E., Sub-Prior; Stephen Z. Wozniczka, O.S.P.P.E., Shrine Dir.; Zdzislaw Kikowski, O.S.P.P.E.; Piotr Marciniak, O.S.P.P.E.; John Michalak, O.S.P.P.E.; Angelus P. Ferrara, O.S.P.P.E.; Tadeusz Olzacki, O.S.P.P.E.; Albert P. Ostatek, O.S.P.P.E.; Marian Zalecki, O.S.P.P.E.; Michael Zembrzuski, O.S.P.P.E.; Bros. Casimir Pasnik; Didak Turi; Luke Mitura; Peter Lisiecki; Thomas Kupczak.

FAIRLESS HILLS. *St. Anthony Friary*, 607 Wistar Rd., 19030. Tel: 215-943-4810. Franciscan Friars T.O.R. Bro. James Boyle, T.O.R., Local Min.; Revs. Fidelis F. Weber, T.O.R., Guidance Dir.; Neil Saller, T.O.R.; M. Gerald Gordon, T.O.R.; Andre C. Strittmatter, T.O.R.; Donald F. Vuketich, T.O.R.; Gabriel Zeis, T.O.R.; Bros. James A. Boyle, T.O.R.; John T. Carosella, T.O.R.; John Patrick Calvey, T.O.R.; Francis M. Haworth, T.O.R.; Lawrence Hilferty, T.O.R. Faculty residence for priests and brothers who teach at Conwell-Egan Catholic High School.

FLOURTOWN. *Augustinians (O.S.A.)*, St. Genevieve Friary, 1225 Bethlehem Pike, 19031-1902. Tel: 215-836-2830. Revs. Joseph A. Duffey, O.S.A., Contact Person; John P. Hennessy, O.S.A.; William A. Recchuti, O.S.A. Total in Residence 3.

HAVERTOWN. *Augustinians (O.S.A.)*, St. Denis Friary, 2401 Denis Ln., 19083-1698. Tel: 610-446-0202. Rev. James J. McCartney, O.S.A., Contact Person. Total in Residence 6.

LANGHORNE. *Society of Mary, Marist Fathers*, St. Mary's Hospital, 19047. Tel: 215-750-2558. Rev. George Wallace, S.M., Contact.

LAVEROCK. *Brothers of Charity (F.C.)*, Triest Hall, 7720 Doe Ln., 19038. Tel: 215-887-6361; 887-6372. Total in Residence 6.

MALVERN. *Augustinians (O.S.A.)*, Malvern Prep School Community, 19335. Tel: 610-644-5454; 647-8281. Rev. Harry J. Erdlen, O.S.A., Prior.

PAOLI. *Daylesford Abbey*, 220 S. Valley Rd., 19301-1900. Tel: 610-647-2530; Fax: 610-651-0219. Legal Title: *Norbertine Fathers of PA, Inc.* Rt. Rev. Jerome G. Tremel, O.Praem., Abbot/Admin.; Very Rev. Robert F. Kelly, O.Praem., Prior; Revs. Theodore J. Antry, O.Praem., Vocation Dir.; Edward J. Smith, O.Praem., Treas.; Maurice C. Avicolli, O.Praem.; Jeffrey T. Cesarone, O.Praem.; Andrew D. Ciferni, O.Praem.; John V. Cimino, O.Praem.; William R. Craig, O.Praem.; Salvatore H. Cuccia, O.Praem.; John A. D'Antonio, O.Praem.; William J. Fischer, O.Praem.; Martin A. Frigo, O.Praem.; Thomas A. Hagendorf, O.Praem.; Joseph A. Kelly, O.Praem.; Edward J. Kimpel, O.Praem.; Joseph C. Laenen, O.Praem.; David T. Lawlor, O.Praem.; John M. Logan, O.Praem., Abbot Emeritus; Revs. Thomas O. Meulemans, O.Praem.; Domenic A. Rossi, O.Praem.; Thomas J. Rossi, O.Praem.; Nicholas R. Terico, O.Praem.; Charles T. Urban, O.Praem.; Bros. Blase G. Corso, O.Praem.; John B. Ginder, O.Praem.; William J. Kelly, O.Praem.; Joseph W. Mulholland, O.Praem. Priests 28; Brothers 4.

SPRINGFIELD. *Servants of Charity (S.C.)*, Don Guanella Village, 1795 S. Sproul Rd., 19064. Tel: 610-328-3406. Rev. Romano DiRuscio, S.C., Contact Person.

VILLANOVA. *Fray de Leon Community*, Villanova University, 19085. Tel: 610-519-4469. Augustinians. Rev. Edward T. Hastings, O.S.A., Contact.

Order of St. Augustine, St. Thomas of Villanova, 109 Willowburn Rd., 19085-1313. Tel: 610-527-0856. Rev. Donald F. Reilly, O.S.A.

Provincial Offices of the Order of St. Augustine, Province of St. Thomas of Villanova, P.O. Box 338, 19085-0338. Tel: 610-527-3330; Fax: 610-520-0618. Very Rev. John E. Deegan, O.S.A., Prior Prov.; Revs. Anthony P. Burrascano, O.S.A., Treas., Mission Procurator, Vicar for Admin.; Alfred E. Murphy, O.S.A., Prov. Archivist; John E. Rotelle, O.S.A., Contact Person, Prov. Sec., Dir. Communications, Augustinian Press; Joseph A. Jordan, O.S.A., Dir. Augustinian Seminary Guild; Richard D. Appicci, O.S.A., Mission Office; Robert J. Guessetto, O.S.A., Coord. Vocation Activities. Tel: 610-525-7890, St. Augustine Friary, 214 Ashwood Rd., P.O. Box 338, 19085. Tel: 610-527-0325. Bro. John J. Del Casale, O.S.A. Total in Residence 12.

St. John Stone Friary, 37 Aldwyn Ln., 19085. Tel: 610-527-2307; Fax: 610-527-2315. Revs. John E. Deegan, O.S.A., Prior Prov.; Kail C. Ellis, O.S.A.; John E. Rotelle, O.S.A.; Michael J. Scanlan, O.S.A.; T. Shawn Tracy, O.S.A., Prior; Francis E. Chambers, O.S.A.

St. Thomas Monastery, 19085. Tel: 610-645-7500. Revs. Richard D. Appicci, O.S.A.; John P. Betoni, O.S.A.; Andrew J. Boyle, O.S.A.; John E. Bresnahan, O.S.A.; George F. Burnell, O.S.A.; Edward J. Burns, O.S.A.; Donald X. Burt, O.S.A.; Jan H. Busch, O.S.A.; George J. Callaghan, O.S.A.; Angus N. Carney, O.S.A.; John F. Casey, O.S.A.; Laurence J. Conneen, O.S.A.; Russell J. DeSimone, O.S.A.; Edward J. Dixey, O.S.A., Prior; Edmund J. Dobbin, O.S.A., Pres., Villanova University; John M. Driscoll, O.S.A.; Gerard M. Duff, O.S.A.; Henry J. Eagan, O.S.A.; Francis A. Eigo, O.S.A.; John J. Farrell, O.S.A.; Francis A. Farsaci, O.S.A.; John J. Fitzgerald, O.S.A.; Charles R. Flynn, O.S.A.; Stephen R. Fogarty, O.S.A.; Dennis J. Gallagher, O.S.A.; John J. Gallagher, O.S.A.; Karl A. Gersbach, O.S.A.; Joseph J. Gildea, O.S.A.; Dante L. Girolami, O.S.A.; John J. Hagen, O.S.A.; Joseph A. Jordan, O.S.A., Treas.; Patrick J. Kenny, O.S.A.; Charles P. Laferty, O.S.A.; Joseph F. Laverty, O.S.A.; Bernard A. Lazor, O.S.A.; John F. Lipp, O.S.A.; Neil J. McGettigan, O.S.A.; Francis X. McGuire, O.S.A.; William A. McGuire, O.S.A., Treas.; John J. McKenzie, O.S.A.; Thomas J. Mahony, O.S.A.; Lee J. Makowski, O.S.A.; Francis L. Melcher, O.S.A.; William J. Murray, O.S.A.; James L. Nolan, O.S.A.; John M. Quinn, O.S.A.; Patrick J. Rice, O.S.A.; George F. Riley, O.S.A.; Joseph C. Schnaubelt, O.S.A.; Albert C. Shannon, O.S.A.; Joseph L. Shannon, O.S.A.; Thomas J. Shea, O.S.A.; Ralph V. Shuhler, O.S.A.; Ralph C. Shurer, O.S.A.; Arthur F. Smith, O.S.A.; John P. Stack, O.S.A.; Robert E. Steinman, O.S.A.; Michael P. Sullivan, O.S.A.; Henry B. Syvinski, O.S.A.; William C. Van Breda, O.S.A.; Dennis G. Wilde, O.S.A.; Bros. Nicholas Osuna, O.S.A.; James E. Farrell, O.S.A.; George J. Phillips, O.S.A. Total Staff 16; Total in Residence 64.

WILLOWBURN. *Order of St. Augustine*, St. Thomas of Villanova Prov. Friary, 109 Willowburn Rd., 19085. Tel: 215-527-0856. Rev. Edward L. Hamel, O.S.A.

WYNDMOOR. *Christian Brothers (F.S.C.)*, LaSalle High School Community, 8605 Cheltenham Ave., 19038. Tel: 215-233-3030. Bro. Timothy Ahern, F.S.C., Contact Person. Total in Residence 16.

Oblates of St. Francis de Sales (O.S.F.S.), Villa De Sales Novitiate, 8501 Flourtown Ave., 19038. Tel: 215-836-1472. Very Rev. Nicholas R. Waseline, O.S.F.S., Contact Person.

Villa de Sales Novitiate, 8501 Flourtown Ave., 19038. Tel: 215-836-1472. Novitiate of the Oblates of St. Francis DeSales, Wilmington-Philadelphia Province.

[AA] CONVENTS AND RESIDENCES OF SISTERS

PHILADELPHIA. *Annunciation Community*, 3501 Lansing St., 19136. Tel: 215-331-9239.

Assumption Hall, Sisters of St. Joseph, 8900 Norwood Ave., 19118. Tel: 215-247-3665; 248-2564. Sr. Joan Daly, S.S.J., Contact. Residence for Norwood-Fontbonne Academy Faculty.

Bernardine Franciscan Sisters, Casa De Paz, 441 Tomlinson Rd., Apt. E-17, 19116-3226. Tel: 215-464-9409. Sr. Therese Immaculate DiCondina, O.S.F., Contact.

Blessed Trinity Missionary Cenacle, 804 N. 24th St., 19130. Tel: 215-765-2237. Missionary Servants of the Most Blessed Trinity, Ministry in Catholic Social Services and various parish ministries.

Blessed Trinity Mother Missionary Cenacle, 3501 Solly Ave., 19136. Tel: 215-335-7550; Fax: 215-335-7559. Generalate, Novitiate and Candidacy of the Missionary Servants of the Most Blessed Trinity. Mother Boniface Center. Sr. Siena Marie Wahl, M.S.B.T., Gen. Custodian; Sr. Joan Marie Keller, M.S.B.T., Gen. Sec. Total Staff 25; Total in Residence 108.

Carmelite Monastery, 66th Ave. and Old York Rd., 19126. Tel: 215-424-6143; Fax: 215-424-6143. Mother Pia, Prioress.

Carmelite Sisters for the Aged and Infirm (O.Carm.), Sacred Heart Manor, 6445 Germantown Ave., 19119. Tel: 215-236-5268.

Congregation of the Sisters of St. Felix, St. Ignatius Convent, 4401 Haverford Ave., 19104. Tel: 215-222-2296; Fax: 215-222-3078. Sr. Mary Joanne Ustaszewska, Local Min.

Congregation of the Sisters of St. Felix, St. Joseph Convent, 16th & Girard Ave., 19130. Tel: 215-787-9482. Sr. Mary Angela Machowski, Local Supr. Sisters 14.

Convent of the Daughters of Charity, 449 E. Locust Ave., 19144. Tel: 215-438-3536. Sr. Anne Marie Graham, D.C., Supr. Total in Residence 5.

Convent of the Little Sisters of the Assumption, 6300 Drexel Rd., 19151. Tel: 215-877-8655. Total in Residence 6.

Convent of the Missionary Sisters of the Immaculate Heart of Mary, I.C.M., 1242 S. Broad St., 19146. Tel: 215-468-6368. Sr. Anna Verlinden, Supr.

Convent of the Sisters of the Good Shepherd, 8550 Verree Rd., 19111-1353. Sr. Maria Virginia Gordon, R.G.S., Coord. Tel: 342-5820.

Convent Sisters of Mercy, 5700 City Ave., 19131-1209. Sisters provide domestic service for Cardinal's Residence.

Daughters of St. Paul, 9171 A Roosevelt Blvd., 19114. Tel: 215-676-9494. Sr. Marie James Hunt, F.S.P., Contact.

Daughters of St. Paul Convent, 9610 Evans St., 19115. Tel: 215-969-5068. Sr. Marie James Hunt, F.S.P., Supr.

Dominican Sisters of Our Lady of the Rosary, O.P., 606 W. Erie Ave., 19140-4431. Tel: 215-226-3507. Dominican Sisters of Our Lady of the Rosary of Fatima. Sr. M. Angelica Perez, O.P., Local Supr.

Emmaus Convent, 5358 Cedar Ave., 19143. Tel: 215-471-7260. Sisters of Mercy (R.S.M.). Total in Residence 3.

Franciscan Sisters of Allegany (O.S.F.), 2622 Potter St., 19125. Tel: 215-739-6441. Sr. Mary Augustini, O.S.F., Local Min.

Franciscan Sisters of Peace, Cecilian Academy, 6818 Cresheim Rd., 19119. Tel: 215-438-7515.

Grey Nuns of the Sacred Heart, 5220 N. Broad St., 19141. Tel: 215-329-0571. Total Staff 1; Total in Residence 4.

Handmaids of the Sacred Heart of Jesus, 4001 N. 17th St., 19140. Tel: 215-225-2468. Sr. Gloria Petrone, A.C.J., Supr. Total in Residence 7.

Hannah House, Sisters of St. Joseph, 2458 N. 16th St., 19132. Tel: 215-221-0211. Sr. Virginia Jenkins, S.S.J., Contact Person.

Immaculate Heart Convent, 7310 Torresdale Ave., 19136. Tel: 215-332-8299. Sr. Marie de Lourdes, I.H.M., Contact Person. Faculty Residence for Sisters, Servants of the Immaculate Heart of Mary, teaching at St. Hubert High School. Total in Residence 12.

Immaculate Heart Convent, 4904 Chestnut St., 19139. Tel: 215-474-8971. Sr. Mary E. Bur, I.H.M., Supr. Faculty Residence for Sisters, Servants of the Immaculate Heart of Mary, who teach at West Philadelphia Catholic High School. Total Staff 9; Total in Residence 9.

Little Servants of the Holy Family of Seoul, 70th & Old York Rd., 19126. Tel: 215-548-5535. Sr. Andrew Kim, L.S.H.F., Local Supr.

Little Sisters of the Assumption, 832 Ritner St., 19148. Tel: 215-334-8902. Sr. Marie Gervasi, L.S.A., Contact.

Little Sisters of the Poor, Holy Family Home, 5300 Chester Ave., 19143. Tel: 215-729-5753; Fax: 215-729-5158.

Little Workers of the Sacred Hearts, Sacred Hearts Convent, 160 Carpenter Ln., 19119. Tel: 215-843-2266.

Mary Immaculate Convent, 1731 S. 11th St., 19148. Tel: 215-468-9133. Sr. Bernard Agnes, I.H.M., Supr. Faculty Residence for Sisters, Servants of the Immaculate Heart of Mary, who teach at St. Maria Goretti High School and John W. Hallahan High School. Total Staff 28; Total in Residence 28.

Medical Mission Sisters, North American Sector, 8400 Pine Rd., 19111. Tel: 215-742-6100; Fax: 215-342-3948.

Medical Mission Sisters (M.M.S.), 217 E. Price St., 19144. Tel: 215-844-3672. Sr. Barbara Ann Brigham, M.M.S., Contact Person. Total in Residence 6.

Medical Mission Sisters, North American Sector, 8400 Pine Rd., 19111. Tel: 215-742-6100; Fax: 215-342-3948. Sr. Estelle Demers, M.M.S., Sector Coord.; Sr. Jane Gates, M.M.S., District Coord. Sisters in Sector 149.

Missionary Servant of the Most Blessed Trinity, Holy Spirit Missionary Cenacle, 1835 Johnson St., 19145. Tel: 215-467-4871. Sr. Marion Dillon, M.S.B.T., Contact Person.

Missionary Sisters of the Holy Rosary, St. Barbara Convent. 205 Cricket Ave., Ardmore, 19003. Sr. Anna Marino, M.S.H.R.

Missionary Sisters of the Most Sacred Heart, Trinity House, 518 Devereaux Ave., 19111. Tel: 215-342-3498.

Missionary Sisters of the Sacred Heart (Cabrini Sisters), 67th and Callowhill Sts., 19151. Tel: 215-748-1789. Sacred Heart of Jesus Community.

Residence for Retired Sisters. Tel: 215-472-7911. Sr. Patricia Dunleavy, M.S.C., Supr.

Monastery of the Visitation Nuns, 5820 City Ave., 19131-1295. Tel: 215-473-5888. Mother Frances de Sales Paganelli, V.H.M., Supr.; Rev. Joseph A. Duke, S.J., Chap. Total Staff 12; Total in Residence 12.

Mother of Peace House, 2622 Potter St., 19125. Tel: 215-739-6441. Franciscan Sisters of Allegany.

Mt. St. Joseph Convent, 9701 Germantown Ave., 19118-2694. Tel: 215-248-7200. Motherhouse of the Sisters of St. Joseph of Chestnut Hill, Philadelphia. Sr. Margaret Fleming, S.S.J., Supr.

Nativity B.V.M. Convent, Sisters of Christian Charity, 3224 Belgrade St., 19134. Sisters of the Christian Charity.

Nazareth Convent, Religious Sisters of Mercy, 6369 Woodbine Ave., 19151. Tel: 215-477-3022. Sr. Patricia Smith, R.S.M., Contact Person.

Peace Hermitage, Society of Catholic Medical Missionaries, 8400 Pine Rd., 19111. Tel: 215-342-0961. Sr. Jane Burns, S.C.M.M., Contact Person.

Poor Servants, Mother of God, 883 N. Judson St., 19130. Tel: 215-763-8593.

Portiuncula Convent, 4565 Cottman Ave., 19135. Tel: 215-332-0125; 0126. Residence for Sisters of St. Francis of Philadelphia. Total in Residence 5.

Provincial House of the Sisters of the Holy Family of Nazareth. Immaculate Conception Province, 4001 Grant Ave., 19114. Tel: 215-637-6464; Fax: 215-637-8475. Sr. M. Michaelann, Prov. Supr.; Rev. Ronald J. Ferrier, Chap. Total in Residence 184.

Religious Sisters of the Assumption, Assumption Convent, 914 S. 49th St., 19143. Tel: 215-727-9430. Sr. Ann Palmer, Supr.

St. Callistus Convent, Religious Sisters of Mercy, 6714 Lansdowne Ave., 19151.

St. Clare Convent, 7375 Ditman St., 19136. Tel: 215-332-4750.

Faculty Residence for Sisters of St. Francis of Philadelphia.

St. Francis Convent, 1727 S. 11th St., 19148. Tel: 215-463-7343. Residence of Sisters of St. Francis of Philadelphia employed at St. Maria Goretti and Hallahan High Schools, St. Agnes Hospital, Sacred Heart School, (Child/Family Treatment), and Archdiocesan Office.

St. Isaac House, Society of the Daughters of the Heart of Mary. 226 N. Essex Ave., #106, Narberth, 19072. Tel: 610-664-9546. Sr. Kathleen F. Devine, D.H.M., Supr.

St. Joseph Convent, 7300 Torresdale Ave., 19136. Tel: 215-338-4884. Faculty Residence for Sisters of St. Joseph, who teach at St. Hubert and Father Judge High School, St. Vincent's Orphanage and Nazareth Academy.

St. Joseph the Worker Convent, 2846 W. Allegheny Ave., 19132. Tel: 215-228-4030. Sisters of Mercy (R.S.M.). Sr. Mary Urban, Coord.

St. Michael Hall, 9001 Germantown Ave., 19118. Tel: 215-247-3698. Sr. James Agnes, S.S.J., Contact Person. Faculty Residence for Sisters of St. Joseph who staff Chestnut Hill College. Total in Residence 13.

School Sisters of Notre Dame, Nativity Community, 6346 Hegerman St., 19135. Tel: 215-333-5742. Sr. Mary Loraditch, S.S.N.D.

School Sisters of Notre Dame, St. Vincent Community, 7201 Milnor St., 19135. Tel: 215-624-5600; 624-5635. Total in Residence 6.

School Sisters of Notre Dame, 2141 N. Howard St., 19122. Tel: 215-634-2227.

School Sisters of Notre Dame, 158 E. Huntingdon St., 19125. Tel: 215-425-1350.

School Sisters of Notre Dame, Vistation Community, 3978 Constance Rd., 19114. Tel: 215-824-0754. Sr. Bernadette Marie Ravenstahl, S.S.N.D., Contact.

School Sisters of Notre Dame (S.S.N.D.). 4 Colony Blvd., Bldg. 4, Apt. 422, Wilmington, DE, 19802-1461. Sr. Susan Plews, S.S.N.D., Contact Person.

Shalom Convent, 5342-44 Cedar Ave., 19143. Tel: 215-474-5538. Residence of Religious Sisters of Mercy.

Sister Servants of the Holy Spirit of Perpetual Adoration (S.Sp.S.A.P.), Convent of Divine Love, 2212 Green St., 19130. Tel: 215-567-0123. Sr. Mary Victoria, S.Sp.S.A.P., Supr.; Rev. Joseph C. Dieckhaus, Chap.

Sisters of Charity of Nazareth, 1905 Brown St., 19130. Tel: 215-236-0993.

Sisters of Mercy of the Americas, Guadalupe Convent, 966 N. Fifth St., 19123. Tel: 215-413-7575. Total in Residence 4.

Sisters of Notre Dame de Namur, Resurrection Convent, 2037 Vista St., 19152. Tel: 215-745-3872. Total Staff 11; Total in Residence 11.

Sisters of St. Francis of Philadelphia. Franciscan Formation House. 338 Warton St., 19147. Tel: 215-336-8915.

Sisters of St. Francis of Philadelphia, Santa Chiara, 2238 S. 12th St., 19148. Tel: 215-465-2227. Sisters Residence for those who work at St. Agnes Medical Center and Epiphany Church.

Sisters of St. Francis of Philadelphia, St. Agnes Convent, 1900 S. Broad St., 19145. Tel: 215-465-1597. Total in Residence 6; Total Staff 6.

Sisters of St. Francis of Philadelphia (O.S.F.), 1342 Castle Ave., 19148. Tel: 215-755-2352.

Sisters of St. Francis of Philadelphia, Canticle House, 1626 Mifflin St., 19145. Tel: 215-551-2586.

Sisters of St. Joseph, Neumann Hall, 58 E. Northwestern Ave., 19118. Tel: 215-248-7282.

Sisters of St. Joseph of Philadelphia. Divine Shepherd Convent, 927 Bethlehem Pike, Erdenheim, 19038. Tel: 215-836-2082. Total in Residence 6.

Sisters of St. Joseph of Philadelphia, Immaculate Heart of Mary Convent, 823 Cathedral Rd., 19128. Tel: 215-482-8540. Sisters in Residence 7.

Sisters of St. Joseph of Philadelphia, Cecilian Academy, 6818 Cresheim Rd., 19119. Tel: 215-438-7515. Total in Residence 11.

Sisters of St. Joseph of Philadelphia, Fournier Community, Administration, 9701 Germantown Ave., 19118-2694. Tel: 215-248-7234. Sr. Margaret Fleming, S.S.J., Supr. Gen.

Sisters of St. Joseph of Philadelphia, Nazareth House. 931 Bethlehem Pike, Erdenheim, 19038. Tel: 215-836-2613. Total in Residence 5.

Sisters of the Blessed Sacrament, Acacia Community, 3533 N. 19th St., 19140. Total in Residence 5.

Sisters of the Good Shepherd, 5356 Chew Ave., 19138. Tel: 215-843-9411. Neighborhood ministry, mediation program. Total in Residence 3.

Sisters of the Good Shepherd (Contemplative), 715 Susquehanna Rd., 19111. Tel: 215-722-3970. Sr. Jude Ellen Golumbieski, C.G.S., Supr.

Sisters of the Good Shepherd (R.G.S.), 8550 Verree Rd., 19111-1353. Tel: 215-342-5820. Sr. Maria Virginia Gordon, R.G.S., Contact Person.

Sisters of the Good Shepherd (R.G.S.), P.O. Box 44258, 19144. Tel: 215-849-2070. Sr. M. Loretta Clancy, R.G.S., Contact Person. Total in Residence 5.

Sisters of the Holy Child, 4724-26 Cedar Ave., 19143. Tel: 215-729-4084.

Response-Ability Residence, 2362 E. York St. Residence for volunteers for Teacher Service Project sponsored by the Sociert of Holy Child.

Sisters of the Holy Family of Nazareth, Holy Family College Convent, Grant and Frankford Aves., 19114. Tel: 215-637-6262.

Sisters of the Holy Family of Nazareth, Infant Jesus Convent, 2755 Holme Ave., 19152. Tel: 215-338-8992.

Sisters of the Holy Family of Nazareth, Nazareth Hospital Convent, 2723 Holme Ave., 19152-2015. Tel: 215-335-6380. Total in Residence 24.

Sisters of the Holy Redeemer, Emmaus Convent, 1117 Wakeling St., 19124. Tel: 215-288-5564.

Sisters of the Holy Redeemer, Angelus-Formation Community, 705 Medary Ave., 19126. Tel: 215-276-0262. Mailing Address: c/o Sisters of the Holy Redeemer, 521 Moredon Rd., Huntingdon Valley, 19006.

AMBLER. *Sisters of the Holy Family of Nazareth (C.S.F.N.)*, St. Mary's Villa for Children, 701 Bethlehem Pike, Box 388, 19002. Tel: 215-643-7676.

ARDMORE. *Missionary Sisters of the Holy Rosary (M.S.H.R.)*, 205 Cricket Ave., 19003. Tel: 610-896-1786. Sr. Paula Molloy, M.S.H.R., Reg. Supr. Total in Residence 20.

ASTON. *Convent of Our Lady of Angels*. (Formerly Glen Riddle), 609 S. Convent Rd., 19014. Tel: 215-459-4125. Motherhouse of the Sisters of St. Francis of Philadelphia. Sr. Marie Lucey, O.S.F., Congregational Min.

Mt. Alvernia Convent, 602A S. Convent Rd., 19014. Tel: 215-459-5989. Sisters of St. Francis of Philadelphia. Sr. Helen St. Paul, O.S.F., Contact Person. Total in Residence 4.

Sisters of St. Francis of Philadelphia, Our Lady of the Valley Convent, 10 Red Hill Rd., 19014. Sr. Margarita Guggy, O.S.F., Contact.

Sisters of St. Francis of Philadelphia, Portiuncula Convent, 610 Red Hill Rd., 19014. Tel: 610-459-8992. Sisters 15.

Sisters of St. Francis of Philadelphia, Assisi House, 600 Red Hill Rd., 19014. Tel: 610-459-8990. Total Staff 110; Total in Residence 140.

Sisters of St. Francis of Philadelphia, TAU Convent, 886 Concord Rd., 19014. Sr. Kathleen Donovan, O.S.F., Contact. Total in Residence 5.

BENSALEM. *Grey Nuns of the Sacred Heart*, Cornwell Station Apartments, 717 Station Ave., No. 0-120, 19020. Tel: 215-639-1613. Sr. Eileen White, G.N.S.H., Contact Person. Total in Residence 2.

St. Elizabeth Convent, 1663 Bristol Pike, 19020-8502. Tel: 215-244-9900. Motherhouse of the Sisters of the Blessed Sacrament for Indians and Colored People. Sr. Monica Loughlin, S.B.S., Pres.; Sr. Elizabeth Strachan, S.B.S., Local Dir. Total in Residence 135.

St. Michael Hall, 1663 Bristol Pike, 19020-8502. Tel: 215-244-9900; 638-0865.

Sisters of the Blessed Sacrament Novitiate, 1663 Bristol Pike, 19020. Mailing Address: P.O. Box 8502, 19020. Sr. Jacinta Franz, S.B.S., Contact Person; Sr. Amedee Maxwell, S.B.S. Professed Sisters 3; Novices 2; Total in Residence 5.

BRANDAMORE. *Medical Mission Sisters*, P.O. Box 216, 19316. Tel: 215-742-6100. Sr. Kathryn Gates, M.M.S., Personnel Asst.

BRYN MAWR. *Missionary Sisters of the Holy Rosary*, 741 Polo Rd., 19010. Tel: 610-520-1974.

Sisters of the Holy Child, 621 Pembroke Rd. Residence for Sisters of the Holy Child Jesus in varied apostolates.

American Province Archives, 1355 Montgomery Ave., Rosemont, 19010-1698. Tel: 610-527-3486, Ext. 221.

Sisters of the Holy Child Jesus, 105 County Line Rd., 19010. Tel: 610-525-9955. Sr. Susan Slater, S.H.C.J., Contact Person. Residence for sisters who serve at Archdiocesean Offices and St. Joseph Prep. High School and SHCJ Health Office, Havertown.

Society of the Holy Child Jesus, 700 Old Lancaster Rd., 19010. Tel: 610-527-5076. Residence of Sisters of the Holy Child Jesus. Total in Residence 7.

CHELTENHAM. *Daughters of Our Lady of the Sacred Heart*, St. Joseph Convent, 7633 Waters Rd., 19012. Tel: 215-224-2159. Total in Residence 11.

CHESTER. *Bernardine Sisters of St. Francis*, Sacred Heart Convent, 2601 W. Tenth St., 19013. Total in Residence 25.

Bernardine Sisters of St. Francis, Bernardine Center, 2625 W. Ninth St., 19013. Tel: 610-497-3225.

Bernardine Sisters of St. Francis, Blessed Katharine Drexel Convent, 1902 Providence Ave., 19013. Tel: 610-876-4916.

Missionaries of Charity, Gift of Mary, 2714 W. 9th St., 19013. Tel: 610-494-4724. Sr. M. Roberta, M.C., Contact.

COATSVILLE. *Comboni Missionary Sisters*, 41 S. 6th Ave., 19320. Tel: 610-380-9229. Sr. Joan Ramus, C.M.S., Supr.

DARBY. *Religious Sisters of Mercy*, 3 Golf Rd., 19023. Tel: 610-461-7634. Sr. Regina Ward, R.S.M., Coord. Residence of Sisters, majority of whom minister at Mercy Health Corporation.

Sisters of the Divine Redeemer, Divine Redeemer Convent, 1209 Springfield Rd., 19023. Tel: 610-534-1688.

DEVON. *Congregation of the Benedictines of Jesus Crucified, O.S.B.*, Regina Mundi Priory, Inc., 550 S. Waterloo and Fairfield Rds., 19333-1798. Tel: 610-688-5130; Fax: 610-995-0477. Sr. Zita Wenker, O.S.B., Prioress.

DREXEL HILL. *Holy Child Convent*, 453 Shadeland Ave., 19026. Tel: 610-259-1732. Residence of Retired Sisters of the Holy Child Jesus (S.H.C.J.).

St. Joseph Convent, 435 N. Lansdowne Ave., 19026-1190. Tel: 610-622-0440. Sr. Gertrude Friel, S.S.J., Local Coord. Faculty Residence for Sisters of St. Joseph who teach at Archbishop Prendergast High School, Msgr. Bonner High School, and Bishop Neuman and Villanova University.

Sisters of Notre Dame de Namur, 435 N. Lansdowne Ave. Tel: 610-237-4760.

Sisters of the Holy Child Jesus (S.H.C.J.), 620 Edmonds Ave., 19026. Tel: 610-626-8223.

Society of the Holy Child Jesus, Provincial Office, 460 Shadeland Ave., 19026. Tel: 610-626-1400; Fax: 610-626-1454. Sr. Susan Slater, S.H.C.J., Prov. Legal Title: *Society of the Holy Child Jesus American Province, Inc.*

Xavier House, 454 Shadeland Ave., 19026. Tel: 610-623-8568. Sisters of the Holy Child Jesus.

ELKINS PARK. *Dominican Motherhouse, Congregation of St. Catherine de Ricci*, 750 Ashbourne Rd., 19027-2596. Tel: 215-635-6027; Fax: 215-635-2071. Sr. Rita McManus, O.P., Pres.

Dominican Retreat House, Convent of Our Lady of Prouille, 750 Ashborne Rd., 19027-2596. Tel: 215-782-8520; 224-0945. Total Staff 39; Total in Residence 19.

St. Catherine Hall, 750 Ashbourne Rd., 19027-2596. Tel: 215-635-4540. Retirement Residence for Dominican Sisters of St. Catherine de Ricci. Total Staff 5; Total in Residence 27.

ELVERSON. *Daughters of St. Mary of Providence (D.S.M.P.)*, St. Mary of Providence Center, R.D. 2, Box 145, 19520. Tel: 942-4166. Sr. Mary Patricia Whyte, D.S.M.P., Contact Person. Total in Residence 3.

ESSINGTON. *Bernardine Sisters of St. Francis*, St. Margaret Mary Convent, 546 Wanamaker Ave., 19029. Tel: 610-521-3286.

FEASTERVILLE. *Grey Nuns of the Sacred Heart*, 1825 Bridgetown Pike, 19053.

FLOURTOWN. *St. Rita Convent*, 1410 Bethlehem Pike, 19031. Tel: 215-836-1615. Sisters of Mercy of the Americas. Sr. Maureen McCann, R.S.M.

Sisters of St. Joseph of Philadelphia, Mt. St. Joseph Academy, 120 W. Wissahickon Ave., 19031-1922. Tel: 215-233-4368; Fax: 215-233-4734. Sr. Constance Gardner, S.S.J., Contact.

FOX CHASE MANOR. *Sisters of St. Basil (O.S.B.M.)*. Motherhouse of the Sisters of St. Basil. 710 Fox Chase Rd., 19046-4198. Tel: 215-663-9153. Sr. Dorothy Ann Busowski, O.S.B.M., Prov.

GLENSIDE. *Medical Mission Sisters*. (Society of Catholic Medical Missionaries, Inc.), 15 E. Glenside Ave., 19038. Tel: 215-886-4036.

Sisters of St. Francis of Assisi (Milwaukee), 229 Edge Hill Rd., 19038. Tel: 215-866-7388.

GWYNEDD VALLEY. *Sisters of Mercy of the Americas, Annunciation Convent*, Gwynedd Mercy College, Evans Rd., 19437. Tel: 215-646-8894.

Religious Sisters of Mercy, St. Joseph Convent, Evans Rd. & Sumneytown Pike, 19437. Tel: 215-646-5259.

Religious Sisters of Mercy, Treweryn Convent, Gwynedd Mercy College, Sumneytown Pike, 19437.

Tabor Convent-Gwynedd Mercy College, Sumneytown Pike, 19437. Tel: 215-641-5516.

Transfiguration Convent, Gwynedd Mercy Convent, 19437. Tel: 215-641-5512.

Visitation Convent, Gwynedd Mercy College, 19437. Tel: 215-641-5537.

HAVERFORD. *Provincial Residence of the Handmaids of the Sacred Heart of Jesus*, St. Raphaela Center, 616 Coopertown Rd., 19041. Tel: 610-642-5715; Fax: 610-642-3879. Sr. Gloria Petrone, A.C.J., Prov.; Sr. Asunta Thanh, A.C.J., Local Supr.

HOLLAND. *Villa Joseph Marie*, 1180 Holland Rd., 18966. Tel: 215-357-8810. Sr. Magdalene Bagdonas, S.S.C., Supr.; Rev. John A. Cannon, Chap.

HUNTINGDON VALLEY. *Sisters of the Holy Redeemer Provincialate*, 521 Moredon Rd., 19006. Tel: 215-938-0540; Fax: 215-938-7759. Sr. M. Regina Heilman, C.S.R., Prov. Supr.; Revs. Michael C. Bolesta, Chap.; Timothy M. Judge, Chap.

IMMACULATA. *Sisters, Servants of the Immaculate Heart of Mary (I.H.M.)*, Pacis Hall, 19345. Tel: 610-889-1668. Sr. Eliz Seton, I.H.M., Contact. Total in Residence 200; Total Staff 52.

Sisters, Servants of the Immaculate Heart of Mary, (I.H.M.), Camilla Hall, Box 100, 19345. Tel: 610-644-1152.

Sisters, Servants of the Immaculate Heart of Mary (I.H.M.), Gillet Hall, Box 900, 19345-0901. Tel: 610-647-4400. Total in Residence 67.

Villa Maria House of Studies, 19345. Tel: 610-647-2160; Fax: 610-889-4874. Legal Title: *Villa Maria House of Studies, Motherhouse of the Sisters, Servants of the Immaculate Heart of Mary*.

JENKINTOWN. *Grey Nuns of the Sacred Heart*, Immaculate Conception Convent, 600 West Ave., 19046. Tel: 215-884-9145. Sr. Kathleen M. Woody, G.N.S.H., Coord.

Sisters of the Holy Redeemer, C.S.R. (1995), St. Elizabeth Convent, 615 Fox Chase Rd., 19046. Tel: 215-379-0112. Sr. M. Barbara Dietrich, C.S.R., Local Coord.

KENNETT SQUARE. *Sisters of Notre Dame de Namur (S.N.D.deN.)*, 501 Cypress St., 19348. Tel: 610-444-1792. Sr. Edna Maier, S.N.D.deN., Contact Person.

KING OF PRUSSIA. *Bernardine Franciscan Sisters*, Generalate, 403 Allendale Rd., 19406. Tel: 610-337-3864; Fax: 610-337-4359. Sr. Mary Margaret Jackson, O.S.F., Gen. Min.; Sr. Christine Marie Jasinowski, Gen. Sec. General Councilors: Sr. David Ann Niski; Sr. Madonna Marie Harvath; Sr. Maria Korick; Sr. Marilisa Helena de Silva.

LANGHORNE. *Monastery of St. Clare, Poor Clares*. Altar Bread Ministry. 1271 Langhorne-Newton Rd., 19047-1297. Tel: 215-968-5775; Fax: 215-968-6254. Cloistered Contemplative Nuns.

San Damiano Convent, 104 Alberts Way, 19047. Tel: 215-860-7185.

Sisters of St. Francis of Philadelphia, St. Mary Convent, 19047. Tel: 215-757-9494. Total in Residence 8.

Sisters of St. Francis of Philadelphia, Franciscan Residence, 113 Alberts Way, 19047. Tel: 215-860-1059. Sisters serving at St. Mary Medical Center.

LANSDALE. *Mercy Convent*, 500 E. Main St., 19446. Tel: 215-855-5001. Residence for Sisters of Mercy. Sr. Thomasina Marie, Coord.

Religious of the Assumption, Assumption Convent, 559 E. Main St., 19446. Tel: 215-368-4427.

LANSDOWNE. *Sisters of Bon Secours*, 44 S. Lansdowne Ave., 19050. Tel: 610-626-8637. Sisters of Bon Secours caring for elderly women in their home.

MALVERN. *Villa Maria Convent*, 370 Old Lincoln Hwy., 19355. Tel: 215-647-4878. Sisters, Servants of the Immaculate Heart of Mary (I.H.M.). Total in Residence 14.

MEADOWBROOK. *Sisters of the Holy Redeemer*, Emmanuel Convent, 1600 Huntingdon Pike, 19046. Tel: 215-947-2735. Mailing Address: c/o Sisters of the Holy Redeemer, 521 Moredon Rd., Huntingdon Valley, 19006.

MERION. *Religious Sisters of Mercy Convent*, 19066. Tel: 610-664-6650; Fax: 610-664-3429. Sr. Christine McCann, R.S.M., Reg. Pres.; Sr. Juliet Ferrari, R.S.M., Local Coord.; Rev. Michael F. Burbidge, Chap. Motherhouse of the Sisters of Mercy of Merion, PA. Sisters 93; Total Staff 16.

Religious Sisters of Mercy, Agape, 515 Montgomery Ave., 19066. Sisters 3.

MERION STATION. *Religious of the Assumption*. Assumption Convent and Spiritual Center. 227 N. Bowman Ave., 19066. Tel: 610-664-3074; 664-1736. Sr. Anne Francoise, R.A., Supr.; Sr. Francis Joseph, R.A., Center Dir. Total in Residence 10; Total Staff 3.

Religious Sisters of Mercy, St. Anne Convent, 276 Meeting House Ln., 19066.

Religious Sisters of Mercy, Bethany House of Prayer, 272 Meeting House Ln., 19066. Tel: 610-667-3066.

Religious Sisters of Mercy, McAuley Convent (Infirmary), 517 Montgomery Ave., 19066. Tel: 610-660-7841. Rev. Thomas F.X. Wheeler, S.J., Chap.

Religious Sisters of Mercy, Justice Ministry, 515 Montgomery Ave., 19066. Tel: 610-664-6650.

Agape Convent, 515 Montgomery Ave., Merion, 19066.

MORTON. *Sisters of St. Francis of Philadelphia (O.S.F.)*, 2130 Franklin Ave., Ct. No. 3, 19070-1217. Tel: 610-543-0186. Total In Residence 7; Total Staff 7.

NEWTOWN. *Grey Nuns of the Sacred Heart*, 135 S. Sycamore St., 18940. Tel: 215-968-0735. Sr. Patricia Geary, G.N.S.H. Total in Residence 3.

NORRISTOWN. *Immaculate Heart Convent*, 1834 Arch St., 19401. Tel: 610-279-2616. Sr. Judith Trumbore, I.H.M., Supr. Faculty Residence for Sisters, Servants of the Immaculate Heart of Mary, who teach at Kennedy-Kenrick Catholic High School.

Missionaries of Charity, 630 DeKalb St., 19401-3944. Tel: 610-277-5962. Sr. M. Carmelina, M.C., Supr. Social Services.

OVERBROOK. *Little Sisters of the Assumption (L.S.A.)*, 6300 Drexel Rd., 19151. Tel: 215-877-8655; Fax: 215-877-0958. Total in Residence 5.

PROSPECT PARK. *Sisters of St. Francis of Philadelphia*, Claddagh House, 518 13th Ave., 19076. Tel: 610-583-1113.

RADNOR. *Armenian Sisters of the Immaculate Conception*, 440 Upper Gulph Rd., 19087. Tel: 610-688-9360. Sr. Cecile Kehyayan, Supr.

Missionary Sisters of the Sacred Heart of Jesus (Cabrini Sisters), Cabrini College Convent, 610 King of Prussia Rd., 19807-3698. Tel: 610-687-1823. Total in Residence 6.

ROSEMONT. *Daughters of St. Mary of Providence (D.S.M.P.)*, 320 Roberts Rd., 19010. Tel: 610-525-8800. Sr. Martha Scheessele, D.S.M.P., Contact Person. Sisters who work at St. Edmond's Home for Children.

Holy Child Infirmary, 1341 Montgomery Ave., 19010. Tel: 610-525-1329. Total Staff 20; Total in Residence 37.

Sisters of the Holy Child Jesus (S.H.C.J.), Henze House, 40 Rosemont Ave., 19010. Tel: 610-525-5843. Total in Residence 6.

Sisters of the Holy Child Jesus (S.H.C.J.), New Sharon Community, 1341 Montgomery Ave., 19010. Tel: 610-525-9900. Sr. Dorothy Cunnion, S.H.C.J., Coord. Total in Residence 14.

Sisters of the Holy Child Jesus (S.H.C.J.), Carroll House Convent, 1301 Wendover Ave., 19010. Tel: 610-527-1025. Total in Residence 5.

Sisters of the Holy Child Jesus (S.H.C.J.), Gracemere Convent, 1316 Wendover Ave., 19010. Tel: 610-525-5601.

Sisters of the Holy Child Jesus (S.H.C.J.), Midhill Convent, 1355 Montgomery Ave., 19010. Tel: 610-527-3486. Total in Residence 12.

Sisters of the Holy Child Jesus (S.H.C.J.), Rosemont College Convent, 19010. Tel: 610-526-2970. Total in Residence 6.

SELLERSVILLE. *Bernardine Sisters of St. Francis*. House of Contemplation/Prayer. St. Agnes Convent, 427 N. Main St., 18960. Tel: 215-257-0845. Open to lay and religious for days of prayer, hermitage retreats, private retreats, and prayer week-ends. Call to inquire.

SHARON HILL. *Sisters of the Holy Child Jesus (S.H.C.J.)*, Cornelian House, 304 Barker Ave., 19079. Tel: 610-534-2025. Sr. Eileen Algeo, S.H.C.J., Supr. Attended from Holy Spirit Church, Sharon Hill.

SPRINGFIELD. *Daughters of St. Mary of Providence*, Divine Providence Village, 686 Old Marple Rd., 19064. Tel: 610-328-7730.

Immaculate Heart of Mary Convent, 1725 S. Sproul Rd., 19064. Tel: 610-544-0275. Sr. Mariann T. Guiniven, I.H.M., Supr. Faculty Residence for Sisters, Servants of the Immaculate Heart of Mary, who teach in Cardinal O'Hara High School and Archbishop Prendergast High School.

Our Lady of Mercy Convent, 1735 S. Sproul Rd., 19064. Tel: 610-544-0238. Faculty Residence for Sisters of Mercy who teach in Cardinal O'Hara and Archbishop Prendergast High Schools.

St. Anthony Convent, 1715 S. Sproul Rd., 19064. Tel: 610-544-4066. Residence for Sisters of St. Francis of Philadelphia who teach in Cardinal O'Hara High School and other Ministries. Total Staff 6; Total in Residence 6.

St. Joseph Convent, 1705 S. Sproul Rd., 19064. Tel: 610-544-4230. Sr. Joyce Ballerino, S.S.J., Local Coord. Sisters of St. Joseph Faculty House, Cardinal O'Hara High School.

STRAFFORD. *Our Lady of the Assumption Convent*, 139 Fairfield Ln., 19087. Tel: 610-688-7889. Sisters, Servants of the Immaculate Heart of Mary. Sr. Patricia Hughes, I.H.M., Supr.

VILLANOVA. *Sisters of Notre Dame de Namur*, Notre Dame Convent, 560 Sproul Rd., 19085. Tel: 610-688-8810. Residence for Sisters of Notre Dame de Namur who teach at Academy of Notre Dame.

WARMINSTER. *Immaculate Heart of Mary Convent*, 657 York Rd., 18974-2001. Tel: 215-674-0717; 674-0665. Sr. Loretta Therese, I.H.M., Supr. Faculty Residence for Sisters, Servants of the Immaculate Heart of Mary, who teach at Archbishop Wood High School. Total in Residence 8.

Sisters of St. Joseph of Philadelphia, Nativity of Our Lord Convent, 605 W. Street Rd., 18974. Tel: 215-672-0147. Residence of Sisters St. Joseph who teach at Archbishop Wood High School and Nativity Parish.

WYNCOTE. *Handmaids of the Sacred Heart of Jesus*, 2025 Church Rd., 19095. Tel: 215-576-6250. Sr. Rosa Maria Molina, A.C.J., Supr. Total in Residence 15.

WYNNEWOOD. *Sisters of the Holy Child Jesus*, 240 Haverford Rd., 19096. Tel: 610-642-3803. Sr. Carroll Juliano, S.H.C.J., Local Supr.

YARDLEY. *Grey Nuns of the Sacred Heart (G.N.S.H.)*, St. Joseph Community, 1750 Quarry Rd., 19067. Tel: 215-968-4237. Sr. Jean Vogel, G.N.S.H., Supr.

Motherhouse of the Grey Nuns of the Sacred Heart, 1750 Quarry Rd., 19067. Tel: 215-968-4236. Sr. Jean Liston, G.N.S.H., Supr. Gen. Total In Residence 55; Total Staff 76.

YEADON. *St. Michael Convent*, 14 Baily Rd., 19050. Tel: 610-623-3631. Sr. Barbara McGeever, R.S.M., Supr. Residence of Religious Sisters of Mercy who staff Mercy Health Corporation of Southeastern PA.

[BB] RETREAT HOUSES

PHILADELPHIA. *Mother Boniface Center*, 3501 Solly Ave., 19136. Tel: 215-335-7541. Sr. Jennie Catanese, M.S.B.T. Sponsored by Missionary Servants of the Most Blessed Trinity. Mid-week and weekend programs; retreats, days of recollection, scripture study, meetings, workshops and hosting programs.

Urban House of Prayer, 1919 Cambridge St., 19130. Tel: 215-236-8328. Sisters of Notre Dame de Namur. Sr. Marie Bodell, S.N.D.deN., Dir.; Rev. George W. Bur, S.J.

ASTON. *Clare House*, 608 B. Legion Rd., 19014. Tel: 610-459-4077. Sr. Celeste Crine, O.S.F., Dir. Directed and Private Retreats. Staffed by Sisters of St. Francis of Philadelphia. Capacity 4; Total Staff 2; Total Guests 180.

ELKINS PARK. *Dominican Retreat House*, Convent of Our Lady of Prouille, 750 Ashbourne Rd., 19027-2596. Tel: 215-782-8520; 224-0945. Retreat house for laity and religious. Total Staff 19; Total in Residence 19.

FOLSOM. *The Marianist Center*, 901 Morton Ave., Ste. 11, 19033. Tel: 610-532-3116. Bro. Jack Ventura, S.M. Total Staff 7; Total Assisted 700.

HAVERFORD. *Saint Raphaela Center*, 616 Coopertown Rd., 19041. Tel: 610-642-5715; Fax: 610-642-3879/ 610-642-6788. Handmaids of the Sacred Heart of Jesus. Sr. Mercedes Rojo, A.C.J., Dir.

MALVERN. *St. Joseph's in the Hills*, 313 Warren Ave., 19355-0315. Tel: 610-644-0400. Laymen's Retreat League. Revs. Dennis J.W. O'Donnell, Ph.D., Rector. Tel: 610-647-8581; Donald C. Connelly, Asst. Rector. Tel: 610-644-0400. Lay, Clergy and Religious Retreats. Annual Retreatants over 29,000; Daily Capacity 310.

YARDLEY. *Providence Center*, 1750 Quarry Rd., 19067. Tel: 215-968-4236. Lawrence McElroy, Dir.

[CC] CAMPS

JAMISON. *Camp Neumann Conference Center*. Mailing Address: P.O. Box 297, 18929. Tel: 215-343-6552. Summer resident camp for boys and girls.

[DD] NEWMAN CENTERS

PHILADELPHIA. *Newman Apostolate*, Newman Center, 2129 N. Broad St., 19122-1193. Tel: 215-232-3779; 235-1596; Fax: 215-235-7302. Rev. Robert A. McLaughlin, Archdiocesan Dir. E-mail:71107.373@compuserve.com

Full Time Chaplaincies:

University of Pennsylvania, Newman Hall, 3716-20 Chestnut St., 19104-6189. Tel: 215-898-7575; Fax: 215-386-5899. Rev. Charles J. Pfeffer, Newman Chap.; Robert Cardie, M.A., Asst. to the Chap.

Drexel University, Newman Center, 30 S. 33rd St., 19104-2509. Tel: 215-590-8760; Fax: 215-590-8634. Revs. Charles J. Brinkman, Chap.; John A. Freeman, Chap.

Temple University, Newman Center, 2129 N. Broad St., 19122-1193. Tel: 215-232-3779; Fax: 215-235-7302. Rev. Robert A. McLaughlin, Chap.; Sr. Dorothy Giloley, S.S.J., Asst. to the Chap.

West Chester University, Newman Center, 409 Trinity Dr., West Chester, 19382-5362. Tel: 610-436-0891; Fax: 610-436-5258. Rev. Samuel A. Verruni.

Tri-College Newman Cluster-Bryn Mawr, Haverford and Swarthmore Colleges, St. Mary Magdeline Rectory, 2400 N. Providence Rd., Media, 19063-1998. Tel: 610-566-6182; 328-8578. Rev. John A. Freeman, Chap.; Ms. Susan Harte, Asst. to Chap.

Part-time Chaplaincies:

Allegheny University of the Health Sciences, Center City.

Allegheny University of the Health Sciences, East Falls. Rev. Richard R. York, Chap.

St. Bridget's Church, 3667 Midvale Ave., 19129-1712. Tel: 215-844-4126.

Allegheny University Hospitals, Bucks County. Rev. Joseph D. Dougherty.

St. John Bosco Church, 235 E. County Line Rd., Hatboro, 19040-1298. Tel: 215-672-7280.

Allegheny University Hopitals, Elkins Park. Rev. Raymond J. Himsworth, Chap.

St. James Church, 8320 Brookside Rd., Elkins Park, 19027. Tel: 215-635-6210.

Beaver College, Glenside, 19038. Rev. J. Michael Flood, Chap., St. Luke the Evangelist, 2316 Fairhill Ave., Glenside, 19038. Tel: 215-572-0128.

Bucks County Community College, St. Andrew Church, 81 Swamp Rd., Newtown, 18940. Tel: 215-968-2262.

Cheney University, West Chester University Newman Center, 409 Trinity Dr., West Chester, 19382-5362. Tel: 610-436-0891.

Community College of Philadelphia.

Delaware County Community College, Media, 19063. Tel: 610-359-6206. Frank Mulvaney, Contact, Math/ Science Dept.; Rev. Leonard N. Peterson, Chap.

St. Anastasia Church, 3301 West Chester Pike, Newtown Square, 19073. Tel: 610-356-1613; Fax: 610-356-8332.

Delaware Valley College of Science and Agriculture, St. Jude Church, 321 W. Butler Ave., Chalfont, 18914-2329. Tel: 215-822-0179. Rev. Michael J. Gerlach.

Harcum Junior College, Our Mother of Good Counsel, 31 Pennswood Rd., Bryn Mawr, 19010. Tel: 610-525-0147.

Lincoln University, Sacred Heart Church, 101 Church Rd., Oxford, 19363. Tel: 610-932-5040. Rev. William B. Dooner, Chap.

Montgomery County Community College, St. Helena Church, P.O. Box 5085, Center Square, 19422. Tel: 610-275-7711.

Pennsylvania State University - Ogontz Campus, Our Lady Help of Christians, 1500 Marian Rd., Abington, 19001. Tel: 215-886-3456.

Pennsylvania State University - Delaware County Campus, St. Francis de Sales, New Rd., Box 97, Lenni, 19062. Tel: 610-459-2203.

Pennsylvania State University-Great Valley Campus.

Philadelphia College of Pharmacy and Science, St. Francis de Sales Church, 4625 Springfield Ave., 19143. Tel: 215-222-5819.

Philadelphia College of Textiles and Science, St. Bridget Church, 3667 Midvale Ave., 19129-1712. Tel: 215-844-4126. Rev. Richard R. York.

Royborough Memorial-School of Nursing, St. John the Baptist, 146 Rector St., 19127. Tel: 215-482-4600.

Temple University-Ambler Division, St. Alphonsus Church, 33 Conwell Dr., Maple Glen, 19002. Tel: 215-646-4600; Fax: 215-646-0180.

University of the Arts, Assoc. Dean's Office, Broad and Pine Sts., 19102. Tel: 215-875-2236.

St. John the Evangelist Church, 21 S. 13th St., 19107. Tel: 215-563-4145. Dr. Annelte DiMedio, Ph.D., Contact.

Ursinus College, St. Eleanor Church, 647 Locust St., Collegeville, 19426. Tel: 610-489-1647; Fax: 610-489-7469. Rev. John A. Franey, Chap.

Temple University, Ambler Division, St. Alphonsus Church, 33 Conwell Dr., Maple Glen, 19002. Tel: 215-646-4600.

Widener University, Blessed Katherine Drexel Church, 20th and Providence Ave., Chester, 19013. Tel: 610-872-3731. Rev. Clemens J. Gendelmann, Chap.

[EE] MISCELLANEOUS LISTINGS

PHILADELPHIA. *Alpha House Kindergarten*, Grant and Franklin Aves., 19114. Tel: 215-632-3366. Mrs. Sara LaSalle-Tarantin, Prin.

Apostleship of Prayer, St. Joseph's University, 5600 City Ave., 19131. Tel: 610-660-1436; 660-1400. Rev. Herbert F. Smith, S.J., Dir.

Catholic Kolping Society, 5400 Rising Sun Ave., 19120. Tel: 215-324-9332. Rev. Engelbert G. Michel, Praeses; Mrs. Catherine Pinkerton, Pres.; Mr. Alphonse Ellerkamp, Vice-Praeses; Mr. Earl Asimos, Treas.; Mr. Alex Eli, Vice Pres.

Catholic League For Persons With Disabilites, 4110 Glenview St., 19135. Tel: 215-331-2617. Board of Directors 12; Total Membership 100.

Catholics United for the Faith. (St. John Neumann Philadelphia Area Chapter), 183 Hillcrest Ave., 19118. Tel: 215-247-2585. Mrs. Anne M. Wilson, Chm.

The Central Association of the Miraculous Medal, 475 E. Chelten Ave., 19144-5785. Tel: 215-848-1010; Fax: 215-848-1014; 1-800-523-3674. Rev. William J. O'Brien, C.M., Dir.; Mr. Charles P. Kelly, Gen. Mgr. & Contact Person Miraculous Medal Magazine.

CORA Services, 733 Susquehanna Rd., 19111. Tel: 215-342-7660; Fax: 215-745-9857. Sr. Mary Charity Kohl, Admin. Legal Title: *Cora Services, Inc., Philadelphia, Pennsylvania.*

Euphrasia House, Inc., P.O. Box 44258, 19144-3016. Tel: 215-849-3371. Sr. Mary Loretta Clancy, Dir. & Contact Person. Women-in-Transition. Sponsored by: Sisters of the Good Shepherd. Total Staff 7; Total in Residence 5.

Franciscan Volunteer Ministry, Inc., P.O. Box 29276, 19125. Tel: 215-427-3070; Fax: 215-427-3059. E-mail:fvmpd@aol.com
Mr. Michael A. Duffy, Exec. Dir.; Ms. Stephanie A. DeBenedetti, Prog. Dir. Purpose: To create and run a faith-based lay volunteer program in the United States.

Good Shepherd Neighborhood House. Mediation Program. 5356 Chew Ave., 19138. Tel: 215-843-5413. Cheryl Cutrona, Exec. Dir. Legal Title: *Good Shepherd Corporation, Philadelphia, Pennsylvania.*

**Holy Redeemer Physician Services.* c/o Gregory J. Nowak, Esq., Stradley, Ronon, Stevens & Young. 2600 One Commerce Square, 19103-7098.

IHM Center for Literacy and GED Programs, 425 W. Lindley Ave., 19120. Tel: 215-457-2232; Fax: 215-457-2232. Sr. Mary Ellen Eckardt, I.H.M., Ph.D., Dir., 929 S. Farragut St., 19143. Tel: 215-382-0292. Full-time program with courses in Adult Basic Education (ABE); English for Speakers of Other Languages (ESOL) and General Educational Development (GED).

Katherine Kiernan Chateau, Inc., c/o Catholic Social Services, 222 N. 17th St., Ste. 300, 19103. Tel: 215-587-3903; Fax: 215-587-2479.

Ladies of Charity, 222 N. 17th St., 19103. Tel: 215-587-3816. Most Rev. Anthony J. Bevilacqua; Rev. Msgr. James T. McDonough, A.C.S.W., Moderator; Mrs. Dominick Lazanski, Pres.

St. Agnes Foundation, 1900 S. Broad St., 19145. Tel: 215-339-4225. James M. Wilson, Pres.

St. Vincent's Orphan Asylum-St. Vincent's Comprehensive Emergency Shelter Program, 7201 Milnor St., 19135. Tel: 215-MA4-5600; Fax: 215-624-8355. Rev. Eduardo G. Montero, J.C.L. Emergency Shelter 84.

Shrine of Our Lady of Victories at St. Peter Claver, 12th & Lombard Sts., 19147. Tel: 215-735-0799. Rev. William J. Maguire, C.S.Sp., S.T.L., Dir. Archconfraternity of Our Lady of Victories.

Society of Catholic Medical Missionaries Generalate, Inc. (Effective 1991), 8400 Pine Rd., 19111. Tel: 215-742-6100; Fax: 215-342-3948. Sr. Clarita Hackman, M.M.S., Contact Person; Sr. Rita Syron, M.M.S., Pres. Corporation collects funds for charitable and missionary work, for Medical Mission Sisters; Assists in operation of hospitals, clinics and primary health care programs; Assists in care of poor, sick and infirm, in U.S. and overseas; Assists in training and educating men and women in medicine and nursing, and other health professions; Trains candidates for the Community; Provides assisted living care to sick and elder Medical Mission Sisters.

The Warner Perpetual Trust for the Benefit of Catholic Charities, Provident National Bank, P.O. Box 7648, 19101. Tel: 610-585-5698; Fax: 610-358-4275. Legal Title: *The Warner Perpetual Trust for the Benefit of Catholic Charities of the Archdiocese of Philadelphia.*
(The "Perpetual" Trust). Mr. Edward Nemanic, Trust Officer.

ASTON. *Franciscan Ministries Foundation, Inc.*, 609 S. Convent Rd., 19014. Tel: 610-558-7713; Fax: 610-558-1421. Sr. Eileen Valerie, Contact. Tel: 610-558-7701; Robert C. Wallis, Exec. Dir. Purpose: Raises funds to fulfill the needs of the Ministries and Retired Sisters of the Sisters of St. Francis of Philadelphia.

Sisters of St. Francis of Philadelphia, Charitable Trust I and Charitable Trust II, Our Lady of Angels Convent, 19014. Tel: 610-459-2112. Sr. Marie Lucey, O.S.F., Congregational Minister.

BALA CYNWYD. *Mercy Health Corp. of Southeastern PA*, One Bala Plaza, Suite 402, 19004. Tel: 610-660-7440. Sr. Mary Christine McCann, R.S.M., Chm. Bd.; Plato A Marinakos, Pres. Holding company for diversified health care subsidiaries including Mercy Catholic Medical Center, Mercy Haverford Hospital, Mercy Health Plan, Mercy Eastwick, Mercy Elderly Housing and Liberty Health System.

CONSHOHOCKEN. *Conshohocken Catholic School.* (Grades PreK-8), 205 Fayette St., 19428. Tel: 610-828-2007. Mrs. Jacqueline Kerrigan, Prin.

St. Vincent de Paul Society, 210 Harry St., 19428. Tel: 610-825-8125. Most Rev. Louis A. DeSimone, D.D., Spiritual Advisor; Anthony R. George, Pres.; Elizabeth Dart, Admin.; Robert Lanzilotta, Stores Dir. Tel: 215-763-5668.

FLOURTOWN. *Saint Joseph Guild*, Stenton and Wissahickon Aves., P.O. Box 36, 19031-0036. Tel: 215-248-7838; Fax: 215-248-7802. Sr. Ann Marguerite, S.S.J., Dir.

FORT WASHINGTON. *John Paul II Foundation for Peace, Justice & Human Rights*, The Copernicus House, P.O. Box 267, 19034. Tel: 215-646-4101.

GAP. *Our Lady of Consolation, Early Childhood School.* (Grades PreK), 5472 Strasburg Rd., 17527. Tel: 610-857-0511. Mrs. Jeanette M. Kolb, Prin.

GLENSIDE. *Counseling Center at St. Luke's*, Rosemore Gardens #E6, 218 N. Easton Rd., 19038. Tel: 215-887-6919. Billing Address: 2315 Fairhill Ave., 19038. Joanne Conway, Ed.D., Clinical Supvr. Staff: Bonnie Dalzell, M.A., Dir.; Kathleen McCabe, O.S.F., M.A., M.S.; Marie McCloskey, M.A. Board of Advisors: Revs. J. Michael Flood, Ex-officio; William G. Erat; Sr. Helen Frederick, S.S.J.; Jane S. Arnold; Michael S. Piotrowicz, Esq.; Paul E. MacDonald, M.A.; Jane E. Margraff; William K. Mosler, CPA; Charles F. Redican, Jr.

HUNTINGDON VALLEY.

**Holy Redeemer Health System, Inc.*, 727 Welsh Rd., 19006. Tel: 215-938-0180; Fax: 215-938-1237. Mailing Address: Communications Department, c/o 1648 Huntingdon Pike, Meadowbrook, 19046. Sponsor: Sisters of the Holy Redeemer, C.S.R. Michael B. Laign, Pres. & CEO. Parent organization which maintains, manages, and operates the health care system composed of the various corporations sponsored and established by the Sisters of the Holy Redeemer, C.S.R. as follows: Drueding Center; Holy Redeemer, Nazareth & St. Mary Home Health Services; Holy Redeemer Support Services; Holy Redeemer Foundation; HRH Management Corp.; Holy Redeemer Visiting Nurse Agency (NJ); Holy Redeemer Managed Care Org.; HR Physician Services; Redeemer Long Term Care and Elder Serv.; Holy Redeemer Hosp. & Med. Ctr.; Redeemer-Nazareth Med. Supply Co.

**Holy Redeemer Physician Services*, 727 Welsh Rd., Ste. 108, 19006. Tel: 215-938-4600; Fax: 215-938-7309. Mailing Address: Communications Department, c/o 1648 Huntingdon Pike, Meadowbrook, 19046.
Subsidiary of Holy Redeemer Health System, Inc. Sponsor: Sisters of the Holy Redeemer C.S.R. Michelle Urofsky, Pres. Nonprofit corporation formed to establish, operate and maintain family health clinics and practices, laboratories, dispensaries, buildings, and facilities relating to these purposes, and provide the services of physicians and other health care professionals in connection with the provision of health care services at Holy Redeemer Hospital and Medical Center, and other hospitals, clinics and health care facilities.

IMMACULATA. *Enserv Inc.*, King Rd., 19345. Tel: 610-647-4400, Ext. 3147.

KING OF PRUSSIA. *Bernardine Franciscans, Delaware County*, 403 Allendale Rd., 19406. Sr. Jean Anthony Rodgers, Contact Person.

RADNOR.

**Eastern Mercy Health System*, 3 Radnor Corporate Center, Ste. 220, 19087-4592. Tel: 610-971-9770; Fax: 610-688-5443. Daniel F. Russell, Pres. & CEO. Eastern Mercy Health System is a multi-institutional Catholic health system sponsored by ten Regional Communities of the Sisters of Mercy of the Americas and the Franciscan Sisters of St. Joseph(Hamburg, NY). Founded in 1986 for the purpose of preserving and strengthening the Catholic health ministry, Eastern Mercy provides programs, services, and expertise which enhance the sponsorship, stewardship, and strategic positioning of participating health care organizations. Eastern Mercy includes regional health care systems and freestanding health care organizations and services throughout seven states. Eastern Mercy facilities and services include large tertiary hospitals, community acute care hospitals, skilled nursing facilities, residential living facilities, and expansive primary care, home care, and outreach services in diverse rural, urban, and suburban communities throughout the eastern United States.

SWAINTON, NJ.

**Holy Redeemer Multi-Care, Inc.*, 1801 Rte. 9 N., 08210.

**Holy Redeemer Visiting Nurse Agency, Inc.*, 1801 Rte. 9 N., 08210.

YEADON. *Mercy Court*, 550 S. Lansdowne Ave., 19050. Tel: 610-623-3083. Sisters of Mercy. Sr. Mary Carmela, R.S.M., Prog. Dir. Low income apartments for independent living for older adults.

RELIGIOUS INSTITUTES OF MEN REPRESENTED IN THE ARCHDIOCESE

For further details refer to the corresponding bracketed number in the Religious Institutes of Men or Women section.

[0140]—*The Augustinians*(Provs. of St. Thomas Villanova & Our Mother of Good Counsel).—O.S.A.

[0290]—*Brothers of Charity.*—F.C.

[0330]—*Brothers of the Christian Schools.* (Baltimore Prov.).—F.S.C.

[0580]—*Brothers of the Good Shepherd.*—B.G.S.

[]—*Brothers of the Holy Spirit.*—B.H.S.

[0900]—*Canons Regular of Premontre.*—O.Praem.

[0470]—*Capuchin Friars.*—O.F.M.Cap.

[0275]—*Carmelites of Mary Immaculate.*—C.M.I.

[0860]—*Congregation of the Immaculate Heart of Mary (Missionhurst).*—C.I.C.M.

[1330]—*Congregation of the Mission.* (Eastern Prov.).—C.M.

[0950]—*Congregation of the Oratory.*—C.O.

[1000]—*Congregation of the Passion.*—C.P.

[0650]—*Holy Ghost Fathers.* (Eastern Prov.).—C.S.Sp.

[0800]—*Maryknoll Fathers and Brothers.*—M.M.

[0825]—*Missionaries of the Blessed Sacrament.*—M.S.S.

[1110]—*Missionaries of the Sacred Heart.* (American Prov.).—M.S.C.

[0840]—*Missionary Servants of the Most Holy Trinity.*—S.T.

[0920]—*Oblates of St. Francis de Sales.*—O.S.F.S.

[0520]—*Order of Friars Minor.* (Assumption B.V.M. & Most Holy Name Provs.).—O.F.M.

[0480]—*Order of Friars Minor, Conventual.*—O.F.M.Conv.

[0970]—*Order of Our Lady of Mercy.*—O.deM.

[0430]—*Order of Preachers (Dominicans).* (Eastern Prov.).—O.P.

[1310]—*Order of the Holy Trinity.*—O.SS.T.

[1010]—*Pauline Fathers.*—O.S.P.P.E.

[1040]—*Piarist Fathers.*—Sch.P.

[1070]—*Redemptorist Fathers.* (Baltimore Prov.).—C.SS.R.

[1220]—*Servants of Charity.*—S.C.

[0690]—*Society of Jesus (Jesuits).* (Maryland Prov.).—S.J.

[0760]—*Society of Mary (Marianists).*—S.M.

[0780]—*Society of Mary (Marists).*—S.M.

[0560]—*Third Order Regular of Saint Francis.* (Prov. of the Most Sacred Heart).—T.O.R.

RELIGIOUS INSTITUTES OF WOMEN REPRESENTED IN THE ARCHDIOCESE

[1070-13]—*Adrian Dominican Sisters.*

[]—*Armenian Sisters of the Immaculate Conception.*—C.I.C.

[1810]—*Bernardine Sisters of the Third Order of St. Francis.*—O.S.F.
[0330]—*Carmelite Sisters for the Aged and Infirm.*—O.Carm.
[0690]—*Comboni Missionary Sisters.*—C.M.S.
[0270]—*Congregation of Bon Secours.*—C.B.S.
[2250]—*Congregation of the Benedictines of Jesus Crucified.*—O.S.B.
[]—*Contemplative Sister of the Good Shepherd.*—C.G.S.
[0760]—*Daughters of Charity of St. Vincent de Paul.*—D.C.
[]—*Daughters of Mary, Mother of Mercy.*—D.M.M.M.
[0900]—*Daughters of Our Lady of the Sacred Heart.*—F.D.N.S.C.
[0940]—*Daughters of St. Mary of Providence.*—D.S.M.P.
[0810]—*Daughters of the Heart of Mary.*—D.H.M.
[0420]—*Discalced Carmelite Nuns.*—O.C.D.
[1070-17]—*Dominican Sisters.*—O.P.
[1070-23]—*Dominican Sisters.*—O.P.
[1105]—*Dominican Sisters of Hope.*—O.P.
[]—*Dominican Sisters of Our Lady of the Rosary.*—O.P.
[1170]—*Felician Sisters.*—C.S.S.F.
[1180]—*Franciscan Sisters of Alleghany, New York.*—O.S.F.
[1425]—*Franciscan Sisters of Peace.*—F.S.P.
[1840]—*Grey Nuns of the Sacred Heart.*—G.N.S.H.
[1870]—*Handmaids of the Sacred Heart of Jesus.*—A.C.J.
[]—*Little Servants of the Holy Family of Seoul.*—L.S.H.F.
[2300]—*Little Servants Sisters of the Immaculate Conception.*—L.S.I.C.
[2310]—*Little Sisters of the Assumption.*—L.S.A.
[2340]—*Little Sisters of the Poor.*—L.S.P.
[2345]—*Little Workers of the Sacred Hearts.*—P.O.S.C.
[2490]—*Medical Mission Sisters.*—M.M.S.
[2710]—*Missionaries of Charity.*—M.C.
[1360]—*Missionary Franciscan Sisters of the Immaculate Conception.*—M.F.I.C.
[2790]—*Missionary Servants of the Most Blessed Trinity.*—M.S.B.T.
[2730]—*Missionary Sisters of the Holy Rosary.*—M.S.H.R.
[2750]—*Missionary Sisters of the Immaculate Heart of Mary.*—I.C.M.
[2800]—*Missionary Sisters of the Most Sacred Heart of Jesus of Hiltrup.*—M.S.C.
[2860]—*Missionary Sisters of the Sacred Heart*(Eastern Prov.).—M.S.C.
[3060]—*Oblates Sisters of St. Francis de Sales.*—O.S.F.S.
[3730]—*Order of St. Basil the Great.*—O.S.B.M.
[3760]—*Order of St. Clare.*—O.S.C.
[1705]—*Order of St. Francis of Assisi.*—O.S.F.
[0950]—*Pious Society Daughters of St. Paul.*—F.S.P.
[3640]—*Poor Servants of the Mother of God.*—S.M.G.
[3390]—*Religious of the Assumption.*—R.A.
[2519]—*Religious Sisters of Mercy of Alma.*—R.S.M.
[3430]—*Religious Teachers Filippini.*—M.P.F.
[2970]—*School Sisters of Notre Dame.*—S.S.N.D.
[]—*Servants of the Lord and of the Virgin of MATARA.*—V.E.
[3540]—*Sister Servants of the Holy Spirit of Perpetual Adoration.*—S.Sp.S.deA.P.
[2160]—*Sister Servants of the Immaculate Heart of Mary.* (Scanton).—I.H.M.
[3630]—*Sister Servants of the Most Sacred Heart of Jesus.*—S.S.C.J.
[0500]—*Sisters of Charity of Nazareth.*—S.C.N.
[0660]—*Sisters of Christian Charity.*—S.C.C.
[2575]—*Sisters of Mercy of the Americas, Merion, PA.*—R.S.M. [0820]—Daughters of the Holy Spirit.—D.H.S.
[3000]—*Sisters of Notre Dame de Namur.*—S.N.D.deN.
[2670]—*Sisters of Our Lady of Mercy.*—S.O.L.M.
[3893]—*Sisters of Saint Joseph of Chestnut Hill, Philadelphia.*—S.S.J.
[3740]—*Sisters of St. Casimir.*—S.S.C.
[1650]—*Sisters of St. Francis of Philadelphia.*—O.S.F.
[0260]—*Sisters of the Blessed Sacrament for Indians and Colored People.*—S.B.S.
[1020]—*Sisters of the Divine Redeemer.*—S.D.R.
[1830]—*Sisters of the Good Shepherd.*—R.G.S.
[1970]—*Sisters of the Holy Family of Nazareth.*—C.S.F.N.
[2000]—*Sisters of the Holy Redeemer.*—C.S.R.
[2060]—*Sisters of the Most Holy Trinity.*—O.SS.T.
[1490]—*Sisters of the Third Franciscan Order of Syracuse.*—O.S.F.
[2170]—*Sisters, Servants of the Immaculate Heart of Mary (Immaculta).*—I.H.M.
[4060]—*Society of the Holy Child Jesus.*—S.H.C.J.
[4120]—*Ursuline Sisters of the Immaculate Conception.*—O.S.U.
[4190]—*Visitation Nuns.*—V.H.M.

ARCHDIOCESAN CEMETERIES

PHILADELPHIA. *Cathedral*, 48th St. and Lancaster Ave., 19131. Tel: 215-477-8918.
Holy Sepulchre, Cheltham Ave. at Easton Rd., 19150. Tel: 215-247-0691.
New Cathedral, 2nd & Butler St., 19140. Tel: 215-634-3212.

BENSALEM. *Resurrection*, 5201 Hulmeville Rd., 19020. Tel: 215-639-0965.

CHALFONT. *St. John Neumann*, 3797 County Line Rd., 18914. Tel: 215-822-0680.

GLENMOORE. *All Souls*, R.R. 322, 19343.

NEWTOWN. *All Saints*, R.R. 413, Twining Bridge Rd., 18940.

SPRINGFIELD. *SS. Peter and Paul*, Sproul Rd., 19064. Tel: 610-544-4933.

WEST CONSHOHOCKEN. *Calvary*, Gulph & Matsonford Rd., 19428. Tel: 610-525-2214.

WEST GROVE. *Holy Saviour*.

YEADON. *Holy Cross*, Baily Rd., 19050. Tel: 610-626-2206; 215-476-3656.

NECROLOGY

✠ Krol, His Eminence John, (Retired). —Died March 3, 1996.
† Bruder, Rev. Msgr. James I., (Retired). —Died Dec. 22, 1995.
† Cronin, Peter F., (Retired). —Died May 24, 1996.
† Dean, Rev. Msgr. Michael J., (Retired). —Died Jan. 18, 1996.
† Duffy, Joseph F., Linfield, PA, St. Clare. —Died Dec. 7, 1995.
† Farrant, James J., Philadelphia, PA, St. Martin de Porres. —Died Aug. 14, 1996.
† Gallagher, Rev. Msgr. Vincent B., (Retired). —Died April 26, 1996.
† Hiller, George P., (Retired). —Died Sept. 10, 1996.
† Holmes, Richard H., Primos, PA, St. Eugene. —Died Feb. 10, 1996.
† Horner, Thomas P., Philadelphia, PA, St. Mary Assumption. —Died Feb. 25, 1996.
† Iannucci, Edward L., (Retired). —Died Feb. 29, 1996.
† Kline, John L., Scoventry, PA, St. Thomas More. —Died Jan. 5, 1996.
† Lyons, Rev. Msgr. Joseph G., (Retired). —Died Dec. 24, 1995.
† McAndrew, Anthony D., (Retired). —Died July 25, 1996.
† McKenzie, John J., (Retired). —Died April 7, 1996.
† McSherry, Hugh E., (Retired). —Died Dec. 27, 1995.
† Nawn, Henry J., (Retired). —Died Jan. 20, 1996.
† O'Neill, Rev. Msgr. John J., (Retired). —Died Feb. 27, 1996.
† Pichla, John H., (Absent On Leave). —Died Aug. 23, 1996.
† Sakalauskas, Kajetonas, Philadelphia, PA, Our Lady Calvary. —Died June 8, 1996.
† Saldutti, Soccorso J., Croydon, PA, St. Thomas Aquinas. —Died April 21, 1996.
† Sikora, Joseph F., (Retired). —Died July 12, 1996.
† Tallon, William F., (Retired). —Died Dec. 14, 1995.
† Walsh, Edmond W., (Retired). —Died June 5, 1996.
† Wassel, Thomas W., (Retired). —Died April 22, 1996.

Diocese of Phoenix

(Dioecesis Phoenicensis)

Most Reverend

THOMAS J. O'BRIEN, D.D.

Bishop of Phoenix; ordained May 7, 1961; consecrated January 6, 1982; installed January 18, 1982. *Res., 48 E. Wagon Wheel Dr., Phoenix, AZ, 85020. All correspondence to be sent to: 400 E. Monroe, Phoenix, AZ, 85004.*

ESTABLISHED DECEMBER 2, 1969.

Square Miles 43,967.

Comprises the Counties of Maricopa; Mohave; Yavapai & Coconino not to include the territorial boundaries of the Navajo Indian Reservation; Pinal—that portion of land known as the Gila River Indian Reservation in the State of Arizona.

Patroness of Diocese: Our Lady of Guadalupe.

For legal titles of parishes and diocesan institutions, consult the Chancery Office.

Diocesan Office: 400 E. Monroe, Phoenix, AZ, 85004. Tel.: 602-257-0030; Fax: 602-258-3425.

Web site address: http://www.catholicsun.org

STATISTICAL OVERVIEW

Personnel	
Retired Archbishops	1
Bishop	1
Retired Bishops	1
Priests: Diocesan Active in Diocese	95
Priests: Active Outside Diocese	4
Priests: Retired, Sick or Absent	45
Number of Diocesan Priests	144
Religious Priests in Diocese	110
Extern Priests in Diocese	22
Ordinations:	
Diocesan Priests	1
Religious Priests	1
Transitional Deacons	1
Permanent Deacons	6
Permanent Deacons in Diocese	178
Total Brothers	7
Total Sisters	232
Parishes	
Parishes	87
With Resident Pastor:	
Resident Diocesan Priests	63
Resident Religious Priests	18
Without Resident Pastor:	
Administered by Permanent Deacons	4
Administered by Women Religious	1
Completely Vacant	2
Missions	28
Professional Ministry Personnel:	
Brothers	2
Sisters	204
Lay Ministers	340
Welfare	
Catholic Hospitals	1
Total Assisted	212,853
Health Care Centers	2
Total Assisted	98,628
Homes for the Aged	8
Total Assisted	396
Day Care and Extended Day Care Centers	26
Total Assisted	882
Specialized Homes	7
Total Assisted	525
Special Centers for Social Services	11
Total Assisted	2,106,076
Residential Care of Disabled	1
Total Assisted	26
Educational	
Diocesan Students in Other Seminaries	20
Total Seminarians	20
High Schools, Diocesan and Parish	4
Total Students	2,417
High Schools, Private	1
Total Students	1,159
Elementary Schools, Diocesan and Parish	23
Total Students	7,642
Catechesis/Religious Education:	
High School Students	5,653
Elementary Students	27,996
Total Students Under Catholic Instruction	44,887
Teachers in the Diocese:	
Priests	15
Scholastics	2
Brothers	1
Sisters	39
Lay Teachers	530
Vital Statistics	
Receptions into the Church:	
Infant Baptism Totals	10,443
Adult Baptism Totals	506
Received into Full Communion	845
First Communions	6,527
Confirmations	2,800
Marriages:	
Catholic	1,254
Interfaith	544
Total Marriages	1,798
Deaths	3,453
Total Catholic Population	386,821
Total Population	2,915,165

Former Bishops—Most Rev. EDWARD A. MCCARTHY, D.D., installed Bishop of the Diocese of Phoenix, Dec. 2, 1969; transferred Coadjutor Archbishop of Miami, July 7, 1976; installed Sept. 17, 1976.—Most Rev. JAMES S. RAUSCH, D.D., Ph.D., installed March 22, 1977; died May 18, 1981.

Vicar General—Rev. Msgr. RICHARD MOYER, V.G., *Diocesan Center, 400 E. Monroe, Phoenix, 85004.* Tel: 602-257-0030.

Diocesan Office—400 E. Monroe, Phoenix, 85004. Tel: 602-257-0030; Fax: 602-258-3425.

Chancellor—Sr. MARY ANN WINTERS, S.C., *400 E. Monroe, Phoenix, 85004.* Tel: 602-257-0030.

Assistant Chancellor—Rev. MICHAEL L. DISKIN, *400 E. Monroe, Phoenix, 85004.* Tel: 602-257-0030.

College of Consultors—Rev. Msgr. RICHARD W. MOYER, V.G.; Revs. ALAN MALONE, J.V.; TIMOTHY DAVERN, V.F., J.C.L.; PETER DOBROWSKI, V.F.; CHARLES KIEFFER; ROBERT VOSS, V.F.; FRANK BARTEL, V.F.; JOHN COLEMAN, V.F.; DOUGLAS NOHAVA, V.F.

Finance and Administration—Rev. MICHAEL STRALEY, Vicar; TARGE T. MANDT, Dir. Financial Planning; STEVE ATTWOOD, Controller, *400 E. Monroe, Phoenix, 85004.* Tel: 602-257-0030.

Vicars Forane—Revs. FRANK FERNANDEZ, V.F., Chm. SCOTT BRUBAKER, V.F.; PETER DOBROWSKI, V.F.; DOUGLAS NOHAVA, V.F.; ROBERT VOSS, V.F.; ED CALLANAN, V.F.; GERALD YAEGER, V.F.; FRANK BARTEL, V.F.; EARL D'EON, V.F.; TIMOTHY DAVERN, V.F.; J C. ORTIZ, V.F.; JOHN COLEMAN, V.F.

Diocesan Tribunal—Office: *400 E. Monroe, Phoenix, 85004.* Tel: 602-257-0030; Fax: 602-257-5646.

Judicial Vicar—Rev. ALAN MALONE.

Adjutant Judicial Vicars—Revs. PHILIP ACQUARO, C.S.B., J.C.L.; TIMOTHY R. DAVERN, J.C.L.; MICHAEL F. DIEDERICHS, J.C.D.; PAUL OREL, J.C.L.

Diocesan Judges—Revs. PHILIP ACQUARO, C.S.B., J.C.L.; VALENTINE L. BOYLE, O.Carm.; ROBERT J. CARUSO; TIMOTHY R. DAVERN, J.C.L.; MICHAEL F. DIEDERICHS, J.C.D.; PETER DOBROWSKI, V.F.; GREGORY M. KOTNIS, J.C.L.; ALAN MALONE; FRANK P. SIMLIK; PAUL OREL, J.C.L.

Defenders of the Bond—Revs. PHILIP ACQUARO, C.S.B., J.C.L.; VALENTINE L. BOYLE, O.Carm.; ROBERT J. CARUSO; TIMOTHY R. DAVERN, J.C.L.; MICHAEL F. DIEDERICHS, J.C.D.; PETER DOBROWSKI, V.F.; CHARLES G. KIEFFER; GREGORY M. KOTNIS, J.C.L.; ALAN MALONE; PAUL OREL, J.C.L.; FRANK P. SIMLIK.

Advocates—Rev. ROBERT J. CARUSO; SANDRA CONSIGLIO; Revs. TIMOTHY R. DAVERN, J.C.L.; PETER DOBROWSKI, V.F.; Sr. RUTH KARNITZ, S.S.N.D.; Revs. CHARLES G. KIEFFER; PAUL OREL, J.C.L.; FRANK P. SIMLIK; Sr. FRANCES WETZEL, O.P.

Auditors—Revs. PHILIP ACQUARO, C.S.B., J.C.L.; VALENTINE L. BOYLE, O.Carm.; TIMOTHY R. DAVERN, J.C.L.; MICHAEL DIEDERICHS, J.C.D.; Sr. RUTH KARNITZ, S.S.N.D.; Revs. ALAN MALONE; PAUL OREL, J.C.L.; Sr. FRANCES WETZEL, O.P.

Notaries—DOROTHY DALTON; Rev. MICHAEL L. DISKIN; M. ANGELA JIMENEZ; Sr. RUTH KARNITZ, S.S.N.D.; MAUREEN HAMILTON; Sr. M. ANTHONY POERIO, I.B.V.M.; Rev. MARCEL SALINAS, C.M.F.

Presbyteral Council—Most Rev. THOMAS J. O'BRIEN, D.D.; Rev. Msgr. RICHARD W. MOYER, V.G.; Revs. FRANK BARTEL, V.F.; SCOTT BRUBAKER, V.F.; ED CALLANAN, V.F.; NATHAN CASTLE, O.P.; JOHN COLEMAN, V.F.; EARL D'EON, V.F.; TIMOTHY DAVERN, J.C.L., V.F.; MICHAEL DISKIN, Asst. Chancellor; MARK DIPPRE, V.F.; FRANK FERNANDEZ, V.F.; PETER DOBROWSKI, V.F.; EVAN HOWARD, O.F.M., V.F.; CHARLES KIEFFER; ALAN MALONE, J.V.; J. C. ORTIZ, V.F.; DOUGLAS NOHAVA, V.F.; PRUDENCIO RODRIQUEZ, C.M.; ROBERT VOSS, V.F.; GERALD YAEGER, V.F.; Sr. MARY ANN WINTERS, Chancellor.

Diocesan Pastoral Council—Most Rev. THOMAS J. O'BRIEN, D.D.; Rev. Msgr. RICHARD W. MOYER, V.G.; Rev. MICHAEL L. DISKIN, Exec. Sec. RICHARD CURRAN; MONICA DOMINGO; Sr. JOAN FITZGERALD, B.V.M., Chm. RAGUE HIDALGO; TIMOTHY HENLEY; JO HINELINE; SARAH JAKUBISIN; MICHAEL JOHNSEN, Vice Chm. ALMA LANDA; HARVEY LESAN; JORGE LOPEZ; KEVIN MCCARTHY; ART STINE; Rev. MICHAEL MINOGUE; JEANNINE MOYLE; NANCY PERLICK, R.S.M.; SHARON REITMEYER; JACQUELINE RIDEAU; THERESA SCROGGINS; Bro. RICHARD SUTTLE, C.M.F.; CARLOS TEJEDA; NAN TROTTA; KRISTINA WATSON; Sr. MARY ANN WINTERS, S.C., Chancellor.

Arizona Catholic Conference—Rev. Msgr. EDWARD RYLE, M.S.W., Exec. Dir., *400 E. Monroe, Phoenix, 85004.* Tel: 602-257-0030.

Buildings & Property—JOSEPH GALANO, Dir., *Diocesan Center, 400 E. Monroe, Phoenix, 85004.* Tel: 602-257-0030. Rev. Msgr. JOHN J. MCMAHON, Vicar, *4633 N. 54th St., Phoenix, 85018.* Tel: 602-840-5066.

Catholic Community Foundation—Most Rev. THOMAS J. O'BRIEN, D.D., Pres. CARL S. MILLER, Exec. Dir., *400 E. Monroe, Phoenix, 85004.* Tel: 602-257-0030.

Cemeteries—Rev. WILLIAM MCKAY, Admin. GARY L. BROWN, Exec. Dir. St. Francis, Holy Cross, and Queen of Heaven. Office: *1438 W. Broadway, #B-245, Tempe, 85282.* Tel: 602-829-0221., Calvary Cemetery: *201 W. University, Flagstaff, 86001.* Tel: 602-774-9125.

"The Catholic Sun"—(Diocesan Newspaper); Mr. CHRISTOPHER GUNTY, Assoc. Publisher, *400 E. Monroe, Phoenix, 85004.* Tel: 602-257-0030; 257-5565.

Communications—MARGE INJASOULIAN, Dir., *400 E. Monroe, Phoenix, 85004.* Tel: 602-257-0030.

Information Services (Data Processing)—KIM BRISWALTER, Dir., *400 E. Monroe, Phoenix, 85004.* Tel: 602-257-0030.

Stewardship Office—(Charity & Development Appeal); BILL SCHWANEKAMP, Dir., *400 E. Monroe St., Phoenix, 85004.* Tel: 602-257-0030. (Annunities and Trusts); CARL S. MILLER, Exec Dir., *400 E. Monroe St., Phoenix, 85004.* Tel: 602-257-0030. JIM CRUTHOFF, Dir. of Planned Giving. Tel: 602-257-5641.

Ecumenical and Inter-Faith Affairs—Rev. MICHAEL L. DISKIN, Dir., *400 E. Monroe, Phoenix, 85004.* Tel: 602-257-0030.

Ministry of Christian Formation—Sr. DOLORETTE FARIAS, S.S.N.D., Dir., *400 E. Monroe, Phoenix, 85004.* Tel: 602-257-0030.

Diaconate Ministry—Rev. MARCEL SALINAS, C.M.F., Dir., *400 E. Monroe, Phoenix, 85004.* Tel: 602-257-0030. THOMAS KAYSER, Assoc. Continuing Education. Tel: 520-445-3141. Vacant; Assoc. Ministry. Tel: 602-257-0030.

Vocations—Rev. ROBERT CLEMENTS, Dir., *400 E. Monroe, Phoenix, 85004.* Tel: 602-257-0030.

Office of Worship—Rev. SCOTT BRUBAKER, Vicar; Sr. MARY ANTHONY POERIO, I.B.V.M., Dir. TREVOR THOMPSON, Asst. Dir., *400 E. Monroe, Phoenix, 85004.* Tel: 602-257-0030.

Schools—MARY BETH MUELLER, Supt. Schools; MARY CATHERINE KEATING, Asst. Supt., *400 E. Monroe, Phoenix, 85004.* Tel: 602-257-0030.

Catechetical Ministry—Deacon JOHN MEYER, Dir. CAROL GASTELUM, Assoc. Dir. RAQUEL HIDALGO, Hispanics Catachesis Coord., *400 E. Monroe, Phoenix, 85004.* Tel: 602-257-0030.

Youth-Young Adult Campus Ministry—LARRY FRAHER, Dir. MODESTO GARCIA, Asst. Dir. KEVIN STARRS, At-Risk Youth Resources, *400 E. Monroe, Phoenix, 85004.* Tel: 602-257-0030.

The Catholic Scouting Program—Rev. DENNIS O'ROURKE, Liaison, *7923 E. Latham, Scottsdale, 85257.* Tel: 602-945-8437; Fax: 602-945-4335.

Family Life Activities—Sr. DOLORETTE FARIAS, S.S.N.D., *400 E. Monroe, Phoenix, 85004.* Tel: 602-257-0030.

Life Issues—JUDY GIFFORD, Dir. Tel: 602-257-0030.

Mount Claret Retreat Center—Directors: Rev. Msgr. JOHN J. MCMAHON; Rev. EUGENE MAGUIRE; Ms. JO SWIGER, Asst. Dir. Cursillo Movement: Revs. LEO DELGADO, Dir. THEO FUENTES, C.M.F., Assoc. Dir., *4633 N. 54th St., Phoenix, 85018.* Tel: 602-840-5066; Fax: 602-840-5732.

Special Services for Persons with Disabilities—ISABELLA RICE, Acting Dir., *400 E. Monroe, Phoenix, 85004.* Tel: 602-227-0030.

Native American Ministry Office—Rev. JOHN HALL, Vicar, *400 E. Monroe, Phoenix, 85004.* Tel: 602-257-0030.

Ministry of Christian Witness—Rev. Msgr. EDWARD RYLE, *400 E. Monroe, Phoenix, 85004.* Tel: 602-257-0030.

Diocesan Attorney—GREGORY J. LEISSE, *400 E. Monroe, Phoenix, 85004.* Tel: 602-257-0030.

Priests' Assurance Association—*400 E. Monroe, Phoenix, 85004.*

Priest Personnel—Rev. THOMAS ZURCHER, C.S.C., Vicar, *400 E. Monroe, Phoenix, 85004.* Tel: 602-257-0030.

Advisory Board for the Continuing Formation of Priests—Rev. THOMAS ZURCHER, C.S.C., *400 E. Monroe, Phoenix, 85004.* Tel: 602-257-0030.

Priestly Life and Ministry Board—Rev. THOMAS ZURCHER, C.S.C., *400 E. Monroe, Phoenix, 85004.* Tel: 602-257-0030.

Priests' Placement Board—Vacant, *400 E. Monroe, Phoenix, 85004.*

Prisons, Catholic Ministries To—Rev. KLEMENS PEPEL, Dir., *Estrella Jail, 2939 W. Durango, Phoenix, 85009.* Tel: 602-256-5574.

Prison Facilities—State and County Jails; Deacon PETER MURPHY. Tel: 602-591-3243 (Pager). Rev. KLEMENS PEPEL. Tel: 602-256-5574.

Arizona Center for Women—Deacon TOM SWISHER, *342 N. 32nd St., Phoenix, 85008.* Tel: 520-550-2034.

Arizona Correctional Training Center—Rev. EMIL COTE, *179th Ave. and McDowell Rd., Perryville, 85323.* Tel: 602-935-9371, Ext. 2198.

Alhambra Correctional Center—(Diagnostic Center); Deacon TOM SWISHER, Chap., *26th St. and Van Buren, Phoenix, 85008.* Tel: 602-994-0952.

Aspen Correctional Center—Deacon TOM SWISHER, Chap., *24th St. and Fillmore, Phoenix, 85008.* Tel: 520-550-2034.

Federal Correctional Institute—Rev. LAWRENCE QUILICI, Chap., *47900 N. 45th Ave., Phoenix, 85027.* Tel: 602-465-9757.

Arizona State Insitutions—(Juveniles).

Adobe Mountain Juvenile Institute—(Boys & Girls); Rev. PETER TAYLOR, Chap., *Black Canyon Hwy., 280 W. Pinnacle Peak Rd., Phoenix, 85027.* Tel: 602-869-9050, Ext. 270.

County Juvenile Detention Center—*3125 W. Durango, Phoenix, 85009.* Diocesan Prison Ministry Staff.

Propagation of the Faith—Sr. JEAN STEFFES, C.S.A., *400 E. Monroe, Phoenix, 85004.* Tel: 602-257-0030.

Holy Childhood Association—Sr. JEAN STEFFES, C.S.A, *400 E. Monroe, Phoenix, 85004.* Tel: 602-257-0300.

Hispanic Ministry—

Office of Hispanic Ministry—Rev. PRUDENCIO RODRIGUEZ DE YURRE, C.M., Ph.D., Vicar; MICHAEL HERNANDEZ NOWAKOWSKI, Dir., *400 E. Monroe, Phoenix, 85004.* Tel: 602-257-0030.

Office of Human Resources (Personnel)—Vacant; Dir., *400 E. Monroe, Phoenix, 85004.* Tel: 602-257-0030.

Religious, Office of—Sr. JEAN STEFFES, C.S.A., Dir., *400 E. Monroe, Phoenix, 85004.* Tel: 602-257-0030.

CLERGY, PARISHES, MISSIONS AND PAROCHIAL SCHOOLS

CITY OF PHOENIX
(Maricopa County)

1—SS. SIMON AND JUDE CATHEDRAL, Revs. Michael O'Grady, Rector; Christopher Carpenter.
Res., 6351 N. 27th Ave., 85017. Tel: 602-242-1300; Fax: 602-249-3768.
School—Tel: 602-242-1299. Sr. M. Raphael Quinn, I.B.V.M., Prin.
Loreto Sisters 4; Lay Teachers 16; Students 570.
Convent—Tel: 602-242-2544.
Mission—Phoenix, Maricopa Co., Santa Rosa Chapel, 1901 W. Ocotillo, 85017. Tel: 602-433-0658.

2—CORPUS CHRISTI, Revs. Louis A. Sigman; Albert F.H. Hoorman; Deacons Alexander Gaudio; Patrick Flynn; Sr. Frances Ellsperman, O.P., Pastoral Assoc.
Res., 3550 E. Knox, 85044. Tel: 602-893-8770; Fax: 602-893-3291.

3—HOLY FAMILY, Rev. Jorge Canez.
Res., 6802 S. 24th St., 85040. Tel: 602-268-2632.

4—IMMACULATE HEART OF MARY, Revs. Antonio Sotelo; Lawrence Baumann; Graciela Albillar, Parish Admin.
Res., 909 E. Washington St., 85034. Tel: 602-253-6129; Fax: 602-253-4210.

5—MOST HOLY TRINITY, Revs. Eugene Sousa, O.P.; Dominic Briese, O.P.; Bruno Mauricci, O.P.; Paul Tran, O.P.; Deacons Ron Filardi; Guy Goubeaux.
Res., 8620 N. Seventh St., 85020. Tel: 602-944-3375; Fax: 602-943-2323.
School—535 E. Alice Ave., 85020. Tel: 602-943-9058. Ms. Christine Steele, Prin.
Lay Teachers 14; Students 355.
McHugh Hall/Small Hall—8820 N. Seventh St., 85020. Tel: 602-997-6726.
Vietnamese Catholic Community: Rev. Paul Tran.

6—ST. AGNES, Revs. Tiernan O'Callaghan, O.Carm.; John Larkin, O.Carm.; Raymond Bonin, O.Carm. In res., Revs. Ernest Larkin, O.Carm.; Michael Kwiecien, O.Carm.
Res., 1954 N. 24th St., 85008. Tel: 602-244-0349; Fax: 602-244-0054.
School—2311 E. Palm Ln., 85006. Tel: 602-244-1451. Catherine Downey, Prin.
Lay Teachers 10; Students 242.
Convent—1818 N. 23rd St., 85006. Tel: 602-244-1174.

7—SS. ANTHONY AND PIUS X, Revs. J. Saul Madrid; John Auther, S.J.
Church & Res.—909 S. First Ave., 85003. Tel: 602-252-1771; Fax: 602-252-1669.
Missions—Phoenix, Maricopa Co. Attended by St. Pius X only. 809 S. Seventh Ave., 85007; Phoenix, Maricopa Co., Our Lady of Fatima, 1414 S. 17th Ave., 85007. Tel: 602-227-3103; 242-1300. Rev. Francis Peacock, Admin.

8—ST. AUGUSTINE, Revs. Fausto Penafiel; John Ebbesmier; Deacon Charles Heeter.
Res., 3630 N. 71st Ave., 85033. Tel: 602-849-3131; Fax: 602-849-5689.

9—ST. CATHERINE OF SIENA, Revs. Douglas J. Nohava; David Kelash; Deacons George Lazok; Joe Lessard.
Res., 6401 S. Central Ave., 85040. Tel: 602-276-5581; Fax: 602-276-9785.
School—6413 S. Central Ave., 85040. Tel: 602-276-2241. Cynthia Bernacki, Prin.
Lay Teachers 9; Students 210.
Convent—313 W. Alta Vista, 85041. Tel: 602-268-5620.

10—ST. EDWARD CONFESSOR, Rev. Jorge Canez; Deacon Peter Fejes.
Res., 4410 E. Southern Ave., 85040. Tel: 602-438-0043; Fax: 602-438-9305.

11—ST. FRANCIS XAVIER, Revs. Edward E. Callanan, S.J.; Patrick J. Reuse, S.J.; Arthur J. Wehr, S.J.
Res., 4715 N. Central Ave., 85012-1796. Tel: 602-279-9547; Fax: 602-248-8968.
School—Tel: 602-266-5364. Mrs. Kristen Spucces, Prin.
Lay Teachers 26; Students 526.

12—ST. GREGORY, Revs. Michael Straley; Emile Pelletier. In res., Rev. Rob Clements.
Res., 3424 N. 18th Ave., 85015. Tel: 602-264-4488; Fax: 602-264-4489.
School—3440 N. 18th Ave., 85015. Tel: 602-266-9527. Ms. Eileen Marie Ripsen, Prin.
Lay Teachers 19; Students 320.
Convent—3437 N. 18th Ave., 85015. Tel: 602-265-2396. Sisters of the Institute of B.V.M.

13—ST. JEROME, Revs. L. Pierce Hissey; John Shetler; Deacons Robert Dedecker; Michael Phelan.
Church—10815 N. 35th Ave., 85029. Tel: 602-942-5555; Fax: 602-504-9115.
School—Tel: 602-942-5644. Carl Hodus, Prin.
Lay Teachers 11; Students 310.

14—ST. JOAN OF ARC, Revs. Larry W. Weidner; John Cullinan; Gena McGowan, Pastoral Assoc.
Parish Center: 3801 E. Greenway Rd., 85032-4698. Tel: 602-867-9171; Fax: 602-482-7930.

15—ST. JOSEPH, Rev. Frank Fernandez; Deacons Stan Giza; Tony Speranza.
Res., 11001 N. 40th St., 85028. Tel: 602-996-5120; Fax: 602-996-4011 (Call first).

16—ST. LUKE, Rev. Richard A. Milligan.
Res., 19644 N. Seventh Ave., 85027. Tel: 602-582-0561.
Mission—New River, Maricopa Co., Good Shepherd Mission, 45033 N. 12th St., 85027. Tel: 602-465-9740. Rev. Valentine Boyle, O.Carm., Admin.

17—ST. MARK, Rev. David Cooney, S.D.S.; Deacons Lou A. Burgess; Jose Hernandez. In res., Rev. Tulio Maya, S.D.S.
Res., 400 N. 30th St., 85008. Tel: 602-267-0503.
Mission—Phoenix, Maricopa Co., St. Philip the Deacon Catholic Center, 615 N. 20th St., 85006. Tel: 602-253-1076. Deacon Louis Pardini, Admin.

18—ST. MARTIN DE PORRES, Deacon Jose Olivarez, Admin. Sacramental Ministers: Revs. Raymond Ritari; David San Filipo.
Res., 3851 W. Wier Ave., 85041. Tel: 602-276-2466 (Church); Fax: 602-232-2147.

19—ST. MARY'S BASILICA, Rev. Evan Howard, O.F.M. In res., Revs. Lester Mitchell, O.F.M.; Blaise Cronin, O.F.M.; Lucius Grosso, O.F.M.; Luis Baldonado, O.F.M.; Bro. Damien Byrne, O.F.M.
Res., 231 N. Third St., 85004. Tel: 602-252-7651; Fax: 602-256-2773.

20—ST. MATTHEW, Revs. Raymond Ritari; David Sanfilippo; Deacons Tony Beltran; Albert Gonzales.
Res., 320 N. 20th Dr., 85009. Tel: 602-258-1789; Fax: 602-258-6507.
School—2038 W. Van Buren, 85009. Tel: 602-254-0611. Dr. Robert Sherman, Prin.
Sisters 2; Lay Teachers 7; Students 226.
Convent—2106 W. Van Buren, 85009. Tel: 602-253-9124.

21—ST. PAUL, Revs. Eugene O'Carroll; L. Brendon Dorian; Deacons Robert England; Kenneth Marion.
Res., 330 W. Coral Gables Dr., 85023. Tel: 602-942-2608; Fax: 602-993-0228.

22—OUR LADY OF THE VALLEY, Revs. Scott Brubaker; Scott Ritchey.
Church—3220 W. Greenway Rd., 85023. Tel: 602-993-1213; Fax: 602-993-1223.

23—SACRED HEART, Rev. Luis Baldonado, O.F.M.
Church—1421 S. 12th St., 85034. Tel: 602-258-2089.

24—ST. THERESA, Revs. Charles G. Kieffer; Fred Adamson. In res., Revs. Michael L. Diskin; Klemens Dobrowski, (Polish Apostolate).
Res., 5045 E. Thomas Rd., 85018. Tel: 602-840-0850; Fax: 602-840-0871.
School—5001 E. Thomas Rd., 85018. Tel: 602-840-0010. Mrs. Kathleen Stordeur, Prin.
Sisters 1; Lay Teachers 25; Students 564.

25—ST. THOMAS THE APOSTLE, Revs. John Spaulding;

Mark Hebert; Joseph Fichtner, O.S.C.; Deacons Americo Gouveia; Donald Kuban; Kenneth Miller. In res., Rev. Francis A. Peacock.
Res., 2312 E. Campbell Ave., 85016-5397. Tel: 602-954-9089; Fax: 602-956-3454.
School—4510 N. 24th St., 85016. Tel: 602-954-9088. Mr. Fredric Stephen, Prin.
Sisters 1; Lay Teachers 27; Students 583.
Convent—4550 N. 24th St., 85016-5299. Tel: 602-954-8489.

26—ST. VINCENT DE PAUL, Revs. Walter L. Housey, C.M.; John O'M. Sharpe, C.M.; J. Antonio Ruiz, C.M.; John V. Shine, C.M. In res., Rev. Michael J. Boyle, C.M.
Res., 3140 N. 51st Ave., 85031. Tel: 602-247-6871; Fax: 602-247-4457.
School—3130 N. 51st Ave., 85031. Tel: 602-247-8595. Sr. Theresa Marie McDermott, D.C., Prin.
Daughters of Charity 2; Lay Teachers 10; Students 218.
Convent—Tel: 602-247-8916.

OUTSIDE THE CITY OF PHOENIX

Bagdad, Yavapai Co., St. Francis of Assisi,
Mailing Address: P.O. Box 768, 86321. Tel: 520-633-2389.
Church & Rectory: 220 Cook St., 86321.

Bapchule, Pinal Co., St. Peter's, Sr. Anne Fischer, S.S.N.D., Admin.; Deacon Joseph Swisher, Admin.
Mailing Address: P.O. Box 545, Sacaton, 85247. Tel: 520-562-3716.
School—Tel: 520-315-3835; Fax: 520-315-3963. Sr. Martha Mary Carpenter, O.S.F., Prin.
Franciscan Sisters of Christian Charity (Manitowoc, WI) 2; Lay Teachers 3; Students 165.
Missions of Gila River Catholic Community Team—.
Missions—Ak Chin, St. Francis; Blackwater, Holy Family; Sacaton Flats, Our Lady of Victory; Santan, St. Anne; Sacaton, St. Anthony.

Buckeye, Maricopa Co., Saint Henry, Rev. Hugo Gonzalez; Deacon John R. Bilinski.
Res., 128 S. Third St., 85326. Tel: 602-386-6407; Fax: 602-386-4328.
Mission—Harquahala Valley, San Isidoro Labrador.

Bullhead City, Mohave Co., St. Margaret Mary, Rev. Peter P. Dobrowski; Deacon Richard Eckert.
Res., 1691 N. Oatman Rd., 86442. Tel: 520-758-7117; Fax: 520-758-2345.

Camp Verde, Yavapai Co., St. Frances Cabrini, Rev. James Kelly.
Res., P.O. Box 1677, 86322. Tel: 520-567-3543.
Church—608 W. General Crook Trail, 86322. Tel: 520-567-3543.
Mission—Black Canyon City, Yavapai Co., St. Philip Benizi, P.O. Box 138, Black Canyon City, 85324. Tel: 620-374-5392. Rev. Luke Silvestri, Admin.

Carefree, Maricopa Co., Our Lady of Joy, Rev. Msgr. Richard Moyer, V.G.; Rev. Clement Procopio, O.F.M.
Res., P.O. Box 1359, 85377. Tel: 602-488-2229 (Church); 488-3090 (Rectory); Fax: 602-488-1085.

Cashion, Maricopa Co., St. William, Rev. Thomas G. Bielawa, S.D.S., Admin.
Mailing Address: P.O. Box 329, 85329.
Res., 11003 W. Third St., 85329. Tel: 602-936-6115.
Mission—Santa Maria, Our Lady of Guadalupe, 6807 Lower Buckeye Rd., Phoenix, 85043.

Chandler, Maricopa Co., St. Andrew the Apostle, Revs. Joseph I. Hennessy; Camille Prat, S.J.; Deacon Dennis Putnam.
Res., 3450 W. Ray Rd., 85226. Tel: 602-899-1990; Fax: 601-917-8475.

St. Mary's, Revs. George E. Highberger; Joseph McGaffin.
Res., 230 W. Galveston, 85224. Tel: 602-963-3207; Fax: 602-814-9417.
School—200 W. Galveston, 85224. Tel: 602-963-4951. Sr. Mary Norbert Long, Prin.
Sisters of Charity, Seton Hill 2; Lay Teachers 20; Students 494.

St. Benedict, Rev. Patrick Robinson; Deacon Stephen Beard.
Res., 660 N. Beck, 85226.
Church—6400 W. Del Rio St., 85226. Tel: 602-961-1610; Fax: 602-961-1794.

Cottonwood, Yavapai Co., Immaculate Conception, Rev. George F. Pirrung; Deacons James Anderson; Onofre Duran; Ron Pelton.
Mailing Address: P.O. Box 995, 86326.
Res., 421 N. Willard St., 86326. Tel: 520-634-2933.
Mission—Clarkdale, Yavapai Co., St. Cecilia, P.O. Box 366, Clarkdale, 86324-0366. Tel: 520-634-2142. Rev. Michael F. Hurley, Admin.

El Mirage, Maricopa Co., Santa Teresita. (Ventura and Verbena). Rev. George Wuest, S.J.; Deacons Jose Garza; Daniel Hurley.
Res., P.O. Box 67, 85335. Tel: 602-583-8183; Fax: 602-583-2963.

Flagstaff, Coconino Co., Nativity of B.V.M., Rev. J.F. Michael Bain; Deacons William Mosley; Douglas Rade.
Res., 16 W. Cherry Ave., 86001. Tel: 520-774-7348; Fax: 520-774-7349.
School—St. Mary's Regional School, 320 N. Humphrey, 86001. Tel: 520-779-1337. Dr. Marie Axman, Prin.
Institute of the Blessed Virgin Mary 1; Lay Teachers 14; Students 256.

Our Lady of Guadalupe, Rev. Kevin Diaz.
Res., 224 S. Kendrick, 86001. Tel: 520-774-3280; Fax: 520-214-0153.
Convent—202 S. Kendrick, 86001. Tel: 520-774-3680.

St. Pius X, Rev. James Turner; Deacons Laurence Whelan; Jack Boehle.
Office: 2257 E. Cedar Ave., 86004. Tel: 520-779-3296; Fax: 520-779-5124.

Fountain Hills, Maricopa Co., Ascension, Rev. Thomas O'Dea; Deacon George J. Reinert, Parish Mgr.
Church—12615 Fountain Hills Blvd., 85268. Tel: 602-837-1066.
Mission—Rio Verde, St. Dominic.

Gila Bend, Maricopa Co., St. Michael, Rev. Howard Kuhns, C.S.C.
Res., 515 W. Norma St., P.O. Drawer F, 85337. Tel: 520-683-2336.
Church—314 Dodson St., 85337.
Mission—Tohono O'Odham, St. Lucy, Paloma Ranch. (Native American Village). Sr. Barbara Anne Webster, O.S.F., Ministries Asst.

Gilbert, Maricopa Co., St. Anne, Revs. Douglas E. Lorig; Julio Higuera; Bobbi Friedrich, Pastoral Assoc.
Mailing Address: P.O. Box 228, 85299-0228. Tel: 602-892-4970; Fax: 601-892-6736.
Church—440 E. Elliot Rd., 85234-0228.
Mission—Queen Creek, Maricopa Co., Our Lady of Guadalupe, P.O. Box 856, Queen Creek, 85242. Tel: 602-963-3207.

Glendale, Maricopa Co.,

1—OUR LADY OF PERPETUAL HELP, Revs. Patrick O. Colleary; Daniel McBride; Deacons James Marth; Tony Lopez; Robert Myers; Armando Mesquita.
Res., 5614 W. Orangewood Ave., 85301. Tel: 602-939-9785; Fax: 602-934-8854.
School—7521 N. 57th Ave., 85301. Tel: 602-931-7288. Sr. Lucia Daluz, O.S.F., Prin.
Sisters 2; Lay Teachers 9; Students 214.
Chapel—Capilla de Nuestra Senora de Guadalupe, 55th Ave. & Lamar.

2—ST. HELEN, Revs. Robert Skagen; Louis Mraz, O.S.C.; Sr. Patricia Oliver, R.S.M., Pastoral Assoc.; Deacons Joseph Shinske; Robert Rudolph Campas; Paul Csuy; Ted Micek.
Res., 5510 W. Cholla, 85304. Tel: 602-979-4202; Fax: 602-412-1226.

3—ST. JAMES, Rev. Kenneth A. Van De Ven; Deacons Robert Triana; John O'Connor.
Church—19640 N. 35th Ave., 85308. Tel: 602-581-0707; Fax: 602-581-0110.
Res., 18225 N. 35th Dr., 85308. Tel: 602-843-0421.

4—ST. LOUIS THE KING, Revs. John Slobig; Robert Bliven, O.S.C.; Deacon Gene Messer. In res., Rev. Paul Orel.
Mailing Address: 4331 W. Maryland Ave., 85301. Tel: 602-930-1127; Fax: 602-930-1129.
School—Tel: 602-939-4260. Sr. Jean Perry, C.S.A., Prin.
Lay Teachers 10; Students 240.

5—ST. RAPHAEL, Revs. Cyprian Hibner, O.Carm.; James Mueller, O.Carm.; Deacons Forrest Briesch; Stewart Wood; Joseph Liotta.
Res., 5504 W. Acoma, 85306.
Church—5525 W. Acoma, 85306. Tel: 602-938-4227; Fax: 601-978-0305.

Goodyear, Maricopa Co., Saint John Vianney, Revs. Joseph V. Corpora, C.S.C.; John A. Herman, C.S.C.; Deacon Terry M. Boyer.
Office: 539 La Pasada Blvd., 85338. Tel: 602-932-3313; Fax: 602-932-1896.
Res., 11 Loma Linda, Avondale, 85323. Tel: 602-925-0418.

Grand Canyon, Coconino Co., El Cristo Rey, Rev. Francis D. Zagorc, C.S.C., Admin.
Res., Rectory Chapel, Boulder at Albright, P.O. Box 505, 86023. Tel: 520-638-2390.

Guadalupe, Maricopa Co., Our Lady of Guadalupe, Rev. Joseph A. Baur, O.F.M., Admin.; Deacon Santo Bernasconi.
Office: 5445 San Angelo, St. Guadelupe, 85283. Tel: 602-839-2860.
Res., 9004 Calle Maravilla, 85283. Tel: 602-839-2376.

Jerome, Yavapai Co., Holy Family. Unassigned.
Res., St. Cecilia Mission, P.O. Box 366, Clarkdale, 86324. Tel: 520-634-2142.

Kingman, Mohave Co., St. Mary's, Rev. James Alling.
Res., 302 E. Spring St., 86401. Tel: 520-753-3359; Fax: 520-753-2581.
Mission—Dolan Springs, Mohave Co., Our Lady of the Desert, P.O. Box 491, Dolan Springs, 86441. Tel: 520-767-3154.

Lake Havasu City, Mohave Co., Our Lady of the Lake, Rev. Michael Deptula; Deacons Robert B. Treichel; Thomas C. Coe; Robert W. Davey; Eamon Parsons.
Res., 1975 Daytona Dr., 86403. Tel: 520-855-2685; Fax: 602-855-7172.

Laveen, Maricopa Co., St. John The Baptist, Sr. Anne Fischer, S.S.N.D., Admin.; Deacon Tom Swisher, Admin.
Res., P.O. Box 693, 85339-0693. Tel: 520-550-2034.
Mission—Santa Cruz, St. Catherine.
Station—Lone Butte, St. Francis Xavier.

Litchfield Park, Maricopa Co., St. Thomas Aquinas, Revs. Franklin L. Bartel; Ray Greco, O.S.B.; Deacons Tony Scarabino; Chuck Shaw.
Res., 447 S. Litchfield Rd., 85340. Tel: 602-935-2151; Fax: 602-935-5044.

Mesa, Maricopa Co.,

1—ALL SAINTS, Rev. Robert Caruso.
Church—1534 N. Recker Rd., 85205. Tel: 602-985-7655; Fax: 602-396-0837.

2—CHRIST THE KING, Rev. John Coleman; Deacons Joseph August; Philip Van Der Heyden; Stanley Humpal.
Res., 1505 E. Dana Ave., 85204.
Church—1551 E. Dana Ave., 85204. Tel: 602-964-1719; Fax: 602-844-4498.
School—Tel: 602-844-4480. Ms. Janice Merfeld, Prin.
Lay Teachers 9; Students 303.

3—HOLY CROSS, Rev. Dennis Riccitelli.
Res., 1244 S. Power Rd., 85206. Tel: 602-981-2021; Fax: 602-981-6844.

4—QUEEN OF PEACE, Revs. Roman C. Mueller, S.D.S.; Lloyd P. Kramlich, S.D.S.; Paul Portland, S.D.S.; Deacons Buddy Clapham; John Reidel.
Res., 141 N. Macdonald St., 85201. Tel: 602-969-9166; Fax: 602-969-8102.
School—109 N. Macdonald St., 85201. Tel: 602-969-0226. Rev. Karl LeClaire, Prin.
Lay Teachers 9; Students 250.

5—ST. BRIDGET, Rev. John F. Cunningham; Deacons Joe Scaccia; William Shea; Len Liszewski.
Res., 2850 E. Lockwood St., 85213. Tel: 602-924-9138.
Church—2213 N. Lindsay Rd., 85213. Tel: 602-924-9111; Fax: 602-924-3103.

6—ST. TIMOTHY, Revs. Dale J. Fushek; Mark Dippre; Deacons Ollie Babbitts; Thomas Bolduc; Barry Smith; Dutch Hurrish. In res., Rev. Marcel Salinas, C.M.F.
Res., 1730 W. Guadalupe, 85202. Tel: 602-838-8844; Fax: 602-820-7984.
Convent—2754 S. Pennington, 85202.
Sisters 4.
Catholic Life Productions, Inc. dba LIFE TEEN Program—Tel: 602-820-7001. Lin Tropio, Prog. Dir.

Peoria, Maricopa Co., St. Charles Borromeo, Rev. Charles Goraieb; Deacons Dan Herron; Eduardo Molina.
Mailing Address: P.O. Box 819, 85380-0819.
Res., 8617 W. Peoria Ave., 85345. Tel: 602-979-3418.
Church—8615 W. Peoria Ave., 85345. Fax: 602-412-2397.

Prescott, Yavapai Co., Sacred Heart, Revs. Fred LeClaire, C.M.F.; Francis Pyka, C.M.F.; Deacons William Davis; Thomas Kayser; John Lamon.
Res., 150 Fleury Ave., 86301. Tel: 520-445-3141; Fax: 520-717-1074.
School—131 N. Summit Ave., 86301. Tel: 520-445-2621. Marian Bresnen, Prin.
Institute of the Blessed Virgin Mary Sisters 1; Lay Teachers 9; Students 189.
Convent—229 N. Summit St., 86301. Tel: 520-445-7861.
Missions—Congress Junction, Yavapai Co., Good Shepherd of the Desert; Yarnell, Yavapai Co., St. Mary's, P.O. Box 706, Yarnell, 85362. Tel: 520-427-3715. Rev. John Faustina; Chino Valley, Yavapai Co., St. Catherine Laboure, P.O. Box 152, Chino Valley, 86323. Tel: 520-636-4071. Rev. John Salvador.

Prescott Valley, Yavapai Co., St. Germaine, Rev. Gerald Yaeger.
Res., 7997 E. Dana Dr., 86314. Tel: 520-772-6350; Fax: 520-772-4413.
Missions—Mayer, St. Joseph; Humboldt, St. Lawrence.

Scottsdale, Maricopa Co.,

1—BLESSED SACRAMENT, Revs. Eugene Young; Matthew Plathottam.
Res., 11300 N. 64th St., 85254. Tel: 602-948-8370; Fax: 602-951-3844.

2—OUR LADY OF PERPETUAL HELP, Revs. William P. Healy; John Bernbrock, S.J.; Deacon Irving Fleming. In res., Rev. Alan Malone.
Res., 7655 E. Main St., 85251. Tel: 602-947-4331; Fax: 602-874-3798.
School—3801 N. Miller Rd., 85251. Tel: 602-874-3720. Sr. Marian Grace Brandt, S.C., Prin.
Lay Teachers 23; Students 548.
Convent—7634 E. Second St., 85251. Tel: 602-945-3867.

3—ST. BERNADETTE, Rev. Richard Felt; Deacons Alan Bowslaugh; John Meyer; Roy Rooker.
Office: 14415 N. 73rd St., #107, 85260-3130. Tel: 602-905-0221; Fax: 602-905-0249.

4—ST. BERNARD OF CLAIRVAUX, Rev. Robert Voss; Deacon Fred Giesner.
Res., 10755 N. 124th St., 85259. Tel: 602-661-9843; Fax: 602-614-8092.

5—ST. DANIEL THE PROPHET, Revs. Francis R. Zappitelli; Dennis J. O'Rourke. In res., Rev. Patrick Smith.
Res., 7923 E. Latham St., 85257. Tel: 602-945-8437; Fax: 602-945-4335.
School—Tel: 602-949-8034. Sr. Mary Lucilla Wertz, S.C., Prin.
Lay Teachers 10; Students 224.
Convent—7830 E. Roosevelt, 85257. Tel: 602-423-5240.
Korean Catholic Community: Rev. Simon Jeon.

6—ST. MARIA GORETTI, Revs. Blase Myer; Oliver Mohan, O.M.I.; Loren Riebe; Deacons Herve Lemire; Len Zbiegien; Tom Bills; Jim Buchanan.
Res., 8344 E. Edward Ave., 85250.
Church—6261 N. Granite Reef Rd., 85250. Tel: 602-948-8380; Fax: 602-948-8815.

7—ST. PATRICK, Rev. Eric Tellez.
Office: 10815 N. 84th St., 85260. Tel: 602-998-3843; Fax: 602-998-5218.

Sedona, Yavapai Co., St. John Vianney, Rev. J.C. Ortiz; Deacon Bob Anderson.
Res., 180 Soldier Pass Rd., P.O. Box 3909, W. Sedona, 86340. Tel: 520-282-7545; Fax: 520-282-1798.
Chapel—Holy Cross, P.O. Box 1043, West Sedona, 86339. Tel: 520-282-4069.

Seligman, Yavapai Co., St. Francis, Rev. Henry Herrera, C.M.F., Admin.
Res., P.O. Box 308, 86337. Tel: 520-422-3354.
Church—104 Schoney, 86337.
Mission—Ashfork, St. Anne.

Sun City, Maricopa Co., St. Clement of Rome, Revs. Earl D'Eon; Ed Coleman, O.M.I.; Deacons Edward Owen; Irving Dennis.
Res., 15800 Del Webb Blvd., 85351. Tel: 602-974-5867; Fax: 602-974-0562.
St. Elizabeth Seton, Revs. Joseph Gillespie; William Waldron; Richard P. Ciesniewski; William Harnischfeger; Deacon William Tone.
Res., 9728 Palmeras Ln., 85373. Tel: 602-972-2129; Fax: 602-974-0654.
Church of St. Joachim & St. Anne, Revs. Frank P. Simlik; Richard Ryan.
Mailing Address: P.O. Box 748, 85372.
Res., 11625 111th Ave., 85351-3746. Tel: 602-972-1179; Fax: 602-972-1170.

Sun City West, Maricopa Co., Our Lady of Lourdes, Revs. Michael Minogue; Harold Graf; Deacons Lee Hanson; Maurice Arnold; Jack Cummings; George Koch.
Res., 19002 N. 128th Ave., 85375. Tel: 602-546-2767; Fax: 602-214-1246.

Sun Lakes, Maricopa Co., St. Steven, Rev. Emmett J. FitzPatrick.
Mailing Address: 24827 S. Dobson Rd., 85248. Tel: 602-895-9266.
Res., 10324 E. Michigan Ave., 85248. Tel: 602-895-9304.

Tempe, Maricopa Co.,

1—HOLY SPIRIT, Rev. John Hanley; Deacon Frank Danna.
Office: 1815 E. Gemini Dr., 85283. Tel: 602-838-7474; Fax: 602-838-6720.

2—OUR LADY OF MT. CARMEL, Revs. Timothy R. Davern, J.C.L.; Donald Kline.
Res., 2121 S. Rural Rd., 85282. Tel: 602-967-8791; Fax: 602-967-4919.
School—2117 S. Rural Rd., 85282. Tel: 602-967-5567. Dr. Vincent Sheridan, Prin.
Lay Teachers 20; Students 479.
Tongan Catholic Community: Rev. Timothy Davern, Liaison.

3—RESURRECTION, Revs. Thomas F. Hever; Bruce Downs. In res., Rev. Joseph Krijnen.
Res., 3201 S. Evergreen Rd., 85282. Tel: 602-838-0207; Fax: 602-756-1501.

4—ST. MARGARET, Deacon Frank G. Galarza, Admin.
Res., 2435 E. McArthur Dr., 85281. Tel: 602-967-0379; Fax: 602-967-3825.

Missions—Salt River Indian, St. Francis; Lehi, St. Paschal Baylon, P.O. Box 3334, Scottsdale, 85257. Tel: 602-994-0952.

Tolleson, Maricopa Co., Blessed Sacrament, Rev. Bruce Cecil, C.S.C.; Deacon Antonio M. Chavez, Sr.
Res., 312 N. 93rd Ave., P.O. Box 248, 85353. Tel: 602-936-7107; Fax: 602-936-9536.

Wickenburg, Maricopa Co., St. Anthony of Padua, Rev. John Vogt.
Res., 232 N. Tegner St., 85390. Tel: 520-684-2096; Fax: 520-684-3539.
Mission—Aguila, Our Lady of Guadalupe.

Williams, Coconino Co., St. Joseph's, Rev. Seamus S. Crossan.
Res., 900 W. Grant, 86046. Tel: 520-635-2430; Fax: 520-635-2430, Ext. 51.

Chaplains of Public Institutions

PHOENIX. *Arizona State Hospital,* 2500 E. Van Buren St., 85008. Tel: 602-220-6190. Chaplains: Rev. Paul O'Connor, C.S.B.; Sr. Patricia Pieper, D.deN.; Deacons George Valverde; Joseph Shinske.
Good Samaritan Medical Center, 1111 E. McDowell Rd., 85006. Tel: 602-239-4324. Rev. Patrick Adkins, O.S.C.
Maricopa Medical Center, 2601 E. Roosevelt St., 85008. Tel: 602-267-5011. Rev. Tulio Maya, S.D.S., Chap.
St. Joseph's Hospital, P.O. Box 2071, 85001. Tel: 602-406-3275. Ms. Theresa M. Ehrsam, Dir., Chaplaincy Svcs.
St. Luke's Medical Center. Vacant. 1800 E. Van Buren St., 85006. Tel: 602-251-8100.
United States Veterans Affairs Medical Center, 650 Indian School Rd., 85012. Tel: 602-222-6422. Revs. Bernard Young, Chap.; Peter Morello, Chief of Chap. Svcs.; Kenneth Klieber, Chap.

CHANDLER. *Chandler Regional Hospital,* 475 S. Obson Rd., 85224. Tel: 602-821-7639. Sr. Anna Oven, O.P., Chap.

LUKE AIR FORCE BASE. *Luke Air Force Base* 58 FW/HC, 13968 Shooting Star St., 85309-1932. Tel: 602-856-6211. Rev. Redmond Raux, Chap.

PRESCOTT. *United States Veterans Hospital (Prescott),* Veterans Administration Medical Center, 86313. Tel: 520-776-6029, Ext. 6478. Rev. Gerald Caffrey, C.M.F., Chap.

SCOTTSDALE. *Scottsdale Memorial Hospital,* 7400 E. Osborn Rd., 85251. Tel: 602-481-4000; 945-8437. Rev. Patrick Smith, Chap.

Special Assignment:
Reverend Fathers—
Acquaro, Philip, C.S.B., Diocesan Ctr., Tribunal Office, 400 E. Monroe, Phoenix, AZ 85004
Clements, Robert, Vocation Dir., 400 E. Monroe St., Phoenix, AZ 85004. Tel: 602-257-0030
Diskin, Michael, Asst. Chancellor & Ecumenical Officer, Diocesan Center, 400 E. Monroe, Phoenix, AZ
Goulet, Wayne F., 8540 N. Central Ave., #13, Phoenix, AZ 85020
Hall, John, Vicar, Native American Ministry, 400 E. Monroe, Phoenix, AZ 85004
Long, John, O.Carm., Exec. Dir. Kino Institute, 1224 E. Northern Ave., Phoenix, AZ 85020
Malone, Alan, Judicial Vicar, 400 E. Monroe, Phoenix, AZ 85004
McMahon, John, Dir. Mount Claret Retreat Center, 4633 N. 54th St., Phoenix, AZ 85018
Orel, Paul, Diocesan Center Tribunal Office, 400 E. Monroe, Phoenix, AZ
Pepel, Klemens, Dir., Prison Ministry, 400 E. Monroe St., Phoenix, AZ 85004
Prudencio, Rodriguez, C.M., Vicar, Hispanic Ministry, Diocesan Center, 400 E. Monroe, Phoenix, AZ 85004
Ryle, Edward J., Exec. Dir., Arizona Catholic Conference, 400 E. Monroe St., Phoenix, AZ 85004
Salinas, Marcel H., C.M.F., Dir., Diaconate Ministry, 400 E. Monroe, Phoenix, AZ 85004
Sharp, David L., C.S.B., Campus Min., Glendale Community College
Straley, Michael, Vicar, FinanVicar, Financial Admin., 400 E. Monroe, Phoenix, AZ
Taylor, Peter, Adobe Mountain Juvenile Institute (Correctional Institution)

On Duty Outside the Diocese:
Reverend Fathers—
Bormann, Charles
Brogan, Leo T.
Draves-Arpaia, Neil
Lessard, Joseph

On Leave:
Reverend Fathers—
Gauthier, John
Kundert, Rudolph
Mampara, Mathew

Unassigned:
Reverend Fathers—
Boulanger, Andre
Bredemann, George
Briceno, Joseph
Hunt Diaz, Kevin
Lehman, Mark A.
Sherwood, Lan S.

Retired:
Reverend Monsignors—
Donohoe, Robert J., 2345 W. Orangewood Ave., Phoenix, AZ 85021
Reverend Fathers—
Bechtel, Francis, 13840 N. Desert Harbor Dr., #407, Peoria, AZ 85381
Bourbon, Arthur, 11121 Desert Butte, Sun City, AZ 85351
Boyle, Thomas, 325 W. Holly St., Phoenix, AZ 85003
Colton, Bernard, 122A Clanabogan Rd., Omagh, Co. Tyrone, BT 7815 N Northern Ireland
Cullinan, John F., St. Joan of Arc, 3801 E. Greenway Rd., Phoenix, AZ 85032-4698
Diederichs, Michael F., 2002 W. Sunnyside Dr., #3315, Phoenix, AZ 85029-3552
Doran, John, Holy Family Center, 1802 W. St. Mary's Rd., Tucson, AZ 85745
Faustina, John M., St. Mary, P.O. Box 706, Yarnell, AZ 85362
Feit, Matthias, 12036 103rd Ave., Sun City, AZ 85351
Florez, Laurence A., P.O. Box 74, Youngtown, AZ 85363
Glass, Gerald J., 8141 N. 16th St., #7, Phoenix, AZ 85020
Groves, Edmund, St. Paul's Convent, Bushmount, Clonakilty, Co. Cork, Ireland
Hodges, Henry D., 4730 W. Northern Ave., #2083, Glendale, AZ 85302
Kelly, Martin C., 10637 Saratoga Cir., Sun City, AZ 85351
Kotnis, Gregory M., P.O. Box 3081, Lake Havasu City, AZ 86405-3081
Krijnen, Joseph G., Resurrection Parish, 3201 S. Evergreen Rd., Tempe, AZ 85282
Long, Francis C., Box 817, Snowflake, AZ 85937
Maguire, Eugene, 4701 N. 68th St., #103, Scottsdale, AZ 85251
McCready, Daniel A., 918 E. Broadmor, Tempe, AZ 85282
McGovern, Michael A., 10206 Snead Cir., Sun City, AZ 85351
McKay, William E., 6457 E. Dodge St., Mesa, AZ 85205
Mitchell, William J., 1675 Leisure World, Mesa, AZ 85206
Morales, Raul, P.O. Box 1143, Gilbert, AZ 85299
Moynihan, Cornelius A., 18626 Spanish Garden Dr., Sun City West, AZ 85375
O'Hern, Charles A., Sun Terrace, 1825 W. Emelita, #339, Mesa, AZ 85202
O'Reilly, Francis J., Churchfield Lawns, Knock, Co. Mayo, Ireland
Portmann, Frederick, 1255 W. Osborn Rd., Phoenix, AZ 85013
Schwartz, Anthony, Villa Guadalupe Home, 1900 Mark Ave., Gallup, NM 87301
Smith, Paul P., 6301 N. 34th Ln., Phoenix, AZ 85017
Sullivan, John T., Nazareth House, 6333 Rancho Mission Rd., San Diego, CA 92108
Wajda, Edward J., 214 S. Laveen Dr., Chandler, AZ 85226
Walsh, Thomas A., Blessed Sacrament, 11300 N. 64th St., Scottsdale, AZ 85254
Wasielewski, Henry R., P.O. Box 939, Tempe, AZ 85280-0939

Permanent Deacons:
Anderson, Bob, Jr., St. John Vianney, Sedona
Anderson, James, Immaculate Conception, Cottonwood
Anderson, Roy, St. Daniel the Prophet
Arnold, Maurice, (Retired), Our Lady of Lourdes, Sun City West
August, Joe, Christ the King, Mesa
Babbits, Ollie, St. Timothy, Mesa
Barelli, John, St. Thomas the Apostle, Phoenix
Barr, Earl, SS. Simon & Jude Cathedral, Phoenix
Bates, James B., On Leave
Battista, James, Holy Cross, Mesa
Beard, Stephen, St. Benedict, Chandler
Beltran, Anthony N., St. Matthew's, Phoenix
Bernasconi, Santo R., Our Lady of Guadalupe, Guadalupe
Bilinski, John, St. Henry, Buckeye
Bills, Tom, St. Maria Goretti, Scottsdale
Boehle, Jack, St. Pius X, Flagstaff

Bolduc, Thomas, St. Timothy, Mesa
Bolton, Edward L., St. Gregory, Phoenix
Booth, William, Diocese of Pueblo
Bowslaugh, Alan F., St. Bernadette, Scottsdale
Boyer, Terry, St. John Vianney, Avondale/Goodyear
Brett, James, St. Theresa, Phoenix
Briesch, Forrest, St. Raphael, Glendale
Brown, James, Denver, CO
Buchanan, James, St. Patrick, Scottsdale
Burgess, Lou A., St. Mark's, Phoenix
Burgin, Edward, Indian Ministry
Burke, Edward, St. Joseph Hospital, Phoenix
Campas, Rudolph, St. Helen, Glendale
Chavez, Antonio, Blessed Sacrament, Tolleson
Clapham, Buddy, Queen of Peace, Mesa
Coe, Tom, Our Lady of the Lake, Lake Havasu City
Conn, Richard A., Our Lady of Mount Carmel, Tempe
Crowley, Nicholas, St. Anne, Gilbert
Csuy, Paul E., St. Helen, Glendale
Curran, Richard, Diocesan Ministry
Czapinski, Clemens, Blessed Sacrament Scottsdale
Danna, Frank, Holy Spirit, Tempe
Davey, Bob, (Retired)
Davis, William, Sacred Heart, Prescott
DeDecker, Robert, St. Jerome Church, Phoenix
Del Monaco, William, St. Mary, Kingman
Dennis, Irving, St. Clement of Rome, Sun City
Dudzic, Anthony, St. Maria Goretti, Scottsdale
Duran, Onofre, Immaculate Conception, Cottonwood
Eckert, Dick, St. Margaret Mary, Bullhead City
England, Robert E., St. Paul, Phoenix
Fejes, Peter, St. Edward, Phoenix
Filardi, Ron, Archdiocese of Portland
Fleming, Irving, Our Lady of Perpetual Help Church, Scottsdale
Flynn, Patrick F., Corpus Christi, Phoenix
Fronske, Robert, (Retired)
Galarza, Frank, St. Margaret, Tempe
Garza, Jose, Santa Teresita, Surprise
Gaudio, Alexander L., Corpus Christi, Phoenix
Gehringer, William D., (Retired)
Giesner, Fred, St. Bernard, Scottsdale
Giza, Stanley, St. Clement of Rome, Sun City
Gonzales, Albert, St. Matthew, Phoenix
Goubeaux, Guy, Most Holy Trinity, Phoenix
Gouveia, Americo, St. Thomas the Apostle, Phoenix
Guldan, Ranald, St. Daniel the Prophet, Scottsdale
Guzman, Juan, St. Gregory, Phoenix
Hamilton, James, St. Vincent de Paul, Phoenix
Hanson, William, Our Lady of Lourdes, Sun City West
Hayes, Pat, Carrolton, TX
Heeter, Charles, St. Augustine, Phoenix
Henn, Thomas
Hernandez, Jose, St. Mark, Phoenix
Herr, Thomas
Herrmann, Richard E., (Retired)
Herron, Dan, Blessed Sacrament, Tolleson
Hickcox, Edward M., Holy Trinity Newman Center, N.A.U., Flagstaff; Our Lady of Guadalupe
Hintze, Craig, St. Mary, Chandler
Holgin, Alex, Our Lady of Mount Carmel, Tempe
Houser, Joseph, St. Augustine, Phoenix
Hoyt, James, Our Lady of Perpetual Help, Scottsdale
Hude, Harry, Blessed Sacrament, Scottsdale
Hughes, Patrick, Blessed Sacrament, Scottsdale
Humpal, Stanley, Christ the King, Mesa
Humphrey, Charles A., St. Catherine Laboure Mission, Chino Valley
Hurley, Dan A., (Retired)
Hurrish, Dutch, St. Timothy, Mesa
Jacobs, Gary, St. Andrew the Apostle, Chandler
Jimenez, Ramon H., St. Anne's, Gilbert
Kayser, Thomas E., Assoc. Dir. of the Permanent Diaconate, Sacred Heart, Prescott
Kelly, Charles, St. Joseph, Pheonix
Kelly, Vincent D., (Retired)
Kloft, Lee, St. Gregory Parish, Phoenix
Koach, Al, St. Daniel the Prophet, Scottsdale
Koch, George, Our Lady of Lourdes, Sun City West
Kuban, Donald, St. Thomas, Phoenix
Kulinowski, Kenneth, St. Anne, Gilbert
Lamon, John, Sacred Heart Parish, Prescott
Lazok, George, St. Catherine of Sienna, Phoenix
LeClair, Douglas, Sabbatical, St. Paul's University, Ontario, Canada
Lemire, Herve, St. Maria Goretti, Scottsdale
Leone, Robert, All Saints Newman Center, Tempe
Lessard, Joseph, St. Catherine of Sienna, Phoenix
Liotta, Joe, St. Raphael, Glendale
Liszewski, Leonard, St. Briget, Mesa
LoCascio, Phil, St. Joan of Arc, Phoenix
Lopez, Tony, Our Lady of Perpetual Help, Glendale
Lukaszewski, Don, All Saints, Mesa
Mader, Charles J., (Retired)
Marion, Kenneth, (Retired)
Marth, Jim, Our Lady of Perpetual Help, Glendale
Martin, Stephen J., SS. Simon and Jude Cathedral, Phoenix
McCarty, Robert J., On Leave
McNamara, Joseph, All Saints Newman Center, Tempe
Meli, John, (Retired)
Mesquita, Armando, St. Charles Borromeo, Peoria
Messer, Gene, St. Louis the King, Glendale
Meyer, John A., Diocesan Dir. of Catechetical Ministry, St. Bernadette, Scottsdale
Micek, Theodore, St. Jerome, Phoenix
Miller, John, St. Thomas the Apostle Byzantine, Gilbert
Miller, Kenneth, Chap., Kolping Society, St. Thomas the Apostle, Phoenix
Molina, Eddie, Our Lady of Perpetual Help, Glendale
Mosley, William, Nativity of B.V.M., Flagstaff
Murphy, Peter, Prison Ministry, St. Gregory Parish, Phoenix
Myers, Robert P., Our Lady of Perpetual Help, Glendale
Neely, Vincent, All Saints, Mesa
O'Connor, John, St. James, Glendale
O'Toole, Gerald, St. Anne Parish, Gilbert
Olivarez, Jose D., St. Martin de Porres, Phoenix
Orega, Elisandro G., (Retired)
Owen, Edward, (Retired)
Pardini, Louis, Ph.D., St. Philip the Deacon, Phoenix
Pelton, Ron, Immaculate Conception, Cottonwood
Peterson, Daniel, Assoc. Dir., St. Thomas Aquinas, Litchfield Park
Phares, William, St. Charles Borromeo, Peoria
Phelan, Mike, St. Jerome, Phoenix
Phelan, Thomas J., St. Anne, Gilbert
Pintar, Thomas A.
Putnam, Dennis, Diocese of Pueblo
Rade, Douglas, Nativity of the B.V.M., Flagstaff
Raymond, Charles J., St. Daniel the Prophet, Scottsdale
Regan, W. Richard, (Retired)
Rein, Richard, St. Jerome, Phoenix
Reinert, George, (Retired)
Riedel, John, Queen of Peace, Mesa
Rocha, Felix, Tuba City
Rodriguez, Jose, St. Mary, Kingman
Roger, Ray, St. Vincent de Paul, Phoenix
Rooker, Roy, St. Bernadette, Scottsdale
Roy, Alex, St. Francis Indian Mission, Mesa - Chaplain, Indian Hospital
Salamone, James, St. Anne Parish, Gilbert
Sanchez, Harry E., St. Agnes, Phoenix
Santa, Reed, Holy Cross, Mesa
Scaccia, Joe, St. Bridget, Mesa
Scarabino, Anthony G., Diocese of Gallup
Sejba, Jim, Our Lady of Joy, Carefree
Semmler, Raymond, All Saints, Mesa
Shaw, Chuck, St. Thomas Aquinas, Litchfield Park
Shea, Bill, St. Bridget, Mesa
Shinske, Joseph, Chap., Arizona State Hospital, St. Helen's, Glendale
Simeone, Philip, Corpus Christi, Phoenix
Smerke, Tony, Holy Cross, Mesa
Smith, Barry, Diocese of LaPae, Baja California - Mexico
Speranza, Tony, (Retired), St. Joseph Parish, Phoenix
Stevenson, William, Dayton, OH
Swisher, Joseph M., Prison Ministry, St. John & St. Peter
Tone, William, (Retired), St. Elizabeth Seton, Sun City
Treichel, Robert, (Retired)
Triana, Robert, St. James, Glendale
Valverde, W. George, Chap., Arizona State Hospital, Phoenix
Van Der Hayden, Philip, Christ the King, Mesa
Vega, Fernando, On Leave
Vera, Emidio B., (Retired)
Vivio, William, Our Lady of the Valley, Phoenix
Walsh, Franklyn, St. Agnes, Phoenix
Walsh, Thomas, On Leave
West, William A., St. Francis Xavier Church, Phoenix
Whelan, Laurence, St. Pius X, Flagstaff
Wood, Stewart, St. Raphael, Glendale
Zanon, Thomas, On Leave
Zbiegien, Leonard J., St. Maria Goretti, Scottsdale

INSTITUTIONS LOCATED IN THE DIOCESE

[A] HIGH SCHOOLS, DIOCESAN

PHOENIX. *Bourgade Catholic High School*, 4602 N. 31st Ave., 85017. Tel: 602-973-4000. Sr. Mary Delbert Weisensel, S.S.N.D., Prin.; Sr. Kathleen Janiak, R.S.M., Dir. Studies; Mrs. Roberta Walker, Dir. Students; Rev. John Ebbesmier, Chap. Sisters 3; Brothers 1; Lay Teachers 18; Students 300.

St. Mary's High School, 2525 N. Third St., 85004. Tel: 602-254-6371. Mr. Bill Lehman, Prin.; Mrs. Suzanne Fessler, Asst. Prin.; Sr. Jeanette Shean, I.B.V.M., Academic Advisor; Daniel Johansen, Academic Advisor; Rev. Blaise Cronin, O.F.M., Spiritual Dir.; Tom Miller, Counselor. Priests 2; Sisters 2; Lay Teachers 36; Students 750.

Seton Catholic High School. (Diocesan School), 1150 N. Dobson Rd., 85224. Tel: 602-963-1900; Fax: 602-963-1974. Mr. George Majoue, Prin.; Mr. Patrick Goodman, Asst. Prin. & Campus Min. Sisters of Charity of Seton Hill 4; Lay Teachers 27; Students 418.

Xavier College Preparatory, 4710 N. Fifth St., 85012. Tel: 602-277-3772; Fax: 602-279-1346. Sr. M. Joan Fitzgerald, B.V.M., Prin.; Sr. Lynn Winsor, B.V.M., Vice Prin. Sisters 10; Lay Teachers 62; Students 949.

[B] HIGH SCHOOLS, PRIVATE

PHOENIX. *Brophy College Preparatory*, Faculty Res., 4701 N. Central Ave., 85012. Tel: 602-264-5291; Fax: 602-266-3642. Jesuit Fathers. Boys day school. Rev. Edward Reese, S.J., Pres.; Mr. Edwin J. Hearn, Prin.; Mr. John Chambers, Asst. Prin.; Mr. Michael P. Klein, Asst. Prin.; Mr. A. Joseph Helm, Jr., Treas.; Revs. E. Louis Bishop, S.J.; Francis A. Moore, S.J., Devel.; William Kopas, Dean of Students; Revs. Peter J. Pabst, S.J., Rector; Kevin Dilworth, S.J., Min.; John J. Perlite, S.J., Sub-Min.; Joseph J. Fice, S.J.; James R. Menard, S.J.; Anton J. Renna, S.J.; John R. Becker, S.J.; David F. Klein, S.J.; Harry T. Oliver, S.J.; Robert J. Glynn, S.J.; Richard T. Coz, S.J.; Doanh Nguyen; Stephen Hurley, S.J. Priests 15; Scholastics 2; Lay Teachers 62; Students 1,159.

[C] GENERAL HOSPITALS

PHOENIX. *Mercy Services Corporation*, 350 W. Thomas Rd., 85013.
For a complete listing, refer to the Hospitals section.

St. Joseph's Hospital and Medical Center, 350 W. Thomas Rd., P.O. Box 2071, 85001. Tel: 602-285-3000.
For a complete listing, refer to the Hospitals section.

[D] HOMES FOR THE AGED & HANDICAPPED

PHOENIX. *Desert Crest Apartments*, 2101 E. Maryland Ave., 85016. Tel: 602-264-6427.
For a complete listing, refer to the Special Care Facilities section.

Senior Village, 3541 W. Vogel, 85051. Tel: 602-843-3008.
For a complete listing, refer to the Special Care Facilities section.

Sweetwater Gardens Apartments, 2035 E. Sweetwater, 85022. Tel: 602-867-4549.
For a complete listing, refer to the Special Care Facilities section.

AVONDALE. *Vianney Villas Apartments*, 750 S. Fourth St., 85323. Tel: 602-932-2036.
For a complete listing, refer to the Special Care Facilities section.

KINGMAN. *Kingman Heights Apartments*, 1020 Detroit Ave., 86401. Tel: 602-753-2425.
For a complete listing, refer to the Special Care Facilities section.

LAKE HAVASU CITY. *Becket House Apartments*, 865 Cashmere Dr., 86403. Tel: 602-855-7178.
For a complete listing, refer to the Special Care Facilities section.

MESA. *Sun Terrace Apartments*, 1825 W. Emelita Ave., 85202-4031. Tel: 602-964-9866.
For a complete listing, refer to the Special Care Facilities section.

WICKENBURG. *Padua Hills Apartments*, 460 S. West Rd., 85390. Tel: 602-684-7034.
For a complete listing, refer to the Special Care Facilities section.

WILLIAMS. *St. Agnes Apartments*, 200 S. Ninth, 86046. Tel: 602-635-2913.
For a complete listing, refer to the Special Care Facilities section.

[E] CONVENTS AND RESIDENCES OF SISTERS

PHOENIX. *Institute of Blessed Virgin Mary (I.B.V.M.)*. (Regional House), 2521 W. Maryland Ave., 85017. Tel: 602-433-0658; Fax: 602-433-9465. Sisters 4.

Missionaries of Charity, 1414 S. 17th Ave., 85007. Tel: 602-258-5504. Sisters 4.

Sisters of Charity of the Blessed Virgin Mary. (Xavier Convent), 4712 N. Third St., 85012. Tel: 602-264-0445. Sisters 9.

Sisters of Divine Savior, 323 E. Elm St., 85012. Tel: 602-274-0228. Sisters 3.

Sisters of St. Benedict of Phoenix, 6407 W. Indian School Rd., 85033. Tel: 602-848-9608.
Day Care Center. Capacity 8 Children.

Sisters of the Precious Blood, 4550 N. 24th St., 85016. Tel: 602-954-8489.

Union of the Sisters of the Presentation of the Blessed Virgin Mary. (Provincial House), 729 W. Wilshire Dr., 85007. Tel: 602-271-9687; 258-9476; Fax: 602-253-9166. Sr. Catherine Burke, P.B.V.M., Prov. Sisters 4.

GLENDALE. *Eucharistic Missionaries of St. Dominic*, 6910 W. Rancho Dr., 85303. Tel: 602-848-6895. Sisters 2.

MESA. *Sisters of Notre Dame de Namur*. (Casa Guadalupe), 548 W. Third St., 85201. Tel: 602-964-3685.

TEMPE. *Sisters of Charity*. (Seton House), 1014 S. George Dr., 85281. Tel: 602-967-5538. Sisters 2.

[F] MONASTERIES AND RESIDENCES OF PRIEST AND BROTHERS

PHOENIX. *Carmelite Community*, 1717 W. Flower, 85015. Revs. Valentine L. Boyle, O.Carm., (Retired); John G. Long, O.Carm.; Bro. Anton Hagan, O.Carm., (Retired). Priests 2; Brothers 1.

Crosier Community of Phoenix (Canons Regular of the Order of the Holy Cross), 2617 E. Campbell Ave., 85016. Tel: 602-224-0434; Fax: 602-224-0722. Revs. Joseph P. Cain, O.S.C.; Joseph J. Bruemmer, O.S.C.; Richard N. Ohlemacher, O.S.C.; Louis R. Mraz, O.S.C.; Fridolin P. Mischke, O.S.C.; Robert J. Bliven, O.S.C.; Leo W. Kapphahn, O.S.C., Rector; Patrick J. Adkins, O.S.C.; Joseph A. Fichtner, O.S.C.; Charles Kunkel, O.S.C., Prior; Robert Zylla, O.S.C. Priests 11.

Holy Cross Congregation of Casa Santa Cruz, 7126 N. Seventh Ave., 85021. Tel: 602-944-6000. Bro. Remigius Bullinger, C.S.C.; Revs. Eugene A. Burke, C.S.C.; Milton N. Adamson, C.S.C.; John Croston, C.S.C., Supr.; Ambrose J. Wheeler, C.S.C.; Robert L. Kramer, C.S.C., Asst. Supr.; John V. Vanden-Bossche, C.S.C., Supr.; Louis Rink, C.S.C. Priests 7; Brothers 1.

TEMPE. *Dominicans (Dominican Community-Jordan House)*, 1042 E. Campus, 85282. Tel: 602-829-1804. Revs. Nathan G. Castle, O.P., Supr.; Robert Marzullo, O.P.; Joseph O'Brien, O.P.; Daniel Rolland, O.P. Priests 2.

[G] RETREAT HOUSES

PHOENIX. *Mt. Claret Retreat Center*, 4633 N. 54th St., 85018. Tel: 602-840-5066. Rev. Msgr. John J. McMahon, Dir.; Rev. Eugene Maguire, Asst. Dir.; Jo Swiger, Asst. Dir.
Cursillo Movement: Revs. Leo Delgado, C.M.F., Dir.; Theo Fuentes, C.M.F., Asst. Dir. Priests 2.

BLACK CANYON CITY. *Contemplative House of Prayer*. (Our Lady of Solitude), P.O. Box 1140, 85324. Tel: 602-374-9204. Sr. Mary Therese Sedlock, O.S.F., Dir.

SCOTTSDALE. *Franciscan Renewal Center, Inc. (Casa de Paz Y Bien)*, 5802 E. Lincoln Dr., P.O. Box 220, 85252. Tel: 602-948-7460; Fax: 602-948-2325. Donna Gordon, Admin.; Revs. Alexander Manville, O.F.M., Retreat Master; Alonso de Blas, O.F.M.; Gino Piccoli, O.F.M.; Bro. Mario Vasquez, O.F.M. Priests 3; Brothers 1.

[H] NEWMAN CENTERS

PHOENIX. *Office of Youth and Young Adult Ministries*, 400 E. Monroe, 85004. Larry Fraher, Dir.; Modesto Garcia, Assoc. Dir.; Kevin Starr, Youth At Risk Coord. Mesa Community College, Chandler; Gilbert Community College; Glendale Community College; Scottsdale Community College; Paradise Valley Community College; ASU West.

Northern Arizona University, Holy Trinity Newman Center. (Flagstaff), P.O. Box 1946, Flagstaff, 86002-1946. Tel: 602-779-1341. Rev. Kieran Kleczewski, O.S.B., Dir.

American Graduate School of International Management. (Glendale), Thunderbird Campus, 15249 N. 59th Ave., Glendale, 85306. Tel: 602-978-7011. Joaquin Duarte. Tel: 602-978-7184.

Glendale Community College, P.O. Box 1562, Wickenburg, 85358. Tel: 520-684-7779. Rev. David L. Sharp, C.S.B.

Yavapai College, Emery Riddle Aeronautical University. (Prescott), Sacred Heart Parish, 150 Fleury Ave., Prescott, 86301. Tel: 502-445-3141. Mrs. Gail Schimberg.

Arizona State University. (Tempe), All Saints Catholic Newman Center, 230 E. University Dr., P.O. Box 1987, Tempe, 85281. Tel: 602-967-7823. Revs. Nathan Castle, O.P., Dir.; Daniel Rolland, O.P.; Robert Marzullo, O.P.; Deacon Robert Leone, Chap.

Mesa Community College, P.O. Box 1175, Cashion, 85329. Tel: 602-936-4221.

Catholic Committee on Scouting. Tel: 602-945-8437. Rev. Dennis O'Rourke, Chap.

[I] ACADEMIES OF RELIGIOUS TEACHING

PHOENIX. *Kino Institute*, 1224 E. Northern Ave., 85020-4295. Tel: 602-997-7397; Fax: 602-870-8871. Diocesan Center for Religious Studies and Lay Ministry Formation with Library, Media Center & Bookstore. Rev. John G. Long, O.Carm., Exec. Dir.
E-mail:frlong@cathdioc.org
Betty G. Loff, Registrar, Financial Admin. Parish Program Coord.
E-mail:bloff@cathdioc.org
1224 East Northern Ave., 85020-4295.
Faculty and Staff.
E-mail:kino@cathdioc.org
Kathy Brown, Dean, School of Ministry; Pat Julian, Consultant, Spiritual Direction Program; Rev. Michael Kwiecien, O. Carm., Faculty.
E-mail:mikek@carmelnet.org
Revs. Ernest Larkin, O.Carm., Faculty/Advisor; Vernon J. Meyer, Dean, School of Biblical Studies; Margaret Newman, Admin. Assistant; Lisa Padula, Secretary; Joanne Rapp, Coord., Spirituality & Spiritual Direction Programs; Rev. Gilbert Rutz, Faculty; Margaret Wheeler, Admin. Asst.; Teofilo Argueta-Ramirez, Coord.,PROGRAMA DE FORMACION PASTORAL. Tel: 602-252-4301, Centro Pastoral Hispano, 1102 East Hilton Ave., 85034. Library, Media Center & Bookstore. (Kino Institute). Tel: 602-906-9798. Sr. Bibiane Roy, O.P., Coord., Librarian & Mgr.
E-mail:INTERNET:bibianer@aol.com
Sr. Joyce Braun, C.S.A., Bookstore & Library Asst.; Tom Missey, Media Center Asst., University of San Francisco. Diana Stickney, Coord. Tel: 602-997-7397, Survival School. Joe Velazquez, Consultant. Tel: 602-997-7397. Total Staff 16.

[J] MISCELLANEOUS LISTINGS

PHOENIX. *Andre House of Arizona*, 1002 W. Polk, 85007. Hospitality House, Indiana Province of the Congregation of Holy Cross. Mailing Address: P.O. Box 2014, 85001-2014. Tel: 602-255-0580. 213 S. 11th Ave., 85007. Rev. John J. Dougherty, C.S.C., Dir.; Deacon Brent Kruger, C.S.C.; Bro. Richard Armstrong, C.S.C.

Casa De Merced, 222 W. Thomas Rd., #214, 85013. Tel: 602-406-6218. Gloria Munoz, Pres.

Catholic Social Services of Central and Northern Arizona, Inc., 1825 W. Northern Ave., 85021. Tel: 602-997-6105; Fax: 602-331-4071. Christopher Bavasi, Pres.; Paul Martodam, M.P.A., CEO; Kristen Schmidt, M.S.W., Ph.D., Deputy Dir.
Regional Agencies:

Catholic Social Service of Phoenix, 1825 W. Northern Ave., 85021. Tel: 602-997-6105; Fax: 602-870-3891.

West Valley Office, 14010 N. El Mirage Rd., El Mirage, 85523. Tel: 602-937-0500.

Head Start Office, 6503 N. 21st Ave., 85015. Tel: 602-246-0051. Maureen Webster, A.C.S.W., Agency Dir.

East Valley Catholic Social Service, 18 E. University Ave., Mesa, 85201. Tel: 602-964-8771; Fax: 602-964-8865. 24 hour Domestic Violence Hotline Tel: 602-821-1024. Elly Gersten, A.C.S.W., Agency Dir.

Catholic Social Service Flagstaff, 201 West University Ave., Flag Staff, 86001. Tel: 520-774-9125; Fax: 520-774-1105. Bill Klein, M.A., Agency Dir.

Catholic Social Service of Yavapai, 116 N. Summit, Prescott, 86301. Tel: 520-778-2531; Fax: 520-771-9531.

Verde Valley Office, 736 North Main St., Cottonwood, 86326. Tel: 520-634-4254.

Black Canyon Office, Kay Mine Rd., P.O. Box 541, Black Canyon City, 85324. Tel: 520-374-9320. John Allen, M.C., Agency Dir.

Catholic Social Service of Mohave, 1370 Ramar Rd., Ste. D, Bullhead City, 86442. Tel: 520-758-4176; Fax: 520-855-4960.

Lake Havasu Office, 1975 Daytona Blvd., Lake Havasu City, 86403. Tel: 520-855-4960. Marty Adams, M.S.W., Agency Dir.

Westside Head Start, 7400 W. Olive Ave., Ste. 10, Peoria, 85345. Tel: 602-486-9868; Fax: 602-486-9988. 22 Head Start Centers. Nancy Reyes, Agency Dir.

Pregnancy Parenting & Adoption Services, 1825 W. Northern Ave., 85021. Tel: 602-997-6105; Fax: 602-331-4071. Connie Mitchell, A.S.C.W., Dir.

Office of Peace & Justice, 2911 N. 11 Ave., 85013. Tel: 602-279-5551; Fax: 602-279-8475. Marie Sullivan, Dir.
Residential Facilities:

Casa Linda Lodge. Tel: 602-943-6461. Pregnant and parenting teens. Morgan Taylor Kane, M.A., Res. Sup.

Sundance Lodge. Tel: 602-870-0376. Group Transitional living for homeless mothers and their children. Shiela Lucas, Program Coord.

My Sister's Place. Domestic Violence Shelter. Theresa Grates, M.C., Supvr.

Crossroads Shelter. Tel: 602-997-3321. Abused and neglected adolescent girls. Morgan Taylor Kane, M.A., Res. Sup.

Spring Haven Group Home. Tel: 602-841-5195. Abused and neglected adolescent girls. Morgan Taylor Kane, M.A., Res. Sup.

Stepping Stones Group Home. Tel: 602-949-9396. Abused and neglected girls. Morgan Taylor Kane, M.A., Res. Sup.

Aspen House, 304 O'Leary, Flagstaff, 86001. Tel: 520-779-5017. Pregnancy shelter.
Child Care Centers:

Peoria Child Development Center, 11708 N. 80th Ave., Peoria, 85345. Tel: 602-486-7211. Glynis Garelick, Coord.

Carefree Child Development Center, 621 W. Clay St., Flagstaff, 86001. Tel: 520-774-1722. Carol Sullivan, M.A., Coord.

Christ Child Society, P.O. Box 15945, 85060-5945. Tel: 602-893-2711. Pat Wilson, Pres.; Sheila Hill, Treas.

Foundation for Senior Living, 77 E. Thomas Rd., Ste. 100, 85012. Tel: 602-285-1800; Fax: 602-285-1838. John Marron, Chm.; Guy Mikkelsen, Exec. Dir.

Foundation for Senior Adult Living, Inc. Sweetwater Gardens (Apartments for the Handicapped), Phoenix; Kingman Heights Apartments, Kingman.

FSAL Desert Crest. (Desert Crest Apartments).

FSAL Development Corp. (Sun Terrace Apartments, Mesa).

FSAL Management.

FSAL Nursing Care Centers.

FSAL Programs. Adult Day Health Care Centers; In-Home Care Services; Home Safety & Repair Program; Community Action Programs/Senior Centers; Adult Foster Care; Oasis (Older Adult Service & Information System); Pathways Program (Resources and Referral-Care Management).

FSAL Rural Development. Becket House Apartments, Lake Havasu City; Vianney Villas Apartments, Avondale; Padua Hills Apartments, Wickenburg; St. Agnes Apartments, Williams.

Payson Senior Living, Inc. (Pineview Manor Apartments, Payson).

FSL Pathways. Assisted Group Living Program (Nine Houses), Phoenix.

The Malta Center, 2000 N. Seventh St., 85006-2101. Tel: 602-340-1881. Rev. Joseph O'Brien, O.P., Exec. Dir.; John O'Brien, Pres. Pastoral and spiritual resources for persons with AIDS, their family members and caregivers.

Mercy Housing Arizona, 222 W. Thomas, #214, 85013. Tel: 602-406-6218. Gloria Munoz, Pres.

Mercy Properties Arizona, 222 W. Thomas Rd., #214, 85013. Tel: 602-406-6218. Gloria Munoz, Pres.

**Natural Family Planning*, 4945 E. Thomas Rd., 85018. Tel: 602-381-1884. Mrs. Janet Kistler, Dir. & Diocesan Coord. for N.F.P. Svcs. Center provides Natural Family Planning Services, Instructional Series, Introductions for Marriage Preparation, and Chastity Education for Adolescents and Parents and offers classes in Spanish and Mother/Daughter, Father/Son Workshops in Fertility Appreciation. Program is endorsed by the Diocesan Development Plan for N.F.P., National Council of Catholic Bishops.

Plazas de Merced, 222 W. Thomas Rd., #214, 85013. Tel: 602-402-6218; Fax: 602-650-7141. Gloria Munoz, Pres.

St. Joseph the Worker. (Job Service), 213 S. 11th Ave., 85007. Tel: 602-257-4390; Fax: 602-254-3834. Mailing Address: P.O. Box 13503, 85002. Matthew Feeney, Chm. Bd. of Dir.; Janet M. Gray, Dir.; Richard Hoyet, Vice Pres.; Bro. Richard Armstrong, C.S.C., Treas. To assisst homeless and poor people in their efforts to secure and keep full-time, meaningful employment.

St. Mary's Scholarship & Benefit Fund, 2525 N. Third St., 85004. Joe Kealy, Pres.

St. Vincent De Paul Society, P.O. Box 13600, 85002; Fax: 602-495-3029. Nancy Spencer, Pres.; Rev. Msgr. John J. McMahon, Spiritual Advisor.

**Southwest Catholic Health Network Corp.*, 2800 N. Central Ave., Ste. 400, 85004. Tel: 602-263-3066; Fax: 602-263-2098. Katherine J. Byrne, Pres.

GOODYEAR. *St. John Vianney School Development Fund*, 539 La Pasada Blvd., 85338. Tel: 602-932-3313; Fax: 602-932-1896. Rev. Joseph V. Corpora, C.S.C., Pres.

TEMPE. *City of the Lord*, 711 W. University Dr., 85281. Tel: 602-968-5895; Fax: 602-921-9175. James R. Jones, Overall Coord.

RELIGIOUS INSTITUTES OF MEN REPRESENTED IN THE DIOCESE

For further details refer to the corresponding bracketed number in the Religious Institutes of Men or Women section.

[0170]—*Basilian Fathers*. (Western Prov.).—C.S.B.

[0200]—*Benedictine Monks*. (St. Meinrad Archabbey).—O.S.B.

[0600]—*Brothers of the Congregation of Holy Cross*.—C.S.C.

[0400]—*Canons Regular of the Order of the Holy Cross*.—O.S.C.

[0270]—*Carmelite Fathers and Brothers*. (Prov. of St. Elias).—O.Carm.

[0350]—*Cistercian Order of the Strict Observance (Trappists)*.—O.C.S.O.
[0360]—*Claretian Missionaries*. (Western Prov.).—C.M.F.
[1330]—*Congregation of the Mission*. (Prov. of the West).—C.M.
[0520]—*Franciscan Friars*. (Prov. of Santa Barbara).—O.F.M.
[0650]—*Holy Ghost Fathers*. (Western Prov.).—C.S.Sp.
[0690]—*Jesuit Fathers and Brothers*. (California, Oregon, & Chicago Provs.).—S.J.
[0910]—*Oblates of Mary Immaculate*. (Our Lady of Hope).—O.M.I.
[0430]—*Order of Preachers (Dominicans)*. (Western Prov.).—O.P.
[0610]—*Priests of the Congregation of Holy Cross*.—C.S.C.
[1200]—*Society of the Divine Savior*. (North American Prov.).—S.D.S.

RELIGIOUS INSTITUTES OF WOMEN REPRESENTED IN THE DIOCESE

[0230]—*Benedictine Sisters of Pontifical Jurisdiction*. (Duluth, St. Paul, MN).—O.S.B.
[0990]—*Congregation of Divine Providence*. (Pittsburgh, PA).—C.D.P.
[1780]—*Congregation of Sisters of the Third Order of St. Francis of Perpetual Adoration*. (La Crosse, WI).—F.S.P.A.
[3710]—*Congregation of the Sisters of St. Agnes*. (Fond du Lac, WI).—C.S.A.
[1710]—*Congregation of the Third Order of St. Francis of Mary Immaculate*. (Joliet, IL).—O.S.F.
[0760]—*Daughters of Charity*. (Los Altos Hills, CA).—D.C.
[0850]—*Daughters of Mary Help of Christians*. (San Antonio, TX).—F.M.A.
[0810]—*Daughters of the Heart of Mary*. (Holyoke, MA).—D.H.M.
[1070-03]—*Dominican Sisters*. (Sinsinawa, WI).—O.P.
[1070-11]—*Dominican Sisters*. (Sparkill, NY).—O.P.
[1070-13]—*Dominican Sisters*. (Adrian, MI).—O.P.
[1070-24]—*Dominican Sisters*. (Great Bend, KS).—O.P.
[1070-28]—*Dominican Sisters*. (Akron, OH).—O.P.
[1070-30]—*Dominican Sisters*. (Mountain View, CA).—O.P.
[1120]—*Dominican Sisters of Roman Congregation*. (Iowa City, IA).—O.P.
[1140]—*Eucharistic Missionaries of St. Dominic*. (New Orleans, LA).—O.P.
[1230]—*Franciscan Sisters of Christian Charity*. (Manitowoc, WI).—O.S.F.
[1430]—*Franciscan Sisters of Our Lady of Perpetual Help*. (St. Louis, MO).—O.S.F.
[1440]—*Franciscan Sisters of the Poor*. (Brooklyn, NY).—F.S.P.
[2370]—*Institute of the Blessed Virgin Mary (Loretto Sisters)*. (Toronto, Ont., Canada).—I.B.V.M.
[2380]—*Institute of the Blessed Virgin Mary (Loretto Sisters)*. (Rathfarnham, Dublin, Ireland).—I.B.V.M.
[2740]—*Maryknoll Sisters of St. Dominic*. (Maryknoll, NY).—M.M.
[2710]—*Missionaries of Charity*. (Calcutta, India).—M.C.
[2790]—*Missionary Servants of Most Blessed Trinity*.—M.S.B.T.
[3130]—*Our Lady of Victory Missionary Sisters*. (Huntington, IN).—O.L.V.M.
[2970]—*School Sisters of Notre Dame*. (Milwaukee, WI; Irving, TX).—S.S.N.D.
[1680]—*School Sisters of St. Francis*. (Milwaukee, WI).—S.S.S.F.
[1630]—*Sisters of St. Francis of Penance and Charity*. (Redwood City, CA).—O.S.F.
[1680]—*School Sisters of St. Francis*. (Milwaukee, WI).—O.S.F.
[1690]—*School Sisters of the Third Order of St Francis*. (Pittsburgh, PA).—O.S.F.
[0440]—*Sisters of Charity of Cincinnati, Ohio*.—S.C.
[0570]—*Sisters of Charity of Seton Hill, Greensburg, Pennsylvania*.—S.C.
[0430]—*Sisters of Charity of the B.V.M.*—B.V.M.
[2575]—*Sisters of Mercy of the Americas*. (Pittsburgh, PA; Rochester, NY; Burlingame, CA; Chicago, IL; Omaha, NE; Providence, RI).—R.S.M.
[3000]—*Sisters of Notre Dame de Namur*. (Cincinnati, OH).—S.N.D.deN.
[1540]—*Sisters of St. Francis*. (Clinton. IA).—O.S.F.
[1705]—*The Sisters of St. Francis of Assisi*. (Milwaukee, WI).—O.S.F.
[1570]—*Sisters of St. Francis of the Holy Family*. (Dubuque, IA).—O.S.F.
[3830-05]—*Sisters of St. Joseph*. (Brentwood, NY).—C.S.J.
[3830-11]—*Sisters of St. Joseph*. (Nazareth, MI).—S.S.J.
[3830-15]—*Sisters of St. Joseph*. (Concordia, KS).—C.S.J.
[3935]—*Congregation of the Sisters of St. Louis*. (Woodland Hills, CA).—S.S.L.
[3840]—*Sisters of St. Joseph of Carondelet*.—C.S.J.
[3930]—*Sisters of St. Joseph of the Third Order of St. Francis*. (South Bend, IN).—S.S.J.-T.O.S.F.
[1030]—*Sisters of the Divine Savior*. (Milwaukee, WI).—S.D.S.
[3730]—*Sisters of the Order of St. Basil the Great*. (Uniontown, PA).—O.S.B.M.
[3260]—*Sisters of the Precious Blood*. (Dayton, OH).—C.PP.S.
[2090]—*Sisters, Home Visitors of Mary*. (Detroit, MI).—H.V.M.
[2150]—*Sisters, Servants of the Immaculate Heart of Mary*.—I.H.M.
[3330]—*Union of the Sisters of the Presentation of the B.V.M.* (Phoenix, AZ).—P.B.V.M.

NECROLOGY

† Gordon, Rev. Msgr. Bernard, (Retired). —Died June 24, 1996.
† McHugh, Rev. Msgr. Neil, (Retired). —Died Nov. 29, 1995.
† Morgan, Harry, (Retired). —Died Nov. 18, 1995.
† Poirier, Philip, (Retired). —Died Aug. 5, 1996.

Diocese of Pittsburgh

(Dioecesis Pittsburgensis)

Most Reverend

DONALD W. WUERL, S.T.D.

Bishop of Pittsburgh; ordained December 17, 1966; appointed Titular Bishop of Rosemarkie and Auxiliary Bishop of Seattle December 3, 1985; consecrated January 6, 1986; appointed and canonically installed Bishop of Pittsburgh February 12, 1988; liturgically installed March 25, 1988. *Office: 111 Blvd. of the Allies, Pittsburgh, PA, 15222-1618. All official correspondence should be sent to this office.*

Most Reverend

JOHN B. MCDOWELL, PH.D.

Retired Auxiliary Bishop of Pittsburgh; Titular Bishop of Tamazuca; ordained November 4, 1945; appointed July 18, 1966; consecrated September 8, 1966; resigned September 30, 1996. *Mailing Address: c/o Diocese of Pittsburgh, 111 Blvd. of the Allies, Pittsburgh, PA, 15222-1618.*

Most Reverend

WILLIAM J. WINTER, V.G., S.T.D.

Auxiliary Bishop of Pittsburgh and Titular Bishop of Uthina; ordained December 17, 1955; appointed December 27, 1988; consecrated February 13, 1989. *Res., Sacred Heart Church, 310 Shady Ave., Pittsburgh, PA, 15206-4389.*

Most Reverend

DAVID A. ZUBIK

Auxiliary Bishop of Pittsburgh; ordained May 3, 1975; appointed February 18, 1997; installed April 6, 1997. *Res., 111 Blvd. of the Allies, Pittsburgh, PA, 15222-1618.*

ESTABLISHED AUGUST 8, 1843.

Square Miles 4,092.

Comprises the Counties of Allegheny, Beaver, Lawrence, Washington, Greene, and Butler in the State of Pennsylvania.

For legal titles of parishes and diocesan institutions, consult the Legal Office.

Pastoral Center: 111 Blvd. of the Allies, Pittsburgh, PA, 15222-1618. Tel.: 412-456-3000.

STATISTICAL OVERVIEW

Personnel	
Bishop	1
Auxiliary Bishops	2
Retired Bishops	1
Priests: Diocesan Active in Diocese	379
Priests: Active Outside Diocese	25
Priests: Diocesan in Foreign Missions	1
Priests: Retired, Sick or Absent	115
Number of Diocesan Priests	520
Religious Priests in Diocese	134
Extern Priests in Diocese	47
Ordinations:	
Diocesan Priests	5
Permanent Deacons in Diocese	22
Total Brothers	44
Total Sisters	1,909
Parishes	
Parishes	218
With Resident Pastor:	
Resident Diocesan Priests	197
Resident Religious Priests	15
Without Resident Pastor:	
Administered by Priests	6
Professional Ministry Personnel:	
Brothers	1
Sisters	90
Lay Ministers	260
Welfare	
Catholic Hospitals	5
Total Assisted	644,305
Health Care Centers	5
Total Assisted	3,420
Homes for the Aged	11
Total Assisted	1,255
Residential Care of Children	4
Total Assisted	467
Day Care and Extended Day Care Centers	98
Total Assisted	5,292
Specialized Homes	4
Total Assisted	426
Special Centers for Social Services	5
Total Assisted	54,825
Residential Care of Disabled	1
Total Assisted	91
Other Institutions	4
Total Assisted	190
Educational	
Seminaries, Diocesan	1
Students from This Diocese	14
Diocesan Students in Other Seminaries	11
Total Seminarians	25
Colleges and Universities	3
Total Students	13,380
High Schools, Diocesan and Parish	8
Total Students	3,796
High Schools, Private	3
Total Students	664
Elementary Schools, Diocesan and Parish	107
Total Students	29,560
Elementary Schools, Private	3
Total Students	760
Non-residential Schools for the Disabled	2
Total Students	163
Catechesis/Religious Education:	
High School Students	8,509
Elementary Students	50,541
Total Students Under Catholic Instruction	107,398
Teachers in the Diocese:	
Priests	5
Brothers	12
Sisters	158
Lay Teachers	1,966
Vital Statistics	
Receptions into the Church:	
Infant Baptism Totals	9,303
Adult Baptism Totals	454
Received into Full Communion	754
First Communions	9,204
Confirmations	9,181
Marriages:	
Catholic	2,776
Interfaith	1,180
Total Marriages	3,956
Deaths	9,230
Total Catholic Population	753,090
Total Population	2,009,092

Former Bishops—Rt. Rev. MICHAEL J. O'CONNOR, D.D., ord. June 1, 1833; cons. Aug. 15, 1843; transferred to Erie and then to Pittsburgh Dec. 20, 1853; resigned May 23, 1860; entered the Society of Jesus Dec. 22, 1860; died at Woodstock College, MD, Oct. 18, 1872.—Rt. Rev. MICHAEL DOMENEC, C.M., D.D., ord. June 30, 1839; cons. Dec. 9, 1860; transferred to Allegheny, Jan. 11, 1876; resigned July 29, 1877; died at Tarragona, Spain, Jan. 5, 1878.—Rt. Rev. JOHN TUIGG, D.D., ord. May 14, 1850; cons. Bishop of Pittsburgh, March 19, 1876; transferred as Apostolic Administrator of Allegheny 1877; died at Altoona Dec. 7, 1889.—Rt. Rev. RICHARD PHELAN, D.D., ord. May 4, 1854; cons. Aug. 2, 1885; Titular-Bishop of Cibyra and Coadjutor to the Rt. Rev. John Tuigg; succeeded to Bishop Tuigg, Dec. 7, 1889; died Dec. 20, 1904.—Most Rev. J. F. REGIS CANEVIN, D.D., ord. June 4, 1879; cons. Titular Bishop of Sabrata and Coadjutor, Feb. 24, 1903; succeeded to the See of Pittsburgh, Dec. 20, 1904; resigned Nov. 26, 1920; Titular Archbishop of Pelusium; appt. Jan. 9, 1921; died March 22, 1927.—Most Rev. HUGH C. BOYLE, D.D., ord. July 2, 1898; succeeded to the See of Pittsburgh, June 16, 1921; cons. June 29, 1921; died Dec. 22, 1950.—His Eminence JOHN CARDINAL DEARDEN, S.T.D., ord. Dec. 8, 1932; Titular Bishop of Sarepta and Coadjutor Bishop of Pittsburgh; appt. March 13, 1948; cons. May 18, 1948; succeeded to the See, Dec. 22, 1950; assistant at the Pontifical Throne, Oct. 15, 1957; installed at the Archdiocese of Detroit, Dec. 18, 1958; created Cardinal, April 28, 1969; died Aug. 2, 1988.—His Eminence JOHN CARDINAL WRIGHT, S.T.D., ord. Dec. 8, 1935; Titular Bishop of Aegea and Auxiliary of Boston; appt. May 10, 1947; cons. June 30, 1947; transferred to Bishop of Worcester, Jan. 28, 1950; transferred to Pittsburgh, Jan. 23, 1959; created Cardinal, April 28, 1969; to the Roman Curia as Prefect of the Sacred Congregation for the Clergy; appt. April 23, 1969; died Aug. 10, 1979.—Most Rev. VINCENT M. LEONARD, D.D., ord. June 16, 1935; appt. Titular Bishop of Arsacal and Auxiliary, Feb. 28, 1964; cons. April 21, 1964; succeeded to the See, June 1, 1969; resigned June 30, 1983; died Aug. 28, 1994.—Most Rev. ANTHONY J. BEVILACQUA, D.D., M.A., J.C.D., J.D., ord. June 11, 1949; Titular Bishop of Aquae Albae and Auxiliary Bishop of Brooklyn; appt. Oct. 4, 1980; cons. Nov.

24, 1980; Bishop of Pittsburgh; appt. Oct. 10, 1983; installed Dec. 12, 1983; appt. Archbishop of Philadelphia, Feb. 11, 1988; created Cardinal, June 29, 1991.

Pastoral Center—111 Blvd. of the Allies, Pittsburgh, 15222. Tel: 412-456-3000. All official correspondence should be directed to this office.

Chancellor—Sr. MARGARET HANNAN, R.S.M. Tel: 412-456-3129.

Vicars General—Most Rev. WILLIAM J. WINTER, V.G., S.T.D.; Most Rev. DAVID A. ZUBIK, V.G.

Bishop's Office—Most Rev. DONALD W. WUERL, S.T.D.; Rev. PAUL J. ZYWAN, Admin. Sec.; Rev. JAMES A. WEHNER, Master of Ceremonies, Direct all official correspondence to the Bishop at this address: *111 Blvd. of the Allies, Pittsburgh, 15222.* Tel: 412-456-3010.

General Secretary—Most Rev. DAVID A. ZUBIK, D.D., V.G. Tel: 412-456-3131; Fax: 412-456-3197.

Associate General Secretary—Sr. MARGARET HANNAN, R.S.M. Tel: 412-456-3129.

Vicar for Canonical Services—Very Rev. LAWRENCE A. DINARDO, J.C.L., V.E.,address all correspondence to: *111 Blvd. of the Allies, Pittsburgh, 15222-1698.* Tel: 412-456-3135; Fax: 412-456-3173.

Canonical Consultants—Revs. RICHARD M. LELONIS, J.C.L.; JAMES P. MCDONOUGH, J.C.L.

Tribunal Office—Address all correspondence to: *111 Blvd. of the Allies, Pittsburgh, 15222-1698.* Tel: 412-456-3033; Fax: 412-456-3173.

Judicial Vicar—Very Rev. ROBERT J. AHLIN, J.C.L.

Adjutant Judicial Vicar—Very Rev. JAMES R. BEDILLION, J.C.L.

Judges—Revs. JAMES L. AARON, M.S.Ed.; PAUL J. BRADLEY, M.A., M.S.W.; Very Rev. LAWRENCE A. DINARDO, J.C.L., V.E.; Rev. TIMOTHY G. EVANS, M.A., S.T.L.; Very Rev. WILLIAM P. FEENEY, M.Div.; Revs. ROBERT F. GUAY, M.Div.; JAMES E. KUNKEL, S.T.M.; RICHARD M. LELONIS, J.C.L.; JOSEPH R. LEMP, S.T.L.; THOMAS M. O'DONNELL, M.Div.; THEODORE A. RUTKOWSKI, S.T.L.; JOSEPH C. SCHEIB, M.A.; CHARLES W. SPEICHER, Ph.D., S.T.M.; ROBERT R. WERTHMAN, M.Div.; Very Rev. LEO V. VANYO, V.F., J.C.D.

Promoter of Justice—Rev. JEROME A. DIXON, J.C.L.

Defenders of the Bond—Revs. MARTIN F. BARKIN, M.Div.; J. LAWRENCE BRUNEY, M.Div.; ROBERT J. CLARKE, M.Div.; DENNIS J. COLAMARINO, M.Div.; LOUIS L. DENINNO, M.Div.; JEROME A. DIXON, J.C.L.; ROBERT M. FRANCO, M.Ch.A.; JAMES P. MCDONOUGH, J.C.L.; JOHN R. RUSHOFSKY, M.S.Ed.; BENEDETTO P. VAGHETTO, J.C.L.

Director of Cases—Mrs. RITA F. JOYCE, J.D., J.C.L.

Auditors-Assessors—Revs. FRANK D. ALMADE, Ph.D.; CHARLES S. BOBER, S.T.D.; ROBERT J. CEDOLIA, M.A.; DAVID D. DEWITT, M.Div.; KEVIN J. DOMINIK, M.Div.; MARK A. ECKMAN, M.Div.; ANDREW C. FISCHER, M.Div.; JOSEPH F. KEENAN, M.Div.; EDWARD L. KRYSTON, M.Div.; WILLIAM P. O'MALLEY, M.Div.

Advocates—Revs. CARMEN A. D'AMICO, M.Div.; MICHAEL W. DECEWICZ, M.Div.; ANDREW C. FISCHER, M.Div.; JOSEPH F. KEENAN, M.Div.; PAUL J. ZYWAN, M.Div.

Notaries—HELEN LAZAR; DARLENE PETERSON; ANNETTE SEMAN; DARLENE WILCE; MARGARET E. WOJTASZEK.

Secretary for Clergy and Religious—Very Rev. JOHN E. KOZAR, V.E., *111 Blvd. of the Allies, Pittsburgh, 15222.* Tel: 412-456-3060; Fax: 412-456-3188.

Secretary for Education—Rev. KRIS D. STUBNA, S.T.D., *111 Blvd. of the Allies, Pittsburgh, 15222.* Tel: 412-456-3100; Fax: 412-456-3101.

Secretary for Pastoral Life—Rev. RONALD P. LENGWIN, *111 Blvd. of the Allies, Pittsburgh, 15222.* Tel: 412-456-3021; Fax: 412-456-3168.

Secretary for Social Concerns—Rev. FRANK D. ALMADE, Ph.D., *111 Blvd. of the Allies, Pittsburgh, 15222.* Tel: 412-456-3156; Fax: 412-456-3180.

Deans and Deaneries—Most Rev. WILLIAM J. WINTER, V.G., S.T.D., Chm., College of Deans; Central Pittsburgh: Very Rev. LEO V. VANYO, V.F., J.C.D., Northside: Very Rev. THOMAS B. FERRIS, V.F., Northeast Allegheny County: Very Rev. ROBERT G. DUCH, V.F., Northwest Allegheny County: Very Rev. GEORGE C. NEWMEYER, V.F., North Central Allegheny County: Very Rev. JOSEPH M. MELE, V.F., South Pittsburgh: Very Rev. BERNARD M. HARCARIK, V.F., Southeast Allegheny County: Very Rev. HUGH J. LANG, V.F., Southwest Allegheny County: Very Rev. WALTER A. SOBON, V.F., South Hills Allegheny County: Very Rev. ROBERT J. REARDON, V.F., South Central Allegheny County: Very Rev. STEPHEN M. CHERVENAK, V.F., Beaver County: Rev. Msgr. RAYMOND T. SCHULTZ, V.F., Butler County: Very Rev. JAMES F. MURPHY, V.F., Lawrence County: Very Rev. MAURO J. CAUTELA, V.F., Greene County: Very Rev. ALBIN C. MCGINNIS, V.F., Washington County East: Very Rev. WILLIAM P. FEENEY, V.F., Washington County West: Very Rev. PHILIP J. DONATELLI, V.F.

Office for the Delegate for Religious—Sr. ANNE WINSCHEL, C.D.P., Delegate, *2900 Noblestown Rd., Pittsburgh, 15205-4227.* Tel: 412-928-5844.

Priest Council—Most Rev. DONALD W. WUERL, S.T.D., Pres.; Most Rev. WILLIAM J. WINTER, V.G., S.T.D.; Most Rev. DAVID A. ZUBIK, V.G.; Revs. HARRY R. BIELEWICZ; CHARLES S. BOBER, S.T.D., S.T.L.; PAUL J. BRADLEY, M.S.W.; LAWRENCE J. BRUNEY; MICHAEL W. DECEWICZ; Rev. Msgr. DANIEL N. DINARDO, S.T.L.; Very Rev. LAWRENCE A. DINARDO, V.E., M.Ch.A., J.C.L.; Revs. JOHN P. GALLAGHER, S.T.L.; RICHARD A. INFANTE; Very Rev. JOHN E. KOZAR, V.E.; Revs. PAUL M. KUPPE, O.F.M.Cap.; JOHN P. MALONEY; ROBERT MCCREARY, O.F.M.Cap.; THOMAS D. O'NEIL; MICHAEL S. SUSLOWICZ; JOHN P. SWEENEY; DAVID H. TAYLOR; BENEDETTO P. VAGHETTO, J.C.L.; LOUIS F. VALLONE; JAMES G. YOUNG.

College of Consultors—Most Rev. DONALD W. WUERL, S.T.D.; Most Rev. WILLIAM J. WINTER, V.G., S.T.D.; Most Rev. JOHN B. MCDOWELL, V.G., Ph.D.; Most Rev. DAVID A. ZUBIK, D.D., V.G.; Rev. Msgr. DANIEL N. DINARDO, S.T.L.; Revs. PAUL J. BRADLEY, M.S.W.; MICHAEL W. DECEWICZ; JOHN P. GALLAGHER, S.T.L.; JOHN P. MALONEY; JOHN P. SWEENEY; DAVID H. TAYLOR; BENEDETTO P. VAGHETTO, J.C.L.; JAMES G. YOUNG.

Diocesan Development Board—Revs. RONALD P. LENGWIN, Chm. FRANK D. ALMADE, Ph.D.; Mrs. NANCY F. BECK; Sr. PATRICIA CAIRNS, C.S.J.; Mr. MARK D. GAFFEY; Sr. MARGARET HANNAN, R.S.M.; Mr. CHARLES A. KOEMPEL, C.P.A.; Mr. JOSEPH G. LUTTRINGER; Mr. AMBROSE MURRAY; Rev. JOHN M. O'TOOLE; Mr. ROBERT R. RETESHKA; Rev. GEORGE A. WILT.

Diocesan Finance Council—Most Rev. DONALD W. WUERL, S.T.D., Pres.; Most Rev. DAVID A. ZUBIK, V.G., Chm.; Sr. MARGARET HANNAN, R.S.M.; Mr. MICHAEL J. HANNON; Mr. MARTIN G. MCGUINN; Mr. HARRY F. MURRAY; Mr. FRED O'BRIEN; Very Rev. ROBERT J. REARDON, V.F.; Mr. FRANK J. SCHNEIDER; Mr. LEO W. YOCHUM.

Diocesan Pastoral Council—Most Rev. DONALD W. WUERL, S.T.D., Chm.; Most Rev. WILLIAM J. WINTER, V.G., S.T.D.; Most Rev. DAVID A. ZUBIK, V.G.; Ms. BARBARA ANTROM; Dr. JOHN A. BAMONTE; Mr. EDWARD BERNOT; Ms. MARY ANN BOBER; Mr. BRAD CATON; Very Rev. STEPHEN M. CHERVENAK, V.F.; Bro. JOHN DEMPSEY, S.M.; Rev. PHILIP N. FARRELL; Mrs. LILLIAN GERMAINE; Mr. RICHARD P. JACOB; Mrs. KATHY KRISFALUSY; Mrs. CHARLES KUDZMA; Mr. ELBERT KUHNS; Mrs. ANNE LAYCHAK; Mr. JOHN LAYTON; Sr. DELIA MARIE MCNEIRNEY, I.H.M.; Rev. STEVEN M. PALSA; Mr. JAMES PARHAM; Sr. MARY PRICE, S.C.; Sr. MARY CABRINI PROCOPIO, C.S.S.F.; Mrs. MONA RUSH; Mr. DONALD SHAW; Ms. JEAN SMALL; Mr. JAMES WEILAND.

Priest Personnel Board—Most Rev. DONALD W. WUERL, S.T.D.; Most Rev. JOHN B. MCDOWELL, Ph.D.; Most Rev. WILLIAM J. WINTER, V.G., S.T.D.; Most Rev. DAVID A. ZUBIK, V.G.; Revs. ROBERT J. CLARKE; CARMEN A. D'AMICO; JOHN P. GALLAGHER; JOHN R. HANEY; JOHN J. KEANE; Very Rev. JOHN E. KOZAR, Chm.; Very Rev. HUGH J. LANG, V.F.; Rev. ALBERT J. SEMLER, Exec. Sec.

Diocesan Administration

Administrative Procedures, Office for—Very Rev. LAWRENCE A. DINARDO, J.C.L., V.E., Admin. Tel: 412-456-3135.

Adult and Family Catechesis, Office for—Rev. RONALD D. LAWLER, O.F.M.Cap., Ph.D., Dir. Tel: 412-456-3117.

Archives and Records Center—Mr. KENNETH A. WHITE, Dir.; Mr. BURRIS E. ESPLEN, Archivist, *125 N. Craig St., Pittsburgh, 15213-1555.* Tel: 412-621-6217.

Bishop, Office of the Diocesan—Revs. PAUL J. ZYWAN, Admin. Sec. JAMES A. WEHNER, Master of Ceremonies. Tel: 412-456-3010.

Bishop Boyle Center—Mr. JOSEPH W. BELECHAK, Mgr., *120 E. 9th Ave., Homestead, 15120-1600.* Tel: 412-462-8516.

Black Catholic Ministries, Office for—Mrs. MARGARETTA STOKES TUCKER, Dir. Tel: 412-456-3170.

Budget and Planning - Secretariat for Education, Office for—Mr. ROY CARTIER, Dir. Tel: 412-456-3108.

Building Commission—Mr. GENE T. ODATO, Chm., *4721 5th Ave., Pittsburgh, 15213.* Tel: 412-621-6206.

Building Services, Office for—Mrs. DARLENE M. HOLZER, Mgr. Tel: 412-456-3016.

Campus Ministry, Office for—Rev. ROBERT L. SEEMAN, Dir., *Newman Center, 342 Normal Ave., Slippery Rock, 16057.* Tel: 412-794-6620.

Canonical Services, Office for—Very Rev. LAWRENCE A. DINARDO, J.C.L., V.E.; Revs. RICHARD M. LELONIS, J.C.L., Consultant; JAMES P. MCDONOUGH, S.T.L., J.C.L., Consultant. Tel: 412-456-3135.

Cardinal Wright Center—Rev. EDWARD J. BURNS, Dir.; Ms. DIANE GASBARRO, Mgr., *10745 Babcock Blvd., Gibsonia, 15044.* Tel: 412-961-6884.

Catechesis, Office for—Tel: 412-456-3114.

Catechetical Ministries, Office for—Ms. SHARON T. TYBOROWSKI, Dir. Tel: 412-456-3110.

Catholic Charities—Sr. PATRICIA CAIRNS, C.S.J., Exec. Dir., *212 9th St., Pittsburgh, 15222.* Tel: 412-456-6999., Allegheny County: *212 9th St., Pittsburgh, 15222.* Tel: 412-456-6999., Beaver County: *1260 N. Brodhead Rd., Monaca, 15601.* Tel: 412-775-0758., Butler County: *300 S. Washington St., Butler, 16001.* Tel: 412-287-4011., Greene County: *195 E. High St., Waynesburg, 15370.* Tel: 412-627-6410., Lawrence County: *20 S. Mercer St., New Castle, 16101.* Tel: 412-658-5526., Washington County: *331 S. Main St., Washington, 15301.* Tel: 412-228-7722., Roselia Center: *624 Clyde St., Pittsburgh, 15213.* Tel: 412-682-4410; 4411. Services for single pregnant women. Maryhouse Residence for Women: *1113 Creedmoor Ave., Pittsburgh, 15226.* Tel: 412-563-3312., St. Joseph's House of Hospitality, Inc.: *1635 Bedford Ave., Pittsburgh, 15219.* Tel: 412-471-0666., Ozanam Cultural Center: *1833 Wylie Ave., Pittsburgh, 15219.* Tel: 412-281-4046.

Catholic Cemeteries Assoc.—Ms. ANNABELLE MCGANNON, Exec. Dir., *718 Hazelwood Ave., Pittsburgh, 15217-0360.* Tel: 412-521-9133.

Catholic Schools, Department for—Dr. ROBERT L. PASERBA, Ed.D., Supt.-Schools; Sr. MURIEL YOUNG, C.D.P., Asst. Supt.-Elementary Schools; Mrs. ANNA MARIE CATANZARO, Asst. Supt.-Secondary Schools; Dr. RONALD T. BOWES, D.A., Asst. Supt.-Planning & Devel. Tel: 412-456-3090.

Educational Consultants—Sr. BENITA DEMATTEIS, O.S.B.; Sr. URSULA KELLY, S.S.N.D.; Sr. CATHERINE ANN KOLLER, C.D.P.; Sr. LORETTA KRALL, C.S.J.; Mr. WILLIAM C. LLOYD; Sr. M. DENISE MAHER, C.S.J.; Sr. IRENE MARY WILBURN, S.C., *135 1st Ave., Pittsburgh, 15222.* Tel: 412-456-3070.

Chaplaincies, Office for—Rev. JOHN J. KEANE, Dir., *4721 5th Ave., Pittsburgh, 15213.* Tel: 412-621-6209.

Charismatic Prayer Groups—Rev. JOHN P. SWEENEY, Moderator, *St. Titus Parish, 952 Franklin St., Aliquippa, 15001.* Tel: 412-378-8561.

Chief Financial Officer—Mr. CHARLES A, KOEMPEL, C.P.A. Tel: 412-456-3137.

Clergy and Ministerial Formation, Department for—Rev. EDWARD J. BURNS, Dir., *St. Paul Seminary, 2900 Noblestown Rd., Pittsburgh, 15205-4227.* Tel: 412-928-5840.

Clergy Personnel, Dept. for—Rev. ALBERT J. SEMLER. Tel: 412-456-3060.

Communications, Office for—Mr. ROBERT R RETESHKA, Dir.; Mr. RAYMOND G. FLECKENSTEIN, Dir. of Communication Services. Tel: 412-456-3020.

Cultural Diversity, Commission on—Rev. RONALD P. LENGWIN, Chm. Tel: 412-456-3021.

Data Automation, Office for—Mr. JOHN F. ZDILLA, Dir. Tel: 412-456-3152.

Deaf Persons, Office for—Mrs. KAREN M. MCGANN, Coord.; Rev. WALTER G. RYDZON, Chap., *48 S. 14th St., Pittsburgh, 15203-1548.* Tel: 412-481-9550 (Voice); 481-9552 (TTY).

Development Office—Mr. MARK D. GAFFEY, Dir. Tel: 412-456-3085.

Diaconate, Office for the—Rev. EDWARD J. BURNS, Dir., *St. Paul Seminary, 2900 Noblestown Rd., Pittsburgh, 15205-4227.* Tel: 412-928-5840.

Diocesan National Black Catholic Congress Leadership Team—Ms. BARBARA ANTROM, Team Leader, *324 Baker Ave., Clairton, 15025.* Tel: 412-233-3492.

Diocesan Purchasing Commission—Mr. JAMES W. PEARCE, Exec. Dir., *2900 Noblestown Rd., Pittsburgh, 15205.* Tel: 412-922-6400.

Disabilities, Department for Persons with—Ms. GRACE T. HARDING, Dir., *48 S. 14th St., Pittsburgh, 15203-1548.* Tel: 412-481-9550 (Voice); 481-9552 (TTY).

Ecumenical and Interfaith Commission—Rev. RONALD P. LENGWIN, Chm. Tel: 412-456-3021.

Educational Media, Department for—Mr. CHARLES BEAUDRY, Dir., *St. Paul Seminary, 2900 Noblestown Rd., Pittsburgh, 15205-4227.* Tel: 412-928-5817.

Educational Special Events, Office for—Sr. M. IGNATIUS ROONEY, R.S.M., Dir. Tel: 412-456-3075; or 928-5830.

Electronic Media, Office for—Mrs. NANCY K. LIPPERT, Dir., *St. Paul Seminary, 2900 Noblestown Rd., Pittsburgh, 15205-4227.* Tel: 412-928-5923.

Employment Development and Community Concerns, Office for—Mr. JOSEPH A. CARR, Dir. Tel: 412-456-3164.

Evangelization and Christian Initiation, Office for—Rev. M. ERIC DISKIN, M.Div., Dir. Tel: 412-456-3083.

Family Life and Family Concerns, Office for—Mrs. MAUREEN H. WOOD, Dir. Tel: 412-456-3160.

Financial Services, Office for—Mr. JOSEPH G. LUTTRINGER, Dir. Tel: 412-456-3025. Central Accounting Dept.: Tel: 412-456-3032. Parish Accounting Dept.: Tel: 412-456-3025. Auditing Dept.: Tel: 412-456-3028.

Foundation, Catholic Diocese of Pittsburgh—Mr. MARK D. GAFFEY, Dir. Tel: 412-456-3085.

Fund Raising, Office for—Mr. MARK D. GAFFEY, Dir. Tel: 412-456-3085.

Gilmary Diocesan Center—Mr. RONALD W. RAGAN, Dir., *601 Flaugherty Run Rd., Coraopolis, 15108-3899.* Tel: 412-264-8400.

Insurance/Employee Benefits, Office for—Mr. DAVID S. STEWART, Mgr. Tel: 412-456-3045.

Justice and Peace Commission—Ms. VERONICA MORGAN-LEE, Ph.D., Chm. Tel: 412-456-3162.

Learning Media Center—Mr. CHARLES BEAUDRY, Dir., *St. Paul Seminary, 2900 Noblestown Rd., Pittsburgh, 15205-4227.* Tel: 412-928-5817.

Legal Office—Mr. WILLIAM A. STEIDLE, JR., ESQ., Gen. Counsel. Tel: 412-456-3126.

Mental Retardation and Special Religious Education, Office for Persons with—Mrs. ELEANOR G. MARSHALL, Coord., *48 S. 14th St., Pittsburgh, 15203-1548.* Tel: 412-481-9550.

Ministries, Institute for—Rev. EDWARD J. BURNS, Supvr.; Sr. PATRICIA ROGAN, O.S.F., Asst. Dir., *St. Paul Seminary, 2900 Noblestown Rd., Pittsburgh, 15205-4227.* Tel: 412-928-5827.

Missions, Office for—Very Rev. JOHN E. KOZAR, V.E., Dir. Tel: 412-456-3065.

Music Ministry, Office for—Rev. JAMES J. CHEPPONIS, Dir. Tel: 412-456-3042.

Natural Family Planning Advisory Committee—Ms. ROSE STANEK, Coord. Tel: 412-456-3160.

Parish Services, Office for—Sr. MARILYN HOEING, O.S.F., Dir. Tel: 412-456-3057.

Payroll, Office for—Mr. JOHN G. CVETIC, Mgr. Tel: 412-456-3006.

Personnel, Office for—Mrs. DARLENE M. HOLZER, Mgr. Tel: 412-456-3016.

Persons with Physical Disabilities, Office for—Rev. PATRICK F. RAGER, Pastoral Counselor. Tel: 412-461-6393.

Pilgrimage Office—Very Rev. JOHN E. KOZAR, V.E., Dir. Tel: 412-456-3065.

Pornography, Commission to Counter—Mrs. NORMA NORRIS, Chm. Tel: 412-456-3160.

Pre-Ordination Formation, Department for—Rev. EDWARD J. BURNS, Dir., *St. Paul Seminary, 2900 Noblestown Rd., Pittsburgh, 15205-4227.* Tel: 412-928-5840.

Property Planning and Development, Office for—Mr. GENE T. ODATO, Dir., *4721 5th Ave., Pittsburgh, 15213.* Tel: 412-621-6206.

Public Affairs, Department for—Rev. RONALD P. LENGWIN, Dir. Tel: 412-456-3021.

Religious Education/CCD, Department for—Mr. BRIAN M. KEANE, Dir. Tel: 412-456-3112.

Research and Planning, Office for—Mr. JOHN P. FLAHERTY, Dir. Tel: 412-456-3146.

Retired Priests, Office for—Very Rev. THOMAS J. KRAM, V.E., Vicar. Tel: 412-881-3675.

Retired Priests, Residences for—Sr. GABRIELLA SECHI, O.S.H.J., Admin., *St. John Vianney Manor, 2600 Morange Rd., Pittsburgh, 15205.* Tel: 412-928-0825. Rev. FRANCIS L. PUCCI, Dir., *Cardinal Dearden Center, 4721 5th Ave., Pittsburgh, 15213.* Tel: 412-687-8038.

St. Paul Seminary—Revs. EDWARD J. BURNS, Rector; ROBERT P. CONNOLLY, Vice Rector; Sr. JUDITH WORDEN, R.S.M., Coord. of Apostolic Work; Sr. M. IGNATIUS ROONEY, R.S.M., Admin. Asst. to Rector, *St. Paul Seminary, 2900 Noblestown Rd., Pittsburgh, 15205.* Tel: 412-921-5800.

Social Awareness, Department for—Tel: 412-456-3161.

Social Programs and Community Development, Department for—Mr. W. JOHN HANNIGAN, M.S.W., Dir. Tel: 412-456-3162.

Society for the Propagation of the Faith—Very Rev. JOHN E. KOZAR, V.E., Dir. Tel: 412-456-3065.

Television and Radio Production—Refer to Electronic Media, Office for.

Theological Commission—Rev. JOSEPH J. KLEPPNER, S.T.L., Ph.D., Chm. Tel: 412-775-6363.

Vision Impairments, Office for Persons with—Ms. KAREN MCGANN, Dir.; Rev. Msgr. PAUL M. LACKNER, Chap., *48 S. 14th St., Pittsburgh, 15203-1548.* Tel: 412-481-9550.

Vocations, Office for—Rev. EDWARD J. BURNS, Dir., *St. Paul Seminary, 2900 Noblestown Rd., Pittsburgh, 15205-4227.* Tel: 412-928-5836.

Worship, Office for—Rev. M. ERIC DISKIN, Dir. Tel: 412-546-3041.

Worship Commission—Rev. M. ERIC DISKIN, Chm. Tel: 412-456-3041.

Youth and Young Adult Ministry, Office for—Mrs. JOYCE A. GILLOOLY, Dir.; Mr. CRAIG COPPAWAY, Coord.-Programs; Rev. EDWARD M. CZEMERDA, Coord.-Spiritual Formation; Mr. GARY SLIFKEY, Coord.-Leadership Training, *Gilmary Diocesan Center, 601 Flaugherty Run Rd., Coraopolis, 15108-3899.* Tel: 412-264-9530.

CLERGY, PARISHES, MISSIONS AND PAROCHIAL SCHOOLS

CITY OF PITTSBURGH, PROPER (Allegheny County)

1—ST. PAUL CATHEDRAL (1834), Very Rev. Leo V. Vanyo, V.F., Rector; Revs. Martin R. Conley; John J. Coll, S.J. In res., Rev. Paul J. Zywan.
Res., 108 N. Dithridge St., 15213. Tel: 412-621-4951; Fax: 412-621-4951.
School—142 N. Craig St., 15213. Tel: 412-621-7023. Sisters of Mercy of the Diocese of Pittsburgh 5; Lay Teachers 8; Students 151.

2—ST. AGNES. Closed. For sacramental records contact St. Paul Cathedral.

3—ST. ANN (Hungarian). Closed. See St. Stephen.

4—ST. AUGUSTINE (German). Closed. See Our Lady of the Angels.

5—ST. BEDE (1922), Rev. Edward M. Bryce. In res., Revs. Joseph C. Beck; Peter Mushi, A.J.
Res., 509 S. Dallas Ave., 15208. Tel: 412-661-7222; Fax: 412-661-9337.
School—6920 Edgerton Ave., 15208. Tel: 412-661-9425.
Lay Teachers 18; Students 290.

6—ST. BENEDICT THE MOOR (1889) (African American), Rev. Carmen A. D'Amico.
Res., 91 Crawford St., 15219. Tel: 412-281-3141; Fax: 412-391-7151.
School—2900 Webster Ave., 15219. Tel: 412-682-3755; Fax: 412-682-4058.
Sisters of St. Joseph 4; Lay Teachers 7; Students 229.
Convent—Tel: 412-621-0519.

7—ST. CATHERINE OF SIENA (Beechview) (1902), Revs. Aloysius Berk; Louis Deninno.
Res., 1901 Broadway, South Hills Sta., 15216. Tel: 412-531-2135.
School—(Grades K-8) 1915 Broadway Ave., 15216. Tel: 412-561-0399.
Sisters of St. Joseph 2; Lay Teachers 10; Students 142.
Catechesis/Religious Programs—Tel: 412-561-8242.
Students 254.

8—ST. CHARLES LWANGA (1992). Consolidated from the following churches: Corpus Christi, Holy Rosary, Mother of Good Counsel, Our Lady Help of Christians, Our Lady of the Most Blessed Sacrament and SS. Peter & Paul. Revs. David H. Taylor; James W. Garvey.
School—Holy Rosary, 7120 Kelly St., 15208. Tel: 412-731-2567; Fax: 412-731-3476.
Lay Teachers 14; Students 296.

9—CORPUS CHRISTI. Closed. See St. Charles Lwanga.

10—ST. ELIZABETH OF HUNGARY (Slovak). Closed. See St. Patrick-St. Stanislaus Kostka.

11—EPIPHANY (1903), Revs. Thomas F. Manion, Admin.; Garry G. Patriquin, Hospital Chaplain.
Res., 1018 Centre Ave., 15219. Tel: 412-471-0257.

12—OUR LADY HELP OF CHRISTIANS (Italian). Closed. See St. Charles Lwanga.

13—HOLY FAMILY (Polish). Closed. See Our Lady of the Angels.

14—HOLY ROSARY. Closed. See St. Charles Lwanga.

15—ST. HYACINTH (Polish). Closed. See St. Regis.

16—IMMACULATE CONCEPTION (1834) (Italian), Revs. Dale E. DeNinno, Admin.; William P. Siple; Robin S. Evanish. In res., Rev. Paul A. Holzer, (Retired).
Res., 4712 Liberty Ave., 15224. Tel: 412-682-5353; Fax: 412-682-6766.
School—Tel: 412-621-5199.
Sisters of the Holy Spirit, Pittsburgh 3; Lay Teachers 17; Students 446.

17—IMMACULATE HEART OF MARY (1897) (Polish), Rev. Joseph E. Swierczynski.
Res., 3058 Brereton Ave., 15219. Tel: 412-621-5170.
School—3029 Paulowna St., 15219. Tel: 412-621-1545.
Lay Teachers 10; Students 168.

18—ST. JOACHIM. Closed. See St. Rosalia.

19—ST. JOHN THE BAPTIST. Closed. See Our Lady of the Angels.

20—ST. JOSEPH (1872) (German), Revs. Dale E. DeNinno, Admin.; William R. Siple; Robin S. Evanish. In res., Rev. Paul A. Holzer, (Retired).
Res., 4712 Liberty Ave., 15224. Tel: 412-682-2354; Fax: 412-682-6766.

21—ST. KIERAN. Closed. See St. Matthew.

22—ST. LAWRENCE O'TOOLE (East End) (1897), Rev. James G. Graham. In res., Rev. Arthur R. Merrell.
Res., 5323 Penn Ave., 15224. Tel: 412-363-1771.

23—ST. MARTIN (West End). Closed. See Guardian Angels.

24—ST. MARY'S (Lawrenceville). Closed. See Our Lady of the Angels.

25—ST. MARY ASSUMPTION (Lawrenceville). Closed. See St. Matthew.

26—ST. MARY OF MERCY (1870), Revs. John M. O'Toole; Francis A. Siler. In res., Rev. Msgr. Francis A. Glenn, (Retired); Revs. Ronald P. Lengwin; William M. Miller.
Res., 202 Stanwix St., 15222. Tel: 412-261-0110; Fax: 412-261-0113.

27—ST. MATTHEW (1993). Consolidated from St. Kieran and St. Mary Assumption. Rev. Robert K. Yetsko, T.O.R.
Res., 5322 Carnegie St., 15201. Tel: 412-781-6701; Fax: 412-781-1331.
Catechesis/Religious Programs—Tel: 412-781-5192.
Students 130.

28—MOTHER OF GOOD COUNSEL (Italian). Closed. See St. Charles Lwanga.

29—OUR LADY OF THE ANGELS (1993). Consolidated from St. Augustine, Holy Family, St. John the Baptist and St. Mary. Revs. Paul M. Kuppe, O.F.M.Cap.; Gervase Degenhardt, O.F.M.Cap.; John Getsy, O.F.M.Cap. In res., Revs. Ralph Zehe, O.F.M.Cap.; Kenan Crowley, O.F.M.Cap.; Michael Joyce, O.F.M.Cap.
Res., 225 37th St., 15201. Tel: 412-682-6888; 682-0929 (office); Fax: 412-682-6889. [CEM]
School—St. John Neumann Regional Catholic Elementary School. See Consolidated Schools under Institutions Located in the Diocese. Tel: 412-682-5096; Fax: 412-682-0811.

30—OUR LADY OF THE MOST BLESSED SACRAMENT. Closed. See St. Charles Lwanga.

31—ST. LOUISE DE MARILLAC (1961), Revs. Thomas E. Kredel; David M. Cillo; John M. Bachkay. In res., Rev. Anthony Mghanga.
Res., 312 McMurray Rd., 15241. Tel: 412-833-1010; Fax: 412-833-6624.
School—310 McMurray Rd., 15241. Tel: 412-835-0600.
Felician Sisters 3; Lay Teachers 25; Students 561.
Catechesis/Religious Programs—Tel: 412-835-1155.
Students 1,056.

32—ST. PATRICK (Strip District). Closed. See St. Patrick-St. Stanislaus Kostka.

33—SS. PETER AND PAUL (East Liberty). Closed. See St. Charles Lwanga.

34—ST. PHILOMENA Squirrel Hill. Closed. See St. Bede.

35—ST. RAPHAEL (1911), Revs. Joseph V. Kurutz; Domenic Mancini. In res., Rev. John Charnoki.
Res., 1118 Chislett St., E., 15206. Tel: 412-661-3100; Fax: 412-363-3577.
School—1154 Chislett St., 15206. Tel: 412-661-0288.
Sisters of St. Joseph 2; Lay Teachers 16; Students 272.
Convent—1101 Jancey St., 15206. Tel: 412-661-6569.

36—ST. REGIS (1993). Merged with St. Hyacinth. Rev. William J. Cheetham.
Res., 3235 Parkview Ave., 15213. Tel: 412-681-9365; Fax: 412-681-1175.

37—ST. ROSALIA. Merged with St. Joachim. Revs. Joseph W. Reschick; Gary W. Oehmler.
Res., 411 Greenfield Ave., 15207. Tel: 412-421-5766; Fax: 412-421-4529.
School—Tel: 412-521-3005.
Sisters of the Immaculate Heart of Mary 7; Lay Teachers 21; Students 360.

38—SACRED HEART (1872), Most Rev. William J. Winter, V.G.; Revs. Francis J. Murhammer; John A. Reifsnyder; Miles Eric Diskin.
Res., 310 Shady Ave., 15206. Tel: 412-661-0187; Fax: 412-661-7932.
School—325 Emerson St., 15206. Tel: 412-441-1582.
Sisters of Charity 3; Lay Teachers 21; Students 465.

39—ST. STANISLAUS (Strip District) (Polish). Closed. See St. Patrick-St. Stanislaus Kostka.

40—ST. PATRICK-ST. STANISLAUS KOSTKA (1993). Consolidated of St. Stanislaus, St. Patrick and St. Elizabeth of Hungary. Revs. Thomas G. Schaefer, C.S.Sp.; Jean Claude Mbemba, C.S.S.P.
Parish Office: 1711 Liberty Ave., 15222. Tel: 412-471-4767; Fax: 412-471-1209.
Res., 57 21st St., 15222. Tel: 412-471-0434.

41—ST. STEPHEN (1993). Merged with St. Ann. Rev.

Cornelius W. McCaulley, S.T.L.
Mailing Address: 5115 Second Ave., 15207.
Res., 131 E. Elizabeth St., 15207. Tel: 412-421-9210.
School—134 E. Elizabeth St., 15207. Tel: 412-421-9447.
Sisters of Charity 1; Lay Teachers 10; Students 155.

SOUTH SIDE

42—St. Adalbert (Polish). Closed. See Prince of Peace.

43—St. Basil (1907) (German), Revs. Robert J. Meyer; Robert J. Miller. In res., Rev. Joseph C. Scheib.
Res., 1735 Brownsville Rd., 15210. Tel: 412-882-9763; Fax: 412-882-2476.
School—1803 Concordia St., 15210. Tel: 412-884-4434.
Sisters of Divine Providence 3; Lay Teachers 13; Students 301.
Catechesis/Religious Programs—Tel: 412-881-4440.
Students 410.
Convent—30 W. Willock Rd., 15227. Tel: 412-881-0638.

44—St. Canice (Knoxville). Closed. See St. John Vianney.

45—St. Casimir (Lithuanian). Closed. See Prince of Peace.

46—St. George (Allentown). Closed. See St. John Vianney.

47—Guardian Angels (West End) (1994). Merged with St. James and St. Martin. Revs. Robert J. Clarke; Mark A. Thomas.
Res., 1030 Logue St., 15220. Tel: 412-921-4077; Fax: 412-922-4945. [CEM]
School—Elizabeth Seton Elementary. See Holy Innocents (West End). Tel: 412-331-4529.

48—St. Henry. Closed. See St. John Vianney.

49—Holy Angels (1903), Rev. J. David Crowley, M.A.
Res., 408 Baldwin Rd., 15207. Tel: 412-461-6906; Fax: 412-461-0961.
Catechesis/Religious Programs—Tel: 412-461-8500.
Students 430.

50—Holy Innocents (1900), Revs. Donald N. Buchleitner; John B. Corbett.
Res., 3011 Landis St., 15204. Tel: 412-331-0268.
School—Elizabeth Seton Elementary, 3021 Landis St., 15204. Tel: 412-331-4529.
Sisters 1; Lay Teachers 20; Students 396.

51—St. James (West End). Closed. See Guardian Angels.

52—St. John the Evangelist. Closed. See Prince of Peace.

53—St. Josaphat (Polish). Closed. See Prince of Peace.

54—St. John Vianney (Hilltop) (1994). Consolidation of the the following churches: St. Canice, St. George, St. Henry, and St. Joseph. Revs. Charles S. Bober; Douglas A. Boyd; John E. Hissrich; Vincent F. Kolo; Mark A. Eckman.
823 Climax St., 15210. Tel: 412-381-8300; Fax: 412-431-3790. [CEM 2][JC]
School—Bishop Leonard Catholic School, 430 Cathedral Ave., 15210. Tel: 412-381-3541; Fax: 412-381-8611.
Catechesis/Religious Programs—Tel: 412-381-5581.
Students 465.

55—St. Justin (Mt. Washington) (1917), Rev. Walter C. Rydzon.
Res., 539 Boggs Ave., 15211. Tel: 412-381-9878.

56—St. Mary of the Mount (Mt. Washington) (1877), Rev. Louis F. Vallone; Deacon Robert Barth.
Res., 403 Grandview Ave., 15211. Tel: 412-381-0212; Fax: 412-381-9921.
School—Bigham St. & Grandview Ave., 15211. Tel: 412-431-4645.
Sisters of the Immaculate Heart of Mary 4; Sisters of Divine Providence 1; Lay Teachers 10; Students 237.

57—St. Matthew (Slovak). Closed. See Prince of Peace.

58—St. Michael (German). Closed. See Prince of Peace.

59—Our Lady of Loreto (1959), Rev. James W. Dolan.
Res., 1905 Pioneer Ave., 15226. Tel: 412-341-6161.

60—St. Pamphilus (1960), Rev. James T. Merlino, O.F.M. In res., Rev. R. Stephen Almango, O.F.M.
Res., 948 Tropical Ave., 15216. Tel: 412-341-1000; Fax: 412-341-6956.
Church—1000 Tropical Ave., 15216. Tel: 412-531-8449; Fax: 412-531-0660.

61—St. Peter. Closed. See Prince of Peace.

62—St. Pius X (1954), Rev. Thomas M. Marpes. In res., Revs. Richard M. Lelonis; Michael Mukasa (Uganda).
Res., 3040 Pioneer Ave., 15226. Tel: 412-563-5423.
School—Brookline Regional Catholic School, (Grades PreK-8) 2690 Waddington Ave., 15226. Tel: 412-563-0858; 341-6163.
Lay Teachers 25; Students 523.
Catechesis/Religious Programs—Tel: 412-563-1588.
Students 140.

63—Prince of Peace (1992). Consolidated from the following churches: St. Adalbert, St. Casimir, St. John the Evangelist, St. Josaphat, St. Matthew, St. Michael and St. Peter. Rev. Bernard M. Harcarik, V.F. Team Ministers: Revs. John B. Lendvai; David J. Jastrab; John F. Walsh.
Res., 81 S. 13th St., 15203-1897. Tel: 412-431-8380; Fax: 412-431-0209. [CEM 6]

64—Resurrection (Brookline), Revs. Joseph P. Grosko; Victor J. Rocha; Deacon Richard Very. In res., Rev. Paul Mwangi.
Res., 1100 Creedmoor Ave., 15226. Tel: 412-563-4400; Fax: 412-563-4403.
Catechesis/Religious Programs—Tel: 412-343-7111.
Students 218.

65—St. Vincent (Esplen). Closed. See St. John of God, McKees Rocks.

66—St. Wendelin (Carrick) (1873), Revs. Thomas M. O'Donnell; Joseph G. Luisi.
Res., 2728 Custer Ave., 15227. Tel: 412-882-1480. [CEM]
School—Bishop John B. McDowell Regional School, 3198 Schieck St., 15227. Tel: 412-884-5676.
Catechesis/Religious Programs—Tel: 412-882-3414.
Students 160.

NORTH SIDE

67—St. Ambrose. Merged with St. Boniface to form Holy Wisdom.

68—Annunciation. Closed. See Incarnation of the Lord.

69—St. Boniface. Merged with St. Ambrose to form Holy Wisdom.

70—St. Cyril of Alexandria (1924), Very Rev. Thomas B. Ferris, V.F. In res., Rev. Charles L. Christen.
Res., 3854 Brighton Rd., 15212. Tel: 412-761-1552; Fax: 412-761-1059.
School—Tel: 412-761-5043.
Sisters of Mercy of the Diocese of Pittsburgh 3; Lay Teachers 13; Students 261.
Catechesis/Religious Programs—Tel: 412-734-0505. Jean M. DiDonato, D.R.E.
Students 155.
Convent—3830 Parviss St., 15212. Tel: 412-766-8338.

71—St. Francis Xavier. Closed. See Risen Lord.

72—St. Gabriel Archangel (Slovak). Closed. See Risen Lord.

73—Holy Wisdom (1994), Very Rev. Lawrence A. DiNardo, M.Ch.A., J.C.L., V.E.; Rev. Msgr. Donald W. Kraus; Rev. Eugene J. Dougherty.
Res., 1025 Haslage Ave., 15212-3429. Tel: 412-231-1116; Fax: 412-231-1072. [CEM]

74—Incarnation of the Lord (1993). Consolidated from Annunciation and Nativity of Our Lord. Rev. Joseph F. Keenan; Sr. Catherine Fedewa, C.F.S.N., Pastoral Assoc. In res., Rev. Matthew Ekwuribe (Nigeria).
Res., 4071 Franklin Ave., 15214. Tel: 412-931-2911; Fax: 412-931-2832.
School—4072 Franklin Rd., 15214. Tel: 412-931-2330.
Sisters 1; Lay Teachers 9; Students 192.

75—St. Joseph. Closed. See St. Peter.

76—St. Leo. Closed. See Risen Lord.

77—Our Lady Queen of Peace. Closed. See St. Peter.

78—Most Holy Name of Jesus (Troy Hill) (1868) (German), Revs. W. David Schorr; James L. Aaron. In res., Revs. Dominic Dery; Andre Quenum.
Res., 1700 Harpster St., 15212-4393. Tel: 412-231-2994. [CEM]
School—1515 Tinsbury St., 15212. Tel: 412-322-6226.
Lay Teachers 10; Students 163.
Catechesis/Religious Programs—Tel: 412-231-3002.
Students 155.

79—Nativity of Our Lord. Closed. See Incarnation of the Lord.

80—St. Nicholas (Croatian). Closed. See St. Nicholas.

81—St. Peter (1993). Consolidated from St. Cyprian, St. Mary's, Mary Immaculate & Our Lady, Queen of Peace, St. Joseph, St. Peter and St. Wenceslaus. Revs. Benjamin Walker, O.S.B.; John-Mary Tompkins, O.S.B.
Res., 720 Arch St., 15212. Tel: 412-321-0711; Fax: 412-321-7807. [CEM]
School—711 W. Commons St., 15212. Tel: 412-231-8248; Fax: 412-231-0835.
Lay Teachers 11; Students 157.

82—Regina Coeli (Italian). Closed. For sacramental records contact St. Cyril of Alexandria.

83—Risen Lord (1993). Consolidated from the following churches: St. Francis Xavier, St. Gabriel Archangel, St. Leo and Our Lady of Perpetual Help. Revs. Vincent Velas; Robert Schweitzer.
Res., 3250 California Ave., 15212. Tel: 412-761-1507; Fax: 412-761-1508.
School—(Grades K-8). Tel: 412-766-7828.
Sisters 1; Lay Teachers 6; Students 93.

84—St. Wenceslaus. Closed. See St. Peter.

OUTSIDE THE CITY OF PITTSBURGH

Aleppo Township, Allegheny Co., St. Mary (1852), Rev. Msgr. John C. McCarren.
Res., 444 Glenfield Rd., Sewickley, 15143. Tel: 412-741-6460. [CEM]

Aliquippa, Beaver Co., St. Titus (1994). Merged with St. Joseph, West Aliquippa. Revs. John P. Sweeney; Robert J. Grecco. In res., Rev. Edward R. Day.
Res., 952 Franklin Ave., 15001. Tel: 412-378-8561. [JC 2]
School—107 Sycamore St., 15001. Tel: 412-378-7940.
Sisters of St. Joseph 1; Lay Teachers 11; Students 165.
Catechesis/Religious Programs—Tel: 412-378-8665.
Students 200.

Allison Park, Allegheny Co., St. Ursula (1908), Revs. Garret D. Dorsey; Ernest Strelinski, P.A.
Res., 3937 Kirk Ave., 15101. Tel: 412-486-6700.
School—Tel: 412-486-5511.
Sisters 1; Lay Teachers 15; Students 224.
Catechesis/Religious Programs—Tel: 412-486-3374.
Students 445.

Ambridge, Beaver Co.,

1—St. Veronica. Closed. See Good Samaritan.

2—Divine Redeemer. Closed. See Good Samaritan.

3—St. Stanislaus. Closed. See Good Samaritan.

4—Church of Christ the King. Closed. See Good Samaritan.

5—Holy Trinity, (Croatian). Closed. See Good Samaritan.

6—Good Samaritan, (1994). Consolidated from the following churches: St. Veronica, Divine Redeemer, St. Stanislaus, Christ the King and Holy Trinity. Revs. John Bauer; John Skirtich; Mark Thomas, S.T.L.
Res., 725 Glenwood Ave., 15003. Tel: 412-266-6565; Fax: 412-266-5570. [CEM][JC]
School—Tel: 412-266-1670.
Catechesis/Religious Programs—Tel: 412-266-2194.
Students 433.

Aspinwall, Allegheny Co., St. Scholastica, Rev. Robert G. Duch, Ph.D.
Res., 309 Brilliant Ave., 15215. Tel: 412-781-0186.
School—205 Brilliant Ave., 15215.
Sisters of the Third Order of St. Francis 1; Lay Teachers 13; Students 211.
Catechesis/Religious Programs—Third & Maple Sts., Pittsburgh, 15215. Tel: 412-781-0288; Fax: 412-781-4316.
Students 273.

Avella, Washington Co., St. Michael (1917), Rev. Pierre G. Sodini, S.T.L.
Res., 95 Highland Ave., P.O. Box 145, 15312. Tel: 412-587-3570. [CEM]

Baden, Beaver Co., St. John the Baptist (1866), Rev. Joseph J. Dascenzo.
Res., Linmore Ave., P.O. Box 171, 15005. Tel: 412-869-2280; Fax: 412-869-0305. [CEM]

Bairdford, Allegheny Co., St. Victor (1919), Revs. C. William Hausen; Roland Ripoli, O.S.B.
Res., Box 149, 15006. Tel: 412-265-2070; Fax: 412-265-6316.
Catechesis/Religious Programs—Tel: 412-265-4040.
Students 459.

Baldwin Boro, Allegheny Co., St. Albert the Great (1956), Revs. Charles W. Speicher, Ph.D.; Edward Kryston; Deacon Robert J. Becker. In res., Rev. Msgr. Daniel A. Gearing.
Res., 3171 Churchview Ave., 15227. Tel: 412-884-7744.
School—Bishop John B. McDowell Regional School, (Grades PreK-8) 3198 Schieck St., 15227. Tel: 412-884-5676; Fax: 412-884-8610.
Lay Teachers 18; Students 285.
Catechesis/Religious Programs—Tel: 412-884-8282. Anita Bridge, D.R.E.
Students 382.

Beaver, Beaver Co., SS. Peter and Paul (1830), Rev. Msgr. Raymond T. Schultz, V.F.; Rev. Daniel B. Dixon. In res., Rev. Regis R. Alberth.
Res., 200 Third St., 15009. Tel: 412-775-4111. [CEM]
School—370 E. End Ave., 15009. Tel: 412-774-4450.
Sisters of Divine Providence 1; Lay Teachers 11; Students 173.
Catechesis/Religious Programs—Students 361.

Beaver Falls, Beaver Co., Divine Mercy (1994). Consolidated from St. Mary and Holy Trinity. Rev. William P. O'Malley. In res., Rev. Paul J. Savage, S.T.L.
Res., 605 Tenth St., 15010. Tel: 412-846-4585; Fax: 412-846-7814. [CEM]
School—609 Tenth St., 15010. Tel: 412-846-5955.
Lay Teachers 12; Students 170.
Catechesis/Religious Programs—Tel: 412-846-8133.
Students 175.

Holy Trinity (Polish). Closed. See Divine Mercy.

St. Philomena (1948), Rev. J. Francis Frazer.
Res., 3908 Sixth Ave., 15010. Tel: 412-843-7375.
School—Tel: 412-846-2272.
Lay Teachers 8; Students 163.

Bellevue, Allegheny Co., Assumption of the Blessed Virgin Mary on the Beautiful River (1903), Revs. Robert J. Boyle; John P. Hickey; Paul W. Merkovsky.
Res., 45 N. Sprague Ave., 15202. Tel: 412-766-6660; Fax: 412-766-4836.
School—35 N. Jackson Ave., 15202. Tel: 412-761-7887.
Lay Teachers 21; Students 307.
Catechesis/Religious Programs—Pittsburgh, Tel: 412-766-4046.
Students 431.

Bentleyville, Washington Co., St. Luke. Closed. See Ave Maria, Ellsworth.

Bessemer, Lawrence Co., St. Anthony (1909), Rev. James A. Downs.
Res., W. Poland Ave., P.O. Box 3, 16112. Tel: 412-667-7737. [CEM]

Bethel Park, Allegheny Co., St. Germaine (1957), Rev. Nicholas A. Pesanka; Sr. Mary Faith Balawejder, C.S.S.F., Pastoral Assoc.
Res., 7003 Baptist Rd., 15102. Tel: 412-833-0661; Fax: 412-833-4036.
School—7001 Baptist Rd., 15102. Tel: 412-833-0223.
Felician Sisters 3; Lay Teachers 13; Students 170.
Catechesis/Religious Programs—Tel: 412-833-6662.
Students 228.

St. Thomas More (1953), Revs. Kenneth R. White; David J. Bonnar; J. Edward Suhoza.
Res., 126 Fort Couch Rd., Pittsburgh, 15241. Tel: 412-833-0031; Fax: 412-833-5995.
School—134 Fort Couch Rd., Pittsburgh, 15241. Tel: 412-833-1412.
Lay Teachers 17; Students 253.
Catechesis/Religious Programs—Tel: 412-835-6996; Fax: 412-833-5995.
Students 525.

St. Valentine (1931), Revs. John A. Harvey; F. Raymond Trance; David D. DeWitt.
Res., 2710 Ohio St., 15102. Tel: 412-835-4415; Fax: 412-835-4417.
School—(Grades PreK-8) 2709 Mesta St., 15102. Tel: 412-835-3780.
Sisters of St. Francis 1; Lay Teachers 17; Students 357.
Catechesis/Religious Programs—Tel: 412-831-6466.
Students 733.

Blawnox, Allegheny Co., St. Edward (1938), Rev. Russell J. Maurer. In res., Rev. Thomas M. Kirby.
Res., 450 Walnut St., Pittsburgh, 15238. Tel: 412-828-4066.
Catechesis/Religious Programs—Tel: 412-828-7310.
Students 135.

Bobtown, Greene Co., St. Ignatius of Antioch (1924), Rev. Alvin Gutierrez.
Res., Box 63, 15315. Tel: 412-839-7122.
Catechesis/Religious Programs—Tel: 412-839-7208; 943-3844.
Students 112.
Mission—Greensboro, Greene Co., Holy Family, Greensboro, 15338.

Boyers, Butler Co., St. Alphonsus (1841). Merged with Epiphany, St. Paschal and St. Louis, W. Sunbury. Rev. Albert C. Koser.
Mailing Address: P.O. Box 46, 16020.
Res., 2709 W. Sunbury Rd., 16020. Tel: 412-791-2393. [CEM][JC 3]
Catechesis/Religious Programs—Students 200.

Braddock, Allegheny Co., Good Shepherd, Revs. Albert L. Zapf; Robert J. Zajdel. In res., Rev. Joseph D. Karabin.
Res., 416 Verona St., 15104. Tel: 412-271-1515.
School—1025 Braddock Ave., 15104. Tel: 412-271-2492. Joanne Schleifer, Prin.
Sisters 3; Lay Teachers 8; Students 155.
Convent—Tel: 412-271-1736.

Braddock Hills, Allegheny Co., Sacred Heart (1897) (Polish), Rev. Albert L. Zapf, Admin.
Res., 1600 Brinton Rd., 15221-4902. Tel: 412-829-2161.

Brentwood, Allegheny Co., St. Sylvester (1927), Revs. Robert R. Werthman; Leroy A. DiPietro; Very Rev. Robert J. Ahlin; Deacon Joseph R. Mueller.
Res., 3754 Brownsville Rd., 15227. Tel: 412-882-8593; Fax: 412-882-0153.
School—30 W. Willock Rd., 15227. Tel: 412-882-9900.
Sisters of Divine Providence 2; Lay Teachers 11; Students 227.
Catechesis/Religious Programs—Tel: 412-881-4142.
Students 332.

Bridgeville, Allegheny Co.,

1—St. Agatha, (1894). Closed. See Holy Child.

2—Holy Child, (1994). Consolidated from St. Agatha and St. Anthony. Revs. Frederick L. Cain; Pierce M. Falkenhan; John E. Dinello. In res., Rev. George T. DeVille, Chap., Mayview State Hospital.
Res., 212 Station St., 15017. Tel: 412-221-5213. [CEM]
School—Tel: 412-221-4720.
Sisters 2; Lay Teachers 16; Students 276.
Catechesis/Religious Programs—Tel: 412-221-6514. Mrs. Cherie Drobycki.
Students 430.
Convent—509 Coulter St., 15017. Tel: 412-221-8930.

3—St. Anthony, (1915) (Lithuanian). Closed. See Holy Child.

4—St. Barbara, (1894), Rev. William F. Kohler.
Res., 45 Prestley Rd., 15017-1971. Tel: 412-221-5152. [CEM]

Bulger, Washington Co., St. Ann (1917), Rev. Rudolph M. Silvers.
Res., 967 Grant St., Box 488, 15019-0488. Tel: 412-796-3791.

Burgettstown, Washington Co., Our Lady of Lourdes (1916), Rev. Richard J. Tusky.
Res., 621 S. Main St., 15021. Tel: 412-947-3363; Fax: 412-947-9348. [CEM]
School—620 Main St., 15021. Tel: 412-947-5076.
Lay Teachers 10; Students 183.

Butler, Butler Co.,

1—St. Fidelis of Sigmaringen, (1995), Revs. James F. Murphy; George Palick.
Res., 125 Buttercup Rd., 16001. Tel: 412-482-2690; Fax: 412-482-2315.
Catechesis/Religious Programs—Tel: 412-482-2362. Mrs. Edythe M. Schirra.
Students 482.

2—St. Michael the Archangel, (1909) (Italian-French), Rev. Matthew R. Cirilli.
Res., 432 Center Ave., 16001. Tel: 412-282-4107; Fax: 412-282-9365. [CEM]
School—Butler Consolidated Schools. See separate listing.
Catechesis/Religious Programs—Tel: 412-282-3156.
Students 225.

3—St. Paul, (1867), Revs. Hugh M. Gloninger; James L. Armstrong; Deacons Raymond C. Rice; Gerald C. Stein, (Retired). In res., Rev. Henry S. Preneta (GBG) Hospital Chaplain.
Res., 128 N. McKean St., 16001. Tel: 412-287-1759.
School—Butler Consolidated Schools. See separate listing. Tel: 412-285-4276; Fax: 412-285-4896.
Catechesis/Religious Programs—Andrea Sleigh.
Students 375.

4—St. Peter, (1821) (German), Rev. Jack Nanz.
Res., 127 Franklin St., 16001. Tel: 412-287-2743; Fax: 412-287-8447. [CEM]
School—Butler Consolidated Schools. See separate listing. Tel: 412-285-4276.
Catechesis/Religious Programs—201 Franklin St., 16001. Tel: 412-285-3249.
Students 320.

5—St. Wendelin, (1863), Rev. Wendel Moliski, O.F.M.Cap.
Res., 210 St. Wendelin Rd., 16001. Tel: 412-287-0820. [CEM]
School—(Grades PreK-6) 211 St. Wendelin Rd., 16001. Tel: 412-285-4986.
Lay Teachers 6; Students 97.
Catechesis/Religious Programs—Students 106.

Cabot, Butler Co., St. Joseph (1904), Rev. Louis J. Petruha, O.F.M.Cap.; Sr. Natalie Lann, C.S.J., Pastoral Assoc.
Res., 315 Stoney Hollow Rd., 16023. Tel: 412-352-2149; Fax: 412-352-7174.
Catechesis/Religious Programs—Tel: 412-352-3030.
Students 363.

California, Washington Co., St. Thomas Aquinas (1888), Rev. Timothy F. Whalen, M.A.
Res., 213 Fourth St., 15419. Tel: 412-938-3204; Fax: 412-938-0434. [CEM]

Canonsburg, Washington Co., St. Patrick (1993). Merged with St. Genevieve. Revs. Philip J. Przybyla; James E. Seeger; Patrick Hynes; Deacon Joseph C. Meyer, Jr.
Res., 317 W. Pike St., 15317. Tel: 412-745-6560; Fax: 412-746-1112. [CEM]
School—Hutchinson & Murdock Sts., 15317. Tel: 412-745-7977.
Priests 3; Sisters of St. Francis 1; Lay Teachers 11; Students 187.
Catechesis/Religious Programs—Tel: 412-745-3787.
Students 592.

St. Genevieve (Polish). Closed. See St. Patrick.

Carmichaels, Greene Co., St. Hugh (1951), Rev. Francis A. Nazimek.
Res., 408 Rte. 88, 15320. Tel: 412-966-7270.
Catechesis/Religious Programs—Students 146.

Carnegie, Allegheny Co.,

1—St. Elizabeth Ann Seton, (1992) (Italian-German). Consolidated from the following churches: Holy Souls, St. Ignatius de Loyola, Immaculate Conception, St. Joseph, St. Luke and St. Vincent de Paul, Walkers Mill. Revs. Rudolph F. Smoley; Robert M. Staszewski.
Res., 206 Mary St., 15106-2489. Tel: 412-276-1011; Fax: 412-276-0816.
Catechesis/Religious Programs—127 Finley Ave., 15106. Tel: 412-279-8118.
Students 103.

2—Holy Souls. Closed. See St. Elizabeth Ann Seton.

3—St. Ignatius de Loyola, (Polish). Closed. See St. Elizabeth Ann Seton.

4—Immaculate Conception, (Polish). Closed. See St. Elizabeth Ann Seton.

5—St. Joseph, (German). Closed. See St. Elizabeth Ann Seton.

6—St. Luke. Closed. See St. Elizabeth Ann Seton.

Castle Shannon, Allegheny Co., St. Anne (1889), Revs. Donald P. Breier; Michael L. Yaksick; Dam Nguyen. In res., Rev. Msgr. Charles O. Rice, Pastor Emeritus.
Res., 400 Hoodridge Dr., Pittsburgh, 15234. Tel: 412-531-5964; Fax: 412-531-6136. [CEM]
School—4040 Willow Ave., Pittsburgh, 15234. Tel: 412-561-7720; Fax: 412-561-7927.
Lay Teachers 16; Students 274.
Catechesis/Religious Programs—Tel: 412-561-0101.
Students 490.

Cecil, Washington Co., St. Mary (1909), Rev. Msgr. Robert P. Garland.
Res., 10 St. Mary's Ln., Box 285, 15321. Tel: 412-221-1560. [CEM]
Catechesis/Religious Programs—Tel: 412-221-0595.
Students 218.

Center Township, Beaver Co., St. Frances Cabrini (1961), Revs. Joseph J. Kleppner, S.T.L., Ph.D.; Chuck Baptiste; Daniel B. Dixon.
Res., 115 Trinity Ave., Aliquippa, 15001. Tel: 412-775-6363.
Catechesis/Religious Programs—Tel: 412-775-3848.
Students 605.

St. Andrew, Butler Co., (1964), Rev. Paul G. Spisak.
Res., 1660 N. Main St., Ext., Butler, 16001. Tel: 412-287-7781; Fax: 412-287-7346.

Charleroi, Washington Co.,

1—St. Jerome. Closed. See Mary Mother of the Church.

2—SS. Cyril and Methodius, (Slovak). Closed. See Mary Mother of the Church.

3—Mary Mother of the Church, (1892). Consolidated from SS. Cyril & Methodius, St. Jerome and Mother of Sorrows. Rev. John A. Marcucci, Team Ministry Moderator. Team Ministers: Revs. David F. Dzermejko; Joseph E. Feltz.
Res., 624 Washington Ave., 15022-1989. Tel: 412-483-5533; Fax: 412-483-0122. [CEM]
Catechesis/Religious Programs—Tel: 412-483-2402.
Students 603.

4—Mother of Sorrows, (Italian). Closed. See Mary Mother of the Church.

Chicora, Butler Co., Mater Dolorosa, Rev. Bartley A. Sorensen.
Res., P.O. Box 243, 16025. Tel: 412-445-2275.
Catechesis/Religious Programs—Students 200.

Chippewa Township, Beaver Co., Christ the Divine Teacher (1969), Rev. Harry R. Sangl.
Res., 116 Thorndale Dr., Beaver Falls, 15010. Tel:

412-846-7540.
Catechesis/Religious Programs—Tel: 412-847-4750.
Students 275.

Churchill Borough, Allegheny Co., St. John Fisher (1960), Rev. Carl J. Gentile.
Res., 33 Lewin Ln., Pittsburgh, 15235. Tel: 412-241-4722.
Catechesis/Religious Programs—Tel: 412-241-4653.
Students 137.

Clairton, Allegheny Co., St. Clare of Assisi (1994). Consolidated from the following churches: St. Joseph, St. Paulinus and St. Clare. Revs. Peter P. Murphy; David J. Kriss.
Office: 314 Wilson Ave., 15025. Tel: 412-233-7870. [CEM]
School—336 Wilson Ave., 15025. Tel: 412-233-7598.
Catechesis/Religious Programs—Students 200.
St. Joseph. Closed. See St. Clare of Assisi.
St. Paulinus. Closed. See St. Clare of Assisi.

Clarksville, Washington Co., St. Thomas (1992), Rev. Thomas R. Miller.
Res., R.D. No. 1, 15322. Tel: 412-377-2588. [CEM]

Conway, Beaver Co., Our Lady of Peace (1941), Revs. Roy Schuster, O.F.M.Cap.; Mark Carter, O.F.M.Cap.; Bernard Finerty, O.F.M.Cap.
Res., 1000 Third Ave., 15027. Tel: 412-869-3024.
Catechesis/Religious Programs—Tel: 412-869-4723.
Students 345.

Coraopolis, Allegheny Co., St. Joseph (1891), Revs. Lawrence V. Holpp; Timothy Dawes.
Res., 1304 Fourth Ave., 15108. Tel: 412-264-6162. [CEM]
School—Tel: 412-264-6141.
Felician Sisters 3; Lay Teachers 8; Students 205.
Catechesis/Religious Programs—1313 Fifth Ave., 15108. Tel: 412-262-2828.
Students 171.

Coylesville, Butler Co., St. John, Rev. Raymond C. Boccardi, Admin.
Res., 455 Clearfield Rd., Fenelton, 16034. Tel: 412-287-7590. [CEM]
Catechesis/Religious Programs—Students 200.

Crafton, Allegheny Co., St. Philip (1839) (Irish), Revs. James J. Schmitt; Kenneth R. Keene, Parochial Vicar.
Res., 50 W. Crafton Ave., Pittsburgh, 15205. Tel: 412-922-6300; Fax: 412-920-7310. [CEM]
School—52 W. Crafton Ave., Pittsburgh, 15205. Tel: 412-928-2742.
Sisters of Charity 3; Lay Teachers 18; Students 320.
Catechesis/Religious Programs—Tel: 412-928-2744.
Students 394.

Cranberry Township, Butler Co., St. Ferdinand (1961), Revs. John P. Gallagher; Joseph P. Newell; Deacon John J. Walsh; Barbara McCarthy, Pastoral Assoc.
Res., 2535 Rochester Rd., 16066-6496. Tel: 412-776-2888; Fax: 412-776-2378.
Catechesis/Religious Programs—Tel: 412-776-9177. Clara Kana, D.R.E.
Students 1,761.

Creighton, Allegheny Co., Holy Family (East Deer Twp.) (1949), Rev. Robert F. Rishel.
Res., 787 Freeport Rd., 15030. Tel: 412-224-1626.

Darlington, Beaver Co., St. Rose of Lima (1871), Rev. James B. Krah.
Res., 3357 Constitution Blvd., 16115. Tel: 412-843-0152.
Catechesis/Religious Programs—Students 184.
Mission—New Galilee, Beaver Co., St. Ann, New Galilee, 16141.

Donora, Washington Co.,

1—St. Charles. Closed. See Our Lady of the Valley.

2—St. Dominic, (Slovak). Closed. See Our Lady of the Valley.

3—Holy Name of the Blessed Virgin Mary. Closed. See Our Lady of the Valley.

4—Our Lady of the Valley, (1992). Consolidated from the following churches: St. Charles, St. Dominic, Holy Name of the Blessed Virgin Mary and St. Philip Neri. Revs. Raymond R. Rhoden, Team Ministry Moderator; John L. O'Shea, Team Minister.
Res., 571 Thompson Ave., 15033. Tel: 412-379-7777; 379-4777; Fax: 412-379-6242. [CEM]
Catechesis/Religious Programs—Second St. Ext. & Park Manor Rd., 15033. Tel: 412-379-5977.
Students 205.

5—St. Philip Neri, (Italian). Closed. See Our Lady of the Valley.

Duquesne, Allegheny Co., Holy Name. Closed. See Christ the Light of the World.
St. Joseph (1897) (German), Rev. L. James Susany. In res., Rev. Joseph Kariuki (Kenya).
Res., 817 W. Grant Ave., 15110. Tel: 412-466-1304. [CEM]
School—Duquesne Consolidated Schools. See separate listing. Tel: 412-466-3895.
Christ the Light of the World (1994). Consolidated from St. Hedwig and Holy Name. Rev. Dennis Colamarino.
Res., 32 S. First St., 15110. Tel: 412-469-0196. [CEM]
Catechesis/Religious Programs—Students 154.

East McKeesport, Allegheny Co., St. Robert Bellarmine (1952), Revs. John G. Oesterle; Malcolm McDonald.
Res., 1313 Fifth Ave., 15035. Tel: 412-824-2644; 824-2635; Fax: 412-824-2635.
Catechesis/Religious Programs—Tel: 412-824-3688.
Students 282.

East Pittsburgh, Allegheny Co., St. William. Closed. See Holy Cross.
St. Helen (Slovak). Closed. See Holy Cross.
Holy Cross (1994). Consolidated from St. William and St. Helen. Rev. Miroslaus A. Wojcicki.
Res., 905 Main St., 15112. Tel: 412-829-1146.
Convent—(Allison Park) 515 Howard St., 15112. Tel: 412-829-0815. Sisters of Divine Providence Sisters 4.

Elizabeth, Allegheny Co., St. Michael (1849), Revs. Timothy G. Evans; Edward R. Day.
Res., 101 McLay Dr., 15037. Tel: 412-751-0663; Fax: 412-751-2161. [CEM]
School—Sixth & Bayard St., 15037. Tel: 412-384-9400.
Lay Teachers 7; Students 140.
Catechesis/Religious Programs—Students 329.

Ellsworth, Washington Co., Ave Maria (1994). Consolidated from St. Luke and St. Clement. Rev. Mark J. Skertich.
Mailing Address: P.O. Box 590, 15331. Tel: 412-239-2227; Fax: 412-239-2272.
Res., 126 Church St., Bentleyville, 15314. Tel: 412-239-3591. [CEM]
School—Ave Maria School, Tel: 412-239-2226; Fax: 412-239-2272.
Catechesis/Religious Programs—Students 156.

Ellwood City, Lawrence Co., St. Agatha (1895), Rev. Paul Henne.
Res., 124 Fifth St., 16117. Tel: 412-758-7587. [CEM]
Catechesis/Religious Programs—Tel: 412-752-1271.
Students 280.
Purification of the Blessed Virgin Mary (1914) (Italian), Revs. Mauro Cautela; Nicholas A. Spirko.
Res., 415 Fourth St., 16117. Tel: 412-758-4411; Fax: 412-758-5563.
School—(Grades K-6). Tel: 412-758-5591; Fax: 412-752-1466.
Sisters 3; Lay Teachers 11; Students 258.
Catechesis/Religious Programs—Tel: 412-758-5562; Fax: 412-752-1466.
Students 392.

Elrama, Allegheny Co., St. Isaac Jogues (1950), Rev. Robert Andrew Kohuch.
Res., Box 600, 15038. Tel: 412-384-4406.

Emsworth, Allegheny Co., Sacred Heart (1891), Revs. Ralph J. Poirier, C.S.Sp.; Francis P. Meenan, C.S.Sp.; John P. Skaj, C.S.Sp.
Res., 154 Orchard Ave., Pittsburgh, 15202. Tel: 412-761-6651; Fax: 412-766-8298.
Catechesis/Religious Programs—Tel: 412-761-3806. Linda McKenzie, D.R.E.
Students 207.

Etna, Allegheny Co., All Saints (1902), Revs. John Vojtek; Jim Orr.
Res., 19 Wilson St., Pittsburgh, 15223-1798. Tel: 412-781-0530; Fax: 412-784-8769.
Preschool—20 Wilson St., Pittsburgh, 15223. Tel: 412-781-4692.
Students 36.
School—19 Dewey St., Pittsburgh, 15223. Tel: 412-782-0939. Bernadine Srocki, M.Ed, Ed.D, Prin.
Lay Teachers 11; Students 183.
Catechesis/Religious Programs—19 1/2 Dewey St., Pittsburgh, 15223. Tel: 412-782-3307. Sr. Mary Catherine Blooming, H.M., D.R.E.
Students 274.
Social Service—Tel: 412-781-2044. Sr. Florence Klaniecki, C.S.F.N., Ph.D.

Evans City, Butler Co., St. Matthias (1939), Rev. William J. Ritzert.
Res., 417 E. Main St., 16033. Tel: 412-538-5331.
Catechesis/Religious Programs—Tel: 412-538-5331.
Students 174.

Finleyville, Washington Co., St. Francis of Assisi (1893), Rev. John Gudewicz.
Res., 3609 Washington Ave., 15332. Tel: 412-348-7145. [CEM]
Catechesis/Religious Programs—Tel: 412-348-6190.
Students 225.

Forest Hills, Allegheny Co., St. Maurice (1949), Rev. Robert M. Franco, M.Ch.A.
Res., 2001 Ardmore Blvd., Pittsburgh, 15221. Tel: 412-271-0809; Fax: 412-271-2415.
School—Tel: 412-351-5403.
Sisters of Mercy (Pittsburgh) 4; Lay Teachers 17; Students 458.
Catechesis/Religious Programs—Tel: 412-352-5404; Fax: 412-271-2415.
Students 200.

Franklin Park Borough, Allegheny Co., Saints John and Paul (1994), Rev. Msgr. Daniel N. DiNardo.
Res., 2586 Wexford-Bayne Rd., Sewickley, 15143. Tel: 412-935-2104; Fax: 412-935-8320.
Catechesis/Religious Programs—Tel: 412-935-7153. Phyllis Haney, D.R.E.
Students 796.
St. John Neumann (1979), Revs. William R. Bovard; Robert R. Coyne.
Res., 1543 Old Orchard Rd., Pittsburgh, 15237. Tel: 412-366-2020; Fax: 412-366-2866.
Catechesis/Religious Programs—2230 Rochester Rd., Pittsburgh, 15237. Tel: 412-366-5885.
Students 1,000.

Fredericktown, Washington Co., St. Michael the Archangel. Closed. See St. Oliver Plunkett, Marianna.

Freedom, Beaver Co., St. Felix (1906) (Italian), Rev. Leon Leitem, O.F.M.Cap.
Res., 450 13th St., 15042. Tel: 412-775-1476. [CEM]
Catechesis/Religious Programs—Tel: 412-728-4421.
Students 140.

Glade Mills, Butler Co., Holy Sepulcher (1944), Rev. John P. Maloney. In res., Rev. Gregory Mallya (Tanzania).
Res., 1304 E. Cruikshank Rd., Butler, 16001. Tel: 412-586-7610; Fax: 412-586-7247.
School—Tel: 412-586-5022.
Lay Teachers 9; Students 188.
Catechesis/Religious Programs—Tel: 412-586-7276.
Students 421.

Glassport, Allegheny Co., St. Cecilia. Closed. See Queen of the Rosary.
Queen of the Rosary (1994). Consolidated from Holy Cross and St. Cecilia. Rev. Casimir Kedzierski.
Res., 530 Michigan Ave., 15045. Tel: 412-672-7209; Fax: 412-672-6390.
School—St. Joseph Regional School. See separate listing. 15133. Tel: 412-678-0659.
Catechesis/Religious Programs—Tel: 412-672-7910.
Students 190.

Glenshaw, Allegheny Co., St. Bonaventure (1957), Revs. George C. Newmeyer; James R. Gretz, Jr.; James R. Torquato.
Res., 2001 Mount Royal Blvd., 15116. Tel: 412-486-2606; Fax: 412-492-9329.
School—Tel: 412-486-2608.
Sisters of Divine Providence 1; Lay Teachers 25; Students 483.
Catechesis/Religious Programs—Tel: 412-486-0800.
Students 462.
St. Mary (1834), Revs. Walter J. Benz, V.F.; Paul Grunebach; John McKenna.
Res., 2510 Middle Rd., 15116. Tel: 412-486-4100; Fax: 412-486-4150. [CEM]
School—Tel: 412-486-7611.
Sisters of Divine Providence 1; Lay Teachers 24; Students 427.
Catechesis/Religious Programs—Tel: 412-486-5521; 492-9344. D.R.E.: Rose Stegman, (Elementary); Eileen Arena, (Adult Educ. & High School).
Students 714.

Green Tree, Allegheny Co., St. Margaret (1938), Revs. Harry E. Nichols; Philip N. Farrell.
Res., 310 Mansfield Ave., Pittsburgh, 15220. Tel: 412-921-0745.
School—915 Alice St., Pittsburgh, 15220. Tel: 412-922-4765.
Lay Teachers 20; Students 337.
Catechesis/Religious Programs—Tel: 412-921-7999.
Students 328.

Harmarville, Allegheny Co., St. Francis of Assisi, Rev. Hugh J. McCormley.
Res., 2599 Freeport Rd., Pittsburgh, 15238. Tel: 412-828-3123.

Harwick, Allegheny Co., Our Lady of Victory (1944), Rev. Alfred C. Cicola. In res., Rev. Gregory C. Swiderski.
Res., 1319 Low Grade Rd., Box 198, 15049. Tel: 412-274-8575.
Catechesis/Religious Programs—Tel: 412-274-6445.

Students 216.

Herman, Butler Co., St. Mary of the Assumption (1842), Rev. James Kurtz, O.F.M.Cap.
Res., 16039. Tel: 412-285-3285; Fax: 412-285-3285. [CEM]
School—Tel: 412-283-2129.
Sisters of Divine Providence 1; Lay Teachers 9; Students 146.
Catechesis/Religious Programs—Students 158.

Hillsville, Lawrence Co., St. Lawrence (1904) (Italian), Rev. James A. Downs.
Res., Martin Kelly Speer Rd., Box 23, 16132. Tel: 412-667-7721. [CEM]

Holiday Park, Allegheny Co., Our Lady of Joy (1968), Revs. Robert J. Cedolia, Admin.; Frank V. Marchukonis, Pastor Emeritus.
Res., 2000 O'Block Rd., Pittsburgh, 15239. Tel: 412-795-3388.
Catechesis/Religious Programs—Tel: 412-795-4389.
Students 840.

Homestead, Allegheny Co.,

1—St. Anne. Closed. See St. Maximilian Kolbe, Munhall.

2—St. Anthony. Closed. See St. Maximilian Kolbe, Munhall.

3—St. Mary Magdalene. Closed. See St. Maximilian Kolbe, Munhall.

4—SS. Peter and Paul, (Lithuanian). Closed. See St. Maximilian Kolbe, Munhall.

Hopewell Township, Beaver Co., Our Lady of Fatima, Revs. Thomas J. McKenna; David E. Scharf.
Res., 4001 Broadhead Rd., Aliquippa, 15001. Tel: 412-375-7626.
School—Lay Teachers 7; Students 147.
Catechesis/Religious Programs—Tel: 412-378-8020; Fax: 412-375-0219.
Students 547.

Imperial, Allegheny Co., St. Columbkille (1908), Revs. Dennis M. Buranosky; Domenic Mancini.
Res., 103 Church Rd., 15126. Tel: 412-695-7325. [CEM]
Catechesis/Religious Programs—Tel: 412-695-2146.
Students 412.

Industry, Beaver Co., St. Christine. Closed. See St. Blaise, Midland.

Ingram, Allegheny Co., Ascension (1967), Rev. Walter A. Sobon.
Res., 114 Berry St., Pittsburgh, 15205. Tel: 412-921-1230; Fax: 412-922-1279.
Catechesis/Religious Programs—Brian M. Keane, D.R.E.
Students 260.

Jefferson Boro, Allegheny Co., St. Thomas A Becket (1957), Rev. Gerard D. Kelly.
Res., 509 Gill Hall Rd., Jefferson Boro, Clairton, 15025. Tel: 412-655-2885; Fax: 412-655-0615.
Catechesis/Religious Programs—139 Gill Hall Rd., 15025. Tel: 412-653-4322.
Students 384.

Kennedy Township, Allegheny Co., St. Malachy (1953), Revs. John D. Brennan; Paul R. Staud; James Chepponis.
Res., 343 Forest Grove Rd., Coraopolis, 15108. Tel: 412-771-5483.
School—Tel: 412-771-4545.
Sisters of the Holy Family of Nazareth 1; Lay Teachers 15; Students 297.
Catechesis/Religious Programs—Tel: 412-771-7480.
Students 450.

Koppel, Beaver Co., Queen of Heaven (1992). Consolidated from St. Monica, Wampum and St. Theresa, Koppel. Rev. Joseph R. Lemp, S.T.L.
Res., 6421 Sixth Ave., P.O. Box A, 16136-0601. Tel: 412-846-5702; Fax: 412-846-2219. [CEM]
Catechesis/Religious Programs—Tel: 412-846-9559.
Students 175.
St. Teresa. Closed. See Queen of Heaven.

Lawrence, Washington Co., St. Elizabeth. Closed. See St. Mary, Cecil.

Liberty Boro, Allegheny Co., St. Eugene. Closed. See St. Mark, Port Vue.

Library, Allegheny Co., St. Joan of Arc (1923), Revs. Phillip Pribonic; Kenneth Kezmarsky.
Res., 6414 Montour St., 15129. Tel: 412-833-2400; Fax: 412-835-1764.
School—6470 Library Rd., 15129. Tel: 412-833-2433.
Lay Teachers 13; Students 195.
Catechesis/Religious Programs—Tel: 412-835-3724.
Students 508.

Lyndora, Butler Co., St. John (1904) (Slovak). Closed. See St. Fidelis of Sigmaringen, Butler.
St. Stanislaus Kostka (1919) (Polish). Merged with St. Conrad, Meridian, and St. John, Lyndora, to form St. Fidelis, Butler.

McDonald, Washington Co., St. Alphonsus (1892), Rev. Edward J. Trzeciakowski.
Res., 219 W. Lincoln Ave., 15057. Tel: 412-926-2984.
Catechesis/Religious Programs—Students 264.

McKeesport, Allegheny Co.,

1—St. Martin de Porres, (1993). Consolidated from St. Mary, Holy Trinity, Sacred Heart and St. Peter. Revs. John R. Rushofsky; James E. Kunkel; Deacon Ken Gleason.
Res., 704 Market St., 15132. Tel: 412-672-9763; Fax: 412-672-2817. [CEM 3]
Schools—St. Joseph Regional School, Tel: 412-678-0659.; McKeesport Central Catholic School, Tel: 412-672-7440; 672-4612; Fax: 412-672-6158.
Catechesis/Religious Programs—Tel: 412-672-7440.
Students 135.

2—St. Peter. Closed. See St. Martin de Porres.

3—St. Mary, (German). Closed. See St. Martin de Porres.

4—St. Mary Czestochowa, (1893) (Polish), Rev. Francis B. Lachowicz.
Res., 2515 Versailles Ave., 15132. Tel: 412-672-0765. [CEM]
School—McKeesport Central Catholic School. See separate listing.
Catechesis/Religious Programs—2412 Versailles Ave., 15132. Tel: 412-751-2873.
Students 150.

5—Holy Trinity. Closed. See St. Martin de Porres.

6—St. Pius V, (1903). Merged with St. Stephen. Rev. John J. Keane, Admin.
Res., 2911 Versailles Ave., 15132. Tel: 412-673-8878.
School—McKeesport Central Catholic School. See separate listing. Tel: 412-672-4612.

7—St. Stephen, (1899) (Hungarian). Closed. See St. Pius V.

8—Sacred Heart, (Croatian). Closed. See St. Martin de Porres.

9—St. Perpetua. Closed. See St. Patrick, Versailles.

McKees Rocks, Allegheny Co.,

1—St. Mary Help of Christians, (German). Closed. See St. John of God.

2—St. Francis de Sales. Closed. See St. John of God.

3—St. John of God, (1993). Consolidated from the following churches: St. Francis de Sales, SS. Cyril & Methodius, St. Maria Goretti Chapel, St. Mark, St. Mary Help of Christians, Mother of Sorrows and St. Vincent, Pittsburgh. Team Ministers: Revs. Paul C. Householder; Lawrence R. Smith; William R. Terza, Team Moderator. In res., Revs. Regis J. Ryan; Christopher Mbogu (Nigeria).
Res., 810 Chartiers Ave., 15136. Tel: 412-771-5646; Fax: 412-331-0678. [CEM][JC 2]
School—See Consolidated Schools under Institutions Located in the Diocese. Tel: 412-331-0220.
Catechesis/Religious Programs—Tel: 412-331-8627. Mr. John Fatula, D.R.E.
Students 248.

4—St. Maria Goretti Chapel. Closed. See St. John of God.

5—Mother of Sorrows, (Italian). Closed. See St. John of God.

6—St. Mark, (Slovak). Closed. See St. John of God.

7—SS. Cyril and Methodius, (Polish). Closed. See St. John of God.

Fredericktown, Washington Co., St. Oliver Plunkett (1994). Consolidated from Saints Mary & Ann, Marianna, and St. Michael Archangel, Fredericktown. Rev. Edward S. Litavec.
Res., Box 638, Marianna, 15333. Tel: 412-377-0128. [CEM]
Catechesis/Religious Programs—Students 170.

Mars, Butler Co., St. Kilian (1920), Rev. John W. Rebel.
Res., Clarke & Cherry Sts., P.O. Box 394, 16046. Tel: 412-625-1665.
Catechesis/Religious Programs—Hook St., 16046. Tel: 412-625-1288.
Students 250.

Meadowlands, Washington Co., Our Lady of the Miraculous Medal (1949), Rev. Ferdinand F. Lech.
Res., Box 366, 15347. Tel: 412-222-1911. [JC]

Meridian, Butler Co., St. Conrad. Merged with St. John and St. Stanislaus Kostka, Lyndora to form St. Fidelis, Butler.

Midland, Beaver Co., St. Blaise (1994), Rev. Dennis J. Bradley.
Res., 772 Ohio Ave., 15059. Tel: 412-643-4050; Fax: 412-643-6533.
Catechesis/Religious Programs—757 Penn Ave., 15059. Tel: 412-643-4663.
Students 275.

Millvale, Allegheny Co.,

1—St. Ann. Closed. See Holy Spirit.

2—St. Anthony, (German). Closed. See Holy Spirit.

3—Holy Spirit, (1994). Consolidated from St. Anthony and St. Ann. Revs. John R. Weber, C.S.Sp.; John L. Marini, C.S.Sp. In res., Rev. Joseph F. Rengers, C.S.Sp.
Res., 608 Farragut St., Pittsburgh, 15209. Tel: 412-821-4424.
School—100 Howard St., Pittsburgh, 15209. Tel: 412-821-4805; Fax: 412-821-4714.
Lay Teachers 10; Students 199.
Catechesis/Religious Programs—Tel: 412-821-2099; Fax: 412-821-9305.
Students 315.

4—St. Nicholas, (Croatian). Closed. See the new St. Nicholas.

5—St. Nicholas, (1994) (Croatian). Merged. Very Rev. Romildo Hrboka, T.O.R.; Rev. Grgo Sikiric, T.O.R.
Administrative Center: 24 Maryland Ave., Pittsburgh, 15209. Tel: 412-821-3438; Fax: 412-821-8726. [JC 2]

Monaca, Beaver Co., St. John the Baptist (1888), Revs. Philip J. De Carlo; Nicholas M. Mastrangelo.
Res., 1409 Pennsylvania Ave., 15061. Tel: 412-775-3940. [CEM]
School—Virginia Ave. & 15th St., 15061. Tel: 412-775-5774.
Sisters of Divine Providence 2; Lay Teachers 10; Students 264.
Catechesis/Religious Programs—Students 378.

Monongahela, Washington Co., Transfiguration (1865), Revs. William P. Feeney; Paul P. Leger, Pastor Emeritus.
Res., 722 W. Main St., 15063. Tel: 412-258-7742; Fax: 412-258-8733. [CEM]
School—731 Chess St., 15063. Tel: 412-258-3199.
Lay Teachers 7; Students 155.
Madonna Catholic Middle School—.
Lay Teachers 5; Students 86.
Catechesis/Religious Programs—Students 185.
St. Anthony (1905) (Italian-Slavic), Rev. Bernard P. Shulik, Admin. In res., Rev. Armand Yeaglin, O.F.M.Cap. Tel: 412-258-2563.
Res., 225 Park Ave., 15063. Tel: 412-258-9710.
Catechesis/Religious Programs—St. Anthony School, Chass St., 15063.
Students 150.

Monroeville, Allegheny Co., St. Bernadette (1955), Revs. Michael W. Decewicz; Michael A. Caridi; Richard A. Infante.
Res., 245 Azalea Dr., 15146. Tel: 412-373-0050; Fax: 412-374-8113.
School—(Grades PreK-8). Tel: 412-372-7255.
Sisters 2; Lay Teachers 13; Students 381.
Catechesis/Religious Programs—Tel: 412-373-1797.
Students 745.
North American Martyrs (1960), Revs. Anthony G. DeLuca; Donald R. Bischof; Deacon Regis C. Cunningham.
Res., 2526 Haymaker Rd., 15146. Tel: 412-373-0330.
School—(Grades K-6). Tel: 412-373-0889.
Lay Teachers 8; Students 142.
Catechesis/Religious Programs—Tel: 412-372-8149.
Students 324.

Moon Township, Allegheny Co., St. Margaret Mary (1956), Rev. John Ayoob.
Res., One Parish Pl., 15108-2697. Tel: 412-264-2573; Fax: 412-264-4327.
Catechesis/Religious Programs—Tel: 412-264-9368.
Students 679.

Mt. Lebanon, Allegheny Co., St. Bernard (1919), Revs. George A. Wilt; Thomas V. Manning; Thomas R. Wilson.
Res., 311 Washington Rd., Pittsburgh, 15216. Tel: 412-561-3301; Fax: 412-563-0211.
School—(Grades PreK-8) 315 Washington Rd., Pittsburgh, 15216. Tel: 412-341-5444; Fax: 412-563-6021.
Lay Teachers 20; Students 480.
Catechesis/Religious Programs—Tel: 412-561-0199.
Students 1,080.
St. Winifred (Pittsburgh) (1960), Rev. Jeremiah T. O'Shea. In res., Rev. John K. Takyi (Ghana).
Res., 550 Sleepy Hollow Rd., Pittsburgh, 15228. Tel: 412-344-5010; Fax: 412-563-7279.
Catechesis/Religious Programs—Tel: 412-563-1414.
Students 429.

Munhall, Allegheny Co.,

1—St. Margaret. Closed. See St. Maximilian Kolbe.

2—St. Maximilian Kolbe, (1992). Consolidated from

the following churches: St. Margaret, Munhall; St. Michael, Munhall; St. Anne, Homestead; St. Anthony, Homestead; St. Mary Magdalene, Homestead; SS. Peter & Paul, Homestead. Rev. Henry R. Krawczyk. In res., Revs. Mark W. Glasgow; James McDonough.
Res., 605 Ninth Ave., 15120-1996. Tel: 412-461-1054; Fax: 412-462-1744. [CEM 3]

3—ST. MICHAEL, (Slovak). Closed. See St. Maximilian Kolbe.

4—ST. RITA, (1936), Rev. Alvin J. Adams.
Res., 218 W. Schwab Ave., 15120. Tel: 412-461-4204.

5—ST. THERESA OF LISIEUX, (1925), Very Rev. Hugh J. Lang; Rev. Howard W. Campbell. In res., Rev. Joseph C. Girdis, (Retired).
Res., One St. Theresa Ct., 15120. Tel: 412-462-8161; Fax: 412-462-4817.
School—Three St. Theresa Ct., 15120. Tel: 412-462-8163.
Sisters of Charity 2; Lay Teachers 21; Students 445.
Catechesis/Religious Programs—Tel: 412-461-7680.
Students 240.

Muse, Washington Co., Holy Rosary (1963), Rev. Edward R. Schleicher.
Res., Orchard St., Box 447, 15350-0447. Tel: 412-745-3531.
Catechesis/Religious Programs—Students 130.

Natrona, Allegheny Co., St. Joseph (1992). Merged with St. Ladislaus and St. Mathias. Rev. Donald J. Sotak.
Res., 96 Pond St., 15065-2630. Tel: 412-224-1336. [CEM]
High School—St. Joseph Catholic High School, 800 Montan Ave., Natrona Heights, 15065. Tel: 412-224-5552.
Catechesis/Religious Programs—Students 175.
St. Ladislaus (Polish). Closed. See St. Joseph.
St. Mathias. Closed. See St. Joseph.

Natrona Heights, Allegheny Co., Blessed Sacrament. Closed. See Our Lady of the Most Blessed Sacrament.
Our Lady of the Most Blessed Sacrament (1992) (Polish-Slovak). Consolidated from Most Blessed Sacrament and Our Lady of Perpetual Help. Revs. Stan M. Gregorek; Aaron J. Kriss; John J. Batykefer.
Res., 1526 Union Ave., 15065-2008. Tel: 412-226-4900; Fax: 412-224-3559.
Catechesis/Religious Programs—Tel: 412-224-3339.
Students 425.
Our Lady of Perpetual Help. Closed. See Our Lady of the Most Blessed Sacrament.

Nemacolin, Greene Co., Our Lady of Consolation, Rev. Michael S. Suslowicz.
Res., P.O. Box 206, 15351. Tel: 412-966-7909.

Neshannock, Lawrence Co., St. Camillus (1959), Rev. David A. Driesch. In res., Rev. Francis C. Graff.
Res., 314 W. Englewood Ave., New Castle, 16105. Tel: 412-652-9471.
Catechesis/Religious Programs—Tel: 412-652-9497.
Students 565.

New Bedford, Lawrence Co., St. James (1844), Rev. Joseph R. McCaffrey.
Res., P.O. Box 207, 16140. Tel: 412-964-8276; Fax: 412-964-1108. [CEM]
Catechesis/Religious Programs—Students 230.

New Brighton, Beaver Co., Holy Family (1994). Consolidated from St. Joseph and SS. Cyril and Methodius. Rev. Harry E. Parsons.
Catechesis/Religious Programs—Students 216.
SS. Cyril and Methodius (Slovak). Closed. See Holy Family.

New Castle, Lawrence Co.,

1—MARY, MOTHER OF HOPE, (1993). Consolidated from St. Mary and Madonna of Czestochowa. Revs. Victor J. Molka, Jr.; Robert M. Miller.
Res., 124 N. Beaver St., 16101. Tel: 412-658-2564; Fax: 412-658-9024. [CEM][JC]
Catechesis/Religious Programs—Tel: 412-656-1017.
Students 329.

2—ST. MARY. Closed. See Mary, Mother of Hope.

3—ST. JOSEPH THE WORKER, (1888), Very Rev. Norbert J. Campbell.
Res., 1111 S. Cascade St., 16101. Tel: 412-658-1683. [JC]
Catechesis/Religious Programs—Tel: 412-654-9739.
Students 450.

4—ST. VITUS, (1901) (Italian), Revs. John D. Petrarulo; J. Lawrence Bruney; John J. Baver.
Res., 910 S. Mercer St., 16101. Tel: 412-652-3422; Fax: 412-654-9364. [CEM][JC]
School—915 S. Jefferson St., 16101. Tel: 412-654-9297.
Apostles of the Sacred Heart of Jesus 5; Lay Teachers 14; Students 272.
Catechesis/Religious Programs—Tel: 412-654-9371.
Students 494.

5—MADONNA OF CZESTOCHOWA. Closed. See Mary, Mother of Hope.

6—ST. MICHAEL, (Slovak). Closed. See St. Vincent de Paul.

7—SS. PHILIP AND JAMES, (Polish). Closed. See St. Vincent de Paul.

8—ST. LUCY, (Italian). Closed. See St. Vincent de Paul.

9—ST. MARGARET. Closed. See St. Vincent de Paul.

10—ST. VINCENT DE PAUL, (1993). Consolidated from the following churches: St. Lucy, St. Michael, SS. Philip & James, St. Margaret and Holy Cross, West Pittsburgh. Revs. Benedetto P. Vaghetto, J.C.L.; Daniel Vallecorsa, M.A., S.T.L.
Res., One Lucymont Dr., 16102. Tel: 412-652-5829; Fax: 412-656-0413. [CEM 2]
Catechesis/Religious Programs—Clayton St., 16102. Tel: 412-654-2822.
Students 260.

North Oakland, Butler Co., St. Joseph (1872), Rev. Bartley A. Sorensen, Admin.
Res., Main St., P.O. Box 243, Chicora, 16025. Tel: 412-445-2275. [CEM]
Catechesis/Religious Programs—Students 98.

North Rochester, Beaver Co., St. Pudentiana. Closed. See St. Cecilia, Rochester.

Oakdale, Allegheny Co., St. Patrick (1866), Rev. William J. Schwartz.
Res., 7322 Noblestown Rd., 15071. Tel: 412-693-9260; Fax: 412-693-9247. [CEM]

Oakmont, Allegheny Co., St. Irenaeus (1908), Rev. William G. Blough.
Res., 387 Maryland Ave., 15139. Tel: 412-828-3065.
School—Tel: 412-828-8444. Ms. Mary Frances Panian, Prin.
Lay Teachers 9; Students 211.
Catechesis/Religious Programs—634 Fourth St., 15139. Tel: 412-828-9450.
Students 264.

O'Hara Township, Allegheny County, St. Joseph (1845), Rev. Walter W. Dworak.
Res., 330 Dorseyville Rd., Pittsburgh, 15215. Tel: 412-963-8885. [CEM]
Catechesis/Religious Programs—342 Dorseyville Rd., Pittsburgh, 15215. Tel: 412-963-9252.
Students 471.

Overbrook, Allegheny Co., St. Norbert (1914) (German), Revs. Michael C. MacVeigh; Joseph P. Pudichery.
Res., 2413 Off Saw Mill Run Blvd., Pittsburgh, 15234. Tel: 412-881-1316; 881-2474.
Catechesis/Religious Programs—Tel: 412-882-2040.
Students 87.

Penn Hills, Allegheny Co., St. Bartholomew (1950), Revs. James S. Ruggiero; Thomas J. Galvin; Richard J. Mueller.
Res., 111 Erhardt Dr., Pittsburgh, 15235. Tel: 412-242-3374; Fax: 412-242-1488.
School—Tel: 412-242-2511; Fax: 412-242-0114.
Sisters 4; Lay Teachers 18; Students 373.
Catechesis/Religious Programs—Tel: 412-242-7207. Sr. M. Mildred Moroz, D.R.E.
Lay Teachers 35; Students 285.
St. Gerard Majella (1964), Rev. Richard J. Czapinski.
Res., 121 Dawn Dr., Verona, 15147. Tel: 412-793-3333.
Catechesis/Religious Programs—Tel: 412-793-3959.
Students 298.
St. Susanna (1960), Rev. Raymond Michael Utz.
Res., 200 Stotler Rd., Pittsburgh, 15235-3598. Tel: 412-731-7465; Fax: 412-798-0479.
Catechesis/Religious Programs—Tel: 412-793-9448.
Students 149.

Perrysville, Allegheny Co., St. Teresa of Avila (1867), Revs. Thaddeus S. Maida; Lawrence F. Stebler; David G. Poecking.
Res., 1000 Avila Ct., Pittsburgh, 15237. Tel: 412-367-9001; Fax: 412-366-8415. [CEM]
School—800 Avila Ct., Pittsburgh, 15237. Tel: 412-364-4216; Fax: 412-364-1172.
Lay Teachers 25; Students 418.
Catechesis/Religious Programs—Tel: 412-366-1077.
Students 772.

Peters Township, Washington Co., St. Benedict the Abbot (1962), Revs. Philip J. Donatelli; John E. Forbidussi; Deacon John Layton.
Res., 120 Abington Dr., McMurray, 15317. Tel: 412-941-9406; Fax: 412-941-9517.
Catechesis/Religious Programs—Tel: 412-941-9517.
Students 1,257.

Pitcairn, Allegheny Co., St. Michael (1895), Rev. James E. Somma.
Church—750 Wall Ave., 15140. Tel: 412-373-3400.
Res., 740 Wall Ave., 15140. Tel: 412-373-2610.

Pleasant Hills, Allegheny Co., St. Elizabeth (1942), Revs. Roy H. Conley; Edward Kunco; Thomas A. Wagner.
Res., Grove Pl., Pittsburgh, 15236. Tel: 412-881-7728; Fax: 412-882-8320.
School—Tel: 412-881-2958.
Sisters 2; Lay Teachers 30; Students 702.
Catechesis/Religious Programs—Tel: 412-882-5023. D.R.E.: Kathleen Probo; Tisha Bridges.
Students 715.
Chapel of Convenience—St. David, Baldwin Boro., Pittsburgh.

Port Vue, Allegheny Co., St. Joseph. Closed. See St. Mark.
St. Mark (1993), Rev. Gerald S. Mikonis.
Administration Center: 1101 Romine Ave., 15133; St. Joseph Worship Site: 1125 Romine Ave., 15133.
Res. & St. Eugene Worship Site—3210 Liberty Way, Liberty Borough, 15133. Tel: 412-678-6275.
School—St. Joseph Regional School. See Consolidated Schools under Institutions Located in the Diocese. Tel: 412-678-0659.
Catechesis/Religious Programs—Michelle Smith, D.R.E.
Students 207.

Prospect, Butler Co., St. Christopher (1974), Rev. Matthew Tosello.
Res., 229-232 N. Franklin St., 16052. Tel: 412-865-2430; Fax: 412-865-2430.
Catechesis/Religious Programs—Tel: 412-865-9840.
Students 118.

Rankin, Allegheny Co., Visitation of the Blessed Virgin Mary (Croatian). Closed. See Word of God, Swissvale.

Renton, Allegheny Co., St. Januarius (1950), Rev. Richard R. Ragni.
Res., 1450 Renton Rd., 15239. Tel: 412-793-4439.

Reserve Township, Allegheny Co., St. Aloysius (1892), Rev. William G. Rutledge.
Res., 3616 Mt. Troy Rd., Pittsburgh, 15212. Tel: 412-821-2351.
School—3614 Mt. Troy Rd., Pittsburgh, 15212. Tel: 412-821-5444.
Lay Teachers 10; Students 173.
Catechesis/Religious Programs—Tel: 412-821-2792.
Students 150.

Richeyville, Washington Co., St. Agnes (1929), Rev. Francis Z. Jurewicz.
Res., Box 406, 15358. Tel: 412-632-5858.

Richland Township, Allegheny Co., Saint Richard (1992), Rev. Kenneth E. Oldenski.
Res., 3841 Dickey Rd., Gibsonia, 15044. Tel: 412-444-1971; Fax: 412-444-6001.
Catechesis/Religious Programs—Students 477.

Robinson Township, Allegheny Co., Holy Trinity (Moon Run) (1944), Revs. Robert W. Herrmann; William J. Scholz. In res., Rev. John Fitzgerald.
Res., 5718 Steubenville Pike, P.O. Box 15567, Pittsburgh, 15244. Tel: 412-787-2140; 787-2143; Fax: 412-787-3799.
School—(Grades PreK-8). Tel: 412-787-2656; Fax: 412-787-9487.
Sisters of St. Francis. (Mt. Prov., Pittsburgh) 2; Lay Teachers 23; Students 429.
Catechesis/Religious Programs—Tel: 412-859-3467.
Students 420.

Rochester, Beaver Co., St. Cecilia (1856). Merged with St. Pudentiana. Revs. Ward Stakem, O.F.M.Cap.; William Gillum, O.F.M.Cap.; Marvin Justi, O.F.M.Cap.
Res., 303 Jackson St., 15074. Tel: 412-775-0801; Fax: 412-774-3056. [CEM]
Catechesis/Religious Programs—Tel: 412-774-2761.
Students 298.

Roscoe, Washington Co., St. Joseph (1904), Rev. Timothy F. Whalen, Admin. In res., Rev. George J. Moneck.
Res., Box 486, 15477. Tel: 412-938-2324.

Ross Township, Allegheny Co., St. Sebastian (North Hills) (1952), Revs. Paul J. Bradley; Brian J. Welding; Kenneth A. Sparks.
Res., 311 Siebert Rd., Pittsburgh, 15237. Tel: 412-364-8999; Fax: 412-364-6330.
School—307 Siebert Rd., Pittsburgh, 15237. Tel: 412-364-7171.
Sisters 7; Lay Teachers 25; Students 505.
Catechesis/Religious Programs—Tel: 412-366-4000.
Students 408.

Russellton, Allegheny Co., Transfiguration (1916), Rev.

Robert W. Habe.
Res., 15 Poma St., 15076. Tel: 412-265-1030. [CEM]
School—(Grades K-6) McKrell Rd., 15076. Tel: 412-265-3350.
Lay Teachers 7; Students 97.
Catechesis/Religious Programs—Tel: 412-265-4860.
Students 242.

Scott Township, Allegheny Co., SS. Simon and Jude (1955), Revs. Richard E. Ward; Patrick C. Barkey. In res., Rev. Kris D. Stubna.
Res., 1607 Greentree Rd., Pittsburgh, 15220. Tel: 412-563-3189; Fax: 412-563-8524.
School—1625 Greentree Rd., Pittsburgh, 15220. Tel: 412-563-1353.
Lay Teachers 20; Students 340.
Catechesis/Religious Programs—Tel: 412-563-1199.
Students 285.

Our Lady of Grace (1947), Revs. Theodore A. Rutkowski; Ray A. Gualtieri; Michael Maranowski.
Res., 310 Kane Blvd., Pittsburgh, 15243. Tel: 412-279-7070.
School—1734 Bower Hill Rd., Pittsburgh, 15243. Tel: 412-279-6611.
Lay Teachers 24; Students 388.
Catechesis/Religious Programs—1730 Bower Hill Rd., Pittsburgh, 15243. Tel: 412-276-0277.
Students 567.

Sewickley, Allegheny Co., St. James (1863), Revs. Raymond Froehlich; Louis F. Pascazi. In res., Rev. Harold E. Baily.
Res., 200 Walnut St., 15143. Tel: 412-741-6650. [CEM]
School—Broad & Bank Sts., 15143. Tel: 412-741-5540.
Sisters of St. Joseph 3; Lay Teachers 12; Students 225.
Catechesis/Religious Programs—Tel: 412-741-6766.
Students 335.

Sharpsburg, Allegheny Co., St. John Cantius (1906) (Polish), Rev. Andrew C. Fischer.
Res., 220 9th St., 15215. Tel: 412-781-6119; Fax: 412-781-4461.

St. Mary (1994), Rev. Patrick M. Cooke, C.S.Sp.
Res., 210 Penn St., Pittsburgh, 15215. Tel: 412-781-2857. [CEM]
Catechesis/Religious Programs—Tel: 412-781-5150.
Students 147.

Madonna of Jerusalem (1904) (Italian), Rev. Andrew C. Fischer.
Res., 220 Ninth St., 15215. Tel: 412-781-6119; Fax: 412-781-4461.

Slippery Rock, Butler Co., St. Peter, Rev. Donald C. Fisher.
Res., 670 S. Main St., 16057. Tel: 412-794-2880; Fax: 412-794-1255. [CEM]
Catechesis/Religious Programs—Tel: 412-794-5101.
Students 245.
Mission—Forestville, Butler Co., St. Anthony, P.O. Box 6, Forestville, 16035. Tel: 412-735-2638.

South Park Township, Allegheny Co., Nativity (1905), Rev. F. Terrence Fedigan. In res., Revs. Innocent Jooji (Nigeria); Paschal Kabura (Uganda).
Res., 5802 Curry Rd., Pittsburgh, 15236. Tel: 412-655-3000.
School—(Grades PreK-8) 5811 Curry Rd., Pittsburgh, 15236. Tel: 412-653-1500; Fax: 412-653-2619.
Sisters 1; Lay Teachers 14; Students 175.
Catechesis/Religious Programs—Tel: 412-655-1565.
Students 412.

Springdale, Allegheny Co., St. Alphonsus (1900), Rev. George E. Saladna, S.T.L., S.S.L.
Res., 249 James St., 15144-1699. Tel: 412-274-5084.
Catechesis/Religious Programs—Tel: 412-274-6456.
Students 165.

Swissvale, Allegheny Co.,

1—St. Anselm. Closed. See Word of God.

2—Word of God, (1994) (Irish-Croatian). Consolidated from the following churches: St. Anselm, St. Barnabus and Visitation of the Blessed Virgin Mary, Rankin. Revs. Frank J. Drabiska; Charles T. Geiselhart; Paul Cwynar.
Res., 7446 McClure Ave., Pittsburgh, 15218. Tel: 412-241-1372; Fax: 412-241-0168.
School—7438 McClure Ave., Pittsburgh, 15218. Tel: 412-371-8587.
Sisters of Charity 3; Lay Teachers 18; Students 394.
Catechesis/Religious Programs—Tel: 412-351-0670.
Students 155.

3—Saint Barnabas, (Slovak). Closed. See Word of God.

4—Madonna del Castello, (1920) (Italian), Rev. John J. Cassella, M.Div.
Res., 2021 S. Braddock Ave., Pittsburgh, 15218. Tel: 412-271-5666.

Tarentum, Allegheny Co., Holy Martyrs (1992) (Slovak). Consolidated from St. Clement and Sacred Heart, St. Peter. Rev. Donald Chortos.
Res., 353 W. Ninth Ave., 15084. Tel: 412-224-0770; Fax: 412-224-7070. [CEM][JC 2]
Catechesis/Religious Programs—216 W. 9th Ave., 15084. Tel: 412-224-1234.
Students 254.

Sacred Heart - St. Peter. Closed. See Holy Martyrs.
St. Clement. Closed. See Holy Martyrs.

Turtle Creek, Allegheny Co., St. Colman (1882), Revs. John A. Geinzer; John W. Markell.
Res., 100 Tri-Boro Ave., 15145. Tel: 412-823-2564.
School—(Grades PreK-8) 547 Hunter St., 15145. Tel: 412-823-4871; Fax: 412-823-6326.
Sisters of Mercy of the Americas 2; Lay Teachers 15; Students 352.
Catechesis/Religious Programs—Tel: 412-823-9114.
Students 275.

Unity, Allegheny Co., St. John the Baptist (1915), Revs. Joseph M. Mele; Kevin J. Dominik; Martin F. Barkin.
Res., 444 St. John St., Pittsburgh, 15239. Tel: 412-793-4511; 793-4580; Fax: 412-793-4311. [CEM]
School—418 Unity Center Rd., Pittsburgh, 15239. Tel: 412-793-0555; Fax: 412-793-4001.
Servants of the Immaculate Heart of Mary 2; Lay Teachers 20; Students 371.
Catechesis/Religious Programs—Tel: 412-795-6376.
Students 627.

Upper St. Clair, Allegheny Co., St. John Capistran (1968), Very Rev. Robert J. Reardon.
Res., 1610 McMillan Rd., Pittsburgh, 15241. Tel: 412-221-6275.
Catechesis/Religious Programs—Tel: 412-221-5445.
Students 334.

Verona, Allegheny Co., St. Joseph (1866), Rev. Msgr. John J. Seli; Rev. Trieu Ngoc Le.
Res., 825 Second Ave., 15147. Tel: 412-795-5114. [CEM]
School—Tel: 412-828-7213.
Lay Teachers 13; Students 235.
Catechesis/Religious Programs—Tel: 412-828-7715.
Students 240.

Versailles, Allegheny Co., St. Denis. Closed. See St. Patrick.

McKeesport, Allegheny Co., St. Patrick (1993). Merged with St. Denis and St. Perpetua, McKeesport. Rev. Gerald Lutz.
Res., 310 32nd St., 15132. Tel: 412-673-4110; Fax: 412-678-7259. [CEM]

Wampum, Lawrence Co., St. Monica. Closed. See Queen of Heaven, Koppel.

Washington, Washington Co., Immaculate Conception (1854), Revs. James G. Young; Frank M. Kurimsky; Kevin F. McKnight; Theodore P. Zabowski; Deacon Leon Abraham.
Res., 119 W. Chestnut St., 15301. Tel: 412-225-1425. [CEM 3]
School—111 W. Spruce St., 15301. Tel: 412-225-1680.
Sisters 1; Lay Teachers 25; Students 600.
Catechesis/Religious Programs—135 W. Chestnut St., 15301. Tel: 412-225-0382.
Students 845.

St. Hilary (1919), Rev. Thomas D. O'Neil.
Res., 320 Henderson Ave., 15301. Tel: 412-222-4087.
School—Tel: 412-222-8750.
Lay Teachers 5; Students 49.
Catechesis/Religious Programs—Students 135.

Waynesburg, Greene Co., St. Ann (1839), Rev. Albin C. McGinnis.
Res., 232 E. High St., 15370. Tel: 412-627-7568. [CEM]
Catechesis/Religious Programs—Students 225.

West Aliquippa, Beaver Co., St. Joseph. Closed. See St. Titus, Aliquippa.

West Mifflin, Allegheny Co.,

1—St. Agnes, (1867), Rev. Michael J. Polak.
Res., 622 St. Agnes Ln., 15122. Tel: 412-466-2655. [CEM]
School—635 St. Agnes Ln., 15122. Tel: 412-466-6238.
Sisters of the Holy Spirit 5; Lay Teachers 6; Students 185.

2—Holy Spirit, (1963), Rev. Daniel A. Valentine.
Res., 2603 Old Elizabeth Rd., 15122-2598. Tel: 412-466-5048; Fax: 412-466-4983.
Catechesis/Religious Programs—Tel: 412-466-1264.
Students 399.

3—Holy Trinity, (1901) (Slovak), Rev. Edward P. Bunchek.
Res., 529 Grant Ave. Ext., 15122. Tel: 412-466-6545. [CEM]
School—Duquesne Consolidated Schools. See separate listing.

4—Resurrection, (1936), Rev. Robert G. Turner.
Res., 3909 Donna Ave., 15122. Tel: 412-461-8087.
School—James LaVelle, One Majka Dr., 15122. Tel: 412-462-4344.
Lay Teachers 11; Students 270.
Catechesis/Religious Programs—Tel: 412-461-4049.
Students 150.

West Pittsburg, Lawrence Co., Holy Cross. Closed. See St. Vincent de Paul, New Castle.

West Sunbury, Butler Co., St. Louis. Closed. See St. Alphonsus, Boyers.

West View, Allegheny Co., St. Athanasius (1905), Revs. Robert A. Norton; James M. Bachner. In res., Rev. Edward F. McSweeney.
Res., 7 Chalfonte Ave., Pittsburgh, 15229. Tel: 412-931-4624; Fax: 412-939-3516.
School—2 Wentworth Ave., Pittsburgh, 15229. Tel: 412-931-6633. Ms. Gabrielle Yingling, Prin.
Lay Teachers 13; Students 164.
Catechesis/Religious Programs—Tel: 412-931-3670. Mary Mercer, D.R.E.
Students 439.

Wexford, Allegheny Co., St. Alexis (1961), Rev. Steven Palsa. In res., Rev. Harry Petrie.
Res., 10090 Old Perry Hwy., 15090. Tel: 412-935-4343; Fax: 412-935-1270.
School—(Grades PreK-5). Tel: 412-935-3190.
Lay Teachers 15; Students 300.
Catechesis/Religious Programs—Tel: 412-935-0877.
Students 320.

St. Alphonsus (1840), Revs. William H. Schroeder; Richard J. Thompson.
Res., 201 Church Rd., 15090. Tel: 412-935-1151. [CEM]
School—Tel: 412-935-1152.
Sisters of the Holy Spirit 1; Lay Teachers 19; Students 530.
Catechesis/Religious Programs—Students 360.

Whitehall, Allegheny Co., St. Gabriel of the Sorrowful Virgin (1944), Revs. John R. Haney; Alan E. Morris. In res., Rev. Thomas F. Carey.
Res., 5200 Greenridge Dr., Pittsburgh, 15236. Tel: 412-881-8115; 881-8117.
School—Tel: 412-882-3353.
Sisters 2; Lay Teachers 21; Students 565.
Catechesis/Religious Programs—Tel: 412-881-7950.
Students 461.

White Oak Boro, Allegheny Co., St. Angela (1958), Rev. Stephen M. Chervenak; Sr. Patricia Marie Buranosky, O.S.F., Pastoral Assoc.
Res., 1732 Fawcett Ave., White Oak, 15131. Tel: 412-672-2365.
School—1640R Fawcett Ave., White Oak, 15131. Tel: 412-672-2360; Fax: 412-672-0880.
Lay Teachers 14; Students 315.
Catechesis/Religious Programs—Tel: 412-672-0913.
Students 270.

Wildwood, Allegheny Co., St. Catherine of Sweden (1953), Revs. Regis M. Farmer; Miroslaw.
Res., 2308 W. Hardies Rd., 15091. Tel: 412-443-2087; 961-0399; 443-5876; Fax: 412-443-3633.
Catechesis/Religious Programs—Students 702.

Wilkinsburg, Allegheny Co., St. James (1869), Rev. Warren W. Metzler.
Res., 718 Franklin Ave., Pittsburgh, 15221. Tel: 412-241-1392; Fax: 412-241-6625.
School—721 Rebecca Ave., Pittsburgh, 15221. Tel: 412-242-3515.
Lay Teachers 15; Students 201.

Wilmerding, Allegheny Co., St. Jude the Apostle (1994). Consolidated from St. Aloysius and St. Leocadia. Rev. John J. O'Malley.
Mailing Address: 201 Caldwell Ave., 15148. Tel: 412-823-1117.
Res., 405 Westinghouse Ave., 15148. Tel: 412-823-8390. [CEM]

St. Leocadia (Polish). Closed. See St. Jude the Apostle.

Wireton, Allegheny Co., St. Catherine of Siena (1911), Rev. John R. Huber.
Res., 20 McGovern Blvd., 15001. Tel: 412-457-7026.
Catechesis/Religious Programs—Tel: 412-457-0106.
Students 229.

Zelienople, Butler Co., St. Gregory (1906), Rev. Charles B. Bergman.

Res., 2 W. Beaver St., 16063. Tel: 412-452-7245; Fax: 412-452-4064. [CEM]
School—115 Pine St., 16063. Tel: 412-452-9731. Lay Teachers 8; Students 150.
Catechesis/Religious Programs—Students 266.

Chaplains of Public Institutions

Hospitals

ALLEGHENY COUNTY. *Allegheny General Hospital.* Tel: 412-359-3131. Revs. Frank A. Mitolo Tel: 412-359-4269; Charles L. Christen, Asst. Chap.
Allegheny Valley Hospital. Tel: 412-224-5100. Rev. Gregory Swiderski Tel: 412-274-6171.
Braddock General Hospital. Tel: 412-636-5000. Rev. Joseph D. Karabin Tel: 412-271-1515.
Children's Hospital. Tel: 412-647-5326. Sr. Nora Egan Tel: 412-372-6758.
Eye and Ear Hospital. Tel: 412-647-2345. Revs. Samuel J. Esposito. Tel: 412-621-5679; Patrick George, T.O.R. Tel: 412-782-4755; Sr. Mary Kay Hammond, C.S.J. Tel: 412-882-7593; Revs. Carlo Napoli, T.O.R. Tel: 412-782-4755; Richard Terdine. Tel: 412-621-5679; Michael McDermott. Tel: 412-621-0364.
Forbes Health Metropolitan Health Center. Tel: 412-247-2424. Rev. Warren W. Metzler Tel: 412-241-1392.
Forbes Regional Health Center. Sr. Monique Dietz, L.B. Tel: 412-781-4022; Rev. James E. Somma Tel: 412-373-2610.
Magee-Women's Hospital. Tel: 412-647-1000. Sr. Nora Egan, C.S.J. Tel: 412-372-6758.
McKeesport Hospital. Tel: 412-664-2000. Rev. John M. Elanjileth (ROM). Tel: 412-673-5552.
Montefiore Hospital. Tel: 412-648-6000. Rev. Samuel J. Esposito. Tel: 412-621-5679; Sr. Mary Kay Hammond, C.S.J. Tel: 412-882-7593; Revs. Patrick George, T.O.R. Tel: 412-782-4755; Carlo Napoli, T.O.R. Tel: 412-782-4755; Richard Terdine. Tel: 412-621-5679; Michael McDermott. Tel: 412-621-0364.
Ohio Valley General Hospital. Tel: 412-777-6161. Rev. Regis J. Ryan Tel: 412-771-5646.
Passavant Hospital. Tel: 412-367-6700. Sr. Caritas Marshall, C.S.J. Tel: 412-364-5938; Rev. W. Peter Horton. Tel: 412-366-9256.
Presbyterian-University Hospital. Tel: 412-647-2020. Revs. Patrick George, T.O.R. Tel: 412-782-4755; Carlo Napoli, T.O.R. Tel: 412-782-4755; Samuel J. Esposito. Tel: 412-621-5679; Sr. Mary Kay Hammond, C.S.J. Tel: 412-882-7593; Revs. Richard Terdine. Tel: 412-621-5679; Michael McDermott. Tel: 412-621-0364.
St. Francis Central. Tel: 412-562-3000. Rev. Barry Patriquin.
St. Francis Medical Center. Tel: 412-622-4343. Rev. Bonaventure Stefun, O.F.M.Cap. Tel: 412-471-4390; Sr. Mary Joseph Trimbur, O.S.F. Tel: 412-622-4741; Rev. Robert Craig, O.F.M.Cap. Tel: 412-682-6103.
St. Margaret Memorial Hospital. Tel: 412-784-4000. Rev. Thomas M. Kirby. Tel: 412-826-9048.
Sewickley Valley Hospital. Tel: 412-741-6000. Rev. Harold E. Baily Tel: 412-741-8836.
Shadyside Hospital. Tel: 412-623-2121. Rev. Gilbert Poznakowski Tel: 412-621-5679.
West Penn Hospital. Tel: 412-578-5000. Rev. John M. Jordan.

BEAVER COUNTY. *Medical Center, Beaver Inc.* Tel: 412-728-7000. Rev. Marvin Justi, O.F.M.Cap. Tel: 412-774-6046.

BUTLER COUNTY. *Butler Memorial Hospital.* Tel: 412-283-6666. Sr. Mary Sheehan, I.H.M. Tel: 412-283-2640.

GREENE COUNTY. *Greene County Memorial.* Tel: 412-627-3101. Rev. Albin C. McGinnis. Tel: 412-627-7568.

LAWRENCE COUNTY. *Ellwood City Hospital.* Tel: 412-752-0081. Rev. Paul Henne. Tel: 412-758-7587.
Jameson Memorial Hospital. Tel: 412-658-9001. Rev. Frank G. Erdeljac. Tel: 412-535-4786.

WASHINGTON COUNTY. *Canonsburg Hospital.* Tel: 412-745-6100. Rev. Ladis J. Cizik. Tel: 412-941-4360.
Mon Valley Hospital. Tel: 412-258-2000. Rev. Armand Yeaglin, O.F.M.Cap. Tel: 412-258-2563.
Washington Hospital. Tel: 412-225-7000. Deacon Leon B. Abraham. Tel: 412-948-3559.

Veterans Administration Hospitals

ALLEGHENY COUNTY. *Veterans Administration - Aspinwall.* Tel: 412-688-6000, Ext. 6729. Revs. Ralph Zehe, O.F.M.Cap. Tel: 412-682-0929; Emitt Schuler, O.F.M.Cap. Tel: 412-531-4545.
Veterans Administration - Oakland. Tel: 412-683-3000. Revs. Ralph Zehe, O.F.M.Cap. Tel: 412-682-6430; Mark W. Glasgow. Tel: 412-461-1054; Emitt Schuler, O.F.M.Cap. Tel: 412-531-4545.

BUTLER COUNTY. *Deshon Veterans Hospital.* Tel: 412-287-4781. Rev. William J. Ritzert. Tel: 412-538-5331.

Rehabilitation, Nursing and Geriatric Care Facilities

ALLEGHENY COUNTY. *Forbes Health Center/Center for Gerontology/Hospice.* Tel: 412-665-3232. Rev. Joseph C. Beck. Tel: 412-661-7222.
Harmarville Rehabilitation Center. Tel: 412-781-5700. Rev. Thomas M. Kirby. Tel: 412-826-9048.
Kane Regional Center - Glen Hazel. Tel: 412-422-6800. Rev. Joseph Beck. Tel: 412-661-7222; Sr. Donna Marie Mulligan, S.C. Tel: 412-461-0968.
Kane Regional Center - McKeesport. Tel: 412-675-8600. Rev. Kenan Crowley, O.F.M.Cap. Tel: 412-682-6888.
Kane Regional Center - Ross. Tel: 412-369-2000. Rev. Ernest Strzelinski.
Kane Regional Center - Scott. Tel: 412-429-3000. Rev. Richard Conboy, S.T.L. Tel: 412-429-3040.
Leader - Bethel Park. Tel: 412-831-6050. Rev. Thomas F. Carey. Tel: 412-881-8115.
Leader - Greentree Tel: 412-344-7744. Rev. Thomas F. Carey. Tel: 412-881-8115.
Marian Manor. Tel: 412-563-6866. Rev. Henry Szarnicki. Tel: 412-563-2011.
Mt. Lebanon Manor Convalescent Center. Tel: 412-257-4444. Rev. Thomas F. Carey. Tel: 412-881-8115.
Southwestern Nursing and Rehabilitation Center. Tel: 412-466-0600, Ext. 5989. Rev. Thomas F. Carey. Tel: 412-881-8115.
Woodhaven Convalescent Center. Tel: 412-856-4770. Rev. Joseph C. Beck. Tel: 412-661-7222.

BEAVER COUNTY. *Beaver Valley Geriatric Center.* Tel: 412-775-7100. Rev. Paul J. Savage. Tel: 412-846-4585.

BUTLER COUNTY. Tel: 412-282-1800. Sr. Mary Sheehan, I.H.M. Tel: 412-283-2640.

GREENE COUNTY. *Curry Memorial Home.* Tel: 412-627-3153. Rev. Albin C. McGinnis. Tel: 412-627-7568.
Franklin Care Center. Tel: 412-852-2020. Rev. Albin C. McGinnis. Tel: 412-627-7568.

LAWRENCE COUNTY. *Almira Home.* Tel: 412-652-4131. Rev. Francis C. Graff. Tel: 412-652-9471.
Belvedere Retirement Home. Tel: 412-924-2191. Rev. Francis C. Graff. Tel: 412-652-9471.
Golden Hill Nursing Home. Tel: 412-654-7791. Rev. Francis C. Graff. Tel: 412-652-9471.
Haven Convalescent Home. Tel: 412-654-8833. Rev. Francis C. Graff. Tel: 412-652-9471.
Highland Hall Care Center. Tel: 412-658-4781. Rev. Francis C. Graff. Tel: 412-652-9471.
Hill View Manor. Tel: 412-658-1521. Rev. Francis C. Graff. Tel: 412-652-9471.
Indian Creek Nursing Center. Tel: 412-652-6340. Rev. Francis C. Graff. Tel: 412-652-9471.
Jack Rees Nursing and Rehabilitation Services. Tel: 412-652-3863. Rev. Francis C. Graff. Tel: 412-652-9471.
The Overlook Medical Clinic. Tel: 412-946-3511. Rev. Francis C. Graff. Tel: 412-652-9471.

Mental Health Facilities

ALLEGHENY COUNTY. *Mayview State Hospital.* Tel: 412-257-6500. Rev. George T. Deville. Tel: 412-221-5213.
Western Psychiatric Hospital. Tel: 412-624-2100. Rev. Michael McDermott. Tel: 412-621-0364.

Correctional Institutions

ALLEGHENY COUNTY. *Allegheny County Jail.* Tel: 412-350-2000. Revs. Dan Walsh, C.S.Sp.; Arthur Merrell. Tel: 412-683-9890.
Dismas House. Tel: 412-231-2927. Rev. James G. Salberg. Tel: 412-287-7781.
Shuman Center. Tel: 412-661-6806. Rev. Arthur R. Merrell. Tel: 412-683-9890.
State Correctional Institution of Pittsburgh Tel: 412-761-1955. Rev. James G. Salberg.

BEAVER COUNTY. *Beaver County Jail.* Rev. Msgr. Raymond T. Schultz. Tel: 412-775-4111.

BUTLER COUNTY. *Butler County Jail.* Rev. Hugh M. Gloninger. Tel: 412-287-1759.

GREENE COUNTY. *State Correctional Institution at Waynesburg.* Tel: 412-627-6185. Rev. George Moneck. Tel: 412-938-2324; Sr. Yvonne Dursh, O.S.F. Tel: 412-882-3470.
Waynesburg County Jail. Rev. Albin C. McGinnis. Tel: 412-627-7568.

LAWRENCE COUNTY. *Lawrence County Jail.* Rev. James Downs. Tel: 412-667-7737.
Youth Development Center. Tel: 412-656-7300. Rev. Joseph McCaffrey. Tel: 412-964-8276; Sr. Noreen Sterns, H.M.

WASHINGTON COUNTY. *Washington County Jail.* Rev. Frank Kurimsky. Tel: 412-561-7557.

On Duty Outside the Diocese:
Reverend Fathers—
Arnott, John J., St. Anthony, P.O. Box 63, Bethel, VT 05032
Bleichner, Howard P., Theological College of Catholic Univ., 401 Michigan Ave. N.E., Washington, DC 20017
Brylinski, Bruce C., 303 Horton St., Grayson, KY 41143-1318
Cellini, Ronald R., St. Peter Parish, P.O. Box 1254, Beauford, SC 29902
Connolly, Brian W., 810 Matson Pl., Cincinnati, OH 45204
Costello, Bernard B., Sabbatical Studies
Fay, William J., St. Vincent Seminary, Frasier Purchase Rd., Latrobe, PA 15650
Friday, Robert M., Catholic Univ., Curley Hall, Washington, DC 20064
Guay, Robert F., Sabbatical Studies
Hebda, Bernard A., Palazzo Delle Congregazioni, Piazza pio XII, 10, Rome, Italy 00193
Johnson, David R., P.O. 236, Louisville, KY 40201-0236
Lauer, Eugene F., Univ. of Notre Dame, 1201 Hesburgh Library, Notre Dame, IN 46556
Manion, Thomas F., St. Paul Church, P.O. Box 268, Crownpoint, NM 87313
Mazurek, James K., SS. Cyril & Methodius Seminary, Orchard Lake, MI 48324
Ogrodowski, William M., North American College, 00120 Vatican City State, Rome, Italy
Paone, Ernest C., 1556 Glacier Rd., Oceanside, CA 92054
Roos, H. Jules, Centro de Obras Sociales, Apartado 473, Chimbote, Peru
Taylor, Augustus R., Jr., 1812 W. 48th St., Los Angeles, CA 90062

Graduate Studies:
Reverend Fathers—
Dalton, George R., Casa Santa Maria, Vatian City State, 00120 Italy

---

Military Chaplains:
Reverend Fathers—
Brzek, Jon J., P.O. Box 8026, Camp Lejeune, NC 28547-8026
Dansak, Thomas E., Chaplain's Office, PSC. Box 8033
Fix, Donald P., 2446 Montclair St., San Diego, CA 92104
Hennessy, Joseph P., 7WG/HC, 158 Ave. B, Dyess AFB, TX 79607-1458
Johnson, David R., Immaculate Conception, P.O. Box 1609, Denham Springs, LA 70726
Laboon, Joseph D., VA Medical Center, 1601 Perdido St., New Orleans, LA 70146
Lamonde, Joseph R., Commarforpac, Box 64105, Camp Smith, HI 96861
Malinsky, Gregory J., 3490 Quail Lake Rd., Colorado Springs, CO 80906
Sagala, James F., Veterans Administration Medical Center, Tremont Ave., East Orange, NJ 07019
Valko, Robert A., CHC USNR, Chap. Office, Naval Sub Base, 140 Sylvester St., San Diego, CA 92106
Yagesh, Richard C., DPTNAVSCI USMERMARCAD, Kings Point, NY 11024-1699

Absent on Sick Leave:
Reverend Fathers—
Lavery, Phillip M.
Rager, Patrick F.
Sweeney, E. Daniel

Retired:
Reverend Monsignors—
Darkowski, Leon S., 235 The Boulevard, Pittsburgh, PA 15210
Dravecky, Michael A., 1471 Guffey Rd., North Huntingdon, PA 15642
Findlan, Joseph G., St. John Vianney Manor, 2600 Morange Rd., Pittsburgh, PA 15205
Gearing, Daniel A., St. Albert the Great, 3171 Church Ave., Pittsburgh, PA 15227
Glenn, Francis A., St. Mary of Mercy, 202 Stanwix St., Pittsburgh, PA 15222
Keefer, Oliver D., Vincentian Home, Perrymont Rd., Pittsburgh, PA 15237
Lackner, Paul M., Cardinal Dearden Center, 4721 Fifth Ave., Pittsburgh, PA 15213-2915
Meenan, Joseph S., Cloverleaf Estates W, 494 Canterbury Cir., Carnegie, PA 15106
Rice, Charles O., St. Anne Church, 400 Hoodridge Dr., Pittsburgh, PA 15234-1794
Rooney, Francis J., St. John Vianney Manor, 2600 Morange Rd., Pittsburgh, PA 15205
Seli, John J., Cape Hacienda #202, 6655 Ridgewood Ave., Cocoa Beach, FL 32931
Sojka, Ferdinand M., St. John Vianney Manor, 2600 Morange Rd., Pittsburgh, PA 15205
Reverend Fathers—
Beck, Leo J., St. John Vianney Manor, 2600 Morange Rd., Pittsburgh, PA 15205
Biondi, Nicholas A., St. John Vianney Manor, 2600 Morange Rd., Pittsburgh, PA 15205
Bolvary, Paul L., Pe'cs Berfseuy'u.16, F632, Hungary
Burchianti, Leo R., St. John Vianney Manor, 2600 Morange Rd., Pittsburgh, PA 15205
Carey, Thomas F., St. Gabriel Sorrowful Virgin, 5200 Greenridge Dr., Pittsburgh, PA 15236

Cercone, Raymond A., c/o R.D. 3, Box 46, Eighty Four, PA 15330-9712
Charnoki, John J., St. Raphael, 1118 Chislett St., Pittsburgh, PA 15206-1304
Conner, Glenn T., St. John Vianney Manor, 2600 Morange Rd., Pittsburgh, PA 15205
Cvelbar, Joseph, St John Vianney Manor, 2600 Morange Rd., Pittsburgh, PA 15205
Deblasio, Dominck A., 605 Market St., Freeport, PA 16229
Denapoli, Ettore J., 743 Muddy Creek Dr., Slippery Rock, PA 16057
Dismachek, Francis M., St. John Vianney Manor, 2600 Morange Rd., Pittsburgh, PA 15205
Dompka, John A., 1150 Tranter, Green Tree, PA 15220
Erkens, William J., Westminster Place, 1215 Hulton Rd., Oakmont, PA 15139
Farina, Edward, James P. Wall Home, 1028 Benton Ave., Pittsburgh, PA 15212
Filip, Francis B., St. John Vianney Manor, 2600 Morange Rd., Pittsburgh, PA 15205
Fording, John D., St. John Vianney Manor, 2600 Morange Rd., Pittsburgh, PA 15205
Gelati, Dario, Via Vela, 46030 Sustinente (MN), Italy
Getty, Roy G., Cardinal Dearden Center, 4721 Fifth Ave., Pittsburgh, PA 15213-2915
Gibson, John W., 12 Lawrence St., P.O. Box 252, Lawrence, PA 15055
Girdis, Joseph C., St. Therese, 1 St. Therese Ct., Munhall, PA 15120
Goralka, Albert A., 301 W. Ninth Ave., Tarentum, PA 15084
Griffith, John O., R.D. No. 2, Box S-27, McDonald, PA 15057
Gubanich, Michael T., 106 S. Pine St., Ellsworth, PA 15331
Henry, Leo G., St. John Vianney Manor, 2600 Morange Rd., Pittsburg, PA 15205
Holzer, Paul A., Immaculate Conception & St. Joseph, c/o 4712 Liberty Ave., Pittsburgh, PA 15224-1794
Horner, Thomas J., St. John Vianney Manor, 2600 Morange Rd., Pittsburgh, PA 15205
Hutnik, William J., Cardinal Dearden Center, 4721 Fifth Ave., Pittsburgh, PA 15213-2915
Jackovic, George V., 124 Bennington Dr., Canonsburg, PA 15317
Jones, Patrick F., St. Jude the Apostle, 405 Westinghouse Ave., Wilmerding, PA 15148-1123
Jozwiak, Stanislaus J., 2103 Fawcett Ave., White Oak, PA 15131-1819
Kato, Stephen M., St. Stephen Rectory, 2125 Beacon St., McKeesport, PA 15132
Kernan, Michael H., Cardinal Dearden Center, 4721 Fifth Ave., Pittsburg, PA 15213-2915
Kilarecki, George W., Vincentian Home, Perrymont Rd., Pittsburgh, PA 15237
Klein, John P., 105 Mulberry St., Coraopolis, PA 15108
Kopecky, Joseph A., 1503 Sylvan Ave., Natrona Heights, PA 15065-1642
Kuczynski, Francis I., Vincentian Home, Perrymont Rd., Pittsburgh, PA 15237
Kuenzig, Aloysius A., 2715 Custer Ave., Pittsburgh, PA 15227
Kuenzig, Peter A., 2715 Custer Ave., Pittsburgh, PA 15227
Lackner, Francis J.X., St. Bernard, 311 Washington Rd., Pittsburgh, PA 15216
Luteri, Evaristo, St. John Vianney Manor, 2600 Morange Rd., Pittsburgh, PA 15205
Majda, Francis A., 1809 Hanna St., New Castle, PA 16101
Malinak, Joseph G., 6000 N. Ocean Blvd., Ft. Lauderdale, FL 33308
Maliszewski, Edward C., P.O. Box 1075, Monroeville, PA 15146-1075
Marconyak, Albert J., Little Sisters of the Poor, 1028 Benton Ave., Pittsburgh, PA 15212
Massung, Francis G., St. John Vianney Manor, 2600 Morange Rd., Pittsburgh, PA 15205
Mastrangelo, Joseph A., 1111 S. Mercer St., New Castle, PA 16101
McColligan, Raymond A., 98 S.W. 15th Ct., Boynton Beach, FL 33426
McIlvane, Donald W., Pittsburgh Area Religion and Race Council, 1817 Investment Bldg., Pittsburgh, PA 15222
Michaels, John L., St. John Vianney Manor, 2600 Morange Rd., Pittsburgh, PA 15205
Miller, Joseph W., Vincentian Home, Perrymont Rd., Pittsburgh, PA 15237
Molnar, Richard L., 237 E. Eugene St., Munhall, PA 15120
Murphy, Thomas R., 6346 Walnut St., Pittsburgh, PA 15206
Nee, Thomas M., St. John Vianney Manor, 2600 Morange Rd., Pittsburgh, PA 15205
O'Brien, Bernard P., 2217 Los Angeles Ave., Pittsburgh, PA 15216
O'Brien, John, Cardinal Dearden Center, 4721 Fifth Ave., Pittsburgh, PA 15213-2915
O'Connell, Thomas C., Vincentian Home, Perrymont Rd., Pittsburgh, PA 15237
Palko, John A., St. Martin de Porres, c/o 705 Shaw Ave., McKeesport, PA 15132-2334
Paluse, Richard V., 37 Forsythe Rd., Pittsburgh, PA 15220
Parme, George J., St. John Vianney Manor, 2600 Morange Rd., Pittsburgh, PA 15205
Petrie, Harry F., St. Alexis, 10090 Old Perry Hwy., Wexford, PA 15090-9320
Pietrzynski, Boleslaus J., Vincentian Home, Perrymont Rd., Pittsburgh, PA 15237
Plantes, Francis P., St. John Vianney Manor, 2600Morange Rd., Pittsburgh, PA 15205
Pucci, Francis L., Cardinal Dearden Center, 4721 Fifth Ave., Pittsburgh, PA 15213-2915
Roach, Charles B., 8990 E. Washington St., Chagrin Falls, OH 44023
Rodgers, Francis M., St. John Vianney Manor, 2600 Morange Rd., Pittsburgh, PA 15205
Rodgers, Thomas M., Cardinal Dearden Center, 4721 Fifth Ave., Pittsburgh, PA 15213-2915
Romero, Oswald E., Cardinal Dearden Center, 4721 Fifth Ave., Pittsburgh, PA 15213-2915
Scanlon, John J., 1337 Fifth Ave., North Versailles, PA 15137
Schirra, Peter M., 421 Marsh Hill Rd., McHenry, MD 21541
Sedlak, Valentine G., Cardinal Dearden Center, 4721 Fifth Ave., Pittsburgh, PA 15213-2915
Smith, Thomas E., 621 Swallow Dr., Casselberry, FL 32707
Soisson, Clifford F., St. John Vianney Manor, 2600 Morange Rd., Pittsburgh, PA 15205
Stuparitz, George P., St. John Vianney Manor, 2600 Morange Rd., Pittsburgh, PA 15205
Szarnicki, Zygmunt V., St. John Vianney Manor, 2600 Morange Rd., Pittsburgh, PA 15205
Turlik, Andrew J., St. John Vianney Manor, 2600 Morange Rd., Pittsburgh, PA 15205
Unger, John M., St. John Vianney Manor, 2600 Morange Rd., Pittsburgh, PA 15205
Vecchio, Michael J., 502 Sewickley Heights Dr., Sewickley, PA 15143
Vollmer, Raymond A., 148 Monastery Ave., Pittsburgh, PA 15203-1432
Weirauch, William P., 181 44th St., Pittsburgh, PA 15201
Wichmanowski, Walter F., St. John Vianney Manor, 2600 Morange Rd., Pittsburgh, PA 15205
Zolnierzak, Stanislaus J., St. John Vianney Manor, 2600 Morange Rd., Pittsburgh, PA 15205

Permanent Deacons:
Abraham, Leon B., Immaculate Conception, Washington
Bane, John J., St. Bernard, Mount Lebanon
Barth, Robert V., Catholic Cemeteries
Becker, Robert J., St. Albert the Great, Baldwin Boro
Brabender, Herbert C., Allegheny General Hospital
Brueckner, Joseph P., St. Teresa, Perrysville
Cunningham, Regis C., North American Martyrs, Monroeville
Giconi, Mario W.
Gleason, Kenneth V., The Intersection, McKeesport
Hathaway, Ralph B., St. Bernard, Mount Lebanon
Layton, John, St. Benedict the Abbot, Peters Township
McKelvey, Albert T.
Meyer, Joseph C., St. Patrick, Canonsburg
Mueller, Joseph R., St. Sylvester, Brentwood
O'Keefe, Charles L., Little Sisters of the Poor
Rice, Raymond C., St. Paul, Butler
Rubio-Roman, Silverio, St. Victor, Bairdford
Schaefer, Jerome R., St. Fidelis, Meridian/Lyndora
Schaffner, Thomas A., St. Fidelis, Meridian/Lyndora
Stein, Gerald C., St. Paul, Butler
Very, Richard, Resurrection, Brookline

INSTITUTIONS LOCATED IN THE DIOCESE

[A] SEMINARIES, RELIGIOUS OR SCHOLASTICATES

PITTSBURGH. *Saint Paul Seminary*, College & Pre-Theology, 2900 Noblestown Rd., 15205. Tel: 412-921-5800. Revs. Edward J. Burns, Rector; Robert P. Connolly, Vice Rector & Dir. Spiritual Formation; Sr. Judith Worden, R.S.M., Coord. Apostolic Works; Sr. Ignatius Rooney, R.S.M., Admin. Asst. to the Rector. In res., Rev. Albert J. Semler. Priests 2; Sisters 2; Students (attending Duquesne University) 14.

[B] COLLEGES AND UNIVERSITIES

PITTSBURGH. *Carlow College*, 3333 5th Ave., 15213. Tel: 412-578-6000.
For a complete listing, refer to the Colleges and Universities section.
Duquesne University of the Holy Ghost, 600 Forbes Ave., 15282. Tel: 412-396-6000; Fax: 412-396-5785.
For a complete listing, refer to the Colleges and Universities section.
La Roche College, 9000 Babcock Blvd., 15237. Tel: 412-367-9300.
For a complete listing, refer to the Colleges and Universities section.

[C] HIGH SCHOOLS, DIOCESAN

PITTSBURGH. *Canevin Catholic High School*, 2700 Morange Rd., 15205. Tel: 412-922-7400. Mr. John Maurer, Headmaster; Rev. Alvin J. Adams, Chap. Priests 2; Sisters 1; Lay Teachers 36; Students 545.
Central District Catholic High School. (Boys), 4720 Fifth Ave., 15213. Tel: 412-621-8189; Fax: 412-631-0758. The school is a Diocesan institution under the care of the Christian Brothers. Bro. Lawrence Monroe, F.S.C., Prin. Priests 1; Brothers 11; Lay Teachers 48; Students 857.
North Catholic High School. (Coed), 1400 Troy Hill Rd., 15212. Tel: 412-321-4823; Fax: 412-321-0599. Priests 2; Brothers 3; Sisters 6; Lay Teachers 30; Students 560.
Oakland Catholic High School, 144 N. Craig St., 15213.

BADEN. *Quigley Catholic High School*, 200 Quigley Dr., 15005. Tel: 412-869-2188; 343-6722. Rev. David C. Menegay, Prin. Priests 2; Sisters 1; Lay Teachers 19; Students 221.

MCKEESPORT. *Serra Catholic High School*, 200 Hershey Dr., 15132. Tel: 412-751-2020.
Under the direction of the Franciscan Friars (Province of the Immaculate Conception). Rev. Michael Dominic Ledoux, O.F.M., Headmaster. Priests 3; Brothers 2; Sisters 3; Lay Teachers 18; Students 330.

MT. LEBANON. *Seton-LaSalle Catholic High School*, 1000 McNeilly Rd., 15226. Tel: 412-561-3583; Fax: 412-561-9097.
Under care of Christian Brothers and Sisters of Charity. Rev. Mark A. Eckman, Chap.

[D] HIGH SCHOOLS, PRIVATE

PITTSBURGH. *Mt. Alvernia High School*, 146 Hawthorne Rd., 15209. Tel: 412-821-3858. Sisters of St. Francis. Dorothy K. McGinley, Prin. Sisters 5; Lay Teachers 13; Students 149.
Vincentian High School, Peebles Rd. & McKnight Rd., 15237. Tel: 412-364-1616. Vincentian Sisters of Charity 5; Lay Teachers 15; Students 192.

CORAOPOLIS. *Our Lady of the Sacred Heart High School*, 1504 Woodcrest Ave., 15108. Tel: 412-264-5140. Felician Sisters, C.S.S.F. State approved day high school. Sr. Mary Francine Horos, C.S.S.F., Prin. Priests 1; Sisters 3; Lay Teachers 25; Students 310.

[E] ELEMENTARY SCHOOLS, DIOCESAN

PITTSBURGH. *St. Agnes Diocesan School*, 120 Robinson St., 15213. Sr. Elizabeth Ann Herbert, R.S.M., Prin. Sisters 2; Lay Teachers 10; Students 215.

[F] CONSOLIDATED SCHOOLS

PITTSBURGH. *Prince of Peace Catholic School*, 85 S. 14th St., 15203. Sisters 3; Lay Teachers 9; Students 190.
St. John Neumann Regional, Catholic Elementary, 250 44th St., 15201. Sisters 3; Lay Teachers 18; Students 348.

AMBRIDGE. *Glenwood*, 8th Ave., 15003. Serving Good Samaritan Parish. Students 214.

BUTLER. *Butler Catholic School.* St. Michael. (Grades 1-3), 130 Glenn Ave., 16001. St. Paul. (Grades K, 4-8), 515 E. Locust St., 16001. Sisters 2; Lay Teachers 25; Students 465. Serving the parishes of St. Paul, St. Michael, St. Fidelis, St. Andrew, and St. Peter's, Butler. Butler Montessori School, St. Paul Bldg., 515 E. Locust St., 16001.

DUQUESNE. *Duquesne Catholic School.* (Grades PreK-8), 12 Norman St., 15110. Serving the Parishes of Christ the Light of the World and St. Joseph, Duquesne. Lay Teachers 7; Students 135.

ELLSWORTH. *Ave Maria School*, Box 590, 15331. Serving the parishes of Ave Maria: St. Luke, Bentleyville; St. Clement, Ellsworth; and St. Joseph, Cokeburg. Lay Teachers 8; Students 220.

MCKEES ROCKS. *St. John of God School.* (Grades PreK-8), 115 Margaret St., 15136. Lay Teachers 13; Students 252.

MCKEESPORT. *McKeesport Central Catholic*, 2412 Versailles Ave., 15132. Tel: 412-672-4612. Serving the parishes of St. Stephen, St. Mary, German; St. Pius V, St. Mary Czestochowa, St. Denis, Versailles; St. Perpetua, Holy Trinity, Sacred Heart and St. Peter, McKeesport. Felician Sisters, C.S.S.F. 2; Lay Teachers 7; Students 150.

PORT VUE. *St. Joseph Regional School.* (Grades PreK-8), 1125 Romine Ave., 15133. Mrs. Elizabeth M. Kinol, Prin. Serving the parishes of Queen of Rosary, St. Martin de Porres, St. Mark, St. Patrick. Lay Teachers 20; Students 426.

[G] ELEMENTARY SCHOOLS, PRIVATE

PITTSBURGH. *Carlow College Campus School.* (Grades PreK-8), 3333 5th Ave., 15213. Sisters of Mercy. Sisters 2; Lay Teachers 26; Students 280.

Mount Gallitzin Academy, 1020 State St., 15005. Tel: 412-562-3745. Rosemary L. Corsetti, Esquire. Purpose: to engage in educational activities and the operation of educational program of the Sisters of St. Joseph. Funds, distributions, gifts, bequests, endowments, grants, and contributions from other charitable organizations and student tuitions will be used to support applicant organization's programs and ministry outreach.

ALLISON PARK. *Providence Heights Alpha School,* 9000 Babcock Blvd., 15101. Tel: 412-366-4455. Sisters of Divine Providence. Ms. Karen Lehman, Prin.; Sisters 7; Lay Teachers 12; Students 204.

BADEN. *Mt. Gallitzin Academy,* 15005. Tel: 412-869-2505; 869-2151. Sisters of St. Joseph. Sr. Norma Zanieski, C.S.J., Prin. Sisters 11; Lay Teachers 9; Students 275.

[H] DEPARTMENT OF SPECIAL EDUCATION

PITTSBURGH. *The De Paul Institute,* Castlegate Ave., 15226. Tel: 412-561-4848. Day school for children with hearing losses and speech and language disabilities. James R. Farwell, Exec. Dir.; Sr. Virginia Pascaretta, S.C., Educational Dir. Sisters 5; Lay Teachers 16; Students 73.

St. Anthony School Programs, 2718 Custer Ave., 15227. Tel: 412-882-1333; Fax: 412-882-1668. Resource rooms for students with special needs in 6 elementary schools and 2 high schools. Kim Scanlon Lieb, Exec. Dir. Lay Teachers 14; Students 90.

NEW BRIGHTON. *McGuire Memorial Home for Retarded Children,* 2119 Mercer Rd., 15066. Tel: 412-843-3400. Sisters 9; Lay Staff 212; Residents 91.

[I] CHILD CARE INSTITUTIONS

PITTSBURGH. *Franciscan Child Day Care Center,* 1401 Hamilton Rd., 15234-2399. Tel: 412-882-5085.
For a complete listing, refer to the Special Care Facilities section.

Mt. Alvernia Day Care & Learning Center, Kindergarten, 146 Hawthorne Rd., 15209.
For a complete listing, refer to the Special Care Facilities section.

Providence Child Care Center, 400 Hoodridge Dr., 15234. Tel: 412-562-3745.
For a complete listing, refer to the Special Care Facilities section.

Vincentian Child Care, Inc., 8200 McKnight Rd., 15237. Tel: 412-366-8588.
For a complete listing, refer to the Special Care Facilities section.

ALLISON PARK. *Providence Connections, Inc.,* Corporate Office, 9000 Babcock Blvd., 15101. Tel: 412-931-5241; Fax: 412-635-5416.
For a complete listing, refer to the Special Care Facilities section.

EMSWORTH. *Holy Family Institute,* 8235 Ohio River Blvd., 15202. Tel: 412-766-4030.
For a complete listing, refer to the Special Care Facilities section.

[J] GENERAL HOSPITALS

PITTSBURGH. *Mercy Hospital of Pittsburgh,* 1400 Locust St., 15219. Tel: 412-232-8111.
For a complete listing, refer to the Hospitals section.

Mercy Providence Hospital, 1004 Arch St., 15212. Tel: 412-323-5600; Fax: 412-323-5685.
For a complete listing, refer to the Hospitals section.

Pittsburgh Mercy Foundation, Forbes-Stevenson Bldg., 1401 Locust St., Ste. 2, 3rd Fl., 15219-5125.
For a complete listing, refer to the Hospitals section.

Pittsburgh Mercy Health System, Inc., 1400 Locust St., 15219. Tel: 412-232-7510.
For a complete listing, refer to the Hospitals section.

St. Francis Central Hospital, 1200 Centre Ave., 15219. Tel: 412-562-3301.
For a complete listing, refer to the Hospitals section.

St. Francis Medical Center, 400 45th St., 15201. Tel: 412-622-4343.
For a complete listing, refer to the Hospitals section.

St. Francis Nursing Center-East, 745 N. Highland Ave., 15206. Tel: 412-362-6622.
For a complete listing, refer to the Hospitals section.

**St. Francis Health System,* 4401 Penn Ave., 15224-1890. Tel: 412-633-4343.
For a complete listing, refer to the Hospitals section.

CRANBERRY TOWNSHIP. *St. Francis Nursing Center-North,* One St. Francis Way, 16066. Tel: 412-772-5350.
For a complete listing, refer to the Hospitals section.

NEW CASTLE. *St. Francis Hospital of New Castle,* 1000 S. Mercer St., 16101. Tel: 412-658-3511.
For a complete listing, refer to the Hospitals section.

[K] SPECIAL HOSPITALS AND SANATORIA FOR INVALIDS

PITTSBURGH. *Villa De Marillac Nursing Home,* 5300 Stanton Ave., 15206. Tel: 412-361-2833.
For a complete listing, refer to the Special Care Facilities section.

Vincentian Home Inc., 111 Perrymont Rd., 15237. Tel: 412-366-5600.
For a complete listing, refer to the Special Care Facilities section.

[L] HOMES FOR THE AGED

PITTSBURGH. *Home for the Aged of the Little Sisters of the Poor,* 1028 Benton Ave., 15212. Tel: 412-761-5373.
For a complete listing, refer to the Special Care Facilities section.

Marian Hall Home, Inc., 934 Forest Ave., 15202. Tel: 412-761-1999; 761-2556.
For a complete listing, refer to the Special Care Facilities section.

Marian Manor Corp., 2695 Winchester Dr., 15220-4099. Tel: 412-563-6866 (Admin.); 563-1244 (Nursing Service).
For a complete listing, refer to the Special Care Facilities section.

St. Joseph Nursing and Health Care Center, Inc., 5324 Penn Ave., 15224-1798. Tel: 412-665-5100.
For a complete listing, refer to the Special Care Facilities section.

St. Paul Manor, 148 Monastery Ave., 15203. Tel: 412-381-4744.
For a complete listing, refer to the Special Care Facilities section.

St. Pius X Residence, Inc., 2681 Waddington Ave., 15226. Tel: 412-563-5040; Fax: 412-563-3776.
For a complete listing, refer to the Special Care Facilities section.

**St. Francis Plaza, Inc.,* 451 44th St., 15201-1122. Tel: 412-683-6252; Fax: 412-683-4269.
For a complete listing, refer to the Special Care Facilities section.

ALLISON PARK. *Regency Hall Nursing Home, Inc.,* 9399 Babcock Blvd., 15101. Tel: 412-366-8540; Fax: 412-369-9789.
For a complete listing, refer to the Special Care Facilities section.

*BADEN. *Villa St. Joseph of Baden, Inc.,* State St., 15005. Tel: 412-869-2151.
For a complete listing, refer to the Special Care Facilities section.

[M] PERSONAL PRELATURES

PITTSBURGH. *Opus Dei.* (Prelature of the Holy Cross and Opus Dei.), 5090 Warwick Terr., 15213. Tel: 412-683-8448. Legal Title: *The Work of God, Inc.* Revs. Francis J. Hoffman, J.C.D.; Joseph Landauer.

[N] MONASTERIES AND RESIDENCES OF PRIESTS AND BROTHERS

PITTSBURGH. *Congregation of the Oratory of St. Philip Neri,* The Pittsburgh Oratory, 4450 Bayard St., 15213. Tel: 412-681-3181. Very Rev. Bryan F. Summers, C.O., Provost; Revs. Drew P. Morgan, C.O.; David S. Abernethy, C.O.; Joseph C. Linck, C.O. Total Staff 5.

Consolata Fathers, 7110 Thomas Blvd., 15208. Tel: 412-241-3995; Fax: 412-247-5173. Revs. Alex Moreschi, I.M.C., Supr.; Alphonsus Mwariri, I.M.C., Admin. Priests 3.

Croatian Commissariate, T.O.R., 24 Maryland Ave., 152090. Tel: 412-821-3438; Fax: 412-821-8276. Very Rev. Romildo Hrboka, Commissary Prov. Councillors: Revs. Gabriel Badurina, T.O.R.; Grgo Sikiric, T.O.R.

Franciscan Friars, T.O.R., Queen of Peace Friary, 5324 Carnegie St., 15201. Tel: 412-782-4755. Very Rev. Edmund F. Carroll, T.O.R., Min. Prov. in res. Tel: 412-781-1232 (Office); Rev. Patrick Donahoe, T.O.R.; Bro. Albert Gentile, T.O.R., Local Min. Hospital Ministry: Revs. Carlo Napoli, T.O.R.; Patrick George, T.O.R.; Bernard Tickerhoof, T.O.R., Retreat Ministry. In res., Revs. Canice Crawford, T.O.R.; Patrick Donahoe, T.O.R.

Marianist Community, 1400 Troy Hill Rd., 15212. Tel: 412-321-7234. Bro. William Grundish, Dir.; Rev. James R. McKay, S.M., Chap.; Bros. Al Gillis; Bernard Hartman. Priests 1; Brothers 5.

St. Augustine Friary, 221 36th St., 15201. Tel: 412-682-6430; Fax: 412-682-6148. Revs. Gregory Chervenak, O.F.M.Cap., Guardian; Robert Craig, O.F.M.Cap., Vicar; Jerome Dunn, O.F.M.Cap.; Paul Farkas, O.F.M.Cap.; Francis Fugini, O.F.M.Cap., Sec. Archives & Annals, Coord. for Missions and Provincial Fund Raising; Aidan Lucko, O.F.M.Cap.; Brendan Malloy, O.F.M.Cap., Communications Dir., Prov. Spiritual Asst. S.F.O.; Roland Raible, O.F.M.Cap.; Bertin Roll, O.F.M.Cap., Dir. Archconfraternity of Christian Mothers; Pascal Schaller, O.F.M.Cap.; Scott Seethaler, O.F.M.Cap.; DeSales Young, O.F.M.Cap.; Bros. David Cira, O.F.M.Cap.; Richard Lubomski, O.F.M.Cap.; Charles O'Connor, O.F.M.Cap.; Thomas Tomasunas, O.F.M.Cap.; Joseph Day, O.F.M.Cap.; Joseph Savey, O.F.M.Cap.

St. Conrad Friary. 9448 Babcock Blvd., Allison Park, 15101. Tel: 412-364-8240; Fax: 412-366-8331. Revs. Robert L. McCreary, O.F.M.Cap., Dir. Novices & Guardian; John Petrikovic, O.F.M.Cap., Graduate Studies,Gregorian Univ., Rome; Blaise J. Fusco, O.F.M.Cap., Chaplain, Jubilarian; Myles Schmitt, O.F.M.Cap., Jubilarian Confessor; W. David Nestler, O.F.M.Cap., Asst. Dir. Novices, Vicar; John Berchmans Schmidt, O.F.M.Cap., Jubilarian.

St. Francis Friary, 2905 Castlegate Ave., 15226. Tel: 412-531-4545. Revs. Thomas A. Dutkiewicz, Vicar, Confessor, St. Mary of Mercy Church, Pittsburgh; Ronald Lawler, Dir. Office for Adult & Family Catechesis; Emil William Fischer, Preaching Ministry, Guardian; Emett Schuler, VA Chap.; Maurice Sheehan. Residents 6.

St. John Vianney Manor, 2600 Morange Rd., 15205. Tel: 412-928-0825; 928-0908. Retired priests' residence. In res., Revs. Leo J. Beck; Nicholas A. Biondi; Leo R. Burchianti; Glenn T. Conner; Joseph Cvelbar; Francis M. Dismachek; Rev. Msgr. Joseph G. Findlan; Revs. John D. Fording; Leo G. Henry; Thomas J. Horner; George W. Kilarecki; Evarisro Luteri; Francis G. Massung; John L. Michaels; Thomas M. Nee; Thomas C. O'Connell; George J. Parme; Francis P. Plantes; Francis M. Rodgers; Rev. Msgr. Francis J. Rooney; Rev. F. Clifford Soisson; Rev. Msgr. Ferdinand M. Sojka; Revs. George P. Stuparitz; Zygmunt V. Szarnicki; Andrew J. Turlik; John M. Unger; Walter F. Wichmanowski; Stanislaus J. Zolnierzak. Total in Residence 28; Total Staff 8.

St. Patrick Friary, 1711 Liberty Ave., 15222. Tel: 412-471-4310. Revs. William Graham, O.F.M.Cap., Vicar; Bonaventure Stefan, O.F.M.Cap., Chap., St. Francis Medical Center, Pittsburgh; Edward Laurent, O.F.M.Cap., Supr., Dir. of St. Fidelis Devel. Office; Philip Fink, O.F.M.Cap., Prov.

St. Paul of the Cross Monastery. Retreat Center, Passionist Overseas Missions. 148 Monastery Ave., S.S., 15203. Tel: 412-381-1188. Very Rev. Xavier Vitacolonna, C.P., Local Supr.; Bro. Matthew Krawchyk, C.P., Asst. Local Supr.; Revs. Timothy Fitzgerald, C.P.; Henry Kavanagh; Gerald Laba, C.P.; John F. McMillan, C.P., Dir. Confraternity of the Passion; Edwin Moran, C.P.; Anthony Neary, C.P.; Clement Pavlick, C.P.; Vincent Segotta, C.P.; Jerome Vereb, C.P.; Mark Ward, C.P., Assoc. Retreat Dir.; Michael Salvagna, C.P., Retreat Dir.; Dan Sullivan, C.P.; Bros. Leo Di Fiore, C.P., Passionist Overseas Missions; Joseph Holzer, C.P.; Benedict Palese, C.P.
Mission Band: Revs. Vincent Segotta, C.P.; Timothy Fitzgerald, C.P.; Edwin Moran, C.P.
Retreat Center: Revs. Michael Salvagna, C.P., Dir. Tel: 412-381-7676; Mark Ward, C.P.
Passionist Overseas Missions: Bro. Leo Di Fiore, C.P., Rel. Admin. Coord. Tel: 412-381-1189. Total Assisted 5,000; Residents 19; Total Staff 15.

Society of The Divine Word, 207 Lytton, 15213. Tel: 412-683-4030. Rev. Walter Ostrowski, S.V.D., Mission Dir. Tel: 412-683-0640. In res., Rev. Leo Dusheck, S.V.D.

Third Order Regular of Saint Francis - Province of the Most Sacred Heart of Jesus, 215 57th St., 15201-2338. Tel: 412-781-1232; Fax: 412-781-1219. Very Rev. Edmund F. Carroll, T.O.R., Prov. Min., Queen of Peace Friary, 5324 Carnegie St., Pittsburg, 15201. Tel: 412-782-4755. Residents 6; Total Staff 2.

AVALON. *Holy Family Friary.* (Friars Minor), The Franciscans. Vice-Province of the Most Holy Savior, 232 S. Home Ave., Pittsburgh, 15202. Tel: 412-761-2550; 761-8470; Fax: 412-761-2959. Friars David Kohut, O.F.M., Prov.; Lawrence Pollack, O.F.M.; Jerome Pavlik, O.F.M.; David A. Moczulski, O.F.M.; Matthew Brozovic, O.F.M.; Daniel Barrett, O.F.M.; Gilbert Maga, O.F.M.; George Poser, O.F.M.; Thomas Gerchak, O.F.M.; Joseph Gonchar, O.F.M.; Micah Muhlen, O.F.M.; Mark Hudak, O.F.M. Friars 10.

BEAVER FALLS. *Our Lady of Peace Monastery,* 71 Darlington Rd., 15010. Tel: 412-843-6110. Rev. Bruno Raspudic, O.F.M., Supr.

BEN AVON. *St. Anthony Friary and Mission House.* 226 Rostrevor Pl., Pittsburgh, 15202-1919. Tel: 412-761-4831. Franciscan Fathers of the Assumption of the

Blessed Virgin Mary Province (Order of Friars Minor). Revs. Jerome B. Staniszewski, O.F.M., Guardian & Dir. Missions; Sylvester E. Makarewicz, O.F.M., Vicar, (On Medical Leave); Marcel M. Pasiecznik, O.F.M.; Michael Lacienski, O.F.M.; Rembert Badarzynski, O.F.M.; James Heinsch, O.F.M.; Bro. Ladislaus Wyka, O.F.M. Fathers 6; Brothers 1.

BETHEL PARK. *Holy Ghost Fathers and Brothers Provincialate*, 6230 Brush Run Rd., 15102. Tel: 412-831-0302. Very Rev. Christopher P. Promis, C.S.Sp., Prov.; Rev. Henry J. Koren, C.S.Sp., Archivist. Residents 6; Total Staff 2.

HERMAN. *St. Mary's Friary*, 16039. Tel: 412-285-3285. Capuchin Friars. Revs. Louis Petruha, O.F.M.Cap., Guardian; DePaul Ripko, O.F.M.Cap.; Wendel Moliski, O.F.M.Cap.; James Kurtz, O.F.M.Cap., Vicar; Lester Knoll, O.F.M.Cap.; Joachim Strupp, O.F.M.Cap.; Bros. James Townsend, O.F.M.Cap.; Robert Herrick, O.F.M.Cap.

MCKEESPORT. *Franciscan Friars*. Faculty Res. Serra Catholic High School, 200 Hershey Dr., 15132. Tel: 412-751-1250. Friars John-Michael Pinto, O.F.M., Guardian; Alexis Anania, O.F.M.; Michael Dominic W. Ledoux, O.F.M., Vicar; Sean Mary Fitzwater, T.O.R.; Jack W. Hoak, O.F.M.

ROCHESTER. *St. Cecilia Friary*, 303 Jackson St., 15074. Tel: 412-775-0801; 774-6046. Capuchin Friars. Revs. Ward Stakem, O.F.M.Cap.; William Gillum, O.F.M.Cap.; Leon Leitem, O.F.M.Cap.; Roy Schuster, O.F.M.Cap.; Mark Carter, O.F.M.Cap.; Bernard Finerty, O.F.M.Cap. In res., Rev. Marvin Justi, O.F.M.Cap., Vicar.

[O] CONVENTS AND RESIDENCES FOR SISTERS

PITTSBURGH. *Convent of Mercy*, 3333 Fifth Ave., 15213. Tel: 412-578-6225. Motherhouse of Sisters of Mercy of the County of Allegheny. Established in 1843. Sr. Georgine Scarpino, R.S.M.; Rev. Robert J. George, Chap. Sisters 224; Total Professed Sisters 224.

Holy Family Manor, 301 Bellevue Rd., 15229-2194. Tel: 412-931-6996. Residence for Retired Sisters. Sisters 57.

Jesus Redeemer Convent, 285 Bellevue Rd., 15229-2195. Tel: 412-931-5388.

Ladies of Bethany, 1004 Oglethorpe Ave., 15201-2151. Tel: 412-781-4022. Other Convents, 1200 Greenhill Rd., 15209. Tel: 412-821-1690. 276 Bruin Rd., Petrolia, 16050. Tel: 412-753-2294.

Motherhouse and Novitiate of the Vincentian Sisters of Charity, 8200 McKnight Rd., 15237. Tel: 412-364-3000; Fax: 412-364-9055. Sr. Rita Gesue, V.S.C., Supr. Gen.; Rev. Blaise J. Fusco, O.F.M.Cap., Chap.

Nativity Convent, 4100 Vinceton St., 15214. Tel: 412-931-2299. North American Union of the Sisters of Our Lady of Charity, Inc. Sr. Thomas Aul, Local Supr. Sisters 14.

Our Lady of Sorrows Convent of the Passionist Nuns, 2715 Churchview Ave., 15227. Tel: 412-881-1155. Motherhouse and Novitiate of the Religious of the Passion. (Passionist Nuns). Mother Mary Ann, C.P., Supr. Professed Sisters 9; Novices 1.

St. Benedict Monastery, Benedictine Sisters of Pontifical Jurisdiction, 4530 Perrysville Ave., 15229-2296. Tel: 412-931-2844; Fax: 412-931-8970. Motherhouse and Novitiate of the Benedictine Sisters in the Diocese. Sr. Roberta Campbell, O.S.B., Prioress. Sisters 90.

Benedictine Center, Inc. Sr. Roberta Campbell, O.S.B., Pres.

Sisters of St. Francis of the Providence of God, St. Francis Convent Motherhouse, 3603 McRoberts Rd., 15234-2398. Tel: 412-882-9911. Sr. Joanne Brazinski, O.S.F., Gen. Supr.; Rev. Thomas Kram, Chap. Sisters 119.

Sisters of the Holy Family of Nazareth of Western Pennsylvania, 285 Bellevue Rd., 15229-2195. Tel: 412-931-4775. Sr. Maria Kruszewski, C.S.F.N., Prov. Supr. Tel: 412-931-4778; Fax: 412-931-9746. Legal Title: *Sisters of the Holy Family of Nazareth of Western Pennsylvania*. Professed Sisters in Provincialate 43; Total Professed Sisters 161.

ALLISON PARK. *The Sisters of Divine Providence*, Providence Heights Motherhouse, 9000 Babcock Blvd., 15101-2793. Tel: 412-931-5241. Motherhouse and Novitiate of the Sisters of Divine Providence in the Diocese (Pittsburgh Province). Sr. Mary Ellen Rufft, C.D.P., Prov. Dir. & Pres.; Rev. Frank D. Almade. In Motherhouse 113; In Province (including Puerto Rico) 281.

BADEN. *St. Joseph Convent*, 15005. Tel: 412-869-2151; 761-3700; Fax: 412-869-3336. Motherhouse of Sisters of St. Joseph. Rev. David C. Menegay, M.A., M.S.Ed., Chap. In Community 333 (Final Professed); Temporary 2; Novices 3.

BELLEVUE. *Mount Assisi Convent*. Motherhouse of the School Sisters of the Third Order of St. Francis, 934 Forest Ave., Pittsburgh, 15202. Tel: 412-761-6004. In res., Rev. James R. Bedillion. Sisters 91; Residents 65; Total Staff 25.

CORAOPOLIS. *Our Lady of the Sacred Heart Convent*. 1500 Woodcrest Ave., Pittsburgh, 15108. Tel: 412-264-2890; 269-2881; Fax: 412-264-7047.

Provincial House and Novitiate of the Felician Sisters of Pennsylvania C.S.S.F. Sr. Mary Cabrini Procopio, C.S.S.F., Prov. Min.; Rev. Arthur L. Garbin, Chap. Professed 148; Total in Residence 88; Total Staff 29.

Infirmary of St. Joseph Hall, 1500 Woodcrest Ave., 15108. Tel: 412-264-2890; 269-2881. Rev. Richard L. Conboy, Chap.

ELIZABETH. *Divine Redeemer Motherhouse*, 999 Rock Run Rd., 15037. Tel: 412-751-8600; Fax: 412-751-0355. Motherhouse and Novitiate of the Sisters of the Divine Redeemer. Sr. M. Monica Kosztolnyik, S.D.R., Prov. In res., Rev. George T. Leech, Chap. In the Community 60.

EMSWORTH. *Mother Frances Convent*. 140 Allegheny Ave., Pittsburgh, 15202-1402. Tel: 412-766-6702.

MILLVALE. *St. Francis Convent*. Mt. Alvernia, 146 Hawthorne Rd., Pittsburgh, 15209. Tel: 412-821-2200; Fax: 412-821-3318. Sisters of St. Francis of Millvale, PA. Motherhouse and Novitiate of the Order in the Diocese. In the Community: Professed Sisters 232; Juniors 1; Associates 37; In the Motherhouse: Professed Sisters 98. Attended by Capuchin Fathers from St. Augustine, Pittsburgh.

ROSS TOWNSHIP. *Motherhouse, Sisters of the Holy Spirit (S.H.S.)*. 5246 Clarwin Ave., Pittsburgh, 15229. Tel: 412-931-1917. Sr. Marita Juras, S.H.S., Gen. Supr.; Very Rev. David A. Zubik, Chap. Professed Sisters 68; Total in Community 68.

VILLA MARIA. *Sisters of the Humility of Mary*, Villa Maria Community Center, P.O. Box 914, 16155. Tel: 412-964-8861; Fax: 412-964-8082. Sr. Celine Metzger, H.M., Major Supr.; Rev. Frank Erdeljac. Tel: 412-535-4786. Professed Sisters 261; Candidates 2; Novices 2; Residents 90; Total Staff 125.

[P] RETREAT HOUSES

PITTSBURGH. *Martina Spiritual Renewal Center, Inc.*, 5244 Clarwin Ave., 15229. Tel: 412-931-9766. Conducted by Sisters of the Holy Spirit.

Purpose: To provide a facility to individuals and groups for retreats and spiritual programs. Sr. Marita Juras, S.H.S., Pres.; Sr. Mary Richard Mehelich, S.H.S., Dir.; Sr. Madalyn Chlebowski, S.H.S., Assoc. Dir.

St. Paul of the Cross Retreat Center, 148 Monastery Ave., 15203. Tel: 412-381-7676; 381-7677; Fax: 412-431-3044. Revs. Michael Salvagna, C.P., Dir.; Mark Ward, C.P., Asst. Dir. Assocs.: Mrs. Bonnie Coluccio; Dr. Susan Stangl; Dr. Salvatore Mascari.

**The Burning Bush: Franciscan House of Prayer*, 32-40 Pius St., 15203-1617. Tel: 412-381-3819.

Purposes: A Franciscan-oriented House of Prayer and retreat facility for contemplation, rest, prayer and spiritual nourishment; facility for formation and prayer of Secular Franciscan Order Members. Contact Persons: Fred Koerner, S.F.O.; Sr. Damian Tosi, O.L.C. Total in Residence 3.

ALLISON PARK. *Kearns Spirituality Center*, 9000 Babcock Blvd., 15101-2713. Tel: 412-366-1124; Fax: 412-635-5416. Sisters of Divine Providence. Sr. Agnes Raible, C.D.P., Dir.

Conference room for 250; overnight accommodations for 60; dining facilities for 200. Total Staff 7.

BETHEL PARK. *Holy Ghost Animation Center*, 6230 Bush Run Rd., 15102. Tel: 412-835-3510. Revs. Francis X. Hanley, C.S.Sp., Dir.; Henry J. Koren, C.S.Sp.; James F. Pergl, C.S.Sp.; John S. Rondeau, C.S.Sp.; William J. Joyce, C.S.Sp.; Daniels DeDominicis, C.S.Sp.; John P. McAndrew, C.S.Sp.; John M. Jendzura. Total in Residence 8; Total Staff 20.

CORAOPOLIS. *Gilmary Diocesan Center*, 601 Flaugherty Run Rd., 15108-3899. Tel: 412-264-8400; Fax: 412-264-8415. Ronald W. Ragan, Dir.

Overnight facilities for 219; meeting rooms for one-day programs; separate adult and youth facilities; 138 seat dining room, 150 seat chapel, indoor heated swimming pool, gymnasium, outdoor volleyball and basketball courts and ballfield.

Office for Adolescent Formation & Youth Ministry. Joyce Gillooly, Dir. Tel: 412-264-9530: Fax: 412-264-9539. Total Staff 11.

GIBSONIA. *John Cardinal Wright Vocation and Prayer Center*, 10745 Babcock Blvd., 15044. Mrs. Diane Gasbarro, Mgr. Total Staff 10.

[Q] OFFICES FOR CAMPUS MINISTRY

PITTSBURGH. *Office of Chaplaincies*, 4721 Fifth Ave., 15213. Tel: 412-621-6209. Rev. John J. Keane, Dir.

SLIPPERY ROCK. *Office for Campus Ministry*, 342 Normal Ave., 16057. Tel: 412-794-6620. Rev. Robert L. Seeman, Dir., Art Institute of Pittsburgh. (Pittsburgh), Downtown Campus Ministry, 135 1st Ave. #118, Pittsburgh, 15222. Tel: 412-456-3118. Rev. Joseph Linck, C.O., Carlow College, 3333 5th Ave., Pittsburgh, 15213. Tel: 412-578-6069. Nellene Groetsch, Carnegie-Mellon University, Ryan Catholic Newman Center, 4450 Bayard St., Pittsburgh, 15213. Tel: 412-681-3181. Rev. Bryan F. Summers, C.O.; Sr. Bernadette Young, C.D.P.; Rev. David S. Abernathy, C.O.; Drew Morgan, C.O., Chatham College, Ryan Catholic Newman Center, 4450 Bayard St., Pittsburgh, 15213. Tel: 412-681-3181. Rev. Bryan F. Summers, C.O.; Sr. Bernadette Young, C.D.P.; Revs. David S. Abernethy; Drew Morgan, C.O., Duquesne University, Campus Ministry, Pittsburgh, 15282. Tel: 412-434-6020. Revs. Donald McEachin, C.S.Sp.; Raymond D. French, C.S.Sp.; Jocelyn Gregoire, C.S.Sp.; Sr. Bernadette Campbell, O.P., Geneva College, Rte. 18 College Hill, Beaver Falls, 15010. Tel: 412-773-3839. Patrick Corcoran, Dir., La Roche College, Campus Ministry, 9000 Babcock Blvd., Pittsburgh, 15237. Tel: 412-367-9300, Ext. 141. Rev. W. Peter Horton, Pennsylvania State University, Beaver Campus, Broadhead Rd., Monaca, 15061. Tel: 412-773-3839. Mr. Patrick W. Corcoran, Point Park College, Downtown Campus Ministry, 135 1st Ave., Rm. 118, Pittsburgh, 15222. Tel: 412-456-3118. Rev. Joseph Linck, C.O., Robert Morris College, Moon Township Campus, St. James, 200 Walnut St., Sewickly, 15143. Tel: 412-741-0836; 262-8313. Rev. Harold E. Baily, Robert Morris College, Pittsburgh Campus, Downtown Campus Ministry, 600 5th Ave., Pittsburgh, 15219. Tel: 412-227-6800. Rev. Joseph Linck, C.O., University of Pittsburgh, Ryan Catholic Newman Center, 4450 Bayard St., Pittsburgh, 15213. Tel: 412-681-3181. Revs. Bryan F. Summers, C.O., Dir.; David S. Abernethy, C.O.; Drew Morgan, C.O.; Sr. Bernadette Young, C.D.P., California University (California), 213 4th St., California, 15419. Tel: 412-938-4573. Faye E. Abbondanza; Rev. Timothy F. Whalen, Westminster College, 314 W. Englewood Ave., New Wilmington, 16105. Tel: 412-946-8761. Rev. David A. Driesch, Slippery Rock University, Newman Center (Slippery Rock), 342 Normal Ave., 16057. Tel: 412-794-8459. Rev. Robert L. Seeman, Dir.; Ms. Diane Magliocca, Campus Min., Washington and Jefferson College (Washington), Newman Center, 1 S. College St., Washington, 15301. Tel: 412-228-7044. Rev. Kevin McKnight, Chap., Waynesburg College (Waynesburg), St. Ann Church, 32 S. Cumberland St., Waynesburg, 15370. Tel: 412-627-8191. Rev. Albin C. McGinnis.

[R] MISCELLANEOUS LISTINGS

PITTSBURGH. *Archivists for Congregations of Women Religious*, ACWR National Office, c/o Mercy Archives, 3333 Fifth Ave., 15213-3165. Tel: 412-578-6213; Fax: 412-578-6180. Sr. Patricia A. Hodge, R.S.M., Contact Person.

Purpose: Education and archival historical research in support of activities and projects conducted by the Roman Catholic Religious Congregations of Women.

The Capuchin Franciscan Volunteer Corps, Inc., 220 37th St., 15201. Tel: 412-682-6011. Province of St. Augustine of the Capuchin Order. Rev. William Talentino, O.F.M.Cap., Dir.

Purpose: To promote, train, supervise and support Catholic lay missions and missionaries throughout the world, especially in conjunction with the ministries and fraternities of the Capuchin Order.

Cardinal Tardini Charitable Trust, 111 Blvd. of the Allies, 15222. Tel: 412-456-3000.

Catholic Business Alliance, 107 Shannon Dr., 15238. Tel: 412-967-0613; Fax: 412-255-9868. Mr. Frederick P. O'Brien, Contact Person.

Purpose: To devote talents and resources to assist Catholic Charities, special Diocesan projects approved by the Bishop, and enrich spiritual life of membership.

Catholic Diocese of Pittsburgh Foundation, 111 Blvd. of the Allies, 15222. Tel: 412-456-3085.

The Catholic Historical Society of Western Pennsylvania, Synod Hall, 125 N. Craig St., 15213. Tel: 412-531-5725. Mr. Anthony P. Joseph, Jr., Pres.

Purpose: To promote the teaching of the Catholic Church in the United States, especially the Church in Western Pennsylvania; to recognize the growth, development and contribution of the Catholic Church by the preservation of artifacts, records and documents related to that history; to make available the results of research and study.

Chimbote Foundation, 2900 Noblestown Rd., 15205.

Congregations of Religious Women Charitable Trust, 285 Bellevue Rd., 15229. Sr. Michele Collins, C.S.F.N., Chm.

Elizabeth Seton Center Inc., 1900 Pioneer Ave., 15226. Tel: 412-561-8400. Sr. Barbara Ann Boss, S.C., Exec. Dir. Day Care Programs for Children and Adults; Senior Citizens Center; Suzuki School of Music. Sisters of Charity 15; Total Assisted 1,030; Total Staff 55.

The Epiphany Association, 948 Tropical Ave., 15216. Tel: 412-341-7494; Fax: 412-341-7495. Total Staff 4.

Holy Family Foundation, 8325 Ohio River Blvd., Ste. 200, 15202-1594. The Holy Family Foundation was formed in 1992 to promote & support the public charitable works & educational purposes of Holy Family Institute.

Jesuit Community of Pittsburgh. Corpus Christi Pastoral Center. 1550 Lincoln Ave., 15206. Tel: 412-361-2167. Rev. Robert B. Cullen, S.J. Total Assisted 5.

Mount Nazareth Center, Inc., 285 Bellevue Rd., 15229-2195. Tel: 412-931-9761; Fax: 412-931-7255. Mr. Fred D. Just, Exec. Dir. Tel: 412-931-1039.

Mt. Nazareth Learning Center. Child Care: Infants; Toddlers; Pre-School; Kindergarten. Tel: 412-931-9761; 931-9241.

Nazareth Housing Services. Housing Counseling; Low Income Home Ownership. Tel: 412-931-3510.

Nazareth Family Services. Family Counseling; Family Life Education. Tel: 412-931-1026. Total Assisted 1,050; Total Staff 32.

North Catholic Endowment Fund, 111 Blvd. of the Allies, 15222.

Pension Plan for the Diocese of Pittsburgh. (Lay Pension Plan), 111 Blvd. of the Allies, 15222. Tel: 412-456-3137; Fax: 412-456-3130. Mr. Charles A. Koempel, Dir.

Pittsburgh Catholic Publishing Associates. Purpose: To promote for Catholics and other readers an understanding of the mission and teachings of the Church and its role in the community. 135 First Ave., Ste. 200, 15222-1506. Tel: 412-471-1252. Mr. Michael Aquilina, Editor; Ms. Carmella A. Weismantle, Comptroller.
Purpose: To promote for Catholics and other readers an understanding of the mission and teachings of the Church and its role in the community.

Pittsburgh Diocese Knights of Columbus Bishop Wright Project, (Incorporated), 2718 Custer Ave., 15227. Tel: 412-882-1333. Project for benefit of St. Anthony School for Programs and McGuire Memorial.

Priests' Benefit Plan of the Diocese of Pittsburgh, 111 Blvd. of the Allies, 15222. Tel: 412-456-3137; Fax: 412-456-3139. Rev. Thomas Kram, Chm.
Purpose: To provide certain retirement and health-related benefits to eligible priests.

St. Joseph's House of Hospitality, Inc., 1635 Bedford Ave., 15219. Tel: 412-471-0666. A subsidiary of Catholic Charities. Mrs. Mary Land Hine, M.P.A., Dir.; Rev. Robert J. Drake, Chap. Seton Hill Sisters of Charity 4; Residents 60; Total Assisted 140; Total Staff 18.

Maryhouse Residence for Women, 1113 Creedmoor Ave., 15226. Tel: 412-563-3312. Residents 30; Sisters of St. Francis 1.

St. Regis Residence for Ladies. (Non-Sectarian), 50 Congress St., 15219. Tel: 412-281-9888. Accommodations for 73 boarders, and is under the direction of a Board of Lay Managers. Rose Smith, Mgr. Permanent Residents 35; Staff 6.

Saint Thomas More Society, 300 Four PPG Pl., 15222-5404. Tel: 412-338-4750. Mr. Brian O'Connor, Pres.

St. Vincent de Paul Society, 1917 Brownsville Rd., 15210.

Sisters of Mercy Continuing Support Trust Fund, 3333 Fifth Ave., 15213. Sr. Georgine Scarpino, Pres.

Sisters of St. Francis of the Providence of God Ministries Corporation, 3603 McRoberts Rd., 15234-2398. Tel: 412-882-9911. Sr. Marian Blodis, O.S.F., Pres.
Program: Franciscan Spirit and Life Center.

Society of Saint Vincent de Paul, Council of Pittsburgh, 1243 N. Franklin St., 15233. Tel: 412-321-1071; Fax: 412-321-9131. Pete Jeffrey, Pres.; Rev. Thomas Rodgers, Spiritual Advisor.

**The Burning Bush*, 32 Pius St., 15203-1617.

Toner Trust, Catholic Institute of Pittsburgh, 111 Blvd. of the Allies, 15222.

Trust for Theological Studies, 111 Blvd. of Allies, 15222. Most Rev. John B. McDowell, Ph.D., D.D., V.G.

Vincentian Sisters of Charity Collaborative Services, 8200 McKnight Rd., 15237. Tel: 412-364-3000. Sr. Rita Gesue, Pres.
Purpose: To provide coordination and supervision of organizations providing long term care services delivered by nursing facilities.

ALLISON PARK. *Divine Providence Foundation*, 9000 Babcock Blvd., 15101. Tel: 412-931-5241; Fax: 412-635-5416. Sr. Mary Ellen Rufft, C.D.P., Pres.
Purpose: To perform, foster, and support acts of Christian charity among the sick and ailing.

Sisters of Divine Providence Charitable Trust, 9000 Babcock Blvd., 15101-2793. Tel: 412-931-5241; Fax: 412-635-5416. Sr. Mary Ellen Rufft, C.D.P., Pres.

BADEN.

**Girls Hope of Pittsburgh, Inc.*, 1020 Baden St., 15005. Tel: 412-869-2868. Sr. Donna Marie Tahaney, Contact Person.
Purpose: To provide a supportive home environment and a quality education through college for girls who have potential for leadership but who because of poverty, abuse, neglect or abandonment cannot remain in their own homes. Total Assisted 20; Total Staff 5.

CLAIRTON. *Sisters Place, Inc.*, 460 Reed St., 15025. Tel: 412-233-3903; Fax: 412-233-3904.
Purpose: To provide hospitality, housing and advocacy to women and children who are homeless or of low income. Sr. Cynthia Serjak, R.S.M., Pres.; Kathi Boyle, Exec. Dir.

ELIZABETH. *Divine Redeemer Health Care Ministeries Corp.*, 999 Rock Run Rd., 15037; Fax: 412-751-0355.

Sisters of Divine Redeemer Charitable Trust, 999 Rock Run Rd., 15037. Tel: 412-751-8600; Fax: 412-751-0355.

MCKEESPORT. *Auberle*, 1101 Hartman St., 15132. Tel: 412-673-5800. Mr. Lynn M. Knezevich, Exec. Dir.
Purpose: To provide services to at risk children and their families. Total in Residence 150; Total Staff 200.

Pauline Auberle Foundation, 1101 Hartman St., 15132. Tel: 412-673-5800. Raymond M. Niedenberger, Exec. Dir. Continues mission of Pauline Auberle Foundation while providing support to Auberle through fundraising, rental agreements, and overall management and leadership services. Total Staff 13.

VILLA MARIA. *The Center for Learning*, Evergreen Rd., Box 910, 16155. Tel: 800-767-9090; 412-964-8083; Fax: 888-767-8080. Educational Development Center and Publisher of values-based instructional materials: Religion for Catholic schools and parishes; English/Language Arts, Social Studies, Novel/Drama and Elementary Curriculum Units for all schools. Sr. Rose Schaffer, H.M., M.A., Pres. & CEO; Sr. Bernadette Vetter, H.M., M.A., Vice Pres. Owned and operated by the Sisters of the Humility of Mary. Directed by an Ecumenical Lay Board. Shipping-business office in Villa Maria. Administrative-Editorial Office, 21590 Center Ridge Rd., Rocky River, OH, 44116. Tel: 216-331-1404; Fax: 216-331-5414.
E-Mail: cfl@stratos.net

Sisters of the Humility of Mary Charitable Trust, Villa Maria Community Center, P.O. Box 313, 16155. Tel: 412-964-8861. Sr. Mildred Ely, H.M., Contact.

Villa Maria Education Center, 16155. Sr. Rose Marie Kramer, H.M., Dir. A center for adolescents and pre-adolescents which provides programs to foster the development of strong spiritual and personal values, self-worth, respect for others, and social awareness. Total Assisted 2,230; Total Staff 5.

Villa Maria Residential Services. (Villa Maria Apartments), P.O. Box 230, 16155. Tel: 412-964-8099; Fax: 412-964-8082. Housing for low & moderate income for senior citizens 62 & over. Sr. Mary Ida Schaffer, H.M., Pres. & CEO. Apartments 37.

WILDWOOD. *Christ Child Society of Pittsburgh*, P.O. Box 213, 15091. Tel: 412-682-4102. Mrs. Madeleine Steinman, Contact; Rev. Frank D. Almade, Chap.
Purpose: To foster a personal love of Christ expressed in service for needy children and youths.

RELIGIOUS INSTITUTES OF MEN REPRESENTED IN THE DIOCESE

For further details refer to the corresponding bracketed number in the Religious Institutes of Men or Women section.

[0200]—*Benedictine Monks.* (St. Vincent Archabbey).—O.S.B.

[0330]—*Brothers of the Christian Schools.* (Prov. of Baltimore).—F.S.C.

[0470]—*The Capuchin Friars.* (Prov. of St. Augustine).—O.F.M.Cap.

[1000]—*Congregation of the Passion.* (Eastern Prov.).—C.P.

[0390]—*Consolata Missionaries.*—I.M.C.

[]—*Croatian Franciscans.* Croatian Commissariate.—T.O.R.

[0520]—*Franciscan Friars.* (Provs. of Assumption B.V.M. & Immaculate Conception; Custodies of Most Holy Savior).—O.F.M.

[0650]—*Holy Ghost Fathers.* (Eastern Prov.).—C.S.Sp.

[0690]—*Jesuit Fathers and Brothers.* (Maryland Prov.).—S.J.

[0950]—*Oratorians.*—C.O.

[0430]—*Order of Preachers (Dominicans).* Province of St. Joseph.—O.P.

[0760]—*Society of Mary (Marianists).* (Cincinnati Prov.).—S.M.

[0420]—*Society of the Divine Word.*—S.V.D.

[0560]—*Third Order Regular of Saint Francis.* (Prov. of Sacred Heart of Jesus).—T.O.R.

RELIGIOUS INSTITUTES OF WOMEN REPRESENTED IN THE DIOCESE

[0130]—*Apostles of the Sacred Heart of Jesus.*—A.S.C.J.

[0230]—*Benedictine Sisters of Pontifical Jursidiction.*—O.S.B.

[]—*Daughters of Mary, Mother of the Church.*—D.M.

[1070-24]—*Dominican Sisters.*—O.P.

[]—*Dominican Sisters, Congregation of the Most Holy Rosary.*

[1170]—*Felician Sisters.*—C.S.S.F.

[1190]—*Franciscan Sisters of Atonement.*—S.A.

[2575]—*Institute of the Sisters of Mercy of the Americas.* (Pittsburgh, PA; Erie, PA; Scranton, PA).—R.S.M.

[]—*Ladies of Bethany.*—L.B.

[2340]—*Little Sisters of the Poor.*—L.S.P.

[2720]—*Mission Helpers of the Sacred Heart.*—M.H.S.H.

[3071]—*North American Union Sisters of Our Lady of Charity.*—O.L.C.

[3050]—*Oblate Sisters of the Sacred Heart of Jesus.*—O.S.H.J.

[3170]—*Religious of the Passion of Jesus Christ.*—C.P.

[3430]—*Religious Teachers Filippini*(St. Lucy Filippini Prov.).—M.P.F.

[2970]—*School Sisters of Notre Dame.*—S.S.N.D.

[1690]—*School Sisters of St. Francis.*—O.S.F.

[0570]—*Sisters of Charity of Seton Hill, Greensburg, Pennsylvania.*—S.C.

[0990]—*Sisters of Divine Providence.*—C.D.P.

[1660]—*Sisters of Saint Francis of the Providence of God.*—O.S.F.

[3830-13]—*Sisters of Saint Joseph.*—C.S.J.

[1620]—*Sisters of St. Francis of Millvale, Pennsylvania.*—O.S.F.

[3840]—*Sisters of St. Joseph of Carondelet.* St. Paul, MN & Albany, NY Prov.—C.S.J.

[1020]—*Sisters of the Divine Redeemer.*—S.D.R.

[1970]—*Sisters of the Holy Family of Nazareth.*—C.S.F.N.

[2040]—*Sisters of the Holy Spirit.*—S.H.S.

[2110]—*Sisters of the Humility of Mary.*—H.M.

[2160]—*Sisters, Servants of the Immaculate Heart of Mary.*—I.H.M.

[4120-03]—*Ursuline Nuns of the Congregation of Paris.*—O.S.U.

[]*Ursuline Sisters of the Immaculate Conception.* (Cleveland).—O.S.V.

[4160]—*Vincentian Sisters of Charity.*—V.S.C.

DIOCESAN CEMETERIES

PITTSBURGH. *Catholic Cemeteries Association, Inc.*, Central Office, 718 Hazelwood Ave., 15217-2807. Tel: 412-521-9133; Fax: 412-521-7019.

Braddock Catholic, 1560 Brinton Rd., 15221-4899. Tel: 412-271-5950; Fax: 412-271-8219.

Calvary Cemetery & Mausoleum, 718 Hazelwood Ave., 15217-2807. Tel: 412-421-9959; Fax: 412-521-7019.

North Side Catholic Cemetery & Mausoleum, 204 Cemetery Ln., 15237-2722. Tel: 412-931-2206; Fax: 412-931-2229.

St. Mary, c/o Calvery Cemetery, 718 Hazelwood Ave., 15217-2807. Tel: 412-421-9959; Fax: 412-521-7019.

St. Stanislaus & St. Anthony, 700 Soose Rd., 15209-1544. Tel: 412-821-4324; Fax: 412-821-4718.

Queen of Heaven Cemetery & Mausoleum, 2900 Washington Rd., Bridgeville, 15017-1793. Tel: 412-831-3360; 941-7601; Fax: 412-942-2550.

Resurrection Cemetery & Mausoleum, R.D. #4, Box 398, Corapolis, 15108-9804. Tel: 412-695-2999; Fax: 412-695-3032.

Sacred Heart, 97 Sacred Heart Rd., Monongahela, 15063-9605. Tel: 412-258-2885; Fax: 412-258-2275.

Good Shepherd Cemetery & Mausoleum, 733 Patton St., Monroeville, 15146-4530. Tel: 412-271-5330; Fax: 412-823-9083.

New Saint Joseph Cemetery & Mausoleum, 1443 Lincoln Hwy., North Versailles, 15137-2448. Tel: 412-823-9111; Fax: 412-823-6655.

Holy Souls, c/o Resurrection Cemetery, R.D. #4, Box 398, Coraopolis, 15108-9804. Tel: 412-695-2999; Fax: 412-695-3032.

Our Lady of Hope Cemetery & Mausoleum, R.D. #4, Box 288, Tarentum, 15084-9517. Tel: 412-224-2785; Fax: 412-224-0211.

Mount Carmel Cemetery & Mausoleum, 7601 Mt. Carmel Rd., Verona, 15147. Tel: 412-241-1260; Fax: 412-241-5041.

NECROLOGY

† Dempsey, Joseph G., Harmarville, PA, St. Francis. —Died June 11, 1996.

† Garber, George T., Bulger, PA, St. Ann. —Died Jan. 18, 1996.

† Kress, Sylvester J., Carnegie, PA, St. Joseph. —Died March 20, 1996.

† Murphy, Robert M., Wilkinsburg, PA, St. James. —Died May 2, 1996.

Diocese of Portland (In Maine)

(Dioecesis Portlandensis)

Most Reverend

JOSEPH JOHN GERRY, O.S.B.

Bishop of Portland; ordained June 12, 1954; ordained Titular Bishop of Praecausa and Auxiliary Bishop of Manchester April 21, 1986; appointed Bishop of Portland December 21, 1988; installed February 21, 1989. *Res., 199 Western Promenade, Portland, ME, 04102. Mailing Address: P.O. Box 11559, Portland, ME, 04104-7559.*

Most Reverend

EDWARD CORNELIUS O'LEARY, D.D.

Bishop Emeritus; ordained June 15, 1946; appointed Titular Bishop of Moglaena and Auxiliary November 17, 1970; consecrated January 25, 1971; succeeded to See December 4, 1974; installed December 18, 1974; resigned September 27, 1988. *Res., Cathedral Residence, 307 Congress St., Portland, ME, 04101.*

Most Reverend

MICHAEL RICHARD COTE, D.D.

Auxiliary Bishop of Portland; ordained June 29, 1975; ordained Titular Bishop of Cebarades and Auxiliary Bishop of Portland July 27, 1995. *Mailing Address: P.O. Box 11559, Portland, ME, 04104-7559.*

ESTABLISHED JULY 29, 1853.

Square Miles 33,040.

Comprises the State of Maine.

Corporate Title: *Roman Catholic Bishop of Portland, a Corporation Sole.*

For the legal titles of other diocesan-related institutions, please consult Chancery.

Chancery: 510 Ocean Ave., P.O. Box 11559, Portland, ME, 04104-7559. Tel.: 207-773-6471; Fax: 207-773-0182.

STATISTICAL OVERVIEW

Personnel	
Bishop	1
Auxiliary Bishops	1
Retired Bishops	1
Priests: Diocesan Active in Diocese	127
Priests: Active Outside Diocese	6
Priests: Retired, Sick or Absent	61
Number of Diocesan Priests	194
Religious Priests in Diocese	54
Extern Priests in Diocese	11
Ordinations:	
Diocesan Priests	2
Transitional Deacons	3
Permanent Deacons	1
Permanent Deacons in Diocese	11
Total Brothers	26
Total Sisters	501
Parishes	
Parishes	139
With Resident Pastor:	
Resident Diocesan Priests	106
Resident Religious Priests	15
Without Resident Pastor:	
Administered by Priests	17
Administered by Lay People	1
Missions	54
New Parishes Created	1
Closed Parishes	2
Professional Ministry Personnel:	
Brothers	1
Sisters	15
Lay Ministers	75
Welfare	
Catholic Hospitals	3
Total Assisted	221,072
Health Care Centers	1
Total Assisted	83
Homes for the Aged	8
Total Assisted	946
Day Care and Extended Day Care Centers	4
Total Assisted	530
Specialized Homes	4
Total Assisted	79
Special Centers for Social Services	7
Total Assisted	2,715
Educational	
Diocesan Students in Other Seminaries	14
Total Seminarians	14
Colleges and Universities	1
Total Students	4,785
High Schools, Diocesan and Parish	1
Total Students	231
High Schools, Private	2
Total Students	574
Elementary Schools, Diocesan and Parish	18
Total Students	3,919
Elementary Schools, Private	1
Total Students	164
Catechesis/Religious Education:	
High School Students	3,899
Elementary Students	16,879
Total Students Under Catholic Instruction	30,465
Teachers in the Diocese:	
Priests	4
Sisters	28
Lay Teachers	273
Vital Statistics	
Receptions into the Church:	
Infant Baptism Totals	3,141
Adult Baptism Totals	270
Received into Full Communion	513
First Communions	3,271
Confirmations	2,712
Marriages:	
Catholic	874
Interfaith	503
Total Marriages	1,377
Deaths	2,963
Total Catholic Population	220,983
Total Population	1,227,927

Former Bishops—The first Bishop-Elect, Very Rev. J. COSKERY V.G.,of Baltimore, declined the nomination.—Rt. Rev. DAVID W. BACON, D.D., cons. April 22, 1855; died Nov. 5, 1874.—Rt. Rev. JAMES AUGUSTINE HEALY, D.D., cons. June 2, 1875; died Aug. 5, 1900.—His Eminence WILLIAM CARDINAL O'CONNELL, cons. Bishop of Portland, May 19, 1901; named Coadjutor Archbishop of Boston, Feb. 8, 1906; succeeded to the See of Boston, Aug. 30, 1907; created Cardinal, Nov. 27, 1911; died April 22, 1944.—Rt. Rev. LOUIS S. WALSH, D.D., cons. Oct. 18, 1906; died May 12, 1924.—Rt. Rev. JOHN GREGORY MURRAY, D.D., ord. April 14, 1900; cons. April 28, 1920; transferred to the Archdiocese of St. Paul, Oct. 29, 1931; died Oct. 11, 1956.—Most Rev. JOSEPH EDWARD MCCARTHY, D.D., ord. July 4, 1903; cons. Aug. 24, 1932; died Sept. 8, 1955.—Most Rev. DANIEL JOSEPH FEENEY, D.D., LL.D., Bishop of Portland; ord. May 21, 1921; appt. Titular Bishop of Sita and Auxiliary of Portland, June 22, 1946; cons. Sept. 12, 1946; Apostolic Administrator of the Diocese; appt. July 27, 1948; Coadjutor *"cum jure successionis"*; appt. March 4, 1952; succeeded to See, Sept. 8, 1955; died Sept. 15, 1969.—Most Rev. PETER LEO GERETY, D.D., ord. June 29, 1939; appt. March 4, 1966; cons. June 1, 1966; appt. Apostolic Administrator, Feb. 18, 1967; succeeded to See, Sept. 15, 1969; transferred Archdiocese of Newark, NJ, April 2, 1974.—Most Rev. EDWARD C. O'LEARY, D.D., ord. June 15, 1946; Titular Bishop of Moglaena and Auxiliary Bishop of Portland; appt. Nov. 17, 1970; cons. Jan. 25, 1971; Apostolic Administrator; appt. June 29, 1974 ninth Bishop of Portland, Dec. 4, 1974; installed Dec. 18, 1974; resigned Sept. 27, 1988.

Vicar General—Most Rev. MICHAEL R. COTE.

Chancery—510 Ocean Ave., P.O. Box 11559, Portland, 04104-7559. Tel: 207-773-6471; Fax: 207-773-0182. Office Hours: Mon.-Fri. 9-4:30. Closed Holidays.

Co-Chancellors—Rev. MICHAEL J. HENCHAL, J.C.L.; Sr. RITA-MAE BISSONNETTE, R.S.R., J.C.L.

Bishop's Delegate for Clergy—Rev. PAUL F. STEFANKO, J.C.L.

Public Affairs—Mr. MARC R. MUTTY.

Diocesan Tribunal—510 Ocean Ave., P.O. Box 11559, Portland, 04104-7559. Tel: 207-773-6471.

Officialis—Rev. PAUL F. STEFANKO, J.C.L.

Promoter of Justice—Rev. MARK P. NOLETTE, J.C.L.

Defenders of the Bond—Sr. RITA-MAE BISSONNETTE, R.S.R., J.C.L.; Sr. CLAUDIA BARBRE, R.S.M., J.C.L.; Rev. PAUL F. STEFANKO, J.C.L.; Sr. ANN KEEVAN, C.S.J., J.C.D.; Rev. MARK P. NOLETTE, J.C.L.; Most Rev. MICHAEL R. COTE, J.C.L., D.D.; Mr. GEORGE G. PAVLOFF, J.C.D.

Advocates—Sr. CLAUDIA BARBRE, R.S.M., J.C.L.; Sr. ANN KEEVAN, C.S.J., J.C.D.; Revs. MARK P. NOLETTE, J.C.L.; PAUL F. STEFANKO, J.C.L.; Mr. GEORGE G. PAVLOFF, J.C.D.; Sr. RITA-MAE BISSONNETTE, R.S.R.

Office Coordinator—Rev. PAUL F. STEFANKO, J.C.L.
Notaries—Mrs. NAJLIA KERRIGAN; Mrs. FRANCESCA M. FORTIN.
Associate Judges—Rev. Msgr. RAYMOND F. BEGIN, S.T.L., J.C.D.; Rev. JOSEPH J. KOURY, J.C.D.; Sr. RITA-MAE BISSONNETTE, R.S.R., J.C.L.; Revs. MARK P. NOLETTE, J.C.L.; Most Rev. MICHAEL R. COTE, J.C.L., D.D.; Mr. GEORGE G. PAVLOFF, J.C.D.
Guardian—Rev. MICHAEL J. HENCHAL, J.C.L.
Deans—Rev. Msgr. ROBERT G. LAVOIE, V.F.; Very Revs. JOHN F. O'HARA, V.F.; RENE T. MATHIEU, V.F.; NORMAND P. RICHARD, V.F.; STEPHEN F. CONCANNON, V.F.; NORMAND CARPENTIER, V.F.; DONALD W. JACQUES, V.F.; ANTONIO AMATO, V.F.; PAUL A. PLANTE, V.F.; GEORGES J. PLANTE, V.F.; LEOPOLD G. NICKNAIR, V.F.; JEAN PAUL LABRIE, V.F.; BRIAN D. BLANCHETTE, V.F.; PAUL E. COTE, V.F.; LAURENT R. LAPLANTE, V.F.; CLEMENT D. THIBODEAU, V.F.; FRANK J. MURRAY, V.F.; JOSEPH J. KOURY, V.F.
Diocesan Consultors—Rev. Msgr. VINCENT A. TATARCZUK; Revs. THOMAS M. MURPHY; GEORGES J. PLANTE, V.F.; CLEMENT D. THIBODEAU; RENE T. MATHIEU; MICHAEL J. HENCHAL, J.C.L.; Most Rev. MICHAEL R. COTE, J.C.L., D.D.; Revs. FRANCIS P. MORIN; JAMES J. MORRISON.

Diocesan Offices and Directors

Campaign for Human Development—Ms. GLORIA A. DUGAN, L.C.S.W., *P.O. Box 10660, Portland, 04104.* Tel: 207-781-8550; Fax: 207-781-8560.
Catholic Stewardship Appeal—Mr. DAVID P. TWOMEY, C.P.A., Dir.; Mrs. ANNETTE DIMILLO, Coord., *510 Ocean Ave., P.O. Box 11559, Portland, 04104-7559.* Tel: 207-773-6471.
Catholic Relief Services—Ms. ANN P. FOLEY, *510 Ocean Ave., P.O. Box 11559, Portland, 04104-7559.* Tel: 207-773-6471.
Catholic Schools Office—Sr. ROSEMARY T. DONOHUE, S.N.D., Supt., Schools, *510 Ocean Ave., P.O. Box 11559, Portland, 04104-7559.* Tel: 207-773-6471.
Catholic Scouting—CHARLES MATTHEW, Co-Chm., *6 Cottage St., Fairfield, 04937.* CARL PARADIS, Co-Chm., *7 Valee Ave, Waterville, 04901.* JOYCE ROSSIGNOL, Girl Scout Liaison, *P.O. Box 812, Waterville, 04901.*
Catholic Charismatic Renewal Diocesan Liaison—Rev. RICHARD P. RICE, *66 North Ave., Sanford, 04073.*
Catholic Charities Maine—Central Services: GLORIA DUGAN, L.C.S.W., A.C.S.W., Exec. Dir.; Mr. PAUL L. MORGAN, Contracting Dir.; Ms. BONNIE BAGLEY, Services Dir.; Ms. SANDRA BOYD, Operations Dir.; Mr. PAUL LUISE, Pub. Rels. Dir., *P.O. Box 10660, Portland, 04104.* Tel: 207-781-8550; Fax: 207-781-8560. PETER J. TURNER, M.B.A., Finance Dir. JUDY KLEIN-GOLDEN, Human Resources Dir.; Mr. NORMAND D. HOULE, Information Technology Dir., *P.O. Box 10660, Portland, 04104.* Tel: 207-781-8550; Fax: 207-781-8560.
Clergy Benefit Plan-Clergy Pension Plan—Prudential Committee: Rev. Msgr. VINCENT A. TATARCZUK, Chm., *P.O. Box 218, Raymond, 04071.* Most Rev. JOSEPH J. GERRY, O.S.B., Pres.; Rev. Msgr. VINCENT A. TATARCZUK, Chm. Bd.; Revs. J. JOSEPH FORD, Treas. JAMES E. KNOX, V.F., Sec. Members: Rev. Msgr. PAUL D. GLEASON; Revs. CLAUDE J. ALBERT; RICHARD R. OUELLETTE; LIONEL G. CHOUINARD; GEORGES J. PLANTE, V.F.; MARCEL G. CHOUINARD; JOHN L. DOUGHER; TIMOTHY NADEAU; JOHN E. HARRIS; MICHAEL J. HENCHAL, J.C.L., Ex-Officio; Mrs. SALLY I. NELSON, Plan Admin.; Mr. JOHN R. ROSSIGNOL, Plan Accountant.
Diocesan Archivist—Sr. THERESE PELLETIER, S.C.I.M.
Diocesan Board of Education—Vacant; Chm.; Sr. ROSEMARY T. DONOHUE, S.N.D., Exec Sec. ANNE E. PELLETIER, Recording Sec. Members: Sr. ANNE-MARIE BOURQUE, R.S.M.; Rev. STEPHEN CONCANNON; PRISCILLA DENTON; Mr. CHARLES KENNEDY; Mr. MICHAEL WELCH; Mr. JAMES A. WARD; Rev. RICHARD ST. CYR; Rev. JAMES KEEGAN, S.J.; Sr. EDWARD MARY KELLEHER, R.S.M.; Rev. RICHARD MCLAUGHLIN; Mr. PAUL MCKENNEY; NOREEN MINKLER; Mrs. DORIS OUELLETTE.
Diocesan Bureau of Housing—Most Rev. JOSEPH J. GERRY, O.S.B., Bishop of Portland/Pres.; Mr. DAVID P. TWOMEY, Treas. ROBERT C. ROBINSON, ESQ., Clerk, *P.O. Box 11559, Portland, 04104-7559.*
Diocesan Council of Priests—Rev. Msgr. VINCENT A. TATARCZUK; Revs. NORMAND E. CARPENTIER; GERARD G. GOSSELIN; ALFRED JACQUES; RENALD D. LABARRE; GEORGES J. PLANTE; PAUL PLANTE; RENE T. MATHIEU, Chm. CLEMENT D. THIBODEAU; MICHAEL J. MCDONALD; FRANCIS P. MORIN; JAMES L. NADEAU; RONALD N. SCHMIT; PHILIP A. TRACY; ROBERT C. VALLAINCOURT; JOHN KEEGAN, S.J.; JAMES J. MORRISON, V.F.; PAUL F. STEFANKO, J.C.L.; MARK NOLETTE. Ex Officio: Revs. MICHAEL J. HENCHAL, J.C.L.; THOMAS M. MURPHY; Most Rev. MICHAEL R. COTE, J.C.L., D.D.
Diocesan Director of Pastoral and Educational Services—Sr. PATRICIA C. FLYNN, R.S.M., *Chancery Office, 510 Ocean Ave., P.O. Box 11559, Portland, 04104-7559.*
Diocesan Finance Council—Most Rev. JOSEPH J. GERRY, O.S.B.; Most Rev. MICHAEL R. COTE; Rev. CLAUDE ALBERT; Mrs. GEORGETTE BERUBE; Mr. WILLIAM STOLOSKI; Mr. MICHAEL MCNAMARA; JOHN DECKRO, Vice-Chm. MARTIN F. MORGAN, JR.; Rev. JAMES J. MORRISON; KEVIN O'NEIL; CHARLES PRINN; WILLIAM RICHARDS; RICHARD RODERICK, Chm. GREGORY ST. ANGELO; Sr. MARY DENIS SCHWARTZ, R.S.M. Ex Officio Members: Rev. MICHAEL J. HENCHAL, J.C.L. Staff: DAVID P. TWOMEY, C.P.A.; Mr. ANTHONY SILVIA; Mr. JOHN R. ROSSIGNOL.
Diocesan Office of Catechetics and Initiation—BARBARA A. SMITH, Diocesan Dir.; Mrs. KATHY DYER, Region I Resource Person, *25 Coolidge Ave., Caribou, 04736.* Tel: 207-496-0520. Sr. CATHERINE GREEN, R.S.M., Region II Resource Person, *492 Main Rd., Hampden, 04444.* Tel: 207-947-5381. Region III Resource Persons: AGNES DINN; JAMES DINN, *24 Hayford St., Farmingdale, 04344.* Tel: 207-622-2874. BARBARA A. SMITH, Region IV Resource Person, *Chancery Office, 510 Ocean Ave., P.O. Box 11559, Portland, 04104-7559.* Tel: 207-773-6471.
Diocesan Office of Public Affairs—Mr. MARC R. MUTTY, Dir., *510 Ocean Ave., P.O. Box 11559, Portland, 04104-7559.*
Diocesan Office of Family Life & Natural Family Planning Program and Respect Life Office—Mr. STEPHEN J. BEIRNE, Dir., *P.O. Box 11559, Portland, 04104-7559.* Tel: 207-773-6471.
Diocesan Office of Ministry to Persons with Disabilities—Sr. CLAIRE BLAIS, C.S.J., *P.O. Box 11559, Portland, 04104-7559.*
Bishop's Delegate for Priests—Rev. PAUL F. STEFANKO, J.C.L., Dir., *510 Ocean Ave., P.O. Box 11559, Portland, 04104-7559.* Tel: 207-773-6471.
Diocesan Office of Small Christian Communities—Sr. PATRICIA C. FLYNN, R.S.M., Coord., *P.O. Box 11559, Portland, 04104-7559.* Tel: 207-773-6471.
Diocesan Office for Worship—Mrs. SUZANNE PROULX POWELL, Dir., *510 Ocean Ave., P.O. Box 11559, Portland, 04104-7559.* Tel: 207-773-6471.
Diocesan Office of Youth Ministry—Mrs. JEANNE S. BIGELOW, Dir. Youth Ministry Regional Coordinators: Region I, KAREN OUELLETTE. Tel: 207-834-8355; Fax: 207-834-6835. Region II, WILLIAM ROMANO, *P.O. Box 623, Waterville, 04901.* Tel: 207-862-6149; Fax: 207-862-4041. Region III, MICHELLE CHURCH, *RFD #2, Box 181, Gardiner, 04345.* Tel: 207-588-0305; Fax: 207-588-0305.
Financial Management—Mr. DAVID P. TWOMEY, Finance Officer; Mr. ANTHONY SILVA, Controller; Mr. JOHN ROSSIGNOL, Asst. Controller, *510 Ocean Ave., P.O. Box 11559, Portland, 04104-7559.* Tel: 207-773-6471.
General Counsel—Mr. ROBERT C. ROBINSON, *12 Portland Pier, P.O. Box 568, Portland, 04112.*
Liturgical Commission—Members: Revs. RENALD LABARRE; RIGINALD BRISSETTE; MARC B. CARON; Mr. KEVIN BIRCH; Rev. MICHAEL J. HENCHAL, J.C.L.; SUZANNE PROULX POWELL, Exec. Sec.
Maine Diocesan Council of Catholic Women—Most Rev. JOSEPH J. GERRY, Episcopal Chm.; Rev. LAWRENCE CONLEY, V.F., Diocesan Moderator, *St. Catherine Parish, 29 Paris St., Norway, 04268-1132.* Mrs. DOROTHY TURMELLE, Diocesan Pres.
Newman Apostolate—Rev. JOSEPH J. KOURY, J.C.D., Coord. Assoc. Pastors: Revs. ALBIN A. ANDRUS; JOSEPH E. DANIELS; LARCH FIDLER, IV; CLAUDE GENDREAU; ERNEST L'HEUREUX; GERALD A. LEVESQUE; JOHN MARQUIS, S.M.; RAYMOND P. MELVILLE; JOHN F. O'HARA. Pastoral Assocs.: Sr. MARY SWEENEY; Sr. LINE RIOUX; Sr. SYLVIA COMER.
Vicar for Religious—Most Rev. MICHAEL R. COTE, F.I.C.
Personnel Board—Revs. JOHN SKEHAN; REGINALD R. BRISSETTE; STEPHEN CONCANNON; MICHAEL J. HENCHAL, J.C.L.; REAL J. NADEAU; MARCEL DUMOULIN; FRANK MURRAY; PAUL F. STEFANKO, J.C.L.; RICHARD OUELLETTE; CHRISTOPHER LAROCHE. Officio Members: Most Revs. JOSEPH J. GERRY, Pres. MICHAEL R. COTE, Vice Pres.; Rev. EDWARD A. THOMSON, Dir., Seminarians.
Pontifical Association of Holy Childhood—Ms. ANN P. FOLEY, Dir., *510 Ocean Ave., P.O. Box 11559, Portland, 04104-7559.* Tel: 207-773-6471.
Pontifical Society for the Propagation of the Faith—Ms. ANN P. FOLEY.
Seminarians, Director of—Rev. EDWARD A. THOMSON, *510 Ocean Ave., P.O. Box 11559, Portland, 04104-7559.* Tel: 207-773-6471.
Vocations—Revs. THOMAS M. MURPHY, Diocesan Dir. DANIEL GREENLEAF, Asst. Dir., *510 Ocean Ave., P.O. Box 11559, Portland, 04104-7559.* Tel: 207-773-6471.

CLERGY, PARISHES, MISSIONS AND PAROCHIAL SCHOOLS

CITY OF PORTLAND
(Cumberland County)

1—CATHEDRAL OF THE IMMACULATE CONCEPTION, Rev. James A. Nadeau, Rector. In res., Most Revs. Edward C. O'Leary, (Retired); Michael R. Cote; Revs. William Modlin; Edward J. O'Brien; Paul R. Marquis; Robert E. Lee; Harold Nicknair; Daniel E. Pollard; John J. Scahill; Michael J. McDonald; Albin Andrus; Patrick J. Barrett.
Res., 307 Congress St., 04101. Tel: 207-773-7746 (Rectory); 774-5101 (Res.); Fax: 207-879-5547.
School—14 Locust St., 04101. Tel: 207-775-1491. Sr. Elizabeth Cobb, R.S.M., Prin.
Sisters of Mercy 2; Lay Teachers 4; Students 112.
Catechesis/Religious Programs—Tel: 207-772-0276. Donna Lebel, D.R.E.
Students 102.

2—ST. DOMINIC'S, Rev. Frank Morin.
Office—42 Gray St., 04102. Tel: 207-773-8146.
Catechesis/Religious Programs—Students 6.

3—ST. JOSEPH'S, Revs. Patrick Glavin, O.F.M.Cap.; Don Bosco Duquette, O.F.M.Cap.; Theodosius Corley, O.F.M.Cap.
Res., 673 Stevens Ave., 04103. Tel: 207-797-7026; Fax: 207-797-2679.
School—697 Stevens Ave., 04103. Tel: 207-797-7073. Ms. Lori Ann Lee, Prin.
Sisters of Mercy 1; Lay Teachers 16; Students 185.
Catechesis/Religious Programs—Tel: 207-797-9509.
Students 326. D.R.E.: Eleanor Bernabei; Sylvia Harlow.

4—ST. LOUIS (Polish), Rev. John Bambol, O.F.M.Conv.
Res., 279 Danforth St., 04102. Tel: 207-773-4176.

5—ST. PATRICK'S, Revs. Coleman P. O'Toole; John D. Civiello.
Res., 1342 Congress St., 04102. Tel: 207-772-6325.
School—1251 Congress St., 04102. Tel: 207-772-2521. Sr. Anne-Marie Bourque, Prin.
Sisters of Mercy 3; Lay Teachers 9; Students 231.
Catechesis/Religious Programs—Tel: 207-772-3521. Cynthia McGarry, D.R.E.
Students 85.

6—ST. PETER'S (Italian), Rev. Kieran Monahan, O.F.M.; Bro. Mark Brown, O.F.M.
Res., 72 Federal St., 04101. Tel: 207-773-0748; Fax: 207-879-0557.
Catechesis/Religious Programs—Bro. Mark Brown, D.R.E.
Students 140.

7—SACRED HEART, Rev. Frank P. Morin. Pastoral Assocs. Sr. Line Rioux, C.S.J., D.R.E. In res., Revs. John Audibert; Robert Bouchard.
Res., 80 Sherman St., 04101-2216. Tel: 207-772-6182; 772-7877.
Catechesis/Religious Programs—Sr. Line Rioux, C.S.J., D.R.E.
Students 55.

8—ST. CHRISTOPHER'S (Peaks Island), Rev. Robert Bouchard.
Res., 107 Island Ave., 04108-1125. Tel: 207-766-2585.
Mission—Long Island, Great Diamond Island.

9—ST. PIUS X, Revs. Arthur H. Pare, S.J., Pastor; Robert F. Regan, S.J., Pastoral Assoc. In res., Rev. John W. Keegan, S.J.
Res., 492 Ocean Ave., 04103. Tel: 207-775-3032; Fax: 207-874-7514.
Catechesis/Religious Programs—Tel: 207-775-2185. Donna Beattie, D.R.E.
Students 285.

OUTSIDE THE CITY OF PORTLAND

Ashland, Aroostook Co., St. Mark's, Rev. Mark P. Nolette.
Res., School St., P.O. Box E, 04732-0545. Tel: 207-435-3591. [CEM]
Catechesis/Religious Programs—Tel: 207-435-6440. Carol H. Bushey, D.R.E.
Students 90.
Mission—Portage, Our Lady of the Lakes.

Auburn, Androscoggin Co., St. Louis, Rev. Richard D. Bertrand, S.J.; Sr. Irene Platt, C.O.C., Pastoral Assoc. & D.R.E.
Res., 24 Dunn St., 04210. Tel: 207-784-4146. [JC]
Catechesis/Religious Programs—Tel: 207-784-0012.
Students 130.
Parish Center—101 Second St., 04210. Tel: 207-784-0012.

St. Philip's, Rev. Roger P. Chabot.
Res., 365 Turner Rd., 04212-8410. Tel: 207-784-6486; Fax: 207-784-6487.
Catechesis/Religious Programs—Students 90.

Sacred Heart, Rev. Maurice T. Lebel; Sr. Elizabeth Platt, C.O.C., Pastoral Assoc. & RCIA Coord.
Res., 267 Minot Ave., 04210. Tel: 207-782-8096.

Catechesis/Religious Programs—Sandra Tardiff, D.R.E., Tel: 207-782-4005.
Students 249.

Augusta, Kennebec Co., St. Mary's, Rev. Paul R. Kerns. In res., Rev. D. Joseph Manship.
Res., 41 Western Ave., P.O. Box 547, 04332. Tel: 207-623-8823; Fax: 207-623-8433. [CEM 2]
School—56 Sewall St., 04332. Tel: 207-623-3491; Fax: 207-626-5818. Sr. Barbara Brennan, R.S.M., Prin.
Sisters of Mercy 2; Lay Teachers 11; Students 251.
Catechesis/Religious Programs—Sr. Theresa Rand, R.S.M., D.R.E.
Students 150.

St. Andrew's, Rev. Edward A. Thomson.
Res., St. Andrew St., R.F.D. 10, Box 1350, 04330. Tel: 207-623-8543; Fax: 207-626-0287.
Catechesis/Religious Programs—Tel: 207-623-3159. Diane Vasseur, D.R.E.
Students 181.

St. Augustine's, Rev. Lionel G. Chouinard.
Res., 1 Kendall St., 04330. Tel: 207-622-2184; Fax: 207-621-4064. [CEM 2]
School—24 Washington St., 04330. Tel: 207-622-1771. Sr. Rachel Boucher, Prin.
Sisters of the Presentation of Mary 2; Lay Teachers 10; Students 189.
Catechesis/Religious Programs—Lisa Couture, D.R.E.
Students 86.

Bangor, Penobscot Co., St. John's, Revs. James P. Brewer; Daniel P. Greenleaf; Robert J. Sullivan, S.J.; Sr. Patricia Mooney, R.S.M., Pastoral Assoc.; Sr. Celestine Theriault, R.S.M., Pastoral Assoc.
Res., 207 York St., 04401. Tel: 207-942-6941; Fax: 207-947-5984.
School—166 State St., 04401. Tel: 207-942-0955. Mrs. Susan Inman, Prin.
Lay Teachers 16; Students 127.
Catechesis/Religious Programs—Tel: 207-947-8263. Joan Winstead, D.R.E.
Students 370.

St. Mary's, Rev. Frank J. Murray.
Res., 768 Ohio St., 04401-3106. Tel: 207-945-5018.
School—Tel: 207-947-7063. Sr. Margaret Walsh, R.S.M., Prin.
Lay Teachers 7; Students 145.
Catechesis/Religious Programs—Tel: 207-942-1643.
Students 600.

Bar Harbor, Hancock Co., Holy Redeemer, Rev. Joseph W. Cahill.
Res., 21 Ledgelawn Ave., 04609. Tel: 207-288-3535.
Catechesis/Religious Programs—Tel: 207-288-3421.
Students 55.

Bath, Sagadahoc Co., Immaculate Conception, Rev. Joseph R. Mckenna.
Res., 144 Lincoln St., 04530. Tel: 207-443-3423.
Catechesis/Religious Programs—Tel: 207-443-4987. Nancy Lewis, D.R.E.
Students 200.

Belfast, Waldo Co., St. Francis of Assisi, Rev. Constanzo J. Piscilli, Admin.
Mailing Address: P.O. Box 189, 04915-0189.
Res., 81 Court St., 04915. Tel: 207-338-6688.
Catechesis/Religious Programs—Tel: 207-338-4423. Sr. Aline Roy, D.R.E.
Students 145.
Mission—Isleboro, St. Mary of the Isles.

Benedicta, Aroostook Co., St. Benedict's, Rev. Joseph Blattner.
Res., 04733. Tel: 207-365-4128. [CEM]
Catechesis/Religious Programs—Tel: 207-365-4269. Anna Robinson, D.R.E.
Students 59.
Mission—Sherman Station, Penobscot Co., St. Joseph's Church, P.O. Box 27, Sherman Station, 04733.

Berwick, York Co., Our Lady of Peace, Rev. Hilary J. Cameron.
Res., 25 Berwick St., 03901-2109. Tel: 207-698-1072.
Catechesis/Religious Programs—Students 175.

Biddeford, York Co., St. Andre's, Rev. Reginald R. Brissette.
Res., 73 Bacon St., 04005. Tel: 207-282-3333. [JC]
School—St. James School. See St. Joseph's for details.
Catechesis/Religious Programs—Tel: 207-282-7434.
Students 75.

St. Joseph's, Revs. Ronald D. LeBarre; Michael J. Seavey; Sr. June Rita Fortier, S.C.I.M.
Office—6 St. Mary St., P.O. Box 408, 04005.
Res., 43 Center St., 04005. Tel: 207-282-9352; Fax: 207-286-8679.
School—New Consolidated School - St. James, (Grades K-8) P.O. Box 5039, 25 Graham St., 04007. Tel: 207-282-4084. Ms. Marie Klement, Prin.
Sisters 1; Lay Teachers 28; Students 486.
Catechesis/Religious Programs—Tel: 207-282-4812. Nancy P. Labbe, D.R.E. & Pastoral Assoc.
Students 332.

St. Mary's, Rev. John Andrew Allen, Pastor.
Res., P.O.Box 515, 04005. Tel: 207-284-5363; Fax: 207-286-8679. [CEM]
School—St. James School. See St. Joseph's for details. Tel: 207-282-4084.
Catechesis/Religious Programs—Tel: 207-282-4812.
Students 127.
Mission—Biddeford Pool, York Co., St. Brendan.

Bingham, Somerset Co., St. Peter's, Rev. Robert V. Paskey, S.J.
Res., Owens St., Box No. 667, 04920. Tel: 207-672-3912.
Catechesis/Religious Programs—Students 71.
Mission—West Forks, SS. Philip & James.

Boothbay Harbor, Lincoln Co., Our Lady, Queen of Peace, Rev. Royal J. Parent.
Res., 82 Atlantic Ave., 04538. Tel: 207-633-2680.
Catechesis/Religious Programs—Students 47.

Bradley, Penobscot Co., St. Ann, Rev. Richard A. Nadeau.
Res., Box 137, 04411. Tel: 207-827-2087. [JC]
Catechesis/Religious Programs—Tel: 207-827-7643. Mary Shorette, D.R.E.
Students 66.

Brewer, Penobscot Co., St. Joseph's, Rev. Ronald N. Schmit.
Res., 531 N. Main St., 04412. Tel: 207-989-5388. [JC]
Catechesis/Religious Programs—Tel: 207-989-5343.
Students 189.

St. Teresa's, Rev. Rudolph J. Leveille.
Res., 440 S. Main St., 04412. Tel: 207-989-7049.
Catechesis/Religious Programs—Tel: 207-989-6129.
Students 67.

Bridgton, Cumberland Co., St. Joseph, Rev. Joseph E. Whitlock.
Mailing Address: P.O. Box 310, 04009-0310. Tel: 207-647-2334.
Catechesis/Religious Programs—Tel: 207-647-8154.
Students 101.
Mission—Fryeburg, Oxford Co., St. Elizabeth Ann Seton, P.O. Box 332, Fryeburg, 04037. Tel: 207-935-4245.

Brownville Junction, Piscataquis Co., St. Francis Xavier, Rev. Myles Cyr, O.M.I., Admin.
Res., Front St., Box 385, 04415. Tel: 207-965-2341.
Catechesis/Religious Programs—Deborah Moulton, D.R.E.
Students 60.
Mission—Milo, St. Paul.

Brunswick, Cumberland Co., St. John the Baptist, Revs. Kenneth Thibodeau, S.M.; Edward Sheehan, S.M.; Kenneth Ridgeway, S.M. In res., Rev. Robert McDonald, S.M.
Res., 39 Pleasant St., 04011. Tel: 207-725-8756; Fax: 207-798-4792. [CEM]
School—St. John's School, 37 Pleasant St., 04011. Tel: 207-725-5507. Sr. Angela Krippendorff, Prin.
Lay Teachers 21; Students 220.
Catechesis/Religious Programs—Tel: 207-729-5966. Carolyn Ruggles, D.R.E.
Students 210.
Mission—Pejepscot, Topsham Co., St. Andrew, Rte. 196, Pejepscot, 04086.

St. Charles, Rev. Donald W. Jacques.
Office: 132 McKeen St., 04011. Tel: 207-725-2624.
Catechesis/Religious Programs—Students 194.
Missions—Bailey Island, Precious Blood; South Harpswell, St. Mary-by-the-Sea.

Bucksport, Hancock Co., St. Vincent de Paul, Rev. John F. O'Hara, V.F.
Res., 158 Franklin St., P.O. Box S, 04416. Tel: 207-469-3322. [CEM]
Catechesis/Religious Programs—Mary O'Shea, D.R.E.
Students 83.

Calais, Washington Co., Immaculate Conception, Rev. Brian D. Blanchette.
Res., 17 Calais Ave., 04619. Tel: 207-454-3413.
Catechesis/Religious Programs—Leah McLean, D.R.E.
Students 120.

Camden, Knox Co., Our Lady of Good Hope, Rev. Gerard G. Gosselin.
Res., 7 Union St., 04843. Tel: 207-236-4785; Fax: 207-236-9422.
Catechesis/Religious Programs—Students 162.
Mission—North Haven, Our Lady of Peace.
Station—Vinalhaven, Our Lady of Peace.

Cape Elizabeth, Cumberland Co., St. Bartholomew, Rev. John J. Feeney; Sr. Ruth Hayden, Pastoral Assoc.
Res., 8 Two Lights Rd., 04107. Tel: 207-799-5528; Fax: 207-799-1532.
Catechesis/Religious Programs—Tel: 207-767-3436.
Students 406.

Caribou, Aroostook Co., Holy Rosary, Revs. Leopold G. Nicknair; Christopher J. LaRoche. In res., Rev. Msgr. Gilman J. Chaloult.
Res., 31 Thomas Ave., P.O. Box 625, 04736. Tel: 207-498-2536.
Catechesis/Religious Programs—Tel: 207-498-8655. D.R.E.: Michael McCormack; Ronald Willey; Jacqueline Lambert.
Students 346.
Mission—Washburn, St. Catherine.

Sacred Heart, Rev. Bernand L. Nicknair.
Res., R.F.D. 4, 04736. Tel: 207-498-2763.
Catechesis/Religious Programs—Lou Ann Kelly, D.R.E.
Students 117.

Daigle, Aroostook Co., Holy Family, Rev. Jean Paul Labrie.
Res., 11 E. Main St., Fort Kent, 04743. Tel: 207-834-5656. [CEM]
Catechesis/Religious Programs—Students 20.

Dexter, Penobscot Co., St. Ann's, Very Rev. Antonio Amato, V.F.
Res., 59 Free St., 04930. Tel: 207-924-7104.
Catechesis/Religious Programs—Students 90.

Dover-Foxcroft, Piscataquis Co., St. Thomas, Rev. Joachim Thanh.
Res., 45 High St., 04426. Tel: 207-564-2842.
Catechesis/Religious Programs—Louise DuLac, D.R.E.
Students 57.
Mission—Sangerville, Holy Family.

Eagle Lake, Aroostook Co., St. Mary's, Rev. James R. Albert.
Res., Church St., 04739. Tel: 207-444-5119.
Catechesis/Religious Programs—Mildred Pelletier, D.R.E.
Students 30.

East Millinocket, Penobscot Co., St. Peter's, Rev. George W. Beaudet.
Res., 56 Cedar St., P.O. Box 400, 04430. Tel: 207-746-3861.
Catechesis/Religious Programs—Tel: 207-746-3333. Julie Fiske, D.R.E.
Students 160.

Eastport, Washington Co., St. Joseph, Rev. Paul M. Sullivan, S.J.
Res., 51 Washington St., 04631. Tel: 207-853-2825. [JC]
Catechesis/Religious Programs—Students 27.
Mission—Pembroke, St. John the Evangelist.

Ellsworth, Hancock Co., St. Joseph's, Rev. Leo James Michand.
Res., 231 Main St., 04605. Tel: 207-667-2342. [CEM]
Catechesis/Religious Programs—Sandra Nelson, D.R.E.
Students 175.
Missions—Green Lake, Our Lady of the Lake; Winter Harbor, St. Margaret.

Fairfield, Somerset Co., Immaculate Heart of Mary, Rev. Marcel L. Dumoulin.
Res., 21 High St., 04937. Tel: 207-453-6131.
Catechesis/Religious Programs—Tel: 207-453-7940.
Students 137.

Falmouth, Cumberland Co., Holy Martyrs, Rev. Msgr. Charles M. Murphy, S.T.D.; Mrs. Judith Dominick, Pastoral Assoc.
Catechesis/Religious Programs—266 Foreside Rd., 04105. Tel: 207-781-4573; Fax: 207-781-3961.
Students 325.

Farmington, Franklin Co., St. Joseph's, Rev. Gerald A. Levesque.
Mailing Address: c/o The Pastoral Center, 13 Middle St., 04938-1598. Tel: 207-778-2778; Fax: 207-778-0268.
Catechesis/Religious Programs—David Levensalor, D.R.E.
Students 149.

Fort Fairfield, Aroostook Co., St. Denis, Rev. William J. Carrigg, Admin.
Res., 43 Main St., 04742-1223. Tel: 207-473-7329. [CEM 2]
Catechesis/Religious Programs—Students 73.

Fort Kent, Aroostook Co., St. Louis, Rev. Jean Paul Labrie.
Res., 11 E. Main St., 04743. Tel: 207-834-5656. [CEM]
Catechesis/Religious Programs—Tel: 207-834-3984. Rita Desjardins, D.R.E.
Students 649.

Frenchville, Aroostook Co., St. Luce's (Upper), Rev. Angelo LeVasseur.

Mailing Address: P.O. Box F, Upper Frenchville, 04784. Tel: 207-543-7313. [CEM]
Catechesis / Religious Programs—Tel: 207-543-5150. Marie Textor, D.R.E.
Students 203.

Gardiner, Kennebec Co., St. Joseph's, Rev. Clement D. Thibodeau.
Res., One Lincoln Ave., 04345-2188. Tel: 207-582-2385. [CEM]
Catechesis / Religious Programs—Tel: 207-582-1149.
Students 328.

Gorham, Cumberland Co., St. Anne, Rev. Ernest L. L'Heureux.
Res., 299 Main St., 04038. Tel: 207-839-4857; 839-3082; Fax: 207-839-3082.
Catechesis / Religious Programs—Tel: 207-839-3082. Claire Sirois, D.R.E.
Students 486.
Mission—East Sebago, Our Lady of Sebago.

Grand Isle, Aroostook Co., St. Gerard-Mt. Carmel, Rev. Richard R. Ouellette.
Res., 04746. Tel: 207-895-3436. [CEM]
Catechesis / Religious Programs—Verna Beaulieu, D.R.E.
Students 94.

Gray, Cumberland Co., St. Gregory, Rev. Msgr. Raymond F. Begin.
Res., 24 N. Raymond Rd., P.O. Box 345, 04039-0345. Tel: 207-657-4241.
Catechesis / Religious Programs—Tel: 207-926-3229.
Students 87.

Greenville, Piscataquis Co., Holy Family, Rev. Anthony Rotunno.
Res., Pritham Rd., P.O. Box 478, 04441. Tel: 207-695-2262.
Catechesis / Religious Programs—Tel: 207-695-2009. Lucy Fay, D.R.E.
Students 37.
Mission—Rockwood, Somerset Co., St. Joseph's. [CEM]

Hallowell, Kennebec Co., Sacred Heart, Rev. Richard G. Lonsdale.
Res., 12 Summer St., 04347. Tel: 207-623-3424.
Catechesis / Religious Programs—Tel: 207-623-3807. Mary Bourque, D.R.E.
Students 76.

Hamlin, Aroostook Co., St. Joseph, Rev. Joseph S. Chasse, S.M.
Res., 336 Main St., Van Buren, 04785. Tel: 207-868-2718. [CEM]
Catechesis / Religious Programs—Tel: 207-868-2835.
Students 361.

Hampden, Penobscot Co., St. Matthew, Rev. George W. Hickey.
Res., 70 Western Ave., P.O. Box 280, 04444. Tel: 207-862-3517.
Catechesis / Religious Programs—Mrs. Nancy Oldershaw, D.R.E.
Students 186.

Houlton, Aroostook Co., St. Mary's, Rev. Philip Cyr.
Res., 110 Military St., 04730. Tel: 207-532-2871.
Catechesis / Religious Programs—Students 291.

Howland, Penobscot Co., St. Leo, Rev. Andre L. Houle, O.M.I.
P.O. Box 329, 04448. Tel: 207-732-3495.
Catechesis / Religious Programs—Tel: 207-732-4171.
Students 67.

Indian Township, Washington Co., St. Ann (1929), Rev. Michael Sheridan.
Church—P.O. Box 358, 04668. Tel: 207-796-5013.
Mission—Indian Township, St. Theresa's Chapel.

Island Falls, Aroostook Co., St. Agnes, Rev. Joseph H. Blattner.
Mailing Address: P.O. Box 27, Benedicta, 04733. Tel: 207-365-4128. [CEM]
Catechesis / Religious Programs—Students 20.
Mission—Patten, St. Paul.

Jackman, Somerset Co., St. Anthony, Rev. Richard C. Malo.
Res., 04945. Tel: 207-668-2881. [CEM]
Catechesis / Religious Programs—Students 48.

Jay, Franklin Co., St. Rose of Lima, Rev. George C. Pelletier.
Res., 1 Church St., 04239. Tel: 207-897-2173; Fax: 207-897-2478.
Catechesis / Religious Programs—Students 194.

Kennebunk, York Co., St. Martha's, Rev. Laurant R. Laplante.
Res., 34 Portland Rd., P.O. Box 510, 04043. Tel: 207-985-6252.
Catechesis / Religious Programs—Mrs. Rosanne Smith, D.R.E.
Students 286.
Mission—Kennebunk, St. Monica's.

Kittery, York Co., St. Raphael's, Rev. Robert D. Lariviere.
Res., 8 Whipple Rd., 03904-1758. Tel: 207-439-0442; Fax: 207-439-0442.
Catechesis / Religious Programs—Faith Formation Center, 6 Whipple Rd., 03904-1739. Tel: 207-439-2642.
Students 145.

Lewiston, Androscoggin Co.,

1—St. Joseph's, Rev. Richard McLaughlin.
Res., 253 Main St., 04240. Tel: 207-784-5328; Fax: 207-795-5078. [JC]
School—393 Main St., 04240. Tel: 207-784-8811; Fax: 207-783-9522. Mrs. Therese Daddario, Prin. Religious 1; Lay Teachers 9; Students 246.
Catechesis / Religious Programs—Tel: 207-782-2286. Mildred Whittingham, D.R.E.
Students 158.

2—Holy Cross, Revs. Rene T. Mathieu; Mark S. Reinhardt.
Res., 16 Ste. Croix St., P.O. Box 1540, 04241-1540. Tel: 207-782-9463; Fax: 207-782-5968. [JC]
School—17 Baird St., 04241. Tel: 207-783-9323. Mrs. Patricia Berthiaume, Prin.
Sisters of Presentation of Mary 2; Lay Teachers 29; Students 565.
Catechesis / Religious Programs—Tel: 207-783-7241. Ms. Ruth Oakley, D.R.E.
Students 280.

3—Holy Family, Revs. Claude Albert; Joseph E. Daniels; Germaine Marquis, Pastoral Assoc. In res., Rev. Rene G. Lavoie.
Res., 607 Sabattus St., 04240. Tel: 207-782-8928; Fax: 207-782-3179.
Catechesis / Religious Programs—Tel: 207-783-7330. Linda Grandmaison, D.R.E.
Students 376.

4—St. Mary's, Rev. Richard D. Bertrand, S.J.
Res., 88 Oxford St., 04243-3061. Tel: 207-783-1585.
Catechesis / Religious Programs—Tel: 207-784-0012. Rosetta Girouard, D.R.E.
Students 93.

5—St. Patrick's, Revs. Real J. Nadeau; Andrew Dubois.
Pastoral Center: 135 Ash St., 04240. Tel: 207-777-1200; Fax: 207-782-0110.
Res., 220 Bates St., 04240. Tel: 207-782-1997. [CEM]
Catechesis / Religious Programs—Fax: 207-786-9223. Hugh Keene, D.R.E.
Students 62.

6—SS. Peter and Paul, Revs. Real J. Nadeau; Andrew Dubois.
Res., 135 Ash St., 04240. Tel: 207-777-1200; Fax: 207-786-9223.
School—250 Bates St., 04240. Tel: 207-782-0721; Fax: 207-782-0110. Mrs. Donna Sawyer, Prin.
Lay Teachers 10; Students 165.
Catechesis / Religious Programs—Mrs. Marie Badeau, D.R.E.
Students 45.

Limerick, York Co., St. Matthew, Rev. Hubert J. Paquet.
Res., R.R. 1, Box 155, 04048. Tel: 207-793-2244.
Catechesis / Religious Programs—Tel: 207-642-3231. D.R.E.: Marc Hildreth; Robert Fournier.
Students 270.

Limestone, Aroostook Co., St. Louis, Rev. William J. Carrigg, Admin.
Res., 302 Main St., 04750-1116. Tel: 207-325-4843.
Catechesis / Religious Programs—Diane Edgecomb, D.R.E.
Students 125.

Lincoln, Penobscot Co., St. Mary, Revs. George Sirois, O.M.I.; Roger Cyr; Deacon Thomas Krapf.
Res., 168 Main St., 04457. Tel: 207-794-6333.
Catechesis / Religious Programs—Jane LeBrun, D.R.E.
Students 123.
Missions—Kingman, St. James; Winn, Sacred Heart; Danforth, St. Ann; Vanceboro, Guardian Angel.

Lisbon, Androscoggin Co., St. Anne's. Merged with Holy Family and SS. Cyril and Methodius to form Holy Trinity, Lisbon Falls.

Lisbon Falls, Androscoggin Co., Holy Trinity (1995), Revs. Anthony F. Kuzia, C.M., Pastor; Julian Szumilo, C.M.
Res., 51 Main St., 04252-1597. Tel: 207-353-6725; 353-2792 (Office). [CEM 3]
Catechesis / Religious Programs—Students 180.
SS. Cyril and Methodius (Slovak). Merged with St. Anne's and Holy Family to form Holy Trinity, Lisbon Falls.

Lubec, Washington Co., Sacred Heart, Rev. Richard A. Lembo.
Res., 19 Church St., 04652. Tel: 207-733-2214.
Catechesis / Religious Programs—Students 15.
Mission—Campobello, St. Timothy's, New Brunswick, Canada.

Lyman, York Co., St. Philip, Rev. Thomas M. Lee.
Res., 169 Rte. 35, 04005. Tel: 207-499-2940. [JC]
Catechesis / Religious Programs—Lucille Prescott, D.R.E.
Students 181.

Machias, Washington Co., Holy Name of Jesus, Rev. Raymond P. Melville.
Res., 11 Free St., P.O. Box 248, 04654. Tel: 207-255-3731.
Catechesis / Religious Programs—Nikki Cester, D.R.E.
Students 70.
Mission—Cherryfield, St. Michael's.

Madawaska, Aroostook Co., St. David's, Rev. Richard R. Ouellette.
Res., Rte. 2, Box 85, 04756. Tel: 207-728-3366. [CEM]
Catechesis / Religious Programs—Tel: 207-728-4356. Therese Albert, D.R.E.
Students 101.
St. Thomas Aquinas, Rev. Michael L. Doucette.
Mailing Address: P.O. Box 128, 04756. Tel: 207-728-7531; Fax: 207-728-4217. [CEM]
Catechesis / Religious Programs—D.R.E.:, Tel: 207-728-7135. Ann Marie Clavette.
Students 323.

Madison, Somerset Co., St. Sebastian, Rev. Georges J. Plante.
Res., 149 Main St., 04950-1599. Tel: 207-696-3203. [CEM]
Catechesis / Religious Programs—Elisabeth Crowley, D.R.E.
Students 92.

Mars Hill, Aroostook Co., St. Joseph, Rev. Thomas Lequin.
Mailing Address: St. Mary's Rectory, P.O. Box 813, Presque Isle, 04769. Tel: 768-3671.
Church—Tel: 207-429-9805.
Catechesis / Religious Programs—P.O. Box 197-A, 04758. Tel: 207-429-9074. Julie Tweedie, D.R.E.
Students 42.

Mechanic Falls, Androscoggin Co., Our Lady of Ransom, Rev. Harold D. Moreshead.
Res., 117 Elm St., P.O. Box 206, 04256. Tel: 207-345-2691.
Catechesis / Religious Programs—D.R.E.: Sandy Ferland; Sheila Priola; Ellen Morrison.
Students 135.
Mission—Mechanic Falls, Oxford Co., St. Mary, P.O. Box 206, Oxford, 04256.

Mexico, Oxford Co., St. Theresa, Rev. Joseph Lange.
Res., 3 Brown St., 04257. Tel: 207-364-2593. [JC]
Catechesis / Religious Programs—Katherine Bisson, D.R.E.
Students 45.
Mission—Dixfield, St. Joseph.

Millinocket, Penobscot Co., St. Martin of Tours, Rev. Normand P. Richard.
Res., 18 Colby St., 04462. Tel: 207-723-5902.
Catechesis / Religious Programs—Tel: 207-723-9904. Paula Miller, D.R.E.
Students 280.

Newcastle, Lincoln Co., St. Patrick, Rev. Raymond Picard.
Mailing Address: P.O. Box 598, 04553. Tel: 207-563-3240.
Catechesis / Religious Programs—St. Patrick's Parish Ctr., Academy Hill Rd., 04553. Tel: 207-563-6038.
Students 90.

Northeast Harbor, Hancock Co., St. Ignatius, Rev. Joseph W. Cahill; Deacon Joseph LaPlante.
Res., 21 Ledgelawn Ave., Bar Harbor, 04609. Tel: 207-288-3535.
Catechesis / Religious Programs—436 Seawall Rd, 04679. Tel: 207-244-0445.
Students 35.
Missions—Islesford, Our Lady Star of the Sea; Manset, St. Peter's.

North Vassalboro, Kennebec Co, St. Bridget's, Rev. Donald R. Daigle.
Mailing Address: P.O. Box 159, 04962. Tel: 207-873-3204.
Catechesis / Religious Programs—Tel: 207-445-4802. Mrs. Ann Morgan, D.R.E.
Students 104.
Mission—China Lake, St. Peter.

Whitefield, Lincoln Co., St. Denis, Rev. Eugene F. Gaffey; Deacon Joseph Reid.
Res., 298 Grand Army Rd, North Whitefield, 04353-3419. Tel: 207-549-7425. [CEM]
Catechesis / Religious Programs—Students 155.

Norway, Oxford Co., St. Catherine of Sienna, Rev. Lawrence J. Conley.
Res., 29 Paris St., 04268. Tel: 207-743-2606.
Catechesis / Religious Programs—Armand Bonneau, D.R.E.
Students 248.
Mission—Bethel, Oxford Co., Our Lady of the Snows, Rte. 26, Bethel, 04217. Tel: 207-824-2933.

Oakland, Kennebec Co., St. Theresa, Rev. Germain H. Bureau.
Res., 25 Church St., 04963. Tel: 207-465-3856.
Catechesis/Religious Programs—Tel: 207-465-7951. Sr. Cecile Grenier, D.R.E.
Students 240.
Mission—Belgrade Lakes, St. Helena.

Old Orchard Beach, York Co., St. Margaret's, Rev. Normand E. Carpentier.
Res., 6 Saco Ave., P.O. Box 289, 04064. Tel: 207-934-2322.
Catechesis/Religious Programs—Tel: 207-934-4232.
Students 189.
Chapel—Old Orchard, St. Luke's.

Old Town, Penobscot Co.,

1—HOLY FAMILY, Rev. Robert C. Vaillancourt.
Res., 262 S. Main St., 04468. Tel: 207-827-4000. [JC]
Catechesis/Religious Programs—Tel: 207-827-2377.
Students 233.

2—ST. JOSEPH'S. Closed. See Holy Family.

3—ST. MARY'S. Closed. See Holy Family.

4—ST. ANN CHURCH, INDIAN ISLAND, Rev. Timothy J. Nadeau.
Mailing Address: P.O. Box 560, 04468. Tel: 207-827-2172. [CEM]
Catechesis/Religious Programs—D.R.E.: Mrs. Terry Paul; Eugene Loring.
Students 40.

Oquossoc, Franklin Co., Our Lady of the Lakes, Very Rev. Paul E. Cote, V.F.
Res., Box 333, 04964. Tel: 207-864-3795.
Catechesis/Religious Programs—Students 28.
Missions—Rangeley, St. Luke; Stratton, St. John, Tel: 207-246-3277; Sugarloaf U.S.A., Richard H. Bell Memorial Chapel, Tel: 207-246-3277.

Orono, Penobscot Co., St. Mary's, Rev. Timothy Nadeau, Pastor.
Res., 89 Main St., 04473. Tel: 207-866-3372. [JC]
Catechesis/Religious Programs—Students 40.

Our Lady of Wisdom Personal Campus Parish, Rev. Joseph J. Koury; Sr. Mary Sweeney, S.C.
Res., University of Maine, 83 College Ave., 04473. Tel: 207-866-2155; Fax: 207-866-4543.
Catechesis/Religious Programs—Margaret Hallee, D.R.E.
Students 118.
Newman Campus Ministry Center—Tel: 207-866-2155; Fax: 207-866-4543.

Perry, Washington Co., St. Ann (Pleasant Point), Rev. John J. Caskins, S.J.
Res., 04667. Tel: 207-853-4718. [CEM]
Catechesis/Religious Programs—Students 30.

Pittsfield, Somerset Co., St. Agnes, Rev. C. James Martel; Deacon David Scammon.
Res., 5 High St., P.O. Box 369, 04967. Tel: 207-487-2777.
School—6 Pine St., 04967. Tel: 207-487-3899. Sr. Linda Mae Plourde, Prin.
Sisters of Presentation 2; Lay Teachers 5; Students 52.
Catechesis/Religious Programs—Students 130.

Presque Isle, Aroostook Co., Nativity of B.V.M., Rev. Thomas Lequin.
Res., 6 Roberts St., P.O. Box 813, 04769-0813. Tel: 207-768-3671. [CEM 2]
Catechesis/Religious Programs—Tel: 207-764-0161. Marcia Hartt, D.R.E.
Students 287.

Richmond, Sagadahoc Co., St. Ambrose, Rev. Paul M. Pare.
Res., 27 Kimball St., P.O. Box 38, 04357. Tel: 207-737-4713.
Catechesis/Religious Programs—Madleine Brodeur, D.R.E.
Students 100.
Mission—Litchfield, Kennebec Co., St. Leo, Litchfield, 04350. Tel: 207-268-4727.

Rockland, Knox Co., St. Bernard's, Rev. Valmont R. Gilbert.
Res., 150 Broadway, 04841. Tel: 207-594-4322; Fax: 207-594-4322. [CEM]
Catechesis/Religious Programs—Tel: 207-594-5204. Mrs. Kathleen DuBay, D.R.E.
Students 175.
Mission—Thomaston, Knox Co., St. James.

Rumford, Oxford Co., St. Athanasius-St. John, Rev. Alfred Jacques.
Res., 126 Maine Ave., 04276. Tel: 207-364-4555. [JC]
School—115 Maine Ave., 04276. Tel: 207-364-2528. Walter Buotte, Prin.
Lay Teachers 13; Students 169.
Catechesis/Religious Programs—Mary Theriault, D.R.E.
Students 171.
Mission—Roxbury Pond, St. Mary's Chapel.

Sabattus, Androscoggin Co., Our Lady of the Rosary, Rev. John F. Harris; Sr. Lucille Fournier, O.P., Pastoral Assoc.
Res., 65 High St., 04280. Tel: 207-375-6951.
Catechesis/Religious Programs—Students 42.
Mission—Greene, St. Francis, Tel: 207-946-5758.

Saco, York Co., Most Holy Trinity, Revs. George B. Mulligan, C.S.C.; Patrick Walsh, C.S.C.; Sr. Rita Bujold, C.S.J., Pastoral Assoc. In res., Rev. James F. Murphy, C.S.C.
Res., 271 Main St., Box 310, 04072. Tel: 207-282-3321; Fax: 207-284-2274.
Catechesis/Religious Programs—Tel: 207-282-6392.
Students 384.

Notre Dame de Lourdes, Rev. Richard E. St. Cyr.
Res., 16 Cutts Ave., 04072. Tel: 207-282-1392; Fax: 207-282-1392. [JC]
School—50 Beach St., 04072. Tel: 207-283-3111. Sr. Florence Falardeau, Prin.
Sisters of the Presentation of Mary 2; Sisters of the Holy Rosary 1; Lay Teachers 8; Students 179.
Catechesis/Religious Programs—Tel: 207-282-0911. Marcel Bertrand, D.R.E.
Students 75.

St. Agatha, Aroostook Co., St. Agatha's, Rev. Michael P. Gendreau.
Res., 04772. Tel: 207-543-7447; Fax: 207-543-6119.
Catechesis/Religious Programs—Tel: 207-543-6119. Nancy Dionne, D.R.E.
Students 90.
Mission—Madawaska, Aroostook Co., St. Michael's Chapel, Birch Point Rd., Madawaska, 04756. Tel: 207-728-7845. [CEM 2]

St. Francis, Aroostook Co., St. Charles, Rev. Philip A. Tracy.
Res., 04774. Tel: 207-398-3530. [CEM]
Catechesis/Religious Programs—Students 124.
Mission—Allagash Plantation, St. Paul.

St. John, Aroostook Co., St. John, Rev. Philip A. Tracy.
Mailing Address: P.O. Box 68, St. Francis, 04774. [CEM]

Sanford, York Co., Holy Family, Rev. Richard P. Rice. Pastoral Assts. Sr. Bonita Cote, F.C.S.C.J., D.R.E.
Res., 66 North Ave., 04073. Tel: 207-324-2420. [JC]
School—St. Thomas Consolidated School. For Holy Family, St. Ignatius and Notre Dame, Springvale. Norman Provost, Prin.
Sisters 1; Lay Teachers 11; Students 242.
Catechesis/Religious Programs—Students 108.

St. Ignatius Martyr, Rev. Raymond D. Auger; Gerald Coutu, Patoral Assoc. & D.R.E.
Res., 10 St. Ignatius St., 04073. Tel: 207-324-6040; Fax: 207-324-6041. [CEM]
Catechesis/Religious Programs—Tel: 207-324-6231. Gerald Coutu, D.R.E.
Students 187.

Scarborough, Cumberland Co., St. Maximilian Kolbe, Rev. Stephen F. Concannon.
Mailing Address: P.O. Box 57, 04074. Tel: 207-883-2597; Fax: 207-883-4246.
Catechesis/Religious Programs—Tel: 207-883-1742. Kathy Sparda, D.R.E.
Students 598.
Mission—Pine Point, Scarborough Co., St. Jude, Rte. 9, Pine Point, 04074.

Sinclair, Aroostook Co., St. Joseph, Rev. Michael P. Gendreau.
Res., St. Agatha, 04772. Tel: 207-543-7447; Fax: 207-543-6119. [CEM]
In res., P.O. Box 69, 04779. Tel: 207-243-7563
Catechesis/Religious Programs—P.O. Box 69, Sinclaire, 04779. Tel: 207-243-7563.
Students 23.

Skowhegan, Somerset Co., Notre Dame De Lourdes, Rev. Marcel G. Chouinard; Sr. Claudette Darisse, S.A.S.V., Pastoral Assoc.
Res., 222 Water St., P.O. Box 369, 04976. Tel: 207-474-2039. [CEM]
Catechesis/Religious Programs—Tel: 207-474-9844. Ann Barriault, D.R.E.
Students 250.

South Berwick, York Co., St. Michael, Rev. Philip Michael Tracy; Sr. Jacqueline Moreau, R.S.M., Pastoral Assoc. & D.R.E.
Res., 29 Young St., 03908. Tel: 207-384-4241; Fax: 207-384-4289. [CEM]
Catechesis/Religious Programs—Students 158.

South Portland, Cumberland Co., Church of the Holy Cross, Revs. Paul E. Coughlin, Pastor; Frederick H. Morse, Pastorial Assoc.
Mailing Address: 30 Emery St.; P.O. Box 2708, 04116-2708.
Res., 11 Aspen Ave., 04106. Tel: 207-799-4611; 772-7489.
School—436 Broadway, 04106. Sr. Maura Murphy, R.S.M., Prin.
Sisters of Mercy 2; Lay Teachers 13; Students 243.
Catechesis/Religious Programs—Tel: 207-799-8345. D.R.E.: Carol Kilroy; Constance Libby.
Students 218.

St. John the Evangelist, Rev. Paul E. Coughlin. In res., Rev. Frederick H. Morse.
Res., 11 Aspen Ave., 04106. Tel: 207-772-7489.
Catechesis/Religious Programs—Sr. Marie Roy, D.R.E.
Students 175.

Springvale, York Co., Notre Dame, Rev. Armand R. Neault.
Res., 10 Payne St., Box 278, 04083. Tel: 207-324-6630. [CEM]
Catechesis/Religious Programs—Rebecca Carlson, D.R.E.
Students 346.

Stockholm, Aroostook Co., St. Therese, Rev. Bernand L. Nicknair.
Res., R.F.D. 4, Caribou, 04736.
Church—04783. Tel: 207-498-2763.
Catechesis/Religious Programs—Loudy Ann Kelly, D.R.E.
Students 69.

Stonington, Hancock Co., St. Mary Star of the Sea, Revs. John O'Hara; George McCormick (CAM).
Res., Thurlow Hill, Box 25, 04681. Tel: 207-367-2343.
Mission—Castine, Hancock Co, Our Lady of Holy Hope, Pleasant St., Box 413, Castine, 04421. Tel: 207-326-8228.

Van Buren, Aroostook Co., St. Bruno - St. Remi, Revs. Joseph S. Chasse, S.M.; David Lajoie, S.M.; Marcel Lajoie, S.M.
Res., 336 Main St., 04785. Tel: 207-868-2718. [CEM]
Catechesis/Religious Programs—Tel: 207-868-2835. Rebecca Devost, D.R.E.
Students 350.
Mission—Van Buren, Aroostock Co., St. Rose Chapel.

St. Remi. Merged with St. Bruno. For further details see separate listing under St. Bruno.

Wallagrass, Aroostook Co., St. Joseph's, Rev. James R. Albert.
Church—RR 1; P.O. Box 1205, Soldier Pond, 04781. Tel: 207-444-5135. [CEM 3]
Res., Church St., P.O. Box 249, Eagle Lake, 04739. Tel: 207-444-5119. [CEM]
Catechesis/Religious Programs—Students 40.

Waterville, Kennebec Co., Holy Spirit. Merged parishes are St. Francis de Sales, Sacred Heart, and Notre Dame, Waterville to form Holy Spirit Parish, Waterville. Revs. James S. Plourde; Claude R. Gendreau.
Res., 70 Pleasant St., 04901-5405. Tel: 207-872-2281; Fax: 207-877-0675. [JC]
Catechesis/Religious Programs—Tel: 207-872-2264; Fax: 207-877-0675. D.R.E.: Rachel Matthews; Monica Bolduc.
Students 332.

Sacred Heart. Closed. See Parish of the Holy Spirit.

Notre Dame. Closed. See Parish of the Holy Spirit.

Wells, York Co., St. Mary, Rev. J. Joseph Ford.
Res., Eldredge Rd., P.O. Box 368, 04090. Tel: 207-646-5605; Fax: 207-646-9437.
Catechesis/Religious Programs—Students 303.
Mission—Ogunquit, All Saints.

Westbrook, Cumberland Co., St. Edmund (Prides Corner), Rev. Albert B. Colpitts.
Res., 355 Bridgton Rd., 04092. Tel: 207-797-8233.
Catechesis/Religious Programs—Tel: 207-797-4539. Mrs. Sandra Bois, D.R.E.
Students 155.

St. Hyacinth, Rev. Msgr. Robert G. Lavoie; Sr. Christine Plouffe, O.P., Pastoral Assoc.
Res., 295 Brown St., 04092. Tel: 207-854-2003. [CEM]
Catechesis/Religious Programs—Tel: 207-854-8214; 854-8019. D.R.E.: Frances Gray; Rosalie Aube.
Students 150.

St. Mary's, Rev. John L. Dougher.
Res., 625 Main St., 04092. Tel: 207-854-2753; Fax: 207-856-7318. [JC]
Catechesis/Religious Programs—Tel: 207-854-8669. Larry Guertin, D.R.E.
Students 195.

Wilton, Franklin Co., St. Mary. Closed. For further details see separate listing for St. Joseph, Farmington.

Windham, Cumberland Co., Our Lady of Perpetual Help, Rev. Donald R. Proulx; Deacon Charles O'Connell.
Res., Rte. 302, 919 Roosevelt Tr., P.O. Box 1030, 04062-1030. Tel: 207-892-8288.
Catechesis/Religious Programs—Tel: 207-892-8922.
Students 237.
Mission—East Raymond, St. Raymond, Rte. 85 at

Crescent Lake, East Raymond, 04071.

Winslow, Kennebec Co., St. John the Baptist, Rev. Paul A. Plante; Mrs. Elaine Gordon, Pastoral Assoc.
Res., 47 Monument St., 04901. Tel: 207-872-2373. [JC]
School—36 1/2 Garand St., 04901. Tel: 207-872-7115. Mr. Kevin Scully, Prin.
Lay Teachers 7; Students 130.
Catechesis/Religious Programs—Students 300.

Winterport, Waldo Co., St. Gabriel, Rev. George W. Hickey.
Res., St. Matthew's, 70 Western Ave., P.O. Box 280, Hampden, 04444. Tel: 207-862-3517.
Catechesis/Religious Programs—Darlene Duffy, D.R.E.
Students 70.

Winthrop, Kennebec Co., St. Francis Xavier, Rev. Sylvio J. Levesque.
Res., 10 Lake St., 04364. Tel: 207-377-2922. [JC]
Catechesis/Religious Programs—Tel: 207-377-6844. Nancy Lynn Yocono, D.R.E.
Students 212.
Mission—Monmouth, Kennebec Co., St. Stanislaus.

Woodland, Washington Co., St. James the Greater, Rev. Michael Sheridan, Sacramental Min.; Ms. Patricia Phillips, Parish Coord.
Res., 24 Summit St., P.O. Box 369, 04694. Tel: 207-427-6908.
Catechesis/Religious Programs—Tel: 207-427-3236. Mrs. Lisa Howard, D.R.E.
Students 90.

Yarmouth, Cumberland Co., Sacred Heart, Rev. Richard A. O'Donnell. Pastoral Assocs.: John Munroe; Cherie Piper.
Res., 33 Main St., 04096. Tel: 207-846-5584. [CEM]
Catechesis/Religious Programs—Tel: 207-846-6003. D.R.E.: Ann Peacock; Cherie Piper; John Munroe.
Students 302.
Mission—Freeport, St. Jude's.

York Harbor, York Co., St. Christopher-by-the-Sea, Rev. James J. Morrison.
Res., 1 Lilac Ln., P.O. Box 1225, 03911. Tel: 207-363-2111; Fax: 207-363-1586.
Catechesis/Religious Programs—Tel: 207-363-4177; Fax: 207-363-1586. Rose Cronin, D.R.E.
Students 399.
Mission—York Beach, St. Mary, Star of the Sea.

Chaplains of Public Institutions

PORTLAND. *Maine Medical Center.* Tel: 207-871-0111. Chaplains: Revs. Paul R. Marquis; Donald McAllister; Albin Andrus; Mrs. Anne Monaghan.
Mercy Hospital. Tel: 207-879-3358. Rev. Donald McAllister; Mrs. Agnes LaStoria; Sr. M. Michael Connelly, R.S.M.
St. Joseph's Manor. Tel: 207-797-0600. Rev. Robert E. Lee.

AUGUSTA. *Augusta Mental Health Institute.* Vacant. Tel: 207-289-7334.
Kennebec Valley Medical Center. Tel: 207-626-1000. Mrs. Dolores Coffin, Pastoral Assoc.

BANGOR. *Eastern Maine Medical Center.* Taylor Hospital, Bangor Convalescent Center, Tel: 207-942-6941. Rev. Robert J. Sullivan, S.J.
St. Joseph's Hospital. Tel: 207-947-8311. Rev. Richard V. Rokos; Sr. Mary Edmund, C.S.S.F., Pastoral Assoc.

BIDDEFORD. *Southern Maine Medical Center.* Tel: 207-283-3663. Sr. Jacqueline Vezina, R.H.S.J.

LEWISTON. *Central Maine Medical Center.* Tel: 207-795-0111. Mrs. Kathleen O'Wril.
St. Mary's Regional Medical Center. Rev. Bertrand R. Poussard, Campus Ave., P.O. Box 291, 04243-0291. Tel: 207-777-8520. Sr. Madeline Normand, P.M.; Sr. Huguette Allard, S.G.M.; Mr. Kenneth Rancort.

SOUTH PORTLAND. *Maine Youth Center* Tel: 207-828-4921. Rev. William Modlin.
Men's Correctional Center Tel: 207-828-4921. Rev. William Modlin.

THOMASTON. *Maine State Prison.* Tel: 207-828-4921. Rev. William Modlin.

TOGUS. *Dept. of Veteran Affairs.* Tel: 207-622-1134, Ext. 5176. Rev. Francis J. Kane.

WARREN. *Super Maximum Facility & Minimum Facility.* Tel: 207-828-4921. Rev. William Modlin.

WATERVILLE. *Mid-Maine Medical Center.* Tel: 207-872-1000. Mrs. Angeline Hubert.

Special or Other Diocesan Assignment:
Reverend Fathers—
Henchal, Michael J., P.O. Box 11559, Portland, ME 04104-7559
Skehan, John R., P.O. Box 11559, Portland, ME 04104-7559
Stefanko, Paul F., P.O. Box 11559, Portland, ME 04104-7559

On Duty Outside the Diocese:
Reverend Fathers—
Carrigan, Fredrick, 342 Willis Ave., P.O. Box 172, Bronx, NY 10454

Military Chaplains:
Reverend Fathers—
Cote, David P., USAF Academy, 2330 Faculty Dr., Bolder, CO 80840
Goudreau, Joseph L., 24AU Lee Ave., Ft. Myers, VA 22211. Tel: 703-696-3532
Morency, Raymond P., 3509 Lake Ave., Apt. 1052, Columbus, SC 29206. Tel: 803-782-2141
Welch, Bernard J., USCG Tracen, 1 Munro Ave., Cape May, NJ 08204-5001. Tel: 609-523-8542/898-6974; Fax: 609-898-6848

Awaiting Assignment:
Reverend Fathers—
Modlin, William F., Cathedral Residence, 307 Congress St., Portland, ME 04101

Sabbatical:
Reverend Fathers—
Caron, Antonin R.
Caron, Marc, Divine Word College, 1025 Michigan Ave., N.W., Washington, DC 20017. Tel: 202-529-7654
Cyr, Joel
Girouard, Robert J.

Retired:
Reverend Monsignors—
Chaloult, Gilman S., 31 Thomas Ave., Caribou, ME 04736
Gleason, Paul D., P.O. Box 1938, Hampton, NH 03842. Tel: 613-926-5442
Tatarczuk, Vincent A., P.O. Box 218, Raymond, ME 04071. Tel: 207-655-3672
Ward, Edward F., c/o Roman Catholic Diocese, P.O. Box 11559, Portland, ME 04104-7559. Tel: 207-773-6471
Reverend Fathers—
Auger, Gaston E., Box 476, West Kennebunk, ME 04094. Tel: 207-985-7059
Barrett, Patrick J., St. John's Rectory, 11 Aspen Ave., South Portland, ME 04106. Tel: 207-772-7489
Berube, Louis, P.O. Box 8054, Lewiston, ME 04243. Tel: 207-777-1692
Bill, J. Armand, 402A Sandpiper Dr., Fort Pierce, FL 34948. Tel: 407-467-1011
Burns, T. Lee, 3103 Vesper Ave., Sarasota, FL 34232. Tel: 813-377-4961
Carrier, Herve G., P.O. Box 3061, Lewiston, ME 04243-3061
Carrier, Joseph S., 133 S. Main St., Auburn, ME 04210. Tel: 207-786-2231
Cormier, Norman R., Pleasant Hill Rd., R.R. 1, Box 441, Limerick, ME 04048-9735. Tel: 207-793-2377
Cournoyer, Napoleon, D'Youville Pavilion, 102 Campus Ave., Lewiston, ME 04240
Davis, John P., 68 Webster Ave., Lewiston, ME 04240
Franck, Marc E., Mount St. Joseph Home, 7 Highwood St., Rm 5, Waterville, ME 04901
Frechette, Leonard A., 43 Center St., Biddeford, ME 04005. Tel: 207-284-7513
Gorham, Peter P., P.O. Box 515, Ellsworth, ME 04605-0515
Goudreau, George W., P.O. Box 28, Rumford, ME 04276
Gower, James M., Holy Redeemer Parish, P.O. Box 86, Bar Harbor, ME 04609. Tel: 207-288-3535
Harvey, Richard R., 12 Bayberry Rd., Brewer, ME 04412-1202. Tel: 207-989-8007
Huot, Leopold J., 19 Lambert St., Biddeford, ME 04005. Tel: 207-282-4325
Knox, James, 31 Clearview Dr., Scarborough, ME 04074-8319. Tel: 207-883-9652
Lauzon, Raymond J., Pranceskona Vienuolynus, Vilniaus 2, Kretinga, 5700 Lithuania
Lavoie, Rene G., Holy Family Rectory, 607 Sabattus St., Lewiston, ME 04240
Lavoie, Robert R., Mt. St. Joseph Home, Highwood St., Waterville, ME 04901
Lee, Robert E., Cathedral Residence, 307 Congress St., Portland, ME 04101. Tel: 207-773-6980
Letourneau, Francis E., P.O. Box 5577, Orlando, FL 32855-5577
Marquis, J. Alphee, Northern Maine Medical Center, 143 E. Main St., Fort Kent, ME 04743. Tel: 207-834-3155
Martel, Robert T., Mount St. Joseph Home, Highwood St., Waterville, ME 04901. Tel: 207-873-0006
McCarthy, Richard C., 58 Pitt St., Portland, ME 04103. Tel: 207-772-1211
McDonald, Michael J., Cathedral Residence, 307 Congress St., Portland, ME 04101. Tel: 207-774-9541
McGarrigle, Michael, 76 Ward Cir., Brunswick, ME 04011-9343. Tel: 207-725-5764
McInnis, Richard W., 16 Lochness Rd., Rumford, ME 04276. Tel: 207-364-8717
Mulkern, Stephen M., P.O. Box 474, New Harbor, ME 04554. Tel: 207-677-2881
Nicknair, Harold, Cathedral Residence, 307 Congress St., Portland, ME 04101. Tel: 207-828-8835
O'Brien, Edward J., Cathedral Residence, 307 Congress St., Portland, ME 04101. Tel: 207-773-7746
Ouellette, Roger J., Mount St. Joseph Home, Highwood St., Waterville, ME 04901. Tel: 207-873-0432
Pare, Paul U., 27 Marion St., Biddeford, ME 04005. Tel: 207-282-4155
Patenaude, Gilbert A., 47 River St., Augusta, ME 04330. Tel: 207-622-3832
Patenaude, Laurent O., Mount St. Joseph Home, Highwood St., Waterville, ME 04901. Tel: 207-873-4873
Pollard, Daniel, Cathedral Residence, 307 Congress St., Portland, ME 04101. Tel: 207-772-0172
Proulx, Roger F., Mount St. Joseph Home, Highwood St., Waterville, ME 04901. Tel: 207-872-4903
Romani, Joseph, 264 Eastern Promenade, Portland, ME 04101. Tel: 207-773-2449
Scahill, John J., Cathedral Residence, 307 Ccngress St., Portland, ME 04101
Sims, Henry F.H., Park Danforth, Apt. 415, Stevens Ave., Portland, ME 04103. Tel: 207-878-2843
Soucy, D. Wilfrid, Robin Dr., New Port Richey, FL 33552. Tel: 813-842-1497
St. Pierre, Romeo A., 15 Garden Cir. N., Caribou, ME 04736. Tel: 207-498-6049
Sullivan, John L., Mount St. Joseph, Highwood St., Waterville, ME 04901
Tracy, George E., 1229 Broadway, Ste. 400, Bangor, ME 04401-2596. Tel: 207-941-2400; Fax: 207-941-2401
Vallely, James P., Proctor Ave., Goose Rocks Beach, ME 04046. Tel: 207-967-2718

INSTITUTIONS LOCATED IN THE DIOCESE

[A] COLLEGES AND UNIVERSITIES

STANDISH. *Saint Joseph's College*, 278 Whites Bridge Rd., 04084-5263. Tel: 207-893-7711; Fax: 207-893-7867.
For a complete listing, refer to the Colleges and Universities section.

[B] HIGH SCHOOLS, REGIONAL

LEWISTON. *St. Dominic Regional High School*, 179 Blake St., 04240. Tel: 207-782-6911. Mr. G. Michael Welch, Prin. Sisters 1; Lay Teachers 20; Students 231.

[C] HIGH SCHOOLS, PRIVATE

PORTLAND. *Catherine McAuley High School*, 631 Stevens Ave., 04103. Tel: 207-797-3802. Sr. Edward Mary Kelleher, R.S.M., Prin. Sisters of Mercy 9; Lay Teachers 18; Girls 229.
Cheverus High School, 267 Ocean Ave., 04103. Tel: 207-774-6238.
Faculty resides at St. Ignatius Residence. See separate listing for details. Rev. John W. Keegan, S.J., Pres.; Mr. John H.R. Mullen, Prin.; Revs. Calvin M. Goodwin, S.J.; John Michalowski, S.J., Supr.; James F. Talbot, S.J.; John J. Hanwell, S.J.; John W. Keegan, S.J.; Bro. Bill Quegan, S.J. Lay Teachers 22; Students 345.

[D] ELEMENTARY SCHOOLS, PRIVATE

WATERVILLE. *Mount Merici Elementary School*, 142 Western Ave., 04901. Tel: 207-873-3773. Susan Cote, Prin. Lay Teachers 11; Students 164.

[E] DIOCESAN HUMAN RELATIONS SERVICES

FALMOUTH. *Catholic Charities Maine.* Mailing Address: P.O. Box 10660, Portland, 04104. 356 U.S. Rte. 1, 04105. Tel: 207-781-8550. Most Revs. Joseph J. Gerry, O.S.B., Pres.; Michael R. Cote, Vice Pres.; Mr. Gregory W. Boulos, Chm.; Mr. Gregory M. Smith, C.P.A., Treas.; Ms. Gloria A. Dugan, Exec. Dir.; Peter J. Turner, Finance Dir.; Ms. Judith Klein-Golden, Human Resources Dir. Tel: 207-781-8550.
Office of Social Justice and Peace, 562 Congress St., Portland, 04101. Tel: 207-879-1130 Ext. 279. Mr.

Paul Christian, Dir.

Parish Social Ministry, P.O. Box 748, Caribou, 04736. Tel: 207-498-2575. Mr. Leo Paquin, Coord.

Arnie Hanson Center, 65 India St., Portland, 04101. Tel: 207-871-7452. Lawrence Hames, Dir.

Evodia House, 79 Allen Ave., Portland, 04103. Tel: 207-878-5251. Lawrence Hames, Dir.

St. Francis House, 88 Third St., Auburn, 04210. Tel: 207-784-2011. Anita Perrier, Program Dir.

The Fellowship House, 95 Blake St., Lewiston, 04240. Tel: 207-784-2901. Anita Perrier, Dir.

St. Elizabeth's Child Development Center, 87 High St., Portland, 04101. Tel: 207-871-7444. Daniel Murphy, Dir.

St. Louis Child Care Center, 116 Hill St., P.O. Box 645, Biddeford, 04005. Tel: 207-282-3790. William J. Hager, Dir.

Catholic Charities Maine Family Child Care, 15 Westminster St., Lewiston, 04240. Tel: 207-786-0925. Carolyn Davis, Dir.

Portland Office-Satellite Office, 562 Congress St., P.O. Box 4042, Portland, 04101. Tel: 207-871-7443.

Fairfield Office-Satellite Office, 66 Western Ave., P.O. Box 378, Fairfield, 04937-0378. Tel: 207-453-4365.

Child Development Center - Peaks Island, Central Ave., P.O. Box 07, Peaks Island, 04108. Tel: 207-766-2854. Janine Blatt, Dir.

St. Louis Child Care Center, 60 School St., Saco, 04072. Tel: 207-282-0478. William J. Hager, Dir.

Catholic Charities Maine Counseling Services, 562 Congress St., Portland, 04101. Tel: 207-775-5671. Cecile Gagne, Dir.

Refugee Resettlement Services, 562 Congress St., Portland, 04101. Tel: 207-871-7437. Doris Hohman, Dir.

Birthline Pregnancy Support Services, 562 Congress St., Portland, 04101. Tel: 207-871-7464. Cheryl Klein, Dir.

Birthline Satellite Offices: 15 Westminster St., Lewiston, 04240. Tel: 207-784-0157. 66 Western Ave., P.O. Box 378, Fairfield, 04937-0378. Tel: 207-453-4365.

SEARCH (Seek Elderly Alone, Renew Courage, and Hope), 15 Westminster St., Lewiston, 04240. Tel: 207-784-0157. Ann Corbin, Dir.

Holy Innocents' Adult and Family Services, 562 Congress St., P.O. Box 797, Portland, 04104. Tel: 207-871-1161; 282-3371.

Catholic Charities Maine Adult and Family Services, Sagadohoc Block, Rm. 3-Satellite Office, Bath, 04530. Tel: 207-443-9608. 66 Western Ave., P.O. Box 378, Fairfield, 04937. Tel: 207-453-4365.

Jessie Albert Memorial Dental Center, 15 Commercial St., Bath, 04530. Tel: 207-443-9721. Deanna Grosso-Keith, D.M.D.

Northeastern Maine Adult and Family Services, P.O. Box 748, Caribou, 04736. Tel: 207-498-2575.

Chester Dental Center, R.R. 1, Box 341 A, Lincoln, 04458. Tel: 207-794-8185. Gary Steinberg, D.M.D.

Northeastern Maine Adult and Family Services-Satellite Office, 6 Lowell St., P.O. Box 343, Calais, 04619. Tel: 207-454-0491.

St. Michael's Center Emergency Foster Care, 1066 Kenduskeag Ave., Bangor, 04401. Tel: 207-941-2855. Mr. Lawrence Bois, Dir. Legal Title: *St. Michael's Center Emergency Foster Care, Juvenile Jail Diversion Program and Home Based Family Services and Tracker Services.*

Educational Services for Blind and Visually Impaired Children, 1066 Kenduskeag Ave., Bangor, 04401. Tel: 207-941-2855. Jean Small, Dir.

Downeast Big Brothers - Big Sisters, 1066 Kenduskeag Ave., Bangor, 04401. Tel: 207-941-2855.

Educational Services for Blind and Visually Impaired Children-Satellite Office, 562 Congress St., Portland, 04101. Tel: 207-871-7440. Legal Title: *Educational Services for Blind and Visually Impaired Children, Instructional Materials Center.*

Therapeutic Foster Care, 15 Westminster St., Lewiston, 04240. Tel: 207-784-0157. Alfred Millette, Dir.

The Christopher Home, P.O. Box 748, Caribou, 04736. Tel: 207-498-2575. Dixie Dumond, Dir.

Juvenile Jail Diversion Program, P.O. Box 748, Caribou, 04736. Tel: 207-498-2575.

Group Home After Care, P.O. Box 748, Caribou, 04736. Tel: 207-498-2575.

Educational Services for Blind and Visually Impaired Children-Satellite Office, P.O. Box 748, Caribou, 04736. Tel: 207-498-2575.

Emergency Foster Care, Caribou, 04736. Tel: 207-498-2575.

Educational Services for Blind and Visually Impaired Children-Satellite Office, 15 Westminster St., Lewiston, 04240. Tel: 207-786-0925.

Educational Services for Blind and Visually Impaired Children-Satellite Office, 66 Western Ave., P.O. Box 378, Fairfield, 04937-0378. Tel: 207-453-4365.

[F] SPECIAL RESIDENTIAL SERVICES

PORTLAND. *McAuley Residence, Inc.*, 194 Spring St., 04102. Tel: 207-773-5289. Transitional Housing and support services for women with or without children. Sr. Carol Lachance, R.S.M., Dir.

AUBURN. *St. Joseph Child Care Center*, 270 Minot Ave., 04210. Tel: 207-782-2711. Ms. Constance R. Ouellette, Dir.

BANGOR. *St. Andre's Group Home for Single Mothers with Infants*, 87 Ohio St., 04401. Tel: 207-945-5021. Group Home Parenting Services for single mothers with infants. Eileen Ward, Program Supvr.

BIDDEFORD. *St. Andre Home, Inc.*, Admin. Office, 283 Elm St., 04005-3093. Tel: 207-282-3351. Dr. Gregory C. Foltz, Exec. Dir. Pregnant and Parenting Young Women, Adoption Services, Service to Troubled Teens, Infant Foster Care Homes, Emergency Placement; Public Information-Education; Community Outreach Services.

St. Andre's Group Home for Pregnant and Parenting Young Women. Mailing Address: 283 Elm Street, 04005. 168 Prospect St., 04005. Tel: 207-284-7436. Sr. Simonne Janelle, S.C.I.M., Supr.

LEWISTON. *St. Andre's Group Home for Troubled Girls.* Mailing Address: 283 Elm St., Biddeford, 04005. 188 Sabattus St., 04240. Suzanne Dionne, Supvr.

[G] HOMES FOR THE AGED

PORTLAND. *Deering Pavilion Apartment House for Senior Citizens*, 880 Forest Ave., 04103. Tel: 207-797-8777.

For a complete listing, refer to the Special Care Facilities section.

St. Joseph's Manor, 1133 Washington Ave., 04103. Tel: 207-797-0600.

For a complete listing, refer to the Special Care Facilities section.

BANGOR. *St. Xavier's Home*, 119 Somerset St., 04401. Tel: 207-942-4815.

For a complete listing, refer to the Special Care Facilities section.

BIDDEFORD. *St. Andre Health Care Facility*, 407 Pool St., 04005-9716. Tel: 207-282-5171.

For a complete listing, refer to the Special Care Facilities section.

LEWISTON. *Marcotte Congregate Housing Inc.*, 100 Campus Ave., 04240. Tel: 207-786-0062.

For a complete listing, refer to the Special Care Facilities section.

**Marcotte Nursing Home - D'Youville Pavilion*, 102 Campus Ave., 04240. Tel: 207-777-4200.

For a complete listing, refer to the Special Care Facilities section.

WATERVILLE. *Mt. St. Joseph Holistic Care Community*, Highwood St., 04901. Tel: 207-873-0705.

For a complete listing, refer to the Special Care Facilities section.

Seton Village Inc., 1 Carver St., 04901. Tel: 207-873-0178.

For a complete listing, refer to the Special Care Facilities section.

[H] GENERAL HOSPITALS

*PORTLAND. *Mercy Hospital*, 144 State St., 04101. Tel: 207-879-3000.

For a complete listing, refer to the Hospitals section.

BANGOR. *St. Joseph Hospital*, 360 Broadway, 04401. Tel: 207-262-1000.

For a complete listing, refer to the Hospitals section.

BUCKSPORT. *Bridgewell, Inc.*, Box 836, 04416.

For a complete listing, refer to the Hospitals section.

*LEWISTON. *St. Mary's Regional Medical Center*, Campus Ave., P.O. Box 291, 04243-0291. Tel: 207-777-8100.

For a complete listing, refer to the Hospitals section.

[I] MONASTERIES AND RESIDENCES OF PRIESTS AND BROTHERS

PORTLAND. *St. Ignatius Residence*, 271 Ocean Ave., 04103-5795. Tel: 207-774-7226. Jesuit Fathers (New England Prov.). Revs. John W. Michalowski, S.J., Supr.; Calvin M. Goodwin, S.J.; James F. Talbot, S.J.; John J. Hanwell, S.J.; Bro. Bill Quegan, S.J. Priests 4; Brothers 1.

ALFRED. *Notre Dame Institute*, Shaker Hill Rd., P.O. Box 159, 04002. Tel: 207-324-6612; Fax: 207-490-2370. Provincial House of Brothers of Christian Instruction. Bro. Francis Blouin, F.I.C., Prov., Tel: 207-324-0067. Bro. James Lacasse, F.I.C., Supr., Tel: 207-324-6612. Bro. Eugene Belisle, F.I.C., Dir., Notre Dame Spiritual Center. Tel: 207-324-6160. Rev. Henry G. Vanasse, F.I.C., Chap., Tel: 207-324-1017. Brothers 20.

AUGUSTA. *St. Paul Retreat House and Cursillo Center.* Oblate Fathers. 136 State St., 04330. Tel: 207-622-6235. Retreat Masters. Revs. Raymond Lebrun, O.M.I.; Michael Lauze, O.M.I., Supr.; Marcel Bolduc, O.M.I., Dir.; Bros. Robert Dutil, O.M.I.; Paul Ricard, O.M.I.; Donat Daigle, O.M.I. Priests 3; Brothers 3.

KENNEBUNKPORT. *St. Anthony's Friary.* Franciscan Vice-Province of St. Casimir in Lithuania,Canada and United States, Office of the Magazine "The Bell of St. Francis" (in Lithuanian language). St. Anthony's Friary, Guest House and St. Anthony's Shrine. P.O. Box 980, 04046. Tel: 207-967-2011. Revs. Placid Barius, O.F.M., Prov. Lithuanian Vice-Province; Leonard Andriekus, O.F.M., Supr., Guardian; George S. Gailiusis, O.F.M., Dir., Gift Shop; Gabriel Baltrusaitis, O.F.M., Vicar of the Friary, Procurator and Dir.- Guest House; Raphael J. Sakalys, O.F.M., Procurator and Mgr. of Magazine Varpelis; John J. Bacevicius, O.F.M., Counsellor; Robert Des Roches, O.F.M., Provincial Spiritual Asst. to Sec. Franciscan Order; Robert Barber, O.F.M., Liturgist; Andrew R. Bisson, Parish Ministry. Priests 9.

LEWISTON. *SS. Peter and Paul Priory*, 27 Bartlett St., 04240. Tel: 207-784-7309; Fax: 207-777-0056. Residence for Dominican Fathers or Friar Preachers. Very Revs. Raymond Corriveau, O.P., Prior; Bernard Fortin, O.P., Sub-Prior; Revs. Jean Marie Lapointe, O.P. (Canada); Maurice Lebrun (Canada); James Donovan, O.P. (Canada); Martin Dionne, O.P.; Rosaire Pelletier, O.P.; Bros. Irenee Richard, O.P.; Robert Beaulieu, O.P.; Bernard Fortin, O.P. Priests 6; Brothers 3.

American Dominican Friars Serving in Canada. Revs. Thomas Demers, O.P.; Thomas R. Potvin, O.P.; Bernard M. Remillard, O.P.; Claude Richard, O.P.

WATERVILLE. *Mt. St. Joseph Priest Retirement Home*, Highwood St., 04901. Tel: 207-873-0705. Revs. Robert R. Lavoie; Robert T. Martel; Roger J. Ouellette; John L. Sullivan; Laurent Patenaude; Marcel Robitaille; Roger Proulx; Mark Franck.

[J] CONVENTS AND RESIDENCES OF SISTERS

PORTLAND. *House of Formation*, 605 Stevens Ave., 04103. Tel: 207-797-6957. Sr. Jean Little, R.S.M., Contact Person.

Mercy Convent, 144 State St., 04101. Tel: 207-773-5560. Sr. Mary Michael Connelly, R.S.M., Supr. Sisters of Mercy of the Americas 5.

Monastery of the Precious Blood, 166 State St., 04101-3794. Tel: 207-774-0861. Sr. Mary Jo Divney, Supr. Adorers of the Precious Blood 5.

Motherhouse of the Sisters of Mercy of the Americas, 605 Stevens Ave., 04103. Tel: 207-797-7861; Fax: 207-797-7861. Sr. Mary Laboure Morin, R.S.M., Pres.; Sr. Margaret Anne Burke, R.S.M., Local Coord. Motherhouse; Rev. Theodosius Corley, O.F.M.Cap., St. Joseph Rectory, Stevens Ave. Sisters in Residence at Motherhouse 84.

St. Catherine's Residence, 242 Walton St., Apt. 207, 04103. Tel: 207-878-8476. Sisters of Mercy of the Americas 2.

St. Patrick, 17 Frances St., 04102. Tel: 207-772-0723. Sisters of Mercy of the Americas 4.

Sisters of Charity, 1137 Washington Ave., 04103. Tel: 207-797-8607. Sisters 5.

Sisters of Mercy of the Americas, 289 Congress St., 04101. Tel: 207-773-8039. Sr. Ellen Turner, R.S.M., Contact Person. Sisters of Mercy of the Americas 3.

Sisters of Our Lady of the Holy Rosary, 20 Thomas St., 04102. Tel: 207-774-3756. Sr. Maureen Bellerose, R.S.R., Reg. Supr., 207-772-3130. Sisters of Our Lady of the Holy Rosary 3.

Sisters of St. Joseph, 38 Malilly Rd., 04103. Tel: 207-775-2466; Fax: 207-773-0182. Sr. Ann Keevan, C.S.J., Contact Person.

ALFRED. *Sisters of Our Lady of the Holy Rosary.* Notre Dame Institute, 04002-0159. Tel: 207-324-0647. Sr. Regina Drody, R.S.R., Coord. Sisters 2.

AUBURN. *Companions of Christ*, 133 Western Ave., 04210. Tel: 207-784-5960. Sr. Elizabeth Platt, C.O.C., Contact Person. Sisters 2.

Sisters of Saint Joseph, 270 Minot Ave., 04210. Tel: 207-782-1548. Sr. Marcelle Roy, C.S.J., Contact Person. Sisters of St. Joseph 1.

AUGUSTA. *St. Augustine*, 5 Kendall St., 04330. Tel: 207-622-2494. Sisters of the Presentation of Mary. Sr. Joan Desmarais, P.M., Supr. Sisters 2.

St. Mary, 8 Lincoln St., 04330. Tel: 207-623-4033. Sr. Theresa Rand, Supr. Sisters of Mercy of the Americas 4.

BANGOR. *St. Joseph Convent*, 360 Broadway, 04401-3900. Tel: 207-262-1000; Fax: 207-262-1922. Sr. Mary Edith St. Jean, C.S.S.F., Contact Person. Felician Sisters 9.

BIDDEFORD. *Marie Fitzbach Convent*, 290 Elm St., 04005. Tel: 207-282-2714. Sr. Jacqueline Bilodeau, S.C.I.M., Supr. Servants of the Immaculate Heart of Mary (Good Shepherd) 7.

Marie Joseph Spiritual Center, R.F.D. 2, Lester Orcutt Blvd., 04005. Tel: 207-284-5671. Sr. Cecile Plasse, P.M., Supr.; Rev. James Murphy, C.S.C., Chap. Sisters of the Presentation of Mary 16.

St. Joseph's Convent, 409 Pool St., 04005. Tel: 207-284-8381. Sr. Claire Ouellette, S.C.I.M., Supr. Section A, B, & C. Sisters of the Immaculate Heart of Mary (Good Shepherd) 50.

BRUNSWICK. *St. John the Baptist Convent*, 37 Pleasant St., 04011. Tel: 207-725-5484. Sr. Angela Krippendorf, O.S.U., Supr. Ursuline Sisters 8.

CASCO. *Community of the Resurrection*, P.O. Box 284, 04015-0284. Tel: 207-627-7184. Sr. Renata Camenzind, Supr. Total in Residence 5.

FORT KENT. *St. Louis*, 12 E. Main St., 04743. Tel: 207-834-5023. Sr. Gloria Ouellette, P.F.M., Supr. Little Franciscans of Mary 3.

HAMPDEN. *Sisters of Mercy of the Americas*, 692 Main Rd., 04444. Tel: 207-947-5381. Sr. Catherine Green, R.S.M.

HOULTON. *Marie Claire Residence*, 7 Cleveland St., 04730. Tel: 207-532-2324. Sr. Carol Martin, P.F.M., Contact Person. Little Franciscans of Mary 3.

INDIAN ISLAND. *St. Ann's Convent*. Penobscot Reservation, P.O. Box 566, Old Town, 04468. Tel: 207-827-4862. Sr. Janet Campbell, R.S.M., Prin. & Supr., Indian Island School. Tel: 207-827-4285. Sisters of Mercy of the Americas 2.

KENNEBUNK. *Sisters of St. Joseph*, 215 Sea Rd., 04043. Tel: 207-967-5986. Sr. Claire Blais, C.S.J. Sisters 4.

KITTERY. *St. Raphael Convent*, 6 Whipple Rd., 03904-1739. Tel: 207-439-2322. Sr. Maureen Hurley, D.W., Coord. Sisters 3.

LEWISTON. *Daughters of Wisdom*, 169 College St., Apt. #1, 04240. Tel: 207-777-1912. Sr. Cecile Bouchard, D.W., Contact Person.

Dominican Sisters of the Roman Congregation, 18 Tampa St., 04240. Tel: 207-782-7480; Fax: 207-753-1945. Sr. Monique Belanger, O.P., Prioress. Sisters 7.

Dominican Sisters of the Roman Congregation, 347 Pine St., 04240. Tel: 207-782-9780. Sr. Monica Dubois, O.P., Supr. Sisters 2.

Grey Nuns of Montreal Residence, 98 Campus Ave., 04240. Tel: 207-782-6849. The Society of the Grey Nuns of Montreal. Sr. Huguette Allard, S.G.M. Sisters 3.

Holy Cross, 15 Baird Ave., 04240. Tel: 207-782-0263. Sr. Nora Dumais, Supr. Sisters of the Presentation of Mary 6.

Holy Family, 2 Rideout Ave., 04240. Tel: 207-783-0693. Sr. Jeanne Page, P.M., Supr. Sisters of Presentation 3.

House of Discernment, 67 Webster St., 04240. Tel: 207-786-3723. Sr. Margaret Camire, Supr. Sisters of Presentation 3.

Sisters of Charity, Sisters' Residence, 98 Campus Ave., 04240. Tel: 207-784-2349. Sisters 10.

Sisters of St. Joseph, 121 Webber Ave., 04240. Tel: 207-783-9069. Sr. Laurette Levasseur, C.S.J., Contact Person. Sisters 2.

OAKLAND. *St. Theresa Community*, 30 Church St., 04963. Tel: 207-465-7605. Sr. Anne Xavier Loubert, C.S.J., Contact Person. Sisters of St. Joseph 2.

OLD ORCHARD BEACH. *Sisters of Our Lady of the Holy Rosary*. Regional House, 25 Portland Ave., 04064. Tel: 207-934-0592. Sr. Olla Laplante, Superior. Sisters 4.

ORLAND. *Missionary Sisters of the Immaculate Conception*. P.O. Box 836, 04416. Tel: 207-469-7616. Sr. Miriam Devlin, S.M.I.C., Contact Person. Sisters 2.

PITTSFIELD. *St. Agnes*, 9 High St., 04967-1213. Tel: 207-487-5040. Sr. Sylvia Lariviere, P.M., Supr. Sisters of Presentation 3.

PLEASANT POINT. *St. Ann's Convent*, P.O. Box 126, 04667. Tel: 207-853-2944. Sr. Maureen Wallace, R.S.M., Supr. Sisters of Mercy of the Americas 2.

PRESQUE ISLE. *St. Mary's Convent*, 331 Main St., 04769. Tel: 207-762-7711. Sr. Mary O'Donnell, R.S.M., Contact Person. Diocesan Sisters of Mercy 2.

ROCKLAND. *St. Bernard's Convent*, 152 Broadway, 04841. Tel: 207-594-7271. Sr. Jeanne Miller, S.A., Contact Person. Franciscan Sisters of the Atonement (Graymoor, NY) 2.

SABATTUS. *Dominican Sisters*, Lisbon Rd., R.F.D. No. 1, Box 3125, 04280-9761. Tel: 207-375-6583. Sr. Lucille Fournier, O.P., Prioress. Dominican Sisters of the Roman Congregation 8.

SACO. *Bay View Community*, 187 Bay View Rd., 04072. Tel: 207-283-3636. Sr. Cecile Labrecque, S.C.I.M., Supr.; Rev. James E. Connor, Chap., Tel: 207-284-8863. Servants of the Immaculate Heart of Mary (Good Shepherd Sisters) 34.

Notre Dame de Lourdes, 27 Thornton Ave., 04072. Tel: 207-284-8943. Sr. Florence Farladeau, Supr. & Prin. Sisters of the Presentation of Mary 3.

Provincial Residence, 313 Seaside Ave., 04072-3410. Tel: 207-284-6429; Fax: 207-282-7376. Servants of the Immaculate Heart of Mary. Sr. Theresa Rounds, S.C.I.M., Prov. Supr. Sisters 3.

Religious Hospitallers of St. Joseph, 44 High St., 04072. Tel: 207-282-3585. Sr. Mary Annunciata, R.H.S.J., Coord. Sisters 3.

ST. AGATHA. *Our Lady of Wisdom Convent*, 380 Main St., P.O. Box 138, 04772-0138. Tel: 207-543-7523. Sr. Yvette Raymond, D.W., Coord. Daughters of Wisdom 7.

SANFORD. *Daughters of the Charity of the Sacred Heart of Jesus*, 20 Lenox St., 04073-3221. Tel: 207-324-4931. Sr. Bonita A. Cote, F.C.S.C.J., Contact Person. Sisters 2.

St. Ignatius, 14 St. Ignatius St., 04073. Tel: 207-324-2034. Sr. St. Benoit Plante, O.S.U., Supr. Sisters 5.

SCARBOROUGH. *Sisters of Notre Dame*, 9 Coach Lantern Ln., 04074. Tel: 207-885-0791. Sr. Rosemary Donahue, S.N.D., Contact Person.

SOUTH PORTLAND. *Holy Cross Convent*, 30 Emery St., 04106. Tel: 207-799-1175. Sr. Annemarie Kiah, Contact Person & Supr. Sisters of Mercy of the Americas 3.

Our Lady of Mercy Convent, 265 Cottage Rd., 04106. Tel: 207-767-5804. Sr. M. Eunice Boyd, R.S.M., Supr. Gen. Diocesan Sisters of Mercy of Portland 9.

St. John the Evangelist Convent, 29 Aspen Ave., 04106. Tel: 207-773-2862. Sr. Elaine Lachance, S.C.I.M., Supr. Servants of the Immaculate Heart of Mary (Good Shepherd) 5.

STANDISH. *Marian Hall*, 04084. Tel: 207-892-5542. St. Joseph's College, 278 Whites Bridge Rd., 04084-5263. Tel: 207-892-6766. Sr. Regina Marie Houston, R.S.M., Contact Person. Sisters of the Americas 6.

VAN BUREN. *St. Bruno Convent*, 300 Main St., 04785. Tel: 207-868-5266. Sr. Dorina Chasse, S.C.I.M., Supr. Servants of the Immaculate Heart of Mary 10.

WATERVILLE. *Blessed Sacrament Convent*, 101 Silver St., 04901. Tel: 207-872-7072. Servants of the Blessed Sacrament. Sr. Catherine Marie Caron, S.S.S., Supr. Sisters 10.

Mt. Merici Convent, 142 Western Ave., 04901-4617. Tel: 207-873-3515. Sr. Agnes Marie Proulx, O.S.U., Prioress. Ursuline Sisters 15.

Mt. St. Joseph Fontbonne Community, Highwood St., 04901. Tel: 207-873-5377. Sr. Cecile Roux, C.S.J., Coord. Sisters of St. Joseph 13.

Mt. St. Joseph Sisters' Residence, Highwood St., 04901. Tel: 207-873-4804. Sr. Yvette Poulin, C.S.J., Coord. Sisters of St. Joseph 3.

Sisters of St. Joseph, 24 Glen Ave., 04901. Tel: 207-873-5247. Sr. Dorine Moreau, C.S.J., Coord. Sisters of St. Joseph 4.

Ursuline Sisters Infirmary, 142 Western Ave., 04901. Tel: 207-873-1931. Sr. Aimee Bouffard, O.S.U., Supr. Ursuline Sisters 19.

Ursuline Sisters' Residence, 140 1/2 Western Ave., 04901. Tel: 207-872-9375. Sr. Theresa Pelletier, O.S.U., Contact Person. Sisters 3.

WINDHAM. *St. George Hall*. St. Joseph College, 278 Whites Bridge Rd., Standish, 04084-5263. Tel: 207-893-6690. Sr. Michele T. Aronica, R.S.M. Sisters of Mercy of the Americas 5.

WINSLOW. *Inter-Community*. Sisters of St. Joseph/Mercy. 17 Boston Ave. #2, 04901. Tel: 207-877-7896. Sisters 2.

Provincialate of the Sisters of St. Joseph, 93 Halifax St., 04901. Tel: 207-872-2878. Sr. Dorothy Bujold, Coord. Sisters 4.

[K] HERMITAGES

ORLAND. *John of the Cross Monastery Hermitage*, 166 Upper Falls Rd., 04472. Tel: 207-469-3456. Sr. Margaret Dorgan, D.C.M. Carmelite Sisters 2.

ST. ALBANS. *Divine Mercy Hermitage*, 57 Byrant Rd., 04971. Tel: 207-938-3730. Sr. Margaret Mary Cuddeback; Sr. Bonnie Emmanuel Bryant, Hermit.

THORNDIKE. *Transfiguration Hermitage*, R.R. 1, Box 398, 04986-9709. Tel: 207-568-3731. Sr. Elizabeth Wagner, Contact Person.

[L] RETREAT HOUSES

ALFRED. *Notre Dame Spiritual Center*, P.O. Box 159, 04002-0159. Tel: 207-324-6160. Bro. Eugene Belisle, F.I.C., Dir.

AUGUSTA. *St. Paul Retreat House and Cursillo Center*. (Men and Women). Oblates of Mary Immaculate. 136 State St., 04330. Tel: 207-622-6235. Revs. Marcel Bolduc, O.M.I.; Raymond Lebrun, O.M.I.; Michael Lauze, O.M.I., Supr./Dir.; Bros. Robert Dutil, O.M.I.; Paul Ricard, O.M.I.; Donat Daigle. Fathers 3; Brothers 3.

BIDDEFORD. *Marie Joseph Spiritual Center*, R.F.D. #2, Lester Orcutt Blvd., 04005. Tel: 207-284-5671. Sr. Cecile Plasse, P.M., Supr.; Rev. James F. Murphy, C.S.C., Chap. Sisters of the Presentation of Mary.

PEAKS ISLAND. *Mother of the Good Shepherd Monastery by the Sea*, 235 Pleasant Ave., 04108. Tel: 207-766-2717. Servants of the God of St. Augustine. Rt. Rev. A.M. Seamus Kuebler, O.A.S., Abbot; Bro. Nicholas Druin. Purpose is to especially pray and minister to priests and brothers.

SACO. *Bay View Villa, Guest and Retreat House*, 187 Bay View Rd., 04072. Tel: 207-283-3636. Servants of the Immaculate Heart of Mary. Sr. Anita Therrien, S.C.I.M., Dir. Guests 30.

UPPER FRENCHVILLE. *Christian Life Center*. P.O. Box C, 04784. Tel: 207-543-6193. Rev. Angelo LeVasseur, Dir.

[M] NEWMAN CENTERS

PORTLAND. *University of Southern Maine*. Portland Campus c/o Sacred Heart Rectory, 80 Sherman St., 04101-2216.

Gorham Campus: Rev. Ernest L. L'Heureux, Chap.

Westbrook College. Res. St. Joseph Church, 673 Stevens Ave., 04103. Revs. Theodosius Corley, O.F.M.Cap.; Patrick Glavin, O.F.M.Cap.; Don Bosco Duquette, O.F.M.Cap.

BIDDEFORD. *University of New England*. Res. St. Joseph Rectory, P.O. Box 408, 04005. Rev. Michael J. Seavey, Chap.

BRUNSWICK. *Bowdoin College*. Newman Center, 04011. Tel: 207-725-8541. Rev. W. Larch Fidler, IV.

CASTINE. *Maine Maritime Academy*, 158 Franklin St., P.O. Box S, 04416. Tel: 207-469-3322. Rev. John F. O'Hara, V.F., Chap.

FARMINGTON. *University of Maine at Farmington*. c/o The Pastoral Center, 13 Middle St., 04938. Rev. Gerald A. Levesque, Chap.

FORT KENT. *University of Maine at Fort Kent*. St. Louis Rectory, 11 E. Main St., 04743.

LEWISTON. *Bates College*, 163 Wood St., 04240. Tel: 207-786-8272. Rev. W. Larch Fidler, IV.

MACHIAS. *University of Maine at Machias*, 9 O'Brien Ave., 04654. Rev. Raymond P. Melville.

ORONO. *University of Maine*. Our Lady of Wisdom Parish, 83 College Ave., 04473-1596. Tel: 207-866-2155; Fax: 207-866-4543. Rev. Joseph J. Koury; Sr. Mary Sweeney, S.C., Pastoral Assoc.

PRESQUE ISLE. *University of Maine at Presque Isle*. St. Mary's Rectory, 6 Roberts St., P.O. Box 813, 04769. Tel: 207-768-3671.

SOUTH PORTLAND. *Southern Maine Technical College*. Holy Cross Rectory, 444 Broadway, 04106. Tel: 207-799-4611. Rev. Albin A. Andrus.

STANDISH. *Saint Joseph's College*. Campus Ministry Office., 04084-5263. Tel: 207-893-7791. Rev. Thomas M. Murphy; Sr. Sylvia Comer, R.S.M., Chap.

WATERVILLE. *Colby College*, Mid Maine Campus Ministry, 04901. Tel: 207-872-3559. Dean of Students Office, Colby College. Rev. John E. Marquis, S.M., Chap.

Thomas College, Mid Maine Campus Ministry, 04901. Tel: 207-872-3559. Dean of Students Office, Colby College. Rev. John E. Marquis, S.M., Chap.

[N] MISCELLANEOUS LISTINGS

PORTLAND. *St. Elizabeth's Child Development Center*, 87 High St., 04101. Tel: 207-871-7444. Daniel Murphy.

BANGOR. *St. Michael's Center*, 1066 Kenduskeag Ave., 04401. Tel: 207-941-2855. Emergency Foster Care Juvenile Jail Diversion Program, Home Based Family Services, and Case Management Services.

RELIGIOUS INSTITUTES OF MEN REPRESENTED IN THE DIOCESE

For further details refer to the corresponding bracketed number in the Religious Institutes of Men or Women section.

[0320]—*Brothers of Christian Instruction*.—F.I.C.
[0470]—*The Capuchin Friars*. (Prov. of St. Mary).—O.F.M.Cap.
[1330]—*Congregation of the Mission*.—C.M.
[0480]—*Conventual Franciscans*.—O.F.M.Conv.
[0520]—*Franciscan Friars*. (Custody of St. Casimer).—O.F.M.
[0690]—*Jesuit Fathers and Brothers*. (New England Prov.).—S.J.
[0780]—*Marist Fathers*. (Boston Prov.).—S.M.
[0910]—*Oblates of Mary Immaculate*. (Prov. of St. John the Baptist).—O.M.I.
[0430]—*Order of Preachers (Dominicans)*. (Canadian Prov.).—O.P.
[0610]—*Priests of the Congregation of the Holy Cross*. (Eastern Prov.).—C.S.C.

RELIGIOUS INSTITUTES OF WOMEN REPRESENTED IN THE DIOCESE

[]—*Community of the Resurrection*.
[]—*Companions of Christ*.—C.O.C.
[3100]—*Congregation of Our Lady of the Holy Rosary*.—R.S.R.
[2230]—*Congregation of the Infant Jesus*.—C.I.J.
[0750]—*Daughters of Charity of the Sacred Heart of Jesus*.—F.C.S.C.J.
[0960]—*Daughters of Wisdom*.—D.W.
[]—*Diocesan Carmelites of Maine*.—D.C.M.
[]—*Diocesan Sisters of Mercy*.—R.S.M.
[1120]—*Dominican Sisters of the Roman Congregation*.—O.P.
[1170]—*Felician Sisters*.—C.S.S.F.
[1190]—*Franciscan Sisters of the Atonement*.—S.A.
[2575]—*Institute of the Sisters of Mercy of the Americas*.—R.S.M.

[2280]—*Little Franciscan of Mary.*—P.F.M.
[2760]—*Missionary Sisters of the Immaculate Conception of the Mother of God.*—S.M.I.C.
[3440]—*Religious Hospitallers of Saint Joseph.*—R.H.S.J.
[3500]—*Servants of the Blessed Sacrament.*—S.S.S.
[3550]—*Servants of the Immaculate Heart of Mary.*—S.C.I.M.
[0490]—*Sisters of Charity of Montreal (Grey Nuns).*—S.G.M.
[0610]—*Sisters of Charity of St. Hyacinthe (Grey Nuns).*—S.C.S.H.
[3000]—*Sisters of Notre Dame de Namur.*—S.N.D.deN.
[3750]—*Sisters of St. Chretienne.*—S.S.Ch.
[3870]—*Sisters of St. Joseph (Lyons, France).*—C.S.J.
[0150]—*Sisters of the Assumptions.*—S.A.S.V.
[0110]—*The Sisters of the Precious Blood.*—A.P.B.
[3310]—*Sisters of the Presentation of Mary.*—P.M.
[4110]—*Ursuline Nuns (Roman Union).* (Northeastern Prov.).—O.S.U.
[0640]—*Sisters of Charity of St. Vincent de Paul.* Halifax.—S.C.

DIOCESAN CEMETERIES

BANGOR. *Mount Pleasant*, 449 Ohio St., 04401. Tel: 207-947-4322. Mr. William Foley.

BIDDEFORD. *St. Joseph*, West St., P.O. Box 391, 04005. Tel: 207-282-0747. Mr. Paul Garriepy.

LEWISTON. *St. Peter*, Switzerland Rd., 04240. Tel: 207-782-8721.

SOUTH PORTLAND. *Calvary*, 1461 Broadway, 04106. Tel: 207-773-5796. Mr. Thomas Nee.

WATERVILLE. *St. Francis*, 78 Grove St., 04901. Tel: 207-872-2770. Mr. Clarence Hebert.

NECROLOGY

† Anderson, John M., (Retired). —Died April 19, 1996.

† Fitzpatrick, Rev. Msgr. David K., Lewiston, ME, St. Patrick's Church. —Died Aug. 12, 1996.

† Gosselin, Antonio A., (Retired). —Died Feb. 14, 1996.

Archdiocese of Portland in Oregon

(Archidioecesis Portlandensis in Oregon)

Most Reverend

FRANCIS E. GEORGE, O.M.I., PH.D., S.T.D.

Archbishop of Portland in Oregon; Profession of Perpetual Vows September 8, 1961; ordained December 21, 1963; appointed Bishop of Yakima July 10, 1990; Episcopal Ordination and Installation September 21, 1990; appointed Archbishop of Portland in Oregon April 30, 1996; installed May 27, 1996.

Most Reverend

KENNETH D. STEINER, D.D.

Archdiocesan Administrator; ordained May 19, 1962; appointed Titular Bishop of Avensa and Auxiliary December 6, 1977; ordained March 2, 1978. *Office: 2838 E. Burnside St., Portland, OR, 97214.*

Most Reverend

CORNELIUS M. POWER, D.D., J.C.D.

Former Archbishop of Portland in Oregon; ordained June 3, 1939; appointed Bishop of Yakima February 5, 1969; consecrated May 1, 1969; appointed Archbishop of Portland in Oregon January 22, 1974; retired July 3, 1986.

ERECTED AS A VICARIATE-APOSTOLIC DECEMBER 1, 1843.

CREATED ARCHDIOCESE OF OREGON CITY, JULY 24, 1846; NAME CHANGED BY PAPAL DECREE TO "ARCHDIOCESE OF PORTLAND IN OREGON," SEPTEMBER 26, 1928.

Square Miles 29,717.

Comprises that part of the State of Oregon lying between the summit of the Cascades and the Pacific Ocean.

For legal titles of parishes and archdiocesan institutions, consult the Archdiocesan Pastoral Center.

Archdiocesan Pastoral Center: 2838 E. Burnside St., Portland, OR, 97214-1895. Tel.: 503-234-5334; Fax: 503-234-2545.

Web site address: http://www.archdpdx.org/

E-mail address: @archdpdx.org

STATISTICAL OVERVIEW

Personnel	
Archbishop	1
Retired Archbishops	1
Auxiliary Bishops	1
Abbots	2
Retired Abbots	1
Priests: Diocesan Active in Diocese	106
Priests: Active Outside Diocese	5
Priests: Diocesan in Foreign Missions	2
Priests: Retired, Sick or Absent	43
Number of Diocesan Priests	156
Religious Priests in Diocese	184
Extern Priests in Diocese	22
Ordinations:	
Diocesan Priests	5
Transitional Deacons	3
Permanent Deacons in Diocese	16
Total Brothers	77
Total Sisters	532
Parishes	
Parishes	125
With Resident Pastor:	
Resident Diocesan Priests	79
Resident Religious Priests	37
Without Resident Pastor:	
Administered by Priests	8
Administered by Lay People	1
Missions	26
Pastoral Centers	1
Professional Ministry Personnel:	
Brothers	3
Sisters	30
Lay Ministers	155
Welfare	
Catholic Hospitals	9
Total Assisted	1,505,996
Health Care Centers	4
Total Assisted	1,068
Homes for the Aged	4
Total Assisted	1,356
Day Care and Extended Day Care Centers	4
Total Assisted	1,614
Specialized Homes	8
Total Assisted	6,262
Special Centers for Social Services	14
Total Assisted	1,018,765
Residential Care of Disabled	3
Total Assisted	32
Educational	
Seminaries, Diocesan	1
Students from This Diocese	20
Students from Other Diocese	103
Diocesan Students in Other Seminaries	2
Students Religious	31
Total Seminarians	53
Colleges and Universities	2
Total Students	5,149
High Schools, Diocesan and Parish	3
Total Students	1,598
High Schools, Private	6
Total Students	3,045
Elementary Schools, Diocesan and Parish	41
Total Students	8,849
Elementary Schools, Private	1
Total Students	372
Catechesis/Religious Education:	
High School Students	3,091
Elementary Students	11,532
Total Students Under Catholic Instruction	33,689
Teachers in the Diocese:	
Priests	54
Brothers	7
Sisters	154
Lay Teachers	1,404
Vital Statistics	
Receptions into the Church:	
Infant Baptism Totals	4,918
Adult Baptism Totals	676
Received into Full Communion	703
First Communions	3,809
Confirmations	2,012
Marriages:	
Catholic	789
Interfaith	605
Total Marriages	1,394
Deaths	2,075
Total Catholic Population	282,593
Total Population	2,725,200

Former Bishops—Most Rev. FRANCIS NORBERT BLANCHET, D.D., First Vicar Apostolic of Oregon Territory; cons. July 25, 1845, Titular Bishop of Drasa; appt. Archbishop of Oregon City, July 24, 1846 when the Vicariate was erected into an ecclesiastical province; resigned 1880; died June 18, 1883.—Most Rev. CHARLES JOHN SEGHERS, D.D., cons. June 29, 1873; Bishop of Vancouver Island, British Columbia; coadjutor to the Archbishop of Oregon City, Dec. 10, 1878; Archbishop, Dec. 20, 1880; resigned 1884 and; transferred to Vancouver Island, British Columbia; died Nov. 28, 1886.—Most Rev. WILLIAM H. GROSS, C.SS.R., D.D., Archbishop of Oregon City; cons. Bishop of Savannah, GA April 27, 1873 promoted by His Holiness Leo XIII Feb. 1, 1885 from Savannah to the Archiepiscopal See of Oregon City; died Nov. 14, 1898.—Most Rev. ALEXANDER CHRISTIE, D.D., Archbishop of Oregon City; cons. June 29, 1898, Bishop of Vancouver Island, B. C. promoted by His Holiness Leo XIII February 12, 1899 from Vancouver Island to the Archiepiscopal See of Oregon City; died April 6, 1925.—Most Rev. EDWARD D. HOWARD, D.D., LL.D., Titular Archbishop of Albule; ord. June 12, 1906; cons. Titular Bishop of Isauria and Auxiliary Bishop of Davenport, April 6, 1924; appt. to the See of Oregon City, April 30, 1926 asst. at the Pontifical Throne, May 2, 1939; transferred to the Titular See of Albule and as Archbishop of Portland in Oregon, Dec. 9, 1966; died Jan. 2, 1983.—Most Rev. ROBERT

JOSEPH DWYER, D.D., Ph.D., ord. June 11, 1932; cons. Bishop of Reno, August 5, 1952; appt. Archbishop of Portland in Oregon, Dec. 9, 1966; resigned Jan. 22, 1974; died March 24, 1976.—Most Rev. CORNELIUS MICHAEL POWER, D.D., J.C.D., ord. June 3, 1939; appt. Bishop of Yakima, Feb. 5, 1969; cons. May 1, 1969; appt. Archbishop of Portland in Oregon, Jan. 22, 1974; retired July 3, 1986.—Most Rev. WILLIAM J. LEVADA, S.T.D., ord. Dec. 20, 1961; appt. Titular Bishop of Capri and Auxiliary Bishop of Los Angeles, March 29, 1983; appt. Archbishop of Portland in Oregan, July 1, 1986; installed Sept. 21, 1986; appt. Coadjutor Archbishop of San Francisco, Aug. 17, 1995; transferred Oct. 24, 1995.

Office of the Archbishop

Archdiocesan Pastoral Center—2838 E. Burnside St., Portland, 97214-1895. Tel: 503-234-5334; Fax: 503-234-2545.

Vicars and Directors

Vicar for Clergy—Rev. CHARLES LIENERT.

Vicar for Finance—Rev. PAUL PERI.

Department Directors—

Business Affairs—PATRICK REILLY.

Clergy—Rev. CHARLES LIENERT.

Education—ROBERT MIZIA.

Chancellor/Public Services—MARY JO TULLY.

Pastoral Services—Rev. MICHAEL MASLOWSKY.

Vicariate For Southeast Asians—Rev. VINCENT MINH, C.SS.R., Episcopal Vicar, *5404 N.E. Alameda Dr., Portland, 97213.* Tel: 503-249-5892.

Chancellor—MARY JO TULLY.

College of Consultors—Most Rev. KENNETH D. STEINER; Rev. Msgr. FRANK CAMPBELL; Very Rev. PATRICK BRENNAN; Revs. JOSEPH BROWNE, C.S.; DONALD BUXMAN; ARTHUR DERNBACH; JOSEPH JACOBBERGER; CHARLES LIENERT; GREGORY MOYS; PAUL PERI.

Area Vicars—Downtown Portland: Rev. JOSEPH JACOBBERGER, North Portland: Rev. CATHAL BRENNAN, Northeast Portland: Rev. ROBERT KRUEGER, Southeast Portland: Rev. PETER KIRWIN, O.F.M., East Portland Suburban: Rev. JOSEPH S. MCMAHON, South Portland Suburban:; Vacant; West Portland Suburban: Rev. RICHARD ROSSMAN, Beaverton Suburban: Rev. WAYNE FORBES, Yamhill County: Rev. THOMAS FARLEY, Tualatin Valley: Rev. CARL FLACH, Columbia County: Rev. ELWIN SCHWAB, North Coast: Rev. MARK BACHMEIER, Marion County:; Vacant; Metropolitan Salem: Rev. GEORGE WOLF, Santiam: Rev. GREGORY MOYS, Albany-Corvallis: Most Rev. KENNETH D. STEINER, Metropolitan Eugene: Rev. TIMOTHY MOCKAITIS, Middle Coast: Rev. JACK WELLS, South Coast: Rev. JOHN MCGUIRE, Douglas County: Rev. WILLIAM RYAN, O.S.A., Southern Oregon: Rev. JAMES CLIFFORD.

Personnel Board—Rev. PAUL F. PERI, Chm.; Very Rev. PATRICK BRENNAN; Rev. Msgr. FRANK CAMPBELL; Revs. BERTRAM GRIFFIN; JOSEPH JACOBBERGER; CHARLES LIENERT, (Ex Officio); JACK MOSBRUCKER.

Tribunal

Judicial Vicar—Dirs.: Rev. THOMAS YURCHAK; LINDA WEIGEL, J.C.L. Tel: 503-233-8381.

Adjutant Judicial Vicar—Rev. CARL FLACH.

Judges—Revs. CARL J. FLACH; CARL GIMPL; GARY JACOBSON; THOMAS YURCHAK, J.C.L.

Defenders of the Bond—Rev. ARTHUR DERNBACH; LINDA WEIGEL, J.C.L.

Auditors—Rev. CARL J. FLACH; KATHLEEN TRUMAN; PEG WILLS.

Notaries—Rev. JOSEPH JACOBBERGER; JANET MCQUISTON; MARGARET PALMER.

Advocates—All priests with Archdiocesan assignments and pastoral ministers by appointment.

Archdiocesan Offices and Agencies

Archives—MARY A. GRANT, Archivist. Tel: 503-233-8334., *2838 E. Burnside St., Portland, 97214-1895.*

Building Commission—Most Rev. FRANCIS E. GEORGE, O.M.I.; Revs. THEODORE WEBER, Chm. PAUL PERI; JOSEPH HEUBERGER; ALEXANDER PLASKER, O.S.B.; A. P. DIBENEDETTO, F.A.I.A.; JOHN BROCKAMP; ROBERT STOCHOSKY; DELIA WILSON; DONALD BENZ; JOSEPH PELLICANO; EDWARD CURTIN; PATRICK REILLY, Ex-Officio; KEN SCOTT, Sec. Tel: 503-234-5334.

Business Affairs—PATRICK REILLY, Dir., *2838 E. Burnside St., Portland, 97214-1895.* Tel: 503-234-5334.

Campus Ministry—Rev. MICHAEL MASLOWSKY, Dir., *2838 E. Burnside St., Portland, 97214-1895.* Tel: 503-234-5334.

Catholic Charities, Inc.—DENNIS KEENAN, Exec. Dir., *231 S.E. 12th Ave., Portland, 97214-9813.* Tel: 503-231-4866.

Catholic Deaf Ministry—Sr. LINDA ROBY, B.V.M., Dir., *2838 E. Burnside St., Portland, 97214-1895.* Tel: 503-233-8398 (V-TDD).

"Catholic Sentinel"—(Official Newspaper of the Archdiocese), Most Rev. FRANCIS E. GEORGE, O.M.I., Publisher-in-Chief; JOHN J. LIMB, Publisher; ROBERT PFOHMAN, Editor, *5536 N.E. Hassalo, Portland, 97213-3638.* Tel: 503-281-1191.

Catholic Youth Organization—WILMA OUHL, Exec. Dir., *Oregon Plaza, 825 N.E. 20th St., Ste. 320, Portland, 97232.* Tel: 503-231-9484.

Cemeteries—Rev. PAUL PERI, V.G., Dir. TIM CORBETT, Supt., *Mt. Calvary Cemetery, 333 S.W. Skyline Blvd., Portland, 97221.* Tel: 503-292-6621.

Clergy Personnel—Rev. CHARLES LIENERT, Vicar for Clergy, *2838 E. Burnside St., Portland, 97214-1895.* Tel: 503-233-8366.

Communications, Office of—BUD BUNCE, Dir., *2838 E. Burnside St., Portland, 97214-1895.* Tel: 503-233-8373.

Continuing Education for Clergy—Rev. PAUL PERI, Dir. Board Members: Revs. EDMOND BLIVEN; DONALD BUXMAN; J. PATRICK MOORE; TIMOTHY MURPHY; SCOTT VANDEHEY, *2838 E. Burnside St., Portland, 97214-1895.* Tel: 503-234-5334.

Development Office—BOB GIACOVELLI, Dir., Devel. Assoc. Dirs.: JONATHAN WEAVER; GILBERT WHITE, *2838 E. Burnside St., Portland, 97214-1895.* Tel: 503-233-8333.

Ecumenical and Interreligious Affairs—Rev. RICHARD SIRIANNI, Dir. MARY JO TULLY, Assoc. Dir., *3123 N.E. 24th Ave., Portland, 97212.* Tel: 503-281-5777.

Education, Religious—Bro. ROBERT RODRIGUES, O.F.M., Dir. Religious Education Field Consultant: CATHY SHANNON, *2838 E. Burnside St., Portland, 97214-1895.* Tel: 503-234-5334.

Family Life Office—BURNS SEELEY, Consultant for Marriage and Family Life, *2838 E. Burnside St., Portland, 97214-1895.* Tel: 503-233-8341.

Finance Council—Most Rev. FRANCIS E. GEORGE, O.M.I., Chair; Rev. PAUL PERI; Rev. PATRICK WALSH; ARTHUR SCHULTE, JR., Ph.D.; LEO C. SHERRY, JR.; MYRON FLECK; ROGER CONKLING; HENRIETTA SAALFELD; PATRICK REILLY; LEONARD VUYLSTEKE; DENNIS FERGUSON; EDWARD HERINCKX, *2838 E. Burnside St., Portland, 97214-1895.* Tel: 503-233-8350.

Financial Services—LEONARD VUYLSTEKE, Dir., *2838 E. Burnside St., Portland, 97214-1895.* Tel: 503-233-8359.

Hispanic Ministeries—RAUL VELAZQUEZ, Dir., *2838 E. Burnside St., Portland, 97214.* Tel: 503-233-8324.

Historical Commission—JOSEPH SCHIWEK, JR., *2838 E. Burnside St., Portland, 97214-1895.*

Holy Childhood, Pontifical Association of—MARY JO TULLY, Dir., *2838 E. Burnside St., Portland, 97214-1895.* Tel: 503-233-8323.

Immigration Counseling Services—Mrs. MARGARET GODFREY, Dir., *434 N.W. 6th Ave., Ste. 202, Portland, 97209.* Tel: 503-221-1689.

Justice and Peace—FRANK FROMHERZ, Dir., *2838 E. Burnside St., Portland, 97214-1895.* Tel: 503-233-8361.

Ministry Formation—Rev. MICHAEL MASLOWSKY, Dir., *2838 E. Burnside St., Portland, 97214-1895.* Tel: 503-233-8391.

Mission Office—MARY JO TULLY, Dir., *2838 E. Burnside St., Portland, 97214-1895.* Tel: 503-233-8323.

Office for People with Disabilities—DOROTHY DESMARTEAU-COUGHLIN, Dir. RUTH HAYES-BARBA, Assoc. Dir., *2838 E. Burnside St., Portland, 97214-1895.* Tel: 503-233-8396 (V/TTY).

Oregon Catholic Conference—Most Rev. FRANCIS E. GEORGE O.M.I., Pres.; Most Rev. THOMAS J. CONNOLLY (BAK), Vice Pres.; Most Rev. KENNETH STEINER; ROBERT CASTAGNA, Exec. Dir., *2838 E. Burnside St., Portland, 97214-1895.* Tel: 503-233-8387.

Oregon Catholic Press—Most Rev. FRANCIS E. GEORGE, O.M.I., Publisher-in-Chief; JOHN J. LIMB, Publisher; DAN HUMPHRIES, Gen. Mgr., *5536 N.E. Hassalo, Portland, 97213.* Tel: 503-281-1191.

Pastoral Services, Evangelization, Pastoral Councils, Charismatic Renewal—Rev. MICHAEL MASLOWSKY, Dir., *2838 E. Burnside St., Portland, 97214-1895.* Tel: 503-233-8385.

Permanent Diaconate—Rev. RICHARD HUNEGER, Dir., *2838 E. Burnside St., Portland, 97214-1895.* Tel: 503-234-5334.

Pro-Life Activities—ROBERT CASTAGNA, Exec. Dir., Oregon Catholic Conference, *2838 E. Burnside St., Portland, 97214-1895.* Tel: 503-233-8387.

Project Rachel—231 S.E. 12th Ave., Portland, 97214-9813. Tel: 1-800-249-8074.

Propagation of the Faith, Pontifical Society for the—MARY JO TULLY, Dir., *2838 E. Burnside St., Portland, 97214-1895.* Tel: 503-233-8322.

St. Mary's Home for Boys—EMMA DENNIS, Exec. Dir., *16535 S.W. Tualatin Valley Hwy., Beaverton, 97006.* Tel: 503-649-5651.

School Office—ROBERT MIZIA, Supt. Tel: 503-233-8300. Bro. WILLIAM CAMPBELL, S.M., Asst. Supt., School Personnel/Technology; Sr. RITA RAE SCHNEIDER, R.S.M., Asst. Supt., Faith Formation/Curriculum, *2838 E. Burnside St., Portland, 97214-1895.*

Vocations—Rev. LIAM CARY, Dir., *2838 E. Burnside St., Portland, 97214-1895.* Tel: 503-233-8368.

Worship—2838 E. Burnside St., Portland, 97214-1895. Tel: 503-234-5334.

Youth Ministry—DONALD CIFFONE, Dir., *2838 E. Burnside St., Portland, 97214-1895.* Tel: 503-233-8395.

CLERGY, PARISHES, MISSIONS AND PAROCHIAL SCHOOLS

CITY OF PORTLAND
(Multnomah County)

1—CATHEDRAL OF THE IMMACULATE CONCEPTION (1851), Revs. Joseph Jacobberger; Luan Tran; Deacon John Ries. In res., Rev. Gary Jacobson.
Res., 1716 N.W. Davis St., 97209. Tel: 503-228-4397; Fax: 503-242-2568.
School—110 N.W. 17th Ave., 97209. Tel: 503-227-4297; Fax: 503-243-3819.
Order of Servants of Mary 2; Lay Teachers 10; Students 220.

2—ST. AGATHA (1911), Rev. Cosmas White, O.S.B. In res., Rev. Matt Burger, O.S.B.
Res., 1403 S.E. Nehalem St., 97202. Tel: 503-236-4747.
School—(Grades K-8). Tel: 503-234-5500.
Sisters 1; Lay Teachers 11; Students 155.

3—ALL SAINTS (1917), Rev. John Kerns.
Res., 3847 N.E. Glisan, 97232. Tel: 503-232-4305; Fax: 503-234-9685.
School—601 N.E. 39th Ave., 97232. Tel: 503-236-6205; Fax: 503-236-0781.
Lay Teachers 21; Students 358.
Catechesis/Religious Programs—Students 33.

4—ST. ANDREW (1907), Rev. Robert W. Krueger.
Res., 806 N.E. Alberta St., 97211. Tel: 503-281-4429.

5—ST. ANTHONY (1917), Rev. Michael Maslowsky.
Res., 3725 S.E. 80th Ave., 97206. Tel: 503-771-6039; Fax: 503-775-6119.

6—ASCENSION (1892), Rev. Peter Kirwin, O.F.M. In res., Bros. Mark Schroeder, O.F.M.; Jeff Macnab, O.F.M.; Robert Rodrigues, O.F.M.
Church: 7507 S.E. Yamhill, 97215. Tel: 503-256-3897; Fax: 503-257-4681.
Res., 404 S.E. 68th, 97215. Tel: 503-253-8305.
Catechesis/Religious Programs—Students 110.

7—ASSUMPTION (1909), Rev. Joseph Baccellieri.
Res., 7406 N. Smith St., 97203. Tel: 503-286-0203.

8—ST. BIRGITTA (1954), Rev. Joseph P. Browne, C.S.C.
Res., 11820 N.W. St. Helens Rd., 97231-2319. Tel: 503-286-3929.
Chapel—Portland, Chapel of Our Lady of Sinj.

9—BLESSED SACRAMENT (1913), Rev. Cathal Brennan; Sr. Raphael Balduc, O.S.F., Pastoral Assoc.
Office: 4610 N. Maryland Ave., 97217. Tel: 503-284-4689. [CEM]
Res., 4620 N. Maryland Ave., 97217. Tel: 503-281-6758.

10—ST. CHARLES (1914), Rev. Jacob Mosbrucker. Pastoral Assocs.: Barbara Hays; Martha Stephenson.
Parish Center: 5310 N.E. 42nd, 97218. Tel: 503-281-6461.
School—Archbishop Howard School, (Grades PreK-8) 5309 N.E. Alameda Dr., 97213. Tel: 503-281-1912.
Lay Teachers 11; Students 272.

11—CHURCH OF KOREAN MARTYRS (1990) (Korean), Rev. Peter Sung Hwan Jeong.
Res., 10840 S.E. Powell Blvd., 97266. Tel: 503-762-6880; Fax: 503-760-6601.

12—ST. CLARE (1913), Rev. Donald A. Durand.
Res., 8535 S.W. 19th Ave., 97219. Tel: 503-244-1037.
School—Tel: 503-244-7600.
Sisters of Charity 1; Lay Teachers 14; Students 227.

13—ST. ELIZABETH OF HUNGARY (1953), Revs. John B. Wironen, C.S.C.; William E. Wickham, C.S.C., Chap. VA Hospital.
Res., 4112 S.W. Sixth Ave. Dr., 97201. Tel: 503-222-2168.

14—ST. FRANCIS OF ASSISI, Rev. John J. Morris, S.J., Moderator; Valerie Chapman, Pastoral Admin.; Silivelio Alaalatoa, Pastoral Assoc.; Joe Rastatter, Soc. Min.
Res., 330 S.E. 11th Ave., 97214. Tel: 503-232-5880.

15—HOLY CROSS (1901), Rev. Cathal Brennan; Pat Campbell Dent, Pastoral Assoc.
Res., 5227 N. Bowdoin St., 97203. Tel: 503-289-2834; Fax: 503-283-7056.

School—Tel: 503-289-3010; Fax: 503-286-5006. Sisters 4; Lay Teachers 8; Students 200.
Chapel—Christ The Teacher, University of Portland, 5000 N. Willamette Blvd., 97203. Tel: 503-283-7311; Fax: 503-283-7399.

16—HOLY FAMILY (1931), Rev. Robert Barricks. 3732 S.E. Knapp, 97202. Tel: 503-774-1428; Fax: 503-774-1854.
Res., 3708 S.E. Flavel St., 97202.
School—Tel: 503-774-8871. Sandy Stanton, Prin. Lay Teachers 14; Students 212.

17—HOLY REDEEMER (1906), Revs. Richard Schiblin, C.S.S.R.; Vincent Minh, C.S.S.R.; Anthony Phuc Nguyen, C.S.S.R.; Joseph K. Nuttman, C.S.S.R.; Ivan Dawson, C.Ss.R.
Res., 25 N. Portland Blvd., 97217. Tel: 503-285-4539; Fax: 503-285-8216.
School—Tel: 503-283-5197.
Sisters of the Holy Names of Jesus and Mary 8; Lay Teachers 28; Students 405.

18—HOLY ROSARY PARISH & DOMINICAN PRIORY (1894), Very Rev. Anthony Patalano, O.P., Prior; Revs. Gerald Albert Buckley, O.P.; Paul Raftery, O.P.; Thomas J. McGreevy, O.P. In res., Revs. Paul A. Duffner, O.P.; Dominic Hoffman, O.P.; Christopher H. Moschini, O.P.
Res., 375 N.E. Clackamas St., 97232. Tel: 503-235-3163; Fax: 503-235-3164.
Confraternity of the Most Holy Rosary—P.O. Box 3617, 97208. Tel: 503-236-8393; Fax: 503-236-8394.
Catechesis/Religious Programs—Students 187.

19—ST. IGNATIUS (1907), Revs. L. Michael Pope, S.J.; Stephen M. Hess, S.J.
Res., 3400 S.E. 43rd Ave., 97206. Tel: 503-777-1491. [JC]
School—3330 1/2 S.E. 43rd St., 97206. Tel: 503-774-5533; Fax: 503-788-1134.
Sisters of the Holy Names of Jesus and Mary 4; Lay Teachers 15; Students 252.
Convent—4130 S.E. Brooklyn, 97206. Tel: 503-231-6538. Sisters of the Holy Names of Jesus and Mary

20—IMMACULATE HEART OF MARY (1888), Rev. Nicolaus Marandu.
Res., 2926 N. Williams Ave., 97227-1628. Tel: 503-287-3724.

21—ST. JOHN FISHER (1959), Rev. Wayne A. Forbes.
Res., 7007 S.W. 46th Ave., 97219. Tel: 503-246-4686; Fax: 503-452-8570.
School—Tel: 503-246-3234; Fax: 503-246-4117. Lay Teachers 13; aides 7; Students 261.
Catechesis/Religious Programs—Tel: 503-244-5784.
Students 261.

22—CHURCH OF ST. JOSEPH THE WORKER (1885), Rev. Jack Krall.
Res., 2310 S.E. 148th, 97233. Tel: 503-761-8710; Fax: 503-761-8545.

23—ST. MARY MAGDALENE (1911). (The Madeleine). Rev. Richard D. Sirianni.
Res., 3123 N.E. 24th Ave., 97212. Tel: 503-281-5777; Fax: 503-281-5787.
School—3240 N.E. 23rd Ave., 97212. Tel: 503-288-9197. Bernadette Kunnen, Prin.
Sisters of the Holy Names of Jesus and Mary 1; Lay Teachers 12; Students 265.

24—CHURCH OF ST. MICHAEL, THE ARCHANGEL (1894), Rev. Bertram F. Griffin; Celeste Granato, Pastoral Min.
Res., 424 S.W. Mill St., 97201. Tel: 501-228-8629.

25—OUR LADY OF SORROWS (1917), Rev. Robert Beltrami, O.F.M.
Res., 5221 S.E. Knight St., 97206. Tel: 503-775-6731.
School—Tel: 503-771-3592; Fax: 503-774-5390. Sisters 4; Lay Teachers 7; Students 174.

26—ST. PATRICK (1885), Rev. Frank Knusel, Admin.
Res., 1623 N.W. 19th Ave., 97209. Tel: 503-222-4086.

27—ST. PETER (1911), Rev. Dale T. Waddill.
Office: 8648 S.E. Foster Rd., 97266. Tel: 503-777-3321.
Res., 5736 S.E. 86th St., 97266. Tel: 503-777-1026.

28—ST. PHILIP NERI (1912) (Italian), Revs. Stephen E.M. Bossi, C.S.P.; Vincent Sampietro, C.S.P.; Joseph J. Scott, C.S.P. Pastoral Assocs.: Kim Armbruster; Claire Meyer; Charlene Scales; Liz Anctil-Frane.
Res., 2408 S.E. 16th Ave., 97214. Tel: 503-231-4955; Fax: 503-234-5088.

29—ST. PIUS X (Cedar Mill) (1953), Revs. Neil J. Moore; Heiko T. Junge; Deacon Robert Little.
Office: 1280 N.W. Saltzman Rd., 97229. Tel: 503-644-5264; Fax: 503-626-6540.
School—1260 N.W. Saltzman Rd., 97229. Tel: 503-644-3244; Fax: 503-646-6568.
Lay Teachers 13; Students 270.
Catechesis/Religious Programs—Tel: 503-644-3063.
Students 442.

30—QUEEN OF PEACE (1924), Rev. Amancio Rodrigues.
Res., 2434 N. Farragut St., 97217. Tel: 503-283-1100; Fax: 503-289-2144.

31—ST. RITA (1924), Rev. Richard Boyle, O.S.M.
Mailing Address: 10029 N.E. Prescott St., 97220. Tel: 503-252-3403; Fax: 503-256-9682.

32—ST. ROSE OF LIMA (1911), Rev. Richard J. Huneger.
Res., 2727 N.E. 54th Ave., 97213. Tel: 503-281-5318; Fax: 503-284-8350.
School—Archbishop Howard School, Tel: 503-281-1912; Fax: 503-284-8350.
Lay Teachers 12; Students 274.

33—SACRED HEART (1893), Rev. Benedict Suing, O.S.B.
Res., 3910 S.E. 11th Ave., 97202. Tel: 503-231-9636.

34—ST. STANISLAUS (1907) (Polish), Rev. Richard G. Philiposki, S.Ch.
Res., 3916 N. Interstate Ave., 97227-1063. Tel: 503-281-7532; Fax: 503-281-7532.

35—ST. STEPHEN (1907), Rev. Morton Park.
Res., 1112 S.E. 41st Ave., 97214. Tel: 503-234-5019; Fax: 503-239-5985.
School—4235 S.E. Salmon, 97214. Tel: 503-235-7040; Fax: 503-239-5985.
Lay Teachers 6; Students 117.

36—ST. THERESE OF THE CHILD JESUS (1955), Revs. Louis J. Urbanski; Nicholas E. Nilema, A.L.C.P. (Tanzania).
Res., 1260 N.E. 132nd Ave., 97230. Tel: 503-256-5850; Fax: 503-253-3560.
School—Tel: 503-253-9400; Fax: 503-253-9571.
Dominican Sisters of Mission San Jose 2; Lay Teachers 15; Students 275.

37—ST. THOMAS MORE (1936), Rev. Arthur P. Dernbach; Deacon Edward Morin.
Res., 3525 S.W. Patton Rd., 97221. Tel: 503-222-2055.
School—Tel: 503-222-6105.
Sisters of St. Francis 1; Lay Teachers 15; Students 225.

38—ST. VINCENT DE PAUL (1919). (Downtown Chapel). Revs. Richard F. Berg, C.S.C.; Stephen J. Sedlock, C.S.C.; Gary N. Smith, S.J.
Res., 601 W. Burnside St., 97209. Tel: 503-228-0746; Fax: 503-402-1607.

OUTSIDE THE CITY OF PORTLAND

Albany, Linn Co., Our Lady of Perpetual Help (1885), Rev. John C. Betts. Pastoral Assocs.: Ellen Ketsdever; Kathleen Gyovai; Sharon Tebb.
Res., 728 Ellsworth St., 97321. Tel: 503-926-1449; Fax: 503-926-2191.
School—815 S. Broadalbin, Tel: 503-928-7474.
Sisters 2; Lay Teachers 4; Students 149.
Catechesis/Religious Programs—Tel: 503-926-9327.
Students 280.

Aloha, Washington Co., St. Elizabeth Ann Seton (1982), Rev. James Galluzzo.
Res., P.O. Box 5938, 97006. Tel: 503-649-9044; 649-6211.
Catechesis/Religious Programs—Students 185.

Ashland, Jackson Co., Our Lady of the Mountain (1959), Revs. Anthony Rosevear, O.P.; Raymond Finerty, O.P., Newman Center; Brendan McAnerney, O.P.
Res., 987 Hillview Dr., 97520. Tel: 541-482-1146; Fax: 541-488-5174.
Catechesis/Religious Programs—Students 200.

Astoria, Clatsop Co., St. Mary, Star of the Sea (1874), Rev. Mark V. Bachmeier.
Res., 1465 Grand Ave., 97103. Tel: 503-325-3671. [JC]
School—Tel: 503-325-3771.
Lay Teachers 8; Students 96.
Mission—Hammond, Clatsop Co., St. Francis de Sales.

Bandon, Coos Co., Holy Trinity (1883), Rev. William E. Karath.
Res., 355 Oregon Ave., Box 1037, 97411. Tel: 541-347-2309; Fax: 541-347-9256. [CEM]
Mission—Port Orford, Curry Co., St. John the Baptist, P.O. Box 884, Port Orford, 97465.

Beaverton, Washington Co., St. Cecilia (1876), Revs. Dennis J. O'Donovan; Richard Thompson; Luke O'Donnell, O.S.B.
Res., 5105 S.W. Franklin Ave., 97005. Tel: 503-644-2619; Fax: 503-626-7204.
School—Tel: 503-644-7647; Fax: 503-626-7204.
Sisters 1; Lay Teachers 14; Students 268.
Catechesis/Religious Programs—Tel: 503-644-0203; Fax: 503-626-7205.
Students 608.
Holy Trinity (1962), Rev. John Waldron.
Res., 13715 S.W. Walker Rd., 97005. Tel: 503-643-9528; Fax: 503-644-8426.
School—Tel: 503-644-5748; Fax: 503-644-8486.
Lay Teachers 18; Students 280.
Catechesis/Religious Programs—Tel: 503-646-0331.
Students 119.

Brookings, Curry Co., Star of the Sea (1923), Rev. Edmund K. Ryan, O.P. In res., Rev. M. Brendan O'Down, (Retired).
Mailing Address: Box 1066, 97415.
Res., 820 Old County Rd., 97415. Tel: 541-469-2313; Fax: 541-469-2683.
Mission—Gold Beach, Curry Co., St. Charles Borromeo, 94323 Gauntlet, P.O. Box 33, Gold Beach, 97444. Tel: 541-247-2453. Rev. Thomas Mannion.

Canby, Clackamas Co., St. Patrick (1882), Rev. Thomas D. Yurchak.
Res., 498 N.W. Ninth, P.O. Box 730, 97013. Tel: 503-266-9411. [CEM]
Preschool—Tel: 503-263-8584. Theresa Jensen, Dir. Lay Teachers 1; Children 8.
Catechesis/Religious Programs—488 N.W. 9th, 97013. Tel: 503-266-2401.
Students 349.

Central Point, Jackson Co., Shepherd of the Valley (1978), Rev. James Clifford, O.S.A.
Office: 600 Beebe Rd., 97502. Tel: 541-664-1050; Fax: 541-664-9312.

Coos Bay, Coos Co., St. Monica (1888), Rev. Terry J. O'Connell.
Mailing Address: 696 Donnelly Ave., 97420-1553. Tel: 541-267-7421.
Church—Sixth St. between Donnelly & Bennett, 97420. Tel: 503-267-7421.

Coquille, Coos Co., Holy Name (1915), Rev. John F. McGuire.
Res., 12 N. Dean St., 97423. Tel: 541-396-3849; Fax: 541-396-4620.
Missions—Myrtle Point, Coos Co., Sts. Ann and Michael, 209 Second St., Myrtle Point, 97458. Tel: 541-396-3849; Powers, Coos Co., St. Bridget, 580 Third & Spruce, Powers, 97466.

Cornelius, Washington Co., St. Alexander (1881), Revs. Martin R. Senko, Admin.; Erasto Guzman-Chavez (Mexico) Co-Admin.; Alfonso Martinez.
Mailing Address: P.O. Box 644, 97113.
Res., 183 N. 11th, 97113. Tel: 503 359-0304. [CEM]
Catechesis/Religious Programs—Students 126.

Corvallis, Benton Co., St. Mary (1861), Most Rev. Kenneth D. Steiner, D.D.; Rev. Martin L. King; Deacon Francis Potts; Gloria J. Holt, Contact Person.
Res., 501 N.W. 25th St., 97330. Tel: 541-757-1988; Fax: 541-757-2788. [CEM]
Catechesis/Religious Programs—Tel: 541-757-1675.
Students 626.

Cottage Grove, Lane Co., Our Lady of Perpetual Help (1897), Rev. James Dowd; Sr. Elizabeth Hecker, S.N.J.M., Pastoral Assoc.
Res., 1025 N. 19th St., 97424. Tel: 541-942-3420.
Mission—Creswell, St. Philip Benizi.

Dallas, Polk Co., St. Philip (1920), Rev. Gerald Quintal.
Office: 825 S.W. Mill St., 97338. Tel: 503-623-2440. [JC]

Estacada, Clackamas Co., St. Aloysius (1924), Rev. David L. Clark, Admin.
Res., 297 N.W. Broadway, P.O. Box 1199, 97023. Tel: 503-630-2416. [JC]

Eugene, Lane Co.,

1—ST. JUDE, (1969), Rev. Peter A. Roerig.
Office: 4330 Willamette, 97405. Tel: 541-344-1191; Fax: 541-345-6001.

2—ST. MARK, (1962), Rev. Daniel Reynolds.
Res., 1760 Echo Hollow Rd., 97402. Tel: 541-689-0725.

3—ST. MARY, (1887), Revs. Scott Vandehey; James Stange.
Res., 1062 Charnelton St., 97401. Tel: 541-342-1139; Fax: 541-334-6996. [CEM]
Catechesis/Religious Programs—Students 167.

4—ST. PAUL, (1955), Rev. Timothy Mockaitis.
Res., 1201 Satre St., 97401. Tel: 541-686-2345; Fax: 541-686-0037.
School—Tel: 541-344-1401.
Sisters 1; Lay Teachers 18; Students 268.
Catechesis/Religious Programs—Students 127.

5—ST. PETER, (1955), Rev. David Ronald Cullings.
Res., 1150 Maxwell Rd., 97404. Tel: 541-688-1051; Fax: 541-689-0782. [JC]

6—ST. THOMAS MORE, (1915). (University Parish). Rev. Jose Pimentel, O.P.; Sr. Janet Ryan, S.N.J.M., Pastoral Assoc. In res., Revs. Augustine Thompson, O.P.; Vincent Lopez, O.P.; Vincent Benoit, O.P.; Christopher Terry, O.P.
Res., 1850 Emerald St., 97403. Tel: 541-343-7021; 346-4468; Fax: 541-686-8028.

Florence, Lane Co., St. Mary, Our Lady of the Dunes (1951), Rev. Donald K. Gutmann.

Res., 85060 U.S. Hwy. 101 S., Box 2640, 97439. Tel: 541-997-2312.

Forest Grove, Washington Co., St. Anthony (1908), Rev. Dave Gutmann; Sandra S. Zajdel, Pastoral Assoc., Tel: 503-357-8147; Lois Boogaard, Bus. Mgr.
Res., 1660 Elm St., 97116. Tel: 503-357-2989; Fax: 503-357-2217.
Catechesis / Religious Programs—Tel: 503-357-8147.
Students 160.

Gervais, Marion Co., Sacred Heart-St. Louis (1847), Rev. Kenneth Jacques, O.S.B.
Res., 680 Elm Ave., P.O. Box 236, 97026. Tel: 503-792-4231; Fax: 503-792-3749. [CEM]
School—Tel: 503-792-4541. Judy Howard, Prin.
Sisters 1; Lay Teachers 4; Students 115.

Grand Ronde, Yamhill Co., St. Michael (1860), Rev. James Crunican.
Res., 48520 S.W. Hebo Rd., 97347. Tel: 503-843-2206.

Grants Pass, Josephine Co., St. Anne (1896), Revs. Karl G. Schray; Todd Molinari.
Res., 1131 N.E. 10th St., 97526. Tel: 541-476-2240; Fax: 541-476-2194.
Parish Center—1133 N.E. 10th St., 97526. Tel: 541-479-4848.
School—(Grades K-6). Tel: 541-479-1582. Mr. Frankie Bytheway, Prin.
Sisters 1; Lay Teachers 7; Students 130.
Kelly Youth Center—1129 N.E. 10th St., 97526. Tel: 541-476-5802.
Catechesis / Religious Programs—Students 164.
Mission—Cave Junction, Josephine Co., St. Patrick, 407 W. River St., Cave Junction, 97523. Tel: 541-592-3658.
Station—Rogue River Catholic Community, Tel: 541-582-1373.

Gresham, Multnomah Co., St. Anne (1957), Rev. J. Michael Morrissey.
Res., 1015 S.E. 182nd Ave., 97233-5099. Tel: 503-665-4935; Fax: 503-661-2116.
Catechesis / Religious Programs—Students 240.

St. Henry (1913), Revs. Joseph S. McMahon; Slider Stevernol; Robert J. Palladino. In res., Rev. Charles J. Lienert.
Office: 346 N.W. First St., 97030. Tel: 503-665-9129; Fax: 503-665-8238.
Catechesis / Religious Programs—Students 190.

Hillsboro, Washington Co., St. Matthew (1902), Revs. Carl J. Flach; J. Patrick Moore.
Res., 447 S.E. 3rd Ave., 97123-4499. Tel: 503-648-1998; Fax: 503-648-4489. [CEM]
School—Tel: 503-648-2512.
Lay Teachers 11; Students 235.
Catechesis / Religious Programs—Tel: 503-648-6213.
Students 301.

Independence, Polk Co., St. Patrick (1908), Rev. Victoriano Perez.
Office: 1275 E St., 97351. Tel: 503-838-1242; Fax: 503-838-6873.
Res., 1258 E St., 97351. Tel: 503-838-5137.

Jordan, Linn Co., Our Lady of Lourdes (1885), Rev. W. Thomas Jones, S.M.
Res., 39043 Jordan Rd., 97374. Tel: 503-394-2437. [CEM]
Mission—Lyons, Linn Co., St. Patrick.

Junction City, Lane Co., St. Helen (1916), Rev. Joseph Black.
Res., 1350 W. Sixth Ave., 97448. Tel: 541-998-8053; Fax: 541-998-9474. [CEM]

Keizer, Marion Co., St. Edward (1967), Rev. Philip M. Hemming.
Office: 5303 River Rd., N., 97303. Tel: 503-393-5323. [CEM]
Catechesis / Religious Programs—Tel: 503-463-5439.
Students 161.

Lake Oswego, Clackamas Co., Our Lady of the Lake (1890), Revs. Rock Sassano; Xavier Panneer Selvam.
Mailing Address: 650 A Avenue, 97034-2943. Tel: 503-636-7687; Fax: 503-636-9415. [CEM]
School—715 A Ave., 97034-2943. Tel: 503-636-2121; Fax: 503-635-7760. Joan M. Codd, Prin.
Sisters 1; Lay Teachers 19; Students 251.
Catechesis / Religious Programs—Students 600.

Lebanon, Linn Co., St. Edward (1903), Rev. Paul P. Maher, O.M.I.; Deacon Richard E. Triska.
Office (Mailing Address): 100 Main St., 97355. Tel: 503-258-5333.
Res., 251 Second St., 97355. Tel: 503-258-5333.
Catechesis / Religious Programs—Students 190.

Lincoln City, Lincoln Co., St. Augustine (1925), Rev. Mell Stead.
Res., 1139 N.W. Hwy. 101, 97367. Tel: 541-994-2216.

McMinnville, Yamhill Co., St. James (1876), Rev. Thomas B. Farley.
Res., 1145 E. First St., 97128. Tel: 503-472-5232; Fax: 503-472-4414. [CEM]
School—Tel: 503-472-2661.
Lay Teachers 9; Students 122.
Catechesis / Religious Programs—Students 120.
Mission—Dayton, Yamhill Co., St. Martin de Porres, 407 Ferry St., Dayton, 97114. Tel: 503-864-2378; Fax: 503-864-3211.

Medford, Jackson Co., Sacred Heart of Jesus (1928), Revs. Mark Cach; Kelly Vandehey.
Res., 449 S. Ivy St., 97501. Tel: 541-779-4661; Fax: 541-732-0633. [JC]
School—Tel: 541-772-4105. David-Paul Zuber, Prin.
Lay Teachers 12; Students 154.
Mission—Jacksonville, Jackson Co., St. Joseph, 280 N. 4th, Jacksonville, 97530.
Catechesis / Religious Programs—Students 382.

Milwaukie, Clackamas Co., Christ the King (1960), Revs. Lawrence Walling, O.S.M.; Kevin Fitzpatrick, O.S.M.
Res., 7414 S.E. Michael Dr., 97222. Tel: 503-659-1475; Fax: 503-652-9447.
School—Tel: 503-654-0601; Fax: 503-654-0168. Ruth Gill, Prin.
Lay Teachers 14; Students 245.
Catechesis / Religious Programs—Tel: 503-659-2760.
Students 199.

St. John the Baptist (1912), Rev. Bruce Brown; Sr. Rae Skinner, S.N.J.M., R.C.I.A. Dir. In res., Rev. Joseph J. Neuville.
Res., 10955 S.E. 25th, 97222. Tel: 503-654-5449; Fax: 503-653-9567.
School—10956 S.E. 25th, 97222. Tel: 503-654-0200.
Lay Teachers 14; Students 205.
Catechesis / Religious Programs—Tel: 503-659-2760.
Students 230.

Molalla, Clackamas Co., St. James (1962), Rev. Edward Altstock.
Res., 301 Frances St., 97038. Tel: 503-829-2080; Fax: 503-829-2806.
Catechesis / Religious Programs—Students 175.

Monroe, Benton Co., St. Rose (1883), Rev. Joseph Black; William J. Richardson, Jr., Admin.
Mailing Address: P.O. Box 516, 97456.
Res., 00470 S. Fifth, 97456. Tel: 541-847-5454. [CEM]

Mt. Angel, Marion Co., St. Mary (1880), Revs. Edmund Smith, O.S.B.; Emmanuel W. Clark, O.S.B.
Res., Box 465, 97362. Tel: 503-845-2296; Fax: 503-845-2297. [CEM 2]
Catechesis / Religious Programs—Tel: 503-845-9248.
Students 275.
Mission—Scotts Mills, Marion Co., Holy Rosary. [CEM]

Myrtle Creek, Douglas Co., All Souls (1952), Rev. William A. Ryan, O.S.A.
Res., 1242 N.E. Spruce St., P.O. Box 810, 97457. Tel: 503-863-3271. [JC]
Mission—Glendale, Douglas Co., Holy Family, Marshall Ave., Glendale, 97442.

Newberg, Yamhill Co., St. Peter (1909), Rev. Gregory A. Gage; Lee Allard, Pastoral Assoc.
Res., 608 S. Columbia St., 97132. Tel: 503-538-4312.

Newport, Lincoln Co., Sacred Heart Parish (1889), Rev. Jack M. Wells.
Res., 927 N. Coast Hwy., P.O. Box 843, 97365. Tel: 541-265-5101; Fax: 541-265-7582. [JC]
Mission—Siletz, Lincoln Co., St. Mary, 231 E. Logsden Rd, Siletz, 97380.

North Bend, Coos Co., Holy Redeemer (1906), Rev. Patrick J. Kiernan.
Res., 2250 16th St., 97459. Tel: 541-756-6901; Fax: 541-756-3234. [JC]
Catechesis / Religious Programs—Tel: 541-756-0161.
Students 240.

North Plains, Washington Co., St. Edward (1913), Rev. Msgr. Frank Campbell.
Res., P.O. Box 507, 97133. Tel: 503-644-1932. [CEM]

Oakridge, Lane Co., St. Michael (1941), Rev. Charles W. Weiss, S.J.
Res., 76387 Crestview St., P.O. Box 422, 97463. Tel: 541-782-3262.
Mission—Dexter, Lane Co., St. Henry, 38925 Dexter Rd., P.O. Box 65, Dexter, 97431. Tel: 541-937-3033. Rev. Joseph E. Perri, S.J.

Oregon City, Clackamas Co., St. John the Apostle (1842), Rev. Donald R. Buxman.
Res., 417 Washington St., 97045. Tel: 503-656-3474; Fax: 503-656-0486. [CEM]
School—Tel: 503-656-5123. Alan Loboy, Prin.
Lay Teachers 10; Students 190.
Catechesis / Religious Programs—Tel: 503-656-7755.
Students 258.

Rainier, Columbia Co., Nativity B.V.M. (1909), Rev. Emmett B. Painter, S.J.
Res., 204 E. C St., P.O. Box 340, 97048. Tel: 503-556-5641.
Mission—Clatskanie, Columbia Co., St. John the Baptist.

Redland, Clackamas Co., St. Philip Benizi (1969), Rev. Theodore R. Weber.
Res., 18211 S. Henrici Rd., Oregon City, 97045. Tel: 503-631-2882.
Catechesis / Religious Programs—Tel: 503-631-7124.
Students 185.

Reedsport, Douglas Co., St. John the Apostle (1924), Rev. Daniel Kolasinski.
Res., 12 St. Johns Way, 97467. Tel: 541-271-5621.

Rockaway, Tillamook Co., St. Mary by the Sea (1927), Rev. William A. Maat, O.S.B.
Res., P.O. Box 390, 97136. Tel: 503-355-2345. [JC]
Church—275 S. Pacific St., Tel: 503-355-2661 (Office).

Roseburg, Douglas Co., St. Joseph (1867), Rev. Ray Elam, O.S.A.
Res., 800 W. Stanton St., 97470. Tel: 541-673-5157; Fax: 541-672-5022. [CEM]
School—Tel: 541-672-1751.
Lay Teachers 7; Students 123.
Catechesis / Religious Programs—Tel: 541-672-7239.
Students 201.
Station—Glide, Tel: 541-496-3999.

Roy, Washington Co., St. Francis of Assisi (1908), Rev. Stephen Breitenstein.
Res., 39135 N.W. Harrington Rd., Banks, 97106. Tel: 503-324-2231. [CEM]
School—39085 N.W. Harrington Rd., Banks, 97106. Tel: 503-324-2182.
Sisters of St Mary of Oregon 2; Lay Teachers 7; Students 128.

St. Helens, Columbia Co., St. Frederic (1910), Rev. Elwin C. Schwab.
Res., 175 S. 13th St., 97051. Tel: 503-397-0148.

St. Louis, Marion Co., St. Louis. Closed. For sacramental records contact Sacred Heart-St. Louis, Gervias.

St. Paul, Marion Co., St. Paul (1839), Rev. Charles D. Borho, Admin.
Res., 20217 Christie St. N.E., P.O. Box 454, 97137. Tel: 503-633-4611. [CEM]
School—20327 Christie St., N.E., P.O. Box 188, 97137. Tel: 503-633-4622. Sr. Mary Simeon Werner, F.S.P.A., Prin.
Sisters 3; Lay Teachers 4; Students 102.

Salem, Marion Co., St. Joseph (1864), Revs. Carl Gimpl; Petrus Binh Hoang; Claudio Manuel Salazar (Mexico).
Res., 721 Chemeketa St. N.E., 97301. Tel: 503-581-1623; Fax: 503-581-7271. [JC]
School—Tel: 503-581-2147.
Sisters of the Holy Names of Jesus and Mary 2; Sisters of St. Mary 1; Lay Teachers 45; Students 275.
Catechesis / Religious Programs—Tel: 503-585-5095.
Students 272.
Mission—Salem, Marion Co., San Jose.

Queen of Peace (1963), Rev. George Wolf. Pastoral Assocs.: Sr. Joan Jett, S.N.J.M.; Darlene Joynt.
Office: P.O. Box 3016, 97302. Tel: 503-364-7202; Fax: 503-364-5882.
School—4227 Lone Oak Rd., S.E., Tel: 503-362-3443; Fax: 503-362-0462.
Lay Teachers 10; Students 168.
Catechesis / Religious Programs—Tel: 503-362-7615. D.R.E.: Tricia Boyle, Preschool-Elem.; Sheila Mousel, Youth Min., Young Adult (Grades 9-12); Monique Ierardi.
Students 270.

St. Vincent de Paul (1925), Rev. Patrick McNamee; Sr. Joyce Barsotti, S.S.M.O.; Raoul Van Landuyt, Pastoral Assoc.; Kimberly Allain, Pastoral Assoc.
Res., 1025 Columbia St., 97303. Tel: 503-363-4589; Fax: 503-363-9493. [JC]
School—Tel: 503-363-8457; Fax: 503-363-1516.
Sisters 1; Lay Teachers 10; Students 104.
Catechesis / Religious Programs—1015 Columbia St. N.E., 97303. Tel: 503-363-2166.
Students 181.

Sandy, Clackamas Co., St. Michael (1898), Revs. Aiden J. Mayo; Robert J. Palladino.
Res., 18090 S.E. Langensand Rd., 97055. Tel: 503-668-4446; Fax: 503-668-5018.
Mission—Welches, Clackamas Co., St. John, Tel: 503-622-6338.

Scappoose, Columbia Co., St. Wenceslaus (1911), Rev. Stephen Clovis.
Parish Office: Tel: 503-543-7495.
Res., 51555 Old Portland Rd., 97056. Tel: 503-543-2110; Fax: 503-543-5159. [CEM]

Catechesis/Religious Programs—Tel: 503-534-7425.
Students 105.

Scio, Linn Co., St. Bernard (1912), Rev. Kevin O'Conner, O.M.I.
Res., P.O. Box 45, 97374. Tel: 503-394-2625.
Mission—Jefferson, Marion Co., St. Thomas, 647 Third St., Jefferson, 97352. Tel: 503-327-2343.

Seaside, Clatsop Co., Our Lady of Victory (1913), Rev. Michael Lau.
Res., 120 Ocean Way, 97138. Tel: 503-738-6161.
Parish Office—Tel: 503-738-6161.
Mission—Arch Cape, Clatsop Co., St. Peter the Fisherman, 1605 Upland Dr., P.O. Box 117, Arch Cape, 97102. Tel: 503-436-2876.

Shady Cove, Jackson Co., Our Lady of Fatima (1955), Rev. William McHugh, O.M.I.
Res., 37 Church Ln., P.O. Box 116, 97539. Tel: 541-878-2479.

Shaw, Marion Co., St. Mary (1906), Rev. Charles P. Taaffe.
Mailing Address: P.O. Box 338, Aumsville, 97325-0338.
Res., 9168 Silver Falls Hwy., S.E., Aumsville, 97325. Tel: 503-362-6159. [CEM]

Sheridan, Yamhill Co., Good Shepherd (1908), Rev. James Crunican.
Res., 127 N.E. Hill St., 97378. Tel: 503-843-2206.

Sherwood, Washington Co., St. Francis (1925), Rev. Thomas McCarthy, S.J.
Mailing Address: P.O. Box 279, 97140. Tel: 503-625-6186; Fax: 503-625-6187.
Res., 400 S. Pine St., 97140. Tel: 503-625-6185.
Church—400 N.E. Oregon St., 97140. Tel: 503-625-5914.
Catechesis/Religious Programs—Tel: 503-625-6187.
Students 237.

Silverton, Marion Co., St. Paul (1914), Rev. Ed Coleman; Deacon Loris A. Buccola.
Res., 1410 Pine St., 97381. Tel: 503-873-2044. [CEM]

Springfield, Lane Co., St. Alice (1947), Rev. Patrick Walsh.
Res., 1520 F St., 97477. Tel: 541-747-7041.

Stayton, Marion Co., Immaculate Conception (1903), Rev. Gregory Moys.
Res., 525 E. Santiam, Box 535, 97383. Tel: 503-769-2656; Fax: 503-769-5621. [CEM]
School—Tel: 503-769-2718.
Sisters of St. Mary of Oregon 1; Lay Teachers 14; Students 242.
Catechesis/Religious Programs—1077 N. Sixth St., 97383. Tel: 503-769-2557.
Students 151.

Sublimity, Marion Co., St. Boniface (1879), Revs. Galdino Monteiro, S.F.X. (India); William M. O'Malley, S.J.
Res., 375 E. Church St., 97385. Tel: 503-769-5664. [CEM]
Missions—Mill City, Marion Co., St. Catherine of Siena, First & Ivy, Mill City, 97360.; Detroit, Marion Co., St. Christopher, Santian Ave., Detroit, 97342.

Sutherlin, Douglas Co., St. Francis Xavier (1957), Rev. J. Brendan Fleming.
Res., P.O. Box 1048, 97479-1048. Tel: 541-459-4042 (Office); 459-7599 (Rectory).
Mission—Drain, Douglas Co., St. John the Apostle, P.O. Box 457, Drain, 97435-0457. Tel: 541-836-2891.

Sweet Home, Linn Co., St. Helen (1953), Rev. Andrew Harris, O.M.I.
Res., 815 Fifth Ave., 97386. Tel: 541-367-2530.
Mission—Brownsville, Linn Co., Holy Trinity, 104 Blakely Ave., Brownsville, 97327.

Tigard, Washington Co., St. Anthony (1910), Revs. Leslie M. Sieg, O.F.M., Parish Admin.; Peter Makalla, A.L.C.P.
Res., 9905 S.W. McKenzie St., 97223. Tel: 503-639-4179; Fax: 503-624-2364. [CEM]
School—Tel: 503-639-4979; Fax: 503-620-5117. Jeananne Bloudek, Prin.
Lay Teachers 14; Students 311.
Catechesis/Religious Programs—Students 351.

Tillamook, Tillamook Co., Sacred Heart (1890), Rev. John Henderson, O.F.M.Conv.
2411 Fifth St., 97141. Tel: 503-842-6647; Fax: 503-815-1865. [CEM]
Mission—Cloverdale, Tillamook Co., St. Joseph, P.O. Box 9, Cloverdale, 97112. Tel: 503-392-3685. Rev. Joseph Obersinner, S.J., Admin.

Tualatin, Clackamas Co., Church of the Resurrection (1981), Rev. Richard Rossman.
Mailing Address: 21060 S.W. Stafford Rd., 97062. Tel: 503-638-1579; Fax: 503-638-8754.
Catechesis/Religious Programs—Students 338.

Veneta, Lane Co., St. Catherine of Siena (1954), Rev. Joseph Black, Moderator; Gene Modrich, Parish Admin.
Res., 25181 E. Broadway, P.O. Box 277, 97487. Tel: 503-541-3933.

Verboort, Washington Co., Visitation B.V.M. (1875), Rev. Joseph Heuberger.
Res., 4285 N.W. Visitation Rd., Forest Grove, 97116. Tel: 503-357-3860. [CEM]
School—Tel: 503-357-6990.
Sisters of St. Mary of Oregon (S.S.M.O.) 2; Lay Teachers 7; Students 150.

Vernonia, Columbia Co., St. Mary (1923), Rev. Ron Millican; Lani Vandehey, Admin.
Church—960 Missouri Ave., 97064. Tel: 503-429-8841; Fax: 503-429-8841.

Waldport, Lincoln Co., St. Anthony (1949), Rev. Gerard Steckler, S.J., Admin.
Res., P.O. Box 770, 97394. Tel: 503-563-3246.

Wilsonville, Clackamas Co., St. Cyril (1926), Rev. Paul Peri; Deacon Jim Myers.
Res., 9210 S.W. Fifth St., 97070. Tel: 503-682-2332; Fax: 503-682-0898.
Catechesis/Religious Programs—Students 135.

Woodburn, Marion Co., St. Luke (1899), Revs. David Zegar; Juan Pablo Padilla Ruiz (Mexico); Deacon Jerry McKenzie.
Office: 417 Harrison St., 97071. Tel: 503-981-5011; Fax: 503-981-5012.
Res., 521 W. Lincoln St., 97071. [CEM]
School—529 Harrison St., 97071. Tel: 503-981-7441.
Sisters 4; Lay Teachers 6; Students 181.
Mission—Hubbard, Marion Co., St. Agnes, 3052 D St., Hubbard, 97032.
Catechesis/Religious Programs—Tel: 503-981-5011; Fax: 503-981-5012.
Students 141.

Yamhill, Yamhill Co., St. John (1910), Revs. David Gutmann, Admin.; John Kindall, S.J.; Beth Heesacker, Pastoral Assoc.
Mailing Address: P.O. Box 580, 97148. Tel: 503-662-4291.

SOUTHEAST ASIAN VICARIATE

1—SOUTHEAST ASIAN VICARIATE, Multnomah Co., (1982), 5404 N.E. Alameda Dr., 97213. Tel: 503-249-5892; Fax: 503-249-1776. Revs. Vincent Minh, C.S.S.R., Episcopal Vicar; John B. Hong-Phuc, C.S.S.R.; James Pham-Van-Ninh, S.E.; Joseph Nguyen Duc Hau, S.E.
Catechesis/Religious Programs—Students 700.

Chaplains of Public Institutions

PORTLAND. *Department of Veterans' Affairs Medical Center,* 3710 S.W. U.S. Veterans' Hospital Rd., Box 1034, 97207. Tel: 503-220-8262, Ext. 7027, 7021. Rev. William E. Wickham, C.S.C.
Oregon Health Sciences University, St. Elizabeth, 4112 Sixth Ave. Drive, 97201. Tel: 503-222-2168. Rev. John B. Wironen, C.S.C.

ROSEBURG. *U.S. Veterans' Administration Hospital,* 913 N.W. Garden Valley Blvd., 97470-6513. Tel: 541-440-1000, Ext. 4720. Rev. Leroy Calkins, O.S.M., V.A.M.C.

SALEM. *Mill Creek Correctional Facility,* 5485 Turner Rd., 97310-9400. Tel: 503-378-2333. Rev. James Jacobson, S.J.
Oregon State Correctional Institution, 3405 Deer Park Dr. S.E., 97310. Tel: 503-373-0147. Rev. Michael Sprauer.
Oregon State Penitentiary, 2605 State St., 97310. Tel: 503-378-2333; Fax: 503-378-3897. Rev. James Jacobson, S.J.
Oregon Women's Correction Center, 2809 State St., 97310. Tel: 503-378-2441. Rev. Michael Sprauer.
Santiam Correctional Institution, 4005 Aumsville Hwy. S.E., 97310-9112. Tel: 503-378-2333. Rev. James Jacobson, S.J.
Youth Correctional Facility, 2450 Strong Rd., 97310. Tel: 503-986-0421; Fax: 503-378-2175. Rev. Ted Frison.

SHERIDAN. *Federal Correctional Institution,* 27072 Ballston Rd., 97378-9601. Tel: 503-843-4442, Ext. 254. Rev. LeRoy Maus.

WHITE CITY. *U.S. Veternan's Affiars Domiciliary,* 97503. Tel: 541-826-2111, Ext. 3321. Revs. Joseph E. Shirey, S.J.; Paschal Donald Salisbury, O.P.

WOODBURN. *MacLaren Youth Correctional Facility,* 2630 N. Pacific Hwy., 97071. Tel: 503-981-9531, Ext. 316. Rev. Ted Frison.

Special Assignment:
Reverend Fathers—
Brennan, Patrick
Carey, Raymond, Mount Angel Seminary, St. Benedict, OR 97373
Johnston, Michael, North American College, 00120 Vatican City, Rome Italy

---

On Duty Outside the Archdiocese:
Reverend Fathers—
Adams, Daniel
Coleman, James, Padres de Santiago Apostol, Castilla 919, Santa Cruz
Dare, Glenn, Diocese of Sacramento
Killingsworth, Bradley, Parroquia Fatima, Castilla 919, Santa Cruz
Olsen, Kenneth, #302-2250 Manor Pl., Comox, BC V9M 1C4 Canada

---

Military Chaplains:
Reverend Fathers—
Wallace, Richard, P.O. Drawer B, 246 B Main St., Havelock, NC 28532

Absent on Leave:
Reverend Fathers—
Chun, Francis, P.O. Box 66277, Portland, OR 97266
McHugh, Donald

Retired:
Reverend Fathers—
Alvares, Augustine, 12075 Mount Hamilton Rd., San Jose, CA 95140
Batory, Stephen
Beno, Joseph, 484 S. 17th St., P.O. Box 1012, St. Helens, OR 97051
Bianco, Hamilcar, c/o Marcia Paseti, 2684 Christy St., Tracy, CA 94376
Bliven, Edmond, 3311 S.W. First Ave., Portland, OR 97201
Brouillard, John, 17704 N.W. Shadyfir Loop, Space 39, Beaverton, OR 97006
Chao, Joseph, 4595-A St. John Vianney Way, Beaverton, OR 97007
Cieslinski, Robert, St. John Vianney Residence, 4630-D S.W. St. John Vianney Way, Beavertown, OR 97007
Cohan, Francis J., Mailing Address: P.O. Box 26, Sheridan, OR 97378
Cormier, Joseph, 3600 S.W. 170th Ave., Beaverton, OR 97006
Cunniff, Vincent, 4655-D S.W.,St. John Vianney Way, Beaverton, OR 97007
Denman, Donald, St. John Vianney Residence, 4630-B S.W. St. John Vianney Way, Beaverton, OR 97007
DePra, Italo, 1148 Third Ave. #62, Chula Vista, CA 91911
Domin, John M., 14645 S.W. Farmington, Beaverton, OR 97007
Engel, John, 17704 N.W. Shadyfir Loop, Space 39, Beaverton, OR 97006
Fritz, Norbert, 15134 S.E. 122nd, Clackamas, OR 97015
Gothe, Marcus, 4655-B S.W. St. John Vianney Way, Beaverton, OR 97007
Grammond, Maurice, Mailing Address: P.O. Box 8475, Portland, OR 97207
Harrington, Emmet, 4926 S.W. Corbett, #207, Portland, OR 97201
Harris, James M., 14295 S.W. Jenkins Rd., Space 23, Beaverton, OR 97005
Hume, Kenneth, 19453 Stillmeadow Dr., Oregon City, OR 97045
Hwang, Bernard, O.S.B., 19526 Lazy Creek Ln., Oregon City, OR 97045
Johnson, William, 3060 S.E. Stark St., Portland, OR 97214
Kennedy, Alan, St. John Vianney Residence, 4655-A S.W. St. John Vianney Way, Beaverton, OR 97007
Kies, Emil, Mailing Address: P.O. Box 5869, Charleston, OR 97420
Linehan, Cornelius, 8736 N.E. Russell Pl., Portland, OR 97220
Linehan, Jeremiah, 6908 N.E. Tillamook St., Portland, OR 97210
McKean, Louis, P.O. Box 1121, Chula Vista, CA 91912
McMahon, Joseph M., 4525-B St. John Vianney Way, Beaverton, OR 97007
Neuville, Joseph, St. John The Baptist, 10955 S.E. 25th Ave., Milwaukie, OR 97222
Reedy, John J., St. John Vianney Residence, 4630-A S.W. St. John Vianney Way, Beaverton, OR 97007
Ridi, Pio, 6806 N. Sedro, Portland, OR 97203
Rodakowski, Louis, P.O. Box 177, Vida, OR 97488
Saalfeld, Lawrence, La Salle Center, 11999 S.E. Fuller Rd., Milwaukie, OR 97222
Schaefers, Francis J., 4465 S.W. 148th St., Beaverton, OR 97007
Schlatter, Glen, 1867 Kingsley Rd., Apt. 91, Eugene, OR 97401

Stipe, Jack H., St. John Vianney Residence, 4525-D S.W. St. John Vianney Way, Beaverton, OR 97007
Thielen, Martin, 4655-C S.W. St. John Vianney Way, Beaverton, OR 97007
Van Der Zanden, Edmund, 4525-C S.W. St. John Vianney Way, Beaverton, OR 97007
Vandehey, Ervin S., St. John Vianney Residence, 4630-C S.W. St. John Vianney Way, Beaverton, OR 97007
Williams, Alfred, 85 S.W. Lexington Way, Beaverton, OR 97006
Wiseman, Thomas, c/o Raymond Heuberger, P.O. Box 243, Sublimity, OR 97385
Wraszczak, Chester, 850 S.E. 169th Dr., Portland, OR 97233

Permanent Deacons:
Buccola, Loris, St. Paul, Silverton
Chapin, Robert L., Jr., St. Anne, Grants Pass
Conley, Roger, St. Vincent de Paul, Salem
Filardi, Ronald, Sacred Heart, Medford
Little, Robert, St. Pius X, Portland
McKenzie, Gerald, St. Luke, Woodburn
Mendez, Jose R., St. Luke, Woodburn; St. Joseph, Salem
Morin, Edward, St. Thomas More, Portland
Myers, James, St. Cyril, Wilsonville
Potts, Francis, St. Mary, Corvallis
Ries, John D., The Cathedral, Portland
Soper, Leonard, St. Benedict Lodge, McKensie Bridge
Stenbeck, John H., St. Joseph, Roseburg
Stromberg, Alton, Our Lady of Victory, Seaside
Triggs, Donald J., St. Mary, Corvallis
Triska, Richard, St. Edward, Lebanon

INSTITUTIONS LOCATED IN THE ARCHDIOCESE

[A] SEMINARIES, RELIGIOUS, ARCHDIOCESAN OR SCHOLASTICATES

PORTLAND. *Franciscan Formation Community*, 827 N.E. Alberta, 97211. Tel: 503-287-9223. Bro. Thomas M. Nichols, O.F.M., Dir. Priests 2; Brothers 1; Postulants 6.

Jesuit Novitiate of St. Francis Xavier, 3301 S.E. 45th Ave., 97206. Tel: 503-774-5699. Rev. Patrick J. Lee, S.J., Dir. Novices; Bro. Wayne M. Gsell, S.J., Socius/Minister. In res., Rev. John J. Kindall, S.J. Priests 1; Brothers 1; Novices 10.

ST. BENEDICT. *Mount Angel Seminary*, 97373. Tel: 503-845-3951; Fax: 503-845-3126. Rt. Rev. Peter Eberle, O.S.B., Abbot & Chancellor; Very Rev. Patrick Brennan, Pres. & Rector; Rev. Nathan Zodrow, O.S.B., Vice Rector, Asst. Public Rels., Dir. of Personal Formation; Marina Keys, Admin. Asst. & Contact Person; Dr. Ernest Skublics, S.T.B., S.T.L, Ph.D., Academic Dean; Revs. Gregory Duerr, O.S.B., Spiritual Dir.; Dave Rogerson, O.S.B. (SEA), Formation Dir. College III-IV; William Hammelman, O.S.B., Formation Dir. Pre-Theology; Liem Nguyen, O.S.B., Formation Dir. ESLI & Theology I; Philip Waibel, O.S.B., Dir. Pastoral Education; Mr. John Degnin, Dir. Devel.; Revs. Odo Recker, O.S.B., Admissions Dir. & Registrar; Richard Paperini, Coordinator Liturgy; Richard Paperini, Formation Dir. Theology III-IV; Sr. Ida VanHoomisen, S.N.J.M., Coordinator of Field Education & Apostolic Ministry; Rev. William Miller, S.J., Formation Dir., Theology I & II; Mr. Thomas Bolton, Alumni Dir.; Rev. Vitaliano Ola'aiga, Formation Dir., College I-II. Priests 26; Sisters 6; Brothers 5; Lay Teachers 17.

[B] COLLEGES AND UNIVERSITIES

*PORTLAND. *University of Portland*, 5000 N. Willamette Blvd., 97203. Tel: 503-283-7911.
For a complete listing, refer to the Colleges and Universities section.

MARYLHURST. *Marylhurst College*, 97036. Tel: 503-636-8141.
For a complete listing, refer to the Colleges and Universities section.

[C] HIGH SCHOOLS, DIOCESAN

PORTLAND. *Central Catholic High School.* (Coed), 2401 S.E. Stark St., 97214. Tel: 503-235-3138; Fax: 503-233-0073. Rev. Timothy Murphy, Pres.; Ron Edwards, Prin.; Revs. Stephen M. Clovis; Ron Millican. Priests 3; Sisters 4; Lay Teachers 69; Students 821.

MEDFORD. *St. Mary's School.* (Coed), 816 Black Oak Dr., 97504. Barbara W. Callaway, Prin.; Rev. Thomas J. Whelan, O.S.A. Priests 1; Sisters 1; Lay Teachers 29; Lay Staff 13; Students 331.

STAYTON. *Regis High School.* (Coed), P.O. Box 65, 97383. Tel: 503-769-2159. Mr. Douglas J. Wasko, Prin. Lay Teachers 15; Students 238.

Regis High School Foundation, P.O. Box 65, 97383.

[D] HIGH SCHOOLS, PRIVATE

PORTLAND. *Jesuit High School.* (Coed), 9000 S.W. Beaverton-Hillsdale Hwy., 97225. Tel: 503-292-2663. The Society of Jesus. Revs. William E. Hayes, S.J., Pres.; Anton T. Harris, S.J., Rector, Admin. & Contact Person; Mr. Richard M. Gedrose, Prin.; Mrs. Sandra Satterberg, Academic Vice Prin.; Mr. Steve Beaird, Vice Pres. Development; Mr. Jerry Hahn, Vice Prin. Student Affairs; Mrs. Shirley Poppe, Admissions Dir.; Mr. Donald Clark, Campus Min. Faculty: Revs. Kevin G. Connell, S.J.; Frank D. Masterson, S.J.; David S. Olivier, S.J.; Lawrence F. Robinson, S.J.; Bruce J. Schmidlkofer, S.J. In res., Revs. Joseph R. DeJardin, S.J.; Gordon L. Keys, S.J.; Edward P. McTighe, S.J.
School: Priests 7; Lay Staff 95; Students 1,016.
Community: Priests 10.

St. Mary's Academy. (Girls), 1615 S.W. Fifth Ave., 97201. Tel: 503-228-8306. Patricia A. Thompson, Prin. Sisters 5; Lay Teachers 44; Students 525.

BEAVERTON. *Valley Catholic Middle & High Schools.* (Coed), 4275 S.W. 148th Ave., 97007. Tel: 503-644-3745. Sisters of St. Mary of Oregon. Mr. Charles E. Lee, Prin. Sisters 8; Lay Teachers 38; Students 450.

EUGENE. *Marist High School.* (Coed), 1900 Kingsley Rd., 97401. Tel: 541-686-2234; Fax: 541-342-6451. Revs. Vincent Benoit, O.P.; Vincent Lopez, O.P., Prin.; Christopher Terry, O.P. Priests 3; Lay Teachers 49; Students 540.

MILWAUKIE. *LaSalle High School.* (Coed), 11999 S.E. Fuller Rd., 97222. Timothy Edwards, Prin. Sisters 1; Lay Teachers 37; Students 571.

SALEM. *Salem Catholic Schools Foundation*, P.O. Box 13207, 97309. Tel: 503-371-9068.

[E] ELEMENTARY SCHOOLS, AREA

EUGENE. *O'Hara Area Elementary Catholic School*, 715 W. 18th, 97402. Paul C. Hepler, Prin. Comprised of students from the following parishes in Eugene: St. Jude, St. Mark, St. Mary, St. Paul, St. Peter, St. Alice and the Newman Center. Lay Teachers 15; Students 329.

[F] ELEMENTARY SCHOOLS, PRIVATE

PORTLAND. *Franciscan Montessori Earth School*, 14750 S.E. Clinton St., 97236. Staffed by Franciscan Sisters of the Eucharist. Mother Francine Cardew, F.S.E., Dir. Franciscan Sisters of the Eucharist 5; Lay Teachers 23; Students 400.

BEAVERTON. *St. Mary of the Valley Grade School*, 4440 S.W. 148th, 97007. Tel: 503-644-9181. Sisters of St. Mary of Oregon. Sr. Marcella Parrish, S.S.M.O., Prin. Sisters 3; Lay Teachers 23; Students 368.

Valley Catholic Middle School. (Grades 7-8), 4440 S.W. 148th, 97007. Sr. Adele Marie, S.S.M.O., Vice Prin. Sisters 1; Lay Teachers 5; Students 104.

[G] SOCIAL AND MINISTERIAL SERVICES

PORTLAND. *Catholic Charities of the Archdiocese of Portland in Oregon*, 231 SE 12th Ave., 97214. Tel: 503-231-4866. Dennis B. Keenan, M.S.W., Exec. Dir.; Richard Deml, C.P.A., Controller; Maureen Hovenkotter, Communications Mgr.; Sr. Mary Dernovek, S.N.J.M., Development Dir.

Catholic Charities Social Service Division of Portland, 231 S.E. 12th Ave., 97214. Tel: 503-231-4866. Douglas Alles, Social Svc. Dir.; Rev. Bruce Cwiekowski, AIDS Ministry Coordinator. Programs include: maternity and aftercare home, adoption, refugee resettlement, Hispanic health outreach, AIDS ministry, ministry to the elderly, Asian social services, and Project Rachel, and Immigration Legal Services.

Catholic Youth Organization/Camp Howard, 825 N.E. 20th, Ste. 320, 97232-2295. Tel: 503-231-9484. Wilma Ouhl, Exec. Dir. Programs include: Youth recreation & camping.

Immigration Counseling Services, 434 N.W. Sixth Ave. #202, 97209. Tel: 503-221-1689. Margaret Godfrey, Exec. Dir. Programs include: Immigration legalization advocacy, court hearing representation.

Catholic Community Services of Lane County, 945 W. Seventh Ave., Eugene, 97402. Tel: 503-345-3642. Jeanne Benson, Exec. Dir. Programs include: Emergency shelter, utilities, and food, single mothers shelter, drug dependent mothers shelter, family shelter, young parents program, family self-sufficiency program.

Catholic Community Services of Mid-Willamette Valley and the Central Coast, 142 Glenbrook N., Keizer, 97307. Tel: 503-390-2600. Jim Seymour, Exec. Dir. Programs include: Center for delinquent youth, developmentally & physically disabled group homes, shelter for displaced youth, counseling center, Hispanic mental health outreach, child abuse prevention program.

Catholic Community Services of Southern Oregon, 440 S. Ivy St., Medford, 97501. Tel: 503-779-0803. Joanna Furmonavicius, Dir. Programs include: Emergency services, health clinics, community education.

[H] CHILD DEVELOPMENT CENTERS

PORTLAND.
**Providence Child Center*, 830 N.E. 47th Ave., 97213. Tel: 503-215-2400. Legal Title: *Sisters of Providence in Oregon.* Ethelyn G. Pankratz, Admin. Sisters 1. Children's Nursing Center providing skilled nursing care and habilitation/rehabilitation services for children who have physical and mental disabilities and multiple care needs. Long-term chronic care, short-term care for respite, transition, or pediatric hospice provided.

Providence Montessori School. Preschool education for children ages 2 1/2 to 6 with a broad array of developmental needs and abilities.

Wee Care. Day-care center for children of employees of Providence Medical Center, ages 6 weeks to 6 years.

[I] RESIDENTIAL SCHOOLS FOR YOUTHS WITH EMOTIONAL-SOCIAL PROBLEMS

BEAVERTON. *St. Mary's Home for Boys, Inc.*, 16535 S.W. Tualatin Valley Hwy., 97006. Tel: 503-649-5651. Residential treatment center for behaviorally & emotionally disturbed children. Emma Dennis, Exec. Dir. Students 100.

[J] GENERAL HOSPITALS

PORTLAND. *Providence Portland Medical Center*, 4805 N.E. Glisan St., 97213. Tel: 503-215-1111.
For a complete listing, refer to the Hospitals section.

Providence St. Vincent Medical Center, 9205 S.W. Barnes Rd., 97225. Tel: 503-297-4411; Fax: 503-291-2468.
For a complete listing, refer to the Hospitals section.

*EUGENE. *Sacred Heart Medical Center*, 1255 Hilyard St., P.O. Box 10905, 97440. Tel: 503-686-7300.
For a complete listing, refer to the Hospitals section.

FLORENCE. *Peace Harbor Hospital*, 400 Ninth St., 97439. Tel: 503-997-8412.
For a complete listing, refer to the Hospitals section.

MEDFORD. *Providence Medford Medical Center*, 1111 Crater Lake Ave., 97504. Tel: 541-732-6611.
For a complete listing, refer to the Hospitals section.

*MILWAUKIE. *Providence Milwaukie Hospital*, 10150 S.E. 32nd Ave., 97222. Tel: 503-652-8300.
For a complete listing, refer to the Hospitals section.

NEWBERG. *Providence Newberg Hospital*, 501 Villa Rd., 97132. Tel: 503-537-1701.
For a complete listing, refer to the Hospitals section.

ROSEBURG. *Mercy Medical Center, Inc.*, 2700 Stewart Pkwy., 97470. Tel: 541-673-0611; Fax: 541-440-4830.
For a complete listing, refer to the Hospitals section.

SEASIDE. *Providence Seaside Hospital*, 725 S. Wahanna Rd., 97138-7735. Tel: 503-717-7000; Fax: 503-717-7505.
For a complete listing, refer to the Hospitals section.

[K] HOMES FOR AGED

PORTLAND. *Mt. St. Joseph Residence and Extended Care Center*, 3060 S.E. Stark St., 97214-3099. Tel: 503-232-6193; Fax: 503-235-2772.
For a complete listing, refer to the Special Care Facilities section.

BEAVERTON. *Maryville Nursing Home*, 14645 S.W. Farmington Rd., 97007. Tel: 503-643-8626.
For a complete listing, refer to the Special Care Facilities section.

MT. ANGEL. *Benedictine Nursing Center*, 540 S. Main St., 97362-9523. Tel: 503-845-6841.
For a complete listing, refer to the Special Care Facilities section.

NORTH BEND. *Evergreen Court for Retirement Living, Inc.*, 451 O'Connell St., 97459. Tel: 541-756-2545.
For a complete listing, refer to the Special Care Facilities section.

St. Catherine's Residence and Nursing Center, 3959 Sheridan Ave., 97459. Tel: 541-756-4151; Fax: 541-756-1049.
For a complete listing, refer to the Special Care Facilities section.

[L] MONASTERIES AND RESIDENCES OF PRIESTS

PORTLAND. *The Grotto, The National Sanctuary of Our Sorrowful Mother*, 85th and N.E. Sandy Blvd., P.O. Box 20008, 97294-0008. Tel: 503-254-7371; 7372 (Monastery). Revs. John M. Topper, O.S.M., Prior & Exec. Dir.; Patrick M. McNamara, O.S.M.; Richard M. Boyle, O.S.M. In res., Rev. Philip M. Brennan, O.S.M. Brothers 2; Sisters 4.

Holy Cross Father & Brother, C.S.C. - University of Portland, 5000 N. Willamette Blvd., 97203. Tel: 503-978-8024. Revs. James Connelly, C.S.C., Supr.; Richard F. Berg, C.S.C.; George C. Bernard, C.S.C.; Frederick Barr, C.S.C.; Thomas Bill, C.S.C.; G. James Brady, C.S.C.; Harry Bride, C.S.C.; Joseph Browne, C.S.C.; Michael M. DeLaney, C.S.C.; Paul Fryberger, C.S.C.; W. Patrick Hannon, C.S.C.; Barry J. Hagan, C.S.C.; Thomas Hosinski, C.S.C.; William Hund, C.S.C.; James King, C.S.C.; John Kurtzke, C.S.C.; M. Terrance, Lally, C.S.C.; Edwin Obermiller, C.S.C.; Dennis O'Hare, C.S.C.; Claude Pomerlau, C.S.C.; Chester Prusynski, C.S.C.; Richard Rutherford, C.S.C.; Jeffrey Schneibel, C.S.C.; Charles D. Sherrer, C.S.C.; Jeffrey Sobosan, C.S.C.; Philip Sopke, C.S.C.; Arthur Schoenfeldt, C.S.C.; Stephen Sedlock, C.S.C.; Adrien Ste. Marie, C.S.C.; David T. Tyson, C.S.C.; Arthur F. Wheeler, C.S.C.; Bros. Ken Allen, C.S.C.; Flugence Dougherty, C.S.C.; Frederick Williams, C.S.C.; Donald Stabrowski, C.S.C.

Holy Rosary Priory, 375 N.E. Clackamas St., 97232. Tel: 503-235-3163.

Jesuit Provincial Office (Oregon Prov.), 2222 N.W. Hoyt, 97210. Tel: 503-226-6977. Very Revs. Robert B. Grimm, S.J., Prov.; Michael A. Tyrrell, S.J., Prov. Treasurer; Revs. Charles E. Schmitz, S.J., Exec. Asst., Socius, Asst. for Special Ministries; Brian L. Ulkrickson, S.J., Dir. of Vocations; L. Paul Fitterer, S.J., Asst. Prov. Secondary Education; Brad R. Reynolds, S.J., Asst. for Formation; John McBride, S.J., 4720 N.E. Broadway, 97213. Rev. David A. Myers, S.J., 5441 San Angelo St., Guadalupe, AZ, 85283. Rev. Kenneth W. Baker, S.J., 86 Riverside Dr., New York, NY, 10024. Rev. Joseph W. Conyard, S.J., 705 N. 94th, Apt. 3, Seattle, WA, 98103. Rev. Anderson E. Bakewell, S.J., P.O. Box 4010, Albuquerque, NM, 87502. Rev. Joseph E. Shirey, S.J., Providence Hospital, 1111 Crater Lake Ave., Medford, 97501. Rev. Kenneth J. Jorgensen, S.J., Albertus Magnus College, 700 Prospect St., New Haven, CT, 06511-1189. Rev. William J. Bichsel, S.J., 1419 1/2 G St., Tacoma, WA, 98405. Rev. James R. Conyard, S.J., Carmelite Monastery, 87609 Green Hill Rd., Eugene, 97402. Rev. George J. Dumais, S.J., 1700 Madeline, Missoula, MT, 59801. Rev. John J. Dunn, S.J., Our Lady of Guadalupe Center, 39100 Orchard Ave., Cherry Valley, CA, 92223-3797. Revs. Harold J. Free, S.J.; Ronald R. Funke, S.J.; Laurence L. Gooley, S.J.; Robert J. Jones, S.J.; James E. Jacobsen, S.J.; Henry H. Kohls, S.J.; Bro. George A. McMonagle, S.J.; Revs. Charles A. Wollesen, S.J.; Wilfred Schoenberg, S.J.; Michael J. Schultheis, S.J.; Thomas J. Sexton, S.J.; Gary N. Smith, S.J.; Joseph L. Showalter, S.J.; Guy Ward, S.J.; Theodore J. Wolf, S.J.; J. Patrick Hurley, S.J.; John V. Murphy, S.J.; Gerard G. Steckler, S.J.; William C. Hausmann, S.J.; Thomas M. McCarthy, S.J.; William M. O'Malley, S.J.; Emmett B. Painter, S.J.; Stephen V. Sunoborg, S.J.; Andrew J. Dofner, S.J.; Anthony P. Via, S.J.; Mark A. Hoelsken, S.J.; Ignatius F. Ohno, S.J.; Bro. James B. Wood, S.J.; Revs. Thomas J. Bunnell, S.J.; Joseph C. Fortier, S.J.; Richard R. Roach, S.J.; Joseph B. Danel, S.J.; William J. Loyens, S.J.; Howard L. Morrison, S.J.; John J. Morris, S.J.; James M. McDonough, S.J.; David G. King, S.J.; Frank E. Case, S.J.; Thomas E. Zeyen, S.J.; John J. Navone, S.J.; Joseph H. Small, S.J.; Timothy R. Clancy, S.J.; Bartholomew J. Murphy, S.J.; J. Gordon Merlandk, S.J.; Roy L. Antunez, S.J.; James K. Voiss, S.J.; Richard S. Bradley, S.J.; John V. Hennessy, S.J.; Arnold R. Beezer, S.J.; James R. Laudwein, S.J.; Dominic Hung Nguyen, S.J.

AMITY. *Brigittine Monastery of Our Lady of Consolation - The Order of the Most Holy Savior*, 23300 Walker Ln., 97101. Tel: 503-835-8080. Bro. Benedict Kirby, O.Ss.S., Prior. Professed 13; Novices 2.

GOLD HILL. *Augustinian Community*, P.O. Box 310, 97525. Tel: 541-855-1333. Revs. James Clifford, O.S.A., Prior; Thomas Whelan, O.S.A.

LAFAYETTE. *The Cistercian (Trappist) Abbey of Our Lady of Guadalupe*, 97127. Tel: 503-852-7174; Fax: 503-852-7748. Order of Cistercians of the Strict Observance. Rt. Revs. Peter McCarthy, O.C.S.O.; Bernard McVeigh, O.C.S.O., (Retired); Revs. John-Baptist Hasbrouck, O.C.S.O., Prior; Dismas Gannon, O.C.S.O.; Romain Payant, O.C.S.O.; Jerome Ebacher, O.C.S.O.; Mark Weidner, O.C.S.O.; Peter Plakut, O.C.S.O.; Howard Curtis, O.C.S.O.; Martin Cawley, O.C.S.O.; Francis King, O.C.S.O.; Timothy Michell, O.C.S.O.; Joseph-Benedict Donnelly, O.C.S.O.; Arnold Weller, O.C.S.O.; Richard Layton, O.C.S.O.; Timothy Clark, O.C.S.O.; Casey Bailey, O.C.S.O. Solemnly Professed 36; Priests 17; Total in Community 39.

ST. BENEDICT. *Mt. Angel Abbey*, 97373. Tel: 503-845-3030; Fax: 503-845-3594. Rt. Rev. Peter Eberle, O.S.B., Abbot; Very Revs. Paul Thomas, O.S.B., Prior; Paschal Cheline, O.S.B., Subprior; Revs. Bruno Becker, O.S.B.; Thomas Aq. Brockhaus, O.S.B.; Isaac Jogues Brown, O.S.B.; Dominic Broxmeyer, O.S.B.; Athanasius Buchholz, O.S.B.; Matthias Burger, O.S.B.; Matthew Butsch, O.S.B.; Emmanuel Clark, O.S.B.; Thien Dang, O.S.B.; Augustine De Noble, O.S.B.; Daniel Hasenoehrl, O.S.B.; Jeremy Driscoll, O.S.B.; Gregory Duerr, O.S.B.; Hugh Feiss, O.S.B.; Richard Galvin, O.S.B.; William Hammelman, O.S.B.; Pius X. Harding, O.S.B.; Stephen Hofmann, O.S.B.; Kenneth Jacques, O.S.B.; Joachim McCann, O.S.B.; Patrick Meagher, O.S.B.; Norbert Novak, O.S.B.; Lawrence Minder, O.S.B.; Liem Nguyen, O.S.B.; David Nicholson, O.S.B.; Bede Partridge, O.S.B.; Alexander Plasker, O.S.B.; Martin Pollard, O.S.B.; Odo Recker, O.S.B.; Leo Rimmele, O.S.B.; Bernard Sander, O.S.B.; Timothy Sander, O.S.B.; Edmund Smith, O.S.B.; Vincent Trujillo, O.S.B.; Philip Waibel, O.S.B.; Jerome Young, O.S.B.; Cosmos White, O.S.B.; Placidus Zach, O.S.B.; Nathan Zodrow, O.S.B. Monks in perpetual vows 64 (divided as follows:); Priests 44; Brothers 20; Monks in triennial vows 64.

[M] CONVENTS AND RESIDENCES FOR SISTERS

PORTLAND. *"Rose Hall" Reparation and Prayer Center*, 2120 S.E. 24th Ave., 97214-5504. Tel: 503-236-4207. Mother Regina Rose, S.R., Dir.

Convent of Our Lady of Angels, 0858 S.W. Palatine Hill Rd., 97219. Tel: 503-635-4534.

Convent of Sisters of Reparation of the Sacred Wounds of Jesus. Novitiate, 2120 S.E. 24th Ave., 97214-5504. Tel: 503-236-4207. Mother Regina Rose, S.R., Supr. Gen.; Sr. Mary of the Angels, S.R., Asst. Sisters 4; Donne Members 80.

Convent of Sisters of Social Service, 21 S.E. Floral Pl., 97214. Tel: 503-232-5806. Sisters 7.

Other Addresses: 14405 S.W. Sexton Mt. Dr., Apt. A, 97005-7493. Tel: 503-641-6509. 5966 D Park Ct., S.E., Salem, 97306-1360.

Convent of the Good Shepherd, 562 N. Portland Blvd., 97217. Tel: 503-283-4931.

Convent of the Society of the Holy Child Jesus, 5431 N. Strong St., 97203. Tel: 503-289-9975.

Franciscan Renewal Center, 0858 S.W. Palatine Hill Rd., 97219. Tel: 503-636-1590. Sr. Mary Jo Chaves, O.S.F.; Sr. Mary Smith, O.S.F.; Sr. Phyllis Morris, O.S.F.; Sr. Mary Gurley, O.S.F.

Holy Cross Convent (1670), 7408 S.E. Alder, 97215. Tel: 503-254-3284. Legal Title: *Vietnamese Adorers of the Holy Cross*. Sr. M. Kim Phuong T. Nguyen, M.T.G., Supr. Sisters 14; Novices 5; Candidates 10. First foundation in the United States in 1976, founded by Bishop Pierre Lambert de la Motte. Represented in the Archdiocese of Portland in Oregon and the Diocese of Arlington.

Sisters of Mercy Convent, 3080 S.E. Stark St., 97214. Tel: 503-236-1972.

BEAVERTON. *Convent, Franciscan Missionary Sisters of Our Lady of Sorrows*, 3600 S.W. 170th Ave., 97006-5099. Tel: 503-649-1634; Fax: 503-649-8382. Sr. Anne Marie, O.S.F., Supr. Gen.; Sr. Carol Ann, O.S.F., Local Supr. Sisters 15.

St. Mary of the Valley Convent, 4440 S.W. 148th Ave., 97007. Tel: 503-644-9181. Motherhouse of the Sisters of St. Mary of Oregon. Sr. Delores Adelman, S.S.M.O., Supr. Gen.; Sr. Sharon Kirk, Local Supr.; Rev. Liam Cary, Chap. Professed Sisters 100.

BRIDAL VEIL. *Convent, Franciscan Sisters of the Eucharist*. Administrative Center, 48100 E. Crownpoint Hwy., 97010. Tel: 541-695-2375. Sr. Mary Michael Costello, F.S.E., Supr. Sisters 7.

EUGENE. *Carmel of Maria Regina*. (Contemplative Order), 87609 Green Hill Rd., 97402. Tel: 503-345-8649. Mother Elizabeth Mary, O.C.D., Prioress. Professed Sisters 11.

MARYLHURST. *Convent of the Holy Names*, 97036. Tel: 503-636-8105. Provincial House of the Sisters of the Holy Names of Jesus & Mary, S.N.J.M. Sr. Eileen Brown, S.N.J.M., Prov. Dir.; Sr. Kathleen Hecht, S.N.J.M., House Admin. Professed Sisters 245; Temporarily professed 3.

MT. ANGEL. *Queen of Angels Monastery*, 840 S. Main St., 97362. Tel: 503-845-6141; Fax: 503-845-6585. Motherhouse of the Benedictine Sisters of Mt. Angel. Sr. Jeanette Von Herrmann, O.S.B., Prioress. Sisters 62; Novitiate 1.

[N] RETREAT HOUSES

PORTLAND. *Loyola Renewal Center*, 3220 S.E. 43rd Ave., 97206. Tel: 503-777-2225; Fax: 503-774-7382. Steve Hill, Dir.; Revs. Mark McGregor, S.J.; John J. Ludvik, S.J.; Bro. Fenton J. Melia, S.J.; Sr. Joanne Maney, S.N.J.M.; Sr. Loretta Schaff, O.S.F.; Jan Al Sever. Priests 2; Brothers 1; Sisters 1; Lay Teachers 2.

BEAVERTON. *Our Lady of Peace Retreat*, 3600 S.W. 170th Ave., 97006-5099. Tel: 503-649-7127; Fax: 503-649-8382. Sr. Carol Ann, O.S.F., Supr.; Sr. M. Joseph, O.S.F., Asst. Supr. Franciscan Missionary Sisters of Our Lady of Sorrows 15.

GOLD HILL. *St. Rita's Retreat Center*, P.O. Box 310, 97525. Tel: 541-855-1333. Rev. Thomas Whelan, O.S.A., Dir. & Contact Person.

MCKENZIE BRIDGE. *St. Benedict Lodge-Dominican Retreat & Conference Center*, 56630 North Bank Rd., 97413. Tel: 541-822-3572. Dominican Retreat & Conference Center. Bro. Daniel Thomas, O.P., Dir. & Contact Person; Rev. David W. Geib, O.P., Chap.; Deacon Leonard Soper; Sr. John Maureen Backenstos, S.N.J.M., Spiritual & Temporal Ministry.

MT. ANGEL. *Benedictine Sisters Shalom Prayer Center*, 97362. Tel: 503-845-6773. Sr. Antoinette Traeger, O.S.B., Dir. Sisters 4.

PACIFIC CITY. *Nestucca Sanctuary*, 97135-0670. Rev. Andrew J. Dufner, S.J., Retreat Dir. & Contact Person.

ST. BENEDICT. *Mount Angel Abbey Retreat House*, 97373. Tel: 503-845-3025. Rev. Isaac Brown, O.S.B., Dir.

[O] SOCIETY OF ST. VINCENT DE PAUL

PORTLAND. *De Paul Treatment Centers, Inc*. Administrative Offices, 1306 S.W. Washington St., 97205. Tel: 503-294-1449. Mailing Address: P.O. Box 3007, 97208. Serves indigent adults and youth with alcoholism and drug addiction. Karla K. McFarland, Exec. Dir.

Adult Treatment Services, 1306 S.W. Washington St., P.O. Box 3007, 97208-3007. Tel: 503-294-1449.

Macdonald Center, 601 W. Burnside, 97209. Tel: 503-222-5720. Mary Sue Richen, Program Dir.

St. Vincent de Paul Rehabilitation Service, Inc., 4867 N.E. Martin Luther King Jr. Blvd., 97211. Tel: 503-281-1289. Training & placement for adults with disabilities. Roy Soards, Exec. Dir.; Bennett Johnson, Dep. Dir. Employees/Trainees 800.

Society of St. Vincent de Paul. Portland Council, 3601 S.E. 27th Ave., 97202. Tel: 503-235-7837. Thomas Sciarretta, Pres.; Janice Pelster, Exec. Dir.

Youth Treatment Services, 4411 N.E. Emerson, 97218. Tel: 503-287-7026. Mailing Address: P.O. Box 3007, 97208. Dan Johnson, Youth Services Manager & Contact Person.

EUGENE. *Society of St. Vincent de Paul*. Archdiocesan Council. 705 S. Seneca St., 97402. Dennis Maricle, Pres.

Society of St. Vincent de Paul. Eugene Council. 705 S. Seneca St., 97402. Tel: 541-687-5820; Fax: 541-683-9423. Donald Lamb, Pres.; Terrence R. McDonald, Exec. Dir.; Rebecca Larson, Contact Person.

MEDFORD. *Society of St. Vincent de Paul*. Rogue Valley Council, P.O. Box 1663, 97501. Tel: 541-772-3828. Gloria Rice, Pres.; Lillian A. Howe, Exec. Dir. & Contact Person.

SALEM.

**Society of St. Vincent de Paul*. Council of Mid-Willamette Valley, 730 Front St. N.E., 97301. Tel: 503-364-1062. Joseph Glandorf, Pres.; Nancy Cooney, Exec. Dir. & Contact Person.

[P] NEWMAN CENTERS

PORTLAND. *University of Portland*, Campus Ministry, 5000 N. Willamette Blvd., 97203. Tel: 503-283-7131. Revs. Philip Sopke, C.S.C., Dir.; Edwin Obermiller, C.S.C., Assoc.; Elizabeth McCabe, Assoc.; Tom Carawan, Assoc.

Southern Oregon State College (Ashland), Walsh Memorial Newman Center, 1150 Ashland St., Ashland, 97520. Tel: 541-482-0825. Rev. Raymond Finerty, O.P., Dir. & Chap.

Oregon State University (Corvallis), Newman Center, 2111 N.W. Monroe St., Corvallis, 97330. Tel: 541-752-6818. Sue Gifford, Pastoral Dir.

University of Oregon (Eugene), Newman Center, 1850 Emerald St., Eugene, 97403. Tel: 541-343-7021; Fax: 541-686-8028. Rev. Jose Pimentel, O.P.; Sr. Janet Ryan, S.N.J.M., Pastoral Assoc.

Lane Community College, 4000 E. 30th Ave., Eugene, 97405. Tel: 541-747-4501, Ext. 2850. Rev. James N. Derringer, Chap., Res., 122 Marion Ln., Eugene, 97404. Tel: 541-688-2605.

Pacific University (Forest Grove). Rev. Dave Gutmann, Chap.; Kathy Yee, Campus Minister, Res. St. Anthony Church, 1660 Elm St., Forest Grove, 97116. Tel: 503-357-8075; Fax: 503-357-2217.

Lewis & Clark (Lake Oswego). Rev. Panneer Selvam, Chap., Our Lady of the Lake Church, 650 A Avenue, Lake Oswego, 97034. Tel: 503-636-7687; Fax: 503-636-9415.

Linfield College (McMinnville). Rev. Thomas Farley, Campus Minister, St. James Church, 1110 E. First St., McMinnville, 97128. Tel: 503-472-5232.

Marylhurst College (Marylhurst), Durocher Center for Campus Ministry. Rev. Henri LaCerte, O.S.B., Chap.; Sr. Elaine Kraft, S.N.J.M., Dir., Marylhurst, 97036. Tel: 503-636-3941, Ext. 351.

Western Oregon State College (Monmouth). Rev. Victor Perez, Chap., Res., 245 W. Main, Monmouth, 97361. Tel: 503-838-1242.

Willamette University (Salem). Rev. Carl Gimpl, Chap., St. Joseph Church, 721 Chemeketa St., N.E., Salem, 97301. Tel: 501-581-1623.

[Q] MISCELLANEOUS

PORTLAND. *Blanchet House of Hospitality*, 340 N.W. Glisan St., 97209. Tel: 503-226-3911. Al Riley, Dir.

**Franciscan Enterprise of Oregon, Inc.*, 4826 N.E. Eighth Ave., 97211. Tel: 503-284-8642; Fax: 503-284-4092. Karen Voiss, Exec. Dir. & Contact Person.

**Franciscan Ministry Network*, 4725 N.E. 9th Ave., 97211. Rev. Matt Tumulty, Exec. Dir. & Contact Person.

Jesuit Development & Communications Office, P.O. Box 4408, 97208. Tel: 503-227-1174. Revs. Charles E. Schmitz, S.J., Dir. Intl. Missions; John V. Murphy, S.J., Assoc. Dir. Devel.; Mr. P. Matthew Senecal, Asst. to the Provincial for Devel. & Communications.

**Jesuit Volunteer Corps: Northwest*, P.O. Box 3928, 97208-3928. Tel: 503-335-8202. Martin Winch, Exec. Dir.

Metro Catholic Broadcasting, KBVM-FM, 88.3, P.O. Box 5888, 97228-5888. Tel: 503-283-7455. Bernie Muller, Gen. Mgr.

Northeast Catholic Counseling Center, 8383 N.E. Sandy Blvd., Suite 205, 97220. Tel: 503-253-0964. Sr. Barbara Kennedy, O.S.M., Dir. & Contact Person. Sisters 2; Lay Counselors 4.

Oregon Catholic Conference, 2838 E. Burnside St., 97214. Tel: 503-233-8387; Fax: 503-235-2630. Most Revs. Francis E. George, O.M.I., Pres.; Thomas J. Connolly, Vice Pres.; Rev. Gregory Moys, Sec.-Treasurer; Mr. Robert Castagna, Gen. Counsel & Exec. Dir.

Paulist Fathers Catholic Center for Evangelization, 2408 S.E. 16th Ave., 97214. Tel: 503-231-4955. Revs. Stephen E. Bossi, C.S.P.; Joseph J. Scott, C.S.P.

St. Andrew Legal Clinic, 807 N.E. Alberta, 97211. Tel: 503-281-1500. Joel K. Overlund, Dir. & Contact Person.

**The Gamelin-Oregon Association-Emilie House*, 5520 N.E. Glisan, 97213-3169. Tel: 503-236-9779; Fax: 503-239-1867. Sisters of Providence. Sr. Alexis Melancon, S.P., Dir. 41 apartments for the elderly and subsidized by the Department of Housing and Urban Development.

BEAVERTON. *Our Lady of Peace Institute in Catholic Teaching*, 3600 S.W. 170th Ave., 97006. Tel: 503-649-7127; Fax: 503-649-8382. Rev. Leo Slatterie, Dir.; Sr. Carol Ann, O.S.F., Coord. & Contact Person; Sr. Anne Marie, O.S.F., Asst. Coord. Staff 7; Students 60.

GRESHAM. *Catholic Engaged Encounter of Oregon, Inc.*, 254 S.E. Paloma Ave., 97080. Marriage Preparation Program providing weekend retreats to engaged couples. Couples served 475; Volunteers 52.

HILLSBORO. *St. Matthew Legal Clinic*, 232 S.E. Lincoln, Ste. H, 97123. Tel: 503-648-1600. Mr. Keith R. Raines, Contact Person.

MARYLHURST. **Cornelia Connelly Pastoral Counseling Center*, Marylhurst College, Aquinas Hall, P.O. Box 251, 97036. Sr. Joan Spearing, S.H.C.J., Dir. & Contact Person.

MT. ANGEL. *Benedictine Foundation of Oregon*, Box 912, 97362. Tel: 503-845-2556. Steven Ritchie, Exec. Dir. & Contact Person.

St. Joseph's Shelter, 925 S. Main, P.O. Box 1005, 97362. Tel: 503-845-6147. Sr. Adele Mansfield, Admin.

RELIGIOUS INSTITUTES OF MEN REPRESENTED IN THE ARCHDIOCESE

For further details refer to the corresponding bracketed number in the Religious Institutes of Men or Women section.

[]—*Apostolic Life Community Of Priests (Holy Spirit Fathers)*.—A.L.C.P.
[0140]—*The Augustinians*.—O.S.A.
[0200]—*Benedictine Monks*. (Mt. Angel, OR).—O.S.B.
[0895]—*Brigittine Monastery of Our Lady of Consolidation*.—O.Ss.S.
[0350]—*Cistercians Order of the Strict Observance (Trappists)*.—O.C.S.O.
[]—*Conventual Franciscans*.—O.F.M.Conv.
[0520]—*Franciscan Friars*. (Prov. of Santa Barbara).—O.F.M.
[0690]—*Jesuit Fathers and Brothers*. (Oregon Prov.).—S.J.
[]—*Missionaries Of The Holy Spirit*.—M.Sp.S.
[0910]—*Oblates of Mary Immaculate*.—O.M.I.
[0430]—*Order of Preachers (Dominicans)*. (Western Prov.).—O.P.
[1030]—*Paulist Fathers*.—C.S.P.
[0610]—*Priests of the Congregation of Holy Cross*.—C.S.C.
[1070]—*Redemptorist Fathers*. (Oakland Prov.).—C.SS.R.
[1240]—*Servites*. (Western Prov.).—O.S.M.
[1260]—*Society of Christ*.—S.Ch.
[]—*Society Of Mary*.—S.M.

RELIGIOUS INSTITUTES OF WOMEN REPRESENTED IN THE ARCHDIOCESE

[0230]—*Benedictine Sisters of Pontifical Jurisdiction*. (Mount Angel, OR).—O.S.B.
[0350]—*Carmelite Sisters (Corpus Christi)*.—O.Carm.
[1920]—*Congregation of the Sisters of Holy Cross*.—C.S.C.
[1780]—*Congregation of the Sisters of the Third Order of St. Francis of Perpetual Adoration*.—F.S.P.A.
[0420]—*Discalced Carmelite Nuns*.—O.C.D.
[1070-12]—*Dominican Sisters*.—O.P.
[]—*Dominican Sisters Of Caldwell, NJ*.—O.P.
[1390]—*Franciscan Missionary Sisters of Our Lady of Sorrows*.—O.S.F.
[]—*Holy Spirit Sisters*.
[1250]—*The Institute of the Franciscan Sisters of the Eucharist*.—F.S.E.
[2575]—*Institute of the Sisters of Mercy of the Americas*. (Omaha, NE).—R.S.M.
[]—*Oblates of Saint Martha*.—O.S.M.
[2519]—*Religious Sisters of Mercy of Alma, MI*.—R.S.M.
[3590]—*Servants of Mary (Servite Sisters)*.—O.S.M.
[]—*Sisters For Christian Community*.—S.F.C.C.
[0430]—*Sisters of Charity of the Blessed Virgin Mary*.—B.V.M.
[3350]—*Sisters of Providence*. (Prov. of the Sacred Heart).—S.P.
[]—*Sisters of Reparation of the Sacred Wounds of Jesus*.—S.R.
[4080]—*Sisters of Social Service of Los Angeles, Inc.*—S.S.S.
[1630]—*Sisters of St. Francis of Penance and Christian Charity*.—O.S.F.
[1650]—*The Sisters of St. Francis of Philadelphia*.—O.S.F.
[1530]—*Sisters of St. Francis of the Congregation of Our Lady of Lourdes, Sylvania, Ohio*.—O.S.F.
[1570]—*Sisters of St. Francis of the Holy Family*. (Dubuque, IA).—O.S.F.
[3890]—*Sisters of St. Joseph of Peace*. (Western Prov.).—C.S.J.P.
[3960]—*Sisters of St. Mary of Oregon*.—S.S.M.O.
[1830]—*The Sisters of the Good Shepherd*.—R.G.S.
[1990]—*Sisters of the Holy Names of Jesus and Mary*.—S.N.J.M.
[4060]—*Society of the Holy Child Jesus*. (American Prov.).—S.H.C.J.
[]—*Vietnamese Adorers of the Holy Cross*.—M.T.G.
[4155]—*Vietnamese Adorers of the Holy Cross*.—M.T.G.

ARCHDIOCESAN CEMETERIES

PORTLAND. *Gethsemani.*
Mount Calvary.

EUGENE. *Mount Calvary.*

SALEM. *St. Barbara.*

NECROLOGY

† Crowe, James Edward, (Retired). —Died March 20, 1996.

† Orso-Manzonetta, Aldo, (Retired). —Died March 22, 1996.

Diocese of Providence

(Dioecesis Providentiensis)

Most Reverend

LOUIS E. GELINEAU, D.D., S.T.L., J.C.L.

Bishop of Providence; ordained June 5, 1954; appointed December 6, 1971; consecrated January 26, 1972. *Res., 30 Fenner St., Providence, RI, 02903-3603. Mailing Address: One Cathedral Square, Providence, RI, 02903-3695.* Tel.: 401-278-4545; Fax: 401-278-4548.

Most Reverend

GEORGE H. PEARCE, S.M., D.D.

Former Archbishop of Suva; ordained February 3, 1947; appointed Titular Bishop of Attalea in Pamphilia February 29, 1956; consecrated June 29, 1956; transferred to Apia June 21, 1966; promoted to Suva June 22, 1967; resigned April 10, 1976; Personal assistant to the Bishop of Providence. *Res. & Mailing Address: 30 Fenner St., Providence, RI, 02903-3603.* Tel.: 401-331-2434.

Most Reverend

ROBERT E. MULVEE, D.D., J.C.D.

Coadjutor Bishop of Providence; ordained June 30, 1957; appointed Auxiliary Bishop of Manchester and Titular Bishop of Summa February 15, 1977; consecrated April 14, 1977; installed Bishop of Wilmington February 19, 1985; consecrated April 11, 1985; appointed Coadjutor Bishop of Providence February 9, 1995

Corporate Title: *Roman Catholic Bishop of Providence.*

ESTABLISHED 1872.

Square Miles 1,085.

Comprises the State of Rhode Island.

Bishop's Office & Chancery Office: One Cathedral Square, Providence, RI, 02903-3695. Tel.: 401-278-4500; Fax: 401-278-4548.

STATISTICAL OVERVIEW

Personnel	
Retired Archbishops	1
Bishop	1
Auxiliary Bishops	1
Retired Bishops	1
Abbots	1
Retired Abbots	1
Priests: Diocesan Active in Diocese	220
Priests: Active Outside Diocese	14
Priests: Diocesan in Foreign Missions	2
Priests: Retired, Sick or Absent	81
Number of Diocesan Priests	317
Religious Priests in Diocese	126
Extern Priests in Diocese	12
Ordinations:	
Transitional Deacons	2
Permanent Deacons in Diocese	83
Total Brothers	123
Total Sisters	759
Parishes	
Parishes	159
With Resident Pastor:	
Resident Diocesan Priests	147
Resident Religious Priests	8
Without Resident Pastor:	
Administered by Priests	3
Administered by Pastoral Teams, etc.	1
Missions	8
Pastoral Centers	14
Professional Ministry Personnel:	
Brothers	3
Sisters	60
Lay Ministers	138
Welfare	
Catholic Hospitals	1
Total Assisted	201,000
Homes for the Aged	13
Total Assisted	862
Residential Care of Children	2
Total Assisted	130
Day Care and Extended Day Care Centers	7
Total Assisted	592
Special Centers for Social Services	10
Total Assisted	68,222
Other Institutions	13
Total Assisted	152,586
Educational	
Seminaries, Diocesan	2
Students from This Diocese	9
Diocesan Students in Other Seminaries	8
Total Seminarians	17
Colleges and Universities	2
Total Students	7,731
High Schools, Diocesan and Parish	4
Total Students	1,752
High Schools, Private	7
Total Students	3,279
Elementary Schools, Diocesan and Parish	48
Total Students	11,735
Elementary Schools, Private	5
Total Students	1,362
Non-residential Schools for the Disabled	3
Total Students	1,500
Catechesis/Religious Education:	
High School Students	9,986
Elementary Students	31,174
Total Students Under Catholic Instruction	68,536
Teachers in the Diocese:	
Priests	55
Brothers	37
Sisters	133
Lay Teachers	1,405
Vital Statistics	
Receptions into the Church:	
Infant Baptism Totals	6,648
Adult Baptism Totals	169
Received into Full Communion	178
First Communions	6,398
Confirmations	4,763
Marriages:	
Catholic	1,943
Interfaith	409
Total Marriages	2,352
Deaths	5,630
Total Catholic Population	637,554
Total Population	1,003,000

Former Bishops—Rt. Rev. THOMAS F. HENDRICKEN, D.D., cons. first Bishop of Providence, April 28, 1872; died June 11, 1886.—Rt. Rev. MATTHEW HARKINS, D.D., cons. second Bishop of Providence, April 14, 1887; died May 25, 1921.—Most Rev. WILLIAM A. HICKEY, D.D., ord. Dec. 22, 1893; appt. Coadjutor Bishop of Providence, *Cum jure successionis,* March 10, 1919; cons. Titular Bishop of Claudiopolis, April 10, 1919; succeeded to the See of Providence, May 25, 1921; died Oct. 4, 1933.—Most Rev. FRANCIS P. KEOUGH, D.D., cons. fourth Bishop of Providence, May 22, 1934; appt. Archbishop of Baltimore, Nov. 29, 1947; died Dec. 8, 1961.—Most Rev. RUSSELL J. MCVINNEY, D.D., appt. May 29, 1948; cons. July 14, 1948 fifth Bishop of Providence; died Aug. 10, 1971.

Vicars General—Most Rev. ROBERT E. MULVEE, D.D., J.C.D.; Rev. Msgr. WILLIAM I. VARSANYI, J.C.D.; Rev. Msgr. SALVATORE R. MATANO, S.T.L., J.C.D.

Episcopal Vicars—

Vicar for Canonical Affairs—Rev. Msgr. WILLIAM I. VARSANYI, J.C.D.

Vicar for Education—Rev. ROBERT J. MCMANUS, M.A., S.T.D.

Vicar for Judicial Matters—Rev. JOEL A. LECUIVRE, J.C.L.

Vicar for Planning & Finance—Rev. Msgr. WILLIAM J. MCCAFFREY, S.T.B., M.A.

Vicar for Social Ministry—Rev. Msgr. GEORGE L. FRAPPIER, S.T.B., M.A.

Vicar for Spirituality and Evangelization—Rev. JOHN C. ALLARD.

Vicars for Deaneries—Deanery No. I: Rev. JOHN A. KILEY, Deanery No. II: Rev. BERTRAND L. THEROUX, Deanery No. III: Rev. JOHN J. LAVIN, Deanery No. IV: Rev. RAYMOND C. THEROUX, Deanery No. V: Rev. JOSEPH P. HENRY, Deanery No. VI: Rev. EDWARD J. MCGOVERN, Deanery No. VII: Rev. RAYMOND B. MALM, Deanery No. VIII: Rev. WILFRID G. GREGOIRE, Deanery No. IX: Rev. JOHN W. LOLIO.

Bishop's Office & Chancery Office—One Cathedral Sq., Providence, 02903-3695. Office Hours: Mon.-Fri. 9-5. Tel: 401-278-4500; Fax: 401-278-4548.

Vicar General and Vicar for Canonical Affairs—Rev. Msgr. WILLIAM I. VARSANYI, J.C.D. Tel: 401-278-4520.

Moderator of the Curia—Rev. Msgr. SALVATORE R. MATANO, S.T.L., J.C.D. Tel: 401-278-4535.

Chancellor—Rev. Msgr. JACQUES L. PLANTE, M.A. Tel: 401-278-4515.

Co-Chancellor—Rev. Msgr. ROBERT C. EVANS, J.C.L. Tel: 401-278-4517.

Secretary to the Bishop—Rev. PETER J. ANDREWS. Tel: 401-278-4547.

Diocesan Tribunal—One Cathedral Sq., Providence, 02903-3695. Tel: 401-278-4666.

Judicial Vicar—Rev. Msgr. PAUL D. THEROUX, J.C.L.;

Rev. JOEL A. LECUIVRE, J.C.L.
Judges—Revs. JOSEPH A. HOWARTH, J.C.L., S.T.B.; FRANCIS P. KAYATTA, M.A., M.C.L., J.C.L.; DAVID W. MASELLO, M.A., M.Div., J.C.L.; RONALD P. SIMEONE, M.Div., J.C.L.
Assessor and Auditor—Rev. Msgr. ARTHUR A. SULLIVAN, Ph.D.
Promoter of Justice—Rev. Msgr. WILLIAM I. VARSANYI, J.C.D.
Defenders of the Bond—Revs. JOEL A. LECUIVRE, J.C.L.; JOHN J. LAVIN, J.C.D.
Assessors and Counselors—Sr. MADONNA CRAWFORD, R.S.M., M.A.; Mrs. DIANE DIFIORE, B.S.
Notary—Mrs. LINDA L. NASTARI.
Secretary—Rev. JOEL A. LECUIVRE, J.C.L.

Council of Priests—One Cathedral Sq., Providence, 02903-3695. Tel: 401-278-4517.
Officers—Most Rev. LOUIS E. GELINEAU, Pres.; Rev. JOEL A. LECUIVRE, Moderator; Rev. Msgr. ROBERT C. EVANS, J.C.L., Sec. & Treas.
Council Members—Most Rev. ROBERT E. MULVEE; Rev. Msgr. GEORGE L. FRAPPIER, S.T.B., M.A.; Revs. Msgr. SALVATORE R. MATANO, S.T.L., J.C.D.; Rev. Msgr. WILLIAM J. MCCAFFREY, S.T.B., M.A.; Rev. Msgr. JOHN E. TAVARES; Rev. Msgr. WILLIAM I. VARSANYI, J.C.D.; Revs. STEPHEN P. AMARAL; HENRY J. BODAH; RANDOLPH G. CHEW; W. DOUGLAS GRANT; DONALD J. KING; WILLIAM J. LEDOUX; EDWARD J. MCGOVERN; ROBERT C. NEWBOLD, Ph.D., J.D.; JOSEPH M. PROTANO; RAYMOND C. THEROUX; ARMAND V. VENTRE; HENRY P. ZINNO, JR.
College of Consultors—Most Rev. ROBERT E. MULVEE; Rev. Msgr. ROBERT C. EVANS, J.C.L.; Rev. Msgr. GEORGE L. FRAPPIER, S.T.B., M.A.; Rev. Msgr. SALVATORE R. MATANO, S.T.L., J.C.D.; Rev. Msgr. WILLIAM J. MCCAFFREY, S.T.B., M.A.; Rev. Msgr. WILLIAM I. VARSANYI, J.C.D.; Revs. HENRY J. BODAH; ANTHONY D. IWUC; DONALD J. KING; JOEL A. LECUIVRE, J.C.L.; EDWARD J. MCGOVERN; ROBERT C. NEWBOLD, Ph.D., J.D.; RAYMOND C. THEROUX, J.C.L.

Diocesan Finance Council—Most Rev. LOUIS E. GELINEAU, Pres.; Most Rev. ROBERT E. MULVEE; Rev. Msgr. SALVATORE R. MATANO, S.T.L., J.C.D.; Rev. Msgr. WILLIAM I. VARSANYI, J.C.D.; Rev. Msgr. ROBERT C. EVANS, J.C.L.; Rev. Msgr. WILLIAM J. MCCAFFREY, S.T.B., M.A., Sec.; Revs. GEORGE B. MCCARTHY; BERTRAND L. THEROUX; Sr. M. THERESE ANTONE, R.S.M.; Mr. JOSE ALEX ARIZA; Mr. JOHN W. FLYNN; Mr. JAMES C. FORTE; Hon. ANTHONY A. GIANNINI; Ms. MARIE J. LANGLOIS; Ms. GLORIA LINCOURT; Mr. THOMAS J. SKALA; Mr. PAUL J. TAVARES.
Director of Stewardship and Development—Mr. ANTHONY T. GWIAZDOWSKI.
Finance Officer—Mr. JAMES P. SULLIVAN, C.P.A.

Diocesan Offices and Directors

Advisory Board on Major Seminarians—Rev. CHARLES H. DOWNING, Chm.; Rev. Msgr. ROBERT C. EVANS, J.C.L.; Revs. PAUL E. DEMARAIS; ROBERT F. HAWKINS; ROGER A. HOULE; DENNIS J. KIETON; EUGENE R. LESSARD; JOSEPH P. MOORE; MARCEL E. PINCINCE; FRANCIS C. SANTILLI; MARCEL L. TAILLON; CLYDE J. WALSH; HENRY P. ZINNO, JR.

AIDS Ministry—Rev. STEPHEN P. AMARAL, Coord., *Office of Community Affairs, 83 Stewart St., Providence, 02903.* Tel: 401-278-4585; 421-7833.

Apostolate for Deaf and Hearing Impaired—Rev. JOHN BOSCO VALENTE, O.F.M., Chap. for the Deaf, *58 Weybosset St., Providence, 02903.* Tel: 401-331-6510. Sr. GABRIEL M. CLUNE, O.P., Dir., *One Cathedral Sq., Providence, 02903-3695.* Tel: 401-278-4630; 331-3283 (voice & TTD).

Apostolate for the Handicapped—(Legal Title: The Mercy Home and School). Rev. GERARD O. SABOURIN, Dir.; Sr. GABRIEL M. CLUNE, O.P., Dir., *One Cathedral Sq., Providence, 02903-3695.* Tel: 401-278-4630.
SPRED (Special Religious Education)—Ms. COLLEEN TOUCHETTE, *One Cathedral Sq., Providence, 02903-3695.* Tel: 401-658-1174.

Archives—Rev. Msgr. JACQUES L. PLANTE, M.A., Archivist, *One Cathedral Sq., Providence, 02903-3695.* Tel: 401-278-4515.

Black Catholic Ministry—Mrs. LOIS TABELLA, Coord., *One Cathedral Sq., Providence, 02903-3695.* Tel: 401-278-4552.

Building Commission—Revs. RAYMOND P. LUFT, Chm. ROGER C. GAGNE; JOEL A. LECUIVRE; STEPHAN A. SILIPIGNI; KENNETH J. SUIBIELSKI; Sr. MARY PATRICIA MURPHY, R.S.M.; Mr. DONALD J. SULLIVAN, P.E.; Mr. ROBERT W. CAMPAGNONE; Mr. JOSEPH CONNOLLY; Ms. VIRGINIA HESSE; Mr. FRANK R. SPIRITO.

Building Commission, Office of—Mr. DONALD J. SULLIVAN, P.E., Dir., Facilities; Mr. FRANK R. SPIRITO, Facilities Engineer; Mr. MAXIME E. GIROUARD, JR., Environmental Engineer, *One Cathedral Sq., Providence, 02903-3695.* Tel: 401-278-4636.

Catholic Campus Ministry—Rev. ALFRED V. RICCI, *Brown University, P.O. Box 1931, Providence, 02912-1931., Res., 92 Hope St., Providence, 02906.* Tel: 401-421-9137.

Catholic Charity Fund—Mr. ANTHONY T. GWIAZDOWSKI, Exec. Dir.; Rev. Msgr. WILLIAM J. MCCAFFREY, S.T.B., M.A., Moderator, *Diocesan Development Center, 80 St. Mary Dr., Cranston, 02920.* Tel: 401-943-6550.

Catholic Foundation of Rhode Island—Vacant; Dir., *Diocesan Development Center, 80 St. Mary's Dr., Cranston, 02920.* Tel: 401-278-4528.

Catholic Inner City Center—(Legal Title: *Catholic Inner City Apostolate, Inc.);* Mr. JOHN J. BARRY, III, *83 Stewart St., Providence, 02903.* Tel: 201-941-5600.

Catholic-Jewish Relations—Rev. EDWARD H. FLANNERY, Dir., *80 Farnum Pike, Georgiaville, 02917.* Tel: 401-231-8561.

Catholic Mutual Group—Mr. GREGG CARLSON, Claims & Risk Mgr., *One Cathedral Sq., Providence, 02903-3695.* Tel: 401-278-4638; 278-4639.

Catholic Relief Services—Rev. Msgr. WILLIAM I. VARSANYI, J.C.D., Dir., *One Cathedral Sq., Providence, 02903-3695.* Tel: 401-278-4515.

Catholic School Office—Bro. WILLIAM DYGERT, C.S.C., Supt., *One Cathedral Sq., Providence, 02903-3695.* Tel: 401-278-4550.

Catholic Scouting-Boy Scouts, Girl Scouts, Camp Fire—One Cathedral Sq., Providence, 02903-3695. Tel: 401-278-4626.

Catholic Social Services—(Legal Title: *The Diocesan Bureau of Social Service);* Mr. STEPHEN A. BURKE, M.S.W., Exec. Dir., *433 Elmwood Ave., Providence, 02907.* Tel: 401-467-7200; Fax: 401-467-6310.

Catholic Youth Organization—(Legal title: *Catholic Youth Organization of the Diocese of Providence);* Miss LOUISE M. DUSSAULT, Dir., Youth Ministry, *One Cathedral Sq., Providence, 02903-3695.* Tel: 401-278-4626.

Cemeteries—(Legal title: *Catholic Cemeteries);* Rev. Msgr. GALLIANO J. CAVALLARO, Dir., *One Cathedral Sq., Providence, 02903-3695.* Tel: 401-278-4575.

Censors of Books—Rev. Msgr. JOHN F. COX, Ph.D.; Rev. ROBERT C. NEWBOLD, Ph.D., J.D.

Charismatic Renewal—Rev. RAYMOND M. KELLY, *152 Holden St., Providence, 02908.* Tel: 401-421-7070.
Charisnewal RI—Co-Dirs.: Mr. BOB LAFAZIA; Mr. TED CARLSON, *244 Smith St., Providence, 02908.* Tel: 401-751-3345.

Child Care, Office of—Mrs. ALEXANDRA F. MOSER, Exec. Dir., *485 Mt. Pleasant Ave., Providence, 02908.* Tel: 401-274-3094.

Clergy Benefit Fund: Medical and Pension—(Legal Title: *Our Lady, Queen of the Clergy).*
Medical Advisory Board—Rev. Msgr. SALVATORE R. MATANO; Rev. Msgr. WILLIAM I. VARSANYI; Rev. Msgr. GEORGE L. FRAPPIER, Sec.; Revs. PAUL R. GRENON; JOSEPH P. HEANEY; ANTHONY D. IWUC; CHARLES B. MCDERMOTT; JAMES T. TRAINOR; JAMES J. VERDELOTTI.
Pension Advisory Board—Rev. Msgr. SALVATORE R. MATANO; Rev. Msgr. WILLIAM J. MCCAFFREY; Rev. Msgr. WILLIAM I.VARSANYI; Rev. Msgr. GEORGE L. FRAPPIER, Sec.; Rev. DONALD J. KING; Mr. JAMES P. SULLIVAN.

Communications—(Legal title: *Diocesan Catholic Telecommunications Network of Rhode Island);* (News Media, Radio, TV, Public Relations); Mr. WILLIAM G. HALPIN, Dir., *One Cathedral Sq., Providence, 02903-3695.* Tel: 401-278-4600; Fax: 401-278-4649.
Media Services Department—(Media Production, Audio-Visual, Photography, Creative Media Programming and Consultation); Mrs. ANN FORTE, *One Cathedral Sq., Providence, 02903-3695.* Tel: 401-278-4678.
Telecommunications Department—(Produces "Rejoice in Hope" and other Catholic programming, Liaison with State Interconnect and CATV Companies, EWTN Liaison); Miss SUSAN MCCARTHY, Program Coord.; Mr. ANTHONY RIZZINI, Asst. to Dir., Radio & TV Prod., *One Cathedral Sq., Providence, 02903-3695.* Tel: 401-278-4608.

Community Affairs Office—Mr. JOHN J. BARRY, III, Dir., *83 Stewart St., Providence, 02903.* Tel: 401-278-4585; 421-7833.

Council of Religious—Sr. MARIE GEORGETTE CHASSE, R.S.M., Coord. Steering Committee: Bro. ALAN AUBIN, S.C.; Sr. COLETTE AUGER, P.M.; Bro. EDMOND PRECOURT, F.S.C.; Sr. MARTA INES TORO, O.P., *One Cathedral Sq., Providence, 02903-3695.* Tel: 401-278-4633.

Cursillo Movement—Rev. FRANK S. SALMANI, Spiritual Dir., *2 Russo St., Providence, 02904.* Tel: 401-861-5111. Mrs. KATHRYN ROBBIO, Lay Coord., *100 Empress Dr., E. Greenwich, 02818.* Tel: 401-884-2424.

Diaconate (Transitory)—Rev. EUGENE R. LESSARD, *1030 Dexter St., Central Falls, 02863.* Tel: 401-726-2600.

Ecumenical Commission—Rev. LIONEL A. BLAIN, Chm., *1200 Mendon Rd., Woonsocket, 02895.* Tel: 401-766-0626. Revs. JOSEPH D. SCHENICK; EDWARD G. ST. GODARD; Mrs. ANNE MORGAN; Mrs. GRADA SUMNER.

Education and Compliance—Lt. ROBERT N. MCCARTHY, Dir., *433 Elmwood Ave., Providence, 02907.* Tel: 401-941-0760.

Education, Department of—Rev. ROBERT J. MCMANUS, M.A., S.T.D., Vicar for Education, *One Cathedral Sq., Providence, 02903.* Tel: 401-278-4587. Bro. WILLIAM DYGERT, C.S.C., Supt., Schools. Tel: 401-278-4550. Sr. SHEILA DURANTE, R.S.M., Asst. Supt.; Rev. ALFRED V. RICCI, Dir., Campus Min., *Brown Univ.* Tel: 401-863-2344. Mr. JOSEPH P. SINWELL, Dir., Office of Religious Education, C.C.D. Tel: 401-278-4646. Rev. GERARD O. SABOURIN, Dir., Diocesan Apostolate for the Handicapped. Tel: 401-278-4630. Ms. COLLEEN TOUCHETTE, SPRED (Special Religious Education). Tel: 401-658-1174.

Family Life Office—Mr. STEPHEN A. BURKE, Dir., *80 St. Mary's Dr., Cranston, 02920.* Tel: 401-943-7900. Catholic Sexuality Education, Vacant Marriage Preparation, Mrs. RITA DONAHUE,Natural Family Planning, Mr. STEPHEN BURKE; Mrs. STEPHEN BURKE,S.D.R.W. (Ministry with Separated, Divorced, Remarried and Widowed Persons), DOROTHY J. LEVESQUE,Respect Life Programs, Mrs. MARIA PARKER. Tel: 401-943-7900.

Finance Office—(Cf. Planning and Finance Office).

Fiscal Office—Mr. J. TIMOTHY KOCAB, Diocesan Controller, *One Cathedral Sq., Providence, 02903-3695.* Tel: 401-278-4616.

Government Liaison—Rev. ROBERT C. NEWBOLD, Ph.D., J.D., Diocesan Dir.

Grievance Committee—Revs. ROBERT P. PERRON, Chm. GERALD E. BEIRNE, Sec. THOMAS J. FERLAND; ROGER C. GAGNE; JOSEPH P. HEANEY; NICHOLAS I. IACOVACCI; FARRELL E. MCLAUGHLIN; JAMES T. TRAINOR.

Health Care Ministries, Office of—Rev. JOHN E. WATTERSON, Dir., *103 Pine Street, P.O. Box 518, Pawtucket, 02862.* Tel: 401-725-0160; Fax: 401-729-0341.

Hispanic Ministry—Sr. MARTA INES TORO, O.P., Dir.; Mrs. AIDA HIDALGO, Coord., *One Cathedral Sq., Providence, 02903-3695.* Tel: 401-278-4526.

Holy Childhood Association—Rev. Msgr. WILLIAM I. VARSANYI, J.C.D., Dir., *One Cathedral Sq., Providence, 02903-3695.* Tel: 401-278-4519.

Holy Name Society—Rev. ANTHONY D. IWUC, Dir., *391 High St., Central Falls, 02863.* Tel: 401-723-5427.

Insurance Commission—Rev. Msgr. WILLIAM J. MCCAFFREY, S.T.B., M.A., Chm.; Rev. Msgr. WILLIAM J. CAREY; Revs. JOHN T. CARTY; VICTOR M. VIEIRA; ROGER G. CHAMPIGNY; Mr. PETER F. GOLDBECKER; Mr. J. TIMOTHY KOCAB; Mr. MICHAEL MCINTYRE; Ms. SANDRA G. PARRILLO; DONALD J. SULLIVAN, P.E.; ANTHONY J. ROURKE; JAMES P. SULLIVAN, C.P.A., *One Cathedral Sq., Providence, 02903-3695.* Tel: 401-278-4616.

Marriage Preparation—(Cf. Family Life Office).

Media Services Department—(Cf. Communications).

Ministerial Formation—(Continuing Education of Priests, Permanent Deacons, Lay Ministers). Rev. ROBERT J. MCMANUS, M.A., S.T.D., Dir., *One Cathedral Sq., Providence, 02903-3695.* Tel: 401-278-4587.

Ministry with Separated, Divorced, Remarried and Widowed Persons—(Cf. Family Life Office).

Natural Family Planning—(Cf. Family Life Office).

Parish Evangelization and Renewal—Sr. MARTA INES TORO, O.P., Dir., *One Cathedral Sq., Providence, 02903-3695.* Tel: 401-278-4624.

Planning and Finance—Rev. Msgr. WILLIAM J. MCCAFFREY, S.T.B., M.A., Vicar; Mr. JAMES P. SULLIVAN, C.P.A., Finance Officer, *One Cathedral Sq., Providence, 02903.* Tel: 401-278-4540; Fax: 401-831-1947.

Priests, Minister for—Rev. NORMAND J. GODIN, *1045 Douglas Pike, Mohegan, Harrisville, 02830.* Tel: 401-568-7101.

Priests' Eucharistic League—Rev. JOSEPH P. HYNES, Dir., *358 Newport Ave., Pawtucket, 02861.* Tel: 401-722-4470.

Priests' Personnel Board—Rev. Msgr. ROBERT C. EVANS, J.C.L., Dir., *One Cathedral Sq., Providence, 02903-3695.* Tel: 401-278-4640. Rev. DONAT A. BARRETTE, Vice Chm. Group I: Revs. JOHN E. UNSWORTH; JOSEPH A. BESSE,Group II: Rev. DANIEL M. TRAINOR,Group III: Rev. ROGER A. HOULE.

Project Hope/Proyecto Esperanza—(Legal Title: *St. Pious X Salvage Bureau);* Mr. JOHN J. BARRY, III, *740 Dexter St., Center Falls, 02863.* Tel: 401-728-0515.

Propagation of the Faith—(Legal title: *Society for the Propagation of the Faith, Diocese of Providence);* Rev. Msgr. WILLIAM I. VARSANYI, J.C.D., Dir., *One Cathedral Sq., Providence, 02903-3695.* Tel: 401-278-4519.

Religious, Office of—Sr. MARIE GEORGETTE CHASSE, R.S.M., Dir., *One Cathedral Sq., Providence, 02903-3695.* Tel: 401-278-4633.

Religious Education—Mr. JOSEPH P. SINWELL, *34 Fenner St., Providence, 02903.* Tel: 401-278-4646.

Renewal in the Spirit—Rev. JOHN F. RANDALL, *Res., 178 Dexter St., Providence, 02907.* Tel: 401-421-6441.

Resource Development Department—(Annual Appeal, Planned Giving, Bishop's Partnership in Charity); Mr. ANTHONY T. GWIAZDOWSKI, Stewardship & Devel. Dir.; Rev. Msgr. WILLIAM J. McCAFFREY, Moderator, *Diocesan Development Center, 80 St. Mary's Dr., Cranston, 02920.* Tel: 401-943-6550.

Retreat House Program—Sr. JEAN MARIE McGEE, R.S.M., Admin., *Our Lady of Peace Spiritual Life Center, Narragansett, 02882.* Tel: 401-884-7676; 783-2871.

St. Vincent de Paul Society—(Emergency Assistance Network), *83 Stewart St., Providence, 02903.* Tel: 401-421-7833.

Social Ministry Vicariate—Rev. Msgr. GEORGE L. FRAPPIER, S.T.B., M.A., Vicar, *128 Green St., Woonsocket, 02895.* Tel: 401-769-7487.

Spirituality and Evangelization—Rev. JOHN C. ALLARD, Vicar; Sr. MARTA INES TORO, O.P., Dir., Evangelization, *One Cathedral Sq., Providence, 02903-3695.* Tel: 401-278-4625.

Stewardship and Development—Mr. ANTHONY T. GWIAZDOWSKI, Dir., *80 St. Mary's Dr., Cranston, 02920.* Tel: 401-943-6550.

Telecommunications—(Cf. Communications).

Vocations—Revs. MARCEL E. PINCINCE, Vocation Recruiter; PAUL E. DEMARAIS, Spiritual Dir., *485 Mt. Pleasant Ave., Providence, 02908.* Tel: 401-831-8011. Sr. MARIE GEORGETTE CHASSE, R.S.M., Assoc. Dir., Religious, *One Cathedral Sq., Providence, 02903-3695.* Tel: 401-278-4633.

Worship, Office for—Revs. KENNETH J. SUIBIELSKI, Dir. PETER ANDREWS, Assoc. Dir., *One Cathedral Sq., Providence, 02903-3695.* Tel: 401-278-4640.

Diocesan Liturgical Commission—Revs. KENNETH J. SUIBIELSKI, Chm. PETER ANDREWS, Vice Chm. Members: Rev. Msgr. JACQUES L. PLANTE, M.A.; Revs. RONALD E. BRASSARD; JOSEPH A. HOWARTH, J.C.L., S.T.B.; STEVEN A. SILIPIGNI; JOSE OMAR ZULUAGA; Mrs. JOANNE MERCIER.

Hispanic Liturgy Committee—Rev. JOSE OMAR ZULUAGA, Chm. Members: Mr. SILVIO CUELLAR; Mrs. CECILIA MARIN; Mrs. MARY MENDEZ; Mrs. SONIA PFLIEGER.

Liturgical Education Committee—Mrs. JOANNE MERCIER, Chm. Members: Revs. JOHN J. DARCY; TIMOTHY J. GORTON; FARRELL E. McLAUGHLIN; Mr. JOHN SILVIA; Mrs. PEGGY SIMMS; Mr. PAUL T. SULLIVAN.

Liturgy Policy & Guide Committee—Rev. JOSEPH A. HOWARTH, J.C.L., S.T.B., Chm. Members: Revs. RANDOLPH G. CHEW; DAVID W. MASELLO; RICHARD A. VALENTINE.

Music Committee—Rev. RONALD E. BRASSARD, Chm. Members: Revs. PAUL J. DAPONTE; ANTHONY MANCINI; THOMAS J. TREPANIER; Mr. MARK GIRARDIN; Sr. GAIL HIMROD, O.P.; Ms. SHERRY HUMES; Deacon PAUL LAMBERT; Mr. DAVID MARTINEZ; Mrs. LINDA REID; Mr. RONALD TURNQUIST.

Worship Environment Committee—Rev. STEPHAN A. SILIPIGNI, Chm. Members: Revs. JOEL A. LECUIVRE, J.C.L.; FRANCIS W. BROCATO, O.P.; Miss ADE BETHUNE; Mr. ALFRED OAKES.

CLERGY, PARISHES, MISSIONS AND PAROCHIAL SCHOOLS

CITY OF PROVIDENCE
(Providence County)

1—CATHEDRAL OF SS. PETER AND PAUL. Cathedral Sq. (Legal title: SS. Peter and Paul's Church, Providence, Rhode Island). Rev. Francis J. Giudice, Rector. In res., Rev. Msgr. Jacques L. Plante; Revs. Normand W. Valois; Peter J. Andrews; Joseph A. Howarth.
Res., 30 Fenner St., 02903. Tel: 401-331-2434 (Office); 278-4510 (Cathedral Residence).

2—ST. ADALBERT'S (Polish). (Legal Title: Saint Adalbert's Church). Rev. Frederick V. Slota.
Res., 866 Atwells Ave., 02909-2596. Tel: 401-351-9306.
Convent—Tel: 401-831-3336. Sr. Mary Alexander, Supr.
Felician Sisters of St. Francis 3.

3—ST. AGNES. (Legal title: St. Agnes Church). Rev. Norman J. Godin, Admin.
Res., 351 Branch Ave., 02904. Tel: 401-861-7265.

4—ST. ANN'S (Italian). (Legal title: Saint Ann's Catholic Church of Providence, Rhode Island). Rev. Frank S. Salmani. In res., Rev. John J. Davey.
Res., 2 Russo St., 02904. Tel: 401-861-5111.
School—525 Branch Ave., 02904. Tel: 401-331-0891.
Lay Teachers 16; Students 241.
Catechesis/Religious Programs—St. Ann's Parish Center, 45 Greeley St., 02904. Tel: 401-521-5220. Students 150.

5—ST. ANTHONY'S. (Legal title: Saint Anthony's Church Corporation, Rhode Island). Rev. Joseph Protano, Jr.
Res., 549 Plainfield St., 02909. Tel: 401-943-2300.

6—ASSUMPTION OF THE BLESSED VIRGIN MARY. (Legal title: The Church of the Assumption, Providence, Rhode Island). Revs. Daniel M. Trainor; Guillermo L. Corrales Bedoya (Columbia).
Res., 791 Potters Ave., 02907. Tel: 401-941-1248.
Catechesis/Religious Programs—Tel: 401-941-3768.
Students 200.

7—ST. AUGUSTINE'S. (Legal title: Saint Augustine's Church, Providence, Rhode Island). Revs. Barry R.L. Connerton; Bernard A. Healey. In res., Rev. Msgr. Salvatore R. Matano.
Res., 20 Old Rd., 02908. Tel: 401-831-3503; Fax: 401-421-9060.
School—635 Mt. Pleasant Ave., 02908. Tel: 401-831-1213. Mrs. Paul F. Morry, Prin.
Sisters of St. Joseph of Cluny 2; Lay Teachers 25; Students 361.
Catechesis/Religious Programs—Students 326.

8—ST. BARTHOLOMEW'S (Italian). Silver Lake District (Legal title: Saint Bartholomew's Church Corporation). Revs. Joseph F. Pranzo, C.S.; Francis Fiorentin, C.S.
Res., 297 Laurel Hill Ave., 02909. Tel: 401-944-4466; Fax: 401-946-5866.
School—311 Laurel Hill Ave., 02909. Tel: 401-944-5662. Ms. Gertrude Blais, Prin.
Sisters 1; Lay Teachers 9; Students 160.
Catechesis/Religious Programs—Students 160.

9—BLESSED SACRAMENT. (Legal title: The Church of the Blessed Sacrament in Providence Rhode Island). Revs. Charles E. Maher; Robert W. Hayman; Deacon Thomas F. Boutier.
Res., 239 Regent Ave., 02908. Tel: 401-751-7575.
School—240 Regent Ave., 02908. Tel: 401-831-3993. Mrs. Susan Caputo, Prin.
Sisters Faithful Companions of Jesus 1; Lay Teachers 23; Students 328.
Convent—350 Mount Pleasant Ave., 02908. Tel: 401-274-6578.
Sisters Faithful Companions of Jesus 4.

10—ST. CASIMIR'S (Lithuanian). (Legal title: Saint Casimir's Church, Providence, Rhode Island). Rev. Adolph Klimanskis (NOR).
Res., 350 Smith St., 02908. Tel: 401-331-1051.

11—ST. CHARLES BORROMEO (French). (Legal title: Saint Charles Borromeo Roman Catholic Church, Providence, Rhode Island). Revs. John F. Randall; John W. Gray.
Res., 178 Dexter St., 02907. Tel: 401-421-6441.
Catechesis/Religious Programs—Students 265.

12—ST. EDWARD'S. (Legal title: The Church of St. Joseph Geneva Rhode Island). Rev. Richard J. Bushee.
Res., 10 Caxton St., 02904. Tel: 401-331-4035.
Church—997 Branch Ave., 02904.

13—GENESIS COMMUNITY. Closed. For inquiries for parish records contact Cathedral of SS. Peter & Paul, Providence.

14—HOLY CROSS (Italian). (Legal Title: Corporation of the Church of the Holy Cross). Rev. Anthony Mancini, Admin.
Res., 18 King Philip St., 02909. Tel: 401-274-5225; Fax: 401-274-6635.
Catechesis/Religious Programs—636 Hartford Ave., 02909. Tel: 401-751-1144. Mrs. June Carnevale, D.R.E.
Students 193.

15—HOLY GHOST (Italian). (Legal title: Corporation of the Church of the Holy Ghost, Rhode Island). Revs. Ignatius Battaglia, C.S.; Angelo J. Susin, C.S.
Res., 472 Atwells Ave., 02909. Tel: 401-421-3551; Fax: 401-421-3557.
School—35 Swiss St., 02909. Tel: 401-421-4455. Mrs. Carol Wood, Prin.
Sisters of Mercy of the Americas 1; Lay Teachers 8; Students 163.
Day Care Center—Tel: 401-521-9510. Sr. Dorothy I. Porcaro, R.S.M., Dir.
Lay Teachers 8; Children 45.

16—HOLY NAME. (Legal title: Church of the Holy Name of Jesus at Providence, Rhode Island). Revs. Thomas J. Trepanier; Marc-Arthur Jerome (Haiti); Deacon Frederick A. Young.
Res., 99 Camp St., 02906. Tel: 401-272-4515; Fax: 401-272-4616.
School—Tel: 401-351-0533.
Lay Teachers 13; Students 150.

17—ST. JOHN'S. Closed. (Legal title: St. John's Church of Providence Rhode Island). Sacramental records at St. Mary's Church, Providence.

18—ST. JOSEPH'S. (Legal title: St. Joseph's Church Providence Rhode Island). Rev. Msgr. William J. McCaffrey. In res., Revs. John J. Rainone; Alfred V. Ricci.
Res., 92 Hope St., 02906. Tel: 401-421-9137.

19—ST. MARON. (Legal title: Church of St. Maron in Providence). Rev. Msgr. Jacques L. Plante.
Res., One Cathedral Square, 02903.

20—ST. MARY'S. (Legal title: St. Mary's Church Providence Rhode Island). Rev. Roger C. Gagne. In res., Rev. Nicholas J. Iacovacci.
Res., 538 Broadway, 02909. Tel: 401-274-3434.
School—30 Barton St., 02909. Tel: 401-274-5250. Mr. Robert Waldraff, Prin.
Sisters of the Congregation de Notre Dame 1; Lay Teachers 11; Students 192.

21—ST. MICHAEL'S. (Legal title: St. Michael's Providence Rhode Island). Revs. Raymond B. Malm; Dennis A. Reardon.
Res., 239 Oxford St., 02905. Tel: 401-781-7210; Fax: 401-461-6164.
Catechesis/Religious Programs—Students 311.

22—OUR LADY OF CHARITY. (Legal title: Church of Our Lady of Charity of Providence). Rev. Msgr. William I. Varsanyi.
Res., One Cathedral Sq., 02903.

23—OUR LADY OF LOURDES (French). (Legal title: Church of Our Lady of Lourdes). Rev. Robert C. Newbold; Deacon Anthony Wendolowski.
Res., 901 Atwells Ave., 02909. Tel: 401-272-8127.

24—OUR LADY OF MT. CARMEL (Italian). (Legal title: Church of Our Lady of Mount Carmel, Providence). Revs. Raymond P. Luft; Hugo Carmona (Columbia).
Res., 12 Spruce St., 02903. Tel: 401-274-2113.

25—OUR LADY OF THE ROSARY (Portuguese). (Legal title: Church of Our Lady of the Rosary). Revs. Antonio M. Paiva; Domingos da Cunha (Timor).
Res., 463 Benefit St., 02903. Tel: 401-421-5621.
Convent—17 Traverse St., 02903. Tel: 401-751-9342, 401-751-6432. Sr. Fatima Simas, S.S.D., Supr.
Sisters of St. Dorothy 4.

26—ST. PATRICK'S. (Legal title: St. Patrick's Church, Providence, Rhode Island). Rev. Raymond M. Kelly.
Res., 152 Holden St., 02908. Tel: 401-421-7070.
Church—244 Smith St., 02908.
School—Tel: 401-421-9300. Mr. Stephen M. Raymond, Prin.
Sisters 1; Lay Teachers 10; Students 146.

27—ST. PIUS V. (Legal title: Saint Pius Church, Providence, Rhode Island). Very Rev. Kenneth R. Letoile, O.P., Prior; Revs. Henry Camacho, O.P.; Michael P. Trainor, O.P.; Michael DeTemple, O.P. In res., Bro. Denis Swann, O.P.
Res., 55 Elmhurst Ave., 02908. Tel: 401-751-4871; Fax: 401-273-1089.
School—49 Elmhurst Ave., 02908. Tel: 401-421-9750; Fax: 401-455-3928. Sr. Shirley Jeffcott, O.P., Prin.
Dominican Sisters 2; Lay Teachers 14; Students 276.
Catechesis/Religious Programs—Tel: 401-421-2263. Mrs. Louise Toomey, D.R.E.
Students 214.
Convent—30 Elmhurst Ave., 02908. Tel: 401-751-0362.

28—ST. RAYMOND'S. (Legal title: Saint Raymond's Church Corporation). In res., Rev. Peter J. Gower, Admin.
Res., 124 Hillside Ave., Pawtucket, 02860. Tel: 401-722-1610; Fax: 401-351-4224.
Church—1240 N. Main St., 02906. Tel: 401-351-4224; Fax: 401-351-4224.

29—ST. SEBASTIAN. Unassigned. (Legal title: Church of Saint Sebastian).
Res., 67 Cole Ave., 02906. Tel: 401-751-0196.
Catechesis/Religious Programs—Students 123.

30—ST. TERESA OF AVILA. (Legal title: Saint Teresa's Church Providence Rhode Island). Rev. Raymond L. Tetrault.
Res., 18 Pope St., 02909. Tel: 401-831-7714.

31—ST. THOMAS. (Legal title: St. Thomas' Church of Manton Rhode Island). Rev. Joseph R. Paquette; Deacon Albert DePetrillo.
Res., 65 Fruit Hill Ave., 02909. Tel: 401-272-7118.
School—See St. Thomas Regional School. Tel: 401-351-0403.
Catechesis/Religious Programs—Tel: 401-272-1443.
Students 273.
Convent—41 Edendale Ave., 02911. Tel: 401-272-1722.

OUTSIDE THE CITY OF PROVIDENCE

Albion, Providence Co., St. Ambrose's. (Legal title: St. Ambrose Church, Albion, Rhode Island). Rev. Pierre J. Plante.

Res., 191 School St., 02802. Tel: 401-333-1568. [CEM]
Catechesis/Religious Programs—Tel: 401-334-3735.
Students 166.

Ashaway, Washington Co., Our Lady of Victory. (Legal title: Church of Our Lady of Victory, Ashaway). Rev. James V. Farley.
Res., 169B Main St., 02804. Tel: 401-377-8830.
Catechesis/Religious Programs—Tel: 401-377-8435; Fax: 401-377-8830.
Students 96.

Ashton, Providence Co., St. Joseph's. (Legal title: St. Joseph's Church, Ashton, Rhode Island). Rev. John W. Hunt.
Res., Mendon Rd., P.O Box 7005, Cumberland, 02864. Tel: 401-333-4013; Fax: 401-333-4013. [CEM]
Catechesis/Religious Programs—Tel: 401-333-4014.
Students 295.

Barrington, Bristol Co., Holy Angels (Italian). (Legal title: Holy Angel's Church Corporation). Rev. David A. Piacentini.
Res., 341 Maple Ave., 02806. Tel: 401-245-7743.

St. Luke's. (Legal title: Saint Luke's Church Corporation, Barrington). Revs. William R. Jenkinson; David C. Procaccini. In res., Rev. Robert J. McManus.
Res., 108 Washington Rd., 02806-1133. Tel: 401-246-1212.
School—Waldron Ave., 02806. Tel: 401-246-0990; Fax: 401-246-2120. Mrs. Margaret C. Halpin, Prin.
Lay Teachers 19; Students 301.
Catechesis/Religious Programs—Tel: 401-246-1363. D.R.E.: Patricia Grattan, D.R.E. (Grades 1-5); Diane Comerford, D.R.E. (Grades 6-10).
Students 620.

Block Island, Washington Co., St. Andrew's. (Legal title: Saint Andrew's Church Corporation, Block Island). Rev. Donal R. Kehew, Admin.
Res., Spring St., 02807. Tel: 401-466-5519.

Bradford, Washington Co., St. Vincent de Paul. (Legal title: Saint Vincent's Church Corporation, Bradford). Rev. James V. Farley.
Res., P.O. Box 277, 5 Church St., 02808. Tel: 401-377-2289; Fax: 401-377-8830.
Catechesis/Religious Programs—Tel: 401-377-8435.
Students 167.

Bristol, Bristol Co., St. Elizabeth's (Portuguese). (Legal title: Saint Elizabeth's Church of Bristol). Revs. Louis L. Brum (BWN) Admin.; Joseph A. Escobar, O.P.
Res., 577 Wood St., 02809. Tel: 401-253-8366; Fax: 401-253-8438.
School—10 Monroe Ave., 02809. Sr. Cynthia Mello, S.S.D., Prin.
Sisters of St. Dorothy 1; Lay Teachers 11; Students 230.
Catechesis/Religious Programs—Lisa Correira, D.R.E.
Students 630.

St. Mary's. (Legal title: Saint Mary's Church, Bristol, Rhode Island). Rev. John McNulty; Deacons Benjamin Barboza; Bernard G. Theroux.
Res., 330 Wood St., 02809. Tel: 401-253-3300; Fax: 401-253-3300. [CEM]
Catechesis/Religious Programs—Tel: 401-253-2270.
Students 173.
Mission—Prudence Island, Our Lady of Prudence.

Our Lady of Mount Carmel (Italian). (Legal title: Church of Our Lady of Mount Carmel, Bristol). Revs. James J. Verdelotti; Henry P. Zinno, Jr.
Res., 141 State St., 02809. Tel: 401-253-9449; Fax: 401-253-5687. [JC]
School—Maestre Pie Filippini. (Religious Teachers Filippini) 117 State St., 02809. Tel: 401-253-8455; Fax: 401-253-5687. Sr. Concetta Millemaggi, M.P.F., Prin.
Sisters 1; Lay Teachers 10; Students 234.
Catechesis/Religious Programs—131 State St., 02809. Tel: 401-253-3984.
Students 201.

Carolina, Washington Co., St. Mary's. (Legal title: Saint Mary's Church Corporation, Carolina). Rev. John F. Heaney.
Res., P.O. Box 475, 02812. Tel: 401-364-7214.
Catechesis/Religious Programs—Tel: 401-783-1849.
Students 343.
Mission—Charlestown, Washington Co., St. James, 2079 Mat. School House Rd., Charlestown, 02813. Tel: 401-364-7214.

Central Falls, Providence Co.,

1—Holy Trinity. (Legal title: Church of the Holy Trinity, Central Falls). Rev. Robert M. Beirne.
Office: 325 Cowden St., 02863. Tel: 401-723-5326.
Res., 338 Cowden St., 02863. Tel: 401-728-6230.
School—(See St. Elizabeth Ann Seton Academy). Sr. Ann McKenna, R.S.M., Prin.

2—St. Joseph's, (Polish). (Legal title: St. Joseph's Church of Central Falls). Rev. Anthony D. Iwuc.
Res., 391 High St., 02863-3109. Tel: 401-723-5427.

3—St. Matthew's, (French). (Legal title: Saint Matthew's Church of Central Falls). Revs. Eugene R. Lessard; John E. Abreu.
Res., 1030 Dexter St., 02863. Tel: 401-726-2600.
Catechesis/Religious Programs—Tel: 401-722-3717.
Students 132.

4—Notre Dame, (French). (Legal title: Notre Dame Church). Rev. Robert P. Perron. In res., Rev. Robert A. Rochon.
Res., 668 Broad St., 02863. Tel: 401-725-1748. [CEM]
Catechesis/Religious Programs—Tel: 401-725-1749.
Students 140.

Chepachet, Providence Co., St. Eugene's (Glocester). (Legal title: St. Eugene's Church Corporation, Chepachet). Rev. Joseph F. Murphy.
Res., 1251 Putnam Pike, P.O. Box A, 02814. Tel: 401-568-5102.
Catechesis/Religious Programs—Students 170.

Coventry, Kent Co., SS. John and Paul. (Legal title: SS. John and Paul Parish Corporation, Coventry). Revs. Joseph P. Henry; Stephan A. Silipigni; William J. Ledoux.
Res., 341 S. Main St., 02816. Tel: 401-821-5764.
School—Father John V. Doyle School, Tel: 401-821-3756. Mr. J. Robert McDermott, Prin.
Lay Teachers 19; Students 401.
Catechesis/Religious Programs—Tel: 401-821-5785.
Students 1,147.

Our Lady of Czenstochowa (Quidnick) (Polish). (Legal title: Church of Our Lady of Czenstochowa). Rev. John D. Dreher.
Res., 445 Washington St., 02816. Tel: 401-821-7991.

St. Vincent de Paul's (French). (Legal title: Church of Saint Vincent de Paul, Anthony, Rhode Island). Rev. Paul J. Laporte, Admin.; Deacon Edward Sadowski, Jr.
Res., 6 St. Vincent de Paul St., 02816. Tel: 401-821-8719.
Convent—8 St. Vincent de Paul St., 02816. Tel: 401-828-6506. Sr. Alberte Cormier, P.M., Supr.
Sisters of the Presentation of Mary 3.
Catechesis/Religious Programs—2 St. Vincent de Paul St., 02816. Tel: 401-828-3090.
Students 240.

Cranston, Providence Co.,

1—St. Ann. (Legal title: St. Anne's Church, Cranston, Rhode Island). Rev. John G. Greaves.
Res., 1493 Cranston St., 02920. Tel: 401-942-2767.
Catechesis/Religious Programs—Tel: 401-942-0655.
Students 335.

2—Holy Apostles. (Legal title: Holy Apostles Church, Cranston, Rhode Island). Rev. Richard D. Sheahan.
Res., 800 Pippin Orchard Rd., 02921. Tel: 401-946-5586; Fax: 401-946-5066.
Catechesis/Religious Programs—Students 930.

3—Immaculate Conception. (Legal title: Immaculate Conception Church Corporation, Cranston). Rev. Ronald E. Brassard; Deacons Carmine Forlingieri; Raymond J. LaFrance; Thomas J. Lennon; Thomas R. Raspallo.
Res., 237 Garden Hills Dr., 02920. Tel: 401-942-1854; Fax: 401-942-2897.
Catechesis/Religious Programs—Tel: 401-942-1958. D.R.E.: Claudia Bertrand; Richard Raspallo.
Students 526.

4—St. Mark. (Legal title: Saint Mark's Church Corporation of Cranston). Revs. Richard A. Donnelly; M. Kevin Lynch.
Res., 9 Garden Ct., 02920. Tel: 401-942-1616.
Catechesis/Religious Programs—Tel: 401-942-3231.
Students 376.

5—St. Mary, (Italian). (Santa Maria della Civita) (Legal title: Saint Mary's Church, Cranston). Revs. Alfred C. Lonardo; Daniel M. Azzarone; Joseph A. Pescatello; Deacon Peter A. Ceprano. In res., Rev. Joel A. Lecuivre.
Res., 1525 Cranston St., 02920-5297. Tel: 401-942-1492; Fax: 401-946-2531.
School—Tel: 401-944-4107. Mrs. Elizabeth Mizzoni, Prin.
Lay Teachers 18; Students 296.
Catechesis/Religious Programs—Tel: 401-944-1323. D.R.E.: Phyllis Ann Persson; Linda Archetto.
Students 487.

6—St. Matthew. (Legal title: St. Matthew's Church Corporation). Revs. Richard A. Walsh; Raymond J. Ferrick; James T. Ruggieri.
Res., 15 Frances Ave., 02910. Tel: 401-461-7172; Fax: 401-461-7173.
Church—Elmwood & Park Ave., 02910.
School—1301 Elmwood Ave., 02910. Tel: 401-941-8954. Barbara C. Dwyer, Prin.
Sisters of Mercy of the Americas 1; Lay Teachers 15; Students 313.
Catechesis/Religious Programs—Tel: 401-781-4568; Fax: 401-461-7173.
Students 393.

7—St. Paul. (Legal title: Saint Paul's Church of Edgewood). Rev. Ronald J. Bengford. In res., Rev. Robert J. Maynard.
Res., One St. Paul Pl., 02905. Tel: 401-461-5734; Fax: 401-786-3616.
School—1789 Broad St., 02905. Tel: 401-941-2030. Mrs. Jean Patterson, Prin.
Lay Teachers 11; Students 181.
Catechesis/Religious Programs—Tel: 401-941-5576.
Students 347.

Cumberland, Providence Co., St. Aidan. (Legal title: St. Aidan Church Corporation, Cumberland). Rev. Donald L. Depatie.
Res., 1745 Diamond Hill Rd., 02864. Tel: 401-333-5897.
Catechesis/Religious Programs—Tel: 401-333-9030.
Students 305.

St. Joan's. (Legal title: Saint Joan's Church, Cumberland, Rhode Island). Rev. Norman W. Bourdon. In res., Rev. Msgr. Robert C. Evans.
Res., 3357 Mendon Rd., 02864-2195. Tel: 401-658-2084; Fax: 401-658-2086.
Catechesis/Religious Programs—Tel: 401-658-0734.
Students 556.

St. John Baptist Mary Vianney. (Legal title: Saint John Baptist Mary Vianney Church Corporation, Diamond Hill). Rev. J. Raymond Theroux; Deacon Paul H. Lambert.
Res., 3609 Diamond Hill Rd., 02864. Tel: 401-333-6060; Fax: 401-333-0766.
Catechesis/Religious Programs—3587 Diamond Hill Rd., 02864. Tel: 401-333-2347.
Students 550.

East Greenwich, Kent Co., Our Lady of Mercy. (Legal title: Our Lady of Mercy, Greenwich, Rhode Island). Revs. John W. Lolio; Anthony W. Verdelotti.
Res., 65 Third St., 02818. Tel: 401-884-4968; Fax: 401-884-1415. [CEM]
Catechesis/Religious Programs—Tel: 401-884-1061.
Students 936.
Convent—36 Fourth Ave., 02818. Tel: 401-884-9292.

East Providence, Providence Co.,

1—St. Francis Xavier, (Portuguese). (Legal title: Saint Francis Xavier's Church). Rev. Msgr. John E. Tavares; Revs. Thomas J. Ferland; Jay A. Finelli.
Res., 81 N. Carpenter St., 02914. Tel: 401-434-1878; Fax: 401-408-1950.
Catechesis/Religious Programs—Tel: 401-434-3153; 434-9421.
Students 936.

2—St. Martha. (Legal title: St. Martha's Church Corporation, East Providence). Revs. Jude P. McGeough; Normand J. Demers.
Res., 2595 Pawtucket Ave., 02914. Tel: 401-434-4060.
Catechesis/Religious Programs—Tel: 401-434-7030.
Students 350.

3—Our Lady of Loreto, (Italian). (Legal title: Church of Our Lady of Loreto, East Providence). Rev. Stanley T. Nakowicz.
Res., 346 Waterman Ave., 02914. Tel: 401-434-3535.

4—Sacred Heart. (Legal title: Church of the Sacred Heart). Revs. Peter S. DiTullio, S.C.; Fortunato Turati, S.C.
Res., 118 Taunton Ave., 02914. Tel: 401-434-0326; Fax: 401-434-7285.
School—56 Purchase St., 02914. Tel: 401-434-1080.
Sisters 4; Lay Teachers 8; Students 192.
Nursery-Day Care—101 Taunton Ave., 02914. Tel: 401-434-2462.
Staff 8; Children 90.
Catechesis/Religious Programs—Students 116.

Foster, Providence Co., St. Paul the Apostle. (Legal title: St. Paul's Church Corporation, Foster). Rev. Paul A. Charland.
Res., 116A Danielson Pike, 02825-1421. Tel: 401-647-3664.
Catechesis/Religious Programs—Students 305.

Georgiaville, Providence Co., St. Michael's. (Legal title: St. Michael's Church, Georgiaville, Rhode Island). Revs. Richard A. Valentine; Raymond J. Ferrick. In res., Rev. Edward H. Flannery.
Res., 80 Farnum Pike, 02917. Tel: 401-231-5119; Fax: 401-231-0523.

Catechesis/Religious Programs—Tel: 401-231-1340.
Students 517.

Greenville, Providence Co., St. Philip's. (Legal title: St. Philip's Church Greenville Rhode Island). Revs. Gerald E. Beirne; Ronald L. Simoneau; Robert E. Lacombe; Deacons Harris J. Gederman; Carlo J. Sabetti.
Res., 622 Putnam Ave., 02828-1403. Tel: 401-949-1500; Fax: 401-949-3504.
School—618 Putnam Ave., 02828. Tel: 401-949-1130.
Sisters of Mercy of the Americas 1; Lay Teachers 15; Students 245.
Catechesis/Religious Programs—Tel: 401-949-0330. Jean Cedor, D.R.E.
Students 946.

Harrisville, Providence Co., St. Patrick's. (Legal title: St. Patrick's Church, Burrillville, Rhode Island). Rev. Bernard M. O'Reilly, M.A., Ph.D., D.Min.
Res., 45 Main St., 02830. Tel: 401-568-5600. [CEM]
Catechesis/Religious Programs—Tel: 401-568-5580.
Students 175.
Mission—Glendale, St. Louis Chapel.

Hope Valley, Washington Co., St. Joseph's. (Legal title: Saint Joseph's Church, Hope Valley). Rev. Michael J. Leckie.
Res., P.O. Box 388, 1105 Main St., 02832. Tel: 401-539-8311.
Catechesis/Religious Programs—Tel: 401-539-8312.
Students 297.

Jamestown, Newport Co., St. Mark. (Legal title: Saint Mark Church of Jamestown). Rev. William J. O'Neill.
Res., 60 Narragansett Ave., 02835. Tel: 401-423-1421. [CEM]
Catechesis/Religious Programs—Tel: 401-423-1518.
Students 302.

Johnston, Providence Co.,

1—St. Brigid. (Legal title: Saint Brigid's Church of Johnston). Rev. James L. Kelleher.
Res., 1231 Plainfield, 02919. Tel: 401-944-2232.
Catechesis/Religious Programs—Students 170.

2—Our Lady of Grace, (Italian). (Legal title: Church of Our Lady of Grace). Rev. Raymond B. Bastia. In res., Rev. Ronald P. Simeone.
Res., 4 Lafayette St., 02919. Tel: 401-231-2220; Fax: 401-231-3905.
Catechesis/Religious Programs—Tel: 401-231-8959; Fax: 401-231-8959.
Students 237.

3—St. Robert Bellarmine. (Legal title: St. Robert Bellarmine Church Corporation, Johnston). Rev. John G. LaPointe.
Res., 1804 Atwood Ave., 02919-3215. Tel: 401-232-5600.
Catechesis/Religious Programs—Students 480.

4—St. Rocco, (Italian). (Legal title: Saint Rocco Church of Johnston). Revs. Alfred P. Almonte, C.S.; Settimo Basso, C.S.; John A. Corrao, C.S.; Deacon Robert P. Troia. In res., Rev. Hector Sartori, C.S.
Res., 927 Atwood Ave., 02919. Tel: 401-942-5203; Fax: 401-464-6422.
School—931 Atwood Ave., 02919. Tel: 401-944-2993; Fax: 401-944-3019. Sr. Mary Carol Gentile, A.S.C.J., Prin.
Apostles of the Sacred Heart of Jesus 4; Lay Teachers 18; Students 460.
Catechesis/Religious Programs—Tel: 401-944-6040.
Students 350.

Kingston, Washington Co., Christ the King. (Legal title: Christ the King Church Corporation, Kingston). Rev. Joseph D. Creedon.
Res., 180 Old North Rd., 02881. Tel: 401-783-7459; Fax: 401-789-3671.
Catechesis/Religious Programs—Tel: 401-789-0417.
Students 767.

Lincoln, Providence Co., St. Jude. (Legal title: St. Jude's Church, Lincoln). Revs. George P. Behan; Francis W. O'Hara.
Res., 301 Front St., 02865. Tel: 401-725-8140.
Catechesis/Religious Programs—Tel: 401-725-8120. Mrs. Lorraine Marot-Fournier, D.R.E.
Students 689.

Little Compton, Newport Co., St. Catherine of Siena. (Legal title: St. Catherine's Church Corporation, Little Compton). Rev. Gerald W. Hussey.
Res., 74 Simmons Rd., P.O. Box 208, 02837-0208. Tel: 401-635-4420; Fax: 401-635-2214. [CEM]

Manville, Providence Co., St. James. (Legal title: Saint James Church of Manville, Rhode Island). Rev. Richard P. Desaulniers; Deacon Gregory Horton.
Res., 33 Division St., Box 60, 02838. Tel: 401-766-1558; Fax: 401-766-1561. [CEM]
Catechesis/Religious Programs—57 Division St., 02838. Tel: 401-769-2676; Fax: 401-766-1516.
Students 260.

Mapleville, Providence Co., Our Lady of Good Help. (Legal title: Eglise de Notre Dame de Bonsecours). Rev. Timothy J. Lemlin; Deacon Richard J. Lapierre.
Res., 1063 Victory Hwy., Box 158, 02839. Tel: 401-568-5272; Fax: 401-568-5351.
Catechesis/Religious Programs—Mrs. Patricia Ducharme, D.R.E.
Students 317.

Middletown, Newport Co., St. Lucy's. (Legal title: Saint Lucy's Church Corp.). Rev. Eugene J. McKenna.
Res., 909 W. Main Rd., 02842-6351. Tel: 401-847-6153.
Catechesis/Religious Programs—D.R.E.: Sr. Mary T. Burns, C.P.; Sr. Rosemary Burnham, R.S.M.; Sr. Assunta Riley, R.S.M.
Students 548.

Misquamicut, Washington Co., Church of St. Clare. (Legal title: Saint Clare's Church Corporation, Misquamicut). Rev. Edmund H. Fitzgerald.
Res., 4 Saint Clare Way, 02891. Tel: 401-348-8765.
Catechesis/Religious Programs—Tel: 401-596-1838.
Students 195.

Narragansett, Washington Co., St. Thomas More. (Legal title: St. Thomas More Church, Narragansett Pier, Rhode Island). Rev. Ralph R. Hogan; Deacon Paul J. Sullivan.
Res., 53 Rockland St., 02882. Tel: 401-789-7682.
Catechesis/Religious Programs—Tel: 401-783-2113.
Students 285.
Chapel—Bonnet Shores, St. Veronica Summer Chapel.

Nasonville, Providence Co., St. Theresa of the Child Jesus. (Legal title: Church of Saint Teresa of the Child Jesus, Nasonville). Rev. John P. Dery.
Res., 35 Dion Dr., Harrisville, 02830. Tel: 401-568-8280. [CEM]
Catechesis/Religious Programs—Tel: 401-567-0705.
Students 200.

Newport, Newport Co.,

1—St. Augustin's. Unassigned. (Legal title: Saint Augustin's Church of Newport).
Res., 2 Eastnor Rd., 02840. Tel: 401-847-0518.
Catechesis/Religious Programs—Students 143.

2—Jesus Saviour, (Portuguese). (Legal title: Church of Jesus-Saviour, Newport). Rev. John D. Broderick.
Res., One Vernon Ave., 02840. Tel: 401-847-1267.

3—St. Joseph's. (Legal title: Saint Joseph's Church of Newport, Rhode Island). Rev. John J. Lavin. In res., Rev. Francis A. O'Loughlin.
Res., 5 Mann Ave., 02840. Tel: 401-847-0065; Fax: 401-849-2195.
Catechesis/Religious Programs—Tel: 401-847-9248; Fax: 401-849-2195.
Students 330.

4—St. Mary's. (Legal title: St. Mary's, Newport, Rhode Island). Rev. George B. McCarthy.
Res., 12 William St., P.O. Box 547, 02840. Tel: 401-847-0475; Fax: 401-845-9497. [CEM]
Catechesis/Religious Programs—Tel: 401-846-6057.
Students 237.

North Kingstown, Washington Co., St. Francis De Sales. (Legal title: St. Francis de Sales Church Corporation, North Kingstown). Revs. Nicholas P. Smith; Douglas Grant.
Res., 381 School St., 02852. Tel: 401-884-2105; Fax: 401-885-4315.
Catechesis/Religious Programs—Tel: 401-885-3639. D.R.E.: Cathleen Dowd; Sara Kirtlink.
Students 985.

North Providence, Providence Co.,

1—St. Anthony's, (Italian). (Legal title: Saint Anthony's Church Corporation, North Providence). Revs. Edward S. Cardente; C. Brian Lagasse.
Res., 5 Gibbs St., 02904. Tel: 401-353-3120; Fax: 401-353-5126.
Catechesis/Religious Programs—Tel: 401-353-5125. Maryann Pallotta, D.R.E.
Students 540.

2—St. Lawrence's. (Legal title: Saint Lawrence Church of Centredale). Rev. Farrell E. McLaughlin. In res., Rev. Peter G. Young.
Res., 624 Woonasquatucket Ave., 02911-1652. Tel: 401-231-9126; Fax: 401-231-7425.
Catechesis/Religious Programs—Tel: 401-231-5255.
Students 265.

3—Mary, Mother of Mankind. (Legal title: Mary, Mother of Mankind Church Corporation, North Providence). Rev. Edward J. McGovern.
Res., 25 Fourth St., 02911. Tel: 401-231-3542.
Catechesis/Religious Programs—Students 335.

4—Presentation of the Blessed Virgin Mary, (Marieville). (Legal title: Church of the Presentation of the Blessed Virgin Mary). Rev. Louis T. Natalizia. In res., Rev. John W. O'Brien; Deacon Louis A. Vani.
Res., 1081 Mineral Spring Ave., 02904. Tel: 401-722-7140; Fax: 401-722-6617.
Catechesis/Religious Programs—Tel: 401-722-8824.
Students 267.

North Scituate, Providence Co., St. Joseph's. (Legal title: Saint Joseph's Church Corporation, North Scituate). Rev. Francis J. Keefe.
Res., Danielson Pk., P.O. Box 236, 02857. Tel: 401-647-2255; Fax: 401-647-2968.
Catechesis/Religious Programs—Tel: 401-647-2650.
Students 476.

North Tiverton, Newport Co., Holy Ghost. (Legal title: Church of the Holy Ghost, North Tiverton). Rev. Charles P. Quinn; Deacon Raymond E. Levesque.
Res., 311 Hooper St., 02878. Tel: 401-624-8131; Fax: 401-625-5156.
Catechesis/Religious Programs—Tel: 401-624-3664.
Students 410.

Pascoag, Providence Co., St. Joseph's. (Legal title: Saint Joseph's Roman Catholic Church of Pascoag). Rev. Clifford J. Cabral.
Res., 183 Sayles Ave., P.O. Box 188, 02859. Tel: 401-568-2411.
Catechesis/Religious Programs—Students 220.

Pawtucket, Providence Co.,

1—St. Anthony's, (Portuguese). (Legal title: Saint Anthony's Church Corporation, Pawtucket). Rev. John C. Baker; Deacon Manuel Martins.
Res., 32 Lawn Ave., 02860. Tel: 401-723-9138.
Catechesis/Religious Programs—Students 270.

2—St. Cecilia's, (French). (Legal title: Saint Cecilia's Church Corporation). Revs. Roger L. Bacon; Francis C. Santilli.
Res., 1253 Newport Ave., 02861. Tel: 401-722-1101.
School—755 Central Ave., 02861. Tel: 401-723-9463.
Sisters 6; Lay Teachers 11; Students 211.

3—St. Edward's. (Legal title: St. Edward's Church of Pawtucket). Rev. James R. Collins; Deacon Raymond E. Batalon.
Res., 58 Hancock St., 02860. Tel: 401-725-7036.
Catechesis/Religious Programs—61 Hope St., 02860. Tel: 401-725-7831.
Students 187.

4—Immaculate Heart of Mary, (Cape Verdean). (An operation of Church of St. Maron in Providence). Rev. Joaquim P. Francisco, C.S.Sp., Admin.
Res., 35 Clay St., Central Falls, 02863. Tel: 401-725-1126.
Church—291 High St., 02860.
Catechesis/Religious Programs—Students 65.

5—St. John the Baptist, (French). (Legal title: The Church of St. John the Baptist of Pawtucket R.I.). Revs. Bernard C. Lavin; Jose Omar Zuluaga (Colombia); Deacon Raymond M. Lagesse.
Res., 69 Quincy Ave., 02860. Tel: 401-722-9054.

6—St. Joseph's. (Legal title: St. Joseph's Church). Rev. Charles B. McDermott. In res., Rev. John J. McElroy, Pastor Emeritus.
Res., 193 Walcott St., 02860. Tel: 401-724-9190.
Catechesis/Religious Programs—Students 184.

7—St. Leo's. (Legal title: Church of Saint Leo the Great in Pawtucket). Revs. John A. Kiley; Christopher M. Davenport.
Res., 697 Central Ave., 02861. Tel: 401-722-1220; Fax: 401-722-1220.
School—723 Central Ave., 02861. Tel: 401-725-3620. Sr. Marie Lorraine Halpin, R.S.M., Prin.
Sisters 7; Lay Teachers 10; Students 286.
Catechesis/Religious Programs—Tel: 401-722-0744. Mrs. Linda Prew, D.R.E.
Students 275.

8—St. Maria Goretti. (Legal title: St. Maria Goretti Church Corporation, Pawtucket). Rev. Kenneth J. Suibielski; Deacon Lucien Ouellette.
Res., 165 Power Rd., 02860. Tel: 401-725-4355; Fax: 401-729-5711.
Catechesis/Religious Programs—Tel: 401-729-5713.
Students 264.

9—St. Mary's. (Legal title: The Church of the Immaculate Conception of Pawtucket, Rhode Island). Revs. John E. Watterson; Albert A. Kenney; Deacon C. Patrick Sheehy.
Res., 103 Pine St., P.O. Box 518, 02862. Tel: 401-722-5425; Fax: 401-729-0341. [CEM]
School—(Grades PreK-8) 167 George St., 02862. Tel: 401-723-6695. Mrs. Patricia Baumgartel, Prin.

Sisters 1; Lay Teachers 10; Students 193.

10—OUR LADY OF CONSOLATION, (French). (Legal title: Church of Our Lady of Consolation Rhode Island). Rev. Normand L. Courtemanche. In res., Rev. Robert D. Ethier.
Res., 10 Webster St., 02860. Tel: 401-722-2804.
School—Tel: 401-728-4450. Mrs. Marie-Berthe Tanguay, Prin.
Sisters 3; Lay Teachers 8; Students 136.
Catechesis/Religious Programs—Tel: 401-725-2409.
Students 90.

11—SACRED HEART. (Legal title: The Church of the Sacred Heart of Jesus of Pawtucket, Rhode Island). Revs. Richard C. Maynard; William H. Tanguay, Dir., Hmong Apostolate, Tel: 401-723-5480.
Res., 38 Park St., 02860. Tel: 401-722-3226.
Catechesis/Religious Programs—Tel: 401-723-6777.
Students 250.

12—ST. TERESA. (Legal title: Church of Saint Teresa of the Child Jesus, Pawtucket, Rhode Island). Revs. Joseph P. Hynes; Charles H. Galligan; Hugh O'Rourke, S.S.C.
Res., 358 Newport Ave., 02861. Tel: 401-722-4470; Fax: 401-722-2958.
School—150 Wood Haven Rd., 02861. Tel: 401-726-1414. Sr. Barbara Foley, R.S.M., Coord.; Sr. Maureen Sadlier, R.S.M., Prin.
Sisters of Mercy of the Americas 2; Lay Teachers 16; Students 315.
Catechesis/Religious Programs—Students 296.

Point Judith, Washington Co., St. Mary, Star of the Sea. (Legal title: St. Mary, Star of the Sea Church Corporation, Point Judith). Revs. Donald J. Bouressa; William F. Sears.
Res., 52 Coffey Ave., Narragansett, 02882. Tel: 401-783-4449; Fax: 401-783-0986.
Catechesis/Religious Programs—Tel: 401-789-7308; Fax: 401-783-0986.
Students 385.

Portsmouth, Newport Co., St. Anthony's. (Legal title: Saint Anthony's Church of Portsmouth). Rev. Edward D. Johnson.
Res., P.O. Box 570, 2836 E. Main Rd., 02871. Tel: 401-683-0089.

St. Barnabas. (Legal title: St. Barnabas Church Corporation, Portsmouth). Rev. Kevin J. Brassil.
Res., 1697 E. Main Rd., 02871. Tel: 401-683-1343; Fax: 401-683-5056.
Catechesis/Religious Programs—Tel: 401-683-3147.
Students 420.

Riverside, Providence Co., St. Brendan. (Legal title: St. Brendan's Church). Revs. John E. Unsworth; Robert L. Bailey; Marcel L. Taillon.
Res., 60 Turner Ave., 02915. Tel: 401-433-2600; Fax: 401-433-1962.
School—55 Turner Ave., 02915. Tel: 401-433-1290.
Lay Teachers 14; Students 232.
Catechesis/Religious Programs—Tel: 401-433-2680. John D. Sousa, D.R.E.
Students 892.

Rumford, Providence Co., St. Margaret. (Legal title: Saint Margaret's Church Corporation, East Providence Rhode Island). Rev. Thomas L. Keenan.
Res., 1098 Pawtucket Ave., 02916. Tel: 401-438-3230; Fax: 401-438-4221.
School—42 Bishop Ave., 02916. Tel: 401-434-2338; Fax: 401-431-0266. Mr. Felipe M. Felipe, Prin.
Lay Teachers 25; Students 360.
Catechesis/Religious Programs—Tel: 401-336-9733.
Students 430.

Slatersville, Providence Co., St. John the Evangelist. (Legal title: St. John's Church Society, Rhode Island). Revs. Raymond A. Tetreault; Paul T. Hurley.
Res., 63 Church St., 02876. Tel: 401-762-0946; Fax: 401-762-0944. [CEM]
Catechesis/Religious Programs—Tel: 401-762-0966. Mrs. Sara D. Hickey, D.R.E.
Students 566.

Tiverton, Newport Co., St. Christopher. (Legal title: Saint Christopher's Church of Tiverton). Rev. Francis P. Kanda.
Res., 1660 Main Rd., 02878. Tel: 401-624-6644.
Catechesis/Religious Programs—Students 193.

St. Madeleine. (Legal title: Saint Madeleine's Church Corporation of Tiverton). Rev. Joseph F. McDonough, C.S.Sp. In res., Rev. Joseph F. McNamara, C.S.Sp.
Res., 35 Lake Rd., 02878. Tel: 401-624-4226.
Catechesis/Religious Programs—Students 148.

St. Theresa's. (Legal title: St. Theresa's Parish Corporation, Tiverton). Rev. Bertrand N. Richman.
Res., 265 Stafford Rd., 02878. Tel: 401-624-8746.

Valley Falls, Providence Co., St. Patrick. (Legal title: St. Patrick's Church Corporation, Valley Falls, Rhode Island). Revs. David T. Perry; Joseph E. Davis.
Res., 301 Broad St., Cumberland, 02864. Tel: 401-725-0344; 725-7802. [CEM]
Catechesis/Religious Programs—Tel: 401-725-0344.
Students 265.

Our Lady of Fatima (Portuguese). (Legal title: Church of Our Lady of Fatima, Valley Falls). Rev. Victor M. Vieira.
Res., Fatima Dr., Cumberland, 02864. Tel: 401-723-6719; Fax: 401-723-1698.
Catechesis/Religious Programs—Tel: 401-724-3454.
Students 481.

Wakefield, Washington Co., St. Francis. (Legal title: Saint Francis Church). Rev. Robert A. Allaire.
Mailing Address: c/o St. Francis Church, P.O. Box 330, 02880. Tel: 401-783-4411.
Res., 114 High St., P.O. Box 330, 02880. Tel: 401-783-4411. [CEM]
Catechesis/Religious Programs—Tel: 401-789-1370.
Students 498.
Mission—Matunuck, St. Romuald. 61 Atlantic Ave.

Warren, Bristol Co.,

1—ST. ALEXANDER, (Italian). (Legal title: Saint Alexander's Church Corporation, Warren). Rev. David W. Masello, Admin.
Res., 221 Main St., 02885. Tel: 401-245-6369. [CEM]
Catechesis/Religious Programs—Tel: 401-245-4332.
Students 55.

2—ST. CASIMIR, (Polish). (Legal title: Saint Casimir's Church of Warren). Rev. Matthew J. Strumski.
Res., 228 Child St., 02885-9998. Tel: 401-245-4422.

3—ST. JEAN BAPTISTE, (French). (Legal title: The Church of Saint Jean Baptiste of Warren Rhode Island). Rev. Emile A. Robert.
Res., 328 Main St., 02885. Tel: 401-245-8392. [CEM]
Catechesis/Religious Programs—Students 275.

4—ST. MARY OF THE BAY. (Legal title: Church of Saint Mary of the Bay). Revs. Bertrand L. Theroux; Timothy J. Gorton.
Res., 645 Main St., 02885. Tel: 401-245-7000. [CEM]
Catechesis/Religious Programs—Tel: 401-245-2644.
Students 413.
Convent—430R Water St., 02885. Tel: 401-245-8629. Sisters of Mercy of the Americas

5—ST. THOMAS THE APOSTLE, (Portuguese). (Legal title: Saint Thomas the Apostle Church Corporation). Rev. Joel D. Oliveira (BO) Admin.
Res., 500 Metacom Ave., 02885. Tel: 401-245-4469.
Catechesis/Religious Programs—Tel: 401-245-4488.
Students 163.

Warwick, Kent Co.,

1—ST. BENEDICT, (Conimicut). (Legal title: St. Benedict's Church, Conimicut). Paul R. Grenon.
Res., 135 Beach Ave., P.O. Box 9485, 02889. Tel: 401-737-9492; Fax: 401-739-0974.
Catechesis/Religious Programs—70 Transit St., 02889. Tel: 401-738-2545.
Students 270.

2—ST. CATHERINE, (Apponaug). (Legal title: Saint Catherine's Roman Catholic Church of Warwick, Rhode Island). Rev. Roger G. Champigny; Deacon John F. Baker.
Res., 3252 Post Rd., 02886. Tel: 401-737-4455.
Catechesis/Religious Programs—Tel: 401-737-6234. D.R.E.: Margaret Boylan; Martha Capaldi.
Students 274.

3—ST. CLEMENT'S. (Legal title: St. Clement Church Corporation, Warwick). Rev. Daniel J. Gray.
Res., 111 Long St., 02886. Tel: 401-739-7213; 739-7591; Fax: 401-739-9668.
Catechesis/Religious Programs—Tel: 401-737-1330.
Students 202.

4—ST. FRANCIS OF ASSISI, (Hillsgrove). (Legal title: Saint Francis Church Corporation, Hillsgrove). Rev. Henry J. Bodah; Deacon Kevin P. Masse.
Res., 596 Jefferson Blvd., 02886. Tel: 401-737-5191. [JC]
School—610 Jefferson Blvd., 02886. Tel: 401-737-2721. Mrs. Judith A. Costa, Prin.
Sisters of St. Joseph 1; Lay Teachers 11; Students 157.
Convent—639 Jefferson Blvd., 02886. Tel: 401-737-6014.

5—ST. GREGORY THE GREAT. (Legal title: St. Gregory the Great Church Corporation, Warwick). Revs. John C. Halloran; Roger M. Fortin; Deacons Robert V. Stone; Noel Edsall.
Res., 41 Sandro Dr., 02886. Tel: 401-884-1666; Fax: 401-884-1666.
Catechesis/Religious Programs—Tel: 401-884-0797.
Students 462.

6—ST. KEVIN. (Legal title: St. Kevin's Church Corporation, Warwick). Revs. Robert F. Hawkins; Francis W. O'Hara.
Res., 333 Sandy Ln., 02889. Tel: 401-737-2638.
School—39 Cathedral Rd., 02889.
Sisters of Notre Dame de Namur 2; Lay Teachers 18; Students 393.
Catechesis/Religious Programs—Carole Flynn, D.R.E.
Students 434.

7—ST. PETER'S, (Pawtuxet). (Legal title: St. Peter's Church, Warwick, Rhode Island). Revs. Peter M. Cavanaugh; Paul J. DaPonte. In res., Rev. Msgr. John F. Cox, Pastor Emeritus.
Res., 350 Fair St., 02888. Tel: 401-467-4895; Fax: 401-785-9282.
School—Sisters of Mercy of the Americas 2; Lay Teachers 18; Students 294. Co-Principals: Sr. Mary Angelus, R.S.M.; Sr. Kathleen Farley, R.S.M.
Catechesis/Religious Programs—120 Mayfair Rd., 02888. Tel: 401-781-9243.
Students 271.

8—ST. RITA'S, (Oakland Beach). (Legal title: Saint Rita's Church Corporation, Oakland Beach). Rev. Bertil J. Anderson.
Res., 722 Oakland Beach Ave., 02886. Tel: 401-738-1800.

9—ST. ROSE OF LIMA, (Greenwood). (Legal title: Saint Rose's Church Corporation, Warwick). Rev. Robert L. Marciano.
Res., 171 Inman Ave., 02886. Tel: 401-739-0212; Fax: 401-732-4144.
School—200 Brentwood Ave., 02886. Tel: 401-739-6937.
Lay Teachers 10; Students 240.
Catechesis/Religious Programs—Tel: 401-737-4632; Fax: 401-737-4632.
Students 234.

10—ST. TIMOTHY'S, (Hoxsie). (Legal title: Saint Timothy's Church Corporation, Warwick). Revs. James J. Hamilton, Admin.; David E. Green.
Res., 1799 Warwick Ave., 02889. Tel: 401-739-9552; Fax: 401-739-9553.
Catechesis/Religious Programs—101 Lake Shore Dr., 02889. Tel: 401-738-9079.
Students 355.

11—ST. WILLIAM'S, (Norwood). (Legal title: Saint William's Church Corporation, Norwood). Rev. Randolph G. Chew; Deacon Thomas P. O'Hara.
Res., 200 Pettaconsett Ave., 02888. Tel: 401-781-7226; Fax: 401-781-4177.
Catechesis/Religious Programs—Tel: 401-781-0343; Fax: 401-781-4177.
Students 325.

Westerly, Washington Co., Immaculate Conception. (Legal title: Church of the Immaculate Conception of Westerly, Rhode Island). Revs. Wilfrid G. Gregoire; Douglas S. Sweet.
Res., 111 High St., 02891. Tel: 401-596-2130.
Catechesis/Religious Programs—Tel: 401-596-0900. Mrs. Sylvia M. Gulla, D.R.E.
Students 495.

St. Pius X. (Legal title: St. Pius X Parish Corporation, Westerly). Revs. Lawrence E. Toole; Raymond N. Suriani.
Res., 44 Elm St., 02891. Tel: 401-596-2535.
School—32 Elm St., 02891. Tel: 401-596-5735.
Lay Teachers 11; Students 200.
Catechesis/Religious Programs—Students 206.

West Warwick, Kent Co.,

1—CHRIST THE KING, (Centreville) (French). (Legal title: Church of Christ the King, West Warwick). Rev. George L. Allard. In res., Rev. David F. Ricard, Chap., Kent County Memorial Hospital, Warwick.
Res., 120 Legris Ave., 02893. Tel: 401-821-9228. [JC]
Catechesis/Religious Programs—130 Legris Ave., 02893. Tel: 401-823-3443. D.R.E.: Mrs. Janice Rousselle; Mrs. Laurie Masse.
Students 221.

2—OUR LADY OF GOOD COUNSEL, (French). (Legal title: Church of Our Lady of Good Counsel, Warwick RI). Rev. Paul R. Lemoi.
Res., 60 Pleasant St., 02893. Tel: 401-821-6428. [CEM]
Catechesis/Religious Programs—Tel: 401-822-1869.
Students 135.

3—SACRED HEART CHURCH, (Natick) (Italian). (Legal title: Church of the Sacred Heart, Natick RI). Rev. Robert J. Giardina.
Res., 820 Providence St., 02893. Tel: 401-821-4184; Fax: 401-828-8838.
Catechesis/Religious Programs—Tel: 401-828-5202.

Students 200.

4—ST. ANTHONY, (Riverpoint) (Portuguese). (Legal title: Saint Anthony's Church Corporation, River Point). Rev. Reinaldo M. Cardoso.
Res., 10 Sunset Ave., 02893. Tel: 401-821-8342.
Catechesis/Religious Programs—Students 164.

5—ST. JAMES, (Arctic). (Legal title: Saint James Church of Arctic). Revs. James P. Hynes; Kevin R. Fisette.
Res., 1270 Main St., P.O. Box 1346, 02893. Tel: 401-821-7323; Fax: 401-821-7323.
Catechesis/Religious Programs—Tel: 401-828-5059.
Students 165.

6—ST. JOHN'S, (Arctic) (French). (Legal title: St. John the Baptist Church of Centreville, Rhode Island). Revs. Alphonse O. Lethiez (Haiti); Barry M. Meehan.
Res., 20 Washington St., P.O. Box 111, 02893. Tel: 401-821-7661; Fax: 401-826-7274. [CEM]
School—St. John the Baptist School, 17 St. John St., 02893. Tel: 401-821-5285; Fax: 401-826-2950. Sr. Claudette Brunelle, P.M., Prin.; Sr. Claire Marie, P.M., Supr.
Sisters of the Presentation of Mary 5; Lay Teachers 12; Students 212.
Catechesis/Religious Programs—Students 141.

7—ST. JOSEPH'S, (Natick). (Legal title: St. Joseph's Church, Natick RI). Rev. Charles H. Downing; Deacons Laurence O. Gagnon; Robert L. Gallo, Hispanic Ministry.
Res., 854 Providence St., 02893-1140. Tel: 401-821-4072.
School—(Grades PreK-8) Wakefield St., 02893. Tel: 401-821-3450.
Religious 1; Deacons 1; Lay Teachers 20; Students 268.
Catechesis/Religious Programs—Students 192.

8—ST. MARY, (Crompton). (Legal title: St. Mary's Church, Crompton Rhode Island). Rev. Paul F. Reynolds.
Res., 70 Church St., 02893. Tel: 401-821-5555; 822-1006. [CEM]
Catechesis/Religious Programs—Tel: 401-828-8756.
Students 239.

9—SS. PETER AND PAUL. (Legal title: SS. Peter and Paul's Church, Phoenixville, Rhode Island). Rev. Richard A. Bucci, Admin.
Res., 48 Highland St., 02893. Tel: 401-821-2198. [CEM]
Catechesis/Religious Programs—Students 80.

Wickford, Washington Co., St. Bernard's. (Legal title: St. Bernard's Roman Catholic Church of Wickford, Rhode Island). Rev. Gerard O. Sabourin.
Office: 415 Tower Hill Rd., 02852. Tel: 401-295-0387.
Catechesis/Religious Programs—Tel: 401-295-5235. D.R.E. Sr. Roberta Giampaoli; Mrs. Carol Maddock; Mrs. Michelle Jacomb.
Students 405.
Mission—Exeter, Washington Co., Blessed Kateri Tekakwitha, 84 Exeter Rd., Exeter, 02822. Tel: 401-295-0234.

Woonsocket, Providence Co.,

1—ST. AGATHA'S. (Legal title: Saint Agatha's Church Corporation, Woonsocket). Revs. John C. Allard; Gerard J. Caron; Deacon Eugene Garceau. In res., Rev. Joseph P. Heaney.
Res., 34 Joffre Ave., 02895. Tel: 401-767-2950.
Catechesis/Religious Programs—Students 122.

2—ST. ALOYSIUS, (French). (Legal title: Saint Aloysius Church of Woonsocket). Rev. Frederic D. Dean.
Res., 323 Rathbun St., 02895. Tel: 401-762-1100.

3—ST. ANN'S, (French). (Legal title: St. Ann's Church Corporation of Woonsocket RI). Revs. Roger A. Houle; Edward L. Pieroni.
Res., 82 Cumberland St., 02895. Tel: 401-766-0370; Fax: 401-765-6321. [JC]
Catechesis/Religious Programs—Tel: 401-766-5771.
Students 200.
Convent—120 Gaulin Ave., 02895. Tel: 401-766-2485. Sr. Adrienne Gendron, P.M., Supr.
Sisters of the Presentation of Mary 4.

4—ST. ANTHONY'S, (Italian). (Legal title: Saint Anthony's Church, Woonsocket RI). Rev. Douglas J. Spina. In res., Rev. Msgr. George L. Frappier.
Res., 128 Greene St., 02895. Tel: 401-766-2640.
Catechesis/Religious Programs—Students 75.

5—ST. CHARLES. (Legal title: St. Charles Borromeo's Church, Woonsocket RI). Rev. D. Bryan Finerty.
Res., 190 N. Main St., 02895. Tel: 401-766-0176. [CEM]
Catechesis/Religious Programs—Students 74.

6—HOLY FAMILY, (French). (Legal title: Church of the Holy Family). Revs. Edward G. St. Godard; James H. Duhaime.
Res., 414 S. Main St., 02895. Tel: 401-762-0830.
Catechesis/Religious Programs—Tel: 401-762-3441.
Students 260.

7—ST. JOSEPH'S. (Legal title: Saint Joseph's Church, Woonsocket). Revs. Lionel A. Blain; Maurice L. Brindamour.
Res., 1200 Mendon Rd., 02895-3999. Tel: 401-766-0626.
Catechesis/Religious Programs—1210 Mendon Rd., 02895. Tel: 401-766-8233. Jeannine Allard, D.R.E.
Students 473.
Station—Woonsocket Health Center, Tel: 401-765-2100.

8—OUR LADY OF VICTORIES, (French). (Legal title: Church of Notre Dame des Victoires). Revs. Roger A. Houle, Admin.; Edward L. Pieroni.
Res., 170 Spring St., 02895. Tel: 401-762-0333.
Catechesis/Religious Programs—Students 73.

9—OUR LADY, QUEEN OF MARTYRS. (Legal title: Our Lady, Queen of Martyrs Church Corporation, Woonsocket). Revs. Joseph D. Schenick; Barry J. Gamache.
Res., 1409 Park Ave., 02895-6597. Tel: 401-762-5117; Fax: 401-765-8875.
Catechesis/Religious Programs—Tel: 401-767-2576.
Students 391.

10—PRECIOUS BLOOD, (French). (Legal title: The Church of the Precious Blood of Woonsocket, Rhode Island). Revs. John C. Allard, Admin.; Gerard J. Caron. In res., Revs. Henri D. Morin; Albert H. Brindamour.
Res., 94 Carrington Ave., 02895. Tel: 401-762-0326; 883-6600. [CEM]

11—SACRED HEART. (Legal title: Church of the Sacred Heart Woonsocket RI). Rev. Dennis J. Kieton, Admin.; Deacon Armand R. Brissette, Jr.
Res., 415 Olo St., 02895. Tel: 401-766-3150; Fax: 401-766-6864.
Catechesis/Religious Programs—Tel: 401-766-3151.
Students 104.

12—ST. STANISLAUS, (Polish). (Legal title: Saint Stanislaus Kostka Church of Woonsocket). Rev. Boguslaw T. Gibowski, Admin.
Res., 174 Harris Ave., 02895. Tel: 401-762-0021.

Chaplains of Public Institutions

PROVIDENCE. *Miriam Hospital,* 164 Summit Ave., 02906. Tel: 401-274-3700. Rev. Peter J. Gower, Res., 124 Hillside Ave., Pawtucket, 02860.
Rhode Island Hospital, 593 Eddy St., 02902. Tel: 401-277-4000. Rev. John J. Rainone, Res., 92 Hope St., 02906. Rev. John W. O'Brien, Res., 1081 Mineral Spring Ave. N., 02904. Rev. Jose Q. Dos Reis, Res., 2615 Warwick Ave., Warwick, 02889. Rev. Gerald G. Harbour; Sr. Perpetua Lester, R.S.M., Res., 367 Kenyon Ave., Pawtucket, 02861. Ms. Janice Hart, Chap.
Roger Williams Hospital. Pastoral care provided by local parishes. 825 Chalkstone Ave., 02908. Tel: 401-456-2000.
Summit Medical Center, 1085 N. Main St., 02906. Tel: 401-272-9600. Rev. Edward P. Doyle, O.P., Res., St. Thomas Aquinas Priory at Providence College, 02918. Tel: 401-856-1000.
Veterans Administration Hospital, Davis Park, 02908. Tel: 401-273-7100. Rev. Francis J. Crowley (BO).

CRANSTON. *Department of Corrections.* Sr. Theresa Foley, S.S.J., 9 Alma Ave., East Providence, 02916. Archdeacon George Yany, 111 Cross St., Central Falls, 02863. Sr. Agnes Bonville, R.S.M., 716 Brayton Ave., Somerset, MA 02726.
Rhode Island State Institutions, Eleanor Slater Hospital, 02893. Rev. Gerard Bernard, M.S.C., Res., 33 Andrews Ave., Apt. B, West Warwick, 02893. Tel: 401-826-0446. Rev. John E. Watterson, Res., 103 Pine St., P.O. Box 518, Pawtucket, 02862. Tel: 401-722-5425.

NEWPORT. *Newport Hospital.* Rev. Francis A. O'Loughlin, Res., 5 Mann Ave., 02840. Tel: 401-847-0065.

NORTH SMITHFIELD. *Landmark Medical Center, Fogarty Unit.* Pastoral care provided by local parishes.

PASCOAG. *Rhode Island-Zambarano State Hospital.* Vacant. Pastoral care provided by Office of Health Ministries. Wallum Lake, 02859.

PAWTUCKET. *Memorial Hospital of Rhode Island.* Pastoral care provided by local parishes.

WAKEFIELD. *South County Hospital.* Pastoral care provided by local parishes. 100 Kenyon Ave., 02880. Tel: 401-782-8000.

WARWICK. *Kent County Memorial Hospital.* Rev. David F. Ricard, Res., 120 Legris Ave., West Warwick, 02893.

WESTERLY. *The Westerly Hospital.* Pastoral care provided by local parishes. 25 Wells St., 02891. Tel: 401-596-6000.

WOONSOCKET. *Landmark Medical Center, Woonsocket Unit.* Pastoral care provided by local parishes.

On Duty Outside the Diocese:
Reverend Monsignors—
Theroux, Paul D., National Conference of Catholic Bishops, Washington, DC
Reverend Fathers—
Berthelette, Ernest H., Chap., U.S. Air Force
Bolton, Paul J., Chap., U.S. Army
Brodeur, Dennis A., 477 N. Lindbergh Blvd., St. Louis, MO 63141
Collins, Raymond F., Catholic University of America, Washington, DC
Darcy, John J., Edifice Deschatelets, 175 Main St., Ottawa, Ontario Canada K1S 1C3
Gallagher, William M., One Cathedral Sq., Providence, RI 02903-3695
Haberek, Jerome A., Chap., U.S. Army
Kelley, Edward J., Chap., U.S. Army
LaMontagne, Bernard L., St. Mary of Woods, IN 47876
Lynch, Cornelius B., Society of St. James
Montecalvo, Carlo F., Chap., U.S. Air Force
O'Neill, Thomas D., Diocese of Victoria
Pincince, Gerald P., 191 Hadley Rd., Sugar Hill, NH 03585
Prendiville, Edmond P., St. Paul Church, 9240 Damascus Rd., Damascus, MD 20872
Rochon, Robert A., St. Ann's Hospital, Fall River, MA

Absent on Leave:
Reverend Fathers—
Abruzzese, Joseph A.
Archambault, Paul A.
Blais, Robert L.
Carpentier, Robert A.
Desrosiers, Alfred A.
LaMountain, Michael V.
Lepire, Roland M.
Scagnelli, Peter J.

Retired:
Reverend Monsignors—
Brock, Edmund J., St. Antoine Residence, 400 Mendon Rd., North Smithfield, RI 02895
Carey, William J., P.O. Box 16, Jamestown, RI 02835
Cavallaro, Galliano J., 50 Park Row West #712, Providence, RI 02903
Cerrito, Albert J., 402 Elm Ave., Port Charlotte, FL 33952
Cox, John F., 350 Fair St., Warwick, RI 02888
Dunn, Louis W., St. John Vianney Residence, 493 Mt. Pleasant Ave., Providence, RI 02908
Dziob, Michael W., St. John Vianney Residence, 493 Mt. Pleasant Ave., Providence, RI 02908
Egan, Edward F., St. John Vianney Residence, 493 Mt. Pleasant Ave., Providence, RI 02908
Fagnant, Donat J., 2 Abbot St., Cumberland, RI 02864-8202
Ferland, Oscar R., 190 Usquepaugh Rd., West Kingston, RI 02892
Geoghegan, Arthur T., 1900 S. Ocean Ave., Ft. Lauderdale, FL 33316
Guilbault, Oscar A., 860 N. Quidnessett Rd., North Kingstown, RI 02852
Lloyd, Paul A., Jeanne Jugen Residence, 964 Main St., Pawtucket, RI 02860
Metsy, Norman G., 6467 Oak Shore Dr., Panama City, FL 32404
Murray, William F., P.O. Box 1366, Mashpee, MA 02649
Struck, John W., 7 Seawind Ter., Westerly, RI 02891
Sullivan, Arthur A., 35 Sweetfern Rd., Warwick, RI 02888
Reverend Fathers—
Beaulieu, Raymond, P.O. Box 433, Jamestown, RI 02835
Belhumeur, Roger E., 1650 Douglas Ave., North Providence, RI 02904
Besse, Joseph A., 70 Landmark Ave., Warwick, RI 02886
Boland, Edward F., St. John Vianney Residence, 493 Mt. Pleasant Ave., Providence, RI 02908
Borkowski, John A., 19 Helen Ave., Freehold, NJ 07728
Brindamour, Albert H., Precious Blood Rectory, 94 Carrington Ave., Woonsocket, RI 02895-4594
Carmone, Anthony F., P.O. Box 9177, Port Charlotte, FL 33949-9177
Carnevale, Thomas J., 2543 W. Main Rd., Portsmouth, RI 02871
Carty, John T., 43 Phillips Rd., East Greenwich, RI 02818-0472
Dailey, Ronald G., 182 Eldridge St., Cranston, RI 02910
Davey, John J., 2 Russo St., Providence, RI 02904
de Serpa, Roberto, Rua Recreio dos Artistas 46-10.D, 9700 Angra do Heroismo, Terceira, Azores
DeLellis, Francis V., 190 S. Weeden Rd., Wakefield, RI 02880

Deneault, Normand J., St. John Vianney Residence, 493 Mt. Pleasant Ave., Providence, RI 02908
Diogo, Louis M., 26 Meadow Rd., Swansea, MA 02777
Doucet, Ovila T., Jeanne Jugan Residence, 964 Main St., Pawtucket, RI 02860
Doyle, John V., 49 Sherwood Valley Ln., Coventry, RI 02816
Dyer, Raymond E., Mt. St. Rita Health Center, 15 Sumner Brown Rd., Cumberland, RI 02864
Ethier, Robert D., 10 Webster St., Pawtucket, RI 02860
Farrell, John F., Box 689, West Kingstown, RI 02892
Fioretti, Jerome, 309 Spring St., Newport, RI 02840
Freitas, Fernando P., 29 Bullocks Pt. Ave., Apt. 3A, Riverside, RI 02915-5341
Gagne, Rene E., St. John Vianney Residence, 493 Mt. Pleasant Ave., Providence, RI 02908
Gallagher, Joseph T., P.O. Box 80066, South Dartmouth, MA 02748
Gillen, Timothy L., St. Clare Home, 309 Spring St., Newport, RI 02840
Gorman, George F., St. John Vianney Residence, 493 Mt. Pleasant Ave., Providence, RI 02908
Hart, Thomas B., P.O. Box 921, Portsmouth, RI 02871
Hazebrouck, Maurice L., 41 Hazebrouck St., Cumberland, RI 02864
Heaney, Joseph P., St. Agatha Rectory, 34 Joffre Ave., Woonsucket, RI 02895
Horgan, Joseph E., 25 Leading St., Johnston, RI 02919
Hunt, Patrick J., 23 Willis Dr., Cumberland, RI 02964
Iacovacci, Nicholas J., St. Mary Rectory, 538 Broadway, Providence, RI 02909
King, Donald J., St. John Vianney Residence, 493 Mt. Pleasant Ave., Providence, RI 02908
Lacasse, Roger, St. Ann Rectory, 82 Cumberland St., Woonsocket, RI 02895
Lambert, Joseph J., St. John Vianney Residence, 493 Mt. Pleasant Ave., Providence, RI 02908
Marot, Roger L., Father Marot CYO Center, 53-77 Federal St., Woonsocket, RI 02895
Maynard, Leon C., St. John Vianney Residence, 493 Mt. Pleasant Ave., Providence, RI 02908
Maynard, Robert J., 1 St. Paul Pl., Cranston, RI 02905
McElroy, John J., 193 Walcott St., Pawtucket, RI 02860
Mendonsa, August F., 106 Allerton Ave., East Providence, RI 02914
Micarelli, Edmond C., 3589 LaAires Ct., Bldg. 107, Apt. C-2, Greenacres, FL 33463
Moniz, Hyacinth, 825 Wakefield St., Box 84, West Warwick, RI 02893
Morin, Henri D., 94 Carrington Ave., Woonsocket, RI 02895
Murphy, Joseph F., Putnam Pike, P.O. Box A, Chepachet, RI 02814
Murphy, William F., St. John Vianney Residence, 493 Mount Pleasant Ave., Providence, RI 02908
Narewski, Peter J., St. John Vianney Residence, 493 Mt. Pleasant Ave., Providence, RI 02908
Pyne, William F., St. Antoine Residence, 400 Mendon Rd., North Smithfield, RI 02896
Rafferty, Raymond J., St. James Well, Greenmore, County Louth, Ireland
Randall, Robert J., 2322 Oliver Hazzard Perry Hwy., Wakefield, RI 02880
Raspallo, Domenic, 38 Oaklawn Ave., Cranston, RI 02920
Robitaille, Henry J., 5 Costilla Lane, Spanish Lakes River Front, Port St. Lucie, FL 34952
Santurri, Joseph, Residenza Maria Marcella, Via della Vignaccia, 197 (Aurelio), 00163 Rome, Italy
Shanley, Joseph D., 167 Blackstone St., Woonsocket, RI 02895
Silva, James M., c/o One Cathedral Sq., Providence, RI 02903
Sullivan, Timothy J., 309 Spring St., Newport, RI 02840
Szymanski, Bronislaus, Pl. Jana Pawla II, 1, Lomza, 18-400 Poland
Thadeu, Joseph S., 62 Griffith Dr., East Providence, RI 02915
Thomson, Paul van K., P.O. Box 814, Wakefield, RI 02880
Trainor, James T., St. John Vianney Residence, 493 Mt. Pleasant Ave., Providence, RI 02908
Turillo, B. Samuel, 215 Old Succotash Rd., South Kingstown, RI 02880
Valois, Normand W., 30 Fenner St., Providence, RI 02903
Walsh, Clyde J., St. John Vianney Residence, 493 Mt. Pleasant Ave., Providence, RI 02908
Young, Peter G., 624 Woonasquatucket Ave., North Providence, RI 02911

Permanent Deacons:
Alessio, Robert G., Immaculate Conception, Westerly
Andrade, Charles, St. Patrick, Providence
Archambault, Bernard L., St. Joseph's, Woonsocket
Bacon, Normand J., St. Patrick, Harrisville
Baker, John F., St. Catherine, Warwick
Barboza, Benjamin, St. Mary, Bristol
Batalon, Raymond E., St. Edward, Pawtucket
Bisbano, Paul, Our Lady of Mount Carmel, Bristol
Bouchard, Thomas, St. Joseph, Woonsocket
Boutier, Thomas F., Blessed Sacrament, Providence
Braga, Joseph F., St. Joseph, North Scituate
Brissette, Armand, Jr., St. Joseph's, Woonsocket
Callahan, Raymond F., St. Mary's, West Warwick
Carpenter, Robert A., Raleigh, NC
Ceprano, Peter A., St. Mary, Cranston
Conley, James E., St. Mary of the Bay, Warren
Cordeiro, Manuel, St. Patrick, Providence
Corey, John A., St. Kevin, Warwick
Dadlez, Mark A., St. Alexander, Warren
Daidone, Salvatore A., Christ the King, Jacksonville, FL
DePetrillo, Albert, St. Thomas, Providence
DePietro, Ronald H., St. Francis de Sales, North Kingstown
DiOrio, Dominic P., Holy Angels, Barrington
Dufour, John, St. Joan, Cumberland
Edsall, Noel, St. Francis de Sales, North Kingstown
Ferrerira, Thomas, Diocese of Sacramento
Forlingieri, Carmine, Immaculate Conception, Cranston
Gagnon, Laurence O., Sr., St. Joseph, West Warwick
Gallo, Robert L., Sacred Heart, West Warwick
Garceau, Eugene, St. Agatha, Woonsocket
Garcia, Luis, Assumption, Providence
Gauthier, Clovis, Our Lady of Consolation, Pawtucket
Gederman, Harris J., St. Philip, Greenville
Gomez, Oscar, St. Teresa, Providence
Goulart, Joseph, Sr., St. Catherine's, Little Compton
Holder, Lawrence C., Diocese of Orlando, FL
Horton, Gregory, St. James, Manville
Johnson, Loring F., Assumption, Providence
Keogh, Richard B., Christ the King, Kingston
LaFleur, Norman R., St. John the Evangelist, Slatersville
LaFrance, Raymond J., St. Francis de Sales, North Kingstown
Lagesse, Raymond M., St. John's, Pawtucket
Lambert, Paul H., St. John Vianney, Cumberland
Lapierre, Richard J., Our Lady of Good Help, Mapleville
Lennon, Thomas J., Immaculate Conception, Cranston
Levesque, Raymond E., Holy Ghost, Tiverton
Lucian, Robert C., Diocese of St. Augustine, FL
MacLure, Robert, St. Patrick, Providence
Martins, Jesse L., St. Theresa, Tiverton
Martins, Manuel, Sacred Heart, Pawtucket
Masse, Kevin P., St. Francis, Warwick
Masse, Paul, St. John the Evangelist, Slatersville
Maynard, Jacques, St. Mary's, West Warwick (Crompton)
McAdam, Robert, St. Augustine's, Providence
Millard, Charles E., M.D., St. Mary of the Bay, Warren
Morisseau, Robert M., St. Benedict, Warwick
Mulcahy, Robert, St. Joseph's, Woonsocket
Napolitano, Michael D., Our Lady of Good Counsel, West Warwick
Nicholson, Robert E., St. Teresa, Pawtucket
Nova, Leocadio, St. Aloysius, Woonsocket
O'Hara, Thomas P., St. William, Warwick
Ouellette, Lucien, St. Maria Goretti, Pawtucket
Ragosta, Armand, St, Mary, Cranston
Raspallo, Thomas R., Immaculate Conception, Cranston
Riccio, Raymond L., St. Rocco, Johnston
Rico, Jose, St. Charles Borromeo, Providence
Sabetti, Carlo J., St. Philip, Greenville
Sadowski, Edward J., Jr., St. Vincent de Paul, Coventry
Sardinha, John, St. Elizabeth's, Bristol
Sheehy, C. Patrick, St. Mary, Pawtucket
Sinesi, Rugiero A., Christ the King, West Warwick
Small, William A., St. Michael, Esmond
Stone, Francis J., St. Peter, Warwick
Stone, Robert V., St. Peter, Warwick
Sullivan, Paul J., St. Thomas More, Narragansett
Tanguay, Paul A., Sacred Heart, East Providence
Theroux, Bernard G., St. Mary, Bristol
Theroux, Paul A., St. Francis of Assisi, Wakefield
Tribelli, Anthony A., St. Ann's, Cranston
Troia, Robert, St. Rocco's, Thornton
Tumminelli, Joseph P., St. Robert Bellamine, Johnston
Turbitt, Robert A., II, SS. John and Paul, Coventry
Turcotte, Joseph G., St. Francis of Assisi, Wakefield
Urrico, Francis X., St. Bernard, North Kingstown
Vani, Louis A., Presentation of the Blessed Virgin Mary, North Providence
Wendoloski, Anthony, Jr., Our Lady of Lourdes, Providence
West, Harry A., Jr., St. Teresa, Providence
Young, Frederick A., Holy Name, Providence

INSTITUTIONS LOCATED IN THE DIOCESE

[A] SEMINARIES, DIOCESAN

PROVIDENCE. *Seminary of Our Lady of Providence*, (House of Formation for College Students), 485 Mt. Pleasant Ave., 02908. Tel: 401-331-1316. Revs. Francis P. Kayatta, Formation Team/Spiritual Dir.; Marcel E. Pincince, Vocation Recruiter; Paul E. Desmarais, Spiritual Dir. Legal Title: *Seminary of Our Lady of Providence*. Students 5.

COVENTRY. *The Society of St. John Vianney*, House of Formation, 455 Washington St., 02816. Tel: 401-821-8714. Rev. Joseph P. Moore (BGP), Moderator. Legal Title: *Our Lady of Providence Preparatory Seminary*. Candidates 4.

[B] COLLEGES AND UNIVERSITIES

PROVIDENCE. *Providence College*, River Ave. & Eaton St., 02918. Tel: 401-865-1000; Fax: 401-865-2057. *For a complete listing, refer to the Colleges and Universities section.*

NEWPORT. *Salve Regina University*, 02840-4192. Tel: 401-847-6650; Fax: 401-847-0372. *For a complete listing, refer to the Colleges and Universities section.*

[C] HIGH SCHOOLS, DIOCESAN

PAWTUCKET. *St. Raphael Academy*, 123 Walcott St., 02860. Tel: 401-723-8100; 723-8740. Rev. Francis C. Santilli, Chap.; Bro. Thomas Casey, F.S.C., Prin. Conducted by the Brothers of the Christian Schools with the Religious of the Holy Union of the Sacred Hearts, Sisters of Mercy of the Americas, and Sisters of St. Chretienne. Legal Title: *Saint Raphael's Academy*. Brothers 5; Sisters 4; Lay Teachers 34; Students-Boys 268; Girls 252.

WAKEFIELD. *The Prout School*, 4640 Tower Hill Rd., 02879. Tel: 401-884-0264; 789-9262; Fax: 401-782-2262. Bro. Edmund Precourt, F.S.C., Prin. Legal Title: *The Prout School*. Brothers 1; Sisters 1; Lay Teachers 29; Students-Boys 188; Girls 159.

WARWICK. *Bishop Hendricken High School*, 2615 Warwick Ave., 02889. Tel: 401-739-3450; Fax: 401-732-8261. Revs. Kevin R. Fisette, Chap.; Jose Q. dos Reis, Chap. of the Brothers; Bro. Kevin Cawley, C.F.C., Pres. & Prin. Congregation of Christian Brothers. Legal Title: *Bishop Hendricken High School*. Priests 1; Brothers 8; Sisters 2; Lay Teachers 48; Boys 832.

[D] HIGH SCHOOLS, REGIONAL

PAWTUCKET. *Bishop Francis P. Keough Regional High School*, 145 Power Rd., 02860. Tel: 401-726-0335. Jeanne H. Leclerc, Prin. Sisters 1; Lay Teachers 10; Girls 65.

[E] HIGH SCHOOLS, PRIVATE

PROVIDENCE. *La Salle Academy*. (Grades 7-12), 612 Academy Ave., 02908. Tel: 401-351-7750; 351-9353 (Residence); Fax: 401-453-6315. Bro. A. Jerome Corrigan, F.S.C., Pres.; Mr. Raymond Pasi, Prin. Conducted by the Brothers of the Christian Schools. Legal Title: *St. John De La Salle Institution*. Priests 1; Brothers 8; Sisters 1; Lay Teachers 75; Students 1,155.

COVENTRY. *St. Xavier Academy*, 2 Saint Vincent de Paul St., 02816. Tel: 401-826-2130. Friends of St. Xavier. Mrs. Kathleen Siok, Prin. Lay Teachers 11; Girls 60.

EAST PROVIDENCE. *St. Mary Academy*. (Grades 7-12). Bayview, 3070 Pawtucket Ave., Riverside, 02915. Tel: 401-434-0113; Fax: 401-483-5936. Sisters of Mercy of the Americas and Sisters of St. Joseph. Sr. Elizabeth McAuliffe, R.S.M., Pres.; Ms. Colleen Gribbon, Prin. Sisters 15; Lay Teachers 51; Girls 668.

GREENVILLE. *Immaculate Conception Academy*, 60 Austin Ave., 02828. Tel: 401-949-2820. Ms. Maria Bracket, Prin.; Rev. David Chaves, L.C., Chap. Boarding School Students 42.

PORTSMOUTH. *Portsmouth Abbey School*, Cory's Ln., 02871. Tel: 401-683-2000. Rt. Rev. F. Marc Serna,

O.S.B., Headmaster. Legal Title: *Order of St. Benedict in Portsmouth, Rhode Island*. Priests 9; Brothers 3; Lay Teachers 38; Students 305.

WARREN. *Our Lady of Fatima High School*. (Grades 7-12), 360 Market St., Rte. 136, 02885. Tel: 401-245-4449. Sr. Mary Margaret Souza, S.S.D., Prin. Sisters of St. Dorothy. Sisters 4; Lay Teachers 11; Students 150.

WOONSOCKET. *Mt. St. Charles Academy*. (Grades 7-12), 02895-5599. Tel: 401-769-0310; Fax: 401-762-2327. Bros. Robert R. Croteau, S.C., Pres.; Clifford M. King, S.C., Prin. Brothers of the Sacred Heart. Legal Title: *Mount Saint Charles Academy, Inc.* Brothers 16; Sisters 1; Lay Teachers 41; Students 825.

[F] ELEMENTARY SCHOOLS, PRIVATE

PROVIDENCE. *San Miguel School*, 12 Carter St., 02907. Tel: 401-467-9777. Bro. Lawrence Goyette, F.S.C. Students 50.

CUMBERLAND. *Mercymount Country Day School*, Wrentham Rd., 02864. Tel: 401-333-5919. Sr. Martha Mulligan, R.S.M., Prin. Sisters of Mercy of the Americas. Sisters 4; Lay Teachers 24; Students 347.

EAST PROVIDENCE. *St. Mary Academy*. Day Pupils. Bayview, 3070 Pawtucket Ave., Riverside, 02915. Tel: 401-438-4635. Sisters of Mercy of the Americas. Sr. Norma Fleming, R.S.M., Prin. Sisters 4; Lay Teachers 12; Students 288.

NEWPORT. *St. Joseph of Cluny Sisters' School, Inc.* (Grades K-8). Day School, Brenton Rd., 02840. Tel: 401-847-6043. Sr. Yvonne Kelly, S.J.C., Prin. Sisters 3; Lay Teachers 15; Students 235.

PORTSMOUTH. *St. Philomena School*, Cory's Lane, 02871. Tel: 401-683-0268. Sisters Faithful Companions of Jesus. Sr. Ann Marie Walsh, F.C.J., Prin. Teaching Sisters 1; Lay Teachers 32; Students 444.

[G] REGIONAL ELEMENTARY SCHOOLS

PROVIDENCE. *Bishop McVinney Regional School*, 155 Gordon Ave., 02905. Tel: 401-781-2370. (Grades PreK-3). Elementary Division: Sr. Lillian Dempsey, C.P., Prin. Sisters 3; Lay Teachers 7; Students 180.

Middle Division. (Grades 4-8), 155 Harrison St., 02907. Tel: 401-331-5714. Sr. Theresina Scully, C.P., Prin. Sisters 1; Lay Staff 8; Students 170.

Catholic Association for Regional Education, 155 Harrison St., 02907. Tel: 401-331-5714. Sr. Theresina Scully, C.P., Exec. Dir. Sisters 4; Lay Teachers 16; Students 350.

St. Thomas Regional School, 15 Edendale Ave., 02911. Tel: 401-351-0403. Patricia A. Wolfert, Prin. Sisters 3; Lay Teachers 12; Students 269.

CENTRAL FALLS. *St. Elizabeth Ann Seton Academy*, 909 Lonsdale Ave., 02863. Tel: 401-728-6230. Sr. Ann McKenna, R.S.M., Prin. Sisters 4; Lay Teachers 19; Students 270.

CRANSTON. *Cranston-Johnston Catholic Regional School*, 43 Poplar Dr., 02920. Tel: 401-942-7245. Deacon Thomas R. Raspallo, Prin. Sisters 2; Lay Teachers 25; Students 425.

EAST GREENWICH. *Our Lady of Mercy Regional School*. (Grades PreK-6), Fourth Ave., 02818. Tel: 401-884-1618. Mrs. Ann Gail Shahinian, Prin. Sisters 5; Lay Teachers 19; Students 331.

PAWTUCKET. *Woodlawn Catholic Regional School*. (Grades K-8), 61 Hope St., 02860. Tel: 401-723-3759. Sr. Martha M. Serbst, R.S.M., Prin. Sisters 5; Lay Teachers 5; Students 270.

PORTSMOUTH. *All Saints Academy, The Newport County Catholic Regional School*. (Grades K-8), 2836 E. Main Rd., 02871. Tel: 401-683-1377. Sr. Marie Baldi, S.U.S.C., Prin. Sisters 3; Lay Teachers 8; Students 155.

WAKEFIELD. *Monsignor Matthew F. Clarke Regional School*. (Grades PreK-6), Tower Hill Rd., 02879. Tel: 401-789-0860. Sr. Aideen Langan, C.P., Prin. Sisters 1; Lay Teachers 16; Students 360.

WARWICK. *Overbrook Academy at Our Lady of Providence Center*. (Boarding School), 836 Warwick Neck Ave., 02889. Tel: 401-737-2850. Miss Bertha Del Toro, Prin./Dir.; Rev. Davis Chaves, L.C., Chap. Students 89.

WEST WARWICK. *Notre Dame Regional School*. (Grades K-8), 59 Pleasant St., 02893. Tel: 401-821-6334. Mary McElroy, Prin. Sisters 1; Lay Teachers 11; Students 197.

[H] THE GREATER WOONSOCKET CATHOLIC REGIONAL SCHOOL SYSTEM

Member Schools

WOONSOCKET. *Father Holland Catholic Regional Elementary School*. (Grades PreK-6). 180 Sayles Ave., Pascoag, 02853. Tel: 401-568-4589. Students 153. Mailing Address: Regional Administration, P.O. Box 487, 1 Social St., 02895. Tel: 401-762-1095. Shawn A. Carpon, Prin.

Good Shepherd Catholic Regional Middle School. (Grades 6-8), 1210 Mendon Rd., 02895. Tel: 401-767-5906. Mrs. Marianne Alger, Admin.; Mrs. Louise P. Kane, Prin. Lay Teachers 9; Students 195.

Monsignor Gadoury Regional Primary School. (Grades PreK-3), 1371 Park Ave., 02895. Tel: 401-767-5902. Constance McClure, Prin. Lay Teachers 6; Students 156.

Our Lady of Victories Regional Primary School. (Grades K-3), 148 Spring St., 02895. Tel: 401-767-5904. Mr. Armand B. Houle, Prin. Lay Teachers 9; Students 202.

St. Joseph Intermediate Regional School. (Grades 4-5), 1210 Mendon Rd., 02895. Tel: 401-767-5907. Mrs. Paula A. Hurteau, Prin. Lay Teachers 6; Students 129.

[I] CHILD CARING FACILITIES

PROVIDENCE. *Group Home for Adolescent Boys*, (Whitemarsh House), 20 Eighth St., 02906. Tel: 401-351-7230. Bro. John McHale, O.L.P., Dir. Boys 60.

NARRAGANSETT. *Ocean Tides*, 635 Ocean Rd., 02882-1314. Tel: 401-789-1016. Bros. Brendan Gerrity, F.S.C., Pres.; Timothy Balfe, F.S.C., Dir. Social Svcs.; John Norton, F.S.C., Court Liaison. Legal Title: *Ocean Tides, Inc.* Brothers 6; Lay Teachers 14; Lay Staff 27; Students 70.

[J] DAY NURSERIES

PROVIDENCE. *The Nazareth Home-Carter Day Nursery*, 239 Public St., 02905. Tel: 401-751-9752. Nicole F. Curran, M.S., Dir.; Mrs. Alexandra Moser, B.A., Exec. Dir. Legal Title: *Nazareth Home*. Day care provided for 126 children.

St. Vincent Day Care Center, 485 Mt. Pleasant Ave., 02908. Tel: 401-274-3094. Mrs. Alexandra F. Moser, B.A., Exec. Dir./Program Dir. Legal Title: *Saint Vincent de Paul Infant Asylum*. Day care provided for 71 children.

MANVILLE. *Mount St. Francis Day Care Center*, 57 Division St., 02838. Tel: 401-767-2829. Mrs. Alexandra Moser, B.A., Exec. Dir. & Program Dir. Legal Title: *Mont St. Francois of Woonsocket, RI*. Day care provided for 121 children three years old through Kindergarten full day.

NEWPORT. *Garrettson Memorial Day Care Nursery*, 299 Spring St., 02840. Tel: 401-846-6470. Mary Ann Altrui, M.S.W., Dir. Legal Title: *The Saint Clare Home*. Day care & licensed kindergarten provided for 90 children between the ages of 2-6 years old. Lay Teachers 12.

[K] GENERAL HOSPITALS

PROVIDENCE. *St. Joseph Corporate Care*, Occupational Health and Safety Services. Tel: 401-456-4020.
For a complete listing, refer to the Hospitals section.

St. Joseph Health Services of Rhode Island - St. Joseph Hospital for Specialty Care, 21 Peace St., 02907. Tel: 401-456-3000.
For a complete listing, refer to the Hospitals section.

NORTH PROVIDENCE. *St. Joseph Health Services of Rhode Island - Our Lady of Fatima Hospital*, 200 High Service Ave., 02904. Tel: 401-456-3000.
For a complete listing, refer to the Hospitals section.

[L] VISITING AND NURSING OF THE SICK

PROVIDENCE. *Holy Spirit Convent*, 43 Westerly Ave., 02909. Tel: 401-946-5639. Daughters of the Holy Spirit. Sr. Louis Ernest Brodeur, D.H.S., Contact Person. Sisters 2; Visiting Sisters 2; Visits 210; Number of patients 67.

[M] HOMES FOR AGED

PROVIDENCE. *St. Joseph Living Center*, 153 Dean St., 02903. Tel: 401-272-3335.
For a complete listing, refer to the Special Care Facilities section.

CUMBERLAND. *Mount St. Rita Health Centre*, 15 Sumner Brown Rd., 02864. Tel: 401-333-6352.
For a complete listing, refer to the Special Care Facilities section.

NEWPORT. *St. Clare Home*, 309 Spring St., 02840. Tel: 401-849-3204; Fax: 401-849-5780.
For a complete listing, refer to the Special Care Facilities section.

NORTH KINGSTOWN. *Scalabrini Villa*, 860 N. Quidnessett Rd., 02852. Tel: 401-884-1802.
For a complete listing, refer to the Special Care Facilities section.

NORTH SMITHFIELD. *St. Antoine Residence*, 400 Mendon Rd., 02895. Tel: 401-767-3500.
For a complete listing, refer to the Special Care Facilities section.

PAWTUCKET. *Jeanne Jugan Apartments*, 310 Sayles Ave., 02860.
For a complete listing, refer to the Special Care Facilities section.

Jeanne Jugan Residence, 964 Main St., 02860. Tel: 401-723-4314; Fax: 401-727-2885.
For a complete listing, refer to the Special Care Facilities section.

WOONSOCKET. *Saint Francis House*, 167 Blackstone St., 02895. Tel: 401-762-5255.
For a complete listing, refer to the Special Care Facilities section.

[N] CAMPS AND COMMUNITY CENTERS

PROVIDENCE. *McAuley House*, 163 Niagara St., 02907. Tel: 401-941-9013. Legal Title: *The McAuley Corporation*. Sr. Maris Stella LaLiberte, R.S.M., Dir. Total under care annually 25,000.

McAuley Village, 325 Niagara St., 02907-2000. Tel: 401-467-3630. Legal Title: *The McAuley Corporation*. Sr. Dolores Crowley, R.S.M., Exec. Dir. Sisters of Mercy 2; Families assisted 22; Children in day care center 46.

St. Francis Chapel & City Ministry Center, 58 Weybosset St., 02903. Tel: 401-331-6510. Rev. David I. Covertino, O.F.M., Guardian & Dir.

St. Martin de Porres Multi-Purpose Center, 160 Cranston St., 02907. Tel: 401-274-6783. Legal Title: *St. Martin de Porres Center*. Wayne B. Houle, Dir. Total under care 2,100.

CHEPACHET. *Mater Spei Day Camp*, Box W, 02814. Tel: 401-568-2473. Maria Piccirilli, Dir.

COVENTRY. *Pawtuxet Valley C.Y.O. Center*, 6 St. Vincent de Paul St., 02816. Tel: 401-822-0573. Mailing Address: P.O. Box 247, West Warwick, 02893. Marie Lachapelle, Dir.

CRANSTON. *Providence County C.Y.O. Center*, 804 Dyer Ave., 02920. Tel: 401-942-6571. Patricia Kane, Dir.

PAWTUCKET. *Father Barry CYO Center*, 38 Denver St., 02860. Tel: 401-723-5111; 723-5119. Legal Title: *Father Barry CYO Center*. Ms. Colette M. Savaria, Dir.

PEACE DALE. *St. Dominic Savio Youth Center*, Broad Rock Rd., P.O. Box 67, 02883. Tel: 401-783-4055; 783-9123; Fax: 401-789-4630. Legal Title: *St. Dominic Savio Boys' Center*. Rev. Stephen P. Amaral, Spiritual Dir.; Mr. Marc G. Giguere, Dir.

Tower Hill Camp, Broad Rock Rd., P.O. Box 67, 02883. Tel: 401-783-9123; Fax: 401-789-4630. Legal Title: *Rhode Island Home for Working Boys*. Rev. Stephen P. Amaral, Spiritual Dir.; Mr. Marc G. Giguere, Dir. Campers 600.

PORTSMOUTH. *Newport County C.Y.O. Center*. 25 Metropolitan Dr., P.O. Box 310, Riverside, 02915. Tel: 401-433-5528. Maria E. Piccirilli, Reg. Dir.

RIVERSIDE. *East Bay C.Y.O. Center*, 25 Metropolitan Park Dr., 02915. Tel: 401-433-4327. Kerry O'Connell, Dir.

WARWICK. *Our Lady of Providence Center*, 836 Warwick Neck Ave., 02889. Tel: 401-739-6850. Legal Title: *OLP Center, Inc.* Mrs. Paulette M. Turcotte, Dir.

West Bay C.Y.O. Center, 165 Beach Ave., P.O. Box 9222, 02889-9998. Tel: 401-737-2033. Deacon Robert M. Morisseau, Reg. Dir.

WOONSOCKET. *Fr. Marot CYO Center*, 53 Federal St., 02895. Legal Title: *CYO of Northern Rhode Island*. Co-Directors: Miss Fern Dery; Mr. Roland Berard; Rev. Roger L. Marot, Spiritual Dir.

[O] PERSONAL PRELATURES

PROVIDENCE. *Opus Dei, Mathewson House*, 224 Bowen St., 02906. Tel: 401-272-7834. Rev. Michael J. Manz.

[P] MONASTERIES AND RESIDENCES OF PRIESTS AND BROTHERS

PROVIDENCE. *Brothers of Our Lady of Providence*, 164 Massachusetts Ave., 02907. Tel: 401-461-6638. Office, 20 Eighth St., 02906. Tel: 401-351-7230. Bro. John McHale, O.L.P., Supr. Brothers 2.

St. Francis Friary, 58 Weybosset St., 02903. Tel: 401-331-6510; Fax: 401-453-0034. Legal Title: *St. Francis Weybosset Street Chapel, Inc.* Franciscan Friars. Revs. David I. Convertino, O.F.M., Guardian; Robert J. Sandoz, O.F.M., Vicar; John J. Marino, O.F.M.; Severin Brady, O.F.M.; Gerald H. Brennan, O.F.M.; Hugh Eller, O.F.M.; Stephen Lynch, O.F.M.; Eugene F. Malek, O.F.M.; Jude R. Murphy, O.F.M.; John B. Valente, O.F.M. Priests 10; Novices 7.

St. John Vianney Residence, 493 Mt. Pleasant Ave., 02908. Tel: 401-331-9870. Residence for Senior Priests. Rev. Edward J. McGovern, Coord. Residents: Rev. Msgr. Louis W. Dunn; Rev. Msgr. Michael W. Dziob; Rev. Msgr. Edward F. Egan; Revs. Edward F. Boland; Normand J. Deneault; Rene E. Gagne; George F. Gorman; Donald J. King; Joseph J. Lambert; Leon C. Maynard; William F. Murphy; Peter J. Narewski; James T. Trainor; Clyde J. Walsh. Priests 13.

St. Pius Priory, 55 Elmhurst Ave., 02908. Tel: 401-751-4871; Fax: 401-273-1089. Legal Title: *Dominican Fathers*. Very Rev. Kenneth Letoile, O.P., Prior; Revs. Henry A. Camacho, O.P.; Michael deTemple, O.P.; Michael P. Trainor, O.P.; Bro. Denis Swann, O.P. Priests 4; Brothers 1.

St. Thomas Aquinas Priory at Providence College, 02918-0001. Tel: 401-865-2101. Legal Title: *Priory of St. Thomas Aquinas*. Dominican Friars.
Assigned & Residing in the Priory: Very Rev. Robert J. Hennessey, O.P., Prior; Most Rev. Ernest B. Boland, O.P., Retired Bishop of Multan; Revs. J. Iriarte Andujar, O.P.; Richard J. Barranger, O.P.; Albino F. Barrera, O.P.; Robert E. Bond, O.P.; Francis W. Brocato, O.P. (Chicago Prov.); Daniel J. Cassidy, O.P.; Edward L. Cleary, O.P. (Chicago Prov.); George L. Cochran, O.P.; Paul M. Conner, O.P. (Oakland Prov.); Thomas M. Coskren, O.P.; John F. Cunningham, O.P.; G. Adrian Dabash, O.P.; James J. Davis, O.P.; Vincent DeLucia, O.P.; John Martin Diggins, O.P.; Edward P. Doyle, O.P.; James A. Driscoll, O.P.; Thomas K. Fergus, O.P.; William David Folsey, O.P.; Joseph J. Guido, O.P.; Kenneth R. Gumbert, O.P. (Oakland Prov.); Ralph T. Hall, O.P.; Leonard P. Hindsley, O.P.; G. Nicholas Ingham, O.P.; Anthony A. Jurgelaitis, O.P.; Terence S. Keegan, O.P.; Bernard F. Langton, O.P.; Joseph L. Lennon, O.P.; Richard A. McAlister, O.P.; James R. McAvey, O.P.; Thomas D. McGonigle, O.P. (Chicago Prov.); J. Stuart McPhail, O.P.; Matthew F. Morry, O.P.; William Paul Marquis, O.P.; Robert D. Myett, O.P.; Francis D. Nealy, O.P.; Mark D. Nowel, O.P.; John S. Peterson, O.P.; Matthew D. Powell, O.P. (Chicago Prov.); James Ferrer Quigley, O.P.; Charles V. Reichart, O.P.; John J. Reid, O.P.; Kevin D. Robb, O.P.; John C. Rubba, O.P.; Paul E. Seaver, O.P.; J. Dominic Skalko, O.P.; A. Philip Smith, O.P.; James T. Sullivan, O.P.; Raphael Van Kets, O.P. (Flanders); Walter C. Wagner, O.P.; Bros. Francis Liebold, O.P.; F. Kevin O'Connell, O.P.
Assigned but Living Outside the Priory: Revs. Stanley R. Azaro, O.P., (Lithuania); Harold R. Barron, O.P., (Heritage Hills Nursing Center); James W.C. Barron, O.P., (St. Vincent Ferrer, River Forest, IL); Walter C. Burke, O.P., (Heritage Hills Nursing Center); Brian Chrzastek, O.P., (Franciscan House, Chicago); Raymond T.A. Collins, O.P., (Heritage Hills Nursing Center); Curtis E. Henritzy, O.P., (The Angelicum, Rome); Dennis C. Kane, O.P., (Heritage Hills Nursing Center); John A. Langlois, O.P., (Fribourg, Switzerland); William J. O'Shaughnessy, O.P., (Heritage Hills Nursing Center); George M. Robillard, O.P., (Heritage Hills Nursing Center). Bishops in Residence 1; Priests in Residence 52; Brothers in Residence 2; Priests residing outside Priory 11.

BRISTOL. *St. Columban's Retirement House*, Box 65, Ferry Rd., 02809. Tel: 401-253-6909. Legal Title: *St. Columban's Foreign Mission Society*. Revs. William F. Sullivan, S.S.C., Supr.; Thomas L. Convery, S.S.C.; Norbert F. Feld, S.S.C.; Brian Gallagher, S.S.C.; Michael Harrison, S.S.C.; John C. Healey, S.S.C.; Rudolph Hoza, S.S.C.; Fintan Keegan, S.S.C.; Thomas A. McCormack, S.S.C.; Joseph McSweeney, S.S.C.; Joseph Murrin, S.S.C.; John O'Doherty, S.S.C.; James Roddy, S.S.C. Priests 13.

HARRISVILLE. *Provincial House*. Brothers of the Sacred Heart, New England Prov. Legal Title: *The Order of the Brothers of the Sacred Heart of New England, Inc.* Mailing Address: 685 Steere Farm Rd., Pascoag, 02859-4601. Tel: 401-568-8686; 568-3361; Fax: 401-568-9810. Bros. Roland Ouellette, S.C., Prov. Supr. of New England Prov.; Louis J. Laperle, S.C., Exec. Asst. for Finances; Fred U. Bouchard, S.C., Local Supr.; Edward Breault, S.C., Prov. Sec.; Paul F. Hebert, S.C., Exec. Asst. for Missions; Charles L. St. Amand, S.C., Exec. Asst. for Dev.; Rev. Albert J. Morel, S.C., Chap. Brothers 28.

MANVILLE. *St. James Residence*, 57 Division St., 02838. Tel: 401-762-0769. Bro. Alan Aubin, S.C., Dir. Brothers of the Sacred Heart 10.

NARRAGANSETT. *Christian Brothers' Center*, 635 Ocean Rd., 02882. Tel: 401-789-0244; Fax: 401-783-5303. Legal Title: *Brothers of the Christian Schools, Long Island-New England Province*. Brothers of the Christian Schools. Bros. William Mann, F.S.C., Prov., Visitor; Daniel Casey, F.S.C., Auxiliary Prov., Education/Continuing-Initial Formation; Robert Hazard, F.S.C., Dir. Formation Ministry; Peter Clifford, F.S.C., Dir. Finance/Development; Rev. Owen F. Goodwin, SS.CC., Chap. Brothers 27; Brothers in the Province 105.

PAWTUCKET. *Brothers of the Christian Schools*, 58 Hancock St., 02860-2629. Tel: 401-725-7815. Bro. Frederick C. Mueller, F.S.C., Dir. Brothers 4.

PORTSMOUTH. *Abbey of St. Gregory the Great* (Cory's Lane), 02871. Tel: 401-683-2000; Fax: 401-683-5888. Legal Title: *Order of St. Benedict in Portsmouth, Rhode Island*. Benedictines of the English Congregation. Rt. Rev. F. Mark Serna, O.S.B., Abbot; Very Rev. R. Ambrose Wolverton, O.S.B., Prior; Rt. Rev. Matthew Stark, O.S.B., Retired Abbot; Revs. Peter Sidler, O.S.B.; H. David Hurst, O.S.B.; Julian Stead, O.S.B.; B. Benedict Lang, O.S.B.; F. Philip Wilson, O.S.B.; R. Maurus Fleming, O.S.B.; A. Damian Kearney, O.S.B.; Michael Stafford, O.S.B.; P. Geoffrey Chase, O.S.B.; Christopher Davis, O.S.B.; Paul McDonald, O.S.B.; T. Edmund Adams, O.S.B.; P. Paschal Scotti, O.S.B. Abbots 2; Priests 14; Brothers 4.

WOONSOCKET. *Brothers of the Sacred Heart*, 800 Logee St., 02895. Tel: 401-769-0313. Bro. Raymond Hetu, S.C., Local Supr. Brothers 9.
St. John's Residence, 159 Earle St., 02895. Tel: 401-766-9677. Bro. John L. Collignon, S.C., Supr. Brothers 8.

[Q] CONVENTS AND RESIDENCES FOR SISTERS

BARRINGTON. *Monastery of Discalced Carmelites*, Nayatt Ave., 02806. Tel: 401-245-3421. Legal Title: *Monastery of Discalced Carmelites at Nayatt, Barrington, RI*. Sr. Genevieve Lawler, O.C.D., Prioress. Professed Sisters 14; Novices 1.

BRISTOL. *Mt. St. Joseph Provincialate*, 13 Monkeywrench Ln., 02809. Tel: 401-253-7835. Sisters of St. Dorothy. Sr. Eileen Egan, S.S.D., Prov. Coord.; Sr. Cynthia Mello, S.S.D., Local Coord. Sisters 5.

CUMBERLAND. *Sisters of Mercy*, Highland View Rd., 02864. Tel: 401-333-2439. Mercycrest Convent, 255 Wrentham Rd., 02864. Tel: 401-333-5283. Sisters 2. Mercyknoll Convent, Highland View Rd., 02864. Tel: 401-333-6804. Sisters 2. Mercy Lodge, House of Hospitality, 6 Sumner Brown Rd., P.O. Box 7651, 02864-0897. Tel: 401-333-2801. Mercymount Convent, Wrentham Rd., 02864. Tel: 401-333-0158. Sisters 4. Sisters 3.
Sisters of Mercy of the Americas, Regional Community of Providence, Highland View Rd., 02864. Tel: 401-333-6333; Fax: 401-333-6450. Legal Title: *Sisters of Mercy of Providence, Inc.* Sr. Barbara Riley, R.S.M., Pres. Counselors: Sr. Carol Mary Morrison, R.S.M.; Sr. Sheila Harrington, R.S.M.; Sr. Patricia Combies, R.S.M.; Sr. Maureen McElroy, R.S.M. Sisters 419; Temporary Vows 5.

NARRAGANSETT. *Sisters of the Cross & Passion Convent*, 24 Castle Rd., 02882. Tel: 401-783-6668. Sisters 3.

NEWPORT. *Benedictines of Jesus Crucified*, 61 Narragansett Ave., 02840-4099. Tel: 401-847-2423. Legal Title: *Benedictines of Jesus Crucified Inc.* Benedictine Sisters of Pontifical Jurisdiction. Convent of the Congregation of the Benedictines of Jesus Crucified, O.S.B. Sr. Marie Agathe Karunaratne, O.S.B., Prioress. Sisters 12.
Cluny Convent, 90 Brenton Rd., 02840-4256. Tel: 401-846-4757; Fax: 401-846-2276. Provincial House. Sr. Marie Cooper, S.J.C., Prov. Supr., St. Joseph Cluny Convent. Tel: 401-847-3637. Sr. Eugenia Brady, S.J.C., Local Supr. Sisters 15; Sisters in Diocese 21; Sisters in Cluny Prov. of U.S.A. & Canada 44.
Corpus Christi Carmel, 516 Broadway, 02840. Tel: 401-847-6165. Corpus Christi Carmelite Sisters. Sr. Teresa Winefride, O.Carm., Supr.; Sr. Emerentiana, O.Carm., Regl. Supr., U.S.A. Sisters 3.
St. Clare Convent, Cutting Memorial, 301 Spring St., 02840. Tel: 401-846-1025. Legal Title: *The Saint Clare Home*. Sr. Simone Leblond, D.H.S., Coord. Daughters of the Holy Spirit 8.

NORTH KINGSTOWN. *Holy Family Convent*, 1 Wright Ln., 02852. Tel: 401-294-3554. Legal Title: *Sisters of the Holy Cross and Passion*. Provincial Office of the Sisters of the Cross and Passion. Sr. Ellen Downes, C.P., Prov. Sisters 2.

NORTH PROVIDENCE. *Franciscan Missionaries of Mary*, 399 Fruit Hill Ave., 02911. Tel: 401-353-5800. Legal Title: *Franciscan Missionaries of Mary*.
Holy Family Community, 399 Fruit Hill Ave., 02911. Tel: 401-353-5800. Sr. Virginia Daly, F.M.M., Supr. Sisters 13.
Our Lady, Queen of Peace, Assisted Living Community, 399 Fruit Hill Ave., 02911. Tel: 401-353-5800. Sr. Philomena Agudo, F.M.M., Supr.; Sr. Rosalie McNaughton, F.M.M., Admin. Sisters 24.
Our Lady of the Lourdes Convent, 385 Fruit Hill Ave., 02911. Tel: 401-353-6381. Sisters 5.
Trinity Community, Assisted Living Community, 399 Fruit Hill Ave., 02911. Tel: 401-353-5800. Sr. Joyce Gardella, F.M.M., Supr. Sisters 20.
Bethany, (House of On-Going Formation), 397 Fruit Hill Ave., 02911. Tel: 401-353-5860. Sr. Josephine J. Iozzo, F.M.M., Dir.
De Chappotin Community, 399 Fruit Hill Ave., 02911. Tel: 401-353-9412. Sisters 6.

NORTH SMITHFIELD. *Franciscan Missionaries of Mary*, Ein Karim Community, 318 Mendon Rd., 02895. Tel: 401-766-8242. Sr. Agnes Begley, F.M.M., Coord. Sisters 4.

PAWTUCKET. *St. John the Baptist Convent*, 85 Slater St., 02860. Tel: 401-722-1850. Sr. Yvette Hubert, F.M.M., Coord. Franciscan Missionaries of Mary 5.

PEACE DALE. *Sisters of the Cross and Passion*, 364 Oakwoods Dr., 02879. Tel: 401-783-5457. Sr. Margaret Mary Hanley, C.P., Coord. Sisters 4.

RIVERSIDE. *St. Mary Convent*, Bay View, 3070 Pawtucket Ave., 02915-5197. Tel: 401-434-0486. Sr. Carmen Demeule, R.S.M., Co-Dir.; Sr. Rita Bartley, R.S.M., Co-Dir. Sisters of Mercy of the Americas 65.

WOONSOCKET. *Emmanuel House*, 67 Highland St., 02895.
Franciscan Apostolic Sisters, 89 Morris St., 02895. Tel: 401-769-9395. Sr. Wilma J. Lopez, F.A.S., Supr. Sisters 4.

[R] RETREAT HOUSES

NARRAGANSETT. *Our Lady of Peace Spiritual Life Center*, Ocean Rd., Box 507, 02882. Tel: 401-884-7676. Legal Title: *Our Lady of Peace Retreat House*. Sr. Jean Marie McGee, R.S.M., Dir. Team Members: Revs. Robert F. Caul; Richard M. Friedrichs.

NEWPORT. *Nazareth Spiritual Enrichment Center*, 12 Cliff Terr., 02840. Tel: 401-847-1654. Sisters of St. Chretienne. Sr. Estelle Plante, S.S.Ch., Dir. Sisters 2.
St. Paul Priory Guest House, 61 Narragansett Ave., 02840-4099. Tel: 401-847-2423. Benedictines of Jesus Crucified, O.S.B. Sr. Marie Agathe Karunaratne, O.S.B., Prioress.

NORTH PROVIDENCE. *Bethany Renewal Center*, 397 Fruit Hill Ave., 02911. Tel: 401-353-5860. Conducted by the Franciscan Missionaries of Mary. Sr. Josephine J. Iozzo, F.M.M., Dir.

[S] NEWMAN CENTERS

PROVIDENCE. *Brown University*, Catholic Chaplain's Office, Box 1931, 02912. Tel: 401-863-2344. Rev. Alfred V. Ricci, Chap.
Johnson & Wales University, Friendship Bldg., 2 Richmond St., 02903. Tel: 401-598-1830. Sr. Francis V. Murphy, S.N.D., Campus Min.
Rhode Island College, Catholic Campus Ministry, Student Union 300, 600 Mt. Pleasant Ave., 02908. Tel: 401-456-8168. Mr. James Montavon, Campus Min.

BRISTOL. *Roger Williams University*, Catholic Chaplain's Office, 1 Old Ferry Rd., 02809. Tel: 401-253-9449. Chaplains: Revs. Timothy J. Gorton; Henry P. Zinno, Jr.

KINGSTON. *University of Rhode Island Catholic Center*, 02881. Tel: 401-792-2324. Chaplains: Revs. John P. Soares; Joseph D. Creedon; Mrs. Carol Maddock, Campus Min.

SMITHFIELD. *Bryant College*, Chaplain's Office, 1150 Douglas Pike, Box 33, 02917-1284. Tel: 401-232-6045. Rev. Pierre J. Plante, Chap.

WARWICK. *Community College of R.I.*, Knight Campus, Chaplain's Office, 400 East Ave., 02886. Tel: 401-825-2226. Ms. Angela M. Anderson, Campus Min., Flanagan Campus, Chaplain's Office, Louisquisset Pike, Lincoln, 02865. Tel: 401-333-7013.

[T] MISCELLANEOUS LISTINGS

PROVIDENCE. *Diocesan Service Corporation*, One Cathedral Square, 02903.
Marian Association of Northern Rhode Island, One Cathedral Sq., 02903.
Miscellaneous Listings for the Diocese of Providence. Mailing address for all Providence listings, Chancery Office: 1 Cathedral Sq., 02903. Tel: 401-278-4500. For further information contact, Rev. Msgr. Jacques L. Plante, Chancellor.
Catholic Charity Fund.
Catholic Information Center of Newport.
Catholic Investment Trust, Inc.
Catholic Teachers' College of Providence.
The Church of the Immaculate Conception, North Providence.
De LaSalle Academy Corporation.
Diocesan Service Corporation.
Homes for Hope Foundation.
House of the Good Shepherd of Providence.
Inter-Parish Loan Fund, Inc.
LaSalle Academy.
Little Sisters of the Assumption of Woonsocket.
The Mercy Home and School.
Mother of Hope Novitiate.
New England Conference of Diocesan Directors of Religious Education.
Our Lady, Queen of the Clergy.
Pius X Salvage Bureau.
Retreat House of the Immaculate Heart of Mary.
The Rhode Island Catholic Orphan Asylum (St. Aloysius Home).
Roman Catholic Bishop of Providence. A Corporation Sole.
St. Benedict's Hearth Corporation, East Providence.
Saint Hedwig's Church Corporation, Providence.
St. John's Church of Providence.
Saint Margaret's Home.
Saint Maria Society.
St. Mary Academy of the Visitation.
Saint Raphael's Industrial Home and School.
St. Vincent de Paul Home, Woonsocket.
Stella Maris Home for Convalescents.
Vision of Hope, Inc.

NARRAGANSETT. *Saint Benilde Community Support Charitable Trust*, 635 Ocean Rd., 02882-1314. Tel: 401-789-0244; Fax: 401-783-5303.

NORTH PROVIDENCE. *Franciscan Missionaries of Mary*, 399 Fruit Hill Ave., 02911.

Mission Resource Center. Tel: 401-353-4470; Fax: 401-353-8779. Sr. Mary Motte, F.M.M., Dir.; Sr. Alma Dufault, F.M.M., Assoc. Dir.

PASCOAG. *Conference of Regional Treasurers*, 685 Steere Farm Rd., 02859-4601. Tel: 401-568-3361; Fax: 401-568-9810. Bro. Louis J. Laperle, S.C., Rep. of CORT I.

Father Andre Coindre Charitable Trust, 685 Steere Farm Rd., 02859-4601. Tel: 401-568-3361; Fax: 401-568-9810. Bro. Louis J. Laperle, S.C., Corp. Sec.

SOUTH KINGSTON. *Hombre Nueva (RI), Inc.*, 47 Crest Ave., 02879. Tel: 203-281-4798. Rev. Juan Sabadell, L.C., Contact Person.

WAKEFIELD. *"Mater Ecclesiae" International Formation Center*, 4780 Tower Hill Rd., 02879. Tel: 401-782-6205; 782-6200. (Regnum Christi Movement). Ms. Gabriela Garza, Dir.; Revs. Jose A. Alonso, L.C., Chap.; Jude Furlong, L.C., Prof. Members 72.

The Legion of Christ (RI) Incorporated, 4780 Tower Hill Rd., 02879. Tel: 203-281-4798. Rev. Juan Sabadell, L.C., Contact Person.

Mater Ecclesiae, Inc., 4780 Tower Hill Rd., 02879. Tel: 203-281-4798. Rev. Juan Sabadell, L.C., Contact Person.

Overbrook, Incorporated, 4780 Tower Hill Rd., 02879. Tel: 203-281-4798. Rev. Juan Sabadell, L.C., Contact Person.

WEST WARWICK. *Tides Family Services*, Family Counseling, 1599 Main St., 02893. Tel: 401-822-1360. Bro. Michael Reis, F.S.C., Pres./Treas.
Branch Offices: Tides Outreach Project, 260 Highland Ave., Providence, 02906. Tides' Hispanic Outreach Project, 400 Dexter Ave., Central Falls, 02863. Staff 29; Assisted 1,500.

RELIGIOUS INSTITUTES OF MEN REPRESENTED IN THE DIOCESE

For further details refer to the corresponding bracketed number in the Religious Institutes of Men or Women section.

[0200]—*Benedictine Monks*.—O.S.B.
[]—*Brothers of Our Lady of Providence*.—O.L.P.
[0330]—*Brothers of the Christian Schools*. (New England-Long Island Prov.).—F.S.C.
[1100]—*Brothers of the Sacred Heart*.—S.C.
[0310]—*Congregation of Christian Brothers*.—C.F.C.
[0520]—*Franciscan Friars*. (Prov. of the Most Holy Name).—O.F.M.
[0650]—*Holy Ghost Fathers*. (Eastern Prov.).—C.S.Sp.
[0730]—*Legionaires of Christ*.—L.C.
[1210]—*Missionaries of St. Charles (Scalabrinians)*.—C.S.
[1110]—*Missionaries of the Sacred Heart*.—M.S.C.
[0430]—*Order of Preachers (Dominicans)*. (Prov. of St. Joseph).—O.P.
[1220]—*Servants of Charity*.—S.C.
[0370]—*Society of St. Columban*.—S.S.C.

RELIGIOUS INSTITUTES OF WOMEN REPRESENTED IN THE DIOCESE

[0130]—*Apostles of the Sacred Heart of Jesus*.—A.S.C.J.
[0230]—*Benedictine Sisters of Pontifical Jurisdiction*.—O.S.B.
[2250]—*Benedictines of Jesus Crucified*.—O.S.B.
[0350]—*Carmelite Sisters (Corpus Christi)*.—O.Carm.
[3090]—*Congregation of Our Lady, Help of Clergy*.—C.L.H.C.
[0940]—*Daughters of St. Mary of Providence*.—D.S.M.P.
[0820]—*Daughters of the Holy Spirit*.—D.H.S.
[0420]—*Discalced Carmelite Nuns*.—O.C.D.
[1070-15]—*Dominican Sisters*.—O.P.
[1170]—*Felician Sisters*.—C.S.S.F.
[]—*Franciscan Apostolic Sisters*.—F.A.S.
[1370]—*The Franciscan Missionaries of Mary*.—F.M.M.
[3790]—*Institute of the Sisters of St. Dorothy*.—S.S.D.
[2340]—*Little Sisters of the Poor*.—L.S.P.
[3450]—*Religious of Jesus and Mary*.—R.J.M.
[2070]—*Religious of the Holy Union of the Sacred Hearts*.—S.U.S.C.
[3430]—*Religious Teachers Filippini*.—M.P.F.
[3650]—*Servants of Our Lady, Queen of the Clergy*.—S.R.C.
[2575]—*Sisters of Mercy of the Americas*.—R.S.M.
[3000]—*Sisters of Notre Dame de Namur*.—S.N.D.deN.
[3720]—*Sisters of Saint Anne*.—S.S.A.
[3750]—*Sisters of St. Chretienne*.—S.S.CH.
[3815]—*Sisters of St. Jeanne d'Arc*.—S.J.A.
[3860]—*Sisters of St. Joseph of Cluny*.—S.J.C.
[3830]—*Sisters of St. Joseph of Springfield*.—S.S.J.
[2980]—*Sisters of the Congregation of Notre Dame*.—C.N.D.
[3180]—*Sisters of the Cross and Passion*.—C.P.
[3310]—*Sisters of the Presentation of Mary*.—P.M.
[]—*Sisters of the Presentation of Mary*.
[3320]—*Sisters of the Presentation of the B.V.M*.—P.B.V.M.
[4040]—*Society of St. Ursula*.—S.U.
[4048]—*Society of the Sisters, Faithful Companions of Jesus*.—F.C.J.

DIOCESAN CEMETERIES

PROVIDENCE. *St. Patrick's*.
BARRINGTON. *Maria Del Campo*.
CRANSTON. *St. Ann's*.
CUMBERLAND. *Resurrection*.
EAST PROVIDENCE. *Gate of Heaven*.
MIDDLETOWN. *St. Columba*.
PAWTUCKET. *Mount St. Mary's*.
St. Francis.
WEST GREENWICH. *St. Joseph*.

NECROLOGY

† Cardoza, Joseph A., Newport, RI, Jesus Savior Church. —Died Oct. 9, 1996.
† Cassidy, James J., Cumberland, RI, Mt. St. Rita Health Centre. —Died Feb. 4, 1996.
† Condon, John P., Newport, RI, St. Augustin Rectory. —Died Jan. 3, 1996.
† deCampos, Jacinto A., Providence, RI, Our Lady of Rosary Church. —Died March 18, 1996.
† Fay, John P., (Retired). —Died March 24, 1996.
† Maguire, Peter J., (Retired). —Died July 8, 1996.
† Page, Russell B., Chepachet, RI, St. Eugene Rectory. —Died Oct. 10, 1996.

Diocese of Pueblo

(Dioecesis Pueblensis)

Most Reverend

ARTHUR N. TAFOYA, D.D.

Bishop of Pueblo; ordained May 12, 1962; appointed July 1, 1980; consecrated September 10, 1980; installed September 10, 1980. *Mailing Address: 1001 Grand Ave., Pueblo, CO, 81003.* Tel.: 719-544-9861; Fax: 719-544-5202.

Most Reverend

CHARLES A. BUSWELL, D.D.

Retired Bishop of Pueblo; ordained July 9, 1939; appointed August 8, 1959; consecrated September 30, 1959; installed October 6, 1959; retired September 18, 1979. *Res., 13 Tartan Ln., Pueblo, CO, 81001.*

DIOCESAN PATRON: St. Therese of the Child Jesus. Secondary Patroness: Our Lady of Guadalupe.

ERECTED A DIOCESE NOVEMBER 15, 1941.

Square Miles 48,155.

Comprises the 29 Counties of Alamosa, Archuleta, Baca, Bent, Conejos, Costilla, Crowley, Custer, Delta, Dolores, Fremont, Gunnison, Hinsdale, Huerfano, Kiowa, La Plata, Las Animas, Mesa, Mineral, Montezuma, Montrose, Otero, Ouray, Prowers, Pueblo, Rio Grande, Saguache, San Juan and San Miguel in the southern part of the State of Colorado.

For legal titles of parishes and diocesan institutions, consult the Business Office.

Catholic Pastoral Center: 1001 N. Grand Ave., Pueblo, CO, 81003. Tel.: 719-544-9861; Fax: 719-544-5202.

STATISTICAL OVERVIEW

Personnel	
Bishop	1
Retired Bishops	1
Priests: Diocesan Active in Diocese	38
Priests: Active Outside Diocese	4
Priests: Diocesan in Foreign Missions	1
Priests: Retired, Sick or Absent	33
Number of Diocesan Priests	76
Religious Priests in Diocese	40
Extern Priests in Diocese	1
Ordinations:	
Permanent Deacons in Diocese	6
Total Brothers	13
Total Sisters	93
Parishes	
Parishes	54
With Resident Pastor:	
Resident Diocesan Priests	34
Resident Religious Priests	19
Without Resident Pastor:	
Administered by Priests	4
Administered by Permanent Deacons	1
Administered by Women Religious	1
Missions	61
Professional Ministry Personnel:	
Sisters	10
Lay Ministers	48
Welfare	
Catholic Hospitals	5
Total Assisted	877,712
Homes for the Aged	4
Special Centers for Social Services	1
Total Assisted	2,997
Educational	
Diocesan Students in Other Seminaries	6
Total Seminarians	6
High Schools, Diocesan and Parish	1
Total Students	225
High Schools, Private	1
Total Students	100
Elementary Schools, Diocesan and Parish	4
Total Students	1,027
Elementary Schools, Private	1
Total Students	223
Catechesis/Religious Education:	
High School Students	2,203
Elementary Students	5,137
Total Students Under Catholic Instruction	8,921
Teachers in the Diocese:	
Sisters	12
Lay Teachers	102
Vital Statistics	
Receptions into the Church:	
Infant Baptism Totals	2,072
Adult Baptism Totals	138
Received into Full Communion	377
First Communions	1,482
Confirmations	875
Marriages:	
Catholic	338
Interfaith	140
Total Marriages	478
Deaths	1,224
Total Catholic Population	104,592
Total Population	487,615

Former Bishops—Most Rev. JOSEPH CLEMENT WILLGING, D.D., First Bishop of Pueblo; ord. June 20, 1908; appt. Dec. 6, 1941; cons. Feb. 24, 1942; Assistant at Pontifical Throne, Feb. 20, 1958; died March 3, 1959.

Catholic Pastoral Center—1001 N. Grand Ave., Pueblo, 81003. Tel: 719-544-9861; 1-800-354-2729; Fax: 719-544-5202. Office Hours: Mon.-Fri. 8-12 & 1-5.

Vicar General—Rev. EDWARD H. NUNEZ, V.G.

Moderator of the Curia—Vacant; Dir.; Rev. MARK A. PLEWKA, J.C.L., Chancellor; Mrs. LORRAINE GUERIN, Vice Chancellor.

Diocesan Tribunal—

Judicial Vicar—Rev. MARK A. PLEWKA, J.C.L.

Adjutant Judicial Vicar—Rev. MICHAEL A. KURZ, J.C.L.; DAVID L. RICKEN, J.C.L.

Promotor Justitiae—Revs. JOSEPH P. MCGUINNESS; DAVID L. RICKEN, J.C.L.

Defensores Vinculi—Revs. RICHARD F. BECKER; ROGER P. DORCY; GEORGE T. HOLLAND; DANIEL R. HUBER; JOSEPH P. MCGUINNESS; EDWARD H. NUNEZ, V.G.; RONALD ROCHE; JEROME A. RYKOWSKI; ERVIN J. SCHMITT.

Judicial Experts—Rev. MARVIN J. KAPUSHION, M.S.W., J.C.L., L.C.S.W.; Dr. MICHAEL MILLARD, Ph.D.

Secretarial to the Tribunal—Ms. DONI NEEDHAM.

Judges—Revs. RICHARD F. BECKER; ROGER P. DORCY; EDWARD H. NUNEZ, V.G.

Ecclesiastical Notaries—Mrs. LORRAINE GUERIN; Ms. DONI NEEDHAM; Rev. MARK T. BETTINGER.

Presbyteral Council-College of Consultors—Ex-Officio: Most Rev. ARTHUR N. TAFOYA, D.D.; Revs. MARK A. PLEWKA, J.C.L.; EDWARD H. NUNEZ, V.G.; CHARLES A. SENA, Vice Chm. & Treas. JESSE PEREZ, Chm. THOMAS M. ADRIANS; ERVIN J. SCHMITT; JAMES F. KOENIGSFELD, V.F.

Deans—Pueblo Deanery: Rev. ROGER P. DORCY, V.F.; Alamosa Deanery: Vacant; Durango Deanery: Rev. MICHAEL MCCLEARY, V.F.; Grand Junction Deanery: Rev. JAMES F. KOENIGSFELD, V.F.; La Junta Deanery: Vacant; Walsenburg Deanery: Rev. BENJAMIN J. BACINO, V.F.

Archivist—Mrs. LORRAINE GUERIN.

Diocesan Offices and Specialists

The Bishop of Pueblo, a Corporation Sole—1001 N. Grand Ave., Pueblo, 81003. Tel: 719-544-9861.

Diocesan Business Office—

Diocesan Director of Business & Finance—Mrs. VIRGINIA JIMENEZ, *1001 N. Grand Ave., Pueblo, 81003.*

Diocesan Office for Development—Mr. THOMAS J. WEAVER, C.F.R.E.

Finance Advisory Council—Mr. ART ESCOBEDO, *P.O. Box 1262, Pueblo, 81002.* Tel: 719-546-0758.

Diocesan Newspaper—"The Chronicle of Catholic Life"; Most Rev. ARTHUR N. TAFOYA, D.D., Publisher, *1001 Grand Ave., Pueblo, 81003.* Tel: 719-544-9861. Managing Editor: *109 Pawnee Ave., Manitou Springs, 80829.* Tel: 719-685-5202.

Coordinator for Schools—Sr. ANDREA VASQUEZ, O.S.B.

Liaison for Organizations—Mrs. RITA ROMERO, Contact Person.

Missions—Dir. Curia, *1001 N. Grand Ave., Pueblo, 81003.* Tel: 719-544-9861.

Holy Childhood, Association—Dir. Curia, *1001 N. Grand Ave., Pueblo, 81003.* Tel: 719-544-9861.

Propagation of the Faith—Dir. Curia, *1001 N. Grand Ave., Pueblo, 81003.* Tel: 719-544-9861.

Family Life Ministries—Mr. LUCIO FLORES, *302 Jefferson St., Pueblo, 81004.* Tel: 719-544-4233.

Migrant Ministry—Sr. ANDREA VASQUEZ, O.S.B., Specialist.

Religious Education / Youth and Young Adult Ministry—Mr. JAMES SCIEGEL, Specialist, Resource Library; Mrs. FRANCES INGO. Tel: 719-544-9861.

Worship—Mrs. PAULA GIORDANO, Contact.

R.C.I.A.—Mr. JIM SCIEGEL, Coord.

Diocesan Liturgical Council—Most Rev. ARTHUR N. TAFOYA, D.D., Contact Person.

Campus Ministry—Mr. LARRY HOWE-KERR, Specialist,

1001 N. Grand Ave., Pueblo, 81003. Tel: 719-544-9861., Mailing Address: *140 Elm Ave., Grand Junction, 81501.*

Vocations—Rev. RAYMOND VANDORPE, C.M., Specialist.

Catholic Social Service, Inc.—Mr. LUCIO FLORES, Dir., *302 Jefferson St., Pueblo, 81004.* Tel: 719-544-4215.

Branch Offices—Catholic Relief Services, Family Counseling Center, 302 Jefferson St., Pueblo, 81004. Tel: 719-544-4215., *Grand Junction Office.* Tel: 970-241-8475., *La Junta Office.* Tel: 719-384-9244.

The Bishop Charles A. Buswell Trust—13 Tartan Ln., Pueblo, 81001. Tel: 719-543-2804.

Boy Scouts of America—Vacant.

Cemetery Committee—Rev. WILLIAM T. GLEESON, Chm., *P.O. Box 40, Capulin, 81124.*

Catholic Charismatic Renewal Center—519 W. 11th St., Pueblo, 81003. Tel: 719-543-7313.

Clergy Benefit Society of the Diocese of Pueblo, Inc.—Vacant.

Clergy Formation Council—Rev. RAYMOND VANDORPE, C.M., *1001 N. Grand Ave., Pueblo, 81003.* Tel: 719-544-9861.

Cursillos in Christianity—Contact: *Chancery, 1001 N. Grand Ave., Pueblo, 81003.* Tel: 719-544-9861.

Diocesan Catechetical Council—Most Rev. ARTHUR N. TAFOYA, D.D., Contact Person, *1001 N. Grand Ave., Pueblo, 81003.* Tel: 719-544-9861.

Diocesan Council of Catholic Women—Rev. RICHARD F. BECKER, Moderator, *1145 S. Aspen Rd., Pueblo, 81006.* Tel: 719-544-1886.

Diocesan Liturgical Council—Most Rev. ARTHUR N. TAFOYA, D.D., Contact, *1001 N. Grand Ave., Pueblo, 81003.* Tel: 719-544-9861.

Diocesan Pastoral Council—Mr. BILL WILLS, *P.O. Box 171, Canon City, 81215.* Tel: 719-275-3649.

Father John Powers Memorial Basketball League, Inc.—Mr. ROBERT J. DOUGLASS, Contact Person, *144 Harvard Ave., Pueblo, 81004.* Tel: 719-544-7192.

John Neumann Catholic School Foundation—330 Lake Ave., Pueblo, 81004. Tel: 719-543-8864.

Due Process Board—Mr. BERNARDINO ALVAREZ, Chm., *2010 E. 13th St., Pueblo, 81001.* Tel: 719-544-4671.

Human Development Commission of the Diocese of Pueblo—Mr. ANDY CARRILLO, Chm., *1638 Laguna St., Pueblo, 81006.* Tel: 719-545-6505.

Campaign for Human Development—Mr. LARRY HOWE-KERR, Chm., *140 Elm Ave., Grand Junction, 81501.*

Nocturnal Adoration Society—Vacant, *311 E. Mesa Ave., Pueblo, 81006.* Tel: 719-545-PRAY.

Presbyteral Council—Most Rev. ARTHUR N. TAFOYA, D.D., Pres.; Revs. JESSE PEREZ, Chm. CHARLIE SENA, Vice Chm. & Treas. TOM ADRIANS; JAMES KOENIGSFELD, V.F.; ERVIN J. SCHMITT; EDWARD H. NUNEZ, V.G., Ex-Officio; MARK A. PLEWKA, J.C.L., Ex-Offico.

Standing Committees—

Clergy Assemblies—Revs. JESSE PEREZ, Chm. WILLIAM DOLL, Sec. JIM BOIES, Treas.

Continuing Education—Revs. J. WILLIAM HUBER, Ph.D., Chm. JOHN FARLEY; JOHN COSTANZO; BOB CARDEN.

Sabbatical—Revs. J. WILLIAM HUBER, Ph.D., Chm. BEN BACINO, V.F.; DANIEL R. HUBER.

Personnel—Revs. TOM ADRIANS, Chm. JESSE PEREZ; JAMES KOENIGSFELD, V.F.; WILLIAM GLEESON; JOHN COSTANZO.

[*]Posada Shelter—Ms. ANNE STATTELMAN, Dir., *1008 N. Grand Ave., Pueblo, 81003.* Tel: 719-545-8776.

Clergy Conference of the Diocese of Pueblo—Rev. THOMAS ADRIANS, *1708 Horseshoe Dr., Pueblo, 81001.* Tel: 719-542-9248.

Las Hermanas de Pueblo—Ms. ROSA LOPEZ, Pres., *USC, 2200 Bonforte Blvd., Pueblo, 81004.* Tel: 719-549-2931.

SEARCH—Ms. SANDY HANSEN, *917 E. Evans, Pueblo, 81004.* Tel: 719-546-1015; 544-8246.

Sisters' Council—Sr. ANDREA VASQUEZ, O.S.B., *1001 N. Grand Ave., Pueblo, 81003-2948.* Tel: 719-544-9861.

Legion of Mary—Mr. JACOB SHAFER, Pres., *1 Hampton Ln., Pueblo, 81001.* Tel: 719-544-4671.

CLERGY, PARISHES, MISSIONS AND PAROCHIAL SCHOOLS

CITY OF PUEBLO
(Pueblo County)

1—SACRED HEART CATHEDRAL, Rev. Anthony A. Wojcinski.
Parish Office: 414 W. 11th St., 81003. Tel: 719-544-5175.

2—CHRIST THE KING, Rev. Thomas M. Adrians.
1708 Horseshoe Dr., 81001. Tel: 719-542-9248.
Convent—11 MacNaughton Rd., 81001. Tel: 719-543-2466; Fax: 719-545-9826.

3—HOLY FAMILY, Revs. Jesse L. Perez; Frank L. Davied, O.F.M.
2827 Lakeview Ave., 81005. Tel: 719-564-2696; Fax: 719-564-4396.
Catechesis/Religious Programs—Joseph DeFrier, D.R.E.
Students 350.
Mission—Rye, Pueblo Co., St. Aloysius. Rev. Marvin J. Kapushion.
Res., P.O. Box 186, Rye, 81069.

4—HOLY ROSARY, Rev. Mark A. Plewka, J.C.L.
Office: 2400 W. 22nd St., 81003. Tel: 719-545-7219.
Res., 2207 W. 22nd St., 81003. Tel: 719-543-0917.

5—OUR LADY OF THE ASSUMPTION, Revs. Ervin J. Schmitt; Edward G. Pettit.
Parish Office: 900 E. Routt, 81004. Tel: 719-543-2168.
Res., 217 E. Mesa Ave., 81006. Tel: 719-543-7576.

6—OUR LADY OF GUADALUPE, Rev. Edward H. Nunez, V.G.
914 E. Second St., 81001. Tel: 719-542-1447.

7—OUR LADY OF THE MEADOWS, Rev. Roger P. Dorcy, V.F.; Deacon Robert J. Myscofski, Pastoral Assoc.
23 Starling Dr., 81005. Tel: 719-561-3580; Fax: 719-561-1271.

8—OUR LADY OF MT. CARMEL, Revs. William Kellett, S.J.; Eugene D. Kelly, S.J.; Harry L. Sanford, S.J.
In res., Deacon Bro. John Fava S.J.
421 Clark St., 81003. Tel: 719-542-5952.

9—ST. ANNE, Rev. James E. Friel.
Res., 2701 E. 12th St., 81001. Tel: 719-545-2644.

10—ST. ANTHONY OF PADUA. Closed. For inquiries for parish records contact the Chancery.

11—ST. FRANCIS XAVIER, Rev. Ronald Roche.
611 Logan Ave., 81004. Tel: 719-564-1125.
Mission—Beulah, Pueblo Co., Our Lady of Lourdes.

12—ST. JOSEPH, Revs. Richard F. Becker; Robert J. Carden.
Office: 1145 S. Aspen Rd., 81006. Tel: 719-544-1886.
Res., 1165 S. Aspen Rd., 81006. Tel: 719-543-0835.

13—ST. LEANDER, Rev. Edward H. Nunez, V.G.
Office: 1438 E. Seventh St., 81001. Tel: 719-544-8411.

14—ST. MARY, Rev. Erwin J. Schmitt; Rev. Edward G. Pettit.
217 E. Mesa Ave., 81006. Tel: 719-543-3601.

15—ST. PATRICK, Revs. Ervin J. Schmitt; Edward G. Pettit.
Res., 304 E. Routt Ave., 81004. Tel: 719-542-4702.

16—ST. PIUS X, Rev. J. William Huber, Ph.D.
Parish Center: 3130 Morris Ave., 81008. Tel: 719-542-4264.
Mission—Pueblo West, Pueblo Co., St. Paul the Apostle, 3130 Morris Ave., 81008. Tel: 719-547-3725.

17—SHRINE OF ST. THERESE, Rev. Vicente Paz en La Casa; Linda Davis, Pastoral Assoc.
300 Goodnight Ave., 81004. Tel: 719-542-1788; Fax: 719-542-2130.

OUTSIDE THE CITY OF PUEBLO

Aguilar, Las Animas Co., St. Anthony, Rev. Edward J. Andary.
P.O. Box 577, 81020. Tel: 719-941-4124. [CEM]
Missions—Trujillo Creek, Mount Carmel; Gulnare, Las Animas Co., San Jose.

Alamosa, Alamosa Co., Sacred Heart, Rev. Gary L. Kennedy.
P.O. Box 547, 81101. Tel: 719-589-3211; 589-5829 (Parish Center).
Station—Mosca, Adams State College, (Alamosa).

Avondale, Pueblo Co., Sacred Heart, Rev. Maurice O. Gallagher.
P.O. Box 278, 81022. Tel: 719-947-3092.
Mission—Boone, Pueblo Co., St. William.

Canon City, Fremont Co., St. Michael, Rev. Daniel R. Huber.
611 N. 11th St., 81212. Tel: 719-275-7549; Fax: 719-275-7540.

Capulin, Conejos Co., St. Joseph, Rev. William T. Gleeson.
Mailing Address: P.O. Box 40, 81124. Tel: 719-274-5304; Fax: 719-274-9865. [CEM]
Missions—La Jara, Conejos Co., Our Lady of the Valley, 19617 S. Hwy. 285, La Jara, 81140. Tel: 719-274-5647; Manassa, Conejos Co., St. Therese of the Child Jesus, 115 Main St., Manassa, 81141.; Los Sauces, St. Anthony, 18900 County Rd. 28, Los Sauces, 81151.; Romeo, Conejos Co., Our Lady of the Immaculate Conception, 211 Blanca St., Romeo, 81148.

Center, Saguache Co., St. Francis Jerome, Revs. Carlos B. Trujillo; William R. Nelson.
P.O. Box 845, 81125. Tel: 719-754-3969.
Mission—Saguache, St. Agnes, 505 Gunnison, 81129. Tel: 719-655-2530.
Station—Crestone, Tel: 719-256-4778; Fax: 719-256-4719.

Conejos, Conejos Co., Our Lady of Guadalupe, Rev. Felix M. Lopez, C.R.
Mailing Address: P.O. Box 305, Antonito, 81120. Tel: 719-376-5985. [CEM]
Missions—Antonito, Conejos Co., St. Augustine; Lobatos, Sagrada Familia; Ortiz, San Juan Nepomuceno y San Cayetano; San Antonio, San Antonio de Padua; San Rafael, San Pedro y San Rafael; San Miguel, San Miguel.

Cortez, Montezuma Co., St. Margaret Mary, Revs. William K. Connoe; Joseph P. McGuinness.
28 E. Montezuma Ave., 81321. Tel: 970-565-3308.
Mission—Dove Creek, Dolores Co., St. Jude.

Crested Butte, Gunnison Co., Queen of All Saints. Attended by St. Peter Parish, Gunnison. Rev. James F. Koenigsfeld, V.F.
Church—P.O. Box 271, 81224. Tel: 970-641-0808; Fax: 970-641-4592.

Del Norte, Rio Grande Co., Holy Name of Mary, Revs. Carlos B. Trujillo; William R. Nelson.
645 Pine Ave., P.O. Box 97, 81132. Tel: 719-657-3147; Fax: 719-657-2613. [CEM]
Missions—Los Valdeses, St. Francis of Assisi; South Fork, Rio Grande Co., Holy Family; Creede, Mineral Co., Immaculate Conception.

Delta, Delta Co., St. Michael, Rev. Charles A. Sena.
Parish Office: 628 Meeker St., 81416. Tel: 970-874-3300.
Res., 560 Meeker St., 81416. Tel: 970-874-5116.
Mission—Cedaredge, Delta Co., St. Philip Benizi, P.O. Box 713, Cedaredge, 81413. Tel: 970-856-6495.

Durango, La Plata Co., St. Columba, Rev. Michael L. McCleary, V.F.
1830 E. Second Ave., 81301. Tel: 970-247-0044; Fax: 970-385-5737.
School—Tel: 970-247-5527.
Sisters of St. Dominic 2; Lay Teachers 14; Students 310.

Sacred Heart, Rev. Joseph Gallegos, C.R.
254 Fifth Ave., 81301. Tel: 970-247-3997.

Florence, Fremont Co., St. Benedict, Rev. Michael Murray, O.S.B.; Ms. Irene Goergen, Pastoral Assoc.
622 W. Second St., P.O. Box 189, 81226. Tel: 719-784-4879.
Mission—Rockvale, Fremont Co., St. Patrick.

Fruita, Mesa Co., Sacred Heart, Rev. John J. Costanzo, Supvr.; Sr. Barbara Piotrowski S.C., Parish Dir.
Mailing Address: 513 E. Aspen Ave., 81521. Tel: 970-858-9605.

Gardner, Huerfano Co., Sacred Heart, Rev. Benjamin J. Bacino, V.F.
Mailing Address: P.O. Box 86, Walsenburg, 81089. Tel: 719-738-1204.

Grand Junction, Mesa Co., Immaculate Heart of Mary, Revs. James H. Plough; John B. Farley.
776 Bookcliff Ave., 81501. Tel: 970-242-6121; Fax: 970-242-6778.
Mission—Palisade, Mesa Co., St. Ann, P.O. Box 530, Palisade, 81526. Tel: 970-464-5157. Sr. Ann Marie Dunn, O.S.F., Pastoral Assoc.
Stations—Debeque; Collbran.

St. Joseph, Revs. John J. Costanzo; Mark T. Bettinger.
Mailing Address: P.O. Box 246, 81502.
253 White Ave., 81501. Tel: 970-243-0209; Fax: 970-243-7493.
School—Holy Family School.
North: 800 Bookcliff, 81501. Tel: 970-242-6168.; South: 303 Grand Ave., 81501. Tel: 970-241-1489.
Lay Teachers 20; Students 390.

Gunnison, Gunnison Co., St. Peter, Rev. James F. Koenigsfeld, V.F.
303 N. Wisconsin St., 81230. Tel: 970-641-0808; Fax: 970-641-4592.
Mission—Lake City, Hinsdale Co., St. Rose of Lima.

Holly, Prowers Co., St. Frances of Rome, Rev. William P. Doll.
130 S. Fifth St., 81047. Tel: 719-537-6688.
Mailing Address: P.O. Box 130.
Mission—Bristol, Prowers Co., St. Mary.

Ignacio, La Plata Co., St. Ignatius Parish, Rev. Doug Hunt, C.R.
P.O. Box 352, 81137. Tel: 970-563-4241.
Missions—Bayfield, La Plata Co., St. Bartholemew, P.O. Box 214, Bayfield, 81122; Arboles, Archuleta Co., SS. Peter & Rose, R.R. 2, 81137.
Station—Tiffany.

La Junta, Otero Co., La Junta Catholic Parish. (Formerly St. Patrick-Our Lady of Guadalupe). Rev. Thomas R. Hinni, C.M.
222 Lincoln St., Box 1181, 81050. Tel: 719-384-4342; 384-4372; Fax: 719-384-7894.

Lamar, Prowers Co., St. Francis De Sales-Our Lady of

Guadalupe, Rev. Raymond P. Grimes.
600 E. Parmenter St., 81052. Tel: 719-336-7759.

Las Animas, Bent Co., St. Mary, Rev. Philip J. Coury, C.M.
714 Elm St., 81054. Tel: 719-456-0357.

Mancos, Montezuma Co., St. Rita, Revs. William K. Connor; Joseph P. McGuinness.
P.O. Box 150, 81328. Tel: 970-533-7388.
Missions—Dolores, Montezuma Co., Our Lady of Victory Church; Rico, Dolores Co., Immaculate Heart of Mary Chapel.
Station—Mesa Verde, National Park.

Monte Vista, Rio Grande Co., St. Joseph, Revs. Carlos B. Trujillo Tel: 719-852-2673; William R. Nelson; Sr. Johnette Sawyer, O.S.B., Pastoral Assoc.
425 Batterson, P.O. Box 587, 81144. Tel: 719-852-2523.
Stations—Morada; Mountain Meadows, Tel: 719-852-5138; Homelake, Tel: 719-852-5118; High Valley, Tel: 719-852-5711.

Montrose, Montrose Co., St. Mary, Revs. James E. King; James F. Koenigsfeld, V.F.; Thomas N. Munson; Deacon Dennis Putnam.
543 S. Fifth St., 81401. Tel: 970-249-3319; Fax: 970-249-9088.
Convent—(Youth Minister Res.) 529 S. Fifth St., 81401.
Mission—Olathe, Montrose Co., Our Lady of Fatima, Tel: 970-323-6217.

Ouray, Ouray Co., St. Daniel the Prophet, Rev. Nathanael Foshage, O.S.B.
P.O. Box 565, 81427. Tel: 970-325-4373.
Mission—Silverton, San Juan Co., St. Patrick, 1005 Reece, Silverton, 81433.

Pagosa Springs, Archuleta Co., Immaculate Heart of Mary, Rev. John C. Bowe, C.R.
P.O. Box 451, 81147. Tel: 970-264-5702. [CEM]
Missions—Frances, St. Francis; Pagosa Junction, Archuleta Co., St. John Baptist; Trujillo, St. James.
Station—Chromo.

Paonia, Delta Co., Sacred Heart, Rev. Michael N. Smith, S.J., Admin.
235 N. Fork Ave., P.O. Box 988, 81428. Tel: 970-527-3214.
Mission—Hotchkiss, Delta Co., St. Margaret Mary, 331 Bridge St., Hotchkiss, 81419. Tel: 970-872-2117.

Rocky Ford, Otero Co., St. Peter, Rev. Richard L. Weyrmeyer.
1209 Swink Ave., 81067. Tel: 719-254-3565.
Missions—Manzanola, Otero Co., St. Joseph the Worker; Ordway, Crowley Co., St. Peter Church; Fowler, Otero Co., Mary Queen of Heaven, P.O. Box 214, Fowler, 81039.

San Luis, Costilla Co., Sangre de Cristo (1881) (Hispanic), Rev. Patrick M. Valdez, C.R.
Res., P.O. Box 326, 81152. Tel: 719-672-3685. [CEM]
Missions—Blanca, Costilla Co., St. James, Blanca, 81123. Tel: 719-672-3685; Fort Garland, Costilla Co., Holy Family, Fort Garland, 81133; Chama, Costilla Co., Immaculate Conception, Chama, 81153; San Acacio, Costilla Co., San Acacio, San Acacio, 81150; San Pedro, Costilla Co., SS. Peter and Paul, San Pedro, 81153; San Isidro, Costilla Co., St. Isidro; San Francisco, Costilla Co., St. Francis of Assisi, San Francisco, 81153; Garcia, Costilla Co., Sacred Heart of Jesus, Garcia, 81134.
Catechesis/Religious Programs—Students 85.

Silverton, San Juan Co., St. Patrick, Rev. Nathanael Foshage, O.S.B.
Mailing Address: P.O. Box 565, Ouray, 81427. Tel: 970-325-4373.

Springfield, Baca Co., Annunciation, Rev. James P. Walsh, S.J.
140 Kansas St., 81073. Tel: 719-523-6645.
Station—Walsh.

Telluride, San Miguel Co., St. Patrick, Rev. Kevin F. Novack, C.S.P., Admin.
P.O. Box 398, 81435. Tel: 970-728-3387.
Mission—Nucla, Montrose Co., Our Lady of Sorrows, P.O. Box 451, Nucla, 81424.

Trinidad, Las Animas Co., Most Holy Trinity, Trinidad Area Catholic Community (Trinidad Cluster), Revs. Mark D. McKenzie, S.J., Supr.; Eugene C. Renard, S.J.; Harry H. Hoormann, S.J.; Robert A. Hagan, S.J.
235 N. Convent St., 81082. Tel: 719-846-3369; Fax: 719-846-4856. [CEM]
School—237 Church St., 81082.
Sisters 5; Lay Teachers 20; Students 250.
Missions—Weston, Las Animas Co., Our Lord of Esquipula; Vigil, St. Isidore; Branson, Las Animas Co., Blessed Sacrament; Trinchera, Las Animas Co., Sacred Heart; Hoehne, Las Animas Co., St. John Baptist; Segundo, Las Animas Co., St. Ignatius.

Our Lady of Mt. Carmel, Trinidad Area Catholic Community (Trinidad Cluster), Revs. Mark D. McKenzie, S.J., Supr.; Harry H. Hoormann, S.J.; Eugene C. Renard, S.J., V.F.; Robert A. Hagan, S.J.
Mailing Address: 235 N. Convent St., 81082.
Office: 507 Alta St., 81082. Tel: 719-846-6372.
Mission—Cokedale, Las Animas Co., Sacred Hearts of Jesus and Mary.

St. Joseph, Trinidad Area Catholic Community (Trinidad Cluster), Revs. Mark D. McKenzie, S.J., Supr.; Eugene C. Renard, S.J.; Harry H. Hoorman, S.J.; Robert A. Hagan, S.J.
615 Goddard Ave., 81082. Tel: 719-846-6129.

Vineland, Pueblo Co., St. Therese, Revs. Richard F. Becker; Robert F. Carden.
1133 Lane 36, Pueblo, 81006. Tel: 719-948-2410.

Walsenburg, Huerfano Co., St. Mary, Revs. Benjamin J. Bacino, V.F.; Edward J. Andary. In res., Sr. Carol Tlack, Senior Outreach Dir.
P.O. Box 86, 81089. Tel: 719-738-1204. [CEM]
School—Lay Teachers 10; Students 102.
Convent—726 Russell St., 81089.
Missions—La Veta, Huerfano Co., Christ the King; Gardner, Huerfano Co., Sacred Heart; Chama, Huerfano Co., Our Lady of Guadalupe.

Westcliffe, Custer Co., Our Lady of the Assumption, Rev. James Mahrer, O.S.B., Admin.
P.O. Box 359, 81252. Tel: 719-783-2340.

Chaplains of Public Institutions

PUEBLO. *Colorado State Hospital*. Vacant. Tel: 719-546-4434.

CANON CITY. *Fremont Correctional Facility*. Vacant. St. Dismas Chapel.

CROWLEY. *Arkansas Valley Correctional Facility*. Vacant.

FLORENCE. *Federal Correctional Institute at Florence*. Rev. John O'Flynn.

FORT LYON. *Veterans Administration Hospital*. Vacant. Mailing Address: P.O. Box 147, 81038. Tel: 719-456-1260, Ext. 3939.

TRINIDAD. *State Home for the Aged*. Administered by priests from Holy Trinity Parish.

On Duty Outside the Diocese:
Reverend Fathers—
Gini, John E., San Miguel, CA
Haberman, C. Robert, San Rafael, CA
Kurz, Michael A., Calumet City, IL
Norman, Clifford A., Mexico
Ricken, David L., J.C.L., Rome, Italy

Absent on Leave:
Reverend Fathers—
Bonfadini, Leo
Bouchard, Norman
Groves, William
Thill, Richard
Vandenberg, James

Military Chaplains:
Reverend Fathers—
Cerwonka, Clarence G., U.S. Army

Sabbatical:
Reverend Fathers—
King, James E.
Quinn, Thomas J.

Retired:
Reverend Monsignors—
Delaney, Howard L., 7-C Bonnymede, Pueblo, CO 81001
Holland, George T.
Kane, Joseph F., 4214 Minnequa, Apt. C, St. Louis, MO 63118
Stauter, Patrick C., 999 Fortino Blvd., No. 58, Pueblo, CO 81008
Reverend Fathers—
Beno, John R., 315 W. 15th St., Pueblo, CO 81003
Blong, Delbert F., 3336 S. Ammons, Unit 12-103, Lakewood, CO 80227
Cavanagh, Michael J., 56 Wentworth, Westwood, MA 02090
Corbett, Michael E., 2102 D. Chautard Dr., Pueblo, CO 81005
Danowski, Alexander J., 653 Country Court, Grand Junction, CO 81506
Kiernan, John G., 2185 Linda Ln., Grand Junction, CO 81501
Kukucka, Joseph G., 417 Indiana St., Sugar City, CO 81076
Marcantonio, Clement, 2nd General Hospital, APO AG, 09180
McDevitt, James J., St. Vincent's Church, 840 George Bush Blvd., Delray, FL 33483
Mendrick, Paul P., 1312 Lakeview Ave., Apt. 204, Pueblo, CO 81004
Montoya, Jose J., Rowan Nursing Home, 4601 E Asbury Cir., Denver, CO 80222
O'Sullivan, John C., Livingston Baker Apts. #608, 1925 First Ave., Seattle, WA 98101
Powers, William V., 1414 E. 8th St., Pueblo, CO 81001
Racki, Leonard E., 31 Terrace Dr., Pueblo, CO 81001
Rykowski, Jerome A., 2675 Springside Ct. #3B, Grand Junction, CO 81506
Schoening, Sylvester H.
Smigiel, Walter J., 3517 Atlantic Dr., Colorado Springs, CO 80910
Sutton, John H., 310 3rd Ave., Cando, ND 58324
Sweeney, Eugene J., 120 Ashley Dr., Fairhope, AL 36532
Tomalonis, John, P.O. Box 218, Bridgewater, NJ 08807-2714
Wichmann, Edward W., 1225 Central Blvd., Apt. 903, Brownsville, TX 78520

Permanent Deacons:
Boies, James A., Sr.
Booth, William R.
Myscofski, Robert, Our Lady of the Meadows, Pueblo
Pewters, William, St. Joseph, Grand Junction
Putnam, Dennis, Montrose
Swindells, George A., Pueblo

INSTITUTIONS LOCATED IN THE DIOCESE

[A] HIGH SCHOOLS, DIOCESAN

TRINIDAD. *Trinidad Catholic Schools*, 201 Church St, 81082. Tel: 719-846-7541. Mr. Joseph A. Reorda, Prin.(Grades K-12). Sisters 5; Lay Teachers 19; Students 225.

[B] HIGH SCHOOLS, PRIVATE

CANON CITY. *St. Scholastica Academy*, 615 Pike Ave., 81212. Tel: 719-275-7461; Fax: 719-269-9531. Girls boarding and day school. (Grades 6-12). Dr. Diane Arnold, Prin. Benedictine Sisters of Chicago 5; Lay Teachers 15; Students 100.

[C] ELEMENTARY SCHOOLS, PRIVATE

PUEBLO. *John Neumann Catholic Schools*, 330 Lake Ave., 81004. Tel: 719-543-8407. Mrs. Diana Croasdell, Admin.
Elementary School, 2415 E. Orman Ave., 81004. Tel: 719-561-9419; 566-9636. Lay Teachers 14; Students 223.
Middle School, 330 Lake Ave., 81004. Tel: 719-543-8864. Lay Teachers 7; Students 93.
Pre-School, 2415 E. Orman Ave., 81004. Tel: 719-561-9419. Mrs. Rose Mary Runyan, Dir. Lay Teachers 3; Students 84.

[D] GENERAL HOSPITALS

PUEBLO. *St. Mary-Corwin Hospital*, 1008 Minnequa Ave., 81004. Tel: 719-560-4000.
For a complete listing, refer to the Hospitals section.

CANON CITY. *St. Thomas More Hospital and Progressive Care Center*, 1338 Phay Ave., 81212. Tel: 719-269-2000.
For a complete listing, refer to the Hospitals section.

DURANGO. *Mercy Medical Center*, 375 E. Park Ave., 81301. Tel: 970-247-4311; Fax: 970-382-1082.
For a complete listing, refer to the Hospitals section.

FLORENCE. *St. Joseph Manor*, 600 W. Third St., 81226-1117. Tel: 719-269-2000.
For a complete listing, refer to the Hospitals section.

GRAND JUNCTION. *Marillac Clinic, Inc.*, 600 Center Ave., Bldg. 3A, 81501.
For a complete listing, refer to the Hospitals section.
St. Mary Hospital and Medical Center, P.O. Box 1628, 81502. Tel: 970-244-2273; Fax: 970-244-7510.
For a complete listing, refer to the Hospitals section.

[E] MONASTERIES AND RESIDENCES OF PRIESTS AND BROTHERS

CANON CITY. *Holy Cross Abbey*, P.O. Box 1510, 81215-1510. Tel: 719-275-8631; Fax: 719-275-7125. Very Rev. Kenneth C. Hein, O.S.B., Admin. & Novice Master; Rt. Revs. Edward J. Vollmer, O.S.B., Retired Abbot; Warren J. Heidgen, O.S.B., Retired Abbot; Revs. Ignatius J. Smith, O.S.B., Prior & Procurator; Stephen J. Sustrick, O.S.B.; Harold M. Glentzer, O.S.B.; Lambert W. Morrow, O.S.B., Subprior; James A. Mahrer, O.S.B.; William L. Thompson, O.S.B.; Bernard P. Gervais, O.S.B.; Bede J. Butler, O.S.B.; Louis M. Kirby, O.S.B.; Henry W. Lacerte, O.S.B.; Michael D. Murray, O.S.B.; Martin de Porres J. Muheim, O.S.B.; Bros. Bernard A.F.

Best, O.S.B.; Matthew Bach, O.S.B.; David J. Downey, O.S.B.; Rev. John Robinson, O.S.B.; Bros. Aelred Wetli, O.S.B., Latin American Missions; Aloysius A.L. Shaima, O.S.B.; Deacon Paul J. Montez, O.S.B.; Bro. Gregory Legge, O.S.B.; Revs. Barnabas W. Stelzner, O.S.B.; Andrew J. Kemberling, O.S.B. Priests of Monastery 18; Professed Brothers 6; Oblates 2.

TRINIDAD. *Trinidad Area Catholic Community*, 615 E. Goddard Ave., 81082. Tel: 719-846-3360. Business Address: 235 N. Convent St., 81082. Tel: 719-846-3369. Revs. Mark D. McKenzie, S.J., Supr.; Robert A. Hagan, S.J.; Harry H. Hoormann, S.J.; Eugene C. Renard, S.J., V.F.

[F] CONVENTS AND RESIDENCES FOR SISTERS

PUEBLO. *Servants of the Blessed Sacrament*, 311 E. Mesa Ave., 81006. Tel: 719-545-7729. Sr. Elizabeth Madden, S.S.S., Supr. Sisters 6.

MONTROSE. *St. Mary Youth Minister Residence*, 529 S. Fifth St., 81401. Tel: 970-249-9088.

[G] NEWMAN CENTERS

GRAND JUNTION. *Campus Ministry - Diocese of Pueblo*, P.O. Box 246, 81502. Tel: 970-243-2686. Mr. Larry Howe-Kerr, Specialist.

University of Southern Colorado, Campus Ministry. Tel: 719-542-9248. Ms. Sheilagh McGlynn.

Adams State College (Alamosa), United Campus Ministry College Center, Rm. 329, Alamosa, 81102. Tel: 719-589-7516; 274-5304. Mr. Daniel Borg.

Fort Lewis College. Fort Lewis College Center for Campus Ministry, North Complex #7, 1000 Rim Dr., Box 7211, Durango, 81301. Tel: 970-247-7460. Ms. Lisa Sauer, Campus Min.

Mesa State College (Grand Junction), Newman Center, 1135 College Pl., 81501. Tel: 970-241-3670. Sr. Kathy Lentsch, O.S.F., Campus Min.

Western State College (Gunnison), Campus Ministry Center, 600 E. Georgia, Gunnison, 81230. Tel: 970-641-0325. Ms. Janet Johnson, Campus Min.

Otero Junior College (La Junta), P.O. Box 1181, La Junta, 81050. Tel: 719-384-4342. Mr. F. Anthony Gallegos, Contact Person.

Lamar Junior College (Lamar). (Contact Parish, St. Francis de Sales), 600 E. Parmenter, Lamar, 81052. Tel: 719-336-7759.

Trinidad State Junior College Campus Ministry (Trinidad), 600 Prospect, Trinidad, 81082. Tel: 719-846-5624. Mr. Allen Bachoroski, Contact Person.

[H] MISCELLANEOUS

PUEBLO.

**Catholic Diocese of Pueblo Foundation*, 1001 N. Grand Ave., 81003.

Deacon Candidate Formation Council, 1001 N. Grand Ave., 81003.

John Neumann Catholic School (Administration & Middle School), 330 Lake Ave., 81004. (John Neumann Catholic Schools housed at Seton Education Center).

Pueblo Community Soup Kitchen, Inc., 422 W. Seventh, 81003. Tel: 719-545-6540. Mrs. Myrtle Huff, Coord.

S.E.T. of Pueblo, Inc., 1902 E. Orman Ave., 81004. Sr. Jacqueline Riggio, S.C., Contact Person. Purpose: A ministry providing for low-income, disadvantaged, and underserved through Service, Empowerment and Transformation.

St. Anthony Community, 18 Dartmouth, 81005. Tel: 719-566-1620.

SEARCH of Pueblo, 917 E. Evans, 81004. Tel: 719-544-8246.

Serra Club of Pueblo, 3216 Baltimore Ave., 81008. Tel: 719-542-8133. Mrs. Sophie Ruskin, Pres.

Sisters for Christian Community, 1081 S. Lynx Dr., 81007. Tel: 719-547-2416. Sallie Watkins, Sec.

CENTER. *Artes Del Valle (Hispanic Craft Cooperative)*, P.O. Box 627, 81125. Tel: 719-589-4769; 754-3191. Artes del Valle is under the auspices of St. Francis Jerome Church, Center.

DURANGO. *Mercy Health Foundation*, 375 E. Park Ave., 81301. Tel: 970-382-1273. Affiliate of Catholic Health Initiatives.

GRAND JUNCTION. *Grand Valley Catholic Outreach*, 240 White Ave., 81501. Tel: 970-241-3658. P.O. Box 246, 81502.

Grand Valley Peace and Justice, 253 White Ave., P.O. Box 246, 81501. Tel: 970-243-4378. Mrs. Bev Goodrich, Dir.

St. Mary's Hospital Foundation, 2635 N. 7th St., P.O. Box 1628, 81502-1628.

St. Mary's Rehabilitation Center, Inc., P.O. Box 1628, 81502.

PAGOSA SPRINGS. *Archuleta Housing Corporation*, 713 San Juan Ave. P.O. Box 355, 81147-0355. Tel: 970-264-2195.

[I] RETREAT WORK

CRESTONE. *Spiritual Life Institute of America, Inc.*, P.O. Box 219, 81131. Tel: 719-256-4778; Fax: 719-256-4719. Revs. William McNamara, O.C.D.; David Denny, Prior. Priests 2; Brothers 2; Sisters 3.

MONTROSE. *Spes in Deo Franciscan Family Retreat Center, Inc.*, 21661 Hwy. 550, 81401. Tel: 970-249-3526. M. Joyce Martin, Pres., Bd. of Directors.

WHITEWATER. *Whitewater Community, Inc.*, 8250 Kannah Creek Rd., 81527. Tel: 970-241-3847. Sisters 2.

RELIGIOUS INSTITUTES OF MEN REPRESENTED IN THE DIOCESE

For further details refer to the corresponding bracketed number in the Religious Institutes of Men or Women section.

[0200]—*Benedictine Monks*.—O.S.B.

[1330]—*Congregation of the Mission*. (Missouri Prov.).—C.M.

[0260]—*Discalced Carmelite Monks*.—O.C.D.

[0690]—*Jesuit Fathers and Brothers*. (Missouri Prov.).—S.J.

[]—*Order Franciscan Minor*.—O.F.M.

[]—*Order of Mary Immaculate*.—O.M.I.

[]—*Paulist Fathers*

[1300]—*Theatine Fathers*. (Rome, Italy).—C.R.

RELIGIOUS INSTITUTES OF WOMEN REPRESENTED IN THE DIOCESE

[0230]—*Benedictine Sisters of Pontifical Jurisdiction*. (Chicago, IL; Covington, KY; Colorado Springs, CO; Yankton, SD).—O.S.B.

[1710]—*Congregation of the Third Order of St. Francis of Mary Immaculate, Joliet, IL*.—O.S.F.

[0420]—*Discalced Carmelite Nuns*.—O.C.D.

[1070-13]—*Dominican Sisters*.—O.P.

[1070-24]—*Dominican Sisters*.—O.P.

[]—*Guadalupanas Missionaries of the Holy Spirit*.

[2575]—*Institute of the Sisters of Mercy of the Americas*.—R.S.M.

[2960]—*Notre Dame Sisters*.—N.D.

[3130]—*Our Lady of Victory*.—O.L.V.M.

[3580]—*Servants of Mary*.—O.S.M.

[3500]—*Servants of the Blessed Sacrament*.—S.S.S.

[]—*Sisters for Christian Community*.—S.F.C.C.

[0440]—*Sisters of Charity of Cincinnati, Ohio*.—S.C.

[0480]—*Sisters of Charity of Leavenworth, Kansas*.—S.C.L.

[2360]—*Sisters of Loretto At the Foot of the Cross*.—S.L.

[1570]—*Sisters of St. Francis of the Holy Family*.—O.S.F.

[3830-15]—*Sisters of St. Joseph*.—C.S.J.

[3830-18]—*Sisters of St. Joseph*.—C.S.J.

[1720]—*Sisters of the Third Order Regular of St. Francis of the Congregation of Our Lady of Lourdes*.—O.S.F.

[]—*Sisters of Whitewater Community*.

[4060]—*Society of the Holy Child Jesus*.—S.H.C.J.

CEMETERIES, DIOCESAN AND PAROCHIAL

PUEBLO. *Gate of Heaven*. Legal Title: *Gate of Heaven Section, Roselawn Cemetery Assoc.*

AGUILAR. *St. Anthony*. (St. Anthony Parish).

CAPULIN. *St. Anthony; St. Francis; St. Joseph; and Capulin*. (St. Joseph Parish).

CONEJOS. *Conejos; Las Mesitas; San Antonio; Ortiz; and Labatos*. (Our Lady of Guadalupe Parish).

DEL NORTE. *St. Francis of Assisi*. (Holy Name of Mary Parish).

FRUITA. *Fruita Catholic*. (Sacred Heart Parish).

PAGOSA SPRINGS. *St. John the Baptist; St. Andrew Avelino; St. Francis; and St. James*. (Immaculate Heart of Mary Parish).

RYE. *Mount Olivet*. (St. Daniel Mission Parish). Legal Title: *The Rye Mount Olivet Cemetary*.

SAN LUIS. *San Luis; San Pedro; San Acacio; San Francisco; and Chama*. (Sangre de Cristo Parish).

TRINIDAD. *Trinidad Catholic*. Legal Title: Trinidad Catholic Cemetery Assoc. (Holy Trinity Parish).

WALSENBURG. *St. Mary*. Legal Title: St. Mary Cemetery Association, Inc. (St. Mary Parish).

WESTCLIFFE. *Silver Cliff Assumption Catholic*. (Our Lady of the Assumption Parish).

NECROLOGY

† McGrath, John, (Retired). —Died Aug. 18, 1996.

† Scheets, Thomas, Pueblo, CO, St. Leander's Parish. —Died Aug. 7, 1996.

† Stovik, Louis C., Pueblo, CO, St. Leander's Parish. —Died Aug. 7, 1996.

Diocese of Raleigh

(Dioecesis Raleighiensis)

Most Reverend

F. JOSEPH GOSSMAN, D.D., J.C.D.

Bishop of Raleigh; ordained December 17, 1955; appointed Titular Bishop of Aguntum and Auxiliary Bishop of Baltimore July 15, 1968; ordained Bishop, September 11, 1968; appointed Fourth Bishop of Raleigh April 8, 1975; installed May 19, 1975. *Res., 1601 Westbridge Ct., Raleigh, NC, 27606. Office: 300 Cardinal Gibbons Dr., Raleigh, NC, 27606.* Tel.: 919-821-9702.

Most Reverend

GEORGE E. LYNCH, D.D.

Retired Auxiliary Bishop of Raleigh; Titular Bishop of Satafi; ordained May 29, 1943; appointed October 20, 1969; consecrated January 6, 1970; retired July 10, 1985. *Res., P.O. Box 3, Woodlawn Station, Bronx, NY, 10470.*

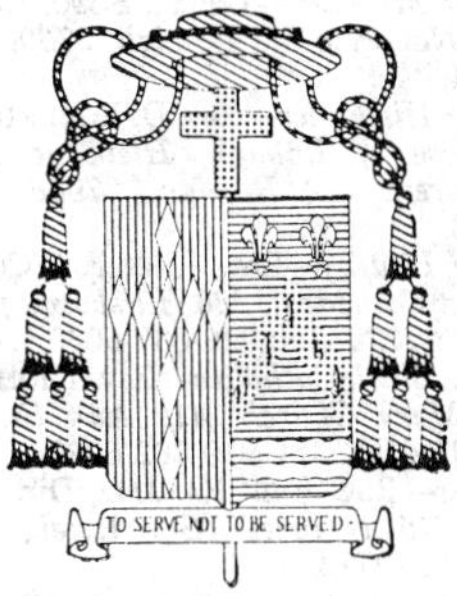

ESTABLISHED AS VICARIATE-APOSTOLIC OF NORTH CAROLINA BY POPE PIUS IX, MARCH 3, 1868.

ESTABLISHED AS DIOCESE OF RALEIGH BY POPE PIUS XI, DECEMBER 12, 1924.

Square Miles 31,875.

Comprises the following Counties in the State of North Carolina: Alamance, Beaufort, Bertie, Bladen, Brunswick, Camden, Carteret, Caswell, Chatham, Chowan, Columbus, Craven, Cumberland, Currituck, Dare, Duplin, Durham, Edgecombe, Franklin, Gates, Granville, Greene, Halifax, Harnett, Hertford, Hoke, Hyde, Johnston, Jones, Lee, Lenoir, Martin, Moore, Nash, New Hanover, Northampton, Onslow, Orange, Pamlico, Pasquotank, Pender, Perquimans, Person, Pitt, Robeson, Sampson, Scotland, Tyrrell, Vance, Wake, Warren. Washington, Wayne and Wilson.

For legal titles of parishes and diocesan institutions, consult the Chancery.

Catholic Center: 300 Cardinal Gibbons Dr., Raleigh, NC, 27606. Tel.: 919-821-9700; Fax: 919-821-9705.

Web site address: http://www.raldioc.org

E-mail address: chancery@raldioc.org

STATISTICAL OVERVIEW

Personnel	
Bishop	1
Retired Bishops	1
Priests: Diocesan Active in Diocese	46
Priests: Active Outside Diocese	4
Priests: Retired, Sick or Absent	21
Number of Diocesan Priests	71
Religious Priests in Diocese	50
Extern Priests in Diocese	16
Ordinations:	
Diocesan Priests	5
Permanent Deacons in Diocese	22
Total Brothers	8
Total Sisters	82
Parishes	
Parishes	70
With Resident Pastor:	
Resident Diocesan Priests	39
Resident Religious Priests	15
Without Resident Pastor:	
Administered by Priests	13
Administered by Women Religious	6
Missions	13
Pastoral Centers	9
Professional Ministry Personnel:	
Sisters	24
Lay Ministers	63
Welfare	
Catholic Hospitals	1
Total Assisted	6,000
Day Care and Extended Day Care Centers	6
Total Assisted	556
Special Centers for Social Services	10
Total Assisted	30,890
Educational	
Diocesan Students in Other Seminaries	28
Total Seminarians	28
High Schools, Diocesan and Parish	1
Total Students	439
Elementary Schools, Diocesan and Parish	17
Total Students	4,833
Catechesis/Religious Education:	
High School Students	2,964
Elementary Students	12,147
Total Students Under Catholic Instruction	20,411
Teachers in the Diocese:	
Brothers	4
Sisters	12
Lay Teachers	268
Vital Statistics	
Receptions into the Church:	
Infant Baptism Totals	2,572
Adult Baptism Totals	202
Received into Full Communion	423
First Communions	2,519
Confirmations	1,164
Marriages:	
Catholic	372
Interfaith	498
Total Marriages	870
Deaths	669
Total Catholic Population	125,652
Total Population	3,549,378

Former Bishops of Diocese—Most Rev. WILLIAM J. HAFEY, D.D., cons. June 24, 1925; transferred to the See of Scranton, PA, Oct. 2, 1937; installed Nov. 15, 1937; died May 12, 1954.—Most Rev. EUGENE J. MCGUINNESS, D.D., cons. Dec. 21, 1937; transferred to the See of Oklahoma City and Tulsa, OK, Dec. 8, 1944; installed Jan. 10, 1945; died Dec. 27, 1957.—Most Rev. VINCENT S. WATERS, D.D., cons. May 15, 1945; installed June 6, 1945; died Dec. 3, 1974.

Former Bishops of Vicariate-Apostolic—His Eminence JAMES CARDINAL GIBBONS, cons. Aug. 16, 1868, Titular Bishop of Adramyttum, first Vicar-Apostolic; transferred to Richmond, VA, July 30, 1872; promoted to the See of Baltimore, Oct. 3, 1877; created Cardinal-Priest of S. Maria in Trastevere, June 7, 1886; died March 24, 1921.—Most Rev. JOHN J. KEANE, cons. Bishop of Richmond and Vicar-Apostolic of North Carolina, Aug. 25, 1878; transferred to the Titular See of Jasso, Aug. 12, 1888; elevated to the Archepiscopal Dignity with the title of Archbishop of Damascus, Jan. 9, 1897; transferred to the See of Dubuque, July 24, 1900; resigned April 3, 1911; appt. Titular Archbishop of Cios, April 28, 1911; died June 23, 1918.—Rt. Rev. H. P. NORTHROP, cons. Titular Bishop of Rosalia and Vicar-Apostolic of North Carolina, Jan. 8, 1882; transferred to Charleston, Jan. 27, 1883; died June 7, 1916.—Rt. Rev. LEO HAID, O.S.B., Vicar Apostolic of North Carolina and Abbot-Ordinary of Belmont Abbey; cons. Titular Bishop of Messene, July 1, 1888; died July 24, 1924.

Office of the Bishop—715 Nazareth St., Raleigh, 27606. Tel: 919-821-9702; Fax: 919-821-9755.

Vicar General—Rev. Msgr. JAMES E. MCSWEENEY, *715 Nazareth St., Raleigh, 27606.*

Vicar General & Moderator of the Curia—Very Rev. GERALD L. LEWIS, *715 Nazareth St., Raleigh, 27606.* Tel: 919-821-9702.

Chancellor—JOHN P. RIEDY, *715 Nazareth St., Raleigh, 27606.* Tel: 919-821-9704.

Vice Chancellor for Canonical Affairs—Rev. GIRARD M. SHERBA, J.C.L., *715 Nazareth St., Raleigh, 27606.* Tel: 919-821-9756.

Chancery—715 Nazareth St., Raleigh, 27606. Tel: 919-821-9703; Fax: 919-821-9705.

Deans—Albermarle: Rev. TERRENCE COLLINS, Cape Fear: Rev. THOMAS P. HADDEN, Fayetteville: Rev. THOMAS J. GAUL, New Bern: Rev. FRANCIS MOESLEIN, Piedmont: Rev. JOHN MCGEE, O.S.F.S, Raleigh: Rev. JOHN F. O'CONNOR, Tar River: Rev. JAMES M. LABOSKY.

Diocesan Attorney—CHARLES F. POWERS, III, *P.O. Box 1471, Raleigh, 27602.* Tel: 919-828-0684.

Diocesan Consultors—Revs. THOMAS P. HADDEN; JOSEPH G. VETTER; JOHN F. O'CONNOR; FRANCIS R. MOESLEIN; MICHAEL P. SHUGRUE; GERALD L. LEWIS.

Diocesan Tribunal—715 Nazareth St., Raleigh, 27606. Tel: 919-821-9700. All rogatorial commissions should be directed to the Tribunal.

Advocates—Sr. BARBARA MARIE CADY, S.U.; DORIS S. ALBERNAZ; DONALD J. BALFE; ROBERT W. BARTOLDUS; BRUCE G. BEEZER, Ed.D.; BARBARA A. BLAIR; JOAN M. DOWD; ROBERT S. DOWD; ROSEMARY DUDASH; TEA DUDLEY; NOELIE H. DUHE, M.P.A.; JOHN R. HALADA; BARBARA HAROLD; JOY M. HARSEN, M.P.H.; MARGARET E. HAST; Rev. Msgr. JOHN L. HUBISZ, Ph.D.; SHIRLEY M. HUX; MICHAEL A. KIRK-DUGAN, J.D.; DOLORES MACK; EDWARD W.

MACK; JOSEPH E. MARTIN; LEE J. MCLURE; MARCELENE A. MCLURE; NANCY T. MILLER; PATRICIA A. MOYLAN, J.D.; ANN M. SAUNDERS; BARTOLO J. SPANO, Ph.D.; JEFFREY D. STRONG; MARY L. WILSON.

Defenders of the Bond—Revs. JOSEPH MULRONEY J.C.L.; ALBAN HARMON, C.P., J.C.L.

Diocesan Judges—Rev. Msgr. JAMES E. MCSWEENEY; Revs. JAMES F. BUTLER; THOMAS P. HADDEN; JEFFREY A. INGHAM; WILLIAM L. PITTS.

Director of the Tribunal—Sr. PATRICIA M. WILSON, S.C.

Notaries—VIKKI NEWELL; ANNE SPEICHER.

Officialis—Rev. GIRARD M. SHERBA, J.C.L.

Promotor of Justice—Vacant.

Priests' Council—Revs. PAUL W. BRANT, S.J.; DAVID BROCKMAN; TERRENCE COLLINS; THOMAS J. GAUL; THOMAS P. HADDEN; JAMES M. LABOSKY; GERALD L. LEWIS; JOHN MCGEE, O.S.F.S.; FRANCIS R. MOESLEIN; JOHN O'CONNOR, Chm. JOHN RANALLI; DOUGLAS REED, O.F.M.Conv.; JAVAN SAXON; GIRARD M. SHERBA; MICHAEL SHUGRUE; JOSEPH G. VETTER.

Sisters' Council—Sr. MARGARET HARIG, S.N.D.

Vicar for Priests—Rev. JOSEPH G. VETTER, *Sacred Heart Church, 5269 Dosher Cutoff, S.E., Southport, 28461.*

Vicars for Religious—Sr. DAMIAN MARIE JACKSON, O.S.F., *711 Mason Rd., Durham, 27712.*

Diocesan Divisions and Departments

Business Services Division—RUSSELL ELMAYAN, Dir., *Catholic Center, 715 Nazareth St., Raleigh, 27606.* Tel: 919-821-9722.

Computer Services—WILLIAM TROWEL. Tel: 919-821-9719.

Fiscal Services—ROBERT P. ZIMMER. Tel: 919-821-9725.

Development Office—DEBORAH ROSSI. Tel: 919-821-9721.

Property/Construction—ARTHUR WESCHE. Tel: 919-821-9726.

Communications Division—FRANK MOROCK, Dir., *Catholic Center, 715 Nazareth St., Raleigh, 27606.* Tel: 919-821-9732.

Evangelization Office—TERRENCE JACKSON, Dir. Tel: 919-821-9746.

Freeman Media Resource Center—TERRI RING. Tel: 919-821-9743.

Graphic Services—TAMMY S. STANLEY. Tel: 919-821-9735.

NC Catholic Newspaper—JOHN STRANGE, Editor. Tel: 919-821-9736.

Campus Ministry—Rev. PHILLIP LEACH, Dir., *Newman Catholic Student Center, 218 Pittsboro St., Chapel Hill, 27516-2738.* Tel: 919-929-3730.

Catholic Schools—MICHAEL J. FEDEWA, Supt. Tel: 919-821-9748.

Faith Development—MARY DOWLING. Tel: 919-821-9771.

Marriage Preparation—Mrs. LINDA BEDO. Tel: 919-821-9753.

Youth Ministry—MARIA MYERS. Tel: 919-821-9770.

Young Adult Ministry—CATHY RUSIN. Tel: 919-821-9771.

Adult Faith Development—ROBERT JONES. Tel: 919-821-9740.

African-American Ministry—Sr. MAXINE TOWNS, S.A., *St. Alphonsus Center, 810 N. Reid St., Wilson, 27893.* Tel: 919-821-9762.

Hispanic Ministry—TERESA SOTO, *Catholic Center, 715 Nazareth St., Raleigh, 27606.* Tel: 919-821-9764.

Vicar for Hispanics—Rev. D. ROBERTO KEENAN, *c/o Diocese of Raleigh, Hispanic Ministry, 715 Nazareth St., Raleigh, 27606.* Tel: 919-821-9738.

Office of Liturgy—Rev. JOHN F. O'CONNOR, *Sacred Heart Cathedral, 226 Hillsborough St., Raleigh, 27603-1724.* Tel: 919-832-6030.

Vicar for Black Catholics—Rev. THOMAS P. HADDEN, *St. Mary Church, 412 Ann St., Wilmington, 28401-4596.* Tel: 910-762-5491.

Vocations—Rev. JOHN RANALLI, Dir., *Catholic Center, 715 Nazareth St., Raleigh, 27606.* Tel: 919-821-9713.

Catholic Social Ministries—KATHLEEN WALSH, A.C.S.W., Dir., *Catholic Center, 715 Nazareth St., Raleigh, 27606.* Tel: 919-821-9752.

Peace and Justice—Sr. JOAN JURSKI, O.S.F., *Catholic Center, 715 Nazareth St., Raleigh, 27606.* Tel: 919-821-9751.

Senior Housing—LINDA BEDO, *Catholic Center, 715 Nazareth St., Raleigh, 27606.* Tel: 919-821-9753.

Regional Offices—

Albemarle Deanery Office—Vacant; Dir., *123 Market St., Hertford, 27944.* Tel: 919-426-7717.

Cape Fear Deanery Office—DIANE PISCZEK, M.Ed., Dir., *2805 Market St., Wilmington, 28403.* Tel: 910-251-8130.

Fayetteville Deanery Office—DOROTHY ANN PYLE, Dir., *111 Boone Trail, Fayetteville, 28306.* Tel: 910-424-2020.

New Bern Deanery Office—MICHAEL MILES, C.C.S.W., Dir., *P.O. Box 1251, New Bern, 28560.* Tel: 919-638-2188.

Piedmont Deanery—SUSAN GILBERTSON, M.S.W., *P.O. Box 647, Durham, 27702.* Tel: 919-286-1964.

Raleigh Deanery—RODERICK B. O'CONNOR, C.C.S.W., *400 Oberlin Rd., Ste. 350, Raleigh, 27605.* Tel: 919-832-0225.

Tar River Deanery—ELAINE FRANZETTI, M.S.W., *P.O. Box 8241, Greenville, 27835-8241.* Tel: 919-355-5111.

Miscellaneous Offices—

Apostleship of Prayer—Rev. MICHAEL H. JORDAN, S.J., *P.O. Box 461, Erwin, 28339.* Tel: 910-897-2277.

Apostleship of the Sea—Rev. FRANCIS R. MOESLEIN, *St. Egbert Church, 1706 Evans St., Morehead City, 28557.* Tel: 919-726-3559.

Boy Scouts—MARYANN TYRER, *3128 Turtle Point Dr., Fayetteville, 28304.*

Censor Librorum—Rev. Msgr. JAMES E. MCSWEENEY.

Engaged Encounter—Marriage Preparation and Enrichment Office, *Catholic Center, 715 Nazareth St., Raleigh, 27606.* Tel: 919-821-9753.

Holy Childhood Pontifical Association—Rev. WILLIAM L. PITTS; Sr. THERESE CHURCH, *209 S. Lumina Ave., Wrightsville Beach, 28480.* Tel: 910-256-2471.

Marriage Encounter—ROGER BOLSER; TERESA BOLSER, *1604 Laughridge Dr., Cary, 27511.* Tel: 919-319-9100.

Personnel Director—LEO TAPLER, *Catholic Center, 715 Nazareth St., Raleigh, 27606.* Tel: 919-821-9711.

Propagation of the Faith—Rev. WILLIAM L. PITTS; Sr. THERESE CHURCH, *209 S. Lumina Ave., Wrightsville Beach, 28480.* Tel: 910-256-2471.

CLERGY, PARISHES, MISSIONS AND PAROCHIAL SCHOOLS

CITY OF RALEIGH
(Wake County)

1—CATHEDRAL OF THE SACRED HEART (1924), Very Rev. John F. O'Connor, Rector.
Office: 226 Hillsborough St., 27603-1724. Tel: 919-832-6030; Fax: 919-833-4667.
Res., 15 N. McDowell St., 27603. Tel: 919-836-1790; Fax: 919-833-4667.
School—Tel: 919-832-4711. Sr. Marilyn Muldoon, O.S.U., Prin.
Ursaline Sisters 1; Lay Teachers 15; Students 265.
Catechesis/Religious Programs—Gail Halada, D.R.E.
Students 153.
Convent—219 W. Edenton St., 27603. Tel: 919-832-1109.

2—CATHOLIC STUDENT CENTER, NORTH CAROLINA STATE UNIVERSITY (1974), Rev. Alan J. Dash; Deacon John Hubisz.
Res., Aquinas House, 600 Bilyeu St., 27606. Tel: 919-833-9668.

3—OUR LADY OF LOURDES (1954), Revs. Jeffrey A. Ingham; Thanh N. Nguyen; Deacon Myles J. Charlesworth.
Office: 2718 Overbrook Dr., 27608. Tel: 919-782-1973; Fax: 919-571-9957.
Res., 2912 Anderson Dr., 27608. Tel: 919-781-9784.
School—2710 Overbrook Dr., 27608. Tel: 919-782-1670. Sr. M. Therese Grady, S.N.D., Prin.
Sisters of Notre Dame 3; Lay Teachers 19; Students 576.
Catechesis/Religious Programs—D.R.E.: Alexandra Stocking, (Adult); Donna Ashcraft, (PreK-8).
Students 293.

4—ST. FRANCIS OF ASSISI (1982), Revs. Daniel Kenna, O.F.M.; James Falduti, O.F.M.; Mark Reamer, O.F.M.; Bro. Sean O'Brien, O.F.M.
Res., 11401 Leesville Rd., 27613. Tel: 919-847-8205; Fax: 919-870-1790.
Catechesis/Religious Programs—Tel: 919-847-8205; Fax: 919-870-1790. D.R.E.: Loretta Jean Schorr, (Adult); Peggy Dunbeck, (Preschool-8); Colleen McCarthy, (High School); Ann Murray, (Family).
Students 1,250.

5—ST. JOSEPH (1968), Rev. JaVan J. Saxon.
Res., 630 Peartree Ln., 27610. Tel: 919-231-6364; Fax: 919-231-9884.
Catechesis/Religious Programs—Tel: 919-231-6364; Fax: 919-231-9884. Mary Jo Clark, D.R.E.
Students 68.

6—ST. LUKE THE EVANGELIST (1985), Rev. David D. Brockman.
Res., 12317 Bayleaf Church Rd., 27614-9165. Tel: 919-870-1490.
Church—12333 Bayleaf Church Rd., 27614-9165. Tel: 919-848-1533; Fax: 919-848-0662.
Catechesis/Religious Programs—Tel: 919-847-4973.
Students 238.

7—ST. RAPHAEL (1966), Revs. Robert S. Curry, S.J.; J. Michael Flynn, S.J.; William J. Kelley, S.J. Pastoral Assocs.: Sr. Patricia Cornell, C.S.C.; Sr. Dolores Glick, M.H.S.H.; Deacon Robert T. Madey.
Res., 5801 Falls of Neuse Rd., 27609. Tel: 919-876-1581; Fax: 919-872-3723.
St. Raphael Catholic School & Early Childhood Center—Tel: 919-876-3526. Rosalie Innacelli, Prin.
Students 234.
Catechesis/Religious Programs—Tel: 919-876-1668; Fax: 919-872-3723. D.R.E.: Mary Lynn Whittaker; Ela Milewska.
Students 923.

OUTSIDE THE CITY OF RALEIGH

Ahoskie, Hertford Co., St. Charles Borromeo (1944), Rev. James F.X. Healey, S.J.
Res., 507 W. First St., P.O. Box 605, 27910. Tel: 919-332-2939.
Catechesis/Religious Programs—Gloria Shriver, D.R.E.
Students 15.
Mission—Scotland Neck, Halifax Co., St. Anne.

Apex, Wake Co., St. Andrew the Apostle (1984), Revs. William F. Schmidt, S.A.; Edward Gallagher, S.A.; Kenneth Cienik, S.A.
Res., 1520 Cone Ave., 27502. Tel: 919-362-0414; Fax: 919-362-5778.
Catechesis/Religious Programs—Tel: 919-362-1673. Noelle Marino-Ruiz, D.R.E.
Students 1,289.

Burgaw, Pender Co., St. Joseph (1908), Rev. Christopher Balas, O.F.M.Conv.
Res., 220 Inlet Dr., Scotts Hill, Wilmington, 28405. Tel: 910-686-7724. [CEM]
Church—Rte. 1, Box 1714, 28425.
Catechesis/Religious Programs—Tel: 910-392-4778. Sr. Frances Acton, O.S.F., D.R.E.
Students 33.
Mission—Wallace, Transfiguration, Wallace.

Burlington, Alamance Co., Blessed Sacrament (1928), Revs. Juniper Alwell, O.F.M.Conv.; Daniel Quackenbush, O.F.M.Conv.; Michael Lorentsen, O.F.M.Conv. In res., Bro. Raymond Sobocinski, O.F.M.Conv.
Mailing Address: P.O. Box 619, 27216. Tel: 910-226-8796; Fax: 910-227-2896.
Res., 408 W. Davis St., 27215.
School—Tel: 910-570-0019. Mr. Thomas A. Kraft, Prin.
Lay Teachers 30; Students 360.
Catechesis/Religious Programs—Tel: 910-226-8796; Fax: 910-227-2896. Miss Sheila Murphy, D.R.E.
Students 284.

Buxton, Dare Co., Our Lady of the Seas, Rev. Andre Izac.
Mailing Address: P.O. Box 753, 27920. Tel: 919-995-6370.

Carolina Beach, New Hanover Co., Immaculate Conception (1925), Rev. Jim Behan, O.S.F.S.
Mailing Address: P.O. Box 726, 28428. Tel: 910-791-1003; Fax: 910-791-0083.
Church—6336 Myrtle Grove Rd., 28428.
Catechesis/Religious Programs—Students 55.

Cary, Wake Co., St. Michael the Archangel (1962), Revs. John A. Wall; Robert T. Schriber.
Res., 804 High House Rd., 27513. Tel: 919-467-6026.
Catechesis/Religious Programs—Tel: 919-467-7900. Stephen O. Edwards, D.R.E.
Students 950.

Castle Hayne, New Hanover Co., St. Stanislaus Kostka (1914) (Polish), Rev. Douglas Reed, O.F.M.Conv.
Res., 220 Inlet Dr.,Scotts Hill, Wilmington, 28405-6824. Tel: 910-686-7724; Fax: 910-675-2336. [CEM]
Church—4849 Castle Hayne Rd., 28429-4849. Tel: 910-675-3116 (Office); 675-3116 (Hall); Fax: 910-675-2336.

Chapel Hill, Orange Co., St. Thomas More (1940), Revs. Michael G. Clay, D.Min.; John L. Gillespie; Harry B. Zerner, S.J. Pastoral Assocs: Ms. Theresa Keller; Sr. Marie St. Paul Alspaugh, S.S.J.
Res., 740 Gimghoul Rd., 27514-3844. Tel: 919-942-1040; Fax: 919-942-6193.
School—920 Carmichael St., 27514. Tel: 919-929-1546; Fax: 919-929-1783. Sr. Marie St. Leger, S.S.J., Prin.
Sisters 1; Lay Teachers 31; Students 395.
Catechesis/Religious Programs—Tel: 919-933-1041; Fax: 919-942-6193. Mrs. Jan Vallero, D.R.E.
Students 592.

Newman Catholic Student Center, University of North Carolina (1968), Revs. Phillip M. Leach; Edward P. Mahoney; Sr. Margaret Harig, S.N.D., Pastoral Assoc.
Res., 218 Pittsboro St., 27516-2738. Tel: 919-929-3730; Fax: 919-929-3778.
Catechesis/Religious Programs—Tel: 919-933-1041.
Students 114.

Clinton, Sampson Co., Immaculate Conception (1910), Revs. John Williams; Steven Carlson.
Mailing Address: P.O. Box 859, 28329. Tel: 910-592-1384.
Missions—Mount Olive, Wayne Co., St. Mary, (1916) 311 W. Main St., Mount Olive 28365. Tel: 919-658-4023; Mount Olive, Wayne Co., Posada Guadalupana, (1993) 1501 Meadow View, Mount Olive, 28365.
Stations—Duplin Co., Carolina Turkeys; San Juan, Old Hwy. 701, Ingold, Tel: 910-592-1384.

Dunn, Harnett Co., Sacred Heart (1916), Rev. Trent L. Watts.
Mailing Address: P.O. Box 535, 28335. Tel: 910-891-1972.
Res., 209 S. Ellis Ave., 28334. Tel: 910-892-3414.
Catechesis/Religious Programs—Tel: 910-892-5982. Mrs. Jan Rebman, D.R.E.
Students 58.

Durham, Durham Co.,

1—Holy Cross, (1938) (African American), Rev. David E. Barry, S.J. In res., Rev. Harry B. Zerner, S.J.
Res., 1400 S. Alston Ave., 27707. Tel: 919-682-4852; Fax: 919-956-7174.
Catechesis/Religious Programs—Tel: 919-688-6160; Fax: 919-596-7174. Helen Hudson, D.R.E.
Students 140.

2—Holy Infant, (1970), Revs. John E. McGee, O.S.F.S.; Richard E. Cleary, O.S.F.S.
Res., 5000 South Park Dr., 27713-9470. Tel: 919-544-7135; Fax: 919-544-1799. [CEM]
Catechesis/Religious Programs—Tel: 919-544-7135; Fax: 919-544-1799. Linda Bowling, D.R.E.
Students 256.

3—Immaculate Conception, (1906), Revs. David J. McBriar, O.F.M.; John J. Heffernan, O.F.M.; Patrick E. Tuttle, O.F.M.; Deacons Laurence DeCarolis; Forrest Evans.
Res., 725 Burch Ave., 27701. Tel: 919-682-3449; Fax: 919-682-7999.
School—Immaculata, 721 Burch Ave., 27701. Tel: 919-682-5847. Mr. William Abel, Prin.
Lay Teachers 29; Students 363.
Catechesis/Religious Programs—Barbara Pegg, D.R.E.
Students 323.

4—St. Matthew, (1990), Rev. Thomas S. Tully.
Res., 1001 Mason Rd., 27712. Tel: 919-479-1001; Fax: 919-479-4848.
Catechesis/Religious Programs—Lynn Sale, D.R.E.
Students 217.
Mission—Butner, Granville Co., St. Bernadette, 1001 Mason Rd., 27712. Tel: 919-479-1001; Fax: 919-479-4848.

Edenton, Chowan Co., St. Anne (1858), Rev. Eugene M. Grabowski.
Mailing Address: P.O. Box 422, 27932. [CEM]
Church—207 N. Broad St., 27932. Tel: 919-482-2617.
Mission—Columbia, All Souls.

Elizabeth City, Pasquotank Co., Holy Family (1915), Rev. Thomas R. Davis.
Mailing Address: P.O. Box 1525, 27906-1525. Tel: 910-338-2521; Fax: 919-753-4367.
Res., 1453 N. Road St., 27909. Tel: 910-335-4419.
Catechesis/Religious Programs—Mrs. Doreen Warren, D.R.E.
Students 220.
Station—Currituck, Currituck Senior Citizens Center.

Farmville, Pitt Co., St. Elizabeth (1931) (Lebanese), Sr. Grace Campbell, I.H.M., Pastoral Admin.
Mailing Address: P.O. Box 189, 27828. Tel: 919-753-4367; Fax: 919-753-4367.
Catechesis/Religious Programs—Tel: 919-753-4367; Fax: 919-753-4367.
Students 7.

Fayetteville, Cumberland Co., St. Ann (1940) (African American), Rev. Ernest Ruede.
Office:—365 N. Cool Spring St., 28301. Tel: 910-483-3216; Fax: 910-483-3216.
Res., 1100 Clarendon St., Apt. 301, 28305. Tel: 910-483-5871.
School—Tel: 910-483-3902; Fax: 910-483-3216. Sr. JoAnne Goecke, D.C., Prin.
Daughters of Charity 3; Lay Teachers 11; Students 199.
Catechesis/Religious Programs—Tel: 910-483-3216; Fax: 910-483-3216. Michael Patterson, D.R.E.
Students 121.
Convent—1933 Martindale Dr., 28304. Tel: 910-484-1675.

St. Elizabeth Ann Seton (1981), Rev. Willard Rucinski, O.S.F.S.
Res., 700 Carnegie St., 28311. Tel: 910-488-8274.
Catechesis/Religious Programs—Brenda Bissonnette, D.R.E.
Students 190.

St. Patrick (1829), Revs. John G. Durbin, S.T.L.; Robert Staley; Deacon Louis Hanemann.
Mailing Address: 2840 Village Dr., 28304. Tel: 910-323-2410; Fax: 910-323-3006.
Res., 433 Holly Ln., 28305. Tel: 910-484-8253.
School—1620 Marlborough Rd., 28304. Tel: 910-323-1865; Fax: 910-484-1573. Mr. Tom Manion, Prin.
Lay Teachers 11; Students 257.
Catechesis/Religious Programs—Tel: 910-323-3006; Fax: 910-323-3006. Tim McHale, D.R.E.
Students 596.

Fuquay-Varina, Wake Co., St. Bernadette (1987), Rev. Francis G. Maloney; Sr. Claudia Bronsing, Pastoral Admin.; Deacon Anthony Meier.
Mailing Address: 1005 Wilbon Rd., 27526-9702. Tel: 919-552-8758; Fax: 919-552-1846.
Catechesis/Religious Programs—Tel: 919-552-8758. Mrs. Michele Dexter, D.R.E.
Students 156.
Raleigh Deanery Hispanic Office—Tel: 919-552-2922. Sr. Kelin Lee Bethea, O.P., Hispanic Min.

Garner, Wake Co., St. Mary, Mother of the Church (1966), Rev. Francis G. Maloney; Deacon Leo Tapler.
Res., 1008 Vandora Springs Rd., 27529. Tel: 919-772-5777.
Catechesis/Religious Programs—Tel: 919-779-4017. Joan Enderle, D.R.E.
Students 313.

Goldsboro, Wayne Co., St. Mary (1889), Revs. John T. Gavin, O.S.F.S.; Joseph E. Tustin, O.S.F.S.
Res., 1000 N. Jefferson Ave., 27530-3141. Tel: 919-734-5033; Fax: 919-580-0730.
School—Tel: 919-735-1931; Fax: 919-735-1917. Lynn P. Magoon, Prin.
Sisters, Servants of the Immaculate Heart of Mary 3; Lay Teachers 13; Students 304.
Catechesis/Religious Programs—Tel: 919-734-5033; Fax: 919-580-0730. Mrs. Carole M. Sears, D.R.E.
Students 262.

Greenville, Pitt Co., St. Gabriel (1936), Rev. Thomas McCann, C.P.; Lucille Gorham, Pastoral Assoc.
Res., 1120 W. Fifth St., 27834. Tel: 919-758-1504; Fax: 919-758-1479.
Catechesis/Religious Programs—Students 35.

St. Peter's, Revs. Joseph R. Jones, C.P.; Alban Harmon, C.P.
Res., 2700 E. Fourth St., 27858. Tel: 919-757-3259; Fax: 919-752-1499.
School—Tel: 919-752-3529; Fax: 919-752-7604. Bro. Simon Jaworski, O.S.F., Prin.
Franciscan Brothers (Brooklyn) 2; Lay Teachers 27; Students 520.
Catechesis/Religious Programs—Tel: 919-757-3259; Fax: 919-752-1499. Sarah McPherson, D.R.E.
Students 494.

Hampstead, Pender Co., St. Jude the Apostle, Rev. Casimir Sabol, O.F.M.Conv.
Mailing Address: P.O. Box 1790, 28443.
Res., 220 Inlet Dr., Scotts Hill, Wilmington, 28405. Tel: 910-686-7724.

Havelock, Craven Co., Annunciation (1953), Rev. Frederick R. Flaherty, M.S.
Mailing Address: Drawer B, 28532-0177. Tel: 919-447-2112.
School—Tel: 919-447-3137. Mrs. June Pietras, Prin.
Lay Teachers 20; Students 236.
Catechesis/Religious Programs—246 E. Main St., 28532. Tel: 919-447-2436. Mrs. Maureen McInerney, D.R.E.
Students 233.

Henderson, Vance Co., St. James the Greater (1925). Consolidated St. Paul and St. Catherine of Siena, Oxford merged to form St. James the Greater. Rev. J. William Long.
Res., 3275 Hwy. 158 Bypass, 27536. Tel: 919-438-3124.
Catechesis/Religious Programs—Tel: 919-438-3124. Donna Gaul, D.R.E.
Students 130.
Mission—Warrenton, Warren Co., St. Joseph, Norlina Rd., Warrenton, 27589. Tel: 919-438-3124.

Hillsborough, Orange Co., Holy Family (1989), Sr. Marie Therese Bugge, O.S.U., Pastoral Admin.
Mailing Address: P.O. Box 1061, 27278. Tel: 919-732-1030.
Catechesis/Religious Programs—Students 71.

Hope Mills, Cumberland Co., Good Shepherd (1981), Rev. Thomas J. Gaul.
Res., 116 Oak St., 28348. Tel: 910-425-1590.
Catechesis/Religious Programs—Tel: 910-425-5617. Mary Packer, D.R.E.
Students 340.

Jacksonville, Onslow Co., Shrine of the Infant of Prague, Church of the Holy Spirit (1941), Revs. Denis Hackett, O.F.M.Conv., Admin.; John Ruffo, O.F.M. Conv.
Mailing Address: P.O. Drawer 556, 28541. Tel: 910-347-4196; Fax: 910-347-9338.
Res., 330 Mildred Ave., 28540. Tel: 910-347-4171.
School—St. Francis of Assisi, Tel: 910-353-1300; 455-0838; Fax: 910-353-1305. Michele Estep, Prin.
Lay Teachers 27; Students 343.
Catechesis/Religious Programs—Tel: 910-455-1296. Sr. Cecilia McClain, S.C., D.R.E.
Students 604.

Kill Devil Hills, Dare Co., Holy Redeemer, Rev. Terrence Collins.
Mailing Address: P.O. Box 327, 27948-0327.
Office: 1206 N. Virginia Dare Tr., 27948. Tel: 919-441-8115.
Res., 109 Sunrise View, Kitty Hawk, 27949.
Mission—Nags Head, Holy Trinity.
Stations—Ocracoke, Annunciation.; Corolla, Corolla Chapel.

Kinston, Lenoir Co., Holy Trinity-Our Lady of the Atonement (1921) (African American-Hispanic), Revs. Girard M. Sherba, J.C.L.; Paul W. Brant, S.J.; Sr. Maria DiBello, R.S.M., Pastoral Assoc.
Mailing Address: P.O. Box 1455, 28503-1455. Tel: 919-523-8898; Fax: 919-527-9495.
Res., 28501. Tel: 919-523-4377; Fax: 919-527-9495.
Church—512 W. Vernon Ave., 28501.
Catechesis/Religious Programs—P.O. Box 1455, 28503. Tel: 919-523-8898; Fax: 919-527-9495. Sandra Murphy, D.R.E.
Students 91.

Laurinburg, Scotland Co., St. Mary, Rev. Kevin Fahey.
Mailing Address: P.O. Box 1148, 28353-1148. Tel: 910-276-1478.

Lumberton, Robeson Co., St. Francis De Sales (1938), Revs. Thomas Watkins; E. Fernando Torres (Columbia).
Mailing Address: P.O. Box 2249, 28359-2249. Tel: 910-739-4723; Fax: 910-739-5443.
Res., 2000 Elizabethtown Rd., 28358. Tel: 910-739-4723; Fax: 910-739-5443.
Mission—Red Springs, Robeson Co., St. Andrew, 506 E. 4th Ave., Red Springs 28377. Tel: 910-843-3440; Fax: 910-739-5443.

Morehead City, Carteret Co., St. Egbert (1929), Rev. Francis R. Moeslein; Deacon Albert Feneis.
Parish Hall—1706 Evans St., 28557. Tel: 919-726-3559.
Res., 1612 Evans St., 28557. Tel: 919-726-2535.
School—Tel: 919-726-3418. Mrs. Lesley Ferguson, Prin.
Lay Teachers 7; Students 148.
Catechesis/Religious Programs—Tel: 919-726-9696.
Students 92.

New Bern, Craven Co., St. Paul (1821), Revs. Stephen C. Worsley; Mark J. Betti; Deacon William Hunt.
Church—3005 Country Club Rd., 28562. Tel: 919-638-1984; Fax: 919-638-2144. [CEM]
School—3007 Country Club Rd., 28562. Tel: 919-633-0100; Fax: 919-633-4457. Sr. Susan Therese Armbruster, I.H.M., Prin.
Sisters, Servants of the Immaculate Heart of Mary 3; Lay Teachers 9; Students 310.
Catechesis/Religious Programs—Tel: 919-633-3030. Sr. Mildred McClain, S.C., D.R.E.
Students 201.

Newton Grove, Sampson Co., Our Lady of Guadalupe (1871), Rev. Joseph J. Yaeger.
Office: P.O. Box 100, 28366. Tel: 910-594-0287.
Res., 211 Irwin Dr., 28366-0100. Tel: 910-594-0152. [CEM]
Catechesis/Religious Programs—Ann Herring, D.R.E.
Students 130.

Pinehurst, Moore Co., Sacred Heart (1919), Revs. Robert T. Lawson; Roch T. Drozdzik.
Mailing Address: P.O. Box 1768, 28374. Tel: 910-295-6550; Fax: 910-295-6450.
Catechesis/Religious Programs—Tel: 910-295-6878. Mrs. Barbara Kemple, D.R.E.
Students 80.
Mission—Robbins, Moore Co., Blessed Juan Diego, Woodmen of the World Bldg., Salisbury & Fourcher St., Robbins, 27325.

Plymouth, Washington Co., St. Joan of Arc (1959), Sr. Margaret Gallagher, I.H.M., Pastoral Admin.
Mailing Address: P.O. Box 822, 27962. Tel: 919-793-4052.

Raeford, Hoke Co., St. Elizabeth of Hungary (1959), Sr. M. Carol Loughney, I.H.M., Pastoral Admin.
Res., 124 Palmer St., 28376-9322. Tel: 910-875-8803.
Catechesis/Religious Programs—Students 50.

Riegelwood, Columbus Co., Christ the King (1964), Rev. Giacomo G. Ghisalberti (GBG) Admin.
Mailing Address: P.O. Box 155, 28456. Tel: 910-655-3313.
Mission—Elizabethtown, Bladen Co., Our Lady of Snows, Tel: 910-862-4998. [JC]

Roanoke Rapids, Halifax Co., St. John the Baptist (1931), Rev. Robert F. Shea.
Res., 115 E. Ninth St., 27870. Tel: 919-537-4667.
Catechesis/Religious Programs—Charles Boykin, D.R.E.
Students 71.

Rocky Mount, Nash & Edgecombe Cos., Our Lady of Perpetual Help (1912), Revs. Joseph M. LaForge; Frank Stange.
Mailing Address: 331 Hammond St., 27804. Tel: 919-972-0452.
Res., 501 Hammond St., 27804. Tel: 919-972-1949; Fax: 919-972-4780.
School—Tel: 919-972-1971. Sr. Mary Paula Hughes, C.S.J., Prin.
Sisters, Servants of the Immaculate Heart of Mary 2; Lay Teachers 6; Students 131.
Catechesis/Religious Programs—Tel: 919-972-0498. Dianne Young, D.R.E.
Students 185.

Roxboro, Person Co., SS. Mary and Edward (1935), Rev. Paul P. Milcetich, O.S.F.S.
Res., 611 N. Main St., 27573-5040. Tel: 910-599-4122.

Sanford, Lee Co., St. Stephen (1932), Rev. John J. Forbes.
Res., 2402 Wicker St. Ext., P.O. Box 4659, 27331-4659. Tel: 919-776-1532; Fax: 919-776-9537.
Catechesis/Religious Programs—Tel: 919-776-3843.
Students 241.

Shallotte, Brunswick Co., St. Brendan the Navigator (1983), Rev. Francis P. Simeone, O.S.F.S.
Mailing Address: Box 911, 28459-9999. Tel: 910-754-8544.
Church & Office: 5105 Ocean Hwy. W., 28459.
Catechesis/Religious Programs—Students 62.

Siler City, Chatham Co., St. Julia (1961), Rev. Daniel M. Quackenbush, O.F.M.Conv.
Mailing Address: 1002 W. Third St., 27344. Tel: 919-742-5584.

Smithfield, Johnston Co., St. Ann (1935), Rev. Joseph G. Mulroney, J.C.L.
Res., 113 N. Seventh St., 27577. Tel: 919-934-2084; Fax: 919-934-4639.
Catechesis/Religious Programs—Students 142.

Southern Pines, Moore Co., St. Anthony of Padua (1895), Rev. James F. Butler; Sr. Mary Anne Pierson, M.S.B.T., Pastoral Assoc.
Mailing Address: P.O. Box 29, 28388-0029.
Res., 175 E. Connecticut Ave., 28387. Tel: 910-692-6613.
Catechesis/Religious Programs—Tel: 910-692-6241. Mrs. Catherine Jensen, D.R.E.
Students 215.

Southport, Brunswick Co., Sacred Heart (1941), Rev. Joseph G. Vetter; Deacon Eugene Gillis (CHL); Patricia Ciemnicki, Pastoral Assoc.
Mailing Address: 5269 Dosher Cutoff, S.E., 28461. Tel: 910-457-6173.
Res., 213 Yaupon Dr., 28461. Tel: 910-457-0223.
Catechesis/Religious Programs—Tel: 910-457-6173. Patricia Novotny, D.R.E.
Students 96.

Swansboro, Onslow Co., St. Mildred (1947), Rev. Emile Dusseault, M.S.
Mailing Address: P.O. Box 338, 28584-0338. Tel: 910-326-4370.
Res., 616 Sabiston Dr., 28584. Tel: 910-326-4370. [CEM]
Catechesis/Religious Programs—Tel: 910-326-5589. Laura Leblanc, D.R.E.
Students 237.

Tarboro, Edgecombe Co., St. Catherine (1934), Rev. William Murphy, C.P.
Res., 1004 St. David St., 27886. Tel: 919-823-3866.

Wake Forest, Wake Co., St. Catherine of Siena (1940), Rev. Richard W. Turner, Admin.
Church—701 S. Main St., 27587. Tel: 919-556-4104.
Catechesis/Religious Programs—Mr. Timothy S. McHale, D.R.E.
Students 205.
Station—Louisburg, Louisburg College Chapel.

Washington, Beaufort Co., Mother of Mercy (1963), Rev. Donald G. Baribeau, M.S.
Res., 112 W. Ninth St., 27889. Tel: 919-946-2941; Fax: 919-946-1399.
Church—111 W. Ninth St., 27889.
Catechesis/Religious Programs—Tel: 919-946-8808. Ms. Blossom von Struve, D.R.E.
Students 80.

Wendell, Wake Co., St. Eugene (1948), Rev. Robert Diegelman.
Mailing Address: P.O. Box 188, 27591. Tel: 919-365-7114.
Catechesis/Religious Programs—Midge Hernandez, D.R.E.
Students 218.

Whiteville, Columbus Co., Sacred Heart (1938), Rev. Albert Gondek, O.S.F.S.
Res., 402 N. Lee St., 28472. Tel: 919-642-3895.
Catechesis/Religious Programs—Students 56.

Williamston, Martin Co., Holy Trinity, Sr. Elizabeth Bullen, I.H.M., Pastoral Admin.
Mailing Address: P.O. Box 894, 27892-0894. Tel: 919-792-4091.
Church—Hwy. 17-13 Bypass, 27892.

Wilmington, New Hanover Co., St. Mark (1978), Revs. Matthew D. Hendrick; Ryszard Kolodziej.
Church—1011 Eastwood Rd., 28403.
Res., 145 Tanbridge Rd., 28405. Tel: 910-392-0720; Fax: 910-392-6777.
Catechesis/Religious Programs—Mrs. Mollie Berry, D.R.E.
Students 609.

St. Mary (1821), Revs. Thomas P. Hadden; Bernard E. Shlesinger, III.
Res., 405 Ann St., 28401-4592. Tel: 910-762-5491; Fax: 910-762-9664. [JC]
School—Tel: 910-762-6517. Barbara Bourne, Prin.
Lay Teachers 17; Students 301.
St. Thomas Preschool—Tel: 910-762-7764. Lydia Braye, Dir.
Lay Teachers 6; Students 72.
Catechesis/Religious Programs—Tel: 910-251-9992. Sr. Barbara Marie Cady, S.U., D.R.E.
Students 585.

Wilson, Wilson Co., St. Alphonsus De Liguori. Closed. For sacramental records contact St. Therese, Wilson.

Church of St. Therese (1923), Very Rev. James M. Labosky, V.F.; Sr. Mary Owen Kleinhenz, S.N.D., Pastoral Assoc.
Church and Office: 700 Nash St., N.E., 27893-3047. Tel: 919-237-3019; Fax: 919-237-2042.
Res., 200 Gray St., N.E., 27893-3710. Tel: 919-237-0143.
School—(Grades PreK-4). Tel: 919-237-5342; Fax: 919-237-2042.
Sisters 3; Lay Teachers 12; Students 126.
Catechesis/Religious Programs—Tel: 919-237-3019; Fax: 919-237-2042.
Students 242.

Wrightsville Beach, New Hanover Co., St. Therese (1939), Rev. William L. Pitts.
Res., 209 S. Lumina Ave., 28480. Tel: 910-256-2471; Fax: 910-256-2471.
Catechesis/Religious Programs—Tel: 910-395-2259. Mrs. Martha Vesligaj, D.R.E.
Students 150.

Special Assignment:
Reverend Fathers—
Mahoney, Edward P., Duke University, Durham, NC 27706
Ranalli, John, 300 Cardinal Gibbons Dr., Raleigh, NC 27606

On Duty Outside the Diocese:
Reverend Fathers—
Fitzgerald, R. Martin, 72 ABW/HC, 6170 Arnold St., Ste. 6, Tinker, AFB 73145-8100

Graduate Studies:
Reverend Fathers—
Garneau, James F., 300 Taylor St. N.E., Apt. L-22, Washington, DC 20017-1530
Rhodes, Ronald E., 66 Clifford St., Boston, MA 02119-2121. Tel: 617-445-9786

Absent on Leave:
Reverend Fathers—
Butler, Michael
Dorsel, John F.
Klaus, Joseph J.

Awaiting Assignment:
Reverend Fathers—
Watkins, Thomas

Retired:
Reverend Monsignors—
Jones, James, 2228 Fox Horn Rd., New Bern, NC 28562. Tel: 919-635-5318
Koch, Frederick A., St. Joseph of the Pines Villa, 592 Central Ave., Apt. D-7, Southern Pines, NC 28387
McSweeney, James E., 233 Hanover Pl., Cary, NC 27511-6624
Murphy, Francis, St. Joseph of the Pines Villa, Apt. C-13, Southern Pines, NC 28387. Tel: 919-692-8289
Reverend Fathers—
Bryon, Paul J., 5305 Quail Meadow Dr., Raleigh, NC 27609. Tel: 919-876-7232
Carcich, G. John, 592 Central Dr., Villa F1, Southern Pines, NC 28387
Chase, Chan, 415 Redd Rd., Apt. 16B, El Paso, TX 79932
Creel, Jesse, St. Albans, 120-32 193rd St., Jamaica, NY 11412-3637. Tel: 708-525-0880
Donohue, Raymond, St. Joseph of the Pines, 592 Central Ave., Apt. F-3, Southern Pines, NC 23837
Giacomini, Antonio, O.F.M.Cap., Stratford Arms, Apt. 9-B, Greenville, NC 27858
Harper, John, St. Joseph of the Pines, 590 Central Dr., Room 540, Southern Pines, NC 28387
Jacobs, Allen A., St. Joseph of the Pines, Knollwood Campus, 590 Central Dr., Southern Pines, NC 28387-2899. Tel: 910-693-3704
Keaney, James P., 1316 E. Ninth St., Roanoke Rapids, NC 27870. Tel: 919-535-4093
Ketchersid, Corbin W., 117 H Feldspar Ln., Fayetteville, NC 28314. Tel: 910-488-1797
Mulholland, Charles H., 5305 Quail Meadow Dr., Raleigh, NC 27609. Tel: 919-876-7232
O'Brien, John G., 5273 Atlantic View, St. Augustine, FL 32084
Parker, Kenneth, 704 McIntosh Rd., Carthage, NC 28327. Tel: 910-245-4640
Richardson, John L., 1889 Norwood St. S.W., Schooner's Pointe, Ocean Isle Beach, NC 28469

Permanent Deacons:
Barnes, Frank, St. Rafael, Raleigh
Broering, Harry, Mother of Mercy, Washington
Charlesworth, Myles, Our Lady of Lourdes, Raleigh
DeCarolis, Lawrence, Immaculate Conception, Durham
Dorsey, Timothy, St. Mary, Goldsboro
Evans, Forest, Immaculate Conception, Durham
Feneis, Al, St. Egbert, Morehead City
Foggie, Willie, St. Eugene, Wendell
Gillis, Eugene, Sacred Heart, Southport
Goodrow, Joseph, Infant of Prague, Jacksonville
Hanemann, Louis, St. Patrick, Fayetteville
Hubisz, John, N.C.S.U. Aquinas House, Raleigh
Hunt, William, St. Paul, New Bern
Kuntz, Edward
Madey, Robert, St. Raphael, Raleigh
McGahran, Robert, St. Brendan, Shallotte
Meier, Anthony, St. Bernadette, Fuquay-Varina
Newton, Philip, St. Luke, Raleigh
Schoebel, James, St. Anthony, Southern Pines
Tapler, Leopold, Catholic Center, Raleigh
Wobser, Don, Holy Redeemer, Kill Devil Hills
Woodhall, Johnathan, St. Anthony, Southern Pines

INSTITUTIONS LOCATED IN THE DIOCESE

[A] HIGH SCHOOLS

RALEIGH. *Cardinal Gibbons Memorial High School*, 2401 Crusader Dr., 27606. Tel: 919-834-1625. Bro. Michel Bettigole, O.S.F., Prin. Lay Teachers 35; Students 508.

[B] CHILD CARE CENTERS

RALEIGH. *St. Joseph Pre-School*, 624 Peartree Ln., 27610.
St. Raphael Catholic School and Early Childhood Center, 5801 Falls of the Neuse Rd., 27609. Mrs. Rosalie P. Innacelli, Dir. Lay Teachers 14; Students 234.

APEX. *Saint Andrew Early Childhood Center*, 3008 Old Raleigh Rd., 27502. Tel: 919-387-8656. Eileen Vaughan, Dir. Total Staff 20; Students 122.

CARY. *St. Michael Early Childhood Center*, 804 High House Rd., 27513. Ms. Elana O'Connell, Dir. Total Staff 17; Students 128.

GARNER. *St. Mary Child Development Center*, 1008 Vandora Springs Rd., 27529. Tel: 919-772-0009. Ms. Karen Williams, Dir. Lay Teachers 7; Total Staff 14; Students 120.

WILMINGTON. *St. Thomas Child Development Center*, 109 S. Second St., 28401. Lydia Davis Braye, Dir. Total Staff 11; Lay Teachers 9; Students 65.

[C] GENERAL HOSPITALS

SOUTHERN PINES. *St. Joseph of the Pines Hospital*, 590 Central Dr., 28387. Tel: 910-692-2212.
For a complete listing, refer to the Hospitals section.

[D] CATHOLIC SOCIAL SERVICES

RALEIGH. *Catholic Social Ministries of the Diocese of*

Raleigh, Inc., 300 Cardinal Gibbons Dr., 27606-2198. Tel: 919-821-9750. Kathleen Walsh, A.C.S.W, Diocesan Dir.
Regional Office, 400 Oberlin Rd. #350, 27605. Tel: 919-832-0225. Roderick B. O'Connor, C.C.S.W.
Regional Office, 2805 Market St., Wilmington, 28403. Tel: 910-251-8130. Diane Pisczek, M.Ed.
Regional Office, 1424 Broad St., P.O. Box 647, Durham, 27702. Tel: 919-286-1964. Susan Gilbertson, C.C.S.W.
Regional Office, 111 Boone Trail, Fayetteville, 28306. Tel: 910-424-2020. Dorothy Ann Pyle, C.C.S.W.
Regional Office, 502 Middle St., P.O. Box 1251, New Bern, 28560. Tel: 919-638-2188. Michael Miles, C.C.S.W.
Regional Office, 7A Landmark St., P.O. Box 8241, 27858. Tel: 919-355-5111. Elaine Franzetti, C.C.S.W.
Regional Office, 123 Market St., Hertford, 27944. Tel: 919-426-7717.
Peace and Justice Office, 300 Cardinal Gibbons Dr., 27606-2198. Tel: 919-821-9751. Sr. Joan Jurski, O.S.F.
Senior Housing Office, 300 Cardinal Gibbons Dr., 27606-2198. Tel: 919-821-9774. Linda Bedo. Total Staff 27; Total Assisted 30,890.

[E] MONASTERIES AND RESIDENCE OF PRIESTS AND BROTHERS

RALEIGH. *De Porres House*, 304 E. Park Dr., P.O. Box 12927, 27605-2927. Tel: 919-833-1893; Fax: 919-833-1449. Revs. James Burke, O.P.; James D. Campbell, O.P.; Arthur R. Kirwin, O.P.; Michael M. Burke, O.P.; Martin J. Iott, O.P.; Jude Siciliano, O.P.
Dominican Community, De Porres House, 4918 Oak Park, 27612. Tel: 919-571-8123. Revs. James Burke, O.P.; Michael M. Burke, O.P.; James D. Campbell, O.P.; Martin J. Iott, O.P.; Arthur R. Kirwin, O.P.; Jude Siciliano, O.P.

BURLINGTON. *Conventual Franciscans*, Blessed Sacrament Church, 408 W. Davis St., P.O. Box 619, 27216. Tel: 910-226-8796; Fax: 910-227-2896. Bro. Raymond Sobocinski. Total in Residence 4.

CHAPEL HILL. *Jesuit Residence, Robert Southwell House*, 211 McCauley St., 27516-2721. Rev. Mark B. Thesing, C.S.C. Total in Residence 1.

DURHAM. *Jesuit Community*, 1400 S. Alston Ave., 27707. Tel: 919-682-4852.
Jesuits in Eastern North Carolina: Revs. James F.X. Healey, S.J.; Michael H. Jordan, S.J.; Harry B. Zerner, S.J.; Robert Curry, S.J.; William J. Kelley, S.J.; Michael J. Flynn, S.J.; David E. Barry, S.J.

GREENVILLE. *St. Peter Friary*, 2606 E. Fifth St., 27858. Franciscan Brothers of Brooklyn. Bro. Simon Jaworski, O.S.F.

WILMINGTON. *Conventual Franciscans O.F.M.Conv.*, Duns Scotus Friary, 220 Inlet Dr., Scots Hill, 28405. Tel: 910-686-7724. Bro. Paul Hardison, O.F.M.Conv. In res., Revs. Casimir Sabol, O.F.M.Conv.; Christopher Balas, O.F.M.Conv.; Douglas Reed, O.F.M.Conv.

[F] CONVENTS AND RESIDENCES FOR SISTERS

RALEIGH. *Cathedral Convent-Ursuline Sisters*, 219 W. Edenton St., 27603. Tel: 919-832-9035.
Sisters of Charity of Seton Hill, 2433 Milburnie Rd., 27610.
Sisters of Divine Providence, 109 Autumn Chase Dr., 27613. Tel: 919-571-0325.
Sisters of Notre Dame, 3905 Yew Circle, 27612. Tel: 919-781-3739. Sisters 3.
Sisters of the Holy Cross, 1213-E Manassas Ct., 27609. Tel: 919-872-3418. Sisters 2.

AHOSKIE. *Sisters of St. Louis—California Region*, 409 W. Church St., 27910. Tel: 919-332-2220.

CARRBORO. *Sisters of Notre Dame*, 606 N. Greensboro St. C-3, 27510. Tel: 919-933-0655.

CARY. *Sisters of Mercy of the Americas*, 129 Carmichael Ct., 27511. Tel: 919-481-4402.
Sisters of St. Francis of Sylvania, Ohio, 1204-C Village Greenway, 27511. Tel: 919-460-6218.

CHAPEL HILL. *St. Thomas More Sisters' Residence*, 301 Colony Woods Dr., 27514. Tel: 919-929-1547. Sisters 3.
Sisters, Servants of the Immaculate Heart of Mary, 5 Lanark Rd., 27514.

DURHAM. *Dominican Congregation of St. Catherine De-Ricci*, 711 Mason Rd., 27712. Tel: 919-477-1285; Fax: 919-477-9485.
Sisters of St. Francis of Philadelphia, 711 Mason Rd., 27712. Tel: 919-477-1285; Fax: 919-477-9485.

FARMVILLE. *Sisters, Servants of the Immaculate Heart of Mary*, P.O. Box 189, 27828-0189. Tel: 919-753-4367.

FAYETTEVILLE. *Daughters of Charity*, Marguerite Naseau House, 1933 Martindale Dr., 28304. Tel: 910-484-1675. Daughters of Charity of St. Vincent de Paul.

FUQUAY-VARINA. *Adrian Dominicans of the Most Holy Rosary*, St. Dominic's, 609 Tilley St., 27526. Mailing Address: P.O. Box 757, 27526. Tel: 919-557-5783.
Sisters of Saint Francis, 125 Church St., 27526. Tel: 919-557-5372.

GOLDSBORO. *St. Mary's Convent*, 1603 Edgerton St., 27530. Tel: 919-735-0838. Sisters, Servants of the Immaculate Heart of Mary.

GREENVILLE. *Daughters of Wisdom*, 303 Oak St., 27858. *Other Residence*: 110-B Eric Ct., 27858. Tel: 919-758-5349. Sisters 2.

JACKSONVILLE. *Holy Spirit Convent*, 3 East Dr., 28546. Tel: 910-353-1200. Total in Residence 4.

KILL DEVIL HILLS. *Sisters of Charity*, 521 Wax Myrtle Dr., 27948. Tel: 919-480-3570. Sr. Margarita M. Brewer, S.C.; Sr. Mary Kay Bush, S.C.; Sr. Francis Agnes Anthony, S.C.

KINSTON. *Sisters of Mercy*, 716 West Rd., 28501. Tel: 919-523-9490.

NEW BERN. *St. Paul Convent*, 3003 Country Club Rd., 28562. Tel: 919-637-3726. Total in Residence 3.
Sisters of Charity of Seton Hill, 1307 B Stallings Pkwy., 28562.

PLYMOUTH. *Sisters, Servants of the Immaculate Heart of Mary*, P.O. Box 822, 27962. Tel: 919-793-4052.

RAEFORD. *St. Elizabeth of Hungary Parish House*, 124 Palmer St., 28376. Tel: 910-875-8803. Sisters 1.

ROCKY MOUNT. *Our Lady of Perpetual Help Convent*, 328 Hammond St., 27804. Tel: 919-446-4515. Sisters, Servants of the Immaculate Heart of Mary. Total in Residence 2.

ROLESVILLE. *Sisters For Christian Community*, P.O. Box 517, 27571.

SANFORD. *St. Mark's Convent*, 807 Valley Rd., 27330. Tel: 919-776-5350. Sisters of St. Joseph of St. Mark 2.

SOUTHERN PINES. *Missionary Servants of the Most Blessed Trinity*, 565 N. May St., 28387-5611. Tel: 910-692-4032.
St. Joseph of the Pines Convent, 590 Central Dr., 28387. Tel: 910-692-6848. Sisters of Providence 3.

TARBORO. *Congregation of St. Agnes*, 701 Cedar Ln., 27886. Tel: 919-823-8801.

WILLIAMSTON. *Sisters, Servants of the Immaculate Heart of Mary*, 503 E. Simmons Ave., 27892. Tel: 919-792-4091.

WILMINGTON. *Sisters of St. Francis of Philadelphia*, 5009 Lord Tennyson Rd., 28405. Tel: 910-392-4778.
Sisters of St. Ursula, 216 S. Fifth Ave., 28401. Tel: 910-763-6770. Sisters 4.

WILSON. *Franciscan Sisters of the Atonement*, 810 N. Reid St., 27893.
Sisters of Notre Dame, 911 Branch St. N.W., 27893-2925. Total in Residence 3.

[G] RETREAT HOUSES

RALEIGH. *Madonna House*, 424 Rose Ln., 27610. Tel: 919-231-4049. Miss Theresa Davis, Dir.

DURHAM. *Avila Retreat Center*, 711 Mason Rd., 27712. Tel: 919-477-1285; Fax: 919-477-9485. Sr. Damian Marie Jackson, O.S.F., Dir. Total Staff 8; Total in Residence 2.

[H] COLLEGE CAMPUS MINISTRY CENTERS

RALEIGH. *Catholic Student Center*, North Carolina State University, Aquinas House, 600 Bilyeu St., 27606. Tel: 919-833-9668. Rev. Alan J. Dash.

CHAPEL HILL. *Newman Catholic Student Center*, University of North Carolina, 218 Pittsboro St., 27516. Revs. Phillip M. Leach; Edward P. Mahoney.

DURHAM. *Catholic Student Center for Students at Duke University*, Box 99057, 27708-9057. Tel: 919-684-8959. Rev. Michael P. Shugrue.
North Carolina Central University, 1400 S. Alston Ave., 27707. Tel: 919-682-4852. Rev. David E. Barry, S.J.

ELON COLLEGE. *Elon College*, 2960 Campus Box, 27244-2010. Tel: 910-226-8796. Mailing Address: Catholic Campus Ministry, Campus Box 2960, 27244-2010. Tel: 910-538-2741. Rev. Michael Lorentsen, O.F.M.Conv., Campus Min.

GREENVILLE. *Catholic Student Center for Students at East Carolina University*, P.O. Box 2605, 27836-2605. Center, 953 E. 10th St., 27858. Tel: 919-757-3760. Office, 955 E. 10th St., 27858. Tel: 919-757-1991. Rev. Paul Vaeth, C.P.

WILMINGTON. *Catholic Student Center*, University of North Carolina at Wilmington, 4802 College Acres Dr., 28403. Tel: 910-791-7167. Rev. William L. Pitts.

[I] MISCELLANEOUS

RALEIGH. *Catholic Housing Corporation*, 300 Cardinal Gibbons Dr., 27606.
Catholic Parish Outreach, 408 Capital Blvd., 27603. Tel: 919-834-9680. Total Staff 81; Total Assisted 16,306.
The Clergy Retirement Plan of Diocese of Raleigh, 300 Cardinal Gibbons Dr., 27606.
Vocations Office, 300 Cardinal Gibbons Dr., 27606. Tel: 919-821-9713; Fax: 919-821-9705. Rev. John A. Ranalli, Dir.

NORTH TOPSAIL BEACH. *Marianist Family Ministry, Inc.*, Christian Family Living Center, 2006 Wicker St., 28460. Tel: 910-328-1584. Joseph Dicostanzo. Total Staff 230; Total in Residence 1,704.

PINEHURST. *St. Joseph of the Pines Home Health Agency*, 95 Aviemore Dr., 28374. Tel: 910-295-3920. Legal Title: *St. Joseph of the Pines, Inc.* Lorena Moree, Exec. Dir. & Chief Oper. Officer.
Serving Moore, Lee, Hoke, Anson, Harnett, Davidson, Randolph, Montgomery, Robeson, Scotland, Chatham, Richmond, Mecklenburg and Cumberland Counties. Home Health Agencies 14; Long Term Care Facilities 2; Adult Day Care Center 1; Acute Care Beds 4; Retirement Villas, Low-income Housing for elderly.

SMITHFIELD. *Short Journey Center*, 2323 Cleveland Rd., 27577. Tel: 919-934-7463; Fax: 919-934-7464.

SOUTHERN PINES. *St. Joseph of the Pines Retirement Villa*, 592 Central Dr., 28387. Tel: 910-692-6455. Mrs. Denise Davidson, Dir. Total Staff 7; Total in Residence 75.

RELIGIOUS INSTITUTES OF MEN REPRESENTED IN THE DIOCESE

For further details refer to the corresponding bracketed number in the Religious Institutes of Men or Women section.

[0470]—*The Capuchin Friars.*—O.F.M.Cap.
[1000]—*Congregation of the Passion.*—C.P.
[0480]—*Conventual Franciscans.*—O.F.M.Conv.
[0520]—*Franciscan Friars.*—O.F.M.
[0530]—*Franciscan Friars of the Atonement.*—S.A.
[0690]—*Jesuit Fathers and Brothers.* (Maryland & New York Provs.).—S.J.
[0720]—*The Missionaries of Our Lady of La Salette.*—M.S.
[0920]—*Oblates of St. Francis De Sales.* (American Prov.).—O.S.F.S.
[0430]—*Order of Preachers (Dominicans).*—O.P.
[0610]—*Priests of the Congregation of Holy Cross.*—C.S.C.

RELIGIOUS INSTITUTES OF WOMEN REPRESENTED IN THE DIOCESE

[3710]—*Congregation of the Sisters of Saint Agnes.*—C.S.A.
[3935]—*Congregation of the Sisters of St. Louis.*—S.S.L.
[1920]—*Congregation of the Sisters of the Holy Cross.*—C.S.C.
[0760]—*Daughters of Charity of St. Vincent de Paul.*—D.C.
[0960]—*Daughters of Wisdom.*—D.W.
[1070-13]—*Dominican Sisters.*—O.P.
[1070-17]—*Dominican Sisters.*—O.P.
[1190]—*Franciscan Sisters of the Atonement.*—S.A.
[2575]—*Institute of the Sisters of Mercy of the Americas.* (Belmont, NC; Merion, PA; Hartford, CT).—R.S.M.
[]—*Mission Helpers of the Sacred Heart.*—M.H.S.H.
[2790]—*Missionary Servants of the Most Blessed Trinity.*—M.S.B.T.
[]—*Sisters for Christian Community.*—S.F.C.C.
[0570]—*Sisters of Charity of Seton Hill, Greensburg, Pennsylvania.*—S.C.
[0990]—*Sisters of Divine Providence.*—C.D.P.
[2990]—*Sisters of Notre Dame.* (Chardon, OH).—S.N.D.
[3340]—*Sisters of Providence.*—S.P.
[1650]—*Sisters of St. Francis of Philadelphia.*—O.S.F.
[3830]—*Sisters of St. Joseph.*—S.S.J.
[3910]—*Sisters of St. Joseph of St. Mark.*—S.J.S.M.
[1830]—*Sisters of the Good Shepherd.* (Silver Spring, MD).—R.G.S.
[1990]—*Sisters of the Holy Names of Jesus and Mary.*—S.N.J.M.
[2150]—*Sisters, Servants of the Immaculate Heart of Mary.*—I.H.M.
[2160]—*Sisters, Servants of the Immaculate Heart of Mary.*—I.H.M.
[2170]—*Sisters, Servants of the Immaculate Heart of Mary.*—I.H.M.
[4048]—*Society of Sisters Faithful Companions of Jesus.*—F.C.J.
[4040]—*Society of St. Ursula.*—S.U.
[]—*Ursuline Sisters.*—O.S.U.

NECROLOGY

† O'Toole, Eugene J., Bordentown, NJ, Bordentown Correctional Center. —Died March 5, 1996.
† Waters, James E., (Retired). —Died March 29, 1996.

Diocese of Rapid City

(Dioecesis Rapidopolitana)

(Vacant See)

Chancery Office: 606 Cathedral Dr., P.O. Box 678, Rapid City, SD, 57709. Tel.: 605-343-3541; Fax: 605-348-7985.

FORMERLY THE DIOCESE OF LEAD.

ERECTED AUGUST 4, 1902; SEE TRANSFERRED TO RAPID CITY, AUGUST 1, 1930.

Square Miles 43,000.

Comprises the Counties of Bennett, Butte, Corson, Custer, Dewey, Fall River, Gregory, Haakon, Harding, Jackson, Jones, Lawrence, Lyman, Meade, Mellette, Pennington, Perkins, Stanley, Shannon, Todd, Tripp and Ziebach in the State of South Dakota.

For legal titles of parishes and diocesan institutions, consult the Chancery Office.

STATISTICAL OVERVIEW

Personnel	
Priests: Diocesan Active in Diocese	27
Priests: Active Outside Diocese	2
Priests: Retired, Sick or Absent	11
Number of Diocesan Priests	40
Religious Priests in Diocese	32
Extern Priests in Diocese	4
Ordinations:	
Transitional Deacons	1
Permanent Deacons in Diocese	31
Total Brothers	11
Total Sisters	82
Parishes	
Parishes	68
With Resident Pastor:	
Resident Diocesan Priests	24
Resident Religious Priests	16
Without Resident Pastor:	
Administered by Priests	24
Administered by Permanent Deacons	1
Administered by Women Religious	1
Completely Vacant	2
Missions	38
Pastoral Centers	4
Welfare	
Residential Care of Children	1
Total Assisted	6
Day Care and Extended Day Care Centers	1
Total Assisted	20
Specialized Homes	2
Total Assisted	1,471
Special Centers for Social Services	2
Total Assisted	2,377
Educational	
Diocesan Students in Other Seminaries	14
Total Seminarians	14
High Schools, Diocesan and Parish	1
Total Students	265
High Schools, Private	1
Total Students	171
Elementary Schools, Diocesan and Parish	1
Total Students	535
Elementary Schools, Private	2
Total Students	371
Catechesis/Religious Education:	
High School Students	1,986
Elementary Students	4,280
Total Students Under Catholic Instruction	7,622
Teachers in the Diocese:	
Priests	3
Brothers	1
Sisters	9
Lay Teachers	91
Vital Statistics	
Receptions into the Church:	
Infant Baptism Totals	728
Adult Baptism Totals	51
Received into Full Communion	99
First Communions	761
Confirmations	521
Marriages:	
Catholic	122
Interfaith	134
Total Marriages	256
Deaths	439
Total Catholic Population	42,320
Total Population	211,591

Former Bishops—Most Rev. JOHN STARIHA, D.D., cons. October 28, 1902; retired March 29, 1909 and named Titular Bishop of Antipatride; died in Laibach, Austria, Nov. 28, 1915.—Most Rev. JOSEPH F. BUSCH, D.D., cons. May 19, 1910; transferred to Saint Cloud, MN, Feb. 21, 1915; died May 31, 1953.—Most Rev. JOHN J. LAWLER, S.T.D., cons. Titular Bishop of Greater Hermopolis and Auxiliary Bishop of St. Paul, Minnesota, May 19, 1910; transferred to the See of Lead, Jan. 29, 1916; died March 11, 1948.—Most Rev. LEO F. DWORSCHAK, D.D., cons. Titular Bishop of Tium and Coadjutor Bishop of Rapid City "cum jure successionis," Aug. 22, 1946; transferred to Fargo, ND, April 10, 1947.—Most Rev. WILLIAM T. MCCARTY, C.SS.R., D.D., appt. Titular Bishop of Anaea and Delegate to the Military Vicar, Jan. 2, 1943; appt. Coadjutor Bishop of Rapid City "cum jure successionis," April 10, 1947; succeeded to March 11, 1948; retired Sept. 17, 1969; appt. Titular Bishop of Rotdon; died Sept. 14, 1972.—Most Rev. HAROLD J. DIMMERLING, D.D., appt. Bishop of Rapid City, Sept. 17, 1969; ord. May 2, 1940; cons. Oct. 30, 1969; died Dec. 13, 1987.—Most Rev. CHARLES J. CHAPUT, D.D., appt. Bishop of Rapid City, April 11, 1988; appt. Archbishop of Denver, Feb. 18, 1997.

Vicar General—Rev. Msgr. MICHAEL B. WOSTER, J.C.L.

Chancery Office—606 Cathedral Dr., P.O. Box 678, Rapid City, 57709. Tel: 605-343-3541; Fax: 605-348-7985. Office Hours: Mon.-Fri. 8-5 Address all official business to this office.

Chancellor—Sr. M. CELINE ERK, O.S.B.

Vice-Chancellor—KERRY KOBER.

Diocesan Tribunal—918 5th St., Rapid City, 57701. Tel: 605-343-8685; Fax: 605-348-1050.

Officialis—Rev. Msgr. MICHAEL B. WOSTER.

Diocesan Consultors—Revs. JOHN HATCHER, S.J.; MICHEL MULLOY; PETER WILKE; ARNOLD KARI; BRIAN LANE; KERRY PRENDIVILLE.

Deaneries—Rev. PETER KOVARIK, Piedmont: Rev. GARY ORESHOSKI, Belle Fourche: Rev. MARK MCCORMICK, Hot Springs: Rev. DALE KUTIL, Ft. Pierre: Rev. JOE ZELLER, Timber Lake: Rev. MICHAEL HIGHT, Presho:

Presbyteral Council—Rev. BRIAN LANE, Pres.

Vicar for Retired Priests—Rev. D. CRAIG COWER.

Permanent Diaconate Program, Sioux Spiritual Center—Rev. JOHN HATCHER, S.J., *HCR 77, Box 271, Howes, 57748.* Tel: 605-985-5906.

Development and Stewardship Program—GRANT TROTTER, Dir.

Continuing Education of Clergy—Rev. Msgr. MICHAEL B. WOSTER.

Vocation Program—Rev. ARNOLD KARI, Dir.

Diocesan Finance Manager—JOHN BELL.

Diocesan Finance Council—Most Rev. CHARLES J. CHAPUT, O.F.M.Cap., Pres.; Rev. Msgr. MICHAEL B. WOSTER; Sr. CELINE ERK, O.S.B.; Rev. RAY DEISCH; CHRIS SCHMID; SHIRLEY STEC; JEFFREY VIKEN; ARTHUR KROETCH; RAY HILLENBRAND; PETE LIEN, JR.; JOHN BELL, Sec.; Mrs. SUSAN WILLIAMS; FRANK SHORT; JERRY GERDES.

Holy Childhood Pontifical Association—Rev. PAUL DAHMS.

Propagation of the Faith—Rev. PAUL DAHMS.

Beginning Experience—918 5th St., Rapid City, 57701. Tel: 605-343-8685.

Birthright—918 5th St., Rapid City, 57701. Tel: 605-343-8685.

Blue Army—918 5th St., Rapid City, 57701. Tel: 605-343-8685.

Catholic Relief Service—Rev. PAUL DAHMS, Dir.

Couple to Couple—918 5th St., Rapid City, 57701.

Cursillo—918 5th St., Rapid City, 57701.

Engaged Encounter—918 5th St., Rapid City, 57701.

Health Panel—Box 678, Rapid City, 57709.

Marriage Encounter—918 5th St., Rapid City, 57701.

Native Concerns Office—PHYLLIS DECORY, Dir., *606 Cathedral Dr., Rapid City, 57701.* Tel: 605-343-3541.

Pro-Life Commission—SUE JIMMERSON, Chm., *606 Cathedral Dr., Rapid City, 57701.*

Right to Life—918 5th St., Rapid City, 57701.

Director of Ongoing Formation—Rev. Msgr. WILLIAM J. O'CONNELL.

Vicar of Education—THOMAS LANE.

Supt. of Schools—DICK THOMPSON.

Director of Rural Life—Rev. Msgr. MICHAEL B. WOSTER.

Office of Family Life—HARRIET YOUNG, Dir., *918 5th St., Rapid City, 57701.* Tel: 605-343-8685.

Diocesan Office of Religious Education—SEAN INNERST, Dir.

Campaign for Human Development—Rev. PAUL DAHMS, Dir.

West River Catholic Newspaper—EILEEN SULLIVAN ROTERT, Editor.

West River Catholic Youth Office—GLEN GAUER, Dir.

Archives—Sr. CELINE ERK, O.S.B.

CLERGY, PARISHES, MISSIONS AND PAROCHIAL SCHOOLS

CITY OF RAPID CITY
(Pennington County)

1—CATHEDRAL OF OUR LADY OF PERPETUAL HELP (1890), Revs. Peter B. Wilke, Rector; Don Hickerson; Karl Pikus; Timothy Hoag; Deacons Tom Lane; George Gladfelter. Pastoral Ministers (Hospital/Hospice): Sr. Kathleen Clancy, O.S.F.; Patricia Petit.
Church—520 Cathedral Dr., 57701-5499. Tel: 605-342-0507.
School—St. Elizabeth Seton Central School. See separate listing under Institutions Located in the Diocese.
Catechesis/Religious Programs—Bro. Ward O'Connell, C.F.X., D.R.E.
Students 349.
Chapel—Immaculate Conception.

2—BLESSED SACRAMENT (1947), Rev. Michael Mulloy; Deacon Ken Hill.
Res., 4500 Jackson Blvd., 57702-4999. Tel: 605-342-3336.
Catechesis/Religious Programs—Tel: 605-342-8730.
Students 744.

3—ST. THERESE THE LITTLE FLOWER (1941). Formerly known as The Church of St. John the Evangelist. Revs. Daniel Juelfs; Benjamin Reese; Bro. Ronald Lang, C.F.X., Pastoral Assoc.; Deacon Claude Sauer.
Res., 532 Adams St., 57701. Tel: 605-342-1556.
Catechesis/Religious Programs—Tel: 605-348-6272.
Students 273.

4—ST. ISAAC JOGUES (1949) (Native American), Revs. Joseph C. Gill, S.J.; Bernard D. Fagan, S.J.; Deacons James Garnett; Leroy Decory.
Res., 220 Wright St., P.O. Box 1304, 57709. Tel: 605-343-3257.
Catechesis/Religious Programs—Tel: 605-343-2165.
Students 170.
Mother Butler Center—Catechetical and Social Center for Indians. Tel: 605-343-2165.
Mission—Rapid City, Pennington Co., Indian Health Service, Sioux San Hospital and Pennington County Jail.

OUTSIDE THE CITY OF RAPID CITY

Belle Fourche, Butte Co., St. Paul (1905), Rev. David Orians.
Res., 855 Fifth St., 57717-1701. Tel: 605-892-3226. [JC]
Also attends St. Mary, Newell and St. Joseph's, Mud Butte.
Catechesis/Religious Programs—Tel: 605-392-3226.
Students 136.

Bison, Perkins Co., Blessed Sacrament (1918), Rev. Leo Hausmann.
Res., P.O. Box 297, 57620. Tel: 605-244-5546. [JC]
Missions—Drew, Perkins Co., St. James, Tel: 605-244-5546; Cox, Harding Co., St. Agnes; Ralph, Harding Co., St. Isidore; Reva, Harding Co., Our Lady of the Prairie.

Bonesteel, Gregory Co., Immaculate Conception (1906), Rev. James Becht.
Res., P.O. Box 376, 57317-0376. Tel: 605-654-2204. [CEM]
Also attends Church of Anthony, Fairfax and St. Francis Xavier, Ponca Creek.
Catechesis/Religious Programs—Students 89.

Buffalo, Harding Co., St. Anthony (1917). Attended by Blessed Sacrament, Bison. Revs. Leo Hausman; Andrew Morvay, (Retired).
Res., P.O. Box 297, Bison, 57620. Tel: 605-244-5546. [JC]
Catechesis/Religious Programs—Students 63.
Missions—Cox, Harding Co., St. Agnes; Ralph, Harding Co., St. Isidore; Reva, Harding Co., Our Lady of the Prairie.

Burke, Gregory Co., Sacred Heart (1905). Attended by St. Joseph, Gregory.
Res., P.O. Box 354, 57523. Tel: 605-775-2532. [CEM]
Catechesis/Religious Programs—Students 89.

Clearfield, Tripp Co., St. Boniface. Closed. For sacramental records contact Immaculate Conception, Winner.

Colome, Tripp Co., St. Isidore (1909). Attended by Immaculate Conception, Winner. Deacon Michael Curtin, Pastoral Asst.
Res., P.O. Box 405, 57528-0405. Tel: 605-842-1437.
Catechesis/Religious Programs—Students 68.

Custer, Custer Co., St. John the Baptist (1911), Rev. Bryan Sorensen.
Res., P.O. Box 632, 57730-0632. Tel: 605-673-4426.
Also attends St. Rose of Lima, Hill City.
Catechesis/Religious Programs—Tel: 605-673-4426.
Students 135.

Deadwood, Lawrence Co., St. Ambrose (1877), Rev. Paul G. Dahms.
Res., 760 W. Main St., P.O. Box 320, 57732-0320. Tel: 605-578-1519. [CEM]
Catechesis/Religious Programs—732 Main St., 57732-0320. Tel: 605-578-1921.
Students 107.

Eagle Butte, Dewey Co., All Saints (1911) (Native American), Revs. John Klingler, S.C.J.; Thomas Westhoven, S.C.J.; Bro. Frank Presto, S.C.J.; Deacon Theodore Knife.
Res., P.O. Box 110, 57625-0110. Tel: 605-964-3391; Fax: 605-964-3300. [JC]
Catechesis/Religious Programs—Students 90.
Missions—Bridger, Ziebach Co., Immaculate Conception; Cherry Creek, Ziebach Co., St. Joseph; Dupree, Ziebach Co., Sacred Heart; Promise, Dewey Co., St. Catherine; Red Scaffold, Ziebach Co., Sacred Heart; Ridgeview, Dewey Co., St. Joseph; Thunder Butte, Ziebach Co., St. Luke; White Horse, Dewey Co., St. Therese.

Edgemont, Fall River Co., St. James (1893). Attended by St. Anthony, Hot Springs. Deacon Earl Witte, (Retired).
Mailing Address: P.O. Box 969, Hot Springs, 57747-0969. Tel: 605-745-3393.
Mission—Ardmore, St. Aloysius, Tel: 605-662-7706.

Fairfax, Gregory Co., St. Anthony's (1904). Attended by Immaculate Conception, Bonesteel.
Mailing Address: c/o P.O. Box 376, Bonesteel, 57317-0376. [CEM]
Catechesis/Religious Programs—Students attend religious education at Immaculate Conception, Bonesteel.

Faith, Meade Co., St. Joseph (1917), Rev. Dennis Riss.
Res., P.O. Box 307, 57626-0307. Tel: 605-967-2201. [CEM]
Catechesis/Religious Programs—Students 68.
Missions—Red Owl, Meade Co., St. Anthony; Plainview, Meade Co., Our Lady of Victory.

Fort Pierre, Stanley Co., St. John (1905), Rev. Dale Kutil.
Res., 206 W. Main, P.O. Box 670, 57532-0670. Tel: 605-223-2176. [JC]
Catechesis/Religious Programs—Tel: 605-223-2492.
Students 120.

Gregory, Gregory Co., St. Joseph (1905), Rev. Msgr. William J. O'Connell.
Res., 414 Church St., 57533. Tel: 605-835-9290. [CEM]
Catechesis/Religious Programs—Mary Vale Hall, 411 Church St., Tel: 605-835-9396.
Students 138.

Hermosa, Custer Co., St. Michael's. Attended by Our Lady of Perpetual Help Cathedral, Rapid City.

Hill City, Pennington Co., St. Rose of Lima (1898). Attended by St. John the Baptist, Custer. Rev. Bryan Sorensen.
Res., P.O. Box 632, Custer, 57730. Tel: 605-673-4426.
Catechesis/Religious Programs—Tel: 605-574-2479.
Students 60.

Hot Springs, Fall River Co., St. Anthony's (1890), Rev. Mark McCormick.
Res., P.O. Box 969, 57747-0969. Tel: 605-745-3393.
Catechesis/Religious Programs—Students 267.
Missions—Oelrichs, Fall River Co., St. Martin, 7th & Main Sts., Oelrichs, SD 57763.; Edgemont, Fall River Co., St. James, 310 3rd St., Edgemont, SD 57735. Tel: 605-662-7706. Deacon Earl F. Witte.; Ardmore, Fall River Co., St. Aloysius, 57735.

Kadoka, Jackson Co., Our Lady of Victory (1908), Rev. Robert D. Baden; Deacon Eugene A. Heckathorne.
Res., P.O. Box 159, 57543-0159. Tel: 605-837-2219.

Kennebec, Lyman Co., St. Michael's (1906). Attended by St. Mary, Lower Brule.
Mailing Address: P.O. Box 185, Lower Brule, 57548-0185. Tel: 605-473-5335; Fax: 605-473-5453. [CEM]

Kenel, Corson Co., Assumption of the Blessed Virgin Mary (1879) (Native American). Attended by St. Bernard, McLaughlin.
Res., P.O. Box 539, McLaughlin, 57642-0539. Tel: 605-823-4401.

Kyle, Shannon Co., Our Lady of Sorrows (1910) (Native American), Rev. Joseph Damhorst, S.J.; Deacon Lawrence Whiting, (Retired).
Res., P.O. Box 398, 57752-0398. Tel: 605-455-2888.
Missions—Allen, Bennett Co., St. John of the Cross; Medicine Root, Shannon, St. Stephens, Tel: 605-455-2723; Wanblee, Bennett Co., St. Ignatius Loyola.

Lead, Lawrence Co., St. Patrick's (1878), Rev. William A. Zandri.
Res., 141 S. Siever St., 57754. Tel: 605-584-2002. [CEM][JC]
Catechesis/Religious Programs—Students 105.

Lemmon, Perkins Co., St. Mary's (1909), Rev. Ronald B. Garry; Deacons Carl Orthman; Bill Dustman.
Res., P.O. Box 210, 57638. Tel: 605-374-3767. [JC]
Catechesis/Religious Programs—Peggy Falvey, D.R.E.
Students 132.
Missions—Morristown, Corson Co., Sacred Heart; Watauga, Corson Co., St. Michael.

Lower Brule, Lyman Co., St. Mary's (1923) (Native American), Revs. Yvon Sheehy, S.C.J.; James L. Walters, S.C.J.
Office: P.O. Box 185, 57568. Tel: 605-473-5335; Fax: 605-473-5453. [CEM]

Manderson, Shannon Co., St. Agnes (1901) (Native American). Attended by Our Lady of Sorrows, Kyle. Rev. Ronald Seminara, S.J.
Res., P.O. Box 88, 57756. Tel: 605-867-5776. [CEM]
Missions—Wounded Knee, Shannon Co., Sacred Heart; Rockyford, Shannon Co., St. Peter's.

Martin, Bennett Co., Our Lady of the Sacred Heart (1918), Rev. John J. Hennessy, S.J.; Deacon Calvin Clifford.
Mailing Address: P.O. Box 567, 57551. Tel: 605-685-6232. [CEM][JC]
Catechesis/Religious Programs—Tel: 605-685-6274.
Students 90.

McIntosh, Corson Co., St. Bonaventure's (1913), Rev. Msgr. William O'Connell; Rev. Steve Biegler.
Res., P.O. Box 320, 57641. Tel: 605-273-4334. [CEM]
Catechesis/Religious Programs—Students 60.

McLaughlin, Corson Co., St. Bernard (1918), Rev. Msgr. William O'Connell; Rev. Steven Biegler; Deacons Vern Rath; Michael Kills Pretty Enemy; Paul Keller.
Res., P.O. Box 539, 57642. Tel: 605-823-4401.
Catechesis/Religious Programs—Tel: 605-823-4210.
Sisters of St. Francis of the Immaculate Conception 2; Lay Teachers 14; Students 79.
Missions—Bullhead, Corson Co., St. Aloysius; Wakpala, Corson Co., St. Bede; Kenel, Corson Co., Our Lady of the Assumption Parish; McIntosh, Corson Co., St. Bonaventure.

Mission, Todd Co., St. Thomas the Apostle (1933) (Native American). Attended by St. Francis, Mission. Rev. Paul Strittmatter, S.J.; Deacon Marlon J. Leneaugh.
Church—P.O. Box 151, 57555. Tel: 605-856-4618. [CEM]
Catechesis/Religious Programs—Tel: 605-856-2273. Gladys Bordeaux, D.R.E.
Students 82.
Mission—Okreek, Todd Co., St. Peter's, P.O. Box 499, St. Francis, 57572. Tel: 605-747-2362.

Morristown, Corson Co., Sacred Heart (1912). Attended by St. Mary's, Lemmon.
Mailing Address: P.O. Box 210, Lemmon, 57638. Tel: 605-374-3767. [JC]

Murdo, Jones Co., St. Martin (1906). Attended by Christ the King, Presho.
Mailing Address: P.O. Box 399, Presho, 57568. Tel: 605-669-2436. [CEM]
Catechesis/Religious Programs—Tel: 605-895-2534.
Students 57.

Newell, Butte Co., St. Mary Star of the Sea (1910). Attended by St. Paul, Belle Fourche.
Mailing Address: P.O. Box 72, 57760. Tel: 605-456-2221.
Catechesis/Religious Programs—Students 64.
Mission—Mud Butte, Meade Co., St. Joseph's Catholic Church, (1921) Mud Butte, 57758.

New Underwood, Pennington Co., St. John the Evangelist (1921), Rev. Reuben Valades.
Res., P.O. Box 305, 57761. Tel: 605-754-6446. [JC]
Mission—Lakeside, Meade Co., St. Margaret.

Norris, Melette Co., Sacred Heart (1955). Attended by St. Agnes, Parmelee. Rev. Glendon R. Welshons, S.J.
Res., 14CR 76, Box 11A, Belvidere, 57521-9701. Tel: 605-747-2118. [JC]

Oglala, Shannon Co., Our Lady of the Sioux. Attended by Holy Rosary Mission, Pine Ridge. Sr. Monica Witte, O.S.F., Pastoral Coord.
Res., P.O. Box 140, 57764. Tel: 605-867-5673.

Parmelee, Todd Co., St. Agnes, Rev. Glendon R. Welshons, S.J.
Res., P.O. Box 115, 57566. Tel: 605-747-2118.

Catechesis/Religious Programs—Students 90.
Missions—Upper Cutmeat, Sacred Heart; He Dog, St. Patrick Hall; Black Pipe-Corn Creek, St. Joseph Hall.

Philip, Haakon Co., Sacred Heart (1907), Rev. Arnold A. Kari.
Res., 307 W. Elm, P.O. Box 309, 57567. Tel: 605-859-2664. [JC]
Catechesis/Religious Programs—Students 129.
Missions—Milesville, Haakon Co., St. Mary; Midland, Haakon Co., St. William.

Piedmont-Black Hawk, Meade Co., Our Lady of the Black Hills (1916), Rev. Peter Kovarik; Deacon Walt Wilson.
Res., HCR 80, Box 481, 57769. Tel: 605-787-5168. [JC]
Catechesis/Religious Programs—Students 185.

Pine Ridge, Shannon Co., Sacred Heart (1890) (Lakota), Rev. Albert Thelen, S.J.
Res., P.O. Box 359, 57770. Tel: 605-867-5551; Fax: 605-867-1291. [JC]
Catechesis/Religious Programs—Students 15.

Porcupine, Shannon Co., Church of Christ the King (1901) (Native American). Attended by Our Lady of Sorrows, Kyle. Rev. Ronald S. Seminara, S.J.
Res., P.O. Box 398, Kyle, 57752-0398. Tel: 605-867-1614; 455-2888. [CEM]
School—Our Lady of Lourdes Mission School, Tel: 605-867-5568; Fax: 605-867-5874. Cynthia Hillman, Prin.
Sisters 3; Lay Teachers 10; Students 174.
Missions—On the Creek, Shannon Co., St. Paul, P.O. Box 7, 57772. Tel: 605-867-1614. [CEM]
Manderson, Shannon Co., St. Agnes, P.O. Box 88, Manderson, 57756. Tel: 605-867-5776. [CEM]
Manderson, Shannon Co., St. Peter's, P.O. Box 88, Manderson, 57756. [CEM]
Wounded Knee, Sacred Heart.

Presho, Lyman Co., Christ the King (1906), Rev. Michael Hight.
Res., P.O. Box 399, 57568-0399. Tel: 605-895-2534. [CEM]
Catechesis/Religious Programs—Students 46.
Missions—Murdo, Jones Co., St. Martin of Tours; Draper, Jones Co., St. Anthony of Padua.

Reliance, Lyman Co., St. Mary's (1911). Attended by St. Mary's, Lower Brule.
Mailing Address: P.O. Box 185, Lower Brule, 57548-0185. Tel: 605-473-5335; Fax: 605-473-5453. [CEM]

Rosebud, Todd Co., St. Bridget, Rev. James H. Ryan, S.J.
Res., P.O. Box 340, 57570-0340. Tel: 605-747-2496.
Catechesis/Religious Programs—Students 148.
Mission—Soldier Creek, St. Rose.

St. Francis, Todd Co., St. Charles (1886), Rev. David Gau, S.J.; Deacon Ben Black Bear, Jr.
Res., Box 499, 57572. Tel: 605-747-2533; Fax: 605-747-5057. [CEM]
Catechesis/Religious Programs—Tel: 605-747-2567.
Students 652.
Missions—See listing under Indian Missions for Rosebud Reservation, St. Francis regarding details on personnel and missions.; Spring Creek, St. Patrick, Tel: 605-747-2362.

Spearfish, Lawrence Co., St. Joseph (1907), Rev. Kerry Prendiville.
Res., P.O. Box 844 5th St., 57783-2005. Tel: 605-642-2306; Fax: 605-642-1024.
Catechesis/Religious Programs—Students 500.

Sturgis, Meade Co., St. Francis of Assisi (1840), Rev. Gary Oreshoski; Deacons Roger Heidt; Roland Gravel.
Res., 1049 Howard St., 57785-1999. Tel: 605-347-3579. [CEM]
Catechesis/Religious Programs—Tel: 605-347-3996. Pat Roe, D.R.E.
Students 273.

Timber Lake, Dewey Co., Holy Cross (1910), Rev. Joseph E. Zeller.
Res., P.O. Box 70, 57656-0070. Tel: 605-865-3653. [JC 3]
Catechesis/Religious Programs—Students 147.
Missions—Isabel, Dewey Co., St. Mary; Trail City, Corson Co., Holy Rosary.

Wall, Pennington Co., St. Patrick's (1917), Rev. Robert D. Baden.
Res., P.O. Box 405, 57790-0405. Tel: 605-279-2542. [JC]
Catechesis/Religious Programs—Students 83.

Wanblee, Jackson Co., Ignatius Loyola (1920) (Native American), Rev. Joe Damhorst, S.J.
Res., P.O. Box 229, 57577. Tel: 605-462-6170. [CEM]
Mission—Potatoe Creek, Jackson Co., St. Henry.

Watauga, Corson Co., St. Michael (1912). Attended by St. Mary's, Lemmon.
Mailing Address: P.O. Box 210, Lemmon, 57638-0210. Tel: 605-473-3767. [CEM]

White River, Mellette Co., St. Ignatius (1899) (Native American), Rev. Charles R. Baumann, S.J.
Res., P.O. Box 245, 57579-0245. Tel: 605-259-3381. [CEM]
Catechesis/Religious Programs—Tel: 605-259-3313.
Students 50.
Mission—Wood, Melette Co., Our Lady of Good Counsel, Wood, 57585.

Sacred Heart, Melette Co., (1919), Rev. Charles R. Baumann, S.J.
Res., P.O. Box 245, 57579-0245. Tel: 605-259-3381. [JC]

Winner, Tripp Co., Immaculate Conception (1910), Rev. Brian Lane; Deacon Michael Curtin.
Res., 302 W. Fourth, P.O. Box 765, 57580. Tel: 605-842-3520.
Catechesis/Religious Programs—Students 200.
Mission—Keyapaha, St. Ann.

INDIAN MISSIONS

Eagle Butte, Dewey Co., Cheyenne River Reservation (1911) (Native American), Revs. John Klingler, S.C.J.; Thomas Westhoven, S.C.J.; Bro. Frank Presto.
Mailing Address: All Saints, P.O. Box 110, 57625. Tel: 605-964-3391; Fax: 605-964-3300.
Missions—Bridger, Ziebach Co., Immaculate Conception; Dupree, Ziebach Co., Sacred Heart; Promise, Dewey Co., St. Catherine; Ridgeview, Dewey Co., St. Joseph; Cherry Creek, Ziebach Co., St. Joseph; Thunder Butte, Ziebach Co., St. Luke; Red Scaffold, Ziebach Co., Sacred Heart; White Horse, Ziebach Co., St. Therese.

Lower Brule, Lyman Co., Lower Brule Reservation (1895) (Native American), Revs. Yvon Sheehy, S.C.J.; James L. Walters, S.C.J.
Mailing Address: P.O. Box 185, 57548. Tel: 605-473-5335; 473-5215; Fax: 605-473-5453. [CEM]

Pine Ridge, Shannon Co., Holy Rosary (Pine Ridge Reservation) (1888) (Native American), Revs. David L. Smith, S.J.; Earl Kurth, S.J.; Joseph Damhorst, S.J., (Kyle, Wamblee); William Pauly, S.J., Supr., (Pine Ridge).; Paul Manhart, S.J., (Kyle, Wamblee); Ron Seminara, S.J., (Manderson, Wounded Knee, Porcupine).; William G. McKenney, S.J.; Kevin C. Schneider, S.J., Red Cloud School Supt.; Peter J. Klink, S.J.; Albert Thelon, S.J., (Sacred Heart, Pine Ridge).
Mailing Address:Pine Ridge P.O., 57770. Tel: 605-867-5491; Fax: 605-967-1291.
Priests 11; Lay Teachers 42; Brothers 5.
School—Red Cloud Indian School, Tel: 605-867-5491; Fax: 605-867-1291. Sr. Monica O.S.F., Coord. Sisters of St. Francis of Penance and Christian Charity 2; Sisters of Charity of Cincinnati 1; School Sisters of Notre Dame of St. Louis 1; Congregation of Notre Dame 2; Lay Teachers 42; Students: Elementary 110; Middle School 87; High School 171.
Missions—Cuny Table, Shannon Co., St. Joseph; Oglala, Shannon Co., Our Lady of Sioux, P.O. Box 140, Oglala, 57764. Tel: 605-867-5673; No Water, Shannon Co., Our Lady of Good Counsel; Slim Butte, Shannon Co., Our Lady of Lourdes; Red Shirt Table, Shannon Co., St. Bernard.

St. Francis, Todd Co., Rosebud Reservation (1886) (Native American). St. Francis Mission and Rosebud Educational Society. Revs. James A. Strzok, S.J., Supr.; John A. Hennessy, S.J., Our Lady of the Sacred Heart, Martin.; Charles R. Baumann, S.J., Sacred Heart Church, White River.; James S. Ryan, S.J., St. Bridget Church, Rosebud.; Paul Strittmatter, S.J., Mission.; Richard T. Jones, S.J., St. Francis.; Kenneth T. Walleman, S.J.; Glendon R. Welshons, S.J.; Christian Keeler, S.J.; David Gau, S.J.; Deacons Ben Black Bear, Jr.; Marlon Leneaugh.
Mailing Address: P.O. Box 499, 57572-0499. Tel: 605-747-2361; Fax: 605-747-5057. [CEM]
Priests 9; Permanent Deacons 2; Brothers 1; Sisters 5.
Catechesis/Religious Programs—Students 621.
Missions—St. Francis, St. Charles; Okreek, St. Peter; Soldier Creek, St. Rose; Spring Creek, St. Patrick; Parmelee, St. Agnes; Upper Cutmeat, Sacred Heart; Rosebud, St. Bridget; White River, St. Ignatius; Two Strike, Immaculate Conception; Wood, Our Lady of Good Counsel; Norris, Sacred Heart; Mission, St. Thomas. Rev. Paul Strittmatter, S.J.

Standing Rock, Corson Co., Standing Rock Reservation (1918), Revs. Frank Reitter, S.M.; Philip Parent, S.M.
St. Bernard's Church: P.O. Box 539, McLaughlin, 57642. Tel: 605-823-4401.
Catechesis/Religious Programs—Tel: 605-823-4210.
Students 149.
Missions—Wakpala, Corson Co., St. Bede; Bullhead, Corson Co., St. Aloysius; Kenel, Corson Co., Assumption of the Blessed Virgin Mary Church.

Chaplains of Public Institutions

ELLSWORTH. *Ellsworth AFB*. Rev. Joseph Motsay, 28th BW/HC, Ellsworth AFB, 57706.

On Duty Outside the Diocese:
Reverend Fathers—
Novotny, Richard

Retired:
Reverend Fathers—
Birdsall, John M., 2110-C St. Martin Dr., Rapid City, SD 57702
Corry, John J., 2110-C St. Martin Dr., Apt. 107, Rapid City, SD 57702
Cower, D. Craig, 824 Columbus, #204, Rapid City, SD 57701-3578
Jordan, Collins P., c/o Lionel Bordeaux, Mission, SD 57555
Lambert, William, 163 Vondera St., Robertsville, MO 63072
Morvay, Andrew, P.O. Box 85, Buffalo, SD 57720-0085
Philbin, William, 1102 City Springs Rd. #104, Rapid City, SD 57702-0223
Plante, Richard A., 255 Texas, Rapid City, SD 57701-7648
Scadron, Christopher, 319 N. Beaver, Flagstaff, AZ 86001
Scherer, Gerald N., P.O. Box 268, Hermoso, SD 57744-0268
Staricek, Andrew, P.O. Box 7, Bison, SD 57620-0007

Permanent Deacons:
Black Bear, Ben, Jr., St. Francis Mission, St. Francis
Clifford, Calvin, Martin
Condon, Harold, Dupree
Coy, Patrick, Hill City
Curtin, Michael, St. Isidore, Colome
DeCory, Leroy, Rapind City
Dustman, Bill, Lemmon
Garnet, James W., Rapid City
Gladfelter, George, Rapid City
Grant, Albert, Hot Springs
Gravel, Edward, Sturgis
Hairy Chin, Francis, (Retired), Hot Springs
Heckathorne, Eugene A., Kadoka
Heidt, Roger, Sturgis
Hill, Ken, Rapid City
Jetson, David, Rapid City
Keller, Paul, McLaughlin
Kills Pretty Enemy, Michael, McLaughlin
Knife, Theodore, Faith
Lane, Thomas, Silver City
Leneaugh, Marlon, Mission
McGeeney, Joe, (Retired)
Murray, Chet, (Retired), Rapid City
Orthman, Carl, Lemmon
Rath, Vern, McLaughlin
Richards, Reno, Allen Mission District
Sauer, Claude, (Retired), St. Therese, Rapid City
Usera, Luis, Colorado
Whiting, Lawrence, Kyle
Wilson, Walt, Piedmont
Witte, Earl Joseph, St. James, Edgemont

INSTITUTIONS LOCATED IN THE DIOCESE

[A] DIOCESAN CATHOLIC SCHOOL SYSTEM

RAPID CITY. *St. Thomas More High School*, 300 Fairmont Blvd., 57701. Tel: 605-343-8484; Fax: 605-348-1315. Richard Thompson, Supt. Students 265; Total Staff 27.

St. Elizabeth Seton Catholic Central School, 431 Oakland, 57701. Tel: 605-348-1477. Students 535; Staff 31.

[B] MONASTERIES AND RESIDENCES OF PRIESTS & BROTHERS

BETHLEHEM. *Holy Nativity Monastery*, 57708. Tel: 605-787-4606. Revs. Louis Marie, Supr.; Maron Morgan; Anthony Kramer; Elias Havel; Martin Ferland. Priests 5.

EAGLE BUTTE. *Sacred Heart Community House*, P.O. Box 110, 57625-0110. Tel: 605-964-3391; Fax: 605-964-3300. Revs. John Klinger, S.C.J., Coord.; Thomas Westhoven, S.C.J.; Bro. Frank Presto, S.C.J. Priests 2; Brothers 1.

HOWES. *Kino Jesuit Community*, HCR 77 Box 271, 57748-9505. Tel: 605-985-5906; Fax: 605-985-5908. Revs. John E. Hatcher, S.J.; Stephen F. Mitten, S.J. In res., Revs. Joseph C. Gill, S.J.; Bernard D. Fagan, S.J.; Thomas J. Tierney, S.J.; Stephen F. Mitten, S.J. Priests 5.

LOWER BRULE. *SCJ Community House*, P.O. Box 185, 57548-0185. Tel: 605-473-5335; 473-5487. Revs. Yvon Sheehy, S.C.J.; James L. Walters, S.C.J. Priests 2; Total in Residence 2; Total Staff 2.

PINE RIDGE. *Jesuit Community of Holy Rosary Mission*, 57770-0001. Tel: 605-867-5491. Revs. William Pauly, S.J., Supr.; David L. Smith, S.J., Supr.; Kevin C. Schneider, S.J.; Earl J. Kurth, S.J.; Joseph Damhorst, S.J.; Peter J. Klink, S.J.; Paul Manhart, S.J.; Albert R. Thelan, S.J.; Ronald Seminara, S.J.; William G. McKenney, S.J. Priests 10; Brothers 5; Total in Residence 15; Total Staff 2.

[C] CONVENTS AND RESIDENCES FOR SISTERS

RAPID CITY.

**Benedictine Convent of St. Martin*, 2110 C St. Martin Dr., 57702-9392. Tel: 605-343-8011. Motherhouse and Novitiate of the Sisters of St. Benedict. Sr. Florence McManamen, O.S.B., Prioress. Sisters 44; Total Staff 2.

Benedictine Convent of St. Martin Retirement Trust, 2110-C St. Martin Dr., 57702-9392. Tel: 605-343-8011. Sr. Mary Wegher, Trustee & Contact Person.

Kateri Convent, 624 Adams, 57701-0809. Tel: 605-343-6261. Oblate Sisters of the Blessed Sacrament 2.

PORCUPINE. *Our Lady of Lourdes School Convent*, P.O. Box 7, 57772-0007. Notre Dame Sisters 2.

[D] MISCELLANEOUS

RAPID CITY. *The Catholic Education Fund, Inc.*, P.O. Box 678, 57709-0678.

Catholic Parish Association Contingency Fund, Inc., 1116 St. Charles St., 57701.

Catholic Social Service of the Diocese of Rapid City, 918 5th St., 57701. Tel: 605-348-6086. James Kinyon, Dir.

Priest Retirement and Aid Association, 824 Columbus St., #204, 57701-3578. Most Rev. Charles J. Chaput, O.F.M.Cap., Pres.; Rev. D. Craig Cower, Exec. Sec.; Rev. Msgr. Michael Woster; Revs. Raymond Deisch, Vice Pres.; Dale Kutil; Leo Hausmann.

St. Martin's Community Center, 2110 C St. Martin Dr., 57702-9392. Tel: 605-343-8011; Fax: 605-399-2723. Sr. Jane Frances Mullaney, O.S.B., Dir.

St. Martin's Learning Center, 2110-C St. Martin Dr., 57702-9392. Tel: 605-343-2243. Sr. Carol Kovarik, O.S.B., Dir. Sisters 2; Students 20.

Western South Dakota Catholic Foundation, Inc., P.O. Box 678, 57709-8303.

EAGLE BUTTE. *Sacred Heart Center*, 121 Landmark St., P.O. Box 2000, 57625-2000. Tel: 605-964-6062; Fax: 605-964-3300. Bro. Francis J. Presto, S.C.J., Dir. Total Assisted 500; Total Staff 28.

HOWES. *The Diocese of Rapid City Mahpiya na Maka Okoigna*. Sioux Spiritual Center, HCR 77, P.O. Box 271, 57748-9505. Tel: 605-985-5906. Revs. John E. Hatcher, S.J.; Stephen E. Mitten, S.J. Total in Residence 3.

MANDERSON. *St. Francis Home*, P.O. Box 122, 57756-0122. Tel: 605-455-2781. Sr. Geraldine Clifford, O.S.F., Minister; Sr. Colleen Mahoney, O.S.F. Sisters of St. Francis Marycrest. Home for abandoned and abused children (Licensed) 2-12 years of age.

RELIGIOUS INSTITUTES OF MEN REPRESENTED IN THE DIOCESE

For further details refer to the corresponding bracketed number in the Religious Institutes of Men or Women section.

[1350]—*Brothers of St. Francis Xavier*.—C.F.X.

[1130]—*Congregation of the Priests and Brothers of the Sacred Heart*.—S.C.J.

[0690]—*Jesuit Fathers and Brothers*.—S.J.

RELIGIOUS INSTITUTES OF WOMEN REPRESENTED IN THE DIOCESE

[0230]—*Benedictine Sisters of Pontifical Jurisdiction*. (Yankton & Rapid City, SD; Bismarck, ND).—O.S.B.

[1070-13]—*Dominican Sisters*. (Adrian, Michigan).—O.P.

[]—*Franciscan Sisters of Little Falls, MN*.

[2960]—*Notre Dame Sisters*. (Omaha, NE).—N.D.

[3010]—*Oblate Sisters of the Blessed Sacrament*. (Marty, SD).—O.S.B.S.

[2970]—*School Sisters of Notre Dame*. (St. Louis, MO; Dubuque, IA).—S.S.N.D.

[]—*School Sisters of Notre Dame*. (Mankato, MN).

[1680]—*School Sisters of St. Francis*. (Milwaukee, WI).—S.S.S.F.

[3580]—*Servants of Mary*. (Omaha, NE).—O.S.M.

[0660]—*Sister of Christian Charity*. (Wilmette, IL).—S.C.C.

[]—*Sisters of Charity of Cincinnati (Ohio)*.—S.C.

[1540]—*Sisters of St. Francis*. (Dubuque, Iowa).—O.S.F.

[1630]—*Sisters of St. Francis of Penance and Christian Charity*. (Denver, CO).—O.S.F.

[]—*Sisters of St. Francis of Perpetual Adoration*. (Colorado Springs, CO).

[2980]—*Sisters of the Congregation of Notre Dame*. (St. Louis, MO; Ridgefield, CT; Montreal).—C.N.D.

[1030]—*Sisters of the Divine Savior*. (Milwaukee, WI).—S.D.S.

[3320]—*Sisters of the Presentation of the B.V.M.* (Aberdeen, SD; Dubuque, IA; Fargo, ND; Fitchburg, MA).—P.B.V.M.

DIOCESAN CEMETERIES

RAPID CITY. Catholic Cemeteries (all Diocesan) are located in the following parishes: Bear Butte, Belle Fourche, Bonesteel, Buffalo, Burke, Cherry Creek, Cheyenne Agency, Clearfield, Colome, Custer, Dallas, Deadwood, Dupree, Eagle Butte, Fairfax, Faith, Gregory, Glencross, Kadoka, Kenel, Kennebec, Lemmon, McIntosh, Martin Mission, Murdo, Pine Ridge, Porcupine, Presho, Reliance, St. Francis, Sturgis, Timber Lake, Trail City, Wakpala, Watauga, Winner, and Witten.

NECROLOGY

† O'Connor, Patrick J., Burke, SD, Sacred Heart Church. —Died Sept. 22, 1996.

Diocese of Reno

(Dioecesis Renensis)

Most Reverend

PHILLIP F. STRALING, D.D.

Bishop of Reno; ordained March 19, 1959; appointed Bishop of San Bernardino July 18, 1978; installed November 6, 1978; appointed Bishop of Reno; installed June 29, 1995. *515 Court St.:, Reno, NV, 89501.*

Pastoral Center: 515 Court St., Reno, NV, 89501. Mailing Address: P.O. Box 1211, Reno, NV, 89504. Tel.: 702-329-9274; Fax: 702-348-8619.

ERECTED AS THE DIOCESE OF RENO BY HIS HOLINESS POPE PIUS XI MARCH 27, 1931. CANONICAL ERECTION OF THE DIOCESE AUGUST 19, 1931; REDESIGNATED DIOCESE OF RENO-LAS VEGAS BY POPE PAUL VI, OCTOBER 13, 1976; REDESIGNATED DIOCESE OF RENO BY HIS HOLINESS POPE JOHN PAUL II MARCH 21, 1995.

Square Miles 70,852.

Legal Title: "The Roman Catholic Bishop of Reno and His Successors, a Corporation Sole."

Comprises the Counties of: Carson City, Churchill, Douglas, Elko, Eureka, Humboldt, Lander, Lyon, Mineral, Pershing, Storey, and Washoe.

PATRONS OF THE DIOCESE: *Our Lady of the Snows (August 5); The Holy Family (Sunday in the Octave of Christmas); Established through an Apostolic brief dated August 24, 1933.*

For legal titles of parishes and diocesan institutions, consult the Pastoral Center.

STATISTICAL OVERVIEW

Personnel	
Bishop	1
Priests: Diocesan Active in Diocese	18
Priests: Active Outside Diocese	2
Priests: Retired, Sick or Absent	6
Number of Diocesan Priests	26
Religious Priests in Diocese	12
Extern Priests in Diocese	7
Ordinations:	
Permanent Deacons	1
Permanent Deacons in Diocese	8
Total Brothers	3
Total Sisters	38
Parishes	
Parishes	28
With Resident Pastor:	
Resident Diocesan Priests	17
Resident Religious Priests	8
Without Resident Pastor:	
Administered by Permanent Deacons	1
Administered by Women Religious	2
Missions	8
New Parishes Created	2
Professional Ministry Personnel:	
Brothers	1
Sisters	6
Lay Ministers	13
Welfare	
Catholic Hospitals	1
Total Assisted	118,017
Health Care Centers	3
Total Assisted	9,539
Day Care and Extended Day Care Centers	1
Total Assisted	215
Special Centers for Social Services	5
Total Assisted	130,000
Educational	
Diocesan Students in Other Seminaries	3
Total Seminarians	3
High Schools, Diocesan and Parish	1
Total Students	450
Elementary Schools, Diocesan and Parish	4
Total Students	1,135
Catechesis/Religious Education:	
High School Students	729
Elementary Students	4,195
Total Students Under Catholic Instruction	6,512
Teachers in the Diocese:	
Priests	1
Brothers	1
Sisters	3
Lay Teachers	78
Vital Statistics	
Receptions into the Church:	
Infant Baptism Totals	1,651
Adult Baptism Totals	111
Received into Full Communion	168
First Communions	1,171
Confirmations	474
Marriages:	
Catholic	209
Interfaith	99
Total Marriages	308
Deaths	408
Total Catholic Population	103,136
Total Population	515,419

Former Bishops—Most Rev. THOMAS K. GORMAN, D.D., D.Sc.Hist., ord. Bishop, July 22, 1931; appt. Coadjutor Bishop of Dallas "cum jure successionis," Feb. 8, 1952; succeeded to the See, Aug. 19, 1954; resigned Aug. 27, 1969; died Aug. 16, 1980.—Most Rev. ROBERT J. DWYER, D.D., Ph.D., ord. June 11, 1932; appt. May 20, 1952; cons. Aug. 5, 1952; elevated to Archiepiscopal Dignity and promoted to Portland in Oregon, Dec. 14, 1966; resigned Jan. 22, 1974; died March 24, 1976.—Most Rev. JOSEPH GREEN, D.D., ord. July 14, 1946; appt. Titular Bishop of Trisipa and Auxiliary of Lansing, June 22, 1962; cons. Aug. 28, 1962; appt. Bishop of Reno, March 10, 1967; resigned Dec. 6, 1974; died Aug. 31, 1982.—Most Rev. NORMAN F. MCFARLAND, D.D., J.C.D., ord. June 15, 1946; appt. Titular Bishop of Bida and Auxiliary of San Francisco, June 5, 1970; ord. Bishop, Sept. 8, 1970; appt. Apostolic Admin., Dec. 6, 1974; appt. Bishop of Reno, Feb. 10, 1976; transferred to Orange, Dec. 29, 1986; appt. Bishop of Orange, Feb. 24, 1987.—Most Rev. DANIEL F. WALSH, D.D., ord. March 30, 1963; appt. Titular Bishop of Tigia and Auxiliary of San Francisco; ord. Bishop, Sept. 24, 1981; appt. Bishop of Reno-Las Vegas, June 9, 1987; installed Aug. 6, 1987; appt. first Bishop of the newly established Diocese of Las Vegas, March 21, 1995; installed June 28, 1995.

Bishop's Office—

Bishop—Most Rev. PHILLIP F. STRALING.

Secretary—HELEN SCHMITT, , Ext. 28.

Vicar-General—Rev. Msgr. THOMAS A. MEGER.

Chancellor—Bro. MATTHEW CUNNINGHAM, F.S.R., , Ext. 29.

Secretary—JOAN TOPOIAN, , Ext. 10.

Tribunal—

Judicial Vicar/Officialis—Very Rev. JOHN A. SULLIVAN.

Canon Lawyer—SHARON PARKER, J.C.L., , Ext. 11.

Secretary/Notary—CARMEN GODOY, , Ext. 19.

Secretary—MONICA O'BRIEN, , Ext. 25.

Promoter of Justice—Rev. GEORGE WOLF.

Defenders of the Bond—Revs. ROBERT A. BOWLING; ALBERT M. FOSSELMAN.

Advocates—Bro. MATTHEW CUNNINGHAM, F.S.R.; Revs. JAMES SETELIK; CHARLES DURANTE; Sr. MARIE MCGLOIN, S.A.

Education, Department of—

Superintendent of Schools—Bro. MATTHEW CUNNINGHAM, F.S.R., , Ext. 29.

Secretary—KAY BACIGALUPI.

Department of Catechetical, Youth Ministry and Respect Life—Rev. FRANCIS MURPHY, Dir., , Ext. 34. NORA MCDONNELL, Sec., , Ext. 13.

Department of Religious Education-Audio/Visual—MARCIE ROSS, , Ext. 35.

Curia—Most Rev. PHILLIP F. STRALING; Bro. MATTHEW CUNNINGHAM, F.S.R.; Mr. KEVIN DAY; Rev. Msgr. THOMAS A. MEGER, V.G., Moderator; Rev. JOHN SULLIVAN; Ms. BARBARA VERDI; Mr. TIM WANNER; Mr. MARTIN BRANDTNER.

Department of Development—Mr. MARTIN BRANDTNER, Dir., , Ext. 15. MARISSA KRAUS, Sec., , Ext. 37.

Diaconate—Rev. GERALD HANLEY.

Diocesan Communications Committee—Most Rev. PHILLIP F. STRALING; Rev. ROBERT BOWLING; Bro. MATTHEW CUNNINGHAM, F.S.R.; Rev. Msgr. LEO MCFADDEN; Rev. GEORGE WOLF; Ms. DIANA SEIXAS.

Diocesan Board of Consultors—Most Rev. PHILLIP F. STRALING; Rev. Msgr. THOMAS MEGER; Revs. ARIEL ARIAS; JAMES SETELIK; KEVIN SCHINDLER-MCGRAW, O.F.M.Conv.; JOHN BAIN; JOHN CORONA; CHARLES DURANTE; ROBERT BOWLING; GEORGE WOLF.

Diocesan Development Committee—Most Rev. PHILLIP F. STRALING; Mr. LEROY ARRASCADA; Rev. ROBERT BOWLING; Mr. BOB CAPURRO; Bro. MATTHEW CUNNINGHAM, F.S.R.; Mr. KEVIN DAY; Rev. Msgr. LEO MCFADDEN; Mr. PETER PARKER; Rev. ROBERT SIMPSON; Mr. TIM WANNER.

Finance Office—

Finance Committee—Most Rev. PHILLIP F. STRALING; Rev. Msgr. THOMAS MEGER; Ms. VIRGINIA ZORIO; Mr. ED HOUSTON; Mr. BOB ARMSTRONG; Bro. MATTHEW CUNNINGHAM, F.S.R.; Mr. TIM WANNER.

Business Manager—TIM WANNER, , Ext. 20.

Personnel Administrator—CINDI MITCHELL, , Ext. 24.

Administrative Assistants—JUDY LUBICH; SUE BARNES; MARISSA KRAUS, , Ext. 23, 22 & 37.

Frontier of the Faith—Tel: 702-348-6628. *310 W. 2nd St., Reno, NV, 89503., Mail: P.O. Box 10930, Reno, NV, 89510.*

Director—BETTIE ENGEBRETSON.

Secretary—ANNETTE EISELE.

Office of Hispanic Ministry—JOSE OJEDA, Dir., , Ext. 36. NORA MCDONNELL, Sec., , Ext. 13.

Institute of Ministry & Leadership Formation—Ms. BARBARA VERDI, Dir., , Ext. 18. BOBBIE GAREBEDIAN, Sec., , Ext. 14.

Missionary Co-Op 1997—Bro. MATHEW CUNNINGHAM, F.S.R.

Natural Family Planning—Sr. M. JULIANNA JERVIS, O.P.

"Northern Nevada Catholic" Newspaper—DIANA SEIXAS, Editor-in-Chief, *2995 Skyline Blvd., Ste. 205, Reno, NV, 89509.* Tel: 702-828-4125; Fax: 702-828-9333.

Our Mother of Sorrows Cemetery—*310 W. 2nd St., Reno, NV, 89503.* Tel: 323-0133., *Mail: P.O. Box 8505, Reno, NV, 89507;* Fax: 323-1229. SOPHIE MITCHELL, Oper. Mgr.; Sr. OFELIA ROIBAS, Staff.

Presbyterial Council—Revs. JOHN BAIN; ROBERT BOWLING; JOHN CORONA; CHARLES DURANTE; JIM SETELIK; GEORGE WOLF, Ex-Officio Member; ARIEL ARIAS; KEVIN SCHINDLER-MCGRAW, O.F.M.Conv.; Rev. Msgr. THOMAS A. MEGER.

Priests' Personnel Board—Most Rev. PHILLIP F. STRALING; Rev. Msgr. THOMAS MEGER; Revs. CHARLES DURANTE; JERRY HANLEY; GEORGE WOLF, Ex-Officio Member; Bro. MATTHEW CUNNINGHAM, F.S.R.

Prison Ministry—Carson City Area: CHARLOTTE FARRELL. Tel: 702-882-5615.

Property Management—TIM WANNER.

Respect Life—Most Rev. PHILLIP F. STRALING; Rev. FRANCIS MURPHY, Dir.; Mr. ROSS BARKER; Mr. JOE BENSON; Ms. SANDRA BENSON; Mr. GONZALO CASTELLANOS; Ms. WINNIE CAVILIA; Ms. MARY CLARK; Mrs. PAT GLENN; Mr. KEVIN HEGERLE; Sr. M. JULIANNA JERVIS, O.P.; Ms. MAUREEN KECK; Rev. MICHAEL MAHONE; Ms. KAREN MORAN; Rev. JIM SETELIK; Mrs. DOTTIE SHORT; Rev. ROBERT SIMPSON.

Seminary Board—Most Rev. PHILLIP F. STRALING; Rev. CHARLES DURANTE; Rev. Msgr. THOMAS A. MEGER, V.G.; Rev. ROBERT SIMPSON.

Vocations Board—Rev. ARTHUR HERKOWSKI, Chm.; Sr. SANDRA DICIANNO; Revs. OMAR BOTIA; CHARLES SHELTON, O.F.M.Conv.; Mr. ROSS BARKER; Mr. DICK PENNDORF; Ms. CONNIE WEST.

CLERGY, PARISHES, MISSIONS AND PAROCHIAL SCHOOLS

CITY OF RENO
(Washoe County)

1—ST. THOMAS AQUINAS CATHEDRAL (1907), Revs. Kevin Schindler-McGraw, O.F.M.Conv., Rector; Charles Shelton, O.F.M.Conv.; Viktor Perez, O.F.M.Conv.
Res., 310 W. Second St., 89503-5398. Tel: 702-329-2571; Fax: 702-329-2456.
Catechesis/Religious Programs—Tel: 702-972-5427. D.R.E.: Jose Ramiro Cortez, (English & Spanish).
Students 125.

2—OUR LADY OF THE SNOWS (1939), Rev. Msgr. Thomas Meger, V.G.; Rev. Robert E. Buchanan.
Office: 1138 Wright St., 89509. Tel: 702-323-6894; Fax: 702-323-6749.
School—1125 Lander St., 89509. Tel: 702-322-2773. Mary E. Clark, Prin.
Lay Teachers 12; Students 264.
Catechesis/Religious Programs—Sr. M. Carmen Baca, D.R.E.
Students 458.

3—OUR LADY OF WISDOM (1965), Rev. Frank Hoffmann.
Office: 1101 N. Virginia St., 89503. Tel: 702-322-4336; Fax: 702-322-3616.

4—ST. ALBERT THE GREAT (1948), Rev. Robert A. Simpson.
Mailing Address: 1259 St. Albert Dr., 89503.
Res., 1250 Wyoming Ave., 89503. Tel: 702-747-0722; Fax: 702-746-3976.
Catechesis/Religious Programs—Tel: 702-747-4750. D.R.E.: Debra Hull, (Grades K-6); Kathy McCane, (Grades 7-12).
Students 393.

5—ST. ROSE OF LIMA, Rev. Thomas Donnelly.
Mailing Address: P.O. Box 18790, 89511-0790. Tel: 702-849-2885.

6—ST. THERESE CHURCH OF THE LITTLE FLOWER (1947). (St. Jude Shrine). Revs. Robert A. Bowling, V.F.; Norman King; Omar Botia; Cyril Apassa; Tom Cronin, Chap., Washoe Medical Center.
Office: 875 E. Plumb Ln., 89502. Tel: 702-322-2255; Fax: 702-322-0048.
Res., 339 Urban Rd., 89509.
School—1300 Casazza Dr., 89502. Tel: 702-323-2931. Sr. Margaret Oates, R.S.M., Prin.
Sisters of Mercy 4; Lay Teachers 5; Students 293.
Catechesis/Religious Programs—Tel: 702-322-3415; Fax: 702-322-0048. Sr. Carol Bettencourt, S.H.F., D.R.E.
Students 395.

OUTSIDE THE CITY OF RENO

Battle Mountain, Lander Co., St. John Bosco (1940), Rev. Lorenzo T. Torrente, Pastoral Admin.
Mailing Address: P.O. Box 428, 89820.
Office & Res.—384 S. Reese St., 89820. Tel: 702-635-2576.
Catechesis/Religious Programs—Karen Wagner, D.R.E.
Students 131.
Mission—Austin, St. Augustine.

Carlin, Elko Co., Sacred Heart (1910), Rev. Joseph Nuttman, C.Ss.R., Pastoral Admin.
Mailing Address: P.O. Box 235, 89822.
Office: 562 Fourth St., 89822. Tel: 702-754-6425; Fax: 702-754-2942.
Res., 315 Peters, 89822.

Carson City, Corpus Christi (1949), Rev. Ariel Arias.
Res., 5335 Snyder Ave., 89701. Tel: 702-882-1967; Fax: 702-882-2435.

St. Teresa's of Avila (1858), Revs. Gerald T. Hanley; Charles Durante; Deacons Bob Evans; Craig LaGier; Wendell Schumacher; Dennis Schreiner.
Res., 108 N. Minnesota St., 89703. Tel: 702-882-1968; Fax: 702-883-7063.
School—567 S. Richmond Ave., 89703. Tel: 702-882-2079; Fax: 702-882-6135. Mrs. Judith Elges, Prin.
Lay Teachers 7; Students 229.
Catechesis/Religious Programs—400 W. King St., Ste. 104, 89703. Tel: 702-882-2130. Mary Ann Randall D.R.E.
Students 620.

Dayton, Lyon Co., St. Ann, Rev. Francis Murphy, Presbyteral Mod.; Deacon Roger Porcella, Parish Life Coord.
Mailing Address: P.O. Box 309, 89403. Tel: 702-246-7578; Fax: 702-246-3789.

Elko, Elko Co., St. Joseph's (1917), Rev. James J. Setelik, Jr.; Sr. Diana White, S.H.F., Pastoral Assoc.
Office: 1035 C St., 89801. Tel: 702-738-6432; Fax: 702-738-0898 (Office Hrs. Only).
Res., 986 Highland Dr., 89801.
Catechesis/Religious Programs—Janie Bauer, D.R.E.
Students 550.
Missions—Wells, St. Thomas Aquinas, 619 Sixth St., P.O. Box 369, Wells, 89835. Tel: 702-752-3400. Sr. Carolyn Whited, S.H.F., Pastoral Assoc.; Jackpot, Elko Co., Blessed Miguel Pro, Box 462, Jackpot, 89825. Sr. Rosemary Boessen, R.S.M., Pastoral Assoc.

Eureka, Eureka Co., St. Brendan's (1872), Rev. Joseph Nuttman, C.Ss.R, Pastoral Admin.
Mailing Address: P.O. Box 305, 89316.
Res., 1022 O'Neill Ave., 89316. Tel: 702-237-5278.

Fallon, Churchill Co., St. Patrick (1920), Rev. Stanley T. Wisniewski, S.J.
Mailing Address: P.O. Box 170, 89407.
Res., 375 Tedford Ln., 89406.
Church—850 W. Fourth St., 89406. Tel: 702-423-2846; Fax: 702-423-5210.
Catechesis/Religious Programs—Tel: 702-423-5210. D.R.E.: Candy Cramer; Patty Fleming.
Students 200.

Fallon Naval Air Station Base Chapel (1977), Rev. Alfonso E. Erestain.
Office: Naval Air Station, 4755 Pasture Rd., Bldg. 351, 89496-5000. Tel: 702-426-2813; Fax: 702-426-2959.

Fernley, Lyon Co., St. Robert Bellarmine (1957), Rev. Martin Perrier, Presbyteral Mod.; Sr. M. Christopher Schmidt, S.H.F., Parish Life Coord.
Mailing Address: P.O. Box 473, 89408.
Office: 190 S. West St., 89408. Tel: 702-575-4011; Fax: 702-575-7601.
Missions—Empire, St. Joseph the Worker; Silver Springs, Our Lady of the Blessed Sacrament.

Gardnerville, Douglas Co., St. Gall (1917), Rev. John J. Corona; Sr. Dorothy Sanchez, F.S.P.A., Pastoral Assoc.
Mailing Address: P.O. Box 788, 89410.
Office: 1343 Centerville Rd., 89410. Tel: 702-782-2852; Fax: 702-782-2622.
Res., 1740 Lavender Ct., Minden, 89423.
Catechesis/Religious Programs—Tel: 702-782-3784. Debbie Posnien, D.R.E., Tel: 702-782-3784.
Students 258.

Hawthorne, Mineral Co., Our Lady of Perpetual Help (1938), Rev. Warren Freret, Pastoral Admin.
Mailing Address: P.O. Box 850, 89415. Office 804 A St., 89415. Tel: 702-945-2020; Fax: 702-945-1772.
Res., 794 A St., 89415.
Mission—Gabbs, St. Michael, Gabbs, 89409.

Incline Village, Washoe Co., St. Francis of Assisi (1965), Rev. Michael Q. Mahone.
Mailing Address: P.O. Box 4226, 89450. Tel: 702-831-0490; Fax: 702-831-2045.
Church—Mt. Rose Hwy. at Kelly Dr., 89450.

Lovelock, Pershing Co., St. John the Baptist (1875), Rev. Thomas Zagorski, O.F.M.Conv.
Mailing Address: 1045 Franklin Ave., 89419-0177. Tel: 702-273-2189; Fax: 702-273-2189.
Res., 1045 Franklin Ave., 89419-0177.
Church—1085 Franklin Ave., 89419-0177.

Sparks, Washoe Co., Holy Cross Catholic Community (1967), Rev. George C. Wolf; Francine McMillen, Pastoral Assoc.
Res., 3175 Goldy Way, 89434. Tel: 702-358-2544; Fax: 702-358-8239.
Catechesis/Religious Programs—Tel: 702-358-8239. D.R.E.: Mary Diebel, (Liturgy of the Word & Grades 1-5); JoElla Barrie, (Post Confirmation & Grades 6-7); Fran McMillen, (Confirmation & Grades 8-10).
Students 381.

Immaculate Conception (1932), Revs. John J. O'Brien, S.A.C.; Timothy Twomey, S.A.C. In res., Rev. John Coen, S.A.C.
Res., 590 Pyramid Way, 89431. Tel: 702-358-5977; Fax: 702-359-3951.
Catechesis/Religious Programs—D.R.E.: Rhonda Gregoire, (Elementary), Tel: 702-425-3939; Monique Jacobs, (High School), Tel: 702-746-1694.
Students 245.

Stead, Washoe Co., St. Michael's (1967), Very Rev. John A. Sullivan, J.C.L.
Res., 14075 Mt. Vida St., Reno, 89506. Tel: 702-972-7462; Fax: 702-972-9373.

Sun Valley, Washoe Co., St. Peter Canisius (1976), Rev. Larry Morrison, Pastoral Admin.
Res., 225 E. Fifth Ave., 89433. Tel: 702-673-2029; Fax: 702-673-2028.

Virginia City, Storey Co., St. Mary in the Mountains (1862), Rev. Bernard Michalik, O.F.M.Conv.
Mailing Address: P.O. Box 510, 89440.
Res., Taylor St. & E St., 89440. Tel: 702-847-9099; Fax: 702-847-0466.

Winnemucca, Humboldt Co., St. Paul (1883), Rev. Joseph Richard.
Mailing Address: 350 Melarkey St., 89445.
Res., Fourth St. & Melarkey St., 89445. Tel: 702-623-2928; Fax: 702-623-4153. [JC]
Catechesis/Religious Programs—Tina Vavra, D.R.E.
Students 330.
Missions—Paradise Valley, Humboldt Co., St. Alphonsus; McDermitt, Humboldt Co., Sacred Heart.

Yerington, Lyon Co., Holy Family (1901), Rev. Thomas E. Wright.
Mailing Address: P.O. Box 839, 89447.
Res., 37 N. West St., 89447. Tel: 702-463-2882; Fax: 702-463-2162.
Church—43 N. West St., 89447.
Mission—Smith Valley, Lyon Co., St. John the Baptist, Hwy. 208, Smith Valley, 89430. Tel: 702-465-2222.

Zephyr Cove, Douglas Co., Our Lady of Tahoe (1966), Rev. John K. Bain.
Mailing Address: P.O. Box 115, 89448.
Res., 630 Don Dr., 89448. Tel: 702-588-2080; Fax: 702-588-0211.
Catechesis/Religious Programs—Kathleen Deiton, D.R.E., Tel: 702-588-3670.
Students 130.

On Duty Outside the Diocese:
Reverend Fathers—
Aitcheson, William M., 11 Irving Ave., Colonial Beach, VA 22443
Quilici, Lawrence, 7954 N. Jacqueline Pl., Tucson, AZ 85741. Tel: 520-579-3635

Leave of Absence:
Reverend Fathers—
Vieages, Harold

Retired:
Reverend Monsignors—
McFadden, Leo E., 3363 Spring Creek Cir., Reno, NV 89509
Reverend Fathers—
Avella, William, 40 Penrose Ln., Yerlington, NV 89447. Tel: 702-463-3958
Fanning, Gerard F., Ballymakenny (East Rand), Drogheda, County Louth
Fosselman, Albert, P.O. Box 5617, Incline Village, NV 89450. Tel: 702-831-5590
Herkowski, Arthur, Blessed Sacrament, 2576 Sunny Slope Dr., Sparks, NV 89434. Tel: 702-331-2857

Permanent Deacons:
Batson, Randol G., St. Mary's Regl. Medical Ctr., 235 W. Sixth St., Reno, NV 89520. Tel: 702-323-2041
Evans, Robert, 700 W. Adeline, Carson City, NV 89701. Tel: 702-883-2341
Lagier, Craig, 1217 Calaveras, Carson City, NV 89703. Tel: 702-883-9740
Porcella, Roger, 986 Ridgeview Dr., Carson City, NV 89705. Tel: 702-267-5110
Ruggiero, Robert L., 4697 W. Leonisio Dr., Sun Valley, NV 89433. Tel: 702-674-3086
Schmitt, Ron, 1095 E. York Way, Sparks, NV 89434
Schreiner, Dennis, 1809 Pyrenees, Carson City, NV 89703. Tel: 702-882-6864
Schumacher, Wendell, 52 Loire St., Carson City, NV 89703. Tel: 702-882-1883

INSTITUTIONS LOCATED IN THE DIOCESE

[A] HIGH SCHOOLS, DIOCESAN

RENO. *Bishop Manogue High School*, 400 Bartlett St., 89512. Tel: 702-329-0011. Dr. Carl Shaff, Pres.; Robert D. Sullivan, Prin.; Stephen F. Reger, Controller. Brothers 1; Sisters 1; Lay Teachers 29; Students 350.

[B] GENERAL HOSPITALS

RENO. *St. Mary's Regional Medical Center*, 235 W. Sixth St., 89520-0108. Tel: 702-323-2041; Fax: 702-789-3963.

For a complete listing, refer to the Hospitals section.

[C] DAY NURSERIES

RENO. *Holy Child Day Home*, 440 Reno Ave., 89509. Tel: 702-329-2979; Fax: 702-329-8531. Mrs. Karen L. Barreras, Dir.; Lay Teachers 32; Boys 105; Girls 110.

[D] MONASTERIES AND RESIDENCES FOR PRIESTS AND BROTHERS

RENO. *Brothers of Our Lady of the Holy Rosary Monastery*, 1725 S. McCarran Blvd., 89502. Tel: 702-358-6806. Bros. Philip Napolitano, F.S.R., Supr.; Matthew Cunningham, F.S.R., Asst. Supr.; Edward Zuber, F.S.R. Brothers 3.

[E] CONVENTS AND RESIDENCES FOR SISTERS

RENO. *Carmelite Monastery (O.C.D.)*, 1950 La Fond Dr., 89509-3099. Tel: 702-323-3236; Fax: 702-322-1532. Carmelite Sisters.

Convent of the Society Devoted to the Sacred Heart (S.D.S.H.), 232 Sunnyside Dr., 89503. Tel: 702-747-2290. Discalced Carmelite Nuns. Sacred Heart Sisters. Sisters 4.

Little Flower Convent (S.M.), 1280 Casazza St., 89502. Tel: 702-322-5966. Sisters of Mercy. Sr. Sandra DiCianno, S.M., Contact Person. Sisters 4.

Monastery of Our Lady of the Mountains, 1950 LaFond Dr., 89509-3099. Tel: 702-323-3236; Fax: 702-322-1532. Sr. Maria, O.C.D., Prioress. Discalced Carmelite Nuns. Professed Nuns 15.

St. Mary's Convent (O.P.), 411 W. Sixth St., 89503. Tel: 702-323-5196. Sr. Kristen Wombacher, Supr. Sisters of St. Dominic. Sisters 6.

Sisters of the Holy Family Convent, S.H.F., 6730 S. McCarran Blvd., 89509. Tel: 702-827-5370. Sr. Carmen Bacha, S.H.F.; Sr. Carol Bettencourt, S.H.F.; Sr. Christopher Schmidt, S.H.F. Holy Family Sisters. Sisters 3.

GARDNERVILLE. *Franciscan Sisters of Perpetual Adoration*, 1450 Douglas, P.O. Box 788, 89410. Tel: 702-782-8405. Sr. Dorothy Sanchez, F.S.P.A. 1.

SPARKS. *Sisters of St. Philip Neri*, 135 Pascus Pl., 89431. Tel: 702-331-0708. Sisters 3.

[F] CAMPUS MINISTRY

RENO. *University of Nevada, Newman Club*. Served by Our Lady of Wisdom, 1101 N. Virginia St., 89503. Tel: 702-322-4336. Rev. Frank Hoffman, Chap.

[G] CATHOLIC COMMUNITY SERVICES

RENO. *Adoption*, 275 E. Fourth St., 89501. Tel: 702-322-7073. Mailing Address: P.O. Box 5099, 89513-5099. Linda Maisel, Dir.

Emergency Assistance, 275 E. Fourth St., 89501. Tel: 702-322-7073. Mailing Address: P.O. Box 5099, 59513-5099. Ida Yoas, Dir.

Holy Child Day Home, 440 Reno Ave., 89509. Tel: 702-329-2979; Fax: 702-329-8537. Karen Barreras, Dir.

St. Vincent's Dining Room, 505 W. Third, 89503. Tel: 702-329-5363. Mailing Address: P.O. Box 5099, 89513-5099. Ray Trevino, Dir.

St. Vincent's Shelter, 1815, 1835, 1865, and 1867 Montello St.; 1550-1570 E. Ninth St., 89512. Tel: 702-322-7073. Mailing Address: P.O. Box 5099, 89513-5099. Frank C. Spanos, Mgr.

St. Vincent's Thrift Shop, 275 E. Fourth St., 89501. Tel: 702-322-9824. Mailing Address: P.O. Box 5099, 89513-5099. Tillie Molina, Mgr.

RELIGIOUS INSTITUTES OF MEN REPRESENTED IN THE DIOCESE

For further details refer to the corresponding bracketed number in the Religious Institutes of Men or Women section.

[0960]—*Brothers of the Congregation of Our Lady of the Holy Rosary*.—F.S.R.

[0480]—*Conventual Franciscans*.—O.F.M.Conv.

[0690]—*Jesuit Fathers and Brothers*.—S.J.

[1070]—*Redemptorist Fathers*.—C.Ss.R.

[0990]—*Society of the Catholic Apostolate*. (Irish Prov.).—S.A.C.

RELIGIOUS INSTITUTES OF WOMEN REPRESENTED IN THE DIOCESE

[1780]—*Congregation of the Sisters of the Third Order of St. Francis of Perpetual Adoration*.—F.S.P.A.

[0420]—*Discalced Carmelite Nuns*.—O.C.D.

[1070-04]—*Dominican Sisters*.—O.P.

[1190]—*Franciscan Sisters of the Atonement*.—S.A.

[2523]—*Sisters of Mercy of Ardagh and Clonmacnois*.—R.S.M.

[2575]—*Sisters of Mercy of the Americas*. (Omaha Region).—R.S.M.

[]—*Sisters of St. Philip Neri*. (Madrid, Spain).

[1960]—*Sisters of the Holy Family*.—S.H.F.

[1990]—*Sisters of the Holy Names of Jesus and Mary*.—S.N.J.M.

DIOCESAN CEMETERIES

RENO. *Our Mother of Sorrows Cemetery & Mausoleum*, 2700 N. Virginia St., 89503. Mailing Address: P.O. Box 8505, 89507. Tel: 702-323-0133. Sophia Mitchell, Operations Mgr.

NECROLOGY

(No Deaths)

Diocese of Richmond

(Dioecesis Richmondiensis)

Most Reverend

WALTER F. SULLIVAN, D.D.

Bishop of Richmond; ordained May 9, 1953; appointed Titular Bishop of Selsey and Auxiliary Bishop of Richmond October 20, 1970; consecrated December 1, 1970; appointed Apostolic Administrator of Richmond April 30, 1973; succeeded to the See, June 6, 1974. *Res., 800 Cathedral Pl., Richmond, VA, 23220. Office: 811 Cathedral Pl., Suite B, Richmond, VA, 23220-4801.*

ESTABLISHED IN 1820.

Square Miles 36,711.

Comprises the State of Virginia, with the exception of the Counties of Arlington, Clarke, Culpeper, Fairfax, Fauquier, Frederick, King George, Lancaster, Loudoun, Madison, Northumberland, Orange, Page, Prince William, Rappahannock, Richmond, Shenandoah, Spottsylvania, Stafford, Warren and Westmoreland.

For legal titles of parishes and diocesan institutions, consult the Chancery Office.

The Chancery: 811 Cathedral Pl., Richmond, VA, 23220-4801. Tel.: 804-359-5661; Fax: 804-358-9159.

STATISTICAL OVERVIEW

Personnel	
Bishop	1
Abbots	1
Priests: Diocesan Active in Diocese	117
Priests: Active Outside Diocese	16
Priests: Retired, Sick or Absent	28
Number of Diocesan Priests	161
Religious Priests in Diocese	39
Extern Priests in Diocese	8
Ordinations:	
Diocesan Priests	4
Transitional Deacons	1
Permanent Deacons	1
Permanent Deacons in Diocese	22
Total Brothers	11
Total Sisters	269
Parishes	
Parishes	141
With Resident Pastor:	
Resident Diocesan Priests	100
Resident Religious Priests	10
Without Resident Pastor:	
Administered by Priests	32
Administered by Permanent Deacons	1
Administered by Women Religious	7
Administered by Lay People	4
Missions	13
Welfare	
Catholic Hospitals	9
Total Assisted	438,670
Health Care Centers	1
Total Assisted	31,570
Homes for the Aged	15
Total Assisted	1,583
Residential Care of Children	1
Total Assisted	88
Day Care and Extended Day Care Centers	5
Total Assisted	605
Specialized Homes	1
Total Assisted	12
Special Centers for Social Services	4
Total Assisted	9,938
Residential Care of Disabled	5
Total Assisted	198
Educational	
Total Seminarians	7
High Schools, Diocesan and Parish	5
Total Students	995
High Schools, Private	4
Total Students	956
Elementary Schools, Diocesan and Parish	23
Total Students	5,102
Elementary Schools, Private	1
Total Students	412
Catechesis/Religious Education:	
High School Students	4,850
Elementary Students	17,818
Total Students Under Catholic Instruction	30,133
Teachers in the Diocese:	
Priests	3
Sisters	26
Lay Teachers	588
Vital Statistics	
Receptions into the Church:	
Infant Baptism Totals	3,245
Adult Baptism Totals	152
Received into Full Communion	982
First Communions	3,377
Confirmations	1,500
Marriages:	
Catholic	463
Interfaith	639
Total Marriages	1,102
Deaths	1,458
Total Catholic Population	183,304
Total Population	4,561,480

Former Bishops—Rt. Rev. PATRICK KELLY, D.D., first Bishop; cons. Aug. 24, 1820; translated Waterford and Lismore in 1822; died Oct. 8, 1829.—Rt. Rev. RICHARD V. WHELAN, D.D., second Bishop; cons. March 21, 1841; translated Wheeling, July 23, 1850; died July 7, 1874.—Rt. Rev. JOHN MCGILL, D.D., cons. Nov. 10, 1850; died Jan. 14, 1872.—His Eminence JAMES CARDINAL GIBBONS, D.D., cons. August 16, 1868 Bishop of Adramyttum, and Vicar-Apostolic of North Carolina; translated the See of Richmond, July 30, 1872; translated the See of Baltimore, Oct. 3, 1877; created Cardinal Priest of S. Maria in Trastevere, June 7, 1886; died March 24, 1921.—Rt. Rev. JOHN J. KEANE, D.D., cons. Aug. 25, 1878; resigned August, 1888 rector of the Catholic University, Washington, DC; transferred to Archbishopric of Dubuque, July 24, 1900; died June 27, 1918.—Rt. Rev. AUGUSTINE VAN DE VYVER, D.D., cons. Oct. 20, 1889; died Oct. 16, 1911.—Rt. Rev. DENIS JOSEPH O'CONNELL, D.D., cons. May 3, 1908 Titular Bishop of Sebaste and Auxiliary Bishop of San Francisco; appt. Bishop of Richmond, Jan. 19, 1912; resigned Jan. 15, 1926 and appointed Titular Archbishop of Marianne; died Jan. 1, 1927.—Most Rev. ANDREW J. BRENNAN, D.D., ord. December 17, 1904; cons. Titular Bishop of Thapsus and Auxiliary Bishop of Scranton, April 25, 1923; appt. Bishop of Richmond, May 28, 1926; resigned April 14, 1945; appt. Titular Bishop of Telmissus; died May 23, 1956.—Most Rev. PETER L. IRETON, D.D., ord. June 20, 1906; appt. Titular Bishop of Cime Coadjutor Bishop and Apostolic Administrator of Richmond, August 3, 1935; cons. October 23, 1935; named Bishop of Richmond, April 14, 1945; named Assistant at the Pontifical Throne, May 21, 1956; died April 27, 1958.—Most Rev. JOHN J. RUSSELL, D.D., ord. July 8, 1923; appt. Bishop of Charleston, Jan. 28, 1950; cons. March 14, 1950; appt. Bishop of Richmond, July 3, 1958; retired April 3, 1973; died March 17, 1993.

Central Administrative Offices

All Diocesan Offices are located at: 811 Cathedral Place, Richmond, VA 23220-4801. Tel: 804-359-5661; Fax: 804-358-9159, unless otherwise indicated

Vicars General—Revs. THOMAS F. SHREVE, V.G., J.C.L.; ROBERT M. PERKINS, V.G.

Episcopal Vicars—Revs. THOMAS J. CAROLUZZA, Eastern Vicariate; CHARLES A. KELLY, Central Vicariate; JAMES GREALISH, Western Vicariate.

Vicar for the Hispanic Apostolate—Rev. MICHAEL S. SCHMIED; ELISA MONTALVO, Dir.

Vicar for Ecumenism—Rev. RAYMOND A. BARTON.

Chancellor—Mrs. ANNE C. EDWARDS.

Department Moderators—Mr. JOHN F. BARRETT; Ms. DIANE BIALKOWSKI; Dr. STEPHEN M. COLECCHI.

Diocesan Tribunal—Sr. PATRICIA MCGREEVY, O.S.B., M.C.H.A., J.C.L., Dir.

Judicial Vicar—Rev. WILLIAM V. SULLIVAN, J.C.L., M.Ch.A.

Judges—Revs. MARTIN E. LAVIN, J.C.L.; J. SCOTT DUARTE, J.C.L.; J. KENNETH RUSH, D.Min.; JAMES GREALISH, B.A.; R. FRANCIS MUENCH, J.C.L.; Sr. PATRICIA MCGREEVY, O.S.B., M.C.H.A., J.C.L.

Defenders of the Bond—Revs. MICHAEL M. DUFFY, J.C.L.; KEVIN J. O'BRIEN, S.T.B.; Deacon JOHN H. THOMAS; H. ROBERTA SMALL, J.C.L.

Roanoke Office—P.O. Box 21784, Roanoke, 24018-0180.

Tidewater Office—145 Dupre Ave., Norfolk, 23503-3423. Tel: 804-588-2941.

Ecclesiastical Notaries—Mrs. BARBARA A. LEE; ANTHONY K. SPRATLEY.

Auditors—Ms. VALERIE MCAVOY.

Vicar for Priests—Rev. ROBERT M. PERKINS.

Vicar for Priestly Formation—Rev. CHARLES A. KELLY.

Vocation Director for Promotion and Recruitment—Rev. MICHAEL MCCARRON.

Department of Pastoral Services—Ms. DIANE BIALKOWSKI, Moderator.

Office of Christian Formation—Sr. KATHLEEN SWEENEY, S.S.N.D., Dir. Assoc. Dirs.: Mr. DENNIS BEEMAN; Ms. PATRICIA NOVAK.

Office of Catholic Schools—Ms. DIANE BIALKOWSKI, Supt.; Bro. JOHN FOX, C.F.X.; Ms. MAUREEN MCCABE, Asst. Supt., Schools.

Office of Campus and Young Adult Ministry—Bro. COSMAS RUBENCAMP, C.F.X., Dir.; Sr. DIANE GUY, S.N.D., Assoc. Dir.

Department of Social Action—Dr. STEPHEN M. COLECCHI, Moderator.

Office of Justice and Peace—Dr. STEPHEN M. COLECCHI, Dir. Assoc. Dirs.: Mr. MICHAEL E. STONE; Dr. KATHLEEN T. KENNEY.

Appalachian Office—Sr. GWEN HENNESSEY, Dir., *P.O. Box 660, St. Paul, 24283.* Tel: 540-762-5050.

Migrant Ministry—JAMES ALBRIGHT, Dir., *P.O. Box*

584, Accomac, 23301. Tel: 804-787-7862.
Office of Refugee Resettlement—Mrs. MARILYN BRESLOW, Exec. Dir.
Richmond Regional Dir.—KATHLEEN JACKSON.
Norfolk Regional Dir.—JANE COOK, Interim Dir., *1801 Ashland Ave., Norfolk, 23509.* Tel: 804-623-9131.
Roanoke Regional Dir.—Mrs. BARBARA SMITH, *1106 9th St. S.E., Roanoke, 24013.* Tel: 540-342-7561.
Ministry with Older Adults—Ms. MARY ELLEN COX, Coord. Tel: 804-227-3116.
Office of Black Catholics—Sr. CORA BILLINGS, R.S.M., Dir.
Office of Communications—Mr. BOB EDWARDS, Dir.
Department of Administrative Services—Mr. JOHN F. BARRETT, Moderator.
Office of Finance—Mr. JOHN F. BARRETT, Dir.; Mr. EDWARD L. SHRINER, C.P.A., Controller.
Office of Personnel—Mr. MICHAEL BECHELLI, Dir.; Ms. ETTA SHEPPERD, Assoc. Dir.
Management Information Services—Mrs. JOAN PARDUE, Dir.; Mrs. KAREN BISHOP, Programmer/Analyst.
Office of Development—Ms. CAROLE KAHWAJY.
Office of Stewardship—Rev. PASQUALE J. APUZZO.
Office of General Services—Mrs. SUSAN R. TEAL.
Office of Risk Management—Mr. WILLIAM J. WHELAN, Dir.
Theological Consultant—Bro. PHILIP DOUGHERTY, C.F.X.

Diocesan Councils

Apostleship of the Sea—Rev. SANTIAGO C. FRIAS, *155 W. Government Ave., Norfolk, 23503.* Tel: 804-480-3433.
Board of Conciliation and Arbitration—Vacant.
Campaign for Human Development—Mr. MICHAEL STONE, Diocesan Dir.
Catholic Relief Services—Dr. KATHLEEN KENNEY.
Catholic Historical Society of the Roanoke Valley—Mrs. MARY C. MAIER, *2609 Hillcrest Ave. N.W., Roanoke, 24012.*
Catholic Daughters of America—Ms. MARIAN E. NOWLAND, State Regent, *4617 Seminary Rd., Apt. 207, Alexandria, 22304.*
Catholic Golden Age—Ms. JEAN CAHEN, *2821 Hilliard Rd., Richmond, 23228.*
"Catholic Virginian" (Diocesan Newspaper)—Mr. CHARLES MAHON, Editor, *P.O. Box 26843, Richmond, 23261.* Tel: 804-359-5654; Fax: 804-359-5689. Mr. STEPHEN S. NEILL, Assoc. Editor; Mrs. JUDITH LINDFORS, Business Mgr./Circulation Dir.
Council of Catholic Women—Mrs. MARGARET DISNEY, *3801 Cedar Grove Rd., Richmond, 23235.*
Catholic Women's Club—Mrs. JOE F. CLARA, Pres., *4536 Phomcroft Dr., Glen Allen, 23060.*
Cemeteries—Rev. FREDERICK J. FEUSAHRENS, Dir. Tel: 804-329-0473.
Charismatic Communities—Mr. ROBERT BROWN, *HC02, Box 205, Buckingham, 23921.* Tel: 804-969-1755.
Councilium Board for Education—MAUREEN MCCABE, *811 Cathedral Pl., Richmond, 23220.* Tel: 804-359-5661.
Council of Priests—See Presbyteral Council.
Cursillio—Rev. JAMES KAUFFMANN, Spiritual Dir., *P.O. Box 396, Ladysmith, 22501.* Tel: 804-448-9064. Lay Co-Dirs.: JAMES MCGROGAN; ALBERTA MCGROGAN, *Rte. 1, Box 65-A, Fairfield, 24435.* Tel: 540-348-5939.
Commonwealth Catholic Charities—1512 Willow Lawn Dr., Richmond, 23230-0565. Tel: 804-285-5900. Rev. DAVID J. BERGNER, S.D.S., Exec. Dir.; Dr. STEPHEN M. COLECCHI, Diocesan Dir.
Catholic Charities of Hampton Roads, Inc.—4855 Princess Anne Rd., Virginia Beach, 23462. Tel: 757-467-7707. Mrs. MARGARET ROBERTSON, Exec. Dir.
Ecumenical Officer—Rev. RAYMOND A. BARTON, *208 E. Jefferson St., Charlotesville, 22901.*
Finance Council—Mr. H. GREGORY KILDUFF, *8936 River Crescent, Suffolk, 23433-1110.*
Haitian Ministry Commission—Bro. COSMOS RUBENCAMP, Exec. Sec., *811 Cathedral Pl., Richmond, 23220.* Tel: 804-359-5661.
Holy Childhood Association—Rev. THOMAS F. SHREVE, J.C.L., V.G.
Knights of Columbus—THOMAS J. HOGAN, State Deputy, *3126 Barkley Dr., Fairfax, 22031.*
Nocturnal Adoration Society—Rev. DONALD F. SCALES, *300 N. Sheppard St., Richmond, 23220.*
Diocesan Pastoral Council—Mr. JOSEPH GUION, *949 W. Ferry Plantation Rd., Virginia Beach, 23455.*
Pax Christi Richmond—Mr. JOHN GALLINI, *2425 Triton Dr., Richmond, 23235.*
Pax Christi Virginia—Vacant.
Presbyteral Council—Rev. THOMAS MAGRI, Chm., *10 Harrison Ave., Williamsburg, 23185-3530.* Tel: 804-220-9375.
Promoter of Justice—Vacant.
Propagation of the Faith—Rev. THOMAS F. SHREVE, J.C.L., V.G.
Respect Life—MICHAEL E. STONE, Coord.
Diocesan AIDS Task Force—Dr. STEPHEN LENTON, Chm., *P.O. Box 7087, Richmond, 23221-0087.*
Richmond Catholic Heritage Foundation—Rev. WILLIAM H. CARR, *St. Bede Church, 10 Harrison Ave., Williamsburg, 23185.*
Secular Carmelite Communities—
Community of the Holy Spirit—SUNNI COWLING, O.C.D.S., Pres., *1211 Mt. Erin Dr., Richmond, 23231.*
Community of Our Lady of the Annunication—TIRA KNIPSEL, O.C.D.S., Pres., *1288 Alanton Dr., Virginia Beach, 23454.*
Serra Club of Richmond—Mr. JAMES POLLOCK, Pres., *10800 Dominion Fairways Dr., Glen Allen, 23060.*
Scouting—Rev. ADRIAN HARMENING, Chap. Tel: 804-342-1319. Mr. JOHN CONRON, Diocesan Lay Chm. Tel: 804-272-5075.

CLERGY, PARISHES, MISSIONS AND PAROCHIAL SCHOOLS

CITY OF RICHMOND

1—CATHEDRAL OF THE SACRED HEART, Most Rev. Walter F. Sullivan, D.D.; Rev. Charles A. Kelly, Rector. In res., Rev. Robert Perkins.
Bishop's Office: 811 Cathedral Pl., 23220-4801. Tel: 804-359-5661.; Cathedral Office: 823 Park Ave., 23220. Tel: 804-359-5651; Fax: 804-359-8043. [JC]
Church—18 N. Laurel, 23220.

2—CHURCH OF THE EPIPHANY (Chesterfield Co), Rev. Thomas F. Shreve.
Mailing Address: 11000 Smoketree Dr., 23236-3144. Tel: 804-794-0222; 0223; Fax: 804-378-2013.
Mission—Amelia, Good Samaritan, P.O.Box 759, Amelia, 23002.

3—HOLY ROSARY, Rev. Arthur Dennis Conrad.
Mailing Address: P.O. Box 23116, 23223.
Parish Office: 1209 N. 33rd St., 23223. Tel: 804-222-1105; Fax: 804-226-2204.
Res., 917 Old Denny St., 23221. Tel: 804-222-3565.
Church—N. 33rd & S St., 23223.
Child Care Center—1218 N. 34th St., 23223. Tel: 804-222-2590. Ms. Deborah Longs, Dir.
Students 120.

4—OUR LADY OF LOURDES (Henrico Co.), Revs. J. Anthony Warner; Frank Wiggins; Thomas McDonnell, S.J.
Res., 8200 Woodman Rd., 23228-3237. Tel: 804-264-4990; 262-7315; 7314; Fax: 804-262-7337. [JC]
School—Tel: 804-262-1770. Lucy R. Reilley, Prin.
Lay Teachers 19; Students 302.

5—SACRED HEART, Rev. David Stokes, S.J.
Mailing Address: 1415 Perry St., 23224-2057.
Res., 1409 Perry St., 23224. Tel: 804-230-6430; 232-8964 (Office); Fax: 804-231-9931. [JC]
Church—1401 Perry St., 23224.

6—ST. AUGUSTINE (Chesterfield Co.), Rev. Michael S. Schmied. In res., Rev. Ricardo Seidel.
Mailing Address: 4400 Beulah Rd., 23237-1850.
Res., 9608 Verlinda Ct., 23237. Tel: 804-778-4842.
Church—Corner of Hopkins & Beulah Rd., 23237. Tel: 804-275-7962; Fax: 804-271-4604.

7—ST. BENEDICT, Revs. Donald Scales, O.S.B. Tel: 804-254-8841; Augustine W. Ludwig, O.S.B.
Res., 3007 Hanover Ave., 23221. Tel: 804-254-8839. [JC]
Church—300 N. Sheppard St., 23221-2407. Tel: 804-254-8810; Fax: 804-355-5112.
School—3100 Grove Ave., 23221. Tel: 804-254-8850. Mary Claire Robinson, Prin.
Lay Teachers 15; Students 254.
Mission—St.Joseph Tridentine Community, Tel: 804-342-1319. Rev. Adrian Harmening, O.S.B.

8—ST. BRIDGET (Henrico Co.), Revs. Thomas G. Miller; Remi Sojka.
Church—6006 Three Chopt Rd., 23226-2797. Tel: 804-282-9511; Fax: 804-285-7227.
School—6011 York Rd., 23226. Tel: 804-288-1994. Mrs. Bettijo Loving, Prin.
Sisters 1; Lay Teachers 30; Students 472.

9—ST. EDWARD THE CONFESSOR, Revs. Ronald A. Ruth; Terry A. Lenning; George Cosmos, Pastoral Assoc.
Mailing Address: 2700 Dolfield Rd., 23235-2618. Tel: 804-272-2948; Fax: 804-560-3565.
Res., 10908 Ashburn Rd., 23235-2618. Tel: 804-330-0772.
Church—Hugeunot Rd. & Dolfield Dr., 23235.
School—Regional School St. Edward-Epiphany, 10701 Huguenot Rd., 23235. Tel: 804-272-2881. Ms. Georgette Richards, Prin.

10—ST. ELIZABETH, Sr. Cora Marie Billings, R.S.M., Pastoral Coord.
Mailing Address: 1301 Victor St., 23222-3935. Tel: 804-329-4599; Fax: 804-321-0741. [JC]
Church—2712 Second Ave., 23222.
School—All Saints, 3418 Noble Ave., 23222. Tel: 804-329-7524. Mr. Kenneth Soistman, Prin.

11—ST. KIM TAEGON, Rev. Dominic Hwa In Hwang.
Mailing Address: 3103 Maury St., 23224-3542. Tel: 804-232-0993; Fax: 804-232-0995.
Church—3100 Logandale Ave., 23224.

12—ST. MARY, Rev. Walter G. Lewis.
Mailing Address: 9505 Gayton Rd., 23229-5319. Tel: 804-740-4044; Fax: 804-740-2197.
School—Tel: 804-740-1048. Hazel Lewane, Prin.
Lay Teachers 21; Students 274.

13—ST. PATRICK, Rev. Arthur D. Conrad, Admin.
Mailing Address: 213 N. 25th St., 23223-7115. Tel: 804-648-0504; Fax: 804-648-5216.
School—2600 E. Grace St., 23223. Tel: 804-648-3621. Sr. Patricia Endres, D.C., Prin.

14—ST. PAUL, Rev. Frederick J. Feusahrens. In res., Rev. George E. Zahn.
Mailing Address: 909 Rennie Ave., 23227. Tel: 804-329-0473; 329-5512; Fax: 804-321-6454.
School—All Saints, 3418 Noble Ave., 23227. Tel: 804-329-7524. Mr. Kenneth Soistman, Prin.

15—ST. PETER, Rev. Robert A. Brownell.
Mailing Address: P.O. Box 933, 23207-0933. Tel: 804-643-4315; Fax: 804-788-9109.
Res., 4030 Forest Hill Ave., Apt. 27, 23225. Tel: 804-231-3941. [JC]
Church—800 E. Grace St., 23219.

16—CHURCH OF THE VIETNAMESE MARTYRS, Rev. Joseph Thang Xuan Pham.
Mailing Address: 67 Clopton St., 23225-3957. Tel: 804-231-4835; Fax: 804-231-4685.

OUTSIDE THE CITY OF RICHMOND

Abingdon, Christ the King, Rev. Robert L. Krenik.
Mailing Address: P.O. Box 1201, 24212-1201.
Res., 124 Park Blvd., Marion, 24354. Tel: 540-783-7282; 628-2941; Fax: 540-783-7282.
Church—Hwy. 11 E., Exit 19 off I-81, 24212.

Appomattox, Our Lady of Peace, Rev. Robert Dillon; Deacon William K. Hayes.
Res., P.O. Box 11, 24522-0011. Tel: 804-352-0104; 352-2653 (Rectory).
Church—Intersection of Rte. 631 & Rte. 627, 24522.

Ashland, Hanover Co., St. Ann, Rev. William V. Sullivan.
Res., 202 Thompson St., 23005-1514. Tel: 804-752-5902.
Church—105 S. Snead St., 23005-1811. Tel: 804-798-5039; Fax: 804-798-5072.

Bedford, Holy Name of Mary, Rev. James J. Begley; Deacon Francis J. Ports.
Mailing Address: 1307 Oakwood St., 24523-1613. Tel: 540-586-8988; Fax: 540-587-9080.
Res., 1531 Newton Cir., 24523. Tel: 540-586-9271.
Church—1301 Oakwood St., 24523.

Big Stone Gap, Wise Co., Sacred Heart, Rev. Anthony Rodrigues. In res., Rev. Leslie Schmidt, Glmy.
Mailing Address: 1821 Holton Ave., 24219-2611. Tel: 540-523-1588; Fax: 540-523-1602.

Blacksburg, Montgomery Co., St. Mary & Newman Community, Revs. Donald H. Lemay; James M. Cowles, Campus Min.; Deacon Mike Ellerbrock.
Mailing Address: 706 Harding Ave., 24060-3618. Tel: 540-552-1091; Fax: 540-953-2962.
Res., 703 Harding Ave. N.E., 24060. Tel: 540-951-2136.
Newman Community: 203 Otey St., 24060. Tel: 540-951-0032.

Blackstone, Nottoway Co., Immaculate Heart of Mary, Mrs. Therese Mansfield, Pastoral Coord.
Mailing Address: P.O. Box 266, 23824-0266. Tel: 804-292-5535.
Church—819 S. Main St., 23824.

Bristol, St. Anne, Rev. Thomas A. Ianucci; Deacon Harry Hall.
Mailing Address: 350 Euclid Ave., 24201-4014. Tel: 540-669-8200; Fax: 540-669-3523. [CEM]
Res., 922 Chester St., 24201. Tel: 540-466-4776.
School—300 Euclid Ave., 24201. Tel: 540-669-0048. Mrs. Jean Green, Prin.
Lay Teachers 21; Students 199.

Brookneal, Campbell Co., St. Elizabeth of Hungary, Rev. Matthias Newell.
Mailing Address: 905 John Randolph Blvd., South Boston, 24592-2943. Tel: 804-572-2285; Fax: 804-575-5653.
Res., 3302 W. Main St., South Boston, 24592. Tel: 804-572-3313.

Church—374 Juniper Cliff Rd., 24528. Tel: 804-572-2285.

Buckingham, Church of the Nativity, Rev. Robert Dillon.
Mailing Address: P.O. Box 241, 23921-0241. Tel: 804-969-2168 (Rectory).
Church—Rte. 60 E., 23921.

Buckner, Immaculate Conception, Rev. Rodney Rodis.
Mailing Address: P.O. Box 40, Mineral, 23117-0040. Tel: 540-894-4266; Fax: 540-894-4993.
Res., 106 Loving St., Louisa, 23093. Tel: 540-967-2465.
Church—1107 Frederick Hall Rd., 23024.

Cape Charles, Northampton Co., St. Charles, Rev. J. Michael Breslin.
Mailing Address: 545 Randolph Ave., 23310-3305. Tel: 804-331-1724.

Charlottesville, Albemarle Co., Church of the Holy Comforter, Revs. Raymond A. Barton; Joseph Torretto.
Mailing Address: 208 E. Jefferson St., 22902-5105. Tel: 804-295-7185; Fax: 804-295-7001.
Res., 660 Evergreen Ave., 22902. Tel: 804-977-5859.
Church of the Incarnation, Rev. William E. La Fratta.
Office: 635 Hillsdale Dr., 22901-1716. Tel: 804-973-4381; Fax: 804-973-1757.
Res., 2414 Commonwealth Dr., 22901. Tel: 804-973-4384.
St. Thomas Aquinas, Revs. Gregory Salomone, O.P.; Gregory Keeler, O.P.; Aaron Laushway, O.P.; Jordan Lenaghan, O.P.
Mailing Address: 331 Kent Rd., 22903.
Office: Tel: 804-293-6472; 293-8081; Fax: 804-296-1941.
Res., 308 Alderman Rd., 22903. Tel: 804-977-5658.
Church—401 Alderman Rd., 22903.

Chesapeake, Prince of Peace, Rev. Christian Haydinger.
Mailing Address: 621 Cedar Rd., 23320-8300. Tel: 757-547-0356; 547-3903; Fax: 757-436-6477.
Res., 303 Elberon Ct., 23320. Tel: 757-547-2951.
St. Mary, Sr. Bernice McCourt, S.N.D., Pastoral Coord.
Mailing Address: P.O. Box 174-B, 23221-0174. Tel: 757-488-2663; 548-8426 (Rectory); Fax: 757-485-3699.
Church—536 Homestead Rd., 23321.
St. Therese of Lisieux, Rev. James C. Griffin.
Mailing Address: 4137 Portsmouth Blvd., 23321-2127. Tel: 757-488-2553; 2554; Fax: 757-465-4086.
Res., 3908 Parkway Rd., 23321. Tel: 757-488-5413.

Chincoteague, Accomack Co., St. Andrew, Rev. John A. Prinelli.
Mailing Address: P.O. Box 229, 23336-0229. Tel: 757-336-5432; Fax: 757-336-3515.
Res., 6319 Mumford St., 23336.
Church—6288 Church St., 23336.

Christiansburg, Holy Spirit Catholic Church, Rev. Louis Benoit.
Mailing Address: P.O. Box 98, 24073.
Church—Our Savior Lutheran Church, Cambria Rd., Pearisburg, 24073. Tel: 540-382-8046; 921-3547.

Clarksville, Mecklenburg Co., St. Catherine of Siena, Rev. James Fosnot.
Mailing Address: P.O. Box 1537, 23927.
Res., 810 Market St., 23927.
Church—Ninth and Virginia Ave., 23927. Tel: 804-374-8408; 447-3622; Fax: 804-447-4729.

Clifton Forge, Alleghany Co., St. Joseph, Rev. Lawrence Mullaney.
Mailing Address: 620 Jefferson Ave., 24422-1715. Tel: 540-863-5371; Fax: 540-863-8963. [CEM]

Clintwood, Dickenson Co., St. Joseph, Rev. Robert B. Rademacher, Glmy.
Mailing Address: Box 1250, 24228-1250. Tel: 540-926-4123; Fax: 540-926-6304.
Church—Main St., 24228.

Colonial Heights, St. Ann, Rev. William F. Condon. In res., Rev. John P. Blankenship.
Mailing Address: 17111 Jefferson Davis Hwy., 23834-5396. Tel: 804-526-2548; Fax: 804-526-1922.
Res., 12861 Percival St., Chester, 23831. Tel: 804-796-9342.

Columbia, Fluvanna Co., St. Joseph, Rev. Gerald A. Przywara; Deacon Albert J. Carini.
Mailing Address: P.O. Box 808, 23038-0808. Tel: 804-589-5201; Fax: 804-589-5201.
Res., 15 Dogleg Rd., Palmyra, 22963. Tel: 804-589-5200.

Covington, Alleghany Co., Church of the Sacred Heart, Rev. David L. Nott.
Office: 214 W. Locust St., 24426-1537. Tel: 540-962-6541; Fax: 540-962-2147.
Res., 222 W. Locust St., 24426-1537. Tel: 540-965-5821.

Crewe, Nottoway Co., St. John the Baptist, Ms. Therese Mansfield, Pastoral Coord.
Mailing Address: 102 Oliver Ave., 23930-1410. Tel: 804-645-7509; Fax: 804-292-5535.
Mission—Meherrin, Sacred Heart, P.O. Box 62, Meherrin, 23954.

Danville, Pittsylvania Co., Sacred Heart, Rev. David V. McGuire.
Mailing Address: 288 W. Main St., 24541-2848. Tel: 804-792-9456; Fax: 804-792-9463.
Res., 154 College Ave., 24541. Tel: 804-792-0081.
School—540 Central Blvd., 24541. Tel: 804-793-2656; Fax: 804-793-2658. Marguerite S. Hancock, Prin.
Lay Teachers 23; Students 281.

Dinwiddie County, St. John, Rev. John J. Martinez, S.J.
Mailing Address: 7215 Squirrel Level Rd., Petersburg, 23805-7035. Tel: 804-861-0123; Fax: 804-861-0123.
Church—Squirrel Level Rd. & Flank Rd., Petersburg, 23805.

Elkton, Rockingham Co., Holy Infant, Rev. Daniel Bain.
Mailing Address: 101 W. Marshall Ave., 22827-1221. Tel: 540-298-1341; Fax: 540-298-1341.
Church—Rte. 33 & Rte. 340, 22827.

Emporia, Greensville Co., St. Richard, Rev. Leo Cervantes.
Mailing Address: 117 Laurel St., 23847-2506. Tel: 804-634-3524; Fax: 804-634-3524.
Mission—Lawrenceville, St. Bernard.
St. Peter the Apostle, Rev. Leo Cervantes.
Mailing Address: 117 Laurel St., 23847-2506. Tel: 804-634-3524.
Church—Rt. 46 & Rt. 626, Valentines, 23887.

Farmville, Prince Edward Co., St. Theresa, Rev. Joseph H. Metzger, III.
Mailing Address: 709 Buffalo St., 23901-1726. Tel: 804-392-3934; Fax: 804-392-1611.
Res., 400 Putney St., 23901. Tel: 804-392-8900.
Church—709 Buffalo St., 23901.

Fincastle, Botetourt Co., Church of the Transfiguration, Sr. Eveline Murray, Pastoral Coord.
Mailing Address: P.O. Box 416, 24090-0416. Tel: 540-473-2656; Fax: 540-473-2193.
Church—3650 Roanoke Rd., 24090.

Fort Monroe, St. Mary Star of the Sea, Rev. Joseph L. Clark.
Res., 7 Frank Ln., 23651-1010. Tel: 757-722-9855; 722-3138; Fax: 757-726-0083.
School—St. Mary Star of the Sea, 14 N. Willard Ave., Hampton, 23663. Tel: 757-723-6358. Sr. Mary Rose Bingham, O.P., Prin.
Sisters 2; Lay Teachers 15; Students 265.

Franklin, Southampton Co., St. Jude, Rev. Carl De Souza.
Mailing Address: 1014 Clay St., 23851-1309. Tel: 757-569-9600; Fax: 757-562-6974.
Mission—Wakefield, Infant of Prague.

Gate City, Scott Co., St. Bernard, Revs. Robert V. Cameron, Glmy.; John Garvey, Glmy. In res., Bro. Bob Hoffman, Glmy.
Mailing Address: 105 Linda St., 24251. Tel: 540-386-9665.
Mission—Dungannon, St. Patrick.

Gloucester, St. Therese, the Little Flower, Rev. John E. Ridgell.
Mailing Address: P.O. Box 669, 23061.
Office: Tel: 804-693-5939; 693-9043 (Hall); Fax: 804-693-4766.
Res., 8051 Belroi Rd., 23061. Tel: 804-693-3380.
Church—6262 Main St., 23061.

Glen Allen, Henrico Co., St. Michael, Rev. John E. Leonard.
Parish Office: 4491 Springfield Rd., 23060. Tel: 804-527-1037; Fax: 804-527-1039.

Hampton

1—Immaculate Conception, Rev. Robert E. French.
Mailing Address: P.O. Box 7382, 23666-0382.
Res., 123 Tanglewood Dr., 23666. Tel: 757-826-0050.
Church—2150 Cunningham Dr., 23666. Tel: 757-826-0393; 826-0455; Fax: 757-825-0855.

2—St. Joseph, Rev. Joseph J. Majewski, C.SS.R. In res., Revs. J. Nicholas Helldorfer, C.SS.R.; Donald Winter, C.SS.R.
Mailing Address: P.O. Box 4126, 23664-0126.
Res., 410 Buckroe Ave., 23664-0126. Tel: 757-851-1711.
Church—414 Buckroe Ave., 23664-0126. Tel: 757-851-8800; Fax: 757-851-1875.

3—St. Rose of Lima, Rev. R. Francis Muench.
Mailing Address: P.O. Box 1380, 23661-0380.
Office: 2114 Bay Ave., 23661. Tel: 757-245-5513; Fax: 757-245-1277.
Res., 2108 Bay Ave., 23661. Tel: 757-245-6313.

4—Our Lady of Viet Nam Chapel, Rev. Anthony Trang Kim Ngo.
Mailing Address: 1806 Ashland Ave., Norfolk, 23509. Tel: 757-722-2657.
Chapel—1307 LaSalle Ave., 23661.

Harrisonburg, Rockingham Co., Blessed Sacrament, Revs. Kenneth E. Wood; John A. Grace.
Mailing Address: P.O. Box 226, 22801-0226.
Res., 843 Meadowlark Dr., 22801. Tel: 540-433-5666.
Church—154 N. Main St., 22801. Tel: 540-434-4341; 434-8601; Fax: 540-434-0849.

Highland Springs, Henrico Co., St. John, Rev. James R. Guttendorf.
Mailing Address: P.O. Box 190, 23075-0190. Tel: 804-737-8028; Fax: 804-328-4683.
Res., 903 W. Nine Mile Rd., 23075. Tel: 804-737-4077.
Church—813 W. Nine Mile Rd., 23075.

Hopewell, St. James Church, Revs. Paul D. Jenkins, Pastor Emeritus; Michael Duffy.
Mailing Address: 510 W. Poythress St., 23860-2508.
Res., 102 N. Fifth Ave., 23860. Tel: 804-452-0375.
Church—500 W. Poythress St., 23860. Tel: 804-458-9223; 458-9286 (evening); Fax: 804-458-1216.
Mission—Claremont, St. Anne.

Hot Springs, Bath Co., The Shrine of the Sacred Heart, Rev. David L. Nott.
Mailing Address: Box B, 24445-0047. Tel: 540-839-2603.

Hurt, Pittsylvania Co., St. Victoria, Rev. Robert J. McEleney, Admin.
Mailing Address: P.O. Box 640, 24563-0640. Tel: 804-324-4824; Fax: 804-324-4759.
Res., 305 Victoria Dr., 24563.

Ladysmith, Caroline Co., St. Mary of the Annunciation, Rev. James F. Kauffmann.
Mailing Address: P.O. Box 396, 22501.
Office & Church—(intersection Rt. 609 & Rt. 629) 10306 Ladysmith Rd., 22501. Tel: 804-448-9064; 358-2427 (Rectory); Fax: 804-358-7025.

Lexington, Rockbridge Co., St. Patrick, Rev. N. Alan Lipscomb.
Mailing Address: P.O. Box 725, 24450-0725. Tel: 540-463-3533; Fax: 540-463-6384.
Res., 221 W. Nelson St., 24450. Tel: 540-463-6819.
Church—219 W. Nelson St., 24450.

Lynchburg, Campbell Co., Holy Cross, Rev. J. Kenneth Rush; Mrs. Judith Pasicznyk, Pastoral Assoc.
Office: 710 Clay St., 24504-2530. Tel: 804-846-5245; Fax: 804-846-7022. [CEM]
Res., 3766 Fort Ave., 24501.
Church—700 Clay St., 24504.
School—Regional School, 2125 Langhorne Rd., 24501. Tel: 804-845-8862. Mr. John P. Jones, Prin.
Lay Teachers 18; Students 254.
High School—Tel: 804-847-5436.
Students 77; Lay Teachers 13.
St. Thomas More, Rev. Kevin O'Brien.
3015 Roundelay Rd., 24502-2036. Tel: 804-237-5911; 237-8855 (Rectory); Fax: 804-846-7022.

Marion, Smyth Co., St. John the Evangelist Church, Rev. Robert L. Krenik.
124 Park Blvd., 24354. Tel: 540-783-7282.
Church—120 Park Blvd., 24354.

Martinsville, Henry Co., St. Joseph, Rev. Martin Lavin.
Mailing Address: 704 E. Church St., 24112-3107. Tel: 540-638-4779; 638-1192; Fax: 540-638-2218.
Res., 9 Booker Rd., 24112. Tel: 540-632-3710.

Mathews, Mathews Co., Church of Francis de Sales, Rev. B. Daniel Bond.
Mailing Address: P.O. Box 158, 23109-0158. Tel: 804-725-2776; 725-5463.
Church—Rte. 647 & Lover's Ln., 23109.

Mechanicsville, Hanover Co., Church of the Redeemer, Rev. John M. DeGiorgio.
Mailing Address: 8218 N. Mayfield Ln., 23111. Tel: 804-746-4911; Fax: 804-746-8465.
Res., 7438 Shire Pkwy., 23111. Tel: 804-730-1844; 730-0224.
Church—8275 Meadowbridge Rd., 23111. Tel: 804-746-0633.

Middlesex County, Church of the Visitation, Rev. B. Daniel Bond.
Mailing Address: P.O. Box 38, Topping, 23169-0038. Tel: 804-758-5160.
Res., Box 34, Cobbs Creek, 23035. Tel: 804-725-5463; Fax: 804-725-5463.
Church—Rte. 33, Harmony Grove, 23035.

Mineral, St. Jude, Rev. Rodney Rodis.
Mailing Address: P.O. Box 40, 23117-0040. Tel: 540-894-4266.
Res., 106 Loving St., Louisa, 23093. Tel: 540-967-2465.
Church—1937 Jefferson Hwy., 23117.

Moneta, Bedford Co., Resurrection, Sr. Elizabeth Bagen, G.N.S.H., Pastoral Coord.
Mailing Address: 15353 Moneta Rd., 24121-9804.
Church—Rte. 122, 24121. Tel: 540-297-5530; Fax: 540-297-6316.

New Bohemia, Prince George Co., Church of the Sacred Heart, Rev. James E. Gallagher.

Mailing Address: 4415 County Dr., Petersburg, 23805-7567. Tel: 804-732-6385; Fax: 804-732-6385. [CEM]

Newport News, Newport Co.,

1—CATHOLIC COMMUNITY OF THE KOREAN MARTYRS, Rev. Andrew Lee.
Mailing Address: 8 Evelyn Dr., 23602-3318. Tel: 804-875-1202.

2—OUR LADY OF MOUNT CARMEL, Revs. Michael McCarron; Peter Tran; Michael Renninger; Deacon Paul Larkin.
100 Harpersville Rd., 23601-2324. Tel: 757-595-0385; 0386; 0387; Fax: 757-599-9285.
School—Tel: 757-596-2754. Sr. Mary Camille Poole, O.P., Prin.
Sisters of St. Dominic 4; Lay Teachers 16; Students 392.

3—ST. JEROME, Revs. Joseph B. Majewski; J. Ven Ilano.
Mailing Address: 116 Denbigh Blvd., 23602. Tel: 757-877-5021; 874-3268; Fax: 757-898-1437.

4—ST. VINCENT DE PAUL, Rev. Michael D. McCarron, Admin.
Mailing Address: P.O. Box 258, 23607. Tel: 757-245-4234; Fax: 757-245-0039.
Church—230 33rd St., 23607.

Norfolk, Norfolk City Co.,

1—BLESSED SACRAMENT, Rev. Julian B. Goodman.
Mailing Address: 170 Painter St., 23505-4557. Tel: 757-423-8305; Fax: 757-451-3335. [JC]
Res., 110 W. Severn Rd., 23505. Tel: 757-423-2176.
Church—Newport Ave. & Painter St., 23505.

2—CHRIST THE KING, Rev. Joseph P. Lehman.
Mailing Address: 1803 Columbia Ave., 23509-1200.
Res., 1804 Ashland Ave., 23509. Tel: 757-622-1120; 622-9196; Fax: 757-627-8808.
School—3401 Tidewater Dr., 23509. Tel: 757-625-4951. Mrs. Patricia Suraci, Prin.
Lay Teachers 19; Students 301.

3—HOLY TRINITY, Rev. Lou Ruoff; Rev. Msgr. Santiago C. Frias.
Mailing Address: 155 W. Government Ave., 23503-2905. Tel: 757-480-3433; Fax: 757-480-8749. [JC]
Res., 175 W. Government Ave., 23503. Tel: 804-480-2430.
School—154 W. Government Ave., 23503. Tel: 757-583-1873. Ms. Deneane Nofplot, Prin.
Lay Teachers 17; Students 230.

4—SACRED HEART, Rev. John J. Dorgan.
Office: 520 Graydon Ave., 23507-1711. Tel: 757-625-6763; Fax: 757-627-1965.

5—BASILICA OF ST. MARY, Rev. Walter C. Barrett, Rector.
Office: 1000 Holt St., 23504-4241. Tel: 757-622-4487; Fax: 757625-7969. [JC]
Church—232 Chapel St., 23504.
School—St. Mary's Academy, 921 Holt St., 23504. Tel: 757-622-7246. Sr. Barbara Boyle, S.N.D., Prin.
Sisters 1; Lay Teachers 18; Students 211.
Convent—1000 Holt St., 23504. Tel: 757-627-5213.

6—OUR LADY OF LAVANG, Rev. Anthony Trang Kim Ngo.
1806 Ashland Ave., 23509.
Church—409 Compostella Rd., 23518. Tel: 757-622-5345.

7—ST. PIUS X, Rev. Williams J. Dale.
Res., 1615 Longdale Dr., 23518. Tel: 757-855-3297.
Church—7800 Halprin Dr., 23518-4408. Tel: 757-583-0291; Fax: 757-583-0293.
School—7813 Nalprin Dr., 23518. Tel: 757-588-6171; Fax: 757-587-6580. Sr. Anne Carroll, I.H.M., Prin.
Sisters Servants of the Immaculate Heart of Mary 2; Lay Teachers 26; Students 525.

Norge, James City Co., St. Olaf, Patron of Norway, Donna Young Whitley, Pastoral Coord.
Mailing Address: P.O. Box 370, 23127-0370. Tel: 757-564-3819; Fax: 757-565-1099.

Norton, Wise Co., St. Anthony, Rev. Joseph C. Facura.
Mailing Address: 1009 Virginia Ave., 24273. Tel: 540-679-2336; Fax: 540-679-4501.
Mission—Coeburn, St. Mary.
Station—Wise, Clinch Valley College of the University of Virginia.

Onley, Accomac Co., St. Peter's the Apostle, Rev. Daniel L. Kelly.
Res., P.O. Box 860, 23418-0860. Tel: 757-787-4592; Fax: 757-787-2899.

Palmyra, Fluvanna Co., Ss. Peter & Paul, Rev. Gerald A. Przywara; Deacon Albert J. Carini.
Mailing Address: Rte. 2, Box 142, 22963. Tel: 804-589-5200; 5201; Fax: 804-589-5201.

Pearisburg, Giles Co., Holy Family, Rev. Louis R. Benoit.
Res., 516 Mason Court Dr., 24134-1832. Tel: 540-921-3547; Fax: 540-726-3907.

Pennington Gap, Lee Co., Church of the Holy Spirit, Rev. Anthony Rodrigues.
Mailing Address: P.O.Box 923, Jonesville, 24263.
Res., 1821 Holton Ave., Big Stone Gap, 24219. Tel: 540-523-6546; Fax: 540-523-1602.
Church—1010 Morgan Ave., 24277.

Petersburg, Prince George Co., St. Joseph, Rev. Robert M. Spener.
Mailing Address: P.O. Box 2006, 23804-1306.
Office: 11 N. Market St., PA 23804. Tel: 804-733-3115; Fax: 804-862-9931.
Res., 19 Centre Hill Ct., 23804. Tel: 804-732-5127. [CEM]
School—Sr. Joan Drega, D.C., Prin., Tel: 804-732-3931. Daughters of Charity of St. Vincent de Paul 4; Lay Teachers 10; Students 192.

Pocahontas, Tazewell Co., St. Elizabeth (1896), Rev. Daniel O. Brady.
Mailing Address: P.O. Box 608, 24635-0608. Tel: 540-988-4626; Fax: 540-988-4626.

Portsmouth, Holy Angels, Rev. James E. Gordon.
Office: 34 Afton Pkwy., 23702-2739. Tel: 757-485-2142; 2143; Fax: 757-485-3699.
Church of the Resurrection, Rev. James V. Carr.
Res., 3420 Wilshire Rd., 23703. Tel: 757-484-7336.
Church—3501 Cedar Ln., 23703. Tel: 757-484-7335; 484-7408; Fax: 757-484-5857.
School—Portsmouth Catholic Elementary School, 2301 Oregon Ave., 23701. Tel: 757-488-6744. Ms. Thea Haubrich, Prin.
St. Paul, Revs. Joseph S. Slowik; Robert J. Walsh.
Res., 518 High St., 23704-3516. Tel: 757-397-7066; 7067; Fax: 757-393-4334. [CEM]
Church—522 High St., 23704.

Powhatan, St. John Neumann, Rev. J. Morton Biber; Deacon John H. Thomas Tel: 804-379-9811.
Church—2480 Batterson Rd., 23139-7513. Tel: 804-598-3121; Fax: 804-598-1467.
Mission—Cartersville, St. Catherine.

Quinque, Green Co., Shepherd of the Hills, Rev. Robert E. Dillon.
Mailing Address: P.O. Box 83, 22965-0083. Tel: 804-985-3929.
Res., 101 W. Marshall Ave., Elkton, 22827. Tel: 540-298-1341.
Church—Rte. 633.

Quinton, New Kent Co., St. Elizabeth Ann Seton, Sr. Agnes Seebach, O.S.U.
Mailing Address: P.O. Box 245, 23141-0245. Tel: 804-932-4125; Fax: 804-932-8126.
Church—2631 Pocahontas Trail, 23141.

Radford, St. Jude, Rev. James Grealish.
Mailing Address: 1740 Tyler Rd., Christiansburg, 24073-6154. Tel: 540-639-5341; Fax: 540-639-4738.

Richlands, Tazewell Co., St. Mary, Rev. Thomas R. Collins.
P.O.Box 696, 24641-0696. Tel: 540-963-8545; 935-2815 (Grundy).
Mission—Grundy, St. Joseph.

Roanoke, Our Lady of Nazareth, Revs. Kenneth G. Stofft; Timothy Huffman.
Mailing Address: 2505 Electric Rd., S.W., 24018-3599. Tel: 540-774-0066 (Office); 774-0857 (Residence); Fax: 540-774-2148.
St. Andrew, Roanoke Co., Rev. Steven R. Rule.
Res., 3025 Bancroft Dr., 24014. Tel: 540-345-7018.
Church—631 N. Jefferson St., 24016-1401. Tel: 540-344-9814; Fax: 540-344-7879. [JC]
St. Gerard, Roanoke Co., Rev. Wayne L. Ball.
809 Orange Ave., N.W., 24016-1117. Tel: 540-343-7744; Fax: 540-776-0903.
School—Roanoke Catholic Regional Elementary, 620 N. Jefferson St., P.O. Box 11926, 24022. Tel: 540-982-3756. Ms. Karen Mabry, Prin.

Rocky Mount, Franklin Co., Francis of Assisi, Sr. Fidelis Rubbo, O.S.F., Pastoral Coord.
Mailing Address: 616 Glennwood Dr., 24151-2111. Tel: 540-483-9591; 483-8981; Fax: 540-489-6504.

St. Paul, Wise Co., St. Therese, Rev. Paul Maier.
Mailing Address: P.O. Box 56, 24283-0056. Tel: 540-762-5932.
Res., 3107 Sixth Ave., Lebanon, 24283.

Salem, Our Lady of Perpetual Help, Rev. Gregory Kandt.
Mailing Address: 314 Turner Rd., 24153-2308. Tel: 540-387-0491; Fax: 540-389-8237.
Res., 1408 Kathryn Ln., 24153. Tel: 540-387-1020.

Scottsville, Albemarle Co., St. George, Rev. Ralph Hamlet.
Mailing Address: P.O. Box 375, Lovingston, 22949-0375. Tel: 804-263-8509; Fax: 804-263-8509.
Missions—Lovingston, St. Mary, Tel: 804-263-4008; Amherst, Amherst Co., Catholic Community of Amherst, Amherst, 24521. Tel: 804-496-9557.

Smithfield, Good Shepherd, Rev. Thomas B. Nee.
Mailing Address: P.O.Box 840, 23431-0840.
Res., 202 S. Broad St., Suffolk, 23434. Tel: 757-365-0579; 925-0731; Fax: 757-538-0103.
Church—300 Smithfield Blvd., 23430.

South Boston, Halifax Co., St. Paschal Baylon, Rev. Matthias Newell.
Mailing Address: 905 John Randolph Blvd., 24592-2943.
Res., 3302 N. Main St., 24592. Tel: 804-575-1607; 572-2285 (Office).

South Hill, Mecklenburg Co., Good Shepherd, Rev. James Fosnot.
Mailing Address: P.O. Box 621, 23970-0621. Tel: 804-374-8408; 447-3622; Fax: 804-447-4729.
Church—1664 N. Mecklenburg Ave., 23970.

Staunton, Augusta Co., St. Francis of Assisi, Rev. John Adam Abe.
Res., 126 N. New St., 24401. Tel: 540-886-9121.
Church—121 N. Augusta, 24401-3636. Tel: 540-886-2262; Fax: 540-885-5743.

Suffolk, St. Mary of the Presentation, Rev. Thomas B. Nee.
Office: 202 S. Broad St., 23434-5715. Tel: 757-539-5732; Fax: 757-538-0103.
Church—200 S. Broad St., 23434.

Tabb, York Co., Blessed Kateri Tekawitha, Rev. Thomas J. Quinlan.
Church & Office: 3800 Big Bethel Rd., 23693. Tel: 804-766-3800; Fax: 804-868-8079.

Tappahannock, Essex Co., St. Timothy, Rev. Richard D. Dollard.
Mailing Address: P.O. Box 129, 22560-0129.
Church—Rte. 17 & Airport Rd., 22560. Tel: 804-443-2760; Fax: 804-443-2022.

Tazewell, St. Theresa, Rev. Daniel O. Brady.
Mailing Address: P.O. Box 345, 24651-0345. Tel: 540-988-4626; Fax: 540-988-4626.
Church—304 Tazewell Ave., 24651.

Virginia Beach

1—CHURCH OF THE ASCENSION, Rev. James E. Parke. In res., Rev. Robert Gloisten.
Res., 4853 Princess Anne Rd., 23462-4446. Tel: 757-495-1886; 495-3833 (Rectory); Fax: 757-495-1516.
Catechesis/Religious Programs—Students 482.

2—CHURCH OF THE HOLY APOSTLES, Virginia Co. Anglican-Roman Catholic Congregation of Hampton Roads. Rev. Charles Faul.
Church—1598 Lynnhaven Pkwy., 23456-2008. Tel: 757-427-0963; Fax: 757-427-9434.

3—CRISTO REY HISPANIC APOSTOLATE, Virginia Co., Sr. Barbara Gerwe, D.C., Pastoral Coordinator.
405 S. Parliament Dr.,Ste. 101, 23462-6311. Tel: 757-490-7896; Fax: 757-518-9638.

4—HOLY FAMILY, Virginia Co., Rev. Richard T. Mooney.
Parish Center: 1279 N. Great Neck Rd., 23454-2117. Tel: 757-481-5702; 340-5161; Fax: 757-481-3989.

5—HOLY SPIRIT, Virginia Co., Revs. Thomas J. Caroluzza; Rolo Castillo; Deacon John T. Glynn.
Office: 1396 Lynnhaven Pkwy., 23456-2798. Tel: 757-468-3600; 3601; 3602; Fax: 757-468-3602.
Res., 3345 Clubhouse Rd., 23452. Tel: 804-340-3933.

6—ST. GREGORY THE GREAT, Virginia Co., Revs. Paschal Kneip, O.S.B.; Damian Abbaticchio, O.S.B.; John Peck; Luke Policicchio, O.S.B.; Anselm Ober, O.S.B.; Deacon Raymond Check.
Res., 5347 Virginia Beach Blvd., Box 8, 23462. Tel: 757-497-8330; 497-7235; Fax: 757-490-1492.
School—5343 Virginia Beach Blvd., 23462-1896. Tel: 757-497-1811. Sr. Rose Marie Adams, I.H.M., Prin.
Sisters 3; Lay Teachers 28; Students 694.

7—ST. JOHN THE APOSTLE CHURCH, Virginia Co., Rev. Dwight E. Shrader.
Church—800 Los Conaes Way, 23456-6421. Tel: 757-426-2180; Fax: 757-426-6857.

8—ST. LUKE, Virginia Co., Rev. Eugene J. Teslovic.
Res., 2304 Salem Rd., 23456-1215. Tel: 757-427-5776; Fax: 757-427-2260.

9—ST. MARK, Virginia Co., Rev. Daniel N. Klem.
Mailing Address: 1505 Kempsville Rd., 23464-7210.
Res., 4901 Whitewood Ln., 23464. Tel: 757-479-1010; 479-0414; 467-4932; Fax: 757-479-9453.

10—ST. MATTHEW, Virginia Co., Rev. Timothy A. Drake.
Office: 3314 Sandra Ln., 23464-1736. Tel: 757-420-6310; Fax: 757-420-6311.
Res., 806 Bridgeport Place, 23464. Tel: 757-523-1723.
School—3316 Sandra Ln., 23464. Tel: 757-420-2455. Ms. Barbara White, Prin.
Lay Teachers 28; Students 526.

11—ST. NICHOLAS, Virginia Co., Rev. James M. Noto.
Res., 3340 Old Kirkwood Dr., 23452-5807. Tel: 757-498-7834.
Office & Church—712 Little Neck Rd., 23452. Tel: 757-340-7231; Fax: 757-340-2727.

12—STAR OF THE SEA, Virginia Co., Revs. James E. Dorson; Robert L. Cummins.
Office: 1404 Pacific Ave., 23451-3439. Tel: 757-428-8547; 425-6583; Fax: 757-428-0788.
Res., 322 Arctic Ave., 23451. Tel: 757-425-9026.

School—311 Arctic Crescent, 23451. Tel: 757-428-8400. Sr. Mary Anne Bolger, I.H.M., Prin. Sisters 2; Lay Teachers 15; Students 265.

Waynesboro, Augusta Co., St. John the Evangelist, Rev. William S. O'Brien.
Mailing Address: 344 Maple Ave., 22980-4706.
Office: Tel: 540-949-6145; 6146; Fax: 540-932-8512.
Res., 320 Maple Ave., 22980. Tel: 540-943-4051.
Church—300 Maple Ave., 22980.
Station—Fishersville, Woodrow Wilson Rehabilitation Center.

West Point, King William Co., Our Lady of the Blessed Sacrament, Rev. James M. Arsenault.
Mailing Address: 3510 King William Ave., 23181-0589.
Church—3570 King William Ave., 23181. Tel: 804-843-3125; Fax: 804-843-3125. [CEM]

Williamsburg, York Co., St. Bede's, Revs. William H. Carr; Antonio R. Malabad; John J. Wagner, III; Patrick Golden. In res., Rev. Thomas Magri, Campus Min., Tel: 757-220-9375.
Mailing Address: 10 Harrison Ave., 23185-3530. Tel: 757-229-3642; 3631; Fax: 757-229-5361.
Res., 610 College Ter., 23185. Tel: 804-288-4233.
Church—500 Richmond Rd., 23185.

Woodlawn, Carroll Co., St. Joseph's, Rev. Charles W. Brickner.
Mailing Address: 99 Joy Ranch Rd., 24381. Tel: 540-236-7814.
Missions—Patrick Springs, Church of the Risen Lord; Floyd, Floyd Co., Church of All Saints.

Wytheville, St. Mary's, Rev. Brian Rafferty.
Mailing Address: P.O. Box 7, 24382. Tel: 540-228-3322. [CEM]
Church—370 E. Main St., 24382.
Mission—Pulaski, St. Edward, Tel: 540-980-6511.

Yorktown, York Co., St. Joan of Arc, Rev. Don Michael Hanna.
Office: 315 Harris Grove Ln., 23692-4014. Tel: 804-898-5570; Fax: 804-898-0737.

Chaplains of Public Institutions

RICHMOND. *McGuire VA Medical Center*. Vacant.
MCV Hospital. Revs. George Zahn; Blaise Perrello.

HAMPTON. *VA Medical Center,* Chaplain Service, Bldg. 69, 23667. Tel: 804-722-9961, Ext. 3600. Revs. Lloyd F. Stephenson; Donald J. Cavey.

NORFOLK. *Depaul Medical Center*. The following are attended by Sacred Heart Church: Children's Hospital of the King's Daughters; Norfolk General Hospital. 150 Kingsley Ln., 23505. Tel: 804-889-5000. Rev. Jerome Turner.

PETERSBURG. *Federal Correctional Institution*. Rev. J. P. Blankenship.

SALEM. *Salem VA Medical Center.* Tel: 540-982-2463. Rev. Wayne Ball, Chap.

Special Assignment:
Reverend Fathers—
Lane, Mark

On Duty Outside the Diocese:
Reverend Fathers—
Bostwick, John, Franklin, LA
Funk, Virgil C., Washington, DC
McNally, Stephen, Bonn, Germany
Murphy, Dennis, Providence, RI
Natale, Samuel, New York
Slattery, Joseph A., Pretoria, South Africa
Smith, Russell E., Emmitsburg, Maryland
Thuy, Pham Quang
Williams, McKinley

Graduate Studies:
Reverend Fathers—
Keeney, Timothy, North American College, Rome

Military Chaplains:
Reverend Fathers—
D'Aurora, Joseph
Dang, Chin Van
Hickman, J. Stephen
Huan, Joseph Van Tran
Kanicki, Philip A.
Moran, Edward C.

Sabbatical:
Reverend Fathers—
Fisher, Charles M.

Retired:
Reverend Monsignors—
Michael, Chester P., Route 2, Box 225, Afton, VA 22920
Reverend Fathers—
Beardsley, Frederick, 5910 Kensington Ave., Richmond, VA 23226
Bowers, Vernon J., Mailing Address: U.S. Post Office, Ware Neck, VA 23178
Cassidy, Patrick, 628 Toll Gate Ln., Petersburg, VA 23865
Chmura, Stanislaus, 717 Cooper Ave., Inverness, FL 34450
Connelly, William P., 4605 Truman Ln., Virginia Beach VA 23445
Dinga, William, 1324 Debree Ave., Norfolk, VA 23517
Dinges, Anthony, 102 Oliver Ave., Crewe, VA 23920
Ditty, James, 1316 Mill Lake Quarter, Chesapeake, VA 23320
Farley, Laurence F., 127 W. Birch St., Hazelton, PA 18201
Gallagher, Paul V., 34 Oakland Dr., Pulaski, VA 24301
Gaughan, Paul, St. John's Rectory, 800 Los Conaes Way, Virginia Beach, VA 23456
Gormley, George J., Our Lady of the Valley, Roanoke, VA 24016
Henry, Thomas, Our Lady of Peace, Charlottesville, VA 22901
Jenkins, Paul, St. James Rectory, 102 N. 5th Ave., Hopewell, VA 23860
Kloepfer, John S., P.O. Box 1472, Clarksville, VA 23927
McIntyre, Raymond T., 62 Manhattan Dr., Ashley, PA 18706
Naro, Carl J., Rte. 1, Box 151, Wingina, VA 24599
Naylor, Ronald J., 1060 Birnam Woods Dr., Virginia Beach, VA 23466
Pereira, Albert F., 4713 Clintwood Dr., Portsmouth, VA 23703
Rodriguez, D. Andres G., San Martin de Tabara, Zamora, Spain
Ruth, Robert F.
Stickle, William, 144 Bay Cliff Trail, Kill Devil Hills, NC 27948
Stockert, Donfred H., 183 Hitchcock Ave., Highland Springs, VA 23075
Van Den Boogaard, Henry, Sun City, FL
Walsh, Robert J., 518 High St., Portsmouth, VA 23704
Warner, Anthony, Our Lady of Lourdes Rectory, 8200 Woodman Rd., Richmond, VA 23228
Warren, Robert, P.O. Box 6194, Charlottesville, VA 22906
Welch, Thomas David, 305 Victoria Dr., Hurt, VA 24563

Permanent Deacons:
Birx, Charles R., St. Jude, Radford
Carini, Albert J., St. Joseph, Columbia
Cartwright, Gordon, Lynchburg, VA
Check, Raymond P., St. Gregory the Great, Virginia Beach
Cortezano, Alfredo, NAS, Norfolk
Dwyer, Bruce K., St. Joseph, Woodlawn
Ellerbrock, Michael, St. Mary, Blacksburg
Fournier, Keith, Virginia Beach, VA
Glynn, John, Holy Spirit, Virginia Beach
Hall, Harry, St. Anne, Bristol
Hanzlik, Edward, Sacred Heart, New Bohemia
Hayes, William, Our Lady of Peace, Appomattox
Horbowy, Thaddeus, FCI, Petersburg
Kwon, Peter H., Dr., St. Jerome, Newport News Korean Community
Larkin, Paul V., Langley AFB
McCormick, Daniel F., St. Mark, Virginia Beach
Menting, Peter J., Good Samaritan, Amelia
Pinto, Richard, Langley AFB
Ports, Francis J., Holy Name of Mary, Bedford
Roderique, Raymond, Forest, VA
Thomas, John H., Diocesan Tribunal
Weir, Robert, Virginia Beach, VA

INSTITUTIONS LOCATED IN THE DIOCESE

[A] HIGH SCHOOLS, DIOCESAN

LYNCHBURG. *Holy Cross Regional School,* 2125 Langhorne Rd., 24501. Tel: 804-847-5436. John P. Jones, Prin. Lay Teachers 34; Students 368.

NEWPORT NEWS. *Peninsula Catholic High School,* 600 Harpersville Rd., 23601. Tel: 757-596-7247; Fax: 757-591-9718. Mr. William R. Hammond, Prin. Lay Teachers 28; Students 315.

PETERSBURG. *St. Vincent de Paul High School,* 240 Wagner Rd., 23803-9232. Tel: 804-733-4305; Fax: 804-862-3634. Daughters of Charity of Saint Vincent de Paul. Dr. Patricia A. Crisci, Prin. Sisters 1; Lay Teachers 17; Students 172.

ROANOKE. *Roanoke Catholic School,* 621 N. Jefferson St., 24016. Tel: 540-982-3532. Ms. Karen Mabry, Prin. Lay Teachers 40; Students 490.

VIRGINIA BEACH. *Catholic High School,* 4552 Princess Anne Rd., 23462. Tel: 804-467-2881; Fax: 804-467-0284. Rev. William L. Pitt, Prin. Priests 3; Lay Teachers 34; Students 452.

[B] HIGH SCHOOLS, PRIVATE

RICHMOND. *Benedictine High School,* 304 N. Sheppard St., 23221. Tel: 804-342-1300. A Military High School in the Charge of the Benedictine Monks. Rt. Rev. Benedict R. McDermott, O.S.B., Pres.; Mr. David A. Bouton, Headmaster; Rev. Adrian W. Harmening, O.S.B.; Bro. Clement M. Carney. Brothers 1; Lay Teachers 23; Students 247.
Saint Gertrude High School, 3215 Stuart Ave., 23221. Tel: 804-358-9114; Fax: 804-355-5682. Sr. Charlotte Lange, O.S.B., Prin. Benedictine Sisters 1; Lay Teachers 27; Students 255.

POWHATAN. *Blessed Sacrament High School at Belmead,* P.O. Box 519, 23139. Tel: 804-598-4729. Dr. Lou Ross Hopewell, Prin. Religious 2; Lay Teachers 10; Students 90.

WILLIAMSBURG. *Walsingham Academy Upper School,* P.O. Box 8702, 23187-8702. Tel: 804-229-6026. (Grades 8-12). Private Day School for Boys and Girls. Sr. Virginia Marie Kauffmann, R.S.M., Prin. Sisters of Mercy 5; Lay Teachers 25; Students 251.

[C] ELEMENTARY SCHOOLS, DIOCESAN

CHARLOTTESVILLE. *Charlottesville Catholic Elementary School.* (Grades K-2), 301-B Jefferson St., 22902. Tel: 804-359-5661. Sr. Susan Mudd, O.S.U., Ed.D., Prin. Lay Teachers 3; Students 31.

[D] ELEMENTARY SCHOOLS, PRIVATE

WILLIAMSBURG. *Walsingham Academy Lower School,* P.O. Box 8702, 23187-8702. (Grades PreK-7). Day School for Boys and Girls. Sr. Mary Jeanne Oesterle, R.S.M., Prin. Sisters 2; Lay Teachers 34; Students 412.

[E] GENERAL HOSPITALS

RICHMOND. *St. Mary's Hospital,* 5801 Bremo Rd., 23226. Tel: 804-285-2011.
For a complete listing, refer to the Hospitals section.

NEWPORT NEWS. *Mary Immaculate Hospital,* 2 Bernardine Dr., 23602-4499. Tel: 757-886-6600.
For a complete listing, refer to the Hospitals section.

NORFOLK. *Bon Secours - De Paul Medical Center, Inc.,* 150 Kingsley Ln., 23505. Tel: 804-889-5000.
For a complete listing, refer to the Hospitals section.

NORTON. *St. Mary's Hospital, Inc.,* P.O. Box 620, 24273. Tel: 540-679-9100.
For a complete listing, refer to the Hospitals section.

PORTSMOUTH. *Maryview Medical Center,* 3636 High St., 23707. Tel: 804-398-2200.
For a complete listing, refer to the Hospitals section.

[F] ORPHANAGES AND INFANT HOMES

RICHMOND. *St. Joseph's Villa,* 8000 Brook Rd., 23227-1338. Tel 804-553-3200; Fax: 804-553-3259.
For a complete listing, refer to the Special Care Facilities section.

NORFOLK. *St. Mary's Infant Home,* 317 Chapel St., 23504. Tel: 804-622-2208.
For a complete listing, refer to the Special Care Facilities section.

ROANOKE. *The Achievement Center-St. Vincent's Home, Inc.*. Mailing Address: P.O. Box 12368, 24025. Tel: 540-982-0128.
For a complete listing, refer to the Special Care Facilities section.
De Paul Family Services, Inc., 4502 Starkey Rd., S.W., 24014. Tel: 540-989-7355.
For a complete listing, refer to the Special Care Facilities section.

[G] CHILD LEARNING CENTERS

RICHMOND. *Holy Angels,* 1307 Lakeside Ave., 23228. Tel: 804-266-7200. Sr. Juliana Paladini, Dir. Comboni Missionary Sisters 4; Lay Teachers 2; Children 35.
Holy Rosary Child Care Center, 1218 N. 34th St., Box 8046, 23223. Tel: 804-222-2590. Mrs. Deborah Longs, Dir. Children 120.

NORFOLK. *Christ the King Extended Care,* 3401 Tidewater Dr., 23509. Tel: 804-627-0119. Mrs. Uli Williford, Admin. Children 80.

[H] HOMES FOR THE AGED

RICHMOND. *Marywood Apartments,* 1261 Marywood Ln., 23229. Tel: 804-740-5567.
For a complete listing, refer to the Special Care Facilities section.
Our Lady of Hope Health Center, Inc., 13700 N. Gayton Rd., 23233.
For a complete listing, refer to the Special Care Facilities section.
St. Francis Home, Inc., 2511 Wise St., 23225-3952. Tel: 804-231-1043; Fax: 804-231-1065.
For a complete listing, refer to the Special Care

Facilities section.

St. Joseph's Home for the Aged, 1503 Michael Rd., 23229. Tel: 804-288-6245.
For a complete listing, refer to the Special Care Facilities section.

St. Mary Wood's, 1257 Marywood Ln., 23229. Tel: 804-741-8624.
For a complete listing, refer to the Special Care Facilities section.

CHARLOTTESVILLE. *Our Lady of Peace*, 751 Hillsdale Dr., 22901. Tel: 804-973-1155.
For a complete listing, refer to the Special Care Facilities section.

HAMPTON. *Seton Manor*, 215 Marcella Rd., 23666. Tel: 804-827-6512.
For a complete listing, refer to the Special Care Facilities section.

LYNCHBURG. *McGurk House Apartments*, 2425 Tate Springs Rd., 24501.
For a complete listing, refer to the Special Care Facilities section.

Nott Homes, Inc., 3009-3011 Roundelay Rd., 24502.
For a complete listing, refer to the Special Care Facilities section.

NEWPORT NEWS. *St. Francis Nursing Center*, 4 Ridgewood Pkwy., 23602.
For a complete listing, refer to the Special Care Facilities section.

NORFOLK. *Madonna Home*, 814 W. 37th St., 23508. Tel: 757-623-6662.
For a complete listing, refer to the Special Care Facilities section.

ROANOKE. *Our Lady of the Valley Retirement Community*, 650 N. Jefferson St., 24016. Tel: 540-345-5111.
For a complete listing, refer to the Special Care Facilities section.

SUFFOLK. *Bon Secours-Maryview Nursing Care*, 4775 Bridge Rd., 23435. Tel: 757-686-0488.
For a complete listing, refer to the Special Care Facilities section.

VIRGINIA BEACH. *Marian Manor*, 5345 Marian Ln., 23462. Tel: 804-456-5018.
For a complete listing, refer to the Special Care Facilities section.

Russell House, 900 First Colonial Rd., 23454. Tel: 804-481-0770.
For a complete listing, refer to the Special Care Facilities section.

[I] HOME FOR HANDICAPPED ADULTS

RICHMOND. *St. Joseph's Villa Housing Corp*, 8000 Brook Rd., 23227-1399. Tel: 804-553-3283; Fax: 804-553-3259.
For a complete listing, refer to the Special Care Facilities section.

[J] SERVICES FOR THE DISABLED

RICHMOND. *Hollybrook I & II*. St. Joseph Villa, 7700 Brook Rd., 23229. Tel: 804-553-3283. Ms. Margaret Hill, Housing Mgr. Residents 80.

Outreach in Love. c/o Epiphany Church, 11000 Smoketree Dr., 23236. Tel: 804-794-0222. Lynda D. Heithaus, Coord. Religious education for people with disabilities.

Seans Place, 713 N. First St., 23219. Tel: 804-344-8164. Mr. Pete Jones, Prog. Coord.

[K] SPECIALIZED SERVICES

RICHMOND. *Commonwealth Catholic Charities*, 1512 Willow Lawn Dr., 23230-0565. Tel: 804-285-5900. Rev. David J. Bergner, S.D.S., Exec. Dir. Satellite Offices: 820 Campbell Ave., S.W., Roanoke, 24016. Tel: 540-344-5107. Woodbrook Shopping Center, 1859-C3 Seminole Trail, Charlottesville, 22901. Tel: 804-974-6880. Connections, One Skyline Pl., Suite 1106, 5205 Leesburg Pike, Falls Church, 22041-3802. Tel: 703-820-1151. Family & Child Center, 3321 S. Crater Rd., Suite C, Petersburg, 23805. Tel: 804-862-3733. Elizabeth Ann Seton Center, 1512 Willow Lawn Dr., 23230-0565. Tel: 804-285-5987. Managed Home Care for the Elderly, 1512 Willow Lawn Dr., 23230-0565. Tel: 804-285-5900. Connections, 302 McClanahan St., S.W., Roanoke, 24014. Tel: 540-342-0411. Total Assisted 6,919.

Elizabeth Ann Seton Center, 1512 Willow Lawn Dr., 23230. Tel: 804-285-5900. Legal Title: *Catholic Charities of Richmond, Inc.* Mrs. Nikki Jones, Dir. Total Assisted 378.

CHARLOTTESVILLE. *Elizabeth Ann Seton Center*. Office, P.O. Box 6565, Richmond, 23230. Tel: 804-974-6880. Ms. Jane Hotchkiss, Dir.

VIRGINIA BEACH. *Catholic Charities of Hampton Roads, Inc.*, 4855 Princess Anne Rd., 23462. Tel: 757-467-7707; Fax: 757-495-3206. Margaret M. Robertson, Exec. Dir.
Branch Offices: 12829 Jefferson Ave., Suite 101, Newport News, 23608. Tel: 757-875-0060. 1301 Colonial Ave., Norfolk, 23517. Tel: 757-625-2568. 3804 Poplar Hill Rd., Suite A, Chesapeake, 23321. Tel: 757-484-0703. 1300 Jamestown Rd., Williamsburg, 23185. Tel: 757-253-2847. Total Assisted 3,500.

[L] ETHNIC AND SPECIAL MINISTRIES

RICHMOND. *Ethnic and Special Ministries*. (See Central Administration Offices), Office for the Hispanic Apostolate.
Hispanic.

Office for Hispanic Catholics of Tidewater - Cristo Rey Hispanic Apostolate, 405 S. Parliament Dr., Suite 101, Virginia Beach, 23462-6311. Tel: 757-490-7896. Sr. Barbara Gerwe, D.C., Pastoral Coord.

Blessed Sacrament Church, 154 N. Main St., Harrisonburg, 22801. Tel: 540-434-4341; 434-8601 (Spanish).

St. Peter the Apostle, P.O. Box 860, Onley, 23418. Tel: 804-787-4592 (Spanish).

Centro Catolico Guadalupe, Richmond, 9608 N. Verlinda Ct., 23237. Tel: 804-796-4944. Rev. Ricardo Seidel, Dir.
Hispanic.

Catholic Community of the Korean Martyrs. Parish Center, 8 Evelyn Dr., Newport News, 23602. Tel: 804-875-1202. Rev. Andrew Lee.

Filipino Apostolate, 5405 Homeward Dr., Virginia Beach, 23464. Rev. Leo O. Manalo.

St. Kim Taegon Church, 3100 Logandale Ave., 23224. Tel: 804-232-0993. Rev. Dominic Hwa In Hwang.
Vietnamese.

Our Lady of Lavang Vietnamese Community of Tidewater, Pastoral Center: 1806 Ashland Ave., Norfolk, 23509. Tel: 804-622-5345. Rev. Anthony Trang Kim Ngo.

Church of the Vietnamese Martyrs, 67 W. Clopton St., 23225. Tel: 804-231-4835. Rev. Joseph Than Xuan Pham.

Our Lady of Viet Nam Chapel. Rev. Anthony Trang Kim Ngo, Mailing Address: 1806 Ashland Ave., Norfolk, 23509. Tel: 804-622-5345. Chapel, 1307 LaSalle Ave., Hampton.
DEAF:

Our Lady of Lourdes, 8200 Woodman Rd., 23228. Tel: 804-262-7315.

Basilica of St. Mary, 1000 Holt St., Norfolk, 23504-4241. Tel: 804-622-4487.

St. Joseph, 414 Buckroe Ave., Hampton, 23664. Tel: 804-851-8800.

St. Francis of Assisi, 121 N. Augusta, Staunton, 24401-3636. Tel: 540-886-2262.

Church of the Incarnation, 635 Hillsdale Dr., Charlottesville, 22901-1716. Tel: 804-973-4381.

Our Lady of Mt. Carmel, 100 Harpersville Rd., Newport News, 23601-2325. Tel: 804-595-0385.
TRIDENTINE MASS.

St. Joseph Tridentine Chapel, Ministry of the St. Benedict Church. Tel: 804-358-0088. Rev. Adrian W. Harmening, O.S.B.

St. Benedict Chapel, Ministry of St. Gregory the Great Church, Chesapeake. Tel: 804-497-8330. Rev. Damian Abbaticchio, O.S.B.
Missionaries of the Holy Family.

General Missions Office - M.S.F., Inc., 260 W. Euclid Blvd., Box 918, West Point, 23181. Rev. John Brieffies, M.S.F., Pres.

[M] MONASTERIES AND RESIDENCES OF PRIESTS AND BROTHERS

RICHMOND. *Mary Mother of the Church Abbey*, 12617 River Rd., 23233. Tel: 804-784-3508. Benedictine Monks. Rt. Rev. Benedict R. McDermott, O.S.B.; Revs. Theophile W. Brown, O.S.B., Prior, Novice Master; Thomas C. Byrne, O.S.B.; Thomas W. Stumpf, O.S.B.; Adrian W. Harmening, O.S.B., Procurator; Donald F. Scales, O.S.B.; Augustine W. Ludwig, O.S.B.; Augustine W. Cunningham, O.S.B.; Bros. Clement Carney, O.S.B.; Matthew Miller, O.S.B.; James Casey, O.S.B.; Joseph Hammock, O.S.B.; David Owen, O.S.B., Procurator, Sub-Prior; Nicholas Fry, O.S.B. Priests 8; Brothers 6.

WEST POINT. *Missionaries of the Holy Family, General Mission Office—M.S.F., Inc.*, P.O. Box 918, 23181. Tel: 804-843-2622. Revs. John Brieffies, M.S.F., Pres. & Dir.; Henry van den Boogaard, M.S.F., (Retired).

[N] CONVENTS AND RESIDENCES FOR SISTERS

RICHMOND. *Benedictine Sisters of Virginia*. St. Gertrude Convent, 3215 Stuart Ave., 23221. Tel: 804-355-7227. Sisters 3.

Comboni Missionary Sisters, Provincial House, 1307 Lakeside Ave., 23228. Tel: 804-266-2975; 262-8827. Sr. Ruth Bryden, C.M.S., Provincial. Sisters 21.

Daughters of Charity. St. Patrick School Community, 207 N. 26th St., 23223. Tel: 804-649-7437. Sr. Clara Pedo, Supr.

CROZET. *Cistercian Nuns of the Strict Observance (Virginia)*, 3365 Monastery Dr., 22932. Tel: 804-823-1452; Fax: 804-823-6379. Mother Marion Rissetto, Supr. Legal Title: *Cistercian Nuns of the Strict Observance in Virginia, Inc. Our Lady of the Angels Monastery*. Professed 9.

NEWPORT NEWS. *Bernardine Sisters of the Third Order of St. Francis*, 8E Ridgewood Pkwy., 23602. Tel: 757-886-6398; 886-6765; Fax: 757-886-6751. Sr. Barbara Ann, Local Min. Sisters 13.

Bethlehem Monastery of the Poor Clare Nuns, 28 Harpersville Rd., 23601. Tel: 804-596-5942. Observing the Primitive Rule of St. Clare, Constitutions of the Poor Clare Federation of Mary Immaculate (strictly cloistered, solemn vows). Mother Mary Colette, Abbess. Solemnly Professed 12; Novices 1; Postulants 1. Attended by Our Lady of Mt. Carmel Church, Newport News.

NORFOLK. *Sisters Servants of the Immaculate Heart of Mary*. St. Pius X Convent, 7813 Halprin Dr., 23518. Tel: 804-587-8657. Sr. Anne Carroll, I.H.M., Supr. Sisters 4.

NORTON. *Poor Servants of the Mother of God*, P.O. Box 620, 24273. Tel: 540-679-0477; Fax: 540-679-7549. Sr. Mary Coughlan, S.M.G., Sister in charge. Sisters 6.

PETERSBURG. *Daughters of Charity*. St. Joseph Convent, 123 Franklin St., 23803. Tel: 804-732-8501. Sisters 4.

PORTSMOUTH. *Sisters of Bon Secours*, 412 West Rd., 23707. Tel: 804-397-3869. Sr. Rita Thomas, Pres. Sisters 3.

ROCKVILLE. *Monastery of the Visitation Monte Maria*, 12221 Bienvenue Rd., 23146. Tel: 804-749-4885. Mother Margaret Mary McGuire, Supr. Visitation Sisters 17; Novices 3.

VIRGINIA BEACH. *Sisters Servants of I.H.M.* St. Gregory the Great Convent, 5349 Virginia Beach Blvd., 23462. Tel: 804-497-7517. Sr. Miriam Cotton, Supr.; Sr. Brenda Anne Query, Supr.

WILLIAMSBURG. *Sisters of Mercy*. Walsingham Academy, P.O. Box 8702, 1100 Jamestown Rd., 23187-8702. Tel: 757-229-2642. Sr. Rose Morris, R.S.M. Sisters 8.

[O] RETREAT HOUSES

RICHMOND. *The Dwelling Place*, 601 Holly Grove Ln., 23235. Tel: 804-323-3360.
Conducted by: Patricia Carreras; Audrey Stech.

Richmond Hill. Ecumenical Center, 2209 E. Grace St., 23235. Tel: 804-783-7903. Rev. Benjamin Campbell, Pastoral Dir.

CHUCKATUCK. *The Well*, 18047 Quiet Way, 23430. Tel: 757-255-2366. Co-Directors: Sr. Nancy Healy, S.F.C.C.; Diane Weymouth.

GATE CITY. *Nazareth House of Prayer*, Rt. 2, Box 277, 24251-8828. Tel: 540-386-7428. Sr. Corrine Myers, R.S.M.; Sr. Catherine Laboure Busam, O.S.F.

HAMPTON. *Holy Family Retreat House*, 1414 N. Mallory St., P.O. 3151, 23663. Tel: 804-722-3997. Rev. Peter E. Sousa, C.SS.R., Supr. & Dir. Asst. Retreat Directors: Revs. Gerard H. Schrieber, C.SS.R.; Bernard J. Power, C.SS.R.; Joseph A. Gribbon, C.SS.R.

LYNCHBURG. *Tabor Retreat Center*, 2125 Langhorne Rd., 24501. Tel: 804-846-6475. Chris Barrett, Dir.

MONTPELIER. *Shalom House*. Retreat Center, P.O. Box 196, 23192. Tel: 804-883-6149. Ms. Catherine Cawley, Dir.

ROANOKE. *Madonna House*, 828 Campbell Ave., S.W., 24016. Tel: 540-343-8464. Ms. Linda Owen, Dir.

[P] MISCELLANEOUS

RICHMOND. *Sacred Heart Center, Inc.*, 1400 Perry St., 23224. Tel: 804-230-4399. Ms. Jeanine Harper, Exec. Dir. Neighbouring Communities Day Care, After School Care, Adult Education and Social Services.

St. Francis Home of Richmond Foundation, Ltd., 2511 Wise St., 23224.

Transitional Housing. Flagler Home-St. Joseph's Villa, 8000 Brook Rd., 23227-1399. Rebecca Lee, Dir. Women & Children in residence 70.

NEWPORT NEWS. *Family Focus*. (Community Churches sites for day and evening programs.), c/o Bernardine Sisters, 8E Ridgewood Pkwy., 23602.

NORFOLK. *Catholic Worker Hospitality House*, 1321 W. 38th St., 23508. Tel: 804-423-5420. Coordinators: Steve Baggerly; Kim Williams.

PORTSMOUTH. *Catholic Elementary Education Foundation of Hampton Roads*, 2301 Oregon Ave., 23701. Sr. Carol Durkin, Chm.

Maryview Psychiatric Hospital, 3636 High St., 23707. Allan D. Erbe, Admin. Beds 54.

ROANOKE. *Catholic Historical Society of the Roanoke Valley*, 624 N. Jefferson St., 24016. Tel: 504-982-0152. Mary C. Mauer, Contact.

St. Francis House, Inc., P.O. Box 2215, 24009. Tel: 540-345-9090. Eileen Stone, Dir. Food Distribution and Social Services.

RELIGIOUS INSTITUTES OF MEN REPRESENTED IN THE DIOCESE

For further details refer to the corresponding bracketed number in the Religious Institutes of Men or Women section.

[0200]—*Benedictine Monks.* (Latrobe, PA).—O.S.B.
[1350]—*Brothers of St. Francis Xavier.*—C.F.X.
[0630]—*Congregation of the Missionaries of the Holy Family.*—M.S.F.
[0570]—*The Glenmary Home Missioners.*—Glmy.
[0650]—*Holy Ghost Fathers.*—C.S.Sp.
[0690]—*Jesuits Fathers and Brothers.*—S.J.
[0430]—*Order of Preachers (Dominicans).* (Province of St. Joseph).—O.P.
[1070]—*Redemptorist Fathers.* (Baltimore Prov.).—C.SS.R.

RELIGIOUS INSTITUTES OF WOMEN REPRESENTED IN THE DIOCESE

[0230]—*Benedictine Sisters of Pontifical Jurisdiction.*—O.S.B.
[1810]—*Bernardine Sisters of the Third Order of St. Francis.*—O.S.F.
[0670]—*Cistercian Nuns of the Strict Observance.*—O.C.S.O.
[0690]—*Comboni Missionary Sisters.*—C.M.S.
[0270]—*Congregation of Bon Secours.*—C.B.S.
[1070-09]—*Congregation of St. Catherine of Siena, Racine.*—O.P.
[1070-07]—*Congregation of St. Cecelia, Nashville.*—O.P.
[1070-02]—*Congregation of St. Mary of the Springs, Columbus.*—O.P.
[1070-13]—*Congregation of the Most Holy Rosary, Adrian.*—O.P.
[1070-06]—*Congregation of the Most Holy Rosary, Newburg.*—O.P.
[3830-05]—*Congregation of the Sisters of St. Joseph of Brentwood, NY.*—C.S.J.
[1920]—*Congregation of the Sisters of the Holy Cross.*—C.S.C.
[0760]—*Daughters of Charity of St. Vincent de Paul.*—D.C.
[0820]—*Daughters of the Holy Spirit.*—D.H.S.
[0960]—*Daughters of Wisdom.*—D.W.
[1180]—*The Franciscan Sisters.*—O.S.F.
[1840]—*Grey Nuns of the Sacred Heart.*—G.N.S.H.
[2575]—*Institute of the Sisters of Mercy of the Americas.*—R.S.M.
[2340]—*Little Sisters of the Poor.*—L.S.P.
[2490]—*Medical Mission Sisters.*—S.C.M.M.
[2480]—*Medical Missionaries of Mary.*—M.M.M.
[2720]—*Mission Helpers of the Sacred Heart.*—M.H.S.H.
[2790]—*Missionary Servants of the Most Blessed Trinity.*—M.S.B.T.
[3760]—*Order of St. Clare.*—P.C.C.
[3640]—*Poor Servants of the Mother of God.*—S.M.G.
[3465]—*Religious of the Sacred Heart of Mary.* (Eastern American Prov.).—R.S.H.M.
[2970]—*School Sisters of Notre Dame.*—S.S.N.D.
[1070-03]—*Sinsinawa Dominican Congregation of the Most Holy Rosary.*—O.P.
[]—*Sisters for Christian Community.*—S.F.C.C.
[0500]—*Sisters of Charity of Nazareth.*—S.C.N.
[0590]—*Sisters of Charity of St. Elizabeth, Convent Station.*—S.C.
[0990]—*Sisters of Divine Providence.* (Our Lady of Divine Providence Prov.).—C.D.P.
[2990]—*Sisters of Notre Dame.*—S.N.D.
[3000]—*Sisters of Notre Dame de Namur.*—S.N.D.deN.
[3950]—*Sisters of Saint Mary of Namur.*—S.S.M.N.
[1530]—*Sisters of St. Francis of the Congregation of Our Lady of Lourdes, Sylvania, Ohio.*—O.S.F.
[3840]—*Sisters of St. Joseph of Carondelet.*—C.S.J.
[2980]—*Sisters of the Congregation of Notre Dame.*—C.N.D.
[1990]—*Sisters of the Holy Names of Jesus and Mary.*—S.N.J.M.
[3260]—*Sisters of the Precious Blood.*—C.P.P.S.
[2170]—*Sisters, Servants of the Immaculate Heart of Mary.* (Immaculata, PA).—I.H.M.
[4110]—*Ursuline Nuns (Roman Union).* (Eastern Prov.).—O.S.U.
[4130]—*Ursuline Sisters of the Congregation of Tildonk, Belgium.*—O.S.U.
[4190]—*Visitation Nuns.*—V.H.M.

DIOCESAN CEMETERIES

RICHMOND. *Holy Cross,* First Ave. & Daniels St., 23222. Tel: 804-321-5936.
Mount Calvary, 1400 S. Randolph St., 23220. Tel: 804-355-5271.

LYNCHBURG. *Holy Cross,* Bedford Ave. Mailing Address: 710 Clay St., 24504. Tel: 804-846-5245.

NORFOLK. *St. Mary's,* 722 E. 30th St., 23504. Tel: 804-627-2874.

PORTSMOUTH. *Portsmouth Catholic,* Elm Ave. & Portsmouth Blvd. Mailing Address: P.O. Box 155, 23705. Tel: 804-488-1723.

ROANOKE. *St. Andrew,* 3601 Salem Tpke., N.W., 24017. Tel: 703-342-9180.

NECROLOGY

(No Deaths)

Diocese of Rochester

(Dioecesis Roffensis)

Most Reverend

MATTHEW H. CLARK, D.D.

Bishop of Rochester; ordained December 19, 1962; appointed Bishop of Rochester April 23, 1979; consecrated May 27, 1979; installed June 26, 1979. *Res., 1150 Buffalo Rd., Rochester, NY, 14624.*

Most Reverend

DENNIS W. HICKEY, D.D., V.G.

Retired Auxiliary Bishop of Rochester; ordained June 7, 1941; appointed Titular Bishop of Rusuccuru and Auxiliary January 5, 1968; consecrated March 14, 1968; retired December 11, 1989. *Res., 415 Ames St., Rochester, NY, 14611.*

Most Reverend

JOSEPH L. HOGAN, S.T.D., D.D.

Retired Bishop of Rochester; ordained June 6, 1942; appointed Bishop of Rochester October 6, 1969; consecrated November 28, 1969; installed November 28, 1969; retired November 28, 1978. *Res., 123 Maple Ave., Victor, NY, 14564.*

Established March 3, 1868.

Square Miles 7,107.

Comprises the Counties of Monroe, Livingston, Wayne, Ontario, Seneca, Cayuga, Yates, Steuben, Chemung, Tioga, Schuyler and Tompkins in the State of New York.

For legal titles of parishes and diocesan institutions, consult the Pastoral Center.

Legal Title of Diocese: The Diocese of Rochester.

Pastoral Center: 1150 Buffalo Rd., Rochester, NY, 14624-1890. Tel.: 716-328-3210; 800-388-7177; Fax: 716-328-3149.

E-mail address: dor@mail-frontiernet.net

STATISTICAL OVERVIEW

Personnel	
Bishop	1
Retired Bishops	2
Abbots	1
Priests: Diocesan Active in Diocese	171
Priests: Active Outside Diocese	7
Priests: Diocesan in Foreign Missions	1
Priests: Retired, Sick or Absent	98
Number of Diocesan Priests	277
Religious Priests in Diocese	65
Extern Priests in Diocese	10
Ordinations:	
Diocesan Priests	2
Transitional Deacons	2
Permanent Deacons	6
Permanent Deacons in Diocese	106
Total Brothers	35
Total Sisters	675
Parishes	
Parishes	161
With Resident Pastor:	
Resident Diocesan Priests	143
Resident Religious Priests	5
Without Resident Pastor:	
Administered by Priests	9
Administered by Permanent Deacons	1
Administered by Women Religious	2
Administered by Lay People	1
Missions	20
Professional Ministry Personnel:	
Sisters	110
Lay Ministers	307
Welfare	
Catholic Hospitals	3
Total Assisted	450,000
Health Care Centers	4
Total Assisted	1,500
Homes for the Aged	3
Total Assisted	8,000
Residential Care of Children	1
Total Assisted	400
Specialized Homes	7
Total Assisted	500
Special Centers for Social Services	3
Total Assisted	120,000
Residential Care of Disabled	1
Total Assisted	200
Educational	
Seminaries, Diocesan	3
Students from This Diocese	3
Diocesan Students in Other Seminaries	9
Total Seminarians	12
Total Students	12
High Schools, Private	7
Total Students	3,508
Elementary Schools, Diocesan and Parish	51
Total Students	15,574
Elementary Schools, Private	5
Total Students	780
Non-residential Schools for the Disabled	1
Total Students	97
Catechesis/Religious Education:	
High School Students	3,600
Elementary Students	32,153
Total Students Under Catholic Instruction	55,736
Teachers in the Diocese:	
Priests	12
Brothers	9
Sisters	69
Lay Teachers	971
Vital Statistics	
Receptions into the Church:	
Infant Baptism Totals	6,291
Adult Baptism Totals	329
Received into Full Communion	518
First Communions	5,420
Confirmations	4,958
Marriages:	
Catholic	1,501
Interfaith	783
Total Marriages	2,284
Deaths	4,236
Total Catholic Population	363,672
Total Population	1,484,426

Former Bishops—Rt. Rev. Bernard J. McQuaid, D.D., cons. July 12, 1868; died Jan. 18, 1909.—Most Rev. Thomas F. Hickey, D.D., ord. March 25, 1884; cons. May 24, 1905; succeeded to the See, Jan. 18, 1909; appt. assistant at the Pontifical Throne, May 4, 1925 made Archbishop of the Titular See of Viminacium, Oct. 30, 1928; died Dec. 10, 1940.—Most Rev. John Francis O'Hern, D.D., ord. Feb. 17, 1901; appt. Bishop of Rochester, Jan. 8, 1929; cons. March 19, 1929; died May 22, 1933.—His Eminence Edward Cardinal Mooney, appt. Aug. 28, 1922; transferred to Detroit, May 26, 1937; installed Archbishop of Detroit, Aug. 3, 1937; created Cardinal, Feb. 18, 1946; died Oct. 25, 1958.—Most Rev. James E. Kearney, D.D., ord. Sept. 19, 1908; appt. Bishop of Salt Lake, Utah, July 1, 1932; cons. Oct. 28, 1932; transferred to Rochester, July 31, 1937; installed Nov. 11, 1937; retired Oct. 26, 1966; died Jan. 12, 1977.—Most Rev. Fulton J. Sheen, D.D., ord. Sept. 30, 1919; appt. Titular Bishop of Cesariana and Auxiliary of New York, May 28, 1951; cons. June 11, 1951; appt. to Rochester, Oct. 26, 1966; installed Dec. 15, 1966; resigned Oct. 15, 1969; appt. Titular Archbishop of Newport; died Dec. 9, 1979.

Pastoral Office Administration

Pastoral Center—1150 Buffalo Rd., Rochester, 14624-1890. Tel: 716-328-3210; 800-388-7177 (Toll Free within Diocese); Fax: 716-328-3149.

Vicar General and Pastoral Office Moderator—Rev. John M. Mulligan.

Chancellor—Rev. Kevin E. McKenna, J.C.D.

Judicial Vicar—Rev. Louis A. Sirianni, I.C.L.

Secretaries to the Bishop—Rev. Timothy T. Brown; Mrs. JoAnn Anderson.

Diocesan Consultors—Most Rev. Dennis W. Hickey, D.D., V.G.; Revs. John M. Mulligan, V.G.; Dennis Shaw; Jack Philipps; Robert Ring; Gerry Appelby; Kevin E. McKenna, J.C.D.; Daniel Holland.

Synod Office—Ms. Kathleen M. Cannon, Dir.

Consultative Bodies—

Bishop's Stewardship Council—Most Rev. Matthew H. Clark; David Peartree; Patrick Fox; Rev. John M. Mulligan, V.G.; Mr. Daniel E. Gill, Chm.; Mr. Joseph P. Bell; Jose Coronas, Finance Chm.; Mr. R. Carlos Carballada; Rev. Peter A. Deckman; Mr. Thomas R. Frey; Bert Garza; Ms. Susan Holliday; Mr. Louis Langie, Jr.; Mr. Thomas McDermott; Barbara Kelley, Devel. Chm.; Sr. Rosemary St. Peter, S.S.J.; Sr. Ann Miller, R.S.M.; Mrs. Jane Napier; Katherine Keough; Mr. Mario Rodriquez; Mr. Larry Kirwin; Ms. Kathleen Whelehan; Mr. James Ryan; Sr. Patricia Schoelles, S.S.J.; Ms. Edna Soltero; Matthew Augustine; Ms. Judy Toyer; Mr. Robert Turissini; Rev. Robert Werth; Germaine Knapp; Sally True.

Priests' Council—Rev. JACK PHILIPPS, Chm.
Regional Coordinator—Rev. TIMOTHY BROWN, Liaison.
Commission of Women—MARY KESSLER, Liaison.
Clergy Relief Society—Most Rev. MATTHEW H. CLARK, D.D., Pres.; Revs. ROBERT KRECKEL, Vice Pres. THOMAS H. WHEELAND, Treas. JOHN FIRPO, Sec. RICHARD R. BRICKLER; JOHN H. HAYES; CHARLIE MANNING; WILLIAM B. LEONE; GENE SWEENEY; RAY BOOTH.
"Catholic Courier"—Tel: 716-328-4340. KAREN FRANZ, Gen. Mgr. & Editor Board of Directors: Most Rev. MATTHEW H. CLARK, Pres.; Rev. JOHN MULLIGAN, Vicar General & V.P.; Rev. KEVIN E. MCKENNA, J.C.D., Sec.; Mr. WILLIAM KEDLEY, Treas.; Most Rev. DENNIS W. HICKEY; Revs. JOHN FORNI; WILLIAM SPILLY; Mr. RICHARD CHAPMAN; Mr. MARTIN MOLL; Mrs. DELORES LOFTUS; Mrs. BARBARA KILEY; Mr. THOMAS FLYNN; Sr. ROBERTA TIERNEY, S.S.N.D.; Mr. RICHARD HARE.
Diocesan Missions Office (Propagation Of The Faith)—Rev. ROBERT C. BRADLER. Tel: 716-436-9200. World and Diocesan Missions.

Internal Support Ministries

Office of Development—
Director of Development—Mr. MARK S. SEEBERG.
Director of Major Gifts—Mrs. MARY L. CONSLER.
Director of Annual Giving—Mr. THOMAS C. D'AGOSTINO.
Administrative Assistant—Mrs. NANCY A. NASH.
Donor Relations Coordinator—Mrs. MICHELE GAMET.
Office of Communications—
Director of Communications—Ms. ELIZABETH BROWN.
Communications Assistant—Ms. PAMELA KINGSLEY.
Department of Financial Services—
Chief Financial Officer—Mr. JAMES M. RINEFIERD.
Controller—Mr. PAUL VISCA.
Manager of Buildings and Properties—Mr. ERIC PATCHKE.
Diocesan Building Commission—ERIC PATCHKE, Sec. DAVID ANDREWS; JOSEPH KIZINSKI; WILLARD STEANE; Sr. ESTELLE MARTIN, R.S.M.; WILLIAM MATTHEWS; Rev. WILLIAM J. AMANN; SANDY MCGREEVY; Rev. JOHN V. ROSSE.
Holy Sepulchre Cemetery—Most Rev. MATTHEW H. CLARK, D.D., Pres.; Rev. PETER T. BAYER, Vice Pres. & Treas. & Sec.; Mr. E. ROBERT VOGT, Dir. & Asst. Treas.; Mr. MARTIN BIRMINGHAM; Mr. ALFRED M. HALLENBECK; Mr. WILLIAM MCGINN; Sr. MARIE MICHELLE PEARTREE, S.S.J.; Mr. JAMES M. RINEFIERD; Mr. LARRY O. STID; Mrs. MICHAEL TOMAINO; Rev. THOMAS WHEELAND.
Information Systems And Research—
Diocean Director—Ms. JOAN A. ZAIA.
AS/400 Coordinator—Mrs. LYNNE SUORSA.
Parish Computer Coordinator—Mr. TOM VEEDER; MAUREEN EASTERLY.
Department of Legal Services—
Director—Rev. KEVIN E. MCKENNA, J.C.D., Chancellor.
Secretary—Mrs. BEVERLY KELLY.
Due Process—
Board of Arbitration—Rev. KEVIN E. MCKENNA, J.C.D., Contact.
Council of Conciliation—Mr. RICHARD PELINO, *18 Nettlecreek Rd., Fairport, 14450.* Tel: 716-223-2857.
Diocesan Archives—Rev. WILLIAM GRAF, Dir. Archival Services, *219 Stenson St., Rochester, 14606.* Tel: 716-458-6079. Rev. ROBERT F. MCNAMARA, Archivist, *4536 St. Paul Blvd., Rochester, 14617.* Tel: 716-338-1602. Sr. CONNIE DERBY, R.S.M., Exec. Asst., *1150 Buffalo Rd., Rochester, 14624.* Tel: 716-328-3210.

External Ministries

Faith Development Ministry—Sr. MARY ANN BINSACK, R.S.M., Dir.
Catholic Schools Office—Mr. TIMOTHY W. DWYER, Supt., Schools.
Assistant Superintendent of Business and Finance—Mr. DAVID MEISENZAHL.
Assistant Superintendents—Sr. PATRICIA CARROLL, S.S.J., Asst. Supt., Government Svcs & Admin.; Sr. VIRGINIA STEINWACHS, S.S.J., Asst. Supt., Human Resources; Sr. MARGARET MANCUSO, S.S.J., Asst. Supt., Curriculum & Instruction; Ms. MARY CAFFREY, Asst. Supt., Assessment & Staff Devel.; Sr. ANNE GUERIN, S.S.J., Asst. Supt., School Advancement; Sr. ELAINE ENGERT, S.S.J., Asst. Supt., WIN Programs.
Department of Evangelization and Catechesis—Ms. MARIBETH MANCINI, Dir.
Coordinator for Sacramental Catechesis—Mrs. BARBARA CARROLL.
Catechetical Consultant—Mrs. MARY BRITTON.
AV Resource Librarian—Mrs. MARY ELLEN FITZGIBBONS.
Coordinator of Youth Ministry—MICHAEL THEISEN.
Coordinator of Young Adult, Adult & Family Faith Formation—KAREN RINEFIERD.
Parish Support Ministries—
Director—Ms. KATHLEEN M. CANNON. Tel: 716-328-3228, Ext. 387 TDD (English). Tel: 716-328-3210 (Spanish).
Office Of Black Ministries—Ms. JACQUELYN DOBSON Dir.
Office of Spanish Apostolate—Bro. LUIS RUBERTE, H.Ch., Dir., Field Office: *873 N. Clinton Ave., Rochester, 14605.* Tel: 716-232-4844.
Hispanic Pastoral Institute—Bro. LUIS RUBERTE, Dir.
Urban Subsidy Program—Ms. JACQUELYN DOBSON.
Office of Asian Pacific Ministry—Ms. HA NGUYEN.
Office of Pastoral Council Formation—Deacon CLAUDE LESTER.
Tribunal—Revs. LOUIS A. SIRIANNI, M.Div., J.C.L., Judicial Vicar; KEVIN E. MCKENNA, J.C.D., Promoter of Justice; Mr. JOHN SKVORAK, J.C.L., Judge Sr. DOROTHY SCHLUETER, R.S.M., Certified Clinical Psychologist; Ms. LINDA SARACENI, Sec.
Case Instructors—Ms. PATRICIA A. KEOUGH; Deacon GEORGE W. BURNETT.
Pro-Synodal Judges—Revs. R. RICHARD BRICKLER; ROBERT COLLINS; DONALD J. CURTISS, J.C.L.; RONALD GAESSER; WILLIAM GRAF, D.Min.; JOHN S. HAYES; JOHN LYNCH; ROBERT F. O'NEILL, M.Ch.A., M.Div.
Defenders of the Bond—Revs. WILLIAM J. GORDINIER, M. GERARD HAFNER; WILLIAM LUM.
Office Of Ecumenical And Interreligious Affairs—Deacon BRIAN MCNULTY.
Commission for Ecumenical and Interreligious Affairs—Deacon BRIAN MCNULTY.
Commission on Christian/Jewish Relations—Rev. JOSEPH P. BRENNAN; Deacon BRIAN MCNULTY.
Director Office of Liturgy—Ms. JOAN WORKMASTER; Ms. VIRGINIA MILLER, Assoc. Dir.
Liturgical Commission—Sr. CHRIS J. TREICHEL, O.S.F., Chm. CHARLES DISPENZA, Vice Chm.; Ms. JOAN WORKMASTER, Exec. Sec.; Sr. ESTELLE MARTIN, R.S.M., Environment & Art Rep.; Rev. DANIEL MCMULLIN, Music Rep.
Catholic Charities of the Diocese of Rochester—JACK BALINSKY, Exec. Dir. PATRICK FOX, Chm., Board of Directors, *1150 Buffalo Rd., Rochester, 14624.* Tel: 716-328-3210.
Campaign for Human Development—JACK BALINSKY.
Catholic Relief Services—JUDY TAYLOR.
Communications Manager—JUDY TAYLOR.
Consistent Life Ethic Coordinator—SUZANNE SCHNITTMAN.
Catholic Charities Regional Offices—
Catholic Charities Community and Residential Services—PAUL T. PICKERING, Exec. Dir., *1945 E. Ridge Rd., Ste. 24, Rochester, 14622.* Tel: 716-339-9800.
Administrative Services—BARBARA POLING, Dir.
Community Services—LUCY DECHAINE, Dir.
Finances—JAMES CROWLEY, Dir.
Residential Services—KATHLEEN TERMINE, Dir.
AIDS Community Follow-up Program—JANE HALLINEN, Dir.
Community Awareness Program—LYN ZYLA.
Catholic Family Center—Ms. CAROLYN A. PORTANOVA Pres. & CEO; Ms. JUDITH AZOFF, VP, Admin. Svcs. RITA AUGUSTINE, VP, Prog. Svcs. BEVERLY LUDKE, VP, Human Resources; BARBARA MURPHY, VP, Finance; MICHAEL COONEY, Chm., Regl. Board of Directors. All offices at: *25 Franklin St., Rochester, 14604.* Tel: 716-546-7220 unless otherwise indicated.
Departments of Catholic Family Center—
Catholic Youth Organization (CYO)—DWAYNE MAHONEY, Dir. Tel: 716-262-7008.
Children and Family Services—KAREN EMERTON, Dir. Tel: 716-262-7100.
Elder Services—IRENE COVENY, Dir. Tel: 716-262-7058.
Employee Assistance & Counseling—WENDY STRAUSS, Dir. Tel: 716-262-7034.
Homeless & Housing Services—MAUREEN SCHNORR, Dir. Tel: 716-463-5452. NORMAN ROBERTS. Tel: 716-423-9590.
Office of Social Policy & Research—BRIAN A. KANE, Dir. Tel: 716-262-7021.
Refugee and Immigration Services—EDWARD A. PATANE, Dir. Tel: 716-262-7082.
Restart Substance Abuse Services—CARL A. HATCH, Dir. Tel: 716-546-3046.
Wayne County—M. JOSH MCCROSSEN, Dir. Tel: 315-331-4867.
Finger Lakes Social Ministries—Serving Yates, Ontario, Wayne, Seneca and Cayuga Counties. GIOVINA CAROSCIO, Exec. Dir. SCARLETT EMERSON, Parish and Community Devel. Coord. ALMA KUNES, Prog. Coord. LUANN IRWIN, Chm., Regl. Board of Directors, Main office: *One Franklin Sq., Geneva, 14456.* Tel: 315-789-2686., Satellite offices at: *29 William St., Auburn, 13021.* Tel: 315-252-0018., *4440 E. Ridge Rd., Williamson, 14589.* Tel: 315-589-2600.
Catholic Charities of the Southern Tier—Serving Chemung, Schuyler, Steuben, Tompkins and Tioga Counties. ANTHONY BARBARO, Exec. Dir.; Sr. PATRICIA PRINZING, Chm., Board of Directors, All offices at: *1700 College Ave., Elmira, 14901.* Tel: 607-734-9784.
Departments of Catholic Charities of the Southern Tier—
Emergency Services—NORMAN WHITE, Dir. Tel: 607-734-4898.
Food Bank of the Southern Tier—JOHN P. FARRER, Dir. Tel: 607-796-6061.
Gateways Community Living Program—TONY PHILLIPS, Dir. Tel: 607-733-8387.
Justice and Peace—KATHLEEN DUBEL, Dir. Tel: 607-734-5893.
Tioga Teens & Family Outreach—JOE FEDEROWICZ, Dir. Tel: 607-687-8607.
Transitions Counseling—AMY DENENBERG, Dir. Tel: 607-936-4695.
Catholic Charities of Livinston County—TIM MCMAHON, M.S.W., Exec. Dir. WILLIAM DERBY, Ph.D, Pres., Regl. Board of Directors, *10 Clinton St., Mt. Morris, 14510.* Tel: 716-658-4466.
Departments of Catholic Charities of Livingston County—
Livingston County Rural Outreach—Sr. NANCY O'BRIEN, Dir.
Community of Caring—GAIL WRATNY-FEATHERS, Dir.
Bishop Sheen Ecumenical Housing Foundation—ALLYNN SMITH, Exec. Dir. SHARON CONHEADY, Pres., Board of Directors, *835 East Ave., Rochester, 14607.* Tel: 716-461-4263.
Camp Stella Maris—RAYMOND TETTE, Exec. Dir. JAY TRAVERS, Pres., Board of Directors, *3052 E. Lake Rd., Livonia, 14487.* Tel: 716-346-2243; 346-2251.
DePaul Mental Health Services, Inc.—MARK H. FULLER, Exec. Dir. ELLEN KREMER, Pres., Board of Directors, *1931 Buffalo Rd., Rochester, 14624.* Tel: 716-426-8000.
Kinship Family and Youth Services, Inc.—JOSEPH WEIDER, Exec. Dir. SARAH HEINEMAN, Pres., Board of Directors, *204 Main St., Hornell, 14843.* Tel: 607-324-0909.
Mercy Center with the Aging—Sr. ANNE MALOY, R.S.M., M.S.W., Dir.; Sr. GRATIA L'ESPERANCE, R.S.M., M.Div., Asst. Dir., *327 Warrington Dr., Rochester, 14618-1536.* Tel: 716-244-5190.
Providence Housing Development Corporation—MAGGIE BRINGEWATT, Exec. Dir. JACK BALINSKY, Pres., Board of Directors, *1150 Buffalo Rd., Rochester, 14624.* Tel: 716-328-3210.
St. Ann's Home and The Heritage—Sr. MARIE MICHELLE PEARTREE, Pres. ANTHONY J. MALONE, P.E., Pres., Board of Directors, *1500 Portland Ave., Rochester, 14621.* Tel: 716-342-1700.
St. Joseph's Villa—M. JUDITH MCKAY, Exec. Dir. JOHN HORVATH, Pres., Board of Directors, *3300 Dewey Ave., Rochester, 14616.* Tel: 716-865-1550.
Human Resources—Mrs. PATRICE BEADLE, Dir.
Department of Personnel Services—Mrs. BARBARA PEDEVILLE.
Department of Priest Personnel—Rev. ROBERT P. RING, Dir.
Coordinator of Clergy Services—Mrs. SANDRA GROCKI.
Priests' Personnel Board—Revs. ROBERT P. RING, Chm. R. RICHARD BRICKLER; MICHAEL F. CONBOY; DAVID J. FARAONE; R. WILLIAM E. GRAF; THOMAS P. MULL; JOHN V. ROSSE.
Intern Process—Rev. EDWARD L. PALUMBOS, Dir., *3003 Dewey Ave., Rochester, 14616.* Tel: 716-663-3230.
Ministry To Priests—Rev. R. RICHARD BRICKLER, *330 Gregory St., Rochester, 14620.* Tel: 473-4271.
Priests' Retirement Committee—Revs. ROBERT P. RING, Chm. THOMAS F. BRENNAN; JOSEPH M. EGAN; Mrs. SANDRA GROCKI; L. JOHN HEDGES; ELMER W. HEINDL; JAMES F. SLATTERY; DANIEL P. TORMEY; FRANCIS H. VOGT; JOHN T. WALSH.
Priests' Sabbatical Committee—Mrs. JUDITH ANN KOLLAR, Chm.; Revs. R. RICHARD BRICKLER; PETER A. DECKMAN; KEVIN E. MCKENNA, J.C.D.; ROBERT P. RING; GEORGE WIANT.
Office Of Vocations—Rev. JOHN A. DESOCIO, Dir., Becket Hall: *314 Gregory St., Rochester, 14620.* Tel: 716-461-2890.
Office Of Seminarians—Rev. JOHN A. DESOCIO, Dir., Becket Hall: *314 Gregory St., Rochester, 14620.* Tel: 716-461-2890.
Vicar for Religious—Vacant.
Deacon Personnel—Vacant.

CLERGY, PARISHES, MISSIONS AND PAROCHIAL SCHOOLS

METROPOLITAN ROCHESTER
(Monroe County)

1—SACRED HEART CATHEDRAL (1910), Most Rev. Matthew H. Clark, D.D.; Revs. Thomas P. Mull; Paul J. Tomasso; Francis Fusare.
Res., 296 Flower City Pk., 14615. Tel: 716-254-3221; Fax: 716-254-8970.
School—Tel: 716-458-8088; Fax: 716-458-7155. Sr. M. Stephanine Riley, S.S.J., Prin.
Lay Teachers 21; Students 421; Preschool 83.
Catechesis/Religious Programs—Students 200.
Convent—287 Flower City Pk., 14615. Tel: 716-254-5048.

2—ST. AMBROSE (1921), Rev. Michael J. Schramel; Nancy Giordano, Pastoral Assoc.
Res., 25 Empire Blvd., 14609. Tel: 716-288-5000; Fax: 716-654-7658.
School—Tel: 716-288-0580. Rebecca Maloney, Prin.
Lay Teachers 25; Students 424.
Catechesis/Religious Programs—Tel: 716-288-1620. Mary Kay Oberst, D.R.E.
Students 334.
Convent—61 Waldo Ave., 14609. Tel: 716-288-9149.

3—ST. ANDREW (1914), Rev. Timothy E. Horan; Deacon William Schmitz; Sr. Anne Marie Lennon, R.S.M., Pastoral Assoc. In res., Rev. Robert Donovan.
Res., 923 Portland Ave., 14621. Tel: 716-342-8686.
School—Tel: 716-467-9201; Fax: 716-467-4191. Sr. Mary Alice O'Brien, R.S.M., Prin.
Lay Teachers 10; Students 254.
Catechesis/Religious Programs—Tel: 718-342-6665. Sr. Lucille Nalbone, M.P.F., D.R.E.
Students 56.

4—ST. ANNE (1930), Rev. Frank E. Lioi. In res., Revs. Joseph M. Sasso; Thomas J. Hoctor; Gary L. Tyman.
Res., 1600 Mt. Hope Ave., 14620-4598. Tel: 716-271-3260; Fax: 716-271-7160.

5—CHURCH OF THE ANNUNCIATION (1917) (Italian), Rev. Robert F. O'Neill; Deacon Victor Yanaitis.
Res., 1754 Norton St., 14609. Tel: 716-544-1050.
Catechesis/Religious Programs—Students 50.

6—ST. ANTHONY OF PADUA (1906) (Italian-Vietnamese), Revs. Paul J. Tomasso; Daniel McMullin; Louis Nhien.
Res., 60 Lorimer St., 14608. Tel: 716-458-1180.

7—ST. AUGUSTINE (1898). Merged with Our Lady of Good Counsel and St. Monica to form Roman Catholic Community of the 19th Ward.
Res., 410 Chili Ave., 14611. Tel: 716-328-2442.

8—BLESSED SACRAMENT (1902), Rev. Bruce F. Ammering. In res., Rev. George Norton.
Res., 259 Rutgers St., 14607. Tel: 716-271-7240.
Catechesis/Religious Programs—Deacon David Paluskiewicz, D.R.E.
Students 61.

9—ST. BONIFACE (1860) (German), Revs. R. Richard Brickler; Desmond O'Neill (Australia).
Res., 330 Gregory St., 14620. Tel: 716-473-4271.
School—(Grades PreK-6). Tel: 716-271-6370. Sr. Mary Smith, S.S.N.D., Prin.
School Sisters of Notre Dame 2; Lay Teachers 12; Students 175.

10—ST. BRIDGET (1854), Rev. Anthony P. Mugavero.
Res., 1089 Joseph Ave., 14621. Tel: 716-467-2725.
Church—175 St. Bridget's Dr., 14605. Tel: 716-454-4236; Fax: 716-454-0835.
Catechesis/Religious Programs—Students 56.

11—ST. CECILIA (1949), Revs. Walter F. Cushing; Dennis Bonsignore; Sr. Marie Therese S.S.N.D., Pastoral Assoc.
Res., 2732 Culver Rd., 14622. Tel: 716-467-4286; Fax: 716-338-2349. [CEM]
Catechesis/Religious Programs—Tel: 716-338-1051.
Students 182.

12—ST. CHARLES BORROMEO (1925), Revs. Edward L. Palumbos; Douglas Della Pietra; Francis E. Blighton. In res., Rev. Elmer W. Heindl.
Res., 3003 Dewey Ave., 14616. Tel: 716-663-3230; Fax: 716-663-8055.
School—64 Maiden Ln., 14616. Tel: 716-663-1220.
Students 305.
Catechesis/Religious Programs—Tel: 716-663-8000. Margaret A. Gray, D.R.E.
Students 400.

13—CHRIST THE KING (1955), Revs. Robert B. Hale, C.S.B.; Richard C. Kinsky, C.S.B.; Joseph A. Trovato, C.S.B.
Res., 445 Kings Hwy., 14617. Tel: 716-266-1288; Fax: 716-266-1074.
School—Tel: 716-467-8730. Colleen D'Hondt, Prin.
Sisters of St. Joseph 1; Lay Teachers 19; Students 260; Preschool 55.
Catechesis/Religious Programs—Tel: 716-338-1146. Mrs. Mary Ann Obark, D.R.E.
Lay Teachers 25; Students 405.

14—CORPUS CHRISTI (1888), Revs. James B. Callan, Admin.; Enrique Cadena (Mexico); Mary Ramerman, Pastoral Assoc.
Res., 80 Prince St., 14605. Tel: 716-325-2424; Fax: 716-262-3576.
Church—864 Main St. E., 14605.
Catechesis/Religious Programs—Tel: 716-232-3032; Fax: 716-262-3576. Mimi Youngman, D.R.E.
Students 329.

15—ST. FRANCIS ASSISI (1929) (Spanish-Italian), Revs. Paul J. Tomasso; Daniel McMullin; Deacon Carlos Vargas.
Res., 77 Whitney St., 14611. Tel: 716-436-6693.
Catechesis/Religious Programs—Students 80.

16—ST. FRANCIS XAVIER. (Canonically merged in 1985 and now known as Holy Redeemer-St. Francis Xavier). All inquiries should be directed to the listed address: 34 Teresa St., 14605-1696.

17—ST. GEORGE (1907) (Lithuanian), Rev. Charles L. Mockevicius.
Res., 545 Hudson Ave., 14605. Tel: 716-232-4111.

18—GUARDIAN ANGELS (1960), Mr. Dean Condon, Admin.; Deacon Anthony Mercadel.
Res., 2061 E. Henrietta Rd., 14623. Tel: 716-334-1412.
Diocesan Child Care and Preschool—.
Lay Teachers 3; Students 91.
Catechesis/Religious Programs—Tel: 716-334-6412. Mrs. Gail Brooks, D.R.E.
Students 200.

19—ST. HELEN (1940), Rev. John A. Firpo; Deacons Christopher Fisher; Richard Schuler, Pastoral Assoc.
Res., 310 Hinchey Rd., 14624. Tel: 716-235-1210; Fax: 716-235-2417.
School—Quadrant School, 150 Lettington Dr., 14624. Tel: 716-235-2391. Carol Robinson, Prin.
Lay Teachers 19; Students 306.
Catechesis/Religious Programs—Tel: 716-235-2407. Patricia Flass, S.S.J., D.R.E.
Students 153.

20—HOLY APOSTLES (1884), Revs. Paul J. Tomasso; Daniel McMullin.
Res., 7 Austin St., 14606. Tel: 716-254-7170.

21—HOLY CROSS (1863), Revs. Thomas H. Wheeland; Frederick F. Eisemann; Peter Enyan-Boadu; Sr. Kathleen Mary O'Connell, Pastoral Assoc.; Sr. Rita Biel, Parish Visitor.
Res., 4492 Lake Ave., 14612. Tel: 716-663-2244; Fax: 716-663-2244.
School—4488 Lake Ave., 14612. Tel: 716-663-6533; Fax: 716-663-7948. Sr. Marilyn Reeves, Prin.
Sisters of Mercy 2; Lay Teachers 26; Students 516.
Catechesis/Religious Programs—Tel: 716-621-8133. Karen Henrichs, D.R.E.
Students 330.
Convent—4490 Lake Ave., 14612. Tel: 716-663-5351.

22—HOLY FAMILY (1864) (German). Deacon Patrick M. Shanley, Admin. In res., Most Rev. Dennis W. Hickey, D.D.; Rev. Louis A. Sirianni.
Res., 415 Ames St., 14611. Tel: 716-328-3110.
School—899 Jay St., 14611. Tel: 716-328-4800. Sr. Lorraine Burns, S.S.N.D., Prin.
Lay Teachers 15; Students 225.

23—HOLY GHOST (1875), Rev. Alexander H. Bradshaw; Sr. Janice Nadeau, S.S.N.D., Pastoral Assoc.
Res., 220 Coldwater Rd., 14624. Tel: 716-247-3535; Fax: 716-247-4223. [CEM]
Catechesis/Religious Programs—Tel: 716-426-1289. Catherine Fechtor, D.R.E.
Students 45.

24—HOLY NAME OF JESUS (1964), Rev. John V. Rosse; Deacon Richard Lombard. In res., Peter T. Bayer.
Res., 15 St. Martin's Way, 14616. Tel: 716-621-4040; Fax: 716-621-6343.
Catechesis/Religious Programs—Tel: 716-621-6343.
Students 270.

25—HOLY REDEEMER-ST. FRANCIS XAVIER (1867-1888). Merged in 1985. Revs. Dennis Shaw; Laurence Tracy; Deacons Agenol Rodriguez; John Erb.
Res., 34 Teresa St., 14605. Tel: 716-482-3211; Fax: 716-325-5771.
Church—300 Bay St., 14605.

26—HOLY ROSARY (1889), Rev. Lawrence V. Murphy; Deacon James Fitch.
Res., 414 Lexington Ave., 14613. Tel: 716-458-4422.
School—420 Lexington Ave., 14613. Tel: 716-254-8180. Miss Mary Beth Fuehrer, Prin.
Lay Teachers 8; Students 120.
Catechesis/Religious Programs—Students 75.

27—IMMACULATE CONCEPTION (1849), Rev. Michael G. Upson.
Office: 445 Frederick Douglass St., 14608. Tel: 716-325-3893; Fax: 716-325-2082.

28—ST. JAMES (1949), Rev. John A. Lynch.
Res., 109 Brockley Rd., 14609. Tel: 716-482-9796.
School—Northeastern Quadrant Catholic School.

29—ST. JOHN EVANGELIST (1914), Rev. William V. Spilly. Pastoral Associates: Sr. Chris Treichel, O.S.F.; Patricia Curtis. In res., Rev. Edward A. Zimmer.
150 Floverton St., 14610. Tel: 716-482-6211.
Res., 549 Humboldt St., 14610. Tel: 716-482-6210; Fax: 716-482-8213.
School—Tel: 716-654-9437; Fax: 716-654-8787.
Lay Teachers 14; Students 183; Pre-School 58.
Catechesis/Religious Programs—Students 65.

30—ST. JOHN EVANGELIST (1865) (Greece), Revs. Joseph F. D'Aurizio; Stanley Kacprzak.
Res., 2400 Ridge Rd., W., 14626. Tel: 716-225-8980; Fax: 716-723-9825.
School—2376 Ridge Rd., W., 14626. Tel: 716-225-3450. Mr. Robert Edelman, Prin.
Lay Teachers 22; Students 335.
Catechesis/Religious Programs—Tel: 716-225-4200.
Students 750.

31—ST. JOSEPH (1836). Closed. For inquiries for parish records contact Our Lady of Victory.

32—ST. JUDE THE APOSTLE (1968), Rev. John J. Steger.
Res., 4100 Lyell Rd., 14606. Tel: 716-247-5262; Fax: 716-429-5111.
Catechesis/Religious Programs—Tel: 716-247-5275.
Students 233.

33—OUR LADY OF GOOD COUNSEL (1928). Merged with St. Augustine and St. Monica to form Roman Catholic Community of the 19th Ward.
Res., 75 Ernestine St., 14619. Tel: 716-235-1130.

34—OUR LADY OF LOURDES (1928), Rev. John L. O'Connor.
Res., 150 Varinna Dr., 14618. Tel: 716-473-9656.
School—Seton Catholic School, (Grades PreK-6). See St.Thomas More for Grades 7 & 8. 165 Rhinecliff Dr., 14618. Tel: 716-473-6604.
Sisters 2; Lay Teachers 30; Students 360.
Catechesis/Religious Programs—Tel: 716-244-2361. Sr. Lucille Lenhard, D.R.E.
Students 264.

35—OUR LADY OF MERCY (1957), Rev. Stanley G. Kacprzak. Pastoral Assocs: Roni Antenucci; Patricia Boyce.
Res., 36 Armstrong Rd., 14616. Tel: 716-865-0775; Fax: 716-865-9403.
Catechesis/Religious Programs—Tel: 716-865-2917. Sr. Kathryn Wahl, D.R.E.
Students 150.

36—OUR LADY OF MOUNT CARMEL (1909), Revs. Dennis Shaw; Laurence Tracy; Sr. Julia Norton, R.S.M.; Deacons Nemesio Martinez; Felix Medero.
Res., 53 Ontario St., 14605. Tel: 716-232-1133; Fax: 716-325-5771.
Catechesis/Religious Programs—Tel: 716-224-01777. Bernard Grizzard, D.R.E.
Students 77.
Convent—59 Ontario St., 14605. Tel: 716-454-6766.
St. Martin's Soup Kitchen—Tel: 716-325-6500.

37—OUR LADY OF PERPETUAL HELP (1905), Rev. Neil Miller; Sr. Livia Ann Ruocco, R.S.M., Pastoral Assoc.; Sr. Francisca Aguillon, O.L.C., Hispanic Pastoral Assoc. In res., Rev. Anthony Mugavero.
Res., 1089 Joseph Ave., 14621. Tel: 716-467-2725.
Catechesis/Religious Programs—Students 55.

38—OUR LADY QUEEN OF PEACE (1960), Rev. Joseph A. Hart; Sr. Jacqulyn Reichart, R.S.M., Pastoral Assoc.; Sr. Jeanne Marie Collins, R.S.M., Pastoral Assoc.; Deacon Albert Bergeron.
Res., 95 Warren Ave., 14618-4311. Tel: 716-244-3010; Fax: 716-242-7733.
601 Edgewood Ave., 14618-4329.

39—OUR LADY OF VICTORY-ST. JOSEPH (1848), Rev. Winfried M. Kellner.
Res., 210 Pleasant St., 14604. Tel: 716-454-2244.

40—OUR MOTHER OF SORROWS (1829) (Irish), Revs. Thomas R. Statt; Richard J. Shatzel; Sr. Mary Doran, S.S.J., Pastoral Assoc. In res., Rev. Raymond G. Heisel.
Res., 5000 Mt. Read Blvd., 14612. Tel: 716-663-5432; Fax: 716-663-5435. [CEM]
School—1701 Latta Rd., 14612. Tel: 716-621-3495. Lori Leone, Prin.
Lay Teachers 27; Students 398.
Catechesis/Religious Programs—Tel: 716-621-3495. Mrs. Claudia Adams, D.R.E.
Students 618.

41—ST. LAWRENCE (1959), Revs. Frank J. Falletta; Dennis R. Sewar; Donald J. Haycock, C.S.C.
Res., 1000 N. Greece Rd., 14626. Tel: 716-723-1350; Fax: 716-723-1361.

School—Tel: 716-225-3870; Fax: 716-225-1336. Sr. Diane Dennie, Prin.
Lay Teachers 21; Students 493.
Catechesis/Religious Programs—Tel: 716-225-7320. Rosanne Young, D.R.E.
Students 880.

42—ST. LUCY (1912). Closed. For inquiries for parish records contact Immaculate Conception Church.

43—ST. MARGARET MARY (1929), Rev. John J. Quinn. In res., Rev. John T. Walsh.
Res., 401 Rogers Pkwy., 14617. Tel: 716-342-2100.
School—Northeast Quadrant School at St. Margaret Mary's, (Grades PreK-6) 400 Rogers Pkwy., 14617. Tel: 716-266-0413. Ms. Kathleen Carroll, Prin.
Lay Teachers 25; Students 300.
Catechesis/Religious Programs—Tel: 716-342-7114.
Students 420.

44—ST. MARK (1964), Rev. Thomas M. Erdle; Deacons James L. Chatterton; Thomas Kluchko.
Res., 54 Kuhn Rd., 14612. Tel: 716-225-3710; Fax: 716-227-6824.
Catechesis/Religious Programs—Mary Margaret Chatterton, D.R.E.
Students 550.

45—ST. MARY (1834), Rev. James Lawlor.
Res., 15 St. Mary's Place, 14607. Tel: 716-232-7140; Fax: 716-232-6289.
Catechesis/Religious Programs—Students 101.

46—EMMANUEL CHURCH OF THE DEAF OF THE DIOCESE OF ROCHESTER (1981), Rev. Raymond Fleming.
Res., 75 Ernestine St., 14619. Tel: 716-235-1812 (Voice); 235-3849 (TTY).

47—ST. MICHAEL (1872) (German-Hispanic), Revs. Dennis J. Shaw; Laurence Tracy.
Res., 869 Clinton Ave., N., 14605. Tel: 716-325-4040; Fax: 716-325-5771.

48—ST. MONICA (1898) (Irish). Merged with Our Lady of Good Counsel and St. Augustine to form Roman Catholic Community of the 19th Ward. In res., Revs. Ray Fleming; Frederick Helfrich; Richard O'Connell.
Res., 34 Monica St., 14619. Tel: 716-235-3322.
School—841 Genesee St., 14611. Tel: 716-235-4140. Sr. Mary Marvin, R.S.M., Prin.
Lay Teachers 12; Students 191.

49—ROMAN CATHOLIC COMMUNITY OF THE 19TH WARD. Consolidation of Our Lady of Good Counsel, St. Augustine, and St. Monica. Rev. Robert Werth; Lourdes Perez-Albuerne, Business Mgr.
Res., 34 Monica St., 14619. Tel: 716-235-3322.

50—ST. PATRICK (1832). Closed. (Old Cathedral). Records from 1832 thru May 1978 can be obtained from St. Anthony of Padua Church. Any information after that time contact St. Francis of Assisi.
1150 Buffalo Rd., 14624.

51—SS. PETER AND PAUL (1843), Revs. Paul Tomasso; Daniel McMullin.
Res., 720 Main St., W., 14611. Tel: 716-436-3110; Fax: 716-436-0373.

52—ST. PIUS TENTH (1954), Revs. Gerald T. Connor; Lance M. Gonyo; Deacon John E. Zierle.
Res., 3032 Chili Ave., 14624. Tel: 716-247-2566; Fax: 716-247-2511. [CEM]
School—(Grades PreK-6). Tel: 716-247-5650; Fax: 716-247-7409. Mr. Stephen Oberst, Prin.
Sisters of St. Joseph 2; Lay Teachers 20; Students 451.
Catechesis/Religious Programs—3000 Chili Ave., 14624. Tel: 716-247-5269; Fax: 716-247-7409. Ms. Ann Hastee, D.R.E.
Students 470.

53—ST. PHILIP NERI (1929) (Italian), Rev. Timothy Horan, Temporary Admin.
Res., 1782 Clifford Ave., 14609. Tel: 716-482-2400.

54—MOST PRECIOUS BLOOD (1930), Rev. William E. Graf.
Res., 219 Stenson St., 14606. Tel: 716-458-6079.

55—ST. SALOME (1925), Rev. William G. Darling.
Res., 4282 Culver Rd., 14622. Tel: 716-323-1160.
Catechesis/Religious Programs—Students 171.

56—ST. STANISLAUS (1890) (Polish), Revs. Mitchell Zygadlo; Valentine A. Jankowiak; Sr. Theresa Collins, S.S.J.
Res., 34 St. Stanislaus St., 14621. Tel: 716-467-3068; Fax: 716-546-3503.

57—ST. THEODORE (1924), Revs. Daniel F. Holland; Michael J. Volino. Pastoral Assocs: Sr. Catherine Pfleger, R.S.M.; Sr. Barbara Bartkowiak, O.S.F.; Sr. Mary Jean Smith, S.S.J.; Deacon Anthony Caruso.
Res., 168 Spencerport Rd., 14606. Tel: 716-429-6811; Fax: 716-429-7726.
Catechesis/Religious Programs—Tel: 716-429-5650.
Students 483.

58—ST. THERESA (1927) (Polish), Rev. Mitchell Zygadlo.
Res., 34 St. Stanislaus St., 14621. Tel: 716-546-3503.

59—ST. THOMAS THE APOSTLE (1922), Revs. Robert C. Bradler; Ralph J. Fraats; Deacon Thomas H. Beck. In res., Rev. Robert F. McNamara.
Res., 4536 St. Paul Blvd., 14617. Tel: 716-342-2323.
Catechesis/Religious Programs—Tel: 716-342-1704. Mr. David Higbee, D.R.E.
Students 200.

60—ST. THOMAS MORE (1953), Rev. Robert L. Collins; Deacon Stephen Carroll; Sr. Ellen Galvin, S.S.J., Pastoral Assoc. In res., Revs. John S. Whalen; Richard J. Orlando; William I. Onuh (Nigeria).
Res., 2617 East Ave., 14610. Tel: 716-381-4200; Fax: 716-381-6327.
School—Siena Catholic Academy, (Grades 7-8). See Our Lady of Lourdes for Grades PreK-6. Tel: 716-381-1220.
Lay Teachers 27; Students 320.
Catechesis/Religious Programs—Tel: 716-381-0470.
Students 105.

OUTSIDE METROPOLITAN ROCHESTER

Addison, Steuben Co., St. Catherine of Siena (1854), Rev. Gerald T. O'Connor.
Res., 49 Maple St., 14801. Tel: 607-359-2115. [CEM]
Catechesis/Religious Programs—Students 60.

Apalachin, Tioga Co., St. Margaret Mary (1955), Rev. David F. Simon; Patricia Federowicz, Pastoral Assoc.; Deacon Joseph F. Federowicz.
Res., 1110 Pennsylvania Ave., 13732. Tel: 607-625-3191; Fax: 607-625-5717.
Catechesis/Religious Programs—Tel: 607-625-3192.
Students 200.

Auburn, Cayuga Co.,

1—HOLY FAMILY, (1834), Rev. Conrad J. Sundholm.
Res., 85 North St., 13021. Tel: 315-252-9576; Fax: 315-255-1506.
School—Cayuga County Catholic School, Tel: 315-253-8327.
Catechesis/Religious Programs—Tel: 315-252-9578.
Students 82.

2—SACRED HEART, (1955), Rev. Paul Brennan.
Res., 90 Melrose Rd., 13021. Tel: 315-252-7271; Fax: 315-255-0716. [JC]
School—St. Joseph School. A consolidation of the following parishes: Holy Family; Sacred Heart; and St. Alphonsus. Tel: 315-253-8327; Fax: 315-253-2401.
Catechesis/Religious Programs—Tel: 315-253-2712.
Students 350.
Mission—Owasco, Cayuga Co., St. Ann, (1912) 90 Melrose Rd., 13021. Tel: 315-252-7271.

3—ST. MARY, (1868) (Irish), Rev. Robert J. Schrader. In res., Rev. James C. Enright.
Res., 15 Clark St., 13021. Tel: 315-252-9545.
Catechesis/Religious Programs—17 Clymer St., 13021. Tel: 315-252-3439.
Students 332.

4—ST. ALPHONSUS, (1853), Revs. Foster P. Rogers; Paul J. Freemesser. In res., Revs. Clarence W. Gardner, Pastor Emeritus; William J. Gaynor; Joseph T. Gaynor.
Res., 10 Lewis St., 13021-2708. Tel: 315-252-7261; Fax: 315-252-7262. [JC]
School—Cayuga County Catholic School (St. Joseph's Campus). A consolidation of the following parishes: Holy Family; Sacred Heart; and St. Alphonsus. Tel: 315-253-8327.
Catechesis/Religious Programs—Tel: 315-253-6147. Marie Venaglia, D.R.E.
Students 152.

5—ST. ALOYSIUS. Closed. For inquiries for parish records contact the Chancery.

6—ST. HYACINTH, (1905) (Polish), Revs. Robert M. Grzybowski, O.F.M.Conv.; Callistus Juras, O.F.M.Conv., Pastoral Assoc.; Deacon Gary DiLallo. In res., Rev. Matthew Swizdor, O.F.M.Conv.
Res., 61 Pulaski St., 13021. Tel: 315-252-7297; Fax: 315-255-3781. [JC]
School—St. Joseph School. A consolidation of the following parishes: Holy Family; Sacred Heart; St. Alphonsus; and St. Hyacinth. Tel: 315-253-8327.
Catechesis/Religious Programs—Tel: 315-252-5132.
Students 152.

7—ST. FRANCIS OF ASSISI, (1907) (Italian), Rev. Robert L. Beligotti. In res., Rev. C. Richard Nangle.
Res., 185 Clark St., 13021. Tel: 315-252-7593; Fax: 315-252-7593. [JC]
Catechesis/Religious Programs—Students 100.

Aurora, Cayuga Co., St. Patrick (1858), Rev. Paul J. Ryan; Deacon John Prave.
Res., Main St., Box 296, 13026-0296. Tel: 315-364-7197. [CEM]

Avon, Livingston Co., St. Agnes (1866), Rev. James C. Burke. In res., Rev. James T. Wolfe.
Res., 108 Prospect St., 14414. Tel: 716-226-2100; Fax: 716-226-6436. [CEM]
School—Tel: 716-226-8500. Mrs. Vicki Rose, Prin.
Lay Teachers 7; Students 69.
Catechesis/Religious Programs—Tel: 716-226-3232.
Students 229.

Bath, Steuben Co., St. Mary (1860), Rev. Robert W. Hammond.
Res., 32 E. Morris St., 14810. Tel: 607-776-3327; Fax: 607-776-3409. [CEM]
Catechesis/Religious Programs—36 E. Morris St., 14810.
Students 175.

Bradford, Steuben Co., St. Stanislaus (1922) (Polish), Revs. Gerald T. O'Connor; Andrew J. Kalafsky.
Res., Main St., P.O. Box 153, 14815-0153. Tel: 607-583-4920.
Mission—Campbell, Steuben Co., St. Joseph, (1870) P.O. Box 153, 14815-0153.
Catechesis/Religious Programs—Students 110.

Brockport, Monroe Co., Nativity of the Blessed Virgin Mary (1848), Rev. Roy J. Kiggins.
Res., 152 Main St., 14420-1972. Tel: 716-637-4500; Fax: 716-637-4232. [CEM]
School—Holley & Utica St., 14420. Tel: 716-637-2100; Fax: 716-637-7420.
Lay Teachers 8; Students 134.
Catechesis/Religious Programs—Tel: 716-637-8490.
Students 250.

Caledonia, Livingston Co., St. Columba (1884), Rev. Walter Plominski, Admin.
Res., 198 North St., 14423. Tel: 716-538-2126. [CEM]
Catechesis/Religious Programs—Students 84.
Mission—Mumford, Monroe Co., St. Patrick, (1854) Church St., 14511.

Canandaigua, Ontario Co., St. Mary (1844), Revs. Walter L. Wainwright; Brian C. Cool.
Res., 95 N. Main St., Canadaigua, 14424. Tel: 716-394-1220; Fax: 716-396-3230. [CEM]
School—16 Gibson St., 14424. Tel: 716-394-4300. Mrs. Eileen O'Neill, Prin.
Lay Teachers 13; Students 208.
Catechesis/Religious Programs—16 Gibson St., 14424. Tel: 716-394-4590.
Students 673.

Canisteo, Steuben Co., St. Joachim (1880), Rev. Daniel W. Heintz.
Res., 32 W. Main St., 14823. Tel: 607-698-4034.
Catechesis/Religious Programs—Students 101.

Cato, Cayuga Co., St. Patrick (1875), Rev. William B. Leone; Deacon John Tomandl; Sr. Virginia Taylor, R.S.M., Pastoral Assoc.
Res., 2667 Hamilton St., P.O. Box 266, Weedsport, 13166. Tel: 315-834-6266.
Catechesis/Religious Programs—Tel: 315-834-9203. Walter Sheehan, D.R.E.
Students 500.

Cayuga, Cayuga Co., St. Joseph (1870), Rev. Paul J. Ryan; Deacon John Prave.
Springfield Cove, P.O. Box 139, Union Springs, 13160.
Res., Main St., Box 296, Aurora, 13026. Tel: 315-364-7197.

Churchville, Monroe Co., St. Vincent De Paul (1869), Rev. William F. Laird, Admin.
Res., 11 N. Main St., Drawer I, 14428. Tel: 716-293-1400. [CEM]
Catechesis/Religious Programs—Tel: 315-293-1180.
Students 83.

Clifton Springs, Ontario Co., St. Felix (1856). Merged with St. Francis to form St. Felix / St. Francis Parish Cluster. Rev. Edward J. Dillon.
Res., 12 Hibbard Ave., 14432. Tel: 315-462-2961. [CEM]

St. Felix / St. Francis Parish Cluster, Rev. Edward J. Dillon.
Office: 12 Hibbard Ave., 14432. Tel: 315-462-2961. [CEM 2]

Clyde, Wayne Co., St. John the Evangelist (1852), Rev. Leo J. Reinhardt; Deacon Gregory J. Kiley.
Res., 114 Sodus St., 14433. Tel: 315-923-3941. [CEM]
Catechesis/Religious Programs—Tel: 315-923-7315; Fax: 315-923-3941. Mary DeLisio, D.R.E.
Students 130.
Mission—Savannah, Wayne Co., St. Patrick, (1875) Grand Ave., Savannah, 13146. Tel: 315-365-3244.

Cohocton, Steuben Co., St. Pius V (1861) (German), Rev. Charles T. Manning.
Res., 35 Maple Ave., P.O. Box 387, 14826. Tel: 716-384-5500. [CEM 2]

Catechesis/Religious Programs—Students 80.
Mission—Perkinsville, Steuben Co., Sacred Heart of Jesus, (1838) Chapel St., P.O. Box 389, Perkinsville, 14529. Tel: 716-728-5665.

Corning, Steuben Co., St. Mary (1848), Revs. Michael F. Conboy; Michael R. Brown; Deacons Raymond Defendorf; Ronald Verkon; Sr. Joan Cawley, S.S.J., Pastoral Assoc. In res., Rev. Francis R. Davis.
Mailing Address: c/o 222 Dodge Ave., 14830. Tel: 607-936-4689; Fax: 607-936-0222. [CEM]
Catechesis/Religious Programs—Mary Ann Hinkley, D.R.E.
Students 75.

St. Patrick (1903), Revs. Michael F. Conboy; Michael R. Brown; Deacons Raymond Defendorf; Ronald Verkon.
Office: c/o 222 Dodge Ave., 14830. Tel: 607-936-4689; Fax: 607-936-0222.
Res., 155 State St., 14830. Tel: 607-962-0422. [JC]
Catechesis/Religious Programs—Mary Ann Hinkley, D.R.E.
Students 159.

St. Vincent de Paul (1913), Revs. Michael F. Conboy; Michael R. Brown; Deacons Ray Defendorf; Ron Verkon; Sr. Edna Slyck, R.S.M., Pastoral Assoc.
Res., c/o 222 Dodge Ave., 14830. Tel: 607-936-4688; Fax: 607-936-0222. [JC]
Catechesis/Religious Programs—Students 154.

Dansville, Livingston Co., St. Mary (1845), Rev. Stephen Kraus.
Res., 40 Elizabeth St., 14437. Tel: 716-335-2700. [CEM]
School—Tel: 716-335-6800.
Lay Teachers 8; Students 164.
Catechesis/Religious Programs—Tel: 716-335-8700.
Students 245.

Dryden, Tompkins Co., Holy Cross (1962), Rev. John H. Hayes.
Res., 375 S. George Rd., Freeville, 13068. Tel: 607-844-8314. [CEM]
Catechesis/Religious Programs—Tel: 607-844-8358.
Students 230.

East Bay, Wayne Co., St. John Fisher (1935). Closed. All inquiries for mission records can be made at St. Mary Magdalen, Wolcott.

East Bloomfield, Ontario Co., St. Bridget (1850), Rev. John J. Philipps; Deacon Claude Lester.
Res., 15 Church St., 14443. Tel: 716-657-7626. [CEM]
Catechesis/Religious Programs—Students 157.

East Rochester, Monroe Co., St. Jerome (1905) (Italian), Rev. Albert L. Delmonte; Sr. Clare Brown, Pastoral Assoc.
Res., 207 S. Garfield St., 14445. Tel: 716-586-3231; Fax: 716-586-0537.
Catechesis/Religious Programs—206 West Ave., 14445. Tel: 716-586-1625.
Students 340.

Elmira, Chemung Co.,

1—Sts. Peter and Paul of Eastside Catholic Parish, (1848), Rev. Patrick L. Connor; Sr. Kathleen Bayer, R.S.M., Pastoral Assoc.
Office: 161 High St., 14901. Tel: 607-732-2132.
Res., 950 Lake St., 14901. Tel: 607-732-2455.
School—Holy Family Catholic Schools. Serving the parishes in Elmira. See St. Mary, St. Casimir, and Our Lady of Lourdes for details.

2—St. Patrick, (1871), Rev. Joseph P. McCaffrey; Sr. Maureen Mylott, S.C., Pastoral Assoc.
Res., 604 Park Pl., 14901. Tel: 607-733-0300.
School—Holy Family Catholic Schools. Serving the parishes in Elmira. See St. Mary, St. Casimir, and Our Lady of Lourdes for details. Tel: 607-734-4414.

3—St. Mary, (1871), Revs. William Donnelly; Michael R. Brown; Lance M. Gonyo.
Res., 224 Franklin St., 14904. Tel: 607-734-6254.
School—Holy Family Primary. See St. Casimir and Our Lady of Lourdes for Intermediate and Jr. High. 421 Fulton St., 14904. Constance Dunn, Prin.
Lay Teachers 6; Students 190.

4—St. John the Baptist of Eastside Catholic Parish, (1866) (German), Rev. Patrick L. Connor; Sr. Kathleen Bayer, R.S.M., Pastoral Assoc.
Office: 161 High St., 14901. Tel: 607-732-1994.
Res., 950 Lake St., 14901. Tel: 607-732-2455.
Church—325 Lake St., 14901.
School—Holy Family Catholic Schools. Serving the parishes in Elmira. See St. Mary, St. Casimir, and Our Lady of Lourdes for details.

5—St. Casimir, (1890) (Polish), Rev. Christopher E. Linsler.
Res., 1004 Davis St., 14901. Tel: 607-734-1622.
School—Holy Family Jr. High. See St. Mary and Our Lady of Lourdes for Primary and Intermediate. 1008 Davis St., 14901. Tel: 734-0336. Mrs. Elizabeth Berliner, Prin.
Lay Teachers 7; Students 140.

6—St. Cecilia of Eastside Catholic Parish, (1904), Rev. Patrick L. Connor; Sr. Kathleen Bayer, R.S.M., Pastoral Assoc.
Office: 161 High St., 14901. Tel: 607-732-1994.
Res., 950 Lake St., 14901. Tel: 607-732-2455.
School—Holy Family Catholic Schools. Serving the parishes in Elmira. See St. Mary, St. Casimir, and Our Lady of Lourdes for details.

7—St. Anthony, (1908) (Italian). Clustered with St. Patrick's Church. Rev. Joseph J. McCaffrey.
Res., 604 Park Pl., 14901. Tel: 607-733-0300; Fax: 607-733-3606.
School—Holy Family Catholic Schools. Serving the parishes in Elmira. See St. Mary, St. Casimir, and Our Lady of Lourdes for details. Tel: 607-734-4414.
Catechesis/Religious Programs—Tel: 607-737-0536.
Students 185.

8—Our Lady of Lourdes, (1940), Rev. Paul J. McCabe.
Res., 120 Fairmont Rd., 14905. Tel: 607-732-6261.
School—Holy Family Intermediate. See St. Mary and St. Casimir for Primary and Junior High. 301 Demarest Pkwy., 14905. Miss Brenda Lisi, Prin.
Lay Teachers 10; Sisters 2; Students 130.

Elmira Heights, Chemung Co., St. Charles Borromeo (1904), Rev. Christopher E. Linsler; Deacon William P. Dougherty. In res., Revs. William D. Tobin; Edward J. Foy.
Res., 132 Oakwood Ave., 14903. Tel: 607-734-7619.
Catechesis/Religious Programs—Tel: 607-734-1622.
Students 163.

Fairport, Monroe Co., Assumption of the Blessed Virgin Mary (1866), Revs. Edward Golden; Paul Walsh, C.S.B.; Deacon Ronald J. Tocci. In res., Rev. Charles F. Adams, O.F.M.
Res., 20 East Ave., 14450. Tel: 716-388-0040; Fax: 716-388-0248. [CEM]
Catechesis/Religious Programs—Assumption School of Religion, 10 Baumer Place, 14450. Tel: 716-223-0525. Sr. Catherine Judge, D.R.E.
Students 913.

Church of the Resurrection (1973), Rev. Louis A. Vasile; Mrs. Donna Fitch, Pastoral Assoc.; Deacon Daniel Kinsky.
Res., 52 Mason Rd., 14450. Tel: 716-223-6686.
Church—63 Mason Rd., 14450. Tel: 716-223-5500; Fax: 716-223-6958.
Catechesis/Religious Programs—Tel: 716-223-5592.
Students 250.

St. John of Rochester (1962), Revs. James E. Boyle; Michael C. Hogan; Sr. Kathleen A. Wayne, R.S.M.; Deacon Thomas J. Cleary.
Ministry Bldg.: 8 Wickford Way, 14450.
Res., 18 Wickford Way, 14450. Tel: 716-248-5993.
School—10 Wickford Way, 14450. Tel: 716-248-8836; Fax: 716-248-8839. Mrs. Marilyn Tripp, Prin.
Lay Teachers 13; Students 170.
Catechesis/Religious Programs—Tel: 716-248-8850.
Students 800.

Fleming, Cayuga Co., St. Isaac Jogues (1946), Rev. Albert Shamon, Admin.
Res., 5 S. Marvine Ave., Auburn, 13021. Tel: 315-255-2912; Fax: 315-255-2912.

Geneseo, Livingston Co., St. Mary (1854), Revs. William Gordinier; J. Walter Carron, Pastor Emeritus. In res., Rev. Eugene McFarland Tel: 716-243-2551.
Office: 13 North St., 14454. Tel: 716-243-1100.
Res., 4 Avon Rd., 14454. Tel: 716-243-2422. [CEM]
Catechesis/Religious Programs—Tel: 716-243-2422.
Students 212.

Geneva, Ontario Co., St. Francis de Sales (1835), Rev. Ronald P. Harley.
Res., 130 Exchange St., 14456. Tel: 315-789-0930; Fax: 315-781-1985. [CEM][JC 2]
School—Consolidated School. See St. Stephen and St. Francis de Sales.
Catechesis/Religious Programs—Students 340.

St. Stephen (1904). Consolidated with the following parishes: St. Francis de Sales and St. Stephen. Rev. Msgr. Gerard C. Krieg; Rev. Brian E. Jeffers.
Res., 48 Pulteney St., 14456. Tel: 315-789-1124; Fax: 315-789-1271. [JC]
School—(Grades PreK-8) 17 Elmwood Ave., 14456. Tel: 315-789-1828. Mrs. Elaine Morrow, Prin.
Sisters of St. Joseph 1; Lay Teachers 17; Students 285.
Catechesis/Religious Programs—21 High St., 14456. Tel: 315-781-2624. Walter Savaria, D.R.E.
Students 180.

Groton, Tompkins Co., St. Anthony (1873), Rev. Robert M. Egan. In res., Rev. Joseph M. McNamara, Pastor Emeritus.
Res., 312 Locke Rd., R.D. 2, 13073. Tel: 607-898-5135. [CEM]
Catechesis/Religious Programs—Students 140.

Hamlin, Monroe Co., St. Elizabeth Ann Seton (1982), Rev. William Amann; Deacons Ramon Datz; John Holmes.
Res., 3747 Brick Schoolhouse Rd., 14464. Tel: 716-964-8627; Fax: 716-964-8627.
Catechesis/Religious Programs—Tel: 716-964-8200.
Students 259.

Hammondsport, Steuben Co., St. Gabriel (1845), Sr. Anne Michelle McGill, Pastoral Admin.
Res., 78 Shethar St., 14840. Tel: 607-569-3501; Fax: 607-569-3226. [CEM]

Henrietta, Monroe Co., Church of the Good Shepherd (1911), Revs. Michael A. Bausch; John M. Mulligan, V.G.; Sr. Barbara Stinard, R.S.M., Pastoral Assoc.; Deacon Eugene Edwards.
Res., 3318 E. Henrietta Rd., 14467. Tel: 716-334-3518; Fax: 716-334-6015.
School—3288 E. Henrietta Rd., 14467. Tel: 716-334-5100. Marie Arcuri, Prin.
Lay Teachers 12; Students 210.
Catechesis/Religious Programs—Tel: 716-334-3023.
Students 650.

Hilton, Monroe Co., St. Leo (1884), Rev. John J. Glogowski; Deacon James P. Steiger.
Res., 167 Lake Ave., 14468. Tel: 716-392-2710; Fax: 716-392-9254.
Catechesis/Religious Programs—Tel: 716-392-9694.
Students 392.

Honeoye, Ontario Co., St. Mary, Our Lady of the Hills (1868), Rev. Edward B. Zenkel.
Res., Rt. 20A, Box 725, 14471. Tel: 716-229-5007. [CEM]
Catechesis/Religious Programs—Students 80.

Honeoye Falls, Monroe Co., St. Paul of the Cross (1870), Lawrence A. Gross; Deacon Albro C. Wilson, Jr.
Res., 29 Monroe St., 14472. Tel: 716-624-1443. [CEM]
Catechesis/Religious Programs—Students 118.

Hornell, Steuben Co., St. Ann (1866), Revs. Elmer J. Schmidt, (Retired); James Jaeger; Deacon Robert W. McCormick.
Res., 31 Erie Ave., P.O. Box 605, 14843. Tel: 607-324-0410. [CEM][JC 2]
School—Tel: 607-324-0733. Sr. Dolores Ann Stein, Prin.
Lay Teachers 18; Students 190.
Catechesis/Religious Programs—Tel: 607-324-7121. Marianne Logan, D.R.E.
Students 203.

St. Ignatius Loyola (1931), Rev. Jeremiah P. Moynihan.
Res., 343 Canisteo St., 14843. Tel: 607-324-5811.

Horseheads, Chemung Co., St. Mary Our Mother (1866), Revs. Thomas W. Burr; Scott M. Kubinski; Deacon Daniel R. Hurley. In res., Rev. Robert C. MacNamara, (Retired).
Res., 816 W. Broad St., 14845. Tel: 607-739-3817; Fax: 607-739-5628. [CEM]
School—811 Westlake St., 14845. Tel: 607-739-9157; Fax: 607-739-2532.
Lay Teachers 14; Students 270.
Catechesis/Religious Programs—Tel: 607-739-8214.
Students 674.

Interlaken, Seneca Co., St. Francis Solanus (1875), Rev. Nelson J. Ruppert, O.F.M.Cap.
Mailing Address: c/o Holy Cross Rectory, P.O. Box 337, Ovid, 14521-0337. Tel: 607-532-8337; Fax: 607-869-9825.
Res., St. Fidelis Friary, 7790 County Rd. 153, 14847. Tel: 607-532-4423; Fax: 607-869-9825.
Church—Orchard St., 14847. Tel: 607-532-8337; Fax: 607-869-9825.

Ithaca, Tompkins Co., St. Catherine of Siena (1960), Rev. Ronald E. Gaesser.
Res., St. Catherine Cir., 14850. Tel: 607-257-2493; Fax: 607-257-5901.
Catechesis/Religious Programs—Students 158.

Immaculate Conception (1848), Revs. Bernard L. Carges; Eugene P. Sweeney; Deacon James D. Hankey.
Res., 113 N. Geneva St., 14850. Tel: 607-273-6121; Fax: 607-273-0185. [CEM 2]
School—320 W. Buffalo St., 14850. Tel: 607-273-2707. Diana Baker, Prin.
Sisters of St. Joseph 1; Lay Teachers 12; Students 205.
Catechesis/Religious Programs—Tel: 607-273-0303.
Students 265.

King Ferry, Cayuga Co., Our Lady of the Lake, King Ferry (1868), Rev. Paul J. Ryan; Deacon John Prave.
Spring Port Cove, P.O. Box 139, Union Springs, 13160.
Res., Main St., P.O. Box 296, Aurora, 13026. Tel:

315-364-7197. [CEM]

Lansing, All Saints (1913), Rev. Ronald E. Gaesser; Mary E. Wintish, R.S.M., Pastoral Assoc.
Res., 347 Ridge Rd., 14882. Tel: 607-533-7344.
Catechesis/Religious Programs—Students 90.

Leicester, Livingston Co., St. Thomas Aquinas (1897), Rev. Richard J. Beligotti.
Res., 175 Main St. Box 195, 14481. Tel: 716-382-3400.
Catechesis/Religious Programs—Students 120.
Mission—Retsof, Livingston Co., St. Lucy, (1912).

Lima, Livingston Co., St. Rose (1848), Rev. James F. Doyle.
Res., 1985 Lake Ave., 14485. Tel: 716-624-1005. [CEM]
Catechesis/Religious Programs—Students 80.

Livonia, Livingston Co., St. Joseph (1911), Rev. William A. Trott.
Res., 14 Washington St., P.O. Box 77, 14487. Tel: 716-346-3815; Fax: 716-346-3815. [CEM]
Catechesis/Religious Programs—41 Spring St., 14487. Tel: 716-346-2500.
Students 208.
Mission—Conesus, Livingston Co., St. William, P.O. Box 77, 14487. Tel: 716-346-3757.

Livonia Center, Livingston Co., St. Michael (1848). Closed. For inquiries for parish records contact St. Mary's, Honeoye.

Lyons, Wayne, St. Michael (1852) (Italian), Rev. William M. Barrett.
Res., 3 Holley St., 14489. Tel: 315-946-4182; Fax: 315-946-4736.
Catechesis/Religious Programs—Students 81.

Macedon, Wayne Co., St. Patrick (1883), Rev. Robert Scott Bourcy; Deacon Dominick N. Abballe.
Res., 52 Main St., 14502. Tel: 315-986-5671. [CEM]

Marion, Wayne, St. Gregory (1914), Rev. Robert Gaudio; Dr. Denise Mack, P.A.
Res., 136 Church St., Palmyra, 14522. Tel: 315-597-4571.
Office: 3806 Union St., 14522. Tel: 315-926-4323.
Catechesis/Religious Programs—Students 132.

Mendon, Monroe Co., St. Catherine of Siena (1902), Revs. Charles J. Latus; John P. Norris; Deacon Fernando V. Ona, M.D.; Sr. Ruth Maier, S.S.J., Pastoral Assoc.
Res., 26 Mendon-Ionia Rd., 14506. Tel: 716-624-4990; Fax: 716-624-4996.
Catechesis/Religious Programs—Karen Dietz, S.S.J., D.R.E.
Students 387.
Convent—15 Mendon-Ionia Rd., 14506. Tel: 624-1538.

Montezuma, Cayuga Co., St. Michael (1865). Closed. For inquiries for parish records contact St. Joseph, Weedsport.

Moravia, Cayuga Co., St. Patrick (1872), Rev. Robert J. Downs.
Res., 51 Grove St., P.O. Box 111, 13118. Tel: 315-497-0626. [CEM]

Mount Morris, Livingston Co., St. Patrick (1869), Rev. Daniel J. Condon.
Res., 46 Stanley St., 14510. Tel: 716-658-2110. [CEM]
Parish Center, 33 Murray St., Mt. Morris, 14510.

Naples, Ontario, St. Januarius (1876), Rev. Philip J. Billotte.
Res., 180 N. Main St., P.O. Box 459, 14512. Tel: 716-374-2414; Fax: 716-374-2415.
Catechesis/Religious Programs—Students 83.

Newark, Wayne Co., St. Michael (1863), Revs. Peter C. Clifford; John Gagnier; Deacon Thomas Cass. In res., Rev. Joseph M. McDonnell, Pastor Emeritus.
Res., 401 Main St., 14513. Tel: 315-331-6753.
School—320 S. Main St., 14513. Tel: 315-331-2297. Mrs. Kathleen Peters, Prin.
Lay Teachers 20; Students 327.
Catechesis/Religious Programs—Tel: 315-331-3408. Rose Leisenring, D.R.E.
Students 265.

Newark Valley, Tioga County, St. John the Evangelist (1880), Rev. William A. Moorby; Deacon Warren M. Rutan.
Res., 24 Rock St., P.O. Box 458, 13811. Tel: 607-642-3328.
Catechesis/Religious Programs—Tel: 607-642-3258.
Students 121.
Mission—Catatonk, Tioga Co., St. Francis of Assisi, (1930) P.O. Box 458, 13811. Tel: 607-659-5959.

North Chili, Monroe Co., St. Christopher (1968), Rev. Bernard F. Dollen.
Res., 3350 Union St., 14514. Tel: 716-594-1400.
Catechesis/Religious Programs—Tel: 716-594-1441.
Students 540.

Nunda, Livingston Co., Holy Angels (1854), Rev. Daniel J. Condon.
Res., 46 Stanley St., Mount Morris, 14510. Tel: 716-468-3450; 658-2110.

Odessa, Schuyler Co., St. Benedict (1965), Rev. David L. Bonin.
Res., 905 N. Decatur St., Watkins Glen, 14891. Tel: 607-535-2786.
Church—Speedway, 14869. Tel: 607-594-2226.
Parish Center, 21 Massachusetts St., Nunda, 14517. Tel: 716-658-3450.

Ontario, Wayne Co., St. Mary of the Lake (1869), Rev. Robert G. Kreckel; Deacon Gerald J. Skerrett.
Res., 5823 Walworth Rd., P.O. Box 499, 14519. Tel: 315-524-2611; Fax: 315-524-7421. [CEM]
Catechesis/Religious Programs—Tel: 315-524-7241.
Students 405.

Ovid, Seneca Co., Holy Cross (1849), Rev. Nelson J. Ruppert, O.F.M.Cap.
Res., 7227 S. Main St., P.O. Box 337, 14521-0337. Tel: 607-869-2261; Fax: 607-869-9825. [CEM]
Catechesis/Religious Programs—Students 57.

Owego, Tioga Co., St. Patrick (1842), Rev. Eugene R. Weis.
Res., 300 Main St., 13827. Tel: 607-687-1068. [CEM]
School—Tel: 607-687-1770. Mrs. Loretta Hayton, Prin.
Lay Teachers 6; Students 139.
Catechesis/Religious Programs—Tel: 607-687-1331.
Students 241.

Painted Post, Steuben Co., Immaculate Heart of Mary (1952), Revs. Michael F. Conboy; Michael R. Brown; Deacons Ron Verkon; Raymond Defendorf; Sr. Mary Kay Ryan, S.S.J., Pastoral Assoc.
Mailing Address: c/o 222 Dodge Ave., Corning, 14830. Tel: 607-936-4688; Fax: 607-936-0222.
Res., 115 State St., Corning, 14830. Tel: 607-962-0422; Fax: 607-936-0222. [CEM][JC]

Palmyra, Wayne Co., St. Anne (1850), Revs. Robert Gaudio; Francis H. Vogt, Pastor Emeritus.
Res., 136 Church St., 14522. Tel: 315-597-4571. [CEM]
Catechesis/Religious Programs—Tel: 315-597-4571. Angelika Sternowski, D.R.E.
Students 140.

Penfield, Monroe Co., Holy Spirit (1965), Revs. Frederick W. Bush; Ronald A. Antinarelli. In res., Rev. Francis M. Feeney.
Res., 1355 Hatch Rd., Webster, 14580. Tel: 716-671-5520.
Catechesis/Religious Programs—Tel: 716-671-5680.
Students 273.

St. Joseph (1860), Revs. Kevin P. Murphy; Lee P. Chase; Deacons Kenneth A. Scarciotta; Thomas Ecker; Sr. Patricia M. Switzer, R.S.M., Pastoral Assoc. In res., Revs. L. John Hedges; Edward Steinkirchner.
Res., 43 Gebhardt Rd., 14526. Tel: 716-586-0674. [CEM]
School—35 Gebhardt Rd., 14526. Tel: 716-586-6968; Fax: 716-586-4619.
Sisters 1; Lay Teachers 24; Students 394.
Catechesis/Religious Programs—Tel: 716-586-2281. Andrew Desmarias, D.R.E.
Students 1,024.

Penn Yan, Yates Co., St. Michael (1850), Revs. Charles Mulligan, Co-Pastor; Peter Deckman, Co-Pastor; Deacon Claude Curtin.
Res., 312 Liberty St., 14527. Tel: 315-536-7459; Fax: 315-536-7450. [CEM 2]
School—210 Keuka St., 14527. Tel: 315-536-6112. Sr. Ann Lafferty, S.S.J., Prin.
Lay Teachers 7; Students 138.
Catechesis/Religious Programs—210 Keoka St., Tel: 315-536-3794.
Students 110.
Mission—Dundee, Yates Co., St. Andrew, (1877) 312 Liberty St., P.O. Box 12, Dundee, 14837.

Phelps, Ontario Co., St. Francis / (1869). Merged with St. Felix to form St. Felix / St. Francis Parish Cluster. Rev. Edward J. Dillon.
Res., 12 Church St., 14532. Tel: 315-548-5331. [CEM]

Pittsford, Monroe Co., St. Louis (1911), Rev. James A. Schwartz; Deacon Thomas J. Driscoll. In res., Revs. John A. Reddington; James F. Slattery.
Res., 64 S. Main St., 14534. Tel: 716-586-5675; Fax: 716-387-9888.
School—11 Rand Pl., 14534. Tel: 716-586-5200. Sr. Barbara Hamm, R.S.M., Prin.
Sisters 1; Lay Teachers 20; Students 397.
Catechesis/Religious Programs—64 S. Main St., 14534. Tel: 716-381-4455.
Students 326.

Church of the Transfiguration (1983), Rev. Gerald J. Appelby; Deacon Michael Piehler; Barbara Swiecki, Pastoral Min.
Res., 50 W. Bloomfield Rd., 14534. Tel: 716-248-2427; Fax: 716-385-9870.
Catechesis/Religious Programs—Tel: 716-248-2465. Mary Presutti, D.R.E.
Students 825.

Rexville, Steuben Co., St. Mary (1845) (Irish), Rev. Daniel W. Heintz.
Res., 32 W. Main St., Canisteo, 14823. Tel: 607-698-4034. [CEM]

Rush, Monroe Co., St. Joseph (1863), Rev. John M. Mulligan, V.G., Sacramental Min.; Sr. Alice Cooney, S.S.J., Pastoral Admin.
Res., 1209 Rush West Rush Rd., 14543. Tel: 716-533-1719.
Catechesis/Religious Programs—Tel: 716-533-1760.
Students 216.

Scipio Center, Cayuga Co., St. Bernard (1867), Rev. Robert J. Downs.
Mailing Address: 2814 Center Rd., P.O. Box 157, 13147. Tel: 315-364-8172.
Res., 51 Grove St., P.O. Box 111, Moravia, 13118. Tel: 315-497-0626. [CEM]

Scottsville, Monroe Co., St. Mary of the Assumption (1853), Rev. Kevin McKenna; Deacon Michael Mahoney, Admin.
Res., 99 Main St., P.O. Box 23, 14546. Tel: 716-889-3100; Fax: 716-889-7806. [CEM]
Catechesis/Religious Programs—Tel: 716-889-8440; Fax: 716-889-7806.
Students 170.

Seneca Falls, Seneca Co., St. Patrick (1831), Rev. David Gramkee.
Res., 97 W. Bayard St., 13148. Tel: 315-568-5203; Fax: 315-568-5203. [CEM]
School—Tel: 315-568-6295.
Lay Teachers 16; Students 176.
Catechesis/Religious Programs—81 W. Bayard St., 13148. Tel: 315-568-2573.
Students 202.

Shortsville, Ontario Co., St. Dominic (1885), Rev. William J. Cosgrove; Deacon Edward A. Smith.
Res., 6 Canandaigua St., 14548. Tel: 716-289-4164. [CEM]
Catechesis/Religious Programs—Students 220.

Sodus, Wayne Co., Epiphany (1922), Rev. David J. Faraone.
Res., 105 W. Main St., 14551. Tel: 315-483-6111; Fax: 315-483-0327.
Catechesis/Religious Programs—Ann Wilkins, D.R.E.
Students 150.
Mission—Sodus Point, Wayne Co., St. Rose, (1886).

Spencerport, Monroe Co., St. John the Evangelist (1850), Rev. William C. Michatek; Deacon Larry Van Etten. In res., Rev. Paul G. Wohlrab.
Res., 60 Martha St., 14559. Tel: 716-352-5481. [CEM]
School—55 Martha St., 14559. Tel: 716-352-4550. Mr. Christopher Meagher, Prin.
Lay Teachers 16; Students K-8 213; Students PreK 26.
Catechesis/Religious Programs—Tel: 716-352-0225. Shirley Curatolo, D.R.E.
Students 686.

Stanley, Ontario Co., St. Theresa (1875), Rev. Mark A. Miller.
Res., 2050 Main St., P.O. Box 416, 14561. Tel: 716-526-5566. [CEM]
Catechesis/Religious Programs—Students 130.
Mission—Rushville, Ontario Co., St. Mary, (1869) Gilbert St., 14561.

Trumansburg, Tompkins Co., St. James the Apostle (1857), Rev. Eugene O'Hara, O.F.M. Cap.
Res., 17 Whig St., 14886. Tel: 607-387-6781. [CEM]

Union Springs, Cayuga Co., St. Michael's (1851), Rev. Paul J. Ryan; Deacon John Prave.
Springport Cove, P.O. Box 135, 13160.
Res., Main St., Box 296, Aurora, 13026. Tel: 315-364-7197. [CEM]

Van Etten, Chemung Co., St. Pius the Tenth (1954), Rev. Thomas H. Watts.
Mailing Address: c/o 132 Main St., 14889. Tel: 607-589-4494; Fax: 607-565-2014.
Res., 503 Clark St., Waverly, 14892. Tel: 607-565-2014; Fax: 607-565-2014.

Victor, Ontario Co., St. Patrick (1856), Rev. George Wiant.
Res., 115 Maple Ave., 14564. Tel: 716-924-7111; Fax: 716-742-3296. [CEM]
Catechesis/Religious Programs—115 Maple Ave., 14564. Tel: 716-924-2800.
Students 327.

Waterloo, Seneca Co., St. Mary (1868), Rev. James R. Cosgrove.
Res., 25 Center St., 13165. Tel: 315-539-2944. [CEM]

School—Tel: 315-539-3772. Sr. Brian Madigan, Prin.
Sisters of St. Joseph 2; Lay Teachers 10; Students 198.
Catechesis/Religious Programs—Tel: 315-539-8146.
Students 280.

Watkins Glen, Schuyler Co., St. Mary of the Lake (1846) (Irish-Italian), Rev. David L. Bonin.
Res., 905 N. Decatur St., 14891. Tel: 607-535-2786. [CEM 2]
Catechesis/Religious Programs—Tel: 607-535-2227.
Students 176.

Waverly, Tioga Co., St. James (1881), Rev. Thomas H. Watts. In res., Rev. William A. Burns.
Res., 503 Clark St., 14892. Tel: 607-565-2014; Fax: 607-565-2014. [CEM]
Catechesis/Religious Programs—Students 129.

Wayland, Steuben Co., St. Joseph's (1881) (German), Rev. Paul R. Schnacky; Deacon Daniel Slattery.
Res., 206 Fremont St., 14572-1298. Tel: 716-728-2228. [CEM]
School—209 Fremont St., 14572. Tel: 716-728-5700.
Sisters 1; Lay Teachers 7; Students 180.
Catechesis/Religious Programs—Tel: 716-728-2228.
Students 187.

Webster, Monroe Co., Holy Trinity (1861), Revs. Thomas F. Nellis; William M. Hart, (Retired); George Heyman; Deacons Leo Kester; Raymond R. Mielcarek.
Res., 1460 Ridge Rd., 14580. Tel: 716-265-1616. [CEM]
School—1456 Ridge Rd., 14580. Tel: 716-265-2002. Mrs. Mary Lou Kime, Prin.
Lay Teachers 14; Students 190.
Catechesis/Religious Programs—Tel: 716-265-4750.
Students 376.

St. Paul (1967), Rev. Raymond Booth. In res.,
Res., 783 Hard Rd., 14580. Tel: 716-671-2100.
Catechesis/Religious Programs—Tel: 716-671-2110. Scott Rutan, D.R.E.
Students 710.

Weedsport, Cayuga Co., St. John (1865), Rev. William B. Leone; Deacon John Tomandl; Sr. Virginia Taylor, R.S.M., Pastoral Assoc.
Res., 2667 Hamilton St., P.O. Box 266, 13166. Tel: 315-834-6266.

St. Joseph (1854), Rev. William B. Leone; Deacon John Tomandl; Sr. Virginia Taylor, R.S.M., Pastoral Assoc.
Res., 2667 Hamilton St., P.O. Box 266, 13166. Tel: 315-834-6266. [CEM]
Catechesis/Religious Programs—Tel: 315-834-9203. Walter Sheehan, D.R.E.
Students 175.

Webster, Monroe Co., St. Rita (1950), Revs. John T. Reif; Donald E. McCarthy, C.S.B.; Deacons Richard Mahany; Stan Douglas.
Res., 1008 Maple Dr., 14580. Tel: 716-671-1100; Fax: 716-671-1105 (call first).
School—Tel: 716-371-3132. Sr. Katherine Ann Rappl, R.S.M., Prin.
Sisters of Mercy 1; Lay Teachers 13; Students 250.
Catechesis/Religious Programs—Tel: 716-671-2079.
Students 697.

Wolcott, Wayne Co., St. Thomas the Apostle (1882), Rev. John V. Forni.
Res., 11956 Washington St., 14590-1133. Tel: 315-594-9430. [CEM]
Mission—Fair Haven, Cayuga Co., St. Jude Chapel, (1962). All inquiries for sacramental records for St. Thomas and St. Jude prior to July 1, 1985 can be made at St. Joseph, P.O. Box 266, Weedsport, NY 13166. Wolcott 14590.

St. Mary Magdalene (1940), Rev. John V. Forni.
Res., 11956 Washington St., 14590-1133. Tel: 315-594-9430.

Chaplains of Public Institutions

Health Care Facilities

ROCHESTER. *Genesee Hospital*. Sr. M. de Chantal, R.S.M.; Rev. George Norton, 224 Alexander St., 14607.
Highland Hospital. Sr. Susan M. Schantz, S.S.J., 1000 South Ave., 14620.
Monroe Community Hospital. Rev. William Onuh, 435 E. Henrietta Rd., 14620. Tel: 716-473-4080.
Rochester General Hospital. Rev. William Endres, 1425 Portland Ave., 14621.
St. Ann's Home/Heritage. Rev. Peter T. Bayer, 1500 Portland Ave., 14621.
St. Mary's Hospital. Rev. P. Frederick Helfrich, 89 Genesee St., 14611.
Strong Memorial Hospital. Revs. Donald J. Curtiss; Matthew A. Kawiak, 601 Elmwood Ave., 14642.

AUBURN, CAYUGA CO. *Mercy Health and Rehabilitation Center*. Cayuga Co. Sr. Mary Gertrude Dumas, O.S.F.; Rev. Paul Freemesser, 3 St. Anthony St., 13021.

BATH, STEUBEN CO. *Soliders' Home and Veterans' Hospital*. Attended by the Catholic Chaplains' Office, Steuben County. Tel: 607-776-2111, Ext. 221.

CANANDAIGUA, ONTARIO CO. *Veteran's Hospital*. Attended by the Catholic Chaplains' Office, Ontario County. Tel: 716-394-2000, Ext. 394.

ELMIRA, CHEMUNG CO. *St. Joseph Hospital*. Chemung Co. Rev. Richard T. Farrell; Sr. Margot Mann, S.S.J., 555 E. Market St., 14901. Tel: 607-733-6541.

HORNELL, STEUBEN CO. *St. James Mercy Hospital*. Steuben Co. Rev. Jeremiah P. Moynihan; Sr. Augustine Malley, R.S.M., 411 Canisteo St., 14843.

State Facilities

ROCHESTER. *Finger Lakes DDSO - Rochester Site*, 620 Westfall Rd., 14620. Tel: 716-461-8676. Sr. Elaine Hollis, S.S.J.
Rochester Psychiatric Center, 1600 South Ave., 14620. Rev. Thomas D. Hoctor.

AUBURN. *Auburn Correctional Facility*, 135 State St., 13021. Revs. John D. Dillon; James C. Enright.

ELMIRA. *Elmira Correctional Facility, Center and Camp Monterey*, P.O. Box 500, 14920. Tel: 607-734-3901. Mr. Peter G. Ladley; Mr. Michael Stanley.

GENESEO, LIVINGSTON CO. *Finger Lakes DDSO - Geneseo Site*, 3 Park St., 14454-1217. Tel: 716-243-6405. Deacon Edward Sergent.

INDUSTRY. *State Agricultural & Industrial School, Div. of Youth*. Vacant. 14474. Tel: 716-533-1700.

MORAVIA, CAYUGA CO. *Cayuga Correctional*, Rt. 38A, 13118. Tel: 315-497-1110. Deacon Gregory Kiley.

NEWARK, WAYNE CO. *Finger Lakes DDSO - Newark Site*, 703 E. Maple Ave., 14513. Tel: 315-331-1700. Deacon Edward Sergeant.

PINE CITY. *Southport Correctional Facility*, P.O. Box 2000, 14871-2000. Tel: 607-734-0850. Mrs. Theresa Stanley, Chap.

RED CREEK. *Butler Correctional Facility*, P.O. Box 388, 13143. Tel: 315-754-6216. Rev. Robert G. Smith.

SONYEA, LIVINGSTON CO. *Groveland Correctional Facility*, Rt. 36, P.O. Box 50, 14556. Tel: 716-658-2871, Ext. 362. Sr. Elizabeth Conheady, S.S.J.; Rev. William Onuh.
Livingston Correctional Facility and Seneca Correctional Facility, Rt. 36, P.O. Box 49, 14556. Deacon Nemesio Martinez.

WILLARD, SENECA CO. *Drug Treatment Center*, 7116 County Rd. 132, P.O. Box 303, 14588. Tel: 607-532-4423. Rev. Vincent Panepinto.

County Jail Chaplains

ROCHESTER. *Livingston County Jail*. Vacant. 4 Church St., Geneseo, 14454. Tel: 716-243-1100.
Monroe County Jail. Deacons Stan Grenn; William Baker; Brian Mahoney.
Tompkins County Jail. Vacant.
Yates County Jail. Vacant.

On Duty Outside the Diocese:
Reverend Fathers—
Bartollotta, Victor W., Jr., Bishop Lynch High School, 9750 Ferguson Rd., Dallas, TX 75228-3891
Celso, Thomas B., 163 Patterson, Newark, NY 14513-9119
Curran, Charles E., Southern Methodist University, 4125 Woodcreek Dr., Dallas, TX 75220
Fleming, Terence K., 1200 Seventh Ave. N., St. Petersburg, FL 33733
McMahon, Gerard J., St. David, 2523 Jackson St., Scranton, PA 18504. Tel: 717-344-9745
Metzger, Edwin B., St. Jude, P.O. Box 65, Athi River, Kenya
Murphy, David M. q, St. Charles Borromeo Church, 51 Hall St., Waltham, MA 02154

Military Chaplains:
Reverend Fathers—
Brown, Lewis E., CHC, USNR, Regional Support Group, 9170 2nd St., Ste. 120, Norfolk, VA 23511-2393

Absent on Leave:
Reverend Fathers—
Corriveau, Kip
DiSano, Frank E.
Lum, William
Schwab, Donald F.
Stacy, Ronald W.
Walczak, Melvin

Unassigned:
Reverend Fathers—
Emo, Eugene
Frederick, Ronald P.

Retired:
Reverend Monsignors—
Boyle, Charles V., 1500 Portland Ave., Rm. 813, Rochester, NY 14621
Cirrincione, Joseph A., Mailing Address: 81 Whitney St., Rochester, NY 14611
Cocuzzi, George A., St. Raymond Rectory, 1759 Castle Hill Ave., Bronx, NY 10462-4297
Duffy, John F., St. Pius X Home, 714 E. Brighton Ave, Apt. 208, Syracuse, NY 13205-2299
Gefell, Gerard J., 2332 Humphrey Rd., Cape Vincent, NY 13618
Gefell, Joseph G., 2332 Humphrey Rd., Cape Vincent, NY 13618
Murphy, J. Emmett, SSJ Convent Infirmary, 4199 East Ave., Rochester, NY 14618-3733
Quinn, Richard M., Sisters of Mercy Infirmary, 1437 Blossom Rd., Rochester, NY 14610
Roche, William M., Our Lady of Mt. Carmel Rectory, 300 Fulton St., Redwood City, CA 94062
Shannon, William H., Sisters of St. Joseph Motherhouse, 4095 East Ave., Rochester, NY 14618
Sullivan, Joseph J., S.S.J. Convent Infirmary, 4199 East Ave., Rochester, NY 14618-3733
Whalen, Leslie G., St. Ann's Home, 1500 Portland Ave., Rm. 834, Rochester, NY 14621

Reverend Fathers—
Alletto, Nicholas P., Lakeshore Nursing Home, 425 Beach Ave., Rochester, NY 14612
Brennan, Joseph P., 251 Bay Village Dr., Rochester, NY 14609
Burns, William A., St. James Rectory, 503 Clark St., Waverly, NY 14892
Calimeri, Anthony F., P.O. Box 24, Phelps, NY 14532
Callan, L. James, 500 Cook Rd., Hamlin, NY 14464
Carron, J. Walter, SSJ Convent Infirmary, 4199 East Ave., Rochester, NY 14618-3733
Cloonan, Joseph F., 4383 Cascade Way, Paso Robles, CA 93446
Dailey, Joseph W., 1471 Long Pond Rd., Apt. 420, Rochester, NY 14626
Davis, Francis R., St. Mary's Rectory, 155 State St., Corning, NY 14830
Donovan, Joseph D., S.S.J. Convent Infirmary, 4199 East Ave., Rochester, NY 14618-3733
Donovan, Robert, St. Andrews Rectory, 923 Portland Ave., Rochester, NY 14621. Tel: 716-342-8686
Egan, Joseph M., 3195 S. Main St., Horseheads, NY 14845
Ehmann, Benedict A., Holy Apostles Rectory, 7 Austin St., Rochester, NY 14606
Elsemann, Frederick F., 151 Sheppler St., Rochester, NY 14612
Erb, Francis J., P.O. Box 665, Savona, NY 14879
Feeney, Francis M., Holy Spirit Rectory, 1355 Hatch Rd., Webster, NY 14580
Foy, Edward J., St. Charles Borromeo Rectory, 130 Oakwood Ave., Elmira Heights, NY 14903
Gardner, Clarence W., St. Alphonsus Rectory, 10 Lewis St., Auburn, NY 13021
Gaynor, Joseph T., St. Alphonsus Rectory, 10 Lewis St., Auburn, NY 13021
Gaynor, William J., St. Alphonsus Rectory, 10 Lewis St., Auburn, NY 13021
Grace, Patrick J., 3742 Wildwood Rd., San Diego, CA 92107
Halloran, Emmet, St. Mary's Rectory, 95 N. Main St., Canandaigna, NY 14424
Hanna, Austin B., Sisters of Mercy Infirmary, 1437 Blossom Rd., Rochester, NY 14610
Hart, William M., 1450 Ridge Rd., Webster, NY 14580
Hayes, John S., S.S.J. Convent Infirmary, 4199 East Ave., Rochester, NY 14618-3733
Hedges, L. John, St. Joseph's Rectory, 43 Gebhardt Rd., Penfield, NY 14526
Heindl, Elmer W., St. Charles Borromeo Rectory, 3003 Dewey Ave., Rochester, NY 14616
Heisel, Raymond G., Our Mother of Sorrows Rectory, 5000 Mt. Read Blvd., Rochester, NY 14612
Hempel, John L., 109 Edgewood Ct., Forest Lakes, Oldsmar, FL 34677
Hogan, Michael C., St. John of Rochester Rectory, 18 Wickford Way, Fairport, NY 14450
Holberton, William B., 555 Spring St., Apt. 806, Bethlehem, PA 18018
Hurley, John D., St. Ann's Home, 1500 Portland Ave., Rochester, NY 14621
Jankowiak, Valentine A., St. Stanislaus, 34 St. Stanislaus St., Rochester, NY 14621
Kalafsky, Andrew J., St. Anthony of Padua Friary, P.O. Box 414, Watkins Glen, NY 14891
Kanka, Robert, St. Ann's Rectory, 31 Erie Ave., P.O. Box 605, Hornell, NY 14843
Kelly, Gerald G., 434 Pine Glen Ln., Apt. B1, Lake Worth, FL 33463
MacNamara, Robert C., St. Mary Our Mother

Rectory, 816 W. Broad St., Horseheads, NY 14845
Marvin, James J., 294 E. Lake Rd., P.O. Box 463, Honcoye, NY 14471
McCarthy, Charles L., 1101 Crystal Lake Dr., Apt. 505, Pompano Beach, NY 33064
McDonald, Elmer J., 6145 Sun Blvd., #505B, St. Petersburg, FL 33715
McDonnell, Joseph M., St. Michael's Rectory, 401 S. Main St., Newark, NY 14513
McFarland, Eugene H., St. Mary Rectory, 13 North St., Geneseo, NY 14454
McNamara, Elmer A., Mailing Address: St. Mark, P.O. Box 371, Kendall, NY 14476
McNamara, Joseph M., St. Anthony Rectory, 312 Locke Rd., R.D. 2, Groton, NY 13073
McNamara, Robert F., St. Thomas the Apostle Rectory, 4536 St. Paul Blvd., Rochester, NY 14617
Meng, Robert A., 7 Harwood Ln., East Rochester, NY 14445
Mockevicius, Charles L., 1156 Plank Rd., Webster, NY 14580
Mockevicius, Dominic, 1156 Plank Rd., Webster, NY 14580
Morgan, John A., 1986 Edgemont Dr., Camarillo, CA 93010
Nacca, John J., Holy Family Cathedral, 122 W. 8th St., P.O. Box 3208, Tulsa, OK 74101
Nangle, C. Richard, St. Francis Rectory, 185 Clark St., Auburn, NY 13021
Nolan, Norbert L., 120 Holyoke St., Bldg. 4, Apt. 2, Rochester, NY 14615
Norris, John P., St. Catherine of Siena Rectory, 26 Mendon-Ionia Rd., Mendon, NY 14506
Nowak, Bernard, 601 Seneca Manor Dr., Apt. 14L, Rochester, NY 14621
O'Brien, Bartholomew J., 103A Biltmore Dr., Horseheads, NY 14845
O'Connell, James F., St. Ann's Home, Rochester, NY
O'Connell, Richard C., St. Monica Rectory, 34 Monica St., Rochester, NY 14619
Orlando, Richard J., St. Thomas More Rectory, 2617 East Ave., Rochester, NY 14610
Reddington, John A., St. Louis Rectory, 46 S. Main St., Pittsford, NY 14534
Roach, John E., 9005 State Rd. 53, Naples, NY 14512
Sansom, Lawrence W., 571 Elmwood Terrace, Apt. B, Rochester, NY 14620
Sasso, Joseph, 8112 Oatka Trail, LeRoy, NY 14482
Schifferli, Jerome F., 7 Washington St., Box 311, Livonia, NY 14487
Schmidt, Elmer J., St. Ann Rectory, 31 Erie Avenue, Hornell, NY 14843
Shamon, Albert J., 5 S. Marvine Ave., Auburn, NY 13021
Slattery, James F., St. Louis Rectory, 60 S. Main St., Pittsford, NY 14534
Steinkirchner, Edward E., St. Joseph's Rectory, 43 Gebhardt Rd., Penfield, NY 14526
Tormey, Daniel, American Catholic University, Louvain College, Naamestraat 100, 3000 Leuven Belgium
Ventura, Gennaro J., 8247 Dutch Hollow Rd., Wayland, NY 14572
Vogt, Francis H., 115 Throop St., Palmyra, NY 14522
Vogt, Otto J., Our Lady of Lourdes Rectory, 150 Varinna Dr., Rochester, NY 14618-3733
Wahl, Raymond J., S.S.J. Convent Infirmary, 4199 East Ave., Rochester, NY 14618-3733
Walsh, John T., St. Margaret Mary Rectory, 401 Rogers Pkwy., Rochester, NY 14617
Whalen, John S., St. Thomas More Rectory, 2617 East Ave., Rochester, NY 14610
Wohlrab, Paul G., St. John the Evangelist Rectory, 60 Martha St., Spencerport, NY 14559
Zimmer, Edward A., St. John the Evangelist Rectory, 549 Humboldt St., Rochester, NY 14610

Permanent Deacons:
Abballe, Dan, St. Patrick, Macedon
Almeter, Robert C., Diocese of Syracuse
Aman, Leo, St. Charles Borromeo, Rochester
Antenucci, John, Holy Apostles/St. Anthony Cluster, Rochester
Baker, William, Monroe County Jail Min.
Beck, Thomas, St. Thomas the Apostle, Rochester
Bergeron, Albert, Our Lady Queen of Peace, Rochester
Birx, Charles, Richmond Diocese
Bowers, Owen F., St. Agnes, Avon
Burnett, George, (On leave)
Campanelli, Michael, (Retired)
Carrol, Stephen, St. Thomas More, Rochester
Caruso, Anthony, St. Theodore
Casey Lawrence B., Church of the Transfiguration, Pittsford
Cass, K. Thomas, St. Michael's, Newark
Chatterton, James, St. Mark's
Cleary, Thomas J., St. John of Rochester, Fairport
Clement, Paul F., Groveland Correctional Facility, Sonyea
Coccia, Angelo, Holy Family, Rochester
Coffey, William, St. Mary's, Rochester
Curtin, Claude, St. Michael's, Penn Yan
Datz, Ramon, St. Elizabeth Ann Seton, Hamlin
Defendorf, Raymond, St. Mary & St. Patrick, Corning
DiLallo, Gary R., St. Hyacinth, Auburn
Dispenza, Charles, St. Bridget's, Rochester
Dizer, Robert, Inactive
Doughtery, William P., St. Charles Borromeo, Elmira Heights
Douglas, Stanley, St. Rita's, Webster
Doyle Gregory J., Matt Talbot Ministry, Rochester
Driscoll, Thomas J., St. Louis, Pittsford
Dwyer, Joseph, St. Charles Borromeo, Rochester
Ecker Thomas R., St. Joseph, Penfield
Edwards, Eugene L., Jr., Good Shepherd, Henrietta
Erb, John, Holy Redeemer/St. Francis, Rochester
Federowicz, Joseph F., Elmira Psychiatric Center, Elmira
Fisher, Christopher, St. Helen's, Gates
Fitch, James E., Holy Rosary, Rochester
Fuerst, Eugene C., Medical Leave
Giugno, John M, Most Precious Blood, Rochester
Glasgow, Joseph H., Fitz, Roman Catholic Community of the 19th Ward, Rochester
Graff, Stephen J., Matt Talbot Ministry, Rochester
Graybill, Patrick A., Out of Diocese
Grenn, Stanley J., St. Augustine, FL
Haber, Francis, St. Mary's of the Lake, Watkins Glen
Hankey, James D., Immaculate Conception, Ithaca
Hoerner, Gerard A., St. Mary's, Dansville
Holmes, John, Jr., St. Elizabeth Ann Seton, Hamlin
Hunt, William R., New Bern, NC
Hurley, Daniel R., St. Mary Our Mother, Horseheads
Kester, Leo A., (Retired)
Kiley, Gregory, Cayuga Correctional Facility
Kinsky, Daniel M., Church of the Resurrection, Fairport
Kluchko, Thomas J., St. Mark, Rochester
Kohlmeier, Charles P., Mercy Prayer Center
Krupiarz, Michael J., Holy Redeemer/St. Francis, Rochester
Lawson, Gregg K., Naperville, IL
Lebron, Juan, Holy Redeemer/St. Francis
Lester, Claude E., St. Bridget/St. Joseph, Bloomfield
Lombard, Richard J., Holy Name of Jesus, Rochester
Mahany, Richard E., St. Rita's, Webster
Mahoney, Brian, Monroe County Jail
Mahoney, Michael, St. Mary of the Assumption, Scottsville
Mangione, Michael, St. Anthony / St. Patrick, Elmira
Marini, Anthony, Diocese of St. Petersburg
Martinez, Nemesio, Livingston Correctional Facility, Sonyea
Maune, William D., Park Forest, IL
McCormick, Robert W., St. Ann's, Hornell
McGuire, Michael R., St. Januarius, Naples; St. Patrick, Elmira
McNulty, Brian J., 19th Ward RCC
Medero, Felix, Community of Hope, Rochester
Melendez, Eliseo, Clinton Correctional Facility
Mercadel, Anthony J., Guardian Angels, Rochester
Mielcarek, Raymond, Holy Trinity, Webster
Morin, Kenneth, (Inactive)
Ona, Fernando V., St. Catherine's, Mendon
Palma, David, Migrant Ministry, Marion
Paluskiewicz, David L., Blessed Sacrament, Rochester
Piehler, Michael J., Transfiguration, Pittsford
Prave, John J., Cayuga Team Ministry, Union Springs
Rodriguez, Agenol, Holy Redeemer, Rochester
Rutan, Warren, St. John the Evangelist, Newark Valley
Sampson, Gregory R., St. Anne, Rochester
Scarciotta, Kenneth A., St. Joseph's, Penfield
Schmitz, William F., St. Andrew's, Rochester
Schrage, Thomas, Parish Support Ministry
Schuler, Richard, St. Helen, Rochester
Schultz, Klaus D., 19th Ward RCC
Sergeant, Edward R., Newark Development Center, Newark
Shanley, Patrick M., Holy Family, Rochester
Skerritt, Jerry, St. Mary's of the Lake, Ontario
Slattery, Daniel P., Groveland Correction Facility
Smith, Edward A., St. Dominic's, Shortsville
Srode, Walter E., Albany Diocese
Steiger, James P., St. Leo, Hilton
Stowell, Robert, St. Mary's, Elmira
Swift, John G., Our Lady Queen of Peace, Rochester
Tocci, Ronald, Church of the Assumption
Tomandl, John D., Northern Cayuga Cluster
Van Etten, Laurence A., St. John the Evangelist, Spencerport
Vargas, Carlos H., St. Francis of Assisi, Rochester
Verkon, Ronald, Corning-Painted Post RCC
Welch, George J., Our Lady of Lourdes, Elmira
Wilson, Albro C., Jr., St. Paul of the Cross, Honeoye Falls
Yanaitis, Victor M., Church of the Annunciation, Rochester
Zierle, John E., St. Pius Tenth, Rochester

INSTITUTIONS LOCATED IN THE DIOCESE

[A] GRADUATE SCHOOL OF THEOLOGY

ROCHESTER. *St. Bernard's Institute*, 1100 S. Goodman St., 14620. Tel: 716-271-3657.

For a complete listing, refer to the Colleges and Universities section.

[B] HIGH SCHOOLS

ROCHESTER. *The Aquinas Institute*, 1127 Dewey Ave., 14613. Tel: 716-254-2020. Revs. Albert R. Gaelens, C.S.B., Prin.; Richard A. Wahl, C.S.B.; Dennis J. Kauffman, C.S.B. Under the direction of the Basilian Fathers. Priests 3; Lay Teachers 58; Students 862.

Bishop Kearney High School. (Coed), 125 Kings Hwy., 14617-5596. Tel: 716-342-4000; Fax: 716-342-4694. Conducted by the Congregation of Christian Brothers in association with the School Sisters of Notre Dame, Wilton Province. Bro. Raymond J. Vercruysse, C.F.C., Pres.; Louis D'Angelo, Prin.; Mrs. Donna Gmelin, Asst. Prin. Brothers 5; Sisters 1; Lay Teachers 34; Students 540.

McQuaid Jesuit High School, 1800 S. Clinton Ave., 14618. Tel: 716-473-1130; Fax: 716-256-6171. Jesuit Fathers. Rev. James J. Fischer, S.J., Pres.; Mr. Franklin L. Kamp, Prin.; Revs. Thomas F. McManus, S.J., Asst. Treas.; Frederick G. Betti, S.J.; John P. Carriero, S.J.; John M. Costello, S.J.; James R. Dolan, S.J.; Joseph DeMaio, O.Carm.; Jack Healy, O.Carm.; Leon J. Hogenkamp, S.J.; William J. McCurdy, S.J.; William C. McCusker, S.J.; Francis J. McNamara, S.J., Alumni Dir.; James P. Malone, S.J.; Brian Murphy, O.Carm.; Lawrence J. Wroblewski, S.J. Priests 15; Lay Teachers 36; Students 744.

Nazareth Schools: The Hall; The Academy, 1001 Lake Ave., 14613. Tel: 716-458-8583; Fax: 716-647-8717. Sisters of St. Joseph 16; Lay Teachers 60; Students 691.

Our Lady of Mercy High School. (Grades 7-12), 1437 Blossom Rd., 14610. Tel: 716-288-7120. Mrs. Evelyn J. Kirst, Prin. Sisters of Mercy 13; Lay Teachers 58; Students 576.

ELMIRA. *Notre Dame High School*, 1400 Maple Ave., 14904. Tel: 607-734-2267; Fax: 607-737-8903. Sr. Mary Walter Hickey, R.S.M., Prin.; Rev. Vincent McDonough, S.J., Chap. Sisters of Mercy 10; Lay Teachers 21; Students 362.

GENEVA. *De Sales High School*. (Incorporated under the laws of the State of New York), 14456. Tel: 315-789-5111. Edward J. Tracey, Prin. Sisters of St. Joseph 1; Lay Teachers 14; Students 160.

[C] JUNIOR HIGH SCHOOLS

ROCHESTER. *All Saints Catholic Jr. High*, 170 Spencerport Rd., 14606. Total Staff 16; Students 151.

Monroe County Catholic Schools, 1150 Buffalo Rd., 14624.

Northeastern Catholic Jr. High, 125 Kings Hwy. S., 14617. Total Staff 20; Students 280.

[D] ELEMENTARY SCHOOLS, PRIVATE

ROCHESTER. *Corpus Christi School*, 546 Oxford St., 14607. Tel: 716-473-3937. Sr. Eileen Daly, S.S.J., Prin. Sisters 4; Lay Teachers 8; Students 175.

Holy Family Catholic School System-Diocese of Rochester, 421 Fulton St., 14904.

Nazareth Hall Elementary School. (Coed), 180 Raines Park, 14613. Tel: 716-458-3786. Sr. Mary Anne Laurer, Dir. Sisters of St. Joseph 6; Lay Teachers 15; Students 230.

Nazareth Hall Middle School. (Coed), 1001 Lake Ave., 14613. Tel: 716-647-8716. Sr. Elizabeth Snyder, Dir. Sisters of St. Joseph 3; Lay Teachers 8; Students 120.

School of the Holy Childhood, 100 Groton Pkwy., 14623. Tel: 716-359-3710. Day Programs and School for Mentally Retarded Children and Adults. Sr. M. Seraphine, S.S.J., Dir. Sisters of St. Joseph 6; Lay Teachers 21; Children 96; Adults 76.

EAST ROCHESTER. *Trinity Montessori School*, 501 S. Garfield St., 14445. Tel: 716-586-1044. Sr. Clare

Francis Mogenhan, S.S.J., Admin. Sisters 4; Lay Teachers 14; Students 89.

[E] HOMES FOR AGED

ROCHESTER. *St. Ann's Home for the Aged*, 1500 Portland Ave., 14621. Tel: 716-342-1700.
For a complete listing, refer to the Special Care Facilities section.
St. Ann's Nursing Home Co., Inc., 1450 Portland Ave., 14621.
For a complete listing, refer to the Special Care Facilities section.

[F] CHILD CARE INSTITUTIONS

ROCHESTER. *St. Joseph's Villa of Rochester*, 3300 Dewey Ave., 14616. Tel: 716-865-1550.
For a complete listing, refer to the Special Care Facilities section.

[G] CAMPS

LIVONIA. *Camp Stella Maris*, Conesus Lake, 4395 E.Lake Rd., 14487. Tel: 716-346-2243; Fax: 716-346-6921. Conesus Lake, 3052 E. Lake Rd., 14487. Tel: 716-346-2243; Fax: 716-346-6921. Mr. Raymond Tette, Exec. Dir.; Matthew J. Flanigan, Camp Dir.; Jay Travers, Board Pres.
Purpose: Residential camping under Catholic auspices, for boys and girls (ages 7-14) of all faiths. Encampment period: Eight weeks during summer (July/August). Rental of facility available September-June for family/youth development retreats. ACA accredited. Day Camp Center for boys and girls (ages 5-10). Encampment period: Eight weeks during July/August in conjuction with resident camp. Adventure-Based Learning Experience (ABLE) high and low challenge ropes courses ideal for building trust, confidence, cooperation, teamwork, self-esteem, communication, and leadership skills.

[H] GENERAL HOSPITALS

ROCHESTER. *St. Mary's Hospital*, 89 Genesee St., 14611. Tel: 716-464-3000.
For a complete listing, refer to the Hospitals section.
AUBURN. *Mercy Health & Rehabilitation Center Nursing Home Co., Inc.*, (1972) St. Anthony St., 13021. Tel: 315-253-0351; Fax: 315-258-3904.
For a complete listing, refer to the Hospitals section.
ELMIRA. *St. Joseph's Hospital*, 555 E. Market St., 14902. Tel: 607-733-6541.
For a complete listing, refer to the Hospitals section.
St. Joseph's Hospital Foundation, Inc., 555 E. Market St., 14902. Tel: 607-737-7004; Fax: 607-737-7837.
For a complete listing, refer to the Hospitals section.
HORNELL. *St. James Mercy Hospital*, 411 Canisteo St., 14843. Tel: 607-324-8000.
For a complete listing, refer to the Hospitals section.

[I] MONASTERIES AND RESIDENCES OF PRIESTS AND BROTHERS

ROCHESTER. *Basilian Residence*, 3497 East Ave., 14618. Tel: 716-586-4600. Revs. T. Paul Broadhurst, C.S.B.; Albert W. Cylwicki, C.S.B., Supr.; Leo A. Hetzler, C.S.B., Councilor; Leo J. Klem, C.S.B.; John R. Lee, C.S.B.; William C. Marceau, C.S.B.; Robert G. Miller, C.S.B.; John C. Murray, C.S.B.; John A. Poluikis, C.S.B., Councilor. In res., Revs. Nathaniel Karisa (Kenya); Dominic Ngugi Kaihu (Kenya).
Priests of the Region Serving Elsewhere: Rev. William J. Sheehan, C.S.B., Collegio San Clemente, Via Labicana, 95, 00184, Rome, Italy. Rev. George Kosicki, C.S.B., Divine Mercy International, Eden Hill, Stockbridge, MA, 01263. Rev. J. Gareth Poupore, C.S.B., 16 Village Trail, Honeoye Falls, 14472. Rev. Donald E. McCarthy, C.S.B., St. Rita's Church, 1008 Maple Dr., Webster, 14580. Basilian Fathers of Fisher House, 224 Fairport Rd., East Rochester, 14445. Tel: 716-381-9283. Revs. Paul F. English, Rector. Tel: 716-264-9185; John R. Cavanaugh. Tel: 716-385-1353; Paul F. Walsh, C.S.B.
Becket Hall, 314 Gregory St., 14620. Tel: 716-461-2890; Fax: 716-328-3149. Residence for Pre-Theologate candidates. Rev. John A. DeSocio, Dir. Students 4.
Residence of Basilian Fathers-The Aquinas Institute, 402 Augustine St., 14613. Tel: 716-254-1190. Revs. Dennis J. Kauffman, C.S.B., Supr.; Peter J. Etlinger, C.S.B.; Albert R. Gaelens, C.S.B.; Thomas M. Miller, C.S.B.; Richard A. Wahl, C.S.B. Priests 5.
St. George's Rectory, 545 Hudson Ave., 14605. Tel: 716-232-4111. Rev. Charles Mockevicius, O.F.M., Admin.
Whitefriars Priory, 625 Colebrook Dr., 14617. Tel: 716-266-2560. Revs. Brian Murphy, O.Carm.; Joseph DeMaio, O.Carm.; Jack Healy, O.Carm., Prior; Matthew Temple, O.Carm.
INTERLAKEN. *St. Fidelis Friary*, 7790 County Rd. 153, 14847. Tel: 607-532-4423. Capuchin Friars-Province of St. Mary (Order of Friars Minor Capuchin). Revs. Eugene O'Hara, O.F.M.Cap., Supr.; Nelson J. Ruppert, O.F.M.Cap., Vicar; Oliver J. O'Connor, O.F.M.Cap., Preaching Ministry; Julian Phelan, O.F.M.Cap., Preaching Ministry. Priests 4.
PIFFARD. *Abbey of the Genesee*, 14533. Tel: 716-243-0660; 243-2220 (Retreat House). The Order of Cistercians of the Strict Observance (Trappists). Rt. Rev. John Eudes Bamberger, O.C.S.O., Abbot; Revs. Francis R. Steger, O.C.S.O., Prior; Thomas Aquinas Bond, O.C.S.O.; John J. Denburger, O.C.S.O.; Marcellus R. Earl, O.C.S.O.; Raymond J. Fournier, O.C.S.O.; Jerome J. Machar, O.C.S.O.; Robert J. Moore, O.C.S.O.; Regis C. Tompkins, O.C.S.O.; Justin R. Sheehan, O.C.S.O.; Joseph F. Stanton, O.C.S.O.; Aelred W. Wentz.
Absent on Leave: Rev. Michael M. Hayden, O.C.S.O. Professed Monks 26; Priests 13; Novices 2; Oblates 1; Total in Community (Piffard) 42.
PINE CITY. *Mount Saviour Monastery*, 231 Monastery Rd., 14871-9770. Tel: 607-734-1688; Fax: 607-734-1689. Very Rev. Martin Boler, O.S.B., Prior; Revs. James Cronin, O.S.B.; James Kelly, O.S.B.; Gerald Ragis, O.S.B. (BUR); Timothy Courcy, O.S.B.
Priests of the province serving elsewhere: Rev. Paul Geraghty, O.S.B., Montreal Archdiocese. Professed Monks 16; Professed Priests 6; Total in Community 16.
WATKINS GLEN. *St. Anthony of Padua Friary*, Lakeview Ave., P.O. Box 41, 14891. Tel: 607-535-2686. Franciscan Friars. Rev. Austin J. Budnick, O.F.M. Affiliated with the Assumption of the B.V.M. Province, with headquarters in Pulaski, Wisconsin. Priests 1.

[J] CONVENTS AND RESIDENCES FOR SISTERS

ROCHESTER. *Nazareth Convent*, 16 Lake View Park, 14613-1798. Tel: 716-458-3443. Sr. Ann Vincent DeRitis, Local Coord. Sisters 42.
North American Union-Sisters of Our Lady of Charity, OLC Holy Angels Convent, 1280 N. Winton Rd., 14609-5897. Tel: 716-654-8600. Sr. Frances Aguillon, Local Supr. Professed Sisters 5.
St. Joseph Convent Infirmary, 4199 East Ave., 14618-3733. Tel: 716-381-4064. Infirmary and home for retired Sisters of Saint Joseph of Rochester, Inc. Sr. Mary Ida Lynch, S.S.J., Local Coord.; Sr. Mary Margaret Merkel, S.S.J., Admin.; Rev. Donald J. Curtiss, Chap. Sisters 75; Priests 6.
Sisters of Mercy of the Americas Regional Community of Rochester, 1437 Blossom Rd., 14610. Tel: 716-288-2710. Sr. Ann Miller, Pres. In res., Rev. Matthew Kawlak. Tel: 716-288-6272. Professed Sisters 212; Temporary Professed 1; Perpetual Vows 212.
Sisters St. Joseph Motherhouse, 4095 East Ave., 14618-3798. Tel: 716-586-1000; Fax: 716-586-1193. Motherhouse of the Sisters of St. Joseph of the Diocese of Rochester. Sr. Rosemary St. Peter, Congregational Pres.; Rev. Msgr. William H. Shannon, Chap. Professed Sisters in Community 442.
Spirit House, Inc., 72 Dorvid Rd., 14617. Tel: 716-544-5698. Sr. Mary Ann Ayers, R.S.M., Dir.
ELMIRA. *Monastery of Mary the Queen, Dominican Nuns*, 1310 W. Church St., 14905. Tel: 607-734-9506. Sr. Mary of the Sacred Heart, O.P., Prioress. Solemn Vows 12; Perpetual Vows 1.
PITTSFORD. *Monastery of Our Lady and St. Joseph Carmelite Monastery*, 1931 W. Jefferson Rd., 14534. Tel: 716-427-7094. Discalced Carmelite Nuns. Mother Miriam of the Angels, O.C.D., Prioress. Professed Nuns with Solemn Vows 9; Externs with Simple Vows 1.

[K] RETREAT HOUSES

ROCHESTER. *Mercy Prayer Center*, 65 Highland Ave., 14620. Conducted and subsidized by Sisters of Mercy. Total in residence 3; Total Staff 6.
S.S.J. Spirituality Center, 402 Rogers Pkwy., 14617. Tel: 716-336-4370. Mary Louise Heffernan, S.S.J., Dir.; Total in residence 4; Total Staff 7.
CANANDAIGUA. *Notre Dame Retreat House*, Box 342, 5151 Foster Rd., 14424. Tel: 716-394-5700. Revs. Frederick C. Brinkman, C.SS.R., Dir.; Timothy F. Keating, C.Ss.R.; Leo F. Dunn, C.Ss.R.
CORNING. *Anawim Community Center*, 122 E. First St., 14830. Tel: 607-936-4965. Rev. Richard Rusk (MET), Admin.

[L] MISCELLANEOUS LISTINGS

ROCHESTER. *Apostleship of Prayer*, Diocesan Pastoral Center, 1150 Buffalo Rd., 14624. Tel: 716-328-3210. Rev. Thomas P. Mull; Mary Kessler, Diocesan Dir. Tel: 716-328-3210.
Archivist, 219 Stenson St., 14606 Tel: 716-458-6079. Rev. William E. Graf, Dir. of Archives and Records, 4536 St. Paul Blvd., 14617. Tel: 716-338-1602. Rev. Robert F. McNamara, Archivist.
Catherine McAuley Housing, 1694 St. Paul St., 14621. Tel: 716-338-7070. Sr. Janet Korn, R.S.M., Pres.
Catholic Charismatic Renewal, 127 W. Meadows Dr., 14616. Tel: 716-321-1265. Diocesan Liaison Team: Don Germano; Louise Dale; David Valone; Robert Cirre; Rev. William A. Moorby, Spiritual Advisor.
Catholic Committee on Scouting, 1150 Buffalo Rd., 14624. Tel: 716-328-3210. Michael Theisen.
Censores Librorum, 1150 Buffalo Rd., 14624. Revs. Joseph A. Hart; Benedict A. Ehmann; Rev. Msgr. William H. Shannon; Rev. William E. Graf.
Dunn Tower Apartments, Inc., 100 Dunn Tower Dr., 14606. Ann R. Huber, Mgr.
Family Rosary For Peace, Inc., P.O. Box 11007, 14611. Tel: 716-235-6955. Rev. Msgr. Joseph A. Cirrincione; Rev. George Norton, Sec.
Holy Childhood Association, 1150 Buffalo Rd., 14624. Tel: 716-436-9200. Rev. Robert Bradler, Dir.
Marriage Encounter Apostolate. (Worldwide). 214 E. William St., Bath, 14810. Tel: 607-776-4870. John and Belinda Brasley; Rev. John Murray, C.S.B.
Melita House for Pregnant Women, 124 Evergreen St., 14605. Tel: 716-232-3656. Sisters of Mercy of Rochester. Contact Persons: Michele Hannagan; Peggy Wyand-Block. Total Staff 6; Total assisted in residence 22; Total assisted in aftercare 100.
Providence Housing Development Corporation, 1150 Buffalo Rd., 14624.
Rochester Catholic Worker Bethany House, 169 St. Bridget's Dr., 14605. Tel: 716-454-4197. Donna Ecker, Contact Person. Total staff 4.
St. Francis de Sales Deaf Assn., 75 Ernestine St., 14619. Tel: 716-235-1812 (Voice); 235-3849 (TTY). Rev. Raymond H. Fleming, Dir.
St. Joseph's House of Hospitality, 402 South Ave., 14620. Tel: 716-232-3262. Mailing Address: Box 1062, 14603. Tel: 716-232-3262. Sr. Marilyn Pray, S.S.J., Contact Person.
St. Joseph's Villa Foundation, 3300 Dewey Ave., 14616. Tel: 716-865-1550. Judith Van Bramer, Dir. of Development.
St. Theodore's Apartment Housing Development Fund Co., Inc. (Dunn Tower II Apts.), 200 Dunn Tower Dr., 14606.
OWEGO. *Tioga County Rural Ministry, Inc.*, 60 North Ave., 13827. Tel: 607-687-3021. Sr. Lisette O'Brien, R.S.M., Pres. Total Staff 3; Total assisted 3,220.
SPENCERPORT. *Legion of Mary*, 60 Martha St., 14559. Tel: 716-352-9052. Rev. Paul G. Wohlrab, Spiritual Dir. - Rochester Comitium, Rochester Comitium, 191 Furlong St., Rochester, 14621-3959. Tel: 716-266-8087. Mrs. Vera Calnan, Pres.

[M] CAMPUS MINISTRY

ROCHESTER. *Diocesan Office of Campus Ministry*, Newman Community, University of Rochester, Interfaith Chapel, Wilson Blvd., 14627-0508. Tel: 716-275-4322. Rev. Gary Tyman. Tel: 716-442-1402.
Campus Ministry Office, Eastman School of Music, 4245 East Ave., 14618. Dr. Joseph G. Kelly. Tel: 716-389-2726; Joelle LaPorte.
Nazareth College of Rochester, 4245 East Ave., 14618. Tel: 716-586-2525, Ext. 331; Fax: 716-586-2452. Sr. Kathleen Weider, S.S.J., Dir., Campus Min. Tel: 716-586-2525 Ext. 331; Deacon Leo Aman.
Catholic Campus Parish, Rochester Institute of Technology, Interfaith Center, 40 Lomb Memorial Dr., 14623. Tel: 716-475-2136. Rev. Joseph Catarise. Tel: 716-475-2135; Sr. Marlene Vigna, R.S.M. Tel: 716-475-2138.
Monroe Community College - Office of the Catholic Chaplain, 1000 E. Henrietta Rd., 14623. Tel: 716-292-2558, Ext. 292. Joan Ann Kirkeby-Prosser.
St. John Fisher College, 3690 East Ave., 14618. Tel: 716-385-8368. Rev. Paul F. English, C.S.B., Dir., Campus Ministry; Deirdre Hetzler.
State University College at Brockport, the Newman Oratory of Brockport, NY, Inc., 101 Kenyon St., 14420. Tel: 716-637-5036. Rev. Theodore J. Auble. Tel: 716-637-5036; Sandra Shields; Victorine Edwards.
State University College at Geneseo (Geneseo), Newman Parish, Interfaith Center, 11 Franklin St., Box 265, Geneseo, 14454. Tel: 716-243-1460. Rev. James E. Hewes; David Desmond.
The Cornell Catholic Community, Inc. (Ithaca), Cornell University, G-22 Anabel Taylor Hall, Ithaca, 14853. Tel: 607-255-4228; Fax: 607-255-7793. Revs. Michael Mahler, Dir., Campus Ministry. Tel: 607-255-6013; Richard Murphy. Tel: 607-255-1078; Dr. Edward J. Ondrako; Sr. Donna M. Fannon, M.H.S.H.; Sr. Margaret Brogden, M.H.S.H.; Ms. Dawn Redlin, Business Mgr. Tel: 607-255-6012.
The Catholic Community of Ithaca College, Muller Chapel, Ithaca College, 453 Danby Rd., Ithaca, 14850. Tel: 607-274-3103. Rev. Thomas Valenti. Tel: 607-274-3184.
Elmira College, 1 Park Place, Elmira, 14901. Tel: 607-735-1824, Ext. 1824. Rev. Severine Yagaza.
Finger Lakes Community College c/o St. Mary's Church, 95 N. Main St., Canandaigua, 14424. Rev. Brian Cool; Thomas Tanchick, Youth Minister. Tel: 716-394-1220.
Corning Community College c/o Eastside Catholic Parish, 161 High St., Elmira, 14901. Rev. Mary Skinner. Tel: 607-734-1688.

Hobart and William Smith College, St. Stephen's Church, 48 Pulteney St., Geneva, 14456. Rev. Msgr. Gerald C. Krieg. Tel: 315-789-1124.

Keuka College c/o St. Michael's Church, 312 Liberty St., Penn Yan, 14527. Revs. Charles Mulligan; Peter Deckman. Tel: 315-536-4411.

Roberts Wesleyan College c/o St. Christopher's Church, 3350 Union St., North Chili, 14514. Rev. Bernard Dollen. Tel: 716-594-1400.

Wells College, c/o St. Patrick Church, Main St., P.O. Box 116, Aurora, 13026-0296. Rev. Paul J. Ryan. Tel: 315-364-7197; Gregory Wesley, Assoc. Chap.

Cayuga Community College, P.O. Box 1000, Auburn, 13021. Sr. Chris Lloyd, S.S.J., Chap. Tel: 315-255-1743.

PENN YAN. *St. Michael's Church*, Keuka College, 312 Liberty St., 14527. Tel: 315-536-7459; Fax: 315-536-7450. Revs. Charlie Mulligan; Peter Deckman.

RELIGIOUS INSTITUTES OF MEN REPRESENTED IN THE DIOCESE

For further details refer to the corresponding bracketed number in the Religious Institutes of Men or Women section.

[0170]—*Basilian Fathers*.—C.S.B.
[0200]—*Benedictine Monks*.—O.S.B.
[0470]—*The Capuchin Friars*. (Province of St. Mary).—O.F.M.Cap.
[0270]—*Carmelite Fathers and Brothers*.—O.Carm.
[0350]—*Cistercians Order of the Strict Observance (Trappists)*.—O.C.S.O.
[0310]—*Congregation of Christian Brothers*. (Eastern Prov.).—C.F.C.
[1140]—*Congregation of the Sacred Hearts of Jesus and Mary*.—SS.CC.
[0480]—*Conventual Franciscans*. (Buffalo & Immaculate Conception Provinces).—O.F.M.Conv.
[0520]—*Franciscan Friars*. (Assumption B.V.M. Prov.).—O.F.M.
[0690]—*Jesuit Fathers and Brothers*. (New York Province).—S.J.
[0610]—*Priests of the Congregation of Holy Cross*.—C.S.C.
[1070]—*Redemptorist Fathers*. (Baltimore Province).—C.SS.R.
[0760]—*Society of Mary (Marianists)*.—S.M.
[1060]—*Society of the Precious Blood*.—C.PP.S.
[0560]—*Third Order Regular of Saint Francis*.—T.O.R.

RELIGIOUS INSTITUTES OF WOMEN REPRESENTED IN THE DIOCESE

[3110]—*Congregation of Our Lady of the Retreat in the Cenacle*.—R.C.
[0760]—*Daughters of Charity of St. Vincent de Paul*.—D.C.
[0420]—*Discalced Carmelite Nuns*.—O.C.D.
[1050]—*Dominican Contemplative Nuns*.—O.P.
[1070-13]—*Dominican Sisters (Adrian, MI)*.—O.P.
[1070-05]—*Dominican Sisters (Amityville, NY)*.—O.P.
[2575]—*Institute of the Sisters of Mercy of the Americas*. (Rochester, NY).—R.S.M.
[2470]—*Maryknoll Sisters of St. Dominic*.—M.M.
[]—*Misioneras Guadalupanas del Espiritu Santo*.
[3070]—*North American Union Sisters of Our Lady of Charity*.—N.A.U.-O.L.C.
[3430]—*Religious Teachers Filippini*.—M.P.F.
[2970]—*School Sisters of Notre Dame*.—S.S.N.D.
[3950]—*Sisters of Saint Mary of Namur*.—S.S.M.N.
[1800]—*Sisters of St. Francis of the Third Order Regular (Williamsville, New York)*.—O.S.F.
[3830-14]—*Sisters of St. Joseph (Rochester)*.—S.S.J.
[3840]—*Sisters of St. Joseph of Carondolet*.—C.S.J.
[3730]—*Sisters of the Order of St. Basil the Great*.—O.S.B.M.
[1490]—*Sisters of the Third Franciscan Order*.—O.S.F.
[3620]—*Sisters, Servants of Mary Immaculate*.—S.S.M.I.
[2160]—*Sisters, Servants of the Immaculate Heart of Mary*.—I.H.M.

DIOCESAN CEMETERIES

ROCHESTER. *Holy Sepulchre*.

REGIONAL CEMETERIES

AUBURN. *St. Joseph's*.
CORNING. *St. Mary*.
ELMIRA. *SS. Peter and Paul's*.
GENEVA. *St. Mary's and St. Patrick's*.

NECROLOGY

† Brennan, Thomas F., Corning, NY, St. Mary's Church. —Died July 30, 1996.
† Hogan, Joseph F., (Retired). —Died March 22, 1996.
† Matuszewski, Leo J., (Retired). —Died Nov. 8, 1996.
† McHale, Michael A., Rochester, NY, Rochester Institute of Technology. —Died Dec. 25, 1995.
† O'Shea, Daniel, New York, NY, General Theological Seminary. —Died Sept. 1, 1996.
† Tobin, William, Elmira Heights, NY, St. Charles Borromeo Rectory. —Died Oct. 29, 1996.
† Trott, William, Livonia, NY, St. Joseph. —Died Oct. 2, 1996.
† Vogt, George, (Retired). —Died June 27, 1996.

Diocese of Rockford

(Dioecesis Rockfordiensis)

Most Reverend

THOMAS G. DORAN, D.D., J.C.D.

Bishop of Rockford; ordained December 20, 1961; appointed Bishop of Rockford April 19, 1994; consecrated June 24, 1994; installed June 24, 1994. *Res., 1243 N. Court St., Rockford, IL, 61103.*

Most Reverend

ARTHUR J. O'NEILL, D.D., V.G.

Retired Bishop of Rockford; ordained March 27, 1943; appointed Bishop of Rockford August 19, 1968; consecrated October 11, 1968; installed October 11, 1968; retired April 19, 1994. *Res., 14 Country Club Beach, Rockford, IL, 61103.* Tel.: 815-877-5078.

ESTABLISHED SEPTEMBER 23, 1908.

Square Miles 6,457.

Comprises Jo Daviess, Stephenson, Winnebago, Boone, McHenry, Carroll, Ogle, DeKalb, Kane, Whiteside and Lee Counties in the State of Illinois.

For legal titles of parishes and diocesan institutions, consult the Chancery Office.

Diocesan Chancery: 1245 N. Court St., P.O. Box 7044, Rockford, IL, 61126-7044. Tel.: 815-962-3709; Fax: 815-968-2824.

STATISTICAL OVERVIEW

Personnel	
Bishop	1
Retired Bishops	1
Abbots	1
Retired Abbots	2
Priests: Diocesan Active in Diocese	113
Priests: Active Outside Diocese	4
Priests: Retired, Sick or Absent	28
Number of Diocesan Priests	145
Religious Priests in Diocese	61
Extern Priests in Diocese	6
Ordinations:	
Diocesan Priests	2
Transitional Deacons	5
Permanent Deacons	15
Permanent Deacons in Diocese	100
Total Brothers	15
Total Sisters	366
Parishes	
Parishes	101
With Resident Pastor:	
Resident Diocesan Priests	85
Resident Religious Priests	7
Without Resident Pastor:	
Administered by Priests	8
Administered by Pastoral Teams, etc.	1
Missions	6
Pastoral Centers	48
Professional Ministry Personnel:	
Sisters	24
Lay Ministers	84
Welfare	
Catholic Hospitals	4
Total Assisted	477,646
Health Care Centers	1
Total Assisted	375
Homes for the Aged	4
Total Assisted	504
Day Care and Extended Day Care Centers	1
Total Assisted	56
Specialized Homes	1
Total Assisted	246
Special Centers for Social Services	10
Total Assisted	285,345
Residential Care of Disabled	2
Total Assisted	71
Educational	
Diocesan Students in Other Seminaries	22
Total Seminarians	22
High Schools, Diocesan and Parish	6
Total Students	3,462
High Schools, Private	2
Total Students	761
Elementary Schools, Diocesan and Parish	41
Total Students	11,451
Catechesis/Religious Education:	
High School Students	4,959
Elementary Students	21,105
Total Students Under Catholic Instruction	41,760
Teachers in the Diocese:	
Priests	13
Sisters	30
Lay Teachers	754
Vital Statistics	
Receptions into the Church:	
Infant Baptism Totals	6,411
Adult Baptism Totals	356
Received into Full Communion	457
First Communions	6,290
Confirmations	3,535
Marriages:	
Catholic	1,005
Interfaith	605
Total Marriages	1,610
Deaths	2,153
Total Catholic Population	280,652
Total Population	1,201,303

Former Bishops—Most Rev. PETER J. MULDOON, D.D., ord. Dec. 18, 1886; cons. Titular Bishop of Tamassus and Auxiliary Bishop of Chicago, July 25, 1901; appt. Bishop of Rockford, Sept. 28, 1908; made Assistant to the Pontifical Throne, June 8, 1921; died Oct. 8, 1927.—Most Rev. EDWARD F. HOBAN, S.T.D., ord. July 11, 1903; cons. Titular Bishop of Colonia and Auxiliary Bishop of Chicago, Dec. 21, 1921; appt. Bishop of Rockford, Feb. 10, 1928; appt. Assistant at the Pontifical Throne, Nov. 25, 1937; appt. Titular Bishop of Listra and Coadjutor Bishop of Cleveland, Nov. 16, 1942; succeeded to the See of Cleveland, Nov. 2, 1945; died Sept. 22, 1966.—Most Rev. JOHN J. BOYLAN, D.D., Ph.D., ord. July 28, 1915; appt. Nov. 21, 1942; cons. Feb. 17, 1943; died July 19, 1953.—Most Rev. RAYMOND P. HILLINGER, D.D., ord. April 2, 1932; appt. Nov. 3, 1953; cons. Dec. 29, 1953; appt. Titular Bishop of Derbe and Auxiliary Bishop of Chicago, June 27, 1956; died Nov. 13, 1971.—Rt. Rev. DONALD M. CARROLL, D.D., appt. June 27, 1956; resigned Sept. 25, 1956.—Most Rev. LORAS T. LANE, D.D., ord. March 19, 1937; appt. Titular Bishop of Bencenna and Auxiliary of Dubuque, May 29, 1951; cons. Aug. 20, 1951; appt. to Rockford, Oct. 11, 1956; died July 22, 1968.

Diocesan Chancery—1245 N. Court St., P.O. Box 7044, Rockford, 61126-7044. Tel: 815-962-3709; Fax: 815-968-2824. Address all official business to this office. Office Hours: Mon.-Fri. 9-5.

Vicars General—Most Rev. ARTHUR J. O'NEILL, D.D., V.G.; Rev. Msgr. DAVID D. KAGAN, J.C.L., V.G.; Rev. Msgr. THOMAS C. BRADY, P.A., V.G., Ph.D., *1245 N. Court St., P.O. Box 7044, Rockford, 61126.* Tel: 815-962-3709.

Moderator of the Curia—Rev. Msgr. DAVID D. KAGAN, J.C.L., V.G.

Episcopal Vicars and Secretary—

Vicar for Catholic Education—Very Rev. F. JAMES LARSON.

Vicar for Clergy and Religious—Rev. Msgr. MICHAEL A. BINSFELD.

Vicar for Ministry to Hispanics—Very Rev. WILLIAM R. SCHUESSLER.

Vicar for Social Ministries—Very Rev. LEO J. BARTEL.

Vicar for Spiritual Formation—Very Rev. KARL P. GANSS.

Secretary for Finance and Administration—Mr. WAYNE LENELL, C.P.A., Ph.D.

Chancellor—Rev. Msgr. CHARLES W. MCNAMEE, J.C.L.

Vice Chancellor—Rev. Msgr. MICHAEL A. BINSFELD.

Bishop's Secretary for Retired Priests—Rev. Msgr. CHARLES W. MCNAMEE, J.C.L.

Secretary to the Bishop/Master of Ceremonies—Rev. GLENN L. NELSON.

Diocesan Tribunal—850 N. Church St., Rockford, 61103. Tel: 815-963-8960; Fax: 815-963-9962. Address all official business to this office.

Judicial Vicar—Rev. Msgr. DAVID D. KAGAN, J.C.L.

Secretary and Director of the Tribunal—Sr. AUDREY STRAUB, S.S.N.D., J.C.L.

Secretary for Administrative Processes—Rev. ROBERT J. SWEENEY.

Promoter of Justice—Rev. Msgr. JOHN J. MITCHELL.

Defender of the Bond—Sr. AUDREY STRAUB, S.S.N.D., J.C.L.

Pro Synodal Judges—Rev. Msgr. RAYMOND J. WAHL, P.A., J.C.D.; Rev. Msgr. CHARLES W. MCNAMEE, J.C.L.; Revs. GERALD P. KOBBEMAN; WILLIAM A. KRIEGSMANN; FRANCIS E. MCDONNELL.

Advocates—Rev. THOMAS J. MONAHAN, Ph.D.; Sr. ELAINE KERSCHER, O.S.F.; Sr. BEVERLY JEANNE HOWE, O.P.
Experts—Rev. LAWRENCE M. URBANIAK, Ph.D.; Mr. MICHAEL M. KAGAN, M.A.
Notaries—Mrs. MARGARET CACCIATORE; Mrs. DENISE GEORGE; Mrs. DONNA HAYES.
Diocesan Consultors—Rev. Msgr. THOMAS C. BRADY; Rev. Msgr. DAVID D. KAGAN; Rev. Msgr. THOMAS L. DZIELAK; Rev. Msgr. DANIEL J. HERMES; Rev. Msgr. JOHN J. MITCHELL; Rev. Msgr. WILLIAM H. SCHWARTZ; Rev. Msgr. RAYMOND J. WAHL; Very Rev. F. JAMES LARSON; Revs. WILLIAM J. CLAUSEN; GERALD P. KOBBEMAN; ANDREW J. PLESA; RICHARD M. RUSSO.
Deans—Aurora Deanery: Rev. Msgr. EDWARD S. WRIGHT, DeKalb Deanery: Very Rev. FRANCIS P. KENNEDY, Elgin Deanery: Very Rev. ROBERT B. HOFFMAN, Freeport Deanery: Very Rev. P. WILLIAM MCDONNELL, McHenry County Deanery: Rev. Msgr. PHILIP E. O'NEIL, Rockford Deanery: Rev. Msgr. JOHN J. MITCHELL, Sterling Deanery: Very Rev. THOMAS E. BALES.
Vicaress for Religious Women—Sr. JAMES MARIE O'CONNOR, S.S.N.D., *1245 N. Court St., P.O. Box 7044, Rockford, 61126.* Tel: 815-962-3709; Fax: 815-968-2824.

Diocesan Offices and Directors

Black Catholic Ministry—Vacant, *1526 S. Main St., Rockford, 61102.* Tel: 815-965-6993.
Campaign for Human Development—Mr. THOMAS MCKENNA, Dir., *921 W. State St., Rockford, 61102.* Tel: 815-965-0895.
Catholic Charismatic Renewal Services—Mr. RON BERGMAN, Diocesan Liaison, *1910 Bracknel Blvd., Rockford, 61103.* Tel: 815-654-4111.
Catholic Office of the Deaf—Rev. GLENN L. NELSON, Dir., *1245 N. Court St., P.O. Box 7044, Rockford, 61126.* Tel: 815-962-3709; 962-2994 (TDD).
Catholic Relief Services—Mr. THOMAS MCKENNA, *921 W. State St., Rockford, 61102.* Tel: 815-965-0895; Fax: 815-965-6141.
Cemeteries—Mr. HARRY KOPLIN, Dir., *8616 W. State St., Winnebago, 61088.* Tel: 815-965-1637; Fax: 815-965-9632.
Censores Librorum—Rev. Msgr. CHARLES W. MCNAMEE, J.C.L.; Rev. FRANCIS E. MCDONNELL.
Charities—Mr. BRISTON FERNANDES, Dir. Offices: *921 W. State St., Rockford, 61102.* Tel: 815-965-0895; Fax: 815-965-6141., *1700 N. Farnsworth Ave., Aurora, 60505., 1315 Pleasant St., DeKalb, 60115., 566 Dundee Ave., Elgin, 60120., 813 S. State Ave., Freeport, 61032., 202 Summit St., Galena, 61036., 5215 W. Bull Valley Rd., McHenry, 60050., 801 W. 11th St., Sterling, 61081.*
Satellite Offices—860 Biester Dr., 206 C, Belvidere, 61008., 105 1/2 W. 1st St., Dixon, 61021.
Clergy Relief Society, Priests' Retirement Committee—Rev. Msgr. CHARLES W. MCNAMEE, J.C.L., Exec. Sec., *1245 N. Court St., P.O. Box 7044, Rockford, 61126* Tel: 815-962-3709; Fax: 815-968-2824.
Communications—Mr. OWEN PHELPS, JR., Dir., *921 W. State St., Rockford, 61102.* Tel: 815-963-3471; Fax: 815-968-2808.
Conciliation and Arbitration Office—Mr. HENRY J. CLOSE, Chm., *124 N. Water St., Ste. 300, P.O. Box 4749, Rockford, 61110.* Tel: 815-968-7591.
Council of Catholic Women, Diocesan—Rev. Msgr. THOMAS L. DZIELAK, Moderator, *708 10th Ave., Rock Falls, 61071.* Tel: 815-625-4508. Mrs. DORIS WITKOWSKI, Pres., *10478 Geneva St., Roscoe, 61073.* Tel: 815-623-2289.
Cursillo Movement—Rev. HAROLD L. NILGES, Dir., *340 Stott St., Genoa, 60135.* Tel: 815-784-2355.
Development Office—Mr. DAVID HOUGAN, Dir., *921 W. State St., Rockford, 61102.* Tel: 815-964-6711.
Divine Worship, Office for—(and RCIA Resources)—Rev. JOHN A. SLAMPAK, Dir., *921 W. State St., Rockford, 61102.* Tel: 815-963-0344; Fax: 815-963-9747.
Ecumenism, Office of—Rev. ROBERT JACKSON, Dir., *1005 Julien St., Belvidere, 61008.* Tel: 815-544-7788.
Education—Very Rev. F. JAMES LARSON, Vicar; Sr. PATRICIA DOWNEY, O.P., Supt., Schools; Sr. JEANETTE LANDUYT, O.P., Assoc. Supt.; Ms. PEG BOWMAN, Dir., Dept. of Catechesis, *1260 N. Church St., Rockford, 61103.* Tel: 815-962-7791.
Ethicist for Health Care Issues, Diocesan—Rev. TIMOTHY L. DOHERTY, *921 W. State St., Rockford, 61102.* Tel: 815-963-4007; Fax: 815-962-2966.
Evangelization—Very Rev. KARL P. GANSS, Dir., *302 Fisk Ave., Dekalb, 60115.* Tel: 815-758-5432; Fax: 815-758-2487.
Family Life & Youth Ministry—Dirs.: Mr. DON GRAMER; Mrs. DON GRAMER, *7708 E. McGregor Rd., Rockford, 61102.* Tel: 815-965-5011.
Finance and Administration—Mr. WAYNE LENELL, C.P.A., Ph.D., Sec., Fin. & Admin., *921 W. State St., Rockford, 61102.* Tel: 815-964-5231; Fax: 815-964-5501.
Hispanic Ministry Offices—Very Rev. WILLIAM R. SCHUESSLER, Vicar, *921 W. State St., Rockford, 61102.* Tel: 815-962-8042. Offices in Diocese: Aurora Deanery: *Centro Cristo Rey, 315 N. Root St., Aurora, 60505* DeKalb Deanery: *Centro Cuerpo de Cristo, 308 Fisk Ave., DeKalb, 60115.* Elgin Deanery: *Centro Jesus Resucitado, 90 N. Kennedy Dr., Carpentersville, 60110.* McHenry Deanery: *Centro San Jose, 207 E. Brainard St., Harvard, 60033.* Rockford Deanery: *Centro Sembrador, 921 W. State St., Rockford, 61102.* Sterling Deanery: *Tu C.A.S.A., 202 W. 6th St., Sterling, 61081.*
Holy Childhood Association—Rev. NEAL KAMINSKI, O.F.M., Dir., *921 W. State St., Rockford, 61102.* Tel: 815-962-2934; Fax: 815-962-2966.
Investment and Loan—Mr. WAYNE LENELL, Sec., Fin. & Admin., *921 W. State St., Rockford, 61102.* Tel: 815-964-5231.
Lay Volunteer Recruitment—Very Rev. KARL P. GANSS, Contact Person, *302 Fisk Ave., DeKalb, 60115.* Tel: 815-758-5432; Fax: 815-758-2487.
Legion of Mary—Rev. WILLIAM P. COLLINS, Dir., *517 Elm St., Rockford, 61102.* Tel: 815-968-0865.
Liturgical Commission, Diocesan—Rev. JOHN A. SLAMPAK, Dir., *921 W. State St., Rockford, 61102.* Tel: 815-963-0344.
Men Religious—Rev. NEAL KAMINSKI, O.F.M., Vicar, *921 W. State St., Rockford, 61102.* Tel: 815-962-2934; Fax: 815-962-2966.
Ministry Formation, Office of—Mr. JOHN MCGRATH, Dir., *921 W. State St., Rockford, 61102.* Tel: 815-962-8873; Fax: 815-962-2966.
Ministry to Priests Program—Rev. Msgr. MICHAEL A. BINSFELD, Vicar, Clergy Sabbaticals and Diocesan Priests' Retreats, *1226 N. Church St., Rockford, 61103.* Tel: 815-965-5767; Fax: 815-965-5768.
Newman-Campus Ministry—Rev. STEPHEN J. KNOX, Dir., *512 Normal Rd., DeKalb, 60115.* Tel: 815-758-6667.
Newspaper—"The Observer"; Mr. OWEN PHELPS, JR., Mng. Editor, *921 W. State St., Rockford, 61102.* Tel: 815-963-3471.
Permanent Diaconate Program—Mr. THOMAS WELCH, Dir., *1266 N. Church St., Rockford, 61103.* Tel: 815-965-5837; Fax: 815-965-5768.
Priests' Eucharistic League—Rev. LAWRENCE M. URBANIAK, Dir., *15012 St. Patrick's Rd., Woodstock, 60098.* Tel: 815-338-7883.
Priest Personnel—Rev. Msgr. MICHAEL A. BINSFELD, Vicar, Clergy and Religious, *1226 N. Church St., Rockford, 61103.* Tel: 815-965-5767; Fax: 815-965-5768.
Pro-Life Activities, Office of—Rev. MICHAEL J. BOLGER, Dir., *229 W. Washington Pl., Freeport, 61032.* Tel: 815-232-7622.
Propagation of the Faith—Rev. NEAL KAMINSKI, O.F.M., Dir., *921 W. State St., Rockford, 61102.* Tel: 815-962-2934; Fax: 815-962-2966.
Research and Planning—Mr. MICHAEL CIESLAK, Dir., *921 W. State St., Rockford, 61102.* Tel: 815-963-7799; Fax: 815-962-2966.
Rural Life Conference—Mr. THOMAS MCKENNA, Dir., *921 W. State St., Rockford, 61102.* Tel: 815-965-0895.
Scouts—Rev. Msgr. WILLIAM H. SCHWARTZ, Dir., *1243 N. Church St., Rockford, 61103.* Tel: 815-965-2765.
Seton Center—Mr. RONALD DITOMASSI, Building Dir., *921 W. State St., Rockford, 61102.* Tel: 815-965-2778.
Social Ministries, Office of—Very Rev. LEO J. BARTEL, Vicar, *921 W. State St., Rockford, 61102.* Tel: 815-965-5116; Fax: 815-965-0628.
Vocation—Rev. MARTIN G. HEINZ, Dir., *850 N. Church St., Rockford, 61103.* Tel: 815-963-1009; Fax: 815-963-9962.

CLERGY, PARISHES, MISSIONS AND PAROCHIAL SCHOOLS

CITY OF ROCKFORD
(Winnebago County)

1—ST. PETER CATHEDRAL (1922), Rev. Msgr. William H. Schwatrz, Rector; Rev. Mark A. Campobello; Deacons Charles Cooper; Martin Czerniewski. In res., Revs. Timothy Doherty; Martin G. Heinz.
Res., 1243 N. Church St., 61103. Tel: 815-965-2765; 658-6060 (Rectory); Fax: 815-965-0743.
School—1231 N. Court St., Tel: 815-963-3620. Mr. Kevin Hart, Prin.
Lay Teachers 13; Students 288.
Catechesis/Religious Programs—Students 102.

2—ST. ANTHONY OF PADUA (1909) (Italian), Rev. Luke Poczworowski, O.F.M.Conv. In res., Rev. Dominic Wisz, O.F.M.Conv.; Deacons Sam Cassaro; Frank Barone.
Res., 1010 Ferguson St., 61102. Tel: 815-965-2761; Fax: 815-965-3244.
Catechesis/Religious Programs—Students 157.

3—ST. BERNADETTE (1957), Rev. Matthew T. Rudden.
Res., 2400 Bell Ave., 61103. Tel: 815-968-0904.
Church—Rockton Ave. & Bell Ave., 61103.
School—2300 Bell Ave., Tel: 815-968-2288. Mrs. Elizabeth Adams-Young, Prin.
Lay Teachers 13; Students 302.
Catechesis/Religious Programs—2300 Bell Ave., 61103. Tel: 815-968-2289.
Students 76.

4—ST. EDWARD (1929), Rev. Msgr. Raymond J. Wahl; Rev. James J. Murphy, Pastor Emeritus; Deacons Lambert Verstynen; Eugene Reilly.
Res., 3026 11th St., 61109. Tel: 815-398-1249.
School—3020 S. 11th St., Tel: 815-396-2631. Mr. John Fitzsimmons, Prin.
Lay Teachers 10; Students 274.
Catechesis/Religious Programs—Tel: 815-229-0282. Miss Rheta Zellner, D.R.E.
Students 255.

5—HOLY FAMILY (1963), Rev. Msgr. Daniel J. Hermes; Rev. Max J. Striedl, Jr.; Deacon Bob Bracken.
Office: 4401 Highcrest Rd., 61107. Tel: 815-398-4280; Fax: 815-398-4287.
School—4407 Highcrest Rd., Tel: 815-398-5331; Fax: 815-398-5902. Mr. Anthony Smerko, Prin.
Lay Teachers 29; Students 585.
Catechesis/Religious Programs—Tel: 815-397-9395. Joellen Lansing, D.R.E.
Students 753.

6—ST. JAMES (1853), Rev. David E. Beauvais. In res., Rev. Edgar Smigiel, O.F.M.
Res., 428 N. Second St., 61107. Tel: 815-962-1214; Fax: 815-962-1236. [JC]
School—409 N. First St., Tel: 815-962-8515; Fax: 815-962-8526. Ms. Margo Shifo, Prin.
Lay Teachers 15; Students 299.
Catechesis/Religious Programs—Tel: 815-962-5588. Sandra Lundy, D.R.E.
Students 269.

7—ST. MARY, Rev. William P. Collins.
Res., 517 Elm St., 61102. Tel: 815-968-0865.

8—ST. PATRICK (1919), Rev. Ronald A. Jones. Pastoral Assocs.: Mr. Scott Suma; Sr. Alyce Kelly, O.P.; Deacon Ron Graw.
Res., 2505 School St., 61101. Tel: 815-965-9539. [JC]
Catechesis/Religious Programs—Tel: 815-964-6591.
Students 65.

9—SS. PETER AND PAUL (1911), Rev. Michael E. Morrissey.
Res., 617 Lincoln Ave., 61102. Tel: 815-962-7171.
Catechesis/Religious Programs—Students 204.

10—ST. RITA (1914), Rev. William R. Wentink; Deacons Alex Hainchek; Robert Martin.
Res., 6254 Valley Knoll Dr., 61109-1898. Tel: 815-398-0853; Fax: 815-397-7499.
School—6284 Valley Knoll Dr., 61109-1898. Tel: 815-398-3466. Mrs. Beverly Sanders, Prin.
Lay Teachers 13; Students 309.
Catechesis/Religious Programs—Tel: 815-398-6483. Mrs. Barbara Malueg, D.R.E.
Students 344.

11—ST. STANISLAUS KOSTKA (1912) (Polish), Rev. John J. Mikula, O.F.M.Conv. In res., Rev. Hippolite Kuras, O.F.M.Conv.
Res., 201 Buckbee, 61104. Tel: 815-965-3913.

OUTSIDE THE CITY OF ROCKFORD

Algonquin, McHenry Co., St. Margaret Mary (1954), Revs. Michael J. Tierney; Wieslaw Grzela; Sr. Jeannine Randolph, S.L.W., Pastoral Assoc.
Parish Office: 111 S. Hubbard St., 60102. Tel: 847-658-7625; Fax: 847-658-7882.
School—113 Hubbard St., Tel: 847-658-5313. Mrs. Kathleen McMahon, Prin.
Lay Teachers 12; Students 229.
Catechesis/Religious Programs—Tel: 847-658-9339. Mrs. Sharon Prykop, D.R.E.
Students 1,097.

Amboy, Lee Co., St. Patrick (1857), Rev. Francis Daleiden, O.S.B.
Res., 32 N. Jones Ave., 61310. Tel: 815-857-2315; Fax: 815-857-2315. [CEM]
Catechesis/Religious Programs—Fax: 815-857-2314.
Students 247.

Apple River, Jo Daviess Co., St. Joseph, Rev. Everett J. Hiller.
Res., 107 Webster St., P.O. Box 3867, 61001. Tel: 815-594-2312. [CEM]

Aurora, Kane Co.,

1—ANNUNCIATION OF THE BLESSED VIRGIN MARY, (1875), Rev. Mario Pedi, O.S.B.; Deacons Raymond Johnson;

Harold Poss.
Res., 1820 Church Rd., 60504. Tel: 630-851-1436; Fax: 630-851-4316. [CEM]
School—1840 Church Rd., Tel: 630-851-4300. Mrs. Nancy Morton, Prin.
Lay Teachers 10; Students 296.
Catechesis/Religious Programs—Students 83.

2—HOLY ANGELS, (1892), Revs. Gerald P. Kobbeman; Mark A. Campobello; Deacons Tim White; Tom Hawksworth; Luke Cordes, (Retired).
Res., 720 Hardin Ave., 60506-4997. Tel: 630-897-1194; Fax: 630-897-1370.
School—720 Kensington Pl., 60506. Tel: 630-897-3613; Fax: 630-897-8233. Springfield Dominicans, Tel: 217-787-0491; Fax: 217-787-8169. Sr. Paul Mary Janssens, O.P., Prin.; Sr. Kathleen Gallagher, O.P., Asst. Prin.
Sisters 5; Lay Teachers 29; Students 737.
Catechesis/Religious Programs—Students 400.

3—ST. JOSEPH, (1899), Rev. Eric R. Barr; Deacon Norbert Szudarski, Pastoral Assoc., Tel: 630-897-0484. In res., Rev. Robert J. McClellan.
Mailing Address: P.O. Box 4395, 60507.
Res., 405 St. Joseph Ave., 60505. Tel: 630-844-3780; Fax: 630-844-1338. [CEM]
School—706 High St., 60507. Tel: 630-844-3781. Mr. Michael Brehm, Prin.
Lay Teachers 23; Students 393.
Catechesis/Religious Programs—Tel: 630-844-3782.
Students 86.

4—ST. MARY, (1872) (Irish), Rev. William F. Morrissey; Sr. Dorothy Hofer, O.S.F., Pastoral Assoc.; Deacons Richard Groom; William Rees; Mrs. Christine Rees. In res., Revs. David R. Engbarth; Joseph M. Lessard.
Res., 430 E. Downer Pl., 60505-3475. Tel: 630-892-0480; Fax: 630-892-8664.
Catechesis/Religious Programs—432 E. Downer Pl., Tel: 630-859-3922.
Students 57.

5—ST. NICHOLAS, (1862) (Hispanic), Rev. David R. Engbarth; Deacon Raymond Kramer, (Retired).
Mailing Address: 308 High St., 60505. Tel: 630-898-8707; Fax: 630-585-6423. [CEM]
Res., 30 E. Downer Pl., 60505. Tel: 630-906-6227.
School—Archbishop Romero School, 312 N. High St., Tel: 630-898-8690; Fax: 630-898-8866. Mrs. Jean Scanlan, Prin.
Lay Teachers 9; Students 218.
Catechesis/Religious Programs—Sr. Regina Marie, R.S.M., D.R.E.
Students 280.

6—OUR LADY OF GOOD COUNSEL, (1909), Rev. Edward F. Gillespie; Deacon James J. Valesano.
Res., 620 S. Fifth St., 60505. Tel: 630-851-1100; Fax: 630-851-4069.
School—601 Talma St., Tel: 630-851-4400. Sr. Nancy Ulrich, O.S.F., Prin.; Lucille Plachetka, Vice Prin.
Students 455.
Catechesis/Religious Programs—Students 62.

7—ST. PETER, Rev. Edwin F. Millen.
Res., 925 Sard Ave., 60506. Tel: 630-896-6816.
School—915 Sard Ave., Tel: 630-892-1283. Sr. Margaret Fabrizius, O.P., Prin.
Sisters 3; Lay Teachers 4; Students 114.

8—ST. RITA OF CASCIA, (1927), Rev. Robert J. Willhite.
Res., 750 W. Old Indian Trail Rd., 60506. Tel: 630-892-5918.
School—770 W. Old Indian Trail, Tel: 630-892-0020; Fax: 630-892-4236. Ms. Elizabeth Baney, Prin.
Lay Teachers 14; Students 326.
Catechesis/Religious Programs—Tel: 630-892-9507. Judith Feiden, D.R.E.
Students 330.

9—SACRED HEART, (1861) (French), Rev. Timothy R. Piasecki; Deacon Richard Groom.
Res., 771 Fulton St., 60505. Tel: 630-898-4165. [CEM]
School—Archbishop Romero School, Tel: 630-898-8690.
Catechesis/Religious Programs—Tel: 630-898-4165. Jo Dresden, D.R.E.
Students 210.

10—ST. THERESE OF JESUS, (1925), Rev. Joseph T. Muller, M.S.C.
Res., 271 N. Farnsworth Ave., 60505. Tel: 630-898-5422; Fax: 630-898-5327.
School—255 N. Farnsworth Ave., Tel: 630-898-0620. Ms. Michelle Sunnen, Prin.
Sisters 1; Lay Teachers 8; Students 183.
Catechesis/Religious Programs—Students 190.

Batavia, Kane Co., Holy Cross (1854), Rev. Stephen St. Jules; Mrs. Nancy Brenski, Pastoral Assoc.
Res., 2300 Main St., 60510. Tel: 708-879-4750; Fax: 708-879-9502. [JC]
Catechesis/Religious Programs—Tel: 708-879-4751. D.R.E.: Mrs. Diane Downey; Mr. Bill Crow.
Students 930.

Belvidere, Boone Co., St. James, Rev. Bernard J. Mullane.
Office: 535 Caswell St., 61008. Tel: 815-547-6397.
Res., 514 Caswell St., 61008. Tel: 815-547-6397. [CEM]
School—320 Logan Ave., 61008. Tel: 815-547-7633; Fax: 815-544-2294. Mrs. Barbara Majernik, Prin.
Lay Teachers 12; Students 210.
Catechesis/Religious Programs—Tel: 815-544-3698. Frank Zimmerman.
Students 442.

Byron, Ogle Co., St. Mary (1895), Rev. John A. Slampak; Deacon Bob Smits, Jr.
Res., P.O. Box 910, 232 E. Second St., 61010. Tel: 815-234-7431; Fax: 815-234-2133. [CEM]
Catechesis/Religious Programs—Tel: 815-234-5349. Marilyn Herrmann, D.R.E.
Students 329.

Carpentersville, Kane Co., St. Monica (1957), Revs. L. Thomas Risley; Robert Camacho; Deacons John Bach; Robert Demming; J. Michael Frazier; Dennis Garber; J. Aimie LaPlante.
Res., 90 N. Kennedy Dr., 60110-1695. Tel: 847-428-2646; Fax: 847-428-0039. [JC]
Catechesis/Religious Programs—Tel: 847-428-7562. Marilyn Ernst, D.R.E.
Students 415.

Cary, McHenry Co., SS. Peter & Paul (1904), Revs. Donald M. Ahles; Miroslaw Reikowski; Deacon Thomas Welch.
Res., 410 N. First St., 60013. Tel: 847-516-2636.
School—416 North First St., 60013. Tel: 847-639-3041. Sr. Katrina Lamkin, O.P., Prin.
Dominican Sisters 1; Lay Teachers 12; Students 283.
Catechesis/Religious Programs—Tel: 847-639-0414; Fax: 847-639-3474. Rosellyn Gilfether, D.R.E.
Students 1,200.

Crystal Lake, McHenry Co., St. Elizabeth Ann Seton (1978), Rev. Stephen K. Potter.
Office: 800 McHenry Ave., 60014. Tel: 815-459-3033; Fax: 815-459-3040.
Res., 445 Dartmoor Dr., 60014. Tel: 815-459-6223.
Catechesis/Religious Programs—Tel: 815-459-3096; Fax: 815-459-3040. Mrs. Renee Bhatia, D.R.E.
Students 1,033.

St. Thomas the Apostle, Revs. Geoffrey Wirth; Timothy Seigel; Mrs. Kathy Fuller, Pastoral Assoc.; Deacon Robert Nebel.
Res., 200 Washington St., 60014. Tel: 815-455-5407.
Pastoral Center: 272 King St., 60014. Tel: 815-455-5400; Fax: 815-455-2733.
School—265 King St., Tel: 815-459-0496; Fax: 815-459-0591. Mrs. Susan Polischuk, Prin.
Lay Teachers 24; Students 446.
Catechesis/Religious Programs—Tel: 815-455-9787. Janet Kayser, D.R.E.
Students 1,851.

DeKalb, DeKalb Co., Christ the Teacher, University Parish of Northern Illinois University (1963), Rev. Stephen J. Knox; Deacon James Dombek. Pastoral Assocs.: Andrea Rusin; Terrence Beer.
Office: 512 Normal Rd., 60115. Tel: 815-758-6667; Fax: 815-758-2053.
Catechesis/Religious Programs—Dr. Laura Bird, D.R.E.
Students 126.

St. Mary (1861), Very Rev. Karl P. Ganss; Rev. Richard A. Rosinski. In res., Rev. Casimiro Fiut, C.SS.R. (Poland).
Office: 302 Fisk Ave., 60115.
Res., 321 Pine St., 60115. Tel: 815-758-5432; Fax: 815-758-2487. [CEM]
School—210 Gurler Rd., Tel: 815-756-7905. Sr. Dorothy Bertsch, S.M.P., Prin.
Sisters 2; Lay Teachers 21; Students 415.
Catechesis/Religious Programs—Tel: 815-758-8405.
Students 375.

Dixon, Lee Co., St. Anne (1928), Rev. Harlan B. Clapsaddle; Sr. Lorraine Pratt, S.S.N.D., Pastoral Min.; Deacon James P. Ferolo.
Res., 1104 N. Brinton Ave., 61021. Tel: 815-288-3131; Fax: 815-288-3139.
School—1112 N. Brinton Ave., Tel: 815-288-5619; Fax: 815-288-3139. Sr. Marcianne Bzdon, S.S.N.D., Prin.
Lay Teachers 10; Students 165.
Catechesis/Religious Programs—Students 120.

St. Patrick (1856), Rev. John L. Stringini.
Office: 612 S. Highland, 61021. Tel: 815-284-7719; Fax: 815-284-4758. [JC]
School—St. Mary Elementary & Junior High, (Grades PreK-8) 704 Peoria Ave., Tel: 815-284-6986; Fax: 815-288-2940. Mr. James Braida, Prin.
Lay Teachers 16; Students 256.
Catechesis/Religious Programs—Tel: 815-284-2867. Sr. Elaine Marie Klugiewicz, D.R.E.
Students 275.

Dundee, Kane Co., St. Catherine of Siena (1914), Rev. William M. McKinstra.
Office: 845 W. Main St., 60118. Tel: 847-426-2217; Fax: 847-426-1130.
Res., 833 Royal Ln., 60118. Tel: 847-426-6253.
School—Tel: 847-426-4808. Sr. Helen Martin, O.P., Prin.
Sisters 2; Lay Teachers 14; Students 286.
Catechesis/Religious Programs—Tel: 847-426-4712.
Students 452.
Mission—Gilbert, Kane Co., St. Mary, c/o 845 W. Main St., West Dundee, 60118. Tel: 847-836-8315. [CEM]

Durand, Winnebago Co., St. Mary (1862) (Irish), Rev. Thomas J. Monohan.
Mailing Address: St. Mary's Church. St. Mary's & St. Patrick's Cemeteries are jointly administered by St. Mary's Church, Durand. 606 W. Main St., 61024. Tel: 815-248-2490; Fax: 815-248-9100.
Catechesis/Religious Programs—Students 146.
Mission—Irish Grove Rd., Stephenson Co., St. Patrick. [CEM]

East Dubuque, Jo Daviess Co., St. Mary (1868), Rev. Raymond O. Holmgren.
Res., 170 Montgomery Ave., 61025. Tel: 815-747-3221. [JC]
School—701 Rte. 35 N., 61025. Tel: 815-747-3010. Mr. Michael Powers, Prin.
Lay Teachers 9; Students 150.
Catechesis/Religious Programs—Students 110.

Elburn, Kane Co., St. Gall (1870) (Irish), Rev. Richard W. Paddock; Sr. Valerie Sepenski, O.S.F., Pastoral Assoc. & D.R.E.
Res., 120 W. Shannon, P.O. Box S, 60119. Tel: 630-365-6030; Fax: 630-365-5483. [CEM]
Catechesis/Religious Programs—Tel: 630-365-9166.
Students 320.

Elgin, Kane Co.,

1—ST. JOSEPH, (1887) (German-Spanish), Revs. Jerome L. Leake; John P. Earl; Deacons John Sauceda; Armando Martinez.
Res., 272 Division St., 60120. Tel: 847-931-2800; Fax: 847-931-2810.
School—274 Division St., Tel: 847-931-2804. Mr. Gene Traversa, Prin.
Lay Teachers 10; Students 263.
Catechesis/Religious Programs—Tel: 847-931-2808.
Students 354.

2—ST. LAURENCE, (1929), Rev. Joseph F. Kulak.
Office: 226 Orchard St., 60123. Tel: 847-468-6900; Fax: 847-468-6904.
Res., 1213 Oakdale Dr., 60123. Tel: 847-468-6900.
School—572 Standish St., 61203. Tel: 847-468-6100; Fax: 847-468-6104. Mrs. Phyllis Jensen, Prin.
Lay Teachers 13; Students 257.
Catechesis/Religious Programs—Tel: 847-468-6900.
Students 248.

3—ST. MARY, (1851), Revs. Thomas J. Dempsey; David A. Peck.
Parish Office—397 Fulton St., 60120.
Res., 390 Fulton St., 60120. Tel: 847-888-2828; Fax: 847-888-2883.
School—103 S. Gifford St., Tel: 847-695-6609; Fax: 847-695-6623. Mr. Carl Macaione, Prin.
Lay Teachers 10; Students 241.
Catechesis/Religious Programs—Tel: 847-888-2718. Mary Beth Mitchell, D.R.E.
Students 241.

4—ST. THOMAS MORE, (1959), Rev. Richard M. Russo; Deacons Thaddeus Ciochon; William Joynt.
Office: 215 Thomas More Dr., 60123. Tel: 847-888-1682; Fax: 847-888-3198. [JC]
School—1625 W. Highland Ave., Tel: 847-742-3959. Mr. David Knott, Prin.
Lay Teachers 13; Students 292.
Catechesis/Religious Programs—Tel: 847-888-4887. Mr. Ron Becker, D.R.E.
Students 444.

Elizabeth, Jo Daviess Co., St. Mary (1889), Rev. Ronald J. Conro.
Res., 112 E. Washington St., Box 246, 61028. Tel: 815-858-3422. [CEM]

Freeport, Stephenson Co.,

1—ST. CATHERINE. Closed. For inquiries for parish records contact the Chancery.

2—ST. JOSEPH, (1862) (German), Rev. John W. Cahill. In res., Rev. Michael J. Bolger.
Res., 229 W. Washington Pl., 61032. Tel: 815-232-7622; Fax: 815-235-4690. [CEM]
School—Freeport Catholic Elementary School, 202 W. Pleasant St., Tel: 815-232-6416. Mr. David Burke, Prin.; Mr. Randall Musser, Assis. Prin.

Lay Teachers 12; Students 254.
Catechesis/Religious Programs—Tel: 815-235-4324.
Students 58.

3—ST. MARY, (1846), Rev. Joseph L. Lutz.
Office: 813 S. State Ave., 61032. Tel: 815-235-7544; Fax: 815-232-8561.
Res., 704 S. State Ave., 61032. Tel: 815-235-7544; Fax: 815-232-8561. [CEM]
Catechesis/Religious Programs—Students 58.

4—ST. THOMAS AQUINAS, (1921), Very Rev. P. William McDonnell; Deacon H. Donald Brunette.
Res., 1400 Kiwanis Dr., 61032. Tel: 815-232-3225. [JC]
Catechesis/Religious Programs—Mary L. Gerbode, D.R.E.
Students 272.

Fulton, Whiteside Co., Immaculate Conception (1863), Rev. Kenneth J. Anderson.
Res., 703 12th Ave., 61252. Tel: 815-589-3542.
Mission—Albany, Whiteside Co., St. Patrick, 1445 Waller Rd., 61230. Tel: 309-887-4072.
Catechesis/Religious Programs—Students 110.

Galena, Jo Daviess Co., St. Mary (1851) (German), Rev. Daniel D. Tranel; Miss Socorro Vasquez de Velasco, Pastoral Assoc.
Res., 406 Franklin St., 61036. Tel: 815-777-0134. [CEM]
Catechesis/Religious Programs—Tel: 815-777-2219. Patricia Schuler, D.R.E.
Students 180.

St. Michael (1832) (Irish), Rev. Daniel D. Tranel, Admin.
Res., 227 S. Bench St., 61036. Tel: 815-777-2053. [CEM]
Catechesis/Religious Programs—Tricia Tranel, D.R.E.
Students 159.

Geneva, Kane Co., St. Peter (1912), Rev. James W. McLoughlin; Deacon Joseph McCafferty; Mrs. Lois Bushman, Pastoral Assoc. In res., Rev. David W. Huber.
Office: 1891 Kaneville Rd., 60134. Tel: 630-232-0124; Fax: 630-232-9262.
Res., 1771 Kaneville Rd., 60134. Tel: 630-208-1625. [JC]
School—1881 Kaneville Rd., Tel: 630-232-0476; Fax: 630-208-5681. Mrs. Deborah Bray, Prin.
Lay Teachers 10; Students 315.
Catechesis/Religious Programs—Tel: 630-232-7659. Sr. Mary Stella Schellenberger, S.S.C.M, D.R.E.
Students 1,150.
Convent—Tel: 630-879-2921.

Genoa, DeKalb Co., St. Catherine of Genoa (1912), Rev. Harold L. Nilges; Sr. Marianne Nilges, O.S.F., Pastoral Assoc.
Res., 340 S. Stott St., 60135. Tel: 815-784-2355. [CEM]
Catechesis/Religious Programs—Tel: 815-784-2045. Janet Elwer, D.R.E.
Students 266.

Hampshire, Kane Co., St. Charles Borromeo (1878), Rev. Thomas E. Brantman.
Res., 297 E. Jefferson St., P.O.Box 505, 60140-0505. Tel: 847-683-2391; Fax: 847-683-7499. [CEM]
School—(Grades PreK-8) 288 E. Jefferson St., Tel: 847-683-3450. Mrs. Kimberly Kohler Freitag, Prin.
Lay Teachers 11; Students 139.
Catechesis/Religious Programs—Tel: 847-683-1536. Sandra Iwanski, D.R.E.
Students 303.

Hanover, Jo Daviess Co., St. John the Evangelist, Rev. Michael A. Librandi.
Res., 103 Savanna Rd., 61041. Tel: 815-591-2258; 244-2577; Fax: 815-244-3974.

Harmon, Lee Co., St. Flannen (1898), Rev. Thomas P. Dolan.
Res., P.O. Box 130, 61042. Tel: 815-359-7819. [CEM]

Hartland, McHenry Co., St. Patrick (1837), Rev. Lawrence M. Urbaniak; Deacon Arthur Holt.
Res., 15012 St. Patrick Rd., Woodstock, 60098. Tel: 815-338-7883. [CEM]
Catechesis/Religious Programs—Students 78.

Harvard, McHenry Co., St. Joseph (1866), Rev. Richard R. Kramer; Sr. Alice Lamping, C.S.C., Pastoral Assoc.
Res., 206 E. Front St., 60033. Tel: 815-943-6406; Fax: 815-943-1604. [CEM]
School—201 N. Division St., Tel: 815-943-6933. Mrs. Marilyn Knapp, Prin.
Lay Teachers 7; Students 131.
Catechesis/Religious Programs—Beverly O'Leary, D.R.E.
Students 172.

Huntley, McHenry Co., St. Mary (1873), Rev. Robert M. Garrity.
Res., 10911 N. Woodstock St., P.O. Box 835, 60142. Tel: 847-669-3137. [CEM]
Catechesis/Religious Programs—Students 180.

Johnsburg McHenry Co., St. John the Baptist (1841), Rev. Robert A. Balog; Deacon Patrick Callahan.
Res., 2302 W. Church St., McHenry, 60050. Tel: 815-385-1477; Fax: 815-363-3333. [CEM]
School—Tel: 815-385-3959; Fax: 815-363-3337. Pamela Dvonch, Prin.
Sisters 1; Lay Teachers 12; Students 231.
Catechesis/Religious Programs—Tel: 815-385-4870. Sr. Clara Bauman, O.P., D.R.E.
Students 496.

Lee, Lee Co., St. James (1878), Rev. Louis J. Pesut.
Res., P.O. Box 108, 60530. Tel: 815-824-2053. [CEM]
Catechesis/Religious Programs—Students 76.

Lena, Stephenson Co., St. Joseph (1870), Rev. Salvatore J. Guagliardo.
Res., 410 W. Lena St., 61048. Tel: 815-369-2810. [CEM]
Catechesis/Religious Programs—Tel: 815-443-2892. Louise Kloepping, D.R.E.
Students 126.

Loves Park, Winnebago Co., St. Bridget (1946), Rev. Msgr. John J. Mitchell; Rev. Daniel J. Deutsch. In res., Rev. John J. Calkins.
Res., 600 Clifford Ave., 61111. Tel: 815-633-6311; Fax: 815-633-6314.
School—604 Clifford Ave., 61111. Tel: 815-633-8255. Sr. Mary Ann Hettel, S.S.C.M., Prin.
Lay Teachers 20; Students 448.
Catechesis/Religious Programs—Tel: 815-633-4006.
Students 323.

McHenry, McHenry Co., Church of Holy Apostles (1989), Rev. Robert N. Sherry.
Church—5211 W. Bull Valley Rd., 60050. Tel: 815-385-5673; Fax: 815-385-6045.
Catechesis/Religious Programs—Tel: 815-385-4273. Jeanne Fraser, D.R.E.
Students 562.

St. Mary (1894) (German), Rev. Thomas E. Burr; Sr. Eleanor King, S.S.S.F., Pastoral Assoc.
Res., 1401 N. Richmond Rd., 60050. Tel: 815-385-0024; Fax: 815-385-7809. [CEM]
School—Montini-Middle Grades, 1405 N. Richmond Rd., 60050. Tel: 815-385-1022. School Sisters of St. Francis, Tel: 815-385-0407. Mrs. Louise Whitaker, Prin.
Lay Teachers 9; Students 214.
Catechesis/Religious Programs—Tel: 815-385-2959. RoseMarie Riedl, D.R.E.
Students 384.

St. Patrick (1840) (Irish), Rev. James V. McKitrick; Deacon John H. Waterman.
Res., 3500 W. Washington St., 60050. Tel: 815-385-0025. [CEM 2]
School—Montini Primary Center, Tel: 815-385-5380. Mrs. Louise Whitaker, Prin.; Mrs. Luann Gavula, Asst. Prin.
Sisters 1; Lay Teachers 10; Students 251.
Catechesis/Religious Programs—Tel: 815-385-2959. RoseMarie Riedl, D.R.E.
Students 459.

Maple Park, DeKalb Co., St. Mary (1850), Rev. William J. Clausen.
Res., 123 S. Sycamore, P.O. Box 280, 60151. Tel: 815-827-3218.
Novak Center: 205 S. Sycamore St. [CEM 2]
Catechesis/Religious Programs—Students 93.

Marengo, McHenry Co., Sacred Heart (1902), Rev. Msgr. Philip E. O'Neil.
Res., 323 N. Taylor St., 60152. Tel: 815-568-7878; Fax: 815-568-7929. [CEM]
Catechesis/Religious Programs—Tel: 815-568-6230. D.R.E.: Robert Olsen; Christine Murphy.
Students 422.

Maytown, Lee Co., St. Patrick (1840), Rev. Thomas P. Dolan.
Res., P.O. Box 130, Harmon, 61042. Tel: 815-359-7819. [CEM]

Menominee Jo Daviess Co., Nativity of the Blessed Virgin Mary (1864), Rev. Bernard F. Dittman, Admin.
Res., 15406 W. Creek Valley Rd., East Dubuque P.O., 61025. Tel: 815-747-3676. [CEM]
School—15390 W. Creek Valley Rd., Tel: 815-747-3670. Sr. Janette Wicker, O.P., Prin.
Sisters 2; Lay Teachers 4; Students 86.

Morrison, Whiteside Co., St. Mary (1904), Very Rev. Leo J. Bartel.
Office: 126 E. Lincolnway, P.O. Box 248, 61270. Tel: 815-772-3095; Fax: 815-772-4890.
Res., 611 Greenwood Dr., 61270. Tel: 815-772-3095.
Catechesis/Religious Programs—Students 116.

Mount Carroll, Carroll Co., SS. John and Catherine (1923). Attended by Savanna. Rev. Joseph F. Jarmoluk.
Res., 314 S. Main St., P.O. Box 193, 61053. Tel: 815-244-1835 (Church).
Catechesis/Religious Programs—Students 76.

North Aurora, Kane Co., Blessed Sacrament (1970), Rev. Msgr. Edward S. Wright, V.F.; Sr. Rose Marie Weber, O.S.F., Pastoral Assoc. & D.R.E.
Res., 801 Oak St., 60542-1063. Tel: 630-897-1029; Fax: 630-897-1062.
Catechesis/Religious Programs—Students 283.

Oregon, Ogle Co., St. Mary (1862), Rev. William A. Budden.
Mailing Address: P.O. Box 419, 61061. Tel: 815-732-2234; Fax: 815-732-4742.
Res., 303 N. Fourth St., 61061. [CEM]
Catechesis/Religious Programs—Students 156.

Pecatonica, Winnebago Co., St. Mary (1872) (Irish-German), Rev. Robert J. Sweeney; Deacon Warren LaMont.
Res., 126 W. Fifth St., P.O. Box 656, 61063. Tel: 815-239-1271. [CEM]
Catechesis/Religious Programs—Students 119.

Polo, Ogle Co., St. Mary's (1856), Rev. Donald F. Smithes; Deacon John Gilmour.
Res., 211 N. Franklin Ave., 61064. Tel: 815-946-2535. [CEM]
Catechesis/Religious Programs—Students 90.

Prophetstown, Whiteside Co., St. Catherine (1917), Rev. Daniel E. Peters, Admin.
Res., 308 E. Third St., 61277. Tel: 815-537-2077.
Catechesis/Religious Programs—Doris Cox, D.R.E.
Students 140.
Mission—Erie, Whiteside Co., St. Ambrose.

Richmond, McHenry Co., St. Joseph (1930), Rev. Joseph W. Kaiser; Deacons Richard Ward; Lawrence Geinosky.
Res., 10519 Main St., 60071. Tel: 815-678-7421. [CEM]
Catechesis/Religious Programs—Tel: 815-678-6961. Patricia Donovan, D.R.E.; Mary Ann Beggs, Asst. D.R.E.
Students 120.

Rochelle, Ogle Co., St. Patrick (1868), Pastoral Team: Very Rev. Francis P. Kennedy; Sr. Judith Hermann, R.S.M.; Deacon Higinio Perez.
Res., 250 Kelley Dr., 61068. Tel: 815-562-2370; Fax: 815-562-5250. [CEM]
Catechesis/Religious Programs—Tel: 815-562-7677. Judy Snyder, D.R.E.
Students 417.

Rock Falls, Whiteside Co., St. Andrew (1950), Rev. Msgr. Thomas L. Dzielak.
Res., 708 10th Ave., 61071. Tel: 815-625-4508; Fax: 815-625-1569. [JC]
School—701 11th Ave., 61071. Tel: 815-625-1456. Mr. Philip D. Bellini, Prin.
Lay Teachers 7; Students 150.
Catechesis/Religious Programs—Students 161.

St. Charles, Kane Co., St. John Neumann (1977), Very Rev. Robert B. Hoffman; Rev. Robert W. Jones; Deacons Martin Hetzel; Paul Iwanski; Ronald Williams.
Res., 2900 E. Main St., 60174. Tel: 630-377-2797; Fax: 630-377-2834.
Catechesis/Religious Programs—Tel: 630-377-2803. Karen Dix, D.R.E.
Students 1,461.

St. Patrick (1851), Revs. Joseph B. Linster; Paul C. White; Sr. Dorothy Dempsey, Pastoral Assoc.
Res. & Church: 408 Cedar St., 60174. Tel: 630-584-0092; Fax: 630-513-2246.
School—State St. & Fifth St., Tel: 630-584-6367; Fax: 630-584-9759. Mr. Joseph Battisto, Prin.
Sisters 1; Lay Teachers 24; Students 540.
Catechesis/Religious Programs—Tel: 630-513-2247. Sr. Joelyn Hayes, D.R.E.
Students 1,350.
Mission—St. Charles, Kane Co., St. Patrick, 6N491 Crane Rd., 60175.

Sandwich, DeKalb Co., St. Paul (1925), Rev. John A. Kraemer.
Res., 110 N. Eddy St., 60548. Tel: 815-786-9266. [CEM]
Catechesis/Religious Programs—Tel: 815-786-8964.
Students 210.

Savanna, Carroll Co., St. John the Baptist (1884), Rev. Joseph F. Jarmoluk.
Res., 318 Chicago Ave., 61074. Tel: 815-273-3961. [CEM]
Catechesis/Religious Programs—Tel: 815-273-3582.
Students 113.

Scales Mound, Jo Daviess Co., Holy Trinity (1863), Rev. Ronald J. Conro.
Mailing Address: 112 E. Washington, Box 246, Elizabeth, 61028. Tel: 815-858-3422. [CEM 2]

Shannon, Carroll Co., St. Wendelin (1870). Attended by St. Mary, Freeport. Rev. Joseph L. Lutz.
18 S. Linn St., P.O. Box 23, 61078. Tel: 815-864-2548 (Church). [CEM]

Catechesis/Religious Programs—Students 60.

Somonauk, DeKalb Co., St. John the Baptist (1865), Rev. Donald D. DeSalvo.
Res., 320 S. Depot St., Box 276, 60552. Tel: 815-498-2010. [CEM]
Catechesis/Religious Programs—Tel: 815-498-2627.
Students 220.

South Beloit, Winnebago Co., St. Peter (1909), Rev. Msgr. Thomas C. Brady; Deacon Peter Calgaro, Pastoral Assoc. In res., Rev. Vytautas Gorinas.
Res., 620 Blackhawk Blvd., 61080. Tel: 815-389-2024; Fax: 815-389-2024.
School—320 Elmwood Ave., Tel: 815-389-3193. Sr. David Ennis, C.S.A., Prin.
Lay Teachers 11; Students 117.
Catechesis/Religious Programs—Tel: 815-389-9091. Carla Horwedel, D.R.E.
Students 330.
Mission—Roscoe, Winnebago Co., Church of the Holy Spirit, P.O. Box 478, Roscoe, 61073. Tel: 815-623-8742.

Spring Grove, McHenry Co., St. Peter (1900), Rev. Andrew J. Plesa.
Church—2206 Main St., P.O. Box 129, 60081. Tel: 815-675-2288; Fax: 815-675-6774. [CEM]
Catechesis/Religious Programs—Tel: 815-675-2576.
Students 337.

Sterling, Whiteside Co., Sacred Heart (1870), Rev. Francis E. McDonnell.
Res., 2224 Avenue J, 61081. Tel: 815-625-0631; 625-1134; Fax: 815-625-1138. [CEM]
Catechesis/Religious Programs—Students 128.

St. Mary (1898), Very Rev. Thomas E. Bales; Deacons Raphael Rios; John Kellen; Jane Olson, Pastoral Assoc. In res., Rev. Carlos Hoffner, M.S.
Res., 507 Ave. B, 61081. Tel: 815-625-0640; Fax: 815-625-1684. [CEM]
School—6 W. Sixth St., Tel: 815-625-2253. Mrs. Rebecca Scmitt Tel: 815-284-2926.
Lay Teachers 14; Students 221.
Catechesis/Religious Programs—600 Ave. B, 61081. Tel: 815-625-6688.
Students 253.

Stockton, Jo Daviess Co., Holy Cross (1893) (German), Rev. Aloysius J. Neumann.
Res., 216 E. Benton Ave., 61085. Tel: 815-947-2545. [CEM]
Catechesis/Religious Programs—Students 160.

Sublette, Lee Co., Our Lady of Perpetual Help, Rev. Edward R. Hughes.
Mailing Address: Box 80, West Brooklyn, 61378. Tel: 815-628-3901. [CEM]
Catechesis/Religious Programs—Students 78.

Sycamore, De Kalb Co., St. Mary (1885), Rev. Frank J. Timar, M.S.C.
Res., 244 Waterman St., 60178. Tel: 815-895-3275; Fax: 815-895-4561. [CEM]
School—222 Waterman St., Tel: 815-895-5215. Ms. Janine M. Bolchazy, Prin.
Lay Teachers 10; Students 151.
Catechesis/Religious Programs—Tel: 815-895-3726.
Students 268.

Tampico, Whiteside Co., St. Mary (1875), Rev. Vincent J. Shindelar.
Res., 105 Benton St., P.O. Box 155, 61283. Tel: 815-438-5425. [CEM]

Virgil, Kane Co., SS. Peter and Paul (1909), Rev. Thomas W. Neville; Deacon Clark Reynolds.
Res., 5 N. 939 Meredith Rd., P.O. Box 26, 60182. Tel: 630-365-6618. [CEM]
Catechesis/Religious Programs—Students 120.

Walton, Lee Co., St. Mary (1913), Rev. Thomas P. Dolan.
Res., P.O. Box 130, Harmon, 61042. Tel: 815-359-7819. [CEM]

Warren, Jo Daviess Co., St. Ann, Rev. Everett J. Hiller.
Res., 608 Railroad St., P.O. Box 665, 61087. Tel: 815-745-2312. [CEM]
Catechesis/Religious Programs—Students 94.

West Brooklyn, Lee Co., St. Mary, Rev. Edward R. Hughes.
Mailing Address: P.O. Box 80, 61378. Tel: 815-628-3901. [CEM]

Wonder Lake, McHenry Co., Christ the King (1949), Rev. Dorrance E. Tranel.
Res., 5006 E. Wonder Lake Rd., 60097. Tel: 815-653-2561. [CEM]
Catechesis/Religious Programs—Tel: 815-653-2581. Ms. Maureen Mclain, D.R.E.
Students 283.

Woodstock, McHenry Co., Resurrection (1978), Rev. Eugene Majewski, C.R.
Mailing Address: 2918 S. Country Club Rd., 60098. Tel: 815-338-7330; Fax: 815-338-7365.
Res., 6022 Shenandoah Dr., Crystal Lake, 60012. Tel: 815-356-5834.
Catechesis/Religious Programs—Nancy Neumeister, D.R.E.
Students 136.

St. Mary (1853), Rev. Msgr. Al F. Harte; Revs. Al F. Harte; James E. Swarthout; Deacons Robert Dolan; Eugene Wedoff.
Res., 312 Lincoln Ave., 60098. Tel: 815-338-3377; Fax: 815-338-3497. [CEM]
School—313 Tryon St., Tel: 815-338-3598; Fax: 815-338-3408. Mrs. Lisa M. Gott, Prin.
Lay Teachers 22; Students 398.
Catechesis/Religious Programs—Tel: 815-338-3413. Mrs. Connie Soucek, D.R.E.
Students 444.

Chaplains of Public Institutions

ELGIN. *Elgin State Hospital*. Vacant. 750 S. State St., 60123.

MOOSEHEART. *School of the Loyal Order of Moose*, 301 Fifth Ave., 60539. Rev. John T. Heraty, Chap.

ST. CHARLES. *Illinois State Youth Center*. Records kept at St. Patrick, St. Charles. Chapel of the Immaculate Conception.

Special Assignment:
Reverend Monsignors—
Binsfeld, Michael A., Vice-Chancellor, Vicar for Clergy and Religious, 1226 N. CHurch St., Rockford, IL 61103. Tel: 815-965-5767
Kagan, David D., Vicar Gen./Moderator of the Curia, 1245 N. Court St., P.O. Box 7044, Rockford, IL 61126. Tel: 815-962-3709
McNamee, Charles W., Chancellor, 1245 N. Court St., P.O. Box 7044, Rockford, 61103. Tel: 815-962-3709
Reverend Fathers—
Larson, F. James, Vicar for Catholic Education, 1260 N. Church St., Rockford, IL 61103
Nelson, Glenn L., Secretary to the Bishop, 1245 N. Court St., P.O. Box 7044, Rockford, IL 61126. Tel: 815-962-3709
Schuessler, William R., Vicar for Ministry to Hispanics, 921 W. State St., Rockford, IL 61102. Tel: 815-962-8042

Active Outside the Diocese:
Reverend Fathers—
Donahugh, Donald E., 100 Gifford Pond Ln., Port Arthur, TX 77642
Falcone, Emillo, Chap., PSC 02, Box 7192, APO AE, NY 09012
Myers, William F., St. Joachim, 19150 S.W.-117th Ave., Miami, FL 33117. Tel: 305-247-8268
Simonini, Michael F., St. Bernard, 1617 W. Pine St., Appleton, WI 54914. Tel: 414-739-0331

On Health Leave:
Reverend Fathers—
Holdren, John C.

On Disability Leave:
Reverend Fathers—
Fitzgibbons, Al L.
Joffe, William I.
Vlasz, Melvyn J.

Absent on Leave:
Reverend Fathers—
Tripodi, Frank J.
Wakitsch, Randal J.
Waser, Frank A.

Retired:
Reverend Monsignors—
Healey, Joseph T., 2505 Whitehall Circle, Rockford, IL 61107. Tel: 815-399-8579
Reverend Fathers—
Becker, Anthony J., 202 Cherry St., Apt. B-7, Mendota, IL 61342
Calkins, John J., 600 Clifford Ave., Loves Park, IL 61111. Tel: 815-633-6311
Draude, Frank C., 7 Sabadell Ln., Hot Springs Village, AR 71909. Tel: 501-922-1109
Gorinas, Vytautas, 620 Blackhawk Blvd., South Beloit, IL 61080. Tel: 815-389-2134
Knott, William P., 15528 W. Sky Hawk Dr., Sun City West, AZ 85375. Tel: 602-214-2520
Kriegsmann, William A., 1439 Rohde, Berkeley, IL 60163. Tel: 708-544-3039
London, Lawrence, Vianney Oaks, 7712 E. McGregor Rd., Rockford, IL 61102. Tel: 815-963-4820
McCarren, Charles K., 5208 East Dr., Loves Park, IL 61111. Tel: 815-877-2702
McGowan, John J., Health Center, 5100 John Ryan Blvd., #108, San Antonio, TX 78245. Tel: 512-677-8855
Peterson, William F., 147 Shadowood Dr., Martinez, GA 30907. Tel: 706-860-4738
Petit, Clement P., 4444 Brendenwood Rd., #306, Rockford, IL 61107. Tel: 815-395-8099
Petit, Edmund P., 616 Redwood Dr., Aurora, IL 60506. Tel: 630-897-8052
Ratazak, Bernard A., Vianney Oaks, 7712 E. McGregor Rd., Rockford, IL 61102. Tel: 815-965-0910
Regnier, William H., Cor Mariae Center, 3330 Maria Linden Dr., Rockford, IL 61114. Tel: 815-633-4573
Rennell, Albert F., 1060 N. Farnsworth Ave., Apt. 1104, Aurora, IL 60505. Tel: 708-898-0664
Richter, Norbert M., Vianney Oaks, 7712 E. McGregor Rd., Rockford, IL 61102. Tel: 815-965-4112
Schlade, Joseph F., 1109 N. Ashland Ave., Chicago, IL 60622. Tel: 312-384-7967
Sherman, Charles E., Vianney Oaks, 7712 E. McGregor Rd., Rockford, IL, IL 61102. Tel: 815-962-6731
Thennes, Clarence J., 659 E. Jefferson St., Freeport, IL 61032. Tel: 815-232-6181
Verstynen, Robert J., 1094 Tulip Ln., #5, Rockford, IL 61107. Tel: 815-394-0447

Permanent Deacons:
Bach, John, St. Monica, Carpentersville
Balsamo, Robert, St. Mary, Elgin
Barone, Frank, St. Anthony of Padua, Rockford
Battista, James, Holy Cross, Mesa, AZ
Berard, Samuel, St. Parick, Dixon
Boyes, Eugene, St. Mary, DeKalb
Bracken, Robert, Holy Family, Rockford
Brandenburg, Robert, St. Patrick, Dixon
Brunette, Donald J., St. Thomas, Freeport
Buga, John, Port Richey, FL
Burch, Michael, St. Mary, DeKalb
Calgaro, Peter, St. Peter, South Beloit; Church of the Holy Spirit, Roscoe; St. James, Rockford
Callahan, Donald J., St. James, Belvidere
Callahan, Patrick, St. John the Baptist, Johnsburg
Cassaro, Sam, St. Anthony of Padua, Rockford
Ciochon, Thaddeus, St. Thomas More, Elgin
Cooper, Charles, St. Peter Cathedral, Rockford
Cordes, Luke, Holy Angels, Aurora
Cristoforo, Michael, St. Rita, Rockford
Czerniewski, Martin, St. Peter Cathedral, Rockford
Dean, William, St. James, Rockford
Demming, Robert, St. Monica, Carpentersville
DeMong, Laverne, St. Joseph, Lena
Devine, John E., Houston, TX
Dolan, Robert J., St. Mary, Woodstock
Dombek, James, Christ the Teacher, DeKalb
Ferolo, James, St. Anne, Dixon
Frazier, J. Michael, St. Monica, Carpentersville
Freund, Walter, McHenry
Garber, Dennis, St. Monica, Carpentersville
Geinosky, Lawrence, St. Joseph, Richmond
Gerdeman, Richard, St. Bernadette, Rockford
Giambalvo, Michael, St. Laurence, Elgin
Gilmour, John, St. Mary, Polo
Goetz, Claude E., Manitowoc, WI
Grassmayer, Simon, St. Margaret Mary, Algonquin
Graw, Ronald, St. Patrick, Rockford
Groom, Richard, Sacred Heart and St. Mary, Aurora
Hainchek, Alex J., St. Rita, Rockford
Hawksworth, Thomas, Holy Angels, Aurora
Hetzel, Martin, St. John Neumann, St. Charles
Hoefler, Ben, Springfield
Holt, Arthur, St. Patrick, Hartland
Hurley, Dan A., Surprise, AZ
Iwanski, Paul, St. John Neumann, St. Charles
Johnson, Raymond R., Annunciation, Aurora
Joynt, William, St. Thomas More, Elgin
Kellen, John, St. Mary, Sterling
Kohler, John, St. Catherine, Genoa
Kramer, Raymond J., St. Nicholas, Aurora
LaMont, Warren R., St. Mary, Pecatonica
LaPlante, Joseph A., St. Monica, Carpentersville
Liegel, Gregory H., Sun City Center, FL
Linstad, Richard E., Sr., Moutain Home, AK
Magee, Ronald, St. James, Rockford
Maher, Patrick, St. Margaret Mary, Algonquin
Martin, Richard, St. Rita of Cascia, Aurora
Martin, Robert H., St. Rita, Rockford
Martinez, Armondo, St. Joseph, Elgin
McCafferty, Joseph, St. Peter, Geneva
McElroy, Robert D., Safety Harbor, FL
Milano, Robert, St. Patrick, Amboy
Mosley, William, Flagstaff, AZ
Muehler, Gerald, St. Mary, Huntley
Mulcahey, Richard, St. Mary, Durand
Murphy, Melvin J., St. Anne, Dixon
Nebel, Robert E., St. Thomas the Apostle, Crystal Lake
Olson, James D., St. James, Belvidere
Patton, James, St. Elizabeth Ann Seton, Crystal Lake
Perez, Higinio, St. Patrick, Rochelle
Phelan, Joseph, Church of Holy Apostles, McHenry
Plazewski, Robert, St. Lawrence, Elgin
Porter, John, Rockford

Poss, Harold, Annunciation of the B.V.M., Aurora
Prendergast, John, Schoolcraft, MI
Real, Robert, St. Laurence, Elgin
Rees, William, St. Mary, Aurora
Reilly, Eugene, St. Edward, Rockford
Reynolds, Clark, S.S. Peter and Paul, Virgil
Rios, Rafael V., St. Mary, Sterling
Sauceda, John, St. Joseph, Elgin
Smith, Daniel, St. James, Belvidere
Smits, Robert, St. Mary, Byron
Statter, Ralph, Crystal Lake
Steinhable, George C., Jr., Chicago
Stredde, John C., Montgomery
Szudarski, Norbert, St. Joseph, Aurora
Trost, Ray, Hampshire
Valesano, James J., Our Lady of Good Counsel, Aurora
Verstynen, Lambert, St. Edward, Rockford
Vondra, Edward, St. Matthew, Boyne City, MI
Ward, Richard, St. Joseph, Richmond
Washburn, Dale C., Edgewater, FL
Waterman, John, St. Patrick, McHenry
Wedoff, Eugene, St. Mary, Woodstock
Welch, Thomas, SS. Peter and Paul, Cary
Wessing, Reinhart P., Appleton, WI
White, Thomas, Holy Angels, Aurora
Whitehead, William, Jr., St. Catherine of Siena, Dundee
Williams, Ronald, St. John Neumann, St. Charles
Zitkus, Lawrence, St. Catherine of Genoa, Genoa

INSTITUTIONS LOCATED IN THE DIOCESE

[A] SEMINARIES, RELIGIOUS OR SCHOLASTICATES

AURORA. *Marmion Abbey*, Butterfield Rd., 60504. Tel: 630-897-7215. Rt. Rev. Vincent Bataille, O.S.B., Abbot; Very Rev. Kenneth Theisen, O.S.B., Prior. Priests 33; Brothers 11.

WOODSTOCK. *Resurrection Center Retreat House*, 2710 S. Country Club Rd., 60098. Tel: 815-338-1032; Fax: 815-338-1017. Mr. James F. Ivers, Dir.; Rev. Richard Grek, C.R., Coord., Adult Programs in Spirituality.

[B] HIGH SCHOOLS, DIOCESAN

ROCKFORD. *Boylan Central Catholic High School*, 4000 St. Francis Dr., 61103. Tel: 815-877-0531; Fax: 815-877-2544. Sr. M. Anthony Marelli, O.P., Prin.; Mr. Vincent E. McGuire, Asst. Prin., Student Affairs; Rev. F. William Etheredge, Spiritual Dir. & Chm., Dept. of Religious Studies; Mr. William C. Thumm, Dean of Students; Mr. Howard Willis, Guidance Dir. Priests 4; Sisters 2; Lay Teachers 81; Students 1,313.

AURORA. *Aurora Central Catholic High School*, 1255 N. Edgelawn Dr., 60506. Tel: 630-907-0095; Fax: 630-907-1076. Mr. Robert Stewart, Prin.; Mr. Warren Smith, Area Supt. Priests 3; School Sisters of St. Francis 3; Lay Teachers 27; Students 459.

ELGIN. *St. Edward Central Catholic High School*, 335 Locust St., 60123. Tel: 847-741-7535; Fax: 847-741-8658. Mr. Frank Bockman, Supt.; Miss Jacqueline Hyzy, Prin.; Mr. Thomas Rapp, Asst. Prin.; Rev. David Peck, Asst. Prin. & Spiritual Dir. Priests 3; Lay Teachers 38; Students 612.

FREEPORT. *Aquin Central Catholic Junior-Senior High School*, 1419 S. Galena Ave., 61032. Tel: 815-235-3154. Mr. David Burke, Supt. Prin.; Rev. Michael J. Bolger, Asst. Prin. & Chm. Religious Studies Dept. Lay Teachers 15; Students 180.

STERLING. *Newman Central Catholic High School; Newman Middle School*, 1101 St. Mary's Rd., 61081-9002. Tel: 815-625-0500; Fax: 815-625-8444. Mr. Philip Bellini, Supt.; Mr. Donald E. Loftus, Prin.; Rev. Daniel Peters, Asst. Prin./Spiritual Dir. Lay Teachers 29; Students 344.

WOODSTOCK. *Marian Central Catholic High School*, 1001 McHenry Ave., 60098. Tel: 815-338-4220; Fax: 815-338-4253. Mr. Thomas E. Landers, Supt.; Mr. John Burke, Prin.; Rev. Paul M. Lipinski, Asst. Prin. & Spiritual Dir.; Mr. James Dvorak, Dean of Students. Priests 4; Sisters 1; Lay Teachers 38; Students 692.

[C] HIGH SCHOOLS, PRIVATE

AURORA. *Marmion Academy*, 1000 Butterfield Rd., 60504. Tel: 630-897-6936; Fax: 630-897-7086. Boarding and Day School. Rt. Rev. Vincent Bataille, O.S.B., Abbot & Pres.; Rev. Basil Yender, O.S.B., Headmaster. Benedictines 18; Lay Teachers 32; Students 430.

Rosary High School, 901 N. Edgelawn Ave., 60506. Tel: 630-896-0831; Fax: 630-896-8372. Sr. M. Megan Farrelly, O.P., Prin.; Sr. Mary Joseph Weigand, O.P., Asst. Prin.; Sr. Karen Marie, O.P., Chm., Religious Studies. Sisters of St. Dominic 10; Lay Teachers 28; Girls 416.

[D] GENERAL HOSPITALS

ROCKFORD. *Saint Anthony College of Nursing*, 5658 E. State St., 61108. Tel: 815-395-5090.
For a complete listing, refer to the Hospitals section.

Saint Anthony Medical Center, 5666 E. State St., 61108. Tel: 815-226-2000.
For a complete listing, refer to the Hospitals section.

AURORA. *Mercy Health Corporation*, 1325 N. Highland Ave., 60506. Tel: 630-859-2222.
For a complete listing, refer to the Hospitals section.

BELVIDERE. *Saint Joseph Hospital*, 1005 Julien St., 61008. Tel: 815-544-3411; Fax: 815-547-5977.
For a complete listing, refer to the Hospitals section.

ELGIN. *St. Joseph Hospital*, 77 N. Airlite St., 60123. Tel: 847-695-3200.
For a complete listing, refer to the Hospitals section.

[E] SCHOOLS FOR EXCEPTIONAL ADOLESCENTS AND ADULTS

FREEPORT. *St. Vincent Home for Children*, 659 E. Jefferson St., 61032. Tel: 815-232-6181; Fax: 815-232-6143. Mrs. Susan M. Murray, Exec. Dir.; Rev. Clarence J. Thennes, Chap. Sisters 2.

St. Vincent's Community Living Facility and Supported Living Program. Mrs. Alria Cole, Admin. Patients assisted annually 29.

[F] SCHOOLS FOR EXCEPTIONAL CHILDREN

FREEPORT. *Saint Francis School for Exceptional Children*, 1209 S. Walnut Ave., 61032. Tel: 815-235-3174; Fax: 815-232-4667. Mr. John McCoy, L.C.S.W., Admin. Students 42.

[G] HOMES FOR AGED AND ADULT DAY CARE CENTERS

ROCKFORD. *Cor Mariae Center*, 3330 Linden Dr., 61114.
For a complete listing, refer to the Special Care Facilities section.

St. Anne Center, 4405 Highcrest Rd., 61107. Tel: 815-229-1999.
For a complete listing, refer to the Special Care Facilities section.

St. Anne Place, 4444 Brendenwood Rd., 61107. Tel: 815-399-6167.
For a complete listing, refer to the Special Care Facilities section.

Vianney Oaks, 7712 E. McGregor Rd., 61102. Tel: 815-965-0910.
For a complete listing, refer to the Special Care Facilities section.

AURORA. *Fox Knoll (Retirement Community)*, 421 N. Lake St., 60506. Tel: 630-844-0380.
For a complete listing, refer to the Special Care Facilities section.

McAuley Manor, 400 W. Sullivan Rd., 60506. Tel: 630-859-3700; Fax: 630-264-1862.
For a complete listing, refer to the Special Care Facilities section.

FREEPORT. *St. Joseph Adult Day Care Center*, 659 E. Jefferson St., 61032. Tel: 815-232-6181; Fax: 815-232-6143.
For a complete listing, refer to the Special Care Facilities section.

St. Joseph Home for the Aged, 659 E. Jefferson St., 61032. Tel: 815-232-6181; Fax: 815-232-6143.
For a complete listing, refer to the Special Care Facilities section.

[H] MONASTERIES AND RESIDENCES OF PRIESTS AND BROTHERS

AURORA. *Marmion Abbey-St. Augustine's Abbey*, Butterfield Rd., 60504. Tel: 630-897-7215; Fax: 630-897-0393, Ext. 59. Legal Title: *Marmion*. Rt. Revs. Vincent Bataille, O.S.B., Abbot; Gerald Benkert, O.S.B., Abbot Emeritus; David J. Cyr, O.S.B., Abbot Emeritus; Very Rev. Kenneth Theisen, O.S.B., Prior; Revs. Barnabas Lundergan, O.S.B.; Andrew Wahmhoff, O.S.B.; Bede Stocker, O.S.B.; Alcuin Deck, O.S.B.; Bro. Anselm Mangano, O.S.B., Subprior; Revs. Luke Bohr, O.S.B.; Augustine Jones, O.S.B.; Martin Witting, O.S.B.; Hugh Schuck, O.S.B.; Terence Stanton, O.S.B.; Matthias Zinkan, O.S.B.; Bernard Schaefer, O.S.B.; Gregory Obee, O.S.B.; Philip Kremer, O.S.B.; Mario Pedi, O.S.B.; Francis Daleiden, O.S.B.; David Palmatier, O.S.B.; Basil Yender, O.S.B.; Joel Rippinger, O.S.B.; Carlos Quintana, O.S.B.; Christian Pusateri, O.S.B.; Michael Burrows, O.S.B.; John Brahill, O.S.B.; Thomas McLaughlin, O.S.B.; Kenneth Theisen, O.S.B.; Mathew F. Kowalski, O.S.B.; Rene Otzoy Colaj, O.S.B.; Cristobal Coche Quic; George Glover, O.S.B.; Frederick Peterson, O.S.B. Priests 33; Brothers 11.

Missionaries of the Sacred Heart Community, 305 S. Lake St., 60507. Tel: 630-892-2371; Fax: 630-892-1678. Provincial Administrative Office of the Missionaries of the Sacred Heart. Very Rev. Mark McDonald, M.S.C., Prov. & Local Supr.; Rev. Edward Ball, M.S.C.; Very Rev. Thomas Cain, M.S.C.; Revs. James Campbell, M.S.C.; Peter E. Campbell, M.S.C.; Thomas Carney, M.S.C.; Robert Cell, M.S.C.; Raymond Diesbourg, M.S.C.; Ronald Leinen, M.S.C., Ph.D.; Thomas Murphy, M.S.C.; Gerald Paul, M.S.C.; Leo Petit, M.S.C.; Bros. Eugene Thomas, M.S.C.; Nicholas Lanese, M.S.C.; Michael Tomcics, M.S.C. Priests 13; Brothers 3.

Priests of the Province Serving Elsewhere - In Bogota, Colombia: Very Rev. Howard Fath, M.S.C., Sectional Supr.; Revs. Javier Bautista, M.S.C.; Joseph Jablonski, M.S.C.; German Barona, M.S.C.; Tito Medina, M.S.C.; Michael Miller, M.S.C.; Wilson Tascon, M.S.C. In Papua New Guinea: Revs. Steve Boland, M.S.C.; Thomas Burns, M.S.C.; David DeLuca, M.S.C.; Henry Einhaus, M.S.C.; Anthony Gendusa, M.S.C.; Joseph Gleixner, M.S.C., Regional Supr.; Bernard Miller, M.S.C.; Leon Weisenberger, M.S.C.; Bros. Anton Freitas, M.S.C.; James Miller, M.S.C.; Patrick O'Hara, M.S.C.; Joseph Tesar, M.S.C.; Daniel Rakow, M.S.C. In Namibia: Rev. Francis Westhoff, M.S.C. In Slovakia: Rev. Hilary Fischer, M.S.C.

MCHENRY. *Villa Desiderata Retreat House*, 3015 N. Bayview Ln., 60050. Tel: 815-385-2264. Rev. Michael Cashen, Dir. & Retreat Master; Bro. Patrick Drohan, C.S.V., Facilities Mgr.

[I] CONVENTS AND RESIDENCES FOR SISTERS

ROCKFORD. *The Poor Clares of Rockford*, Corpus Christi Monastery, 2111 S. Main St., 61102. Tel: 815-963-7343. Franciscan Colettine Poor Clares. Mother Mary Annette Lepine, P.C.C., Abbess; Rev. Neal Kaminski, O.F.M., Chap., Res., 2223 S. Main St., 61102. Tel: 815-964-7606. Cloistered Sisters 30; Extern Sisters 2.

AURORA. *McAuley Convent*, 400 W. Sullivan Rd., 60506. Tel: 630-859-3700. Sisters of Mercy. Mrs. Mary A. Burnell, Admin.; Sr. Nadine Hargadon, R.S.M., Convent Coord. Bed Capacity 31.

BATAVIA. *Holy Heart of Mary Novitiate*, 717 N. Batavia Ave., 60510. Tel: 708-879-1296. Servants of the Holy Heart of Mary. Sr. Linda K. Hatton, S.S.C.M., Supr. & Formation Directress. Professed Sisters 7; Candidate 1; Novices 1.

ST. CHARLES. *Our Lady of Creek Bend*, 37 W. 584 Dean St., 60175. Tel: 630-584-5699. Felician Sisters Residence. Sisters 4.

[J] COMMUNITY SERVICES

ROCKFORD. *Fourth Street Bridge Youth Shelter*, 405 S. Fourth St., 61104. Tel: 815-965-3700. Karen Johnston, M.S., Program Admin. Total Staff 15; Total assisted 246.

Martin House, 1020 S. Main St., 61101. Tel: 815-963-6967. Mr. John P. McCoy, Admin.; Rev. William P. Collins, Chap.

St. Elizabeth's Community Center, 1536 S. Main St., 61102. Tel: 815-969-6526. Mr. Anthony T. Burns, Exec. Dir. Total Staff 16; Total assisted 20,200.

AURORA. *Hesed House, Inc.*, 659 S. River St., 60506. Tel: 630-897-2156. Sr. Rose Marie Lorentzen, B.V.M., Exec. Dir. Ecumenical Center for ministry to the poor. Total assisted 218,972.

Public Action to Deliver Shelter, Inc. (PADS), 659 S. River St., 60506. Tel: 630-897-2165. Sr. Rose Marie Lorentzen, B.V.M., Exec. Dir. Ecumenical advocacy, overnight and transitional shelters and daytime drop-in center for homeless persons. Total assisted 45,673.

[K] RETREAT HOUSES

ROCKFORD. *Bishop Lane Retreat House*, 7708 E. McGregor Rd., 61102. Tel: 815-965-5011. Don & Lorrie Gramer, Admins.

[L] FOUNDATIONS

ROCKFORD. *Boylan Educational Foundation, Inc.*, 4000 St. Francis Dr., 61103; Fax: 815-877-2544.

The Catholic Foundation for the People of the Diocese of Rockford, 921 W. State St., 61102. Tel: 815-964-6711. Mr. Michael Burch, Exec. Dir.

AURORA. *Aurora Catholic Education Foundation*, P.O. Box 234, 60507.

Mercy Services Foundation of Aurora, 1325 N. Highland Ave., 60506. Tel: 630-801-2663. Ms. Joann S. Rebeck, Exec. Dir.

CRYSTAL LAKE. *St. Thomas the Apostle School Foundation, Inc.*, 272 King St., 60014.

DEKALB. *Newman Center of Northern Illinois University Educational Program*, 512 Normal Rd., 60115; Fax: 815-753-2053. Legal Title: *Newman Center of Northern Illinois University Educational Program and Development Fund, Inc.* Total Staff 16.

ELGIN. *St. Edward Central Catholic High School Education Foundation*, 100 Perry St., 60123. Peg Mueller, Dir. Devel.

FREEPORT. *Education Through the 90's Foundation*, 1419 S. Galena Ave., 61032. The foundation provides financial support for the Freeport catholic school system.

Freeport Catholic Education Foundation, 1419 S. Galena Ave., 61032. The foundation provides financial support for the Freeport catholic school system.

STERLING. *Sauk Valley Catholic Education Foundation*, 1101 St. Mary's Rd., 61081.

Sauk Valley Area Religious Education Center, 1101 St. Mary Rd., 61081.

SYCAMORE. *St. Mary's of Sycamore Foundation, Ltd.*, 244 Waterman St., 60178.

WOODSTOCK. *McHenry County Catholic Education Foundation*, 1005 McHenry Ave., 60098. Mr. Thomas Landers, Exec. Officer.

St. Mary's of Woodstock School Foundation, Inc., 312 Lincoln Ave., 60098.

[M] NEWMAN CENTERS

DEKALB. *Newman Foundation for Catholic Students of Northern Illinois University*, 512 Normal Rd., 60115. Tel: 815-758-6667. Rev. Stephen J. Knox. Pastoral Assocs.: Mr. Terry Beer; Ms. Rose Drance; Ms. Andrea Rusin; Mrs. Sandy Kowalkowski, Dir., Alumni Devel. Assoc.

[N] MISCELLANEOUS

ROCKFORD. *Catholic Office of the Deaf*, 1245 N. Court St., P.O. Box 7044, 61126.

The Vineyard Books and Gifts, Highcrest Center, 1638 N. Alpine Rd., 61107. Tel: 815-398-4030; Fax: 815-398-8477. Joann Toti, Mgr.

AURORA.

**Joseph Corporation of Illinois, Inc.*, P.O. Box 525, 60507. Tel: 630-820-7400; Fax: 630-820-7402. (Ecumenical not-for-profit housing developer). MaryAnn Shanley-Wencel, Exec. Dir.; Sr. Mary Catherine Daly, R.S.M., Admin. Asst.; Sr. Margaret Barrett, R.S.M., Project Dir.; Sr. Kathleen Braun, S.S.S.F., Housing Counselor.

MOUNT CARROLL. *Samaritan Homecare / Hospice*. Sponsor: Mercy Health Services, Sisters of Mercy, Regional Community of Detroit, 102 E. Washington St., 60153. Tel: 815-244-2749. Katherine McCann, R.N., Supvr.; Gary Baum, Pres.

ST. CHARLES. *Queen of Americas Guild*, 345 Kautz Rd., P.O. Box 851, 60174. Tel: 708-584-1822; Fax: 708-584-0648. Mr. Frank Smoczynski, Pres.; Mr. Stephen Banaszak, Vice Pres.; Mr. Alan Napleton, Sec. & Dir.; Beverly Smoczynski, Treas. & Dir.

Board of Directors: Revs. Christopher Rengers, O.F.M.Cap.; Jacob Joerger, O.P.; George Hastrich; Sr. M. Theresa Alonso, M.C.M.; Mrs. Ruth Sloan.

STERLING. *St. Vincent DePaul Society*. St. Mary's Conference, 600 Ave. B, 61081. Total Staff 16; Total assisted 2,719.

STOCKTON. *Christ in the Wilderness*, 7500 S. Randecker Rd., 61085-8922. Sr. Lorraine Mark, C.S.J., Dir., Center of Solitude and Prayer.

RELIGIOUS INSTITUTES OF MEN REPRESENTED IN THE DIOCESE

For further details refer to the corresponding bracketed number in the Religious Institutes of Men or Women section.

[0200]—*Benedictine Monks*. (Marmion Abbey, Aurora).—O.S.B.

[1320]—*Clerics of St. Viator*.—C.S.V.

[1080]—*Congregation of the Resurrection*. (Chicago Prov.).—C.R.

[0480]—*Conventual Franciscans*. (St. Bonaventure Province).—O.F.M.Conv.

[0520]—*Franciscan Friars*. (Assumption of the B.V.M. Prov.).—O.F.M.

[]—*Institute of Christ the King Sovereign Priest (Provincial House-Italy)*.

[0690]—*Jesuit Fathers-Chicago Province of the Society of Jesus*.—S.J.

[0720]—*The Missionaries of Our Lady of La Salette*.—M.S.

[1110]—*Missionaries of the Sacred Heart*.—M.S.C.

[]—*Redemptorist Missionaries (Provincial House-Belgium)*.—S.Ss.R.

RELIGIOUS INSTITUTES OF WOMEN REPRESENTED IN THE DIOCESE

[]—*Auxiliaries of the Blessed Sacrament*.—A.S.B.

[0230]—*Benedictine Sisters*.—O.S.B.

[0350]—*Carmelite Sisters (Corpus Christi)*.—O.Carm.

[2100]—*Congregation of the Humility of Mary*.—C.H.M.

[1920]—*Congregation of the Sisters of the Holy Cross*.—C.S.C.

[1710]—*Congregation of the Third Order of St. Francis of Mary Immaculate*.—O.S.F.

[1070-02]—*Dominican Sisters*.—O.P.

[1070-03]—*Dominican Sisters*.—O.P.

[1070-10]—*Dominican Sisters*.—O.P.

[1070-13]—*Dominican Sisters*.—O.P.

[1070-01]—*Dominican Sisters of St. Catharine*.—O.P.

[1170]—*Felician Sisters*.—C.S.S.F.

[2575]—*Institute of the Sisters of Mercy of the Americas*. (Chicago, IL).—R.S.M.

[]—*Mexican Passionist Sisters*.—C.F.P.

[2865]—*Missionaries of the Sacred Heart & Our Lady of Guadalupe*.—M.S.C.Gpe.

[2790]—*Missionary Servants of the Most Blessed Trinity*.—M.S.B.T.

[3760]—*Poor Clare Colettines*.—P.C.C.

[2970]—*School Sisters of Notre Dame*.—S.S.N.D.

[1680]—*School Sisters of St. Francis*.—O.S.F.

[3520]—*Servants of the Holy Heart of Mary*.—S.S.C.M.

[0430]—*Sisters of Charity of the Blessed Virgin Mary*.—B.V.M.

[2360]—*Sisters of Loretto at the Foot of the Cross*.—S.L.

[2450]—*Sisters of Mary of the Presentation*.—S.M.P.

[3360]—*Sisters of Providence of Saint Mary-of-the-Woods, Indiana*.—S.P.

[3710]—*Sisters of St. Agnes*.—C.S.A.

[1760]—*Sisters of St. Francis*.—O.S.F.

[1705]—*The Sisters of St. Francis of Assisi*.—O.S.F.

[1640]—*Sisters of St. Francis of Perpetual Adoration*.—O.S.F.

[1570]—*Sisters of St. Francis of the Holy Family*.—O.S.F.

[1660]—*Sisters of St. Francis of the Providence of God*.—O.S.F.

[3830-02]—*Sisters of St. Joseph*.—C.S.J.

[3830-15]—*Sisters of St. Joseph*.—C.S.J.

[3930]—*Sisters of St. Joseph of the Third Order of St. Francis*.—S.S.J.-T.O.S.F.

[1970]—*Sisters of the Holy Family of Nazareth*.—C.S.F.N.

[2350]—*Sisters of the Living Word*.—S.L.W.

[1770]—*Sisters of the Third Order of St. Francis*. (Peoria, Illinois).—O.S.F.

[3530]—*Spirit Missionary Sisters*.—S.Sp.S.

DIOCESAN CEMETERIES

ROCKFORD. *Calvary-St. Mary's / St. James*.

AURORA. *Mount Olivet*.

BATAVIA. *Geneva-St. Charles Resurrection*.

ELGIN. *Mount Hope*.

NECROLOGY

† Bajo, Philip, (Retired). —Died Feb. 5, 1996.

† Eye, Rev. Msgr. Sylvester J., P.A., (Retired). —Died April 4, 1996.

† Gordon, Raymond P., (Retired). —Died May 15, 1996.

† Kilduff, John J., (Retired). —Died Dec. 10, 1995.

† Tuchlinsky, John F., (Retired). —Died July 24, 1996.

Diocese of Rockville Centre

(Dicecesis Petropolitana In Insula Longa)

Most Reverend

JAMES J. DALY, D.D.

Retired Auxiliary Bishop of Rockville Centre and Vicar General; ordained May 22, 1948; appointed Titular Bishop of Castra Nova and Auxiliary to the Bishop of Rockville Centre February 28, 1977; ordained Bishop May 9, 1977. *Res., Church of St. Joseph, 59 Church St., Kings Park, NY, 11754.* Tel.: 516-269-6455.

Most Reverend

EMIL A. WCELA, D.D.

Auxiliary Bishop of Rockville Centre and Episcopal Vicar of Eastern Vicariate; appointed Titular Bishop of Filaca and Auxiliary to the Bishop of Rockville Centre October 21, 1988; ordained Bishop December 13, 1988. *Res., Eastern Vicariate - Diocese of Rockville Centre, P.O. Box 780, Riverhead, NY, 11901.* Tel.: 516-369-0071.

Most Reverend

JOHN R. McGANN, D.D.

Bishop of Rockville Centre; ordained June 3, 1950; appointed Titular Bishop of Morosbisdus and Auxiliary to the Bishop of Rockville Centre November 12, 1970; ordained Bishop January 7, 1971; appointed Bishop of Rockville Centre May 3, 1976; installed June 24, 1976. *Res., St. Agnes Cathedral, 29 Quealy Pl., Rockville Centre, NY, 11570.* Tel.: 516-766-0205.

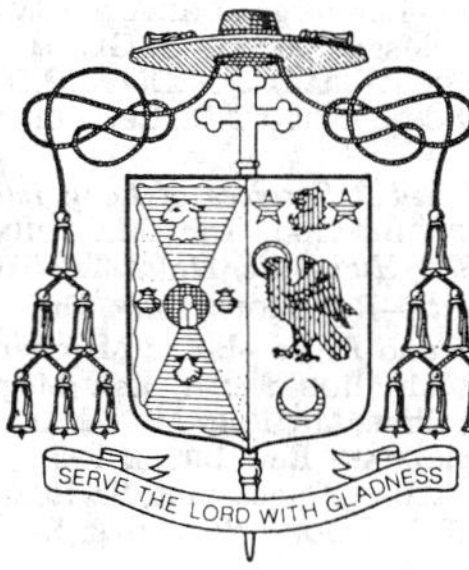

Chancery Office: 50 N. Park Ave., Rockville Centre, NY, 11570. Tel.: 516-678-5800; Fax: 516-678-1786.

Most Reverend

JOHN C. DUNNE, D.D.

Auxiliary Bishop of Rockville Centre and Episcopal Vicar of Central Vicariate; appointed Titular Bishop of Abercorn and Auxiliary to the Bishop of Rockville Centre October 21, 1988; ordained Bishop December 13, 1988. *Res., Central Vicariate - Diocese of Rockville Centre, P.O. Box 39, Farmingdale, NY, 11735-0039.* Tel.: 516-249-1700.

ESTABLISHED APRIL 6, 1957.

Square Miles 1,222.

THE ROMAN CATHOLIC DIOCESE OF ROCKVILLE CENTRE, NEW YORK.

Comprises the Counties of Nassau and Suffolk (excepting Fishers Island) in the State of New York.

For legal titles of parishes and diocesan institutions, consult the Chancery Office.

STATISTICAL OVERVIEW

Personnel	
Bishop	1
Auxiliary Bishops	3
Priests: Diocesan Active in Diocese	283
Priests: Active Outside Diocese	44
Priests: Diocesan in Foreign Missions	2
Priests: Retired, Sick or Absent	129
Number of Diocesan Priests	458
Religious Priests in Diocese	95
Extern Priests in Diocese	63
Ordinations:	
Diocesan Priests	3
Transitional Deacons	1
Permanent Deacons	9
Permanent Deacons in Diocese	196
Total Brothers	104
Total Sisters	1,543
Parishes	
Parishes	134
With Resident Pastor:	
Resident Diocesan Priests	131
Resident Religious Priests	3
Without Resident Pastor:	
New Parishes Created	1
Professional Ministry Personnel:	
Sisters	14
Lay Ministers	4
Welfare	
Catholic Hospitals	4
Total Assisted	611,462
Homes for the Aged	4
Total Assisted	4,556
Residential Care of Children	4
Total Assisted	8,904
Day Care and Extended Day Care Centers	103
Total Assisted	4,723
Specialized Homes	3
Total Assisted	71
Special Centers for Social Services	38
Total Assisted	194,219
Residential Care of Disabled	15
Total Assisted	121
Other Institutions	95
Total Assisted	214,898
Educational	
Seminaries, Diocesan	1
Students from This Diocese	16
Students from Other Diocese	25
Students Religious	5
Total Seminarians	21
Colleges and Universities	2
Total Students	4,586
High Schools, Diocesan and Parish	4
Total Students	3,754
High Schools, Private	9
Total Students	7,169
Elementary Schools, Diocesan and Parish	63
Total Students	27,675
Elementary Schools, Private	4
Total Students	1,110
Non-residential Schools for the Disabled	3
Total Students	210
Catechesis/Religious Education:	
High School Students	4,599
Elementary Students	105,134
Total Students Under Catholic Instruction	154,258
Teachers in the Diocese:	
Priests	10
Brothers	65
Sisters	236
Lay Teachers	1,729
Vital Statistics	
Receptions into the Church:	
Infant Baptism Totals	21,957
Adult Baptism Totals	545
First Communions	17,641
Confirmations	15,199
Marriages:	
Catholic	6,037
Interfaith	1,231
Total Marriages	7,568
Deaths	11,564
Total Catholic Population	1,347,096
Total Population	2,880,184

Former Bishops—Most Rev. WALTER P. KELLENBERG, D.D., first Bishop of Rockville Centre; ord. June 2, 1928; appt. Titular Bishop of Joannina and Auxiliary Bishop of New York, Aug. 25, 1953; cons. Oct. 5, 1953; appt. Bishop of Ogdensburg, Jan. 19, 1954; appt. first Bishop of Rockville Centre, April 16, 1957; installed May 27, 1957; died Jan. 11, 1986.

Vicar General—Most Rev. EMIL A. WCELA, D.D.

Episcopal Vicars—Western Vicariate: Rev. Msgr. JOHN A. ALESANDRO, S.T.L., J.C.D., J.D., Eastern Vicariate: Most Rev. EMIL A. WCELA, D.D., Central Vicariate: Most Rev. JOHN C. DUNNE, D.D.

Chancery—50 N. Park Ave., Rockville Centre, 11570. Tel: 516-678-5800; Fax: 516-678-1786(Building); 516-764-3316(Chancery).

Chancellor—Rev. Msgr. FRANCIS J. SCHNEIDER, J.C.D.

Vice-Chancellors—Sr. LUCY M. BLYSKAL, C.S.J., M.A., J.C.D.; Rev. Msgr. ALAN J. PLACA, J.D.; Rev. ROBERT J. BRENNAN, M.Div.

Secretary to the Bishop—Rev. Msgr. ROBERT J. BRENNAN, M.Div.

Diocesan Tribunal—50 N. Park Ave., Rockville Centre, 11570.

Officialis—Rev. Msgr. MICHAEL MANZELLI, S.T.L., J.C.D., M.A.

Vice-Officiales—Revs. THOMAS V. ARNAO, J.C.L.; ROBERT O. MORRISSEY, J.C.D.; Rev. Msgr. EDWARD A. SWEENEY, J.C.D.Cand.

Diocesan Judges—Sr. LUCY BLYSKAL, C.S.J., J.C.D.; Rev. Msgr. THOMAS D. CANDREVA, S.T.L., J.C.D.; Rev. Msgr. DOMENICK T. GRAZIADIO, M.A.; Revs. JAMES F. PEREDA, J.C.D.Cand.; RICHARD P. KOPINSKI, M.A., M.S.; Rev. Msgr. JOHN C. NOSSER, M.S.; Rev. Msgr. GEORGE P. GRAHAM, J.C.D., Ph.D.; Rev. Msgr. THOMAS E. MOLLOY, S.T.B., J.C.D.; Rev. Msgr. RICHARD C. BAUHOFF, J.C.D.; Rev. Msgr. CHARLES A. GUARINO, J.C.D.; Rev. Msgr. FRANCIS S. MIDURA, M.Ch.A.; Rev. Msgr. JOHN C. TUTONE, J.C.D.

Promoter of Justice—Rev. DONALD F. DIEDERICH, J.C.D.

Defender of the Bond—Sr. LOIS KELLER, R.S.M., J.C.L.

Adjunct Defender of the Bond—Rev. ABRAHAM PORUNNOLIL, J.C.L.

Post Annulment Counseling Coordinator—Mrs. MARGARET WILSON, M.A.

Medical Experts—Sr. PATRICIA BERLINER, Ph.D., *101-18 104th St., Ozone Park, 11416.* Dr. CHRISTOPHER DEEG, Ph.D., *7 Dix Hills Ct., Dix Hills, 11746.* Dr. ERIC R. LUTKER, Ph.D., *283 Commack Rd., Commack, 11725.* Dr. MARY ANN O'DONOHUE, Ph.D., *66 Leamington St., Lido Beach, 11561.* Dr. SIMEON RYAN, Ph.D., *53 Morris Pkwy., Valley Stream, 11580.*

Procurator-Advocates—Deacons JOSEPH T. BARTOLOTTO; EDWARD BILLIA; ROBERT P. BROYLES; Rev. WILLIAM G. BRESLAWSKI; Sr. MARY JANE BRUSTMAN, C.I.J.; Sr. IMELDA BUETOW, R.G.S.; Mrs. BARBARA BUTLER; Deacon FRANCISCO CALES; Mrs. VIRGINIA CONLIN; Sr. MIRIAM HONORA CORR, C.S.J.; Rev. THOMAS C. COSTA; Deacon FRANK COVE; Sr. LUCILLE D'AMELIO, O.P.; Deacon GREGORY D'ANGELO; Mr. RICHARD J. DEMARCO; Rev. JOHN DERASMO; Ms. ANITA DOS SANTOS; Rev. Msgr. JOHN P. DREASEN; Rev. LAWRENCE T. DUNCKLEE; Rev. Msgr. CHARLES R. FINK; JOHN J. FITZGERALD; Deacons ANDREW GARGIULO; RONALD GILLETTE; Sr. MARGARET ANN HARTIGAN, R.S.M.; Deacon ROBERT HESCHL; Sr. BONNIE KELLY, C.S.J.; Sr. JANE LYONS, C.I.J.; Rev. JAMES P. MANNION, JR.; Sr. CAROLANN MASONE, O.P.; Rev. Msgr. JAMES M. MCDONALD; Sr. PATRICIA A. MCDONNELL, C.S.J.; Rev. Msgr. JOHN J. MIRECKI; Revs. JOSEPH MIRRO; JOHN R. MOORE; Mrs. NANCY NEWBERT; Sr. MERCY POSTHAUER, O.P.; Sr. MARIETTE QUINN, I.H.M.; Sr. MARY RONALD, C.S.F.N.; Deacon PETER SCHULTZ; Revs. THOMAS J. ST. PIERRE; ANTHONY STRAGANELLI; Sr. MARIA STAPLETON, C.S.J.; Rev. JOSEPH W. STAUDT; Mrs. ANN-MARY STREIDER; Sr. KATHLEEN T. SULLIVAN, C.S.J.; Deacon GARY SWANE; Sr. EUGENIA A. TRAVERS, O.P.; Rev. Msgr. EDMOND J. TRENCH; Sr. JANE LYONS, C.I.J.; Sr. PATRICIA TURLEY, C.S.J.; Sr. CAROLANN MASONE, O.P.; Mrs. VIRGINIA CONLIN; Sr. MONA GURRETTE, D.W.; Sr. ELLEN ZAK, C.S.F.N.; Rev. ANDRZEJ ZGLEJSZEWSKI.

Notaries—Sr. RUTH BORGERSEN, R.S.M., M.A.; Mrs. C. GATZ; Sr. MARGARET GERARD VON ACHEN, O.P., M.A., M.S.; Mrs. H. HOWE; Mrs. G. ROHE; Mrs. T. TUZZOLINO.

Archives—Ms. JEAN WASSONG.

College of Consultors—Most Rev. JOHN R. MCGANN, D.D.; Most Rev. JOHN C. DUNNE, D.D.; Most Rev. EMIL A. WCELA, D.D.; Rev. Msgr. JOHN A. ALESANDRO; Rev. Msgr. DANIEL E. FAGAN; Rev. Msgr. THOMAS S. KANE; Rev. Msgr. FRANCIS J. SCHNEIDER; Rev. Msgr. JOHN J. SKELLY; Rev. Msgr. DANIEL J. HURLEY; Revs. BRIAN MCKEON; BRIAN J. MCNAMARA; JOSEPH MIRRO; FREDERICK J. PELLEGRINI, S.J.

Senate of Priests—Most Rev. JOHN R. MCGANN, D.D.; Most Rev. JOHN C. DUNNE, D.D.; Most Rev. EMIL A. WCELA, D.D.; Rev. Msgr. JOHN A. ALESANDRO; Rev. Msgr. ROBERT EMMET FAGAN; Revs. WILLIAM BRESLAWSKI; WILLIAM E. KOENIG; Rev. DANIEL E. FAGAN; Rev. Msgr. DANIEL J. HURLEY; Rev. Msgr. THOMAS S. KANE; Revs. BRIAN A. MCKEON; BRIAN J. MCNAMARA; JOSEPH A. MIRRO; FREDERICK PELLEGRINI, S.J.; Rev. Msgr. FRANCIS J. SCHNEIDER; Rev. Msgr. JOHN J. SKELLY.

Deans and Assistant Deans—Deanery 1, Rockville Centre: Rev. Msgr. DONALD T. BENNETT,

Deanery 2, North Hempstead: Rev. Msgr. JOHN J. SKELLY,

Deanery 3, Oyster Bay: Rev. Msgr. JOHN J. MCCANN,

Deanery 4, Belmont: Rev. Msgr. JOHN R. DREASEN,

Deanery 5, Hicksville: Rev. Msgr. JAMES E. BOESEL,

Deanery 6, Five Towns: Rev. Msgr. CHARLES R. FINK,

Deanery 7, Seaford: Rev. Msgr. ROBERT E. GUGLIELMONE,

Deanery 8, Huntington: Rev. Msgr. PATRICK J. ARMSHAW,

Deanery 9, Babylon: Rev. Msgr. ROBERT J. SACCACIO,

Deanery 10, Islip: Rev. Msgr. JOHN J. ROWAN,

Deanery 11, North Brookhaven: Rev. Msgr. JOHN A. MCGUIRE,

Deanery 12, South Brookhaven: Rev. Msgr. JAMES MCDONALD,

Deanery 13, Peconic: Rev. Msgr. JOHN P. SULLIVAN,

Deanery 14, Smithtown; Rev. Msgr. CHARLES A. GUARINO.

Diocesan Offices and Directors

Director of Administration—Mr. HENRY DWYER. Tel: 516-678-5800.

Apostleship of Prayer—Rev. Msgr. JAMES M. MCDONALD, Dir.

Catholics of African Ancestry—Vacant.

Building Office—Mr. CHESTER STRZEPEK, Dir.

Diocesan Building Commission—Rev. Msgr. JOHN A. ALESANDRO, Chm.; Rev. Msgr. RONALD HAYDE; Rev. Msgr. DANIEL A. PICCIANO; Rev. Msgr. BRENDAN P. RIORDAN; Mr. EDWARD FITZPATRICK; Mr. JOSEPH MCCORMACK; Mr. EUGENE SOUTHER, ESQ.; Mr. CHESTER STRZEPEK; Mr. CHARLES V. VACHRIS.

Campus and Young Adult Ministry—Rev. Msgr. DONALD M. BECKMANN, D.Min., Diocesan Dir./Pastor, Campus Parish, *50 N. Park Ave., Rockville Centre, 11510.* Tel: 516-678-5800. Ms. MARY BETH REYNOLDS, Prog. Coord., Young Adult Min.

Office of Catechesis—GEORGE RAND, Dir.; Sr. ANNE MARIE DEAN, C.S.J., Central Vicariate, Catechetical Coord., DRE Personnel Service; Sr. JOAN MARY FINN, O.P., Coord. Pastoral Ministry for the Deaf; Sr. SALLY RYAN, R.S.M., Western Vicariate, Catechetical Coord. Pastoral Ministry for persons with Disabilities; Ms. DIANE VELLA, Eastern Vicariate, Catechetical Coord. Adult Catechesis. Secretarial Staff: Mrs. THERESA ALBANESE; Mrs. MARY BENNETT; Mrs. ELEANOR SHERIDAN; Mrs. PATRICIA DALY, Dept. Mgr.

Office of Worship—Rev. Msgr. RONALD E. HAYDE, M.Div., Dir.; Sr. SHEILA BROWNE, R.S.M., Coord., Catechumenate and Ligurgical/Musical Support Svcs. Secretarial Staff: Mrs. MARION HAWKEY; Mrs. MICHELE KASHUBA; Mrs. CAROL QUARANTO; Mrs. PATRICIA DALY, Dept. Mgr.

Catholic Charities—Rev. Msgr. JOHN D. GILMARTIN, Diocesan Dir., *90 Cherry Ln., Hicksville, 11801-6232.* Tel: 516-733-7000.

Catholic Press Association of the Diocese of Rockville Centre, Inc., Publisher of "The Long Island Catholic"—ELIZABETH O'CONNOR, Editor, *99 N. Village Ave., P.O. Box 9009, Rockville Centre, 11571-9009.* Tel: 516-594-1000.

Catholic Relief Service—Sr. CATHERINE KELLY, S.S.J.

Cemeteries—Mrs. ELLEN WOODBURY, Dir., *Catholic Cemeteries, P.O. Box 182, Westbury, 11590.* Tel: 516-334-7998.

Censors of Books—Rev. Msgr. JOHN A. ALESANDRO, S.T.L., J.C.D.; Rev. Msgr. FRANCIS X. GLIMM, S.T.L.; Rev. Msgr. GEORGE P. GRAHAM, M.Div., J.C.D.; Rev Msgr. FRANCIS J. SCHNEIDER, J.C.D.; Rev. ROBERT J. SMITH, S.T.D.

Charismatic Renewal Services of Long Island, Inc.—Mr. STEPHEN BENTHAL, Dir.; Mr. JOHN BOUCHER, *P.O. Box 7338, Hicksville, 11802.* Tel: 516-822-1163.

Hatian Apostolate—Rev. MOISE AIME, Dir.

Office of Justice and Peace—Board Members: Mrs. ALICE BOYLE; Mr. ROB SMITH; Rev. Msgr. JOHN D. GILMARTIN, Chm.; Mr. JOHN MCNAMARA; Mrs. MARGARET MELKONIAN; Rev. BRUCE REED; Rev. Msgr. DENNIS M. REGAN, Consultant; Sr. ROSE SHERIDAN, C.S.J., Staff; Rev. JOHN W. WHITE; Rev. GERALD S. TWOMEY.

Commission on Parish Boundaries—Rev. Msgr. JOHN F. BENNETT, Chm.; Rev. WILLIAM GILL; Rev. Msgr. JOHN A. MCGUIRE; Rev. Msgr. ROBERT T. MULLIGAN; Rev. Msgr. FRANCIS J. SCHNEIDER; Rev. Msgr. THOMAS SPADARO; Mr. CHET STRZEPEK, Exec. Sec.

Consultation Service for Religious Personnel, Inc.—Sr. THOMAS MORE, R.G.S., Exec. Dir., *984 N. Village Ave., Rockville Centre, 11570.* Tel: 516-678-2135.

Office of Bishop's Annual Appeal—JOHN J. KELLY, Dir.

Office of Development—JOHN J. KELLY, Dir.

Stewardship Office—JERRY LOCEY, Dir. LOIS TYLUS, Assoc. Dir., *P.O. Box 532, Rockville Centre, 11571.* Tel: 516-763-6795; Fax: 516-763-6799.

Office of Religious Retirement Fund—JOHN J. KELLY, Dir.

Office of Permanent Deacons—Deacon GERARD WILSON, Dir.

Diocesan Commodities, Corp.—Mr. CHET STRZEPEK, Gen. Mgr. Tel: 516-764-2130.

Diocesan Service, Inc.—Risk Mgmt. & Insurance, *253 Sunrise Hwy., Rockville Centre, 11570.* Tel: 516-678-1000.

Diocese of Rockville Centre Protected Self Insurance Program—50 N. Park Ave., Rockville Centre, 11570. Tel: 516-678-5800.

Diocesan Campaign for Human Development—Rev. Msgr. JOHN D. GILMARTIN, Dir.

Due Process Committee (Conciliation-Arbitration)—Sr. LUCY BLYSKAL, C.S.J., J.C.D., Exec. Sec.

Ecumenism, Office of Ecumenical & Interreligious Affairs—50 N. Park Ave., Rockville Centre, 11570. Tel: 516-678-5800. Rev. Msgr. DONALD M. BECKMANN, D.Min., Dir.

Education Dept.—Sr. JOANNE CALLAHAN, O.S.U., M.A., P.D., Supt., Schools; JOANNE O'BRIEN, M.A., M.Ed., Ed.D., Assoc. Supt., Schools; Sr. MARIE CHAMINADE, O.P., Ed.D., Asst. Supt., Government Affairs; ROSEMARY DAMM, M.A., Dir., Curriculum & Instruction; Mr. BIAGIO M. ARPINO, M.S., P.D., Dir., Teacher Personnel; Sr. TERESA RORKE, C.S.J., M.S., P.D., Dir., Regional School Planning; Sr. CATHERINE STARE, S.C., M.S., M.A., Dir., Curriculum & Testing; Sr. ANTOINETTE DE AVEIRO, O.P., M.S., Dir., Early Childhood Programs.

Finance Council—Mr. HARRY DWYER, Chm.; Rev. Msgr. JOHN ALESANDRO; Rev. Msgr. JAMES KELLY; Mr. D. DESMOND MCCARTHY; Mr. KEVIN MURPHY; Rev. Msgr. JOHN ROWAN.

Health Care Ministry—Rev. Msgr. ALAN J. PLACA, Sec. to the Bishop for Health Affairs. Tel: 516-678-5800. Bro. CAMPION LALLY, O.S.F., Exec Dir.; Sr. PATRICIA HARTIGAN, O.P., Dir., Pastoral Planning.

Chaplaincy Services & Pastoral Health Ministries—Sr. EILEEN DONOVAN, O.P., Dir. Tel: 516-678-5800.

Diocesan Medical Ethics Commission—Rev. Msgr. ALAN J. PLACA, Exec. Sec. *Members*—Rev. Msgr. DENNIS M. REGAN, S.T.D., Chm.; Rev. Msgr. JOHN A. ALESANDRO, J.C.D.; Sr. ALICE O'SHAUGHNESSY, M.D.; Sr. EILEEN DONOVAN, O.P.; DAVID J. FLEMING, ESQ.; Rev. Msgr. GEORGE P. GRAHAM, J.C.D.; Sr. AUDREY HARSEN, O.P.; VINCENT DI RUBBIO; Mrs. DONNA M. O'BRIEN; Mr. PATRICK J. SCOLLARD; Bro. CAMPION LALLY, O.S.F.; Rev. EUGENE F. MURPHY; Mr. BARRY ZEMAN; Rev. VINCENT RUSH; Mr. LEWIS GROSSMAN; Rev. ROBERT S. SMITH, S.T.D.; JAMES B. TORMEY, M.D.; ROBERT F. VIZZA, Ph.D.; DANIEL P. WALSH; ROBERT J. SMITH, Chm.

Family Ministry, Office of—RICK HINSHAW, Dir. Coords.: Dr. NANCY BENVENGA; Mrs. PATRICIA FLYNN; Ms. PATRICIA MCDONOUGH; Sr. JUDITH O'BRIEN; Mrs. MAUREEN RUSSELL.

Respect Life Coordinator—RICK HINSHAW.

Finance Office—Mr. KEVIN T. MURPHY, Chief Fiscal Officer; Mr. DENNIS J. MEEKINS, Dir., Diocesan Accounting.

Holy Childhood Association—Sr. CATHERINE G. KELLY, S.S.J.

Holy Name Societies, Diocesan Union of—Rev. JOHN P. HALPIN, Spiritual Dir.

Information Bureau—JOHN KAL, Dir., Communications, *P.O. Box 9009, Rockville Centre, 11570.* Tel: 516-594-1000.

Manager of Employee Benefits—JOHN CALAMARI.

Manager of Property and Casualty Insurance—JAMES A. WALLACE. Tel: 516-678-5800.

Lawyers' Guild—Rev. Msgr. GEORGE P. GRAHAM, M.Div., Moderator/Dir.

Legion of Mary—Rev. GERALD FITZSIMMONS, S.M.M.

Nocturnal Adoration Society—Rev. Msgr. JAMES M. MCDONALD.

Physicians' Guild—Rev. EUGENE F. MURPHY.

Director for Priest Personnel—Rev. Msgr. FRANCIS J. CALDWELL, M.S.W.

Priests Personnel Assignment Board—Most Rev. JOHN R. MCGANN, D.D.; Most Rev. JOHN C. DUNNE, D.D.; Most Rev. EMIL A. WCELA, D.D.; Rev. Msgr. JOHN A. ALESANDRO, D.D., J.C.D.; Rev. Msgr. RICHARD C. BAUHOFF, J.C.D.; Rev. Msgr. FRANCIS J. CALDWELL, M.S.W.; Rev. Msgr. EDWARD DONNELLY; Rev. Msgr. JAMES P. KELLY; Revs. BRIAN J. INGRAM; CHARLES E. PAPA; KENNETH H. WINKLER.

Priests Personnel Policy Board—Rev. Msgr. FRANCIS J. CALDWELL, M.S.W.; Rev. Msgr. ROBERT GUGLIELMONE; Rev. Msgr. CHARLES R. FINK; Revs. JOSEPH DEGROCCO; ANTHONY M. STANGANELLI; Rev. JOHN WHITE, Chm.

Ministry to Priests-Internship Program-Sabbatical—Rev. Msgr. FRANCIS J. CALDWELL, M.S.W., Dir.

St. Pius X Priests' Residence and Vicar for Senior Priests—Rev. ROBERT BLYMAN, M.D.

Vocations Office—Rev. THOMAS J. HAROLD.

Priests' Sickness, Disability and Retirement Board—Most Rev. JOHN R. MCGANN, D.D., Chm.; Most Rev. JOHN C. DUNNE, D.D.; Rev. Msgr. JOHN A. ALESANDRO; Rev. Msgr. CHARLES A. GUARINO; Rev. Msgr. ROBERT GUGLIELMONE; Revs. ROBERT Y. BLYMAN; ROBERT J. CLERKIN; THOMAS W. GROENEWOLD; Rev. Msgr. JOHN P. MARTIN; Rev. Msgr. FRANCIS J. CALDWELL, Dir., Priest Personnel; Rev. Msgr. THADDEUS ROONEY; Rev. Msgr. JAMES SWIADER.

Prison Ministry and Criminal Justice, Office of—Pastoral Team: Bro. JOHN MOYLAN, O.S.F., Dir.; Sr. VIRGINIA WATERS, F.S.P.; Revs. WILLIAM R. SCRILL; RALPH FERRO; Bro. LARRY BACKUS, C.S.C.; Sr. MICHELLE BREMER, C.S.F.N., *1767 Deer Park Ave., Deer Park, 11729.* Tel: 516-242-8631. For individual institutions see separate listing.

Mission Office—Sr. CATHERINE G. KELLY, S.S.J., Dir.

Telicare of the Diocese of Rockville Centre—Rev. Msgr. THOMAS J. HARTMAN, Dir.; Mr. MICHAEL O'LEARY, Gen. Mgr. Tel: 516-538-8700.

Research & Planning, Diocesan Office of—Mr. CHESTER J. STRZEPEK, M.S., P.D., Dir.

Resettlement Council (Immigration Matters)—Catholic Charities-See separate listing.

Seminary of the Immaculate Conception Board of Governors—Most Rev. JOHN R. MCGANN, D.D., Chm.; Most Rev. EMIL A. WCELA, D.D., Vice Chm.; Most Rev. RENE A. VALERO; Rev. Msgr. F. J. SCHNEIDER, S.T.L., J.C.D.; Rev. Msgr. OTTO L. GARCIA; Rev. Msgr. VINCENT A. KEANE; Rev. DONALD J. HARRINGTON, C.M.; Rev. JOSEPH LEVESQUE, C.M.; Rev. ROBERT J. WHELAN; JUDITH HEALY, Ph.D.; Mr. JAMES T. MCCARTHY; Dr. IRENE IMPELLIZZERI; Mrs. HILDA BROSKY; Mr. KEVIN T. MURPHY; Sr. JOHN RAYMOND MCGANN, C.S.J.; Mr. EDWARD B. FITZPATRICK, JR.; Rev. Msgr. VINCENT F. FULLAM, S.T.D.; Revs. MICHAEL TEDONE; THOMAS J. HAROLD.

Shrines and Pilgrimages—Rev. Msgr. RONALD E. HAYDE, Liaison.

Spanish Apostolate, Diocesan—Sr. CAROLANN MASONE, O.P., Dir.

Vicar for Hispanics—Rev. Msgr. PABLO M. RODRIQUEZ.

Vicars for Religious—Sr. MARIA REGINA LOURES, I.H.M.; Bro. PATRICK MURPHY, O.S.F.

Women's Commission—JOSEPHINE E. MISCIOSCIA, Co-Chm. MARYBETH ZEMAN, Co-Chm. PATRICIA MIZZI; MARY ANN O'CONNOR; PATRICIA A. RIEGGER; MARY

J. WEILER; ANITA L. YOUNG; Rev. VINCENT T. RUSH, Sec.

Youth Ministries, Office of—Mr. MICHAEL G. MCCARTHY, Dir.; Rev. KEVIN SMITH, Chap., Scouting; Mr. AUSTIN CANNON, Prog. Coord., Scouting; Mrs. MARIANNE COLLINS, Prog. Coord., C.Y.O. -Support.

CLERGY, PARISHES, MISSIONS AND PAROCHIAL SCHOOLS

VILLAGE OF ROCKVILLE CENTRE (Nassau County)

1—ST. AGNES CATHEDRAL (1894), Most Rev. John R. McGann, D.D.; Revs. German Villabon, O.S.A.; William E. Koenig; Thomas W. Groenewold; Deacons Thomas McDaid; Vincent Smyth. In res., Rev. Msgr. Frank J. Caldwell; Rev. Msgr. Ronald E. Hayde; Rev. Msgr. Robert J. Brennan.
Res., 29 Quealy Pl., 11570. Tel: 516-766-0205; Fax: 516-763-0745.
School—Tel: 516-678-5550; Fax: 516-678-0437. Sr. Kathleen Carlin, Prin.
Sisters of St. Dominic 3; Lay Teachers 39; Students 887.
Catechesis/Religious Programs—Tel: 516-678-2306. Mrs. Donna Eschenauer, D.R.E.
Students 1365.

2—CAMPUS PARISH OF LONG ISLAND (1972), Rev. Msgr. Donald M. Beckmann, D.Min.
Res., Office. (For details, please refer to Campus Ministries and Newman Centers located under the Institution section.) 50 N. Park Ave., 11570. Tel: 516-678-5800, Ext. 613.

OUTSIDE VILLAGE OF ROCKVILLE CENTRE

Amityville, Suffolk Co., St. Martin's (1897), Rev. Msgr. Robert J. Saccacio; Revs. Richard T. Stelter; Francis Sang.
Res., 37 Union Ave., 11701. Tel: 516-264-0124; Fax: 516-264-0139.
School—Tel: 516-264-7166.
Sisters of St. Dominic (Union Ave.) 4; Lay Teachers 21; Students 524.
Catechesis/Religious Programs—Tel: 516-691-1617.
Students 388.

Babylon, Suffolk Co., St. Joseph's (1877), Rev. Msgr. Ronald A. Richardson; Revs. John R. Moore; Thomas G. McCormick; Thomas P. Maloney; Deacons Michael J. Leyden; John F. Sullivan. In res., Rev. John J. Gorman.
Res., 39 N. Carll Ave., 11702-2701. Tel: 516-669-0068; Fax: 516-669-9175. [CEM]
Catechesis/Religious Programs—Tel: 516-587-4717. Marianne Mione, D.R.E.
Students 1,507.
Missions—Oak Beach, Suffolk Co. (Summer) 11702; West Gilgo Beach, Suffolk Co. (Summer) 11702.

Baldwin, Nassau Co., St. Christopher (1915), Rev. Msgr. John F. Bennett; Rev. Msgr. Joseph F. Lawlor, Pastor Emeritus; Revs. Gennaro DiSpigno; Michael G. Boyle; Deacons Charles Muscarnera; Joseph Pellegrino.
Res., 11 Gale Ave., 11510. Tel: 516-223-0723; Fax: 516-867-5678.
School—21 Pershing Blvd., 11510. Tel: 516-223-4404. Sr. Dolores McLaughlin, Prin.
Sisters of St. Joseph 4; Lay Teachers 18; Students 423.
Catechesis/Religious Programs—Tel: 516-223-5813. D.R.E.: Mrs. Julianne Markey; Mrs. Gail Milne.
Students 1,098.

Bay Shore, Suffolk Co., St. Patrick's (1883), Rev. Msgr. Robert Emmet Fagan; Revs. Joseph W. Staudt, Pastoral Assoc.; Robert Giuntini; Deacons Joseph Peralta; Michael Mahoney. In res., Rev. Msgr. James F. Coffey, Pastor Emeritus; Rev. Msgr. Richard P. Hendel, (Retired).
Res., 9 N. Clinton Ave., 11706. Tel: 516-665-4911; Fax: 516-665-8388. [CEM]
School—6 N. Clinton Ave., 11706. Tel: 516-665-0569. Ms. Cathleen Quinn, Prin.
Lay Teachers 22; Students 515.
Catechesis/Religious Programs—Tel: 516-665-4914.
Students 1,190.

Bayville, Nassau, St. Gertrude's (1959), Revs. Peter Kaczmarek; Martin W. Curley.
Res., 28 School St., 11709. Tel: 516-628-1113; Fax: 516-628-9032.
Catechesis/Religious Programs—Tel: 516-628-2432.
Students 520.

Bellmore, Nassau Co., St. Barnabas the Apostle (1912), Rev. Peter C. Dooley; Rev. Msgr. Daniel J. Potterton, Pastor Emeritus; Revs. Edward J. Muhs, Pastor Emeritus; Brian Ingram; Robert Petekiewicz; Deacons Bernard Sherlock; Paul Bedell.
Res., 2320 Bedford Ave., 11710. Tel: 516-785-0054; Fax: 516-221-7789.
Schools—St. Elizabeth Ann Seton Regional School, Bellmore Campus, 2341, Washington Ave., Tel: 516-785-5709; Fax: 516-785-4468.; St. Elizabeth Ann Seton Regional School, East Meadow Campus, 600 Newbridge Road, East Meadow, Tel: 516-785-7006; Fax: 516-784-7008. See Regional Schools under Institutions Located in the Diocese.
Catechesis/Religious Programs—Tel: 516-785-0130.
Students 1,200.

Bellport, Suffolk Co., Mary Immaculate (1905), Rev. Msgr. Bernard J. Ryan; Rev. Constantino Nieva; Deacon Arthur J. Dooling.
Res., 16 Brown's Ln., 11713. Tel: 516-286-0154; Fax: 516-286-2937.
School—Holy Angels Regional School, Patchogue, Tel: 516-475-4220. See Regional Schools under Institutions Located in the Diocese.
Catechesis/Religious Programs—Tel: 516-286-3504.
Students 420.

Bethpage, Nassau Co., St. Martin of Tours (1923), Revs. Raymond Collins, C.SS.R.; Thomas Schmidt, C.SS.R.; Kevin MacDonald, C.SS.R.; Vincent Crotty, C.SS.R.
Res., 40 Seaman Ave., 11714. Tel: 516-931-0818; Fax: 516-931-0559.
School—St. John Baptist de LaSalle Regional School, Bethpage/Farmingdale. See Regional Schools under Institutions Located in the Diocese. Tel: 516-931-0983.
Catechesis/Religious Programs—208 Broadway, 11714. Tel: 516-822-9768. Mrs. Elizabeth Lukaschek, D.R.E.
Students 400.

Blue Point, Suffolk Co., Our Lady of the Snow (1917), Revs. Diarmuid F. McGann; Richard M. Scanlon, Pastor Emeritus; Deacons Robert Gronenthal; Steve Kramer; Frank Hartmann.
Res., 175 Blue Point Ave., 11715. Tel: 516-363-6385; Fax: 516-363-7394.
School—Prince of Peace Regional School, Sayville, Tel: 516-589-3426. See Regional Schools under Institutions Located in the Diocese.
Catechesis/Religious Programs—Tel: 516-363-6394.
Students 900.

Bohemia, Suffolk Co., St. John Nepomucene (1919), Revs. James L. Wood; Louis L. Reuss, Pastor Emeritus; Charles N. Mangano; Deacons Richard Wanser; James Bohuslaw. In res., Rev. Bartholomew J. Galvin, M.M.
Res., 1140 Locust Ave., 11716. Tel: 516-589-0540; Fax: 516-244-8086. [CEM]
School—Prince of Peace Regional School, Sayville. See Regional Schools under Institutions Located in the Diocese. Tel: 516-589-0422.
Catechesis/Religious Programs—1150 Locust Ave., 11716. Tel: 516-567-1765.
Students 1,450.

Brentwood, Suffolk Co., St. Anne's (1895), Revs. Thomas J. St. Pierre; Gerald S. Twomey; James J. Hannon; Deacons Jesus Alvarado; Juan Diaz; Terence A. Rasanen; Thomas R. Samson.
Res., 88 Second Ave., 11717. Tel: 516-273-8113; Fax: 516-436-7914.
School—Our Lady of Providence Regional School, Central Islip, Tel: 516-234-6324; Fax: 516-234-6360. See Regional Schools under Institutions Located in the Diocese.
Catechesis/Religious Programs—Tel: 516-231-7344. Ms. Virginia Conzo, D.R.E.
Students 818.

St. Luke (1965), Revs. William R. Logan; Camilo Lugo; Deacons Wenceslao Rivera; Richard A. Luken.
Res., 266 Wicks Rd., 11717. Tel: 516-273-1110; Fax: 516-951-2779. [JC]
School—Our Lady of Providence Regional School, Central Islip, Tel: 516-234-6535. See Regional Schools under Institutions Located in the Diocese.
Catechesis/Religious Programs—Tel: 516-273-4333.
Students 912.

Bridgehampton, Suffolk Co., Queen of the Most Holy Rosary (1922), Rev. Patrick J. Callan.
Mailing Address: P.O. Box 3035, 11932. Tel: 516-537-0156; Fax: 516-537-7116.
School—Stella Maris Regional School, Sag Harbor, Tel: 516-725-2525; Fax: 516-725-4587. See Regional Schools under Institutions Located in the Diocese.

Brookville, Nassau Co., St. Paul the Apostle (1962), Revs. Mario Costa; Arthur C. Anderson.
Res., Cedar Swamp Rd., Brookville, Glen Head, 11545. Tel: 516-935-1880; Fax: 516-938-3683.
Catechesis/Religious Programs—Tel: 516-938-4531. D.R.E.: Sr. Regina Kraft; Mr. Len Tufaro.
Students 471.

Carle Place, Nassau Co., Church of Our Lady of Hope (1987), Rev. Msgr. Francis S. Midura; Rev. Francis S. Midura; Deacons Lawrence V. Hammel; John T. Hickey; Thomas B. Rich; Raymond J. Tirelli.
Church—Cherry Ln. & Broadway, P.O. Box 352, 11514-0352. Tel: 516-334-6288; Fax: 516-997-4622.
School—St. Brigid/ Our Lady of Hope Regional School, 101 Maple Ave., Westbury, 11590.
Catechesis/Religious Programs—Tel: 516-334-4781. Margaret V. Cecere, D.R.E.
Students 865.

Cedarhurst, Nassau Co., St. Joachim (1894), Rev. Paul Rahilly; Deacon Frank J. Bono.
Res., 614 Central Ave., 11516. Tel: 516-569-1845; Fax: 516-569-0117.
School—620 Central Ave., 11516. Tel: 516-569-2290.
Sisters of St. Joseph 3; Lay Teachers 11; Students 248.
Catechesis/Religious Programs—Tel: 516-295-0878.
Students 204.

Centereach, Suffolk Co., Assumption of the Blessed Virgin Mary (1955), Rev. Msgr. Joseph K. Curley; Revs. Lawrence T. Duncklee; Ramon Joseph.
Res., 20 Chestnut St., 11720. Tel: 516-585-8760; Fax: 516-585-3601.
Catechesis/Religious Programs—Tel: 516-588-6408. Mrs. Miriam Selig, D.R.E.
Students 1,282.

Center Moriches, Suffolk Co., St. John the Evangelist (1898), Rev. John J. Corcoran, Pastor Emeritus; Rev. Msgr. James M. McDonald, Pastor; Rev. Kevin W. Gruber, Assoc. Pastor; Deacons Galvin Murphy; Chris Vigliotta.
Res., 25 Ocean Ave., 11934. Tel: 516-878-0009; Fax: 516-874-2466.
School—Our Lady, Queen of Apostles Regional School, Center Moriches. See Regional Schools under Institutions Located in the Diocese. Tel: 516-878-1033; Fax: 516-878-1059.
Catechesis/Religious Programs—Tel: 516-878-4141.
Students 1600.

Centerport, Suffolk Co., Our Lady Queen of Martyrs (1966), Rev. Msgr. T. Peter Ryan; Rev. Harold J. Heindel; Sr. Eileen Corcoran, O.P. In res., Rev. Msgr. Joseph F. Colligan, Pastor Emeritus.
Res., Prospect and Mill Dam Rds., P.O. Box 609, 11721. Tel: 516-757-8184; Fax: 516-262-0155.
School—Trinity Regional School, East Northport, Tel: 516-261-5130; Fax: 516-266-5345. See Regional Schools under Institutions Located in the Diocese.
Catechesis/Religious Programs—Tel: 516-757-0720. Margaret Dritto, D.R.E.
Students 1004.

Central Islip, Suffolk Co., St. John of God (1904), Revs. Joseph P. Granata; Gerald F. Di Giralamo, S.A.; William F. Brisotti. Pastoral Assocs.: Sr. Catherine Peluso, O.P.; Sr. Agnes Claudia Allen, C.S.J., (Spanish Apostolate); Deacon Ronald J. Gillette. In res., Revs. Augustine J. Sheehan, Chap. Northport Veterans' Hospital; John P. Halpin, Chap., Pilgrim Psychiatric Center.
Res., 84 Carleton Ave., 11722. Tel: 516-234-6535; Fax: 516-234-7474. [CEM]
School—Our Lady of Providence Regional School, Central Islip. See Regional Schools under Institutions Located in the Diocese. Tel: 516-234-6324.
Catechesis/Religious Programs—Tel: 516-234-4040. Sonia Repole, D.R.E.
Students 539.
Parish Outreach Office—Tel: 516-234-1884. Elizabeth B. Bures.
Convent—330 St. John St., 11722. Tel: 516-234-6533. Sisters of St. Joseph

Commack, Suffolk Co., Christ the King (1959), Revs. George J. Hein; Sabbas Rodrigues; Simon Fernando; Jeffrey J. Madley.
Res., Indian Head Rd., P.O. Box 284, 11725. Tel: 516-864-1623; Fax: 516-864-8891.
School—Holy Family Regional School, Commack, Tel: 516-543-0202; Fax: 516-543-0203. See Regional Schools under Institutions Located in the Diocese.
Catechesis/Religious Programs—Tel: 516-864-3696. Mrs. Viola Fusco, D.R.E.
Students 1,020.

Copiague, Suffolk Co., Our Lady of the Assumption (1928), Revs. Michael Flynn; Peter Karpiel; Edward Sullivan.
Res., Molloy St., 11726. Tel: 516-842-5211; 842-5476; Fax: 516-789-5326.
Catechesis/Religious Programs—Ruth Durago, D.R.E.
Students 920.

Coram, Suffolk Co., St. Frances Cabrini (1953), Revs.

Nicholas J. Figliola; Siby J. Alenchery; Deacon Carmen L. Pagrotta.
Res., 134 Middle County Rd., 11727. Tel: 516-732-8445; Fax: 516-732-8130.
School—Holy Angels Regional School, Patchogue, Tel: 516-475-0422. See Regional Schools under Institutions Located in the Diocese.
Catechesis/Religious Programs—Tel: 516-698-3149. Sr. Dorothy Schnell, C.S.J., D.R.E.
Students 867.

Cutchogue, Suffolk Co., Sacred Heart (1901), Revs. Peter A. Allen; John P. Henry, Pastor Emeritus; Deacon John Bopp.
Res., 27700 Main Rd., P.O. Box 926, 11935-0926. Tel: 516-734-6722; Fax: 516-734-7906. [CEM]
School—Our Lady of Mercy Regional School, Tel: 516-734-5166. See Regional Schools under Institutions Located in the Diocese.
Catechesis/Religious Programs—Tel: 516-734-2568.
Students 375.
Mission—Mattituck, Suffolk Co., Our Lady of Good Counsel, Main Rd., 11952.

Our Lady of Ostrabrama (1909) (Polish), Rev. Msgr. John F. Cwalina, Pastor Emeritus; Rev. Msgr. John C. Nosser; Rev. Msgr. Tadeus Niewczas (Poland).
Res., Depot Ln., Box 997, 11935. Tel: 516-734-6446; Fax: 516-734-4117.
School—North Fork Regional Catholic School, Cutchogue, Tel: 516-734-5166. See Regional Schools under Institutions Located in the Diocese.
Catechesis/Religious Programs—Students 85.

Davis Park, Fire Island Suffolk Co., Most Precious Blood (1962). (Summer Mission). Rev. Msgr. Donald M. Beckmann, D.Min., Admin.
Mailing Address: St. Martha's, 546 Greengrove Ave., Uniondale, 11553. Tel: 516-481-2550.
Res., Spindrift Walk, Fire Island, 11728. Tel: 516-597-6525.

Deer Park, Suffolk Co., SS. Cyril and Methodius (1956), Rev. Msgr. Brendan P. Riordan; Revs. Joseph Baidoo; Forrest T. Parkinson; Donald C. Hayden. In res., Rev. Msgr. Alan J. Placa.
Res., 125 Half Hollow Rd., 11729-4288. Tel: 516-667-4044; Fax: 516-667-6237.
School—(Grades K-8). Tel: 516-667-6229.
Sisters of St. Joseph 2; Lay Teachers 27; Students 640; Nursery 70.
Catechesis/Religious Programs—Tel: 516-667-6264.
Students 598.

Dix Hills, Suffolk Co., St. Matthew (1965), Rev. Msgr. Saverio C. Mattei; Rev. Msgr. Leo J. Goggin, Pastor Emeritus; Revs. Lawrence A. Chadwick; Anthony Nguyen Phuoc Anh (Vietnam); Deacons James M. McQuade; Arnold Quaranta; Frank Gariboldi.
Res., 35 N. Service Rd., 11746. Tel: 516-499-8520.
School—Holy Family Regional School. See Regional Schools under Institutions Located in the Diocese. Tel: 516-453-0202.
Catechesis/Religious Programs—Tel: 516-499-8521. Mr. Anthony C. D'Amico, D.R.E.
Students 1,287.

East Hampton, Suffolk Co., Most Holy Trinity (1894), Rev. Donald J. Desmond, Pastor; Rev. Msgr. Christopher Huntington, Pastor Emeritus; Sr. Eileen Marie Connor, O.P., D.R.E.
Res., 57 Buell Ln., 11937. Tel: 516-324-0134; Fax: 516-329-3552. [CEM]
School—Stella Maris Regional School, Sag Harbor. See Regional Schools under Institutions Located in the Diocese. Tel: 516-725-2525; Fax: 516-725-4587.
Catechesis/Religious Programs—Tel: 516-324-7994; Fax: 516-329-3552.
Students 375.
Convent—79 Buell Ln., 11937. Tel: 516-324-1444.
Mission—Amagansett, Suffolk Co., St. Peter the Apostle, Main St., Amagansett, 11930. Tel: 516-324-0134; Fax: 516-329-3552.

East Islip, Suffolk Co., St. Mary's (1898), Rev. Steven J. Peterson; Rev. Msgr. Peter A. Chiara, Pastor Emeritus; Revs. Lucian Fernandes; Vincent Marteja; Deacon Gerard R. Wilson; Dorothy Horstmann, Pastoral Assoc.
Res., 20 Harrison Ave., 11730. Tel: 516-581-4266; Fax: 516-581-0112.
School—Tel: 516-581-3304; Fax: 516-581-7509. Biagio Arpino, Prin.
Lay Teachers 42; Students 950.
Catechesis/Religious Programs—Tel: 516-581-3304. D.R.E.: Susan Fullam; Sr. Katy Hamm.
Students 1,820.

East Meadow, Nassau Co., St. Raphael (1941), Revs. Thomas J. Haggerty; Aaron Vellaramparampil; Joseph E. Nohs; Sr. Judith Enterlin, C.S.J., Pastoral Assoc.
Res., 600 Newbridge Rd., 11554. Tel: 516-785-0236; Fax: 516-783-9578.
School—St. Elizabeth Ann Seton Regional School, East Meadow Campus. See Regional Schools under Institutions Located in the Diocese. Tel: 516-785-7006; Fax: 516-785-7008.
Catechesis/Religious Programs—Tel: 516-221-9096. D.R.E.: Sr. Elizabeth Mc Neill, R.S.M.; Sr. Karen Kaelin, C.S.J.
Students 1,500.

East Northport, Suffolk Co., St. Anthony of Padua (1951), Revs. Richard P. Hoerning; James Atkins; Edward R. D'Andrea; Deacons Robert Braun; Martin W. Duggan. In res., Revs. James A. Kirrane (BRK); Lawrence J. O'Leary.
Res., 20 Cheshire Pl., 11731-2591. Tel: 516-261-1077; Fax: 516-757-0572.
School—Trinity Regional School, East Northport. See Regional Schools under Institutions Located in the Diocese. Tel: 516-261-5130.
Catechesis/Religious Programs—Tel: 516-261-1306. D.R.E.: Mrs. Judith Corbellini; Mrs. Eileen Schlee; Mrs. Marguerite Goglia.
Students 1,130.

East Patchogue, Suffolk Co., St. Joseph the Worker (1955), Revs. Thomas March, O.F.M.Cap.; William Winters, O.F.M.Cap.; Joseph Shea, O.F.M.Cap.
Res., 510 Narragansett Ave., 11772. Tel: 516-286-9133; Fax: 516-286-9145.
School—Holy Angels Regional School, Patchogue. See Regional Schools under Institutions Located in the Diocese. Tel: 516-475-0422; Fax: 516-475-2036.
Catechesis/Religious Programs—Mrs. Therese Marsh, D.R.E.
Students 652.

East Rockaway, Nassau Co., St. Raymond's (1909), Rev. Msgr. William W. Jablonski; Rev. William V. Singleton, Pastor Emeritus. Pastoral Assocs.: Revs. Antonio S. Pascual; Michael A. Carroll; Deacons Robert C. Campbell; Richard W. LaRossa; Gregory D'Angelo; Guy Donza. In res., Rev. James P. Moyna.
Res., 263 Atlantic Ave., 11518. Tel: 516-593-5000; Fax: 516-887-0554.
School—Tel: 516-593-9010; Fax: 516-593-0986.
Sisters, Servants of the Immaculate Heart of Mary 4; Lay Teachers 18; Students 382.
Catechesis/Religious Programs—Tel: 516-593-9075. Mrs. Evelyn Contaldi, D.R.E.
Students 826.

Elmont, Nassau Co., St. Boniface, Revs. John R. Dreasen, V.F.; Mathew Kottaram (India); Douglas Dower; George Punti; Sr. Evelyn Lamoureux, D.W., Human Services. In res., Rev. Francis Odufuye (Nigeria).
Res., 631 Elmont Rd., 11003. Tel: 516-354-0715.
School—Sr. Mary Brown, Prin. Sisters of St. Dominic 11; Lay Teachers 15; Students 297.
Catechesis/Religious Programs—Sr. Eileen Corcoran, O.P., D.R.E.
Students 900.

St. Vincent de Paul (1951), Revs. Joseph M. Hickey, M.A., M.S.Ed., P.D.; Augustine Fernando; Bruce Reed, M.Div. In res., Rev. Francis J. Schneider, J.C.D., M.Div.; Deacon Thomas Divita.
Res., 1500 DePaul St., 11003. Tel: 516-352-2127; Fax: 516-352-3099.
Catechesis/Religious Programs—Tel: 516-352-2265. Ms. Mary Alice Burchell, M.A., D.R.E.
Students 626.

Farmingdale, Nassau Co., St. Kilian (1896), Rev. Msgr. Charles W. Swiger; Revs. Angel V. Resultay (Philippines); Charles P. Romano; Lawrence Kupferman; Leo Peter Prengaman, S.J.; Deacons Frank D. Barone; Lucio Cotone; Herman Rodenburg; Donald Zirkel. In res., Most Rev. John C. Dunne.
Res., 485 Conklin St., 11735. Tel: 516-249-0127; Fax: 516-249-7131.
School—St. John Baptist de LaSalle Regional School, Bethpage/Farmingdale. See Regional Schools under Institutions Located in the Diocese. Tel: 516-931-0983 (Bethpage); 516-694-3610 (Farmingdale); Fax: 516-931-1502 (Bpg); 516-694-3614 (Fmdl).
Catechesis/Religious Programs—Tel: 516-694-0633; Fax: 516-454-8612. Mrs. Joanne Kolasa, D.R.E.
Students 1,246.

Farmingville, Suffolk Co., Church of the Resurrection (1988), Rev. Thomas F. Mulvanerty; Deacons Daniel Macellaro; Walter Williams.
Church—50 Granny Rd., 11738. Tel: 516-696-0232; Fax: 516-696-0271.
Catechesis/Religious Programs—Tel: 516-696-0270.
Students 698.

Floral Park, Nassau Co., St. Hedwig's (Polish), Revs. Francis E. Filmanski; Chester Diadia.
Res., 1 Depan Ave., 11001. Tel: 516-354-0042.

Our Lady of Victory (1921), Rev. Msgr. Charles J. Nosser; Revs. Gene Vollmer; Charles N. Srion (Thailand); Deacon Lawrence P. Mulligan.
Res., 2 Floral Pkwy., 11001-3198. Tel: 516-354-0482; 354-0479; Fax: 516-354-7450.
School—2 Bellmore St., 11001. Tel: 516-352-4466; 354-2150; Fax: 516-352-4467. Sr. Maria Wittenborn, S.C., Prin.
Religious 5; Lay Teachers 28; Students 444.
Catechesis/Religious Programs—Tel: 516-352-0510. Sr. Barbara Kaiser, C.S.J., D.R.E.
Students 1250.

Franklin Square, Nassau Co., St. Catherine of Sienna (1908), Rev. Msgr. William Costello; Revs. Anthony M. Stanganelli; Marian Bicz; Dennis Whelan.
Res., 33 New Hyde Park Rd., 11010. Tel: 516-352-0146; Fax: 516-326-7427.
School—Holzhimer, Tel: 516-437-2733. Mrs. Diane Staudinger, Prin.
Sisters of St. Dominic 2; Lay Teachers 25; Students 397.
Catechesis/Religious Programs—Tel: 516-354-4554.
Students 1,425.

Freeport, Nassau Co., Our Holy Redeemer (Hispanic), Revs. Richard Figliozzi; James Nunes; Gregory Semeniuk, C.M. In res., Revs. Michael Manzelli; William Henesy; Deacons James Dunne; Francisco Cales; Bruce A. Burnham.
Res., 37 S. Ocean Ave., 11520. Tel: 516-378-0665; Fax: 516-546-1416.
Catechesis/Religious Programs—Tel: 516-546-1057; Fax: 516-546-1416.
Students 660.

Garden City, Nassau Co., St. Joseph's (1901), Rev. Msgr. Donald T. Bennett; Revs. Richard F. Delaney; Robert J. Clerkin. In res., Rev. Msgr. John A. Alesandro.
Res., 130 Fifth St., 11530. Tel: 516-747-3535; Fax: 516-746-0719.
School—450 Franklin Ave., 11530. Tel: 516-747-2730. Sr. Mary O'Donnell, O.P., Prin.
Lay Teachers 24; Students 432.
Catechesis/Religious Programs—Tel: 516-741-7787. D.R.E.: Doris Petrocelli, (Grades PreK-4); Susan Mirabella, (Grades 5-12).
Students 975.

St. Anne (1929), Revs. Brian A. McKeon; Richard R. Donovan; Deacons Edward Cunningham; Jack McGowan. In res., Revs. Joseph J. D'Angelo; James C. Miller.
Res., 35 Dartmouth St., 11530. Tel: 516-352-5904; Fax: 516-352-1360.
School—25 Dartmouth St., 11530. Tel: 516-352-1205. Miss Jacqueline Lucarelli, Prin.
Religious of the Sacred Heart of Mary 3; Lay Teachers 21; Students 471.
Catechesis/Religious Programs—Tel: 516-488-1032. Sr. Kathleen Corr, O.P., D.R.E.
Students 647.

Glen Cove, Nassau Co., St. Patrick's (1856), Rev. Msgr. John J. McCann; Revs. Thomas J. McCarthy; Robert J. Coyle; Henry I. Benack, Hospital Chap.; Sr. Frances Gritte, S.C.H., Pastoral Assoc.
Res., 235 Glen St., 11542. Tel: 516-676-0276; Fax: 516-674-9137. [CEM]
School—All Saints Regional Catholic School, Glen Cove. See Regional Schools under Institutions Located in the Diocese. Tel: 516-676-0762; Fax: 516-676-0660.
Catechesis/Religious Programs—Tel: 516-671-7223; Fax: 516-674-9137. Ms. Catherine Bilquin, D.R.E.
Students 413.

St. Rocco (1937) (Italian), Rev. Domenick T. Graziadio; Rev. Msgr. Domenick T. Graziano; Rev. Cletus Ogu.
Res., 18 Third St., 11542. Tel: 516-676-2482; Fax: 516-676-2117.
School—All Saints Regional Catholic School, Glen Cove. See Regional Schools under Institutions Located in the Diocese. Tel: 516-676-0762; Fax: 516-676-0660.
Catechesis/Religious Programs—Students 290.

Glen Head, Nassau Co., St. Hyacinth (1909) (Polish), Revs. Richard Kopinski; Paul Mijas; Joseph Kozlowski, Pastor Emeritus; Deacon Robert J. Heintz.
Res., 319 Cedar Swamp Rd., 11545. Tel: 516-676-0361; Fax: 516-674-4728.
School—All Saints Regional Catholic School, Glen Cove. See Regional Schools under Institutions Located in the Diocese. Tel: 516-671-3033.
Catechesis/Religious Programs—Miss Eileen Meserole, D.R.E.
Students 170.

Great Neck, Nassau Co., St. Aloysius (1876), Revs. Thomas Candreva, S.T.L., J.C.D.; Kenneth G. Murphy; Rodrigo Velasquez (Columbia); John Seung Chi Baek (Korea).
Res., 592 Middle Neck Rd., 11023. Tel: 516-482-2770; Fax: 516-829-3504.
Catechesis/Religious Programs—Tel: 516-482-5660.
Students 183.

Greenlawn, Suffolk Co., St. Francis of Assisi (1966) (Haitian), Rev. Msgr. Patrick J. Armshaw; Rev.

Thomas W. Coby. In res., Rev. Malachy C. Flaherty, O.F.M.Cap.; Deacon Allan Longo.
Res., 29 Northgate Dr., 11740. Tel: 516-757-7435; Fax: 516-757-0469.
School—Trinity Regional School, East Northport. See Regional Schools under Institutions Located in the Diocese. Tel: 516-261-5130; Fax: 516-266-5345.
Catechesis/Religious Programs—Tel: 516-754-6436. Mrs. Theresa DeMayo, D.R.E.
Students 640.

Greenport, Suffolk Co., St. Agnes (1886), Rev. Msgr. John P. Sullivan; Sr. Sheila Molloy, O.S.U.
Res., Front St., 11944. Tel: 516-477-0048; Fax: 516-477-8519. [CEM]
School—Our Lady of Mercy, Cutchogue. See Regional Schools under Institutions Located in the Diocese. Tel: 516-734-5166.
Catechesis/Religious Programs—Tel: 516-477-1422.
Students 168.

Hampton Bays, Suffolk Co., St. Rosalie's (1901), Revs. William J. Gill; Patrick A. Bergin, M.M.
Res., 31 Montauk Hwy., 11946. Tel: 516-728-0031; Fax: 516-728-2559.
School—Our Lady of the Hamptons Regional School. See Regional Schools under Institutions Located in the Diocese. Tel: 516-283-9140.
Catechesis/Religious Programs—Tel: 516-728-9461. Sarah Cunliffe, D.R.E.
Students 527.
Mission—East Quogue, 31 Montauk Hwy., 11946. Tel: 516-653-4471.

Hauppauge, Suffolk Co., St. Thomas More (1967), Revs. Ellsworth R. Walden; Ralph Sommer; Deacons Alfred Pankus; Robert Weisz.
Res., 115 Kings Rd., 11788. Tel: 516-234-5551; Fax: 516-234-6412.
School—Holy Family Regional School, Commack. See Regional Schools under Institutions Located in the Diocese. Tel: 516-678-5800.
Catechesis/Religious Programs—119 Kings Rd., 11788. Tel: 516-234-0397. D.R.E.: Mrs. Mary Ellen Carroll; Mrs. Patricia Chapin.
Students 926.

Hempstead, Nassau Co., Our Lady of Loretto (1870), Rev. Msgr. Pablo M. Rodriguez; Revs. James M. Kissane; Fruto Rosales; Sr. Teresa Logue, S.C., Pastoral Assoc.; Sr. Mary Therese Von Holdt, B.V.M.; Deacon Jose Roa; Mr. Kevin Hickson; Ms. Cathie Blackman.
Res., 104 Greenwich St., 11550. Tel: 516-489-3675; Fax: 516-485-8371.
School—St. Martin de Porres Regional School, Uniondale. See Regional Schools under Institutions Located in the Diocese. Tel: 516-481-3303.
Catechesis/Religious Programs—Tel: 516-489-3675.
Students 318.

St. Ladislaus (1915) (Polish), Rev. Msgr. Edward Wawerski. In res., Revs. Denis J. Sheridan; John Siebor.
Res., 18 Richardson Pl., 11550. Tel: 516-489-0368; Fax: 516-292-9193.
School—St. Martin de Porres Regional School, Uniondale. See Regional Schools under Institutions Located in the Diocese.

Hewlett, Nassau Co., St. Joseph's (1872), Rev. Msgr. Charles R. Fink; Deacons Thomas Costello; Pat Acquafredda. In res., Rev. Eugene J. McManus.
Res., 1346 Broadway, 11557. Tel: 516-374-0290; Fax: 516-374-2598.
Catechesis/Religious Programs—1355 Noel Ave., 11557. Tel: 516-569-6080. Frances Acquafredda, D.R.E.
Students 429.

Hicksville, Nassau Co., St. Ignatius Loyola (1859), Revs. Edward L. Tarrant; Frederic J. Harrer, Pastor Emeritus; John V. Tunny; Gerard A. Gordon.
Res., 129 Broadway, 11801. Tel: 516-931-0056; Fax: 516-939-0852.
School—20 Cherry St., 11801. Tel: 516-931-0831. Ms. Jacqueline Burdi, Prin.
Lay Teachers 23; Students 410.
Catechesis/Religious Programs—Tel: 516-935-6873. Jane E. Schreiber, D.R.E.
Students 630.

Holy Family (1951), Rev. Msgr. Edward J. Donnelly; Revs. Jeffrey W. Johnston; Julian Casjar.
Res., 5 Fordham Ave., 11801. Tel: 516-938-3846; Fax: 516-938-6241.
School—Tel: 516-938-3881; Fax: 516-938-5041. Sr. Eileen McMahon, O.P., Prin.
Sisters of Saint Dominic 3; Lay Teachers 24; Students 592.
Catechesis/Religious Programs—Tel: 516-938-3854. Mrs. Carol Nealon, D.R.E.
Students 1034.

Our Lady of Mercy, Rev. Msgr. James E. Boesel; Rev. Msgr. John D. Mott; Revs. Charles A. Gartner; Peter Liu; Robert S. Hewes.
Res., 500 S. Oyster Bay Rd., 11801. Tel: 516-931-4351; Fax: 516-433-8702.
School—Tel: 516-433-7040; Fax: 516-433-6809. Sr. Mary Joanne Deegan, R.S.M., Prin.
Sisters of Mercy 10; Lay Teachers 23; Students 682.
Catechesis/Religious Programs—Sr. Suzanne LePre, D.R.E.
Students 777.
Youth Ministry—.
Lay Teachers 10; Students 115.

Holbrook, Suffolk Co., Good Shepherd (1970), Revs. Thomas L. Spadaro; Paul J. Rogers; Robert C. Scheckenback; Deacon Robert Hernandez.
Res., 1370 Grundy Ave., 11741. Tel: 516-588-7689; Fax: 516-588-7603.
School—Prince of Peace Regional School, Sayville. See Regional Schools under Institutions Located in the Diocese.
Catechesis/Religious Programs—Tel: 516-981-3889. D.R.E.: Sr. Lillian Delorme, O.P.; Sr. Margaret Mary Caulson, I.H.M.
Students 2,500.

Huntington Suffolk Co., St. Patrick's (1849), Rev. John Denniston; Rev. Msgr. Martin J. Flynn, Pastor Emeritus; Rev. Msgr. James B. Richter; Revs. Thomas Edamattam (India); Ernest E. Robinson; Deacons Robert R. Maro; Jules Gagnon. In res., Rev. Owen Shelley, O.F.M.Cap., Chap.
Res., 400 Main St., 11743-3298. Tel: 516-673-5320; Fax: 516-673-4102. [CEM]
School—360 Main St., 11743-3298. Tel: 516-673-5325. Sr. Helen Ann Ebbitt, Prin.
Sisters 2; Lay Teachers 24; Students 600.
Catechesis/Religious Programs—Tel: 516-673-5323. D.R.E.: Sr. Frances Viola; Mrs. Peggy Troisi.
Students 1300.

Huntington Station, Suffolk Co., St. Hugh of Lincoln (1913), Rev. Msgr. Vincent Rush; Revs. Joseph Arevalo; L. Damian Cooper; Deacons Edward W. Billia; Vito B. Taranto; Thomas Reilly.
Res., 21 E. Ninth St., 11746. Tel: 516-427-0638; Fax: 516-427-1319.
Parish Center—1450 New York Ave., 11746.
School—Trinity Regional School, East Northport. See Regional Schools under Institutions Located in the Diocese. Tel: 516-261-5130; Fax: 516-266-5345.
Catechesis/Religious Programs—Tel: 516-271-6081. Miss Eileen McNamara, D.R.E.
Students 1,022.

Inwood, Nassau Co., Our Lady of Good Counsel (1910), Rev. Peter A. Libasci.
Res., 63 Wanser Ave., 11096. Tel: 516-239-0953; Fax: 516-239-0386.
Catechesis/Religious Programs—Sr. Kathleen Schaetzle, C.S.J., D.R.E.
Students 335.

Island Park, Nassau Co., Sacred Heart (1938), Rev. John J. Tutone.
Res., 282 Long Beach Rd., 11558. Tel: 516-432-0655; Fax: 516-897-7567.
Catechesis/Religious Programs—Tel: 516-431-7877. Mrs. Carmel Caracciolo, D.R.E.
Students 395.

Islip Terrace, Suffolk Co., St. Peter the Apostle (1962), Revs. Gerard A. Ringenback; Felix Weerasinghe, Pastoral Assoc.
Res., 94 Valley Stream St., 11752. Tel: 516-277-9448; Fax: 516-224-1594.
School—Our Lady of Providence Regional School, Central Islip. See Regional Schools under Institutions Located in the Diocese.
Catechesis/Religious Programs—Tel: 516-581-5715. Sr. Ellen Zak, C.S.F.N., D.R.E.
Students 800.

Kings Park, Suffolk Co., St. Joseph's (1888), Rev. Msgr. Alex F. Manly; Revs. Francis P. Vattakudiyil; Paul A. Dolan; Deacon W. Donald Bennettson.
Parish Center—59 Church St., 11754. Tel: 516-269-6635; Fax: 516-269-7508.
School—Holy Family Regional School, Commack. See Regional Schools under Institutions Located in the Diocese. Tel: 516-543-0202; Fax: 516-543-0203.
Catechesis/Religious Programs—Tel: 516-269-4383.
Students 1,750.

Lake Ronkonkoma, Suffolk Co., St. Elizabeth Ann Seton (1988), Rev. Patrick J. Whitney; Deacons Robert Gaudioso; Joseph Gioglio.
Res., 800 Portion Rd., 11779. Tel: 516-737-4388; Fax: 516-737-4389.
Catechesis/Religious Programs—Tel: 516-737-8915. D.R.E.: Mrs. Michelle Hahn; Mrs. Therese Boucher.
Students 1,000.

Levittown Nassau Co., St. Bernard (1948), Rev. Msgr. George P. Graham, J.C.D., Ph.D.; Revs. Orsete Dias; Paul G. Driscoll, M.A.; Tony Lacson, J.C.D. In res., Rev. Martin J. Hall, M.A.
Res., 3100 Hempstead Tpke., 11756. Tel: 516-731-4220; Fax: 516-731-4355.
School—Tel: 516-731-4322.
Lay Teachers 19; Students 379.
Catechesis/Religious Programs—Tel: 516-731-8511.
Students 1,250.

Lindenhurst, Suffolk Co., Our Lady of Perpetual Help (1871), Rev. Msgr. Daniel S. Hamilton; Revs. Vitalis Pedzik; Edward M. Seagriff; Richard F. Kammerer; Edward J. Walsh.
Res., 210 S. Wellwood Ave., 11757-4989. Tel: 516-226-7725; Fax: 516-225-9597.
School—Tel: 516-226-0208.
Sisters of St. Dominic 2; Lay Teachers 27; Students 680.
Catechesis/Religious Programs—Diana Castellano, Coord. Program Admin.; Biagio Arpino, Coord. Teaching Training & Curriculum Planning.
Students 2,106.

Long Beach, Nassau Co., St. Ignatius Martyr (1926), Revs. Thomas P. O'Donnell; Richard A. Nilsson, Pastoral Assoc. In res., Rev. Msgr. Edward A. Sweeny.
Res., 721 W. Broadway, 11561. Tel: 516-432-0045; Fax: 516-432-0358.
School—Long Beach Regional Catholic School, Long Beach. See Regional Schools under Institutions Located in the Diocese. Tel: 516-432-8900.
Catechesis/Religious Programs—Tel: 516-432-6788; Fax: 516-432-0358.
Students 600.

St. Mary of the Isle (1915), Rev. Thomas E. Donohoe; Deacon John P. Dunlop; Sr. Frances Monuszko, O.P., Dir. St. Mary of the Isle Community Center.
Res., 315 E. Walnut St., 11561. Tel: 516-432-0157; Fax: 516-897-0566.
School—Long Beach Regional Catholic School, Long Beach. See Regional Schools under Institutions Located in the Diocese. Tel: 516-432-8900.
Catechesis/Religious Programs—Tel: 516-432-0157. Claire Schirtzer, M.A., D.R.E.
Students 421.

Lynbrook, Nassau Co., Our Lady of Peace (1941), Revs. Lawrence M. Penzes; Mark P. Rowan; Deacon Aniello Squitieri. In res., Rev. Antony Asir.
Res., 25 Fowler Ave., 11563. Tel: 516-599-6414; Fax: 516-596-1847.
School—Tel: 516-593-4884.
Sisters of Mercy 1; Lay Teachers 16; Students 350.
Catechesis/Religious Programs—Tel: 516-593-5150.
Students 622.

Malverne, Nassau Co., Our Lady of Lourdes (1926), Revs. Donald M. Baier; Edwin J. Collins, Pastor Emeritus; John F. Whelan; John F. Wymes; John F. Meade; Deacon Frank Cove.
Res., 65 Wright Ave., 11565. Tel: 516-599-1269; Fax: 516-887-9517.
School—76 Park Blvd., 11565. Tel: 516-599-7328. Mr. John A. McQuillan, Prin.
Lay Teachers 15; Students 300.
Catechesis/Religious Programs—Tel: 516-599-7222; Fax: 516-599-2256. Mrs. Margaret DeStefano, D.R.E.
Students 471.

Manhasset, Nassau Co., St. Mary's (1853), Rev. Msgr. John J. Skelly; Rev. Msgr. John J. Wiest, Pastor Emeritus; Revs. Joseph D. Casaclang; Kevin M. Smith; Anthony E. Refalo.
Res., 1300 Northern Blvd., 11030. Tel: 516-627-0385; Fax: 516-627-6070.
School—1340 Northern Blvd., 11030. Tel: 516-627-0184; Fax: 516-627-3795.
Sisters of the Immaculate Heart of Mary 4; Lay Teachers 27; Students 412.
High Schools—(Coed) 25 Second St., 11030. Tel: 516-627-2711; Fax: 516-627-3209.; 51 Clapham Ave., 11030.
Sisters of the Immaculate Heart of Mary 6; Marist Brothers 4; Lay Teachers 50; Students 857.
Catechesis/Religious Programs—Tel: 516-627-4028.
Students 1031.

Manorhaven, Nassau Co., Our Lady of Fatima (1948), Revs. Kenneth T. Nee; Joseph Minturn. In res., Rev. Lino S. Gonsalves (GOA).
Res., 6 Cottonwood Pl., Pt. Washington, 11050. Tel: 516-767-0781; Fax: 516-767-2981.
Catechesis/Religious Programs—Tel: 516-944-8322.
Students 275.

Manorville, Suffolk Co., St. Peter & Paul, Rev. John J. McGratty; Eda Lorello, Pastoral Assoc.; Deacons Joseph Guntert; John C. Pettorino.
Res., 781 Wading River Rd., P.O. Box 207, 11949. Tel: 516-369-1273; Fax: 516-369-1273.

Massapequa, Nassau Co., St. Rose of Lima (1952), Rev. Msgr. Daniel J. Hurley; Revs. Lawrence A. Sheehan, S.J.; John M. Derasmo; Thomas P. Tuite; Deacons Thomas J. Forbes; Thomas J. Quinn; Frank J. Flood; Francis B. McGuiness; Dennis R. O'Connor.

Res., 2 Bayview Ave., 11758-7299. Tel: 516-798-4992; Fax: 516-795-7836.
School—Tel: 516-541-1546. Sr. Kathleen Gallina, Prin.
Sisters of St. Dominic 1; Lay Teachers 26; Students 548.
Catechesis/Religious Programs—Tel: 516-541-1712.
Students 2,162.

Massapequa Park, Nassau Co., Our Lady of Lourdes (1955), Revs. Robert E. Mason; Thomas J. Reynolds; Anthony J. Heinlein; Deacons Domenick Valdano; Steve Delligatti.
Res., 855 Carmans Rd., 11762. Tel: 516-541-3270; Fax: 516-797-9851.
School—Tel: 516-798-7926.
Lay Teachers 21; Students 390.
Catechesis/Religious Programs—379 Linden St., 11762. Tel: 516-799-5179.
Students 715.

Mastic Beach, Suffolk Co., St. Jude (1949), Revs. Joseph A. Mirro; Steven A. Berbig; Steven Camp; Franklin Salazar; Deacons Thomas Gross; Thomas Gillen; Luis Giraldo.
Res., 89 Overlook Dr., 11951. Tel: 516-281-5743; Fax: 516-395-5786.
School—Our Lady, Queen of Apostles Regional School, Center Moriches. See Regional Schools under Institutions Located in the Diocese.
Catechesis/Religious Programs—Tel: 516-281-2835. Virginia Struckhoff, D.R.E.
Students 1,720.
Parish Human Services Center—89 Overlook Dr., 11951. Tel: 516-281-5634. Helen Mahon, Coord.

Medford, Suffolk Co., St. Sylvester (1948), Revs. Charles E. Papa; Michael F. Holzmann; Edward J. Kealey; Deacons George J. Riegger; Francis P. Roettinger.
Res., 68 Ohio Ave., P.O. Box 336, 11763. Tel: 516-475-4506; Fax: 516-475-1057.
School—Holy Angels Regional School, Patchogue. See Regional Schools under Institutions Located in the Diocese. Tel: 516-475-0422.
Catechesis/Religious Programs—Tel: 516-475-8191. Mrs. Patricia A. Desmond, D.R.E.
Students 1,350.

Melville, Suffolk Co., St. Elizabeth (1962), Revs. Bruce J. Powers; Michael A. Vetrano; Deacons Richard Johnston; Joseph Mercolino.
Res., 181 Wolf Hill Rd., 11747. Tel: 516-271-4455; Fax: 516-271-1415.
School—Trinity Regional School, East Northport. See Regional Schools under Institutions Located in the Diocese. Tel: 516-261-5130; Fax: 516-266-5345.
Catechesis/Religious Programs—Students 822.

Merrick, Nassau Co., Cure of Ars (1926), Rev. Msgr. James P. Swiader; Rev. Robert A. Romeo; Sr. Miriam Michael Joos, O.P., Pastoral Assoc. In res., Revs. Thomas V. Arnao; John P. Murray.
Res., 2323 Merrick Ave., 11566. Tel: 516-623-1400; Fax: 516-623-1107.
School—St. Elizabeth Ann Seton Regional School, Bellmore/East Meadow. See Regional Schools under Institutions Located in the Diocese. Tel: 516-679-1990; Fax: 516-679-2082.

Mineola, Nassau Co., Corpus Christi (1901) (Portuguese), Revs. Kenneth H. Winkler; Tomaz Gomide; Robert J. Batule; Rev. Msgr. Eugene F. Murphy; Rev. Thomas F. Murphy; Deacon John C. Reinhart. In res., Rev. Msgr. Lawrence D. Costello, Pastor Emeritus.
Res., 155 Garfield Ave., 11501. Tel: 516-746-1223; Fax: 516-294-5311.
School—120 Searing Ave., 11501. Tel: 516-746-2966. Sr. Laura Helbig, O.P., Prin.
Sisters of St. Dominic 4; Lay Teachers 14; Students (Nursery to 8th) 427.
Catechesis/Religious Programs—Tel: 516-294-0631. D.R.E.: Mrs. Ursula Bordonaro; Mrs. Joan O'Brien.
Students 693.

Montauk, Suffolk Co., St. Therese of Lisieux (1950), Rev. Raymond H. Nugent, M.Div.
Res., 55 S. Etna Ave., P.O. Drawer 5027, 11954. Tel: 516-668-2200.
School—Stella Maris Regional School, Sag Harbor. See Regional Schools under Institutions Located in the Diocese. Tel: 516-725-2525.
Day Care/Nursery School—Tel: 516-668-5353.
Children (3 & 4 years old) 64.
Catechesis/Religious Programs—Students 165.

Nesconset, Suffolk Co., Church of the Holy Cross (1988), Pastoral Team: Revs. Joseph M. Schlafer; William G. Breslawski; Sr. Jane Halligan, S.S.N.D., Pastoral Assoc.
Res., 95 Old Nichols Rd., 11767. Tel: 516-265-2200; Fax: 516-265-2229.
Catechesis/Religious Programs—Mrs. Judith Pickel, D.R.E.
Students 633.

New Hyde Park, Nassau Co., Holy Spirit (1893), Rev. Msgr. John T. Heinlein; Revs. Chuck Romano; John T. Daley. In res., Rev. Robert O. Morrissey.
Res., 500 Jericho Tpke., 11040. Tel: 516-354-0359; Fax: 516-354-2611 (Rectory).
School—13 S. Sixth St., 11040. Tel: 516-354-5566. Sr. Angela LiVecchi, O.P., Prin.
Sisters of St. Dominic (Amityville) 4; Lay Teachers 27; Students 510.
Catechesis/Religious Programs—13 S. 6th St., 11040. Tel: 516-354-2363.
Students 480.

Notre Dame (1941), Revs. Peter Pflomm; John Murray, Pastor Emeritus; William T. Slater; James P. Carmody; Anthony Kim (Korea); Sr. Judith A. Golden, O.P., Pastoral Assoc.; Deacon Gilbert McGaffney.
Res., 45 Mayfair Rd., 11040. Tel: 516-352-7203; Fax: 516-326-7988.
School—Tel: 516-354-5618; Fax: 516-326-7988. Sr. Lorraine McDonald, O.P., Prin.
Sisters of St. Dominic (Amityville) 5; Lay Teachers 27; Students 608.
Catechesis/Religious Programs—25 Mayfair Rd., 11040. Tel: 516-437-5604. D.R.E.: Sr. Mary Jane Coleman, R.S.M.; Sr. Alice Reichmeider, O.P.
Students 903.

North Merrick, Nassau Co., Sacred Heart (1952), Revs. Thomas G. Gallagher; James F. Drew; Deacon Daniel J. Delargy. In res., Rev. Brian Brinker, Chap. at Nassau County Medical Center.
Res., 1921 Old Mill Rd., 11566. Tel: 516-379-1356; Fax: 516-379-1610.
School—Tel: 516-378-5797; Fax: 516-378-5797. Sr. Mary Morrin, C.S.J., Prin.
Sisters of St. Joseph 5; Lay Teachers 14; Students 307.
Catechesis/Religious Programs—Tel: 516-868-9406. Mrs. Cecelia Lerro, D.R.E.
Students 1000.

Northport, Suffolk Co., St. Philip Neri (1894), Revs. Thomas J. Colgan; William Dailey; Michael O'Farrell; Deacons John F. Burkhart; Andrew Schneider. In res., Rev. Michael J. O'Farrell.
Res., 344 Main St., 11768. Tel: 516-261-7753; Fax: 516-261-7420. [CEM]
School—Trinity Regional School, East Northport. See Regional Schools under Institutions Located in the Diocese.
Catechesis/Religious Programs—Tel: 516-261-7800. Lorraine Cortina, D.R.E.
Students 510.

Ocean Beach, (Fire Island) Suffolk Co., Our Lady of the Magnificat (1921), Revs. Ronald Hayde; Robert Morrissey.
Mailing Address: P.O. Box 445, 11770. Tel: 516-583-5868.

Oceanside, Nassau Co., St. Anthony (1927), Revs. Kirk R. Reynolds, S.J.; Frederick J. Pellegrini, S.J.; Conrad R. Dietz; Martin F. Kirby; Pierce A. Brennan, S.J.; Matthew F. Roche, S.J.; Sr. Gena Travers, O.P., Pastoral Assoc.; Deacon James W. Flannery; Anna Maria Sirianni.
Res., 110 Anchor Ave., 11572. Tel: 516-764-0048; 764-0665; Fax: 516-764-7726.
Catechesis/Religious Programs—Tel: 516-678-3388. Sr. Virginia Weigman, O.P., D.R.E.
Students 700.

Oyster Bay, Nassau Co., St. Dominic's (1895), Rev. Msgr. Charles A. Ribaudo; Rev. Msgr. James E. Collins, Pastor Emeritus; Revs. Malcolm J. Burns; Paul F. Butler.
Res., 96 Anstice St., 11771. Tel: 516-922-4488; Fax: 516-922-9491.
School—35 School St., 11771. Tel: 516-922-4233; Fax: 516-624-7613.
Sisters of the Immaculate Heart of Mary 2; Lay Teachers 14; Students 317.
High School—110 Antice St., 11771. Tel: 516-922-4888; Fax: 516-922-4898.
Sisters of the Immaculate Heart of Mary 1; Lay Teachers 36; Students 454.
Catechesis/Religious Programs—Tel: 516-922-7788; Fax: 516-922-4898.
Students 561.

Patchogue, Suffolk Co., St. Francis de Sales (1888) (Hispanic). Unassigned. Deacons Martin McIndoe; Fernando J. Quinones.
Res., 7 Amity St., 11772. Tel: 516-475-0161; Fax: 516-475-1481. [CEM]
School—Holy Angels Regional School, Patchogue. See Regional Schools under Institutions Located in the Diocese. Tel: 516-475-0422.
Catechesis/Religious Programs—Tel: 516-289-4339; Fax: 516-475-1481.
Students 450.

Our Lady of Mt. Carmel, Revs. Robert J. O'Connell; Alexander L. Sledzaus, Pastor Emeritus; Alfredo Sobalvarro, Assoc. Pastor. In res., Rev. Edward J. Werring.
Res., 495 New North Ocean Ave., 11772. Tel: 516-475-4739.
School—Holy Angels Regional School, Patchogue. See Regional Schools under Institutions Located in the Diocese.
Catechesis/Religious Programs—Kathleen Reid, M.A., D.R.E.
Students 781.

Plainview, Nassau Co., St. Pius X (1955), Revs. Hugh D. Cannon; Robert A. McGuire, Dir. of Spirit Life Center, Tel: 516-938-7119. In res., Rev. Brian J. McNamara, Chap. St. Anthony's High School.
Res., 1 St. Pius Ct., 11803. Tel: 516-938-3959; Fax: 516-433-6138.
School—St. John Baptist de LaSalle Regional School, Bethpage/Farmingdale. See Regional Schools under Institutions Located in the Diocese. Tel: 516-931-0983 (Bethpage); 516-694-3610 (Farmingdale).
Catechesis/Religious Programs—Tel: 516-822-0919.
Students 312.

Point Lookout, Nassau Co., Our Lady of the Miraculous Medal, Revs. William Gomes; Andrew J. Gallagher, Pastor Emeritus.
Res., 75 Parkside Dr., 11569. Tel: 516-431-2772; Fax: 516-432-8669.
School—Long Beach Regional Catholic School, Long Beach. See Regional Schools under Institutions Located in the Diocese. Tel: 516-432-8900; Fax: 516-432-8926.

Port Jefferson, Suffolk Co., Infant Jesus 1903, Rev. Msgr. Dennis M. Regan; Revs. Abraham Z. Porunnolil; Michael J. Rieder; Irene Moynihan, Pastoral Assoc.; Deacons Patrick C. Gerace; William J. Powers; Richard E. Waldmann.
Res., 110 Myrtle Ave., 11777. Tel: 516-473-0165; Fax: 516-331-8094.
School—Our Lady of Wisdom Regional School, Port Jefferson. See Regional Schools under Institutions Located in the Diocese. Tel: 516-473-1211.
Catechesis/Religious Programs—Tel: 516-928-0447. Mrs. Barbara Saulino, D.R.E.
Students 1,400.

St. Gerard Majella (1968), Revs. William A. Hanson, Co-Pastor; Christopher J. Heller, Co-Pastor; Deacon Thomas O'Connor.
Res., 300 Terryville Rd., Port Jefferson Station, 11776. Tel: 516-473-2900; Fax: 516-473-0015.
School—Our Lady of Wisdom Regional School, Port Jefferson. See Regional Schools under Institutions Located in the Diocese.
Catechesis/Religious Programs—Tel: 516-928-2550. Eda Lorello, D.R.E.
Students 1,157.

Port Washington, Nassau Co., St. Peter of Alcantara (1901), Rev. Msgr. Walter E. Simmons; Revs. William O'Rourke, Ph.D.; Richard G. Henning, M.A., M.Div.
Res., 1327 Port Washington Blvd., 11050. Tel: 516-883-6675; Fax: 516-944-7461.
School—Tel: 516-944-3772.
Sisters 7; Lay Teachers 19; Students 610.
Catechesis/Religious Programs—Tel: 516-883-5584. Mrs. Elizabeth Eleanor Miller, D.R.E.
Students 410.
Convent—1317 Port Washington Blvd., 11050. Tel: 516-762-1282. Sisters, Servants of the Immaculate Heart of Mary (Scranton, PA)

Riverhead, Suffolk Co., St. John the Evangelist (1861), Revs. Thomas S. Kane; Paul R. Bie. In res., Most Rev. Emil A. Wcela; Rev. Msgr. John Lovett; Rev. Msgr. Martin Bowe.
Res., 546 St. John's Pl., 11901. Tel: 516-727-2030. [CEM]
School—Tel: 516-727-4144.
Sisters of St. Dominic (Amityville) 1; Lay Teachers 9; Students 254.
Catechesis/Religious Programs—Tel: 516-727-6774.
Students 468.

St. Isidore's (1903) (Polish), Rev. Msgr. John Mirecki; Rev. Joseph Walas (Poland) Pastoral Assoc.
Res., 622 Pulaski St., 11901. Tel: 516-727-2114; Fax: 516-369-3566. [CEM]
School—515 Marcy Ave., 11901. Tel: 516-727-1650; Fax: 516-727-3945. Sr. Linda Joseph Chichi, C.S.F.N., Prin.
Sisters of the Holy Family of Nazareth 3; Lay Teachers 8; Students 252.

Rocky Point, Suffolk Co., St. Anthony of Padua (1948), Revs. Joseph C. Coschignano; Michael Maffeo.
Res., 614 Rte. 25A, 11778. Tel: 516-744-2609; Fax: 516-744-5782.
Catechesis/Religious Programs—Tel: 516-821-0872.
Students 1,100.

Ronkonkoma, Suffolk Co., St. Joseph's (1910), Revs. Donald R. Shane; Caetano F.X. Costa; Santiago Dineros; Angelo Ditta; Deacons James Altonji; Michael J. DeBellis; Joseph Dougherty; John Erdman; Joseph Maffeo.

Res., 45 Church St., 11779. Tel: 516-588-8456; Fax: 516-471-2569.
School—25 Church St., 11779. Tel: 516-588-4760. Mrs. Marie Salvietti, Prin.
School Sisters of Notre Dame 1; Lay Teachers 24; Students 500.
Catechesis/Religious Programs—Tel: 516-981-1805. D.R.E.: Linda Cussen; Beth Rivalsi.
Students 1,479.

Roosevelt, Nassau Co., Queen of the Most Holy Rosary (1919), Rev. Msgr. Thomas E. Molloy, J.C.D.; Sr. Kathleen O'Donnell, S.C., Pastoral Assoc.; Deacon Louis Sandberg. In res., Rev. Ralph Ferro.
Res., 196 W. Centennial Ave., 11575. Tel: 516-378-1315; Fax: 516-378-5754.
Catechesis/Religious Programs—200 W. Centennial Ave., 11575. Tel: 516-623-1391. Mrs. Ellen Zaffonte, D.R.E.
Students 335.

Roslyn, Nassau Co., St. Mary's (1871), Rev. Msgr. Richard C. Bauhoff; Deacon Edward M. Case.
Res., 110 Bryant Ave., P.O. Box 387, 11576-0387. Tel: 516-621-2222; Fax: 516-621-7892.
School—All Saints Regional Catholic School, Glen Cove. See Regional Schools under Institutions Located in the Diocese. Tel: 516-676-0762.
Catechesis/Religious Programs—Tel: 516-621-6798. Sr. Frances Birmingham, O.P., D.R.E.
Students 306.

Sag Harbor, Suffolk Co., St. Andrew's (1859), Rev. Andrew P. Blake; Sr. Lucille D'Amelio, O.P., Pastoral Assoc. In res., Rev. Manuel Quesada, South Fork Spanish Apostolate.
Res., 122 Division St, P.O. Box 1080, 11963-0034. Tel: 516-725-0123; Fax: 516-725-3310. [CEM]
School—Stella Maris Regional School, Sag Harbor. See Regional Schools under Institutions Located in the Diocese. Tel: 516-725-2525; Fax: 16-725-4587.
Catechesis/Religious Programs—Tel: 516-725-5805.
Students 131.

St. James, Suffolk Co., SS. Philip and James (1907), Rev. Msgr. Charles A. Guarino, V.F.; Revs. Daniel P. Sheridan; Brian D. McQuade; Deacons Charles Brown; Kenneth Maher; Frank Crivello; Robert Heschl. In res., Rev. Ladislaus Cser, S.J.
Res., 454 North Country Rd., 11780. Tel: 516-584-5454; Fax: 516-862-9675.
School—(Grades Pre-8). Tel: 516-584-7896; Fax: 516-584-3258. Mr. Anthony Giordano, Prin.
Lay Teachers 17; Students 429.
Catechesis/Religious Programs—Tel: 516-584-5486. Sr. Mary Regina Tierney, O.P., D.R.E.
Students 1,175.

Saltaire, Suffolk Co., Our Lady Star of the Sea, Mission Chapel. (Summer Mission). Rev. Richard R. Viladesau, S.T.D., Admin.
Res., Our Lady of the Blessed Sacrament, 34-24 203 St., Bayside, 11361. Tel: 718-229-5929.

Sayville, Suffolk Co., St. Lawrence the Martyr (1895), Rev. Msgr. John Rowan; Revs. Sean J. Gann; Ronald Rebaldo; Deacons Edward W. Smith; William F. Fullam, Jr.
Res., 27 Handsome Ave., 11782. Tel: 516-589-0042; 589-8135; 589-3887; Fax: 516-589-5318. [CEM]
School—Prince of Peace Regional School, Sayville. See Regional Schools under Institutions Located in the Diocese. Tel: 516-589-3926.
Catechesis/Religious Programs—Tel: 516-589-3160. Mrs. Lorraine Gallagher, D.R.E.
Students 1,200.

Sea Cliff, Nassau Co., St. Boniface Martyr (1898), Rev. Michael J. Torpey; Sr. Kathleen P. Murphy, O.P., Pastoral Assoc.
Res., 12 Main Ave., 11579-1312. Tel: 516-676-0676; Fax: 516-674-6742.
School—All Saints Regional Catholic School, Glen Cove. See Regional Schools under Institutions Located in the Diocese.
Catechesis/Religious Programs—Tel: 516-671-0418. Julia Byrne, D.R.E.
Students 422.

Seaford, Nassau Co., St. William, the Abbot (1928), Rev. Msgr. Thomas G. Leavey; Revs. John Hien; Peter Garry; Peter Dugandzic; Deacons William Brennan; Thomas Buchenberger; Michael Metzdorff. In res., Rev. James F. Pereda.
Res., 2000 Jackson Ave., 11783. Tel: 516-785-1266; Fax: 516-785-4824.
School—2001 Jackson Ave., 11783. Tel: 516-785-6784. Mrs. Anna Guardino, Prin.
Ursuline Sisters 2; Lay Teachers 23; Students 564.
Catechesis/Religious Programs—Tel: 516-679-9558. D.R.E.: Mrs. Georgette Levesque; Mrs. Susan Martin.
Students 1,378.

Maria Regina (1954), Revs. James A. Brassil; John Malone; Andrew L. Millar; Lawrence B. Rafferty. In res., Rev. Francis M. Casey.
Res., 3945 Jerusalem Ave., 11783. Tel: 516-798-2415; Fax: 516-798-7493.
School—4045 Jerusalem Ave., 11783. Tel: 516-541-1229.
Sisters of Mercy 3; Lay Teachers 25; Students 603.
Catechesis/Religious Programs—3945 Jerusalem Ave., 11783. Tel: 516-541-0921.
Students 1,250.

St. James (1951), Revs. Daniel A. Picciano; Francis Samuel; Richard P. Whitney; Deacons Robert J. Haley, (Retired); James G. Beirne; John G. Leahy.
Res., 80 Hicksville Rd., 11783. Tel: 516-731-3710; Fax: 516-731-4828.
School—St. John Baptist de LaSalle Regional School, Bethpage/Farmingdale. See Regional Schools under Institutions Located in the Diocese. Tel: 516-931-0983.
Catechesis/Religious Programs—Tel: 516-796-2979; Fax: 516-731-4828. Sr. Rosemary Traynor, D.R.E.
Students 1,550.

Selden, Suffolk Co., St. Margaret of Scotland (1948), Revs. Christopher Aridas; John Worthley; John J. Mullen, Pastor Emeritus; Deacons William E. Kogler; Biagio Muratore; Phil Paolicelli; Joseph Scollan.
Res., 81 College Rd., 11784. Tel: 516-732-3131; Fax: 516-732-8827.
School—Holy Angels Regional School, Patchogue. See Regional Schools under Institutions Located in the Diocese. Tel: 516-475-0422.
Catechesis/Religious Programs—Tel: 516-698-0798; Fax: 516-732-8827. D.R.E.: Cathy DePasquale; Barbara Mahon; Marilynne Schaefer; Peggy Scheiner.
Students 2,050.

Setauket, Suffolk Co., St. James (1949), Revs. Donald Diederich, J.C.D.; John Barrett, Ph.D.; John Fitzgerald; Thomas F. McGlade, Pastor Emeritus; Philip Reehil, Pastor Emeritus; Deacons Gerry Coates; Thomas Owens; Joseph Ingulli.
Res., 429 Rte. 25-A, 11733. Tel: 516-941-4141; Fax: 516-751-6607. [CEM]
School—Our Lady of Wisdom Regional School, Port Jefferson. See Regional Schools under Institutions Located in the Diocese. Tel: 516-473-1211.
Catechesis/Religious Programs—Tel: 516-751-7287.
Students 1,265.

Shelter Island, Suffolk Co., Our Lady of the Isle, Rev. Charles Dougherty, C.P. In res., Revs. Blaine Brezinski, C.P.; Malcolm Cornwell, C.P.
Res., Shelter Island Heights, Box 3027, 11965. Tel: 516-749-0001; Fax: 516-749-4218. [CEM]
School—Stella Maris Regional School, Sag Harbor. See Regional Schools under Institutions Located in the Diocese.

Shoreham, Suffolk Co., St. Mark (1973), Revs. Theodore J. Howard; William E. McCarthy; Deacons Albert Vigliotta; Donald Donovan.
Res., 105 Randall Rd., 11786. Tel: 516-744-2800; Fax: 516-821-1628.
Catechesis/Religious Programs—Tel: 516-821-0550. Sr. Virginia Dunne, D.W., D.R.E.
Students 828.

Smithtown, Suffolk Co., St. Patrick (1952) (Irish/Italian), Revs. Paul Walsh; Vincent Liu; Frank J. Parisi; Deacons Richard Sanders; Fred Jackman; Robert Dejewski.
Res., 280 E. Main St., 11787. Tel: 516-265-2271; Fax: 516-360-0381. [CEM]
School—Tel: 516-724-0285; Fax: 516-724-4958. Sr. Aquinata McGrath, Prin.
Sisters of St. Joseph 5; Lay Teachers 23; Students 686.
Catechesis/Religious Programs—Tel: 516-724-7454. Maureen Moore, D.R.E.
Students 1,451.

Sound Beach, Suffolk Co., St. Louis de Montfort (1971), Rev. Msgr. John A. McGuire; Rev. Yhomas P. Murray, Pastoral Assoc.; Deacons Joseph T. Bartlotto; Peter F. Schultz; Gary F. Swane; Montford D. Naylor.
Mailing Address: P.O. Box 923, 11789. Tel: 516-744-8566; Fax: 516-744-8611.
Res., New York Ave., 11764.
School—Our Lady of Wisdom Regional School, Port Jefferson. See Regional Schools under Institutions Located in the Diocese. Tel: 516-473-1211.
Catechesis/Religious Programs—Tel: 516-744-9515. Mr. John McNamara, D.R.E.
Students 2,010.

Southampton, Suffolk Co., Sacred Hearts of Jesus and Mary (1896), Rev. Msgr. Edmond J. Trench; Deacon John W. McGauvran.
Res., 168 Hill St., 11968. Tel: 516-283-0097; Fax: 516-283-3836. [CEM]
School—Our Lady of the Hamptons Regional School. See Regional Schools under Institutions Located in the Diocese. Tel: 516-283-9140.
Catechesis/Religious Programs—Students 360.

Our Lady of Poland (1918) (Polish), Rev. Stanley Kondeja.
Res., 35 Maple St., 11968. Tel: 516-283-0667; Fax: 516-287-4146.
School—Our Lady of the Hamptons Regional School. See Regional Schools under Institutions Located in the Diocese. Tel: 516-283-9140; Fax: 516-287-3958.
Catechesis/Religious Programs—Students 234.

Southold, Suffolk Co., St. Patrick's (1865), Revs. George J. Michell; Martin J. Osborne, Pastor Emeritus.
Res., Main Rd., P.O. Box 1117, 11971-1401. Tel: 516-765-3442; Fax: 516-765-9631. [CEM]
School—Our Lady of Mercy, Cutchogue. See Regional Schools under Institutions Located in the Diocese. Tel: 516-734-5166.
Catechesis/Religious Programs—Tel: 516-765-2338.
Students 200.

Syosset, Nassau Co., St. Edward Confessor (1952), Rev. Joseph C. McComiskey; Rev. Msgr. Walter Rudnicki (Poland); Rev. Robert W. Dahlke, S.J.
Res., 205 Jackson Ave., 11791-4218. Tel: 516-921-4420; Fax: 516-921-4549.
School—2 Teibrook Ave., 11791. Tel: 516-921-7767; Fax: 516-496-0001. Sr. Margaret A. Hartigan, R.S.M., Prin.
Sisters of Mercy (Brooklyn) 2; Lay Teachers 16; Students 270.
Parish Social Ministry Office:—Tel: 516-921-5628; Fax: 516-364-7326. Ms. Dawn Ravella, Dir.
Youth Ministry Office—Tel: 516-921-7631. Mr. Frank Maiello.
Catechesis/Religious Programs—Tel: 516-364-1790. Mrs. Mary Jane Mastrodomenico, D.R.E.
Students 738.

Uniondale, Nassau Co., St. Martha (1949), Rev. Edward Fitzpatrick. In res., Rev. Msgr. Donald M. Beckman; Revs. Zachary Callahan; Gregory Semeniuk.
Res., 546 Greengrove Ave., 11553. Tel: 516-481-2550.
School—St. Martin de Porres Regional School, Uniondale. See Regional Schools under Institutions Located in the Diocese.
Catechesis/Religious Programs—Tel: 516-481-6608. Sr. Eileen Curley, R.S.M., D.R.E.
Students 251.

Valley Stream, Nassau Co., Holy Name of Mary (1902), Rev. Msgr. Daniel E. Fagan; Revs. Theodore J. LeTure, Pastor Emeritus; James L. Maltese; Thomas M. Moriarty, Jr.; Deacon Anthony Cuseo.
Res., 55 E. Jamaica Ave., 11580. Tel: 516-825-1450; Fax: 516-825-1906.
School—90 S. Grove St., 11580. Tel: 516-825-4009. Sr. Elizabeth Marie Lynch, C.S.J., Prin.
Lay Teachers 18; Students 315.
Catechesis/Religious Programs—90 Grove St., 11580. Tel: 516-825-1810. Sr. Barbara Shea, O.P., D.R.E.
Students 1,175. Parish Outreach 90 Grove St., 11580. Tel: 516-825-0177; Fax: 516-825-5092. Sr. Margie Kelly, O.S.S., Dir.

Blessed Sacrament (1950), Revs. Gregory J. Cappuccino; John J. Dillon; Frank M. Nelson; Aloysius P. Pakianather (Sri Lanka); Deacons Anthony M. Cedrone; Salvatore A. Marino; Sr. Josann Gallagher, Dir. Family Services.
Res., 201 N. Central Ave., 11580. Tel: 516-568-1027; Fax: 516-872-1499.
School—50 Rose Ave., 11580. Tel: 516-825-7334. Melanie Maione, Prin.
Sisters of St. Joseph 2; Lay Teachers 23; Students 369.
Catechesis/Religious Programs—Tel: 516-561-1407. D.R.E.: Lucille Vavosa; Neil Griffin.
Students 1080.

Wading River, Suffolk Co., St. John Baptist (1922), Revs. Joseph T. Mundy; John P. Vitsas, Pastor Emeritus; Deacons Frederick Finter; Gregory Senholzi.
Res., 1488 North Country Rd., 11792. Tel: 516-929-4339; Fax: 516-369-6961.

Wantagh, Nassau Co., St. Frances de Chantal (1952), Revs. Robert E. Guglielmone; Joseph DeGrocco; James Mannion; Deacons Robert O'Donovan; Thomas Bast. In res., Rev. David G. Farley, (Retired).
Res., 1309 Wantagh Ave., 11793. Tel: 516-785-2333; Fax: 516-826-7645.
School—St. Elizabeth Ann Seton Regional School, Bellmore/East Meadow. See Regional Schools under Institutions Located in the Diocese. Tel: 516-785-5709; Fax: 516-785-4468.
Catechesis/Religious Programs—Tel: 516-785-2242; Fax: 516-826-7645. D.R.E.: Sr. Patricia Doran, C.S.J.; Mary Golden, (Grades K-8).
Students 1,669.

West Babylon, Suffolk Co., Our Lady of Grace, Rev. Msgr. James McNamara; Revs. Thomas Saloy; Gerald Cestare; Deacons Peter DiGiuseppe; John Mostler; John Morrow; Charles Graff; George

Proper; Joseph T. Deegan. In res., Rev. James Vlaun.
Res., 702 Albin Ave., 11704. Tel: 516-587-5185; Fax: 516-587-1427.
Catechesis/Religious Programs—Tel: 516-661-9353. D.R.E.: Sr. Janet Whelan; Sr. Ann Higgins; Lee Abseck.
Students 2,109.

Westbury, Nassau Co., St. Brigid (1850), Revs. Thomas C. Costa; Claude J. D'Souza; Martin Klein; Francis X. Gaeta; Deacons Robert P. Broyles; William F.X. Byrne; John Falls; Felix Matheis; James Morris.
Res., 75 Post Ave., 11590. Tel: 516-334-0021; Fax: 516-334-0082.
School—St. Brigid/ Our Lady of Hope Regional School, 101 Maple Ave., 11590. Tel: 516-333-0580; Fax: 516-333-0590. Mrs. Christine Lombardi, Prin. School Sisters of Notre Dame 1; Lay Teachers 28; Students 400.
Catechesis/Religious Programs—Tel: 516-333-9434. D.R.E.: Stephanie Clagnaz; Jennifer Gallagher.
Students 1,000.

Westhampton Beach, Suffolk Co., Immaculate Conception (1891), Rev. Msgr. Joseph M. Murray; Rev. Patrick F. Holland, C.S.Sp.
Res., Main Rd., 11978. Tel: 516-288-1423.
School—Our Lady, Queen of Apostles Regional School, Center Moriches. See Regional Schools under Institutions Located in the Diocese.
Catechesis/Religious Programs—Tel: 516-288-4188. Sr. Virginia Baeder, D.R.E.
Students 330.

West Hempstead, Nassau Co., St. Thomas, the Apostle (1931), Rev. Msgr. James P. Lisante; Revs. Brian Patrick Barr; Andrzej Zglejszewski; Rev. Msgr. Frank Maniscalco; Rev. Thomas Fusco.
Res., 24 Westminster Rd., 11552. Tel: 516-489-8585; Fax: 516-292-2651.
School—12 Westminster Rd., 11552. Tel: 516-481-9310; Fax: 516-481-8769. Sr. Mary Casey, O.P., Prin.
Sisters 2; Lay Teachers 17; Students 375.
Catechesis/Religious Programs—Tel: 516-538-7460. Mrs. Marilyn Meehan, D.R.E.
Students 875.
Mission—Lakeview, Nassau Co., Chapel, Nassau Blvd. & Hempstead Ave., 11552. Tel: 516-483-4091.

West Islip, Suffolk Co., Our Lady of Lourdes (1956), Revs. Joseph C. Lukaszewski; Francis X. Eisele; Michael Hands; John A. Brendel, Pastor Emeritus; Deacons Richard Barry; John Teufel. In res., Rev. James C. Vlaun.
Res., 455 Hunter Ave., 11795. Tel: 516-661-3224; Fax: 516-661-7143.
School—44 Toomey Rd., 11795. Tel: 516-587-7200. Regina A. Cioffi, Prin.
Lay Teachers 15; Students 340.
Catechesis/Religious Programs—Tel: 516-661-5440. D.R.E.: Sr. Diane Liona; Sr. Nancy Campkin.
Students 1,616.

Williston Park, Nassau Co., St. Aidan's (1929), Rev. Msgr. James P. Kelly; Revs. Donald E. Babinski; Stephen Pietrowski; Rev. Msgr. Charles E. Bermingham, Pastor Emeritus; Rev. Msgr. Robert J. Kirwin, Pastor Emeritus; Deacons Herman J. Determann; Richard T. Blake; Salvatore Villani. In res., Rev. Thomas J. Harold.
Res., 505 Willis Ave., 11596. Tel: 516-746-6585; Fax: 516-746-6055.
Schools—(Grades Nursery-3) 525 Willis Ave., 11596. Tel: 516-746-6270.; (Grades 4-8) 510 Willis Ave., 11596. Tel: 518-747-6150. Eileen Oliver, Prin.
Sisters 3; Lay Teachers 28; Students 555.
Catechesis/Religious Programs—Tel: 516-747-3272. D.R.E.: Sr. Jo Ann Bonauro, S.C.; Sr. Mary Sullivan, S.H.C.J.
Students 1,025.
Convent—16 Pembroke St., 11596. Tel: 518-741-6869. Sisters of Charity

Woodbury, Nassau Co., Holy Name of Jesus (1962), Rev. Msgr. Anthony J. Savastano; Rev. John Oravecz.
Res., 690 Woodbury Rd., 11797-2504. Tel: 516-921-2334; Fax: 516-921-2408.
Catechesis/Religious Programs—Tel: 516-921-2334. Sr. Laboure D.R.E.
Students 207.

Wyandanch, Suffolk Co., Our Lady of the Miraculous Medal (1934), Rev. John I. Cervini; Deacons Bernard Taylor; Richard Lamb. In res., Rev. Msgr. John D. Gilmartin.
Res., 1434 Straight Path, 11798. Tel: 516-643-7568; Fax: 516-643-5935.
Gerald Ryan Outreach Center, Inc.—Tel: 516-643-7591; Fax: 516-491-7285. Mrs. Ann Druckenmiller, Dir.; Sr. Elizabeth Myles, C.S.J., Religious Education & Youth Ministry, Tel: 516-643-3364.

Chaplains of Public Institutions

ROCKVILLE CENTRE. *Mercy Medical Center,* 50 North Park Ave., Tel: 516-678-5800, Ext. 521. Sr. Eileen Donovan, O.P., Dir., Chaplaincy, Chaplains: Revs. Denis Sheridan; Asir Antony; Sr. Mary Alice Aschenbach, C.I.J., Dir.; Sr. Aidan Fahey, R.S.M.; Sr. Mary Morrow, D.W.; Sr. Norma Jean Lokcinski, C.I.J.; Sr. Bernadette Foley, C.I.J; Deacon Robert Walsh; Patricia Pannullo.
Mercy Hospice, Tel: 516-255-2360. Sr. Dolores Castellano.

AMITYVILLE. *Brunswick Hospital,* 366 Broadway, 11701. Tel: 516-789-7000; 264-0124; 842-8488. Rev. Robert A. Hyatt.
South Oaks Psychiatric Hospital, Sunrise Hwy., 11701. Tel: 516-264-4000. Rev. Robert A. Hyatt, Res., Our Lady of Consolation Home, Tel: 516-598-0497.

BAY SHORE. *Southside Hospital,* Montauk Hwy., 11706. Tel: 516-435-3484. Revs. Harold E. McBride, S.M.M.; Peter McCrann.

BETHPAGE. *Mid-Island Hospital.* Tel: 516-520-0222. Rev. Kevin McDonald, C.S.S.R.

CENTRAL ISLIP. *Central Islip State Hospital,* 11722. Tel: 516-234-6262. Rev. John Halpin Tel: 516-234-6535.

EAST MEADOW. *Nassau County Medical Center,* 2201 Hempstead Tpke., 11554. Tel: 516-572-3195; 542-2069. Revs. Brian J. Brinker; John P. Murray; Sr. Maureen Chase.
Nassau County Police Department. Rev. Msgr. John A. Alesandro; Rev. Joseph J. D'Angelo.
Nassau County, Fire Chiefs, Council of. Rev. Vincent A. Kennedy.

GLEN COVE. *North Shore Community Hospital at Glen Cove.* Tel: 516-676-5000. Rev. Henry Benack.

HUNTINGTON. *Huntington Hospital,* 11743. Tel: 516-351-2000. Rev. Owen Shelley, O.F.M.Cap.

KINGS PARK. *Kings Park State Hospital,* 11754. Tel: 516-544-2691. Rev. Thomas Houle, O.F.M.Cap.

MANHASSET. *North Shore Univ. Hospital,* 1554 Northern Blvd., 11030. Tel: 516-562-0100. Revs. Antony Xavier; Ande Tensae, O.F.M.Cap., Res., North Shore Hospital, Tel: 516-562-4713.

MELVILLE. *Long Island Developmental Center,* Box 788, 11747. Tel: 516-385-2700. Rev. Malachy C. Flaherty, O.F.M.Cap., Res., St. Francis of Assisi, 29 Northgate Dr., Greenlawn, 11740. Tel: 516-751-7435.

MINEOLA. *Winthrop Hospital,* First St., 11501. Tel: 516-663-0333. Rev. Msgr. Eugene F. Murphy; Rev. Augustine Fahnbulleh, Res., Corpus Christi, 155 Garfield Ave., 11501-2583. Tel: 516-746-1223.

NESCONSET. *Nesconset Nursing Home,* 11767. Tel: 516-361-8800. Rev. Aidan Neenan, O.F.M.Cap.

NORTHPORT. *Veteran's Hospital,* 11768. Tel: 516-261-4400. Revs. Eugene T. Jarcynski, C.S.C.; Charles L. Mockevicius; Augustine Sheehan; Gerald DiGiralamo.

PATCHOGUE. *Brookhaven Memorial Hospital,* 100 Hospital Rd., 11772. Tel: 516-654-7100. Bro. James Maloney, O.F.M.Cap.

PLAINVIEW. *Central General Hospital,* 888 Old Country Rd., 11083. Tel: 516-681-8900. Rev. Jose Simon Palliparambil, Res., Church of Our Lady of Mercy, 500 S. Oyster Bay Rd., Hicksville. Tel: 516-931-4351.

PORT JEFFERSON. *Maryhaven Centre of Hope,* 11777. Tel: 516-474-3400. Sr. Maryaline Zierle, O.P.
Mather Memorial Hospital, 11777. Tel: 516-473-1320, Ext. 4007. Sr. Ann McHugh, O.S.U.; Rev. Thomas Jones.
St. Charles Hospital, Port Jefferson, New York, 11777. Tel: 516-474-6000. Rev. Thomas Jones; Sr. Martha Winum, D.W.; Sr. Mona Guerrette, D.W.; Rev. James Miller, Res., St. Gerard Majella, 300 Terryville Rd., Port Jefferson Station, 11776.

ROSLYN. *St. Francis Hospital,* 11576. Sr. Lois Ann Van Delft, F.M.M., Dir.; Revs. Gabriel Miah; Joseph Maniangatt; Sr. Rita Sculti, O.P.; Sr. Nancy Exconde, F.M.M.; Bro. John Lesica, C.F.X.; Sr. Mari Garesche, F.M.M.; Sr. Noreen O'Malley, F.M.M.

ST. JAMES. *St. James Nursing Home,* 11780. Tel: 516-862-8000. Rev. Aidan Neenan, O.F.M.Cap.

SAYVILLE. *Good Samaritan Nursing Home,* 11782. Tel: 516-567-6600. Sr. Elizabeth Toohig, S.C.; Rev. Francis Nuss.

SMITHTOWN. *Community Hospital of Western Suffolk,* Smithtown By-Pass, Rte. 111, 11787. Tel: 516-979-9800. Deacon Fred Jackman.
St. John's Episcopal Hospital, 11787. Tel: 516-360-2000. Rev. Frederick Hill, O.F.M.Cap., Res., St. Patrick, 280 E. Main St., 11787. Tel: 516-862-3000; 979-1292.

STONY BROOK. *L.I. State Veterans' Home.* Tel: 516-444-8500. Rev. Charles F. Kohli.
Stony Brook University Hospital, SUNY at Stony Brook, 11790. Tel: 516-444-2765. Revs. Robert S. Smith, Dir. Chaplaincy Svcs.; John Keegan, M.M.; Sr. Marjorie Devlin.

UNIONDALE. *Holly Patterson Home for Nassau Community Aged and Infirm,* 875 Jerusalem Ave., 11553. Tel: 516-572-1500. Revs. Michael Reid; John H. McCabe, Res., Holy Trinity High School, Hicksville. Tel: 516-433-2900.

VALLEY STREAM. *Franklin Medical Center Hospital,* 11580. Tel: 516-256-6000. Rev. Francis Odufuye; Mrs. Carol Breslin, Res., St. Boniface Rectory, 631 Elmont Rd., Elmont, 11003-4028. Tel: 516-825-8800.

WEST BRENTWOOD. *Pilgrim Psychiatric Center,* P.O. Box A, 11717. Tel: 516-434-5134. Rev. Lawrence J. O'Leary; Sr. Mary Summerville, C.S.J.; Rev. John Halpin.

WEST ISLIP. *Consolation Nursing Home,* 11795. Tel: 516-587-1600. Rev. Robert Hyatt; Sr. M. Alicia Lanni, O.P.
Good Samaritan Hospital, 11795. Tel: 516-376-3000. Revs. Vincent Cunningham, S.M.M.; Bernard M. Blood, S.M.M.; Lawrence Bellew, C.P.; Sr. Gertrude O'Brien, D.W.; Sr. Ellen Moore, O.P.; Sr. Felicia Moore, R.G.S.; Sr. Doris Marie Deane; Rev. Paul J. Dahm,
Good Samaritan Hospice Program, 175 Beach Dr., 11795. Tel: 516-376-3850. Sr. Dorothy Monks; Sr. Joyce Osgood.

Prison Ministry

DEER PARK. *Office of Prison Ministry and Criminal Justice Affairs,* 1767 Deer Park Ave., 11729. Tel: 516-242-8631. Bro. John Moylan, O.S.F., Pastoral Team.

HICKSVILLE. *Nassau County Correctional Center*. Vacant. C.S. 1072, 11802. Tel: 516-572-4145; 572-3621.

RIVERHEAD. *Suffolk County Correctional Facility*. Vacant. One Center Dr., 11901. Tel: 516-852-2294.

YAPHANK. *Suffolk County Minimum Security Facility*. Vacant. Box 69, 11980. Tel: 516-852-4713.

Absent on Leave:
Reverend Fathers—
Ball, Matthew J.
Burke, William P.
Dillon, John
Flaherty, Kevin S.
Gabriele, John J.
Gress, Warren
Hart, James
Heenan, Michael F.
Houghton, Timothy
Huneke, Robert D.
Lennon, Charles
Mann, Peter
McDonnell, Stephen
Meyer, John D.
Morrelly, Leonard
Morris, Stephen P.
Nirrengarten, Andrew
Passamonte, Philip B.
Petriano, Thomas
Zach, Kenneth M.

Priests Released from Diocesan Assignment:
Reverend Monsignors—
Maniscalco, Francis
Reverend Fathers—
Alarcon, Felix
Bogert, James
Bowman, James
Carlo, Raymond
DeVita, Thomas F.
Duvelsdorf, Peter L.
Ehrhart, Charles, Chap. Major
Gallagher, William G.
Hanson, Donald M.
Mahoney, John F.
McMullen, Francis R.
Miraglia, Salvatore J.
Newman, Louis I.
Trapani, Anthony, Lt., CHC, USNR
Viladesau, Richard R.
Walsh, Kevin

Military Chaplains:
Reverend Fathers—
Bowman, James C.
Erhart, Charles M., U.S.M.C.A.-N.B.G.
Trapini, Anthony

Graduate Studies:
Reverend Monsignors—
Sweeny, Edward, St. Paul's, Ottawa, Canada
Reverend Fathers—
Miller, James, Catholic University, Washington, DC
Pereda, James F., Rome, Italy

Sick Leave:
Reverend Fathers—
Connolly, Andrew
Hagan, Vincent

Staiger, Charles

Retired:
Reverend Monsignors—
Ballweg, Lawrence
Bermingham, Charles E.
Chiara, Peter A.
Coffey, James F.
Colligan, Joseph F.
Collins, James E.
Costello, Lawrence
Cwalina, John F.
Flynn, Martin J.
Glimm, Francis X.
Goggin, Leo J.
Hendel, Richard P.
Huntington, Christopher
Kane, Arthur J.
Kirwin, Robert J.
Lawlor, Joseph F.
Margiotta, Vincent S.
McCarren, Edgar P.
Potterton, Daniel J.
Rooney, Thaddeus
Soave, Alfred
Stegmann, Raymond V.
Villar, Demetrio
Wiest, John J.
Reverend Fathers—
Barry, Ronald
Branigan, Patrick G.
Brendel, John A.
Buckley, Harold P.
Byrne, John J.
Casey, Francis M.
Collins, Edwin
Corali, Serafino A.
Cser, Ladislaus, S.J.
Curley, Robert
Curry, Thomas P.
Daley, John T.
David, Raymond J.
De Vita, James C.
Delaney, William I.
Dolan, James J.
Drab, John
Farley, David G.
Flaherty, Malachy, O.F.M.Cap.
Flaherty, William H.
Flynn, Edward J.
Gallagher, Andrew J.
Gartner, Charles
Gfroerer, Gerard J.
Gorman, John J.
Govern, William H.
Hall, Martin
Harrer, Frederic J.
Henesy, William
Henry, John P.
Hourihane, Francis
Kayser, Robert
Kennedy, Vincent A.
Korycki, Walter R.
Kozlowski, Joseph P.
LeTure, Theodore J.
Loy, Vincent P.
McGlade, Thomas F.
McManus, Eugene
Meade, James C.
Mockevicius, Charles L.
Monteleone, Raphael D.
Muhs, Edward
Mullen, John J.
Murphy, William T.
Murray, John E.
Navarroli, Frederick
O'Brien, Denis J.
O'Farrell, Michael J.
Osborne, Martin
Pai, Simon
Parrini, Warren
Pazo, John T.
Power, Virgil
Powers, Vincent J.
Reehil, Philip J.
Reidy, Martin F.
Reuss, Louis L.
Scanlon, Richard
Serrano, John J.
Shanahan, Edward J.
Sheehan, Lawrence
Singleton, William
Sledzaus, Alexander L.
Spinner, Hubert
Swiatocha, Bruno
Tortora, Raymond
Traynor, John
Vitsas, John P.
Wickman, Robert
Wilutis, John P.
Wodziak, Michael

Yang, Paul

Permanent Deacons:
Acquafredda, Patrick, St. Joseph, Hewlett
Altonji, James F., St. Joseph, Ronkonkoma
Alvarado, Jesus, St. Anne, Brentwood
Ashe, James C., Our Lady of Poland, Southampton
Barone, Frank D., Farmingdale, St. Kilian
Barry, Richard C., Our Lady of Lourdes, West Islip
Bartolotto, Joseph T., St. Louis De Montfort, Sound Beach
Bast, Thomas J., St. Frances de Chantal, Wantagh
Bedell, Paul, St. Barnabas Apostle, Bellmore
Beirne, James G., Seaford, St. James
Bennettson, Donald W., St. Joseph's, Kings Park
Biggin, James A., St. Martin of Tours, Bethpage
Billia, Edward W., St. Hugh of Lincoln, Huntington Station
Blake, Richard T., St. Aidan, Williston Park
Bohuslaw, James, St. John Nepomucene, Bohemia
Bono, Frank J., St. Joachim, Cedarhurst
Bopp, John T., Sacred Heart, Cutchogue
Bowe, Martin J., St. John the Evangelist, Riverhead
Braun, Robert G., St. Anthony of Padua, East Northport
Brennan, William V., St. William the Abbot, Seaford
Brown, Charles, SS. Philip & James, St. James
Broyles, Robert, St. Bridgid, Westbury
Buchenberger, Thomas E., St. William the Abbot, Seaford
Burkart John F., St. Philip Neri, Northport
Burnham, Bruce A., Our Holy Redeemer, Freeport
Byrne, William F., St. Brigid, Westbury
Cales, Francisco, Our Holy Redeemer, Freeport
Campbell, Robert, St. Raymond, East Rockaway
Capobianco, Eugene, St. Martin of Tours, Bethpage
Case, Edward M., St. Mary, Roslyn
Cavallaro, John, Outreach Project, Brentwood
Cedrone, Anthony M., Blessed Sacrament, Valley Stream
Cepeda, Jose A., Our Lady of Assumption, Copiague
Coates, Gerard, St. James, Setauket
Coleman, Thomas, St. Martha, Uniondale
Connolly, George P., Our Lady of Perpetual Help, Lindenhurst
Costello Thomas P., St. Joseph, Hewlett
Cotone, Louis, St. Kilian, Farmingdale
Cove, Francis K., Our Lady of Lourdes, Malverne
Crivello, Frank, Sts. Philip & James, St. James
Cunningham, Edward F., St. Anne, Garden City
Cuseo, Anthony W., Holy Name of Mary, Valley Stream
D'Angelo, Gregory R., St. Raymond, East Rockaway
DeBellis, Michael J., St. Joseph, Ronkonkoma
Deignan, Thomas F., SS. Cyril and Methodius, Deer Park
Dejewski, Robert, St. Patrick, Smithtown
Delargy, Daniel, Sacred Heart, North Merrick
Delligatti, Stephen F., Our Lady Lourdes, Massapequa Park
Determann, Herman J., St. Aidan, Williston Park
Diaz, Juan, St. Anne, Brentwood
Diaz-Granados, Francisco, St. Francis de Sales, Patchogue
DiGiovanna, James R., St. Catherine of Siena, Franklin Square
DiGiuseppe, Peter A., Our Lady Grace, West Babylon
DiVita, Thomas, St. Vincent Paul, Elmont
Donovan, Donald T., St. Mark, Shoreham
Donza, Gaetano, St. Raymond, East Rockaway
Dooling Arthur J., Mary Immaculate, Bellport
Dougherty, Joseph M., St. Joseph, Ronkonkoma
Duggan, Martin, St. Anthony of Padua, East Northport
Dunlop, John P., St. Mary of the Isle, Long Beach
Dunne, James A., Our Holy Redeemer, Freeport
Erdman, John P., St. Joseph, Ronkonkoma
Evers, Jeffrey, SS. Cyril & Methodius, Deer Park
Falls, John D., St. Brigid, Westbury
Ferri, Richard, St. Martin of Tours, Amityville
Finter, Frederick E., St. John the Baptist, Wading River
Flannery, James W., St. Anthony, Oceanside
Flood, Frank J., St. Rose of Lima, Massapequa
Fodale, John E., St. Catherine of Siena, Franklin Square
Forbes, Thomas J., St. Rose of Lima, Massapequa
Fullam, William F., Jr., St. Lawrence the Martyr, Sayville
Gagnon, Jules O. A., St. Patrick, Huntington
Gargiulo, Andrew T., Our Lady of Perpetual Help, Lindenhurst
Gariboldi, Frank, St. Matthew, Dix Hills
Gaudioso, Robert, St. Elizabeth Ann Seton, Lake Ronkonkoma
Gerace, Patrick C., Infant Jesus, Port Jefferson
Giambalvo, Anthony M., Ss. Cyril and Methodius, Deer Park
Gillen, Thomas J., St. Jude's, Mastic Beach
Gillette, Ronald J., St. John of God, Central Islip
Gioglio, Joseph G., Elizabeth Ann Seton, Lake Ronkonkoma
Giraldo, Luis D., St. Jude, Mastic Beach
Graff, Charles J., Our Lady of Grace, West Babylon
Gronenthal, Robert W., Our Lady of Snow, Blue Point
Gross, Thomas A., Jr., St. Jude, Mastic Beach
Guntert, Joseph F., Ss. Peter and Paul Mission Chapel, Manorville
Hammel, Lawrence V., Our Lady of Hope, Carle Place
Heintz, Robert, St. Hyacinth, Glen Head
Hernandez, Robert, Good Shepherd, Holbrook
Heschl, Robert J., Sts. Philip & James, St. James
Hickey, John, Our Lady of Hope, Carle Place
Huber, Charles F., SS. Cyril & Methodius, Deer Park
Ingulli, Joseph, St. James, Setauket
Jackman, Frederick, St. Patrick, Smithtown
Johnston, Richard J., St. Elizabeth, Melville
Kogler, William E., St. Margaret of Scotland, Selden
Kramer, Steven L., Our Lady of the Snow, Blue Point
Lamb, Richard W., Our Lady of the Miraculous Medal, Wyandanch
LaRossa, Richard W., St. Raymond, East Rockaway
Leahy, John G., St. James, Seaford
Lewis, Clinton, St. Martha, Uniondale
Leyden, Michael J., St. Joseph, Babylon
Logsdon, Patrick B., Queen of the Most Holy Rosary, Roosevelt
Longo, Allan D., St. Francis of Assisi, Greenlawn
Lovett, John J., St. John the Evangelist, Riverhead
Luken, Richard A., St. Luke, Brentwood
Macellaro, Daniel A., Resurrection, Farmingdale
Maffeo, Joseph R., St. Joseph, Ronkonkoma
Maher, Kenneth, SS. Philip & James, St. James
Mahoney, Michael A., St. Patrick, Bay Shore
Marino, Salvatore A., Blessed Sacrament, Valley Stream
Maro, Robert R., St. Patrick, Huntington
Matheis, Felix J., St. Brigid, Westbury
McDaid, Thomas P., St. Agnes, Rockville Centre
McGaffney, Gilbert, Notre Dame, New Hyde Park
McGauvran, John W., Sacred Hearts of Jesus and Mary, Southampton
McGowan, John, St. Anne, Garden City
McGuinness, Francis B., St. Rose of Lima, Massapequa
McGuirk, Eugene G., St. Hedwig, Floral Park
McIndoe, Martin B., St. Francis de Sales, Patchogue
McKenna, Michael A., St. Boniface, Elmont
McQuade, James J., St. Matthew, Dix Hills
Mercolino, Joseph T., St. Elizabeth, Melville
Metzdorff, Michael C., St. William the Abbot, Seaford
Micucci, Raymond R., St. Boniface, Elmont
Mildeberger, William H., Jr., St. Boniface, Elmont
Montesano, Joseph A., Our Lady Queen of Martyrs, Centerport
Morris, James P., St. Brigid, Westbury
Morrow, John W., Our Lady of Grace, West Babylon
Mostler, John F., Our Lady of Grace, West Babylon
Mulligan, Lawrence P., Our Lady of Victory, Floral Park
Muratore, Biagio V., St. Margaret of Scotland, Selden
Murphy, Galvin C., St. John the Evangelist, Center Moriches
Muscarnera, Charles, St. Christopher, Baldwin
Mystkowski, Joseph J., Our Lady of Mt. Carmel, Patchogue
Naylor, Montford D., St. Louis de Montfort, Sound Beach
O'Connor, Dennis R., St. Rose of Lima, Massapequa
O'Connor, Thomas F., St. Gerard Majella, Port Jefferson Station
O'Donovan, Robert S., St. Frances de Chantal, Wantagh
Odin, Frank A., Our Lady Perpetual Help, Lindenhurst
Owens, Thomas F., St. James, Setauket
Pagnotta, Carmen, St. Frances Cabrini, Coram
Pankus, Alfred, St. Thomas More, Hauppauge
Paolicelli, Philip, St. Margaret of Scotland, Selden
Pellegrino, Joseph C., St. Christopher, Baldwin
Peralta, Joseph F., St. Patrick, Bay Shore
Pettorino, John C., SS. Peter and Paul, Manorville
Pickel, James D., St. Martin of Tours, Amityville
Powers, William J., Infant Jesus, Port Jefferson
Quaranta, Arnold T., St. Matthew, Dix Hills
Quinn, Thomas J., St. Rose of Lima, Massapequa
Quinones, Fernando J., St. Francis de Sales, Patchogue
Rasanen, Terence A., St. Anne, Brentwood

Reilly, Thomas J., St. Hugh of Lincoln, Huntington Station
Reinhart, John C., Corpus Christi, Mineola
Rich, Thomas B., Our Lady of Hope, Carle Place
Riegger, George J., St. Sylvester, Medford
Rivera, Wenceslao, St. Luke, Brentwood
Roa, Jose, Our Lady of Loretto, Hempstead
Rodenburg, Herman I., St. Kilian, Farmingdale
Roettinger, Francis P., St. Sylvester, Medford
Samson, Thomas R., St. Anne, Brentwood
Sandberg, Louis C., Queen of the Most Holy Rosary, Roosevelt
Sanders, Richard W., St. Patrick's, Smithtown
Schneider, Andrew M., St. Philip Neri, Northport
Schultz, Peter F., St. Louis de Montford, Sound Beach
Scollan, Joseph M., St. Margaret of Scotland, Selden
Senholzi, Gregory B., St. John the Baptist, Wading River
Sherlock, Bernard F., St. Barnabas Apostle, Bellmore
Shortell, Michael V., St. Martha, Uniondale
Smith, Edward W., St. Lawrence the Martyr, Sayville
Smith, Robert, St. Rosalie, Hampton Bays
Smyth, Vincent P., St. Agnes, Rockville Centre
Squiteri, Aniello, Our Lady of Peace, Lynbrook
Stampfli, William J., St. Martin of Tours, Amityville
Sullivan, John F., St. Joseph, Babylon
Sullivan, Kenneth R., St. Rose of Lima, Massapequa
Swane, Gary, St. Louis de Montfort, Sound Beach
Taranto, Vito, St. Hugh, Huntington
Taylor, Bernard H., Our Lady Miraculous Medal, Wyandanch
Teufel, John G., Our Lady of Lourdes, West Islip
Tirelli, Raymond J., Our Lady of Hope, Carle Place
Trodden, John E., Our Lady of Hope Chapel, Central Islip
Valdaro, Dominick, Our Lady Lourdes, Massapequa Park
Vargas, Daniel E., Our Lady of Assumption, Copiague
Vigliotta, Albert C., St. Mark, Shoreham
Vigliotta, Crescenzo T., St. John the Evangelist, Center Moriches
Villani, Salvatore B., St. Aidan, Williston Park
Waldmann, Richard E., Infant Jesus, Port Jefferson
Walsh, Robert P., Mercy Hospital, Rockville Centre
Wanser, Richard, St. John Nepomucene, Bohemia
Weigel, John A., Maria Regina, Seaford
Weisz, Robert D., St. Thomas More, Hauppauge
Wetzel, Edward V., St. Martin of Tours, Amityville
Whitfield, Gerard F., Maria Regina, Seaford
Williams, Walter B., Jr., Resurrection, Farmingville
Wilson, Gerard R., St. Mary, East Islip
Zirkel, Donald E., St. Kilians, Farmingdale

INSTITUTIONS LOCATED IN THE DIOCESE

[A] SEMINARIES, DIOCESAN

HUNTINGTON. *Diocesan Seminary of the Immaculate Conception*, Lloyd Harbor, 11743. Tel: 516-423-0483. Rev. Msgr. Vincent F. Fullam, J.D. (BRK), Rector; Most Rev. John R. McGann, D.D., Chm., Board of Governors; Rev. Robert J. Smith, S.T.D., Vice Rector and Academic Dean; Sr. Kieran Hartigan, R.S.M., P.D., Assoc. Dean; Revs. Thomas M. Fusco, M.Div., Dir. Pastoral Formation and Dean of Seminarians; Cornelius H. Mahoney, M.Div., Dir. Spiritual Formation (M.Div. Program); Sr. Alice Patricia Dolan, C.S.J., M.A., Dir. Spiritual Formation (M.A. Program); Mrs. Joan Innvar, Registrar; Jiri Lipa, Ph.D., Librarian; Mrs. Bernadette M. Grodman, Business Officer; Sr. Mary Alice Piil, C.S.J., Ph.D.; Sr. Maria Pascuzzi, C.S.J., S.S.L., S.T.D.; Sr. Josephine Daspro, C.S.J., M.A.; Revs. Michael J. Curran, S.T.D. (BRK); Peter I. Vaccari, S.T.L. (BRK); Gerard Luttenberger, C.M., S.T.D.; Roland Faley, T.O.R., S.T.D., Moderator of Liturgy; Joseph R. Gibino, Ph.D. (BRK). Priests 9; Sisters 5; Seminarians 54; (MA) 115.

[B] COLLEGES AND UNIVERSITIES

ROCKVILLE CENTRE. *Molloy College*, 1000 Hempstead Ave., 11571-5002. Tel: 516-678-5000; 800-229-1020. *For a complete listing, refer to the Colleges and Universities section.*

PATCHOGUE. *St. Joseph's College*, 155 W. Roe Blvd., 11772-2399. Tel: 516-447-3200; Fax: 516-654-1782. *For a complete listing, refer to the Colleges and Universities section.*

[C] HIGH SCHOOLS, DIOCESAN

NASSAU COUNTY

HICKSVILLE. *Holy Trinity*, 98 Cherry Ln., 11801. Tel: 516-433-2900. Mr. James J. Boglioli, Prin.; Rev. Joseph J. Nixon, Chap. In res., Rev. Msgr. Thomas J. Hartman; Revs. John H. McCabe; Michael Reid. Sisters 13; Lay Teachers 80; Students 1,575.

SUFFOLK COUNTY

WEST ISLIP. *St. John the Baptist*, 1170 Montauk Hwy., 11795. Tel: 516-587-8000. Walter D. Lace, Prin.; Rev. James C. Vlaun, Chap. In res., Revs. Francis B. Nuss; Robert G. Fulton. Sisters 13; Priests 1; Lay Teachers 59; Students 920.

[D] HIGH SCHOOLS, PRIVATE

BRENTWOOD. *Academy of St. Joseph*. Independent; (Coed school grades PreK-6; Girl's school grades 7-12), Brentwood Rd., 11717. Tel: 516-273-2406; 273-4023; Fax: 516-231-4155. Directed by the Sisters of St. Joseph. Sr. Valerie Scholl, C.S.J., Dir.; Sr. Joanne Forker, C.S.J., Prin. Sisters of St. Joseph 20; Lay Teachers 33; Students 450.

HEMPSTEAD. *Sacred Heart Academy*. College preparatory-girls, 47 Cathedral Ave., 11550. Tel: 516-483-7383; Fax: 516-483-1016. Sr. Edyth Fitzsimmons, C.S.J., Prin. Sisters 31; Lay Teachers 48; Students 750.

MINEOLA. *Chaminade High School (Boys)*. Directed by the Society of Mary (Marianists), 11501. Tel: 516-742-5555. Bros. George E. Endres, S.M., Pres.; Michael J. McAward, S.M., Prin.; Mr. Salvatore Trentacoste, Asst. Prin.; Bros. Michael J. Gillen, S.M., Dir. Guidance; Thomas J. Cleary, S.M., Dean of Students; James W. Conway, S.M., Dir. Student Svcs.; Rev. Garrett J. Long, S.M., Chap. Brothers 22; Priests 3; Lay Teachers 45; Students 1,600.

OAKDALE. *LaSalle Center*. Global Learning Community (K-Grade 12), 11769. Tel: 516-589-0900; Fax: 516-563-7277. Directed by the De La Salle Christian Brothers. Mr. Donald Puleio, Comptroller; Rosemary Barone, Dir. of Admissions. Brothers 11; Sisters 2; Lay Teachers 38; Students: Upper School 280; Middle School 65; Primary School 160; Pre-School 60.

OLD WESTBURY. *School of the Holy Child Middle / Upper School*. Detox and counseling services for drop-in clients and 3-day stay. 25 Store Hill Rd., 11568. Tel: 516-626-9300. Directed by the Sisters of the Holy Child of Jesus. Grace Cavallo, Head of the School; Miss Elizabeth McCann, Prin. Lay Teachers 21; Students 109.

RIVERHEAD. *Mercy High School*. (Coed), 1225 Ostrander Ave., 11901. Tel: 516-727-5900. Directed by the Sisters of Mercy. Sr. Mary Elaine, R.S.M., Prin.; Sr. Marie E. Parrino, R.S.M., Asst. Prin./Dean of Students; Sr. Mary Christi, R.S.M., Asst. Prin. Sisters of Mercy (Brooklyn) 14; Other Sisters 3; Lay Teachers 27; Students 375.

SOUTH HUNTINGTON. *St. Anthony High School*. College Prep. 275 Wolf Hill Rd., 11747-1394. Tel: 516-271-2020. Directed by the Franciscan Brothers. Franciscan Fathers of Brooklyn. Bro. Peter Dawson, O.S.F., Prin. Brothers 23; Priests 1; Intercommunity Sisters 16; Lay Teachers 92; Students 2,125.

SYOSSET. *Our Lady of Mercy Academy*. Girls-day students. 815 Convent Rd., 11791. Tel: 516-921-1047. Directed by the Sisters of Mercy. Sr. Virginia Bertschi, R.S.M., Prin. Sisters of Mercy 15; Lay Teachers 26; Students 405.

UNIONDALE. *Kellenberg Memorial High School*, 1400 Glenn Curtiss Blvd., 11553. Directed by the Society of Mary. Rev. Philip K. Eichner, S.M., Pres.; Bros. Kenneth M. Hoagland, S.M., Prin.; Richard Hughes, Asst. Prin. Academics; Mr. Kenneth Conrade, Asst. Prin. Admissions; Rev. Albert Bertioni, S.M., Asst. Prin. Guidance; Mr. Kevin A'Hearn, Dean of Students & Asst. Prin. Latin School; Bro. Roger Poletti, S.M., Asst. Prin. Activities; Rev. Thomas Cardone, S.M., Chap.; Mrs. Marina Trentacoste, Dean of Women; Mr. Richard Kotlarz, Supvr. of Building Maintenance and Landscaping; Bro. Donald Nussbaum, S.M.; Mr. James Jones, Supvr. Cleaning Maintenance; Mrs. Catherine Zabrouski, Financial Supvr. Priests 3; Brothers 8; Lay Teachers 68; Students 1,580.

[E] REGIONAL SCHOOLS

BELLMORE. *St. Elizabeth Ann Seton Regional School*. Supported by the following parishes: St. Barnabas, Bellmore; St. Raphael, East Meadow; Cure of Ars, Merrick; St. Frances de Chantal, Wantagh.

Bellmore Campus, 2341 Washington Ave., 11710. Tel: 516-785-5709. Dr. Eileen Kilbride, Prin. Sisters 1; Lay Teachers 24; Students 560.

East Meadow Campus, 600 Newbridge Ave., East Meadow, 11554. Tel: 516-785-7006. Sr. William Noreen, S.C.H., Prin. Sisters 4; Lay Teachers 24; Students 550.

BETHPAGE. *St. John Baptist de LaSalle Regional School*. Supported by the following parishes: St. Martin of Tours, Bethpage; St. Kilian, Farmingdale; St. Pius X, Plainview; St. James, Seaford.

Bethpage Campus, Central Ave., 11714. Tel: 516-931-0983. Dr. Victor Lana, Headmaster. Lay Teachers 20; Students 286.

Farmingdale Campus, 50 Cherry St., Farmingdale, 11735. Tel: 516-694-3610. Mrs. Susan Anaischik, Prin. Sisters 1; Lay Teachers 25; Students 458.

CENTER MORICHES. *Our Lady, Queen of Apostles Regional School*, 2 St. Johns Pl., 11934. Tel: 516-878-1033. Sr. Eileen Martin, S.C., Prin. Lay Teachers 16; Students 342. Supported by the following parishes: St. John Evangelist, Center Moriches; St. Jude, Mastic Beach; Immaculate Conception, Westhampton Beach; Ss. Peter & Paul, Manorville.

CENTRAL ISLIP. *Our Lady of Providence Regional School*, 82 Carleton Ave., 11722. Tel: 516-234-1113; 234-6324; Fax: 516-234-6360. Sr. Judith Burchyns, C.S.J., Prin.-Upper School; Sr. Stephen Mary Puglisi, C.S.J., Prin.-Lower School. Sisters 4; Lay Teachers 30; Students 620. Supported by the following parishes: St. Anne, Brentwood; St. Luke, Brentwood; St. John of God, Central Islip; St. Peter the Apostle, Islip Terrace.

COMMACK. *Holy Family Regional School*, Indian Head Rd., P.O. Box 729, 11725. Tel: 516-543-0202. Ms. Agatha Cavoli, Prin. Sisters 3; Lay Teachers 20; Students 445. Supported by the following parishes: Christ the King, Commack; St. Matthew, Dix Hills; St. Thomas More, Hauppauge; St. Joseph, Kings Park.

CUTCHOGUE. *Our Lady of Mercy Regional School*, P.O. Box 970 - Main St., 11935. Tel: 516-734-5166. Sr. Mary Christi, Prin. Lay Teachers 8; Students 144. Supported by the following parishes: Sacred Heart, Cutchogue; Our Lady of Ostrabrama, Cutchogue; St. Agnes, Greenport; and St. Patrick, Southold.

EAST NORTHPORT. *Trinity Regional School*, 1025 Fifth Ave., 11731. Tel: 516-261-5130. Ms. Jeanne Morcone, Prin. Sisters 7; Lay Teachers 38; Students 853. Supported by the following parishes: Our Lady Queen of Martyrs, Centerport; St. Anthony of Padua, East Northport; St. Francis of Assisi, Greenlawn; St. Hugh of Lincoln, Huntington Station; St. Elizabeth, Melville; St. Philip Neri, Northport.

Satellite campuses exist at: 1450 New York Ave., Huntington Station, 11746. Tel: 516-549-7450. 364 Main St., Northport, 11768. Tel: 516-261-8520.

GLEN COVE. *All Saints Regional Catholic School*, 12 Pearsall Ave., 11542-3052. Tel: 516-676-0762. Sisters 1; Lay Teachers 24; Students 373. Supported by the following parishes: St. Boniface, Sea Cliff; St. Hyacinth, Glen Head; St. Mary, Roslyn; St. Patrick, Glen Cove; St. Rocco, Glen Cove.

Primary School. (Grades Nursery-3), 319 Cedar Swamp Rd., Glen Head, 11545-2298. Tel: 516-671-3033.

Upper Campus. (Grades 4-8), 12 Pearsall Ave., 11542-3052. Tel: 516-676-0762. Sr. Maureen Vellon, R.S.H.M., Prin.

LONG BEACH. *Long Beach Catholic Regional School*. (Grades PreK-8), 735 W. Broadway, 11561. Tel: 516-432-8900. Sr. Patricia Koehler, O.P., Prin. Sisters 3; Lay Teachers 19; Students 389. Supported by the following parishes: St. Ignatius, Long Beach; St. Mary of the Isle, Long Beach, and Our Lady of the Miraculous Medal, Point Lookout.

PATCHOGUE. *Holy Angels Regional School*. (Grades K-8), Division St., 11772. Tel: 516-475-0422. Sr. Elise Bier, R.S.M., Prin. Sisters 2; Lay Teachers 15; Students 400. Supported by the following parishes: Mary Immaculate, Bellport; St. Frances Cabrini, Coram; St. Joseph the Worker, E. Patchogue; St. Sylvester, Medford; Our Lady of Mount Carmel, Patchogue; St. Frances de Sales, Patchogue, and St. Margaret of Scotland, Selden.

PORT JEFFERSON. *Our Lady of Wisdom Regional School*, 114-116 Myrtle Ave., 11777. Tel: 516-473-1211. Mrs. Angela Orofino, Prin. Lay Teachers 18; Students 323. Supported by the following parishes: Infant Jesus, Port Jefferson; St. Louis de Montfort, Sound Beach; St. James, Setauket; St. Gerard Majella, Port Jefferson Station.

SAG HARBOR. *Stella Maris Regional School*, Division St., 11963. Tel: 516-725-2525. Judith Curtin, Prin. Sisters 2; Lay Teachers 22; Students 250. Supported by the following parishes: St. Therese of Lisieux, Montauk; Most Holy Trinity, East Hampton; St. Andrew, Sag Harbor; Queen of the Most Holy Rosary, Bridgehampton; Our Lady of the Isle, Shelter Island.

SAYVILLE. *Prince of Peace Regional School*, 200 Main

St., 11782. Tel: 516-589-3426. Sr. Mary Kelly, S.S.N.D., Prin. Sisters 2; Lay Teachers 15; Students 320. Supported by the following parishes: Our Lady of Snow, Blue Point; St. John Nepomucene, Bohemia; Good Shepherd, Holbrook; St. Lawrence, Sayville.

SOUTHAMPTON. *Our Lady of the Hamptons Regional School.* (Grades K-8), 160 N. Main St., 11968. Tel: 516-283-9140. 31 Montauk Hwy., Hampton Bays, 11946. Tel: 516-723-3740. Nursery and PreK. Sr. Kathryn Schlueter, C.S.J., Prin. Sisters 3; Lay Teachers 15; Students 357. Supported by the following parishes: St. Rosalie, Hampton Bays; Our Lady of Poland, Southampton, and Sacred Hearts Jesus Mary, Southampton.

UNIONDALE. *St. Martin de Porres Regional School*, 530 Hempstead Blvd., 11553. Tel: 516-481-3303. Lay Teachers 20; Students 315. Supported by the following parishes: Our Lady of Loretto, Hempstead; St. Ladislaus, Hempstead; St. Martha, Uniondale.

[F] ELEMENTARY SCHOOLS, PRIVATE

MANHASSET. *Our Lady of Grace Montessori School and Center.* (Grades PreK-1), 29 Shelter Rock Rd., 11030. Tel: 516-365-9832; Fax: 516-365-9329. Sisters, Servants of the Immaculate Heart of Mary 5; Lay Teachers 13; Students 200.

OLD WESTBURY. *School of the Holy Child-Lower.* (Grades N-5), 25 Store Hill Rd., 11568. Tel: 516-626-9300. Mrs. Grace Cavallo, Prin. Lay Teachers 24; Students 127.

[G] SPECIALIZED CHILD CARE AGENCIES

NESCONSET. *Cleary Deaf Child Center, Inc.*, 301 Smithtown Blvd., 11767. Tel: 516-588-0530 (Voice and TTY); Fax: 516-588-0016.
For a complete listing, refer to the Special Care Facilities section.

PORT JEFFERSON. *Maryhaven Center of Hope*, Myrtle ave., 11777. Tel: 516-474-4100; Fax: 516-474-4110.
For a complete listing, refer to the Special Care Facilities section.

SEA CLIFF. *St. Christopher-Ottilie Corp.*, 101 Downing Ave., 11579. Tel: 516-643-8800.
For a complete listing, refer to the Special Care Facilities section.

SYOSSET. *St. Mary's Children and Family Services*, 525 Convent Rd., 11791-3864. Tel: 516-921-0808.
For a complete listing, refer to the Special Care Facilities section.

WADING RIVER. *Little Flower Children's Services*, 11792. Tel: 516-929-6200.
For a complete listing, refer to the Special Care Facilities section.

[H] CATHOLIC CHARITIES

HICKSVILLE. *Catholic Charities Central Administration*, 90 Cherry Ln., 11801-6299. Tel: 516-773-7000; Fax: 516-733-7099. Rev. Msgr. John D. Gilmartin, Ph.D., Diocesan Dir. Tel: 516-733-7013; Laura A. Cassell, Chief Operating Officer. Tel: 516-733-7012; William McNamara, Special Assistant. Tel: 516-733-7023; John K. Bingham, Esq., Asst. Diocesan Dir. Tel: 516-733-7037; Janine Klein, Dir. Finance. Tel: 516-733-7015; Michael S. H. Young, Dir. Admin. Services. Tel: 516-733-7040; Donna Murphy O'Brien, Dir. Health Services. Tel: 516-733-7008; Robert A. Murphy, Dir. Housing. Tel: 516-733-7075; Sr. Geraldine Bowes, O.P., Dir. Human Services. Tel: 516-733-7060; Thomas J. Ulrich, Dir. Parish Social Ministry. Tel: 516-789-5230; Revs. John W. White, Dir. Education & Development. Tel: 516-733-7044; James E. Claffey, C.M., Dir. Immigrant Svcs. Tel: 516-789-5210.

Administrative Services, 90 Cherry Ln., 11801-6299. Tel: 516-733-7000. Carol Ann Radziewicz, Human Resource Admin. Tel: 516-733-7005; Robert J. Manfredi, MIS Admin. Tel: 516-733-7003; Helene Canberg, Communications/PR Specialist. Tel: 516-733-7043; Barbara Cody, Communications/PR Specialist. Tel: 516-733-7042; John Gonta, Purchasing/Facilities Admin. Tel: 516-733-7090.

Finance, 90 Cherry Ln., 11801-6299. Tel: 516-733-7000. Jo Ann Parda, Financial Admin. Tel: 516-733-7017; Maureen Angelillo, Payroll Mgr. Tel: 516-733-7030.

Health Services, 90 Cherry Ln., 11801-6299. Tel: 516-733-7000.

Alcohol & Substance Abuse Services, 155 Indian Head Rd., Commack, 11725. Tel: 516-543-6200. Kathleen Ayers, Program Admin.
Outpatient Clinics: P.O. Box 156, 119 Main St., Bridgehampton, 11932. Tel: 516-537-1159. Wayne Cavaliere, Contact, 155 Indian Head Rd., Commack, 11725. Tel: 516-543-6200. Simone Tomassoni, Contact, Talbot House Alcohol Crisis Center, 30-C Carlough Rd., Bohemia, 11716. Tel: 516-589-4144. Robert Howard, Contact.

Mental Health Services, 90 Cherry Ln., 11801-6299. Tel: 516-733-7000. Ann Russo, Sr. Program Admin. Tel: 516-733-7059.
Community Support Services (For deinstitutionalized people with chronic mental illness): 269 W. Main St., Bay Shore, 11706. Tel: 516-665-5320. Kate Bishop, Contact, 1729 N. Ocean Ave., Medford, 11763. Tel: 516-654-2966. Denis Demers, Contact.
Mental Health Clinics (Suffolk): 21 Fourth Ave., Ste. 234, Bay Shore, 11706. Tel: 516-665-6707. Adelaide Corvelle, Contact, 1727 N. Ocean Ave., Medford, 11763. Tel: 516-654-1919. Carmen Marrin, Contact.
St. Anthony's Guidance Clinics (Nassau): 124 Greenwich St., Hempstead, 11550. Tel: 516-292-8280. Phyllis Friedlin, Contact, 259 Mineola Blvd., Mineola, 11501. Tel: 516-248-7100. Patricia Quinn, Contact.

HIV/AIDS Services, 333 N. Main St., Freeport, 11520. Tel: 516-623-7400.

Special Dental Services Program, 333 N. Main St., Freeport, 11520. Tel: 516-623-7400. Daniel Maiden, Dental Coord., 1080 Sunrise Hwy., Amityville, 11701. Tel: 516-854-1069.

Ministry of Health, 143 Schleigel Blvd., Amityville, 11701. Tel: 516-789-5207. Marie Burns, R.N., Contact.

Housing Services, 90 Cherry Ln., 11801-6299. Tel: 516-733-7000. James Verity, Pastoral Care Coord. Tel: 516-733-7082; Lynn Reddy, Housing Coord. Tel: 516-733-7081.

Senior Housing: St. Agnes Village, 100 St. Agnes Rd., Uniondale, 11553. Tel: 516-485-4721. St. Joseph's Village, 2000 Boyle Rd., Selden, 11784. Tel: 516-736-0524. Bishop Kellenberg Gardens, 2477 Long Beach Rd., Oceanside, 11572. Tel: 516-766-0777. Peternana Terrace, 45 Wallace St., Freeport, 11520. Tel: 516-378-4072. Bishop Ryan Village, 10 Squiretown Rd., Hampton Bays, 11946. Tel: 516-728-2413. George Link Jr. Apts., George Link Jr. Cir., Coram, 11727. Tel: 516-732-6878. Mary's Manor, 60 Doughty Blvd., Inwood, 11696. Tel: 516-239-4291. Msgr. Henry J. Reel, 590 Christopher Ct., Medford, 11763. Tel: 516-475-6504.

Human Services, 90 Cherry Ln., 11801-6299. Tel: 516-733-7000.

Food and Nutrition (FAN) Program, 90 Cherry Ln., 11801-6299. Tel: 516-733-7000. Robert H. Horn, Program Admin. Tel: 516-733-7051.
Food Center Locations: 66 N. 19th St., Wyandanch, 11798. Tel: 516-491-4166. 61-C Brightside Ave., Central Islip, 11722. Tel: 516-232-2797. 127 Bedell St., Hempstead, 11550. Tel: 516-489-9660. St. Hugh of Lincoln, 21 E. Ninth St., Huntington Station, 11746. Tel: 516-549-5606. 23A Nassau Ave., Inwood, 11696. Tel: 516-371-5640. Blanco Dr., Mastic Beach, 11951. Tel: 516-399-5141. 400 Hallett Ave., Riverhead, 11901. Tel: 516-369-9246.
Health Services:

Office for Persons with Disabilities, 143 Schleigel Blvd., Amityville, 11701. Tel: 516-789-5219. Services for Persons Blind/Visually Impaired. Tel: 516-789-5213. Paul Sauerland, Contact, Services for Persons Deaf and Hard of Hearing. Tel: 516-789-5219. Bro. Alan J. Thomas, O.F.M., Contact.

Office of Mental Health Residences. Tel: 516-665-5092. Esther Lowengart, Program Coord.
Residence for people who are psychiatrically impaired: Siena Residence, 12 Mechanicsville Rd., Bay Shore, 11706. Tel: 516-968-8007. Anita DiMatteo, Contact.
Residences for children who are seriously emotionally disturbed: Teaching Family Home Program, 759 Stewart Ave., Bethpage, 11714. Tel: 516-938-2338. Bobby & April Walsh, Contacts, 4 Pleasant Ave., Farmingdale, 11735. Tel: 516-293-3153. Toinette & Tony Wheeler, Contacts, 2280 Sunrise Hwy., Islip, 11751. Tel: 516-581-6760. Mary & Bill Toomey, Contact.

Residential Services, 269 W. Main St., Bay Shore, 11706. Tel: 516-665-3434. Diane Ammirati, Program Admin.
Community residences for people who are developmentally disabled: Alhambra House, 3 Forest Pl., Huntington Station, 11746. Tel: 516-673-5240. Sr. Dolores Lawson, Contact, Caritas Residence P.O. Box 2383, 4 Hilton Ct., Aqueboque, 11931. Tel: 516-722-5366. Carolyn Giallorenzo, Contact, Christopher Residence, 70 McKeon Ave., Valley Stream, 11580. Tel: 516-825-8282. Lynn Baumgarten, Contact, Msgr. R. Emmet Fagan Residence, 1504 DePaul St., Elmont, 11003. Tel: 516-358-2559. John Sheridan, Contact, Rev. Thomas Helfrick Residence, 1 E. Moriches Blvd., East Moriches, 11940. Tel: 516-878-2965. Mako Residence, 380 Ed's Rd., Southold, 11971. Tel: 516-675-1783. Neumann Residence. (For Deaf Adults), 30 Brinkerhoff Ln., Mahasset, 11030. Tel: 516-627-5038. Sr. Jane Mullen, Contact, Bishop Ryan Residence, 258 Deauville Blvd., Copiague, 11726. Tel: 516-691-2126. Sr. Clare Romeo, Contact, Seton Residence, 3 Lombardi Pl., Amityville, 11701. Tel: 516-598-8216. Sr. Margaret Stadelman, Contact, Ted Hansler Residence, 24 Gardiners Ln., Hampton Bays, 11946. Tel: 516-728-8125. John Garvey, Contact, Joseph Virdone Residence, 27 North Carll Ave., Babylon, 11702. Tel: 516-661-2826. Sr. Ursula Sheridan, Contact.

Maternity Services, 29 Kirkwood Ave., Merrick, 11566. Tel: 516-223-7888. Sr. Lesley Block, Program Mgr., Parent Training Program, 29 Kirkwood Ave., Merrick, 11566. Tel: 516-223-7888.
Residence for Pregnant Women: Regina Residence, 29 Kirkwood Ave., Merrick, 11566. Tel: 516-223-7888. Sr. Lesley Block, Contact.
Residence for Mothers and Babies: Malta House, 39 Spruce St., Brentwood, 11717. Tel: 516-223-7888.

Senior Services, 90 Cherry Ln., 11801-6299. Tel: 516-733-7000. Liivia Westervelt, Program Admin. Tel: 516-733-7057, Bi-County Alliance of Senior Clubs, 90 Cherry Ln., 11801-6299. Tel: 516-733-7074. Mary McGrath, Contact, Link-Age Case Management, 90 Cherry Ln., 11801-6299. Tel: 516-733-7057. Esther Green, Contact, Meals-On-Wheels (Nassau). (For Seniors and People with AIDS), 124 Greenwich St., Hempstead, 11550. Tel: 516-485-7555. Jackie Blount, Contact, Meals-On-Wheels (Suffolk), 555 Albany Ave., Amityville, 11701. Tel: 516-842-4123. MaryAnn McGrenra, Contact.
Senior Community Service Centers: 555 Albany Ave., Amityville, 11701. Tel: 516-842-7331. Dennis Sullivan, Contact, 379 Linden St., Massapequa Park, 11762. Tel: 516-797-5357. Marline Evangelista, Contact, 619 Fenworth Blvd., P.O. Box 183, Franklin Square, 11010. Tel: 516-481-3322. Susan Weilhoefer, Contact, P.O. Box 243, 25 Nassau Ln., Island Park, 11558. Tel: 516-432-3388. Marie Frangella, Contact, 80 Anchor Ave., Oceanside, 11572. Tel: 516-764-9792. Margaret Keffel, Contact, P.O. Box 524, 2197 Jackson Ave., Seaford, 11783. Tel: 516-679-8373. Patricia Nadeau, Contact, Immigrant Services, 143 Schleigel Blvd., Amityville, 11701-1399. Tel: 516-733-7000. Carmen Maquilon, Legal Svcs. Tel: 516-789-5225; Gloria Jordan, M.S.W., Social Svcs.

Parish Social Ministry, 143 Schleigel Blvd., Amityville, 11701. Tel: 516-789-5200. Judy Mazzarella, Developer; Specialist. Tel: 516-789-5221; Brian Paradine, Employment Services. Tel: 516-789-5237.
Parish Social Ministry Developers—Western Vicariate: Patricia Oliviero, Deanery 1 & 5. Tel: 516-789-5237; Bridget Sheehan, Deanery 2 & 3. Tel: 516-789-5229.
Central Vicariate: Nancy Healey, Deanery 7 & 9. Tel: 516-789-5209; Tom Burns, Deanery 8 & 14. Tel: 516-789-5228.
Eastern Vicariate: Joy Mele, Developer Assoc., Deanery 10 & 12. Tel: 516-789-5239; Sr. Mary Anne Owens, Deanery 11 & 13. Tel: 516-654-0365; Chris Reimann, Public Policy Coord. Tel: 516-789-5220; Sr. Rose Sheridan, Public Policy Specialist. Tel: 516-789-5298; Richard Koubek, Public Policy Educ. Specialist. Tel: 516-789-5298.

[I] DIOCESAN HOSPITALS

NASSAU COUNTY

ROCKVILLE CENTRE. *Mercy Medical Center*, 1000 N. Village Ave., 11570. Tel: 516-255-0111.
For a complete listing, refer to the Hospitals section.
Mercy Medical Center, 1000 N. Village Ave., 11570. Tel: 516-255-2331.
For a complete listing, refer to the Hospitals section.

OLD BROOKVILLE. *The St. Francis-Mercy Corporation*, Northern Blvd., 11545-1111. Tel: 516-562-6904.
For a complete listing, refer to the Hospitals section.

ROSLYN. *St. Francis Hospital*, 100 Port Washington Blvd., 11576. Tel: 516-562-6000.
For a complete listing, refer to the Hospitals section.

SUFFOLK COUNTY

PORT JEFFERSON. *The St. Charles Corporation*, 200 Belle Terre Rd., 11777. Tel: 516-474-6000.
For a complete listing, refer to the Hospitals section.
St. Charles Hospital, Port Jefferson, New York, 11777. Tel: 516-474-6000.
For a complete listing, refer to the Hospitals section.

WEST ISLIP. *The Samaritan Corporation*, 1000 Montauk Hwy., 11795. Tel: 516-376-4001.
For a complete listing, refer to the Hospitals section.

[J] RESIDENCES FOR AGED

AMITYVILLE. *Dominican Village, Inc.*, 565 Albany Ave., 11701. Tel: 516-842-6091.
For a complete listing, refer to the Special Care Facilities section.

HUNTINGTON. *St. Joseph's Guest Home for the Aged, Inc.*, 350 Cuba Hill Rd., 11743. Tel: 516-368-9528.
For a complete listing, refer to the Special Care Facilities section.

WEST ISLIP. *Our Lady of Consolation Geriatric Care Center*, 111 Beach Dr., 11795. Tel: 516-587-1600; Fax: 516-587-5960.
For a complete listing, refer to the Special Care Facilities section.

[K] HOSPICES

SAYVILLE. *Good Samaritan Nursing Home*, 11782. Tel: 516-244-2400.
For a complete listing, refer to the Special Care Facilities section.

UNIONDALE. *Mercy Hospice*, St. Pius X Service Center, 122o front St., 11553. Tel: 516-485-3060.
For a complete listing, refer to the Special Care Facilities section.

WEST ISLIP. *Good Samaritan Hospice*, 1000 Montauk Hwy., 11795. Tel: 516-376-4001.
For a complete listing, refer to the Special Care Facilities section.

[L] SOCIETY OF ST. VINCENT DE PAUL

BETHPAGE. *Central Council*, Diocese of Rockville Centre, 249 Broadway, 11714. Tel: 516-822-3132. Rev. Msgr. Patrick Armshaw, Spiritual Dir.; James J. Reilly, Pres.; Robert S. Ellis, Exec. Dir. Total Assisted 40,630; Total Staff 103; Volunteers 864.

[M] HOME HEALTH SERVICES

HAMPTON BAYS. *Dominican Sisters Family Health Service*, 103 W. Montauk Hwy., P.O. Box 209, 11946. Tel: 516-728-0181; Fax: 516-728-2943. Montauk Hwy. & Cross Hwy., P.O. Box 866, 11930. Tel: 516-267-1090. Mrs. Joanna O'Connell, R.N., B.S., Admin. Suffolk Offices.

WESTBURY. *Nursing Sisters Home Visiting Service, Inc.* Administrative Office, 1600 Stewart Ave., 11590. Tel: 516-683-1370. Sr. Agnes Stumpf, C.I.J., Exec. Dir.; Sr. Dolores Wisniewski, C.I.J., Assoc. Exec. Dir., Corporate Office, 310 Prospect Park W., Brooklyn, 11215. Tel: 516-683-1370. Sr. Mary Nadine Casey, C.I.J., Pres.
Nursing Service Offices: Kings County, 310 Prospect Park W., Brooklyn, 11215. Tel: 718-965-7339. Mrs. Elise Mattia, Supvr., Nassau County, 1600 Stewart Ave., 11590. Tel: 516-683-1300. Sr. Sheila Bianchi, C.I.J., Supvr.; Mrs. Jayne Wheeler, Supvr., Suffolk County, 3241 Rte. 112, Medford, 11763. Tel: 516-696-1002. Mrs. Lee Fink, Supvr.

[N] MONASTERIES AND RESIDENCES OF PRIESTS AND BROTHERS

BAY SHORE. *Montfort Missionaries*, 26 S. Saxon Ave., 11706. Tel: 516-666-7500. Headquarters of magazine "Queen of All Hearts" and "Montfort Publications". Tel: 516-665-0726. Revs. Roger M. Charest, S.M.M., Mng. Editor; George J. Werner, S.M.M., Supr., Preaching Team; Bernard M. Blood, S.M.M., Preaching Team; Vincent P. Cunningham, S.M.M., Hospital Chap.; William M. Dilgen, S.M.M., Marriage Encounter; J. Patrick Gaffney, S.M.M., Assoc. Edit.; Preaching Team; Maurice A. Landry, S.M.M.; Ronald L. Lloyd, S.M.M. (England); James Manning, S.M.M., Preaching Team; Harold E. McBride, S.M.M., Hospital Chap.; Peter J. McCrann, S.M.M., Hospital Chap.; Eugene J. Moynihan, S.M.M.; Theodore Murphy, S.M.M., Hospital Chap. Priests 13.
Montfort Missionaries - Retreat Center, 26 S. Saxon Ave., 11706.

EASTPORT. *Shrine of Our Lady of the Island*, Montfort Misionaries; Eastport-Manor Rd., 11941. Tel: 516-325-0661. Revs. William J. Vigliotta, S.M.M., Dir.; Raymond Graham, S.M.M.; Bro. Christopher Golla, S.M.M.

GLEN COVE. *St. Josaphatis Monastery, Novitiate and Retreat House*, East Beach Dr., 11542. Tel: 516-671-0545; Fax: 516-676-7465. Basilian Fathers. Revs. Mauricio Popadiuk, O.S.B.M. (Brazil), Supr. & Master of Novices; Hilarion Bebedik, O.S.B.M.; Theodosius Ilnicki, O.S.B.M., Asst. Master of Novices; Julian Katrij, O.S.B.M.; Atanasius B. Pekar, O.S.B.M.

HEWLETT. *Marianist Community*, 335 Daub Ave., 11557. Tel: 516-374-1027. Rev. Joseph Lynch, S.M.

MINEOLA. *Provincial Residence and Novitiate*, 240 Emory Rd., 11501. Tel: 516-742-5555. Society of Mary (Marianists). Bro. George E. Endres, S.M., Prov.; Rev. Thomas A. Cardone, S.M., Asst. Prov. & Asst. Religious Life; Bro. Kenneth M. Hoagland, S.M., Asst. Education; Rev. Philip K. Eichner, S.M., Asst. Temporalities; Bro. Michael J. Gillen, S.M., Councilor; Rev. Francis T. Keenan, S.M., Councilor; Bro. Michael J. McAward, S.M., Councilor. In res., Revs. Ernest P. Lorfanfant, S.M.; Garrett J. Long, S.M.; Francis T. Keenan, S.M.

OYSTER BAY. *St. Francis Monastery, Novitiate and Apostolic Center*, Planting Fields Rd., R.F.D. 1, Box 1365, 11771-1302. Tel: 516-922-3545. Franciscan Brothers. Bros. Patrick Murphy, Co-Vicar for Religious, Diocese of Rockville Centre. Tel: 516-922-3886; Roman Morris, O.S.F., Dir., St. Francis Center. Tel: 516-922-3708. Brothers 6.
Vincentian Community, 104 Anstice St., 11771. Revs. Gerard H. Luttenberger, C.M.; Timothy J. Lyons, C.M.

SMITHTOWN. *St. Ann's Friary*, Eckerncamp Dr., 11787. Capuchin Fathers (Prov. St. Mary). Revs. Matthias Wesnofske, O.F.M.Cap., Supr.; Aidan Neenan, O.F.M.Cap.

UNIONDALE. *St. Pius X Residence*, 1220 Front St., 11553. Tel: 516-485-4200. Revs. Robert Blyman, Vicar for Senior Priests; Robert Fulton, Admin. In res., Revs. John J. Byrne; Serafino A. Corali; Edward J. Flynn; Vincent A. Kennedy; John J. Serrano; Edward D. Shillito; John P. Wilutis; Gerard J. Gfroerer; John P. Vitsas; Edward J. Shanahar.; Raymond J. David; Thomas P. Curry; Hubert Spinner; Robert Blyman; Rev. Msgr. Alfred Soave.

WEST HEMPSTEAD. *Maryknoll Residence*, 813 Myrna Dr., 11552. Tel: 516-489-7799. Rev. Alphonse A. Schiavone, M.M., Dir.

[O] CONVENTS AND RESIDENCES FOR SISTERS

ROCKVILLE CENTRE. *St. Joseph's Villa*, 984 N. Village Ave., 11570. Tel: 516-678-4860. Congregation of the Infant Jesus (Nursing Sisters of the Sick Poor). Professed Sisters 31.

AMITYVILLE. *Queen of the Rosary, Motherhouse*, 555 Albany Ave., 11701-1197. Tel: 516-842-6000; Fax: 516-842-0240. Sisters of St. Dominic. Legal Titles: *Dominican Sisters Community Support Corporation; Amityville Dominican Sisters, Inc.* Sr. Mary Hughes, O.P., Prioress. Co-Administrators: Sr. Mary A. Sullivan; Sr. Helen Zalak; Rev. Msgr. Domenick J. Adessa, Chap. Total in Residence 140.

BAY SHORE. *New Jerusalem*, 106 N. Penataquit Ave., 11706-6939. Tel: 516-968-8859. Sisters 6.

BLUE POINT. *Ursuline Sisters, St. Ursula Center*, Middle Rd., P.O. Box 86, 11715. Tel: 516-363-6544. Congregation of Tidonk. Sr. Philomena O'Brien, O.S.U., Retreat Dir.; Sr. Ursula Liebold, O.S.U., Coord.

BRENTWOOD. *Maria Regina Convent*, 1725 Brentwood Rd., Bldg. 1, 11717-5589. Tel: 516-273-4500. Sisters of St. Joseph. Sr. Marie de Montfort Shields, C.S.J., Local Supr. Sisters 165.
Saint Joseph Convent, Motherhouse, Brentwood Rd., 11717. Tel: 516-273-4531; Fax: 516-273-1345. Sisters of Saint Joseph Generalate. Sr. Angela Gannon, Gen. Supr.; Sr. Miriam Lucille Montella, Gen. Sec.; Sr. Joan Larkin, Gen. Treas.; Sr. Edna McKeever, C.S.J., Community Archivist.
Saint Joseph Convent, Brentwood Rd., 11717. Tel: 516-273-4531. Sisters 1,025.
Saint Joseph Novitiate, Brentwood Rd., 11717. Tel: 516-434-9834. Sr. Maryann Rogers, C.S.J., Coord.

CORAM. *Daughters of Wisdom*, 2 Welling Way, 11727-1005. Sisters 4.

DIX HILLS. *Contemplative Sisters of the Good Shepherd*, 151 Burrs Ln., P.O. Box 8020, 11746-9020. Tel: 516-643-1071. Sr. Helen Lussier, Supr. Sisters 20.
Sisters of the Good Shepherd, Madonna Heights, 151 Burrs Ln., P.O. Box 8020, 11746-9020. Tel: 516-643-8800. Coordinators: Sr. Yvette Arnold; Sr. Karen Keegan. Sisters 28. Legal Title: *Sisters of the Good Shepherd, Huntington, NY, Inc.*

FRANKLIN SQUARE. *Spiritual Life Center*, 1031 Mosefan St., 11010. Tel: 516-328-7438. Sisters of St. Dominic. Sr. Kathleen Murphy, O.P., Dir. Sisters 2.

HAMPTON BAYS. *St. Joseph's Villa Retreat and Renewal Center*, 81 Lynn Ave., 11946. Tel: 516-728-6447. Sisters of St. Joseph 2.

HUNTINGTON. *Missionary Sisters of St. Benedict*, 350 Cuba Hill Rd., 11743. Tel: 516-368-9528. Sr. Mary Boniface Slota, O.S.B., Supr. Sisters 22.

ISLIP. *Daughters of Wisdom (Provincial House)*, 385 Ocean Ave., 11751-4600; Fax: 516-277-3274. Sr. Evelyn Eckhardt, D.W., Prov. Administration offices. Sisters 4.
Daughters of Wisdom Islip Community, 385 Ocean Ave., 11751-4600. Sisters 5.

MEDFORD. *Inter-Community*, 97 Robinson Ave., 11763. Sisters 2.

OCEANSIDE. *St. Anthony's Parish House*, 111 Anchor Ave., 11572. Dominican Sisters (Amityville).

OLD WESTBURY. *Sisters of the Holy Child Jesus*, 25 Store Hill Rd., 11568; Fax: 516-626-7914. 28 Central Dr., 11545.

RONKONKOMA. *Religious of Our Lady of the Retreat in the Cenacle*, 310 Cenacle Rd., 11779-2203.
Provincial House, P.O. Box 2429, 11779-2203. Tel: 516-471-6270. Sr. Marian Hahn, Prov. Professed Sisters 3.
Cenacle Retreat House. Tel: 516-588-8366. Sr. Emma K. Finkbohner, Admin. Coord. Professed Sisters in Residence 60.
Cenacle Formation House, 312 Cenacle Rd., 11779-2203. Tel: 516-737-8491. Professed Sisters 2; Novices in Residence 3.

ROOSEVELT. *Oblate Sisters of the Most Holy Redeemer*, Mother of Good Counsel Home, 290 Babylon Tpke., P.O. Box 329, 11575-0329. Tel: 516-223-1013; Fax: 516-223-4254. Sr. Celina Ardila, O.SS.R., Exec. Dir. Mother of Good Counsel Home is a small group home for pregnant and parenting teenage mothers and their infants.

SEAFORD. *St. Angela Convent*, 3905 Maple St., 11783. Ursuline Sisters of Tildonk.

SELDEN. *Providence Newman Center*, 76 College Rd., 11784. Sr. Grace Maria Dolan, C.S.J.
Sisters of St. Joseph, 2316 Hampton Ave., 11783. Tel: 516-826-1773. Sisters 5.

SOUND BEACH. *Our Lady of Perpetual Help Convent*, 49 Hilltop Dr., Box 926, 11789. Tel: 516-744-2477. Sr. Alice Benedict, D.W., Admin./Coord. Daughters of Wisdom 23.

WATER MILL. *Siena Spirituality Center*, P.O. Box 660, 11976. Tel: 516-726-4740; Fax: 516-726-1930. Dominican Sisters (Amityville) 8.

[P] RETREAT HOUSES

BLUE POINT. *St. Ursula Retreat Center, Inc.*, Middle Rd. and Blue Point Ave., P.O. Box 86, 11715-0086. Tel: 516-363-6544; 363-2422 (Retreat Center). Directed by Ursuline Sisters of Tildonk. Sr. Philomena O'Brien, O.S.U., Retreat Dir. Weekend retreats; private retreats; directed retreats; days and evenings of prayer. Sr. Ursula Liebold, O.S.U., Coord. of Sisters. Total in residence 14.

MANHASSET. *St. Ignatius Retreat House, Inisfada*, Box 756, 11030. Tel: 516-621-8300. The Society of Jesus. Revs. Leo J. Daly, S.J., Dir.; Timothy A. Curtin, S.J.; James J. Dinneen, S.J.; Peter F. O'Brien, S.J.; Vincent J. Ritchie, S.J.; Bernard E. Shannon, S.J. Sisters 2; Total Staff 12; Total in Residence 9.

MELVILLE. *St. Joseph's Prayer Center*, 167 Wolf Hill Rd., 11747. Tel: 516-421-3369. Sr. Mary Dymphna Murray, R.S.M., Admin. Dir.; Rev. James J. Wheeler, S.J., Apostolic Dir. Total Staff 20.

MOUNT SINAI. *House of the Holy Innocents, Inc.*, 722 Mt. Sinai-Coram Rd., Box 174, 11766. Tel: 516-331-1745.

OYSTER BAY. *St. Francis Center, Inc.*, R.F.D. No. 1, Box 1365, Planting Fields Rd., 11771-1302. Tel: 516-922-3708. Directed by Franciscan Bros. of Brooklyn. Bro. Roman Morris, O.S.F., Dir.

RONKONKOMA. *Cenacle Retreat House*, 310 Cenacle Rd., 11779-2203. Tel: 516-588-8366. Religious of the Cenacle. Sr. Mary Jane Laffan, Ministry Coord. Ministry Staff 12.

SAG HARBOR. *Cormaria Retreat House*, 11963. Tel: 516-725-4206. Directed by the Religious of the Sacred Heart of Mary. Sr. Ann Thaddeus Marino, R.S.H.M., Retreat Dir. Religious of the Sacred Heart of Mary 4; Total Staff 5.

SHELTER ISLAND HEIGHTS. *St. Gabriel's Youth House*, 64 Burns Rd., P.O. Box 3015, 11965. Tel: 516-749-0850; Fax: 516-749-3154. A Youth Retreat Ministry directed by the Passionists. Retreats available for youth and young adult; women, men and married couples. Private retreats available at 3 bedroom, waterfront, "Star of the Sea" House of Prayer. Mr. Robert A. Scott, Retreat Dir.; Sr. Maureen Kervick, S.S.J., Dir. Admin. Retreat Team: Ms. Patricia Krupski; Rev. Blaine Brezinski, C.P.

[Q] CAMPUS MINISTRIES AND NEWMAN CENTERS

ROCKVILLE CENTRE. *The Campus Parish of Long Island*. Office of Campus and Young Adult Ministry, 50 N. Park Ave., 11570. Tel: 516-678-5800. Rev. Msgr. Donald M. Beckmann, D.Min., Pastor & Dir. Canonical institute of non-territorial campus parishes.
Adelphi University, Rm. 316, University Center, Chaplain's Center, Garden City, 11530. Tel: 516-877-3116. Rev. Joseph J. D'Angelo; Sr. Marilyn Nichols, S.S.J.
Hofstra University. Chaplains' Office, Student Center 213, Hempstead, 11550. Tel: 516-463-6920. Rev. Msgr. Donald M. Beckmann, D.Min.; Sr. Kathleen Riordan, O.P.
Nassau Community College. Stewart Avenue-Math Department, Garden City, 11530-6793. Tel: 516-572-7611. Mr. Gene Zirkel; Deacon Thomas Rich.
LIU/C.W. Post College and New York Institute of Technology - Old Westbury. Interfaith Center, Brookville, 11548. Tel: 516-299-2229. Rev. Edward J. Brown, M.S.
Southampton Campus of Long Island University. Box 301, East Quogue, 11942. Tel: 516-728-2022. Rev. William J. Gormley, C.M.
Suffolk Community College. 533 College Rd., Selden, 11784. Tel: 516-451-4369. Sr. Grace Dolan, C.S.J.
SUNY at Farmingdale. Memorial Hall, Rm. 211,

Melville Rd., Farmingdale, 11735. Tel: 516-420-2638. Rev. Edward J. Werring.

SUNY at Old Westbury. Box 210, Old Westbury, 11568. Tel: 516-876-3000, Ext. 3380. Mrs. Barbara Tutunjian.

SUNY at Stony Brook - Catholic Campus Ministry. Interfaith Center, 158 Humanities, Stony Brook, 11794-8033. Tel: 516-632-6562. Sr. Margaret Ann Landry, R.S.H.M.; Rev. John Fitzgerald.

SUNY at Stony Brook. University Hospital, H.S.C.-L3-122, Stony Brook, 11794-8033. Rev. Robert S. Smith, Dir.

Young Adult Ministry. 50 N. Park Ave., 11570. Tel: 516-678-5800, Ext. 616. Ms. Mary Beth Reynolds.

[R] MISCELLANEOUS

ROCKVILLE CENTRE.

**Women Helping Women*, 255 Merrick Rd., 11570.

AMITYVILLE. *Amityville Dominican Sisters, Inc.*, 555 Albany Ave., 11701. Tel: 516-842-6000. Sr. Mary Hughes, O.P., Pres.; Sr. Francis Ann Gorman, O.P., Vice Pres.; Sr. Barbara C. Suessmann, O.P., Sec. & Treas.

Dominican Sisters Community Support Corp., 555 Albany Ave., 11701. Tel: 516-842-6000. Sr. Mary Hughes, O.P., Pres.; Sr. Francis Ann Gorman, O.P., Vice Pres.; Sr. Barbara C. Suessmann, O.P., Sec. & Treas.

BAY SHORE. *Pronto of Long Island, Inc.*, 128 Pine Aire Dr., 11706. Tel: 516-231-8290. Contact Persons: Sr. Mary Schramm, O.S.U.; Mrs. Nilda Alvarez.

BELLMORE. *Damien-Dutton Society for Leprosy Aid, Inc.*, 616 Bedford Ave., 11710. Tel: 516-221-5829; 800-448-6166; Fax: 516-221-5909. Howard E. Crouch, Pres.; Betty Campbell, Vice Pres.

BROOKVILLE. *Sisters, Lovers of the Holy Cross*. St. Paul's Cottage, Cedar Swamp Rd., 11545. Sr. Maria Lien Tran, Pres.

CENTERPORT. *Mt. Alvernia, Inc.*, Prospect Rd., P.O. Box 301, 11721. Tel: 516-261-5730. Directed by the Franciscan Brothers. Bro. Bryan Murphy, O.S.F., Dir.

Camp Alvernia.

Alvernia Center for Environmental Studies.

DEER PARK. *Aid to the Church in Need*. United States Office. Mailing Address: P.O. Box 576, 11729. Tel: 800-628-6333; 516-242-8321; Fax: 516-243-1922. 2017 Deer Park Ave., 11729. Mr. Robert W. Lulley, National Dir.

FARMINGVILLE. *Religious Computer Systems*, P.O.Box 508, 11738-0508. Tel: 516-732-7270; Fax: 516-732-6591. Sr. Jane Muller, O.P. Social Security and computer services for Religious institutions under sponsorship of the Amityville Dominicans.

HICKSVILLE. *Hope Community of Hicksville, Inc.*, 46 Miller Rd., 11801. Total Assisted 50.

ISLIP. *Wisdom Charitable Trust*, 385 Ocean Ave., 11751. Tel: 516-277-2660.

NEW HYDE PARK. *Apostleship of Prayer, National Office for the U.S.*, 3 Stephen Ave., 11040-3130. Tel: 516-328-9777; Fax: 516-328-6039. Rev. John H. Rainaldo, S.J., National Dir. Total Staff 4.

OAKDALE. *Saint John De La Salle of New York, Inc.*, 500 Montauk Hwy., 11769. Tel: 401-789-0244. Bro. Michael J. McKenery, F.S.C.

RONKONKOMA. *Catholic Press Association of the United States and Canada, Inc.*, 3555 Veterans Memorial Hwy., Unit O, 11779. Tel: 516-471-4730. Mr. Christopher J. Gunty, Pres.; Mr. Owen P. McGovern, Exec. Dir.

UNIONDALE. *TELIcare of the Diocese of Rockville Centre*. 1200 Glenn Curtiss Blvd., 11553. Michael P. O'Leary, Gen. Mgr.

WEST BABYLON. *Christa House, Inc.*, P.O.Box 1633, 11704. Tel: 516-889-0586. Sr. Patricia A. Ryan, C.S.J.

WYANDANCH. *Gerald J. Ryan Outreach Center, Inc.*, 1434 Straight Path, 11798; Fax: 516-491-7285. Total Assisted 15,600; Total Staff 3.

The Opening Word Program, Inc., 1434 Straight Path, 11798. Tel: 516-643-0541. Directed by the Sisters of St. Dominic. Sr. Mary Ryan, O.P., Exec. Dir.; Sr. Margaret Briody, Treas.; Sr. Mary Hughes, O.P., Chairperson.

RELIGIOUS INSTITUTES OF MEN REPRESENTED IN THE DIOCESE

For further details refer to the corresponding bracketed number in the Religious Institutes of Men or Women section.

[0330]—*Brothers of the Christian Schools*.—F.S.C.
[0600]—*Brothers of the Congregation of Holy Cross*.—C.S.C.
[0470]—*The Capuchin Friars*. (St. Mary Prov.).—O.F.M.Cap.
[1330]—*Congregation of the Mission-Vincentians*. (Eastern Prov.).—C.M.
[1000]—*Congregation of the Passion*. (Prov. of St. Paul of the Cross).—C.P.
[0490]—*Franciscan Brothers of Brooklyn*.—O.S.F.
[0690]—*Jesuit Fathers and Brothers*. (N.Y. Prov.).—S.J.
[0770]—*The Marist Brothers*.—F.M.S.
[0800]—*Maryknoll*.—M.M.
[0720]—*Missionaries of Our Lady of La Salette*.—M.S.
[0870]—*Montfort Missionaries*.—S.M.M.
[0430]—*Order of Preachers-Dominicans*.—O.P.
[1070]—*Redemptorist Fathers*.—C.SS.R.
[0760]—*Society of Mary*. (Provs. of N.Y.; Meribah).—S.M.

RELIGIOUS INSTITUTES OF WOMEN REPRESENTED IN THE DIOCESE

[3110]—*Congregation of Our Lady of the Retreat in the Cenacle*.—R.C.
[1920]—*Congregation of the Sisters of the Holy Cross*.—C.S.C.
[0960]—*Daughters of Wisdom*.—D.W.
[1070-05]—*Dominican Sisters*.—O.P.
[1070-11]—*Dominican Sisters*.—O.P.
[1070-15]—*Dominican Sisters*.—O.P.
[1070-16]—*Dominican Sisters*.—O.P.
[1370]—*Franciscan Missionaries of Mary*.—F.M.M.
[1180]—*Franciscan Sisters of Allegany, New York*.—O.S.F.
[1425]—*Franciscan Sisters of Peace*.—F.S.P.
[2575]—*Institute of the Sisters of Mercy of the Americas*. (Brooklyn, NY).—R.S.M.
[0210]—*Missionary Benedictine Sisters*.—O.S.B.
[3030]—*Oblate Sisters of M.H. Redeemer*.—O.S.S.R.
[2070]—*Religious of the Holy Union of the Sacred Hearts*.—S.U.S.C.
[3465]—*Religious of the Sacred Heart of Mary*.—R.S.H.M.
[2970]—*School Sisters of Notre Dame*.—S.S.N.D.
[0640]—*Sisters of Charity of St. Vincent de Paul*. (Halifax).—S.C.
[0650]—*Sisters of Charity of St. Vincent de Paul, of New York*.—S.C.
[0430]—*Sisters of Charity of the Blessed Virgin Mary*.—B.V.M.
[2990]—*Sisters of Notre Dame de Namur*.—S.N.D.
[3830]—*Sisters of St. Joseph*.—C.S.J.
[2980]—*Sisters of the Congregation de Notre Dame*.—C.N.D.
[3180]—*Sisters of the Cross and the Passion*.—C.P.
[1830]—*Sisters of the Good Shepherd*.—R.G.S.
[1970]—*Sisters of the Holy Family of Nazareth*.—C.S.F.N.
[2240]—*Sisters of the Infant Jesus*.—C.I.J.
[2160]—*Sisters, Servants of the Immaculate Heart of Mary*.—I.H.M.
[4060]—*Society of the Holy Child Jesus*.—S.H.C.J.
[4130]—*Ursuline Sisters of the Congregation of Tildonk, Belgium*.—O.S.U.

DIOCESAN CEMETERIES

CENTRAL ISLIP. *Queen of All Saints*, 115 Wheeler Rd., 11722. Tel: 516-234-8297.

CORAM. *Holy Sepulchre*, 3443 Rte. 112, 11727. Tel: 516-732-3460.

WESTBURY. *Holy Rood*, Old Country Rd., Box 182, 11590. Tel: 516-334-7990.

NECROLOGY

† Borcino, Raymond F., (Retired). —Died March 2, 1996.
† Cannizzaro, Francis J., Inwood, NY, Our Lady of Good Counsel. —Died June 16, 1996.
† Lynch, Rev. Msgr. John J., Southampton, NY, Sacred Hearts of Jesus and Mary. —Died April 11, 1996.
† Mulligan, Rev. Msgr. Robert T., Rockville Center, NY, St. Agnes Cathedral. —Died Nov. 4, 1996.
† Nedd, Edward S., (Retired). —Died Nov. 22, 1995.
† Rogers, Alfred J., (Retired). —Died Jan. 13, 1996.
† Schaefer, Rev. Msgr. Frederick F., Patchogue, NY, St. Francis de Sales. —Died Aug. 20, 1996.
† Shanahan, Patrick E., West Babylon, NY, Our Lady of Grace. —Died Nov. 26, 1995.

Diocese of Sacramento

(Dioecesis Sacramentensis)

Most Reverend

WILLIAM K. WEIGAND, D.D.

Bishop of Sacramento; ordained May 25, 1963; appointed Bishop of Salt Lake City September 3, 1980; ordained and installed November 17, 1980; appointed Bishop of Sacramento November 30, 1993; installed January 27, 1994. *Mailing Address: Diocesan Pastoral Center, 2110 Broadway, Sacramento, 95818-2541.* Tel.: 916-733-0200.

Most Reverend

FRANCIS A. QUINN, D.D., ED.D.

Retired Bishop of Sacramento; ordained June 15, 1946; appointed Titular Bishop of Numana and Auxiliary Bishop of San Francisco April 28, 1978; Episcopal ordination June 29, 1978; appointed Bishop of Sacramento December 18, 1979. *Office: 2110 Broadway, Sacramento, CA, 95818-2541.* Tel.: 916-733-0200 (Office).

ERECTED BY HIS HOLINESS, LEO XIII, MAY 28, 1886.

Square Miles 42,597.

Legal Title: "Roman Catholic Bishop of Sacramento, a Corporation Sole."

Comprises the Counties of Amador, Butte, Colusa, El Dorado, Glenn, Lassen, Modoc, Nevada, Placer, Plumas, Sacramento, Shasta, Sierra, Siskiyou, Solano, Sutter, Tehama, Trinity, Yolo and Yuba in the State of California.

CO-PATRONS OF DIOCESE: St. Patrick; Our Lady of Guadalupe.

For legal titles of parishes and diocesan institutions, consult the Diocesan Pastoral Center.

Diocesan Pastoral Center: 2110 Broadway, Sacramento, CA, 95818-2541. Tel.: 916-733-0200; Fax: 916-733-0215.

Web site address: http://www.cwo.com/~diocsacr

E-mail address: CREATEPEAC@aol.com

STATISTICAL OVERVIEW

Personnel	
Bishop	1
Retired Bishops	1
Abbots	1
Priests: Diocesan Active in Diocese	117
Priests: Active Outside Diocese	6
Priests: Retired, Sick or Absent	40
Number of Diocesan Priests	163
Religious Priests in Diocese	73
Extern Priests in Diocese	27
Ordinations:	
Diocesan Priests	2
Transitional Deacons	1
Permanent Deacons	15
Permanent Deacons in Diocese	106
Total Brothers	35
Total Sisters	208
Parishes	
Parishes	98
With Resident Pastor:	
Resident Diocesan Priests	89
Resident Religious Priests	8
Without Resident Pastor:	
Administered by Priests	1
Missions	43
Professional Ministry Personnel:	
Brothers	2
Sisters	34
Lay Ministers	61
Welfare	
Catholic Hospitals	8
Total Assisted	442,028
Health Care Centers	3
Total Assisted	11,303
Homes for the Aged	1
Total Assisted	118
Residential Care of Children	2
Day Care and Extended Day Care Centers	3
Total Assisted	341
Special Centers for Social Services	7
Total Assisted	951,089
Educational	
Diocesan Students in Other Seminaries	23
Seminaries, Religious	2
Total Seminarians	23
High Schools, Diocesan and Parish	4
Total Students	1,688
High Schools, Private	3
Total Students	2,364
Elementary Schools, Diocesan and Parish	48
Total Students	13,710
Catechesis/Religious Education:	
High School Students	1,739
Elementary Students	14,356
Total Students Under Catholic Instruction	33,880
Teachers in the Diocese:	
Priests	8
Scholastics	2
Brothers	7
Sisters	27
Lay Teachers	685
Vital Statistics	
Receptions into the Church:	
Infant Baptism Totals	8,401
Adult Baptism Totals	705
Received into Full Communion	640
First Communions	6,045
Confirmations	4,788
Marriages:	
Catholic	969
Interfaith	599
Total Marriages	1,568
Deaths	2,626
Total Catholic Population	425,000
Total Population	2,854,000

Former Bishops—Rt. Rev. EUGENE O'CONNELL, D.D., cons. Titular Bishop of Flaviopolis and appt. Vicar Apostolic of Marysville, Feb. 3, 1861; appt. First Bishop of Grass Valley, March 22, 1868; resigned March 17, 1884 and appt. Titular Bishop of Joppa; died Dec. 4, 1891.—Rt. Rev. PATRICK MANOGUE, D.D., cons. Titular Bishop of Ceremos, Coadjutor to Bishop O'Connell of Grass Valley, Jan. 16, 1881; succeeded to the See of Grass Valley on Bishop O'Connell's resignation, March 17, 1884; became the first Bishop of Sacramento, May 1886; died Feb. 27, 1895.—Rt. Rev. THOMAS GRACE, D.D., cons. June 16, 1896; died Dec. 27, 1921.—Rt. Rev. PATRICK J. KEANE, D.D., ord. June 20, 1895; cons. Bishop of Samaria, Dec. 14, 1920; appt. to See of Sacramento, March 17, 1922; died Sept. 1, 1928.—Most Rev. ROBERT J. ARMSTRONG, D.D., Litt.D., ord. Dec. 10, 1910; cons. March 12, 1929; died Jan. 14, 1957.—Most Rev. JOSEPH T. MCGUCKEN, D.D., S.T.D., LL.D., ord. Jan. 16, 1928; cons. Titular Bishop of Sanavo and Auxiliary Bishop of Los Angeles, March 19, 1941; Coadjutor Bishop of Sacramento, Oct. 26, 1955; succeeded to Jan. 14, 1957, as Bishop of Sacramento; promoted to the See of San Francisco, Feb. 21, 1962; died Oct. 6, 1983.—Most Rev. ALDEN J. BELL, D.D., M.S.S.W., ord. May 14, 1932; appt. Titular Bishop of Rhodopolis and Auxiliary Bishop of Los Angeles, April 18, 1956; cons. June 4, 1956; appt. Bishop of Sacramento, March 30, 1962; retired March 15, 1979; died Aug. 28, 1982.—Most Rev. JOHN S. CUMMINS, D.D., ord. Jan. 24, 1953; appt. Titular Bishop of Lambesi and Auxiliary Bishop of Sacramento, Feb. 26, 1974; cons. May 26, 1974; appt. Bishop of Oakland, May 3, 1977.—Most Rev. FRANCIS A. QUINN, D.D., Ed.D., ord. June 15, 1946; appt. Titular Bishop of Numana and Auxiliary Bishop of San Francisco, April 28, 1978; Episcopal Ordination, June 29, 1978; appt. Bishop of Sacramento, Dec. 18, 1979; retired Nov. 30, 1993.—Most Rev. ALPHONSE GALLEGOS, O.A.R., D.D., ord. May 24, 1958; appt. Titular Bishop of Sassabe and Auxiliary Bishop of Sacramento, Sept. 1, 1981; cons. Nov. 4, 1981; died Oct. 6, 1991.—Most Rev. WILLIAM K. WEIGAND, D.D., ord. May 25, 1963; appt. Bishop of Salt Lake City, Sept. 3, 1980; ord. Bishop, Nov. 17, 1980; appt. Bishop of Sacramento, Nov. 30, 1993.

Diocesan Pastoral Center—2110 Broadway, Sacramento, 95818-2541. Office Hours: Mon.-Fri. 8:30-4:30. Tel: 916-733-0200; Fax: 916-733-0215.

Vicar General and Moderator of the Curia—Rev. ROBERT P. WALTON, Diocesan Pastoral Center. Tel: 916-733-0200.

Chancellor—Sr. EILEEN ENRIGHT, R.S.M.

Vice Chancellor—Rev. MARTIN BRUSATO, Diocesan Pastoral Center.

Secretary to the Bishop—Rev. MARTIN BRUSATO, Diocesan Pastoral Center.

Vicar Episcopal for Theological and Canonical Affairs—Rev. CHARLES S. MCDERMOTT, S.T.D., *2110 Broadway, Sacramento, 95818-2541.* Tel: 916-733-0200.

Vicar for Priests—Rev. MICHAEL CORMACK, *615 Vine Ave., Roseville, 95678.* Tel: 916-783-5212.

Vicar for Religious—Sr. PATRICIA SIMPSON, O.P., *2110 Broadway, Sacramento, 95818-2541.* Tel: 916-733-0244.

Vicar for Deacons—Deacon GERALD PAULY, *1908 46th St., Sacramento, 95819.* Tel: 916-451-3738.

Vicars Forane—Revs. AIDAN O'REILLY, (Siskiyou); MICHAEL CANNY, (Shasta); THOMAS SEABRIDGE, (Lower Valley West); BRENDAN MCKEEFRY, (Lower Valley East); BERNARD BURNS, (Ridge); JOHN MOLUMBY, (Northern Mines); Rev. Msgr. JAMES C. KIDDER, (Southern Mines); Revs. DANIEL LOONEY, (Yolo); MICHAEL DOWNEY, (Solano); NICHOLAS DUGGAN, (Southern Suburbs); T. BRENDAN O'SULLIVAN, (Center Suburbs); LEO MCALLISTER, (American River); MICHAEL CORMACK, (Northern Suburbs); VINCENT BRADY, (City).

Vicar for Hispanics—Rev. HUMBERTO GOMEZ, *2110 Broadway, Sacramento, 95818-2541.* Tel: 916-733-0177.

Diocesan Tribunal—Please direct all requests to the Tribunal. Mailing Address: *2110 Broadway, Sacramento, 95818-2541.* Tel: 916-733-0225.

Judicial Vicar—Vacant.

Adjutant Judicial Vicars—Revs. JOHN FOLMER, J.C.D.; CHARLES S. MCDERMOTT, S.T.D.

Director of the Tribunal—JOANNE FANKHAUSER.

Pro-Synodal Judges—Rev Msgr. PATRICK M. NOLAN; Rev Msgr. ALBERT G. O'CONNOR; Revs. RODOLFO DELGADO, J.C.L.; JOHN FOLMER, J.C.D.; WILLIAM MACCARTHY; CORNELIUS O'DONNELL, J.C.B.

Promotor of Justice—Rev. CHARLES S. MCDERMOTT, S.T.D.

Defenders of the Bond—Rev. Msgr. JAMES C. KIDDER; Revs. JOHN BOLL; BRENDAN MCKEEFRY; JOHN CANTWELL; KIERAN MCMAHON, J.C.L.

Approved Advocates—SUSAN BOONE; CAROL SCOTT.

Notaries—MARGARITA CASTRO; CAROL CHEEVER.

Civil Law—LOUIS N. DESMOND, ESQ., Diocesan Attorney.

College of Consultors—Rev. Msgr. JAMES CHURCH; Revs. MICHAEL J. CORMACK; HUMBERTO GOMEZ; POLYCARPO GUMAPO; MICHAEL KIERNAN; PATRICK O'CONNOR; ROBERT P. WALTON.

Diocesan Offices and Directors

AIDS, Ministry to—Rev. JOHN HEALY, Coord., *4001 J St., Sacramento, 95819.* Tel: 916-453-4753.

Alcoholism Advisory Board—Revs. MICHAEL CORMACK. Tel: 916-783-5211. THOMAS MAGUIRE. Tel: 209-274-4911. Dr. WILLIAM MERZ. Tel: 916-353-6623.

Apostleship of Prayer—Rev. RICHARD DOHENY, Dir., *P.O. Box 1180, Fair Oaks, 95628.* Tel: 916-967-1229.

Archives—Rev. WILLIAM BREAULT, S.J., Pro-Tem Archivist, *2110 Broadway, Sacramento, 95818-2541.* Tel: 916-733-0100.

Black Catholic Council—CHARLES FARRELL, *Office, 2110 Broadway, Sacramento, 95818-2541.* Tel: 916-733-0160.

Building Committee—Direct inquiries to: Mr. THOMAS MCNAMARA, Staff, *Diocesan Pastoral Center, 2110 Broadway, Sacramento, 95818-2541.* Tel: 916-733-0277.

California Catholic Conference—1010 - 11th St., Ste. 200, Sacramento, 95814. Tel: 916-443-4851; Fax: 916-443-5629. Most Rev. JOHN S. CUMMINS, Pres.; Most Rev. SYLVESTER RYAN, Vice Pres.; Most Rev. MICHAEL DRISCOLL, Sec./Treas.; Rev. Msgr. E. JAMES PETERSEN, (FRS), Exec. Dir.; Mr. DAVID A. POLLARD, Assoc. Dir., Legislative and Public Policy; Mr. ROBERT TEEGARDEN, Assoc Dir., Education; CAROL HOGAN, Assoc. Dir., Communications; Rev. ALEJANDRO CASTILLO, S.V.D., Assoc. Dir., Hispanic Affairs; Mr. RICHARD MOCKLER, Exec. Dir., Catholic Charities; Mr. RICHARD STRAWN, California Support Fund.

California Association of Catholic Hospitals—1121 L St., 409, Sacramento, 95814. Tel: 916-444-3386.

Campus Ministry—Rev. MICHAEL NEWMAN, S.D.S., Diocesan Dir., *Newman Catholic Ctr., 346 Cherry St., Chico, 95926.* Tel: 916-342-5180.

Catholic Faith Formation—Sr. MAURA POWER, R.S.M., Dir., *2110 Broadway, Sacramento, 95818-2541.* Tel: 916-733-0123.

Catholic Charities Sacramento, Inc.—Rev. EDWARD LEWIS, Pres., *2110 Broadway, Sacramento, 95818-2541.* Tel: 916-733-0200.

Cemeteries—Rev Msgr. PATRICK M. NOLAN, Dir., *6700 21st Ave., P.O. Box 245346, Sacramento, 95820.* Tel: 916-452-5951.

Censor Librorum—Rev. CHARLES S. MCDERMOTT, S.T.D., *2110 Broadway, Sacramento, 95818-2541.* Tel: 916-733-0200.

Communications and Media—Rev. JAMES T. MURPHY, Dir., *2110 Broadway, Sacramento, 95818-2541.* Tel: 916-733-0258.

Council of Priests—Most Rev. WILLIAM K. WEIGAND, D.D., Pres. Please direct all inquiries to: Rev. MICHAEL KIERNAN, Chm. Tel: 916-365-8573. Rev. Msgr. JAMES CHURCH; Revs. JOHN BOLL; RONAN BRENNAN; MARTIN BRUSATO; MICHAEL CORMACK; HUMBERTO GOMEZ; POLYCARPO GUMAPO; MICHAEL KIERNAN; THOMAS MAGUIRE; JULIAN MEDINA; MARTIN MORONEY; PATRICK O'CONNOR; BRENDAN O'SULLIVAN; GILBERTO PENA; EDUINO SILVEIRA; ROBERT P. WALTON; Deacon WILLIAM RIEHL, Deacon Observer Direct all correspondence to: *2110 Broadway, Sacramento, 95818-2541.*

Deaf and Hard of Hearing (Office of Catholic Faith Formation)—JEAN NELSON, Coord. of Support Services; JAMES ANDERSON, Pastoral Minister for Deaf and Hard of Hearing, *2110 Broadway, Sacramento, 95818-2541.* Tel: 916-733-0123; TDD 733-0144.

Detention Service—Rev. LIAM P. MCSWEENEY, *CA Youth Authority, 3001 Ramona Ave., Sacramento, 95826.* Tel: 916-739-2000.

Development—Mr. LAWRENCE LARSON, Diocesan Dir., *2110 Broadway, Sacramento, 95818-2541.* Tel: 916-733-0266.

Diocesan Pastoral Council—Please direct all inquiries to: Rev. EDWARD LEWIS, Staff. Tel: 707-644-8396. or Office of the Bishop:Tel: 916-733-0200. VIDA RYAN, Staff; GIL AZEVEDO; Mr. ANTONIO BARBOSA; EVELIA BERUMEN; Mr. HENRY BOYER; Mrs. BARBARA COELHO; Mrs. BELEN "BEL" CORPUZ; Mr. EUGENE EVEN; CHARLES FARRELL; TILLIE FERNANDEZ; Sr. MAUREEN FITZGERALD; ROBERT GILBRIDE; Revs. HUMBERTO GOMEZ; POLYCARPO GUMAPO; Mr. EVERETT LAYNE; Rev. EDWARD LEWIS; Sr. NANCY MCINERNEY; Mr. HAROLD MYERS; JOHN ROE; MARY ROSE; VIDA RYAN; JESSIE SHIELDS; ANTONIA TAMAYO; Rev. ROBERT P. WALTON; MARY ANN WESLEY; Most Rev. WILLIAM K. WEIGAND, D.D.; ROSEMARY WITHERBY.

Diocesan Priests' Trust Fund—Most Rev. WILLIAM K. WEIGAND, D.D., Pres. Ex Officio Direct inquiries to: Rev. Msgr. MURROUGH WALLACE, Treas., *St. Theresa Church, 1041 Lyons Ave., South Lake Tahoe, 96150.* Tel: 916-544-3533.

Disability Ministry—Mr. ROBERT BRENNAN, *2110 Broadway, Sacramento, 95818-2541.* Tel: 916-733-0123.

Divorced and Separated, Ministry to—Direct inquiries to: *Family Life Office, 2110 Broadway, Sacramento, 95818-2541.* Tel: 916-733-0155.

Due Process Conciliation, Council of—Rev. Msgr. MURROUGH WALLACE, Chm.; Rev. ALFRED KASTER; Dr. WILLIAM MARIANO; ELAINE MASSEY; Sr. MAURA POWER, R.S.M.,Direct all correspondence to: Rev. CHARLES S. MCDERMOTT, S.T.D., *2110 Broadway, Sacramento, 95818-2541.* Tel: 916-733-0200.

Office of Arbitration—Revs. CHARLES S. MCDERMOTT, Chm. DANIEL CASEY; MICHAEL CORMACK; FRED OLIVER; Mrs. SHEILA NOLAN, Office: *2110 Broadway, Sacramento, 95818-2541.* Tel: 916-733-0200.

Eastern Catholic Churches—Rev. CHARLES S. MCDERMOTT, Liaison Officer, *2110 Broadway, Sacramento, 95818-2541.* Tel: 916-733-0200.

Ecumenism—Rev. Msgr. JAMES C. KIDDER, *5145 Golden Foothill Pkwy., #100, El Dorado Hills, 95762.* Tel: 916-933-6532.

Evangelization (Office of Catholic Faith Formation)—THOMAS FAUSSONE, *2110 Broadway, Sacramento, 95818-2541.* Tel: 916-733-0123.

Family Life—Vacant, *2110 Broadway, Sacramento, 95818-2541.* Tel: 916-733-0155.

Finance Council—Members: Mr. NEIL MCALLISTER, JR.; Sr. M. MICHAEL MURPHY, R.S.M.; Rev. MICHAEL CORMACK; Mr. MICHAEL PROFUMO; Mr. CHARLES SYLVA; Mr. PETE PADILLA; Ms. JULIE NAUMAN; Mr. DAVID RICHIE. Ex Officio: Rev. ROBERT P. WALTON; Mr. THOMAS J. MCNAMARA, *Chancery Office, 2110 Broadway, Sacramento, 95818-2541.* Tel: 916-733-0277.

Investment Review Committee—Direct inquiries to: Mr. THOMAS MCNAMARA, *2110 Broadway, Sacramento, 95818-2541.* Tel: 916-733-0277.

Finance Office—Mr. THOMAS MCNAMARA, Dir., *2110 Broadway, Sacramento, 95818-2541.* Tel: 916-733-0277.

Gospel Justice Resource Ctr., Catholic Reg. Commission—GEORGIANN LYGA, Prog. Dir., *2110 Broadway, Sacramento, 95818-2541.* Tel: 916-733-0255.

Hispanic Apostolate—Rev. HUMBERTO GOMEZ, Vicar for Hispanics, *2110 Broadway, Sacramento, 95818-2541.* Tel: 916-733-0177.

Holy Childhood Association—Mr. THOMAS BUTLER, *2110 Broadway, Sacramento, 95818-2541.* Tel: 916-733-0110.

Hospitals, Diocesan Liaison for Catholic—Rev. JOHN J. HEALY, *4001 J St., Sacramento, 95819.* Tel: 916-453-4753.

Lay Ministry—Sr. ANITA MINIHANE, R.S.M., *2110 Broadway, Sacramento, 95818-2541.* Tel: 916-733-0250.

Marriage Preparation Center—Vacant; Dir., *2110 Broadway, Sacramento, 95818-2541.* Tel: 916-733-0155.

Newspapers—"Catholic Herald" and "El Heraldo Catolico"; Ms. JULIE SLY, General Editor; JOSE RAMIREZ, Editor, El Heraldo, Office: *5890 Newman Ct., P.O. Box 19312, Sacramento, 95819.* Tel: 916-452-3344.

Ongoing Education of Clergy—Rev. T. BRENDAN O'SULLIVAN, Dir., *St. Anthony Church, 660 Florin Rd., Sacramento, 95831.* Tel: 916-428-5678.

Opus Sanctorum Angelorum—Rev. J. DERMOT DWYER, Spiritual Dir., *P.O. Box 752, Colfax, 95713.* Tel: 916-346-2286.

Permanent Diaconate Program—Sr. PATRICIA SIMPSON, O.P., Dir.; Deacon WILLIAM RIEHL; Sr. STEPHANA O'LEARY, S.S.S., Asst. Dir., Office: *2110 Broadway, Sacramento, 95818-2541.* Tel: 916-733-0244.

Priests' Diocesan Aid Society—Ex-Officio Officer: Most Rev. WILLIAM K. WEIGAND, D.D.,Please direct inquiries to: Rev. Msgr. JAMES F. CHURCH, Sec./Treas., *2428 Bell St., Sacramento, 95825.* Tel: 916-455-3001.

Priests' Personnel Board, Diocesan—Please direct all inquiries to: Rev. VINCENT BRADY, Sec., *1017 11th St., Sacramento, 95814.* Tel: 916-444-3071. Revs. MARTIN BRUSATO; ROY DONER; WILLIAM KINANE, Chm. PATRICK MCGRATH; GERALD RYLE; ENRIQUE SANCHEZ; ROBERT P. WALTON.

Propagation of the Faith—Rev. Msgr. JAMES CHURCH, Dir., *2110 Broadway, Sacramento, 95818-2541.* Tel: 916-733-0100.

Properties Committee—Please direct all inquiries to: Mr. THOMAS MCNAMARA, Staff, *2110 Broadway, Sacramento, 95818-2541.* Tel: 916-733-0277.

Radio and Television—See Communications and Media.

Research and Planning—Sr. EILEEN ENRIGHT, R.S.M., Chancellor, *2110 Broadway, Sacramento, 95818-2541.* Tel: 916-733-0200.

Respect Life—MARIE SHEAHAN BROWN, Diocesan Coord., *Family Life Office, 2110 Broadway, Sacramento, 95818-2541.* Tel: 916-733-0155.

Retired Priests—Rev. MICHAEL CORMACK, Coord., *615 Vine Ave., Roseville, 95678.* Tel: 916-783-5211.

Schools—Mr. THOMAS BUTLER, Supt.; Mr. DOMINIC PUGLISI, Assoc. Supt., *2110 Broadway, Sacramento, 95818-2541.* Tel: 916-733-0110.

Vocations—Revs. JAMES T. MURPHY, Dir. HUMBERTO GOMEZ, Dir., Hispanic Seminarians, *2110 Broadway, Sacramento, 95818-2541.* Tel: 916-733-0258.

Worship, Office of—Revs. KIERAN MCMAHON, Dir. Pro-Tem; MARK AVILA, O.M.V., Assoc. Dir., *2110 Broadway, Sacramento, 95818-2541.* Tel: 916-733-0220.

Lay Organizations—

Beginning Experience—TERESA BENNETT, Pres., *P.O. Box 161761, Sacramento, 95816.* Tel: 916-535-5057. BRENDA FRENCH, Pub. Rels.

Catholic Alumni Club—SERGE BOULANGER, Pres., *P.O. Box 1777, Sacramento, 95609-1777.* Tel: 916-944-4882; 863-3040.

Catholic Daughters of the Americas—SHIRLEY GODFREY, *6600 Greenhaven Dr., Sacramento, 95831.* Tel: 916-428-5044.

Charismatic Renewal—Rev. Msgr. ANDREW V. COFFEY, Bishop's Liaison; Deacon JERRY PAULY, Assoc. Liaison. Tel: 916-451-3738. Mr. MICHAEL DONEEN, Treas.

Cursillo Movement—Office: *2110 Broadway, Sacramento, 95818-2541.* Tel: 916-733-0181.

Daughters of Isabella—WANDA SOUZA, *700 2nd St., 58, Galt, 95682.* Tel: 209-745-1746. ANITA RADOSEVICH. Tel: 209-745-1914.

Diocesan Council of Catholic Nurses—Mrs. ELEANOR HAVEY, *4935 61st St., Sacramento, 95820.* Tel: 916-457-8649.

Diocesan Council of Catholic Women—Rev. Msgr. EDWARD J. KAVANAGH, Moderator; Mrs. MILDRED ROWE, Pres.

Handicapables—CHRISTINE SHOWER. Tel: 916-375-1040.

Italian Catholic Federation—Rev. MARTIN BRUSATO, Chap., *2110 Broadway, Sacramento, 95818-2541.* Tel: 916-733-0200.

Knights of Peter Claver and Ladies Aux.—Mr. FRED MCLAURIN, Sacramento, Area Deputy, *P.O. Box 13471, Sacramento, 95813.* Tel: 916-971-4954. Mrs. NOELLA M. FRANCIS, Area Deputy, Ladies Div., *7375 Putnam Way, Sacramento, 95822.* Tel: 916-427-7041.

Knights of Columbus—Mr. CHARLES E. NULK, Northern California Chapter Pres., *5336 Spilman Ave., Sacramento, 95819*. Tel: 916-451-6308.
Legion of Mary Comitium—Rev. Msgr. CORNELIUS P. HIGGINS, *3027 Olive Glen Ct., Sacramento, 95821*. Tel: 916-487-9493. BETTY FRIES, Pres., *6090 S. Land Park Dr., Apt. 2, Sacramento, 95822*. Tel: 916-422-7437. Three Curiae attached: Marysville-Yuba City, North Sacramento, Solano.
Marriage Encounter Worldwide—Contact Family Life Office, *2110 Broadway, Sacramento, 95818-2541*. Tel: 916-733-0155.
Scouting, Catholic Committe on—Rev. ROBERT MARSICEK, S.D.S., Diocesan Chap., *9079 Greenback Ln., Orangevale, 95662-4703*. Tel: 916-989-7400.
Secular Franciscan Order—*St. Francis Church, 1112 26th St., Sacramento, 95816*. Tel: 916-443-8084.
Secular Order of Discalced Carmelites—*P.O. Box 2865, Sacramento, 95812*.
Serra Club of Sacramento—YOUNG D. STEWART, Pres., *5903 Via Casitas, Carmichael, 95608*. Tel: 916-332-8732.
Young Ladies Institute—Mrs. PATRICIA CARVO, District 7 Deputy, *2768 Lincoln Rd., Yuba City, 95991*. Tel: 916-673-7147.
St. Thomas More Society—HERB BOLZ, Pres. Tel: 916-753-6094. Rev. CHARLES S. MCDERMOTT. Tel: 916-733-0200.

CLERGY, PARISHES, MISSIONS AND PAROCHIAL SCHOOLS

CITY OF SACRAMENTO
(Sacramento County)

1—CATHEDRAL OF THE BLESSED SACRAMENT (1889), Most Rev. William K. Weigand; Revs. Vincent Brady, Rector; Michael McKeon; Deacons Don De Haven; John Masla. In res., Rev. Martin Brusato.
Res., 1017 Eleventh St., 95814. Tel: 916-444-3071; Fax: 916-443-2749. Catechetical Center Cathedral Parish Hall Conducted by parish CCD and Daughters of Charity of Canossa.
Res., 1949 North Ave., 95838. Tel: 916-925-4001.
Social Service Center—Tel: 916-444-3070.
Catechesis/Religious Programs—Tel: 916-444-5364.
Students 135.

2—ALL HALLOWS (1942), Rev. Polycarpo Gumapo; Deacons Michael Donovan; George Kriske.
Res., 5500 13th Ave., 95820. Tel: 916-456-7206; Fax: 916-456-7325.
School—5700 13th Ave., 95820. Tel: 916-457-5621. Stephanie C. Jones, Prin.
Lay Teachers 10; Students 288.
Catechesis/Religious Programs—Tel: 916-736-0204.
Students 34.
Station—California State Youth Authority Center, 3001 Ramona Ave., 95820. Tel: 916-733-2350; Fax: 916-227-2511. Rev. William P. McSweeney, Chap.

3—HOLY SPIRIT (1940), Rev. Charles Brady; Deacon Bernard J. Weeks. In res., Rev. Msgr. E. James Petersen (FRS).
Res., 3159 Land Park Dr., 95818. Tel: 916-443-5442; Fax: 916-446-9015.
School—3920 W. Land Park Dr., 95822. Tel: 916-448-5663. Sr. Jean Marie Gorman, R.S.M., Prin.
Sisters 1; Lay Teachers 11; Students 315.
Convent—Tel: 916-448-3578. Sisters of Mercy (Auburn, CA)
Catechesis/Religious Programs—Tel: 916-448-8257.
Students 28.

4—IMMACULATE CONCEPTION (1909), Rev. Mark L. Mosher; Deacons Gerald Pauly; Ramon Vega.
Parish Office: 3263 First Ave., 95817. Tel: 916-452-6866; Fax: 916-452-3879.
Res., 2549 32nd St., 95817. Tel: 916-452-6866.
School—3263 First Ave., 95817. Tel: 916-452-7308. Lee Shoemaker, Prin.
Sisters 2; Lay Teachers 8; Students 195.
Catechesis/Religious Programs—Students 60.

5—OUR LADY OF GUADALUPE SHRINE (1958) (Mexican), Revs. Roberto Jaramillo; Rodolfo Delgado, Admin.; Deacon Jose Ramirez.
Res., 711 T St., 95814. Tel: 916-442-3211; Fax: 916-442-3679.
Catechesis/Religious Programs—730 S St., 95814. Tel: 916-446-3500.
Students 619.

6—OUR LADY OF LOURDES (1957), Rev. Anthony Traynor; Deacon James Lalonde.
Res., 1951 North Ave., 95838. Tel: 916-925-5313; Fax: 916-922-0625.
Catechesis/Religious Programs—Students 150.
Convent—1949 North Ave., 95838. Tel: 916-925-4001; Fax: 916-925-8897. Daughters of Charity of Cannosa

7—PRESENTATION OF THE BLESSED VIRGIN MARY (1961), Revs. Simon D. Twomey; Michael Carroll. In res., Rev. Msgr. Cornelius Higgins, Pastor Emeritus; Rev. William Feeser.
Mailing Address: P.O. Box 214208, 95821-0208.
Res., 4123 Robertson Ave., 95821. Tel: 916-481-7441; Fax: 916-481-2841.
School—3100 Norris Ave., 95821. Tel: 916-482-0351; Fax: 916-482-0377. Theresa Altieri, Prin.
Lay Teachers 13; Students 329.
Parish Center—3110 Norris Ave., 95821.
Catechesis/Religious Programs—Tel: 916-482-8883. Susan B. McLeod.
Students 70.

8—SACRED HEART OF JESUS (1926), Rev. Michael O'Hara; Sr. Mary Martin, R.S.M., Pastoral Assoc., Tel: 916-452-4830; Deacons Gilbert Parra; William Riehl.
Res., 1040 39th St., 95816. Tel: 916-452-4136.
School—Sacred Heart, 3933 I St., 95816. Tel: 916-456-1576. Maureen Douglass, Prin.
Sisters of Mercy (Auburn, CA) 1; Lay Teachers 11; Students 310.
Catechesis/Religious Programs—Tel: 916-454-3640. Sr. O'Meara, R.S.M., D.R.E.
Students 315.

9—ST. ANNE (1961), Revs. Januarius E. Rodrigues; R. Francis Stevenson; Deacons Pedro Manriquez; Modesto Chavarria.
Res., 7724 24th St., 95832. Tel: 916-422-8380; Fax: 916-422-7538.
School—7720 24th St., 95832. Tel: 916-422-3142. Mr. Francis T. McNamara, Prin.
Lay Teachers 8; Students 241.
Catechesis/Religious Programs—Tel: 916-422-2419.
Students 226.

10—ST. ANTHONY (1974), Rev. T. Brendan O'Sullivan; Deacons James Healy; Richard Koppes.
Res., 660 Florin Rd., 95831. Tel: 916-428-5678; Fax: 916-428-0312.
Catechesis/Religious Programs—Tel: 916-392-6362.
Students 270.

11—ST. CHARLES BORROMEO (1960), Revs. Michael McFadden; Erwin C. Mesiona. In res., Rev. James T. Murphy.
Res., 7584 Center Pkwy., 95823. Tel: 916-421-5177; Fax: 916-392-4831.
School—7580 Center Pkwy., 95823. Tel: 916-421-6189. Sr. Maureen Fitzgerald, Prin.
Sisters 5; Lay Teachers 9; Students 323.
Catechesis/Religious Programs—Students 323.
Convent—(Motherhouse, Hamden, CT). Tel: 916-421-7174. Apostles of the Sacred Heart of Jesus

12—ST. ELIZABETH (1909) (Portuguese), Rev. Eduino Silveira.
Res., 1817 12th St., 95814. Tel: 916-442-2333.

13—ST. FRANCIS OF ASSISI (1894), Rev. Richard Juzix, O.F.M.; Deacon Richard Driggs.
1066 26th St., 95816. Tel: 916-443-8084; Fax: 916-443-7356.
School—2500 K St., 95816. Tel: 916-442-5494; Fax: 916-442-1390. Ms. Barbara O'Donnell, Prin.
Lay Teachers 15; Students 335.
Catechesis/Religious Programs—Students 215.

14—ST. IGNATIUS (1954), Revs. Christopher M. Cartwright, S.J.; Paul F. Belcher, S.J.; Kevin Ballard, S.J.; Deacon Jackson Gualco. In res., Rev. Gerald H. Robinson, S.J., Dir., Ignatian Institute for Family Life.
Res., 3235 Arden Way, 95825. Tel: 916-482-9666; Fax: 916-482-6573.
School—3245 Arden Way, 95825. Tel: 916-488-3907. Cassandra Saenz, Prin.
Lay Teachers 15; Students 354.
Catechesis/Religious Programs—Students 160.
Ignatian Institute for Family Life—Tel: 916-482-9666; Fax: 916-482-6573.

15—ST. JOSEPH'S (1924), Revs. Robert A. Copsey; Andrew Koziczuk (Poland); Sr. Ellen Philbin, R.S.M., Parish Min.; Deacon Henry Garcia. In res., Rev. Humberto Gomez.
Res., 1717 El Monte Ave., 95815. Tel: 916-925-3584; Fax: 916-925-1045.
School—1718 El Monte Ave., 95815. Tel: 916-925-1465. Mrs. Marsha J.B. Cornelius, Prin.
Sisters of Mercy (Auburn, CA) 1; Lay Teachers 8; Students 297.
Catechesis/Religious Programs—Tel: 916-924-8541.
Students 140.

16—ST. MARY (1906) (Italian), Revs. Philip Massetti; Enrico Tunesi, O.S.J.; Deacon Luigi Del Gaudio.
Res., 1333 58th St., 95819. Tel: 916-452-0296; Fax: 916-452-3908.
School—5815 N St., 95819. Tel: 916-452-1100. Sr. Joan O'Sullivan, P.B.V.M., Prin.
Sisters 1; Lay Teachers 12; Students 332.
Convent—5801 N St., 95819. Tel: 916-451-5881. Sisters of the Presentation of the Blessed Virgin Mary (Monastereven, Ireland)
Catechesis/Religious Programs—Tel: 916-452-4115.
Students 467.

17—ST. PAUL (1958), Revs. Nicholas Duggan; John Hee-Wan Jeong; Deacon Charles Morrison.
Res., 7200 Gardner Ave., P.O. Box 292280, 95829. Tel: 916-381-5200; Fax: 916-381-0332.
Korean Catholic Community—Tel: 916-363-1008. John Bae, Contact Person.

18—ST. PETER (1955), Rev. Sidney Peter Hall; Deacons Deogracia "Ray" Ramos; Alejandro Reynoso.
Res., 6210 McMahon Dr., 95824. Tel: 916-455-3001; Fax: 916-455-4721.
School—6200 McMahon Dr., 95824. Tel: 916-455-2915; Fax: 916-455-2915.
Sisters 4; Lay Teachers 6; Students 276.
Catechesis/Religious Programs—Students 197.
Convent—5870 62nd St., 95824. Tel: 916-457-0182. Sisters Servants of the Blessed Sacrament (Guadalajara, Mexico)

19—ST. PHILOMENE (1948), Rev. Msgr. James F. Church; Rev. Msgr. Patrick M. Nolan, Pastor Emeritus; Rev. Terry A. Fulton; Deacons Charles Cheever; Keith Burke.
Res., 2428 Bell St., 95825. Tel: 916-481-6757; Fax: 916-481-1603.
School—2320 El Camino Ave., 95825. Tel: 916-489-5466; Fax: 916-481-1603. Mr. Charles Suarez, Prin.
Lay Teachers 13; Students 127.
Catechesis/Religious Programs—Tel: 916-488-6091.
Students 127.

20—ST. ROBERT (1955), Rev. Kieran M. McMahon; Deacon Martin Rodriguez. In res., Rev. Mark Avila, O.M.V.
Res., 2243 Irvin Way, 95822. Tel: 916-451-1475.
School—2251 Irvin Way, 95822. Tel: 916-452-2111. Gail Sherman, Prin.
Lay Teachers 12; Students 313.

21—ST. ROSE (1942), Rev. Msgr. Edward J. Kavanagh; Rev. Francis Lawlor. In res., Rev. Charles S. McDermott.
Res., P.O. Box 5037, Oak Park Station, 95817. Tel: 916-421-1414; Fax: 916-421-0460.
School—St. Patrick, 5945 Franklin Blvd., 95824. Tel: 916-421-4963; Fax: 916-421-3849. Dave Hoffman, Prin.
Lay Teachers 16; Students 379.
Catechesis/Religious Programs—Tel: 916-392-5679.
Students 525.

22—VIETNAMESE CATHOLIC MARTYRS (Vietnamese), Rev. Jude Ban Nguyen; Deacon Anthony Huy Nguyen.
Res., 10371 Jackson Rd., 95827. Tel: 916-366-3162.
Catechesis/Religious Programs—Students 664.

OUTSIDE THE CITY OF SACRAMENTO

Alturas, Modoc Co., Sacred Heart (1883), Rev. Rodney L. Hall.
Res., 507 E. Fourth St., 96101. Tel: 916-233-2119.
Catechesis/Religious Programs—Students 28.
Missions—Cedarville, Modoc Co., St. James, Bonner & Garfield, Cedarville, 96104; Alturar; Cedarville; Eaglesville; Fort Bidwell; Lake City; Likely; Paris Creek.

Anderson, Shasta Co., Sacred Heart (1949), Rev. Michael F. Kiernan; Deacon Michael Evans.
Res., 3141 St. Stephen's Dr., P.O. Box 547, 96007. Tel: 916-365-8573; Fax: 916-365-8573.
School—(Grades PreK-5) 3167 St. Stephen's Dr., 96007. Tel: 916-365-1429; Fax: 916-365-8573. Mrs. Margaret Heyfron, Prin.
Lay Teachers 7; Students 170.
Catechesis/Religious Programs—Students 180.
Missions—Cottonwood, Shasta Co., St. Anne, 2nd and Main Sts., Cottonwood, 96022; Shingletown, Shasta Co., Mary Queen of Peace, Shingletown Ridge Rd., Shingletown, 96088. Tel: 916-474-1870.

Antelope, Sacramento Co., St. Clare (1992), Rev. Colin Macdonald.
Res., 4313 Shandwick Dr., 95843. Tel: 916-721-4771; Fax: 916-721-4288.
Catechesis/Religious Programs—Students 40.

Auburn, Placer Co., St. Joseph (1861), Revs. John Molumby; Glenn Dare; Deacon Ed Morgado.
Res., 1162 Lincoln Way, 95603. Tel: 916-885-2956; Fax: 916-823-6676. [CEM]
School—11610 Atwood Rd., 95603. Tel: 916-885-4490; Fax: 916-885-0182. Mrs. Joan Walthers, Prin.
Sisters 1; Lay Teachers 8; Students 296.
Catechesis/Religious Programs—Tel: 916-885-0362.
Students 241.

Mission—Auburn, Placer Co., St. Teresa of Avila, (1994) 11600 Atwood Rd., 95603.
Station—Forest Hill.

Benicia, Solano Co., St. Dominic (1854), Revs. Anthony Petrarca, O.P.; Dominic DeLay, O.P.; Deacon Ed Lazarek. In res., Revs. John Morris, O.P.; Bede Wilks, O.P.
Res., 475 E. I St., P.O. Box 756, 94510. Tel: 707-747-7220; Fax: 707-745-5642. [CEM]
School—935 E. 5th St., 94510. Tel: 707-745-1266. Mr. Mike Wallace, Prin.
Lay Teachers 13; Students 342.
Catechesis/Religious Programs—433 East I St., 94510. Tel: 707-747-7240.
Students 554.

Burney, Shasta Co., St. Francis of Assisi (1949), Rev. Eric D. Lofgren.
Res., 37464 Juniper Ave., P.O. Drawer 160, 96013. Tel: 916-335-2372.
Catechesis/Religious Programs—Students 68.
Mission—Bieber, Lassen Co., St. Stephen, Hwy. 299, Bieber, 96009.
Station—Fall River Mills.

Carmichael, Sacramento Co., Our Lady of the Assumption (1952), Rev. Leo McAllister; Deacons Michael Tateishi; Thomas Ferreira; James Meucci. In res., Revs. Anthony B. Warnakula; William Broderick, (Retired).
Res., 5057 Cottage Way, 95608. Tel: 916-481-5115; Fax: 916-481-4026.
School—5055 Cottage Way, 95608. Tel: 916-489-8958. Sr. Mary Ellen Beck, I.B.V.M., Prin.
Sisters 1; Lay Teachers 9; Students 307.
Catechesis/Religious Programs—Tel: 916-488-4626.
Students 306.
Convent—Tel: 916-488-8188. Ladies of Loretto (Toronto, Canada)

St. John the Evangelist (1960), Revs. John Lagomarsino, S.S.C., Parochial Admin.; Tongele Ngbatana; Sr. Eileen Mary O'Connor, R.S.M., Pastoral Assoc.; Deacon James Weeks. In res., Rev. Patrick O'Rafferty.
Res., 5751 Locust Ave., 95608. Tel: 916-483-8454; Fax: 916-481-8326.
School—5701 Locust Ave., 95608. Tel: 916-481-8845. Dr. Jacqueline Pajda, Prin.
Lay Teachers 14; Students 320.
Catechesis/Religious Programs—Tel: 916-483-4628. Sr. Celine Heneghan, R.S.M., D.R.E.
Students 324.
Convent—Tel: 916-482-0163.

Chico, Butte Co., Our Divine Savior (1967), Revs. Roy R. Doner; Joseph Huyen Van Nguyen; Deacon Jude Duvernay.
Res., Office, 566 E. Lassen Ave., 95973. Tel: 916-343-4248; Fax: 916-343-3538.
Catechesis/Religious Programs—Tel: 916-345-6201.
Students 225.

St. John the Baptist (1878), Revs. Gilberto Pena-Martinez; Brent Nall; Deacons Antonio Ramirez; Jesus Campos Padilla; James Burkett; Stephen Schwartz.
Res., 435 Chestnut St., 95928. Tel: 916-343-8741; Fax: 916-345-8602.
School—(Grades K-8) 435 Hazel St., 95928. Tel: 916-342-2502. Colleen Waugh, Prin.
Lay Teachers 13; Students 280.
Catechesis/Religious Programs—Students 461.
Mission—Durham, Butte Co., St. James, P.O. Box 562, 95938. [JC]

Citrus Heights, Sacramento Co., Holy Family (1949), Revs. John Cantwell; Jose Karikattil; Rev. Msgr. Vito Mistretta, Pastor Emeritus; Deacon William Lubinsky.
Res., 7817 Old Auburn Rd., 95610. Tel: 916-723-2494; Fax: 916-723-0199.
School—Tel: 916-722-7788. Sr. Arlene Connelly, I.B.V.M., Prin.
Lay Teachers 15; Students 573.
Preschool—Patricia Peterson, Preschool Dir., Tel: 916-722-4620.
Lay Teachers 7; Students 72.
Catechesis/Religious Programs—Tel: 916-721-8329. Marsha Candela, D.R.E.
Students 280.

Clarksburg, Yolo Co., St. Joseph (1893), Rev. Daniel Madigan.
Res. and Church—32890 S. River Rd., 95612. Tel: 916-665-1132; Fax: 916-665-9264.

Colfax, Placer Co., St. Dominic (1951), Rev. Dermot Dwyer, Admin.
Res., 58 E. Oak St., P.O. Box 752, 95713. Tel: 916-346-2286; Fax: 916-346-2286. [CEM]
Catechesis/Religious Programs—Students 129.

Colusa, Colusa Co., Our Lady of Lourdes (1870), Rev. Edward Pepka, Admin.
Res., 745 Ware Ave., 95932. Tel: 916-458-4170; Fax: 916-458-8728. Rev. Heriberto Serrano; Deacon Miguel Fernandez.; Res., 627 8th St., P.O. Box 1346, Williams, 95987. Tel: 916-473-5043.
Church—4th St., 95932. Tel: 916-458-7901.
School—(Grades PreK-8). Tel: 916-458-8208. Mrs. Barbara Genera, Prin.
Lay Teachers 7; Students 174.
Catechesis/Religious Programs—Students 90.
Mission—Princeton, Colusa Co., St. Joseph, 1st and Center St., Princeton, 95970.
Station—Sycamore, Our Lady of Sorrows. [CEM]

Corning, Tehama Co., Immaculate Conception (1947), Revs. Miguel Silva; Thomas L. Seabridge.
Res., 814 Solano St., 96021. Tel: 916-824-5879. [JC]
Catechesis/Religious Programs—Students 101.
Mission—Tehama, Tehama Co., St. Stanislaus, 4th & D St., Tehama, 96090.

Davis, Yolo Co., St. James (1912), Rev. Daniel A. Looney; Rev. Msgr. Andrew V. Coffey, Pastor Emeritus; Rev. Richard J. Blinn, S.J.; Deacon Paul Taloff.
Res., 200 W. 14th St., 95616. Tel: 916-756-3636; Fax: 916-756-5342. [JC]
School—1215 B St., 95616. Tel: 916-756-3946; Fax: 916-753-9765. Mary Kay Bolz, Prin.
Lay Teachers 13; Students 302.
Catechesis/Religious Programs—Tel: 916-756-9000. Linda O'Hara, D.R.E.
Students 380.
Catholic Student Community Center—514 C St., 95616. Tel: 916-753-7393; Fax: 916-753-2794. Sr. Mary Pat White, R.S.C.J.

Dixon, Solano Co., St. Peter (1877), Revs. Maurice O'Brien; John J. Kyne, Pastor Emeritus; Deacons Robert H. Ikelman; John King.
Res., 105 S. 2nd St., 95620. Tel: 916-678-9424; Fax: 916-678-9432.
Catechesis/Religious Programs—Students 240.

Downieville, Sierra Co., Immaculate Conception (1853), Rev. Goodwin Xavier.
Res., Flume St., P.O. Box 48, North San Juan, 95960. Tel: 916-292-3227.
Church—Church St., 95936. Tel: 916-289-3102.
Missions—North San Juan, Nevada Co., St. John, 10047 Flume St., 95960. Deacon George Lucas; Sierra City, Sierra Co., St. Thomas, 108 Butte Aly, Sierra City, 96125; Challenge, Yuba Co., St. Anthony, La Porte Rd., Challenge, 95925. Tel: 916-675-2001; Malakoff Diggins, Nevada Co., St. Columcille.

Dunsmuir, Siskiyou Co., St. John the Evangelist (1900), Rev. Cornelius O'Donnell.
Res., 5605 Shasta Ave., 96025. Tel: 916-235-4705; Fax: 916-235-4759. [JC]

El Dorado Hills, El Dorado Co., Holy Trinity (1992), Rev. Msgr. James C. Kidder.
Church—5145 Golden Foothill Pkwy. #100, 95762. Tel: 916-933-6532; Fax: 916-933-6532.
Catechesis/Religious Programs—Students 383.

Elk Grove, Sacramento Co., St. Joseph (1962), Rev. Msgr. Albert G. O'Connor. In res., Rev. Robert Walton; Deacon Paul Imrisek.
Res., 9961 Elk Grove-Florin Rd., 95624. Tel: 916-685-3681; Fax: 916-685-7254.
Catechesis/Religious Programs—Tel: 916-685-5636.
Students 567.
Mission—Rancho Murieta, P.O. Box 552, 95683.

Good Shepherd Catholic Church (1994), Rev. Philip Wells.
Res., 6310 Thresher Ct., 95758. Tel: 916-684-5722; Fax: 916-684-4472.
Catechesis/Religious Programs—Students 285.

Fairfield, Solano Co., Holy Spirit (1950), Revs. Michael Downey; Luciano Valenzuela (Philippines); Mario Nunez; Sr. Maura O'Sullivan, O.C.I.A., Pastoral Assoc.; Sr. Elizabeth Curtis, C.H.F., Pastoral Assoc.
Res., 1050 N. Texas St., P.O. Box X, 94533. Tel: 707-425-3138; Fax: 707-425-2029. [CEM]
School—(Grades K-8). Tel: 707-422-5016. Sr. Mairead Langley, C.H.F., Prin.
Sisters 3; Lay Teachers 11; Students 356.
Catechesis/Religious Programs—Tel: 707-425-9042; Fax: 707-425-2029. Suselia Hernandez, D.R.E.
Students 746.
Convent—Tel: 707-425-3572. Sisters of the Holy Faith (Dublin, Ireland)

Our Lady of Mount Carmel, (1979). (Carmelite Fathers). Revs. Kevin McBrien, O.Carm.; Neal McNanna, O.Carm.; Deacon Len Trueworthy.
Parish Office—Tel: 707-422-7767; Fax: 707-422-7946.
Res., 698 Berkeley Way, 94533. Tel: 707-426-3639; Fax: 707-436-3619.
Church—2700 Dover Ave., 94533.
Catechesis/Religious Programs—Tel: 707-422-2814.
Students 273.

Fair Oaks, Sacramento Co., St. Mel (1948), Revs. Richard Doheny; Carroll Keating, S.J.; Rev. Msgr. William Horgan, Pastor Emeritus; Deacon Patrick Henning. In res., Rev. Edward F. Collins (DAV).
Res., 4745 Pennsylvania Ave., P.O. Box 1180, 95628. Tel: 916-967-1229; Fax: 916-967-5659.
School—Tel: 916-967-2814. Janet Nagel, Prin.
Lay Teachers 11; Students 305.
Catechesis/Religious Programs—Tel: 916-966-4314.
Students 230.

Folsom, Sacramento Co., St. John the Baptist (1857), Revs. Ignatius Haran; Thomas Ryan; Deacons Leslie White; Dennis Merino.
Mailing Address: Office:, 307 Montrose Dr., 95630. Tel: 916-985-2065; Fax: 916-985-7579.
Res., 107 Joseph Way, 95763-0235. [CEM]
School—St. John's-Notre Dame, Tel: 916-985-4129. Sr. Anne Maria Ryan, P.B.V.M., Prin.
Lay Teachers 14; Students 314.
Catechesis/Religious Programs—Tel: 916-985-7338.
Students 435.
Station—Folsom State Prison, P.O. Box W, Represa, 95671. Tel: 916-985-2561. Rev. Denis P. Keaney, Chap.
Mailing Address: Folsom State Prison, P.O. Box 29, Represa, 95671. Tel: 916-985-8610, Ext. 6425. Deacon Dennis Merino, Chap.

Fort Jones, Siskiyou Co., Sacred Heart (1921), Rev. John Lawrence.
Res., 101 Carlock St., P.O. Box 126, 96032-0126. Tel: 916-468-2605; Fax: 916-468-5577.
Missions—Etna, Siskiyou Co., St. Mary, 386 Center St., Etna, 96027; Happy Camp, Siskiyou Co., All Saints, 1321 Indian Creek Rd., Happy Camp, 96093; Sawyer's Bar, Siskiyou Co., St. Joseph, Sawyer's Bar Rd., Etna, 96027.

Galt, Sacramento Co., St. Christopher (1885), Rev. Martin Brusato.
Res., 526 Third St., P.O. Box 276, 95632. Tel: 209-745-1389; Fax: 209-745-2773.
Catechesis/Religious Programs—Students 373.

Grass Valley, Nevada Co., St. Patrick (1855), Revs. Nicholas Phelan; Alfred D. Kaster; Sr. Geneva Paluka, R.S.M., Pastoral Min.; Deacons Carlos Astesana; James Chatigny; Milton Stackhouse; Brian Moore.
Res., 235 Chapel St., 95945. Tel: 916-273-2347. [CEM]
School—Mt. St. Mary's, Tel: 916-273-4694; Fax: 916-273-1724. Lydia Blecksmith, Prin.
Lay Teachers 9; Students 216.
Preschool/Day Care—Tel: 916-273-6244.
Lay Teachers 5; Students 38.
Catechesis/Religious Programs—Students 201.

Gridley, Butte Co., Sacred Heart (1926), Rev. Julian Medina.
Res., 1560 Hazel St., P.O. Box 205, 95948. Tel: 916-846-2140; Fax: 916-846-5615.
Catechesis/Religious Programs—Tel: 916-846-5091.
Students 315.
Convent—1515 Hazel St., 95948.
Mission—Live Oak, Sutter Co., Our Lady of Guadalupe, 9660 Broadway, Live Oak, 95953.

Ione, Amador Co., Sacred Heart (1932), Rev. Thomas Relihan.
Res., Church and Washington Sts., P.O. Box 4, 95640. Tel: 209-274-2158. [CEM][JC]
Catechesis/Religious Programs—Students 60.
Missions—Ione, Preston School of Industry, California Youth Authority, 201 Waterman Rd., 95640. Tel: 209-274-4771, Ext. 250. Rev. Michael O'Halloran, O.P.; Ione, Amador Co., Mule Creek State Prison, P.O. Box 409099, 95640. Tel: 209-274-4911. Rev. Thomas J. Maquire, Chap.

Isleton, Sacramento Co., St. Therese's (1953), Rev. Enrique Sanchez.
Res., P.O. Box 697, 95641. Tel: 916-777-6871.
Church—4th St. and Jackson Blvd., 95641.
Catechesis/Religious Programs—Students 79.

Jackson, Amador Co., St. Patrick's (1864), Rev. Paul C. Ricks; Deacons William Thompson; Don Gercich.
Res., 115 Court St., P.O. Box 923, 95642. Tel: 209-223-0168; Fax: 209-223-2548. [CEM 2]
Catechesis/Religious Programs—170 New York Ranch Rd., 95642. Tel: 209-223-2145.
Students 133.
Missions—Buckhorn, Amador Co., Our Lady of the Pines, Tiger Creek Rd., Pioneer, 95660; Volcano, Amador Co., St. Bernard, Plug-Emigrant St., Volcano, 95689.

Knights Landing, Yolo Co., St. Paul (1949), Rev. Thomas A. Batch; Rev. Msgr. Cornelius P. Higgins, Pastor Emeritus; Deacon Antonio Gonzalez.
Res., 222 Sycamore Way, P.O. Box 176, 95645. Tel: 916-735-6478.
Catechetical Center—6th and Locust Sts., 95645.
Mission—Zamora, Yolo Co., St. Agnes, 95645.

Lincoln, Placer Co., St. Joseph (1892) (Hispanic), Revs.

Manuel B. Soria; James Rockenstein, O.F.M.; Deacons Jesus Rodriguez; Roberto Ruiz; Kenneth Boone.
Res., 585 D St., 95648. Tel: 916-645-2102; Fax: 916-645-1422. [JC]
Catechesis/Religious Programs—412 6th St., 95648. Tel: 1-919-645-7754.
Students 160.
Missions—Nicolaus, Sutter Co., St. Boniface, 1028 Marcum Rd., Nicolaus, 95659. Tel: 916-656-2368; Wheatland, Yuba Co., St. Daniel, 214 Main St., Wheatland, 95692. Tel: 916-633-0344.
Shrine—Our Lady of Guadalupe, 3rd and K Sts., 95648.

Marysville, Yuba Co., St. Joseph (1852), Revs. Leon Juchniewicz; Guillermo Rodriguez; Deacons Jesus Munoz; David Perez.
Res., 319 Seventh St., 95901. Tel: 916-742-6461; Fax: 916-742-0346. [CEM]
School—(Grades K-8) 715 C St., 95901. Tel: 916-743-4484. Mrs. Janet Wales, Prin.
Lay Teachers 9; Students 245.
Catechesis/Religious Programs—Tel: 916-742-7100.
Students 164.
Mission—Dobbins, Sacred Heart Church, 95953.

Maxwell, Colusa Co., Sacred Heart (1881), Revs. John Myles; Heriberto Serrano.
Res., 45 Elm St., P.O. Box 607, 95955. Tel: 916-438-2432. [CEM]
Missions—Arbuckle, Colusa Co., Holy Cross, 408 Laurel St., Arbuckle, 95912; Williams, Colusa Co., Annunciation, 617 8th St., Williams, 95987. Tel: 916-473-2925; Stonyford, Colusa Co., St. Mary of the Mountain, 2nd & Geary Sts., Stonyford, 95979.

McCloud, Siskiyou Co., St. Joseph (1933), Rev. Cornelius O'Donnell.
213 Colombero Dr., P.O. Box 518, 96057. Tel: 916-235-4705.
Res., 5605 Shasta Ave., Dunsmuir, 96025. Tel: 916-235-4705. [JC]

Mount Shasta, Siskiyou Co., St. Anthony (1954), Rev. Aidan O'Reilly.
Res., P.O. Box 467, 96067. Tel: 916-926-4477.
Church—Pine and Alma Sts., 96067.
Catechesis/Religious Programs—Tel: 916-926-3061.
Students 95.

Nevada City, Nevada Co., St. Canice (1851), Revs. James McKnight; Edward Mello, Pastor Emeritus.
Res., 317 Washington St., P.O. Box 1597, 95959. Tel: 916-265-2049. [CEM]
Church—Coyote St., 95959.
Catechesis/Religious Programs—Tel: 916-265-2712.
Students 146.

North Highlands, Sacramento Co., St. Lawrence (1955), Rev. Gerald Ryle.
Res., 4325 Don Julio Blvd., 95660. Tel: 916-332-4777; Fax: 916-332-8325.
School—(Grades K-8) 4325 Don Julio Blvd., 95660. Tel: 916-332-4779. Mr. James Gabrielli, Prin.
Lay Teachers 11; Students 298.
Catechesis/Religious Programs—Students 385.

Orangevale, Sacramento Co., Divine Savior (1987), Revs. Robert R. Marsicek, S.D.S.; Neil W. Seidl, S.D.S. In res., Rev. J. Patrick Ritter, S.D.S.
Office: 9079 Greenback Ln., 95662. Tel: 916-989-7400; Fax: 916-989-7410.
Res., 8680 Hickory Leaf Pl., 95662. Tel: 916-989-5425.
Catechesis/Religious Programs—Tel: 916-989-7407.
Students 432.
Counseling Center—Tel: 916-989-7414.

Orland, Glenn Co., St. Dominic (1919), Revs. Thomas L. Seabridge; Miguel Silva.
Res., 822 A St., P.O. Box 816, 95963. Tel: 916-865-4550; 916-865-7080 (Spanish Tel.); Fax: 916-865-8451.
Catechesis/Religious Programs—Tel: 916-865-7115.
Students 40.
Mission—Hamilton City, Glenn Co., St. Mary, 400 Los Robles, 95951.

Oroville, Butte Co., St. Thomas the Apostle (1864), Rev. Troy David Powers; Rev. Msgr. Paul Degnan, Pastor Emeritus.
Res., 1330 Bird St., 95965. Tel: 916-533-0262; Fax: 916-533-1148.
School—1380 Bird St., 95965. Tel: 916-534-6969. Mr. Paul Weber, Prin.
Lay Teachers 7; Students 141.
Catechesis/Religious Programs—Students 98.

Paradise, Butte Co., St. Thomas More (1949), Revs. Brendan Mckeefry; James O'Brien.
Res., 767 Elliott Rd., 95969. Tel: 916-877-4501; Fax: 916-877-5633.
School—771 Elliott Rd., 95969. Tel: 916-877-5328; Fax: 916-877-1485. Mrs. Colleen Waugh, Prin.
Lay Teachers 11; Students 172.
Catechesis/Religious Programs—Tel: 916-877-5633; 916-877-6023.
Students 126.

Placerville, El Dorado Co., St. Patrick's (1855), Revs. John Sullivan; Robert H. Taylor, S.J.; Deacon Stan S. Rudger.
Res., 3109 Sacramento St., 95667. Tel: 916-622-0373. [CEM]
Catechesis/Religious Programs—Tel: 916-622-7692.
Students 615.
Convent—3122 Sacramento St., 95667. Tel: 916-622-1983. Sr. Thomas Marie Heavey, S.A., Supr.
Mission—Georgetown, El Dorado Co., St. James, 2831 Harkness St., Georgetown, 95634. Tel: 916-333-9432.

Portola, Plumas Co., Holy Family (1929), Rev. Bernard J. Burns.
Res., 108 Taylor Ave., P.O. Box 1077, 96122. Tel: 916-832-5006.
Catechesis/Religious Programs—Students 80.
Mission—Loyalton, Sierra Co., Holy Rosary, 4th St., 96118.

Quincy, Plumas Co., St. John (1947), Rev. Stephan Borlang; Deacon William Kearns.
Res., 170 Lawrence St., P.O. Box 510, 95971. Tel: 916-283-0890; Fax: 916-283-4204.
Catechesis/Religious Programs—Students 103.
Mission—Greenville, Plumas Co., St. Anthony.
Station—Buck's Lake, Quincy.

Rancho Cordova, Sacramento Co., St. John Vianney (1958), Rev. Martin J. Moroney; Deacons Walter Little; Phil Moseley. In res., Revs. John Folmer; John Hee-Wan Jeong.
Res., 10497 Coloma Rd., 95670. Tel: 916-362-1385; Fax: 916-361-8102.
School—10499 Coloma Rd., 95670. Tel: 916-363-4610; Fax: 916-363-3243. Mrs. Vicky Andrews, Prin.
Lay Teachers 12; Students 321.
Catechesis/Religious Programs—Tel: 916-362-3827.
Students 230.

Red Bluff, Tehama Co., Sacred Heart (1867), Revs. Sean O'Leary; Malachy Conway.
Res., 515 Main St., 96080. Tel: 916-527-2209; Fax: 916-529-2586. [CEM]
Parish Hall: 2355 Monroe St., 96080. Tel: 916-527-1351.
School—2255 Monroe St., 96080. Tel: 916-527-6727. Mrs. Kate Grimes, Prin.
Lay Teachers 9; Students 198; Preschool 44.
Catechesis/Religious Programs—Students 241.

Redding, Shasta Co., Our Lady of Mercy (1980), Revs. Michael Canny; Walter Dev Burke; Deacon Anthony Short.
Office: 2600 Shasta View Dr., 96002. Tel: 916-222-3424; Fax: 916-221-5717.
Catechesis/Religious Programs—Students 237.

St. Joseph (1907), Rev. Msgr. Russell G. Terra; Deacons David Gasman; Frank Lopez; Michael Mangas.
Res., 2040 Walnut Ave., 96001. Tel: 916-243-3463; Fax: 916-243-2747. [CEM]
School—2460 Gold St., 96001. Tel: 916-243-2302; Fax: 916-243-2747. Mr. Tom Schwerdt, Prin.
Lay Teachers 13; Students 351.
Catechesis/Religious Programs—Tel: 916-243-7999.
Students 60.
Mission—Shasta Lake City, Shasta Co., St. Michael, 3440 Shasta Dam Blvd., 96019.

Rio Vista, Solano Co., St. Joseph (1885), Revs. Patrick M. McGrath; William K. Walsh, Pastor Emeritus.
Res., 130 S. 4th St., 94571. Tel: 707-374-2155. [CEM 2]
Catechesis/Religious Programs—Tel: 707-374-5071.
Students 114.

Rocklin, Placer Co., SS. Peter and Paul (1981), Rev. Michael J. Dillon.
Res., 4450 Granite Dr., P.O. Box 824, 95677. Tel: 916-624-5827; Fax: 916-624-5924.
Catechesis/Religious Programs—Tel: 916-624-3093.
Students 644.

Roseville, Placer Co., St. Rose (1907), Revs. Daniel J. Casey; Robert Brooks; Deacons William H. Boudier; Peter M. Silott; Juan Tamayo. In res., Rev. Michael J. Cormack, Pastor Emeritus.
Res., 615 Vine Ave., 95678. Tel: 916-783-5211; Fax: 916-783-5212.
School—633 Vine Ave., 95678. Tel: 916-782-1161. Marie Giorgi, Prin.
Sisters 2; Lay Teachers 14; Students 310.
Catechesis/Religious Programs—Tel: 916-786-0650.
Students 485.

South Lake Tahoe, El Dorado Co., St. Theresa (1951), Rev. Msgr. Murrough C. Wallace; Revs. Michael O'Reilly; John J. Grace, Pastor Emeritus.
Res., 1041 Lyons Ave., 96150. Tel: 916-544-3533; Fax: 916-544-4662.
School—1081 Lyons Ave., 96150. Tel: 916-544-8944. Dr. Jeannette Holmes, Prin.
Catechesis/Religious Programs—Tel: 916-544-4788.
Students 240.
Mission—Camp Sacramento, El Dorado Co., Our Lady of the Sierras.

Susanville, Lassen Co., Sacred Heart (1912), Rev. Noel Lynch.
Res., 120 N. Union St., P.O. Box 501, 96130. Tel: 916-257-3230; Fax: 916-257-9213.
Catechesis/Religious Programs—Msgr. Moran Hall, 140 N. Weatherlow St., 96130. Tel: 916-257-8008.
Students 86.
Station—Herlong.

Sutter Creek, Amador Co., Immaculate Conception (1864), Revs. Liam MacCarthy; Ronan P. Brennan, Pastor Emeritus.
Res., 130 Spanish St., P.O. Box 127, 95685. Tel: 209-267-5602. [CEM]
Catechesis/Religious Programs—Spanish & Amelia Sts., 95685. Tel: 209-267-0447.
Students 95.
Mission—Plymouth, Amador Co., St. Mary of the Mountains, Church St., Plymouth, 95669.

Tahoe City, Placer Co., Corpus Christi (1961), Rev. Patrick J. O'Connor.
Church & Res.—905 W. Lake Blvd., Hwy. 89 S., P.O. Box 1878, 96145. Tel: 916-583-4409; Fax: 916-583-1408.
Catechesis/Religious Programs—Tel: 916-583-4637.
Students 100.
Mission—Olympic Valley, Placer Co., Queen of the Snows, 1550 Squaw Valley Rd., 96145.
Station—Tahoma.

Truckee, Nevada Co., Assumption of the Blessed Virgin Mary (1870), Revs. Stanley Poltorak; Francisco Hernandez-Tovar; Deacon Ray Craig.
Res., 10124 E. St., Hwy. 267 N., P.O. Box 34014, 96160. Tel: 916-587-3595; Fax: 916-582-8648.
Catechesis/Religious Programs—Students 200.
Mission—Kings Beach, Placer Co., Our Lady of the Lake, 8363 Steelhead, Kings Beach, 96143. Tel: 916-546-2291.

Tulelake, Siskiyou Co., Holy Cross (1949), Rev. Patrick Henry, Admin.
Res., 765 First St., 96134. Tel: 916-667-2727.
Church—P.O. Box 266, 96134.
Mission—Dorris, Siskiyou Co., Our Lady of Good Counsel, W. 3rd St., Dorris, 96023.

Vacaville, Solano Co., St. Joseph (1992), Rev. Vincent O'Reilly.
Res., 1791 Marshall Rd., 95689. Tel: 707-447-2354; Fax: 707-447-9322.
School—Notre Dame, 1781 Marshall Rd., 95687. Tel: 707-447-1460; Fax: 707-447-1498. Maryalice Clare, Prin.
Catechesis/Religious Programs—Students 250.

St. Mary (1947), Revs. Benedict DeLeon; Eugenio Lopez; Deacon Gary McSwain; Rev. Lawrence Ryan, Pastor Emeritus.
Res., 350 Stinson Ave., 95688. Tel: 707-448-2390; Fax: 707-448-2818.
Catechesis/Religious Programs—Students 728.
Catechetical Center—300 Hemlock St., 95688. Tel: 707-446-1881.
Students 718.

Vallejo, Solano Co., St. Basil (1941), Revs. William P. Storan; Rustico Centino; Deacon Michael Carlomagno.
Res., 1200 Tuolumne St., 94590. Tel: 707-644-5251; Fax: 707-644-1423.
School—1230 Nebraska St., 94590. Tel: 707-642-7629; Fax: 707-642-8635. Mrs. Susan M. Hill, Prin.
Lay Teachers 12; Students 356; Preschool 82.
Catechesis/Religious Programs—Tel: 707-644-8309.
Students 358.

St. Catherine of Siena (1964), Revs. William P. Kinane; Jesus Soriano.
Res., 3450 Tennessee St., P.O. Box 5390, 94591. Tel: 707-553-1355; Fax: 707-557-6896.
School—(Grades K-8) 3460 Tennessee St., 94591. Tel: 707-643-6691; Fax: 707-647-4441. Mrs. Flavia R. Lorega, Prin.
Lay Teachers 14; Students 343.
Catechesis/Religious Programs—Tel: 707-643-1951.
Students 353.

St. Vincent Ferrer (1855), Revs. Edward J. Lewis; Leonardo Pahamtang (Philippines); Gerardo Rubio (Tijuana, Mexico); Tobias Vereker.
Res., 925 Sacramento St., 94590. Tel: 707-644-8396; Fax: 707-644-1330.

School—420 Florida St., 94590. Tel: 707-642-4311; Fax: 707-642-1329. Sr. Jude Stockholm, O.P., Prin.
Sisters 1; Lay Teachers 11; Students 350.
Catechesis/Religious Programs—Tel: 707-643-0188.
Students 862.
Mission—South Vallejo, Solano Co., St. Louis Bertrand. Fax: 707-644-8396.

Walnut Grove, Sacramento Co., St. Anthony (1931), Rev. Edward Mello.
Res., 2nd St. and Walnut Ave., P.O. Box 436, 95690. Tel: 916-776-1330.

Weaverville, Trinity Co., St. Patrick (1853), Rev. Keith Canterbury; Deacon Everett Layne.
Res., P.O. Box 1219, 96093. Tel: 916-623-4383.
Church—102 Church St., 96093.
Missions—Hayfork, Trinity Co., Holy Trinity; Lewiston, Trinity Co., St. Gilbert.

Weed, Siskiyou Co., Holy Family (1933), Rev. John Hannan.
Res., 1051 N. Davis Ave., P.O. Box 248, 96094. Tel: 916-938-2076.

West Sacramento, Yolo Co., Holy Cross (1913), Rev. John Kouba, S.D.S.; Deacon Thomas Perrin, S.D.S.; Bro. William Hoefgen, S.D.S.; Deacon Raul Leon.
Res., 1321 Anna St., 95605. Tel: 916-371-1211; Fax: 916-371-9277.
School—800 Todhunter Ave., 95605. Tel: 916-371-1313. Mrs. Julie Brehl, Prin.
Sisters 2; Lay Teachers 6; Students 202.
Catechesis/Religious Programs—Students 160.
Convent—Tel: 916-371-1931; 933-0971. Sisters of Mercy (Auburn, CA)

Our Lady of Grace (1949), Rev. Edward O'Hara.
Res., 911 Park Blvd., 95691. Tel: 916-371-4814.
School—1990 Linden Rd., 95691. Tel: 916-371-9416; 371-9715; Fax: 916-371-1319. Sr. Michael Henry Moulin, D.H.S., Prin.
Sisters 1; Lay Teachers 9; Students 287.
Convent—Tel: 916-371-9715.

Westwood, Lassen Co., Our Lady of the Snows (1929), Rev. Thomas Carrigan.
Res., 307 Fifth St., P.O. Box 905, 96137. Tel: 916-256-3344; Fax: 916-256-3344.
Church—425 Cedar St., 96137.
Catechesis/Religious Programs—Tel: 916-596-4261.
Students 78.
Mission—Chester, Plumas Co., Christ the King, Melissa St., Chester, 96020.

Willows, Glenn Co., St. Monica (1877), Rev. Mathias J. O'Callaghan.
Res., 1129 W. Wood St., 95988. Tel: 916-934-3314; Fax: 916-934-3205. [CEM]
Catechesis/Religious Programs—Students 230.
Catechetical School—1151 W. Wood St., 95988. Tel: 916-934-5916.
Students 194.

Winters, Yolo Co., St. Anthony (1913), Rev. Joseph P. Ternullo; Deacons Alejandro Arroyo; Colby Smith.
Res., 303 Main St., P.O. Box 986, 95694. Tel: 916-795-2230; Fax: 916-795-5470.
Church—301 Main St., 95694.
Parish Center—511 Main St., 95694.
Catechesis/Religious Programs—Students 100.
Mission—Esparto, Yolo Co., St. Martin, 25633 Grafton Rd., Esparto, 95627. Tel: 916-787-3750.

Woodland, Yolo Co., Holy Rosary (1871), Revs. John E. Boll; Colm O'Kelly; Rodrigo Ojeda; Deacons Edward Kull; Gonzalo Chavez; Antonio Fernandez; Robert Link.
Res., 318 Court St., 95695. Tel: 916-662-2805; Fax: 916-662-0796. [CEM]
School—505 California St., 95695. Tel: 916-668-2442. Jeanni Venturini, Prin.
Lay Teachers 11; Students 282.
Catechesis/Religious Programs—Tel: 916-662-5394. Nancy Johnson.
Students 500.
Mission—Yolo, Yolo Co., Our Lady of Guadalupe.

Yreka, Siskiyou Co., St. Joseph (1855), Rev. William Hold.
Res., 314 Fourth St., P.O. Box 570, 96097. Tel: 916-842-3842.
Catechetical Center—308 Fourth St., 96097. Tel: 916-842-4874.
Catechesis/Religious Programs—Students 72.
Mission—Hawkinsville, Siskiyou Co., Immaculate Conception.

Yuba City, Sutter Co., St. Isidore (1952), Revs. Joseph E. Bishop; Joseph Huong. In res., Rev. Vincent A. Meskenas (BEL).
Res., 222 Clark Ave., 95991. Tel: 916-673-1573; Fax: 916-673-2512.
School—200 Clark Ave., 95991. Tel: 916-673-2217; Fax: 916-673-2217. Miss Sheila S. Garlock, Prin.
Lay Teachers 11; Students 291.
Catechesis/Religious Programs—Students 450.

Chaplains of Public Institutions

SACRAMENTO. *California Youth Authority,* Northern Reception Center-Clinic, 3001 Ramona Ave., 95826. Tel: 916-739-2104. Rev. William P. McSweeney, Res., 929 Fulton Ave., No. 441, 95825. Tel: 916-488-4149.
Mule Creek State Prison. P.O. Box 409099, Ione, 95640. Tel: 209-274-4911. Rev. Thomas Maguire, Res., P.O. Box 578, Plymouth, 95669. Tel: 209-245-4331.
Sutter General Hospital, 2801 L St., 95816. Tel: 916-454-2222. Rev. H. James McFarland, S.J.
Sutter Memorial Hospital, 52nd & F Sts., 95819. Tel: 916-454-3333. Rev. H. James McFarland, S.J.
University of California, Davis Medical Center, 2315 Stockton Blvd., 95817. Tel: 916-453-2011. Rev. William J. Dinelli, Res., 4315 Martin Luther King Jr. Blvd., 95820.

FOLSOM. *Folsom State Prison Annex.* Vacant. P.O. Box 29, Represa, 95671.
State Prison. P.O. Box W, Represa, 95671. Tel: 916-985-2561. Rev. Denis P. Keaney, Res., 1521 Lake Vista Ln., 95630. Tel: 916-933-4980.

PRESTON. *School of Industry,* California Youth Authority. Tel: 209-274-4771, Ext. 250. Rev. Michael O'Halloran, O.P., Res., 201 Waterman Rd., Ione, 95640.

SUSANVILLE *California Correctional Center.* Attended by Lassen County. P.O. Box 790, 96130. Tel: 916-257-2181, Ext. 180.
Sierra Army Depot. Attended by Army & Navy Chaplains and Sacred Heart Parish.

VACAVILLE. *California Medical Facility, Solano Co.* P.O. Box 4000, 95696. Tel: 707-448-6841, Ext. 2378. Rev. Innocent Emechete, Chap., Res., 105 S. Second St., Dixon, 95620.
California Medical Facility, South, P.O. Box 4000, 95696. Tel: 707-448-6841, Ext. 3137. Rev. Paul Schloeder, Chap.

Special Assignment:
Reverend Fathers—
O'Callaghan, Matthias J., Chap. to Police Officers, St. Monica Parish, 1129 W. Wood St., Willows, CA 95988
O'Halloran, Michael, O.P., Chap. for Law Enforcement, 201 Waterman Rd., Ione, CA 95640
Seabridge, Thomas L., Liaison for Arts and Shrines, St. Dominic Parish, P.O. Box 816, Orland, CA 95963. Tel: 916-865-4550
Silveira, Eduino, Chap. to Sheriff Deputies, St. Elizabeth Church, 1817 12th St., Sacramento, CA 95814
Traynor, Anthony, Chap. to Firefighters & Sacramento Metro Airport, Our Lady of Lourdes Church, 1951 North Ave., Sacramento, CA 95838

On Duty Outside the Diocese:
Reverend Fathers—
Dermody, Thomas, San Diego
Leslie, Patrick, Santa Rosa

Military Chaplains:
Reverend Fathers—
Higgins, Richard B., U.S. Air Force
Mennis, James F., U.S. Navy

Awaiting Assignment:
Reverend Fathers—
Walsh, Michael

Absent on Leave:
Reverend Fathers—
Steinauer, Carl J.

Retired and in Senior Ministry:
Reverend Monsignors—
Coffey, Andrew, 520 C St., Davis, CA 95616
Degnan, Paul, 1540 Bird St., Oroville, CA 95965
Higgins, Cornelius, 3027 Olive Glen Ct., Sacramento, CA 95821
Horgan, William, Carrigan Wood, Brosna, Tralee, Co. Kerry, Ireland
Mistretta, Vito F., 7760 Woodchuck Way, Citrus Heights, CA 95610
Nolan, Patrick, P.O. Box 215231, Sacramento, CA 95821
O'Neill, Patrick J., 350 Locust Dr., Apt. #L-104, Vallejo, CA 94591
Peters, Roy V., 469 Ena Rd. #3010, Honolulu, HI 96815
Poole, James D., 7515 Soules Way, Sacramento, CA 95823
Schons, Gerard, 627 3rd St., Galt, CA 95632
Terwilliger, John G., 3865 J St., Apt. #354, Sacramento, CA 95816
Reverend Fathers—
Albrecht, Walter H., 722 State St., Aberdeen, WA 98520
Brennan, Ronan P., 2007 Country Villa, Auburn, CA 95603
Broderick, William, 5057 Cottage Way, Carmichael, CA 95608
Connelly, Robert J., P.O. Box 5037, Oak Park Sta., Sacramento, CA 95817
Cormack, Michael J., 7413 Timberrose, Roseville, CA 95747
Delahunty, Thomas P., 3247 Sandhurst Ct., Cameron Park, CA 95682
Grace, John J., 3035 Berkeley Ave., South Lake Tahoe, CA 96150
Gurnell, Anthony, P.O. Box 627, Cayucos, CA 93430
Kyne, John J., Box 143, Corning, CA 96021
Lanigan, Patrick J., 1182 Hartford Pl., Fairfield, CA 94533
Lenehan, Vincent, 2251 Northrop Ave., Sacramento, CA 95825
Lyons, Vincent, 1147-A Porter St., Vallejo, CA 94590
Maio, Anthony V., 110 Village Ct., Vacaville, CA 95687
Mello, Edward, 3250 Blue Oaks Dr., #203, Auburn, CA 95602
Moloney, Bean
O'Brien, Thomas, 30 Woodlawn Park, Killarney, Co. Kerry, Ireland
O'Dowd, Brendan
O'Rafferty, Patrick, 5751 Locust Ave., Carmichael, CA 95608
Ramos, Cipriano, 338 Elm St., Roseville, CA 95678
Ryan, Lawrence A., P.O. Box 8050, Santa Cruz, CA 95061
Van Snellenberg, John, 3700 Valle Verde Dr., Napa, CA 94558
Walsh, William K., 50 River Rd., #30, Rio Vista, CA 94571
Wdowiak, Boleslaw, c/o Alta Sierra, 11564 Tammy Way, Grass Valley, CA 95949

Permanent Deacons:
Adams, James V., Chatsworth, CA
Arroyo, Alejandro, St. Anthony, Winters
Astesana, Carlos, St. Patrick's, Grass Valley
Boone, Kenneth, St. Patrick, Weaverville
Boudier, William, St. Rose, Roseville
Burke, Keith, Presentation, Sacramento
Burkett, James, St. John, Chico; St. Mary, Vacaville
Cabrera, Domingo, St. Vincent Ferrer, Vallejo
Carlomagno, Michael, St. Basil, Vallejo
Cavanagh, Paul, St. Vincent Ferrer, Vallejo
Chatigny, James, St. Patrick, Grass Valley
Chavarria, Modesto, St. Anne, Sacramento
Chavez, Gonzalo, Holy Rosary, Woodland
Cheever, Charles, St. Philomene, Sacramento
Christiansen, George, Unassigned
Colenzo, Sam, St. James, Davis
Craig, Ray, Assumption, Truckee
Cronley, Michael, St. Anthony, Sacramento
DeHaven, Donald, Cathedral of the Blessed Sacrament, Sacramento
Del Gaudio, Lou, St. Mary, Sacramento
Donovan, Michael, All Hallows, Sacramento
Driggs, Richard, St. Francis of Assisi, Sacramento
Duvernay, Anthony, Our Divine Savior, Chico
Evans, Michael, Sacred Heart, Anderson
Fernandez, Antonio, Holy Rosary, Woodland
Fernandez, Miguel, Our Lady of Lourdes, Colusa
Ferreira, Thomas, Our Lady of Assumption, Carmichael
Fracolli, Gary, St. Lawrence, North Highlands
Garcia, Henry, St. Joseph, Sacramento
Gasman, David H., St. Joseph's, Redding
Gercich, Don, St. Patrick, Jackson
Godinez, Rafael, Unassigned
Gonzalez, Antonio, St. Paul, Knights Landing
Gualco, Jack, St. Ignatius, Sacramento
Healy, James, St. Anthony's, Sacramento
Helgeson, Raymond, Stubenville
Henning, Patrick, St. Mel, Fair Oaks
Hernandez, Jesus, St. Vincent Ferrer, Vallejo
Ikelman, Robert, St. Peter, Dixon
Imrisek, Paul, St. Joseph, Elk Grove
Kearns, William, St. John, Quincy
King, John, St. Peter, Dixon
Koppes, Richard, St. Anthony, Sacramento
Kriske, George, All Hallows, Sacramento
Kull, Carl, Holy Rosary, Woodland
LaLonde, James, Our Lady of Lourdes, Sacramento
Layne, Everett H., Holy Trinity (Mission of Weaverville)
Lazarek, Edward, St. Dominic, Benicia
Leon, Raul, Holy Cross, West Sacramento
Lewandowski, Daniel
Link, Robert, Holy Rosary, Woodland
Little, Walter, St. John Vianney, Rancho Cordova
Lobo, Pete, St. Catherine, Vallejo
Lopez, Frank, St. Joseph, Redding
Lubinsky, William, Holy Family, Citrus Heights
Lucas, George, Immaculate Conception, North San Juan

Magallanes, Jesus, Sacred Heart, Anderson
Mangas, Michael, St. Joseph, Redding
Mangoba, Leo, St. Vincent Ferrer, Vallejo
Manriquez, Pedro, St. Anne, Sacramento
Masla, John, Cathedral of the Blessed Sacrament, Sacramento
McGill, Thomas, Tucson, AZ
McSwain, Gary, ID
Merino, Dennis, St. John the Baptist, Folsom
Meucci, James, Assumption, Carmichael
Moore, Brian, St. Patrick, Grass Valley
Morgado, Edwin, St. Joseph, Auburn
Morris, Douglas, Austin, TX
Morrison, Charles, St. Paul, Sacramento
Moseley, Philip, St. John Vianney, Rancho Cordova
Munoz, Jesus, St. Joseph, Marysville
Nguyen, Anthony, Vietnamese Catholic Martyrs, Sacramento
Niekamp, Lawrence, Our Divine Savior, Oragevale
Padilla, Jesus, St. John the Baptist, Chico
Parra, Gilbert, Sacred Heart, Sacramento
Pauly, Gerald, Immaculate Conception, Sacramento; Vicar for Deacons
Perez, Ben, St. Catherine, Vallejo
Perez, David, St. Joseph's, Marysville
Ramirez, Antonio, St. John, Chico
Ramirez, Jose, Our Lady of Guadalupe, Sacramento
Ramos, Ray, St. Peter, Sacramento
Rasmussen, Charles, Trinity, El Dorado Hills
Redling, Ralph, Kelseyville, CA
Reyna, Pedro, Sacred Heart, Maxwell
Reynoso, Alejandro, St. Peter, Sacramento
Riehl, William, Sacred Heart, Sacramento
Rodriquez, Jesus, St. Joseph, Lincoln
Rodriquez, Martin, St. Robert, Sacramento
Rudger, Stanley, St. Patrick, Placerville
Ruiz, Roberto, St. Joseph's, Lincoln
Sanchez, Miquel, Holy Spirit, Fairfield
Schaeffer, William, Abbey of New Clairvaux, Vina
Schwartz, Steve, St. John, Chico
Sheldon, Lawrence, Our Lady of Mt. Carmel, Fairfield
Shields, Floyd, McClellan Air Force Base
Short, Sam, Our Lady of Mercy, Redding
Silott, Peter, St. Rose, Roseville
Sims, Robert, St. Vincent Ferrer, Vallejo
Smith, Colby, St. Anthony, Winters
Stackhouse, Milton, (Retired)
Symkowick, Joseph, Newman Catholic Community, CSUS, Sacramento
Taloff, Paul, St. James, Davis
Tamayo, Juan, St. Rose, Roseville
Tateishi, Michael, Our Lady of the Assumption, Carmichael
Thompson, William, St. Patrick, Jackson
Trueworthy, Len, Our Lady of Mt. Carmel, Fairfield
Vega, Ramon, Immaculate Conception, Sacramento
Weeks, James, Holy Spirit, Sacramento
Weeks, James B., St. John the Evangelist, Carmichael
White, Les, St. John the Baptist, Folsom
Wortman, Richard, St. Philip (Byzantine), Sacramento
Wroblicky, Theodore, St. Andrew the Apostle (Ukrainian)
Yang, Gnia, Hmong Community
Zellmer, Gary, Washington

INSTITUTIONS LOCATED IN THE DIOCESE

[A] SEMINARY, RELIGIOUS

LOOMIS. *Mount St. Joseph Novitiate and Seminary*, 6530 Wells Ave., P.O. Box 547, 95650. Tel: 916-652-6336. Novitiate of Oblates of St. Joseph. Revs. John C. Warburton, O.S.J., Rector; Brian Crawford, O.S.J.; Bro. Marcello DiNardo, O.S.J. Priests 1; Brothers 1.

VINA. *Abbey of New Clairvaux, Trappist Seminary*, P.O. Box 80, 96092. Tel: 916-839-2161; Fax: 916-839-2332. Rt. Rev. Thomas X. Davis, O.C.S.O., J.C.L., Abbot. In res., Revs. Timothy VanderVennet, O.C.S.O., S.T.L.; Lawrence A. Glaser, O.C.S.O.; Joseph Wittbrod, O.C.S.O.; Paul Jerome Konkler, O.C.S.O.; Harold Meyer, O.C.S.O.; Anthony Bellesorte, O.C.S.O.; Mark Scott, O.C.S.O., S.S.L.; John Baptist Porter, O.C.S.O.; Paul Mark Schwan, O.C.S.O.; Edwin J. McCabe, O.C.S.O., Trappist Monastery, Lantao Island, P.O. 5, Hong Kong. Rev. Maurus Pei, O.C.S.O. Seminarians 2.

[B] HIGH SCHOOLS, DIOCESAN

SACRAMENTO. *St. Francis High School*. (Girls), 6051 M St., 95819. Tel: 916-452-3461; Fax: 916-452-1591. Apostles of the Sacred Heart of Jesus (Hamden, CT). Sr. Catherine Sedgeman, A.S.C.J., Prin. Sisters 5; Priests 1; Lay Teachers 53; Girls 788.

PALO CEDRO. *Bishop Quinn High School*, 21893 Old 44 Dr., 96073. Tel: 916-547-2900; Fax: 916-547-5349. Dr. Raymond L. John, Principal.

Bishop Quinn High School, 21893 Old 44 Dr., 96073.

RED BLUFF. *Mercy High School*, 233 Riverside Way, 96080. Tel: 916-527-8313. Michael J. Steinbrecher, Ed.D., Prin. Lay Teachers 17; Students 154.

VALLEJO. *St. Patrick-St. Vincent High School*, 1500 Benicia Rd., 94591. Tel: 707-644-4425; Fax: 707-644-3107. Sr. Sue Pixley, O.P., Principal. Sisters 3; Lay Teachers 41; Students 651.

[C] HIGH SCHOOLS, PRIVATE

SACRAMENTO. *Christian Brothers High School of Sacramento, Inc.*, 4315 Martin Luther King Jr. Blvd., 95820. Tel: 916-733-3630. Mr. Mark L. Warren, Pres.; Bro. A. Stephen Rusyn, F.S.C., Prin. Brothers 6; Sisters 3; Lay Teachers 66; Students 935.

Jesuit High School. Mailing Address: P.O. Box 254647, 95865. Tel: 916-482-6060. 1200 Jacob Ln., Carmchael, 95608. (Boys). Revs. Edwin B. Harris, S.J., Pres.; Alfred E. Naucke, S.J., Rector; Reynold J. Gato, S.J., Dir. Devel.; Francis G. Hernandez, S.J.; John A. Kelly, S.J.; Richard L. McCurdy, S.J.; Charles R. Olsen, S.J.; Lorenzo J. Palafox, S.J.; John T. Quinn, S.J.; A. Francis Stiegeler, S.J., Prin.; William K. Stolz, S.J.; George V. Wanser, S.J.; Carlton E. Whitten, S.J. Jesuit Priests 13; Brothers 3; Scholastics 2; Lay Teachers 55; Boys 1,000.

Loretto High School. (Girls), 2360 El Camino Ave., 95821. Tel: 916-482-7793. Religious of the Institute of the Blessed Virgin Mary. Sr. Helen Timothy, I.B.V.M., Prin. Sisters 2; Lay Teachers 46; Girls 412.

[D] ELEMENTARY SCHOOLS, DIOCESAN

PALO CEDRO. *Saint Francis Middle School*, 21945 Old 44 Dr., 96073. Dr. Raymond John, Principal. Students 133; Total Staff 9.

[E] DAY NURSERY AND CHILD CARE HOMES

SACRAMENTO. *Grace Day Home*, 1909 7th St., 95814. Tel: 916-442-6557. Ms. Nancy DeArmond, Exec. Dir. Lay Staff 34; Children 150.

St. Patrick Children's Home, Inc., 5945 Franklin Blvd., 95824. Tel: 916-421-1620. Rev. Msgr. Edward J. Kavanagh, Exec. Dir.; Colleen Maloney, Financial Officer.

Three Residential Group Homes for Boys and Girls: Lopresti, 5036 Lemon Hill Ave., 95828. Farley, 7580 El Terraza Dr., 95828. McMahon, 8529 Florin Rd., 95828. Total residents 24; Total Assisted 31; Total Staff 62.

St. Patrick's Child Care Centers, 5945 Franklin Blvd., 95824. Tel: 916-422-0123. Sandra Patitucci, Dir. Children (ages 2-5) 68; Children in after school care program 32; Total Assisted 99; Total Assisted 64.

St. Patrick's Infant Toddler Program, 5945 Franklin Blvd., 95824. Tel: 916-422-0123. Children (ages 6 weeks-2 years) 24; Total Assisted 27.

St. Patrick's Infant-Toddler Program, 8201 Florin Rd., 95828. Tel: 916-383-3254. Sandra Patitucci, Dir. Children (ages 6 weeks-2 years 9 months) 34; Total Assisted 94. State funded for low income families-12 children ages 2-5. Private care: non-state funded.

[F] HOMES FOR SENIOR CITIZENS

SACRAMENTO. *Mercy-McMahon Terrace*, 3865 J St., 95816. Tel: 916-733-6510; Fax: 916-733-6515.

For a complete listing, refer to the Special Care Facilities section.

[G] GENERAL HOSPITALS

SACRAMENTO. *Mercy General Hospital*, 4001 J St., 95819. Tel: 916-453-4545.

For a complete listing, refer to the Hospitals section.

CARMICHAEL. *Mercy American River Hospital*, 4747 Engle Rd., 95608. Tel: 916-484-2222.

For a complete listing, refer to the Hospitals section.

FOLSOM. *Mercy Hospital of Folsom*, 1650 Creekside Dr., 95630. Tel: 916-983-7400.

For a complete listing, refer to the Hospitals section.

MT. SHASTA. *Mercy Medical Center*, 914 Pine St., P.O. Box 239, 96067. Tel: 916-926-6111.

For a complete listing, refer to the Hospitals section.

RANCHO CORDOVA. *Mercy Healthcare Sacramento*, 10540 White Rock Rd., 95670. Tel: 916-851-2000.

For a complete listing, refer to the Hospitals section.

RED BLUFF. *Mercy Healthcare North dba St. Elizabeth Community Hospital*, 2550 Sr. Mary Columba Dr., 96080-4397. Tel: 916-529-8000; Fax: 916-529-8009.

For a complete listing, refer to the Hospitals section.

REDDING. *Mercy Medical Center*, Clairmont Heights, P.O. Box 496009, 96049. Tel: 916-225-6000.

For a complete listing, refer to the Hospitals section.

SUSANVILLE. *Lassen Community Hospital*, 560 Hospital Ln., 96130. Tel: 916-257-5325.

For a complete listing, refer to the Hospitals section.

[H] MONASTERIES AND RESIDENCES OF PRIESTS AND BROTHERS

CARMICHAEL. *Jesuit High School Community of Sacramento*.

(California Prov., Los Gatos). Mailing Address: P.O. Box 254647, Sacramento, 95865. Tel: 916-482-6060. 1200 Jacob Ln., 95608. Revs. Alfred E. Naucke, S.J., Rector; William F. Breault, S.J.; Robert G. Dolan, S.J.; Reynold J. Gatto, S.J.; Edwin B. Harris, S.J.; Francis G. Hernandez, S.J.; John A. Kelly, S.J.; Richard L. McCurdy, S.J.; Charles R. Olsen, S.J.; Lorenzo J. Palafox, S.J.; John T. Quinn, S.J.; A. Francis Stiegeler, S.J.; William K. Stolz, S.J.; George V. Wanser, S.J.; Carlton E. Whitten, S.J.; Bros. Justin DeChance, S.J.; Charles Onorato, S.J.; Mr. James Sanders, S.J.; Mr. Michael Taylor, S.J.; Mr. Mark Zangrando, S.J. Priests 15; Brothers 3; Scholastics 2.

CITRUS HEIGHTS. *Christ the King Retreat*, 6520 Van Maren Ln., 95621. Tel: 916-969-0685; Fax: 916-725-4812. The Passionists (Chicago, IL). A community residence for the Passionist priests and brothers who conduct missions and retreats. Very Rev. Donald A. Webber, C.P., Supr.; Revs. Neil J. Parsons, C.P.; Thomas More Newbold, C.P.; James G. Strommer, C.P.; Joseph Mitchell, C.P., Retreat Dir.; James Busch, C.P.; Cedric Pisegna, C.P.; Raymond McDonough, C.P.; Bro. Carl Hund, C.P. Priests 8; Brothers 1.

VINA. *Abbey of New Clairvaux, Trappist*, P.O. Box 80, 96092. Tel: 916-839-2161; Fax: 916-839-2332. Cistercian Abbey, Cistercians of the Strict Observance. Rt. Rev. Thomas X. Davis, O.C.S.O., J.C.L., Abbot; Revs. Joseph J. Wittbrod, O.C.S.O., Prior; Timothy VanderVennett, O.C.S.O., S.T.L.; Lawrence A. Glaser, O.C.S.O.; Paul Jerome Konkler, O.C.S.O.; Harold K. Meyer, O.C.S.O.; Anthony R. Bellesorte, O.C.S.O.; Mark A. Scott, O.C.S.O.; John Baptist Porter, O.C.S.O.; Paul Mark Schwan, O.C.S.O., Trappist Monastery, Lantao Island, P.O. 5, Peng Chau, Hong Kong. Rev. Maurus Pei, O.C.S.O. Priests 10; Professed Brothers 17.

[I] CONVENTS AND RESIDENCES FOR SISTERS

SACRAMENTO. *Apostles of the Sacred Heart of Jesus*, St. Francis High School Convent, 5945 M St., 95819. Tel: 916-457-1768; Fax: 916-452-1591. Sisters 4. St. Charles Borromeo Convent, 7580 Center Pkwy., 95823. Tel: 916-421-7174; Fax: 916-421-3954. Sisters 4.

Canossian Daughters of Charity, Our Lady of Lourdes Convent, 1949 North Ave., 95838. Tel: 916-925-4001. Sisters 4.

Presentation Sisters, St. Mary's Convent, 5801 N St., 95819. Tel: 916-451-5881. Sisters 4.

Religious of the Cenacle, 1964 Ethan Way #15, 95825. Tel: 916-924-3913; 971-1777 (Office).

Religious of the Virgin Mary, 1123 W St., 95818. Tel: 916-447-7008. Sisters 5.

Sister Servants of the Blessed Sacrament, St. Peter's Convent, 5870 62nd St., 95824. Tel: 916-457-0182. Sisters 5; Total Staff 4; Total Assisted 58.

Sisters of Social Service, 2514 U St., 95818-1821. Tel: 916-455-5841. Sisters 2. 3257 11th Ave., 95817. Tel: 916-455-1106.

Other Locations: 6016 Homesweet Way, Carmichael, 95608. Tel: 916-489-0803. 5349 Sedona Ct., Carmichael, 95608. Tel: 916-489-3714. Jericho, 926 J St., Ste 410, 95814. Catholic Social Service, 745 Georgia St., Vallejo, 94590. Tel: 707-644-8909.

Sisters of St. Dominic, St. Martin de Porres Convent, 379 Bell Ave., 95838. Tel: 916-929-4375. Sisters 2.

Sisters of St. Francis of Penance and Christian Charity, 2245 Woodside Ln., 95824. Tel: 916-442-6557.

Other Locations: 3208 58th St., 95820. Tel: 916-452-0666. St. Francis Manor, 2515 J. St. #608, 95816. 3141 32nd Ave., 95824. 3886 H St., 95816-1935.

Sisters of the Holy Rosary of Fatima, 1708 U St., 95818. Tel: 916-442-8646. Sisters 2.

Sisters of the Sacred Hearts of Jesus & Mary, St. Paul's Convent, P.O. Box 292280, 95829. Tel: 926-381-5200. Sisters 2.

AUBURN. *Institute of the Sisters of Mercy of the Americas*.

Auburn Regional Community. Motherhouse: 535 Sacramento St., 95603-5699. Tel: 916-887-2000; Fax: 916-885-6581. Sr. Susan McCarthy, R.S.M., Pres. Sisters in Community 24; Sisters in Diocese 88.

Russell House, 2223 L St., Sacramento, 95816-4926. Tel: 916-446-9251. Sisters 6.

McAuley Convent, 3846 H St., Sacramento, 95816-4613. Tel: 916-455-2843. Sisters 4.

Sisters of Mercy, 5625 Frontier Way, Carmichael, 95608. Tel: 916-489-0844. Sisters 5.

Our Lady of Fatima Convent, 1715 El Monte Ave., Sacramento, 95815-2904. Tel: 916-924-8541. Sisters 2.
Holy Spirit Convent, 3920 W. Land Park Dr., Sacramento, 95822-1123. Tel: 916-448-3578. Sr. Brenda O'Keeffe. Sisters 1.
Mercy Convent, 750 41st St., Sacramento, 95819-2738. Tel: 916-457-8274. Sisters 7.
Mercy San Juan, 6620 Oakbrook Dr., Fair Oaks, 95628. Tel: 916-962-7144. Sisters 8.
Mercy Convent, 2254 Gold St., Redding, 96001-2420. Tel: 916-225-7590. Sisters 6.
Mercy Residence, 8637 Posadera Ave., Orangevale, 95662-3329. Tel: 916-987-1436. Sisters 2.
Holy Cross Convent, 800 Todhunter Ave., West Sacramento, 95605-2299. Tel: 916-371-1931. Sisters 5.
Sisters of Mercy, 212 Bittercreek Dr., Folsom, 95630-2353. Tel: 916-983-9268. Sisters 2.
Sisters of Mercy, 848 39th St., Sacramento, 95816. Tel: 916-454-1723. Sisters 3.
Sisters of Mercy, 1396 Oakwood Ave., Vallejo, 94591. Tel: 707-552-9882. Sisters 2.
Sisters of Mercy, 2101 Shoreline Dr., #146, Alameda, 94501. Tel: 510-521-7756. Sisters 2. ISL, P.O. Box 53147, Chicago, IL, 60653-0147. Tel: 773-324-3321. Sr. Eileen Barrett, (Sept.-June), Mt. St. Joseph Convent West Indies, 82 Manchester Rd., Mandeville P.O., Manchester, Jamaica. Tel: 809-962-2170; Fax: 809-963-0135. Sr. Anne Chester, (Sept.-April), 1100 39th St., #214, Sacramento, 95816-5527. Tel: 916-457-5509. Sr. Teresa Gahan, Franciscan Center, 1784 LaCross Ave., St. Paul, MN, 55119-4808. Tel: 612-739-7953. Sr. Mary Corita Keane, (Sept.-May), Sisters of Mercy, 800 41st St., Sacramento, 95819. Tel: 916-454-3658. Sisters 2. P.O. Box 162791, Sacramento, 95816. Tel: 916-373-9563. Sr. Anna Marie Sliman, P.O. Box 1522, Mt. Shasta, 96067-9510. Tel: 916-926-6644. Sr. Mary Virginia Sullivan, 1180 Matmore Rd., #32, Woodland, 95776-6341. Tel: 916-662-6840. Sr. Sally Dominic Torres, 4740 Appian Way, #10, El Sobrante, 94803. Tel: 510-222-8415. Sr. Frances Walshe.

CARMICHAEL. *Dominican Sisters*, 8633 Fair Oaks Blvd., #30, 95608-2592. Congregation of the Most Holy Rosary, Sinsinawa, WI. Sisters 2.
Religious of the Institute of the Blessed Virgin Mary, Assumption Convent, 5055 Cottage Way, 95608. Tel: 916-488-8188. Sisters 5.
Other Locations: 3606 Chadsworth Way, Sacramento, 95821. Tel: 916-485-6384. Sisters 4.

DAVIS. *Society of the Sacred Heart*, 406 E. Eighth St., 95616. Tel: 916-753-8344.

FAIR OAKS. *Sisters of Mercy*, St. Mel's Convent, P.O. Box 1180, 95628. Tel: 916-967-9504. Sisters 3.

FAIRFIELD. *Sisters of the Holy Faith*, Holy Spirit Convent, 1050 N. Texas St., 94533. Tel: 707-425-3572. Sisters 5.

GEORGETOWN. *Discalced Carmelite Nuns*, P.O. Box 1720, 95634. Tel: 916-333-1617. Carmel of the Holy Family. Sisters 16.

MARYSVILLE. *Sisters of St. Mary of Oregon*, Our Lady of the Lake Conent, 1801 Ellis Lake Dr., #173, 95901. St. Mary of Oregon, 4440 S.W. 148th Ave., Beaverton, OR, 97007.

PLACERVILLE. *Franciscan Sisters of the Atonement*, St. Patrick's Convent, 3122 Sacramento St., 95667. Tel: 916-622-1983.

POLLOCK PINES. *Ursuline Sisters*, 6305 Sierra Springs Dr., 95726. Tel: 916-644-3319.

WEST SACRAMENTO. *Daughters of the Holy Spirit*, Our Lady of Grace Convent, 1990 Linden Rd., 95691. Tel: 916-371-9715. Sisters 2; Total Staff 5; Total Assisted 60.

[J] RETREAT HOUSES

SACRAMENTO. *Pendola Center*, 2110 Broadway, 95818-2541. Tel: 916-733-0123. Center located in Sierra-Nevada foothills near Camptonville. Summer camp for boys and girls 7-16. Available for teenage and young adult retreats, school midweek retreats, field trips. Contact: Stephen Tholcke, Dir. of Pendola Center, Dept. of Catholic Faith Formation.

APPLEGATE. *Our Lady of the Oaks Villa*, P.O. Box 128, 95703. Tel: 916-878-2776. For Jesuit Fathers, Brothers and Scholastics. Rev. Philip P. Callaghan, S.J., Priest in charge, Res. University of San Francisco, 2130 Fulton St., San Francisco, 94117. Tel: 415-666-6940.

AUBURN. *Marian Retreat Center*, 535 Sacramento St., 95603. Tel: 916-887-2019. Sr. Katherine Doyle, R.S.M., Dir.

CITRUS HEIGHTS. *Christ the King Retreat Center*, 6520 Van Maren Ln., 95621. Tel: 916-969-4706. Rev. Joseph O. Mitchell, C.P., Dir. Associate Directors: Revs. Raymond McDonough, C.P.; Donald Webber, C.P.; Bro. Carl Hund; Mr. Thomas Borkowski, Admin.

[K] CAMPUS MINISTRIES AND NEWMAN CENTERS

CHICO. *Director of Campus Ministry*, 346 Cherry St., 95928. Tel: 916-342-5180; Fax: 916-342-3016. Rev. Michael J. Newman, S.D.S.
California State University (Sacramento), Newman Catholic Community. Rev. D. Joseph McCarthy, Dir., 5900 Newman Ct., Sacramento, 95819. Ms. Mary Ann Williams, Admin. Asst., Tel: 916-454-4198; Fax: 916-454-4180.
California State University (Chico), Newman Catholic Community. Rev. Michael J. Newman, S.D.S., Diocesan Dir. of Campus Ministry; Ms. Marge Flynn, Sec., 346 Cherry St., 95928. Tel: 916-342-5180; Fax: 916-342-3016.
University of California (Davis), Newman Catholic Community, 514 C St., Davis, 95616. Tel: 916-753-7393; Fax: 916-753-2794. Co-Directors: Rev. Liam MacCarthy; Sr. Mary Pat White, R.S.C.J.; Ms. Cyndi Smit, Sec.

[L] CATHOLIC SOCIAL WELFARE ACTIVITIES

SACRAMENTO. *Catholic Charities of Sacramento, Inc.* Diocese of Sacramento. 5890 Newman Ct., 95819. Roman Catholic Bishop of Sacramento, a Corporation Sole. Rev. Edward J. Lewis, Pres. of the Bd.
Adult Reading Program, 3300 3rd Ave., 95817. Tel: 916-456-7323.
Clothing Program, 3333 Third Ave., 95817.
Food Distribution Center Program, 3333 Third Ave., 95817. Tel: 916-456-1980.
Homeless Haven (Transitional Housing Program), 3333 Third Ave., 95817. Tel: 916-456-1980.
Mother-Baby Program, 3333 Third Ave., 95817. Tel: 916-456-1980.
Sacramento Food Bank Services, Inc., 3333 Third Ave., 95817. Tel: 916-456-1980; 452-3663.
Catholic Social Service, Sacramento, Central Office, 5890 Newman Ct., 95819. Tel: 916-452-7481. Richard Mata, Pres., Bd. of Dirs.; Adrienne F. Rogers, Exec. Dir.
Sacramento, Camellia City Senior Center, 1121 - Ninth St., 95814. Tel: 916-442-9014. Denise Nelson, Center Dir. Day Center, In-Home Visiting, Money management program, meals, housing assistance, health screening, information and referral.
Sacramento, Counseling Services, School-Based Counseling Program, 8928 Volunteer Ln., Ste. 230, 95826. Robert Carvalho-Lehman, L.C.S.W., Dir., Counseling Dept. Tel: 916-368-3260.
Sacramento, Centro Guadalupe. Advocacy, Information and Referral, Licensed Bilingual Counseling, Bilingual Food Closet, Parenting Classes, Community Pals, Employment Assistance, Adult Homeless Education Program. Sylvia Villalobos, Center Dir., 730 S St., 95814. Tel: 916-443-5367.
Refugee Resettlement Services, 5890 Newman Ct., 95819. Tel: 916-452-1445. Cau Lao, Refugee Dept. Dir.
Immigration Services & Citizenship Dept., 5890 Newman Ct., 95819. Tel: 916-452-7481. Adela Avila, Program Dir. Total Staff 50; Total Assisted 110,337
Mercy Education Resource Center, 6007 Folsom Blvd. #200, 95819. Tel: 916-737-6026. Sponsored by the Sisters of Mercy Auburn Regional Community. Provides Marriage counseling and individual counseling, and psycho-educational assessment. Sr. Anne Sekul, R.S.M., Dir.
Mercy/Charities Housing California, 10540 White Rock Rd., Ste. 135, 95670. Tel: 916-851-2034; Fax: 916-851-2076. Sr. Mary Monica Burns, R.S.M. Provides potentially homeless or otherwise disadvantaged persons with housing facilities and supportive services especially designed to meet their physical, social and psychological needs.
Housing developments also located in San Francisco, San Rafael, San Jose, Santa Cruz, Red Bluff, Fairfax, Daly City, Mill Valley and Belmont.
Society of St. Vincent de Paul, Sacramento District Council, 95609-0564. Mailing Address: P.O. Box 564, Carmichael, 95609-0564. Main Office: 2620 Fulton Ave., 95821. Tel: 916-972-1253. Mr. George Lukoskie, Pres.
St. Vincent de Paul Thrift Store, 2620 Fulton Ave., 95821. Tel: 916-972-1212. Mr. Arturo Guerro, Mgr.

CHICO. *Grand Council, Catholic Ladies Relief Society of the Sacramento Diocese*, 2581 California Park Dr., #111, 95928. Mrs. Betty Cichrillo, Pres.

REDDING. *Northern Valley Catholic Social Service*, 1733 Oregon St., 96001. Tel: 916-241-0552. Jan Mauer Watkins, Exec. Dir. Foster family agency; adolescent family life programs; information and referral; counseling program; low-income housing program; independent living skills for foster youth; foster care education; HIV/AIDS program; Supported living services for developmentally disabled; and developmentally disabled housing.
Pine Street Place (Transitional Shelter).
Wilshire Place (Developmentally Disabled Housing).
Hartford Place (Developmentally Disabled Housing).
Offices: 1020 Market St., 96001. 1216 Sheridan Ave., Chico, 95926. 2445 Oroville Dam Blvd., Ste.5, Oroville, 95965.

ROSEVILLE. *Society of St. Vincent DePaul*, 139 Riverside, 95678. Tel: 916-781-3303; (dining room & thrift store) 781-3368; (food locker) 781-3335. Mr. Dave Sorensen, Pres.

VALLEJO. *Catholic Social Service of Solano County*, Central Office, 745 Georgia St., 94590. Tel: 707-644-8909. Mr. Faison C. Jordan, Jr., Exec. Dir. Sisters of Social Service 1; Lay Workers 11.
Outreach Offices: 2700 Dover Ave., Fairfield, 94533. Tel: 707-422-3466. 40 Eldrige Ave., Ste. 9A, Vacaville, 95688.
Society of St. Vincent de Paul Solano District Council, P.O. Box 931, 94590. Mr. Michael Hayes, Pres.

[M] YOUTH AND YOUNG ADULT MINISTRIES

SACRAMENTO. *Department of Catholic Faith Formation*, 2110 Broadway, 95818. Tel: 916-733-0123. Sr. Maura Power, R.S.M., Dir.; Linda Shumate, Asst. Admin. for Catechetics; Sr. Maria Padilla, R.S.M., Consultant, Hispanic Catechesis; Ms. Amanda Trujillo, Coord. Hispanic Youth/Young Adult Ministry; Mrs. Cheryl Tholcke, Coord. Youth Ministry; Mrs. Margaret Walrath, Consultant/Ministry to Deaf; Mr. Stephen Tholcke, Dir. Pendola Center; Mr. Robert Brenner, Coord. For The Ministry To Persons With Disabilitites.

ORANGEVALE. *Catholic Committee on Scouting*, 9079 Greenback Ln., 95662. Rev. Robert R. Marsicek, S.D.S., Diocesan Chap.

[N] CAMPS

SACRAMENTO. *Pendola Center*, Office, 2110 Broadway, 95818-2541. Tel: 916-733-0123; 736-3652; Fax: 916-733-0195. Located at Camptonville, Yuba County. Mr. Stephen F. Tholcke, Dir. Diocesan youth & young adult retreat center (September-April). Summer camp for boys and girls 7-16 (June, July, August). Outdoor school (September, October, November).

[O] MISSIONARY ORGANIZATIONS

SACRAMENTO. *Friends of Leprosy Patients*, P.O. Box 2655, 95812. National Headquarters. Most Rev. William K. Weigand, D.D., Ed.D., Bishop of Sacramento, Honorary Chm.; R.B. Roberts, Pres.

[P] MISCELLANEOUS

SACRAMENTO. *Catholic Charities of California, Inc.*, Cathedral Sq., 1010 11th St., Ste. 200, 95814. Tel: 916-443-4851; Fax: 916-443-4731. Mr. Frank Hudson, Pres.; Sr. Ray Monda DuVall, Vice Pres.; Rev. Msgr. Gregory A. Cox, Sec. & Treas.; Richard Mockler, Exec. Dir.
**Loaves & Fishes*, P.O. Box 2161, 95812.
Loaves & Fishes Dining Room, 1321 N. C St., 95812. Tel: 916-446-0874. LeRoy Chatfield, Exec. Dir.
Mustard Seed.
Brother Martin's Courtyard.
Maryhouse, 1321 N. C St., 95814. Tel: 916-446-4962. Joan Burke, Dir.
MercyClinic, 1321 N. C St., 95814. Tel: 916-446-3345.
Friendship Park, 1300 N. C St., 95814. Tel: 916-443-7378. Rev. Chris Hartmire.
**Stanford Settlement*, 450 W. El Camino, 95833-2299. Tel: 916-927-1303; Fax: 916-922-1694. Sr. Jeanne Felion, S.S.S., Dir. Assisted annually 10,000.

RELIGIOUS INSTITUTES OF MEN REPRESENTED IN THE DIOCESE

For further details refer to the corresponding bracketed number in the Religious Institutes of Men or Women section.

[]—*Assumptionist Fathers*.—A.A.
[0330]—*Brothers of the Christian Schools*. (Moraga, CA).—F.S.C.
[0270]—*Carmelite Fathers & Brothers*. (Barrington, IL).—O.Carm.
[0350]—*Cistercians Order of the Strict Observance-Trappists*.—O.C.S.O.
[0370]—*Columban Fathers*.—S.S.C.
[]—*Congregation of Mother Coredemptrix*.—C.M.C.
[1000]—*Congregation of the Passion*. (Chicago, IL).—C.P.
[0520]—*Franciscan Friars*. (Prov. of St. Barbara).—O.F.M.
[]—*Holy Ghost Fathers*.—C.S.Sp.
[0690]—*Jesuit Fathers and Brothers*. (California Prov., Los Gatos, CA).—S.J.
[0930]—*Oblates of St. Joseph*. (Santa Cruz, CA).—O.S.J.
[]—*Oblates of the Virgin Mary*.—O.M.V.
[0430]—*Order of Preachers-Dominicans*. (Oakland).—O.P.

[]—*St. Patrick Missionary Society*.—S.P.S.
[1200]—*Society of the Divine Savior*. (Milwaukee, WI).—S.D.S.
[]—*Society of the Most Holy Trinity*.—S.O.L.T.

RELIGIOUS INSTITUTES OF WOMEN REPRESENTED IN THE DIOCESE

[0130]—*Apostles of the Sacred Heart of Jesus*. (Hamden, CT).—A.S.C.J.
[3110]—*Congregation of Our Lady of the Retreat in the Cenacle*. (Chicago, IL).—R.C.
[1940]—*Congregation of the Sisters of the Holy Faith*.—C.H.F.
[0730]—*Daughters of Charity of Canossa*.—Fd.CC. (Rome, Italy).
[0820]—*Daughters of the Holy Spirit*. (Putnam, CT).—D.H.S.
[0420]—*Discalced Carmelite Nuns*.—O.C.D.
[1070-03]—*Dominican Sisters*. (Sinsinawa, WI).—O.P.
[1070-04]—*Dominican Sisters*. (San Rafael, CA).—O.P.
[1190]—*Franciscan Sisters of the Atonement*. (Garrison, NY).—S.A.
[2370]—*Institute of the Blessed Virgin Mary (Loretto Sisters)*.—I.B.V.M.
[2575]—*Institute of the Sisters of Mercy of the Americas*.—R.S.M.
[]—*Religious of the Virgin Mary*. (Quezon City, Philippines).—R.V.M.
[3499]—*Sister Servants of the Blessed Sacrament*.—S.S.B.S.
[]—*Sisters of Mercy of Cashel*.—R.S.M.
[4080]—*Sisters of Social Service of Los Angeles, Inc.*.—S.S.S.
[1630]—*Sisters of St. Francis of Penance and Christian Charity*. (Redwood City, CA).—O.S.F.
[]—*Sisters of St. Joseph of Carondelet*.—C.S.J.
[3960]—*Sisters of St. Mary of Oregon*.—S.S.M.O.
[1960]—*Sisters of the Holy Family*. (San Jose, CA).—S.H.F.
[]—*Sisters of the Holy Name of Jesus & Mary*.—S.N.J.M.
[]—*Sisters of the Holy Rosary of Fatima*. (Salvatierra, Mexico).—H.R.F.
[3680]—*Sisters of the Sacred Hearts of Jesus and Mary*. (Essex).—S.H.J.M.
[]—*Society of the Holy Child Jesus*.
[4070]—*Society of the Sacred Heart*.—R.S.C.J.
[3330]—*Union of the Sisters of the Presentation of the Blessed Virgin Mary*.—P.B.V.M.
[4110]—*Ursuline Nuns*.—O.S.U.

DIOCESAN CEMETERIES

SACRAMENTO. *St. Joseph*, 2615 21st St., 95818. Tel: 916-455-8324.
St. Mary's Cemetery & Mausoleum, 6700 21st Ave., 95820. Tel: 916-452-4831.

CITRUS HEIGHTS. *Calvary Cemetery & Mausoleum*, 7101 Verner Ave., P.O. Box 41303, 95841. Tel: 916-969-6541.

VALLEJO. *All Souls Cemetery & Mausoleum*, Glen Cove Rd., 94590. Tel: 707-644-5209.
St. Vincent, 550 Glen Cove Rd., 94590. Tel: 707-644-5209.

NECROLOGY

† Carney, John J., (Retired). —Died Dec. 12, 1996.

† Fagundes, Rev. Msgr. Valdemiro M., Rio Vista, CA, St. Elizabeth Parish. —Died Sept. 22, 1996.

† Lucas, Eugene, Rio Vista, CA, St. Joseph Parish. —Died Dec. 10, 1996.

Diocese of Saginaw

(Dioecesis Saginavensis)

Most Reverend

KENNETH E. UNTENER, S.T.D., D.D.

Bishop of Saginaw; ordained June 1, 1963; ordained and installed as Bishop of Saginaw November 24, 1980. *Res., 5800 Weiss St., Saginaw, MI, 48603-2799.*

ESTABLISHED FEBRUARY 26, 1938.

Square Miles 6,955.

Comprises the following Counties in the State of Michigan: Arenac, Bay, Clare, Gladwin, Gratiot, Huron, Isabella, Midland, Saginaw, Sanilac and Tuscola.

For legal titles of parishes and diocesan institutions, consult the Chancery Office.

Chancery: 5800 Weiss St., Saginaw, MI, 48603-2799. Tel.: 517-799-7910; Fax: 517-797-6670.

STATISTICAL OVERVIEW

Personnel	
Bishop	1
Priests: Diocesan Active in Diocese	85
Priests: Active Outside Diocese	4
Priests: Retired, Sick or Absent	33
Number of Diocesan Priests	122
Religious Priests in Diocese	15
Extern Priests in Diocese	5
Ordinations:	
Permanent Deacons in Diocese	14
Total Brothers	2
Total Sisters	146
Parishes	
Parishes	110
With Resident Pastor:	
Resident Diocesan Priests	77
Resident Religious Priests	8
Without Resident Pastor:	
Administered by Priests	13
Administered by Permanent Deacons	1
Administered by Women Religious	10
Administered by Lay People	1
Professional Ministry Personnel:	
Sisters	7
Lay Ministers	2
Welfare	
Catholic Hospitals	1
Total Assisted	123,402
Health Care Centers	1
Total Assisted	10,325
Homes for the Aged	1
Total Assisted	100
Residential Care of Children	3
Total Assisted	96
Day Care and Extended Day Care Centers	7
Total Assisted	138
Specialized Homes	1
Total Assisted	43
Special Centers for Social Services	5
Total Assisted	1,240
Educational	
Diocesan Students in Other Seminaries	4
Total Seminarians	4
High Schools, Diocesan and Parish	3
Total Students	1,014
Elementary Schools, Diocesan and Parish	32
Total Students	5,478
Catechesis/Religious Education:	
High School Students	3,257
Elementary Students	11,157
Total Students Under Catholic Instruction	20,910
Teachers in the Diocese:	
Sisters	20
Lay Teachers	335
Vital Statistics	
Receptions into the Church:	
Infant Baptism Totals	2,300
Adult Baptism Totals	257
Received into Full Communion	224
First Communions	2,136
Confirmations	3,934
Marriages:	
Catholic	653
Interfaith	332
Total Marriages	985
Deaths	1,621
Total Catholic Population	141,207
Total Population	685,532

Former Bishops—Most Rev. WILLIAM F. MURPHY, S.T.D., J.C.L., LL.D., ord. June 13, 1908; appt. first Bishop of Saginaw, March 17, 1938; cons. May 17, 1938; died Feb. 7, 1950.—Most Rev. STEPHEN S. WOZNICKI, D.D., second Bishop; ord. Dec. 22, 1917; appt. Titular Bishop of Pelte and Auxiliary Bishop of Detroit, Dec. 13, 1937; cons. Jan. 25, 1938; transferred to Saginaw, March 28, 1950 Assistant at the Pontifical Throne, Dec. 22, 1967; resigned and transferred to the Titular See of Tiava, Oct. 30, 1968; died Dec. 10, 1968.—Most Rev. FRANCIS F. REH, S.T.L., J.C.D., third Bishop; ord. Dec. 8, 1935; appt. Bishop of Charleston, June 4, 1962; cons. June 29, 1962; transferred to the Titular See of Macrinna in Maurentania; Rector Pontifical North American College in Rome, Sept. 5, 1964; transferred to Saginaw, Dec. 18, 1968; installed Feb. 26, 1969; retired April 29, 1980; died Nov. 14, 1994.

Delegate to Senior Priests—Rev. Msgr. EUGENE A. FORBES, P.A., S.T.L., J.C.D., *4699 S. 11 Mile Rd., Auburn, 48611-9535.* Tel: 517-662-6480.

Vicars General—Rev. JAMES F. GAVIT, J.C.D., *2120 Erie St., Saginaw, 48601-4497.* Tel: 517-753-3865. Rev. THOMAS E. SUTTON, *2711 Mackinaw St., Saginaw, 48602-3145.* Tel: 517-799-2334.

Episcopal Vicars—

Vicar for Hispanics—MARIA CEPEDA, Pastoral Minister, Coord., *Our Lady of Guadalupe Chapel & Center, 1619 Broadway, Bay City, 48708-8538.* Tel: 517-894-0661.

Vicar for Religious—Sr. JANET FULGENZI, O.P., Ph.D., *5800 Weiss St., Saginaw, 48603-2799.* Tel: 517-799-7910.

Vicar of Administration—Rev. THOMAS E. SUTTON, *c/o 5800 Weiss St., Saginaw, 48603-2799.*

Vicar for Canonical Affairs—Rev. JAMES F. GAVIT, J.C.D., *c/o 5800 Weiss St., Saginaw, 48603-2799.*

Vicars for Vicariates—Revs. ROBERT SHINE, Vicariate 1; MICHAEL DUNCKEL, Vicariate 2; WOLFGANG STREICHARDT, Vicariate 3; GEORGE SEROUR, Vicariate 4; FREDERICK J. KAWKA, Vicariate 5; JOHN SARGE, Vicariate 6; ROBERT H. BYRNE, Vicariate 7; JAMES HELLER, Vicariate 8; DONALD DUEWEKE, Vicariate 9; WILLIAM RUTKOWSKI, Vicariate 10; LEONARD WILKUSKI, Vicariate 11; THOMAS KOWALCZYK, Vicariate 12.

Chancery—5800 Weiss St., Saginaw, 48603-2799. Tel: 517-799-7910; Fax: 517-797-6670.

Chancellor—THOMAS P. SCHROEDER.

Administrative Assistant to the Chancellor—CONNIE HUISKENS.

Administrative Assistant to the Bishop—LEONA JONES.

Director of Finance—Mr. LEONARD A. MELESKI.

Administrative Assistant—BARBARA PINE.

General Accountant—MARY JANE TACEY.

Finance Council—THOMAS OUELLETTE, Chm.

Catholic Services Appeal—ADRIENNE JESCHKE, Coord., *5800 Weiss St., Saginaw, 48603-2799.* Tel: 517-799-7910.

Diocesan Building Commission—DICK RANKL, Chm., *5800 Weiss St., Saginaw, 48603-2799.* Tel: 517-799-7910.

Tribunal—5800 Weiss St., Saginaw, 48603-2799. Tel: 517-799-7910.

Judicial Vicar—Rev. RICHARD M. FILARY, J.C.L.

Defenders of the Bond—Very Rev. JAMES F. GAVIT, J.C.D.; Rev. ROBERT J. DELAND, J.C.L.

Judges—Revs. THOMAS E. SUTTON, J.C.L.; EUGENE A. FORBES, J.C.D.; ROBERT J. MEISSNER; ROBERT W. DAVEY, M.A.; RICHARD M. FILARY, J.C.L.

Promoter of Justice—Rev. JAMES F. GAVIT, J.C.D.

Notaries—NANCY HAHN LERCZAK; PATRICIA D. PRESTON.

Advocate—Rev. ROBERT W. DAVEY, M.A.

Diocesan Council—Sr. HONORA REMES, D.C., Chm., *5800 Weiss, Saginaw, 48603-2799.* Tel: 517-799-7910.

Diocesan Presbyteral Council—Rev. JAMES HELLER, Chm., *P.O. Box 1092, Bay City, 48706-1092.*

Diocesan Consultors—Revs. ROBERT S. GOHM; PETER J. GASPENY; JAMES HELLER; RANDY J. KELLY; ROBERT H. BYRNE; JACK HAMMER.

Clergy Personnel Board—Rev. WILLIAM TAYLOR, Chm., *1525 S. Washington, Saginaw, 48601-2895.* Tel: 517-755-8020.

Diocesan Council of Catholic Women—Mrs. BETTY LAFAVE, Pres., *754 Frank St., Caro, 48723.* Rev. DONALD J. EPPENBROCK, Moderator, *5366 Main St., Box 399, Lexington, 48450-0399.* Tel: 313-359-8101.

Office of Communication—Mrs. CATHERINE HAVEN, Dir., *5800 Weiss St., Saginaw, 48603-2799.* Tel: 517-797-6666.

Mission Office—Rev. ROBERT W. DAVEY, Dir. & Vicar for Missions; IRENE G. ALVA, Assoc. Dir., *5800 Weiss St., Saginaw, 48603-2799.* Tel: 517-797-6631.

Office of Education-Formation—Dr. MARIAN MIKOLAIZYK, Supt. of Schools, *5800 Weiss St., Saginaw, 48603-2799.* Tel: 517-797-6651. DANIEL GAST, Dir. Religious Education Formation; MARIAN MIKOLAIZYK, Schools Consultant.

Director of Family-Youth Ministry—PEGGY MCCOURTNEY.

Family Life Ministry—Refer to: Catholic Family Service, *5800 Weiss St., Saginaw, 48603-2799.* Tel: 517-797-6638.

Evangelization Ministry—Contact Office of Education.

Black Catholic Concerns—Mr. RICK NIX, *5800 Weiss St.,*

Saginaw, 48603-2799. Tel: 517-799-7910.

Ecumenism Ministry—Rev. GEORGE SEROUR, *8370 Unionville Rd., Sebewaing, 48759-9553.* Tel: 517-883-2746.

Ministry to Charismatic Renewal—MARGE FOBEAR, Dir., *Charismatic Renewal Center, 127 N. Warren St., P.O. Box 1287, Saginaw, 48606-1287.* Tel: 517-754-9351.

Ministry to Priests—Rev. ROBERT S. GOHM,Saginaw Diocesan Center, *5800 Weiss St., Saginaw, 48603-2799.* Tel: 517-799-7910.

Office of Church Ministries—Rev. ROBERT S. GOHM, Dir. of Church Ministries Office, Ministry to Priests Program, Continuing Education for Priests; Rev. THOMAS MOORE, O.S.F.S., Dir. Seminarians & Vocation Dir.; Sr. ROBERTA KOLASA, S.J., Dir., Diocesan Ministries Institute; Sr. JOSEPHINE GAUGIER, O.P., English Language Lay Ministry Program.

Office of Christian Service—CHRISTINE DOBY, Dir., *5800 Weiss St., Saginaw, 48603-2799.* Tel: 517-797-6672.

Office of Liturgy—MARY SELLARS MALLOY, Dir., *5800 Weiss St., Saginaw, 48603-2799.* Tel: 517-797-6664.

Catholic Family Services—THOMAS CONKLIN, Exec. Dir., *5800 Weiss St., Saginaw, 48603-2799.* Tel: 517-797-6636.

Saginaw Counseling Center—THOMAS CONKLIN, Dir., *710 N. Michigan Ave., Saginaw, 48602-4372.* Tel: 517-753-8446.

Bad Axe Counseling Center—123 Scott St., Bad Axe, 48413-1329. Tel: 517-269-7931.

Bay City Counseling Center—512 N. Lincoln St., Bay City, 48708-6615. Tel: 517-892-2504.

Midland Counseling Center—220 W. Main St., Midland, 48640-5165. Tel: 517-631-4711.

Mt. Pleasant Counseling Center—120 S. University St., Mt. Pleasant, 48858-2305. Tel: 517-773-9328.

Caro Counseling Center—124 E. Burnside St., Caro, 48723-1213. Tel: 517-673-5352.

Sandusky Counseling Center—119 E. Sanilac, Sandusky, 48471-1147. Tel: 810-648-2304.

Latin American Affairs Department—Mr. GILBERTO GUEVARA, Dir., *405 Hayes St., Saginaw, 48602.* Tel: 517-755-4477.

St. Francis Home (for elderly)—Sr. JANE MARIE LEBIEDZINSKI, C.S.S.F., Admin., *915 N. River Rd., 48609-6865.* Tel: 517-781-3150.

St. Vincent Home-Boysville of Michigan (for children)—Mr. RICK L. BOONE, M.S.W., North Reg. Dir., *925 N. River Rd., 48609-6866.* Tel: 517-781-0490.

St. Vincent de Paul Store—Mr. THOMAS M. SCHREMS, Mgr., *122 S. Hamilton St., Saginaw, 48602-2013.* Tel: 517-793-9585.

Organizations and Services—

Association of Saginaw Priests—Rev. JOHN A. EDERER, Pres., *2168 N. Winn Rd., Mt. Pleasant, 48858-9730.*

Catholic Cemeteries—Mr. JOSEPH LUGHERMO, Dir., *5800 Weiss St., Saginaw, 48603-2799.* Tel: 517-797-6627.

Catholic Newspaper—KATHLEEN A. SOCHA, Editor, *1520 Court St., P.O. Box 1405, Saginaw, 48605-1405.* Tel: 517-793-7661.

Censor—Rev. Msgr. FRANCIS J. MURRAY, *5965 W. Michigan Ave., Saginaw, 48603-7500.* Tel: 517-791-5002.

Clergy Benefit Society—Rev. ROBERT BYRNE, *1035 N. River Rd., Saginaw, 48609-6864.* Tel: 517-868-4081.

Conciliation-Arbitration—Mr. PATRICK KALTENBACH, Conciliation Clerk, *8th Fl., Second Natl. Bank, Saginaw, 48607.* Tel: 517-753-3461.

Holy Childhood Association—Rev. ROBERT W. DAVEY, *5800 Weiss St., Saginaw, 48603-2799.*

Marriage Encounter—Rev. JOSEPH A. SCHABEL, Spiritual Dir. Tel: 517-753-8446.

St. Vincent de Paul Society—Mr. DONALD RUBIS, Pres., *523 Michigan Ave., Bay City, 48708.* Tel: 517-893-5772.

Office of Stewardship/Development—ANNETTE O'BRIEN, *5800 Weiss St., Saginaw, 48603-2799.* Tel: 517-797-6679.

CLERGY, PARISHES, MISSIONS AND PAROCHIAL SCHOOLS

CITY OF SAGINAW
(Saginaw County)

1—ST. MARY CATHEDRAL (1853), Sr. Honora Remes, D.C., Pastoral Admin.; Rev. Robert Gohm.
Res., 615 Hoyt Ave., 48607-1713. Tel: 517-752-8119; Fax: 517-752-2165. [CEM]

2—HOLY FAMILY, Rev. William R. Taylor. In res., Rev. Robert Gohm.
Res., 1525 S. Washington Ave., 48601-2895. Tel: 517-755-8020. [CEM]

3—HOLY ROSARY. Closed. For inquiries for parish records contact the Chancery.

4—SS. SIMON AND JUDE, Rev. Robert Schramm, O.S.F.S.; Sr. Teresita Weind, S.N.D.deN., Pastoral Assoc. In res., Revs. John S. Mancini, O.S.F.S.; Thomas M. Moore, O.S.F.S.
Res., 2395 S. Outer Dr., 48601-6643. Tel: 517-752-7424; Fax: 517-753-8601.

5—OUR LADY HELP OF CHRISTIANS. Closed. For inquiries for parish records contact the Chancery.

6—OUR LADY OF MOUNT CARMEL. Closed. For inquiries for parish records contact the Chancery.

7—SACRED HEART. Closed. For inquiries for parish records contact the Chancery.

8—ST. ANDREW, Rev. Donald L. Christensen.
Res., 612 N. Michigan Ave., 48602-4387. Tel: 517-754-0487; Fax: 517-754-0308.

9—ST. ANTHONY OF PADUA, Rev. Walter Balduck, O.F.M.Cap. In res., Rev. Art Cooney, O.F.M.Cap.
Res., 3680 S. Washington Rd., 48601-4997. Tel: 517-752-1971; Fax: 517-752-1441. [JC]

10—ST. CASIMIR, Rev. John S. Sarge.
Res., 2122 S. Jefferson Ave., 48601-3498. Tel: 517-752-6648; Fax: 517-752-6691. [JC]

11—ST. GEORGE, Rev. John S. Sarge; Nanette Navarre, Pastoral Assoc.
Res., 2120 Erie St., 48601-4497. Tel: 517-753-3865; Fax: 517-753-6903. [JC]

12—ST. HELEN, Rev. Robert J. Meissner.
Res., 2445 N. Charles St., 48602-5096. Tel: 517-793-0618; Fax: 517-793-5487. [JC]
School—Sr. Corinne Weiss, S.J., Prin. Servants of Jesus 1; Lay Teachers 11; Students 313.

13—ST. JOHN VIANNEY, Rev. Dale A. Orlik.
Church—6400 McCarty Rd., 48603-9621. Tel: 517-790-5086.
Res., 6228 Wild Oak Dr., 48603-1059. Tel: 517-792-6582; Fax: 517-790-1681.

14—ST. JOSEPH, Rev. Daniel Anholzer, O.F.M.Cap.
Res., 910 N. Sixth Ave., 48601-1103. Tel: 517-753-4418.
Convent—903 N. Seventh St., 48601. Tel: 517-752-5470.
Sisters 6.

15—SS. PETER AND PAUL, Rev. Robert J. DeLand; Sr. Janet Brown, O.P., Pastoral Assoc.
Res., 4735 W. Michigan Ave., 48603-6370. Tel: 517-799-5448; Fax: 517-799-1495.
School—Sr. Anne Breitag, O.P., Prin. Sisters 1; Lay Teachers 10; Students 201.

16—ST. RITA. Closed. For inquiries for parish records contact the Chancery.

17—ST. STEPHEN, Revs. Patrick Jankowiak; Thomas E. Sutton.
Res., 2711 Mackinaw St., 48602-3146. Tel: 517-799-2334; Fax: 517-793-3611.
School—Barbara Geary, Prin. Sisters 3; Lay Teachers 16; Students 502.

18—ST. THOMAS AQUINAS, Revs. Robert Konopa, O.F.M.; Leonard Stunek, O.F.M.
Res., 5376 State Rd., 48603-3771. Tel: 517-799-2460; Fax: 517-799-2464. [JC]
School—Bernardine Sisters of Third Order of St. Francis. (Farmington, MI). Sr. Ann De Guise, O.S.F., Prin.
Sisters 3; Lay Teachers 16; Students 478.

OUTSIDE THE CITY OF SAGINAW

Albee, Saginaw Co., St. Mary, Rev. Kenneth E. Yaroch.
Res., 5661 Fergus Rd., Rte. 2, St. Charles, 48655-9624. Tel: 517-770-4453.

Alma, Gratiot Co., St. Mary, Rev. David Parsch.
Res., 517 N. Prospect Ave., 48801-1694. Tel: 517-463-5370; Fax: 517-463-8297.
School—220 W. Downie St., 48801. Tel: 517-463-4579. Mrs. Mary Jo Fachting, Prin.
Lay Teachers 7; Students 239.

Argyle, Sanilac Co., St. Joseph, Rev. Msgr. William J. Gruden.
Res., 4960 N. Ubly Rd., 48410-0007. Tel: 517-658-8145; Fax: 517-658-8105. [CEM]
Mission—Freiburg, Sanilac Co., St. Ignatius.

Auburn, Bay Co., St. Joseph, Rev. Charles H. O'Neil.
Res., 84 W. Midland Rd., P.O. Box 34, 48611-0034. Tel: 517-662-6861; Fax: 517-662-0064.
School—Area School. Sr. Lucy Ann Quinn, Prin.

AuGres, Arenac Co., St. Mark, Rev. Noel T. Rudy.
Res., 415 S. Court St., 48703-9598. Tel: 517-876-7925; Fax: 517-876-7778.

Bad Axe, Huron Co., Sacred Heart, Rev. Jack J. Leipert.
Res., 311 Whitelam St., 48413-1205. Tel: 515-269-7729; Fax: 517-269-4010. [CEM]

Bannister, Gratiot Co., St. Cyril, Rev. R.K. LeFleur.
Res., 517 E. Main St., 48807-9762. Tel: 517-862-5270; Fax: 517-862-4534.

Bay City, Bay Co.,

1—HOLY TRINITY, Rev. Patrick C. O Connor.
Res., 1008 S. Wenona Ave., 48706-5094. Tel: 517-893-4073; Fax: 517-893-7087.
School—Tel: 517-892-3018. Sally Preston, Prin.
Lay Teachers 6; Students 159.

2—ST. BONIFACE, Rev. James W. Bessert.
Res., 510 N. Lincoln Ave., 48708-6694. Tel: 517-893-4851; Fax: 517-893-1781.

3—ST. HEDWIG, Rev. Richard M. Filary.
Res., 1504 S. Kiesel, 48706-5240. Tel: 517-893-1072; Fax: 517-893-4710.

4—ST. HYACINTH, Rev. Gerald F. Kukla.
Res., 1515 Cass Ave., 48708-8740. Tel: 517-895-5581; Fax: 517-895-5583. [CEM]
School—Sr. Alice Ann Gradowski, C.S.S.F., Prin. Felician Sisters (Livonia, MI) 2; Lay Teachers 3; Students 83.
Convent—1507 Michigan Ave., 48708.

5—ST. JAMES, (1983), Rev. Peter J. Gaspeny.
Res., 710 Columbus Ave., 48708-6483. Tel: 517-893-4693; Fax: 517-893-1504. [CEM]
School—Sr. Maureen Donovan, S.C., Prin. Sisters of Charity of Cincinnati, OH 3; Lay Teachers 5; Students 230.
Convent—200 S. Farragut St., 48708.

6—ST. JOSEPH, Rev. Raymond S. Fron.
Res., 1005 Third St., 48708-6006. Tel: 517-895-5783; Fax: 517-895-8837.

7—ST. MARIA GORETTI, Rev. James F. Gavit.
Res., 2872 N. Euclid Rd., 48706-1342. Tel: 517-684-1523; Fax: 517-684-8286.

8—ST. MARY, Rev. James Heller.
Res., 501 N. Walnut St., P.O. Box 1092, 48706-1092. Tel: 517-892-6031; Fax: 517-892-4005.

9—ST. STANISLAUS, Revs. Loren M. Kalinowski; Francis Arthur, O.F.M.
Res., 1503 Kosciuszko Ave., Ste. 100, 48708-8027. Tel: 517-893-6421; Fax: 517-893-3985.
School—Sr. Mary Elise Milostan, C.S.S.F., Prin. Felician Sisters (Livonia, MI) 2; Lay Teachers 3; Students 148.

10—ST. VINCENT DE PAUL, Rev. James Fitzpatrick.
Res., 4505 Two Mile Rd., 48706-2799. Tel: 517-684-1170; Fax: 517-684-4925.

11—OUR LADY OF GUADALUPE CHAPEL AND CENTER, Mrs. Maria Cepeda, Vicar for Hispanics.
Res., 1619 Broadway, 48708-8538. Tel: 517-894-0661.

12—OUR LADY OF THE VISITATION, Rev. Emmett L. Marceau.
Res., 1106 State St., 48706-3697. Tel: 517-684-5184; Fax: 517-684-5189.
School—Visitation Academy, 1110 State St., 48706. John Leaman, Prin.
Sisters 1; Lay Teachers 3; Students 80.

Beal City, Isabella Co., St. Joseph the Worker, Rev. John F. Cotter.
Res., 2163 N. Winn Rd., Mt. Pleasant, 48858-9730. Tel: 517-644-2041; Fax: 517-644-2026. [CEM]
School—Sr. Jean Birkman, O.P., Prin. Sisters 1; Lay Teachers 5; Students 126.

Beaver, Bay Co., St. Valentine, Rev. Richard C. Ratajczak.
Res., 999 S. 9 Mile Rd., Kawkawlin, 48631-9756. Tel: 517-662-6843. [CEM]
School—1010 S. 9 Mile Rd., Kawkawlin, 48631. Tel: 517-662-6966; Fax: 517-662-0152.
Felician Sisters (Livonia, MI) 1; Lay Teachers 2; Students 63.

Birch Run, Saginaw Co., Sacred Heart, Rev. Mason L. Vaughn.
Res., 12157 Church St., 48415-8706. Tel: 517-624-9098; Fax: 517-624-9427.

Bridgeport, Saginaw Co., Assumption of the Blessed Virgin Mary, Rev. Daniel Nowak, O.F.M.
Res., 7945 Bell Rd., P.O. Box 602, 48722-0602. Tel: 517-777-1200; Fax: 517-777-6280.
St. Christopher, Rev. Robert W. Davey.
Res., 3926 Williamson Rd., Saginaw, 48601-5839. Tel: 517-777-2605; Fax: 517-777-9691.

Caro, Tuscola Co., Sacred Heart, Rev. Michael J. Bell.
Res., 140 Atwood, 48723-1742. Tel: 517-673-2346. [CEM]
Convent—919 W. Frank St., 48723. Tel: 517-673-7813.

Carrollton, Saginaw Co., St. John the Baptist, Rev. J.J. Fleming; Sr. Virginia Scally, S.N.D.deN., Pastoral Admin.
Res., 545 Maple Ridge, P.O. Box 248, 48724-0248. Tel: 517-752-9350; Fax: 517-753-4943.
St. Josaphat, Rev. Richard E. Jozwiak.
Res., 469 Shattuck Rd., Saginaw, 48604-2391. Tel:

517-753-2497; Fax: 517-753-2498.
School—Betty MacArthur, Prin. Lay Teachers 9; Students 221.

Caseville, Huron Co., St. Roch, Rev. Dennis Kucharczyk.
Res., 6253 Main St., 48725. Tel: 517-856-4933.

Cass City, Tuscola Co., St. Pancratius, Rev. Paul W. Bala.
Res., 4292 S. Seeger St., 48726-1423. Tel: 517-872-3336; Fax: 517-872-1852.

Chesaning, Saginaw Co., Our Lady of Perpetual Help, Rev. Joseph M. Griffin.
Res., 404 S. Wood, 48616-1399. Tel: 517-845-6894; Fax: 517-845-7787. [CEM]
School—802 Lockwood St., 48616. Carol Klemko, Prin.
Lay Teachers 8; Students 143.

Clare, Clare Co., St. Cecilia, Rev. Joseph Ryan.
Res., 902 N. McEwan St., 48617-1297. Tel: 517-386-7681. [CEM]
School—Pam Dickerson, Prin. Lay Teachers 4; Students 109.

Coleman, Midland Co., St. Philip Neri, Rev. John Mullet.
Res., 5199 W. Shaffer Rd., P.O. Box M, 48618-0512. Tel: 517-465-1768; Fax: 517-465-6311.
Mission—Edenville, Gladwin Co., St. Anne.

Croswell, Sanilac Co., St. Patrick, Rev. Wolfgang Streichardt.
Res., 105 W. Sanborn Ave., 48422-1399. Tel: 810-679-3849; Fax: 810-679-3903. [CEM]
Mission—Peck, Sanilac Co., St. John. [CEM]

Essexville, Bay Co., St. John the Evangelist, Rev. John F. Gentner. In res., Rev. Msgr. Olin J. Murdick; Rev. Michael H. Wolf.
Res., 1600 Hudson St., 48732-1377. Tel: 517-892-1893; Fax: 517-894-5558.
School—619 Main St., 48732. Sue Grzegorczyk, Prin.
Sisters 1; Lay Teachers 6; Students 120.

Fisherville, Bay Co., St. Anthony, Rev. Msgr. Eugene A. Forbes, J.C.D., V.G., P.A.
Res., 4699 S. 11 Mile Rd., Auburn, 48611-9535. Tel: 517-662-6480; Fax: 517-662-4335. [CEM]
School—Auburn Area Catholic, West Campus, 1492 W. Midland Rd., Auburn, 48611-9560. Tel: 517-662-6581; Fax: 517-662-4335.

Frankenmuth, Saginaw Co., Blessed Trinity, Rev. Frederick J. Kawka.
Res., 958 E. Tuscola Rd., 48734-9770. Tel: 517-652-3259; Fax: 517-652-2206.

Freeland, Saginaw Co., St. Agnes, Rev. Lawrence M. Pashak.
Res., 335 Johnson, 48623-9006. Tel: 517-695-5652; Fax: 517-695-6275.

Gagetown, Tuscola Co., St. Agatha, Rev. George Serour, Sacramental Min.; Sr. Joan Maher, M.Ss.P., Admin.
Res., 4618 South St., Box 139, 48735-0139. Tel: 517-665-9966.

Gladwin, Gladwin Co., Sacred Heart, Rev. Julius A. Spleet.
Res., 300 N. Silverleaf St., 48624-1697. Tel: 517-426-7154; Fax: 517-426-0896.
School—Sr. Mary Elizabeth Klier, O.S.F., Prin.
Bernardine Sisters of Third Order of St. Francis (Farmington, MI) 2; Lay Teachers 3; Students 117.

Harbor Beach, Huron Co., Our Lady of Lake Huron, Rev. Edward J. Konieczka; Sr. Eileen Houlihan, I.H.M., Pastoral Assoc.
Res., 413 S. First St., 48441-1325. Tel: 517-479-3393. [CEM]
School—Mr. Lawrence E. Kish, II, Prin. Lay Teachers 7; Students 170.
Convent—406 S. First St., 48441.

Harrison, Clare Co., St. Athanasius, Rev. Stephen J. Fillion.
Res., 1010 Byfield Dr., P.O. Box 528, 48625-0528. Tel: 517-539-6232.

Helena, Huron Co., St. Anthony, Rev. Michael G. Dunckel.
Res., 4190 Parisville Rd., Ruth, 48470-9759. Tel: 517-479-6781. [CEM]

Hemlock, Saginaw Co., St. Mary, Rev. James Krasman, O.F.M.
Res., 151 St. Mary's Dr., 48626-9614. Tel: 517-642-5606; Fax: 517-642-5240. [CEM]
St. Mary Center—245 St. Mary's Dr., 48626.

Ithaca, Gratiot Co., St. Paul the Apostle, Rev. John F. Ederer.
Res., 621 E. Center St., 48847-1596. Tel: 517-875-3654.
Mission—Perrinton, Gratiot Co., St. Martin De Porres.

Kawkawlin, Bay Co., Sacred Heart, Rev. Chester J. Pilarski.
Res., 2510 S. Fraser Rd., 48631-9115. Tel: 517-684-1402; Fax: 517-684-0038.

Kinde, Huron Co., St. Mary-St. Edward, Rev. Kevin Kerbawy.
Res., 1709 Moeller Rd., P.O. Box 68, 48445-0068. Tel: 517-874-4744.

Lexington, Sanilac Co., St. Denis, Rev. Donald J. Eppenbrock.
Res., 5366 Main St., P.O. Box 399, 48450-0399. Tel: 810-359-5400; Fax: 810-359-5833. [CEM]

Linwood, Bay Co., St. Anne, Rev. Thomas M. Kowalczyk.
Res., 315 Center St., P.O. Box 397, 48634-0397. Tel: 517-697-4443.
School—Tel: 517-697-3100. Sr. Rose Ellen Dzwieleski, O.S.F., Prin.
Bernardine Sisters of Third Order of St. Francis (Farmington, MI) 3; Lay Teachers 6; Students 171.

Maple Grove, Saginaw Co., St. Michael, Rev. Donald G. Dueweke.
Res., 17994 Lincoln Rd., New Lothrop, 48460-9600. Tel: 517-845-7011; Fax: 517-845-4729. [CEM]

Marlette, Sanilac Co., St. Elizabeth, Rev. Richard Bokinskie.
Res., 6785 W. Marlette St., 48453-1296. Tel: 517-635-7581; Fax: 517-635-5808.

Mayville, Tuscola Co., St. Joseph, Rev. Richard Bokinskie.
Mailing Address: 315 Wohmer Rd., P.O. Box 283, 48744-0283.

Merrill, Saginaw Co., Sacred Heart, Rev. John J. Thome.
Res., 419 S. Midland St., 48637-0099. Tel: 517-643-5366. [CEM]

Midland, Midland Co., Assumption Blessed Virgin Mary, Rev. Henry P. DuRussel.
Res., 3516 Monroe, Rd. 8, 48642. Tel: 517-631-4447; Fax: 517-631-4323.

Blessed Sacrament, Revs. John R. Johnson; Robert J. Howe.
Res., 3109 Swede Ave., 48642-3888. Tel: 517-835-6777; Fax: 517-835-2451.
School—Brian Frankovich, Prin. Lay Teachers 12; Students 249.

St. Brigid, Rev. Leonard F. Wilkuski.
Res., 207 Ashman St., 48640-5185. Tel: 517-835-7121; Fax: 517-835-9141.
School—130 W. Larkin St., 48640-6579. Tel: 517-835-9481; Fax: 517-835-9141. Christine Szatkowski, Prin.
Lay Teachers 7; Students 141.

Mount Pleasant, Isabella Co., Sacred Heart, Revs. Thomas J. McNamara; Craig Albrecht; Joseph F. Favara. In res., Rev. Donald E. Henkes (MEM).
Res., 302 S. Kinney, 48858-2773. Tel: 517-772-1385; Fax: 517-773-9118. [CEM]
School—(Grades PreK-6) 200 S. Franklin St., 48858-2529. Suzanne Hovey, Prin.
Sisters 1; Lay Teachers 12; Students 314.
High School—Sacred Heart Academy, (Grades 7-12) 316 E. Michigan, 48858-2640. Tel: 517-772-1457.
Sisters 1; Lay Teachers 12; Students 306.

St. Mary University Parish, Rev. Jeffrey Donner.
Res., 1405 S. Washington, 48858-4280. Tel: 517-773-3931.

Munger, Bay Co., St. Norbert, Rev. James R. Carlson.
Res., 126 W. Munger Rd., 48747-9767. Tel: 517-659-2193; Fax: 517-659-3417.

Nine Mile, Bay Co., St. Mary, Rev. Joseph K. Miller.
Res., 739 W. Cody-Estey Rd., Pinconning, 48650-8925. Tel: 517-879-5596; Fax: 517-879-6151. [CEM]

Oakley, Saginaw Co., St. Michael, Rev. Xavier G. Goulet, O.F.M. Conv.
Res., Box 75, 48649-0075. Tel: 517-845-3545; Fax: 517-845-5499. [CEM]

Palms, Sanilac Co., St. Patrick, Rev. Ronald Wagner, Sacramental Min.; Sr. Theresa Carlow, S.N.D.deN., Pastoral Admin.
Res., 1801 Palms Rd., 48465. Tel: 810-376-4853.

Parisville, Huron Co., St. Mary, Rev. Michael G. Dunckel.
Res., 4190 Parisville Rd., Ruth, 48470-9759. Tel: 517-864-3523; Fax: 517-864-3164. [CEM]

Pigeon, Huron Co., St. Francis Borgia, Rev. Barney Janowicz.
Res., 25 Moeller St., Box U, 48755. Tel: 517-453-2151. [CEM]

Pinconning, Bay Co., St. Agnes, Rev. Joseph Miller, Sacramental Min.; Barbara J. Walker, Pastoral Admin.
Res., 216 E. Fifth St., P.O. Box 325, 48650-0325. Tel: 517-879-2151; Fax: 517-879-2151. [CEM]

St. Michael, Rev. Ramon Matuszewski.
Res., 225 Jennings St., 48650-9408. Tel: 517-879-2141; Fax: 517-879-6633.
School—Joan Turmell, Prin. Lay Teachers 10; Students 156.

Pinnebog, Huron Co., St. Felix, Rev. Dennis Kucharczyk, Sacramental Min.; Sr. Mary Schwartz, S.S.J., Pastoral Min.
Res., 3515 Limerick, Kinde, 48445-9723. Tel: 517-874-5833. [CEM]

Port Austin, Huron Co., St. Michael, Rev. Robert W. Shine.
Res., 8637 Garfield, P.O. Box 298, 48467-0298. Tel: 517-738-7521; Fax: 517-738-5886. [CEM]
Parish Center—8661 Independence Ave., P.O. Box 350, 48467.

Port Sanilac, Sanilac Co., St. Mary, Rev. Ronald J. Dombrowski.
Res., 7066 W. Main St., P.O. Box 467, 48469-0467. Tel: 810-622-9904; Fax: 810-622-7953. [CEM]
Mission—Forestville, Sanilac Co., St. John Chrysostom.

Rapson, Huron Co., St. Joseph, Rev. John Weiss.
Res., 3455 Rapson Rd., Rt. 3, Bad Axe, 48413-9149. Tel: 517-269-8084. [CEM]
Mission—Smiths Corners, Hurenco Co., Holy Trinity. [CEM]

Reese, Tuscola Co., St. Elizabeth, Rev. James R. Carlson.
Res., 12835 E. Washington, 48757-9712. Tel: 517-868-4081. [CEM]
School—Robin Andress, Prin. Lay Teachers 5; Students 95.

Rosebush, Isabella Co., St. Henry, Sr. Ellen McDonald, O.P., Pastoral Admin.; Rev. Thomas J. McNamara, Sacramental Min.
Res., P.O. Box 67, 48878-0067. Tel: 517-433-2229. [CEM]
School—James Cardon, Prin. Lay Teachers 4; Students 69.
Mission—Leaton, Isabella Co., St. Charles.

Ruth, Huron Co., SS. Peter and Paul, Rev. Ronald F. Wagner.
Res., 7115 Atwater Dr., P.O. Box 55, 48470-0055. Tel: 517-864-3650. [CEM]
School—Richard Smith, Prin. Sisters 1; Lay Teachers 4; Students 116.

Ryan, Midland Co., St. Patrick, Sr. Elaine Raymond, M.S.S.P., Pastoral Admin.; Rev. John Thome, Sacramental Min.
Res., 4708 N. Meridian Rd., Rte. 2, Merrill, 48637-9546. Tel: 517-643-5652; Fax: 517-643-5652, Ext. 111. [CEM]

St. Charles, Saginaw Co., Immaculate Conception, Rev. Joseph J. Kearns.
Res., 708 Sanderson St., 48655-1895. Tel: 517-865-9460. [CEM]
School—H. Ross Klemko, Prin. Lay Teachers 4; Students 51.
Convent—712 Sanderson St., 48655. Tel: 517-865-6166.

St. Louis, Gratiot Co., St. Joseph, Rev. John E. Hammer.
Office: 605 S. Franklin, 48880-1747. Tel: 517-681-5080; Fax: 517-681-2887.
Res., 409 Butternut St., 48880-1747.
Mission—Irishtown, Gratiot Co., St. Patrick. [CEM]

Sandusky, Sanilac Co., St. Joseph, Rev. Stanislaus Surman.
Res., 511 N. Sandusky Rd., P.O. Box 249, 48471-0249. Tel: 810-648-2085.

Sanford, Midland Co., St. Agnes, Rev. Frank Voris, O.F.M.Cap.
Res., 2500 W. River Rd., 48657-9497. Tel: 517-687-5657; Fax: 517-687-2450.

Sebewaing, Huron Co., Holy Family, Rev. George J. Serour.
Res., 8370 Unionville Rd., 48759-9553. Tel: 517-883-2746; Fax: 517-883-2810. [CEM]

Shepherd, Isabella Co., St. Vincent De Paul, Rev. William J. Rutkowski, Admin.
Res., 168 Wright, 48883-9079. Tel: 517-828-5720. [CEM]
School—Gail Schmidt, Prin. Lay Teachers 4; Students 127.
Mission—Winn, Isabella Co., St. Leo. [CEM]

Shields, Saginaw Co., Holy Spirit, Rev. Robert H. Byrne.
Res., 1035 N. River Rd., Saginaw, 48609-6864. Tel: 517-781-2457; Fax: 517-781-5518.

Standish, Arenac Co., Resurrection of the Lord, Rev. Gerald E. Balwinski.
Res., 423 Cedar, Box 306, 48658-0306. Tel: 517-846-9565; Fax: 517-846-9566. [CEM]

Ubly, Huron Co., St. Columbkille, Rev. Randy Kelly.
Res., 4470 Washington St., 48475-9801. Tel: 517-658-8824; Fax: 517-658-2088. [CEM]

St. John the Evangelist, Rev. Randy Kelly.
Res., 4470 Washington St., 48475-9701. Tel: 517-658-8824; Fax: 517-658-2088. [CEM]

Vassar, Tuscola Co., St. Frances Xavier Cabrini, Rev. Richard T. Szafranski.
Res., 165 W. Maple St., 48768-1203. Tel: 517-823-2911; Fax: 517-823-2999.

Mission—Millington, Tuscola Co., St. Bernard.

Wilmot, Tuscola Co., St. Michael, Rev. Paul Bala.
Res., 1951 Kingston Rd., Deford, 48729. Tel: 517-683-2475; Fax: 517-683-2556. [CEM]

Zilwaukee, Saginaw Co., St. Matthew, Rev. Thomas J. Fleming.
Res., 511 W. Cornell, Saginaw, 48604-1311. Tel: 517-755-7336.

Chaplains of Public Institutions

BAY CITY. *Bay Medical Center and Bay Osteopathic Hospital,* 1201 S. Erie, 48706. Sr. Beth Pero, S.S.J.

On Duty Outside the Diocese:
Reverend Fathers—
Falsey, James E., P.O. Box 89, Nulato, AK 99765
Friske, Joseph P., Damaschkestr. 20, 8000 Munchen 82, Germany
Loos, Frederick C., Ave. Naucalpan #84, Col. La Canada, Naucalpan, Mexico, C.P. 53570
Sikorski, Harold R., Recife, Brazil

Military Chaplains:
Reverend Fathers—
Boucher, Edward, U.S.N.R, 508 Long Lake Dr., Pensacola, FL 32506

Retired:
Reverend Monsignors—
Murdick, Olin J.
Murray, Francis
Reverend Fathers—
Bauer, Joseph O.
Bur, Stanislaus
Eickholt, Henry C.
Favara, Joseph F.
Frego, Max
Ganley, Charles
Greiner, Lawrence
Hart, Harry J.
Hoogterp, John P.
Howard, T. Cyril
Klimas, George H.
Kryszak, Marian
LaMarre, Theodore E.
Maher, Michael L.
McEachin, Cornelius
Navarre, Robert G.
Rabideau, Richard L.
Roach, Joseph W.
Schabel, Joseph A.
Sierminski, Vernon
Skornia, Bernard L.
Torok, Bela E.
Trombley, J. Edward
Van Mullekom, Richard
Welna, Floyd
Welsmiller, Francis F.
Wolf, Michael H.
Woloszyk, Ignatius J.

Permanent Deacons:
Alder, David P., On Duty Outside the Diocese
Alex, Frank, St. Anne, Edenville; & St. Philip Neri, Coleman
Arnold, Michael, St. Valentine Church, Beaver
Belanger, Stanley, (Retired)
Belmer, Floyd, Holy Family Church, Saginaw
Cremin, John J., St. Mary, Alma
DeNeut, Gerard H., St. Matthew, Zilwaukee
Emmeot, Dale, Blessed Sacrament Church, Midland
Fussman, Lawrence, Sacred Heart Church, Mount Pleasant
Hudson, Francis W., St. Brigid, Midland
Jankowiak, Michael, Blessed Sacrament, Midland
Kasprzyk, David, On Duty Outside the Diocese
Kebblish, Edward, Assumption B.V.M., Midland
Keller, George, Bay County Jail Ministry
Kuhr, Lambert, Jr., (Retired), Out of the Diocese
Masserang, Lawrence, Blessed Trinity, Frankenmuth
Middleton, Allan, St. Cecilia, Clare
Moeggenberg, John, St. Brigio, Midland
Stilwell, Lee, St. Norbert, Munger
Wilberding, John, St. Vincent dePaul, Shepherd
Winkler, Frank, (Retired)

INSTITUTIONS LOCATED IN THE DIOCESE

[A] HIGH SCHOOLS, INTER-PAROCHIAL

SAGINAW. *Nouvel Catholic Central High School,* 2555 Wieneke Rd., 48603. Stanley DeVoir, Prin.; John Cuhbertson, Asst. Prin.; Sharon Jordan, Campus Min. Lay Teachers 32; Students 498.

BAY CITY. *All Saints Central High School,* 217 S. Monroe St., 48708; Fax: 517-892-7188. Thomas Grange, Prin. Felician Sisters 1; Lay Teachers 20; Students 210.

[B] MIDDLE SCHOOLS

BAY CITY. *Holy Family Middle School,* 1503 Kosciuszko Ave., Ste. 200, 48708. Tel: 517-892-8332. Barbara Rakowski, Prin.; Elizabeth Schwedler, Pastoral Counselor. Lay Teachers 10; Students 157.

[C] ELEMENTARY SCHOOLS, PRIVATE

SAGINAW. *Francis F. Reh Academy,* 2201 Owen St., 48601. Tel: 517-753-2349. Sr. Diane Hoffman, O.P., Prin. Religious 3; Lay Teachers 7; Students 173.

AUBURN. *Auburn Area Catholic Schools,* East Campus: 114 Midland Rd., 48611. Tel: 517-662-6431. West Campus: 1492 W. Midland Rd., 48611. Tel: 517-662-6581. Sr. Lucy Ann Quinn, O.P., Prin. Lay Teachers 7; Students 152.

[D] CHILDREN'S HOMES

SAGINAW. *St. Vincent Home-Boysville of Michigan, Inc.,* 925 N. River Rd., 48609. Tel: 517-781-2780; Fax: 517-781-5422.
For a complete listing, refer to the Special Care Facilities section.

[E] GENERAL HOSPITALS

SAGINAW. *St. Mary's Medical Center of Saginaw, Inc.,* 830 S. Jefferson Ave., 48601-2594.
For a complete listing, refer to the Hospitals section.

[F] HOMES FOR AGED

SAGINAW. *St. Francis Nursing Home,* 915 N. River Rd., 48609 Fax: 517-781-3791.
For a complete listing, refer to the Special Care Facilities section.

[G] MONASTERIES AND RESIDENCES OF PRIESTS AND BROTHERS

SAGINAW. *Queen of Angels Friary and Retreat House,* 3400 S. Washington Rd., P.O. Box 2026, 48605. Tel: 517-755-2149. Capuchin Friars of the Province of St. Joseph (Detroit) of the Capuchin Order of Friars Minor Capuchin.
Retreat Team: Revs. Robert Malloy, O.F.M.Cap., Dir.; Walter Balduck, O.F.M.Cap.; Francis Voris, O.F.M.Cap.; Bro. James Gleason, O.F.M.Cap. In res., Rev. Vernon Wagner, O.F.M.Cap. Priests 4.

[H] CONVENTS AND RESIDENCES FOR SISTERS

SAGINAW. *Franciscan Sisters of St. Clare, F.S.S.C.,* 4875 Shattuck Rd., 48603-2962. Tel: 517-797-0593; Fax: 517-797-0527. Sr. Dianne Doughty, F.S.S.C., Community Coord. Sisters 4.
Motherhouse and Novitiate of the Mission Sisters of the Holy Spirit, 1030 N. River Rd., 48609. Tel: 517-781-0934. Sr. Margo Tafoya, M.S.Sp., Community Coord. Sisters 12.

ALMA. *Motherhouse and Novitiate of the Religious Sisters of Mercy of Alma, Michigan,* 1835 Michigan Ave., P.O. Box 564, 48801. Tel: 517-463-6035. Mothers Mary Quentin Sheridan, R.S.M.; Mary McGreevy, R.S.M., Vicar. Sisters 13.

[I] MISCELLANEOUS LISTINGS

SAGINAW. *Emmaus House,* 733 S. 14th St., 48601. Tel: 517-755-7538. Co-Directors, Emmaus House: Sr. Marietta Fritz, S.N.D.deN.; Sr. Deb Morris; Sr. Karin Swanson.
Jail Ministry, 1325 Cherry St., 48601. Tel: 517-755-3305. Sr. Mary Ruth Rault, D.C., Chap.
Holy Spirit Sisters Charitable Trust, 1030 N. River Rd., 48609. Sr. Margo Tafoya, M.S.Sp., Pres.
St. Mary's Medical Center of Saginaw, Inc., 830 S. Jefferson Ave., 48601.
Seton Health Corporation of East Central Michigan, 830 S. Jefferson Ave., 48601. Fred Fraizer, Pres. & CEO.

ALMA. *Religious Sisters of Mercy of Alma Corporation,* 1835 Michigan Ave., 48801. Tel: 517-463-6035. Mothers Mary Quentin Sheridan, R.S.M., Pres.; Mary McGreevy, R.S.M., Vice Pres.
Sacred Heart Mercy Health Care Center, 7320 N. Alger Rd., 48801. Tel: 517-463-3451; 463-8464. Sr. Mary Judith O'Brien, R.S.M.

BAY CITY. *Bay County Jail Ministry,* 1100 Stanton St., 48708. Tel: 517-893-7985. Deacon George F. Keller, Chap.
Retrouvaille Program of the Saginaw Diocese, 915 Columbus Ave., 48708. Tel: 517-684-5206. Dave & Vickie Murray, Contact Persons.
Society of St. Vincent de Paul, 523 Michigan Ave., 48708. Mr. Donald Rubis, Pres.
Member Conferences: Bay City-Holy Trinity, St. Hyacinth, St. James, St. Joseph's, St. Mary, St. Stanislaus, Visitation, St. Vincent de Paul; Essexville-St. John.

RELIGIOUS INSTITUTES OF MEN REPRESENTED IN THE DIOCESE

For further details refer to the corresponding bracketed number in the Religious Institutes of Men or Women section.

[0470]—*The Capuchin Friars.* (St. Joseph Prov.).—O.F.M.Cap.
[0480]—*Conventual Franciscans.*—O.F.M.
[0520]—*Franciscan Friars.* (Assumption Prov.).—O.F.M.
[0920]—*Oblates of St. Francis De Sales.*—O.S.F.S.

RELIGIOUS INSTITUTES OF WOMEN REPRESENTED IN THE DIOCESE

[1810]—*Bernadine Sisters of Third Order of St. Francis.*—O.S.F.
[0760]—*Daughters of Charity of St. Vincent de Paul.* (Evansville).—D.C.
[1070-03]—*Dominican Sisters.* (Sinsinawa, WI).—O.P.
[1070-09]—*Dominican Sisters.* (Racine, WI).—O.P.
[1070-13]—*Dominican Sisters.* (Adrian, MI).—O.P.
[1070-14]—*Dominican Sisters.* (Grand Rapids).—O.P.
[1070-26]—*Dominican Sisters.* (Oxford, MI).—O.P.
[1170]—*Felician Sisters.*—C.S.S.F.
[]—*Franciscan Sisters of St. Clare.*—F.S.S.C.
[2740]—*Mission Sisters of the Holy Spirit.*—M.S.Sp.
[3130]—*Our Lady of Victory Missionary Sisters.* (Huntington, IN).—O.L.V.M.
[3560]—*Servants of Jesus.*—S.J.
[0440]—*Sisters of Charity of Cincinnati, Ohio.*—S.C.
[2519]—*Sisters of Mercy of Alma, Michigan.*—R.S.M.
[2575]—*Sisters of Mercy of the Americas.* (Detroit, MI).—R.S.M.
[3000]—*Sisters of Notre Dame de Namur.* (Boston, MA; Cincinnati, OH).—S.N.D.deN.
[1570]—*Sisters of St. Francis of the Holy Family.* (Dubuque, IA).—O.S.F.
[3830-11]—*Sisters of St. Joseph.* (Nazareth, MI).—S.S.J.
[1030]—*Sisters of the Divine Savior.* (Milwaukee, WI).—S.D.S.
[1990]—*Sisters of the Holy Name of Jesus and Mary.* (Spokane, WA).—S.N.J.M.
[2110]—*Sisters of the Humility of Mary.*—H.M.
[3260]—*Sisters of the Precious Blood (Dayton, Ohio).*—C.PP.S.
[2150]—*Sisters, Servants of the Immaculate Heart of Mary.* (Monroe).—I.H.M.

DIOCESAN CEMETERIES

SAGINAW. *St. Andrew's, Mt. Olivet & Calvary.*
BAY CITY. *St. Patrick's & Calvary.*
MIDLAND. *Calvary.*

NECROLOGY

† Mahoney, Rev. Msgr. Charles A., (Retired). —Died Oct. 28, 1996.

Diocese of St. Augustine

(Dioecesis Sancti Augustini)

Most Reverend

JOHN J. SNYDER, D.D.

Bishop of St. Augustine; ordained June 9, 1951; appointed Titular Bishop of Forlimpopuli December 19, 1972; consecrated February 2, 1973; appointed Bishop of St. Augustine October 2, 1979; installed December 5, 1979. *Res., Cathedral-Basilica of Saint Augustine, 35 Treasury St., St. Augustine, FL, 32084.* Tel.: 904-824-2806; Fax: 904-260-8736. *Please address all official mail to: Catholic Center, P.O. Box 24000, Jacksonville, FL, 32241-4000.* Tel.: 904-262-3200; Fax: 904-260-8736.

Square Miles 11,032.

Florida, east of the Apalachicola River, was erected by Pope Pius IX into a Vicariate-Apostolic in the year 1857, and in 1870 into the Diocese of St. Augustine.

Comprises all of the northeastern Counties of the State of Florida including Alachua, Baker, Bradford, Clay, Columbia, Dixie, Duval, Flagler, Gilchrist, Hamilton, Lafayette, Levy, Nassau, Putnam, St. Johns, Suwannee and Union Counties.

For legal titles of parishes and diocesan institutions, consult the Catholic Center.

Catholic Center: P.O. Box 24000, Jacksonville, FL, 32241-4000. Tel.: 904-262-3200; Fax: 904-262-0698.

Web site address: http://staugustine.ml.org/

STATISTICAL OVERVIEW

Personnel	
Bishop	1
Priests: Diocesan Active in Diocese	71
Priests: Active Outside Diocese	13
Priests: Retired, Sick or Absent	6
Number of Diocesan Priests	90
Religious Priests in Diocese	20
Extern Priests in Diocese	20
Ordinations:	
Diocesan Priests	3
Transitional Deacons	1
Permanent Deacons in Diocese	22
Total Brothers	2
Total Sisters	119
Parishes	
Parishes	50
With Resident Pastor:	
Resident Diocesan Priests	46
Resident Religious Priests	4
Without Resident Pastor:	
Missions	9
Welfare	
Catholic Hospitals	1
Total Assisted	254,166
Homes for the Aged	2
Total Assisted	1,034
Special Centers for Social Services	6
Total Assisted	40,000
Residential Care of Disabled	4
Total Assisted	21
Other Institutions	3
Total Assisted	218
Educational	
Diocesan Students in Other Seminaries	13
Total Seminarians	13
High Schools, Diocesan and Parish	2
Total Students	1,720
Elementary Schools, Diocesan and Parish	23
Total Students	6,985
Non-residential Schools for the Disabled	1
Total Students	110
Catechesis/Religious Education:	
High School Students	1,090
Elementary Students	8,350
Total Students Under Catholic Instruction	18,268
Teachers in the Diocese:	
Priests	1
Brothers	1
Sisters	17
Lay Teachers	386
Vital Statistics	
Receptions into the Church:	
Infant Baptism Totals	2,000
Adult Baptism Totals	258
Received into Full Communion	462
First Communions	2,230
Confirmations	1,803
Marriages:	
Catholic	408
Interfaith	335
Total Marriages	743
Deaths	907
Total Catholic Population	115,975
Total Population	1,502,699

Former Bishops—Rt. Rev. AUGUSTIN VEROT, S.S., D.D., cons. April 25, 1858; Vicar-Apostolic of Florida; translated to the See of Savannah in July, 1861; appt. Bishop of St. Augustine March, 1870; died June 10, 1876.—Rt. Rev. JOHN MOORE, D.D., cons. May 13, 1877; died July 30, 1901.—Rt. Rev. WILLIAM JOHN KENNY, D.D., ord. Jan. 15, 1879; cons. May 18, 1902; died Oct. 23, 1913.—Rt. Rev. M. J. CURLEY, D.D., cons. June 30, 1914; promoted to See of Baltimore Aug. 10, 1921; died May 16, 1947.—Most Rev. PATRICK BARRY, D.D., ord. June 9, 1895; appt. Feb. 22, 1922; cons. May 3, 1922; died Aug. 13, 1940.—Most Rev. JOSEPH P. HURLEY, D.D., ord. May 25, 1919; appt. Aug. 16, 1940; cons. Oct. 6, 1940 Received Personal title of Archbishop Aug. 18, 1950; died Oct. 30, 1967.—Most Rev. PAUL F. TANNER, D.D., ord. May 30, 1931; appt. Titular Bishop of Lamasba, Oct. 18, 1965; appt. Bishop of Saint Augustine, Feb. 21, 1968; retired April 21, 1979 Remained as Administrator to Dec. 4, 1979. died July 29, 1994.

Catholic Center—11625 Old St. Augustine Rd., Jacksonville, 32258., Mailing Address: P.O. Box 24000, Jacksonville, 32241-4000. Office Hours: Mon.-Fri. 9-4:30. Tel: 904-262-3200; Fax: 904-262-0698.

Vicar General and Moderator of Curia—Rev. Msgr. VINCENT J. HAUT, V.G., M.S.W.

Chancellor—Rev. KEITH R. BRENNAN, J.C.D.

Secretary to the Bishop—NANCY KELLY.

Secretary to the Chancellor—JUDY T. PINSON.

Fiscal Office—IRENE G. PULEO, Fiscal Mgr.

Diocesan Tribunal—P.O. Box 24000, Jacksonville, 32241-4000. Tel: 904-262-3200.

Judicial Vicar—Rev. JOHN R. REYNOLDS, J.C.L.

Associate Judges—Rev. Msgr. DANIEL B. LOGAN; Rev. PETER H. COLASURDO, J.C.L.

Defenders of the Bond—Revs. PETER H. COLASURDO, J.C.L.; JAMES R. BODDIE, JR.; KEITH R. BRENNAN, J.C.D.; RALPH L. BESENDORFER, J.C.D.

Advocates—Revs. GREGORY J. FAY; DONAL SULLIVAN.

Promotor of Justice—Rev. Msgr. PATRICK M. MADDEN, S.T.L.

Executive Secretary—VERONICA DOSKOCIL.

Secretary—MARY C. SLEEPER.

Diocesan Consultors—Rev. Msgr. JOHN J. LENIHAN, M.S.W.; Rev. Msgr. EUGENE C. KOHLS, P.A., J.C.D.; Rev. Msgr. VINCENT HAUT, V.G., M.S.W.; Revs. ROBERT J. BAKER, S.T.D., V.F.; JAMES R. BODDIE, JR.; DANIEL CODY; ROLAND M. JULIEN, V.F.; MICHAEL J. LARKIN.

Diocesan Pastoral Council—JAMES A. RICHARDSON, II, Chm., *Diocese of St. Augustine Catholic Center, P.O. Box 24000, Jacksonville, 32241-4000.* Tel: 904-262-3200; Fax: 904-262-0698.

Presbyteral Council—Revs. JAMES R. BODDIE, JR., Chm.; JOHN H. TETLOW, Vice Chm.; KEITH R. BRENNAN, J.C.D., Chancellor & Treas.; THOMAS WILLIS, Sec.; Rev. Msgr. VINCENT J. HAUT, V.G., M.S.W.; Rev. Msgr. DANIEL B. LOGAN; Revs. JOHN PHILLIPS; NOEL COX, C.S.Sp.; WILLIAM A. KELLY, V.F.; JAMES O'NEAL; ROLAND M. JULIEN, V.F.; WILLIAM HOCHHEIM; THOMAS SULLIVAN, V.F.

Deans—St. Augustine Deanery: Rev. ROBERT J. BAKER, S.T.D., V.F., Gainesville Deanery: Rev. ROLAND M. JULIEN, V.F., North Jacksonville Deanery: Rev. THOMAS SULLIVAN, V.F., South Jacksonville Deanery: Rev. WILLIAM A. KELLY, V.F.

Building Commission—Most Rev. JOHN J. SNYDER, Chm.; Rev. Msgr. VINCENT J. HAUT, V.G., M.S.W., Vice Chm.; Rev. KEITH R. BRENNAN, J.C.D., Chancellor; Rev. Msgr. DANIEL B. LOGAN; Rev. THOMAS CODY; ARTHUR TODD; Revs. MICHAEL J. LARKIN; GREGORY J. FAY.

Catholic Foundation of Diocese of St. Augustine—Most Rev. JOHN J. SNYDER; Rev. Msgr. VINCENT J. HAUT, V.G., M.S.W.; Rev. Msgr. JOHN J. LENIHAN, M.S.W.; Rev. KEITH R. BRENNAN, J.C.D., Chancellor; Dr. GASTON ACOSTA-RUA; JOHN CRAWFORD; ROBERT T. SHIRCLIFF; GEORGE HELOW; WARREN POWERS; PETER STRAIN; JAMES P. DOLAN; RICARDO MORALES; FRANCIS SCHOLTZ; MARTHA BARRETT; S. P. BRAUD, III; JACK DEMETREE; PHIL SMITH; ERNEST P. BONO; DIANNE T. RICE; DENIS PLUMB; IRENE G. PULEO, Fiscal Mgr., *P.O. Box 24000, Jacksonville, 32241-4000.* Tel: 904-262-3200.

Finance Committee—REESE BOHN; ROBERT A. DEVEREUX; Mr. CLYDE E. LOWER; Rev. Msgr. MORTIMER DANAHER; Rev. Msgr. VINCENT J. HAUT, V.G., M.S.W.; Revs. KEITH R. BRENNAN, J.C.D.; LUKE MCLOUGHLIN; IRENE G. PULEO, Fiscal Mgr. PATRICIA JEREMIAH; MARY ALICE PHELAN; TIMOTHY LANE; MARIA ALLEN; FRANCIS N. SCHOLTZ, *P.O. Box 24000, Jacksonville, 32241-4000.* Tel: 904-262-3200.

Health Insurance Committee, Diocesan—Rev. KEITH R. BRENNAN, J.C.D.; Rev. Msgr. VINCENT J. HAUT, V.G., M.S.W.; Rev. MICHAEL R. HOULE; PATRICIA A. TIERNEY; WILLIAM J. TIERNEY; IRENE G. PUELO; JANET P. MORTON; SANDRA WARD; Sr. MAUREEN KELLEY, O.P., *P.O. Box 24000, Jacksonville, 32241-4000.* Tel: 904-262-3200.

Stewardship Council, Diocesan—Most Rev. JOHN J. SNYDER; Rev. ROBERT MCDERMOTT; Rev. JAMES R. BODDIE, JR.; Rev. Msgr. JAMES J. HESLIN; Rev. JOSEPH FINLAY; LANE CAMPAU; DANIEL L. TALAGA; FRANCIS SCHOLTZ; DENIS M. PLUMB; LANE CAMPAU;

WILLIAM HELTEMES; GERALD WEEDON; PAT THOMAS; MICHAEL CASCONE, JR.; BETSY BERGMAN; JOHN WOMBOUGH; KENNETH DAVIDSON, *P.O. Box 24000, Jacksonville, 32241-4000.* Tel: 904-262-3200.

Diocesan Offices and Directors

Alcohol and Other Drug Abuse Commission—WILLIAM J. TIERNEY, Convener, *P.O. Box 24000, Jacksonville, 32241-4000.* Tel: 904-262-3200.

Apostleship of the Sea—Deacon DALE WAMSTAD, O.F.M., *Providence Center, 134 E. Church St., Jacksonville, 32202-3130.* Tel: 904-356-3104.

Archives of Diocese—Rev. KEITH R. BRENNAN, J.C.D., Chancellor, *P.O. Box 24000, Jacksonville, 32241-4000.* Tel: 904-262-3200.

Assisted Suicide Task Force—T. JAMES GALLAGHER, M.D., Chm., *P.O. Box 24000, Jacksonville, 32241-4000.* Tel: 904-262-3200.

Bioethics Commission—T. JAMES GALLAGHER, M.D., Chm., *P.O. Box 24000, Jacksonville, 32241-4000.* Tel: 904-262-3200.

Black, African, Caribbean and Native American Ministries—Rev. JAMES R. BODDIE, JR., Vicar of the Black Apostolate; ELLA SIMMONS, Dir., *P.O. Box 24000, Jacksonville, 32241-4000.* Tel: 904-262-3200.

Campaign for Human Development—Rev. EDWARD K. ROONEY, Dir., *1606 Blanding Blvd., Middleburg, 32068.* Tel: 904-282-0439.

Campus Ministry—Sr. LUCILLE CLYNES, D.W., Dir. PETER W. MORGAN, Campus Minister, *Jacksonville University, Jacksonville, 32211.* Tel: 904-744-3950, Ext 2258; 646-2638.

Christian Formation—Sr. LUCILLE CLYNES, D.W, Dir., *P.O. Box 24000, Jacksonville, 32241-4000.* Tel: 904-262-3200.

Catholic Burse Endowment Fund, Inc.—(Education of Priests), *P.O. Box 24000, Jacksonville, 32241-4000.* Tel: 904-262-3200.

Catholic Charities Bureau, Inc.—WILLIAM J. TIERNEY, Exec. Dir., *P.O. Box 24000, Jacksonville, 32241-4000.* Tel: 904-262-3200. See Separate Listing for more details.

Catholic Relief Services—WILLIAM J. TIERNEY, Dir., *P.O. Box 24000, Jacksonville, 32241-4000.* Tel: 904-262-3200.

Catholic Women, Council of—Rev. LUKE McLOUGHLIN, Spiritual Moderator, *St. Matthew Church, 1773 Blanding Blvd., Jacksonville, 32210.* Tel: 904-388-8698.

Charismatic Renewal—Rev. Msgr. HAROLD F. JORDAN, Diocesan Coord., *Mission of Nombre de Dios, 30 Ocean Ave., St. Augustine, 32084.* Tel: 904-824-3045.

Civil Institutions—Rev. JOSEPH MANIANGAT, M.A., *St. Mary Parish, P.O. Box 1120, Macclenny, 32063.* Tel: 904-259-6414.

Communications Commission—ART MARSHALL, Chm., *P.O. Box 24000, Jacksonville, 32241-4000.* Tel: 904-262-3200.

Communications, Office of—KATHLEEN BAGG-MORGAN, Dir., *P.O. Box 24000, Jacksonville, 32241-4000.* Tel: 904-262-3200.

Continuing Education for Priests—Rev. Msgr. R. JOSEPH JAMES, Dir., *9401 Staples Mill Rd., Jacksonville, 32244.*

Cursillos de Cristiandad—Rev. Msgr. R. JOSEPH JAMES, Spiritual Dir., *Mary Queen of Heaven, 9401 Staples Mill Rd., Jacksonville, 32244.* Tel: 904-777-3168. Rev. TIMOTHY R. LOZIER, Asst. Spiritual Dir., *St. Augustine Parish, P.O. Box 13888, Gainesville, 32604.* Tel: 904-372-3533.

Disabilities, Ministry of Persons with—DAN JOHNSON, Dir., *P.O. Box 24000, Jacksonville, 32241-4000.* Tel: 904-262-3200.

Ecumenism—Rev. Msgr. JOHN J. LENIHAN, M.S.W., Chm., *3619 Toledo Rd., Jacksonville, 32217.* Tel: 904-733-1630.

Educational Services—PATRICIA A. TIERNEY, M.S.Ed., Supt. Schools, *P.O. Box 24000, Jacksonville, 32241-4000.* Tel: 904-262-3200.

The Guardian of Dreams—Mr. LOUIS WALSH, Chm., *P.O. Box 24000, Jacksonville, 32241-4000.* Tel: 904-262-3200; Fax: 904-262-0698.

Family Life, Diocesan Center for—NANCY C. FISHER, R.N., Dir.; Rev. DANIEL CODY, Consultant, *P.O. Box 24000, Jacksonville, 32241-4000.* Tel: 904-262-3200. Regional Office: St. Vincent Medical Center. Tel: 904-387-7474.

Farmworker Services Program—Mrs. CHIQUI MALDONADO, Dir., *40 Sanford St., St. Augustine, 32084.* Tel: 904-829-6300.

Florida Catholic Conference—D. MICHAEL McCARRON, Ph.D., Exec. Dir., *890 Tallahassee Bank Bldg., P.O. Box 1638, Tallahassee, 32302-1638.* Tel: 904-222-3803.

Health Care Task Force—LEONARD SPILLANE, Chm., *P.O. Box 24000, Jacksonville, 32241-4000.* Tel: 904-262-3200.

Hispanic Ministry—Rev. LUIS FLOREZ, Dir.; Deacon JAMES SWANSON, Coord., *P.O. Box 53257, Jacksonville, 32201.* Tel: 904-262-3200; 353-3243.

Holy Childhood Association, The—Rev. BRIAN EBURN, Dir., *P.O. Box 24000, Jacksonville, 32241-4000.* Tel: 904-262-3200.

Holy Name Societies—Rev. Msgr. PATRICK M. MADDEN, S.T.L., Spiritual Dir., *Sacred Heart Rectory, 5752 Blanding Blvd., Jacksonville, 32244.* Tel: 904-771-2152.

Investment Commission—Rev. Msgr VINCENT J. HAUT, M.S.W., V.G.; Rev. KEITH R. BRENNAN, J.C.D., Chancellor; IRENE G. PUELO, Fiscal Mgr. JAMES DOLAN; THOMAS TIERNEY; TIMOTHY LANE; ROBERT A. DEVEREAUX.

Justice and Peace Commission—ELIZABETH O'BRIEN, Chm., *P.O. Box 24000, Jacksonville, 32241-4000.* Tel: 904-262-3200.

Justice and Reconciliation, Ministry for—Sr. DOROTHEA MURPHY, R.S.M., Coord.; Rev. GROVER B. TIPTON, Chap., *1717 N.E. 9th, Suite 123, Gainesville, 32609.* Tel: 904-372-6006.

Legalization—NANCY VALDIVIESO, Dir., *P.O. Box 24000, Jacksonville, 32241-4000.* Tel: 904-272-3200., *Providence Center, P.O. Box 53257, Jacksonville, 32201.* Tel: 904-354-5904.

Legion of Mary—Rev. JOSE MANIYANGAT, Spiritual Dir., *P.O. Drawer 5040, Jacksonville, 32247-5040.* Tel: 904-398-1963.

Liturgy Office—Revs. THOMAS WILLIS, Chm. LUCILLE BARRETT, Vice-Chm.; Dr. GLENN KUHNEL, Exec. Sec., *P.O. Box 24000, Jacksonville, 32241-4000.* Tel: 904-262-3200.

Planned Giving Office—Mrs. DENIS PLUMB, Dir., *P.O. Box 24000, Jacksonville, 32241-4000.* Tel: 904-262-3200.

Marriage Encounter—NANCY C. FISHER, R.N., Exec. Dir. Exec. Team: SUSAN SHIELDS; BILL SHIELDS, *1851 King St., Room 103, Jacksonville, 33204.* Tel: 904-387-7474.

Parish Social Ministry—Sr. MARLENE PAYETTE, S.S.J., Dir., *Providence Center, 134 E. Church St., Jacksonville, 32202-3130.* Tel: 904-354-3416.

Priests' Spirituality Committee—Rev. DONAL P. SULLIVAN, *P.O. Box 276, Green Cove Springs, 32043.* Tel: 904-284-3811.

Propagation of the Faith—Rev. BRIAN EBURN, Dir., *P.O. Box 24000, Jacksonville, 32241-4000.* Tel: 904-262-3200.

Refugee Resettlement—WILLIAM C. BEITZ, Dir., *Providence Center, 134 E. Church St., Jacksonville, 32202-3130.* Tel: 904-354-3416.

Respect Life Activities—BONNIE SEAVER, Dir.; Rev. THOMAS S. WILLIS, Spiritual Moderator, *P.O. Box 24000, Jacksonville, 32241-4000.* Tel: 904-262-3200.

Rural Life Director—MICHAEL PENDERGRAFT, *P.O. Box 863, Chiefland, 32626.* Tel: 904-493-1561.

St. Vincent de Paul Societies—Rev. Msgr. MORTIMER DANAHER, Moderator, *742 Arlington Rd., Jacksonville, 32211.* Tel: 904-724-0080.

Scouts—Revs. JAMES R. BODDIE, JR., Chap. EDWARD MURPHY, Asst. Chap., *P.O. Box 24000, Jacksonville, 32241-4000.* Tel: 904-262-3200.

Seminarians—Rev. JOHN H. TETLOW, Dir., *P.O. Box 24000, Jacksonville, 32241-4000.* Tel: 904-262-3200.

Stewardship, Office of—FRANCIS N. SCHOLTZ, Dir., *P.O. Box 24000, Jacksonville, 32241-4000.* Tel: 904-262-3200.

Vicar for Clergy—Rev. RALPH L. BESENDORFER, J.C.D., *P.O. Box 24000, Jacksonville, 32241-4000.* Tel: 904-262-3200.

Vicar for Religious—Sr. MAUREEN KELLEY, O.P., *P.O. Box 24000, Jacksonville, 32241-4000.* Tel: 904-262-3200.

Vicar for Senior Priests—Rev. Msgr. EUGENE C. KOHLS, P.A., J.C.D., *P.O. Box 5040, Jacksonville, 32247-5040.* Tel: 904-387-2554.

Vocations—Rev. JOHN H. TETLOW, Dir., *P.O. Box 24000, Jacksonville, 32241-4000.* Tel: 904-262-3200.

Youth and Young Adult Ministry—Ms. CINDEE CASE, Dir., *P.O. Box 24000, Jacksonville, 32241-4000.* Tel: 904-262-3200.

CLERGY, PARISHES, MISSIONS AND PAROCHIAL SCHOOLS

CITY OF ST. AUGUSTINE
(St. John County)

1—CATHEDRAL OF ST. AUGUSTINE (1565). (A Minor Basilica). Revs. Robert J. Baker; Jeremiah F. Lambe, C.S.Sp.; Timothy M. Lindenfelser; Edward N. Booth; Deacons Thomas Richards; John Pelletier. In res., Rev. Msgr. Harold F. Jordan; Revs. Rene Robert, Chap. to the Catholic Deaf; Terry Smith, C.S.Sp.; John H. Tetlow.
Res., 35 Treasury St., 32084. Tel: 904-824-2806; Fax: 904-824-0761. [CEM]
School—Cathedral Parish School, (Grades K-8) 259 St. George St., 32084. Tel: 904-824-2861; Fax: 904-824-2862. Sr. Mary Victor Azar, S.S.J., Prin.
Sisters 1; Lay Teachers 26; Students 383.
Cathedral Parish Early Education Center—(Preschool and After School Care) 10 San Sebastian Ave., 32084. Tel: 904-829-2933. Kathleen Tiews, Dir.
Lay Teachers 5; Students 93.
Catechesis/Religious Programs—Tel: 904-829-3338. Sr. Nicole Cayer, S.S.J., D.R.E.
Students 220.
Missions—St. Augustine, St. Johns Co., Prince of Peace, San Marco Ave., 32084. Tel: 904-824-2806; St. Augustine, St. Johns Co., St. Benedict the Moor, Martin Luther King Ave., 32084. Tel: 904-824-2806.

2—MISSION OF NOMBRE DE DIOS AND SHRINE OF OUR LADY OF LA LECHE (1565), Rev. Msgr. Harold F. Jordan, Dir.
Office: 30 Ocean Ave., 32084. Tel: 904-824-3045; Fax: 904-829-0819.
Res., 35 Treasury St., 32084. Tel: 904-824-3045; Fax: 904-824-0761.

3—ST. ANASTASIA (1988), Rev. Seamus O'Flynn; Sr. Enda Egan, Pastoral Assoc.; Deacons Bob Lucian; Bob Robertson.
Res., One Hawaiian Blvd., 32084. Tel: 904-471-3747; 471-5364 (Office); Fax: 904-471-7448.
Catechesis/Religious Programs—Susan Seasholtz, D.R.E.
Students 116.

4—SAN SEBASTIAN (1968), Rev. Peter Colasurdo.
Res., 1112 State Rd. 16, 32095. Tel: 904-824-6625; Fax: 904-829-0459.
Catechesis/Religious Programs—Deacon James Swanson, D.R.E.
Students 81.

OUTSIDE THE CITY OF ST. AUGUSTINE

Atlantic Beach, Duval Co., St. John the Baptist (1967), Rev. Joseph Meehan; Deacon Harold Brodeur. In res., Rev. D. Terrence Morgan.
Mailing Address: P.O. Drawer 330005, 32233. Tel: 904-246-6014; Fax: 904-246-1219.
Catechesis/Religious Programs—Tel: 904-246-6014; Fax: 904-246-1219. Carole Fuchs, D.R.E.
Students 301.

Branford, Suwannee Co., San Juan Mission (Independent), Rev. Gerald A. Vallee.
Mailing Address: P.O. Box 949, 32008. Tel: 904-935-2632; Fax: 904-935-2632.

Bunnell, Flagler Co., St. Stephen (1957), Rev. Frederick Parke.
Mailing Address: 4600 Belle Terre Pkwy., Palm Coast, 32164.
Res., Rte. 100, 32110. Tel: 904-445-2246; Fax: 904-445-7808.

Callahan, Nassau Co., Our Lady of Consolation (1974), Rev. Ralph L. Besendorfer, J.C.D.
Res., 11625 Old St. Augustine Rd., Jacksonville, 32258. Tel: 904-262-3200; Fax: 904-262-0698.
Catechesis/Religious Programs—Edith Tasso, D.R.E.
Students 52.

Chiefland, Levy Co., St. John the Evangelist (1982), Rev. Michael Pendergraft.
Res., P.O. Box 863, 32644-0863. Tel: 352-493-1561; Fax: 352-493-9258.
Mission—Cross City, Dixie Co., Holy Cross, Cross City, 32628. Tel: 352-498-5671.

Crescent City, Putnam Co., St. John the Baptist (1910), Rev. Brian Eburn; Sr. Bridie Ryan, Pastoral Assoc.
Res., P.O. Box 908, 32112. Tel: 904-698-2055; Fax: 904-698-4146. [CEM]
Catechesis/Religious Programs—Students 54.

Elkton, St. John Co., St. Ambrose (1875) (Minorcan), Rev. Patrick Carroll, C.S.Sp., Admin.
Res., 6070 Church Rd., 32033. Tel: 904-692-1366; Fax: 904-692-1136. [CEM]
Mission—Bakersville, St. Johns Co., Our Lady of Good Counsel, 5005 Church Rd., Bakersville, 32092. [CEM]

Fernandina Beach, Amelia Island, Nassau Co., St. Michael's (1872), Revs. Mark S. Waters; Neil Cornelli.
Res., 505 Broome St., 32034. Tel: 904-261-3472; Fax: 904-321-1901.
Catechesis/Religious Programs—Tel: 904-261-3472; Fax: 904-321-1901. Janice Balota, Pastoral Assoc.
Students 250.

Flagler Beach, Flagler Co., Santa Maria Del Mar (1970), Rev. John O'Flaherty; Deacon Charlie Karr.
Res., 801 N. Central Ave., P.O. Box 130, 32136. Tel: 904-439-2791; Fax: 904-439-2791. [CEM]

Gainesville, Alachua Co.,

1—ST. PATRICK'S, (1887), Revs. Roland M. Julien; Paul V. Donnelly; Michael Thompson.
Res., 500 N.E. 16th Ave., 32601. Tel: 352-372-4641; 376-0575; Fax: 352-376-0575.
School—Tel: 352-376-9878; Fax: 352-371-6177. Elaine Baumgartner, Prin.
Lay Teachers 26; Students 509.
Catechesis/Religious Programs—Tel: 352-376-9878, Ext. 60. Diane St. Onge, D.R.E.
Students 72.
Mission—Hawthorne, Alachua Co., St. Philip Neri, U.S. 301 S., Hawthorne, 32640.

2—HOLY FAITH, (1973), Revs. Michael S. Williams; Erlindo N. Molon, Pastoral Assoc.
Res., 700 N.W. 39 Rd., 32607. Tel: 352-376-5405; Fax: 352-375-7568.
Catechesis/Religious Programs—Tel: 352-374-4708; Fax: 352-375-7568. Carmen M. Delgado, D.R.E.
Students 334.

3—QUEEN OF PEACE, (1987), Rev. Jeffrey A. McGowan.
Church—10900 S.W. 24th Ave., 32607. Tel: 352-332-6279; Fax: 352-331-7347.
Catechesis/Religious Programs—Tel: 352-332-6279; Fax: 352-331-7347. Dan Talaga, D.R.E.
Students 308.

4—ST. AUGUSTINE, (1923), Revs. John D. Gillespie; John M. Phillips; Timothy R. Lozier. In res., Rev. Anthony S. Michaelraj (India).
Res., 1738 W. University Ave., P.O. Box 13888, 32604. Tel: 352-372-3533; Fax: 352-378-9010.
Catechesis/Religious Programs—Tel: 352-372-3533; Fax: 352-378-9010. Kelli Brew, D.R.E.
Students 323.

Green Cove Springs, Clay Co., Sacred Heart (1874), Rev. Donal Sullivan.
Res., 614 W. Bay St., P.O. Box 276, 32043. Tel: 904-284-3811.
Catechesis/Religious Programs—Tel: 904-284-3811. Mrs. Sherry Latta-Raines, D.R.E.
Students 82.

High Springs, Alachua Co., St. Madeleine (1925), Rev. Noel Cox, C.S.Sp.
Mailing Address: P.O. Box 892, 32643.
Res., 3330 E. Martin Luther King Blvd., 32643. Tel: 904-454-2358; Fax: 904-454-4985.
Catechesis/Religious Programs—Students 72.

Interlachen, Putnam Co., St. John's Mission (1968), Rev. John J. Heerey (BRK).
Res., P.O. Box 207, 32148. Tel: 904-684-2528. [JC]

Jacksonville, Duval Co.,

1—ASSUMPTION, (South Jacksonville) (1913), Rev. Msgr. Eugene C. Kohls; Revs. Jose Maniyangat; James O'Neal; Deacon David MacNamara. In res., Rev. Luis Florez, Dir., Hispanic Apostolate.
Res., 2403 Atlantic Blvd., P.O. Box 5040, 32247-5040. Tel: 904-398-1963; Fax: 904-398-6115.
School—Tel: 904-398-1774; Fax: 904-398-6712. Mrs. Maureen Matthes, Prin.
Lay Teachers 29; Students 645.
Catechesis/Religious Programs—Tel: 904-398-1963; Fax: 904-398-6115. Sr. Lyn Payette, S.S.J., D.R.E.
Students 80.

2—BLESSED TRINITY, (1957), Rev. Denis O'Regan.
Res., 10472 Beach Blvd., P.O. Box 16466, 32245. Tel: 904-641-1414; Fax: 904-641-1414.
Catechesis/Religious Programs—Tel: 904-641-0515; Fax: 904-641-1414. Mrs. Margaret Arp, D.R.E.
Students 231.

3—CHRIST THE KING, (1954), Rev. Msgr. Mortimer Danaher; Revs. Brian Carey, C.S.Sp.; Thanh T. Nguyen. In res., Rev. John H. Tetlow.
Res., 742 Arlington Rd., 32211. Tel: 904-724-0080; Fax: 904-721-2326.
School—Tel: 904-724-2954; Fax: 904-721-8004. Mrs. Janet Morton, Prin.
Sisters 1; Lay Teachers 27; Students 632; Teachers Aids 5.
Catechesis/Religious Programs—Tel: 904-724-0080; Fax: 904-721-2326.
Students 632.

4—CRUCIFIXION, (1974) (African American), Rev. Cletus M. Watson, T.O.R.; Deacon Henry Bellinger, (Retired).
Res., 454 W. 63rd St., 32208. Tel: 904-768-0261.
Church of the Crucifixion Rectory: 6079 Bagley Rd., 32209-1800. Tel: 904-765-5284; Fax: 904-765-1680.

5—HOLY FAMILY, (1974), Rev. Msgr. Daniel B. Logan.
Office: 9800 Baymeadows Rd., 32256. Tel: 904-641-5838; Fax: 904-641-9704.
Catechesis/Religious Programs—Tel: 904-641-5838; Fax: 904-641-9704. Mrs. Judy Resta, D.R.E.
Students 174.

6—HOLY ROSARY, (1921), Revs. Glenn D. Parker, C.SS.R.; Alfred A. Sieradski, C.SS.R.
Res., 746 W. 41st St., 32206. Tel: 904-764-3241; Fax: 904-765-4995.
School—Sisters of Notre Dame. (Toledo Prov.) 4920 Brentwood Ave., 32206. Tel: 904-765-6522; 353-6933; Fax: 904-765-4995. Sr. Patricia Marie McClain, S.N.D., Prin.
Sisters 4; Lay Teachers 9; Students 160.

7—HOLY SPIRIT, (1966), Rev. Msgr. James J. Heslin; Deacon Gjet Bajraktari.
Res., 11665 Fort Caroline Rd., 32225. Tel: 904-641-7244; Fax: 904-641-7266.
School—(Grades PreK-5). Tel: 904-642-9165. Therese Moore, Prin.
Lay Teachers 8; Students 162.
Catechesis/Religious Programs—Judy Altmiller, D.R.E.
Students 328.

8—IMMACULATE CONCEPTION, (1854), Revs. Antonio Leon; Warren Keene; Richard Powers, S.J.
Res., 121 E. Duval St., P.O. Box 100, 32201. Tel: 904-359-0331; Fax: 904-356-8133. [CEM]

9—MARY QUEEN OF HEAVEN, (1988), Rev. Msgr. R. Joseph James.
Res., 3804 Bandera Circle S., 32244. Tel: 904-777-1272; Fax: 904-778-7691.
Catechesis/Religious Programs—9401 Staples Mill Dr., 32244. Tel: 904-777-3168; Fax: 904-778-7691.
Students 126.

10—MOST HOLY REDEEMER, (1962), Rev. Thomas S. Willis
Res., 3523 Normandy Blvd., 32221-6701. Tel: 904-786-1192; Fax: 904-786-4224.
Catechesis/Religious Programs—Sharon Tomore, D.R.E.
Students 111.

11—OUR LADY OF THE ANGELS, (1917), Rev. Joseph Notarpole.
Res., 430 Crystal St., 32254. Tel: 904-389-4878; Fax: 904-389-4878.

12—PRINCE OF PEACE, (1970), Rev. Michael J. Larkin.
Res., 3320 Bennett Rd., 32216. Tel: 904-733-6860; Fax: 904-367-0215.
Catechesis/Religious Programs—Tel: 904-733-6018.
Students 93.

13—RESURRECTION, (1959), Revs. Thomas Cody; Daniel Shasky.
Res., 3383 University Blvd. N., 32277. Tel: 904-744-0833; Fax: 904-744-7235.
School—Tel: 904-744-1266; Fax: 904-744-7235. Katherine Boice, Prin.
Lay Teachers 16; Students 300.
Catechesis/Religious Programs—Tel: 904-744-5800; Fax: 904-744-7235. Noreen Rocha, D.R.E.
Students 222.

14—SACRED HEART, (1959), Rev. Msgr. Patrick M. Madden; Revs. Alan E. Bower; Conrad Cowart.
Res., 5752 Blanding Blvd., 32244. Tel: 904-771-2152; Fax: 904-771-5800.
School—Sisters of Mercy (Clonakilty, Ireland), Tel: 904-771-5800; Fax: 904-771-5800. Sr. Josephine O'Leary, R.S.M., Prin.
Sisters 1; Lay Teachers 28; Students 609.
Catechesis/Religious Programs—Tel: 904-771-2152. Sr. Mary of Mercy, D.R.E.
Students 227.

15—ST. JOSEPH'S, (1883), Revs. Daniel Cody; Patrick Soares, C.S.Sp.
Res., 11730 Old St. Augustine Rd., 32258-2002. Tel: 904-268-5422; Fax: 904-292-0248. [CEM]
School—Tel: 904-268-6688; Fax: 904-268-8989. Mrs. Carolyn Backherms, Prin.
Lay Teachers 25; Students 602.
Catechesis/Religious Programs—Tel: 904-268-5422; Fax: 904-292-0248. Carole Ginzl, D.R.E.
Students 834.

16—ST. MATTHEW'S, (Lake Shore) (1949), Rev. Luke McLoughlin. In res., Rev. John R. Reynolds, J.C.L.
Res., 1773 Blanding Blvd., 32210. Tel: 904-388-8698; Fax: 904-384-1233.
School—Tel: 904-387-4401. David Yazdiya, Prin.
Lay Teachers 12; Students 302.
Catechesis/Religious Programs—Tel: 904-388-1207. D.R.E.: Dr. Susan Napier; Onie Rodriguez, (Youth).
Students 113.

17—ST. PATRICK, (1959), Rev. Robert T. McDermott.
Res., 1429 Broward Rd., 32218. Tel: 904-768-2593; Fax: 904-786-2144.
School—Sisters of Mercy, (Grades K-8). Tel: 904-768-6323; Fax: 904-768-2144. Sr. Carmel O'Callahan, C.S.M., Prin.
Lay Teachers 14; Students 271.
Catechesis/Religious Programs—Tel: 904-757-4720.
Students 217.

18—ST. PAUL'S, (1923), Revs. Thomas K. Sullivan; James J. Corry, C.S.Sp.
Res., 2609 Park St., P.O. Box 40705, 32203. Tel: 904-387-2554; Fax: 904-388-6871.
School—Tel: 904-387-2841; Fax: 904-387-1781. Mrs. Ana Voss, Prin.
Lay Teachers 14; Students 252.
Catechesis/Religious Programs—Students 47.

19—ST. PIUS THE FIFTH, (1919) (African American), Rev. James R. Boddie, Jr.
Res., 2110 Blue Ave., 32209. Tel: 904-354-1501; Fax: 904-354-7240.
School—1470 W. 13th St., 32209. Tel: 904-354-2613; Fax: 904-356-4522. Sr. Elise Kennedy, S.S.J., Prin.
Sisters 2; Lay Teachers 10; Students 193.
Catechesis/Religious Programs—Tel: 904-354-1501; Fax: 904-354-7240.
Students 55.

20—SAN JOSE, (1959), Rev. Msgr. John J. Lenihan; Revs. Thomas Walsh; Anthony P. Palazzolo; Rodolfo Godinez Fuentes.
Res., 3619 Toledo Rd., 32217. Tel: 904-733-1630; Fax: 904-733-7973.
School—Sisters of Mercy, Tel: 904-733-2510. Sr. Eithne Lowther, R.S.M., Prin.
Sisters 2; Lay Teachers 24; Students 525.
Catechesis/Religious Programs—Nancy Cronin, D.R.E.
Students 390.

21—SYRIAC ANTIOCHIAN-RITE MISSION ST. EPHREM, (1986), Rev. Mansour Mattosha.
Res., 9645 Baymeadows Rd., Apt. #733, 32256. Tel: 904-739-8941.

Jacksonville Beach, Duval Co., St. Paul's (1930), Revs. William A. Kelly; Robert L. Napier; Wayne Price.
Res., 224 N. Fifth St., 32250. Tel: 904-249-2600; Fax: 904-249-0422.
School—Tel: 904-249-5394; Fax: 904-241-2911. Mrs. Rosemary Spraggins, Prin.
Lay Teachers 25; Students 503.
Catechesis/Religious Programs—Tel: 904-249-2660. Mary Coleman, D.R.E.
Students 589.

Keystone Heights, Clay Co., St. William (1948), Rev. Moises Palaroan.
Res., P.O. Box 721, 32656. Tel: 352-473-4136; Fax: 352-473-4119. [JC]
Catechesis/Religious Programs—P.O. Box 781, 32656. Tel: 904-473-4223.
Students 143.

Korona, Flagler Co., St. Mary's (1914) (Polish), Revs. John O'Flaherty; Walter C. Bayer (Poland); Deacon Charlie Karr.
Mailing Address: P.O. Box 1537, Bunnell, 32110-1537. Tel: 904-439-2537.
Res., 801 N. Central Ave., P.O. Box 130, Flagler Beach, 32036. Tel: 904-439-2791. [CEM]

Lake City, Columbia Co., Epiphany (1965), Rev. Anthony G. Sebra; Sr. Mary Esther Flanagan, S.S.J., Pastoral Assoc.
Res., Malone Dr., Rte. 10, Box 161-B, 32025. Tel: 904-752-4470; Fax: 904-752-4652.
School—Tel: 904-752-2320; Fax: 904-752-4652. Mr. Mark Akerman, Prin.
Lay Teachers 8; Students 140.
Catechesis/Religious Programs—Tel: 904-752-3018; Fax: 904-752-4652.
Students 61.

Live Oak, Suwannee Co., St. Francis Xavier, Rev. Michael E. Morse.
Res., P.O. Box 1179, 32060. Tel: 904-364-1108; Fax: 904-364-1108.
Catechesis/Religious Programs—Tel: 904-362-7287. Nancy Roberts, D.R.E.
Students 83.
Mission—Jasper, Hamilton Co., St. Therese of Lisieux, P.O. Box 890, Jasper, 32052. Tel: 904-364-1108.

Macclenny, Baker Co., St. Mary's (1960), Rev. Joseph Maniangat.
Res., 104 Jacqueline Cir., P.O. Box 1120, 32063. Tel: 904-259-6414; Fax: 904-259-6414. [JC]
Catechesis/Religious Programs—Tel: 904-259-3217; Fax: 904-259-6414. Janet DeBoe, D.R.E.
Students 42.
Chaplaincy—Northeast Florida State Hospital, Macclenny; Union Correctional Institute, Raiford; and Florida State Prison, Starke. Tel: 904-259-6414; Fax: 904-259-6414.

Middleburg, Clay Co., St. Luke's (1982), Rev. Edward Rooney.
Res., 1606 Blanding Blvd., 32068. Tel: 904-282-0439; Fax: 904-291-9711.
Catechesis/Religious Programs—Students 330.

Orange Park, Clay Co., St. Catherine's (1877), Rev. Msgr. Vincent J. Haut, V.G.; Revs. Alex Ducci; Raymond J. Carlo. In res., Revs. Felicien K. Houndjame; William Butler, C.S.Sp.
Res., 1649 Kingsley Ave., 32073. Tel: 904-264-0577; Fax: 904-264-7999.
Catechesis/Religious Programs—Tel: 904-264-2470; Fax: 904-264-7999. Bro. Kenney Gorman, D.R.E.

Students 929.
Mission—Orange Park, Clay Co., Moosehaven Chapel, 1700 Park Ave., 32073. Tel: 904-278-1210.

Palatka, Putnam Co., St. Monica's (1837), Rev. Joseph F. Finlay; Sr. Martha Costello, O.P., Pastoral Min.
Office: 114 S. 4th St., 32177. Tel: 904-325-9777; Fax: 904-329-1960. [CEM]
Catechesis / Religious Programs—Tel: 904-325-7777; Fax: 904-325-1960. Rev. Joseph F. Finlay, D.R.E.
Students 105.

Palm Coast, Flager Co., St. Elizabeth Ann Seton (1979), Revs. Frederick Parke; Edward Murphy; Sr. Mary Ryan, I.H.M., Pastoral Min.; Deacons Richard Arsenault; James Casapulla; Robert McDermott.
Res., 4600 Belle Terre Pkwy., 32164. Tel: 904-445-2246; Fax: 904-445-7808.
Catechesis / Religious Programs—Tel: 904-446-5854. D.R.E. Mrs. Roasaire Downey; Mrs. Dee Casapulla.
Students 650.

Ponte Vedra Beach, St. John Co., Our Lady Star of the Sea (1972), Rev. Msgr. T. Leo Danaher.
Mailing Address: 545 Hwy. A1A N., 32082. Tel: 904-285-2698; Fax: 904-285-2502.
Catechesis / Religious Programs—Tel: 904-273-0590.
Students 436.

St. Augustine Shores, St. John Co., Corpus Christi (1975), Rev. William C. Mooney; Deacon Joseph Cross.
Res., P.O. Box 3064, St. Augustine, 32085. Tel: 904-797-4842.
Catechesis / Religious Programs—Tel: 904-797-4842; Fax: 904-797-2746.
Students 127.

Starke, Bradford Co., St. Edward's (1941), Rev. William A. Hochheim.
Res., 441 N. Temple Ave., 32091-3207. Tel: 904-964-6155.
Catechesis / Religious Programs—Tel: 904-964-6237. Sr. Anne Doyle, R.M.S.
Students 44.

Switzerland, St. John Co., San Juan Del Rio (1977), Rev. Gregory J. Fay.
Res., 1714-3 State Rd., No. 13, 32259. Tel: 904-287-1589; 287-0519 (Office); Fax: 904-287-0519.
Catechesis / Religious Programs—Tel: 904-287-2270.
Students 230.

Williston, Levy Co., Holy Family (1970), Rev. James T. Moss.
Res., Rte. 3, Box 50, 32696. Tel: 352-528-2893; Fax: 352-528-6002.
Catechesis / Religious Programs—Students 60.
Mission—Inglis, Levy Co., St. Anthony the Abbot, P.O. Box 1070, Inglis, 34449.

Special Assignment:
Reverend Fathers—
Brennan, Keith R., Chancellor, The Catholic Center, P.O. Box 24000, Jacksonville, FL 32241-4000. Tel: 904-262-3200
Foley, Patrick H.
Revilla, Francisco
Tipton, Grover B., Chap. of Prison Ministry

Graduate Studies:
Reverend Fathers—
Glisson, Nicholas J.

On Duty Outside the Diocese:
Reverend Monsignors—
Conesa, Diego, Diocese of St. Petersburg
Reverend Fathers—
Brown, Raymond E., S.S., 418 N.E. 105th St., Miami Shores, FL 33138
Fernandez, Marcellus, 706 E. Brandon Blvd., Brandon, FL 33511
Morgan, D. Terrence, North American College, Rome, Italy
Russo, Caesar, P.O. Box 343, Bronx, NY 10470
Walsh, Flannan J.
Young, Dennis M., Chap., V.A. Medical Center, Augusta, GA

Military Chaplains:
Reverend Fathers—
Brault, Gilles R.
Camarda, Ronald A.
Dux, John H.

Absent on Sick Leave:
Reverend Fathers—
Gagan, Philip R.
Pollard, John L.

Retired:
Reverend Monsignors—
Dawson, Joseph, 301 Elizabeth, Folkston, GA 31537
Haryasz, Francis S., 397 Village Drive St., Augustine, FL 32095
Reverend Fathers—
Barry, Joseph A., Presbyterian Apartments, 1045 Oak St., Apt. #206, Jacksonville, FL 32204
Couture, Fernand, Hwy. 17, Orange Park, FL 32073

INSTITUTIONS LOCATED IN THE DIOCESE

[A] HIGH SCHOOLS, DIOCESAN

ST. AUGUSTINE. *St. Joseph Academy*, 155 State Rd. 207, 32095. Tel: 904-824-0431. Day School. Deacon James F. Delaney, Chap.; Mr. Edward L. Locks, Prin. Lay Teachers 16; Students 230.

JACKSONVILLE. *Bishop Kenny High School*, 1055 Kingman Ave., P.O. Box 5544, 32247. Tel: 904-398-7545; Fax: 904-398-5728. Rev. Michael R. Houle, M.A., M.Ed., M.Div., Pres.; Miss Jane Marnett, M.S., Prin.; Robert West, M.Ed., Vice Prin. & Athletic Dir.; Mrs. Karen Crews, M.Ed., Asst. Prin. for Curriculum; Dave Williams, M.Ed., Dean of Students. Priests 1; Sisters 2; Lay Teachers 70; Students 1,340.
San Juan del Rio Catholic School, 1714-2 State Rd. 13, 32259. Tel: 904-287-8081.

[B] ELEMENTARY SCHOOLS, INTERPAROCHIAL

MIDDLEBURG. *Annunciation School*. (Grades K-3), 1610 Blanding Blvd., 32068. Interparish school composed of students from Sacred Heart, Green Cove Springs; St. Catherine's, Orange Park; and St. Luke, Middleburg. Susan Powell, Prin. Students 193.

[C] CATHOLIC CHARITIES

ST. AUGUSTINE. *Catholic Charities Regional Office*, 40 Sanford St., P.O. Box 543, 32085. Tel: 904-829-6300. Becky Stringer, Exec. Dir.

GAINESVILLE. *Catholic Charities Regional Office*, 1717 N.E. 9th St., 32609. Tel: 352-372-0294. Leonard Spillane, Dir.

JACKSONVILLE. *Catholic Charities Bureau, Inc.*, 11625 Old St. Augustine Rd., P.O. Box 24000, 32241-4000. Mr. William J. Tierney, Diocesan Dir. Tel: 904-262-3200.
Catholic Charities Regional Office, 134 E. Church St., 32202. Tel: 904-354-4846; Fax: 904-354-4718. William C. Beitz, Dir.
New Hope Program, 134 East Church St., 32202. Tel: 904-354-3464. Deacon Stanley Grenn, Dir.
Office of Aging Services, 134 E. Church St., 32202. Tel: 904-354-4846. Ms. Kathryn Strayer, L.I.C.S.W., Dir. Office of Aids Ministry, 134 East Church St., 32202. Tel: 904-354-4718. Sr. Marlene Payette, S.S.J., Dir.
Office of Justice and Peace, 11625 Old St. Augustine Rd., P.O. Box 24000, 32241. Tel: 904-262-3200. Delena Stephens, Dir.

[D] SPECIAL APOSTOLATES

ST. AUGUSTINE. *Religious Education for Catholic Deaf and Blind*, 207 N. San Marco Ave., 32084. Tel: 904-823-4407 (Voice/TDD). Rev. Rene Robert, Chap. Tel: 904-825-0359 (Voice/TDD); Kathy Waller, Pastoral Worker and Teacher. Tel: 904-823-4407. Florida School for the Deaf and Blind.

JACKSONVILLE. *L'Arche Harbor House I, II, III, and IV*, 700 Arlington Rd., 32211. Tel: 904-725-7740; Fax: 904-725-1346. Dorothy B. Klein, Exec. Dir. Total Staff 15; Total in Residence 21. A community residence with mentally retarded adults.
Morning Star School, 725 Mickler Rd., 32211. Mrs. Teri Aschliman, Prin. A school for exceptional children. Lay Teachers 11; Students 110.

[E] GENERAL HOSPITALS

JACKSONVILLE. *St. Vincent's Medical Center, Inc.*, 1800 Barrs St., P.O. Box 2982, 32203. Tel: 904-387-7300.
For a complete listing, refer to the Hospitals section.

[F] HOMES FOR AGING

JACKSONVILLE. *All Saints Home*, 5838 Blanding Blvd., 32246.
For a complete listing, refer to the Special Care Facilities section.
St. Catherine Laboure Manor, 1750 Stockton St., 32204. Tel: 904-308-4700.
For a complete listing, refer to the Special Care Facilities section.

[G] CATHOLIC CHARITIES OFFICE OF HOUSING

JACKSONVILLE. *Jacksonville, Family Housing Management Co.*, 134 E. Church St., 32202. Tel: 904-632-1255. Sandra B. Bonna, Dir., Jacksonville, Office of Housing Development, 134 E. Church St., 32202. Tel: 904-632-1255. Leo V. Rabuck, Dir.
Hurley Manor I, 3333 University Blvd. N., 32277. Tel: 904-744-6022. Norma Sullivan, Res. Mgr. Parent Co., Catholic Charities Housing Association of Jacksonville, Inc. T. William Glocker, Pres.
Hurley Manor II, 3335 University Blvd. N., 32277. Tel: 904-744-9348. Norma Sullivan, Res. Mgr. Parent Co., Diocesan Housing Bureau, Inc. Alton W. Yates, Pres.
Barry Manor, 1000 Husson Ave., Palatka, 32277. Tel: 904-328-5137. Patsy Sutton, Res. Mgr. Parent Co., Palatka Retirement Villas, Inc. Bernice Trotman, Pres.
St. Clare House, 2064 Dellwood Ave., 32204.
Providence Center, 134 E. Church St., 32202. Tel: 904-632-1255.

[H] MONASTERIES AND RESIDENCES OF PRIESTS AND BROTHERS

JACKSONVILLE. *Maryknoll Fathers & Brothers*, 2243 Saragossa Ave., 32217-2685. Tel: 904-739-1112. In res., Revs. Dennis Cleary, M.M.; Henry Murphy, M.M. Total in Residence 2.

[I] CONVENTS AND RESIDENCES FOR SISTERS

ST. AUGUSTINE. *Motherhouse of the Sisters of St. Joseph of St. Augustine, Florida*, 241 St. George St., P.O. Box 3506, 32085. Sr. Florence Bryan, S.S.J., Gen. Supr. Professed Sisters 116.
The Sisters of St. Joseph Continuing Community Support Trust Fund.

[J] RETREAT HOUSES

JACKSONVILLE. *Loretto House of Prayer*, 4118 Loretto Rd., 32223. Sr. Eileen Marie Flanagan, Dir.
Marywood Center for Spirituality and Ministry Formation, 1714-5 State Rd. 13, 32259. Tel: 904-287-2525; Fax: 904-287-9738. Mr. David E. Nowak, Dir.; Ms. Patricia McHugh, Conference Coord.; Sr. Kathleen Power, Prog. Coord.; Mr. Tim Kennedy, Plant Mgr. Total Staff 10; Total in Residence 1.

KORONA. *Carmelite Fathers House of Prayer*, Star Rte., Box 70, 32110. Rev. Joseph F. Zawada, O.C.D. Total Staff 4.

[K] MISCELLANEOUS

GAINESVILLE. *The Center for the Study of the Passion of Christ and the Holy Shroud*, 1738 W. University, 32603. Mrs. Gerry DeGraff, Exec. Sec.

ORLANDO. *The Florida Catholic Aids Network*, P.O. Box 1800, 32802. Tel: 904-354-4846, Ext. 229; Fax: 904-354-4718. Sr. Marlene Payette, S.S.J., Contact.

ST. PETERSBURG. *Pax Christi Florida, Inc.* Regional branch of the International Catholic Peace Movement. P.O. Box 10747, 33733-0747. Tel: 813-327-5045.

[L] NEWMAN CENTERS

ST. AUGUSTINE. *Flagler College Newman Center*, c/o Cathedral of St. Augustine, 35 Treasury St., 32084. Rev. Robert J. Baker, S.T.D.

GAINESVILLE. *University of Florida-St. Augustine Parish and Student Center*, 1738 W. University Ave., P.O. Box 13888, 32604. Tel: 904-372-3533. Revs. John D. Gillespie; Timothy R. Lozier; John M. Phillips. In res., Rev. Anthony S. Michaelraj (India).

JACKSONVILLE. *Jacksonville University and University of North Florida Catholic Campus Ministry*, 32211. Tel: 904-744-3950, Ext. 7258. Mr. Pete Morgan, Dir. Catholic Campus Ministry.

RELIGIOUS INSTITUTES OF MEN REPRESENTED IN THE DIOCESE

For further details refer to the corresponding bracketed number in the Religious Institutes of Men or Women section.

[1350]—*Brothers of St. Francis Xavier*.—C.F.X.
[1330]—*Congregation of the Mission*.—C.M.
[0260]—*Discalced Carmelite Friars*.—O.C.D.
[0650]—*Holy Ghost Fathers*.—C.S.Sp.
[0800]—*Maryknoll*.—M.M.
[1070]—*Redemptorist Fathers*.—C.SS.R.
[0370]—*Society of St. Columban*.—S.S.C.
[0560]—*Third Order Regular of St. Francis*.—T.O.R.

RELIGIOUS INSTITUTES OF WOMEN REPRESENTED IN THE DIOCESE

[0760]—Daughters of Charity of St. Vincent de Paul (Eastern Prov.)— D.C.
[0230]—*Benedictine Sisters of Pontifical Jurisdiction*.—O.S.B.

[2515]—*Cashel Mercy Sisters.*—C.M.S.
[0960]—*Daughters of Wisdom.*—D.W.
[1070-13]—*Dominican Sisters.*—O.P.
[2490]—*Medical Mission Sisters.*—M.M.S.
[2720]—*Mission Helpers of the Sacred Heart.*—M.H.S.H.
[2170]—*Servants of the Immaculate Heart of Mary.*—I.H.M.
[]—*Sisters for Christian Community.*—S.F.C.C.
[2517]—*Sisters of Mercy.*—S.M.
[2600]—*Sisters of Mercy.* (Cork and Ross).—S.M.
[2990]—*Sisters of Notre Dame.* (Toledo Prov.).—S.N.D.
[3900]—*Sisters of St. Joseph of St. Augustine, FL.*—S.S.J.
[1530]—*Sisters of St. Francis of the Congregation of Our Lady of Lourdes, Sylvania, OH.*—O.S.F.

NECROLOGY

† Burns, Rev. Msgr. John P., Jacksonville, FL, St. Matthews. —Died April 25, 1996.
† Gordon, Thomas, Keystone Heights, FL, St. William. —Died May 6, 1996.

Diocese of St. Cloud

(Dioecesis S. Clodoaldi)

Most Reverend

JOHN F. KINNEY, D.D., J.C.D.

Bishop of St. Cloud; ordained February 2, 1963; appointed Titular Bishop of Caorle and Auxiliary Bishop of St. Paul and Minneapolis November 16, 1976; consecrated January 25, 1977; appointed Bishop of Bismarck June 28, 1982; installed August 23, 1982; appointed Bishop of St. Cloud May 9, 1995; installed July 6, 1995. *Office: 214 Third Ave. S., P.O. Box 1248, St. Cloud, MN, 56302-1248.* Tel.: 320-251-2340.

Most Reverend

GEORGE H. SPELTZ

Former Bishop of St. Cloud; ordained June 2, 1940; appointed Auxiliary Bishop of Winona and Titular Bishop of Claneus February 13, 1963; consecrated March 25, 1963; appointed Coadjutor of St. Cloud April 4, 1966; succeeded January 31, 1968; resigned January 13, 1987. *Res., 224 Third Ave. S., St. Cloud, MN, 56302.* Tel.: 320-251-3871.

Corporate Title: *"The Diocese of St. Cloud."*

ERECTED AS THE VICARIATE OF NORTHERN MINNESOTA, FEBRUARY 12, 1875.

CREATED AS THE DIOCESE OF ST. CLOUD, SEPTEMBER 22, 1889.

Square Miles 12,251.

Comprises the Counties of Stearns, Sherburne, Benton, Morrison, Mille Lacs, Kanabec, Isanti, Pope, Stevens, Traverse, Grant, Douglas, Wilkin, Otter Tail, Todd and Wadena in the State of Minnesota.

For legal titles of parishes and diocesan institutions, consult the Chancery Office.

Chancery: 214 Third Ave. S., P.O. Box 1248, St. Cloud, MN, 56302. Tel.: 320-251-2340; Fax: 320-251-0470.

STATISTICAL OVERVIEW

Personnel	
Bishop	1
Retired Bishops	1
Abbots	1
Retired Abbots	1
Priests: Diocesan Active in Diocese	100
Priests: Active Outside Diocese	4
Priests: Diocesan in Foreign Missions	2
Priests: Retired, Sick or Absent	39
Number of Diocesan Priests	145
Religious Priests in Diocese	131
Extern Priests in Diocese	6
Ordinations:	
Transitional Deacons	1
Permanent Deacons	5
Permanent Deacons in Diocese	32
Total Brothers	68
Total Sisters	595
Parishes	
Parishes	141
With Resident Pastor:	
Resident Diocesan Priests	86
Resident Religious Priests	16
Without Resident Pastor:	
Administered by Priests	39
Professional Ministry Personnel:	
Sisters	11
Lay Ministers	53
Welfare	
Catholic Hospitals	4
Total Assisted	156,327
Homes for the Aged	11
Total Assisted	1,229
Day Care and Extended Day Care Centers	2
Total Assisted	100
Specialized Homes	6
Total Assisted	122
Special Centers for Social Services	6
Total Assisted	22,644
Residential Care of Disabled	5
Total Assisted	62
Other Institutions	1
Total Assisted	85
Educational	
Diocesan Students in Other Seminaries	4
Seminaries, Religious	1
Students Religious	7
Total Seminarians	11
Colleges and Universities	2
Total Students	3,689
High Schools, Diocesan and Parish	1
Total Students	536
High Schools, Private	1
Total Students	176
Elementary Schools, Diocesan and Parish	35
Total Students	6,149
Non-residential Schools for the Disabled	1
Total Students	25
Catechesis/Religious Education:	
High School Students	7,877
Elementary Students	17,783
Total Students Under Catholic Instruction	36,246
Teachers in the Diocese:	
Priests	43
Brothers	10
Sisters	60
Lay Teachers	612
Vital Statistics	
Receptions into the Church:	
Infant Baptism Totals	2,529
Adult Baptism Totals	73
Received into Full Communion	214
First Communions	2,980
Confirmations	2,702
Marriages:	
Catholic	761
Interfaith	368
Total Marriages	1,129
Deaths	1,417
Total Catholic Population	147,415
Total Population	433,427

Former Bishops—Rt. Rev. RUPERT SEIDENBUSCH, O.S.B., D.D., cons. Bishop of Halia, Vicar-Apostolic of Northern Minnesota, May 30, 1875; resigned Nov. 15, 1888; died June 2, 1895.—Rt. Rev. OTTO ZARDETTI, D.D., cons. Oct. 20, 1889; transferred to Bucharest, Roumania, and raised to the Archiepiscopal Dignity, Feb. 23, 1894; died May 9, 1902.—Rt. Rev. MARTIN MARTY, O.S.B., D.D., cons. Bishop of Tiberias, Feb. 1, 1880; Bishop of Sioux Falls, 1889; transferred to St. Cloud, Jan. 21, 1895; died Sept. 19, 1896.—Rt. Rev. JAMES TROBEC, D.D., ord. Sept. 8, 1865; cons. Bishop of St. Cloud, Sept. 21, 1897; resigned April 15, 1914 and; Titular Bishop of Lycopolis; died Dec. 14, 1921.—Most Rev. JOSEPH F. BUSCH, D.D., ord. July 28, 1889; appt. Bishop of Lead, S. D., April 9, 1910; cons. May 19, 1910; transferred to See of St. Cloud, Jan. 19, 1915; died May 31, 1953.—Most Rev. PETER W. BARTHOLOME, D.D., ord. June 12, 1917; appt. Titular Bishop of Lete and Coadjutor Bishop of St. Cloud "cum jure successionis", Dec. 6, 1941; cons. March 3, 1942; succeeded to See May 31, 1953; appt. Assistant at the Pontificial Throne July 23, 1954; resigned Jan. 31, 1968; died June 17, 1982.—Most Rev. GEORGE H. SPELTZ, D.D., Ph.D., appt. Auxiliary Bishop of Winona and Titular Bishop of Claneus February 13, 1963; cons. March 25, 1963; appt. Coadjutor of St. Cloud April 4, 1966 succeeded Jan. 31, 1968; resigned Jan. 13, 1987.—Most Rev. JEROME HANUS, O.S.B., D.D., appt. Bishop of St. Cloud, July 6, 1987; ord. and installed Aug. 24, 1987; appt. Coadjutor Archbishop of Dubuque, IA, Aug. 23, 1994.

Chancery—P.O. Box 1248, 214 Third Ave. S., St. Cloud, 56302. Tel: 320-251-2340; 320-252-9879 (after hours); Fax: 320-251-0470. Office Hours: Mon.-Fri. 9-12 & 1-4:30.

Vicar General—Rev. Msgr. DANIEL J. TAUFEN, S.T.L.

Chancellor—Rev. SEVERIN SCHWIETERS.

Assistant Chancellor—Rev. ROBERT E. ROLFES, J.C.L.

Diocesan Tribunal—316 Seventh Ave. N., St. Cloud, All marriage cases are to be directed to: *The Tribunal, Box 576, St. Cloud, 56302.* Tel: 320-251-6557.

Judicial Vicar—Rev. VIRGIL HELMIN, J.C.L.

Adjutant Judicial Vicar—Revs. ROBERT E. ROLFES, J.C.L.; WILLIAM VOUK, III, J.C.L.

Promoter Justitiae—Rev. Msgr. DANIEL J. TAUFEN, S.T.L.

Defensor Vinculi—Revs. NICHOLAS LANDSBERGER; ALFRED HELTEMES; GREGORY LIESER; THOMAS OLSON.

Pro-Synodal Judges—Revs. ROBERT C. HARREN, J.C.L.; ROBERT E. ROLFES, J.C.L.; PAUL SCHMELZER; ROBERT LANDSBERGER; WILLIAM VOUK, III, J.C.L.; JONATHAN LICARI, O.S.B.

Notaries—Revs. SEVERIN SCHWIETERS; VIRGIL HELMIN, J.C.L.; ROBERT E. ROLFES, J.C.L.; WILLIAM VOUK, III, J.C.L.; JILL LENTNER; DIANA SKAJA.
Advocates—Revs. JOSEPH KORF; MARVIN ENNEKING; LEON SLOMINSKI.
Marriage Counseling—Caritas Family Services, Mr. THOMAS KEAVENY, L.I.C.S.W., Dir., *Pastoral Center, Diocese of St. Cloud, 305 N. Seventh Ave., St. Cloud, 56303.* Tel: 320-252-4121.

Diocesan Consultors—Rev. Msgr. DANIEL J. TAUFEN, S.T.L.; Revs. TIMOTHY BALTES; GERALD DALSETH; RAYMOND DONNAY; JAMES HAHN; JOSEPH KORF; RICHARD LEISEN; VINCENT LIESER; KENNETH RIEDEMANN; DAVID RIEDER; EBERHARD SCHEFERS; RAYMOND STEFFES, O.S.C.

Deans—St. Cloud: Rev. TIMOTHY BALTES, St. Joseph: Rev. VINCENT LIESER, Alexandria: Rev. KENNETH RIEDEMANN, Cold Spring: Rev. JOHN CASKEY, Fergus Falls: Rev. JOSEPH KORF, Foley: Rev. FRANCIS BRITZ, Little Falls: Rev. LAURN VIRNIG, Melrose: Rev. RALPH ZIMMERMAN, Morris: Rev. ARLIE SOWADA, Princeton: Rev. MARK OSTENDORF, Sauk Centre: Rev. BERNARD KAHLHAMER, Wadena: Rev. DAVID RIEDER.

Diocesan Corporate Board—Most Rev. JOHN KINNEY, Pres.; Rev. Msgr. DANIEL J. TAUFEN, S.T.L., Vice Pres. SEVERIN SCHWIETERS, Sec. ROBERT C. HARREN, J.C.L.; ALFRED HELTEMES.

Diocesan Finance Council—Rev. SEVERIN SCHWIETERS, Finance Officer; Rev. Msgr. DANIEL J. TAUFEN, S.T.L.; Rev. ROBERT E. ROLFES, J.C.L.; Mr. LEE TORBORG; Sr. KATHLEEN KALINOWSKI, O.S.B.; Mr. JOHN LEISEN; Mr. RICHARD GRUBER; Mr. THOMAS REIF; Mrs. SHARON HESS; Mrs. LUANN POPP; Mr. LOREN LIESEMEYER.

Due Process Service—Rev. ROBERT C. HARREN, J.C.L., Chm.; Mr. JAMES O'TOOLE.

Presbyteral Council—Revs. JOSEPH KORF, Chm. TIMOTHY BALTES, Vice Chm. JOHN CASKEY, Sec. KENNETH RIEDEMANN; FRANCIS BRITZ; RALPH ZIMMERMAN; MARK OSTENDORF; LLOYD HAUPT; BERNARD KAHLHAMER; VINCENT LIESER; GREGORY MASTEY; DAVID RIEDER; ARLIE SOWADA; DOMINIC RUIZ, O.S.B.; LAURN VIRNIG; Rev. Msgr. DANIEL J. TAUFEN, S.T.L.,Address correspondence to: *Presbyteral Council of the Diocese of St. Cloud, Our Lady of Victory, Church 207 Vine St. N., Fergus Falls, 56537-2041.*

Pastoral Council—MARY THERESE ANDERSON, Chm.; Revs. KENNETH RIEDEMANN; GREGORY MASTEY; ROGER KASPERICK, O.S.B.; Deacon BERNARD GRUENES; Sr. MARIE DONAHUE, S.S.N.D.; Sr. MARY TERESE WOIDA, O.S.B.; ROSEMARY BORGERT; Mrs. MARCELLA BRIOL; Mrs. JEAN COOL; CHARLOTTE KREBS; JEROME FISCHER; CAROL STEIDL; NANCY HENDRICKX; KATIE HENNEMANN; DELORES HOFFMAN; JOSEPH MALINOWSKI; KATHY MOELLER; PAT QUACKENBUSH; JENNIFER SCHNEIDER; ALFRED SCHWALBE; VIRGINIA TERHAAR; Mrs. LEMAY BECHTOLD, Exec. Sec.

Diocesan Offices and Programs

Apostleship of Prayer and Enthronement of the Sacred Heart—Rev. RICHARD WEY, Dir., *11 Eighth Ave. S., St. Cloud, 56301.*

Boy Scouts—Rev. LEROY SCHEIERL, Dir., *St. Francis DeSales, P.O. Box 69, Belgrade, 56312-0069.*

Building Commission—Revs. EBERHARD SCHEFERS, Chm. THOMAS OLSON; LEROY SCHOLZ; Sr. COLLEEN HAGGERTY, O.S.B.; JEANNE CHRISTIANSON; DONALD KAINZ,Address correspondence to: Rev. EBERHARD SCHEFERS, *Church of St. Francis Xavier, P.O. Box 150, Sartell, 56377-0150.*

Campaign for Human Development—Rev. Msgr. DANIEL J. TAUFEN, S.T.L., Dir., *P.O. Box 1248, St. Cloud, 56302.*

Campus Ministry—Rev. KEVIN ANDERSON, *Newman Center, 396 First Ave. S., St. Cloud, 56301.*

Catholic Charities—Mr. STEVEN BRESNAHAN, Dir., *1730 Seventh Ave. S., St. Cloud, 56301.* Tel: 320-252-0412. Caritas Family Services: Adoption, Counselling (Individual, Family, Financial, Pregnancy), Food Shelf and Women's Guild Clothing, P.M.I.'s, Refugee Resettlement, Services to Widowed and Divorced. Supervisors: JAMES WAGNER, *207 Seventh Ave. N., St. Cloud, 56303.* Tel: 320-252-1280. DONNA JOHNSON, *305 Seventh Ave. N., St. Cloud, 56303.* Tel: 320-252-4121.
Women's Guild—JOYCE STOCK, Coord., *207 Seventh Ave. N., St. Cloud, 56303.* Tel: 320-253-3454.

Catholic Relief Services—Rev. RICHARD LEISEN, Dir., *P.O. Box 39, Paynesville, 56362.* Tel: 320-252-0412.

Catholic Women, Council of—Rev. HAROLD J. KOST, Moderator, *Holy Family Church, Belle Prairie, Rte. 4, Little Falls, 56345.* DELORES HOFFMAN, Pres., *Rte. 3, Box 141, Pierz, 56364.*

Cemeteries Assumption-Calvary—Rev. WILLIAM GARDING, Gen. Mgr., Office: *2341 Roosevelt Rd., St. Cloud, 56301.* Tel: 320-251-5511.

Censores Librorum—Revs. PAUL ZYLLA, S.T.D.; ROBERT C. HARREN, J.C.L.; Rev. Msgr. DANIEL J. TAUFEN, S.T.L.

Charismatic Renewal, Bishop's Liaison To—Rev. GERALD MISCHKE, *St. Mary's Parish, P.O. Box 308, Holdingford, 56340-0308.*

Clerical Aid Association—Most Rev. JOHN F. KINNEY, Pres.; Rev. Msgr. DANIEL J. TAUFEN, S.T.L., Sec.; Revs. SEVERIN SCHWIETERS, Treas. Directors: SYLVESTER KLEINSCHMIDT; RICHARD LEISEN; ALEXANDER LUDWIG; EUGENE DOYLE; EUGENE MEEMKEN; SILVERIUS SCHMITT, Address mail to: *The Chancery, P.O. Box 1248, St. Cloud, 56302.*

Commission for the Catholic Mission Among the Colored People and Indians—Rev. RAYMOND STEFFES, O.S.C., Dir., *P.O. Star Route, Onamia, 56359.*

Communications Office—(Radio, Television, Public Information, CTNA Affiliate), ROSEMARY BORGERT, Dir., *Pastoral Center, Diocese of St. Cloud, 305 N. Seven Ave., St. Cloud, 56303.* Tel: 320-251-0558.

Continuing Formation of Priests—Rev. VINCENT LIESER, Dir., *St. John Seminary, Collegeville, 56321.*

Development Office—Rev. ROBERT E. ROLFES, J.C.L., Vicar for Devel.; Mr. MARK LEASE, Dir. Devel.

Diocesan Education Council—Sr. KATHERINE KALHOFF, S.S.N.D.; Deacon GREGORY STEELE; JOAN HEIPER; AIMEE BATES; NOELLA FATH; GERALYN NATHE-EVANS; JOANNE KRAVA.

Office of Catholic Education Ministries—Sr. CATHERINE KALLHOFF, S.S.N.D., Supt. Education; LINDA KAISER, School Consultant; LORI DAHLHOFF, Consultant for Ministries/Persons with Disabilities and Cathechist Formation; JAN HAARMAN, Consultant Religious Education and Faith Formation; TIMOTHY WELCH, Consultant Media/Computer and Ministry Formation Program; PAT MALOVRH, Office Coord. JEFFREY KASTER, Consultant for the Formation of Youth; CLAIRE CAUCCI, Media Coord., Address all correspondence to: *Catholic Education Ministries, Pastoral Center, Diocese of St. Cloud, 305 N. Seventh Ave., St. Cloud, 56303.* Tel: 320-251-0111.

Diocesan Ecumenical Commission—Rev. ALBERT HOLMES, Chm., Address all correspondence to: *P.O. Box 158, Bertha, 56437-0158.*

Diocesan Priests Pension Plan Trustees—Most Rev. JOHN KINNEY; Rev. Msgr. DANIEL J. TAUFEN, S.T.L.; Revs. RICHARD LEISEN; ALEXANDER LUDWIG; KENNETH BRENNY; SILVERIUS SCHMITT; SEVERIN SCHWIETERS; STANLEY WIESER; LLOYD HAUPT.

Eucharistic League—Rev. RAYMOND SCHULZETENBERG, Dir., *S.S. Peter & Paul Church, Gilman, 56333.*

Family Life Bureau—CHRISTINE CODDEN, Dir., *Pastoral Center, Diocese of St. Cloud, 305 N. Seventh Ave., St. Cloud, 56303.* Tel: 320-252-4721.

Holy Childhood Association—Rev. RICHARD WEY, Dir., *11-Eighth Ave., S., St. Cloud, 56301.*

Koinonia Program of Central Minnesota—Rev. DAVID MACIEJ, *33 24 Ave. N., St. Cloud, 56303.*

Legion of Decency—Rev. ROBERT E. ROLFES, J.C.L., *P.O. Box 1248, St. Cloud, 56302.*

Legion of Mary—Rev. RAYMOND STEFFES, O.S.C., *Crosier Monastery, Onamia, 56359.*

Natural Family Planning—Mrs. KAY EK, Dir., *316 Seventh Ave. N., St. Cloud, 56303.* Tel: 320-252-2100.

Newspaper "St. Cloud Visitor"—Sr. NANCY BAUER, O.S.B., Editor & Business Mgr., *Pastoral Center, Diocese of St. Cloud, 305 N. Seventh Ave., Box 1068, St. Cloud, 56302.*

Permanent Diaconate Program—Deacon MICHAEL KEABLE, Dir.; Rev. LEROY KREMER, Vicar for Permanent Deacons, *Our Lady of Lourdes Church, 208 W. Broadway, Little Falls, 56345.* Deacon STEPHEN YANISH, Pres., Diaconal Community, *305 Seventh Ave. N., St. Cloud, 56303.* Tel: 612-252-4721.

Personnel Committee—Revs. GREGORY LIESER, Dir., *930 31st Ave. N., St. Cloud, 56303.* JONATHAN LICARI, O.S.B.; MARVIN ENNEKING; LEROY KREMER; DAVID RIEDER; LEROY SCHOLZ; Rev. Msgr. DANIEL J. TAUFEN.

Respect Life Program—Rev. THOMAS KNOBLACH, *St. Ann's Church, 514 S.E. First St., Wadena, 56482.* Tel: 218-631-1593.

Propagation of the Faith—Rev. RICHARD WEY, Dir., *11 Eighth Ave. S., St. Cloud, 56301.* Tel: 320-251-1100; Fax: 320-251-2061.

Rural Life Program—Mr. THOMAS KEAVENY, Dir. Catholic Community Services, *305 Seventh Ave. N., St. Cloud, 56303.* Tel: 320-252-4121.

Spanish Migrant Program—Rev. ALAN WIELINSKI, Dir., *St. Leonard's Church, P.O. Box 378, Pelican Rapids, 56572.*

TEC (Central Minnesota TEC) (Together Encountering Christ)—Rev. KENNETH OPAT, O.S.C., Coord., *516 School St., Anoka, 55303.* Tel: 612-323-8178; Fax: 612-421-4230.

Vocations—Rev. DONALD WAGNER, Dir., *305 Seventh Ave. N., St. Cloud, 56303.* Tel: 320-251-5001.

Worship, Office of—Mr. GARY FELDHEGE, Dir., *Pastoral Center, Diocese of St. Cloud, 305 N. Seventh Ave., St. Cloud, 56303.* Tel: 320-255-9068.

CLERGY, PARISHES, MISSIONS AND PAROCHIAL SCHOOLS

CITY OF ST. CLOUD
(Benton, Stearns, Sherburne Counties)

1—ST. MARY'S CATHEDRAL OF ST. CLOUD, Rev. Steven Binsfeld.
Res., 25 Eighth Ave., S., 56301. Tel: 320-251-1840; Fax: 320-253-5001.
School—Tel: 320-252-2740; Fax: 320-252-5360.
School Sisters of Notre Dame 3; Lay Teachers 6; Students 114.

2—HOLY ANGELS. Closed. For inquiries for parish records contact the Chancery.

3—HOLY SPIRIT, Rev. Virgil A. Helmin.
Office: 2405 Walden Way, 56301. Tel: 320-251-3764; Fax: 320-252-5143.
School—St. Elizabeth Ann Seton. Inter-Parochial school. See separate listing.

4—ST. ANTHONY OF PADUA, Revs. Robert C. Harren; David Maciej.
Res., 33 24th Ave., N., 56303. Tel: 320-251-5966; Fax: 320-251-0664.
School—St. Elizabeth Ann Seton Inter-Parochial School. See separate listing.

5—ST. AUGUSTINE, Rev. Simon Bischof, O.S.B.; Deacon Jeff Hennes.
Office: 443 Second St., S.E., 56304. Tel: 320-251-8335; Fax: 320-251-8364.
Res., 210 Fifth Ave., S.E., 56304.
School—Tel: 320-251-2376.
Sisters of Notre Dame 1; Lay Teachers 12; Students 208.

6—ST. JOHN CANTIUS, Rev. Peter Snyers; Deacon Fred Reker
Res., 1515 N. Third St., 56303. Tel: 612-251-4455; Fax: 612-251-1513. [JC]

7—ST. MICHAEL, Rev. Edwin J. Kraemer; Deacon Bernard Gruenes.
Res., 1036 Co. Rd. 4, 56303. Tel: 320-251-6923; Fax: 320-202-1104.
School—Sts. Peter & Paul & Michael Inter-Parochial School. See separate listing.

8—ST. PAUL, Rev. Timothy Baltes; Deacon Michael Keable. In res., Rev. Christopher Trussel.
Res., 1125 11th Ave., N., 56303. Tel: 320-251-4831.
School—Sts. Peter & Paul & Michael Inter-Parochial School. See separate listing.

9—ST. PETER, Rev. Gregory Lieser.
Res., 930 31st Ave., N., 56303. Tel: 320-252-2113. [JC]
School—Sts. Peter & Paul & Michael Inter-Parochial School. See separate listing.

10—CHRIST CHURCH, Rev. Kevin Anderson.
Res., 396 S. First Ave., 56301. Tel: 612-251-2712.

OUTSIDE THE CITY OF ST. CLOUD

Albany, Stearns Co., Seven Dolors, Rev. Corwin Collins, O.S.B.
Res., Box 277, 56307. Tel: 320-845-2705. [CEM]
School—Tel: 320-845-2011.
Lay Teachers 8; Students 128.

Alexandria, Douglas Co., St. Mary's, Revs. Alexander P. Ludwig; Gregory J. Mastey.
Res., 411 Hawthorne St., P.O. Box 669, 56308. Tel: 320-763-5781; Fax: 320-763-4833. [CEM]
School—Lay Teachers 9; Students 197.

Avon, Stearns Co., St. Benedict's, Rev. James Reichert, O.S.B.; Deacon Brian Krebs.
Church—P.O. Box 98, 56310. Tel: 320-356-7121. [CEM]

Battle Lake, Otter Tail Co., Our Lady of the Lake, Rev. Paul Folsom.
Res., 409 Lake Ave., N., P.O. Box 671, 56515. Tel: 218-864-5619.

Becker, Sherbune Co., Immaculate Conception, Rev. Mark G. Ostendorf; Deacon Gregory Steele.
Res., 12100 Sherburne Ave., Box 426, 55308. Tel: 612-261-4242.

Belgrade, Stearns Co., St. Francis De Sales, Rev. LeRoy Scheierl.
Res., 541 Martin Ave., P.O. Box 69, 56312. Tel: 320-254-8218. [CEM]

Belle Prairie, Morrison Co., Holy Family, Rev. Harold J. Kost.
Res., R.R. 4, Little Falls P.O., 56345. Tel: 320-632-5720. [CEM]

Belle River, Douglas Co., St. Nicholas, Rev. Jeff Ethen.
Church—9473 County Rd. 3, N.E., Carlos, 56319.

Tel: 612-852-7041. [CEM]

Bertha, Todd Co., St. Joseph's, Rev. Albert Holmes.
Res., 56437. Tel: 218-924-2605. [CEM]

Big Lake, Sherburne Co., Our Lady of the Lake, Rev. Nicholas Dressen.
Res., 55309. Tel: 320-263-2863; Fax: 320-263-3187. [CEM]

BlueGrass, Wadena Co., St. Hubert's, Rev. Peter Kirchner, Jr.
Res., 20 Brown St., N., P.O. Box C, Verndale, 56481. Tel: 218-445-5786.

Bluffton, Otter Tail Co., St. John the Baptist, Rev. Kevin Schwartz.
Res., 56518. Tel: 218-385-2608. [CEM]

Bowlus, Morrison Co., St. Stanislaus Kostka, Rev. Silverius J. Schmitt.
Res., 428 Main St., 56314. Tel: 320-584-5313. [CEM]

Braham, Isanti Co., St. Peter & Paul, Rev. Nicholas M. Zimmer.
Res., 55006. Tel: 320-396-3105.

Brandon, Douglas Co., Church of St. Ann, Rev. Eugene Lemm.
Res., 56315. Tel: 320-524-2462. [CEM]

Breckenridge, Wilkin Co., St. Mary of the Presentation, Rev. Leo Moenkedrick.
Res., 221 N. Fourth St., 56520-1496. Tel: 218-643-5173. [CEM 2]
School—Tel: 218-643-5443.
Lay Teachers 11; Students 140.

Brennyville, Benton Co., St. Elizabeth, Rev. Thomas Olson.
Res., 16426 125 Ave., N.E., Foley, 56329. Tel: 320-355-2454. [CEM]

Brooten, Stearns Co., St. Donatus, Rev. James Statz.
Res., 33932 County Rd. 18, Sauk Centre, 56378. Tel: 612-352-2521; 346-2431.

Browerville, Todd Co., Christ the King, Rev. Kenneth Thielman; Deacon Vincent Leisen.
Res., 56438. Tel: 320-594-2291. [CEM]
School—Tel: 320-594-6114.
Lay Teachers 6; Students 73.

Brown's Valley, Traverse Co., St. Anthony's, Rev. Arlie Sowada.
Res., Box 359, 56219. Tel: 320-695-2621. [CEM]

Buckman, Morrison Co., St. Michael's, Rev. Ronald Dockendorf.
Res., 56317. Tel: 612-468-2316. [CEM]

Butler, Otter Tail Co., Holy Cross, Rev. Kevin Schwartz.
Res., P.O.Box 36, Bluffton, 56518. Tel: 218-385-2608.

Cambridge, Isanti Co., Christ the King, Rev. James David Hahn.
Res., 227 N. Fern, 55008. Tel: 320-689-1221. [CEM]

Chokio, Stevens Co., St. Mary's, Rev. Jerome G. Nordick.
Res., 56221. Tel: 320-324-2680. [CEM]

Clarissa, Todd Co., St. Joseph, Rev. Eugene A. Meemken; Deacon Vern Thelen.
Res., 107 S. John St., P.O. Box 5, 56440. Tel: 218-756-2205. [CEM]

Clear Lake, Sherburne Co., St. Marcus, Rev. LeRoy Scholz.
Res., 55319. Tel: 320-743-2481. [CEM]

Cold Spring, Stearns Co., St. Boniface, Rev. Julian Schmiesing, O.S.B.; Deacons Elmer Eichers; John Salchert; Bruce Maltzen.
Res., 418 Main St., 56320. Tel: 320-685-3280. [CEM]
School—Tel: 612-685-3541.
Lay Teachers 15; Students 229.

Collegeville, Stearns Co., St. John the Baptist, Rev. Jonathan Licari, O.S.B.
Res., 56321. Tel: 320-363-2765. [JC]

Dent, Otter Tail Co., Sacred Heart, Rev. Leo Otto.
Res., 56528. Tel: 218-758-2700. [CEM]

Donnelly, Stevens Co., St. Theresia. Closed. For inquiries for parish records contact the Chancery.

Duelm, Benton Co., St. Lawrence's, Rev. Elmer J. Torborg.
Res., 10915 Duelm Rd., N.E., Foley, 56329. Tel: 320-968-7502.

Dumont, Traverse Co., St. Peter's, Rev. Tony Salzbrunn.
Res., 201 Ninth St., S., Wheaton, 56296. Tel: 320-563-4421.

Eden Valley, Stearns Co., The Church of the Assumption, Rev. Virgil Braun.
Res., 55329. Tel: 320-453-2788. [CEM]

Elbow Lake, Grant Co., St. Olaf, Rev. Andrew Marthaler.
Res., 18 Sixth Ave., N., 56531. Tel: 218-685-4318. [CEM]

Elizabeth, Otter Tail Co., St. Elizabeth, Rev. Alan Wielinski.
Res., 56533. Tel: 218-736-5230. [CEM]

Elk River, Sherburne Co., The Church of St. Andrew, Rev. Robert J. Kieffer; Deacons Frederick St. Jean; Cecil Adams.
Res., 566 Fourth St., 55330. Tel: 320-441-1483; Fax: 320-441-2336. [CEM]
School—Tel: 320-441-3202; Fax: 320-441-2262.
Lay Teachers 13; Students 295.

Elmdale, Morrison Co., St. Edward's, Rev. Todd Schneider.
Res., P.O. Box 188, Upsala, 56384. Tel: 320-573-2975. [CEM]

Elrosa, Stearns Co., SS. Peter and Paul, Rev. LeRoy Scheierl.
Res., 56325. Tel: 320-697-5541. [CEM]

Farming, Stearns Co., St. Catherine's, Rev. Gunther Rolfson, O.S.B.
Res., Rte. 1, Richmond P.O., 56368. Tel: 320-548-3467. [CEM]

Fergus Falls, Otter Tail Co., Our Lady of Victory, Rev. Joseph Korf.
Res., 207 Vine St., N., 56537. Tel: 218-736-2429; Fax: 218-736-4407.
School—Tel: 218-736-6661; Fax: 218-736-4407.
Lay Teachers 8; Students 147.

Flensburg, Morrison Co., Sacred Heart, Rev. Anthony Kroll.
Res., 56328. Tel: 320-632-6930. [CEM 2]

Foley, Benton Co., St. John's, Rev. Alfred J. Heltemes.
Res., 56329. Tel: 320-968-7913. [CEM]
School—St. John's Area School. Consolidation of the following parishes: St. John's, Foley; St. Lawrence, Brennyville; St. Joseph, Morrill; SS. Peter & Paul, Gilman; St. Louis, Foreston; St. Patrick of Minden Township. Tel: 320-968-7972.
Lay Teachers 7; Students 115.

Foreston, Mille Lacs Co., St. Louis Bertrand, Rev. James Cashman, O.S.C.
Res., P.O. Box 128, 56330. Tel: 320-294-5460; 294-5588; Fax: 320-294-5588. [CEM]

Foxhome, Wilkin Co., St. Joseph. Closed. For inquiries for parish records contact the Chancery.

Freeport, Stearns Co., Sacred Heart, Rev. Roger Klassen, O.S.B.
Res., 56331. Tel: 320-836-2143. [CEM]
School—Tel: 320-836-2591.
Sisters of St. Benedict 2; Lay Teachers 3; Students 63.

Gilman, Benton Co., SS. Peter and Paul, Rev. Raymond A. Schulzetenberg.
Res., 56333. Tel: 320-387-2255. [CEM]
School—St. John's. (Foley) Area School.

Glenwood, Pope Co., Sacred Heart, Rev. Thomas G. Becker; Deacon Frank Schmainda.
Res., 105 N. Franklin, 56334. Tel: 320-634-3813. [CEM]

Greenwald, Stearns Co., St. Andrew's, Rev. Kenneth J. Popp.
Res., 56335. Tel: 612-987-3160. [CEM]
School—Tel: 612-987-3133.
Lay Teachers 3; Students 28.

Grey Eagle, Todd Co., St. Joseph's, Rev. Joel Nathe.
Res., P.O. Box 366, 56336. Tel: 320-285-2544. [CEM]

Harding, Morrison Co., Holy Cross, Rev. Roger Thoennes.
Res., P.O. Rte. 4, Pierz, 56364. Tel: 320-277-3701. [CEM]

Henning, Otter Tail Co., Church of St. Edward of Henning, Rev. Albert Holmes.
Res., 56551. Tel: 218-583-2490. [CEM]

Herman, Grant Co., St. Charles, Rev. Jerome Nordick.
Res., P.O. Box 187, Chokio, 56221. Tel: 320-324-2680.

Hillman, Morrison Co., St. Rita's, Rev. Nathan Packard.
Res., Rte. 2, Box 308, 56338. Tel: 320-277-3807. [CEM]

Holdingford, Stearns Co., St. Hedwig's, Revs. Gerald Mischke, Co-Pastor; Anthony Oelrich, Co-Pastor.
Res., 56340. Tel: 320-746-2231; Fax: 320-746-2884. [CEM]

St. Mary's, Revs. Gerald Mischke, Co-Pastor; Anthony Oelrich, Co-Pastor.
Res., 56340. Tel: 320-746-2231; Fax: 320-746-2884. [CEM]

Isanti, Isanti Co., St. Elizabeth Ann Seton, Rev. Richard McGuire.
Res., 109 Fifth Ave., S., 55040. Tel: 320-444-5226. [CEM]

Jacob's Prairie, Wakefield Township, Stearns Co., St. James, Rev. Michael Kwatera, O.S.B.
Res., 25042 County Rd. 2, Cold Spring, 56320. Tel: 612-685-3479. [CEM]

Kensington, Grant Co., Our Lady of the Runestone, Rev. Kenneth Riedemann.
Res., R.R. 2, Box 31, Lowry, 56349-9519. Tel: 320-283-5273.

Kent, Wilkin Co., St. Thomas, Rev. Stanley Wieser.
Res., 56553. Tel: 218-557-8312. [CEM]

Kimball, Stearns Co., Church of Saint Anne, Rev. Frank S. Tomasiewicz; Deacon Stephen Yanish.
Res., P.O. Box 99, 55353. Tel: 320-398-3860. [CEM]

Lake Henry, Stearns Co., St. Margaret's, Rev. Leo Leisen.
Res., Roscoe, 56371. Tel: 320-243-4574. [CEM]

Lake Reno, Pope Co., St. John Nepomuk, Rev. Kenneth Riedemann.
Res., R.R. #2, Box 31, Lowry, 56349. Tel: 320-283-5273. [CEM]

Lastrup, Morrison Co., St. John Nepomuk, Rev. Roger Thoennes.
Res., 56344. Tel: 320-468-2111. [CEM]

Little Falls, Morrison Co., St. Mary, Rev. Nicholas Landsberger.
Res., 305 Fourth St., S.E., 56345. Tel: 320-632-5640. [CEM 3]
School—See Inter-Parochial Schools under Institutions Located in the Diocese.

Our Lady of Lourdes, Rev. Leroy M. Kremer; Deacon Bruce Geyer.
Res., 208 W. Broadway, 56345. Tel: 320-632-8243.
School—See Inter-Parochial Schools under Institutions Located in the Diocese.

Long Prairie, Todd Co., St. Mary of Mt. Carmel, Rev. Mark Stang.
Res., 56347. Tel: 320-732-2635. [CEM]
School—Sisters of St. Benedict 1; Lay Teachers 7; Students 123.

Luxemburg, Stearns Co., St. Wendelin's, Rev. Leon Slominski.
Res., 22714 State Hwy. 15, St. Cloud, 56301. Tel: 320-251-6944. [CEM]
School—Tel: 612-251-9175.
Sisters 1; Lay Teachers 5; Students 100.

Maine, Otter Tail Co., Church of Saint James at Maine, Rev. Paul Folsom.
Res., 409 Lake Ave., N., P.O. Box 671, Battle Lake, 56515. Tel: 218-864-5619. [CEM]

Mayhew Lake, Benton Co., Annunciation, Rev. Francis Britz.
Res., 9965 Mayhew Lake Rd. N.E., Sauk Rapids, 56379. Tel: 320-252-1729. [CEM]

Meire Grove, Stearns Co., St. John's, Rev. Kenneth J. Popp.
Res., Greenwald, 56335. Tel: 320-987-3160. [CEM]
School—Tel: 612-987-3491.
Lay Teachers 3; Students 43.

Melrose, Stearns Co., St. Mary's, Rev. Ralph G. Zimmerman.
Res., 211 S. Fifth Ave., E., 56352-1427. Tel: 320-256-4207; Fax: 320-256-4208.
School—Tel: 320-256-4257.
Lay Teachers 15; Students 210.

Menahga, Wadena Co., The Church of the Assumption of Our Lady of Menahga, Rev. Kevin Schwartz.
Res., St. John the Baptist, Bluffton, 56518. Tel: 218-385-2608. [CEM]

Milaca, Mille Lacs Co., St. Mary's, Rev. Richard John, O.S.C.
Res., 625 3rd Ave. S.E., 56353. Tel: 320-983-3255. [CEM]

Millerville, Douglas Co., Seven Dolors, Rev. Eugene Lemm.
Res., 16921 County Rd. 7, N.W., Brandon, 56315. Tel: 320-876-2240. [CEM]

Mora, Kanabec Co., St. Mary's, Rev. Eugene G. Belair.
Res., 55051. Tel: 320-679-1593. [CEM]
Mission—Ogilvie, Kanabec Co., St. Kathryn.

Moran, Todd Co., St. Isidore, Rev. Eugene Meemken.
Res., St. Joseph's Church, P.O. Box 5, Clarissa, 56440. Tel: 218-756-2205. [CEM]

Morrill, Morrison Co., St. Joseph's, Rev. Thomas F. Olson.
Res., P.O. Rte. 3, Foley, 56329. Tel: 612-355-2585. [CEM]

Morris, Stevens Co., Assumption of the Blessed Virgin Mary, Rev. Gerald Dalseth.
Res., 207 E. Third, Box 287, 56267. Tel: 320-589-3003. [CEM]
School—Tel: 612-589-1704.
Lay Teachers 7; Students 91.

Motley, Morrison Co., St. Michael's, Rev. Robert Landsberger.
Res., 56466. Tel: 218-352-6143.

New Munich, Stearns Co., Immaculate Conception, Rev. Landelin Robling, O.S.B.
Res., 652 Main St., Box 131, 56356. Tel: 320-837-5217. [CEM]

North Prairie, Morrison Co., Holy Cross, Rev. Silverius J. Schmitt.
Res., Bowlus, 56314. Tel: 320-584-5313. [CEM]

Ogilvie, Kanabec Co., St. Kathryn's, Rev. Eugene Belair.
Res., 201 Forest Ave., E., Mora, 55051. Tel: 320-679-1593.

Onamia, Mille Lacs Co., The Church of the Holy Cross of Onamia, Rev. William McNiff, O.S.C.
Res., 56359. Tel: 320-532-3122. [CEM]

Opole, Stearns Co., Our Lady of Mt. Carmel, Revs. Gerald Mischke, Co-Pastor; Anthony Oelrich, Co-Pastor.
Res., St. Mary's Rectory, Holdingford, 56340. Tel: 320-746-2231. [CEM]

Osakis, Douglas Co., Immaculate Conception, Rev. Victor Kinzer.
Res., 56360. Tel: 312-859-2390. [CEM]
School—St. Agnes, Tel: 320-859-2130.
Lay Teachers 5; Students 81.

Padua, Stearns Co., Church of St. Anthony of Padua, Rev. James Statz.
Res., 33932 County Rd. 18, Sauk Centre, 56378. Tel: 320-352-2521. [CEM]

Parkers Prairie, Otter Tail Co., Church of St. William, Rev. Jeff Ethen.
Res., 56361. Tel: 218-338-2761.

Paynesville, Stearns Co., St. Louis, Rev. Richard Leisen.
Res., 505 Burr St., Box 39, 56362. Tel: 320-243-4413; Fax: 320-398-7885. [CEM]

Pearl Lake, Stearns Co., Holy Cross, Rev. John Caskey; Deacon Andrew Kunkel.
Res., 10651 County Rd. 8, Kimball, 55353. Tel: 320-398-7986; Fax: 320-398-7885. [CEM]
School—Tel: 612-398-7885.
Lay Teachers 4; Students 66.

Pelican Rapids, Otter Tail Co., St. Leonard's, Rev. Alan Wielinski.
Res., 56572. Tel: 218-863-5161. [CEM]

Perham, Otter Tail Co., St. Henry's, Rev. David J. Rieder.
Res., Box 216, 56573. Tel: 218-346-4240. [CEM]
School—Area School, Tel: 218-346-6190.
Lay Teachers 8; Students 120.
St. Stanislaus, Rev. David J. Rieder; Deacon Donald Tzinski.
Res., P.O. Box 216, 56573. Tel: 218-346-4240. [CEM]

Pierz, Morrison Co., St. Joseph's, Rev. Kenneth Brenny.
Res., 56364. Tel: 320-468-6033. [CEM]
School—See Inter-Parochial School under Institutions Located in the Diocese.

Princeton, Mille Lacs Co., St. Edward's, Rev. Mark Willenbring.
Res., 804-S. Seventh Ave., 55371. Tel: 320-389-2115. [CEM]

Randall, Morrison Co., St. James, Rev. Alvin Quade.
Res., Box 225, 56475. Tel: 320-749-2720. [CEM]

Rice, Benton Co., Immaculate Conception, Rev. Marvin Enneking.
Res., 130 First Ave., N.E., P.O. Box 189, 56367. Tel: 612-393-2725.

Richmond, Stearns Co., SS. Peter and Paul's, Rev. Dominic Ruiz, O.S.B.; Deacon Joe Stefancin.
Res., P.O. Box 69, 56368. Tel: 320-597-2575. [CEM]
School—Tel: 612-597-2565.
Lay Teachers 7; Students 115.

Rockville, Stearns Co., Mary of the Immaculate Conception, Rev. Robert E. Rolfes.
Res., 56369. Tel: 320-251-7801. [CEM]

Roscoe, Stearns Co., St. Agnes, Rev. Leo Leisen.
Res., 56371. Tel: 320-243-4574. [CEM]

Royalton, Morrison Co., Holy Trinity, Rev. Laurn Virnig.
Res., 56373. Tel: 320-584-5484. [CEM]

Rush Lake, Otter Tail Co., St. Lawrence, Rev. Leo Otto, O.P.
Res., Box 68, Dent, 56528. Tel: 218-758-2700. [CEM]

St. Anna, Stearns Co., Immaculate Conception, Revs. Gerald Mischke, Co-Pastor; Anthony Oelrich, Co-Pastor.
Res., St. Mary's Rectory, Holdingford, 56340. Tel: 320-746-2231. [CEM]

St. Anthony, Stearns Co., St. Anthony's, Rev. William Vouk, III.
Res., 24328 Trobec St., Albany, 56307. Tel: 320-845-2416. [CEM]

St. Augusta, Stearns Co., St. Mary Help of Christians, Rev. Robert D. Schmainda.
Res., 24588 County Rd. 7, St. Cloud, 56301. Tel: 320-252-1799; Fax: 320-252-1992. [CEM]
School—Tel: 320-251-3937.
Sisters of St. Benedict 2; Lay Teachers 5; Students 161.

St. Francis, Stearns Co., St. Francis of Assisi, Rev. William Vouk, III.
Res., 44055 State Hwy. 238, Freeport P.O., 56331. Tel: 320-573-2203. [CEM]

St. Joseph, Stearns Co., St. Joseph's, Rev. Florian Muggli, O.S.B.
Res., 56374. Tel: 320-363-7505. [CEM]
School—Lay Teachers 13; Students 170.

St. Martin, Stearns Co., St. Martin's, Rev. Landelin Robling, O.S.B.
Res., 119 Maine St., Box 290, 56376. Tel: 320-548-3550. [CEM]

St. Nicholas, Stearns Co., St. Nicholas, Rev. John Caskey. In res., Rev. Bernard Mischke, O.S.C.
Res., 15862 County Rd. 165, Watkins, 55389. Tel: 320-398-7986. [CEM]

St. Rosa, Stearns Co., St. Rose of Lima, Rev. Arthur H. Hoppe.
Res., 28905 County Rd. 17, Freeport P.O., 56331-9610. Tel: 320-836-2151. [CEM]

St. Stephen, Stearns Co., St. Stephen's, Rev. John Miller.
Res., 56375. Tel: 320-251-1520. [CEM]

St. Wendel, Stearns Co., St. Columbkille's, Revs. Gerald Mischke, Co-Pastor; Anthony Oelrich, Co-Pastor.
Res., St. Mary's Rectory, Holdingford, 56340. Tel: 320-746-2231. [CEM]

Sartell, Stearns Co., St. Francis Xavier, Rev. Eberhard Schefers; Deacon Jerome Schwarzbauer.
Res., P.O. Box 150, 56377. Tel: 320-252-1363; Fax: 320-259-7090.
School—Tel: 612-252-9940.
Lay Teachers 11; Students 175.

Sauk Centre, Stearns Co., Our Lady of the Angels, Rev. Bernard Kahlhamer; Deacon Lawrence Kaas.
Res., 211 S. Seventh, 56378. Tel: 320-352-3502. [CEM]
St. Paul's, Rev. Timothy Wenzel.
Res., 304 Sinclair Lewis Ave., 56378. Tel: 320-352-2196.
School—Holy Family School. Inter-Parochial School: St. Paul's Sauk Centre, Our Lady of Angels, Sauk Center. 231 Sinclair Lewis Ave., 56378. Tel: 320-352-6535.
Lay Teachers 19; Students 398.

Sauk Rapids, Benton Co., Sacred Heart, Revs. Eugene Doyle; James Herzing.
Res., 308 Third Ave., S., 56379. Tel: 320-251-8115; Fax: 320-251-8115. [CEM]
School—324 Third Ave., S., 56379. Tel: 320-251-2854; Fax: 320-251-0705.
Sisters 2; Lay Teachers 15; Students 287.
St. Patrick, Rev. Elmer Torborg.
Res., 7286 Duelm Rd. N.E., 56379. Tel: 320-252-2069.

Sedan, Pope Co., Immaculate Conception Church, Rev. Frank Poncelet.
Res., Rte. 3, Box 78, Glenwood, 56334. Tel: 320-334-5489.

Sobieski, Morrison Co., St. Stanislaus, Rev. Raymond N. Donnay.
Res., P.O. R.F.D. 3, Little Falls, 56345. Tel: 320-632-5086. [CEM]

Spring Hill Stearns Co., St. Michael's, Rev. Leo Leisen.
Res., 100 Lillie Ave., Roscoe, 56371. Tel: 320-243-4574. [CEM]

Staples, Todd Co., Sacred Heart, Rev. Lauren A. Germann; Deacon Robert Shaffer.
Res., 310 Fourth St., N., 56479. Tel: 218-894-2296.
School—Tel: 218-894-2077.
Lay Teachers 7; Students 113.

Swanville, Morrison Co., St. John the Baptist, Rev. Thomas C. Meyer.
Res., 22 1st. St., P.O. Box 68, 56382. Tel: 320-547-2920; Fax: 320-547-2578. [CEM]

Tintah, Traverse Co., St. Gall's, Rev. Andrew Marthaler.
Res., 56583. Tel: 218-369-2188. [CEM]

Upsala, Morrison Co., St. Mary, Rev. Todd Schneider.
Res., 308 S. Main St., P.O. Box 188, 56384. Tel: 320-573-2132. [CEM]

Urbank, Otter Tail Co., Sacred Heart, Rev. Jeff Ethen.
Res., Rte. 2, Box 133, P.O. Parkers Prairie, 56361. Tel: 218-267-2661. [CEM]

Verndale, Wadena Co., St. Frederick's, Rev. Peter K. Kirchner, Jr.
Res., 56481. Tel: 218-445-5786. [CEM]

Villard, Pope Co., St. Bartholomew's, Rev. Joseph Vandeberg.
Res., St. Alexius Church, West Union, 56389. Tel: 320-352-2563.

Vineland, Mille Lacs Co., St. Therese, Little Flower Indian Mission, Rev. Raymond Steffes, O.S.C.
Res., P.O. Onamia, 56359. Tel: 320-532-3614.

Wadena, Wadena Co., St. Ann's, Rev. Thomas Knoblach.
Res., 514 First St., S.E., 56482. Tel: 218-631-7149; Fax: 218-631-1593. [CEM]
School—Tel: 218-631-2631.
Lay Teachers 10; Students 143.

Wahkon, Mille Lacs Co., Sacred Heart, Rev. Nathan Packard.
Res., 56386. Tel: 320-495-3324.

Waite Park, Stearns Co., St. Joseph's, Rev. Ronald Weyrens; Deacon Richard Midas.
Res., 106 Seventh Ave., N., 56387. Tel: 320-251-5231; Fax: 320-251-3010. [CEM]
School—Tel: 612-251-4741.
Lay Teachers 8; Students 130.

Ward Springs, Todd Co., St. Bernard's, Rev. Joel Nathe.
Res., P.O. Box 366, Grey Eagle, 56336. Tel: 320-285-2544.

West Union, Todd Co., St. Alexius, Rev. Joseph Vandeberg.
Res., 56389. Tel: 320-352-2563. [CEM]
Mission—Villard, Pope Co., St. Bartholomew.

Wheaton, Traverse Co., Ave Maria, Rev. Tony Salzbrunn.
Res., 201 Ninth St. S., 56296. Tel: 320-563-4421. [JC]

Zimmerman, Sherburne Co., St. Pius X, Rev. Antonio Marfori.
Res., Box 152, 55398. Tel: 320-856-4401.

Chaplains of Public Institutions

ST. CLOUD. *Minnesota State Reformatory for Men*. Rev. Joel Kelly, O.S.B., Res., St. John's Abbey, Collegeville, 56321.
U.S. Veteran's Hospital, 56301. Rev. Alfred Stangl.

CAMBRIDGE. *Cambridge State School and Hospital*. Vacant. 55008.

FERGUS FALLS. *State Hospital Chapel*. Vacant. 56537.

SAUK CENTRE. *State Home School for Girls*. Rev. Kenneth Thielman.

Special Assignment:
Reverend Fathers—
Eccleston, John
Garding, William
Lieser, Vincent
Rolfes, Robert, Asst. Chancellor
Schwieters, Severin, Chancellor of the Diocese
Stangl, Alfred
Taufen, Daniel, V.G.
Thoennes, James
Trussel, Chris
Wagner, Donald

On Duty Outside the Diocese:
Reverend Fathers—
Kalkman, Richard, 23 Diaz Ave., San Francisco, CA 94132
Majerus, Daniel, 8722 Timberbriar, San Antonio, TX 78250
Maus, LeRoy, 734 24th St., N.E., McMinnville, OR 97128
Vos, William, Maryknoll Fathers, P.O. Box 578, Musoma, Tanzania, Africa
Walz, Richard, Maracay, Venezuela

Absent on Leave:
Reverend Fathers—
Belland, David, P. O. Box 354, Waite Park, MN 56387
Sauer, Alban, 1120 11th Ave. N., St. Cloud, MN 56303

Retired:
Reverend Monsignors—
Kleinschmidt, Anthony, Josephinum College, Worthington, OH 43085
Reverend Fathers—
Bednark, Walter, 23189 State Hwy. 4, Paynesville, MN 56362
Botz, Lawrence, Box 95, Elrosa, MN 56325
Ebner, Frank, 10339 Parrish Ave. N.E., Elk River, MN 55330
Ekman, Robert, St. Benedict's Center, 1810 S.E. Minnesota Blvd., St. Cloud, MN 56304
Fadrowski, Stanislaus, 1934 Michigan Ave., Englewood, FL 34224
Finnegan, Roscoe L., 715 Farney Rd., Las Cruces, NM 88005
Fridgen, Joseph, P.O. Box 364, Grey Eagle, MN 56336-0366
Furlan, William, 320 Fourth Ave. S., Sauk Rapids, MN 56379
Gall, Sylvester, 520 First St. N.E., Apt. 80, Sartell, MN 56377
Haupt, Lloyd, 929 Brenda Lee Dr., St. Cloud, MN 56303
Heid, Richard, Box 256, Brandon, MN 56315
Illies, Wilfred, 2000 15th Ave. S.E., St. Cloud, MN 56304
Kampsen, Frederick, 884 S. Third Ave. W., Melrose, MN 56352
Kleinschmidt, Sylvester, 412 First St. S., Apt. 1,

Sauk Centre, MN 56378
Kloeckner, William, 10540 Co. Rd. 34 N.W., Alexandria, MN 56308
Lang, Raymond, 1615 15th Ave. S.E. #342, St. Cloud, MN 56304
Minette, James, 101 Enterprise Dr., Apt. 163, Rohnert Park, CA 94928
Morslander, Edward, 500 Third St. S. #164, Waite Park, MN 56387
Otto, Leo, R.R. 3, Box 118, Perham, MN 56573
Pavelis, Harold, Box 88, Concord, CA 94522
Pecovnik, Karel, Parkers Prairie, MN 56361
Peterka, Theodore, Russell Arms 209, 315 Division St., Sauk Rapids, MN 56379
Podrosky, Alfred, 117 Bechwood Dr., Monongahela, PA 15063
Ramacher, Edward, Unit 220 Edgewater S., HC2, Pequot Lakes, MN 56472
Rieder, Donald, 1615 15th Ave., S.E., Apt. 328, St. Cloud, MN 56304
Riley, Patrick, 3034 Fulton Cir., Clearwater, MN 55320
Santo, Vincent, 907 Sinclair Lewis Ave., Sauk Centre, MN 56378
Schmelzer, Paul, 213 Third St., S., St. Cloud, MN 56301
Schwinghammer, Claude, Park Gardens, 114 First St. N., Apt. 219, Waite Park, MN 56387
Sobieck, Elmer, P.O. Box 281, St. Joseph, MN 56374
Speiser, Allan, 101 Riverside Dr. S.E. Apt. 224, St. Cloud, MN 56304
Vogel, Arthur, 617 Pinecone Rd., Apt. 308, Sartell, MN 56377
Vogrin, Joseph, Parkers Prairie, MN 56361
Wey, Richard, Rte. 1, Box 31A, Cushing, MN 56443
Wiersgalla, Joseph, St. Benedict's Center, 1810 S.E. Minnesota Blvd., St. Cloud, MN 56304
Zylla, Paul, 1615-15th Ave., S.E. #251, St. Cloud, MN 56304

Permanent Deacons:
Adams, Cecil, St. Andrew, Elk River
Bates, Kenneth, Country Manor, Sartell
Cichoski, Jerome, Morris
Eichers, Elmer, St. Boniface, Cold Spring
Fromm, Jeffrey, SS. Peter & Paul, Richmond
Geyer, Bruce, Our Lady of Lourdes, Little Falls
Gruenes, Bernard, St. Michael, St. Cloud
Hennes, James C., St. Augustine, St. Cloud
Kaas, Lawrence, Our Lady of the Angels, Sauk Centre
Kaebs, Brian, St. Benedict, Avon
Keable, Michael, St. Paul, St. Cloud
Kosiba, Leo, St. Mary, St. Cloud
Kruchten, Kenneth R., (Retired)
Kunkel, Andrew, Holy Cross, Pearl Lake
Leisen, Vincent, Christ the King, Browerville
Maltzen, Bruce, St. Boniface, Cold Spring
Midas, Richard, St. Joseph, Waite Park
Reker, Fred, St. John Cantius, St. Cloud
Roth, Jerome
Salchert, John, St. Boniface, Cold Spring
Schmainda, Frank, Sacred Heart, Glenwood
Schwarzbauer, Jerome, St. Francis Xavier, Sartell
Scott, John W., (Retired)
Shaffer, Robert, Sacred Heart, Staples
St. Jean, Fred, St. Andrew, Elk River
Steele, Gregory J., Immaculate Conception, Becker
Thielen, Vern, St. Joseph, Clarissa
Tzinski, Donald, St. Henry and St. Stanislaus, Perham
Weinhandl, Thomas, St. Michael, Motley
Woods, John, St. Peter, St. Cloud
Yanish, Stephen, St. Anne's, Kimball

INSTITUTIONS LOCATED IN THE DIOCESE

[A] SEMINARIES, RELIGIOUS OR SCHOLASTICATES

COLLEGEVILLE. *St. John's Seminary*, 56321. Tel: 320-363-2100; Fax: 320-363-2504. Revs. Dale Launderville, O.S.B., Rector; Jonathan Licari, O.S.B., Vice Rector; Vincent Lieser, Dir. Spiritual Formation. Students 25. Legal Title: *St. John's Seminary*.

[B] COLLEGES AND UNIVERSITIES

COLLEGEVILLE. *St. John's University*, (1857), 56321-2000. Tel: 320-363-2011; Fax: 320-363-2504.
For a complete listing, refer to the Colleges and Universities section.

ST. JOSEPH. *College of St. Benedict*, (1913) 37 S. College Ave., 56374-2099. Tel: 320-363-5407 (Public Affairs); Fax: 320-363-5136 (Public Affairs).
For a complete listing, refer to the Colleges and Universities section.

[C] HIGH SCHOOLS, DIOCESAN

ST. CLOUD. *Cathedral High and John XXIII Middle School*, 312 Seventh Ave. N. Box 1579, 56302. Tel: 320-251-3421; Fax: 320-253-5576. Mr. James McConnell, Chief Admin.; Mr. Raymond Aafedt, Prin.; Mr. Thomas P. Raiche, Middle School Coord.; Rev. Christopher Trussel. Priests 1; Sisters 1; Lay Teachers 53; Students 741.

Cathedral High School Education Foundation, 312 Seventh Ave. N. P.O. Box 1579, 56302. Jeannette Stack, Chm.

[D] HIGH SCHOOLS, PRIVATE

COLLEGEVILLE. *St. John's Preparatory School*. College Preparatory. P.O. Box 4000, 56321. Tel: 320-363-3315; Fax: 320-363-3513. Rev. Mark Thamert, O.S.B., Pres. Students 176.

[E] INTER-PAROCHIAL SCHOOLS

ST. CLOUD. *St. Elizabeth Ann Seton School*. (Grades K-3), Primary: 1615 Eleventh Ave. S., 56301. Tel: 320-251-1988. Bonnie Massmann, Prin. Lay Teachers 10; Students 160. Middle: (Grades 4-6), 2410 First St. N., 56303. Tel: 320-251-6231. Dan Hollenhorst, Prin. Lay Teachers 8; Students 119. Consolidation of schools of the following parishes: Holy Spirit, St. Cloud; St. Anthony, St. Cloud.

Sts. Peter, Paul and Michael School. (Grades K-4), Primary: 925 N. 30th Ave., 56303. Tel: 320-251-4737. Principals: Mrs. Sharon Bichler; Michael Mullin. Lay Teachers 25. Middle: (Grades 5-8), 1215 N. 11th Ave., 56303. Tel: 320-251-5295. Lay Teachers 24; Students 675. Consolidation of the following parishes: St. Michael; St. Paul; St. Peter, St. Cloud.

FOLEY. *St. John's Area School*. (Grades K-6), 215 7 Ave. South, 56329. Tel: 320-968-7972. Julie Mueller, Prin. Consolidation of the following parishes: St. John of Foley; St. Lawrence, Duelm; St. Elizabeth, Brennyville; St. Joseph, Morrill; SS. Peter and Paul, Gilman; St Louis, Foreston; St. Patrick of Minden Township. Lay Teachers 8; Students 115.

LITTLE FALLS. *Mary of Lourdes Elementary and Middle School*. (Grades K-4), Primary: 307 Fourth St., S.E., 56345. Tel: 320-632-5408. Janet Stone, Prin. Benedictine Sister 1; Lay Teachers 12; Students 193; Preschool Students 40. Middle: (Grades 5-8), 205 N.W. Third St., 56345. Tel: 320-632-6742. Debra J. Meyer, Prin. Lay Teachers 9; Students 125. Consolidation of following parishes: St. Mary, Little Falls and Our Lady of Lourdes, Little Falls.

PIERZ. *Holy Trinity School*, Box 427, 56364. Tel: 320-468-6446. Ms. Barbara Sufka, Admin. Prin.; Rev. Kenneth Brenny, Pres.-Corporate Board. Lay Teachers 15; Students 185. Consolidation of the following parishes: St. Michael's, Buckman; Holy Cross, Harding; St. John Nepomuk, Lastrup; St. Joseph, Pierz.

SAUK CENTRE. *Holy Family School*. (Grades K-6), 231 Sinclair Lewis Ave., 56378. Tel: 320-352-6535. Lynn Peterson, Prin. Consolidation of the following parishes: St. Paul's, Sauk Centre; Our Lady of the Angels, Sauk Centre. Lay Teachers 19; Students 398.

[F] HOMES FOR EMOTIONALLY DISTURBED AND HANDICAPPED

ST. CLOUD. *Caritas Family Services, Catholic Charities Community Services*, 305 N. Seventh Ave., 56303. Tel: 320-252-4121; Fax: 320-259-8761.
For a complete listing, refer to the Special Care Facilities section.

Community Services of Catholic Charities, 205 Seventh Ave. N., 56303. Tel: 320-259-8757; Fax: 320-240-3339.
For a complete listing, refer to the Special Care Facilities section.

Day Treatment Services, 1712 Seventh Ave. S., 56301. Tel: 320-251-3647.
For a complete listing, refer to the Special Care Facilities section.

In-Home Family Services, Catholic Charities Community Services, 700 Mall Germain, 56302. Tel: 320-251-1404; Fax: 320-252-8180.
For a complete listing, refer to the Special Care Facilities section.

LaPaz Community Inc., 1730 Seventh Ave., S., 56301. Tel: 320-253-9470.
For a complete listing, refer to the Special Care Facilities section.

St. Cloud Children's Home of the Diocese of St. Cloud, 1726 Seventh Ave. S., 56301. Tel: 320-251-8811; Fax: 320-251-3198.
For a complete listing, refer to the Special Care Facilities section.

St. Elizabeth Home, 306 15th Ave., N., 56301. Tel: 320-252-8350.
For a complete listing, refer to the Special Care Facilities section.

COLD SPRING. *Mother Teresa Home*, 101 Tenth Ave., 56320. Tel: 320-685-8626.
For a complete listing, refer to the Special Care Facilities section.

St. Ann's Home, 103 10th Ave. N., 56320. Tel: 320-685-7898.
For a complete listing, refer to the Special Care Facilities section.

St. Luke's Home, 411 Eighth Ave. N., 56320. Tel: 320-685-7750.
For a complete listing, refer to the Special Care Facilities section.

COLD SPRINGS. *Bethany Home*, 13 8th Ave. S., 56320. Tel: 320-685-7899.
For a complete listing, refer to the Special Care Facilities section.

FERGUS FALLS. *Catholic Charities Intensive Treatment Unit*, Box 1006, 56538-1006. Tel: 218-739-9325; Fax: 218-739-2242.
For a complete listing, refer to the Special Care Facilities section.

LITTLE FALLS. *St. Camillus Place*, 1100 S.E. Fourth St., 56345. Tel: 320-632-6894.
For a complete listing, refer to the Special Care Facilities section.

WAITE PARK. *St. Francis Home*, 25 Second St. N., 56387. Tel: 320-251-7630.
For a complete listing, refer to the Special Care Facilities section.

[G] GENERAL HOSPITALS

ST. CLOUD. *St. Cloud Hospital*, 1406 Sixth Ave. N., 56303. Tel: 320-251-2700.
For a complete listing, refer to the Hospitals section.

ALBANY. *Albany Area Hospital*, 300 Third Ave., 56307. Tel: 320-845-2121.
For a complete listing, refer to the Hospitals section.

BRECKENRIDGE. *St. Francis Medical Center*, 415 Oak St., 56520. Tel: 218-643-3000.
For a complete listing, refer to the Hospitals section.

LITTLE FALLS. *St. Gabriel's Hospital*, 815 S.E. Second St., 56345. Tel: 320-632-5441; Fax: 320-632-1190.
For a complete listing, refer to the Hospitals section.

[H] HOMES FOR AGED

ST. CLOUD. *St. Benedict's Center*, 1810 Minnesota Blvd., S.E., 56304. Tel: 320-252-0010; Fax: 320-654-2351.
For a complete listing, refer to the Special Care Facilities section.

ALBANY. *Mother of Mercy Nursing Home and Retirement Center*, Box 676, 56307. Tel: 320-845-2195.
For a complete listing, refer to the Special Care Facilities section.

BRECKENRIDGE. *St. Francis Home*, 56520. Tel: 218-643-7661.
For a complete listing, refer to the Special Care Facilities section.

COLD SPRING. *Assumption Court*, 615 1st St. N., 56320. Tel: 320-685-4110.
For a complete listing, refer to the Special Care Facilities section.

Assumption Home, 715 N. First St., 56320. Tel: 320-685-3693; Fax: 320-685-7044.
For a complete listing, refer to the Special Care Facilities section.

John Paul Apartments, 200 Eighth Ave. N., 56320. Tel: 320-685-4429.
For a complete listing, refer to the Special Care Facilities section.

LITTLE FALLS. *Alverna Apartments*, 300 Eighth Ave., S.E., 56345. Tel: 320-632-1246.
For a complete listing, refer to the Special Care Facilities section.

St. Otto's Care Center, 920 S.E. 4th St., 56345. Tel: 320-632-9281; Fax: 320-632-1120.
For a complete listing, refer to the Special Care Facilities section.

MORRIS. *Villa of St. Francis Nursing Home*, 1001 Scott Ave., 56267. Tel: 320-589-1133.
For a complete listing, refer to the Special Care Facilities section.

PARKERS PRAIRIE. *St. William's Living Center*, P.O. Box 30, 56361. Tel: 218-338-4671; Fax: 218-338-5917.
For a complete listing, refer to the Special Care Facilities section.

PIERZ. *St. Mary's Villa Inc.*, 56364. Tel: 320-468-6405.
For a complete listing, refer to the Special Care Facilities section.

STAPLES. *Mary Rondorf Retirement Home of Sacred Heart Parish*, 56479. Tel: 218-894-2124.
For a complete listing, refer to the Special Care Facilities section.

[I] MONASTERIES AND RESIDENCES OF PRIESTS AND BROTHERS

ST. CLOUD. *Crosier Community of St. Cloud*, 930 N. 31st Ave., 56303. Tel: 320-654-1388. Legal Title: *Crosier Community of St. Cloud*.

COLLEGEVILLE. *St. John's Abbey, of the Order of St.*

Benedict and St. John's University, School of Theology, Seminary, Prepatory School and Novitiate. P.O. Box 2015, 56321-2015. Tel: 612-363-2011. Rt. Rev. Timothy Kelly, O.S.B., Abbot and Chancellor; Very Revs. Geoffrey Fecht, O.S.B., Prior; Alan Reed, O.S.B., Subprior; Revs. Henry Anderl, O.S.B.; Knute Anderson, O.S.B.; Thomas Andert, O.S.B.; Alexander Andrews, O.S.B.; Burkard Arnheiter, O.S.B.; Timothy Backous, O.S.B., College Chap.; Rudolph Baumberger, O.S.B.; Peregrin Berres, O.S.B.; Luigi Bertocchi, O.S.B.; Michael Bik, O.S.B.; Paschal Botz, O.S.B.; Allan Bouley, O.S.B.; Silvan Bromenshenkel, O.S.B.; Vitus Bucher, O.S.B.; Alto Butkowski, O.S.B.; Jerome Coller, O.S.B.; Alberic Culhane, O.S.B.; Cosmas Dahlheimer, O.S.B.; Godfrey Diekmann, O.S.B.; Arnold Dittberner, O.S.B.; Ian Dommer, O.S.B.; Nicholas Doub, O.S.B.; Daniel Durken, O.S.B.; John Patrick Earls, O.S.B.; Richard Eckroth, O.S.B.; Gall Fell, O.S.B.; Melchior Freund, O.S.B.; Bernard Friedl, O.S.B.; Cyril Gorman, O.S.B.; Nathanael Hauser, O.S.B.; Henry Bryan Hays, O.S.B.; William G. Heidt, O.S.B.; Antony Hellenberg, O.S.B.; Francis Hoefgen, O.S.B., Guestmaster; Eric Hollas, O.S.B., HMML Dir.; Roger Kasprick, O.S.B.; Philip Kaufman, O.S.B.; Joel Kelly, O.S.B.; Emmanuel Kelsch, O.S.B.; Chrysostom Kim, O.S.B.; John Klassen, O.S.B., Formation Dir.; Roger Klassen, O.S.B.; Revs. Jude Koll, O.S.B.; Robert Koopmann, O.S.B.; John Kulas, O.S.B.; Michael Kwatera, O.S.B.; Dale Launderville, O.S.B., Dean at the School of Theology, Rector of Seminary; Emeric Lawrence, O.S.B.; Donald LeMay, O.S.B.; Nathan Libaire, O.S.B., Study Leave; Jonathan Licari, O.S.B.; Luke Mancuso, O.S.B.; Omer Maus, O.S.B.; Brennan Maiers, O.S.B.; J. Patrick McDarby, O.S.B.; Finian McDonald, O.S.B.; Kilian McDonnell, O.S.B.; Rene McGraw, O.S.B.; Aloysius Michels, O.S.B.; Dustan Moorse, O.S.B.; Michael Naughton, O.S.B., Dir. Liturgical Press; Benedict Nordick, O.S.B.; Virgil O'Neill, O.S.B.; Cassian Osendorf, O.S.B.; Michael Patella, O.S.B.; Roman Paur, O.S.B.; Raymond Pedrizetti, O.S.B.; Robert Pierson, O.S.B., Dir. Vocations; Anthony Ruff, O.S.B., Study Leave; Dominic Ruiz, O.S.B., Sts. Peter & Paul Church; Jan Santich, O.S.B.; Bartholomew Sayles, O.S.B.; Sebastian Schramel, O.S.B.; Francisco Schulte, O.S.B.; Paul Schwietz, O.S.B.; Kevin Seasoltz, O.S.B.; Gregory Sebastian, O.S.B.; Cyprian Seitz, O.S.B.; Gervase Soukup, O.S.B.; Gregory Soukup, O.S.B.; Luke Steiner, O.S.B.; Columba Stewart, O.S.B.; James Studer, O.S.B.; Edwin Stueber, O.S.B.; Benjamin Stein, O.S.B.; Don Talafous, O.S.B.; Allen Tarlton, O.S.B.; Donald Tauscher, O.S.B.; Gordon Tavis, O.S.B., Treas.; Vincent Tegeder, O.S.B., Archivist; Mark Thamert, O.S.B., Pres., St. Johns Preparatory School; Wilfred Theisen, O.S.B.; Hilary Thimmesh, O.S.B.; Simeon Thole, O.S.B.; Thomas Thole, O.S.B.; James Tingerthal, O.S.B., Dir. Special Events; Jerome Tupa, O.S.B.; Daniel Ward, O.S.B.; Blane Wasnie, O.S.B.; Magnus Wenninger, O.S.B.; Robert Wieber, O.S.B., Study Leave; Andrew Winczewski, O.S.B.; Hugh Witzmann, O.S.B.; Bruce Wollmering, O.S.B.; Angelo Zankl, O.S.B.; Germain Loeber, O.S.B, Chap.

On Special Assignments: Rev. Gerard Farrell, O.S.B., 302 Nassau St., Princeton, NJ, 08540. Tel: 609-924-5638. Rev. Barnabas Laubach, O.S.B., St. Bernardine Hospital, 2101 N. Waterman Ave., San Bernardino, CA, 92404. Tel: 909-883-8711. Rev. Paul Marx, O.S.B., Leave of Exclaustration.

Priests of the Abbey Serving Abroad: Revs. George Wolf; Cletus Connors, O.S.B., St. Augustine Monastery, Box N-3940, Nassau, Bahamas. Tel: 809-364-1511; Fax: 809-364-1265. Very Rev. Mel Taylor, O.S.B., Prior; Rev. Fintan Bromenshenkel, O.S.B., St. Augustine Monastery, Box N-3940, Nassau, Bahamas. Tel: 809-364-1511; Fax: 809-364-1265. Mary Mother of the Church Abbey, 12617 River Rd., Richmond, VA, 23233. Revs. Theophile Brown, O.S.B.; Neal Henry Lawrence, O.S.B., St. Anselm Priory 6-22, 4-Chome, Kamiosaki, Shinagawa-Ku, Tokyo, Japan, 141. Rev. Thomas Wahl, O.S.B., St. Anselm Priory, 6-22, 4-Chome, Kamiosaki, Shinagawa-Ku, Tokyo, Japan, 141. Rev. Peter Kawamura, O.S.B.; Very Rev. Kieran Nolan, O.S.B., Prior; Rev. William Skudlarek, O.S.B. Japan, St. Anselm Priory, 6-22, 4-Chome, Kamiosaki, Shinagawa-Ku, Tokyo, Japan, 141. Rev. Cyprian Weaver, O.S.B., Benedictine Wimmer Priory, 1 Lane 96, Ming Chih Rd., Sec. 3, Taishan, Taipei, Hsien Republic of China, Taiwan, 24302. Rev. Aelred Tegels Germany. Community Priests 157; Professed Brothers 67; Novices 5; Claustral Oblate 1.

ONAMIA. *Crosier Monastery*, 56359. Tel: 320-532-3103; Fax: 320-532-3103, Ext. 214. Legal Title: *Crosier Fathers of Onamia*. Very Rev. Raymond A. Steffes, O.S.C., Prior.; Revs. William T. McNiff, O.S.C., Sub Prior; Joseph Brennan, O.S.C.

Priests Elsewhere: Revs. Clement N. Gustin, O.S.C., Buhl; James Cashman, O.S.C., Foreston; John J. Fleischhacker, O.S.C., McGregor; Richard T. John, O.S.C., Milaca; Henry A. Miller, O.S.C., Fort Ripley-St. Mathias; Bernard C. Mischke, O.S.C., St. Nicholas.

The National Shrine of St. Odilia is sponsored and maintained by the Crosier Fathers of Onamia. Priests in Residence 3; Priests Elsewhere 6; Brothers in Residence 7.

[J] CONVENTS AND RESIDENCES FOR SISTERS

LITTLE FALLS. *St. Francis Convent*, 116 Eighth Ave., S.E., 56345. Tel: 320-632-2981. Motherhouse of Franciscan Sisters of Little Falls, MN. Sr. Rose Margaret Schneider, Community Min.; Rev. John Eccleston, Chap. Sisters 88; Novices 1; Total in Community 259.

ST. JOSEPH. *Congregation of the Sisters of the Holy Cross (C.S.C.)*, 12543 Old Collegeville Rd., 56374. Sr. Kathleen Moroney, C.S.C., Treas.

St. Benedict's Monastery, 104 Chapel Ln., 56374-0220. Tel: 320-363-7100. Motherhouse and Formation House for all but the Dependent Priories of the Sisters of the Order of Saint Benedict. Sr. Ephrem Hollermann, O.S.B., Prioress; Sr. Elaine Schroeder, O.S.B., Coord. Eucharistic Presiders. Sisters 118; Total in Community 439.

SAUK RAPIDS. *St. Clare's Monastery*. Major Papal Cloister, 56379. Tel: 320-251-3556. Franciscan Poor Clare Nuns. Mother Mary Peter, O.S.C, Abbess. Cloistered Nuns: Solemn Professed 13; Extern Sisters: Perpetual Professed 3; Novices 1.

[K] RETREAT HOUSES

ST. FRANCIS. *Pacem in Terris Center for Spirituality*, Hermitage Retreats, P.O. Box 418, 55070. Tel: 612-444-6408; Fax: 612-444-9649. Mrs. Shirley Wanchena, S.F.O., Dir.

[L] NEWMAN CENTERS

ST. CLOUD. *Newman Center, Inc.*, 396 First Ave., S., 56301. Tel: 320-251-3260; 251-2712 (Home). Rev. Kevin Anderson.

MORRIS. *Newman Catholic Student Center*, 306 E. Fourth St., 56267. Tel: 320-589-1947. Directors of Campus Ministry: Jeff Schaffer; Carol Schaffer.

[M] MISCELLANEOUS

ST. CLOUD. *Domus Transitional Housing of Catholic Charities*, 217 Sixth Ave., N., 56301. Tel: 320-259-9270. 321 & 323 Fourteenth Ave., 56301. Mr. Steven P. Bresnahan; Harvey Schmitt.

Key Row Community, Inc.; Key Row-Little Falls, Inc.; Key Row-Milaca, Inc., 1730 Seventh Ave., S., 56301. Tel: 320-253-9470. Organizations providing low-cost housing to Elderly and Families Little Falls, Milaca, Morris, Wheaton and St. Cloud. Mr. Steven P. Bresnahan, Exec. Dir.; Harvey Schmitt, Dir. Housing Svcs.

Sacred Music Inc. of the Diocese of St. Cloud, Box 1248, 56302.

St. Joseph's Apartment, Inc. Located in St. Joseph and Sauk Centre, MN. 1730 Seventh Ave., S., 56301. Tel: 320-259-8757. Mr. Steven P. Bresnahan, Exec. Dir.; Harvey Schmitt, Dir. Housing Svcs.

St. Therese Center for Special Ministry, 823 First St., S., 56301. Tel: 320-251-8064. Rev. John H. McManus, O.M.I.; Sr. Georganne Burr, O.S.B.; Laura Polipnick, L.P.N.

Services to Aging of Catholic Charities, 1252 Thirty-Second Ave., N., 56303. Tel: 320-252-2048; Fax: 320-253-7464. Mr. Steven P. Bresnahan, Exec. Dir.; Sr. Grace Donovan, O.S.B., Dir. Aging Svcs. Legal Title: *Services to Aging of Catholic Charities: Senior Dining/Meals on Wheels, Caregivers, Share-A-Home, Foster Grandparent Program.*

The Society of the Homeless Orphan of the Diocese of St. Cloud, St. Cloud Children's Home, 1730 Seventh Ave., S., 56301. Tel: 320-252-0412.

Valley Vista Apartments of Browns Valley Inc., 1730 Seventh Ave., S., 56301. Tel: 320-253-9470. Mr. Steven P. Bresnahan, Exec. Dir.; Harvey Schmitt, Dir. Housing Svcs.

ALEXANDRIA. *Carmelite Hermits of Adoration, Inc.*, 7005 E. State Hwy. 27, 56308. Sr. Imelda, Prioress. Sisters 2.

BROWNS VALLEY.

**Browns Valley Health Center*, S. Jefferson St., R.R.1 Box 182 D., 56219; Fax: 320-695-2166.

LITTLE FALLS. *Franciscan Sisters Health Care, Inc.*, 116 Eighth Ave. S.E., 56345-2981. Tel: 320-632-3601. Sr. Rose Margaret Schneider, O.S.F., Pres.

Franciscan Sisters of Little Falls, MN Charitable Trust, 116 Eighth Ave. S.E., 56345. Tel: 320-632-2981.

MORRIS. *St. Francis Health Services*, 801 Nevada, Ste. 100, 56267. Tel: 320-589-2004.

**Prairie Community Services.*

ONAMIA. *National Shrine of St. Odilia*, 56359. Tel: 320-532-3103. Sponsored and maintained by The Crosiers of Onamia.

ST. JOSEPH. *Monastic Interreligious Dialogue*, St. Benedict's Convent, 104 Chapel Ln., 56374-2020. Sr. Katherine Howard, O.S.B., Contact Person.

RELIGIOUS INSTITUTES OF MEN REPRESENTED IN THE DIOCESE

For further details refer to the corresponding bracketed number in the Religious Institutes of Men or Women section.

[0200]—*Benedictine Monks*. (Collegeville, MN).—O.S.B.

[0400]—*Canons Regular of the Order of the Holy Cross*. (Province of St. Odilia).—O.S.C.

RELIGIOUS INSTITUTES OF WOMEN REPRESENTED IN THE DIOCESE

[0230]—*Benedictine Sisters of Pontifical Jurisdiction*.—O.S.B.

[1920]—*Congregation of the Sisters of the Holy Cross*.—C.S.C.

[1310]—*Franciscan Sisters of Little Falls, Minnesota*.—O.S.F.

[3760]—*Order of St. Clare*.—O.S.C.

[2970]—*School Sisters of Notre Dame*. (Northwestern Prov.).—S.S.N.D.

[1710]—*Sisters of St. Francis of Mary Immaculate*.—O.S.F.

[1570]—*Sisters of St. Francis of the Holy Family*.—O.S.F.

NECROLOGY

† Hohn, Francis, (Retired). —Died Dec. 31, 1995.

† Ringwelski, Raymond, (Retired). —Died Nov. 4, 1996.

† Vossberg, Roger, (Retired). —Died May 1, 1996.

Archdiocese of St. Louis

(Archidioecesis S. Ludovici)

His Eminence

JOHN JOSEPH CARDINAL CARBERRY, D.D., S.T.D., J.C.D., PH.D.

Former Archbishop of St. Louis; ordained July 28, 1929; appointed Titular Bishop of Elis and Coadjutor of Lafayette in Indiana May 3, 1956; consecrated July 25, 1956; succeeded to See November 20, 1957; transferred to Columbus January 16, 1965; appointed Archbishop of St. Louis February 17, 1968; installed March 25, 1968; created Cardinal April 28, 1969; retired July 31, 1979. *All communications to His Eminence should be addressed to: The Catholic Center, 4445 Lindell Blvd., St. Louis, MO, 63108-2497.*

Most Reverend

GEORGE J. GOTTWALD, D.D.

Former Auxiliary Bishop of St. Louis; ordained June 9, 1940; appointed Titular Bishop of Cedamusa and Auxiliary Bishop of St. Louis June 10, 1961; consecrated August 8, 1961; retired August 1, 1988. *All communications should be addressed to: The Catholic Center, 4445 Lindell Blvd., St. Louis, MO, 63108-2497.*

Most Reverend

CHARLES R. KOESTER, D.D.

Retired Auxiliary Bishop of St. Louis; ordained December 20, 1941; appointed Titular Bishop of Suacia and Auxiliary Bishop of St. Louis January 5, 1971; consecrated February 11, 1971; retired July 15, 1990. *All communications should be addressed to: The Catholic Center, 4445 Lindell Blvd., St. Louis, MO, 63108-2497.*

Most Reverend

JUSTIN F. RIGALI, J.C.D.

Archbishop of St. Louis; ordained April 25, 1961; appointed Titular Archbishop of Bolsena June 8, 1985; ordained Bishop September 14, 1985; appointed Archbishop of St. Louis January 25, 1994; installed March 16, 1994.

The Catholic Center: 4445 Lindell Blvd., St. Louis, MO, 63108-2497. Tel.: 314-533-1887; Fax: 314-533-1889.

Most Reverend

PAUL A. ZIPFEL, D.D.

Auxiliary Bishop of St. Louis; ordained March 18, 1961; appointed Titular Bishop of Walla Walla and Auxiliary Bishop of St. Louis May 16, 1989; consecrated June 29, 1989. *Res., 676 W. Lockwood Blvd., Webster Groves, MO, 63119.*

Most Reverend

EDWARD K. BRAXTON, PH.D, S.T.D.

Auxiliary Bishop of St. Louis; ordained May 13, 1970; appointed Titular Bishop of Macomades Rusticiana and Auxiliary Bishop of St. Louis March 28, 1995; consecrated May 17, 1995. *Res., 4431 Lindell Blvd., St. Louis, MO, 63108.*

DIOCESE JULY 18, 1826; ARCHDIOCESE JULY 20, 1847.

Square Miles 5,968.

Comprises that portion of the State of Missouri bounded on the north by the northern line of the County of Lincoln; on the west by the western lines of the Counties of Lincoln, Warren, Franklin and Washington; on the south by the southern lines of the Counties of Washington, St. Francois and Perry; on the east by the Mississippi River.

Heavenly Patrons—Saint Louis, King, Saint Vincent de Paul and Saint Rose Philippine Duchesne.

For legal titles of parishes and archdiocesan institutions, consult the Catholic Center.

STATISTICAL OVERVIEW

Personnel	
Retired Cardinals	1
Archbishop	1
Auxiliary Bishops	2
Retired Bishops	2
Abbots	1
Retired Abbots	1
Priests: Diocesan Active in Diocese	354
Priests: Active Outside Diocese	18
Priests: Diocesan in Foreign Missions	6
Priests: Retired, Sick or Absent	103
Number of Diocesan Priests	481
Religious Priests in Diocese	397
Extern Priests in Diocese	6
Ordinations:	
Diocesan Priests	2
Religious Priests	1
Transitional Deacons	6
Permanent Deacons	10
Permanent Deacons in Diocese	196
Total Brothers	187
Total Sisters	2,340
Parishes	
Parishes	227
With Resident Pastor:	
Resident Diocesan Priests	203
Resident Religious Priests	24
Without Resident Pastor:	
Missions	9
Welfare	
Catholic Hospitals	12
Total Assisted	1,144,665
Homes for the Aged	17
Total Assisted	23,709
Residential Care of Children	10
Total Assisted	1,433
Day Care and Extended Day Care Centers	17
Total Assisted	1,253
Specialized Homes	14
Total Assisted	5,639
Special Centers for Social Services	24
Total Assisted	128,650
Residential Care of Disabled	1
Total Assisted	53
Educational	
Seminaries, Diocesan	2
Students from This Diocese	33
Students from Other Diocese	39
Diocesan Students in Other Seminaries	4
Seminaries, Religious	5
Students Religious	49
Total Seminarians	86
Colleges and Universities	2
Total Students	12,462
High Schools, Diocesan and Parish	14
Total Students	6,509
High Schools, Private	15
Total Students	8,684
Elementary Schools, Diocesan and Parish	148
Total Students	41,532
Elementary Schools, Private	6
Total Students	2,328
Non-residential Schools for the Disabled	8
Total Students	270
Catechesis/Religious Education:	
High School Students	631
Elementary Students	22,504
Total Students Under Catholic Instruction	95,006
Teachers in the Diocese:	
Priests	40
Sisters	210
Lay Teachers	3,378
Vital Statistics	
Receptions into the Church:	
Infant Baptism Totals	7,734
Adult Baptism Totals	906
Received into Full Communion	731
First Communions	7,772
Confirmations	7,284
Marriages:	
Catholic	1,926
Interfaith	1,548
Total Marriages	3,474
Deaths	4,520
Total Catholic Population	568,300
Total Population	2,063,163

Former Bishops—Rt. Rev. JOSEPH ROSATI, C.M., Bishop of St. Louis; cons. Bishop of the Titular See of Tenagra and constituted Coadjutor of Bishop DuBourg of Louisiana at Donaldsville, LA, March 25, 1824. When the See of Louisiana was divided Bishop Rosati was made Bishop of St. Louis and Administrator of New Orleans. He died while on business in Rome on September 25, 1843.—Most Rev. LOUIS WILLIAM VALENTINE DUBOURG, Archbishop of the Cardinalatial See of Besancon; cons. in Rome, Sept. 24, 1815, Bishop of Louisiana, Upper and Lower, took his first residential seat in St. Louis, Jan. 6, 1818. On July 18, 1826, the Diocese of Louisiana was divided and the Sees of St. Louis and New Orleans erected. Bishop DuBourg, having resigned the See of Louisiana, was transferred to the Diocese of Montauban in France, Aug. 13, 1826, and made Archbishop of the Cardinalatial See of Besancon, Feb. 15, 1833, where he died Dec. 12 of the same year.—Most Rev. PETER RICHARD KENRICK, D.D., Archbishop of St. Louis; cons. Nov. 30, 1841, Bishop of Drasa and Coadjutor to.—Rt. Rev. BISHOP ROSATI, Bishop of St. Louis, 1843; Archbishop, 1847; Titular Archbishop of Marcianopolis, May 21, 1895; died March 4, 1896.—Most Rev. JOHN JOSEPH KAIN, D.D., Archbishop of St. Louis; cons. Bishop of Wheeling, WV on May 23, 1875; Titular Archbishop of Oxyrynchia and Coadjutor "cum jure successionis" of Archbishop of St. Louis, 1893; Administrator of Archdiocese of St. Louis, Dec. 14, 1893; created Archbishop of St. Louis on May 21, 1895; died Oct. 13, 1903.—His Eminence JOHN CARDINAL GLENNON, D.D., Archbishop of St. Louis; born June 14, 1862; ord. Dec. 20, 1884; appt. Titular Bishop of Pinara and Coadjutor to the Bishop of Kansas City, March 14, 1896; cons. June 29, 1896; transferred to St. Louis, April 27, 1903, as Coadjutor to the Archbishop of St. Louis "cum jure successionis"; Archbishop of St. Louis, Oct. 13, 1903; Pallium received May 14, 1905; Assistant at the Pontifical Throne, June 21, 1921; created Cardinal Priest, Feb. 18, 1946; died March 9, 1946.—His Eminence JOSEPH CARDINAL RITTER, D.D., Archbishop of St. Louis; born July 20, 1892; ord. May 30, 1917; appt. Titular Bishop of Hippo, Feb. 3, 1933 and Auxiliary Bishop of Indianapolis; cons. March 28, 1933; appt. Archbishop of Indianapolis, Nov. 11, 1944; appt. Archbishop of St. Louis, July 20, 1946 assistant at the Pontifical Throne, Oct. 5, 1956; created Cardinal, Priest Jan. 16, 1961; died June 10, 1967.—His Eminence JOHN JOSEPH CARDINAL CARBERRY, D.D., S.T.D., J.C.D., Ph.D., Archbishop of St. Louis; ord. July 28, 1929; appt. Titular Bishop of Elis and Coadjutor of Lafayette in Indiana, May 3, 1956; cons. July 25, 1956; succeeded to See, Nov. 20, 1957; transferred to Columbus, Jan. 16, 1965; appt. Archbishop of St. Louis, Feb. 17, 1968; installed March 25, 1968; created Cardinal, April 28, 1969; retired July 31, 1979.—Most Rev. JOHN L. MAY, D.D., Archbishop of St. Louis; ord. May 3, 1947; appt. Auxiliary Bishop of Chicago, June 21, 1967; cons. Aug. 24, 1967; transferred to Mobile, Oct. 8, 1969; installed as Bishop of Mobile, Dec. 10, 1969; appt. Archbishop of St. Louis, Jan. 29, 1980; installed March 25, 1980; resigned Dec. 9, 1992; died March 24, 1994.

The Catholic Center—4445 Lindell Blvd., St. Louis, 63108-2498. Tel: 314-533-1887; Fax: 314-533-1889. Office Hours: Mon.-Fri. 8:30-4.

Vicars General—Most Rev. PAUL A. ZIPFEL, D.D., V.G.; Most Rev. EDWARD K. BRAXTON, Ph.D., S.T.D., V.G.; Rev. Msgr. JOSEPH F. NAUMANN, V.G.; Rev. Msgr. JOHN R. GAYDOS, V.G.

Moderator of the Curia—Most Rev. PAUL A. ZIPFEL, D.D., V.G.

Chancellor—Rev. Msgr. RICHARD F. STIKA, *4445 Lindell Blvd., St. Louis, 63108.* Tel: 314-533-1887.

Secretary to the Archbishop—Rev. Msgr. RICHARD F. STIKA.

Associate Secretary to the Archbishop—Rev. EDWARD J. STANGER.

Masters of Ceremonies to the Archbishop—Rev. Msgr. RICHARD F. STIKA; Rev. PAUL J. NIEMANN.

Master of Ceremonies to the Cathedral of St. Louis—Rev. EDWARD J. STANGER.

Chief Financial Officer—Mr. VINCENT M. JONES.

Metropolitan Tribunal—4445 Lindell Blvd., St. Louis, 63108. Tel: 314-533-1887; Fax: 314-533-0049.

Judicial Vicar—Rev. JOHN B. SCHAMLEFFER, J.C.L., M.C.L.

Adjutant Judicial Vicars—Revs. MICHAEL P. JOYCE, C.M., J.C.D.; MARK S. RIVITUSO, J.C.L., M.C.L.

Judge—Deacon J. GERARD QUINN, J.C.L.

Defenders of the Bond—Sr. CHARLOTTE RIGALI, C.S.J., J.C.D.; Rev. JAMES J. RAMACCIOTTI, J.C.L.

Director of Advocate Services—Rev. CHARLES C. DEISTER.

Auditors—Revs. PHILIP J. BENE; MICHAEL P. BOEHM; JOHN A. BROCKLAND; WILLIAM W. MCCUMBER.

Promoter of Justice—Rev. JEROME D. BILLING, J.C.L.

Notaries—Mrs. ELIZABETH KWIATKOWSKI; Mrs. JOYCE KOETTING; Mrs. PATRICIA LANASA.

Archdiocesan Consultors—Most Rev. PAUL A. ZIPFEL, D.D., V.G.; Most Rev. EDWARD K. BRAXTON, Ph.D., S.T.D., V.G.; Rev. Msgr. JOSEPH F. NAUMANN, V.G.; Rev. Msgr. JOHN R. GAYDOS, V.G.; Rev. Msgr. PAUL G. ANTHONY; Rev. Msgr. ROBERT P. JOVANOVIC; Rev. Msgr. RICHARD J. LUBELEY; Rev. Msgr. GEORGE J. LUCAS, V.G.; Rev. Msgr. EDWARD J. SUDEKUM; Rev. Msgr. WALTER M. WHITED; Rev. Msgr. JOHN J. LEYKAM.

Deaneries/Deans—North St. Louis: Rev. Msgr. JAMES T. TELTHORST, V.F., South St. Louis: Very Rev. GERALD MEIER, V.F., Northwest County: Very Rev. ROBERT J. HERMANN, V.F., Northeast County: Very Rev. JOHN P. HESS, V.F., Southwest County: Rev. Msgr. JEROME J. BUCHHEIT, V.F., Southeast County: Rev. Msgr. THOMAS DEMPSEY, V.F., St. Charles: Very Rev. DONALD SCHRAMM, V.F., Festus: Very Rev. MICHAEL DONALD, V.F., Ste. Genevieve: Very Rev. JOHN JOHNSON, V.F., Washington: Very Rev. ROBERT HEIMOS, V.F.

Vicar for Administration—Rev. Msgr. JOHN R. MAGUIRE.

Co-Vicar for Religious—Sr. EVA MARIA ACKERMAN, O.S.F.

Archdiocesan Offices and Directors

Archdiocesan Board of Conciliation and Arbitration—Rev. Msgr. DONALD E. RAU, Chm.; Ms. EILEEN SEARLS, Sec.; Mr. JAMES BURTON, Treas.; Rev. BERNARD NIENHAUS; Mr. BERNARD HUGER; Sr. JOAN MARIE GLEASON, C.S.J.

Archdiocesan Building and Boundary Commission—Rev. Msgr. RICHARD J. GALLAGHER, Exec. Sec.; Rev. Msgr. RICHARD J. LUBELEY; Rev. Msgr. ROBERT J. MUESENFECHTER.

Catholic Family Service—Mr. RICHARD E. HENNICKE, A.C.S.W., Exec. Dir., *7800 Kenrick Rd., St. Louis, 63119.* Tel: 314-968-8010. See MISCELLANEOUS section for more information.

Archdiocesan Development Appeal—See MISCELLANEOUS section for more information.

Catholic Information Center—Rev. VALENTINE YOUNG, O.F.M.Cap., Dir. Tel: 314-621-6555; 231-9991. See MISCELLANEOUS section for more information.

Catholic Office of Disability Ministry—LORRAINE FAHEY, Dir., *7800 Kenrick Rd., St. Louis, 63119.* Tel: 314-961-4320, Ext. 190; Fax: 314-918-0878. Also see MISCELLANEOUS section.

Catholic Relief Services—Rev. Msgr. BERNARD H. SANDHEINRICH, Dir., *4140 Lindell Blvd., St. Louis, 63108.* Tel: 314-371-4980.

Catholic Cemeteries of St. Louis—Rev. Msgr. ROBERT MCCARTHY, Dir., *6901 Mackenzie Rd., St. Louis, 63123.* Tel: 314-352-5300. See CEMETERIES section for more information.

Central Purchasing—Rev. Msgr. RICHARD J. GALLAGHER, Dir., *7800 Kenrick Rd., St. Louis, 63119.* Tel: 314-961-4320, Ext. 163.

Catholic Charities—Mr. JOHN LALLY, Pres. JOHN W. MCCARTHY, Assoc. Dir., Finance, *4532 Lindell Blvd., St. Louis, 63108.* Tel: 314-367-5500; Fax: 314-367-6927. See MISCELLANEOUS section for more information.

Cardinal Ritter Institute-Archdiocesan Office for Services to the Elderly—JOHN M. LALLY, CEO; ARTHUR J. KORTE, COO-Svcs. MICHAEL J. LALLY, COO-Residences, *4483 Lindell Blvd., St. Louis, 63108.* Tel: 314-652-3600. See SERVICES FOR THE ELDERLY section for more information.

Catholic Commission on Housing—Rev. RICHARD J. QUIRK, Exec. Dir., *4140 Lindell Blvd., St. Louis, 63108.* Tel: 314-371-4980. See MISCELLANEOUS section for more information.

Catholic Community Services—Sr. BETTY BRUCKER, F.S.M , Exec. Dir., *325 N. Newstead, St. Louis, 63108* Tel: 314-531-0511. See MISCELLANEOUS section for more information.

Archdiocesan Deaf Ministry—Rev. VICTOR A. BARNHART, Dir.; See MISCELLANEOUS section for more information.

Archdiocesan Orphan Board-(Managers of the Roman Catholic Orphan Asylums)—Mr. JOHN SIMON, JR., Pres., *4532 Lindell Blvd., St. Louis, 63108* Tel: 314-367-5500.

Catholic Services for Children and Youth—WILLIAM J. MURPHY, Admin., *4140 Lindell Blvd., St. Louis, 63108.* Tel: 314-371-4980. See MISCELLANEOUS section for more information.

Archdiocesan Data Center—Mr. GERALD F. LAWLER, Dir. Mgmt. Information Systems, *4140 Lindell Blvd., St. Louis, 63108.* Tel: 314-371-0124.

Office for Ecumenical & Interreligious Affairs—Rev. VINCENT A. HEIER, Dir., *462 N. Taylor, St. Louis, 63108.* Tel: 314-531-9700; Fax: 314-531-2269.

Archdiocesan Liturgical Commission—GEORGE WATSON, Chm.; Rev. PAUL J. NIEMANN, Sec. Ex Officio Members: Rev. JOHN FOLEY, S.J.; JOSEPH MILNER; GLORIA GREENE; JOHN A. ROMERI; ANA ANITA ATOK; ROBERT BARRINGER; Deacon GEORGE BEINKE; Rev. JOHN BROCKLAND; Rev. TED BRUG; GLENN BYER; MARY KAY CHRISTIAN; JIM COMBS; Sr. CATHY DOHERTY, S.S.N.D.; RUBY DOUTHET; Bro. STEVE ERSPAMER, S.M.; CAROL FAGAN; KATHY GIBLER; Sr. GABRIEL MARY HOARE, S.L.; LEA KOESTERER; JOAN MAHER; SHARON MCGINNIS; CHRISTOPHER ORF; Sr. VIRGINIA MARIE PERKINS, O.S.U.; BETH PILARSKI; THOMAS POELKER; Sr. GABRIELLA ROGENSKI, C.D.P.; BRENDA SOBOLESKI; JAMES WICKMAN; SANDRA WILSON.

Archdiocesan Office of Worship—Rev. PAUL J. NIEMANN, *7800 Kenrick Rd., St. Louis, 63119.* Tel: 314-961-4320, Ext. 117.

Archdiocesan Human Rights Office/HRO System—Mr. THOMAS M. NOLAN, Dir.; Rev. Msgr. JOHN A. SHOCKLEE, M.A., Dir., Emeritus, *462 N. Taylor, St. Louis, 63108.* Tel: 314-652-6100; Fax: 314-531-2269.

Commission on Human Rights—

Domestic Social Development Divisions—

Black & Native American Missions Program—

International Justice & Peace Division—

Campaign for Human Development—

Parish Social Concerns & Social Concerns Education—

Committee on Women in the Church—

Black Catholic Congress/African American Catholics—

Catholic Legal Assistance Ministry—Tel: 314-454-6964.

Immigration Law Project—Tel: 314-454-6867.

General & Management—

Council of Catholic Youth—Mr. MICHAEL P. KALIST, Exec. Dir.; Rev. BRETT SCHOTT, Spiritual Moderator, *4140 Lindell Blvd., St. Louis, 63108.* Tel: 314-371-4980, Ext. 110.

Holy Childhood, Pontifical Association—Rev. Msgr. BERNARD H. SANDHEINRICH, Dir., *4140 Lindell Blvd., St. Louis, 63108.* Tel: 314-371-4980.

Holy Name Society—Rev. MARVIN C. KOPFF, Spiritual Dir.; Mr. JOSEPH A. RYAN, SR., Pres., *Mailing Address: Holy Name Society, P.O. Box 109435, St. Louis, 63119-6435.*

Latin American Apostolate, Archdiocese of St. Louis—Rev. Msgr. BERNARD H. SANDHEINRICH, Dir., *4140 Lindell Blvd., St. Louis, 63108.* Tel: 314-371-4980.

Hospitals/Office of Health Ministry—Rev. Msgr. ROBERT M. KRAWINKEL, Ph.D., Coord., *925 Cella Rd., St. Louis, 63124.* Tel: 314-993-4442. See HOSPITALS section for more information.

The Legion of Mary—JEAN M. LEONHARDT, Pres., *324 Algonquin Dr., Ballwin, 60311.* Tel: 314-230-0347. Spiritual Dirs.: Revs. ROBERT C. LISS; EDWARD HILGEMAN.

Pan y Amor—Rev. Msgr. BERNARD H. SANDHEINRICH, Dir., *4140 Lindell Blvd., St. Louis, 63108.* Tel: 314-371-4980.

Archdiocesan Newspaper "The St. Louis Review"—Rev. Msgr. DENNIS M. DELANEY, Editor; Mr. PAUL P. PENNICK, Mng. Editor; Mr. THOMAS L. COURTAWAY, Comptroller & Circulation Mgr., *462 N. Taylor, St. Louis, 63108.* Tel: 314-531-9700; Fax: 314-531-2269.

Archdiocesan Office of Stewardship & Development—Mr. FRANK J. COGNATA, JR., Dir., *4445, St. Louis, 63108.* Tel: 314-533-1887.

Archdiocesan Charitable Bequest Council—See MISCELLANEOUS section for more information.

Office for the Continuing Formation of Priests—Rev. ROBERT W. FINN, Dir., *7800 Kenrick Rd., St. Louis, 63119.* Tel: 314-961-4320, Ext. 428.

Priests' Mutual Benefit Society—Rev. Msgr. JOHN R. MAGUIRE, Pres.; Rev. Msgr. JOHN T. RONQUEST, Exec. Sec.; Rev. MARVIN KOPFF, Archbishop's Rep.-Retired Priests.

Priests' Purgatorial Society—Rev. Msgr. RICHARD F. STIKA, Pres.

Pro-Life—Mrs. MOLLY CORCORAN KERTZ, Dir./Coord., *462 N. Taylor Ave., St. Louis, 63108.* Tel: 314-531-3666.

Regina Cleri—Sr. GERALDINE VOGEL, Admin.; Rev. MARVIN KOPFF, Archbishop's Rep., *7850 Kenrick Rd., St. Louis, 63119.* Tel: 314-968-2240.

Society for the Propagation of the Faith—Rev. Msgr. BERNARD H. SANDHEINRICH, Dir., *4140 Lindell Blvd., St. Louis, 63108.* Tel: 314-371-4980.

Today and Tomorrow Education Foundation—BRIDGET FLOOD, Exec. Dir., *4140 Lindell Blvd., St. Louis, 63108.* Tel: 314-371-4980, Ext. 269.

Criminal Justice Ministry—1408 S. Tenth St., St. Louis, 63104. Tel: 314-241-8062.

Office of Communications—Rev. Msgr. DENNIS DELANEY, Dir., *462 N. Taylor Ave., St. Louis, 63108.* Tel: 314-531-9700; Fax: 314-531-2269.

St. Vincent de Paul Society of St. Louis—Mr. ROBERT J. O'REILLY, II, Pres.; Mr. ROBERT GRONEMEYER, Pres. Emeritus; Mr. ROBERT E. O'DONNELL, Exec. Sec.; Mr. RICHARD KLOHR, III, Vice Pres.; Mr. GLENNON CURRAN, Treas.; Rev. JAMES CORMACK, C.M., Spiritual Advisor; ROSE MARIE VOELKER, Sec., Office: *4141 Forest Park Blvd., St. Louis, 63108.* Tel: 314-531-2183; Fax: 314-531-6712.

Society of St. Vincent de Paul, Council of the United States—(Territory: United States)—Most Rev. J. TERRY STEIB, S.V.D., Bishop of Memphis, Spiritual Advisor; JOSEPH H. MUELLER, Pres. RITA W. PORTER, Exec. Sec./Dir., *58 Progress Pkwy., Hazelwood, 63043-3706.* Tel: 314-576-3993; Fax: 314-576-6755. See MISCELLANEOUS section for more information.

Schools/Catholic Education Office—Mr. GEORGE HENRY, Supt., *4140 Lindell Blvd., St. Louis, 63108.* Tel: 314-371-4980. See SCHOOLS section for more information.

St. Louis Roman Catholic Theological Seminaries, Inc.—Rev. Msgr. RICHARD F. STIKA, Sec., *4445 Lindell Blvd., St. Louis, 63108.* Tel: 314-533-1887.

Kenrick-Glennon Seminary (St. Louis Roman Catholic Theological Seminary-Kenrick School of Theology)—Rev. Msgr. GEORGE J. LUCAS, Pres./Rector.

Cardinal Glennon College—Rev. EDWARD M. RICE, Dir., *5200 Glennon Dr., St. Louis, 63119.* Tel: 314-644-0266. See SEMINARIES section for more information.

Archdiocesan Vocation Office—Rev. WILLIAM G. KEMPF, Dir. Asst. Dirs.: Rev. MICHAEL T. BUTLER; Sr. JEANETTE HEMMER, C.PP.S, *5200 Glennon Dr., St. Louis, 63119.* Tel: 314-647-5270.

Archdiocesan Pastoral Council—In transition—

Archdiocesan Council of Priests—Most Rev. JUSTIN RIGALI; Most Rev. PAUL A. ZIPFEL, D.D., V.G.; Most Rev. EDWARD K. BRAXTON, D.D., V.G.; Rev. Msgr. JOSEPH F. NAUMANN, V.G.; Rev. Msgr. JOHN R. GAYDOS, V.G.; Revs. DALE WUNDERLICH, S. City Deanery: JOHN G. DEMPSEY, Ex-Officio/Personnel Dir. RICHARD BOCKSKOPF, N.W. County Deanery: ROBERT W. FINN, Ex-officio/Continuing Formation of Priests; MARK DOLAN, N.E. County Deanery: NORBERT ERNST, Festus Deanery/Chm.: JAMES WILLIAMS, N. City Deanery: Rev. Msgr. GEORGE J. LUCAS, Rector, Kenrick Glennon Seminary; Revs. PAUL TELKEN, Washington Deanery: ROBERT ROSEBROUGH, S.W. County Deanery: DONALD RECK, S.J.,

Religious-Teaching; Very Rev. JAMES CORMACK, C.M., Religious-Parish; Revs. JOHN SEPER, Ste. Genevieve Deanery/Sec.: DENNIS STEHLY, S.E. County Deanery/ Vice Chm.: Rev. Msgr. RICHARD F. STIKA, Chancellor; Revs. ROBERT OSBORNE, S.M., Religious-Other; MICHAEL HENNIG, St. Charles Deanery.

Office of Priests' Personnel—Rev. JOHN G. DEMPSEY, Dir., *4532 Lindell Blvd., St. Louis, 63108.* Tel: 314-367-5530.

Archdiocesan Priests' Personnel Board—Rev. JOHN G. DEMPSEY, Personnel Dir.; Rev. Msgr. CHARLES J. FORST; Rev. Msgr. WILLIAM A. DRENNAN; Rev. Msgr. JAMES T. TELTHORST; Rev. Msgr. JAMES E. PIEPER; Revs. KENNETH BROWN; PAUL J. ROTHSCHILD.

Archdiocesan Office of Urban and Community Affairs—Rev. Msgr. SALVATORE E. POLIZZI, Dir. Consultors: Dr. GEORGE D. WENDEL; LOUIS G. BERRA, *6052 Waterman, St. Louis, 63112.* Tel: 314-721-6340.

Archdiocesan Office of the Permanent Diaconate—Deacon MARTIN TOWEY, Ph.D. Dir., *7800 Kenrick Rd., St. Louis, 63119.* Tel: 314-961-4320, Ext. 401. Committee: Deacons EUGENE BARRON; STANLEY M. PETERSON, JR.; ROBERT C. RIEGEL; MARTIN TOWEY, Ph.D.; Mrs. BONNIE FORSTER; Mrs. JOAN HANSON; Mr. RICHARD HENNICKE; Mrs. ANGELA MENARD; Mrs. CAROL HERDLER; Rev. PHILIP G. KRAHMAN.

Archdiocesan Office of Laity and Family Life—Mrs. MARIA RODGERS O'ROURKE, Dir., *7800 Kenrick Rd., St. Louis, 63119.* Tel: 314-961-4320, Ext. 404.

Catholic Services Agencies Building—Mr. ROBERT J. FAHEY, Admin. & Bldg. Mgr., *4140 Lindell Blvd., St. Louis, 63108.* Tel: 314-371-4980.

Archdiocesan Pastoral Center—Deacon ROBERT SNYDER, Admin., *7800 Kenrick Rd., St. Louis, 63119.* Tel: 314-961-4320, Ext. 114.

CLERGY, PARISHES, MISSIONS AND PAROCHIAL SCHOOLS

CITY OF ST. LOUIS
(St. Louis County)

1—ST. LOUIS CATHEDRAL (1896), Rev. Msgr. James T. Telthorst; Rev. Msgr. John R. Maguire, Senior Priest; Rev. Timothy R. Cook. In res., Most Rev. Edward K. Braxton, V.G.
Res., 4431 Lindell Blvd., 63108. Tel: 314-533-2824; Fax: 314-533-2844.
School—Tel: 314-531-3375. Mary Lou Storment, Prin.
Sisters 1; Lay Teachers 12; Students 221.
Catechesis / Religious Programs—Students 265.

2—EPIPHANY OF OUR LORD (1911), Revs. Dale P. Wunderlich; Charles W. Barthel; Deacon Edward Flint.
Res., 6596 Smiley Ave., 63139. Tel: 314-781-1199; Fax: 314-645-8760.
School—Tel: 314-781-5626. Mr. Tom Archer, Prin.
Sisters of St. Dominic 2; Sisters of Notre Dame 1; Lay Teachers 21; Students 427.
Catechesis / Religious Programs—Students 427.

3—HOLY FAMILY (1898), Revs. Robert G. Leibrecht; Michael Freymuth.
Res., 4125 Humphrey St., 63116. Tel: 314-772-8292.
School—Tel: 314-771-2007. Mary Ann Kauffman, Prin.
Lay Teachers 12; Students 202.
Catechesis / Religious Programs—Students 200.

4—HOLY GUARDIAN ANGELS. Closed. For inquiries for parish records contact the Chancery.

5—HOLY INNOCENTS (1893), Revs. George P. Brennan; Vincent A. Heier; Deacon Fred Hummel.
Res., 4923 Odell St., 63139. Tel: 314-776-6440; Fax: 314-776-6441.
School—Tel: 314-771-2188.
Lay Teachers 9; Students 132.

6—IMMACULATE CONCEPTION-ST. HENRY (1865), Rev. John Gavin, O.S.A.; Deacon James McGrath. In res., Rev. Francis Lawlor, O.S.A.
Res., 3120 Lafayette Ave., 63104. Tel: 314-776-1333.

7—IMMACULATE HEART OF MARY (1951), Revs. H. John Reiker; Robert H. Babka. In res., Rev. Msgr. Dennis M. Delaney.
Res., 4092 Blow St., 63116. Tel: 314-481-7543.
School—4070 Blow St., 63116. Tel: 314-832-1678. Mrs. Christina Cheak, Prin.
Lay Teachers 21; Students 356.
Catechesis / Religious Programs—Students 360.

8—MOST BLESSED SACRAMENT (1907), Rev. Michael J. Witt; Deacons Albert X. Vaughn; Cliff Gholston.
Res., 5017 Northland Ave., 63113. Tel: 314-367-5244.
School—Bishop Healy School, 2727 N. Kingshighway, 63113. Tel: 314-361-5696.
Sisters 1; Lay Teachers 20; Students 370.

9—MOST HOLY NAME OF JESUS. Merged with Most Holy Trinity.

10—MOST HOLY ROSARY (1891). Closed. See St. Elizabeth, Mother of John the Baptist.

11—MOST HOLY TRINITY (1848), Revs. Richard H. Creason; Richard A. Buchheit; Deacon Robert S. Smerek.
Res., 3519 N. Fourteenth St., 63107-3796. Tel: 314-241-9165.
School—1435 Mallinckrodt St., 63107-3796. Tel: 314-231-9014. David Chiodini, Prin.
Sisters 1; Lay Teachers 12; Students 157.
Convent—Tel: 314-621-6835.
Sisters 1.

12—OUR LADY OF MOUNT CARMEL. Closed. For inquiries for parish records contact the Chancery.

13—OUR LADY OF PERPETUAL HELP. Merged with Most Holy Trinity.

14—OUR LADY OF SORROWS (1907), Revs. Michael Campbell; Mitchell Doyen; John R. Vien; Rev. Msgr. James J. Holland, Senior Priest; Deacons Robert Wertz; Robert H. Schnable.
Res., 5020 Rhodes Ave., 63109. Tel: 314-351-1600; Fax: 314-351-1602.
School—S. Kingshighway, 63109. Tel: 314-353-1451.
Sisters of Notre Dame 2; Lay Teachers 38; Students 550.
Catechesis / Religious Programs—Students 550.

15—OUR LADY OF THE HOLY CROSS (1864), Rev. Patrick K. Hambrough; Deacon Donald Driscoll.
Res., 8115 Church Rd., 63147. Tel: 314-381-0323.
School—1018 Baden Ave., 63147. Tel: 314-383-4782; Fax: 314-383-5982.
Sisters 3; Lay Teachers 8; Students 140.

16—RESURRECTION OF OUR LORD (1930), Revs. Thomas W. Wyrsch; Robert W. Argent, Senior Priest.
Res., 3900 Meramec St., 63116. Tel: 314-832-7023.
School—3800 Meramec St., 63116. Tel: 314-772-6745; Fax: 314-772-6745. Ms. Kathy Sodlacek, Prin.
Sisters 2; Lay Teachers 9; Students 173.

17—VISITATION-ST. ANN'S SHRINE (1881), Rev. James E. Williams, Admin.
Res., 4515 Evans Ave., 63113. Tel: 314-535-8804.
School—Bishop Healy at Blessed Sacrament, Tel: 314-367-5696.

18—ST. ADALBERT/ST. PHILIP NERI. See St. Simon of Cyrene.

19—ST. AGATHA (1871), Rev. James Rodis.
Res., 3239 S. 9th St., 63118. Tel: 314-772-1603; Fax: 314-772-7609.

20—ST. AGNES. Closed. For inquiries for parish records contact the Chancery.

21—ST. ALOYSIUS GONZAGA (1892) (Italian), Rev. Ralph E. Stroot; Deacon Richard C. Lake.
Res., 5608 N. Magnolia Ave., 63139. Tel: 314-647-2541. [JC]
School—5628 N. Magnolia Ave. 63139. Tel: 314-647-7056; 645-2363 (Preschool). Sr. Michele Intravia, O.S.U., Prin.
Sisters 2; Lay Teachers 8; Students 173.
Preschool—5625 S. Magnolia, 63139.
Extended Day Care—.
Lay Teachers 5; Students 50.

22—ST. ALPHONSUS LIGUORI (1867), Revs. Maurice Nutt, C.SS.R.; Richard Potts, C.SS.R.; Deacons Leslie A. Johnson; Henry Buckner. In res., Bro. Terrance Burke, C.SS.R.
Res., 1118 N. Grand Blvd., 63106. Tel: 314-533-0304; Fax: 314-533-4260.

23—ST. AMBROSE (1903) (Italian), Revs. Thomas J. Santen; James J. Ramacciotti; Michael J. Palmer; Sr. Patricia Kofron, A.S.C.J., Pastoral Assoc.; Deacon John J. Stoverink.
Res., 5130 Wilson Ave., 63110. Tel: 314-771-1228; Fax: 314-771-0454.
School—5110 Wilson Ave., 63110. Tel: 314-772-1437; Fax: 314-771-4560. Sr. Patricia Brady, A.S.C.J., Prin.
Apostles of the Sacred Heart of Jesus 4; Lay Teachers 19; Students 344.
Catechesis / Religious Programs—Students 344.

24—ST. ANN, MOTHER B.V.M.. Closed. For inquiries for parish records contact the Chancery.

25—ST. ANTHONY OF PADUA (1863), Revs. Benet A. Fonck, O.F.M.; Kenneth Rosswog, O.F.M. Pastoral Assocs.: Bros. Loyola Freightman, O.F.M.; Richard Baranski, O.F.M.
Res., 3140 Meramec St., 63118. Tel: 314-353-7470; Fax: 314-353-0958.
School—4235 Compton Ave., 63118. Tel: 314-752-3397. Ms. Joan Feldmann, Prin.
Sisters of St. Joseph of Carondelet 1; Lay Teachers 11; Students 199.

26—ST. BARBARA. Closed. See St. Augustine for details.

27—ST. AUGUSTINE (1992), Rev. Robert J. Gettinger.
Center: 1371 Hamilton Ave., 63112. Tel: 314-385-1934; Fax: 314-385-2949. Consolidation of St. Barbara, St. Rose of Lima, St. Edward, St. Mark and Notre Dame de Lourdes (Wellston).

28—ST. BONIFACE (1859) (German), Rev. Robert J. Samson; Deacon Earl Tresch.
Res., 7622 Michigan Ave., 63111. Tel: 314-638-1438; Fax: 314-638-1438.

29—ST. BRIDGET OF ERIN (1853) (African American), Rev. Msgr. Richard A. Buchheit.
Res., 2401 Carr St., 63106. Tel: 314-231-8870; Fax: 314-231-3780.
School—Central Catholic/St. Nicholas School, 1106 N. Jefferson Ave., 63106. Tel: 314-231-6254.
Sisters 2; Lay Teachers 14; Students 309.

30—ST. CECILIA (1906), Rev. Francis X. Blood. In res., Rev. Gregory G. Kirsch.
Res., 5418 Louisiana Ave., 63111. Tel: 314-351-1318.
Church—Eiler & Alaska Ave., 63111.
School—906 Eichelberger Ave., 63111. Tel: 314-353-2455. Sr. Suzanne Laughlin, O.P., Prin.
Lay Teachers 11; Students 220.

31—ST. CRONAN (1878), Revs. Joseph D. Ross; James Krings.
Res., 1203 S. Boyle Ave., 63110. Tel: 314-289-9545; Fax: 314-289-9546.

32—ST. EDWARD, KING. Closed. See St. Augustine for details.

33—ST. ELIZABETH, MOTHER OF JOHN THE BAPTIST (1891) (African American), Revs. Carl J. Scheble; Emmanuel Ogunnaike, M.S.P. (Nigeria); Deacons Nathaniel E. Shipp; Jesse Bell.
Res., 4330 Shreve Ave., 63115. Tel: 314-381-4145; Fax: 314-381-2212.
School—St. Engelbert "FOCUS" Consolidated School, 4720 Carter Ave., 63115. Tel: 314-389-0401. Ms. Barbara Soete, Prin.
Religious 4; Lay Teachers 9; Students 212.
St. Engelbert "FOCUS" Day Care Ctr.—4746 Carter Ave., 63115. Tel: 314-389-0720. Ms. Belinda Palmer, Dir.
Lay Teachers 18; Students 105.

34—ST. FRANCIS DE SALES (1867), Rev. Richard J. Bockskopf; Deacon Thomas A. Buhr. In res., Rev. John P. Comer.
Res., 2653 Ohio Ave., 63118. Tel: 314-771-3100; Fax: 314-776-4088.

35—ST. FRANCIS XAVIER (1841). (College). Revs. Leonard E. Kraus, S.J.; Glenn Mueller, S.J.; Deacon Bro. Anthony I. Messineo, T.O.R.S.Carm.
3628 Lindell Blvd., 63108. Tel: 314-977-7300; Fax: 314-977-7315.
Catechesis / Religious Programs—Students 151.

36—ST. GABRIEL THE ARCHANGEL (1934), Rev. Msgr. John R. Gaydos; Revs. Charles E. Burgoon; C. Eugene Morris; Edwin J. Burmester; Deacon Phillip Gerdes.
Res., 6303 Nottingham Ave., 63109. Tel: 314-353-6303; Fax: 314-353-7704.
School—4700 Tamm Ave., 63109. Tel: 314-353-1229.
Lay Teachers 33; Students 560.

37—ST. HEDWIG, Rev. Msgr. Joseph W. Baker.
Res., 3202 Pulaski St., 63111. Tel: 314-481-2486.

38—ST. JAMES THE GREATER (1860) (Irish-Italian), Rev. Msgr. Edward J. Deutschmann; Rev. David E. Rauch.
Res., 6401 Wade Ave., 63139. Tel: 314-645-0167.
School—1360 Tamm Ave., 63139. Tel: 314-647-5244. Ms. Karen Battaglia, Prin.
Lay Teachers 12; Students 220.
Catechesis / Religious Programs—Students 318.

39—ST. JOAN OF ARC (1941), Rev. Msgr. Lawrence J. Walsh; Revs. Paul J. Rothschild; John G. Dempsey; Deacons Daniel H. Henroid; Wayne Bryant.
Res., 5800 Oleatha St., 63139. Tel: 314-832-2838; Fax: 314-352-9350.
School—Tel: 314-752-4171. Mrs. Judy Talleur, Prin.
Lay Teachers 30; Students 490.

40—ST. JOHN THE APOSTLE AND EVANGELIST (1847), Rev. Msgr. Bernard E. Granich.
Res., 15 Plaza Sq., 63103. Tel: 314-421-3467.

41—ST. JOHN THE BAPTIST (1914), Revs. John J. Ghio; Edward R. Goldian, S.J.; Bro. Padraic Campbell, O.S.F. In res., Rev. Msgr. Joseph F. Naumann, V.G.
Res., 4200 Delor St., 63116. Tel: 314-353-1255.
School—4170 Delor St., 63116. Tel: 314-481-6654.
Sisters of the Most Precious Blood, O'Fallon 1; Lay Teachers 21; Students 404.
High School—5021 Adkins St., 63116. Tel: 314-351-5604; Fax: 314-351-3050. Bro. David A. Migliorino, O.S.F., Prin.
Sisters 3; Lay Teachers 29; Students 440.
Catechesis / Religious Programs—Students 844.

42—ST. JOHN NEPOMUK (1854) (Czech), Rev. Joseph J. Portucheck.
Res., 1625 S. 11th St., 63104. Tel: 314-231-0141.

43—SHRINE OF ST. JOSEPH, CAPUCHIN FATHERS (1844) (German). Unassigned.
Res., 1220 N. 11th St., 63106. Tel: 314-231-9407; Fax: 314-231-0802.

44—ST. JOSEPH (1904) (Croatian), Revs. Joseph M. Abramovic, O.F.M.; Ivo Sivric, O.F.M.
Res., 2112 S. 12th St., 63104. Tel: 314-771-0958.

45—ST. LIBORIUS. Closed. For inquiries for parish records contact the Chancery.

46—BASILICA OF ST. LOUIS, THE KING (1770), Rev. Msgr. Bernard H. Sandheinrich; Revs. Michael L. Seidel; Richard J. Quirk.
Res., 209 Walnut St., 63102. Tel: 314-231-3250; Fax: 314-231-4280.

47—ST. MARGARET OF SCOTLAND (1899), Rev. Kenneth Brown.
Res., 3854 Flad Ave., 63110. Tel: 314-776-0363.
School—3864 Castlemen, 63110. Tel: 314-776-7837.
Sisters 4; Lay Teachers 9; Students 237.

48—ST. MARK, EVANGELIST. Closed. See St. Augustine for details.

49—ST. MARY MAGDALEN (1919), Revs. Dennis E. Doerhoff; Thomas C. Bryon; Deacon J. Gerard Quinn.
Res., 4924 Bancroft Ave., 63109. Tel: 314-352-2111; Fax: 314-481-7661.
School—4911 Sutherland Ave., 63109. Tel: 314-832-3360; Fax: 314-481-7661.
Lay Teachers 16; Students 246.

50—SS. MARY AND JOSEPH (1821), Rev. Robert L. Szydlowski; Rev. Msgr. Fenton J. Runge, Senior Priest.
Res., 6304 Minnesota Ave., 63111. Tel: 314-481-6304.

51—ST. MARY OF VICTORIES, Rev. Msgr. Donald E. Rau.
Res., 744 S. 3rd St., 63102. Tel: 314-231-9062.

52—ST. MATTHEW, APOSTLE (1893), Revs. Matthew D. Ruhl, S.J.; Jeffrey Harrison, S.J.; Robert L. Sullivan, S.J.; Robert Luchi, S.J.
Res., 2715 N. Sarah St., 63113. Tel: 314-531-6443.

53—ST. NICHOLAS (1865), Rev. Richard R. Andrus, S.V.D.; Bro. Lawrence Camilleri, S.V.D.; Deacon Stanley Peterson. In res., Rev. Edward Wald, S.V.D., (Retired).
Res., 701 N. 18th St., 63103. Tel: 314-231-2860; Fax: 314-231-9127.
School—Central Catholic/St. Nicholas School, 1805 Lucas St., 63103. Tel: 314-421-1822.
Lay Teachers 40; Students 400.
Chapel—Christ the King.

54—ST. PATRICK (1981), Revs. Valentine Young, O.F.M.Cap.; Simon R. Conrad, O.F.M.Cap.; Canice Froelich, O.F.M.Cap.; Simeon Gallagher, O.F.M.Cap.
Res., 1000 N. 7th St., 63101. Tel: 314-231-9991.
Shrine—Shrine of St. Joseph, Tel: 314-231-9407.

55—SS. PETER AND PAUL (1849), Rev. Bruce H. Forman; Deacons Philip Gerdes; Joseph T. Haefner; Thomas Gorski.
Res., 1919 S. 7th Blvd., 63104. Tel: 314-231-9923; Fax: 314-231-9923.

56—ST. SIMON OF CYRENE (1993), Rev. Gerald T. Will; Deacons Raymond V. Mroczkowski; Fred Dodson.
Res., 5076 Durant Ave., 63115. Tel: 314-385-0068; Fax: 314-385-5339.

57—ST. PIUS THE FIFTH (1905) (Irish), Revs. Michael J. Lydon; Brett T. Schott; Chau Pham, S.V.D.; Deacon Walter W. Christ. Pastoral Assocs.: Sr. Paulette Weindell, C.PP.S.; Sr. Dorothy Ann Katke, C.PP.S.
Res., 3310 S. Grand Blvd., 63118. Tel: 314-772-1525; Fax: 314-772-5615.
School—3530 Utah, 63118. Tel: 314-773-8770. Robert Bolland, Interim Prin.
Sisters 3; Lay Teachers 8; Students 184.

58—ST. RAPHAEL THE ARCHANGEL (1950), Rev. Msgr. William A. Drennan; Rev. Matthew L. O'Toole. In res., Rev. Edward J. Stanger.
Res., 6047 Bishops Pl., 63109. Tel: 314-352-8100; Fax: 314-353-6603.
School—Tel: 314-352-9474. Mrs. Susan Brown, Prin.
Lay Teachers 13; Students 186.
Catechesis/Religious Programs—Students 265.

59—ST. ROCH, Rev. Msgr. Salvatore E. Polizzi; Rev. Lawrence A. Herzog. In res., Rev. Msgr. Adrian I. Dwyer.
Res., 6052 Waterman Ave., 63112. Tel: 314-721-6340; Fax: 314-721-1656.
School—6040 Waterman Ave., 63112. Tel: 314-721-2595. Mrs. Gloria Openlander, Prin.
Lay Teachers 15; Students 195.

60—ST. ROSE OF LIMA. Closed. See St. Augustine for details.

61—ST. STANISLAUS KOSTKA (1880) (Polish), Rev. Msgr. Ted L. Wojcicki.
Res., 1413 N. 20th St., 63106. Tel: 314-421-5948.

62—ST. STEPHEN, PROTOMARTYR (1926), Very Rev. Gerald A. Meier, V.F.; Rev. John J. Wetmore.
Res., 3949 Wilmington Ave., 63116. Tel: 314-481-1133; Fax: 314-481-6036.
School—3929 Wilmington Ave., 63116. Tel: 314-752-4700. Sr. Mary Eschbacher, C.S.J., Prin.
Lay Teachers 14; Students 277.

63—ST. TERESA OF AVILA (1865), Rev. Robert E. Zinser.
Res., 3636 N. Market St., 63113. Tel: 314-371-1190; Fax: 314-531-1047.
Missionaries of Charity—3629 Cottage, 63113. Tel: 314-533-2777.

64—ST. THOMAS OF AQUIN (1882), Rev. Msgr. Richard J. Gallagher.
Res., 3949 Iowa Ave., 63118. Tel: 314-772-2644.

65—ST. VINCENT DE PAUL (1841), Rev. James B. Cormack, C.M.; Sr. Jackie Toben, S.S.N.D., Pastoral Assoc.; Mr. Dennis Wells, Pastoral Assoc.
Res., 1408 S. Tenth St., 63104. Tel: 314-231-9328; Fax: 314-621-2232.

66—ST. WENCESLAUS (1895) (Bohemian), Very Rev. Joseph Paul Roelke, M.S.F.; Deacon George W. Miller. In res., Bro. Kenneth J. Schwartz, M.S.F.
Res., 3014 Oregon Ave., 63118-1498. Tel: 314-865-1020; Fax: 314-664-8260.
Catechesis/Religious Programs—Notre Dame Elementary School, 3022 Oregon Ave., 63118-1498. Tel: 314-776-0883.
Students 154.

CHURCHES IN ST. LOUIS COUNTY

Affton, St. Dominic Savio (1956), Revs. Edward F. Feuerbacher; Richard J. Heman; Deacon James L. Murphy.
Res., 6120 Pebble Hill Dr., 63123. Tel: 314-353-7629.
Church—7748 MacKenzie Rd., 63123.
School—Tel: 314-832-4161. Sr. Ann Gregory Bischof, C.P., Prin.
Lay Teachers 16; Students 248.

St. Timothy (1958), Revs. David A. Walter; Bryan Kuchar; Deacons Philip Caruana; Gene Hoffmann.
Res., 816 Union Rd., St. Louis, 63123. Tel: 314-631-4244; Fax: 314-631-4250.
School—824 Union Rd., St. Louis, 63123. Tel: 314-631-0991; 638-4557. Michael Talleur, Prin.
Lay Teachers 12; Students 249.
Catechesis/Religious Programs—Students 265.

Seven Holy Founders (1927), Revs. Timothy Kremen, O.S.M.; Francis Martin, O.S.M.; John Fontana, O.S.M.; Deacon Charles Lombardo.
Office: 6820 Aliceton Ave., St. Louis, 63123. Tel: 314-638-3938; Fax: 314-638-0613.
Church—6741 Rock Hill Rd., St. Louis, 63123. Tel: 314-631-3938.
School—6737 Rock Hill Rd., St. Louis, 63123. Tel: 314-631-8149. Miss Barbara Peach, Prin.
Lay Teachers 28; Students 532.
Catechesis/Religious Programs—Tel: 314-631-2333.
Students 172.

Ballwin, Holy Infant (1954), Rev. Msgr. Jerome J. Buchheit; Revs. Joseph G. Kempf; Joseph R. Monahan; Deacons John A. O'Leary; Kenneth C. Clemens.
Res., 627 Dennison Dr., 63021. Tel: 314-227-7440; Fax: 314-227-7441.
School—Tel: 314-227-0802; Fax: 314-227-9184. Sr. Rosario Delaney, R.S.M., Prin.
Sisters of Mercy (Meath Mercy Generalate, Ireland) 4; Lay Teachers 27; Students 782.
Catechesis/Religious Programs—Students 592.

Bellefontaine Neighbors, Our Lady of Good Counsel (1951), Revs. Donald R. Wester; John E. Vogler.
Res., 1160 St. Cyr Rd., St. Louis, 63137. Tel: 314-867-1441; Fax: 314-867-1442.
School—1134 St. Cyr Rd., St. Louis, 63137. Tel: 314-867-2400. Sr. Barbara Thomas, A.S.C.J., Prin.
Sisters 4; Lay Teachers 12; Students 202.
Convent—1142 St. Cyr Rd., St. Louis, 63137. Tel: 314-868-3067.

Bel-Ridge, St. Thomas More (1955), Revs. Norbert A. Mersinger; Donald J. Burke; Deacons Singleton Harris; Edward C. Fronick.
Res., 3425 St. Thomas More Pl., St. Louis, 63121. Tel: 314-428-7900.

Berkeley, Holy Ghost (1923), Rev. Aloysius A. Forst.
Res., 6314 Garfield Ave., 63134. Tel: 314-522-1200.

Bissell Hills, St. Jerome (1952), Revs. Mark A. Dolan; Mark S. Rivituso, J.C.L.
Res., 10235 Ashbrook Dr., St. Louis, 63137. Tel: 314-868-2310; Fax: 314-868-3919.
School—Tel: 314-867-2100.
Lay Teachers 21; Students 325.

Brentwood, St. Mary Magdalen (1912), Revs. Bernard J. Wilkins; Clark B. Maes; Deacon Leroy Martin.
Res., 2618 Brentwood Blvd., 63144. Tel: 314-961-8400.
School—8762 Magdalen Ave., 63144. Tel: 314-961-0149. Mrs. Alice Rygelski, Prin.
Sisters 1; Lay Teachers 11; Students 176.
Catechesis/Religious Programs—Students 160.

Bridgeton, St. Mary (1852), Rev. William J. Baier.
Res., 4603 Long Rd., 63044. Tel: 314-731-0593. [CEM]
School—4601 Long Rd., 63044. Tel: 314-731-3147.
Lay Teachers 14; Students 125.

St. Lawrence the Martyr (1960), Rev. James E. Murphy; Deacons Wm. Walbridge; Simon Bachu; R. Fielding Harrison. In res., Rev. Msgr. Michael F. Regan.
Res., 4335 DuPage Dr., 63044. Tel: 314-739-0496; Fax: 314-739-2768.
School—4329 DuPage Dr., 63044. Tel: 314-739-3123.

Chesterfield, Ascension (1923), Rev. Msgr. Joseph Pins; Revs. Richard Nelke; Gary Wolken; R. John Schwaig; Deacons Larry Hutti; Frank Chauvin; William P. Wunderlich; Robert Brooks; Robert Keeney.
Res., 230 Santa Maria Dr., 63005. Tel: 314-532-3304; Fax: 314-532-3518.
School—238 Santa Maria Dr., 63005. Tel: 314-532-1151. Mrs. Laurie Ann O'Connor, Prin.
Lay Teachers 23; Students 542.
Catechesis/Religious Programs—Tel: 314-532-1136; 532-9344 (Adult Education).
Students 710.

Incarnate Word (1965), Revs. Robert J. Hermann; Eugene E. Utrup; James J. Byrnes; Deacons Jerome Toohey; Glennon Bourbon.
Res., 13416 Olive Blvd., 63017. Tel: 314-576-5366; Fax: 314-576-2046.
School—Tel: 314-878-3207. Lucia Signorelli, Prin.
Sisters 2; Lay Teachers 20; Students 350.
Catechesis/Religious Programs—Tel: 314-878-0442. Mrs. Denise DeFord, D.R.E.
Students 300.

Clayton, St. Joseph (1842), Rev. Msgr. Jerome F. Wilkerson; Rev. Gerald J. Kleba.
Res., 106 N. Meramec Ave., 63105. Tel: 314-726-1221; Fax: 314-726-1229.
Catechesis/Religious Programs—Tel: 314-727-9059. Mrs. Kathleen Wolfersberger, D.R.E.
Students 125.

Concord Village, St. Simon the Apostle (1959), Revs. William B. Ahrens; James B. Wilke; Rev. Msgr. John T. Ronquest; Deacon Carl Beckman.
Res., 11011 Mueller Rd., St. Louis, 63123. Tel: 314-842-3848.
School—11019 Mueller Rd., St. Louis, 63123. Tel: 314-842-0181.
Lay Teachers 23; Students 474.
Catechesis/Religious Programs—Students 145.

Crestwood, St. Elizabeth of Hungary (1956), Rev. Thomas J. Haley; Deacon Robert Snyder. In res., Revs. Donald Hoffman; John M. Kilcullen.
Res., 1420 S. Sappington Rd., 63126. Tel: 314-968-0760.
School—1414 S. Sappington Rd., 63126. Tel: 314-962-9698. Sr. Charlotte Flarlong, Prin.
Sisters 1; Lay Teachers 14; Students 182.
Catechesis/Religious Programs—Students 76.
Convent—1405 S. Sappington Rd., 63126. Tel: 314-961-2630.

Creve Coeur

1—ST. ANSELM (1966), Revs. Gerard Garrigan, O.S.B.; R. Benedict Allin, O.S.B.; D. Ralph Wright, O.S.B.; Deacon William J. McKenna; Miss Barbara Peiffer, Pastoral Assoc.
Res., 530 S. Mason Rd., St. Louis, 63141. Tel: 314-878-2120; Fax: 314-878-2199.
Catechesis/Religious Programs—Students 316.

2—ST. JOHN BOSCO (1972), Rev. Patrick J. O'Laughlin. In res., Rev. Msgr. Rowland Gannon; Rev. David T. Thomas; Deacon Charles W. Georges.
Res., 12934 Marine Ave., St. Louis, 63146. Tel: 314-434-1312.
Catechesis/Religious Programs—Tel: 314-878-6492.
Students 212.

3—ST. MONICA (1872), Rev. Msgr. Nicholas A. Schneider; Rev. Dennis M. Doyle; Deacons John W. Baker; Michael H. Dalton; Robert K. Gamache; Millard R. Miller. In res., Rev. Charles C. Deister.
Res., 12136 Olive Blvd., 63141-6629. Tel: 314-434-4211; Fax: 314-434-5978. [CEM]
School—12132 Olive Blvd., 63141-6698. Tel: 314-434-2173; Fax: 314-434-7689. Mrs. Susan E. Rohman, Prin.
Lay Teachers 27; Students 406.

4—OUR LADY OF THE PILLAR (1938), Revs. William R. Wightman, S.M.; Herbert W. Pieper, S.M.; Deacons William Hayes; Norman B. Werner. In res., Rev. J. Donald Cahill, S.M.
Res., 401 S. Lindbergh Blvd., St. Louis, 63131. Tel: 314-993-2280; Fax: 314-993-6462.
School—Tel: 314-993-3353.

Franciscan Sisters of Our Lady of Perpetual Help 3; Lay Teachers 9; Students 218.
Convent—403 S. Lindbergh Blvd., 63131. Tel: 314-993-3666.

5—ST. RICHARD (1963), Rev. C. Robert Dorhauer. In res., Rev. Msgr. Vernon E. Gardin.
Res., 11223 Schuetz Rd., St. Louis, 63146. Tel: 314-432-6224; Fax: 314-432-6030.
School—11211 Schuetz Rd., St. Louis, 63146. Tel: 314-872-3152. Mr. Michael R. Corley, Prin.
Sisters 2; Lay Teachers 14; Students 167.

Des Peres, St. Clement (1951), Rev. Msgr. James E. Pieper; Rev. Mark G. Whitman. In res., Rev. William H. Thurmer.
Res., 1510 Bopp Rd., St. Louis, 63131. Tel: 314-965-0709.
School—1508 Bopp Rd., St. Louis, 63131. Tel: 314-822-1903. Mary Christina Reichardt, Prin.
Lay Teachers 28; Students 425.

Ellisville, St. Clare of Assisi (1963), Revs. Richard E. Hanneke; Charles M. Frankey.
Res., 15642 Clayton Rd., 63011. Tel: 314-394-7307; Fax: 314-394-6264.
School—Tel: 314-227-8654. Mrs. Denny Bram, Prin.
Sisters 1; Lay Teachers 15; Students 298.
Catechesis / Religious Programs—Tel: 314-394-4368.
Students 542.

Eureka, Sacred Heart (1889), Rev. Alexander R. Anderson.
Res., 350 E. Fourth St., 63025. Tel: 314-938-5048.
School—Tel: 314-938-4602. Patricia J. Corley, Prin.
Sisters 2; Lay Teachers 8; Students 221.
Catechesis / Religious Programs—Students 210.

Fenton, St. Paul (1878), Rev. Richard F. Everding; Rev. Msgr. Robert J. Mueserfechter; Rev. Eugene Robertson; Deacon John Weatherholt.
Res., 15 Forest Knoll, 63026. Tel: 314-343-1234; Fax: 314-343-4809. [CEM]
School—465 New Smizer Mill Rd., 63026. Tel: 314-343-4333.
Religious 2; Lay Teachers 21; Students 406.
Catechesis / Religious Programs—Tel: 314-343-1678.
Students 509.

Ferguson, Good Shepherd (1958), Rev. Gregory R. Mikesch.
Res., 921 Smith Ave., 63135. Tel: 314-521-1008; Fax: 314-521-1034.
School—1050 Smith Ave., 63135. Tel: 314-524-4332.
Sisters 2; Lay Teachers 12; Students 230.

Sts. John and James (1882), Rev. Timothy M. Foley; Deacon L. Jerome Marren.
Res., 140 N. Elizabeth Ave., 63135. Tel: 314-522-0275.
School—150 N. Elizabeth Ave., 63135. Tel: 314-522-3888.
Catechesis / Religious Programs—Students 314.

Our Lady of Guadalupe (1954), Rev. A. John Schuler.
Res., 17 Hawkesbury Dr., 63121. Tel: 314-522-9264; Fax: 314-522-8461.
School—1115 S. Florissant Rd., 63121. Tel: 314-524-1948. Sharon J. Morgenthaler, Prin.
Lay Teachers 9; Students 168.
Catechesis / Religious Programs—Students 190.

Florissant

1—NORTH AMERICAN MARTYRS (1954), Revs. Kevin F. Hederman; Robert G. Ditch; Deacons Robert J. Powers; Peter Gounis.
Res., 1400 S. Lafayette Ave., 63031. Tel: 314-837-9304.
School—Tel: 314-831-2440.
Lay Teachers 8; Students 188.
Catechesis / Religious Programs—Students 275.

2—OUR LADY OF FATIMA (1950), Rev. Thomas J. Schaab; Deacon Andrew Neimeyer.
Res., 4550 Washington St., 63033. Tel: 314-837-9366; Fax: 314-837-9367.
School—4500 Washington St., 63033. Tel: 314-921-0437.
Lay Teachers 12; Students 215.

3—ST. ANGELA MERICI (1962), Revs. Ferdinand J. Wesloh; Charles P. Tichacek.
Res., 14005 Davey Dr., 63034. Tel: 314-838-6565; Fax: 314-838-6566.
School—3860 N. Highway 67, 63034. Tel: 314-831-8012.
Lay Teachers 22; Students 442.

4—ST. CHRISTOPHER (1967), Rev. Donald L. Dyer; Deacons Kenneth M. Potzman; George A. Graham; George Blase. In res., Rev. Louis P. Dierker.
Res., 11575 Old Halls Ferry Rd., 63033. Tel: 314-839-2427; Fax: 314-839-2428.

5—ST. DISMAS (1956), Revs. Robert W. Burkemper; Rickey J. Valleroy; Deacon Herbert B. Gettemeier.
Res., 2650 Parker Rd., 63033. Tel: 314-837-3410; Fax: 314-837-6628.
School—1220 Paddock Dr., 63033. Tel: 314-837-0369.
Lay Teachers 14; Students 223.
Catechesis / Religious Programs—St. Thomas the Apostle, 500 St. Catherine, 63033. Tel: 314-921-3023.
Students 330.

6—ST. FERDINAND (1788), Revs. Gary Gebelein; Michael G. Murphy; Glennon Goellner; Deacon Raymond C. Hennicke.
Res., 1765 Charbonier Rd., 63031. Tel: 314-837-3165; Fax: 314-837-3166.
School—Tel: 314-921-2201; Fax: 314-921-2253.
Sisters of Loretto at the Foot of the Cross 1; Sisters of the Most Precious Blood 1. Lay Teachers 20; Students 325.
Catechesis / Religious Programs—Students 430.

7—SACRED HEART (1866) (German), Very Rev. John Paul Hess; Rev. Thomas C. Miller.
Res., 751 N. Jefferson St., 63031. Tel: 314-837-3757; Fax: 314-837-8897.
School—501 St. Louis St., 63031. Tel: 314-831-3372. Mrs. Susan Gieseke, Prin.
Religious 2; Lay Teachers 24; Students 489.

8—ST. NORBERT (1965), Revs. James W. Schaefer; Brian P. Smith; Deacon Robert Klostermann.
Res., 16455 New Halls Ferry Rd., 63031. Tel: 314-831-3874; Fax: 314-831-3875.
School—Tel: 314-839-0948. Sr. Agnes Marie Keena, B.V.M., Prin.
Sisters 2; Lay Teachers 25; Students 481.
Catechesis / Religious Programs—Tel: 314-830-0841. Sr. Therese Flerlage, O.S.F., D.R.E.
Students 290.

9—ST. SABINA (1960), Revs. Donald L. Buhr; Kevin G. Callahan; Deacons Harold A. Strauss; Joseph Marcinkiewicz, Jr.; Alvin Dietz; Paul Porterfield.
Res., 1365 Harkee Dr., 63031. Tel: 314-837-1365; Fax: 314-837-7680.
School—1625 Swallow Dr., 63031. Tel: 314-837-6524. Sr. Joan Galli, C.S.J., Prin.
Sisters 2; Lay Teachers 14; Students 243.
Catechesis / Religious Programs—Students 385.

10—ST. THOMAS THE APOSTLE (1963), Rev. Vincent Bommarito; Deacons Joseph Morris; Charles Holmes.
Res., 500 Clemens Dr., 63033. Tel: 314-838-4017.
School—3500 St. Catherine St., 63033. Tel: 314-921-7313. Marlynne Huenneke, Prin.
Lay Teachers 24; Students 387.

11—TRANSFIGURATION (1965), Revs. Joseph W. Banden; Henry J. Garavaglia; Deacon Joseph Peacock.
Res., 6685 Lakeside Hills Dr., 63033. Tel: 314-741-2309; Fax: 314-355-7527.
School—12555 Partridge Run Dr., 63033. Tel: 314-741-0413. Carol Werner, Prin.
Lay Teachers 10; Students 181.
Convent—12613 Partridge Run Dr., 63033. Tel: 314-741-6568.

Gardenville, St. George (1915), Revs. Harold H. Voelker; Joseph J. Adragna; Deacons Roy E. Schulze; Robert Penberthy.
Res., 4980 Heege Rd., St. Louis, 63123. Tel: 314-352-3544.
School—4974 Heege Rd., St. Louis, 63123. Tel: 314-832-6432.
Lay Teachers 21; Students 261.

Glasgow Village, St. Pius X (1954), Rev. James C. Marshall; Deacons Tom Dowd; Frank Shake.
Res., 335 Shepley Dr., St. Louis, 63137. Tel: 314-867-1139.

Glen Owen, St. Sebastian. See St. Sebastian, St. Louis County.

Grantwood, Our Lady of Providence (1954), Revs. Robert F. Johnston; Glennon Doherty, Pastoral Assoc.; Deacons Gerald Prives; Christian Winkelmann. In res., Rev. John Heil.
Res., 8866 Pardee Rd., St. Louis, 63123. Tel: 314-843-3570; Fax: 314-843-8033.
School—8874 Pardee Rd., St. Louis, 63123. Tel: 314-842-2073. Mary Jo Masterson, Prin.
Lay Teachers 13; Students 252.

Glencoe, St. Alban Roe (1980), Rev. Msgr. Edmund O. Griesedieck; Deacons Anthony D. Falbo; Thomas L. Eultgen.
Res., 2001 Shepard Rd., 63038 Tel: 314-458-2977; Fax: 314-273-5425.
Catechesis / Religious Programs—Tel: 314-458-2460. Jill McKendry, D.R.E.
Students 724.

Hathaway Manor, St. Casimir. Closed. For inquiries for parish records contact the Chancery.

Hazelwood, St. Bartholomew (1959), Revs. David M. Novak; Thomas M. Robertson.
Res., 8370 Latty Ave., 63042. Tel: 314-524-4422; Fax: 314-524-7036.
Parish Center—8390 Latty Ave., 63042. Tel: 314-524-3117.

Our Lady of Mercy (1964), Rev. Gregory J. Lockwood; Deacon Robert De Pyper.
Res., 1607 Ville-Maura Ln., 63042. Tel: 314-739-9369; Fax: 314-739-1242.

St. Martin de Porres (1962), Revs. G. Timothy Vowels; John Brockland.
Res., 615 Dunn Rd., 63042. Tel: 314-895-1100; Fax: 314-895-5992.
School—631 Undercliff, 63042. Tel: 314-895-3600.
Lay Teachers 13; Students 203.
Kinderhaus—627 Undercliff, 63042.

Jennings

1—CORPUS CHRISTI/ST.LUCY (1915), Revs. James J. Foster; William J. Wigand; Deacons Harry Nieman; Raymond Audrain.
Res., 8449 Corpus Christi Ln., St. Louis, 63136. Tel: 314-388-0123.
School—2120 Switzer Ave., St. Louis, 63136. Tel: 314-388-0468.
Sisters 1; Lay Teachers 15; Students 246.
Catechesis / Religious Programs—Students 255.

2—ST. FRANCES XAVIER CABRINI (1965), Rev. Msgr. Robert L. McCarthy.
Res., 8450 Lucas-Hunt Rd., 63136. Tel: 314-385-0009; Fax: 314-385-0009.

3—ST. LOUISE DE MARILLAC (1935), Rev. James J. Foster.
Res., 8449 Jennings, St. Louis, 63136. Tel: 314-388-0123.

4—ST. LUCY. See Corpus Christi/St. Lucy, Jennings for details.

Kinloch, Holy Angels (1931), Rev. Edward J. Schramm; Deacon Frank Nesbitt; Judy Brown, Pastoral Assoc.
Res., 8122 Scott St., 63140. Tel: 314-522-0863; Fax: 314-521-3208.
School—Tel: 314-521-0877.
Lay Teachers 8; Students 119.

Kirkwood, St. Peter (1832), Revs. John J. Brennell; Michael P. Boehm; Deacons Joseph Sulze; Richard Hesse. In res., Rev. Theodore Burghoff.
Res., 243 W. Argonne Dr., 63122. Tel: 314-966-8600; Fax: 314-966-5721. [CEM]
School—215 N. Clay St., 63122. Tel: 314-821-0460.
Lay Teachers 33; Students 457.
Catechesis / Religious Programs—Tel: 314-822-1347.
Students 239.

St. Gerard Majella (1955), Revs. Herbert C. Hauck; Matthew M. Mitas; Deacons Tim Dolan; James Burton.
Res., 1969 Dougherty Ferry Rd., 63122. Tel: 314-965-3985; Fax: 314-965-7650.
School—2005 Dougherty Ferry Rd., 63122. Tel: 314-822-8844. Jane Koberlein, Prin.
Lay Teachers 17; Students 301.
Catechesis / Religious Programs—Tel: 314-822-4814.
Students 321.

Ladue, Church of the Annunziata (1929), Rev. Msgr. Robert M. Krawinkel; Rev. Jerome R. Keaty.
Res., 925 Cella Rd., St. Louis, 63124. Tel: 314-993-4422; Fax: 314-994-7877.
Catechesis / Religious Programs—Students 182.

Lemay

1—MARY QUEEN OF THE UNIVERSE (1956), Revs. John W. Siesle; Donald J. Koch; Deacon Eugene Czarnecki.
Res., 4230 Ripa Ave., St. Louis, 63125. Tel: 314-638-3030.
School—4220 Ripa Ave., St. Louis, 63125. Tel: 314-638-2520.
Sisters 1; Lay Teachers 17; Students 204.

2—MOST PRECIOUS BLOOD (1961), Rev. Msgr. Charles Forst; Rev. Patrick D. Ryan.
Res., 3635 Union Rd., St. Louis, 63125. Tel: 314-487-6456; Fax: 314-487-5358.
School—Tel: 314-892-5349. Roseanne Burgoon, Prin.
Lay Teachers 12; Students 169.

3—ST. ANDREW (1905), Revs. Edward J. Hilgeman; Paul J. Spielman; Deacon Robert Karsznia.
Res., 309 Hoffmeister Ave., St. Louis, 63125. Tel: 314-631-0691.
School—Sisters of Notre Dame, 321 Hoffmeister Ave., St. Louis, 63125. Tel: 314-631-5135; 631-2010. Sr. Josephine Winkeler, C.S.J., Prin.
Catechesis / Religious Programs—317 Hoffmeister Ave., St. Louis, 63125. Tel: 314-631-5135.
Students 240.

4—ST. BERNADETTE (1947), Rev. Mark S. Ebert; Rev. Msgr. Edward C. Eichor; Deacon Michael Coppage.
Res., 68 Sherman Rd., Jefferson Barracks, 63125. Tel: 314-892-6882; Fax: 314-892-7716.
School—74 Kearney St., Jefferson Barracks, 63125. Tel: 314-892-8379; Fax: 314-892-4281.
Sisters of Notre Dame 1; Lay Teachers 8; Students 152.

5—ST. MARTIN OF TOURS, Revs. Arthur J. Althoff; Nicholas Smith; Deacon Terry McNamee; Mrs. Leslie Walrath, Pastoral Assoc.
Res., 610 W. Ripa Ave., 63125. Tel: 314-544-5664.

School—618 W. Ripa Ave., 63125. Tel: 314-544-5793. Mrs. Joanne Geels, Prin.
Lay Teachers 11; Students 216.

6—ST. MATTHIAS (1959), Rev. William J. Kester; Deacons John F. Smith; Joseph Hercules; Gary J. Kuenz.
Res., 796 Buckley Rd., St. Louis, 63125. Tel: 314-892-5109.
School—800 Buckley Rd., St. Louis, 63125. Tel: 314-892-7500.
Lay Teachers 14; Students 194.
Convent—798 Buckley Rd., St. Louis, 63125.

Manchester, St. Joseph (1865), Revs. Gerard R. Welsch; Jeffrey Knight.
Res., 567 St. Joseph Ln., 63021. Tel: 314-227-5247; Fax: 314-391-8393. [CEM]
School—555 St. Joseph Ln., 63021. Tel: 314-391-1253. Phyllis Fredrickson, Prin.; Milissa Milan, Asst. Prin.
Sisters of Notre Dame 1; Lay Teachers 36; Students 657.
Catechesis/Religious Programs—Tel: 314-391-1404.
Students 650.

Christ, Prince of Peace (1971), Revs. Joseph E. Wormek; Robert Corbett.
Res., 415 Weidman Rd., 63011. Tel: 314-391-1307; Fax: 314-391-1319.
School—417 Weidman Rd., 63011. Tel: 314-394-6840. Sr. Kathleen Donnelly, O.P., Prin.
Dominican Sisters 2; Lay Teachers 23; Students 365.
Catechesis/Religious Programs—Tel: 314-391-1560.
Students 201.

Maplewood, Immaculate Conception (1904), Rev. Thomas J. Ripper, M.S.; Sr. Georgeann Hanson, S.L., Pastoral Assoc.; Deacon Edwin Dingman.
Res., 2934 Marshall Ave., 63143. Tel: 314-645-3307; Fax: 314-645-0672. [JC]
Additional Residence for Priests—2900 Marshall, 63143. Tel: 314-645-5904. Revs. Joseph C. Shea, M.S.; Peter D. Kohler.

Maryland Heights, St. Blaise (1961), Revs. Richard J. Bockskopf; Stephen Puricell; Deacon Jacob W. Dorhauer.
Res., 3130 Parkwood Ln., 63043. Tel: 314-739-0230.
School—Tel: 314-739-1934.
Sisters 3; Lay Teachers 12; Students 238.
Catechesis/Religious Programs—Tel: 314-739-9796. Virginia Gerdes, D.R.E.
Students 300.

Mattese, Assumption (1839), Rev. Msgr. Thomas J. Dempsey, V.F.; Revs. Francis F. Koeninger; Richard J. Schilli; Deacons Frederick J. Mueller, Jr.; Richard B. Levac.
Res., 4725 Mattis Rd., St. Louis, 63128. Tel: 314-487-7970; Fax: 314-892-5513. [CEM]
School—Tel: 314-487-6520. Margaret Adams, Prin.
Lay Teachers 25; Students 451.
Catechesis/Religious Programs—Tel: 314-487-2149. Carol Aliperti, D.R.E.
Students 193.

Mary, Mother of the Church (1971), Rev. Msgr. Edward Reilly; Rev. Steve Robeson; Deacon Eugene W. Caton.
Res., 5901 Kerth Rd., St. Louis, 63128. Tel: 314-894-1373; Fax: 314-894-3801.
Catechesis/Religious Programs—Ed Lewandowski, D.R.E.
Students 359.

Mehlville, St. Margaret Mary Alacoque (1962), Revs. Dennis Stehly; Alan J. Knaup; Philip Bene.
4900 Ringer Rd., St. Louis, 63129. Fax: 314-487-2522.
Res., 5056 Faust Ct., St. Louis, 63129. Tel: 314-487-2522.
School—Tel: 314-487-1666.
Lay Teachers 32; Students 700.
Catechesis/Religious Programs—Students 400.

Normandy, Ascension-St. Paul (1955), Rev. Stephen G. Joyce; Ms. Leodia Gooch, Pastoral Min.; Deacon Albert Bernsen.
Res., 7005 Ascension Dr., 63121. Tel: 314-385-6750; Fax: 314-385-6965.
School—3801 Nelson Dr., 63121. Tel: 314-261-1592. Jo Ann Gaynor, Prin.
Lay Teachers 18; Students 275.

St. Ann (1854), Rev. James T. Edwards; Deacon Norman Jansen.
Res., 7530 Natural Bridge Rd., 63121. Tel: 314-385-5090. [CEM]
School—Tel: 314-381-0113. Sr. Gloria Clapperton, Prin.
Lay Teachers 16; Students 261.

Oakville, St. Francis of Assisi (1927), Revs. Robert Behnen, O.F.M.; Blane O'Neill, O.F.M.; Aloys Jost, O.F.M.; Deacons Alan Ecker; George R. Fink; Lawrence Kelly. In res., Revs. Silas Musholt, O.F.M.; Valerian Schott, O.F.M.; Ermin Micka, O.F.M.; Charles Reuter, O.F.M.
Res., 4556 Telegraph Rd., St. Louis, 63129. Tel: 314-487-5736; Fax: 314-487-3701.
School—4550 Telegraph Rd., St. Louis, 63129. Tel: 314-892-3918; Fax: 314-892-3918. Marilyn Koncen, Prin.
Franciscan Sisters of Our Lady of Perpetual Help 2; Lay Teachers 34; Students 720.
Catechesis/Religious Programs—Students 270.

Queen of All Saints (1972), Rev. Msgr. Robert P. Jovanovic, M.Ed.; Revs. John L. Hallemann, Senior Assoc.; Henry J. Breier; Deacon Richard W. Coffman.
Res., 6603 Christopher Dr., 63129-4919. Tel: 314-846-8207; Fax: 314-846-0636.
School—Tel: 314-846-0506. Sr. JoDonna Grimes, S.S.N.D., Prin.
Students 400.
Catechesis/Religious Programs—Marge Schumer, D.R.E.
Students 720.

Overland, All Souls, Revs. John F. Blomberg; Frank D'Amico; Deacon Arnold Krieger.
Res., 9550 Tennyson Ave., 63114. Tel: 314-427-0442.
School—9600 Tennyson Ave., 63114. Tel: 314-429-5319.
Sisters of Notre Dame 1; Lay Teachers 12; Students 165.

Our Lady of the Presentation (1915), Rev. Dennis R. Port.
Res., 8860 Tudor Ave., St. Louis, 63114. Tel: 314-427-0486; Fax: 314-423-3020.
School—8840 Tudor Ave., St. Louis, 63114. Tel: 314-428-8191; Fax: 314-423-1213.
Lay Teachers 24; Students 297.

Pagedale, St. Catherine of Siena (1909), Rev. Victor A. Barnhart, Admin.
Res., 6815 Page Ave., St. Louis, 63133-1505. Tel: 314-721-3069 (Voice); 727-2747 (TDD); Fax: 314-727-2747.

Pine Lawn, St. Paul the Apostle. Merged to form Ascension-St. Paul, Normandy.

Richmond Heights, Immacolata (1945), Revs. Michael J. Sheridan; Gary J. Faust; Louis Roedig.
Church—8900 Clayton Rd., 63117. Tel: 314-991-5700; Fax: 314-991-4769.
School—8910 Clayton Rd., 63117. Tel: 314-991-1924. Mr. Salvatore Latragna, Prin.
Lay Teachers 20; Students 278.

Little Flower, St. Teresa of the Infant Jesus (1926), Revs. James J. Benz; Philip G. Krahman; Deacon Stephen Murray.
Res., 1264 Arch Terrace, 63117. Tel: 314-645-1445; Fax: 314-645-3258.
School—1275 Boland Pl., 63117. Tel: 314-781-4995. Clare Ortmeier, Prin.
Sisters 3; Lay Teachers 13; Students 205.

St. Luke the Evangelist (1914), Revs. Richard L. Stoltz; William G. Kempf; Rev. Msgr. John J. Kennedy.
Res., 7230 Dale Ave., St. Louis, 63117. Tel: 314-644-2144.
School—1414 Bellevue Ave., St. Louis, 63177. Tel: 314-781-2072; Fax: 314-781-7411.
Lay Teachers 13; Students 193.

Riverview Gardens, St. Catherine of Alexandria (1921), Revs. Thomas M. Robertson; John L. Eckhard; Deacon Edwin Schulte.
Res., 321 Chambers Rd., St. Louis, 63137. Tel: 314-867-8515.
School—10014 Diamond Dr., St. Louis, 63137. Tel: 314-869-0515. Sr. Patricia Dalton, S.S.N.D., Prin.
Sisters 2; Lay Teachers 10; Students 216.

St. Ann, St. Gregory (1942), Rev. John I. Caffe. In res., Deacon William F. Priesmeyer.
Res., 3500 St. Luke Ln., 63074. Tel: 314-428-3346.
School—3400 St. Gregory Ln., 63074. Tel: 314-429-0964.
Lay Teachers 9; Students 105.

St. Kevin (1953), Revs. John J. Leykam; Andrew J. O'Connor.
Res., 10909 St. Henry Ln., 63074. Tel: 314-427-6336; Fax: 314-427-5333.
School—10901 St. Henry Ln., 63074. Tel: 312-427-7074. Margaret Fortner, Prin.
Lay Teachers 16; Students 282.

St. Louis County, St. Sebastian (1953), Rev. Jim R. French; Deacon Herbert L. Ehrhard.
Res., 9950 Glen Owen Dr., St. Louis, 63136. Tel: 314-868-0730; Fax: 314-868-0731.
School—1826 Chambers Rd., St. Louis, 63136. Tel: 314-869-1923.
Lay Teachers 15; Students 197.

Sappington, St. Catherine Laboure (1953), Rev. Patrick J. Keeley, C.M. Pastoral Associates: Rev. Raymond Ross, C.M.; Deacon George Tichacek.
Res., 9740 Sappington Rd., St. Louis, 63128. Tel: 314-843-3245; Fax: 314-843-3196.
School—9750 Sappington Rd., St. Louis, 63128. Tel: 314-843-2819; Fax: 314-843-7687. William Braun, Prin.
Lay Teachers 24; Students 497.
Catechesis/Religious Programs—Students 167.

Shrewsbury, Cure of Ars (1966), Rev. Clarence P. Good.
Res., 670 S. Laclede Station Rd., St. Louis, 63119. Tel: 314-962-5883.

St. Michael (1895), Revs. Edmond J. Fitzgibbon; Martin J. Mulvihill; Bernard Suellentrop; Deacon Stephen Arnold.
Res., 7622 Sutherland Ave., St. Louis, 63119. Tel: 314-647-5611; Fax: 314-781-9211.
School—7630 Sutherland Ave., St. Louis, 63119. Tel: 314-647-7159.
Sisters 1; Lay Teachers 17; Students 238.

Spanish Lake, St. Aloysius (1871), Rev. Gerald T. Nienhaus; Deacon Walter J. Ruegg.
Res., 12110 Larimore Rd., St. Louis, 63138. Tel: 314-741-3690; Fax: 314-741-6468.
School—12122 Larimore Rd., St. Louis, 63138. Tel: 314-741-0294.
Sisters 1; Lay Teachers 8; Students 144.
Catechesis/Religious Programs—Students 127.

Our Lady of Loretto (1959), Revs. Stephen Gira, C.R.; Steven R. Thoma, C.R.; Deacons Francis Droesch; James Michael Buckley.
Res., 11725 Bellefontaine Rd., St. Louis, 63138. Tel: 314-741-7700; Fax: 314-741-7700.
School—1650 Redman Ave., St. Louis, 63138. Tel: 314-741-0400. Mrs. Marie Moritz, Prin.
Sisters of Notre Dame 1; Lay Teachers 14; Students 206.

Sunset Hills, St. Justin Martyr (1964), Revs. Bernard J. Schloemer; Leo T. Lewis.
Res., 11962 Bardmont Dr., St. Louis, 63126. Tel: 314-843-8482; Fax: 314-843-8507.
School—11914 Eddie and Park Rd., St. Louis, 63126. Tel: 314-843-6447. Sr. Ann Martinek, Prin.
Sisters of St. Francis of Clinton, Iowa 2; Lay Teachers 11; Students 247.

University City

1—ALL SAINTS (1901), Rev. Donald L. Molitor; Deacon Franklin J. Fick.
Res., 6403 Clemens Ave., 63130. Tel: 314-721-6403.

2—CHRIST THE KING (1927), Rev. John A. Ditenhofer. In res., Rev. John Jay Hughes; Deacon E. Ray Kiely.
Res., 7316 Balson Ave., 63130. Tel: 314-721-8737; Fax: 314-721-8737.
School—7324 Balson Ave., 63130. Tel: 314-725-5855; Fax: 314-725-5981. Sr. Rosella McNamee, R.S.M., Prin.
Sisters of Mercy 3; Lay Teachers 11; Students 222.

3—OUR LADY OF LOURDES (1916), Rev. Msgr. Edward J. Sudekum; Rev. Msgr. Norbert J. Dietz; Rev. Lawrence C. Brennan; Sr. Margaret Marie Vitt, O.S.U., Pastoral Assoc.; Deacon Albert X. Vaughn.
Res., 7148 Forsyth Blvd., 63105. Tel: 314-726-6200; Fax: 314-726-6201.
School—7157 Northmoor Ave., 63105. Tel: 314-726-3352.
Lay Teachers 19; Students 243.

4—ST. PATRICK (1940), Revs. Eugene Bendel; Theodore R. Brug.
Res., 8665 Olive Blvd., 63132. Tel: 314-993-1277.

Valley Park, Sacred Heart (1903), Revs. Robert T. Rosebrough; Thomas M. Begley; Sr. Donna Fischer, S.S.N.D., Pastoral Assoc.; Deacons Ewald Winker; Larry Damato; Allen F. Love.
Res., 10 Ann Ave., 63088. Tel: 314-225-5268; Fax: 314-225-1952. [CEM]
School—12 Ann Ave., 63088. Tel: 314-225-3824. Sharon Baumgartner, Prin.
Lay Teachers 22; Students 321.
Catechesis/Religious Programs—Students 453.

Vinita Park, St. Rita (1919), Rev. David L. Wichlan; Deacon Louis J. Reynoso.
Res., 8240 Washington St., St. Louis County, 63114. Tel: 314-428-4845.

Warson Woods, Ste. Genevieve Du Bois (1956), Rev. John B. Shamleffer. In res., Rev. Msgr. John P. Holland, Senior Priest.
Res., 1575 N. Woodlawn Ave., 63122. Tel: 314-966-3780; Fax: 314-966-4687.
School—Tel: 314-821-4245. Helen Petropoulos, Prin.
Sisters 1; Lay Teachers 13; Students 215.

Webster Groves, Annunciation (1950), Revs. Denny M. Schaab; John G. Klocker, Senior Priest.
Res., 12 W. Glendale Rd., 63119. Tel: 314-962-5955; Fax: 314-961-0643.
School—16 W. Glendale, 63119. Tel: 314-961-7712. Mary Rath, Prin.
Lay Teachers 15; Students 222.

Holy Redeemer (1886), Revs. Joseph M. Simon; Stephen G. Puricelli; Deacon Richard Wessels. In res., Rev. Mark L. Fuller.
Res., 17 Joy Ave., 63119. Tel: 314-962-0038; Fax: 314-962-2084.
School—341 E. Lockwood, 63119. Tel: 314-962-8989. Cynthia Hasten, Prin.

Lay Teachers 16; Students 212.
Catechesis/Religious Programs—Tel: 314-962-1487.
Students 200.

Mary, Queen of Peace (1922), Rev. Msgr. Thomas J. Woracek; Rev. Msgr. Richard J. Lubeley, Senior Priest; Rev. John J. Borcic; Deacons Robert C. Riegel; Paul McKee. In res., Most Rev. Paul A. Zipfel, V.G.
Res., 676 W. Lockwood Blvd., 63119. Tel: 314-962-2311; Fax: 314-968-9885.
School—680 W. Lockwood Ave., 63119. Tel: 314-961-2891. Sr. Ann Sullivan, S.L., Prin.
Sisters of Loretto at the Foot of the Cross 2; Lay Teachers 28; Students 515.
Catechesis/Religious Programs—Students 144.

Wellston, Notre Dame De Lourdes. Closed. See St. Augustine, St. Louis for details.

West Overland, St. Jude (1953), Rev. Joseph L. Parisi; Deacon Eugene D. Barron.
Res., 2218 N. Warson Rd., St. Louis, 63114. Tel: 314-428-2262.

Woodson Terrace, St. William (1953), Rev. Eugene P. Selzer; Deacon John J. Buckley.
Res., 9311 Stansberry Ave., 63134. Tel: 314-428-7371; Fax: 314-428-1158.
School—9330 Stansberry Ave., 63134. Tel: 314-427-6444.
Lay Teachers 3; Students 70.

CHURCHES OUTSIDE ST. LOUIS CITY AND ST. LOUIS COUNTY

Apple Creek, Perry Co., St. Joseph's (1828) (German), Rev. John D. Bolderson.
Res., Perryville Rte. 2, 63775. Tel: 314-788-2330. [CEM][JC 2]
School—(Grades K-8). Nancy Heberlie, Prin.
Lay Teachers 3; Students 61.

Arnold, Jefferson Co., Immaculate Conception (1840), Revs. Earl Meyer, O.F.M.Cap.; Gilmary Tallman, O.F.M.Cap.; Deacons Joseph C. Streckfuss; Bradford M. Buchek.
Res., 2300 Church Rd., P.O. Box 217, 63010. Tel: 314-296-5289. [CEM]
School—Holy Child School. Consolidated with St. David, Arnold. Tel: 314-296-0055; Fax: 314-296-5639. Mrs. Marlene DiMaggio, Prin.
Lay Teachers 22; Students 349.
Catechesis/Religious Programs—Tel: 314-296-5598. Joyce Ott, D.R.E.
Students 396.

St. David (1963), Rev. Thomas Schmidt; Deacon Thomas G. Politte.
Res., 2334 Tenbrook Rd., 63010. Tel: 314-296-5485; Fax: 314-296-5526.
School—Holy Child Consolidated School. See Immaculate Conception for details. Tel: 314-296-0055.
Catechesis/Religious Programs—Students 190.

Augusta, St. Charles Co., Immaculate Conception (1851), Rev. Msgr. Charles G. Clavenna.
Res., 5912 Hwy. 94 S., 63332. Tel: 314-482-4455. [CEM]

Belgique, Perry Co., Nativity of the Blessed Virgin Mary. Closed. For inquiries for parish records contact the Chancery.

Berger, Franklin Co., St. Paul (1853) (German), Rev. Daniel E. Mosley.
Res., 603 Miller St., New Haven, 63068. Tel: 573-237-3372. [CEM]

Biehle, Perry Co., St. Maurus (1870) (German), Rev. Joseph B. Eilers.
Res., Rte. 7, Box 237, Perryville, 63775. Tel: 573-547-5246. [CEM][JC]
School—Tel: 573-547-6123.
Lay Teachers 3; Students 13.

Bloomsdale, Ste. Genevieve Co., St. Agnes (1822), Rev. Raymond J. Oge.
Res., P.O. Box 124, 63627. Tel: 314-483-2555. [CEM]
School—Tel: 314-483-2506. Sr. Donna Marie Kist, C.PP.S., Prin.
Sisters of the Most Precious Blood (O'Fallon, MO) 1; Lay Teachers 10; Students 153.

Bonne Terre, St. Francois Co., St. Joseph's (1872), Rev. John H. Schneider.
Res., 15 St. Joseph St., 63628. Tel: 573-358-2112; Fax: 573-358-4233. [CEM]
School—(Grades K-6). Tel: 573-358-5947. William Martim, Prin.
Lay Teachers 4; Students 44.
Mission—French Village, St. Francois Co., St. Anne, P.O. Box 307 French Village, 63036. Tel: 573-358-2112.

Brewer, Perry Co., Christ the Savior (1907), Rev. Felipe J. Martinez, C.M.
Res., Rte. 4, Box 347, Perryville, 63775. Tel: 573-547-2677.

Catawissa, Franklin Co., St. James (1913), Rev. Hubert E. Creason.
Res., P.O. Box 447, 63015. Tel: 314-271-6038; 257-3993. [CEM]
Mission—Armagh, Franklin Co., St. Patrick, Hwy. NN & Rock Church Rd., 63015. [CEM]

Clover Bottom, Franklin Co., St. Ann's (1883) (Polish-German), Rev. John E. Majewski. In res., Rev. Michael E. Turek.
Res., Clover Bottom, 7851 State Rd. YY, Washington, 63090-9627. Tel: 314-239-3222. [CEM]

Coffman, Ste. Genevieve Co., St. Catherine of Alexandria (1929). Attended by River Aux Vases. Rev. F. Joseph Reilly.
Res., 18411 RAV Church Rd., Ste. Genevieve, 63670. Tel: 314-883-2923. [CEM]

Concord Hill, Warren Co., St. Ignatius (1857) (German), Rev. Finbarr Dowling, O.S.B.
Res., 701 Mill Rd., Marthasville, 63357. Tel: 314-932-4445. [CEM 2]
School—703 Mill Rd., 63357. Tel: 314-932-4444. Barbara McDermott, Prin.
Sisters of Notre Dame 2; Sisters of Mercy 1; Lay Teachers 2; Students 55.
Mission—Case, Warren Co., St. Anthony, 701 Mill Rd., 63357.

Cottleville, St. Charles Co., St. Joseph (1873), Rev. Msgr. Walter M. Whited; Revs. Erich A. Fechner; Timothy P. Cronin; Deacon Ronald Bachista.
Res., 1355 Motherhead Rd., St. Charles, 63304. Tel: 314-441-0055; Fax: 314-441-7708. [CEM]
School—1351 Motherhead Rd., St. Charles, 63304. Tel: 314-441-7978; Fax: 314-441-9932. Ms. Mary Ellen Schraeder, Prin.
Sisters 1; Lay Teachers 34; Students 778.
Catechesis/Religious Programs—Tel: 314-447-5239. Mrs. Barbara Blackburn, D.R.E.
Students 979.

Crystal City, Jefferson Co., Sacred Heart (1881), Revs. Michael L. Donald; John A. Keenoy; Deacon Gerard G. Stoverink.
Res., 555 Bailey Rd., 63019. Tel: 314-937-4662; Fax: 314-931-0422. [CEM]
School—Tel: 314-931-5701.
Lay Teachers 11; Students 144.
Catechesis/Religious Programs—Students 177.

Dardenne, St. Charles Co., Immaculate Conception, Revs. Robert J. Reiker; K. Robert Smoot; James R. Komaska; Deacons Don Schiffman; Charles Drayton.
Res., 7701 Hwy. N, O'Fallon, 63366. Tel: 314-561-4459; Fax: 314-561-3883. [CEM]
School—Tel: 314-561-4450.
Lay Teachers 12; Students 263.
Catechesis/Religious Programs—Tel: 314-561-1974.
Students 528.

De Soto, Jefferson Co., St. Rose of Lima (1885), Revs. Ronald J. Hopmeir; Robert J. Suit; Deacon Edward J. Boyer.
Res., 504 S. Third St., 63020. Tel: 314-337-2212; Fax: 314-337-2394. [CEM]
School—Tel: 314-586-3594; Fax: 314-337-7855. Sr. Rosemary Meiman, O.S.U., Prin.
Sisters 2; Lay Teachers 8; Students 104.
Catechesis/Religious Programs—Tel: 314-337-2212; Fax: 314-337-7855.
Students 150.

Dutzow, Warren Co., St. Vincent de Paul (1856), Rev. Stephen F. Bauer.
Res., 7602 S. Hwy. 94, Marthasville, 63357. Tel: 314-433-2678. [CEM]
School—Tel: 314-433-2466.
Lay Teachers 10; Students 173.
Catechesis/Religious Programs—Students 165.

Elsberry, Lincoln Co., Sacred Heart (1905), Rev. James P. Grady.
Res., 714 Lincoln St., 63343. Tel: 573-898-2202; Fax: 573-898-2202.

Farmington, St. Francois Co., St. Joseph (1890), Revs. Eugene Robertson; Thomas J. Wissler; Deacons William J. Greif; Albin A. Gegg.
Res., 5 S. Carleton, 63640 Tel: 573-756-4250. [CEM 2]
School—501 Ste. Genevieve Ave., 63640. Tel: 573-756-6312.
Students 164.

Festus, Jefferson Co., Our Lady, Rev. John V. Kerber.
Res., 1550 St. Mary Ln., 63028. Tel: 314-937-5513; 931-4702 (toll-free).
School—Sisters of Notre Dame 2; Lay Teachers 8; Students 200.

Flint Hill, St. Charles Co., St. Theodore (1883), Rev. Albert A. Mattler.
Res., P.O. Box 246, 63346. Tel: 314-332-9269. [CEM]
School—Tel: 314-332-9465.
Lay Teachers 6; Students 93.

Gildehaus, Franklin Co., St. John the Baptist (1839), Revs. William J. Leach; Kevin V. Schmittgens.
Res., 5567 Gildenhaus Rd., Gildenhaus, 63089. Tel: 314-583-2488. [CEM]
School—Tel: 314-583-2392. Ruth O. Himmelberg, Prin.
Lay Teachers 8; Students 195.

Hawk Point, Lincoln Co., St. Mary (1919) (Bohemian), Rev. Bernard Nienhaus.
Res., P.O. Box 205, 63349. Tel: 314-338-4331. [CEM 2]

Herculaneum, Jefferson Co., Church of the Assumption of B.V.M. (1916), Rev. Robert F. Fleiter.
Res., 329 Station St., 63048-1328. Tel: 314-475-5305. [CEM]

High Ridge, Jefferson Co., St. Anthony of Padua (1921), Revs. Eugene R. Sinz; Richard H. Suren; Deacons Bill Gearon; Paul Crafts; Dick Shelby; Joe Otzenberger.
Res., 3009 High Ridge Blvd., 63049. Tel: 314-677-4868; Fax: 314-677-2781.
School—3005 High Ridge Blvd., 63049. Tel: 314-677-3585. Mr. Robert Cowell, Prin.
Lay Teachers 10; Students 167.
Catechesis/Religious Programs—Students 174.

Hillsboro, Jefferson Co., Church of the Good Shepherd (1934), Rev. Michael E. Dieckmann.
Res., 703 Third St., 63050-4342. Tel: 314-789-3356; Fax: 314-789-9986. [CEM]
School—Tel: 314-789-2300. Mrs. Michel Wendell, Prin.
Lay Teachers 6; Students 84.

House Springs, Jefferson Co., Our Lady, Queen of Peace, Revs. Norbert A. Ernst; Larry T. Huber, Jr.; Deacon Thomas Gerling.
Res., 4696 Notre Dame Ln., 63051. Tel: 314-671-3062; Fax: 314-671-0003. [CEM 2]
School—Tel: 314-671-0247. Sr. Louise Schmid, O.P., Prin.
Sisters 2; Lay Teachers 8; Students 210.
Catechesis/Religious Programs—Students 240.

Imperial, Jefferson Co., St. John (1869), Rev. Edward L. Heim.
Res., 4525 Hwy. 21, 63052. Tel: 314-296-8061; Fax: 314-296-8067. [CEM]
School—Tel: 314-296-8112. Sr. Ann Muckerman, S.S.N.D., Prin.
Lay Teachers 10; Students 160.

Josephville, St. Charles Co., St. Joseph (1852), Rev. Raymond B. Liermann.
Res., 1390 Josephville Rd., Wentzville, 63385. Tel: 314-332-6676. [CEM]
School—1410 Josephville Rd., Wentzville, 63385. Tel: 314-327-7174. Barbara Rygelski, Prin.
Lay Teachers 4; Students 92.

Kimmswick, Jefferson Co., St. Joseph's, Rev. Andrew J. Sigmund; Deacons Kenneth A. Henning; Glennon P. Politte, Sr.
Res., 63053. Tel: 314-464-1013. [CEM]
School—Tel: 314-464-9027. Pat Kirk, Prin.
Students 230.
Catechesis/Religious Programs—Students 330.

Krakow, Franklin Co., St. Gertrude's (1845), Rev. Dennis B. Zacheis.
Res., 6535 State Rd. YY, Washington, 63090. Tel: 314-239-4216; Fax: 314-451-0221. [CEM]
School—Tel: 314-239-2347. Marilyn Traffas, Prin.
Lay Teachers 16; Students 280.

Lawrenceton, Ste. Genevieve Co., St. Lawrence's (1872). Attended by St. Agnes Rectory. Rev. Raymond J. Oge.
Bloomsdale, 63627. Tel: 314-483-2555. [CEM]

Luebbering, Franklin Co., St. Francis of Assisi (1874), Rev. John B. McEntee.
Res., 100 Luebbering Rd., 63061-9705. Tel: 314-629-1717. [CEM]

Millwood, Lincoln Co., St. Alphonsus (1850), Rev. John L. Mayer.
Res., 24 St. Alphonsus, Silex, 63377. Tel: 573-384-6223. [CEM]
School—Tel: 573-384-5305.
Lay Teachers 5; Students 75.
Catechesis/Religious Programs—Students 180.

Moselle, Franklin Co., St. Mary's (1905) (German), Rev. Lawrence J. Schieber.
Res., 1587 Hwy. AM, Villa Ridge, 63089. Tel: 314-451-4685. [CEM]

Neier, Franklin Co., St. Joseph's (1881), Rev. Gerald T. Simpson.
Res., 2401 Neier Rd., Union, 63084. Tel: 314-583-2806. [CEM]

New Haven, Franklin Co., Assumption (1892) (German), Rev. Daniel E. Mosley.
Res., 63068. Tel: 314-237-3372. [CEM]

New Melle, St. Charles Co., Immaculate Heart of Mary (1945), Rev. Joseph A. Weber; Shawn Mueller, Pastoral Assoc.
Res., 26 W. Hwy. D, Box 100, 63365. Tel: 314-398-5270; Fax: 314-398-5577. [CEM]
Catechesis/Religious Programs—Sandra Robor, D.R.E.

Students 190.

O'Fallon, St. Charles Co., Assumption (1871) (German), Revs. Robert D. Boisaubin; Ronald J. Rubbelke. In res., Rev. Paul Link, C.PP.S.
Res., 115 W. Third St., 63366. Tel: 314-240-3721; Fax: 314-240-3722. [CEM]
School—Tel: 314-240-4474. Sr. Patricia Cody, O.P., Prin.
Lay Teachers 24; Students 432.
Catechesis/Religious Programs—Tel: 314-978-3857.
Students 340.

St. Barnabas (1961), Rev. Daniel M. Hogan.
Res., 1415 N. Main St., 63366. Tel: 314-272-4555.

Old Mines, Washington Co., St. Joachim's (1723), Rev. Theodore X. Pieper; Deacon Steven Politte.
Res., Rte. 1, P.O. Box 1110, Cadet, 63630. Tel: 573-438-6181; Fax: 573-438-6181. [CEM]
School—Tel: 573-438-3973. Joyce Politte, Prin.
Lay Teachers 7; Students 54.

Old Monroe, Lincoln Co., Immaculate Conception (1857), Rev. Gregory L. Schmidt; Deacon Anthony Trautman.
Res., 110 Maryknoll Rd., 63369. Tel: 314-661-5002. [CEM]
School—120 Maryknoll Rd., 63369. Tel: 314-665-5463. Mrs. Mary Dixon, Prin.
Sisters of the Third Order Regular of St. Francis (Oldenburg, IN) 1; Lay Teachers 8; Students 155.
Convent—122 Maryknoll Rd., Tel: 314-665-5303.

Ozora, Ste. Genevieve Co., Sacred Heart (1898), Rev. James J. Pavlik.
Res., 17742 State Rte. N., St. Mary, 63673. Tel: 314-543-2209. [CEM]
School—Tel: 314-543-2997.
Lay Teachers 3; Students 27. Sisters of the Most Precious Blood. Mrs. Kathleen Grither, Prin.

Pacific, Franklin Co., St. Bridget Church (1841) (Irish), Rev. Richard V. Coerver.
Res., 111 W. Union St., 63069. Tel: 314-271-3993. [CEM]
School—Tel: 314-257-4533.
Lay Teachers 6; Students 107.

Park Hills, St. Francois Co., Immaculate Conception (1903), Rev. Ambrose F. Stratman.
Res., Box 66, 63601-0066. Tel: 573-431-2427. [CEM][JC]
Mission—Bismarck, St. Francois Co., St. John, (1879). Deacon Walter Roderick. 215 High St., P.O. Box 95, Belgrade, 63622. Tel: 573-766-5311. [CEM][JC]

Perryville, Perry Co., St. Vincent De Paul (1818), Revs. Kevin P. Fausz, C.M.; Gerard P. Kelly, C.M.; George K. Billings, C.M.
Res., 1000 Rosati Court, 63775. Tel: 573-547-4591; Fax: 573-547-4145. [CEM 4]
School—Tel: 573-547-6503. Robert Rousseau, Prin.
Daughters of Charity of St. Vincent de Paul 1; Lay Teachers 22; Students 324.
Junior-Senior High School—Tel: 573-547-2560. Sr. Mary Bryan Owens, S.S.N.D., Prin.
Daughters of Charity of St. Vincent de Paul 1; Lay Teachers 22; Students 324.
Catechesis/Religious Programs—Parish School of Religion, 1021 W. St. Joseph, 63775. Tel: 314-547-4503.
Students 285.
Missions—Highland, Perry Co., St. Joseph, 1701 W. St. Joseph, Perryville, 63775. Tel: 314-547-6533; Crosstown, Perry Co., St. James.
Catechesis/Religious Programs—Parish School of Religion, 1021 W. St. Joseph, 63775. Tel: 314-547-4503.
Students 285.

Portage Des Sioux, St. Charles Co., St. Francis (1809) (French-German), Rev. Michael J. Sandweg.
Res., P.O. Box 128, 63373. Tel: 314-899-0906. [CEM]
School—Tel: 314-753-2345.
Sisters 2; Lay Teachers 1; Students 30.
Mission—West Alton, St. Charles Co., Immaculate Conception, West Alton, 63386.
Catechesis/Religious Programs—Students 150.

Port Hudson, Franklin Co., Holy Family (1872), Rev. James M. Sullivan.
Res., 124 Holy Family Church Rd., New Haven, 63068. Tel: 573-459-6441. [CEM]
Catechesis/Religious Programs—Students 150.
Mission—Gerald, Franklin Co., St. Gerald.

Potosi, Washington Co., St. James (1829), Rev. George Galovich.
Res., 201 N. Missouri Ave., 63664. Tel: 314-438-4686; 1-800-533-8163 (toll-free); Fax: 314-438-2100. [CEM]

Richwoods, Washington Co., St. Stephen's (1841), Rev. Robert C. Liss.
Res., H.C.R. 63, Box 1, 63071-9701. Tel: 573-678-2207. [CEM]

River Aux Vases, Ste. Genevieve Co., SS. Phillip and James (1840), Rev. F. Joseph Reilly.
Res., 18411 RAV Church Rd., Ste. Genevieve, 63670. Tel: 314-883-2923. [CEM]

St. Charles, St. Charles Co.,

1—St. Charles Borromeo, (1792), Revs. Richard J. Tillman; Xavier R. Albert; Donald E. Henke.
Res., 601 N. 4th St., 63301. Tel: 314-946-6370; 946-1893; Fax: 314-946-3189.
School—431 Decatur, 63301. Tel: 314-946-2713.
Sisters of Notre Dame 2; Lay Teachers 19; Students 335.
Catechesis/Religious Programs—Tel: 314-946-2916.
Students 200.
Chapel—Convent of the Sacred Heart, Regis Hall, Tel: 314-946-6456.

2—St. Cletus, (1965), Revs. James P. Callahan; William McCumber; Deacon Frank Prideaux.
Res., 2705 Zumbehl Rd., 63301. Tel: 314-946-6327; Fax: 314-946-6466.
School—Tel: 314-946-7756.
Lay Teachers 20; Students 300.
Catechesis/Religious Programs—Tel: 314-946-5936.
Students 250.

3—St. Elizabeth Ann Seton, (1975), Revs. Kevin J. Mahoney; Timothy P. Elliott; Donald L. Neuner.
Res., 2 Seton Ct., 63303. Tel: 314-946-6717; Fax: 314-946-9263.
School—Tel: 314-946-6716.
Sisters 1. Lay Teachers 37; Students 728.
Catechesis/Religious Programs—Nancy Burian, D.R.E.
Students 500.

4—Sts. Joachim and Ann, (1981), Revs. Dennis J. Doyle; James L. Gahan; Patrick Christopher.
Mailing Address: 4112 McClay Rd., 63304. Tel: 314-441-7503.
School—4110 McClay Rd., 63304. Tel: 314-441-4835; Fax: 314-441-9534. Sr. Barbara Siderewicz, O.S.F., Prin.
Sisters 2. Lay Teachers 26; Students 673.
Catechesis/Religious Programs—Tel: 314-926-0021.
Students 719.

5—St. Peter, (1850), Revs. Arthur F. Bromschwig; Donald D. Carey; Deacon Thomas J. Willbrand. In res., Rev. Msgr. Raymond A. Hampe.
Res., 324 S. Third St., 63301. Tel: 314-946-6641; Fax: 314-946-9789. [CEM]
School—222 Jackson St., 63301. Tel: 314-947-9669.
Lay Teachers 20; Students 326.

6—St. Robert Bellarmine, (1964), Revs. Fred A. Meyer; Tony Dattilo.
Res., 1424 First Capitol Dr., S., 63303. Tel: 314-946-6799.
School—Tel: 314-946-1474. Cathy Wayland, Prin.; Sue Finley, Asst. Prin.
Lay Teachers 8; Students 153.
Catechesis/Religious Programs—Students 233.

St. Clair, Franklin Co., St. Clare, Rev. Paul E. Telken.
Res., Box 526, 63077. Tel: 314-629-0315. [CEM]
School—Sisters of Notre Dame 1; Lay Teachers 5; Students 102.

Ste. Genevieve, Ste. Genevieve Co., Ste. Genevieve's (1759), Revs. John J. Johnson; John M. Seper; Deacon George Wood.
Res., 49 Du Bourg Pl., 63670. Tel: 573-883-2731; Fax: 573-883-2907. [CEM]
School—40 N. Fourth St., 63670. Tel: 573-883-2403.
Lay Teachers 21; Students 304.
High School—Valle High School, Tel: 573-883-7496.
Sisters 1; Lay Teachers 14; Students 158.

St. Mary's, Ste. Genevieve Co., Immaculate Conception, Rev. Richard C. Kasznel.
Res., P.O. Box 27, 63673. Tel: 314-543-2536. [CEM]
Convent—Mailing Address: P.O. Box 85, 63673.
Ursuline Sisters 3.

St. Paul, St. Charles Co., St. Paul (1850), Rev. Msgr. John J. Hickel.
Rectory: Tel: 314-978-1400.; Parish Center: Tel: 314-978-1900.
Res., P.O. Box 66069, 63366. [CEM]
School—P.O. Box 66070, 63366. Tel: 314-978-1818. Mary Price, Prin.
Lay Teachers 11; Students 213.

St. Peters, St. Charles Co., All Saints (1815), Revs. Michael L. Henning; Mark C. Ullrich; Robert C. Lane; Deacon Gerald Knobbe.
Res., 7 McMenemy Rd., 63376. Tel: 314-397-1440; Fax: 314-397-1421. [CEM]
School—Tel: 314-397-1477. Rae Ann Kielty, Prin.
Lay Teachers 25; Students 411.
Catechesis/Religious Programs—Tel: 314-397-6995. Ms. Marya Pohlmeier, D.R.E.
Students 525.

Sereno, Perry Co., Our Lady of Victory (1908), Rev. Francis H. Agnew, C.M., Admin.
Res., Rte. 3, Box 135, Perryville, 63775. Tel: 314-547-6812. [JC]

Silver Lake, Perry Co., St. Rose of Lima (1885), Rev. Kevin P. Fausz, C.M.
Res., 1000 Rosati Ct., Perryville, 63775. [CEM]
St. Mary's Seminary—Perryville, 63775. Tel: 314-547-4591; Fax: 314-547-4145.

Sullivan, Franklin Co., St. Anthony (1891), Rev. Theodore J. Brunnert; Deacons Michael Sabo; Allen Kaufman.
Res., 201 W. Springfield Ave., 63080. Tel: 573-468-6101. [CEM]
School—101 W. Springfield Ave., 63080. Tel: 573-468-4423. Barbara Kelley, Prin.
Lay Teachers 6; Students 94.

Church of the Holy Martyrs of Japan (1879), Rev. Robert A. Marshall, Admin.
Church—8244 Hwy. AE, 63080. Tel: 573-627-3378. [CEM]

Tiff, Washington Co., St. Joseph's (1723), Rev. Theodore X. Pieper, Admin.
Res., R.R.I. Box 1110, Cadet, 63630. Tel: 573-438-6181; Fax: 573-438-6181. [CEM]

Troy, Lincoln Co., Sacred Heart (1891), Rev. Donald C. Schramm; Sr. Mary Ann Fisher, C.S.J., Pastoral Min.; Deacon Thomas Burkemper.
Res., 80 Main St., 63379. Tel: 314-528-8219. [CEM]
School—Tel: 314-528-6684. Sr. Jeannette Fenewald, S.S.N.D., Prin.
Lay Teachers 10; Students 196.
Catechesis/Religious Programs—Students 244.

Union, Franklin Co., Immaculate Conception (1866), Revs. Jerome D. Billing; Peter M. Blake.
Res., 100 N. Washington Ave., 63084. Tel: 314-583-5144. [CEM]
School—6 W. State St., 63084. Tel: 314-583-2641.
Sisters 2; Lay Teachers 11; Students 243.

Warrenton, Warren Co., Holy Rosary (1868), Rev. Eugene P. Brennan.
Res., 724 E. Booneslick Rd., 63383. Tel: 314-456-3698. [CEM]
School—716 E. Booneslick Rd., 63383. Tel: 314-456-2882. Sr. Mary Ann Boes, Prin.
Sisters of St. Joseph of Carondelet 1; Lay Teachers 9; Students 200.
Catechesis/Religious Programs—Students 200.

Washington, Franklin Co., St. Francis Borgia (1834) (German), Revs. John M. Costello; Michael E. Oslance; Deacons Gilbert Holtmeyer; Leon Noelker.
Res., 311 W. Second St., 63090. Tel: 314-239-6701. [CEM]
School—225 Cedar St., 63090. Tel: 314-239-2590.
Lay Teachers 30; Students 433.

Our Lady of Lourdes (1958), Very Rev. Robert L. Heimos, V.F.
Res., 1014 Madison Ave., 63090. Tel: 314-239-3520; Fax: 314-239-7682.
School—950 Madison Ave., 63090. Tel: 314-239-5292.
Sisters of Notre Dame 1; Lay Teachers 18; Students 326.
Catechesis/Religious Programs—Students 482.

Weingarten, Ste. Genevieve Co., Our Lady Help of Christians (1872), Rev. John Suren.
Res., 13370 Hwy. 32, Ste. Genevieve, 63670-9402. Tel: 314-883-3796. [CEM]

Wentzville, St. Charles Co., St. Patrick (1905), Revs. Leo J. Spezia; Donald A. Glastetter; Deacon Paul H. Chavaux.
Res., 405 S. Church St., 63385. Tel: 314-332-9225; Fax: 314-332-9225. [CEM]
School—701 Church St., 63385. Tel: 314-332-9913. Mrs. Nancy Repking, Prin.
Lay Teachers 14; Students 220.
Catechesis/Religious Programs—Tel: 314-332-9036.
Students 300.

West Alton, St. Charles Co., Immaculate Conception. Closed. See St. Francis, Portage des Sioux.

Zell, Ste. Genevieve Co., St. Joseph (1845), Rev. Msgr. James E. Hanson.
Res., 11824 Zell Rd., Ste. Genevieve, 63670. Tel: 314-883-3481. [CEM]
School—Tel: 314-883-5097.
Adorers of the Blood of Christ (Ruma, IL) 1; Lay Teachers 4; Students 62.

Korean Ministry

Ellisville, St. Andrew Kim Korean Catholic Community Church (Korean), Rev. Joseph Mun, Byung Hak (South Korea).
Res., 82 Henry Ave., P.O. Box 1184, 63011.

Chaplains of Public Institutions

St. Louis. *Christian Hospital Northeast-Northwest*, 11133 Dunn Rd., 63136. Tel: 314-355-2300. Rev. James L. Winzerling, Res. Chap.

Lammert International Airport. Tel: 314-427-8787. Rev. Edward B. Hemkens.
Regional Hospital, 5535 Delmar Blvd., 63112. Tel: 314-361-1212. Rev. Francis J. Shine, C.M., Chap.
St. Anthony Medical Center. Tel: 314-525-1000. Rev. Donald J. Hoffman. Tel: 314-968-0760.
St. John's Mercy Medical Ctr. Tel: 314-569-6470. Rev. Philip G. Krahman. Tel: 314-645-1445.
Saint Louis University Hospital. Tel: 314-525-1000. Rev. Gregory G. Kirsch. Tel: 314-351-1318.
St. Mary's Health Ctr. Tel: 314-768-8000. Revs. James A. Krings. Tel: 314-289-9545; James N. Rutkowski.

KIRKWOOD. *St. Joseph Hospital.* Tel: 314-966-1596. Rev. Mark L. Fuller. Tel: 314-962-0038.

ST. CHARLES. *St. Joseph Health Center.* Tel: 314-947-5000. Rev. Msgr. Raymond A. Hampe. Tel: 314-946-6641.

WASHINGTON. *St. John's Hospital.* Tel: 314-239-8000. Rev. Timothy J. Toohey. Tel: 314-239-8081.

Special Assignment:
Reverend Monsignors—
Lucas, George J., Pres. & Rector, Kenrick-Glennon Seminary, 5200 Glennon Dr., St. Louis, MO 63119. Tel: 314-644-0266
O'Brien, Joseph M., Dir. Special Projects & Chap., St. Agnes Home, 10341 Manchester Rd., St. Louis, MO 63122. Tel: 314-367-5500; 966-8085
Stika, Richard F., Chancellor, 4510 Lindell, St. Louis, MO 63108. Tel: 314-367-4437
Reverend Fathers—
Aten, Robert L., Contemplative Heart of Mary Hermitage, Centerville, MO. Tel: 573-648-2467
Dalton, Donald T., Ursuline Provincialate, 210 Glennon Heights Rd., Crystal City, MO 63019. Tel: 314-937-6206
Kopff, Marvin C., Archbishop's Liaison with Retired Priests & Chap. Retired Sisters of the Most Precious Blood. Tel: 413-968-2240
Mannion, Martin K., St. Vincent Home, 7401 Florissant Rd., St. Louis, MO 63121. Tel: 314-261-3246

Sabbatical:
Reverend Fathers—
Chochol, Ronald C., Ph.D.

On Duty Outside the Archdiocese:
Reverend Monsignors—
Dolan, Timothy M., Rome, Italy
Ratermann, David A., Cochabamba, Bolivia
Reverend Fathers—
Blattner, Joseph H., Benedicta, ME
Bozada, Mark N., O.P., Dominican Novitiate, Oakland, Ca
Fidler, W. Larch, IV, Brunswick, ME
Hayden, Patrick T., La Paz, Bolivia
Kopfensteiner, Thomas R., Fordham University, Bronx, NY
Lampert, Robert E., Oblate School of Theology, San Antonio, TX
Means, David A., Anchorage, AK
Menner, Robert J., Riberalta, Bolivia
Michler, James, La Paz, Bolivia
Schmidt, Dennis C., Columbia, MO
Siebert, Anthony G., Belize, Central America
Somos, Joseph, Chicago, IL
Stretch, Daniel P., La Paz, Bolivia
Vollmer, Gary l., Las Vegas, NV

Military Chaplains:
Reverend Fathers—
Banken, Robert L., Lt.
Breig, Gary R.
Deken, John C.
Keutzer, Walter
Kovalcin, John A.
Swetnam, R. William
Zinzer, Walter A.

Absent on Sick Leave:
Reverend Fathers—
Brinkman, Don G.
Fitzgerald, Alfred J.
Valentine, Leroy A.

Leave of Absence:
Reverend Fathers—
Christian, Norman H.
Haberkern, Thomas A.
Knight, Robert D.
Siefert, John S.

Retired:
Reverend Monsignors—
Behrmann, Elmer H., 2012 Clermont Crossing Dr., Apt. G, St. Louis, MO 63146
Boessen, Bernard H., Regina Cleri, 7850 Kenrick Rd., St. Louis, MO 63119
Byrne, Henry L., No. 7, Newberry Ct., St. Peters, MO 63376
Byrne, John T., 13900 Clayton Rd., Manchester, MO 63011
Chiodini, Jasper J., Regina Cleri, 7850 Kenrick Rd., St. Louis, MO 63119
Dwyer, Adrian I., 6052 Waterman, St. Louis, MO 63112
Finley, James J., 4607 Poepping, St. Louis, MO 63123
Gannon, Rowland E., 12934 Marine Ave., St. Louis, MO 63146-2234
Glynn, Gerard N., 9814a Greenery Ln., St. Louis, MO 63132
Hartnett, James R., 2013 Trailcrest Ln., St. Louis, MO 63122
Hesseldenz, Clarence H., 5126 Shaw Pl. #A, Waldorf, MD 20602-1519
Holland, James J., 5020 Rhodes Ave., St. Louis, MO 63109-3589
Holland, John P., 1575 N. Woodland Ave., St. Louis, MO 63122-1462
Kennedy, John J., 665 S. Skinker #10E, St. Louis, MO 63105
Krieger, Wilfred L., 4286 Putting Green Dr., San Antonio, TX 78217
Kurtz, George J., Regina Cleri, 7850 Kenrick Rd., St. Louis, MO 63119
Marschner, Aloysius J., Regina Cleri, 7850 Kenrick Rd., St. Louis, MO 63119
Meyer, Louis F., 4908 Sutherland, St. Louis, MO 63109
Molloy, Patrick J., Regina Cleri, 7850 Kenrick Rd., St. Louis, MO 63119
Nibberich, Lawrence C., Regina Cleri, 7850 Kenrick Rd., St. Louis, MO 63119
O'Brien, Joseph T., P.O. Box 54764, St. Petersburg, FL 33739
O'Connell, James P., 60 Plaza Sq., Apt. 1207, St. Louis, MO 63103
Obmann, Russell J., 5851 Itaska Ave., St. Louis, MO 63109-3117
Overman, Robert F., 1711 Parkhaven, San Antonio, TX 78232
Peet, Arthur V., Regina Cleri, 7850 Kenrick Rd., St. Louis, MO 63119
Regan, Michael F., 4335 DuPage Dr., Bridgeton, MO 63044-1606
Ronquest, John T., St. Simon Rectory, 11011 Mueller Rd., St. Louis, MO 63123
Rotrige, Henry J., 2143 Crownhill Rd., San Diego, CA 92109
Schilly, Adolph M., Regina Cleri, 7850 Kenrick Rd., St. Louis, MO 63119
Shocklee, John A., 3225 N. Florissant Ave., St. Louis, MO 63107
Sommer, Jerome, Regina Cleri, 7850 Kenrick Rd., St. Louis, MO 63119
Sullivan, Donald E., Regina Cleri, 7850 Kenrick Rd., St. Louis, MO 63119
Reverend Fathers—
Bell, Ira J., Regina Cleri, 7850 Kenrick Rd., St. Louis, MO 63119
Boul, Walter, Regina Cleri, 7850 Kenrick Rd., St. Louis, MO 63119
Britt, William J., Regina Cleri, 7850 Kenrick Rd., St. Louis, MO 63119
Bukauskas, Anthony, 11 Bertha Ln., Union, MO 63084
Burmester, Edwin J., St. Gabriel, 6303 Nottingham, St. Louis, MO 63109
Byrne, John H., 7601 Watson Rd., St. Louis, MO 63119
Campbell, John R., 5375 Kenrick Park Dr., St. Louis, MO 63119
Cooper, Thomas T., Regina Cleri, 7850 Kenrick Rd., St. Louis, MO 63119
Deutsch, Bernard F., 101 Winter Harbor Rd., Ocean City, MD 21842
Dierker, Louis P., 11575 Old Halls Ferry Rd., St. Louis, MO 63033
Figge, Edwin H., 753 Rozier, Apt. 10, Ste. Genevieve, MO 63670
Flynn, James A., 6875 N.W. 9th St., Margate, FL 33063
Gambon, John A., 300 Eastlane Dr., Washington, MO 63090
Gerst, Lawrence G., 1371 Hamilton, St. Louis, MO 63112
Gibson, Michael P., 665 S. Skinker Blvd., St. Louis, MO 63105
Haar, George B., Regina Cleri, 7850 Kenrick Rd., St. Louis, MO 63119
Hrdlicka, Lambert A., 4243 LaSalette Dr., St. Louis, MO 63123
Huels, Vincent P., 555 Bluff Park Dr., Florissant, MO 63031
Huhn, Donald W., 303-107 Racquet Club Rd., Fort Lauderdale, FL 33326
Julius, James A., 1800 Beach Dr., Gulf Port, MS 39507
Kersgieter, Paul J., 2605 Mullanphy Ln., Florissant, MO 63031
Knoll, Urban H., 628 S. Fourth St., St. Charles, MO 63301
Kraus, Robert J., 318 Jefferson St., Apt. 25, Jefferson City, MO 65101
Leibinger, Arthur B., P.O. Box 122, Bloomsdale, MO 63627
Lessard, Joseph P., P.O. Box 322, Prairie DuRocher, IL 62277
Matyas, Francis B., Regina Cleri, 7850 Kenrick Rd., St. Louis, MO 63119
McLain, J. Clyde, Regina Cleri, 7850 Kenrick Rd., St. Louis, MO 63119
Mersinger, Arthur J., Regina Cleri, 7850 Kenrick Rd., St. Louis, MO 63119
Morse, John A., 525 Mill rd., Marthasville, MO 63357
Noser, J. Homer, 7677 Watson Rd., Apt. 302, St. Louis, MO 63119
O'Brien, Joseph A., Regina Cleri, 7850 Kenrick Rd., St. Louis, MO 63119
Ottoline, Robert A., Regina Cleri, 7850 Kenrick Rd., St. Louis, MO 63119
Phelan, John R., Regina Cleri, 7850 Kenrick Rd., St. Louis, MO 63119
Regan, William D., Regina Cleri, 7850 Kenrick Rd., St. Louis, MO 63119
Rehme, Albert A., 362 Rue Bonne Terre (TDL), Bonne Terre, MO 63628
Ruff, Charles R., Regina Cleri, 7850 Kenrick Rd., St. Louis, MO 63119
Ryan, Joseph J., 1526 Chevy Chase, Sun City Center, FL 33573
Scheer, Joseph O., 2800 Olive St., Apt. 4M, St. Louis, MO 63103
Schlattmann, Edward B., Regina Cleri, 7850 Kenrick Rd., St. Louis, MO 63119
Schmaltz, Albert F., 1279 Josephville Rd., Wentzville, MO 63385
Schneider, John G., 1607 Tomkins St., St. Charles, MO 63301
Sommer, Jerome, Regina Cleri, 7850 Kenrick Rd., St. Louis, MO 63119
Thurmer, William H., 1510 Bopp Rd., St. Louis, MO 63131-4137
Unterreiner, Glennon T., 6825 Natural Bridge, St. Louis, MO 63121
Vogler, John E., 7530 Natural Bridge, Normandy, MO 63121
Wetzel, William I., Col., 770 Carolyn Ave., Summerland Key, FL 33042-5646
Winkler, Clarence E., Regina Cleri, 7850 Kenrick Rd., St. Louis, MO 63119
Wolf, Joseph B., 1970 Greenpoint Dr., Apt. 103, St. Louis, MO 63122

Permanent Deacons:
Arnold, Steven J.
Audrain, Raymond J.
Bachista, Ronald J.
Bachu, Simon W.
Baker, John W., M.D.
Bansbach, Paul, On Duty Outside the Archdiocese
Barron, Eugene D.
Basler, James H.
Bauwens, Gerard, On Duty Outside the Archdiocese
Beckman, Carl H.
Beinke, George A.
Bell, Jesse H.
Bernsen, Albert B.
Blase, George A.
Bourbon, Glennon L., Sr.
Boyer, Edward J.
Bryant, Wayne T.
Buchek, Bradford M.
Buck, George D.
Buckley, James Mike
Buckley, John J.
Buckner, Henry A., Sr.
Buhr, Thomas A.
Burkemper, Thomas B.
Burton, James L.
Caruana, Philip P.
Casseau, William U.
Caton, Eugene W.
Chauvin, Charles Frank
Chavaux, Paul H.
Chitwood, Dennis M.
Christ, Walter W.
Clemens, Kenneth C., Jr.
Coffman, Richard W.
Coppage, Michael J., Jr.
Cox, Joseph E.
Crafts, R. Paul
Czarnecki, Eugene J.
Dalton, Michael H.
Damato, Larry (PAT)
DePyper, Robert R.
Dickerson, Raymond A.

Dietz, Alvin J.
Dingman, Edwin H.
Dodson, Fred
Dolan, Timothy C.
Dorhauer, Jacob W.
Dowd, Thomas L.
Drayton, Charles E.
Driscoll, Donald L.
Droesch, Francis A.
Dunning, John W., On Duty Outside the Archdiocese
Ecker, Alan E.
Efken, Donald C.
Ehrhard, Herbert L.
Eultgen, Thomas L.
Falbo, Anthony D. (HRT)
Fick, Franklin J.
Fink, George Russ
Flint, Edward G.
Forster, Thomas E.
Fronick, Edward C.
Gabbert, William L.
Gamache, Robert K. (DEN)
Gawedzinkski, Norbert L.
Gearon, William A.
Gegg, Albin A.
Geiser, Gerald J.
Georges, Charles W.
Gerdes, Philip J.
Gerling, Thomas J. (JC)
Gettemeier, Herbert B.
Gholston, Clifford
Gorski, Thomas (ARL)
Gounis, Peter E.
Graham, George A.
Grant, Maurice A., Sr.
Greif, William J.
Gunsaullus, Roland J.
Haefner, Joseph Tom
Hanses, Eugene J.
Harris, Singleton L.
Harrison, R. Fielding
Hayes, William R.
Heitert, Donald C.
Hengen, Philip R.
Hennicke, Raymond C.
Henning, Kenneth A.
Henroid, Daniel H.
Hercules, Joseph E.
Hesse, Richard P.
Hirtz, Frederick J., On Duty Outside the Archdiocese
Hoffmann, Eugene A.
Holmes, Charles E.
Holtmeyer, Gilbert C.
Hummel, Fred J.
Hutti, Lawrence J., Jr.
Janson, Norman F.
Johnson, Leslie A.
Jurek, Thomas F., On Duty Outside the Archdiocese
Karsznia, Robert A.
Kaufman, Allen G.
Keeney, Robert J.
Kelly, Lawrence C.
Kennedy, Joseph M.
Kenney, T. Michael, III
Kiely, E. Ray
Klempert, Michael L.
Klostermann, Robert, Sr.
Knobbe, Gerald E.
Krieger, Arnold F.
Kuenz, Gary J.
Lake, Richard C.
Levac, Richard B.
Lombardo, Charles W.
Longmeyer, Harold
Love, Allen F.
Luke, Herbert, M.D.
Macauley, Edward C.
Marcinkiewicz, Joseph, Jr.
Marren, L. Jerome
Martin, Leroy A., Jr.
McGrath, James E.
McKee, Paul R.
McKenna, William J.
McNamee, George W., On Duty Outside the Archdiocese
McNamee, Terrance M.
Menard, Louis A.
Messineo, Anthony L.
Miller, George W.
Miller, Millard Ray
Morris, Joseph C.
Mroczkowski, R. V.
Mueller, Frederick J.
Murphy, James L.
Murphy, Thomas P.
Murphy, Thomas O.
Murray, Stephen L.
Nesbitt, Frank E.
Nieman, Harry
Niemeyer, Andrew C.
Noelker, Leon R.
O'Leary, John A.
Otzenberger, Joseph M.
Peacock, Joseph C.
Penberthy, Robert S.
Peterson, Stanley M., Jr.
Politte, Glennon P., Sr.
Politte, Stephen A.
Politte, Thomas G.
Porterfield, Paul D.
Potzman, Kenneth M.
Powers, Robert J.
Prideaux, Frank W.
Priesmeyer, W., Jr.
Prives, Gerald J.
Quinn, J. Gerard
Reynoso, Louis J.
Riegel, Robert C.
Roberson, Robert L.
Roderick, Walter L.
Ruegg, Walter J.
Sabo, Michael C.
Schiffman, Donald J.
Schnable, Robert H.
Schuld, Gerald C.
Schulte, Edwin
Schultheis, Glennon J.
Schulze, Roy E.
Shake, Frank R.
Shelby, Richard L.
Shipp, Nathaniel E.
Sinak, William S.
Smerek, Robert S.
Smith, James R.
Smith, John F.
Snyder, Robert J.
Snyder, Robert C.
Stoverink, Gerard G.
Stoverink, John J.
Strauss, Harold A.
Streckfuss, Joseph C.
Sulze, Joseph W.
Sutton, Ronald L.
Tichacek, George A.
Toohey, Jerome V.
Towey, Martin G.
Trautman, Anthony G.
Tresch, Earl K.
Vaughn, Albert X.
Walbridge, William F.
Weatherholt, Harold J.
Werner, Norman B.
Wertz, Robert E.
Wessels, Richard H.
Willbrand, Thomas J.
Winkelmann, Christian H.
Winker, Ewald
Wood, George F.
Wunderlich, William P.

INSTITUTIONS LOCATED IN THE ARCHDIOCESE

[A] SEMINARIES, ARCHDIOCESAN

ST. LOUIS. *Kenrick-Glennon Seminary*. (St. Louis Roman Catholic Theological Seminary), KENRICK SCHOOL OF THEOLOGY, 5200 Glennon Dr., 63119. Tel: 314-644-0266; Fax: 314-644-3079. Rev. Msgr. George J. Lucas, M.A., Rector; Revs. Thomas M. Molini, M.A., Vice Rector, Dir. of Formation; Lawrence C. Brennan, S.T.D., Academic Dean; J. Dennis Martin, C.M., M.A., Dir. of Spiritual Life; Rev. Msgr. William J. Lyons, S.T.L., Dir. Pre-Theology; Mr. William J. Matula, B.A., Business Officer; Revs. John F. Clark, C.M., M.A.; Robert F. Coerver, C.M., S.T.D., Prof. Emeritus; Glennon C. Doherty, M.A.; John P. Heil, S.S.D.; Gregory J. Lockwood, S.T.D. (Candidate); Donald F. Molitor, M.A.; James J. Ramacciotti, J.C.L.; James E. Swift, C.M., S.T.D.; Sr. Zoe Glenski, D.C., Ph.D.; Sr. Maribeth Howell, O.P., Ph.D.; Susanne M. Harvath, Ph.D.; Glenn C.J. Byer, Ph.D.; Andrew J. Sopko, Ph.D.; Lawrence J. Welch, Ph.D.; Mr. Peter F. Hesed, M.A.; Deacon George W. Miller, B.S.; Howard M. Graber, Ph.D., Rabbi. Priests 16; Sisters 2; Students 63; St. Louis Students 21. CARDINAL GLENNON COLLEGE, 5200 Glennon Dr., 63119. Tel: 314-644-0266. Revs. Edward M. Rice, Dir.; Michael T. Butler, Assoc.; Rev. Msgr. William J. Lyons, Spiritual Dir.; Sr. Pat Dalton, S.S.N.D.; Mrs. Marlynne Huenneke; Mrs. Jeanine Burton; Ms. Helen Marx, Exec. Sec. Priests 3; Sisters 1; Lay Teachers 3; Students 18; St. Louis Students 12; Belleville Students 4; Peoria, IL 2.

[B] SEMINARIES, RELIGIOUS, OR SCHOLASTICATES

ST. LOUIS. *Aquinas Institute of Theology*, 3642 Lindell Blvd., 63108. Tel: 314-977-3882; Fax: 314-977-7225. Rev. Charles E. Bouchard, O.P., Pres.; Sr. Diane Kennedy, O.P., Dean; Rev. Albert Glade, O.P., Business Mgr. & Dir. Student Affairs; Eileen Wickham, Inst. Advancement; Scott Hippert, Admissions and Public Rels.; Revs. Richard Peddicord, O.P.; Joseph P. Gillespie, O.P.; Donald Goergen, O.P.; Gregory J. Heille, O.P.; Thomas Esselman, C.M.; Harry M. Byrne, O.P.; Frank C. Quinn, O.P.; Sr. Marygrace Peters, O.P.; Sr. Joan Delaplane, O.P.; Sr. Mary Margaret Pazdan, O.P.; Sr. Carla Mae Streeter, O.P.; Sr. Catherine Vincie, R.S.H.M. Priests 10; Sisters 9; Lay Teachers 6; Total Enrollment 180.

St. John Neumann House. Redemptorist College Seminary Residence, 3737 Washington Blvd., 63108. Tel: 314-531-2777; Fax: 314-531-5726. Revs. Gary Lauenstein, C.Ss.R., Rector and Superior; Joseph Nolen, C.Ss.R., Dir. of Formation; David Polek, C.Ss.R., Vocation Dir.; Wm. Emmett Collins, C.Ss.R.; Jack Hacker, C.Ss.R. Priests 6; Total Enrollment 5.

[C] COLLEGES AND UNIVERSITIES

ST. LOUIS. *Fontbonne College*, 6800 Wydown Blvd., 63105. Tel: 314-862-3456.

For a complete listing, refer to the Colleges and Universities section.

Saint Louis University, 221 N. Grand Blvd., DB 261, 63103-2097. Tel: 314-977-2222.

For a complete listing, refer to the Colleges and Universities section.

[D] RELIGIOUS EDUCATION

ST. LOUIS. *Paul VI Institute of Catechetical and Pastoral Studies*, 4140 Lindell Blvd., 63108. Tel: 314-371-4980, Ext. 74; Fax: 314-371-0267. Rev. Msgr. John M. Unger, Dir.; Sr. Marianne Almon, S.S.N.D., Admin. Total Enrollment 2,000.

[E] HIGH SCHOOLS, ARCHDIOCESAN

ST. LOUIS. *Bishop DuBourg High School*, 5850 Eichelberger St., 63109. Tel: 314-832-3030. A Co-Educational School Staffed by Diocesan Priests, Religious and Lay Teachers. Mr. Thomas Jokerst, Prin. Associate Principals: Dr. Gerald Gruszka; Ms. Cathy Fetter. Priests 4; Sisters 4; Lay Teachers 54; Students 898.

Cardinal Ritter College Prep, 5421 Thekla Ave., 63120. Tel: 314-381-7980; Fax: 314-381-8050. Co-Educational High School Staffed by Religious and Laity. Mrs. Carmele U. Hall, Pres. & Prin. Priests 1; Sisters 2; Lay Teachers 23; Students 250.

Rosati-Kain High School, 4389 Lindell Blvd., 63108. Tel: 314-533-8513. Conducted for Girls by Diocesan Priest, the Sisters of St. Joseph and the School Sisters of Notre Dame. Sr. Joan Andert, S.S.N.D., Prin.; Patrice Johannes, Assoc. Prin. Priests 1; Sisters 5; Lay Teachers 23; Girls 427.

Saint Mary's High School, 4701 S. Grand Blvd., 63111. Tel: 314-481-8400. For Boys, Staffed by Brothers of Mary and Archdiocesan Priests. Rev. Mitchell Doyen, Admin.; Mr. Kevin Hacker, B.A., M.Ed., Prin. Priests 4; Brothers 1; Sisters 2; Lay Teachers 28; Total Enrollment 468.

FESTUS. *St. Pius X High School*, 1030 St. Pius Dr., 63028. Tel: 314-937-3695; 931-7487. A Co-Educational High School Conducted by Diocesan Priests and Lay Faculty. Miss Adele Greaving, Prin. Priests 3; Lay Teachers 27; Students 435.

FLORISSANT. *St. Thomas Aquinas-Mercy High School*, 845 Dunn Rd., 63031. Tel: 314-837-1144. A Co-Educational High School Conducted by One Diocesan Priest, a Vincentian Priest, and Lay Men and Women. Mr. Paul Frein, Prin.; Patricia Moore, Asst. Prin. Priests 2; Lay Teachers 30; Students 515.

MANCHESTER. *John F. Kennedy Catholic High School*, 500 Woods Mill Rd., 63011. Tel: 314-227-5900. A Co-Educational High School Staffed by Diocesan Priests. Randy Berzon, Prin. Priests 1; Lay Teachers 25; Students 400.

O'FALLON. *St. Dominic High School*, 31 St. Dominic Dr., 63366. Tel: 314-240-8303; Fax: 314-240-9884. A Co-Educational High School Conducted by Diocesan Priests and Sisters of the Third Order of St. Dominic. Sr. Mary H. Bender, S.S.N.D., Admin.; Sr. Carolyn, O.P., Prin. Priests 2; Sisters 3; Lay Teachers 37; Students 607.

ST. CHARLES. *Duchesne High School*, 2550 Elm St., 63301-1494. Tel: 314-946-6767. A Co-Educational College Prep High School Conducted by Archdiocesan Priests and Catholic Lay Staff. Under the Auspices of the Catholic Education Office. Sponsored by Seven Parishes in and around St. Charles, MO. Mr. Charles L. Nolan, Admin.; Mr. Donald C. Burkhart, Prin.; Revs. James L. Gahan; Donald E. Henke. Priests 2; Sisters 1; Lay Teachers 42; Students 617.

SPANISH LAKE. *Rosary High School*, 1720 Redman Ave., 63138. Tel: 314-741-1333. A Co-Educational High School Staffed by Archdiocesan Priests, Religious and Lay Teachers. Daniel J. Matusiak, Ed.D., Prin.; Sr. Geraldine Neier, S.S.N.D., Asst. Prin.; Mr. Richard Barrett, Asst. Prin. Priests 1; Sisters 2; Lay Teachers 32; Students 546.

WASHINGTON. *St. Francis Borgia Regional High School*, 1000 Borgia Dr., 63090. Tel: 314-239-7871; Fax: 314-239-1198. A Co-Educational High School Staffed by Diocesan Priests and School Sisters of Notre Dame. Rev. Michael E. Turek, Admin.; Mr. George Wingbermuehle, Prin. Priests 2; Sisters 2; Lay Teachers 38; Students 590.

[F] HIGH SCHOOLS, PRIVATE

ST. LOUIS. *Christian Brothers College High School (C.B.C.)*, 6501 Clayton Rd., 63117. Tel: 314-721-1200; Fax: 314-721-2471. Bro. Lawrence Humphrey, F.S.C., Pres.; Mr. James B. Gerdes, Prin. Brothers 9; Lay Teachers 60; Students 963.

Cor Jesu Academy, 10230 Gravois, 63123. Tel: 314-842-1546. Apostles of the Sacred Heart. Sr. Sheila O'Neill, A.S.C.J., Prin. Priests 1; Sisters 11; Lay Teachers 30; Students 534.

De Smet Jesuit High School, 233 N. New Ballas Rd., 63141. Tel: 314-567-3502. Dr. Gregory A. Densberger, Ph.D., Prin.; Rev. Richard L. Bailey, S.J., Pres. Priests 8; Sisters 2; Brothers 1; Students 1,120.

Incarnate Word Academy, 2788 Normandy Dr., 63121. Tel: 314-725-5850; Fax: 314-725-2308. Sisters of Charity of Incarnate Word of San Antonio. Mrs. Julie C. Sheridan, Prin. Lay Teachers 41; Support Staff 14; Students 480.

Notre Dame High School, 320 E. Ripa Ave., 63125. Tel: 314-544-1015. Sr. Shelley Hogan, S.S.N.D., Prin. Sisters 10; Lay Teachers 40; Girls 514.

St. Elizabeth Academy, 3401 Arsenal St., 63118. Tel: 314-771-5134. Sisters of the Most Precious Blood. Sr. Theresa Austin, C.PP.S., Pres.; Sr. Linda Zechmeister, C.PP.S., Prin. Sisters 6; Lay Teachers 18; Students 275.

St. Joseph's Academy, 2307 S. Lindbergh Blvd., 63131. Tel: 314-965-7205; Fax: 314-965-9114. Sr. Nancy Folkl, C.S.J., Prin. Sisters of St. Joseph of Carondelet 6; Lay Teachers 46; Girls 610.

St. Louis University High School, George H. Backer Memorial, 4970 Oakland Ave., 63110. Tel: 314-531-0330. Revs. Richard E. Hadel, S.J., Supr.; Robert T. Costello, S.J., Pres.; Martin Hagan, S.J.; Jeffrey D. Harrison; James G. Knapp, S.J.; Gerald R. Sheahan, S.J.; Bros. Thomas C. Thornton, S.J.; Richard H. Witzofsky, S.J. In res., Rev. Frank Reale, S.J. Priests 6; Scholastics 1; Brothers 2; Admin. 4; Lay Teachers 71; Students 1,000.

CREVE COEUR. *Chaminade College Preparatory School Inc.*, 425 S. Lindbergh Blvd., 63131-2799. Tel: 314-993-4400; Fax: 314-993-4403. Residents and Day Students. Society of Mary. Rev. Ralph A. Siefert, S.M., Pres.; James E. Gerker, Prin.; Michael Thro, Campus Min. Priests 2; Brothers 4; Lay Teachers 61; Students 525.

St. Louis Priory School, 500 S. Mason Rd., 63141-8500. Tel: 314-434-3690; Fax: 314-576-7088. Rev. J. Gregory Mohrman, O.S.B., Headmaster; Rt. Rev. W. Thomas Frerking, O.S.B.; Revs. Christopher Hanson, O.S.B.; M. Paul Kidner, O.S.B.; J. Laurence Kriegshauser, O.S.B.; Joseph Marino, O.S.B.; Bede Price, O.S.B.; D. Ralph Wright, O.S.B. Priests 8; Brothers 2; Lay Teachers 40; High School Students 219; Students Grades 7-8 135.

FRONTENAC. *Villa Duchesne/Oak Hill*, 801 S. Spoede Rd., 63131. Tel: 314-432-2021.
(Girls: PreK-12; Boys: PreK-6). Religious of the Sacred Heart. Mrs. Renee Allen, Prin. (7-12); Dr. Harry Trumfio, Prin. (PreK-6); Sr. Ann Caire, R.S.C.J., Headmistress. Sisters 6; Lay Faculty 78; Elementary School Students (PreK-6) 396; High School Students (7-12) 390.

KIRKWOOD. *Ursuline Academy*, 341 S. Sappington Rd., 63122. Tel: 314-966-4556. Ursuline Nuns of the Roman Union. Dr. Patricia Hensley, Prin. Sisters 3; Lay Teachers 50; Students 570.

Vianney High School, 1311 S. Kirkwood Rd., 63122. Tel: 314-965-4853; Fax: 314-965-1950.
E-mail: archstl856@connectinc.com
Conducted for Boys by the Society of Mary (Marianists). Revs. Richard Wosman, S.M., Pres.; J. Donald Cahill, S.M.; Robert R. Osborne, S.M. Priests 3; Brothers 6; Lay Teachers 42; Students 700.

TOWN AND COUNTRY. *Visitation Academy*, 3020 N. Ballas Rd., 63131. Tel: 314-432-5353; Fax: 314-432-7210. Mrs. Patricia Hurst, M.A., (PreK-6). Visitation Sisters 3; Lay Teachers 16; Students 247.

WEBSTER GROVES. *Nerinx Hall High School*, 530 E. Lockwood, 63119. Tel: 314-968-1505; Fax: 314-962-6556. Sr. Barbara Roche, S.L., Pres.; Dr. Mary Schenkenberg, Prin.; Mrs. Deborah Kirchner, Dean of Students. Sisters of Loretto at the Foot of the Cross 7; Lay Teachers 53; Students 560.

[G] ELEMENTARY SCHOOLS, PRIVATE

CHESTERFIELD. *Linda Vista Catholic School*, 1633 Kehrs Mill Rd., 63005. Tel: 314-532-3315. Conducted by the Sisters of the Most Precious Blood.
Preschool Classes for 3-6 Year Olds, Grades 1-6. Lay Teachers 28; Students 234.

CREVE COEUR. *Chaminade College Preparatory*. (Middle School), Residents and Day Students, 425 S. Lindbergh Blvd., 63131. Tel: 314-993-4400; Fax: 314-993-4403.
(Boys Grades 7-12). Society of Mary. Rev. Ralph A. Siefert, S.M., Pres.; Mr. Michael T. Bander, Prin. Priests 2; Lay Teachers 24; Students 260.

St. Louis Priory School, 500 S. Mason Rd., 63141-8500. Tel: 314-434-3690; Fax: 314-576-7088.
(Boys Grades 7-8).
Corporate Title: The Abbey of St. Mary and St. Louis. Rev. Gregory Mohrman, O.S.B., Headmaster. Priests 3; Brothers 2; Lay Teachers 24; Students 135.

FRONTENAC. *Oak Hill School*, 801 S Spoede Rd., 63131. Tel: 314-432-2021.
(Grades PreK-6) (Coed). Dr. Harry Trumfio, Prin.; Sr. Ann Caire, R.S.C.J., Headmistress. Sisters 2; Lay Teachers 34; Students 400

Villa Duchesne, 801 S. Spoede Rd., 63131. Tel: 314-432-2021.
(Girls 7-12). Mrs. Renee Allen, Prin.; Sr. Ann Caire, R.S.C.J., Headmistress. Sisters 5; Lay Teachers 44; Girls 379.

NORMANDY. *Mount Providence School*, 8351 Florissant Rd., 63121. Tel: 314-524-8046. Sr. Barbara Horenkamp, C.D.P., Prin.; Rev. John Vogler, Chap. Sisters of Divine Providence of the St. Louis Province 4; Lay Teachers 12; Students 135.

ST. CHARLES. *Academy of the Sacred Heart*. (Coed), 619 N. 2nd St., 63301. Tel: 314-946-6127; Fax: 314-949-6659. Religious of the Sacred Heart. Sr. Margaret Caire, Headmistress; Mrs. Kathy Hopper, Prin. Sisters 11; Lay Teachers 44; Students 655.

TOWN AND COUNTRY. *Visitation Accdemy*, 3020 N. Ballas Rd., 63131. Tel: 314-432-5353. Principals: Patricia Hurst, M.A., (PreK-6); Maxine Adlersfluegel, Ph.D., (7-12); Mrs. Isabelle Lenhardt, M.Ed.; M.Ed. Admin., Head of School. Visitation Sisters 8; Lay Teachers 66; Students 628.

[H] DEPARTMENT OF SPECIAL EDUCATION

ST. LOUIS. *Catholic Guidance Center*, 4472 Lindell Blvd., 63108. Tel: 314-533-3454. Psycho-Educational Testing Facility and also Administrative Office for the Archdiocesan Department of Special Education, Serving Children with Developmental Disabilities, Mental Retardation or Learning Disabilities. Rev. Msgr. Vernon E. Gardin, Ph.D., Exec. Dir. Children Tested During Year 300.
Special Ungraded Day Classes, Schools and Residential School, PSR for Disabled and with Mental Retardation Children or Major Learning Disabilities (ages 5-16). Located in the Following Parish Schools: Holy Innocents (2 LD Classes); Sacred Heart (2 MR Classes); St. Christopher (5 LD Classes); Our Lady of Guadalupe (1 LD Class); Annunziata (6 LD Classes); St John the Baptist (3 LD Classes); St. George (3LD Classes). Total Number of Children Served 270; Total Number in PSR for Handicapped 120.

St. Joseph's Vocational Center, 5341 Emerson Ave., 63120. Tel: 314-261-8600. Diane Marquart, Coord. A Vocational Training Program for Developmentally Disabled Young Adults (Ages 15-22). Lay Teachers 1; Students 50.

St. Mary's Special School for Exceptional Children, 5341 Emerson Ave., 63120. Tel: 314-261-8533; Fax: 314-381-2002. Dawn M. Schenk, M.A., Admin. Dir.; Rev. Msgr. Vernon E. Gardin, Exec. Dir. A Residential Facility for children with mental retardation & other developmental disabilities (ages 5-21); Early Intervention Prog. for children (ages 0-35 months) with developmental disabilities; Independent Supported living Prog. serving clients with mental retardation & other developmental disabilities (age 14 & up); Vocational Placement Svcs. for clients (age 16 & up). Religious 1; Lay Staff 67; Students 80.

Special Religious Education Ministry, 4472 Lindell Blvd., 63108. Tel: 314-533-3454. Department of Special Education. Mary Beth Schulte, Coord. Provides catholic religious educ. for children with disabilities in public special programs. (ages 7-21) & for adults with disabilities living in institutions or in their own homes. Lay Teachers 35; Total Enrollment 105.

UNIVERSITY CITY. *St. Joseph Institute for the Deaf*, 1483 82nd Blvd., 63132. Tel: 314-993-1507 (Voice/TDD); Fax: 314-993-9890. School for the Deaf (School for Handicapped). J. Michael Keller, Pres.; Sr. Joyce Buckler, C.S.J., Ed.D., Prin. Sisters 10; Lay Teachers 15; Students 110. Audio/oral day & residential school for hearing-impaired children from birth-8th grade. Early intervention therapy for children 0-5; pre- & elementary school offering intense speech & academic prog.

[I] SERVICES FOR THE ELDERLY

ST. LOUIS. *Cardinal Ritter Institute*, 4483 Lindell Blvd., 63108. Tel: 314-652-3600. Archdiocesan Office Provides Social Services, Health Services and Housing Services for the Elderly. Legal Title: *Cardinal Ritter Institute, Inc.* Mr. John M. Lally, CEO; Arthur J. Korte, Dir. & COO. Total Clients Served 24,542.

Cardinal Ritter Institute Residential Services, Inc., 4483 Lindell Blvd., 63108. Tel: 314-652-3600. Provides housing Mgmt. & other svcs. for residential facilities for the elderly. Mr. John M. Lally, CEO; Michael J. Lally, Dir. & COO.

Alexian Court Apartments. (Legal Title: Alexian Brothers Services, Inc.), 2636 Chippewa St., 63118. Tel: 314-771-5604.
Sponsored by Alexian Brothers of Missouri, Inc., Managed by Cardinal Ritter Institute.

Our Lady of Life Apartments, Inc., 7655 Watson Rd., 63119. Tel: 314-968-9447. Rev. Marvin C. Kopff.

St. John Neumann Apartments, Inc., 8424 Lucas Hunt Rd., 63136. Tel: 314-385-0707.

St. Joseph Apartments, Inc., 7677 Watson Rd., 63119. Tel: 314-962-0969.

St. Patrick Apartments, Inc., 555 Bluff Parks Dr., 63031. Tel: 314-839-3212.

San Luis Apartments, Inc., 4483 Lindell Blvd., 63108. Tel: 314-534-4730.

Santa Ana Apartments, Inc., 3737 Ashby Rd., 63074. Tel: 314-428-7385.

Visitation Senior Apartments, Inc., 1911 N. Taylor Ave., 63113. Tel: 314-652-3600.

Holy Infant Apartments, Inc., 7663 Watson Rd., 63119. Tel: 314-962-7878.

St. Agnes Apartments, Inc., 2840 Wisconsin, 63118. Tel: 314-664-1255. St. Peter Residence for Seniors, 333 S. Second St., St. Charles, 63301-6401. Tel: 314-947-7004. Property of St. Peter Parish, Managed by Cardinal Ritter Institute. Santa Maria Apartments, 12565 Santa Maria Ct., Hazelwood, 63042. Tel: 314-739-7220. Mary Queen and Mother Center, 7601 Watson Rd., 63119. Tel: 314-961-8485. Mother of Perpetual Help Residence, 7609 Watson Rd., 63119. Tel: 314-961-8000.

Cardinal Ritter Institute Residential Services Inc., 4483 Lindell Blvd., 63108. Tel: 314-652-3600. Provides Housing Management and Other Services for Residential Facilities for the Elderly. Mr. John M. Lally, CEO; Michael J. Lally, Dir. and COO.

Corporate Action for the Care of the Elderly, Inc., 7601 Watson Rd., 63119. Tel: 314-961-8485. Association Composed of Representatives of 14 Religious Communities and The Cardinal Ritter Institute. Corporal Work of Mercy in the Metro St. Louis Area. Bro. Thomas Keusenkothen, C.F.A., Pres.

St. Elizabeth Adult Day Care Center, 3401 Arsenal St., 63118. Tel: 314-772-5107; Fax: 314-772-3674. Conducted by the Sisters of the Most Precious Blood to Provide Day Care for the Elderly. Sr. John Antonio Miller, C.PP.S., Dir.

St. Elizabeth East Adult Day Care Center, 3227 S. Ninth St., 63118. Tel: 314-771-1591.

St. Elizabeth West Adult Day Care Center, 7240 Anna, 63143. Tel: 314-644-6585.

St. Elizabeth North Adult Day Care Center, 2545 Dorwood, 63136. Tel: 314-867-6511. For all: Total Assisted 210; Total Staff 35.

[J] CHILD GUIDANCE

ST. LOUIS. *Central Intake*, 4140 Lindell Blvd., 63108. Tel: 314-371-0047; 371-0051; 371-0053 (Managed Care Ref. only). Sally Nelson, A.C.S.W., L.C.S.W., Dir. of Central Intake. Provides evaluation & referral svcs. for Child Help (formerly Catholic Charities Children's Network or Catholic Charities Children's Services Network) & handles managed care referrals for entire Catholic Charities Federation of St. Louis. Total Assisted 2,300; Total Staff 2.

Child Center of Our Lady, 7900 Natural Bridge Rd., 63121. Tel: 314-383-0200; Fax: 314-383-6334. Psychiatric Treatment Center. Milton T. Fujita, M.D., CEO & Medical Dir. Legal Title: *Child Center of Our Lady of Grace, Inc.* Patients assisted annually 218 (Children, Adolescents, Parents and Families).

[K] GENERAL HOSPITALS

ST. LOUIS. *Alexian Brothers Hospital*, 3933 S. Broadway, 63118. Tel: 314-865-3333.
For a complete listing, refer to the Hospitals section.

Incarnate Word Hospital, 3545 Lafayette, 63104. Tel: 314-865-6500; Fax: 314-865-6526.
For a complete listing, refer to the Hospitals section.

Saint Louis University Hospital, 3635 Vista Ave., P.O. Box 15250, 63110-0250. Tel: 314-577-8000, Ext. 8066; Fax: 314-577-8003 (Exec. Office).
For a complete listing, refer to the Hospitals section.

St. Mary's Health Center, 6420 Clayton Rd., 63117.

Tel: 314-768-8000; Fax: 314-768-8011.
For a complete listing, refer to the Hospitals section.

BRIDGETON. *De Paul Health Center*, 12303 De Paul Dr., 63044. Tel: 314-344-6000.
For a complete listing, refer to the Hospitals section.

CREVE COEUR. *St. John's Mercy Medical Center*, 615 S. New Ballas Rd., 63141. Tel: 314-569-6000; Fax: 314-569-6910.
For a complete listing, refer to the Hospitals section.

KIRKWOOD. *St. Joseph Hospital of Kirkwood*, 525 Couch Ave., 63122. Tel: 314-966-1601.
For a complete listing, refer to the Hospitals section.

LAKE ST. LOUIS. *St. Joseph Hospital West*, 100 Medical Plaza, 63367. Tel: 314-625-5200; Fax: 314-625-5314.
For a complete listing, refer to the Hospitals section.

ST. CHARLES. *St. Joseph Health Center*, 300 First Capitol Dr., 63301. Tel: 314-947-5000; Fax: 314-947-5090.
For a complete listing, refer to the Hospitals section.

WASHINGTON. *St. John's Mercy Hospital*, 200 Madison Ave., 63090. Tel: 314-239-8000.
For a complete listing, refer to the Hospitals section.

[L] SPECIAL HOSPITALS

ST. LOUIS. *Cardinal Glennon Children's Hospital*, 1465 S. Grand Blvd., 63104. Tel: 314-577-5600; Fax: 314-268-6468.
For a complete listing, refer to the Special Care Facilities section.

SSM Rehabilitation Institute, 6420 Clayton Rd., #600, 63117. Tel: 314-768-5300; Fax: 314-768-5355.
For a complete listing, refer to the Special Care Facilities section.

[M] PROTECTIVE INSTITUTIONS

Day Care Centers

ST. LOUIS. *Guardian Angel Settlement Association*, Mailing Address: P.O. Box 2055, 63158. Tel: 314-231-3188. Fonda Fantroy, Exec. Dir. Founded by the Daughters of Charity of St. Vincent de Paul.
Child Day Care Services.

DeSales Day Care, 2652 Ohio, 63118. Tel: 314-771-6417.

St. Patrick's Day Care, 1200 N. 6th St., 63106. Tel: 314-421-2816.

Social Services, 1401 La Salle St., 63104. Tel: 314-231-3188. Casework & Case Mgmt.; Emergency Svcs.; Senior Prog., Summer Youth Employment Prog.; Neighborhood Activities; Art, Gardening & Environmental Prog.; Paralegal on staff. For all: Total Assisted 15,340; Total Staff 31.

Sacred Heart Villa, 2108 Macklind Ave., 63110. Tel: 314-771-2224. Sr. Barbara Ann Matazzaro, A.S.C.J., Dir. Full-Time Care From 6:30-5:30 for Children 3-5 Years Old. Conducted by the Apostles of the Sacred Heart of Jesus. Total Assisted 125; Total Staff 22.

Stella Maris Child Center, 5654 Delmar Blvd., 63112. Tel: 314-367-7950. Ann Bingham, Dir. Conducted by a Board of Directors and Staff of Lay Teachers. Licensed Capacity 132; Total Assisted 200; Total Staff 50.

Visitation Child Development Center, 1421 N. Taylor, 63113. Tel: 314-533-8411. E. Nancy Norman, Dir. Learning Center and Day Care Service for 2-6 Year Old Children; Kindergarten Included. Conducted by Visitation Parish. Total Assisted 2; Total Staff 5.

FERGUSON. *Villa St. Joseph Child Care and Education Center*, 205 Brotherton Ln., 63135. Tel: 314-521-4424. Sr. Joan Phyllis Dyreks, O.S.F., Dir. Operated by the Franciscan Sisters of Our Lady of Perpetual Help. Total Assisted 60; Total Staff 14.

IMPERIAL. *Queen of Apostles Center*, 800 Montebello Camp Rd., 63052. Tel: 314-464-0163. Apostles of the Sacred Heart of Jesus 5; Children 52.

KINLOCH. *St. Martin's Child Center*, 8140 Scott Ave., P.O. Box 9722, 63140. Tel: 314-524-4719. Ms. Lula Stallings, Exec. Dir. Day care for children 2-6 years, 2-12 Summer only. Legal Title: *St. Martin Child Center, Inc.* Bed Capacity 63.

KIRKWOOD. *Carmelite Child Development Center*, 1111 N. Woodlawn Ave., 63122. Provides child development, child care and child education and services. Full Day 106; Kindergarten 24; Total Staff 15.

St. Joseph Educational Child Care Center, 1132 S. Glenwood Ave., 63122. Tel: 314-821-6636. Operated by the St. Joseph Hospital in Kirkwood.

[N] HOMES FOR CHILDREN

ST. LOUIS. *Boys Hope/Girls Hope of St. Louis, Inc.*, 755 S. New Ballas Rd., Ste. 120, 63141. Tel: 314-692-7477; Fax: 314-692-7810.
For a complete listing, refer to the Special Care Facilities section.

Marian Hall Agencies, 1340 Partridge Ave., 63130. Tel: 314-726-3339.
For a complete listing, refer to the Special Care Facilities section.

Marian Hall Emergency Shelter, 325 N. Newstead, 63108. Tel: 314-531-0511.
For a complete listing, refer to the Special Care Facilities section.

St. Joseph's Home for Boys, 4753 S. Grand Blvd., 63111-1459. Tel: 314-481-9121; Fax: 314-481-5605.
For a complete listing, refer to the Special Care Facilities section.

FLORISSANT. *Father Dunne's News Boys Home*, 853 Dunn Rd., 63031. Tel: 314-837-0513.
For a complete listing, refer to the Special Care Facilities section.

Marygrove Services, Inc., 2705 Mullanphy Ln., 63031. Tel: 314-837-1702; Fax: 314-837-5319.
For a complete listing, refer to the Special Care Facilities section.

NORMANDY. *St. Vincent Home for Children*, 7401 Florissant Rd., 63121. Tel: 314-261-6011.
For a complete listing, refer to the Special Care Facilities section.

[O] HOMES FOR AGED

ST. LOUIS. *Alexian Brothers Lansdowne Village*, 4624 Lansdowne, 63116. Tel: 314-351-6888; Fax: 314-351-5825.
For a complete listing, refer to the Special Care Facilities section.

Alexian Brothers Sherbrooke Village, 4005 Ripa Ave., 63125. Tel: 314-544-1111; Fax: 314-544-5134.
For a complete listing, refer to the Special Care Facilities section.

Chariton Apartments, 4249 Michigan Ave., 63111. Tel: 314-352-7600.
For a complete listing, refer to the Special Care Facilities section.

Fusz Pavilion, 3601 Lindell Blvd., 63108. Tel: 314-534-1201.
For a complete listing, refer to the Special Care Facilities section.

Little Sisters of the Poor, Home for the Aged, 3225 N. Florissant Ave., 63107. Tel: 314-421-6022.
For a complete listing, refer to the Special Care Facilities section.

Mary, Queen and Mother Nursing Center, 7601 Watson Rd., 63119.
For a complete listing, refer to the Special Care Facilities section.

Mother of Good Counsel Home, 6825 Natural Bridge Rd., (St. Louis Co.), 63121. Tel: 314-383-4765.
For a complete listing, refer to the Special Care Facilities section.

Regina Cleri Home, 7850 Kenrick Rd., 63119. Tel: 314-968-2240.
For a complete listing, refer to the Special Care Facilities section.

EUREKA. *Price Memorial*, Forby Rd., P.O. Box 476, 63025. Tel: 314-587-3200.
For a complete listing, refer to the Special Care Facilities section.

St. Joseph Hill Infirmary, Inc., St. Joseph Rd., 63025. Tel: 314-587-3661.
For a complete listing, refer to the Special Care Facilities section.

KIRKWOOD. *St. Agnes Home for the Elderly*, 10341 Manchester Rd., 63122. Tel: 314-965-7616; Fax: 314-965-3179.
For a complete listing, refer to the Special Care Facilities section.

MEHLVILLE. *Nazareth Living Center*, 2 Nazareth Ln., 63129. Tel: 314-487-3950.
For a complete listing, refer to the Special Care Facilities section.

ST. CHARLES. *St. Joseph Carmelite Home*, 723 First Capitol Dr., 63301. Tel: 314-946-4140.
For a complete listing, refer to the Special Care Facilities section.

[P] MONASTERIES AND RESIDENCES OF PRIESTS AND BROTHERS

ST. LOUIS. *The Abbey of St. Mary and St. Louis*, 500 S. Mason Rd., 63141-8500. Tel: 314-434-2557; Fax: 314-434-0795. Benedictines of the English Congregation. Rt. Rev. W. Thomas Frerking, O.S.B., Abbot; Very Rev. M. Paul Kidner, O.S.B., Prior; Rt. Rev. J. Luke Rigby, O.S.B.; Very Rev. Timothy Horner, O.S.B.; Revs. D. Ralph Wright, O.S.B.; R. Benedict Allin, O.S.B.; P. Finbarr Dowling, O.S.B.; J. Laurence Kriegshauser, O.S.B.; J. Gregory Mohrman, O.S.B.; Gerard Garrigan, O.S.B.; Joseph Marino, O.S.B.; Christopher Hanson, O.S.B.; Bede Price, O.S.B. Priests 13; Brother Monks 4; Oblates 1; Total Staff 21.

Bellarmine House of Studies, 3737 Westminster, 63108. Tel: 314-652-8862. Jesuit Residence for Students in the College of Philosophy and Letters of St. Louis University. Rev. Ralph G. Huse, S.J., Rector; Bro. Pablo Hernandez, S.J., Treas.; Revs. Louis J. McCabe, S.J.; Perard C. Monestine, S.J.; William T. Oulvey, S.J.; Bro. Thomas Naughton, S.J., Asst. Rector. Priests 4; Brothers 3; Students 15; Total Staff 3.

De Smet Jesuit High School Community, 233 N. New Ballas Rd., 63141. Tel: 314-567-3500. Revs. John D. Arnold, S.J., Rector; Richard L. Bailey, S.J.; John J. Bergin, S.J.; Robert E. Bosken, S.J.; John V. Craig, S.J.; Michael H. Durso, S.J.; Charles F. Ferrara, S.J.; Bro. Donald E. Lee, S.J.; Revs. Michael A. Marchlewski, S.J.; Thomas F. McQueeny, S.J.; William J. Snyders, S.J.; Bro. Henry E. Welch, S.J.; Rev. Martin J. Whealen, S.J. Total in Residence 13; Total Staff 1.

Dominican Community of St. Louis. St. Louis Bertrand Priory - Province of St. Albert the Great. 97 Waterman St., 63112. Tel: 314-361-4445. Revs. Kevin David O'Rourke, O.P.; Benedict M. Ashley, O.P.; Ralph A. Powell, O.P.; Joseph P. Gillespie, O.P.; Eric A. Reiran, O.P.; Stanley A. Drongowski, O.P.
Assigned but living elsewhere: Rev. Charles E. Bouchard, O.P., 2001 26th Ave. S., Nashville, TN, 37212. Tel: 615-297-9686.

Franciscan Brothers, of the St. Francis Monastery-Brooklyn, New York, at St. John the Baptist Parish, 4200 Delor St., 63116. Tel: 314-353-1255. Religious Brothers of the Third Order Regular of Saint Francis (Generalate, Saint Francis Monastery, Brooklyn, NY). Bro. Padraic Campbell, O.S.F., Coord. Brothers in Congregation 120; Brothers in Archdiocese of St. Louis 2.

Franciscan Friary of St. Anthony of Padua. (Franciscan Province of the Sacred Heart-Provincial Headquarters), 3140 Meramec St., 63118-4339. Tel: 314-353-7470. Legal Title: *The Franciscan Fathers of the State of Missouri.* Very Rev. Kurt Hartrich, O.F.M., Prov. Minister; Rev. John Doctor, O.F.M., Prov. Vicar; Bro. Richard Baranski, O.F.M., Pastoral Assoc.; Revs. Maynard Billig, O.F.M., Priest's Confessor; Michael Crosby, O.F.M., Dir. of Office of Friar Formation; Allan DaCorte, O.F.M., Prov. Treas.; Bro. Patrick Darnell, O.F.M.; Revs. David Eckelkamp, O.F.M., Province Ministry to Retired Friars; Benet Fonck, O.F.M., Admin.; Thomas Gardner, O.F.M., Prov. Promotor for Missions, Commissary of the Holy Land & Exec. Dir. Franciscan O.F.M. Conference; Bros. Loyola Freightman, O.F.M.; Leo Geurts, O.F.M., Co-Dir. Franciscan Connection; James Hickey, O.F.M., Devel. Office; Donald Lachowicz, O.F.M., Dir. St. Jane Catholic Community Center; Revs. Christopher Lambert, O.F.M., Province Sec.; Andrew Lewandowski, O.F.M., Chap. for Benedictine Nuns; Bros. Damian Pfeifer, O.F.M.; Daniel Piasecki, O.F.M., AIDS Ministry; Dennis Pryor, O.F.M.; Revs. John Rausch, O.F.M., Chap. Franciscan Sisters of Mary; Kenneth Rosswog, O.F.M., Parochial Vicar; Bros. David Schulte, O.F.M.; William Schulte, O.F.M., Dir. Office of Public Rels. & Devel.; Revs. Thomas Shaughnessy, O.F.M., Co-Dir. Franciscan Connection; Ladislas Siekaniec, O.F.M.; Floribert Veverka, O.F.M., Sen. Parochial vicar; Martin Wolter, O.F.M., Chap. Little Portion, Eureka Springs, AR; Columban Yelovich, O.F.M. Priests 17; Brothers 11.
Military Chaplains: Rev. Joseph Carlos, CHC, USNR, 810 E. OceanView Ave., #305, Norfolk, VA, 23503. Rev. Charles E. Gunti, O.F.M., (Lt. Col.) Chap., 27 St. Lo Dr., Ft. Carson, CO, 80913. Friars of Sacred Heart Province Serving Abroad: Rev. Robert J. Karris, O.F.M., Curia Generalizia dei Frati Minori, Via Santa Maria Mediatrice, 25, Rome, Italy, 00165. Rev. Gilberto Cavazos, O.F.M., Antonianum, Via Merulana 124, Rome, Italy, 00185. Rev. Albert Haase, 133 Waterloo Rd., Kowloon, Hong Kong, 11136. Bro. Jeffrey Haller, O.F.M., Franciscan Friary, 133 Waterloo Rd., Kowloon, Hong Kong. Rev. Basil Tsung-Li-Chuen, O.F.M., Catholic Mission Church, Kanchuang Rd. 305, Tashi Taoyuan, Taiwan, ROC. Rev. Francis Li-Chung-Lun, O.F.M.; Bro. Thomas Courtney, O.F.M., Couvent de Terre Sainte, Bab Thouma, Damascus, Syria. Rev. Louis Antl, O.F.M., Penitenzieri, Pazza S. Giovanni in Laterano, 4, Vatican City, Italy, 00120. Rev. James Perluzzi, O.F.M., Curia Generalizia dei Frati Minori, Via Santa Maria Mediatrice, 25, Rome, Italy, 00165. Friars Attached to the Province but Residing Elsewhere: Rev. Edd Anthony, O.F.M., Franciscan Canticle, 370 W. Arenas Rd., Palm Springs, CA, 92262. Rev. Bernon Gensert, O.F.M., Good Shepherd Manor, 10127 Guadalupe Tr., N.W., P.O. Box 10248, Albuquerque, NM, 87184. Rev. Bernadine Hahn, O.F.M., St. Thomas More Parish, 4804 Grover St., Omaha, NE, 68106. Rev. Michael Hill, O.F.M., St. Joseph Church, 1294 Makawao Ave., Makawao, HI, 96768. Rev. Kenneth Kieffer, O.F.M., 1782 Troy Ln., Oceanside, CA, 92054. Rev. Michael Lanning, O.F.M., Holy Trinity Rectory, 213 W. 82nd St., New York, NY, 10024. Rev. Leon Reuter, O.F.M., St. Joseph, 125 E. Broadway, Shelbyville, IN, 46176. Bro. Ronald Witkewitz, O.F.M., 10030 Clifton Pk., Evergreen Park, IL, 60642. Rev. Allan Wolter, O.F.M., Old Mission, 2201 Laguna St., Santa Barbara, CA, 93105-3697. Rev. Eric Kahn, O.F.M., House of Prayer, 648 S. Assisi Way, Republic, 65738. Rev.

Theodosius Schelich, O.F.M., Chap. St. Francis Hospital, 1215 E. Union, Litchfield, IL, 62056.

Hallahan House, 4511 W. Pine Blvd., 63108-2191. Tel: 314-361-7765 (day); 758-7125 (night). Revs. Robert F. Weiss, S.J., Supr.; Gregory H. Jacobsmeyer, S.J., Min.; James J. Dougherty, S.J.; Thomas J. Hogan, S.J.; L. Gene Martens, S.J.; Raymond M. Tully, S.J.; Ralph E. Vonderhaar, S.J.; Bros. Stephen F. O'Brien, S.J.; Julius F. Petrk, S.J.

Jesuit Community Corporation at St. Louis University - Jesuit Hall, 3601 Lindell Blvd., 63108-3393. Tel: 314-658-2588; Fax: 314-535-0402. Revs. A. James Blumeyer, S.J., Rector; James H. Baker, S.J.; Lawrence H. Biondi, S.J.; John E. Blewett, S.J.; Joseph E. Brown, S.J.; Harold C. Bradley; Robert A. Brungs, S.J.; J. Richard Burtschi, S.J.; Lucius F. Cervantes, S.J.; Maria Joseph Christie, S.J. (India); Francis X. Cleary, S.J.; J. Eugene Coomes, S.J.; Daniel T. Costello, S.J.; Anthony C. Daly, S.J.; Denis E. Daly, S.J.; Lowrie J. Daly, S.J.; Terrence E. Dempsey, S.J.; Philip T. Derrig, S.J.; Everett A. Diederich, S.J.; Michael J. Doody, S.J.; Paul J. Duffy, S.J. (Australia); Adelmo P. Dunghe, S.J.; Richard W. Dunphy, S.J.; William B. Faherty, S.J.; David L. Fleming; Philip C. Fischer, S.J.; John B. Foley, S.J.; William Foley; Ignatius Futo, S.J.; Chester E. Gaiter, S.J.; George E. Ganss, S.J.; Michael J. Garanzini, S.J.; Eugene E. Grollmes, S.J.; Francis J. Guentner, S.J.; Martin Hagan, S.J.; Garth L. Hallett, S.J.; Marcus A. Haworth, S.J.; W. Charles Heiser, S.J.; John F. Kavanaugh, S.J.; George V. Kennard, S.J.; John Killoren; E. Edward Kinerk, S.J.; Harry R. Klocker, S.J.; Gregory N. Konz, S.J.; Leonard E. Kraus, S.J.; Gerhardt B. Lehmkuhl, S.J.; Edwin L. Lisson, S.J.; Michael K. May, S.J.; John L. McCarthy, S.J.; J. Barry McGannon, S.J.; Frederick G. McLeod, S.J.; Maurice B. McNamee, S.J.; Glenn R. Mueller, S.J.; W. W. Mueller; Jerome Odbert; Edward C. O'Brien, S.J.; Martin D. O'Keefe, S.J.; Walter J. Ong, S.J.; John W. Padberg, S.J.; Martin E. Palmer, S.J.; Claude Pavur, S.J.; Robert L. Phillips, S.J.; Robert Poirier; Nicholas F. Pope, S.J.; Paul C. Reinert, S.J.; Raymond H. Reis, S.J.; Ralph C. Renner, S.J.; Lars Reuter; Anthony J. Rochel, S.J.; Albert C. Rotola, S.J.; John C. Ruoff, S.J.; Bernard C. Schulte, S.J.; Albert H. Schulz, S.J.; James A. Sebesta, S.J.; John F. Sheehan, S.J.; Richard F. Smith, S.J.; John F. Snyder, S.J.; Paul V. Stark, S.J.; William V. Stauder, S.J.; Linus J. Thro, S.J.; Derick Turton, S.J.; John Valenta; James V. Veltrie, S.J.; John J. Walsh, S.J.; Laurence E. Walsh, S.J.; Raymond L. Windle, S.J. Priests 86; Brothers 3; Scholastics 1.

The Jesuits of the Missouri Province, 4511 W. Pine Blvd., 63108-2191. Tel: 314-361-7765. Missouri Province of the Society of Jesus. Very Rev. E. Edward Kinerk, S.J., Prov.; Revs. Louis J. McCabe, S.J., Exec. Asst.; Robert F. Weiss, S.J., Treas.; Frank E. Reale, S.J., Asst. for Jesuits in Training & Asst. for Secondary Education; Robert L. Sullivan, S.J., Asst. for Jesuits in Pastoral & Intl. Apostolates; William T. Oulvey, S.J., Asst. for Province Planning & Vocation Dir.; L. Gene Martens, S.J., Assoc. Dir. Jesuit Devel. Office; Mrs. Danielle Harper, Asst. for Social Ministries; Ms. Mary Flick, Dir. Publications & Editor, The Jesuit Bulletin, Panorama. Tel: 314-361-7765; Rev. William B. Faherty, S.J., Prov. Archivist. Priests 287; Students in Major Seminary 24; Novices 1; Brothers 32.

Missouri Province Jesuit Priests Not Listed Elsewhere: Rev. John R. Daly, S.J., 1630 S. Lewis Pl., Tulsa, OK, 74104. Tel: 918-749-0876. 2426 Alto Cerro Cir., San Diego, CA, 92109-1501. Tel: 619-274-0057. Rev. Joseph L. Herbert, S.J., 1085 Zang, Golden, CO, 80401. Tel: 303-233-3046. Rev. William J. Kane, S.J., St. Clement Hospital, 325 Spring St., Red Bud, IL, 62278. Tel: 618-282-3831. Rev. Urban J. Kramer, S.J., St. Francis Hospital, 6161 S. Yale Ave., Tulsa, OK, 74139. Tel: 918-494-2200. Rev. H. James McFarland, S.J., 330 N St., Apt. #34, Sacramento, CA, 95814. Tel: 916-448-8510. Rev. John F. O'Shea, S.J. R.R. #2, Box 188, Valley Falls, KS, 66088-9415. Tel: 913-945-3582. Rev. Frederick E. Schuller, S.J., Saints Peter & Paul Church, 1436 N. 67th Ave. E., Tulsa, OK, 74115-5666. Tel: 918-838-0646. Total in Residence 180; Total Staff 9.

La Salette Missionaries, 4650 S. Broadway, 63111-1398. Tel: 314-353-5000; Fax: 314-353-4582. Missionaries of Our Lady of La Salette, Province of Mary Queen. Very Rev. Dennis J. Meyer, M.S., Prov. Supr.; Bro. Timothy A. Schultz, M.S., Prov. Treas.; Revs. Joseph C. Shea, M.S., Foreign Mission Procurator. Tel: 314-353-5000; John Nuelle, M.S.

Provincial Vocation Office. Tel: 314-353-5000.

La Salette Ministries Development Center. Tel: 314-752-0760. Rev. Edward J. Brunnert, M.S., Dir.

La Salette Spirituality Center. Tel: 314-353-5000. Revs. James R. Dunphy, M.S.; Dennis J. Meyer; Edward J. Brunnert; James P. O'Reilly, M.S., (Retired); Laval L. Landry, M.S., (Retired); Louis L. VanDane, M.S.; Bros. Timothy A. Schultz, M.S.; Thomas Murphy, M.S.

Priests and Brothers of the Province Serving in the Foreign Missions: Diocese of Morondava, Madagascar: Most Rev. Bernard Ratsimamotoana, M.S., D.D., Bishop of Morondava (Malgash), Eglise Catholique, B.P. 132, 619. Very Rev. Marc Ranaivsoon, M.S., Prov. Supr.; Revs. Arthur A. Lueckenotto, M.S.; Jeremy J. Morais, M.S.; Donald Pelletier, M.S.

Diocese of Cordoba, Argentina: Revs. John M. Garvey, M.S.; John M. McCarthy, M.S.

Rome, Italy: Generalate, Missionari di N.S. de La Salette, Piazza Madonna della Salette, 3. Tel: (06) 53-04-51. Very Rev. Isidro Perin, M.S.; Revs. Raphael Rakatonocliarimanana, M.S., Vicar Gen.; Gerald Lebanowski, General Councillor & Gen. Sec.; Antoni Skalb, Gen. Councillor; Rene Gelinas, Gen. Councillor; Orlando Sapuay; Bolivar Hauck, M.S., Gen. Treas.; Jean Stern, M.S., Procurator to Holy See. Priests 37; Brothers 6; Oblates 2; Total Staff 4.

Leo Brown Jesuit Community, 5047 Washington Pl., 63108. Tel: 314-367-8013. Revs. Michael D. Barber, S.J.; Timothy S. Godfrey, S.J., Supr.; Thomas E.J. Kelly, S.J.; Donald W. Reck, S.J.; Bro. Donald R. Schlichter; Revs. Thomas J. Melancon, S.J.; John J. Vowells.

Marianist Community. P.O. Box 718, Eureka, 63025. Tel: 314-938-5470. Rev. Jose Ramirez, S.M., Dir. Priests 1; Brothers 4.

Maryknoll House, 4542 W. Pine Blvd., 63108. Tel: 314-361-7729. Revs. Stephen L. Schroeppel, M.M.; Robert A. Lilly, M.M.

Provincialate of the Society of Mary, Province of St. Louis, P.O. Box 23130, 63156-3130. Tel: 314-367-0390; Fax: 314-361-3131. 4538 Maryland Ave., 63108-1911. Rev. Timothy Dwyer, S.M.; Bros. Jerome Bommer, S.M., Asst. Prov.; Richard Dix, S.M., Temporalities; Rev. John Moder, S.M., Councillor.

Priests of the Province on Special Assignment: Rev. Gerald C. Haby, S.M., St. Michael Church, 310 Denman Dr., Mt. Pleasant, TX, 75455-4157. Rev. Edward M. Jach, S.M., 1600 Madison Rd., Cincinnati, OH, 45206-1815. Rev. Bernard M. Rochon, S.M., St. Timothy Parish, 1515 Saltillo St., San Antonio, TX, 78207-6898. Rev. James Tobin, S.M., 1033 W. Loyola Ave., #804, Chicago, IL, 60626-5218. Rev. Adolf Windisch, S.M., 300 College Park, Dayton, OH, 45469-0300. Rev. David Paul, S.M., 911 B. Geyer Ave., 63104-3921. Rev. Lawrence Doersching, S.M., 175 Phelan Ave., San Francisco, CA, 94112-1897.

Priests of the Province Serving Outside the USA: Rev. David Fleming, S.M., Supr. Gen., Marianisti, Via Latina 22, Rome, Italy, 00179.

Priests of the Province Serving in the Missions: Rev. William A. Christensen, S.M., IIRD, Ground Floor No. 3/14 Iqbal Rd., Block-A, Bangladesh, Dhaka-1207. Rev. James Schimelpfening, S.M., Nirmal Deep, P.B. 144, Ranchi 834 001, Bihar, India. Rev. Lawrence E. Jordan, S.M., Colegio San Jose Obrero, Apartado 459, Trujillo, Peru. Rev. William J. Morris, S.M., Universidad Santa Maria, Apartado 1350, Arequipa, Peru. Rev. Michael Barber, S.M., Comunidad Marianista, Apartado 839, 96400 Coatzacoalcos, Veracruz, Mexico. Rev. Quentin Hakewerth, S.M., Noviciado Marianista, Apartado 1152 - Adm. 1, Queretaro, QRO, Mexico, 76000.

Special Status: Revs. Anthony Pogorelc, S.M.; Gregory Benkowski, S.M.; Paul Donoghue, S.M. Total in Residence 69; Total Staff 24.

St. Alphonsus Rectory of the Redemptorist, 1118 N. Grand Blvd., 63106. Tel: 314-533-0304. Revs. Maurice Nutt, C.SS.R.; Richard Potts, C.SS.R. In res., Bro. Terrance Burke, C.SS.R. Total Staff 4.

St. Bonaventure Friary (Province of Our Lady of Consolation), 4012 Washington Blvd., 63108. Tel: 314-533-3179. Revs. David Lenz, O.F.M.Conv., Guardian; Formation Dir.; Wayne Hellmann, O.F.M.Conv.; Angelus LaFleur, O.F.M.Conv.; Hans Christoffersen, O.F.M.Conv.; Bro. Steven McMichael, O.F.M.Conv., Solemn Profession. Priests 4; Solemn Professed 5; Candidates 5.

St. Crispin's Friary, 3731 Westminster Pl., 63108. Tel: 314-531-4506. Revs. Christopher Popravak, O.F.M.Cap.; Christian Fey, O.F.M.Cap., Vicar Librarian; Julian Haas, O.F.M.Cap.; Mark Schenk, O.F.M.Cap., Guardian; Gerald Wintz, O.F.M.Cap.

St. Dominic Priory, 3601 Lindell Blvd., 63108. Tel: 314-658-2588. Revs. Philip J. Lamberty, O.P.; Arthur L. Kinsella, O.P.; Charles R. Malatesta, O.P.; Patrick F. Norris, O.P.; Frank C. Quinn, O.P., Subprior; Rodney T. Adams, O.P.; Thomas M. Condon, O.P.; Albert G. Glade, O.P.; Gregory J. Heille, O.P.; Albert S. Moraczewski, O.P.; Richard A. Peddicord, O.P., Prior; Michael A. Mascari, O.P. Total in Residence 30.

St. Louis University High School Jesuit Community, #3 Lawn Pl., 63110. Tel: 314-652-5425; Fax: 314-531-8446. Revs. James G. Knapp, S.J., Supr.; Robert T. Costello, S.J.; Richard E. Hadel, S.J.; Ralph D. Houlihan, S.J.; Frank E. Reale, S.J.; Gerald R. Sheahan, S.J.; Bros. C. Thomas Thornton, S.J.; Richard H. Witzofsky, S.J.; Barton T. Geger, S.J. Priests 6; Brothers 2; Scholastics 1.

St. Matthew Jesuit Community, 2715 N. Sarah St., 63113-2940. Tel: 314-531-6443. Revs. Matthew D. Ruhl, S.J., Supr.; Jeffrey Harrison, S.J.

St. Patrick Friary, 1000 N. 7th St., 63101. Tel: 314-231-9991. Revs. Valentine Young, O.F.M.Cap., Supr.; Simon R. Conrad, O.F.M.Cap.; Canice Froehlich, O.F.M.Cap.; Simeon Gallagher, O.F.M.Cap.; Didacus Dunn, O.F.M.Cap.; Bro. Eugene Pellegrino. Priests 4.

Servants of the Paraclete, St. Michael's Community, 13270 Maple Dr., 63127. Tel: 314-965-0860; Fax: 314-965-7202. Revs. Mario D'Agostini, s.P.; Joseph McNamara, s.P.; Richard Brown, s.P., St. John Vianney Renewal Center; Michael Foley, S.P., Fr. Servant, Clinical Prog. Dir., Eime Rd., 63023. Tel: 314-677-1828; Fax: 314-285-5895. Priests 3.

Vincentian Bellerive Residence, 73 Bellerive Acres, 63121. Tel: 314-389-4394. Very Rev. Lawrence F. Asma, C.M., Supr.; Revs. James T. Beighlie, C.M.; Edward J. Virgets, C.M.; Jules G. Yallaly, C.M.; John V. Farris, C.M.

Vincentian Henrietta Residence, 42 Henrietta Pl., 63104. Tel: 314-776-6148. Very Rev. Romain G. Morales, C.M., Supr.; Revs. John A. Shaughnessy, C.M.; Francis J. Shine, C.M.; Wilbert H. Bruns, C.M.; Joseph E. Begue, C.M.; Daniel P. Kearns, C.M.; Bro. Dave Goodman, C.M.

Vincentian Residence, 2904 Arsenal St., 63118. Tel: 314-773-7633. Revs. Ignatius M. Melito, C.M., Supr.; John F. Gagnepain, C.M.; James E. Swift, C.M.; Bro. F. Joseph Hess, C.M.; Revs. Edward J. Mullin, C.M.; Michael P. Joyce, C.M.; Daniel A. Ricci, C.M. Attached But Not In Residence: Revs. Glennon E. Figge, C.M., Daughters of Charity, Mater Dei Prov. House, Evansville, IN; Daniel E. Harris, C.M., St. John's Seminary Theologate, Camarillo, CA 93012; Patrick J. McDevitt, C.M., Loyola Univ., Baltimore, MD; John E. Rybolt, C.M., Paris, France; Daniel R. Schulte, C.M., Houston, TX.

Vincentian-St. Lazare Residence, 2912 Arsenal St., 63118. Tel: 314-771-1869; Fax: 314-771-2410. Revs. John F. Clark, C.M., Supr.; William A. Bogel, C.M.; Bro. James E. Donlevy, C.M.; Rev. Richard J. Janson, C.M.; Bro. Kenneth J. Lund, C.M.; Revs. J. Dennis Martin, C.M.; Mark S. Pranaitis, C.M.; Paul O. Schneebeck, C.M., Contact Person; Joseph J. Snoha, C.M.; Thomas E. Esselman, C.M.

White House Retreat Jesuit Community, 7400 Christopher Dr., 63129-5799. Tel: 314-846-2575. Office, 3601 Lindell Blvd., 63108-3393. Tel: 314-533-8903. Rev. Luke J. Byrne, S.J., Dir. & Supr.; Bro. George R. Hale, S.J., Min. & Treas. Associate Directors: Revs. Robert A. Doyle, S.J.; Robert L. Holmes, S.J.; David W. Koesterer, S.J.; Philip D. Kraus, S.J.

ARNOLD. *Immaculate Conception Friary*, 2300 Church Rd., P.O. Box 217, 63010. Tel: 314-296-5301. Revs. Gilmary Tallman, O.F.M.Cap., Vicar; Earl R. Meyer, O.F.M.Cap., Supr. In res., Bro. John Schmeidler, O.F.M.Cap.

CENTERVILLE. *Contemplative Heart of Mary Hermitage*. Rev. Robert L. Aten, Mailing Address: R.R. #1 309-C, Lesterville, 63654. Tel: 573-648-2467.

EARTH CITY. *Congregation of the Mission Midwest Province (Vincentians)*, 13663 Rider Tr. N., 63045-1512. Tel: 314-344-1184; Fax: 314-344-2989. Very Rev. William E. Hartenbach, C.M., Prov.; Revs. Michael P. Joyce, C.M.; Ignatius M. Melito, C.M., Communications Coord.; David J. Nygren, C.M.; Christopher S. Robinson, C.M.; Bro. F. Joseph Hess, C.M., Treas.

Vincentian Foreign Mission Society, 13663 Rider Tr. N., 63045-1512. Tel: 314-344-1184. Office for Vincentian Foreign Missions' Personnel and Projects. Rev. James P. Graham, C.M., Dir.

EUREKA. *Franciscan Brothers House of Studies*, Forby Rd., P.O. Box 129, 63025. House of Studies of Franciscan Missionary Brothers of the Sacred Heart of Jesus. Bro. John Spila, O.S.F., Dir. Brothers 3.

Our Lady of the Angels Monastery, St. Joseph Rd., 63025; Fax: 314-938-4960. Generalate of Franciscan Missionary Brothers of the Sacred Heart of Jesus. Bros. Bernardo Trosa, O.S.F., Dir. General; Matthew Gallagher, O.S.F.; Rev. Josef Lukaszczyk, Chap. Professed Brothers 13.

Apostolate: Price Memorial Nursing Home and St. Joseph's Hill Infirmary/Black Madonna Shrine, Adult Boarding Facility at Camilus Hall Boarding Home, Merkle Knipprath Nursing home, Joliet Diocese and Countryside Villas Retirement Center, Clifton, IL 60927.

HIGH RIDGE. *Society of Our Mother of Peace*, Sons of Our Mother of Peace, Maria Fonte Solitude, P.O. Box 322, 63049. Tel: 314-677-3235. Rev. Placid Guste, S.M.P., Supr. Priests 2; Brothers 3; Total in Residence 5; Total Staff 3.

LIGUORI. *Liguori Mission House/Redemptorists*, Ten Liguori Dr., 63057. Tel: 314-464-6999; Fax: 314-464-6765. Very Rev. Norman J. Muckerman, C.SS.R.; Revs. Charles C. Bueche, C.SS.R.; Thomas Cosgrove, C.SS.R.; Thomas Duggan, C.SS.R.; Paul Farrell, C.SS.R.; James J. Higgins, C.SS.R.; William Hogan, C.SS.R.; Victor Karls, C.SS.R.; Harry Korte, C.SS.R.; Wilfrid Lowery, C.SS.R.; William McKee, C.SS.R.; Bro. Gabriel Medic, C.SS.R.; Revs. James Patterson, C.SS.R.; Allan Weinert, C.SS.R.; Robert Pagliari, C.SS.R.; Henry McKeever, C.SS.R.; James Nugent, C.SS.R.; Carl Schwarz, C.SS.R.; Robert Rossbach, C.SS.R. Priests 18; Brothers 1.

St. Clement Health Care Center, 300 Liguori Dr., 63057. Tel: 314-464-3666; Fax: 314-464-4717. The Redemptorists. Revs. Edmund T. Langton, C.SS.R., Rector; George J. Corbett, C.SS.R.; Francis A. Flanagan, C.SS.R.; Albert A. Fuytinck, C.SS.R.; Evan B. Gautreau, C.SS.R.; Robert M. Gaydos, C.SS.R.; James S. Kelly, C.SS.R.; Arthur B. Klyber, C.SS.R.; Bruno V. Lischwe, C.SS.R.; Orville C. Mailloux, C.SS.R.; Dwaine J. Marsch, C.SS.R.; Thomas E. Monaghan, C.SS.R.; Henry F. Porten, C.SS.R.; Gerard F. Resch, C.SS.R.; Henry A. Schultz, C.SS.R.; Paul E. Schwarz, C.SS.R.; Anthony A. Stuebben, C.SS.R.; Raymond F. Walter, C.SS.R.; Alvin O. Billimek, C.SS.R.; Norbert E. Delort, C.SS.R.; Francis J. Ryan, C.SS.R.

OAKVILLE. *St. Francis Friary*, 4550 Telegraph Rd., 63129. Tel: 314-487-5736. Franciscan Fathers. Revs. John Sullivan, O.F.M.; Robert Benhen, O.F.M.; Blane O'Neill, O.F.M.; Charles Reuter, O.F.M., Chap. Poor Clare Monastery; Valerian Schott, O.F.M., (Retired); Ermin Micka, O.F.M., (Retired).

PERRYVILLE. *Congregation of The Mission*, St. Mary's Seminary, 63775-1599. Tel: 314-547-6533; Fax: 314-547-2204. U.S. Motherhouse of the Congregation of the Mission (Vincentian Fathers, Prov. of the Midwest). Very Rev. Arthur L. Trapp, C.M., Supr.; Revs. Charles T. Herbst, C.M.; Charles F. Rice, C.M.; Robert J. Brockland, C.M.; Clarence J. Bogetto, C.M.; Francis A. Byrne, C.M.; John P. Tackaberry, C.M.; Willis F. Darling, C.M.; Alphonse X. Hoernig, C.M.; Charles F. Shelby, C.M.; Gilmore H. Guyot, C.M.; Bernard FitzGerald, C.M.; Charles D. Saunders, C.M.; Kenneth E. Grass, C.M.; Francis Germovnik, C.M.; Nicholas E. Persich, C.M.; Robert J. Zimney, C.M.; Louis J. Derbes, C.M.; James P. Graham, C.M.; John F. Zimmerman, C.M.; Oscar Lukefahr, C.M.; James A. Fischer, C.M.; Bros. Peter Baxter, C.M.; Harvey Goertz, C.M.; Richard A. Hermann, C.M.; Mark Howard Argus, C.M.; John Mangogna, C.M.; Matthew J. Teel, C.M.; Raymond J. Tochtrop, C.M.; Richard Zoellner, C.M. Fathers 22; Professed Brothers 8; Total Staff 5.

[Q] PERSONAL PRELATURES

KIRKWOOD. *Opus Dei.* (Legal Name: Prelature of the Holy Cross and Opus Dei), Wespine Study Center, 100 E. Essex Ave., 63122. Tel: 314-821-1608; Fax: 314-821-4722. Revs. Michael E. Giesler; Gregory J. Coyne.

[R] CONVENTS AND RESIDENCES FOR SISTERS

ST. LOUIS. *Augustinian Nuns of Contemplative Life.* Mother of Good Counsel Convent, 4328 Westminster Pl., 63108. Tel: 314-533-2054. Legal Title: *Augustinian Cloistered Nuns, Inc.* Total in Residence 6.

Benedictine Convent of Perpetual Adoration, 8300 Morganford Rd., 63123. Tel: 314-638-6427; Fax: 314-638-2028 (Community); 638-7360. Generalate, Novitiate and Healthcare Community of Benedictine Sisters of Perpetual Adoration, under Pontifical Jurisdiction. Sr. Mary Jane Romero, Prioress Gen.
Four other interdependent monasteries: Clyde, MO; Tucson, AZ; Sand Springs, OK; and Dayton, WY. Membership in St. Louis Community 65; Total in Congregation 141; Novices 5.

Congregation of Mary, Queen of the World Community, 4540 Lindell Blvd., 63108. Tel: 314-361-8211. Sr. Jacinta Tran, C.M.R., Local Supr.

Daughters of Our Mother of Peace, 5587 Page Blvd., 63112. Tel: 314-382-2592. Sr. Maryjoy Lambert, S.M.P., Supr. Sisters 5.

Daughters of St. Paul Convent, 9804 Watson Rd., 63126. Tel: 314-965-3571. Sisters 4.

Franciscan Sisters of Mary Administrative Offices, 1100 Bellevue Ave., 63117-1883. Tel: 314-768-1824; Fax: 314-768-1880. Offices of the Franciscan Sisters of Mary & Convent. Sr. Jacqueline Motzel, F.S.M., Pres.; Rev. John Rausch, O.F.M., Chap. Professed Sisters in Archdiocese 154; In Residence 106.

Franciscan Sisters of Mary Novitiate, 1100 Bellevue Ave., 63117-1883. Tel: 314-768-1824; Fax: 314-768-1880.

Franciscan Sisters of Our Lady of Perpetual Help, 201 Brotherton Ln., 63135. Tel: 314-522-6800; Fax: 314-521-7179. Motherhouse and Novitate of Franciscan Sisters of Our Lady of Perpetual Help. Sr. Monica Marie Laws, O.S.F., Supr. Gen.; Rev. Larry Nickels, O.F.M., Res. Chap. Total Sisters in the Community 158; In Residence 12; Total Assisted 43; Total Staff 10.

Heart of Mary Center, 5306 Winona Ave., 63109. Tel: 314-351-4049. Sr. Anita Baird, D.H.M., Supr. Daughters of the Heart of Mary 5.

Incarnate Word Convent, 7800 Natural Bridge Rd., 63121. Tel: 314-385-8739. Regional House of the St. Louis Province of the Sisters of Charity of the Incarnate Word of San Antonio. Sr. Kathleen Coughlin, C.C.V.I., Prov. Supr.; Sr. Rose Mary Politte, C.C.V.I., Coord. Sisters 3.

Loretto Center, 590 E. Lockwood, 63119-3279. Tel: 314-963-1887. Sr. Anthony Mary Sartorius, S.L., Coord. Sisters 30; Total Staff 24.

Medical Mission Sisters, 2800 Olive St., 63103. Sr. Joan Coughlin, Local Contact. Sisters 3.

Missionaries of Charity, 3629 Cottage, 63113. Tel: 314-533-2777. Sr. M. Manorama, M.C., Supr. Sisters 6; Total Assisted 22,237.
Missionaries of Charity also in: Peoria, IL; Chicago, IL; Detroit, MI; Memphis, TN; Dallas, TX; Little Rock, AR; Baton Rouge, LA; Lafayette, LA.

Monastery of St. Clare of the Immaculate Conception, 200 Marycrest Dr., 63129-4813. Tel: 314-846-2618. Poor Clare Nuns. Mother Mary Leo Hoffman, O.S.C., Abbess Cloistered Nuns 9.

Mount Grace Convent and Chapel of Perpetual Adoration, 1438 E. Warne Ave., 63107. Tel: 314-381-2654. Sister Servants of the Holy Spirit of Perpetual Adoration (Generalate, Bad Driburg, Germany). Sr. M. Margaret, Supr., 1438 E. Warne Ave., 63107. Attended by Divine Word Fathers. 1446 E Warne Ave., 63107. Sisters 28.

Notre Dame Hall, 3753 W. Pine Blvd., 63108. Tel: 314-531-9881. School Sisters of Notre Dame (Motherhouse Sancta Maria in Ripa, St. Louis). Interprovincial Novitiate for School Sisters of Notre Dame, 4950 Heege Rd., 63123. Tel: 314-481-8634. Sisters 10.

Provincial House, Society of the Sacred Heart-United States Province, 4389 W. Pine Blvd., 63108. Tel: 314-652-1500; Fax: 314-534-6800. Total in Residence 7; Total Staff 4. Province Corporations: California Province of the Society of the Sacred Heart, Inc.; Ladies of the Sacred Heart of St. Louis, Missouri; Society of the Sacred Heart, Chicago Province, Inc.; Religious of the Sacred Heart, Washington Province, Inc.; Religious of the Sacred Heart, New York Province, Inc.; Religious of the Sacred Heart in Massachusetts, Inc.

St. Joseph's Convent of Mercy, 611 S. New Ballas Rd., 63141. Sr. Michael Marie Flannery, R.S.M., Coord. Sisters of Mercy of the Americas. Sisters 45.

St. Joseph's Provincial House, 6400 Minnesota Ave., 63111-2399. Tel: 314-481-8800; Fax: 314-481-2366; 351-3111. Prov. House of the Sisters of St. Joseph of Carondelet. Sr. Barbara Dreher, C.S.J., Prov. Dir. Co-Administrators: Sr. Eileen Hoffer, C.S.J.; Sr. Catherine Lucien Mattler, C.S.J. Sisters in Province 650; In Archdiocese 416.

Sancta Maria in Ripa, 320 E. Ripa Ave., 63125-2897. Tel: 314-544-0455; Fax: 314-544-6754. Motherhouse of the School Sisters of Notre Dame, St. Louis Province. Sr. Kathleen Wegman, Prov. Leader; Rev. John M. Unger, Chap. Sisters in Diocese 418.
Caroline Conference and Retreat Center.
Liturgical Fabric Arts.
Maria Center.
Resource Development.

Sisters of Mercy of the Americas, Regional Community of St. Louis, 2039 N. Geyer Rd., 63131-3399. Tel: 314-966-4313. Sr. Richard Mary Burke, R.S.M., Reg. Pres. Regional Sisters in Archdiocese 93.
Convent Corporations:
Sisters of Mercy of the St. Louis Regional Community, Inc.
St. Joseph's Convent of Mercy of St. Louis.
Education Institutions:
Sisters of Mercy Education System, St. Louis, Inc., Begin Literacy Program.
Sisters of Mercy - ARISE, Las Milpas, Inc.
Health Institutions:
Sisters of Mercy Health System, St. Louis, Inc.
Other: Mercy Center, Conference/Renewal Ministry.

Sisters of St. Francis of the Martyr St. George. Mother of Good Counsel Home, 6825 Natural Bridge Rd., 63121. Tel: 314-383-4765; Fax: 314-383-7256. Sisters 15.

Society of the Helpers of the Holy Souls, 3432A Crittenden, 63118. Tel: 314-771-7482. Sr. Patricia A. Hottinger, S.H.

Villa Gesu, 11755 Riverview Dr., 63138. Tel: 314-741-6830. School Sisters of Notre Dame. Health Care and Retirement Center for Sisters of the St. Louis Province. Sr. Marina Langhorst, S.S.N.D., Supr.; Sr. Joan DiProspere, S.S.N.D., Admin.; Rev. Elvan Maschmann, O.F.M., Chap. Sisters 126.

CHESTERFIELD. *Missionary Sisters of St. Peter Claver*, 667 Woods Mill Rd., S., P.O. Box 1058, 63006-1058. Tel: 314-434-8084. Sr. M. Aidan Daly, S.S.P.C., Supr. Sisters 7.

CRYSTAL CITY. *Ursuline Provincialate*, 210 Glennon Heights Rd., 63019. Tel: 314-937-6206; Fax: 314-937-7627. Central Province of the Nuns of Roman Union. Sr. Pauline Lorch, O.S.U., Prov. Prioress. Sisters 13.

ELLISVILLE. *Immaculate Conception Monastery Passionist Nuns*, 15700 Clayton Rd., 63011-2300. Tel: 314-227-5275. Mother Mary Salvador, C.P., Supr. Professed Religious 12. Cloistered Contemplatives.

FLORISSANT. *Contemplative Sisters of the Good Shepherd*, 2711 Mullanphy Ln., 63031. Tel: 314-837-1719. Sr. Magdalen Clark, C.G.S. Sisters 26.

Pallottine Missionary Sisters-Queen of Apostles Province, 15270 Old Halls Ferry Rd., 63034-1661. Tel: 314-837-7100. Provincialate & novitiate & renewal center of the Missionary Sisters of the Catholic Apostolate. Sr. Elisabeth Heptner, S.A.C., Prov. Professed Sisters 5. Convent Frascati, 1932 W. Linda Ln., Lonedell, 63060-9739. Tel: 314-629-5610. Professed Sisters 3.

FRONTENAC. *Congregational Office of the Sisters of St. Joseph of Carondelet*, 2307 S. Lindbergh Blvd., 63131. Tel: 314-966-4048. Congregational Leadership Team: Sr. Marie Damien Adams, C.S.J.; Sr. Lynn M. Levo, C.S.J.; Sr. Rose McLarney, C.S.J.; Sr. Judy Molosky, C.S.J.; Sr. Toni Marie Nash, C.S.J. Sisters 5.

Religious of the Sacred Heart Convent, 801 S. Spoede Rd., 63131. Sisters 7.

HIGH RIDGE. *Society of Our Mother of Peace, Daughters of Our Mother of Peace*, Maria Fonte Solitude, P.O. Box 322, 63049. Tel: 314-677-3235. Sr. Mary Perpetua Spranger, S.M.P. Sisters 14; Total in Residence 8.

KIRKWOOD. *Carmelite Sisters of the Divine Heart of Jesus Provincial House and Novitiate*, 10341 Manchester Rd., 63122. Tel: 314-965-1638; Fax: 314-822-3154. Sr. M. Angelina Finnell, Prov. Supr. Sisters 9; Novices 4; Postulants 2. We are a house of formation where young women are taught to be religious. Besides our child care center we have St. Agnes Home, a nursing home.

LADUE. *Carmel of St. Joseph*, 9150 Clayton Rd., 63124-1898. Tel: 314-993-6899; Fax: 314-993-5039. Discalced Carmelites.
Chapel of the Precious Blood. Mother Mary Joseph, O.C.D., Prioress; Rev. Kevin D. Horrigan, Res. Chap. Professed 8; Extern Sisters 1.

LIGUORI. *Monastery of St. Alphonsus*, 200 Liguori Dr., 63057-9999. Tel: 314-464-1093. Order of the Most Holy Redeemer (Redemptoristine Nuns). Professed 17; Novices 1; Postulants 1.

LONEDELL. *Pallottine Missionary Sisters-Frascati Community*, 1932 W. Linda Ln., 63060-9739. Sisters 3.

NORMANDY. *Convent of the Immaculate Heart*, 7626 Natural Bridge Rd., 63121. Tel: 314-383-0300. A residence for aged & infirm Good Shepherd Sisters of the St. Louis Prov.

Good Shepherd Provincialate, 7654 Natural Bridge Rd., 63121. Tel: 314-381-3400. Sr. M. Nora Patricia O'Flannigan, R.G.S., Prov. Sisters 9; Total Staff 5.

Pelletier Trust, a Charitable Trust of the Sisters of the Good Shepherd.

Marillac Provincial House, 7800 Natural Bridge Rd., 63121-4694. Tel: 314-382-2800; Fax: 314-382-8392. Daughters of Charity of St. Vincent de Paul. Provincial House and Place of Retirement for Daughters of Charity. Sr. Nannette Gentile, D.C., Visitatrix; Sr. Germaine Price, D.C., Asst.; Very Rev. William A. Bogel, C.M., Dir.; Rev. Edward J. Virgets, C.M., Chap. for Retirement Villa. Sisters in Archdiocese 108; In Residence 85.

Mount Providence, 8351 Florissant Rd., 63121. Tel: 314-524-3803; Fax: 314-524-7203. Motherhouse of the Sisters of Divine Providence of the St. Louis Prov. Sr. Janet Folkl, C.D.P., Prov. Legal Titles: *Sisters of Divine Providence of Missouri*; *Sisters of Divine Providence of Missouri Charitable Trust.* Sisters 59.

O'FALLON. *St. Mary's Institute*, 204 N. Main St., 63366-2299. Tel: 314-240-3420; 240-6010; Fax: 314-272-5031. Motherhouse of the Sisters of the Most Precious Blood.
Chapel of St. Joseph. Sr. Andree Fries, C.PP.S., Supr. Gen. Sisters in Archdiocese 271.

ST. CHARLES. *Franciscan Sisters of Mary*, 567 Jackson St., 63301-2667. Tel: 314-946-7258. Sisters 3.

Religious of the Sacred Heart, 301 Decatur St., 63301; Fax: 314-949-6659. Sisters 4.

Religious of the Sacred Heart, 800 N. 5th St., 63301. Sisters 5.

Religious of the Sacred Heart Regis Hall, 221 Decatur St., 63301. Tel: 314-946-6456; 946-6527. Sisters 19.

ST. LOUIS COUNTY. *Religious of the Sacred Heart*, 13644 Conway Rd., 63141. Tel: 314-434-7687. Sisters 2.

13648 Conway Rd., 63141. Tel: 314-878-1882. Sisters 5.

Religious of the Sacred Heart, 541 S. Mason Rd., 63141. Tel: 314-878-6705. Sisters 5.

TOWN AND COUNTRY. *Monastery of the Visitation, St. Louis*, 3020 N. Ballas Rd., 63131. Tel: 314-432-5353. Sr. Anne Madeleine Godefroy, V.H.M., Supr. Residence of Visitation Nuns Teaching or Living at the Monastery of the Visitation. Sisters 25.

[S] HOMES FOR MEN AND WOMEN

ST. LOUIS. *Cathedral Tower*, 325 N. Newstead Ave., 63108. Tel: 314-531-0511.
For a complete listing, refer to the Special Care Facilities section.

Father Dempsey's Hotel, Inc., 3427 Washington Ave., 63103.
For a complete listing, refer to the Special Care Facilities section.

Father Jim's Home, 3427 Washington Ave., 63103. Tel: 314-535-7221.
For a complete listing, refer to the Special Care Facilities section.

Queen of Peace Center, 325 N. Newstead Ave., 63108. Tel: 314-531-0511.
For a complete listing, refer to the Special Care Facilities section.

Rosati Group Home, Inc., 4532 Lindell Blvd., 63108. Tel: 314-367-5500.
For a complete listing, refer to the Special Care Facilities section.

Rosati Stabilization Center, 4224 N. Grand Ave., 63107. Tel: 314-534-6624.
For a complete listing, refer to the Special Care Facilities section.

St. Martha's Hall, P.O. Box 4950, 63108. Tel: 314-533-1313.
For a complete listing, refer to the Special Care Facilities section.

St. Philippine Duchesne Shelter, 1015 Goodfellow Blvd., 63112. Tel: 314-454-1012.
For a complete listing, refer to the Special Care Facilities section.

Villa Maria Center, 8351 Florissant Rd., 63121. Tel: 314-521-2255.
For a complete listing, refer to the Special Care Facilities section.

NORMANDY. *Maria Droste Residence*, 7660 Natural Bridge Rd., 63121. Tel: 314-383-5553.
For a complete listing, refer to the Special Care Facilities section.

[T] RETREAT HOUSES

ST. LOUIS. *The Cenacle*, 7654 Natural Bridge Rd., 63121-4989. Tel: 314-381-7070. Congregation of Our Lady of the Retreat in the Cenacle. Sr. Agnes Sauer, R.C., Supr. Sisters 6.

Mercy Center, 2039 N. Geyer Rd., 63131. Tel: 314-966-4686. Mary Ann Kaletta, Admin. Conference and Renewal Ministry. Operated by the Sisters of Mercy of the Americas, Province St. Louis.

White House Retreat, Office: 3601 Lindell Blvd., Ste. 204, 63108. Tel: 314-533-8903. 7400 Christopher Dr., 63129. Tel: 314-846-2575. Rev. Luke J. Byrne, S.J., Dir. Associate Directors: Revs. Robert A. Doyle, S.J.; Leonard M. Murray, S.J.; Robert L. Holmes, S.J.; David W. Koesterer, S.J.; Philip D. Kraus, S.J.; Robert L. Murphy, S.J.; Bro. George R. Hale, S.J. Total Staff 8.

DITTMER. *Il Ritiro-The Little Retreat*, Eime Rd., P.O. Box 38, 63023. Tel: 314-285-3759; Toll Free from St. Louis: 274-0554; Fax: 314-285-1530. Operated by the Franciscan Friars. Revs. Bertin Miller, O.F.M., Exec. Dir.; Nathan McNally, O.F.M., Retreat Dir.; Dismas Bonner, O.F.M.; Gavin Griffith, O.F.M.; Damien Dougherty; Leonard Paskert; Rev. Michael Crosby. Total in Residence 12; Total Staff 6.

Vianney Renewal Center, 6476 Eime Rd., P.O. Box 130, 63023. Tel: 314-274-5226; 677-1828; Fax: 314-274-1430. Operated by the Servants of the Paraclete. Rev. Richard Brown, s.P., Dir. of Prog.

EUREKA. *Marianist Retreat & Conference Center*, P.O. Box 718, 63025. Tel: 314-938-5390. Center for Formation and Growth in the Christian Life. Conducted by the Society of Mary. Revs. Joseph Uvietta, S.M., Dir.; Jose Ramirez, S.M. Total in Residence 5; Total Staff 18.

FLORISSANT. *Pallottine Renewal Center*, 15270 Old Halls Ferry Rd., 63034. Tel: 314-837-7100. Pallottine Missionary Sisters. Sr. Bernadita Peterson, S.A.C., Admin.

GLENCOE. *La Salle Institute*, 2101 Rue de la Salle, 63038. Tel: 314-938-5374; Fax: 314-587-9792. Community: Tel: 314-938-6142. Bro. Marvin Becker, Dir. Community 6.

HIGH RIDGE. *Society of Our Mother of Peace-Maria Fonte Solitude*, P.O. Box 322, 63049. Tel: 314-677-3235. Sr. Mary Perpetua, S.M.P.; Rev. Placid Guste, S.M.P.

[U] CAMPS AND COMMUNITY CENTERS

HILLSBORO. *Don Bosco Camp*, 4870 Jarvis Rd., 63050. J. Kevin McInnis, Dir.

[V] NEWMAN CENTERS

ST. LOUIS. *University of Missouri, St. Louis, Newman House*, 63121. Tel: 314-385-3455. Deacon Dennis Chitwood, Dir.

Washington University Newman Centers, Washington University Newman Chapel, 6352 Forsyth Blvd., 63105-2269. Tel: 314-725-3358; Fax: 314-727-6053. Rev. Gary G. Braun, Archdiocesan Dir. of Campus Ministries. In res., Rev. Msgr. William J. Lyons. Total in Residence 2; Total Staff 15.

[W] MISCELLANEOUS

ST. LOUIS. *Alexian Brothers of Missouri, Inc.*
Alexian Brothers of St. Louis, Inc.
Alexian Brothers Services, Inc.

Almost Home, 203 Brotherton Lane, 63135-3105. Tel: 314-521-3832. Transitional living prog. for teenage mothers & their children who are homeless. Sr. Irene Radtke, F.S.M., Dir. Total Assisted 47; Total Staff 7.

**American Academy of Natural Family Planning*, 615 S. New Ballas Rd., 63141. Tel: 314-991-5766. Mrs. Diane Daly.

Anna Trust, 6400 Minnesota Ave., 63111. A Charitable Trust Fund Established to Support the Religious and Charitable Purposes of the Sisters of St. Joseph of Carondelet, St. Louis Province.

Archdiocesan Charitable Bequest Council, 4445 Lindell Blvd., 63108. Tel: 314-533-1887; Fax: 314-533-1889. Mr. Frank J. Cognata, Jr., Dir.; Mr. Anthony D. O'Connor; Mr. Roger E. Cammon; Mr. David T. Keifer; Mr. Fred L. Vilbig; Mr. Timothy Wichmer; Mr. James G. Blase; Ms. Christi S. Fingal; Rev. Richard E. Hanneke, Archbishop's Rep., Planned Giving.

Archdiocesan Development Appeal, 4140 Lindell Blvd., 63108. Tel: 314-371-4980, Ext. 166. Mary Morfeld, Exec. Dir.

Archdiocesan Stewardship Education Committee, 4445 Lindell Blvd., 63108. Tel: 314-533-1887; Fax: 314-533-1889. Mr. Frank J. Cognata, Jr., Dir.; Mrs. Teresa R. Manna, Assoc.; Mrs. Sue Toland; Mr. Bob Barrett; Ms. Dee Harvill; Mr. John Kennedy; Mr. Tom Coerver; Ms. Michele DeVous; Revs. Michael Henning; Michael Donald.

Aware, Inc., St. Anthony's Medical Center, 10010 Kennerly Rd., 63128. Tel: 314-525-1622. Donna Kallal, Pres.; Mrs. Colleen George, Vice Pres.

B.R.E.M. Catholic Social Ministry, 1371 Hamilton Ave., 63112. Tel: 314-383-4666; Fax: 314-383-5366. Ms. Dorothy Kastigar, Dir. Provides Employment Counseling and Referrals, Health Outreach, and Referrals for Food, Clothing and Housing. Also Provides Community Education, Leadership, Development, Family Support and Community Development Services.

Birthright, 2206 S. Brentwood Blvd., 63144. Tel: 314-962-5300. Shirley E. Ducey, Admin. Dir.
Branch Offices: 215 Clarkson Exec. Pkwy., 63011. Tel: 314-227-2266. 6500 Chippewa, 63109. Tel: 314-962-3653. 3435A Bridgeland, 63044. Tel: 314-227-8775. 205 N. 5th St., St. Charles, 63301. Tel: 314-724-1200. 4144 Lindell, 63108. Tel: 314-946-4900.

Boys Hope, 12120 Bridgeton Square Dr., 63044. Tel: 314-298-1250. Rev. Paul G. Sheridan, S.J., Pres. & CEO. A College Preparatory Residential Child Care Agency Serving Abandoned, Abused and Neglected Children. Total Assisted 200; Total Staff 50.
With affiliated programs in: Baton Rouge; Chicago; Cincinnati; Denver; Detroit; Jacksonville; Nevada; New Orleans; New York; Northeast Ohio; Orange County, CA; Phoenix; Pittsburgh.

Cardinal Glennon Children's Hospital Foundation, 477 N. Lindbergh Blvd., 63141. Tel: 314-994-7800. Member of the S.S.M. Health Care System.

Caritas Center - Ladies of Charity Service Center, 7500 Natural Bridge Rd., 63121. Tel: 314-383-4207. Legal Title: *Charity Service Center*. Aid for the Needy. Sr. Louise Scheessele, D.C., Dir. Total Assisted 13,226; Total Staff 52.

The Caroline Trust, 320 E. Ripa Ave., 63125-2897. Tel: 314-554-0455; Fax: 314-544-6754. Supports the Religious and Charitable Purposes of the School Sisters of Notre Dame and Provides Support for the Aged, Infirm and Disabled Sisters of the Province.

Carondelet Health System, 13801 Riverport Dr., Ste. 300, 63043-4810. Tel: 314-770-0333; Fax: 314-770-0444. Gary F. Christiansen, Pres. Tel: 314-770-0333.

Catholic Charities Foundation, 4532 Lindell Blvd., 63108. Tel: 314-367-5500. Mr. John M. Lally, M.S.W., L.C.S.W., CEO. A Charitable Fund Established to Support the Activities of Catholic Charities.

Catholic Charities Volunteer Department, 4532 Lindell Blvd., 63108. Tel: 314-367-5500. The Recruiting and Referral Office for Volunteers Serving the Needs of the Various Programs Affiliated with Catholic Charities in Conjunction with the St. Vincent Pallotti Center for Apostolic Development which Develops and Enhances Lay Volunteer Ministry by Bringing Together Clergy, Religious and Laity.

Catholic Commission on Housing, 4140 Lindell Blvd., 63108. Tel: 314-371-0138. Rev. Richard J. Quirk, Exec. Dir. An Agency of the Catholic Charities Federation that Assists Low and Moderate Income Families in Buying their First Home.

Catholic Community Services Administration, 325 N. Newstead, 63108-2728. Tel: 314-531-0511. Sr. Betty Brucker, F.S.M., Exec. Dir. An Agency of the Catholic Charities Federation. A Consolidation of Catholic Outreach Services, Catholic Health Outreach Program and the Archbishop's Commission on Community Health.

Midtown Catholic Community Services, 1202 S. Boyle Ave., 63110-3814. Tel: 314-534-1180.

Rural Catholic Community Services, P.O. Box 668, Festur, 63028-0668. Tel: 314-931-5859. c/o St. Joachim, Rte. 1, Box 1110, Cadet, 63630-9717. Tel: 573-438-6182.

Father Tolton Catholic Community Services, 2011 E. Linton Ave., 63107-1134. Tel: 314-534-5323.

St. Jane Catholic Community Services, 7005 Ascension Dr., 63121-3427. Tel: 314-383-6539.

St. Joseph Catholic Community Services, 6322 Minnestoa, 63111-2553. Tel: 314-351-6407.

Southside Catholic Community Services, 2216 Sidney St., 63104-2833. Tel: 314-773-6100.

St. Charles County Catholic Community Services, 202 Main St., O'Fallon, 63366-2203. Tel: 314-978-8189.

Vietnamese Immigrant Health Center, 2651 Keokuk St., Bldg. A, 63118-4624. Tel: 314-664-8990. Catholic Community Services - Friends of Moms. At Joint Neighborhood Ministry, 2911 McNair Ave., 63118-1632. Tel: 314-771-3987. For all: Total Assisted 55,886; Total Staff 49.

Catholic Deaf Ministry, 6815 Page Ave., 63133-1505. Tel: 314-721-3069; 727-2747 (TDD). Provides Services for Deaf and Hearing Impaired Persons.

Catholic Family Services, 7800 Kenrick Rd., 63119. Tel: 314-968-8010. Richard Hennicke, Exec. Dir. Provides professional counseling (individual & small groups) to individuals & families experiencing stress. Family Life Outreach & Parent Education available. Fees based on ability to pay.
District Offices:

South, 7800 Kenrick Rd., 63119. Tel: 314-968-8010.

Northwest, 4450 Washington, Florissant, 63033. Tel: 314-831-1533.

West County, 504 Woods Mill Rd., Manchester, 63011. Tel: 314-391-9966.

St. Charles, 1360 S. Fifth, St. Charles, 63302. Tel: 314-946-6014.

North City, Monsanto YMCA, 63112. Tel: 314-367-4646.

Crystal City/Festus, 305 W. Main, Festus, 63028. Tel: 314-937-2157; 937-2163; 1-800-652-8055.

Franklin Warren Counties, P.O. Box 342, Union, 63084. Tel: 314-583-1800.

St. Vincent Church, 1000 Rosati Ct., Perryville, 63775. Tel: 314-547-4591; 1-800-652-8055. For all: Total Assisted 12,562; Total Staff 49.

The Catholic Health Association of the United States, 4455 Woodson Rd., 63134. Tel: 314-427-2500; Fax: 314-427-0029.
Established June 24, 1915. John E. Curley, Jr., Pres. & CEO.

Catholic High School Association, 4140 Lindell Blvd., 63108. Tel: 314-371-4980. Mr. George Henry, Supt.

Focus Foundation (Federation of Catholic Urban Schools), 4140 Lindell Blvd., 63108. Tel: 314-371-4980. Sr. Margaret McCulloch, B.V.M., Dir.

Today and Tomorrow Educational Foundation, 4140 Lindell Blvd., 63108. Tel: 314-371-4980. Bridgett Flood, Dir.

Catholic Information Center, 1000 N. Seventh St., 63101. Tel: 314-621-6555; 231-9991. Rev. Valentine Young, O.F.M.Cap., Dir.

Catholic Kolping Society of America, 4035 Keokuk St., 63116. Tel: 314-776-5312. Otto J. Eichhorn, Treas.

Catholic Leadership Development, 4140 Lindell Blvd., 63108. Tel: 314-727-2350. Mailing Address: 43 Aberdeen Pl., 63105. Gerty O'Leary, Dir.
Participants are nominated by pastors and Catholic leaders and are committed to learning and active project work.

Catholic Office of Disability Ministry, 7800 Kenrick Rd., 63119-5004. Tel: 314-961-4320, Ext. 190; Fax: 314-918-0878. Lorraine Fahey, Dir.

Catholic Services for Children and Youth, 4140 Lindell Blvd., 63108. Tel: 314-371-4980. William J. Murphy, M.S.W., Dir. Child Welfare Agency Providing Adoption, Foster Family Care, Outreach Counseling in Own Home, Social Services for Residential Treatment Centers and Services for Unmarried and Single Parents. Total in Residence 3,400; Total Staff 60.

Central Bureau of the CCUA, 3835 Westminster Pl.,

63108-3472. Tel: 314-371-1653. Rev. John H. Miller, C.S.C., Dir. and Editor of the Social Justice Review.

Chiara Corporation, 1100 Bellevue, 63117. Tel: 314-768-1817; Fax: 314-768-1880. Mr. John O'Shaughnessy, Contact Person. Ministries that promote, enhance and provide for the spiritual, religious, physical or mental well-being of members of society in accordance with the religious and charitable purposes of the Franciscan Sisters of Mary.

Child Center Foundation, 7900 Natural Bridge Rd., 63121; Fax: 314-383-6334. John K. Brooks, Chm. Bd.

Child Center Foundation provides financial support to the Child Center of Our Lady, a residential, day treatment, and outpatient services facility serving severely emotionally disturbed children and their families.

Daughters of Charity Healthcare Foundation of St. Louis, 7806 Natural Bridge Rd., 63121-4626. Tel: 314-383-5444. Michael Anderson, Contact Person.

Daughters of Charity National Health System, P.O. Box 45998, 63145-5998. 4600 Edmundson Rd., 63134. Tel: 314-253-6700; Fax: 314-253-6807. Donald A. Brennan, Pres./CEO.

The Daughters of Charity National Health System is sponsored by four of the United States Provinces of the Daughters of Charity: Northeast Prov., Albany, NY; Southeast Prov., Emmitsburg, MD; East Central Prov., Evansville, IN; and West Central Prov., St. Louis, MO.

Daughters of Charity National Health System-West Central Inc., 7806 Natural Bridge Rd., 63121. Tel: 314-383-5444. James S. Kramer, Regl. Exec. & CEO.

Daughters of Charity West Central Region Foundation, 7806 Natural Bridge Rd., 63121-4626. Tel: 314-383-5444. Michael Anderson, Contact Person. Provides funds for the poor & underserved; will fund projects related to health education, wellness & prevention, primary medical svcs. & social svcs.

Dial Help, 325 N. Newstead, 63108. Tel: 314-371-4357; 800-666-9990. Mrs. Mary Carroll, Admin.; Mr. Chris MacLellan, Dir. Information and Referral Service Operated by Catholic Charities.

Dismas House of St. Louis, 5025 Cote Brilliante Ave., 63113. Tel: 314-361-2802; Fax: 314-361-8780. Rev. Joseph M. Kohler, Exec. Dir.

Eucharistic Missionaries of St. Theresa, 4431 Lindell Blvd., 63108. Tel: 314-533-2824. Sr. Theresa Caracheo Espinal, M.E.S.T.

Franciscan Sisters of Mary, 1100 Bellevue Ave., 63117-1883. Tel: 314-768-1824; Fax: 314-768-1880.

Good Shepherd Programs, Inc., 7654 Natural Bridge Rd., 63121. Operates the Maria Droste Residence.

Gregorian University Foundation, 3601 Lindell Blvd., 63108. Tel: 314-977-2598; Fax: 314-977-7211. Rev. John F. Snyder, S.J., Vice Chm. Bd. of Trustees.

Hispanic Ministry of the Archdiocese of St. Louis, 5418 Louisiana, 63111. Tel: 314-351-1318. Rev. Francis X. Blood, Contact; Sr. Alicia Alvarado, O.P., Asst. Coord.

Institute for Theological Encounter with Science & Technology (ITEST), 221 N. Grand Blvd., 63103. Tel: 314-977-2703; Fax: 314-977-7264. Rev. Robert A. Brungs, S.J., Dir.

Institute of Jesuit Sources, 3700 W. Pine St., 63108. Tel: 314-977-7257; Fax: 314-977-7263. Rev. John W. Padberg, S.J., Dir.

Intercommunity Housing Association, 590 E. Lockwood, 63119-3279. Provides safe, affordable housing & supportive svcs. for economically disadvantaged & working poor families in St. Louis.

The Jesuits of the Missouri Province, Office of Development: 4517 W. Pine Blvd., 63108. Tel: 314-361-7765; Fax: 314-758-7163. Mr. Ray Markham, Dir.; Rev. L. Gene Martens, S.J., Assoc. Dir. Legal Title: *The Jesuits of the Missouri Prov.*

Ladies of Charity of St. Catherine Laboure, 10211 Gregory Ct., 63128. Affiliate with Ladies of Charity of the United States & the Assoc. of Intl. Charities of St. Vincent de Paul. Mary Ann Morovitz, Pres.

Ladies of Charity of St. Vincent-Guardian Angel. St. Vincent's Church, 1408 S. Tenth St., 63104. Affiliate with Ladies of Charity of the United States & the Assoc. of Intl. Charities of St. Vincent de Paul. Natalie Cox, Pres.

Ladies of Charity of the United States of America, P.O. Box 31697, 63131-1697. Most Rev. Paul Zipfel, Auxiliary Bishop of St. Louis; Doris C. Hoag, National Pres.

LCUSA continues, expands, and improves the charitable works of the local associations of the LCUSA, which number 73.

Mary and Joseph Trust, 1100 Bellevue Ave., 63117-1883. Tel: 314-768-1817.

McAuley Charitable Trust, 2039 N. Geyer Rd., 63131-3399. Tel: 314-966-4313. The Sisters of Mercy of the Americas, Regional Community of St. Louis. Sr. Katherine Marie Glosenger, R.S.M., Contact Person.

Migration and Refugee Services, 2840 Wisconsin Ave., 63118. Tel: 314-771-2570; Fax: 314-771-6406. Mr. Richard Hayde, Resettlement Dir. To Facilitate the Settlement of Refugees.

The Missionaries of Our Lady of La Salette, Provincialate, 4650 S. Broadway, 63111-1398. Total in Residence 13; Total Staff 4.

Missionaries of the Kingship of Christ, P.O. Box 2234, 63109. Tel: 314-353-5002. Rev. Msgr. Louis F. Meyer, Spiritual Dir., Madonna House, 4908 Sutherland Ave., 63109. Tel: 314-352-5822.

A Pontifical Secular Institute.

The Museum of Western Jesuit Missions, 700 Howdershell Rd., Box 1095, 63031. Rev. William B. Faherty, S.J., Curator. Total in Residence 1; Total Staff 10.

National Christian Life Community of the United States of America (CLC), 3601 Lindell Blvd., Rm. 202 (Jesuit Hall), 63108-3393. Tel: 314-977-7370. Joan Felling, Pres. Founded c. 1540 & approved 1584, a public, intl. assn. of the Faithful of Pontifical Right which builds small Faith-Communities for mission & Svc. to the church. It uses the Spiritual Exercises of Saint Ignatius of Loyola as its specific source & characteristic instrument for its spirituality. Membership equally open to primarily catholic christian men, women, youth & young adults, clergy, brothers & sisters.

Network of Sacred Heart Schools, Inc., 4389 W. Pine Blvd., 63108. Tel: 314-652-1500; Fax: 314-534-6800. Sr. Barbara Dawson, Prov.

Notre Dame Ministry Corporation, 320 Ripa Ave., 63125. Tel: 314-544-0455. Sr. Barbara Marie McInturff, S.S.N.D. Includes: Notre Dame High School, Notre Dame Preschool, Notre Dame Travel & Notre Dame Tutorial Center.

Oblate House of Studies, 3741 Laclede Ave., 63108-3317. Tel: 314-534-2451. Rev. Allen Maes, O.M.I.

Our Lady's Inn, 1050 Julia, 63104. Tel: 314-241-6050. Julie Peetz, Contact Person. A residential shelter for pregnant women who have no home, who are being abused, who have no one who cares, and/or who are being pressured to abort their baby. We provide living facilities, food, clothing, counseling, and vocational guidance.

Perpetual Help Charitable Trust, 201 Brotherton Ln., 63135; Fax: 314-521-7179. Established by the Franciscan Sisters of Our Lady of Perpetual Help to Support the Religious and Charitable Purposes of the Franciscan Sisters of Our Lady of Perpetual Help. Total assisted 614; Total Staff 349.

Review for Religious, 3601 Lindell Blvd., Rm. 428, 63108. Tel: 314-977-7363; Fax: 314-977-7362. Total Staff 6.

Sacred Heart Program, Inc., 3900 Westminster Pl., 63108. Tel: 314-533-0320; 888-7CONTACT. Gary Kolarcik, Exec. Dir. The Sacred Heart Program produces "Contact," a nationwide broadcast designed to help society's "strugglers" - the spiritually, physically or financially impoverished.

St. Charles Lwanga Center, 5021 Northland Ave., 63113-1014. Tel: 314-367-7929. Provides spiritual formation and lay leadership training with evangelization outreach for the Black Catholic Community, those working in the community and all interested persons. Gloria N. Green, Dir. Total Staff 4.

St. Francis de Sales Association, 228 Chestnut Ave., 63119. Mrs. Martha Smith, Western Regl. Dir. Promotes Christian Living of the Baptismal Commission According to the Spirituality of St. Francis de Sales.

St. Francis Home Care, Inc., 477 N. Lindbergh, 63141. Tel: 314-994-7800.

St. John's Mission, 4517 W. Pine Blvd., 63108. Tel: 314-361-7765; Fax: 314-758-7163.

St. Louis Catholic Charismatic Renewal, 7800 Kenrick Rd., 63119. Tel: 314-961-3420, Ext. 418; Fax: 314-961-4320, Ext. 444. Rev. Dennis Chitwood, Liaison; Ramona Neumann, Coord. for Centre & Renewal. Tel: 314-961-4320 Ext. 419. Ctr. with books & tapes, prayer time, ministry times, retreats for parishes, leaders training,small faith groups, conferences, special events & days of renewal.

St. Louis Health Care Network, 477 N. Lindbergh, 63141. Tel: 314-994-7800.

A Member of the SSM Health Care System.

St. Louis Roman Catholic Landmark Corp., 4445 Lindell Blvd., 63108. Maintains, Supports, Repairs and Preserves the St. Louis Roman Catholic Cathedral Located at Lindell and Newstead.

St. Martha's Hall, P.O. Box 4950, 63108. Tel: 314-533-1313. Provides Emergency Shelter, Counseling, Advocacy to Abused Women and their Children. Michelle Schiller-Baker, Dir. Total Assisted 340; Total Staff 10.

St. Mary's Health Center Foundation, 6420 Clayton Rd., 63117. Tel: 314-768-8067. Member of the S.S.M. Health Care System.

St. Patrick Center, 1200 N. 6th St., 63106. Tel: 314-621-1283. An Agency in Downtown St. Louis, Housing a Wide Range of Social Services for Mentally Ill and/or Chemically Dependent Homeless Persons and for Residents in the Area at Risk of Becoming Homeless. Total Assisted 7,000; Total Staff 55.

St. Paul Books and Media, 9804 Watson Rd., 63126. Tel: 314-965-3512; Fax: 314-821-8401. Total in Residence 3.

St. Vincent de Paul Educational Foundation Perryville, 1010 A Rosati Ct., 63775. Develops, Promotes and Sustains Catholic Education in Perry County. Rev. Kevin Fausz, C.M., Moderator.

St. Vincent Pallotti Center for Apostolic Development, 4532 Lindell Blvd., 63108. Tel: 314-367-5500. (See Catholic Charities Volunteer Department).

Seminar on Jesuit Spirituality, 3700 W. Pine St., 63108. Tel: 314-977-7257; Fax: 314-977-7263. Rev. John W. Padberg, S.J., Chm. Total Staff 3.

Sisters of Mercy Education System, Inc., 2039 N. Geyer Rd., 63131; Fax: 314-966-2298.

Serves the Mission of the Sisters of Mercy in its Charitable Ministry and Education Services.

Society of St. Vincent DePaul, Council of the United States, 58 Progress Pkwy., 63043-3706. Most Rev. J. Terry Steib, S.V.D., Bishop of Memphis, Spiritual Advisor; Joseph H. Mueller, Pres.; Rita W. Porter, Exec. Sec./Dir., Tel: 314-576-3993; Fax: 314-576-6755.

SSM Health Care, 477 N. Lindbergh, 63141. Tel: 314-994-7800. Member of the S.S.M. Health Care System.

SSM Rehabilitation Institute Foundation, 6420 Clayton Rd. #600, 63117. Tel: 314-768-5300. Member of the S.S.M. Health Care System.

Theology Digest, 3634 Lindell Blvd., 63108. Tel: 314-658-2857; 658-2859. Total Staff 2.

The Vincentian Press Religious Supply, 1405 S. Ninth St., 63104. Rev. Joseph E. Begue, C.M., Dir. Total Staff 3.

We & God Spirituality Center, 3601 Lindell Blvd., 63108. Tel: 314-977-2696.

**Women for Faith and Family*, P.O. Box 8326, 63132. Mrs. Helen Hull Hitchcock, Pres.

ARNOLD. *AJT, Inc.*, 320 E. Ripa Ave., 63125. 2488 Birch Ln., 63010. Tel: 314-296-1882. Sr. Alene Faul, S.S.N.D., Ph.D., Pres.; Rev. J. Patrick Gaffney, S.M.M., Vice Pres.; Betty A. Studley, Sec.-Treas. Exclusively Religious, Literary Educational and Charitable Related to the Integration of Religious, Charitable and Educational Service Resources to Provide Materials to Existing Religious Instruction, Specifically the Development of Bible Study Computer Study Computer Software Programs.

BRIDGETON. *DePaul Health Care Foundation*, 12303 DePaul Dr., 63066. Tel: 314-344-6000. Member of the S.S.M. Health Care System.

CADET. *Rural Parish Workers of Christ the King*, R.R. 1, Box 1667, 63630. Tel: 314-586-5171. Miss Natalie Villmer, Gen. Dir. A Secular Institute of the Archdiocese of St. Louis. Workers 5; Total Assisted 2,500; Total in Residence 6; Total Staff 7.

EARTH CITY. *Congregation of the Mission International Fund*, 13663 Rider Tr. N., 63045-1512. Tel: 314-344-1184; Fax: 314-344-2989. Bro. F. Joseph Hess, C.M.

Lazarist Trust Fund, 13663 Rider Tr. N., 63045-1512. Tel: 314-344-1184; Fax: 314-344-2989.

FLORISSANT. *Marygrove, Inc.*, 2705 Mullanphy, 63031. Total Assisted 936; Total Staff 125.

KIRKWOOD. *St. Joseph Hospital of Kirkwood Foundation*. 525 Couch Ave., St. Louis, 63122. Tel: 314-966-1644. A Member of the SSM Health Care System.

LIGUORI. *Liguori Mission House, The Redemptorists*, 10 Liguori Dr., 63057. Tel: 314-464-6999; Fax: 314-464-6765. Rev. William McKee, C.SS.R.

O'FALLON. *Centers for Professional and Pastoral Services*, 204 N. Main St., 63366. Tel: 314-240-6010. Sponsored by Sisters of the Most Precious Blood of O'Fallon, MO. Sr. Andree Fries, C.PP.S.

Charitable Trust, Sisters of the Most Precious Blood of O'Fallon, MO, 204 N. Main St., 63366. Trust fund for support of retired Sisters of the Most Precious Blood.

St. Dominic Endowment Fund, St. Dominic High School, 31 St. Dominic Dr., 63366. Tel: 314-272-6277; Fax: 314-240-8303. Sr. Mary H. Bender, S.S.N.D., Treas. Sponsored by Sisters of the Most Precious Blood of O'Fallon, MO.

PERRYVILLE. *The Association of the Miraculous Medal*, 1811 W. St. Joseph St., 63775. Tel: 573-547-8343; Fax: 573-547-1389. Rev. Charles F. Shelby, C.M., Dir.

Catholic Home Study Service, P.O. Box 363, 63775. Tel: 573-547-4084. Rev. Oscar Lukefahr, C.M., Dir.

Ladies of Charity of St. Vincent de Paul Parish, 1000 Rosati Ct., 63775. Affiliate with Ladies of Charity of the United States & the Assoc. of Intl. Charities of St. Vincent de Paul. Dorothy Barry, Pres.

PEVELY. *Vision of Peace Ministries*, Abby Ln., P.O. Box 69, 63070. Tel: 314-475-3697. Sr. Catherine Vetter, C.C.V.I., Pres. Bd. of Dir. Total in Residence 2; Total Staff 2.

ST. CHARLES. *Duchesne High School Endowment Fund*

Inc., 2550 Elm St., 63301. Tel: 314-946-6767. Mr. Charles L. Nolan, Admin. Receives Bequests and Gifts from Various Donors for the Express Purpose of Aiding and Benefitting Duchesne High School, St. Charles, and by Investment and Use of Such Bequests and Gifts and Income therefrom Aids and Benefits the High School in Fulfilling its Educational Purposes.

St. Joseph Health Center and St. Joseph Hospital West Foundation, 300 First Capitol Dr., 63301. Tel: 314-947-5612; Fax: 314-947-5090. Member of the S.S.M. Health Care System; governed by 25 member fiduciary board of directors.

RELIGIOUS INSTITUTES OF MEN REPRESENTED IN THE ARCHDIOCESE

For further details refer to the corresponding bracketed number in the Religious Institutes of Men or Women section.

[0120]—*Alexian Brothers*. (Chicago).—C.F.A.
[0140]—*The Augustinians. (Prov. of Our Mother of Good Counsel)*.—O.S.A.
[0200]—*Benedictine Monks. (English, Swiss American Congregation)*.—O.S.B.
[0330]—*Brothers of the Christian Schools. (St. Louis Prov.)*.—F.S.C.
[0600]—*Brothers of the Congregation of Holy Cross*.—C.S.C.
[0470]—*The Capuchin Friars*. (Kansas City, MO).—O.F.M.Cap.
[1330]—*Congregation of the Mission. (Midwest Prov.)*.—C.M.
[0630]—*Congregation of the Missionaries of the Holy Family*. (Europe).—M.S.F.
[1000]—*Congregation of the Passion. (Western Prov. of Holy Cross)*.—M.S.F.
[1130]—*Congregation of the Priests of the Sacred Heart*.—S.C.J.
[1080]—*Congregation of the Resurrection*. (Rome, Italy).—C.R.
[0480]—*Conventual Franciscans. (Our Lady of Consolation Prov.)*.—O.F.M.Conv.
[0520]—*Franciscan Friars. (Croatian Franciscan Commissariat, Sacred Heart Prov.)*.—O.F.M.
[0540]—*Franciscan Missionary Brothers of the Sacred Heart of Jesus*. (Eureka, MO).—O.S.F.
[0690]—*Jesuit Fathers and Brothers*. (Missouri Prov.).—S.J.
[0800]—*Maryknoll*.—M.M.
[0830]—*Mill Hill Missionaries*.—M.H.M.
[0720]—*The Missionaries of Our Lady of La Salette*.—M.S.
[0870]—*Monfort Missionaries*.—S.M.M.
[0910]—*Oblates of Mary Immaculate*.—O.M.I.
[0430]—*Order of Preachers*.—O.P.
[0610]—*Priests of the Congregation of Holy Cross*.—C.S.C.
[1070]—*Redemptorist Fathers*. (St. Louis Prov.).—C.SS.R.
[0700]—*St. Joseph's Society of the Sacred Heart*.—S.S.J.
[1230]—*Servants of the Paraclete*.—s.P.
[1240]—*Servites*. (Chicago).—O.S.M.
[0760]—*Society of Mary*. (St. Louis Prov.).—S.M.
[0420]—*Society of the Divine Word*. (Northern Prov.).—S.V.D.
[]—*Sons of Our Mother*.—S.M.P.

RELIGIOUS INSTITUTES OF WOMEN REPRESENTED IN THE ARCHDIOCESE

[0100]—*Adorers of the Blood of Christ*. (Ruma, IL; Wichita, KS).—A.S.C.
[0130]—*Apostles of the Sacred Heart of Jesus*.—A.S.C.J.
[0160]—*Augustinian Cloistered Nuns*.—O.S.A.
[0230]—*Benedictine Sisters of Pontifical Jurisdiction*. (Atchison; Columbia; Fort Smith; Olivetan; Yankton).—O.S.B.
[0360]—*Carmelite Sisters of the Divine Heart of Jesus*. (Carmel).—D.C.J.
[3110]—*Congregation of Our Lady of the Retreat in the Cenacle*.—R.C.
[0220]—*Congregation of the Benedictine Sisters of Perpetual Adoration of Pontifical Jurisdiction*.—O.S.B.
[0460]—*Congregation of the Sisters of Charity of the Incarnate Word*.—C.C.V.I.
[]—*Daughters of Calvary*.—C.M.F.C.
[0760]—*Daughters of Charity of St. Vincent de Paul*.—D.C.
[]—*Daughters of Our Mother of Peace*.—S.M.P.
[0810]—*Daughters of the Heart of Mary*.—D.H.M.
[0420]—*Discalced Carmelite Nuns*.—O.C.D.
[1070-01]—*Dominican Sisters*.—O.P.
[1070-11]—*Dominican Sisters*. (Sparkill).—O.P.
[1070-13]—*Dominican Sisters*. (Akron).—O.P.
[1070-28]—*Dominican Sisters*. (Akron).—O.P.
[]—*Eucharist Missionaries of St. Theresa*.—M.E.S.T.
[1370]—*Franciscan Missionaries of Mary*.—F.M.M.
[1310]—*Franciscan Sisters of Little Falls, Minnesota*.—O.S.F.
[1415]—*Franciscan Sisters of Mary*.—F.S.M.
[1430]—*Franciscan Sisters of Our Lady of Perpetual Help*.—O.S.F.
[2340]—*Little Sisters of the Poor*.—L.S.P.
[2470]—*Maryknoll Sisters of St. Dominic*.—M.M.
[2490]—*Medical Mission Sisters*.—S.C.M.M.
[2710]—*Missionaries of Charity*.—M.C.
[0390]—*Missionary Carmelites of St. Teresa*.—C.M.S.T.
[3990]—*Missionary Sisters of St. Peter Claver*.—S.S.P.C.
[3040]—*Oblate Sisters of Providence*.—O.S.P.
[3760]—*Order of St. Clare*.—O.S.C.
[2010]—*Order of the Most Holy Redeemer*.—O.SS.R.
[0950]—*Pius Society Daughters of St. Paul*.—F.S.P.
[3170]—*Religious of the Passion of Jesus Christ*.—C.P.
[3465]—*Religious of the Sacred Heart of Mary*.—R.S.H.M.
[2970]—*School Sisters of Notre Dame*.—S.S.N.D.
[0500]—*Sisters of Charity of Nazareth*.—S.C.N.
[0590]—*Sisters of Charity of St. Elizabeth, Convent Station*.—S.C.
[0630]—*Sisters of Charity of St. Vincent de Paul*.—S.V.Z.
[0430]—*Sisters of Charity of the Blessed Virgin Mary*.—B.V.M.
[0660]—*Sisters of Christian Charity*.—S.C.C.
[]—*Sisters of Christian Community*.—S.F.C.C.
[0990]—*Sisters of Divine Providence*.—C.D.P.
[2360]—*Sisters of Loretto at the Foot of the Cross*. (St. Louis Prov.).—S.L.
[2570]—*Sisters of Mercy*.—R.S.M.
[2580]—*Sisters of Mercy of the Americas*.—R.S.M.
[2630]—*Sisters of Mercy of the Holy Cross*.—S.C.S.C.
[3000]—*Sisters of Notre Dame de Namur*.—S.N.D.deN.
[1540]—*Sisters of Saint Francis, Clinton, Iowa*.—O.S.F.
[1540]—*Sisters of St. Francis of the Martyr St. George*.—O.S.F.
[3830]—*Sisters of St. Joseph*.—C.S.J.
[1830]—*Sisters of the Good Shepherd*.—R.G.S.-C.G.S.
[2350]—*Sisters of the Living Word*.—S.L.W.
[3270]—*Sisters of the Most Precious Blood*. (O'Fallon, MO).—C.PP.S.
[3150]—*Sisters of the Pallottine Missionary Society*.—S.A.C.
[3540]—*Sisters Servants of the Holy Spirit of Perpetual Adoration*.—S.Sp.S.deA.P.
[2150]—*Sisters, Servants of the Immaculate Heart of Mary*.—I.H.M.
[]—*Society of Helpers of the Holy Souls*.—S.H.
[4070]—*Society of the Sacred Heart*.—R.S.C.J.
[4110]—*Ursuline Nuns*.—O.S.U.
[4120-05]—*Ursuline Nuns, of the Congregation of Paris*. (Maple Mount).—O.S.U.
[4190]—*Visitation Nuns*.—V.H.M.

ARCHDIOCESAN CEMETERIES

ST. LOUIS. *Calvary*, 5239 W. Florissant Ave., 63115. Tel: 314-381-1313.
Resurrection, 7301 Watson Rd., 63119.
SS. Peter and Paul, 7030 Gravois Ave., 63116.
CREVE COEUR. *St. Monica*, Olive Street Rd., 63141.
DARDENNE. *Our Lady of the Miraculous Medal*, Freymuth & Orf Rd., 63366.
FLORISSANT. *Sacred Heart*, Graham Rd., 63033.
St. Ferdinand, Graham Rd., 63031.
GLENCOE. *Holy Cross*, 16200 Manchester Rd., 63038.
KIRKWOOD. *St. Peter*, Geyer & W. Monroe Ave., 63122.
LEMAY. *Mount Olive*, 3906 Mount Olive St., 63125.
ST. CHARLES. *St. Charles Borromeo*, Randolph St., 63301.

NECROLOGY

† Brauner, Omer H., (Retired). —Died Feb. 2, 1996.
† Eckhoff, Rev. Msgr. Frederick C., (Retired). —Died Nov. 10, 1996.
† Flavin, Rev. Msgr. Cornelius J., (Retired). —Died Oct. 18, 1996.
† Houlehin, John J., (Retired). —Died Oct. 24, 1996.
† Kuenz, Robert B., (Retired). —Died Jan. 2, 1996.
† Richmond, Joseph J., (Retired). —Died March 25, 1996.
† Santen, Raymond, (Retired). —Died March 22, 1996.
† Sievers, V. Paul, (Retired). —Died April 5, 1996.

Archdiocese of St. Paul and Minneapolis

(Archidioecesis Paulopolitana et Minneapolitana)

Most Reverend

HARRY J. FLYNN, D.D.

Archbishop of Saint Paul and Minneapolis; ordained May 28, 1960; appointed Coadjutor of Lafayette April 19, 1986; consecrated June 24, 1986; appointed Bishop of Lafayette May 13, 1989; appointed Coadjutor Archbishop of Saint Paul and Minneapolis February 22, 1994; appointed Archbishop of Saint Paul and Minneapolis September 8, 1995.

Most Reverend

J. RICHARD HAM, M.M., D.D.

Retired Auxiliary Bishop of Saint Paul and Minneapolis; ordained June 12, 1948; appointed Titular Bishop of Putzia of Numidia and Auxiliary Bishop of Guatemala November 28, 1967; consecrated January 6, 1968; appointed Auxiliary Bishop of Saint Paul and Minneapolis October 7, 1980; resigned October 30, 1990. *Res., St. Teresa Residence,, Maryknoll, NY, 10545.*

Most Reverend

JOHN R. ROACH, D.D.

Retired Archbishop of Saint Paul and Minneapolis; ordained June 8, 1946; appointed Titular Bishop of Cenae and Auxiliary Bishop of Saint Paul and Minneapolis July 12, 1971; consecrated September 8, 1971; appointed Archbishop of Saint Paul and Minneapolis May 21, 1975; installed July 16, 1975; resigned September 8, 1995. *Office: 226 Summit Ave., St. Paul, MN, 55102.* Tel.: 612-291-4400.

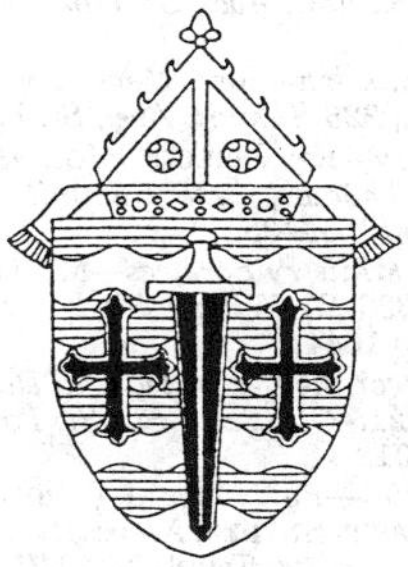

Most Reverend

LAWRENCE H. WELSH, D.D.

Auxiliary Bishop of Saint Paul and Minneapolis; ordained May 26, 1962; appointed Bishop of Spokane November 7, 1978; consecrated November 14, 1978; resigned April 17, 1990; appointed Titular Bishop of Aulona and Auxiliary Bishop of Archdiocese of Saint Paul and Minneapolis November 5, 1991. *Office: 226 Summit Ave., St. Paul, MN, 55102.* Tel.: 612-291-4400.

DIOCESE ESTABLISHED, JULY 19, 1850. ARCHDIOCESE ESTABLISHED, MAY 4, 1888.

Square Miles 6,187.

Comprises the following twelve Counties of the State of Minnesota: Ramsey, Hennepin, Anoka, Carver, Chisago, Dakota, Goodhue, Le Sueur, Rice, Scott, Washington and Wright.

Corporate Title: The Archdiocese of Saint Paul and Minneapolis.

For legal titles of parishes and archdiocesan institutions, consult the Chancery.

Chancery: 226 Summit Ave., St. Paul, MN, 55102. Tel.: 612-291-4400; Fax: 612-290-1629.

Web site address: http://www.mtn.org/archcom/

E-mail address: archcom@archspm

STATISTICAL OVERVIEW

Personnel	
Archbishop	1
Retired Archbishops	1
Bishop	1
Auxiliary Bishops	1
Retired Bishops	1
Priests: Diocesan Active in Diocese	236
Priests: Active Outside Diocese	12
Priests: Diocesan in Foreign Missions	3
Priests: Retired, Sick or Absent	94
Number of Diocesan Priests	345
Religious Priests in Diocese	146
Extern Priests in Diocese	32
Ordinations:	
Diocesan Priests	7
Permanent Deacons	8
Permanent Deacons in Diocese	166
Total Brothers	66
Total Sisters	1,189
Parishes	
Parishes	222
With Resident Pastor:	
Resident Diocesan Priests	179
Resident Religious Priests	29
Without Resident Pastor:	
Administered by Priests	14
Missions	5
Pastoral Centers	4
Closed Parishes	1
Professional Ministry Personnel:	
Brothers	2
Sisters	76
Lay Ministers	545
Welfare	
Catholic Hospitals	3
Total Assisted	132,555
Homes for the Aged	4
Total Assisted	684
Residential Care of Children	1
Total Assisted	4,000
Specialized Homes	4
Special Centers for Social Services	5
Educational	
Seminaries, Diocesan	2
Students from This Diocese	48
Students from Other Diocese	95
Total Seminarians	48
Colleges and Universities	3
Total Students	14,324
High Schools, Diocesan and Parish	7
Total Students	4,302
High Schools, Private	4
Total Students	2,340
Elementary Schools, Diocesan and Parish	88
Total Students	27,133
Elementary Schools, Private	1
Total Students	259
Catechesis/Religious Education:	
High School Students	21,404
Elementary Students	63,595
Total Students Under Catholic Instruction	133,405
Teachers in the Diocese:	
Priests	6
Brothers	11
Sisters	107
Lay Teachers	2,324
Vital Statistics	
Receptions into the Church:	
Infant Baptism Totals	11,838
Adult Baptism Totals	439
Received into Full Communion	1,337
First Communions	10,305
Confirmations	7,294
Marriages:	
Catholic	2,454
Interfaith	1,471
Total Marriages	3,925
Deaths	4,860
Total Catholic Population	733,961
Total Population	2,681,324

Former Bishops—Rt. Rev. JOSEPH CRETIN, D.D., cons. Jan. 26, 1851; died Feb. 22, 1857.—Most Rev. THOMAS L. GRACE, O.P., D.D., cons. July 24, 1859; resigned July 31, 1884; named Titular Bishop of Menith, and later, Titular Archbishop of Siunia; died Feb. 22, 1897.—Most Rev. JOHN IRELAND, D.D., cons. Dec. 21, 1875; Bishop of Maronea, and Coadjutor to.—Most Rev. THOMAS L. GRACE, O.P., D.D., succeeded to the See of St. Paul, July 31, 1884; appt. Archbishop, May 15, 1888; died Sept. 25, 1918.—Most Rev. AUSTIN DOWLING, D.D., Archbishop of St. Paul; ord. June 24, 1891; appt. Bishop of Des Moines, Iowa, Jan. 31, 1912; cons. April 25, 1912 Nominated Archbishop of St. Paul, Feb. 1, 1919; died Nov. 29, 1930.—Most Rev. JOHN GREGORY MURRAY, S.T.D., ord. April 14, 1900; appt. Titular Bishop of Flavias, Auxiliary to the Bishop of Hartford, Nov. 15, 1919; cons. April 28, 1920; transferred to the Diocese of Portland, May 29, 1925; appt. Archbishop of St. Paul, Oct. 29, 1931; died Oct. 11, 1956.—Most Rev. WILLIAM O. BRADY, D.D., Archbishop of St. Paul; ord. Dec. 21, 1923; appt. Bishop of Sioux Falls, June 10, 1939; cons. Aug. 24, 1939; appt. Titular Archbishop of Selymbria and Coadjutor "cum jure successionis" of St. Paul, June 16, 1956; succeeded to See, Oct. 11, 1956; died Oct. 1, 1961.—Most Rev. LEO C. BYRNE, D.D., Coadjutor Archbishop "cum jure successionis" of Saint Paul and Minneapolis; ord. June 10, 1933; appt. titular Bishop of Sabidia and Auxiliary of St. Louis, May 21, 1954 cons. June 29, 1954; transferred to Wichita, "cum jure successionis" 1961; appt. Apostolic Administrator of Wichita, Feb. 25, 1963; promoted to St. Paul and Minneapolis, Aug. 2, 1967; died Oct. 21, 1974.—Most Rev. LEO BINZ, D.D., ord. March 15, 1924; appt. Titular Bishop of Pinara and Coadjutor Bishop of Winona, Nov. 21, 1942; cons. Dec. 21, 1942; Titular Archbishop of Silyum and Coadjutor to the Archbishop of Dubuque "cum jure successionis," Oct. 15, 1949; Archbishop of Dubuque, Dec. 2, 1954; appt. Archbishop of Saint Paul, Dec. 16, 1961; resigned May 21, 1975; died Oct. 9, 1979.—Most Rev. JOHN R. ROACH, D.D., Archbishop of St. Paul and Minneapolis; ord. June 8, 1946; appt. Titular Bishop of Cenae and Auxiliary Bishop of St. Paul and Minneapolis, July 12, 1971; cons. Sept. 8, 1971; appt. Archbishop of St. Paul and Minneapolis, May 21, 1975; resigned Sept. 8, 1995.

Chancery—226 Summit Ave., St. Paul, 55102. Tel: 612-291-4400; Fax: 612-290-1629. Office Hours: Mon.-Fri. 9-5 All Official business should be directed to this office.

Vicar General and Moderator of the Curia—Rev. KEVIN M. MCDONOUGH, J.C.D.
Vicar General—Most Rev. LAWRENCE H. WELSH.
Chancellor for Civil Affairs—Mr. WILLIAM S. FALLON, J.D.
Chancellor for Canonical Affairs—Sr. M. DOMINICA BRENNAN, O.P., J.C.L.
Vice Chancellor—Rev. AUSTIN T. WARD.
Assistant Chancellor—Bro. VINCENT H. CHAMPINE, O.P.
Delegate for Marriage Dispensations—Bro. VINCENT H. CHAMPINE, O.P.

Episcopal Vicars—
For Eastern Vicariate—Rev. KEVIN M. MCDONOUGH, J.C.D.
For Western Vicariate—Most Rev. LAWRENCE H. WELSH.
For Southern Vicariate—Most Rev. HARRY J. FLYNN.
For Hispanic Vicariate—Most Rev. LAWRENCE H. WELSH.
For Canonical Affairs—Rev. KEVIN M. MCDONOUGH, J.C.D.
For African-American Catholics—Rev. KEVIN M. MCDONOUGH, J.C.D.
For Retired Priests—Rev. CHARLES M. EGGERT.
For Marriages—Revs. KEVIN M. MCDONOUGH, J.C.D.; AUSTIN T. WARD.
Vicar for Religious—Sr. DORIS RAUENHORST, O.P.

Archdiocesan Divisions—
Administration and Financial Services—Rev. AUSTIN T. WARD, Dir.
Christian Formation and Education—THOMAS MCCARVER, Dir.
Ministry Personnel—
Outreach—Mrs. JANET KROCHESKI, Dir.
Community Services—Rev. Msgr. J. JEROME BOXLEITNER, Dir.
Resource Development—JAMES MULLIN, Dir.
Due Process Dir.—Sr. M. DOMINICA BRENNAN, O.P., J.C.L.
Administrative Asst. to the Vicar General and to the Moderator of the Curia—Mrs. JUDY DELANEY.
Special Asst. to Archbishop Flynn—Mr. MERTON J. LASSONDE.
Archivist—Mr. STEVEN T. GRANGER; Mr. PATRICK ANZELC, Asst.
Controller—Mr. THOMAS J. BAKER.
Assistant Controller—Mr. SCOTT J. DOMEIER.
Department of Human Resources, Pension Plan, General Insurance Program and Personnel Director—Deacon WILLIAM G. UMPHRESS.

Metropolitan Tribunal—328 W. Kellogg Blvd., St. Paul, 55102-1997. Tel: 612-291-4466.
Judicial Vicar—Rev. JOSEPH L. WAJDA, J.C.L.
Adjutant Judicial Vicars—Revs. RONALD J. BOWERS, J.C.D; KEVIN M. MCDONOUGH, J.C.D.

Associate Judges—Rev. Msgr. WILLIAM BAUMGAERTNER; Rev. Msgr. ELLSWORTH KNEAL, J.C.D.; Revs. LEO J. TIBESAR, M.A.; MICHAEL V. TEGEDER; Deacon PAUL W. CARLSON; Sr. DOMINICA BRENNAN, O.P., J.C.L.; Mrs. RUTH DUHAMEL, J.C.L.; Mrs. MARILIES YOUNG, J.U.D.
Defenders of the Bond—Revs. JEROME W. FEHN; LAWRENCE R. JOHNSON; ROBERT B. WELLISCH; Deacon JOHN J. SALCHERT; Bro. VINCENT H. CHAMPINE, O.P.; Mr. ROBERT MANUELE, J.D.
Ecclesiastical Attorneys—Rev. PATRICK J. WALL, O.S.B.
Ecclesiastical Notaries—Mrs. LINDA BOTKIN; Mrs. KAREN NEDEAU.

Archdiocesan Consultors—Most Rev. LAWRENCE H. WELSH; Rev. Msgr. RICHARD E. PATES; Revs. GEORGE J. GRAFSKY; KEVIN M. MCDONOUGH, J.C.D.; JOSEPH J. ARACKAL, V.C.; A. MICHAEL SAUBER; ROBERT T. CASSIDY; PETER C. WITTMAN.

Presbyteral Council—Most Rev. HARRY J. FLYNN; Most Rev. LAWRENCE H. WELSH; Rev. Msgr. RICHARD E. PATES; Revs. KEVIN M. MCDONOUGH, J.C.D.; TIMOTHY J. WOZNIAK, Exec. Dir. MICHAEL J. KRENIK; JEROME F. KEISER; JOSEPH H. HITPAS, O.M.I.; THOMAS H. BRIOSCHI; FREDERICK F. CAMPBELL; JOSEPH J. ARACKAL, V.C.; GEORGE J. GRAFSKY; THOMAS M. KOMMERS; ROBERT T. CASSIDY; CHARLES L. FROEHLE; HAROLD J. TASTO; ROBERT L. HAZEL; LEO J. TIBESAR; MARTIN B. SHALLBETTER; PETER F. CHRISTENSEN; CHARLES M. EGGERT.

Corporate Board—Most Rev. HARRY J. FLYNN; Most Rev. LAWRENCE H. WELSH; Revs. KEVIN M. MCDONOUGH, J.C.D.; AUSTIN T. WARD; Rev. Msgr. AMBROSE V. HAYDEN; THOMAS HOLLORAN; MARY FREY; CHERYL O'SHAUGHNESSY; JERRY HALLORAN; WILLIAM S. FALLON.

Censores Librorum—Rev. FREDERICK F. CAMPBELL, Chm., Bd., *St. John the Evangelist, Hopkins, 55343.* Rev. Msgr. RICHARD J. SCHULER; Revs. DENNIS J. DEASE; CHARLES L. FROEHLE; JAMES A. LAVIN; DAVID W. SMITH; ARTHUR L. KENNEDY.

Archdiocesan Offices and Directors

Advisory Board on Natural Family Planning—Deacon JAMES F. BASKFIELD, Liaison, *328 W. Kellogg Blvd., St. Paul, 55102.* Tel: 612-291-4438.

Allocations Committee—Rev. AUSTIN T. WARD, Dir., *226 Summit Ave., St. Paul, 55102.* Tel: 612-291-4400.

Apostleship of Prayer—Rev. Msgr. CLARENCE J. STEINER, *324 S. Prior Ave., St. Paul, 55105.*

Archbishop Ireland Educational Fund, Inc.—Most Rev. HARRY J. FLYNN, D.D., Pres., *226 Summit Ave., St. Paul, 55102.*

Archdiocesan AIDS Ministry Office—Sr. JOANNE LUCID, B.V.M., Dir., *Riverside Medical Center, Riverside at 25th Ave. S., Minneapolis, 55454.* Tel: 612-672-4345.

Archdiocesan Council of Catholic Women—Rev. Msgr. JAMES D. HABIGER, Moderator; ELAINE MONITOR, Pres., *328 W. Kellogg Blvd., St. Paul, 55102.* Tel: 612-291-4545.

Archdiocesan Director of Youth—Mr. GREGORY WEINAND.

Archdiocesan Finance Council—Deacon THOMAS DOLAN, Chm., *226 Summit Ave., St. Paul, 55102.* Tel: 612-291-4492.

Building Commission—Rev. Msgr. AMBROSE V. HAYDEN, Coord., *226 Summit Ave., St. Paul, 55102.*

Campus Ministry—Rev. GREGORY TOLAAS, Dir., *University of St. Thomas, 2115 Summit Ave., P.O. Box 5028, St. Paul, 55105.*

Catholic Youth Ministry Services—Mr. GREGORY WEINAND, Dir., *328 W. Kellogg Blvd., St. Paul, 55102.* Tel: 612-290-1644.

Catholic Center for the Separated and Divorced—STEVE KING, Dir., *215 Old Sixth St., St. Paul, 55102.* Tel: 612-222-3001.

Catholic Charities—Rev. Msgr. J. JEROME BOXLEITNER, Dir.; Rev. LARRY SNYDER, Assoc. Dir., *404 S. 8th St., Minneapolis, 55404.* Tel: 612-340-7500.

Catholic Commission on Social Justice—JULIE SMENDZIOL-O'BRIEN, Chm. RON KRIETEMEYER, Dir., *328 W. Kellogg Blvd., St. Paul, 55102.* Tel: 612-291-4477.

Catholic Committee on Scouting—Deacon DONALD RINKENBERGER, Church of St. Joseph the Worker: *Maple Grove, 55369.* Tel: 612-559-9178.

Catholic Education and Formation Ministries—THOMAS MCCARVER, Dir., *328 W. Kellogg Blvd., St. Paul, 55102.* Tel: 612-291-4500.

Cemeteries—Mr. JOHN CHEREK, Dir., *400 Selby Ave., St. Paul, 55102.* Tel: 612-228-9991.

Center for Ministry—Sr. FRAN DONNELLY, B.V.M., Dir., *244 Dayton Ave., St. Paul, 55102.* Tel: 612-290-1616.

Charismatic Renewal Office—COLIN LAVERGNE, Dir., *3927 E. Lake, Minneapolis, 55406.* Tel: 612-721-2543.

Christ Child Services, Inc.—226 Summit Ave., St. Paul, 55102. Tel: 612-291-4400.

Christian Sharing Fund—SARA MCGRATH JOHNSON, *328 W. Kellogg Blvd., St. Paul, 55102.* Tel: 612-291-4477.

Commission on Bio-Medical Ethics—Dr. RICHARD BERQUIST, Chm., *University of St. Thomas, 2115 Summit Ave., St. Paul, 55105.* Tel: 612-647-5000.

Commission on Chemical Health—Rev. BRYAN O'ROURKE, Chm., *Church of St. Mary of the Lake, 105 N. Forestview Ln., Plymouth, 55441.* Tel: 612-545-1447.

Commission on Women—PHYLLIS A. WILLERSCHEIDT, Exec. Coord., *328 W. Kellogg Blvd., St. Paul, 55102.* Tel: 612-291-4495.

Commission for Black Catholics—HERBERT GIBBS, Chm.; Sr. SHARON M. HOWELL, C.S.J., Exec. Sec., *2115 Summit Ave., Mail #5006, St. Paul, 55105.* Tel: 612-962-6462.

Commission for Ecumenism and Interreligious Affairs—Rev. ARTHUR L. KENNEDY, Chm., *University of St. Thomas, 2115 Sumit Ave., P.O. Box 5022, St. Paul, 55105.* Tel: 612-647-5300.

Commission for Family Life—Deacon JAMES F. BASKFIELD, Exec. Sec., *328 W. Kellogg Blvd., St. Paul, 55102.* Tel: 612-291-4438.

Commission on Pastoral Health Care—Sr. MARY HEINEN, C.S.J., Chm., *1884 Randolph Ave., St. Paul, 55105.* Tel: 612-690-7028.

Commission on Ministry—PATTI BRADY, Chm., *244 Dayton Ave., St. Paul, 55102.* Tel: 612-290-1616.

Common Bond Communities—Mr. JOSEPH A.L. ERRIGO, JR., Pres., *328 W. Kellogg Blvd., St.Paul, 55102.* Tel: 612-291-1750.

Communications Office—TIMOTHY ANDERSON, Acting Dir., *226 Summit Ave., St. Paul, 55102.* Tel: 612-291-4411.

Consultation Services Center for Priests, Brothers and Sisters—Sr. DOLORE ROCKERS, O.S.F., Ph.D., Dir., *633 N. Snelling Ave., St. Paul, 55104.* Tel: 612-644-0112.

Council of Religious—Sr. DORIS RAUENHORST, O.P., Ex-Officio, *244 Dayton Ave., St. Paul, 55102.*

Cursillo—Rev. EUGENE POULIOT, Spiritual Advisor; AL SCHROEDER, Lay Dir. MARY SCHROEDER, Lay Dir., *1575 W. 200th St., Jordan, 55352.* Tel: 612-492-6257.

Holy Childhood, Pontifical Association—Deacon LAWRENCE J. SWIRTZ, Dir., *328 W. 6th St., St. Paul, 55102.*

Legion of Mary—St. Paul Curia and Comitium, Rev. Msgr. RICHARD J. SCHULER, *548 Lafond Ave., St. Paul, 55103.* Tel: 612-293-1710. North Minneapolis Curia, Rev. FRANCIS L. FRIED, *1315 2nd St. N.E., Minneapolis, 55413.* Tel: 612-379-9736. South Minneapolis Curia, Rev. MICHAEL SAUBER, *535 S. Lewis St., Shakopee, 55379.* Tel: 612-445-1319.

Marriage Encounter—JEANNE STOESSEL, Exec. Dir., *953 Lake Dr., St. Paul, 55120.* Tel: 612-454-3238.

Migration and Refugee Services—Mr. THOMAS KOSEL, Admin., *215 Old Sixth St., St. Paul, 55102.* Tel: 612-222-3001.

Ministry to Hmong—Rev. ROBERT B. WELLISCH; Deacon VA THAI LO, *Twin Cities Hmong Catholic Community, 68 W. Exchange St., St. Paul, 55102.* Tel: 612-771-4644.

Ministry to Koreans—Rev. ANDREW LIM, *Church of St. Andrew Kim, 1449 Cleveland Ave., St. Paul, 55108.* Tel: 612-642-9822.

Ministry to Vietnamese—Rev. MATTHIAS CHUONG, C.M.C., *Church of St. Joseph Hien, 1800 Dupont Ave. N., Minneapolis, 55411.* Tel: 612-522-5006.

Nazareth Hall College and Seminary, Inc.—Most Rev. HARRY J. FLYNN, D.D., Pres.

Newman Centers—University of Minnesota, Minneapolis and St. Paul Campus, Rev. STEPHEN BOSSI, C.S.P., Dir., *1701 University Ave. S.E., Minneapolis, 55414.* Tel: 612-331-3437. Hamline University, Macalster College, St. Olaf College, Rev. DAVID HASCHKA, S.J., Campus Min., *1550 Summit Ave., St. Paul, 55105.* Tel: 612-644-9041.

Newspaper—"The Catholic Bulletin"; Mr. DENNIS W. HEANEY, Publisher/Gen. Mgr.; Mr. ROBERT ZYSKOWSKI, Editor, *244 Dayton Ave., St. Paul, 55102.* Tel: 612-291-4444.

Office of the Deaf—Rev. WILLIAM J. KENNEY, *701 Fillmore St. N.E., Minneapolis, 55413.* Tel: 612-623-4019; 378-1344 (TTD).

Office of Indian Ministry—Rev. JAMES C. NOTEBAART, Dir., *3045 Park Ave., Minneapolis, 55407.* Tel: 612-824-7616.

Office for Social Justice—Mr. RON KRIETEMEYER, Admin., *328 W. Kellogg Blvd., St. Paul, 55102.* Tel: 612-291-4477.

Office of Due Process—Sr. M. DOMINICA BRENNAN, O.P., J.C.L., Dir., *226 Summit Ave., St. Paul, 55102.* Tel: 612-291-4437.

Office of Ecumenism—Rev. ARTHUR L. KENNEDY, Ecumenical Officer, *University of St. Thomas, 2115 Summit Ave., P.O. Box 5022, St. Paul, 55105.* Tel: 612-962-5050.

Office of Evangelization—Rev. MARTIN M.P. FLEMING, *328 W. Kellogg Blvd., St. Paul, 55102.* Tel: 612-291-4488.

Office of Human Resources—Deacon WILLIAM G. UMPHRESS, Dir., *328 W. Kellogg Blvd., St. Paul, 55102.* Tel: 612-291-4499.

Office of Pastoral Planning—Mr. ROBERT J. BURKE, Dir., *328 W. Kellogg Blvd., St. Paul, 55102.* Tel: 612-291-4544.

Office of Presbyteral Personnel Resources—Rev. PAUL JAROSZESKI, Exec. Sec., *226 Summit Ave., St. Paul, 55102.* Tel: 612-291-4430.

Parish Pastoral Council Assistance Center—Mr. ROBERT J. BURKE, Dir., *328 W. Kellogg Blvd., St. Paul, 55102.* Tel: 612-291-4544.

Pastoral Council—Most Rev. HARRY J. FLYNN, D.D., Chm.; Mr. MERTON J. LASSONDE, Exec. Sec., *226 Summit Ave., St. Paul, 55102.* Tel: 612-291-4400.

Permanent Deacon Assembly—Deacon DANIEL D. KIRCHOFFNER, Pres., *2220 Summit Ave., St. Paul, 55105.* Tel: 612-962-6875.

Permanent Deacon Office—Deacon PETER A. D'HEILLY, Dir., *2220 Summit Ave., St. Paul, 55105.* Tel: 612-962-6875.

Presbyteral Council—Rev. PETER WITTMAN, Exec. Dir., *226 Summit Ave., St. Paul, 55102.* Tel: 612-291-4400.

Propagation of the Faith—Deacon LAWRENCE J. SWIRTZ, Dir., *328 W. Kellogg Blvd., St. Paul, 55102.* Tel: 612-222-6556.

Resource Development Office—Mr. JAMES MULLIN, Dir., *328 W. Kellogg Blvd., St. Paul, 55102.* Tel: 612-290-1610.
Annual Catholic Appeal—MARY NICHOLSON, Dir.
Endowment Campaign—Mr. JAMES MULLIN, Consultant.

Respect Life—Mrs. JANET KROCHESKI, Dir., *328 W. Kellogg Blvd., St. Paul, 55102.* Tel: 612-291-4505.

Rural Life Conference—Mr. DALE R. HENNEN, *105 3rd*

St. N.W., Montgomery, 56069. Tel: 612-364-7323.

Sacerdotal Union of Daily Adoration—Rev. ALBERT F. BYRNE, *2590 Margaret St., N. St. Paul, 55109.*

Seton Center—MICHELLE BAILEY, Admin., *Spruce Tree Center, Ste. 400, 1600 University Ave., St. Paul, 55104.* Tel: 612-641-1180. Outpatient social and medical services for unwed women and young couples.

Society of St. Vincent De Paul, Archdiocesan Council—Ms. BERNICE MARUSKA, Pres., *1008 Arcade St., St. Paul, 55102.* Tel: 612-771-0358.

To Encounter Christ (TEC)—PAM GEEMSCHEID DEMORETT, Coord., *1201 S.E. 5th St., Minneapolis, 55414.* Tel: 612-331-3644.

Venezuelan Missions—Revs. MARK DOSH; PATRICK J. RYAN; DENNIS DEMPSEY, *El Buen Pastor Parroquia San Francisco de Asis, Apartado 272, Puerto Ordaz, Estado Bolivar, Venezuela, 8015.*

Vocation Office—Dir., Vocations: Revs. STAN P. MADER; JOHN L. UBEL, *2220 Summit Ave., St. Paul, 55105.* Tel: 612-962-6890.

Worship Board—Mr. FRANK WINKELS, Chm., *244 Dayton Ave., St. Paul, 55102.* Tel: 612-290-1625.

Worship Center—VICKI KLIMA, Dir.; Mr. MICHAEL SILHAVY, Assoc. Dir., Music, *244 Dayton Ave., St. Paul, 55102.* Tel: 612-290-1625.

CLERGY, PARISHES, MISSIONS AND PAROCHIAL SCHOOLS

METROPOLITAN ST. PAUL
(Ramsey County)

1—CATHEDRAL OF ST. PAUL (1850), Revs. John Estrem, Rector; Timothy L. Norris.
Res., 239 Selby Ave., 55102. Tel: 612-228-1766.

2—ASSUMPTION (1856) (German), Rev. John M. Malone.
Res., 51 W. Seventh St., 55102. Tel: 612-224-7536; Fax: 612-224-8514.

3—BLESSED SACRAMENT (1916), Revs. Thomas R. McDonough; Orlando Tatel.
Res., 1801 La Crosse Ave., 55119. Tel: 612-735-3707; Fax: 612-578-1125.
School—1800 Ames Ave., 55119. Tel: 612-735-3676.
Lay Teachers 9; Students 128.
Catechesis/Religious Programs—977 E. 5th St., 55106. Tel: 612-771-9152.
Students 150.

4—HOLY CHILDHOOD (1946), Rev. Gordon M. Doffing.
Res., 1457 Midway Pkwy., 55108. Tel: 612-644-7495.
School—1435 Midway Pkwy., 55108. Tel: 612-644-2791. Sharon Brennan, Prin.
Sisters 3; Lay Teachers 10; Students 149.
Catechesis/Religious Programs—Tel: 612-644-5645. Sr. Thelma Vetsch, S.S.N.D., D.R.E.
Students 23.

5—HOLY SPIRIT (1936), Rev. Michael L. Papesh; Deacons William Umphress; W. Richard Barrett.
Res., 512 S. Albert St., 55105. Tel: 612-698-3353; Fax: 612-698-1605.
School—1406 Randolph Ave., 55105. Tel: 612-698-7233. Brigid M. O'Donnell, Faith Formation Dir.
Catechesis/Religious Programs—Tel: 612-699-7258; Fax: 612-698-1605.
Students 388.

6—THE IMMACULATE HEART OF MARY (1949), Rev. Charles F. Burns, S.J.; Sr. Mary Claire Inhofer, O.S.B., Pastoral Assoc. In res., Revs. David J. Haschka, S.J. Tel: 612-644-9041; Richard M. Rice, S.J. Tel: 612-644-9024; Robert F. O'Connor, S.J. Tel: 612-644-9018; Philip Dreckman, S.J. Tel: 612-646-2938.
Office: Tel: 612-699-7722; Fax: 612-642-5103.
Res., 1550 Summit Ave., 55105. Tel: 612-644-5458.
School—IHM-St. Luke. See St. Luke, St. Paul for details. Tel: 612-224-4836.

7—MATERNITY OF THE BLESSED VIRGIN (1949), Revs. John G. Donahue; Francis R. Dudley.
Res., 1414 N. Dale St., 55117. Tel: 612-489-8825; Fax: 612-488-4055.
School—Maternity of Mary-St. Andrew, 592 Arlington Ave., 55117. Tel: 612-489-1459.
Sisters 1; Lay Teachers 22; Students 307.
Catechesis/Religious Programs—Tel: 612-489-8827; Fax: 612-488-4055. Mary Weyandt, D.R.E.
Students 193.

8—THE NATIVITY OF OUR LORD (1922), Rev. Patrick D. Lannan; Rev. Msgr. Clarence J. Steiner; Revs. John W. Kelley; William Baer; Richard C. O'Connor (NU); Deacon Gerald L. Devine.
Office: 1900 Wellesley, 55105. Tel: 612-696-5401; Fax: 612-696-5458.
School—1900 Stanford Ave., 55105. Tel: 612-699-1311; Fax: 612-696-5420.
Sisters of St. Joseph 1; Lay Teachers 38; Students 810. Principals: Mrs. Margo Weiberg; Kate Wollan.
Catechesis/Religious Programs—Tel: 612-696-5454; Fax: 612-696-5458.
Students 100.

9—OUR LADY OF GUADALUPE (1931) (Mexican), Rev. Hugo L. Montero.
Res., 401 Concord Street, 55107. Tel: 612-228-0506.
Catechesis/Religious Programs—Students 212.

10—SACRED HEART (1881) (German), Revs. John Dombrowski, O.F.M.; Alois Gabrus, O.F.M.; Deacon Wayne Wittman. In res., Revs. Fabian F. Burdiek, O.F.M.; Nicholas W. Meyer, O.F.M.; Michael Cusato, O.F.M.; William Schmidt, O.F.M.; Bros. Gary Jeriha, O.F.M.; Robert Gross, O.F.M.; Francis Gonser, O.F.M.; Lester Kochlin, O.F.M.; Michaek Luke Ubben, O.F.M.
Res., 840 E. Sixth St., 55106. Tel: 612-776-2741; Fax: 612-776-2743.
School—Trinity Catholic School. (South Campus). Collaborative School with St. Patrick & St. Casimir Parishes in St. Paul. 835 E. Fifth St., 55106. Tel: 612-776-2773; Fax: 612-776-2764.
Catechesis/Religious Programs—Tel: 612-774-7505. Janet Rogalla, D.R.E.
Students 236.

11—ST. ADALBERT (1881) (Polish-Vietnamese), Revs. Timothy J. Kernan; Peter Quangle; Deacon Bill Falvey; Maggie Rein, Pastoral Assoc. In res., Revs. Peter Quang Le; Michael J. Stevens.
Res., 265 Charles Ave., 55103. Tel: 612-228-9002.
Catechesis/Religious Programs—Tel: 612-228-9002.
Students 61.
Frogtown Resource Center—262 Edmund Ave., 55103. Tel: 612-293-1931.

12—ST. AGNES (1887) (German), Rev. Msgr. Richard J. Schuler. Rev. Robert J. Altier; Deacons Jerome J. Bilder; Harold Hughesdon; Bernard Pedersen.
Res., 548 Lafond Ave., 55103. Tel: 612-293-1710; Fax: 612-227-4229.
School—530 Lafond Ave., 55103. Tel: 612-227-1886. Mr. John Boone, Prin.
Sisters of Notre Dame 2; Lay Teachers 14; Students 257.
High School—Tel: 612-228-1161. Mr. William Peper, Prin.
Sisters of Notre Dame 1; Lay Teachers 22; Students 334.
Catechesis/Religious Programs—Students 70.

13—ST. AMBROSE (1915) (Italian), Rev. Thomas J. Pingatore.
Res., 711 Bradley St., 55101. Tel: 612-776-4957.
Catechesis/Religious Programs—Tel: 612-483-1910. Jeanne Kelcher, D.R.E.
Students 55.

14—ST. ANDREW (1895), Rev. Roger F. Carroll; Deacon Thomas Konkel.
Res., 1051 Como Ave., 55103. Tel: 612-488-6775.
School—Maternity of Mary/St. Andrew. Consolidated. See Maternity of the Blessed Virgin for details. Tel: 612-489-1459.

15—ST. ANDREW KIM (1990) (Korean), Rev. Andrew Lim (Korea).
Res., 1449 N. Cleveland Ave., 55108. Tel: 612-642-9822; Fax: 612-642-0140. [JC]

16—ST. BERNARD (1890) (German), Revs. Michael F. Anderson; Jose Gutierrez; Stanley V. Sledz; Deacon Sonny Laqui.
Res., 197 W. Geranium Ave., 55117. Tel: 612-488-6733; Fax: 612-488-9466.
Childcare Center—(33 Months thru Kindergarten). 1160 Woodbridge St., 55117. Tel: 612-489-9203; Fax: 612-488-9466. Victoria Aulik, Dir.
Lay Teachers 7; Students 30.
School—(Grades PreK-8) 180 W. Rose Ave., 55117. Tel: 612-489-8086. Dennis Donovan, Prin.
Lay Teachers 20; Students 300.
High School—170 W. Rose Ave., 55117. Tel: 612-489-1338. John O'Neill, Prin.
Lay Teachers 23; Students 370.

17—ST. CASIMIR (1892) (Polish), Rev. Patrick T. Casey; Teresa Borer, Pastoral Musician; Tony Schreiner, Business Mgr.
Res., 934 E. Geranium Ave., 55106. Tel: 612-774-0365; Fax: 612-774-0508.
School—Trinity Catholic School. Collaborative School with St. Patrick & Sacred Heart Parishes in St. Paul. Tel: 612-776-5169; Fax: 612-774-9943.
Catechesis/Religious Programs—Tel: 612-776-5641.
Students 179.

18—ST. CECILIA (1912), Rev. Paul A. Jaroszeski.
Res., 2357 Bayless Pl., 55114. Tel: 612-644-4502; Fax: 612-647-1445.

19—ST. COLUMBA, Revs. Paul A. LaFontaine; Thomas Tam (Vietnam).
Res., 1327 Lafond Ave., 55104. Tel: 612-645-9179; Fax: 612-645-9170.
School—1330 Blair Ave., 55104. Tel: 612-644-1807.
Lay Teachers 12; Students 250.

20—ST. FRANCIS DE SALES (1884) (German), Rev. James P. Burns. In res., Rev. Karl M. Wittman, (Retired).
Res., 650 Palace Ave., 55102-3593. Tel: 612-228-1169; Fax: 612-224-7744.
School—St. Francis-St. James United School, 426 S. Osceola St., 55102. Tel: 612-228-1167; Fax: 612-228-0169.
Sisters of Notre Dame 3; Lay Teachers 18; Students 235.

21—ST. GREGORY THE GREAT (1951), Revs. Thomas P. Hunstiger; Gerald G. Grieman.
Parish Center: Tel: 612-698-1745; Fax: 612-699-5151.
Res., 1668 Montreal Ave., 55116-2499. Tel: 612-698-9794; Fax: 612-699-5151.
School—Highland Catholic School. See listing under Institutions located in the Archdiocese for details. Tel: 612-690-2477; Fax: 612-699-1869.
Catechesis/Religious Programs—1668 Montreal Ave., 55116. Tel: 612-698-1745; Fax: 612-699-5151.
Students 160.

22—ST. JAMES (1887), Rev. John E. Mitchell.
Res., 496 View St., 55102. Tel: 612-227-7029.
School—St. Francis-St. James United School, (Grades K-8). See St. Francis De Sales for details. Tel: 612-228-1167.
Catechesis/Religious Programs—Tel: 612-222-3959.
Students 240.

23—ST. JOHN OF ST. PAUL (1886) (Irish), Rev. Joseph P. Fink. In res., Rev. Richard M. Hogan.
Res., 977 E. Fifth St., 55106. Tel: 612-771-3690; Fax: 612-771-7919.
Catechesis/Religious Programs—Blessed Sacrament School. Blessed Sacrament and St. John's combine religious education. 1800 Ames Ave., 55106. Tel: 612-735-3676.
Students 155.

24—ST. LEO (1945), Revs. Gerald G. Grieman; Thomas P. Hunstiger; Deacons Richard Stevenson; Gerald Scherkenbach.
Res., 2055 Bohland Ave., 55116. Tel: 612-698-5581; Fax: 612-698-9526.
School—Highland Catholic School. See listing under Institutions located in the Archdiocese for details. Tel: 612-690-2477; Fax: 612-699-1869.
Catechesis/Religious Programs—Highland Catholic Community, 1668 Montreal Ave., Tel: 612-698-5583; Fax: 612-698-9526.
Students 282.

25—ST. LOUIS KING OF FRANCE (1868) (French), Revs. Paul F. Morrissey, S.M.; James D. Duffy, S.M.
Res., 506 Cedar St., 55101. Tel: 612-224-3379; Fax: 612-224-0017.

26—ST. LUKE (1888), Rev. David Haschka, S.J.; Deacon Thomas Dzik.
Center: 1079 Summit Ave., 55105. Tel: 612-227-7669; Fax: 612-227-0847.
School—IHM-St. Luke, 1065 Summit Ave., 55105. Tel: 612-224-4836; Fax: 612-224-0097.
Sisters 2; Lay Teachers 23; Students 397.
Catechesis/Religious Programs—Students 172.

27—ST. MARK (1889), Revs. Jerome F. Keiser; Stan Mader; Deacon Robert Conlin. In res., Rev. Anthony Andrade, O.S.B.
Res., 2001 Dayton Ave., 55104. Tel: 612-645-5717.
School—1983 Dayton Ave., 55104. Tel: 612-644-3380; Fax: 612-644-1923.
Sisters 2; Lay Teachers 22; Students 443.

28—ST. MARY (1865), Revs. Joseph Hitpas, O.M.I.; Daniel Taillez, O.M.I., (France) Hmong Chap.; Joseph Menker, O.M.I., Chap., Ramsey Hospital; Robert Allie, O.M.I., Chap., Ramsey Hospital.
Res., 261 E. 8th St., 55101. Tel: 612-222-2619.

29—ST. MATTHEW (1886) (German), Revs. Stephen J. Adrian; Martin L. Warren (England); Deacon John Murphy.
Church—490 Hall Ave, 55107. Tel: 612-224-9793; Fax: 612-292-0925.
Res., 507 Hall Ave., 55107. Tel: 612-224-1037.
School—497 Humboldt Ave., 55107. Tel: 612-224-6912. Sr. Leonius Skarr, O.P., Prin.
Sisters 1; Lay Teachers 15; Students 220.

30—ST. PASCAL BAYLON (1946), Rev. Thomas H. Brioschi; Deacons Joseph Schmitz; Richard Pashby.
Res., 1757 Conway St., 55106. Tel: 612-774-1585; Fax: 612-774-9152.
School—1770 E. 3rd St., 55106. Tel: 612-776-0092.
Sisters 2; Lay Teachers 21; Students 434.
Catechesis/Religious Programs—Tel: 612-774-0655.
Students 178.

31—ST. PATRICK (1884), Rev. Jerome B. Hackenmueller.
Res., 1095 De Soto St., 55101. Tel: 612-774-8675; Fax: 612-774-9106.

School—Trinity Catholic School - North & South Campus. Collaborative School with St. Patrick, St. Casimir & Sacred Heart Parishes in St. Paul. Tel: 612-776-2763 (South); 776-5169 (North); Fax: 612-774-9943 (North); 776-2764 (South).

32—St. Peter Claver (1892) (African American), Rev. Kevin M. McDonough.
Res., 375 N. Oxford St., 55104. Tel: 612-646-1797.

33—St. Stanislaus (1872) (Czech), Rev. John C. Clay.
Res., 398 Superior St., 55102. Tel: 612-292-0303.
Catechesis/Religious Programs—395 Superior St., 55102. Tel: 612-292-1913.
Students 164.

34—Highland Catholic Community (1926). Consolidation of St. Therese, St. Leo, and St. Gregory. Revs. Thomas P. Hunstiger, Co-Pastor; Gerald G. Grieman, Co-Pastor.
Parish Center—1850 Mississippi River Blvd. S., 55116-2644. Tel: 612-698-3371; Fax: 612-698-8042.
School—Highland Catholic School. See listing under Institutions located in the Archdiocese for details. Tel: 612-690-2477; Fax: 612-699-1869.
Catechesis/Religious Programs—Tel: 612-698-5583; Fax: 612-698-9526.
Students 72.

35—St. Thomas The Apostle (1954), Rev. Richard P. Wirth; Deacon Ervin Barrett.
Res., 2119 Stillwater Ave., 55119. Tel: 612-738-0677.
Catechesis/Religious Programs—Tel: 612-738-2995.
Students 219.

36—St. Vincent de Paul (1888), Rev. Chue Ying Vang; Deacon Va Thai Lo.
Res., 651 Virginia St., 55103. Tel: 612-488-6737; Fax: 612-487-6790. [CEM]

OUTSIDE METROPOLITAN ST. PAUL

Cottage Grove, Washington Co., St. Rita (1966), Rev. Thomas P. Fitzgerald; Deacons Jack Nicklay; Steve Koop.
8694 80th St. S., 55016. Tel: 612-459-4596; Fax: 612-459-5364.
Catechesis/Religious Programs—Students 740.

Lake Elmo, Washington Co., Guardian Angels (1885), Revs. Michael M. Arms; Mark J. Underdahl; Sr. Dorothy Mrock, O.S.F.; Deacon Larry Murphy.
Res., 8260 Hudson Blvd., 55042. Tel: 612-738-2223; Fax: 612-738-2453. [CEM]
Catechesis/Religious Programs—Tel: 612-738-2223; Fax: 612-738-2453. Roy Dick, D.R.E.
Students 1,308.

Little Canada, Ramsey Co., St. John the Evangelist (1851), Revs. Robert J. Fitzpatrick; Marc. T. Maus; Sr. Anne Becker, S.S.N.D., Dir. Pastoral Ministry.
Res., 380 Little Canada Rd., St. Paul, 55117. Tel: 612-484-2708; Fax: 612-484-0567. [CEM]
School—2621 McMenemy St., 55117. Tel: 612-484-3038; Fax: 612-484-3187.
Lay Teachers 13; Students 287.
Catechesis/Religious Programs—Tel: 612-484-0048. Jean Conant Winter, D.R.E.
Students 700.

Mahtomedi, Washington Co., St. Jude of the Lake (1939), Rev. Jerry C. Vandrovec.
Res., 700 Mahtomedi Ave., 55115. Tel: 612-426-3245; Fax: 612-426-3246.
School—600 Mahtomedi Ave., 55115. Tel: 612-426-2562. Ann Austin McCormick, Prin.
Lay Teachers 9; Students 223.
Catechesis/Religious Programs—Tel: 612-426-4469.
Students 744.

Maplewood, Ramsey Co., Holy Redeemer (1880) (Italian), Rev. Austin T. Ward.
Res., 2555 Hazelwood Ave., St. Paul, 55109. Tel: 612-777-1321.

Presentation of the Blessed Virgin Mary (1946), Revs. Charles V. Lachowitzer; Gregory J. Schaffer; Deacon Jack Veiman.
Res., 1725 Kennard St., 55109. Tel: 612-777-8116; Fax: 612-777-8743.
School—1695 Kennard St., 55109. Tel: 612-777-5877.
Lay Teachers 21; Students 419.
Catechesis/Religious Programs—Tel: 612-777-6041; Fax: 612-777-8743.
Students 285.

St. Jerome (1940), Rev. Kenneth F. Ludescher.
1894 McMenemy Rd., 55117. Tel: 612-771-1928.
Church—380 Roselawn Ave. E., 55117. Tel: 612-771-1209; Fax: 612-771-3623.
Res., 1725 Kennard, 55109. Tel: 612-771-1209; Fax: 612-771-3623.
School—384 E. Roselawn Ave., 55117. Tel: 612-771-8494.
Lay Teachers 13; Students 245.

Mendota, Dakota Co., St. Peter (1840) (Native American-French-English), Rev. Kevin I. Clinton; Deacon Jim Seaton. In res., Revs. Gilbert J. Gustafson; Richard H. Jeub.
Res., P.O. Box 50679, 55150. Tel: 612-452-4030; Fax: 612-456-0646. [CEM]
Catechesis/Religious Programs—Tel: 612-452-4551; Fax: 612-456-0646. Ellen Casey, D.R.E.
Students 339.

New Brighton, Ramsey Co., St. John the Baptist (1906) (Polish), Revs. William Murtaugh; James M. Grogan; Deacons Joseph McPherson; Russel Evans.
Parish Center—835 2nd Ave., N.W., 55112. Tel: 612-633-8333; Fax: 612-633-7404.
Res., 812 1st Ave., N.W., 55112. [CEM]
School—845 2nd Ave., N.W., 55112. Tel: 612-633-1522.
Sisters 1; Lay Teachers 19; Students 403.
Catechesis/Religious Programs—Tel: 612-633-1540; Fax: 612-633-7404.
Students 530.

North St. Paul, Ramsey Co., St. Peter (1888), Revs. Albert F. Byrne; Stanley Maslowski; George Kolath (India); Deacon James Hepp.
Res., 2590 N. Margaret St., 55109. Tel: 612-777-8304; Fax: 612-777-0497. [CEM]
School—2602 N. Margaret St., 55109. Tel: 612-777-3091; Fax: 612-777-7750.
Sisters 1; Lay Teachers 18; Students 435.
Catechesis/Religious Programs—Tel: 612-777-8304; Fax: 612-777-0497.
Students 420.

Oakdale, Washington Co., Transfiguration (1939), Rev. James D. Smith; Deacon Dan Kirchoffner.
Res., 6133 15th St. N., 55128. Tel: 612-738-2646; Fax: 612-578-8816.
School—935 Ferndale Ave., Maplewood, 55119. Tel: 612-739-0550; Fax: 612-578-2782. Ted Zarembski, Prin.
Lay Teachers 12; Students 258.
Catechesis/Religious Programs—Tel: 612-738-3276. Susan Brady, D.R.E.
Students 850.

Roseville, Ramsey Co., Corpus Christi (1939), Rev. Robert C. Nygaard.
Res., 2131 N. Fairview Ave., 55113-5499. Tel: 612-639-8888; Fax: 612-639-8288.
Catechesis/Religious Programs—Tel: 612-639-8888; Fax: 612-639-8288. D.R.E.: Colleen Ciaccio; Alisa Weber.
Students 253.

St. Rose of Lima (1939), Revs. Walter L. Sochacki; Minh Xuan Vu.
Res., 2048 N. Hamline Ave., 55113. Tel: 612-645-9389; Fax: 612-646-4187.
School—2072 Hamline Ave. N., 55113. Tel: 612-646-3832.
Sisters 3; Lay Teachers 19; Students 333.
Catechesis/Religious Programs—Tel: 612-646-8029; Fax: 612-646-4187. Deb McPherson, D.R.E.
Students 350.

Shoreview, Ramsey Co., St. Odilia (1960), Revs. Richard McGuire, O.S.C.; Jerome Schik, O.S.C.; Marven Tellers, O.S.C.; Deacons John Flood; Jerome Ciresi.
3495 N. Victoria St., 55126. Tel: 612-484-6681; Fax: 612-484-0780.
School—(Grades K-8). Tel: 612-484-3364; Fax: 612-484-0780. Mr. Robert Grose, Prin.
Lay Teachers 31; Students 644.
Catechesis/Religious Programs—Tel: 612-484-2777; Fax: 612-484-0780. Katie Gebhard, D.R.E.
Students 1,165.

West St. Paul, Dakota Co., St. Joseph (1942), Revs. Frederick F. Campbell; Michael J. Miller.
Res., 1154 Seminole Ave., 55118. Tel: 612-457-2781; Fax: 612-451-1272.
School—1138 Seminole Ave., 55118. Tel: 612-457-8550; Fax: 612-451-1272.
Lay Teachers 44; Students 790.
Catechesis/Religious Programs—Tel: 612-457-8841.
Students 285.

St. Michael (1879), Rev. Gerald L. Dvorak.
Res., 337 E. Hurley, 55118. Tel: 612-457-2334; Fax: 612-451-1668.
School—E. Haskell & Sperl, 55118. Tel: 612-457-2510.
Sisters 6; Lay Teachers 9; Students 220.

White Bear Lake, Ramsey Co., St. Mary of the Lake (1881), Rev. Roger P. Pierre; Deacons Sherm Stromen; Joe Thill.
Res., 4741 Bald Eagle Ave., 55110. Tel: 612-429-7771; Fax: 612-429-9539. [CEM]
School—4690 Bald Eagle Ave., 55110. Tel: 612-429-5378. Mary Kane, Prin.
Lay Teachers 10; Students 297.
Catechesis/Religious Programs—Tel: 612-429-8001. D.R.E.: Helen Welter; Mary Beth Jambor.
Students 742.

St. Pius X (1954), Revs. Michael J. Krenik; Mark Shane Wasinger; Deacon Edward F. Feffer.
Res., 3878 Highland Ave., 55110. Tel: 612-429-5337; Fax: 612-429-9359.
School—Tel: 612-429-5338; Fax: 612-429-9359.
Lay Teachers 19; Students 307.
Catechesis/Religious Programs—Tel: 612-429-5994.
Students 326.

METROPOLITAN MINNEAPOLIS
(Hennepin County)

1—The Basilica of St. Mary Co-Cathedral (1907), Revs. Michael O'Connell, Rector; Dale J. Korogi; Deacons George H. Babcock; Del Ferguson; Thomas Kasbohn.
Res., 88 N. 17th St., 55403-1295. Tel: 612-333-1381; Fax: 612-333-7230. [CEM]
Catechesis/Religious Programs—Tel: 612-333-1381; Fax: 612-333-7230.
Students 424.

2—All Saints (1916) (Polish), Rev. George J. Kovalik.
Res., 435 4th St., N.E., 55413. Tel: 612-379-4996.
School—Northeast Regional Catholic School. See Elementary Schools, Consolidated, Parochial under Institutions located in the Archdiocese for details. Tel: 612-789-8851.

3—Annunciation (1922), Rev. Kenneth J. Pierre.
Res., 509 W. 54th St., 55419. Tel: 612-824-0787; Fax: 612-823-8467.
School—525 W. 54th St., 55419. Tel: 612-823-4394.
Sisters 1; Lay Teachers 23; Students 365.

4—Ascension (1890), Rev. Robert L. Hazel. In res., Rev. Luke Mikschl, S.T.
Res., 1723 Bryant Ave., N., 55411. Tel: 612-529-9684; Fax: 612-529-7618.
School—1726 Dupont Ave., N., 55411. Tel: 612-521-3609.
Sisters 3; Lay Teachers 11; Students 230.

5—Christ the King (1938), Rev. John M. Hofstede.
5029 Zenith Ave., S., 55410. Tel: 612-920-5030; Fax: 612-920-1179. [JC]
School—Cooperative program with St. Thomas the Apostle, Minneapolis. Tel: 612-927-8673; 922-0655; Fax: 612-927-7426.

6—Holy Cross (1886) (Polish), Revs. David T. Ostrowski, O.S.B.; Stanislaw Rakiej, S.Ch.
Res., 1621 University Ave., N.E., 55413. Tel: 612-789-7238; Fax: 612-789-5769.
School—Northeast Regional Catholic School. See Elementary Schools, Consolidated, Parochial under Institutions located in the Archdiocese for details. Tel: 612-789-8851; Fax: 612-789-8773.

7—Holy Name (1916), Rev. Ronald E. Clubb.
Res., 3637 11th Ave., S., 55407. Tel: 612-724-5465; Fax: 612-724-5466.
School—Risen Christ Catholic School. See Elementary Schools, Consolidated, Parochial under Institutions located in the Archdiocese for details. Tel: 612-822-5329.

8—Holy Rosary (1878), Revs. Charles M. Santoro, O.P.; Edward W. Leahy, O.P.; Sr. Martha Wiegand, O.P., Pastoral Assoc.; Deacon Thomas E. Dolan.
Res., 2424 18th Ave., S., 55404. Tel: 612-724-3651; Fax: 612-728-8944.
School—Risen Christ Catholic School. See Elementary Schools, Consolidated, Parochial under Institutions located in the Archdiocese for details. Tel: 612-822-5329.
Convent—1614 E. 24th St., 55404. Tel: 612-724-2620.
Dominican Sisters (Sinsinawa, WI) 6.

9—Incarnation (1909), Rev. Robert Monaghan.
Res., 3817 Pleasant Ave., 55409-1296. Tel: 612-822-2101; Fax: 612-822-7928.
School—Risen Christ Catholic School. See Elementary Schools, Consolidated, Parochial under Institutions located in the Archdiocese for details.

10—Our Lady of Lourdes (1877) (French-Canadian), Rev. William J. Ward.
Res., One Lourdes Pl., 55414. Tel: 612-379-2259.
School—Northeast Regional Catholic School. See Elementary Schools, Consolidated, Parochial under the Institutions located in the Archdiocese for details.

11—Our Lady of Mount Carmel (1938) (Italian), Rev. William J. Kenney.
Res., 701 Fillmore St., N.E., 55413. Tel: 612-331-1746; Fax: 612-378-1344.
School—Northeast Regional Catholic School. See Elementary Schools, Consolidated, Parochial under the Institutions located in the Archdiocese for details.

12—Our Lady of Peace (1991), Rev. Msgr. Richard E. Pates; Deacon Jack Weiland.
Res., 5425 11th Ave., S., 55417. Tel: 612-823-8253; Fax: 612-823-5102.
School—5435 11th Ave., S., 55417. Tel: 612-824-3455; Fax: 612-823-5102.
Lay Teachers 23; Students 395.

13—OUR LADY OF PERPETUAL HELP. Closed. For inquiries for parish records contact the Chancery.

14—OUR LADY OF VICTORY (1945), Rev. Terrence M. Hayes.
Res., 5155 Emerson Ave., N., 55430. Tel: 612-529-7788; Fax: 612-529-3343.
Church—52nd and Fremont Aves., 55430.
School—St. Elizabeth Seton, 5140 Fremont Ave., N., 55430. Tel: 612-529-7781.
Sisters 1; Lay Teachers 21; Students 360.
Catechesis/Religious Programs—Tel: 612-287-9180.
Students 140.

15—ST. ALBERT THE GREAT (1935), Rev. Cletus J. Wessels, O.P. In res., Revs. Paul J. Johnson, O.P.; Brendan J. McMullen, O.P.; James R. Motl, O.P.; John G. O'Connell, O.P.; C. A. Kilroy, O.P.; Robert M. Kelly, O.P.; Jay M. Harrington; Joseph E. Bidwill, O.P.; Bro. Vincent H. Champine, O.P. In res., Revs. Edward W. Leahy, O.P.; Charles M. Santoro, O.P.
Res., 2833 32nd Ave., S., 55406. Tel: 612-724-3644; Fax: 612-724-5057.
Parish Center—2836 33rd Ave., S., 55406. Tel: 612-724-3643; Fax: 612-722-9726.
School—Risen Christ Catholic School. See Elementary Schools, Consolidated, Parochial under Institutions located in the Archdiocese for details. Tel: 612-822-5329.

16—ST. ANNE (1884) (French), Rev. Michael G. Monogue.
Res., 2627 Queen Ave., N., 55411. Tel: 612-529-0503; Fax: 612-529-5860.
School—St. Elizabeth Seton. (Consolidated). 5140 Fremont Ave., N., 55430-3496. Tel: 612-529-7781; Fax: 612-529-3343.

17—ST. ANTHONY OF PADUA (1849), Rev. Joseph G. Kivel.
Res., 804 Second St., N.E., 55413. Tel: 612-379-2324.
School—Northeast Regional Catholic School. See Elementary Schools, Consolidated, Parochial under the Institutions located in the Archdiocese for details.

18—ST. AUSTIN (1937), Rev. Gregory T. Welch; Deacon James C. Dondelinger.
Res., 4050 Upton Ave., N., 55412. Tel: 612-529-9561; Fax: 612-529-8787.
School—St. Elizabeth Seton, 5140 Fremont Ave., N., 55430. Tel: 612-529-7781; Fax: 612-529-3343.
Sisters 1; Lay Teachers 19; Students 360.

19—ST. BONIFACE (1858) (German), Rev. Mathias Spier, O.S.B.
Res., 629 Second St., N.E., 55413. Tel: 612-379-2761.
School—Northeast Regional Catholic School. See Elementary Schools, Consolidated, Parochial under the Institutions located in the Archdiocese for details. Tel: 612-789-8851.

20—ST. BRIDGET (1915), Rev. Killian J. Perry, T.O.R. In res., Revs. Vincent J. Spinos, T.O.R.; J. Patrick Quinn, T.O.R.
Res., 3811 Emerson Ave., N., 55412. Tel: 612-529-7779; Fax: 612-529-8451.
School—5140 Fremont Ave., N., 55430-3497. Tel: 612-529-7719. Joyce Klevens, Prin.
Sisters 1; Lay Teachers 20; Students 360.

21—ST. CHARLES BORROMEO (1938), Revs. Francis R. Kittock; Mark A. Huberty; Deacon Dennis Neumann.
Res., 2420 St. Anthony Blvd., 55418. Tel: 612-781-6529; Fax: 612-781-9723.
School—2727 Stinson Blvd., 55418. Tel: 612-781-2643; Fax: 612-788-7768.
Lay Teachers 25; Students 372.

22—ST. CLEMENT (1902), Rev. Earl C. Simonson.
Res., 911 24th Ave., N.E., 55418. Tel: 612-789-3533.
School—Northeast Regional Catholic School. See Elementary Schools, Consolidated, Parochial under the Institutions located in the Archdiocese for details. Tel: 612-789-8851.

23—SS. CYRIL & METHODIUS (1891) (Slovak), Rev. Francis L. Fried.
Res., 1315 2nd St., N.E., 55413. Tel: 612-379-9736.
School—Northeast Regional Catholic School. See Elementary Schools, Consolidated, Parochial under the Institutions located in the Archdiocese for details. Tel: 612-789-8851.

24—ST. FRANCES CABRINI (1946), Rev. Leo J. Tibesar; Marie Rossa, Admin.
Res., 1500 Franklin Ave., S.E., 55414-3697. Tel: 612-339-3023; Fax: 612-339-0734.
Catechesis/Religious Programs—Students 160.

25—ST. HEDWIG (1914) (Polish), Rev. Theodore C. Guminga.
Res., 129 29th Ave., N.E., 55418. Tel: 612-789-4830.
School—Northeast Regional Catholic School. See Elementary Schools, Consolidated, Parochial under the Institutions located in the Archdiocese for details.

26—ST. HELENA (1913), Rev. Richard R. Villano.
3204 E. 43rd St., 55406. Tel: 612-729-7344.
Res., 4320 33rd Ave., S., 55406. Tel: 612-729-2252; Fax: 612-724-8695.
School—3200 E. 44th St., 55406. Tel: 612-729-9301.
Lay Teachers 12; Students 187.

27—ST. JOAN OF ARC (1946), Rev. George P. Wertin.
Res., 4537 3rd Ave., S., 55409. Tel: 612-823-8205; Fax: 612-825-7028.
Catechesis/Religious Programs—Tel: 612-823-8205; Fax: 612-825-7028. Kathy Itzin, D.R.E.
Students 575.

28—ST. JOSEPH HIEN, Revs. Matthias Chuong, C.M.C. (Vietnam); Isidore M. Bac, C.M.C. (Vietnam); Deacon Joseph Nhac Phuc Nguyen.
Res., 1814 Dupont Ave., N., 55411. Tel: 612-522-5006.

29—ST. LAWRENCE (1887), Revs. James F. Wiesner, C.S.P.; John J. Behnke, C,S.P.; Deacon Paul Carlson. In res., Revs. Paul S. Rospond, C.S.P.; Charles A. Martin, C.S.P.; Wilfred A. Brimley, C.S.P.; James B. Corbett, C.S.P., (Retired).
Res., 1201 5th St., S.E., 55414. Tel: 612-331-7941; Fax: 612-378-1771.

30—ST. LEONARD OF PORT MAURICE (1941) (African American), Rev. James DeBruycker.
Res., 3949 Clinton Ave., 55409. Tel: 612-825-5811; 347-2260.

31—ST. OLAF (1941), Revs. John E. Forliti; Ralph J. Goman; Kevin T. Kenney; Leon F. Klimczyk, S.J.; Deacon Stephen Boatwright.
Res., 215 S. 8th St., 55402. Tel: 612-332-7471; Fax: 612-332-3412.

32—ST. PHILIP (1906) (Polish), Rev. Peter C. Njoku (Nigeria).
Res., 2507 Bryant Ave., N., 55411. Tel: 612-529-3125.

33—ST. STEPHEN (1885), Revs. Patrick E. Griffin; Lawrence E. Hubbard.
Parish Center—2211 Clinton Ave., 55404. Tel: 612-874-0311; Fax: 612-874-0313.
School—Risen Christ Catholic School. See Elementary Schools, Consolidated, Parochial under Institutions located in the Archdiocese for details. Tel: 612-822-5329.

34—ST. THOMAS THE APOSTLE (1908), Rev. Stephen R. O'Gara.
Res., 2914 W. 44th St., 55410. Tel: 612-922-0041; Fax: 612-922-1921.
School—Combined program with Christ the King, Minneapolis. 2900 W. 44th St., 55410. Tel: 612-922-0655.
Lay Teachers, Both Campuses; 21; Students 412.

35—VISITATION (1946), Rev. Francis A. Pouliot; Deacon Peter A. D'Heilly.
Res., 4500 Lyndale Ave., S., 55409. Tel: 612-822-3139.
School—4530 Lyndale Ave., S., 55409. Tel: 612-827-3861.
Sisters of St. Benedict 1; Lay Teachers 7; Students 121.

OUTSIDE METROPOLITAN MINNEAPOLIS

Blaine, Anoka Co., St. Timothy's (1943), Rev. Harold J. Tasto; Deacons Joseph Kenney; Kevin Jents.
Res., 707 89th Ave., N.E., 55434. Tel: 612-784-1329; Fax: 612-784-0652.
Catechesis/Religious Programs—Students 995.

Bloomington, Hennepin Co., Nativity of the Blessed Virgin Mary (1949), Revs. Robert E. Johnson; Brendan J. McMullen, O.P.; Deacons James McLaughlin; Rob Warhol.
Office: 9900 Lyndale Ave., S., 55420. Tel: 612-881-8671; Fax: 612-881-8692.
School—9901 Bloomington Fwy., 55420. Tel: 612-881-8160; Fax: 612-881-3032.
Lay Teachers 24; Students 455.
Catechesis/Religious Programs—Tel: 612-881-1451. Rose Ann Stans, D.R.E.
Students 250.

St. Bonaventure (1959), Revs. Regis T. Schlagheck, O.F.M.Conv.; Joseph West, O.F.M.Conv.; Deacon Patrick Casey. In res., Revs. Ken Bartsch, O.F.M. Conv., Chap.; Urban S. Wagner, O.F.M.Conv.
Res., 901 E. 90th St., S., 55420. Tel: 612-854-4733.
Catechesis/Religious Programs—Tel: 612-854-7062.
Students 419.

St. Edward (1967), Revs. Martin B. Shallbetter; J. Kevin Finnegan; Deacon Willard F. Dornfeld.
Res., 9401 Nesbitt Ave., S., 55437. Tel: 612-835-9220; Fax: 612-835-0156.
Catechesis/Religious Programs—Tel: 612-835-3272; Fax: 612-835-0156.
Students 758.

Brooklyn Center, Hennepin Co., St. Alphonsus (1959), Revs. Thomas Donaldson, C.SS.R.; Arthur Rossie, C.SS.R.; Martin Stillmock, C.SS.R.; Edward Monroe, C.SS.R.; Deacons Jerome H. Bisek; Bobby May; David Holst; Bro. Raymond Bowersox, C.SS.R. In res., Rev. David Shannon, C.SS.R.
Res., 7025 Halifax Ave., N., 55429. Tel: 612-561-5100; Fax: 612-561-0336.
School—Benedictine Sisters, 7031 Halifax Ave., N., 55429. Tel: 612-561-5101.
Lay Teachers 17; Students 286.
Catechesis/Religious Programs—4111 71st Ave., N., 55429. Tel: 612-561-5102. Barbara Walhood, D.R.E.
Students 1,018.

Brooklyn Park, Hennepin Co., St. Gerard (1970), Revs. Anthony Criscitelli, T.O.R.; Bradley Baldwin, T.O.R.
Res., 9600 Regent Ave., N., 55443. Tel: 612-424-8770; Fax: 612-424-4327.
Catechesis/Religious Programs—Tel: 612-424-8600; Fax: 612-424-4327. Brian Richards, D.R.E.
Students 699.

Burnsville, Dakota Co., Mary, Mother of the Church (1965), Revs. James C. Zappa, Jr.; William G. Pelant; Deacons Peter Huberty; George Nugent; Barry Haller, Business Admin.
Church—3333 Cliff Rd., 55337. Tel: 612-890-0045; Fax: 612-890-0789.
Catechesis/Religious Programs—D.R.E.: Kathleen Groh; Marcia Berra.
Students 1,116.

Church of the Risen Savior (1970), Revs. Thomas H. Sieg; James Gorman; Deacon Richard Stevens; Lawrence Blake, Admin.
Office: 1501 E. County Rd. 42, 55306. Tel: 612-431-5222; Fax: 612-431-5221.
Catechesis/Religious Programs—D.R.E.: Karen Fitzpatrick; Barbara Skierecki; Susan Ford.
Students 1,686.

Columbia Heights, Anoka Co., Immaculate Conception (1923), Rev. Paul G. Moudry; Deacon Larry Palkert.
Res., 4030 Jackson St., N.E., 55421. Tel: 612-788-9062; Fax: 612-788-0202.
School—4053 N.E. Quincy, 55421. Tel: 612-788-9065; Fax: 612-788-0202.
Sisters of St. Francis 3; Lay Teachers 14; Students 340.
Catechesis/Religious Programs—Tel: 612-788-9067; Fax: 612-788-0202.
Students 300.

Coon Rapids, Anoka Co., Church of the Epiphany (1964), Revs. Bernard A. Reiser; Thomas W. Wilson; James L. Lamm, Admin.
Res., 1900 111th Ave., N.W., 55433. Tel: 612-755-1020; Fax: 612-755-8069. [CEM]
School—11001 Hanson Blvd., 55433. Tel: 612-754-1750. Michael Strauss, Prin.
Lay Teachers 40; Students 767.
Catechesis/Religious Programs—11001 Hanson Blvd., 55433. Tel: 612-755-5010. Dennis Schommer, D.R.E.
Students 1,720.

Crystal, Hennepin Co., St. Raphael (1951), Revs. Mark R. Juettner; Thomas E. McCabe; Thomas Rayer (India).
Res., 7301 Bass Lake Rd., 55428. Tel: 612-537-8401; Fax: 612-537-4878.
School—Tel: 612-537-6242; Fax: 612-537-4878.
Sisters 1; Lay Teachers 22; Students 480.
Catechesis/Religious Programs—Tel: 612-533-3770. Paulette Schatz, D.R.E.
Students 520.

Eagan, Dakota Co., St. Thomas Becket (1989), Rev. Thomas M. Kommers; Deacon Paul Tatone.
Res., 4455 S. Robert Tr., 55123. Tel: 612-683-0689; 683-9808 (Parish Center); Fax: 612-683-0361.
Catechesis/Religious Programs—Students 350.

St. John Neumann (1977), Revs. Robert M. Schwartz; John J. Mitchell.
Res., 4030 Pilot Knob Rd., 55122. Tel: 612-454-2079; Fax: 612-454-0860.
Catechesis/Religious Programs—Students 1,486.

Eden Prairie, Hennepin Co., Pax Christi (1981), Rev. J. Timothy Power; Deacons Mike Gerdts; Howard Wirtz.
Res., 12100 Pioneer Tr., 55347. Tel: 612-941-3150; Fax: 612-941-7942.
Catechesis/Religious Programs—Tel: 612-941-6007; Fax: 612-941-7942.
Students 1,575.

Edina, Hennepin Co., Our Lady of Grace (1946), Revs. Robert T. Cassidy; Robert L. Valit; Deacon Donald Pendergast. In res., Rev. Jerome W. Fehn.
Res., 5071 Eden Ave., 55436. Tel: 612-929-3317; Fax: 612-929-4612.
School—5051 Eden Ave., 55436. Tel: 612-929-5463; Fax: 612-929-8170.
Lay Teachers 27; Students 501.
Catechesis/Religious Programs—Tel: 612-929-3317; Fax: 612-929-4612.
Students 350.

St. Patrick (1857) (Irish), Revs. Ambrose J. Mahon; William A. Brown.

Res., 6820 St. Patrick's Ln., 55439. Tel: 612-941-3164; Fax: 612-941-7371.
Catechesis/Religious Programs—Tel: 612-941-1407. Sue Kelley, D.R.E.
Students 829.

Fridley, Anoka Co., St. William (1963), Rev. Patrick A. Kennedy, Admin.; Deacon Jim Wagner.
Res. and Admin. Center: 6120 5th St., N.E., 55432. Tel: 612-571-5600; Fax: 612-571-6924.
Catechesis/Religious Programs—Students 330.

Golden Valley, Hennepin Co., Good Shepherd (1946), Rev. Theodore C. Campbell.
Res., 145 Jersey Ave., S., 55426. Tel: 612-544-0649; Fax: 612-544-9896. [JC]
School—Tel: 612-545-4285; Fax: 612-545-1896.
Lay Teachers 18; Students 319.
Catechesis/Religious Programs—Students 150.

St. Margaret Mary (1946), Rev. Timothy Hodapp; Deacon John Winkelman.
Res., 2301 Zenith Ave., N., 55422. Tel: 612-588-9466; Fax: 612-588-0190.
Catechesis/Religious Programs—Students 137.

Ham Lake, Anoka Co., Saint Paul (1981), Rev. Timothy F. Nolan; Deacons Bill Beck; Don McPhee.
Res., 1740 Bunker Lake Blvd., N.E., 55304. Tel: 612-757-6910; Fax: 612-757-6920.
Catechesis/Religious Programs—Tel: 612-757-6910; Fax: 612-757-6920. Bob Peach, D.R.E.
Students 779.

Lino Lakes, Anoka Co., St. Joseph (1891), Revs. Timothy Morin; Kenneth G. LaVan.
Office: 171 Elm St., 55014. Tel: 612-784-3015; Fax: 612-784-3699. [CEM]
Catechesis/Religious Programs—D.R.E.: Shirley Gormley; Christine Kroner; Kenneth Schaan; Jeanne Degerstrom.
Students 1,320.

New Hope, Hennepin Co., St. Joseph (1858), Rev. Donald J. Piche.
Res., 8701 36th Ave., N., 55427. Tel: 612-544-3352. [CEM]
Parish Center & Office—Tel: 612-544-3352; Fax: 612-544-3435.
Catechesis/Religious Programs—D.R.E.: Mary Greving; Connie Thomas; Larry Thomas.
Students 797.

Plymouth, Hennepin Co., St. Mary of the Lake (1935), Rev. Bryan A. O'Rourke; Deacon William Schiller.
Res., 105 Forestview Ln., N., 55441. Tel: 612-545-1443; Fax: 612-797-0996.
Catechesis/Religious Programs—Students 220.

Richfield, Hennepin Co., Assumption of the B.V.M. (1876), Rev. Michael Tix; Deacon Robert Smith.
Res., 305 E. 77th St., 55423. Tel: 612-866-5019; Fax: 612-866-5274.
School—Blessed Trinity Nicollet & Penn Campus, Tel: 612-866-6906; Fax: 612-869-0277;866-5080.
Students 409.
Catechesis/Religious Programs—Tel: 612-866-5019; Fax: 612-866-5274.
Students 170.

St. Peter (1943), Rev. Rodger R. Bauman.
Res., 6740 Nicollet Ave., S., 55423. Tel: 612-866-5089; Fax: 612-866-5080.
School—Consolidation of Assumption, St. Peter & St. Richard. 6720 Nicollet Ave., S., 55423.
Lay Teachers 12; Students 436.
Catechesis/Religious Programs—Tel: 612-866-3257.
Students 164.

St. Richard (1952), Rev. Gregory L. Esty; Deacons William J. Berghoff; Byron Rudolphi.
Office: 7540 Penn Ave., S., 55423. Tel: 612-869-2426; Fax: 612-869-0277.
Res., 7601 Penn Ave., S., 55423. Tel: 612-869-2426; Fax: 612-869-0277.
School—Blessed Trinity Catholic School. Consolidation of Assumption, St. Peter & St. Richard. Tel: 612-866-6906; Fax: 612-869-0277.
Lay Teachers 22; Students 403.
Catechesis/Religious Programs—Students 308.

Robbinsdale, Hennepin Co., Sacred Heart (1911), Rev. Robert E. Zasacki; Deacon Thomas Coleman.
Office: 4087 W. Broadway, 55422. Tel: 612-537-4561; Fax: 612-537-5426.
Res., 4510 40-1/2 Ave., N., 55422. Tel: 612-537-4561; Fax: 612-537-5426.
School—4050 Hubbard, 55422. Tel: 612-537-1329; Fax: 612-537-5426.
Lay Teachers 20; Students 229.
Catechesis/Religious Programs—Cyrilene Brouillard, D.R.E.
Students 229.

St. Louis Park, Hennepin Co., Most Holy Trinity (1943), Rev. Dennis Thompson, O.F.M.Conv.
Res., 4017 Utica Ave., 55416. Tel: 612-926-7516; Fax: 612-926-2222.
School—3946 Wooddale Ave., 55416. Tel: 612-926-2222.
Lay Teachers 9; Students 101.

Holy Family (1926), Rev. Thomas W. Dufner; Deacon Alfred R. Kattar.
Res., 5900 W. Lake St., 55416. Tel: 612-929-0113; Fax: 612-915-1474.
School—Park Valley Catholic School, Tel: 612-545-4285. Joint Venture with Good Shepherd, Golden Valley.
Catechesis/Religious Programs—Tel: 612-929-0113.
Students 300.

OUTSIDE TWIN-CITY METROPOLITAN AREA

Albertville, Wright Co., St. Albert (1904), Rev. Frank Ryan, O.M.I.
Mailing Address: P.O. Box 127 55301. Tel: 612-497-2474. [CEM]
Catechesis/Religious Programs—P.O. Box 67, 55301. Tel: 612-497-3782.
Students 264.

Annandale, Wright Co., St. Ignatius (1882), Rev. J. Christopher Russell.
Res., 55302. Tel: 320-274-8828. [CEM]
Catechesis/Religious Programs—Tel: 320-274-5064.
Students 313.

Anoka, Anoka Co., St. Stephen (1856), Revs. Michael Paquet, O.S.C.; Michael Van Sloun, O.S.C.; Dale Ettel, O.S.C.; Deacons Peter Bednarczyk; Dominic Ehrmantraut. In res., Revs. David E. Gallus, O.S.C.; Ken Opat, O.S.C.; Gene Plaisted, O.S.C.
Office: 2020 Fifth Ave., N., 55303. Tel: 612-421-2471; Fax: 612-421-4230. [CEM]
School—506 Jackson, 55303. Tel: 612-421-3236.
Lay Teachers 25; Students 445.
Catechesis/Religious Programs—Tel: 612-421-2471.
Students 1,050.

Bayport, Washington Co., St. Charles (1943), Rev. Jonathan P. Shelley.
Res., 409 N. 3rd St., 55003. Tel: 612-439-4511; Fax: 612-430-9717. [CEM]
School—St. Croix Catholic School. See Elementary Schools, Consolidated, Parochial under Institutions located in the Archdiocese for details. Tel: 612-439-5581.

Bellechester, Goodhue Co., St. Mary (1860) (Luxembourgian), Rev. Frank J. Wampach, Admin.
Res., 223 Chester Ave., 55027. Tel: 612-923-4305. [CEM]

Belle Creek, Goodhue Co., St. Columbkill (1860), Rev. Bruce Peterson.
Res., Goodhue Rte. 2, Box 90, 55027. Tel: 612-258-4307. [CEM]
Mission—Goodhue, Goodhue Co., Holy Trinity, Rt. 2, P.O. Box 90, 55027. Tel: 612-923-4472.

Belle Plaine, Scott Co., Our Lady of the Prairie (1972). Unassigned.
Res., 212 N. Chestnut St., 56011. Tel: 612-873-2323; Fax: 612-873-2323. [CEM 2]
School—Tel: 612-873-6564; Fax: 612-873-6564.
Sisters 1; Lay Teachers 5; Students 63.
Catechesis/Religious Programs—Tel: 612-873-2323; Fax: 612-873-2323. Kathy Koepp, D.R.E.
Students 400.

Buffalo, Wright Co., St. Francis Xavier (1915), Rev. Charles L. Froehle; Deacon Richard Boisclair.
Res., 9 N.W. 3rd St., 55313. Tel: 612-682-1183; Fax: 612-682-0485. [CEM 2]
School—Tel: 612-682-1295. Dianna Vossen, Prin.
Lay Teachers 13; Students 241.
Catechesis/Religious Programs—Tel: 612-682-1295. Sharon Kelly, D.R.E.
Students 590.

Cannon Falls, Goodhue Co., St. Pius V (1856), Rev. Roger J. Hessian, Admin.
Res., 410 W. Colvill Ave., P.O. Box 367, 55009-0367. Tel: 507-263-2578. [CEM]
Catechesis/Religious Programs—Tel: 507-263-4800 (Grades PreK-8); 263-4680 (Grades 9-12).
Students 309.

Carver, Carver Co., St. Nicholas (1868), Rev. Gerard J. Rowan.
Res., 412 W. Fourth St., Box 133, 55315. Tel: 612-448-2345. [CEM 2]

Cedar, Anoka Co., St. Patrick (1894), Rev. Michael J. Kennedy; Sharon L. Murray, Admin.; Deacon Terry Scherer.
Res., 19921 Nightingale St., N.W., Oak Grove, 55011-9243. Tel: 612-753-2011; Fax: 612-753-9803. [CEM]
Catechesis/Religious Programs—Tel: 612-753-2036; Fax: 612-753-9803. Joseph Draper, D.R.E.
Students 536.

Cedar Lake, Scott Co., St. Patrick (1856) (Irish), Rev. Sebastien Bakatuinamina, C.I.C.M.
Res., Cedar Lake Twp., 24425 Old Hwy. 13 Blvd., Jordan, 55352. Tel: 612-492-6276. [CEM]
Catechesis/Religious Programs—Students 221.
Mission—Spring Lake Twp., Scott Co., St. Catherine, (1865) 4500 E. 220th St., Prior Lake 55372. Tel: 612-447-2180. [CEM]

Centerville, Anoka Co., St. Genevieve (1854) (French Canadian), Rev. Richard J. Wolter.
Res., 7087 Goiffon Ave., 55038. Tel: 612-429-7937. [CEM]
Catechesis/Religious Programs—Tel: 612-426-1818.
Students 169.

Chanhassen, Carver Co., St. Hubert (1865) (German), Revs. Stephen D. Ulrick; Paul L. Magee; Deacon Robert Wagner.
Res., 7707 Great Plains Blvd., 55317. Tel: 612-934-9106; Fax: 612-934-8209. [CEM]
School—Tel: 612-934-6003.
Lay Teachers 25; Students 322.
Catechesis/Religious Programs—Tel: 612-934-6387.
Students 850.

Chaska, Carver Co., Guardian Angels (1858), Rev. Timothy Rudolphi.
Res., 218 W. 2nd St., 55318. Tel: 612-448-4100; Fax: 612-448-3076. [CEM]
School—Tel: 612-448-2562; Fax: 612-448-3281.
Lay Teachers 10; Students 204.
Catechesis/Religious Programs—Tel: 612-448-3478.
Students 215.

Clearwater, Wright Co., St. Luke (1870), Rev. Ramon J. Buckley.
Mailing Address: P.O. Box 249, 55320-0249.
Res., 425 Spring St., 55320. Tel: 612-558-6341. [CEM]

Cleveland, Le Sueur Co., Church of the Nativity of the Blessed Virgin Mary (1865) (Irish-German). Unassigned.
Res., 56017-0187. Tel: 507-931-5409. [CEM]

Coates, Dakota Co., St. Agatha (1870), Rev. James W. Whalen, Temp. Admin.
Res., University of St. Thomas, 2115 Summit Ave., St. Paul, 55105. Tel: 612-645-2400. [CEM]

Cologne, Carver Co., St. Bernard (1859), Rev. Gerald E. Keefe.
Res., 212 Church St., E., 55322. Tel: 612-466-2031. [CEM]
School—300 Church St., E., 55322. Tel: 612-466-5917.
Sisters of Notre Dame 2; Lay Teachers 3; Students 63.

Corcoran, Hennepin Co., St. Thomas the Apostle (1896), Rev. George R. Kinney.
Res., 20,000 County Rd. 10, Hamel, 55340. Tel: 612-420-2385; Fax: 612-420-4710. [JC 4]
Catechesis/Religious Programs—Tel: 612-420-2385; Fax: 612-420-4710. Lori Palmode, D.R.E.
Students 314.

Dayton, Hennepin Co., St. John the Baptist (1862) (French Canadian), Rev. John M. Siebenaler.
Res., 55327. Tel: 612-428-2828. [CEM 2][JC]
Catechesis/Religious Programs—Tel: 612-856-3122.
Students 159.

Deephaven, Hennepin Co., St. Therese (1946), Rev. John M. Bauer; Deacon James F. McDonald.
Res., 18323 Minnetonka Blvd., 55391. Tel: 612-473-4422; Fax: 612-423-2685.
School—18325 Minnetonka Blvd., 55391. Tel: 612-473-4355.
Sisters 5; Lay Teachers 12; Students 268.
Catechesis/Religious Programs—Tel: 612-473-2891; 473-5455. Margaret Stimmler, D.R.E.
Students 610.

Delano, Wright Co., St. Joseph (1902) (Polish), Rev. Thomas G. Boedy, S.J.; Deacon Joseph Frederick.
Church—401 River St., P.O. Box 470, 55328-0470. Tel: 612-972-2077; Fax: 612-972-6177. [CEM]
School—Delano Catholic Elementary School, Tel: 612-972-2528; Fax: 612-972-6177.
Catechesis/Religious Programs—Tel: 612-972-2976; Fax: 612-972-6177.
Students 320.

St. Mary of Czestochowa (1884) (Polish), Rev. James T. Livingston.
Office & Res.: 1867 95th St., S.E., 55328. Tel: 612-955-1139. [CEM]

St. Peter (1865) (German), Rev. Thomas G. Boedy, S.J.; Deacon Joseph Frederick.
Offices: 204 River St., 55328. Tel: 612-972-2077; Fax: 612-972-6177. [CEM 2]
School—Delano Catholic Elementary School, Tel: 612-972-2528.
Lay Teachers 10; Students 110.
Catechesis/Religious Programs—235 S. 2nd St., 55328. Tel: 612-972-2976; Fax: 612-972-6177.
Students 320.

Elysian, Le Sueur Co., St. Andrew Holy Trinity, Waterville, MN (1894), Rev. Michael W. Ince, Admin.

Church—Box 261, 56028. Tel: 507-267-4928.

Excelsior, Lake Minnetonka, Hennepin Co., St. John the Baptist (1903), Rev. James G. Wolnik; Deacons John MacKenzie; James Baskfield; Gary Hoffman.
Res., 680 Mill St., 55331. Tel: 612-474-8868; Fax: 612-474-5962. [CEM][JC]
School—Tel: 612-474-5812.
Lay Teachers 13; Students 153.
Catechesis/Religious Programs—Students 286.

Faribault, Rice Co., Immaculate Conception (1856), Rev. George J. Freeman; Deacon R. Daniel Wesley.
Res., 4 Second Ave., S.W., 55021-6029. Tel: 507-334-2266. [CEM]
School—Catholic School of Faribault. See Elementary Schools, Consolidated, Parochial under Institutions located in the Archdiocese for details. Tel: 507-334-7704.
Catechesis/Religious Programs—Tel: 507-334-9142.
Students 300.

Fairbault, Rice Co., Sacred Heart (French-German). Merged with St. Lawrence, Fairbault, and renamed Sacred Heart - St. Lawrence of Fairbault in 1996.

Faribault, Rice Co., St. Lawrence (1869) (German). Merged with Sacred Heart, Fairbault, and renamed Sacred Heart - St. Lawrence of Fairbault in 1996.

Sacred Heart - St. Lawrence of Fairbault. Sacred Heart, Fairbault, and St. Lawrence, Fairbault, were merged and renamed in 1996. Rev. David W. Kohner.
Res., 520 4th Ave., N.W., 55021-4227.

Farmington, Dakota Co., St. Michael, Rev. Eugene A. Pouliot.
Res., 622 5th St., 55024-0227. Tel: 612-463-3360; Fax: 612-463-2339.
Center: 421 Walnut, P.O. Box 227, 55024.
Church—412 Spruce, 55024. [CEM]
Catechesis/Religious Programs—Students 423.

Forest Lake, Washington Co., St. Peter (1904), Revs. Robert J. Sipe; Jerome C. Kern; Deacons Gary Houle; Ralph L'Allier, Pastoral Min.
Res., 1250 S. Shore Dr., 55025. Tel: 612-464-3578; Fax: 612-464-5494. [CEM]
School—Tel: 612-464-2610. Marylou Evanoff, Prin.
Lay Teachers 23; Students 296.
Catechesis/Religious Programs—D.R.E.: Judy Foster; Susan Fast.
Students 1,000.

Hamel, Hennepin Co., St. Anne (1879), Rev. Allen J. McIntrye.
Res., 200 Hamel Rd., Box 256, 55340. Tel: 612-478-6644. [CEM]

Hampton, Dakota Co., St. Mathias (1900), Rev. Valerius U. Messerich, O.F.M.
Res., 23315 Northfield Blvd., 55031-9701. Tel: 612-437-9030; Fax: 612-437-5848. [CEM]
School—Tel: 612-437-5282.
Lay Teachers 7; Students 93.

Hancock Township, Carver Co., Assumption. Closed. For inquiries for parish records contact the Chancery.

Hassan Township, Hennepin Co., St. Walburga (1856) (German), Rev. Michael McGlauchlin; Deacons Merlin Williams; Dominic Ehrmentrant.
Res., 12020 Fletcher Ln., Rogers, 55374. Tel: 612-428-2081; Fax: 612-428-4032. [CEM 2]

Hastings, Dakota Co., St. Elizabeth Ann Seton (1987), Revs. Eugene J. McGlothlin, O.S.B.; Blane H. Wasnie, O.S.B., D.R.E.; Stephen G. Beauclair, O.S.B.; Deacon Michael A. Humbert.
Res., 2035 W. Fifteenth St., 55033. Tel: 612-437-4254; Fax: 612-438-2948. [CEM][JC]
School—Tel: 612-437-3098. Barbara Vergenz, Prin.
Lay Teachers 23; Students 476.
Catechesis/Religious Programs—Tel: 612-437-9191.
Students 960.

Hazelwood, Rice Co., Annunciation of the B.V.M. (1863), Rev. James E. Holl.
Res., 4996 Hazelwood Ave., Northfield, 55057. Tel: 612-652-2625. [CEM]

Heidelberg, Le Sueur Co., St. Scholastica (1856) (German-Czech), Rev. Richard P. Roedel.
Res., Rte. 1, Box 218, New Prague, 56071. Tel: 612-758-4292. [CEM]

Hopkins, Hennepin Co., St. John the Evangelist (1950). Unassigned.
Res., 6 Interlachen Rd., 55343. Tel: 612-935-5536.
School—John Ireland Schools. See Elementary Schools, Consolidated, Parochial under Institutions located in the Archdiocese for details. Tel: 612-938-3442.

St. Joseph's (1926), Rev. John M. Long; Deacon Francis J. Tangney.
Res., 1310 Main St., 55343. Tel: 612-935-0111; Fax: 612-935-4539. [CEM]
School—John Ireland Schools. See Elementary Schools, Consolidated, Parochial under Institutions located in the Archdiocese for details. Tel: 612-938-3442; Fax: 612-938-3457.
Catechesis/Religious Programs—Tel: 612-935-7004; 935-5059.
Students 260.

Hugo, Washington Co., St. John the Baptist (1902), Rev. Daniel W. Friberg; Deacon Thomas Barrett.
Res., 14383 N. Forest Blvd., 55038. Tel: 612-426-1004. [CEM]
Catechesis/Religious Programs—Tel: 612-429-9170. Alice Christiansen, D.R.E.
Students 232.

Inver Grove Heights, Dakota Co., St. Patrick (1856) (Irish), Rev. Timothy L. Corbley; Deacon Harlan Christensen.
Res., 3535 72nd St., E., 55076. Tel: 612-455-6624; Fax: 612-455-8984. [CEM]
Catechesis/Religious Programs—Tel: 612-455-5900.
Students 620.

Jordan, Scott Co., St. John the Baptist (1858), Rev. James M. Perkl.
Res., 313 E. 2nd St., P.O. Box 97, 55352. Tel: 612-492-2640. [CEM][JC]
School—215 E. 2nd St., 55352. Tel: 612-492-2030.
Lay Teachers 15; Students 218.
Catechesis/Religious Programs—Students 306.

Kenyon, Goodhue Co., St. Michael (1944), Rev. Dennis C. Kampa, Admin.
Church—108 Bullis St., 55946. Tel: 507-789-6120.
Res., 451 5th St., S.W., Box 368, Pine Island, 55963. Tel: 507-356-4944. [CEM]

Kilkenny, Le Sueur Co., St. Canice (1858) (Irish), Rev. Ronald W. Dahlheimer.
Res., 56052. Tel: 507-595-2561. [CEM]

Lake St. Croix Beach, Washington Co., St. Francis Of Assisi (1938), Rev. Thomas J. Hallsten, O.S.B.
Res., 16770 13th St., 55043. Tel: 612-436-7817; Fax: 612-436-6524.
Catechesis/Religious Programs—Students 288.

Lakeville, Dakota Co., All Saints (1889), Revs. Eugene W. Tiffany; Jeffrey H. Huard.
Res., P.O. Box 518, 55044. Tel: 612-469-4481; Fax: 612-469-4484. [CEM]
School—Tel: 612-469-3332; Fax: 612-469-4484. Jackie Sauber, Prin.
Lay Teachers 12; Students 190.
Catechesis/Religious Programs—20965 Holyoke Ave., 55044. Bonnie Serio, D.R.E.
Students 900.

Le Center, Le Sueur Co., St. Mary (1899), Rev. Raymond G. Monsour.
Res., 165 N. Waterville Ave., 56057. Tel: 507-357-4838. [CEM]
Catechesis/Religious Programs—Tel: 507-357-6633.
Students 337.

Le Sueur, Le Sueur Co., St. Anne (1852), Rev. Kenneth L. O'Hotto.
Res., 217 N. 3rd St., 56058. Tel: 612-665-2047. [CEM 2]
School—Tel: 612-665-2489.
Lay Teachers 8; Students 100.
Catechesis/Religious Programs—503 N. 4th St., 56058. Tel: 612-665-3811.
Students 188.

Lexington, Le Sueur Co., St. Joseph (1903) (Polish), Rev. Richard P. Roedel.
Res., Rte. 1, Box 218, New Prague, 56071. Tel: 612-758-4292. [CEM]

Lindstrom, Chisago Co., St. Bridget of Sweden (1948), Rev. Charles A. Brambilla.
Res., Box 754, 55045. Tel: 612-257-2474; Fax: 612-257-1498.
Catechesis/Religious Programs—Students 575.

Long Lake, Hennepin Co., St. George (1917), Rev. Timothy Dolan; Deacon John Reed.
Church—133 N. Brown Rd., 55356. Tel: 612-473-1247. [CEM]
Res., Tel 612-473-1248.

Lonsdale, Rice Co., Immaculate Conception (1903), Rev. Stanley F. Kozlak.
Res., 55046. Tel: 507-744-2829. [CEM]
School—Lonsdale, New Market, Veseli Area School. See Elementary Schools, Consolidated, Parochial under Institutions located in the Archdiocese for details. Tel: 507-744-2394.
Catechesis/Religious Programs—Students 206.

Loretto, Hennepin Co., SS. Peter and Paul (1867). Unassigned.
Mailing Address: P.O. Box 96, 55357. Tel: 612-479-0535; Fax: 612-479-4383.
Res., 125 Railway St., 55357. [CEM]
School—Tel: 612-479-0540; Fax: 612-479-4046.
Lay Teachers 10; Students 150.
Catechesis/Religious Programs—Tel: 612-479-0538; Fax: 612-479-4046.
Students 300.

Maple Grove, Hennepin Co., St. Joseph the Worker (1870), Rev. John F. Parkos; Deacon Donald S. Rinkenberger.
Church—7180 Hemlock Ln., 55369-5597. Tel: 612-425-6505; Fax: 612-425-6587.
Catechesis/Religious Programs—Tel: 612-425-9801. Stephen R. Robach, D.R.E.
Students 1,254.

Maple Lake, Wright Co., St. Timothy (1882). Unassigned. Deacon Ron Freeman.
Res., 8 N. Oak Ave., Box 281, 55358. Tel: 320-963-3726. [CEM 3]
School—Tel: 320-963-3417. Sr. Anita Kolles, S.S.N.D., Prin.
Lay Teachers 7; Students 83.
Catechesis/Religious Programs—Students 236.

Marysburg, Le Sueur Co., Immaculate Conception (1857) (Irish), Rev. Daniel R. Dernek (WIN) Admin.
Res., Rte. 1, Box 196, Madison Lake, 56063. Tel: 507-243-4157. [CEM]

Marystown, Scott Co., St. Mary of the Purification (1855), Rev. John R. Gilbert.
Res., 15850 Marystown Rd., Shakopee, 55379-9138. Tel: 612-445-3469; 2647 (Parish). [CEM]
School—Shakopee Area Catholic School. See Elementary Schools, Consolidated, Parochial under Institutions located in the Archdiocese for details.

Miesville, Dakota Co., St. Joseph (1873) (German-Irish), Rev. Marvin J. Klaers. In res., Rev. Michael F. O'Connor.
Office: 23955 Nicolai Ave., E., Hastings, 55033. Fax: 612-437-3526.
Res., 8433 239th St., E., Hastings, 55033. Tel: 612-437-5520. [CEM]
Church—55033. Tel: 612-437-3526.
Catechesis/Religious Programs—Tel: 612-437-3506.
Students 155.

Minnetonka, Hennepin Co., Immaculate Heart of Mary (1946), Revs. Patrick J. Hipwell; Richard Huber; Deacon David Huibregtse.
Res., 13505 Excelsior Blvd., 55345. Tel: 612-935-1432; Fax: 612-935-0474.
Catechesis/Religious Programs—Tel: 612-935-7077. D.R.E.: Sr. Arlene Pomje, C.S.J.; Deacon Patrick Casey.
Students 445.

Montgomery, Le Sueur Co., Holy Redeemer (1881), Revs. George J. Grafsky; Glen T. Jenson.
Res., 206 Vine Ave., W., 56069. Tel: 507-364-7981; Fax: 507-364-8660. [CEM]
School—205 Vine Ave., W., 56069. Tel: 507-364-7383.
Sisters of St. Benedict 1; Lay Teachers 12; Students 151.
Catechesis/Religious Programs—Students 153.

Monticello, Wright Co., St. Henry (1904), Rev. Marc T. Maus; Deacon George Lukach.
Office: 501 W. 4th St., 55362. Tel: 612-295-2402; Fax: 612-295-2345. [CEM]
Catechesis/Religious Programs—Tel: 612-295-2345. D.R.E.: Gary Russell; Karen Jendro.
Students 1,016.
Convent—Sisters of the Presentation. Tel: 612-295-2345; Fax: 612-295-2345.

Mound, Hennepin Co., Our Lady of the Lake (1909), Rev. Michael V. Tegeder.
Res., 2385 Commerce Blvd., 55364. Tel: 612-472-1284; Fax: 612-472-1284. [CEM]
School—Tel: 612-472-3400. Miss Kim Doyle, Prin.
Lay Teachers 21; Students 235.
Catechesis/Religious Programs—Tel: 612-472-4848.
Students 310.

New Market, Scott Co., St. Nicholas (1893) (German), Rev. George A. Welzbacher.
Res., 51 Church St., P.O. Box 9, 55054. Tel: 612-461-2403. [CEM]
School—Lonsdale, New Market, Veseli Area School. See Elementary Schools, Consolidated, Parochial under Institutions located in the Archdiocese for details. Tel: 507-744-2394.

New Prague, Scott Co., St. Wenceslaus (1857), Rev. William J. Paron; Deacon Leonard J. Shanbour.
Res., 215 E. Main St., 56071. Tel: 612-758-3225. [CEM]
School—Tel: 612-758-3133. John Harty, Prin.
Lay Teachers 21; Students 337.
Catechesis/Religious Programs—Tel: 612-758-2276. Sr. Margaret Schreiber, O.P., D.R.E.
Students 352.

New Trier, Dakota Co., St. Mary (1856), Rev. Marvin J. Klaers.
Res., 8433 239th St., E., Hampton, 55031. Tel: 612-437-5520. [CEM]
School—Tel: 612-437-5546.
Lay Teachers 3; Students 48.

North Branch, Chisago Co., St. Gregory (1874), Rev.

James T. Schoenberger; Deacon Thomas P. Langlois; Elizabeth R. Langlois, Pastoral Min.
Res., P.O. Box 609, 55056. Tel: 612-674-4056. [CEM]
Catechesis/Religious Programs—Tel: 612-674-7382.
Students 296.

Northfield, Rice Co., St. Dominic (1869), Most Rev. Paul V. Dudley, D.D.; Rev. Dennis D. Evenson.
Office: 216 N. Spring St., 55057. Tel: 507-645-8816; Fax: 507-645-8818.
Res., 116 N. Linden, 55057. Tel: 507-663-0154. [CEM]
School—Tel: 507-645-8136.
Sisters of Notre Dame 1; Students 213.
Catechesis/Religious Programs—Tel: 507-645-8816.
Students 350.

Norwood, Carver Co., Ascension (1859) (German), Rev. Paul C. Ardolf.
Res., 55368. Tel: 612-467-3351. [CEM 2]
Catechesis/Religious Programs—Students 197.

Osseo, Hennepin Co., St. Vincent de Paul (1855) (French), Revs. Curtis F. Lybarger; Robert A. Patterson; Deacons Sherman H. Otto; Bernard Dols.
Res., 9100 93rd Ave., N., Brooklyn Park, 55445-1407. Tel: 612-425-2210; Fax: 612-425-7898. [CEM]
School—Tel: 612-425-3970; Fax: 612-425-2674.
Lay Teachers 11; Students 228.
Catechesis/Religious Programs—D.R.E.: Arlys Lingen; Renee Paske; Bruce Baumann; Carol Ekstrom.
Students 1,500.

Pine Island, Goodhue Co., St. Michael (1878), Rev. Dennis C. Kampa.
Res., 55963. Tel: 507-356-4944. [CEM]
Catechesis/Religious Programs—Tel: 507-356-4280.
Students 272.
Mission—Kenyon, St. Michael.

Prior Lake, Scott Co., St. Michael (1912), Rev. Richard Banker.
Res., 16311 Duluth Ave., S.E., 55372. Tel: 612-447-2491; Fax: 612-447-2489. [CEM 2]
School—Tel: 612-447-2124; Fax: 612-447-2124 (call before sending).
Sisters 1; Lay Teachers 21; Students 370.
Catechesis/Religious Programs—Tel: 612-447-2486; Fax: 612-447-2489. D.R.E.: Janel Boegeman; Tom Donlon; Margaret Breunig.
Students 570.

Red Wing, Goodhue Co., St. Joseph (1865), Rev. Thomas J. Walker.
Res., 426 8th St., 55066. Tel: 612-388-1133. [CEM]
School—Tel: 612-388-9493. Marion Willis, Prin.
Ursuline Sisters 1; Lay Teachers 6; Students 86.
Catechesis/Religious Programs—Tel: 612-388-6000.
Students 635.

Rogers, Hennepin Co., St. Martin (1912) (German), Rev. Michael McGlauchlin; Deacon Merlin Williams.
Office: 21304 Church Ave., 55374-9445. Tel: 612-428-2585. [CEM]
School—Tel: 612-428-2355.
Lay Teachers 7; Students 132.
Catechesis/Religious Programs—Students 153.

Rosemount, Dakota Co., St. Joseph (1865), Rev. Francis J. Roach.
Res., 14375 S. Robert Tr., 55068. Tel: 612-423-4402; Fax: 612-423-4403. [CEM]
School—Tel: 612-423-1658.
Sisters 1; Lay Teachers 9; Students 231.
Catechesis/Religious Programs—Tel: 612-423-3131. Sr. Mary Louise McKenna, D.R.E.
Students 600.

Rush City, Chisago Co., Sacred Heart (1872) (Irish), Rev. Ralph F. Huar.
Res., 55069. Tel: 320-358-4370; Fax: 320-358-4479. [CEM]

St. Benedict, Scott Co., St. Benedict, Rev. Elgar Bockenfeld, O.F.M.
Res., Rte. 1, P.O. Box 93, New Prague, 56071. Tel: 612-738-4642. [CEM]

St. Bonifacius, Hennepin Co., St. Boniface (1859) (German), Rev. James T. Livingston.
Res., 4025 Main St., P.O. Box 68, 55375. Tel: 612-446-1054. [CEM]

St. Henry, Le Sueur Co., Church of St. Henry, Rev. Frederick C. Meyer.
Mailing Address: P.O. Le Sueur, R.R. No. 1, Box 52, 56058. Tel: 507-357-4990. [CEM]

St. Michael, Wright Co., St. Michael (1857), Rev. Leonard Siebenaler; Deacons Maynard Warne; Donald Becker.
Res., 55376. Tel: 612-497-2745; Fax: 612-497-2745. [CEM]
School—Tel: 612-497-3887.
Sisters 1; Lay Teachers 9; Students 204.
Catechesis/Religious Programs—Students 469.

St. Paul Park, Washington Co., St. Thomas Aquinas (1885), Rev. Timothy J. Wozniak.
Res., 920 Holly Ave., 55071. Tel: 612-459-2131; Fax: 612-459-8765. [CEM]
Catechesis/Religious Programs—Students 449.

St. Thomas, Le Sueur Co., St. Thomas (1858) (Irish), Rev. Richard P. Ruedel.
Res., Rte. 1, Box 218, New Prague, 56071. Tel: 612-758-4292. [CEM]

Savage, Scott Co., St. John the Baptist (1854), Revs. Peter C. Wittman; Rinaldo B. Custodio; Deacon Tom Michaud.
Res., 55378. Tel: 612-890-9465; Fax: 612-890-3006. [CEM]
School—Tel: 612-890-6604; Fax: 612-890-3006.
Lay Teachers 33; Students 703.
Catechesis/Religious Programs—Tel: 612-890-9434; Fax: 612-890-3006. D.R.E.: Amy Kusber; Andi Little.
Students 920.

Shakopee, Scott Co., St. Mark (1856) (German), Rev. William F. Stolzman; Deacon Alan Schroeder.
Res., 350 S. Atwood St., 55379-1238. Tel: 612-445-1229; Fax: 612-445-9639. [CEM][JC]
School—Shakopee Area Catholic School. See Elementary Schools, Consolidated, Parochial under Institutions located in the Archdiocese for details. Tel: 612-445-3387.
Catechesis/Religious Programs—305 S. Scott St., 55379. Tel: 612-445-3488.
Students 350.

St. Mary (1865), Rev. A. Michael Sauber; Deacon James L. Thornton.
Res., 535 S. Lewis St., 55379. Tel: 612-445-1319; 445-3234. [CEM][JC]
School—Shakopee Area Catholic School. See Elementary Schools, Consolidated, Parochial under Institutions located in the Archdiocese for details. Tel: 612-445-3387; 445-3159.
Catechesis/Religious Programs—Shakopee Area Religious Education. This is a consolidation of three parish programs. 305 S. Scott St., 55379. Tel: 612-445-3488. D.R.E.: Laura Shupe; Karen Martin.
Students 570.

Shieldsville, Rice Co., St. Patrick (1856) (Irish-Czech), Rev. George Grafsky.
Res., 7525 Dodd Rd., Faribault, 55021. Tel: 507-334-6002. [CEM]

South St. Paul, Dakota Co., Holy Trinity (1918) (Polish), Rev. John M. LeVoir.
Res., 752 5th Ave., S., 55075. Tel: 612-455-1228.
Office: 749 6th Ave., S., 55075. Tel: 612-455-1302.
School—745 6th Ave., S., 55075. Tel: 612-455-8557.
Lay Teachers 21; Students 352.
Catechesis/Religious Programs—Students 224.

St. Augustine (1896), Rev. Raymond J. Zweber.
Res., 302 5th Ave., N., 55075. Tel: 612-451-1212.
Catechesis/Religious Programs—Tel: 612-451-1560; 451-0685. D.R.E.: Sr. Bernadine Frischmon, O.S.B.; Margaret V. Root Kustritz.
Students 198.

St. John Vianney (1946), Rev. Martin A. Beckman; Deacon Fred de los Reyes.
Res., 789 17th Ave., N., 55075. Tel: 612-451-1863; Fax: 612-451-1864.
School—1815 Bromley, 55075. Tel: 612-451-8395.
Lay Teachers 12; Students 200.
Catechesis/Religious Programs—Students 290.

Stillwater, Washington Co., St. Mary (1865), Rev. Patrick J. Wall, Admin.; Deacon Peter Bellavance.
Res., 407 S. 5th St., 55082. Tel: 612-439-1270. [JC]
School—St. Croix Catholic School. See Elementary Schools, Consolidated, Parochial under Institutions located in the Archdiocese for details. Tel: 612-439-5581.
Catechesis/Religious Programs—Tel: 612-439-7142.
Students 163.

St. Michael (1853), Revs. Michael C. Skluzacek; Jonathan Shelley.
Res., 611 S. Third St., 55082. Tel: 612-439-4400; Fax: 612-430-3271. [JC]
Church—611 S. Third St., 55082. Tel: 612-430-2536.
Office: 218 E. Willard St., 55082.
School—St. Croix Catholic School. See Elementary Schools, Consolidated, Parochial under Institutions located in the Archdiocese for details. Tel: 612-439-5581. Martin Weisbeck, Prin.
Catechesis/Religious Programs—Tel: 612-439-7142; Fax: 612-439-7705. William Klein, D.R.E.
Students 900.

Taylors Falls, Chisago Co., St. Joseph's (1873), Rev. Albert J. Shanley, M.S.; Deacon Kevin Madden.
Res., 500 River St., 55084. Tel: 612-465-7345. [CEM][JC]
Mission—Franconia, Chisago Co., St. Francis Xavier, 55084.

Union Hill, Le Sueur Co., St. John the Evangelist, Rev. Elgar Bockenfeld, O.F.M.
Res., Rte. 1, P.O. Box 93, New Prague, 56071. Tel: 612-758-4642. [CEM]

Vermillion, Dakota Co., St. John the Baptist (1881), Rev. Joseph J. Arackal, V.C.
Res., 106 W. Main St., 55085. Tel: 612-437-5652; Fax: 612-437-1933. [CEM]
School—111 W. Main St., 55085. Tel: 612-437-2644.
Franciscan Clarist Sisters 2; Lay Teachers 5; Students 81.

Veseli, Rice Co., Most Holy Trinity (1874) (Czech), Rev. John G. Lapensky.
Res., 9845 Main St., 55046. Tel: 507-744-2823. [CEM 2]
School—Lonsdale, New Market, Veseli Area School. See Elementary Schools, Consolidated, Parochial under Institutions located in the Archdiocese for details. Tel: 507-744-2394.
Catechesis/Religious Programs—Students 198.

Victoria, Carver Co., St. Victoria (1856) (German), Rev. Robert L. White.
Res., Box 8, 55386. Tel: 612-443-2661; Fax: 612-443-2661. [CEM]
Catechesis/Religious Programs—Tel: 612-443-3536.
Students 170.

Waconia, Carver Co., St. Joseph (1859), Rev. Martin J. Siebenaler.
Res., 32 E. 1st St., 55387. Tel: 612-442-2384; Fax: 612-442-4500. [CEM]
School—Tel: 612-442-4500.
Lay Teachers 12; Students 157.
Catechesis/Religious Programs—Tel: 612-442-4871.
Students 150.

Watertown, Carver Co., Immaculate Conception (1863) (German-Irish), Rev. Robert J. Boller.
Res., 109 Angel Ave., N.W., P.O. Box 548, 55388. Tel: 612-955-1458. [CEM]
Catechesis/Religious Programs—113 Angel Ave., N.W., Tel: 612-955-1777. Marianne Kaufmann, D.R.E.
Students 287.

Waterville, Le Sueur Co., Holy Trinity (1892), Rev. Michael W. Ince.
Res., 506 Common St., 56096. Tel: 507-362-4311. [CEM]
Catechesis/Religious Programs—Tel: 507-362-8396.
Students 112.

Waverly, Wright Co., St. Mary (1884), Rev. William F. Martin.
Res., P.O. Box 278, 55390. Tel: 612-658-4319. [CEM]
Catechesis/Religious Programs—Tel: 612-658-4118.
Students 290.

Wayzata, Hennepin Co., Holy Name (1865), Rev. Arnold Weber, O.S.B.; Deacons Joe Wierschem; Nelson Hickman.
Res., 155 County Rd., 24, 55391. Tel: 612-473-9620 (rectory); Fax: 612-473-0598. [CEM]
School—Tel: 612-473-3675; Fax: 612-473-4715.
Lay Teachers 22; Students 362.
Catechesis/Religious Programs—Tel: 612-473-7901.
Students 880.

St. Bartholomew (1916), Rev. Stephen J. LaCanne.
Office: 630 E. Wayzata Blvd., 55391. Tel: 612-473-6601; Fax: 612-473-0980.
School—(Grades PreK-6). Tel: 612-473-6189.
Lay Teachers 12; Students 245.
Catechesis/Religious Programs—Students 250.

Zumbrota, Goodhue Co., St. Paul (1900), Rev. Frank J. Wampach.
Office: 749 S. Main St., 55903. Tel: 507-732-5324. [CEM][JC]
Res., 223 Chester Ave., Bellechester, 55027. Tel: 612-923-4305.
Catechesis/Religious Programs—Students 160.

Chaplains of Public Institutions

ST. PAUL. *Bethesda Medical Center*. Deacon Jerome J. Bilder.
Gillette Children's Hospital. Revs. Joseph Menker, O.M.I.; Robert Allie, O.M.I.
HealthEast, Inc. Rev. Gerald K. Foley (CR).
Midway Hospital. Attended by Church of St. Mark, St. Paul.
Ramsey County Correctional Facilities. Rev. Edward J. Flahavan.
Ramsey County Home. Vacant. 1735 Kennard St., 55109.

St. John's Hospital. (Lutheran), 840 E. 6th St., 55106. Rev. Fabian F. Burdiek, O.F.M.
St. Paul-Ramsey Hospital, 261 E. 8th St., 55101. Revs. Joseph Menker, O.M.I.; Robert Allie, O.M.I.
United Hospitals, Inc. Vacant.
MINNEAPOLIS. *Abbot-Northwestern Hospital,* 3617 38th Ave., S., 55066. Revs. Robert A. Patterson; Clement J. Burke (DUB).
Hennepin County Courts. Rev. James Jackson, 2055 Bohland Ave., St. Paul, 55116.
Hennepin County Medical Center, 2421 Third Ave., S., 55404. Rev. James R. DeBruycker.
Metropolitan Medical Center. Rev. James Cassidy, Chap.
Minneapolis Children's Medical Center, 3617 38th Ave., S., 55406. Rev. Robert A. Patterson.
Minnesota Soldiers' Home. Rev. Eugene J. Abbott.
Riverside Medical Center, 2450 Riverside Ave., 55454. Rev. Leo J. Tibesar.
University of Minnesota Hospitals. Rev. Meinrad Dindorf, O.S.B., Chap., 2001 Dayton Ave., St. Paul, 55104.
Veterans Administration Medical Center, 54th and 48th Aves., S., 55417. Rev. William K. Gamber.
ANOKA. *Anoka State Hospital.* Vacant. 516 School St., 55303.
EDINA. *Fairview-Southdale Hospital.* Rev. Jerome W. Fehn, Chap.
FARIBAULT. *Faribault State School and Hospital.* Attended by Immaculate Conception Parish. Braille and Sight Saving School, Minnesota School for the Deaf, (Retardation).
GOLDEN VALLEY. *North Memorial Hospital.* Rev. Leo D. Krautkremer, 4003 Bryant Ave., N., Minneapolis, 55412.
LINO LAKES. *Minnesota Correctional Facility.* Rev. Msgr. J. Jerome Boxleitner, Chap., 1121 E. 46th St., Minneapolis, 55407.
ST. LOUIS PARK. *Methodist Hospital.* Rev. Jerome W. Fehn, Chap.
SHAKOPEE. *Women's State Reformatory.* Rev. James T. Schoenberger, Church of St. Gregory, North Branch.
STILLWATER. *Minnesota State Prison.* Rev. Gregory A. Skrypek.

Special Assignment:
Reverend Fathers—
Abbott, Eugene J.
Flahavan, Edward J., Chap., Ramsey County Correctional Facilities
Fleming, Martin M.P., Office of Evangelization
Gamber, William K., Chap., V.A. Medical Center
Hubbard, Lawrence E., Hispanic Ministry
Jackson, James, Chap., Hennepin County Courts
Jeub, Richard H., Chancery, Pro Tem.
Johnson, Lawrence R., Chancery Pro Tem.
Kapoun, Robert E., Chancery Pro Tem
Kozlak, Stanley F., Chancery Pro Tem.
Lepak, Roy C., Hermit, Cotton, MN
McConville, James P., Chancery Pro Tem.
Notebaart, James C., Office of Indian Ministry
Snyder, Larry J., Catholic Charities
Stevens, Michael J., Catholic Education Center
Wajda, Joseph L., Tribunal
Walsh, Harry A., Chancery, Pro Tem.
Whittier, William O., Chancery Pro Tem

On Duty Outside the Archdiocese:
Reverend Monsignors—
Namie, James B., Maronite Chancery, P.O. Box 280036 - Dyker Heights Station, Brooklyn, NY 11228-0002
Reverend Fathers—
Brandes, John F., Parroquia San Lucas Toliman, Dept. Solola 07013, Guatemala
Bury, Harold J., P.O. Box 20310, Cleveland, OH 44120
Dempsey, Dennis K., El Buen Pastor Parroquia San Francisco de Asis, Apartado 272, Puerto Ordaz, Estado Bolivar, 8015 Venezuela
Dosh, Mark B., El Buen Pastor Parroquia San Francisco de Asis, Apartado 272, Puerto Ordaz, Estado Bolivar, 8015 Venezuela
O'Connell, Marvin R., University of Notre Dame, IN
Ryan, Patrick J., El Buen Pastor Parraquia San Francisco de Asis, Apartado 272, Puerto Ordaz, Estado Bolivar, 8015 Venezuela
Slusser, Michael S., Dept. of Theology, Duquesne Univ., Pittsburgh, PA 15282

Military Chaplains:
Reverend Fathers—
Himmelsbach, James R., U.S. Army
Smith, John B., U.S. Army
Vakoc, Henry T., U.S. Army

Graduate Studies:
Reverend Fathers—
Byron, J. Michael
Conlin, Daniel C.

Retired:
Reverend Monsignors—
Baumgaertner, William L., 2190 Summit Ave., St. Paul, MN 55105
Dillon, David A., 1011 Feltl Ct., No. 910, Hopkins, MN 55343
DuLac, Henri J., 1011 Feltl Ct., No. 628, Hopkins, MN 55343
Fleming, Francis J., 2115 Summit Ave., Mail #4337, St. Paul, MN 55105
Gilligan, Francis J., Regina Retirement Home, 1175 Nininger Rd., Hastings, MN 55033
Hayden, Ambrose V., 2190 Summit Ave., St. Paul, MN 55105
Hessian, Patrick J., P.O. Box 7598, Silver Spring, MD 20907
Kneal, Ellsworth, 2260 Summit Ave., St. Paul, MN 55105
Lavin, James M., 2115 Summit Ave., St. Paul, MN 55105
Murphy, Terrance J., 2115 Summit Ave., St. Paul, MN 55105
Probst, Robert L., College of St. Thomas, 2115 Summit Ave., St. Paul, MN 55105
Sankovitz, John P., 2115 Summit Ave., St. Paul, MN 55105
Steiner, Clarence J., 324 Pior Ave. S., St. Paul, MN 55105
Sweeney, John A., 179 N. McKnight Rd., No. 210, St. Paul, MN 55119
Reverend Fathers—
Baglio, Joseph L., 2190 Summit Ave., St. Paul, MN 55105
Barthelme, Frederick J., 1204 W. Linden St., Stillwater, MN 56071
Bigot, Ross G., 2190 Summit Ave., St. Paul, MN 55105
Blais, Melvin J., Gallery Towers-Unit 703, 26 W. 10th St., St. Paul, MN 55102
Broker, Ralph H.
Brown, John T., Box 10, Cannon Falls, MN 55009
Buchanan, John J., 2190 Summit Ave., St. Paul, MN 55105
Burns, Donald W., 2067 Sheperd Rd. #205, St. Paul, MN 55116
Cody, Nicholas A., P.O. Box 22, Cross Lake, MN 56442
Colon, Vincent A., 2350 Springside Dr., Maplewood, MN 55119
Conroy, Thomas J.
Decowski, Frank J.
DeSutter, Gilbert J., 24571 W. Cedar Lake Dr., Jordan, MN 55352
Dobihal, Robert F., 2067 Shepard Rd., Apt. 202, St. Paul, MN 55116
Dolan, Leo A., 2190 Summit Ave., St. Paul, MN 55105
Dudley, Francis R., Maternity of B.V.M., St. Paul, MN
Dufresne, Oliver J., P.O. Box 3848, Minneapolis, MN 55403
Dunn, John P., 1926 Norfolk Ave., St. Paul, MN 55116
Dynes, Leo J., 627 Linden Ave., Kilkenny, MN 56052
Egan, Harvey F., 121 S. Washington, No. 512, Minneapolis, MN 55401
Eggert, Charles M., 2190 Summit Ave., St. Paul, MN 55105
Endres, Gilbert J.
Fitzpatrick, John P., Rte. 1, P.O. Box 825, Ogilvie, MN 56358
Gamber, William K.
Gannon, Joseph T., 2190 Summit Ave., St. Paul, MN 55105
Garvey, Thomas J., 1041 16th Ave., S.E., Minneapolis, MN 55414
Gessner, Henry E., 433 W. 5th St., Waconia, MN 55387
Grzeskowiak, Edward S.
Guillemette, Joseph H., 330 S. Exchange St., St. Paul, MN 55102
Hamel, Robert F., 2136 Reaney, St. Paul, MN 55119
Hayes, Francis R., 1500 Douglas Dr., N., Minneapolis, MN 55422
Hermes, Roger J., 4405 Bay Lane, St. Paul, MN 55110
Houle, Cecil T., 4368 Buckingham Ct., Vadnais Heights, MN 55110
Howley, Leo W., 1101 Sibley Memorial Hwy., Unit 111, St. Paul, MN 55118
Huber, Leo R.
Janski, Jerome J., 16551 S. Temple Dr., St. Paul, MN 55345
Jenniges Leonard J., RR. 2, Sanborn, MN 56083
Jirik, Charles C., 1422 Emerson Ave., N., Minneapolis, MN 55411
Joyce, John E., Rt. 1, Henderson, MN 56044
Jude, Robert J., P.O. Box 219, Maple Lake, MN 55358
Karels, Agdus S., 513 N.W. 4th St., Ortonville, MN 56278
Keane, Robert E., 5921 14th Ave. S., Minneapolis, MN 55417
Keller, Lawrence E., 1212 Larpenteur Ave., E., St. Paul, MN 55109
Klein, Bernard C.
Kolar, Thomas F., 2750 N. Victoria St., Room 225, Roseville, MN 55113
Kubat, Alphonse M., 2190 Summit Ave., St. Paul, MN 55105
Larkin, Richard
Louis, Anthony M., 8000 Bass Lake Rd., Rm. 232W, New Hope, MN 55428
Mahoney, Richard J.
McGrade, William H., 6541 Golden Valley Rd. #302, Golden Valley, MN 55427
McNulty, William C., 86 Wilkin St., #209, St. Paul, MN 55102
Mertz, Frederick A., 391 Laurel Ave., #102, St. Paul, MN 55102
Mertz, William H., 4115 Beaver Dam Rd., Eagan, MN 55152
Moorman, Raymond J., 3220 S. Yosemite Ave., S., St. Louis Park, MN 55416
Moudry, Richard P., 11113 Hyland Ter., Eden Prairie, MN 55344
Mycue, Gordon E., 5805 Winnetka Ave., N., New Hope, MN 55428
Payant, Remi J., 2190 Summit Ave., St. Paul, MN 55105
Remes, James A.
Riley, John F., 2190 Summit Ave., St. Paul, MN 55105
Robertson, Thomas J., 2154 Upper Roy Lake, Nisswa, MN 56468
Ryan, T. Kenneth, c/o Catholic Digest, P.O. Box 3090, St. Paul, MN 55165
Salt, Donald L., 2190 Summit Ave., St. Paul, MN 55105
Schmitzer, Richard C., 14047 81st Ave., N., Maple Grove, MN 55369
Schnitzius, Donald J., 2190 Summit Ave., St. Paul, MN 55105
Seefeldt, Wilbert T., 15442 Red Oaks Rd., S.E., Prior Lake, MN 55372
Streff, Joseph N.
Stromberg, James S.
Thurner, Robert M., Chancery, Pro Tem., 2190 Summit Ave., St. Paul, MN 55105
Vrana, Francis R., 14840 62nd St., N., No. 205, Stillwater, MN 55082
Wagner, Alfred S., 2190 Summit Ave., St. Paul, MN 55105
Westhoff, Donald F., 20 E. Exchange B-208, St. Paul, MN 55101
Whalen, James W., University of St. Thomas
Wirth, John J., 330 S. Exchange, St. Paul, MN 55102
Wittman, Karl M.
Zweber, Clement J., P.O. Box 962, Lakeville, MN 55044

Permanent Deacons:
Adrian, Mathias, Retired, St. Paul
Asenbrenner, Francis
Babcock, George H., Basilica of St. Mary, Minneapolis
Barrett, Ervin F., St. Thomas the Apostle, St. Paul
Barrett, Thomas F., St. John the Baptist, Hugo
Barrett, W. Richard, Holy Spirit, St. Paul
Baskfield, James F., St. John the Baptist, Excelsior
Beck, William E., St. Paul, Ham Lake
Becker, Donald L., St. Michael, St. Michael
Beckfeld, William F., St. Bartholomew, Wayzata
Bednarczyk, Peter, Unassigned
Bellavance, Peter G., St.Mary, Stillwater
Berghoff, William J., St. Richard, Richfield
Bernard, Charles V., Leave of Absence
Bilder, Jerome J., St. Agnes, St. Paul
Bisek, Jerome H., St. Alphonsus, Brooklyn Center and AIDS Ministry
Blissenbach, Gerald, Medical leave
Boatwright, Stephen, St. Olaf, Minneapolis
Boisclair, A. Richard, St. Francis, Buffalo
Bramwell, Robert, St. Thomas, Corcoran
Brown, Fredrick L., (Retired)
Campbell, Kevin A., Leave of absence
Carlson, Paul, St. Lawrence, Minneapolis and Metropolitan Tribunal
Carlson, Roger B., Assignment pending
Casey, Patrick J., St. Bonaventure, Bloomington
Cate, Allan, Leave of Absence
Christensen, Harlan L., St. Patrick, Inver Grove Heights
Ciresi, Jerome D., St. Odilia, Shoreview
Coleman, Thomas F., Sacred Heart, Robbinsdale
Conlin, Robert E., St. Mark, St. Paul
D'Heilly, Peter, Dir., Center for Diaconate and

Visitation, Minneapolis
DeLosReyes, Alfredo L., St. John Vianney, S. St. Paul
Devine, Gerald L., Nativity, St. Paul
DeVinney, Charles A., Unassigned
Dinzeo, Anthony J., Bethesda Hospital
Dolan, Thomas E., Holy Rosary, Minneapolis
Dols, Bernard R., St. Vincent de Paul, Osseo
Dondelinger, James, St. Austin, Minneapolis
Donnelly, Patrick T., (Retired)
Dornfeld, Willard, St. Edward, Bloomington
Dubay, Frank X., Diocese of Venice, FL
Dzik, Thomas W., St. Luke, St. Paul
Ehrmantraut, Dominic, St. Stephen, Anoka and St. Walburga, Fletcher
Erpenbach, William L., Sacred Heart, St. Lawrence, Faribault
Evans, Russell, St. John the Baptist, New Brighton
Falvey, William E., St. Adalbert, St. Paul
Feffer, Edward F., St. Pius X, White Bear Lake
Ferguson, Delmar F., Basilica, Minneapolis
Flood, John J., St. Odilia, Shoreview
Frederick, Joseph J., Delano Catholic Community
Freeman, Ronald, St. Timothy, Maple Lake
Gerdts, Michael G., Pax Christi, Eden Prairie
Getz, Ronald L., Retired
Giesen, Robert F., Leave of Absence
Goodwin, Donald, Unassigned
Gruber, Leonard L., St. Dominic, Northfield
Hanten, Nick, Retired
Hathaway, Donald F., Indian Ministry, Minneapolis
Heidenreich, Michael, Diocese of Las Vegas, NV
Hepp, James E., St. Peter, N. St. Paul
Hickman, Nelson, Holy Name, Medina
Hoffman, Gary, St. John Excelsior
Holst, David, St. Alphonsus, Brooklyn Park
Houle, Gary J., St. Peter, Forest Lake
Huberty, Peter J., Mary, Mother of the Church, Burnsville
Hughesdon, Harold, St. Agnes, St. Paul
Huibregtse, David, Immaculate Heart of Mary, Minnetonka, AIDS Ministry
Humbert, Michael, St. Elizabeth Ann Seton, Hastings; Cretin-Derham Hall High School, St. Paul
Janes, Edward, St. Peter, Richfield
Jents, Kevin, St. Timothy, Blaine
Kasbohm, Thomas F., Basilica of St. Mary, Minneapolis
Kattar, Alfred R., Holy Family, St. Louis Park
Kenney, Joseph G., St. Timothy, Blaine
Keys, Thomas, St. John the Evangelist, Little Canada
Kirchoffner, Daniel D., Transfiguration, Maplewood
Konkel, Thomas A., St. Andrew, St. Paul
Koop, Steven E., St. Rita, Cottage Grove
Kuhns, James C., (Retired)
L'Allier, Ralph, St. Peter, Forest Lake
Lagui, Marciano I., St. Bernard, St. Paul
Langlois, Thomas, St. Gregory the Great, North Branch
Lee, Joseph, Office of Indian Ministry
Lewis, Charles, (Retired)
Lo, Va Thai, Hmong Community, St. Vincent de Paul, St. Paul
Lukach, George, St. Henry, Monticello
MacKenzie, John M., St. John the Baptist, Excelsior
Madden, Kevin, St. Joseph, Taylors Falls; St. Francis, Franconia
Maltzen, Bruce H., Diocese of St. Cloud
Mangan, John T., Minnesota Veteran's Home
Mann, George A., Unassigned
Mantel, James F., Immaculate Conception, Watertown
May, Bobby, St. Alphonsus, Brooklyn Center
McDonald, James F., St. Therese, Deephaven
McLaughlin, James, Nativity, Bloomington
McPhee, Don, St. Paul, Ham Lake
McPherson, Joseph T., St. John the Baptist, New Brighton
Medlicott, James V., Retired
Michaud, Thomas P., St. John, Savage
Murphy, James W., St. John, Hopkins
Murphy, John L., St. Matthew, St. Paul
Murphy, Lawrence J., Guardian Angels, Lake Elmo
Neumann, Dennis J., St. Charles Borromeo, St. Anthony
Nguyen, Nhac Phuc, St. Joseph Hien, Minneapolis
Nicklay, John, St. Rita, Cottage Grove
Nicolosi, Dr. Charles, Leave of Absence
Nugent, George J., Mary, Mother of the Church, Burnsville
O'Connor, Robert, United Hospital
O'Keefe, Clyde, (Retired)
Otto, Sherman H., St. Vincent de Paul, Osseo
Palkert, Lawrence, Immaculate Conception, Columbia Heights
Pashby, Richard E., St. Pascal, St. Paul
Pederson, Bernard A., St. Agnes, St. Paul
Pendergast, Donald, Our Lady of Grace, Edina
Rajcich, G. Michael, St. Bridget, Lindstrom
Reed, John A., St. George, Long Lake
Rinkenberger, Donald, St. Joseph the Worker, Maple Grove
Rollings, Virgil, (Retired)
Rudolphi, Byron W., Jr., St. Richard, Richfield
Scherer, Terrance P., St. Patrick, Cedar
Scherkenbach, Gerald A., St. Leo, St. Paul
Schiller, William C., St. Mary of the Lake, Plymouth
Schmitz, Joseph, Woodbury Health Care Center
Schneider, Frank J., St. Jerome, Maplewood
Schramer, Joseph J., Campus Ministry, University of St. Thomas
Schroeder, Allan, St. Mark, Shakopee
Seaton, James B., St. Peter, Mendota
Semlak, Thomas L., St. Casimir, St. Paul
Shambour, Leonard, St. Wenceslaus, New Prague
Shupe, Russell, St. Michael, Prior Lake
Smith, James, (Retired)
Smith, Robert B., Assumption, Richfield
Stevenson, Richard E., St. Leo the Great, St. Paul
Stickney, Stephen S., Sabbatical
Stiles, Thomas G., St. Columba, St. Paul
Stipe, Bruce, Leave of Absence
Straub, Arthur J., Leave of Absence
Stromen, Sherman, St. Mary of the Lake, White Bear Lake
Swirtz, Lawrence, Propagation of the Faith
Tangney, Francis J., St. Joseph, Hopkins
Tatone, Paul M., St. Thomas Becket, Eagan
Thell, Frank J., St. Paul Police Chap.
Thill, Joseph, St. Mary of the Lake, White Bear Lake
Thornton, James, St. Mary, Shakopee
Tift, J. Neil, Cathedral, St. Paul
Trombley, Robert, Leave of Absence
Umphress, William G., Holy Spirit, St. Paul
Urbanski, Roger G., (Retired)
Valdez, Carl R., Hispanic Ministry
Veiman, John, Presentation, Maplewood
Vivier, Louis J., Leave of Absence
Wagner, James M., St. William, Fridley
Wagner, Robert C., St. Hubert, Chanhassen
Warhol, Robert W., Nativity of B.V.M., Bloomington
Warne, Maynard E., St. Michael, St. Michael
Weiland, John D., Our Lady of Peace
Wesley, R. Daniel, Immaculate Conception, Faribault
Wierschem, Joseph G., Holy Name, Medina
Wilkinson, Delvin L., Leave of Absence
Williams, Merlin J., St. Walburga, Fletcher; St. Martin, Rogers
Winkelman, John W., Ascension, Minneapolis
Winn, Luther E., (Retired)
Wirtz, Howard, Pax Christi, Eden Prairie; St. Joseph's Home for Children
Wittman, Wayne C., Sacred Heart, St. Paul
Witucki, Richard P., St. Bartholomew, Wayzata
Woznick, Gregory, On Leave from Duluth
Yaeger, Loren, Leave of Absence
Yekaldo, Fred D., St. Ambrose, St. Paul

INSTITUTIONS LOCATED IN THE ARCHDIOCESE

[A] SEMINARIES, ARCHDIOCESAN

ST. PAUL. *St. John Vianney Seminary*, 2115 Summit Ave., 55105. Tel: 612-962-6825; Fax: 612-962-6835. Rev. Peter F. Christensen, Rector. Spiritual Directors-Counselors: Revs. Paul D. Sirba; Xavier Thelakkatt (India); John Ubel, Counselor; Mrs. Theresa Thurmes, Apostolic Life Coord.; John Daniewicz, D.R.E.; Tim Anderson, Promotions Coord. Students 74.

The Saint Paul Seminary, School of Divinity of the University of St. Thomas, 2260 Summit Ave., 55105. Tel: 612-962-5050; Fax: 612-962-5790. Legal Title: *The Saint Paul Seminary*. Rev. Phillip J. Rask, Ph.D., Rector; Mrs. Jan Viktora, M.A., Asst. Academic Dean; Revs. Dominic Serra, S.L.D.; Thomas Krenik, D.Min., Spiritual Dir.; Jerome M. Dittberner, S.T.D.; Rev. Msgr. Ellsworth Kneal, J.C.D., Prof. Emeritus; Revs. Paul F. Feela, M.A., Dir. Worship; Peter E. Feldmeier, Ph.D.; Ms. Mary Martin, M.A., Theological Librarian; Revs. James R. Motl, O.P., Ph.D.; Ronald Bowers, J.C.D., Vice Rector; Dr. Thomas Fisch, Ph.D.; Dr. Victor J. Klimoski, Ph.D., Academic Dean; Rev. John Echert, S.S.L.; Sr. Christine Athans, B.V.M., Ph.D.; Dr. Gene Scapanski, S.T.D.; Rev. William C. McDonough, S.T.D.; Sr. Carol Rennie, O.S.B., M.A., Dir. Student Life; Dr. David Jenkins, D.Mus., Dir. Liturgical Music; Sr. Paul Therese Saiko, S.S.N.D., M.A.; Sr. Katarina Schuth, O.S.F., Ph.D.; Rev. Robert C. Nygaard; Rev. Msgr. John A. Sweeney; Revs. Gerald Keefe; Douglas Dandurand (SC). MDIV/Seminarians 65; MDIV/non-Sems 7; Pastoral Studies Division 38; Pastoral Studies (non-degree) 6; Doctor of Ministry 31 ; Priests 13; Sisters 4; Lay Staff 23.

[B] SEMINARIES, RELIGIOUS, OR SCHOLASTICATES

ST. PAUL. *Jesuit Novitiate*, 1035 Summit Ave., 55105. Tel: 612-224-5593. Revs. Michael G. Harter, S.J., Supr. and Novice Director; John M. Paul, S.J., Novice Dir.; Bro. John J. Masterson, S.J., Asst. to Novice Dir. Priests 2; Novices 11.

[C] COLLEGES AND UNIVERSITIES

ST. PAUL. *College of St. Catherine*, 2004 Randolph Ave., 55105. Tel: 612-690-6000.
For a complete listing, refer to the Colleges and Universities section.

University of St. Thomas, 2115 Summit Ave., 55105. Tel: 612-962-5000; Fax: 612-962-6504.
For a complete listing, refer to the Colleges and Universities section.

MINNEAPOLIS. *The College of St. Catherine-Minneapolis*, 601 25th Ave. S., 55454. Tel: 612-690-7702.
For a complete listing, refer to the Colleges and Universities section.

[D] HIGH SCHOOLS, PAROCHIAL

ST. PAUL. High Schools are maintained in the following parishes (for particulars refer to the individual parish). City of St. Paul: St. Agnes, St. Bernard.

[E] HIGH SCHOOLS, ARCHDIOCESAN

ST. PAUL. *Hill-Murray School*, 2625 Larpenteur Ave. E., 55109-5098; Fax: 612-770-5262. Joseph M. Peschges, Pres. Lay Teachers 55. Students 760.

The Saint Thomas Academy, 55120. Tel: 612-454-4570. Mr. John B. Greving, Headmaster; Rev. John E. Pilaczynski, O.M.I. Priests 1; Lay Professors 63; Students 694.

MINNEAPOLIS. *De La Salle High School*, Christian Brothers, One De La Salle Dr., 55401. Bro. Michael Collins, F.S.C., Pres.; Barry C. Lieske, Prin. Brothers 6; Sisters 1; Lay Teachers 22; Students 372.

Totino-Grace High School, 1350 Gardena Ave., N.E., 55432. Tel: 612-571-9116. Bro. Milton Barker, F.S.C., Pres.; Kathleen M. Murphy, Prin. Brothers 2; Lay Teachers 60; Students 1,029.

ST. LOUIS PARK. *Benilde-St. Margaret's Jr. & Sr. High School*, 2501 Hwy. 100 S., 55416. Tel: 612-927-4176. Mr. James F. Hamburge, Pres.; Mr. Robert C. Tift, Prin.; Mary Andersen, Asst. Prin. Sisters 2; Lay Teachers 63; Students 920.

[F] HIGH SCHOOLS, PRIVATE

ST. PAUL. *Convent of the Visitation School*. Day School for Girls. 2455 Visitation Dr., 55120. Tel: 612-454-6474; Fax: 612-454-7144. K. Michele Clarke, Head of School. Sisters 3; Lay Teachers 33; Students 256.

Cretin-Derham Hall, 550 S. Albert St., 55116. Tel: 612-690-2443; Fax: 612-696-3393. Co-Sponsors: Brothers of the Christian Schools and Sisters of St. Joseph of Carondelet. Richard Engler, Pres. & Prin. Sisters 6; Brothers 3; Lay Teachers 80; Students 1,245.

FARIBAULT. *Bethlehem Academy*, 55021. Tel: 507-334-3948. Sisters 3; Lay Teachers 16; Students 205.

Faribault B.A., Inc., 55021. Tel: 507-334-3948. Sisters of St. Dominic (Sinsinawa, WI). Sisters 3; Lay Teachers 16; Students 205.

RICHFIELD. *Academy of Holy Angels*, 6600 Nicollet Ave., S., 55423-2498. Tel: 612-798-2600; Fax: 612-798-2610. Dr. Jill M. Reilly, Prin. Priests 1; Sisters 3; Lay Teachers 50; Students 650.

[G] ELEMENTARY SCHOOLS, PRIVATE

MENDOTA HEIGHTS. *Convent of the Visitation School*, 2455 Visitation Dr., 55120. Tel: 612-454-6474; Fax: 612-454-7144. K. Michele Clarke, Head of School. Sisters of The Visitation of Holy Mary 1; Lay Teachers 29; Students 244.

[H] ELEMENTARY SCHOOLS, CONSOLIDATED, PAROCHIAL

ST. PAUL. *Highland Catholic School*. (Grades K-8), 2017 Bohland Ave., 55116. Lay Teachers 25; Students 470. Serving the parishes of St. Leo, St. Therese and St. Gregory.

IHM/St. Luke's Consolidated School. (Grades PreK-8), 1065 Summit Ave., 55105. Tel: 612-224-4836. Sisters 2; Lay Teachers 17; Students 351. Serving the parishes of Immaculate Heart of Mary and St. Luke.

Trinity Catholic School, 835 E. Fifth St., 55106. Sisters 3; Lay Teachers 17; Students 325. Serving the parishes of Sacred Heart, St. Casimir and St. Patrick.

MINNEAPOLIS. *Northeast Regional Catholic School*, 1630 Fourth St, N.E., 55413; Fax: 612-789-8773. Sisters 2; Lay Teachers 13; Students 225. Serving the parishes of St. Cyril & Methodius, Holy Cross, St.

Anthony, All Saints, Our Lady of Lourdes, St. Hedwig, St. Clement, St. Boniface, St. Maron, St. Constantine, Our Lady of Mt. Carmel and St. Lawrence.

Risen Christ Catholic School. (Grades K-2), East Campus: 1120 E. 37th St., 53407. Tel: 612-729-2336. Sisters 1; Lay Teachers 8; Students 199. (Grades 3-8), West Campus: 3800 Pleasant Ave., 55409. Tel: 612-822-5329. Sisters 1; Lay Teachers 14; Students 276. Serving the parishes of Holy Name, Holy Rosary, Incarnation, St. Albert the Great and St. Stephen.

FARIBAULT. *Consolidated Catholic School of Faribault.* (Grades PreK-6), 15 S.W. Third Ave., 55021. Lay Teachers 20; Students 368. Serving the parishes of Immaculate Conception, St. Lawrence and Sacred Heart.

HASTINGS. *St. Elizabeth Ann Seton School*, 600 Tyler St., 55033. Mrs. Barbara Vergenz, Admin. Lay Teachers 24; Students 475.

HOPKINS. *John Ireland Schools.* (Grades PreK-8), 1320 Main Street, 55343. Tel: 612-938-3442. Sisters 2; Lay Teachers 21; Students 244. Serving the parishes of St. John the Evangelist, St. Joseph and Immaculate Heart of Mary.

LONSDALE. *Lonsdale, New Market, Veseli Area Catholic School*, 108 First Ave., S.E., P.O. Box 10, 55046. Sisters 1; Lay Teachers 11; Students 198. Serving the parishes of Veseli, New Market and Lonsdale.

RICHFIELD. *Blessed Trinity Catholic School of Richfield, Minnesota*, 7540 Penn Ave., S., 55423. Tel: 612-866-6906. Rev. Gregory L. Esty, Pres. Lay Teachers 20; Students 450. Serving the parishes of Assumption, St. Peter's and St. Richard's.

SHAKOPEE. *Shakopee Area Catholic School.* (Grades PreK-8), 305 S. Scott, 55379. Tel: 612-445-3387. Notre Dame Sisters 1; Lay Teachers 21; Students 509. Serving the parishes of St. Mark, St. Mary, St. Mary of the Purification.

STILLWATER. *St. Croix Catholic Educational Programs*, 218 E. Willard St., 55082. Tel: 612-439-4400. Rev. Michael C. Skluzacek, Pres. Lay Teachers 21; Students 391. Serving the parishes of St. Michael's, St. Mary's, and St. Charles.

St. Croix Catholic School. (Grades K-8), 621 S. Third St., 55082. Tel: 612-439-5581. Mr. Marty Weisbeck, Prin. Lay Teachers 21; Students 383. Serving the parishes of St. Charles, Bayport; St. Mary, Stillwater; St. Michael, Stillwater.

[I] HOMES FOR CHILDREN

MINNEAPOLIS. *St. Joseph's Home for Children*, 1121 E. 46th St., 55407. Tel: 612-827-6241.

For a complete listing, refer to the Special Care Facilities section.

[J] GENERAL HOSPITALS

HASTINGS. *Regina Medical Center*, 1175 Nininger Rd., 55033. Tel: 612-480-4100.

For a complete listing, refer to the Hospitals section.

NEW PRAGUE. *Queen of Peace Hospital*, 302 Second St., N.E., 56071. Tel: 612-758-4431; Fax: 612-758-5009.

For a complete listing, refer to the Hospitals section.

SHAKOPEE. *St. Francis Regional Medical Center*, 1455 St. Francis Ave., 55379. Tel: 612-403-3000; Fax: 612-403-3820.

For a complete listing, refer to the Hospitals section.

[K] SPECIAL HOSPITALS AND SANATORIA FOR INVALIDS

ST. PAUL. *Our Lady of Good Counsel Home*, 2076 St. Anthony Ave., 55104. Tel: 612-646-2797.

For a complete listing, refer to the Special Care Facilities section.

[L] SOCIAL SERVICE AGENCIES

ST. PAUL. *Home of the Good Shepherd*, 5100 Hodgson Rd., 55126. Tel: 612-484-0221; Fax: 612-486-1616. Helen Chargo, Admin. Diversified programs providing services for women and children. Sisters 7; Lay Staff 33.

[M] HOMES FOR AGED

ST. PAUL. *Bethany Convent for Retired Sisters*, 1870 Randolph, 55105. Tel: 612-690-7050.

For a complete listing, refer to the Special Care Facilities section.

Franciscan Health Community, 1925 Norfolk Ave., 55116. Tel: 612-696-8400.

For a complete listing, refer to the Special Care Facilities section.

Holy Family Residence, 330 S. Exchange St., 55102. Tel: 612-227-0336.

For a complete listing, refer to the Special Care Facilities section.

HASTINGS. *Regina Convalescent and Nursing Care and Retirement Center*, 55033. Tel: 612-480-4333.

For a complete listing, refer to the Special Care Facilities section.

[N] MONASTERIES AND RESIDENCES OF PRIESTS AND BROTHERS

ST. PAUL. *Oblate Provincial Offices*, 267 E. Eighth St., 55101. Tel: 612-292-8622; Fax: 612-292-8769. Revs. David A. Kalert, O.M.I., Prov.; Thomas J. Singer, O.M.I., Personnel Dir.; Robert F. Moosbrugger, O.M.I., Treas.; Edward C. Coleman, O.M.I.; Terence J. Figel O.M.I.; Thomas J. Hayes, O.M.I.; Michael J. Hussey, O.M.I.; Maynard C. Kegler, O.M.I.; Thomas M. Killeen, O.M.I.; John F. Louis, O.M.I.; William E. Nadeau, O.M.I.; James J. Pillar, O.M.I.; Dale M Schlitt, O.M.I.; Jerome A. Ward, O.M.I.; John A. Weissler, O.M.I.; James J. Wynne, O.M.I. Total in Residence 59; Total Staff 16.

Oblate Residence, 104 N. Mississippi River Blvd., 55104. Tel: 612-645-3560. Bro. Gerald Decker, O.M.I., Dir. of House; Revs. Patrick J. Babin, O.M.I.; Edward C. Coleman, O.M.I.; James Datko, O.M.I.; Donald L. Dietz; Thomas J. Hayes, O.M.I.; Michael J. Hussey, O.M.I.; Maynard C. Kegler, O.M.I.; Robert Kell, O.M.I.; Thomas M. Killeen, O.M.I.; John F. Louis, O.M.I.; Leo M. Miller, O.M.I.; Wm. E. Nadeau, O.M.I.; James J. Pillar, O.M.I.; Laurence E. Rosebaugh; Dale M. Schlitt, O.M.I.; Jerome A. Ward, O.M.I.; Paul W. Wilhelm, O.M.I.; James J. Wynne, O.M.I. In res., Bro. Lorenzo Williams, O.M.I.; Revs. David A. Kalert, O.M.I., Prov.; Thomas Singer, O.M.I.; Paul Ischler, O.M.I.; Stanley Sergot, O.M.I.; Robert Moosbrugger, O.M.I.

Special Assignments: Military Chaplains: Rev. Terence J. Figel, O.M.I., Chaplaincy, 1461 Starlifter Cir., Scott AFB, IL, 62225.

MINNEAPOLIS. *La Storta Jesuit Community*, 2201 Pillsbury Ave., S., 55404. Tel: 612-871-1612; Fax: 612-871-0947. Revs. Dennis R. Karamitis, S.J.; Robert H. Fitzgerald, S.J.; Matthew L. Linn, S.J., Supr.; Robert P. Neenan, S.J.; Aloysius F. Schmitz, S.J.; Francis J. Burke, S.J.; Thomas G. Boedy, S.J.; Leon F. Klimczyk, S.J.; John A. Mazzitello, S.J.; John M. Ginsterblum, S.J.; Bro. Lee A. McNamee, S.J.

Maryknoll Fathers and Brothers, Catholic Foreign Mission Society of America, 10345 Portland Ave. S., 55420. Tel: 612-884-7743; Fax: 612-884-7744. Rev. Dennis T. Dunne, Dir.

Paulist Fathers, 1201 Fifth St., S.E., 55414. Tel: 612-331-7941; Fax: 612-378-1771. Revs. John J. Behnke, C.S.P.; Wilfred A. Brimley, C.S.P., (Retired); James B. Corbett, C.S.P., (Retired); James F. Wiesner, C.S.P. Total in Residence 6.

St. Albert the Great Priory, 2833 32nd Ave., S., 55406. Tel: 612-724-3644; Fax: 612-724-5057. Rev. Jay M. Harrington, O.P., Prior. Order of Preachers (Dominicans). Province of St. Albert the Great.

ANOKA. *Crosier Community of Anoka*, 516 School St., 55303-2349. Tel: 612-421-7115. In res., Revs. Dale Ettel, O.S.C.; David E. Gallus, O.S.C.; Kenneth Opat, O.S.C., Supr.; Michael Paquet, O.S.C.; Eugene D. Plaisted, O.S.C.; Michael Van Sloun, O.S.C.

SHOREVIEW. *Crosier Community of Shoreview*, 3500 Vivian Ave., 55126-3852. Tel: 612-490-3352. Revs. Jerome Schik, O.S.C.; Dale Ehrman, O.S.C.; Marven Tellers, O.S.C.; Richard McGuire, O.S.C.; Thomas O'Brien, O.S.C.; Thomas Carkhuff, O.S.C.; Bro. Augustine Schloesser, O.S.C.

Crosier Provincial House Province of St. Odilia, 3470 Vivian Ave., 55126. Tel: 612-787-0832. In res., Very Rev. John J. Neville, O.S.C., Prov.

[O] CONVENTS AND RESIDENCES FOR SISTERS

ST. PAUL. *Contemplative Sisters of the Good Shepherd*, 5104 Hodgson Rd., 55126-1229. Tel: 612-482-5240. Sr. Teresita Mater, Supr. Sisters 15.

Convent of the Good Shepherd, 5100 Hodgson Rd., 55126-1297. Tel: 612-484-0221; Fax: 612-486-1600. Sr. Joan Spiering, Pres. Sisters of the Good Shepherd 38. Contemplative Sisters of the Good Shepherd, 5104 Hodgson Rd., 55126-1229. Tel: 612-482-5240; Fax: 612-486-1600. Sisters 22.

Franciscan Sisters of Little Falls, MN (O.S.F.), 727 E. Margaret St., 55106. Tel: 612-772-1740. Sr. Jean Schwieters, O.S.F., Formation Min. Professed 3; Novices 1.

Franciscan Sisters of St. Paul, Franciscan Regional Center, 1388 Prior Ave., S., 55116. Tel: 612-690-1501; Fax: 612-690-2509. Sr. Antonice Delury, O.S.F., Reg. Dir. Sisters 14.

Monastery of the Visitation, 2455 Visitation Dr., 55120. Tel: 612-683-1700. Sr. Mary Denise Villaume, V.H.M., Supr. Visitation Nuns 19.

St. Mary's Mission House, 265 Century Ave., 55125. Tel: 612-738-9704. Missionary Sisters of St. Peter Claver. Sr. Maria Moryl, S.S.P.C., Supr. Sisters 10; Novices 3.

St. Paul's Priory, 2675 Larpenteur Ave., E., 55109. Tel: 612-777-8181; Fax: 612-777-4442. Benedictine Sisters of Pontifical Jurisdiction. Sr. Marie Fujan, O.S.B., Prioress; Sr. Mary Lou Dummer, O.S.B., Subprioress. Sisters 94.

Sisters of St. Joseph of Carondelet, 1884 Randolph Ave., 55105. Tel: 612-690-7000; Fax: 612-690-7039. Province Leadership Team: Sr. Margaret Belanger, C.S.J.; Sr. Margaret L. Kvasnicka, C.S.J.; Sr. Ann V. Walton, C.S.J. Sisters of Province 473; Total Staff 91.

Carondelet Center; St. Joseph School of Music; Carondelet-Suzuki Talent Education School; Editorial Development Associates; Project One-Fifty; Sisters Care; Free Store; Derham Community; Vineyard; Carondelet LifeCare Ministries/St. Mary's Health Clinics; Youth & Family Center, Inc.; Holy Family Hospital; Cardondelet LifeCare Corporation; Sisters of St. Joseph of Carondelet Ministries Foundation, St. Paul Province; Learning in Style; INSTEP, Women at the Well; Adult Literacy; The College of St. Catherine; Minnesota Center for Health Care Ethics; Wisdom Ways: A Resource Center for Spirituality.

Sisters of the Good Shepherd - St. Paul Province, 5100 Hodgson Rd., 55126. Tel: 612-484-0221; Fax: 612-486-1611. Sr. Joan Spiering, Prov. Supr.

MINNEAPOLIS. *Congregation of the Handmaids of the Holy Child Jesus*, 1705 Bryant Ave., S., 55411. Tel: 612-521-3127. Sr. Rosemary I. Essien, Pres.; Sr. Mary O. Abue, Vice Pres.; Sr. Carolyn O. Onyeoziri, Sec. & Treas.; Sr. Geraldine Inyang.

St. Clare's Monastery of the Infant Jesus, 8650 Russell Ave. S., 55431-1998. Tel: 612-881-4766. Sr. Mary Catherine Martin, O.S.C., Abbess. Franciscan Poor Clare Nuns. Professed Nuns 16.

Visitation Monastery of Minneapolis, 1527 Fremont Ave., N., 55411. Tel: 612-521-6113. Sr. Mary Margaret McKenzie, V.H.M., Supr.

LAKE ELMO. *Carmel of Our Lady of Divine Providence*, 8251 De Montreville Tr. N., 55042-9547. Tel: 612-777-3882. Sr. Paula of the Eucharist, O.C.D., Prioress; Rev. John M. Burns, Chap. Discalced Carmelite Nuns. Professed 9; Postulants 1; Novices 3.

WAYZATA. *Franciscan Clarist Congregation, F.C.C.*, Vimala Province, Convent of St. Therese House, 17931 Minnetonka Blvd., 55391. Tel: 612-473-4771. Sr. Mary Vandanakara, Coord. Total in Residence 6.

[P] SECULAR INSTITUTES

ST. PAUL. *Missionaries of the Kingship of Christ*, The Chancery, 226 Summit Ave., 55102. Tel: 612-291-4400. Sr. M. Dominica Brennan, O.P. Secular Institute of Pontifical Right for women and men founded in Italy in 1919.

[Q] RETREAT HOUSES AND CENTERS OF SPIRITUALITY

ST. PAUL. *Benedictine Center - St. Paul's Priory*, 2675 E. Larpenteur Ave., 55109. Tel: 612-777-7251; Fax: 612-777-4442. Patricia Roberts, Dir. Total Staff 6.

Catholic Youth Ministry Services, 328 W. Kellogg, 55102. Tel: 612-291-4500. Mr. Gregory T. Weinand, Dir.

Loyola, 389 N. Oxford St., 55104. Tel: 612-641-0008. Rev. Richard M. Rice, S.J.; Sr. Elizabeth Kerwin, C.S.J., Dir. Total Staff 7.

Maryhill Retreat Center, 260 Summit Ave., 55102. Tel: 612-224-3615. Daughters of the Heart of Mary Sisters 14.

BUFFALO. *Christ the King Retreat Center*, 621 First Ave., S., 55313. Tel: 612-682-3453. Revs. Aloysius Svobodny, O.M.I.; James L. Datko; John H. McManus, O.M.I.; James D. Deegan, O.M.I., Dir.; Dennis L. Deis, O.M.I.; Bro. Anthony Szklarski, O.M.I., Bus. Mgr. Total in Residence 6; Total Staff 24.

FRONTENAC. *Villa Maria Center*, 29847 County Blvd. 2, 55026. Tel: 612-345-4582. Sr. Carolyn Marie Brockland, O.S.U., Prioress; Sr. Chabanel Mathison, O.S.U., Dir. Ursuline Sisters of the Roman Union 14.

LAKE ELMO. *Jesuit Retreat House*, 8243 Demontreville Tr., N., 55042. Tel: 612-777-1311. Revs. Gerald E. Goetz, S.J., Dir.; Edward S. Sthokal, S.J., Asst. Total in Residence 2; Total Staff 5.

MARINE ON ST. CROIX. *Christian Brothers Retreat Center*, 15525 St. Croix Tr., N., 55047. Tel: 612-433-2486. Bro. Charles Kelly, F.S.C., Admin. Total in Residence 8; Total Staff 12.

PRIOR LAKE. *Franciscan Retreat House*, 16385 Saint Francis Ln., 55372. Tel: 612-447-2182. Bro. Ambrose Eischens, O.F.M.Conv., Dir. of Retreats; Revs. Mark F. Mindrup, O.F.M.Conv.; Ambrose Finnegan, O.F.M.Conv.; Simeon Yates, O.F.M.Conv.; Howard Hansen, O.F.M.Conv., (Community Guardian); Francisco Gomez, O.F.M.Conv.; Bro. Louis Fouquette, O.F.M.Conv.

WAYZATA. *Cenacle Retreat House*, 1221 Wayzata Blvd., 55391-1942. Tel: 612-473-7308. Sr. Laura Koberlein, R.C., Supr.; Sr. Mary Peters, R.C., Coord. of Ministry; Rev. Matthew L. Linn, S.J. Cenacle Religious 4; Lay Directors 50.

[R] HOMES FOR DISABLED

ST. PAUL. *Guild Supported Housing Services*, 289 E. Fifth St., 55101. Tel: 612-291-0067.

For a complete listing, refer to the Special Care Facilities section.

Our House of Minnesota, Inc. I, 1846 Dayton Ave., 55104. Tel: 612-644-6650.

For a complete listing, refer to the Special Care Facilities section.

Our House of Minnesota, Inc. II, 1846 Portland, 55104. Tel: 612-644-2411.

For a complete listing, refer to the Special Care Facilities section.

[S] MINNESOTA CATHOLIC CONFERENCE (M.C.C.)

ST. PAUL. *Minnesota Catholic Conference,* 475 University Ave. W., Ste. B, 55103. Tel: 612-227-8777; Fax: 612-227-2675. Rev. David F. McCauley (FAR), Exec. Dir.; Thomas J. Pearson, Dir. Education Dept.; Timothy J. Rudnicki, Dir. Social Concerns Dept. Total Staff 7. The M.C.C. is a Minnesota Corporation, the purpose of which is to promote the general welfare of the people of the State of Minnesota. All Catholic Bishops of the State of Minnesota constitute Ex Officio the Board of Directors.

[T] ASSOCIATIONS OF THE FAITHFUL

ST. PAUL. *The Companions of Christ,* 2137 Marshall Ave., 55104. Tel: 612-642-5933. Jeffrey Huard, Mod. Total in Residence 11.

Franciscan Brothers of Peace, Inc., Queen of Peace Friary, 1289 Lafond Ave., 55104. Tel: 612-646-8586. Bros. Michael Gaworski, F.B.P., Founder; Paul O'Donnell, F.B.P., Guardian Overall. Total Assisted 18; Total in Residence 9; Total Staff 2.

LAKE ELMO. *Hermits of the Most Blessed Virgin Mary of Mount Carmel,* 8249 De Montreville Tr., N., 55042-9545. Tel: 612-779-7351. Carmel of the Blessed Virgin Mary. Revs. John M. Burns, Prior; Joseph V. Vaccaro. Priests 2; Brothers 5.

WEST ST. PAUL. *Community of Christ the Redeemer,* 110 Crusader Ave., 55118. Tel: 612-451-6114. Mr. James C. Kolar, Pres.

NET Ministries, Inc., 110 Crusader Ave., W., 55118-4427. Tel: 612-450-6833; Fax: 612-450-9984. Mr. Mark Berchem, Exec. Dir. Total Staff 24.

[U] CAMPS AND COMMUNITY CENTERS

ST. PAUL. *Catholic Youth Ministry Services,* 328 W. Kellogg, 55102. Tel: 612-290-1644. Mr. Gregory T. Weinand, Dir.

MCGREGOR. *Catholic Youth Camps, Inc.* Mailing Address: Administrative Office: 2131 Fairview Ave. N., Ste. 200, Roseville, 55113. Tel: 612-636-1645. Mr. Jerome J. Meeds, Camp. Dir., Location: HCR 3, Box 655, 55760. Tel: 218-426-3383. Total Assisted 1,535; Total Staff 55.

[V] NEWMAN CENTERS

MINNEAPOLIS. *University of Minnesota Newman Center and Chapel,* 1701 University Ave., S.E., 55414. Tel: 612-331-3437. Rev. Paul S. Rospond, C.S.P., Dir.; Robert Hayden, Admin. Campus Ministers: Rev. Charles A. Martin, C.S.P.; Sr. Jeri Cashman, O.P.; Bro. Fintan Moore, C.F.C.; Tom Conry. Total Staff 8.

[W] MISCELLANEOUS LISTINGS

ST. PAUL. *Carondelet Lifecare Ministries/St. Mary's Health Clinics,* 1884 Randolph Ave., 55105-1700. Tel: 612-690-7020. Sr. Mary Madonna Ashton, Pres. Neighborhood Clinics 11; Patient visits 5,063; Total Staff 11.

Christian Brothers Youth Home, 1540 Lincoln Ave., 55105. Tel: 612-699-0736. Bro. Michael Lee Anderson, F.S.C., Dir.; Mr. Pat McGuire. Total Assisted 15; Total Staff 2.

Missionary Oblates of Mary Immaculate, 267 E. Eighth St., 55101. Tel: 612-292-8622. Legal Title: *Missionary Oblates of Mary Immaculate Central United States Province - Continuity of Care Charitable Trust.*

Nativity of Our Lord Endowment Fund, 1900 Wellesley Ave., 55105. Tel: 612-699-0309; Fax: 612-696-5458. Rev. Patrick D. Lannan, Vice Pres. Total Assisted 2,000; Total Staff 15.

Oblate Media and Communication Corporation, 267 E. Eighth St., 55101. Tel: 612-292-8622. Rev. David A. Kalert, O.M.I., Pres. Oblates of Mary Immaculate, Central U.S. Province.

St. Joseph's Hospital Sponsor, Inc., 1884 Randolph Ave., 55105. Sr. Margaret L. Kuasnicka, C.S.J., Pres.

Sisters of St. Joseph of Carondelet Ministries Foundation, St. Paul Province, 1884 Randolph Ave., 55105. Tel: 612-690-7026. Sr. Irene O'Neill, C.S.J., Dir.

**The Archdiocese of St. Paul and Minneapolis Catholic Community Foundation,* 328 W. Kellogg Blvd., 55102. Tel: 612-290-1610. Mr. James Mullin, Exec. Dir.

MINNEAPOLIS. *Catholic Eldercare, Inc.,* 817 Main St., N.E., 55413. Tel: 612-379-1370. Michael J. Shasky, COO.
Skilled Nursing Facility, 150 Beds; Assisted Living Apartments for Elderly Adults, 52 Units; Home Health Care for the Elderly, 250 Assisted. Total Assisted 500; Total Staff 300.

**Samaritan Homes, Inc.,* 4639 Blaisdell Ave., S., 55409. Tel: 612-824-2911. Bros. Paul O'Donnell, F.B.P., Pres.; Anthony Sweere, F.B.P., Vice Pres. & Sec.; Dominic Marie Hart, F.B.P., Guardian.

To Encounter Christ of the Archdiocese of St. Paul-Minneapolis, Minnesota, Inc., 1201 S.E. Fifth St., 55414. Tel: 612-331-3644. Pam Germscheid DeMorett, Prog. Coord.

Twin Cities Catholic Alumni Club, Mailing Address: P.O. Box 581321, 55458-1321. Tel: 612-338-1288. Teddi Tri, Club Pres.

Youth and Family Center Inc., 4405 E. Lake St., 55406. Sr. Martha Merriman, C.S.J., Dir.; Sr. Betty Wurm, C.S.J., Dir. Counseling Center. Total Assisted 150; Total Staff 3.

MAPLEWOOD. *Maple Tree: Priory Childcare Center,* 1695 Century Ave., N., 55109. Tel: 612-770-0766. Sr. Marie Fujan, Prioress - St. Paul Priory; Sr. Mary Lou Dummer, Pres. Total Assisted 67; Total Staff 21.

SHAKOPEE. *St. Gertrude's Health Center,* 1850 Sarazin St., 55379. Tel: 612-403-3499. Ron Gilsrud, Admin.; Barry J. Halm, Pres.; David H. Amundson, Treas.; Sr. Kathleen Hofer, CEO.

SHOREVIEW. *Crosier Missions,* 3510 Vivian Ave., 55126-3852. Tel: 612-486-7456. Rev. David E. Gallus, O.S.C., Dir. Total in Residence 15; Total Staff 1.

WEST ST. PAUL. *St. Paul's Outreach, Inc.,* 110 Crusader Ave., 55118. Tel: 612-451-6114. Mr. Gordon C. DeMarais, Pres.; Dr. James C. Kolar, Vice Pres.; Patrick D. Menke, Sec. & Treas.

RELIGIOUS INSTITUTES OF MEN REPRESENTED IN THE ARCHDIOCESE

For further details refer to the corresponding bracketed number in the Religious Institutes of Men or Women section.

[0200]—*Benedictine Monks.* (St. John's Abbey).—O.S.B.
[0330]—*Brothers of the Christian Schools.* (Winona Province).—F.S.C.
[0400]—*Canons Regular of the Order of the Holy Cross.*—O.S.C.
[0470]—*The Capuchin Fathers.* (Prov. of St. Joseph).—O.F.M.Cap.
[0480]—*Conventual Franciscans.* (Prov. of Our Lady of Consolation).—O.F.M.Conv.
[0520]—*Franciscan Friars.* (Prov. of Sacred Heart).—O.F.M.
[0690]—*Jesuit Fathers and Brothers.* (Wisconsin Prov.).—S.J.
[0780]—*Marist Fathers.* (American Prov.).—S.M.
[0800]—*Maryknoll.*—M.M.
[0720]—*The Missionaries of Our Lady of La Salette.*—M.S.
[0910]—*Oblate Fathers of Mary Immaculate.* (Central Prov.).—O.M.I.
[0430]—*Order of Preachers (Dominicans).* (Prov. of St. Albert the Great).—O.P.
[1030]—*Paulist Fathers.*—C.S.P.
[1070]—*Redemptorist Fathers.* (St. Louis Prov.).—C.SS.R.
[1060]—*Society of the Precious Blood.* (Cincinnati Prov.).—C.PP.S.
[0560]—*Third Order Regular of St. Francis.* (Prov. of the Immaculate Conception).—T.O.R.
[]—*Vincentian Congregation.* (India).—V.C.

RELIGIOUS INSTITUTES OF WOMEN REPRESENTED IN THE ARCHDIOCESE

[0230]—*Benedictine Sisters of Pontifical Jurisdiction.* (Crookston, St. Paul, St. Joseph, Duluth, MN).—O.S.B.
[3110]—*Congregation of Our Lady of the Retreat in the Cenacle.*—R.C.
[3710]—*Congregation of the Sisters of St. Agnes.*—C.S.A.
[1780]—*Congregation of the Sisters of the Third Order of St. Francis of Perpetual Adoration.* (Eastern Region).—F.S.P.A.
[0810]—*Daughters of the Heart of Mary.*—D.H.M.
[0420]—*Discalced Carmelite Nuns.*—O.C.D.
[1070-03]—*Dominican Sisters.*—O.P.
[1070-10]—*Dominican Sisters.*—O.P.
[1070-23]—*Dominican Sisters.*—O.P.
[1170]—*Felician Sisters.*—C.S.S.F.
[1310]—*Franciscan Sisters of Little Falls, Minnesota.*—O.S.F.
[1485]—*Franciscan Sisters of St. Paul, MN.*—O.S.F.
[2575]—*Institute of the Sisters of Mercy of the Americas.* (Dubuque, IA; Detroit, MI; Omaha, NE).—R.S.M.
[2340]—*Little Sisters of the Poor.*—L.S.P.
[3990]—*Missionary Sisters of St. Peter Claver.*—S.S.P.C.
[3760]—*Order of St. Clare.*—O.S.C.
[3230]—*Poor Handmaids of Jesus Christ.*—P.H.J.C.
[2970]—*School Sisters of Notre Dame.*—S.S.N.D.
[1680]—*Schools Sisters of St. Francis.*—O.S.F.
[3590]—*Servants of Mary (Servite Sisters).*—O.S.M.
[3520]—*Servants of the Holy Heart of Mary.*—S.S.C.M.
[0520]—*Sisters of Charity of Our Lady, Mother of Mercy.*—S.C.M.M.
[0430]—*Sisters of Charity of the Blessed Virgin Mary.*—B.V.M.
[0660]—*Sisters of Christian Charity.*—S.C.C.
[1705]—*The Sisters of St. Francis of Assisi.*—O.S.F.
[1530]—*Sisters of St. Francis of the Congregation of Our Lady of Lourdes, Sylvania, Ohio.*—O.S.F.
[1570]—*Sisters of St. Francis of the Holy Family.*—O.S.F.
[3840]—*Sisters of St. Joseph of Carondelet.*—C.S.J.
[3880]—*Sisters of St. Joseph of Medaille.*—C.S.J.
[3930]—*Sisters of St. Joseph of the Third Order of St. Francis.*—S.S.J.-T.O.S.F.
[1020]—*Sisters of the Divine Redeemer.*—S.D.R.
[1830]—*The Sisters of the Good Shepherd.*—R.G.S.
[2110]—*Sisters of the Humility of Mary.*—H.M.
[3320]—*Sisters of the Presentation of the B.V.M.* (Dubuque, IA; Sioux Falls, SD).—P.B.V.M.
[1720]—*Sisters of the Third Order Regular of St. Francis of the Congregation of Our Lady of Lourdes.*—O.S.F.
[2150]—*Sisters, Servants of the Immaculate Heart of Mary.*—I.H.M.
[4110]—*Ursuline Nuns (Roman Union).*—O.S.U.
[4190]—*Visitation Nuns.*—V.H.M.

ARCHDIOCESAN CEMETERIES

ST. PAUL. *Calvery.*
The Catholic Cemeteries, Central Office, 244 Dayton Ave., 55102. Tel: 612-227-6543.

MINNEAPOLIS. *St. Anthony & St. Mary.*

MENDOTA HEIGHTS. *Resurrection.*

NEW HOPE. *Assumption & Gethsemane.*

PARISH CEMETERIES

SHAKOPEE, MN. *Catholic Cemeteries of Shakapee, Minnesota, Inc.* A corporation formed by the Church of St. Mark and the Church of St. Mary, both of Shakopee, to consolidate separate cemeteries. 535 S. Lewis St., 55379.

NECROLOGY

† Koziol, Thaddeus R., (Retired). —Died April 7, 1996.
† Luger, Arnold E., (Retired). —Died Nov. 19, 1995.
† Tomlinson, Donald F., (Retired). —Died Nov. 9, 1995.
† Zlotkowski, Clarence L., (Retired). —Died Oct. 3, 1996.

Diocese of St. Petersburg

(Dioecesis Sancti Petri in Florida)

Most Reverend

ROBERT N. LYNCH

Fourth Bishop of St. Petersburg; ordained May 13, 1978; appointed Fourth Bishop of St. Petersburg December 5, 1995; consecrated and installed January 26, 1996. *Office: P.O. Box 40200, St. Petersburg, FL, 33743-0200.*

Most Reverend

W. THOMAS LARKIN, D.D.

Retired Bishop of St. Petersburg; ordained May 15, 1947; appointed Second Bishop of St. Petersburg April 24, 1979; ordained Bishop May 27, 1979; installed June 28, 1979; retired November 28, 1988.

ESTABLISHED JUNE 17, 1968.

Square Miles 3,177.

Comprises the Counties of Citrus, Hernando, Hillsborough, Pasco and Pinellas in the State of Florida.

For legal titles of parishes and diocesan institutions, consult the Chancery.

Chancery: P.O. Box 40200, St. Petersburg, FL, 33743-0200. Tel.: 813-344-1611; Fax: 813-345-2143.

STATISTICAL OVERVIEW

Personnel	
Bishop	1
Retired Bishops	2
Retired Abbots	1
Priests: Diocesan Active in Diocese	99
Priests: Active Outside Diocese	10
Priests: Retired, Sick or Absent	21
Number of Diocesan Priests	130
Religious Priests in Diocese	147
Extern Priests in Diocese	70
Ordinations:	
Diocesan Priests	2
Transitional Deacons	4
Permanent Deacons in Diocese	71
Total Brothers	50
Total Sisters	350
Parishes	
Parishes	72
With Resident Pastor:	
Resident Diocesan Priests	60
Resident Religious Priests	12
Without Resident Pastor:	
Missions	5
Pastoral Centers	1
New Parishes Created	1
Welfare	
Catholic Hospitals	2
Total Assisted	589,704
Health Care Centers	7
Total Assisted	38,129
Homes for the Aged	7
Total Assisted	1,610
Day Care and Extended Day Care Centers	13
Total Assisted	1,432
Specialized Homes	2
Total Assisted	208
Special Centers for Social Services	36
Total Assisted	396,211
Educational	
Diocesan Students in Other Seminaries	11
Total Seminarians	11
Colleges and Universities	1
Total Students	7,179
High Schools, Diocesan and Parish	5
Total Students	1,847
High Schools, Private	2
Total Students	978
Elementary Schools, Diocesan and Parish	40
Total Students	10,792
Elementary Schools, Private	4
Total Students	1,239
Non-residential Schools for the Disabled	2
Total Students	133
Catechesis/Religious Education:	
High School Students	2,443
Elementary Students	18,891
Total Students Under Catholic Instruction	43,513
Teachers in the Diocese:	
Priests	14
Brothers	4
Sisters	60
Lay Teachers	803
Vital Statistics	
Receptions into the Church:	
Infant Baptism Totals	4,423
Adult Baptism Totals	712
Received into Full Communion	567
First Communions	4,963
Confirmations	3,403
Marriages:	
Catholic	1,068
Interfaith	987
Total Marriages	2,055
Deaths	4,319
Total Catholic Population	353,117
Total Population	2,287,817

Former Bishops—Most Rev. CHARLES B. MCLAUGHLIN, D.D., ord. June 6, 1941; appt. Titular Bishop of Risinium and Auxiliary of Raleigh, Jan. 13, 1964; appt. First Bishop of St. Petersburg, May 8, 1968; installed June 17, 1968; died in Office, Dec 14, 1978.—Most Rev. W. THOMAS LARKIN, D.D., ord. May 15,1947; Second Bishop of St. Petersburg; appt. April 24, 1979; ord. Bishop, May 27, 1979; installed June 28, 1979; retired Nov. 28, 1988.—Most Rev. JOHN C. FAVALORA, D.D., Third Bishop of St. Petersburg; ord. Dec. 20, 1961; appt. Bishop of Alexandria, June 16, 1986; ord. and installed July 29, 1986; appt. Third Bishop of St. Petersburg, March 7, 1989; installed May 16, 1989; installed Third Archbishop of Miami, Dec. 20, 1994.

Diocesan Offices

Chancery—6363 Ninth Ave. N., St. Petersburg, 33710. Tel: 813-344-1611; Fax: 813-345-2143. *Mailing Address: P.O. Box 40200, St. Petersburg, 33743-0200.*

Notre Dame Building—6533 Ninth Ave. N., St. Petersburg, 33710. Tel: 813-345-3338; Fax: 813-347-6508. *Mailing Address: P.O. Box 43022, St. Petersburg, 33743-3022.*

Tribunal—905 S. Prospect Ave., Clearwater, 34616. Tel: 813-446-2326; 442-8884; Fax: 813-446-4287. *Mailing Address: P.O. Box 1460, Clearwater, 34617.*

Catholic Media Center—2816 Morrison Ave., Tampa, 33629. Tel: 813-289-4562 (Hillsborough); 823-5346 (Pinellas). *Mailing Address: P.O. Box 18081, Tampa, 33679.*

WBVM Radio—Tampa. Tel: 813-289-8040.

Office of the Bishop; Most. Rev. ROBERT N. LYNCH

Executive Secretary—Mrs. SUE TULLY.

Diocesan Curia

Vicar General and Moderator of the Curia—Rev. Msgr. BRENDAN MULDOON, V.G.; Mrs. JOAN MORGAN, Sec.

Chancellor—Rev. ROBERT C. GIBBONS, J.C.L.; Mrs. SOPHIE CARROLL, Sec. & Notary; Mrs. LISA MOBLEY, Archivist.

Judicial Vicar—Very Rev. DACIAN DEE, J.C.D.

Tribunal Staff—Rev. WILLIAM SWENGROS, J.C.L., Vice Judicial Vicar; Revs. STEPHEN DAMBRAUSKAS, J.C.L., Defender of the Bond; ROBERT C. GIBBONS, J.C.L., Promoter of Justice; RONALD AUBIN, J.C.L., Judge; Mr. ANTHONY ELLUL, J.C.D., Judge; Deacon KAZIMIEREZ MIELCAREK, Ph.D., Auditor. Notaries: Mrs. SARAH DURST; Mrs. LOUISE KNOCHELMANN; Mrs. MARY SUE OLIVER.

Vicar for Clergy—Rev. Msgr. JOHN NEFF, *St. Paul Church, 12708 N. Dale Mabry Hwy., Tampa, 33624.* Tel: 813-961-3023.

Personnel Board—Revs. ARTHUR PROULX, Chm. DENNIS HUGHES; ROBERT MORRIS; Rev. Msgr. J. BERNARD CAVERLY. Ex-Officio: Rev. Msgr. JOHN NEFF; Rev. Msgr. BRENDAN MULDOON; Rev. ROBERT C. GIBBONS, J.C.L.

Incardination Commission—Rev. Msgr. JOHN NEFF, Chm.; Rev. ROBERT C. GIBBONS, J.C.L., Exec. Sec.; Revs. THOMAS EARNER, V.F.; JOSEPH PELLEGRINO; Rev. Msgr. BRENDAN MULDOON; Rev. MICHAEL LYDON.

Vocations Office—Rev. MICHAEL O'BRIEN, Dir. Vocations, *Notre Dame Building.* Asst. Dirs.: Revs. LEONARD PIOTROWSKI; ARTHUR PROULX; Sr. PHYLLIS SHAUGHNESSY, O.S.C.

Permanent Diaconate Office—Revs. THOMAS MADDEN, Dir. ALAN WEBER, Assoc. Dir., *Notre Dame Building;* Deacon JOSEPH BROWN, Asst. Dir.

Vicar for Religious—Very Rev. JUDE DUFFY, O.F.M.Cap.,

Most Holy Redeemer Church, 10110 Central Ave., Tampa, 33612. Tel: 813-933-2859. Sr. EUGENE MARIE SCHNEIDER, O.S.F., Sec., *Notre Dame Building.*

Our Lady of Good Counsel Camp—Rev. JAMES JOHNSON, Dir., *8888 E. Gobbler Dr., Floral City, 32636.* Tel: 904-726-2198.

Department of Apostolates

Executive Director—Rev. ROBERT C. GIBBONS, J.C.L.

Black Catholics, Office of—Rev. CALLIST NYAMBO, Dir.; Ms. YVONNE NELLUM, Coord., *Catholic Media Center.*

Charismatic Renewal, Office of—Dr. RONALD NOVOTNY, Coord., *709 Bayview Ave., Clearwater, 34619.* Tel: 813-797-3311. Rev. ANTONIO DIEZ, Spanish Speaking Spiritual Moderator, *6819 Krycul Ave., P.O. Box 418, Riverview, 33569.* Tel: 813-677-2175.

Cursillo—Rev. Msgr. JOHN MCNULTY, P.A., Moderator, *Notre Dame Building.* Tel: 813-345-3338.

Spanish Cursillo—Deacon JOHN SIERRA, Dir., *St. Paul Church, 12708 N. Dale Mabry Hwy., Tampa, 33624.* Tel: 813-961-3023.

Cursillo Center—1706 11th Ave., Tampa, 33675. Tel: 813-248-3942.

Ecumenical and Inter-Religious Affairs—Rev. Msgr. J. BERNARD CAVERLY, *St. Raphael Church, 1376 Snell Isle Blvd. N.E., St. Petersburg, 33704.* Tel: 813-821-7989.

Evangelization, Office of—Rev. Msgr. JOHN SCULLY, P.A., Dir., *Chancery.*

Haitian Apostolate—Rev. CHRISTOPHER FITZGERALD, I.C., Dir., *P.O. Box 1218, Seffner, 33584.* Tel: 813-682-9115.

Hispanic Apostolate—Rev. DEMETRIO LORDEN, Co-Dir., *P.O. Box 16397, Temple Terrace, 33687.* Tel: 813-988-1593. Rev. CHRISTOPHER FITZGERALD, I.C., Co-Dir., *P.O. Box 1218, Seffner, 33584.* Tel: 813-682-9115. Deacon JUAN SIERRA, Assoc. Dir., *2021 E. Busch Blvd., Tampa, 33612.* Tel: 813-931-3005.

St. Casimir Lithuanian Apostolate—Rev. STEPHEN ROPOLAS, O.F.M., Dir., *555 68th Ave., St. Petersburg Beach, 33706.* Tel: 813-367-2408.

Miserere Guild, Inc.—Rev. Msgr. J. BERNARD CAVERLY, Dir., *St. Raphael Church, 1376 Snell Isle Blvd. N.E., St. Petersburg, 33704.* Tel: 813-821-7989.

Calvary Catholic Cemetery—Mr. GREG TSCHIDERER, Mgr., *11801 U.S. Hwy. 19 N., Clearwater, 34624-7407.* Tel: 813-572-4355.

Prison and Jail Ministry—Rev. MICHAEL PERRY, O.de.M., Dir., *5650 Seventh Ave. N., St. Petersburg, 33710.* Tel: 813-345-4766.

Propagation of the Faith—Rev. Msgr. JOHN SCULLY, P.A., Diocesan Dir., *Chancery Building.*

Rural Life Ministry—Very Rev. CHRISTOPHER FITZGERALD, I.C., Dir., *P.O. Box 1218, Seffner, 33584.* Tel: 813-681-9115.

Sea, Apostleship of the—

Port of St. Petersburg—Rev. BERNARDINE SMITH, T.O.R., Chap., *515 4th St., St. Petersburg, 33701.* Tel: 813-896-2191.

Port of Tampa—Rev. THOMAS STOKES, S.M., *Our Lady of Perpetual Help Church, 1711 E. 11th Ave., Tampa, 33605.* Tel: 813-248-5701.

Department of Catholic Formation and Education

Executive Director—Dr. BARBARA MCCONVILLE, Ph.D., *Notre Dame Building.*

Catholic Schools Office—Rev. ROBERT KROLL, O.F.M., Supt.; Sr. VIRGINIA CHIAMBALERO, O.P., Assoc. Supt.; Ms. MARY BRYAN, Assoc. Supt. for Curriculum.

Family Life Office—Deacon JOE GROTE, Dir.

Spanish Marriage Encounter—Rev. DEMETRIO LORDEN, Coord. Tel: 813-988-1593 (Tampa).

Library, Father William F. Balfe Memorial—Vacant.

Religious Education Office—Mr. BRIAN A. LEMOI, Dir.

Respect Life Office—Mrs. SHARON ILER, Coord.; Rev. Msgr. JOHN MCNULTY, P.A., Bishop's Delegate to Pro-Life Activities.

Scouting Office—Revs. ANTON DECHERING, Dir., *1600 54th Ave. S., St. Petersburg, 33712.* Tel: 813-867-3663. JAMES JOHNSON, Assoc. Dir. Tel: 352-726-1670.

Worship, Office of—Rev. JOHN TAPP, Dir.

Youth Ministry Office—Mr. THOMAS J. MIKLUSICAK, Dir.

Department of Communications

Executive Director—Mr. JOSEPH MANNION, *Notre Dame Building.*

Catholic Television Mass—MARY JO MURPHY, Producer.

Diocesan Radio - WBVM 90.5 FM & WLMS 88.3 FM—Mr. THOMAS DERZYPOLSKI, Station Mgr., *Media Center, Tampa.* Tel: 813-289-8040; 800-223-WBVM.

"The Florida Catholic" Newspaper—Mr. STEPHEN SIMS, Editor, *Notre Dame Building, St. Petersburg.* Tel: 813-345-3338.

Circulation & Subscription—P.O. Box 3551, Orlando, 32802. Tel: 407-423-3438.

Department of Temporal Affairs

Department of Temporal Affairs—Chancery Building; Rev. ROBERT C. GIBBONS, Chief Financial Officer; Mr. PAUL A. WARD, JR., Exec. Dir.; Mr. JOSEPH CORSETTI, Asst. to the Exec. Dir.; Mr. JOSEPH G. GABAY, Controller; Mr. H. ARTHUR MCQUILLEN, Admin. Asst.; Mrs. CHARLOTTE MYERS, Personnel; Mr. MICHAEL DENNIN, Data Processing; Mrs. CAROL PILARSKI, Data Processing.

Finance Council—Mr. THEO CHIVE, Chm.; Mr. C. DAVID CARLEY; Rev. Msgr. BRENDAN MULDOON; Mr. JAMES QUINLAN, SR.; Mrs. LAURA KRUEGER BROCK; Revs. JACOB MONTELEONE; ROBERT C. GIBBONS; Mr. FRED DOBBINS; Mr. GREGORY C. JEWELL; Mr. WILLIAM G. TAPP; Mr. PATRICK WALSH.

Insurance, Health & Welfare Administration—Mr. DONALD BRASIER, Insurance Mgr.; Mrs. KAE YAUCHLER, Admin. Asst.

Department of Real Estate

Chancery Building—Mr. JAMES A. SEBESTA, Exec. Dir.; Mr. RONALD G. BENTO, Real Estate Mgr.; Mr. STEVE B. ZIENTEK, Real Estate Planning.

Department of Facilities and Construction Management

Notre Dame Building—Mrs. DENISE DIGRUCCIO, Dir.

Department of Social Ministries

Notre Dame Building—6533 Ninth Ave. N., St. Petersburg, 33710. Tel: 813-345-3338. *Mailing Address: P.O. Box 43022, St. Petersburg, 33743-3022.* Mr. ARNOLD ANDREWS, Exec. Dir.

Pastoral Offices and Consultative Bodies to the Diocesan Curia

Presbyteral Council—Most Rev. ROBERT N. LYNCH, Pres.; Rev. Msgr. BRENDAN MULDOON, V.G., Vice Pres.; Very Rev. RALPH ARGENTINO, V.F., Chm.; Rev. Msgr. JOHN NEFF; Rev. ROBERT GIBBONS, J.C.L.; Very Revs. DACIAN DEE, J.C.D.; ROBERT DONLAN, V.F.; JUDE DUFFY, O.F.M.Cap., V.F.; JAMES JOHNSON, V.F.; JAMES LARA, V.F.; JOSEPH PELLEGRINO, V.F.; GERARD POWERS, V.F.; Revs. RICHARD ALLEN; JOHN CIPPEL; JOSEPH DOYLE, S.J.; BRENDAN LAWLOR; THOMAS MADDEN; JACOB MONTELEONE; ROBERT MORRIS; MICHAEL MUHR; ERIC PETERS; ROBERT SCHNEIDER; PETER SCHWEITZER; WILLIAM SWENGROS; GREGG TOTTLE.

College of Consultors—Rev. Msgr. BRENDAN MULDOON, V.G.; Rev. ROBERT C. GIBBONS, J.C.L., Sec.; Rev. Msgr. JOHN NEFF; Very Rev. DACIAN DEE, J.C.D.; Revs. RALPH ARGENTINO; ROBERT DONLAN, V.F.; JUDE DUFFY, O.F.M.Cap., V.F.; JAMES JOHNSON, V.F.; JAMES LARA, V.F.; JOSEPH PELLEGRINO, V.F.; GERARD POWERS, V.F.; GREGG TOTTLE.

Vicars Forane—Very Revs. RALPH ARGENTINO, V.F., Lower Pinellas Deanery; JOSEPH PELLEGRINO, V.F., Upper Pinellas Deanery; JUDE DUFFY, O.F.M.Cap., V.F., West Hillsborough Deanery; JAMES LARA, V.F., East Hillsborough Deanery; GERARD POWERS, V.F., Pasco Deanery; ROBERT DONLAN, V.F., Hernando Deanery; JAMES JOHNSON, V.F., Citrus Deanery.

Cemetery Board—Rev. Msgr. J. BERNARD CAVERLY, Chm.; Mr. TERRENCE BRETT; Mrs. ELEANOR KIRBY; Mr. CHARLES MARSICANO; Mr. GREG TSCHIDERER.

Committees for Priestly Life & Ministry—

Continuing Formation—Appointed Members: Revs. MICHAEL O'BRIEN, Chm. LEONARD PLAZEWSKI; ARTHUR PROULX; JOHN CIPPEL; JAMES MERKEL; Rev. Msgr. JOHN NEFF, Ex-Officio.

Commission for Women Religious—Sr. PATRICIA CAULFIELD, O.P.; Sr. DOROTHY DWYER, O.S.F.; Sr. MARY RENETTA GRAFF, S.N.D.; Sr. MARY DAVID HYDRO, O.S.B.; Sr. MARGARET MCGINLEY, I.H.M.; Sr. PHYLLIS SHAUGHNESSY, O.S.C.; Sr. JOSEPHINE MARIE STREVA, O.S.F.; Sr. VIRGINIA TURNER, S.N.D.; Very Rev. JUDE DUFFY, O.F.M.Cap., Ex-Officio.

Diocesan Liturgical Commission—Rev. JOHN TAPP, Chm.; Revs. DAVID DEJULIO; COLMAN COOKE; LEONARD PLAZEWSKI; ROBERT SCHNEIDER; Deacon JOSEPH KRZANOWSKI; Mr. CLARK BOKOR; Ms. MARIA ESPINOSA; Dr. WILLIAM PICHER; Mr. CHRISTOPHER BERKE; Sr. LISA-JUDENE ERAZMUS, O.S.B.; Ms. MARCY SCHWABENBAUER.

Housing Board—Most Rev. W. THOMAS LARKIN, Chm.; Rev. Msgr. BRENDAN MULDOON; Mr. DOUGLAS B. CONNOR; Mr. THOMAS W. ASHTON; Mr. RICHARD A. LEANDRI; ALBERT M. SALEM, JR., ESQ.; Mr. JAMES A. SEBESTA; Mrs. ETHEL SHARP; Mr. JOSEPH SOROTA, JR.

Diocesan Board of Catholic Formation & Education—Mrs. JUDY FLYNN; Mr. STEVE CHUMBRIS; Rev. GERARD POWERS; Sr. ADELE LUBER, S.S.N.D.; Mrs. JOANN WHITE; Mr. MELVIN DENNARD; Mr. HAROLD JACKSON. Ex-Officios: Mrs. ROSANNE M. SMITHWICK; Mr. CHUCK SULLIVAN; Mr. EDWARD TAYLOR; Mrs. MARIE HOUGH; Dr. BARBARA MCCONVILLE; Rev. Msgr. BRENDAN MULDOON, V.G.

Permanent Diaconate Board—Rev. Msgr. JOHN F. NEFF; Revs. DAVID BANKS; THOMAS MADDEN, Chm. JACOB MONTELEONE; ARTHUR PROULX; ALAN WEBER; Deacons JOSEPH BROWN; JERRY CRALL; AUGUSTIN ORTIZ; LIONEL ROBERTS; Mrs. PAT KRZANOWSKI.

Realty Advisory Board—Rev. Msgr. BRENDAN MULDOON, V.G.; Mr. RONALD G. BENTO; E. THOMAS FISHER, JR., Esq.; Mr. EUGENE MOHLER; Mr. JAMES A. SEBESTA; Mr. STEVE B. ZIENTEK; Mr. JERRY GANEY; Mr. ROBERT E. SCHWEIGER; Mr. VERNON SHEA.

Organizations Serving the Diocese

Archdiocese of Miami, Diocese of St. Petersburg, and Diocese of Venice Pension Plan—

Pension Plan Administrator—Gabriel, Roeder. Smith & Co., West Broward Professional Bldg., 7320 Griffin Rd., Fort Lauderdale, 33314. Tel: 305-791-5888.

Catholic Charities, Diocese of St. Petersburg, Inc.

Central Services—6533 Ninth Ave. N., St. Petersburg, 33710. Tel: 813-893-1313; 800-260-2294 (Evenings & Weekends). Mr. ARNOLD ANDREWS, Exec. Dir.

Pious Foundations

Catholic Education Foundation, Inc.—6533 Ninth Ave. N., St. Petersburg, 33710. Tel: 813-345-3338., *Mailing Address: P.O. Box 43022, St. Petersburg, 33743-3022.*

Organizations of the Catholic Faithful

Catholic Daughters of America—Mrs. ROSE TOMASSI, National Dir. Tel: 813-360-8508. Mrs. ROSE MONCHECOURT, State Regent. Tel: 813-934-6209.

Diocesan Council of Catholic Women—Rev. HAROLD BUMPUS, Diocesan Moderator. Tel: 352-489-4889.

Deanery Chaplains—Revs. ROBERT SCHAEUFELE, Lower Pinellas; Rev. AIDEN FOYNES, Upper Pinellas; Revs. PATRICK IRWIN, East Hillsborough; MICHAEL MUHR, West Hillsborough; FELIX SANCHEZ, Pasco; RAYMOND LETTRE, Hernando; THOMAS MORGAN, Citrus.

Family of St. Jerome, "Familian Sancti Hieronymi"—Mr. JAN G. HALISKY, P.A., Praeses Generalis, *507 S. Prospect Ave., Clearwater, 34616.*

Knights of Columbus—Rev. ROBERT RITTMEYER, Chap. Tel: 813-782-2813.

Society of St. Vincent de Paul—

Council of St. Petersburg Diocese—P.O. Box 13938, Tampa, 33681-0938. Tel: 813-832-5486. Mr. MARVIN ROPERT, Pres.

Hernando/Citrus St. Vincent de Paul Society District Council—Mr. CESAR LANDAETA, Pres. Tel: 904-688-9070.

Hillsborough District Council—Mr. JOSEPH LATINA, Pres. Tel: 813-985-1012.

Ozanam District Council (Pasco Deanery)—Mr. DENNIS HOLT, Pres. Tel: 813-966-2046.

Lower Pinellas District Council—Mr. WILLIAM REAGOR, Pres. Tel: 813-345-0212.

Upper Pinellas District Council—Mr. WALTER HAINS, Pres. Tel: 813-442-7370.

CLERGY, PARISHES, MISSIONS AND PAROCHIAL SCHOOLS

CITY OF ST. PETERSBURG

(Pinellas County)

1—CATHEDRAL OF ST. JUDE THE APOSTLE (1950), Very Rev. David T. DeJulio, Rector; Revs. Joel M. Kovanis; Robert Gately (COL); Arcangelo Manzi, O.de.M.; Sr. Jean Charles Birney, O.P., Pastoral Assoc.

Res., 5815 Fifth Ave. N., P.O. Box 40928, 33743. Tel: 813-347-9702; Fax: 813-343-8370.

School—Tel: 813-347-8622; Fax: 813-343-0305. Sr. Patricia Caulfield, O.P., Prin.

Sisters 1; Lay Teachers 28; Students 471.

Catechesis/Religious Programs—Tel: 813-345-8780; Fax: 813-343-8370. Sr. Joseph Eilese Hukle, O.P., D.R.E.

Students 356.

2—BLESSED TRINITY (1961), Rev. Anton Dechering; Deacon Lionel Roberts; Sr. Jean Barrett, O.S.F., Pastoral Assoc.

Res., 1600 54th Ave. S., 33712. Tel: 813-867-3663; Fax: 813-864-2679.

School—St. Paul Interparochial School. See Elementary Schools, Interparochial under Institutions Located in the Diocese. Tel: 813-823-6144.

Catechesis/Religious Programs—Tel: 813-867-2421; Fax: 813-864-2679. Mrs. Patricia Wiand, D.R.E.

Students 234.

3—Holy Cross (1965), Revs. Robert L. Schaeufele; Richard Jankowski. In res., Rev. Michael O'Brien.
Res., 7851 54th Ave. N., 33709. Tel: 813-546-3315; 541-2242; Fax: 813-547-2005.
Catechesis/Religious Programs—Tel: 813-547-2004; Fax: 813-547-2005.
Students 252.

4—Holy Family (1959), Revs. Robert J. Schneider; Jerome E. Diffley, Pastor Emeritus; Paul Pecchie; Sr. Jamesann McCue, I.H.M., Dir., Pastoral Assoc.; Deacons Michael Columbus; Gene Loffredo.
Res., 200 78th Ave. N.E., 33702. Tel: 813-526-5783; Fax: 813-521-2545.
School—250 78th Ave. N.E., 33702. Tel: 813-526-8194; Fax: 813-527-6567. Sr. Florence Ann Marino, I.H.M.
Sisters 1; Lay Teachers 15; Students 241.
Catechesis/Religious Programs—Tel: 813-525-8489. D.R.E.: Walt Smith; Anne P. Perez, (Adult and Elementary).
Students 400.

5—St. Joseph (1922), Rev. Arthur Proulx. In res., Rev. Peter Young.
Res., 2624 Union St., S., 33712. Tel: 813-822-2153; Fax: 813-823-5820.
Preschool—Immaculate Conception, Tel: 813-822-2156; Fax: 813-553-9133.
Lay Teachers 6; Students 188.
Catechesis/Religious Programs—Tel: 813-822-8427.
Students 73.
Mission—St. Petersburg, Pinellas Co., Vietnamese Martyrs Mission, Tel: 813-822-7344. Rev. Peter Young.

6—St. Mary Our Lady of Grace (1921), Revs. Bernardine J. Smith, T.O.R.; Brian J. Miller, T.O.R.; Thomas M. Scanlon, T.O.R.
Res., 515 Fourth St., S., 33701. Tel: 813-896-2191; Fax: 813-895-6279.
St. Mary's Center—.

7—St. Paul (1929), Revs. Robert C. Gibbons; Timothy J. Sherwood.
Res., 1800 12th St. N., 33704. Tel: 813-822-3481; Fax: 813-822-1754.
School—St. Paul Interparochial School. See Elementary Schools, Interparochial under Institutions Located in the Diocese. Tel: 813-823-6144; Fax: 813-896-0609.
Catechesis/Religious Programs—Tel: 813-822-3481; Fax: 813-822-1754.
Students 80.
Mission—St. Petersburg, The Mercy of God Polish Mission, 1358 20th Ave. N., 33704. Tel: 813-823-6997. Rev. Wiktor Dziedziech.

8—St. Raphael (1961), Revs. J. Bernard Caverly; John Gerth; Deacon Joseph Grote. In res., Rev. Jose Gonzalez.
Res., 1376 Snell Isle Blvd., N.E., 33704. Tel: 813-821-7989; Fax: 813-823-8824.
School—Tel: 813-821-9663. Mrs. Carole Huff, Prin.
Lay Teachers 16; Students 281.
Catechesis/Religious Programs—Tel: 813-821-7989. Rhona Beettam, D.R.E.
Students 136.

9—Transfiguration (1959), Rev. John Bolger. Deacons: Revs. Gerald McGory; Raphael Quiles.
Res., 4000-43 St. N., 33714. Tel: 813-525-0262; Fax: 813-522-1328.
School—Tel: 813-527-2880; Fax: 813-522-1328. Mrs. Joanne Claire, Prin.
Lay Teachers 12; Students 222.
Catechesis/Religious Programs—Students 65.

OUTSIDE THE CITY OF ST. PETERSBURG

Beverly Hills, Citrus Co., Our Lady of Grace (1966), Rev. Henry J. Riffle, O.S.B.; Deacon Romulo Postadan.
Res., 6 Roosevelt Blvd., 34465. Tel: 352-746-2144; Fax: 352-746-6892.
School—Central Catholic School of Citrus County, Lecanto. See Elementary Schools, Interparochial under Institutions Located in the Diocese. Tel: 352-746-2020; Fax: 352-746-3448.
Catechesis/Religious Programs—Tel: 352-746-2144; Fax: 352-746-6892. Margaret Lynch, D.R.E.
Students 123.

Brandon, Hillsborough Co., Church of the Nativity (1960), Revs. James Lara; George Rozycki; Edward P. Nichols, Jr.; Deacon Jim Pescatore.
Church—705 E. Brandon Blvd., 33511. Tel: 813-681-4608; Fax: 813-653-9482.
Res., 705 E. Westbrook, 33511. Tel: 813-684-0256. [JC]
School—Tel: 813-689-3395; Fax: 813-681-5406. Sr. Irene St. Jean, C.S.C., Prin.
Sisters of Holy Cross (Pittsfield, NH) 2; Lay Teachers 33; Students 758.
Catechesis/Religious Programs—Tel: 813-689-9101; Fax: 813-684-1880. Ann Marie Sullivan, D.R.E.
Students 1,023.

Brooksville, Hernando Co., St. Anthony (1892), Rev. Robert R. Donlan; Sr. Loretta Lonsdorf, O.S.M., Pastoral Asst.
Res., 20428 Cortez Blvd., 34601-5601. Tel: 352-796-2096; Fax: 352-796-7144.
School—Notre Dame Interparochial School. See Elementary Schools, Interparochial under Institutions Located in the Diocese. Tel: 352-683-0755; Fax: 352-683-3924.
Catechesis/Religious Programs—Tel: 352-796-4434, Ext. 20; Fax: 352-796-7144. Sr. Patricia Saunders, O.P., D.R.E.
Students 230.
Mission—Ridge Manor, Hernando Co., St. Anne, 4241 Treiman Blvd., Ridge Manor, 33525. Tel: 352-583-2550. Rev. Bruno Szymusiak.

Citrus Springs, Citrus Co., St. Elizabeth Ann Seton (1976), Rev. Harold Bumpus; Rev. Msgr. George Cummings, Pastor Emeritus; Deacon Thomas Metty.
Res., 1460 W. St. Elizabeth Pl., 34434. Tel: 352-489-4889.
School—Central Catholic School of Citrus County. See Elementary Schools, Interparochial under Institutions Located in the Diocese. Lecanto, Tel: 352-746-2020; Fax: 352-746-3448.
Catechesis/Religious Programs—Tel: 352-489-4889. Mrs. Claire Mangine, D.R.E.
Students 50.

Clearwater, Pinellas Co.,

1—All Saints, (1987), Rev. Gregory J. Andrews.
Office 2801 Curlew Rd., 34621. Tel: 813-789-1025; Fax: 813-784-8025.
School—Guardian Angels Interparochial School. See Elementary Schools, Interparochial under Institutions Located in the Diocese. Tel: 813-799-6724.
Catechesis/Religious Programs—Students 170.

2—Light of Christ, (1966), Revs. Timothy J. Allman; Ronald Poirier; Deacon James Hassett. In res., Rev. Keith McKee (Canada).
Mailing Address: P.O. Box 6115, 34618. Tel: 813-441-4545; Fax: 813-441-8771.
Res., 2176 Marilyn St., 34625.
School—St. Cecelia Interparochial School. See Elementary Schools, Interparochial under Institutions Located in the Diocese. Tel: 813-461-1200; Fax: 813-446-9140.
Pre-School—Tel: 813-442-4797; Fax: 813-441-8771. Mrs. Barbara Barko, Dir.
Lay Teachers 16; Students 120.
Catechesis/Religious Programs—Tel: 813-442-7081. William Woodard, D.R.E.
Students 604.

3—St. Brendan, (1978), Rev. Edward J. Mulligan.
Res., 245 Dory Passage, 34630. Tel: 813-443-5485; Fax: 813-442-5896.
School—St. Cecelia Interparochial School. See Elementary Schools, Interparochial Under Institutions Located in the Diocese. Tel: 813-447-3494; Fax: 813-442-4810.

4—St. Cecelia, (1924), Revs. Aiden Foynes; Peter Schweitzer; Kenneth Bischko, T.O.R.; Francis X. Sarjeant, S.J. In res., Rev. John Anoia; Deacon Kazimierez Mielcarek.
Res., 820 Jasmine Way, 34616. Tel: 813-447-3494; Fax: 813-442-4810.
School—St. Cecelia Interparochial School. See Elementary Schools, Interparochial under Institutions Located in the Diocese. Tel: 813-461-1200; Fax: 813-446-9140.
Catechesis/Religious Programs—Mr. J. Patrick Finan, D.R.E.
Students 368.

5—St. Michael the Archangel, (1980), Revs. James E. Russo; Francis Dionne; Nino Viviano; Sr. Theresa Betz, S.N.D., Pastoral Assoc.
Res., 2281 State Rd. 580, 34623. Tel: 813-797-2375; Fax: 813-791-8287.
Catechesis/Religious Programs—Mrs. Katie White, D.R.E.
Students 373.

Crystal River, Citrus Co., St. Benedict (1953), Rev. James Merkel; Deacon James Pullar.
Mailing Address: 455 S. Suncoast Blvd., 34429. Tel: 352-795-4478; 4479; Fax: 352-795-4160.
School—Central Catholic School of Citrus County. See Elementary Schools, Interparochial under Institutions Located in the Diocese. Lecanto, Tel: 352-746-2020; Fax: 352-746-3448.
Catechesis/Religious Programs—Deacon James Pullar, D.R.E.
Students 97.

Dade City, Pasco Co., St. Rita (1912), Rev. Felix Sanchez. In res., Rev. Anselm Harry Morrison, A.A.
Mailing Address: P.O. Box 944, 33526-0944.
Office: 14404 14th St., 33523. Tel: 352-567-2894; Fax: 352-523-0039.
Res., 14325 13th St., 33523. Tel: 352-521-3145.
School—St. Anthony Interparochial School. See Elementary Schools, Interparochial under Institutions Located in the Diocese. San Antonio, Tel: 352-588-3041; Fax: 352-588-3142.
Catechesis/Religious Programs—Lillie Dennard, D.R.E.
Students 427.

Dunedin, Pinellas Co., Our Lady of Lourdes (1958), Revs. Thomas Madden; Thomas M. Conmy, C.S.C.; Ken Slattery.
Res., 750 San Salvador Dr., 34698. Tel: 813-733-3606; Fax: 813-733-8305.
School—Tel: 813-733-3776; Fax: 813-733-3776. Mr. Craig Mousseau.
Sisters of Notre Dame (Chardon Ohio) 1; Lay Teachers 18; Students 316.
Catechesis/Religious Programs—Tel: 813-733-0872; Fax: 813-733-8305. Sr. Mary Deborah Carlin, S.N.D., D.R.E.
Students 462.

Gulfport, Pinellas Co., Most Holy Name of Jesus (1960), Revs. Raymond O'Neill; Gerald Hendry; Deacon Glenn Pickart.
Res., 5800 15th Ave., S., 33707. Tel: 813-347-9989; Fax: 813-343-6420.
School—Tel: 813-347-1774. Sr. M. Francis Elizabeth, O.P., Prin.
Sisters 2; Lay Teachers 13; Students 207.
Catechesis/Religious Programs—Tel: 813-347-7803. Sr. Jean Clemenger, O.P., D.R.E.
Students 90.

Holiday, Pasco Co., St. Vincent De Paul (1969), Revs. Colman M. Cooke; Emil Styczen; Sr. Josephine Rooney, O.S.C., Pastoral Assoc.
Res., 4843 Mile Stretch Dr., P.O. Box 3865, 34690. Tel: 813-938-1974; Fax: 813-938-1975.
School—Bishop Larkin Interparochial School. See Elementary Schools, Interparochial under Institutions Located in the Diocese. Hudson, Tel: 813-862-6981.
Catechesis/Religious Programs—Tel: 813-934-8035. Sr. Lucia Brady, O.S.C., D.R.E.
Students 243.

Homosassa, Citrus Co., St. Thomas the Apostle (1987), Rev. David A. Banks; Deacon Richard Meyer.
Res., 7040 S. Suncoast Blvd., 34446. Tel: 352-628-7000; Fax: 352-628-4723.
School—Central Catholic School of Citrus County. See Elementary Schools, Interparochial under Institutions Located in the Diocese. Lecanto.

Hudson, Pasco Co., St. Michael (1971), Revs. Desmond Daly; Paul Goudreau; Seamus Collins, O.P.; Deacons Forrest E. Evans; Robert Simpson.
Res., 8014 State Rd. #52, 34667. Tel: 813-868-5276; Fax: 813-862-9187.
School—Bishop Larkin Catholic Interparochial School. See Elementary Schools, Interparochial under Institutions Located in the Diocese. Tel: 813-862-6981; Fax: 813-869-9893.
Catechesis/Religious Programs—Tel: 813-863-9742. Mary Alber, D.R.E.
Students 502.

Indian Rocks Beach, Pinellas Co., St. Jerome (1956), Very Rev. Msgr. Brendan Muldoon, V.G.; Revs. Leonard Piotrowski; Sean O'Sullivan, I.C. In res., Very Rev. Dacian Dee, J.C.D., V.E.
Mailing Address: P.O. Box 100, 33785.
Res., 10895 Hamlin Blvd., Largo, 33774. Tel: 813-595-4610; Fax: 813-596-6792.
Catechesis/Religious Programs—Tel: 813-595-3100. Sandra Bonilla, D.R.E.
Students 843.

Inverness, Citrus Co., Our Lady of Fatima (1955), Revs. James B. Johnson; Desmond Gill, Pastor Emeritus; Deacon Martin Fallon. In res., Rev. Nehmatallah El-Hayek.
Mailing Address: 550 U.S. Hwy. 41 S., 34450. Tel: 352-726-1670; Fax: 352-344-8384.
Res., 518 Desota Ave., 34450. Tel: 352-726-1670.
School—Central Catholic School of Citrus County. See Elementary Schools, Interparochial under Institutions Located in the Diocese. Tel: 352-746-2020; Fax: 352-746-3448.
Catechesis/Religious Programs—D.R.E.: Sr. Mary Charia Ripple, S.S.N.D.; Sr. Constance Coulter, S.S.N.D.
Students 303.

Land O'Lakes, Pasco Co., Our Lady of the Rosary (1952), Rev. Ronald B. Aubin; Deacon Augustin Ortiz.
Res., P.O. Box 1229, 34639. Tel: 813-949-4565; Fax: 813-948-1981.
School—Most Holy Redeemer Interparochial School. See Elementary Schools, Interparochial under Institutions Located in the Diocese. Tampa, Tel: 813-933-4750; Fax: 813-933-3181.
Catechesis/Religious Programs—Tel: 813-949-2699; Fax: 813-948-1981. Mrs. Clara Cappadoro, D.R.E.
Students 396.

Largo, Pinellas Co.,

1—ST. CATHERINE OF SIENA, (1976), Revs. Michael J. Finnegan; Thomas M. Dieter (JOL); John O'Donovan (Ireland). Pastoral Assocs.: Tel: 813-531-1690. Sr. Ann Gertrude, S.S.J.; Sr. Therese Ganly, S.S.J.; Deacon Michael Slattery.
Res., 1955 S. Belcher Rd., Clearwater, 34624. Tel: 813-531-7721.
School—St. Cecelia Interparochial School. See Elementary Schools, Interparochial under Institutions Located in the Diocese. Tel: 813-461-1200.
Catechesis/Religious Programs—Tel: 813-531-7721. Sr. Frances Hance, S.S.J., D.R.E.
Students 394.

2—ST. JUSTIN MARTYR, (1987), Rev. Michael Lydon; Sr. Kathleen Francis Honc, O.S.F., Pastoral Asst.
Res., 10725 Ridge Rd., 34648. Tel: 813-397-3312; Fax: 813-393-6653.
Catechesis/Religious Programs—Rosemary Mandery, D.R.E.
Students 175.

3—ST. MATTHEW, (1985), Rev. Thomas Spillett; Deacon John DiVito.
Mailing Address: P.O. Box 10097, 33773.
Office: 9111 90th Ave., N., 33777. Tel: 813-393-1288; Fax: 813-398-2683.
Catechesis/Religious Programs—Ruth Appel, D.R.E.
Students 343.

4—ST. PATRICK, (1958), Rev. Msgr. John M. McCall; Revs. Robert Morris; Vincent Morton.
Res., 2121 16th Ave. S.W., P.O. Box 167, 34640. Tel: 813-584-2318; Fax: 813-586-5413.
School—Tel: 813-581-4865; Fax: 813-581-7842. Mrs. Patricia Coyle, Prin.
Lay Teachers 14; Students 270.
Catechesis/Religious Programs—Tel: 813-584-6697. Annetta Wallace, D.R.E.
Students 306.

Lecanto, Citrus Co., St. Scholastica (1987), Rev. Thomas Morgan; Deacons Terrence E. Knox; Stephen Kurylowicz.
Res., 4301 W. Homosassa Trail, 34461-9106. Tel: 352-746-9422; 563-2296; Fax: 352-746-2335.
School—Central Catholic School of Citrus County. See Elementary Schools, Interparochial under Institutions Located in the Diocese. Tel: 352-746-2020.
Catechesis/Religious Programs—Tel: 352-746-9422; Fax: 352-746-2335. D.R.E.: Jane Osterling; Judy Bescher.
Students 335.

Masaryktown, Pasco Co., St. Mary, Our Lady of Sorrows (1931), Rev. James A. Bucaria.
Mailing Address: P.O. Box 9675, 34609-0106. Tel: 352-796-2792; Fax: 352-544-0398.
School—Notre Dame Interparochial School. See Elementary Schools, Interparochial under Institutions Located in the Diocese. Spring Hill, Tel: 352-683-0755.

New Port Richey, Pasco Co., Our Lady Queen of Peace (1913), Revs. Gerard E. Powers, V.F.; Gerard Murphy; Luis B. Rios Cappiello; Deacons Roger Lind (RVC); John Liggan (NY).
Res., 5340 High St., 34652. Tel: 813-849-7521; Fax: 813-849-4814.
School—Bishop Larkin Interparochial School. See Elementary Schools, Interparochial under Institutions Located in the Diocese. Hudson, Tel: 813-862-6981; Fax: 813-869-9893.
Catechesis/Religious Programs—Tel: 813-842-9396.
Students 473.

St. Thomas Aquinas (1980), Revs. Thomas F. Earner; Patrick Rebel; Deacons Melvin Dunphy; Lee Brennan.
Res., 8320 State Rd. 54, 34653. Tel: 813-372-8600; Fax: 813-376-2330.
St. Thomas Early Childhood Development Center—Tel: 813-376-2330.
School—Bishop Larkin Interparochial School. See Elementary Schools, Interparochial under Institutions Located in the Diocese. Hudson, Tel: 813-862-6981; Fax: 813-862-9187.
Catechesis/Religious Programs—Tel: 813-376-1622; Fax: 813-376-7204. Sr. Sabrina Burton, D.R.E.
Students 624.

Palm Harbor, Pinellas Co., St. Luke the Evangelist (1985), Revs. Donald F. Leininger; Michael O'Neill; Theodore Costello. Pastoral Assocs.: Sr. Madeleine Donnelly; Sr. Bridget Mulligan; Sr. Bridget Finn; Deacon James Blaney.
Res., 2757 Alderman Rd., 34684. Tel: 813-786-3648; Fax: 813-789-9556.
St. Luke Early Childhood Center—Tel: 813-787-2914; Fax: 813-789-9556.
School—Guardian Angels Interparochial School. See Elementary Schools, Interparochial under Institutions Located in the Diocese. Clearwater.
Students 172.
Catechesis/Religious Programs—Tel: 813-787-2845. Sr. Madeleine Donnelly, O.S.C., D.R.E.
Students 920.

Pinellas Park, Pinellas Co., Sacred Heart (1910), Revs. Ralph Argentino; Peter Busch, T.O.R.; Paul Mizener, O.F.M.Conv.; Deacons Louis Izzo; L. Roger Cartier.
Res., 8001 46th St., N., 34665. Tel: 813-541-4447; Fax: 813-541-2073.
School—7951 46th Way N., 34665. Tel: 813-544-1106; Fax: 813-541-2073. Ms. Christina Meadows, Prin.
Sisters 2; Lay Teachers 16; Students 259.
Catechesis/Religious Programs—Tel: 813-541-4133. Dr. Gregory Dalle-Tezze, D.R.E.
Students 275.

Plant City, Hillsborough Co., St. Clement (1912), Revs. Hugh F. Lagan; Seamus Hatton, C.SS.R.; Jaime Viso; Deacon John Anderson.
Res., 1104 Alexander St., 33566. Tel: 813-752-8251; Fax: 813-759-2721.
Catechesis/Religious Programs—Tel: 813-752-8252. Jo Ann Parolini, D.R.E.
Students 275.

Port Richey, Pasco Co., St. James the Apostle (1984), Rev. Michael Devine; Deacon Paul G. Metilly.
Res., 8400 Monarch Dr., 34668. Tel: 813-869-3130; Fax: 813-869-8886.
School—Bishop Larkin Interparochial School. See Elementary Schools, Interparochial under Institutions Located in the Diocese. Hudson, Tel: 813-862-6981.
Catechesis/Religious Programs—Tel: 813-869-3132. Sr. Eileen Derrick, O.S.F., D.R.E.
Students 410.

Ridge Manor, Hernando Co., St. Anne (1965),
Res., 4142 Tremain Blvd., Hwy. 301, 33525. Tel: 352-583-2550. Rev. Bruno Szymusiak.

Riverview, Hillsborough Co., Resurrection (1983), Rev. Antonio Diez.
Mailing Address: P.O. Box 418, 33569.
Res., 6819 Krycul Ave., 33569. Tel: 813-677-2175; Fax: 813-671-7844.

Ruskin, Hillsborough Co., St. Anne (1956), Rev. Edward Lamp; Sr. Marian Stenken, S.C.N., Pastoral Assoc., D.R.E. In res., Rev. Msgr. Augustine Ndeukoya.
Office: 106 11th Ave., N.E., 33570. Tel: 813-645-1714; Fax: 813-645-5570.
Catechesis/Religious Programs—Mrs. Margaret Van Wagner, D.R.E.
Students 275.

Safety Harbor, Pinellas Co., Espiritu Santo (1960), Rev. Gregg Tottle. Pastoral Assocs.: Sr. Rose Bernhardt, O.S.F.; Sr. Paulamarie Lacy, S.N.D.; Sr. Nanette Herman, S.N.D.; Deacons Dominic P. Friscia; Vincent Alterio; Robert McElroy.
Res., 2405 Philippe Pkwy., P.O. Box 176, 34695. Tel: 813-726-8477; Fax: 813-799-2062.
School—St. Cecelia Interparochial School. See Elementary Schools, Interparochial under Institutions Located in the Diocese. Clearwater, Tel: 813-461-1200.
Catechesis/Religious Programs—Tel: 813-726-6742.
Students 900.

St. Joseph, Pasco Co., Sacred Heart (1888), Rev. Arthur M. Villemaire; Deacon William Connors.
Res., 32145 St. Joe Rd., Dade City, 33525. Tel: 352-588-3641; Fax: 352-588-5299. [CEM]
School—St. Anthony Interparochial School. See Elementary Schools, Interparochial under Institutions Located in the Diocese. San Antonio, Tel: 352-588-3041; Fax: 352-588-3142.
Catechesis/Religious Programs—Joyce Joyner, D.R.E.
Students 105.
Sacred Heart Child Care Center—32245 St. Joe Rd., Dade City, 33525. Tel: 352-588-4060; Fax: 352-588-4311. Mrs. Toni Watkins.

St. Pete Beach, Pinellas Co., St. John (1939), Revs. John C. Murphy; Julio B. Rivero, T.O.R.; Deacon Gene Powell. In res., Rev. Msgr. Patrick Trainor, P.A.; Revs. Vincent M. Shea, O.S.M.; William Weibler; Ray Hughes, C.R.
Res., 445 82nd Ave., 33706. Tel: 813-360-1147; Fax: 813-367-4418.
School—500 84th Ave., 33706. Tel: 813-360-1113; Fax: 813-367-8734. Sr. Joan Brennan, S.C., Prin.
School Sisters of Notre Dame (Baltimore, MD) 1; Lay Teachers 14; Students 255.
Catechesis/Religious Programs—D.R.E.: Robert Davis; Sharon Davis.
Students 90.

San Antonio, Pasco Co., St. Anthony of Padua (1884), Rev. Dennis E. Hughes.
Res., 32832 Massachusetts Ave., P.O. Box 578, 33576. Tel: 352-588-3081. [CEM]
School—St. Anthony Interparochial School. See Elementary Schools, Interparochial under Institutions Located in the Diocese. Tel: 352-588-3041; Fax: 352-588-3142.
Catechesis/Religious Programs—Tel: 352-588-3081.
Students 108.

Seffner, Hillsborough Co., St. Francis of Assisi (1987), Very Rev. Christopher Fitzgerald, I.C., V.F.; Rev. Dai Viet Mai, I.C.; Deacons Joseph Brown; Jerome Thomas.
Res., P.O. Box 1218, 33583. Tel: 813-681-9115; Fax: 813-689-4148.
Catechesis/Religious Programs—Joan McCollum, D.R.E.
Students 249.

Seminole, Pinellas Co., Blessed Sacrament (1959), Revs. James Gordon, I.C.; G. Richard Pilger, I.C.; Michael Ferran, I.C.
Res., 11565 66th Ave. N., 34642. Tel: 813-391-4661.
School—Tel: 813-391-4060; Fax: 813-391-5638. Jane Moerschbacher, Prin.
Lay Teachers 18; Students 300.
Catechesis/Religious Programs—Students 147.

Spring Hill, Hernando Co., St. Theresa (1968), Rev. Msgr. John Scully; Rev. Francis Ferrara; Deacon Gerard Uzzi.
Res., 1107 Commercial Way, 34606. Tel: 352-683-2849; Fax: 352-683-3437.
School—Notre Dame Interparochial School. See Elementary Schools, Interparochial under Institutions Located in the Diocese.
Catechesis/Religious Programs—Margaret Uhl, D.R.E.
Students 300.

St. Frances Xavier Cabrini (1980), Revs. John A. Cippel; Merrell Dickey; Raymond Lettre. In res., Rev. Andrew Beaudoin, S.S.S.
Mailing Address: 5030 Mariner Blvd., 34609. Tel: 352-683-9666; Fax: 352-688-2660.
School—Notre Dame Interparochial School. See Elementary Schools, Interparochial under Institutions Located in the Diocese. Tel: 352-683-0755.
Catechesis/Religious Programs—Jeanne Schneider, D.R.E.
Students 780.

Saint Joan of Arc (1988), Rev. Anthony D'Angelo.
Res., 13485 Spring Hill Dr., 34609. Tel: 352-688-0663, Ext. 34.
School—Notre Dame Interparochial School. See Elementary Schools, Interparochial under Institutions Located in the Diocese.

Sun City Center, Hillsborough Co., Prince of Peace, Rev. Msgr. Diego Conesa; Deacon Angelo Pignataro.
Res., 1002 Fordham Dr., 33573. Tel: 813-634-2328; Fax: 813-633-9244.
Mailing Address: 702 Valley Forge Blvd., 33573-5353. Tel: 813-634-2328; Fax: 813-633-9244.
Catechesis/Religious Programs—Students 12.
Mission—Wimauma, Hillsborough Co., Our Lady of Guadalupe Catholic Mission, P.O. Box 1022, Wimauma, 33598. Tel: 813-633-2384. Rev. Philip Scott.

Tampa, Hillsborough Co.,

1—BLESSED SACRAMENT, (1960) (Spanish), Rev. Marciano G. Martin, C.PP.S.
Res., 1205 Windermere Way, 33619. Tel: 813-626-2984; Fax: 813-626-2984.
Catechesis/Religious Programs—1603 Carnegie Cr., 33619. Tel: 813-626-9564.
Students 65.

2—CHRIST THE KING, (1941), Revs. Michael Muhr; Edwin Palka; Timothy Moffatt, T.O.R.
Res., 821 S. Dale Mabry Hwy., P.O. Box 10395, 33679-0395. Tel: 813-876-5841; Fax: 813-873-2426.
School—Tel: 813-876-8770; Fax: 813-879-0315. Sr. Joanne Holloman, F.M.A., Prin.
Daughters of Mary Help of Christians 3; Lay Teachers 29; Students 533.
Catechesis/Religious Programs—Tel: 813-870-2509. Linda A. Waggoner, D.R.E.
Students 571.

3—EPIPHANY, (1963), Rev. Ignatius Tuoc; Deacon Richard McIntosh.
Mailing Address: P.O. Box 11246, 33680. Tel: 813-258-3440.
Res., 2510 E. Hanna Ave., 33610. Tel: 813-238-5060; 234-8693.
Catechesis/Religious Programs—Tel: 813-238-1751. Suzy Mackey, D.R.E.
Students 39.
Mission—Tampa, Hillsborough Co., St. Joseph Vietnamese Mission, 2510 E. Hanna Ave., 33610. Tel: 813-238-5060.

4—GOOD SHEPHERD, (1966), Rev. Richard Allen.
Res., 6624 Travis Blvd., 33610. Tel: 813-626-7588; Fax: 813-626-5882.
Catechesis/Religious Programs—6410 E. Hillsborough Ave., 33610. Tel: 813-626-9991.
Students 57.

5—INCARNATION, (1962), Revs. Eric Hunter; Felician Napoli, O.F.M.; Paul Hervey; Deacon Joseph Krzanowski.

Res., 5124 Gateway Dr., 33615. Tel: 813-885-7861; Fax: 813-886-3624.
School—Tel: 813-884-4502; Fax: 813-885-3743. Mrs. Carolyn Goslee, Prin.
Lay Teachers 28; Students 581.
Catechesis/Religious Programs—Tel: 813-887-5110. Barbara Catineau, D.R.E.
Students 469.

6—MOST HOLY REDEEMER, (1937), Revs. Jude Duffy, O.F.M.Cap.; John V. Salvas, O.F.M.Cap. Pastoral Assocs.: Bro. Nicholas Mormando, O.F.M.Cap.; Deacons Lowell L. Hecht, Jr.; J. Manuel Rodriguez.
Res., 10110 Central Ave., 33612. Tel: 813-933-2859; Fax: 813-933-8258.
School—Most Holy Redeemer Interparochial School. See Elementary Schools, Interparochial under Institutions Located in the Diocese. Tel: 813-933-4750; Fax: 813-933-3181.
Catechesis/Religious Programs—Miss Marie O'Driscoll, D.R.E.
Students 150.

7—OUR LADY OF PERPETUAL HELP, (1890), Revs. Thomas A. Stokes, S.M.; Robert Fahey, S.M.; Richard Colbert, S.M.
Res., 1711 11th Ave., 33605. Tel: 813-248-5701.
Catechesis/Religious Programs—Students 81.

8—SACRED HEART, (1860), Revs. Richard W. McGowan, S.J.; Thomas Hidding, S.J.; Patrick H. Koch, S.J.; Robert Nilon, S.J.; Bro. J. Fillmore Elliot, S.J.
P.O. Box 1524, 33601. Tel: 813-229-1595; Fax: 813-221-2350.
School—Tel: 813-229-0618; Fax: 813-223-7667. Rev. Patrick Koch, S.J., Prin.
Sisters 1; Lay Teachers 17; Students 235.
Catechesis/Religious Programs—Students 32.

9—ST. JOSEPH, (1896), Revs. James H. Geiger, C.SS.R.; Joseph Gorney, C.SS.R.; Jerome A. Murphy, C.SS.R.; George Phillips, C.SS.R.
Mailing Address: P.O. Box 4298, 33677.
Res., 3012 Cherry St., 33607. Tel: 813-877-5729; Fax: 813-877-5720.
School—Tel: 813-879-7720; Fax: 813-873-0804.
Daughters of Mary Help of Christians (Paterson, NJ) 5; Lay Teachers 13; Students 235.
Catechesis/Religious Programs—Students 155.

10—ST. LAWRENCE, (1959), Rev. Msgr. Laurence E. Higgins, P.A.; Revs. Joseph Kutipurath, O.De.M.; Edward C. Keating, O.F.M.
Res., 3410 W. Hillsborough Ave., 33614. Tel: 813-875-4040; Fax: 813-876-0491.
School—Tel: 813-879-5090; Fax: 813-879-6886.
Lay Teachers 31; Students 611.
Catechesis/Religious Programs—Students 247.

11—ST. MARK THE EVANGELIST, (1996), Rev. Austin M. Mullen.
Res., 17531 Edinburgh Dr., 33647. Tel: 813-907-9717; Fax: 813-907-9617.

12—ST. MARY, (1966), Revs. Robert Morris; Robert Young.
Res., 15520 North Blvd., 33613. Tel: 813-961-1061; Fax: 813-961-3782.
School—Most Holy Redeemer Interparochial School. See Elementary Schools, Interparochial under Institutions Located in the Diocese. Tel: 813-933-4750.
Catechesis/Religious Programs—Tel: 813-963-2079. Sr. Nancy Christopher, O.S.F., D.R.E.
Students 361.

13—ST. PATRICK, (1958), Revs. Venard Moffitt, T.O.R.; Colman McGarrill, T.O.R.; Angelus Migliore, T.O.R.; Deacon John M. Edgerton.
Parish Office: 4212 Fair Oaks Ave., 33611. Tel: 813-839-5337; Fax: 813-831-2778. [JC]
School—4518 S. Manhattan Ave., 33611. Tel: 813-839-5056; Fax: 813-832-5907. Mr. Robert Kenel, Prin.
Lay Teachers 20; Students 384.
Catechesis/Religious Programs—Tel: 813-839-4958. Marcia Seheult, D.R.E.
Students 193.

14—ST. PAUL, (1963), Rev. Msgr. John F. Neff; Revs. Terrance Sowada; Ramon Hernandez (Cuba); Greg Kovalesky, Pastoral Assoc.; Deacons Juan Sierra; Ron Rojas.
Mailing Address: 12708 N. Dale Mabry, 33618. Tel: 813-961-3023; Fax: 813-962-8780.
School—Most Holy Redeemer Interparochial School. See Elementary Schools, Interparochial under Institutions Located in the Diocese. Tel: 813-933-4750; Fax: 813-933-3181.
Catechesis/Religious Programs—Tel: 813-961-3023, Ext. 230. Sr. Barbara Jean Rosswurm, D.R.E.
Students 830.

15—ST. PETER CLAVER, (1893) (African American), Rev. Callist N. Nyambo.
Res., 1203 N. Nebraska Ave., 33602. Tel: 813-223-7098; Fax: 813-223-6520.
School—(Grades K-5). Tel: 813-224-0865; Fax: 813-223-1982. Sr. Thomas Joseph McGoldrick, S.S.J., Prin.
Lay Teachers 7; Students 120.

16—ST. TIMOTHY, (1985), Revs. John G. Tapp; Eric Peters; Deacon Jerry L. Crall.
Res., 4015 Ragg Rd., 33624. Tel: 813-968-1077; Fax: 813-961-9429.
School—Most Holy Redeemer Interparochial School. See Elementary Schools, Interparochial under Institutions Located in the Diocese. Tel: 813-933-4750.
Catechesis/Religious Programs—Tel: 813-961-1716; Fax: 813-961-9429. Mary Olson, D.R.E.
Students 709.

Tarpon Springs, Pinellas Co., St. Ignatius (1956), Very Rev. Joseph A. Pellegrino, V.F.; Revs. John J. Blum; Walter G. Michalik, C.S.C.; Louis DeTommaso, O.F.M.
Mailing Address: P.O. Box 1306, 34688-1306.
Res., 715 E. Orange St., 34689. Tel: 813-937-4050; Fax: 813-943-0676.
School—Guardian Angels Interparochial School, Clearwater. See Elementary Schools, Interparochial under Institutions Located in the Diocese. Tel: 813-799-6724; Fax: 813-724-9018.
Catechesis/Religious Programs—Tel: 813-934-4163. Diane Magoulis, D.R.E.
Students 595.

Temple Terrace, Hillsborough Co., Corpus Christi (1958), Revs. Brendan Lawlor; Demetrio L. Lorden; Leonard J.M. Plazewski.
Res., 9715 N. 56th St., 33617. Tel: 813-988-1593; Fax: 813-985-3583.
School—Tel: 813-988-1722. Mr. Paul F. Archer, Prin.
Lay Teachers 18; Students 318.
Catechesis/Religious Programs—Tel: 813-985-3335. Mrs. Jannifer Regnery, D.R.E.
Students 587.

Valrico, Hillsborough Co., St. Stephen (1987), Revs. Patrick Irwin; Tom Anastasia.
Church—5049 Bell Shoals Rd., 33594. Tel: 813-689-4900.
Catechesis/Religious Programs—Tel: 813-689-7174. Joyce Morgan, D.R.E.
Students 915.

Zephyrhills, Pasco Co., St. Joseph, Revs. Jacob A. Monteleone; John Hays. In res., Revs. Robert Rittmeyer; Edward DeRussy; Deacon Raymond A. Haberle.
Church—5316 11th St., 33540. Tel: 813-782-2813; Fax: 813-788-1036.
School—St. Anthony Interparochial School, San Antonio. See Elementary Schools, Interparochial under Institutions Located in the Diocese. Tel: 352-588-3041; Fax: 352-588-3142.
Catechesis/Religious Programs—Tel: 813-788-2510. Mrs. Patricia Knopp, D.R.E.
Students 197.

On Duty Outside the Diocese:
Reverend Fathers—
Galan, Juan Cerro
Garcia, Avelino
Kane, John
Mahony, John
McDonough, Donat Michael
Plourde, Peter
Waters, Joseph

Absent on Leave:
Reverend Fathers—
Ryan, Greg

Military Chaplains:
Reverend Fathers—
McCahon, Joseph F.S., U.S.A.F.
Plourde, John, U.S.A.F.

Retired:
Reverend Monsignors—
Cummings, George
DuBois, William
Trainor, Patrick
Reverend Fathers—
Colgan, John
Cottrell, James
D'Angelo, Rocco
Dambrauskas, Stephen
Dauss, Francis
Diffley, Jerome
Estibalez, Inocencio
Gardner, Simeon
Gill, Desmond
Goodman, Frank
Jozwiak, Zygmunt
Kearney, William
Malin, George
O'Toole, Charles
Obert, Martin
Rinaldo, Alexander
Rittmeyer, Robert
Simon, Bernard

Permanent Deacons:
Alterio, Vincent
Anderson, John (NY)
Bevvino, Frank J., Jr., On Duty Outside the Diocese
Blaney, James (RVC)
Brennan, Lee
Breznak, Charles
Brown, Joseph
Buga, John (PSC)
Buttles, Edward
Cajaio, Henry
Cartier, Roger L. (NOR)
Ciarciaglino, Joseph (PSC)
Columbus, Michael
Connors, William
Crall, Jerry
Culkin, John (ALB)
Demers, Emile (Canada)
Desjardins, Roland (ORL)
Diaz, William
DiVito, John
Dunphy, Melvin (WOR)
Edgerton, John (NY)
Evans, Forrest
Friscia, Dominic
Grote, Joseph
Haberle, Raymond
Hassett, James
Hecht, Lowell, Jr.
Izzo, Louis
Knox, Terrence (MIA)
Krzanowski, Joseph
Kurylowicz, Stephen
Liggan, John (NY)
Lind, Roger F. (RVC)
Loffredo, Eugene E. (HRT)
Marini, Anthony (ROC)
McElroy, Robert (RCK)
McGory, Gerald
McIntosh, Richard
Metilly, Paul (FR)
Metty, Thomas
Meyer, Richard (TR)
Moschetto, Samuel (BO)
Ortiz, Samuel
Pescatore, James (RVC)
Pickart, Glenn
Pignatoro, Angelo
Polcari, Joseph (MIA)
Postadan, Romulo (NEW)
Powell, Eugene
Pullar, James
Quiles, Rafael (CLV)
Roberts, Lionel (BRK)
Rodriguez, Manuel
Rojas, Ronald (PCE)
Schott, Thomas (OKL)
Shiel, Thomas (NY)
Sierra, John
Simpson, Robert C. (RVC)
Slattery, Michael
Thomas, Jerome
Tibbetts, Albert
Uzzi, Gerard (PAT)
Vance, Ronald, On Duty Outside the Diocese
Wallace, Barry
Yarawsky, William

INSTITUTIONS LOCATED IN THE DIOCESE

[A] COLLEGES

ST. LEO. *Saint Leo College.* Mailing Address: P.O. Box 2187, 33574. Tel: 352-588-8200.
For a complete listing, refer to the Colleges and Universities section.

[B] HIGH SCHOOLS, DIOCESAN

ST. PETERSBURG. *St. Petersburg Catholic High School,* 6333 Ninth Ave., N., 33710. Tel: 813-344-4065. Rev. Gerald Hendry, Chap. Priests 3; Sisters 2; Lay Teachers 35; Students 471.

CLEARWATER. *Clearwater Central Catholic High School,* 2750 Haines Bayshore Rd., 34620. Tel: 813-531-1449; Fax: 813-535-7034. Sr. Mary Dion Horrigan, S.N.D., Prin. Priests 1; Sisters of Notre Dame (Chardon, Ohio) 3; Sisters of Providence (Indiana)

1; Lay Teachers 43; Students 655.

TAMPA. *Tampa Catholic High School*, 4630 N. Rome Ave., 33603. Tel: 813-870-0860. Rev. Richard Colbert, S.M., Dir. Pastoral Svcs.; Bro. James J. MacDonald, C.F.C., Prin. Priests 1; Congregation of Christian Brothers (New Rochelle, NY) 4; Sisters 1; Lay Teachers 47; Students 721.

[C] HIGH SCHOOLS, PRIVATE

TAMPA. *Academy of the Holy Names High School*, 3319 Bayshore Blvd., 33629. Tel: 813-839-5371; Fax: 813-839-1486. Dr. Claire M. Helm, Pres.; Sr. Anne Celine Turner, S.N.J.M., Prin. Legal Titles: *Academy of the Holy Names of Florida, Inc.*; *Academy of the Holy Names Foundation, Inc.* Sisters 8; Lay Teachers 30; Students 309.

Jesuit High School, 4701 N. Himes Ave., 33614. Tel: 813-877-5344; Fax: 813-872-1853. Revs. Michael F. Kennelly, S.J., Rector; Joseph Doyle, S.J., Pres.; Mr. Michael D. Trainor, Prin.; Bro. A. Joseph Martin, S.J., Minister; Revs. Richard G. Hartnett, S.J., Alumni Chap.; John Kaack, S.J., Chap.; John J. Cazenavette, S.J.; Brian Garry, S.J.; Rodney T. Kissinger, S.J.; Michael E. Chesney, S.J.; Donald W. Saunders, S.J. Legal Titles: *Jesuit High School of Tampa, Inc., FKA*; *St. Louis Catholic, Benevolent and Educational Association, Inc.*; *Jesuit High School Foundation, Inc.* Priests 11; Brothers 1; Lay Teachers 50; Students 671.

[D] ELEMENTARY SCHOOLS, INTERPAROCHIAL

ST. PETERSBURG. *St. Paul Interparochial School.* (Grades PreK-8), 1900 12th St. N., 33704. Tel: 813-823-6144; Fax: 813-896-0609. Sr. Kathleen Stagnaro, O.S.F., Prin. Serving Blessed Trinity and St. Paul. Sisters 2; Lay Teachers 13; Students 287.

CLEARWATER. *Guardian Angels Catholic School.* (Grades K-6), 2270 Evans Rd., 34623. Tel: 813-799-6724. Cindy H. Mann, Prin. Serving All Saints, St. Ignatius, St. Luke and St. Michael the Archangel. Lay Teachers 15; Students 263.

St. Cecelia Interparochial School. (Grades K-8), 400 S. Hillcrest Ave., 34616. Tel: 813-461-1200. Mrs. Helen S. Marston, Prin. Serving Espiritu Santo, Light of Christ, St. Brendan, St. Catherine of Siena and St. Cecelia. Lay Teachers 37; Students 756.

HUDSON. *Bishop Larkin Interparochial School.* (Grades K-6), 8014 State Rd. 52, 34677. Tel: 813-862-6981. Serving Our Lady Queen of Peace, St. James, St. Michael the Archangel, St. Thomas Aquinas and St. Vincent de Paul. Lay Teachers 15; Students 272.

LECANTO. *Central Catholic School of Citrus County*, 4341 W. Homosassa Trail, 34461. Tel: 352-746-2020. Patricia V. Dvorscak, Prin. Serving Our Lady of Fatima, Our Lady of Grace, St. Benedict, St. Elizabeth Ann Seton, St. Scholastica and St. Thomas the Apostle. Lay Teachers 16; Students 270.

SAN ANTONIO. *St. Anthony Interparochial School.* (Grades K-8), 32902 Massachusetts Ave., P.O. Box 847, 33576-0847. Tel: 352-588-3041. Concetta A. Rizzo, Prin. Serving Sacred Heart, St. Anthony, St. Joseph and St. Rita. Sisters 1; Lay Teachers 13; Students 225.

SPRING HILL. *Notre Dame Interparochial School.* (Grades PreK-8), 1117 Suzanne Dr., 34607. Tel: 352-683-0755. Mary Johnson, Prin. Serving St. Anne Mission, St. Anthony, St. Frances Xavier Cabrini, St. Joan of Arc, St. Mary and St. Theresa. Sisters 3; Lay Teachers 18; Students 404.

TAMPA. *Most Holy Redeemer Interparochial School.* (Grades K-8), 302 E. Linebaugh Ave., 33612. Tel: 813-933-4750. Fred Coffaro, Prin.; Marcella Walker, Asst. Prin. Serving Most Holy Redeemer, Our Lady of the Rosary, St. Mary, St. Paul and St. Timothy. Lay Teachers 25; Students 497.

[E] ELEMENTARY SCHOOLS, PRIVATE

TAMPA. *Academy of the Holy Names Elementary.* (Grades PreK-8), 3319 Bayshore Blvd., 33629. Tel: 813-839-5371; Fax: 813-837-5710. Dr. Claire Helm, Pres. Principals: Sr. Ann Regan, S.N.J.M.; Dr. Carmen Caltagirone. Legal Titles: *Academy of the Holy Names of Florida, Inc.*; *Academy of the Holy Names Foundation, Inc.* Sisters of the Holy Names of Jesus and Mary (Albany) 8; Lay Teachers 34; Students 531.

Mary Help of Christians School. (Grades 6-8). (Boys), 6400 E. Chelsea St., 33610-5699. Tel: 813-626-6191. Salesians of St. John Bosco. (Resident and Day School). Revs. Frank R. Wolfram, S.D.B., Dir.; John Nazzaro, S.D.B., Prin.; Kenneth Germaine, S.D.B., Admin.; Lawrence Urban, S.D.B., Youth Dir.; August P. Bosio, S.D.B.; Bros. Dominic Casaraghi, S.D.B.; John Versaggi, S.D.B.; Joseph Ackroyd, S.D.B.; Salvatore Sammarco, S.B.D. Legal Title: *Salesian Society, Inc.* Priests 3; Brothers 2; Lay Teachers 8; Students 130.

Villa Madonna School, 315 W. Columbus Dr., 33602. Tel: 813-229-1322. Sr. Cecilia Besi, F.M.A., Prin. Legal Title: *Salesian Sisters of Tampa, Inc.* Daughters of Mary Help of Christians 10; Lay Teachers 28; Students 543.

[F] PRESCHOOLS AND DAY CARE CENTERS

ST. PETERSBURG. *Immaculate Conception Pre-School.* Ages 1-5, Extended Care. Lower Pinellas Deanery, 2100 26th Ave. S., 33712. Tel: 813-822-2156; Fax: 813-553-9133. Mrs. Rita A. Jackson, Dir.; Mrs. Mary Calloway, Asst. Dir.; Rev. Arthur Proulx, Admin. Lay Teachers 19; Children 180.

CLEARWATER. *Light of Christ Preschool.* Ages 2-5, Extended Care. Upper Pinellas Deanery, 2176 Marilyn St., 34625. Tel: 813-442-4797. Mrs. Barbara Barko, Sunday School & Preschool Dir.; Rev. Timothy Allman, Pastor. Lay Teachers 8; Students 90.

Little Nazareth Early Childhood Center. Ages 3-4. Upper Pinellas Deanery, 820 Jasmine Way, 34616. Tel: 813-447-3494. Mrs. Sandra A. Barbeau, Dir.; Very Rev. Aiden Foynes. Lay Teachers 2; Children 32.

DADE CITY. *Sacred Heart Child Care Center.* Infant-PreK, Extended Care. Pasco Deanery, 32245 Saint Joe Rd., 33525. Tel: 904-588-4060. Mrs. Toni Watkins, Dir.; Rev. Arthur Villemaire. Children 150.

LARGO. *St. Jerome Early Childhood Center.* Ages 3-4. 10895 Hamlin Blvd., 33774. Tel: 813-596-9491. Denise Roach, Dir.; Rev. Msgr. Brendan Muldoon, V.G. Children 116.

NEW PORT RICHEY. *St. Thomas Aquinas Early Childhood Center*, 8320 State Rd. 54, 34653. Tel: 813-376-2330. Mrs. Cindy McKallip, Dir.; Rev. Thomas F. Earner; Pamela Bruno, Sec. Lay Teachers 2; Children 79.

PALM HARBOR. *St. Luke Early Childhood Center.* Ages 2-4, Extended Care. 2757 Alderman Rd., 34684. Tel: 813-787-2914; Fax: 813-789-9556. Ms. Carol Hussin, Dir.; Rev. Donald F. Leininger. Children 172.

SAN ANTONIO. *Holy Name Academy Child Care Center dba Bendictine Sisters of Florida.* (aka Holy Name Academy, Inc.) Ages 2-5, Extended Care. 12117 Wichers Rd., 33576. Tel: 352-588-8325; Fax: 352-588-8319. Sr. Roberta Bailey, O.S.B., Admin. Sisters 1; Lay Teachers 5; Children 70.

TAMPA. *St. Paul Preschool.* Ages 3-4. 12708 N. Dale Mabry Hwy., 33618-2802. Tel: 813-962-6535, Ext. 241. Mrs. Maureen Miller, Dir.; Rev. Msgr. John Neff. Lay Teachers 6; Children 108.

St. Timothy Preschool, 4015 Ragg Rd., P.O. Box 340129, 33694-0129. Tel: 813-960-4857. Mrs. Charlotte Blackburn, Dir.; Rev. John Tapp. Students 113.

TARPON SPRINGS. *St. Ignatius Early Childhood Center.* Ages 2-6. 725 E. Orange St., P.O. Box 1306, 34688-1306. Tel: 813-934-4163. Mrs. Jean Lanes, Dir.; Rev. Joseph Pellegrino. Lay Teachers 7; Children 67.

[G] SCHOOLS FOR EXCEPTIONAL CHILDREN

PINELLAS PARK. *Morning Star School*, 4661 80th Ave., N., 33781. Tel: 813-544-6036. Sr. Mary Louis, A.S.C.J., Prin. Apostles of the Sacred Heart of Jesus (Hamden, CT) 2; Lay Teachers 9; Students 55.

TAMPA. *Morning Star School*, 210 E. Linebaugh Ave., 33612. Tel: 813-935-0232; 932-2321. Miss Jeanette Friedheim, Prin. Lay Teachers 10; Students 84.

[H] SCHOOLS FOR THEOLOGICAL AND SPIRITUAL TRAINING

ST. PETERSBURG. *Pastoral Institute of the Diocese of St. Petersburg*, 6533 Ninth Ave. N., 33710. Mailing Address: P.O. Box 43022, 33743-3022. Tel: 813-345-3338. Dr. Barbara McConville, Exec. Dir.

CLEARWATER. *The Cenacle of Our Lady of Divine Providence.* School of Spirituality. 702 Bayview Ave., 34619. Tel: 813-724-9505; Fax: 813-724-9421. Ronald W. Novotny, Ph.D., Dir. Lay Teachers 3.

[I] DAY CARE CENTERS

TAMPA. *Peter Claver Day Care Center, Inc.*, 1431 Tampa Park Plaza, 33605. Tel: 813-229-7632. Total Staff 15; Total Assisted 81.

[J] CATHOLIC CHARITIES

ST. PETERSBURG. *Catholic Charities, Diocese of St. Petersburg, Inc.* Mailing Address: 6533 Ninth Ave., N., Ste. 1, E., 33710. Tel: 813-893-1313. Provides Counseling Services to Individuals, Families and Children; Pregnancy Related Services; Adoption Placement; Daystar Life Centers; Foster Home Placement; Family Life Education; Gerontology Services; Refugee and Immigration Services; Child Care Services; Basic Education Program; Emergency Care Services; AIDS Volunteer; Campaign for Human Development; Catholic Relief Services; Disabilities Services.

Pinellas County Regional Offices:

Central Services, 6533 Ninth Ave., N., Ste. 1, E., 33710. Tel: 813-345-9126. Mr. Arnold Andrews, Exec. Dir.

[K] GENERAL HOSPITALS

ST. PETERSBURG. *St. Anthony's Hospital, Inc.*, 1200 Seventh Ave., N., 33705. Tel: 813-825-1100.
For a complete listing, refer to the Hospitals section.

TAMPA. *St. Joseph's Hospital, Inc.*, 3001 W. Martin Luther King Blvd., 33607.
For a complete listing, refer to the Hospitals section.

[L] RETIREMENT AND HEALTH CARE CENTERS

*ST. PETERSBURG. *Bon Secours-Maria Manor Nursing Care Center, Inc.*, 10300 Fourth St., N., 33716. Tel: 813-576-1025.
For a complete listing, refer to the Hospitals section.

CLEARWATER. *The Tepeyac Corporation dba Clinica Guadalupana*, 1215 Drew St., Ste. 7B, 34615. Tel: 813-461-7730.
For a complete listing, refer to the Hospitals section.

[M] RETIREMENT HOUSING

ST. PETERSBURG. *Holy Cross Housing dba Casa Santa Cruz*, 7851 54th Ave. N., 33709.
For a complete listing, refer to the Hospitals section.

CLEARWATER. *St. Michael's Housing Corporation dba Casa Miguel*, 2285 State Rd. #580, 34623. Tel: 813-797-8551.
For a complete listing, refer to the Hospitals section.

TAMPA. *Christ the King Housing II, Inc. dba Kings Manor*, 2946 W. Columbus Dr., 33607. Tel: 813-875-0139; Fax: 813-875-6061.
For a complete listing, refer to the Hospitals section.

Christ the King Housing, Inc. dba Kings Arms, 4125 N. Lincoln Ave., 33607. Tel: 813-873-0234.
For a complete listing, refer to the Hospitals section.

St. Patrick's Housing Corporation dba Patrician Arms, 4516 S. Manhattan Ave., 33611. Tel: 813-835-8227.
For a complete listing, refer to the Hospitals section.

[N] SENIOR CENTERS

LARGO. *Bethlehem Centre, Inc.*, 10895 Hamlin Blvd., 34644. Tel: 813-596-9394. Senior Center Offering Daily Programming of a Social, Educational, Remedial, and Religious Nature; Luncheon on Tuesday and Friday, Counseling; Alzheimer's Support Group. Mrs. Patricia Morgan, Dir. Total Staff 3.

[O] MONASTERIES AND RESIDENCES OF PRIESTS AND BROTHERS

ST. PETERSBURG. *Missionaries of Africa*, 5757 Seventh Ave. N., 33710. Tel: 813-343-1001; Fax: 813-343-4395. Rev. Paul J. Heon, M.Afr.; Bro. Philip J. Nadeau, M.Afr.; Revs. Jean C. Robitaille, M.Afr., Coord.; Constant H. Durette, M.Afr.; Joseph Sys, M.Afr.; Charles Tardiff, M.Afr.; Aime F. Lacasse, M.Afr.; Kevin J. Barrett, M.Afr.

Notre Dame Residence, 1101 66th St. N., 33710. Tel: 813-384-0546.

St. Anthony Friary. Franciscan Residence and Retirement Community. 357 Second St., N., 33701; Fax: 813-821-8067. Revs. Roch A. Coogan, O.F.M., Guardian; Roy Gasnick, O.F.M., Vicar; Venard Murphy, O.F.M.; Bros. Richard James, O.F.M.; Michael Madden, O.F.M.; Marion Ressel, O.F.M.; Valerian Vaverchack, O.F.M.

Full-time Active Ministry: Revs. James Jones, O.F.M.; Arthur Murray, O.F.M.; Thomas K. Murphy, O.F.M.

Retirement Community: Revs. Patrick Adams, O.F.M.; Edward Burke, O.F.M.; Declan Bailey, O.F.M.; Theodore A. Blackowski, O.F.M.; Arnold Brown, O.F.M.; Simeon Capizzi, O.F.M.; Peter Carr, O.F.M.; Paul Feichter, O.F.M.; Louis Foley, O.F.M.; Martin A. Hanhauser; Laurence A. Hardy, O.F.M.; Clement Healy; Leonard E. Lencewicz; Neil Padden, O.F.M.; Raphael McDonald, O.F.M.; Alexis P. Morris; James P. Mulhern, O.F.M.; Columba Murphy, O.F.M.; Maurice O'Hara, O.F.M.; James Schwantner, O.F.M.; Bernard Weinholtz, O.F.M.; Bros. John V. Krieg, O.F.M.; John Reeder, O.F.M.; Francis X. Tokar, O.F.M.

St. Peter Nolasco Residence, 5650 Seventh Ave. N., 33710. Tel: 813-345-4766. Revs. Arcangelo Manzi, O.de.M., Supr. of the House; Michael Perry, O.de.M.; Benedict Ptacek, O.de.M.; Oscar Kozyra, O.de.M.; Bro. Richard Henry, O.de.M. Total Staff 4; Total in Residence 4.

BELLEAIR BLUFFS. *St. James Friary*, 2433 Indian Ave., 33770-2032. Tel: 813-585-2521; Fax: 813-585-2460. Franciscan Friars Ministry of the Word (New York). Revs. Edward Flanagan, O.F.M.; Roderic Petrie, O.F.M.; Martin Bednar, O.F.M.

CLEARWATER. *Pius X Friary*, 2305 Williams Dr., Morning Estates, 34624. Tel: 813-530-0153. Franciscan Friars of Atonement (Garrison, NY).

KENNEBUNKPORT, ME. *Franciscan Friary*, Vice-Province of St. Casimir, 04046.

PINELLAS PARK. *Priests of the Sacred Heart*, 6701 82nd Ave., N., 34665. Tel: 813-541-2661; Fax: 813-547-0408. Bro. Timothy Murphy, S.C.J., Coord.; Most Rev. Joseph A. DePalma, S.C.J., Retired Bishop of DeAar, S.Africa; Revs. Joseph Poirier, S.C.J., (Staff); Joseph Doscher, S.C.J., (Staff); Thomas Simcox, S.C.J., (Retired); Leonard Tadyszak, S.C.J., (Retired); Raymond Vega, S.C.J., (Retired); Kenneth Mitchell, S.C.J., (Retired); Michael van der Peet, S.C.J., (Retired); Bros. Paul Schneeberger, S.C.J., (Retired); Gabriel Kersting, S.C.J., (Retired). Total Staff 3; Total in Residence 11.

ST. LEO. *St. Leo Abbey*, 33574. Tel: 352-588-2881; 588-5150. Very Rev. Simeon J. Thole, O.S.B., Apostolic Admin.; Rt. Rev. Marion Bowman, O.S.B., Retired Abbot; Revs. Francis A. Flood, O.S.B., Prior; Andrew Metzger, O.S.B.; Paul Romfh, O.S.B.; Gregory Traeger, O.S.B.; Damian Duquesnay, O.S.B.; Richard Hugli, O.S.B.

On Duty Outside the Monastery: Rt. Rev. Patrick Shelton, O.S.B., Retired Abbot; Revs. James Hoge, O.S.B.; Robert Velten, O.S.B.; Jude Krogol, O.S.B.; Henry Riffle, O.S.B.; David Draim, O.S.B.; Vincent Morton, O.S.B. Priests 14; Brothers 20; Internal Oblates 1.

SEMINOLE. *Capuchin Franciscan Residence*, 7171 128th St. N., 33776. Tel: 813-397-0011. Rev. Joseph Testagrossa, O.F.M.Cap., Admin.

[P] CONVENTS AND RESIDENCES FOR SISTERS

ST. PETERSBURG. *St. Anthony Hospital Convent*, 631 11th St. N., 33705. Tel: 813-825-1142. Franciscan Sisters of Allegany (Allegany, NY).

HOLIDAY. *St. Clare's Convent*, 2109 Tilogia Court, 34690. Sr. Josephine Rooney, O.S.C., Regl. Supr.

St. Clare Sisters Retreat Ministry. Tel: 813-786-3821. Total in Residence 18.

ST. LEO. *Holy Name Monastery*, P.O. Box 2450, 33574-2450. Mailing Address: P.O. Box H, 33574-4002. Tel: 352-588-8320.

Motherhouse and Novitiate of the Benedictine Sisters of Florida. Legal Title: *Holy Name Academy, Inc.* Sr. Germaine Bevans, O.S.B., Prioress. Professed Sisters 26; Temporary Promises 2.

TAMPA. *Franciscan Sisters of Mary*, 8501 Anglers Pointe Dr., 33637-1833. Tel: 813-988-0893.

St. Clare Convent, 2924 Curtis St., 33614. Tel: 813-870-4272. Franciscan Sisters of Allegany (Allegany, NY).

St. Elizabeth Convent, 3000 Perry Ave., 33603. Tel: 813-229-1978. Franciscan Sisters of Allegany. Total Staff 3; Total in Residence 20.

Sisters of the Holy Cross, 6703-A Jamesville Dr., 33617. Tel: 813-989-2647.

Sisters of the Holy Cross, 13301 B Whitestone Dr., 33617. Tel: 813-989-0649. Sisters 3.

Villa Madonna Convent, 2611 N. Massachusetts Ave., 33602. Tel: 813-223-2209. Daughters of Mary Help of Christians (Haledon, NJ). Total Staff 10; Total in Residence 10.

[Q] RETREAT CENTERS

CLEARWATER. *Our Lady of Divine Providence, House of Prayer, Inc.*, 702 Bayview Ave., 34619. Tel: 813-797-7412.

Ministries of the Marian Servants of Divine Providence:

Our Lady of Divine Providence House of Prayer.

Our Lady's House of Peace. Retreat House.

Providence House. Retreat House.

The Cenacle of Our Lady of Divine Providence School of Spirituality. Affiliated with Franciscan University of Steubenville.

Living His Life Abundantly. Media Ministry.

ST. LEO. *St. Leo Abbey Retreat Center*, P.O. Box 2350, 33574. Tel: 352-588-2009. Bro. Dennis McCarthy, O.S.B., Dir.

TAMPA. *Franciscan Center, Retreat House*, 3010 Perry Ave., 33603. Tel: 813-229-2695. Franciscan Sisters of Allegany. Sr. Catherine Cahill, O.S.F., Admin.; Sr. Mary Fleming, O.S.F., Asst. Admin.; Sr. Jo Streva, O.S.F., Coord. Public Rels. and Scheduling. Retreat Team: Sr. Regina Kane, O.S.F.; Sr. Juliana Mohr, O.S.F., Coord. Support Svcs.; Sr. Colleen Brady, O.S.F.

[R] SUMMER CAMPS

ST. PETERSBURG. *Our Lady of Good Counsel Camp*. Mailing Address: 8888 E. Gobbler Dr., Floral City, 34436. Tel: 352-726-2198; Fax: 352-726-3212. Rev. James Johnson, Dir., Our Lady of Fatima Church, 550 US Hwy 41, S., Inverness, 34450. Tel: 352-726-1910; Fax: 352-344-8384.

[S] CAMPUS MINISTRY

ST. PETERSBURG. *St. Petersburg Eckerd College*, 5650 7th Ave. N., 33710. Tel: 813-864-8470. Bro. Richard Henry, O.de.M., Chap.

TAMPA. *Catholic Student Center, University of South Florida*, 13005 N. 50th St., 33617. Tel: 813-988-3727. Rev. Alan Weber, Chap.

University of Tampa, P.O. Box 1524, 33601-1524. Tel: 813-229-1595. Rev. Thomas Hidding, S.J., Chap.

[T] MISCELLANEOUS

ST. PETERSBURG. *Catholic Charities Housing, Inc.*, 6533 Ninth Ave. N., 33710.

Chancery Office, 6363 Ninth St., 33743. For detailed information on the following listings contact the Chancery Office.

Allegany Health System Foundation, Inc.

Catholic Charities Housing, Inc.

Catholic Education Foundation, Inc.

Catholic Media Ministry, Inc.

Christopher Assurance, Inc.

Franciscan Sisters of Allegany Health System, Inc.

Regis Manor, Inc.

WBVM, 90.5 FM, Inc., Clearwater.

Catholic Charities Foundation of Tampa Bay, Inc.

Epiphany Housing of Tampa, Inc., c/o P.O. Box 40200, 33743-0200. Most Rev. Robert N. Lynch, Chm.

St. Anthony's Ancillary Services, Inc., 1200 7th Ave. N., 33705.

St. Anthony's Professional Buildings and Services, Inc., 1200 7th Ave. N., 33705.

PALM HARBOR. *St. Vincent Ministry to Priests, Inc.*, 970 Pine Hill Rd., 34683-3013. Tel: 813-784-6462; Fax: 813-787-3741. Rev. Kevin Scallon, C.M.

RELIGIOUS INSTITUTES OF MEN REPRESENTED IN THE DIOCESE

For further details refer to the corresponding bracketed number in the Religious Institutes of Men or Women section.

[0140]—*The Augustinians*. (Villanova, PA).—O.S.A.

[0190]—*Basilian Salvatorian Fathers*. (Methuen, MA).—B.S.O.

[0200]—*Benedictine Monks*. (St. Leo, FL).—O.S.B.

[1350]—*Brothers of St. Francis Xavier*. (Ellicott City, MD).—C.F.X.

[0470]—*The Capuchin Friars*. (White Plains, NY; Union City, NJ).—O.F.M.Cap.

[0350]—*Cistercians Order of the Strict Observance (Trappists)*. (Spencer, MA).—O.C.S.O.

[1320]—*Clerics of St. Viator*. (Arlington Heights, IL).—C.S.V.

[0310]—*Congregation of Christian Brothers*. (New Rochelle, NY).—C.F.C.

[0220]—*Congregation of the Blessed Sacrament*. (Cleveland, OH).—S.S.S.

[0630]—*Congregation of the Missionaries of the Holy Family*. (Santiago, Chile).—M.S.F.

[1130]—*Congregation of the Priests of the Sacred Heart*. (Hales Corner, WI).—S.C.J.

[0520]—*Franciscan Friars*. (New York, NY; Pulaski, WI; Kennebunkport, ME; Dublin, Ireland).—O.F.M.

[0530]—*Franciscan Friars of the Atonement*. (Garrison, NY).—S.A.

[0650]—*Holy Ghost Fathers*. (Dublin, Ireland).—C.S.Sp.

[0300]—*Institute of Charity*. (Peoria, IL).—I.C.

[0690]—*Jesuit Fathers and Brothers*. (New Orleans, LA; Baltimore, MD).—S.J.

[0780]—*Marist Fathers*. (Washington, DC).—S.M.

[0800]—*Maryknoll*.—M.M.

[0850]—*Missionaries of Africa*. (Washington, DC).—M.Afr.

[0910]—*Oblates of Mary Immaculate*. (Washington, DC; St. Paul, MN).—O.M.I.

[0970]—*Order of Our Lady of Mercy*. (Cleveland, OH).—O.deM.

[0430]—*Order of Preachers (Dominicans)*. (Dublin, Ireland).—O.P.

[0610]—*Priests of the Congregation of the Holy Cross*. (Notre Dame, IN; Bridgeport, CT).—C.S.C.

[1060]—*Redemptorist Fathers*. (New York, NY).—C.SS.R.

[0700]—*St. Joseph's Society of the Sacred Heart*. (Baltimore, MD).—S.S.J.

[1190]—*Salesians of Don Bosco*. (New Rochelle, NY).—S.D.B

[]—*Scarboro Foreign Missions*. (Scarboro, Ontario, Canada).—S.F.M.

[1060]—*Society of the Precious Blood*. (Dayton, OH).—C.PP.S.

[0560]—*Third Order Regular of Saint Francis*. (Pittsburgh, PA).—T.O.R.

RELIGIOUS INSTITUTES OF WOMEN REPRESENTED IN THE DIOCESE

[0130]—*Apostles of the Sacred Heart of Jesus*. (Hamden, CT).—A.S.C.J.

[0230]—*Benedictine Sisters of Pontifical Jurisdiction*. (St. Leo, FL).—O.S.B.

[3110]—*Congregation of Our Lady of Retreat in the Cenacle*. (Lake Ronkonkoma, NY).—R.C.

[3710]—*Congregation of the Sisters of St. Agnes*.—C.S.A.

[1920]—*Congregation of the Sisters of the Holy Cross*.—C.S.C.

[1730]—*Congregation of the Sisters of the Third Order of St. Francis, Oldenburg, IN*.—O.S.F.

[0850]—*Daughters of Mary Help of Christians*. (Haledon, NJ).—F.M.A.

[]—*Daughters of Mary Immaculate*. (Vietnam).—F.M.I.

[1070-01]—*Dominican Sisters*.—O.P.

[1070-02]—*Dominican Sisters*.—O.P.

[1070-05]—*Dominican Sisters*.—O.P.

[1070-11]—*Dominican Sisters*.—O.P.

[1070-13]—*Dominican Sisters*.—O.P.

[1120]—*Dominican Sisters of the Roman Congregation*.—O.P.

[1140]—*Eucharistic Missionaries of St. Dominic*.—O.P.

[1370]—*Franciscan Missionaries of Mary*.—F.M.M.

[1180]—*Franciscan Sisters of Allegany, New York*.—O.S.F.

[1310]—*Franciscan Sisters of Little Falls, Minnesota*.—O.S.F.

[1370]—*Franciscan Sisters of Mary*. (Bronx, NY).—F.M.M.

[1415]—*Franciscan Sisters of Mary*. (St. Louis, MO).—F.S.M.

[]—*Handmaids of the Holy Child Jesus*. (Nigeria).—H.H.C.J.

[2575]—*Institute of the Sisters of Mercy of the Americas*. (Merion, PA; Chicago, IL; New York, NY; Detroit, MI).—R.S.M.

[2420]—*Marist Missionary Sisters (Missionary Sisters of the Society of Mary)*.—S.M.S.M.

[2470]—*Maryknoll Sisters of St. Dominic*.—M.M.

[2490]—*Medical Mission Sisters*. (Philadelphia, PA).—S.C.M.M.

[2480]—*Medical Missionaries of Mary*.—M.M.M.

[2720]—*Mission Helpers of the Sacred Heart*. (Baltimore, MD).—M.H.S.H.

[]—*Missionarias Hijas de la Madre de la Luz*. (Mexico).—M.H.M.L.

[1360]—*Missionary Franciscan Sisters of the Immaculate Conception*. (Newton, MA).—O.S.F.

[0242]—*Missionary Sisters of the Society of Mary*.—S.M.S.M.

[3760]—*Order of St. Clare*. (Evansville, IN; Greenville, SC).—O.S.C.

[3770]—*Order of St. Clare*.—O.S.C.

[4180]—*Religious Venerini Sisters*.—M.P.V.

[2970]—*School Sisters of Notre Dame*. (Baltimore, MD; Wilton, CT).—S.S.N.D.

[1680]—*School Sisters of St. Francis*. (Milwaukee, WI).—S.S.S.F.

[3590]—*Servants of Mary (Servite Sisters)*.—O.S.M.

[0440]—*Sisters of Charity of Cincinnati, Ohio*. (Mt. St. Joseph, OH).—S.C.

[0500]—*Sisters of Charity of Nazareth*.—S.C.N.

[0590]—*Sisters of Charity of Saint Elizabeth, Convent Station*.—S.C.

[0570]—*Sisters of Charity of Seton Hill*. (Greensberg, PA).—S.C.

[0650]—*Sisters of Charity of St. Vincent dePaul*.—S.C.

[1930]—*Sisters of Holy Cross*. (Pittsfield, NH).—C.S.C.

[]—*Sisters of Mary, Mother of God*. (Tampa, FL).—S.M.M.G.

[2575]—*Sisters of Mercy of The Americas*.—R.S.M.

[2990]—*Sisters of Notre Dame*. (Chardon, OH).—S.N.D.

[3000]—*Sisters of Notre Dame de Namur*. (Boston, MA).—S.N.D.deN.

[3360]—*Sisters of Providence*. (St. Mary of the Woods, IN.).—S.P.

[3893]—*Sisters of Saint Joseph of Chestnut Hill, Philadelphia*.—S.S.J.

[3720]—*Sisters of St. Anne*.—S.S.A.

[]—*Sisters of St. Anne Bangalore*.—S.A.B.

[3750]—*Sisters of St. Chretienne*. (Wrentham, MA).—S.S.Ch.

[3770]—*Sisters of St. Clare*.—O.S.C.

[1510]—*Sisters of St. Francis*.—O.S.F.

[1630]—*Sisters of St. Francis of Penance and Christian Charity*.—O.S.F.

[1650]—*Sisters of St. Francis of Philadelphia*.—O.S.F.

[1570]—*Sisters of St. Francis of the Holy Family*.—O.S.F.

[3830-11]—*Sisters of St. Joseph.*—S.S.J.
[3830-14]—*Sisters of St. Joseph.*—S.S.J.
[3840]—*Sisters of St. Joseph of Carondelet.* (St. Louis, MO).—C.S.J.
[3880]—*Sisters of St. Joseph of Medaille.*—C.S.J.
[3890]—*Sisters of St. Joseph of Peace.* (Englewood Cliffs, NJ).—C.S.J.P.
[3900]—*Sisters of St. Joseph of St. Augustine, Florida.*—S.S.J.
[1970]—*Sisters of the Holy Family of Nazareth.* (Philadelphia, PA).—C.S.F.N.
[1990]—*Sisters of the Holy Names of Jesus and Mary.* (Albany, NY).—S.N.J.M.
[3730]—*Sisters of the Order St. Basil the Great.* (Uniontown, PA).—O.S.B.M.
[1490]—*Sisters of the Third Franciscan Order.*—O.S.F.
[2150]—*Sisters, Servants of the Immaculate Heart of Mary.*—I.H.M.
[2160]—*Sisters, Servants of the Immaculate Heart of Mary.*—I.H.M.
[4190]—*Visitation Nuns.* (Wheeling, WV; Washington, DC).—V.H.M.

DIOCESAN CEMETERIES

CLEARWATER. *Calvary Catholic,* 11801 U.S. Hwy. 19 N., 34624-7407.

NECROLOGY

† Larkin, James A., Dunedin, FL, Our Lady of Lourdes Church. —Died July 1, 1996.

† Maguire, Francis X., St. Petersburg, FL, Transfiguration Church. —Died Nov. 8, 1996.

Diocese of Salina

(Dioecesis Salinensis)

Most Reverend

GEORGE K. FITZSIMONS, D.D.

Bishop of Salina; ordained March 18, 1961; appointed Titular Bishop of Pertusa and Auxiliary Bishop of Kansas City-St. Joseph May 27, 1975; Episcopal ordination July 3, 1975; appointed Bishop of Salina March 22, 1984; installed May 29, 1984. *Address all official communications to: P.O. Box 980, Salina, KS, 67402.*

Chancery Office: 103 N. Ninth, P.O. Box 980, Salina, KS, 67402-0980. Tel.: 913-827-8746; Fax: 913-827-6133.

FORMERLY DIOCESE OF CONCORDIA.

ESTABLISHED AUGUST 2, 1887.

SEE TRANSFERRED TO SALINA DECEMBER 23, 1944.

Square Miles 26,685.

(New boundaries established by Apostolic Letters dated July 1, 1897).

Bounded on the west by Colorado, on the north by Nebraska, on the east by the east lines of Washington, Riley, Geary and Dickinson Counties, and on the south by the south lines of Dickinson, Saline, Ellsworth, Russell, Ellis, Trego, Gove, Logan and Wallace Counties in the State of Kansas.

For legal titles of parishes and diocesan institutions, consult the Chancery Office.

STATISTICAL OVERVIEW

Personnel	
Bishop	1
Retired Bishops	1
Priests: Diocesan Active in Diocese	54
Priests: Active Outside Diocese	1
Priests: Retired, Sick or Absent	13
Number of Diocesan Priests	68
Religious Priests in Diocese	19
Ordinations:	
Diocesan Priests	1
Total Brothers	1
Total Sisters	213
Parishes	
Parishes	92
With Resident Pastor:	
Resident Diocesan Priests	40
Resident Religious Priests	8
Without Resident Pastor:	
Administered by Priests	40
Administered by Women Religious	3
Administered by Lay People	1
Welfare	
Homes for the Aged	4
Total Assisted	326
Educational	
Diocesan Students in Other Seminaries	7
Total Seminarians	7
High Schools, Diocesan and Parish	4
Total Students	397
High Schools, Private	1
Total Students	305
Elementary Schools, Diocesan and Parish	12
Total Students	1,887
Catechesis/Religious Education:	
High School Students	2,142
Elementary Students	6,171
Total Students Under Catholic Instruction	10,909
Teachers in the Diocese:	
Priests	9
Sisters	6
Lay Teachers	205
Vital Statistics	
Receptions into the Church:	
Infant Baptism Totals	983
Adult Baptism Totals	111
Received into Full Communion	211
First Communions	978
Confirmations	693
Marriages:	
Catholic	235
Interfaith	225
Total Marriages	460
Deaths	588
Total Catholic Population	52,114
Total Population	328,480

Former Bishops—Rt. Rev. RICHARD SCANNELL, D.D., cons. in Nashville, Tenn., Nov. 30, 1887; transferred to Omaha, Jan. 30, 1891; died Jan. 8, 1916.—Rt. Rev. JOHN J. HENNESSY, D.D., Apostolic Administrator, 1891-98, Bishop of Wichita.—Rt. Rev. THADDEUS BUTLER, D.D., Bishop-elect; died July 17, 1897.—Rt. Rev. JOHN F. CUNNINGHAM, D.D., cons. Sept. 21, 1898; died June 23, 1919.—Most Rev. FRANCIS J. TIEF, D.D., cons. Mar. 30, 1921; retired and appointed Titular Bishop of Nisa, June 11, 1938; died Sept. 22, 1965.—Most Rev. FRANK A. THILL, D.D., cons. Oct. 28, 1938; transferred to Salina, Dec. 23, 1944; died May 21, 1957.—Most Rev. FREDERICK W. FREKING, D.D., cons. Nov. 30, 1957; transferred to LaCrosse, Dec. 30, 1964.—Most Rev. CYRIL J. VOGEL, D.D., ord. Bishop, June 17, 1965; died Oct. 4, 1979.—Most Rev. DANIEL W. KUCERA, O.S.B., Ph.D., D.D., ord. May 26, 1949; appt. Titular Bishop of Natchez and Auxiliary Bishop of Joliet, June 6, 1977; cons. July 21, 1977; appt. Bishop of Salina, March 11, 1980; installed May 7, 1980; transferred to Archbishop of Archdiocese of Dubuque, February 23, 1984.

Chancery Office—103 N. Ninth, P.O. Box 980, Salina, 67402-0980. Tel: 913-827-8746; Fax: 913-827-6133.

Vicar General and Chancellor—Rev. Msgr. JAMES E. HAKE, J.C.L., *Res., Immaculate Conception Church, P.O. Box 167, Minneapolis, 67467.*

Diocesan Finance Officer—Rev. JEROME L. MORGAN, *Res., St. Wenceslaus, Box 528, Wilson, 67490.* Mr. GREG LUST, Asst. Finance Officer & Business Mgr., *P.O. Box 980, Salina, 67402-0980.* Rev. Msgr. GILBERT LANDOLL, Financial Consultant.

Diocesan Tribunal—103 N. Ninth, P.O. Box 980, Salina, 67402-0980. Tel: 913-827-8746; Fax: 913-827-6133.

Judicial Vicar-Officialis—Rev. RALPH ASCHENBRENNER.

Associate Judges—Rev. Msgr. ARMAND GIRARD, J.C.L.; Rev. Msgr. JAMES E. HAKE, J.C.L.; Revs. KENNETH P. LOHRMEYER, J.C.L.; DANIEL SCHEETZ, J.C.L.

Defenders of the Bond—Rev. Msgr. ARMAND GIRARD, J.C.L.; Rev. Msgr. JAMES E. HAKE, J.C.L.; Revs. KENNETH P. LOHRMEYER, J.C.L.; DANIEL SCHEETZ, J.C.L.

Auditors-Notaries—MARY ANN HUFFMAN; JENNY KEELER; FRANCES SCHNEIDER; DARLENE STREIT.

Promoter of Justice and Guardians—Rev. Msgr. ALFRED J. WASINGER; Rev. Msgr. GILBERT LANDOLL.

Procurators and Advocates—Revs. NORBERT DLABAL; ROGER K. MEITL; JEROME L. MORGAN; WILLIAM SURMEIER; JOHN WOLESKY; Sr. MARY LOU ROBERTS, C.S.J.

Diocesan Finance Council—Most Rev. GEORGE K. FITZSIMONS, D.D.; Rev. JEROME L. MORGAN; BILL BECKMEYER; DONALD P. DIEDERICH; JOHN GRAHAM; GREG LUST; LORRAINE McCLAIN; JOHN NORTON.

College of Consultors—Rev. Msgr. JAMES E. HAKE, J.C.L.; Revs. NORBERT DLABAL; MERLIN KIEFFER; MELVIN LONG; JEROME L. MORGAN; DONALD D. ZIMMERMAN.

Episcopal Vicars—Western District: Rev. JAMES HOOVER, West Central District: Rev. DONALD D. ZIMMERMAN, East Central District: Rev. JEROME L. MORGAN, Eastern District: Rev. LOUIS MATTAS.

Council of Priests—Revs. WILLIAM SURMEIER, Chm. HENRY BAXA, Treas. BARRY BRINKMAN; MERLIN KIEFFER, NORBERT DLABAL, Sec. JOSEPH POPELKA, Recording Sec.; Rev. Msgr. JAMES E. HAKE, J.C.L.; Revs. FRANK COADY; FRANK GRINKO, O.F.M.Cap.; JAMES HOOVER; MELVIN LONG, Vice-Chm. JEROME L. MORGAN; RANDALL WEBER; DONALD D. ZIMMERMAN.

Diocesan Pastoral Council—Most Rev. GEORGE K. FITZSIMONS, D.D.; PAT SCHMIDTBERGER, Pres.; Sr. MARY LOU ROBERTS, C.S.J., Moderator; GENE LORSON, Vice Chm.; Rev. Msgr. RAYMOND MENARD; Revs. JAMES HOOVER; JEROME L. MORGAN; JOSEPH POPELKA; MARK WESELY; Sr. ROSALIA COSTELLA, C.S.A ; Sr. KENNETH STRUCKHOFF, C.S.A.; Sr. MARY JO THUMMEL, C.S.J.; Sr. MARILYN WALL, C.S.J. Laity: DALLAS BREEN; MARITA CAMPBELL, Sec. MELVA DORTLAND; MONICA DUSIN; ROSEANN FELDER; JERRY FREITAG; JAMES GUILFOYLE; MARY JO HEATH; LEROY HERRMAN; HAROLD KOSTER; RON LAGER; MARLENE MONTGOMERY; DARREL SCHMEIDLER; MARLA SCHMIDT; HOWARD ROME; JOAN WESSEL.

Personnel Board—Most Rev. GEORGE K. FITZSIMONS, D.D.; Revs. LEROY METRO, Chm. BARRY BRINKMAN; AL DWYER; RANDALL WEBER; MELVIN LONG; Rev. Msgr. JAMES E. HAKE, J.C.L., Ex Officio.

Seminary Board—Most Rev. GEORGE K. FITZSIMONS, D.D.; Revs. NORBERT DLABAL; STEVE HEINA; GALEN LONG; LEROY METRO; KEITH WEBER; KEVIN WEBER; JOHN WOLESKY.

Diocesan Offices and Directors

Art and Architecture Commission—Rev. JEROME L. MORGAN, Chm.; Rev. Msgr. JAMES E. HAKE, J.C.L., Vice Chm.; Rev. Msgr. JOHN GEORGE WEBER; Revs. FRANK COADY; JOHN MOEDER; DONALD D. ZIMMERMAN; Mr. GREG LUST; Mr. STEVE HOLKE.

Catholic Charities, Inc. & Family Life, Board—Most Rev. GEORGE K. FITZSIMONS, D.D.; Sr. BETH STOVER, C.S.J., Dir.; Revs. ALOYSIUS BRUNGARDT; RON GILARDI, O.F.M.Cap.; DAMIAN RICHARDS; Sr. MARY LOU ROBERTS, C.S.J., L.B.S.W.; MIKE STOTTMANN, Pres. DARLENE STOTTMANN; JIM LEDUC; SUSAN LEDUC, Sec. RICHARD BACHAMP; TANYA BACHAMP; RENZIE POE; LULA POE; RON RIPPE; DEB RIPPE; GUY STEIER; JULIE STEIER; Dr. BILL SIBILLA; JUDY SIBILLA; BOB SCHUMACHER; BERNIE SCHUMACHER.

Catholic Charities Outreach Office—JOAN PERKINS, Sec. JANET RUSSELL, L.S.C.S.W., Adoption Counselor; Rev. WILLIAM SURMEIER, M.S., Pastoral Counselor; Sr. ANN WALTERS, C.S.A., M.S., Pastoral Counselor, *2707 Vine #17, P.O. Box 811, Hays, 67601.* Tel: 913-625-2644; Fax: 913-625-6497.

Catholic Charities of Salina, Inc.—Sr. BETH STOVER,

C.S.J., Dir.; Sr. MARY LOU ROBERTS, C.S.J., L.B.S.W., Social Worker; BONNIE FREY, L.S.C.S.W., Adoption Worker; BILL WHITE, L.S.C.S.W., Counselor; BONNIE OTEY, Sec., *425 W. Iron, P.O. Box 1366, Salina, 67401.* Tel: 913-825-0208; Fax: 913-826-9708.

Catholic Community Annual Appeal—P.O. Box 980, Salina, 67402-0980; Fax: 913-827-6133.

Office of Catholic Formation—Rev. Msgr. JAMES E. HAKE, J.C.L., Dir., *103 N. Ninth, P.O. Box 825, Salina, 67402.* Tel: 913-827-8746; Fax: 913-827-6133.

Coordinator of Office of Catholic Formation—Sr. BARBARA ELLEN APACELLER, C.S.J.

Director of Religious Education—Sr. BARBARA ELLEN APACELLER, C.S.J.

Superintendent of Schools—Sr. CLARISSA TENBRINK, A.S.C.

Consultant for Religious Education & Media—(Grades K-8), PEGGY HERBERT.

Consultant for Religious Education—(Grades 9-12), Sr. BARBARA ELLEN APACELLER, C.S.J.

Director of Adult Education—Rev. FRANK COADY.

Valueing Your Sexuality—PEGGY HEBERT, Dir.

Audio-Visual—VIRGINIA ANDERES.

Catholic Youth Organization and Youth Ministry—Sr. BARBARA ELLEN APACELLER, C.S.J., *P.O. Box 980, Salina, 67402.*

Office of Communications—P.O. Box 980, Salina, 67402.

Diocesan Council of Education—NADINE KARLIN, Pres. MARY JO THUMMEL, C.S.J.; CAROL AHLVERS; ROBERT BOLIG; PAT BRECKUNITCH; JERRY CASEY; STEVE JUENEMANN; ARVILLA JUENEMANN, Vice Pres. MARY POPELKA; ANGIE BAALMAN; JAMES OSS; STACY KOHLMEIER; LAURA JO MEYER; Revs. HENRY BAXA; ALOYSIUS BRUNGARDT; GALEN LONG; LARRY GRENNAN. Ex Officio from Chancery Staff: Rev. Msgr. JAMES E. HAKE, J.C.L.; Sr. BARBARA APACELLER, C.S.J.; Sr. CLARISSA TENBRINK, A.S.C.

Due Process Board—Revs. KENNETH P. LOHRMEYER, J.C.L., Chm. NORBERT DLABAL; Sr. BETH STOVER, C.S.J.; Mr. NICK COMPAGNONE; MARY JO HEATH; Mr. LEROY HERRMAN; Rev. Msgr. JAMES E. HAKE, J.C.L., Clerk.

Family Life Office—Sr. MARY LOU ROBERTS, C.S.J., Acting Dir.; Rev. ALOYSIUS BRUNGARDT, Moderator.

Family Ministry Advisory Board—Sr. MARY LOU ROBERTS, C.S.J.; Revs. ALOYSIUS BRUNGARDT; NORBERT DLABAL; MERLIN KIEFFER; LOREN WERTH; Sr. CAROLYN JUENEMANN; SHEILA MARCOTTE, Sec.

Holy Childhood, Pontifical Association—Rev. Msgr. JAMES E. HAKE, J.C.L., Dir., *P.O. Box 980, Salina, 67402.*

Office of Liturgy—Rev. FRANK COADY, Dir., *P.O. Box 980, Salina, 67402.* Tel: 913-827-8746; Fax: 913-827-6133.

Newspaper—"The Register, Northwestern Kansas Edition"; Rev. Msgr. RAYMOND MENARD, Editor; Mr. GREG LUST, Business Mgr., *P.O. Box 1038, Salina, 67402.*

Priests' Continuing Formation Committee—Revs. KENNETH P. LOHRMEYER, J.C.L., Chm. BARRY BRINKMAN; STEVE HEINA; MELVIN LONG. Ex Officio: Most Rev. GEORGE K. FITZSIMONS, D.D.; Rev. Msgr. JAMES E. HAKE, J.C.L.

Propagation of the Faith—Rev. Msgr. JAMES E. HAKE, J.C.L., Dir., *P.O. Box 980, Salina, 67402.* Tel: 913-827-8746.

Rural Life Conference—Rev. Msgr. JOHN GEORGE WEBER, Dir., *926 E. Republic, Salina, 67432.* Tel: 913-823-1322.

Salina Diocesan Clergy Health and Retirement Association, Inc.—Board of Trustees: Most Rev. GEORGE K. FITZSIMONS, D.D., Pres., *103 N. Ninth, P.O. Box 980, Salina, 67402-0980.* Revs. AL BRUNGARDT; NORBERT DLABAL; JEROME MORGAN; LOREN WORTH; LOUIS MATTAS; BRAD STERRETT; Mr. GREG LUST.

Salina Diocesan Council of Catholic Women (S.D.CC.W.)—MELVA DORTLAND, Pres., *2985 Vineyard Rd., Gorham, 67640.* Rev. KEVIN WEBER, Moderator, *P.O. Box 980, Salina, 67402.*

Scouting—Rev. DONALD P. MCCARTHY, *625 Freeman Ave., Oakley, 67748.*

Vocations—

Diocesan Director of Vocations—Rev. KEVIN WEBER.

Spiritual Formation for Newly Ordained Priests—Rev. FRANK COADY.

Spiritual Dir. for Seminarians & Newly Ordained Priests—Rev. LEROY METRO.

CLERGY, PARISHES, MISSIONS AND PAROCHIAL SCHOOLS

CITY OF SALINA
(Saline County)

1—CATHEDRAL OF THE SACRED HEART (1876), Revs. Alvin J. Werth; Fred Gatschet; Sr. Mary Augustine, C.S.J., Pastoral Assoc. In res., Rev. Msgr. Raymond Menard.
Res., 118 N. Ninth St., 67401. Tel: 913-823-7221. [JC]
School—(Grades PreK-6) 406 W. Iron Ave., 67401. Tel: 913-825-4798. Pat Breckunitch, Prin.
Sisters of St. Joseph 1; Lay Teachers 8; Students 173.
Catechesis/Religious Programs—Tel: 913-823-2713. Peggy Hebert, D.R.E.
Students 100.

2—ST. ELIZABETH ANN SETON (1982), Rev. LeRoy Metro.
Res., 1000 Burr Oak Ln., 67401. Tel: 913-825-5282. [JC]
Catechesis/Religious Programs—Alvarez Squires, D.R.E.
Students 230.

3—ST. MARY'S (1959), Revs. Keith Weber; Allen Scheer.
Res., 230 E. Cloud St., 67401. Tel: 913-827-5575; Fax: 913-827-8997. [JC]
School—(Grades PreK-6) 304 E. Cloud St., 67401. Tel: 913-827-4200. Mr. Nick Compagnone, Prin.
Lay Teachers 22; Students 441.
Catechesis/Religious Programs—Mrs. Nancy Main, D.R.E.
Students 298.

OUTSIDE THE CITY OF SALINA

Abilene, Dickinson Co., St. Andrew's (1874), Rev. Louis S. Mattas.
Res., 102 N.W. 4th, P.O. Box 398, 67410. Tel: 913-263-1570. [CEM]
School—(Grades PreK-5). Tel: 913-263-2453. Dennis McCall, Prin.
Lay Teachers 6; Students 71.
Catechesis/Religious Programs—Tel: 913-263-1570. Alice Bartow, D.R.E.
Students 202.

Angelus, Sheridan Co., St. Paul's (German). Attended by St. Joseph's Church, Oakley.
Mailing Address: 625 Freeman Ave., Oakley, 67748. Tel: 913-672-3828.
Church—Tel: 913-824-3256. [CEM]
Catechesis/Religious Programs—Students 40.

Antonino, Ellis Co., Our Lady Help of Christians (1905). Attended by St. Joseph, Hays.
Mailing Address: P.O. Drawer 1000, Hays, 67601. Tel: 913-625-7356; Fax: 913-625-7394.

Atwood, Rawlins Co., Sacred Heart (1879), Rev. Damian Richards.
Res., Sacred Heart, 508 N. Railroad Ave., 67730. Tel: 913-626-3335. [CEM][JC 3]
Catechesis/Religious Programs—Tel: 913-626-3431. Sharon McDougal, D.R.E.
Students 150.

Aurora, Cloud Co., St. Peter's (1884), Rev. Henry Kieffer; Rev. Msgr. James Hake, Parish Dir./Pastoral Admin.
Res., Tel: 913-464-3754. [CEM][JC]
Catechesis/Religious Programs—Tel: 913-464-3461.
Students 57.

Beardsley, Rawlins Co., St. John's, Mailing Address:St. Francis, 67756.
Church—Atwood, 67730. [CEM]

Belleville, Republic Co., St. Edward's (1901), Rev. John A. Moeder.
Res., 1827 Q St., P.O. Box 99, 66935. Tel: 913-527-5559. [CEM]
Catechesis/Religious Programs—Sacred Hearts Center, 1813 Q St., 66935. Tel: 913-527-5819. Bev Lapo, D.R.E.
Students 150.

Beloit, Mitchell Co., St. John the Baptist (1869), Revs. Henry R. Baxa; Albert D. Dwyer; Sr. Mary Stanislaus Porter, Pastoral Assoc.
Res., 701 E. Court St., 67420. Tel: 913-738-2851. [CEM]
School—(Grades PreK-6). Tel: 913-738-3941. William F. Orth, Prin.
Sisters of St. Joseph 1; Lay Teachers 8; Students 138.
High School—(Grades 7-12). Tel: 913-738-2942. Bertha Johnson, Prin.
Priests 1; Lay Teachers 11; Students 79.
Catechesis/Religious Programs—Tel: 913-738-2851.
Students 121.

Bird City, Cheyenne Co., St. Joseph's (1911). Attended by St. Francis, St. Francis. Rev. Randall D. Weber.
Church—67731. Tel: 913-332-2680.

Brookville, Saline Co., St. Joseph's (1884). Attended by Sacred Heart Cathedral, Salina.
Mailing Address: 118 N. 9th, Salina, 67401.
Church—67425. [CEM]

Catharine, Ellis Co., St. Catherine's (1892), Rev. Earl Befort, O.F.M.Cap.
Mailing Address: P.O. Drawer 1000, Hays, 67601. Tel: 913-625-7356. [CEM]

Cawker City, Mitchell Co., SS. Peter and Paul (1878) (German). Attended by St. Boniface, Tipton. Jeanie Munsch, Pastoral Assoc.
Church—Tel: 913-781-4319; 373-4455. [CEM]
Catechesis/Religious Programs—1202 Holly, 67430. Tel: 913-781-4835.
Students 54.

Chapman, Dickinson Co., St. Michael's (1883), Carolyn Juenemann, C.S.J., Parish Dir./Pastoral Admin.; Rev. Richard E. Lutgen, Supvr.
Res., P.O. Box 217, 67431. Tel: 913-922-6509. [CEM]
Catechesis/Religious Programs—Tel: 913-922-6509. Loretta Fisher, D.R.E.
Students 105.

Claudell, Smith Co., St. Francis (1914). Attended by SS. Philip & James, Phillipsburg.
Mailing Address: R.R. #3, Box 144A, Phillipsburg, 67661. Tel: 913-543-5367.

Clay Center, Clay Co., SS. Peter and Paul (1879), Rev. Loren J. Werth.
Res., 730 Court St., 67432. Tel: 913-632-5011. [CEM]
Catechesis/Religious Programs—Tel: 913-632-3204. Cyndy Schwensen, D.R.E.
Students 145.

Clifton, Washington Co., St. Mary's (French-German). Attended by St. John the Baptist, Clyde.
Mailing Address: 204 N. High, Clyde, 66938. Tel: 913-446-3474; Fax: 913-446-2268.
Church—Tel: 913-455-3384. [CEM]
Catechesis/Religious Programs—Tel: 913-455-2291. Mrs. Linda Kantack, D.R.E.
Students 45.

Clyde, Cloud Co., St. John the Baptist's (1880) (French-German), Rev. Francis Coady; Brenda Koch, Pastoral Assoc. & D.R.E.
Res., 204 N. High, 66938. Tel: 913-446-3474; Fax: 913-446-2268. [CEM]
Catechesis/Religious Programs—Students 111.

Colby, Thomas Co., Sacred Heart, Rev. Steven C. Heina; Sr. Rosalyn Juenemann, C.S.J., Pastoral Assoc. & D.R.E.
Res., 585 N. French Ave., 67701. Tel: 913-462-2179. [CEM]
School—(Grades PreK-5). Tel: 913-462-2813. Mr. Ladislado Hernandez, Prin.
Lay Teachers 7; Students 104.
Catechesis/Religious Programs—Students 300.

Collyer, Trego Co., St. Michael's (1893) (German), Rev. Basil Torrez.
Res., Ainslie Ave., Box 174, 67631. Tel: 913-769-5272. [CEM][JC]
Catechesis/Religious Programs—Melissa Metcalf, D.R.E.
Students 63.

Concordia, Cloud Co., Our Lady of Perpetual Help (1887), Rev. Barry Brinkman.
Office: 232 E. Fifth, P.O. Box 608, 66901. Tel: 913-243-1099.
Res., 420 Kansas, P.O. Box 608, 66901. Tel: 913-243-4658. [CEM]
Catechesis/Religious Programs—Tel: 913-243-1410. Laura Jo Meyer, D.R.E.
Students 339.

Cuba, Republic Co., St. Isidore's (1873) (Czech). Attended by St. Edward, Belleville.
Mailing Address: P.O. Box 99, Belleville, 66935.
Church—. [CEM]

Damar, Rooks Co., St. Joseph's (1912). Attended by Immaculate Heart of Mary, Hill City.
Mailing Address: 10 N. 10th Ave., Hill City, 67642. Tel: 913-839-4343. [CEM]
Catechesis/Religious Programs—Tel: 913-839-4360. Gil Berland, D.R.E.
Students 75.

Delphos, Ottawa Co., St. Paul's. Attended by Immaculate Conception, Minneapolis.
Church—67436.

Densmore, Norton Co., St. Mary's. Closed. For inquiries for parish records contact the Chancery.

Dorrance, Russell Co., St. Joseph's (1902) (German-Irish). Attended by St. Wenceslaus, Wilson. Rev. Jerome Morgan.
Mailing Address: P.O. Box 528, Wilson, 67490. Tel: 913-658-3361. [CEM]
Catechesis/Religious Programs—Tel: 913-666-4419. Susan Thielen, D.R.E.
Students 72.

Downs, Osborne Co., St. Mary's (1903). Attended by St. Aloysius, Osborne.
Mailing Address: P.O. Box 267, Osbourne, 67473.
Church—1312 Prentice, 67437. Tel: 913-454-3551.

Ellis, Ellis Co., St. Mary's (1870), Rev. Galen J. Long; Sr. Doris M. Flax, Pastoral Assoc.
Church—703 Monroe, 67637. Tel: 913-726-4522.
School—(Grades PreK-6). Tel: 913-726-3185. Rev. Donald McCarthy, Prin.

Sisters of St. Joseph 2; Lay Teachers 8; Students 78.
Catechesis/Religious Programs—Mary Reiter, D.R.E.
Students 135.

Ellsworth, Ellsworth Co., St. Bernard's (1909), Rev. Daniel L. Scheetz.
Res., 911 Kansas St., 67439. Tel: 913-472-3136.

Elmo, Dickinson Co., St. Columba's. Attended by St. John the Evangelist, Herington.
712 N. Broadway, Herington, 67449. [CEM]

Esbon, Jewell Co., Sacred Heart (1887). Attended by St. Theresa's, Mankato.
Mailing Address: P.O. Box 265, Mankato, 66956.
Church—Tel: 913-378-3939. [CEM]

Fort Riley, Riley Co., Fort Riley Catholic Community. Attended by Archdiocese for the Military Services.

Glasco, Cloud Co., St. Mary's. Attended by St. John's, Beloit.
Mailing Address: 701 E. Court St., Beloit, 67420.
Church—301 E. First St., P.O. Box 554, 67445. [CEM]

Goodland, Sherman Co., Our Lady of Perpetual Help (1887), Rev. Daryl Olmstead.
Church—307 W. 13th, 67735. Tel: 913-899-7205.
Catechesis/Religious Programs—Tel: 913-899-5407. John Eisenbart, D.R.E.
Students 209.

Gorham, Russell Co., St. Mary's (1984), Rev. Daniel L. Scheetz, Supvr.; Sr. Mary Jo Thummel, C.S.J., Admin.
Res., Box 135, 67640. Tel: 913-637-5241. [CEM]
Catechesis/Religious Programs—St. Mary's Parish Center, 161 Chicago, 67640. Tel: 913-637-5224. Pam Novak, D.R.E., Tel: 913-637-5273.
Students 70.

Grainfield, Gove Co., St. Agnes (1910) (German). Attended by Sacred Heart, Park. Rev. Mark Berland.
Mailing Address: P.O. Box 78, Park, 67751-0078. Tel: 913-673-4684. [JC]
Catechesis/Religious Programs—Tel: 913-673-5510. Kathryn Kraus, D.R.E.
Students 64.

Greenleaf, Washington Co., Sacred Heart (1890). Attended by St. John the Baptist, Hanover. Rev. Edward Oen, C.PP.S. Pastoral Assocs.: Lawrence Hogan; James Donigan.
Mailing Address: P.O. Box 395, Hanover, 66945. Tel: 913-337-2207.
Church—Tel: 913-747-2862. [CEM]

Grinnell, Gove Co., Immaculate Conception (1888) (German). Attended by St. Joseph's Oakley. Rev. Roger Meitl, Parish Dir./Pastoral Admin.
Mailing Address: 625 Freeman Ave., Oakley, 67748. [CEM]
Catechesis/Religious Programs—Fax: 913-824-3388. Sr. Kenneth Struckhoff, D.R.E.
Students 63.

Gypsum, Saline Co., St. Patrick's, Rev. John A. Wolesky. Parish Directors/Pastoral Administrators: Mr. James Karber; Mrs. Alan (Debie) Martin.
Office: c/o Salina Regina Medical Center, P.O. Box 5201, Salina, 67402-5201. Tel: 913-452-6368.
Res., 118 N. Ninth, Salina, 67401. [CEM]

Hanover, Washington Co., St. John the Baptist (1868) (Bohemian), Rev. Edward J. Oen, C.PP.S.
Res., Box 395, 66945. Tel: 913-337-2207. [CEM]
School—(Grades 1-8). Tel: 913-337-2782. Sr. Vivian Boucher, C.S.J., Prin.
Sisters of St. Joseph 1; Lay Teachers 8; Students 105.

Hays, Ellis Co., Immaculate Heart of Mary (1967), Revs. Donald D. Zimmerman; Carl Kramer; Joseph Popelka. Pastoral Assocs.: Sr. Rosalia Costello, C.S.A.; Betty Lou Whalen.
Res., 18th and Vine, 67601. Tel: 913-625-7339. [JC]
Catechesis/Religious Programs—D.R.E.: Dorothy Jacobs; Pat Legleiter.
Students 747.

St. Joseph's (1885), Revs. Michael Scully, O.F.M.Cap.; Curtis Carlson, O.F.M.Cap.; Paulinus I. Karlin, O.F.M.Cap. In res., Most Rev. Firmin Schmidt, O.F.M.Cap., (Retired); Rev. Bennett Collucci.
Res., P.O. Drawer 1000, 67601. Tel: 913-625-7356; Fax: 913-625-7394. [JC]
School—(Grades K-5). Tel: 913-625-3131. Dolores McKibbin, Prin.
Lay Teachers 16; Students 152.
Catechesis/Religious Programs—Tel: 913-628-2311. D.R.E.: Martha A. Brungardt; Jerry Michaud; Renee Michaud.
Students 243.

St. Nicholas of Myra (1983), Arvilla Juenemann, Admin.; Rev. William J. Surmeier.
Office: 2901 E. 13th, P.O. Box 932, 67601. Tel: 913-628-1446; Fax: 913-628-6627.
Res., 2405 A Henry Dr., 67601. Tel: 913-628-6658.
Catechesis/Religious Programs—Tel: 913-628-2188. Sr. Martina Stegman, O.P., D.R.E.
Students 251.

Herington, Dickinson Co., St. John the Evangelist, Rev. Donald F. Pfannenstiel.
Res., 712 N. Broadway, 67449. Tel: 913-258-2013. [CEM]
Catechesis/Religious Programs—D.R.E.: Linda Polston; Beth Blackwell.
Students 80.

Herndon, Rawlins Co., Assumption (1880). Attended by Sacred Heart, Atwood. Rev. Damian Richards.
Mailing Address: 508 N. Railroad Ave., Atwood, 67730
Church—Box 247, 67739. Tel: 913-322-5560. [CEM]
Catechesis/Religious Programs—Students 49.

Hill City, Graham Co., Immaculate Heart of Mary (1958), Rev. Donald P. McCarthy.
Res., 10 N. 10th Ave., 67642. Tel: 913-421-2535.
Catechesis/Religious Programs—Tel: 913-421-2665. Joyce Tauber, D.R.E.
Students 126.

Holyrood, Ellsworth Co., St. Mary's (1886). Attended by St. Bernard's, Ellsworth. Rev. Daniel L. Scheetz.
Mailing Address: 911 Kansas, Ellsworth, 67439. Tel: 913-472-3136.

Hope, Dickinson Co., St. Phillip's. Attended by St. John's Herington.
Mailing Address: 712 N. Broadway, Herington, 67449.
Church—67451. Tel: 913-366-7353.

Hoxie, Sheridan Co., St. Frances Xavier Cabrini (1949), Rev. Merlin Kieffer.
Res., 924 N. 17th, Box 38, 67740. Tel: 913-675-3300. [CEM]
Catechesis/Religious Programs—Verlene Feldt, D.R.E.
Students 161.

Jamestown, Cloud Co., St. Mary's (1873). Closed. For sacramental records contact Our Lady of Perpetual Help, Concordia.

Junction City, Geary Co., St. Francis Xavier's, Revs. Albert M. DeSanctis; Beryl Gibson.
Res., 218 N. Washington, P.O. Box 399, 66441. Tel: 913-238-2998; Fax: 913-238-4731. [CEM]
School—(Grades PreK-8) 280 N. Jefferson St., 66441. Tel: 913-238-2841. Mr. James Oss, Prin. (Elementary & High School).
Priests 1; Lay Teachers 11; Students 165.
High School—Lay Teachers 14; Students 80.
Catechesis/Religious Programs—Students 300.

Kanopolis, Ellsworth Co., St. Ignatius Loyola (1947) (Mexican). Attended by St. Bernard's, Ellsworth. Rev. Daniel L. Scheetz.
Mailing Address: 911 Kansas, Ellsworth, 67439.
Church—Tel: 913-472-4628. [JC]

Kimeo, Washington Co., St. Michael's. Closed. For inquiries for parish records contact the Chancery.

Leoville, Decatur Co., Immaculate Conception (1885). Attended by Sacred Heart Parish, Selden.
Mailing Address: P.O. Box 57, Selden, 67757. Tel: 913-386-4496.
Church—Tel: 913-386-4409. [CEM]
Catechesis/Religious Programs—Jill Reichert, D.R.E.
Students 73.

Lincoln, Lincoln Co., St. Patrick's (1870), Rev. Ralph L. Aschenbrenner.
Res., 206 N. Fifth, Box 327, 67455. Tel: 913-524-4823. [CEM 2]
Catechesis/Religious Programs—Tel: 913-524-3043. Linda Workman, D.R.E.
Students 61.

Logan, Phillips Co., St. John's (1888). Attended by St. Thomas, Stockton. Rev. James P. Grennan.
Mailing Address: 722 Main St., Stockton, 67669. [CEM]
Catechesis/Religious Programs—Jean Kiser, D.R.E.
Students 69.

Manhattan, Riley Co., Seven Dolors (1880), Revs. Lawrence E. Grennan; Mark Wesely; Sr. Janis Wagner, C.S.J., Pastoral Assoc.
Res., 731 Pierre St., Box 844, 66502. Tel: 913-565-5000; Fax: 913-565-5003.
School—(Grades PreK-8) 306 S. Juliette, 66502. Tel: 913-565-5050. Tom Schmitz, Prin.
Lay Teachers 19; Students 262.
Catechesis/Religious Programs—D.R.E.: Connie Ranker; Sandra Nilges; Maggie Haag.
Students 200.

St. Isidore (1963), Rev. Brad Sterrett; Rev. Msgr. Armand Girard, (Retired).
Res., 711 Denison St., 66502. Tel: 913-539-7496; Fax: 913-539-0220.

St. Thomas More Parish (1981), Rev. Melvin T. Long.
Church Office—2900 Kimball Ave., 66502. Tel: 913-776-5151.
Catechesis/Religious Programs—Tel: 913-776-1398.
Students 369.

Mankato, Jewell Co., St. Theresa of Infant Jesus (1949), Rev. Kenneth P. Lohrmeyer.
Res., 422 N. Commercial, Box 265, 66956. Tel: 913-378-3939. [CEM]

McDowell, Geary Co., St. Joseph. Closed. For inquiries for parish records contact the Chancery.

Meredith, Cloud Co., St. Peter's. Closed. Sacramental records are located at St. Peter.

Miltonvale, Cloud Co., St. Anthony's. Attended by SS. Peter and Paul, Clay Center.
Mailing Address: 730 Court St., Clay Center, 67432. Tel: 913-632-5011.
Church—Tel: 913-427-2253.

Minneapolis, Ottawa Co., Immaculate Conception of the Blessed Virgin Mary, Rev. Msgr. James E. Hake.
Res., 216 Cherry St., Box 167, 67467. Tel: 913-392-2079; 392-2013 (Church Hall).
Catechesis/Religious Programs—Students 66.

Morrowville, Washington Co., SS. Peter and Paul (1887). Attended by St. Augustine's, Washington.
410 B St., Washington, 66968. Tel: 913-325-2346. [CEM]

Munden, Republic Co., St. George's (1887) (Czech). Attended by St. Edward's, Belleville.
Mailing Address: P.O. Box 99, Belleville, 66935. [CEM]

Munjor, Ellis Co., St. Francis of Assisi (1876), Rev. William J. Surmeier.
Mailing Address: P.O. Box 932, Hays, 67601.
Church—883 Moscow, 67601. Tel: 913-625-5314. [CEM]

New Almelo, Norton Co., St. Joseph's (1878). Attended by St. Francis of Assisi, Norton. Sr. Veronica Roy, C.S.J., Pastoral Assoc.
Res., 67652. Tel: 913-567-4875. [CEM]

Niles, Ottawa Co., Sacred Heart. Closed. Sacramental records are located at Immaculate Conception.

Norton, Norton Co., St. Francis of Assisi (1878), Rev. John Walsh.
Res., 108 S. Wabash, Box 148, 67654. Tel: 913-877-2234.
Catechesis/Religious Programs—Cathy Hanchett, D.R.E.
Students 128.
Mission—New Almelo, Norton Co., St. Joseph's Church, HC-1 Box 175, New Almelo, 67652. Tel: 913-567-4875.

Oakley, Logan Co., St. Joseph's (1890), Rev. Roger K. Meitl.
Res., 625 Freeman Ave., 67748. Tel: 913-672-3828. [CEM]
School—(Grades K-5) 725 Freeman Ave., 67748. Tel: 913-672-4451. Mr. Ladislado Hernandez, Prin.
Priests 1; Lay Teachers 7; Students 75.
Catechesis/Religious Programs—St. Joseph Parish Annex, 405 E. Seventh, 67748. Tel: 913-672-4443. Phyllis Temaat, D.R.E.
Students 75.

Oberlin, Decatur Co., Sacred Heart (1888), Rev. James F. Hoover; Sr. Marilyn Wall, C.S.J., Pastoral Admin. & Dir.
Res., 210 E. Washington, 67749. Tel: 913-475-3103. [JC]
Catechesis/Religious Programs—Angela Corcoran, D.R.E.
Students 86.

Ogden, Riley Co., St. Patrick's (1866). Attended by Seven Dolors, Manhattan.
Res., P.O. Box A, 66517. Tel: 913-565-5090. [CEM]

Osborne, Osborne Co., St. Aloysius (1881), Rev. Roger W. Hough.
Res., Box 267, 67473. Tel: 913-346-5582. [CEM]
Catechesis/Religious Programs—Rhonda Reed, D.R.E.
Students 163.
Mission—Downs, Osborne Co., St. Mary's.

Park, Gove Co., Sacred Heart (1898) (German), Rev. Mark Berland.
Res., P.O. Box 78, 67751. Tel: 913-673-4684. [CEM]
Catechesis/Religious Programs—D.R.E.: Gloria Pfannenstiel; Sandii Ostmeyer; Pam Nemechek.
Students 123.

Pfeifer, Ellis Co., Holy Cross. Closed. For sacramental records contact St. Fidelis, Victoria.

Phillipsburg, Phillips Co., SS. Philip and James (1875), Rev. Kerry Ninemire.

Res., R.R. #3, Box 144A, 67661. Tel: 913-543-5577; 543-5367.
Catechesis/Religious Programs—Janie Harger, D.R.E.
Students 100.
Mission—Claudell, Phillips Co., St. Francis.

Plainville, Rooks Co., Sacred Heart (1890), Rev. Aloysius B. Brungardt.
Res., 206 N. Washington, P.O. Box 100, 67663. Tel: 913-434-4658. [CEM]
School—Tel: 913-434-2157.
Sisters 1; Lay Teachers 7; Students 123.
Catechesis/Religious Programs—Students 107.

Russell, Russell Co., St. Mary's (1886), Rev. Charles Steier.
Res., 28 Kansas St., 67665. Tel: 913-483-2871. [CEM]
Catechesis/Religious Programs—Tel: 913-483-4359. D.R.E.: Kathy Hoss; Donna Vicek.
Students 194.

St. Francis, Cheyenne Co., St. Francis (1912) (German), Rev. Randall D. Weber.
Res., 625 S. River St., P.O. Box 1170, 67756. Tel: 913-332-2680.
Catechesis/Religious Programs—Myra Douthit, D.R.E.
Students 107.
Missions—Bird City, Cheyenne Co., St. Joseph's, 203 N. Bird, Bird City, 67731. Tel: 913-734-2287; Beardsley, Rawlins Co., St. John's, Rte. 2, 67756. Tel: 913-626-3946.

St. Joseph, Cloud Co., St. Joseph's. Closed. For sacramental records contact St. John the Baptist, Clyde.

St. Peter, Graham Co., St. Anthony's (1894) (German). Attended by St. Michael's, Collyer. Rev. Basil Torrez; Sr. Clarice Richmeier, C.S.J., Pastoral Assoc.
Mailing Address: Box 174, Collyer, 67631. Tel: 913-769-5272. [CEM]

Schoenchen, Ellis Co., St. Anthony's (1877). Attended by St. Joseph's, Hays.
Res., 215 W. 13th, P.O. Drawer 1000, Hays, 67601. Tel: 913-625-7356; Fax: 913-625-7394. [CEM]

Seguin, Sheridan Co., St. Martin's (1910). Attended by St. Frances Xavier Cabrini, Hoxie.
Mailing Address: P.O. Box 38, Hoxie, 67740. Tel: 913-675-3300. [CEM]

Selden, Sheridan Co., Sacred Heart (1906), Rev. James F. Hoover.
Res., Box 57, 67757. Tel: 913-386-4496. [CEM]

Sharon Springs, Wallace Co., Holy Ghost (1907), Rev. Francis Stuart, O.S.B.
Res., 403 N. Main St., 67758. Tel: 913-852-4984.
Catechesis/Religious Programs—Shirley Blaesi, D.R.E.
Students 60.
Mission—Wallace, Wallace Co., St. Peter.

Smith Center, Smith Co., St. Mary's (1959). Attended by St. Theresa, Mankato.
403 W. Hwy. 6, Box 263, 66967. Tel: 913-282-6888.
Catechesis/Religious Programs—Mrs. Stacey Rempe, D.R.E.
Students 55.

Solomon, Dickinson Co., Immaculate Conception (1886), Rev. John Lahey.
Res., 3599 N. Field Rd., 67480. Tel: 913-655-2221. [CEM]
Catechesis/Religious Programs—Marcia Storer, D.R.E.
Students 78.

Stockton, Rooks Co., St. Thomas (1878), Rev. James P. Grennan.
Res., 722 Main St., 67669. Tel: 913-425-6656. [CEM]

Tipton, Mitchell Co., St. Boniface's (1874), Rev. Norbert F. Dlabal.
Res., Box 87, 67485. Tel: 913-373-4455. [CEM]
High School—Tel: 913-373-5635.
Priests 1; Lay Teachers 6; Students 33.
Catechesis/Religious Programs—Students 99.

Victoria, Ellis Co., St. Fidelis (1876), Rev. Frank X. Grinko, O.F.M.Cap.
Res., 900 Cathedral Ave., 67671. Tel: 913-735-2777; 735-9456; Fax: 913-735-9455. [CEM]
Church Office—601 10th St., 67671. Tel: 913-735-2777.
Catechesis/Religious Programs—Tel: 913-735-9244. Eugenie Ricklefs, D.R.E.
Students 234.

Vincent, Ellis Co., St. Boniface (1908) (German-Russian). Attended by St. Fidelis, Victoria. Rev. Frank X. Grinko, O.F.M.Cap.
601 10th St., Victoria, 67671. Tel: 913-735-2777; 735-9456. [CEM]

WaKeeney, Trego Co., Christ the King (1933), Rev. Joseph H. Scheetz.
Res., 412 N. Ninth St., 67672. Tel: 913-743-2330. [CEM]
Catechesis/Religious Programs—Tel: 913-743-2339. Verna Flax, D.R.E.
Students 210.

Walker, Ellis Co., St. Ann's (1904) (German-Russian). Attended by St. Fidelis, Victoria.
Mailing Address: 601 10th St., Victoria, 67671. Tel: 913-735-2777.

Wallace, Wallace Co., St. Peter's (1877). Attended by Holy Ghost Church, Sharon Springs.
Mailing Address: P.O. Box 190, 67761.

Washington, Washington Co., St. Augustine's, Rev. Paul Becquet, C.PP.S.
Res., 410 B St., 66968. Tel: 913-325-2346. [JC]
Catechesis/Religious Programs—Marilyn Pachta, D.R.E.
Students 49.

Wilson, Ellsworth Co., St. Wenceslaus (1882) (Slovak), Rev. Jerome Morgan.
Res., P.O. Box 528, 67490. Tel: 913-658-3361. [CEM]
Catechesis/Religious Programs—Tel: 913-658-3474. Mrs. Steve Dlabal, Sr., D.R.E.
Students 57.
Mission—Dorrance, Russell Co., St. Joseph.

Zurich, Rooks Co., St. Ann's. Attended by Sacred Heart, Plainville. Rev. Aloysius B. Brungardt.
Res., P.O. Box 8, 67676. Tel: 913-662-3212. [CEM]

On Duty Outside the Diocese:
Reverend Fathers—
Dallen, James, W. 818 21st Ave., Spokane, WA 99203

Retired:
Reverend Monsignors—
Girard, Armand, St. Isidore's Catholic Student Center, 711 Denison, Manhatten, KS 66502
Hecker, Adolph J., 2505 Henry, Hays, KS 67601
Kruse, Clement, 205 E. 25th St. Terrace, Hays, KS 67601
Landoll, Gilbert J., 507 N. Broadway, Apt. G., P.O. Box 475, Abilene, KS 67410
Lemoine, Vincent P., P.O. Box 141, Winterset, IA 50273
Sinner, Emil E., 209 24th St., Box 549, Wilson, KS 67490
Weber, John George, 926 E. Republic, Salina, KS 67401
Reverend Fathers—
Conklin, Christopher J., Mailing Address: P.O. Box 454, Concordia, KS 66901
Dion, Maurice B., 214 E. North St., Hanover, KS 66945
Kilian, William T., St. Joseph Church, P.O. Box 68, Damar, KS 67632
Kuhn, Herbert C., Catholic Care Center, 6700 E. 45th St. N., Wichita, KS 67226
Moeder, August L., P.O. Box 74, 217 Grant, Quinter, KS 67752
Pierce, Larry E., P.O. Box 237, Oakley, KS 67748

INSTITUTIONS LOCATED IN THE DIOCESE

[A] HIGH SCHOOLS, INTER-PAROCHIAL

SALINA. *Sacred Heart Junior-Senior High School*, 230 E. Cloud, 67401. Tel: 913-827-4422. John Krajicek, Prin. Sisters 2; Priests 1; Lay Teachers 20; Total 205.

[B] HIGH SCHOOLS, PRIVATE

HAYS. *Thomas More Prep-Marian*, 1701 Hall, 67601. Tel: 913-625-6577; Fax: 913-625-3912. Rev. Michael Scully, O.F.M.Cap., Pres. Legal Title: *Thomas More Prep-Marian Inc.* Four-year Catholic High School, with college preparatory programs conducted by Capuchin Friars and Sisters of St. Agnes; residency programs for boys and girls; special program for candidates for Priesthood and Religious Life. Capuchin Friars 3; Lay Teachers 27; Students 305.
Endowment Foundation of Thomas More Prep-Marian, Inc. Dennis Bieker, Pres.

[C] HOMES FOR AGED

CONCORDIA. *Mount Joseph Senior Community*, 66901. Tel: 913-243-1347; Fax: 913-243-1907.
For a complete listing, refer to the Special Care Facilities section.

HAYS. *St. John's New Horizons*, 2225 Canterbury, 67601. Tel: 913-628-8742.
For a complete listing, refer to the Special Care Facilities section.

MANHATTAN. *St. Joseph Senior Community, Inc.*, 2423 Kimball Ave., 66502. Tel: 913-539-7671.
For a complete listing, refer to the Special Care Facilities section.

VICTORIA. *St. John's Rest Home*, 701 Seventh St., 67671. Tel: 913-735-2208.
For a complete listing, refer to the Special Care Facilities section.

[D] MONASTERIES AND RESIDENCES OF PRIESTS AND BROTHERS

HAYS. *St. Bonaventure's Friary*, 506 W. 6th St., 67601. Tel: 913-625-4483. Revs. Blaine E. Burkey, O.F.M.Cap., Guardian; Earl J. Befort, O.F.M.Cap.; William Kraus, O.F.M.Cap., Vicar & Provincial Vocation Dir. Tel: 913-628-2482; John R. Toepfer, O.F.M.Cap. Priests 4.
St. Joseph's Friary, P.O. Drawer 1000, 67601. Tel: 913-625-7356. Revs. Michael Scully, O.F.M.Cap.; Paulinus I. Karlin, O.F.M.Cap.; Curtis Carlson, O.F.M.Cap. In res., Rev. Fidelis McManus, O.F.M.Cap.; Most Rev. Firmin Schmidt, O.F.M.Cap., (Retired); Rev. Bennett Collucci, O.F.M.Cap.

VICTORIA. *St. Fidelis Friary*, 67671. Tel: 913-735-9456; Fax: 913-735-9455. Revs. Felix Petrovsky, O.F.M.Cap.; Ronald Gilardi, O.F.M.Cap., Vicar; Berard Tomassetti, O.F.M.Cap.; Frank X. Grinko, O.F.M.Cap., Pastor & Guardian; Harold Vogler, O.F.M.Cap., (Retired); Bro. Augustine Rohde, O.F.M.Cap. Total in Residence 6.

[E] CONVENTS AND RESIDENCES FOR SISTERS

SALINA. *Medaille Center*, 148 N. Oakdale St., 67401. Tel: 913-827-3685. Sisters of St. Joseph. Sr. Rose Beatrice Dreiling, C.S.J., Coord. Sisters 14.

CONCORDIA. *Nazareth Motherhouse for the Sisters of St. Joseph, Concordia*, Administration Offices, 215 Court St., P.O. Box 279, 66901 Tel: 913-243-2149. Rev. Msgr. Alfred Wasinger, Chap.; Sr. Christine Doman, C.S.J., Pres. Professed Sisters 247; Novices 2; Postulants 1; In Community 247.
Saint Joseph Foundation for Apostolic and Charitable Purposes.

[F] RESIDENCES FOR RETIRED SISTERS

CONCORDIA. *St. Marys Convent*, 830 W. 11th St., 66901. Tel: 913-243-2550. Residence for Retired Sisters. Sr. Frances Cabrini Wahlmeier, Admin. Sisters 36.

[G] RETREAT CENTERS

CONCORDIA. *Manna House of Prayer*, 323 E. Fifth St., Box 675, 66901. Tel: 913-243-4428. Sr. Bette Moslander, C.S.J., Dir. Total Staff 10; Total in Residence 10.

VICTORIA. *Capuchin Center for Spiritual Life*, 900 Cathedral Ave., 67671. Tel: 913-735-9393; Fax: 913-735-9455. Rev. Ron Gilardi, O.F.M.Cap.

[H] NEWMAN CENTERS

HAYS. *Comeau Catholic Campus Center at Fort Hays State University*, Office: 506 W. Sixth, 67601. Tel: 913-625-7396. Rev. John R. Toepfer, O.F.M.Cap., Chap., Capuchin Vocation Office. Tel: 913-628-2482. Rev. Bill Kraus, O.F.M.Cap., Dir., St. Bonaventure Friary. Tel: 913-625-4483. Revs. Blaine Burkey, O.F.M.Cap., Guardian; Bill Kraus, O.F.M.Cap., Vicar; Earl Befort, O.F.M.Cap.; John Toepfer, O.F.M.Cap. Total Staff 3.

MANHATTAN. *St. Isidore's Catholic Student Center*. Kansas State University. 711 Denison, 66502. Tel: 913-539-7496. In res., Rev. Brad Sterrett, Chap.; Rev. Msgr. Armand Girard, (Retired). Total Staff 8; Total in Residence 2.

[I] MISCELLANEOUS

SALINA. *Marymount Diocesan Activities Center, Inc.*, P.O. Box 980, 67402-0980. Tel: 913-827-8746; Fax: 913-827-6133. Rev. Msgr. James E. Hake, Pres.
Marymount Memorial Educational Trust Fund, P.O. Box 980, 67402-0980. Tel: 913-827-8746; Fax: 913-827-6133. Most Rev. George K. Fitzsimons, D.D., Trustee.
Sacred Heart Junior-Senior School Endowment Fund, P.O. Box 6318, 67401. Tel: 913-825-4011.
Salina Catholic Diocese Education Endowment, Inc., 103 N. Ninth St., P.O. Box 980, 67402-0980. Tel: 913-827-8746; Fax: 913-827-6133.
Salina Catholic Diocese Gift & Annuity Fund, Inc., 103 N. Ninth St., P.O. Box 980, 67402-0980. Tel: 913-827-8746; Fax: 913-827-6133.
Salina Catholic Diocese Seminary Burses, Inc., 103 N. Ninth St., P.O. Box 980, 67402-0980. Tel: 913-827-8746; Fax: 913-827-6133.

RELIGIOUS INSTITUTES OF MEN REPRESENTED IN THE DIOCESE

For further details refer to the corresponding bracketed number in the Religious Institutes of Men or Women section.

[0470]—*The Capuchin Friars.* (Province of Mid-America).—O.F.M.Cap.

[0200]—*Monks of St. Benedict.* (Conception, MO).—O.S.B.

[1060]—*Society of the Precious Blood.* (Kansas City Prov.).—C.PP.S.

RELIGIOUS INSTITUTES OF WOMEN REPRESENTED IN THE DIOCESE

[0100]—*Adorers of the Blood of Christ.*—A.S.C.

[3710]—*Congregation of the Sisters of Saint Agnes.*—C.S.A.

[1070-24]—*Dominican Sisters.*—O.P.

[3580]—*Servants of Mary.*—O.S.M.

[]—*Sisters of St. Benedict.*—O.S.B.

[3830-15]—*Sisters of St. Joseph.*—C.S.J.

NECROLOGY

† Sander, Rev. Msgr. Edward, Lincoln, KS, St. Patrick's. —Died Jan. 3, 1996.

Diocese of Salt Lake City

(Dioecesis Civitatis Lacus Salsi)

Most Reverend

GEORGE H. NIEDERAUER

Bishop of Salt Lake City; ordained April 30, 1962; appointed Bishop of Salt Lake City November 3, 1994; ordained January 25, 1995. *Office: 27 C St., Salt Lake City, UT, 84103.* Tel.: 801-328-8541, Ext. 304; Fax: 801-328-0324.

Most Reverend

JOSEPH LENNOX FEDERAL, D.D.

Retired Bishop of Salt Lake City; ordained December 8, 1934; appointed Auxiliary Bishop of Salt Lake City February 5, 1951; consecrated Titular Bishop of Appiaria April 11, 1951; made Coadjutor Bishop of Salt Lake City, *cum jure successionis*, May 8, 1958; succeeded to the See, March 31, 1960; retired April 1980. *Office: 27 C St., Salt Lake City, UT, 84103.* Tel.: 801-328-8641, Ext. 307.

ESTABLISHED AS A VICARIATE-APOSTOLIC ON NOV. 23, 1886.

ERECTED A DIOCESE ON JANUARY 27, 1891.

Square Miles 84,990.

Originally comprised all Utah and the Counties of Eureka, Lander, Lincoln, White Pine, Nye, Elko and Clark in the State of Nevada. By Apostolic Constitution dated March 27, 1931, the Nevada section was separated from the Salt Lake Diocese and incorporated in the Reno Diocese. The name was changed to Diocese of Salt Lake City on March 31, 1951.

Comprises the State of Utah.

Patron of the Diocese of Salt Lake City: St. Mary Magdalene.

For legal titles of parishes and diocesan institutions, consult the Chancery Office.

Diocesan Offices and Organizations: 27 C St., Salt Lake City, UT, 84103. Tel.: 801-328-8641; Fax: 801-328-9680.

STATISTICAL OVERVIEW

Personnel	
Bishop	1
Retired Bishops	1
Abbots	1
Priests: Diocesan Active in Diocese	39
Priests: Active Outside Diocese	5
Priests: Diocesan in Foreign Missions	1
Priests: Retired, Sick or Absent	9
Number of Diocesan Priests	54
Religious Priests in Diocese	32
Extern Priests in Diocese	9
Ordinations:	
Permanent Deacons in Diocese	25
Total Brothers	12
Total Sisters	68
Parishes	
Parishes	43
With Resident Pastor:	
Resident Diocesan Priests	31
Resident Religious Priests	8
Without Resident Pastor:	
Administered by Priests	3
Administered by Lay People	1
Missions	19
Professional Ministry Personnel:	
Sisters	16
Lay Ministers	22
Welfare	
Homes for the Aged	1
Total Assisted	449
Day Care and Extended Day Care Centers	6
Total Assisted	291
Special Centers for Social Services	2
Total Assisted	201,635
Educational	
Diocesan Students in Other Seminaries	6
Total Seminarians	6
High Schools, Diocesan and Parish	2
Total Students	1,195
Elementary Schools, Diocesan and Parish	10
Total Students	2,697
Catechesis/Religious Education:	
High School Students	1,396
Elementary Students	6,540
Total Students Under Catholic Instruction	11,834
Teachers in the Diocese:	
Priests	3
Brothers	2
Sisters	6
Lay Teachers	223
Vital Statistics	
Receptions into the Church:	
Infant Baptism Totals	2,328
Adult Baptism Totals	397
Received into Full Communion	314
First Communions	1,628
Confirmations	1,063
Marriages:	
Catholic	280
Interfaith	230
Total Marriages	510
Deaths	581
Total Catholic Population	81,021
Total Population	1,964,000

Former Bishops—Rt. Rev. LAWRENCE SCANLAN, D.D., ord. June 24, 1868; appt. Vicar-Apostolic of Utah, Jan. 25, 1887; cons. Titular Bishop of Larandum, June 29, 1887; named first Bishop of Salt Lake, Jan. 30, 1891; died May 10, 1915.—Rt. Rev. JOSEPH S. GLASS, C.M., D.D., LL.D., second Bishop; ord. Aug. 15, 1897; cons. Aug. 24, 1915; died Jan. 26, 1926.—Most Rev. JOHN J. MITTY, D.D., third Bishop; ord. Dec. 22, 1906; cons. Sept. 8, 1926; made Coadjutor Archbishop of San Francisco, cum jure successionis, Feb. 4, 1932; Titular Archbishop of Egina; succeeded to the See, March 5, 1935.—Most Rev. JAMES E. KEARNEY, D.D., ord. Sept. 19, 1908; appt. July 4, 1932; cons. Oct. 28, 1932; appt. Bishop of Rochester, July 31, 1937; installed Nov. 11, 1937.—Most Rev. LEO J. STECK, D.D., ord. June 8, 1924; appt. Auxiliary Bishop of Salt Lake, March 3, 1948; cons. Titular Bishop of Ilium, May 20, 1948; died June 19, 1950.—Most Rev. DUANE G. HUNT, D.D., LL.D., ord. June 27, 1920; appt. Aug. 6, 1937; cons. Oct. 28, 1937; appt. assistant at the Pontifical Throne; appt. May 25, 1946; died March 31, 1960.—Most Rev. WILLIAM KEITH WEIGAND, D.D., ord. May 25, 1963; appt. Sept. 3, 1980; ord. Bishop, Nov. 17, 1980; transferred to the See of Sacramento; installed Jan. 27, 1994.

Diocesan Pastoral Center—27 C. St., Salt Lake City, 84103. Tel: 801-328-8641; Fax: 801-328-9680.

Office of the Bishop—SHIRLEY MARES, Sec. Tel: 801-328-8641, Ext. 304; Fax: 801-328-0324.

Vicar General and Moderator of the Curia—Rev. Msgr. J. TERRENCE FITZGERALD, Ext. 305.

Chancellor—Deacon SILVIO MAYO, Ext. 315.

Diocesan Offices

African American, Hmong, Korean, Native American—Sr. LORRAINE MASTERS, O.L.V.M., Dir., Ext. 335.

Apostleship of Prayer—Rev. MATTHEW O. WIXTED, Dir., *112 S. Allen St., Midvale, 84047.* Tel: 801-255-3721.

Archives—Mrs. BERNICE MOONEY, Dir., Ext. 346. Rev. Msgr. JEROME STOFFEL, Dir., Emeritus, Ext. 351.

Campus Ministry—Rev. CASSIAN LEWINSKI, O.P., *170 S. University St., Salt Lake City, 84102.* Tel: 801-359-6066.

Catholic Community Services—Sr. MARGO CAIN, C.S.C., Exec. Dir., *2300 W. 1700 S., Salt Lake City, 84104.* Tel: 801-977-9119; Fax: 801-977-9224. MARY ANN SHEA, Bd. Pres.

Catholic Foundation of Utah—Mrs. NANCY GILES, Pres.; Mr. KURT SIMPSON, Exec. Dir., Ext. 306.

Catholic Relief Services—Deacon SILVIO MAYO, Ext. 315.

Catholic Schools Offices—Rev. JOSEPH MAYO, Supt., Ext. 330.

Cemetery—Mount Calvary—JENNINGS H. MEASE, Dir. Tel: 801-355-2476.

Chancery—LINDA MARTINEZ, Sec., Ext. 317.

College of Consultors—Rev. Msgr. ROBERT J. BUSSEN; Rev. Msgr. J. TERRENCE FITZGERALD; Rev. Msgr. JOHN J. HEDDERMAN; Rev. Msgr. M. FRANCIS MANNION; Rev. VICTOR G. BONNELL; Rev Msgr. ROBERT R. SERVATIUS; Rev. Msgr. JOHN J. SULLIVAN.

Communications Media Office—Vacant, Ext. 334.

Cursillo—FLORENTINO J. VALLES, *P.O. Box 1801, Salt Lake City, 84110.* Tel: 801-484-9068.

Deans—Wasatch Deanery: Rev. Msgr. ROBERT R. SERVATIUS, Southeastern Deanery: Rev. WILLIAM WHEATON, Northern Deanery: Rev. VICTOR G. BONNELL, Salt Lake Deanery: Rev. GERALD P. LYNCH, Southwestern Deanery: Rev. PAUL S. KUZY, C.PP.S.

Diaconate Formation—Sr. ELLEN MARY TYLER, C.S.C., Dir., Ext. 320. Sr. MARIA MOLINA, S.N.D., Assoc. Dir., Ext. 338. Deacon STEVE KIRTS, Ext. 313.

Diocesan Development Drive—Mr. KURT SIMPSON, Dir.

Diocesan Lay Volunteers—Sr. ELLEN MARY TAYLOR, C.S.C., Dir.

Development Office—KURT SIMPSON, Dir., Ext. 306.

Diocesan Office for Persons with Disabilities—BIBIAN J. RENDON, Ext. 345.

Diocesan Pastoral Council—MILLIE SPARKS, Pres.

Ecunemical Commission—Rev. Msgr. M. FRANCIS MANNION, Chm. Tel: 801-328-8941. Revs. CASSIAN LEWINSKI, O.P.; VICTOR BONNELL.
Engaged Encounter—BOB TOOMEY; RENEE TOOMEY. Tel: 801-487-3195.
Family Life-Natural Family Planning—Mrs. VEOLA MARTINEZ-BURCHETT, Ext. 337.
Finance Council—Most Rev. GEORGE H. NIEDERAUER, Ex-Officio; Rev. Msgr. J. TERRENCE FITZGERALD; Rev. Msgr. JOHN J. HEDDERMAN; Rev. COLIN F. BIRCUMSHAW; CAROL BROCKMAN; Deacon SILVIO MAYO; BOB EVANS; MARY ANN SHEA; JOSEPH ZVONEK; BARBARA WOODBURY; GEORGE BEATON.
Finance Office—BARBARA WOODBURY, Comptroller, Ext. 309.
Government Liaison—DEE ROWLAND, Ext. 336.
Hispanic Diaconate—Sr. MARIA MOLINA, S.N.D., Ext. 338.
Hispanic Evangelization & Leadership Formation—Deacon GERMAN TORO, Ext. 331.
Hispanic Affairs—JUANCARLOS R. QUESADACESPEDES.
Holy Childhood Association—Deacon SILVIO MAYO, Dir., Ext. 315.
Lay Ministries—Sr. ELLEN MARY TAYLOR, C.S.C., Ext. 320. Sr. MARIA MOLINA, S.N.D., Assoc. Dir.
Liturgy Office—MAXINE KAISER, Ext. 321.
Liturgical Commission—Rev. COLIN F. BIRCUMSHAW, Chm.
Marriage Encounter—MIKE FULTON; NANCY FULTON. Tel: 801-576-0418.
Ministry to Correctional Institutions—Revs. REYES G. RODRIQUEZ, Dir., *2119 S. 400 E., Salt Lake City, 84115.* Tel: 801-487-1000. MICHAEL ARKINS, S.S.S. Tel: 801-968-2369. JOSEPH KOCHITHARA. Tel: 801-485-5610. FRANCIS B. PELLIGRINO. Tel: 801-966-5111. MICHAEL SCIUMBATO. Tel: 801-896-5539.
Ministry to Priests Program—Clergy Continuing Education. Rev. WILLIAM H. FLEGGE, Dir., *172 North 500 West Provo, Utah, 84601.* Tel: 801-314-5001. Team: Revs. WILLIAM WHEATON; ANDRZEJ SKRZYPIEC; CLARENCE SANDOVAL.
Newspaper—"Intermountain Catholic," BARBARA S. LEE, Editor Ext. 340. ERIKA MARTINEZ, Staff Writer; LON SCHIFFBAUER, Business Mgr.
Peace and Justice Commission—DEE ROWLAND, Dir., Ext. 336.
People's Eucharistic League—Blessed Sacrament Fathers.
Diaconate—Co-Dirs.: Deacons SILVIO MAYO, Ext. 315. DOUGLAS SLIGER. Tel: 801-479-8815.
Presbyteral Council—Rev. Msgr. ROBERT R. SERVATIUS, Pres.; Revs. GERALD P. LYNCH, Vice Pres. COLIN F. BIRCUMSHAW, Sec.
Priests' Mutual Benefit Society (Retirement)—Most Rev. GEORGE H. NIEDERAUER, Chm. Ex-Officio Bd. of Dirs.: Rev. Msgr. J. TERRENCE FITZGERALD, Vice Chm.; Rev. Msgr. JOHN J. HEDDERMAN, Sec./Treas.; Revs. DONALD HOPE; VICTOR G. BONNELL; GERALD LYNCH COLIN BIRCUMSHAW; Rev. Msgr. JOHN J. SULLIVAN.
Priests' Personnel Board—Most Rev. GEORGE H. NIEDERAUER; Rev. VICTOR G. BONNELL; Rev. Msgr. J. TERRENCE FITZGERALD; Revs. JAMES SEMPLE; GERALD P. LYNCH; CLARENCE SANDOVAL; JOSEPH M. MAYO, Ext. 304.
Real Estate Office—RICHARD SALVITTI, Ext. 319.
Religious Education—DAN JOHN, Dir., Ext. 325.
Respect Life—Mrs. VEOLA MARTINEZ-BURCHETT, Ext. 337.
Retreat Movement—Sr. DANILE KNIGHT, O.S.B., Dir., *1794 Lake St., Ogden, 84401.* Tel: 801-392-9231.
Retrovivaille—MIKE BEDARD; SUE BEDARD. Tel: 801-773-4587.
Sisters' Council—Executive Team: Sr. GEORGITA CUNNINGHAM, R.S.M.; Sr. JUDINE SUTER, O.S.B.; Sr. MARIANNE ROHRER, S.A.; Sr. CATHERINE KAMPHAUS, C.S.C.; Sr. CLAUDE CRINNION, S.H.F.; Sr. LORRAINE MASTERS, O.L.V.M.
Society for the Propagation of the Faith—Deacon SILVIO MAYO, Dir., Ext. 315.
Tribunal—
Judicial Vicar—Rev. Msgr. JOHN J. HEDDERMAN, J.C.L., Ext. 318.
Secretary & Notary—VIOLA MCGEHEE, Ext. 316.
Adjutant Judicial Vicars—Revs. ROBERT T. MORIARITY; GERALD P. LYNCH; LANGES SILVA, Ext. 312.
Promotor of Justice—Rev. COLIN F. BIRCUMSHAW.
Defenders of the Bond—Rev. Msgr. J. TERRENCE FITZGERALD; Rev. Msgr. ROBERT R. SERVATIUS; Rev. Msgr. JOHN J. SULLIVAN; Rev. JOSEPH M. MAYO.
Judges—Rev. Msgr. JOHN J. HEDDERMAN; Revs. GERALD P. LYNCH; ROBERT T. MORIARITY; WALTER RIENDEAU, S.S.S.; LANGES SILVA.
Vocation Office—Rev. GERALD P. LYNCH, Dir.; Sr. JEREMIA JANUSCHKA, O.S.B., Assoc. Dir., Ext. 324.
Youth Ministry—MARY FASIG, Dir., Ext. 327.

CLERGY, PARISHES, MISSIONS AND PAROCHIAL SCHOOLS

SALT LAKE CITY
(Salt Lake County)

1—CATHEDRAL OF THE MADELEINE (1866), Rev. Msgr. M. Francis Mannion, Rector. In res., Most Rev. George H. Niederauer; Revs. David J. Bittmenn; Langes Silva.
Res., 331 E. S. Temple St., 84111. Tel: 801-328-8941; Fax: 801-328-9680.
Catechesis/Religious Programs—Tel: 801-328-1241; Fax: 801-364-6504.
Students 90.

2—OUR LADY OF GUADALUPE (Hispanic), Revs. Patrick F. Carley; Langes Silva; Sr. Rosario Lara, Pastoral Assoc.
Res., 715 W. 300 N., 84116. Tel: 801-364-2019.
Catechesis/Religious Programs—Students 178.

3—OUR LADY OF LOURDES (1913), Rev. James Semple. In res., Rev. James A. Janda.
Res., 1085 E. Seventh S. St., 84102. Tel: 801-322-3330; Fax: 801-363-6007. [CEM]
School—1065 E. Seventh S. St., 84102. Tel: 801-364-5624. Edward Campos, Prin.
Sisters of the Holy Cross 1; Daughters of Charity 1; Lay Teachers 15; Students 268.
Catechesis/Religious Programs—Students 55.

4—SACRED HEART (1917) (Hispanic), Rev. Leonidas Lopez; Deacon Tom Otero.
Res., 948 S. 2nd East St., 84111. Tel: 801-363-8632.
Catechesis/Religious Programs—174 E. 900 S., 84111.
Students 150.

5—ST. AMBROSE (1948), Rev. Msgr. John J. Hedderman; Rev. Joseph Kochithara.
Res., 2315 Redondo Ave., 84108. Tel: 801-485-5610; 484-3642.
School—J. E. Cosgriff Memorial School, 2335 Redondo Ave., 84108. Tel: 801-486-3197; Fax: 801-484-8270. Mr. F. Timothy Carr, Prin.
Lay Teachers 19; Students 289.
Catechesis/Religious Programs—Tel: 801-485-9324.
Students 390.

6—ST. ANN (1917), Rev. Msgr. John J. Sullivan; Deacon Mansueto Flaim. In res., Rev. Reyes G. Rodriguez.
Res., 2119 S. 400 E., 84115. Tel: 801-487-1000.
School—430 E. 2100 S., 84105. Tel: 801-486-0741; Fax: 801-486-0742. Constance M. Smith, Prin.
Sisters of Charity of the Incarnate Word 1; Lay Teachers 12; Students 290.
Catechesis/Religious Programs—Tel: 801-261-5943.
Students 122.

7—ST. CATHERINE OF SIENA (1981), Revs. Cassian Lewinski, O.P.; Michael S. Fonse, O.P.
Res., 170 S. University, 84102. Tel: 801-359-6066; Fax: 801-359-4547.
Catechesis/Religious Programs—Students 70.

8—ST. PATRICK'S (1892), Rev. Gerald P. Lynch.
Res., 1072 W. Fourth South St., 84104-1261. Tel: 801-596-7233. [CEM]
Catechesis/Religious Programs—Tel: 801-596-7255. Maureen Malley, D.R.E.
Students 84.

9—ST. THOMAS MORE (1981), Rev. Terence M. Moore; Deacon Steven Kirts.
Res. & Parish Center: 3015 E. Creek Rd., Sandy, 84093. Tel: 801-942-5285 (Office); 942-7678 (Rectory); Fax: 801-942-5287.
Catechesis/Religious Programs—Students 296.

10—ST. VINCENT DE PAUL (1925), Rev. George F. Davich. In res., Rev. Thomas J. Kaiser.
Res., 1375 E. Spring Ln., 84117. Tel: 801-272-9216; Fax: 801-273-1156.
School—1385 E. Spring Ln., 84117. Tel: 801-277-6702. Antoinette Houston, Prin.
Lay Teachers 15; Students 346.
Catechesis/Religious Programs—Tel: 801-272-2132.
Students 179.

SUBURBAN SALT LAKE CITY

1—IMMACULATE CONCEPTION, Salt Lake Co., (1890). Unassigned.
Res., P.O. Box 151, Copperton, Bingham Canyon, 84006. Tel: 801-569-2706.

2—ST. FRANCIS XAVIER, Salt Lake Co., (1955), Revs. Joseph M. Mayo; Francisco Gomez; Deacon Mel Sanchez.
Res., P.O. Box 18631, 84118. Tel: 801-968-2123; Fax: 801-966-1639.
School—See separate listing under Elementary Schools, Regional in the Diocese.
Catechesis/Religious Programs—Students 600.

3—OUR LADY OF LOURDES, Salt Lake Co., (1916), Rev. Andrzej Skrzypiec (Poland).
Res., P.O. Box 38, 84044. Tel: 801-250-6349; Fax: 801-250-3860. [JC]
Catechesis/Religious Programs—8585 W. 3010 S., 84044. Tel: 801-250-6052.
Students 100.

4—ST. THERESE OF THE CHILD JESUS, Salt Lake Co., (1925), Revs. Stanislaw Herba; Francisco Gomez; Deacon Stanley Stott.
Office: 112 S. Allen St., 84047. Tel: 801-255-3721.
Res., 130 S. Allen St., 84047. Tel: 801-255-0340.
Catechesis/Religious Programs—Tel: 801-561-0431.
Students 250.

5—ST. JUDE, Salt Lake Co., (1975) (Maronite Rite), Rev. Gebran Bou-Merhi.
Res., 4893 Wasatch St., 84107. Tel: 801-268-2820.

6—BLESSED SACRAMENT, Salt Lake Co., (1972), Rev. Msgr. Robert R. Servatius; Deacon Russell Langner.
Res., 9757 S. 1700 E., 84092. Tel: 801-571-5517; Fax: 801-571-2071.
School—1745 E. 9800 S., 84092. Tel: 801-572-5311; Fax: 801-572-0251. Sr. Catherine Kamphaus, C.S.C., Prin.
Holy Cross Sisters 1; Lay Teachers 14; Students 313.
Catechesis/Religious Programs—1745 E. 9800 S., 84092. Tel: 801-571-2071.
Students 458.
Mission—Draper, Salt Lake Co., St. John the Baptist, 9757 S. 1700 E., 84092. Tel: 801-571-8594.
Station—Alta, Our Lady of the Snows.

7—ST. MARTIN DE PORRES, Salt Lake Co., (1982), Rev. Michael J. Arkins, S.S.S.; Bro. David Phelan, S.S.S. In res., Rev. Tom O'Mahony, S.S.S.
Mailing Address: 4976 Valois Cir., 84118. Tel: 801-969-8857; Fax: 801-966-9675.
Church—4914 S. 2200 W., 84118. Tel: 801-968-2369.
Catechesis/Religious Programs—Students 150.

8—ST. JOSEPH THE WORKER, Salt Lake Co., (1969), Rev. John B. Hart.
Res., P.O. Box 98, 84084. Tel: 801-255-8902; Fax: 801-255-5003.
Catechesis/Religious Programs—Tel: 801-961-4062.
Students 325.

9—SS. PETER AND PAUL, Salt Lake Co., (1972), Rev. Francis B. Pellegrino; Deacon Lynn Johnson.
Res., P.O. Box 70308, 84170. Tel: 801-966-5111; 966-5119; Fax: 801-966-5119.
Catechesis/Religious Programs—Tel: 801-969-7116.
Students 175.

OUTSIDE SALT LAKE CITY

American Fork, Utah Co., St. Peter's (1969), Rev. James E. Blaine, Parochial Admin.
Res., 626 N. 600 East, 84003. Tel: 801-756-7771.
Catechesis/Religious Programs—Tel: 801-756-2747.
Students 75.

Bountiful, Davis Co., St. Olaf (1944), Rev. Rudolph A. Daz.
Res., 276 E. 1700 South, 84010. Tel: 801-295-3621; Fax: 801-295-3621.
School—1793 S. Orchard Dr., 84010. Tel: 801-295-5341; Fax: 801-295-5915.
Lay Teachers 10; Students 213.
Catechesis/Religious Programs—Students 245.

Brigham City, Box Elder Co., St. Henry (1950), Revs. F. Warren Schoeppe, S.J.; Francisco Pires (Brazil); Deacons Bob Bambrick; Dick Werling.
Res., P.O. Box 872, 84302. Tel: 801-723-2941.
Catechesis/Religious Programs—Tel: 801-723-1215.
Students 190.
Mission—Tremonton, Box Elder Co., Santa Ana, 760 W. 600 N., Tremonton, 84337.

Cedar City, Iron Co., Christ the King (1934), Rev. Michael J. Winterer.
Res., 70 N. 200 West, P.O. Box 626, 84720. Tel: 801-586-8298; Fax: 801-865-5960.
Catechesis/Religious Programs—Students 88.
Missions—Panguitch, Garfield Co., St. Gertrude, S. Main St., Panguitch, 84759. Tel: 801-676-8406; Bryce Canyon, Garfield Co., St. Dominic, Pink Cliff, 84717.
Stations—Beryl Junction.; Brian Head. (Winter).

East Carbon, Carbon Co., Good Shepherd (1947), Rev. Joseph W. Morris, S.J.
Res., P.O. Box 99, 84520. Tel: 801-888-3306.
Convent—105 2nd E., P.O. Box 5, 84520. Tel: 801-888-5528.
Mission—Green River, Emery Co., St. Michael, 140 N. Long St., Green River, 84525. Tel: 801-564-3320.

Eureka, Juab Co., St. Patrick's (1885) (Irish), Rev. Walter A. Riendeau, S.S.S.
Res., P.O. Box 387, Payson, 84651. Tel: 801-465-4782. [JC]

Helper, Carbon Co., St. Anthony's (1944), Rev. Erik J. Richtsteig.
Res., 5 S. Main, 84526. Tel: 801-472-5661. [JC]
Catechesis/Religious Programs—Students 70.

Huntsville, Weber Co., St. Florence Catholic Community (1990), Rev. Henry J. Piacitelli, C.M., Admin.
Mailing Address: 514-24th St., Ogden, 84401-1594. Tel: 801-622-2495.
Church: Tel: 801-745-5673.
Catechesis/Religious Programs—Students 66.

Kanab, Kane Co., St. Christopher's (1953), Rev. Anthony L. Vollmer, C.PP.S.
Res., 39 W. 200 S., #106, 84741. Tel: 801-644-5652; Fax: 801-644-3413.
Station—North Rim, Grand Canyon.

Layton, Davis Co., St. Rose of Lima (1948), Rev. Victor G. Bonnell; Deacons Robert Quintana, (Retired); John Weis.
Mailing Address: 210 South Chapel St., P.O. Box 557, 84041.
Res., 321 Whitesides St., 84041. Tel: 801-544-4269.
Catechesis/Religious Programs—400 East 500 North, 84041. Tel: 801-544-5425.
Students 387.

Logan, Cache Co., St. Thomas Aquinas (1941), Rev. Clarence J. Sandoval; Sr. Marilyn Mark, O.S.B., Pastoral Assoc.
Res., 795 N. 800 East, 84321. Tel: 801-752-1478.
Catechesis/Religious Programs—Students 202.

Milford, Beaver Co., St. Bridget (1948), Rev. Eugenio Yarce.
Res., 210 S. 1st West, P.O. Box 785, 84751. Tel: 801-387-2732.
Missions—Delta, Millard Co., St. John Bosco, P.O. Box 924, Delta, 84624. Tel: 801-364-3710; Fillmore, Millard Co., Holy Family, 390 N. Main St., Fillmore, 84631.

Moab, Grand Co., St. Pius X (1955), Rev. Kenneth Vialpando.
Res., 122 W. 400 North, P.O. Box 357, 84532. Tel: 801-259-5211.
Catechesis/Religious Programs—Tel: 801-259-0384.
Students 70.
Mission—LaSal, Grand Co., Sacred Heart, Hwy. 46/Main, 84530. Tel: 801-686-2255.

Monticello, San Juan Co., St. Joseph (1935), Rev. Kenneth Vialpando. In res., Deacon Joseph Reed.
Res., P.O. Box 518, 84535. Tel: 801-587-2322. [JC]
Catechesis/Religious Programs—Students 61.
Station—Blanding, Halls Crossing.

Ogden, Weber Co.,

1—HOLY FAMILY, (1979), Rev. Lawrence P. Sweeney.
Res., P.O. Box 3070, 84409. Tel: 801-479-1112; Fax: 801-479-1126. [JC]
Catechesis/Religious Programs—Students 205.

2—ST. JAMES, (1966), Rev. Donald E. Hope; Deacons Bud J. Wardle; Tony Lopez. In res., Rev. John E. Norman.
Res., 495 N. Harrison Blvd., 84404. Tel: 801-782-5393.
Catechesis/Religious Programs—Tel: 801-782—7372.
Students 280.

3—ST. JOSEPH'S, (1875), Revs. Colin F. Bircumshaw; Julio E. Sanchez; Charles E. Cummins; Deacons John Conniff; Thomas Buller.
Res., 514 24th St., 84401. Tel: 801-399-5627; Fax: 801-399-5918.
School—See separate listing under Elementary Schools, Regional located in the Diocese. Tel: 801-393-6051; Fax: 801-393-6086. R. Louise Price, Prin.
Catechesis/Religious Programs—Tel: 801-621-3602.
Students 424.
Mission—Huntsville, Weber Co., St. Florence, 6481 E. Hwy. 39, 84317. Tel: 801-745-5673.

4—ST. MARY'S, (1957), Revs. Martin Rock, S.J.; Neale W. Herrlich, S.J.; John Ferguson, S.J.
Res., P.O. Box 9196, 84409. Tel: 801-621-7961; Fax: 801-394-1244.
Catechesis/Religious Programs—Tel: 801-621-2274.
Students 315.

Park City, Summit Co., St. Mary of the Assumption (1881), Revs. Robert J. Bussen; Reyes Rodriquez; Deacon Lowell Palm.
Res., P.O. Box 669, 84060. Tel: 801-649-9676; Fax: 801-647-9678.
Catechesis/Religious Programs—Students 270.
Mission—Heber City, Wasatch Co., St. Lawrence, 1st West Center, Heber City, 84032. Tel: 801-654-1168.

Payson, Utah Co., San Andres (1986), Rev. Walter A. Riendeau, S.S.S.
Mailing Address: P.O. Box 387, 84651. Tel: 801-465-4782.
Church—315 E. 100 N., 84651.
Catechesis/Religious Programs—Students 91.
Missions—Nephi, Utah Co., Our Lady of Victory Mission, c/o San Andres, 84651. Eureka, Utah Co., St. Patrick Parish, c/o San Andres, 84651.

Price, Carbon Co., Notre Dame de Lourdes (1918), Rev. William Wheaton; Deacon Deane L. Foote.
Res., 160 N. Carbon Ave., 84501. Tel: 801-637-1846. [JC]
Catechesis/Religious Programs—Tel: 801-637-7917.
Students 124.
Mission—Huntington, Emery Co., San Rafael, P.O. Box 603, Huntington, 84528. Tel: 801-687-2999.

Provo, Utah Co., St. Francis of Assisi (1892), Revs. William Flecce; Javier G. Virgen.
Res., 172 N. 500 West St., 84601. Tel: 801-374-5001; Fax: 801-375-4751.
Catechesis/Religious Programs—Students 261.
Mission—American Fork, Utah Co., St. Peter's, 634 N. 600 E., American Fork, 84003. Tel: 801-756-7771.

Richfield/Monroe, Sevier Co., St. Elizabeth's (1947), Rev. Michael R. Sciumbato; Deacon James McElfresh.
Res., 5995 N. Hwy. 89, Monroe, 84754. Tel: 801-896-5539.
Catechesis/Religious Programs—Students 87.
Missions—Torrey, Wayne Co., St. Anthony of the Desert, Sandcreek Rd., Torrey, 84775. Tel: 801-425-3319; Ephraim, Sanpete Co., St. Jude, 160 E. Center St., Ephraim, 84627. Tel: 801-283-6242. Sr. Brenda Cousins, C.S.C., Pastoral Assoc.
Stations—Marysvale, Richfield, Tel: 801-528-6000; Central Utah Correctional Facility, Gunnison, Tel: 801-528-6257; Fax: 801-528-6259. [JC]

Roosevelt, Duchesne Co., St. Helen's (1940) (Native American), Rev. Thomas L. Culleton.
Res., 433 E. 200 North, P.O. Box 415, 84066. Tel: 801-722-2975; 722-2975. [CEM]
Missions—Duchesne, Duchesne Co., Holy Spirit, Duchesne, 94066.; Fort Duchesne, Uintah Co., Blessed Kateri Tekakwitha, P.O. Box 533, 84026. Tel: 801-722-4734. Sr. Margaret Usuka, S.N.D., Dir.
Station—Roosevelt, Tabiona.

St. George, Washington Co., St. George's (1955), Rev. Paul S. Kuzy, C.PP.S.; Deacon John O'Brien.
Mailing Address: P.O. Box 188, 84771. Tel: 801-673-2604.
Res., 165 N. 200 West, 84770. Tel: 801-673-7354.
Catechesis/Religious Programs—Students 89.
Station—Zion National Park. (Lodge). Tel: 801-772-3256.

Tooele, Tooele Co., St. Marguerite's (1910), Revs. Matthew O. Wixted; Hernando Diaz; Sr. Marianne Rohrer, Pastoral Assoc.; Deacon James Garcia.
Res., 15 S. 7th St., 84074. Tel: 801-882-3860; Fax: 801-882-3866.
Pre-School—Tel: 801-882-0081. Mrs. Janet Barbiero, Coord.
Catechesis/Religious Programs—Students 339.
Mission—Wendover, Tooele Co., San Felipe, 606 E. Aria Blvd., Wendover, 84083. Tel: 801-665-7710; 665-2339.

Vernal, Uintah Co., St. James the Greater (1948), Rev. Jan Bednarz.
Res., 138 N. 100 West St., 84078. Tel: 801-789-3016. [JC]
Catechesis/Religious Programs—Tel: 801-789-3034.
Students 155.
Station—Dutch John, Flaming Gorge.

Chaplains of Public Institutions

SALT LAKE CITY. *County Youth Detention Center*. Rev. Michael Arkins, S.S.S.
Decker Lake Youth Center. Rev. Francis Pellegrino.
Oxbow Correctional Facility. Rev. Joseph Kochithara.
Salt Lake County Jail. Rev. Reyes G. Rodriguez.
Veterans Administration Hospital, 500 Foothill Dr., 84113. Tel: 801-581-2121. Rev. Gebran Bou-Mehri; Sr. Julie Maher.

DRAPER. *State Penitentiary*. Rev. James E. Blaine, P.O. Box 142, American Fork, 84003. Tel: 801-756-7771.

GUNNISON. *State Penitentiary*. Rev. Javier G. Virgen.

On Duty Outside the Diocese:
Reverend Fathers—
Curran, Patrick J., 872 Farmington Ave., Hartford, CT 06119
Fischer, Louis A., 3444 Pringle St. No. 5, San Diego, CA 92110
Gaeta, David R., 102 Gilmore Dr., Kelly AFB, TX 78241-5813
Govorchin, Vincent, 240 Nice Ln. #203, Newport Beach, CA 92663
Tkach, Norman A., 858 N. 6th St., Banning, CA 92220

Retired:
Reverend Monsignors—
Benvegnu, Mark O.
Kenny, James T.
Pollock, Robert C.
Stoffel, Jerome C.
Reverend Fathers—
Curnutte, William G.
Fischer, Louis A.
Fogarty, James
Freegard, Charles E.
Kaiser, Thomas J.
Mobley, William A.
Spellen, Lawrence M.

Permanent Deacons:
Aguilar, James, Sabbatical
Bambrick, Robert W., St. Henry's, Brigham City
Buller, Thomas M., St. Joseph's, Ogden
Conniff, John J., St. Joseph's, Ogden
Cummings, Owen, Cathedral of the Madeleine, Salt Lake City
Flaim, Mansueto, St. Ann's, Salt Lake City
Foote, Deane L., Notre Dame de Lourdes Parish, Price
Garcia, James D., St. Marguerite's, Tooele
Glodowski, Robert J., On Duty Outside the Diocese
Johnson, Lynn R., Sts. Peter and Paul, Salt Lake City
Kirts, Steven W., St. Thomas More, Sandy
Lopez, Anthony J., St. James, Ogden
Mayo, Silvio, Unassigned
McElfresh, James L., St. Elizabeth, Richfield
O'Brien, John, St. George, St. George
O'Connell, Charles L., On Duty Outside the Diocese
Otero, Tranquilino, Sacred Heart, Salt Lake City
Palm, Lowell L., St. Lawrence, Heber
Quintana, Robert J., Hispanic Ministry, Davis & Weber Counties; St. Rose of Lima, Layton
Reed, Joseph W., St. Joseph, Monticello
Roscoe, Lt. Col. John H., On Duty Outside the Diocese
Sanchez, Mel J., St. Francis Xavier
Sliger, Douglas R., St. Florence, Huntsville
Stott, Stanley L., St. Therese, Midvale
Wardle, Bud J., St. James, Ogden
Weis, John C., St. Rose of Lima, Layton
Werling, Richard E., St. Henry's, Brigham City

INSTITUTIONS LOCATED IN THE DIOCESE

[A] SEMINARIES, RELIGIOUS, OR SCHOLASTICATES

HUNTSVILLE. *Abbey of Our Lady of the Holy Trinity*, 1250 S. 9500 E., 84317. Tel: 801-745-3784. Rt. Rev. Leander Dosch, O.C.S.O., Abbot and Dir. of Studies; Bro. Lawrence Baumbach, O.C.S.O., Novice Master. Priests 16; Brothers 9; Oblate 1; Candidates 2.

[B] HIGH SCHOOLS, DIOCESAN

SALT LAKE CITY. *Judge Memorial Catholic High School*, 650 S. 11th E., 84102. Tel: 801-363-8895. Day School. (Coed). Bro. Harold Hathaway, C.S.C., Pres.; Ms. Renee Genereaux, Prin.; Revs. James P. McHugh, O.S.F.S.; David J. Bittmenn. Priests 1; Brothers 1; Lay Teachers 62; Students 975.

OGDEN. *St. Joseph Catholic High School*, 1790 Lake St., 84401. Tel: 801-394-1515. Revs. John E. Norman, Prin.; Charles Cummins. Priests 2; Lay Teachers 17; Students 220.

[C] ELEMENTARY SCHOOLS, REGIONAL

KEARNS. *St. Francis Xavier Regional School*, 4501 W. 5215 S., 84118. Tel: 801-966-1571. Revs. Joseph M. Mayo; Francisco Gomez; Jim Mello, Prin. Lay Teachers 15; Students 282.

OGDEN. *St. Joseph Regional School*, 2980 Quincy St., 84401. Tel: 801-393-6051. Revs. Colin Bircumshaw; Julio Sanchez; Charles E. Cummins; R. Louise Price, Prin. Lay Teachers 24; Students 394.

PRICE. *Notre Dame Regional School*. (Grades PreK-9), 210 N. 6th E., 84501. Tel: 801-637-2850. Daughters of Charity. Rev. William Wheaton, Admin.; Sr. Stella J. Burns, D.C., Prin. Sisters 2; Lay Teachers 10; Students 206.

[D] FOUNDATIONS

MURRAY. *Holy Cross Ministries*. Mailing Address: P.O. Box 57672, 84157-0672.
For a complete listing, refer to the Hospitals section.

OGDEN. *The St. Benedict's Foundation*, 319 E. Ridgeline Dr., 84405-6925. Tel: 801-479-1800; Fax: 801-479-3216.
For a complete listing, refer to the Hospitals section.

[E] HOMES FOR AGED

SALT LAKE CITY. *St. Joseph Villa*, 451 Bishop Federal Ln., 84115-2295. Tel: 801-487-7557.
For a complete listing, refer to the Special Care Facilities section.

[F] MONASTERIES AND RESIDENCES OF PRIESTS AND BROTHERS

SALT LAKE CITY. *Oblate House*, 554 E St., 84103. Tel: 801-359-8201. Oblates of St. Francis de Sales. Rev. James P. McHugh, O.S.F.S., Contact Person. Total in Residence 3.

HUNTSVILLE. *Abbey of Our Lady of the Holy Trinity of the Order of Cistercians*, 1250 S. 9500 E., 84317. Tel: 801-745-3784. Rt. Rev. Leander Dosch, O.C.S.O., Abbot; Revs. David Altman, O.C.S.O.; Casimir Bernas, O.C.S.O.; Patrick Boyle, O.C.S.O.; Charles Cummings, O.C.S.O.; Malachy Flaherty, O.C.S.O.; Bartholomew Gottemoller, O.C.S.O.; Brendan Hanratty, O.C.S.O.; Alan Hohl, O.C.S.O.; David Kinney, O.C.S.O.; Thomas Porter, O.C.S.O.; Joseph Schroer, O.C.S.O.; Baldwin Shea, O.C.S.O. Legal Title: *Abbey of Our Lady of the Holy Trinity of the Order of Cistercians of the Strict Observance.*
Residing Elsewhere: Revs. Emmanuel Spillane, O.C.S.O.; Cletus Dollinger, O.C.S.O.; Gregory Santos, O.C.S.O. Priests 13; Brothers 11; Total in Community 24.

[G] CONVENTS, MONASTERIES AND RESIDENCES FOR SISTERS

SALT LAKE CITY.
**Carmel of the Immaculate Heart of Mary Monastery*, 5714 Holladay Blvd., 84121. Tel: 801-277-6075; Fax: 801-277-4263. Mother Margaret Mary Miller, O.C.D., Prioress. Professed Cloistered Sisters 6; Professed Out-Sisters 1.
Convent of Mary Queen of Peace, 347 E. S. Temple, 84111. Tel: 801-364-7535. Our Lady of Victory Missionary Sisters 1.
Our Lady of Lourdes Convent, 675 S. 11th E., 84102. Tel: 801-583-1204. Sisters of the Holy Cross 3.
Our Lady of the Wasatch Convent, 2335 Redondo Ave., 84108. Tel: 801-467-4984. Sisters of the Holy Cross 3.
Queen of Peace Convent, 1583 S. 19th E., 84108. Tel: 801-583-4661. Legal Title: *Sisters of the Holy Cross, Inc.* Sisters 2.
St. Joseph Villa Convent, 451 Bishop Federal Ln., 84115-2295. Tel: 801-487-7557. Congregation of Sisters of Charity of the Incarnate Word 7; Total Assisted 37; Total Staff 10.
St. Vincent de Paul Convent, 1385 E. Spring Ln., 84117-6797. Tel: 801-277-7890. Sisters of the Holy Family 1; Sisters of the Holy Cross 1; Sisters for Christian Community 1.
Sisters of Notre Dame, 27 C St., 84103. Tel: 801-328-8641. Sr. Maria Molina, S.N.D., Dir. Office of Hispanic Diaconate, 5306 Cobble Creek Rd., #15-I, 84117. Sisters 1.

EAST CARBON CITY. *Good Shepherd Convent*. Mailing Address: P.O. Box 5, 84520. Tel: 801-888-5528. Our Lady of Victory Missionary Sisters 2.

HELPER. *Convent of St. Anthony*, 30 S. Main St., 84526. Tel: 801-472-5468. Total Assisted 100; Total in Residence 2.

MOAB. *St. Pius X Convent*, Holiday Haven, No. 62, 400 N. 500 West 7 #4, 84532. Tel: 801-259-8657. Our Lady of Victory Missionary Sisters 1.

OGDEN. *Mount Benedict Priory*, Shalom Convent, 309 E. 5450 S., 84405. Tel: 801-479-6030. Sisters of St. Benedict 3. St. Benedict's Convent, 5462 S. 200 E., 84405. Tel: 801-479-8107. Sisters 4. St. Benedict's Convent, 665 S. 1100 E., Salt Lake City, 84102. Tel: 801-582-1042. Sisters 1. Our Lady of the Mountains Convent, 1794 Lake St., 84401. Tel: 801-392-1476. Sisters 2. 484 N. 300 E., Logan, 84321. Tel: 801-753-7445. Sisters 1.

PRICE. *Home of the Daughters of Charity*, 48 W. 200 N., 84501. Tel: 801-637-0163. Daughters of Charity. Sr. Ellen Van Zandt, D.C., Sr. Servant. Sisters 3.

RICHFIELD. *Peace House-Casa de Paz*, 840 Sunset Dr., 84701. Tel: 801-896-8527. Total in Residence 1.

WEST JORDAN. *St. Joseph the Worker Convent*, 7405 S. Redwood Rd., 84084. Tel: 801-561-4090. Total in Residence 1; Total Staff 1.

[H] NEWMAN CENTERS

SALT LAKE CITY. *University of Utah, Newman Center*. St. Catherine of Siena University Parish. 170 S. University, 84102. Tel: 801-359-6066. Revs. Cassian Lewinski, O.P.; Michael S. Fones. Total Students in Residence 10; Total Staff 5.

EPHRAIM. *St. Jude Mission*, 160 E. Center, 84627. Tel: 801-283-6242. Rev. Michael R. Sciumbato, Pastoral Admin.; Sr. Brenda Cousins, C.S.C., Pastoral Assoc. Total Assisted 500; Total Staff 4.

LOGAN. *St Thomas Aquinas, Newman Center*. (Utah State University), 795 N. 800 E., 84321. Tel: 801-752-1478. Rev. Clarence J. Sandoval; Sr. Marilyn Mark, O.S.B., Campus Min. Total in Residence 1; Total Staff 2.

OGDEN. *Weber State University, Newman Center*, 3738 Custer Ave., 84403. Tel: 801-399-9531. Rev. Charles T. Cummins, Dir. Total in Residence 3; Total Staff 1.

PRICE. *College of Eastern Utah, Newman Club*, 454 E. 400 North, 84501. Tel: 801-637-6785. Rev. William Wheaton. Total Staff 1.

ST. GEORGE. *Dixie College, Newman Center*. Tel: 801-673-2604; 673-7354. Mailing Address: St. George Church, P.O. Box 188, 84771. Rev. Paul S. Kuzy, C.PP.S., Dir., 165 N. 200 W., 84770.

[I] RETREAT HOUSES

OGDEN. *Our Lady of the Mountains*, 1794 Lake St., 84401. Tel: 801-392-9231. Sr. Danile Knight, O.S.B., Dir. Total Staff 6; Total in Residence 1.

[J] CATHOLIC COMMUNITY SERVICES

SALT LAKE CITY. *Catholic Community Services*, 2300 W. 1700 S., 84104. Tel: 801-977-9119; Fax: 801-977-8227. Mary Anne Shea, Board Pres.; Sr. Margo Cain, C.S.C., Exec. Dir., Northern Utah Office: 622 23rd St., Ogden, 84401. Tel: 801-394-5944; Fax: 801-394-5948. Mr. Matthew M. Minkevitch, B.A., Dir.
Marillac House, 2300 W. 1700 S., 84104. Tel: 801-977-9119; Fax: 801-363-3621. Gail Reinert, Dir. Tel: 801-359-0830.
St. Mary's Home For Men, 1206 W. 200 S., Box 941, 84110. Tel: 801-328-1894; Fax: 801-328-1895. Three daily family style meals. 40 beds for homeless, fundless, sober men. Work obligation, Inc., non-profit organization, 1972. Mr. John G. Bash, Dir.
St. Vincent de Paul Center, 437 W. 200 S., 84101. Tel: 801-534-1500; Fax: 801-596-8532. Mr. Robert D. Mayo, Dir.
Marillac Transitional Housing Services, Inc., 2300 W. 1700 S., 84104. Gail Reinert, Dir.
William K. Weigand Resource Center, 235 Rio Grande St., 84101. Tel: 801-363-7710; Fax: 801-363-7647. Mr. Robert D. Mayo, Dir.
Villa Maria, 2300 W. 1700 S., 84104. Gail Reinert, Dir. Tel: 801-359-0830. Home for Single Pregnant Adults.
Shelter Plus Housing, 622 23rd St., Ogden, 84401. Matthew M. Minkevitch, B.A., Dir. Housing for people with AIDS/HIV. Total Assisted 191,451; Total Staff 71.
The Madeleine Choir School, 331 East South Temple, 84111.

RELIGIOUS INSTITUTES OF MEN REPRESENTED IN THE DIOCESE

For further details refer to the corresponding bracketed number in the Religious Institutes of Men or Women section.

[0600]—*Brothers of the Congregation of the Holy Cross*.—C.S.C.
[0220]—*Congregation of the Blessed Sacrament*.—S.S.S.
[1330]—*Congregation of the Mission*. (Province of the West).—C.M.
[0520]—*Franciscan Friars*. (Santa Barbara Province).—O.F.M.
[0690]—*Jesuit Fathers and Brothers*. (California Prov.).—S.J.
[0920]—*Oblates of St. Francis de Sales*.—O.S.F.S.
[0350]—*Order of Cistercians of the Strict Observance (Trappists)*.—O.C.S.O.
[0430]—*Order of Preachers (Dominicans)*. (Western Province).—O.P.
[1060]—*Society of the Precious Blood*.—C.PP.S.

RELIGIOUS INSTITUTES OF WOMEN REPRESENTED IN THE DIOCESE

[0230]—*Benedictine Sisters of Pontifical Jurisdiction*.—O.S.B.
[0470]—*Congregation of the Sisters of Charity of the Incarnate Word, Houston, Texas*.—C.C.V.I.
[1920]—*Congregation of the Sisters of the Holy Cross*.—C.S.C.
[0760]—*Daughters of Charity of St. Vincent de Paul*. (Province of the West).—D.C.
[0420]—*Discalced Carmelite Nuns*.—O.C.D.
[1070-09]—*Dominican Sisters*.—O.P.
[1070-13]—*Dominican Sisters*.—O.P.
[1190]—*Franciscan Sisters of the Atonement*.—S.A.
[2575]—*Institute of the Sisters of Mercy of the Americas*.—R.S.M.
[3130]—*Our Lady of Victory Missionary Sisters*.—O.L.V.M.
[]—*Sisters for Christian Community*.—S.F.C.C.
[3000]—*Sisters of Notre Dame de Namur*.—S.N.D.deN.
[3840]—*Sisters of St. Joseph of Carondelet*.—C.S.J.
[1960]—*Sisters of the Holy Family*.—S.H.F.
[3330]—*Union of the Sisters of the Presentation of the Blessed Virgin Mary*.—P.B.V.M.

DIOCESAN CEMETERIES

SALT LAKE CITY. *Mount Calvary Catholic*, Office, 275 U St., 84103. Tel: 801-355-2476. Mr. Jennings H. Mease, Dir.; Harriet Malloy, Sec.

NECROLOGY

† Benvegnu, Mark O., (Retired). —Died Dec. 17, 1995.
† Freegard, Charles E., (Retired). —Died April 9, 1996.

Diocese of San Angelo

(Dioecesis Angeliana)

Most Reverend

MICHAEL D. PFEIFER, O.M.I.

Bishop of San Angelo; ordained December 21, 1964; consecrated and installed Bishop of San Angelo July 26, 1985. *Res., P.O. Box 1829, San Angelo, TX, 76902.*

ESTABLISHED OCTOBER 16, 1961.

Square Miles 37,433.

Comprises 29 Counties in the State of Texas as follows: Andrews, Brown, Callahan, Coke, Coleman, Concho, Crane, Crockett, Ector, Glasscock, Howard, Irion, Kimble, McCulloch, Martin, Menard, Midland, Mitchell, Nolan, Pecos, Reagan, Runnells, Schleicher, Sterling, Sutton, Taylor, Terrell, Tom Green and Upton.

For legal title of parishes and diocesan institutions, consult the Chancery Office.

The Chancery: P.O. Box 1829, San Angelo, TX, 76902. Tel.: 915-651-7500; Fax: 915-651-6688.

Web site address: http://home.navisoft.com/sanangelo

E-mail address: WtAngelus@aol.com

STATISTICAL OVERVIEW

Personnel	
Bishop	1
Priests: Diocesan Active in Diocese	28
Priests: Active Outside Diocese	11
Priests: Retired, Sick or Absent	12
Number of Diocesan Priests	51
Religious Priests in Diocese	17
Extern Priests in Diocese	6
Ordinations:	
Permanent Deacons in Diocese	45
Total Sisters	39
Parishes	
Parishes	49
With Resident Pastor:	
Resident Diocesan Priests	24
Resident Religious Priests	12
Without Resident Pastor:	
Administered by Priests	9
Administered by Women Religious	2
Administered by Lay People	1
Administered by Pastoral Teams, etc.	1
Missions	24
Professional Ministry Personnel:	
Sisters	20
Lay Ministers	13
Educational	
Diocesan Students in Other Seminaries	6
Total Seminarians	6
Elementary Schools, Diocesan and Parish	3
Total Students	908
Catechesis/Religious Education:	
High School Students	4,242
Elementary Students	8,560
Total Students Under Catholic Instruction	13,716
Teachers in the Diocese:	
Sisters	5
Lay Teachers	57
Vital Statistics	
Receptions into the Church:	
Infant Baptism Totals	2,212
Adult Baptism Totals	179
Received into Full Communion	255
First Communions	1,989
Confirmations	1,157
Marriages:	
Catholic	333
Interfaith	109
Total Marriages	442
Deaths	577
Total Catholic Population	81,807
Total Population	675,907

Former Bishops—Most Rev. THOMAS J. DRURY, D.D., LL.D., ord. June 2, 1935; appt. Oct. 16, 1961; cons. and installed Jan. 24, 1962; transferred to Corpus Christi, July 19, 1965; died July 22, 1992.—Most Rev. THOMAS TSCHOEPE, D.D., ord. May 30, 1943; appt. Bishop Jan. 12, 1966; cons. Mar. 9, 1966; transferred to Dallas, Aug. 27, 1969.—Most Rev. STEPHEN A. LEVEN, D.D., ord. June 10, 1928; cons. Feb. 8, 1956, Auxiliary of San Antonio; appt. to San Angelo Oct. 22, 1969; retired April 16, 1979; died June 28, 1983.—Most Rev. JOSEPH A. FIORENZA, ord. May 29, 1954; appt. Sept. 4, 1979; ord. and installed October 25, 1979; transferred to Galveston-Houston, Dec. 18, 1984.

Vicar General—Rev. Msgr. TIMOTHY J. MURPHY, J.C.L.

Chancery Office—804 Ford, San Angelo, 76905. Tel: 915-651-7500; Fax: 915-651-6688. Office Hours: Mon.-Fri. 9-12 & 1-5, *Mailing Address: Box 1829, San Angelo, 76902.*

Chancellor—Rev. Msgr. LARRY J. DROLL, J.C.L.

Diocesan Tribunal—P.O. Box 1829, San Angelo, 76902.
Judicial Vicar—Rev. Msgr. TIMOTHY J. MURPHY, J.C.L., *P.O. Box 1829, San Angelo, 76902.*
Judges—Revs. WILLIAM DUBUISSON, O.M.I., J.C.L., Adjutant Judicial Vicar; TOM BARLEY, J.C.L.; Very Rev. MAURICE J. VOITY.

Promotor Justitiae—Rev. JAMES PLAGENS.

Defensores Vinculi—Rev. Msgr. LARRY J. DROLL, J.C.L.; Rev. CHARLES GREENWELL; Very Rev. MARK WOODRUFF.

Diocesan Consultors—Rev. Msgr. LARRY J. DROLL; Very Rev. BERNARD L. GULLY; Rev. RAYMOND CORR, O.P.; Rev. Msgr. TIMOTHY J. MURPHY; Very Revs. WILLIAM DU BUISSON, O.M.I.; TOM BARLEY.

Priests' Personnel Committee—Rev. Msgr. LARRY J. DROLL, Chm.

Presbyteral Council—Rev. TOM BARLEY, J.C.L., Chm.; Rev. Msgr. TIMOTHY J. MURPHY; Rev. Msgr. LARRY J. DROLL; Revs. TERENCE BRENON; JAMES PLAGENS; MARK WOODRUFF; WILLIAM DU BUISSON, O.M.I.; Revs. JAMES BRIDGES; JOHN RAYMOND CORR, O.P.; JOSEPH UECKER, C.PP.S.

Vicar for Women Religious—Sr. MALACHY GRIFFIN, O.P.

Diocesan Offices and Directors

Accounting Office—Mr. DAVID MAYRAND.

Office of Parish Pastoral Leadership—Rev. JAMES PLAGENS.

Campaign for Human Development—Mr. LES MAIMAN.

Catholic Relief Services—Mr. LES MAIMAN.

Catholic University, Friends of—Rev. Msgr. TIMOTHY J. MURPHY.

Communications Office—Very Rev. MAURICE J. VOITY.

Continuing Education of the Clergy—Very Rev. MARK WOODRUFF.

Cursillos de Cristiandad—Rev. BERNARD GULLY.

Deans—Very Revs. CHARLES GREENWELL, San Angelo Deanery: MARK WOODRUFF, Midland-Odessa Deanery: FRED NAWARSKAS, Abilene Deanery.

Diocesan Liturgical Commission—Rev. JAMES PLAGENS.

Holy Childhood, Pontifical Association—Miss MARY SUE BREWER.

Newspaper—"West Texas Angelus"; Very Rev. MAURICE J. VOITY, Editor.

Office of Evangelization—Rev. FRANCIS X. FREY.

Office of Education and Formation—Sr. JOAN MARKUS, S.S.N.D.

Permanent Deacon Director—Deacon ALAN NEFF.

Priests' Pension Plan—Board of Directors: Rev. Msgrs. TIMOTHY J. MURPHY; LARRY J. DROLL; Very Rev. CHARLES GREENWELL; Rev. Msgr. FRED NAWARSKAS; Rev. BENEDICT ZIENTEK.

Propagation of the Faith—Rev. Msgr. TIMOTHY J. MURPHY.

Rural Life—Deacon LEROY BEACH, Dir.

Schools—Sr. JOAN MARKUS, S.S.N.D., Supt.

Seminarians, Director of—Rev. DAVID ESPITIA.

Vocations—Rev. DAVID ESPITIA, Dir.

CLERGY, PARISHES, MISSIONS AND PAROCHIAL SCHOOLS

CITY OF SAN ANGELO
(Tom Green County)

1—CATHEDRAL OF THE SACRED HEART (1884), Very Rev. Maurice Voity, Rector.
Office: 19 S. Oakes St., 76903. Tel: 915-658-6567; Fax: 915-651-5813.
School—Angelo Catholic School, Sacred Heart Campus, (Grades 2-6). Tel: 915-655-3325; Fax: 915-655-1286. Sr. Kathleen Kudlac, O.S.F., Prin.
Sisters 1; Lay Teachers 8; Students 199.
Catechesis/Religious Programs—Sr. Carol Markus, S.S.N.D., D.R.E.
Students 280.
Sacred Heart Cathedral-Parish Educational Endowment Fund, Inc.—Tel: 915-658-6567.

2—HOLY ANGELS (1961), Very Rev. Charles C. Greenwell.
Parish Office: 2202 Rutgers Ave., 76904. Tel: 915-949-3308; 944-8967.
School—Angelo Catholic School, (Grades PreK-1). Holy Angels Campus 2315 A & M Ave., Tel: 915-655-3325. Sr. Kathleen Kudlac, O.F.M., Prin.
Lay Teachers 5; Students 101.

Catechesis/Religious Programs—Tel: 915-942-8192. Mrs. Judy Feist, D.R.E., (Grades 1-6).
Students 495.

3—St. Margaret (1967), Rev. James Chaumont; Deacons Ray Smith; Dan Pena.
Res., 2619 Era St., 76905. Tel: 915-651-4633.
Catechesis/Religious Programs—Dee Ann Kemp, D.R.E.
Students 124.
Mission—Robert Lee, Coke Co., Our Lady of Guadalupe.

4—St. Mary's (1930), Rev. Terence Brenon; Deacons Lazaro Sevier; Mario Torres; Roy Ibarra; Jerry Trevino. In res., Rev. George Fey, C.PP.S.
Res., 7 West Ave. N., 76903. Tel: 915-655-6278.
Catechesis/Religious Programs—Minnie Ibarra, D.R.E.
Students 361.

5—St. Joseph (1942) (Hispanic), Rev. John Raymond Corr, O.P.; Deacons Manuel Maldonado; John Munoz.
Res., 301 W. 17th, 76903. Tel: 915-653-5006; Fax: 915-659-2795.
Catechesis/Religious Programs—Tel: 915-658-8759. Michael R. Wyse, D.R.E.
Students 502.

OUTSIDE THE CITY OF SAN ANGELO

Abilene, Taylor Co.,

1—Sacred Heart, (1891), Rev. Robert Bush; Deacon William Smith.
Res., 837 Jeanette St., 79602. Tel: 915-677-7951; Fax: 915-677-7710.
Catechesis/Religious Programs—Tel: 915-673-0697. Sr. Mary Rose Keegan, S.M., D.R.E.; Penny Pope, D.R.E.
Students 509.
Mission—Clyde, Callahan Co., Sts. Joachim and Ann. Deacon Peter Ballaro. [CEM]

2—Holy Family, (1976), Rev. Msgr. Frederick Nawarskas; Sr. Dolores Siebenmorgen, S.S.N.D., Pastoral Assoc.; Deacons Paul Klein; Gerald Schwalb.
Res., 5410 Buffalo Gap Rd., P.O. Box 5970, 79606. Tel: 915-692-1820; Fax: 915-698-5131.
Catechesis/Religious Programs—Joe Burns, D.R.E.
Students 440.

3—St. Francis of Assisi, (1906) (Hispanic), Revs. Joseph Uecker, C.PP.S.; David Matz, C.PP.S.; Deacon Jose Sanchez.
Res., 826 Cottonwood St., 79601. Tel: 915-672-6695.
Catechesis/Religious Programs—D.R.E.: Virginia Camacho; Norma Collazo.
Students 350.

4—St. Vincent Pallotti, (1963), Revs. Joseph H. Uecker, C.PP.S. Tel: 915-673-7048; David Matz, C.PP.S; Sr. Rebecca Otter, O.P., Pastoral Assoc., Tel: 915-672-5933.
Res., 2525 Westview, 79603. Tel: 915-672-1794.
Catechesis/Religious Programs—D.R.E.: Ofilia Rodriguez; Minerva Garcia.
Students 365.

Andrews, Andrews Co., Our Lady of Lourdes (1957), Rev. Bernard L. Gully.
Res., 201 N.E. Ave. K, 79714. Tel: 915-523-4215.
Catechesis/Religious Programs—Tel: 915-524-2789.
Students 621.

Ballinger, Runnels Co., St. Mary Star of the Sea (1892), Rev. Louis Moeller; Deacons Henry Martinez; D.J. Goetz.
Res., 608 Sixth St., 76821. Tel: 915-365-2687. [JC]
Catechesis/Religious Programs—D.R.E.: Shawn Nagel; Dolly Martinez.
Students 280.
Mission—Bronte, Coke Co., St. James, Bronte, 76933.

Big Lake, Reagan Co., St. Margaret of Cortona (1949), Rev. Joel Byrne, O.F.M.
Res., 107 First St., 76932. Tel: 915-884-2645. [JC]
Catechesis/Religious Programs—Tel: 915-884-6874. Lorenzo Florez, D.R.E.
Students 158.
Mission—Rankin, Upton Co., St. Thomas.

Big Spring, Howard Co., Immaculate Heart of Mary (1961), Rev. Christopher Coleman, M.S.C.; Deacons Wayne Rock; David King.
Res., 1009 Hearn St., 79720. Tel: 915-267-4124; Fax: 915-267-7844.
Catechesis/Religious Programs—Mrs. Ruth Salazar, D.R.E.
Students 241.

Sacred Heart (1948), Rev. Cornelius J. Scanlan, O.M.I.
Res., 508 N. Aylford, 79720. Tel: 915-263-7884; Fax: 915-263-3621.
Mailing Address: P.O. Box 2101, 79721-2101.
Catechesis/Religious Programs—Tel: 915-267-9092. Margie Rodriguez, D.R.E.
Students 144.

St. Thomas (1887), Rev. Cornelius Scanlan, O.M.I. In res., Rev. Adolfo L. Valenzuela.
Res., 605 N. Main St., P.O. Box 627, 79721. Tel: 915-263-2864; Fax: 915-263-3621.
Catechesis/Religious Programs—Miss Mary Chavez, D.R.E.
Students 120.

Brady, McCulloch Co., St. Patrick's (1876), Mr. Noe Rocha, Pastoral Coord.
Res., P.O. Box 1188, 76825. Tel: 915-597-2324.
Catechesis/Religious Programs—Mercy James, D.R.E.
Students 208.
Mission—Melvin, McCullogh Co., St. Francis Xavier.

Brownwood, Brown Co., St. Mary's (1896) (Hispanic), Rev. Msgr. Benedict Zientek; Deacon John Specht.
Res., 1105 Main Ave., 76801. Tel: 915-646-7455.
Catechesis/Religious Programs—Tel: 915-646-9630. Bryan Scott Boyce, D.R.E.
Students 348.

Carlsbad, Tom Green Co., St. Therese of the Child Jesus (1957), Revs. Terry Brenon, Supvr.; Miguel Dinio, O.P.
Mailing Address: P.O. Box 416, 76934-0416. Tel: 915-465-8062.
Catechesis/Religious Programs—Students 66.
Mission—Sterling City, Sterling Co., St. Paschal Baylon.
Station—San Angelo State School for the Mentally Retarded.

Coleman, Coleman Co., Sacred Heart (1950), Rev. Lawrence S. Cyr, C.PP.S. In res., Rev. Austin C. Herrmann, C.PP.S.
Res., 303 E. College, 76834. Tel: 915-625-5773.
Catechesis/Religious Programs—201 San Saba, 76834. Tel: 915-625-2031. Sr. Esperanza Razura, A.S.C., D.R.E.
Students 170.

Colorado City, Mitchell Co., St. Ann's (1943), Rev. Ray Wilhelm, O.M.I.; Sr. Guadalupe Rodriguez, C.C.V.I., Pastoral Assoc. & D.R.E.
Res., P.O. Box 966, 79512. Tel: 915-728-3252; Fax: 915-728-3252.
Catechesis/Religious Programs—Tel: 915-728-5865.
Students 237.
Mission—Loraine, Mitchell Co., San Jose.

Crane, Crane Co., Good Shepherd, Sr. Laureanna Perez, D.C., Pastoral Coord.; Sr. Doris Moore, D.C.; Deacons Julio Carrasco; Apolonio Gutierrez.
Mailing Address: P.O. Box 1294, 79731.
Res., 1109 S. Virginia St., 79731. Tel: 915-558-2718.
Church—9th & S. Virginia St., 79731.
Catechesis/Religious Programs—Mary Garcia, D.R.E.
Students 231.

Eden, Concho Co., St. Charles (1927) (Hispanic-German), Rev. Michael Rodriguez; Deacons Leroy Beach; Joe Lopez.
Res., P.O. Box 575, 76837. Tel: 915-869-8311.
Catechesis/Religious Programs—Students 111.
Missions—Millersview, Concho Co., Our Lady of Guadalupe; Eola, Concho Co., St. Philip.

Eldorado, Schleicher Co., Our Lady of Guadalupe (1924), Rev. Jeremiah McCarthy, M.S.C.
Res., P.O. Box 211, 76936. Tel: 915-853-2663.
Catechesis/Religious Programs—Tel: 915-853-3366. D.R.E.: Sylvia Belman; Nell Edmiston; Rosie Diaz; Martha Acosta; Lucy Rodriguez; Patty Furr.
Students 289.
Missions—Knickerbocker, Tom Green Co., Immaculate Conception, P.O. Box 36, Knickerbocker, 76939. Tel: 915-944-2820; Mertzon, Irion Co., St. Peter's, 324 N. Commerce, P.O. Box 772, Tel: 915-835-2000.

Fort Stockton, Pecos Co., St. Joseph's (1875) (Hispanic), Rev. Joe Vasquez; Deacons Andres Hernandez; Cosme Ureta, Jr.
Res., 403 S. Main, 79735. Tel: 915-336-5027.
Catechesis/Religious Programs—Tel: 915-336-5037. Elizabeth C. Rojo, D.R.E.
Students 385.

St. Agnes (1953) (Hispanic), Rev. Charles Geller; Sr. Miriam Tracey, M.S.H.R., Pastoral Assoc.; Sr. Maria O'Connor, M.S.H.R.; Deacon Simon Franco.
Mailing Address: Rte. 1, Box 105, 79735. Tel: 915-336-2724. [CEM]
Catechesis/Religious Programs—D.R.E.: Lillian Subia; Arabella Granado.
Students 385.
Missions—Coyanosa, Pecos Co., St. Isidore; Imperial, Pecos Co., Our Lady of Lourdes. Deacon Jose Esparza

Junction, Kimble Co., St. Theresa of the Child Jesus (1959), Rev. Quirino Cornejo.
Res., P.O. Box 486, 76849. Tel: 915-446-3393; Fax: 915-396-2076.
Catechesis/Religious Programs—Students 42.

McCamey, Upton Co., Sacred Heart (1935), Rev. Barry L. McLean.
Res., Drawer G, 79752. Tel: 915-652-8214; Fax: 915-652-8216.
Catechesis/Religious Programs—Tel: 915-652-8810. Margie Sanchez, D.R.E.
Students 110.
Mission—Iraan, Pecos Co., St. Francis of Assisi, Tel: 915-652-8216.

Menard, Menard Co., Sacred Heart (1873), Rev. Quirino H. Cornejo.
Res., P.O. Box 788, 76859. Tel: 915-396-4906; Fax: 915-396-2076.
Catechesis/Religious Programs—Students 84.

Midland, Midland Co.,

1—St. Ann's, (1896), Rev. Msgr. Timothy J. Murphy; Mr. Thomas Burke, Pastoral Assoc.; Deacon Hubert Collins.
Res., 1908 W. Texas Ave., 79701. Tel: 915-682-6303; Fax: 915-684-4528.
School—(Grades PreK-6) 2000 W. Texas Ave., Tel: 915-684-4563; Fax: 915-687-2468. Mrs. Barbara Ransbottom, Prin.
Religious 1; Lay Teachers 30; Students 401.
Catechesis/Religious Programs—Tel: 915-687-0941. Marge Hellinghausen, D.R.E.
Students 826.

2—Our Lady of Guadalupe, (1961), Revs. Robert Vreteau, O.M.I.; Gilbert Rodriguez; Deacon Jesse Guajardo, Pastoral Assoc.
Res., 1401 E. Garden Ln., P.O. Box 7, 79702. Tel: 915-682-2581; Fax: 915-682-9364.
Catechesis/Religious Programs—Tel: 915-683-8908. D.R.E.: Sr. Regina Javier, O.N.D.; Sr. Luisita Iglesias, O.N.D.
Students 844.

3—Our Lady of San Juan de Los Lagos, (1984) (Spanish), Very Rev. Robert Vreteau, O.M.I.; Rev. Gilbert Rodriguez.
Res., 1008 W. New Jersey, 79701. Tel: 915-682-8698.
Catechesis/Religious Programs—Tel: 915-682-2100. D.R.E.: Isabel Rey; Luiz Martinez.
Students 363.

4—St. Stephen's, (1982), Rev. James P. Bridges.
Mailing Address: 1008 Neely Ave., 79707. Tel: 915-520-7394; Fax: 915-520-7395.
Parish Office: 4601 Neely Ave., 79707.
Catechesis/Religious Programs—Tel: 915-520-3065. Karla Blake, D.R.E.
Students 301.

Miles, Runnels Co., St. Thomas (1962), Rev. Stephen Kennelly (Ireland); Sr. Madeleine Zimmerer, C.D.P., Pastoral Assoc.
Res., P.O. Box 306, 76861. Tel: 915-468-3171.
Catechesis/Religious Programs—Students 154.

Odessa, Ector Co.,

1—Holy Redeemer, (1961) (Spanish), Rev. Frank Chavez; Deacons Ignacio Cisneros; Antonio Gonzales; Pedro Santoya.
Res., 2633 Conover, 79763. Tel: 915-332-5560; Fax: 915-332-6631.
Catechesis/Religious Programs—Tel: 915-332-9231. D.R.E.: Anita Diaz; Sr. Marie Unterreiner; Isabel Garza, (Elementary).
Students 944.

2—St. Anthony, (1948) (Mexican), Revs. David Lee Herrera; Luis Zepeda; Sr. Jovita Perez, Pastoral Assoc.; Deacon Barney Rodriguez.
Office: 1321 W. Monahans St., 79763. Tel: 915-337-6314; Fax: 915-333-3631.
Catechesis/Religious Programs—Tel: 915-337-0241. D.R.E.: Belinda Urias; Yolanda Chavarria; Irene Nunez.
Students 368.

3—St. Elizabeth Ann Seton, (1982), Very Rev. Mark Woodruff; Deacon Alan Neff, Pastoral Assoc.
Res., 1506 Alpine, 79762. Tel: 915-367-4657 (Office); 366-8629 (Rectory).
Catechesis/Religious Programs—Tel: 915-367-4668. Rebecca McIlwain, D.R.E.
Students 395.
Mission—Odessa, Our Lady of San Juan.

4—St. Joseph, (1948) (Mexican), Revs. David Lee Herrera; Luis Zepeda; Sr. Jovita Perez; Deacons Abel Campos; Eufracio Hernandez; Jesus Mercado.
Res., 907 S. Dixie St., 79761. Tel: 915-337-2213; Fax: 915-333-3631.
Catechesis/Religious Programs—Tel: 915-337-4734. D.R.E.: Monica Lopez; Mary Rivas; Polo Ramirez.
Students 630.
Mission—Odessa, Ector Co., St. Martin de Porres, 2821 E. Hammett, 79766.

5—St. Mary's, (1938), Rev. Francis Frey.
Res., 612 E. 18th St., 79761. Tel: 915-332-5334.
School—(Grades PreK-6) 1703 N. Adams, 79761. Tel: 915-337-6052. Sr. Kathleen Murray, D.C., Prin.
Sisters 3; Lay Teachers 14; Students 207.
Catechesis/Religious Programs—Tel: 915-332-1844. Sr. Doris Moore, D.C., D.R.E.

Students 323.

Olfen, Runnels Co., St. Boniface (1901), Rev. Stephen Kennelly; Rev. Msgr. Kevin Heyburn.
Res., P.O. Box 96, Rowena, 76875-0096. Tel: 915-442-2893. [CEM]
Church—1118 County Rd.234, Rowena, 76875.

Ozona, Crockett Co., Our Lady of Perpetual Help (1929) (Hispanic), Very Rev. William Du Buisson, O.M.I.; Rev. Ray Gallagher.
Res., P.O. Box 1069, 76943. Tel: 915-392-3353.
Catechesis/Religious Programs—Tel: 915-392-3429. D.R.E.: Juanita Delgado; Mabel Hernandez. Students 278.
Mission—Sheffield, Crockett Co., Good Shepherd.

Rowena, Runnels Co., St. Joseph's (1906), Revs. Stephen Kennelly; Kevin J. Heyburn; Sr. Madeleine Zimmerer, C.D.P., Pastoral Assoc.
Res., P.O. Box 96, 76875. Tel: 915-442-3521; Fax: 915-442-4602. [CEM]
Catechesis/Religious Programs—Mrs. Ina Albarado, D.R.E.
Students 148.

St. Lawrence, Glasscock Co., St. Lawrence, Rev. Tom Barley.
Res., 2400 FM 2401, Garden City, 79739. Tel: 915-397-2300. [CEM]
Catechesis/Religious Programs—Tel: 915-397-2777. Deborah Pelzel, D.R.E.
Students 257.
Mission—Midkiff, Upton Co., St. Thomas.

Sanderson, Terrell Co., St. James (1916) (Hispanic), Rev. Joe Vasquez.
Res., 409 N. Second St., P.O. Box 520, 79848. Tel: 915-345-2354.
Catechesis/Religious Programs—Tel: 915-345-2354. Lee Warrington, D.R.E.
Students 95.

Sonora, Sutton Co., St. Ann's (1927), Very Rev. William Du Buisson, O.M.I.; Rev. Raymond Gallagher.
Office: 311 W. Plum St., P.O. Box 1397, 76950. Tel: 915-387-2278; Fax: 9115-387-2278.
Res., 105 Oakwood, Box 1397, 76950. Tel: 915-387-5966.
Catechesis/Religious Programs—Students 305.

Stanton, Martin Co., St. Joseph's (1882), Rev. Tom Barley; Deacon Ernie Sanchez.
Res., P.O. Box 846, 405 N. Convent St., 79782-0846. Tel: 915-756-3743.
Catechesis/Religious Programs—Teri Marquez, D.R.E.
Students 244.
Mission—Lenorah, Martin Co., St. Isidore.

Sweetwater, Nolan Co., Holy Family (1885), Rev. Michael Goode, C.PP.S. In res., Rev. Bernard P. Degan, C.M.
Mailing Address: P.O. Box 847, 79556.
Res., 507 Crane St., 79556. Tel: 915-235-2694; Fax: 915-235-3483.
Catechesis/Religious Programs—D.R.E.: Margaret Torres; Mary Petrie; Diane Miller.
Students 186.
Mission—Merkel, Taylor Co., Our Mother of Mercy, P.O. Box 206, Merkel, 79536. Tel: 915-928-5239.

Immaculate Heart of Mary (1962) (Hispanic), Rev. Hendrik Laenen, O.M.I.
Res., 511 W. Alabama, 79556. Tel: 915-235-5271; 235-3318 (Office); Fax: 915-235-0258.
Catechesis/Religious Programs—Students 135.
Mission—Roscoe, Nolan Co., St. Albert the Great.

Wall, Tom Green Co., St. Ambrose (1941), Rev. Msgr. Larry J. Droll.
Res., P.O. Box 228, 76957. Tel: 915-651-7551; Fax: 915-651-6605. [CEM]
Catechesis/Religious Programs—D.R.E.: Dolores Gully; Mary Kay Ripple; Sylvia Chappa.
Students 280.
Mission—Mereta, Tom Green Co., Holy Family, Tel: 915-468-3101.

Winters, Runnels Co., Our Lady of Mt. Carmel (1962), Rev. Sam F. Homsey, C.PP.S.
Res., 119 W. College, 79567. Tel: 915-754-4626.
Catechesis/Religious Programs—Tel: 915-754-4893. Dinell Jacob, D.R.E.
Students 88.

On Duty Outside the Diocese:
Reverend Fathers—
Chengazhacheril, George
D'Mello, Lawrence
Esquivez, Miguel
Lynes, James
McCaffrey, Daniel

Military Chaplains:
Reverend Fathers—
Diab, Thomas, 64 FTW/HC, 231 Reece Blvd., Reece AFB, TX 79489-5051
Hicks, Steven, 15th NEU, Box 555365, Camp Pendleton, CA 92055-5365
Regan, Richard, 750 SPTS/HC, 1080 Lockheed, Box 049, Sunnyvale, CA 94088-1236

Absent on Leave:
Reverend Fathers—
Colacicco, Frank, St. Isidore Church, 445 LaGanda, CA 94526
Espitia, David, Box 1829, San Angelo, TX 76902
Lotief, Cecil, P.O. Box 912, Hays, KS 67601
McNulty, Theodore, 620 S. 5th, Aurora, IL 60505
Plagens, James, Box 1829, San Angelo, TX 76902
Wade, Hubert, 3019 W. Frennch Pl., San Antonio, TX 78228

Retired:
Reverend Fathers—
Aaron, James R., Catholic Care Center, 6700 E. 45th, Wichita, KS 67226
Braun, Serran R., 4908 Blue Ridge, San Angelo, TX 76904
Coleman, James, Padua Place, 100 Peter Baque Rd., San Antonio, TX 78209
Cowan, Vincent, Box 1243, Fort Stockton, TX 79735
Diersing, Leo, 102 Hamilton, Ballinger, TX 76821
Droll, Louis J., 114 Parque Vista Dr., Georgetown, TX 78626
Femenia, Nicholas, P.O. Box 37056, San Antonio, TX 78237
Kelly, Robert M., Box 601, Center Moriches, NY 11934
Larue, Charles, Padua Place, 80 Peter Baque Rd., San Antonio, TX 78209
Schultz, Russell, 80 Peter Baque Rd., San Antonio, TX 78209
Valladares, Herman, Leon, Spain
Vergauwen, Peter, 80 Peter Baque, San Antonio, TX 78209

Permanent Deacons:
Bacon, James, Sacred Heart, McCamey
Ballaro, Peter, Sts. Joachim & Ann Mission, Clyde
Ballero, Peter, Sacred Heart, Abilene
Beach, Leroy, Our Lady of Guadalupe, Millersview
Beach, Leroy, St. Charles, Eden
Camacho, Isaac, Holy Family, Abilene
Campos, Abel, San Jose, Odessa
Campos, Abel, St. Joseph, Odessa
Carrasco, Julio, Good Shepherd, Crane
Cisneros, Ignacio, Holy Redeemer Church, Odessa
Collins, Hubert, St. Ann's Church, Midland
Crochet, Larry, Austin
Decuir, Harold, Sacred Heart, San Angelo
Esparza, Jose, Our Lady Of Lourdes, Imperial
Franco, Simon, St. Agnes, Ft. Stockton
Giovannitti, Thomas, Our Lady of Guadalupe
Goetz, D. J., St. Mary's, Ballinger
Gonzales, Antonio, Holy Redeemer Church, Odessa
Guajardo, Jesse, Our Lady of Guadalupe, Midland
Gutierrez, Apolonio, Good Shepherd, Crane
Hernandez, Andres, St. Agnes Church, Ft. Stockton
Hernandez, Eufracio, San Jose, Odessa
Ibarra, Roy, St. Mary, San Angelo
King, David, Immaculate Heart of Mary Church, Big Spring
Klein, Paul, Holy Family Church, Abilene
Lopez, Joseph, St. Philip's Church, Eola
Maldonado, Manuel, St. Joseph, San Angelo
Martinez, Enrique, St. James, Bronte
Mercado, Jesus, San Jose, Odessa
Munoz, John, St. Joseph, San Angelo
Neff, Alan, St. Elizabeth Ann Seton, Odessa
Pena, Daniel, St. Margaret, San Angelo
Rock, Wayne, Immaculate Heart of Mary Church, Big Spring
Rodriguez, Barney, St. Anthony's Church, Odessa
Samaniego, Enemencio, St. Ann, Sonora
Sanchez, Ernie, St. Joseph Church, Stanton
Sanchez, Pedro, St. Francis, Abilene
Santoya, Pedro, Holy Redeemer, Odessa
Schwalb, Gerald, Holy Family, Abilene
Sevier, Lazaro, St. Mary, San Angelo
Smith, Raymond, St. Margaret, San Angelo
Smith, William, Sacred Heart Church, Abilene
Specht, John, St. Mary, Brownwood
Torres, Mario, St. Mary, San Angelo
Trevino, Jerry, St. Mary, San Angelo
Ureta, Cosme, St. Joseph Church, Ft. Stockton
Yanez, Horacio, St. Thomas, Big Spring
Youngblood, Jack C., Worcester Diocese

INSTITUTIONS LOCATED IN THE DIOCESE

[A] MONASTERIES AND RESIDENCES OF PRIESTS & BROTHERS

CHRISTOVAL. *Mount Carmel Hermitage*, Box 337, 76935-0337. Tel: 915-896-2249. Hermits of the Most Blessed Virgin Mary of Mt. Carmel. Rev. Fabian Maria Rosette, H.O.Carm. Hermits 3.

[B] CONVENTS AND RESIDENCES FOR SISTERS

SAN ANGELO. Holy Redeemer Parish.
Carmelite Nuns of the Ancient Observance, Monastery of Our Lady of Grace, One Saint Joseph Pl., 76905. Tel: 915-651-4959.
Dominican Sisters, 3526 Juanita, 76901. Tel: 915-944-7605. Congregation of the Most Holy Rosary. Sinsinawa Dominicans. Total in Residence 1; Total Staff 1. 2113 N. 7th, Abilene, 76903.
School Sisters of St. Francis, 1217 Lester Lane, 76903.
Sisters of Charity of the Incarnate Word, Mailing Address: 555 Smith Blvd., 76905. Tel: 915-655-3294. Sisters 1.
Sisters of the Living Word, 2627 Era St., 76901. 3111 W. Beauregard, Apt. B, 76904-4901.

ABILENE. *Marist Sisters*, 810 Peach, 79602.
School Sisters of Notre Dame, P.O. Box 5970, 79605. 2627 Era St., San Angelo, 76905. 2625 San Fernando, Odessa, 79763-2128.

COLEMAN. *Adorers of the Blood of Christ*, 210 E. Pecan, 76834.

FT. STOCKTON. *Missionary Sisters of the Lady of the Holy Rosary*, Rt. 1, Box 105, 79735. 1111 W. 13th St., Odessa, 79763.

MIDLAND. *Congration of the Humility of Mary, CHM*, 1190-A N. Carrizo, #A, 79701.
Oblates of Notre Dame, 1400 Garden Ln., 79701.

ODESSA. *Daughters of Charity*, 3525 Oakridge Dr., 79762. Tel: 915-362-7358. P.O. Box 1294, Crane, 79721. Sisters 6; Total Staff 18.
Missionary Catechists of Divine Providence, 1321 W. Monahans, 79761.

ROWENA. *Sisters of Divine Providence*, Mailing Address: P.O. Box 132, 76875. Tel: 915-442-4021. 3301B Moss St., Midland, 79701. 1717 Idlewild St., Abilene, 79602. Sisters 1.

[C] ST. VINCENT DE PAUL SOCIETY

SAN ANGELO. *Catholic Outreach Services*, 12 N. Chadbourne, 76903. Tel: 915-658-4124. Thrift Store Social Services.

ABILENE. *St. Vincent De Paul Society*, 1241 Walnut, 79601. Tel: 915-677-6871.
St. Vincent De Paul Thrift Store. Total Assisted 12,000; Total Staff 3.

BIG SPRING. *St. Vincent De Paul Society*, 1009 Hearn, 79720.
Food Distribution. Families 663; People 1,953.

MIDLAND. *St. Vincent De Paul Society*. Mailing Address: P.O. Box 711, 79702-0711. Total Staff 2.

ODESSA. *Catholic Charities Community Services Odessa, Inc.*, 606 W. 10th, 79761. Tel: 915-332-1387.

STANTON. *St. Vincent De Paul Society*. Mailing Address: P.O. Box 158, 79782.

[D] CAMPUS MINISTRY

SAN ANGELO. *Catholic Newman Center*, 2451 Dena Dr., 76904. Tel: 915-949-8033. Sr. Marie Malachy Griffin, O.P., Campus Min. Total Staff 1.

[E] MISCELLANEOUS

SAN ANGELO. *Christ the King Retreat Center*, 802 Ford, 76905. Tel: 915-651-5352. Rev. Andy Wueste, O.M.I., Dir. Total in Residence 1; Total Staff 11.

RELIGIOUS INSTITUTES OF MEN REPRESENTED IN THE DIOCESE

For further details refer to the corresponding bracketed number in the Religious Institutes of Men or Women section.

[1330]—*Congregation of the Mission*. (St. Louis Province).—C.M.

[0520]—*Franciscan Friars*. (Province of St. John the Baptist).—O.F.M.

[1110]—*Missionaries of the Sacred Heart*. (Cork Ireland Prov.).—M.S.C.

[0910]—*Oblates of Mary Immaculate*. (Southern American Prov.).—O.M.I.

[0430]—*Order of Preachers (Dominicans)*. (Southern Prov.).—O.P.

[1070]—*Redemptorist Fathers*. (New Orleans Prov.).—C.Ss.R.

[1060]—*Society of the Precious Blood*. (Kansas City Prov.).—C.PP.S.

RELIGIOUS INSTITUTES OF WOMEN REPRESENTED IN THE DIOCESE

[]—*Adorers of the Blood of Christ*.—A.S.C.

[0320]—*Carmelite Nuns of the Ancient Observance*.—O.Carm.

[1010]—*Congregation of Divine Providence of San Antonio, Texas.*—C.D.P.
[0460]—*Congregation of Sisters of Charity of the Incarnate Word.*—C.C.V.I.
[]—*Congregation of the Humility of Mary.*—C.H.M.
[1070-13]—*Congregation of the Most Holy Rosary.*—O.P.
[0760]—*Daughters of Charity of St. Vincent De Paul.*—D.C.
[1070-03]—*Dominican Sisters.*—O.P.
[1070-24]—*Dominican Sisters.*—O.P.
[2430]—*Marist Sisters / Congregation of Mary.*—S.M.
[2690]—*Missionary Catechists of Divine Providence, San Antonio, Texas.*—M.C.D.P.
[2730]—*Missionary Sisters of Our Lady of the Holy Rosary.*—M.S.H.R.
[2960]—*Oblates of Notre Dame.*—O.N.D.
[]—*Oblates of Notre Dame.* (Midland, TX).
[2970]—*School Sisters of Notre Dame.*—S.S.N.D.
[1690]—*School Sisters of the Third Order of St. Francis.* (Pittsburgh, PA).—O.S.F.
[1570]—*Sisters of St. Francis of the Holy Family.*—O.S.F.
[2350]—*Sisters of the Living Word.*—S.L.W.

NECROLOGY

† Waldron, John, Midland, TX, St. Stephen. —Died Dec. 20, 1995.
† Wilde, Rev. Msgr. Alvin, Midland, TX, Our Lady of San Juan Church. —Died June 22, 1996.

Archdiocese of San Antonio

(Archidioecesis Sancti Antonii)

Most Reverend

PATRICK F. FLORES, D.D.

Archbishop of San Antonio; ordained May 26, 1956; appointed Titular Bishop of Italica and Auxiliary of San Antonio March 18, 1970; consecrated May 5, 1970; appointed Bishop of El Paso April 4, 1978; installed May 29, 1978; promoted Archiepiscopal See of San Antonio August 28, 1979; installed October 13, 1979. *Res., 2600 W. Woodlawn Ave., San Antonio, TX, 78228. All official communications to the Most Reverend Archbishop should be addressed to the Chancery Office, P.O. Box 28410, San Antonio, TX, 78228-0410.* Tel.: 210-734-2620.

Most Reverend

BERNARD F. POPP, D.D.

Retired Auxiliary Bishop of San Antonio; ordained February 24, 1943; appointed Titular Bishop of Capsus and Auxiliary Bishop of San Antonio June 7, 1983; consecrated July 25, 1983. *Res., 4535 Lord Rd., San Antonio, TX, 78220. Mailing Address: P.O. Box 28410, San Antonio, TX, 78228-0410.* Tel.: 210-734-2620.

ESTABLISHED AUGUST 28, 1874.

CREATED AN ARCHBISHOPRIC, AUGUST 3, 1926.

Square Miles 27,841.

The San Antonio Archdiocese comprises Atascosa, Bandera, Bexar, Comal, Dimmit, Edwards, Frio, Gillespie, Gonzales, Guadalupe, Karnes, Kendall, Kerr, Kinney, La Salle (that part of La Salle County north of the Nueces River), Maverick, McMullen (that part of McMullen County north of the Nueces River), Medina, Real, Uvalde, Val Verde, Wilson and Zavala.

For legal titles of parishes and archdiocesan institutions, consult the Chancery Office.

Chancery Office: 2718 W. Woodlawn Ave., P.O. Box 28410, San Antonio, TX, 78228-0410. Tel.: 210-734-2620; Fax: 210-734-0231.

STATISTICAL OVERVIEW

Personnel	
Archbishop	1
Auxiliary Bishops	1
Retired Bishops	1
Priests: Diocesan Active in Diocese	118
Priests: Active Outside Diocese	12
Priests: Retired, Sick or Absent	25
Number of Diocesan Priests	155
Religious Priests in Diocese	230
Extern Priests in Diocese	48
Ordinations:	
Diocesan Priests	5
Religious Priests	3
Transitional Deacons	1
Permanent Deacons	13
Permanent Deacons in Diocese	240
Total Brothers	96
Total Sisters	879
Parishes	
Parishes	143
With Resident Pastor:	
Resident Diocesan Priests	90
Resident Religious Priests	50
Without Resident Pastor:	
Administered by Priests	3
Missions	39
Pastoral Centers	3
Professional Ministry Personnel:	
Brothers	8
Sisters	39
Lay Ministers	121
Welfare	
Catholic Hospitals	5
Total Assisted	90,983
Health Care Centers	2
Total Assisted	14,476
Homes for the Aged	8
Total Assisted	497
Residential Care of Children	2
Total Assisted	180
Day Care and Extended Day Care Centers	13
Total Assisted	1,496
Specialized Homes	5
Total Assisted	2,538
Special Centers for Social Services	7
Total Assisted	296,813
Other Institutions	1
Total Assisted	80
Educational	
Seminaries, Diocesan	1
Students from This Diocese	7
Students from Other Diocese	27
Diocesan Students in Other Seminaries	7
Seminaries, Religious	11
Students Religious	35
Total Seminarians	49
Colleges and Universities	4
Total Students	11,090
High Schools, Diocesan and Parish	3
Total Students	1,139
High Schools, Private	6
Total Students	2,262
Elementary Schools, Diocesan and Parish	38
Total Students	11,569
Elementary Schools, Private	4
Total Students	1,594
Catechesis/Religious Education:	
High School Students	12,138
Elementary Students	35,035
Total Students Under Catholic Instruction	74,876
Teachers in the Diocese:	
Priests	41
Scholastics	1
Brothers	26
Sisters	164
Lay Teachers	1,509
Vital Statistics	
Receptions into the Church:	
Infant Baptism Totals	13,709
Adult Baptism Totals	463
Received into Full Communion	735
First Communions	9,868
Confirmations	5,646
Marriages:	
Catholic	2,312
Interfaith	528
Total Marriages	2,840
Deaths	4,875
Total Catholic Population	652,413
Total Population	1,828,740

Former Bishops—Rt. Rev. ANTHONY DOMINIC PELLICER, D.D., cons. Dec. 8, 1874; died April 14, 1880.—Rt. Rev. JOHN C. NERAZ, D.D., cons. May 8, 1881; died Nov. 15, 1894.—Rt. Rev. JOHN ANTHONY FOREST, D.D., cons. Oct. 28, 1895; died March 11, 1911.—Most Rev. JOHN W. SHAW, D.D., Coadjutor Bishop of San Antonio; appt. Feb. 7, 1910; cons. Titular Bishop of Castabala, April 14, 1910; succeeded to the See of San Antonio, March 11, 1911; made assistant at the Pontifical Throne, Sept., 1916; promoted to the See of New Orleans, Jan. 25, 1918; died Nov. 2, 1934.—Most Rev. ARTHUR JEROME DROSSAERTS, D.D., LL.D., Bishop of San Antonio; appt. July 18, 1918; cons. Dec. 8, 1918; named Archbishop, Aug. 3, 1926; assistant at the Pontifical Throne, Aug. 19, 1934; died Sept. 8, 1940.—Most Rev. ROBERT E. LUCEY, S.T.D., Bishop of Amarillo; appt. February 10, 1934; cons. May 1, 1934; promoted to the Archiepiscopal See of San Antonio, Jan. 23, 1941; died Aug. 1, 1977.—Most Rev. FRANCIS J. FUREY, Titular Bishop and Auxiliary of Philadelphia; appt. Aug. 24, 1960; cons. Dec. 22, 1960; promoted to Coadjutor and Apostolic Administrator "sede plena" of San Diego, July 25, 1963; promoted to Archiepiscopal See of San Antonio, June 4, 1969; Pallium conferred, Dec. 15, 1969; died April 23, 1979.

Vicar General and Moderator of the Curia—Rev. Msgr. LAWRENCE STUEBBEN, V.G.

Chancery Office—2718 W. Woodlawn Ave., P.O. Box 28410, San Antonio, 78228-0410. Tel: 210-734-2620; Fax: 210-734-0231. Office Hours: Mon.-Fri. 8:30-5.

Chancellor and Judicial Vicar—Rev. Msgr. PATRICK J. MURRAY, J.C.L., P.A.

Archives—Bro. EDWARD J. LOCH, S.M., Archivist.

Administrative Asst. to the Archbishop—Rev. Msgr. LAWRENCE J. STUEBBEN, V.G.

Office of the Archbishop—Secretaries to the Archbishop: MYRTLE G. SANCHEZ; CARMEN IRUEGAS, *2718 W. Woodlawn Ave., P.O. Box 28410, San Antonio, 78228-0410.*

Office of the Synod—Sr. JANET MARIE ABBACCHI, S.S.N.D., Coord., *P.O. Box 28410, San Antonio, 78228-0410.* Tel: 210-734-2620; Texas: 1-800-SYNOD-98.

College of Consultors—Most Rev. BERNARD F. POPP, D.D., V.G.; Most Rev. JOHN W. YANTA, D.D., V.G.; Rev. Msgr. PATRICK J. MURRAY, J.C.L., P.A.; Rev. Msgr. LAWRENCE STUEBBEN, V.G.; Rev. Msgr. JOHN FLYNN, V.U.; Rev. Msgr. THOMAS FLANAGAN; Rev. Msgr. EUGENE O'CALLAGHAN; Revs. DAVID GARCIA; STUART JULEEN.

Deans—In Metropolitan Area: North: Very Rev. GERALD HAMMEL, S.M., V.U., Central: Rev. Msgr. BALTHASAR JANACEK, V.U., Northwest: Rev. JOE AVILES, V.U., Northeast: Rev. JOHN O'DONOGHUE, V.U., Western: Very Rev. GILBERT OBIN, C.I.C.M., Southwest: Very Rev. LAWRENCE BRUMMER, O.F.M., V.U., Southeast: Very Rev. LAWRENCE JANEZIC, O.F.M., V.U., In Rural Area: Del Rio: Very Rev. RAMIRO CORTEZ, O.M.I., Floresville: Very Rev. WILLIAM MCNAMARA, V.F., Fredericksburg: Very Rev. MICHAEL BOULETTE, V.F., Hondo: Very Rev. WALLIS STILES, V.F., Pleasanton: Very Rev. MICHAEL YARBROUGH, V.F., Seguin: Very Rev. Msgr. EUGENE O'CALLAGHAN, V.F., Uvalde: Very Rev. PABLO SILICIA, V.F.

Vicars for Religious—Rev. Msgr. THOMAS FRENCH, *Incarnate Word Residence, 4515 Broadway, San Antonio, 78209.* Tel: 210-822-0385. Sr. CHARLENE WEDELICH, C.D.P., *P.O. Box 28410, San Antonio, 78228-0410.* Tel: 210-734-2620.

Vicar for Priests—Vacant.

Vicar for Retired Priests—Rev. Msgr. ALEXANDER WANGLER.

Archdiocesan Presbyteral Council—Most Rev. PATRICK F. FLORES, D.D.; Most Rev. BERNARD F. POPP, D.D., V.G.; Most Rev. JOHN W. YANTA, D.D.; Rev. Msgr. PATRICK J. MURRAY, J.C.L.; Rev. EDWARD BERNAL, Chm.; Rev. Msgr. LAWRENCE STUEBBEN, V.G.; Very Revs. JOHN O'DONOGHUE, V.U.; GERALD HAMMEL, S.M., V.U.; WALLIS STILES, V.F.; Rev. Msgr. EUGENE O'CALLAGHAN, V.F.; Rev. Msgr. ROY RIHN; Rev. Msgr. BALTHASAR JANACEK, V.U.; Very Revs. GILBERT OBIN, C.I.C.M., V.F.; JOE AVILES, V.U.; LAWRENCE JANEZIC, O.F.M., V.U.; LAWRENCE BRUMMER, O.F.M., V.U.; RAMIRO CORTEZ, O.M.I., V.F.; MICHAEL BOULETTE, V.F.; WILLIAM MCNAMARA, V.F.; MICHAEL YARBROUGH, V.F.; Rev. Msgr. PABLO SILICIA, V.F.; Rev. MICHAEL DEGEROLAMI.

Women's Commission—Mrs. MARTHA BRINKMANN, Chm., *P.O. Box 28410, San Antonio, 78228-0410.*

Archdiocesan Tribunal—*P.O. Box 28410, San Antonio, 78228-0410.* Tel: 210-734-2620, Ext. 135.

Judicial Vicar—Rev. Msgr. PATRICK J. MURRAY, J.C.L., P.A.

Adjutant Judicial Vicar—Rev. Msgr. TERENCE NOLAN, J.C.L.

Assistant Director—Mrs. MARY DELATTE.

Judges—Rev. Msgr. PATRICK J. MURRAY, J.C.L., P.A.; Rev. Msgr. JOHN FLYNN; Rev. Msgr. BERNARD MULLANEY; Rev. Msgr. TERENCE NOLAN, J.C.L.; Rev. Msgr. JAMES HENKE; Rev. Msgr. JAMES JANISH; Revs. EMMET CAROLAN; MICHAEL KENNY; JOSEPH LOPEZ.

Promotor Justitiae—Rev. Msgr. J. L. MANNING, J.C.D., P.A.

Defenders of the Bond—Revs. KEVIN RYAN; DENNIS DARILEK; PATRICK CRONIN; PAUL CLEARY; ROGELIO MARTINEZ; JOHN MAKOTHAKAT, J.C.D.; JOSEPH REYNA, J.C.L.; ADOLFO VALDIVIA, J.C.L.; Rev. Msgr. THOMAS MURPHY.

Approved Advocates—Rev. Msgr. J. L. MANNING, J.C.D., P.A.; Rev. Msgr. CHARLES PUGH; Rev. Msgr. JOSEPH DEANE; Rev. Msgr. LAMBERT BILY, V.U.; Revs. JOHN O'DONOGHUE, M.Ed.; Sr. ELIZABETH MCCULLOUGH, C.D.P.; STEVE GENGENBACHER; Rev. LESLIE A. VANCE, J.C.L.; Mrs. CARMEN MASON; Sr. BERNICE A. LINDSEY, O.S.B.; Mrs. ADRIAN FERRARO SEAWRIGHT; Mrs. EDNA BONO, M.S.W.

Notaries—Mrs. MARY DELATTE; Mrs. SUE FORBRICH; Mrs. CLAUDIA MENCK; Mrs. LORETTA REYES; Mr. EDWIN RYAN.

Interdiocesan Appellate Court—*P.O. Box 28410, San Antonio, 78228-0410.* Tel: 210-736-9444; 736-2620, Ext. 145, 147.

Moderator—Most Rev. PATRICK F. FLORES, D.D.

Judicial Vicar—Rev. FRED SACKETT, O.M.I., J.C.D.

Judges—Revs. MICHAEL A. JAMAIL, J.C.D. (BEA); LESLIE A. VANCE, J.C.L.; ALBERT HUBERTUS; TIMOTHY A. GOLLOB (DAL); Sr. MARGARET A. RAMSDEN, S.F.C.C., J.C.L.

Defenders of the Bond—Revs. RAY WILHELM, O.M.I., J.C.L.; WARREN A. BROWN, O.M.I., J.C.L.; RICHARD F. VAUGHAN (AMA); JAMES M. KOTARA; DENISE J. DOYLE, J.C.D., Ph.D.; LAURA L. LEFAVE, J.C.L.

Notary—DONNA MILLS.

Due Process: Councils of Conciliation and Arbitration—Mr. GEORGE VOLZ, K.C.S.G., Chm., *503 Mary Louise Dr., San Antonio, 78201.* Tel: 210-732-5670.

Diocesan Administration

Administrative Services Department—Rev. Msgr. LAWRENCE J. STUEBBEN, V.G., Dir., *P.O. Box 28410, San Antonio, 78228-0410.* Tel: 210-734-2620.

Archives—Bro. EDWARD J. LOCH, S.M., *P.O. Box 28410, San Antonio, 78228-0410.* Tel: 210-734-2620.

Archdiocesan Business Manager and Finance Officer—Mr. DAVID CASTILLEJA, *P.O. Box 28410, San Antonio, 78228-0410.* Tel: 210-734-2620; Fax: 210-734-2774.

Archdiocesan Development Office—Mr. CHRIS GRASSO, Dir., *P.O. Box 28410, San Antonio, 78228-0410.* Tel: 210-734-2620; Fax: 210-734-0231.

Archdiocesan Finance Council—Mrs. CARMEN RIVERO; Mrs. CARMEN TREVINO; Mr. C. J. KRAUSE; Mr. JOHN FENSKE Mr. VINCENT BEAULLIEU; Mr. TIM BRANIFF; Mr. ROGER CUMPIAN; Mr. JEFF PRUETT; Mr. DENNIS BIEDIGER; Mrs. JOAN LENNON; Mrs. MARY LOU BENAVIDES; Mr. LAWRENCE ERNST; Mr. AUGUST LUBANSKI; Deacon ROBERT KUSENBERGER.

Archdiocesan Debt Review Committee—Mr. DAVID CASTILLEJA, Sec.; Mr. RICHARD TREVINO, JR.; Mr. LOUIS SANCHEZ; Mr. GEORGE VOLZ; Mr. ALEX STEWART; Mr. JOHN D. SPECIA; Mr. S. F. DANYSH; Mrs. JENNITA POSTON; Mrs. DORA ANN VERDE; Mr. JOHN F. KRAMER.

Building Board—Messrs. EDWARD TSCHOEPE; COSMO F. GUIDO; JACK LOPEZ; DAN CERNA; STEVE PERSYN.

Lay Pension Plan—Mr. RENE WILKES, Mgr., *P.O. Box 28410, San Antonio, 78228-0410.* Tel: 210-734-2620.

Archdiocesan Cemeteries Office—Most Rev. BERNARD F. POPP, D.D., V.G., Dir.; Mr. ALBERT J. SANCHEZ, Supt., *746 Castroville Rd., San Antonio, 78207.* Tel: 210-432-2303.

Computer Center—CHUCK HUGHES, *P.O. Box 28410, San Antonio, 78228-0410.* Tel: 210-734-2620.

Director of Accounting—DELIA THOMAS, *P.O. Box 28410, San Antonio, 78228-0410.* Tel: 210-734-2620.

Parish Accounting System—Ms. ROSE RODRIGUEZ. Tel: 210-734-2420.

Print/Mail Room—MARIA HINJOSA. Tel: 210-734-2620; Fax: 210-734-0231.

Department of Educational Services—Sr. THERESE SAN MIGUEL O.S.F., Dir., *P.O. Box 28410, San Antonio, 78228-0410.* Tel: 210-734-2620.

Archdiocesan Schools Office—Mr. DALE HOYT, Supt., *P.O. Box 28410, San Antonio, 78228-0410.* Tel: 210-734-2620.

Archdiocesan Catechetical-Religious Education Center—BONNIE LE MELLE ABADIE, Dir., *P.O. Box 28410, San Antonio, 78228-0410.* Tel: 210-734-2620.

Office of Catholic Youth Ministry-CYO—Mr. PAT PERILLO, Dir., *P.O. Box 28410, San Antonio, 78228-0410.* Tel: 210-734-2620.

Catholic Committee on Scouting (Boys)—Rev. JOE AVILES, V.U., Chap. ALBERT REITER, Chm., *13023 El Marro, San Antonio, 78233-5835.* Tel: 210-653-5404.

Catholic Committee on Girl Scouting—Deacon BOB HENNESSY, Chap. FRAN POTEET, Chm., *4807 Lambeth Dr., San Antonio, 78228.* Tel: 210-734-7960.

Campus Ministry (Newman Apostolate)—Sr. GLORIA URRABAZO, M.C.D.P., Dir. SAC, St. Philip's, UTSA, Palo Alto, Texas Lutheran, Schreiner College, Kerrville, Trinity, UT Health Science Center, S.W. Texas Junior College-Uvalde. *Catholic Student Center, 312 Courtland, San Antonio, 78212.* Tel: 210-736-3752.

Family Life Office—Mr. STEVE GENGENBACHER, Dir., *P.O. Box 28140, San Antonio, 78228-0410.* Tel: 210-734-2620.

Life Concerns Ministry—Mr. GENE TOWNSEND, Life Concerns Advocate, *P.O. Box 28140, San Antonio, 78228-0410.* Tel: 210-734-2620.

Natural Family Planning Office—Mrs. HENRIETTA O'CONNOR, Dir., *P.O. Box 28410, San Antonio, 78228.* Tel: 210-734-2620.

Office of Worship—Rev. Msgr. JAMES HENKE, Chm., Liturgy Commission; DOLORES MARTINEZ, Dir., *P.O. Box 28410, San Antonio, 78228-0410.* Tel: 210-734-2620.

Missions Awareness Office—(Holy Childhood Pontifical Assn.; Propagation of the Faith); MARY WISNIEWSKI Dir., *P.O. Box 28410, San Antonio, 78228-0410.* Tel: 210-734-2620.

Catholic Adult Faith Enrichment (C.A.F.E.)—Bro. JOSEPH ESPARZA, C.S.C., Consultant, *P.O. Box 28140, San Antonio, 78228-0410.* Tel: 210-734-2620.

Department of Personnel Services—Most Rev. JOHN W. YANTA, D.D., *P.O. Box 28410, San Antonio, 78228-0410.* Tel: 210-734-2620.

Priests Personnel Board—Most Rev. JOHN W. YANTA, D.D., Chm.; Rev. Msgr. BALTHASAR JANACEK, V.U.; Rev. Msgr. LIAM BROSNAM; Revs. JOE AVILES, V.U.; NORMAN ERMIS; Rev. Msgr. ALBERT HUBERTUS; Rev. Msgr. DERMOT BROSNAN; Revs. STUART JULEEN; ANTHONY CUMMINS; PHILLIP HENNING; JOE LOPEZ.

Office for Priests—Most Rev. JOHN W. YANTA, D.D., *P.O. Box 28410, San Antonio, 78228-0410.* Tel: 210-734-2620.

Catholic Consultation Center—LILLIAN YONKERS, Exec. Dir., *11103 West Ave., Ste. 202, San Antonio, 78213.* Tel: 210-377-1133; Fax: 210-377-1230.

Assumption-St. John's Seminary—Rev. DAVID CRUZ,(LUB.) '86; *P.O. Box 28240, San Antonio, 78284.* Tel: 210-734-5137.

Permanent Diaconate Program—Rev. JOHN O'DONOGHUE, Dir., *2600 W. Woodlawn Ave., P.O. Box 28240, San Antonio, 78284-2701.* Tel: 210-734-0114.

Vocation Office—Rev. CARLOS VELAZQUEZ, Dir.; Sr. CECILIA ANN CAVAZOS, M.C.D.P., Assoc. Dir., *2600 W. Woodlawn Ave., P.O. Box 28240, San Antonio, 78228-0410.* Tel: 210-734-0553.

Pro-Life Office—Most Rev. JOHN YANTA, D.D., Dir.; Mr. PETER MONOD DE FROIDVILLE, Assoc. Dir., *P.O. Box 28410, San Antonio, 78228-0410.* Tel: 210-734-2620; Fax: 210-734-0231.

Catholic Television of San Antonio—(CTSA) Channel 22; Sr. CHARLENE WEDELICH, C.D.P., Interim Dir. Fax: 210-734-2939.

Today's Catholic Newspaper—Mrs. MARTHA PACK BRINKMAN, Editor. Fax: 210-734-2939.

Department of Social and Community Services—Rev. MICHAEL DEGEROLAMI, Dir., *P.O. Box 28410, San Antonio, 78228-0410.* Tel: 210-734-2620.

Office of Social Concerns—Rev. MICHAEL DEGEROLAMI, Dir. CARMEN BADILLO, Assoc. Dir., *P.O. Box 28410, San Antonio, 78228-0410.* Tel: 210-734-2620.

Campaign for Human Development—Mrs. IRMA CARDENAS, Dir. Tel: 210-734-2620.

Ministry to Hearing Impaired—CHERYL VAN LEEUWEN RIOS, *223 E. Summit, San Antonio, 78212.* Tel: 210-731-8404 (Voice); 731-9208 (TDD).

Ministry to Persons with Disabilities—BECKY VILLARREAL, *815 McDougal, San Antonio, 78223.* Tel: 210-533-3120.

Bexar County Detention Ministries—Sr. MARGARET CAREW, C.C.V.I. Tel: 210-270-6328. Sr. TERESA CARTER, C.S.B. Tel: 210-270-6329. Deacon GILBERT PRATT. Tel: 210-270-6457. Rev. LEN BRONIAK, C.SS.R. Tel: 210-270-6320., *200 N. Comal, San Antonio, 78207.* Rev. KEVIN MANION, C.M.F., *600 Mission Rd., San Antonio, 78210.* Tel: 210-531-1189. Deacon A. C. CAMERO; FABIAN DOMINGUEZ, *State Jail, 6535 Cagnon Rd., San Antonio, 78252.* Tel: 210-675-6620. Each works in a different area of the jails.

St. Peter and Joseph's Home—(See Protective Institutions).

Seton Home—(See Protective Institutions).

Health Ministry Committee—Rev. MICHAEL DEGEROLAMI.

Catholic Charities, Archdiocese of San Antonio—VALERIE TREVINO, Interim Dir., *2903 W. Salinas St., San Antonio, 78207.* Tel: 210-433-3256; Fax: 210-433-0851.

Refugee Resettlement Services—Vacant. Tel: 210-433-3256.

Director Immigration Services—JULIE ESCALANTE, ESQ., *2903 W. Salinas St., San Antonio, 78207.* Tel: 210-433-3256.

Diocesan Offices And Directors

Apostleship of Prayer—Vacant.

Archdiocesan Council of Catholic Women—Mrs. EMMA CANNON, *4803 Bill Anders Dr., San Antonio, 78219.* Tel: 210-661-7145. Rev. JOE AVILES, V.U., *1710 Clower, San Antonio, 78201-3597.* Tel: 210-735-5269.

Catholic Center for Charismatic Renewal—Rev. THOMAS FLANAGAN, Dir., Liaison, *1707 S. Flores, San Antonio, 78204.* Tel: 210-226-7545; 7546.

Catholic Lawyers Guild—Rev. Msgr. PATRICK J. MURRAY, J.C.L., P.A., Spiritual Moderator, *P.O. Box 28410, San Antonio, 78228-0410.* Tel: 210-734-2620.

Catholic Physicians Guild—Rev. JOHN A. LEIES, S.M., S.T.D.; MIGUEL BEDOLLA, M.D., Ph.D., Pres., *520 Fordham Ln., San Antonio, 78228.* Tel: 210-436-3227.

Censores Librorum—Revs. FRED SACKETT, O.M.I.; CHARLES NEUMANN, S.M.

Movimiento de Apostolado Familiar & Marriage Encounter (Rural)—Rev. ABRAHAM LA TORRE, (Colombia), *3107 N. St. Mary's St., San Antonio, 78212.* Tel: 210-732-6295.

Movimiento Familiar Cristano (Urban)—Presidents: CHELO MEDINA; JOSE MEDINA, *9215 Brink, San Antonio, 78221.* Tel: 210-924-2972.

Christian Life Communities—Vacant.

Black Catholic Apostolate—Deacon THOMAS WHITE, Dir., *1819 Nevada, San Antonio, 78203.* Tel: 210-532-5358.

Cursillo Movement (Spanish)—Mr. JOE BERRELEZ, *419 S. Moreno, Pearsall, 78061.* Tel: 210-334-4876.

Cursillo Movement (English)—Sr. BERNICE LINDSEY, O.S.B., *416 W. Highland Dr., Boerne, 78006.* Tel:

210-816-8504; 210-922-4061.

Ecumenical Affairs—Rev. J. WILLIS LANGLINAIS, S.M., Dir., *One Camino Santa Maria, P.O. Box 18, San Antonio, 78228-8518.* Tel: 210-436-3092.

Holy Childhood, Pontifical Association—MARY WISNIEWSKI, *P.O. Box 28410, San Antonio, 78228-0410.* Tel: 210-734-2620.

Holy Name Society—ISIDRO LEOS, JR., *363 Pinewood, San Antonio, 78216.* Tel: 210-828-1089.

Pre-Seminary Program—Rev. CARLOS VELAZQUEZ, Dir., *Assumption Seminary, P.O. Box 28240, San Antonio, 78284.* Tel: 210-735-0553.

Priests Eucharistic League—Rev. THOMAS FLANAGAN, Dir., *6097 Kitchener, San Antonio, 78240.* Tel: 210-696-0896.

Propagation of the Faith—MARY WISNIEWSKI, *P.O. Box 28410, San Antonio, 78228-0410.*

Public Relations Council—Col. JOSEPH B. MCSHANE, *1410 Treasure Way, San Antonio, 78209.* Tel: 210-826-3361.

Retreats, Men—Rev. THOMAS OVALLE, O.M.I., Dir., *Oblate Renewal Center, 127 Oblate Dr., San Antonio, 78216.* Tel: 210-349-4173.

Respect Life Program—Rev. SHERRILL SMITH, Moderator, *2127 S. Zarzamora, San Antonio, 78207.* Tel: 210-224-8474.

Rural Life Conference—Vacant.

St. Vincent de Paul Society—Ms. NELL SHARROCK, Pres., Mailing Address: *928 W. Commerce, San Antonio, 78207.* Tel: 210-225-7837.

CLERGY, PARISHES, MISSIONS AND PAROCHIAL SCHOOLS

CITY OF SAN ANTONIO

1—CATHEDRAL OF SAN FERNANDO (1731), Revs. David Garcia; Jose Arturo Cepeda; James L. Emperur, S.J.; Deacons Albert Garza; Doroteo E. Pedroza.
Res., 115 Main Plaza, 78205. Tel: 210-227-1297; Fax: 210-271-0149.
Catechesis/Religious Programs—Sr. Clara Ruiz, H.C.G., D.R.E. Students 713.
Mission—San Antonio, Bexar Co., San Francesco di Paola, 205 Piazza Italia, 78207. Tel: 210-227-0548. Rev. Balthasar J. Janacek.

2—BLESSED SACRAMENT (1956), Rev. John O'Donoghue; Deacons Joe Fertitta; Wayne Chycinski; Joseph Jorgensen.
Office: 600 Oblate Dr., 78216. Tel: 210-824-7231; Fax: 210-822-2144.
School—Sr. Eileen Gurecky, Prin. Sisters of Incarnate Word and Blessed Sacrament 2; Lay Teachers 11; Students 298; Day Care 108.
Catechesis/Religious Programs—Students 261.

3—CHRIST THE KING (1928) (Hispanic), Rev. Richard Pena; Esther Rodriguez, Admin.; Deacon Rudy Pena.
Res., 2623 Perez St., 78207. Tel: 210-433-6301; Fax: 210-435-2736.
Catechesis/Religious Programs—Sr. Adelina Esquivel, M.C.M., D.R.E. Students 239.

4—DIVINE PROVIDENCE (1981), Rev. P. John Mannion, M.S.C.; Deacons Jose Suniga; Juan G. Martinez.
Church—5667 Old Pearsall Rd., 78242-2335. Tel: 210-623-3970; Fax: 210-623-3978.
Catechesis/Religious Programs—Sr. Eileen Howley, P.B.V.M., D.R.E. Students 669.

5—HOLY FAMILY (1963) (Hispanic), Revs. James Kotara; Antonio Hernandez; Deacons Armando Scott; Manuel Carranza; Javier Tamez.
Res., 152 Florencia, 78228-5899. Tel: 210-433-8216.
Catechesis/Religious Programs—Tel: 210-433-3006. Ester Mango, D.R.E. Students 333.

6—HOLY NAME (1961) (Polish/Hispanic), Rev. Franciszek Kurzaj; Deacon David L. Herbert.
Res., 3814 Nash Blvd., 78223. Tel: 210-333-5020; 5021.
School—Tel: 210-333-7356; Fax: 210-333-7642. Mrs. Miriam Christiansen, Prin. Lay Teachers 21; Students 335.
Catechesis/Religious Programs—Tel: 210-333-3613; Fax: 210-333-5021. Margaret Miksch, D.R.E. Students 212.

7—HOLY REDEEMER (1910) (African American), Rev. Norbert Rosso, C.S.Sp.; Deacon Thomas White.
Res., 1819 Nevada, 78203. Tel: 210-532-5358.

8—HOLY ROSARY (1948) (Hispanic), Revs. John J. Manahan, S.M.; Bernard Meyer, S.M. Pastoral Assocs.: Bros. James Droste, S.M.; James McCaffrey, S.M.; Robert Hatesohl, S.M.; Deacons Felipe Barajas; Earl Colley.
Res., 159 Camino Santa Maria, 78228. Tel: 210-433-3241; Fax: 210-433-2133.
School—155 Camino Santa Maria, 78228. Tel: 210-433-4312. Sr. Bernice Mallory, S.H.Sp., Prin. Sisters 2; Deacons 1; Lay Teachers 17; Students 225.
Catechesis/Religious Programs—Sr. Joyce Des Jardines, S.S.N.D., D.R.E. Students 270.

9—HOLY SPIRIT (1964), Rev. Anthony Pesek; Rev. Msgr. Lawrence F. Walsh.
Res., 758 W. Ramsey Rd., 78216. Tel: 210-341-1395; Fax: 210-341-8438.
School—770 W. Ramsey Rd., 78216. Tel: 210-349-1169; Fax: 210-349-1247. Mrs. Joann Gawlik, Prin. Lay Teachers 32; Students 415.
Catechesis/Religious Programs—Tel: 210-341-1397. Pat Keene, D.R.E. Students 641.

10—HOLY TRINITY (1987), Rev. Douglas Fater; Deacon Jerry Micek.
Res., 20523 Huebner Rd., 78258. Tel: 210-497-4200; Fax: 210-497-4285.
Catechesis/Religious Programs—Gail Zitz, D.R.E. Students 313.

11—IMMACULATE CONCEPTION (1933) (Hispanic), Rev. Msgr. Leo Martinez; Deacons Ignacio T. Martinez; Antonio R. Munoz.
Res., 314 Merida St., 78207. Tel: 210-225-2986; Fax: 210-225-2987.
Catechesis/Religious Programs—Students 100.

12—IMMACULATE HEART OF MARY (1912) (Hispanic), Revs. Ignacio Blanco, C.M.F.; Robert Alvarado, C.M.F.; Connie Bonilla, Admin.; Deacons Jorge Bonilla-Valentin; Alfredo Cervantes. In res., Revs. Peter Caballe, C.M.F.; Michael Cecere, C.M.F.; George Sturm, C.M.F.; Richard Trevino, C.M.F.
Res., 617 S. Santa Rosa Blvd., 78204. Tel: 210-226-8268; 8269; Fax: 210-222-1479.
Catechesis/Religious Programs—Teresa Soria, D.R.E. Students 125.

13—OUR LADY OF THE ANGELS (1947) (Hispanic), Revs. Luis Gerardo Arraiza, O.F.M.Cap. (Spain); Gregorio Goicoechea, O.F.M.Cap. (Spain); Deacon Albert Ramirez.
Res., 1214 Stonewall St., 78211. Tel: 210-924-6591; Fax: 210-924-6593.
Catechesis/Religious Programs—Mary Jessie Rodriguez, D.R.E. Students 450.

14—OUR LADY OF THE ATONEMENT CATHOLIC (1983). (A Personal Parish for the Anglican Common Identity). Rev. Christopher G. Phillips.
Res., 8015 Shady Hollow Ln., 78255. Tel: 210-695-3332.
Church—15415 Red Robin Rd., 78255. Tel: 210-695-2944; Fax: 210-695-9679.
School—Atonement Academy, Tel: 210-695-2240. Lay Teachers 8; Students 62.

15—OUR LADY OF GOOD COUNSEL (1952) (Hispanic), Revs. Paul Van Coillie, C.I.C.M., D.R.E.; Celestin Tongotani, C.I.C.M.; Deacon Robert Cruz.
Res., 1204 Castroville Rd., 78237. Tel: 210-432-0873.
Catechesis/Religious Programs—Remolino Center, 107 Remolino, 78237. Students 455.

16—OUR LADY OF GRACE (1938), Rev. Msgr. Terence Nolan; Rev. Thomas Kavanaugh, C.M.; Deacon Robert Schonhoff.
Res., 223 E. Summit Ave., 78212. Tel: 210-734-7285; Fax: 210-734-8334.

17—OUR LADY OF GUADALUPE (1911) (Hispanic), Revs. James L. Lambert, S.J.; Martin L. Elsner, S.J.; Samuel Rosales, S.J.; Bro. Alexander Gussio, S.J.; Deacons Joe Camero; Robert Galvan; Leon Kattengell; Carlos Sandoval.
Res., 1321 El Paso St., 78207. Tel: 210-226-4064; Fax: 210-226-4973.
Catechesis/Religious Programs—Rev. Michael Bouzigard, S.J. Students 80.
Mission—San Antonio, Bexar Co., Santa Cruz, 1303 Tampico, 78207.

18—OUR LADY OF MT. CARMEL AND ST. THERESE, DISCALCED CARMELITE FATHERS (1926) (Hispanic), Revs. John Suenram, O.C.D., Supr.; Ralph Reyes, O.C.D.; Michael Okuroski, O.C.D.; Louis Scagnelli, O.C.D.; Christopher Timoney, O.C.D.; James A. Curiel, O.C.D.; Deacon Dan Cisneros.
Res., 906 Kentucky Ave., 78201-6097. Tel: 210-735-9126; Fax: 210-735-1389 (parish); 738-0818 (res.).
School—905 Kentucky Ave., 78201. Tel: 210-732-9207; Fax: 210-732-3214. Sr. Eileen Mannion, S.H.Sp., Prin. Sisters of the Holy Ghost 3; Lay Teachers 10; Students 265.
Catechesis/Religious Programs—Sr. Dympna Clark, S.H.Sp., D.R.E. Students 314.

19—OUR LADY OF PERPETUAL HELP (1913) (Hispanic), Rev. John R. Cody, C.SS.R. Pastoral Assocs.: Sr. Consuelo Morales, M.P.S.; Sr. Monica Rodriguez, M.P.S.
Res., 618 S. Grimes St., 78203. Tel: 210-532-7031; Fax: 210-534-1280.
Catechesis/Religious Programs—Tel: 210-534-7193. Students 151.

20—OUR LADY OF SORROWS (1915) (Hispanic), Rev. Lambert S. Bily; Deacon Jesse Fraga. In res., Revs. Abraham LaTorre; Marian Piekarczyk, S.D.S., (Poland) Dir. Polish Catholic Mission.
Res., 3107 N. St. Mary's St., 78212. Tel: 210-732-6295; 736-6719 (Polish).
Catechesis/Religious Programs—Donna Salas, D.R.E. Students 160.

21—PRINCE OF PEACE (1980), Rev. Patrick Cronin; Deacons Art Marin; Pino Sanabria; Tom Neal.
Res., 7893 N. Grissom Rd., 78251. Tel: 210-681-8330; Fax: 210-681-2286.
Catechesis/Religious Programs—Tel: 210-681-5063. Shirley Jones, D.R.E. Students 1,370.

22—RESURRECTION OF THE LORD, Rev. Paul A. Raaz; Deacon Thomas Swift.
Offices & Mailing Address: 7990 W. Military Dr., 78227. Tel: 210-675-1470.
Res., 7151 Cypress Grove, 78227.
Catechesis/Religious Programs—Students 558.

23—SACRED HEART (1899) (Hispanic), Revs. Walter O. D'heedene, C.I.C.M.; Mark Rayalipunna, C.I.C.M.; Deacon Valentine Gallegos.
Res., 2114 W. Houston St., 78207-3496. Tel: 210-227-5059; Fax: 210-227-6209.
Catechesis/Religious Programs—Tel: 210-227-9763. Sr. Juanita Ramirez, D.R.E. Students 215.

24—ST. AGNES (1923) (Hispanic), Rev. Msgr. Peter O'Callaghan; Deacon Leon Guerrero. In res., Very Rev. Lawrence Stuebben, V.G.
Res., 804 Ruiz St., 78207. Tel: 210-227-8258.
Catechesis/Religious Programs—Tel: 210-226-4441. Sr. Margaret Mary Barrett, D.R.E. Students 483.

25—ST. ALPHONSUS (1925) (Hispanic), Rev. Jose Luis Sandoval; Sr. Adele Massaro, Pastoral Assoc.
Res., 2004 Chihuahua St., 78207. Tel: 210-433-9365; Fax: 210-433-9365.
Catechesis/Religious Programs—Tel: 210-432-3176. Terry Boone, D.R.E. Students 67.

26—ST. ANN (1912) (Hispanic), Revs. Richard B. Williams, O.P.; Cayet Mangiaracina, O.P.; Deacon Richard Hormachea.
Res., 210 St. Ann St., 78201. Tel: 210-734-6687; Fax: 210-738-1755.
School—Tel: 210-735-2341. David Fernandez, Prin. Sisters 3; Lay Teachers 6; Students 146.
Catechesis/Religious Programs—Tel: 210-733-9681. Students 350.

27—ST. ANTHONY MARY CLARET (1988), Rev. Albert Hubertus.
Res., 6150 Roft Rd., 78253. Tel: 210-688-9033; Fax: 210-688-3575.
Catechesis/Religious Programs—Linda Burrage, D.R.E. Students 508.

28—ST. ANTHONY OF PADUA (1957), Rev. William J. Collins, M.S.C.; Sr. Dorothea O'Meara, C.S.B., Admin.; Deacon Gilbert Wiessler.
Res., 102 Lorenz Rd., 78209. Tel: 210-824-1743; Fax: 210-824-0167.
Catechesis/Religious Programs—Tel: 210-824-6740. Mrs. Carmen Ortiz, D.R.E. Students 251.

29—ST. BENEDICT (1958) (Polish/Hispanic), Rev. Edward A. Pavlicek, Jr.; Most Rev. Bernard F. Popp, D.D.; Deacon Dan Kearns.
Res., 4535 Lord Rd., 78220. Tel: 210-648-0123; Fax: 210-648-1722.
School—Mrs. Frances Grams, Prin. Lay Teachers 13; Students 177.
Catechesis/Religious Programs—Tel: 210-648-4632. Deborah Desjean, D.R.E. Students 207.

30—ST. BONAVENTURE (1959) (Hispanic), Revs. Raymond Schuster; Toby Guerrero; Deacons Fidel Hinojosa; Amador Gonzalez; Edward Patino.
Res., 1918 Palo Alto Rd., 78211. Tel: 210-922-1685; Fax: 210-922-7821.
Catechesis/Religious Programs—Tel: 210-922-1882. Mrs. Diane Guerra, D.R.E. Students 500.

31—St. Brigid (1972), Revs. Thomas Flanagan; Francis M. Landwermeyer, S.J.; Jeannette Easley, Pastoral Admin.; Deacons Thomas Billimek; Pasquale M. Benigno; George G. Alberty, Jr.; Roy Amo; Peter Gutierrez.
Res., 6907 Kitchener Rd., 78240. Tel: 210-696-0896; Fax: 210-696-7319.
Catechesis/Religious Programs—Charlene Staedtler, D.R.E.
Students 320.

32—St. Cecilia (1919), Rev. Msgr. Joseph Deane; Rev. Robert Bovenzi, C.P.; Phyllis Evans, Pastoral Assoc.; Deacon Fred Quarles. In res., Rev. Kevin Manion, C.M.F.
Res., 125 W. Whittier St., 78210-2897. Tel: 210-533-7109.
School—Dr. Barbara Wagner, Prin. Sisters 7; Lay Teachers 6; Students 260.
Catechesis/Religious Programs—Rose M. Luera, D.R.E.
Students 325.
Mission—San Antonio, Bexar Co., Purisima Concepcion, 807 Mission Rd., 78210.

33—St. Clare (1968) (Hispanic), Rev. Gary German, O.F.M.; Deacons Florencio Moreno, Jr.; Charles F. Pope, Sr.
Res., 7701 Somerset Rd., 78211. Tel: 210-924-5252.
Catechesis/Religious Programs—Mercedes G. Cortes, D.R.E.
Students 222.

34—St. Dominic (1971), Revs. Paul Cleary; Joseph Pena; Deacons Henry Medina; Robert L. Garza; Lionel Garza; Alan Fitzpatrick; Ree Stockton; Jimmie Trevino; Bert Stewart.
Res., 5919 Ingram Rd., 78228. Tel: 210-435-6211; 435-0114; Fax: 210-435-1732.
Catechesis/Religious Programs—Sue Graves, D.R.E.
Students 644.

35—St. Francis of Assisi (1980), Rev. Msgr. James Henke; Deacons Tom Franklin; Anton Svatek; Ed Bozek; Gilbert Pratt; Bruce Bellg.
Res., 4201 De Zavala Rd., 78249-2000. Tel: 210-492-4600; Fax: 210-492-8128.
Education Office—Tel: 210-492-4683.
Catechesis/Religious Programs—Pat Hanavan, D.R.E.
Students 511.

36—St. Gabriel (1958) (Hispanic), Rev. Louis Jaspers, C.I.C.M. (Belgium); Carmen Morales, Admin.; Deacon Frank Castellano.
Res., 747 S.W. 39th St., 78237. Tel: 210-433-3689.
Catechesis/Religious Programs—Tel: 210-432-3354. Mavis Montemayor, D.R.E.
Students 188.

37—St. Gerard Majella (1911), Rev. Gerard F. Siebold, C.SS.R.
Res., 1617 Iowa St., 78203. Tel: 210-533-0161 (Church Office).
School—1619 Iowa St., 78203. Tel: 210-533-9541. Mrs. Peggy Burt, Prin.
Sisters 1; Lay Teachers 11; Students 238.
High School—Archdiocesan Regional, 521 S. New Braunfels Ave., 78203. Tel: 210-533-8061. Maurice Abadie, Prin.
Sisters 1; Lay Teachers 17; Students 204.
Catechesis/Religious Programs—Students 150.

38—St. Gregory's (1955), Rev. Michael B. O'Gorman. Pastoral Assocs.: Sr. M. Carmel O'Callaghan, P.B.V.M.; Sr. Luz Valdez, M.C.M.; Deacons Don Novian; Fred Campos, Jr.
Res., 700 Dewhurst, 78213. Tel: 210-342-5271; Fax: 210-342-0542.
School—Tel: 210-342-0281. Joyce Z. Burc, Prin.
Lay Teachers 35; Students 628.
Catechesis/Religious Programs—Tel: 210-342-3826. Allison Baez, D.R.E.
Students 400.

39—St. Helena (1974), Rev. Leo M. Dolan.
Office: 14714 Edgemont, 78247. Tel: 210-653-3316; Fax: 210-653-3163.
Res., 14527 Angora, 78247. Tel: 210-653-3850.
Catechesis/Religious Programs—Tel: 210-653-3316. D.R.E.: Suzan Roy; Joan Raymond.
Students 747.

40—St. Henry (1904) (Hispanic), Rev. Msgr. Emil J. Wesselsky.
Res., 1619 S. Flores St., 78204. Tel: 210-225-6877.
Catechesis/Religious Programs—Sr. Diana O. Rodriguez, H.C.G., D.R.E.
Students 206.

41—St. James the Apostle (1954) (Hispanic), Rev. Emmit Carolan; Onofre Toscano, Pastoral Assoc.; Deacon John McDonald.
Res., 907 W. Theo Ave., 78225. Tel: 210-922-2136; Fax: 210-923-0940.
School—Tel: 210-924-1201; Fax: 210-924-1201. Sr. Carmen Botello, F.M.A., Prin.
Daughters of Mary Help of Christians 4; Lay Teachers 19; Students 419.
Catechesis/Religious Programs—Tel: 210-922-4061. Mary Toscano, D.R.E.
Students 735.

42—St. John, the Evangelist (1956), Rev. Edward Kelly; Deacons Rosendo Urrabazo; Evan Wittig; Hugo Chavez.
Res., 102 S. Audubon Dr., 78212. Tel: 210-828-2201; Fax: 210-738-0599.
School—128 S. Audubon Dr., 78212. Tel: 210-735-3526. Mrs. Linda Murphy, Prin.
Sisters 2; Lay Teachers 11; Students 304.
Catechesis/Religious Programs—D.R.E.: Gloria Chavez; Lisa Flores.
Students 165.

43—St. John Berchmans (1910) (Hispanic), Revs. Edward M. Bernal; James M. Hynes (Peru); Deacons Jose Diaz; James T. Raso; Librado Cena.
Res., 1147 Cupples Rd., 78226. Tel: 210-434-3247; Fax: 210-432-0431.
School—Tel: 210-433-0411; Fax: 210-433-2335. Sr. Mary Andreen, Prin.
Sisters 3; Lay Teachers 17; Students 262.
Catechesis/Religious Programs—Tel: 210-433-2121. Marta Lucia Salazar, D.R.E.
Students 431.

44—St. John Neumann (1977), Rev. Robert Silverman.
Church—6680 Crestway Dr., 78239. Tel: 210-654-1643; Fax: 210-654-1645.
Catechesis/Religious Programs—Tel: 210-654-3707.
Students 340.

45—St. Joseph (Downtown) (1868) (German), Rev. Thomas J. Fitzgerald, S.S.S. In res., Bro. Martin Hayes, S.S.S.
Res., 623 E. Commerce St., 78205. Tel: 210-227-0126; Fax: 210-227-7690. [CEM]

46—St. Joseph (South San) (1935) (Hispanic), Revs. Eugene Michel, O.F.M.; Lawrence Brummer, O.F.M.; Deacons Leon Mueller; Genaro Herrera. In res., Rev. Michael Haney, O.F.M.
Res., 535 New Laredo Hwy., 78211-1900. Tel: 210-924-4383.
School—2372 W. Southcross St., 78211. Tel: 210-922-0193; 923-7910. Mrs. Margaret Schlueter, Prin.
Brothers 1; Lay Teachers 14; Students 207.
Catechesis/Religious Programs—Tel: 210-924-4383. Mrs. Imelda Morales, D.R.E.
Students 350.

47—St. Jude (1954) (Hispanic), Rev. Jose A. Giganto, O.S.A. In res., Rev. Leonidas Fresno, O.S.A.
Res., 130 S. San Augustine Ave., 78237. Tel: 210-432-8044; Fax: 210-432-1760.
Catechesis/Religious Programs—Tel: 210-432-5786. Rosalinda F. Rodriguez, D.R.E.
Students 358.
Mission—San Antonio, Santa Maria Goretti.

48—St. Lawrence (1959) (Hispanic), Rev. Adolfo A. Valdivia; Deacons Alois Keller; Richard Gonzalez.
Res., 236 E. Petaluma, 78221. Tel: 210-924-4401; Fax: 210-924-4401.
Catechesis/Religious Programs—Students 450.

49—St. Leo (1919) (Hispanic), Revs. Enda McKenna; Jeffery Pehl. Pastoral Assocs.: Sr. Joanne Whalen; Deacons John Landez; Alvino Pacheco; Thomas Torres.
Res., 123 Octavia Pl., 78214. Tel: 210-533-9108; Fax: 210-533-0643.
School—119 Octavia Pl., 78214. Tel: 210-532-3166; Fax: 210-532-5997. Illene Richter, Prin.
Religious 1; Lay Teachers 11; Students 350.
Catechesis/Religious Programs—Tel: 210-532-7317. Lupe Sielski, D.R.E.
Students 350.

50—St. Leonard's (1966) (Hispanic), Revs. Michael Haney, O.F.M.; Jesus Aguirre-Garza, O.F.M.; Deacon Carlos Salinas.
Res., 8510 S. Zarzamora, 78224-2099. Tel: 210-924-6000; Fax: 210-924-5552.
Catechesis/Religious Programs—Students 500.

51—St. Luke (1959), Rev. Patrick J. Ragsdale; Deacon Robert Hennessy.
Office: 4603 Manitou, 78228-1889. Tel: 210-433-2777; Fax: 210-432-2419.
Res., 6014 Horizon, 78228.
School—Tel: 210-434-2011. Dr. Harold A. Kreger, Prin.
Lay Teachers 31; Students 576.
Catechesis/Religious Programs—Tel: 210-436-0339; Fax: 210-433-2778. Deacon Robert Hennessy, D.R.E.
Students 650.

52—St. Margaret Mary (1955) (Hispanic), Revs. Michael Kenny; Anthony Cowan; Deacons Wilfred Lamb; Gerardo Mechler; Charles Roel; Zeke Moczygemba.
Res., 1314 Fair Ave., 78223. Tel: 210-532-6309; Fax: 210-532-6333.
School—Tel: 210-534-6137. Miss Susan Bukala, Prin.
Felician Sisters 2; Lay Teachers 19; Students 498.
Catechesis/Religious Programs—Theresa Pawelek, D.R.E.
Students 358.
Mission—San Antonio, St. Catherine.

53—St. Mark the Evangelist (1976), Rev. Kevin E. Ryan; Dorothea G. Hamlin, Pastoral Admin.; Deacons Paul De Lauter; Ernest Zepeda; Steve Marques.
Res., 1602 Thousand Oaks Dr., 78232-2398. Tel: 210-494-1606; 1607; Fax: 210-494-4957.
Catechesis/Religious Programs—Tel: 210-494-7434.
Students 1,096.

54—St. Martin de Porres (1964) (Hispanic), Rev. Gilbert Obin, C.I.C.M., D.R.E.; Deacon Jose Menchaca.
Res., 1730 Dahlgreen St., 78237. Tel: 210-432-5203.
Catechesis/Religious Programs—Tel: 210-436-2071.
Students 284.

55—St. Mary (1852), Rev. Michael Levy, O.M.I.
Res., 202 N. St. Mary's St., 78205. Tel: 210-226-8381.
School—207 N. St. Mary's St., 78205. Tel: 210-223-8581. Mrs. Beatrice Aleman, Prin.
Sisters 3; Lay Teachers 10; Students 170.

56—St. Mary Magdalen (1940) (Hispanic), Revs. Joe Aviles; Dennis A. Jarzombek.
Res., 1710 Clower St., 78201. Tel: 210-735-5269; Fax: 210-738-0698.
School—Tel: 210-735-1381. Sr. Patricia O'Sullivan, Prin.
Presentation Sisters 3; Incarnate Word Sisters 1; Lay Teachers 10; Students 214.
Catechesis/Religious Programs—Tel: 210-735-5284. Linda Froboese, D.R.E.
Students 771.

57—St. Matthew's (1968), Rev. Msgr. John F. Flynn; Revs. Don C. Shepanski; James G. Galvin; Deacons Tom Fox; Wilbur Hoelschler; Horacio Tudon; Keith Werner.
Res., 10703 Wurzbach Rd., 78230. Tel: 210-696-4161; Fax: 210-696-7624.
School—Tel: 210-696-7433. Cynthia Salinas, Prin.
Sisters 2; Lay Teachers 34; Students 602.
Catechesis/Religious Programs—Fax: 210-696-8858. Sr. Therese Gleitz, D.R.E.
Students 1,618.

58—St. Michael (1866) (Hispanic), Rev. Jesus Murugarren, O.S.A. (Spain); Lillie Ramirez, Admin. Pastoral Assocs.: Juan Garcia; Alice Olivera; Nicholas Farley.
Res., 418 Indiana, 78210. Tel: 210-532-3707; Fax: 210-532-3707. [CEM]
Catechesis/Religious Programs—Students 148.

59—St. Patrick (1893) (Hispanic), Rev. James Conway; Deacon Ray Prevott. In res., Rev. Thomas McSwiggan.
Res., 1114 Willow St., 78208. Tel: 210-226-5223; Fax: 210-227-8616.
Catechesis/Religious Programs—Sr. Alicia Drone, A.S.C., D.R.E.
Students 198.

60—St. Paul (1954) (Hispanic), Revs. Dennis Darilek; Jimmy D. Drennan; Johnny E. Sapia, Admin.; Deacons Clayton Mangold; Daniel Muriada. In res., Rev. Michael DeGerolami.
Res., 350 Sutton Dr., 78228-3199. Tel: 210-733-7152; Fax: 210-733-0929.
School—307 John Adams, 78228. Tel: 210-732-2741. Sr. Virginia Huser, C.D.P., Prin.
Religious Sisters 1; Lay Teachers 23; Students 420.
Catechesis/Religious Programs—Virginia Valenzuela, D.R.E.
Students 500.

61—St. Peter Prince of the Apostles (1923), Rev. Msgr. Thomas Murphy; Teresa Berg, Admin.; Deacons John Dunn; John Spitzer; Raymond Cross.
Res., 111 Barilla Pl., 78209. Tel: 210-822-3367; Fax: 210-828-5826.
School—112 Marcia Pl., 78209. Tel: 210-824-3171; Fax: 210-822-4504. Mary Ann Leopold, Prin.
Lay Teachers 25; Students 473.
Catechesis/Religious Programs—Tel: 210-822-1605. Alma Small, D.R.E.
Students 275.

62—St. Philip of Jesus (1914) (Hispanic), Revs. Pablo Paniagua; John M. Pagel (CHL); Deacons G. T. Zapata; Jose Sanchez.
Res., 131 Bank St., 78204. Tel: 210-226-5024.
School—134 E. Lambert St., 78204. Tel: 210-222-2872; Fax: 210-229-1829. Sr. Celly Ann Amparano, Prin.
Sisters 3; Lay Teachers 9; Aides 3; Students 275.
Catechesis/Religious Programs—Tel: 210-225-6622. Sr. Marian Sturm, I.W.B.S., D.R.E.
Students 131.

63—St. Pius X (1957), Rev. Msgr. Liam P. Brosnan; Rev. Msgr. William C. Martin; Deacon Thomas Crowley.

Office: 3303 Urban Crest, 78209. Tel: 210-824-0139; Fax: 210-829-5125.
Res., 654 Cave Ln., 78209. Tel: 210-826-4064.
School—(Grades PreK-8) 7734 Robin Rest Dr., 78209. Tel: 210-824-6431. Mrs. Celeste Bonsignore, Prin.
Lay Teachers 22; Students 378.
Catechesis/Religious Programs—Diana Carpenter, D.R.E.
Students 361.

64—ST. ROSE OF LIMA (1981), Revs. Juan Alfaro; Virgil Elizondo; Deacons Rey Jasso; Anthony Lira; Chester Ostaszewski.
Res., 9883 Marbach Rd., 78245. Tel: 210-675-1920; Fax: 210-675-6067.
Catechesis/Religious Programs—D.R.E.: Sr. Martha Ruiz, H.C.G.; Sr. Maria Concepcion Garcia, H.C.G.
Students 859.

65—ST. STEPHEN (1965) (Hispanic), Rev. Sherrill Smith; Deacon Henry Dillard.
Res., 2127 S. Zarzamora St., 78207. Tel: 210-224-8474; Fax: 210-224-8474.

66—ST. THOMAS MORE (1964), Rev. John M. Makothakat; Deacon Jerome Ciarrocchi.
Res., 4411 Moana, 78218. Tel: 210-655-5070; Fax: 210-655-8446.
School—4427 Moana, 78218. Tel: 210-655-2882; Fax: 210-655-9603. Mrs. Mary Jane Regel, Prin.
Presentation Sisters 1; Lay Teachers 11; Students 280.
Catechesis/Religious Programs—Tel: 210-654-6824. Mrs. Carol McGuire, D.R.E.
Students 264.

67—ST. TIMOTHY'S (1953) (Hispanic), Rev. Bernard M. Rochon, S.M.; Deacons Pedro M. Soriano; Rudy Medrano; Antonio Caballero; Tomas Alvarado.
Res., 1515 Saltillo St., 78207. Tel: 210-434-2391.

68—ST. VINCENT DE PAUL (1961), Rev. Jose Luis De La Rosa.
Res., 4222 S.W. Loop 410, 78227-4495. Tel: 210-674-1200; Fax: 210-674-1640.
Catechesis/Religious Programs—Tel: 210-674-4291. Cathy Canty, D.R.E.
Students 502.

69—SAN FRANCISCO DE LA ESPADA (1731) (Hispanic), Rev. Lawrence Janezic, O.F.M.; Deacon Ricardo Medina, III.
Res., 10040 Espada Rd., 78214. Tel: 210-627-2064; Fax: 210-527-2064.
Catechesis/Religious Programs—Hope Esparza, D.R.E.
Students 190.
Mission—San Antonio, St. Francis Cabrini.

70—SAN JOSE Y SAN MIGUEL (1720) (Hispanic), Revs. Herbert Jones, O.F.M.; John Abts, O.F.M.; Jesus M. Aguirre-Garza, O.F.M.; Sr. Immaculata Kelly, P.B.V.M., Pastoral Assoc.; Deacon Santiago Rodriguez. In res., Rev. Arturo Miguel O Campo, O.F.M.; Bros. Ben Eastman, O.F.M.; Thomas Eisenmenger, O.F.M.
Res., 701 E. Pyron Ave., 78214. Tel: 210-922-0543; Fax: 210-922-1041 (Friars).
Catechesis/Religious Programs—Kathleen Rollow, D.R.E.
Students 175.

71—SAN JUAN CAPISTRANO (1731) (Hispanic), Rev. Jorge Baistra.
Mailing Address: 9101 Graf Rd., 78214.
Church—78214. Tel: 210-534-3161.
Mission—Southton, St. Ann.

72—SAN JUAN DE LOS LAGOS (1952) (Hispanic), Rev. Galeb Mokarzel, O.M.I.; Bro. Ben Juarez, O.M.I., Pastoral Assoc.; Deacons Albert Salinas; Eleodoro Vasquez.
Res., 3231 El Paso St., 78207. Tel: 210-433-9722.
Catechesis/Religious Programs—Tel: 210-433-2411.
Students 175.

73—SENYOR SANTO NINO DE CEBU (1993) (Filipino), Rev. Ernest Palaming, O.F.M.Cap.
Mailing Address: P.O. Box 33514, 78265. Tel: 210-650-3288.
Res., c/o Rev. Ernest Palaming, O.F.M.Cap., 1730 Dahlgreen St., 78237. Tel: 210-333-7006.

74—VIETNAMESE MARTYERS CATHOLIC CENTER (1976), Rev. Dominic Luong, S.S.S.
Centers—1210 S. W.W. White, P.O. Box 28023, 78208. Tel: 210-359-5923.

OUTSIDE THE CITY OF SAN ANTONIO

Asherton, Dimmit Co., Immaculate Conception (1918) (Hispanic), Rev. Mauricio A. Lopez.
Res., P.O. Box 8, 78827. Tel: 210-468-3343.
Catechesis/Religious Programs—Sr. Maria del Carmen, D.R.E.
Sisters 4; Students 150.
Missions—Big Wells, St. Michael; Catarina, St. Henry.

Bandera, Bandera Co., St. Stanislaus (1855) (Polish), Rev. Msgr. Michael G. McManus.
Res., Box 757, 78003-0757. Tel: 210-460-4712; Fax: 210-796-7641. [CEM]
Catechesis/Religious Programs—Tel: 210-796-3573. Elouise Mangold, D.R.E.
Students 220.
Mission—Medina Lake, Bandera Co., St. Victor's Chapel, Park Rd. 37, Lakehills, 78063. Tel: 210-612-3012.

Boerne, Kendall Co., St. Peter the Apostle (1866) (German), Rev. Anthony O. Cummins; Mary Ann Chandler, Admin.
Mailing Address: 119 Kronkosky, 78006. Tel: 210-816-2233; Fax: 210-816-2143.
Catechesis/Religious Programs—D.R.E.: Val Marko; Rebecca Cash; Jeanette Belter.
Students 650.

Brackettville, Kinney Co., St. Mary Magdalen (1875), Rev. James Cashin; Deacon Robert W. Nelson, D.R.E.
Res., Box 95, 78832. Tel: 210-563-2487. [CEM]
Catechesis/Religious Programs—James Bader, D.R.E.
Students 215.
Mission—Spofford Junction, St. Blaise.

Canyon Lake, Comal Co., St. Thomas the Apostle (1967), Rev. Patrick J. Palmer.
Res., HC 4, Box 402, 78133-4113. Tel: 210-964-3497.

Carrizo Springs, Dimmit Co., Our Lady of Guadalupe (1881) (Hispanic), Rev. Msgr. Pablo A. Sicilia; Deacons Jose F. Perez; Genaro Ramon; Juan Sauceda.
Res., 1107 N. Eighth St., 78834. Tel: 210-876-2239.
Catechesis/Religious Programs—Tel: 210-876-5150.
Students 621.

Castroville, Medina Co., St. Louis (1844), Rev. Mike Horan; Jeri White, Pastoral Assoc.; Deacon Gene Ebner.
Res., 610 Madrid, 78009. Tel: 210-538-2267; Fax: 210-931-9016. [CEM]
School—Tel: 210-931-3544. Vickie Tschirhart, Prin.
Lay Teachers 12; Students 175.
Catechesis/Religious Programs—Tel: 210-931-2556. Jeri White, D.R.E.
Students 419.
Mission—Mico, St. Francis of Assisi (Medina Lake Chapel).

Cestohowa, Karnes Co., Nativity of the Blessed Virgin Mary (1873) (Polish), Revs. Damien Tomiczek, S.D.S.; Gregory Sawicki, S.D.S.
Res., Rte. 1, Box 20, 78113. Tel: 210-745-2633. [CEM]

Charlotte, Atascosa Co., St. Rose of Lima (1909) (Hispanic), Rev. John Wagner.
Mailing Address: P.O. Box 69, 78011. Tel: 210-277-1242.
Catechesis/Religious Programs—Students 169.
Mission—Tilden, St. Joseph, Tel: 512-274-3374.

Comfort, Kendall Co., Sacred Heart (1949), Rev. Joseph P. Petsch.
Church—510 Broadway, 78013. Tel: 210-995-3708; Fax: 210-995-2952.
Res., 104 Daniel St., 78013. Tel 210-995-3501.
Catechesis/Religious Programs—Students 126.

Converse, Bexar Co., St. Monica (1959), Rev. Msgr. Patrick J. Flanagan (Ireland).
Res., 501 North St., P.O. Box 429, 78109. Tel: 210-658-3816.
School—Tel: 210-658-6701. James Mollicone, Prin.
Lay Teachers 19; Students 517; Day Care 251.
Catechesis/Religious Programs—Janice Van Slambrouck, D.R.E.
Students 346.

Cotulla, La Salle Co., Sacred Heart (1884) (Hispanic), Rev. John van Lare, C.M. (Holland); Deacon Jose Patterson.
Res., P.O. Box 560, 78014. Tel: 210-879-2658. [CEM]
Catechesis/Religious Programs—Tel: 210-879-3196. Sr. Petra Salgado, D.R.E.
Students 230.

Crystal City, Zavala Co., Sacred Heart (1917) (Hispanic), Rev. Msgr. Jose Maria Guevara (Peru); Deacons Jose L. Lopez; Jose G. Garza.
Res., 115 E. Kinney St., 78839. Tel: 210-374-3148; Fax: 210-374-2211.
Catechesis/Religious Programs—Tel: 210-374-5547. Deacon Jose G. Garza, D.R.E.
Students 204.

Del Rio, Val Verde Co., Our Lady of Guadalupe (1906) (Hispanic), Revs. Jose Caracoza Perez, M.N.M.; Armando Guerrero Mendoza, M.N.M.; Deacons Eliesar Hernandez; Adrian Falcon.
Res., 509 Garza St., 78840. Tel: 210-775-3713; Fax: 210-775-9161.
Catechesis/Religious Programs—Tel: 210-775-2178. Rev. Armando Mendoza, D.R.E.
Students 480.

Sacred Heart (1895), Rev. Gerard Barrett, O.M.I.; Deacons John C. Graf; Robert C. Kusenberger; David B. Scarbo.
Mailing Address: P.O. Box 1503, 78840.
Office: 302 E. Greenwood, 78840.
Res., 411 Spring St., 78840. Tel: 210-775-2143; Fax: 210-775-2143. [CEM]
Church—304 Mill St., 78840.
School—209 E. Greenwood, 78840. Tel: 210-775-3274. Mrs. Terri Barrera, Prin.
Lay Teachers 17; Students 241.
Catechesis/Religious Programs—Sr. Theresa P. Hereford, D.R.E.
Students 207.

St. Joseph's (1927) (Hispanic), Rev. Roberto Pena, O.M.I.; Deacons Filomeno Salazar; Federico Cuellar.
Res., 510 Wernett St., P.O. Box 1455, 78840. Tel: 210-775-4753; Fax: 210-775-5200.
Catechesis/Religious Programs—Tel: 210-775-5200. D.R.E.: Raymundo Mendoza; Yolanda Mendoza.
Students 750.
Mission—Comstock, Mary, Queen of the Universe.

Devine, Medina Co., St. Joseph's (1897), Rev. Clement De Meersman, C.I.C.M.
Res., 108 S. Washington Dr., 78016. Tel: 210-663-2244. [CEM]
Catechesis/Religious Programs—Janie Saucedo, D.R.E.
Students 210.

D'Hanis, Medina Co., Holy Cross (1847) (Hispanic), Rev. Wallis Stiles.
Res., P.O. Box 426, 78850. Tel: 210-363-7268. [CEM]
Catechesis/Religious Programs—Students 170.

Dilley, Frio Co., St. Joseph's (1899) (Hispanic), Rev. Salvador Pedroza.
Res., 114 E. Frio, P.O. Box N, 78017. Tel: 210-965-1926.
Catechesis/Religious Programs—Josefa Canales, D.R.E.
Students 200.
Mission—Dilley, St. Mary.

Eagle Pass, Maverick Co., Our Lady of Refuge (1859) (Hispanic), Revs. Richard Beck, O.M.I.; Patricio Dominguez, O.M.I.; Deacon Efren Maldonado.
Office: Box 909, 78853-0909. Tel: 210-773-8451; Fax: 210-757-2557.
Res., 810 Ceylon St., Box 909, 78853. Tel: 210-773-8421. [CEM]
School—Tel: 210-773-3531. Sr. Elizabeth Orr, Prin.
Sisters of Charity of the Incarnate Word 1; Lay Teachers 13; Students 183.
Catechesis/Religious Programs—Tel: 210-773-6011. Sr. Irene Mejia, D.R.E.
Students 307.
Missions—Seco Mines, Our Lady of Lourdes, Tel: 210-773-8288; Quemado, Our Lady of Guadalupe, Tel: 210-758-1888.

Sacred Heart (1967) (Hispanic), Rev. Ramiro Cortez, O.M.I.; Deacon Manuel Cardona.
Res., 2055 William St., P.O. Box 806, 78852. Tel: 210-773-2451.
Catechesis/Religious Programs—Tel: 210-773-5013 (Parish Hall); Fax: 210-758-1023. Carmen S. Garcia, D.R.E.
Students 1,030.
Mission—El Indio, Our Lady of San Juan.

St. Joseph's (1967), Rev. John McGrath, O.M.I. Administrators: Jesus de la Garza; Graciela T. Gonzalez.
Res., P.O. Box 246, 78852. Tel: 210-773-6114.
Catechesis/Religious Programs—Tel: 210-773-6515; 773-6536. Mrs. Gloria R. Cantu, D.R.E.
Students 416.

Elmendorf, Bexar Co., St. Anthony (1896) (Hispanic), Rev. William McNamara; Deacon John K. Miller.
Res., P.O. Box 248, 78112. Tel: 210-635-8539; Fax: 210-835-8644. [CEM]
Catechesis/Religious Programs—Anita Casillas, D.R.E.
Students 200.
Mission—Saspamco, Our Lady of Perpetual Help. [CEM]

Falls City, Karnes Co., Holy Trinity (1902) (Polish), Rev. Jan Piotr Klak (Poland).
Res., Box 158, 78113. Tel: 210-254-3539; Fax: 210-254-3530. [CEM]
Catechesis/Religious Programs—Rose Lee Moczygemba, D.R.E.
Students 178.

Floresville, Wilson Co., Sacred Heart (1882), Rev. Victor Carrillo; Rose Marie Pennartz, Admin.; Deacons Scott Donaho; Mike Perez.
Res., 1009 Trail St., 78114. Tel: 210-393-6117. [CEM]

School—Tel: 210-393-2117. Bro. Joseph Ballard, C.S.C., Prin.
Sisters 2; Lay Teachers 8; Students 133.
Catechesis/Religious Programs—Debbie Leal, D.R.E.
Students 325.

Fredericksburg, Gillespie Co., St. Mary's (1846) (German), Revs. Phillip D. Henning; Eduardo D. Morales; Deacons Gregorio Martinez, Jr.; Francisco De La Torre.
Mailing Address: P.O. Box 152, 78624.
Res., 306 W. San Antonio St., 78624. Tel: 210-997-9523; Fax: 210-997-1037. [CEM]
School—Tel: 210-997-3914; 997-2203; Fax: 210-997-2382. Billy Pahl, Prin.
Lay Teachers 19; Students 352.
Catechesis/Religious Programs—Charlene Staedtler, D.R.E.
Students 267.
Mission—Fredericksburg, Our Lady of Guadalupe.

Gonzales, Gonzales Co., St. James (1885), Revs. Francisco A. Macias; Ubaldo Santos, C.M.F.; Deacon Alfonso Moreno.
Res., 417 N. College St., 78629. Tel: 210-672-2945. [CEM]
Catechesis/Religious Programs—Tel: 210-672-6291.
Students 425.
Missions—Gonzales, Gonzales Co., Sacred Heart; Waelder, Gonzales Co., St. Patrick.
Stations—Gonzales, Care Inn of Gonzales.; Ottine, Warm Springs Rehabilitation Hospital, Tel: 210-672-6592.

Harper, Gillespie Co., St. Anthony's (1909), Rev. David C. Meurer.
Res., Box 318, 78631. Tel: 210-864-4026. [CEM]

Helotes, Bexar Co., Our Lady of Guadalupe (1942), Revs. Gerald Hammel, S.M.; Gerald Pleva, S.M.; Deacon Timothy Houlihan.
Res., P.O. Box 36, 78023. Tel: 210-695-8791; Fax: 210-695-9957. [CEM]
Catechesis/Religious Programs—D.R.E.: Nancy Drymala; Jan Growney; Cindy TeJeda; Mary Shrader.
Students 775.

Hobson, Karnes Co., St. Boniface (1901) (Polish), Revs. Damien Tomiczek, S.D.S. (Poland); Gregory Sawicki, S.D.S.
Res., P.O. Box 135, 78117. Tel: 210-780-3559. [CEM]

Hondo, Medina Co., St. John the Evangelist (1892), Rev. Msgr. Vincent Fecher; Deacon Albert Villa; Martina Saathoff, Admin.
Res., 2102 Avenue J, 78861. Tel: 210-741-2236. [CEM]
Catechesis/Religious Programs—Tel: 210-426-2565. D.R.E.: Norma Villa; Barbara Sisneros.
Students 640.
Mission—Yancey, Immaculate Heart of Mary.

Jourdanton, Atascosa Co., St. Matthew's, Rev. Michael H. Yarbrough, Admin.; Deacons Eusebio Guevara; Welton Fiedler.
Mailing Address: Box 670, 78026.
Res., 1700 Campbell, 78026. Tel: 210-769-3687; Fax: 210-769-2861. [CEM]
Catechesis/Religious Programs—D.R.E.: Lydia Brown; Judy Hooge; Sr. Karen Schwane, O.S.U.
Students 134.
Mission—Christine, St. Ignatius.

Karnes City, Karnes Co., St. Cornelius (1917), Rev. Stuart Juleen.
Res., 605 E. Calvert St., 78118. Tel: 210-780-3947.
Catechesis/Religious Programs—Tel: 210-780-3949. Sr. Rose Anthony McClosky, O.L.V.M., D.R.E.
Students 350.
Mission—Fashing, St. Elizabeth.

Kenedy, Karnes Co., Our Lady of Peace (1959), Revs. Patrick P. Bergin (CC); John Flanagan, M.S.F.
Res., 1 Notre Dame Pl., 78119. Tel: 210-583-2417.
Catechesis/Religious Programs—Tel: 210-583-2247. Janie Hernandez, D.R.E.
Students 272.

Kerrville, Kerr Co., Notre Dame (1889), Revs. Michael J. Boulette; Anthony Vilano; Deacon Joseph H. Holmstrom, Jr.
Res., 909 Main St., 78028. Tel: 210-257-5961; Fax: 210-257-5961.
School—923 Main St., 78028. Tel: 210-257-6707; Fax: 210-896-6686. Sr. Conchessa Johnston, C.C.V.I., Prin.
Sisters of Charity of the Incarnate Word 5; Lay Teachers 10; Students 249.
Catechesis/Religious Programs—Tel: 210-896-4233. Mrs. Lou Chamberlain, D.R.E.
Students 255.

Kirby, Bexar Co., St. Joan of Arc (1971), Rev. Leslie A. Vance; Deacons John Buchanan; Joe Kopecky; Robert Galan, Jr.; John X. Huttinger; Joseph P. Nash.
Res., 2829 Ackermann Rd., San Antonio, 78219. Tel: 210-661-5277.
Catechesis/Religious Programs—Tel: 210-661-2220. Mrs. Paulette Petron, D.R.E.
Students 395.

Kosciuszko, Wilson Co., St. Ann's (1898) (Polish), Rev. Edward Wanat, S.D.S.
Res., Rte. 2, Box 76, Stockdale, 78160. Tel: 210-745-2541; Fax: 210-745-2434. [CEM]

LaCoste, Medina Co., Our Lady of Grace (1911) (Hispanic), Rev. Msgr. Thomas M. Palmer.
Res., P.O. Box 39, 78039. Tel: 210-985-3346; Fax: 210-762-3334. [CEM]
Catechesis/Religious Programs—Mary Ann Mangold, D.R.E.
Students 400.

La Pryor, Zavala Co., St. Joseph (1917) (Hispanic), Rev. Jose Luis Balderas; Deacons Gene Orrigan; Juan Gallegos.
Res., P.O. Box 436, 78872. Tel: 210-365-4107.
Mission—Batesville, St. Patrick.

La Vernia, Wilson Co., St. Ann (1917), Rev. Peter McKenna.
Mailing Address: P.O. Box 256, 78121.
Res., 78121. Tel: 210-779-3131.
Catechesis/Religious Programs—D.R.E.: Angela Puchot; Robin Thompson; Ginger McDowell; Pat Recker; Clay Bordner.
Students 341.

Leon Springs, Bexar Co., St. Elizabeth Ann Seton (1961), Rev. Patrick L. Marron.
Res., Leon Springs, 7655 Curres Cir., Boerne, 78015-6503. Tel: 210-698-1941; Fax: 210-698-1983.
Catechesis/Religious Programs—Students 158.

Losoya, Bexar Co., El Carmen Catholic Church (1898) (Hispanic). (Our Lady of Mt. Carmel). Rev. Richard J. McCarthy, C.M., Admin. In res., Rev. Oscar J. Miller, C.M.
Res., 18555 Leal Rd. (Losoya), San Antonio, 78221. Tel: 210-626-2333.
Catechesis/Religious Programs—Tel: 210-626-1063. D.R.E.: Emily Ortiz; Mary Esther Rodriguez.
Students 390.

Lytle, Atascosa Co., St. Andrew (1904), Rev. Francis Vanhee.
Res., P.O. Box 326, 78052. Tel: 210-709-4287. [CEM]
Catechesis/Religious Programs—Students 342.
Missions—Natalia, St. John Bosco; Coal Mine, Immaculate Conception.

Macdona, Bexar Co., Our Lady Queen of Heaven (1944) (Hispanic), Rev. Rudolph T. Carrola.
Res., 9961 Aliann, 78054.
Mailing Address: P.O. Box 94, 78054-0094. Tel: 210-622-3282; Fax: 210-622-3282.

Martinez, Bexar Co., St. Jerome (1925), Rev. Thomas J. O'Brien; Deacon Joe Champagne.
Res., 7955 Real Rd., San Antonio, 78263. Tel: 210-648-2694; Fax: 210-648-3690. [CEM]
Catechesis/Religious Programs—Tel: 210-648-0336. Shirley Bordovsky, D.R.E.
Students 252.

New Braunfels, Comal Co., Holy Family (1964), Rev. James Wasser; Amelia Lankford, Pastoral Assoc.
Res., 245 S. Hidalgo, 78130. Tel: 210-609-5320; Fax: 210-609-5322.
Catechesis/Religious Programs—Tel: 210-608-9615. Loraine Blant, D.R.E.
Students 350.

Our Lady of Perpetual Help (1926), Rev. Richard Oberstar, M.S.F.; Deacons Cayetano Morales; Ramond Ybarra.
Res., 138 W. Austin St., 78130. Tel: 210-625-3534.
Catechesis/Religious Programs—Elizabeth Martinez, D.R.E.
Students 225.
Mission—Hunter, St. John. [CEM]

SS. Peter and Paul (1845), Rev. Msgr. Eugene O'Callaghan, V.F.; Rev. Msgr. Edward Bily; Deacons Fred Fey; Ray Kaufman; Ben Wehman; Frank Fikac; William Schroeder; James Behling.
Res., 386 N. Castell St., 78130. Tel: 210-625-4531; Fax: 210-625-5461. [CEM]
School—Tel: 210-625-3233; Fax: 210-625-3246. Norma A. Miller, Prin.
Lay Teachers 15; Students 344.
Catechesis/Religious Programs—386 N. Castell, 78130. Tel: 210-625-1519. Bill Smith, D.R.E.
Students 675.
Mission—Comal, St. Joseph.

Nixon, Gonzales Co., St. Joseph's (1915), Rev. David G. Zumaya; Deacons Dimas Medina; Daniel Medina, Sr.
Res., 207 S. Washington Ave., 78140-2920. Tel: 210-582-1127. [CEM]
Catechesis/Religious Programs—Students 30.

Panna Maria, Karnes Co., Immaculate Conception of the Blessed Virgin Mary (1854) (Polish), Rev. Jan Piotr Klak (Poland).
Res., P.O. Box 9, 78144. Tel: 210-780-2748. [CEM]
Mission—Helena, St. Helena.

Pearsall, Frio Co., Immaculate Heart of Mary (1891), Rev. Joseph A. Reyna; Deacon Manuel Carrizales.
Res., 422 W. Brazos, P.O. Box AK, 78061. Tel: 210-334-2382. [CEM]
Catechesis/Religious Programs—Tel: 210-334-4879. Esther Martinez, D.R.E.
Students 584.

Pleasanton, Atascosa Co., St. Andrew (1913), Rev. Carlos Davalos; Deacons Norman Phillips; Jose Valenzuela.
Res., 626 Market St., 78064-2747. Tel: 210-569-3356; Fax: 210-281-4902. [CEM]
Catechesis/Religious Programs—Sr. Dorothy Moczygemba, C.S.S.F., D.R.E.
Students 500.
Mission—Campbellton, Sacred Heart.

St. Luke-Loire (1859), Rev. James Hoelscher; Deacons Jose Trevino; Richard Gonzalez.
Res., Rte. 1, P.O. Box 81, 78064. Tel: 210-393-6763.
Catechesis/Religious Programs—Students 153.
Mission—Leming, Our Lady of Guadalupe. [CEM]

Poteet, Atascosa Co., St. Philip Benizi (1897) (Hispanic), Rev. Felix A. Avau, C.I.C.M.
Res., P.O. Box 348, 78065. Tel: 210-742-3796. [CEM]
Catechesis/Religious Programs—Beatrice Bermudez, D.R.E.
Students 240.

Poth, Wilson Co., Blessed Sacrament (1910) (Hispanic/Polish), Rev. Samuel Heitkamp.
Res., P.O. Box 339, 78147. Tel: 210-484-3302. [CEM]
Catechesis/Religious Programs—Tel: 210-484-3303. Cherral Frerich, D.R.E.
Students 396.

Rocksprings, Edwards Co., Sacred Heart of Mary (1900) (Hispanic), Rev. Jeremiah Murphy, M.S.C.
Res., P.O. Box 887, 78880. Tel: 210-683-2165.
Missions—Camp Wood, St. Mary Magdalen; Leakey, St. Raymond of Pennafort.

Runge, Karnes Co., St. Anthony's (1901) (Polish), Revs. Paschal Bergin (CC) Admin.; John Flanagan, M.S.F.
Mailing Address: P.O. Box 188, 78151.
Res., Arsenso St., 78151. Tel: 210-239-4146. [CEM 2]

Sabinal, Uvalde Co., St. Patrick's (1884), Rev. James Dudley, M.S.C.
Res., Box 117, 78881. Tel: 210-988-2255.
Missions—Knippa, St. Joseph; Vanderpool, St. Mary.

St. Hedwig, Bexar Co., Annunciation of the Blessed Virgin Mary (1868) (Polish), Rev. Bill Zadora, S.D.S. (Poland).
Res., P.O. Box 100, 78152. Tel: 210-667-1232; Fax: 210-667-1232. [CEM]
Catechesis/Religious Programs—Sr. Luz Moreno, D.R.E.
Students 300.

Schertz, Guadalupe Co., Church of the Good Shepherd (1972), Rev. Roger P. Robbins; Mrs. Micki Christy, Admin.; Deacons John J. Gorman; Paul La Combe.
Res., P.O. Box 929, 78154. Tel: 210-658-4350.
Catechesis/Religious Programs—Tel: 210-658-6188. D.R.E.: Mrs. Gerry Stift; Mrs. Joan Smith.
Students 375.
Mission—Marion, Immaculate Conception.

Seguin, Guadalupe Co., Our Lady of Guadalupe (1908) (Hispanic), Revs. Gerard Mackin, M.S.F.; James E. Wuerth, M.S.F.; Deacons Nick Carillo; Juan Garza.
Res., 409 W. Krezdorn, 78155-4429. Tel: 210-379-4338. [CEM]
Catechesis/Religious Programs—Tel: 210-379-2818. Mr. George Oliva, D.R.E.
Students 850.

St. James (1873), Rev. Gerald Hubertus.
Res., 510 S. Camp St., 78155. Tel: 210-379-1796; Fax: 210-379-1796. [CEM]
School—510 S. Austin St., 78155. Tel: 210-379-2878; Fax: 210-379-2878. Janice Jessen, Prin.
Sisters 2; Lay Teachers 11; Students 237.
Catechesis/Religious Programs—D.R.E.: Marianne Miller; Terri Broussard.
Students 250.

Selma, Bexar Co., Our Lady of Perpetual Help (1897), Rev. Conor McGrath; Deacons Clifford Friesenhahn; Robert Thayer.
Res., 16075 N. Evans Rd., 78154-3824. Tel: 210-651-6913; Fax: 210-651-5272.
School—Tel: 210-651-6811; Fax: 210-651-6811. Sr. Evelyn Korenek, I.W.B.S., Prin.
Sisters of Incarnate Word and Blessed Sacrament 3; Lay Teachers 18; Students 332.
Catechesis/Religious Programs—Verneanne Wong, D.R.E.
Students 740.

Smiley, Gonzales Co., St. Philip Benizi (1963) (Hispanic), Rev. David Zumaya; Deacons Frank Rojas Pastoral Admin.; John J. Moreno.
Res., P.O. Box 32, 78159-0032. Tel: 210-587-6258.

Somerset, Bexar Co., St. Mary's (1920), Rev. Paul M. Newhouse, C.I.C.M. (Belgium); Deacon Walter Mushalla.
Res., Box 295, 78069. Tel: 210-429-3645. [CEM]
Catechesis/Religious Programs—Mrs. Lydia Stinson, D.R.E.
Students 230.

Spring Branch, Comal Co. (Honey Creek), St. Joseph (1876), Rev. James Janish; Sandy Strange, Pastoral Assoc.; Deacons Johnny Gass; James Legendre. In res., Rev. Mark A. Garrett, O.S.A.
Res., 25781 Hwy. 46 W., 78070-3613. Tel: 210-980-2268; Fax: 210-980-3184. [CEM]
Catechesis/Religious Programs—Sandy Strange, D.R.E.
Students 351.

Stockdale, Wilson Co., St. Mary (1895) (Polish), Rev. Wieslaw Iwaniec.
Res., Box 535, 78160. Tel: 210-996-3415.
Catechesis/Religious Programs—Venice Grantham, D.R.E.
Students 160.

Stonewall, Gillespie Co., St. Francis Xavier (1945), Rev. Joseph G. De La Garza.
Res., Ranch Rd., 1, H.C. 1, Box 425, 78671. Tel: 210-644-2368.

Uvalde, Uvalde Co., Sacred Heart (1883), Revs. Kenneth M. Dakin; Miguel Arango Medina (Colombia); Deacons Hector V. Garcia; Ernest Gonzales; Antonio Hinojosa; Fortunato Hinojosa; Gonzalo Uriegas.
Res., 408 Fort Clark St., 78801. Tel: 210-278-3448; Fax: 210-278-2835. [CEM]
School—Tel: 210-278-2661. Sr. Dolores Aviles, S.T.J., Prin.
Teresian Sisters 3; Lay Teachers 9; Students 168.
Catechesis/Religious Programs—Tel: 210-278-3060. Linda Milam, D.R.E.
Students 956.

Von Ormy, Bexar Co., Sacred Heart (1935) (Hispanic), Rev. Rudolph T. Carrola, Jr.
Res., 13466 IH 35 S., 78073-3302. Tel: 210-622-3457; Fax: 210-622-3457.
Catechesis/Religious Programs—Denise Barker, D.R.E.
Students 100.
Res., P.O. Box 94, Macdona, 78054-0094. Tel: 210-622-3282; Fax: 210-622-3282.

St. Peter the Fisherman (1987) (Hispanic), Rev. Msgr. Charles Pugh.
Res., 24290 Hwy. 16 S., 78073. Tel: 210-276-8778.
Missions—Moore, St. Augustine; Bigfoot, Our Lady of Mt. Carmel.

KOREAN APOSTOLATE

San Antonio, Korean Catholic Community (1991), Rev. Andrew Yong Min Im (Korea); Deacon Philip C. Kim.
Res., 6831 Leyland, 78239. Tel: 210-655-3373.
Church—St. Pius X, 3303 Urban Crest, 78209.

OLD SPANISH MISSIONS

San Antonio, Old Spanish Missions, Rev. Msgr. Balthasar Janacek, Dir.
Mailing Address: c/o Catholic Chancery, P.O. Box 28410, 78228.
Purisima Concepcion—807 Mission Rd., 78210.
San Francisco de la Espada—10040 Espada Rd., 78214.
San Juan Capistrano—9101 Graf Rd., 78214.
San Jose—701 E. Pyron Rd., 78214.

Chaplains of Public Institutions

SAN ANTONIO. *Audie Murphy VA Hospital,* 7400 Merton Minter, 78229. Tel: 210-617-5308. Revs. Harry Martin; George Evans, O.C.S.O.
Baptist Memorial Hospital, 111 Dallas St., 78205. Tel: 210-222-8431. Rev. Edward Murray, O.M.I.; Mrs. Pat Sammis.
Brooke Army Medical Center, P.O. Box 15097, 78212. Tel: 210-650-5518. Rev. James Schellenberg.
Methodist Hospital, 7700 Floyd Curl, 78229. Tel: 210-692-4030. Revs. Aaron Arce, O.P.; Stefan Wiera; Marian Piekarczyk.
St. Luke's Baptist Hospital; University Hospital, 4502 Medical Dr., 78229. Tel: 210-680-2635 (Residence). Revs. George F. Healy, C.S.Sp.; Nicholas Brown, S.C.J.
San Antonio State Hospital, 6711 S. New Braunfels, 78223. Tel: 210-532-8811. Rev. Augustine Amanzeh.
Santa Rosa Hospital System, 519 W. Houston, 78207. Tel: 210-704-2021. Rev. Mark Scheffler, C.Ss.R.; Mr. Richard Woodley.
Southwest General Hospital. Tel: 210-921-2000. Deacon Leon Mueller.

KERRVILLE. *Veterans' Administration Hospital.* Vacant. Tel: 210-896-2020.

Special Assignment:
Reverend Fathers—
Ochoa, Einer M.De J.
Ruiz, Luis E., Sabbatical

On Duty Outside the Archdiocese:
Reverend Fathers—
Dillane, Maurice, Ireland
Garret, Sean, 110 St. Mary St., S.W., Fort Walton Beach, FL 32548. Tel: 904-243-3742
Keane, John F.
Kownacki, Robert, 7224 Balmoral, Chicago, IL 60656. Tel: 312-775-7315
Martinez, Manuel, Federal Bureau of Prisons, 320 1st St. N.W., HOLC Bldg. 254, Washington, DC 20534
O'Rourke, Michael J., O.P., St. Anthony, New Orleans, LA
Rubaj, Leon, Incarnate Word Sister's Convent, 1101 N.E. Water St., Victoria, TX 77901

Military Chaplains:
Reverend Fathers—
Barlow, James P., Chaplain Major, 803 C St., S.E., Washington, DC 20003
Gonzalez, George G., Chap. Major, 6726 Widgeon Dr., Midland, GA 31820
Hernandez, Alfred Ricardo, Col. Catholic Chap., 3240 Old Lawley Toll Rd., Calistoga, CA 94515
Nee, Eugene O., A.P.O., PFC 50, Box RET 667, APO, AE 09494
Tellez, Jairo, Major, U.S.A.F., Germany

Absent on Sick Leave:
Reverend Fathers—
Busteed, Francis

On Leave:
Reverend Fathers—
Crane, Jeff
Currie, Donald
Davila, Johnny
De La Rosa, Vincent
Dietz, Xavier Ortiz
Duran, Jorge
O'Sullivan, Michael
Ruiz, Enrique

Retired:
Reverend Monsignors—
Collins, Thomas J., 8520 Cross Mountain Tr. #302, San Antonio, TX 78255. Tel: 210-698-0682
Costantino, Anthony, 8520 Cross Mountain Tr. #201, San Antonio, TX 78255. Tel: 210-698-3638
Garcia, Raymond, 7458 Louis Pasteur Dr., San Antonio, TX 78229
Goertz, Alois J., 8520 Cross Mountain Tr., #100, San Antonio, TX 78255. Tel: 210-698-9067
Manning, J. Leroy, 8520 Cross Mountain Tr. #1102, San Antonio, TX 78255. Tel: 210-698-3183
Matocha, John L., Box 158B, Mathis, TX 78368. Tel: 512-547-9859
Mullaney, Bernard C., 8520 Cross Mountain Tr. #402, San Antonio, TX 78255. Tel: 210-698-3975
Rihn, Roy, 8520 Cross Mountain Tr. #301, San Antonio, TX 78255. Tel: 210-698-0287
Stuebben, George, 314 Cave Ln., San Antonio, TX 78209. Tel: 210-829-0238
Wangler, Alex, 6701 Blanco Rd., Apt. 110, San Antonio, TX 78216-6111. Tel: 210-342-6063
Reverend Fathers—
Femenia, Nicholas, Mailing Address: P.O. Box 37056, San Antonio, TX 78237
Gitter, Aloysius A., Mailing Address: P.O. Box 98, Harper, TX 78631. Tel: 210-864-4131
Goebel, Bernard M., 150 Beethoven St., San Antonio, TX 78210. Tel: 210-359-9034
Johnson, Robert F., 601 Van Ness Ave., #1052, San Francisco, CA 94102. Tel: 415-674-3572
Martinez, Rogelio, 8520 Cross Mountain Tr. #1101, San Antonio, TX 78255. Tel: 210-698-2243
O'Callaghan, Patrick, Mailing Address: P.O. Box 34413, San Antonio, TX 78265
Vinklarek, Emil T., 601-A Summit, Hwy. 90, Schulenburg, TX 78956. Tel: 409-743-3712

Permanent Deacons:
Alberty, George G., Jr., St. Brigid's, San Antonio
Alvarado, Thomas, St. Timothy's, San Antonio
Amo, Ernest Roy, St. Brigid
Baker, Robert L., On Duty Outside the Archdiocese
Barajas, Felipe, Holy Rosary, San Antonio
Barron, Cyriaco, Jr., On Leave
Bautista, Teofilo, Annunciation of BVM, St. Hedwig
Behling, James, On Duty Outside the Archdiocese
Bellg, Bruce J., St. Francis of Assisi, San Antonio
Bemrich, Richard, (Retired)
Benigno, Pasquale, St. Brigid's, San Antonio
Billimek, Thomas E., St. Brigid's, San Antonio
Bonilla-Valentin, Jorge, Immaculate Heart of Mary, San Antonio
Bozek, Edwin J., Jr., St. Francis of Assisi, San Antonio
Brumley, Denson C., On Leave
Buchanan, John, (Retired)
Caballero, Antonio, St. Timothy, San Antonio
Callaway, George, Jr., St. Anthony Mary Claret, San Antonio
Camero, A. C., Our Lady of Guadalupe & Jail Ministry, San Antonio
Campos, Fred, Jr., St. Gregory the Great, San Antonio
Cardona, Manuel, Sacred Heart, Eagle Pass
Carranza, Manuel G., Jr., Holy Family, San Antonio
Carrillo, Nick L., Our Lady of Guadalupe, Seguin
Carrillo, Victor, Jr., Sacred Heart, Eagle Pass
Carrizales, Manuel, Immaculate Heart of Mary, Pearsall
Carroll, Bernard, On Leave
Castellano, Frank V., St. Gabriel, San Antonio
Cena, Librado, St. John Berchmans, San Antonio
Cervantes, Alfredo, Immaculate Heart of Mary, San Antonio
Champagne, Joseph, St. Jerome, Martinez
Chavez, Hugo V., St. John the Evangelist, San Antonio
Chycinski, Wayne, Blessed Sacrament, San Antonio
Ciarrochi, Jerome, St. Thomas More, San Antonio
Cisneros, Daniel, Our Lady of Mt. Carmel & St. Therese (aka Little Flower), San Antonio
Clancey, Patrick, The Patrician Movement, San Antonio
Colley, Earl M., Holy Rosary, San Antonio
Corrigan, Gene, St. Joseph, La Pryor
Cross, Raymond, St. Peter Prince of Apostles, San Antonio
Crowley, Thomas, St. Pius X, San Antonio
Cruz, Robert, On Leave
Cuellar, Federico, On Leave
De la Torre, Francisco, St. Mary's, Fredericksburg
DeLaGarza, Gustavo, On Leave
DeLauter, Paul, St. Mark Parish, San Antonio
Diaz, Jose G., St. John Berchman, San Antonio
Dillard, Henry, St. Stephen, San Antonio
Donaho, Scott, Jr., Sacred Heart, Floresville
Donias, Justo, Jr., Catholic Charities, Fort Wayne, IN
Droll, Victor, St. Elizabeth's, Pflugerville
Dunn, John N., St. Peter Prince of Apostles, San Antonio
Ebner, Eugene, St. Louis, Castroville
Enriquez, Marcos, On Leave
Espinosa, Jose R., On Leave
Estrada, Melchor, On Leave
Falcon, Adrian, Our Lady of Guadalupe, Del Rio
Fertitta, J. V., Sr., Blessed Sacrament, San Antonio
Fey, Fred, Sts. Peter & Paul, New Braunfels
Fiedler, Welton J., St. Matthew, Jourdanton, TX
Fikac, Frank J., Sts. Peter & Paul, New Braunfels
Fitzpatrick, Alan, St. Dominic, San Antonio
Fox, Thomas J., St. Matthew's, San Antonio
Fraga, Jesse, Our Lady of Sorrows, San Antonio
Franklin, Thomas M., St. Francis of Assisi, San Antonio
Friesenhahn, Clifford, Our Lady of Perpetual Help, Selma
Galan, Roberto L., Jr., St. Joan of Arc, Kirby
Gallegos, Juan, St. Joseph, La Pryor
Gallegos, Valentine, Sacred Heart, San Antonio
Galvan, Robert, Our Lady of Guadalupe, San Antonio
Garcia, Hector, Sacred Heart, Uvalde
Garcia, Roberto, St. Bernard of Clairvaux, Dallas
Garza, Albert G., San Fernando Cathedral, San Antonio
Garza, Jose, Sacred Heart, Crystal City
Garza, Juan, Our Lady of Guadalupe, Seguin
Garza, Lionel, Jr., St. Dominic, San Antonio
Garza, Robert M., St. Dominic, San Antonio
Gass, Johnny J., St. Joseph, Honey Creek, Spring Branch
Gonzales, Ernest L., Sacred Heart, Uvalde
Gonzalez, Amador, St. Bonaventure, San Antonio
Gonzalez, Richard, St. Luke-Loire, Pleasanton
Gorman, John J., Good Shepherd, Schertz
Gorton, Everett D., St. Vincent De Paul, San Antonio
Graf, John E., Sacred Heart, Del Rio
Guerrero, Leon, St. Agnes, San Antonio
Guevara, Eusebio, St. Matthew's, Jourdanton
Gutierrez, Pedro, St. Brigid, San Antonio
Hansbauer, Eugene, On Leave
Hennessy, Robert, St. Luke's, San Antonio
Henson, Archibald, St. Louis, Castroville
Herbert, David L., Holy Name, San Antonio
Hernandez, Elieser, Our Lady of Guadalupe, Del Rio
Hernandez, Jose D., St. Lawrence, San Antonio

Herrera, Genaro M., St. Joseph's (South San), San Antonio
Herrera, Ramon, On Leave
Hinojosa, Antonio, Sacred Heart, Uvalde
Hinojosa, Fidel, St. Bonaventure, San Antonio
Hinojosa, Fortunado, Sacred Heart, Uvalde
Hobbs, John R., San Francisco di Paola, San Antonio
Hoelscher, Wilbur L., St. Matthew's, San Antonio
Hollstein, Albert, (Retired)
Holmstrom, Joseph, Notre Dame, Kerrville
Hormachea, Richard, St. Ann's, San Antonio
Houlihan, Timothy, Our Lady of Guadalupe, Helotes, TX
Hunsucker, Paul, St. Thomas the Apostle, Canyon Lake
Huttinger, John X., St. Joan of Arc, San Antonio
Imburgia, Scott, Permanent Diaconate Office, San Antonio
Jasso, Reynaldo, St. Rose of Lima, San Antonio
Johnson, Hiram B., St. James the Apostle, San Antonio
Jorgensen, J. D., Blessed Sacrament, San Antonio
Joslin, Wayne L., March A.F.B. Chapel, Military
Kaizen, Joseph, On Duty Outside the Archdiocese
Kasavage, Richard, St. Rose of Lima, San Antonio
Kattengell, Leon E., Our Lady of Guadalupe, San Antonio
Kaufman, Raymond, Sts. Peter & Paul, New Braunfels
Kearns, W. Daniel, St. Benedict, San Antonio
Keller, Alois, Jr., St. Lawrence, San Antonio
Kim, Philip C., Korean Community, San Antonio
Knopp, Kenneth P., (Retired)
Kopecky, Joseph, St. Joan of Arc, Kirby
Krupa, Joseph, San Antonio Church of the Holy Spirit
Kusenberger, Robert, Sacred Heart, Del Rio
La Combe, Paul B., Church of Good Shepherd, Schertz, TX
Lamm, Wilfred, St. Margaret Mary, San Antonio
Landez, John, St. Leo & Permanent Diaconate Office, San Antonio
Legendre, James F., St. Joseph, Honey Creek, Spring Branch
Link, John Dennis, Sacred Heart, Uvalde
Lira, Antonio, St. Rose of Lima, San Antonio
Lira, Rodolfo, Toledo, OH
Lopez, Jose Luis, Sacred Heart, Crystal City
Ludolph, Anthony, Schoenstatt Rep., San Antonio
Maldonado, Efren, Our Lady of Lourdes, Seco Mines
Mangold, Clayton, St. Paul, San Antonio
Marin, Arturo, Prince of Peace, San Antonio
Marques, Steven J., St. Mark, San Antonio
Martinez, Gregorio, Jr., St. Mary, Fredricksburg
Martinez, Ignacio, Immaculate Conception, San Antonio
Martinez, Juan G., Divine Providence, San Antonio
McDonald, John, On Leave
Mechler, Gerardo A., St. Margaret Mary, San Antonio
Medina, Damacio, St. Joseph, Nixon
Medina, Daniel G., St. Joseph, Nixon
Medina, Henry, St. Dominic, San Antonio
Medina, Ricardo, San Francisco de la Espada, San Antonio
Medrano, Rudy C., St. Timothy, San Antonio
Menchaca, Joseph, St. Martin De Porres, San Antonio
Merlin Joseph, On Leave
Meyers, Joseph L., Wilford Hall Medical Center, San Antonio
Micek, Jerome, Holy Trinity, San Antonio
Miller, John K., St. Anthony, Elmendorf
Miller, Mark C., Indiana
Moczygemba, Zafirin, St. Margaret Mary, San Antonio
Morales, Cayetano, Our Lady of Perpetual Help, New Braunfels
Moreno, Alfonso, Sacred Heart, Gonzales
Moreno, Florencio, Internship, El Paso, TX
Moreno, John J., St. Philip's, Smiley
Mueller, Leon, St. Joseph (S.S.) & Southwest General Hospital, San Antonio
Munoz Antonio, Immaculate Conception, San Antonio
Muraica, Daniel, St. Paul's & Permanent Diaconate Office, San Antonio
Mushala, Walter A., St. Mary's, Somerset
Nash, Joseph, St. Joan of Arc, Kirby, TX
Navarro, Ruben W., St. Raymond Pennafort, Leakey
Neal, Thomas R., Prince of Peace, San Antonio
Nelson Robert W., St. Mary Magdalene, Brackettville
Neville, Richard F., Jr., Randolph, A.F.B., San Antonio
Novian, Donald, St. Gregory, San Antonio
Olivarez, Jesse, On Leave
Ortega Sylvester, St. Jude, San Antonio
Ortiz, Antonio H., St. Jude, San Antonio
Ostaszewski, Chester R., St. Rose of Lima, San Antonio
Pacheco, Alvino, St. Leo, San Antonio
Paiz, Gabriel, (Retired)
Patino, Edward, St. Agnes, San Antonio
Patterson, Jose, Sacred Heart, Cotolla, TX
Pedroza, Doroteo E., San Fernando, San Antonio
Pena, Rudy, Christ the King, San Antonio
Perez, Jose F., Our Lady of Guadalupe, Carrizo Springs
Perez, Julio T., American Embassy, Luanda, Angola, Africa
Perez, Miguel, Jr., Sacred Heart, Floresville
Phillips, Norman D., St. Andrew, Pleasanton
Pope, Charles F., Sr., St. Clare, San Antonio
Pratt, Gilbert, St. Francis of Assisi & Jail Ministry, San Antonio
Prevott, Raymond, St. Patrick, San Antonio
Pruneda, Esmeraldo, St. Jude, San Antonio
Quarles, Fred J., St. Cecilia, San Antonio
Ramirez, Albert, Our Lady of Angels, San Antonio
Ramirez, Victor, Our Lady of the Angels, San Antonio
Ramon, Genaro, Sr., Our Lady of Guadalupe, Carrizo Springs
Raso, James, St. John Berchman, San Antonio
Reyes, Ramiro, Ligonier, IN
Riojas, Francisco, St. Philip, Smiley
Rodriguez, Santiago, San Jose Mission, San Antonio
Rodriguez, Severo, Jr., On Leave
Salazar, Filomeno, St. Joseph, Del Rio
Salinas, Alberto, San Juan DeLos Lagos, San Antonio
Salinas, Carlos, On Leave
Sanabria, Agripino, Prince of Peace, San Antonio
Sanchez, Jose, St. Philip of Jesus, San Antonio
Sandoval, Carlos, Our Lady of Guadalupe, San Antonio
Sauceda, Juan, Our Lady of Guadalupe, Carrizo Springs
Scarbo, David B., Sacred Heart, Del Rio
Schonhoff, Robert L., Our Lady of Grace, San Antonio
Schroeder, William, Sts. Peter and Paul, New Braunfels
Scott, Armando, Holy Family, San Antonio
Sekinger, Eugene, Military Parochial, Brooks Air Force Base
Seymour, Warren V., St. Raymond of Pennafort, Leakey
Shoemake, William, Christ the King, Belton
Soriano, Pedro, St. Timothy, San Antonio
Spitzer, John L., On Leave
Stewart, Wilbert, St. Dominic, San Antonio
Stockton, Ree, St. Dominic, San Antonio
Stokes, Leslie, On Duty Outside the Archdiocese
Suniga, Jose A., Divine Providence, San Antonio
Svatek, Anton, (Retired)
Swift, Thomas N., Resurrection of the Lord, San Antonio
Tamez, Javier, Holy Family, San Antonio
Thayer, Robert, Our Lady of Perpetual Help, Selma
Tijerina, Salvador, On Leave
Torres, Thomas, St. Leo, San Antonio
Trevino, Jimmie, St. Dominic, San Antonio
Trevino, Jose S., St. Luke-Loire, Pleasanton
Trujillo, Jose M., Mission San Juan Capistrano, San Antonio
Tudon, Horacio R., St. Matthew's, San Antonio
Uriegas, Gonzalo, Sacred Heart, Uvalde
Urrabazo, Rosendo, St. John the Evangelist, San Antonio
Valenzuela, Jose J., St. Andrew's, Pleasanton
Vasquez, Eleodore, San Juan de Los Lagos, San Antonio
Villa, Albert G., St. John the Evangelist, Hondo, TX
Wasniewski, Michael, On Leave
Wehman, Ben, St. Peter and Paul, New Braunfels
Weissler, Gilbert, St. Anthony of Padua, San Antonio
Werner, Keith N., St. Matthew's, San Antonio
White, George, (Retired)
White, Thomas, St. Clair, Holy Redeemer, San Antonio
Wittig, Evan, St. John Evangelist, San Antonio
Wright, Michael, On Duty Outside the Archdiocese
Wuenschel, Douglas, Church of the Holy Spirit, San Antonio
Ybarra, Ray, Our Lady of Perpetual Help, New Braunfels
Zapata, Gumercindo, St. Philip of Jesus, San Antonio
Zapata, Thomas, On Leave
Zavala, Placido, On Leave
Zepeda, Ernest, (Retired)
Zizke, William, Medical Center Hospital

INSTITUTIONS LOCATED IN THE ARCHDIOCESE

[A] SEMINARIES, ARCHDIOCESAN

SAN ANTONIO. *The Assumption-St. John's Seminary*, 2600 W. Woodlawn Ave., P.O. Box 28240, 78228. Tel: 210-734-5137; Fax: 210-734-2324. Legal Title: *The Seminary of the Assumption of the Blessed Virgin Mary-St. John of San Antonio, TX.* Revs. David R. Cruz (LUB), Rector, Admissions & Devel., Admin.; Norman Ermis, Vice Rector & Dir. Internship & Pastoral Year; Gerald McBrearity, S.S., Dir. Spiritual Formation, Dir. of Community Life, Coord. Pre-Theology Program, Liason with O.S.T. Academic Affairs.; Sr. Mary Theresa Cullen, C.S.B., Dir. Pastoral Formation, Coord. Cultural Prog, Coord. Language Program.; Sr. Addie Walker, S.S.N.D., Dir. Liturgical Formation, Coord. Cultural Program; Rev. Jose Lopez, Spiritual Dir. In Res. Priests 4; Sisters 2; Seminarians 34; Domestic Dept.: Josephine Sisters (Mexico City, Mexico) 9.

Permanent Diaconate, 2600 W. Woodlawn, P.O. Box 28240, 78284-2701. Tel: 210-734-0114. Rev. John O'Donoghue, Dir. Assistant Directors: Deacons John Landez; George White.

[B] SEMINARIES, RELIGIOUS OR SCHOLASTICATES

SAN ANTONIO. *Congregation of Holy Cross - Formation Community*, Bro. Charles Andersen Residence, 320 Brahan Blvd., 78215-1020. Tel: 210-233-9117. Bro. Richard Critz, C.S.C., Co-Dir.; Rev. Lawrence A. LeVasseur, C.S.C., Co-Dir. Brothers 1; Seminarians 4.

Dominican Priory of Juan Macias, 210 St. Ann St., 78201. Tel: 210-734-6687. Revs. Richard B. Williams, O.P., Prior; Aaron Arce, O.P.; Cayet Mangiaracina, O.P.; Vicente M. Pena, O.P.; Joseph Determan, O.P.; Bro. John E. Lydon, O.P.

Franciscan Formation Program in San Jose Friary (Casa Juan Diego), 701 E. Pyron Ave., 78214. Tel: 210-922-4976. Revs. Herbert Jones, O.F.M., Dir.; Jesus Aguirre-Garza, O.F.M., Asst. Dir.

George Sexton House of Studies. (Theology), 314 E. King's Hwy., 78212. Tel: 210-735-7318. Missionary Oblates of Mary Immaculate, United States Region. Revs. Robert E. Wright, O.M.I., Supr.; Jerome C. Burnet, O.M.I.; Vaughn Fayle, O.M.I. Scholastics 10.

Immaculate Heart Claretian Seminary, 617 S. Santa Rosa Blvd., 78204. Tel: 210-222-9406; Fax: 210-222-1479. Revs. Lawrence Christian, C.M.F., Formation Dir.; Richard DeTore, C.M.F., Dir.; Paul Keller, C.M.F.

Joseph Gerard House of Studies, 318 Oblate Dr., 78216. Tel: 210-377-3640; 377-0142. Revs. Patrick Guidon, Dir.; Rufus Whitley, O.M.I., Assoc. Dir.; Warren Brown, O.M.I. Post Graduate Candidates 2.

Marianist Formation Community, 3303 W. Woodlawn, 78228. Tel: 210-436-0182. Bro. Fred A.R. Stovall, S.M., Dir.; Revs. John Moder, S.M.; Rudy Vela. Priests 2; Brothers 4.

Missionhurst Formation Community, 1147-A Cupples Rd., 78226. Tel: 210-434-5347. Rev. William Quigley, C.I.C.M., Dir. Formation. Theology 9.

MSF Formation Community, 104 Cas-Hills Dr., 78213-3322. Tel: 210-344-9145. Rev. Alberto T. Trevino, Jr., M.S.F., Dir. Seminarians 7.

Redemptorist Seminary, Liguori House, 1523 Iowa, 78203. Tel: 210-533-0442. Revs. Gerald L. Siebold, C.Ss.R., Supr.; Byron Miller, C.Ss.R., Vocation Dir. and Formation Dir., Vice-Prov. of New Orleans. Students 5.

St. Anthony Mary Claret Seminary, 402 John Adams Dr., 78228-4231. Tel: 210-734-2678; Fax: 210-733-8732. Revs. Stephen Sherwood, C.M.F., Dir.; Daryld Olds, C.M.F.; Steven Niskanen, C.M.F., Voc. Dir. Seminarians 4.

San Damiano Friary, 1104 Kentucky Ave., 78201. Tel: 210-734-4962. Conventual Franciscans Friars Minor Conventual. Revs. Miguel Briseno, O.F.M.Conv., Dir. Vocations; Kenneth Davis, O.F.M.Conv.; Marcos Ayala, O.F.M.Conv.; Bros. Timothy Unser, O.F.M.Conv., Guardian of House of Formation; Joshe Duplissey, O.F.M.Conv.

[C] COLLEGES AND UNIVERSITIES

SAN ANTONIO. *Oblate School of Theology*, (1903) 285 Oblate Dr., 78216-6693. Tel: 210-341-1366; Fax: 210-341-4519.

For a complete listing, refer to the Colleges and Universities section.

Our Lady of the Lake University, 411 S.W. 24th, 78207-4689. Tel: 210-434-6711; Fax: 210-436-0824.

For a complete listing, refer to the Colleges and Universities section.

St. Mary's University of San Antonio, Texas, (1852)

One Camino Santa Maria, 78228-8572. Tel: 210-436-3011.
For a complete listing, refer to the Colleges and Universities section.
The United Colleges of San Antonio, 285 Oblate Dr., 78216.
For a complete listing, refer to the Colleges and Universities section.
University of the Incarnate Word, 4301 Broadway, 78209. Tel: 210-829-6000.
For a complete listing, refer to the Colleges and Universities section.

[D] HIGH SCHOOLS, ARCHDIOCESAN

SAN ANTONIO. *Antonian College Preparatory High School*. (Coed), 6425 West Ave., 78213. Tel: 210-344-9265. Mr. Gilbert L. Saenz, Prin.; Revs. Francis M. Lanwermeyer, S.J.; Richard Detore, C.M.F. Priests 2; Sisters 1; Deacons 1; Lay Teachers 30; Students 480.
Holy Cross High School. (Grades 7-12). (Boys), 426 N. San Felipe, 78228. Tel: 210-433-9395. Brother of the Congregation of Holy Cross. Bro. Stanley Culotta, C.S.C., Prin. Brothers 8; Lay Teachers 21; Sisters 2; Students 455.

[E] HIGH SCHOOLS, REGIONAL

SAN ANTONIO. *St. Gerard Catholic High School*, 521 S. New Braunfels Ave., 78203. Tel: 210-533-8061. Maurice Abadie, Prin. Sisters 1; Lay Teachers 18; Students 205.

[F] HIGH SCHOOLS, PRIVATE

SAN ANTONIO. *Blessed Sacrament Academy*, 1135 Mission Rd., 78210. Tel: 210-532-4731. Sr. M. Odilia Korenek, I.W.B.S., Dir. & Supr.
Second Chance High School, Texas Charter School. Sisters of the Incarnate Word and Blessed Sacrament 2; Lay Teachers 13; Other Sisters 2; Students 180.
Child Development Center. Sisters of the Incarnate Word and Blessed Sacrament 3; Lay Teachers 19; Students 110.
Central Catholic High School, 1403 N. St. Mary's St., 78215-1785. Tel: 210-225-6794. Rev. Joseph A. Tarrillion, S.M., Pres.; Dr. Paul M. Sullivan, Ed.D., Prin.; Revs. Donald Cowie, S.M.; Joseph G. Rasky, S.M. Priests 3; Brothers 9; Lay Teachers 31; Students 449.
Healy-Murphy Center, Inc., 618 Live Oak St., 78202. Tel: 210-223-2944. Sr. Veronica Cahill, S.H.Sp., Prin. & Exec. Dir. Day School for High School Students. Provides an alternative to the Regular School System. Sisters 6; Lay Teachers 44; Counselors 2; Nurses 2; Students 350; Child Development Department: Six weeks-5 yrs 168; On Campus Clinic: Nurse 1; Doctor 1.
Incarnate Word High School, 727 E. Hildebrand Ave., 78212-2598. Tel: 210-829-3100; Fax: 210-829-3120. Mr. Roger Labat, Prin. Sisters 5; Brothers 1; Lay Teachers 50; Students 560.
Providence High School, 1215 N. St. Mary's St., 78215. Tel: 210-224-6651; Fax: 210-224-6214. Sr. Ramona Bezner, C.D.P., Prin. Sisters 4; Lay Teachers 31; Students 498.
St. Anthony Catholic High School, 3200 McCullough Ave., 78212-3099. Tel: 210-731-2500; Fax: 210-731-2515. Revs. Patrick Gitzen, O.M.I.; Richard Hall, O.M.I.; Raul Salas, O.M.I.
Boys boarding department. Dr. Gary L. Short, Prin. Priests 3; Lay Teachers 17; Students 186.
St. Francis Academy, 1807 Centennial Ave., 78211. Tel: 210-923-1421. Sr. Jeanne Marie Ulica, O.S.F., Prin. School Sisters of St. Francis 7; Lay Teachers 14; Students 227.

[G] ELEMENTARY SCHOOLS, PRIVATE

SAN ANTONIO. *Mount Sacred Heart School*. (Grades PreK-8), 619 Mount Sacred Heart Rd., 78216. Tel: 210-342-6711. Coed Montessori. Mrs. Sylvia D. Herrera, Prin.; Rev. James Hubert, C.I.C.M., Chap. Sisters 5; Lay Teachers 28; Students 336.
St. Anthony's School, 205 W. Huisache St., 78212. Tel: 210-732-8801. Robert C. Niehoff, Prin. Lay Teachers 16; Students 224.
St. John Bosco School. (Grades K-8), 5630 W. Commerce St., 78237. Tel: 210-432-8011. Day School. Institute of the Daughters of Mary Help of Christians (Salesian Sisters of St. John Bosco). Sr. Theresa Sironi, F.M.A., Supr.; Mary Anne Oehler, Prin. Sisters 15; Lay Teachers 29; Students 682.
St. Martin Hall, Our Lady of the Lake University of San Antonio, 411 S.W. 24th St., 78207. Tel: 210-434-6711, Ext. 308. Sr. Rita Louise Petsch, C.D.P., Prin. Campus Laboratory School, Preschool Kindergarten and Elementary. Sisters 3; Lay Teachers 19; Students 284.
Westside Catholic Interparish School. (Grades K-8), Mailing Address: P.O. Box 830513, 78283-0513. 314 Merida St., 78207. Tel: 210-224-2450. Mrs. Marianne Mongiollo. Sisters 2; Lay Teachers 7; Students 165.

[H] GENERAL HOSPITALS

SAN ANTONIO. *Incarnate Word Health System*, 9311 San Pedro #1250, 78216-4496. Tel: 210-524-4100.
For a complete listing, refer to the Hospitals section.
Santa Rosa Children's Hospital, 519 W. Houston St., 78207-3198. Tel: 210-704-2011.
For a complete listing, refer to the Hospitals section.
Santa Rosa Health Care System, 519 W. Houston St., 78207-3198. Tel: 210-704-2011.
For a complete listing, refer to the Hospitals section.
Santa Rosa Hospital, 519 W. Houston St., 78207-3198. Tel: 210-704-2011.
For a complete listing, refer to the Hospitals section.
Santa Rosa Northwest Hospital, 2827 Babcock Rd., 78229. Tel: 210-705-6300.
For a complete listing, refer to the Hospitals section.
Santa Rosa Skilled Nursing Facility, 519 W. Houston St., 78207-3198. Tel: 210-704-2011.
For a complete listing, refer to the Hospitals section.

[I] PROTECTIVE INSTITUTIONS

SAN ANTONIO. *Father Flanagan's Boys' Town of San Antonio*, 503 Urban Loop, 78204. Tel: 210-271-1010.
For a complete listing, refer to the Special Care Facilities section.
Providence Home & Family Services, Inc., 2650 Castroville Rd., 78237. Tel: 210-434-2111; Fax: 210-433-2806.
For a complete listing, refer to the Special Care Facilities section.
St. Peter & Joseph Childrens Home, 919 Mission Rd., 78210. Tel: 210-533-1203.
For a complete listing, refer to the Special Care Facilities section.
Seton Home for Homeless, Pregnant Young Women, 1115 Mission Rd., 78210. Tel: 210-533-3504.
For a complete listing, refer to the Special Care Facilities section.
Visitation Hospitality House of San Antonio, Texas and La Posada Transitional Housing, 945 W. Huisache, 78201. Tel: 210-735-6910.
For a complete listing, refer to the Special Care Facilities section.

[J] DAY CARE CENTERS AND KINDERGARTENS

SAN ANTONIO. *Blessed Sacrament Learning Center*, 222 W. Cavallos St., 78204. Tel: 210-223-5013. Sisters of Mercy of the Blessed Sacrament. Sr. Bernadette Gomez, Admin. Sisters 12; Children 57.
Carmelite Learning Center, 2006 Martin Luther King Dr., 78203. Tel: 210-533-0651. Sr. Fatima Cardoza, Carmel,D.C.J., Dir. Carmelite Sisters of the Divine Heart of Jesus 5; Lay Staff 17; In Day Care 120. Attended from St. Patrick's Church.
Immaculate Conception Kindergarten and Nursery, 2407 W. Travis St., 78207. Tel: 210-226-3934. Sr. Maria Del Carmen Sanchez, A.P.G., Dir. Sisters 3; Lay Staff 12; Kindergarted & Nursery Children 95.
St. Anthony Day Care Learning Center; Infant and Toddler Center, 1707 Centennial Blvd., 78211. Tel: 210-924-4443. Sr. Mary Ann Domagalski, M.S.S.A., Admin.; Sr. Lucelia Sanchez, M.S.S.A., Dir. Sisters 2; Lay Staff 28; Children 150.
St. Brigid's Kindergarten, 5118 Loma Linda Dr., 78201. Tel: 210-733-0037. Sr. Stephenie Deegan, C.S.B., Dir. Children 30.
BOERNE. *St. Albert Hall dba St. Albert Early Learning Center*, 216 W. Highland Dr., 78006. Tel: 210-816-2059; 2060; Fax: 210-816-1872. Vanessa Bothe-Hernandez, Dir. Children 160; Staff 25.

[K] HOMES FOR AGED

SAN ANTONIO. *Casa De Padres*, 8520 Cross Mountain Tr., 78255.
For a complete listing, refer to the Special Care Facilities section.
Incarnate Word Motherhouse and Retirement Center, 4707 Broadway, 78209. Tel: 210-829-7561.
For a complete listing, refer to the Special Care Facilities section.
Oblate Madonna Residence, 5722 Blanco Rd., 78216. Tel: 210-341-2350.
For a complete listing, refer to the Special Care Facilities section.
Padua Place, 80 Peter Baque Rd., 78209. Tel: 210-826-7721.
For a complete listing, refer to the Special Care Facilities section.
St. Francis Nursing Home, 630 W. Woodlawn, 78212. Tel: 210-736-3177.
For a complete listing, refer to the Special Care Facilities section.
St. Joseph's Community, 520 Fordham Ln., 78228-4821. Tel: 210-436-3771.
For a complete listing, refer to the Special Care Facilities section.
KENEDY. *John Paul II Nursing Home*, 215 Tilden, P.O. Box 359, 78119. Tel: 210-583-9841.
For a complete listing, refer to the Special Care Facilities section.

[L] BOARDING HOMES

SAN ANTONIO. *Seraphic Sisters Boarding Home for the Aged*, 619 W. Craig Pl., 78212. Tel: 210-736-3177. Sr. Elizabeth Dubicka, S.O.L.S., Dir. Guests 8.

[M] MONASTERIES AND RESIDENCES OF PRIESTS AND BROTHERS

SAN ANTONIO. *Capuchin Franciscan Friars (Spain)*, 1214 Stonewall St., 78211-1554. Tel: 210-924-6591; Fax: 210-924-6593. Revs. Luis G. Arraiza, O.F.M.Cap.; Gregorio Goicoechea, O.F.M.Cap.
Casa Maria Marianist Community, St. Mary's University, One Camino Santa Maria, 78228-8518. Tel: 210-436-3066. Revs. George T. Montague, S.M., Dir. Tel: 210-436-3210; J. Willis Langlinais, S.M. Tel: 210-436-3705; Norbert C. Brockman, S.M. Tel: 210-436-3659; Bros. Joseph Barrett, S.M. Tel: 210-436-3228; Cletus Behlmann, S.M. Tel: 210-434-1331; Edward Loch, S.M. Tel: 210-431-2272; Harold Lootens, S.M. Tel: 210-436-3258; Terrence O'Connor, S.M. Tel: 210-436-3231.
Casa Pasionista Guadalupe, 700 Waverly, 78201. Tel: 210-736-5228; Fax: 210-737-6549. Revs. G. Alexander Steinmiller, C.P.; Robert Bovenzi, C.P.; Clemente Barron, C.P.
Central Catholic Marianist Community, 1403 N. St. Mary's St., 78215-1785. Tel: 210-225-1112. Revs. Donald Cowie, S.M., Dir.; Donald Cowie, S.M.; Joseph Rasky, S.M. Brothers 9.
Chaminade Community House, 10910 Wild Grape, 78230-3459. Tel: 210-641-6354. Marianists. Revs. Conrad J. Kaczkowski, S.M., Supr.; Joseph A. Tarrillion, S.M.; Charles H. Miller, S.M.
De Mazenod House. (Faculty Residence), 7707 Madonna Dr., 78216. Tel: 210-349-8572. Missionary Oblates of Mary Immaculate. Revs. Frederick Sackett, O.M.I., Supr.; Jan Heemrood, O.M.I.; Ken Hannon, O.M.I.; Thomas Ovalle, O.M.I.; Arthur Flores, O.M.I.; William Morrell, O.M.I.; Ronald Young, O.M.I. Priests 7.
Discalced Carmelites (Prov. of St. Therese), 906 Kentucky Ave., 78201-6097. Tel: 210-735-9126. Revs. Ralph Reyes, O.C.D., Supr.; John Magdalene Suenram, O.C.D.; Louis Scagnelli, O.C.D.; Michael Okuroski, O.C.D.; James Anthony Curiel, O.C.D.; Christopher Timoney, O.C.D.; Bro. Bernard O'Neil, O.C.D. Priests 5; Brothers 1; Clerical Students 3.
Harcar House, 6111 Walking Gait, 78240. Tel: 210-680-3685.
Hospital Ministry: Revs. George F. Healy, C.S.Sp.; Nicholas Brown, S.C.J.
Holy Cross Community, 426 N. San Felipe St., 78228. Tel: 210-434-9100. Bro. Stanley Culotta, C.S.C., Dir.; Rev. Patrick Foley, C.S.C. Priests 1; Brothers 8.
Brothers of the Holy Cross, 800 Babcock Rd., Apt. G-1, 78201. Tel: 210-734-8602. Bro. Terrence Muehlenkamp, C.S.C.
Bro. Charles Andersen Residence, 320 Brahan Blvd., 78215. Tel: 210-223-9117. Rev. Lawrence LeVasseur, C.S.C., Dir. Priests 1; Brothers 4; Seminarians 2.
Holy Cross Fathers, 411 S.W. 24th St., 78285. Tel: 210-433-6731. Rev. John Lubbers, C.S.C.
Villas of Castle Hills, 604, 1000 Jackson-Keller Rd., 78213. Tel: 210-377-3997. Bro. David Fitzgerald, C.S.C.
Holy Cross Brothers, 3601 Magic Dr., #1202, 78229-5456. Tel: 210-525-9423. Bro. Peter Mullett, C.S.C.
Holy Cross Brothers, 2519 Broadway, 78215. Bro. William Dooling, C.S.C.
Holy Rosary Marianist Community, 159 Camino Santa Maria, 78228-4997. Tel: 210-433-6137; Fax: 210-433-2133. Rev. John Manahan, S.M.; Bros. James Droste, S.M., Dir.; Michael Brangan, S.M.; James Facette, S.M.; James McCaffery, S.M.
LaRisa Apartments Marianist Community, 800 Babcock Rd., #252, 78201. Tel: 210-735-5952. Brothers 2.
Marianist Formation Community, 3303 W. Woodlawn Ave., 78228. Tel: 210-436-0182. Bro. Fred A.R. Stovall, S.M., Dir.; Revs. Rudy Vela, S.M.; John Moder, S.M. Priests 2; Brothers 4.
Marianist Residence, St. Mary's University, 520 Fordham Ave., 78228-4800. Tel: 210-436-3744; Fax: 210-436-3747. Bro. Herbert Janson, S.M., Dir. Tel: 210-436-3745; Revs. Robert Hogan, S.M.; John A. Leies, S.M. Tel: 210-436-3227; John G. Leies, S.M. Tel: 210-436-3140; Bernard Meyer, S.M. Tel: 210-436-3761; Charles Neumann, S.M. Tel: 210-436-3762; John Rechtien, S.M. Tel: 210-436-2092; Louis Reile, S.M. Tel: 210-436-3764; Paul Ryan, S.M. Tel: 210-436-3766; W. Franz Schorp, S.M. Tel: 210-436-2259. Priests 9; Brothers 22.
Marianist Vocation Ministry, One Camino Santa Maria, 78228-8556. Tel: 210-431-2193; Fax: 210-436-3724. Bro. Michael Sullivan, S.M., Dir.

Missionaries of the Sacred Heart. Sectional Headquarters of the Irish Province for California and Southern States. 237 W. Magnolia, 78212. Tel: 210-402-0354; Fax: 210-402-0346. Revs. William J. Clarkson, M.S.C., Supr.; Patrick O'Shea, M.S.C.; James Harnan, M.S.C.; Stephen White, M.S.C.; Colm Mulligan, M.S.C., P.O. Box 250, Spring Branch Rd., 78070. Tel: 210-885-4853. Sunray Apartments, 7600 Blanco Rd., #508, 78216. Tel: 210-308-8235. Revs. John Finn, M.S.C.; Gerald Grace, M.S.C.

Miscellaneous: Rev. Patrick Stenson, M.S.C., Religious Activities Office, 3700 N. Capitol St. N.W., Washington, DC, 20317. Tel: 202-882-1888. Rev. Aidan O'Donovan, M.S.C., 907 Colony Ridge, Irving, 75061. Tel: 972-590-8512; Fax: 972-986-1322.

Missionhurst Community Residence, 1746 Donaldson, 78228. Tel: 210-432-1384; 435-4210. Revs. Michael Cattaert, C.I.C.M.; Pieter Van Der Paalen, C.I.C.M.

Other Addresses: 6534 Kings Crown, 78233. Tel: 210-653-0832. Revs. Francis Van Hee, C.I.C.M.; James Meuree, C.I.C.M., 7600 Blanco Rd., Apt. 1605, 78216. Tel: 210-344-3813. Rev. Ralph Nuyten, C.I.C.M.

MSF Center & Provincialate, 210 El Rancho Way, 78209. Tel: 210-826-9815. Congregation of the Missionaries of the Holy Family. Very Revs. Robert E. O'Hara, M.S.F., Prov.; John Dowling, M.S.F., Prov. Treas.

Oblate Benson Residence (Southern Prov.), 334 W. Kings Hwy., 78212. Tel: 210-732-5162. Missionary Oblates of Mary Immaculate. Very Rev. Eugene Canas, O.M.I., Prov.; Revs. Gerard Weber, O.M.I. Tel: 210-732-8024; Edward Murray, O.M.I.; William O'Conner, O.M.I. Tel: 210-733-7833; Charles Borgers, O.M.I. Tel: 210-731-9894.

Priests of the Sacred Heart-House of Formation, 133 Thelma Dr., 78212-2517. Tel: 210-826-6091; 6092; Fax: 210-826-8019. Revs. Douglas Watson, S.C.J., Dir.; Nicholas Brown, S.C.J. In res., Rev. Ralph Intranuovo, S.C.J. Students 7.

Provincial Administration Office, Oblates of Mary Immaculate (Southern Prov.), 7711 Madonna Dr., 78216-6696. Tel: 210-349-1475; Fax: 210-349-7411. Very Rev. Eugene Canas, O.M.I., Prov.; Revs. Charles Banks, O.M.I., Vicar Prov.; Jerome Burnet, O.M.I., Prov. Treas.

Chaplains Not Listed Elsewhere: Rev. Donald McNally, O.M.I., Chap., Texas Department of Corrections, Jester III Unit, Rte. 2, Richmond, 77469. Tel: 713-277-7000. Rev. Donald Burnet, O.M.I., 3228 La Madera Way, Antelope, CA, 95843. Tel: 916-643-6021. Rev. Clifford Blackburn, O.M.I., Santa Rosa Hospital, 519 W. Houston St., 78207. Rev. Edward Murray, O.M.I., Audie Murphy VA Hospital, 7400 Merton Minter, 78229. Tel: 210-617-5300. Baptist Memorial Hospital, 111 Dallas St., 78205. Tel: 210-222-8431.

Redemptorists of Texas-Redemptorist Community at St. Gerard, 1617 Iowa St., 78203. Tel: 201-534-4351. (Vice Province of New Orleans). Revs. Thomas Picton, C.SS.R., Supr.; John Cody, C.SS.R.; Jose Chavez, C.SS.R.; Robert Ruhnke, C.SS.R.; Mark Sheffler, C.SS.R.; Leonard Broniak, C.SS.R., Deaf Ministry Team.

St. Anthony Catholic High School House, 3200 McCullough Ave., 78212. Tel: 210-731-8724. Revs. Raul Salas, O.M.I.; Patrick Gitzen, O.M.I.; Richard Hall, O.M.I.; Leo Perez, O.M.I.; Charles Banks, O.M.I.

San Damiano Friary, 1104 Kentucky Ave., 78201. Tel: 210-734-4962. Friars Minor Conventual. Conventual Franciscans. Revs. Miguel Briseno, O.F.M.Conv.; Kenneth Davis, O.F.M.Conv.; Bros. Tim Unser, O.F.M.Conv.; Joshe Duplissey, O.F.M.Conv.

Vincentian Residence, 235 E. Mulberry, Apt. 203, 78212. Tel: 210-733-8765. Rev. Jeff Malpiede, C.M.

[N] CONVENTS AND RESIDENCES FOR SISTERS

SAN ANTONIO. *Bernadine Franciscan Sisters*, 5411 Callaghan Rd., 78228. Tel: 210-684-3445. Sisters 3. 500 N. Santa Rosa Blvd., 78207. Tel: 210-271-3091. Sisters 1. Sr. Therese San Miguel, O.S.F., Coord.

Blessed Sacrament Convent, 222 W. Cevallos St., 78204. Tel: 210-223-5013. Sisters of Mercy of the Blessed Sacrament. Sr. Dolores Munoz, H.M.S.S., Supr. Sisters 13.

Blessed Sacrament Convent, 118 Melba, 78216. Tel: 210-828-0155. Sisters of the Incarnate Word and Blessed Sacrament. Sr. Mary Therese Fritz, Supr. Sisters 2.

Carmelite Convent, 2006 Martin Luther King Dr., 78203. Tel: 210-533-0651. Carmelite Sisters of the Divine Heart of Jesus. Sr. Maria Fatima, Carmel, D.C.J., Supr. Sisters 7.

Cordi-Marian Missionary Sisters, Cordi-Marian Villa, 11624 FM 471, 78253. Tel: 210-688-3099; 688-3889. Convent, Provincial House and Retreat Center. Sr. Catalina Marquez, M.C.M., Prov. Supr.; Sr. Celina Martin, M.C.M., Supr.; Rev. Isidoro Garcia, C.M.F., Chap. Sisters 12.

Cordi-Marian Missionary Sisters Convent and Formation House, 2902 Morales St., 78207. Tel: 210-433-5064. Sr. Mary Elia Jaime, M.C.M., Supr. Sisters 4.

Daughters of Charity Convent, 7603 Somerset Rd., 78211. Tel: 210-927-2795; Fax: 210-922-0332. Daughters of Charity of St. Vincent de Paul. Sr. Patricia Connolly, D.C., Supr. Sisters 5.

The Daughters of St. Paul Convent. (Pontifical F.S.P.), 114 Main Plaza, 78205. Tel: 210-224-8101. Sr. Susan Miriam Wolf, F.S.P., Supr. Sisters 4.

El Carmen Sister's Residence, 1835-1 Martinez-Losoya, 78221. Tel: 210-626-2024. Daughters of Charity of St. Vincent de Paul. Sr. Aileen Marek, D.C., Supr. Sisters 4.

Eucharistic Franciscan Missionary Sisters, 558 Cumberland, 78204. Tel: 210-224-7993. Sr. Teresa Rojas, M.E.F., Supr. Sisters 3.

Felician Sisters, 3910 Meadow Ridge, 78210. Tel: 210-532-3433. Sr. Dorothy Moczygemba, C.S.S.F., Supr. Sisters 3.

5518 King Richard Dr., 78229. Tel: 210-520-9767. Sr. Lucy Korzekwa, C.S.S.F., Supr. Sisters 3.

Franciscan Sisters of Little Falls, MN, 6900 No. Vandiver, Apt. D201, 78209. Tel: 210-822-1074. Sr. Mary Dumonceaux, O.S.F.

Hermanas Catequistas Guadalupanas Convent, 4110 S. Flores St., 78214. Tel: 210-532-9344. Sr. Maria Martha Ruiz, H.C.G., Supr. Sisters 7. 115 Arlington Ct., 78210. Tel: 210-533-2968. Sr. Sofia Arredondo, H.C.G., Supr. Sisters 4.

Holy Rosary Convent, 543 Westminister, 78228. Tel: 210-433-1108. Sr. Joyce des Jardins, S.S.N.D., Correspondent. Sisters 4.

Holy Spirit Motherhouse, 301 Yucca St., 78203. Tel: 210-533-5149. Motherhouse of the Sisters of the Holy Spirit and Mary Immaculate. Sr. Anne Finnerty, S.H.Sp., Gen. Supr. Sisters 58.

Incarnate Word and Blessed Sacrament Convent, 1135 Mission Rd., 78210. Tel: 210-534-8005. Sisters of the Incarnate Word and Blessed Sacrament. Sr. M. Odilia Korenek, Supr. Sisters 8.

Incarnate Word Generalate, 4503 Broadway, 78209. Tel: 210-828-2224. General Administration of the Congregation of Sisters of Charity of the Incarnate Word. Sr. Teresa Stanley, C.C.V.I., Supr. Gen. Sisters 4.

Incarnate Word Motherhouse and Retirement Community, 4707 Broadway, 78209. Tel: 210-829-7561. Mr. Richard Boyd, Exec. Dir.; Sr. Angelica Coleman, C.C.V.I., Admin. Extended Care; Sr. Margaret Mary Curry, C.C.V.I., Admin. Asst.; Sr. Philomena Birmingham, C.C.V.I., Coord. Independent Living; Sr. Agnes Moloney, C.C.V.I., Asst. Coord. Extended Care; Debbie Bowles, Dir. Admissions & Mktg.; Rev. Msgr. Thomas French, Chap. Sisters in Extended Care 40; Senior Independent Living 96.

Institute of the Daughters of Mary Help of Christians, Province of Mary Immaculate, 6019 Buena Vista St., 78237. Tel: 210-432-0089; 0090; Fax: 210-432-4016. Salesian Sisters of St. John Bosco. Sr. Martina Ponce, F.M.A., Prov. Supr.

Missionary Catechists of Divine Providence, St. Andrew's Convent, 2318 Castroville Rd., 78237. Tel: 210-432-0113. Casa Benitia, 4650 Eldridge Ave., 78237. Tel: 210-433-5259. Sisters 3. Casa Guadalupe, 147 School St., 78210. Tel: 210-534-9005. Sisters 3. Catholic Student Center, 312 Courtland St., 78212. Tel: 210-736-3752. Sisters 1. Casa Providencia, 203 Tansyl Dr., 78213. Tel: 210-348-6534. Sisters 3. St. Mary's Catholic School, 207 N. St. Mary's St., 78205. Tel: 210-223-1151. Sisters 1. Immaculate Conception Church, P.O. Box 387, Asherton, 78827-0367. Tel: 210-468-3342. Sisters 1. House of Studies of the Missionary Catechists of Divine Providence & House of Administration. Sr. Carmen Therese Lazo, M.C.D.P., Supr. Gen., House of Initial Formation. Tel: 210-435-4626. Students 2. Sisters 9.

Monastery of the Discalced Carmelite Nuns, 6301 Culebra & St. Joseph Way, 78238-4909. Tel: 210-680-1834. Rev. Mother Therese Leonard, O.C.D., Prioress. Sisters 10.

Mount Sacred Heart Convent, 5922 Blanco Rd., 78216. Tel: 210-344-4805; 344-4193. Provincial House of Sisters of the Sacred Heart of Jesus. Sr. Laura Gonzalez, S.S.C.J., Prov. Sisters 39.

North American Union, Sisters of Our Lady of Charity, P.O. Box 10443, 78210. Tel: 210-534-1231. Sr. Agnes O'Mahoney, O.L.C., Supr. Sisters 11.

Our Lady of Czestochowa, Grotto Shrine and Convent, 138 Beethoven St., 78210. Tel: 210-333-4582; 337-8193 (Convent). Seraphic Sisters of Our Lady of Sorrows. Sr. Inga Michnowicz, S.O.L.S., Supr.; Rev. Bernard Goebel, Chap. Sisters 4.

Our Lady of the Lake Convent, 515 S.W. 24th St., 78207. Tel: 210-434-1866; Fax: 210-431-9965. Sisters of Divine Providence. Sr. Annalee Prather, C.D.P., Coord. Professed Sisters 49. O.L.L. Convent Home for retired Sisters of Divine Providence. Coordinators: Sr. Madonna Sangalli, C.D.P.; Sr. Mona Gavin, S.H.Sp., McCullough Hall Nursing Center and Regan Hall, 603 S.W. 24th St., 78207. Tel: 210-433-6011. Home for retired Sisters of Divine Providence. Sisters 82.

Our Lady of the Pillar Convent, 251 W. Ligustrum Dr., 78228. Tel: 210-433-5501. Centralhouse of the Congregation of the Daughters of Mary Immaculate. Marianist Sisters. Sr. Evangeline Escobar, F.M.I., Prov.; Sr. La Von Kampf, F.M.I., Dir. of Sisters. Sisters 9.

Our Lady of Victory Missionary Sisters Convent, 1114 San Carlos, 78207-6727. Tel: 210-223-5005. Sisters 1.

Presentation Convent, 8931 Callaghan Rd., 78230-4570. Tel: 210-342-2503. Residence of the Community of the Union of the Sisters of the Presentation of the B.V.M. Sr. Mary F. O'Driscoll, P.B.V.M., Supr. Sisters 17.

Religious of Mary Immaculate Convent, 719 Augusta St., 78215. Tel: 210-226-0025; Fax: 210-226-3305. Religious of Mary Immaculate Sisters. Sr. Clara Echeverria, R.M.I., Local Supr. Sisters 12.

St. Anthony Convent, 100 Peter Baque Rd., 78209. Tel: 210-824-4553. Motherhouse and Novitiate of the Missionary Servants of St. Anthony. Sr. Mary Ann Domagalski, M.S.S.A. Sisters 5.

St. Brigid's Convent, 5118 Loma Linda Dr., 78201. Tel: 210-733-0701; 736-1671; Fax: 210-733-3145; 737-3683. Regional House. Sr. Teresa Carter, C.S.B., Regional Coord.

Address matters connected with congregation to the Regional Coord. Sisters 20.

St. James Convent, 907 W. Theo, 78225. Tel: 210-533-9659. Daughters of Mary Help of Christians (Salesian Sisters of St. John Bosco). Sr. Carmen Botello, F.M.A., Supr. Sisters 4.

St. John Bosco Convent, 5630 W. Commerce St., 78237. Tel: 210-432-8011. Daughters of Mary Help of Christians. Sr. Theresa Sirioni, F.M.A., Supr. Sisters 15.

St. Joseph's Convent - S.S.N.D. House of Formation, 2372 W. Southcross, 78211. Sr. Judy Schaefer, S.S.N.D., Coord. Sisters 3; Postulants 1.

St. Teresa's Convent, 138 Fair Ave., 78223-1014. Tel: 210-533-5330; Fax: 210-533-2532. Sr. Carmelina Guzman, S.T.J., Coord. Society of St. Theresa of Jesus 19.

School Sisters of Notre Dame, 132 City, 78204. Tel: 210-271-7433. Sr. Carol George, S.S.N.D., Coord. Sisters 3.

School Sisters of Notre Dame, Convents: Caroline House, 3415 W. Woodlawn, 78228. Tel: 210-435-3234. Sr. M. Emiliana Fecher, S.S.N.D., Correspondent. Sisters 3.

Seraphic Franciscan Sisters of Our Lady of Sorrows Convent. (Grotto Shrine of Our Lady of Czestochowa), 138 Beethoven St., 78210. Tel: 210-337-8193. Sr. Inga Michnowicz, O.L.S., Dir. Seraphic Sisters of Our Lady of Sorrows 4.

Seraphic Sisters of Our Lady of Sorrows Convent, 621 W. Woodlawn Ave., 78212. Tel: 210-734-3364. Sr. Emilia Rzeznik, Supr. Sisters 8.

The Sisters of Perpetual Adoration Convent, 2403 W. Travis St., 78207. Tel: 210-227-5546. Sr. Maria Conception Quesada-Aguirre, A.P.G., Supr. Sisters 7.

The Sisters of the Holy Cross, 800 Babcock Rd., J-5, 78201. Tel: 210-734-5327. Other Address: 404 Faith, 78228. Tel: 210-433-6408. Sisters 3.

Sisters, Servants of the Immaculate Heart of Mary, 1603 Babcock, #270, 78229. Tel: 210-340-3881. Sr. Virginia Celmer, I.H.M.

Stella Maris Convent, 2702 Castroville Rd., 78237. Tel: 210-434-1314. Congregation of Divine Providence, Inc. Sisters 3.

Ursuline Residences, 4812 Vance Jackson Rd., 78230. Tel: 210-344-1800. Ursuline Nuns.

Other Residences Located At: 3500 Oakgate, 78230. Tel: 210-694-5054. 1207 Olive, Jourdanton, 78026. Tel: 210-769-2015. 315 Shadwell, 78228. Tel: 210-737-7421. 1700 Jackson Keller #605, 78213. Tel: 210-344-9463. Sisters 10.

BIG WELLS. *Carmelitas del Sagrado Corazon-OCD*, P.O. Box 266, 78830. Tel: 210-457-2693. Sr. Paula Aramburo, O.C.D., Supr. Sisters 3.

BOERNE. *St. Scholastica Monastery*, 416 W. Highland, 78006. Tel: 210-249-2645; 816-8504. Congregation of Benedictine Sisters, Monastery, Novitiate and Omega Retreat Center. Sr. Mary Agnes Zinni, O.S.B., Prioress. Sisters 23.

HELOTES. *Generalate of the Congregation of Divine Providence*, P.O. Box 197, 78023. Tel: 210-695-8721. Sr. Lora Ann Quinonez, C.D.P., Supr. Gen. Sisters 6.

UVALDE. *Society of St. Teresa of Jesus*. (Teresian Sisters), Mailing Address: 343 N. Crisp St., 78801. Tel: 210-278-6724. Sisters 3.

[O] RETREAT HOUSES

SAN ANTONIO. *Oblate Renewal Center*, Mailing Address: 285 Oblate Dr., 78216-6693. Tel: 210-349-4173; 341-1366. Revs. Thomas Ovalle, O.M.I., Dir.; Kevin

Collins, O.M.I.; Sr. Theresa O'Toole, S.H.Sp.

BOERNE. *Omega Retreat Center*, 216 W. Highland Dr., 78006. Tel: 210-816-8471 (San Antonio); 249-3894 (Boerne). Mr. Andy Anderson, Prog. Coord.

CASTROVILLE. *Moye Center*, 600 London, 78009. Tel: 210-931-2227. Center for Retreats and Renewal. Under the direction of the Sisters of Divine Providence. Sisters 3.

NEW BRAUNFELS. *Spiritan Renewal Center*, 19440 IH 35 N., 78132-4839. Tel: 210-609-2475. Rev. Joseph Gaglione, C.S.Sp., Dir.

[P] CATHOLIC CHARITABLE ORGANIZATIONS AND CLINICS

SAN ANTONIO. *Catholic Charities, Archdiocese of San Antonio*, 2903 W. Salinas St., 78207. Tel: 210-433-3256; Fax: 210-433-0851. Valerie J. Trevino, Interm Dir.

See Curia Section - Department of Social & Community Services.

Daughters of Charity Services of San Antonio, 7607 Somerset Rd., 78211-3752. Tel: 210-921-0071; Fax: 210-922-0332. Mr. Donald Moore, Exec. Dir. Daughters of Charity Svcs.

This corporation operates centers at two locations: De Paul Family Center, 7603 Somerset, 78211. Tel: 210-924-5903. El Carmen Center, 18555-1 Leal Rd., 78221. Tel: 210-626-2121. Sisters 4.

Society of St. Vincent de Paul, 928 W. Commerce, 78207. Tel: 210-225-7837; Fax: 210-225-8878. Ms. Nell Sharrock, Pres.; Mary M. Armstrong, Exec. Dir.

[Q] NEWMAN CENTERS

SAN ANTONIO. *Catholic Campus Ministry*, Catholic Student Center, 312 W. Courtland Pl., 78212-3906. Tel: 210-736-3752. Sr. Gloria Urrabazo, M.C.D.P., Dir. Archdiocesan Campus Ministry: Bros. Michael Winslow, C.S.C., San Antonio College; John E. Lydon, O.P., St. Philip's College & Trinity University; Sr. M. Carmen Salas, M.H.S.H., Palo Alto College and Southwest Texas Junior College,Uvalde.; Mario Macias, University of Texas at San Antonio.

St. Anthony Catholic Student Center, 14523 Roadrunner Way, 78249. Tel: 210-699-9594. Mrs. Beatriz M. Garcia.

Southwest Texas Junior College, 2401 Garner Field Rd., Uvalde, 78801-6297. Tel: 210-278-4401.

Texas Lutheran College, 1000 W. Court St., Seguin, 78155-5999. Tel: 210-372-8000.

Schreiner College, 2100 Memorial Blvd., Kerrville, 78028-5697. Tel: 210-896-5411.

Both Texas Lutheran and Schreiner Colleges are served by Sr. Gloria Urrabazo, M.C.D.P.

[R] PERSONAL PRELATURES

SAN ANTONIO. *Opus Dei (Prelature of the Holy Cross and Opus Dei)*, 345 E. Summit, 78212. Tel: 210-732-3065. Rev. Jose Gomez.

[S] FOUNDATIONS, ENDOWMENTS AND TRUSTS

SAN ANTONIO. *The Archbishop Charity Fund*, P.O. Box 28410, 78228. Tel: 210-734-2620.

Archbishop Flores Charity Fund, P.O. Box 28410, 78228. Tel: 210-734-2620.

Archdiocesan Endowment Fund, P.O. Box 28410, 78228-0410. Tel: 210-734-2620. Rev. Msgr. Patrick Murray, Chancellor; Most Rev. Patrick Flores.

Assumption Seminary Endowment Fund, P.O. Box 28410, 78228-0410. Tel: 210-734-2620. Rev. Msgr. Patrick Murray, Chancellor; Most Rev. Patrick Flores.

Casa de Padres Endowment Fund, P.O. Box 28410, 78228-0410. Tel: 210-734-2620. Rev. Msgr. Patrick Murray, Chancellor; Most Rev. Patrick Flores.

Holy Spirit Trust, 301 Yucca St., 78203. Tel: 210-533-8142. Sisters of the Holy Spirit. Sr. Anne Finnerty, Pres.

Missionary Oblates of Mary Immaculate of Texas Continuing Care Foundation, 7711 Madonna Dr., 78216-6696. Tel: 210-349-1475. Rev. Jerome Burnet, O.M.I., Treas.

National Foundation for Mexican-American Vocations, P.O. Box 7367, 78207-0367. Tel: 210-227-0548. A nonprofit organization to help financially Mexican American Seminarians. Rev. Msgr. Bathasar Janacek, Chm.

St. Peter and Joseph Childrens' Home Endowment Fund, P.O. Box 28410, 78228-0410. Tel: 210-734-2620. Rev. Msgr. Patrick Murray, Chancellor; Most Rev. Patrick Flores.

Seton Home Endowment Fund, P.O. Box 28410, 78228-0410. Tel: 210-734-2620. Rev. Msgr. Patrick Murray, Chancellor; Most Rev. Patrick Flores.

HELOTES. *Providence Trust*, P.O. Box 197, 78023. Tel: 210-695-8721.

Congregation of Divine Providence, Inc. Charitable Trust. Trustees: Sr. Imelda Gonzalez, C.D.P.; Sr. John Martin Ebrom, C.D.P.; Sr. Madonna Sangalli, C.D.P.

[T] MISCELLANEOUS

SAN ANTONIO. *"Today's Catholic"*, Mailing Address: P.O. Box 28410, 78228-0410. 2718 W. Woodlawn Ave., 78228. Tel: 210-734-2620; Fax 210-734-2939. OfficialCatholic newspaper of the Archdiocese of San Antonio. Owned and operated by the San Antonio Archdiocesan Publishing Society. Most Rev. Patrick F. Flores, Publisher; Mrs. Martha Pack Brinkmann, Editor.

Archdiocesan Union of Holy Name Societies, 2610 Perez St., 78207. Tel: 210-433-6301. Rev. Richard Pena, Spiritual Dir.

Benedictine Resource Center, 530 Bandera Rd., 78228-5525. Tel: 210-735-4988; Fax: 210-735-2615. Sr. Mary Agnes Zinni, O.S.B., Pres.; Arturo Chavez, CEO.

Benitia Family Center, 4650 Eldridge Ave., 78237-2600. Tel: 210-433-9300; 432-0113; Fax: 210-432-6739. Sr. Carmen M. Sanchez, M.C.D.P., Dir. Sisters 3.

The Blue Army, 6680 Crestway, 78239. Tel: 210-654-1643. Rev. Robert Silverman, Archdiocesan Chap.

Catholic Eastside Apostolate. Healy-Murphy Center Inc. See High Schools, Private. 618 Live Oak, 78202. Tel: 210-223-2944.

Federation of Catholic Parent Teacher Clubs of the Archdiocese of San Antonio, 6002 Windy Hill Dr., 78242. Tel: 210-645-4500. Ruth Guerrero, Pres.

Focolare Movement, Mailing Address: P.O. Box 15726, 78212; Fax: 210-341-2535. (Work of Mary) (Men and Women), Founded in Trent, Italy, in 1943. International Headquarters is in Rome. Women's Branch, Texas, 10714 Mt. Tipton, 78213. Tel: 210-341-8445. Marigen Lohla, Men's Branch, Texas, 9315 Overton Rd., 78217. Tel: 210-590-8812; Fax: 210-590-8921. Mr. Joe Ting.

Hispanic Telecommunications Network, Inc., 1405 N. Main, #240, 78212. Tel: 210-227-5959; Fax: 210-554-0822. Mr. Jose Roberto Gutierrez, Pres.

Principal Activity is the production of Nuestra Familia, the National Catholic evangelization television series for U.S. Hispanics.

Intercongregational Justice & Peace Office. (Camino a la Paz), Mailing Address: P.O. Box 15765, 78212. 285 Oblate Dr., 78216. Tel: 210-344-6778. Rev. Jeff Malpide, C.M., Dir. Religious 1.

Ladies of Charity of El Carmen, 18555 Leal Rd., 78221. Tel: 210-626-1861. Martina Clakley, Pres.

Las Hermanas U.S.A., P.O. Box 15792, 78212-8992. Tel: 210-434-0947. Promotes the leadership role of Hispanic Women in the church and society. Dolores Florez.

Madonna Neighborhood Center, 1906 Castroville Rd., 78237. Tel: 210-432-2374. Norma J. Funari, Dir. Casework, Day Care, After School Care, Social Services, Adult & Youth Socialization Programs. Emergency Food Pantry, Clothing, Furniture, Counseling, Evening Meal, Summer Recreation.

Marian Center of San Antonio, P.O. Box 831001, 78283-1001. Tel: 210-225-6279; Fax: 210-225-0044. Ms. Therese H. Palacios, Pres.

Marianist Lay Network, 218 S. Josephine Tobin Dr., 78201-5941. Tel: 210-735-0212. Rita J. Bordano, Treas.

Merced Housing of Texas, 3120 W. Ashby St., 78228. Tel: 210-732-5667; Fax: 210-732-2309. Susan R. Sheeran, Regl. Pres. A consortium of religious orders to provide quality, affordable, service orientated housing for the economically poor, to strengthen families and promote healthy communities.

Missionaries of Pastoral Charity Society, 1135 Mission Rd., 78210-4598. Tel: 210-534-8005; Fax: 210-534-6568. Rev. Kenneth C. Myers (El Salvador), Dir.; Sr. Claudia Klesel, I.W.B.S., Office Mgr.

North American Union Sisters of Our Lady of Charity, P.O. Box 10443, 78210.

Oblate Lourdes Grotto Shrine of the Southwest, P.O. Box 96, 78212-1859. Tel: 210-342-9864. Rev. Richard Houlahan, O.M.I., Grotto Dir.

Oblate Missions, 2503 Blanco Rd., 78212-1859. Mailing Address: P.O. Box 96, 78291. Tel: 210-736-1685; Fax: 210-736-1314. Mailing Address: P.O. Box 2904, 78299-2904. Missionary Association of Mary Immaculate; Island of Lepers; Isles of Hope; Children of the Mountain. Most Rev. Philip F. Smith, O.M.I., D.D. (Philippines); Revs. Richard A. Houlahan, O.M.I., Dir.; Saturnino Lajo, O.M.I. (Spain), Spanish Consultant; Edward J. Cronin, O.M.I., Dir. Emeritus.

The Patrician Movement, Main Office: La Villita de San Patricio, 222 E. Mitchell St., 78210. Tel: 210-532-3126.

Field Offices: 1249 S. St. Mary St., 78210. Tel: 210-533-9191. 278 E. Mitchell, 78210. Tel: 210-533-2505. 528 S. Polaris, 78203. Tel: 210-534-4029. 215 Claudia, 78210. Tel: 210-533-0226. A non-profit corporation chartered under the laws of the State of Texas. Rev. Msgr. Dermot N. Brosnan, Exec. Dir.; Deacon Patrick M. Clancey, Ed.D., Admin.; Patrick M. Clancey, Admin. & Contact Person. Provides comprehensive, Residential and Outpatient Substance Abuse Treatment Services. Accredited by the Joint Commission on Accreditation of Healthcare Organizations. Licenced by the Texas Commission on Alcohol and Drug Abuse. 222 E. Mitchell, 78210. Total Assisted 1,750.

Pauline Book and Media Center, 114 Main Plaza, 78205. Tel: 210-224-8101; Fax: 210-224-0938. Sr. Susan Miriam Wolf, F.S.P., Supr. Daughters of St. Paul 4.

Pilgrim Center of Hope - Evangelization Center, 7680 Joe Newton, 78251. Tel: 210-521-3377; Fax: 210-521-0288. Directors: Deacon Tom Fox; Mrs. Mary Jane Fox; Rev. Jasper Mavs, O.F.M.

Pillars of San Fernando Cathedral, 115 Main Plaza, 78205. Tel: 210-734-2620. An organization of benefactors that promotes and helps finance the oldest cathedral-sanctuary in the United States. Most Rev. Bernard Popp, D.D.

Polish American Priest Association (P.A.P.A.), 5035 Bernadine, 78220. Tel: 210-648-1991. Rev. Peter Zenozian (BRK).

Religious of Mary Immaculate. (Pontifical), Villa Maria, 719 Augusta St., 78215. Tel: 210-226-0025; Fax: 210-226-3305. Sr. Clara Echeverria, R.M.I., Local Supr. Residence for Students and Working Girls. Apostolic Work: Counseling & guidance of young women of good moral conduct of any race or religion. Sisters 12; Girls 60.

San Antonio Community Law Center, 405 N. St. Mary's, Atrium 242, 78205. Tel: 210-271-9595; Fax: 210-271-3803. Provides legal assistance to the working poor. Attorneys: Bro. William Dooling, C.S.C.; Charles E. Montemayor.

San Antonio Intercommunity Finance Office, 2818 Castroville Rd., 78237. Tel: 210-341-8884. Sr. Carmen Caputo, C.N.D., Dir.

Secular Franciscan Order, 1214 Stonewall, 78211-1544. Tel: 210-924-6591. Rev. Gregorio J. Goicoechea, O.F.M.Cap., Spiritual Asst.

Serra Club of San Antonio, Inc., 544 Rittiman Rd., 78209. Tel: 210-828-0115. Mr. Charles A. Brown, Pres.

Teleton Navideno, 2903 W. Salinas, 78207. Tel: 210-433-3256. Christmas Telethon-Branch of Catholic Charities of San Antonio, Inc. Mr. Olegario G. Tijerina, Volunteer Admin. Coord.

MOUNTAIN HOME. *Camp Tecaboca*, 78058. Tel: 210-866-3425 (Summer); 713-926-5925 (Off-Season). Mailing Address: (September-May), 1122 Colorado, Ste. 106, Austin, 78701. Bro. Michael Gillespie, S.M.; Deece Eckstein, Dir. Tel: 512-320-0444; 320-0726 (Fax). Texas Catholic Boy's Camp. Operated by the Society of Mary, Province of St. Louis.

RELIGIOUS INSTITUTES OF MEN REPRESENTED IN THE ARCHDIOCESE

For further details refer to the corresponding bracketed number in the Religious Institutes of Men or Women section.

[0140]—*The Augustinians*. (Prov. of Castile).—O.S.A.

[0600]—*Brothers of the Congregation of Holy Cross*.—C.S.C.

[0470]—*The Capuchins Friars*.—O.F.M.Cap.

[0350]—*Cistercian Order of the Strict Observance*.—O.C.S.O.

[0360]—*Claretian Missionaries*. (Western Prov.).—C.M.F.

[0220]—*Congregation of the Blessed Sacrament*.—S.S.S.

[1330]—*Congregation of the Mission*. (Southern Prov.).—C.M.

[0630]—*Congregation of the Missionaries of the Holy Family*.—M.S.F.

[1000]—*Congregation of the Passion*.—C.P.

[1130]—*Congregation of the Priests of the Sacred Heart*.—S.C.J.

[0480]—*Conventual Franciscans*.—O.F.M.Conv.

[0260]—*Discalced Carmelite Fathers*.—O.C.D.

[0520]—*Franciscan Friars*. (Sacred Heart Prov.).—O.F.M.

[0650]—*Holy Ghost Fathers*. (Western Prov.).—C.S.Sp.

[0690]—*Jesuit Fathers and Brothers*. (New Orleans Prov.).—S.J.

[]—*Missionaries of the Nativity of Mary*. (Mexico).—M.N.M.

[1110]—*Missionaries of the Sacred Heart*.—M.S.C.

[0860]—*Missionhurst Congregation of the Immaculate Heart of Mary*.—C.I.C.M.

[0910]—*Oblates of Mary Immaculate*. (Southern Prov.).—O.M.I.

[0430]—*Order of Preachers (Dominican)*. (New Orleans Prov.).—O.P.

[0610]—*Priests of the Congregation of Holy Cross*.—C.S.C.

[1070]—*Redemptorist Fathers*.—C.SS.R.

[0760]—*Society of Mary (Marianists)*.—S.M.

[1200]—*Society of the Divine Savior*.—S.D.S.

[1060]—*Society of the Precious Blood.*—C.PP.S.

RELIGIOUS INSTITUTES OF WOMEN REPRESENTED IN THE ARCHDIOCESE

[0100]—*Adorers of the Blood of Christ.*—A.S.C.
[0230]—*Benedictine Sisters of the Pontifical Jurisdiction.*—O.S.B.
[1810]—*Bernardine Sisters of the Third Order of St. Francis.*—O.S.F.
[]—*Carmelitas del Sagrado Corazon.*—O.C.D.
[0360]—*Carmelite Sisters of the Divine Heart of Jesus.*—Carmel.D.C.J.
[3110]—*Congregation of Our Lady of the Retreat in the Cenacle.*—R.C.
[0460]—*Congregation of Sisters of Charity of the Incarnate Word.*—C.C.V.I.
[3735]—*Congregation of St. Brigid.*—C.S.B.
[0870]—*Congregation of the Daughters of Mary Immaculate (Marianist Sisters).*—F.M.I.
[2200]—*Congregation of the Incarnate Word and Blessed Sacrament.*—I.W.B.S.
[0725]—*Cordi-Marian Sisters.*—M.C-M.
[0760]—*Daughters of Charity of St. Vincent de Paul.*—D.C.
[0850]—*Daughters of Mary Help of Christians.*—F.M.A.
[0420]—*Discalced Carmelite Nuns.*—O.C.D.
[1070-13]—*Dominican Sisters.*—O.P.
[1070-19]—*Dominican Sisters.*—O.P.
[1150]—*Eucharistic Franciscan Missionary Sisters.*—E.F.M.S.
[1170]—*Felician Sisters.*—C.S.S.F.
[1310]—*Franciscan Sisters of Little Falls, MN.*
[1900]—*Hermanas Catequistas Guadalupanas.*—H.C.G.
[1910]—*Hermanas Josefinas.*—H.J.
[3370]—*Hermanas Mercedarias Del Santisimo Sacramento.*—H.M.S.S.
[2720]—*Mission Helpers of the Sacred Heart.*—M.H.S H.
[2770]—*Missionaries of Jesus, Mary and Joseph.*—M.J.M J.
[2690]—*Missionary Catechists of Divine Providence, San Antonio, Texas.*—M.C.D.P.
[2890]—*Missionary Servants of St. Anthony.*—M.S.S.A.
[]—*Missionary Sisters of Our Lady of Perpetual Help.*—M.P.S.
[2760]—*Missionary Sisters of the Immaculate Conception of the Mother of God.*—S.M.I.C.
[3070]—*North American Union of the Sisters of Our Lady of Charity.*—O.L.C.
[]—*Oblate Missionaries of Mary Immaculate.*—O.M.M.I.
[3130]—*Our Lady of Victory Missionary Sisters.*—O.L.V.M.
[0950]—*Pious Society Daughters of St. Paul.*—F.S.P.
[3460]—*Religious of Mary Immaculate.*—R.M.I.
[2970]—*School Sisters of Notre Dame.*—S.S.N.D.
[1680]—*School Sisters of St. Francis.* WI.—S.S.S.F.
[1690]—*School Sisters of the Third Order of St. Francis.*—O.S.F.
[]—*Seraphic Franciscan Sisters of Our Lady of Sorrows.*—O.L.S.
[1010]—*Sisters of Divine Providence of San Antonio, Texas.*—C.D.P.
[2360]—*Sisters of Loretto At the Foot of the Cross.*—S.L.
[3000]—*Sisters of Notre Dame de Namur.*—S.N.D.deN.
[3195]—*Sisters of Perpetual Adoration.*—A.P.G.
[3460]—*Sisters of Providence of Saint Mary-of-the-Woods, Indiana.*—S.P.
[1570]—*Sisters of St. Francis of the Holy Family.*—O.S.F.
[1930]—*Sisters of the Holy Cross.*—C.S.C.
[1960]—*Sisters of the Holy Family.*—S.H.F.
[2050]—*Sisters of the Holy Spirit and Mary Immaculate.*—S.H.Sp.
[3320]—*Sisters of the Presentation of the B.V.M.*—P.B.V.M.
[3670]—*Sisters of the Sacred Heart of Jesus.*—S.S.C.J.
[2150]—*Sisters, Servants of the Immaculate Heart of Mary.*—I.H.M.
[4020]—*Society of St. Theresa of Jesus.*—S.T.J.
[4110]—*Ursuline Nuns (Roman Union).*—O.S.U.

ARCHDIOCESAN CEMETERIES

SAN ANTONIO. *Holy Cross.*
San Fernando No. 1.
San Fernando No. 2.
San Fernando No. 3 (Roselawn).

NECROLOGY

† Janak, Rev. Msgr. Hubert, (Retired). —Died June 26, 1996.
† Kalina, Francis, (Absent on Sick Leave). —Died March 5, 1996.
† Vinklarek, Emil Thomas, (Retired). —Died Oct. 31, 1996.

Diocese of San Bernardino

Most Reverend

GERALD R. BARNES

Bishop of San Bernardino; ordained December 20, 1975; appointed Titular Bishop of Montefiascone and Auxiliary of San Bernardino January 27, 1992; succeeded to the See, December 28, 1995; installed as Second Bishop of San Bernadino March 12, 1996. *Office: 1201 E. Highland Ave., San Bernardino, CA, 92404.*

Chancery: 1201 E. Highland Ave., San Bernardino, CA, 92404. Tel.: 909-475-5300; Fax: 909-475-5833.

DIOCESE ESTABLISHED NOVEMBER 6, 1978.

Square Miles 27,293.

Comprises the Counties of San Bernardino and Riverside.

Legal Titles:

The Roman Catholic Bishop of San Bernardino, a Corporation Sole (Churches, Rectories, Halls, Catechetical Centers, etc.).

Diocese of San Bernardino Education and Welfare Corporation (Schools, Convents, Newman Facilities, etc.).

Diocese of San Bernardino Catholic Charities.

St. Bernardine Plaza.

La Paz Dev. Corp. (Senior Citizens Housing).

San Gorgonio Villa.

Caritas Telecommunications.

A California Non-profit Corporation.

STATISTICAL OVERVIEW

Personnel	
Bishop	1
Priests: Diocesan Active in Diocese	82
Priests: Active Outside Diocese	5
Priests: Retired, Sick or Absent	48
Number of Diocesan Priests	143
Religious Priests in Diocese	75
Extern Priests in Diocese	8
Ordinations:	
Diocesan Priests	1
Transitional Deacons	13
Permanent Deacons	83
Total Brothers	20
Total Sisters	156
Parishes	
Parishes	97
With Resident Pastor:	
Resident Diocesan Priests	64
Resident Religious Priests	29
Without Resident Pastor:	
Administered by Women Religious	3
Administered by Lay People	1
Missions	13
Professional Ministry Personnel:	
Lay Ministers	40
Welfare	
Catholic Hospitals	2
Total Assisted	308,361
Educational	
Seminaries, Diocesan	1
Students from This Diocese	8
Diocesan Students in Other Seminaries	8
Total Seminarians	16
High Schools, Diocesan and Parish	2
Total Students	894
Elementary Schools, Diocesan and Parish	30
Total Students	8,351
Elementary Schools, Private	1
Total Students	51
Catechesis/Religious Education:	
High School Students	8,299
Elementary Students	24,897
Total Students Under Catholic Instruction	42,508
Teachers in the Diocese:	
Priests	1
Sisters	45
Lay Teachers	438
Vital Statistics	
Receptions into the Church:	
Infant Baptism Totals	9,001
Adult Baptism Totals	1,539
Received into Full Communion	678
First Communions	8,230
Confirmations	2,644
Marriages:	
Catholic	1,543
Interfaith	328
Total Marriages	1,871
Deaths	2,331
Total Catholic Population	626,236
Total Population	3,037,303

Former Bishop—Most. Rev. PHILLIP F. STRALING D.D., Bishop of San Bernardino; ord. March 19, 1959; appt. July 18, 1978; cons. Nov. 16, 1978; transferred to See of Reno, June 29, 1995.

Chancellor/Moderator of Curia—Rev. Msgr. DONALD S. WEBBER, J.C.L., *1201 E. Highland Ave., San Bernardino, 92404.* Tel: 909-475-5100; 783-3811.

Bishops Secretary—Mrs. MARIA ECHEVERRIA, *1201 E. Highland Ave., San Bernardino, 92404.* Tel: 909-475-5110; Fax: 909-475-5109.

Chancery—1201 E. Highland Ave., San Bernardino, 92404. Tel: 909-475-5300; Fax: 909-475-5155. Office Hours: Mon.-Fri. 8:30-4:30.

Diocesan Business Manager—Deacon GEORGE M. SCHMIT, *1201 E. Highland Ave., San Bernardino, 92404.* Tel: 909-475-5150.

Presbyteral Council—Most Rev. GERALD R. BARNES; Rev. Msgr. DONALD S. WEBBER, J.C.L.; Very Rev. GEORGE GONZALES; Rev. EFREN MUSGNI, M.S.; Rev. Msgr. PHILIP BEHAN; Rev. MARK KOTLARCZYK; Very Rev. MICHAEL BROOKS, SS.CC.; Rev. RAFAEL PARTIDA; Rev. Msgr. PETER LUQUE; Rev. THOMAS BURDICK; Very Rev. RENO AIARDI, I.M.C.; Rev. KENNETH JENKINS; Very Rev. STEPHEN PORTER; Revs. JOSEPH KRAH; ARTURO BALAGAT; VINCENT CONNOR; ANTHONY FERRERO; FRED GAGLIA.

Diocesan Curia—Most Rev. GERALD R. BARNES; Rev. Msgr. DONALD S. WEBBER, J.C.L.; Sr. MARY JO NELSON, O.L.V.M.; Deacon GEORGE SCHMIT; JIM PESTA; Revs. ALFRED LOPINTO; ROBERT MILLER; PETER BRADLEY; Sr. DOMINIC REANTASSO, SS.CC.; CLARE COLELLA; MARIA ACOSTA; Rev. ROMEO SELECCION, M.S.

Diocesan Tribunal—1201 E. Highland Ave., San Bernardino, 92404. Tel: 909-475-5320.

Judicial Vicar—Rev. Msgr. ROBERT E. LAWRENCE, J.C.L.

Adjutant Judicial Vicar—Rev. Msgr. DONALD S. WEBBER, J.C.L.

Defender of the Bond—Rev. THOMAS WALLACE.

Pro-Synodal Judges—Rev. JOSEPH N. STADLER, J.C.D.; Rev. Msgr. LOURENCO AVILA; Revs. FRANCIS WIESER, J.C.D.; ADRIAN BRINN; ROBERT ERICKSON; ANTHONY T. FERRERO, J.C.L.; GEORGE GONZALES; KENNETH JENKINS; CORNELIUS O'LEARY, Ph.D.; Rev. Msgr. DONALD S. WEBBER, J.C.L.; Rev. Msgr. PHILIP BEHAN, J.C.L.; Revs. MICHAEL BROOKS, SS.CC.; ARTHUR CARRILLO, C.P., J.C.L.

Secretaries—GWEN GIFFORD; GINA GRADIAS.

Notary—GWEN GIFFORD; GINA GRADIAS.

Lay Advocates—SANDRA BOYD; Sr. JOAN BREIDER, O.S.F.; CONSTANCE BROWN; Deacon BUD BURRIS; CLARE COLELLA; SHARON DONOVAN; Deacon MARLIN FILIPEK; FRANCES FITZGERALD; JOHN FITZGERALD; Sr. PATRICIA HAIRE, C.S.J., Ph.D.; DAVID A. HATCHER, JR.; MARGARET HAWES; Deacon LLOYD S. HAWES; ALVIN KELLY; Deacon PHILIP KERMOTT; PHYLLIS KOLBLY; JOAN MCNELIS; Deacon WALTER MELENDREZ; MARY MYERS; Sr. DEANNA O'NEIL, O.S.B.; DEE A. OGDEN, Ph.D.; JAMES E. PESTA; YOLANDA REGALADO; WALDO SANCHEZ; JODY SANCHEZ; STEPHEN SCARPITTA; ROGER C. SCHERER; Sr. ELIZABETH SCULLY, O.F.M.; MARY SULLIVAN-TANSEY; Deacon GEORGE SCHMIT; BETTY SCHMIT; CAROLINA P. TORRES; PATRICIA WOODS.

Vicar for Ethnic Affairs—Most Rev. GERALD R. BARNES. Tel: 909-475-5110.

Vicar for Hispanic Affairs—Most Rev. GERALD R. BARNES. Tel: 909-475-5110.

Vicar for Deacons—Vacant. Tel: 909-475-5160.

Vicar for Native Americans—Rev. RAFAEL PARTIDA. Tel: 619-347-3507.

Vicar for Retired Priests—Rev. Msgr. THOMAS F. MEAGHER. Tel: 909-475-5120.

Vicar for Priests in Special Works—Rev. VINCENT CONNOR. Tel: 909-597-1861.

Vicar for Religious—Sr. CAROLYN GRIES, O.S.B., *1201 E. Highland Ave., San Bernardino, 92404.* Tel: 909-475-5345.

Archivist—Dr. R. BRUCE HARLEY, *1201 E. Highland Ave., San Bernardino, 92404.* Tel: 909-475-5399.

African American Commission Office—EFFIE SHARP, Chm. Tel: 909-475-5194.

Building Committee—1201 E. Highland Ave., San Bernardino, 92404. Tel: 909-475-5440.

Catechetical and Theological Formation—MARCIA HANINGER, Dir., Education Media; PETER R. BRADLEY, Dir., Straling Leadership Institute, *1201 E. Highland Ave., San Bernardino, 92404.* Tel: 909-475-5370.

Permanent Diaconate Office—MARIE ACOSTA; PAT SKORA, Ministry Service Analyst, *1201 E. Highland Ave., San Bernardino, 92404.* Tel: 909-475-5160.

Catholic Charities—Rev. ALFRED LOPINTO, *1450 N. D St., San Bernardino, 92405.* Tel: 909-388-1239.

Detention Ministry—MIKE KENNEDY, Coord. Tel: 909-388-1239.

Catholic Committee on Scouting—(Boy Scouts and Girl Scouts); PHILIP COLELLA, *4862 Pershing Ave., San Bernardino, 92407.* Tel: 909-882-6372. Rev. ANTHONY FERRERO, Chap., *1201 E. Highland Ave., San Bernardino, 92404.* Tel: 909-591-9402.

Campus Ministry—Rev. NED REIDY, C.S.C., Dir., *Christ of the Desert (Newman Center), Palm Desert, 92260.* Tel: 619-346-0089.

Catholic Daughters of America—Mrs. ELIZABETH TICICH, *11461 Courtside St., Victorville, 92392.* Tel: 619-949-4056.

Catholic Deaf Circle—St. Catherines of Alexandria Church, 7050 Brockton Ave., Riverside, 92506. Tel: 909-689-2624 (TDD); 683-0800.

Charismatic Renewal Office—Rev. MICHAEL BARRY, SS.CC., *641 Roberds, San Bernardino, 92411.* Tel: 909-386-7700. ADRIENNE SCHUBERT, Counseling and Prayer.

Council of Catholic Women—MARY JANE THOMAS, *1505 Pamela St., Corona, 91719.* Tel: 909-734-0972.

Cursillo—HANK ESPINOZA. Tel: 909-683-5956.

Diocesan Development Office—1201 E. Highland Ave., San Bernardino, 92404. Tel: 909-475-5460.

Diocesan Ministries Fund Drive—Vacant, *1201 E. Highland Ave., San Bernardino, 92404.* Tel: 909-475-5460.

Diocesan Planning and Increased Offering Campaign—1201 E. Highland Ave., San Bernardino, 92404. Tel: 909-475-5460.

Diocesan Real Property Department—PHILIP SOUSA, *1201 E. Highland Ave., San Bernardino, 92404.* Tel: 909-475-5440.

Ecumencial Commission—Rev. STEVE PORTER, *St. Mary Church, Fontana.* Tel: 909-822-5670.

Education Department—THOMAS J. HEDING, Supr., *1201 E. Highland Ave., San Bernardino, 92404.* Tel: 909-475-5437.

Caritas Telecommunications—CLARE COLELLA, Dir., *1201 E. Highland Ave., San Bernardino, 92404.* Tel: 909-475-5350; Fax: 909-475-5357.

Equestrian Order of Holy Sepulchre of Jerusalem—MARY HUMANN, *1605 Laurel Ave., Upland, 91784.*

Evangelization—Rev. MICHAEL BARRY, SS.CC., Dir., *641 Roberds, San Bernardino, 92411.* Tel: 909-386-7700.

Evangelization and Catechesis for Hispanics—Vacant, *1201 E. Highland Ave., San Bernardino, 92404.* Tel: 909-475-5360.

Centro Junipero Serra—1476 W. 6th St., San Bernardino, 92411. Tel: 909-384-8272.

Centro Maria De La Esperanza—St. Anthony Church, 3074 Madison St., Riverside, 92504. Tel: 909-688-6230.

Centro Sembrador—505 E. Mt. View Ave., Barstow, 92311. Tel: 619-256-1578.

Centro Cristo del Desierto—1030 W. 6th St., Ste. 16, Coachella, 92236. Tel: 619-398-0606.

Centro Tonantzin—13770 Oaks Ave., Chino, 91710. Tel: 909-591-8689.

Valley Missionary Program—Rev. JUAN CONNOR, C.S.C., Dir., Mailing Address: *52-525 Oasis Palm, Coachella, 92236.* Tel: 619-398-9278.

Native American Council—Deacon FRANK ALANIZ. Tel: 619-949-0696.

Italian Catholic Federation—MARGARITE HALSTEAD, Corresponding Office Sec., *4159 Largewood Pl., Riverside, 92506.*

Knights of Columbus—TOM SULLIVAN, Contact Person. Tel: 909-886-1964.

Marian Council—HOWARD LITTLEFIELD. Tel: 909-882-7146.

Missions—Rev. RENO AIARDI, I.M.C., Dir., *1201 E. Highland Ave., San Bernardino, 92404.* Tel: 909-475-5130. Holy Childhood Association: Sr. ROSALINE O'CONNOR, R.S.M., Coord. Society for the Propagation of the Faith; Catholic Relief Services; National and World Apostolates to the Poor *P.O. Box 1416, San Bernardino, 92402.* Tel: 909-475-5530.

Newspaper—"Inland Catholic"; Mr. STEVEN BARRIE, Editor, *1201 E. Highland Ave., San Bernardino, 92404.* Tel: 909-475-5420.

Office of Worship—LINDA VALDIVIA, Sec., *1201 E. Highland Ave., San Bernardino, 92404.* Tel: 909-475-5335.

Human Concerns Commission—JEANETTE ARNQUIST, *28111 Rawlings Rd., Hemet, 92344.*

Human Resources—Mr. JAMES PESTA, Dir., *1201 E. Highland Ave., San Bernardino, 92404.* Tel: 909-475-5570.

Planned Giving (The Catholic Foundation)—Vacant, *1201 E. Highland Ave., San Bernardino, 92404.* Tel: 909-475-5460.

Pope John Paul II, Polish American Society—Mrs. MARY JANE WILSON. Tel: 909-882-4377.

Priests Continuing Education—Rev. ROBERT MILLER, *1201 E. Highland Ave., San Bernardino, 92404.* Tel: 909-475-5340.

Priest Retreats—Rev. ROBERT MILLER, *1201 E. Highland Ave., San Bernardino, 92404.* Tel: 909-475-5340.

Pro Life Committee of Human Concerns Commission—Rev. THOMAS BURDICK, *St. Catherine of Alexandria, 7050 Brockton, Riverside, 92506.* Tel: 909-683-0800.

Seminarians—Most Rev. GERALD R. BARNES, *1201 E. Highland Ave., San Bernardino, 92404.* Tel: 909-475-5110.

Serra Clubs—HOWARD LITTLEFIELD, District Governor, *758 W. 24th St., San Bernardino, 92405.* Tel: 909-882-7146.

Serra Club, Palm Springs—THOMAS LIENBARD, *314 Castellana St., Palm Desert, 92260.* Tel: 619-340-1660.

Serra Club, High Desert—LEWIS KRELOVICH, *37114 San Bruno, Barstow, 92311.* Tel: 619-245-1339.

Serra Club, Riverside—GEORGE MATUS, Pres., *4545 9th St., Riverside, 92501.*

Serra Club, San Bernardino—JOSEPH C. BONADIMAN, Pres., *250 S. Lena Rd., Ste. E, San Bernardino, 92412.* Tel: 909-885-3806.

Serra Club, Murrieta—MARVIN HAYES, *44611 LaPaz Rd., Temecula, 92592.* Tel: 909-676-4804.

TV Apostolate—Wordnet, Inc. Rev. MICHAEL MANNING, S.V.D., *Divine Word Seminary, 11316 Cypress Ave., Ste. 9, Riverside, 92505.* Tel: 909-689-4885.

Vocations—Sr. SARAH SHREWSBURY, O.S.C., *1201 E. Highland Ave., San Bernardino, 92404.* Tel: 909-475-5470.

Engaged Encounter (English)—Coords.: BILL SHANNON; CLAUDIA SHANNON. Tel: 909-465-1434.

Engaged Encounter (Spanish)—Coords.: ALBERTO SANTANA; MONICA SANTANA. Tel: 909-872-0738.

Marriage Encounter—DAN QUAM; THERESA QUAM. Tel: 909-487-9325.

Marriage Enrichment—CHRIS STEVENSON; CHERYL STEVENSON. Tel: 909-989-1893.

Search—(Young Adult Retreats), Rev. VINCENT CONNOR, *15180 Euclid Ave., Chino, 91710.* Tel: 909-597-1861.

Inland Empire Catholic Singles—PHYLLIS PURCELL. Tel: 909-684-2592.

Ministry to the Divorced, Widowed and Separated—SUSAN KLESZWESKI, *Catholic Charities, 1201 E. Highland Ave., San Bernardino, 92404.* Tel: 909-370-0800.

Pre-Cana-Marriage Preparation—Deacon JAMES DALE, *St. Frances de Sales Church, 4268 Lime St., Riverside, 92501.* Tel: 909-686-4004 (Church); 689-4411 (Work); 684-4623 (Residence). Palm Springs: Catholic Charities: *850 S. Palm Canyon Dr., 92264.* Tel: 619-325-9566.

Liturgy Commission—LINDA VALDIVIA, Sec., *1201 E Highland Ave., San Bernardino, 92404.* Tel: 909-475-5335.

Natural Family Planning—SUSAN KLESZEWSKI, M.S.W., L.C.S.W., Dir., *1201 E. Highland Ave., San Bernardino, 92404.* Tel: 909-370-1039.

Family Life Commission—SUSAN KLESZEWSKI, M.S.W., L.C.S.W., *1201 E. Highland Ave., San Bernardino, 92404.* Tel: 909-370-1039.

Project Rachael (Post Abortion Counseling & Ministry) (24 Hr. Hot Line)—Tel: 1-800-794-7863.

A.I.D.S. Inter Faith Aids Council—c/o Catholic Charities. Tel: 909-370-0800. CATHERINE MCMILLAN. Tel: 619-325-9566.

World Apostolate of Fatima (Blue Army)-San Bernardino Division—FERNE C. SCHMITT, Sec. Tel: 909-875-2894.

Apostolate of the Sacred Heart—LUCILLE MCSWEENEY, Coord. Tel: 909-626-4515.

Pregnancy Counseling Center of San Bernardino—Tel: 909-889-4182; (24 Hr. Hot Line) 909-825-6656.

Third Order Franciscans—MARGARET MEDEIROS, Contact, *c/o Queen of Angels Church, 4824 Jones Ave., Riverside, 92505.* Tel: 909-689-3674.

CLERGY, PARISHES, MISSIONS AND PAROCHIAL SCHOOLS

CITY OF SAN BERNARDINO
(San Bernardino County)

1—OUR LADY OF THE ROSARY CATHEDRAL, Revs. Alfred Lo Pinto (BRK) Rector; Louis Abdoo, I.M.C.; Luigi Inverardi, I.M.C.
Office: 265 W. 25th St., 92405. Tel: 909-883-8991; Fax: 909-882-2061.
Res., 2525 Arrowhead Ave., 92405. Tel: 909-883-1141.
School—2620 Arrowhead Ave., 92405. Tel: 909-886-1088.
Lay Teachers 19; Students 348.
Catechesis/Religious Programs—Students 145.

2—CHRIST THE KING (1934), Rev. Miguel Urrea.
Res., 272 E. Rialto Ave., 92408. Tel: 909-885-1476; Fax: 909-885-3926.

3—OUR LADY OF THE ASSUMPTION (1954), Rev. Michael L. Sturn; Deacon G. Dale Plein.
Res., 796 W. 48th St., 92407. Tel: 909-882-2931; Fax: 909-883-4851.
School—Tel: 909-881-2416. Sr. Maura Redington, Prin.
Sisters of Mercy 3; Lay Teachers 8; Students 318.
Catechesis/Religious Programs—Students 280.

4—OUR LADY OF FATIMA (1952), Rev. Edmund Gomez. Pastoral Coord. Sr. Eileen Rafferty, R.S.M.; Sr. Marita Beumer, C.PP.S.
Office: 1000 N. Valencia Ave., 92410. Tel: 909-885-0948; Fax: 909-384-0576.
Catechesis/Religious Programs—Students 105.

5—OUR LADY OF GUADALUPE (1925) (Hispanic), Revs. Ramon Rosales; Martin Rodriguez, O.R.C.; Adolphus Chavez.
Res., 1430 W. Fifth St., 92411. Tel: 909-888-0044; 884-8010; Fax: 909-888-4428.
Catechesis/Religious Programs—1475 W. 7th St., 92411. Tel: 909-381-1628.
Students 711.

6—ST. ANNE (1938), Revs. James Moore; Joseph Phan Nam, C.M.C.; Kathy Jeffries, Pastoral Coord.
Res., 6885 Del Rosa Ave., 92404. Tel: 909-884-6375; Fax: 909-884-8976.
School—6886 Del Rosa Ave., 92404. Tel: 909-885-7472; Fax: 909-884-5870.
Lay Teachers 9; Students 128.
Catechesis/Religious Programs—Tel: 909-884-5400.
Students 198.

7—ST. ANTHONY (1948), Revs. Eric P. Vargas, S.V.D.; Paul Vung Le, S.V.D.
Res., 1640 Western Ave., 92411. Tel: 909-887-3810; Fax: 909-880-0982.
School—1510 W. 16th St., 92411. Tel: 909-887-5413; Fax: 909-887-5413.
Sisters of Mercy 5; Lay Teachers 7; Students 260.
Catechesis/Religious Programs—Students 260.

8—ST. BERNARDINE (1862), Rev. Edmund Gomez; Sr. Marita Beumer, C.PP.S., Pastoral Coord.
Res., 531 North F St., 92410. Tel: 909-884-0104; Fax: 909-885-4634.
Catechesis/Religious Programs—Students 97.

9—ST. PHILLIP THE APOSTLE. Unassigned. (Melkite-Greek Catholic Mission).
Res., 923 W. Congress, 92410.

10—ST. THERESA. Closed. For inquiries for parish records contact the Chancery.

OUTSIDE THE CITY OF SAN BERNARDINO

Adelanto, San Bernardino Co., Christ the Good Shepherd (1962), Rev. Antonio Das Neves.
Res., 17900 Jonathan, P.O. Box 579, 92301. Tel: 619-246-7083; Fax: 619-246-4603.

Alta Loma, San Bernardino Co., St. Peter & St. Paul (1970), Very Rev. Peter Covas; Rev. Jaime Hamame.
Mailing Address: P.O. Box 248, 91701. Tel: 909-987-9312; Fax: 909-980-9404.
School—9135 Banyan Ave., 91701. Tel: 909-987-7908.
Lay Teachers 9; Aides 5; Students 116.
Catechesis/Religious Programs—Tel: 909-980-9423. Dot Flagg, D.R.E.
Students 1,700.
Youth Ministry—Tel: 909-944-8483. Carol Michaud.
Students 300.

Anza, Riverside Co., Sacred Heart (1993), Rev. Bernard J. Carr.
Mailing Address: P.O. Box 390118, 92539.
Res., 56250 Cahuilla Rd., Hwy. 371, 92539. Tel: 909-763-5636; Fax: 909-763-0236.
Catechesis/Religious Programs—Ms. Linda Bahash, D.R.E.
Students 160.
Missions—Anza, Riverside Co., Our Lady of the Snows Cahuilla Indian Reservation,; Anza, Cahuilla Indian Reservation; Riverside Co., Santa Rosa Indian Mission, Santa Rosa Reservation, Tel: 909-659-2708; Santa Rosa Reservation.

Apple Valley, San Bernardino Co., Our Lady of the Desert (1974), Revs. Maurice Cardinal; Vimencio Ignacio; Deacons Carlos Reyes; Robert Rittman.
Office: 18386 Corwin Rd., 92307. Tel: 619-242-4427; Fax: 619-242-1195.
Catechesis/Religious Programs—Tel: 619-242-5819.
Students 526.

Banning, Riverside Co., Precious Blood (1890), Rev. Michael Lama; Deacon Ralph Sepulveda.
Res., 157 W. Nicolet St., 92220. Tel: 909-849-2434; Fax: 909-849-8698.
School—P.O. Box 458, 92220. Tel: 909-849-2433; Fax: 909-849-0843.
Lay Teachers 7; Students 162.
Missions—Banning, Riverside Co., St. Mary, 92220. Tel: 909-849-2434; Morongo Reservation, Riverside Co., Indian Mission, North of Fields Rd., 92220.
Catechesis/Religious Programs—117 W. Nicolet St., Tel: 909-849-1897.
Students 142.

Barstow, San Bernardino Co., St. Joseph (1914), Revs. Einer Ochoa; Amaro Saumell; Deacons Francis Roman; Margarito Saenz; Donald Burgett.
Res., 505 E. Mountain View Ave., 92311. Tel: 619-256-6818; Fax: 619-256-8307.
School—555 E. Mountain View Ave., 92311. Tel: 619-256-2397.
Sisters of Mercy of the Blessed Sacrament 3; Lay Teachers 8; Students 185.
Mission—Baker, San Bernardino Co., Our Lady of the Desert, 92311.

Catechesis/Religious Programs—Students 370.
St. Philip Neri Church (1979), Rev. Joseph Nacu, M.S.
Mailing Address: 909 Armory #409, 92311. Tel: 619-253-5412; Fax: 619-253-2021. [JC]
Catechesis/Religious Programs—Students 75.

Beaumont, Riverside Co., San Gorgonio (1908), Rev. John Robert Domas. In res., Rev. John Yates, C.SS.P.
Res., 1234 Palm Ave., P.O. Box 155, 92223. Tel: 909-845-2849; Fax: 909-845-9259.
Catechesis/Religious Programs—Students 153.

Big Bear Lake, San Bernardino Co., St. Joseph (1931), Rev. Lawrence F. Grajek.
Res., 42242 N. Shore Dr., P.O. Box 1709, 92315. Tel: 909-866-3030; Fax: 909-866-5087. [JC]
Catechesis/Religious Programs—Tel: 909-866-4581.
Students 125.

Bloomington, San Bernardino Co., St. Charles Borromeo (1939) (Hispanic), Rev. Richard Humphrys.
Office: 11342 Spruce St., Box 248, 92316. Tel: 909-877-0792; Fax: 909-877-4304.
Res., 11368 Spruce St., 92316.
Catechesis/Religious Programs—Students 400.

Blythe, Riverside Co., St. Joan of Arc, Rev. Arturo G. Chavez.
Res., 875 E. Chanslorway, 92225. Tel: 619-922-3261; Fax: 619-922-5279.

Cathedral City, Riverside Co., St. Louis (1948), Revs. Michael J. Brooks, SS.CC.; Delfino Lara, SS.CC. (Mexico).
Res., 37-220 Glenn Ave., 92234. Tel: 619-328-2398; Fax: 619-770-4598. [CEM]

Chino, San Bernardino Co., Our Lady of Guadalupe (1902) (Hispanic), Rev. Anthony T. Ferrero.
Res., 5048 D St., 91710. Tel: 909-591-9402; Fax: 909-591-9404.
Catechesis/Religious Programs—Tel: 909-628-3615.
Students 500.
St. Margaret Mary (1947), Rev. Thomas F. Gillespie.
Res., 12686 Central Ave., 91710. Tel: 909-627-8466; Fax: 909-627-8049. [JC]
School—12664 Central Ave., 91710. Tel: 909-591-8419.
Sisters of St. Francis 2; Lay Teachers 13; Students 314.
Catechesis/Religious Programs—Tel: 909-591-7408.
Students 850.

Chino Hills, San Bernardino Co., St. Paul the Apostle (1986), Rev. Michael N. Maher, SS.CC.; Sr. Mary Mackessy, S.N.J.M., Pastoral Assoc.
Office: 14085 Peyton Dr., 91709. Tel: 909-465-5503; Fax: 909-465-1683.
Res., 14860 Cherry Dr., 91709. Tel: 909-597-6154.
Catechesis/Religious Programs—Tel: 909-465-5503, Ext. 16. Lori Muniz, D.R.E.
Students 1,650.

Coachella, Riverside Co., Our Lady of Soledad, Revs. Robert J. Nogosek, C.S.C.; John S. Connor, C.S.C. In res., Revs. Joseph Pawlicki, C.S.C.; Donald F. Guertin, C.S.C.
Res., 52-525 Oasis Palm, 92236. Tel: 619-398-5577; Fax: 619-398-1783.
Catechesis/Religious Programs—Judy Hoy, D.R.E.
Students 500.

Colton, San Bernardino Co., Immaculate Conception (1943), Rev. Michael R. McNally; Deacon Wayn Joslin.
Office: 1106 N. La Cadena Dr., 92324. Tel: 909-825-5110; Fax: 909-825-0912.
Res., 1090 N. La Cadena Dr., 92324. Tel: 909-825-3004. [JC]
Catechesis/Religious Programs—Students 346.
San Salvador (1893) (Hispanic), Rev. Pierre Deglaire, C.S.Sp.
Parish Center: 178 W. K St., 92324. Tel: 909-825-3481; Fax: 909-825-4473.
Church—Seventh St. & L St., 92324.
Catechesis/Religious Programs—Students 451.

Corona, Riverside Co.,

1—CORPUS CHRISTI CHURCH, (1994), Rev. Gerald C. Deluney.
Office: 107 N. McKinley #109, 91719. Tel: 909-272-9043; Fax: 909-272-6821.
Catechesis/Religious Programs—Students 350.

2—ST. EDWARD, (1896), Rt. Rev. Peter Lugue; Revs. John Benjamin; Timothy Jernejcic.
Res., 605 W. Fifth St., 91720. Tel: 909-737-6432; Fax: 909-737-7259.
School—500 S. Merrill St., 91720. Tel: 737-2530.
Lay Teachers 25; Students 550.
Catechesis/Religious Programs—Tel: 909-737-5060.
Students 779.

3—ST. MARY MAGDALENE, (1989), Sr. Maureen Chiccine, R.S.C.J., Pastoral Coord.
Church—8540 Weirick Rd., 91719. Tel: 909-277-1801.
Catechesis/Religious Programs—Students 150.

4—ST. MATTHEW, (1973), Rev. John Wagner; Sandra Boyd, Pastoral Assoc.
Res., 2140 W. Ontario, 91720. Tel: 909-737-1621; Fax: 909-737-9715.
Catechesis/Religious Programs—Lou Ann Tannaz, D.R.E.
Students 775.

Crestline, San Bernardino Co., St. Frances Xavier Cabrini (1946), Rev. John R. Hindman.
Res., 23079 Crest Forest Dr., P.O. Box 3817, 92325. Tel: 909-338-2303; Fax: 909-338-2383.
Catechesis/Religious Programs—Students 75.

Desert Hot Springs, Riverside Co., St. Elizabeth of Hungary (1946), Rev. Edward McGuiness.
Res., 66700 E. Pierson Blvd., 92240. Tel: 619-329-8794; Fax: 619-329-6760.
Catechesis/Religious Programs—Tel: 619-251-9268.
Students 135.

Fontana, San Bernardino Co.,

1—CHURCH OF THE RESURRECTION, (1953), Revs. Leonard Krzywda, C.R.; Ted Wicki, C.R. In res., Rev. Humphrey Ruszel, C.R.
Res., 7650 Tamarind, 92336. Tel: 909-822-4732; Fax: 909-822-0620.
School—17434 Miller Ave., 92335. Tel: 909-822-4431; Fax: 909-822-0617.
Sisters 1; Lay Teachers 10; Students 293.
Catechesis/Religious Programs—Tel: 909-822-2502.
Students 435.

2—ST. GEORGE, (1954), Rev. Philip A. O'Carroll.
Res., 17895 San Bernardino Ave., 92335. Tel: 909-877-1531; Fax: 909-877-6531.

3—ST. JOSEPH, (1930), Revs. Richard F. McGee, C.R.; Henry Ruszel, C.R.; Deacon Michael Juback.
Office: 17080 Arrow Blvd., 92335. Tel: 909-822-0566; Fax: 909-829-1739.
School—8460 Mango Ave., 92335. Tel: 909-822-5423.
Daughters of Divine Charity 3; Lay Teachers 7; Students 272.
Catechesis/Religious Programs—Tel: 909-822-3411.
Students 282.

4—ST. MARY, (1939), Rev. Stephen C. Porter; Deacons Mario Omtierrez; Chuck Faltz; Roberto Cardenai.
Church—14798 Slover Ave., 92337. Tel: 909-822-5670 (English) 909-356-8398 (Spanish) 909-822-1830; Fax: 909-822-6672.
Catechesis/Religious Programs—Tel: 909-872-1830.
Students 450.

5—ST. NICHOLAS, (Byzantine Rite), Rev. Kurt Burnette, Admin.
Res., 9112 Oleander Ave., 92335. Tel: 909-822-9917.

Grand Terrace, San Bernardino Co., Christ the Redeemer (1980), Rev. Msgr. Donald S. Webber.
Res., 12770 Oriole, 92313. Tel: 909-783-3811; Fax: 909-783-4689.
Catechesis/Religious Programs—Students 235.

Guasti, San Bernardino Co., San Secondo d'Asti (1926) (Italian), In res., Rev. Msgr. Thomas Meagher.
Res., 250 N. Turner Ave., P.O. Box 1056, 91743. Tel: 909-390-0011; Fax: 909-390-0012.
Catechesis/Religious Programs—Students 119.

Hemet, Riverside Co., Holy Spirit Parish (1991), Rev. Silvio D'Ostilio, C.S.Sp.; Jamie Allred, Youth Ministry; Joyce Frichtel, Pastoral Assoc.
Res., 26340 Soboba Ave., Box 5268, 92544. Tel: 909-927-8544; Fax: 909-927-8546.
Catechesis/Religious Programs—Students 190.
Our Lady of the Valley (1946), Revs. Louis G. Perreault, C.S.Sp.; Lance R. Bliven, C.S.Sp.; Clement Lachowsky, C.S.Sp.; James H. Burnie, C.S.Sp.; Deacon Jack Henke.
Mailing Address: P.O. Box 2446, 92546.
Res., Parish Office, 780 S. State St., 92543. Tel: 909-929-6131; Fax: 909-929-8009.
Catechesis/Religious Programs—Tel: 909-658-7436. Ella Mae Tufte, D.R.E.
Students 573.

Hesperia, San Bernardino Co., Holy Family, Rev. Msgr. Philip A. Behan; Rev. Robert Guerrero.
Res., 9974 I Ave., 92345. Tel: 619-244-9180; Fax: 619-244-1959.

Highland, San Bernardino Co., St. Adelaide (1956), Rev. John Ryan; Sr. Maura Feely, Admin. Assoc.
Res., 27457 E. Baseline, 92346. Tel: 909-862-8669; Fax: 909-862-1603.
School—27487 E. Baseline, 92346. Tel: 909-862-5851; Fax: 909-862-2877.
Lay Teachers 11; Students 315.
Catechesis/Religious Programs—Tel: 909-862-8184.
Students 400.
Mission—East Highlands, San Bernardino Co., St. John Bosco, 28991 Merris St., Highland, 92346. Tel: 909-425-0931. Rev. John Ryan.

Idyllwild, Riverside Co., Queen of Angels, Rev. Wayne T. Epperley, C.S.Sp.
Res., 54525 N. Circle Dr., P.O. Box 1106, 92549. Tel: 909-659-2708; Fax: 909-659-0208.

Indio, Riverside Co., Our Lady of Perpetual Help (1937), Revs. Rafael A. Partida; Michael Krelovich.
Office: 82-450 Bliss St., 92201. Tel: 619-347-3507; Fax: 619-347-8367.
Res., 45-119 Park St., P.O. Box BB, 92201. Tel: 619-347-5661 (Rectory).
School—82-470 Bliss Ave., 92201. Tel: 619-347-3786; Fax: 619-347-7207.
Lay Teachers 9; Students 176.
Catechesis/Religious Programs—Tel: 619-347-0594.
Students 447.

Joshua Tree, San Bernardino Co., St. Christopher of the Desert (1960), Rev. Robert J. Tomkins.
Res., 61350 Wahl Terr., 92252. Tel: 619-366-8710; Fax: 619-366-2690.
Church—Parish Center, 61261 Sunburst Dr., 92252. Tel: 619-366-8810; Fax: 619-366-2690.

Lake Arrowhead, San Bernardino Co., Our Lady of the Lake (1938), Rev. Robert J. Erickson.
Res., 27642 Rim of the World Dr., P.O. Box 7, Crest Park, 92326. Tel: 909-337-2333; Fax: 909-337-5041. [CEM]
Catechesis/Religious Programs—Students 170.

Lake Elsinore, Riverside Co., St. Frances of Rome (1887), Revs. George Gonzalez; Jose P. Kuruvila, O.I.C.; Deacon Bud Burris.
Res., P.O. Box 215, 92530. Tel: 909-674-6881; Fax: 909-674-6443.
Catechesis/Religious Programs—Students 350.

Lake Tamarisk, Riverside Co., St. Augustine, Rev. Edward L. Franklin (OG).
Mailing Address: P.O. Box 768, Desert Center, 92239. Tel: 619-227-3191; Fax: 619-328-8392.
Res., 43960 Shasta Dr., 92239.

La Quinta, Riverside Co., St. Francis of Assisi (1974), Rev. Jack D. Barker.
Res., 47-225 Washington, P.O. Box 1503, 92253. Tel: 619-564-1255; Fax: 619-564-0763.
Catechesis/Religious Programs—Tel: 619-564-2069.
Students 373.

Loma Linda, San Bernardino Co., St. Joseph the Worker (1944), Rev. Paul R. Gill.
Res., 10816 Mt. View Ave., 92354. Tel: 909-796-2605; Fax: 909-796-0755.
Catechesis/Religious Programs—Tel: 909-796-4308.
Students 185.

Lucerne Valley, San Bernardino Co., St. Paul (1963), Rev. Msgr. John T. Slattery.
Res., 8973 Mesa Rd., P.O. Box 588, 92356. Tel: 619-248-7410; Fax: 619-248-2559.

Mecca, Riverside Co., Our Lady of Guadalupe Shrine (1927), Revs. Pedro E. Amezcua; Saul Ayala.
Mailing Address: P.O. Box 218, 92254. Tel: 619-396-2717; Fax: 619-396-0047. [JC]
Church—65-100 Dale Killer Rd., 92254.
Res., 91-110 5th St., 92254.
Catechesis/Religious Programs—Tel: 909-684-0279; Fax: 909-684-0390.
Students 500.

Montclair, San Bernardino Co., Our Lady of Lourdes, Rev. Robert J. Donat.
Res., 10191 Central Ave., 91763. Tel: 909-626-7278; Fax: 909-626-0562.
School—5303 Orchard St., 91763. Tel: 909-621-4418; 624-5164; Fax: 909-626-0318.
Sisters of the Presentation 3; Lay Teachers 10; Students 280.
Catechesis/Religious Programs—Sr. Angela Callanan, D.R.E.
Students 579.

Moreno Valley, Riverside Co., St. Christopher (1959), Revs. Efren Musngi, M.S.; Enrique La Puebla, M.S.; Romeo Seleccion, M.S.; Deacon Samual Sanchez.
Res., 25075 Cottonwood Ave., 92553. Tel: 909-924-1968; Fax: 909-247-6477.
Catechesis/Religious Programs—D.R.E.: Elizabeth Scretchings; Pat Garza, (High School); Mirca Sanchez, (Spanish).
Students 1,689.

Murrietta, Riverside Co., St. Martha's (1992), Rev. Charles F. Schultz, S.T.D.
Church—37200 Whitewood Rd., 92563. Tel: 909-698-8180; Fax: 909-698-7353.
Catechesis/Religious Programs—Students 1,036.

Needles, San Bernardino Co., St. Ann (1888), Rev. William M. Brunner, S.S.C.

Res., 218 D St., P.O. Box 175, 92363. Tel: 619-326-2721; Fax: 619-326-3068. [JC]
Catechesis/Religious Programs—Students 130.

Norco, Riverside Co., St. Mel (1959), Rev. Arturo Balagat.
Res., 4200 Corona Ave., P.O. Box 700, 91760. Tel: 909-737-7144; Fax: 909-735-8332.

Ontario, San Bernardino Co., Our Lady of Guadalupe (1948) (Hispanic), Revs. Sacramento Perez, O.M.; Francisco Caballero; Edwardo Perez; Deacons Ernesto Vital; Guiseppe Raspa.
Res., 710 S. Sultana St., 91761. Tel: 909-986-6154; Fax: 909-984-1541.
Catechesis/Religious Programs—Students 750.

St. George (1905), Revs. Joseph Krah; Amaro Saumell; Santos Leonel Ortega; Sr. Danielle Daran, R.N., Pastoral Assoc. In res., Rev. Msgr. Timothy Lawlor.
Res., 325 W. E St., 91762. Tel: 909-983-2637; Fax: 909-395-9707. [JC]
School—322 W. D St., 91762. Tel: 909-984-9123.
Lay Teachers 9; Students 303.
Catechesis/Religious Programs—Students 290.

St. Elizabeth Ann Seton (1980), Rev. Msgr. Lourenco Avila.
Res., 2713 S. Grove Ave., 91761. Tel: 909-947-2956; Fax: 909-947-2946.
Catechesis/Religious Programs—Tel: 909-947-5436.
Students 626.

Palm Desert, Riverside Co., Christ of the Desert (1986). (Newman Center). Rev. Ned Reidy, C.S.C.
Res., 73441 Fred Waring Dr., 92260. Tel: 619-346-0089; Fax: 619-340-2245.

Sacred Heart (1956), Revs. Anthony J. Timlin; Peter McCormick, S.P.
Res., 43-775 N. Deep Canyon Rd., 92260. Tel: 619-346-6502; Fax: 619-773-4873.
School—Tel: 619-346-3513. Sr. Joan Griffin, O.S.F., Prin.
Lay Teachers 9; Religious Teachers 2; Students 265.
Catechesis/Religious Programs—Tel: 619-340-0143.
Students 165.

Palm Springs, Riverside Co., Our Lady of Guadalupe (1912) (Cahuilla Indian), Rev. Eugene Speno.
Res., 204 S. El Segundo, P.O. Box 1947, 92263. Tel: 619-325-5809; Fax: 619-327-2049.

Our Lady of Solitude (1929) (Hispanic), Revs. Miguel Ceja; Adrian Brinn; Deacon John Skora.
Res., 151 W. Alejo Rd., 92262. Tel: 619-325-3816; Fax: 619-325-5316. [JC]
Catechesis/Religious Programs—Students 225.

St. Theresa, Rev. Msgr. Malachy M. McGinn.
Res., 2800 E. Ramon Rd., 92264. Tel: 619-323-2669; Fax: 619-322-8581.
School—455 S. Compadre, 92262. Tel: 619-327-4919.
Sisters 4; Lay Teachers 10; Students 320.

Perris, Riverside Co., St. James (1907), Rev. William D. Erstad. In res., Rev. John Niessen.
Office: 269 W. Third St., 92570.
Res., 260 W. Third St., 92570. Tel: 909-657-2380; Fax: 909-943-7290.
School—250 W. Third St., 92570. Tel: 909-657-5226; Fax: 909-657-1793.
Irish Sisters of Mercy 3; Lay Teachers 10; Students 300.
Catechesis/Religious Programs—Tel: 909-657-8809. Sr. Noreen O'Connor, D.R.E.
Students 989.

Phelan, San Bernardino Co., Blessed Junipero Serra Church (1989), Rev. Patrick V. Kirsch.
Mailing Address: P.O. Box 292570, 92329-2570.
Rectory Office: 4471 Sunrise Blvd., 92371. Tel: 619-868-4342; Fax: 619-249-3438.
Catechesis/Religious Programs—Students 142.

Rancho Cucamonga, San Bernardino Co., Our Lady of Mount Carmel (1905), Rev. Alfonso Cerezo.
Res., 10079 Eighth St., P.O. Box 303, 91729-0303. Tel: 909-987-2717; Fax: 909-987-3818.
Catechesis/Religious Programs—Students 410.

Sacred Heart (1953), Rev. Fred R. Gaglia, Ph.D.
Res., 12704 Foothill Blvd., 91739. Tel: 909-899-1049; Fax: 909-899-3229.
School—Tel: 909-899-1601.
Lay Teachers 11; Students 300.
Catechesis/Religious Programs—Students 340.

Redlands, San Bernardino Co., Sacred Heart (1894), Revs. Joseph F. Felker, Admin.; Frank T. Dicristina; Deacons William Keough; Richard Cover.
Res., 115 W. Olive Ave., 92373. Tel: 909-793-2469; Fax: 909-335-1719.
School—215 S. Eureka St., 92373. Tel: 909-792-3958.
Lay Teachers 20; Students 294.
Catechesis/Religious Programs—Tel: 909-798-4167. Dr. Sarah Elder, D.R.E.
Students 443.

St. Mary (1941) (Latino), Rev. Jose Maria Cima.
Res., 1214 Columbia St., 92374. Tel: 909-792-3695; Fax: 909-798-2665. [JC]
Catechesis/Religious Programs—Students 310.

Rialto, San Bernardino Co., St. Catherine of Siena (1949), Rev. Howard A. Lincoln; Deacons Joseph F. Rios; Edwin Chamberlayne; Gonzalo Sotelo. Pastoral Assoc.: Kay Halder; Steve Valenzuela; Horacio Cortez. In res., Rev. Ciro Libanati.
Res., 339 N. Sycamore, 92376-3517. Tel: 909-875-1360; Fax: 909-875-2822.
School—335 N. Sycamore Ave., 92376. Tel: 909-875-7821.
Lay Teachers 9; Students 300.
Catechesis/Religious Programs—Students 280.

St. Thomas More, Rev. Edward A. Dubel, C.R.
Res., 222 E. Easton, P.O. Box 367, 92376. Tel: 909-421-7030; Fax: 909-421-1374.

Riverside, Riverside Co.,

1—Our Lady of Guadalupe Shrine, Revs. Pedro E. Amezcua; Martin S. Rodriguez; Deacons Rudy Ybarra; Joe Ortiz.
Res., 2858 Ninth St., 92507. Tel: 909-684-0279; Fax: 909-684-0390.

2—Our Lady of Perpetual Help, Rev. Ignatius Rodrigues; Deacons Joe Gomeck; Ysidro, Gurrola; Larry Quilliam.
Res., 5250 Central Ave., 92504. Tel: 909-689-8921; Fax: 909-689-3619.
School—6686 Streeter Ave., 92504. Tel: 909-689-2125.
Lay Teachers 12; Students 283.

3—Queen of Angels, Revs. Ronald Rocky, O.F.M.Conv.; Anthony Howard, O.F.M.Conv.
Res., 4824 Jones Ave., 92505. Tel: 909-689-3674; Fax: 909-687-6146.
School—Tel: 909-689-1992.
Lay Teachers 13; Students 220.

4—Sacred Heart, (1945), Rev. Edward J. Connolly.
Res., 9935 Mission Blvd., 92509. Tel: 909-685-5058; Fax: 909-685-1056.
Catechesis/Religious Programs—Tel: 909-685-8510.
Students 980.

5—St. Anthony, (1923), Rev. Eliseo Hernandez.
Res., 3074 Madison St., 92504. Tel: 909-352-8393; Fax: 909-352-8816.

6—St. Catherine of Alexandria, (1946), Revs. Thomas J. Burdick; David Andel.
Res., 7050 Brockton Ave., 92506. Tel: 909-683-0800; Fax: 909-683-4114.
School—3728 Arlington Ave., 92506. Tel: 909-684-1091.
Lay Teachers 16; Students 368.
Catechesis/Religious Programs—Tel: 909-683-6319. Sr. Claudine Wietecha, D.R.E.
Students 480.

7—St. Francis de Sales, (1886), Revs. Louis Marx; Peter Vavro; Jose P. Issac; Deacon James Dale.
Res., 4268 Lime St., 92501. Tel: 909-686-4004; Fax: 909-686-3948. [JC]
School—Tel: 909-683-5083; Fax: 909-683-0249.
Religious 3; Lay Teachers 16; Students 330.
Catechesis/Religious Programs—Tel: 909-784-0987.
Students 267.

8—St. John the Evangelist, (1956), Rev. Michael Fredericks; Rev. Msgr. Edward T. Cronin, Pastor Emeritus.
Res., 3980 Opal St., 92509. Tel: 909-684-6864; Fax: 909-684-3115.
Mission—Belltown, Riverside Co., Our Lady of Guadalupe, 2518 Hall Ave., P.O. Box 3024, Riverside, CA 92509. Tel: 909-788-1464.
Catechesis/Religious Programs—Tel: 909-686-5181.
Students 450.

9—St. Patrick, Rev. James McLaughlin.
Church—6235 Rivercrest Dr., Ste. G, 92507. Tel: 909-697-7727; Fax: 909-697-7729.

10—St. Andrew's Newman Center. Serving Riverside Community College & UCR. Revs. David Farrugia, O.P.; Donald Bramble, O.P.; Francis Goode.
105 W. Big Springs Rd., 92507. Tel: 909-682-8751; Fax: 909-682-3513.
Res., 872 Spruce St., 92507. Tel: 909-784-0160.
Catechesis/Religious Programs—Fax: 909-784-0160. Frances Hodgkinson, D.R.E.
Students 120.

11—St. Thomas the Apostle, (1903), Revs. Robert M. Herbst, O.F.M.Conv.; John R. Heinz, O.F.M.Conv.; Bro. Gerald Villanueva, O.F.M.Conv., Pastoral Assoc.; Rev. John R. Heinz, O.F.M.Conv.
Res., 3774 Jackson St., 92503. Tel: 909-689-1131; Fax: 909-354-7402.
School—9136 Magnolia Ave., 92503. Tel: 909-689-1981.
Sisters 1; Lay Teachers 10; Students 334.
Catechesis/Religious Programs—Tel: 909-689-7180. Nancy Corbitt, D.R.E.
Students 600.
Mission—Riverside, Our Lady of Guadalupe, 9398 Indiana Ave., 92503. Rev. Robert M. Herbst, O.F.M.Conv.

Running Springs, San Bernardino Co., St. Anne in the Mountains (1963), Rev. Ignatius Rasquiuha.
Res., 30480 Fredalba Rd., P.O. Box 2400, 92382. Tel: 909-867-2832; Fax: 909-867-2832.

San Jacinto, Riverside Co., St. Anthony (1890), Rev. Charles Devine; Mr. Chuck Stroud, Pastoral Assoc.
Res., 630 S. Santa Fe Ave., 92583. Tel: 909-654-7911; Fax: 909-654-2309.
School—St. Hyacinth Academy, Tel: 909-654-2013.
Sisters 2; Lay Teachers 8; Students 212.
Catechesis/Religious Programs—Tel: 909-654-3311.
Students 250.

Soboba Indian Reservation, Riverside Co., St. Joseph (1888) (American Indian), Rev. Francis Weiser; Mr. Michael Madrigal, Admin.
Mailing Address: P.O. Box 1027, San Jacinto, 92581. Tel: 909-654-2086; Fax: 909-654-2086. [CEM]

Sun City, Riverside Co., St. Vincent Ferrer (1965), Rev. Gerard J. McGuinness; Deacon Ronald Rehaume. In res., Rev. Michael O'Day.
Res., 27931 Murrieta Rd., 92586-2320. Tel: 909-679-4531; Fax: 909-679-7521.
Catechesis/Religious Programs—Tel: 909-672-4019.
Students 279.

Temecula, Riverside Co., St. Catherine (1979), Revs. Anthony M. DiLeo; Charles Patron; Deacon John Barth.
Res., 41875 C St., 92592. Tel: 909-676-4403; Fax: 909-695-6659.
Catechesis/Religious Programs—Kathleen Igo, D.R.E.
Students 860.

Thermal, San Bernardino Co., San Felipe de Jesus, Revs. Bob Nogosek; John Connor, C.S.C.
Church—67-305 Hwy. 86, 92274. Tel: 619-398-5577; Fax: 619-398-1783.

Trona, San Bernardino Co., St. Madeleine Sophie Barat, Rev. William J. Kiefer.
Res., 83395 Trona Rd., 93562. Tel: 619-372-4717.

Thousand Palms, San Bernardino, St. Philip the Apostle, Rev. Joseph Mawicke; Deacon Charles Burns.
Res., 31-525 Via Pared, P.O. Box 405, 92276. Tel: 619-343-1911; Fax: 619-343-3211.
Catechesis/Religious Programs—Students 82.

Twentynine Palms, San Bernardino Co., Blessed Sacrament, Rev. Baldwin Beyer, O.F.M.Cap., Admin.
Office: 6785 Sage Ave., 92277. Tel: 619-367-3343; Fax: 619-367-0543.
School—6755 Sage Ave., 92277. Tel: 619-367-3341.
Lay Teachers 8; Students 122.
Catechesis/Religious Programs—Virginia Harris, D.R.E.
Lay Teachers 9; Students 120.

Upland, San Bernardino Co., St. Joseph (1922), Revs. John Kavcak, M.S.C.; Ron Larkin, M.S.C.; Tom Burns, M.S.C.; Deacons Charles Pobjoy; Frank Simoni; John Kim.
Res., 877 N. Campus Ave., 91786. Tel: 909-981-8110; Fax: 909-949-8090.
School—905 Campus Ave., 91786. Tel: 909-920-5185; Fax: 909-920-5190.
Sisters of the Presentation 4; Lay Teachers 13; Students 358.
Catechesis/Religious Programs—Tel: 909-982-9518. Liliana Moore, D.R.E.
Students 627.

St. Anthony (1974), Rev. Edmond G. O'Donnell; Deacon Eugene Bello.
Res., 2110 N. San Antonio Ave., P.O. Box 608, 91785. Tel: 909-985-2803; Fax: 909-982-8643.
Church—2110 N. San Antonio Ave., 91785.
Catechesis/Religious Programs—Tel: 909-981-7080. Susan Breen, D.R.E.
Students 355.

Victorville, San Bernardino Co., Holy Innocents (1992), Rev. Mark E. Kottarczyk.
Mailing Address: P.O. Box 1777, 92393. Tel: 619-955-6010; Fax: 619-955-2100.
Catechesis/Religious Programs—Tel: 909-955-6262.
Students 460.

St. Joan of Arc (1922), Revs. Gerardo Mendoza; John Fahnestock.
Res., 15512 Sixth St., 92392. Tel: 619-245-7674; Fax: 619-245-7077.
Catechesis/Religious Programs—15503 5th St., 92392.
Students 491.

Wrightwood, San Bernardino Co., Our Lady of the Snows (1946), Rev. Patrick V. Kirsch.
Mailing Address: P.O. Box 292570, Phelan, 92329. Tel: 619-868-4342; Fax: 619-868-2171.
Rectory Office: 4471 Sunrise Blvd., Phelan, 92371.
Catechesis/Religious Programs—Students 84.

Yucaipa, San Bernardino Co., St. Frances Xavier Cabrini (1953), Rev. Charles E. Miller, Admin.
Res., 12687 California St., 92399. Tel: 909-797-2533; Fax: 909-790-5803.
Catechesis/Religious Programs—Students 150.

Yucca Valley, San Bernardino Co., St. Mary of the Valley, Rev. Raymond J. Rabatsky.
Res., 7495 Church St., 92284-3247. Tel: 619-365-2287; Fax: 619-369-0622.

Chaplains of Public Institutions

SAN BERNARDINO. *San Bernardino City and County Jails*. Vacant.
San Bernardino Community Hospital, 1500 W. 17th St., 92411. Tel: 909-884-6333; 881-4053. Rev. John Gorman.
San Bernardino County Medical Center, 780 E. Gilbert St., 92404. Tel: 909-884-6824. Rev. Dennis Flynn, S.V.D.
San Bernardino Juvenile Hall & Verdemont Boys Ranch. Catholic Charities, 1450 N. D St., 92405. Tel: 909-388-1239. Rev. Alfred Lo Pinto, Coord. Detention Ministry.
San Bernardino Medical Center, 2101 N. Waterman Ave., 92404. Tel: 909-883-8711. Rev. Barnabas Laubach, O.S.B.

BLYTHE. *Chuckawalla Valley State Prison,* P.O. Box 2289, 92226. Tel: 619-922-5300. Rev. John Rusk.

CHINO. *California Institute for Men,* P.O. Box 128, 91710. Tel: 909-681-6497; 597-1821, Ext. 2289; 2689. Rev. Chester Kopec, O.P.
California Youth Authority. P.O. Box 800, Ontario, 91761. Tel: 909-597-1861, Ext. 395. Rev. Vincent Connor, Chap.
Camp Prado. Vacant.
Southern Conservation Center, P.O. Box 128, 91710. Tel: 909-597-1821, Ext. 2289. Rev. Michael Bucaro.

FONTANA. *Kaiser Permanente Hospital,* 9961 Sierra Ave., 92335. Tel: 909-829-5850; 829-5000 (Emergency). Rev. William Marcotte.

FRONTERA. *California Institute for Women,* 16756 Chino-Corona Rd., 91720. Tel: 909-597-1771. Rev. Neil Fuller, S.V.D., Chap.

LOMA LINDA. *Jerry Pettis Memorial Hospital,* 11201 Benton St., 92354. Tel: 909-825-7084. Rev. Msgr. Adolphus Chavez, (Hispanics); Mr. Stephen Elias.
Loma Linda Community Hospital, 25333 Barton Rd., 92354. Tel: 909-796-7311, Ext. 4367. Rev. Leonard Mestas.
Loma Linda University Medical Center, Barton Rd. and Anderson St., 92354. Tel: 909-824-0800. Rev. Leonard Mestas.

NORCO. *California Rehabilitation Center,* Western & Fifth Sts., P.O. Box 1841, 91760. Tel: 909-737-2683, Ext. 4305. Rev. Msgr. Cosimo Corciulo.

PATTON. *Patton State Hospital*. Vacant.

PILOT ROCK. *Crestline*. Vacant. Tel: 909-338-2303.

RIVERSIDE. *Riverside Community Hospital*. Rev. Martin Rodriguez.
Riverside General Hospital 9851 Magnolia Ave., 92503. Tel: 909-358-7100; 689-3674. Bro. Dario Garcia, O.F.M.Conv.
Riverside Juvenile Hall. Vacant.

On Duty Outside the Diocese:
Reverend Fathers—
Buchanan, Robert, Our Lady of Snows, 1138 Wright St., Las Vegas, NV 89509
Frankovich, Frank, Companions of the Cross, 100 Young St., Ottawa, Ontario, Canada KIY 3P7
Kurilec, Robert, USN, 3908 Roebling Ln., Virginia Beach, VA 23452
Lowe, Frank, Capt., Chap., 319 B.W./H.C., Grand Forks A.F.B., ND 58205-6335

Military Chaplains:
Reverend Fathers—
Foley, Francis P., C.H.C., Office of the Chaplain, MCAGCC, Twentynine Palms, CA 92278
Jasinski, John B., Office of the Chaplain, MCLB, Barstow, CA 92311-5000. Tel: 619-269-2630
Menz, Anthony, National Training Center, Center Chapel, P.O. Box 10007, Fort Irwin, CA 92310. Tel: 619-386-3562
Schnipke, Eugene, 831 CSG-HC, George AFB, CA 92394. Tel: 619-269-2630

On Leave:
Reverend Fathers—
Gil, Rudi
Stauber, James

Retired:
Reverend Monsignors—
Andreatta, Tullio, 2245 Fort Stockton Rd., San Diego, CA 92103
Bradley, John J., 3066 Ladera Dr., San Bernardino, CA 92405
Lawlor, Timothy, 325 W. E St., Ontario, CA 91762
Meagher, Thomas, 1011 St. Andrews #4, Upland, CA 91786
Nightengale, Francis, 6458 N. Via Divina, Tucson, AZ 85715-0973
Nolan, Michael, P.O. Box 1643, Upland, CA 91785
O'Leary, Cornelius, 25098 Jaclyn Ave., Moreno Valley, CA 92543
Reverend Fathers—
Baseford, Paul, 485 Foxenwood Dr., Santa Maria, CA 92355
Battle, Lawrence, 73450 Country Club Dr. #190, Palm Desert, CA 92260
Bonacum, Thomas, 124 Box Garner Valley Rd., Mountain Center, CA 92561
Casey, Donald A., P.O. Box 92483, Henderson, NV 89009
Coslowsky, Marion, 733 Belinda Ave., Barstow, CA 92311
Cronin, Edward, 3980 Opal St., Riverside, CA 92509
DePasquale, Dominic, 4673 Braemar Pl., Riverside, CA 92501
Dien, Vincent, 5186 Homestead Pl., Riverside, CA 92504
Dietrich, Edward, 2034 Chia, Palm Springs, CA 92262
Diezel, Joseph J., 5734 N. McVickor, Chicago, IL 60646
Downey, Robert, P.O. Box 292629, Phelan, CA 92329
Fitzwilliam, Ivan, 388 Reposo St., San Jacinto, CA 92582
Ganahl, James, 15767 Tuscola Rd., Apt. 1, Apple Valley, CA 92307
Greiner, Lawrence, 197 Via Lola, Apt. 10, Palm Springs, CA 92262
Guillen, Manuel R., 1535 Third Ave., San Diego, CA 92101
Guillen, Patricio, 2002 S. Magnolia Ave., Ontario, CA 91762
Jalbert, Marcel, 25714 Masa Ct., San Bernardino, CA 92404
Jazbec, Stanley, 6784 Outpost Rd., Joshua Tree, CA 92252
Kiefer, William, 83395 Trona Rd., Trona, CA 93562
Leahy, Anthony, P.O. Box 4027, Oceanside, CA 92051
Leissler, Joseph L., 45-803 Hwy. 74, Palm Desert, CA 92260
Lenoir, Jean, 79-925 Camelback Dr., Bermuda Dunes, CA 92201
Nagler, Robert, 1945 Illion St., San Diego, CA 92110
O'Day, Michael, 28710 Olympia Way, Sun City, CA 92586
O'Donovan, Daniel
O'Keeffe, Patrick, 1201 E. Highland Ave., San Bernardino, CA 92404
O'Sullivan, Brendan, 1001 Encinitas Blvd., San Diego, CA 92024
Roach, Joseph, 9466 Navajo Tr., Morongo Valley, CA 92256
Scanlan, Patrick J., 6333 Rancho Mission Rd., San Diego, CA 92108
Schilly, Joseph, 2772 Sterling Ave., San Benardino, CA 92404
Slattery, John, P.O. Box 588, Lucerne Valley, CA 92356
Snoj, Joseph, 7124 Helman Ave., Alta Loma, CA 91701
Stadler, Joseph, 1977 Lupine, Monterey Park, CA 91755
Strancar, Ignatius, 6333 Rancho Mission Rd., San Diego, CA 92108
Trong, Joseph, 12772 Louise Cir., Garden Grove, CA 92643
Valdes, Luis, 1775 Pennsylvania, Riverside, CA 92507
Vehovec, Valentine, 6333 Rancho Mission Rd., #104, San Diego, CA 92108
Wadell, John, Cl. Fra. Pere Fornes, 13, Muro, Mallorca, Spain 07440
Walters, Vincent, 565 Wisconsin St., San Francisco, CA 94107
Waterfall, Richard A., P.O. Box 409, Palm Springs, CA 92263
White, Kris, 11171 Oakwood Dr., I-305, Loma Linda, CA 92354
Wieser, Francis, 10831 Deerfield Dr., Cherry Valley, CA 92223
Yahn, George, P.O. Box 167, Songnor, Nandi Hills District, Kenya, East Africa
Zaratti, Elio, 6333 Rancho Mission Rd., San Diego, CA 92108

Permanent Deacons:
Acosta, Joseph, Highland
Aguilera, Santos, Hesperia
Basoco, Raymond, On Duty Outside the Diocese
Bello, Eugene, Upland
Borne, Edward, Perris
Brannick, Thomas, Rialto
Burger, Joseph, Ontario
Burgett, Donald, Barstow
Burns, Charles, La Quinta
Burns, Jim, On Duty Outside the Diocese
Burris, Bud, Lake Elsinore
Campbell, Gerald, Cathedral City
Chamberlayne, Edwin, Rialto
Clinton, Jack, Upland
Cohoon, Kenneth, Corona
Conrad, Jack, Alta Loma
Cover, Richard, Redlands
Dale, James R., Riverside
Everard, Ed, On Duty Outside the Diocese
Freeman, Russ, On Duty Outside the Diocese
Fultz, Charles, Upland
Garcia, Joseph, Norco
Gomeck, Joseph, Riverside
Gomez, Manuel, Apple Valley
Gonzalez, Victor, Bermuda Dunes
Grandon, Walter, Anza
Grandon, Wayne, On Duty Outside the Diocese
Gurrola, Ysidro, Riverside
Haproff, David, Corona
Hawes, Lloyd, Chino
Henke, John A., San Jacinto
Heredia, Juan, Palm Desert
Hodnick, Mark, Alta Loma
Hoy, Wayne, Coachella
Jacobs, Gary, Apple Valley
Joslin, Wayne, Moreno Valley
Kafka, Gene, San Bernardino
Keough, William, Redlands
Kermott, Philip P., Banning
Key, Joseph, San Bernardino
Kilbourn, Austin, Moreno Valley
Kim, John, Upland
Meader, James, Twentynine Palms
Melendrez, Walter, Alta Loma
Melton, Harold, Lake Elsinore
Michel, Jesse, Desert Hot Springs
Millen, Arthur, Riverside
Mirci, Philip, Redlands
Neufell, James, Riverside
Olivas, Manuel, Riverside
Ortiz, Joseph, Riverside
Partida, Ralph, Jr., Chino
Plein, Dale, San Bernardino
Pobjoy, Charles, Cucamonga
Quilliam, Lawrence, Riverside
Ramirez, Raymond, Indio
Rehaume, Ronald J., Sun City
Reyes, Carlos, Apple Valley
Rios, Joseph, Redlands
Rittman, Robert, Apple Valley
Robicheaux, Paul, Norco
Rodriquez, Jose, On Duty Outside the Diocese
Roman, Francis, Barstow
Saenz, Margarito, Barstow
Saladin, Jerry, On Duty Outside the Diocese
Salinas, Arcadio, Jr., Cathedral City
Sanchez, Samuel, Moreno Valley
Schmit, George, Upland
Sepulveda, Ralph, Banning
Shalhoub, William J., Yucaipa
Silva, Francisco, Mecca
Simoni, Frank, Upland
Simpson, Jerry, Running Springs
Skora, John, Palm Springs
Soper, Leonard, On Duty Outside the Diocese
Sotelo, Gonzalo, Rialto
Spinney, Don, On Duty Outside the Diocese
Vasquez, Sergio, Coachella
Vital, Ernesto, Upland
Von Ins, Paul, Alta Loma
Wagner, Tom, On Duty Outside the Diocese
Ybarra, Rudy, Riverside
Zambrano, Jose, Corona

INSTITUTIONS LOCATED IN THE DIOCESE

[A] SEMINARIES, RELIGIOUS OR SCHOLASTICATES

RIVERSIDE. *Blessed Junipero Serra House of Formation*, 3325 13th St., 92501. Tel: 909-788-9931; Fax: 909-781-9031. Revs. Jose Sanz, Rector; Rolando Fonsela, Vice Rector.

Divine Word Seminary, 11316 Cypress Ave., 92505. Tel: 909-689-4858; Fax: 909-785-0327. Revs. Walt Miller, S.V.D., Rector; Neil D. Fuller, S.V.D.; Joseph Fertal, S.V.D.; Clifton Etienne, S.V.D.; Michael Manning; John McHenry, S.V.D.; Cosmas A. Meyer, S.V.D.; John Shevlin, S.V.D.; Richard Winters, S.V.D.; Paul Schmidt, S.V.D.; Bro. William Morgan, S.V.D.

[B] HIGH SCHOOLS, DIOCESAN

SAN BERNARDINO. *Aquinas High School*. (Coed), 2772 Sterling Ave., 92404. Tel: 909-886-4659; Fax: 909-886-7717. Revs. Andrew Sotelo, S.J., Prin.; Joseph Schilly. Priests 1; Sisters 1; Lay Teachers 18; Students 291.

RIVERSIDE. *Notre Dame High School*. (Coed), 7085 Brockton Ave., 92506. Tel: 909-369-2810; Fax: 909-781-9020. Mr. Stephen T. Krup, Prin.; Rev. Richard Parker. Priests 1; Sisters 2; Lay Teachers 43; Students 576.

[C] HOMES FOR SENIOR CITIZENS

SAN BERNARDINO. *St. Bernardine Plaza*, 550 W. Fifth St., 92401. Tel: 909-888-0153; Fax: 909-381-1589.
For a complete listing, refer to the Special Care Facilities section.

PALM DESERT. *La Paz Villas*, P.O. Box 1962, 92261. Tel: 619-346-6033.
For a complete listing, refer to the Special Care Facilities section.

[D] GENERAL HOSPITALS AND CLINICS

SAN BERNARDINO. *St. Bernardine Medical Center*, 2101 N. Waterman Ave., 92404. Tel: 909-883-8711; Fax: 909-881-4546.
For a complete listing, refer to the Hospitals section.

APPLE VALLEY. *St. Mary Regional Medical Center*, 18300 Hwy. 18, P.O. Box 7025, 92307. Tel: 619-242-2311; Fax: 619-242-9750.
For a complete listing, refer to the Hospitals section.

[E] MONASTERIES AND RESIDENCES OF PRIESTS AND BROTHERS

CORONA. *Congregation of the Mother Coredemptrix*, 1775 S. Main St., 91720-4961. Tel: 909-737-4125; 340-9880.
Shrine of Presentation (Den Thanh Duc Me Dang Con). Revs. Athanasius M. Bui Anh Tuan, C.M.C.; Camillus M. Nguyen Du Tuan, C.M.C., Dir.; James Vu dai Luong; Joachim Ngo hoang Khoi; Francis Hoang-Anh-Thang, C.M.C.

HEMET. *Congregation of the Sacred Hearts, SS.CC.*, Western U.S. Province, 32481 Sage Rd., 92544. Tel: 909-767-9436.

Holy Ghost Fathers, 309 E. Whittier Ave., 92543. Tel: 909-658-2241. Revs. Joseph Sweeney, C.S.Sp., Supr.; John A. Strmiska, C.S.Sp.; Edmond J. Leonard, C.S.Sp.; James P. O'Reilly, C.S.Sp.; Richard Kissane, C.S.Sp.; Norman Lord, C.S.Sp.; Joseph B. Murphy, C.S.Sp., 25981 Cherry Hills Boulevard, Sun City, 92586-2467. Tel: 909-672-4406. Rev. Kenneth F. Milford, C.S.Sp., 1600-177 San Jacinto St., 92383-5146. Tel: 909-654-7010. Rev. John Yates, C.S.Sp., San Gorgonio Church, P.O. Box 155, Beaumont, 92223-0155. Tel: 909-845-2849; Fax: 909-845-9259. Rev. Daniel C. Murphy.

MORONGO VALLEY. *St. Michael's of Morongo Valley, Inc.*, 9466 Navajo Tr., 92256. Tel: 619-363-6617. Retirement Facility. In res., Revs. Gerald F. Clune (ALB), (Retired); Harry J. Murphy (GBG), (Retired); Richard S. Bradley, S.J., (Retired); Joseph W. Roach, S.A.G., (Retired); John D. Sauter (CIN), (Retired).

RIVERSIDE. *Operarios Del Reino De Cristo, O.R.C.*, 2858 Ninth St., 92507. Tel: 909-684-0279; Fax: 909-684-0309. Rev. Pedro Amezcua, O.R.C., Local Prov.

St. Vincent Ferrer House, 872 Spruce St., 92507. Tel: 909-784-0160; Fax: 909-682-3513. Dominicans. Revs. David Farrugia, O.P.; Lawrence Farrell, O.P.; Donald Bramble; Francis Goode.

VICTORVILLE. *Hospitaller Brothers St. John of God*, P.O. Box 2457, 92392. Tel: 619-241-4917; Fax: 619-241-8911. Bro. Gary Hill, O.H., Pres. Brothers 3; Licensed Beds 61.

[F] CONVENTS AND RESIDENCES FOR SISTERS

SAN BERNARDINO. *Congregation of the Sisters of Mercy*, 4825 H St., 92407.

CALIMESA. *Missionary Sisters of the Immaculate Conception*, 1271 Nugget Ct., 92320; Fax: 909-795-8128. Madonna of the Community 2.

COACHELLA. *Our Lady of Victory Missionary Sisters*, Office: 52-525 Oasis Palm Ave., 92236. Tel: 619-398-5577. Res., 81-860 Shadow Palm, #48, 92201. Tel: 619-347-7034.

GRAND TERRACE. *Sisters of St. Benedict, Holy Spirit Monastery*, 22791 Pico St., 92313-5750. Tel: 909-783-4446. Sr. Mary Esther Steckler, O.S.B., Prioress. Sisters 12.

REDLANDS. *Sisters of Mercy, U.S. Province*, 1075 Bermuda Dr., 92374. Tel: 909-809-4747; Fax: 909-798-5300. Sr. Teresa O'Connell, R.S.M., Prov.

TUSTIN. *Sisters of the Company of Mary (O.D.N.)*, 16791 E. Main St., 92780. Tel: 714-541-3125; Fax: 714-835-0648. Sr. Ernestine Velarde, O.D.N., Maj. Sup. Convent. Vina de Lestonnac Ministry Center, 39300 De Portola Rd., Temecula, 92592. Tel: 909-695-1076.

Vina de Lestonnac Ministry Center, 39300 De Portola Rd., Temecula, 92592. Tel: 909-695-2186; Fax: 909-695-1509.

St. Jeanne de Lestonnac Preschool/Kindergarten & First Grade, 39300 De Portola Rd., Temecula, 92692 Tel: 909-695-3396. Sr. Enedina Badillo, O.D.N.; Sr. Michele Bohan, O.D.N.; Sr. Andrea Calderon, O.D.N.; Sr. Maria de la Torre, O.D.N.; Sr. Josephine Diaz, O.D.N.; Sr. Raphael Garcia, O.D.N.; Sr. Mary Gomez, O.D.N.; Sr. Justine Gonzales, O.D.N.; Sr. Linda Gutierrez, O.D.N.; Sr. Manuela Hernandez, O.D.N.; Sr. Patricia Huber, O.D.N.; Sr. Catalina Ponce, O.D.N.; Sr. Lupe Romero, O.D.N.; Sr. Victoria Ruiz, O.D.N.; Sr. Marve Watkins-King, O.D.N.

YUCAIPA. *Our Lady of Victory Missionary Sisters*, 12755 California St., 92399. Tel: 909-797-6369. Sr. Mary Matilda Spetter, O.L.V.M., D.R.E.; Sr. Elizabeth Hann, O.L.V.M., Ministry to Elderly. Sisters 2.

[G] CAMPS & RETREATS

ARROW BEAR LAKE. *Camp Don Bosco*. (Boys), Near Running Springs Office, 13640 Bellflower Blvd., 92382. Salasian Fathers.

BIG BEAR. *Sacred Heart Retreat Camp*, 896 Cienega Rd., P.O. Box 1795, 92315. Tel: 909-866-5696.

CHERRY VALLEY. *Servants of the Paraclete Guadalupe Retreat Center*, 39100 Orchard Ave., 92223-3797. Tel: 909-845-7777; Fax: 909-845-6271. Revs. Salvatore L. Busca, s.P., Sec. Gen. & Supr.; Gregory McCormick, s.P., Asst. Supr.; Frank James, s.P.

LOS ANGELES. *Camp Mariastella, Inc.* Camp for girls. 2303 S. Figueroa Way, 90007. Tel: 213-745-7870; Fax: 213-747-4499. P.O. Box 99, Wrightwood, 92394. Founded by the Sisters of Social Service.

REDLANDS. *El Carmelo Retreat House*, 926 E. Highland Ave., P.O. Box 446, 92373. Tel: 909-792-1047. Revs. Patrick Sugrue, O.C.D., Sup.; Reginald McSweeney, O.C.D.; Dominic O'Callaghan, O.C.D.; Thomas Koller; Richard Mandoli, O.C.D.; Bro. Boniface Scheerer, O.C.D. Priests 5; Brothers 1; Sisters 4.

RIVERSIDE. *Divine Word Retreat Center*, 11316 Cypress Ave., 92505. Tel: 909-689-4858. Rev. Walt Miller, S.V.D. Dir. of Retreat Center.

RUNNING SPRINGS. *St. Joachin & St. Anne Retreat Center*, P.O. Box 1760, 92382. Tel: 909-867-7362. Robert Fredericks, Guestmaster.

[H] NEWMAN CENTERS

SAN BERNARDINO. *Newman Catholic Fellowship*, 265 W. 25th St., 92405. Tel: 909-883-8991; Fax: 909-882-2061. Rev. Gilles Allard, I.M.C.

PALM DESERT. *Christ of the Desert Newman Center*, 73441 Fred Waring Dr., 92260. Tel: 619-346-0089; Fax: 619-340-2245. Rev. Ned Reidy, C.S.C., Dir.

REDLANDS *University of Redlands Newman Community*, 1200 E. Colton Ave., Box 3080, 92373-0999. Tel: 909-335-4006.

RIVERSIDE *St. Andrews Newman Center*, 105 W. Big Springs Rd., 92507. Tel: 909-682-8751. Directors: Revs. David Farrugia, O.P.; Donald Bramble, O.P. Serving Riverside Community College and University of California at Riverside.

[I] MISCELLANEOUS

SAN BERNARDINO.
**Caritas Telecommunications*, 1201 E. Highland Ave., 92404

RIVERSIDE
**Wordnet, Inc.*, Divine Word Seminary, 11316 Cypress Ave., Ste. 9, 92505. Tel: 909-689-4885. Rev. Michael Manning, S.V.D.

VICTORVILLE. *Casa Venegas*, 16694 Allen St., 92392-3511. Tel: 619-241-6607. Home for homeless.

RELIGIOUS INSTITUTUES OF MEN REPRESENTED IN THE DIOCESE

For further details refer to the corresponding bracketed number in the Religious Institutes of Men or Women section.

[0200]—*Benedictine Monks*. (MN; WA).—O.S.B.

[0470]—*Capuchin Franciscans*.—O.F.M.Cap.

[]—*Congregation of Mother Coredemptrix*.—C.M.C.

[1080]—*Congregation of the Resurrection*.—C.R.

[1140]—*Congregation of the Sacred Hearts of Jesus and Mary*. (Western Prov.).—SS.CC.

[0390]—*Consolata Missionaries*.—I.M.C.

[0480]—*Conventual Franciscans*. (St. Joseph Cupertino Prov.).—O.F.M.Conv.

[0260]—*Discalced Carmelite Friars*. (Western Prov.).—O.C.D.

[0520]—*Franciscan Friars*.—O.F.M.

[0650]—*Holy Ghost Fathers*.—C.S.Sp.

[0670]—*Hospitaller Brothers of St. John of God*.—O.H.

[0690]—*Jesuit Fathers and Brothers*.—S.J.

[0720]—*Missionaries of Our Lady of La Salette*.—M.S.

[1110]—*Missionaries of the Sacred Heart*.—M.S.C.

[0920]—*Oblates of St. Francis de Sales*.—O.S.F.S.

[0970]—*Order of Our Lady of Mercy*.—O.de.M.

[0430]—*Order of Preachers (Dominicans)*. (Holy Name Prov.).—O.P.

[0610]—*Priests of the Congregation of Holy Cross*.—C.S.C.

[1230]—*Servants of the Paraclete*.—s.P.

[0760]—*Society of Mary*.—S.M.

[0420]—*Society of the Divine Word*. (Western Prov.).—S.V.D.

[]—*Western Dominican Fathers and Brothers*.—O.P.

RELIGIOUS INSTITUTES OF WOMEN REPRESENTED IN THE DIOCESE

[0230]—*Benedictine Sisters of Pontifical Jurisdiction*. (Grand Terrace, CA).—O.S.B.

[0700]—*Company of Mary*.—O.D.N.

[3690]—*Congregation of the Sacred Hearts and of Perpetual Adoration*.—SS.CC.

[]—*Congregation of the Sacred Hearts of Jesus and Mary*.—SS.CC.

[0470]—*Congregation of the Sisters of Charity of the Incarnate Word*. Houston, Texas.—C.C.V.I.

[]—*Consolation Sisters*. (Highland CA).—O.S.F.

[0790]—*Daughters of Divine Charity*.—F.D.C.

[0880]—*Daughters of Mary and Joseph*.—D.M.J.

[1070-10]—*Dominican Sisters*.—O.P.

[1070-13]—*Dominican Sisters*.—O.P.

[1070-15]—*Dominican Sisters*.—O.P.

[1070-19]—*Dominican Sisters*.—O.P.

[1070-20]—*Dominican Sisters*.—O.P.

[1070-26]—*Dominican Sisters*.—O.P.

[1230]—*Franciscan Sisters of Christian Charity*.—O.S.F.

[]—*Immaculate Heart Community*.—I.H.M.

[2370]—*Institute of the Blessed Virgin Mary (Loretto Sisters)*.—I.B.V.M.

[2575]—*Institute of the Sisters of Mercy of the Americas*. (Burlington, VT; Hartford, CT).—R.S.M.

[2760]—*Missionary Sisters of the Immaculate Conception of the Mother of God*.—S.M.I.C.

[]—*Oblates of Santa Marta*.—O.S.M.

[3130]—*Our Lady of Victory Missionary Sisters*.—O.L.V.M.

[]—*Religious of the Good Shepherd*.—R.G.S.

[2970]—*School Sisters of Notre Dame*.—S.S.N.D.

[1680]—*School Sisters of St. Francis*.—O.S.F.

[0430]—*Sisters of Charity of the Blessed Virgin Mary*.—B.V.M.

[2360]—*Sisters of Loretto at the Foot of the Cross*.—S.L.

[2549]—*Sisters of Mercy*. (Sligo, Ireland).—R.S.M.

[2590]—*Sisters of Mercy of the Blessed Sacrament*.—H.M.S.S.

[1540]—*Sisters of Saint Francis*. Clinton, Iowa.—O.S.F.

[]—*Sisters of St. Benedict*.—O.S.B.

[3770]—*Sisters of St. Clare*.—O.S.C.

[1720]—*Sisters of St. Francis*.—O.S.F.

[1650]—*The Sisters of St. Francis of Philadelphia.*—O.S.F.

[1550]—*Sisters of St. Francis of the Holy Cross.*—O.S.F.

[3830-03]—*Sisters of St. Joseph.*—C.S.J.

[3840]—*Sisters of St. Joseph of Carondolet.*—C.S.J.

[1990]—*Sisters of the Holy Names of Jesus and Mary.*—S.N.J.M.

[3320]—*Sisters of the Presentation of the B.V.M.*.—P.B.V.M.

[4050]—*Sisters of the Society Devoted to the Sacred Heart.*—S.D.S.H.

[2150]—*Sisters, Servants of the Immaculate Heart of Mary.*—I.H.M.

[4070]—*Society of the Sacred Heart.*—R.S.C.J.

NECROLOGY

† Munnelly, James, Sun City, CA, St. Vincent Ferrer Church. —Died April 15, 1996.

† Rabatsky, Raymond, Yucca Valley, CA, St. Mary of the Valley. —Died June 12, 1996.

† Rice, George, (Retired). —Died March 3, 1996.

Diocese of San Diego

(Dioecesis Sancti Didaci)

Most Reverend

ROBERT H. BROM, D.D.

Bishop of San Diego; ordained December 18, 1963; appointed Bishop of Duluth March 25, 1983; consecrated and installed May 23, 1983; appointed Coadjutor Bishop of San Diego April 22, 1989; appointed Bishop of San Diego July 10, 1990. *Office: P.O. Box 85728, San Diego, CA, 92186-5728.* Tel.: 619-490-8200.

Most Reverend

GILBERT E. CHAVEZ, D.D.

Auxiliary Bishop of San Diego and Titular Bishop of Magarmel; ordained March 19, 1960; appointed April 19, 1974; Episcopal ordination June 21, 1974. *Res., 1535 Third Ave., San Diego, CA, 92101.*

ESTABLISHED JULY 11, 1936.

Square Miles 8,852.

Legal Titles: *The Roman Catholic Bishop of San Diego, a Corporation Sole*—(Churches, Rectories, Halls, Catechetical Centers, etc.) *University of San Diego, a Corporation. Catholic Charities, Diocese of San Diego, a California Non-profit Corporation.*

Comprises the Counties of Imperial and San Diego in the State of California.

For legal titles of parishes and diocesan institutions, consult the Diocesan Office.

Pastoral Center: P.O. Box 85728, San Diego, CA, 92186-5728. Tel.: 619-490-8200; Fax: 619-490-8272.

STATISTICAL OVERVIEW

Personnel	
Bishop	1
Auxiliary Bishops	1
Abbots	1
Retired Abbots	1
Priests: Diocesan Active in Diocese	127
Priests: Active Outside Diocese	9
Priests: Retired, Sick or Absent	76
Number of Diocesan Priests	212
Religious Priests in Diocese	93
Extern Priests in Diocese	98
Ordinations:	
Diocesan Priests	3
Permanent Deacons	7
Permanent Deacons in Diocese	95
Total Brothers	21
Total Sisters	355
Parishes	
Parishes	98
With Resident Pastor:	
Resident Diocesan Priests	85
Resident Religious Priests	13
Without Resident Pastor:	
Missions	20
Pastoral Centers	2
Professional Ministry Personnel:	
Brothers	2
Sisters	53
Lay Ministers	158
Welfare	
Catholic Hospitals	1
Total Assisted	487,930
Health Care Centers	1
Total Assisted	32,727
Homes for the Aged	6
Total Assisted	728
Residential Care of Children	1
Total Assisted	9
Day Care and Extended Day Care Centers	1
Total Assisted	18,021
Specialized Homes	7
Total Assisted	2,849
Special Centers for Social Services	16
Total Assisted	185,463
Residential Care of Disabled	1
Total Assisted	52
Other Institutions	3
Total Assisted	103
Educational	
Seminaries, Diocesan	1
Students from This Diocese	9
Students from Other Diocese	13
Diocesan Students in Other Seminaries	9
Total Seminarians	18
Colleges and Universities	1
Total Students	6,603
High Schools, Diocesan and Parish	3
Total Students	1,820
High Schools, Private	2
Total Students	1,312
Elementary Schools, Diocesan and Parish	43
Total Students	12,934
Elementary Schools, Private	1
Total Students	353
Non-residential Schools for the Disabled	1
Total Students	165
Catechesis/Religious Education:	
High School Students	7,357
Elementary Students	26,023
Total Students Under Catholic Instruction	56,585
Teachers in the Diocese:	
Priests	15
Sisters	49
Lay Teachers	1,101
Vital Statistics	
Receptions into the Church:	
Infant Baptism Totals	12,435
Adult Baptism Totals	566
Received into Full Communion	642
First Communions	9,149
Confirmations	3,665
Marriages:	
Catholic	1,783
Interfaith	574
Total Marriages	2,357
Deaths	2,697
Total Catholic Population	690,783
Total Population	2,782,204

Former Bishops—Most Rev. CHARLES F. BUDDY, D.D., S.T.D., Ph.D., ord. Sept. 19, 1914; appt. Oct. 31, 1936; cons. Dec. 21, 1936; named Asst. at Pontifical Throne, Jan. 12, 1964; died March 6, 1966.—Most Rev. FRANCIS J. FUREY, D.D., Ph.D., LL.D., ord. March 15, 1930; appt. Auxiliary Bishop of Philadelphia, Aug. 24, 1960; cons. Dec. 22, 1960; succeeded to the See of San Diego, March 6, 1966; translated to Archbishop of San Antonio, June 4, 1969; died April 23, 1979.—Most Rev. LEO T. MAHER, D.D., Bishop of San Diego; ord. Dec. 18, 1943; First Bishop of Santa Rosa; appt. Feb. 21, 1962; cons. April 5, 1962; translated to San Diego, Aug. 27, 1969; retired July 10, 1990; died Feb. 23, 1991.

Pastoral Center—3888 Paducan Dr., San Diego, 92117., Mailing Address: P.O. Box 85728, San Diego, 92186-5728. Tel: 619-490-8200; Fax: 619-490-8272. Office Hours: Mon.-Fri. 8:30-4:30.

Auxiliary Bishop and Vicar General—Most Rev. GILBERT E CHAVEZ, D.D., *1535 Third Ave., San Diego, 92101-3192.* Tel: 619-239-0229.

Chancellor/Moderator of the Diocesan Offices—Rev. Msgr. DANIEL J. DILLABOUGH. Tel: 619-490-8310.

Assistants to Bishop Robert H. Brom—Rev. EDWARD P. MCNULTY. Tel: 619-490-8300. Mr. RODRIGO VALDIVIA. Tel: 619-490-8301.

Temporal Affairs—Rev. Msgr. DANIEL J. DILLABOUGH, Dir. Tel: 619-490-8310.

Diocesan Tribunal-First Instance

Judicial Vicar—Rev. Msgr. MARK A. CAMPBELL, B.A., M.Ed., J.C.L.

Adjutant Judicial Vicar—Rev. DAVID N. CROISETIERE, J.C.L., M.C.L.

Promotor of Justice and Defender of the Bond—Rev. Msgr. DANIEL J. DILLABOUGH, S.T.D., J.C.L.

Diocesan Judges—Rev. BRIAN HAYES, J.C.L.; Miss MARY JO GRETSINGER, S.T.L., J.C.L.; EDWARD PETERS, J.D., J.C.D.

Auditor—Rev. LOUIS I. NEWMAN, B.A.

Notaries—Mrs. CONNIE NOEL; Mrs. CHERYL JOHNSTON.

Consultants—Dr. FRANCISCO MERINO, M.D.; PETER MCDADE, Ph.D.

Appellate Division, Second Instance—Special Officers of Mandate: Rev. Msgr. MARK A. CAMPBELL, B.A., M.Ed., J.C.L.; Rev. DAVID N. CROISETIERE, J.C.L., M.C.L.

Defender of the Bond-Second Instance—Rev. Msgr. DANIEL J. DILLABOUGH, S.T.D., J.C.L.

Metropolitan Judges at Second Instance—Rev. Msgr. MARK A. CAMPBELL, B.A., M.Ed., J.C.L.; Rev. Msgr. DAVID N. CROISETIERE, J.C.L., M.C.L.; Rev. BRIAN HAYES, J.C.L.; Miss MARY JO GRETSINGER, S.T.L., J.C.L.; EDWARD PETERS, J.D., J.C.D.

Notaries—Mrs. CONNIE NOEL; Mrs. CHERYL JOHNSTON.

Diocesan Offices and Directors

Archivist—Contact, *Chancellor's Office.* Tel: 619-490-8310.

Canonical Affairs—EDWARD PETERS, J.D., J.C.D., Dir. Tel: 619-490-8314.

Catholic Charities—Sr. RAYMONDA DUVALL, C.H.S., Exec. Dir., *349 Cedar St., San Diego, 92101.* Tel: 619-231-2828.

Cemetery Committee—Rev. Msgr. W. FRANCIS PATTISON, Dir., *Holy Cross Cemetery, 4470 Hilltop Dr., San Diego, 92102.* Tel: 619-264-3127.

Censores Librorum—Rev. Msgr. RICHARD F. DUNCANSON, S.T.D.; Rev. Msgr. JOHN R. PORTMAN, S.T.D.; Revs. DENNIS W. KROUSE, S.T.D.; NORBERT J. RIGALI, S.J., Ph.D.; BERNADEANE CARR, S.T.L.; Mr. TERRY MCGOLDRICK, S.T.D.

Civil Affairs—VINCENT WHELAN, Esq., Dir. Tel: 619-490-8277. ROBERT G. SULLIVAN, Esq., Assoc. Counsel; EDWARD PETERS, Esq. of Counsel.

Computer Services—Ms. JENNA SEMER, Dir. Tel: 619-490-8222.

Ecumenical and Interreligious Affairs—Rev. DENNIS MIKULANIS, S.T.D., Vicar, *990 Saturn Blvd., San Diego, 92154.* Tel: 619-423-0242.

Education—Sr. CLAIRE PATRICE FITZGERALD, C.S.J., Dir. Pro Tem. Tel: 619-490-8241.

San Diego Diocesan Institute for Adult Education and Formation for Ministry—TERRY MCGOLDRICK, S.T.D., Dir. Tel: 619-490-8212.

Catechetical Ministry—Mrs. GINGER INFANTINO, Dir. Tel: 619-490-8234. Sr. M. CRISTINA GONZALEZ, C.V.I., Asst. Dir. for Hispanic Catechesis. Tel: 619-490-8233.

Schools—Sr. CLAIRE PATRICE FITZGERALD, C.S.J., Dir. Tel: 619-490-8241. Sr. TIMOTHEA KINGSTON, C.S.C., Personnel Dir. Tel: 619-490-8243. Mrs. PATRICIA BANNON, Curriculum Dir. Tel: 619-490-8244.

Youth and Young Adult Ministry—MONIQUE MUTHER, M.F.C.C., Dir. Tel: 619-490-8261.

Evangelization and Adult Faith Resources—Sr. GLORIA GALVAN-GRIMALDO, M.G.S.S., Assoc. Dir. for Hispanic Evangelization. Tel: 619-490-8214.

Finance—Mr. H.L. "HAL" GARDNER, Finance Officer. Tel: 619-490-8284. Mr. KAREN TISI, Accounting Supr.

Human Resources—Mr. STEVEN WOOLLEY, Dir. Tel: 619-490-8282.

Liturgy and Spirituality—Mrs. MARY ANN FALLON, Dir. Tel: 619-490-8290.

Marriage and Family Life—Rev. WILLIAM ORTMANN, Dir. Tel: 619-490-8296.

Missions—Rev. Msgr. ANTHONY J. CHYLEWSKI, Dir. Tel: 619-490-8250.

Multicultural Affairs—Mr. RODRIGO VALDIVIA, Dir. Tel: 619-490-8301.

Hispanic Affairs—ENRIQUE MENDEZ, Dir. Tel: 619-490-8249. JOSEPH FERRER, Asst. Dir.

Permanent Diaconate—Deacon JAMES KEELEY, Dir. Assocs.: Deacons THOMAS DOUGHERTY; LOUIS ROCHA; ALVIN MCDANIEL. Tel: 619-490-8216.

Seminary—*St. Francis*—Rev. STEVEN CALLAHAN, Rector, *1667 Santa Paula Dr., San Diego, 92111.* Tel: 619-291-7446.

Social Ministries—Deacon JAMES KEELEY, Dir. Tel: 619-490-8323.

"Southern Cross"—*(Diocesan Newspaper)*—BERNADEANE CARR, S.T.L., Editor. Tel: 619-490-8269.

Stewardship—Mr. RODRIGO VALDIVIA, Dir. Tel: 619-490-8301.

Women Religious—Sr. NANCY KANE, R.S.C.J., Vicar. Tel: 619-490-8289.

Advisory Bodies

Clergy Personnel Board—Rev. Msgr. DANIEL J. DILLABOUGH, Chm. Tel: 619-490-8310.

College of Consultors—Most Rev. GILBERT E. CHAVEZ; Rev. Msgrs. DANIEL J. DILLABOUGH; JOHN A. DICKIE; RAYMOND C. KIRK; EAMONN F. LYNG; W. FRANCIS PATTISON.

Diocesan Pastoral Council—Mr. RODRIGO VALDIVIA, Exec. Coord. Tel: 619-490-8301.

Finance Council—Most Rev. ROBERT H. BROM, Chm.; Mr. EDWARD MCNULTY, Recording Sec.; Rev. Msgr. DANIEL J. DILLABOUGH; Rev. Msgr. THOMAS PRENDERGAST; Sr. MARY JO ANDERSON; Mr. ROBERT BAKER; Mr. THOMAS BLAKE; Mr. JOHN T. BLANKINSHIP JR.; Mr. JOHN D. BOYCE; Mr. JOHN FOWLER; Mrs. ANN GREENBERG; Mr. OSCAR PADILLA; Mr. DAVID SCHAEFER.

Presbyteral Council—Most Revs. ROBERT H. BROM; GILBERT E. CHAVEZ; Rev. Msgr. W. FRANCIS PATTISON, Chm.; Rev. EDWARD P. MCNULTY, Exec. Sec.; Rev. Msgr. DANIEL J. DILLABOUGH; Rev. Msgr. RAYMOND C. KIRK; Rev. Msgr. MARK A. CAMPBELL; Revs. JOSEPH MASAR; PETER MCGUINE; MICHAEL RATAJCZAK; FRANK WAGNER, O.M.I.; ROBERT D. NIKLIBORC; FRANCIS PENKO; EDUARDO GUDINO; CHARLES SHESLO; NICHOLAS DEMPSEY; RAMON MARRUFO; DENNIS MIKULANIS; WILLIAM SPRINGER; WILLIAM ORTMANN; MICHAEL MURPHY; STEVEN CALLAHAN,Liaison for Military Chaplains: Rev. MICHAEL DIAZ, CHC, USNR Retired Priests Representative: Rev. Msgr. WILLIAM A. KRAFT.

Vicars Forane—Cathedral: Rev. Msgr. EDWARD F. BROCKHAUS, El Cajon: Rev. Msgr. MICHAEL GALLAGHER, Escondido: Rev. Msgr. HENRY F. FAWCETT, La Jolla: Rev. Msgr. LAWRENCE M. PURCELL, Oceanside: Rev. RAMON MARRUFO, University: Rev. Msgr. THOMAS PRENDERGAST, El Centro: Rev. JOSEPH MASAR, South Bay: Very Rev. JOSEPH MEL COLLIER.

Miscellaneous

Apostleship of the Sea—Deacon WILLIAM POLLOCK, Port Chap., *3322 Carleton St., San Diego, 92106.* Tel: 619-224-2669.

Charismatic Renewal—SHAWN QUINN, Admin., *1659 B Santa Paula Dr., San Diego, 92111.* Tel: 619-683-2050.

Hispanic Charismatic Renewal Center—NARCISCO GUZMAN, Coord. Tel: 619-683-3893.

Christ Child Society—Rev. NICHOLAS DEMPSEY, Spiritual Advisor. Tel: 619-223-2200.

Cursillo—Deacon JAMES SCULL, Spiritual Advisor; JIM ZAWADZKI, Lay Dir. Tel: 619-460-3171.

Filipino—Rev. BIEN QUANG DO, Spiritual Dir. RAMON DELA CRUZ, Lay Dir. Tel: 619-484-6131.

Hispanic—MOISES ARANDA, Pres. Secretariat. Tel: 619-690-1132.

Holy Childhood Association—Rev. Msgr. ANTHONY J. CHYLEWSKI, Dir., *P.O. Box 711011, San Diego, 92171-1011.* Tel: 619-490-8250.

Propagation of the Faith—Rev. Msgr. ANTHONY CHYLEWSKI, Dir.; Sr. KATHY SCHMITTGENS, S.S.N.D., Dir. Mission Education, *P.O. Box 711011, San Diego, 92171-1011.* Tel: 619-490-8250.

CLERGY, PARISHES, MISSIONS AND PAROCHIAL SCHOOLS

CITY OF SAN DIEGO
(San Diego County)

1—ST. JOSEPH CATHEDRAL, Most Rev. Gilbert E. Chavez, D.D.; Revs. Frank Theriault, C.S.C. (Canada); Robert Campbell, O.P. In res., Revs. Paul Balio (Philippines); William Ortmann.
Res., 1535 Third Ave., 92101-3192. Tel: 619-239-0229; Fax: 619-239-3788.

2—ASCENSION, Rev. James Sassone; Deacon Jim Scull.
Res., 11292 Clairemont Mesa Blvd., 92124-1524. Tel: 619-279-2735.
Catechesis/Religious Programs—Susan Paul, D.R.E. Students 270.

3—BLESSED SACRAMENT, Revs. William F. Rowland, C.J.M.; Oscar Roy, C.J.M. (Canada); James Burson, C.J.M.; Deacon Louis Principe. In res., Rev. Jerry Hamperzonian; Deacon Tony Albers.
Res., 4540 El Cerrito Dr., 92115. Tel: 619-582-5722.
School—Tel: 619-582-3862; Fax: 619-265-9310. Dr. Brian Bennett, Prin.
Lay Teachers 21; Students 534.
Catechesis/Religious Programs—Students 155.

4—CHRIST THE KING (1938), Revs. Eduardo A. Samaniego, S.J.; Wayne Negrete, S.J.; Deacon Jonathan P. Connor. In res., Revs. Gilbert J. Gentile, S.J.; Joe Speiler, S.J.
Res., 29 N. 32nd St., 92102. Tel: 619-231-8906; Fax: 619-238-7060.

5—GOOD SHEPHERD, Revs. Fernando Ramirez; Earl Edward Eggleston; Cavana White; Deacon Ron Diem.
Res., 8200 Gold Coast Dr., 92126-3699. Tel: 619-271-0207; Fax: 619-271-0748.
School—8180 Gold Coast Dr., 92126. Tel: 619-693-1522; Fax: 619-271-0207. Mrs. Chris Corpora, Prin.
Lay Teachers 13; Students 315.
Catechesis/Religious Programs—Tel: 619-271-8769. Mr. Charles McGuire, D.R.E.
Lay Teachers 78; Students 1,205.

6—HOLY FAMILY (Linda Vista), Revs. Bruce Orsborn; Joseph Khuyen Van Lai; Deacons Thomas Dougherty; Paul Davidson.
Res., 1957 Coolidge St., 92111-7098. Tel: 619-277-0404; Fax: 619-277-7978.
School—Tel: 619-277-0222.
Lay Teachers 12; Students 239.
Catechesis/Religious Programs—Students 130.

7—HOLY SPIRIT, Rev. Msgr. Roger A. Lechner; Rev. Doan Van Lai.
Res., 2725-55th St., 92105-5094. Tel: 619-262-2435; Fax: 619-262-8718.

8—IMMACULATA, Most Rev. Robert H. Brom; Rev. Msgr. Daniel J. Dillabough; Rev. Edward McNulty; Sr. Priscilla Lemire, Pastoral Assoc.
Res., U.S.D. Campus, Alcala Park, 92110. Tel: 619-574-5700; Fax: 619-574-5707.
Catechesis/Religious Programs—Students 130.

9—IMMACULATE CONCEPTION, Rev. Msgr. Alphonsus Moloney.
Res., 2540 San Diego Ave., 92110-2840. Tel: 619-295-4148; Fax: 619-297-6916.

10—MISSION BASILICA SAN DIEGO DE ALCALA. (California's First Mission). Rev. Msgr. Thomas Prendergast; Rev. William A. Springer; Deacons Bill Vasquez; Ernest Grosso.
Res., 10818 San Diego Mission Rd., 92108-2498. Tel: 619-283-7319; Fax: 619-283-7762.
Catechesis/Religious Programs—Tel: 619-624-0900.
Students 143.

11—OUR LADY OF ANGELS, Rev. Kenneth Del Priore.
Res., 656 24th St., 92102-2911. Tel: 619-239-1231; Fax: 619-234-5520.
School—Our Lady's School-North Campus, Tel: 619-233-8888; Fax: 619-234-5520.
Sisters 2; Lay Teachers 9; Students 220.
Catechesis/Religious Programs—Sr. Dina Marie Garcia, D.R.E.
Students 400.

12—OUR LADY OF GUADALUPE, Revs. Richard H. Brown, S.J.; James I. Rasura, S.J.; Augusto Berrio, S.J. In res., Rev. Max Oliva, S.J.
Res., 1770 Kearny Ave., 92113-1128. Tel: 619-233-3838; Fax: 619-233-3252.
School—Our Lady's School-South Campus, 744 Beardsley, 92113. Tel: 619-233-8888.
Religious 2; Lay Teachers 3; Students 110.
Catechesis/Religious Programs—Tel: 619-233-3838; Fax: 619-233-3252. Veronica Lopez, D.R.E. Students 220.

13—OUR LADY OF MT. CARMEL (Rancho Penasquitos), Rev. Msgr. Henry F. Fawcett; Rev. Paul Palmitessa; Deacons Bernard Yeatts; John Phelps; H. Thomas Jones.
Res., 13541 Stoney Creek Rd., 92129. Tel: 619-566-3550; 484-1070; Fax: 619-484-3157.
Catechesis/Religious Programs—Students 1300.

14—OUR LADY OF REFUGE (Pacific Beach), Rev. Msgr. William E. Elliott. In res., Rev. Christopher Merris.
Res., 4228 Jewell St., 92109. Tel: 619-274-9670; Fax: 619-274-9671.
Catechesis/Religious Programs—Tel: 619-274-2959. Martin Magana, D.R.E.
Students 118.

15—OUR LADY OF THE ROSARY, Revs. Steven M. Grancini, C.R.S.P.; Louis M. Solcia, C.R.S.P.
Res., 1659 Columbia St., 92101-2584. Tel: 619-234-4820; Fax: 619-234-3559.
Catechesis/Religious Programs—Tel: 619-234-4820. Esther Leuzzi, D.R.E.
Students 145.

16—OUR LADY OF THE SACRED HEART, Revs. Richard L. Perozich; Joseph Phen Van Pham; Deacon Peter Can Nguyen.
Res., 4177 Marlborough Ave., 92105-1412. Tel: 619-280-0515; Fax: 619-280-0517.
School—Tel: 619-284-1715. Sr. Linda Lutz, Prin.
Lay Teachers 8; Students 165.
Catechesis/Religious Programs—Tel: 619-283-9262. Sr. Mary Jo Maes, D.R.E.
Students 600.

17—OUR MOTHER OF CONFIDENCE (University City), Rev. Msgr. Donal C. Sheahan; Deacons William Klopchin; Arnold Hess. In res., Rev. Brian Hayes.
Res., 3131 Governor Dr., 92122. Tel: 619-453-0222; Fax: 619-453-2547.
Catechesis/Religious Programs—Tel: 619-453-3554. D.R.E.: Cathy Whelan; Sr. Frances Franey, S.N.J.M.
Students 357.

18—SACRED HEART (Ocean Beach), Rev. Ronald Hebert; Deacon Giles Schmitt.
Res., 4776 Saratoga, 92107-9990. Tel: 619-224-2746.
School—Tel: 619-222-7252; Fax: 619-222-2836. Mr. Robert Hamm, Prin.
Lay Teachers 12; Students 295.
Catechesis/Religious Programs—Jean Morrow, D.R.E.
Students 70.

19—ST. AGNES (Pt. Loma), Rev. Nicholas Dempsey; Deacon William Pollock.
Res., 1140 Evergreen St., 92106. Tel: 619-223-2200; Fax: 619-226-4009.
Catechesis/Religious Programs—Tel: 619-223-9748. Mrs. Robert Spondike, D.R.E.
Students 119.

20—ST. ANNE, Rev. Robert D. Nikliborc.
Res., 621 Sicard St., 92113-2334. Tel: 619-239-8253.

Catechesis/Religious Programs—Tel: 619-232-5903.
Students 220.

21—ST. BRIGID (Pacific Beach), Rev. Msgr. Sean Murray; Rev. Peter Escalante, Pastor Emeritus.
Res., 4735 Cass St., 92109-2698. Tel: 619-483-3030; Fax: 619-483-7131.
Catechesis/Religious Programs—Tel: 619-483-3032. Sr. Hilda McDonagh, R.S.M., D.R.E.
Students 165.

22—ST. CATHERINE LABOURE, Rev. Msgr. William Cuddihy; Rev. Msgr. Fernando Gutierrez.
Res., 4026 Mt. Abraham Ave., 92111. Tel: 619-277-3133; Fax: 619-277-9181.
Catechesis/Religious Programs—Tel: 619-279-0587. Patricia Doyle, D.R.E.
Students 275.

23—ST. CHARLES, Revs. Dennis Mikulanis; Luis C. Valenciano; Michael Dean Robinson; Deacon Seodello Martinez.
Res., 990 Saturn Blvd., 92154. Tel: 619-423-0242; Fax: 619-423-1966.
School—Tel: 619-423-3701; Fax: 619-423-5331.
Sisters of Mercy 2; Lay Teachers 13; Students 307.
Catechesis/Religious Programs—Students 553.

24—ST. CHARLES BORROMEO, Revs. Michel Froidurot; David N. Croisetiere.
Res., 2802 Cadiz St., 92110-4813. Tel: 619-225-8157; Fax: 619-225-2288.
School—Tel: 619-223-8271.
Sisters 2; Lay Teachers 12; Students 259.
Catechesis/Religious Programs—Students 75.

25—ST. COLUMBA, Rev. Msgr. Patrick J. Mullarkey; Rev. Noel S. Ryan, S.S.C.; Deacons Louis X. Ball; Nick Santiago. In res., Rev. Louis Newman.
Res., 3327 Glencolum Dr., 92123. Tel: 619-277-3863; Fax: 619-279-9053.
School—(Grades PreK-8). Tel: 619-279-1882.
Lay Teachers 14; Students 342.
Catechesis/Religious Programs—Tel: 619-277-3861.
Students 132.

26—ST. DIDACUS, Rev. Scott J. McColl. In res., Rev. Gary Holtey, Chap.
Res., 4772 Felton St., 92116. Tel: 619-284-3472; Fax: 619-284-3484.
School—4630 34th St., 92116. Tel: 619-284-8730; Fax: 619-284-1764.
Lay Teachers 13; Students 280.
Catechesis/Religious Programs—Tel: 619-284-7050. Mrs. Mary J. Curtis, D.R.E.
Students 80.

27—ST. GREGORY THE GREAT (1985), Rev. James N. Poulsen; Deacon L. Ferris Bell.
Mailing Address: P.O. Box 261699, 92196. Tel: 619-695-6799; Fax: 619-695-6639.
Res., 10403 Avenida Magnifica, 92131.
Parish Center: 10650 Treena St., 92131.

28—ST. JEROME (1985), Rev. James V. Caldwell; Deacons Kenneth E. Montoya; Joseph Delano.
Office: 2515 Beyer Blvd., 92154-1502. Tel: 619-423-0405; Fax: 619-423-9363.
Res., 4485 Murrieta Cir., 92154-1713. Tel: 619-428-7978.
Catechesis/Religious Programs—Sr. Roberta Collins, C.S.J.P., D.R.E.
Students 340.

29—ST. JOHN THE EVANGELIST, Rev. Msgr. Anthony A. Giesing. In res., Rev. Manuel Ediza (Philippines).
Res., 1638 Polk Ave., 92103. Tel: 619-291-1660.
Catechesis/Religious Programs—Students 97.

30—ST. JUDE, Rev. Msgr. Edward F. Brockhaus; Rev. Henry Rodriguez; Deacon Manuel Nunez.
Res., 1129 S. 38th St., 92113-3210. Tel: 619-264-2195; Fax: 619-264-8528.
School—1228 S. 38th St., 92113. Tel: 619-264-3154; Fax: 619-264-8050.
Religious 1; Lay Teachers 10; Students 320.
Catechesis/Religious Programs—Tel: 619-264-5651. D.R.E.: Susy Maldonado, (Spanish); Eddie Johnson, (English).
Students 1,375.

31—ST. MARY MAGDALENE (Clairemont), Rev. Msgr. John A. Dickie. In res., Revs. Robert J. Nagler (SB) (Retired); Michael T. White, C.S.Sp.
Res., 1945 Illion St., 92110. Tel: 619-276-1041; Fax: 619-276-0144.
School—Tel: 619-276-6545.
Lay Teachers 33; Students 573.
Catechesis/Religious Programs—Tel: 619-276-6545. Mrs. Phyllis Alcaraz, D.R.E.
Students 125.

32—ST. MAXIMILIAN KOLBE MISSION (Polish). Unassigned. (Quasi Parish).
Res., 1735 Grand Ave., 92109.

33—ST. MICHAEL, Revs. Joseph Mel Collier; Andre Ramos.
Res., 2643 Homedale St., 92139. Tel: 619-470-1977; Fax: 619-470-6357.
School—2637 Homedale St., 92139. Tel: 619-470-4880.
Sisters 2; Lay Teachers 18; Students 332.
Catechesis/Religious Programs—Tel: 619-470-2291. Mr. Louis Costa, D.R.E.
Students 971.

34—ST. PATRICK, Revs. Gary E. Sanders, O.S.A.; Thomas J. McLaughlin, O.S.A.; Bro. Michael T. Bube, O.S.A.
Res., 3585 30th St., 92104. Tel: 619-295-2157; Fax: 619-688-1225.
School—Tel: 619-297-1314.
Lay Teachers 10; Students 254.
Catechesis/Religious Programs—Patricia Lawrence, D.R.E.
Students 110.
Chapel—St. Augustine, 3266 Nutmeg St., 92104. Tel: 619-282-2028.

35—ST. RITA, Rev. Msgr. Francis Pattison; Rev. Juvencio D. Ricafort. In res., Rev. Msgr. Joseph A. Carroll.
Res., 5124 Churchward St., 92114-3797. Tel: 619-264-3165; Fax: 619-264-2907.
School—Tel: 619-264-0109.
Sisters 1; Lay Teachers 11; Students 270.
Catechesis/Religious Programs—Tel: 619-264-4399. Margaret Castro, D.R.E.
Students 409.

36—ST. THERESE, Rev. Msgr. Frederick J. Florek; Rev. Richard E. Huston; Deacons Leo Dube; Robert Ekhaml.
Res., 6016 Camino Rico, 92120-3099. Tel: 619-582-3716; Fax: 619-582-2535.
School—St. Therese Academy, Tel: 619-583-6270; Fax: 619-583-6271.
Sisters 4; Lay Teachers 13; Students 359.
Catechesis/Religious Programs—Tel: 619-582-2585. Sr. Damien Peters, D.F.C., D.R.E.
Students 251.

37—ST. VINCENT DE PAUL, Revs. Nicholas P. Clavin; James Rankin. In res., Rev. Msgr. Anthony Chylewski.
Res., 4077 Ibis St., 92103-1899. Tel: 619-299-3881; Fax: 619-299-9509.
School—Tel: 619-296-2222.
Sisters of Mercy 2; Lay Teachers 9; Students 264.

38—SAN RAFAEL (Rancho Bernardo), Rev. Msgr. Lloyd V. Bourgeois; Rev. Walter Halloran, S.J.
Res., 17252 Bernardo Center, 92128. Tel: 619-487-4314; Fax: 619-487-1498.
Catechesis/Religious Programs—Tel: 619-674-1145. D.R.E.: Sr. Ita O'Neil, O.S.F.; Sr. Joan Derry, S.H.F.
Students 700.

OUTSIDE THE CITY OF SAN DIEGO

Alpine, San Diego Co., Queen of Angels, Rev. Matthew Spahr.
Res., 2569 Victoria Dr., 91901-3662. Tel: 619-445-2145.
Catechesis/Religious Programs—Students 165.

Bonita, San Diego Co., Corpus Christi (1984), Rev. John G. Proctor, Jr.; Deacon James H. Hitch.
Mailing Address: P.O. Box 1349, 91908.
Res., 2934 Degen Dr., 91902. Tel: 619-482-3954; Fax: 619-482-7236. [CEM]
Church—450 Corral Canyon Rd., 91902.
Catechesis/Religious Programs—Tel: 619-482-3957; Fax: 619-482-7236. Deacon James H. Hitch, D.R.E.
Students 482.

Borrego Springs, San Diego Co., St. Richard, Rev. Simon Lefebvre, C.S.V.
Res., P.O. Box 1128, 92004-1128. Tel: 619-767-5701.
Catechesis/Religious Programs—Students 140.

Brawley, Imperial Co., Our Lady of Perpetual Help, Rev. Jorge Moreno.
Res., 1250 B St., P.O. Box 1283, 92227. Tel: 619-344-2226; Fax: 619-344-1557.
Catechesis/Religious Programs—Tel: 619-344-5787. Juan Coronado, D.R.E.
Students 167.

Sacred Heart, Rev. Joseph G. Masar; Deacon Donald L. Spinney.
Res., 402 S. Imperial St., 92227. Tel: 619-344-3171; Fax: 619-344-3171.
School—(Grades K-8). Tel: 619-334-2662; Fax: 619-344-1910.
Lay Teachers 11; Students 140.
Catechesis/Religious Programs—Tel: 619-344-3171. Sr. Dawnna Spinney, D.C.M., D.R.E.
Students 140.

St. Margaret Mary, Rev. Roque P. Vano.
Res., 620 S. 10th St., 92227. Tel: 619-344-3571; Fax: 619-344-3598.
Catechesis/Religious Programs—Tel: 619-344-3451.
Students 491.

Calexico, Imperial Co., Our Lady of Guadalupe, Revs. Bernard A. Rapp; Michael J. Sinor.
Res., 124 E. Fifth St., 92231. Tel: 619-357-1822; Fax: 619-357-0115.
School—Our Lady of Guadalupe Academy, Tel: 619-357-1986; Fax: 619-357-3282.
Sisters, Servants of the Blessed Sacrament 6; Lay Teachers 23; Students 598.
Catechesis/Religious Programs—Tel: 619-357-2532. Sr. Maria Teresa Bandera, C.V.I., D.R.E.
Students 545.

Calipatria, Imperial Co., St. Patrick, Revs. Amador Lopez, O.M.I.; James Kernan, O.M.I.
Res., 133 E. Church St., P.O. Box 238, 92233. Tel: 619-348-2733.
Catechesis/Religious Programs—Tel: 619-348-2454.
Students 166.
Mission—Niland, Imperial Co., Immaculate Heart of Mary, 19 Sixth St., P.O. Box 160, Niland, 92257.

Carlsbad, San Diego Co., St. Elizabeth Seton, Rev. Donald E. Coleman.
Res., 6628 Santa Isabel St., 92009-5148. Tel: 619-438-3393; Fax: 619-438-7739.
Catechesis/Religious Programs—Tel: 619-438-3438. Larry Broding, D.R.E.
Students 270.

St. Patrick, Rev. Msgr. Stephen McCall; Revs. Joseph Mullen, S.J.; Thomas W. Thompson.
Res., 3821 Adams St., 92008-0249. Tel: 619-729-2866; Fax: 619-434-3325.
School—3820 Pio Pico, 92008. Tel: 619-729-1333. Ms. Jean Panno, Prin.
Lay Teachers 16; Students 365.

St. Thomas More (1985), Rev. Peter McGuine.
Mailing Address: P.O. Box 4415, 92018-4415.
Res., 2256 Cameo Rd., 92008. Tel: 619-599-1980; Fax: 619-599-1982.
Church—1910 Shadowridge Dr., Ste. 107, Vista, 92083.
Catechesis/Religious Programs—Students 112.

Chula Vista, San Diego Co.,

1—MOST PRECIOUS BLOOD, Revs. Frank Wagner, O.M.I.; Ernest Sylvestre, O.M.I.
Res., 1245 4th Ave., 91911-3012. Tel: 619-422-2100; Fax: 619-422-1375.
Catechesis/Religious Programs—Tel: 619-422-2159. Sr. Camille Crabbe, C.V.I., D.R.E.
Students 320.

2—OUR LADY OF GUADALUPE, Rev. Mario Vesga; Deacons Daniel Parra; Margarito Lozoya; Raul Hernandez.
Res., 345 Anita St., 91911-4198. Tel: 619-422-3977; Fax: 619-422-1056.
Catechesis/Religious Programs—Tel: 619-427-2774.
Students 400.

3—ST. PIUS X, Rev. Msgr. Donald R. Kulleck; Rev. Paul Bauer; Deacon Dan De Pozo. In res., Rev. James J. Kinzig.
Res., 36 E. Naples St., 91911-2298. Tel: 619-420-9193.
School—37 E. Emerson, 91911. Tel: 619-422-2015; Fax: 619-422-0048. Eileen Hanson, Prin.
Lay Teachers 10; Students 307.
Catechesis/Religious Programs—Tel: 619-426-2263. Lois Richards, D.R.E.
Students 635.

4—ST. ROSE OF LIMA, Rev. Msgr. Richard F. Duncanson; Rev. Msgr. Charles P. Young, Pastor Emeritus; Revs. Michael X. Tran; George Soria; Deacons Oscar Alvarez; Joe Arismendez.
Res., 293 H St., 91910. Tel: 619-427-0230; Fax: 619-427-5786.
School—473 Third Ave., 91910. Tel: 619-422-1121.
Lay Teachers 15; Religious 1; Students 343.
Catechesis/Religious Programs—Tel: 619-426-6717. Sr. Margaret Ann Altmiller, O.L.V.M., D.R.E.
Students 1,208.

Coronado, San Diego Co., Sacred Heart, Rev. Michael F. Murphy; Rev. Msgr. John R. Portman; Rev. Msgr. Jememiah O'Sullivan, Co-Pastor Emeritus; Deacon William Vivio. In res., Rev. John Wheeler.
Res., 672 B Ave., 92118-2299. Tel: 619-435-3167.
School—Benedictine Sisters 2; Lay Teachers 11; Students 251.
Catechesis/Religious Programs—Tel: 619-435-4858.
Students 202.

Del Mar, San Diego Co., St. William of York (1985), Rev. George Byrne.
Res., P.O. Box 2726, 92014-5726. Tel: 619-481-3232; Fax: 619-481-3573.
Catechesis/Religious Programs—Tel: 619-481-4061. Sr. Catherine Osimo, C.S.C., D.R.E.
Students 201.

Descanso, San Diego Co., Our Lady of Light, Rev. Gerald F. Palcheck.
Res., 9136 Riverside Dr., P.O. Box 219, 91916. Tel: 619-445-3620.

Catechesis/Religious Programs—Claire Donivan, D.R.E.
Students 55.
Mission—Descanso, Our Lady of the Pines, 9136 Riverside Dr., 91916.

El Cajon, San Diego Co.,

1—HOLY TRINITY, Revs. Brian M. Corcoran; William A. Kernan; Deacons C. Edwin Donivan; Louis Rocha.
Res., 405 Ballard St., 92019. Tel: 619-444-9425; Fax: 619-444-9426.
School—Tel: 619-444-7529.
Lay Teachers 17; Students 294.
Catechesis/Religious Programs—Students 364.

2—OUR LADY OF GRACE, Rev. Msgr. Michael J. Gallagher; Revs. Burt Boudoin; Joseph Bien Quang Do; Omer LeBlanc, C.J.M.; Deacons R. Walt Woznicki; George Shea; Sr. Carmel Lohan, S.M., Pastoral Asst.
Res., 2766 Navajo Rd., 92020-2183. Tel: 619-469-0133; Fax: 619-469-0575.
School—Sisters 1; Lay Teachers 15; Students 325.
Catechesis/Religious Programs—Tel: 619-466-5656. D.R.E.: Doris Hertzig; Stephanie Hagenburger.
Students 450.

3—ST. KIERAN, Rev. Francis G. Penko; Deacon John Trumble.
Mailing Address: P.O. Box 2428, 92021-0428.
Office: 1510 Greenfield Dr., 92021-0428. Tel: 619-588-6881; Fax: 619-588-5274.
School—1347 Camillo Way, Tel: 619-588-6398. Miss Michaele Durant, Prin.
Lay Teachers 12; Students 194.
Catechesis/Religious Programs—Tel: 619-447-2424.
Students 135.

4—ST. LOUISE DE MARILLAC, Rev. Louis A. Salca.
Res., 2005 Crest Dr., 92021-4309. Tel: 619-444-3076.

5—ST. LUKE, (1985), Rev. Raymond G. O'Donnell; Deacon John Snyder.
Res., 1980 Hillsdale Rd., 92019. Tel: 619-442-1697; Fax: 619-442-2293.
Catechesis/Religious Programs—Tel: 619-442-2515. D.R.E.: Rosalie Camacho; Rev. Jane Alfano.
Students 380.

El Centro, Imperial Co., Our Lady of Guadalupe, Rev. Eduardo Gudino.
Res., 153 E. Brighton Ave., 92243. Tel: 619-352-5535; Fax: 619-352-8003.
Catechesis/Religious Programs—Tel: 619-352-5554. Victor Hernandez, D.R.E.
Students 611.

St. Mary, Rev. Msgr. Thomas J. Vidra.
Res., 795 LaBrucherie, P.O. Box 3425, 92244. Tel: 619-352-4211; Fax: 619-352-7397.
School—Tel: 619-352-7285.
Sister Servants of the Blessed Sacrament 4; Lay Teachers 7; Students 278.
Catechesis/Religious Programs—Tel: 619-353-8260.
Students 258.

Encinitas, San Diego Co., St. John the Evangelist, Rev. Msgr. Timothy Harnett; Rev. Patrick J. Mulcahy.
Res., 1001 Encinitas Blvd., 92024-0457. Tel: 619-753-6254; Fax: 619-753-7118.
School—Tel: 619-753-1893.
Lay Teachers 20; Students 360.

Escondido, San Diego Co., Church of the Resurrection, Revs. Charles Fuld; Jose Edmundo Zarate-Suarez; Deacons James Kostick; Lawrence Michaels; Leopoldo Valdivia.
Res., 1445 Conway Dr., 92027. Tel: 619-747-2322; Fax: 619-747-7079.
Catechesis/Religious Programs—Tel: 619-747-4550. Margaret Butkis, D.R.E.
Students 730.
Comunidad Hispana—Tel: 619-747-4553.

Church of St. Timothy (1985), Rev. James E. Rafferty.
Res., 3110 Quiet Hills Dr., 92029-7304. Tel: 619-489-1200; Fax: 619-489-2731.
Catechesis/Religious Programs—Tel: 619-489-0482. Cheryl Verber, D.R.E.
Students 118.

St. Mary, Revs. Peter Navarra; Victor Maristela.
Res., 1160 S. Broadway Ave., 92025-5815. Tel: 619-745-1611; Fax: 619-745-1238.
School—Tel: 619-743-3431.
Sisters of the Precious Blood 2; Lay Teachers 12; Students 319.
Catechesis/Religious Programs—130 E. 13th Ave., 92025. Tel: 619-745-8255. Susan Ferraris, D.R.E.
Students 1350.

Fallbrook, San Diego Co., St. Peter, Revs. Edward Kaicher; Anthony Stanonik; Deacon Bennett Dean.
Res., 450 S. Stage Coach Ln., 92028. Tel: 619-728-7034; Fax: 619-723-4050.
School—St. Peter's Catholic School, Tel: 619-728-6961; Fax: 619-723-4050.
Lay Teachers 9; Students 185.
Catechesis/Religious Programs—Tel: 619-728-3412.
Students 600.

Holtville, Imperial Co., St. Joseph, Rev. Cecilio T. Moraga, Admin.
Res., 560 Maple Ave., 92250. Tel: 619-356-2147.
Catechesis/Religious Programs—Tel: 619-356-5738. Maria Ayon, D.R.E.
Students 362.

Imperial, Imperial Co., St. Anthony of Padua, Revs. Firmo Mantovani, C.S. (Brazil); Mauro Verzeletti, C.S. (Brazil).
Res., 210 W. Seventh St., 92251. Tel: 619-355-1347; Fax: 619-355-1226.
Catechesis/Religious Programs—Tel: 619-355-1304. Martha P. Rubalcava, D.R.E.
Students 210.
Missions—Heber, Sacred Heart; Seeley, Holy Spirit.

Jacumba, San Diego Co., St. Mary Magdalene (1947), Rev. George A. Carroll, S.J.
Res., 44686 Calexico Ave., P.O. Box 406, 91934-0406. Tel: 619-766-4661.
Catechesis/Religious Programs—Debbie Hebert, D.R.E.
Students 15.
Missions—Cameron Corner, St. Adelaide; Campo Indian Reservation, Our Lady of Mount Carmel.

Jamul, San Diego Co., St. Pius X Rev. Scott Burnia; Deacons H. B. Cody; A. R. McDaniel.
Res., 14107 Lyons Valley Rd., P.O. Box 369, 91935. Tel: 619-669-0085; Fax: 619-669-0087.
Catechesis/Religious Programs—Tel: 619-669-0086. Sr. Anne Egan, R.J.M., D.R.E.
Students 150.

Julian, San Diego Co., St. Elizabeth, Rev. Donal C. Walsh.
Res., P.O. Box 366, 92036-0366. Tel: 619-765-0613; Fax: 619-765-0552.

La Jolla, San Diego Co., All Hallows, Rev. Msgr. Patrick Fox. In res., Revs. William T. Wilson; Daniel Polizzi.
Res., 6602 La Jolla Scenic Dr. S., 92037-5799. Tel: 619-459-2975; Fax: 619-459-9712.
School—2390 Nautilus, 92037. Tel: 619-459-4602.
Sisters 2; Lay Teachers 25; Students 288.
Catechesis/Religious Programs—Patricia Stewart, D.R.E.
Students 60.

Mary, Star of the Sea, Rev. Msgr. Eamonn F. Lyng; Rev. Msgr. James M. Gilfillan, Pastor Emeritus; Deacon William Dalzell.
Res., 7727 Girard Ave., 92037-4480. Tel: 619-454-2631; Fax: 619-454-5968.
School—Stella Maris Academy, 7654 Herschel Ave., 92037. Tel: 619-454-2461; Fax: 619-454-4913.
Lay Teachers 15; Students 232.
Catechesis/Religious Programs—Tel: 619-454-1714. Sr. Christian Koch, D.R.E.
Students 140.

Lakeside, San Diego Co., Blessed Kateri Tekakwitha, Rev. Anthony C. May; Deacon Bill Clarke.
Res., 1054 Barona Rd., 92040-1502. Tel: 619-443-3412.
Catechesis/Religious Programs—Tel: 619-445-8333. Betty Alto, D.R.E.
Students 140.
Missions—Lakeside, Barona, 1054 Barona Rd., 92040-1502. Tel: 619-443-3412; Alpine, Viejas; El Cajon, Sycuan.

Our Lady of Perpetual Help, Rev. Msgr. Neal T. Dolan; Rev. Ben Davison; Deacon Anthony L. Gasparovic.
Res., 13208 Lakeshore Dr., 92040. Tel: 619-443-1412; Fax: 619-443-1733.
School—Tel: 619-443-1440. Mr. Richard Scherer, Prin.
St. Joseph of Carondelet Sisters 1; Lay Teachers 12; Students 227.
Catechesis/Religious Programs—Tel: 619-443-5018. Joan Lopez, D.R.E., (Jr. High School).
Students 462.

La Mesa, San Diego Co., St. Martin of Tours, Rev. John M. Sproul. In res., Rev. Msgr. Patrick O'Neill; Deacon Timothy Treadwell.
Res., 7710 El Cajon Blvd., 91941. Tel: 619-465-5334; Fax: 619-465-7297.
School—Tel: 619-466-3241; Fax: 619-466-0285.
Lay Teachers 14; Students 277.
Catechesis/Religious Programs—Tel: 619-698-8434. Christine Davis, D.R.E.
Students 294.

Lemon Grove, San Diego Co., St. John of the Cross, Rev. Msgr. Raymond C. Kirk; Rev. John D. Cuddigan, S.J.; Deacons Ralph Robbins; Peter Corrao; Frank Santoyo; Martin Villafana. In res., Rev. Donald Buchanan, (Retired).
Res., 8086 Broadway, 91945-2598. Tel: 619-466-3209; Fax: 619-466-9276.
School—8175 Lemon Grove Way, 91945. Tel: 619-466-8624. Sr. Guadalupe Mier Y Teran, H.M.S.S., Prin.
Sisters 2; Lay Teachers 7; Students 327.
Catechesis/Religious Programs—Tel: 619-461-2681. Karen Dey, D.R.E.
Students 586.
Convent—8171 Lemon Grove Way, 91945. Tel: 619-460-4271.
Sisters of Mercy of the Blessed Sacrament 5.

National City, San Diego Co., St. Anthony of Padua, Rev. Willaim T. Lawson.
Res., 1816 Harding Ave., P.O. Box 1507, 91951-1507. Tel: 619-477-4520; Fax: 619-477-8708.
Catechesis/Religious Programs—Angelina Sampo, D.R.E.
Students 355.

St. Mary, Revs. Dionisio Malacintal (PH); Jose Castillo (Columbia).
Res., 411 E. Eighth St., 91950-2395. Tel: 619-474-1501; Fax: 619-474-1502.
Catechesis/Religious Programs—Tel: 619-474-5777.
Students 673.

Oceanside, San Diego Co., St. Margaret, Rev. William F. Gold; Deacon Lewis Beatty.
Res., 4300 Oceanside Blvd., 92056-2999. Tel: 619-941-5560; Fax: 619-941-1857.
Catechesis/Religious Programs—Tel: 619-941-5561. Sr. Yvonne Hawker, O.S.F., D.R.E.
Students 460.

St. Mary Star of the Sea, Revs. John P. Dolan; Humberto C. Zanetti, O.F.M. (Italy); Deacon James A. Roy.
Res., 609 Pier View Way, 92054-2861. Tel: 619-722-1688; Fax: 619-722-2653.
School—Tel: 619-722-7259.
Lay Teachers 16; Students 338.
Catechesis/Religious Programs—Tel: 619-722-1000.
Students 222.

Pala, San Diego Co., Mission San Antonio de Pala, Rev. Paul Marconi, C.R.S.P.
Res., P.O. Box 70, 92059-0070. Tel: 619-742-3317; Fax: 619-742-3040.
Catechesis/Religious Programs—Tel: 619-742-1714.
Students 68.
Convent—Tel: 619-742-1714.
Franciscan Sisters of Philadelphia 4.
Chapels—Rincon Indian Reservation, St. Bartholomew.; Pauma, El Centro Guadalupano, Tel: 619-742-4559; La Jolla Indian Reservation, Our Lady of Refuge.; Pauma Indian Reservation, St. James.

Poway, San Diego Co., St. Gabriel, Rev. Msgr. Joseph Brady.
Res., 13734 Twin Peaks Rd., 92074-0867. Tel: 619-748-5348; Fax: 619-748-5764.
Catechesis/Religious Programs—Tel: 619-748-7475. Sr. Teresa Boland, O.S.F., D.R.E.
Students 675.

St. Michael, Rev. Msgr. Joseph L. Finnerty; Rev. William Mooney; Deacon Franz Schultz.
Res., 15546 Pomerado Rd., 92064-2404. Tel: 619-487-4755; Fax: 619-487-5937.
School—15542 Pomerado Rd., 92064. Tel: 619-485-1303.
Sisters of Mercy of Sligo 2; Lay Teachers 12; Students 304.
Catechesis/Religious Programs—Tel: 619-487-0360. Kathy Wood, D.R.E.
Students 930.

Ramona, San Diego Co., Immaculate Heart of Mary, Rev. Charles W. Sheslo; Deacon Modesto Perez.
Res., 537 E St., 92065. Tel: 619-789-0583; Fax: 619-789-3875.
Catechesis/Religious Programs—Tel: 619-789-6151. Sr. Patricia Elower, P.B.V.M., D.R.E.
Students 450.

Rancho Santa Fe, San Diego Co., Church of the Nativity (1985), Rev. Msgr. Dennis R. Clark.
Mailing Address: P.O. Box 8770, 92067-8770.
Res., 6309 El Apajo Rd., 92067. Tel: 619-756-1911; Fax: 619-756-9562.
Catechesis/Religious Programs—Tel: 619-756-0937. Sr. Rose Schmidt, D.R.E.
Students 287.

San Luis Rey, San Diego Co., Mission San Luis Rey de Francia, Revs. Michel Gagnon, O.F.M.; Vincent Hughes, O.F.M.; Armando Lopez, O.F.M.
Res., 4070 Mission Ave., Oceanside, 92057-6497. Tel: 619-757-3250; Fax: 619-757-3299.

San Marcos, San Diego Co., St. Mark, Rev. Msgr. Thomas P. Healy; Rev. Aurelio P. Crisologo; Deacons Sam Hunt; Dick Jansing.
Res., 1147 Discovery, 92069. Tel: 619-744-1540; Fax: 619-744-3828.
Catechesis/Religious Programs—Tel: 619-744-1130.
Students 490.

Santa Ysabel, San Diego Co., Santa Ysabel Indian

Mission (1818), Rev. William P. Stevenson.
Res., 23013 Hwy. 79, P.O. Box 129, 92070-1010. Tel: 619-765-0810; Fax: 619-765-0810. [CEM]
Missions—Warner Springs, San Diego Co., St. Francis, Hwy. 79, Warner Springs, 92086.; Los Coyotes Reservation, St. Isadore.

Santee, San Diego Co., Guardian Angels, Rev. Michael A. Cunnane.
Res., 9310 Dalehurst Rd., 92071-1010. Tel: 619-448-1213; Fax: 619-448-2980.
Catechesis/Religious Programs—9310 Dalehurst, 92071. Tel: 619-448-1274. Sr. Mary Potter, R.S.M., D.R.E.
Students 512.

San Ysidro, San Diego Co., Our Lady of Mt. Carmel, Revs. Emmett Farrell; Ricardo Mejia, Admin.
Res., 2020 Alaquinas Dr., 92173-2107. Tel: 619-428-1415; Fax: 619-428-5626.
School—Tel: 619-428-2091; Fax: 619-428-8324. Sr. Rebeca Munoz, Prin.
Sisters of the Most Blessed Sacrament 5; Lay Teachers 9; Students 340.
Catechesis/Religious Programs—Tel: 619-428-3686.
Students 290.

Solana Beach, San Diego Co., St. James (Del Mar), Rev. Msgr. Lawrence M. Purcell; Deacons John Gallagher; Al Graff; John Brice; Ted Bear. In res., Rev. John Howard, C.J.M.
Office: 625 S. Nardo Ave., 92075-2398. Tel: 619-755-2545; Fax: 619-755-3845.
School—Tel: 619-755-1777.
Lay Teachers 16; Students 257.
Catechesis/Religious Programs—Tel: 619-755-2545. Sr. Shaun Marie Larkin, S.B.L., Prin.; Robert Kidd, D.R.E.
Students 353.
Mission—Solana Beach, San Diego Co., St. Leo, 936 Genevieve, Tel: 619-481-6788.

Spring Valley, San Diego Co., Santa Sophia, Revs. Michael Ratajczak; Joseph Viet Hoang; Deacons Francis DeMoor; James Kelley.
Res., 9800 San Juan St., 91977. Tel: 619-463-6629; Fax: 619-463-8101.
School—Tel: 619-463-0488; Fax: 619-668-5469.
Lay Teachers 11; Students 291.
Catechesis/Religious Programs—Tel: 619-463-6011. Joe McKnight, D.R.E.
Students 378.

Valley Center, San Diego Co., St. Stephen, Rev. Michael A. Booth.
Res., P.O. Box 1015, 31020 Cole Grade Rd., 92082. Tel: 619-749-3324; Fax: 619-749-6684.
Catechesis/Religious Programs—Tel: 619-749-3352. Penny Phillips, D.R.E.
Students 251.

Vista, San Diego Co., St. Francis, Revs. Ramon R. Marrufo; George A. Dunkley; Deacons Robert P. Mueller; Michael Collins; Frank Mercardante.
Res., 525 W. Vista Way, 92083-5974. Tel: 619-945-8000; Fax: 619-945-8036.
School—Robert Heveron, Prin. Lay Teachers 18; Students 385.
Catechesis/Religious Programs—Rae Arnold, D.R.E. Students 774.

Westmorland, St. Joseph, Rev. Manuel Mesa, O.M.I.
Res., 300 N. Center St., P.O. Box 627, 92281. Tel: 619-344-5267; 344-3721 (Parish Hall).

Winterhaven, Imperial Co., St. Thomas. (Indian Mission). Rev. Duncan W. Monohan.
Res., P.O. Box 1176, 92283-1176. Tel: 619-572-0283.
Mission—Winterhaven, Imperial Co., St. Mary.

Eastern Churches

San Diego, San Diego Co., Our Lady of Perpetual Help. (Ukrainian Catholic). Rev. Andrew Mykyta.
Res., 4014 Winona Ave., 92105. Tel: 619-282-9538.

El Cajon, San Diego Co., St. Peter. (Chaldean Eastern Church). Rev. Michael J. Bazzi.
Res., 1627 Jamacha Way, 92019. Tel: 619-579-7913; 588-9921; Fax: 619-588-8281.
Catechesis/Religious Programs—Tel: 619-447-4842. Khelood Allos, D.R.E.
Students 550.

Chaplains of Public Institutions

Hospitals

SAN DIEGO. *Alvarado, Grossmont and Kaiser Hospitals*. Revs. James Burson, C.J.M. Tel: 619-287-3270; Gary M. Holtey.
Children's Hospital. Rev. Manuel Ediza.
Mercy Hospital. Revs. Ben Bachmeier; Francis W. McDonnell. Tel: 619-260-7020.
Scripps Hospital. Rev. Daniel Polizzi. Tel: 619-457-4123.
Sharp Memorial Hospital. Revs. Manuel Ediza. Tel: 619-541-3475; James V. Corrigan, O.S.A., Clinical Pastoral Ed.
UCSD Medical Center. Rev. Paul Balio. Tel: 619-239-0229.

LA JOLLA. *Veterans Administration Hospital*. Tel: 619-552-8585. Revs. Alfred Fiorino, S.J.; Jerry Hamperzonian.

OCEANSIDE. *Tri City Hospital*. Rev. Peter Nguyen. Tel: 619-945-8000.

Retirement Homes

SAN DIEGO. *Nazareth House*. Rev. Msgr. Patrick J. Kearney. Tel: 619-563-0480.

LA MESA. *Little Flower Haven*. Rev. Philip Bronk, S.T. Tel: 619-466-3163.

Detention Ministries

SAN DIEGO. *Calipatria State Prison*. Tel: 619-348-7000. Rev. Thomas Dermody.
Central Detention Facility and San Diego City Jail. Rev. James I. Rasura, S.J. Tel: 619-233-3838.
East Otay Mesa Detention Facility & George F. Baily Detention Facility. Deacon Sam Martinez. Tel: 619-422-2100.
Juvenile Hall. Monique Muther. Tel: 619-490-8260.
Metropolitan Correction Center. Deacon Nicholas Santiago. Tel: 619-232-4311.
R.J. Donovan Correctional Facility. Rev. Ron Chiasson, O.M.I. Tel: 619-661-6500.

CHULA VISTA. *South Bay Detention Facility*. Rev. James V. Caldwell.

EL CENTRO. *El Centro City Jail*. Deacon Luciano Arias. Tel: 619-337-1031.
El Centro Juvenile Hall & Imperial County Jail. Julia Ullos. Tel: 619-352-2936.

SANTEE. *Las Colinas Women's Detention Facility*. Deacon George Shea. Tel: 619-469-0133.

VISTA. *Vista Detention Facility*. Mr. Manny Robles. Tel: 619-726-8912.

State Conservation Camps

SAN DIEGO. *Rainbow Conservation Camp*. Deacon George Paulicivic. Tel: 619-728-7034.

Special Assignment:
Reverend Monsignors—
Eagen, Brent I., Univ. of San Diego, Alcala Park, San Diego, CA 92110
Reverend Fathers—
Howard, John, C.J.M., 744 Sonrisa St., Solana Beach, CA 92075
Mort, Ernest C., C.S.P., University Admin. of U.S.C.D.
O'Leary, James J., S.J., University of San Diego, Alcala Park, San Diego, CA 92110
Oliva, George M., S.J., Retreat Ministry

On Duty Outside the Diocese:
Reverend Fathers—
Cordileone, Salvatore
Cribbin, James
Flynn, Edward R., 98 San Marino Dr., San Rafael, CA 94901
Foley, J. Patrick
Parrales, Napoleon J., Cementerio Nuevo, Barquisimeto, Venezuela
Reilly, John (Ireland)

Military Chaplains:
Reverend Fathers—
Buchmiller, Ronald J., Ch.C., USN
Diaz, Michael, CHC, USN
Jennings, Tommie, CHC, USNR

Unassigned:
Reverend Monsignors—
Higgins, Michael K., P.O. Box 87225, San Diego, CA 92138. Tel: 619-280-7500; Fax: 619-280-8400
Reverend Fathers—
Gomes-Kelly, John R.
Langille, Justin
Merris, Christopher
Ryland, Raymond

Absent on Sick Leave:
Reverend Fathers—
England, Robert
Moffo, James
Ryan, Alphonsus
Twarog Theodore S.

Leave of Absence:
Reverend Fathers—
Buttimer, Joseph J.
Conwill, Giles A.
Dunleavy, Steven
Huggins, Michael L.
Kennedy, James
Kothuis, Hans
Mason, James H.
Sweeney, Lawrence
White, Robert E.

Retired:
Reverend Monsignors—
Aldasoro, Francisco
Balderas, Luis G.
Bergin, William A.
Bolger, William
Brennan, Joseph F.
Briody, Thomas
Campion, John J.
Coughlan, Michael J.
Creighton, Edward
Dollen, Charles
Egan, Thomas J.
Galindo, Rudolph
Gilfillan, James M.
Hanley, Andrew W.
Kearney, Patrick J.
Kraft, William A.
McDermott, Thomas J.
Mimnagh, Peter F.
Moore, J. Raymond
Murray, Sean
O'Donoghue, James P.
O'Neill, Patrick J.
O'Sullivan, Jeremiah
Portman, John
Rhatigan, John
Topping, Joseph
Young, Charles P.
Reverend Fathers—
Anderson, Arthur Edward
Beatty, John
Borda, Peter Paul
Buchanan, Donald
Capetillo, Modesto
Chase, Maurice
Fischer, Eugene
Goce, Lauro
Holland, Kilian
Houck, Richard
Keenan, John J.
Keith, John C.
Lorenz, Vincent E.
Lucev, John
McDonnell, Francis W.
McDonnell, Joseph T.
McManus, Martin
Nesbitt, John B.
O'Curneen, Hugh
Quinn, John T.
Roll, David H.
Russell, Richard J.
Salada, Urbano
Sierra, Francis A.
Smith, Aquinas
Smith, Michael
Sostrich, John L.
Thompson, J. Noel
Tindall, Harold
Uboldi, Victor
Ullman, Earl L.
Wheeler, John

Permanent Deacons:
Albers, Tony, San Diego
Arias, Luciano, El Centro
Arismendez, Joe, Chula Vista
Arnold, Ron, Vista
Ball, Lou, San Diego
Bear, Ted, Del Mar
Beatty, Lewis, Oceanside
Bell, L. Ferris, San Diego
Brice, John, Leucadia
Chia, Henry, Carlsbad
Clarke, William G., Jamul
Cody, Henry B., Jamul
Collins, Michael, San Marcos
Connor, Jonathan P., San Diego
Corder, Richard G., Olivenhain
Corrao, Jack P., San Diego
Corrao, Peter T., Lemon Grove
Costello, John M., Chula Vista
Dalzell, William, LaJolla
Davidson, Paul, San Diego
Dean, Ben, Fallbrook
Delano, Joe, San Diego
DeMoor, Francis, (Retired), Spring Valley
DePozo, Daniel, Chula Vista
Diem, Ronald H., San Diego
Donivan, Ed, El Cajon
Dougherty, Thomas P., San Diego
Dube, Leo, San Diego
Early, John M., Escondido
Ekhaml, Robert T., San Diego
Enciso, Pedro, Vista
Finn, Kenneth, Escondido
Frazee, Mike, Carlsbad
Gallagher, John V., Solana Beach
Gasparovic, Anthony L., Lakeside

Graff, Albert P., Rancho Santa Fe
Grosso, Ernest, Santee
Gullotta, Daniel, Lakeside, MT
Hernandez, Raul, Chula Vista
Hess, Arnie, San Diego
Hitch, James, Bonita
Hunt, Sam, San Marcos
Jansing, Dick, Lake San Marcos
Jones, Thom, San Diego
Keeley, Jim, Descanso
Klopchin, Bill, San Diego
Kostick, Jim, Escondido
Kutler, Harold, Oceanside
Leach, Dave, San Luis Obispo
Lozoya, Margarito, Chula Vista
Mackey, Bob, Carlsbad
Maher, Thomas M., Jr., Escondido
Martinez, Seodello A., San Diego
Mather, Dick, Oceanside
McDaniel, Al, Jamul
Mercardante, F., Vista
Michaels, Larry, Escondido
Montoya, Ken, San Diego
Mueller, Robert, Vista
Nevins, William J., La Mesa
Newman, Michael C., Ferndale
Nguyen, Peter Can, San Diego
Nunez, Manuel, La Mesa
Osgood, Franklin B., Colorado
Pagliaro, Jesse, Oceanside
Parra, Daniel, San Diego
Paulicivic, George, Sr., Murrieta
Perez, Modesto, San Marcos
Phelps, John, San Diego
Pollock, William, San Diego
Principe, Louis, Lakeside
Robbins, Ralph, El Cajon
Robles, Manny, Vista
Rocha, Louis, El Cajon
Rondeau, Dick, Belpre, KS
Roy, James, Oceanside
Santiago, Nicholas M., San Diego
Santoyo, Juan, La Mesa
Schmitt, Giles V., San Diego
Scull, James, San Diego
Shea, George, El Cajon
Shelton, Carl, San Diego
Shockley, Gordon E., Louisville, KY
Skupnik, Ray, Long Beach
Snyder, John A., Alpine
Threatt, Marvin, Lemon Grove
Treadwell, Timothy, El Cajon
Trumble, John, El Cajon
Valdivia, Leopoldo, Escondido
Vasquez, Bill, San Diego
Vecchitto, Glenn, Chula Vista
Villafana, Martin, San Diego
Vivio, Bill, Coronado
Walling, Robert, Bend, OR
Wood, Joseph, La Jolla
Woznicki, Walter, El Cajon
Yeatts, Bernard, San Diego

INSTITUTIONS LOCATED IN THE DIOCESE

[A] SEMINARIES, DIOCESAN

SAN DIEGO. *St. Francis Seminary*, 1667 Santa Paula Dr., 92111. Tel: 619-291-7446; Fax: 619-291-7011. Rev. Msgr. Steven Callahan, Rector; Revs. Jaime Escobedo; James Flynn. Priests 3; Students 23.

[B] COLLEGES AND UNIVERSITIES

SAN DIEGO. *Austin House - House of Formation*, 1605 28th St., 92102. Tel: 619-233-9141 (Prov. Office).
For a complete listing, refer to the Colleges and Universities section.
University of San Diego, 5998 Alcala Park, 92110-2492. Tel: 619-260-4600.
For a complete listing, refer to the Colleges and Universities section.

[C] HIGH SCHOOLS, DIOCESAN

SAN DIEGO. *Academy of Our Lady of Peace*. (Grades 9-12), 4860 Oregon St., 92116. Tel: 619-297-2266; Fax: 619-297-2473. (Girls). Sr. Dolores Anchondo, C.S.J., Prin. Sisters of St. Joseph of Carondelet 4; Lay Teachers 40; Students 730.
Marian Catholic High School, 1002 18th St., 92154. Tel: 619-423-2121; Fax: 619-423-6910. (Coed). Mrs. Estelle Kassebaum, Prin. Religious 2; Lay Teachers 27; Students 325.
St. Augustine High School, 3266 Nutmeg St., 92104-5199. Tel: 619-282-2184; Fax: 619-282-1203. Conducted By the Augustinians. (Boys). Revs. John R. Sanders, O.S.A., Prin.; Timothy Lamm, O.S.B.; Harry M. Neely, O.S.A.; Walter P. Vogel, O.S.A.; Bro. Stephen McKenna, O.S.A.; Deacon Richard Hardick, O.S.A.
(For information concerning the monastery see separate listing under Monasteries). Priests 4; Brothers 1; Deacons 1; Sisters 1; Lay Teachers 29; Students 580.
University of San Diego High School, 5961 Linda Vista Rd., 92110-1947. Tel: 619-298-8277; Fax: 619-260-1696. (Coed). Richard E. Kelly, Ph.D., Prin.; Rev. Michael White, C.S.Sp. Priests 1; Lay Teachers 77; Students 1,317.

CALEXICO. *Vincent Memorial High*. (Grades 9-12), 525 W. Sheridan, 92231. Tel: 619-357-3461; Fax: 619-357-0902. (Coed). Conducted by Sisters Servants of the Blessed Sacrament. Sisters 2; Lay Teachers 10; Students 181.

[D] SPECIAL SCHOOLS

EL CAJON. *St. Madeleine Sophie's Center for Developmentally Disabled Adults*, 2119 E. Madison Ave., 92019-1111. Tel: 619-442-5129; Fax: 619-442-2590. Frances S. Glasser, Exec. Dir. Sisters 1; Lay Teachers 50; Enrollment 180.

[E] PROTECTIVE INSTITUTIONS

SAN DIEGO. *Nazareth House*, 6333 Rancho Mission Rd., 92108. Tel: 619-563-0480.
For a complete listing, refer to the Special Care Facilities section.

SPRING VALLEY. *Noah Homes*, 12526 Campo Rd., 91978. Tel: 619-660-6200; Fax: 619-660-1481.
For a complete listing, refer to the Special Care Facilities section.

[F] GENERAL HOSPITALS AND CLINICS

SAN DIEGO. *Mercy Hospital and Medical Center dba Mercy Healthcare San Diego*, 4077 Fifth Ave., 92103. Tel: 619-294-8111; Fax: 619-686-3530.
For a complete listing, refer to the Hospitals section.

[G] HOMES FOR SENIOR CITIZENS

SAN DIEGO. *Cathedral Plaza*, 1551 Third Ave., 92101. Tel: 619-234-0093.
For a complete listing, refer to the Special Care Facilities section.
Guadalupe Plaza, 4142 42nd St., 92105. Tel: 619-584-2414.
For a complete listing, refer to the Special Care Facilities section.
Nazareth House Retirement Home, 6333 Rancho Mission Rd., 92108. Tel: 619-563-0480.
For a complete listing, refer to the Special Care Facilities section.
St. John's Plaza. 8150 Broadway Lemon Grove, 91945. Tel: 619-466-5354.
For a complete listing, refer to the Special Care Facilities section.

LA MESA. *Little Flower Haven*, 8585 La Mesa Blvd., 91941. Tel: 619-466-3163.
For a complete listing, refer to the Special Care Facilities section.

[H] MONASTERIES AND RESIDENCES OF PRIESTS AND BROTHERS

SAN DIEGO. *Augustinian Community*, 3266 Nutmeg St., 92104. Tel: 619-282-2028; Fax: 619-282-1203. Revs. John R. Sanders, O.S.A., Prin.; John D. Keller, O.S.A.; Peter J. Marron, O.S.A.; Thomas P. Garrett, O.S.A.; James E. Hannan, O.S.A.; Harry M. Neely, O.S.A., Prior; James A. Mott, O.S.A., Prov.; William H. Sullivan, O.S.A.; Bros. J. Stephen McKenna, O.S.A., Procurator; Michael Harkay, O.S.A., 1605 28th St., 92102. Revs. Walter Vogel, O.S.A., Prior; Richard Hardick, O.S.A., Diaconate; Jerome Bevilacqua, O.S.A.
Monica House - Augustinian Community, 1621 28th St., 92104.

BOULEVARD. *Cedar Pines - Augustinian Community*, 1371 Tierra del Sol Rd., 91905-4694.

CAMARILLO. *Rancho Camarillo - Augustinian Community*, 3771 Mission Oaks Ave., 93012-5034.

OCEANSIDE. *Prince of Peace Abbey, Benet Hill*, 92054. Tel: 619-430-1305; 1306. Benedictine Fathers. Rt. Revs. Charles Wright, O.S.B., Abbot; Claude Ehringer, O.S.B., (Retired), Abbot; Revs. David Carvalho, O.S.B.; Luke Dougherty, O.S.B.; Sharbel Ewen, O.S.B.; Anselm Fister, O.S.B.; Alexis Foyo, O.S.B.; Basil Mattingly, O.S.B.; Aquinas Nichols, O.S.B.; Herbert Palmer, O.S.B.; Stephanos Pedrano, O.S.B.; Bros. Peter Aslin, O.S.B.; Joseph Black, O.S.B.; Thomas Cimini, O S.B.; Anselm Clark, O.S.B.; Anthony Green, O.S.B.; Blaise Heuke, O.S.B.; Clement Kennedy, O.S.B.; Benedict Menezes, O.S.B.; Raphael Meyer, O.S.B.; Mario Quizon, O.S.B.; Daniel Sokol, O.S.B.; Meinrad Taylor, O.S.B.; Timothy Balk, O.S.B., Bro. Oblate. Priests 11; Brothers 12; Novices 2.

SAN LUIS REY. *San Luis Rey*, 4050 Mission Ave., 92068. Tel: 619-757-3651. Franciscan Friars. Rev. Warren J. Rouse, O.F.M., Guardian; Bros. Conrad Duran, O.F.M.; Bede McKinnon, O.F.M.; Maurice Peltier, O.F.M.; Roch Schwab, O.F.M.; Thomas Thing, O.F.M.; Rufino Zaragosa, O.F.M.; Revs. Michel Gagnon, O.F.M.; Vincent Hughes, O.F.M.; Paul Lee; Armando Lopez, O.F.M.; William Shaughnessy, O.F.M.; Mel Bucher. Priests 7; Brothers 6.

[I] CONVENTS AND RESIDENCES FOR SISTERS

SAN DIEGO. *Carmelite Monastery of San Diego, California*. (Discalced), 5158 Hawley Blvd., 92116-1934. Tel: 619-280-5425. Sr. Yvonne Hanke, O.C.D. Sisters 14.
Community of the Holy Spirit, 6151 Rancho Mission Rd., #205, 92108. Tel: 619-584-0809. Sr. Susann Kernaghan. Sisters 18.
Daughters of Divine Charity, 10294 Eagle Rock Ave., 92126. Tel: 619-271-1451. Sisters 3.
Maryknoll Sisters, 2227 31st St., 92104. Tel: 619-283-5678. Sisters 4.
Medical Mission Sisters, 5673 Marne Ave., 92120. Tel: 619-286-6880. Sisters 4. 211 N. Citrus, #123, Escondido, 92027. Tel: 619-480-1372. Sisters 2. 636 Mariposa Cir., Chula Vista, 91911-2511. Tel: 619-482-3109. Sisters 3.
Missionaries of Charity, 3877 Boston Ave., 92113. Tel: 619-263-9566. Sisters 5.
Poor Sisters of Nazareth, 6330 Rancho Mission Rd., 92108. Tel: 619-563-0480. Sisters 8.
Religious of Jesus and Mary, 1510 Third Ave., 92101. Tel: 619-234-0556. Sisters 10.
Religious of the Sacred Heart. Casa Maria Community, Univ. of San Diego, 5998 Alcala Park, 92110-2492. Tel: 619-299-3639. Sisters 5.
School Sisters of Notre Dame, 5202 Santa Margarita Ave., 92114. Tel: 619-264-7011. Sisters 4.
Sisters of Loretto, 6528 Bradford St., 92115. Tel: 619-287-8388. Sisters 2.
Sisters of Mercy (Ireland & South Africa), 10726 Caminito Cascara, #15, 92108. Tel: 619-284-1027. Sisters 2.
Sisters of Mercy of the Americas (Burlingame), 4216 Albatross Dr., 92103. Tel: 619-260-8047. Sisters 2.
Sisters of Social Service, 3525 Third Ave., 92103-4908. Tel: 619-295-1896. Sisters 3.
Sisters of St. Francis (Philadelphia), 17155 Ruette Compana, 92128. Tel: 619-451-2649. Sisters 2.
Sisters of St. Joseph of Carondelet, 4860 Oregon St., 92116. Tel: 619-295-2891; 295-2887. Sisters 4.
Sisters of St. Joseph of Peace, 2880 Caulfield Dr., 92154. Tel: 619-423-7360. Sisters 2.
Sisters of the Holy Family, 6333 College Grove Way, B9, 92115. Tel: 619-286-3371.
Sisters of the Precious Blood, 4202 58th St., 92115. Tel: 619-229-1817. Sisters 2.
Society of the Holy Child Jesus, 6243 Caminito Telmo, 92111. Tel: 619-277-0309. Sisters 3.

CALEXICO. *Sister Servants of the Blessed Sacrament*, 536 Rockwood, 92231. Tel: 619-357-1046. Sisters 9.

CARLSBAD. *Sisters of Charity of the Blessed Virgin Mary*, 2409 La Pluma Ln., 92009. Tel: 619-633-1315. Sr. Mary Kay Dun, Reg. Supr. Sisters 3.
Sisters of St. Francis (Rochester), 7216 San Lucas, 92009. Tel: 619-438-5443.

CHULA VISTA. *Benedictine Sisters of Glendora*, 236 Alvarado, 91910-3610. Tel: 619-422-4567. Sisters 2.
Religious of the Incarnate Word, 153 Rainier Ct., 91911. Tel: 619-420-0231; Fax: 619-691-5939. Sisters 4.

EL CAJON. *Sisters of Mercy (Ireland & South Africa)*, 2766 Navajo Rd., 92020. Tel: 619-465-2233. Sisters 3.

EL CENTRO. *Our Lady of Victory Convent*, 604 El Centro Ave., 92243. Tel: 619-353-6416. Our Lady of Victory Missionary Sisters 3.
Religious of the Incarnate Word, 102 W. Holt, 92243. Tel: 619-353-4146. Sisters 3.

LA JOLLA. *Dominican Sisters of Adrian*, 6570 La Jolla Scenic Dr., 92037. Tel: 619-459-3681. Sisters 2.
Sisters of the Holy Cross, 1001 Kline St., 92037-4426. Tel: 619-454-2861. Sisters 3.

LA MESA. *Carmelite Sisters of the Divine Heart of Jesus*, 8585 La Mesa Blvd., 91941. Tel: 619-466-3163; Fax: 619-466-9642. Sr. M. Angela Therese Lovato, Prov. Supr.; Sr. Mary Alice Prieto, Supr. Sisters 13; Novices 1.
Medical Mission Sisters. District Office, 4817 Palm Ave., Ste. M, 91941. Tel: 619-589-7000; Fax: 619-698-2815. Legal Title: *Society of Catholic Medical Missionaries, Inc.* Sr. Justine Church, M.M.S., Dist. Coord.
Religious of Jesus and Mary, 4197 S. Tropico Dr., 91941-6866. Tel: 619-465-0158. Sr. Rosemary Nicholson, R.J.M., Reg. Supr. Sisters 4.

LAKE SAN MARCOS. *Daughters of Mary and Joseph*, 1545 Via Brisa del Lago, 92069. Tel: 619-744-6578.

LEMON GROVE. *Sisters of Mercy of the Blessed Sacrament*, 8171 Lemon Grove Way, 91945. Tel: 619-460-4271. Sisters 5.

NATIONAL CITY. *Sisters of the Heart of Jesus in the Blessed Sacrament*, 912 Arcadia Pl., 91950. Tel: 619-267-4342. Sisters 3.

OCEANSIDE. *Sisters of the Precious Blood*, 4070 Mission Ave., 92057. Tel: 619-757-2155. Sisters 4.

PALA. *Sisters of St. Francis (Philadelphia)*, P.O. Box M, 92059. Tel: 619-742-1714. Sisters 4.

SAN YSIDRO. *Medical Missionaries of Mary*, 438 Blackshaw Ln., 92173. Tel: 619-690-9237. Sisters 7.
Sister Servants of the Blessed Sacrament, 333 W. Park Ave., 92173. Tel: 619-428-1314. Sisters 6.
Sisters of St. Dominic (Tacoma), 1868 Via las Tonadas, 92173. Tel: 619-428-1629. Sisters 3.

SOLANA BEACH. *Sisters of St. Joseph of Carondelet*, 409 Santa Domingo, 92075. Tel: 619-755-6446. Sr. Suzanne Steffen, Reg. Supr. Sisters 3.

SPRING VALLEY. *Sisters of St. Joseph of Orange*, 10771 Del Rio Rd., 91978. Tel: 619-670-9663. Sisters 3.

VISTA. *Sisters of St. Clare*, 326 Santa Clara Dr., 92083. Tel: 619-945-8025. Sr. Madeline Fitzgerald, Reg. Supr. Sisters 2.

[J] SOCIAL SERVICES

SAN DIEGO.
**Bayside Settlement House*, 2202 Comstock St., 92111-6502. Tel: 619-278-0771; Fax: 619-278-0856. Grover Diemert, Exec. Dir.
Bayside Linda Vista, 2202 Comstock St., 92111. Tel: 619-278-0771; Fax: 619-285-1491.
Catholic Charities, 349 Cedar St., 92101. Tel: 619-231-2828; Fax: 619-234-2272. Sr. RayMonda DuVall, C.H.S., Exec. Dir.
Emergency Services—Main Office: Tel: 619-231-2828. Michele Dunne, Dir., St. Francis Center. Tel: 619-631-2819. Sr. Avis Schons, Dir.
Counseling Services. Peter McDade, Ph.D., Dir.; Ms. Susan Torres-Tacata, Dir. Tel: 619-231-2828, Casa de San Juan. Pregnancy, Parenting, and Adoption. Tel: 619-231-2828. Delia Sables, A.C.S.W., Dir. Tel: 619-231-2828, Foster Grand Parent Program. Tel: 619-231-2828. Sr. Susann Kernaghan, C.H.S., Dir., Foster Grandparent Program, Refugee & Immigrant Svcs., 4575 Mission Gorge Pl., Ste. A, 92120. Tel: 619-287-9454. Dr. Robert Moser, Dir., La Posada de Guadalupe de Carlsbad. Tel: 619-929-2322. El Centro—Imperial Valley Services, 250 W. Orange, El Centro, 92243. Tel: 619-353-6822. House of Hope. Tel: 619-352-1182. Our Lady of Guadalupe Shelter. Tel: 619-357-2894.
Homeless Women's Services.
Rachel's Women's Center, 759 Eighth Ave., 92101. Tel: 619-696-0873. Women's Bean Project. Tel: 619-230-1151.
Joan of Arc Residence, 1510 Third Ave., 92101. Tel: 619-239-2663; 234-0556. Residence for Employed Young Women and College Students 18-62 Years. Sr. Margaret Mary Doucet, R.J.M., Supr. Religious 10; Permanent Residents 60; Capacity 71.
St. Vincent de Paul Village, 3350 E St., 92102. Tel: 619-687-1000; Fax: 619-687-1010. Rev. Msgr. Joseph A. Carroll, Pres. Total Staff 283; Total Assisted Annually 138,975.
Joan Kroc Homeless Center, 1501 Imperial Ave., 92101. Tel: 619-233-8500. Mary Case, Vice Pres.
Bishop Maher Men's Center, 1501 Imperial Ave., 92101. Tel: 619-233-8500.
SHARE Southern California, 3350 E St., 92101. Tel: 619-525-2200.
Josue AIDS Centers, 3350 E St., 92102. Tel: 619-466-4827. Paul Mirabile Center, 1501 Imperial Ave., 92101. Tel: 619-233-8500.
Toussaint Teen Center, 633 State St., 92101. Tel: 619-233-8500, Ext. 3399. Patricia Dean, Village Place, 32-17th St., 92101. Tel: 619-687-1000.
Thrift Stores, 815 33rd St., 92102. Tel: 619-687-1021. Keith MacKay, Vice Pres.

[K] RETREATS

SAN DIEGO. *Spiritual Ministry Center*, 4822 Del Mar Ave., 92107-3407. Tel: 619-224-9444.

ALPINE. *La Providencia Spiritual Renewal Center*, 641 N. Glen Oaks Dr., 91901-2736. Tel: 619-445-4570. Sr. Patricia Hanson, C.S.J.O.

OCEANSIDE. *Prince of Peace Retreat Center*, 92054. Tel: 619-430-1305; 1306. Benedictine Fathers-Benet Hill. Rev. Sharbel Ewen, O.S.B., Guest Master.

PALA. *Pala Rey Youth Camp & Retreat Center*, 10779 Pala Rd., 92059. Tel: 619-742-8767. Bro. Joseph Lockwood, Contact Person.

SAN LUIS REY. *Mission San Luis Rey Retreat*. Mailing Address: P.O. Box 409, 92068. Tel: 619-757-3659; Fax: 619-757-4613. Revs. William Rusty Shaughnessy, O.F.M., Retreat Master; Mel Bucher, O.F.M.; Bro. Rufino Zaragoza, O.F.M.; Sr. Mary Lou Carlson, O.S.F.

[L] CAMPS

SAN DIEGO. *Whispering Winds Catholic Conference Center*, P.O. Box 608054, 92160-8054. Tel: 619-277-9963. Don Kojis, Exec. Dir.

DESCANSO.
**Camp Oliver*. Summer Resident Camp for Girls & Boys ages 6-14. Directed by Sisters of Social Service. (June-Aug.; Available Sept.-June for rental groups). P.O. Box 712525, 2202 Comstock St., Ste. 2, San Diego, 92171. Tel: 619-492-9171. Sr. Ellen Hunter, S.S.S., Dir.

SAN FRANCISCO. *Pala Rey Youth Camp and Retreat Center*, Salesian Society, Provincial Office, 1100 Franklin St., 94109. Bro. Joseph Lockwood.

[M] NEWMAN CENTERS

SAN DIEGO. *San Diego State University Newman Center*, 5855 Hardy Ave., 92115. Tel: 619-583-9181; Fax: 619-265-9310. Revs. Angus Beaton, C.J.M., Dir.; John C. Shinsky, C.J.M.
University of California at San Diego (Campus Ministry), 3115 Bremerton Pl., 92037. Tel: 619-534-2521 (Office); 453-1855 (Res.). Revs. James W. Moran, C.S.P.; Peter M. Abdella, C.S.P.

[N] MISCELLANEOUS

SAN DIEGO.
**Catholic Answers, Inc.*, P.O. Box 17490, 92177. Tel: 619-541-1131; Fax: 619-541-1154. Karl Keating, Pres.
Catholic Committee on Scouting, 3350 E St., 92102. Tel: 619-687-1000. Rev. Msgr. Joseph Carroll, Scout Chap.; Jim Fallon, Coord.; Steve Rostart, Chm.
Pauline Book and Media Center, 5945 Balboa Ave., 92111. Tel: 619-565-9181. Daughters of St. Paul. Sr. Sean Marie David, F.S.P., Supr. Sisters 2.
San Diego Catholic Worker, P.O. Box 127244, 92112. Tel: 619-233-0519. Jane R. Emerson, Pres.
San Diego Central Magnificat, 13106 Roundup Ave., 92129. Tel: 619-484-1058. Mary Ann Silva.

ENCINITAS. *Kraemer Endowment Foundation, Inc.*, 1106 Second St., #126, 92024. Tel: 619-720-9160. Margaret E. Delaney, Exec. Dir.

ESCONDIDO.
**Benedictus*, 1555 Glenna Dr., 92025. Tel: 619-743-8453. Deacon Kenneth J. Finn, Contact Person.

RELIGIOUS INSTITUTES OF MEN REPRESENTED IN THE DIOCESE

For further details refer to the corresponding bracketed number in the Religious Institutes of Men or Women section.

[0140]—*The Augustinians*.—O.S.A.
[0200]—*Benedictine Monks*.—O.S.B.
[0470]—*Capuchin Friars, The*.—O.F.M.Cap.
[0270]—*Carmelite Fathers*.—O.Carm.
[1320]—*Clerics of St. Viator*.—C.S.V.
[0160]—*Clerics Regular of St. Paul*.—C.R.S.P.
[0450]—*Congregation of Jesus and Mary*.—C.J.M.
[0520]—*Franciscan Friars*.—O.F.M.
[0650]—*Holy Ghost Fathers*.—C.S.Sp.
[]—*Holy Ghost Fathers of Ireland*.—C.S.Sp.
[0690]—*Jesuit Fathers and Brothers*.—S.J.
[1210]—*Missionaries of St. Charles (Scalabrinians)*.—C.S.
[0840]—*Missionary Servants of the Most Holy Trinity*.—S.T.
[0910]—*Oblates of Mary Immaculate*.—O.M.I.
[0430]—*Order of Preachers (Dominicans)*.—O.P.
[1030]—*Paulist Fathers*.—C.S.P.
[0610]—*Priests of the Congregation of Holy Cross*.—C.S.C.
[1260]—*Society of Christ*.—S.Ch.
[0370]—*Society of St. Columban*.—S.S.C.

RELIGIOUS INSTITUTES OF WOMEN REPRESENTED IN THE DIOCESE

[0230]—*Benedictine Sisters of Pontifical Jurisdiction*. (Glendora, CA; St. Joseph, MN).—O.S.B.
[0360]—*Carmelite Sisters of the Divine Heart of Jesus*.—Carmel D.C.J.
[2020]—*Community of the Holy Spirit*.—C.H.S.
[3935]—*Congregation of the Sisters of St. Louis, Juilly-Monaghan*.—S.S.L.
[1920]—*Congregation of the Sisters of the Holy Cross*.—C.S.C.
[1710]—*Congregation of the Third Order of St. Francis of Mary Immaculate, Joliet, IL*.—O.S.F.
[0790]—*Daughters of Divine Charity*.—F.D.C.
[0880]—*Daughters of Mary and Joseph*.—D.M.J.
[0420]—*Discalced Carmelite Nuns*.—O.C.D.
[1070-03]—*Dominican Sisters*.—O.P.
[1070-11]—*Dominican Sisters*.—O.P.
[1070-13]—*Dominican Sisters*.—O.P.
[1070-14]—*Dominican Sisters*.—O.P.
[1070-20]—*Dominican Sisters*.—O.P.
[1070-21]—*Dominican Sisters*.—O.P.
[2470]—*Maryknoll Sisters of St. Dominic*.—M.M.
[2490]—*Medical Mission Sisters*.—M.M.S.
[2480]—*Medical Missionaries of Mary*.—M.M.M.
[2710]—*Missionaries of Charity*.—M.C.
[1845]—*Missionary Cathechists Guadalupanas of the Holy Spirit (Mexico)*.—M.G.Sp.S.
[3070]—*North American Unions of Sisters of Our Lady of Charity*.—N.A.U.-O.L.C.
[3190]—*Nuns of the Perpetual Adoration of Blessed Sacrament*.—A.P.
[3130]—*Our Lady of Victory Missionary Sisters*.—O.L.V.M.
[0950]—*Pious Society Daughters of St. Paul*.—F.S.P.
[3242]—*Poor Sisters of Nazareth*.—P.S.N.
[3320]—*Presentation of the Blessed Virgin Mary Sisters*.—P.B.V.M.
[3450]—*Religious of Jesus and Mary*.—R.J.M.
[3449]—*Religious of the Incarnate Word*.—C.V.I.
[3465]—*Religious of the Sacred Heart of Mary*.—R.S.H.M.
[2970]—*School Sisters of Notre Dame*.—S.S.N.D.
[1680]—*School Sisters of St. Francis*.—O.S.F.
[3499]—*Sister Servants of the Blessed Sacrament*.—S.J.S.
[0520]—*Sisters of Charity of Our Lady, Mother of Mercy*.—S.C.M.M.
[0430]—*Sisters of Charity of the Blessed Virgin Mary*.—B.V.M.
[2360]—*Sisters of Loretto At the Foot of the Cross*.—S.L.
[2549]—*Sisters of Mercy*. (Ireland & South Africa).—R.S.M.
[2575]—*Sisters of Mercy of The Americas*. (Burlingame, CA; Omaha, NE; Cincinnati, OH).—R.S.M.
[2590]—*Sisters of Mercy of the Blessed Sacrament*.—H.M.S.S.
[1540]—*Sisters of Saint Francis, Clinton, Iowa*.—O.S.F.
[4080]—*Sisters of Social Service of Los Angeles, Inc.*.—S.S.S.
[3770]—*Sisters of St. Clare*.—O.S.C.
[1705]—*The Sisters of St. Francis of Assisi*.—O.S.F.
[1630]—*Sisters of St. Francis of Penance and Christian Charity*.—O.S.F.
[1650]—*Sisters of St. Francis of Philadelphia*.—O.S.F.
[3830-03]—*Sisters of St. Joseph*.—C.S.J. (Orange).
[3840]—*Sisters of St. Joseph of Carondelet*. (Los Angeles, CA; St. Louis, MO).—C.S.J.
[3890]—*Sisters of St. Joseph of Peace*. (Bellevue, WA).—C.S.J.P.
[]—*Sisters of the Heart of Jesus in the Blessed Sacrament*.
[1960]—*Sisters of the Holy Family*.—S.H.F.
[1990]—*Sisters of the Holy Names of Jesus and Mary*.—S.N.J.M.
[3260]—*Sisters of the Precious Blood (Dayton, Ohio)*.—C.PP.S.
[1720]—*Sisters of the Third Order Regular of St. Francis of The Congregation of Our Lady of Lourdes*.—O.S.F.
[1490]—*Sisters of Third Franciscan Order*.—O.S.F.
[4060]—*Society of the Holy Child Jesus*.—S.H.C.J.
[4070]—*Society of the Sacred Heart*.—R.S.C.J.

DIOCESAN CEMETERIES

SAN DIEGO. *Holy Cross, El Campo, Mission San Diego de Alcala*.

DEL MAR. *Calvary*.

JACUMBA. 3 Indian Reservation cemeteries.

PALA INDIAN MISSIONS. 6 separate Indian burial grounds.

SAN LUIS REY. *Mission San Luis Rey*.

SANTA YSABEL INDIAN MISSIONS. 15 separate Indian burial grounds.

NECROLOGY

† Anderson, James R., (Retired). —Died Feb. 3, 1996.
† Cloonan, John Henry, (Retired). —Died May 16, 1996.
† Dougherty, Harold Gene, (Retired). —Died Aug. 18, 1996.
† LaRiviere, Earl W., (Retired). —Died June 24, 1996.

Archdiocese of San Francisco

(Archidioecesis Sancti Francisci)

Most Reverend

WILLIAM J. LEVADA, S.T.D.

Archbishop of San Francisco; ordained December 20, 1961; appointed Titular Bishop of Capri and Auxiliary Bishop of Los Angeles March 29, 1983; Episcopal ordination May 12, 1983; appointed Archbishop of Portland in Oregon July 1, 1986; installed as Archbishop of Portland in Oregon September 21, 1986; appointed Coadjutor Archbishop of San Francisco August 17, 1995; succeeded to See December 27, 1995. *Office: 445 Church St., San Francisco, CA, 94114.*

Most Reverend

JOHN R. QUINN, D.D.

Archbishop Emeritus of San Francisco; ordained July 19, 1953; appointed Auxiliary Bishop of San Diego and Titular Bishop of Thisiduo October 21, 1967; Episcopal ordination December 12, 1967; transferred to Oklahoma City and Tulsa November 18, 1971; appointed as Archbishop of the Archdiocese of Oklahoma City on February 6, 1973; appointed Archbishop of San Francisco February 22, 1977; installed as Archbishop of San Francisco April 26, 1977; resigned December 27, 1995.

Most Reverend

PATRICK J. MC GRATH, D.D., J.C.D.

Auxiliary Bishop of San Francisco and Titular Bishop of Allegheny; ordained June 7, 1970; appointed December 6, 1988; Episcopal ordination January 25, 1989. *Office: 445 Church St., San Francisco, CA, 94114.*

ESTABLISHED JULY 29, 1853.

Square Miles 1,012.

Legal Title: *The Roman Catholic Archbishop of San Francisco, a Corporation Sole*

Code Address: *Roman, San Francisco.*

Comprises the Counties of San Francisco, San Mateo and Marin in the State of California.

PATRONS OF THE ARCHDIOCESE OF SAN FRANCISCO: St. Francis of Assisi, October 4; St. Patrick, March 17.

For legal titles of parishes and archdiocesan institutions, consult the Chancery Office.

The Chancery Office: 445 Church St., San Francisco, CA, 94114. Tel.: 415-565-3600; Fax: 415-565-3649.

STATISTICAL OVERVIEW

Personnel	
Archbishop	1
Retired Archbishops	1
Auxiliary Bishops	1
Retired Bishops	2
Priests: Diocesan Active in Diocese	148
Priests: Active Outside Diocese	15
Priests: Diocesan in Foreign Missions	1
Priests: Retired, Sick or Absent	59
Number of Diocesan Priests	223
Religious Priests in Diocese	207
Extern Priests in Diocese	50
Ordinations:	
Diocesan Priests	1
Religious Priests	8
Transitional Deacons	6
Permanent Deacons in Diocese	53
Total Brothers	47
Total Sisters	873
Parishes	
Parishes	89
With Resident Pastor:	
Resident Diocesan Priests	75
Resident Religious Priests	14
Without Resident Pastor:	
Missions	6
Pastoral Centers	4
Professional Ministry Personnel:	
Brothers	3
Sisters	66
Lay Ministers	93
Welfare	
Catholic Hospitals	3
Total Assisted	451,997
Homes for the Aged	11
Total Assisted	7,027
Residential Care of Children	2
Total Assisted	368
Day Care and Extended Day Care Centers	2
Total Assisted	154
Specialized Homes	6
Total Assisted	190
Special Centers for Social Services	35
Total Assisted	70,000
Residential Care of Disabled	4
Total Assisted	105
Other Institutions	11
Total Assisted	871,990
Educational	
Seminaries, Diocesan	1
Students from This Diocese	12
Students from Other Diocese	35
Diocesan Students in Other Seminaries	4
Students Religious	12
Total Seminarians	28
Colleges and Universities	3
Total Students	10,930
High Schools, Diocesan and Parish	4
Total Students	3,473
High Schools, Private	9
Total Students	4,105
Elementary Schools, Diocesan and Parish	60
Total Students	19,297
Elementary Schools, Private	6
Total Students	1,817
Catechesis/Religious Education:	
High School Students	2,083
Elementary Students	14,967
Total Students Under Catholic Instruction	56,700
Teachers in the Diocese:	
Priests	35
Scholastics	4
Brothers	10
Sisters	128
Lay Teachers	1,759
Vital Statistics	
Receptions into the Church:	
Infant Baptism Totals	8,424
Adult Baptism Totals	447
Received into Full Communion	337
First Communions	5,172
Confirmations	2,994
Marriages:	
Catholic	1,495
Interfaith	577
Total Marriages	2,072
Deaths	3,567
Total Catholic Population	420,000
Total Population	1,700,000

Former Bishops—Rt. Rev. FRANCIS GARCIA DIEGO Y MORENO, O.F.M., D.D., cons. Bishop of both Californias, Oct. 4, 1840; died in Santa Barbara, April 30, 1846.—Most Rev. JOSEPH SADOC ALEMANY, O.P., D.D., cons. Bishop of Monterey, June 30, 1850; appt. first Archbishop of San Francisco, July 29, 1853; resigned and appt. Titular Archbishop of Pelusio, Dec. 28, 1884; died in Valencia, Spain, April 14, 1888.—Most Rev. PATRICK WILLIAM RIORDAN, D.D., cons. Titular Archbishop of Cabasa and appt. Coadjutor Archbishop of San Francisco *cum jure successionis* Sept. 16, 1883; succeeded to Dec. 28, 1884; died in San Francisco, Dec. 27, 1914.—Most Rev. GEORGE MONTGOMERY, D.D., cons. Titular Bishop of Tmui and appt. Coadjutor Bishop of Monterey and Los Angeles *cum jure successionis* April 8, 1894; succeeded to May 6, 1896; appt. Titular Archbishop of Osimo and Coadjutor Archbishop of San Francisco *cum jure successionis* March 27, 1903; died in San Francisco, Jan. 10, 1907.—Most Rev. EDWARD J. HANNA, D.D., cons. Titular Bishop of Titopolis and appt. Auxiliary Bishop of San Francisco Dec. 4, 1912; appt. Archbishop of San Francisco, June 1, 1915; resigned and; appt. Titular Archbishop of Gortyna, March 2, 1935; died July 10, 1944.—Most Rev. JOHN JOSEPH MITTY, D.D., cons. Bishop of Salt Lake City, June 21, 1926; appt. Coadjutor Archbishop of San Francisco *cum jure successionis,* Jan. 29, 1932; succeeded to March 2, 1935; died Oct. 15, 1961.—Most Rev. JOSEPH T. MCGUCKEN, S.T.D., appt. Auxiliary of Los Angeles, Feb. 4, 1941; cons. Titular Bishop of Sanavo March 19, 1941; appt. Coadjutor Bishop of Sacramento *cum jure successionis,* Oct. 26, 1955; succeeded to Jan. 14, 1957; appt. Archbishop of San Francisco, Feb. 21, 1962; appt. Assistant at the Pontifical Throne, March 19, 1966; retired Feb. 22, 1977; died Oct. 26, 1983.—Most Rev. JOHN R. QUINN, D.D., appt. Auxiliary Bishop of San Diego, Oct. 21, 1967; cons. Titular Bishop of Thisiduo, Dec. 12, 1967; transferred to Oklahoma City and Tulsa, Nov. 18, 1971; appt. Archbishop of the Archdiocese of Oklahoma City, Feb. 6, 1973; appt. Archbishop of San Francisco, April 26, 1977; resigned Dec. 27, 1995.

The Chancery Office—445 Church St., San Francisco, 94114. Tel: 415-565-3600; Fax: 415-565-3649. Open Mon.-Fri. All applications for dispensations, faculties, etc., and all correspondence should be addressed: The Chancery Office.

Vicar General and Moderator of the Curia—Most Rev. PATRICK J. MCGRATH, V.G.

Vicar for Parishes and Pastoral Services—Most Rev. CARLOS A. SEVILLA, S.J., V.G.

Vicar for Administration—Rev. Msgr. ROBERT W. MCELROY, V.G.

Chancellor Pro-Tempore—Rev. GREGORY INGELS, J.C.D.

Administrative Assistant to the Archbishop—Rev. THOMAS S. MERSON.

College of Consultors—Most Rev. PATRICK J. MCGRATH, V.G.; Rev. Msgr. ROBERT W. MCELROY, V.G.; Rev. Msgr. FRANCIS A. LACEY, P.A.; Rev. Msgr. JAMES P. MCKAY; Revs. MAURICE M. MCCORMICK; WILLIAM P. QUINN; ALBERT C. VUCINOVICH.

Deans—Deanery 1 (San Francisco): Rev. WILLIAM P. QUINN, Deanery 2 (San Francisco): Rev. BRUCE A. DREIER, Deanery 3 (San Francisco): Rev. MILTON T. WALSH, Deanery 4 (San Francisco): Rev. Msgr. FRED A. BITANGA, Deanery 5 (San Francisco): Rev. JOSEPH WALSH, Deanery 8 (San Mateo Co.): Rev. MAURICE M. MCCORMICK, Deanery 9 (San Mateo Co.): Rev. VINCENT RING, Deanery 10 (San Mateo Co.): Rev. JAMES H. MACDONALD, Deanery 11 (San Mateo Co.): Rev. JOHN P. PENEBSKY, Deanery 12 (Marin Co.): Rev. PAUL ROSSI, Deanery 13 (Marin Co.): Rev. ALBERT P. VUCINOVICH.

Council of Priests—Rev. CRAIG FORNER, Chm.; Mrs. MARY ELLEN HOFFMAN, Admin. Asst. Tel: 415-565-3670.

Censores Librorum—Rev. Msgr. WARREN HOLLERAN, S.T.D.; Revs. GERALD D. COLEMAN, S.S., S.T.L., Ph.D.; MILTON T. WALSH, S.T.D.

Metropolitan Tribunal

San Francisco Metropolitan Tribunal—445 Church St., San Francisco, 94114. Tel: 415-565-3690; Fax: 415-565-3696.

Judicial Vicar and Director—Rev. RANDOLPH R. CALVO, J.C.D.

Adjutant Judicial Vicars—Revs. WILLIAM E. DUGGAN, J.C.L.; GREGORY INGELS, J.C.D.

Assoc. Director of Tribunal—Sr. NANCY REYNOLDS, S.P., J.C.L.

Promoter of Justice—Rev. Msgr. RICHARD S. KNAPP.

Defenders of the Bond—Revs. STEPHEN A. MERIWETHER, J.C.L.; MAURICE MCCORMICK, J.C.L.

Judges—Sr. NANCY REYNOLDS, S.P., J.C.L.; Sr. LYNN JARRELL, O.S.U., J.C.D.; Rev. Msgr. IGNATIUS WANG, J.C.D.

Tribunal Auditors—Sr. JOANNE O'CONNOR, O.P.; Sr. MARIANNE RASMUSSEN, O.S.F.

Notaries and Secretaries to the Tribunal—Ms. ANNETTE GOLEY; Mrs. REINA A. PARADA; Ms. ELLEN FOSTER.

Department of the Moderator of the Curia

Moderator of the Curia—Most Rev. PATRICK J. MCGRATH, V.G.

Archives—Dr. JEFFREY BURNS, Dir.; Revs. JOHN J. REILLY, Assoc. Dir. HENRY J. TRAINOR, *320 Middlefield Rd., Menlo Park, 94025.* Tel: 415-328-6502; Fax: 415-322-0997.

Campaign for Human Development—(See the Catholic Charities listing under Institutions located in the Archdiocese for details and information.).

Catholic Relief Services—(See the Catholic Charities listing under Institutions located in the Archdiocese for details and information.).

Cemeteries, Office of—Rev. Msgr. JOSEPH SULLIVAN, Dir.; Mrs. KATHERINE ATKINSON, Gen. Mgr., *P.O. Box 1577, Colma, 94014.* Tel: 415-756-2060; Fax: 415-994-8147.

Communications, Office of—Deacon WILLIAM MITCHELL, Dir., *441 Church St., San Francisco, 94114.* Tel: 415-565-3630; Fax: 415-565-3633.

Ecumenism and Interreligious Affairs, Office of—Rev. P. GERARD O'ROURKE, Dir. Tel: 415-565-3645; Fax: 415-565-3633.

Mission Office—(San Francisco Society for Propagation of the Faith); Rev. Msgr. IGNATIUS WANG, Dir. Tel: 415-565-3676; Fax: 415-565-3677.

Public Policy and Social Concerns, Office of—Mr. GEORGE WESOLEK, Dir. Tel: 415-565-3673; Fax: 415-565-3648.

Research and Planning, Office of—Rev. JOSE R. ARONG, O.M.I., Dir. Tel: 415-565-3684.

Respect Life Office—Directors, Respect Life Commission: MARY ANNE SCHWAB; ALICE ASTURIAS; Rev. LAWRENCE C. GOODE, Chm. Tel: 415-565-3672.

Department of the Vicar for Clergy

Vicar for Clergy—Most Rev. PATRICK J. MCGRATH, Pro-Tempore.

Priests Personnel Board—Most Rev. PATRICK J. MCGRATH, D.D., J.C.D., Chm.; Rev. WILLIAM A. O'CONNELL, Exec. Sec.

Priests Personnel, Office of—Rev. WILLIAM A. O'CONNELL, Dir. Tel: 415-565-3605.

Clergy Education, Office of—Rev. JOSEPH WALSH, Dir., *St. Kevin's Church, 704 Cortland Ave., San Francisco, 94110.* Tel: 415-648-5751. TERESITA GALANG, Admin. Asst., *445 Church St., San Francisco, 94114.* Tel: 415-565-3605.

Permanent Diaconate, Office of—Deacon LEON KORTENKAMP, Dir. Tel: 415-565-3620.

Vocations Office—Rev. JOSEPH BRADLEY, Dir.; Sr. LOURDES GONZALEZ, O.J.P., Asst. Dir. Tel: 415-565-3618.

Vicar for Religious—Rev. ANDREW F. MAGINNIS, S.J. Tel: 415-565-3656.

Vicar for Priests—Rev. ANTHONY E. MCGUIRE, *St. Anne Parish, 850 Judah St., San Francisco, 94122.* Tel: 415-665-1600. *415-665-1603.*

Priests Retirement Board—Most Rev. PATRICK J. MCGRATH, Chm. Tel: 415-565-3600. Rev. WILLIAM WORNER, Archbishop's Liaison to Retired Priests, *Serra Clergy House, 455 W. 20th Ave., San Mateo, 94403.* Tel: 415-358-1566.

Department of the Vicar for Administration

Vicar for Administration—Rev. Msgr. ROBERT W. MCELROY, V.G.

Director of Finance/Finance Officer—Mr. RICHARD P. HANNON.

Director of Real Estate—Mr. LES MCDONALD.

Director of Stewardship and Development—Rev. HARRY G. SCHLITT.

Director of Human Resources—Mr. CARL FEIL. Tel: 415-565-3627.

In-House Legal Counsel—Mr. JACK M. HAMMEL.

Pastoral Center Facilities Manager—Mr. LES MCDONALD.

Finance Council—Rev. Msgr. ROBERT W. MCELROY, V.G., Chm.; Mr. DONALD BAIRD; Rev. Msgr. CHARLES J. DURKIN; Mrs. CECILIA HERBERT; Mr. RICHARD HANNON; Mr. JOHN HITCHCOCK, JR.; Mr. FRANK HUDSON; Deacon HENRY JACQUEMET, JR.; Mr. JAMES JENSEN; Deacon GARY WEST.

Investment Committee—Mrs. CECILIA HERBERT, Chm.; Rev. JACQUES DIDIER, M.E.P.; Mr. VICTOR BARRIOS; Mr. JOHN KELLER; Mr. PETER MAIER; Mr. I. P. SICOTTE, JR.

Building and Maintenance Committee—Rev. Msgr. EDWARD MCTAGGART, Chm.; Rev. Msgr. JAMES P. MCKAY, V.G.; Rev. RICHARD S. DEITCH; Mr. JAMES HAGEN; Mr. RICHARD HANNON; Mr. DONALD JUNKIN; Mr. BEN MURPHY; Mr. RALPH MARCHESE. Ex Officio: Mr. CHARLES BARBERINI; Mr. STEVEN BOWERS; Mr. LES MCDONALD.

Real Estate Committee—Rev. Msgr. ROBERT W. MCELROY; Mr. DONALD BAIRD; Mr. JOHN A. CATTALINI; Mr. BILL HALEY; Mr. RICK HANNON; Mr. TERRENCE E. O'BRIEN; Mr. RALPH MARCHESE; Mr. LES MCDONALD; Mr. JOHN WEINGERTHER. Tel: 415-565-3600.

Department of the Vicar for Parishes

Vicar for Parishes—Most Rev. CARLOS A. SEVILLA, S.J., V.G.

Ethnic Ministries, Office of—Ms. NOEMI CASTILLO, Dir. Tel: 415-565-3622.

Chinese Affairs—Sr. MARIA HSU, Fd.CC., Coord. Tel: 415-565-3680.

Hispanic Affairs—Mrs. CECILIA ARIAS-RIVAS, Coord. Tel: 415-565-3668.

Japanese Mission—Mr. HARRY YASUMURA, Liaison, *St. Francis Xavier Church, 1801 Octavia St., San Francisco, 94109.* Tel: 415-346-7309.

Palestinian and Arab Mission—Rev. LABIB KOBTI, *St. Anne Church, 850 Judah St., San Francisco, 94122.* Tel: 415-665-1600; Fax: 415-665-1603.

Polish Mission and Croatian-Slovene Mission—Rev. CZESLAW RYBACKI, S.Ch., Coord., *245 Linden St., San Francisco, 94102.*

St. Michael Korean Church—Rev. STEPHANUS CHEOL SOO SEE, Pastor, *32 Broad St., San Francisco, 94112.* Tel: 415-333-6424; Fax: 415-333-1196.

Tongan Ministry—Rev. SAIMONE MOALA, Coord., *St. Timothy Church, 1515 Dolan Ave., San Mateo, 94401.* Tel: 415-342-2470; Fax: 415-342-8156.

Vietnamese Catholic Ministry—Rev. JOSEPH NGUYEN DUC TRONG, Coord., *3240 Lawton St., San Francisco, 94122.* Tel: 415-759-4293; Fax: 415-664-9775.

Evangelization and Renew, Office of—Vacant.

Family Life, Office of—CARMEN DE LA VEGA NEAFSEY, Dir. Tel: 415-565-3650.

Parish Life, Office of—Rev. DAVID M. PETTINGILL, Dir. Tel: 415-565-3600.

Religious Education, Office of—Sr. CELESTE ARBUCKLE, Asst. Dir. Tel: 415-565-3652.

School of Pastoral Leadership—Co-Directors: CARMEN NEASFEY; Dr. KEN WEARE, Ph.D., *475 Eucalyptus Dr., San Francisco, 94132.* Tel: 415-242-9087; Fax: 415-242-9089.

Worship, Office of—Rev. JOHN TALESFORE, Dir.

Young Adults, Office of—Vacant.

Youth Ministry—(Coordinated by Catholic Youth Organization); Rev. DAVID A. GHIROSO, Exec. Dir. (See separate category under Institutions located in the Archdiocese for details and information.), *Youth Ministry Services, One St. Vincent's Dr., San Rafael, 94903.* Tel: 415-507-2000; Fax: 415-491-0842. Parish-based youth leadership training Program and Services.

Department of Catholic Schools

Superintendent—Sr. GLENN ANN MCPHEE, O.P.; Mr. PAUL BERGEZ, Assoc. Supt. Finance & Devel. JOAN HASTINGS, Assoc. Supt. Personnel & Human Resources; Sr. MARIANNE VIANI, S.N.J.M., Assoc. Supt. Curriculum; LOIS BAUER, Asst. Supt. Administrative Svcs.; Sr. MARCELLA HOLIAN, C.S.J., Asst. Supt. Personnel & Staff Devel., *443 Church St., San Francisco, 94114-1792.* Tel: 415-565-3660.

Archdiocesan Board of Education—ROB AVESON, Chm.; Sr. KATHRYN CAMACHO, S.N.D., Vice Chm. SUSAN BURNS; GERALD BURRONI; CATHERINE DRISCOLL CANNATA; Revs. MANUEL CURSO; BERNARD DABBENE, S.D.B.; JAMES GARCIA; PATRICK GOUGH; MOLLY O'SHEA; JOHN PICETTI.

Roman Catholic Welfare Corporation of San Francisco—Most Rev. WILLIAM J. LEVADA, Pres.; Most Rev. PATRICK J. MCGRATH, Vice Pres.; Rev. Msgr. ROBERT W. MCELROY, Vice Pres.-Sec.; Sr. GLENN ANNE MCPHEE, O.P., Asst. Sec.; Mr. RICHARD HANNON, Treas.; Rev. GREGORY INGELS, Asst. Treas. Tel: 415-565-3600.

CLERGY, PARISHES, MISSIONS AND PAROCHIAL SCHOOLS

CITY OF SAN FRANCISCO
(San Francisco County)

1—CATHEDRAL OF ST. MARY (ASSUMPTION) (1891), Revs. Milton T. Walsh; Richard S. Deitch; Michael Martin; Deacon Joseph Borg.
Cathedral Office: 1111 Gough St., 94109. Tel: 415-567-2020; Fax: 415-567-2040.

2—ST. AGNES (1893), Revs. Russell J. Roide, S.J.; John R. Treacy, S.J.; Francis K. Chung, S.J.; John Sung, S.J.; Mick McCarthy, S.J. In res., Rev. Thomas L. Smolich, S.J.
Res., 1025 Masonic Ave., 94117. Tel: 415-487-8560; Fax: 415-487-8575.

3—ALL HALLOWS (1886). Closed. For sacramental records please contact Our Lady of Lourdes, San Francisco.

4—ST. ANNE (1904), Revs. Anthony McGuire; Dominic Savio Lee; Deacon John Dupre. In res., Revs. Labib Kobti (Latin Patriarchy of Jerusalem); Thomas S. Merson. Joseph P. Bradley.
Res., 850 Judah St., 94122. Tel: 415-665-1600; Fax: 415-665-1603.
School—1320 14th Ave., 94122. Tel: 415-664-7977. Sisters 1; Lay Teachers 21; Students 600.

5—ST. ANTHONY (1893), Revs. Michael Weldon, O.F.M.; Francisco Reyes, O.F.M.; Robert Pfisterer, O.F.M.; Daniel Lackie, O.F.M.; Guglielmo Lauriola, O.F.M. In res., Revs. Floyd A. Lotito, O.F.M., Guardian; Anthony Baumann, O.F.M.; Finian McGinn, O.F.M.; Sergio Santos, O.F.M.; Bro. Javier Reyes, O.F.M.
Res., 3215 Cesar Chavez St., 94110. Tel: 415-647-2704; Fax: 415-647-7282.
Secondary Church—Under the care and administration of the pastor of St. Anthony of Padua parish. Immaculate Conception, 3255 Folsom St., 94110. Tel: 415-824-1762; Fax: 415-824-0129.
High School—St. Anthony, 299 Precita Ave., 94110. Tel: 415-648-2008. Sr. John Ellen Turner, O.P., Prin.
Sisters 5; Lay Teachers 13; Students 275.
School—Immaculate Conception Elementary School, 1550 Treat Ave., 94110. Tel: 415-824-6860; Fax: 415-824-0129.
Sisters of the Third Order of St. Dominic, Congregation of the Queen of the Holy Rosary 2; Lay Teachers 16; Students 254.

6—ST. BENEDICT PARISH AT ST. FRANCIS XAVIER CHURCH (Japanese). (Deaf and Hearing Impaired). Rev. Daniel Adams.
Res., 1801 Octavia, 94109. Tel: 415-567-9855; 567-0438 (TDD); Fax: 415-567-0916.
High School—Marin Catholic High School, 675 Sir Francis Drake Blvd., Kentfield, 94904. Tel: 415-461-8844.
Mission—Menlo Park, St. Anthony, 3500 Middlefield Rd., Menlo Park 94025. Tel: 415-366-4692.

7—St. Boniface (1860) (German), Revs. Louis Vitale, O.F.M.; Terence Cronin, O.F.M.; John Luat Nguyen, O.F.M. Pastoral Assocs.: Bro. Didacus Clavel, O.F.M.; Sr. Graciela Martinez, O.S.F. In res., Revs. Joaquin Moreno, O.F.M.; Stephen Tan Nguyen, O.F.M.; Stephan Kain, O.F.M.; Bros. Regan Chapman, O.F.M.; Robert Brady, O.F.M.; David Bauer, O.F.M.; Angelo Cardanalli, O.F.M.; Kelly Cullen, O.F.M.; Dennis Duffy, O.F.M.; Kurt Rawhauser, O.F.M.; Simon Scanlon.
Res., 133 Golden Gate Ave., 94102. Tel: 415-863-0111; Fax: 415-863-7602.
Catechesis/Religious Programs—Students 180.

8—St. Brendan (1929), Rev. Msgr. Edward P. McTaggart; Rev. William P. Crowley, C.S.Sp. In res., Most Rev. Patrick J. McGrath; Revs. William E. Duggan; Jose Parappully, S.D.B.
Res., 29 Rockaway Ave., 94127. Tel: 415-681-4225; Fax: 415-681-3976.
School—234 Ulloa St., 94127. Tel: 415-731-2665; Fax: 415-731-7207.
Sisters of St. Dominic, Adrian, MI 2; Lay Teachers 20; Students 355.

9—St. Brigid (1863). Closed. For sacramental records please contact St. Vincent de Paul, San Francisco.

10—St. Cecilia (1917), Rev. Msgr. Steven Otellini; Revs. Michael D. Harriman; Lodovico Joseph Landi. In res., Rev. Msgr. John T. Foudy; Rev. Heribert Duquet, M.E.P.
Res., 2555 17th Ave., 94116. Tel: 415-664-8481; Fax: 415-661-2957.
School—660 Vicente St., 94116. Tel: 415-731-8400. Sisters of the Holy Names 5; Lay Teachers 16; Students 581.
Catechesis/Religious Programs—Students 51.

11—St. Charles Borromeo (1887) (Spanish-Filipino), Revs. Jose A. Rodriguez; Victorio Balagapo.
Res., 713 S. Van Ness Ave., 94110. Tel: 415-824-1700; Fax: 415-824-0844.
School—3250 18th St., 94110. Tel: 415-861-7652. Dominican Sisters of the Most Holy Rosary (Philippines) 6; Lay Teachers 5; Students 293.
Catechesis/Religious Programs—Students 269.

12—Corpus Christi (1898), Revs. Bernard J. Dabbene, S.D.B.; Armand Oliveri, S.D.B.; Hugo Santucci, S.D.B.; Salvatore Giacomini, S.D.B.; Aloysius Pestun, S.D.B.; Deacon Tom Ilao.
Res., 62 Santa Rosa Ave., 94112. Tel: 415-585-2291; Fax: 415-585-0773.
School—75 Francis St., 94112. Tel: 415-587-7014; Fax: 415-587-1575.
Salesian Sisters of St. John Bosco (Daughters of Mary Help of Christians) 5; Lay Teachers 8; Students 314.
Catechesis/Religious Programs—Tel: 415-585-3240.
Students 250.

13—St. Dominic (1873), Revs. Roberto Corral, O.P.; Timothy Conlan, O.P.; Xavier M. Lavagetto, O.P.; Bro. Mark Gorski, O.P.; Deacon Fred Swanson. In res., Revs. Reginald Martin, O.P., Prior; Gregory Anderson, O.P.; Felix Cassidy, O.P.; John Klaia, O.P.; Thomas J. Hayes, O.P.; Brian Mullady, O.P.; Paul Raftery, O.P.; Terrance Reilly, O.P.; Peter J. Sanguinetti, O.P.; Bros. Gregory Lira, O.P.; Peter Yost, O.P.
Res., 2390 Bush St., 94115. Tel: 415-567-7824; Fax: 415-567-1608.
School—2445 Pine St., 94115. Tel: 415-346-9500; Fax: 415-346-8001.
Sisters of the Third Order of St. Dominic, Congregation of the Most Holy Name 5; Sisters of Mercy 1; Sisters of the Holy Names of Jesus and Mary 1; Lay Teachers 6; Students 258.

14—St. Edward (1916). Closed. For sacramental records please contact Star of the Sea, San Francisco.

15—St. Elizabeth (1912), Revs. Edwin W. Farrugia; Benjamin Nombrado; Edward Phelan.
Res., 449 Holyoke Ave., 94134. Tel: 415-468-0820; Fax: 415-468-1457.
School—450 Somerset St., 94134. Tel: 415-468-3247; Fax: 415-468-1804.
Lay Teachers 12; Students 293.
Catechesis/Religious Programs—Tel: 415-468-3274; Fax: 415-468-2804.
Students 125.

16—St. Emydius (1913), Revs. Craig Forner; Alex Legaspi; Deacon John W. Hutzler.
Res., 286 Ashton Ave., 94112. Tel: 415-587-7066; Fax: 415-587-6690.
School—301 DeMontfort Ave., 94112. Tel: 415-333-4877. Miss Nell Jeffrey, Prin.
Lay Teachers 10; Students 225.

17—Church of the Epiphany (1914), Revs. Bruce A. Dreier; Mark V. Taheny; Rolando Caverte; Manuel Estrada; Deacons Manuel Ocon; Ding Viray.
Res., 827 Vienna St., 94112. Tel: 415-333-7630; Fax: 415-333-1803.
School—600 Italy Ave., 94112. Tel: 415-337-4030; Fax: 415-337-8583.
Sisters 1; Lay Teachers 22; Students 565.
Catechesis/Religious Programs—Students 350.

18—St. Finn Barr (1926), Revs. Lawrence C. Goode; Cyril O'Sullivan.
Res., 415 Edna St., 94112. Tel: 415-333-3627; Fax: 415-333-4090.
School—419 Hearst Ave., 94112. Tel: 415-333-1800; Fax: 415-452-0177.
Sisters of Mercy (Ireland) 3; Lay Teachers 9; Students 335.

19—St. Francis of Assisi Mission. Closed. For sacramental records please contact SS. Peter and Paul, San Francisco.

20—St. Gabriel (1941), Revs. Harry G. Schlitt; Thomas Moran.
Res., 2535 40th Ave., 94116. Tel: 415-731-6161; Fax: 415-731-1270.
School—2550 41st Ave., 94116. Tel: 415-566-0314. Lay Teachers 22; Students 498.
Catechesis/Religious Programs—Students 65.

21—Holy Cross (1887) (Korean). Closed. For sacramental records please contact St. Michael, San Francisco.

22—Holy Family Chinese Mission (1921). (aka St. Mary's Chinese Catholic Center—1903). Rev. Daniel E. McCotter, C.S.P.; Sr. Prisca Hui, S.N.J.M., Pastoral Assoc.; Ms. Lisa Tom French, Admin.
Res., 910 Broadway, 94133. Tel: 415-929-4690; Fax: 415-929-4699.
School—St. Mary Chinese School, 910 Broadway, 94133. Tel: 415-929-4690; Fax: 415-929-4699. Jerry Dinoto, Prin.
Sisters 6; Lay Teachers 14; Students 345.
Chinese Language School—Tel: 415-929-4694. Stephen Woon Wah Tang, Prin.
Students 650; Chinese Teachers 15; Elementary Students 600; High School Students 50.
Holy Family Association—Loretta Fung, Pres. Pastoral Council; Katy Sid, Pres.

23—Holy Name of Jesus (1925), Revs. William P. Quinn; Raym J. Zohlen; Piers M. Lahey. In res., Rev. Msgr. Ignatius Wang; Rev. Trong Duc Nguyen; Deacon Dennis Rivera.
Res., 3240 Lawton St., 94122. Tel: 415-664-8590; Fax: 415-664-9775.
School—1560 40th Ave., 94122. Tel: 415-731-4077; Fax: 415-731-3328.
Sisters 2; Lay Teachers 18; Students 604.
Catechesis/Religious Programs—Students 140.

24—St. Ignatius (1855), Revs. Charles R. Gagan; James Fleming, S.J.; Thomas G. Piquado, S.J.
Res., 650 Parker Ave., 94118. Tel: 415-422-2188; Fax: 415-387-1867.

25—Immaculate Conception (1912) (Italian). Closed. For sacramental records please contact St. Anthony of Padua, San Francisco.

26—St. James (1888), Rev. Daniel Carter. In res., Rev. George Mullonkal, M.C.B.S.
Res., 1086 Guerrero St., 94110. Tel: 415-824-4232; Fax: 415-824-0605.
School—321 Fair Oaks St., 94110. Tel: 415-647-8972; Fax: 415-647-0166.
Sisters of the Third Order of St. Dominic, Congregation of Queen of the Holy Rosary 5; Lay Teachers 8; Students 239.
Catechesis/Religious Programs—Students 70.

27—St. John the Evangelist (1893), Rev. James E. Meyers, S.S. In res., Revs. Francis Filice; James Tucker, S.S.; Sr. Patricia Galli, R.S.M., Pastoral Assoc.
Res., 19 St. Mary's Ave., 94112-1098. Tel: 415-334-4646; Fax: 415-334-0891.
Parish Center: 98 Bosworth St., 94112. Tel: 415-334-4646; Fax: 415-334-0891.
School—925 Chenery St., 94131. Tel: 415-584-8383; Fax: 415-584-8359.
Lay Teachers 8; Students 283.

28—St. John of God (1967), Revs. William J. Brady; Alan Wilson, O.F.M.Cap., Chap.
Res., 1290 Fifth Ave., 94122. Tel: 415-566-5610; Fax: 415-566-5073.
Catechesis/Religious Programs—Tel: 415-664-9850. Phil Warren, D.R.E.
Students 75.

29—St. Joseph (1861). Closed. For sacramental records please contact St. Patrick, San Francisco.

30—St. Kevin (1922), Rev. Joseph R. Walsh; Deacon Dan Rosen. In res., Rev. Msgr. Joseph P. Sullivan.
Res., 704 Cortland Ave., 94110. Tel: 415-648-5751; Fax: 415-648-4441.
Catechesis/Religious Programs—Tel: 415-282-0277.
Students 117.

31—Old St. Mary's Cathedral (1854), Revs. John J. Foley, C.S.P.; Thomas J. Dove, C.S.P.; Peter G. Shea, C.S.P. In res., Revs. Leo Conlin, C.S.P., (Retired); Philip Cunningham, C.S.P., (Retired); Charles A. Donovan, C.S.P., (Retired); Daniel E. McCotter, C.S.P.; John A. Carr, C.S.P., (Retired); Joseph M. Hanly, C.S.P., (Retired); Edward Maher, C.S.P., (Retired).
Res., 660 California St., 94108. Tel: 415-288-3800; Fax: 415-288-3838.

32—St. Michael Korean Church (1898) (Korean), Rev. Stephanus Cheol Soo Lee.
Res., 32 Broad St., 94112. Tel: 415-333-1194; Fax: 415-333-1196.

33—Mission Dolores Basilica (1776). (San Francisco de Asis). Rev. Msgr. John J. O'Connor; Rev. Santos Rodrigues; Deacon Vicente Cervantes.
Res., 3321 16th St., 94114. Tel: 415-621-8203; Fax: 415-621-2294. [CEM]
School—3371 16th St., 94114. Tel: 415-861-7673. Andreina Gualco, Prin.
Sisters 3; Lay Teachers 8; Students 290.
Catechesis/Religious Programs—Students 81.

34—St. Monica (1911), Revs. Warren L. Woods; Simeon Chang; Jonathan Paala.
Res., 470 24th Ave., 94121. Tel: 415-751-5275; Fax: 415-751-0440.
School—5920 Geary Blvd., 94121. Tel: 415-751-9564.
Sisters of the Holy Names of Jesus and Mary 3; Lay Teachers 7; Students 354.
Catechesis/Religious Programs—Students 114.

35—Most Holy Redeemer (1900), Revs. Zachary J. Shore; Thomas J. Hayes, O.M.I. In res., Rev. William W. Young.
Res., 100 Diamond St., 94114-2414. Tel: 415-863-6259; Fax: 415-552-8786.

36—Nativity (1902) (Polish and Croatian-Slovene), Rev. Czeslew Rybacki, S.Ch.
Res., 245 Linden St., 94102. Tel: 415-252-5799.

37—Notre Dame des Victoires (1856) (French), Revs. Etienne Siffert, S.M.; Phillip d'Auby, S.M.
Res., 566 Bush St., 94108. Tel: 415-397-0113; Fax: 415-397-3217.
School—659 Pine St., 94108. Tel: 415-421-0069. Mary K. Ghisolfo, Prin.
Sisters of St. Joseph of Orange 3; Lay Teachers 16; Students 300.

38—Our Lady of Fatima Byzantine Catholic Church (1954). Catholic Russian Center (Byzantine). Rev. Steven A. Armstrong, S.J.
Res., 101 20th Ave., 94121-1398. Tel: 415-752-2052; Fax: 415-752-6073.

39—Our Lady of Guadalupe. Closed. For sacramental records please contact SS. Peter and Paul, San Francisco.

40—Our Lady of Lourdes (1942), Rev. Kirk Ullery.
Res., 1715 Oakdale Ave., 94124. Tel: 415-285-3377; Fax: 415-285-2191.

41—St. Patrick (1851), Rev. Msgr. Fred A. Bitanga; Rev. Leobardo D. Montoya; Deacons Tom Buenavista; Virgil Capati. In res., Revs. Robert Andrey; Henry J. Trainor.
Res., 756 Mission St., 94103. Tel: 415-421-3730; Fax: 415-512-9730.
Catechesis/Religious Programs—Students 125.

42—St. Paul (1880), Revs. Mario P. Farana; Mamerto Sigaran; Mary Tan, Pastoral Assoc.
Res., 221 Valley St., 94131. Tel: 415-648-7538; Fax: 415-648-4740.
School—180 Fair Oaks St., 94110. Tel: 415-648-2055; Fax: 415-648-1920. Sr. Ann Cronin, B.V.M., Prin.; Patricia Esling, Vice Prin.
Sisters 1; Lay Teachers 9; Students 265.
Catechesis/Religious Programs—1660 Church St., 94131. Tel: 415-826-4484.
Students 115.
Convents—323 29th St., 94131. Tel: 415-648-3211; Fax: 415-648-4740. Sisters of Charity, Blessed Virgin Mary; 316 29th St., 94131. Tel: 415-647-1889. Novitiate of the Missionaries of Charity

43—St. Paul of the Shipwreck (1915), Rev. Efrem Trettel, O.F.M. In res., Rev. Michael Walsh.
Res., 1122 Jamestown Ave., 94124. Tel: 415-468-3434; Fax: 415-468-1400.
School—St. Paul of the Shipwreck Academy, 1060 Key Ave. at Third St., 94124. Tel: 415-467-1798.
Lay Teachers 9; Students 155.

44—St. Peter (1867), Revs. Jose Chavarin; Gustavo Perez; Francis MacPeck, S.J.; Deacons Roger Hernandez; David Gamarra. In res., Rev. Edmund M. Shipp.
Res., 1200 Florida St., 94110. Tel: 415-282-1652; Fax: 415-647-4618.
School—1266 Florida St., 94110. Tel: 415-647-8662. Vicki Butler, Prin.
Sisters 3; Lay Teachers 11; Students 520.

45—SS. Peter and Paul (1884) (Italian), Revs. David T. Purdy, S.D.B.; Austin Conterno, S.D.B.; Salvatore Giacomini, S.D.B.; John Lam, S.D.B.; John O'Brien, S.D.B. In res., Revs. Anthony F. Di Falco, S.D.B.; Gabriel J. Zavattaro, S.D.B.

Res., 666 Filbert St., 94133. Tel: 415-421-0809; Fax: 415-421-0217.
School—632 Filbert St., 94133. Tel: 415-421-5219; Fax: 415-421-1831. Sr. Sandra Neaves, F.M.A., Prin.
Salesian Sisters 5; Lay Teachers 9; Students 324.

46—St. Philip the Apostle (1910), Rev. Michael J. Healy. In res., Revs. P. Gerard O'Rourke; Brendan McBride.
Res., 725 Diamond St., 94114. Tel: 415-282-0141; Fax: 415-282-8962.
School—4174 24th St., 94114. Tel: 415-824-8467. Peg Rybicki, Prin.
Lay Teachers 10; Students 250.

47—Sacred Heart (1885), Rev. Kenneth M. Westray. In res., Rev. Daniel Adams.
Res., 546 Fillmore St., 94117. Tel: 415-861-5460; Fax: 415-861-7839.
School—735 Fell St., 94117. Tel: 415-621-8035; Fax: 415-861-7039. Eileen Murphy, Prin.
Lay Teachers 7; Students 114.
Catechesis/Religious Programs—Students 114.

48—Star of the Sea (1894), Rev. Msgr. Charles J. Durkin; Revs. Benedict Chang; Greg Aherne, S.J. In res., Rev. Calixto Armas.
Res., 4420 Geary Blvd., 94118. Tel: 415-751-0450; Fax: 415-368-5651.
School—360 Ninth Ave., 94118. Tel: 415-221-8558; Fax: 415-221-7547. Mrs. Lynda McCarthy, Prin.
Sisters 3; Lay Teachers 6; Students 320.
Convent—4350 Geary Blvd., 94118. Tel: 415-752-6050. Sisters of St. Joseph of Carondelet

49—St. Stephen (1950), Revs. John C. Wester; Sean Corcoran, C.S.S.P.; John L. Greene; Sr. Petra Keller, S.S.S., Pastoral Assoc.; Deacon Gary West. In res., Rev. Joseph P. O'Reilly.
Res., 601 Eucalyptus Dr., 94132. Tel: 415-681-2444; Fax: 415-681-7843.
School—401 Eucalyptus Dr., 94132. Tel: 415-664-8331. Sr. Paulinea Simms, R.S.M., Prin.
Sisters of Mercy 2; Lay Teachers 10; Students 312.
Catechesis/Religious Programs—Sr. Toni Lynn Gallagher, R.S.M., D.R.E.
Students 46.

50—St. Teresa (1880), Rev. Peter J. Sammon. Pastoral Assocs.: Sr. Kathleen Healy, P.B.V.M.; Sr. Lucia Lodolo, P.B.V.M.; Deacon Charles Allen. In res., Rev. Edward K. Murray.
Res., 390 Missouri St., 94107. Tel: 415-285-5272; Fax: 415-285-8510.
Church—19th & Connecticut Sts., 94107.
Catechesis/Religious Programs—Students 53.

51—St. Thomas, The Apostle (1922), Revs. Kirby C. Hanson; Charles J. Sullivan; Stanley Wu.
Res., 3835 Balboa St., 94121. Tel: 415-387-5545; Fax: 415-221-0868.
School—3801 Balboa St., 94121. Tel: 415-221-2711.
Lay Teachers 10; Students 250.

52—St. Thomas More (1950), Rev. Jerome P. Foley, Chap. In res., Revs. Steven Davies; John Talesfore.
Res., 1300 Junipero Serra Blvd., 94132. Tel: 415-452-9634; Fax: 415-452-9653.

53—St. Vincent de Paul (1901), Revs. John K. Ring; Edward A. Bonhert; Lewis B. O'Neil, S.J.; Sr. M. Antonio Heaphy, P.B.V.M., Pastoral Assoc., Dir. of Religious Formation.
Res., 2320 Green St., 94123. Tel: 415-922-1010; Fax: 415-922-7203.
School—2350 Green St., 94123. Tel: 415-346-0970. George Enes, Prin.
Lay Teachers 10; Students 256.

54—Visitacion, Church of the (1907), Rev. Thomas L. Seagrave.
Res., 655 Sunnydale Ave., 94134. Tel: 415-239-5950; Fax: 415-239-0538.
School—Our Lady of the Visitacion, 785 Sunnydale Ave., 94134. Tel: 415-239-7840.
Daughters of Charity of St. Vincent de Paul 4; Lay Teachers 7; Students 285.
Mission—Brisbane, Our Lady of Guadalupe.

OUTSIDE THE CITY OF SAN FRANCISCO

Belmont, San Mateo Co., Immaculate Heart of Mary (1947), Revs. James H. MacDonald; Clifford A. Martin; Deacons Steven Hackett; Henry Jacquemet. In res., Rev. Msgr. John J. Kenny.
Res., 1040 Alameda de las Pulgas, 94002. Tel: 415-593-6157; Fax: 415-593-1665.
School—1000 Alameda de las Pulgas, 94002. Tel: 415-593-4265. Dr. Margaret Purcell, Prin.
Lay Teachers 12; Students 310.
Catechesis/Religious Programs—Mrs. Genny Pereira, D.R.E.
Students 376.

St. Mark (1965), Rev. Floro B. Arcamo. In res., Revs. Miles O'Brien Riley; William J. Flanagan.
Res., 325 Marine View Ave., 94002. Tel: 415-591-5937; Fax: 415-591-7645.
Catechesis/Religious Programs—Tel: 415-591-7072.
Students 139.

Burlingame, San Mateo Co., St. Catherine of Siena (1908), Revs. James W. Alyward; Zosimo Alvar, Jr.; Didacus Ma. In res., Rev. Msgr. John J. Murphy.
Res., 1310 Bayswater Ave., 94010. Tel: 415-344-6884; Fax: 415-344-1022.
School—1300 Bayswater Ave., 94010. Tel: 415-344-7176; Fax: 415-344-7426. Sr. Antonella Manca, M.S.C. Prin.
Sisters of the Sacred Side of Jesus 4; Lay Teachers 8; Students 322.
Catechesis/Religious Programs—Students 130.

Our Lady of Angels (1926), Revs. Michael Mahoney, O.F.M.Cap.; Martin Haggins, O.F.M.Cap. In res., Revs. Emilian Meade, O.F.M.Cap.; Donal O'Mahony, O.F.M.Cap.; Harold Snider, O.F.M.Cap.
Res., 1721 Hillside Dr., 94010. Tel: 415-347-7768; Fax: 415-347-3550.
School—1328 Cabrillo Ave., 94010. Tel: 415-343-9200. Joan Marino, Prin.
Sisters of Mercy 2; Lay Teachers 14; Students 310.
Catechesis/Religious Programs—Tel: 415-347-3671. Mrs. Kathryn Jones, D.R.E.
Students 305.

Colma, San Mateo Co., Holy Angels (1914), Revs. John J. Cloherty; Arturo Albano; Deacons John Ruiz; Lernito Prudenciado.
Res., 107 San Pedro Rd., 94014. Tel: 415-755-0478; Fax: 415-755-7653.
School—20 Reinter St., 94014. Tel: 415-755-0220.
Sisters 2; Lay Teachers 8; Students 262.
Catechesis/Religious Programs—Tel: 415-992-5539.
Students 430.

Daly City, San Mateo Co., St. Andrew (1968) (Filipino), Revs. Frank R. Piro; Jose Superiaso; Sr. Nancy McLaughlin, P.B.V.M., Pastoral Assoc.; Deacon Felix Amora.
Church—1571 Southgate Ave., 94015. Tel: 415-756-3223; Fax: 415-756-0251.
Rectory 1 Ridgefield Ave., 94015. Tel: 415-756-3223; Fax: 415-756-0251.
Catechesis/Religious Programs—Tel: 415-991-2937. Michele Bussey, D.R.E.
Students 400.

Our Lady of Mercy (Westlake) (1954), Revs. Manuel Curso; John F. Glogowski. In res., Rev. Edward M. Cleary.
Res., 1 Elmwood Dr., 94015. Tel: 415-755-2727.
School—15 Elmwood Dr., 94015. Tel: 415-756-3395. Arlene Fife, Prin.
Sisters 5; Lay Teachers 21; Students 611.
Catechesis/Religious Programs—Tel: 415-755-7353.
Students 184.

Our Lady of Perpetual Help (Westlake) (1925), Rev. Msgr. John R. Pernia; Rev. Antonio Petilla.
Res., 60 Wellington Ave., 94014. Tel: 415-755-9786.
School—80 Wellington Ave., 94014. Tel: 415-755-4438. James Costello, Prin.
Religious 1; Lay Teachers 8; Students 320.
Catechesis/Religious Programs—Tel: 415-755-4010. Sr. Hermina F. Coquia, F.M.M., D.R.E.
Students 320.

East Palo Alto, San Mateo Co., St. Francis of Assisi (1951), Rev. Joseph A. Gordon; Deacon Louis Dixon.
Res., 1425 Bay Rd., 94303. Tel: 415-322-2152; Fax: 415-322-7319.
Catechesis/Religious Programs—Students 300.

Fairfax, Marin Co., St. Rita (1930), Revs. Cornelius Healy; Albert Vucinovich. In res., Rev. Paul A. Perlite; Deacon Peter Kehrlein.
Res., 100 Marinda Dr., 94930. Tel: 415-456-4815; Fax: 415-456-3677.
School—102 Marinda Dr., 94930. Tel: 415-456-1003; Fax: 415-456-7946. Maureen Cassidy, Prin.
Lay Teachers 11; Students 241.
Catechesis/Religious Programs—Students 76.

Foster City, San Mateo Co., St. Luke (1970), Revs. Robert G. Stadler; Irenio Ramoso; Deacon Mar Tano.
Res., 1111 Beach Park Blvd., 94404. Tel: 415-345-6660; Fax: 415-345-8167.
Catechesis/Religious Programs—Tel: 415-574-9191; 573-7409.
Students 244.

Half Moon Bay, San Mateo Co., Our Lady of the Pillar (1868), Revs. Daniel J. Maguire; Agnel Jose de Heredia; Fabio Medina; Deacon John McGhee.
Res., 400 Church St., 94019. Tel: 415-726-4674; Fax: 415-726-0980. [CEM]
Catechesis/Religious Programs—Tel: 415-726-5587.
Students 475.
Missions—Pescadero, San Mateo Co., St. Anthony, P.O. Box 277, Pescadero, 94060. Tel: 415-879-0750; La Honda, San Mateo Co., Our Lady of Refuge, Pescadero, 94060.

Kentfield-Greenbrae, Marin Co., St. Sebastian (1951), Revs. Thomas Parenti; W. Paul O'Dell.
Res., 373 Bon Air Rd., Greenbrae, 94904. Tel: 415-461-0704; Fax: 415-461-2018.
Catechesis/Religious Programs—Students 59.

Lagunitas, Marin Co., St. Cecilia (1937), Rev. Thomas A. Daly.
Rectory: Box 289, 94938. Tel: 415-488-9799; Fax: 415-488-1963.
High School—Marin Catholic, 675 Sir Francis Drake Blvd., Kentfield, 94904.
Mission—Nicasio, St. Mary.

Larkspur, Marin Co., St. Patrick (1915), Rev. John D. Shanahan. In res., Rev. Joseph Eagan, S.J.
Res., 114 King St., 94939. Tel: 415-924-0600; Fax: 415-924-3617.
School—120 King St., 94939. Tel: 415-924-0501; Fax: 415-924-3554. Judy O'Rourke, Prin.
Lay Teachers 9; Students 285.
Catechesis/Religious Programs—Students 150.

Menlo Park, San Mateo Co.,

1—St. Anthony, (1951), Revs. James L. Garcia; Eduardo Mendoza; Deacon Jose Solano.
Res., 3500 Middlefield Rd., 94025. Tel: 415-366-4692; Fax: 415-366-4135.
Catechesis/Religious Programs—Tel: 415-365-6071. Gladys Fields, D.R.E.
Students 670.
Mission—Redwood City, San Mateo Co., St. Joseph the Workman, 400 Heller St., Redwood City, 94063.

2—St. Denis, (1853; Restored 1961), Rev. Msgr. John F. Rodriguez.
Res., 2250 Avy Ave., 94025. Tel: 415-854-5976; Fax: 415-854-3754.
Chapel—Our Lady of the Wayside, 930 Portola Rd., Portola Valley, 94028. Tel: 415-851-5085; Fax: 415-851-1019. Rev. George L. Thomas.
Catechesis/Religious Programs—Tel: 415-854-3754.
Students 350.

3—The Church of the Nativity, (1877), Revs. Clement A. Davenport; William J. Queenan, S.S (TR); Donald S. D'Angelo. In res., Rev. John J. Reilly, Assoc. Dir., Archives, Tel: 415-328-6502.
Res., 210 Oak Grove Ave., 94025. Tel: 415-323-7914; Fax: 415-323-3231.
School—1250 Laurel St., 94025. Tel: 415-325-7304.
Sisters 5; Lay Teachers 10; Students 264.

4—St. Raymond, (1950), Rev. Patrick T. Michaels.
Office: 1100 Santa Cruz Ave., 94025. Tel: 415-323-1755.
Res., 1231 Arbor Rd., 94025. Tel: 415-321-1339; Fax: 415-323-3206.
School—1211 Arbor Rd., 94025. Tel: 415-322-2312; Fax: 415-322-2910. Sr. Ann Bernard O'Shea, C.S.J., Prin.
Sisters 2; Lay Teachers 16; Students 279.
Catechesis/Religious Programs—Tel: 415-323-6353. Sr. Rita McCloskey, D.R.E.
Students 138.

Millbrae, San Mateo Co., St. Dunstan (1940), Revs. Alwyn Furtado, C.S.Sp.; Finnbar Horrigan, C.S.Sp.; Francis Mulloy, C.S.Sp. In res., Rev. William Doolin, C.S.Sp.
Res., 1133 Broadway, 94030. Tel: 415-697-4730; Fax: 415-697-5203.
School—1150 Magnolia Ave., 94030. Tel: 415-697-8119; Fax: 415-697-9295. Bonnie Davis, Prin.
Lay Teachers 14; Students 311.
Catechesis/Religious Programs—Tel: 415-697-7451.
Students 366.

Mill Valley, Marin Co., Our Lady of Mt. Carmel (1910), Revs. Joseph O'Connell; Paul Perry; Deacon Bruce Hall.
Res., 3 Oakdale Ave., 94941. Tel: 415-388-4190; Fax: 415-388-4197.

Novato, Marin Co., St. Anthony of Padua (1968), Revs. Kevin P. Gaffey; Toan Nguyen, S.J.; Deacon Joseph Brumbaugh. In res., Rev. James E. O'Malley.
Res., 1000 Cambridge St., 94947. Tel: 415-883-2177; Fax: 415-883-4049.
Catechesis/Religious Programs—Tel: 415-883-9000. Judith Ann Ross, D.R.E.
Students 370.

Our Lady of Loretto (1892), Revs. John J. O'Neill; Martin Avila; Deacon William Mitchell.
Res., 1806 Novato Blvd., 94947. Tel: 415-897-2171; Fax: 415-897-8251.
School—1811 Virginia Ave., 94947. Tel: 415-892-8621. Ms. Clare Menezes, Prin.
Lay Teachers 13; Students 320.
Catechesis/Religious Programs—Tel: 415-897-6714. D.R.E.: Betty McDonald; Mary Ann Hudick.
Students 370.

Olema, Marin Co., Sacred Heart (1967), Rev. Joseph A. Bravo.
Res., P.O. Box 70, 94950. Tel: 415-663-1139; Fax: 415-663-9660. [CEM]
Mission—Bolinas, St. Mary Magdalen.

Pacifica, Marin Co., Good Shepherd (1951), Rev. Maurice M. McCormick; Deacon Pete Pelimiano.

Res., 901 Oceana Blvd., 94044. Tel: 415-355-2593; Fax: 415-355-1832.
School—909 Oceana Blvd., 94044. Tel: 415-359-4544. Patricia Volan, Prin.
Lay Teachers 14; Students 352.
Catechesis/Religious Programs—Sr. Margaret Riley, O.S.F., D.R.E.
Students 210.

St. Peter, San Mateo Co., (1956), Rev. Leonard J. Calegari. In res., Rev. William A. O'Connell; Deacon Peter Solan.
Res., 700 Oddstad Blvd., 94044. Tel: 415-359-6313; Fax: 415-359-2262.
Catechesis/Religious Programs—Tel: 415-359-5000. D.R.E.: Mrs. Barbara Malone; Mrs. Margaret Anne Kerns.
Students 613.

Portola Valley, San Mateo Co., Our Lady of the Wayside (1941). See St. Denis, Menlo Park.

Redwood City, San Mateo Co., Our Lady of Mount Carmel (1887), Revs. John P. Kavanaugh; Charito Suan; Deacon Paul Moriarty. In res., Rev. Msgr. William M. Roche; Rev. Msgr. Dominique Desjardins (Ottawa) (Retired).
Res., 347 Grand St., 94062. Tel: 415-366-3802; Fax: 415-366-1421.
Parish Center—300 Fulton St., 94062.
School—301 Grand St., 94062. Tel: 415-366-6127; Fax: 415-366-0902.
Lay Teachers 12; Students 298.

St. Matthias (1961), Rev. Msgr. James B. Flynn. In res., Rev. Thomas E. Lacey.
Res., 1685 Cordilleras Rd., 94062. Tel: 415-366-9544; Fax: 415-366-4817.
Catechesis/Religious Programs—St. Matthias Day Care Center, 533 Canyon Rd., 94062. Tel: 415-366-7085; 415-367-1320; Fax: 415-366-1049.
Students 82.

St. Pius (1951), Rev. Msgr. Peter G. Armstrong; Revs. William E. Brown; John P. Penebsky; Deacon Steve Michaelson. In res., Rev. Msgr. James J. Haggarty; Rev. Anthony Chung.
Res., 1100 Woodside Rd., 94061. Tel: 415-361-1411; Fax: 415-369-3641.
School—Tel: 415-368-8327; Fax: 415-368-7031. Rita Carroll, Prin.
Lay Teachers 13; Students 313.
Catechesis/Religious Programs—Tel: 415-368-0429. Joyce Wickstrom, D.R.E.
Students 255.

San Anselmo, Marin Co., St. Anselm (1907), Revs. Peter McDonald; Lawrence J. Finnegan; Deacon Bernard O'Halloran. In res., Revs. Dennis McManus; Richard Bain.
Res., Shady Ln. & Bolinas Ave., 94960. Tel: 415-453-2342; Fax: 415-453-8713.
School—40 Belle Ave., 94960. Tel: 415-454-8667; Fax: 415-454-4730. Marilyn Dineen, Prin.
Lay Teachers 17; Students 258.
Catechesis/Religious Programs—Tel: 415-457-5910. Tom Kavanaugh, D.R.E.
Students 186.

San Bruno, San Mateo Co., St. Bruno (1912), Rev. Ronald A. Burke; Deacon Joseph Lavulo.
Res., 555 San Bruno Ave. W., 94066. Tel: 415-588-2121; Fax: 415-588-6087.
Catechesis/Religious Programs—Tel: 415-588-4509. Mrs. Gloria Flores, D.R.E.
Students 310.

St. Robert (1958), Revs. Vincent D. Ring; James H. Morris; Deacon Rusty Duffey. In res., Rev. Joseph J. Marini.
Res., 1380 Crystal Springs Rd., 94066. Tel: 415-589-2800; Fax: 415-588-3628.
School—345 Oak Ave., 94066. Tel: 415-583-5065.
Lay Teachers 14; Students 326.
Catechesis/Religious Programs—Tel: 415-588-0477.
Students 436.

San Carlos, San Mateo Co., St. Charles (1928), Revs. John A. Ryan; Feliciano Mofan; Deacon Roy Twitty. In res., Rev. Francis Murray; Sr. Pat Hunter, Pastoral Assoc.
Res., 880 Tamarack Ave., 94070. Tel: 415-591-7349; Fax: 415-637-1968.
School—850 Tamarack Ave., 94070. Tel: 415-593-1629; Fax: 415-593-9723. Arlene Bertellotti, Prin.
Lay Teachers 17; Students 315.
Catechesis/Religious Programs—Joanne Thompson, D.R.E.
Students 660.

San Mateo, San Mateo Co.,

1—St. Bartholomew, (1955), Revs. Daniel T. Keohane; John P. Conley; Deacon John Sequeira. In res., Revs. William R. Lowery; George R. Meyer.
Res., 300 Alameda de las Pulgas, 94402. Tel: 415-347-0701; Fax: 415-347-2429.
Catechesis/Religious Programs—Tel: 415-348-3412; Fax: 415-347-3429. Karen Melko, D.R.E.
Students 388.

2—St. Gregory, (1941), Rev. Msgr Robert W. McElroy; Revs. Kevin J. Longworth, S.P.S.; Robert Cipriano; Deacon Fred Iskander. In res., Rev. Peter Karam.
Res., 140 28th Ave., 94403. Tel: 415-345-8506; Fax: 415-345-9329.
School—2701 Hacienda St., 94403. Tel: 415-573-0111; Fax: 415-573-6548. Patricia Teilh, Prin.
Lay Teachers 10; Students 304.
Catechesis/Religious Programs—Tel: 415-574-8716.
Students 317.

3—St. Matthew, (1863), Rev. Msgr. James P. McKay; Revs. William J. Ahlbach; Terence J. Horan; Aquino Padilla; Te Van Nguyen; Deacon Gerald Pera.
Res., One Notre Dame Ave., 94402. Tel: 415-344-7622; Fax: 415-344-4830.
School—901 S. El Camino Real, 94402. Tel: 415-343-1373; Fax: 415-343-2046. Mrs. Theresa Canizzaro, Prin.
Lay Teachers 22; Students 526.
Catechesis/Religious Programs—Tel: 415-344-7622.
Students 366.

4—St. Timothy, (1954), Revs. Kieran J. McCormick; Jorge del Real; Deacons Angel Aguilar; Nicolas Rodriguez. In res., Most Rev. Carlos A. Sevilla, S.J., D.D.
Res., 1515 Dolan Ave., 94401. Tel: 415-342-2468; Fax: 415-342-8156.
School—Tel: 415-342-6567; Fax: 415-342-5913. Mrs. Evelyn Nordberg, Prin.
Lay Teachers 9; Students 273
Catechesis/Religious Programs—Tel: 415-579-0901. Mrs. Irl Bolin, D.R.E.
Students 248.

San Rafael, Marin Co.,

1—Blessed Sacrament, (1951). Closed. For sacramental records please contact St. Isabella, San Rafael.

2—St. Isabella, (Terra Linda) (1961), Revs. Michael J. Keane; Jesus Parina; Rory Murphy. In res., Rev. William L. Knapp (Philippines); Deacon Jerry Friedman.
Res., 1 Trinity Way, P.O. Box 6166, 94903. Tel: 415-479-1560; Fax: 415-479-8303. [CEM]
School—P.O. Box 6188, 94903. Tel: 415-479-3727. Sr. Jeanne Marie, O.P., Prin.
Sisters 1; Lay Teachers 11; Students 277.
Catechesis/Religious Programs—Tel: 415-479-1222. Sharon Grant, D.R.E.
Students 530.

3—St. Raphael, (Terra Linda) (1817), Rev. Msgr. Richard S. Knapp; Revs. Rene Gomez; Joseph Hung; William L. Vaughan; Sr. Dianne Nixon, S.N.J.M., Pastoral Assoc.; Sr. Mary Helen Jathas, S.H.F.
Res., 1104 Fifth Ave., 94901. Tel: 415-454-8141; Fax: 415-454-8193.
School—1100 Fifth Ave., 94901. Tel: 415-454-4455. Sr. Anne Marie Mullin, O.P., Prin.
Sisters of the Third Order of St. Dominic, Congregation of the Most Holy Name 2; Lay Teachers 12; Students 240.
Station—San Quentin, State Prison.

4—St. Sylvester, (Terra Linda) (1961). Closed. For sacramental records please contact St. Raphael, San Rafael.

Sausalito, Marin Co., St. Mary Star of the Sea (1881), Rev. Paul J. Rossi. In res., Rev. Eugene F. Duggan.
Res., 180 Harrison Ave., 94965. Tel: 415-332-1765; Fax: 415-332-4962.

South San Francisco, San Mateo Co.,

1—All Souls, (1913), Revs. William J. Justice; Agustin M. Escalante; Deacon Alex Aragon; Sr. Martha Vega, S.S.S., Pastoral Assoc. In res., Rev. Randolph R. Calvo, J.C.D.
Res., 315 Walnut Ave., 94080. Tel: 415-871-8944; Fax: 415-871-5806.
School—479 Miller Ave., 94080. Tel: 415-583-3562; Fax: 415-952-1167. Eileen Gorman, Prin.
Priests 2; Lay Teachers 13; Students 330.
Catechesis/Religious Programs—Tel: 415-573-5356. Maureen Galeotti, D.R.E.
Students 612.

2—Mater Dolorosa, (1961), Revs. Hugh O'Donnell; Eduardo Dura. In res., Rev. Stephen A. Meriwether.
Res., 307 Willow Ave., 94080. Tel: 415-583-4131; Fax: 415-761-2232.
School—1040 Miller Ave., 94080. Tel: 415-588-8175. William Kovacich, Prin.
Sisters 1; Lay Teachers 10; Students 251.
Catechesis/Religious Programs—Tel: 415-589-4448. Sr. Bernard Joseph, P.B.V.M., D.R.E.
Students 152.

3—St. Augustine, (1970), Revs. Eugene D. Tungol; Domingo B. Orimaco; Felix S. Namocatcat; Deacons Robert Bertolani; Frank Almeida.
Res., 3700 Callan Blvd., 94080. Tel: 415-873-2282; Fax: 415-873-1356.
Catechesis/Religious Programs—Tel: 415-873-2878. Sr. Nona Barairo, D.R.E.
Students 566.

4—St. Veronica, (1951), Revs. Wilton S. Smith; Edward Ludeman; Deacon Roger Beaudry. In res., Revs. Patrick P. McCarthy; Richard Kalkman.
Res., 434 Alida Way, 94080. Tel: 415-588-1455; Fax: 415-588-1481.
School—Tel: 415-589-3909; Fax: 415-589-2826. Joan Coleman, Prin.
Lay Teachers 13; Students 334.

Tiburon, Marin Co., St. Hilary (1951), Rev. Msgr. Francis A. Lacey, P.A.; Rev. Msgr. Robert J. Plocki; Deacon Russell H. Holm.
Res., 761 Hilary Dr., 94920-1498. Tel: 415-435-1122; Fax: 415-435-1862.
School—765 Hilary Dr., 94920. Tel: 415-435-2224; Fax: 415-435-5895. Mrs. Marilyn Lynch, Prin.
Lay Teachers 23; Students 292.
Catechesis/Religious Programs—Tel: 415-435-1639. Elsie Peregrin, D.R.E.
Students 175.

Tomales, Marin Co., Church of the Assumption (1860), Rev. Robert K. White.
Res., 26825 Shoreline Hwy., P.O. Box 82, 94971-0082. Tel: 707-878-2208; Fax: 707-878-2208. [CEM]
Mission—Marshall, Marin Co., St. Helen, (1902) P.O. Box 82, 94971-0082.

Woodside, San Mateo Co., St. Marcella Mission. Closed. For sacramental records please contact St. Denis, Menlo Park.

Chaplains of Public Institutions

San Francisco. *County Jail, Redwood City*. Deacon Paul Moriarty, St. Vincent De Paul Prison Chap.
Kaiser Hospital Redwood City. Revs. Francis Murray; Anthony Chung.
Kaiser Hospital San Francisco. Rev. Steven E. Davies.
Knights of Malta. The Sovereign Military Order of Malta (Western U.S.A. Association of the Sovereign Military Hospitaller Order of St. John of Jerusalem of Rhodes and of Malta—a Nonprofit Corporation). Revs. Egon Javor, O.S.B.; John P. Kavanaugh; Milton T. Walsh.
Laguna Honda Home. Rev. Timothy Enright, C.S.Sp.
Laguna Honda Home. Deacon Pete Palimiano.
St. Mary's Medical Center. Revs. Richard A. Lopez, Contact; Edward K. Murray.
St. Thomas More Society. (Lawyers). Rev. William Duggan.
San Francisco Fire Department. Rev. John L. Greene.
San Francisco General Hospital. Revs. Edmund M. Shipp; George Mullonkal, M.C.B.S.
San Francisco Police Department. Rev. Msgr. John P. Heaney; Rev. Thomas Daly.
Sequoia Hospital. Revs. Francis Murray; Anthony Chung.
Serra Club of San Francisco (Downtown). Rev. Joseph Bradley.
Serra Club of San Francisco (Golden Gate). Rev. Msgr. Edward P. McTaggart.
Sheriff's Honor Camp and Medium Security Facility. Served by St. Vincent de Paul volunteers, Redwood City.
Young Ladies' Institute. Rev. Edward McTaggart, Moderator-ACCW.
Youth Guidance Center. Rev. Daniel E. Carter.

Marin. *Serra Club of Marin*. Rev. Msgr. Thomas I. Kennedy.

Novato. *Serra Club of Marin*. Rev. Piers M. Lahey.

San Mateo. *Serra Club of El Camino Real*. Rev. James J. Ward.
Serra Club of San Mateo. Rev. Msgr. James O. McKay.
Seton Medical Center. Deacon Richard J. Olsen.
Sheriff's Honor Camp and Medium Security Facility. Served by St. Vincent de Paul volunteers, Redwood City.

San Quentin. *California State Prison*. Rev. Denis McManus, C.S.Sp.

Special Assignment:
Reverend Monsignors—
Heaney, John P., San Francisco Police Department Chaplain
Holleran, J. Warren, St. Patrick Seminary
McElroy, Robert W., Vicar for Admin.
Wang, Ignatius, Dir. Propagation of the Faith
Reverend Fathers—
Bain, Richard, Dir. Healing Ministry
Bonsor, Jack, St. Patrick's Seminary
Bradley, Joseph, Vocations
Brennan, Bernard, Chap. Ft. Mason
Calvo, Randolph R., Judicial Vicar, Metropolitan Tribunal, San Francisco
Chung, Anthony, Chap., Kaiser and Sequoia Hospitals, Redwood City
Daly, Thomas A., Marin Catholic High School
Davies, Steven E., Chap., Kaiser Hospital
Duggan, William, Metropolitan Tribunal

Foley, Jerome, Vocations, San Francisco State University
Ghiorso, David A., Catholic Youth Organization
Haberman, Robert, Dominican College
Howell, Stephen H., Junipero Serra High School
Ingels, Gregory, Chancellor pro-tempore
Madden, Thomas, Vallombrosa Center
McCain, William, Studies, North American College, Rome
Meriwether, Stephen A., Metropolitan Tribunal, San Francisco
Merson, Thomas S., Admin. Asst. to the Archbishop
Murray, Edward, St. Mary's Hospital
Murray, Francis, Kaiser and Sequoia Hospitals, Redwood City
Nguyen, Trong Duc, Coord., Vietnamese Ministry
O'Connell, William A., Priest Personnel
O'Rourke, P. Gerard, Ecumenical & Interreligious Affairs
Padazinski, C. Michael, Studies, North American College, Rome
Pettingill, David M., Office of Parish Life
Reilly, John J., Asst. Dir., Archives
Riley, Miles O'Brien, Communications
Sanchez, Joseph, Chap. St. Anne's Home
Schipper, Carl A., St. Patrick's Seminary
Schlitt, Harry G., Archdiocesan Dir. of Stewardship
Smith, Raymond K., Silver Penny Farm
Talesfore, John, Studies
Tarantino, James T., Marin Catholic High School
Trainor, Henry, Archives
Walsh, Joseph, Dir., Clergy Education
Worner, William, Serra Clergy House

On Duty Outside the Archdiocese:
Reverend Fathers—
Coleman, John, VA Hospital, Palo Alto
Fredericks, James L., Loyola-Marymount, Los Angeles
Hagan, James, Mexico
Jocson, Salvador, Portugal
Kaylor, Lee
McElligott, Thomas J., Berkeley
Ochylski, Ronald S., Society of St. Sulpice
Richard, Joseph E., Diocese of Reno
Smith, Raymond K., Silver Penny Farm, Petaluma

Military Chaplains:
Reverend Fathers—
Brennan, Bernard, Fort Mason

Absent on Leave:
Reverend Monsignors—
O'Shea, Patrick J.
Reverend Fathers—
Ervin, Thomas
Hoenisch, Richard
Keegan, A. Peter
Leach, Jerome
Young, William

Retired:
Reverend Monsignors—
Cahill, Daniel R.
Fitzpatrick, Joseph A.
Foudy, John T.
Gallagher, Eugene A.
Heuring, Alvan P. (DUB)
Keane, James P.
Kennedy, Edwin J.
Kennedy, Thomas I.
Kenny, John J.
Murphy, John J.
Plocki, Robert
Reverend Fathers—
Armas, James
Atkins, James
Bitangjol, Albert P.
Burns, Thomas J.
Chang, Simeon
Cleary, Edward M.
Decker, Raymond G.
Duggan, Eugene F.
Duggan, Paul E.
Flanagan, William J.
Foudy, Denis D.
Gluszek, W. Adalbert
Greenlaw, Martin F.
Jaszovsky, Joseph
Keane, Patrick J.
Knapp, William L.
Lacey, Thomas E.
Lee, Joseph Chun Yuan
Lowery, William R.
Marini, Joseph J.
McCaffrey, James L.
McCarthy, Patrick P.
McDonnell, Donald C.
Meyer, George R.
Mihovilovich, John B.
O'Malley, James E.
O'Reilly, Joseph P.
Ojeda, Filemon G.
Perlite, Paul A.
Pyne, Donald E.
Raimondi, Michele
Robello, Louis J.
Rodriguez, Guillermo
Thomas, George L.
Uglesic, Leopold
Walsh, David I.
Ward, John J.
Worner, William H.
Zoph, John L.

Permanent Deacons:
Aguilar, Angel, St. Timothy, San Mateo
Allen, Charles, St. Teresa, San Francisco
Almeida, Frank, St. Augustine, South San Francisco
Amora, Felix, St. Andrew, Daly City
Aragon, Alex, All Souls, South San Francisco
Beaudry, Roger, St. Veronica, South San Francisco
Bertolani, Robert, St. Augustine, South San Francisco
Borg, Joseph, St. Mary Cathedral, San Francisco
Brumbaugh, Joseph, St. Anthony of Padua, Novato
Buenavista, Tom, St. Patrick, San Francisco
Capati, Bill, St. Patrick, San Francisco
Cervantes, Vicente, Mission Dolores, San Francisco
Dixon, Louis, St. Francis of Assisi, East Palo Alto
Duffey, Rusty, St. Robert, San Bruno
Dupre, John, St. Anne, San Francisco
Friedman, Jerome, Nazareth House/St. Isabella, San Rafael
Gamarra, David, St. Peter, San Francisco
Hackett, Steven, Immaculate Heart of Mary, Belmont
Hall, J. Bruce (NEW), Our Lady of Mt. Carmel, Mill Valley
Hernandez, Roger, St. Peter, San Francisco
Holm, Russell, (Retired)
Hutzler, John, St. Emydius, San Francisco
Ilao, Thomas, Corpus Christi, San Francisco
Iskander, Fred, St. Gregory, San Mateo
Jacquemet, Henry, Immaculate Heart of Mary, Belmont
Jee, John, Sabbatical, San Francisco
Kehrlein, Peter, St. Rita, Fairfax
Kortenkamp, Leon, Dir., Permanent Diaconate
Lavulo, Joseph, St. Bruno, San Bruno
McGhee, John, Our Lady of Refuge, La Honda
Michaelson, Steven, St. Pius, Redwood City
Mitchell, William, Archdiocesan Communications Office, San Francisco
Moriarty, Paul K. (RIC), St. Vincent de Paul, San Francisco; Detention Ministry, San Mateo County
O'Halloran, Bernard, St. Anselm, San Anselmo
Ocon, Manuel, Epiphany, San Francisco
Olsen, Richard (SEA), Seton Medical Center
Pelimiano, Pete, Good Shepherd, Pacifica
Pera, Gerald, St. Matthew, San Mateo
Prudenciado, Lernito, Holy Angels, Colma
Rivera, Dennis, Holy Name of Jesus, San Francisco
Rodriguez, Nicolas, St. Timothy, San Mateo
Rosen, Dan, St. Kevin, San Francisco
Ruiz, Juan, Holy Angels, Colma
Sequeira, John, St. Bartholomew, San Mateo
Solan, Peter, St. Peter, Pacifica
Solano, Jose, St. Anthony of Padua, Menlo Park
Soo, Felix, (Retired)
Swanson, Fred, St. Dominic, San Francisco
Tano, Mar, St. Luke, Foster City
Twitty, Roy, St. Charles, San Carlos
Viray, Ricardo, Epiphany, San Francisco
West, Gary, St. Stephen, San Francisco

INSTITUTIONS LOCATED IN THE ARCHDIOCESE

[A] SEMINARIES, ARCHDIOCESAN

MENLO PARK. *St. Patrick Seminary* (1889), 320 Middlefield Rd., 94025. Tel: 415-325-5621; 321-5655 (Library); Fax: 415-322-0997. Major Seminary of the Archdiocese of San Francisco, under the direction of the Society of St. Sulpice. Legal Title: *(1891, 1944): The Roman Catholic Seminary of San Francisco.* Most Rev. William J. Levada, Chancellor; Revs. Gerald D. Coleman, S.S., Ph.D., Pres. & Rector; Ronald D. Witherup, S.S., Ph.D., Academic Dean & Vice Rector; Jack Bonsor, Ph.D., Dean of Students; Sr. Dorothea M. Ross, C.S.J., Dir. Field Educ.; Dr. Cecil White, Ph.D., Librarian; Rev. John F. Mattingly, S.S., M.S.L.S., Emeritus Dir. Library & Liaison to Alumni; Ms. Dorothy Tully, D.A., Registrar.

Faculty in Residence: Revs. Jack Bonsor, Ph.D.; Gerald D. Coleman, S.S., Ph.D.; Frederick J. Cwiekowski, S.S., S.T.D.; Robert V. Gavin, S.S.; John F. Mattingly, S.S., M.S.L.S.; Frank B. Norris, S.S., S.T.D.; James P. Oberle, S.S., Ph.D., Dir. Spiritual Life Prog.; Ronald D. Witherup, S.S., Ph.D.; Rev. Msgr. J. Warren Holleran, S.T.D.; Rev. Carl A. Schipper, Ph.D., Dir. of Pastoral Yr. Priests 9; Religious 2; Lay Teachers 2; Students 51.

[B] SEMINARIES, RELIGIOUS OR SCHOLASTICATES

SAN FRANCISCO. *Capuchi House of Studies,* San Buenavista Friary, 750 Anza St., 94118. Tel: 415-387-7005. Revs. Enda Heffernan, O.F.M.Cap., Guardian; Donal Burke, Sabbatical; Dale Trunk, CPE Student; Alan Wilson, O.F.M.Cap., Hospital Chap.; Bros. Mark Mance, O.F.M.Cap., Prov. Sec. & Treas.; Mark Ortega, Instructor. Priests 4; Brothers 2.

Marianist Seminary, 175 Phelan Ave., 94112. Tel: 415-239-0841; Fax: 415-239-0848. Rev. John McEnhill, S.M., Rector. Priests 1; Brothers 4.

St. Peter Chanel Seminary, College Division, 625 Pine St., 94108. Tel: 415-398-3543. Very Rev. John F. McGregor, S.M., Prov. & Supr.; Bro. Patrick Souza, S.M., Admin. In res., Revs. James L. Pratt, S.M.; Patrick Coyle, S.M.; Francis Springer, S.M.; Bro. John Hunt, S.M.

[C] COLLEGES AND UNIVERSITIES

*SAN FRANCISCO. *University of San Francisco,* 2130 Fulton St., 94117-1080. Tel: 415-422-5555; Fax: 415-422-2303.
For a complete listing, refer to the Colleges and Universities section.

BELMONT. *College of Notre Dame,* 1500 Ralston Ave., 94002. Tel: 415-593-1601; Fax: 415-637-0493.
For a complete listing, refer to the Colleges and Universities section.

SAN RAFAEL. *Dominican College,* 50 Acacia Ave., 94901-2298. Tel: 415-457-4440; Fax: 415-485-3205.
For a complete listing, refer to the Colleges and Universities section.

[D] HIGH SCHOOLS, ARCHDIOCESAN

SAN FRANCISCO. *Archbishop Riordan High School (Boys),* 175 Phelan Ave., 94112. Tel: 415-586-8200. Rev. Timothy M. Kenney, S.M., Prin. Priests 1; Brothers 10; Lay Teachers 39; Students 700.

Sacred Heart Cathedral Preparatory (Coed), 1055 Ellis St., 94109. Tel: 415-775-6626. Bro. Christopher Brady, F.S.C., Prin. Brothers 7; Sisters 3; Lay Teachers 78; Students 1,190.

KENTFIELD. *Marin Catholic College Preparatory (Coed),* 675 Sir Francis Drake Blvd., 94904. Tel: 415-461-8844; Fax: 415-461-7161. Mr. William G. Isetta, Prin.; Revs. James T. Tarantino, Pres.; Thomas A. Daly, Chap. In res., Rev. John J. Ward, (Retired). Priests 2; Dominican Sisters of San Rafael 3; Lay Teachers 48; Students 680.

SAN MATEO. *Junipero Serra High School (Boys),* 451 W. 20th Ave., 94403-1385. Tel: 415-345-8207; Fax: 415-573-6638. Rev. Stephen H. Howell, Pres.; Mr. C. Michael Peterson, Prin.; Rev. John L. Zoph. Priests 2; Sisters 1; Lay Teachers 47; Students 877.

[E] HIGH SCHOOLS, PRIVATE

SAN FRANCISCO. *Convent of the Sacred Heart, High School (Girls),* 2222 Broadway, 94115. Tel: 415-563-2900. Religious of the Sacred Heart. Dr. Mary Magnano Smith, Dir.; Mr. Douglas Grant, Prin. Religious 1; Lay Teachers 27; Students 196.

Immaculate Conception Academy, (Girls), 3625 24th St., 94110. Tel: 415-824-2052. Sr. Mary Catherine Antczak, O.P., Prin. Sisters 5; Lay Teachers 27; Students 295.

Mercy High School (Girls), 3250 19th Ave., 94132. Tel: 415-334-0525. Ms. Dorothy McCrea, Prin. Sisters 6; Lay Teachers 39; Students 525.

St. Ignatius College Preparatory (Coed), 2001 37th Ave., 94116. Tel: 415-731-7500; Fax: 415-731-9704. Revs. Mark F. Toohey, S.J., Rector; Anthony P. Sauer, S.J., Pres.; Samuel Bellino, S.J.; Paul F. Capitolo, S.J.; Harry V. Carlin, S.J., Exec. Vice Pres.; Edward S. Fassett, S.J.; A. Francis Frugoli, S.J.; Gregory M. Goethals, S.J.; Charles A. Hoffman, S.J.; Gerald F. Hudson, S.J.; Michael J. Kotlanger, S.J.; Steven C. Nejasmich, S.J., Prin.; David J. Robinson, S.J.; Warren J. Wright, S.J. Priests 14; Scholastics 4; Brothers 6; Lay Teachers 90; Students 1,472.

ATHERTON. *Sacred Heart Preparatory (Convent of the Sacred Heart)(Girls),* 94027. Tel: 415-322-1866. Religious of the Sacred Heart. Mr. Milton Werner, Ed.D., Dir. Sacred Heart Schools; Mr. Richard Dioli, Prin. Religious 2; Lay Teachers 56; Students 375.

BELMONT. *Notre Dame High School (Girls),* 1540 Ralston Ave., 94002. Tel: 415-595-1913; Fax: 415-595-2116. Ms. Rita Gleason, Prin. Lay Teachers 42; Students 568.

BURLINGAME. *Mercy High School (Girls)*, 2750 Adeline Dr., 94010-5597. Tel: 415-343-3631. Sr. Rosann Fraher, R.S.M., Prin. Sisters 4; Lay Teachers 35; Students 376.

PORTOLA VALLEY. *Woodside Priory School (Coed)*, 302 Portola Rd., 94028. Tel: 415-851-8221. Dr. Frank Cody, Headmaster. Priests 4; Brothers 1; Lay Teachers 37; Students 250. Legal Title: *Benedictine Fathers of the Priory, Inc.*

SAN ANSELMO. *San Domenico School*. (Grades 1-8, Coed; Grades 9-12, Girls. Boarding and Day Students.), 1500 Butterfield Rd., 94960-1099. Tel: 415-454-0200; Fax: 415-454-6604. Sr. Gervaise Valpey, O.P., Head of School; John Bowermaster, Upper School Prin. Chaplains 1; Lay Teachers 22; Students 131.

[F] ELEMENTARY SCHOOLS, ARCHDIOCESAN

SAN FRANCISCO. *St. Brigid Elementary School*. (Grades K-8), 2250 Franklin St., 94109. Tel: 415-673-4523. Sr. Encarnacion Ortega, R.C.M., Prin. Sisters 5; Lay Teachers 7; Students 317.

St. Thomas More School. (Grades K-8), 50 St. Thomas More Way, 94132. Tel: 415-337-0100. Joseph T. Elsbernd, Prin. Lay Teachers 10; Students 330.

[G] ELEMENTARY SCHOOLS, PRIVATE

SAN FRANCISCO. *Schools of the Sacred Heart, Convent of the Sacred Heart Elementary School*. (Grades K-8), 2222 Broadway, 94115. Tel: 415-563-2900. Dr. Mary Magnano Smith, Dir.; Pamela Hayes, Interim Prin. Lay Teachers 33; Students 312.

Schools of the Sacred Heart, Stuart Hall For Boys. (Grades K-8), 2222 Broadway, 94115. Tel: 415-563-2900. Schools of the Sacred Heart. Dr. Mary Magnano Smith, Dir.; Mr. Thomas G. Lengel, Headmaster. Sisters 1; Lay Teachers 22; Students 312.

ATHERTON. *St. Joseph's School*. (Grades PreK-8), 50 Emilie Ave., 94027. Tel: 415-322-9931. Dr. Milton Werner, Dir.; Mr. John Miller, Prin. Sisters 2; Lay Teachers 61; Students 512.

BELMONT. *C.N.D. Early Learning Center*. (Preschool), 1500 Ralston Rd., 94002. Tel: 415-508-3519. Sisters of Notre Dame de Namur. Mrs. Mary O'Keeffe, Dir. Lay Teachers 9; Children 72.

Notre Dame Elementary School, 1500 Ralston Ave., 94002. Tel: 415-591-2209. Sr. Dolores Quigg, S.N.D-.deN., Prin. Sisters 5; Lay Teachers 21; Students 260.

SAN ANSELMO. *San Domenico Early Ed., Lower and Middle School*, 1500 Butterfield Rd., 94960-1099. Tel: 415-454-0200; Fax: 415-454-6604. Sr. Gervaise Valpey, O.P., Head of School; Mathew Heersche, Middle School Prin. (Grades 6-8); Carole Chase, Lower School Prin. (Grades 1-5); Carole Chase, Early Education Prin. (PreK-K). Sisters 2; Chaplains 1; Lay Teachers (Middle and Lower School) 18; (Early Education) 15; Students 578.

[H] ST. VINCENT DE PAUL SOCIETY

SAN FRANCISCO. *Society of St. Vincent de Paul Archdiocesan Council*, 1825 Mission St., 94103. Tel: 415-621-5305; Fax: 415-340-9210. Deborah Payne, Pres. E-mail: vincent@vincent.org

San Francisco District Council of the St. Vincent de Paul Society, 425 Fourth St., 94107. Tel: 415-977-1270; Fax: 415-977-1271. Jack Noonan, Pres.

Thrift Stores:

425 Fourth St., 94107. Tel: 415-908-0250 (For information or pick-up).

1519 Haight St., 94117. Tel: 415-863-3615. 1529 Haight St., 94117. 186 W. Portal Ave., 94127. Tel: 415-664-7119. 5424 Geary Blvd., 94121. Tel: 415-666-0299.

Thrift Store Pickups. Tel: 888-637-7837.

Vehicle Donations. Tel: 1-800-YES-SVDP.

Vehicle Sales. Tel: 415-908-0250.

Vincentian Villa, 1825 Mission St., 94103. Tel: 415-621-5305. Housing project for fixed income seniors and handicapped. Capacity 124.

Arlington Residence, 480 Ellis St., 94102. Tel: 415-673-9600. A safe and sober residential, low cost hotel for men and women in recovery. Rooms 172.

Ozanam Center, 1175 Howard St., 94103. Tel: 415-864-3057. Detox and counseling services for drop-in clients and 3-day stay.

Reception Center. Tel: 415-621-6471; 621-6427.

Rosalie House, 3543 18th St. #4, 94110. Tel: 415-255-2754. An eight week emergency shelter for victims of domestic violence. Beds 20.

San Francisco Vincentian Life, 425 Fourth St., 94107. Tel: 415-977-1270. Supports and develops membership of the Society through parish conferences and involvement in the programs.

South of Market Multi-Service Center, 525 Fifth St., 94103. Tel: 415-597-7970. A 24-hour shelter for homeless men, offering social, physical and counseling services. Beds 200.

Brennan House. Tel: 415-255-2894; 255-0165 (Crisis Hotline). Transitional housing program for the survivors of domestic violence. Program provides in-depth counseling, job rehabilitation, education, children's programs, and support groups. Beds 15.

Riley Center Community Office, 2543 18th St., #4, 94110. Tel: 415-552-2943. Provides drop-in counseling and follow up services for survivors of domestic abuse. Community outreach available.

San Francisco Vincentian Desk, 425 Fourth St., 94107. Tel: 415-908-0250. Sr. Mary Loretta, Contact. Homeless help desk operated out of the San Francisco store.

SAN MATEO. *San Mateo County District Council*. Main Office, St. Vincent de Paul Society. 50 N. B St., 94401. Tel: 415-343-4405; Fax: 415-343-9495. Joe Marchetti, Pres.; Lorraine Moriary, Exec. Dir.

Thrift Stores:

831 Main St., Redwood City, 94062. Tel: 415-366-6367.

113 S. B St., 94401. Tel: 415-347-5101.

344 Grand Ave., South San Francisco, 94080. Tel: 415-589-8445.

6298 Mission St., Daly City, 94014. Tel: 415-871-6844.

2406 El Camino Real, Redwood City, 94063. Tel: 415-369-5898.

Thrift Store Pickups:

South San Francisco. Tel: 415-871-6844.

Tel: 415-342-1860.

Redwood City. Tel: 415-369-2837.

Vehicle Sales. Tel: 415-593-8447.

St. Vincent de Paul Dining Room at St. Francis of Assisi Church. Monday evenings 5-6:30pm, 1425 Bay Rd., East Palo Alto, 94303. Tel: 415-322-2152; Fax: 415-322-7319.

San Mateo Vincentian Life, 50 N. B St., 94401. Tel: 415-343-4403.

Services for the Incarcerated - Hope in Action Ministry, 50 N. B St., 94401. Tel: 415-330-8937. Deacon Paul Moriarty, Chap.

Homeless Services:

Central County. M-F, 10am-12noon, 50 N. B St., 94401. Tel: 415-343-4403.

North County. M-F, 10am-12noon, 344 Grand Ave., South San Francisco, 94080. Tel: 415-589-9039.

South County. M-F, 1:00pm-2:00pm, 2600 Middlefield Rd., Redwood City, 94063. Tel: 415-780-7260; Fax: 415-780-7217.

SAN RAFAEL. *St. Vincent de Paul Society Marin County District Council*, 820 B St., P.O. Box 150527, 94915. Tel: 1-800-637-7837 (For Pick-up Service); Fax: 415-454-3406. Seamus Kilty, Pres. Tel: 415-454-3303.

St. Vincent de Paul Dining Room, 820 B St., 94901-3003. Tel: 415-454-3366.

Marin County Vincentian Life, 820 B. St., 94915. Tel: 415-454-3303.

[I] DAY NURSERIES

SAN FRANCISCO. *Holy Family Day Home*, 299 Dolores St., 94103. Tel: 415-861-5361; Fax: 415-398-1925. Legal Title: *Holy Family Day Home, Inc.* Sr. Ann Maureen Murphy, S.H.F., Dir. Religious 2; Lay Staff 23; Capacity 100.

[J] GENERAL HOSPITALS

SAN FRANCISCO. *St. Mary's Medical Center*, 450 Stanyan St., 94117. Tel: 415-668-1000.

For a complete listing, refer to the Hospitals section.

DALY CITY. *Seton Medical Center*, 1900 Sullivan Ave., 94015. Tel: 415-992-4000.

For a complete listing, refer to the Hospitals section.

MOSS BEACH. *Seton Medical Center Coastside*, 600 Marine Blvd., 94038. Tel: 415-728-5521.

For a complete listing, refer to the Hospitals section.

[K] SENIOR CITIZEN RESIDENCES

SAN FRANCISCO. *Alexis Apartments of St. Patrick's Parish*, 390 Clementina St., 94103.

For a complete listing, refer to the Special Care Facilities section.

Home for the Aged of the Little Sisters of the Poor, St. Anne's Home, 300 Lake St., 94118. Tel: 415-751-6510; Fax: 415-751-0650.

For a complete listing, refer to the Special Care Facilities section.

Madonna Residence, 1055 Pine St., 94109. Tel: 415-928-0743.

For a complete listing, refer to the Special Care Facilities section.

Mercy Terrace Corporation Apartments, 333 Baker St., 94117. Tel: 415-931-2325.

For a complete listing, refer to the Special Care Facilities section.

SAN RAFAEL. *Nazareth House*, 245 Nova Albion Way, 94903. Tel: 415-479-8282.

For a complete listing, refer to the Special Care Facilities section.

[L] RESIDENTIAL GROUP HOMES

SAN FRANCISCO. *The Good Shepherd Gracenter*, 1310 Bacon St., 94134. Tel: 415-586-2822.

For a complete listing, refer to the Special Care Facilities section.

Mount St. Joseph-St. Elizabeth, (1976) 100 Masonic Ave., 94118. Tel: 415-567-8370; Fax: 415-292-5531.

For a complete listing, refer to the Special Care Facilities section.

[M] RETREAT HOUSES

BURLINGAME. *Mercy Center, Spirituality and Conference Center*, 2300 Adeline Dr., 94010. Tel: 415-340-7474; Fax: 415-340-1299. Brenda Aiken, Dir.; Michael Lane, Mgr. of Conference Services; Sue Thourson, Reservation Coord. Staff 21; Overnight capacity 93; Daytime use 300.

MENLO PARK. *Vallombrosa Center* (1946), 250 Oak Grove Ave., 94025. Tel: 415-325-5614. Rev. J. Thomas Madden, Live-in Dir. Legal Title: *Vallombrosa Center, Conference and Retreat Center of the Archdiocese of San Francisco.*

PETALUMA. *Silver Penny Farm Retreat Center*, 5215 Old Lakeville Rd., No. 1, 94954. Tel: 707-762-1498. Rev. Raymond K. Smith, Dir.

REDWOOD CITY. *Mount Alverno Conference and Retreat Center*, 3910 Bret Harte Dr., Box 1028, 94064. Tel: 415-369-0798.

SAN RAFAEL. *Santa Sabina Center*, 25 Magnolia, 94901. Tel: 415-457-7727; Fax: 415-457-2310. Sr. Susannah Malarkey, O.P., Dir. Dominican Sisters Retreat and Conference Center.

[N] MONASTERIES AND RESIDENCES OF PRIESTS AND BROTHERS

SAN FRANCISCO. *Jesuit Community at St. Ignatius College Preparatory*, 2001 37th Ave., 94116-1165. Tel: 415-731-7500; Fax: 415-731-9408. Revs. Mark F. Toohey, S.J.; Samuel P. Bellino, S.J.; Paul F. Capitolo; Harry V. Carlin; Edward S. Fassett; A. Francis Frugoli; Gregory M. Goethals; Rev. Charles A. Hofmann, S.J.; Revs. Gerald F. Hudson; Michael J. Kotlanger; Stephen C. Nejasmich; David J. Robinson; Anthony P. Sauer; Warren J. Wright; Bros. Douglas E. Draper; Louis A. Bueler; Thomas J. Koller; Arthur W. Lee; John E. Maloney; Daniel J. Peterson. Priests 14; Brothers 6; Scholastics 4.

Jesuit Community at University of San Francisco. (Corporate Title: Jesuit Community at University of San Francisco), 650 Parker Ave., 94118-4267. Tel: 415-422-4200; Fax: 415-387-1867. Revs. Edward V. Stackpoole, S.J., Rector; Robert L. McDevitt, S.J., Min.; Joseph T. Angilella, S.J.; Steven A. Armstrong, S.J.; Cameron Ayers, S.J.; Paul J. Bernadicou, S.J.; Cornelius M. Buckley, S.J.; Francis J. Buckley, S.J.; Albert Chan, S.J. (Hong Kong); John W. Clark, S.J.; Denis E. Collins, S.J.; Albert C. Corcoran, S.J.; Robert F. Curran, S.J.; Geoffrey R. Dillon, S.J. (NO); Charles W. Dullea, S.J.; Joseph D. Fessio, S.J.; James J. Fleming, S.J. (NEN); Charles R. Gagan, S.J.; Albert A. Grosskopf, S.J.; Richard A. Hill, S.J.; Pierre P. Jacobs, S.J.; R. Daniel Kendall, S.J.; George V. Kennard, S.J.; Francis E. King, S.J.; John J. LoSchiavo, S.J.; Thomas M. Lucas, S.J.; Andrew F. Maginnis, S.J.; Edward J. Malatesta, S.J.; Robert L. Maloney, S.J.; John H. Martin, S.J.; Robert B. Mathewson, S.J.; Edwin J. McDermott, S.J.; Everett J. Mibach, S.J.; Cornelius J. Monacell, S.J.; Robert L. Niehoff, S.J. (ORE); Richard E. Mulcahy, S.J.; Stephen Olivo, S.J.; Daniel A. O'Sullivan, S.J.; Thomas G. Piquado, S.J.; Robert B. Plushkell, S.J.; Thomas J. Powers, S.J.; Luis H. Quihuis, S.J.; Thomas A. Reed, S.J.; William O. Richardson, S.J.; David C. Robinson, S.J.; Vernon J. Ruland, S.J.; Donald B. Sharp, S.J.; John P. Schlegel, S.J.; Alden J. Stevenson, S.J.; Theodore T. Taheny, S.J.; Peter J. Togni, S.J.; George M. Twigg-Porter, S.J.; Eugene R. Zimmers, S.J.; Michael J. Zimmers, S.J.; Bros. John F. Graham, S.J.; John Keck, S.J. Priests 55; Brothers 2.

Marianist Community, 175 Phelan Ave., 94112. Tel: 415-586-8181. Bro. Thomas Redmond, S.M., Supr.; Revs. Lawrence Doersching, S.M.; Timothy Kenney, S.M.; Joseph Lackner, S.M.; John McEnhill, S.M.; Bros. Thomas Deasy, S.M.; Paul Fennelly, S.M.; Thomas French, S.M.; Thomas Jalbert, S.M.; Timothy Kim, S.M.; James Leaghy, S.M.; Patrick McMahon, S.M.; Richard Olsen, S.M.; Kevin Thomas, S.M.; John Thompson, S.M. Priests 4; Brothers 11.

Maryknoll Fathers and Brothers, Catholic Foreign Mission Society of America, Inc., 2555 Webster St., 94115. Tel: 415-921-1100. Revs. Gerald J. Nagle, M.M., Dir.; Joseph J. Donovan, M.M.; Arthur H. Wille, M.M.; Bro. James J. Fahy, M.M. Priests 5; Brothers 1.

Casa Maryknoll, 453 Miller Ave., South San Francisco, 94080. Tel: 415-952-5500. Revs. Manuel J. Mejia, M.M., Co-Dir.; Juan M. Zuniga, M.M., Co-Dir.

Paris Foreign Mission Society Residence, 930 Ashbury St., 94117. Tel: 415-664-6747. Revs. Jacques R. Didier, M.E.P., Dir.; Maurice J. Duhart, M.E.P. Priests 2.

Provincial Residence. San Francisco Province of the Society of Mary (Marist Fathers), 625 Pine St., 94108. Tel: 415-398-3543; Fax: 415-781-4937. Very Rev. John F. McGregor, S.M., Prov. & Supr.; Revs. James L. Pratt, S.M.; Patrick J. Coyle, S.M.; Francis Springer, S.M.; Bros. Patrick Souza, S.M.; John Hunt, S.M. Priests 24; Deacons 1; Brothers 6; Scholastics 3.

St. Dominic Priory, 2390 Bush St., 94115. Tel: 415-567-7824; Fax: 415-567-1608. Very Rev. Reginald E. Martin, O.P., Prior; Revs. Gregory H. Anderson, O.P.; Felix F. Cassidy, O.P.; Timothy Conlan, O.P.; Roberto Corral, O.P.; Thomas J. Hayes, O.P.; John J. Klaia, O.P.; Xavier Lavagetto, O.P.; Samuel R. Parsons, O.P.; Terrence J. Reilly, O.P.; Joseph P. Sanguinetti, O.P.; Paul Conner, O.P.; Salvatore Di-Nardo, O.P.; Brian T. Mullady, O.P.; Bros. Mark A. Gorski, O.P.; Xavier Lavagetto, O.P.; Gregory R. Lira, O.P.; Peter A. Yost, O.P. In res., Rev. James S. Jenner, O.P. Priests 14; Brothers 3.

Salesian Provincial Residence, 1100 Franklin St., 94109. Tel: 415-441-7144; Fax: 415-563-5394. Revs. William Schafer, S.D.B., Prov.; Mario Mich, S.D.B., Dir.; Bro. Joseph R. Lockwood, S.D.B., Prov. Treas.; Revs. Gael Sullivan, Vice Dir.; Roger Luna, S.D.B.; Steven Whelan, S.D.B.; Gerald Wertz, S.D.B. In res., Revs. Joseph Scanagatta, S.D.B.; James Collins, S.D.B.; George Hacker, S.D.B.; Larry Lorenzoni, S.D.B.; Albert Marshall, S.D.B. Priests 11; Brothers 1.
Military Chaplain: Rev. Robert Delis, S.D.B., Hq. MAG-12, 1st MAW, 96603-8725.

Verbum Dei Community, 1618 Howard St., #B, 94103. Tel: 415-861-8406. Revs. Rodolfo DLC Llamas, V.D.C.; Greg Morgan, V.D.C. Priests 2; Brothers 1.

BURLINGAME. *Capuchin Provincial House,* 1345 Cortez Ave., 94010. Tel: 415-342-4550. Revs. Gerald Barron, O.F.M., Prov.; Peter Banks, O.F.M.Cap.; Bertrand Mulligan, O.F.M.Cap.; Camillus MacRory, O.F.M.Cap.; Flavian Welstead, O.F.M.Cap.; Richard Lopes, O.F.M.Cap.

PORTOLA VALLEY. *Woodside Priory,* 302 Portola Rd., 94028. Tel: 415-851-8220. Very Revs. William J. Sullivan, O.S.B., Prior; Martin J. Mager, O.S.B., Subprior; Revs. Pius L. Horvath, O.S.B.; Egon J. Javor, O.S.B.; Maurus B. Nemeth, O.S.B. Priests 6; Brothers 2. Legal Title: *Benedictine Fathers of the Priory, Inc.*

[O] CONVENTS AND RESIDENCES FOR SISTERS

SAN FRANCISCO. *Carmelite Monastery of Cristo Rey, Discalced Carmelite Nuns,* 721 Parker Ave., 94118-4297. Mother Mary Joseph Chavez, O.C.D., Prioress. Professed Nuns 16.

Daughters of St. Paul, 46 Geary St., 94108. Tel: 415-781-5180. Sr. Laura Rhoderica, F.S.P., Supr. Sisters 4.

Franciscan Missionaries of Mary (F.M.M.), St. Joseph Convent, 46 Harrington St., 94112. Tel: 415-587-8359. Sisters 5.

Missionaries of Charity. (India), 1596 Fulton St., 94117. Tel: 415-563-9446. Sisters 7. Noviciate, 312 29th St., 94131. Tel: 415-647-1889. Sisters 4; Novices 45. 974 Valencia St., 94110. Tel: 415-821-9687. Sisters 5.

Monastery of Perpetual Adoration, Nuns of Perpetual Adoration, 771 Ashbury St., 94117. Tel: 415-566-2743; Fax: 415-564-4469. Mother Rosalba Vargas, A.P., Supr. Cloistered Nuns 24.

Presentation Convent, Motherhouse of the Sisters of the Presentation of B.V.M., 2340 Turk Blvd., 94118. Tel: 415-751-0406. Sr. Rosina Conrotto, P.B.V.M., Pres. Sisters in Archdiocese 91; Total in congregation 155.

St. Francis Convent of Mercy (Sisters of Mercy-Burlingame), 826 30th Ave., 94121. Sisters 2.

Shalom Convent, 416 Stanyan St., 94117. Tel: 415-750-5545. Sisters of Mercy (Burlingame, CA) 4.

Sisters of Social Service, 1850 Ulloa St., 94116. Tel: 415-681-9219. Sisters 5.

Sisters of St. Joseph of Orange, 544 Bush St., 94108. Tel: 415-398-7383. Sisters 3.

Sisters of St. Joseph of Orange, 1737 Silliman St., 94134. Tel: 415-585-0159. Sisters 3.

Sisters of the Good Shepherd, 1310 Bacon St., 94134. Tel: 415-586-2822; Fax: 415-586-0355. Sisters 8.

Sisters of the Holy Family, 174 Stanyan St., Flat #2, 94118. Tel: 415-221-7704. Sisters 4.

Sisters of the Precious Blood, 326 Ewing Ter., 94118. Sisters 2.

Sisters of the Visitation of Japan, 604 Cabrillo St., 94118. Sisters 4. Serving the Archdiocese in Japanese Bible Study and visiting the elderly and sick.

Society of Helpers (Helpers of the Holy Souls), 855 Lincoln Way, 94122. Tel: 415-661-6316. Sr. Veronica Donlon, Local Supr. Sisters 6.

Verbum Dei Community. (Apostolic Institute: Instituto Apostolico Verbum Dei, Loeches, Madrid), 1239 Howard St., 94103. Tel: 415-863-4469. Sr. Maria Teresa Pasadas, V.D.C., Supr.; Sr. Raquel Meora, V.D.C.

ATHERTON. *Religious of the Sacred Heart Oakwood,* 140 Valparaiso Ave., 94027; Fax: 415-326-2251. Sr. Mary McMahon, R.S.C.J., Dir. Sisters 33. Infirmary for elderly Religious of the Sacred Heart.

BURLINGAME. *Regional Community of the Sisters of Mercy of the Americas,* 2300 Adeline Dr., 94010-5599. Tel: 415-340-7410; Fax: 415-347-2550. Sisters 64; Total in congregation 222; Total in Archdiocese 127.

DALY CITY. *Quinhon Missionary Sisters of the Holy Cross,* 298 Southgate Ave., 94015. Tel: 415-992-1560. Sisters 10; Novices 4; Postulants & Aspirants 10.

MENLO PARK. *Corpus Christi Monastery,* 215 Oak Grove Ave., 94025. Tel: 415-322-1801; Fax: 415-322-6816. Nuns of the Order of Preachers. Sr. Mary of the Angels, Prioress. Cloistered Religious 22; Extern Sisters 2.

REDWOOD CITY. *Casa Chiara Community,* 3910 Bret Harte Dr., Box 685, 94064-0685. Tel: 415-366-3968. Franciscan Sisters. Sisters 4.

Provincial House of the Sisters of St. Francis of Penance and Christian Charity, 3910 Bret Harte Dr., P.O. Box 1028, 94064. Tel: 415-369-1725. Legal Titles: *Sisters of St. Francis-Mount Alverno; Sisters of St. Francis Charitable Trust.* Sr. Michele Mangan, C.S.F., Prov. Supr. Sisters 19; Total in Province 110.

SAN RAFAEL. *Carmelite Monastery of the Mother of God, Discalced Carmelite Nuns,* 530 Blackstone Dr., 94093. Mother Anne Marie Vanni, O.C.D., Prioress. Sisters 5.

Dominican Sisters of San Rafael Generalate & Convent, 1520 Grand Ave., 94901-2236. Tel: 415-453-8303; Fax: 415-453-8367. Sr. Kristin Wombacher, O.P., Prioress Gen. Total in Community 161; Total in Archdiocese 93.

Dominican Convent, 1540 Grand Ave., 94901. Tel: 415-454-9221. Sisters 24.

Our Lady of Lourdes Convent (Infirmary), 77 Locust Ave., 94901. Tel: 415-457-3171. Sisters 26.

Our Lady of Mercy Convent, 15 Elmwood Dr., Daly City, 94015. Tel: 415-756-3457. Sisters 6.

Our Lady of Mt. Carmel Convent, 34 Buena Vista Ave., Mill Valley, 94941. Tel: 415-389-0328. Sisters 6.

San Domenico Convent, 1500 Butterfield Rd., San Anselmo, 94960. Tel: 415-453-9172. Sisters 11.

Sacred Heart Convent, 660 Oak St., San Francisco, 94117. Tel: 415-431-2881. Sisters 9.

St. Dominic Convent, 1851 Pierce St., San Francisco, 94115. Tel: 415-922-8817. Sisters 6.

St. Catherine of Siena Convent, 14 Roger Dr., 94901. Tel: 415-453-4330. Sisters 5.

SOUTH SAN FRANCISCO. *Holy Family Convent,* 381 Avalon Dr., 94080. Sisters 3.

[P] SECULAR INSTITUTES

SAN FRANCISCO. *Missionaries of the Kingship of Christ,* 3215 Cesar Chavez St., 94110. A Franciscan secular institute for women.

The Society of Our Lady of the Way, 147 Dorado Ter., 94112-1740. Tel: 415-585-3319. A secular institute for women. Yvonne Claire Artigues, S.O.L.W., Local Contact, 726 Geneva Ave., 94112-3327. Tel: 415-585-7967.

[Q] CATHOLIC CHARITIES

SAN FRANCISCO. *Catholic Charities of the Archdiocese of San Francisco,* 814 Mission St., 3rd Fl., 94103. Tel: 415-281-1200; Fax: 415-281-1394. Mr. Frank C. Hudson, CEO; Mr. A. James Benz, CFO; Mr. Don Diltz, COO; Mrs. Sophie L. Aldrich, Exec. Dir. Devel. & Mktg.; Sr. Irma L. Dillard, Dir. of Human Resources/Volunteers; Mr. Robert Nelson, Dir. of Policy & Media Rels.

Campaign for Human Development, 814 Mission St., 3rd Fl., 94103. Tel: 415-442-6844; Fax: 415-281-1394. Francis C. Hudson, Archdiocesan Dir.

Catholic Relief Services, 814 Mission St., 3rd Fl., 94103. Tel: 415-442-6844; Fax: 415-281-1394.

Mercy/Charities Housing California, 1028A Howard St., 94103. Tel: 415-487-6825; Fax: 415-487-6834. Ms. Jane Graf, Pres.

MENTAL HEALTH AND CLINICAL SERVICES: Charles King, Ph.D., Dir.

Marin Counseling, 179 Los Ranchitos Rd., San Rafael, 94903. Tel: 415-579-0277, Ext. 24; Fax: 415-343-0413.

San Francisco Counseling, 814 Mission St., 5th floor, 94103. Tel: 415-281-1200; Fax: 415-281-1394.

Daly City Counseling, 6755 Mission St., Daly City, 94014. Tel: 415-922-4222; Fax: 415-922-7867.

San Mateo Counseling. Tel: 415-363-2276.

Pregnancy Counseling / Adoption Services, 814 Mission St., 5th floor, 94103. Tel: 415-281-1200; Fax: 415-281-1394.

Grief Care, 2559 40th Ave., 94116. Tel: 415-564-7882; Fax: 415-731-1270.

CHILDREN AND FAMILY SERVICES. Martin Torow, Svc. Dir.

San Francisco Family Services, 812 Mission St., 94103. Tel: 415-281-1200; Fax: 415-281-1230. Hearing Impaired, 1801 Octavia St., 94109. Tel: 415-749-3812; Fax: 415-567-0916.

Peninsula Family Resource Center (PFRC), 520 S. El Camino Real, Ste. 240, San Mateo, 94402. Tel: 415-696-1255; Fax: 415-696-1257.

Richmond Hills Family Center, 6324 Geary Blvd., 94121. Tel: 415-750-5080; Fax: 415-750-5085.

Guerrero House, 899 Guerrero St., 94110. Tel: 415-550-4476; Fax: 415-550-4481.

West Marin Social Services, 65 Third St., Point Reyes Station, 94956. Tel: 415-663-1252; Fax: 415-663-1319.

Adoptions and Foster Care, 814 Mission St., 5th floor, 94103. Tel: 415-281-1200; Fax: 415-281-1394.

Marin Family Services, 179 Los Ranchitos Rd., San Rafael, 94903. Tel: 415-499-1470, Ext. 14; Fax: 415-479-2667.

SOCIAL MINISTRY AND COMMUNITY OUTREACH: Donna Hoang, Dir.

Citizenship, Refugee, Immigration Services (CRIS), 812 Mission St., 94103. Tel: 415-281-1200; Fax: 415-281-1230. 179 Los Ranchitos Rd., San Rafael, 94903. Tel: 415-499-1470; Fax: 415-479-2667.

Detention Ministries, 814 Mission St., 3rd floor, 94103. Tel: 415-442-5207; Fax: 415-281-1394.

St. Joseph's Village, 1415 Howard St., 94103. Tel: 415-442-6836; Fax: 415-281-1394.

HIV Community Housing and Services: Ms. Tiffany Mock-Goeman, Svc. Dir.

HIV Direct Services, 812 Mission St., 94103. Tel: 415-281-1200; Fax: 415-281-1230.

Leland Avenue Project, 141 Leland Ave., 94134. Tel: 415-281-1200; Fax: 415-281-1394.

HIV Money Management, 812 Mission St., 94103. Tel: 415-281-1200; Fax: 415-281-1230.

HIV Housing Services, 812 Mission St., 94103. Tel: 415-281-1200; Fax: 415-281-1230.

**Peter Claver Community,* 1340 Golden Gate Ave., 94115. Tel: 415-749-3800; Fax: 415-563-3153.

Belmont House Aids Hospice, 730 El Camino Real, Belmont, 94002. Tel: 415-802-9426; Fax: 415-802-8385.

Derek Silva Community, 1594 Market St., 94102. Tel: 415-553-8700; Fax: 415-575-3729.

HIV Food & Emergency Services, 600 Columbia Dr., San Mateo, 94402. Tel: 415-579-0277, Ext. 3338; Fax: 415-343-0413.

AGING SERVICES: Pietie Vreman, Dir.

San Francisco Senior Services, 812 Mission St., 94103. Tel: 415-281-1200; Fax: 415-281-1230.

Ombudsman & Meals on Wheels, 600 Columbia Dr., San Mateo, 94402. Tel: 415-579-0277; Fax: 415-343-0413.

San Carlos Adult Day Care, 787 Walnut St., San Carlos, 94070. Tel: 415-595-9325; Fax: 415-593-2316.

Noriega Adult Day Support Center, 3601 Noriega St., 94122. Tel: 415-242-8015; Fax: 415-242-8017.

OMI Senior Center, 446 Randolph St., 94132. Tel: 415-587-1443; Fax: 415-586-7960.

Marine Senior Services, 179 Los Ranchitos, San Rafael, 94903. Tel: 415-499-1470, Ext. 16; Fax: 415-479-2667.

AUXILIARIES:

Auxiliary of Little Children's Aid, P.O. Box 31040, 94131. Tel: 415-442-6888; Fax: 415-281-1394.

Little Children's Aid, Junior Auxiliary, 814 Mission St., 3rd Fl., 94103. Tel: 415-442-6888; Fax: 415-281-1394.

Catholic Charities Auxiliary of San Mateo, 600 Columbia Dr., San Mateo, 94402. Tel: 415-442-6888; Fax: 415-281-1394.

Primrose House of Catholic Charities of San Mateo, 307 Primrose Rd., San Mateo, 94010. Tel: 415-442-6888; Fax: 415-281-1394.

[R] CATHOLIC YOUTH ORGANIZATIONS

SAN FRANCISCO. *Catholic Youth Organization of the Archdiocese of San Francisco,* 1 St. Vincent's Dr., 94903. Tel: 415-507-2000; Fax: 415-491-0842. Rev. David A. Ghiorso, Exec. Dir.; Stewart Clark, Archdiocesan Youth Dir.

CYO Archbishop McGucken Youth Retreat and Conference Center. Location of CYO Camp Armstrong, and CYO Caritas Creek Environmental Education Program. 2136 Bohemian Hwy., Occidental, 95465. Tel: 707-874-0210. Steve Grant, Dir.

CYO Sports & Recreation, 1 St. Vincent Dr., San Rafael, 94903. Tel: 415-507-4290. Provides a variety of organized team sports programs throughout the year for elementary school age children.

CYO Camp Armstrong, 2136 Bohemian Hwy., Occidental, 95465. Tel: 415-507-2000. Paula M. Pardini, Dir. Summer camp located at Archbishop McGucken Youth Center.

CYO Caritas Creek Environmental Education Program, 1 St. Vincent Dr., San Rafael, 94903. Tel: 415-507-2000. Paula Pardini, Dir. An environmental education program located at Archbishop

McGucken Youth Center, serving children grades 5-8.

CYO Mission Day Care, 180 Fair Oaks St., 94110. Tel: 415-826-6880. Liliana Carnero-Rossi, Dir. Provides after-school services for children, summer day camps, and holiday recess camps.

CYO San Francisco Boys and Girls Home, P.O. Box 210399, 94121-0399. Tel: 415-750-5300. Kent Egleson, Exec. Dir. Since 1915. Residential treatment, special education and home-based services for emotionally, behaviorally, and educationally disadvantaged abused children ages 10-18 at residential group homes. Individual psychotherapy and family counseling provided.

St. Vincent's School for Boys, 1 St. Vincent Dr., San Rafael, 94903. Tel: 415-507-2000. Mr. Kent Egleson, Exec. Dir. Since 1855. Residential treatment, special education, foster care, day treatment, and home-based services for emotionally, behaviorally, and educationally disadvantaged boys.

CYO Transportation Services, 699 Serramonte Blvd., Ste. 210, Daly City, 94015. Tel: 415-757-2110. Martin Rea, Dir. Provides school bus transportation for all CYO-related programs and for other nonprofit school and community organizations.

CYO Youth Ministry Services, 1 St. Vincent Dr., San Rafael, 94903. Tel: 415-507-2000. Parish-based youth leadership training programs and services.

[S] NEWMAN CENTERS

SAN FRANCISCO. *Newman Center, San Francisco State University*, St. Thomas More Church, 1300 Junipero Serra Blvd., 94123. Tel: 415-452-9634; Fax: 415-452-9653. Revs. Jerome P. Foley, Chap.; Jack McLean, Campus Min.

Newman Center, University of California Medical Center, 1290 Fifth Ave., 94122. Tel: 415-566-5610. Revs. William J. Brady; Alan Wilson, O.F.M.Cap., Dir., Res., 750 Anza St., 94118-4234. Tel: 415-387-7005.

[T] PERSONAL PRELATURES

SAN FRANCISCO. *Opus Dei*. (Prelature of the Holy Cross and Opus Dei) Delegate Vicariate. 765 14th Ave., 94118. Tel: 415-386-0431. Very Rev. George M. Rossman, Delegate Vicar; Revs. Torlach C. Delargy; Arne A. Panula.

Other Priests in the Archdiocese: Rev. Salvador V. Serrano, 1835 Bay Laurel, Menlo Park, 94025. Tel: 415-327-1675. Rev. Paul A. Donlan, 108 Kipling Dr., Mill Valley, 94941. Tel: 415-388-4531.

[U] MISCELLANEOUS LISTINGS

SAN FRANCISCO.

**All Hallows Community, Inc.*, c/o Mercy Services Corp., 1035 Folsom St., 94103.

Apostleship of Prayer, 2130 Fulton St., 94117. Tel: 415-666-0123. Rev. George Twigg-Porter, S.J., Dir.

Archdiocesan Council of Catholic Women, 445 Church St., 94114. Tel: 415-565-3600. Cathy Mibach, Pres.

Association of Ladies of Charity of St. Vincent de Paul, 2570 Ocean Ave., P.O. Box 194, 94109. Tel: 415-369-6287; Fax: 415-592-2160. Lauren Santucci, Pres.; Linda Ramelot, Vice-Pres.; Liz Watson, Sec.; Diane Croce, Sec.; Marilyn Christen, Treas.; Charlotte Kiesel, Founding Pres. The purpose of the Association is to make known the spirit of St. Vincent de Paul, St. Louise de Marillac and St. Elizabeth Ann Seton by performing corporal works of mercy for the poor and needy of the San Francisco Archdiocese.

California Handicapables, Inc (1965), 1311 Montgomery St., 94133-3521. Tel: 415-474-3821. Miss Nadine Calligiuri, Founder; Sally Tooley, Treas. Provides transportation and lunch along with Mass on the 2nd Saturday of every month at St. Mary's Cathedral, San Francisco.

Catholic Healthcare West, 1700 Montgomery St., Ste. 300, 94111. Tel: 415-397-9000. Mr. Richard J. Kramer, Pres. A nonprofit corporation. CHW is a multi-congregational Health System co-sponsored by the Auburn Regional Community of the Sisters of Mercy; the Burlingame Regional Community of the Sisters of Mercy; the Sisters of St. Dominic of the Congregation of the Most Holy Rosary, Adrian, MI; the Daughters of Charity of St. Vincent de Paul, Province of the West; the Sisters of the Third Order of St. Dominic, Congregation of the Most Holy Name, San Rafael, CA; the Congregation of the Sisters of St. Catherine of Siena of Kenosha, WI. There are 35 affiliated hospitals, retirement homes, long-term care facilities, and related corporations, located in California, Arizona, and Nevada. This organization provides centralized management and support functions for the following affiliated nonprofit organizations in the Archdiocese of San Francisco (other affiliates are listed in their respective dioceses): CHW West Bay, which includes St. Mary's Medical Center, San Francisco; Seton Medical Center Coastside, Moss Beach; Seton Health Services Foundation; Mercy Terrace Corporation; MSC Psychiatric Services Corporation; San Francisco Heart Institute.

Catholic Kolping Society, 440 Taraval St., 94116. Hubert Brinkman, Pres., 1738 Quesada Way, Burlingame, 94010. Catherine Vennemeyer, Treas., 2733 Trousdale Dr., Burlingame, 94010.

Catholics for Truth & Justice, 2555 17th Ave., 94116. Tel: 415-664-8481. Rev. Msgr. Steven D. Ottelini, Chap.

Charismatic Movement, Charismatic Board, 2555 17th Ave., 94116. Tel: 415-664-8481; Fax: 415-661-2957. Rev. L. Joseph Landi, Chm.

Equestrian Order of the Holy Sepulchre of Jerusalem - Northwest Lieutenancy, 3050 24th Ave., 94132. Tel: 415-664-6565. Albert E. Maggio.

Father Raphael Piperni Charitable Trust, 1100 Francklin St., 94109. Tel: 415-441-7144. (The FRPC (R) Trust).

Filipino Cursillo Secretariat, P.O. Box 881601, 94188-1601. Deacon Mar Tano, Spiritual Advisor.

Franciscan Friars of California, Office of Communications, 135 Golden Gate Ave., 94102-3809. Tel: 415-241-2636; Fax: 415-863-8240. Rev. Floyd A. Lotito, O.F.M., Dir.

Holy Childhood Pontifical Association, 445 Church St., 94114. Tel: 415-565-3676; Fax: 415-565-3677. Rev. Msgr. Ignatius Wang, Dir.

Legion of Mary, 415 Edna St., 94112. Tel: 415-333-3627. Rev. Lawrence Goode, Dir.

Mercy/Charities Housing California, 1028 A Howard St., 94103. Housing development for low-income families, elderly, and singles.

Mercy Family Plaza, c/o Mercy/Charities Housing California, 1028 A Howard St., 94103. Thirty-six affordable units for families.

MSC Psychiatric Services. Provides certain psychiatric patient care services.

Mercy Terrace Corporation. Housing project for low- and moderate-income persons and families; also multi-services for residents and community.

Pauline Books & Media, 46 Geary St., 94108. Tel: 415-781-5180. Daughters of St. Paul. Sr. Laura Rhoderica, F.S.P., Supr. Sisters 4.

Philip Rinaldi Charitable Trust, P.O. Box 640009, 94164-0009.

Religious Trust (RETA), Box 7443, 94120. A nonprofit multiple, religious employer health plan with trust fund.

The Ricci Institute for Chinese-Western Cultural History at the Center for the Pacific Rim, University of San Francisco, 2130 Fulton St., 94117-1080. Tel: 415-422-6401; Fax: 415-422-2291. Revs. Edward J. Malatesta, S.J., Dir.; Albert Chan, S.J., Ph.D., Senior Research Fellow; Mark Mir, Research Fellow and Chinese Library Cataloguer; Xiao Wu-Xin, Ed.D., Asst. Dir./Research Fellow.

St. Anthony Foundation, 121 Golden Gate Ave., 94102. Tel: 415-241-2600; Fax: 415-252-1635. Mrs. Jeanne Zarka Brooks, Exec. Dir.; Rev. Giles Valcovich, O.F.M., Chap. A nonprofit, charitable corporation assisting the homeless and low-income.

St. Benedict Center for Deaf and Hearing Impaired at St. Francis Xavier Church.

St. Rose Academy Corporation, Rose Court, 2507 Pine St., 94109. Tel: 415-921-3584.

Shrine of St. Jude Thaddeus, 2390 Bush St., 94115. Rev. Thomas J. Hayes, O.P., Dir.

Sisters of the Presentation Community Support Trust Fund, 2340 Turk Blvd., 94118. Tel: 415-751-0406. Trust used for the religious and charitable needs of the Sisters of the Presentation of the Blessed Virgin Mary. Trustees: Sr. Joanna Bruno, P.B.V.M.; Sr. Pamela Chiesa, P.B.V.M.; Sr. Patricia Anne Cloherty, P.B.V.M.; Sr. Patricia Doyle, P.B.V.M.; Sr. Adele Hancock, P.B.V.M.; Sr. Patricia Marie Mulpeters, P.B.V.M.; Sr. Rose Therese Sousa, P.B.V.M.

Spiritual Programs and Retreats, 704 Cortland Ave., 94110. Rev. Joseph Walsh, Dir.

**The Ordinary Mutual, RRG*, P.O. Box 191867, 94119-1867. Tel: 415-536-8440; Fax: 415-536-8513. Gregory Campbell, Underwriting Mgr.; Rev. Msgr. Thomas J. Keys, Pres. A Risk Retention Group Corporation, incorporated in Vermont, serving the Dioceses of Boise, Tucson, Fresno, Monterey, Oakland, Orange, Sacramento, San Jose, Santa Rosa, and Stockton, and the Archdioceses of Los Angeles and San Francisco.

Together in the Mission of Education (T.I.M.E.), 98 Bosworth St., 94112. Tel: 415-334-4334. Sr. Rita Jovick, P.B.V.M., Devel. Dir.

BURLINGAME. *Music at Kohl Mansion, Inc.*, 2750 Adeline Dr., 94010. Tel: 415-343-8463; Fax: 415-343-2316. Carol Eggers, Contact Person. To develop and promote public knowledge and appreciation of musical arts by sponsoring chamber music concerts and other public performances of music, as well as music education activities.

DALY CITY. *Association of Catholic Student Councils*, 242 Greenview Dr., 94014. Tel: 415-584-9877. Marilyn Thickett, Exec. Dir.

LOS ANGELES. *Christian Live Communities (Sodalities)*, P.O. Box 45041, 90045. Tel: 310-338-7445; Fax: 310-338-3002. Rev. James D. Earps, S.J.

MENLO PARK. *St. Joseph's-St. Patrick's College Alumni Association*, St. Patrick's Seminary, 320 Middlefield Rd., 94025. Tel: 415-327-8956. Mr. Donald C. Carroll, Contact.

Vatican II Institute for Clergy Formation, 320 Middlefield Rd., 94025. Tel: 415-325-9122; Fax: 415-325-6765. Revs. Eugene J. Konkel, S.S., Dir.; Jeremiah Farrell, S.S., Assoc. Dir.

MOUNTAIN VIEW. *Hospital and Health Services Liaison*, St. Joseph's College, P.O. Box 7009, 94039. Tel: 415-694-1400. Rev. Gerald D. Coleman, S.S., Ph.D.

PACIFICA. *Cursillo*, 901 Oceana Blvd., 94044. Tel: 415-355-2593; Fax: 415-355-1832. Rev. Maurice M. McCormick, Chap., Gen. Secretariat.

REDWOOD CITY. *The Catholic Worker Community*, 545 Cassia St., 94063. Tel: 415-366-4415. Lawrence P. Purcell. A foster home for teenagers.

SAN RAFAEL. *Catholic Scouting*, 1 St. Vincent Dr., 94903. Tel: 415-507-2000; Fax: 415-491-0842. Rev. David Ghiorso.

**Center Interfaith Housing*, 164 N. San Pedro Rd., 94903; Fax: 415-453-8367.

Mission Holding Corporation, 1520 Grand Ave., 94901. Governing Board: Sr. Kristin Wombacher, O.P.; Sr. Cathryn deBack, O.P.; Sr. Patricia Simpson, O.P.; Sr. Anne Marie Mullin, O.P.; Sr. Katherine Hamilton, O.P.

Third Order of St. Dominic Support and Charitable Trust Fund, 1520 Grand Ave., 94901. Tel: 415-453-8303; Fax: 415-453-8367. Legal Title: *Third Order of St. Dominic, Congregation of the Most Holy Name, Support and Charitable Trust Fund*. Trust used for the religious and charitable needs of the Sisters of the Third Order of St. Dominic, Congregation of the Most Holy Name. Trustees: Sr. Kristin Wombacher, O.P.; Sr. Cathryn de Back, O.P.; Sr. Patricia Boss, O.P.

[V] CLOSED INSTITUTIONS

SAN FRANCISCO. *All Hallows Church*. For sacramental records please contact Our Lady of Lourdes, 1715 Oakdale Ave., San Francisco 94124. Tel: 415-285-3377; Fax: 415-285-2191.

Holy Cross Korean Church. For sacramental records please contact St. Michael, 32 Broad St., San Francisco, 94112. Tel: 415-333-1194; Fax: 415-333-1196.

Immaculate Conception Church. For sacramental records please contact St. Anthony of Padua, 3215 Cesar Chavez St., San Francisco, 94110. Tel: 415-647-2704; Fax: 415-647-7282.

Our Lady of Guadalupe Church. For sacramental records please contact SS. Peter and Paul, 666 Filbert St., San Francisco, 94133. Tel: 415-421-0809; Fax: 415-421-0217.

St. Brigid Church. For sacramental records please contact St. Vincent de Paul, 2320 Green St., San Francisco 94123. Tel: 415-992-1010; Fax: 415-922-7203.

St. Edward the Confessor Church. For sacramental records please contact Star of the Sea, 4420 Geary Blvd., San Francisco, 94118. Tel: 415-751-0450; Fax: 415-368-5651.

St. Francis of Assisi Church. For sacramental records please contact SS. Peter and Paul, 666 Filbert St., San Francisco, 94133. Tel: 415-421-0809; Fax: 415-421-0217.

St. Joseph Church. For sacramental records please contact St. Patrick, 756 Mission St., San Francisco, 94103. Tel: 415-421-0547; 415-512-9730.

SAN RAFAEL. *Blessed Sacrament Church*. For sacramental records please contact St. Isabella, One Trinity Way, San Rafael, 94901. Tel: 415-479-1560; Fax: 415-479-8303.

St. Sylvester Church. For sacramental records please contact St. Raphael, 1104 Fifth Ave., San Rafael, 94901. Tel: 415-453-2314; Fax: 415-453-5402.

WOODSIDE. *St. Marcella Mission*. For sacramental records please contact St. Denis, 2250 Avy Ave., Menlo Park, 94025. Tel: 415-854-5976; Fax: 415-854-3754.

RELIGIOUS INSTITUTES OF MEN REPRESENTED IN THE ARCHDIOCESE

For further details refer to the corresponding bracketed number in the Religious Institutes of Men or Women section.

[0200]—*Benedictine Monks*. (Hungary).—O.S.B.

[0330]—*Brothers of the Christian Schools*. (Prov. of San Francisco).—F.S.C.

[0470]—*The Capuchin Franciscans*. (Irish Prov.).—O.F.M.Cap.

[0520]—*Franciscan Friars*. (Santa Barbara Prov.).—O.F.M.

[0650]—*Holy Ghost Fathers*.—C.S.Sp.

[0690]—*Jesuit Fathers and Brothers*. (California Prov.).—S.J.

[0780]—*Marist Fathers*. (American Prov.).—S.M.

[0800]—*Maryknoll*.—M.M.
[0910]—*Oblates of Mary Immaculate*.—O.M.I.
[0430]—*Order of Preachers (Dominicans)*. (Western Prov.).—O.P.
[0897]—*Paris Foreign Mission Society*.—M.E.P.
[1030]—*Paulist Fathers*.—C.S.P.
[1170]—*St. Patrick Missionary Society*.—S.P.S.
[1190]—*Salesian Don Bosco*.—S.D.B.
[1260]—*Society of Christ*. (Chicago Prov.).—S.Ch.
[0760]—*Society of Mary (Marianists)*. (Prov. of the Pacific).—S.M.
[1200]—*Society of the Divine Savior*.—S.D.S.
[0420]—*Society of the Divine Word*. (Western Prov.).—S.V.D.
[1290]—*Society of the Priests of Saint Sulpice*. (American Prov.).—S.S.
[]—*Verbum Dei Community*.—V.D.C.

RELIGIOUS INSTITUTES OF WOMEN REPRESENTED IN THE ARCHDIOCESE

[]—*Announcers of the Lord*.—S.A.L.
[]—*Benedictine Sisters of Perpetual Adoration*.—O.S.B.
[]—*Bernardine Franciscan Sisters*.—O.S.F.
[]—*Congregation of Divine Providence*.
[1920]—*Congregation of the Sisters of the Holy Cross*. (Notre Dame, IN).—C.S.C.
[1940]—*Congregation of the Sisters of the Holy Faith*.—C.H.F.
[1710]—*Congregation of the Third Order of St. Francis of Mary Immaculate, Joliet, IL*.—O.S.F.
[0730]—*Daughters of Charity of Canossa*.—F.D.C.C.
[0760]—*Daughters of Charity of St. Vincent de Paul*. (Prov. of the West).—D.C.
[0880]—*Daughters of Mary and Joseph*.—D.M.J.
[0850]—*Daughters of Mary Help of Christians*.—F.M.A.
[0420]—*Discalced Carmelite Nuns*.—O.C.D.
[1050]—*Dominican Contemplative Nuns*.—O.P.
[1070-03]—*Dominican Sisters*.—O.P.
[1070-13]—*Dominican Sisters*.—O.P.
[1370]—*The Franciscan Missionaries of Mary*.—F.M.M.
[1390]—*Franciscan Missionaries Sisters of Our Lady of Sorrows*.—O.S.F.
[]—*Franciscan Missionaries, Our Lady of Peace*.—M.F.P.
[1415]—*Franciscan Sisters of Mary*.—F.S.M.
[]—*Las Hermanas Misioneras*.—M.S.C.Gpe.
[2340]—*Little Sisters of the Poor*.—L.S.P.
[2390]—*Lovers of the Holy Cross Sisters*.—L.H.C.
[]—*Maryknoll Missionary Sisters*.—M.M.
[2720]—*Mission Helpers of the Sacred Heart*.—M.H.S.H.
[2710]—*Missionary Sisters of Charity*.—M.C.
[]—*Missionary Sisters of the Sacred Side*.—M.C.S.
[3190]—*Nuns of the Perpetual Adoration of the Blessed Sacrament*.—A.P.
[]—*Oblates of Jesus the Priest*.—O.S.J.
[0950]—*Pious Society Daughters of St. Paul*.—F.S.P.
[3242]—*Poor Sisters of Nazareth*.—P.S.N.
[3465]—*Religious of the Sacred Heart of Mary*.—R.S.H.M.
[0440]—*Sisters of Charity of Cincinnati, Ohio*.—S.C.
[0430]—*Sisters of Charity of the Blessed Virgin Mary*.—B.V.M.
[]—*Sisters of Mercy (Galaway)*. (Loughrea, Ireland).—S.M.
[2575]—*Sisters of Mercy of the Americas*. (Burlingame, CA).—R.S.M.
[2580]—*Sisters of Mercy of the United States of America*.—R.S.M.
[3000]—*Sisters of Notre Dame de Namur*. (Prov. of CA).—S.N.D.deN.
[3360]—*Sisters of Providence of Saint Mary-of-the-Woods, Indiana*.—S.P.
[4080]—*Sisters of Social Service of Los Angeles, Inc.*.—S.S.S.
[1570]—*Sisters of St. Francis of Holy Family*.—O.S.F.
[1630]—*Sisters of St. Francis of Penance and Christian Charity*.—O.S.F.
[3840]—*Sisters of St. Joseph of Carondelet*. (Los Angeles Prov.).—C.S.J.
[3930-03]—*Sisters of St. Joseph of Orange*.—C.S.J.O.
[3890]—*Sisters of St. Joseph of Peace*.—C.S.J.P.
[1830]—*The Sisters of the Good Shepherd*.—R.G.S.
[1960]—*Sisters of the Holy Family*. (San Francisco, CA).—S.H.F.
[1990]—*Sisters of the Holy Names of Jesus and Mary*. (Provs. of CA; Oregon; Washington).—S.N.J.M.
[2130]—*Sisters of the Immaculate Conception*. (Prov. of Madrid).—R.C.M.
[3260]—*Sisters of the Precious Blood (Dayton, Ohio)*.—C.PP.S.
[3320]—*Sisters of the Presentation of the B.V.M.*—P.B.V.M.
[1720]—*Sisters of the Third Order Regular of St. Francis of the Congregation of Our Lady of Lourdes*.—O.S.F.
[1890]—*Society of Helpers*.—H.H.S.
[]—*Society of Our Lady of the Way*.—S.O.L.W.
[4070]—*Society of the Sacred Heart*.—R.S.C.J.
[3330]—*Union Sisters of the Presentation of the Blessed Virgin Mary*.—P.B.V.M.
[4110]—*Ursuline Nuns (Roman Union)*.—O.S.U.
[]—*Ursuline Sisters of the Immaculate Conception*. (Louisville,KY).—O.S.U.
[]—*Verbum Dei Community*. (Valencia, Spain).—V.D.C.
[4190]—*Visitation Nuns*.—V.H.M.

ARCHDIOCESAN CEMETERIES AND MAUSOLEUMS

SAN FRANCISCO. *Holy Cross Cemetery and Mausoleum*. Mailing Address: P.O. Box 577, Colma, 94014. Tel: 415-756-2060.

MENLO PARK. *Holy Cross*. Mailing Address: P.O. Box 577, Colma, 94014. Tel: 415-756-2060.

SAN RAFAEL. *Mount Olivet*, Box 4368, 94903. Tel: 415-479-9020.

NECROLOGY

✠ Moran, Most Rev. William J., San Rafael, CA, Nazareth House. —Died Aug. 23, 1996.
† Dullea, Rev. Msgr. Edward M., Mill Valley, CA, Our Lady of Mount Carmel. —Died Aug. 8, 1996.
† Isaacs, John S., San Francisco, CA, St. Peter. —Died Dec. 29, 1996.
† Leach, Cyril V., Greenbrae, CA, St. Sebastian. —Died March 19, 1996.
† Muldoon, Charles, (On Duty Outside the Diocese). —Died Oct. 16, 1995.
† Orta-Colomo, Antonio, San Francisco, CA, St. Peter. —Died Sept. 22, 1996.
† Rey, Antonio R., Daly City, CA, Our Lady of Perpetual Help. —Died Feb. 6, 1996.
† Ring, John M., (Retired). —Died April 15, 1996.
† Ryan, Rev. Msgr. Philip F., (Retired). —Died May 2, 1996.
† Skoyles, Arthur W., San Mateo, CA, Serra Clergy House. —Died Sept. 4, 1996.

Diocese of San Jose in California

(Dioecesis Sancti Josephi in California)

Most Reverend

PIERRE DUMAINE, D.D., PH.D.

First Bishop of San Jose; ordained June 15, 1957; appointed Auxiliary Bishop of San Francisco and Titular Bishop of Sarda April 28, 1978; Episcopal ordination June 29, 1978; appointed Bishop of San Jose January 27, 1981; installed as Bishop of San Jose March 18, 1981. *Office: Diocese of San Jose, 900 Lafayette St., Ste. 301, Santa Clara, CA, 95050-4966.*

ESTABLISHED JANUARY 27, 1981.

Square Miles 1,300.

Legal Title: The Roman Catholic Bishop of San Jose, a Corporation Sole.

The Diocese of San Jose comprises the County of Santa Clara in the State of California.

PATRONS OF THE DIOCESE OF SAN JOSE: St. Joseph, Husband of Mary, March 19; St. Clare of Assisi, August 11.

For legal titles of parishes and diocesan institutions, consult the Chancery Office.

Diocese of San Jose: 900 Lafayette St., Ste. 301, Santa Clara, CA, 95050-4966. Tel.: 408-983-0100; Fax: 408-983-0295.

STATISTICAL OVERVIEW

Personnel	
Bishop	1
Priests: Diocesan Active in Diocese	89
Priests: Active Outside Diocese	3
Priests: Retired, Sick or Absent	26
Number of Diocesan Priests	118
Religious Priests in Diocese	211
Extern Priests in Diocese	19
Ordinations:	
Diocesan Priests	1
Permanent Deacons in Diocese	8
Total Brothers	76
Total Sisters	440
Parishes	
Parishes	46
With Resident Pastor:	
Resident Diocesan Priests	39
Resident Religious Priests	5
Without Resident Pastor:	
Administered by Priests	2
Missions	5
Pastoral Centers	1
New Parishes Created	1
Professional Ministry Personnel:	
Brothers	3
Sisters	31
Lay Ministers	96
Welfare	
Catholic Hospitals	3
Total Assisted	245,343
Health Care Centers	1
Total Assisted	85
Homes for the Aged	1
Total Assisted	66
Total Assisted	270
Special Centers for Social Services	41
Total Assisted	66,769
Residential Care of Disabled	2
Total Assisted	89
Educational	
Colleges and Universities	1
Total Students	7,863
High Schools, Diocesan and Parish	2
Total Students	1,631
High Schools, Private	4
Total Students	3,965
Elementary Schools, Diocesan and Parish	30
Total Students	10,974
Elementary Schools, Private	1
Total Students	152
Catechesis/Religious Education:	
High School Students	2,629
Elementary Students	14,687
Total Students Under Catholic Instruction	41,901
Teachers in the Diocese:	
Priests	57
Scholastics	2
Brothers	6
Sisters	8
Lay Teachers	594
Vital Statistics	
Receptions into the Church:	
Infant Baptism Totals	8,818
Adult Baptism Totals	498
Received into Full Communion	497
First Communions	5,053
Confirmations	2,272
Marriages:	
Catholic	1,420
Interfaith	451
Total Marriages	1,871
Deaths	2,049
Total Catholic Population	391,313
Total Population	1,565,253

Diocese of San Jose—900 Lafayette St., Ste. 301, Santa Clara, 95050-4966. Tel: 408-983-0100; Fax: 408-983-0295.

Vicar General—Rev. MICHAEL J. MITCHELL, V.G., Moderator, *Diocese of San Jose, 900 Lafayette St., Ste. 301, Santa Clara, 95050-4966.* Tel: 408-983-0240.

Episcopal Vicars—

Vicar for Canonical Affairs—Rev. MAURICE F. SHEA, S.T.L., J.C.D., *Diocese of San Jose, 900 Lafayette St., Ste. 301, Santa Clara, 95050-4966.* Tel: 408-983-0219.

Vicar for Clergy—Rev. STEPHEN TUTAS, S.M., *Diocese of San Jose, 900 Lafayette St., Ste. 301, Santa Clara, 95050-4966.* Tel: 408-983-0149.

Vicar for Ecumenical and Interreligious Affairs—Rev. EUGENE J. BOYLE, *Dioces of San Jose, 900 Lafayette St., Ste. 301, Santa Clara, 95050-4966.* Tel: 408-983-0161.

Vicar for Parish—Rev. PHILIP MCCRILLIS. Tel: 408-983-0129.

Vicar for Pastoral Ministry—Sr. PATRICIA MARIA MULPETERS. Tel: 408-983-0120.

Vicar for Religious—Rev. DAVID H. SCHUYLER, S.M., S.T.L., J.C.D., *Diocese of San Jose, 900 Lafayette St., Ste. 301, Santa Clara, 95050-4966.* Tel: 408-983-0219.

Chancellor—LINDA BEARIE, *Diocese of San Jose, 900 Lafayette St., Ste. 301, Santa Clara, 95050-4966.* Tel: 408-983-0160.

Diocesan Tribunal—Diocese of San Jose, 900 Lafayette St., Ste. 301, Santa Clara, 95050-4966. Tel: 408-983-0219.

Judicial Vicar—Rev. DAVID H. SCHUYLER, S.M., S.T.L., J.C.D.

Adjutant—Rev. MAURICE F. SHEA, S.T.L., J.C.D.

Judges—Revs. DAVID H. SCHUYLER, S.M., S.T.L., J.C.D.; MAURICE F. SHEA, S.T.L., J.C.D.; HEIN MINH NGUYEN, J.C.D.

Defender of the Bond—Rev. FRANCIS V. CILIA.

Advocates—Sr. JULIE BELLEFEUILLE, S.N.D.; Sr. M. JUDE RISTEY, P.B.V.M. Tel: 408-983-0221. NANCY STEVENS, J.C.L. Tel: 408-983-0223. Sr. ANN MARGUERITE SOUZA, C.S.J., J.C.L. Tel: 408-983-0224.

Notary and Secretary to the Tribunal—Mrs. BELVA M. DICAROLIS. Tel: 408-983-0219.

Bishop's Executive Committee—Most Rev. PIERRE DUMAINE, D.D, Ph.D.; Revs. MICHAEL J. MITCHELL, V.G.; PHILIP MCCRILLIS; STEPHEN TUTAS, S.M.; Sr. PATRICIA MARIE MULPETERS, P.B.V.M.; Sr. MARY CLAUDE POWER, P.B.V.M.; LINDA BEARIE.

Diocesan Consultors—Revs. LUDWIG ANDRE; J. PATRICK BROWNE; BERNARD K. FREYNE; JOSEPH J. MILANI; MICHAEL J. MITCHELL, V.G.; FRANCIS CILIA; ALEXANDER LARKIN; TERRENCE J. SULLIVAN.

Council of Priests—Most Rev. PIERRE DUMAINE, D.D., Ph.D.; Revs. STEPHEN TUTAS, S.M., Liaison; MICHAEL J. MITCHELL, V.G.; HIEN NGUYEN; J. PATRICK BROWNE; BARRY FREYNE; NORMAN SEGOVID; JOHN SANDERSFELD; MATTHEW STANLEY; PHILIP MCCRILLIS; JOSEPH MILANI; LUDWIG ANDRE; MICHAEL O'CONNOR; ROBERT LEGER; FRANCIS CILIA; WARWICK JAMES; DAVID H. SCHUYLER, S.M., S.T.L., J.C.D.; CHARLES MACEDO; TERRANCE SULLIVAN; JEFFREY LABELLE; MATEO SHEEDY.

Council of Religious—Revs. ALBERT BUNSIC, O.C.D.; DAVID H. SCHUYLER, S.M., S.T.L., J.C.D., Liaison; PETER FILICE, S.J.; Bro. RALPH KUDER, C.S.C.; Sr. AILEEN DONOHUE, S.N.D.; Sr. ROSEMARY EVERETT, S.N.J.M.; Sr. PAULE FREEBURG, D.C.; Sr. PETER MCCUSKER, R.S.M.; Sr. MARGARET MCGRAW, C.S.J.; Sr. BARBARA NIXON, S.N.J.M.; Sr. GISELA ENRIQUEZ, M.E.S.S.T., *Diocese of San Jose, 900 Lafayette St., Ste. 301, Santa Clara, 95050-4966.* Tel: 408-983-0161.

Deans—Northern Deanery: Rev. LUDWIG ANDRE, Northwestern Deanery: Rev. TERRENCE J. SULLIVAN, Northeastern Deanery: Rev. WARWICK JAMES, Southwestern Deanery: Rev. FRANCIS CILLA, Central Deanery: Rev. J. PATRICK BROWNE, Southeastern Deanery: Rev. JOHN SANDERSFELD.

Apostleship of Prayer—Rev. JOHN J. SWEENY, *2800 Mission College Rd., Santa Clara, 95051.*

Archives—Mr. TONY MCGILTON, Records Management, *Diocese of San Jose, 2242 Calle Del Mundo, Santa Clara, 95054.* Tel: 408-727-6082.

Special Assistance Ministries Team—Rev. STEPHEN TUTAS, S.M., Chm., *10110 N. DeAnza Blvd., Cupertino, 95014.* Tel: 408-252-7653. Mr. GERALD DOOHER, Ph.D.; Revs. GEORGE MANCHA; JAMES S. TUCKER, S.S.

Building Committee—Mr. ROBERT E. SUMMERS; Revs. FRANCIS V. CILIA; MARK CATALANA; DANIEL DERRY; ROBERT GRAY; MICHAEL J. MITCHELL, V.G.; THOMAS F. MURRAY; STEPHEN E. PERATA; Mr. CHARLES F. BUCKLEY, Consultant.

Canonical Affairs—Rev. MAURICE F. SHEA, S.T.L., J.C.D., *Diocese of San Jose, 900 Lafayette St., Ste. 301, Santa Clara, 95050-4966.* Tel: 408-983-0219.

Charismatic Communities—Revs. ANTHONY PEREIRA, S.D.B.; ANGEL MARIANO, S.J.; Deacon JOSE ALVAREZ, *Charismatic Renewal Center, 3000 El Camino Real, Santa Clara, 95051.* Tel: 408-378-4646.

Catholic Charities—Catholic Charities of Santa Clara County. DEE WISCHMANN, CEO, *2625 Zanker Rd., Ste. 200, San Jose, 95134.* Tel: 408-468-0100; Fax: 408-944-0275.

Chinese Catholic Community—Rev. MATTHEW KOO, *900 Lafayette St., Ste. 301, Santa Clara, 95050-4966.* Tel: 408-983-0211.

Management Information System—TOM ACKERSON, Mgr., *900 Lafayette St., Ste. 301, Santa Clara, 95050-4966.* Tel: 408-983-0163.

Cursillo Movement—Rev. ROBERT LEGER, Chap., *St. Frances Cabrini, 15333 Woodard Rd., San Jose, 95124.* Tel: 408-377-3090.

Permanent Diaconate—Rev. STEPHEN TUTAS, S.M., Dir., *Diocese of San Jose, 900 Lafayette St., Ste. 301, Santa Clara, 95050-4966.* Tel: 408-983-0149.

Education Department—Sr. MARY CLAUDE POWER, P.B.V.M., Supt. of Schools. Asst. Supt. of Schools: Mr. JIM BRENNAN; MARIAN STUCKEY, *Diocese of San Jose, 900 Lafayette St., Ste. 301, Santa Clara, 95050-4966.* Tel: 408-983-0185.

Continuing Clergy Education & Formation—LEONEL NOIA, *1375 E. Santa Clara St., San Jose, 95116.* Revs. ROBERT H. PASSALACQUA; PAUL P. WEISBECK; JON PEDIGO; KEVIN JOYCE; HEIN NGUYEN.

Diocesan Development Office—VALLYN TURNER, Dir., *Diocese of San Jose, 900 Lafayette St., Ste. 301, Santa Clara, 95050-4966.* Tel: 408-983-0245.

Evangelization Committee—Vacant; Chm., *Diocese of San Jose, 900 Lafayette St., Ste. 301, Santa Clara, 95050-4966.*

Finance Office—Rev. MICHAEL J. MITCHELL, V.G., Dir.; Mr. CHARLES BARTON, Controller/Deputy Dir.

Finance Council—Bishop PIERRE DUMAINE, D.D., Ph.D.; WALTER SCHOENDORF; Rev. MICHAEL J. MITCHELL, V.G.; Mr. ROBERT MCADAMS; Mr. DONALD NYMOEN; Mr. MATTHEW O'ROURKE; Mr. EUGENE TOOMEY; DONALD WAITE; Mr. ROBERT E. SUMMERS.

Health Affairs—Sr. PATRICIA MARIE MULPETERS, P.B.V.M., Liaison.

Human Concern Commission—Rev. TIMOTHY KIDNEY, Pres. Tel: 408-983-0137., *Diocese of San Jose, 900 Lafayette St., Ste. 301, Santa Clara, 95050-4966.* Tel: 408-983-0121.

Italian Catholic Federation—Rev. GEORGE ARANHA, Chap., *200 O'Connor Dr., San Jose, 95128.* Tel: 408-294-8953.

Knights of Columbus—ANTHONY J. PERRELLA, Pres., *931 Brookgrove Ln., Cupertino, 95014.* Tel: 408-255-5399.

Legion of Mary—Rev. JOHN J. SWEENY, *Our Lady of Peace, 2800 Mission College Blvd., Santa Clara, 95051.* Tel: 408-988-4585.

Ministry to Priests Program—Revs. STEPHEN TUTAS, S.M., Liaison, *900 Lafayette St., Ste. 301, Santa Clara, 95050.* ROBERT LEGER, Chm. PAUL DUONG; RICHARD GARCIA; DAVID MERCER.

Vicar of Pastoral Ministry—Sr. PATRICIA MARIE MULPETERS, Ministry Institute; ANNE GRYCZ, Assoc. Dir. Scripture & Liturgy; THERESA MAES, Assoc. Dir. Family Life & Pastoral Care; JEANNINE LEICHNER, Assoc. Dir. Catechetical Ministry; CHARMAINE WARMENHOVEN, Assoc. Dir. Special Pastoral Ministries; VINCENT NIMS, Assoc. Dir. Youth & Young Adult Ministry; TERRIE IACINO, Assoc. Dir. Sec. Human Concerns; ROBERT DELANEY, Assoc. Dir. Hispanic Ministry.

Diocesan Clergy Personnel—Revs. STEPHEN TUTAS, S.M., Vicar for Clergy, Chm. CHRISTOPHER BENNETT; Revs. LEO RCONEY; JOSEPH J. MILANI; ALEXANDER LARKIN; BARRY FREYNE; RICHARD GARCIA.

Pastoral Care Advisory Committee—Liaisons: THERESA MAES; CHARMAINE WARMENHOVEN, *Diocese of San Jose, 900 Lafayette St., Ste. 301, Santa Clara, 95050-4966.* Tel: 408-983-0126.

Pastoral Resource Committee for Ministry to the Homosexual—Sr. PATRICIA MARIE MULPETERS, P.B.V.M., Chm., *Diocese of San Jose, 900 Lafayette St., Ste. 301, Santa Clara, 95050-4966.* Tel: 408-983-0160.

Advisory Committee for Ministry with the Deaf and Persons with Disabilities—CHARMAINE WARMENHOVEN, Liaison, *Diocese of San Jose, 900 Lafayette St., Ste. 301, Santa Clara, 95050-4966.* Tel: 408-983-0141 (Voice); 408-983-0292 (TDD).

Personnel Office—LINDA BEARIE, Dir. MARY ANN ARNOLD, Asst. Dir., *Diocese of San Jose, 900 Lafayette St., Ste. 301, Santa Clara, 95050-4966.* Tel: 408-983-0149.

Propagation of the Faith-Holy Childhood Association-Catholic Relief Service—MARGARET COAKER, Dir. Tel: 408-983-0166. Sr. MARY MARIUS MEI, B.V.M., Mission Coord. Tel: 408-983-0166., *Diocese of San Jose, 900 Lafayette St., Ste. 301, Santa Clara, 95050-4966.* Tel: 408-983-0166.

Research and Planning—Sr. PATRICIA MARIE MULPETERS, P.B.V.M., Liaison, *Diocese of San Jose, 900 Lafayette St., Ste. 301, Santa Clara, 95050-4966.* Tel: 408-983-0160.

Respect Life Program—TERRIE IACINO, Assoc. Dir., *Diocese of San Jose, 900 Lafayette St., Ste. 301, Santa Clara, 95050-4966.* Tel: 408-983-0137.

Clergy Retirement Board—Revs. ARTHUR HARRISON, Chm. MICHAEL J. MITCHELL, V.G.; THOMAS AHERN; ROBERT KIEFER; CHARLES MACEDO; Mr. D.J. HIENLEN; Mr. JOHN WHALEN; Rev. JAMES WALSH.

Catholic Telemedia Network—SHIRLEY CONNOLLY, Gen. Mgr., *324 Middlefield Rd., Menlo Park, 94025.* Tel: 415-326-7850; Fax: 415-326-4605.

Vocation Office—Rev. RICHARD GARCIA, Dir., *Diocese of San Jose, 900 Lafayette St., Ste. 301, Santa Clara, 95050-4966.* Tel: 408-983-0149.

Women in the Church Office—Sr. PATRICIA MARIE MULPETERS, P.B.V.M., *Diocese of San Jose, 900 Lafayette St., Ste. 301, Santa Clara, 95050-4966.* Tel: 408-983-0160.

Liturgical Commission—ANNE E. GRYCZ, Liaison; Sr. FRANCIS ALLEN; Sr. PATRICIA DAVIS, P.B.V.M.; Rev. JOSEPH DELGADO; TONY EIRAS; Sr. BETTE GAMBONINI, B.V.M.; Rev. WARWICK JAMES, Chm. BLESSIE LASCOLA; ELIZABETH LILLY; Sr. SHARON MCMILLAN, S.N.D.; RAUL MENDOZA; Sr. JOSEFINA MONTALVO, R.S.C.J.; BARBARA MOUNT; BERNIE NOJADERA; JAY SOMERA; Rev. MATTHEW STANLEY; JUDY SWAZEY; Rev. GARY THOMAS.

"The Valley Catholic" (Diocesan Newspaper)—ROBERTA WARD, Editor; MICHAEL HAWKINS, Business Mgr., *Diocese of San Jose, 900 Lafayette St., Ste. 301, Santa Clara, 95050-4966.* Tel: 408-983-0260.

Consultation Processes: Diocesan and Parish—Sr. PATRICIA MARIA MULPETERS, P.B.V.M., *Diocese of San Jose, 900 Lafayette, Ste. 301, Santa Clara, 95050-4966.* Tel: 408-983-0160.

Ecumenical and Interreligious Affairs—Rev. EUGENE BOYLE, *Diocese of San Jose, 900 Lafayette St., Ste. 301, Santa Clara, 95050-4966.* Tel: 408-983-0161.

CLERGY, PARISHES, MISSIONS AND PAROCHIAL SCHOOLS

CITY OF SAN JOSE

1—ST. JOSEPH CATHEDRAL (1849), Revs. J. Patrick Browne; Abel Lopez; Rick Rodoni. In res., Rev. Fausto Lopez.
Res. and Church—80 S. Market St., 95113. Tel: 408-283-8100; Fax: 408-283-8110.
Catechesis/Religious Programs—Students 238.

2—ST. PATRICK PROTO-CATHEDRAL (1871), Revs. Timothy Kidney; Walter Mallo.
Res., 389 E. Santa Clara St., 95113. Tel: 408-294-8120; Fax: 408-291-6277.
School—51 N. 9th St., 95112. Tel: 408-283-5858; Fax: 408-291-6277.
Lay Teachers 9; Students 323.
Catechesis/Religious Programs—Tel: 408-291-6279; Fax: 408-291-6277.
Students 283.

3—ST. FRANCIS OF ASSISI/EDENDALE (1996), Rev. John Sandersfeld.
Res., 4100 San Felipe Rd., 95135. Tel: 408-223-1562; Fax: 408-223-1759.
Catechesis/Religious Programs—Students 190.

4—EDENVALE CATHOLIC MISSION (1993), Rev. Norman Segovia.
Res., 5278 B Monterey Rd., 95111. Tel: 408-362-9958; Fax: 408-223-1759.

5—FIVE WOUNDS PORTUGUESE NATIONAL CHURCH (1914) (Portuguese), Rev. Leonel C. Noia. In res., Revs. Jack La Rocca; Robert Gray.
Res., 1375 E. Santa Clara St., 95116. Tel: 408-292-2123; Fax: 408-292-0201.
School—1390 Five Wounds Ln., 95116. Tel: 408-293-0425; Fax: 408-971-7607.
Priests 1; Sisters 2; Lay Teachers 12; Students 273.
Catechesis/Religious Programs—Students 620.

6—ST. FRANCES CABRINI (1955), Revs. G. Robert Leger; Robert G. Essig, Pastor Emeritus. In res., Rev. Don Flickinger.
Res., 15333 Woodard Rd., 95124. Tel: 408-879-1120; Fax: 408-377-3587.
School—15325 Woodard Rd., 95124. Tel: 408-377-6545; Fax: 408-377-8491.
Sisters 1; Lay Teachers 25; Students 678.
Catechesis/Religious Programs—Students 270.

7—HOLY CROSS (1911) (Italian), Revs. Antonio DeAngelis, C.S.; Gianantonio Baggio.
Res., 580 E. Jackson St., 95112. Tel: 408-294-2440; Fax: 408-294-8609.
Catechesis/Religious Programs—Students 385.

8—HOLY FAMILY (1905), Revs. Francis V. Cilia; Gregory Kimm; Anthony Mancuso; Sr. Bette Gamboni, Pastoral Assoc.
Res., 4848 Pearl Ave., 95136. Tel: 408-265-4040; Fax: 408-978-9979.
School—4850 Pearl Ave., Tel: 408-978-1355; Fax: 408-978-0290.
Lay Teachers 21; Students 655.
Catechesis/Religious Programs—Tel: 408-265-6201. Virginia Silvers, D.R.E.
Students 377.

9—HOLY SPIRIT (1963), Rev. Paul P. Weisbeck.
Res., 1200 Redmond Ave., 95120. Tel: 408-997-5115; Fax: 408-997-5102.
Catechesis/Religious Programs—Students 256.

10—ST. ANTHONY (1982), Rev. Robert E. Hayes. In res., Rev. Anthony Mancuso.
Mailing Address: P.O. Box 55, New Almaden, 95042. Tel: 408-997-4800; Fax: 408-997-4801.
Catechesis/Religious Programs—Students 177.

11—ST. CHRISTOPHER (1951), Revs. James Walsh; Christopher Bennett.
Office: 2278 Booksin Ave., 95125. Tel: 408-269-2226; Fax: 408-269-2784.
School—Tel: 408-723-7223; Fax: 408-978-5458.
Sisters of the Presentation 2; Lay Teachers 34; Students 625.
Catechesis/Religious Programs—Tel: 408-264-8764; Fax: 408-978-5458.
Students 625.

12—ST. JOHN VIANNEY (1952), Revs. Lawrence Hendel; John Pedigo; Joseph Delgado; Deacon Joseph Alvarez.
Res., 4609 Alum Rock Ave., 95127. Tel: 408-258-7832; Fax: 408-258-6152.
School—4601 Hyland Ave., 95127. Tel: 408-258-7677; Fax: 408-258-5997.
Sisters of the Presentation B.V.M. 3; Lay Teachers 22; Students 624.
Catechesis/Religious Programs—Tel: 408-251-0657; Fax: 408-272-1045.
Students 575.

13—ST. JULIE (1974), Rev. Richard C. Fry; Rev. Msgr. Jose V. Suarez (Philippines). In res., Rev. John Balleza.
Res., 366 St. Julie Dr., 95119. Tel: 408-629-3030; Fax: 408-629-3343.
Catechesis/Religious Programs—Tel: 408-226-3595.
Students 160.

14—ST. LEO THE GREAT (1923), Revs. Richard J. Garcia; Francisco Rios. In res., Revs. Maurice F. Shea; Matthew Koo.
Res., 88 Race St., 95126. Tel: 408-293-3503; Fax: 408-293-3516.
School—Tel: 408-293-4846; Fax: 408-293-5855.
Lay Teachers 10; Students 292.
Catechesis/Religious Programs—Tel: 408-293-1662. Gayle Morrissette, D.R.E.
Students 269.

15—ST. MARIA GORETTI (1961), Revs. Kevin Joyce; Arthur Yabes, S.V.D.; Gerardo Menchaca.
Res., 2980 Senter Rd., 95111. Tel: 408-363-2300; Fax: 408-363-2305.
Catechesis/Religious Programs—Tel: 408-363-2310. Bro. Bill Farrell, S.M., D.R.E.
Students 632.

16—ST. MARTIN OF TOURS (1914), Revs. George A. Aranha; William Pegnan, O.F.M.Cap.
Res., 200 O'Connor Dr., 95128. Tel: 408-294-8953; Fax: 408-294-2624.
School—300 O'Connor Dr., 95128. Tel: 408-287-3630; Fax: 408-287-4313.
Lay Teachers 33; Students 362.
Catechesis/Religious Programs—Students 148.

17—MOST HOLY TRINITY (1961) (Hispanic/Filipino), Revs. Jeffrey LaBelle, S.J.; Angel Mariano, S.J.; Deacons Salvador Alvarez; Vincente Perez.
Res., 2040 Nassau Dr., 95122. Tel: 408-729-0101; Fax: 408-258-4131.
School—Sisters 3; Lay Teachers 10; Students 310.
Catechesis/Religious Programs—Clara R. Morales, D.R.E.
Students 375.

18—OUR LADY OF GUADALUPE (1962) Hispanic, Revs. Damian Gamboa, O.F.M.; James Kyrie, O.F.M.; Walter Gomez.
Office: 2020 E. San Antonio St., 95116. Tel: 408-258-7057; Fax: 408-258-8249.
Catechesis/Religious Programs—Tel: 408-258-0544. Olga Islas-Siem, D.R.E.
Students 725.

19—ST. THOMAS OF CANTERBURY (1967), Rev. Walter M. McMahon.
Res., 1522 McCoy Ave., 95130. Tel: 408-378-1595; Fax: 408-378-1215.
Catechesis/Religious Programs—Students 125.

20—QUEEN OF APOSTLES (1960), Rev. James J. Mifsud, S.M.; Bro. William McCall, S.M. In res., Rev. T. William Bolts, S.M.

Res., 4911 Moorpark Ave., 95129. Tel: 408-253-7560; Fax: 408-253-9530.
School—Tel: 408-252-3659.
Lay Teachers 12; Students 308.

21—OUR LADY QUEEN OF MARTYRS, VIETNAMESE MISSION (1985) (Vietnamese), Revs. Dominic Do van Dinh, Admin.; Peter Chinh Pham.
Office: 389 E. Santa Clara St., 95113. Tel: 408-291-6280; Fax: 408-291-6289.
Catechesis/Religious Programs—Tel: 408-291-6282. Bro. Fortunat Tran Trong An Phong, F.S.C., D.R.E.
Students 1,400.

22—SACRED HEART OF JESUS (1920), Revs. Mateo E. Sheedy; Robert S. Brocato.
Res., 325 Willow St., 95110. Tel: 408-292-0146; Fax: 408-292-0172.
Catechesis/Religious Programs—Tel: 408-292-0146.
Students 400.

23—SANTA TERESA (1967), Rev. Raymond G. Kenny.
Res., 794 Calero Ave., 95123. Tel: 408-629-7777; Fax: 408-629-5260.
Catechesis/Religious Programs—Tel: 408-227-5915; Fax: 408-629-5260.
Students 281.

24—CHURCH OF THE TRANSFIGURATION (1965), Rev. William C. Leininger.
Mailing Address: 4325 Jarvis Ave., 95118. Tel: 408-264-3600; Fax: 408-266-2745.
Catechesis/Religious Programs—Tel: 408-266-2745.
Students 190.

25—ST. VICTOR (1961), Revs. Stephen F. Perata; Robert R. Taheny, S.J.; Candido O. Lim, S.J. (Philippines).
Res., 3108 Sierra Rd., 95132. Tel: 408-251-7055; Fax: 408-251-5528.
School—Tel: 408-251-1740; Fax: 408-251-1492.
Sisters of St. Joseph of Carondelet 2; Lay Teachers 12; Students 317.
Catechesis/Religious Programs—Tel: 408-251-0154; Fax: 408-251-5528.
Students 489.

26—ST. MARY OF THE ASSUMPTION (1975). (Croatian Mission). Rev. Dujo Boban, O.F.M. In res., Rev. Joseph Mikulich, O.F.M.
Res., 901 Lincoln Ave., 95126. Tel: 408-279-0279; Fax: 408-292-5868.
Catechesis/Religious Programs—Students 105.
Croatian Franciscan Fathers Corporation—Tel: 408-279-0279; Fax: 408-292-5868.
Franciscan Fathers—Tel: 408-276-0279; Fax: 408-292-5868.

OUTSIDE THE CITY OF SAN JOSE

Alviso, Santa Clara Co., Our Lady, Star of the Sea (1985) (Mexican-American), Rev. John R. Coleman.
Mailing Address: P.O. Box 426, 95002.
Res., 1385 Michigan Ave., 95002. Tel: 408-263-2121; Fax: 408-263-1182.
Catechesis/Religious Programs—Tel: 408-263-6637; Fax: 408-263-1182.
Students 250.

Campbell, Santa Clara Co., St. Lucy (1947), Revs. Terrence J. Sullivan; Lieu Vu; Robert Passalacqua.
Res., 2350 Winchester Blvd., 95008. Tel: 408-378-2464; Fax: 408-378-5548.
School—76 Kennedy Ave., 95008. Tel: 408-378-7454; Fax: 408-378-4945.
Sisters 3; Lay Teachers 15; Students 317.
Catechesis/Religious Programs—Tel: 408-379-5900; Fax: 408-378-5548.
Students 309.

Cupertino, Santa Clara Co., St. Joseph of Cupertino (1913), Revs. Leo J. Rooney; Joseph J. Milani; Mark Catalana; Peter Luc Phan; Deacon Don McLaughlin. In res., Rev. Michael Mitchell.
Res., 10110 N. DeAnza Blvd., 95014. Tel: 408-252-7653; Fax: 408-252-5263.
School—10120 N. DeAnza Blvd., 95014. Tel: 408-252-6441.
Lay Teachers 13; Students 309.
Catechesis/Religious Programs—Tel: 408-253-0660.
Students 376.

Gilroy, Santa Clara Co., St. Mary (1865), Revs. Daniel Derry; Jeronimo Guitierrez (Mexico); Jean M. Lemay.
Res., 11 First St., 95020. Tel: 408-847-5151; Fax: 408-847-4851. [CEM]
School—7900 Church St., 95020-4499. Tel: 408-842-2827; Fax: 408-847-7679. Christa Hanson, Prin.
Religious 1; Lay Teachers 11; Students 311.
Catechesis/Religious Programs—7950 Church St., 95020. Tel: 408-847-2652; Fax: 408-847-4851. D.R.E.: Carrie Rauch; Hilda Porcella.
Students 1092.

Los Altos, Santa Clara Co., St. Nicholas (1947), Rev. Gary R. Thomas.
Res., 473 Lincoln Ave., 94022. Tel: 415-948-2158; Fax: 408-948-8566.
School—12816 S. El Monte Ave., Los Altos Hills, 94022. Tel: 415-941-4056; Fax: 415-941-3842.
Sisters of Mercy 1; Lay Teachers 9; Students 286.
Catechesis/Religious Programs—Tel: 415-941-7622.
Students 200.
Station—Seven Oaks, Residential Park for the Aged, 1174 Los Altos Ave., 94022. Tel: 415-948-7337.

St. Simon (1955), Revs. Ludwig M. Andre; Joseph Rich. In res., Revs. Thomas Murray; Randy Benas.
Res., 1860 Grant Rd., 94024. Tel: 415-967-8311; Fax: 415-967-8876.
School—1840 Grant Rd., 94024. Tel: 415-968-9952.
Sisters, Servants of the Immaculate Heart of Mary (Immaculata, PA) 2; Lay Teachers 26; Students 611.
Catechesis/Religious Programs—Tel: 415-961-5469.
Students 125.

St. William (1959), Rev. Michael J. Burns.
Res., 611 S. El Monte Ave., 94022-4058. Tel: 415-948-8169; Fax: 415-948-8508.
Catechesis/Religious Programs—Tel: 415-941-1460; Fax: 408-948-8508.
Students 200.

Los Gatos, Santa Clara Co., St. Mary of the Immaculate Conception (1912), Revs. Justin Zawadzki; Anthony Pereira.
Res., 219 Bean Ave., 95030. Tel: 408-354-3726; Fax: 408-354-9302.
School—30 Lyndon Ave., 95030. Tel: 408-954-3944; Fax: 408-395-9151.
Sisters of the Holy Names of Jesus and Mary 2; Lay Teachers 20; Students 279.
Catechesis/Religious Programs—Tel: 408-354-4061; Fax: 408-354-9302.
Students 396.

Milpitas, Santa Clara Co., St. Elizabeth (1968), Revs. Edward Samy; Hien Minh Nguyen. In res., Rev. Joseph B.C. Okorie (Nigeria).
Res., 750 Sequoia Dr., 95035. Tel: 408-262-8100; Fax: 408-946-8703.
Catechesis/Religious Programs—Tel: 408-263-1995.
Students 240.

St. John the Baptist (1877), Revs. Charles F. Dougherty; Victor Pavalkis, Pastor Emeritus; Wilfredo S. Manrique.
Res., 279 S. Main St., 95035. Tel: 408-262-2546; Fax: 408-263-2564. [CEM]
School—360 S. Abel St., 95035. Tel: 408-262-8110; Fax: 408-262-0814.
Augustinian Recollect Sisters 2; Lay Teachers 8; Students 337.
Catechesis/Religious Programs—Tel: 408-262-3955; Fax: 408-262-3955. Linda Jo White, D.R.E.
Students 305.

Morgan Hill, Santa Clara Co., St. Catherine of Alexandria (1909), Revs. Eugene P. O'Donnell; Enrico A. Hernadez.
Res., 17400 Peak Ave., 95037. Tel: 408-779-3959; Fax: 408-779-0289.
School—Tel: 408-779-9950. Sr. Ann Therese Lynch, P.B.V.M., Prin.; Jeanne Smith, Vice Prin.
Lay Teachers 13; Students 298.
Catechesis/Religious Programs—Tel: 408-779-9604. Mrs. Wendy Scherbart, D.R.E.
Students 935.

Mountain View, Santa Clara Co., St. Athanasius (1959), Revs. Diarmuid Casey, C.S.Sp. (Ireland); Kevin B. Corrigan, C.S.Sp. (Ireland). In res., Revs. William O'Neill, C.S.Sp. (Ireland); Desmond McGlade, C.S.Sp. (Ireland).
Res., 160 N. Rengstorff Ave., 94043. Tel: 415-961-8600; Fax: 415-968-5633.
Catechesis/Religious Programs—Tel: 415-967-7900; Fax: 415-968-5633.
Students 330.

St. Joseph the Worker (1901), Revs. Oscar D. Tabujara; Robert B. Moran.
Res., 582 Hope St., 94041. Tel: 415-967-3831; Fax: 415-691-1522.
School—1120 Miramonte Ave., 94041. Tel: 415-967-1839; Fax: 415-691-1530. Kay Ingalls, Prin.
Lay Teachers 12; Students 299.

Palo Alto, Santa Clara Co.,

1—ST. THOMAS AQUINAS, (1901), Revs. Barry Freyne; Matthew Stanley; George Mancha.
Office: 3290 Middlefield Rd., 94306. Tel: 415-494-2496; Fax: 415-494-3780.
School—St. Elizabeth Seton Catholic Community School, 1095 Channing Ave., 94306. Tel: 415-326-9004; Fax: 415-326-2949.
Priests 1; Sisters 2; Lay Teachers 12; Students 252.
Catechesis/Religious Programs—Tel: 415-494-3097.
Students 302.

2—ST. ALBERT THE GREAT, (1961). Merged with St. Thomas Aquinas Parish. In res., Revs. Charles B. Macedo, (Retired); Matthew D. Stanley; George Mancha.
c/o St. Thomas Aquinas: 3290 Middlefield Rd., 94306. Tel: 415-327-8222; Fax: 415-494-3780.
Church—1097 Channing Ave., 94301.

3—ST. ANN CHAPEL, (1951). Merged with St. Thomas Aquinas Parish, Newman Center for Stanford University. In res., Revs. John Hester; William Lenane, (Retired); Eugene Boyle.
Office: c/o St. Thomas Aquinas: 3290 Middlefield Rd., 94306. Tel: 415-494-2496; Fax: 415-494-3780.
Church—1247 Cowper St., 94301.

4—OUR LADY OF THE ROSARY, (1959). Merged with St. Thomas Aquinas Parish.
Office: c/o St. Thomas Aquinas: 3290 Middlefield Rd., 94306. Tel: 415-494-2496; Fax: 415-494-3780.
Church—3233 Cowper St., 94306.

Santa Clara, Santa Clara Co.,

1—CHINESE CATHOLIC COMMUNITY, Rev. Matthew Koo.
Res., 900 Layfayette St., Ste. 301, 95050-4966. Tel: 408-983-0211; Fax: 408-983-0295.

2—ST. CLARE, (1777), Revs. John M. Martin, S.J.; Gerald J. Phelan, S.J.; Ronald J. Sanfilippo, S.J.; Augustine Tsong, S.J.; Bro. Raymond Keefe, S.J. In res., Rev. David Fitch, S.J.
Mailing Address: Box 178, 95052-0178. Tel: 408-248-7786; Fax: 408-248-8150.
School—Tel: 408-246-6797.
Sisters 4; Lay Teachers 10; Students 308.
Catechesis/Religious Programs—Tel: 408-241-0252. Mrs. Diane Madruga, D.R.E.
Lay Teachers 12; Aides 16; Students 208.
Station—Convalescent Hospital. (Mission skilled Nursing Home). Tel: 408-248-3736.

3—ST. JUSTIN, (1951), Revs. Jose Galang; Terrence Davis; Joseph Prendergast.
Res., 2655 Homestead Rd., 95051. Tel: 408-296-1193; Fax: 408-244-9437.
School—Tel: 408-248-1094.
Lay Teachers 15; Students 311.
Catechesis/Religious Programs—Students 280.

4—ST. LAWRENCE THE MARTYR, (1959), Revs. V. Warwick James (South Africa); Victor L. Wilkiemeyer, Pastor Emeritus; Hao Dinh.
Res., 1971 St. Lawrence Dr., 95051. Tel: 408-296-3000; Fax: 408-296-3100.
Schools—(Grades PreK-5) 1977 St. Lawrence Dr., 95051. Tel: 408-296-2260.
Lay Teachers 11; Students 250; (Grades 6-8). Tel: 408-296-3013.
Sisters 1; Lay Teachers 11; Students 197; (Grades 9-12) 2000 Lawrence Ct., 95051. Tel: 408-296-3013.
Sisters 3; Lay Teachers 25; Students 310.
Catechesis/Religious Programs—Students 205.

5—OUR LADY OF PEACE, (1961), Revs. John J. Sweeny; Juan Carranco. In res., Rev. Msgr. Edgar P. McCarren (RVC); Rev. Camilo P. Villanueva.
Res., 2800 Mission College Blvd., 95054. Tel: 408-988-4585; Fax: 408-988-0679.
Catechesis/Religious Programs—Tel: 408-988-7543. Richard Hernandez, D.R.E.
Students 652.

Saratoga, Santa Clara Co., Sacred Heart (1951), Revs. Alexander C. Larkin; Kenneth Silvia, C.S.C. In res., Deacon Thomas Combellick.
Res., 13724 Saratoga Ave., 95070. Tel: 408-867-3634; Fax: 408-867-5339.
School—13718 Saratoga Ave., 95070. Tel: 408-867-9241.
Sisters of Notre Dame de Namur 2; Lay Teachers 18; Students 300.
Catechesis/Religious Programs—Tel: 408-867-1530.
Students 310.

Church of the Ascension (1964), Rev. Paul Duong.
Res., 12033 Miller Ave., 95070. Tel: 408-725-3939; Fax: 408-725-3932.
Catechesis/Religious Programs—Tel: 408-725-3930.
Students 160.

Sunnyvale, Santa Clara Co.,

1—ST. ALBERT CHMIELOWSKI POLISH CATHOLIC PASTORAL MISSION, (1986) (Polish), Rev. Pawel Bandurski, S.Ch. (Poland).
Res., Mass held at St. Cyprian Church. 1133 W. Washington Ave., 94086. Tel: 408-735-9160; Fax: 408-735-9160.

2—STS. ANDREW AND PAUL KOREAN CATHOLIC MISSION OF SAN JOSE, (1981), Rev. John Jong-Man Park.
Res., 531 E. Weddell Dr., 94089-2162. Tel: 408-734-9721; Fax: 408-734-9723.

3—ST. CYPRIAN, (1961), Revs. Mark J. Neary; Raymund J. Field, C.S.V. In res., Rev. Pawel Bandurski, S.Ch.
Res., 1133 W. Washington, 94086. Tel: 408-739-8506; Fax: 408-739-2815.
School—195 Leota Ave., 94086. Tel: 408-738-3444.
Sisters of the Immaculate Heart of Mary (Westchester, PA) 2; Lay Teachers 8; Students 292.

Catechesis/Religious Programs—Tel: 408-739-9417.
Students 62.

4—ST. MARTIN, (1916), Revs. Benito O. Manding; Salvatore Blandino.
Res., 590 Central Ave., 94086. Tel: 408-736-3725; Fax: 408-736-4968.
School—597 Central Ave., 94086. Tel: 408-736-5534.
Lay Teachers 13; Students 334.
Catechesis/Religious Programs—Tel: 408-736-0967.
Students 246.

5—CHURCH OF THE RESURRECTION, (1963), Rev. Michael J. O'Connor. In res., Revs. Nicholas E. Farana; Alexander Alfonso; Bede Marandu.
Res., 725 Cascade Dr., P.O. Box 2040, 94087. Tel: 408-245-5554; Fax: 408-245-5589.
Church—1399 Hollenbeck Ave., P.O. Box 2040, 94087.
School—1395 Hollenbeck Ave., 94087. Tel: 408-245-4571; Fax: 408-245-4576.
Religious 1; Lay Teachers 11; Students 313.
Catechesis/Religious Programs—Students 257.

Chaplains of Public Institutions

SAN JOSE. *Agnews State Hospital*. Rev. Thomas J. Byrne, S.J. Tel: 408-294-9224.
Alexian Brothers Hospital. Revs. Arturo Mateo, M.S.C. Tel: 408-259-5000; Thai Q. Trinh. Tel: 408-259-5000.
Catholic Scouting. Rev. Paul Soukup, S.J. Tel: 408-554-4124.
Detention Ministry for Juveniles. Rev. Jack LaRocca. Tel: 408-280-7744.
Good Samaritan Hospital.
Notre Dame Villa. Rev. Leonard Traverso. Tel: 408-867-3212.
O'Connor Hospital. Revs. Toribio Ives Aniban. Tel: 408-947-2500; Robert Carey, C.S.V. Tel: 408-947-2500.
Santa Clara County Jail. Rev. Francisco Rios. Tel: 408-293-3503.
Santa Clara County Women's Facility. Ms. Marilu Eder.

LOS GATOS. *Presentation Center*. Rev. Antonio Medina, M.G. Tel: 408-354-2346.

MILPITAS. *Elmwood Rehabilitation Center*. Revs. Patrick Kilcoyne. Tel: 408-629-3030; Joseph Okorie. Tel: 415-943-1685; Francisco Rios. Tel: 408-293-3503.
Stanford Medical Center. Rev. John Hester. Tel: 415-723-4000.

PALO ALTO. *Children's Hospital at Stanford*. Vacant. Tel: 415-961-2118.

SANTA CLARA. *Santa Clara Valley Medical Center*. Revs. Alfred Playoust, S.J. Tel: 408-294-9224; Lenox Day, S.J. Tel: 408-294-9224; Eugene Corbett, S.J. Tel: 408-294-9224.

SARATOGA. *Our Lady of Fatima Villa*. Rev. Leonard Traverso. Tel: 408-867-3212.

Special Assignment:
Reverend Fathers—
Boyle, Eugene J., Vicar for Ecumenical & Interreligious Affairs
Garcia, Richard, Vocations Office
Gray, Robert, Finance Dept.
McCrillis, Philip, Vicar for Parish
Mitchell, Michael J., Vicar General
Schuyler, David, S.M., Judicial Vicar & Vicar for Religious
Shea, Maurice, Vicar for Canonical Affairs
Tribunal, Hien Nguyen
Tucker, James, S.S., Pastoral Services
Tutas, Stephen, S.M., Vicar for Clergy

On Duty Outside the Diocese:
Reverend Fathers—
Keulman, Kenneth P., New Orleans, LA
Rubio, Jo, Washington, DC
Tinh, Joseph Nguyen, Heimback-Vlatten, West Germany

Military Chaplains:
Reverend Fathers—
Hendel, Lawrence, Army National Guard. Tel: 408-252-7653
Regan, Richard J., 750 SG/HCM, Box 50, Sunnyvale, CA 94089-1236

Retired:
O'Connor, William
Reverend Monsignors—
Maher, James
McCarren, Edgar
O'Brien, Timothy
Powers, John
Reverend Fathers—
Ahern, Thomas
Baltazar, Ayala
Boyle, Eugene J.
Cottrell, Frank
Essig, Robert
Farana, Nicholas
Harrison, Arthur
Hayden, Guy B.
Hlebs, Milan
Hofmann, Arthur
Kelly, Alfred
Largente, Laurent
Lenane, William
Macedo, Charles
Maher, Raymond
Milani, Joseph
Murray, Thomas
O'Neill, William
Pavalkis, Victor
Peace, John
Re, Angelo
Spika, Anthony L.
Wilkiemeyer, Victor

Permanent Deacons:
Alvarez, Jose, St. John Vianney
Alvarez, Salvador, Most Holy Trinity & St. Catherine of Alexandria
Bunje, Carl, St. Thomas Aquinas
Chavez, Eloy, Our Lady of Guadalupe
Combellick, Thomas, Sacred Heart, Saratoga
Garcia, Bruno, Our Lady of Guadalupe
McLaughlin, Donald, St. Joseph of Cupertino
Perez, Vincente, Most Holy Trinity

INSTITUTIONS LOCATED IN THE DIOCESE

[A] SHRINES

SANTA CLARA. *Shrine of Our Lady of Peace*, 2800 Mission College Blvd., 95054. Tel: 408-988-4585; Fax: 408-988-0679. Rev. John J. Sweeny, Dir.
Staff: Mary Jean Kula; Kathryn Dwyer.
Our Lady of Peace Gift Shop. Tel: 408-980-9825.

[B] COLLEGES AND UNIVERSITIES

SANTA CLARA. *Santa Clara University*, 500 El Camino Real, 95053-0460. Tel: 408-554-4764; Fax: 408-554-2700.
For a complete listing, refer to the Colleges and Universities section.

[C] HIGH SCHOOLS, DIOCESAN

SAN JOSE. *Archbishop Mitty High School*. (Coed), 5000 Mitty Ave., 95129. Tel: 408-252-6610; Fax: 408-252-0518. Mr. Timothy Brosnan, Prin.; Rev. Rick Rodini, Campus Chap. Priests 1; Sisters 2; Lay Teachers 61; Students 1,321; Total Staff 112.

SANTA CLARA. *Saint Lawrence Academy*. (Grades 7-12), 2000 Lawrence Ct., 95051. Tel: 408-296-3013. College Prep Coed. Ron Modeste, Prin.; Gail Harrell, Assoc. Prin. Sisters 3; Lay Teachers 26; Students 310.

[D] HIGH SCHOOLS, PRIVATE

SAN JOSE. *Bellarmine College Preparatory*, 850 Elm St., 95126-1899. Tel: 408-294-9224; Fax: 408-294-1894; 297-2072. Society of Jesus.
Non-Resident Students: Revs. Gerald T. Wade, S.J., Supr.; William H. Muller, S.J., Pres.; James E. Morse, S.J., Treas.; John D. Murphy, S.J., Prin.; Raymond P. Allender, S.J.; Thomas H. Byrne, S.J.; Mario L. Capitolo, S.J.; Ronald M. Clemo, S.J.; Eugene J. Corbett, S.J.; Lenox C. Day, S.J.; Ralph J. Drendel, S.J.; John F. Dullea, S.J.; John L. Flynn, S.J.; Gerald J. Lentz, S.J.; Edward J. McFadden, S.J.; Alfred G. Playoust, S.J.; Michael G. Scully, S.J.; Robert J. Shinney, S.J.; Francis J. Silva, S.J.; William J. Stout, S.J.; William V. Thom, S.J.; Charles J. Tilley, S.J.; Bros. Raymond P. Koeplin, S.J.; Edmund W. Ryan, S.J.; Stephen J. Corder, S.J., Scholastics; Paul T. Mariani, S.J. Priests 17; Scholastics 2; Brothers 2; Lay Teachers 73; Students 1,350.
Notre Dame High School, 596 S. Second St., 95112. Tel: 408-294-1113; Fax: 408-288-8185. Sisters of Notre Dame de Namur.
Non-Resident Students. Anne A. Koch, Prin. Sisters 3; Lay Teachers 34; Students 485.
Presentation High School, 2281 Plummer Ave., 95125. Tel: 408-264-1664; Fax: 408-266-3028. Sisters of the Presentation. Sisters 1; Lay Teachers 42; Teachers 56; Students 680; Total Staff 56.

MOUNTAIN VIEW. *St. Francis High School*, 1885 Miramonte Ave., 94040. Tel: 415-968-1213; Fax: 415-968-3241. Brothers of Holy Cross. Mr. James Bowler, Pres.; Mr. Michael Speckman, Dir. of Activities; Mr. Kevin Makley, Vice Pres.; Mrs. Patty Tennant, Prin.; Angelo Aguiar, Dir. Devel.; Rev. Salvatore M. DiNardo, O.P. Brothers 2; Sisters 1; Lay Teachers 80; Students 1,450; Total Staff 123.

[E] ELEMENTARY SCHOOLS, PRIVATE

LOS GATOS. *Casa Maria Montessori, Preschool & Kindergarten*, 200 Prospect Ave., 95030. Tel: 408-354-8475. Kerry Anne Leonard, Admin. Sisters 2; Lay Teachers 12; Students 152; Total Staff 14.

[F] THE CATHOLIC CHARITIES OF THE DIOCESE OF SAN JOSE

SAN JOSE. *Catholic Charities of Santa Clara County*, 2625 Zanker Rd., 95134. Tel: 408-468-0100; Fax: 408-944-0275. Mailing Address: Sally Vance, 2625 Zanker Rd., 95134. Dee Wischmann, CEO; Sally Vance, Exec. Asst. to CEO; Chris Larsen, Dir. of Devel.; Michael J. Cummins, CFO; Marilou Cristina, Dir of Family Svcs.; Sr. Marilyn Lacey, Dir. of Immigration, Refugee & Youth Svcs.; Chris Block, Dir. of Housing Devel. & Svcs., 195 E. San Fernando, 95112. Tel: 408-282-1125.
FAMILY SERVICES: Ron Ober, Dir., Mental Health & Clinical Svcs.
Children's Counseling Center. Tel: 408-944-0469.
Community Counseling & Education Svcs., 2625 Zanker Rd., 95134. Tel: 408-944-0469.
Focus for Work, 2625 Zanker Rd., Ste. 101, 95134. Tel: 408-944-0591. Eila Latif, Prog. Dir.
Oasis. (Older Adult Mental Health Team), 2625 Zanker Rd., 95134. Tel: 408-955-9170.
COMMUNITY SERVICES:
Foster Grandparent Program, 2625 Zanker Rd., 95134. Tel: 408-944-0668. Jane Contois, Prog. Dir. Number Assisted 85.
Martha's Kitchen, 311 Willow St., 95110. Tel: 408-293-6111. Bro. Joseph Nuuanu, Dir.
Independent Aging Program, 195 E. San Fernando St., 95112. Tel: 408-282-8600. (Respite Care, Case Management, Direct Services).
Long Term Care Ombudsman Program, 2625 Zanker Rd., 95134. Tel: 408-944-0567. Donna DiMinico, Prog. Dir. Number Assisted 8,813.
OLDER ADULT SERVICES:
Multi-Service Senior Center Programming, Eastside Neighborhood Ctr., 2150 Alum Rock Ave., 95112. Tel: 408-251-0215.
John XXIII Multiservice Center, 195 E. San Fernando St., 95112. Tel: 408-295-4116.
Volunteer Services, 2625 Zanker Rd., 95134. Tel: 408-944-0282. Susan Alberto, Mgr.
HOUSING DEVELOPMENT & SERVICE:
Shared Housing Program, 195 E. San Fernando St., 95112. Tel: 408-282-1144. Chris Block, Dir. Number Assisted 1,227.
IMMIGRATION, REFUGEE & YOUTH SERVICES:
Immigration Program, 2625 Zanker Rd., 95134. Tel: 408-944-0691. Number Assisted 5,472. Second Immigration Program Site, 7950 Church St., Gilroy, 95020. Tel: 408-842-4808.
Employment and Education Program & Career Center, 2625 Zanker Rd., 95134. Tel: 408-944-0362. Jane Hills, Dir.
USCC Refugee Resettlement, 2625 Zanker Rd., 95134. Tel: 408-944-0362. Sr. Marilyn Lacey, Dir.
Y.E.S./C.Y.O. Youth Programs, 645 Wool Creek Rd., 95112. Tel: 408-283-6150. Bich-Lien Phan, Dir. Numbers Assisted 436.
NEIGHBORHOOD SERVICE CENTERS:
Eastside Neighborhood Center, 2150 Alum Rock Ave., 95116. Tel: 408-251-0215. Ellen Hertel, Prog. Coord.
John XXIII Neighborhood Center, 195 E. San Fernando St., 95112. Tel: 408-295-4116. Marion Johnson, Prog. Coord. Number Assisted 2,083.
Martha's Kitchen, 311 Willos St., 95110. Tel: 408-293-6111. Bro. Joseph Nuuanu, Dir.
NUTRITION SERVICES:
Senior Nutrition Services, 2625 Zanker Rd., 95134. Tel: 408-944-0282. Judd Ingram, Prog. Mgr.
Burbank Nutrition Site, 2400 Clove Dr., 95128. Tel: 408-293-0623.
Eastside Nutrition Site, 2150 Alum Rock Ave., 95116. Tel: 408-251-0215.
Gilroy Nutrition Site, 7371 Hanna St., Gilroy, 95020. Tel: 408-842-4200.
John XXIII Nutrition Site, 195 E. San Fernando, 95112. Tel: 408-295-6940.
Morgan Hill Nutrition Site, 17666 Crest Ave., Morgan Hill, 95037. Tel: 408-779-1413.
HANDICAPABLES PROGRAM: All Nutrition Sites: Number Assisted 2,665.
Handicapables Program, 4353 Payne Avenue #705, 95114. Tel: 408-243-3160.
AUXILIARIES:
Palo Alto/Los Altos Auxiliary. Tel: 415-948-3425. Patricia A. Sykes, Pres.

[G] DAY NURSERIES

SAN JOSE. *St. Elizabeth's Day Home*, 1544 McKinley Ave., 95126. Tel: 408-295-3456; Fax: 408-295-5917. Emili Willit, Exec. Dir. Lay Staff 40; Children 200.

[H] GENERAL HOSPITALS

SAN JOSE. *Alexian Brothers Hospital*, 225 N. Jackson Ave., 95116. Tel: 408-259-5000.
For a complete listing, refer to the Hospitals section.
O'Connor Hospital, 2105 Forest Ave., 95128. Tel: 408-947-2500.
For a complete listing, refer to the Hospitals section.

MORGAN HILL. *O'Connor Hospital dba Saint Louise Hospital & Health Center*, Admin. Office, 18500 Saint Louise Dr., 95037. Tel: 408-779-1500.
For a complete listing, refer to the Hospitals section.

[I] SPECIAL SANATORIUM AND HOSPITALS

SARATOGA. *Our Lady of Fatima Villa*, 20400 Saratoga-Los Gatos Rd., 95070. Tel: 408-741-2950; Fax: 408-741-4930.
For a complete listing, refer to the Special Care Facilities section.

[J] HOTEL, SENIOR CITIZENS RESIDENCE

SAN JOSE. *Jeanne d'Arc Manor*, 85 S. Fifth St., 95112. Tel: 408-288-7421.
For a complete listing, refer to the Special Care Facilities section.

[K] HOMES FOR THE AGED

MOUNTAIN VIEW. *Villa Siena*, 1855 Miramonte Ave., 94040. Tel: 415-961-6484.
For a complete listing, refer to the Special Care Facilities section.

[L] RETREATS

LOS ALTOS. *Jesuit Retreat House*, 300 Manresa Way, 94022. Tel: 415-948-4491; Fax: 415-948-0640. Revs. Gerald P. McCourt, S.J., Supr.; Philip C. Blake, S.J.; Bernard J. Bush, S.J.; Robert J. Fabing, S.J.; Terence E. Koch, S.J.; Dave J. Morgan, S.J.; James R. Hanley, S.J.; Joseph P. Logan, S.J.; Timothy J. Meier, S.J.; Bro. Lawrence Thoo, S.J. Priests 10.

LOS GATOS. *Presentation Education and Retreat Center*, 19480 Bear Creek Rd., 95030-9519. Tel: 408-354-2346; Fax: 408-354-5226. Retreat and Conference Center for Religious and Laity. Sr. Virginia Pfluger, O.P., Exec. Dir. Capacity 128; Staff 22.
Villa Holy Names, 82 Prospect Ave., 95032. Tel: 408-354-2312. Sr. Jacquelyn Slater, S.N.J.M. Total Staff 2.

[M] MONASTERIES AND RESIDENCES OF PRIESTS AND BROTHERS

SAN JOSE. *Carmelite Monastery, Novitiate*, P.O. Box 3420, 95156-3420. Tel: 408-251-1361. Very Rev. Albert Bunsic, O.C.D., Prior; Revs. Michael Buckley, O.C.D.; Ailbe Doolan, O.C.D.; Donald Kinney, O.C.D., Subprior, Novice Master; Pascal Pierini, O.C.D.; Jan Lundberg, O.C.D.; Bro. Michael Villagomez, O.C.D. Priests 6; Brother 1; Novice 1.
Marianist Community, 10381 Singleton Rd., 95111. Tel: 408-972-2716. Revs. Joseph Stefanelli, S.M.; Timothy Eden, S.M., Prov.; Bros. Eugene Fitzsimmons, S.M.; William Farrell, S.M. Priests 2; Brothers 3.

CUPERTINO. *The Marianist Mission*, 22825 San Juan Rd., P.O. Box 1775, 95015-1775. Tel: 408-253-4841. Rev. Donald F. Bracht, S.M., Dir.
Marianist Provincial Residence. Mailing Address: P.O. Box 1775, 95015-1775. Tel: 408-253-4841; Fax: 408-253-5280. Res., 22825 San Juan Rd., 95014. Tel: 408-253-4841; Fax: 408-253-5280. Bros. Gary E. Morris, S.M., Asst. Prov./Dir. of Education; John Haster, S.M., Asst. for Temporalities & Community Dir. In res., Rev. John Rielly, S.M.; Bros. Stanley Murakami, S.M.; James Riley, S.M. Priests 4; Brothers 4.
Priests of the Pacific Province Working at Other Locations: Rev. Francis Nakagawa, S.M., 12500 Dupont Rd., Sebastopol, 95472. 334 State St., #106, Los Altos, 94022. Rev. Jorge da Silva, 461 Monterey Ave., Los Altos, 95030-5302. Rev. Robert Hughes, S.M., (Sabbatical), c/o 8491 E. Malcomb Dr., Scottsdale, AZ, 82550. Retreat Center 1; Lay Staff Only 22.
Marianist Novitiate Corporation, P.O. Box 1775, 95015-1775.
Marianist Retreat Center, 22622 Marianist Way, 95014. Tel: 408-253-6279; Fax: 408-253-1834. Ms. Michele Latno, Dir. Retreat Center 2; Staff 12.
Villa Saint Joseph, 22840 Mercedes Rd., 95014-3920. Tel: 408-257-4427. Marianist Retirement Home. Rev. Stephen Tutas, S.M., Dir. Priests 2; Brothers 15; Total in Residence 17.

LOS ALTOS. *Maryknoll*, 23000 Cristo Rey Dr., 94022. Tel: 415-967-3822; Fax: 415-965-3473. Rev. Philip F. Sheerin, M.M.; Bro. Charles A. Heschele, M.M. Retirement House for Priests and Brothers. In res., Revs. Edward F. Moore, M.M., Admin.; Joseph J. O'Neill, M.M., Asst. Admin.; Frederick Allen, M.M.; James A. Bodenstedt, M.M.; George M. Buckley, M.M.; James C. Connell; Clyde F. Davis, M.M.; Gilbert J. DeRitis, M.M.; John J. Drew, M.M.; Joseph E. Early, M.M.; Thomas F. Foley, M.M.; Henry J. Felsecker, M.M.; James F. Habenicht, M.M.; Donald J. Haren, M.M.; Leon A. Harter, M.M.; James A. Jackson, M.M.; Walter W. Johnson; Thomas S. Keane, M.M.; Wenceslaus F. Knotek, M.M.; John J. McCabe, M.M.; Stephen J. Maskell, M.M.; John J. Ridyard, M.M.; Michael J. Ruck, M.M.; Alfred E. Smith, M.M.; Norbert M. Verhagen, M.M.; John J. Vinsko, M.M.; James R. Whitmore, M.M.; Bros. Thomas A. Hickey, Asst. Admin.; John Brown, M.M.; Gordon M. Burns, M.M.; Conrad Fleisch, M.M. Priests 34; Brothers 5.

LOS GATOS. *California Province of the Society of Jesus, Jesuit Provincial Office*, P.O. Box 519, 95031. Tel: 408-354-6143. Revs. James N. Chevedden, S.J.; Alfred G. Playoust, S.J.; Robert A. Graham, S.J.; Edward J. Thylstrup, S.J.; Bro. Howard C. Ellis, S.J., Sacred Heart Jesuit Center, P.O. Box 128, 95031-0128. Tel: 408-354-9240. Very Rev. John A. Privett, S.J., Regl. Prov.; Rev. John T. Mitchell, S.J., Exec. Asst.; Bro. Joseph Avila, S.J.; Revs. Philip L. Bourret, S.J.; Bernard I. Brannon, S.J.; Edward T. Burke, S.J.; Joseph R. Caldwell, S.J.; Gilbert M. Chacon, S.J.; Eugene Colosimo, S.J.; Bro. Charles L. Connor, S.J.; Revs. Joseph M. Costa, S.J.; Raymond A. Devlin, S.J.; Patrick D. Doherty, S.J.; Joseph L. Dondero, S.J.; Thomas M. Donohoe, S.J.; Thomas P. Finsterbach, S.J.; Leo J. Hombach, S.J.; Bro. Jack A. Hughes, S.J.; Rev. George J. Koch, S.J.; Bro. Norbert Korte, S.J.; Revs. Thomas W. Leahy, S.J.; William Lester, S.J.; Gerdenio M. Manuel, S.J.; William J. Maring, S.J.; Bro. Thomas A. Marshall, S.J.; Revs. Joseph L. Martin, S.J.; Roger B. McAuliffe, S.J.; Bro. Paul I. McElligott, S.J.; Revs. Vincent T. McGinty, S.J.; Joseph F. Meehan, S.J.; Ralph J. Moholy, S.J.; James J. Monaghan, S.J.; Bro. John R. Moniz, S.J.; Rev. Francisco Pena, S.J.; Bros. Edward J. Rethers, S.J.; Theodore C. Rohrer, S.J.; Revs. Arthur F. Rutledge, S.J.; Arthur J. Schenk, S.J.; Bros. Bernard J. Schenk, S.J.; William W. Snyder, S.J.; Revs. Robert L. St. Clair, S.J.; Donald F. St. Sure, S.J.; Daniel J. Sullivan, S.J.; Francis Wang, S.J.; Bro. Lee H. Williams, S.J.; Revs. Ronald D. Wolf, S.J.; George Wong, S.J. Priests 46; Brothers 13.
Marianists, 461 Monterey Ave., 95030. Tel: 408-395-1816. Rev. Jorge da Silva, S.M.; Bro. Jerome Gorg, S.M.
Sacred Heart Jesuit Center, Box 128, 95031. Tel: 408-354-9240. Legal Title: *California Province of the Society of Jesus dba Sacred Heart Jesuit Center*. Revs. John A. Privett, S.J., Prov.; Gregory D. Aherne, S.J., Supr.; Thomas G. Allender, S.J., Life's Journey, P.O. Box 40168, Phoenix, AZ, 85067. Bros. Joseph Avila; Thomas E. Berney, S.J.; Revs. Philip L. Bourret, S.J. (China); Edward T. Burke, S.J.; J. Ripley Caldwell; Joseph M. Costa, S.J.; Eugene J. Colosimo; Bro. Charles L. Connor, S.J.; Revs. Robert H. Dailey, S.J.; Joseph L. Dondero, S.J.; Thomas M. Donohoe, S.J.; John S. Enright, S.J.; Robert E. Griffin, S.J.; Bro. Jack Hughes, S.J.; Rev. George J. Koch, S.J.; Bro. Norbert J. Korte, S.J.; Revs. Thomas W. Leahy, S.J.; William F. Lester, S.J.; William J. Maring, S.J.; Joseph L. Martin, S.J.; Roger D. McAuliffe, S.J.; Bro. Paul I. McElligott, S.J.; Revs. Vincent T. McGinty, S.J.; Joseph F. Meehan, S.J.; James T. Monaghan, S.J.; Bro. John R. Moniz, S.J.; Revs. Carroll M. O'Sullivan, S.J.; Francisco Otazua-Pena, S.J.; Raymond A. Pallas, S.J.; Bros. Edward J. Rethers, S.J.; Theodore C. Rohrer, S.J.; Revs. Arthur F. Rutledge, S.J.; Benjamin F. Sargent, S.J.; Arthur J. Schenk, S.J.; Bro. Bernard J. Schenk, S.J.; Rev. Edmond J. Smyth, S.J.; Bros. Willard Snyder, S.J.; Leonard J. Sullivan, S.J.; Revs. Donald F. St. Sure, S.J.; Alexander A. Tait, S.J.; Francis X. Wang, S.J. (China); Bro. Lee H. Williams, S.J.; Revs. Ronald D. Wolf, S.J.; George Wong, S.J. (China); John C. Wright, S.J., Villa Serra #336, 1320 Padre Dr., Salinas, 93901. Priests 40; Brothers 13.

SANTA CLARA. *Marianist Community*, 319 Pineview Dr., 95050. Tel: 408-241-7110. Bro. Robert G. Hoppe, S.M., Dir. Priests 1; Brothers 3.

SARATOGA. *St. Patrick's Missionary Society*. (St. Patrick Fathers), 19536 Eric Dr., 95070. Tel: 408-253-3135. Rev. Eamonn Hayden, S.P.S. Priests 1.

[N] CONVENTS AND RESIDENCES FOR SISTERS

SAN JOSE. *Community of the Holy Spirit*, 1275 Naglee Ave., 95126. Tel: 408-275-1710.
Daughters of Charity of St. Vincent de Paul, O'Connor Hospital, Sisters' Residence, 350 O'Connor Dr., 95128. Tel: 408-289-9215. Sisters 13.
Dominican Sisters, Congregation of the Sacred Heart, Houston, 1092 W. San Fernando St., 95126. Tel: 408-294-7151.
Eucharistic Missionaries of the Most Holy Trinity, 815 S. Daniel Way, 95128. Tel: 408-243-3157. Sr. Gisela Enriquez, Supr., 11892 E. Lampson Ave., Garden Grove, 92640. Tel: 714-530-5727. Sr. Virginia Herrera. Sisters 4. Sisters 5.
Pious Disciples of the Divine Master, 2076 Lincoln Ave., 95125. Tel: 408-265-8105. Sr. Connie Marletta, P.D.D.M.; Sr. M. Cornelia DeToffoli, Supr. Sisters 4.
Quinhon Missionary Sisters of the Holy Cross, 1050 St. Elizabeth Dr., 95126. Tel: 408-287-8385.
St. Joseph's Novitiate, Franciscan Hospitaller Sisters of the Immaculate Conception, 300 S. 17th St., 95112-2245. Tel: 408-998-2896; Fax: 408-998-3407. Sr. Lucinda Dias Fonseca, F.H.I.C., Regl. Supr. Sisters 7.
Sinsinawa Dominican Congregation of the Most Holy Rosary, 613 S. Clover Ave., 95128. Sisters 8.
Sisters of Charity of Nazareth, 3208 Neal Ave., 95117. Tel: 408-244-4206.
Sisters of Charity of the Blessed Virgin Mary, 972 Palm St., 95110. Tel: 408-292-4105. Sisters 10.
Sisters of Charity of the Blessed Virgin Mary, 2070 Radio Ave., #4, 92125-3551. Tel: 408-847-5101. Sr. Bette Gambonini, B.V.M.
Sisters of LaSalle, 3867 Silver Creek Rd., 95121-1969. Tel: 408-238-9351. Sr. Theresa Claire Nguyen Thi Sang, Supr. Sisters 13.
Sisters of Loretto at the Foot of the Cross, 635 Bolton Ct., No. 1, 95129. Tel: 408-255-4875. Sisters 2.
Sisters of Notre Dame de Namur, 1976 Jonathan Ave., 95125-2568. Tel: 408-269-1117.
Other Convent Addresses: 918 S. Ninth St., 95112-2470. Tel: 408-293-2159. Sisters 2. 1338 Fruitdale Ave., #B7, 95126-4030. Tel: 408-297-1676. Sisters 4. 1342 Fruitdale Ave., #D2, 95126-4031. Tel: 408-947-0553. 1342 Fruitdale Ave., #D4, 95126-4031. Tel: 408-298-1629. 1342 Fruitdale Ave., #D6, 95126-4031. Tel: 408-293-4326. 2558 Loomis Dr., 95121. Tel: 408-288-5696. Sisters 3. 1147 Leigh Ave. #3, 95126. Tel: 408-998-1034. 1338 Fruitdale Ave., #B1, 95126. Tel: 408-971-0329. 125 Pleasant Ridge Ave., 95127. Tel: 408-259-7278. 1340 Fruitdale Ave., #C2, 95126. Tel: 408-947-1079. 1348 Fruitdale Ave., #G3, 95126. Tel: 408-288-6464. Sisters 65. Sisters 2.
Sisters of St. Charles Borromeo - Scalabrinians, 571 N. 13th St., 95112. Tel: 408-293-4880. Sisters 2.
Sisters of St. Joseph of Carondelet, 3383 Whitman Way, 95132. Tel: 408-259-1993. 101 Glenn Erie Ave., #308, 95125. Tel: 408-295-4047. 850 Meridian #22, 95126. Tel: 408-426-5980. 4350 Geary Blvd., San Francisco, 94118. Tel: 415-752-6050. Sr. Marcella Fabing, C.S.J., Regl. Supr., 19480 Bear Creek Rd., Los Gatos, 95030. Tel: 408-354-2346. 5880 Taormino Ave., 95123. Sisters 2. 1999 Lawrence Ct., Santa Clara, 95051. Tel: 408-248-9048. Sisters 3.
Sisters of the Holy Family, Holy Family Convent, 1050 St. Elizabeth Dr., 95126. Tel: 408-287-8385. St. Elizabeth's Day Home Day Care Center. Children 200. Sisters 14.
Sisters of the Holy Names of Jesus and Mary, Santa Teresa Residence, 218 Truckee Ln., 95136. Tel: 408-225-4956. Sisters 2. P.O. Box 907, Los Gatos, 95031. Tel: 408-354-1654. Sisters 2.
Sisters of the Presentation of the B.V.M., San Jose, 2304 Booksin Ave., 95125. Tel: 408-265-1962.
Other Convent Addresses: 2280A Booksin Ave., 95125. Tel: 408-267-6276. Sisters 2. 2280B Booksin Ave., 95125. Tel: 408-264-9211. Sisters 2. 2282A Booksin Ave., 95125. Tel: 408-264-0188. Sisters 2. 2282B Booksin Ave., 95125. Tel: 408-266-5805. Sisters 2. 4600 Hyland Ave., 95127. Tel: 408-258-8212. Sisters 4. 6864 Avenida Rotella St., 95139. Tel: 408-225-6462. Sisters 2. 462 N. 15th St., 95112. Tel: 408-288-6991. 1565 Main St. #7, Santa Clara, 95050. Tel: 408-248-2588. Sisters 4.
Society of Helpers, 612 N. 3rd St., #8, 95112. Tel: 408-275-8309. Sr. Ascension Higuera, H.H.S.
Society of the Sacred Heart, 362 N. Seventh St., 95112. Tel: 408-297-3634. Sisters 3.

ALVISO. *Society of the Sacred Heart*, P.O. Box 962, 95002. Tel: 408-262-7539. Sr. Josefina Montalvo, R.S.C.J.

CAMPBELL. *Susan House*, 100 El Caminito Ave., 95008-3412. Tel: 408-374-8684. Home for the Developmentally Disabled. Sisters of Notre Dame de Namur 2.

CUPERTINO. *Blessed Virgin Missionaries of Carmel (B.V.M.C.)*, 10130 N. Deanza Blvd., 95014. Tel: 408-257-1022. Sr. Mary James Gonzaga, B.V.M.C., Supr. Sisters 3.
Intercommunity Convent, 10351 S. Blaney Ave., 95014. Tel: 408-725-0898; Fax: 408-252-4848. Sr. Harriet Dow, O.S.F. Sisters 2.
Sisters of Notre Dame de Namur, 21153 Gardena Dr., 95014. Tel: 408-257-0167. Sr. Peter Joseph Navone, 10351 S. Blaney, 95014. Tel: 408-725-0898. Sisters 2. Provincial Residence, 14800 Bohlman Rd., Saratoga, 95070.

GILROY. *Maryknoll Missioners*, 10230-B New Ave., 95020. Tel: 408-847-1055.

LOS ALTOS. *Sisters, Servants of the Immaculate Heart of Mary*, 1840 Grant Rd., 94024. Tel: 415-968-5686. Sr. Mary Glackin, I.H.M., 173 Leota Ave., Sunnyvale, 94086. Tel: 408-738-2795. Sisters 3; Staff 3; Total Assisted 70. Extended Day Care Center, 94086. Sisters 4.

LOS ALTOS HILLS. *Daughters of Charity of St. Vincent de Paul (Laboure Residence), Seton Provincialate*, 26000 Altamont Rd., 94022. Tel: 415-941-4490; Fax: 415-949-3874. Sr. Joyce Weller, D.C., Prov.; Rev. Joseph V. Haley, C.M., Dir. Sisters 39; Total in Province 160; Total in Diocese 51.

Immaculate Heart Monastery of the Poor Clares, 28210 Natoma Rd., 94022. Tel: 415-948-2947. Mother Maura, P.C.C., Abbess. Sisters 19.

Sisters of Mercy, 12816 S. El Monte Ave., 94022. Tel: 415-948-0775. Sr. Laura Murphy, R.S.M. Sisters 4.

LOS GATOS. *Convent of the Holy Names*, Mailing Address: P.O. Box 1906, 95031. 200 Prospect Ave., 95032. Tel: 408-354-1730. Sr. Lolita Krebsbach, S.N.J.M., 82 Prospect Ave., 95032. Tel: 408-354-3747.

Presentation Convent, 19480 Bear Creek Rd., 95030. Tel: 408-354-2346. Presentation Convent Community. Sr. M. Francis Milanesi, P.B.V.M., Community Rep. Sisters 9.

House of Religious Women. Sr. Michele O'Connell, P.B.V.M., Community Rep. Staff 7; Total in Residence 9.

Provincialate of the Sisters of the Holy Names, Mailing Address: P.O. Box 907, 95031. Tel: 408-395-5150; Fax: 408-354-8305. Sr. Sally Slyngstad, S.N.J.M., Prov. Supr. Total in province 281; Total in Diocese 91. Convent, 200 Prospect Ave., P.O. Box 1906, 95031. Tel: 408-354-1730. Seraphine Community, P.O. Box 907, 95031. Tel: 408-354-1654. Villa Community, 82 Prospect Ave., 95032. Tel: 408-354-3747.

MORGAN HILL. *Sisters of the Presentation of the Blessed Virgin Mary*, 220 Spring Ave., 95037. Tel: 408-779-8726. Sr. Paula Baker, P.B.V.M.

MOUNTAIN VIEW. *Dominican Sisters of Oakford (Dedicated to St. Catherine of Siena)*, 1855 Miramonte Ave., 94040. Tel: 415-965-1903. Sr. Ursula Bomholt, O.P., Regl. Supr. Sisters 6; Total in province 19; Total in Diocese 9. Dominican Sisters of Oakford, St. Catherine's Convent, 749 San Diego Ave., Sunnyvale, 94086. Tel: 408-734-3210. Sisters 3.

Medical Mission Sisters, 2430 Alvin St., 94043. Tel: 415-968-2709. Sr. Charlotte Gusmano, M.M.S., Area Contact Person.

Other Residences: Monte Vista Terrace, 1101 Grant Rd., Apt #345, 94040. Tel: 415-961-5571. Monte Vista Terrace, 1101 Grant Rd., Apt. #344, 94040. Tel: 415-969-9843. 233 Carroll St., Sunnyvale, 94086. Tel: 408-245-6580. Fund Raising Office, 1059 El Monte Ave., Ste. C, 94040. Tel: 415-964-4764. Sisters 3.

Sisters of Mercy of Americas (Burlingame), 2685 California St. #205, 94040-1203. Tel: 415-949-3186. Local Contact: Sr. Maria Juanita Van Bommel, R.S.M., 256 LaPala Dr., #14, San Jose, CA 95127. 2225 Sharon Rd. #126, Menlo Park, 94025-6702. Tel: 415-233-1855. Sr. Carolyn Marie Krohn, R.S.M., Sisters of Mercy of the Americas Burlingname Regional Community, 254 N. Rengstorff Ave., 94043. Tel: 415-967-7915. 2685 California St., #205, 94020.

Sisters of Notre Dame de Namur and Franciscan Sisters of Perpetual Adoration, 1151 Phyllis Ave., 94040-3129. Tel: 415-964-3659.

PALO ALTO. *Sisters of Loretto at the Foot of the Hill*, 3980 El Camino Real, #106, 94306. Tel: 415-493-2185. Sr. Jeanette Donnelly, S.L.

Sisters of the Holy Family, 51 Encina Ave., 94301. Tel: 415-326-8156.

SANTA CLARA. *Carmelite Monastery of the Infant Jesus, Discalced Carmelite Nuns*, 1000 Lincoln St., 95050. Tel: 408-296-8412. Sr. Roseanne, O.C.D., Prioress. Sisters 17.

Dominican Sisters of San Rafael, 1565 Main St. #5, 95050. Tel: 408-248-5748. 1156 Santa Clara St. #11, 95050. Tel: 408-554-6431.

Sisters of Charity of the Blessed Virgin Mary, 807 Washington St., 95050-4904. Tel: 408-249-0773. Sr. Ann Marie Dress, B.V.M. Sisters 5.

Sisters of the Holy Names, Santa Clara Residence, 1999 Lawrence Ct., 95051-2128. Tel: 408-248-9048. Sr. Marion Patrick, S.N.J.M. Sisters 6.

Sisters of the Holy Names, Stella Kennedy Residence, 2001 Lawrence Ct., 95051. Tel: 408-248-8855. Sr. Barbara Nixon, S.N.J.M. Sisters 7.

SARATOGA. *Our Lady of Fatima Villa Convent*, 20400 Saratoga-Los Gatos Rd., P.O. Box 442, 95070. Tel: 408-867-9542. Dominican Sisters of St. Catherine of Siena. Miscellaneous: We operate an 85-bed nursing home for lay retired relgious. Sisters 3.

Sisters of Notre Dame de Namur Provincial House, 14800 Bohlman Rd., 95070-6393. Tel: 408-741-0324; Fax: 408-741-5809. Notre Dame Villa, 14800 Bohlman Rd., 95070. Tel: 408-867-3212. Sr. Barbara Thiella, S.N.D., Team Liaison for the Diocese of San Jose. Sisters 17; In province 176; In Diocese 68. 13716 Saratoga Ave., 95070-5499. Tel: 408-867-2660. Sisters 6. Sisters 5.

SUNNYVALE. *Sisters of Notre Dame de Namur*, 505 Granger Ter., #2, 94087. Tel: 408-746-0983. Sr. Katherine Nelson, S.N.D.

[O] NEWMAN CENTERS

SAN JOSE. *The Newman Center/Catholic Campus Ministry*, San Jose State University, 195 E. San Fernando St., 95112. Tel: 408-938-1610; Fax: 408-938-1612. Mailing Address: Catholic Campus Ministry/SJSU, The Newman Community, P.O. Box 720204, 95172-0204. Rev. David Mercer, Assoc. Dir.; Ms. Ginny Hinkle, Associate Dir.

PALO ALTO. *Newman Center, Catholic Community at Stanford*, Stanford University, P.O. Box 2301, 94301. Revs. Patrick LaBelle, O.P., Dir. Campus Ministry; John Paul Forte', O.P.; Nancy Greenfield, Campus Min.; Teresa Pleins, Campus Min.

[P] MISCELLANEOUS LISTINGS

SAN JOSE. *Charities Housing Development Corporation of Santa Clara County*, 195 E. San Fernando St., 95112. Tel: 408-282-1125. Mr. Chris Block.

Giovanni Center, Inc., 85 S. Fifth St., 95112. Tel: 408-288-7436. Carol George, Admin. Lay Staff 3; Residents 40. A California nonprofit charitable, public-benefit, housing project for low-income elderly. Sponsored by the Roman Catholic Bishop of San Jose, a corporation sole.

St. Vincent de Paul Society, District Council of Santa Clara County, 2040 S. 7th St., 95112. Tel: 408-993-9500; Fax: 408-993-0885. Mr. Stephen J. Pehanich, Exec. Dir. Total Assisted 32,000; Total Staff 24.

San Tomas/Charities Housing Corporation, 195 E. San Fernando St., 95112. Tel: 408-282-1125. Mr. Chris Block.

Serra Clubs District 31, 2000 W. Hedding St., 95128. Tel: 408-249-4087. Mr. Sal Sagnitto.

Vietnamese Youth and Culture Association, La Salle Vietnam House, 1103 Maxey Ct., 95132. Tel: 408-926-4665. Brothers of the Christian Schools (San Francisco Prov.). Bro. Tran Trong An Phong, F.S.C., Dir.

LOS ALTOS. *Jesuit Institute for Family Life*, 300 Manresa Way, 94022. Tel: 415-948-4854. Rev. Robert J. Fabing, S.J., Dir.

LOS GATOS. *San Jose Serra Club*, 135 Belridge Dr.y, 95032. Tel: 408-356-6256. John J. McCormack, Pres.

MENLO PARK. *Roman Catholic Communications Corporation of the Bay Area*, The Catholic Telemedia Network of the Bay Area, 324 Middlefield Rd., 94025. Tel: 415-326-7850; Fax: 415-326-4605. Most Revs. John S. Cummins, Chm.; Pierre DuMaine, Vice Chm.; Shirley Connolly, Gen. Mgr.

MOUNTAIN VIEW. *Mountain View Serra Club*, 1745 Crane Ave., 94040. Rev. Tom Carroll, Pres.

St. Joseph the Worker Center, 582 Hope St., 94041. Tel: 415-967-1902. Day Worker Center. Josephine Fregoso deRamirez, Dir.; Rev. Eugene P. O'Donnell, Contact Person. Total Assisted 30.

SANTA CLARA. *The Roman Catholic Welfare Corporation of San Jose*, 900 Lafayette St., Ste. 301, 95050-4966. Tel: 408-983-0240; Fax: 408-983-0295. Rev. Michael J. Mitchell, Contact Person.

St. Joseph Seminary Corporation, 900 Lafayette St., Ste. 301, 95050-4966. Tel: 408-983-0237; Fax: 408-983-0295. Rev. Michael J. Mitchell, Contact Person.

San Jose Cathedral Foundation. (A nonprofit, charitable, public-benefit California corporation.), 900 Lafayette St., Ste. 301, 95050-4966. Tel: 408-983-0100. Most Rev. Pierre DuMaine, Chm. of Bd. & Pres.

SARATOGA. *Notre Dame Plaza Corporation*, 14800 Bohlman Rd., 95070-6399. Tel: 408-741-0324; Fax: 408-741-5809.

RELIGIOUS INSTITUTES OF MEN REPRESENTED IN THE DIOCESE

For further details refer to the corresponding bracketed number in the Religious Institutes of Men or Women section.

[0120]—*Alexian Brothers*.—C.F.A.
[0330]—*Brothers of the Christian Schools*.—F.S.C.
[0600]—*Brothers of the Congregation of Holy Cross (Eastern Province)*.—C.S.C.
[0600]—*Brothers of the Congregation of the Holy Cross (Southwest Province)*.—C.S.C.
[0470]—*Capuchin Friars, The*.—O.F.M.Cap.
[1320]—*Clerics of St. Viator*.—C.S.V.
[1330]—*Congregation of the Mission (Vincentians)*.—C.M.
[0260]—*Discalced Carmelite Friars*.—O.C.D.
[0520]—*Franciscan Friars (Province of St. Barbara)*.—O.F.M.
[0650]—*Holy Ghost Fathers*.—C.S.Sp.
[]—*Institute of Incarnate Word*. (Argentina).—I.V.E.
[0690]—*Jesuit Fathers and Brothers (Society of Jesus-)(California Province)*.—S.J.
[0760]—*Marianists (Society of Mary)*.—S.M.
[0800]—*Maryknoll (Catholic Foreign Mission Society of America, Inc.)*.—M.M.
[1210]—*Missionaries of St. Charles - Scalabrinians (Province of St. John Baptist)*.—C.S.
[1110]—*Missionaries of the Sacred Heart*.—M.S.C.
[0430]—*Order of Preachers (Province of the Most Holy Name of Jesus-Western Dominican Province)*.—O.P.
[1260]—*St. Patrick's Missionary Society*.—S.P.S.
[1260]—*Society of Christ*.—S.Ch.
[0420]—*Society of the Divine Word*.—S.V.D.
[1290]—*Society of the Priests of St. Sulpice*.—S.S.

RELIGIOUS INSTITUTES OF WOMEN REPRESENTED IN THE DIOCESE

[]—*Augustinian Recollects*.—A.R.
[]—*Blessed Virgin Missionaries of Carmel*.—B.V.M.C.
[]—*Caritas Sisters of Miyazaki*.—C.S.M.
[2020]—*Community of the Holy Spirit*.—C.H.S.
[1070-25]—*Congregation of the Dominican Sisters of Saint Catherine of Siena of Kenosha*.—OP.
[1070-04]—*Congregation of the Most Holy Name (Dominican Sisters of San Rafael)*.—O.P.
[2100]—*Congregation of the Humility of Mary*.—C.H.M.
[1070-13]—*Congregation of the Most Holy Rosary (Dominican Sisters)*.—O.P.
[1070-12]—*Congregation of the Queen of the Holy Rosary (Dominican Sisters)*.—O.P.
[1780]—*Congregation of the Sisters of the Third Order of St. Francis of Perpetual Adoration*.—E.S.P.A.
[0760]—*Daughters of Charity of St. Vincent De Paul*.—D.C.
[0420]—*Discaled Carmelite Nuns*.—O.C.D.
[1070-19]—*Dominican Sisters of Houston, Texas (Congregation of the Sacred Heart)*.—O.P.
[1070-30]—*Dominican Sisters of Oakford*..O.P.
[]—*Eucharistic Missionaries of the Most Holy Trinity —M.E.S.S.T.*
[1270]—*Franciscan Hospitaller Sisters of the Immaculate Conception*.—F.H.I.C.
[2470]—*Maryknoll Sisters*.—M.M.
[2490]—*Medical Mission Sisters*.—M.M.S.
[2715]—*Missionary Sisters of Christ the King*.—M.S.C.K.
[2900]—*Missionary Sisters of St. Charles Borromeo (Scalabrini Sisters)*.—M.S.C.S.
[3760]—*Order of St. Clare (Immaculate Heart Monastery of Poor Clares)*.—P.C.C.
[0980]—*Pious Disciples of the Divine Master*.—P.D.D.M.
[0980]—*Quinhon Missionary Sisters of the Holy Cross*.—Q.M.H.C.
[3465]—*Religious of the Sacred Heart of Mary (West American Province)*.—R.S.H.M.
[1070-03]—*Sinsinawa Dominican Congregation of the Most Holy Rosary*.—O.P.
[0500]—*Sisters of Charity of Nazareth (Southern Region)*.—S.C.N.
[0430]—*Sisters of Charity of the Blessed Virgin Mary*.—B.V.M.
[]—*Sisters of LaSalle*.—L.S.
[2360]—*Sisters of Loretto at the Foot of the Cross*.—S.L.
[2516]—*Sisters of Mercy (Ireland)*.—R.S.M.
[2570]—*Sisters of Mercy of the Americas (Regional Community of Burlingame)*.—R.S.M.
[3000]—*Sisters of Notre Dame de Namur (California Province)*.—S.N.D.
[3840]—*Sisters of St. Joseph of Carondelet (Province of St. Louis)*.—C.S.J.
[1960]—*Sisters of the Holy Family*.—S.H.F.
[1990]—*Sisters of the Holy Names of Jesus and Mary (California Province)*.—S.N.J.M.
[3320]—*Sisters of the Presentation of the Blessed Virgin Mary*.—P.B.V.M.
[1760]—*Sisters of the Third Order of Saint Francis of Penance and of Charity*.—O.S.F.
[2170]—*Sisters, Servants of the Immaculate Heart of Mary*.—I.H.M.
[2150]—*Sisters, Servants of the Immaculate Heart of Mary, Monroe, Michigan*.—I.H.M.
[1890]—*Society of Helpers (American Province)*.—H.H.S.
[4070]—*Society of the Sacred Heart*.—R.S.C.J.
[4110]—*Ursuline Nuns (Roman Union (Western Province)*.—O.S.U.

DIOCESAN CEMETERIES AND MAUSOLEUMS

SAN JOSE. *Calvary.* (Santa Clara Co.), 2655A Madden Ave., 95126. Tel: 408-258-2940; Fax: 408-258-5614. Robert E. Summers, Dir.

LOS ALTOS. *Gate of Heaven,* 22555 Cristo Rey Dr., 94024. Tel: 415-428-3730; Fax: 415-428-3733. Robert E. Summers, Dir.

NECROLOGY

† Bergan, William A., (Retired). —Died Dec. 7, 1995.
† Cullen, Leo, (Retired). —Died Oct 21, 1995.
† Deasy, Thomas, (Retired). —Died Feb. 23, 1995.
† Devlin, James J., (Retired). —Died Feb. 13, 1996.
† Essig, Robert, (Retired). —Died Nov. 20, 1996.
† Flaherty, James A., (Retired). —Died Sept. 28, 1995.
† O'Neill, John J., (Retired). —Died Oct. 24, 1995.
† O'Sullivan, Carroll, (Retired). —Died Oct. 24, 1996.
† Pallas, Raymond A., (Retired). —Died March 17, 1996.
† Tait, Alexander A., (Retired). —Died Oct. 1, 1996.

Archdiocese of Santa Fe

(Archidioecesis Sanctae Fidei)

Most Reverend

MICHAEL J. SHEEHAN, S.T.L., J.C.D.

Archbishop of Santa Fe; ordained July 12, 1964; consecrated and installed as First Bishop of Lubbock June 17, 1983; appointed Apostolic Administrator of Santa Fe April 6, 1993; installed as Eleventh Archbishop of Santa Fe September 21, 1993. *Res., Catholic Center, 4000 St. Joseph Pl., N.W., Albuquerque, NM, 87120.*

Archdiocese of Santa Fe Catholic Center: 4000 St. Joseph Pl., N.W., Albuquerque, NM, 87120. Tel.: 505-831-8100.

ESTABLISHED IN 1850.

CREATED AN ARCHBISHOPRIC IN 1875.

Solemnly consecrated to the Immaculate Heart of Mary on October 7, 1945.

Square Miles 61,142.

Comprises the Counties of Colfax, Curry, DeBaca, Guadalupe, Harding, Los Alamos, Mora, Quay, Roosevelt, San Miguel, Santa Fe, Socorro, Taos, Torrance and Union with a part of Bernalillo, Sandoval, Rio Arriba and Valencia Counties.

PATRON OF THE ARCHDIOCESE: St. Francis of Assisi.

For legal titles of parishes and archdiocesan institutions, consult the Chancery Office.

STATISTICAL OVERVIEW

Personnel	
Archbishop	1
Retired Archbishops	1
Abbots	2
Priests: Diocesan Active in Diocese	69
Priests: Active Outside Diocese	4
Priests: Retired, Sick or Absent	38
Number of Diocesan Priests	111
Religious Priests in Diocese	106
Ordinations:	
Diocesan Priests	2
Religious Priests	1
Transitional Deacons	1
Permanent Deacons	5
Permanent Deacons in Diocese	135
Total Brothers	91
Total Sisters	299
Parishes	
Parishes	91
With Resident Pastor:	
Resident Diocesan Priests	59
Resident Religious Priests	25
Without Resident Pastor:	
Administered by Permanent Deacons	2
Administered by Women Religious	3
Administered by Lay People	2
Missions	216
Pastoral Centers	4
Professional Ministry Personnel:	
Brothers	5
Sisters	45
Lay Ministers	190
Welfare	
Catholic Hospitals	4
Total Assisted	16,591
Health Care Centers	1
Total Assisted	5,000
Homes for the Aged	3
Total Assisted	200
Day Care and Extended Day Care Centers	2
Total Assisted	133
Specialized Homes	3
Total Assisted	629
Special Centers for Social Services	5
Total Assisted	210,550
Residential Care of Disabled	1
Total Assisted	16
Educational	
Seminaries, Diocesan	1
Students from This Diocese	2
Students from Other Diocese	29
Diocesan Students in Other Seminaries	21
Total Seminarians	23
Colleges and Universities	1
Total Students	1,600
High Schools, Diocesan and Parish	1
Total Students	1,013
High Schools, Private	2
Total Students	883
Elementary Schools, Diocesan and Parish	18
Total Students	4,762
Catechesis/Religious Education:	
High School Students	5,099
Elementary Students	19,403
Total Students Under Catholic Instruction	32,783
Teachers in the Diocese:	
Priests	3
Brothers	5
Sisters	34
Lay Teachers	404
Vital Statistics	
Receptions into the Church:	
Infant Baptism Totals	6,404
Adult Baptism Totals	243
Received into Full Communion	331
First Communions	5,529
Confirmations	3,270
Marriages:	
Catholic	1,134
Interfaith	222
Total Marriages	1,356
Deaths	2,438
Total Catholic Population	260,313
Total Population	979,742

Former Archbishops—Most Rev. J. B. LAMY, cons. Nov. 24, 1850; created first Archbishop, 1875; resigned July 18, 1885; died Feb. 13, 1888.—Most Rev. J. B. SALPOINTE, D.D., second Archbishop; cons. Bishop of Doryla and Vicar Apostolic of Arizona, June 20, 1869; appt. Coadjutor of Santa Fe "cum jure successionis", April, 22, 1884; promoted to the Titular Archiepiscopal See of Anazarba, Oct. 11 of same year; succeeded to the See of Santa Fe, July 18, 1885; resigned Jan. 7, 1894; Titular Archbishop of Tomi; died July 15, 1898.—Most Rev. P. L. CHAPELLE, cons. Nov. 1, 1891; Archbishop of Santa Fe, Jan 7, 1894; transferred to New Orleans, Dec. 1, 1897; died Aug. 9, 1905.—Most Rev. PETER BOURGADE, D.D., cons. May 1, 1885; Bishop of Thaumacum and Vic. Ap. of Arizona; Bishop of Tucson, May 8, 1897; transferred to Santa Fe, Jan. 7, 1899; died May 17, 1908.—Most Rev. J. B. PITAVAL, D.D., cons. Titular Bishop of Sora and Auxiliary of Santa Fe, July 25, 1902; promoted to the See of Santa Fe, Jan. 3, 1909; resigned Feb., 1918; appt. Titular Archbishop of Amida, July 29, 1918; died May 23, 1928.—Most Rev. ALBERT T. DAEGER, O.F.M., D.D., cons. May 7, 1919; died Dec. 2, 1932.—Most Rev. RUDOLPH ALOYSIUS GERKEN, D.D., cons. Bishop of Amarillo, April 26, 1927; appt. Archbishop of Santa Fe, June 2, 1933; installed as Archbishop of Santa Fe, Aug. 23, 1933; died March 2, 1943.—Most Rev. EDWIN V. BYRNE, D.D., cons. Bishop of Ponce, P.R. transferred to Diocese of San Juan, P.R. promoted to Archbishop of Santa Fe, June 15, 1943; died July 25, 1963.—Most Rev. JAMES P. DAVIS, D.D., cons. Bishop of San Juan, P.R., Oct. 6, 1943; promoted to Archbishop, April 30, 1960; transferred to Archdiocese of Santa Fe, Jan. 3, 1964; retired Oct. 1974; died March 4, 1988.—Most Rev. ROBERT F. SANCHEZ, cons. 10th Archbishop of Santa Fe, July 25, 1974; resigned April 6, 1993.—

All offices are located at the *Archdiocese of Santa Fe Catholic Center, 4000 Saint Joseph Pl., N.W., Albuquerque, NM 87120. Tel. 505-831-8100, unless otherwise indicated.*

Office of the Archbishop

Vicar-General—Very Rev. LEO LUCERO, V.G., *1120 Canyon Rd., Santa Fe, 87501.* Tel: 505-983-8528.

Secretary to the Archbishop—Mrs. JULIE ROMERO. Tel: 505-831-8120.

Office of the Chancellor

Chancellor—Rev. RICHARD OLONA. Tel: 505-831-8158. Vice Chancellors: Sr. NANCY KAZIK, O.S.F. Tel: 505-831-8188. Rev. DONALD STARKEY. Tel: 505-831-8348.

Archivist and Artistic Patrimony—Mrs. MARINA OCHOA, *213 Cathedral Pl., Santa Fe, 87501.* Tel: 505-983-3811., *Albuquerque Office at the Catholic Center.* Tel: 505-831-8174.

Attorney for the Archdiocese—Mr. CHARLES P. REYNOLDS, *201 12th St., N.W., Albuquerque, 87102.* Tel: 505-842-8177.

Communications-Media—Ms. MARY RYLAND, Dir. Tel: 505-831-8180.

Ecumenical Commission and Inter-Religious Affairs—Rev. ERNEST FALARDEAU, S.S.S., Dir., *St. Charles Borromeo Church, 1818 Coal S.E., Albuquerque, 87106.* Tel: 505-242-3462.

Madonna Retreat and Conference Center—Sr. MARIE VIRGINIA LOVATO, S.C., Dir., *4040 St. Joseph Pl., N.W., Albuquerque, 87120.* Tel: 505-831-8196.

Newspaper, Archdiocesan "People of God"—Most Rev. MICHAEL J. SHEEHAN, Publisher; Sr. NANCY KAZIK, O.S.F., Editor, *4000 St. Joseph Pl., N.W., Albuquerque, 87120.* Tel: 505-831-8188.

Parish Bulletin Service, "The Catholic Communicator"—JENNY CHILSON, *P.O. Box 93244, Albuquerque, 87199-3244.* Tel: 505-856-0333; Fax: 505-822-5589.

Human Resources—Mr. WALTER DUGUAY, Dir. Tel: 505-831-8130.

Canonical Services Division

Judicial Vicar—Rev. Msgr. JOSEPH A. PEPE, J.C.D. Tel: 505-831-8177.

College of Consultors—Very Revs. LEO LUCERO, V.G.; GILBERT SCHNEIDER, O.F.M.; Rev. Msgr. SIPIO SALAS; Revs. RAMON ARAGON; JUAN MENDEZ; RICHARD OLONA; FRANCIS EGGERT; MIKE SHEA.

Council of Men & Women Religious—Vacant.

Holy Childhood Association—See Mission Office.

Immaculate Heart of Mary Seminary—Rev. ARTURO MEZA, Rector, *Mt. Carmel Rd., Santa Fe, 87501.* Tel: 505-988-1975.

Mission Office—Rev. ARKAD BICZAK, Dir. Propagation of the Faith; Holy Childhood; Catholic Relief Svcs., *John XXIII Catholic Community, 4831 Tramway Ridge Dr. N.E., Albuquerque, 87111.* Tel: 505-293-0088.

Office of Religious—Sr. NANCY KAZIK, O.S.F., Dir. Tel: 505-831-8188.

Permanent Diaconate Program—Deacon DONATO LUCERO, Dir., *Immaculate Heart of Mary, 3700 Canyon Rd., Los Alamos, 87544.* Tel: 505-662-6193.

Pilgrimage for Vocations—Rev. EDMOND SAVILLA, Dir., *P.O. Box 888, Taos, 87571.* Tel: 505-758-9208.

Presbyteral Council of the Archdiocese of Santa Fe—Most Rev. MICHAEL J. SHEEHAN, Pres.; Rev. RICHARD OLONA, Ex-Officio; Very Rev. LEO LUCERO, V.G., Ex-Officio; Revs. RON CARRILLO, Chm. TIM MARTINEZ, Sec. Exec. Committee Exec. Board Members: Rev. LAMBERT LUNA; Rev. Msgr. DOUG RAUN.

Propagation of the Faith—See Mission Office.

Vicars Forane (Deans)—Very Revs. JOHNNY LEE CHAVEZ, Santa Fe Deanery: LAMBERT LUNA, Albuquerque-Deanery A: RONALD BRUCKNER, Albuquerque-Deanery B: Rev. Msgr. JOAQUIN BAZAN, Albuquerque-Deanery C: Very Revs. VIRGIL FURFARO, Southwest Deanery: CHARLES BROWN, Northwest Deanery: GEORGE SALAZAR, Northeast Deanery: ANTHONY MARTINEZ, Southeast Deanery:

Tribunal—Tel: 505-831-8177.
- *Judicial Vicar*—Rev. Msgr. JOSEPH A. PEPE, J.C.D.
- *Adjutant Judicial Vicar*—Vacant.
- *Promoter of Justice*—Rev. LUCIEN HENDREN, J.C.L.
- *Defenders of the Bond*—Revs. SOTERO SENA; MIKE SHEA; RICK ZERWAS; ROBERT MALLOY; DOUGLAS RAUN.
- *Associate Judges*—Revs. RAMON ARAGON; C. JOHN BRASHER; CRISPIN C. BUTZ, O.F.M.; JOHN R. CONWAY; ARTHUR J. ESPELAGE, O.F.M., J.C.D.; NORMAN R. FALARDEAU, S.S.S.; LUIS JARAMILLO, J.C.L.; ROYCE R. THOMAS, J.C.L.; MANUEL VIERA, O.F.M., J.C.L.; JEROME MARTINEZ Y ALIRE, J.C.L.
- *Notaries*—Mrs. LEDIA APODACA; Ms. PAULA DUVALL; Ms. HELEN WILLS.
- *Delegate for Matrimonial Dispensations*—Rev. Msgr. JOSEPH A. PEPE, J.C.D.; DONALD J. STARKEY,Reverend Deans.

Appeal Court—Tel: 505-831-8177.

Vocation Director—Rev. JOHN CARNEY, Dir. Tel: 505-831-8143. Rev. RICK ZERWAS, Assoc. Dir.; Deacon RUDY ZAMORA, Asst. Dir.

Finance Division

Executive Director of Finance—Mr. TONY SALGADO, C.P.A. Tel: 505-831-8132.

Annual Catholic Appeal—Archdiocesan Annual Appeal Program, Mrs. LINDA J. GARCIA, Operations Mktg. Mgr. Tel: 505-831-8155.

Archdiocese of Santa Fe Catholic Foundation—MARY P. DUNN, Exec. Dir., *4000 St. Joseph Pl., N.W., Albuquerque, 87120.* Tel: 505-831-8246. Non-profit corporation for financial support of Archdiocese of Santa Fe.

Finance Council—Most Rev. MICHAEL J. SHEEHAN, Pres.; Mr. WILLIAM GRADY, Chm.; Very Revs. GILBERT SCHNEIDER, O.F.M.; LEO LUCERO, V.G.; Revs. RICHARD OLONA; JOHN CONWAY; Mr. GIG BRUMMEL; Mr. TONY SALGADO, C.P.A.; Mr. TIM SHEEHAN; Ms. JENNIFER CANTRELL.

Property Managers and Construction Contract Coord.—Mr. JOHN HUCHMALA. Tel: 505-831-8136.

Pastoral Ministries

Executive Director—Ms. FRANCES VOGEL, *4000 St. Joseph Pl., N.W., Albuquerque, 87120.* Tel: 505-831-8151.

AIDS/HIV Ministry of the Archdiocese of Santa Fe—JEFF STROBEL, Dir., *P.O. Box 42311, Albuquerque, 87196.* Tel: 505-243-1847; 800-497-2540.

Campaign for Human Development—Mrs. JOAN LEAHIGH, Coord., *4000 St. Joseph Pl., N.W., Albuquerque, 87192.* Tel: 505-831-8167.

Catholic Committee on Scouting—(Boy Scouts and Girl Scouts). Rev. ROBERT MALLOY, Dir. Scouting, *Queen of Heaven, 5311 Phoenix N.E., Albuquerque, 87110.* Tel: 505-881-1772.

Catholic Schools Office—Sr. MICHELLE MICEK, O.S.F., Supt. Tel: 505-831-8173. Mrs. CELINE RADIGAN, Dir. Program and Fund Devel.

Catholic Social Services of Albuquerque—AILEEN GARRIOTT, Exec. Dir., *2010 Bridge S.W., Albuquerque, 87105., Mailing Address: P.O. Box 25405, Albuquerque, 87125.* Tel: 505-247-9521.

Catholic Social Services of Santa Fe, Inc.—AILEEN GARRIOTT, Exec. Dir., *138 Park Ave., Santa Fe, 87501., Mailing Address: P.O. Box 443, Santa Fe, 87504.* Tel: 505-982-0441.

Cursillo Movement—Rev. CHRYSTOSTOM PARTEE, O.F.M., Coord., *San Diego Friary, P.O. Box 79, Jemez Pueblo, 87024.* Tel: 505-834-7300.

Ministry to the Disabled—Ms. PATRICIA STEFFES, Dir. Tel: 505-831-8174.

Hospital Ministry—Ms. PATRICIA STEFFES, Coord. Tel: 505-831-8151.

Prison & Detention Ministry—PATRICIA STEFFES, Dir. Tel: 505-831-8174.

Archdiocesan Network for Catholic Legislative Advocacy—Mrs. JOAN LEAHIGH. Tel: 505-831-8167.

Liturgical Commission—Most Rev. MICHAEL J. SHEEHAN, Pres. GENE VARELA, Chm., *2307 Camino Artista, Santa Fe, 87505.* Tel: 505-827-7640.

Marriage and Family Life Office—Mrs. REMEDIOS (HEDDY) LONG, Dir. Tel: 505-831-8117.

Ministry to Spanish Speaking—Deacon JUAN BARAJAS. Tel: 505-831-8152.

African American Ministry—Ms. BRENDA DABNEY. Tel: 505-831-8243.

Native American Ministry—Mr. MIKE VALDO. Tel: 505-831-8243.

Newman Centers—
- *ALBQ: Aquinas Newman Center*—Rev. ROBERT KELLER, O.P., Dir., *Univ. of New Mexico, 1815 Las Lomas Rd. N.E., Albuquerque, 87106.* Tel: 505-247-1095.
- *LAS VEGAS: St. Paul Newman Center*—Rev. GEORGE SALAZAR, Coord., *Highlands University, 811 Sixth St., Las Vegas, 87701.* Tel: 505-425-9295.
- *PORTALES: St. Thomas Moore Newman Center*—Very Rev. ANTHONY MARTINEZ, Chap., *Eastern New Mexico University, P.O. Box 2253, Portales, 88130.* Tel: 505-356-5615.
- *SANTE FE: College of Santa Fe*—Rev. JAMES CRONIN, Dir., *St. Michael's Dr., Santa Fe, 87501.* Tel: 505-473-6011.

Office of Worship—Rev. THOMAS MAYEFSKE, Dir. Tel: 505-831-8194.

Peace Pilgrimage—Deacon JOHN LEAHIGH, Coord. Tel: 505-831-8167.

Pro Life Commission—JOAN LEAHIGH, Dir., *4000 St. Joseph Pl., N.W., Albuquerque, 87120.* Tel: 505-831-8167.

RCIA—Rev. THOMAS MAYEFSKE. Tel: 505-831-8194.

Religious Education—Ms. CATHERINE ABEYTA, Dir. Tel: 505-831-8127. Ms. MARYANN HOLLAND, Dir. Catachetical Support, *4000 St. Joseph Pl., N.W., Albuquerque, 87120.* Tel: 505-831-8128.

Schools of Lay Ministry Formation—
- *Albuquerque Deanery A,B,C, "Emmaus Journey"*—FRANCES VOGEL, Coord., *4000 St. Joseph Pl. N.W., Albuquerque, 87120.* Tel: 505-831-8151.
- *Northwest Deanery*—Ms. MARY ANN HOLLAND, Coord., *Ojo Sarco, 87550.* Tel: 505-689-2457.
- *Santa Fe Deanery*—(Jornada de Fe). TERESITA SCULLY, Coord., *8 Enebro Rd., Santa Fe, 87505.* Tel: 505-988-5345.

St. Vincent de Paul Council—Rev. PAUL BACA, Spiritual Dir., *Community of the Risen Savior, 7701 Wyoming N.E., Albuquerque, 87109.* Tel: 505-821-1571.

Social Justice—Mrs. JOAN LEAHIGH. Tel: 505-831-8167.

Stewardship and Evangelization—Deacon JUAN BARAJAS, Dir. Tel: 505-831-8152.

Youth and Young Adult Ministry—Mrs. BERNADETTE JARAMILLO, Dir. Tel: 505-831-8145.

Ministry Resource Center—Mrs. PATRICIA MCINTIRE, Dir. Tel: 505-831-8187.

CLERGY, PARISHES, MISSIONS AND PAROCHIAL SCHOOLS

CITY OF SANTA FE
(Santa Fe County)

1—THE CATHEDRAL OF SAN FRANCISCO DE ASIS (1610), Revs. Salvador Aragon, O.F.M., Rector; Godfrey Blank, O.F.M.; Wayne Gibbeaut, O.F.M.; Cecil Kleber, O.F.M.; Manuel Viera, O.F.M.; Deacon Charles Bates. In res., Rev. Antonio Valdez, O.F.M.
Res., P.O. Box 2127, 87504. Tel: 505-982-5619. [CEM]
School—Tel: 505-982-0331. Sr. Josephine Macias, C.D.P., Prin.
Sisters 1; Lay Teachers 9; Students 187.
Catechesis/Religious Programs—Tel: 505-982-3625. Maria Comito, D.R.E.
Students 150.
Missions—Santa Clara, Rio Arriba Co., Indian Pueblo, 87504-2127; San Ildefonso, Sante Fe Co., Indian Pueblo, 87504-2127; Tesuque, Sante Fe Co., Indian Pueblo, 87504-2127.

2—OUR LADY OF GUADALUPE (1882) (Hispanic American), Rev. Luis Pena; Deacon Anthony Trujillo.
Res., 417 Agua Fria St., 87501. Tel: 505-983-8868. [CEM][JC]
Catechesis/Religious Programs—Tel: 505-988-3336. Connie Smith, D.R.E.
Students 305.
Missions—Tesuque, Santa Fe Co., San Ysidro, 87574; Rio en Medio, Sante Fe Co., Our Lady of Sorrows, 87574.

3—CRISTO REY (1940), Rev. Leo E. Lucero, V.G.; Deacon Randy Rodriguez.
Res., 1120 Canyon Rd., 87501. Tel: 505-983-8528. [JC]
School—Tel: 505-983-8411. Terry Lopez, Prin.
Lay Teachers 7; Students 139.
Mission—Canada de Los Alamos, Santa Fe Co., Our Lady of Guadalupe, Tel: 505-983-8528; Fax: 505-983-8528.
Catechesis/Religious Programs—Students 65.

4—ST. ANNE'S (1942), Rev. R. E. Coughlan; Deacon Joseph L. Black.
Res., 511 Alicia, 87501. Tel: 505-983-4430; Fax: 505-983-7483. [JC]
School—Tel: 505-982-3712. Sr. Phyllis Stowell, S.C.L., Prin.
Sisters 2; Lay Teachers 6; Students 135.
Catechesis/Religious Programs—Students 193.

5—ST. JOHN BAPTIST (1953), Revs. Juan Mendez; Nathan Libaire, O.S.B.; Deacons Andres Carrillo; Tony Rodriguez.
Res., 1301 Osage Ave., 87505. Tel: 505-983-5034; Fax: 505-983-1861.
Catechesis/Religious Programs—D.R.E.: Sr. Rebecca Wolf, Elementary; Juanita Montoya, Confirmation & Adult.
Students 356.

6—SAN ISIDRO (1835) (Hispanic), Rev. Franklin D. Pretto.
Res., Rte. 6, Box 111, 87501. Tel: 505-471-0710; Fax: 505-471-9034. [CEM 2]
Catechesis/Religious Programs—Sr. Lorraine Delisle, S.C., D.R.E.
Students 260.
Mission—La Cienega, Santa Fe Co.

7—SANTA MARIA DE LA PAZ CATHOLIC COMMUNITY (1990), Rev. Jerome J. Martinez y Alire. Pastoral Assocs.: Sr. Emelia Atencio, O.P.; Sr. Paula Gallagher, I.H.M.; Sr. Colleen Shanahan, O.S.F.; Deacon Facundo R. Rodriguez.
Res., 11 College Ave., 87505. Tel: 505-473-4330; 473-4200 (Office); Fax: 505-473-1602.
Catechesis/Religious Programs—Mrs. Patricia Lopez, D.R.E.
Students 643.

OUTSIDE THE CITY OF SANTA FE

Abiquiu, Rio Arriba Co., St. Thomas Apostle (1745) (Hispanic), Rev. Don J. Chavez.
Res., P.O. Box 117, 87510. Tel: 505-685-4462. [CEM 5]
Catechesis/Religious Programs—Tel: 505-685-4462. Sr. Melanie Pursch, O.L.V.M., D.R.E.
Students 174.
Missions—Canones; Medanales; Youngsville; Coyote; Mesa de Poleo; Capulin; Gallina.

Alameda, Bernalillo Co., Nativity of the Blessed Virgin Mary (1911), Rev. Michael J. Shea; Deacon Robert Contreras.
Res., 9502 Fourth St., N.W., 87114. Tel: 505-898-5253. [CEM][JC 2]
Catechesis/Religious Programs—Tel: 505-898-1441. Sr. Frances Biel, C.S.S.F., D.R.E.
Students 590.
Mission—Alameda, Bernalillo Co., Our Lady of Mount Carmel.

Albuquerque, Bernalillo Co.,

1—ANNUNCIATION, (1959), Rev. Ronald L. Bruckner; Deacons Harry Gogan; Victor J. Bachechi. In res., Rev. Msgr. Joseph A. Pepe, J.C.D.
Res., 2600 Vermont N.E., 87110. Tel: 505-293-5462; 298-7553.
Office: 2532 Vermont N.E., 87110. Tel: 505-298-7553; Fax: 505-294-7418.
School—2610 Utah N.E., 87110. Tel: 505-299-6783. Sr. Rose Therese Wich, S.C., Prin.
Lay Teachers 32; Students 517.
Catechesis/Religious Programs—Tel: 505-296-0411. Sr. Sharon Brannen, Fd.C.C., D.R.E.
Students 283.

2—ASCENSION, (1962), Rev. Anthony P. Bolman; Deacons Jesus Medina; Bill Hoefler.
Res., 2150 Raymac Rd., S.W., 87105. Tel: 505-877-8550. [CEM 2]
Catechesis/Religious Programs—Tel: 505-877-8144. Sr. Connie Martinez, Fd.C.C., D.R.E.
Students 303.

3—COMMUNITY OF THE RISEN SAVIOUR, (1979), Revs. Paul M. Baca; Antonio Mondragon. Pastoral Associates: Sr. Marie Luisa Vasquez, O.P.; Deacon Paul Carrico.

Church—7701 Wyoming, N.E., 87109. Tel: 505-821-1571.
Catechesis/Religious Programs—Ann Bazen, D.R.E. Students 853.
Mission—Albuquerque, Bernalillo Co., Prince of Peace, 12500 Carmel, N.E., 87122. Tel: 505-856-7657.

4—HOLY FAMILY, (Hispanic), Revs. Jack Clark Robinson, O.F.M.; Donald Billiard, O.F.M.; Deacons Santos Abeyta; Robert Paiz; Eddie Blea. In res., Revs. Nils Francis Thompson, O.F.M.; Paul Juniet, O.F.M.; Bro. Peter Forton, O.F.M.
Res., 562 Atrisco Dr., S.W., P.O. Box 12127, 87105. Tel: 505-842-5426; Fax: 505-842-9767.
Catechesis/Religious Programs—Tel: 505-842-5448. Sr. Lois Ursula Higgins, O.S.F., D.R.E. Students 250.

5—HOLY GHOST, (1953), Rev. Joe D. Vigil; Deacons Pat Kneafsey; Robert Stromberg; Ubaldo Chavez.
Res., 833 Arizona Ave., S.E., 87108. Tel: 505-265-5957; Fax: 505-255-0115.
School—Tel: 505-256-1563. Noreen Copeland, Prin. Sisters 3; Lay Teachers 14; Students 221.
Catechesis/Religious Programs—Tel: 505-265-1975. Bro. Bruce Michalek, D.R.E. Students 172.

6—IMMACULATE CONCEPTION, (1883) (Hispanic), Revs. Francis E. Renfroe, S.J.; William King, S.J.; Paul V. Osterle, S.J.; Richard Rodriguez, S.J.; Deacons Gilbert Valverde; George Sandoval; Tom Perez.
Res., 619 Copper Ave., N.W., 87102. Tel: 505-247-4272; Fax: 505-243-0402.
School—St. Mary, 227 Seventh St., 87102. Tel: 505-242-6271; Fax: 505-242-4837. Sr. Marianella Domenici, S.C., Prin.
Sisters 2; Lay Teachers 34; Students 610.
Catechesis/Religious Programs—Tel: 505-247-2555.
Students 125.

7—OUR LADY OF FATIMA, (1949), Rev. Francis T. Eggert; Deacons Thomas Jones; Faustin Archuleta; Frank See; Hugh Hackett; Sandy Hall; Charles Duran.
Res., 4020 Lomas, N.E., 87110. Tel: 505-265-5868; Fax: 505-268-0680.
School—Tel: 505-255-6391. Linda Honeyfield, Prin. Lay Teachers 19; Students 289.

8—OUR LADY OF GUADALUPE, (1954), Rev. Ramon Aragon; Deacons Manuel Facio; Jim Delgado; George Valverde.
Res., 1860 Griegos, N.W., 87107. Tel: 505-345-4596.
Catechesis/Religious Programs—Tel: 505-344-7153. Molly C. De Baca, D.R.E.
Students 345.

9—OUR LADY OF LAVANG, (1986) (Vietnamese), Rev. Tin Mahn Bui.
Mailing Address: 2115 Inez N.E., 87110. Tel: 505-275-3079.
Church—8600 Gonzales Rd., S.W., 87105. Tel: 505-839-4738.

10—OUR LADY OF THE ASSUMPTION, (1954), Revs. Luis D. Jaramillo; Michael Cimino; Deacons Rue White; Salvador Nunez.
Office: 811 Guaymas, N.E., 87108. Tel: 505-256-9818; 256-9877; Fax: 505-256-3131.
Res., 8030 Fruit, N.E., 87108. Tel: 505-255-5727.
School—817 Guaymas, N.E., 87108. Tel: 505-256-3167. Robert M. Kaiser, Prin.
Lay Teachers 19; Students 198.
Catechesis/Religious Programs—Robert Shields, D.R.E.
Students 319.

11—OUR LADY OF MOST HOLY ROSARY, (1950) (Hispanic), Revs. Joel P. Garner, O.Praem.; Domenic Rossi, O.Praem.; Deacons Juan Barajas; Harry Beare; Charles Johnson; Frank Perez; Gene Tuma.
Office: 5415 Fortuna Rd., N.W., 87105. Tel: 505-836-5011; Fax: 505-836-7562.
Res., Santa Maria de la Vid Priory, 5825 Coors S.W., 87121. Tel: 505-873-4399.
Catechesis/Religious Programs—Tel: 505-831-2525. D.R.E.: Stephen Tumolo; Sr. Evangeline Salayar, O.S.B.
Students 710.

12—QUEEN OF ANGELS NATIVE AMERICAN CENTER AND ARCHDIOCESAN SHRINE TO KATERI TEKAKWITHA, (1952) (Native American), Rev. Paul Juniet, O.F.M.
Res., I 40 & 12 St., N.W., P.O. Box 6881, 87197. Tel: 505-243-0835.

13—QUEEN OF HEAVEN, (1952), Rev. Robert P. Malloy; Deacons Ruben Barela; Larry Cleveland; Chuck Cullen; Pilar Garcia; Dan Lopez; Julian Padilla.
Office: 5311 Phoenix, N.E., 87110. Tel: 505-881-1772; Fax: 505-883-5222.
Res., 5310 Claremont Ave., N.E., 87110. Tel: 505-881-6719.
School—Tel: 505-881-2484; Fax: 505-837-1123. Mary Cunning, Prin.
Sisters 4; Lay Teachers 26; Students 422.
Catechesis/Religious Programs—Tel: 505-881-0715. Donna Arellanes, D.R.E.
Students 625.

14—SACRED HEART, Rev. Enrique Bravo, C.S.B.; Sr. Teresa Aparicio, O.L.V.M., Pastoral Assoc.; Deacon Alfonso Montoya, (Retired).
Res., 412 Stover Ave., S.W., 87102. Tel: 505-242-0561. [JC]
Catechesis/Religious Programs—JoAnn Garcia, D.R.E.
Students 95.

15—SAINT JOSEPH ON THE RIO GRANDE, (1986), Rev. Frank Prieto; Deacons Don Bruckner; Frank Lucero.
Office: 4080 Saint Joseph Pl., N.W., 87120. Tel: 505-831-8265.
Catechesis/Religious Programs—Tel: 505-831-8346. Harv Weakland, D.R.E.
Students 482.

16—SAN FELIPE DE NERI, (1703) (Hispanic), Rev. Lambert Joseph Luna; Deacons Jose Lucero; Gerald Hietpas; James Robert (Bob) Lewis.
Res., P.O. Box 7007, 87194. Tel: 505-243-4628; Fax: 505-224-9495.
School—2000 Lomas Blvd., N.W., 87104. Tel: 505-242-2411; Fax: 505-242-7355. Sr. Carmel M. Purcell, B.V.M., Prin.
Sisters 1; Lay Teachers 10; Students 214.
Catechesis/Religious Programs—Tel: 505-247-2041; Fax: 505-224-7975. Silvia O. Zapata, D.R.E. Students 116.
Mission—Albuquerque, Bernalillo Co., San Jose de los Duranes, 2110 Los Luceros Rd., N.W., 87104.

17—SAN IGNACIO, (1916) (Hispanic), Deacon Merce Villareal, Admin.
Res., 1300 Walter, N.E., 87102. Tel: 505-243-4287.

18—SAN JOSE, Revs. Avelino Lorenzo, S.D.B.; Paul Tran; Deacons Charles Lucero; Paul Nguyen.
Res., 2401 Broadway, S.E., 87102. Tel: 505-242-3658; Fax: 505-248-0810.
Catechesis/Religious Programs—Sr. Bernice Garcia, O.P., D.R.E.
Students 495.

19—SANTUARIO SAN MARTIN DE PORRES, (1979), Rev. Daniel L. Farris; Deacons Patricio Santistevan; Sotero Montoya.
Res., 8321 Camino San Martin, S.W., 87121. Tel: 505-836-4676.
Catechesis/Religious Programs—Renee Ortiz, D.R.E.
Students 214.

20—SANGRE DE CRISTO, (1972), Rev. Albert J. Podvin; Deacon Lloyd Martinez.
Res., 8901 Candelaria, N.E., 87112. Tel: 505-293-2327; Fax: 505-292-0590.
Catechesis/Religious Programs—Students 261.

21—ST. ANNE, 1929 (Armijo), Rev. Msgr. Joaquin Bazan; Deacons Tibo Chavez; Rene Greivel.
Res., 1400 Arenal Rd., S.W., 87105. Tel: 505-877-3121.
Catechesis/Religious Programs—Tel: 505-873-2188. D.R.E.: Sr. Marcella Campos, C.S.J.; Sr. Gemella Casey, C.S.J.
Students 600.

22—ST. BERNADETTE, (1959), Revs. Thomas A. Zotter; James P. Moore; Deacons Alfred McLane; J. Robert Martinez.
Res., 1800 Martha, N.E., 87112. Tel: 505-298-7557; Fax: 505-271-8099.
Catechesis/Religious Programs—Tel: 505-293-7779; Fax: 505-298-2412. Sr. Maria Orlandini, Fd.CC., D.R.E.
Students 674.

23—ST. CHARLES BORROMEO, (1934), Revs. Robert Chabot, S.S.S.; Roger Bourgeois, S.S.S.; Normand R. Falardeau, S.S.S.; Ernest Falardeau, S.S.S.; Joseph Roy, S.S.S.; Julian Rousseau, S.S.S.; Dennis Ruane, S.S.S.; Robert Stark, S.S.S.; Joseph Thai Minh Tran, S.S.S.; Bro. Peter Mahady, S.S.S.; Deacons Lorenzo Castillo; John Leahigh.
Res., 1818 Coal Pl., S.E., 87106. Tel: 505-242-3462; Fax: 505-247-1292. [JC]
School—Tel: 505-243-5788; Fax: 505-764-8842. Mr. James Ochoa, Prin.
Sisters 2; Lay Teachers 20; Students 365.
Catechesis/Religious Programs—Tel: 505-268-9197. Juanita Gonzales, D.R.E.
Students 202.

24—ST. EDWIN, (1965) (Hispanic), Rev. Jose Hernandez; Deacons Nestor Garcia; Desiderio Luna; Bill Grossman.
Res., 2105 Barcelona, S.W., 87105. Tel: 505-877-2967. [CEM]
Catechesis/Religious Programs—Tel: 505-877-3727.
Students 330.

25—ST. FRANCIS XAVIER, (1928) (Hispanic), Deacon Andrew Chavez, Parish Life Coord.
Res., 817 Arno, S.E., 87102. Tel: 505-243-5201; 224-9474. [JC]

26—ST. JOHN THE APOSTLE, (1984). (John XXIII Catholic Community). Rev. Arkad Biczak; Deacons John Russo; Charles Allen; John Wertz; Alex Trujillo.
Res., 4831 Tramway Ridge Dr., N.E., 87111. Tel: 505-293-0088; Fax: 505-293-7276.
Catechesis/Religious Programs—Tel: 505-293-7756. Jude Fournier, D.R.E.
Students 447.

27—ST. JUDE THADDEUS, (Paradise Hills) (1968), Rev. John R. Conway; Deacons Robert Aragon; Raymond Gonzales.
Mailing Address: 5712 Paradise Blvd., N.W., 87114. Tel: 505-898-0826 (Church); 897-0391 (Res.).
Catechesis/Religious Programs—Tel: 505-897-4006.
Students 335.

28—ST. THERESE OF THE INFANT JESUS SHRINE OF THE LITTLE FLOWER, Revs. John Plans, S.F.; Charles L. Stoeber, S.F.; Deacons Patrick M. Cooney; Esequiel Torres, (Retired); Manuel Montoya.
Res., 300 Mildred, N.W., 87107. Tel: 505-344-8050.
School—Tel: 505-344-4479; Fax: 505-344-3349. Antoinette Crump, Prin.
Lay Teachers 14; Students 270.
Catechesis/Religious Programs—Tel: 505-344-7643.
Students 270.

29—ST. THOMAS AQUINAS UNIVERSITY PARISH, (1954). (Serving the University of New Mexico). Revs. Robert J. Keller, O.P.; Paul Wierenge, O.P.; John Vincent Blake, O.P.; Michael T. Demkovich, O.P.; Bro. Andrew J. Pavlak; Deacon Bruce Eklund.
Res., 1815 Las Lomas Rd., N.E., 87106. Tel: 505-247-1094; Fax: 505-247-2933.
Catechesis/Religious Programs—Fax: 505-247-2933. Michael LaLone, D.R.E.
Students 220.

Anton Chico, Guadalupe Co., San Jose (1857) (Hispanic), Rev. Patrick S. Duffy, O.C.S.O.
Res., Box 99, 87711. Tel: 505-427-1164. [CEM][JC 4]
Catechesis/Religious Programs—Students 186.
Missions—Dilia, Guadalupe Co.; Dahlia, Guadalupe Co.; Plaza de Arriba, Guadalupe Co.; Tecolotito, San Miguel Co.

Arroyo Seco, Taos Co., Holy Trinity (1834) (Spanish), Rev. Vincent P. Chavez; Deacons Patrick DeLozier; Michael L. Kittredge.
Res., Box 189, 87514. Tel: 505-776-2273; Fax: 505-776-2273. [CEM]
Catechesis/Religious Programs—Students 120.
Missions—Arroyo Hondo, Taos Co.; Valdez, Taos Co.; Las Colonias, Taos Co.; San Cristobal, Taos Co.

Belen, Valencia Co., Our Lady of Belen (1793), Rev. David Gallegos, O.S.M.; Allen Sanchez, Pastoral Assoc.; Deacons Felix Barela; Manuel Gallegos; Norbert Sanchez; Robert Sanchez; Rudy Zamora.
Res., 101-A N. 10th St., 87002. Tel: 505-864-8043; Fax: 505-861-0969. [CEM][JC]
School—Tel: 505-864-4724. Dr. Rebecca Lutz, Prin. Sisters 1; Lay Teachers 8; Students 210.
Catechesis/Religious Programs—Tel: 505-864-7869.
Students 560.
Missions—Los Chavez, Valencia Co., 20 Thresher Ln., 87002. Tel: 505-864-9297; Jarales, Valencia Co., P.O. Box 29, Jarales, 87023. Tel: 505-864-4231; Pueblitos, Valencia Co., 7 Wood Dr., 87002. Tel: 505-864-6267; Bosque, Valencia Co., P.O. Box 159, Bosque, 87006. Tel: 505-864-2192.

Bernalillo, Sandoval Co., Our Lady of Sorrows (1699) (Indio-Hispanic), Rev. William E. Sanchez; Deacon Paul Maestas.
Office: P.O. Box 607, 87004. Tel: 505-867-5252; Fax: 505-867-0267.
Res., Camino del Pueblo, 87004. Tel: 505-867-0585. [CEM 3]
Catechesis/Religious Programs—Ursulita Perez, D.R.E.
Students 586.
Missions—Placitas, Sandoval Co.; Algodones, Sandoval Co.; Sandia Indian Pueblo, Sandoval Co.

Cerrillos, Santa Fe Co., St. Joseph (1850), Rev. Donnan Herbe, O.F.M.
Res., Box 98, 87010. Tel: 505-471-1562. [CEM]
Catechesis/Religious Programs—Students 57.
Missions—Golden, Santa Fe Co.; Galisteo, Santa Fe Co.

Chama, Rio Arriba Co., St. Patrick (1963), Rev. Clarence Maes.
Res., 247 Pine St., Box 36, 87520-0036. Tel: 505-756-2926.
Missions—Cebolla, Santo Nino; Canjilon, St. Juan Nepumoceno.

Chimayo, Rio Arriba Co., Holy Family (1955) (Hispanic), Revs. Miguel Mateo, S.F.; Casimiro Roca, S.F.; Jose Maria Conde, S.F.; Deacon Jose Lopez.
Res., P.O. Box 235, 87522. Tel: 505-351-4360; Fax:

505-351-4698. [CEM]
Catechesis/Religious Programs—Tel: 505-351-4131. D.R.E.: Sr. Marianna Ableidinger, F.S.P.A.; Sr. Marilyn Schata, O.L.V.M.; Sr. Priscilla Wilke, O.L.V.M.; Sr. Carol Virnig, O.S.F.
Students 228.
Missions—Truchas, Rio Arriba Co., Holy Rosary; Trampas, Taos Co., San Jose de Gracia; Cundiyo, Rio Arriba Co., Santo Domingo; Cordova, Rio Arriba Co., San Antonio; Rio Chiquito, Rio Arriba Co., Sagrado Corazon; Ojo Sarco, Rio Arriba Co., Santo Tomas; El Valle, Taos Co., San Miguel Archangel; El Santuario, Santa Fe Co., El Santuario Shrine, Tel: 505-351-4889.

Cimarron, Colfax Co., Immaculate Conception Church (1864) (Hispanic-Mexican), Rev. C. John Bresler; Sr. Hildegard Smith, S.C.C., Pastoral Assoc.
Res., Rte. 1, Box 11, 87714. Tel: 505-483-2775. [JC]
Catechesis/Religious Programs—Tel: 505-376-9028. D.R.E.: Mrs. Gloria Martinez; Mr. James Doherty.
Students 80.
Convent—Tel: 505-376-2553.
Sisters of Christian Charity 3.
Missions—Eagle Nest, Colfax Co., St. Mel, 200 Willow Creek, Eagle Nest, 87718. Tel: 505-376-2553; Black Lake, Colfax Co., St. Anthony.

Clayton, Union Co., St. Francis Xavier, Rev. Joe Kuehner; Deacon P. Louis Montoya.
Res., 115 N. First St., 88415. Tel: 505-374-9500.
Catechesis/Religious Programs—118 N. 2nd St., 88415.
Students 120.
Missions—Des Moines, Union Co., Our Lady of Guadalupe, Des Moines, 88418; Folsom, Union Co., St. Joseph, Folsom, 88419; Moses, Union Co., Sacred Heart, Seneca, 88437; Hayden, Quay Co., Holy Trinity, Nara Visa, 88430.

Clovis, Curry Co., Sacred Heart (1908), Rev. Carlos Chavez.
Res., 911 Merriwether St., 88101. Tel: 505-763-6947; Fax: 505-762-5557.
Catechesis/Religious Programs—Mary Ann Lingnau, D.R.E.
Students 281.
Mission—Melrose, Curry Co., P.O. Box 375, Melrose, 88124.

Our Lady of Guadalupe (1945), Rev. Daniel Balizan.
Res., 108 Davis St., 88101. Tel: 505-763-4445; Fax: 505-763-4446. [JC]
Catechesis/Religious Programs—Tel: 505-762-7343. D.R.E.: Helen Gauna; Lindy Esquibel; Sally Romero; Manuel Torres.
Students 210.
Mission—Texico, Curry Co., Box 122, 88135.

Corrales, Sandoval Co., San Ysidro (1966), Rev. Lucian C. Hendren.
Res., Box 460, 87048. Tel: 505-898-1779. [CEM]
Catechesis/Religious Programs—Students 123.

Dixon, Rio Arriba Co., St. Anthony (1929), Joanne M. Dupont, Parish Life Coord.
Res., 5 Church St., P.O. Box 39, 87527-0039. Tel: 505-579-4389. [CEM 2]
Catechesis/Religious Programs—Students 113.
Missions—Velarde, Rio Arriba Co., Nuestra Senora de Guadalupe; Pilar, Taos Co., Nuestra Senora de los Dolores; Lyden, Rio Arriba Co., San Jose.

El Rito, Rio Arriba Co., San Juan Nepomuceno (1832) (Spanish), Rev. Patrick J. Chavez; Deacon Fabian Garcia.
Res., 87530. Tel: 505-581-4714. [CEM][JC 9]
Catechesis/Religious Programs—Students 62.
Missions—La Madera, Rio Arriba Co., Gen. Del., La Madera, 87539; Las Tablas, Taos Co., Gen. Del., Las Tablas, 87539; Ojo Caliente, Rio Arriba Co., Gen. Del., Ojo Caliente, 87549; Petaca, Taos Co., Gen. Del., Petaca, 87539; Servilleta, Taos Co., Gen. Del., Servilleta, 87539; Vallecitos, Rio Arriba Co., Gen. Del., Vallecitos, 87581; Canon de Vallecitos, Rio Arriba Co., Gen. Del., Canon de Vallecitos, 87581; Tres Piedras, Taos Co., Gen. Del., Tres Piedras, 87579; Placitas, Rio Arriba Co., P.O. Box 7, 87530.

Espanola, Rio Arriba Co., Sacred Heart (1950) (Hispanic), Rev. Augustine Moore; Sr. Rosemary Schwer, S.C.C., Pastoral Assoc. & D.R.E.; Sr. Marianne Schwer, S.C.C.; Deacons Ralph Vigil; Diego Herrera; Benjie Lopez.
Res., P.O. Box 69, 87532. Tel: 505-753-4225; Fax: 505-753-3312. [CEM 2]
Catechesis/Religious Programs—Tel: 505-753-9413; Fax: 505-753-1695.
Students 280.
Missions—Hernandez, Rio Arriba Co., 87532. Tel: 505-753-3312; Chili, Rio Arriba Co., 87532; El Guache, Rio Arriba Co., 87532; Guachupanque, Rio Arriba Co., 87532; El Duende, Rio Arriba Co., 87532.

Fort Sumner, De Baca Co., St. Anthony (1958) (Hispanic). Attended by St. Rose of Lima, Santa Rosa. Rev. Sotero Sena.
Res., 114 W. Richard Ave., P.O. Box 370, 88119. Tel: 505-355-2320. [CEM]
Catechesis/Religious Programs—Students 65.

Isleta, Pueblo Bernalillo Co., St. Augustine (1613) (Native American), Rev. Nicholas E. Nirschl, O.Praem.
Res., P.O. Box 463, 87022. Tel: 505-869-3398; 873-4399.
Catechesis/Religious Programs—Josephine Balvea, D.R.E.
Students 150.

Jemez Pueblo, Sandoval Co., San Diego Indian Missions (1608) (Native American-Spanish), Revs. Chrysostom Partee, O.F.M.; Gino Correa, O.F.M.
Res., P.O. Box 79, 87024. Tel: 505-834-7300. [CEM]
School—Indian Mission School, Tel: 505-834-7419. Sr. Barbara Tylkowski, O.S.F., Prin.
Sisters 2; Lay Teachers 7; Students 85.
Catechesis/Religious Programs—Gail Madalena, D.R.E.
Students 60.
Missions—Canyon, Sandoval Co.; Ponderosa, Sandoval Co.; San Ysidro, Sandoval Co.; Santa Ana, Sandoval Co.; Zia, Sandoval Co.

Jemez Springs, Sandoval Co., Our Lady of the Assumption (1947), Very Rev. Liam Hoare, s.P.
Res., 87025. Tel: 505-829-3586; Fax: 505-829-3592. [CEM]

La Joya, Socorro Co., Our Lady of Sorrows (1930) (Spanish), Rev. Vincent A. Nicosia, S.O.L.T.; Deacon Alfred Edwin Esquibel.
Mailing Address: 19 Calle de la Iglesia, 87028. Tel: 505-864-4461; Fax: 505-861-3552.
Res., 1249 Hwy. 304, Veguita, 87062. Tel: 505-864-0745. [CEM]
Missions—Abeytas, Socorro Co., San Antonio; Contreras, Socorro Co., San Jose; Las Nutrias, Socorro Co., San Isidro; Veguita, Socorro Co., San Juan; Sabinal, Socorro Co., San Antonio.

Las Vegas, San Miguel Co., Immaculate Conception (1885), Rev. George V. Salazar, Deacon Reynaldo Cordova.
Res., 811 Sixth St., 87701. Tel: 505-425-7791; Fax: 505-425-6991. [CEM]
Catechesis/Religious Programs—Tel: 505-454-0685. D.R.E.: Rosa de Aragon; Salomon Maese; Carol Corbin.
Students 687.
Mission—San Antonio, San Miguel Co., Los Vigiles (Our Lady of Refuge), 811 6th, 87701.

Our Lady of Sorrows Church (1851) (Hispanic), Revs. Vincent G. Defazio; Tobin Hitt; Deacons Jose Leroy Martinez; Macedon Montoya, Jr.
Res., 403 Valencia St., 87701. Tel: 505-454-1469. [CEM][JC 2]
Catechesis/Religious Programs—Tel: 505-425-6823. Mr. Ray de Aragon, D.R.E.
Students 317.
Missions—Sapello, San Miguel Co., Our Lady of Guadalupe, HC 68, Box 13, Sapello, 87745. Tel: 505-425-3608; Trujillo, San Miguel Co., San Ignacio, Trujillo Rte. Box 428, 87701. Tel: 505-641-5358; Variadero, San Miguel Co., Holy Family, Garita, 88421. Tel: 505-641-5341; Rociada Abajo, San Miguel Co., Santo Nino, Box 688, Rociada Abajo, 87742. Tel: 505-425-8624; Gallinas, San Miguel Co., Santo Nino, Box 63 El Porvenir Rte., Montezuma, 87731. Tel: 505-425-6015.
Chapels—Christ the King, 2609 Encino St., 87701. Tel: 505-425-6894; Montezuma; San Antonio, Rte. Box 90, El Porvenir, 87731. Tel: 505-425-8010; San Ignacio, HC 68 Box 6, Sapello, 87745. Tel: 505-454-1139; Our Lady of Sorrows, Box 39 Anton Chico Rte., 87701. Tel: 505-421-5599; San Geronimo, Box 310 Mineral Hill Rte., 87701. Tel: 505-454-0718; San Antonio, P.O. Box 85, 87701. Tel: 505-425-3405; Lourdes; San Jose, HC 69 Box 17, Rociada, 87742. Tel: 505-425-8672; San Rafael, c/o Al Sanchez Jr., General Delivery, Trementina, 88439. Tel: 505-641-5384; Santo Nino de Atocha, Anton Chico Rte. Box 20, 87701. Tel: 505-425-8014; Ojitos Frios; Manuelitas; Santo Nino, Tel: 505-454-0409.

Los Alamos, Los Alamos Co., Immaculate Heart of Mary (1946), Rev. Charles C. Brown; Deacons Charles Pacheco; Gerald Langner; Don Lucero; Tony Porto; Ray Alcouffe.
Mailing Address: 3700 Canyon Rd., 87544.
Res., 3694 Canyon Rd., 87544. Tel: 505-662-6193.
Catechesis/Religious Programs—Tel: 505-662-7773. Karen McLoughlin, D.R.E.
Students 450.
Mission—White Rock, Los Alamos Co., 196 Meadow, 87544. Tel: 505-672-1270.

Los Lunas, Valencia Co., St. Clement (1961), Rev. Rick Zerwas; Deacons Edward Espinosa; John O'Hare.
Res., P.O. Box 147, 87031. Tel: 505-865-7385. [CEM][JC]
Catechesis/Religious Programs—Tel: 505-865-3018. Sr. Charlotte Moser, O.P., D.R.E.
Students 520.
Mission—Los Lentes, Valencia Co., 87031.

Los Ojos, Rio Arriba Co., San Jose (1883) (Spanish), Rev. Sean Murnan, O.F.M.
Res., Box 6, 87551. Tel: 505-588-7473. [CEM][JC 2]
Catechesis/Religious Programs—Students 69.
Missions—Ensenada, Rio Arriba Co.,; La Puente, Rio Arriba Co.,; Plaza Blanca, Rio Arriba Co.

Mora, Mora Co., St. Gertrude (1851), Rev. Timothy A. Martinez; Bercy Espinoza, Pastoral Assoc.
Res., P.O. Box 599, 87732. Tel: 505-387-2336. [CEM][JC 9]
Catechesis/Religious Programs—Mary Romero, D.R.E.
Students 420.
Missions—Le Doux, Mora Co., 87732; El Carmen, Mora Co., 87732; Lucero, Mora Co., 87732; Santiago-Talco, Mora Co., 87732; Ojo Feliz, Mora Co., 87732; Buenavista, Mora Co., 87732; Golondrinas, Mora Co., 87732; Rainsville, Mora Co., 87732; Chacon, Mora Co., 87732; Holman, Mora Co., 87732; Cleveland, Mora Co., 87732; Guadalupita, Mora Co., 87732; Monte Aplanado, Mora Co., 87732; Turquillo, Mora Co., 87732; La Cueva, Mora Co., 87732; Holman, Mora Co., 87732.

Moriarty, Torrance Co., Estancia Valley Catholic Parish (1972), Rev. Virgil Furfaro; Deacons James A. Baca; Juan S. Lucero.
Res., Box 129, 87035. Tel: 505-832-6655. [CEM][JC]
Catechesis/Religious Programs—Corriene Lucero, D.R.E.
Students 1,213.
Missions—Estancia, Torrance Co.; Tajique, Torrance Co.; Tapia, San Miguel Co.; Edgewood, Santa Fe Co.

Mountainair, Torrance Co., St. Alice. Unassigned.
Res., P.O. Box 206, 87036. Tel: 505-847-2264. [CEM 5][JC]
Catechesis/Religious Programs—Tel: 505-847-0190. D.R.E.: Anne Marie Nunez, (Elementary); Prescilla Quintana.
Students 80.
Missions—Abo, Torrance Co., 87036; Punta de Agua, Torrance Co., 87036; Manzano, Torrance Co., 87036; Torreon, Torrance Co., Torreon, 87061; Willard, Torrance Co., Willard, 87063.

Pecos, San Miguel Co., St. Anthony (1862), Rev. Johnny Lee Chavez.
Res., HC 70, Box 23, 87552. Tel: 505-757-6345. [CEM 5]
Catechesis/Religious Programs—Tel: 505-757-6305.
Students 289.
Missions—Canoncito, Santa Fe Co., 87552; Las Colonias, San Miguel Co., 87552; Glorieta, Santa Fe Co., 87552; Rowe, San Miguel Co., 87552; El Macho, San Miguel Co., 87552.

Pena Blanca, Sandoval Co., Nuestra Senora De Guadalupe (Hispanic-Native American), Revs. Hilaire Valiquette, O.F.M.; Joseph Redinbo, O.F.M.; Deacon Albert Arquero.
Res., P.O. Box 1270, 87041. Tel: 505-465-2226. [CEM]
Catechesis/Religious Programs—Tel: 505-465-2685. Sr. Jeanne Tranel, O.P., D.R.E.
Students 320.
Missions—Cochiti, Sandoval Co., Indian Pueblo; San Felipe, Sandoval Co., Indian Pueblo; Santo Domingo, Sandoval Co., Indian Pueblo; Sile, Sandoval Co.; La Bajada, Sandoval Co.

Penasco, Taos Co., San Antonio de Padua (1866), Rev. Adam Lee Ortega y Ortiz.
Res., 14079 N. Hwy. 75, P.O. Box 460, 87553-0460. Tel: 505-587-2188; 587-2111 (Office); Fax: 505-587-2188. [CEM]
Catechesis/Religious Programs—Tel: 505-587-2216. Joyce Kilgore, D.R.E.
Students 196.
Missions—Chamisal, Taos Co., Santa Cruz Mission; Llano Largo, Taos Co., San Acacio Mission; Rio Lucio, Taos Co., Sagrado Corazon Mission; Vadito, Taos Co., Nuestra Senora de los Dolores Mission; Picuris Indian Pueblo, Taos Co., San Lorenzo Mission; Llano San Juan, Taos Co., San Juan Nepomuceno Mission; Placita, Taos Co., Nuestra Senora de la Asuncion Mission; Rodarte, Taos Co., Santa Barbara Mission.

Peralta, Valencia Co., Our Lady of Guadalupe (1970), Rev. Albert Gallegos, O.S.M.; Deacon Joe Trujillo.
Res., P.O. Box 288, 87042. Tel: 505-869-2189. [CEM]
Catechesis/Religious Programs—Tel: 505-869-6993. D.R.E.: Marlene Monteith; Margaret Trujillo.
Students 356.
Station—Peralta, Valencia.

Pojoaque, Santa Fe Co., N.S. de Guadalupe del Valle de

Pojoaque (1959) (Spanish), Rev. Jose Flavio Santillanes; Deacons John Archuleta; Pedro Garcia.
Res., Rte. 5, Box 216 D, Santa Fe, 87501. Tel: 505-455-2472; Fax: 505-455-3849. [JC]
Catechesis/Religious Programs—Tel: 505-455-2267.
Students 92.
Missions—Nambe, Santa Fe Co., Nambe Indian Pueblo; El Rancho, Santa Fe Co.

Portales, Roosevelt Co., St. Helen (1952), Rev. Anthony Martinez.
Office: Tel: 505-356-4241; Fax: 505-359-1721.
Res., 1600 S. Avenue O, 88130. Tel: 505-359-1557.
Catechesis/Religious Programs—Cornie Moore, D.R.E.
Students 203.
Mission—Portales, Roosevelt Co., University Catholic Center.

Questa, Taos Co., St. Anthony (1841), Rev. William E. Young (NY).
Res., Box 200, 87556. Tel: 505-586-0470; 0471; Fax: 505-586-1755. [CEM 6]
Catechesis/Religious Programs—Students 124.
Missions—Cerro, Taos Co.; Red River, Taos Co.; Costilla, Taos Co.; Amalia, Taos Co.

Ranchos De Taos, Taos Co., San Francisco de Asis (1936) (Hispanic), Rev. John M. Tourangeau.
Res., Box 72, 87557. Tel: 505-758-2754; Fax: 505-758-8022. [CEM]
School—(Grades K-6) P.O. Box 463, 87557. Tel: 505-758-1236. Sr. Grace Aufderbeck, Prin.
Sisters of Charity of Cincinnati 2; Lay Teachers 6; Students 138.
Catechesis/Religious Programs—Nora Perea, D.R.E.
Students 190.
Missions—Talpa, Taos Co., N.S. de San Juan de Los Lagos; Llano Quemado, Taos Co., N.S. del Carmel; Los Cordovas, Taos Co., San Isidro.

Raton, Colfax Co., St. Patrick/St. Joseph (1891), Rev. James L. Vance; Deacon Thomas Alderette.
Res., 105 Buena Vista St., Box 278, 87740. Tel: 505-445-9763. [CEM]
School—401 S. Fourth St., 87740. Tel: 505-445-3862.
Sisters 1; Lay Teachers 7; Students 128.
Catechesis/Religious Programs—104 Buena Vista St., 87740. Tel: 505-445-9563.
Students 214.
St. Patrick's. Consolidated with St. Joseph's to form St. Patrick/St. Joseph.
St. Joseph's. Consolidated with St. Patrick's to form St. Patrick/St. Joseph.

Ribera, San Miguel Co., San Miguel Del Vado (1804) (Hispanic), Rev. John Shedlock.
Res., P.O. Box 488, San Miguel, 87560. Tel: 505-421-2405; 421-2780 (Office). [CEM]
Catechesis/Religious Programs—Students 140.
Missions—San Isidro Norte, San Miguel Co., Ilfield, 87538. [JC]
San Jose, San Miguel Co., San Jose, 87565. [JC]
San Juan, San Miguel Co., San Jose, 87565. [JC]
Bernal, San Miguel Co., Serafina, 87569. [JC]
El Pueblo, San Miguel Co., El Pueblo, 87560. [JC]
La Lagunita, San Miguel Co., Serafina, 87569. [JC]
San Isidro Sur, San Miguel Co., Ilfield, 87538. [JC]

Rio Rancho, Sandoval Co., St. Thomas Aquinas (1974), Rev. Msgr. Douglas A. Raun; Rev. Tien Tri Nguyen; Deacons Aston Bailey; Enrique Padilla.
Res., 1502 Sara Rd., S.E., 87124. Tel: 505-892-1511; Fax: 505-891-3044.
Catechesis/Religious Programs—Tel: 505-892-1497.
Students 1,238.

Roy, Harding Co., Holy Family-St. Joseph (1918) (Hispanic), Rev. Joe Kuehner; Sr. Anthony Ebell, S.S.C.J., Pastoral Assoc.; Deacon Edward Olona.
Res., P.O. Box 37, 87743. Tel: 505-485-2579. [CEM 4]
Missions—Bueyeros, Harding Co.; Gallegos, Harding Co.; Clayton, St. Francis Xavier; Sabinoso, San Miguel Co.; Mosquero, Harding Co.

San Juan Pueblo, Rio Arriba Co. (Indian Pueblo), St. John the Baptist, Deacon Eloy E. Martinez.
Res., P.O. Box 1075, 87566. Tel: 505-852-4179.
Catechesis/Religious Programs—Sr. Clarita Trujillo, D.R.E. & Pastoral Assoc.
Students 358.
Missions—Alcalde, Rio Arriba Co., 87566; Chamita, Rio Arriba Co., 87566; El Guique, Rio Arriba Co., 87566; Ranchitos, Rio Arriba Co., 87566; Estaca, Rio Arriba Co., 87566. [CEM]
Shrine—Our Lady of Lourdes. Pilgrimage shrine.

Santa Cruz, Santa Fe Co., Holy Cross (1695) (Hispanic), Revs. Ron Carrillo, S.F.; Jose Maria Blanch, S.F.
Res., P.O. Box 1228, 87567. Tel: 505-753-3345; Fax: 505-753-7401. [CEM]
School—Tel: 505-753-4644. Sr. Lucille Leannah, O.P., Prin.
Sisters 3; Lay Teachers 13; Students 244.
Catechesis/Religious Programs—Tel: 505-753-4567; Fax: 505-753-7401. D.R.E.: Sr. Angelina Gonzales, O.P., (Elementary); Mrs. Lynda Martinez, (Junior & Senior High).
Students 1,110.
Convent—Box 1137, 87567. Tel: 505-753-3340.
Missions—Cuarteles; La Mesilla; La Puebla; San Pedro; Santo Nino.

Santa Rosa, Guadalupe Co., St. Rose of Lima (1907) (Hispanic), Rev. Sotero A. Sena; Deacon Pat Houlihan, (Retired).
Res., 439 Third St., 88435. Tel: 505-472-3724; Fax: 505-472-3724. [CEM]
Catechesis/Religious Programs—Tel: 505-472-3992. D.R.E.: Sr. Helen Halligan; Sr. Ann Kaufmann.
Students 335.
Missions—Puerto de Luna, Guadalupe Co., 88435; San Ignacio, Guadalupe Co., 88435; Borica, Guadalupe Co., 88435; Cuervo, Guadalupe Co., 88435; Newkirk, Guadalupe Co., 88435; Colonias, Guadalupe Co., 88435; Pintada, Guadalupe Co., 88435; Milagro, Guadalupe Co., 88435.

Socorro, Socorro Co., San Miguel (1615), Rev. Domingo B. Gumpal; Deacons Alfred Gilbert; James Alexander Elsberg.
Res., 403 El Camino Real, N.W., 87801. Tel: 505-835-1620. [CEM 8][JC]
School—Tel: 505-835-3661; Fax: 505-835-4343. Sr. Mary Metro, O.S.F., Prin.
Sisters 2; Lay Teachers 11; Students 136.
Catechesis/Religious Programs—Tel: 505-835-2891. Stella C. Castillo, D.R.E.
Students 280.
Missions—Lemitar, Socorro Co., 87801; Polvadera, Socorro Co., 87801; Luis Lopez, Socorro Co., 87801; San Antonio, Socorro Co., 87801; Alamillo, Socorro Co., 87801; Magdalena, Socorro Co., 87801; Kelly, Socorro Co., 87801; Riley, Socorro Co., 87801.

Springer, Colfax Co., St. Joseph (1882) (Hispanic), Rev. C. John Brasher.
Res., 605 Fifth St., P.O. Box 516, 87747. Tel: 505-483-2775. [JC]
Catechesis/Religious Programs—Martha Lopez, D.R.E.
Students 91.
Missions—Palo Blanco, Colfax Co.; Maxwell, Colfax Co.; Tinaja, Colfax Co.
Station—New Mexico Boys' School. (Detention Facility). Tel: 505-483-2775. Sr. Rose Urban, Chap.

Taos, Taos Co., Nuestra Senora De Guadalupe (1801), Rev. Edmund Savilla; Deacon Donald Martinez.
Res., P.O. Box 888, 87571. Tel: 505-758-2095; Fax: 505-758-2745. [CEM]
Catechesis/Religious Programs—Tel: 505-758-8451. Sr. Kristen McNamara, D.R.E.
Students 311.
Missions—Taos, Taos Co., St. Jerome; Taos Pueblo.
Chapels—El Prado, St. Theresa; Canon, Our Lady of Sorrows; Ranchitos, Immaculate Conception; La Loma, San Antonio; Taos Indian Pueblo.

Tierra Amarilla, Rio Arriba Co., Santo Nino (1966) (Spanish), Rev. Sean Murnan, O.F.M.
Mailing Address: Box 193, 87575. Tel: 505-588-7463. [JC]

Tijeras, Bernalillo Co., Holy Child (1962), Rev. John F. Carney; Deacon Ray Bouffard.
Res., Box 130, 87059. Tel: 505-281-1502; 281-2297 (Office); Fax: 505-281-7794. [CEM 9]
Catechesis/Religious Programs—Students 177.
Missions—Carnuel, Bernalillo Co., Holy Child; Chilili, Bernalillo Co., San Juan de Nepumoceno; Escobosa, Bernalillo Co., San Isidro; San Antonio, Bernalillo Co.; Sedillo, Bernalillo Co., San Isidro; Canoncito, San Lorenzo; Tijeras, San Antonito.

Tome, Valencia Co., Immaculate Conception (1750) (Spanish), Rev. Carl Feil, O.S.M.
Res., P.O. Box 100, 87060-0100. Tel: 505-865-7497; Fax: 505-865-7497. [CEM]
Catechesis/Religious Programs—7 Church Loop, Juan Diego Hall.
Students 196.
Mission—Casa Colorada, Valencia Co., State Hwy. 304 South, 87002.

Tucumcari, Quay Co., St. Anne (1910), Rev. John C. Daniel; Deacon Robert Welch.
Res., 306 W. High St., 88401. Tel: 505-461-2515.
Catechesis/Religious Programs—Tel: 505-461-3568; 461-3058. Nancy Arias, D.R.E.
Students 326.
Missions—Logan, Quay Co., Logan, 88426; Nara Visa, Quay Co., Nara Visa, 88430; San Jon, Quay Co., San Jon, 88434.

Vaughn, Guadalupe Co., St. Mary (1936), Sr. Elena Carney, O.L.V.M., Parish Life Coord.
Res., P.O. Box 276, 88353. Tel: 505-584-2954. [CEM][JC]
Missions—Encino, Torrance Co.; Duran, Torrance Co.; Pastura, Guadalupe Co.; Pinos Wells, Torrance Co.

Villanueva, Our Lady of Guadalupe (1830) (Hispanic), Rev. John Shedlock.
Mailing Address: P.O. Box 39, 87583. Tel: 505-421-2548. [CEM]
Missions—Sena, San Miguel Co., 87533; Cerrito, San Miguel Co., 87533; Gonzales Ranch, San Miguel Co., 87533; Leyba, San Miguel Co., 87533; Aurora, San Miguel Co., 87533.

Wagon Mound, Mora Co., Santa Clara (1882) (Hispanic). Attended by Immaculate Conception, Las Vegas. Sr. Eileen Hussey, O.P., Admin.
Res., P.O. Box 186, 87752. Tel: 505-666-2478. [CEM]
Catechesis/Religious Programs—Students 60.
Missions—Ocate, Mora Co.; Los Hueros, Mora Co.; Los Le Febres, Mora Co.; Watrous, Mora Co.

Priests Serving Private and Public Institutions

SANTA FE. *New Mexico State Penitentiary*. Rev. Ricardo Russo, O.F.M.
St. Vincent's Hospital. Rev. Arthur Jakobiak, Chap.

ALBUQUERQUE. *Lovelace Hospital*. Rev. Steve Sanchez.
Presbyterian Hospital. Revs. David Klein, C.S.B.; Reinaldo Davila, O.F.M.
St. Joseph Medical Center. Revs. Christian O'Brien, O.Praem.; James Huth, O.Praem.
U.S.P.H. Indian Hospital. Rev. Nils Francis Thompson, O.F.M.
University Hospital. Revs. Millan J. Garcia; Reinaldo Davila, O.F.M.
Veterans Administration Medical Center. Vacant. Rev. Julian Rousseau.

LAS VEGAS. *State Hospital*. Attended by Immaculate Conception Parish.

LOS LUNAS. *Correctional Facility (State)*. Deacon Lorenzo Castillo.

SPRINGER. *New Mexico Boys School*. Attended by St. Joseph Parish, Springer.

On Duty Outside the Archdiocese:
Reverend Fathers—
Berg, Timothy
Plotkowski, Jerome

Military Chaplains:
Reverend Fathers—
Flaska, John, U.S. Army

Absent on Leave:
Reverend Fathers—
Ortega, Eduardo

Retired:
Reverend Monsignors—
Burns, Bernard
Hill, Peter
McNiff, James
Stadtmueller, Fred
Reverend Fathers—
Alvarez, Manuel
Amiro, Raymond M.
Anstiss, Arthur
Auman, Robert
Bayer, Leonard
Beach, Robert
Cuesta, Benedicto
Cushing, Alan
Debaenst, Emmanuel
Dennis, Clay
Fitzgerald, John W.
Galli, Clarence
Hendriks, Boniface
Homola, William B.
Hunt, Ted
Kapitz, Donald
Montoya, Ernest
Niemeyer, Elmer L.
Rivera, Guadalupe
Salas, Sipio
Savard, Wilfred

Permanent Deacons:
Abeyta, Santos, Holy Family, Albuquerque
Aird, Gordon, Community of the Risen Savior, Albuquerque
Alcouffe, Raymond, Immaculate Heart of Mary, Los Alamos
Alderette, Thomas, St. Joseph-St. Patrick, Raton
Allen, Charles, John XXIII, Albuquerque
Aragon, Robert, St. Jude Thaddeus, Paradise Hills
Archuleta, Faustin, Our Lady of Fatima, Albuquerque
Archuleta, John, Our Lady of Guadalupe, Pojoaque

Armijo, Vicente, Immaculate Conception, Las Vegas
Arquero, Albert, Nuestra Senora de Guadalupe, Pene Blanca
Baca, James, Estancia Valley Parish, Moriarty
Bachechi, Victor, Annunciation, Albuquerque
Bailey, Aston, St. Thomas Aquinas, Rio Rancho
Ballard, Alphonse L., St. Joseph on the Rio Grande, Albuquerque
Barajas, Juan, Holy Rosary, Albuquerque, Stewardship
Bates, Charles, St. Francis Cathedral, Santa Fe
Beare, Harry, St. Thomas Aquinas, Rio Rancho
Black, Joseph, NM National Guard, Santa Fe
Blea, Edward, Holy Family, Albuquerque
Bouffard, Raymond, Holy Child, Tijeras
Braune, Oscar, Our Lady of Fatima, Albuquerque
Bruckner, Donald G., St. Joseph on the Rio Grande, Albuquerque
Carrillo, Andres, St. John the Baptist, Santa Fe
Castillo, Lorenzo, St. Charles, Albuquerque
Chavez, Andrew, St. Francis Xavier, Albuquerque
Chavez, Tiburci, St. Anne, Albuquerque
Chavez, Ubaldo, Holy Ghost, Albuquerque
Cleveland, Larry, Queen of Heaven; Ministry to Deaf, Santa Fe
Contreras, Robert, Nativity of Blessed Virgin Mary, Alameda
Cooney, Patrick, St. Therese, Albuquerque
Cordova, Raynaldo A., Our Lady of Sorrows, Las Vegas
Cullen, Charles, Queen of Heaven, Albuquerque
Delgado, James P., Our Lady of Guadalupe, Albuquerque
Delozier, Patrick, Holy Trinity, Arroyo Seco
Dimas, Claudio, New Mexico State Penitentiary
Duran, Charles, Our Lady of Fatima, Albuquerque
Eklund, Bruce, St. Thomas Aquinas Newman Center, Albuquerque
Elliott, Robert, Community of the Risen Savior, Albuquerque
Escandon, Jose, St. Bernadette, Albuquerque
Espinosa, Edward, San Clemente, Los Lunas
Esquibel, A. Edwin, Our Lady of Sorrows, La Joya
Facio, Manuel, Our Lady of Guadalupe, Albuquerque
Gagnon, Fabian, St. Joseph on the Rio Grande, Albuquerque; Office of Handicappable, Santa Fe
Gallegos, Manuel A., Our Lady of Belen, Belen
Garcia, Fabian A., San Juan Nepomuceno, El Rito
Garcia, Nestor, St. Edwin, Albuquerque
Garcia, Pedro, Our Lady of Guadalupe, Pojoaque
Garcia, Pilar, Queen of Heaven, Albuquerque
Gilbert, Alfred, San Miguel, Socorro
Gogan, Harry L., Annunciation, Albuquerque
Gonzales, Raymond, St. Jude Thaddeus, Paradise Hills
Greivel, Rene, St. Anne, Albuquerque
Grossman, William L., St. Edwin, Albuquerque
Hackett, Hugh, Our Lady of Fatima, Albuquerque
Hall, Sandy, Our Lady of Fatima, Albuquerque
Herrera, Diego A., Sacred Heart, Espanola
Hietpas, Gerald M., San Felipe de Neri, Albuquerque
Hoefler, William C., Ascension, Albuquerque
Houlihan, William, St. Rose of Lima, Santa Rosa
Johnson, Charles V., Holy Rosary, Albuquerque
Jones, Thomas E., Our Lady of Fatima, Albuquerque
Kazek, Chester, Leave of Absence
Kittredge, Michael, Holy Trinity, Arroyo Seco
Kneafsey, John, Holy Ghost, Albuquerque
Langner, Gerald, Immaculate Heart of Mary, Los Alamos
Leahigh, John, St. Charles, Albuquerque
Lewis, Bob, San Felipe de Neri, Albuquerque
Lopez, Benjamin, Sacred Heart, Espanola
Lopez, Demetrio, Queen of Heaven, Albuquerque
Lopez, Jose O., Holy Family, Chimayo
Lovato, Frank, San Felipe de Neri, Albuquerque
Lucero, Charles
Lucero, Donato, Immaculate Heart of Mary, Los Alamos
Lucero, Frank, St. Joseph on the Rio Grande, Albuquerque
Lucero, John S., St. Joseph-St. Patrick, Raton
Lucero, Jose E., San Felipe de Neri, Albuquerque
Lucero, Juan S., Estancial Valley Parish, Estancia
Luna, Desiderio, St. Edwin, Albuquerque
Maestas, Pablo, Our Lady of Sorrows, Bernalillo
Martinez, Donald J., Our Lady of Guadalupe, Taos
Martinez, Eloy, San Juan, San Juan Pueblo
Martinez, J. Robert, St. Bernadette, Albuquerque
Martinez, Jose Leroy, Our Lady of Sorrows, Las Vegas
Martinez, Lloyd, Sangre de Cristo, Albuquerque
McLane, Alfred, St. Bernadette, Albuquerque
Medina, Jesus, San Jose, Albuquerque
Meyrick, Earl, John XXIII, Albuquerque
Mishler, Richard, Holy Rosary, Albuquerque
Montoya, Alfonso, Sacred Heart, Albuquerque
Montoya, Macedon, Jr., Our Lady of Sorrows, Las Vegas
Montoya, Oswaldo, Our Lady of Guadalupe, Santa Fe
Montoya, P. Louis, St. Francis Xavier, Clayton
Montoya, Sotero, Santuario de San Martin, Albuquerque
Nguyen, Dung (Paul), San Jose, Albuquerque
Nunez, Salvador, Our Lady of the Assumption, Albuquerque
O'Hare, John J., Our Lady of Belen, Belen
Olona, Edward, St. Joseph, Springer
Pacheco, Carlos Felix, Our Lady of Guadalupe, Santa Fe
Pacheco, Charles, Immaculate Heart of Mary, Los Alamos
Padilla, Daniel F., St. John the Baptist, Santa Fe
Padilla, Julian, Queen of Heaven, Albuquerque
Paiz, Robert, Holy Family, Albuquerque
Perez, Frank, Holy Rosary, Albuquerque
Perez, Tomas, Immaculate Conception, Albuquerque
Prentiss, Richard, Kirtland AFB Chapel, Albuquerque
Rodriguez, Antonio, St. John the Baptist, Santa Fe
Rodriguez, Facundo, Santa Maria de la Paz, Santa Fe
Rodriguez, Juan
Rodriguez, Randall, Cristo Rey, Santa Fe
Russo, John L., John XXIII Catholic Community, Albuquerque
Sanchez, Norbert C., Our Lady of Belen, Belen
Sanchez, Robert, Our Lady of Belen, Belen
Sandoval, Alberto, San Antonio de Padua, Penasco
Sandoval, George, Immaculate Conception, Albuquerque
Santistevan, Patrick, San Martin de Porres, Albuquerque
Santistevan, Peter, Our Lady of Sorrows, Bernalillo
Schwenn, Charles E., St. Joseph, Cerrillos
See, Frank C., Our Lady of Fatima, Albuquerque
Stromberg, Robert, Holy Ghost, Albuquerque
Torres, H. Esequiel, St. Therese, Albuquerque
Toya, Patrick, San Diego Mission, Jemez Pueblo
Trujillo, Alex, John XXIII, Albuquerque
Trujillo, Anthony, Our Lady of Guadalupe, Santa Fe
Trujillo, Joseph, Our Lady of Guadalupe, Peralta
Tuma, Eugene, St. Jude Thaddeus, Albuquerque
Vallarreal, Robert, Immaculate Heart of Mary, Los Alamos
Valverde, George, Our Lady of Guadalupe, Albuquerque
Vigil, Ralph, Sacred Heart, Espanola
Villareal, Merce A., Admin., Sacred Heart, Espanola
Welch, Robert, St. Anne, Tucumcari
White, Rue, Our Lady of the Assumption, Albuquerque; Worship, Santa Fe
Zamora, Rudy R., Our Lady of Belen, Belen; Vocations Office, Santa Fe

PILGRIMAGE SHRINES

CHIMAYO. *Santuario de Chimayo*. Attended by Holy Family, Chimayo. 87522.

SAN JUAN. *Our Lady of Lourdes*. (San Juan Pueblo P.O.) P.O. Box 1075, 87566.

INSTITUTIONS LOCATED IN THE ARCHDIOCESE

[A] SEMINARIES, ARCHDIOCESAN

SANTA FE. *Immaculate Heart of Mary Seminary*, College Seminary, Mt. Carmel Rd., 87501. Tel: 505-988-1975. Rev. Arturo Meza (AMA), Rector. In res., Rev. Msgr. Peter J. Hill, (Retired).
Staff Members: Rev. Fernando Rubio-Boitel, Spiritual Dir.; Sr. Maria Armijo, S.F.C.C., Dean of Academics. Seminarians 34.

[B] SEMINARIES, RELIGIOUS OR SCHOLASTICATES

SANTA FE. *Sangre de Cristo Center*, Rte. 4, 87501. Tel: 505-983-7291; Fax: 505-983-7291. Bro. Bernard Lo-Coco, F.S.C., Dir. Associate Directors: Bro. Joseph Schmidt, F.S.C.; Sr. Patrice Kerin, O.S.F.; Bro. John Kidd, F.S.C.; Sr. Julie McCole, O.S.F. Program of refoundation for religious and priests, under the administration of the Christian Brothers. Participants 66 annually. Total Staff 7.

[C] COLLEGES AND UNIVERSITIES

SANTA FE. *College of Santa Fe*, (1947), 87501. Tel: 505-473-6011.
For a complete listing, refer to the Colleges and Universities section.

[D] HIGH SCHOOLS, ARCHDIOCESAN AND PAROCHIAL

ALBUQUERQUE. *St. Pius X High School*, 5301 St. Joseph Dr., N.W., 87120. Tel: 505-831-8400. Revs. Ronald G. Schwenzer, C.S.B., Prin.; Donald F. Hyatt, C.S.B.; Samuel J. Falbo. Priests 3; Religious 1; Lay Teachers 64; Students 1,013.

[E] HIGH SCHOOLS, PRIVATE

SANTA FE. *St. Catherine Indian Boarding School, Inc., Junior-Senior High Boarding School*. (Coed), 801-A Griffin St., 87501. Tel: 505-982-1889. Sr. Patrick Marie Dempsey, Prin. Lay Teachers 15; Sisters 5; Students 195.
St. Michael's High School. (Grades 7-12). (Coed Day School), 100 Siringo Rd., 87505. Tel: 505-983-7353; Fax: 505-982-8722. Bro. Paul Walsh, F.S.C., Prin. Brothers of the Christian Schools 6; Sisters 1; Lay Teachers 36; Students 688.

[F] GENERAL HOSPITALS

ALBUQUERQUE. *St. Joseph Healthcare System*, 7850 Jefferson, N.E., Ste. 100, 87109. Tel: 505-727-2804; Fax: 505-727-2814.
For a complete listing, refer to the Hospitals section.
St. Joseph Medical Center, 601 Dr. Martin Luther King, Jr. Ave., N.E., 87102. Tel: 505-727-2804; Fax: 505-727-2814.
For a complete listing, refer to the Hospitals section.
St. Joseph Northeast Heights Hospital, 4701 Montgomery, N.E., 87109. Tel: 505-727-2804; Fax: 505-727-2814.
For a complete listing, refer to the Hospitals section.
St. Joseph Rehabilitation Hospital, 505 Elm St., N.E., 87102. Tel: 505-727-2804; Fax: 505-727-2814.
For a complete listing, refer to the Hospitals section.
St. Joseph West Mesa Hospital, 10501 Golf Course Rd., N.W., 87114. Tel: 505-727-2804; Fax: 505-727-2814.
For a complete listing, refer to the Hospitals section.

[G] SPECIAL HOSPITALS AND SANATORIA FOR INVALIDS

SANTA FE. *Villa Therese Catholic Clinic*, 219 Cathedral Pl., 87501. Tel: 505-983-8561.
For a complete listing, refer to the Special Care Facilities section.

[H] SHELTER CARE HOMES

ALBUQUERQUE. *Good Shepherd Center, Inc.*, 218 Iron St., S.W., P.O. Box 749, 87103 Tel: 505-243-2527.
For a complete listing, refer to the Special Care Facilities section.
Good Shepherd Manor, 10127 Guadalupe Tr., N.W., P.O. Box 10248, 87184. Tel: 505-898-0177.
For a complete listing, refer to the Special Care Facilities section.
Marie Amadea Shelter for Unwed Mothers, P.O. Box 708, 87103. Tel: 505-242-1516.
For a complete listing, refer to the Special Care Facilities section.

[I] CARE HOMES FOR PHYSICALLY AND MENTALLY HANDICAPPED

ALBUQUERQUE. *Casa Angelica*, 5629 Isleta Blvd., S.W., 87105. Tel: 505-877-5763.
For a complete listing, refer to the Special Care Facilities section.

[J] MONASTERIES AND RESIDENCES OF PRIESTS AND BROTHERS

ABIQUIU. *Monastery of Christ in the Desert*, 87510. Tel: 505-470-4515. Subiaco Congregation. Rt. Rev. Philip Lawrence, O.S.B., Abbot; Revs. Christian Leisy, O.S.B., Sub Prior; Bernard Cranor, O.S.B.; Ezequiel Bas Luna, O.S.B.; Luis Regalado, O.S.B. Monks 35.

ALBUQUERQUE. *Bethany on the Rio Grande*, 2508 Pajarito Rd., S.W., 87105. Tel: 505-873-1487. House of Rest and Recreation for Priests. Mr. Tom Schellenbach, Dir.
Little Brothers of the Good Shepherd, Villa Mathias-Foundation House, 901 Bro. Mathias Pl., N.W., P.O. Box 389, 87103. Tel: 505-243-4238; Fax: 505-764-9721. Brothers 10; Total Staff 3.
San Antonio Provincial Friary Franciscan Friars, 1350 Lakeview Rd., S.W., Box 12315, 87105. Tel: 505-877-5425; Fax: 505-877-2591. Very Rev. Gilbert Schneider, O.F.M., Prov.; Revs. Martin Rademaker, O.F.M., Vicar Prov.; Donald Billiard, O.F.M., Treas. of Prov.; Bro. Gerald Grantner, Archivist; Rev. Crispin Butz, O.F.M., Sec. of Prov. Priests 70; Brothers 18; Temporary Professed 1; Postulants 2; Novices 1. Legal Titles: *San Antonio Provincial Friary Franciscan Friars - Province of Our Lady of Guadalupe; The Province of Our Lady of Guadalupe of Friars Minor, Inc.; Southwest Franciscan Services, Inc.; Southwest Franciscan Missions, Inc.*
Santa Maria de la Vid Priory, 5825 Coors Rd., S.W.,

87121-6700. Tel: 505-873-4399. Canons Regular of Premontre (Norbertine Community). Very Rev. Joel P. Garner, O.Praem., Prior & Vocation Dir.; Revs. Vincent J. DeLeers, O.Praem.; James Huth, O.Praem.; Stan N. Joppe, O.Praem.; Nicholas E. Nirschl; Norbert R. Manders, O.Praem.; Domenic Rossi, O.Praem.; Francis Dorff, O.Praem; Joseph Serano; Christian T. O'Brien, O.Praem. Priests 10. Sponsor of "Center for Spiritual Life".

BERNALILLO. *Southwest Marian Divine Mercy Center*, 161 Sheriffs Posse Rd., P.O. Box 1840, 87004-1840. Rev. Richard J. Drabik, M.I.C., Spiritual Dir. Total in Residence 2; Total Staff 2.

JEMEZ SPRINGS. *The Jemez Program, Our Lady of Lourdes Novitiate*, 87025-0010. Tel: 505-829-3586. Motherhouse for Servants of the Paraclete and Renewal Houses and Treatment Centers for Priests and Brothers. Very Rev. Liam Hoare, s.P., Servant General; Revs. James Sampson, s.P., Supr. Tel: 505-829-3004; Ray Gunzel, s.P.; Paul Valley, s.P.; Fernand Couture; Bros. J. Paul Pelletier, s.P.; Conrad Rydelek, Formation House. Rev. Benedict Livingston, s.P., Dir. of Formation. Novices: Mr. Douglas MacLean; Mr. Toni O'Kane. Priests 6; Brothers 2.

[K] CONVENTS AND RESIDENCES FOR SISTERS

SANTA FE. *Discalced Carmelite Monastery*, Mount Carmel Rd., 87501. Tel: 505-983-7232. Mother Rose Teresa, O.C.D., Prioress; Rev. Anderson E. Bakewell, S.J., Chap.; Solemn Professed Nuns 7; Postulants 2; Extern Sisters 3.

ALBUQUERQUE. *Cristo Rey Provincial House*, 5625 Isleta Blvd., S.W., 87105. Tel: 505-873-2854; Fax: 505-873-0678. Canossian Daughters of Charity. Sr. Paola Canziani, Prov. Supr. Sisters 15.

JEMEZ SPRINGS. *Cor Jesu Monastery*, 87025. Tel: 505-829-3906; Fax: 505-829-3906. Motherhouse and Novitiate of the Handmaids of the Precious Blood. Rev. Mother John Paul, H.P.B., Mother Prioress. Perpetually Professed Sisters 34; First Professed Sisters 1; Novices 1.

RIO RANCHO. *Felician Sisters*, Provincial House & Novitiate, 4210 Meadowlark Ln., S.E., P.O. Box 15096, 87124-1021. Tel: 505-892-8862. Assumption of the Blessed Virgin Mary. Sr. Rosemarie Goins, C.S.S.F., Prov. Min. In res., Revs. Paul Schneider, O.F.M., Chap.; Forest McAllister, O.F.M. Residents 40; Professed Sisters of Province 77; Total Assisted per Month 4,000; Total Staff 65; Postulants 1.

SANTA CRUZ. *Monastery of Our Lady of the Desert*, P.O. Box 690, 87567.

[L] RETREAT HOUSES

ALBUQUERQUE. *Dominican Retreat House*, 2348 Pajarito Rd., S.W., 87105. Tel: 505-877-4211. Center for Retreats. Dominican Sisters (Elkins Park, PA). Sisters 3; Total Staff 3.

Madonna Retreat and Conference Center, 4040 St. Joseph Pl., N.W., 87120. Tel: 505-831-8196. Sr. M. Virginia Louato, S.C., Dir. Total in Residence 2; Total Staff 3.

PECOS. *Our Lady of Guadalupe Benedictine Abbey*, 87552. Tel: 505-757-6415; Fax: 505-757-2285. Retreat House. Rt. Rev. Andrew Miles, O.S.B.; Revs. Paul Meaden, O.S.B.; Samuel Dennis, O.S.B.; Robert Lussier, O.S.B.; Bernard Lebiedz, O.S.B.; Colman Heffern, O.S.B.; Michael Leek, O.S.B.; Wilfrid Tunink, O.S.B.; Very Rev. Mark Norris, O.S.B., Prior. Priests 9; Brothers 9; Sisters 9; Total in Residence 27; Total Staff 16.

[M] NEWMAN CENTERS

ALBUQUERQUE. *St. Thomas Aquinas*, 1815 Las Lomas Rd., N.E., 87106. Tel: 505-247-1094. Revs. Robert Keller, O.P.; Paul Wierenga, O.P. Total in Residence 5; Total Staff 10.

LAS VEGAS. *St. Paul, Highlands University Newman Center*, 909 Eighth St., 87701. Tel: 505-425-7791. Attended by Immaculate Conception Parish, Las Vegas. Rev. George Salazar, Chap.

PORTALES. *University Catholic Center - St. Thomas More Chapel*, P.O. Box 2253, E.N.M.U., 88130. Tel: 505-356-5615. Rev. Anthony L. Martinez, Chap. Total Staff 2.

[N] MISCELLANEOUS LISTINGS

SANTA FE. *St. Michael's High School Foundation*, 2209 Brothers Rd., Ste. 220, 87505. Tel: 505-988-2264. Mr. Arthur Jaramillo, Pres.

ALBUQUERQUE. *Annual Catholic Appeal Foundation of the Archdiocese of Santa Fe*, 4000 St. Joseph Pl., N.W., 87120. Tel: 505-831-8100. Tony Salgado, Contact Person.

Archbishop's School Fund, 4000 St. Joseph Pl., N.W., 87120. Tel: 505-831-8173. Carol Lonski, Pres.

Archdiocese of Santa Fe Catholic Foundation, 4000 St. Joseph Pl., N.W., 87120. Tel: 505-831-8246. Mary P. Dunn, Contact Person.

Brother Mathias Barrett, Inc., P.O. Box 10248, 87184. Total Assisted 40; Total Staff 21.

Brothers of the Good Shepherd Inc. of New Mexico, 901 Brother Mathias Pl., N.W., P.O. Box 389, 87102-7103. Tel: 505-243-4238; Fax: 505-764-9721. Total in Residence 10; Total Staff 3.

Caritas Deus Inc., P.O. Box 389, 87102. Tel: 505-243-2527; Fax: 505-247-2207. Property management nonprofit corporation.

Catholic Charismatic Center, 1412 Fifth St., N.W., 87102. Tel: 505-247-0398. Sr. Martha Jean McGarry, I.H.M., Dir.

Center for Action and Contemplation, P.O. Box 12464, 87195. Tel: 505-242-9588. Rev. Richard Rohr, O.F.M., Founder & Animator. Co-Directors: Wendy Corry; Shari Wightman. Total in Residence 3; Total Staff 7.

Charity Unlimited, Inc., P.O. Box 389, 87102. Tel: 505-243-4238; Fax: 505-764-9721. Property management nonprofit corporation.

Dominican Ecclesial Institute, 1815 Las Lomas, N.E., 87106. Tel: 505-243-0525. Rev. Michael Demkovich, O.P.

Fraternidad de Nuestro Padre Jesus Nazareno, 4000 St. Joseph Pl., N.W., 87120. Rev. Jerome J. Martinez y Alire, Chap.

Good Shepherd Center, Inc. of New Mexico, 218 Iron St., N.W., P.O. Box 749, 87102. Tel: 505-243-2527; Fax: 505-247-2207. Total Staff 12.

Norbertine Community of New Mexico, Inc., 5825 Coors Rd., N.W., 87121-6700. Tel: 505-873-4399. Rev. Joel Garner, O.Praem.

St. Francis Gardens Nursing Home, 904 Las Lomas Rd., N.E , 87102. Tel: 505-727-2804; Fax: 505-727-2814. Owned by Sisters of Charity Healthcare System, Cincinnati, OH. Integrated with St. Joseph Health Care System. Marcia Wegmann, Admin. Beds 135; Priests 2; Total Staff 113.

St. Pius X High School Foundation, Inc., 5301 St. Joseph Dr., N.W., 87120. Tel: 505-831-8406. Nonprofit corporation for the financial support of St. Pius X High School. Rev. Ronald G. Schwenzer, C.S.B.

**St. Bernadette Institute of Sacred Art*, P.O. Box 8249, 87198. Tel: 505-265-9126; Fax: 505-266-4678. Dan Paulos, Contact Person.

Villa Mathias Inc., P.O. Box 389, 87103. Tel: 505-243-4238; Fax: 505-764-9721.

JEMEZ SPRINGS. *Fitzgerald Charitable Trust*, P.O. Box 10, 87025. Tel: 505-829-3586. Rev. Benedict Liningstone, s.P.

RIO RANCHO. *St. Felix Pantry, Inc.*, 4020 Barbara Loop, 87124-1021. Tel: 505-891-8075. Sr. Seraphine Moynier, Contact Person. Total Assisted per Month 3,500; Total Staff 60.

RELIGIOUS INSTITUTES OF MEN REPRESENTED IN THE ARCHDIOCESE

For further details refer to the corresponding bracketed number in the Religious Institutes of Men or Women section.

[0170]—*Basilian Fathers*.—C.S.B.

[0200]—*Benedictine Monks*. (Our Lady of Guadalupe Abbey, Pecos; Abbey of Christ in the Desert, Abiquiu).—O.S.B.

[1350]—*Brothers of St. Francis Xavier*.—C.F.X.

[0330]—*Brothers of the Christian Schools*. (Baltimore, Midwest & De La Salle Provinces).—F.S.C.

[0580]—*Brothers of the Good Shepherd*.—B.G.S.

[0900]—*Canons Regular of Premontre*. (Norbertine Fathers of Pennsylvania & De Pere, Wisconsin).—O.Praem.

[0350]—*Cistercian Order of the Strict Observance*. (GA).—O C.S.O.

[0740]—*Congregation of Marians of the Immaculate Conception*. (St. Stanislaus Kostka Prov.).—M.I.C.

[0220]—*Congregation of the Blessed Sacrament*.—S.S.S.

[0520]—*Franciscan Friars*. (Our Lady of Guadalupe, St. John the Baptist & St. Barbara Provinces).—O.F.M.

[0430]—*Order of Preachers-Dominicans*. (St. Albert the Great Prov.).—O.P.

[1190]—*Salesians of Don Bosco*. (San Francisco Province).—S.D.B.

[1230]—*Servants of the Paraclete*.—s.P.

[1240]—*Servites*. (Eastern Prov.).—O.S.M.

[0690]—*Society of Jesus*. (New Orleans Prov., Oregon Prov., Missouri Prov.).—S.J.

[]—*Society of Our Lady of the Most Holy Trinity*.—S.O.L.T.

[0640]—*Sons of the Holy Family*. (Silver Spring, MD).—S.F.

RELIGIOUS INSTITUTES OF WOMEN REPRESENTED IN THE ARCHDIOCESE

[0200]—*Benedictine Sisters*. (Pecos and Abiquiu, NM).—O.S.B.

[0730]—*Canossian Daughters of Charity*. (Albuquerque, NM).—Fd.C.C.

[1010]—*Congregation of Divine Providence, Allison Park, Texas*.—C.D.P.

[1780]—*Congregation of the Sisters of the Third Order of St. Francis of Perpetual Adoration*. (La Crosse, WI).—F.S.P.A.

[0420]—*Discalced Carmelite Nuns*. (Santa Fe, NM).—O.C.D.

[1070-02]—*Dominican Sisters*. (Columbus, OH).—O.P.

[1070-03]—*Dominican Sisters*. (Sinsinawa, WI).—O.P.

[1070-09]—*Dominican Sisters*. (Racine, WI).—O.P.

[1070-13]—*Dominican Sisters*. (Adrian, MI).—O.P.

[1070-14]—*Dominican Sisters*. (Grand Rapids, MI).—O.P.

[1070-17]—*Dominican Sisters*. (Elkins Park, PA).—O.P.

[1070-21]—*Dominican Sisters*. (Edmonds, PA).—O.P.

[1170]—*Felician Sisters*. (Congregation of Sisters of St. Felix of Cantalice).—C.S.S.F.

[1500]—*Franciscan Sisters of Mary Immaculate of the Third Order of St. Francis of Assisi*. (Amarillo, TX).—F.M.I.

[1430]—*Franciscan Sisters of Our Lady of Perpetual Help*. (St. Louis, MO).—O.S.F.

[1440]—*Franciscan Sisters of the Poor*. (Brooklyn, NY).—S.F.P.

[1860]—*Handmaids of the Precious Blood*. (Jemez Springs, NM).—H.P.B.

[1820]—*Hospital Sisters of the Third Order of St. Francis*. (Springfield, IL).

[3130]—*Our Lady of Victory Missionary Sisters*. (Huntington, IN).—O.L.V.M.

[2519]—*Religious Sisters of Mercy of Alma, Michigan.*.—R.S.M.

[1680]—*School Sisters of St. Francis*. (Milwaukee, WI).—O.S.F.

[]—*Sisters for Christian Community*. (Cincinnati).—S.F.C.C.

[0440]—*Sisters of Charity of Cincinnati, Ohio*. (Mt. St. Joseph, OH).—S.C.

[0480]—*Sisters of Charity of Leavenworth, Kansas*.—S.C.L.

[0590]—*Sisters of Charity of St. Elizabeth of New Jersey*.—S.C.

[0430]—*Sisters of Charity of the Blessed Virgin Mary*. (Dubuque, IA).—B.V.M.

[0660]—*Sisters of Christian Charity*. (Wilmette, IL).—S.C.C.

[2360]—*Sisters of Loretto at the Foot of the Cross*. (Denver, CO).—S.L.

[0230]—*Sisters of Pontifical Jurisdiction*. (Colorado Springs, CO).—O.S.B.

[1705]—*The Sisters of St. Francis of Assisi*. (Milwaukee, WI).—O.S.F.

[1630]—*Sisters of St. Francis of Penance and Christian Charity*. (Sacred Heart Prov.); Holy Name Province).—O.S.F.

[1640]—*Sisters of St. Francis of Perpetual Adoration*. (St. Joseph Province, Colorado Springs, CO).—O.S.F.

[1650]—*Sisters of St. Francis of Philadelphia*. (Aston, PA).—O.S.F.

[1530]—*Sisters of St. Francis of the Congregation of Our Lady of Lourdes, Sylvania, Ohio*.—O.S.F.

[1570]—*Sisters of St. Francis of the Holy Family*. (Dubuque, IA).—O.S.F.

[3830-01]—*Sisters of St. Joseph*. (Boston, MA).—C.S.J.

[3830-11]—*Sisters of St. Joseph*. (Kalamazoo, MI).—S.S.J.

[0260]—*Sisters of the Blessed Sacrament for Indians and Colored People*. (Bensalem, PA).—S.B.S.

[3320]—*Sisters of the Presentation of B.V.M.* (Aberdeen, SD).—P.B.V.M.

[3670]—*Sisters of the Sacred Heart of Jesus*. (San Antonio, TX).—S.S.C.J.

[4100]—*Sisters of the Sorrowful Mothers (Third Order of St. Francis)*. (Broken Arrow, OK).—S.S.M.

[1760]—*Sisters of the Third Order of St. Francis of Penance and Charity*. (Tiffin, OH).—O.S.F.

[1780]—*Sisters of the Third Order of St. Francis of Perpetual Adoration*. (LaCross, WI).

[1720]—*Sisters of the Third Order Regular of St. Francis of the Congregation of Our Lady of Lourdes*. (Rochester, MN).—O.S.F.

[2150-60]—*Sisters, Servants of the Immaculate Heart of Mary*. (Monroe, MI; Scranton, PA).—I.H.M.

[]—*Society of Our Lady of the Most Holy Trinity.* (Robstown, TX).—S.O.L.T.

[4120]—*Ursuline Nuns, of the Congregation of Paris.* (Maple Mount, KY).—O.S.U.

ARCHDIOCESAN CEMETERIES

ALBUQUERQUE. *Archdiocesan Cemetery Association,* 4000 St. Joseph Pl., N.W., 87120. Tel: 505-831-8100. Operates Rosario Cemetery, Santa Fe; Mount Calvary & Gate of Heaven, Albuquerque.

Catholic Cemetery Association, 4000 St. Joseph Pl., N.W., 87120. Tel: 505-831-8100.

NECROLOGY

† Burke, James T., Socorro, NM, San Miguel. —Died Feb. 11, 1996.

† Hesnan, Thomas F., Albuquerque, NM, Annunciation. —Died Dec. 4, 1996.

† Rodriguez, Jose, Santa Fe, NM, St. Anne. —Died Feb. 22, 1996.

† Schneider, Albert A., Espanola, NM, Sacred Heart. —Died June 1, 1996.

Diocese of Santa Rosa in California

(Diœcesis Sanctae Rosae in California)

Most Reverend

G. PATRICK ZIEMANN, D.D.

Bishop of Santa Rosa; ordained April 29, 1967; appointed Titular Bishop of Obba and Auxiliary of Los Angeles on December 29, 1986; ordained Bishop on February 23, 1987; appointed Bishop of Santa Rosa July 14, 1992.

ESTABLISHED FEBRUARY 21, 1962.

Square Miles 11,711.

Comprises six Counties in the State of California-viz., Del Norte, Humboldt, Lake, Mendocino, Napa and Sonoma.

Legal Titles: "The Roman Catholic Bishop of Santa Rosa, a Corporation Sole" and "The Roman Catholic Welfare Corporation of Santa Rosa."

For legal titles of parishes and diocesan institutions, consult the Chancery Office.

Chancery Office: 547 "B" St., P.O. Box 1297, Santa Rosa, CA, 95402. Tel.: 707-545-7610; Fax: 707-542-9702.

STATISTICAL OVERVIEW

Personnel	
Bishop	1
Retired Bishops	1
Priests: Diocesan Active in Diocese	56
Priests: Active Outside Diocese	7
Priests: Retired, Sick or Absent	19
Number of Diocesan Priests	82
Religious Priests in Diocese	19
Extern Priests in Diocese	24
Ordinations:	
Diocesan Priests	3
Transitional Deacons	3
Permanent Deacons in Diocese	21
Total Brothers	42
Total Sisters	101
Parishes	
Parishes	43
With Resident Pastor:	
Resident Diocesan Priests	39
Resident Religious Priests	4
Without Resident Pastor:	
Missions	20
Pastoral Centers	13
Professional Ministry Personnel:	
Sisters	7
Lay Ministers	24
Welfare	
Catholic Hospitals	4
Total Assisted	265,535
Homes for the Aged	2
Total Assisted	60
Residential Care of Children	1
Total Assisted	107
Specialized Homes	1
Total Assisted	19
Special Centers for Social Services	23
Total Assisted	255,000
Residential Care of Disabled	2
Total Assisted	12
Educational	
Diocesan Students in Other Seminaries	11
Total Seminarians	11
High Schools, Diocesan and Parish	3
Total Students	1,034
High Schools, Private	4
Total Students	1,041
Elementary Schools, Diocesan and Parish	13
Total Students	2,991
Elementary Schools, Private	2
Total Students	102
Catechesis/Religious Education:	
High School Students	1,655
Elementary Students	5,744
Total Students Under Catholic Instruction	12,578
Teachers in the Diocese:	
Priests	4
Sisters	14
Lay Teachers	308
Vital Statistics	
Receptions into the Church:	
Infant Baptism Totals	3,097
Adult Baptism Totals	205
Received into Full Communion	118
First Communions	2,431
Confirmations	686
Marriages:	
Catholic	505
Interfaith	287
Total Marriages	792
Deaths	1,052
Total Catholic Population	137,391
Total Population	772,859

Former Bishops—Most Rev. LEO T. MAHER, D.D., ord. Dec. 18, 1943; appt. First Bishop of Santa Rosa, Feb. 21, 1962; cons. April 5, 1962; translated San Diego, Aug. 27, 1969; died Feb. 23, 1991.—Most Rev. MARK J. HURLEY, D.D., Ph.D., J.C.B., L.L.D., ord. Sept. 23, 1944; appt. Titular Bishop of Thunusuda & Auxiliary of San Francisco, Oct. 12, 1967; cons. Jan. 4, 1968; translated Santa Rosa, Nov. 9, 1969; appt. member of the Vatican Secretariat for Non-Believers, consultor to the Congregation for Catholic Education; resigned as Bishop of Santa Rosa, April 15, 1986.—Most Rev. JOHN T. STEINBOCK, D.D., ord. May 1, 1963; Titular Bishop of Midila and Auxiliary Bishop of Orange; appt. May 29, 1984; translated Santa Rosa, March 31, 1987; translated Fresno, Nov. 25, 1991.

Vicar General—Rev. Msgr. THOMAS J. KEYS, *547 "B" St., P.O. Box 1297, Santa Rosa, 95402.* Tel: 707-545-7610.

Deans—Sonoma-North: Rev. DAVID SHAW, Napa: Rev. Msgr. JOHN J. BRENKLE, Sonoma-South: Rev. STEPHEN J. CANNY, Mendocino-Lake: Rev. GEORGE RISDEN, Humboldt-Del Norte: Rev. MICHAEL M. KELLY.

Chancery Office—547 "B" St., P.O. Box 1297, Santa Rosa, 95402. Tel: 707-545-7610; Fax: 707-542-9702. Office Hours: Mon.-Fri. 9-5 All applications for dispensations, faculties, etc., and all correspondence should be addressed to the Chancery Office.

Moderator of Curia—Rev. Msgr. THOMAS J. KEYS, V.G.

Members of the Curia—Rev. Msgr. THOMAS J. KEYS, V.G.; Rev. Msgr. JAMES E. PULSKAMP; Rev. Msgr. JOHN J. BRENKLE; Revs. DAVID SHAW; STEPHEN J. CANNY; GEORGE RISDEN; MICHAEL M. KELLY; DANIEL P. WHELTON.

Chancellor—Rev. Msgr. JAMES E. PULSKAMP.

Vice-Chancellor—Sr. PATRICIA BRANDMEIR, S.N.J.M.

Vicar of Finance—Rev. Msgr. THOMAS J. KEYS, V.G.

Secretary to the Bishop—GUADALUPE GUERRERO, . Fax: 707-545-3810.

Diocesan Tribunal—P.O. Box 1297, Santa Rosa, 95402. Tel: 707-542-9014.

Judicial Vicar—Rev. DANIEL P. WHELTON, J.C.L.

Adjutant Judicial Vicar—Rev. Msgr. JOHN J. BRENKLE, J.C.D.

Promoter of Justice—Rev. STEPHEN J. CANNY.

Defender of the Bond—Rev. DAVID SHAW.

Diocesan Judges—Rev. Msgr. JOHN J. BRENKLE, J.C.D.; Rev. Msgr. JAMES P. GAFFEY; Revs. JOHN CREWS; DANIEL WHELTON, J.C.L.; Sr. MARGUERITE B. STEIN, J.C.L., M.C.L., J.D.

Advocates—Revs. MICHAEL M. KELLY; FERGAL MCGUINNESS; WALTER ROGINA; Sr. MAURA MURPHY, O.S.U.; Deacon RODRIGO AGUDELO; STELLA AGUDELO.

Advocate-Auditor—Sr. ROSE MARY KUKLOK, O.S.B.

Notary—Rev. Msgr. JAMES E. PULSKAMP.

Board of Consultors—Rev. Msgr. THOMAS J. KEYS, V.G.; Rev. Msgr. JAMES E. PULSKAMP; Rev. Msgr. JOHN J. BRENKLE; Revs. DAVID SHAW; STEPHEN J. CANNY; GEORGE RISDEN; MICHAEL M. KELLY.

Ministries Board—Rev. Msgr. THOMAS J. KEYS, V.G.; Rev. Msgr. JAMES E. PULSKAMP; Revs. SEAN MURRAY, C.SS.R.; XAVIER OCHOA; ANGELITO PERIES, C.SS.R.; ALVIN VILLARUEL; Deacons ALLAN BOHNER; JOSEPH REMLEY; Sr. OLIVE MURPHY, S.M.; Sr. ANN PATRICIA O'CONNOR, C.S.J.; GUADALUPE GUERRERO, Sec. MICHELLE HEALY; NANCY MARSDEN; LINDA REMLEY; MAUREEN SHAW; ED BYROM; STANLEY CORDERO; MICHAEL KAMPLAIN.

Diocesan Priests' Council—Rev. Msgr. THOMAS J. KEYS, V.G.; Rev. Msgr. JAMES E. PULSKAMP; Rev. Msgr. JOHN J. BRENKLE; Revs. MICHAEL CLONEY; STEPHEN J. CANNY; ANDREW METCALF; RALPH J. MONTEIRO, O.S.A.; XAVIER OCHOA; TED OSWALD; MICHAEL M. KELLY; HANS RUYGT; DAVID G. SHAW; GEORGE RISDEN; PATRICK STEPHENSON; DANIEL P. WHELTON.

Finance Committee—Rev. Msgr. THOMAS J. KEYS, V.G.; Mr. CONO DI PIETRO; Mr. JOHN KLEIN.

Diocesan Offices and Directors

AIDS Ministry Outreach—NANCY MARSDEN, *P.O. Box 11574, Santa Rosa, 95406.* Tel: 707-528-3887.

Archivist—Rev. Msgr. JAMES E. PULSKAMP, *547 B St., P.O. Box 1297, Santa Rosa, 95402.* Tel: 707-545-7610.

Attorney for the Diocese—Mr. JOHN KLEIN, *P.O. Box 1845, Santa Rosa, 95402.* Tel: 707-546-6767.

Boy Scouts—STANLEY CORDERO, *P.O. Box 11574, Santa Rosa, 95406.* Tel: 707-571-8647.

Building Committee—Rev. Msgr. THOMAS J. KEYS, V.G., Chm.; Rev. MICHAEL J. CLEARY; LEWAIN BEARD; DON LINDSAY; JOHN RYAN; THOMAS FELLENZ; JOHN KLEIN; JOHN MILES; CLYDE SMITH.

Catholic Charities, Central Admin. Office—MAUREEN E. SHAW, A.C.S.W., Diocesan Dir., *2325 Montgomery Dr., P.O. Box 4900, Santa Rosa, 95402.* Tel: 707-528-8712.

Catholic Youth Organization—Rev. Msgr. THOMAS J. KEYS, V.G., Dir., Office: *547 B St., P.O. Box 3268, Santa Rosa, 95402.* Tel: 707-545-7610.

Cemeteries—Rev. Msgr. GERARD FAHEY, Dir., Office: *P.O. Box 2098, 2930 Bennett Valley Rd., Santa Rosa, 95404.* Tel: 707-546-6290.

Clergy Formation—Rev. GARY LOMBARDI, Dir., *35 Liberty St., Petaluma, 94952.* Tel: 707-762-4278.

Detention Ministry, Adult—24A Ursuline Rd., Santa Rosa, 95403. Tel: 707-544-9080.

Detention Ministry, Juvenile—ED BYROM, Dir., *155 N. Pythian Rd., Santa Rosa, 95409.* Tel: 707-537-6300, Ext. 6248.

Development—Rev. Msgr. THOMAS J. KEYS, V.G., Dir., *547 B St., P.O. Box 1297, Santa Rosa, 95402.* Tel: 707-545-7610.

Disabled—Chancery Office, 547 B St., P.O. Box 1297, Santa Rosa, 95402. Tel: 707-545-7610.

Ecumenical and Interreligious Affairs—Rev. THOMAS W. DEVEREAUX, Dir., *208 Matheson St., Healdsburg, 95448.* Tel: 707-433-5536.

Health Affairs—Dr. MICHAEL GOSPE, M.D., Liaison, *170 Sotoyome, Santa Rosa, 95405.* Tel: 707-546-6948.

Hispanic Ministry—Revs. XAVIER OCHOA, Dir. RODOLFO GRAMAJO, Assoc. Dir., *Centro Pastoral Hispano, 81 W. Cotati Ave., Cotati, 94931.* Tel: 707-795-0578.

Cursillos De Cristiandad—Rev. MANUEL CHAVEZ, Spiritual Dir., *491 S. Franklin St., Cloverdale, 95425.* Tel: 707-894-2535.

Los Jovenes—Mr. OSVALDO RODRIGUEZ, *Centro Pastoral Hispano, 81 W. Cotati Ave., Cotati, 94931.* Tel: 707-795-0578.

Movimiento Familiar Cristiano—Deacon RODRIGO AGUDELO, Spiritual Dir., *3727 View Ct., Santa Rosa, 95403.* Tel: 707-526-4892.

Renovacion Carismatica Catolica—Rev. JOSE GONZALEZ, Dir., *408 Matheson St., Healdsburg, 95448.* Tel: 707-433-5536.

Leadership Development—MICHAEL KAMPLAIN, *151 Faught Ct., Santa Rosa, 95403.* Tel: 707-545-5236.

National Council of Catholic Women—Sr. ANTONIA KILLIAN, S.M., Spiritual Dir., *1100 High School Rd., Sebastopol, 95472.* Tel: 707-824-1851.

Native American Affairs—Rev. RALPH MONTEIRO, O.S.A., Liaison, *P.O. Box 429, Hoopa, 95546.* Tel: 916-625-4415.

Newspaper—"Redwood Crozier", Deacon ALLAN BOHNER, Editor, *547 B St., P.O. Box 1297, Santa Rosa, 95402.* Tel: 707-545-7610.

Parish Priest Consultors—Rev. Msgr. WILLIAM HYNES; Rev. Msgr. GERARD FAHEY; Revs. MICHAEL J. CLEARY; THOMAS W. DEVEREAUX.

Parish Social Ministry—NANCY MARSDEN, *P.O. Box 11574, Santa Rosa, 95406.* Tel: 707-528-3887.

Permanent Diaconate—Directors: Deacon JOSEPH REMLEY; LINDA REMLEY, *547 B St., P.O. Box 1297, Santa Rosa, 95402.* Tel: 707-545-7610.

Pontifical Association of Holy Childhood—Deacon RICHARD NAUMANN, *547 B St., P.O. Box 1297, Santa Rosa, 95402.* Tel: 707-545-7610.

Priests' Health and Retirement Board—Rev. Msgr. THOMAS J. KEYS, V.G.; JAMES P. GAFFEY; Revs. APOLINAR HERNANDEZ; GEORGE RISDEN.

Priests' Personnel Committee—Rev. Msgr. THOMAS J. KEYS, V.G.; Rev. Msgr. JAMES E. PULSKAMP; Rev. Msgr. JAMES P. GAFFEY; Revs. ROBERT BLAKE; DANIEL P. WHELTON.

Propagation of the Faith—Deacon RICHARD NAUMANN, *547 B St., P.O. Box 1297, Santa Rosa, 95402.* Tel: 707-545-7610.

Property Committee—Rev. Msgr. THOMAS J. KEYS, V.G., Chm.; Mr. LEWAIN BEARD; Mr. CONO DI PIETRO; Mr. LAWRENCE GIOVANNONI; Mr. HAROLD LOCKWOOD.

Council for Religious—Sr. PATRICIA CARSON, R.S.M.; Sr. MARY TIMOTHY GALLAGHER, O.S.M.; Sr. ANTONIA KILLIAN, S.M.; Sr. THERESE GRISEWOOD, S.M.; Bros. JONATHAN CORD, F.S.C.; RAFAEL WILLEKE, F.S.C.

Religious Education—Sr. OLIVE MURPHY, S.M., Dir. MARIA DE JESUS CERVANTES, Hispanic Catechetical Ministry, *P.O. Box 11574, Santa Rosa, 95406.* Tel: 707-525-8440. MICHELLE HEALY, Assoc. D.R.E. & Coord. of Ministries (North), *222 Dollison St., Eureka, 95501.* Tel: 707-444-3627.

Respect Life—JOSEPH OLSEN; NORA OLSEN, *4525 Heath Cir., Rohnert Park, 94928.* Tel: 707-586-3009.

Schools—Sr. ANN PATRICIA O'CONNOR, C.S.J., Supt. of Schools; Sr. MARION IRVINE, O.P., Asst. Supt. of Schools; Sr. FRANCIS MARIE HANSEN, C.S.J., Consultant, Office: *P.O. Box 6654, Santa Rosa, 95406.* Tel: 707-525-9525.

Serra Club—Rev. HANS RUYGT, Chap., *P.O. Box 786, Ukiah, 95482.* Tel: 707-642-1431.

Vocations—Rev. HANS RUYGT, Dir., *P.O. Box 786, Ukiah, 95482.* Tel: 707-642-1431. Rev. ALVIN VILLARUEL, Assoc. Dir. of Vocations & Seminarians.

Youth Ministry—STANLEY CORDERO, Dir., *P.O. Box 11574, Santa Rosa, 95406.* Tel: 707-571-8647. AGNES BAILEY, Dir., Humboldt & Del Norte Counties, *222 Dollison St., Rm. 212, Eureka, 95501.* Tel: 707-445-1006.

CLERGY, PARISHES, MISSIONS AND PAROCHIAL SCHOOLS

CITY OF SANTA ROSA
(Sonoma County)

1—CATHEDRAL OF ST. EUGENE (1950), Rev. Msgr. James P. Gaffey; Revs. Walter Rogina, Jr.; Bruce Lamb; Jerald F. Thomas; Deacons Richard Naumann; W. Everett Woodruff.
Res., 2323 Montgomery Dr., 95405. Tel: 707-542-6984; Fax: 707-542-1621. [CEM]
School—300 Farmers Ln., 95405. Tel: 707-545-7252; Fax: 707-545-2594. Mrs. Barbara Gasparini, Prin.
Lay Teachers 12; Students 357.
Catechesis/Religious Programs—Tel: 707-542-1525. Diane Drew, D.R.E.
Students 330.

2—HOLY SPIRIT (1964), Rev. Msgr. James E. Pulskamp; Rev. Roger Lamoureux. In res., Rev. Daniel P. McCarthy, Pastor Emeritus.
Res., 1244 St. Francis Rd., 95409. Tel: 707-539-4495.
Catechesis/Religious Programs—Tel: 707-539-3343. Bernard Ciernick, D.R.E.
Students 176.

3—ST. ROSE OF LIMA (1877), Revs. Denis A. O'Sullivan; Gerard Gormley; Perfecto Nacional (Philippines); Ray Rioux. In res., Rev. Msgr. Thomas J. Keys.
Res., 398 10th St., 95401. Tel: 707-542-6448; Fax: 707-542-3359.
School—4300 Old Redwood Hwy., 95403. Tel: 707-545-0379; Fax: 707-545-7150. Kathy Ryan, Prin.
Lay Teachers 14; Students 361.
Catechesis/Religious Programs—Tel: 707-542-3080. Sr. Shelia Coffey, S.M., D.R.E.
Students 367.

4—RESURRECTION (1967), Revs. David Shaw; William Donahue; Deacon Rodrigo Agudelo.
Res., 303 Stony Point Rd., 95401. Tel: 707-544-7272; Fax: 707-544-2901.
Catechesis/Religious Programs—Tel: 707-544-0708. Betty Kovanis, D.R.E.
Students 460.

5—STAR OF THE VALLEY (1981), Rev. Msgr. Gerard Fahey. In res., Rev. Patrick Leslie (SAC).
Res., 615 Wild Oak Dr., 95409. Tel: 707-538-2387; Fax: 707-539-6262.

OUTSIDE CITY OF SANTA ROSA

American Canyon, Holy Family, Rev. Patrick Stephenson; Deacon Michael Simmons.
Res., 402 Donaldson Way, 94589. Tel: 707-645-9331; Fax: 707-645-0424.
Catechesis/Religious Programs—Maria Salas, D.R.E.
Students 96.

Arcata, Humboldt Co., St. Mary's (1883), Rev. Michael M. Kelly; Deacon John Gai.
Res., 1690 Janes Rd., 95521. Tel: 707-822-7696; Fax: 707-822-6931. [CEM]
School—1730 Janes Rd., 95521. Tel: 707-822-3877. Sr. Gretchen Krueger, O.P., Prin.
Sisters 1; Lay Teachers 5; Students 70.
Catechesis/Religious Programs—Kathleen Gigannon, D.R.E.
Students 115.
Mission—Blue Lake, St. Joseph.

Boyes Hot Springs, Sonoma Co., St. Leo (1966), Rev. Msgr. John J. O'Hare; Rev. Aurelio Villa, O.F.M.
Res., 601 Agua Caliente Rd., Sonoma, 95476. Tel: 707-996-8422; Fax: 707-996-3984.
Church—P.O.Box 666, 95416.
Catechesis/Religious Programs—Tel: 707-996-7503. Cindy Vrooman, D.R.E.
Students 280.

Calistoga, Napa Co., Our Lady of Perpetual Help (1915), Rev. J. Lawrence Carolan.
Res., 901 Washington St., 94515. Tel: 707-942-6894.
Catechesis/Religious Programs—D.R.E.: Laverne Oyarzo; Teresa Olguin.
Students 39.

Clearlake, Lake Co., Our Lady, Queen of Peace (1967), Rev. George Risden; Deacon Ralph W. Glendinning.
Res., P.O. Box 460, 95422. Tel: 707-994-6618.
Catechesis/Religious Programs—Lela Davis-Cagnacci, D.R.E.
Students 110.

Cloverdale, Sonoma Co., St. Peter's (1917), Revs. Robert Blake; Manuel Chavez. In res., Rev. Henry Faucher, Pastor Emeritus.
Res., 491 S. Franklin St., 95425. Tel: 707-894-2535.
Catechesis/Religious Programs—Debbi Davis, D.R.E.
Students 102.
Mission—Asti, Our Lady of Mt. Carmel.

Cotati, Sonoma Co., St. Joseph (1913), Rev. Stephen J. Canny.
Res., 150 St. Joseph Way, 94931. Tel: 707-795-4807; Fax: 707-795-7851.
Catechesis/Religious Programs—Tel: 707-795-7678. Georgette Parry, D.R.E.
Students 466.

Crescent City, Del Norte Co., St Joseph (1869), Rev. Diogo C. Baptista.
Res., 319 E St., 95531. Tel: 707-465-1762; Fax: 707-465-1763. [CEM]
School—440 Third St., 95531. Tel: 707-464-3477. Mr. Larry L. Beam, Prin.
Sisters 3; Lay Teachers 4; Students 71.
Catechesis/Religious Programs—Sr. Catherine Niess, O.S.F., D.R.E.
Students 100.
Mission—Klamath, St. Robert and Ann.
Station—Smith River, Our Lady of Guadalupe.

Eureka, Humboldt Co., St. Bernard (1864), Revs. Michael Cloney; Loren Allen.
Res., P.O. Box 169, 95502. Tel: 707-442-6466. [CEM]
School—115 Henderson St., 95502. Tel: 707-443-2226. Mrs. Edith Young, Prin.
Lay Teachers 10; Students 220.
Catechesis/Religious Programs—Lila Bollmann, D.R.E.
Students 70.
Mission—Eureka, St. Joseph.

Sacred Heart (1963), Rev. Donald W. Eagleson; Ann Lynch, Pastoral Assoc.; Deacons James Hercher; Anthony Viegas.
Res., 2085 Myrtle Ave., 95501. Tel: 707-443-8429; Fax: 707-443-8420.
Catechesis/Religious Programs—Debbie Hubard, D.R.E.
Students 135.

Ferndale, Humboldt Co., Church of the Assumption (1878), Rev. Denis Doyle.
Res., P.O. Box 427, 95536. Tel: 707-786-9551. [CEM]
Catechesis/Religious Programs—Angela Jorgensen, D.R.E.
Students 71.
Mission—Petrolia, St. Patrick.

Fort Bragg, Mendocino Co., Our Lady of Good Counsel (1890), Revs. Thomas K. Diaz; David Villalobos.
Res., 255 S. Harold St., 95437. Tel: 707-964-0229.
Catechesis/Religious Programs—Tel: 707-964-5727. D.R.E.: Toni Clark; Caryn Brady.
Students 157.

Fortuna, Humboldt Co., St. Joseph (1909), Rev. Norman J. Simoneau (MAN) Admin.; Deacon Thomas Silva. In res., Rev. James Thottapally (India).
Res., P.O. Box 430, 95540. Tel: 707-725-1148. [CEM]
Catechesis/Religious Programs—2292 Newburg Rd., 95540. Tel: 707-725-1216.
Students 108.
Mission—Loleta, St. Patrick.

Garberville, Humboldt Co., Our Lady of the Redwoods (1950), Rev. Thomas Gowing, Admin.
Res., 515 Maple Ln., 95542. Tel: 707-923-7864.
Mission—Leggett, St. Cecilia, (1954).

Guerneville, Sonoma Co., St. Elizabeth (1916), Rev. Philip J. Ryan, Admin.
Res., 14095 Woodland Dr., 95446-9553. Tel: 707-869-2107.
Catechesis/Religious Programs—Tel: 707-923-7864.
Students 29.
Missions—Monte Rio, St. Catherine; Cazadero, St. Colman.

Healdsburg, Sonoma Co., St. John the Baptist (1884), Revs. Thomas W. Devereaux; Jose Gonzalez (Mexico); Rose Marie Woodruff, Pastoral Assoc. & D.R.E.
Res., 208 Matheson St., 95448. Tel: 707-433-5536; Fax: 707-433-1813.
School—217 Fitch St., 95448. Tel: 707-433-2758; Fax: 707-433-0353.
Lay Teachers 17; Students 309. Principals: Sandra Blasser; Robert Blasser.
Catechesis/Religious Programs—Tel: 707-433-5112.
Students 509.

Hoopa, Humboldt Co., Mission of Blessed Kateri Tekakwitha (1986), Rev. Ralph Monteiro, O.S.A., Admin.
Res., P.O. Box 429, 95546. Tel: 916-625-4415.
Tekakwitha Center—P.O. Box 845, 95546. Tel: 916-625-4464. Sr. Patricia Carson, R.S.M., Dir.

Lakeport, Lake Co., St. Mary (1871), Rev. Ted Oswald.
Res., 801 N. Main St., 95453. Tel: 707-263-4401. [CEM]
School—Holy Family School, 95453. Tel: 707-262-1954.

Sisters 1; Lay Teachers 1; Students 25.
Catechesis/Religious Programs—Tel: 707-263-0606. Hedy Griego, D.R.E.
Students 160.
Missions—Lucerne, Queen of the Rosary; Kelseyville, St. Peter. [CEM]

McKinleyville, Humboldt County, Christ the King (1967), Rev. Stephen MacPherson.
Res., P.O. Box 2367, 95521. Tel: 707-839-2911.
Catechesis/Religious Programs—D.R.E.: Carol Clymo; Alouez Linehan.
Students 112.
Missions—Trinidad, Holy Trinity; Orick, St. Thomas.

Mendocino, Mendocino Co., St. Anthony (1864), Rev. John J. Martin, M.M., Admin.
Res., P.O. Box 665, 95460. Tel: 707-937-5808. [CEM]

Middletown, Lake Co., St. Joseph (1894), Rev. Thomas Keffer, Admin.
Res., P.O. Box 1350, 95461. Tel: 707-987-3676.
Mission—Loch Lomond, Our Lady of the Lake.
Station—Forest Lake, Our Lady of the Pines.

Napa, Napa Co., St. Apollinaris (1957), Revs. Michael J. Cleary; Dermot Kavanagh, C.S.Sp. In res., Rev. Fergal McGuinness.
Res., 3700 Lassen St., 94558. Tel: 707-257-2555; Fax: 707-257-3552.
School—Tel: 707-224-6525. Patricia Granucci, Prin.
Sisters 1; Lay Teachers 16; Students 326.
Catechesis/Religious Programs—Tel: 707-255-7200. Sr. Peggy Cruise, S.M., D.R.E.
Students 421.

St. John the Baptist (1859), Revs. Timothy J. O'Sullivan; Luis Martinez; Robert Castro.
Res., Box 178, 94559. Tel: 707-226-9379; Fax: 707-254-9262.
School—983 Napa St., 94559. Tel: 707-224-8388; Fax: 707-224-0236.
Lay Teachers 10; Students 191. Principals: Charles Stanton; Judy Stanton.
Catechesis/Religious Programs—Tel: 707-255-3533.
Students 261.
Station—Imola, State Hospital, St. Luke's Chapel.

St. Thomas Aquinas (1964), Rev. Msgr. Gerard J. Brady. In res., Rev. Gary Sumpter.
Res., 2725 Elm St., 94558. Tel: 707-255-2949.
Catechesis/Religious Programs—Students 160.

Occidental, Sonoma Co., St. Philip (1964), Rev. Daniel P. Whelton.
Res., P.O. Box 339, 95465. Tel: 707-874-3812.
Catechesis/Religious Programs—Judy Van Gorder, D.R.E.
Students 56.
Mission—Bodega, St. Teresa. [CEM]

Petaluma, Sonoma Co., St. James (1964), Rev. Michael A. Culligan; Deacons Ray Noll; Ken Manz. In res., Rev. Msgr. Joseph Alzugaray.
Res., 125 Sonoma Mt. Pky., 94954. Tel: 707-762-4256.
Catechesis/Religious Programs—Tel: 707-762-9063.
Students 800.

St. Vincent de Paul (1857), Revs. Gary Lombardi; Apolinar Hernandez; Chinh Nguyen.
Res., 35 Liberty St., 94952. Tel: 707-762-4278; Fax: 707-763-8188.
School—Howard & Union Sts., 94952. Tel: 707-762-6426; Fax: 707-762-6791. Sue Kernan, Prin.
Lay Teachers 11; Students 312.
High School—849 Keokuk, P.O. Box 517, 94953. Tel: 707-763-1032; Fax: 707-763-9448. Mr. Edward Kavanaugh, Prin.
Lay Teachers 25; Students 357.
Catechesis/Religious Programs—Camilla Edwards, D.R.E.
Students 250.

Philo, Mendocino Co., St. Elizabeth Seton, Rev. Michaelraj Philominsamy, C.PP.S., Admin.
Res., P.O.Box 248, 95466. Tel: 707-895-2690.

Point Arena, Mendocino Co., St. Aloysius (1950), Rev. Thomas P. O'Sullivan (SAC) Admin.
Res., P.O. Box 66, 95468. Tel: 707-882-2277; Fax: 707-882-2277. [CEM]
Missions—Elk, Blessed Sacrament, (1880); Gualala, Mary, Star of the Sea.

Rohnert Park, Sonoma Co., St. Elizabeth Seton (1981), Rev. John Griffin; Deacons Joseph Remley; Paul Bromham.
Res., 4595 Snyder Ln., 94928. Tel: 707-585-3708.
Catechesis/Religious Programs—Tel: 707-585-8821. Moira Bromham, D.R.E.
Students 225.

Saint Helena, Napa Co., St. Helena (1887), Rev. Msgr. John J. Brenkle; Rev. Oscar Diaz.
Res., 1340 Tainter St., 94574. Tel: 707-963-1228; Fax: 707-963-2894. [CEM]
School—1255 Oak Ave., 94574. Tel: 707-963-4677; Fax: 707-963-4677. Sr. Mary Dorothea Quinn, C.S.J., Prin.
Sisters 2; Lay Teachers 7; Students 138.
Catechesis/Religious Programs—D.R.E.: Heidi Clothier; Sr. Kathleen O'Shea, C.S.J.
Students 178.

Scotia, Humboldt Co., St. Patrick (1930), Rev. Andre Bernard (WOR) Admin.
Res., P.O. Box 98, 95565. Tel: 707-764-5446.

Sebastopol, Sonoma Co., St. Sebastian (1898), Rev. Msgr. William Hynes; Rev. George Aziz, S.J.; Deacon Harry Martin.
Res., 7983 Covert Ln., 95472. Tel: 707-823-2208; Fax: 707-823-1098.
Catechesis/Religious Programs—Tel: 707-823-4966. Barbara Schliemann, D.R.E.
Students 200.

Sonoma, Sonoma Co., St. Francis Solano (1878), Revs. James McSweeney; Andrew Metcalf; Aurelio Villa, O.F.M.
Res., 469 Third St., W., 95476. Tel: 707-996-6759; Fax: 707-939-8128. [CEM]
School—342 W. Napa St., 95476. Tel: 707-996-4994. Francine Maffei, Prin.
Lay Teachers 25; Students 360.
Catechesis/Religious Programs—Tel: 707-996-1578. Will Roll, D.R.E.
Students 409.

Ukiah, Mendocino Co., St. Mary of the Angels (1887), Revs. Hans Ruygt; Rodolfo Gramajo; Mary Leittem-Thomas, Pastoral Assoc.
Res., 900 S. Oak St., 95482. Tel: 707-462-1431; Fax: 707-462-2879. [CEM]
School—991 S. Dora St., 95482. Tel: 707-462-3888; Fax: 707-462-6014. Mary Jo Hons, Prin.
Lay Teachers 12; Students 251.
Catechesis/Religious Programs—Tel: 707-462-1131. Sr. Jane Kelly, P.B.V.M., D.R.E.
Students 265.
Mission—Hopland, St. Francis.

Willits, Mendocino Co., St. Anthony (1923), Rev. Louis J. Nichols (SY) Admin.; Deacon Allan G. Bohner.
Res., 61 W. San Francisco Ave., 95490. Tel: 707-459-2252; Fax: 707-459-9070.
Catechesis/Religious Programs—Tel: 707-459-9127. Margie Shanahan, D.R.E.
Students 76.
Mission—Covelo, Queen of Peace. [CEM]

Windsor, Sonoma Co., Our Lady of Guadalupe (1969), Revs. Vincent O'Neill; Xavier Ochoa; Marge Bailly, Pastoral Assoc.
Mailing Address: 8460 Alden Ln., 95492. Tel: 707-837-8962; Fax: 707-837-9157.
Catechesis/Religious Programs—Tel: 707-837-7617. Louis Gonzalez, D.R.E.
Students 150.

Yountville, Napa Co., St. Joan of Arc (1920), Rev. Mathew Ittiyappara; Deacon Jerry Cain.
Res., Box 2009, 94599. Tel: 707-944-2461.
Catechesis/Religious Programs—Students 52.
Mission—Rutherford, Holy Family.

Chaplains Of Public Institutions

CRESCENT CITY. *Pelican Bay State Prison*. Rev. Joseph Vallooran (India).

ELDRIDGE. *Sonoma Developmental Center*. Rev. Patrick J. Leslie (SAC) Chap.

IMOLA. *Napa State Hospital* 94558. Rev. James Lantsberger, O.M.I., Chap.

PETALUMA. *U.S. Coast Guard Training Center*. Rev. James A. Ingram (ORL) Chap.

YOUNTVILLE. *Veterans Administration Home*. Rev. Paul F. Ledermann (OG) Chap.

Special Assignment:
Reverend Fathers—
Chinchilla, Jose (Mexico)

Military Chaplains:
Reverend Fathers—
Serban, Ron

On Duty Outside the Diocese:
Reverend Fathers—
Boettcher, John
Rioux, Raymond
Talcott, Peter

Graduate Studies:
Reverend Fathers—
Hume, Jorge
Kelly, Michael E.
Logan, Gary

On Leave:
Reverend Fathers—
Martino, Steven
McAllister, Alex
Parker, Thomas

Retired:
Reverend Monsignors—
Fleming, Vincent A.
Monaghan, George D.
Serado, William
Tappe, Walter J.
Tillman, Clyde F.
Tournier, Andre
Reverend Fathers—
Hanratty, Brendan
Healy, John
Keogh, Thomas
McCarthy, Daniel P.
McIntyre, Justin
Munari, Mario
Sheehy, Wilfred
Tracy, Charles

Permanent Deacons:
Agudelo, Rodrigo, Santa Rosa
Bohner, Allan G., Willits
Bond, Ken, Arcata
Bromham, Paul, Rohnert Park
Cain, Jerry B., Yountville
Cook, Irving B., Jr., Lakeport
Duncan, Steve
Gai, John, Aracata
Glendinning, Ralph, Clearlake
Hercher, James, Eureka
Manz, Kenneth, Petaluma
Martin, Harry, Sebastopol
Naumann, Richard, Santa Rosa
Newman, Michael C. (SD), Ferndale
Noll, Ray, Petaluma
Remley, Joseph, Rohnert Park
Ross, Norman, Santa Rosa
Silva, Thomas, Fortuna
Viegas, Anthony, Eureka
Woodruff, W. Everett, Santa Rosa

INSTITUTIONS LOCATED IN THE DIOCESE

[A] SEMINARIES, RELIGIOUS, OR SCHOLASTICATES

NAPA. *Mont La Salle Novitiate*, 4405 Redwood Dr., 94558. Mailing Address: P.O. Box 3470, 94558. Tel: 707-252-3821. Brothers of the Christian Schools. Bro. Richard Moratto, Dir. Brothers 3; Students 3.

[B] HIGH SCHOOLS, DIOCESAN

SANTA ROSA. *Cardinal Newman High School*, 50 Ursuline Rd., 95403. Tel: 707-546-6470. Mr. Thomas C. Beecher, Prin.; Rev. Alvin M. Villaruel. Priests 1; Lay Teachers 29; Students 492.

EUREKA. *St. Bernard's High School*, 222 Dollison St., 95501. Tel: 707-443-2735; Fax: 707-443-4723. Jeffery A. Jacobs, Prin.; Rev. Loren Allen; Craig Brown, Campus Min. Priests 2; Lay Teachers 17; Students 230.

[C] HIGH SCHOOLS, PRIVATE

SANTA ROSA.

**Ursuline High School*, 90 Ursuline Rd., 95403. Tel: 707-524-1130; Fax: 707-542-0131. Ursuline Sisters of the Roman Union. Legal Title: *Santa Rosa Ursuline Corporation*. Sr. Dianne Baumunk, O.S.U., Prin. Sisters 3; Lay Teachers 37; Students 431.

**Ursuline Parent Association of Santa Rosa*.

**Ursuline Memorial Scholarship Fund*.

NAPA.

**Kolbe Academy for Boys and Girls*. High School. 1600 F St., 94559. Tel: 707-255-6412. Mr. Francis Crotty, Admin.; Diane Muth, Prin. Lay Teachers 2; Students 3.

[D] ELEMENTARY SCHOOLS, PRIVATE

NAPA.

**Kolbe Academy for Boys and Girls*, 1600 F St., 94559. Tel: 707-255-6412. Mr. Francis Crotty, Admin.; Diane Muth, Prin. Lay Teachers 6; Students 23.

[E] CATHOLIC CHARITIES

SANTA ROSA. Mailing Address: P.O. Box 4900, 95402. American Romero, Prog. Dir.

**Diocese of Santa Rosa, Catholic Charities*.
Central Administrative Offices, 2325 Montgomery Dr., P.O. Box 4900, 95402. Tel: 707-528-8712. Maureen E. Shaw, A.C.S.W., Diocesan Dir.; Mary Ann McGee, R.N., Assoc. Dir. Programs; Sharon McCarty, Dir. Admin. Svcs./Human Resources; Lia Boatman, Dir. Accounting Svcs.; Frances Caballo,

Development Dir.

Family Support Center, 465 A St., 95401. Tel: 707-542-5426. Mailing Address: P.O. Box 4900, 95402. Jerry Campbell, Prog. Dir.

Homeless Service Center, 600 Morgan St., 95401. Tel: 707-525-0226. Mailing Address: P.O. Box 4900, 95402. Nick Baker, Program Dir.

Professional Foster Care, 3425 Valle Verde Dr., Napa, 94558. Tel: 707-224-3191. Anna Shetka, Program Dir.

I'm Home Alone, 2325 Montgomery Dr., 95405. Tel: 707-528-8712. Mailing Address: P.O. Box 4900, 95402. Michele Osmon, Prog. Dir.

Immigration Services, 516 Morgan St., 95401. Tel: 707-578-6000. Mailing Address: P.O. Box 4900, 95402.

Interfaith Volunteer Caregiver Program, 9470 Mendenhall Ave., Upper Lake, 95485. Tel: 707-275-9161. Mailing Address: P.O. Box 925, Upper Lake, 95485. Louis P. Denny, Prog. Dir.

Rural Food Program, 2325 Montgomery Dr., 95405. Tel: 707-528-8712. Mailing Address: P.O. Box 4900, 95402. Sharon Malm Read, Program Dir.

Phone Friend, 2325 Montgomery Dr., 95405. Tel: 707-528-8712. Mailing Address: P.O. Box 4900, 95402. Michele Osmon, Program Dir.

Alzheimer's Respite/Resource Center, 636 Cherry St., 95401. Tel: 707-528-8712. 1000 N. Gravenstein Hwy., Sebastopol, 95472. Tel: 707-528-8712. Mailing Address: P.O. Box 4900, 95402. Scott Hale, Program Dir.

St. Joseph Nazareth Residence, 2280 Newburg Rd., Fortuna, 95540. Tel: 707-725-3512. Jackie Keller, Prog. Dir. Residents 6.

Professional Counseling Services of Humboldt/Del Norte, 2936 J St., Eureka, 95501. Tel: 707-444-9611. 1151 Main St., Fortuna, 95540. Tel: 707-725-3389. Sr. Patricia Carson, R.S.M., Regional Dir.

Shared Housing Exchange, 2016 Jefferson St., Napa, 94559. Tel: 707-224-4403. Danda Winford, M.A., Prog. Dir.

Teen Mom Program, 3425 Valle Verde Dr., Napa, 94558. Tel: 707-224-3191. Marjorie Lewis, Prog. Dir.

Free-To-Be, 2325 Montgomery Dr., 95405. Tel: 707-528-8712. Mailing Address: P.O. Box 4900, 95402. Sue Bisbee, Program Dir.

Social Justice, 2325 Montgomery Dr., 95405. Tel: 707-528-8712. Mailing Address: P.O. Box 4900, 95402. David Hinkley, Program Dir.

Choix de Vie, 1209 Jefferson St., Napa, 94559. Tel: 707-258-0260. Sr. Teresita Poulin, B.V.M., Prog. Dir.

Counseling Referral, 2016 Jefferson St., Napa, 94559. Tel: 707-224-4403. Danda Winford, Prog. Dir.

Parish/Family Services, 2325 Montgomery Dr., 95405. Tel: 707-528-8712. Mailing Address: P.O. Box 4900, 95402. Ann McGee, Prog. Dir.

Phase Two - Housing Development, 2325 Montgomery Dr., 95405. Tel: 707-528-8712. Mailing Address: P.O. Box 4900, 95402. Sr. Teresita Poulin, B.V.M., Prog. Dir.

Phase Two - Supportive Services, 516 Morgan St., 95401. Tel: 707-577-7696. American Romero, Prog. Dir.

[F] VOLUNTEER SERVICES

EUREKA. *Society of St. Vincent de Paul, District Council of the Redwood Region*, 212 G St., 95501. Tel: 707-443-8676. C. M. Weisel, Pres.

NAPA. *Society of St. Vincent de Paul, District Council of Napa County*, P.O. Box 187, 94558. Tel: 707-257-0387. Hillman Brooks, Pres.

ROHNERT PARK. *Society of St. Vincent de Paul, District Council of Sonoma County*, P.O. Box 1095, 94928. Tel: 707-584-1579. Mr. Joris Bergmann, Pres.; Mr. Paul Bromham, Exec. Dir.; Rev. Msgr. Thomas J. Keys, Spiritual Dir.

[G] GENERAL HOSPITALS

SANTA ROSA. *Santa Rosa Memorial Hospital*, 1165 Montgomery Dr., 95405. Tel: 707-546-3210.
For a complete listing, refer to the Hospitals section.

EUREKA. *St. Joseph Hospital of Eureka*, 2700 Dolbeer St., 95501. Tel: 707-445-8121.
For a complete listing, refer to the Hospitals section.

FORTUNA. *Redwood Memorial Hospital*, 3300 Renner Dr., 95540. Tel: 707-725-3361; Fax: 707-725-7212.
For a complete listing, refer to the Hospitals section.

NAPA. *Queen of the Valley Hospital of Napa*, 1000 Trancas St., 94558. Tel: 707-252-4411; Fax: 707-257-4073.
For a complete listing, refer to the Hospitals section.

[H] RESIDENTIAL TREATMENT CENTERS

ARCATA.

**Butler Valley, Inc.*, Administrative Office, 380 12th St., 95521. Tel: 707-822-0301; Fax: 707-822-3589. 3971 F St., Eureka, 95501. Tel: 707-442-7313. Robert Clayton, Exec. Dir. Staff 23; Residents12.

SONOMA. *Hanna Boys Center*, P.O. Box 100, 95476. Tel: 707-996-6767; Fax: 707-996-4742. Legal Title: *Hanna Boys Center*. For underprivileged, emotionally disturbed and pre-delinquent boys, ages 9 to 18 years. Revs. John S. Crews, Ed.D., Exec. Dir.; Gregory Klaas. Priests 2; Sisters 1; Staff 136; Students 107.

[I] HOMES FOR SENIOR CITIZENS

*SANTA ROSA. *Vigil Light Apartments (The Vigil Light, Inc.)*, 1945 Long Dr., 95405. Tel: 707-544-2810.
For a complete listing, refer to the Special Care Facilities section.

FORTUNA. *St. Joseph Nazareth Residence*, 2280 Newburg Rd., 95540. Tel: 707-725-3512.
For a complete listing, refer to the Special Care Facilities section.

[J] CAMPS AND COMMUNITY CENTERS

DUNCAN MILLS. *St. Joseph Camp*. Brothers of the Christian Schools. Mailing Address: P.O. Box 198, 95430-0198. Tel: 707-865-9941; Fax: 707-865-1025. Bro. Bede Van Duren, F.S.C., Dir. Tel: 707-252-3857.

LEGGETT. *Camp St. Michael*. (Boys - Girls). Mailing Address: P.O. Box 287, Eureka, 95502. Office: 222 Dollison St., Rm. 212, Eureka, 95501. Tel: 707-445-1006 (Business Office); 984-6877 (Campsite Office). Mr. & Mrs. Robert Bailey, Co-Dirs.

MIDDLETOWN. *Camp Salesian*, 95461. Office, Salesian High School, 2851 Salesian Ave., Richmond, 94804. Tel: 510-234-4433.
Conducted by the Salesians of St. John Bosco.

[K] NEWMAN CENTERS

ARCATA. *Newman Community, Humboldt State University*, 700 Union St., 95521. Tel: 707-822-6057; Fax: 707-822-6057. Deacon Kenneth M. Bond.

PENNGROVE. *Newman Hall, Sonoma State University, Intercollegiate Catholic Ministries*, 1798 E. Cotati Ave., 94951. Tel: 707-794-7957. Rev. Stephen Frost (ORG).

[L] HOUSES OF PRAYER AND RETREAT HOUSES

SANTA ROSA. *Angela Center*, 535 Angela Dr., 95403. Tel: 707-528-8578. Sr. Christine Van Swearingen, O.S.U., Dir.

Cardinal Newman Retreat Center, 24 Ursuline Rd., 95403. Tel: 707-579-9200; 525-8440. Sr. Olive Murphy, S.M., Dir.

NAPA. *Christian Brothers Retreat and Conference Center*. Mailing Address: 4401 Redwood Rd., P.O. Box 3720, 94558. Tel: 707-252-3810; 707-252-3811; Fax: 707-252-3818. Linda Lewis, Dir.; Charlotte Horne, Sec.

OAKVILLE. *Carmelite House of Prayer*, P.O. Box 347, 94562. Tel: 707-944-2454. Rev. James Geohegan, O.C.D., Dir.

SEBASTOPOL. *Diocesan House of Prayer*, 1100 High School Rd., 95472. Tel: 707-824-8936. Revs. Sean Murray, C.SS.R.; Angelito Peries, C.SS.R.; Sr. Antonia Killian, S.M.

[M] MONASTERIES AND RESIDENTS FOR PRIESTS AND BROTHERS

NAPA. *De La Salle Institute/Provincial Office*, 4401 Redwood Rd., 94558. Tel: 707-252-0222; Fax: 707-252-0407. Mailing Address: P.O. Box 3720, 94558. Brothers of the Christian Schools. Bro. David Brennan, F.S.C., Pres.

Lasallian Education Corporation.

District of San Francisco Christian Brothers Charitable Trust.

Holy Family Community, 4405 Redwood Rd., 94558-9708. Tel: 707-252-3768. Brothers of the Christian Schools. Bros. Jonathan Cord, F.S.C., Dir.; James Riordan, F.S.C., Sub. Dir. Brothers 21.

Justin Community, 4026 Maher St., 94558-2297. Tel: 707-255-2722. Brothers of the Christian Schools. Brothers 8.

Provincialate Community, 4403 Redwood Rd., 94558. Tel: 707-252-0802; Fax: 707-252-7046. Brothers of the Christian Schools. Bros. David Brennan, F.S.C., Prov.; Stanislaus Campbell, F.S.C., Asst. Prov.; Raphael Willeke, F.S.C., Dir.; Rev. David L. Deibel, Chap. Brothers 10.

OAKVILLE. *Carmelite House of Prayer*. Mailing Address: P.O. Box 347, 94562. Tel: 707-944-2454; 944-2460; Fax: 707-944-8533. Discalced Carmelite Friars. Revs. James Buckley, O.C.D., Supr.; Mark Kristy, O.C.D.; John Lysaght, O.C.D.; Bros. Roger Larre, O.C.D.; Charles Garrity, O.C.D. Priests 3; Brothers 2.

[N] CONVENTS AND RESIDENCES FOR SISTERS

SANTA ROSA. *Memorial Hospital Convent*, 271 Doyle Park Dr., 95405. Tel: 707-525-5235. Sister St. Joseph of Orange. Sisters 8.

Provincialate of Ursuline Nuns, 639 Angela Dr., 95403. Tel: 707-545-6811; Fax: 707-579-8571. Ursulines of the Roman Union - Western Province. Sr. Francis Xavier Porter, O.S.U., Prov.

ARCATA. *St. Mary's Convent*, 1710 Janes Rd., 95521. Tel: 707-822-4293. Sisters 1.

CRESCENT CITY. *Holy Family Convent*, 440 Third St., 95531. Tel: 707-464-3450. Sisters St. Francis of Holy Family. Sisters 3.

EUREKA. *St. Bernard's Convent*, 255 Henderson St., 95501-4313. Tel: 707-442-2454. Sisters St. Joseph of Orange. Sisters 5.

FORTUNA. *Redwood Memorial Hospital Convent*, 3300 Renner Dr., 95540. Tel: 707-725-3361. Sisters St. Joseph of Orange. Sisters 3.

HEALDSBURG. *Ursuline Residence*, 8329 Hwy. 128, 95448. Ursuline Nuns. Sisters 1.

NAPA. *Queen of the Valley Convent*, 1000 Trancas St., 94558. Tel: 707-255-6169; Fax: 707-257-4192. Sisters St. Joseph of Orange. Sisters 6.

St. Apollinaris Convent, 3700 Lassen St., P.O. Box 3012, 94558. Tel: 707-255-2185. Congregation of the Sisters of Mercy - The United States Province. Sisters 3.

Siena Convent, 4038 Maher St., 94558. Tel: 707-255-6110. Dominican Sisters of San Rafael. Sisters 9.

ST. HELENA. *St. Helena Convent*, 1229 Oak Ave., 94574. Tel: 707-963-5530. Sisters St. Joseph of Carondelet. Sisters 3.

SEBASTOPOL. *Hermitage of Christ the King*, 6501 Orchard Station Rd., 95472. Tel: 707-795-8555. Sisters of Christ the King. Sr. Mary Minette, S.C.K., Supr. Sisters 2; Assoc. Sisters 5.

WHITETHORN. *Our Lady of the Redwoods Abbey*, 95589. Tel: 707-986-7419. Cistercian Nuns of the Strict Observance. Sr. Rosemary Ducan, O.C.S.O., Supr. Pro Tem; Rev. Roger De Ganck, O.C.S.O., Chap. Priests 1; Sisters 11.

WINDSOR. *Ursuline Residence*, 9248 Lakewood Dr., 95492. Tel: 707-838-4973. Ursuline Nuns. Sisters 2.

[O] MISCELLANEOUS

SANTA ROSA. *Apostolic Endowment Trust*, P.O. Box 1297, 95402. Tel: 707-545-7610. Rev. Msgr. Thomas J. Keys, Dir.

Loyola Institute for Family Life, 170 A Wikiup Dr., 95403. Tel: 707-526-1167. Robert Dalzell, Dir.

Parish Social Ministry, P.O. Box 11574, 95406.

NAPA.

**Justin-Sienna High School Corporate Board of Trustees, Inc.*, 4026 Maher St., 94558.

SEBASTOPOL. *National Catholic AIDS Network*, 12500 Dupont Rd., 95472. Tel: 707-874-3013; Fax: 707-874-1433. Rev. Rodney J. DeMartini, S.M., Exec. Dir.

RELIGIOUS INSTITUTES OF MEN REPRESENTED IN THE DIOCESE

For further details refer to the corresponding bracketed number in the Religious Institutes of Men or Women section.

[0140]—*Augustinians.*—O.S.A.

[0330]—*Brothers of the Christian Schools.* (San Francisco Prov.).—F.S.C.

[0350]—*Cistercian Order of the Strict Observance.*—O.C.S.O.

[0260]—*Discalced Carmelite Friars.* (Anglo-Irish Prov.).—O.C.D.

[0520]—*Franciscan Friars.*—O.F.M.

[0650]—*Holy Ghost Fathers.*—C.S.Sp.

[0690]—*Jesuit Fathers.*—S.J.

[0780]—*Marist Fathers.*—S.M.

[0800]—*Maryknoll.*—M.M.

[0910]—*Oblates of Mary Immaculate.*—O.M.I.

[0430]—*Order of Preachers.*—O.P.

[0610]—*Priests of the Congregation of the Holy Cross.*—C.S.C.

[1070]—*Redemptorist Fathers.*—C.SS.R.

[1060]—*Society of the Precious Blood.*—C.PP.S.

RELIGIOUS INSTITUTES OF WOMEN REPRESENTED IN THE DIOCESE

[0670]—*Cistercian Nuns of the Strict Observance.*—O.C.S.O.

[1070-03]—*Dominican Sisters.*—O.P.

[1070-04]—*Dominican Sisters.*—O.P.

[1070-13]—*Dominican Sisters.*—O.P.

[2575]—*Institute of the Sisters of Mercy of the Americas.*—R.S.M.

[2470]—*Maryknoll Sisters of St. Dominic.*—M.M.

[1680]—*School Sisters of St. Francis.* (Holy Name Prov.).—O.S.F.

[0430]—*Sisters of Charity of the Blessed Virgin Mary.* (Dubuque, IA).—B.V.M.

[]—*Sisters of Christ the King.*—S.C.K.

[2516]—*Sisters of Mercy.*—S.M.

[0230]—*Sisters of St. Benedict.*—O.S.B.

[1570]—*Sisters of St. Francis of the Holy Family.* (Dubuque IA).—O.S.F.

[3830-03]—*Sisters of St. Joseph.*—C.S.J.

[3840]—*Sisters of St. Joseph of Carondelet.*—C.S.J.
[1990]—*Sisters of the Holy Names of Jesus and Mary.*—S.N.J.M.
[3320]—*Sisters of the Presentation of the B.V.M.*—P.B.V.M.
[1705]—*Sisters of the Third Order of St. Francis of Assisi.*—O.S.F.
[4110]—*Ursuline Nuns.* (Western Prov.).—O.S.U.

DIOCESAN CEMETERIES

SANTA ROSA. *Calvary Catholic.*
EUREKA. *St. Bernard.*
PETALUMA. *Calvary Catholic.*
ST. HELENA *Holy Cross.*
SONOMA. *St. Francis Solano.*

NECROLOGY

† Radvina, Vincent, (Retired). —Died Nov. 30, 1995.
† Rogers, John, Louvain, American College. —Died Nov. 8, 1995.

Diocese of Savannah

(Dioecesis Savannensis)

Most Reverend

J. KEVIN BOLAND, D.D.

Bishop of Savannah; ordained June 14, 1959; appointed Bishop of Savannah February 7, 1995; ordained and installed April 18, 1995.

Most Reverend

RAYMOND W. LESSARD, D.D.

Retired Bishop of Savannah; ordained December 16, 1956; appointed March 5, 1973; consecrated and installed April 27, 1973. *Catholic Pastoral Center: 601 E. Liberty St., Savannah, GA, 31401-5196.* Tel.: 912-238-2320.

ESTABLISHED AS DIOCESE OF SAVANNAH JULY 3, 1850. NAME CHANGED TO DIOCESE OF SAVANNAH-ATLANTA JAN. 5, 1937; REDESIGNATED NOV. 8, 1956.

Square Miles 37,038.

Comprises 90 Counties in the southern part of the State of Georgia.

PATRONS OF THE DIOCESE: I. ST. JOHN THE BAPTIST; II. OUR LADY OF PERPETUAL HELP. This diocese was solemnly consecrated to the Sacred Heart of Jesus, May 7, 1872, and on Dec. 8, 1943, it was solemnly consecrated to the Immaculate Heart of Mary.

For legal titles of parishes and diocesan institutions, consult the Chancery.

Chancery: Catholic Pastoral Center, 601 E. Liberty St., Savannah, GA, 31401-5196. Tel.: 912-238-2320; Fax: 912-238-2335.

Web site address: http://www.interpath.net/~mdoyle/svhhom.html

E-mail address: Diosav@sava.gulfnet.com

STATISTICAL OVERVIEW

Personnel	
Bishop	1
Retired Bishops	1
Priests: Diocesan Active in Diocese	45
Priests: Active Outside Diocese	9
Priests: Retired, Sick or Absent	10
Number of Diocesan Priests	64
Religious Priests in Diocese	30
Extern Priests in Diocese	8
Ordinations:	
Diocesan Priests	1
Transitional Deacons	3
Permanent Deacons in Diocese	37
Total Brothers	18
Total Sisters	146
Parishes	
Parishes	53
With Resident Pastor:	
Resident Diocesan Priests	38
Resident Religious Priests	15
Without Resident Pastor:	
Missions	26
Pastoral Centers	1
Professional Ministry Personnel:	
Brothers	7
Sisters	19
Lay Ministers	12
Welfare	
Catholic Hospitals	3
Total Assisted	305,276
Health Care Centers	8
Total Assisted	163,172
Residential Care of Children	1
Total Assisted	42
Specialized Homes	1
Total Assisted	30
Special Centers for Social Services	21
Total Assisted	280,640
Educational	
High Schools, Diocesan and Parish	2
Total Students	613
High Schools, Private	3
Total Students	2,023
Elementary Schools, Diocesan and Parish	15
Total Students	4,509
Catechesis/Religious Education:	
High School Students	5,105
Elementary Students	1,079
Total Students Under Catholic Instruction	13,329
Teachers in the Diocese:	
Priests	5
Brothers	1
Sisters	30
Lay Teachers	366
Vital Statistics	
Receptions into the Church:	
Infant Baptism Totals	1,408
Adult Baptism Totals	207
Received into Full Communion	412
First Communions	1,406
Confirmations	1,203
Marriages:	
Catholic	183
Interfaith	256
Total Marriages	439
Deaths	584
Total Catholic Population	73,853
Total Population	2,439,868

Former Bishops—Rt. Rev. FRANCIS X. GARTLAND, D.D., first bishop; cons. Nov. 10, 1850; died Sept. 20, 1854.—Rt. Rev. JOHN BARRY, D.D., second bishop; cons. Aug. 2, 1857; died Nov. 21, 1859.—Rt. Rev. AUGUSTIN VEROT, S.S., D.D., cons. April 25, 1858; Vic. Ap. of Florida; transferred to Savannah, July, 1861; returned to Florida as first Bishop of St. Augustine, 1870; died June 10, 1876.—His Eminence IGNATIUS CARDINAL PERSICO, D.D., transferred to this See March 11, 1870; resigned 1872; created Cardinal 1893; died 1895.—Rt. Rev. W. H. GROSS, C.SS.R., D.D., cons. April 27, 1873; promoted to Oregon 1885; died Nov. 14, 1898.—Rt. Rev. THOMAS A. BECKER, D.D., cons. Bishop of Wilmington, Aug. 16, 1868; transferred to Savannah 1886; died July 29, 1899.—Rt. Rev. BENJAMIN J. KEILEY, D.D., cons. June 3, 1900; resigned Feb. 13, 1922; appt. Titular Bishop of Scillium, March 24, 1922; died June 17, 1925.—Most Rev. MICHAEL J. KEYES, S.M., D.D., cons. Oct. 18, 1922; resigned Sept. 23, 1935; appt. Titular Bishop of Areopolis and Assistant at the Pontifical Throne; died July 31, 1959.—Most. Rev. GERALD P. O'HARA, D.D., J.U.D., appt. Titular Bishop of Heliopolis and Auxiliary Bishop of Philadelphia April 26, 1929; cons. May 20, 1929; transferred to See of Savannah, Nov. 16, 1935 received personal title of Archbishop July 12, 1950; appt. Apostolic Nuncio to Ireland, 1951; appt. Apostolic Delegate to Great Britain, 1954; resigned Nov. 11, 1959; died July 16, 1963.—Most Rev. THOMAS J. MCDONOUGH, D.D., J.C.D., cons. April 30, 1947; transferred as Auxiliary from St. Augustine to Savannah, Jan. 2, 1957; succeeded to See, March 2, 1960; promoted to Archbishop of Louisville, March 1, 1967; resigned Sept. 29, 1981.—Most Rev. GERARD L. FREY, D.D., cons. Aug. 8, 1967; transferred to Bishop of Lafayette, LA Nov. 7, 1972; retired May 13, 1989.—Most Rev. RAYMOND W. LESSARD, D.D., cons. April 27,1973; resigned Feb. 7, 1995.

Vicar General—Rev. FRANCIS J. NELSON, *Catholic Pastoral Center, 601 E. Liberty St., Savannah, 31401-5196.* Tel: 912-925-4725.

Chancery—*Catholic Pastoral Center, 601 E. Liberty St., Savannah, 31401-5196.* Tel: 912-238-2320; Fax: 912-238-2335.

Chancellor—Sr. MARY FAITH MCKEAN, R.S.M.

Business Manager—DONALD W. FREW.

Diocesan Tribunal—*Catholic Pastoral Center, 601 E. Liberty St., Savannah, 31401-5196.* Tel: 912-238-2320.

Officialis—Rev. JEREMIAH J. MCCARTHY, J.C.L.

Tribunal Judges—Revs. DOUGLAS K. CLARK, S.T.L.; FRANCIS J. NELSON, J.C.L.; HERBERT J. WELLMEIER; WILLIAM SIMMONS.

Defender of the Bond—Rev. J. GERARD SCHRECK, J.C.D.

Promoter of Justice—Rev. Msgr. DANIEL J. BOURKE, P.A.

Notary—CAROLE BARRAS.

Censor Librorum—Rev. DOUGLAS K. CLARK, S.T.L.

Archivist—Vacant, *Catholic Pastoral Center, 601 E. Liberty St., Savannah, 31401-5196.* Tel: 912-238-2320.

Georgia Catholic Conference—Mr. CHEATHAM HODGES, Exec. Sec., *3200 Deans Bridge Rd., Augusta, 30906.* Tel: 706-798-1719.

Legal Counsel—JOHN BRENNAN, *Catholic Pastoral Center, 601 E. Liberty St., Savannah, 31401-5196.* Tel:

912-238-2320.

Finance Board—Most Rev. J KEVIN BOLAND; Rev. P. JAMES COSTIGAN; Sr. MARY FAITH MCKEAN, R.S.M.; Mr. FERNANDO ARGUELLES; DONALD FREW; JOHN M. BRENNAN; JOSEPH P. BRENNAN; EMMET BOYD; LULA L. HUFF; Mr. E. J. MADDOCKS; FRED MILLER; GREGORY H. SMITH.

Investment Committee—Most Rev. J. KEVIN BOLAND; Rev. P. JAMES COSTIGAN; Mr. DONALD FREW; Mr. ODILO BLANCO; EDWARD J. BROWN, JR.; Sr. MARY FAITH MCKEAN, R.S.M.

Building Committee—Most Rev. J. KEVIN BOLAND; Rev. FRANCIS J. NELSON; DONALD W. FREW; Revs. P. JAMES COSTIGAN; GABRIEL CUMMINGS; Mr. RONALD A. JACOBS; M. SCOTT CLARK; RICHARD SIMMONS; LEON M. HOBBS, III; ROY HUSSEY; JAMES BANNON.

Catholic Cemetery Board—Rev. JAMES M. MAYO; Mr. JOHN M. SCHRODER, SR.; Mrs. GERALDINE WILLIAMS; Mr. DAVID BLANTON; Mr. SCOTT CLARK; Mr. DONALD FREW.

Deans—

Savannah Deanery: Rev. JOHN A. KENNEALLY, V.F., *18412 Whitfield Ave., Savannah, 31406.* Tel: 912-355-1523.

Augusta Deanery: Rev. ALLAN J. MCDONALD, V.F., *P.O. Box 2446, Augusta, 30903.* Tel: 706-722-4944.

Albany Deanery: Rev. EDWARD R. FRANK, V.F., *202 Hillcrest St., N.E., Moultrie, 31768.* Tel: 912-985-8949.

Columbus Deanery: Rev. FRANK PATTERSON, V.F., *320 12th St., Columbus, 31901.* Tel: 706-323-6908.

Macon Deanery: Rev. JOHN CUDDY, V.F., *830 Poplar St., Macon, 31201.* Tel: 912-745-1631.

Statesboro Deanery: Rev. MICHAEL SMITH, V.F., *221 John Paul Ave., Statesboro, 30458.* Tel: 912-681-6726.

Valdosta-Brunswick Deanery: Rev. JOHN O'BRIEN, *800 Gornto Rd., Valdosta, 31602.* Tel: 912-876-4364.

College of Consultors—Current Consultors: Revs. WILLIAM LEAHY; JAMES M. MAYO; FRANCIS J. NELSON, J.C.L.; J. GERARD SCHRECK, J.C.D.; FINBARR P. STANTON; HERBERT J. WELLMEIER.

Council of Priests—Revs. BRETT A. BRANNEN; ROBERT CHANEY; BRIAN LABURT; MICHAEL J. KAVANAUGH; WILLIAM LEAHY; JAMES M. MAYO; FRANCIS J. NELSON, J.C.L.; JOHN FITZPATRICK; CHARLES ROLAND; MARK J. ROSS; J. GERARD SCHRECK, J.C.D.; WILLIAM F. SIMMONS, V.G.; FINBARR P. STANTON; JAMES B. WALKER; HERBERT J. WELLMEIER.

Council of Religious—Sr. CARMEL TURSI, S.B.S., Pres.; Bro. WALTER GLUHM, C.S.C., Vice Pres.; Sr. HELEN EYNON, O.S.F., Sec.-Treas.

Special Vicars—

Religious Vicar—Vacant.

Social Ministry Vicar—Sr. MARIA CIESLINSKI, M.S.B.T., *Catholic Pastoral Center, 601 E. Liberty St., Savannah, 31401-5196.* Tel: 912-238-2320.

Temporal Affairs Vicar—Rev. P. JAMES COSTIGAN, *1420 Monte Sano Ave., Augusta, 30904.* Tel: 706-733-6627.

Diocesan Offices and Directors

Newspaper—"The Southern Cross"; Rev. DOUGLAS K. CLARK, Editor, Business Office: *Catholic Pastoral Center, 601 E. Liberty St., Savannah, 31401-5196.* Tel: 912-238-2320; Fax: 912-238-3339., Printing Office: *601 E. 6th St., Waynesboro, 30830.*

Director of Communications—Mrs. BARBARA KING, *Catholic Pastoral Center, 601 E. Liberty St., Savannah, 31401-5196.* Tel: 912-238-2320; Fax: 912-236-0848.

Superintendent of Schools—Sr. MARY FRANCES SOBCZAK, C.D.P., *Catholic Pastoral Center, 601 E. Liberty St., Savannah, 31401-5196.* Tel: 912-238-2320.

Director of African American Ministry—Deacon FRANK MATHIS, *Catholic Pastoral Center, 601 E. Liberty St., Savannah, 31401-5196.* Tel: 912-238-2320.

Director of Campus Ministry—Rev. MICHAEL SMITH, *221 John Paul Ave., Statesboro, 30458.* Tel: 912-681-6726; Fax: 912-681-6727.

Director of Youth Ministry—Mr. JULIAN HEYMAN, *Catholic Pastoral Center, 601 E. Liberty St., Savannah, 31401-5196.* Tel: 912-238-2320.

Director of Ecumenism and Interreligious Affairs—Deacon FRETWELL G. CRIDER, *P.O. Box 57, Tybee Island, 31328.* Tel: 912-786-8217.

Director of Family Life—Vacant, *Catholic Pastoral Center, 601 E. Liberty St., Savannah, 31401-5196.* Tel: 912-238-2320.

Director of Home Missions—Rev. LAWRENCE A. LUCREE, *332 S. Lee St., Americus, 31709.* Tel: 912-924-3495.

Director of Deanery Migrant Ministry—Rev. JUAN LOPEZ, *P.O. Box 955, Reidsville, 30453.* Tel: 912-557-6570.

Director of Social Ministry—Sr. MARIA CIESLINSKI, M.S.B.T. *601 E. Liberty St., Savannah, 31401-5196.* Tel: 912-238-2320.

Director of Vocations—Rev. ALLAN J. MCDONALD, V.F., *P.O. Box 2446, Augusta, 30903.* Tel: 706-722-4944.

Asst. Director of Vocations—Rev. BRETT A. BRANNEN, *830 Poplar St., Macon, 31201.* Tel: 912-745-1631.

Director of Vocations—Irish Seminarians; Rev. JOHN O'BRIEN, V.F., *800 Gornto Rd., Valdosta, 31602-1699.* Tel: 912-244-2430; Fax: 912-244-5352.

Diocesan Departments and Agencies

Apostleship of the Sea—Rev. K. D. XAVIER, *112 Fell St., Savannah, 31401.* Tel: 912-236-7716.

Campaign for Human Development—Sr. MARIA CIESLINSKI, M.S.B.T., *Catholic Pastoral Center, 601 E. Liberty St., Savannah, 31401-5196.* Tel: 912-238-2320.

Catholic Cemetery Advisory Board—Board Members: DONALD W. FREW; M. SCOTT CLARK; Rev. JAMES M. MAYO; GERALDINE WILLIAMS; DAVID BLANTON; JOHN M. SCHRODER, SR., *601 E. Liberty St., Savannah, 31401-5196.* Tel: 912-238-2320.

Catholic Relief Services—Sr. MARY FAITH MCKEAN, Dir., *Catholic Pastoral Center, 601 E. Liberty St., Savannah, 31401-5196.* Tel: 912-238-2320.

Clergy Welfare Board—Rev. JAMES M. MAYO, *556 E. Gordon St., Savannah, 31401-5196.* Tel: 912-232-7147.

Council of Catholic Women—Rev. JOHN O'BRIEN, Chap., *800 Gornto Rd., Valdosta, 31602-1699.* Tel: 912-244-2430. JOAN SCHAFF, Pres., *398 Penrose Dr., Savannah, 31410.*

Diocesan Communications Commission—Mrs. BARBARA KING, Contact Person, *Catholic Pastoral Center, 601 E. Liberty St., Savannah, 31401-5196.* Tel: 912-238-2320; Fax: 912-236-0848.

Diocesan Consultant On Substance Abuse—Rev. PATRICK J. SHINNICK, *4937 Bloomfield Rd., Macon, 31206.* Tel: 912-788-6386; Fax: 912-788-2837.

Diocesan Liturgical Commission—Vacant, *Catholic Pastoral Center, 601 E. Liberty St., Savannah, 31401-5196.* Tel: 912-238-2320; Fax: 912-238-2335.

Diocesan Scout Chairman—Mr. JULIAN HEYMAN, *Catholic Pastoral Center, 601 E. Liberty St., Savannah, 31401-5196.* Tel: 912-238-2320.

Holy Childhood Association—Sr. MARY FRANCES SOBCZAK, C.D.P., Dir., *Catholic Pastoral Center, 601 E. Liberty St., Savannah, 31406-5196.* Tel: 912-238-2346.

Lay Ministry Formation—Ms. ANN PINCKNEY, *Catholic Pastoral Center, 601 E. Liberty St., Savannah, 31406-5196.* Tel: 912-238-2320.

Natural Family Planning—SALLY KENNEDY, Dir. JAMES ROUTON, M.D., Medical Consultant, *601 E. Liberty St., Savannah, 31401-5196.* Tel: 912-238-2320.

Permanent Diaconate—Deacon GEORGE H. FOSTER, *4568 Betty's Branch Way, Evans, 30809.* Tel: 404-860-2379.

Propagation of the Faith—Mrs. ANN PINCKNEY, *Catholic Pastoral Center, 601 E. Liberty St., Savannah, 31401-5196.* Tel: 912-238-2320.

Refugee Resettlement—Vacant, *601 E. Liberty St., Savannah, 31401-5196.* Tel: 912-238-2320.

Religious Education—Ms. ANN PINCKNEY, *Catholic Pastoral Center, 601 E. Liberty St., Savannah, 31401-5196.* Tel: 912-238-2320.

Stewardship and Development—Ms. PATRICIA SIGNS, Dir., *Catholic Pastoral Center, 601 E. Liberty St., Savannah, 31401-5196.* Tel: 912-238-2320.

CLERGY, PARISHES, MISSIONS AND PAROCHIAL SCHOOLS

CITY OF SAVANNAH
(Chatham County)

1—CATHEDRAL OF ST. JOHN THE BAPTIST, Revs. William O. O'Neill; Douglas K. Clark; Bro. Robert Sokolowski, S.M., Pastoral Assoc.; Deacon Dewain Smith. In res., Rev. Msgr. Felix Donnelly.
Res., 222 E. Harris St., 31401. Tel: 912-233-4709; Fax: 912-238-2335.
School—Notre Dame Academy, Tel: 912-232-5473.
Sisters 2; Lay Teachers 11; Students 139.

2—ST. ANTHONY'S, Rev. Robert E. Chaney; Deacon Fretwell G. Crider. In res., Rev. Xavier Kumbalaparambil.
Res., 112 Fell St., 31401. Tel: 912-232-5258.

3—ST. BENEDICT THE MOOR, Rev. James M. Mayo; Deacons Prince A. Jackson, Jr.; Mike Foley.
Res., 556 E. Gordon St., 31401. Tel: 912-232-7147.

4—MOST BLESSED SACRAMENT, Revs. Jeremiah J. McCarthy; Thomas E. Campbell; Deacon Michael F. Daly. In res., Rev. Msgr. Daniel J. Bourke.
Res., 1003 E. Victory Dr., 31405-2499. Tel: 912-356-6980.
School—Tel: 912-356-6987. Miss Mary Anne Butler, Prin.
Lay Teachers 22; Students 366.

5—MOST PURE HEART OF MARY, Rev. Gabriel Cummings; Deacon Frank Mathis.
Mailing Address: P.O. Box 24308, 31403-4308.
Res., 902 W. 36th St., 31401. Tel: 912-232-4751.

6—SACRED HEART OF JESUS, Rev. John Lyons. Pastoral Assocs.: Sr. Ann Walker, O.S.F.; Sr. Lida Bulf, O.S.F.
Res., 1707 Bull St., 31401. Tel: 912-232-0792; Fax: 912-236-0065.

7—ST. FRANCES XAVIER CABRINI, Rev. Francis J. Nelson; Deacon Louis J. Andruzzi. In res., Rev. Joseph F. Ware.
Res., 11500 Middleground Rd., 31419-1227. Tel: 912-925-4725.

8—ST. JAMES, Revs. John A. Kenneally, V.F.; Robert A. Girardeau.
Res., 8412 Whitfield Ave., 31406. Tel: 912-355-1523; Fax: 912-353-7226.
School—Tel: 912-355-3132. Sr. Jeannine I.H.M., Prin.
Sisters 5 Lay Teachers 17; Students 572.
Mission—Isle of Hope, Our Lady of Good Hope.

9—ST. PETER THE APOSTLE CHURCH, Rev. Patrick O'Brien.
Mailing Address: 7020 Concord Rd., P.O. Box 30859, 31410.
Res., 302 Bryson Dr., 31410. Tel: 912-897-5156; Fax: 912-897-7924.
School—Tel: 912-897-5224. Sr. Assunta Desposito, R.S.M., Prin.
Lay Teachers 14; Students 305.

10—STS. PETER AND PAUL. Unassigned. (Vietnamese Mission).
Res., P.O. Box 5906, 31414. Tel: 912-236-8711.

OUTSIDE THE CITY OF SAVANNAH

Albany, Dougherty Co., St. Teresa, Revs. Finbarr P. Stanton; James P. Dalton.
Res., 421 Edgewood Ln., 31707. Tel: 912-432-0891; 439-2302 (office); Fax: 912-439-0516.
School—417 Edgewood Ln., 31707. Sr. Pauline Hritz, A.S.C., Prin. & Supr.
Adorers of the Blood of Christ 2; Lay Teachers 32; Students 407.

Americus, Sumter Co., St. Mary, Rev. Lawrence A. Lucree.
Res., 332 S. Lee St., P.O. Box K, 31709. Tel: 912-924-3495.
Missions—Montezuma, Macon Co., St. Michael; Buena Vista, Marion Co., St. Mary Magdalen.

Augusta, Richmond Co.,

1—CHURCH OF THE MOST HOLY TRINITY, Revs. Allan J. McDonald; Andrew T. Doris; Daniel Munn; Deacons Joseph F. Colbert; Donald R. McArdle; Ephraim J. Williams. Pastoral Assocs.: Sr. Bridget Lennon, O.S.F.; Mr. Fletcher R. Bingham.
Mailing Address: P.O. Box 2446, 30903. Tel: 706-722-4944; Fax: 706-722-7774.
Res., 303 Broad St., 30901. Tel: 706-724-4367.
School—Immaculate Conception School, Tel: 706-722-9964. Sr. Una Toomey, Prin.
Sisters 5; Lay Teachers 12; Students 215. Missionary Franciscan Sisters of the Immaculate Conception.
Convent & Chapel—Immaculate Conception, 1018 Laney Walker Blvd., 30901. Tel: 706-722-2380.

2—ST. JOSEPH'S, Rev. Michael Ring; Deacon Gregory L. Bernard.
Res., 2607 Lumpkin Rd., 30906. Tel: 706-798-1920.

3—ST. MARY ON THE HILL, Rev. P. James Costigan; Deacons Donald G. Cisick; James J. O'Connell.
Res., 1420 Monte Sano Ave., 30904. Tel: 706-733-6627; Fax: 706-733-4887.
School—1220 Monte Sano Ave., 30904. Tel: 706-733-6193. Ms. Joyce Connelly, Prin.
Lay Teachers 23; Students 504.
Convent—1210 Monte Sano Ave., 30904. Tel: 706-733-4101. Sisters of St. Joseph of Carondelet
Chapels—St. Joseph Hospital; St. Mary on the Hill Convent; Aquinas High School.

4—ST. TERESA OF AVILA, Rev. Walter L. DiFrancesco; Deacon William L. Johnson.
Res., 117 Pleasant Home Rd., 30907-3517. Tel: 706-863-4956.

Bainbridge, Decatur Co., St. Joseph's, Rev. Joel S. Bladt, S.T.; Deacon William N. Halbohn.
Res., 822 Ramsey St., P.O. Box 192, 31717. Tel: 912-248-0030.
Mission—Donalsonville, Seminole Co., Church of the Incarnation.

Blakely, Early Co., Holy Family, Rev. Conrad Schmitt, S.T.
Mailing Address: Box 425, 31723.
Res., 109 Arlington St., P.O. Box 425, 31723. Tel: 912-723-3339.
Mission—Cuthbert, Randolph Co., St. Luke.

Brunswick, Glynn Co., St. Francis Xavier, Revs. Wilfrid Logsdon, O.F.M.Conv.; Cletus Pifher, O.F.M.Conv.;

Bro. Michael Wright, O.F.M.Conv.; Deacons Ntungwa Maasha; George F. Ruehling, III.
Res., 729 Union St., 31520. Tel: 912-265-3249.
School—Tel: 912-265-9470; Fax: 912-265-9471. Ms. Jane O'Day, Prin.
Sisters 1; Lay Teachers 12; Students 252.
Mission—Darien, McIntosh Co., Nativity of Our Lady.

Claxton, Evans Co., St. Christopher, Revs. Laurence B. Goulding, Glmy.; Robert Healy, Glmy.; Sr. Janet Fischer, F.S.P.A., Pastoral Assoc.
Res., 402 S. River St., P.O. Box 890, 30417-0890. Tel: 912-739-3913.
Convent—402 S. River St., 30417. Tel: 912-739-2275. Franciscan Sisters of Perpetual Adoration
Missions—Glennville, Tattnall Co., St. Jude, P.O. Box 772, Glennville, 30427. Tel: 912-654-1908. Bro. Charles Kennedy, Glmy., Pastoral Assoc.; Pembroke, Bryan Co., Holy Cross, P.O. Box 890, 30417-0890.

Columbus, Muscogee Co.,

1—HOLY FAMILY, Revs. Frank Patterson, V.F.; Arthur Weltzer, Pastor Emeritus.
Res., 320 12th St., 31901. Tel: 706-323-6908.

2—OUR LADY OF LOURDES, Rev. George Gonzalez; Deacon Francis P. Benyo.
Res., 1953 Torch Hill Rd., 31903. Tel: 706-689-5720; Fax: 706-687-9579.
School—1973 Torch Hill Rd., 31903. Tel: 706-689-5644. Sr. Mairead Hourigan, O.S.U., Prin.; Sr. Kathleen Supr.
Sisters 3; Lay Teachers 10; Students 170. Ursuline Sisters.
Tel: 706-689-5184.

3—ST. ANNE, Revs. Joseph Gerard Schreck; Joseph A. Smith.
Res., 3544 Trinity Dr., P.O. Box 6606, 31907. Tel: 706-561-8678; Fax: 706-568-0179.
School—3550 Trinity Dr., 31907. Tel: 706-561-8232. Mrs. Patricia Nobes, Prin.
Lay Teachers 15; Students 293.
Mission—Pine Mountain, Harris Co., Christ the King, P.O. Box 32, Hamilton, 31811. Tel: 706-628-5158. Sr. Philomena Fogarty, F.M.M., Pastoral Assoc.
Chapels—St. Francis Hospital.; Pacelli High School.

4—ST. BENEDICT THE MOOR, Rev. Paul T. Brick, S.D.S.
Church—2930 Thomas St., P.O. Box 5705, 31906.
Res., 2939 Ninth St., 31906. Tel: 706-323-8300; Fax: 706-324-7071.
Parish Hall—2935 Ninth St., 31906. Tel: 706-324-1749; Fax: 706-324-7099.

Cordele, Crisp Co., St. Theresa, Rev. Raul Perez.
Res., 807 Third St., S., 31015. Tel: 912-273-3446.

Douglas, Coffee Co., St. Paul's, Rev. Daniel O'Connell. Pastoral Associates: Sr. Mary Saunders, S.A.; Sr. Agnes Rooney, S.A.
Res., 523 E. Ward St., 31533. Tel: 912-384-3560.
Missions—Fitzgerald, Ben Hill Co., St. William; Willacoochee, Atkinson Co., Holy Family.

Dublin, Laurens Co., Immaculate Conception, Revs. Gerald Ragan; Charles Hughes.
Res., 204 N. Church St., 31021. Tel: 912-272-0266.
Chapel—Dublin, VA Hospital.
Mission—Sandersville, Washington Co., St. William.

Hazlehurst, Jeff Davis Co., Good Shepherd, Rev. Herbert Graf, O.F.M.Conv.
Mailing Address: P.O. Box 1468, 31539. Tel: 912-375-5948.
Mission—Baxley, Appling Co., St. Rose of Lima.

Hinesville, Liberty Co., St. Stephen, First Martyr, Rev. Gerard Herman, O.F.M.Conv., V.F.
Res., 399 Woodland Ave., 31313. Tel: 912-876-4364.

Jesup, Wayne Co., St. Joseph, Rev. Florian Tiell, O.F.M.Conv. In res., Rev. Keith O'Neill, O.F.M.Conv.
Res., 1048 E. Cherry St., P.O. Box 176, 31598. Tel: 912-427-9239.

Lakeland, Lanier Co., Queen of Peace, Rev. Christian LeFrois, O.S.B, Admin.
Res., 1332 S. Mill St., P.O. Box 26, 31635. Tel: 912-482-3555.
Missions—Nashville, Berrien Co., St. Mary; Adel, Cook Co., St. Margaret Mary.

Macon, Bibb Co., St. Joseph's, Revs. John Cuddy, V.F.; Brett A. Brannen.
Res., 830 Poplar St., 31201. Tel: 912-745-1631; Fax: 912-745-2254.
School—Sisters of Mercy 1; Lay Teachers 21; Students 382.
Holy Spirit, Rev. Patrick J. Shinnick; Sr. Catherine France, D.C., Pastoral Assoc.; Deacon Daniel W. Bish, Jr.
Res., 4937 Bloomfield Rd., 31206. Tel: 912-784-0178; Fax: 912-788-2837.
Parish Center—4074 Chambers Rd., 31206. Tel: 912-788-6386.
St. Peter Claver, Rev. James B. Walker.
Res., 131 Ward St., 31204. Tel: 912-743-1454.
School—133 Ward St., 31204. Tel: 912-743-3985. Sr. Donna Marie Coward, R.S.M., Prin.
Sisters 3; Lay Teachers 14; Students 190.

McRae, Telfair Co., Holy Redeemer, Rev. Thomas E. Kirkendoll, Jr., Glmy.; Sr. Fran Trochta, C.D.P., Pastoral Assoc.
Res., 201 Telfair, 31055. Tel: 912-868-2002.
Convent—804 Anson St., Eastman, 31023. Tel: 912-374-4031. Congregation of Divine Providence Sisters
Mission—Eastman, Dodge Co., St. Mark, P.O. Box 4304, Eastman, 31023. Tel: 912-374-0238.

Moultrie, Colquitt Co., Immaculate Conception, Rev. Edward R. Frank, V.F.; Deacon Philip J. Walsh.
Res., 202 Hillcrest Ave., S.E., 31768. Tel: 912-985-8949.
Mission—Camilla, Mitchell Co., St. John Vianney, P.O. Box 391, Camilla, 31730. Tel: 912-336-8685.

Perry, Houston Co., St. Patrick, Rev. Michael J. O'Keeffe; Deacons Ralph H. McAtee; Ken Hutnick.
Res., I-75 at 341 S., P.O. Box 612, 31069. Tel: 912-987-4213.
Mission—Fort Valley, Peach Co., St. Juliana.

Port Wentworth, Chatham Co., Our Lady of Lourdes, Rev. Michael J. Kavanaugh; Deacon Raymond G. Pierce.
Res., 501 S. Coastal Hwy., Rte. U.S. 17, P.O. Box 4056, 31407. Tel: 912-964-0219.
Mission—Springfield, St. Boniface, P.O. Box 927, Springfield, 31329. Tel: 912-754-7473. Sr. Rose Ballantine, O.S.F., Pastoral Assoc.

Richmond Hill, Bryan Co., St. Anne, Rev. Herbert J. Wellmeier.
Res., P.O. Box 648, 31324. Tel: 912-756-3338.

St. Marys, Camden Co., Our Lady Star of the Sea, Rev. William J. Leahy.
Res., P.O. Box 290, 31558. Tel: 912-882-4718.
Mission—Folkston, Charlton Co., St. Francis of Assisi, 1609 N. 2nd St., Folkston, 31537. Tel: 912-496-3219.

St. Simons Island, Glynn Co., St. Williams, Revs. Germain Belen, O.F.M.Conv.; John C. Sattler, O.F.M.Conv.
Mailing Address: 2300 Frederica Rd., 31522. Tel: 912-638-2647; Fax: 912-638-7577.
Res., 2300 Frederica Rd., 31522.

Statesboro, Bulloch Co., St. Matthew's, Rev. Michael H. Smith, V.F.
Res., 221 John Paul Ave., 30458. Tel: 912-681-6726; 681-2445; Fax: 912-681-6727.

Swainsboro, Emanuel Co., Holy Trinity, Rev. Michael Langell.
Res., 928 W. Main St., 30401. Tel: 912-237-8722.
Mission—Metter, Candler Co., Holy Family, P.O. Box 231, Metter, 30439. Tel: 912-685-5811. Sr. Paul Marie Westlake, R.S.M., Pastoral Assoc.

Sylvania, Screven Co., Our Lady of the Assumption, Rev. Edward V. Gorny, Glmy.
Res., 121 Ridgecrest Dr., 30467. Tel: 912-564-2312.
Mission—Millen, Jenkins Co., St. Bernadette, P.O. Box 616, Millen, 30442. Tel: 912-982-1445.
Chapel—Bay Branch, St. Joseph.

Thomasville, Thomas Co., St. Augustine's, Rev. Victor Seidel, S.T.; Deacon Howard G. Halladay.
Res., 211 N. Pinetree Blvd., 31792. Tel: 912-226-3624.
Mission—Cairo, Grady Co., St. Elizabeth Ann Seton, 11th Ave. N.W., Cairo, 31728. Tel: 912-377-6996.

Thunderbolt, Chatham Co., Nativity of Our Lord, Rev. Francis C. Higgins.
Mailing Address: P.O. Box 3855, Savannah, 31414.
Res., 3115 E. Victory Dr., 31404. Tel: 912-354-4014; Fax: 912-352-1048.
Chapel—Thunderbolt, St. Mary's Home.

Tifton, Tift Co., Our Divine Saviour, Rev. James A. Kirchner.
Res., 1205 Love Ave., P.O. Box 212, 31793. Tel: 912-382-4600.
Mission—Alapaha, Berrien Co., St. Ann, Tel: 912-532-2216.

Tybee Island, Chatham Co., St. Michael's, Rev. John J. Fitzpatrick; Deacon George C. Hosti.
Res., 802 Lovell Ave., P.O. Box 38, 31328. Tel: 912-786-4505.
School—808 Lovell Ave., P.O. Box 740, 31328. Tel: 912-786-4507. Mr. Michael Orsini, Prin.
Lay Teachers 11; Students 157.

Valdosta, Lowndes Co., St. John the Evangelist, Rev. John O'Brien.
Church Office: 800 Gornto Rd., 31602-1699. Tel: 912-244-2430; Fax: 912-244-5352.
Res., 2402 Berkley Dr., 31602. Tel: 912-244-9920.
Newman Center—412 Baytree Rd., 31602. Tel: 912-247-6707.
School—Sisters of St. Joseph, Tel: 912-244-2556; 244-0050 (Convent). Sr. Pauline Oetgen, C.S.J., Prin.
Sisters 4; Lay Teachers 16; Students 258.

Vidalia, Toombs Co., Sacred Heart, Rev. Mark J. Ross; Deacons Clayton J. Burke, Jr.; Joseph P. Claroni.
Mailing Address: P.O. Box 1086, 30474. Tel: 912-537-7709; Fax: 912-537-4691.
Res., 3119 E. North St., 30474. Tel: 912-537-7709.
Mission—Reidsville, Tattnall Co., St. Andrew the Apostle.

Warner Robins, Houston Co., Sacred Heart, Revs. Fred J. Nijem; Michael C. Lubinsky; Sr. Teresa Baugh, P.B.V.M., Pastoral Assoc.; Deacons Harold P. Kimball; Dennis A. Arcand; Philippe Fleury.
Mailing Address: P.O. Box 5052, 31099. Tel: 912-923-0124; Fax: 912-328-3078.
School—Sisters of Presentation. Mrs. Bonnie Solinsky, Prin.
Sisters 3; Lay Teachers 24; Students 285.

Waycross, Ware Co., St. Joseph's, Rev. Charles W. Roland; Sr. Mary Robers, S.C., Pastoral Assoc.
Res., 2011 Darling Ave., 31501. Tel: 912-283-7700.
Mission—Alma, Bacon Co., St. Raymond.

Waynesboro, Burke Co., Sacred Heart, Rev. Brian LaBurt.
Res., 115 S. Liberty St., 30830. Tel: 706-554-2535.
Mission—Louisville, Jefferson Co., St. Joan of Arc, Tel: 912-625-3433.

Chaplains of Public Institutions

Special Assignment:
Reverend Fathers—
Brown, Wayland Y., 8920 Old Montgomery Rd., Savannah, GA 31406
Canty, Richard J., Memorial Medical Center & Candler General Hospital
Cushing, Robert A., 3890 Russell St., Smyrna, GA 30082-3533. Tel: 404-436-0610
Lopez, Juan, Migrant Ministry. Tel: 912-557-6570
Ryan, Timothy K., 1310 Primrose Dr., Roswell, GA 30076. Tel: 404-667-1313; 667-6305 (Fax)

On Duty Outside the Diocese:
Reverend Fathers—
Healy, Thomas, St. Kilian's Parish, Irishe Katholische Mission, Landsberger Strasse 39, 80339 Munich, Germany. Tel: 0.11.49.89.5003580
Keohane, Donal
Pachence, Ronald A., University of San Diego, San Diego, CA 92110
Schreck, Christopher J., St. Charles Borromeo Seminary, 1000 E. Wynnewood Rd., Wynnewood, PA 19096-3099. Tel: 215-667-3394

Military Chaplains:
Reverend Fathers—
Cerrone, Michael J., U.S.A.
Madden, Ronald, U.S.N.
Minch, Richard, U.S.A.
Quang, John, U.S.N.

Retired:
Reverend Monsignors—
Bourke, Daniel J., P.A., Blessed Sacrament Church, 1003 E. Victory Dr., Savannah, GA 31405. Tel: 912-356-6980
Donnelly, Felix G., Cathedral of St. John the Baptist, P.O. Box 8307, Savannah, GA 31412. Tel: 912-233-4709
LeFrois, Marvin J., 800 Gornto Rd., Valdosta, GA 31602-1699. Tel: 912-253-0041
Reverend Fathers—
Barry, Francis, c/o Mrs. John Blainey, Ross Tara, County Meath, Republic of Ireland
Doris, Andrew T., 2346 McDowell St., Augusta, GA 30904. Tel: 706-736-0593
Dowling, William P.
Payne, Thomas H., c/o Cudmore, 5946 S. 2825 W., Ray, UT 84067
Weltzer, Arthur, 320 12th St., Columbus, GA 31901

Permanent Deacons:
Andruzzi, Louis J., St. Frances Cabrini, Savannah
Arcand, Dennis A., Sacred Heart, Warner Robins
Benyo, Francis P., Our Lady of Lourdes, Columbus
Bernard, Gregory L., St. Joseph's, Augusta
Bish, Daniel W., Jr., Holy Spirit, Macon
Burke, Clayton J., Jr., Sacred Heart, Vidalia
Cisick, Donald G., St. Mary's on the Hill, Augusta
Claroni, Joseph P., Sacred Heart, Vidalia
Colbert, Joseph L., Holy Trinity, Augusta
Crider, Fretwell G., St. Anthony, Savannah
Daly, Michael F., Blessed Sacrament, Savannah
Fleury, Philippe D., Windmeadows Apts., 2712 S.W. 34th St., Apt. 137, Gainesville, FL 32608
Foley, Michael F., St. Benedict the Moor Church, Savannah
Foster, George H., St. Michael, Fort Gordon
Halbohn, William N., St. Joseph Church, Bainbridge
Halladay, Howard G., St. Augustine, Thomasville

Hosti, Charles J., St. Michael, Tybee Island
Houghton, Arthur A., Good Shepherd, Hazlehurst
Hutnick, Kenneth P., St. Juliana Church, Perry
Jackson, Prince A., Jr., St. Benedict the Moor, Savannah
Johnson, William L., St. Teresa of Avila, Augusta
Kimball, Harold P., Sacred Heart, Warner Robins
Maasha, Ntungwa, St. Francis Xavier, Brunswick
Martin, John F., Unassigned
Mathis, Frank, Most Pure Heart of Mary, Savannah
McArdle, Donald R., Holy Trinity, Augusta
McAtee, Ralph H., St. Patrick, Perry
O'Connell, James J., St. Mary on the Hill, Augusta
O'Neill, Robert, Unassigned
Pierce, Raymond G., Our Lady of Lourdes, Port Wentworth
Rowe, John A., Unassigned
Ruehling, George F., III, St. Francis Xavier, Brunswick
Sanchez, Aurelio, Holy Trinity Church, Swainsboro
Smith, Dewain E., Cathedral of St. John the Baptist, Savannah
Walsh, Philip J., Immaculate Conception, Moultrie
White, George H., St. Anthony, Savannah
Williams, Ephraim J., Holy Trinity, Augusta

INSTITUTIONS LOCATED IN THE DIOCESE

[A] HIGH SCHOOLS, DIOCESAN

AUGUSTA. *Aquinas High School*, 1920 Highland Ave., 30904-5305. Tel: 706-736-5516; Fax: 706-736-2678. Mr. John Albert, Prin.; Mrs. Penny Jackson, Asst. Prin. Sisters 3; Lay Teachers 21; Students 261.

COLUMBUS. *Pacelli High School*, 3556 Trinity Dr., 31907. Tel: 706-561-8243; Fax: 706-561-3243. Mr. Richard Fenchak, Prin.; Revs. Carey Lahrs, S.D.S.; J. Gerard Schreck, Diocesan Moderator. Priests 2; Lay Teachers 27; Students 352.

[B] HIGH SCHOOLS, PRIVATE

SAVANNAH. *Benedictine Military School*. (Grades 9-12), 6502 Seawright Dr., P.O. Drawer 13577, 31416. Tel: 912-356-3500; Fax: 912-356-3527. Secondary school conducted by the Dependent Priory of Benedictine Monks of St. Vincent Archabbey, Latrobe, PA. Rev. John Murtha, O.S.B., Pres.; Ms. Kelly Burke, Prin.; Revs. Wilfred M. Dumm, O.S.B.; Ronald P. Gatman, O.S.B.; Anthony P. Wesolowski, O.S.B.; Jeffrey S. Nyardy, O.S.B.; Bros. Gerard J. Klaric, O.S.B.; Timothy J. Brown, O.S.B.; Francis G. Ehnat, O.S.B. Priests 5; Brothers 1; Lay Teachers 27; Boys 409.

Convent and Academy of St. Vincent de Paul, 207 E. Liberty St., 31401. Tel: 912-236-9541; Fax: 912-236-7877. Sisters of Mercy of the Americas. Sr. Helen Marie Buttimer, R.S.M., Prin. Sisters 8; Lay Teachers 25; Girls 354.

MACON. *Mount de Sales Academy*. (Grades 7-12), 851 Orange St., 31201. Tel: 912-751-3240; Fax: 912-751-3241. Sisters of Mercy of the Americas. Sr. Mary Rosina Bayliss, R.S.M., Pres.; Mr. Terrence G. Mermann, Prin. Sisters 2; Lay Teachers 44; Students 612.

[C] CHILD CARE HOMES

SAVANNAH. *St. Mary's Home*, E. Victory Dr., P.O. Box 3627, Sta. B, 31404. Tel: 912-236-7164; Fax: 912-236-7164.

For a complete listing, refer to the Special Care Facilities section.

[D] RESIDENCES FOR SINGLE PREGNANT WOMEN

MACON. *Nazareth Home, Residence for Single Pregnant Women*, 538 Orange St., P.O. Box 204, 31202-0204. Tel: 912-746-9803. Sr. Elyse Staab, D.C., Dir.

[E] GENERAL HOSPITALS

SAVANNAH. *St. Joseph's Hospital*, 11705 Mercy Blvd., P.O. Box 60129, 31419-1791. Tel: 912-925-4100.

For a complete listing, refer to the Hospitals section.

AUGUSTA. *St. Joseph Center For Life, Inc.*, 2260 Wrightsboro Rd., 30910.

For a complete listing, refer to the Hospitals section.

St. Joseph Hospital, Augusta, GA, Inc., 2260 Wrightsboro Rd., 30910. Tel: 706-481-7400; Fax: 706-481-7599.

For a complete listing, refer to the Hospitals section.

COLUMBUS. *St. Francis Hospital*, 2122 Manchester Expwy., P.O. Box 7000, 31908-7000. Tel: 706-596-4000.

For a complete listing, refer to the Hospitals section.

[F] MONASTERIES AND RESIDENCES OF PRIESTS

SAVANNAH. *The Benedictine Priory*, 6502 Seawright Dr., 31406. Tel: 912-356-3520. Dependent Priory of St. Vincent Archabbey, Latrobe, PA. Revs. Wilfred M. Dumm, O.S.B.; Anthony Wesolowski, O.S.B.; Ronald Gatman, O.S.B.; John Murtha, O.S.B.; Jeffrey Nyardy, O.S.B.; Very Rev. Meinrad J. Lawson, O.S.B., Prior; Bros. Gerard J. Klaric, O.S.B.; Timothy Brown, O.S.B.; Francis Ehnat, O.S.B.

[G] CONVENTS AND RESIDENCES FOR SISTERS

SAVANNAH. *Carmelite Monastery*, 11 W. Back St., 31419. Tel: 912-925-8505; Fax: 912-925-8506. Sr. Angela Collins, O.C.D., Prioress. Professed Nuns 5.

Mercy Convent, 11801 McAuley Dr., 31419. Tel: 912-925-3800.

[H] NEWMAN CENTERS

SAVANNAH. *Armstrong State College Newman Group*, 402 Willow Rd., 31419. Tel: 912-925-5993. Mr. Mathew Daly, Campus Min.

Savannah State College Newman Group, 4 Indigo Ct., 31406. Tel: 912-925-5477. Mrs. Ann Lipsey, Campus Min.

MACON. *Mercer University, Wesleyan College Newman Center*, 2737 Gwinette Dr., 31204. Tel: 912-741-7522. Sr. Catherine France, D.C., Campus Min.

STATESBORO. *Georgia Southern University Newman Center*, 221 John Paul Ave., 30458. Tel: 912-681-6728. Ms. Jane Hall, Campus Min.

VALDOSTA. *Valdosta State College Newman Center*. Mailing Address: 800 Gornto Rd., 31602. 412 Baytree Rd., 31602. Tel: 912-247-6707. Mr. Carl Hand, Campus Min.

[I] MISCELLANEOUS

SAVANNAH. *Office of Social Ministry*, 601 E. Liberty St., 31401-5196. Tel: 912-238-2320. Sr. Maria Cieslinski, M.S.B.T., L.I.C.S.W., Dir.

Social Apostolate, 502 E. Liberty St., P.O. Box 8703, 31412. Tel: 912-233-1877. Sr. Mary Therese Brown, O.S.F., Dir.

ALBANY. *St. Clare's Evangelization-Community Center*, 2005 Martin Luther King Dr., P.O. Box 4123, 31706. Tel: 912-883-2566. Sr. Deborah Driscoll, O.S.F., Contact Person.

AUGUSTA. *Catholic Social Services*, 1419 Arsenal Ave., P.O. Box 2823, 30904. Tel: 706-733-8332; Fax: 706-733-7749. Ms. Maxine Miller, Dir.

BRUNSWICK. *Society of St. Vincent de Paul*, 1217 Newcastle St., 31520. Tel: 912-262-6027. Mrs. Pamela Kesegi, Pres.

CLAXTON. *Clothesbasket*, 402 S. River St., 30417. Tel: 912-739-2275. Sr. Janet Fischer, F.S.P.A., Dir.

COLUMBUS. *Holy Family Soup Kitchen*, 320 12th St., 31901. Tel: 706-322-8102; Fax: 706-327-8191. Mrs. Frances Cummings, Dir.

Our Lady of Lourdes, 1953 Torch Hill Rd., 31903. Tel: 706-689-5720. Sr. Kathleen Twomey, O.S.U., Dir.

St. Benedict Social Concerns, 2935 Ninth St., 31906. Tel: 706-323-8300.

St. Vincent de Paul, St. Anne Conference, 2000 Kay Cir., 31907. Tel: 706-568-1592. Paul and Claire Arrington, Dirs.

HAMILTON. *Christ the King (FOCUS)*, Hwy. 27, Box 32, 31811. Tel: 706-628-5158. Sr. Philomena Fogarty, F.M.M., Dir.

MACON. *Macon Social Apostolate (SERVE)*, 570 High Pl., 31201. Tel: 912-745-7165; Fax: 912-745-2254. Ms. Debris Bailey, Dir.

MILLEN. *Catholic Thrift Shop*, P.O.Box 616, 30442. Tel: 912-554-5842. Sr. Mary Ellen Barrette, Dir.

VALDOSTA. *St. Francis Center*, P.O. Box 1331, 31601. Tel: 912-242-8656.

WARNER ROBINS. *Sacred Heart Christian Service Center*, P.O. Box 5052, 31099-5052. Tel: 912-929-3897.

RELIGIOUS INSTITUTES OF MEN REPRESENTED IN THE DIOCESE

For further details refer to the corresponding bracketed number in the Religious Institutes of Men or Women section.

[0200]—*Benedictine Monks*. (St. Vincent Archabbey).—O.S.B.
[0600]—*Brothers of the Congregation of Holy Cross*.—C.S.C.
[0480]—*Conventual Franciscans*. (Prov. of Our Lady of Consolation).—O.F.M.Conv.
[0570]—*Glenmary Home Missioners*. (Glendale, OH).—Glmy.
[0770]—*The Marist Brothers*. (Poughkeepsie, NY).—F.M.S.
[0780]—*Marist Fathers*. (Washington Prov.).—S.M.
[0840]—*Missionary Servants of Most Holy Trinity*. (Dublin).—S.T.
[0610]—*Priests of the Congregation of Holy Cross*.—C.S.C.
[1200]—*Society of the Divine Savior*. (American Prov.).—S.D.S.

RELIGIOUS INSTITUTES OF WOMEN REPRESENTED IN THE DIOCESE

[0100]—*Adorers of the Blood of Christ*.—A.S.C.
[1780]—*Congregation of the Sisters of the Third Order of St. Francis of Perpetual Adoration*.—F.S.P.A.
[0760]—*Daughters of Charity of St. Vincent De Paul*. (Emmitsburg, MD).—D.C.
[0420]—*Discalced Carmelite Nuns*.—O.C.D.
[1070-13]—*Dominican Sisters*.—O.P.
[1370]—*Franciscan Missionaries of Mary*.—F.M.M.
[1470]—*Franciscan Sisters of St. Joseph*.—F.S.S.J.
[1190]—*Franciscan Sisters of the Atonement*.—S.A.
[2080]—*Home Mission Sisters of America*.
[4150]—*Irish Ursuline Nuns*.—O.S.U.
[1360]—*Missionary Franciscan Sisters of the Immaculate Conception*.—O.S.F.
[2790]—*Missionary Servants of the Most Blessed Trinity*.—M.S.B.T.
[0440]—*Sisters of Charity of Cincinnati*.—S.C.
[1000]—*Sisters of Divine Providence of Kentucky*.—C.D.P.
[1010]—*Sisters of Divine Providence of San Antonio, Texas*.—C.D.P.
[2575]—*Sisters of Mercy of the Americas*. (Baltimore, Erie, Portland).—R.S.M.
[3950]—*Sisters of Saint Mary of Namur*.—S.S.M.N.
[1070-18]—*Sisters of St. Dominic of the American Congregation of the Sacred Heart of Jesus*.—O.P.
[3840]—*Sisters of St. Joseph of Carondelet*. (St. Louis, MO).—C.S.J.
[0260]—*Sisters of the Blessed Sacrament for Indians and Colored People*.—S.B.S.
[1720]—*Sisters of the Third Order Regular of St. Francis of the Congregation of Our Lady of Lourdes*.—O.S.F.
[2170]—*Sisters, Servants of the Immaculate Heart of Mary*.—I.H.M.
[3330]—*Union of the Sisters of the Presentation of the Blessed Virgin Mary*.—P.B.V.M.

DIOCESAN CEMETERIES

SAVANNAH. *Catholic Cemetery and Properties*. Mr. Donald W. Frew, Dir.

Catholic Pastoral Center, 601 E. Liberty St., 31401-5196. Tel: 912-238-2320.

AUGUSTA. *Catholic Cemetery*. Rev. Allan McDonald.

Holy Trinity Church, 720 Telfair St., P.O. Box 2446, 30903. Tel: 706-722-4944.

DOUGLAS. *St. Paul's*, c/o 523 Ward St., 31533. Tel: 912-384-3560.

SYLVANIA. *Catholic Cemetery*. Rev. Edward V. Gorny, Glmy.

Our Lady of the Assumption Church, 121 Ridgecrest Dr., 30467. Tel: 912-564-2312.

WILLACOOCHEE. *Catholic Cemetery*. Rev. Daniel P. O'Connell.

NECROLOGY

(No Deaths)

Diocese of Scranton

(Dioecesis Scrantonensis)

Most Reverend

JAMES C. TIMLIN, D.D.

Bishop of Scranton; ordained July 16, 1951; appointed Titular Bishop of Gunugo and Auxiliary Bishop of Scranton August 3, 1976; consecrated September 21, 1976; succeeded to See of Scranton April 24, 1984; installed June 7, 1984. *Office: 300 Wyoming Ave., Scranton, PA, 18503.* Tel.: 717-346-8910.

Most Reverend

JOHN M. DOUGHERTY, D.D., V.G.

Auxiliary Bishop of Scranton; ordained June 15, 1957; appointed Titular Bishop of Sufetula and Auxiliary Bishop of Scranton February 7, 1995; Episcopal ordination received March 7, 1995. *Office: 300 Wyoming Ave., Scranton, PA, 18503.* Tel.: 717-346-8910.

ESTABLISHED MARCH 3, 1868.

Square Miles 8,847.

Comprises the Counties of Luzerne, Lackawanna, Bradford, Susquehanna, Wayne, Tioga, Sullivan, Wyoming, Lycoming, Pike and Monroe in Pennsylvania.

For legal titles of parishes and diocesan institutions, consult the Chancery Office.

Chancery Office: 300 Wyoming Ave., Scranton, PA, 18503. Tel.: 717-346-8910.

STATISTICAL OVERVIEW

Personnel	
Bishop	1
Auxiliary Bishops	1
Abbots	1
Priests: Diocesan Active in Diocese	265
Priests: Active Outside Diocese	17
Priests: Retired, Sick or Absent	84
Number of Diocesan Priests	366
Religious Priests in Diocese	101
Extern Priests in Diocese	3
Ordinations:	
Diocesan Priests	3
Religious Priests	2
Transitional Deacons	2
Permanent Deacons in Diocese	32
Total Brothers	9
Total Sisters	865
Parishes	
Parishes	200
With Resident Pastor:	
Resident Diocesan Priests	189
Resident Religious Priests	7
Without Resident Pastor:	
Administered by Priests	4
Missions	86
Pastoral Centers	25
Professional Ministry Personnel:	
Sisters	67
Welfare	
Catholic Hospitals	7
Total Assisted	697,490
Health Care Centers	3
Total Assisted	98,256
Homes for the Aged	7
Total Assisted	748
Residential Care of Children	7
Total Assisted	962
Day Care and Extended Day Care Centers	2
Total Assisted	148
Specialized Homes	10
Total Assisted	2,532
Special Centers for Social Services	4
Total Assisted	170,109
Residential Care of Disabled	1
Total Assisted	140
Educational	
Seminaries, Diocesan	1
Students from This Diocese	17
Students from Other Diocese	8
Diocesan Students in Other Seminaries	12
Seminaries, Religious	2
Students Religious	48
Total Seminarians	77
Colleges and Universities	4
Total Students	11,059
High Schools, Diocesan and Parish	9
Total Students	3,445
High Schools, Private	2
Total Students	738
Elementary Schools, Diocesan and Parish	60
Total Students	13,491
Elementary Schools, Private	4
Total Students	183
Non-residential Schools for the Disabled	1
Total Students	15
Catechesis/Religious Education:	
High School Students	7,226
Elementary Students	25,202
Total Students Under Catholic Instruction	61,436
Teachers in the Diocese:	
Priests	49
Brothers	2
Sisters	257
Lay Teachers	1,833
Vital Statistics	
Receptions into the Church:	
Infant Baptism Totals	4,911
Adult Baptism Totals	256
Received into Full Communion	289
First Communions	5,025
Confirmations	5,931
Marriages:	
Catholic	1,686
Interfaith	648
Total Marriages	2,334
Deaths	5,093
Total Catholic Population	360,993
Total Population	1,036,320

Former Bishops—First Bishop: Rt. Rev. WILLIAM O'HARA, D.D., cons. July 12, 1868; died Feb. 3, 1899.—*Second Bishop:* Rt. Rev. MICHAEL J. HOBAN, D.D., cons. Coadjutor, March 22, 1896; succeeded to See, Feb. 3, 1899; died Nov. 13, 1926.—*Third Bishop:* Most Rev. THOMAS C. O'REILLY, D.D., ord. June 4, 1898 Elected Dec. 19, 1927, cons. Feb. 16, 1928; installed March 8, 1928; died March 25, 1938.—*Fourth Bishop:* Most Rev. WILLIAM J. HAFEY, D.D., ord. June 16, 1914; appt. First Bishop of Raleigh, April 6, 1925; cons. June 24, 1925; transferred to Scranton as Coadjutor *cum jure successionis* and Apostolic Administrator, Oct. 2, 1937; succeeded to See, March 25, 1938; died May 12, 1954.—*Fifth Bishop:* Most Rev. JEROME D. HANNAN, D.D., ord. May 22, 1921; appt. August 17, 1954; cons. Sept. 21, 1954; died Dec. 15, 1965.—*Sixth Bishop:* Most Rev. J. CARROLL M. MCCORMICK, D.D., ord. July 10, 1932; appt. Titular Bishop of Ruspae and Auxiliary of Philadelphia, Jan. 11, 1947; cons. April 23, 1947; appt. Bishop of Altoona-Johnstown, June 25, 1960; transferred to the See of Scranton, March 4, 1966; installed May 25, 1966; retired Feb. 15, 1983; died Nov. 2, 1996.—*Seventh Bishop:* Most Rev. JOHN J. O'CONNOR, D.D., ord. Dec. 15, 1945; appt. Titular Bishop of Cuzola and Auxiliary Bishop to the Military Vicar April 24, 1979; cons. May 27, 1979; appt. Bishop of Scranton, May 10, 1983; installed June 29, 1983; transferred to the See of New York, Jan. 31, 1984.

Vicar General—Most Rev. JOHN M. DOUGHERTY, D.D., V.G., *300 Wyoming Ave., Scranton, 18503.* Tel: 717-346-8910.

Chancery Office—300 Wyoming Ave., Scranton, 18503. Tel: 717-346-8910.

Moderator of the Curia—Most Rev. JOHN M. DOUGHERTY, D.D., V.G. Tel: 717-346-8910.

Chancellor—Mr. JAMES B. EARLEY. Tel: 717-346-8910; 346-8908.

Secretary to Bishop Timlin—Rev. ANDREW W. KILPATRICK. Tel: 717-346-8910; 346-8956; 344-7231 (After 5 P.M.).

Diocesan Financial Office—JAMES M. QUINN, Dir. Tel: 717-346-8965.

Diocesan Tribunal—300 Wyoming Ave., Scranton, 18503. Tel: 717-346-8944; Fax: 717-346-8991.

Judicial Vicar—Rev. PATRICK J. PRATICO, J.C.D.

Coordinator—JOSEPH V. FOX.

Judges—Very Rev. EDWARD R. LIPTOCK, V.F.; Rev. JOSEPH C. BAMBERA, J.C.L.; CHARLES J. REID, J.D., J.C.L.; Rev. PATRICK J. PRACTICO, J.C.D.; Rev. PETER H. COLASURDO, J.C.L.; LINDA E. PRICE, J.C.L.; Revs. DAVID M. O'CONNELL, C.M., J.C.L.;

JOHN L. SULLIVAN, J.C.L.

Defenders of the Bond—Very Rev. JOSEPH G. QUINN, J.D., J.C.L., V.F.; Rev. JOHN A. BERGAMO, J.C.L.; Very Rev. RICHARD A. BURKE, C.P., J.C.L.; Rev. JAMES J. WALSH, J.C.L.

Promotor of Justice—Rev. JOHN A. BERGAMO, J.C.L.

Auditors—JOSEPH A. BARRETT, Ph.D.; JOSEPH V. FOX; Revs. JOHN A. BERGAMO, J.C.L.; CYRIL D. EDWARDS, M.Div.; BERNARD P. EVANOFSKI; JOSEPH ELSTON; MICHAEL J. SULLIVAN.

Procurator/Advocate—JOSEPH V. FOX.

Psychological Expert—JOSEPH A. BARRETT, Ph.D.

Notaries—ANN WALSH; PATRICIA WALTON.

Diocesan Finance Council—Most Rev. JOHN M. DOUGHERTY, D.D., V.G.; Rev. Msgr. JOHN J. BENDIK; Mrs. ELLEN DERMODY; JOHN D. MCCARTHY; JAMES E. O'BRIEN, JR., ESQ.; MARY THERESA PATERSON, ESQ.; MARY ELLEN COLEMAN; Rev. Msgr. NEIL J. VAN LOON; JAMES M. QUINN; JAMES B. EARLEY; THOMAS MEDICO; Sr. JEAN MOHL, S.C.C.

Diocesan Consultors—Most Rev. JAMES C. TIMLIN, D.D.; Rev. Msgr. F. ALLAN CONLAN; Rev. Msgr. PETER P. MADUS, V.F.; Rev. Msgr. NEIL J. VAN LOON, V.F.; Very Rev. FRANCIS J. CASTELLANO, V.F.; Very Rev. JOSEPH G. QUINN, V.F.; Very Rev. JOSEPH M. ZIOBRO, V.F.; Revs. WILLIAM J. FELDCAMP; PATRICK J. PRATICO; BERNARD A. TOLOCZKO. Ex Officio: Most Rev. JOHN M. DOUGHERTY, D.D., V.G.; Revs. JOSEPH C. BAMBERA; ANDREW W. KILPATRICK, Sec.

Diocesan Pastoral Council—Contact: ELLEN C. DERMODY, Diocesan Dir., Pastoral Planning. Tel: 717-346-8932.

Deans—Scranton-South: Rev. Msgr. LEONARD J. NOVAK, V.F., Scranton-West: Very Rev. PAUL P. COTTONE, V.F., Scranton-North: Rev. Msgr. PETER P. MADUS, V.F., Scranton-Central: Very Rev. JOSEPH G. QUINN, V.F., Carbondale: Very Rev. PETER V. HERHENREADER, V.F., Abingtons: Very Rev. JOSEPH M. BOLES, V.F., Dunmore: Very Rev. EDWARD R. LIPTOCK, V.F., Freeland: Very Rev. MICHAEL J. PICCOLA, V.F., Hazleton: Very Rev. GIRARD F. ANGELO, V.F., Kingston: Rev. Msgr. NEIL J. VAN LOON, V.F., Nanticoke: Very Rev. SANTINO J. FANUCCI, V.F., Old Forge: Very Rev. JOSEPH F. CIPRIANO, V.F., Olyphant: Rev. Msgr. STANLEY W. PIORKOWSKI, V.F., Pittston: Very Rev. JAMES J. PAISLEY, V.F., Plymouth: Very Rev. JOHN L. FABIAN, V.F., West Pittston: Very Rev. DANIEL D. HITCHKO, V.F., Wilkes-Barre Central/South: Rev. Msgr. FRANCIS J. CALLAHAN, V.F., Wilkes-Barre Plains: Very Rev. JOSEPH M. ZIOBRO, V.F., Bradford and Sullivan: Very Rev. RONALD J. HUGHES, V.F., Lycoming: Very Rev. FRANCIS J. CASTELLANO, V.F., Monroe: Very Rev. JOHN B. BOYLE, V.F., Pike: Rev. Msgr. WILLIAM P. WARD, V.F., Susquehanna: Very Rev. THOMAS A. CAPPELLONI, V.F., Tioga: Very Rev. THOMAS P. SHOBACK, V.F., Wayne: Very Rev. EDWARD R. SCOTT, V.F., Ashley-Mountain Top: Very Rev. THOMAS J. O'MALLEY, V.F.

Presbyteral Council—Most Rev. JAMES C. TIMLIN, D.D., Pres.; Revs. JOHN K. MANNO, Chm. J. PETER CRYNES, Vice Chm. JOHN M. LAPERA, Sec.; Rev. Msgr. JOHN J. BENDIK; Rev. Msgr. F. ALLAN CONLAN; Rev. Msgr. GEORGE R. DEMUTH; Rev. Msgr. PHILIP A. GRAY; Rev. Msgr. PETER P. MADUS, V.F.; Rev. Msgr. NEIL J. VAN LOON, V.F.; Rev. Msgr. WILLIAM P. WARD, V.F.; Very Rev. JOSEPH G. QUINN, V.F.; Very Rev. JOSEPH M. ZIOBRO, V.F.; Very Rev. MARIO S. BUTTINI, O.S.J.; Very Rev. FRANCIS J. CASTELLANO, V.F.; Revs. JOHN J. CHMIL; WILLIAM J. FELDCAMP; WILLIAM J. FLYNN, S.S.; GERARD M. GANNON; ANDREW W. KILPATRICK; JOSEPH R. KOPACZ; VINCENT F. LANGAN; HILARY L. MALINOWSKI; JAMES J. MCGARRY; THOMAS D. MCLAUGHLIN; PATRICK J. PRATICO; JOSEPH A. SIDERA, C.S.C.; BERNARD A. TOLOCZKO; JOSEPH O. WEBER; DONALD J. WILLIAMS. Ex Officio: Most Rev. JOHN M. DOUGHERTY, D.D., V.G.; Rev. JOSEPH C. BAMBERA.

Diocesan Building Commission—All plans for building should be sent to Chancery Office, *300 Wyoming Ave., Scranton, 18503.* Most Rev. JOHN M. DOUGHERTY, D.D., V.G.; MICHAEL M. BARBETTI; Rev. Msgr. JOHN J. BENDIK; WILLIAM J. BURKAVAGE; Rev. WILLIAM J. FELDCAMP; Rev. Msgr. ANTHONY C. MARRA; JOSEPH M. O'CONNOR; PAUL S. ROTELLA, ESQ.; Rev. Msgr. NEIL J. VAN LOON, V.F.; DONALD J. WOLFF.

Vicar for Canonical Services—Rev. PATRICK J. PRACTICO, J.C.D., *300 Wyoming Ave., Scranton, 18503.* Tel: 717-346-8944.

Vicar for Priests—Rev. JOSEPH C. BAMBERA, *300 Wyoming Ave., Scranton, 18503.* Tel: 717-346-8939.

Vicars for Religious—Most Rev. JOHN M. DOUGHERTY, D.D., V.G., *300 Wyoming Ave., Scranton, 18503.* Tel: 717-346-8910. Sr. M. GABRIEL KANE, I.H.M. Tel: 717-346-8947.

Diocesan Offices and Directors

Blue Army of Our Lady of Fatima—Rev. JOHN S. MARINKO, Diocesan Spiritual Dir., *120 Willow Ave., Olyphant, 18447.* Tel: 717-489-2023.

Campaign for Human Development Director—Rev. WILLIAM E. PICKARD, *300 Wyoming Ave., Scranton, 18503.* Tel: 717-346-8910.

Campus Ministry—Sr. CATHERINE ANN GILVARY, I.H.M., Dir., *P.O. Box 149, Lycoming College, Williamsport, 17701.* Tel: 717-321-4111.

Catholic Charismatic Renewal—Rev. RICHARD J. LOCH, Spiritual Advisor; ROBERT VALIANTE, Coord., *P.O. Box 3306, Scranton, 18505.* Tel: 717-344-2214.

Catholic Health Care Facilities Director and Representative to Catholic Institutions of Higher Learning—Rev. Msgr. ANDREW J. MCGOWAN, *Mercy Hospital, Scranton, 18501.* Tel: 717-348-7010.

Catholic Relief Services—JAMES B. EARLEY, Chancellor, *300 Wyoming Ave., Scranton, 18503.* Tel: 717-346-8910.

Catholic Social Services—Diocesan Dir., *400 Wyoming Ave., Scranton, 18503.* Tel: 717-346-8935.

Lackawanna County Branch—

Scranton Office—Mr. STEPHEN R. NOCILLA, M.A., Exec. Dir., *400 Wyoming Ave., Scranton, 18503.* Tel: 717-346-8936; Fax: 717-341-1293.

Carbondale Office—39 S. Main St., Carbondale, 18407. Tel: 717-282-0460.

Luzerne County Branch—

Wilkes-Barre Office—Mr. NED DELANEY, M.A., Exec. Dir., *33 E. Northampton St., Wilkes-Barre, 18701.* Tel: 717-824-5766.

Hazleton Office—81 S. Church St., Hazleton. Tel: 717-455-1521.

Lycoming County Branch—

Williamsport Office—Mr. ROBERT MAKOS, M.S.W., L.S.W., Exec. Dir., *1015 Washington Blvd., Williamsport, 17701.* Tel: 717-322-4220.

Mansfield Office—242 S. Main St., Mansfield, 16933. Tel: 717-662-7773.

Monroe County Branch—

Stroudsburg Office—Mrs. MARY LOU MALLOY, A.S.C.W., L.S.W., Exec. Dir., *411 1/2 Main St., Stroudsburg, 18360.* Tel: 717-476-6460.

Milford Office—111 E. High St., Milford, 18337. Tel: 717-296-0388.

Natural Family Planning Coordinator—Diocesan Coord., *400 Wyoming Ave., Scranton, 18503.* Tel: 717-346-8935.

Diocesan Board of Education—JOHN MARX, Pres.; Rev. KEVIN P. MULHERN, Vice Pres.; Sr. ANN MONICA BUBSER, I.H.M., Sec. RUTH A. CONNOLLY, Exec. Sec.

Cemeteries—Mr. WALTER BENNETT, Dir., *1708 Oram St., Scranton, 18504.* Tel: 717-346-8923.

Censor Librorum—Rev. Msgr. DAVID A. BOHR, S.T.D., *St. Pius X Seminary, Dalton, 18414.* Tel: 717-563-1131.

Continuing Education of Priests—Rev. JOSEPH C. BAMBERA, Dir., *300 Wyoming Ave., Scranton, 18503.* Tel: 717-346-8939.

Cursillo Movement—Rev. JAMES R. NASH, Spiritual Moderator, *60 S. Main St., Montrose, 18801.* Tel: 717-735-4834.

Diocesan Commission on Ethics for Catholic Health Care Facilities—Rev. Msgr. DAVID A. BOHR, S.T.D., Chm.; Sr. JOANNE BEDNAR, S.C.C.; J. BRIAN BENESTAD, Ph D.; Deacon THOMAS M. CESARINI; Sr. JEAN COUGHLIN, I.H.M.; Sr. VINCENTIA DORSEY, I.H.M.; Rev. JAMES J. DOYLE, C.S.C.; PATRICK J. FERRARO, M.D.; Rev. ANDREW W. KILPATRICK; Rev. Msgr. ANDREW J. MCGOWAN; JAMES MCKENNA, M.D.; JOANNE ORLOSKI, M.D.; Revs. JAMES A. RAFFERTY, S.T.L.; ROBERT J. SIMON; WILLIAM P. SMEDLEY, M.D.; Rev. JOSEPH B. WILSON, Ph.D.; GLEN YANIK, ESQ.

Diocesan Commission on Ecumenism and Inter-Faith Matters—Rev. PHILIP A. ALTAVILLA, Diocesan Dir.

Diocesan Director of Public Relations—Sr. MARIANNE ADDY, I.H.M., Dir., *300 Wyoming Ave., Scranton, 18503.* Tel: 717-346-8931.

Diocesan Engineer—Mr. TERRY K. STEPHENS, *300 Wyoming Ave., Scranton, 18503.* Tel: 717-341-1287; 341-1295; Fax: 717-346-8992.

Diocesan Historian—Rev. Msgr. JOHN P. GALLAGHER, Ph.D., *1214 Quincy Ave., Dunmore, 18510.* Tel: 717-343-2777.

Diocesan Office for Communications—Mrs. MARIA ORZEL, Exec. Dir., *400 Wyoming Ave., Scranton, 18503.* Tel: 717-346-8953; 800-246-0288; Fax: 717-346-8958.

Diocesan Office of Religious Education—SANDRA CZYZYK, Dir.

Ministry for Persons with Disabilities—MARY RYAN, Dir.

Ministry with Deaf and Hard of Hearing—Sr. MARY BETH MAKUCH, SS.C.M., Dir., *400 Wyoming Ave., Scranton, 18503.* Tel: 717-346-8961., Audio-Visual Resource Center. Tel: 717-346-8911.

Diocesan Office of Development—ANTHONY SHIPULA, Dir., *300 Wyoming Ave., Scranton, 18503.* Tel: 717-346-8903.

Diocesan Office of Ecumenism—Rev. PHILIP A. ALTAVILLA, Dir., *300 Wyoming Ave., Scranton, 18503.* Tel: 717-346-8944.

Diocesan Office of Parish Ministries—Rev. ROBERT J. SIMON, Exec. Dir.; Sr. CATHERINE E. MULKERRIN, C.S.J., Parish Structures Dir. JOAN TUREL, Worship Dir. KATHY YAKLIC, Youth and Young Adult Ministry Dir. MARY ANN PAULUKONIS, Family Life Dir., *300 Wyoming Ave., Scranton, 18503.* Tel: 717-346-8914.

Diocesan Pro-Life Office—Rev. ROBERT J. SIMON, Diocesan Dir., *300 Wyoming Ave., Scranton, 18503.* Tel: 717-346-8904.

Holy Childhood Association—Rev. Msgr. JOHN A. ESSEFF, Dir., *300 Wyoming Ave., Scranton, 18503.* Tel: 717-346-8933.

Holy Name Society—Rev. MARTIN M. BOYLAN, Ph.D., Spiritual Moderator, *300 Wyoming Ave., Scranton, 18503.* Tel: 717-346-8909.

Legion of Mary—Rev. CHARLES P. CONNOR, Diocesan Spiritual Dir., *1403 Jackson St., Scranton, 18504.* Tel: 717-344-2679.

Liturgical Commission—Rev. Msgr. DALE R. RUPERT, Chm.; Rev. ROBERT J. SIMON, Vice Chm. JOAN TUREL, Diocesan Worship Dir.

Marriage Encounter—Rev. JOHN S. MARINKO, S.T.L., Spiritual Advisor, *120 Willow Ave., Olyphant, 18447.* Tel: 717-489-2023.

D.C.C.M.—Rev. MARTIN M. BOYLAN, Ph.D., Spiritual Moderator, *300 Wyoming Ave., Scranton, 18503.* Tel: 717-346-8914.

D.C.C.W.—Rev. Msgr. FRANCIS J. CALLAHAN, Spiritual Moderator, *300 Wyoming Ave., Scranton, 18503.* Tel: 717-346-8921.

Newspaper—"The Catholic Light"; Mr. JEROME M. ZUFELT, Editor, *300 Wyoming Ave., Scranton, 18503.* Tel: 717-346-8918.

Office of Pastoral Planning—ELLEN C. DERMODY, Exec. Dir., *300 Wyoming Ave., Scranton, 18503-1279.* Tel: 717-346-8932.

Diocesan Television Station-CTV—Mrs. MARIA ORZEL, Exec. Dir. JAMES BRENNAN, Mgr., *400 Wyoming Ave., Scranton, 18503.* Tel: 717-346-8953.

Permanent Diaconate Office—Rev. Msgr. DAVID A. BOHR, Dir., *St. Pius X Seminary, 1000 Seminary Rd., Dalton, 18414.* Tel: 717-563-1131.

Pilgrimages—Rev. MICHAEL J. KLOTON, Diocesan Dir., *13 Hudson Rd., Plains, 18705.* Tel: 717-288-1404.

Priests' Eucharistic League—Rev. Msgr. JOHN P. GALLAGHER, Ph.D., *1214 Quincy Ave., Dunmore, 18510.* Tel: 717-343-2777.

Priests Purgatorial Society—Rev. JOSEPH C. BAMBERA, Sec., *300 Wyoming Ave., Scranton, 18503.* Tel: 717-346-8939.

Priests' Retirement Advisory Board—Most Rev. JOHN M. DOUGHERTY, D.D., V.G.; Rev. THOMAS A. FLYNN; Rev. Msgr. JOHN P. GALLAGHER; JAMES M. QUINN; Rev. Msgr. NEIL J. VAN LOON, V.F.; Revs. RICHARD J. POLMOUNTER; JOSEPH C. BAMBERA; JAMES B. EARLEY.

Propagation of the Faith—Rev. Msgr. JOHN A. ESSEFF, Dir., *300 Wyoming Ave., Scranton, 18503.* Tel: 717-346-8933; Fax: 717-346-8948.

Pastoral Formation Institute—Rev. Msgr. DAVID A. BOHR, S.T.D., Dir., *St. Pius X Seminary, 1000 Seminary Rd., Dalton, 18414.* Tel: 717-563-8501.

Renewal—Fatima Center—Mr. JEFFREY SEYMOUR, M.A., *1000 Seminary Rd., Dalton, 18414.* Tel: 717-563-8500.

Retirement Fund for Religious—Dirs.: Sr. MARIANNE ADDY, I.H.M.; Sr. M. GABRIEL KANE, I.H.M. Tel: 717-346-8931; 346-8947.

Schools—RUTH A. CONNOLLY, Ed.D., Supt., *300 Wyoming Ave., Scranton, 18503.* Tel: 717-346-8942. PATRICK G. CAWLEY, Asst. Supt., Curriculum and Staff Devel. Tel: 717-346-8943. DANIEL F. DONOVAN, Asst. Supt., Personnel. Tel: 717-346-8941. Rev. DAVID L. TRESSLER, Asst. Supt., Christian Formation. Tel: 717-455-9431.

Scouts of America—Rev. BERT S. KOZEN, Diocesan Chap., *24 N. Washington St., Canton, 17724.* Tel: 717-673-5253.

Council of Women Religious—Contact: Sr. M. GABRIEL KANE, I.H.M., Vicar for Religious.

Christian Life Communities—Sr. MARYLA FARFOUR, I.H.M., Coord., *333 Wyoming Ave., Scranton, 18503.* Tel: 717-344-9725. Rev. ROBERT J. SIMON, Spiritual Advisor, *301 S. State St., Clarks Summit, 18411.* Tel: 717-586-1741.

Vocations—Rev. ALBERT M. LIBERATORE, Dir.; Sr. M. GABRIEL KANE, I.H.M., Assoc. Dir., *St. Pius X Seminary, 1000 Seminary Rd., Dalton, 18414.* Tel: 717-563-1131.

CLERGY, PARISHES, MISSIONS AND PAROCHIAL SCHOOLS

CITY OF SCRANTON
(Lackawanna County)

1—ST. PETER'S CATHEDRAL (1853), Very Rev. Joseph G. Quinn, V.F.; Rev. Jeffrey J. Walsh. In res., Most Rev. James C. Timlin, D.D.; Rev. Andrew W. Kilpatrick.
Res., Tel: 717-344-7231.

2—ST. ANN'S (1901), Revs. Roger Elliott, C.P.; Patrick Geinzer, C.P.; Alphonsus Coen, C.P.
Res., 1250 St. Ann St., 18504. Tel: 717-342-5166.
School—1228 St. Ann St., 18504. Tel: 717-348-3753.
Sisters of Jesus Crucified 3; Lay Teachers 12; Students 240.

3—ST. ANTHONY OF PADUA (1913) (Italian), Rev. Michael A. Penn. In res., Rev. Robert J. Barone.
Res., 1402 Short Ave., 18508. Tel: 717-342-4190.

4—ST. DAVID'S (1946), Rev. Gerard J. McMahon, Admin.
Res., 2523 Jackson St., 18504. Tel: 717-344-9745.

5—ST. FRANCIS (1920) (Italian), Rev. Msgr. Philip A. Gray.
Res., 630 Genet St., 18505. Tel: 717-346-0797; Fax: 717-346-7187.

6—HOLY CROSS (1897). Merged with St. Patrick's, Scranton.

7—HOLY FAMILY (1891), Rev. Msgr. Constantine V. Siconolfi.
Res., 510 Gibson St., 18509. Tel: 717-342-8548. [CEM]

8—HOLY NAME (1938), Rev. Joseph C. Bambera.
Res., 1414 E. Elm St., 18505. Tel: 717-346-3859; Fax: 717-346-3859.

9—HOLY ROSARY (1871), Rev. Msgr. Joseph P. Kelly.
Res., 316 William St., 18508. Tel: 717-342-4881.
School—312 William St., 18508.
Priests 1; Sisters of the I.H.M. 5; Lay Teachers 11; Students 300.
Missions—Scranton, Lackawanna Co., St. Stanislaus; St. Stephen's.

10—IMMACULATE CONCEPTION (1967), Revs. William D. Campbell; Joseph F. Orloski; Richard E. Fox. In res., Rev. Edward F. Barrett.
Res., 801 Taylor Ave., 18510. Tel: 717-961-5211.

11—ST. CLARE (1967), Rev. Msgr. Joseph A. Fadden.
Res., 2301 N. Washington Ave., 18509. Tel: 717-344-9884.
School—2215 N. Washington Ave., 18509. Tel: 717-343-2790.
Sisters of the I.H.M. 4; Lay Teachers 12; Students 258.

12—ST. JOHN THE BAPTIST (1885) (German). Merged with St. Patrick's, Scranton.

13—ST. JOHN THE EVANGELIST (1886), Rev. Eugene R. Carr.
Res., 516 Fig St., 18505. Tel: 717-343-6026.

14—ST. JOSEPH'S (1894) (Lithuanian), Rev. Msgr. Peter P. Madus, V.F.
Res., 116 Theodore St., 18508. Tel: 717-342-4339; Fax: 717-342-4245. [CEM]

15—ST. JOSEPH'S (1872), Rev. John M. Lapera. In res., Rev. Conan Conaboy, C.P.
Res., 312 Davis St., 18505. Tel: 717-344-1724; Fax: 717-344-1787. [CEM]

16—ST. LUCY'S (1901) (Italian), Very Rev. Paul P. Cottone; Rev. Joseph J. Fanti.
Res., 949 Scranton St., 18504. Tel: 717-347-9421.

17—ST. MARY OF THE ASSUMPTION (1854) (German), Revs. Richard J. Loch; Patrick D. Healey; Joseph Valakuzhy Oommen, O.I.C.
Res., 430 Pittston Ave., 18505. Tel: 717-961-2297; Fax: 717-341-7664. [CEM]
School—430 River St., 18505. Tel: 717-342-9700; Fax: 717-341-7664.
Sisters of Christian Charity 3; Lay Teachers 18; Students 323.

18—ST. MARY'S (1904) (Polish), Rev. Albert E. Oldfield. In res., Rev. P. Lawrence Homer.
Res., 3335 Greenwood Ave., Moosic, 18507. Tel: 717-343-4024. [CEM]
School—Lay Teachers 6; Students 75.

19—ST. MICHAEL'S (1914) (Lithuanian), Rev. Louis J. Campbell.
Res., 1703 Jackson St., 18504. Tel: 717-961-1205; Fax: 717-961-2284.

20—NATIVITY OF OUR LORD (1903), Revs. Joseph R. Kopacz; Michael F. Quinnan. In res., Revs. John C. Ruth; Gustaro Aldolfo Tenorio Pena.
Res., 633 Orchard St., 18505. Tel: 717-344-6159.
School—638 Hemlock St., 18505. Tel: 717-346-9922.
Sisters of the I.H.M. 2; Lay Teachers 23; Students 519.

21—ST. PATRICK'S (1870), Revs. Paul F. Leonard; Charles P. Connor; Philip A. Altavilla; Thomas Yuen.
Res., 1403 Jackson St., 18504. Tel: 717-344-2679; 343-4353; Fax: 717-343-2835.
School—122 S. Summer Ave., 18504. Tel: 717-343-8114.
Sisters of the I.H.M. 2; Lay Teachers 20; Students 531.
Missions—Scranton, Lackawanna Co., Holy Cross; Scranton, Lackawanna Co., St. John the Baptist.
Chapel—Scranton, Immaculate Heart of Mary.

22—ST. PAUL'S (1887), Rev. Msgr. Paul J. Purcell. In res., Rev. William B. Pickard.
Res., 1510 Penn Ave., 18509. Tel: 717-961-1549.
School—1527 Penn Ave., 18509. Tel: 717-343-7880; Fax: 717-343-0069.
Sisters of the I.H.M. 1; Lay Teachers 12; Students 250.

23—SS. PETER AND PAUL (1910) (Polish), Rev. Edward J. Shoback.
Res., 1309 W. Locust St., 18504. Tel: 717-343-7015; Fax: 717-343-7023. [CEM]

24—SACRED HEARTS OF JESUS AND MARY (1885) (Polish), Rev. Msgr. Leonard J. Novak, V.F. In res., Revs. Emil M. Hussack; Walter L. Ferrett.
Res., 1217 Prospect Ave., 18505. Tel: 717-343-6420. [CEM]

25—ST. STANISLAUS (1915) (Polish). Merged with Holy Rosary, Scranton.

26—ST. VINCENT DE PAUL (1925), Rev. Eugene L. Gunning.
Res., 1201 Providence Rd., 18508. Tel: 717-346-9739; Fax: 717-347-3250.

OUTSIDE THE CITY OF SCRANTON

Archbald, Lackawanna Co., St. Thomas Aquinas (1858), Revs. Gerard M. Gannon; Edward P. Lyman.
Res., 411 Church St., 18403. Tel: 717-876-1701. [CEM]

Ashley, Luzerne Co., Holy Rosary (1900) (Slovak), Rev. John F. Samson.
Res., 60 Charles St., 18706. Tel: 717-822-7543.
St. Leo's (1887), Very Rev. Thomas J. O'Malley, V.F.
Res., 33 Manhattan St., 18706. Tel: 717-825-6669; Fax: 717-823-3714.

Athens, Bradford Co., St. Joseph (1852), Rev. Vincent F. Lanagan.
Res., 85 Division St., South Waverly, 18840. Tel: 717-888-2123 (Home); 717-888-2129 (Office).

Avoca, Luzerne Co., St. Mary's (1871), Very Rev. Leo J. McKernan.
Res., 715 Hawthorne St., 18641. Tel: 717-655-8218; 457-3412. [CEM]
School—742 Spring St., 18641. Tel: 717-457-9700; 457-9600.
Lay Teachers 10; Students 160.
SS. Peter and Paul (1909) (Polish), Rev. Mark J. Bochinski.
Res., 912 Vine St., 18641. Tel: 717-457-2483; 457-9806. [CEM]

Bastress, Lycoming Co., Immaculate Conception (1838) (German), Rev. Robert T. Busteed.
Res., R.R. No. 3, Box 122, Williamsport, 17701. Tel: 717-745-3301. [CEM]
School—R.R. #3, P.O.Box 120, Williamsport, 17701. Tel: 717-745-3320.
Sisters of Christian Charity 3; Lay Teachers 6; Students 123.

Bear Creek Township, Luzerne Co., St. Christopher (1962). Merged with Holy Saviour, Wilkes-Barre.
Station—Valley Crest Home.
St. Elizabeth (1938), Rev. Anthony M. Urban.
Res., P.O. Box 25, 18602. Tel: 717-472-3061.
Mission—Thornhurst, Luzerne Co., St. Mark.

Bentley Creek, Bradford Co., St. Ann's (1843), Rev. Richard G. Ghezzi.
Res., R.R. No. 3, Box 138A, Gillett, 16925. Tel: 717-596-2109. [CEM]
Mission—Ridgebury, Bradford Co., Our Lady of Perpetual Help.

Blakeslee, Monroe Co., Christ the King (1976), Rev. Raymond L. Deviney.
Res., P.O. Box 171, 18610. Tel: 717-646-8990.

Blossburg, Tioga Co., St. Andrew's. Merged with St. Mary, Blossburg.
St. Mary's (1874) (Polish), Very Rev. Thomas P. Shoback, V.F.
Res., 138 St. Mary's St., 16912. Tel: 717-638-3241; Fax: 717-638-2952. [CEM]
Missions—Arnot, Tioga Co., St. Stanislaus Kostka; Morris Run, Tioga Co., St. Joseph; Blossburg, Tioga Co., St. Andrew, (1851).

Brodheadsville, Monroe Co., Our Lady Queen of Peace (1968), Rev. William J. McCawley.
Res., P.O. Box 38, 18322. Tel: 610-681-6139; Fax: 717-992-0448.

Bushkill, Pike Co., St. John (1986), Rev. Msgr. Kevin P. O'Neill.
Mailing Address: R.D. 6, Box 6932, East Stroudsburg, 18301. Tel: 717-223-9144.

Buttonwood, Luzerne Co., Exaltation of the Holy Cross (1917) (Polish), Rev. James E. McGahagan.
Res., 420 Main Rd., Buttonwood, Wilkes-Barre, 18702. Tel: 717-823-6242. [CEM]

Canadensis, Monroe Co., St. Bernadette (1967), Rev. Alfred J. Vito.
Res., P.O. Box 14, 18325. Tel: 717-595-2139; Fax: 717-595-6235.
Mission—Promised Land, Monroe Co., Our Lady of Fatima.

Canton, Bradford Co., St. Michael (1853), Rev. Bert S. Kozen; Deacon William H. Graham.
Res., 24 N. Washington St., 17724. Tel: 717-673-5253. [CEM]
Missions—Troy, Bradford Co., St. John Nepomucene. [CEM]
Ralston, Lycoming Co., St. Aloysius.

Carbondale, Lackawanna Co., Our Lady of Mt. Carmel (1882) (Italian), In res., Rev. Michael P. Litcheck.
Res., 15 Fallbrook St., 18407. Tel: 717-282-5172. [CEM]
School—29 Fairview St., 18407. Tel: 717-282-0340.
Lay Teachers 7; Students 169.
St. Rose of Lima (1830), Revs. William J. Feldcamp; Richard J. Cirba; James A. Rafferty.
Res., 6 N. Church St., 18407. Tel: 717-282-2991; Fax: 717-282-7580. [CEM]
School—86 Terrace St., 18407. Tel: 717-282-7930.
Priests 3; Sisters of the I.H.M. 9; Lay Teachers 8; Students 215.

Carverton, Luzerne Co., St. Frances Cabrini (1947), Rev. Joseph O. Weber.
Res., 585 Mt. Olivet Rd., Kingston Township, Tel: 717-696-3737.
Mission—Centermoreland, Luzerne Co., Blessed Sacrament.

Clarks Green, Lackawanna Co., St. Gregory (1974), Rev. Msgr. John H. Louis.
Res., 330 N. Abington Rd., 18411. Tel: 717-587-4808.

Clarks Summit, Lackawanna Co., Our Lady of the Snows (1911), Revs. James J. McGarry; John K. Schaal; Robert J. Simon. In res., Rev. Thomas J. Major.
Res., 301 S. State St., 18411. Tel: 717-586-1741; Fax: 717-586-2504.
Mission—Newton, Lackawanna Co., St. Benedict.

Conyngham, Luzerne Co., St. John Bosco (1964), Rev. John K. Manno.
Res., 2 Charles Ave. P.O. Box 919, 18219. Tel: 717-788-1997; Fax: 717-788-6667.
Parish Center—Tel: 717-788-9933.

Dallas, Luzerne Co., Gate of Heaven (1951), Revs. William F. Cusick; David P. Cappelloni; Deacon Thomas M. Cesarini.
Res., Machell Ave., 18612. Tel: 717-675-2121.

Dalton, Lackawanna Co., Our Lady of the Abingtons (1967), Very Rev. Joseph M. Boles, V.F.
Res., W. Main St., 18414. Tel: 717-563-1622.

Dickson City, Lackawanna Co., St. Thomas the Apostle. Merged with Visitation of the Blessed Virgin Mary (Polish), Dickson City.
Visitation of the Blessed Virgin Mary (1890) (Polish), Rev. Msgr. Stanley W. Piorkowski; Revs. Patrick L. Albert; Stefan Krawontka.
Res., St. Mary's Square, P.O. Box 9038, 18519. Tel: 717-489-2091. [CEM]
School—Tel: 717-489-0061.
Bernardine Sisters of St. Francis 4; Lay Teachers 7; Students 295.
Mission—Dickson City, Lackawanna Co., St. Thomas Apostle, (1889).

Dorrance, Luzerne Co., Our Lady Help of Christians (Polish), Rev. Robert N. Shilala.
Res., R.R. No. 1, Wapwallopen, 18660. Tel: 717-868-5855. [CEM]

Drums, Luzerne Co., Church of the Good Shepherd (1940), Very Rev. Michael J. Piccola, V.F.
Res., P.O. Box 430, 18222. Tel: 717-788-3141; Fax: 717-788-2953.

Dunmore, Lackawanna Co.,

1—ALL SAINTS, (1905) (Slovak), Very Rev. Edward R. Liptock, V.F.
Res., 324 Ward St., 18512. Tel: 717-342-6468. [CEM]

2—CHRIST THE KING, (1949), Rev. Msgr. John P. Gallagher, Ph.D.
Res., 1214 Quincy Ave., 18510. Tel: 717-343-2777.

3—ST. ANTHONY OF PADUA, (1894) (Italian), Rev. Msgr. Anthony C. Marra.
Res., 303 Smith St., 18512. Tel: 717-344-1209.
School—208 Smith St., 18512. Tel: 717-342-1182.
Sisters 2; Lay Teachers 9; Students 201.
Convent—215 Franklin St., 18512. Tel: 717-343-1422. Religious Teachers Filippini

4—ST. CASIMIR, (Polish). Merged with St. Mary of Mount Carmel, Dunmore.
5—ST. MARY OF MOUNT CARMEL, (1856), Revs. John A. Doris; Michael B. Harris.
Res., 322 Chestnut St., 18512. Tel: 717-346-7429; Fax: 717-346-0523. [CEM]
School—325 Chestnut St., 18512.
Sisters of the I.H.M. 2; Priests 1; Lay Teachers 14; Students 292.
Mission—Dunmore, Lackawanna Co., St. Casimir, (1929).
6—ST. ROCCO'S, (1905) (Italian), Rev. Anthony R. Tombasco.
Res., 118 Kurtz St., 18510. Tel: 717-344-1239.

Dupont, Luzerne Co., Sacred Heart of Jesus (1902) (Polish), Rev. Daniel D. Olszewski.
Res., 215 Lackawanna Ave., 18641. Tel: 717-654-3713. [CEM]
School—217 Lackawanna Ave., 18641. Tel: 717-654-8822.
Lay Teachers 11; Students 181.

Duryea, Luzerne Co., Holy Rosary (1893) (Polish), Rev. Charles W. Rokosz. In res., Rev. Francis P. Skitzki.
Res., 127 Stephenson St., 18642. Tel: 717-457-3502. [CEM]
School—110 1/2 Stephenson St., 18642. Tel: 717-457-2553.
Bernardine Sisters 1; Lay Teachers 10; Students 260.
Sacred Heart of Jesus (1889) (German), Rev. Richard J. Kvedrovicz.
Res., 529 Stephenson St., 18642. Tel: 717-457-2253.
Mission—Duryea, Luzerne Co., St. Joseph's, (1909).
St. Joseph's (1909) (Lithuanian). Merged with Sacred Heart of Jesus, Duryea. [CEM].

Dushore, Sullivan Co., St. Basil's (1838), Rev. Patrick J. McLaughlin.
Res., P.O. Box 307, 18614. Tel: 717-928-8865. [CEM]
Missions—Cummiskey, Sullivan Co., St. Francis of Assisi; Overton, Sullivan Co., St. Francis Xavier; Mildred, Sullivan Co., St. Francis of Assisi, (1894). [CEM]
Laporte, Sullivan Co., Sacred Heart; Eagles Mere, Sullivan Co., St. Francis of Assisi.
Shrine—Sugar Ridge, SS. Philip and James Church-St. John Neumann Shrine.

East Stroudsburg, Monroe Co., St. Matthew's (1902), Revs. John A. Bergamo; Thomas J. Sokolowski.
Res., 200 Brodhead Ave., 18301. Tel: 717-421-2342; Fax: 717-421-8414.

Edwardsville, Luzerne Co., SS. Cyril and Methodius (1900) (Slovak). Merged with St. Anthony's, Larksville.

Elkland, Tioga Co., St. Thomas the Apostle (1907), Rev. Gerard M. McGlone.
Res., 111 First St., 16920. Tel: 814-258-5121.
Mission—Westfield, Tioga Co., St. Catherine.

Elmhurst, Lackawanna Co., St. Eulalia (1950), Rev. Msgr. F. Allan Conlan, Ph.D.
Res., P.O. Box 143, 18416. Tel: 717-842-7656.

Exeter, Luzerne Co., St. Anthony of Padua (1928) (Italian), Revs. Silvio Chini, O.S.J.; Francis Siguan, O.S.J.
Res., 28 Memorial Ave., Exeter Boro, Pittston, 18643. Tel: 717-654-2103; Fax: 717-654-8621.
St. Cecilia (1900), Very Rev. Daniel D. Hitchko, V.F.
Res., 1700 Wyoming Ave., 18643. Tel: 717-654-2133; Fax: 717-654-3449. [CEM]
Convent—1690 Wyoming Ave., 18643. Tel: 717-655-8119.
St. John the Baptist (1898) (Polish), Rev. Daniel D. Hitchko, V.F.
Res., 121 Schooley Ave., Exeter Boro, Pittston, 18643. Tel: 717-655-3761. [CEM]

Eynon, Lackawanna Co., St. Mary's Czestochowa (1915) (Polish), Rev. Patrick J. Pratico.
Res., 417 Main St., 18403. Tel: 717-876-2223.
Mission—Eynon, Lackawanna Co., St. Mary of Vilna, (1901).
St. Mary of Vilna (Lithuanian). Merged with St. Mary's Czestochowa, Eynon.

Fairmount Springs, Luzerne Co., St. Martha's (1966). Merged with Our Lady of Mt. Carmel, Lake Silkworth.

Forest City, Susquehanna Co., Sacred Heart of Jesus (1904) (Polish), Rev. Joseph S. Sitko.
Res., 612 Hudson St., 18421. Tel: 717-785-3838.
Missions—Forest City, Susquehanna Co., St. Anthony; Forest City, Susquehanna Co., St. Michael; Forest City, Susquehanna Co., St. Agnes.
St. Joseph's (1904) (Slovenian), Rev. Casimir F. Sulicki.
Res., 741 Delaware St., 18421. Tel: 717-785-3694. [CEM]

Freeland, Luzerne Co.,

1—ST. ANN'S, (1862), Revs. Cyril D. Edwards; Gerard F. Safko; Deacon Cyril J. Kowalchick.
Office: 898 Center St., 18224. Tel: 717-636-3035. [CEM]
Res., 420 Vine St., 18224. Tel: 717-636-2192.
Missions—Freeland, Luzerne Co., St. Anthony's, (1901). [CEM]
Freeland, Luzerne Co., St. Casimir's, (1886). [CEM]
Freeland, Luzerne Co., St. John Nepomucene, (1892). [CEM]
2—ST. ANTHONY'S. Merged with St. Ann's, Freeland.
3—ST. CASIMIR'S. Merged with St. Ann's, Freeland.
4—ST. JOHN NEPOMUCENE. Merged with St. Ann's, Freeland.

Friendsville Susquehanna Co., St. Francis Xavier's (1831), Rev. William J.P. Langan.
Res., 18818. Tel: 717-553-2288. [CEM 3]
Missions—Middletown, Susquehanna Co., St. Patrick; Little Meadows, Susquehanna Co., St. Thomas the Apostle, (1887).
St. Joseph's (1829), Rev. Josepha J. Manarchuck.
Res., Quinn Rd., R.R. #1, Box 1402, 18818. Tel: 717-553-2300. [CEM 2][JC]
Mission—Silver Lake, Susquehanna Co., St. Augustine.

Glen Lyon, Luzerne Co., St. Adalbert's (1889) (Polish), Rev. Edward M. Masakowski.
Res., 31 S. Market St., 18617. Tel: 717-736-6372. [CEM]
Missions—Glen Lyon, Luzerne Co., St. Denis; Glen Lyon, Luzerne Co., St. Michael's, (1909). [CEM]
St. Michael's. Merged with St. Adalbert's, Glen Lyon.

Gouldsboro, Wayne Co., St. Rita (1975), Rev. Martin M. Boylan, Ph.D., Admin.
Res., P.O. Box 537, 18424. Tel: 717-842-4995; Fax: 717-842-5413.
Missions—South Sterling, Wayne Co., St. Mary Magdalene; Newfoundland, Wayne Co., St. Anthony of Padua.

Great Bend, Susquehanna Co., St. Lawrence's (1872), Rev. John J. Kulavich.
Res., 506 Franklin St., 18821. Tel: 717-879-2392. [CEM]
Mission—New Milford, Susquehanna Co., St. John. [CEM]

Harding, Luzerne Co., Church of the Holy Redeemer (1952), Rev. Thomas E. McCann.
Res., R.D. 1, Pittston, 18643. Tel: 717-388-6300.

Harleigh, Luzerne Co., Sacred Heart of Jesus (1903), Very Rev. Girard F. Angelo, V.F.
Res., 1 Church Pl., 18225. Tel: 717-455-1162.
Shrines—National Shrine of the Sacred Heart, (1975).; Men of the Sacred Heart, National Office, (1977), Tel: 717-455-1162.

Harveys Lake, Luzerne Co., Our Lady of Victory (1969), Rev. Louis A. Grippe; Deacon William A. Dervinis.
Res., R.D. #1, Box 309, 18618. Tel: 717-639-1535; Fax: 717-639-1294.

Hawley, Wayne Co., Blessed Virgin Mary, Queen of Peace (1852), Rev. William B. Healey; Deacon Frank Kujawa.
Res., 314 Chestnut Ave., 18428. Tel: 717-226-3183; Fax: 717-226-2126. [CEM]
Mission—Lake Wallenpaupack, Wayne Co., St. Veronica.

Hazleton, Luzerne Co.,

1—ST. GABRIEL'S, (1855), Revs. Michael J. Delaney; John C. O'Bell; Sr. Dora Maria Vizcarra, I.H.M., Pastoral Assoc.
Res., 122 S. Wyoming St., 18201. Tel: 717-454-0212; Fax: 717-459-5187. [CEM]
2—CHURCH OF THE MOST PRECIOUS BLOOD, (1885) (Italian), Revs. Maurice L. Raymond; James J. Alco. In res., Rev. Austin E. Flanagan.
Res., 131 E. Fourth St., 18201. Tel: 717-454-8714; Fax: 717-454-8754.
3—HOLY ROSARY, (1916) (Italian), Rev. Patrick J. Genello.
Res., 240 S. Poplar St., 18201. Tel: 717-454-6693.
4—HOLY TRINITY, (1887) (German), Rev. David L. Tressler, Admin. In res., Rev. Joseph J. Ferrara.
Res., 123 W. Oak St., 18201. Tel: 717-454-5394. [CEM]
School—35 N. Church St., 18201. Tel: 717-455-9645.
Sisters of Christian Charity 2; Lay Teachers 10; Students 213.
Mission—Hazleton, Luzerne Co., Our Lady of Mount Carmel, (1905).
5—HOLY TRINITY, (1907) (Slovak), Rev. Leonard M. Butcavage; Deacon Louis Smolinsky.
Res., 178 N. Wyoming St., 18201. Tel: 717-454-3233; Fax: 717-454-0237. [CEM]
6—ST. JOSEPH'S, (1882) (Slovak), Rev. Msgr. Francis J. Beeda; Rev. Andrew S. Hvozdovic; Deacon Leonard G. Kassick.
Res., 604 N. Laurel St., 18201. Tel: 717-454-0881; Fax: 717-454-1285. [CEM]
School—600 N. Laurel St., 18201. Tel: 717-454-4411.
Sisters of SS. Cyril and Methodius 5; Lay Teachers 7; Students 195.
Mission—Hazleton, Luzerne Co., St. Ladislaus.
7—OUR LADY OF GRACE, (1910) (Italian), Rev. Neil O. Gugliemelli.
Res., 750 N. Vine St., 18201. Tel: 717-454-8797. [CEM]
8—OUR LADY OF MOUNT CARMEL, (1905) (Tyrolese). Merged with Holy Trinity (German), Hazleton.
9—SS. PETER AND PAUL, (1887) (Lithuanian). Merged with Transfiguration, West Hazleton.
10—ST. STANISLAUS, (1893) (Polish), Rev. Louis S. Garbacik.
Res., 652 Carson St., 18201. Tel: 717-454-0662. [CEM]

Honesdale, Wayne Co., St. John the Evangelist (1842), Revs. Kevin P. Mulhern; Wieslaw Ziebacz; Sr. Mary Rose Mitchell, Pastoral Min.; Deacon Mark S. Jennings.
Res., 150 Terrace St., 18431. Tel: 717-253-4561; Fax: 717-253-1058. [CEM 3]
Mission—Rileyville, Wayne Co., St. Joseph.
Chapel—Honesdale, St. Mary Magdalene, (1853).

Hudson, Luzerne Co., St. Joseph's (1889) (Polish), Rev. Victor C. Zawadzki.
Res., 25 Oak St., N.E. Station, Wilkes-Barre, 18705. Tel: 717-823-0238; Fax: 717-822-0394. [CEM]

Hughestown, Luzerne Co., Blessed Sacrament (1945), Rev. Joseph D. Verespy.
Res., 65 Rock St., P.O. Pittston, 18640. Tel: 717-654-6553.

Inkerman, Luzerne Co., St. Mark's (1900), Rev. Albert J. Augustyn.
Res., 1 St. Mark Ln., 18640. Tel: 717-654-0033.

Jackson, Susquehanna Co., St. Martin of Tours (1940), Very Rev. Thomas A. Cappelloni, V.F.
Res., P.O. Box 20, 18825. Tel: 717-756-2541; Fax: 717-756-2105.
Mission—Starrucca, Wayne Co., St. Paul.

Jermyn, Lackawanna Co., Sacred Heart of Mary (1889), Rev. James J. Walsh.
Res., 624 Madison Ave., 18433. Tel: 717-876-1061. [CEM]

Jersey Shore, Lycoming Co., St. Luke's (1902), Rev. John C. Lambert.
Res., 118 Kendall Ave., 17740. Tel: 717-398-2557.

Jessup, Lackawanna Co., St. Mary's Assumption (1904) (Italian), Rev. Andrew R. Gallia.
Res., 516 Third Ave., 18434. Tel: 717-489-4726. [CEM]
St. James. Merged with St. Michael's (Slovak), Jessup.
St. Michael's (1911) (Slovak), Rev. William B. Blake. In res., Rev. Joseph A. Matz; Deacon John Hatala.
Res., 605 Church St., 18434. Tel: 717-489-2252. [CEM]
Missions—Jessup, Lackawanna Co., St. Michael, (1896); Jessup, Lackawanna Co., St. Stanislaus.

Kingston, Luzerne Co., St. Hedwig's (1901) (Polish), Rev. Richard A. Zavacki.
Res., 207 Zerbey Ave., 18704. Tel: 717-287-5634; Fax: 717-287-8566. [CEM]
School—16 Pulaski St., 18704. Tel: 717-288-6051; Fax: 717-287-8566.
Lay Teachers 8; Students 132.
St. Ignatius (1885), Rev. Msgr. Neil J. VanLoon, V.F.; Revs. Glenn E. McCreary; David W. Cramer. In res., Rev. Robert J. Gibson.
Res., 339 N. Maple Ave., 18704. Tel: 717-288-6446. [CEM]
Chapel—St. Ann's, Tel: 717-288-5919.
St. Mary's Annunciation (1902) (Lithuanian), Rev. Joseph J. Lasky.
Res., 258 Zerbey Ave., 18704. Tel: 717-287-5096.

Laflin, Luzerne Co., St. Maria Goretti (1967), Very Rev. James J. Paisley.
Res., 42 Redwood Dr., 18702. Tel: 717-655-8956; Fax: 717-655-1746.

Lake Ariel, Wayne Co., St. Thomas More (1941), Very Rev. Edward R. Scott, V.F.
Mailing Address: Box 188, 18436. Tel: 717-698-5584; Fax: 717-698-8468. [CEM]
Mission—Ledgedale, Wayne Co., St. Mary.

Lake Silkworth, Luzerne Co., Our Lady of Mount Carmel (1923), Rev. Thomas R. Hudak; Deacon Frank J. Sehn.
Res., R.R. 2, Box 265, Lake Silkworth, Hunlock Creek, 18621. Tel: 717-477-5040. [CEM]
Mission—Fairmount Springs, Luzerne Co., St. Martha's, (1966).

Lake Winola, Wyoming Co., St. Mary of the Lake (1986), Rev. Louis T. Kaminski; Deacon Raymond A. Pieretti.
Res., P.O. Box 1, Fairview Rd., 18625. Tel: 717-378-2181.

Larksville, Luzerne Co., St. Anthony of Padua (1908) (Slovak), Rev. Bernard P. Evanofski.
Res., 1 Wilson St., 18704. Tel: 717-287-4018. [CEM]
Mission—Edwardsville, Luzerne Co., SS. Cyril and Methodius, (1900). [CEM]

Lattimer Mines, Luzerne Co., St. Mary's (1903) (Italian). Merged with St. Nazarius, Pardeesville.

Little Meadows, Susquehanna Co., St. Thomas the Apostle (1887). Merged with St. Francis Xavier, Friendsville.

Lords Valley, Pike Co., St. John Neumann (1976), Rev. Charles J. Cummings, Admin.; Deacon John Nash.
Res., Lords Valley, HC8, Box 8390, Hawley, 18428.
Mission—Blooming Grove, Good Shepherd.

Luzerne, Luzerne Co., Sacred Heart (1893) (German), Rev. Robert P. Arnold.
Res., 469 Miller St., P.O. Box 125, 18709. Tel: 717-287-6600.
School—545 Charles St., 18709. Tel: 717-287-3431. Sisters of Christian Charity 2; Lay Teachers 6; Students 144.
St. Ann's (1924) (Lithuanian). Merged with Sacred Heart, Luzerne.
St. John Nepomucene (1907) (Slovak). Merged with Sacred Heart, Luzerne.

Mansfield, Tioga Co., Holy Child (1953), Rev. Joseph P. Rafferty.
Res., 237 S. Main St., 16933. Tel: 717-662-3568.
Mission—Tioga, Tioga Co., St. Mary.

Matamoras, Pike Co., St. Joseph's (1892), Rev. John J. Turi.
Res., 309 Ave. F, 18336. Tel: 717-491-2618.
Mission—Mill Rift, Pike Co., Holy Family.

Mayfield, Lackawanna Co., Sacred Heart of Jesus (1904) (Polish), Rev. Joseph C. Rusin.
Res., 420 Hudson St., 18433. Tel: 717-876-1950. [CEM]

Meshoppen, Wyoming Co., St. Joachim's (1873), Rev. Patrick D. McDowell.
Res., P.O. Box 67, 18630. Tel: 717-833-2114; Fax: 717-833-2115. [CEM]
Mission—Auburn, Susquehanna Co., St. Bonaventure. [CEM]

Mildred, Sullivan Co., St. Francis of Assisi (1894). Merged with St. Basil, Dushore.
Missions—Eagles Mere, Sullivan Co., St. Francis of Assisi; Laporte, Sullivan Co., Sacred Heart.

Milford, Pike Co., St. Patrick's (1946), Rev. Gerald F. Mullally.
Res., 415 Fourth St., P.O. Box W, 18337. Tel: 717-296-7451.
St. Vincent de Paul (1976), Rev. Msgr. William P. Ward; Deacon Albert W. Perreault.
Res., R.R. 3, Box 240, 18337. Tel: 717-686-4545.

Mocanaqua, Luzerne Co., St. Mary, Our Lady of Perpetual Help (1904) (Polish), Rev. Carl T. Prushinski.
Res., 150 Main St., 18655. Tel: 717-542-4157. [CEM]
Mission—Mocanaqua, Luzerne Co., Ascension.

Montdale, Lackawanna Co., Corpus Christi (1942), Rev. William J. Flynn, S.S.
Res., R.R. 1, Box 389, Olyphant, 18447. Tel: 717-254-9502.

Montoursville, Lycoming Co., Our Lady of Lourdes (1942), Rev. Stephen D. McGough.
Res., 800 Mulberry St., 17754. Tel: 717-368-8598.

Montrose, Susquehanna Co., Holy Name of Mary (1898), Rev. James R. Nash.
Res., 60 S. Main St., 18801. Tel: 717-278-1504. [CEM]

Moscow, Lackawanna Co., St. Catherine of Siena (1861), Rev. Michael E. Finn; Deacons John J. Franceschelli; Frank A. Earley. In res., Rev. Scott P. Sterowski.
Res., Church St., 18444. Tel: 717-842-4561.

Mount Pocono, Monroe Co., St. Mary of the Mount (1909), Rev. Msgr. Arthur J. Kaschenbach.
Res., 27 Fairview Ave., 18344. Tel: 717-839-7138.
Mission—Pocono Summit, Monroe Co., St. Joan of Arc.

Mountaintop, Luzerne Co., St. Jude's (1953), Revs. Paul M. Mullen; Joseph J. Evanko; Deacon James E. Bogdan.
Res., 422 S. Mountain Blvd., 18707. Tel: 717-474-6315.
School—Sisters 1; Lay Teachers 19; Students 371.
Missions—Solomon's Gap, Luzerne Co., St. Catherine; Nuangola, Luzerne Co., St. Ann.

Muncy, Lycoming Co., Resurrection (1941), Rev. Phillip J. Sladicka.
Res., 526 S. Main St., 17756. Tel: 717-546-3900.

Nanticoke, Luzerne Co.,

1—Holy Child, (1942) (Polish). Merged with Holy Trinity (Polish), Nanticoke.

2—Holy Trinity, (1894) (Polish), Revs. Bernard A. Toloczko; Joseph J. Kutch.
Res., 520 S. Hanover St., 18634. Tel: 717-735-4833; Fax: 717-735-2281. [CEM]
Mission—Nanticoke, Luzerne Co., Holy Child, (1942).

3—St. Francis of Assisi, (1872), Very Rev. Santino J. Fanucci, V.F.
Res., 173 E. Green St., 18634. Tel: 717-735-6903; 735-7011.

4—St. Joseph's, (1888) (Slovak), Rev. Leo M. Gardzalla.
Res., 107 E. Noble St., 18634. Tel: 717-735-0331. [CEM]

5—St. Mary of Czestochowa, (1901) (Polish), Rev. John S. Krafchak.
Res., 1030 S. Hanover St., 18634. Tel: 717-735-6911. [CEM]

6—St. Stanislaus, (1875) (Polish), Rev. Joseph R. Kakareka.
Res., 38 W. Church St., 18634. Tel: 717-735-0313. [CEM]

Nicholson, Wyoming Co., St. Patrick's (1888), Rev. John V. Polednak.
Res., Main and High Sts., 18446. Tel: 717-942-6602. [CEM]

Old Forge, Lackawanna Co.,

1—St. Lawrence O'Toole, (1895), Rev. Michael J. Kirwin; Deacon Carmine Mendicino.
Res., 620 S. Main St., 18518. Tel: 717-457-2032.

2—St. Mary's, (1897) (Italian), Very Rev. Joseph F. Cipriano, V.F.; Rev. Stanley J. Kurash.
Res., 123 W. Grace St., 18518. Tel: 717-457-5900.
School—216 W. Grace St., 18518.
Daughters of Our Lady of Mercy 2; Lay Teachers 10; Students 190.

3—St. Michael's, (1905) (Polish), Rev. Joseph M. Brozena.
Res., 236 Vine St., 18518. Tel: 717-457-3353.

4—St. Stanislaus, (1903) (Polish), Rev. Cyril J. Rable.
Res., 1267 Franklin St., 18518. Tel: 717-457-5103. [CEM]

Olyphant, Lackawanna Co., Holy Ghost (1888) (Slovak), Rev. John S. Marinko.
Res., 120 Willow Ave., 18447. Tel: 717-489-2023. [CEM]
Convent—126 Willow Ave., 18447. Tel: 717-489-0792. Sisters of SS. Cyril and Methodius
St. Michael the Archangel (1909) (Polish), Rev. Kenneth G. Kizis.
Res., 132 Lincoln St., 18447. Tel: 717-489-0623. [CEM]
St. Patrick's (1875), Rev. John J. Kelley.
Res., 200 Delaware Ave., 18447. Tel: 717-489-0752. [CEM]

Pardeesville, Luzerne Co., St. Nazarius (1966) (Italian), Rev. Joseph W. Bucolo.
Res., R.D. 2, P3D3, Hazleton, 18201. Tel: 717-454-2469.
Mission—Lattimer Mines, Luzerne Co., St. Mary, (1903). Tel: 717-454-4975.

Peckville, Lackawanna Co., Sacred Heart of Jesus (1946), Rev. William F. Purcell.
Res., 1101 Willow St., 18452. Tel: 717-383-3244.

Pittston, Luzerne Co.,

1—Our Lady of Mt. Carmel, (1904) (Italian), Revs. Paul J. Pavese, O.S.J.; Paul A. McDonnell, O.S.J.
Res., 237 William St., 18640. Tel: 717-654-6902.

2—St. Casimir's, (1890) (Lithuanian). Merged with St. John the Evangelist, Pittston.

3—St. John the Baptist, (1892) (Slovak), Rev. Andrew F. Strish; Rev. Msgr. Joseph J. Super, (Pastor Emeritus).
Res., 16 William St., 18640. Tel: 717-654-2112; Fax: 717-654-4210. [CEM 2]
School—12 William St., 18640. Tel: 717-654-0845. Robert Kaluzavich, Prin.
Lay Teachers 9; Students 241.

4—St. John the Evangelist, (1854), Rev. Msgr. John J. Bendik; Rev. Frank S. Homets. In res., Rev. Hugh H. McGroarty.
Res., 35 William St., 18640. Tel: 717-654-0053; Fax: 717-654-3751. [CEM]

5—St. Joseph's, (1909) (Polish). Merged with St. John the Evangelist, Pittston.

6—St. Mary, Help of Christians, (1853), Rev. Richard J. Polmounter; Deacons Joseph J. Gowarty; Leo R. Thompson.
Res., 535 N. Main St., 18640. Tel: 717-654-0263. [CEM]
Mission—Pittston, Luzerne Co., St. Mary of the Assumption, (1863).

7—St. Mary's Assumption, (1863) (German). Merged with St. Mary, Help of Christians, Pittston.
School—41 Carroll St., 18640. Tel: 717-654-8313; Fax: 717-654-8320.
Sisters of Christian Charity 2; Lay Teachers 8; Students 263.

8—St. Rocco, (1919) (Italian), Revs. Raymond Tabon, O.S.J.; Nicholas J. Dininni, O.S.J.
Res., 62 W. Oak St., 18640. Tel: 717-654-2914. [CEM]

Plains, Luzerne Co., Sacred Heart (1883), Rev. Robert E. Burnett.
Res., 115 N. Main St., 18705. Tel: 717-823-3830. [CEM]
SS. Peter and Paul (1898) (Polish), Rev. Joseph A. Greskiewicz. In res., Rev. Michael J. Kloton.
Res., 13 Hudson Rd., 18705. Tel: 717-825-6663; Fax: 717-823-4556. [CEM]
School—12 Hudson St., 18705. Tel: 717-824-9433. Bernardine Sisters of St. Francis 2; Lay Teachers 8; Students 189.

Pleasant Mount, Wayne Co., St. James (1887), Rev. Richard W. Beck.
Res., P.O. Box 53, 18453. Tel: 717-448-2211.
Missions—Hill Top, Wayne Co., St. Cecilia; Lake Como, Wayne Co., Assumption of the B.V.M.; Rock Lake, Wayne Co., St. Juliana's.

Plymouth, Luzerne Co.,

1—Nativity of the Blessed Virgin Mary, (1885) (Polish), Rev. Msgr. Vincent J. Grimalia; Rev. Samuel T. Perrins.
Res., 66 Willow St., 18651. Tel: 717-779-5324; Fax: 717-779-4921. [CEM 2]

2—St. John the Baptist, (1899) (Polish), Rev. Msgr. John C. Masakowski.
Res., 126 Nesbitt St., 18651. Tel: 717-779-9620. [CEM]

3—St. Stephen's, (1886) (Slovak), Very Rev. John L. Fabian, V.F.
Res., 24 Wadhams St., 18651. Tel: 717-779-9610. [CEM]

4—St. Vincent de Paul, (1872), Rev. Joseph F. Houston. In res., Rev. James J. Jacobs; Deacon Peter G. Smith.
Res., 101 Church St., 18651. Tel: 717-779-9508; Fax: 717-779-2332. [CEM]

Pocono Pines, Monroe Co., Our Lady of the Lake (1985), Rev. Thomas J. Maloney.
Res., P.O. Box 0, 18350. Tel: 717-646-6424; Fax: 717-646-1047.

Rock Lake, Wayne Co., St. Juliana's (1838). Merged with St. James, Pleasant Mount.
R.R. 1, Box 117, Pleasant Mount, 18453. Tel: 717-448-2624.

Royal, Susquehanna Co., St. Pius X (1967), Very Rev. Peter V. Herhenreader, V.F.
Res., Box 64, Clifford, 18413. Tel: 717-222-4209.

Sayre, Bradford Co., Church of the Epiphany (1888), Revs. William J. Karle; Glenn E. McCreary.
Res., 304 S. Elmer Ave., 18840. Tel: 717-888-9641.
School—627 Stevenson St., 18840. Tel: 717-888-5802.
Sisters of I.H.M. 2; Lay Teachers 10; Students 213.

Shavertown, Luzerne Co., St. Therese (1926), Revs. J. Peter Crynes; Kenneth M. Seegar.
Res., 64 Davis St., 18708. Tel: 717-696-1144; Fax: 717-696-1210.

Shohola, Pike Co., St. Ann's (1928), Rev. Donald J. Williams.
Res., P.O. Box 86, 18458. Tel: 717-559-7642. [CEM]
Missions—Lackawaxen, Pike Co., St. Mary; Greeley, Pike Co., Sacred Heart.

Simpson, Lackawanna Co., St. Michael's (1903), Rev. Hilary L. Malinowski.
Res., 46 Midland St., 18407. Tel: 717-282-2161. [CEM]
Mission—Simpson, Lackawanna Co., Holy Trinity.

South Waverly, Bradford Co., St. John the Evangelist (1902), Rev. Vincent F. Langan.
Res., 85 Division St., 18840. Tel: 717-888-2123.

South Williamsport, Lycoming Co., St. Lawrence's (1931), Rev. Francis L. Pauselli; Deacon J. Morris Smith.
Res., 344 Winthrop St., 17701. Tel: 717-322-0403; Fax: 717-322-4335.

Stroudsburg, Monroe Co., St. Luke's (1968), Revs. Thomas D. McLaughlin; Carmen J. Perry.
Office: 818 Main St., 18360. Tel: 717-421-9097; 421-9863; Fax: 717-421-6015.
Res., 906 Main St., 18360. Tel: 717-421-8460.

Sugar Notch, Luzerne Co., Holy Family (1901) (Polish), Rev. John S. Terry.
Office: 828 Main St., 18706. Tel: 717-822-8983. [CEM]
Mission—Sugar Notch, Luzerne Co., St. Charles Borromeo.
SS. Peter and Paul (1847) (Lithuanian). Merged with Holy Family, Sugar Notch.

Susquehanna, Susquehanna Co., St. John the Evangelist (1847), Rev. Michael J. Pulicare.
Res., 101 Jackson Ave., 18847. Tel: 717-853-4634.

[CEM]

Swoyersville, Luzerne Co., Holy Name of Jesus (1905). Merged with St. Mary of Czestochowa, Swoyersville.

Holy Trinity (1895) (Slovak), Rev. Michael J. Zipay.
Res., 116 Hughes St. (P.O. Kingston), 18704. Tel: 717-287-6624. [CEM]

St. Mary of Czestochowa (1909) (Polish), Rev. John J. Sempa. In res., Rev. Joseph T. Gilbert; Deacon Peter J. Hoegen; Sr. Ellen Maroney, I.H.M., Pastoral Assoc.
Res., 283 Shoemaker St. (P.O. Kingston), 18704. Tel: 717-287-2139; Fax: 717-287-6474. [CEM]

Tannersville, Monroe Co., Our Lady of Victory (1968), Rev. Henry E. Zapotocki.
Res., Rt. 611, 18372. Tel: 717-629-4572; Fax: 717-629-0335.

Taylor, Lackawanna Co., Immaculate Conception (1898), Rev. Joseph D. Flannery.
Res., 202 Church St., 18517. Tel: 717-562-2390.

St. John the Baptist (1904) (Slovak), Rev. Joseph J. Mattey.
Res., 408 N. Main St., 18517. Tel: 717-562-1341. [CEM]

Throop, Lackawanna Co., St. Anthony's (1911) (Polish). Merged with St. John the Baptist, Throop. Rev. August A. Ricciardi.
Office: 215 Rebecca St., 18519. Tel: 717-489-1963. [CEM]
Res., 520 Charles St., 18512. Tel: 717-489-1682.

St. Bridget's (1916). Merged with St. John the Baptist & St. Anthony's, Throop. Rev. August A. Ricciardi.
Office: 520 Sanderson St., 18512. Tel: 717-489-1682.
Res., 520 Charles St., 18512.

St. John the Baptist (1905) (Slovak). Merged with St. Anthony's, Throop. Rev. August A. Ricciardi.
Office: 520 Sanderson St., 18512. Tel: 717-489-1822. [CEM]
Res., 520 Charles St., 18512. Tel: 717-489-1682.
Missions—Throop, Lackawanna Co., St. Bridget; St. Mary.

Tobyhanna, Monroe Co., St. Ann (1923), Very Rev. John B. Boyle, V.F.
Res., Main St., 18466. Tel: 717-894-8018; Fax: 717-894-9619. [CEM 2]

Towanda, Bradford Co., SS. Peter and Paul (1841), Very Rev. Ronald J. Hughes.
Res., 106 Third St., 18848. Tel: 717-265-2113; Fax: 717-265-2114. [CEM 3]
School—St. Agnes, 102 Third St., 18848. Tel: 717-265-6803; Fax: 717-265-2114.
Lay Teachers 12; Students 255.
Mission—Ulster, Bradford Co., Immaculate Conception.

Tunkhannock, Wyoming Co., Nativity of Blessed Virgin Mary (1884), Rev. Joseph F. Sica.
Res., 99 E. Tioga St., 18657. Tel: 717-836-3275. [CEM 3]

Wanamie, Luzerne Co., St. Mary's (1906) (Lithuanian), Rev. Gerald J. Gurka.
Res., 203 Bellas Rd., Wanamie, Nanticoke, 18634. Tel: 717-735-2153. [CEM]
Mission—Nanticoke, Luzerne Co., St. Joseph.

Waymart, Wayne Co., St. Mary's (1915), Rev. John T. Albosta.
Res., 242 Carbondale Rd., P.O. Box 160, 18472. Tel: 717-488-6440. [CEM]
Mission—Canaan, Wayne Co., St. Patrick.
Station—Wayne Co., Farview State Prison.

Wellsboro, Tioga Co., St. Peter's (1879), Rev. Michael J. Sullivan; Deacon Robert A. Scheib.
Res., 38 Central Ave., 16901. Tel: 717-724-3371; Fax: 717-724-6322. [CEM]
Mission—Morris, Tioga Co., Sacred Heart.

West Hazleton, Luzerne Co., St. Francis of Assisi (1940), Rev. Connell A. McHugh.
Res., 544 N. Broad St., 18201. Tel: 717-454-3072.
Mission—Harwood, Luzerne Co., St. Michael.

Transfiguration (1907) (Polish), Rev. Richard E. Czachor.
Res., 213 W. Green St., 18201. Tel: 717-454-3933; Fax: 717-454-8326. [CEM]
School—217 W. Green St., 18201. Tel: 717-454-6131.
Bernardine Sisters of St. Francis 1; Lay Teachers 9; Students 179.
Mission—Hazleton, Luzerne Co., SS. Peter and Paul.

Weston, Luzerne Co., Sacred Heart (1888), Rev. Joseph P. Bonner.
Res., 18256. Tel: 717-384-4121. [CEM]
Mission—Nuremberg, Luzerne Co., St. Joseph.

West Pittston, Luzerne Co., Immaculate Conception (1910), Rev. Joseph J. Adonizio.
Res., 605 Luzerne Ave., 18643. Tel: 717-654-2753; Fax: 717-654-9244.

West Wyoming, Luzerne Co., Our Lady of Sorrows (1953), Rev. Michael J. Rafferty.
Res., 363 W. 8th St., 18644. Tel: 717-693-1991.

White Haven, Luzerne Co., St. Patrick's (1874), Rev. Salvatore A. Bentivegna, O.S.J.
Res., 530 Elmira St., 18661. Tel: 717-443-9944. [CEM]
Station—White Haven Center, Tel: 717-453-9564.

White Mills, Wayne Co., St. Joseph's (1968), Rev. Michael H. Marchetti.
Mailing Address: Box 153, 18473. Tel: 717-253-0307.
Mission—Beach Lake, Wayne Co., St. Bernard, Tel: 717-729-7247.

Wilkes-Barre, Luzerne Co.,

1—St. Aloysius, (1898), Rev. Msgr. Donald A. McAndrews; Revs. Thomas D. Skotek; Paul A. Miller.
Res., 143 W. Division St., 18702. Tel: 717-823-3791; Fax: 717-826-0233.
School—321 Barney St., 18702. Tel: 717-824-6131.
Lay Teachers 17; Students 260.

2—Blessed Sacrament, (1917), Rev. Joseph A. Kearney; Deacon James P. Feerick.
Res., 213 E. Main St., 18705. Tel: 717-822-9561.
Missions—Wilkes-Barre, Luzerne Co., St. Francis of Assisi; Wilkes-Barre, Luzerne Co., St. John The Baptist
Station—Wilkes-Barre, Geisinger Wyoming Valley Hospital, Tel: 717-826-7300.

3—St. Boniface, (1896) (German), Rev. T. Timothy Delaney; Deacon Francis J. Bradigan.
Res., 225 Blackman St., 18702. Tel: 717-822-8330.

4—St. Casimir's, (1889) (Lithuanian), Revs. James F. Boyle, C.S.C.; Joseph F. Callahan, C.S.C. In res., Rev. James B. Mannis, C.S.C.
Res., 301 Delaney St., Lyndwood, Wilkes-Barre, 18702. Tel: 717-825-2598. [CEM]

5—St. Dominic, (1882), Rev. William R. Culnane.
Res., 155 Austin Ave., 18705. Tel: 717-822-8871.

6—St. Francis of Assisi, (1913) (Lithuanian). Merged with Blessed Sacrament, Wilkes-Barre.

7—Holy Rosary, (1906) (Italian), Rev. Peter D. Menghini.
Res., 363 Park Ave., 18702. Tel: 717-822-1183.

8—Holy Saviour, (1895), Revs. E. Francis Kelly; Robert M. Timchak; Deacon Carl J. Orbon.
Res., 54 Hillard St., 18702. Tel: 717-822-1186; Fax: 717-822-1074.
Mission—Bear Creek Township, Luzerne Co., St. Christopher.
Station—Wilkes-Barre, Valley Crest Home.

9—Holy Trinity, (1893) (Lithuanian), Rev. Theodore L. Obaza.
Res., 416 E. South St., 18702. Tel: 717-823-1081. [CEM 2]

10—St. John the Evangelist, (1927). Merged with Sacred Heart of Jesus, Wilkes-Barre.

11—St. John the Baptist, (1924) (Slovak). Merged with Blessed Sacrament, Wilkes-Barre.

12—St. Joseph, (Georgetown) (1898), Revs. Raymond J. Lynch, O.F.M.; Alvin Black, O.F.M. In res., Rev. Benjamin J. Foerch, O.F.M.
Res., St. Joseph's Friary, 783 E. Northampton St., 18702. Tel: 717-822-8023; Fax: 717-822-2891.

13—St. Joseph's, (1927) (Slovak). Merged with St. Mary's Church of the Immaculate Conception, Wilkes-Barre.

14—St. Mary's Church of the Immaculate Conception, (1845), Rev. Msgr. Thomas V. Banick; Rev. Vincent Dang.
Res., P.O. Box 348, 134 S. Washington St., 18703. Tel: 717-823-4168. [CEM]
Mission—Wilkes-Barre, Luzerne Co., St. Joseph.

15—Maternity of the Blessed Virgin Mary, (1885) (Polish) Rev. Msgr. Alexander T. Kulik; Rev. Mark G. Balczeniuk.
Res., 40 Park Ave., 18702. Tel: 717-824-7832. [CEM 2]

16—St. Nicholas, (1856) (German), Rev. Msgr. Joseph G. Rauscher; Rev. John J. Chmil.
Res., 226 S. Washington St., 18701-2897. Tel: 717-823-7736; 823-5842; Fax: 717-823-0256. [CEM]

17—St. Patrick's, (1920), Rev. J. Duane Gavitt; Deacon Florian J. Gyza.
Res., 316 Parrish St., 18702. Tel: 717-823-1948.

18—Sacred Heart of Jesus, (1896) (Slovak), Very Rev. Joseph M. Ziobro, V.F.; Rev. Daniel J. Doherty; Deacon Joseph F. DeVizia.
Res., 601 N. Main St., 18705. Tel: 717-823-4988; Fax: 717-823-5932. [CEM]
School—607 N. Main St., 18705. Tel: 717-824-0818.
Sisters of SS. Cyril and Methodius 3; Lay Teachers 13; Students 315.
Mission—Wilkes-Barre, Luzerne Co., St. John the Evangelist.

19—St. Stanislaus Kostka, (1908) (Polish), Rev. Joseph M. Horanzy.
Res., 666 N. Main St., 18705. Tel: 717-822-8026. [CEM]

20—St. Therese's, (1929), Rev. Msgr. Francis J. Callahan, V.F. In res., Rev. George A. Jeffrey.
Res., 25 Old River Rd., 18702. Tel: 717-822-1075; 824-3052; Fax: 717-829-4147.

Williamsport, Lycoming Co.,

1—Annunciation, (1865), Rev. Msgr. William J. Fleming; Rev. Joseph Elston.
Res., 410 Walnut St., 17701. Tel: 717-323-9456; 693-0289. [CEM]
School—711 W. Edwin St., 17701. Tel: 717-322-6036, 322-2754.
Sisters of I.H.M. 4; Lay Teachers 6; Students 160.

2—Ascension, (1907), Rev. Joseph B. Wilson, Ph.D., Admin.
Office: 2100 Linn St., 17701. Tel: 717-326-4922.
Res., 2111 Linn St., 17701. Tel: 717-326-4922.

3—St. Boniface's, (1853) (German), Revs. John J. Tamalis; Jacek Bialkowski. In res., Revs. Andrew Kurovsky; Anthony Boothali; Deacon Clair J. Raisch.
Res., 326 Washington Blvd., P.O. Box 1205, 17703. Tel: 717-326-1544.
School—710 Franklin St., 17703. Tel: 717-326-3738.
Sisters of Christian Charity 1; Lay Teachers 7; Students 222.

4—Holy Rosary, (1915) (Polish), Rev. Andrew J. Krusinski.
Res., 313 Arch St., 17701. Tel: 717-323-6316.

5—Mater Dolorosa, (1908) (Italian), Very Rev. Francis J. Castellano, V.F.
Res., 635 Hepburn St., Williampsort, 17701. Tel: 717-326-9769; Fax: 717-327-8141.

6—St. Ann's, (1959), Very Rev. Francis J. Castellano, V.F., Admin.
Res., 1220 Northway Rd., 17701. Tel: 717-322-5935.
School—1225 Northway Rd., 17701.
Sisters of Christian Charity 3; Lay Teachers 7; Students 181.
Mission—Cascade, Lycoming Co., Assumption of the B.V.M.

Wyalusing, Bradford Co., St. Mary's Assumption (1950), Rev. Thomas J. McDermott.
Res., R.R. 4, Box 3, 18853. Tel: 717-746-1006.
Mission—Stowell, Wyoming Co., St. Anthony.

Wyoming, Luzerne Co., St. Joseph's (1914) (Polish), Rev. Walter F. Skiba.
Res., 97 E. Sixth St., 18644. Tel: 717-693-0510. [CEM]

Chaplains of Public Institutions

Clarks Summit. *Clarks Summit State Hospital,* 18411. Tel: 717-586-1741. Rev. James J. McGarry.

Dallas. *State Correctional Institution,* 18612. Tel: 717-675-1101. Deacon Jose A. Munoz.

East Stroudsburg. *East Stroudsburg State University,* P.O. Box 331, 18301. Tel: 717-476-0321. Philip J. Paul, Campus Min.

La Plume. *Keystone Junior College.* Vacant. Dalton, 18440. Tel: 717-945-3059.

Montgomery. *Allenwood Prison.* Prison Camp, 17752. Rev. Roberto Ignacio, 101 Sherman St., Muncy, 17756. Tel: 717-546-8357.

Muncy. *Muncy Prison.* Tel: 717-546-3900. Rev. Philip J. Sladicka, Chap.

Wilkes-Barre. *Geisinger Wyoming Valley Hospital.* Tel: 717-822-9561. Rev. Joseph A. Kearney.
Veteran's Administration Hospital. Tel: 717-824-3521. Rev. Benjamin J. Foerch, O.F.M., Chap.

Williamsport. *Lycoming College,* 17701. Tel: 717-321-4111. Sr. Catherine Ann Gilvary, I.H.M., Campus Min.

Special Assignment:
Reverend Fathers—
Finn, Edward S., Chap., R.D. #1, Box 310A, Equinunk, PA 18417. Tel: 717-224-4380
Hazzouri, Alex J., Villa St. Joseph Residence, Dunmore, PA 18509
Yaszcz, Thomas A., 52 W. Grove St., Nanticoke, PA 18634. Tel: 717-735-8754, Ext. 315

On Duty Outside the Diocese:
Reverend Monsignors—
Jordan, John W., 4320 Holland Ave., Dallas, TX 75219. Tel: 214-630-9414
Kline, Robert R., Mt. St. Mary's College, Emmitsburg, MD 21727. Tel: 301-447-6122
Yarrish, Bernard E., North American College, 00120 Vatican City State. Tel: 011-39-6-684-931
Reverend Fathers—
Fives, Carl J., Mt. St. Mary's College, Emmitsburg, MD 21727. Tel: 301-447-6122
Gabuzda, Richard J., Kenefick #1208, 320 N. 20th St., Omaha, NE 68178. Tel: 402-449-6384
McGee, James J., S.S., Society of St. Sulpice

Plominski, Walter J., Diocese of Rochester, NY
Silvestri, Luke A., St. Philip Benizi Rectory, Box 138, Black Canyon City, AZ 85324
Walsh, John A., 258 Acorn Dr., Longwood, FL 32750. Tel: 407-330-4966
Waznak, Robert J., S.S., Society of St. Sulpice
Wysocki, Joseph A., 5424 Burling Rd., Bethesda, MD 20014
Yenkevich, Daniel J.

Military Chaplains:
Reverend Fathers—
Dormer, David J., Chap., U.S. Army, 1305-B Bastogne Ct., Ft. Wainwright, AK 99703
Hochreiter, Robert S., Chap., U.S. Air Force, PSC 50 Box 672, APO, AE 09494. Tel: 011-44-280-708-287
Kelly, Brian F., 2047 San Remo Dr., Oceanside, CA 92056
Motsay, Joseph R., Chap., U.S.A.F., 9409 B Washington St., Ellsworth, SD 57706. Tel: 605-923-6066
Petruska, William M., U.S. Naval Force Central Command, CHC, U.S.N., Code 010, FPO, AE 09501
Stavoy, Stephen J., Roman Catholic Chap., HMS Sultan, P.O. 123 BY, Hampshire Hans, United Kingdom. Tel: 01-70-55-42-437

Unassigned or Leave of Absence:
Reverend Monsignors—
Gajewski, Chester A., P.O. Box 549, Pocono Lake, PA 18347. Tel: 717-472-9178
Reverend Fathers—
Kringe, Charles J., 708 N. Broad St. W., West Hazleton, PA 18201. Tel: 717-454-1380
Kulik, Francis J.
Purta, Jerome J.
Rossetti, Mark T.

Sabbatical or Graduate Studies:
Reverend Fathers—
Rossi, Walter R., 430 Taylor St., N.E., D-21, Washington, DC 20001. Tel: 202-832-9693

Retired:
Reverend Monsignors—
Burns, Gerald J., Villa St. Joseph Residence, Dunmore, PA 18509
Casey, George T., P.O. Box 1578, Hollywood, FL 33022. Tel: 305-920-0681
Cawley, Thomas J., Villa St. Joseph Residence, Dunmore, PA 18509
Clarke, James T., Villa St. Joseph Residence, Dunmore, PA 18509
Crotti, William A., Villa St. Joseph Residence, Dunmore, PA 18509
Demuth, George R., Holy Family Pavilion, 2510 Adams Ave., Apt. 303, Scranton, PA 18509-1597
Donovan, William L., Villa St. Joseph Residence, Dunmore, PA 18509
Harvan, Michael S., 185 Hickory Rd., Bear Creek Township, Wilkes-Barre, PA 18702. Tel: 717-472-3072
Horan, Thomas C., 137 S. Church St., Carbondale, PA 18407. Tel: 717-282-4291; 698-5366
Kane, Francis A., Holy Family Residence, 2500 Adams Ave., Scranton, PA 18509. Tel: 717-346-2501
Law, Joseph A., Hemlock Farms, Box 2170, Hawley, PA 18428. Tel: 717-775-0912
Lowry, James M., Villa St. Joseph Residence, Dunmore, PA 18509
Mecca, Mark A., St. Mary's Villa, Elmhurst, PA 18416
Meier, Joseph F., 175 N. Vine St., Apt. 2E, Hazleton, PA 18201. Tel: 717-454-8970
Norkunas, Anthony J., 253 S. Meade St., Wilkes-Barre, PA 18702
O'Brien, John J., Villa St. Joseph Residence, Dunmore, PA 18509
Ozalas, Michael C., 106 Venard Rd., Clarks Summit, PA 18411. Tel: 717-587-5149
Pakutka, William J., Villa St. Joseph Residence, Dunmore, PA 18509
Penkala, Edmund S., Villa St. Joseph Residence, Dunmore, PA 18509
Sullivan, Edward T., Villa St. Joseph Residence, Dunmore, PA 18509
Super, Joseph J., 16 William St., Pittston, PA 18640. Tel: 717-654-2112
Reverend Fathers—
Alisauskas, Peter J., Indian Lake, P.O. Box 106, White Haven, PA 18661. Tel: 717-472-3360
Bocianski, Andrew B., St. Mary's Villa, Elmhurst, PA 18416
Breslin, Joseph W., Villa St. Joseph Residence, Dunmore, PA 18509
Brogus, Albert G., 43 James St., Plains, PA 18705
Casey, John W., P.O. Box 1578, Hollywood, FL 33022. Tel: 305-920-0681
Conboy, Joseph T., Villa St. Joseph Residence, Dunmore, PA 18509
Cortese, Patrick S., P.O. Box 366, Mildred, PA 18632
Dacey, Martin J., Villa St. Joseph Residence, Dunmore, PA 18509
Domnick, Alphonsus, T.O.R., Villa St. Joseph Residence, Dunmore, PA 18509
Everling, Robert M., Villa St. Joseph Residence, Dumore, PA 18509
Ferrara, Joseph J., 123 W. Oak St., Hazleton, PA 18201. Tel: 717-455-2188
Fox, Joseph F., 1706 Delaware St., Dunmore, PA 18509. Tel: 717-343-5522
Gaiardo, Martin J., Muberry Tower, 499 Muberry St., Apt. 1216, Scranton, PA 18503. Tel: 717-347-4826
Gallagher, Edward F., Villa St. Joseph Residence, Dunmore, PA 18509
Hines, William F., 2461 S.W. 82nd Ave., Bldg. 2-Apt. 105, Ft. Lauderdale, FL 33324. Tel: 305-423-9301
Hlopko, John J., Lake Rd., P.O. Box 67, Bear Creek, PA 18602. Tel: 717-472-3483
Kalinowski, Stainslaus J., 3020 Cedar Ave., Scranton, PA 18505
Langan, James J., 2420 S.W. 81st Ave., Arrowhead Condominium, Bldg. 7, Apt. 402, Davie, FL 33324
Lewis, Harry J., Villa St. Joseph Residence, Dunmore, PA 18509
Madaj, John A., Fox Manor, R.D. 1, Box 309, Hazleton, PA 18201. Tel: 717-455-0634
Makowski, Edward J., Little Flower Manor, 200 South Meade St., Wilkes-Barre, PA 18702-6221
Maloney, Andrew P., P.O. Box 583, Mountainhome, PA 18342. Tel: 717-595-7679
Markowski, Clement A., Villa St. Joseph Residence, Dunmore, PA 18509
McCarthy, Daniel A., Villa St. Joseph Residence, Dunmore, PA 18509
Merkel, Francis J., Little Flower Manor, 200 S. Meade St., Wilkes-Barre, PA 18702
Mikus, Frank P., Villa St. Joseph Residence, Dunmore, PA 18509
Mulrooney, Charles F., Villa St. Joseph Residence, Dunmore, PA 18509
Mulrooney, F. Harold, 1203 Schlager St., Scranton, PA 18504. Tel: 717-343-8704
Noviello, Anthony A., 385 Montgomery Pike, South Williamsport, PA 17701. Tel: 717-323-6552
O'Haire, John A., Villa St. Joseph Residence, Dunmore, PA 18509
Pace, William J., Villa St. Joseph Residence, Dunmore, PA 18509
Plevyak, Valentine R., Villa St. Joseph Residence, Dunmore, PA 18509
Ryan, Joseph F., P.O. Box 77, Pocono Summit, PA 18346. Tel: 717-839-9260
Saltry, Joseph A., Holy Family Residence, Rm.256, 2500 Adams Ave., Scranton, PA 18509
Sammons, Joseph F., 101 Queen Esther Dr., Sayre, PA 18840
Smith, Arnold R., Villa St. Joseph Residence, Dunmore, PA 18509
Sokolowski, Edward V., 3 Regina Dr., Mountaintop, PA 18707. Tel: 717-472-2269
Soltis, Anthony, 551 Orchard St., Warrior Run, PA 18706
Stalavicz, George P., Little Flower Manor, 200 S. Meade St., Wilkes-Barre, PA 18702
Ulrich, Carl G., Villa St. Joseph Residence, Dunmore, PA 18509
Wayda, Henry A., St. Mary's Villa, Elmhurst, PA 18416
Zawodniak, Edward J., R.R. #2, Box 355, Hickory Tree Rd., Loyalville, Dallas, PA 18612

INSTITUTIONS LOCATED IN THE DIOCESE

[A] SEMINARIES, DIOCESAN

DALTON. *Saint Pius X Seminary.* (Collaborative College/Pre-Theology Seminary), 1000 Seminary Rd., 18414. Tel: 717-563-1131; Fax: 717-563-8520. Rev. Msgr. David A. Bohr, S.T.D., Rector; Rev. Msgr. John A. Esseff, D.Min., M.A., S.T.L., Dir., Apostolic Formation; Rev. Msgr. Dale R. Rupert, Spiritual Dir.; Rev. Albert M. Liberatore, Academic Dean & Dir., Liturgical Formation.
Non-Resident Faculty: Revs. Robert J. Barone, S.T.D.; Michael F. Quinnan, M.A., S.T.L.; James A. Rafferty, S.T.L.; Deacon J. Morris Smith, M.A., Th.D.; Mr. Edward G. Mathews, Jr., M.A., M.Phil., Ph.D. Seminarians 26.

[B] SEMINARIES, RELIGIOUS

PITTSTON. *St. Joseph's Oblate Seminary*, R.R. 4, Box 4, 18640. Tel: 717-654-7542. Very Rev. Mario S. Buttini, O.S.J., Rector; Rev. Gregory T. Finn, O.S.J., Dir. Formations & Vocation; Bro. Victor Cipriani, O.S.J.

[C] COLLEGES AND UNIVERSITIES

SCRANTON. *Marywood College*, 18509. Tel: 717-348-6211.
For a complete listing, refer to the Colleges and Universities section.
University of Scranton, 18510. Tel: 717-941-7533.
For a complete listing, refer to the Colleges and Universities section.
DALLAS. *College Misericordia*, 18612. Tel: 717-674-6400.
For a complete listing, refer to the Colleges and Universities section.
*WILKES-BARRE. *Kings College*, 18711. Tel: 717-826-5900.
For a complete listing, refer to the Colleges and Universities section.

[D] HIGH SCHOOLS, DIOCESAN

SCRANTON. *Bishop Hannan High School*, 330 Wyoming Ave., 18503. Tel: 717-346-4643. Mr. James P. Marcks, Prin.; Rev. Jeffrey J. Walsh, Dir., Religious Formation; Mr. Matthew Rakauskas, Asst. Prin. Priests 4; Sisters Servants of the Immaculate Heart of Mary 6; Lay Teachers 30; Students 427.

CARBONDALE. *Sacred Heart Junior/Senior High School*, 44 S. Church St., 18407. Tel: 717-282-2790. Margaret Hart, Prin.; Rev. James A. Rafferty, Dir., Religious Formation. Priests 1; Sisters 1; Lay Teachers 10; Students 190.

DUNMORE. *Bishop O'Hara High School*, 501 E. Drinker St., 18512. Tel: 717-346-7541. Joseph Casciano, Prin.; Rev. Scott P. Sterowski, Dir., Religious Formation. Sisters, Servants of the Immaculate Heart of Mary; Sisters of SS. Cyril and Methodius. Priests 1; Sisters 3; Lay Teachers 25; Students 353.

EAST STROUDSBURG. *Notre Dame Junior/Senior High School*, 60 Spangenburg Ave., 18301. Tel: 717-421-0466; Fax: 717-476-0629. Jeffrey N. Lyons, Prin.; Rev. Alfred J. Vito, Dir., Religious Formation; Diane Young, Dean of Students. Priests 2; Sisters, Servants of the Immaculate Heart of Mary 2; Lay Teachers 24; Students 372.

HAZLETON. *Bishop Hafey Junior/Senior High School*, 1700 W. 22nd St., 18201. Tel: 717-455-9431. Rev. David L. Tressler, M.S., M.Ed., Prin. & Procurator; Mrs. Kathleen Stark, Vice Prin.; Mr. Michael Stofko, Coord. of Student Affairs; Mr. Richard Smith, Dean of Students; Mr. Thomas A. Kostic, Dir., Religious Formation; Sr. Felice Donelin, S.C.C., Dir.; Mrs. Miriam Jamelli, Jr. High Guidance Counselor; Mr. Thomas Cipriano, Asst. Procurator / Development Dir. Priests 2; Lay Teachers 33; Students 609.

KINGSTON. *Bishop O'Reilly High School*, 316 N. Maple Ave., P.O. Box 1346, 18704. Tel: 717-288-1404. Mrs. Anita M. Sirak, Prin.; Sr. Carol Makravitz, S.C.C., Vice Prin.; Rev. Michael J. Kloton, Dir., Religious Formation & Asst. Prin.; Mrs. Linda Prawdzik, Dir., Guidance; Mr. Ralph Mancuso, Business Mgr. Priests 1; Sisters 2; Lay Teachers 29; Students 409.

PITTSTON. *Seton Catholic High School*, 37 William St., 18640. Tel: 717-654-4831; 655-0208; Fax: 717-654-2599. James J. Redington, Prin.; Rev. Frank S. Homets, Dir., Religious Formation. Sisters 4; Lay Teachers 19; Students 292.

WILKES-BARRE. *Bishop Hoban High School*, 159 S. Penna Blvd., 18701. Tel: 717-829-2424. Mr. Frank Majikes, Prin.; Sr. Mary Ann Cody, I.H.M., Asst. Prin.; Sr. Leonita Duhoski, R.S.M., Dir. of Devel.; Sr. Catherine Ann Morris, SS.C.M., Dir. of Guidance; Rev. Robert M. Timchak, Dir., Religious Formation. Priests 2; Sisters 12; Lay Teachers 32; Students 595.

WILLIAMSPORT. *Bishop Neumann Junior/Senior High School*, 901 Penn St., 17701. Tel: 717-323-9953. Rev. Andrew Kurovsky, Prin.; Sr. Carmelita Smith, S.C.C., Vice Prin.; Sr. Minnette Welding, I.H.M., Dir., Religious Formation. Priests 2; Sisters 4; Lay Teachers 21; Students 250.

[E] HIGH SCHOOLS, PRIVATE

SCRANTON.
**Scranton Preparatory School*, 1000 Wyoming Ave., 18509. Tel: 717-941-7737. Society of Jesus. Revs. Eugene A. Nolan, S.J., Pres.; Royden B. Davis, S.J., Rector; Richard S. McCouch, S.J., Chap.
Faculty: Revs. Michael A. Hricko, S.J.; Leonard A. Martin, S.J.; William J. McGrath, S.J.; Bro. James C. Lemon, S.J. Priests 5; Brothers 1; Lay Teachers 40; Students 680.

MOSCOW. *St. Gregory's Academy*, R.R. 8, Box 8214, 18444. Tel: 717-842-8112; Fax: 717-842-4513. Priestly Fraternity of St. Peter. Rev. Paul Carr, F.S.S.P., Chap.; Alan Hicks, Headmaster. Lay Teachers 10; Students 58.

[F] INTER-PAROCHIAL ELEMENTARY SCHOOLS

CLARKS GREEN. *Our Lady of Peace Elementary School*, 410 N. Abington Rd., 18411. Tel: 717-587-4152. Sr. Alice Marie McCormick, I.H.M., Prin. I.H.M. Sisters 5; Lay Teachers 19; Students 448.

Saint Gregory Early Childhood Center, 330 N. Abington Rd., 18411. Tel: 717-587-4808; Fax: 717-586-4515. Mrs. Antoinette Goldate, Prin. Lay Teachers 3; Students 90.

CRESCO. *Monsignor McHugh Elementary School*, 18326. Tel: 717-595-7463; Fax: 717-595-9639. Sr. Rosemarie Mozzachio, I.H.M., Prin. Sisters, Servants of the Immaculate Heart of Mary 4; Lay Teachers 14; Students 393.

Immaculate Heart of Mary Convent, R.R. 1, Box 568, 18326. Tel: 717-595-7548.

DALLAS. *Gate of Heaven Elementary School*, 40 Machell Ave., 18612. Tel: 717-675-6566; Fax: 717-674-0198. Mrs. Mary Tigue, Prin. Lay Teachers 22; Students 497.

EAST STROUDSBURG. *Notre Dame Elementary School*, 78 Ridgeway St., 18301. Tel: 717-421-3651. Sr. Mary Alice Kane, I.H.M., Prin. I.H.M. Sisters 5; Lay Teachers 20; Students 450.

EXETER. *Wyoming Area Catholic Elementary School*, 1690 Wyoming Ave., 18643. Tel: 717-654-7982. Sr. Marion Tarone, I.H.M., Prin. I.H.M. Sisters 6; Lay Teachers 8; Students 255.

FORTY FORT. *Regis Elementary School*, 1133 Wyoming Ave., 18704. Tel: 717-288-5558. Mrs. Jane Quinn, Prin.

HAZLETON. *Holy Spirit Academy*, 225 E. Fourth St., 18201. Tel: 717-459-0054. Mrs. Alice Flynn, Prin. Priests 3; Sisters 2; Lay Teachers 12; Students 299.

HONESDALE. *Saint Vincent Elementary School*, 329 Cliff St., 18431. Tel: 717-253-1074. Mrs. Sue Delling, Prin. Lay Teachers 10; Students 247.

JESSUP. *La Salle Academy*, 309 First Ave., 18434. Tel: 717-489-2010. Sr. Christopher Godlewski, S.S.C.M., Prin. Sisters 5; Lay Teachers 23; Students 555.

NANTICOKE. *Pope John Paul II Elementary School*, 518 S. Hanover St., 18634. Tel: 717-735-7935. Mr. James A. Jones, Prin. Lay Teachers 14; Students 290.

PLYMOUTH. *Holy Child Elementary School*, 119 Willow St., 18651. Tel: 717-779-2843. Sr. M. Le Roy Prymak, O.S.F., Prin. Sisters 3; Lay Teachers 8; Students 202.

SWOYERSVILLE. *Regis Academy*, 112 Hughes St., 18704. Tel: 717-287-3133. Robert Hines, Prin. Lay Teachers 11; Students 173.

WILKES-BARRE. *Saint Boniface Elementary School*, 221 Blackman St., 18702. Tel: 717-823-0939. Sr. John Marie Hickl, S.C.C., Prin. S.C.C. Sisters 1; Lay Teachers 8; Students 265.

Saint Nicholas-Saint Mary Elementary School, 242 S. Washington St., 18701. Tel: 717-823-8089. Sr. Marie Pauline Demeck, S.C.C., Prin. S.C.C. Sisters 5; Lay Teachers 20; Students 531.

[G] PRESCHOOLS AND CHILD CARE CENTERS

SCRANTON. *Immaculate Care Preschool*, 800 Taylor Ave., 18510. Tel: 717-344-4380. Ann Marie McDonald, Prin.

Marywood Early Childhood Center. Marywood College. 2300 Adams Ave., 18509. Tel: 717-343-7762. Sr. Marilyn Muro, I.H.M., Dir.

MILFORD. *St. Patrick Preschool*, 111 High St., 18337. Tel: 717-296-4721. Rita Straka, Teacher.

St. Vincent de Paul Preschool, R.R. #1, Dingman Hills, Box 240, 18337. Tel: 717-686-3493. Diane C. Quintiliani, Teacher.

MOSCOW. *St. Catherine Preschool*, P.O. Box 250, 18444. Tel: 717-842-4561. Janet Michael, Dir.

MOUNT POCONO. *St. Mary Playschool*, 27 Fairview Ave., 18344. Tel: 717-839-1718. Halina Lombardy, Dir.

MUNCY. *Resurrection Early Childhood Center*, 526 S. Main St., 17756. Tel: 717-546-3900. Michael A. Cillo, Dir.

PITTSTON. *St. Mary's Early Childhood Learning Center*, 535 N. Main Ave., 18640. Tel: 717-654-8188. Sr. Anne Therese Peach, S.C.C., Prin.

[H] RENEWAL CENTERS

CRESCO. *The Immaculate Heart of Mary Spiritual Renewal Center*, R.R. 1, Box 568, 18326. Tel: 717-595-7548; 7549. Sr. Anne Mary Boslett, I.H.M., Dir.

DALTON. *Fatima Renewal Center*, 1000 Seminary Rd., 18414. Tel: 717-563-8500. Diocesan Renewal Center. Jeff Seymour, Retreat Coord.

NANTICOKE. *Holy Family Spiritual Renewal Center*, 151 Newport St., 18634-1300. Martin J. Hudak, Dir.

[I] GENERAL HOSPITALS

SCRANTON. *Mercy Hospital*, 746 Jefferson Ave., 18501. Tel: 717-348-7100.

For a complete listing, refer to the Hospitals section.

CARBONDALE. *Marian Community Hospital*, 100 Lincoln Ave., 18407. Tel: 717-282-1000; Fax: 717-282-7177.

For a complete listing, refer to the Hospitals section.

Marian Community Hospital Foundation, 100 Lincoln Ave., 18407. Tel: 717-281-1000.

For a complete listing, refer to the Hospitals section.

Maxis Medical Services, 100 Lincoln Ave., 18407. Tel: 717-281-1000.

For a complete listing, refer to the Hospitals section.

HAZLETON. *Hazleton-Saint Joseph Medical Center*, 687 N. Church St., 18201. Tel: 717-459-4444.

For a complete listing, refer to the Hospitals section.

MUNCY. *Muncy Valley Hospital*, 215 E. Water St., 17756. Tel: 717-546-4242.

For a complete listing, refer to the Hospitals section.

NANTICOKE. *Mercy Care Corporation, Home Health Agency*, 128 W. Washington St., 18634. Tel: 717-735-9375; Fax: 717-735-9318.

For a complete listing, refer to the Hospitals section.

Mercy Special Care Hospital, 128 W. Washington St., 18634. Tel: 717-735-5000; Fax: 717-735-9220.

For a complete listing, refer to the Hospitals section.

WILKES-BARRE. *Mercy Hospital*, 25 Church St., P.O. Box 658, 18765. Tel: 717-826-3100; Fax: 717-831-8989.

For a complete listing, refer to the Hospitals section.

Mercy Med-Care, Inc., 25 Church St., Box 658, 18765. Tel: 717-826-3100.

For a complete listing, refer to the Hospitals section.

WILLIAMSPORT. *Divine Providence Hospital of the Sisters of Christian Charity*, 1100 Grampian Blvd., 17701. Tel: 717-320-7007.

For a complete listing, refer to the Hospitals section.

**Grampian Health Services, Inc.*, 1201 Grampian Blvd., 17701. Tel: 717-326-8214.

For a complete listing, refer to the Hospitals section.

Providence Foundation, 1100 Grampian Blvd., 17701. Tel: 717-321-5467.

For a complete listing, refer to the Hospitals section.

Providence Health System, Inc., 1100 Grampian Blvd., 17701. Tel: 717-320-7007.

For a complete listing, refer to the Hospitals section.

Sisters of Christian Charity Healthcare Corporation, 1100 Grampian Blvd., 17701. Tel: 717-326-8181.

For a complete listing, refer to the Hospitals section.

**Susquehanna Regional Home Health & Services*, 1201 Grampian Blvd., 17701. Tel: 717-323-9891.

For a complete listing, refer to the Hospitals section.

[J] SPECIAL HOSPITALS

SCRANTON. *St. Joseph's Center*, 2010 Adams Ave., 18509. Tel: 717-342-8379; 961-1549.

For a complete listing, refer to the Special Care Facilities section.

NANTICOKE. *Mercy Health Care Center*, Newport St., 18634. Tel: 717-735-7300.

For a complete listing, refer to the Special Care Facilities section.

[K] SPECIAL EDUCATION SCHOOLS

CLARKS GREEN. *Lourdesmont*, 537 Venard Rd., 18411. Tel: 717-587-4741. Legal Title: *Good Shepherd Corporation of Clarks Summit, PA*. Sr. Mary Joanne Getzendaner, R.G.S., Supr.; Kathleen Serafin, M.S., Prin.; Mr. John A. Antognoli, Ed.D., Exec. Dir. Sisters of the Good Shepherd 7; Staff 106; Total Assisted 503.

FALLS. *St. Michael's Group Home*, Box 405A, 18615. Tel: 717-378-2560. Total Assisted 29; Total Staff 5.

HOBAN HEIGHTS. *St. Michael's School*, Box 370, 18657. Tel: 717-388-6155; Fax: 717-388-6979. Mr. James F. Huff, M.S.W., Dir. Students Assisted 381; Total Staff 171.

TUNKHANNOCK. *St. Michael's Group Home*, 17 Chestnut St., 18657. Tel: 717-836-6360. Total Assisted 15.

St. Michael's Group Home, 28 Putnam St., 18657. Tel: 717-836-4911. Total Assisted 16; Total Staff 4.

WEST PITTSTON. *St. Michael's Group Home*, 225/227 Damon St., 18643. Tel: 717-655-9370. Total Assisted 14; Total Staff 4.

WILLIAMSPORT. *St. Michael's Group Home*, 119 E. Fourth St., 17701. Tel: 717-322-0561. Total Assisted 25; Total Staff 6.

[L] HOMES FOR AGED

SCRANTON. *Home for Aged of the Little Sisters of the Poor, Holy Family Residence*, 2500 Adams Ave., 18509. Tel: 717-343-4065; 346-5788; Fax: 717-347-1941.

For a complete listing, refer to the Special Care Facilities section.

DALLAS. *Mercy Center Nursing Unit, Inc.*, Lake St., Box 370, 18612. Tel: 717-675-2131; Fax: 717-674-5658.

For a complete listing, refer to the Special Care Facilities section.

ELMHURST. *St. Mary's Villa Nursing Home*, 18416. Tel: 717-842-7621; Fax: 717-842-2953.

For a complete listing, refer to the Special Care Facilities section.

WILKES-BARRE. *Little Flower Manor of the Diocese of Scranton*, 200 S. Meade St., 18702. Tel: 717-823-6131.

For a complete listing, refer to the Special Care Facilities section.

[M] MONASTERIES AND RESIDENCES OF PRIESTS AND BROTHERS

SCRANTON. *Saint Ann's Passionist Monastery*, 1230 St. Ann St., 18504. Tel: 717-347-5691. Congregation of the Passion.

Chaplaincies: St. Gabriel's Convent, Clarks Summit, 18411. Very Rev. Richard Burke, C.P., Rector, Monastery & Shrine; Revs. Berard Tierney, C.P.; Vincent Boney, C.P.; Conan Conaboy, C.P.; John Connor, C.P.; Nicolas Gill, C.P.; Peter Grace, C.P.; Henry Kavanaugh, C.P.; Kevin McCloskey, C.P.; Richard Nalepa, C.P.; Cassian Yuhaus, C.P., Exec. Dir., Ministry for Religious Research & Consultancy. Tel: 717-586-9099; Bro. Daniel Turner, C.P. Priests 9; Brothers 1.

St. Gregory's Priory (Priestly Fraternity of St. Peter), 819 N. Webster Ave., 18510. Tel: 717-342-3091; Fax: 717-941-9798. Rev. Daniel W. Oppenheimer, Prior.

BRODHEADSVILLE. *Salesian Monastery*, HC 1, Frantz Rd., Box 455, 18322. Tel: 717-992-0230 (Monastery); 992-3448 (Abbot's Office). Bro. Bernard Seif, S.M.C., Abbot.

ELMHURST. *Priestly Fraternity of St. Peter (F.S.S.P.)*, U.S. Headquarters, Our Lady of Guadalupe Seminary, Griffin Rd., P.O. Box 196, 18416. Tel: 717-842-4000; Fax: 717-842-4001. Revs. Arnaud J. Devillers, F.S.S.P., District Supr.; Michel R. Berger, F.S.S.P., Faculty; James B. Buckley, F.S.S.P., Novice Master; Paul S. Carr, F.S.S.P., Faculty & Chap., St. Gregory's Academy; Dennis Duvelius, F.S.S.P., Admin. Asst. & Dir. of Admissions; John Melnick, Faculty; Daniel W. Oppenheimer, F.S.S.P.; Nathan R. Vail, F.S.S.P., Seminary Rector; Deacon Chad Ripperger, Ph.D., Faculty. Priests 22; Seminarians 46; Novices 13.

Priests Working Elsewhere: Rev. Louis Campbell, St. Michael the Archangel, Latin Mass Community, 1703 Jackson St., Scranton, 18504. Tel: 717-961-1205. Rev. Carlos S. Casavantes, F.S.S.P. (CC), Most Precious Blood, 3502 Saratoga Blvd., Corpus Christi, TX, 78415. Tel: 512-854-3800 (Parish); 854-9481 (Chap. direct). Rev. Pablo Alvarez, F.S.S.P. (LR), Community of St. John the Baptist, 2414 N. Tyler, Apt.312, Little Rock, AR, 72207. Tel: 501-280-9155. Rev. Michael T. Irwin, F.S.S.P. (Y), Queen of the Holy Rosary, 291 Scoville Dr., Vienna, OH, 44473. Tel: 330-856-4204. Revs. Peter J. Gee, F.S.S.P. (KCK); John V. Rizzo, F.S.S.P. (KCK), 208 Sunset Ln., P.O. Box 98, Maple Hill, KS, 66507. Tel: 913-256-4727. Rev. James W. Jackson, F.S.S.P. (TLS), 1720 E. Apache, Tulsa, OK, 74148. Tel: 918-425-0486. Revs. Paul S. Petko, F.S.S.P. (OM); Joseph Poisson, F.S.S.P., 1404 Castelar St., Omaha, NE, 68108. Tel: 402-341-1305. Rev. Karl A. Pikus, F.S.S.P. (RC), 522 Columbus St., Rapid City, SD, 57701. Tel: 605-341-1578. Rev. Karl Claver, F.S.S.P. (DAL), 6228 Winton St., Dallas, TX, 75214. Tel: 214-823-7934. Rev. Joseph Terra, F.S.S.P. (PAT), Our Lady of Fatima Chapel, 32 W. Franklin Ave., Pequannock, NJ, 07440. Tel: 201-694-6727. Rev. Jose Salgado, Our Lady of Mt. Carmel Community, 4697 Field St., Wheat Ridge, CO, 80033-3050. Tel: 303-425-3273. Rev. Mark Fischer, F.S.S.P., 3400 Old Alabama Rd., Alpharetta, GA, 30202. Tel: 770-442-2511.

LITTLE MEADOWS. *St. Joseph's House*, R.R. 1, Box 1418, 18830. Tel: 717-395-3639. Rev. Vincent J. Young, O.M.V., Dir.

MOUNT POCONO. *Diocesan Oratory of Saint Philip Neri - Newman House*, 21 Fairview Ave., 18344. Tel: 717-839-2185. Rev. Peter M.J. Stravinskas, Ph.D., S.T.D., Provost.

PITTSTON. *Eastern Province of the Oblates of St. Joseph*, Rte. 315, R.D. 4, 18640. Tel: 717-654-7542; Fax: 717-654-8621. Very Rev. Mario S. Buttini, O.S.J., Prov.; Revs. Silvio Chini, O.S.J., 1st Councilor; Paul J. Pavese, O.S.J., 2nd Councilor; Joseph Sibilano, O.S.J., Treas. Priests 12.

WILKES-BARRE. *Moreau House*. (House of Formation for the Congregation of Holy Cross - C.S.C.), 415 N. Main St., 18702. Tel: 717-824-8820. Revs. Donald J. Grimes, C.S.C.; Thomas P. Lonney, C.S.C.

St. Joseph's Friary, 783 E. Northampton St., 18702. Tel: 717-822-8023. Revs. Raymond J. Lynch, O.F.M., Guardian; Alvin Black, O.F.M.; Benjamin J. Foerch, O.F.M. Priests 3.

[N] DIOCESAN RESIDENCE FOR RETIRED PRIESTS

DUNMORE. *Villa St. Joseph*, 1600 Green Ridge St., 18509. Tel: 717-343-4791. Most Rev. John M. Dougherty, D.D., V.G. Tel: 717-344-3272. In res., Rev. Msgr. Gerald J. Burns. Tel: 717-343-7161; Rev. Msgr. Thomas J. Cawley. Tel: 717-343-2254; Rev.

Msgr. James T. Clarke. Tel: 717-969-1235; Rev. Msgr. William A. Crotti. Tel: 717-343-7544; Rev. Msgr. William L. Donovan. Tel: 717-963-9383; Rev. Msgr. James M. Lowry. Tel: 717-342-1527; Rev. Msgr. John J. O'Brien. Tel: 717-961-1865; Rev. Msgr. William J. Pakutka. Tel: 717-341-9168; Rev. Msgr. Edmund S. Penkala. Tel: 717-344-6288; Rev. Msgr. Edward T. Sullivan. Tel: 717-341-9203; Revs. Joseph W. Breslin. Tel: 717-341-3315; Joseph T. Conboy. Tel: 717-941-9405; Alphonsus M. Domnick, T.O.R. Tel: 717-341-9176; Martin J. Dacey. Tel: 717-342-1536; Robert M. Everling. Tel: 717-343-4925; Edward F. Gallagher. Tel: 717-348-6873; Harry J. Lewis. Tel: 717-343-5499; Clement A. Markowski. Tel: 717-343-0555; Daniel A. McCarthy. Tel: 717-344-1662; Joseph F. Meighan. Tel: 717-941-0509; Frank P. Mikus. Tel: 717-342-2728; Charles F. Mulrooney. Tel: 717-969-1305; John A. O'Haire. Tel: 717-342-6865; William J. Pace. Tel: 717-961-5856; Valentine R. Plevyak. Tel: 717-969-9109; Arnold R. Smith. Tel: 717-941-3209; Carl G. Ulrich. Tel: 717-341-5898.

[O] CONVENTS AND RESIDENCES FOR SISTERS

SCRANTON. *Immaculate Heart of Mary Center, Marywood*, 2300 Adams Ave., 18509. Tel: 717-342-6850. Sisters, Servants of the Immaculate Heart of Mary. Sr. Anne Munley, I.H.M., Congregation Admin.; Sr. Therese O'Rourke, I.H.M., Asst. to Congregation Admin. & Dir., Apostolic Planning. Tel: 717-346-5401; Sr. Catherine Luxner, I.H.M., Dir., Spiritual Renewal. Tel: 717-346-5402; Sr. Mary Persico, I.H.M., Dir., Temporal Affairs. Tel: 717-346-5405; Sr. Mary Martha Gardiner, I.H.M., Councilor at Large. Tel: 202-529-5654; Sr. Theresa Jordan, I.H.M., Business Mgr. Tel: 717-346-5406; Sr. Annmarie Sanders, I.H.M., Dir., Communications. Tel: 717-346-5404 Ext. 508; Sr. Beatrice Caulson, I.H.M., Dir., Novices/Candidates. Tel: 717-346-5414; Sr. Kathryn Kurdziel, I.H.M., Dir., Vocations. Tel: 717-346-5413; Sr. Amy Zychal, I.H.M., Dir., Devel. Tel: 717-346-5431 Ext. 599; Rev. Robert J. Barone, S.T.D., Chap. Professed Sisters 699.

Marian Convent, Marywood, 18509. Tel: 717-346-1752. Sr. St. Mel Wright, I.H.M., Coord. Tel: 717-346-1752; Sr. Rosemary Goulet, I.H.M., Admin. Tel: 717-346-1752. Sisters, Servants of the Immaculate Heart of Mary 150.

Parish Visitors of Mary Immaculate, 410 S. Main Ave., 18504. Tel: 717-343-7841. Sr. Dolores Marie, P.V.M.I., Supr. Sisters 5.

CLARKS SUMMIT. *St. Gabriel's Monastery*, 631 Griffin Pond Rd., 18411. Tel: 717-586-2791. Religious of the Passion of Jesus Christ; Passionist Nuns (Contemplative). Sr. Helen V. Gallagher, C.P., Supr.; Sr. Colette Greder, C.P., Vicar; Sr. Gail Worcelo, C.P., Councilor. Professed Sisters 15.

DALLAS. *Mercy Center*, Lake St., 18612. Tel: 717-675-2131. Sr. Jayne Pruitt, R.S.M., Admin.; Sr. Ruth Ann Fox, R.S.M., Coord. Sisters 127.

Mercy Center Convent, 18612. Tel: 717-675-2131. Sr. Jayne Pruitt, R.S.M., Admin.; Sr. Ruth Ann Fox, R.S.M., Coord.; Sr. Louise Christofor, R.S.M., Dir. of Nursing; Rev. Francis G. Kulig, Chap. Sisters 115.

Sisters of Mercy of the Americas Regional Community of Dallas, 18612. Tel: 717-675-1966; Fax: 717-675-9051. Sr. Maureen McCann, R.S.M., Pres.; Sr. Catherine McGroaty, R.S.M., Assoc. Tel: 717-675-2048. Sisters 5.

[P] RETREAT HOUSES

CLARKS SUMMIT. *St. Gabriel's Retreat Center*, 631 Griffin Pond Rd., 18411. Tel: 717-586-4957. Religious of the Passion of Jesus Christ; Passionist Nuns (Contemplative).

MOUNT POCONO. *Villa Our Lady Retreat House*, HCR 1, Box 41, 18344-9714. Tel: 717-839-7553. Sr. M. Bonaventa, O.S.F., Supr. Bernadine Sisters 8.

[Q] CAMPS AND COMMUNITY CENTERS

SCRANTON. *Catholic Youth Center*, 500 Jefferson Ave., 18510. Tel: 717-347-3311. Mr. John J. O'Connor, Exec. Dir.; Rev. Cyril D. Edwards, Spiritual Moderator.

TUNKHANNOCK. *Camp St. Andrew*, P.O. Box 679, 18657. Tel: 717-836-2975. Off-Season Mailing Address: 316 William St., 18508. Tel: 717-341-1290. Rev. Msgr. Joseph P. Kelly, Exec. Dir. Regular Camp, Basketball Clinics 1,000 children.

WILKES-BARRE. *Catholic Youth Center*, 36 S. Washington St., 18702. Tel: 717-823-6121. Rev. John S. Terry, Dir.; Mr. Anthony D. English, Jr., Exec. Dir.

[R] MISCELLANEOUS LISTINGS

SCRANTON. *The Catherine McAuley Center*, 747 Madison Ave., 18510. Tel: 717-342-1342; Fax: 717-341-8108. Sr. Therese Marie Marques, R.S.M., Exec. Dir.

The Catherine McAuley Center - Bridge Program, 747 Madison Ave., 18510. Tel: 717-342-1342; Fax: 717-341-8108. Sr. Therese Marie Marques, R.S.M., Exec. Dir.

The Catherine McAuley Center - Maple Street House, 1030 Maple St., 18505. Tel: 717-342-1342. Sr. Therese Marie Marques, R.S.M., Exec. Dir.

The Catherine McAuley Center - Swetland Street House, 747 Madison Ave., 18510. Tel: 717-342-1342. Sr. Therese Marie Marques, R.S.M., Exec. Dir.

The Catherine McAuley House Annex, 115 Ferdinand St., 18508. Tel: 717-342-1342; Fax: 717-341-8108. Sr. Therese Marie Marques, R.S.M., Exec. Dir.

Cross Apartments, 507 Broadway, 18505. Tel: 717-342-1342. Sr. Therese Marie Marques, R.S.M., Exec. Dir.; Sr. Marise Fabie, R.S.M., Dir., Housing.

Frances Warde House, 1646 Capouse Ave., 18509. Tel: 717-342-6962. Sr. Therese Marie Marques, R.S.M., Exec. Dir.; Sr. Marise Fabie, R.S.M., Dir., Housing.

The Guild Studios. Religious Store, 400 Wyoming Ave., 18503. Tel: 800-367-6610. Mrs. Michele D. Keating, Gen. Mgr.

I.H.M. Congregation Charitable Trust, 2300 Adams Ave., 18509. Tel: 717-342-6850. Congregation of the Sisters, Servants of the Immaculate Heart of Mary.

ISECP, Inc., 926 Monroe Ave., 18510. Tel: 717-344-7295; Fax: 717-941-6340. Rev. George J. Schemel, S.J., Dir.

Saint Ann's Media, Inc., 1230 St. Ann St., 18504. Tel: 717-941-0100; Fax: 717-941-0185. Rev. Peter A. Grace, C.P., Dir. Sponsored by the Passionist Fathers.

St. Anthony's Haven, Wyoming & Olive Sts., 18503. Tel: 717-969-0753.

St. Francis of Assisi Kitchen, 500 Penn Ave., 18509. Tel: 717-342-5556. Rev. Msgr. Constantine V. Siconolfi, M.S., Dir.

CLARKS SUMMIT. *Ministry for Religious Research and Consultancy*, 631 Griffin Pond Rd., 18411. Tel: 717-586-9099; Fax: 717-586-9203. Rev. Cassian J. Yuhaus, C.P., Exec. Dir.

DALLAS. *People of God Community of Northeastern PA*, 31 Dorchester Dr., 18612. Tel: 717-826-1810; 675-8286. Glenn G. Yanik, Pres.

Stoneview Studio, Mercy Center, 18612. Tel: 675-1361. Producers of Art: Paintings, Sculpture and Other Media. Sr. Benedicta San Antonio, R.S.M., Dir.

Studio I, Mercy Center, Box 370, 18612. Tel: 717-675-2131; 675-1865. Designing and handcrafting fine jewelry and sculpture. Workshops in jewelry making using the lost wax casting technique: A. Couples - wedding bands/engagement rings. B. All ages interested in learning the art of jewelry making. Sr. Regina Kiel, R.S.M., Designer & Artist.

DICKSON CITY. *Lay Missionaries of the Passion (Passionist Secular Institute)*, 633 Main St., 18519. Tel: 717-489-0795. Dorothy L. Armstrong. Professed Members 7; In Formation 10.

HARLEIGH. *Shrine of the Sacred Heart*, 1 Church Pl., 18225. Tel: 717-455-1162. National Office: Men of the Sacred Heart, P.O. Box 500, 18225. Tel: 717-455-1162.

PITTSTON. *The Gabriel House*, 13 William St., 18640. Tel: 717-654-7157. Anne Marie McCawley, Project Coord.
Residence for low income women.

PLYMOUTH. *The Catherine McAuley House*, 121 Church St., 18651. Tel: 717-779-2801. Sr. Therese Marie Marques, R.S.M., Exec. Dir.; Sr. Marie Larkin, P.B.V.M., Case Mgr.

Emmaus Spirituality Program for Priests, 101 Church St., 18651. Tel: 717-779-7736. Rev. James J. Jacobs, Natl. Dir.

WILKES-BARRE. *Project REMAIN*, 269 S. Washington St., 18701. Tel: 717-829-5373. Sr. Miriam Francis Stadulis, R.S.M., Dir.; Sr. Joan McCabe, R.S.M., Assoc. Dir.

St. Vincent De Paul Kitchen, 39 E. Jackson St., 18702. Tel: 717-829-7796. Ned Delaney, M.A., Exec. Dir.

RELIGIOUS INSTITUTES OF MEN REPRESENTED IN THE DIOCESE

For further details refer to the corresponding bracketed number in the Religious Institutes of Men or Women section.

[1000]—*Congregation of the Passion*. (Union City, NJ).—C.P.

[0520]—*Franciscan Friars*. (Prov. of the Most Holy Name of Jesus).—O.F.M.

[0690]—*Jesuit Fathers and Brothers*. (Maryland Prov.).—S.J.

[0930]—*Oblates of St. Joseph*. (Asti, Italy).—O.S.J.

[]—*Priestly Fraternity of St. Peter*.—F.S.S.P.

[0610]—*Priests of the Congregation of Holy Cross*. (Wilkes-Barre, PA).—C.S.C.

RELIGIOUS INSTITUTES OF WOMEN REPRESENTED IN THE DIOCESE

[1810]—*Bernardine Sisters of the Third Order of St. Francis*.—O.S.F.

[0330]—*Carmelite Sisters of the Aged and Infirm*.—O.Carm.

[]—*Congregation of St. Joseph*.—C.S.J.

[0890]—*Daughters of Our Lady of Mercy*.—D.M.

[2575]—*Institute of the Sisters of Mercy of the Americas*.—R.S.M.

[]—*Little Sisters of the Poor*.—P.S.D.P.

[]—*Marianites of the Holy Cross*.—M.S.C.

[3160]—*Parish Visitors of Mary Immaculate*.—P.V.M.I.

[3240]—*Poor Sisters of Jesus Crucified and the Sorrowful Mother*.—C.J.C.

[3170]—*Religious of the Passion of Jesus Christ*.—C.P.

[3430]—*Religious Teachers Filippini*.—M.P.F.

[0570]—*Sisters of Charity of Seton Hill, Greensburg, PA*.—S.C.

[0660]—*Sisters of Christian Charity*.—S.C.C.

[2990]—*Sisters of Notre Dame*. (Ohio).—S.N.D.

[3780]—*Sisters of Saints Cyril and Methodius*.—SS.C.M.

[]—*Sisters of St. Francis*.—O.S.F.

[1830]—*Sisters of the Good Shepherd*.—R.G.S.

[1970]—*Sisters of the Holy Family of Nazareth*.—C.S.F.N.

[2160]—*Sisters, Servants of the Immaculate Heart of Mary*.—I.H.M.

DIOCESAN CEMETERIES

SCRANTON. *Cathedral*, 1708 Oram St., 18504. Tel: 717-347-9251.

Diocesan Cemeteries Office, 1708 Oram St., 18504. Tel: 717-346-8923. Walter Bennett, Dir.

CARVERTON. *Mount Olivet*, P.O. Box 257, 18644. Tel: 717-696-3636.

DRUMS. *Calvary*, P.O. Box 485, 18222. Tel: 717-788-2150.

MOSCOW. *St. Catherine's*, Main St., P.O. Box 114, 18444. Tel: 717-842-8411.

OLD FORGE. *Holy Cross*, 18518. Tel: 717-347-9251.

WILLIAMSPORT. *Resurrection*, P.O. Box 12, 17754. Tel: 717-368-2727.

NECROLOGY

† Barrett, Rev. Msgr. Francis G., (Retired). —Died May 29, 1996.

† Caglioti, Ralph V., (Retired). —Died May 21, 1996.

† Corcoran, Francis P., Williamsport, PA, St. Boniface's Church. —Died Aug. 11, 1996.

† Fundalewicz, Edward L., Scranton, PA, St. Michael's Church. —Died Nov. 22, 1995.

† Gardzalla, Robert J., (Retired). —Died April 19, 1996.

† Green, John J., (Retired). —Died Sept. 23, 1996.

† Kazlauskas, John J., (Retired). —Died Dec. 17, 1995.

† Matircho, George J., (Retired). —Died March 24, 1996.

† McAndrews, Arthur J., (Retired). —Died April 25, 1996.

† McCloskey, George P., (Military Chaplains). —Died Aug. 20, 1996.

✠ McCormick, Most Rev. J. Carroll, (Retired). —Died Nov. 2, 1996.

† O'Neill, John J., (Retired). —Died Dec. 19, 1995.

† Yashkas, Rev. Msgr. Frank L., (Retired). —Died March 26, 1996.

Archdiocese of Seattle

Archidioecesis Seattlensis

Most Reverend

THOMAS J. MURPHY, D.D., S.T.D.

Archbishop of Seattle; ordained April 12, 1958; appointed Bishop of Great Falls July 5, 1978; appointed Coadjutor Archbishop of Seattle May 26, 1987; succeeded to See August 21, 1991. *Office: 910 Marion St., Seattle, WA, 98104.* Tel.: 206-382-4375; Fax: 206-382-3495. *Res.: Connolly House, 1104 Spring, Seattle, WA, 98104.* Tel.: 206-623-2625.

Most Reverend

RAYMOND G. HUNTHAUSEN, D.D.

Retired Archbishop of Seattle; ordained June 1, 1946; appointed Bishop of Helena, Montana July 8, 1962; consecrated August 30, 1962; appointed Archbishop of Seattle February 25, 1975; installed May 22, 1975; retired August 21, 1991. *Office: 910 Marion St., Seattle, WA, 98104.* Tel.: 206-382-4884; Fax: 206-382-3495.

Legal Title: *"Corporation of the Catholic Archbishop of Seattle."*

ESTABLISHED MAY 31, 1850. NAME CHANGED TO SEATTLE, SEPTEMBER 11, 1907.

CREATED ARCHDIOCESE, JUNE 23, 1951.

Square Miles 24,834.

Comprises the Counties of Clallam, Clark, Cowlitz, Grays Harbor, Island, Jefferson, King, Kitsap, Lewis, Mason, Pacific, Pierce, San Juan, Skagit, Skamania, Snohomish, Thurston, Wahkiakum and Whatcom in the State of Washington.

For legal titles of parishes and archdiocesan institutions, consult The Chancery.

Chancery Office: 910 Marion St., Seattle, WA, 98104. Tel.: 206-382-4560; Fax: 206-382-4840.

Web site address: http://www.seattlearch.org

STATISTICAL OVERVIEW

Personnel	
Archbishop	1
Retired Archbishops	1
Abbots	1
Retired Abbots	2
Priests: Diocesan Active in Diocese	140
Priests: Active Outside Diocese	4
Priests: Retired, Sick or Absent	45
Number of Diocesan Priests	189
Religious Priests in Diocese	132
Extern Priests in Diocese	22
Ordinations:	
Diocesan Priests	1
Religious Priests	1
Transitional Deacons	3
Permanent Deacons in Diocese	82
Total Brothers	31
Total Sisters	674
Parishes	
Parishes	138
With Resident Pastor:	
Resident Diocesan Priests	84
Resident Religious Priests	18
Without Resident Pastor:	
Administered by Priests	24
Administered by Women Religious	8
Administered by Lay People	4
Missions	30
Pastoral Centers	7
New Parishes Created	1
Professional Ministry Personnel:	
Sisters	42
Lay Ministers	420
Welfare	
Catholic Hospitals	9
Total Assisted	1,068,576
Health Care Centers	3
Total Assisted	6,173
Homes for the Aged	7
Total Assisted	1,248
Day Care and Extended Day Care Centers	6
Total Assisted	725
Specialized Homes	4
Total Assisted	2,301
Special Centers for Social Services	22
Total Assisted	98,538
Residential Care of Disabled	1
Total Assisted	50
Other Institutions	11
Total Assisted	293
Educational	
Diocesan Students in Other Seminaries	24
Total Seminarians	24
Colleges and Universities	2
Total Students	7,503
High Schools, Diocesan and Parish	3
Total Students	2,189
High Schools, Private	6
Total Students	2,924
Elementary Schools, Diocesan and Parish	54
Total Students	15,641
Elementary Schools, Private	2
Total Students	674
Catechesis/Religious Education:	
High School Students	6,530
Elementary Students	27,580
Total Students Under Catholic Instruction	63,065
Teachers in the Diocese:	
Priests	40
Brothers	12
Sisters	45
Lay Teachers	1,527
Vital Statistics	
Receptions into the Church:	
Infant Baptism Totals	6,308
Adult Baptism Totals	1,129
Received into Full Communion	703
First Communions	5,562
Confirmations	2,687
Marriages:	
Catholic	1,042
Interfaith	1,174
Total Marriages	2,216
Deaths	2,853
Total Catholic Population	369,050
Total Population	4,282,200

Former Bishops—Rt. Rev. A. M. A. BLANCHET, cons. Bishop of Walla Walla, Sept. 27, 1846; transferred to Nesqually, May 31, 1850; resigned 1879 made Bishop of Ibora; died Feb. 25, 1887.—Rt. Rev. AEGIDIUS JUNGER, D.D., cons. Oct. 28, 1879; died Dec. 26, 1895.—Most Rev. EDWARD JOHN O'DEA, D.D., cons. Bishop of Nesqually, Sept. 8, 1896 See transferred to Seattle, Sept. 11, 1907; died Dec. 25, 1932.—Most Rev. GERALD SHAUGHNESSY, S.M., S.T.D., Bishop of Seattle; appt. July 1, 1933; cons. Sept. 19, 1933; died May 18, 1950.—Most Rev. THOMAS A. CONNOLLY, D.D., cons. Aug. 24, 1939 succeeded, May 18, 1950; retired Feb. 25, 1975; died April 18, 1991.—Most Rev. RAYMOND G. HUNTHAUSEN, D.D., ord. June 1, 1946; appt. Bishop of Helena, Montana, July 8, 1962; cons. Aug. 30, 1962; appt. Archbishop of Seattle, Feb. 25, 1975; installed May 22, 1975; retired Aug. 21, 1991.

Office of the Archbishop

Chancery Office—*910 Marion St., Seattle, 98104.* Tel: 206-382-4560; Fax: 206-382-4840.

Vicars General—Very Rev. GEORGE L. THOMAS, Ph.D., V.G., *910 Marion St., Seattle, 98104.* Tel: 204-382-4888. Very Rev. JAMES D. PICTON, V.G., J.D., *910 Marion St., Seattle, 98104.* Tel: 206-382-4288.

Chancellor—Very Rev. GEORGE L. THOMAS, Ph.D., V.G., *910 Marion St., Seattle, 98104.* Tel: 206-382-4888.

Episcopal Vicars for Ministers—Very Rev. GEORGE L. THOMAS, Ph.D., V.G., *910 Marion St., Seattle, 98104.* Tel: 206-382-4888.

Episcopal Vicar for Parishes and Faith Communities—Very Rev. JAMES D. PICTON, V.G., J.D., *910 Marion St., Seattle, 98104.* Tel: 206-382-4288.

Canonical Consultant—Rev. ANTHONY E. BAWYN, J.C.L.; Sr. BEVERLY DUNN, S.P., J.C.D., *910 Marion St., Seattle, 98104.* Tel: 206-382-4565.

Notaries—Ms CHRISTINE TAYLOR Tel: 206-382-4357. Rev. ANTHONY E. BAWYN, J.C.L. Tel: 206-382-4565. Sr. JOYCE COX, B.V.M. Tel: 206-382-4829.

Coordinator for Religious—Sr. JOYCE COX, B.V.M., *910 Marion St., Seattle, 98104.* Tel: 206-382-4829.

Administrative Assistant to the Archbishops—Mrs. MARILYN MADDEFORD, *910 Marion St., Seattle, 98104.* Tel: 206-382-4886.

College of Consultors—Very Rev. GEORGE L. THOMAS, Ph.D., V.G.; JAMES D. PICTON, V.G., J.D., And Very Reverend Deans.

Deans—Very Rev. GARY MORELLI, Northern: Very Rev. OLIVER DUGGAN, Snohomish: Very Rev. JOSEPH P. MITCHELL, Peninsula: Very Rev. JOHN MCMULLAN, North Seattle: Very Rev. HORACIO YANEZ, Eastside: Very Rev. LESTER MCCLOSKEY, South Seattle: Very Rev. PETER DUGGAN, South King: Very Rev. ALAN MARSHALL, Pierce: Very Rev. ROGER SMITH, South Sound: Very Rev. HANS OLSON, Southern:

Assistant to the Archbishop for Administration and Finance—Mr. PATRICK SURSELY, Dir., *910 Marion St., Seattle, 98104.* Tel: 206-382-4588.

Assistant to the Archbishop for Chancery Management & Pastoral Planning—Mr. DENNIS J. O'LEARY, *910 Marion St., Seattle, 98104.* Tel: 206-382-4834.

Metropolitan Tribunal

Judicial Vicar—Very Rev. JOSEPH H. DOOGAN, J.C.L., *910 Marion St., Seattle, 98104.* Tel: 206-382-4830; Fax: 206-382-2071.

Adjunct Judicial Vicar—Rev. JAMES A. WILLIAMS, J.C.L.

Judges—CHARLENE CRAM; Rev. ANTHONY BAWYN, J.C.L.; JAMES A. BROOKS; Sr. BEVERLY DUNN, S.P., J.C.D.; Rev. BERNARD A. KONDA, J.C.D.; Deacon LAWRENCE J. SULLIVAN.

Defenders of the Bond—Very Rev. JAMES D. PICTON, V.G., J.D.; Sr. ANNE HERKENRATH, S.N.J.M.; CHARLOTTE EDMAN; JOHN F. WILSON, J.D.

Notaries—VALERIE BLESENER; IRENE DELVILLAR; KAREN LEZCANO.

Archdiocesan Offices and Directors

African/American Ministry—SHARON PITRE-WILLIAMS, Dir., *910 Marion St., Seattle, 98104.* Tel: 206-382-2061; Fax: 206-382-2069.

AIDS Ministry—Rev. DAVID JAEGER, Chap., *910 Marion St., Seattle, 98104.* Tel: 206-382-4942.

Adult and Religious Education—Ms. CARLA CALDWELL, *910 Marion St., Seattle, 98104.* Tel: 206-382-4268.

Archdiocesan Council of Catholic Women—Sr. JOYCE COX, B.V.M., Liaison, *910 Marion St., Seattle, 98104.* Tel: 206-382-4829.

Archdiocesan Liturgical Commission—Mr. DENNIS LUCEY, Chm., *910 Marion St., Seattle, 98104.* Tel: 206-382-4878.

Archdiocesan Pastoral Council—Ms. CARLA CALDWELL, Exec. Sec., *910 Marion St., Seattle, 98104.* Tel: 206-382-4268.

Archives—Ms. CHRISTINE TAYLOR, *910 Marion St., Seattle, 98104.* Tel: 206-382-4857.

Asian/Pacific Island Ministry—VERONICA LEASIOLAGI BARBER, Dir., *910 Marion St., Seattle, 98104.* Tel: 206-382-4828; Fax: 206-382-2069.

Campaign for Human Development—Mr. J. L. DROUHARD, Interim Dir., *910 Marion St., Seattle, 98104.* Tel: 206-382-4869; Fax: 206-382-3487.

Campus Ministry—Rev. THOMAS DEMAN, O.P., *Newman Center, U of W, 4502 20th Ave., N.E., Seattle, 98105.* Tel: 206-527-5072.

Catholic Community Services of Western Washington—Mr. MICHAEL REICHERT, Dir., *100 23rd Ave. S., Seattle, 98144.* Tel: 206-328-5696; Fax: 206-328-5699.

Catholic Relief Services—J.L. DROUHARD, Interim Dir., *910 Marion St., Seattle, 98104.* Tel: 206-382-4583.

Catholic Schools—Mr. HARRY PURPUR, Supt., *910 Marion St., Seattle, 98104.* Tel: 206-382-4855.

Catholic Youth Organization—Dr. STEPHEN MCAULIFFE, Dir., *910 Marion St., Seattle, 98104.* Tel: 206-382-4562.

Cemeteries—Mr. RICHARD PETERSON, Dir., *910 Marion St., Seattle, 98104.* Tel: 206-382-9281.

Censores Librorum—Revs. PETER CHIRICO, S.S., S.T.D.; WILLIAM TREACY; MICHAEL RASCHKO, Ph.D.

Chinese, Ministry to—Rev. Msgr. JOHN CHI, Chap., *1531 Bradner Pl., S., Seattle, 98144.* Tel: 206-324-8521.

Development Office—Mr. PAUL LEBLANC, Dir., *910 Marion St., Seattle, 98104.* Tel: 206-382-4836.

Due Process, Office for—Ms. JESSIE DYE, Admin., *910 Marion St., Seattle, 98104.* Tel: 206-382-4592.

Ecumenical and Interreligious Affairs—Sr. JOYCE COX, B.V.M., *910 Marion St., Seattle, 98104.* Tel: 206-382-4829.

Events Planning—Mr. DAVID JONES, *910 Marion St., Seattle, 98104.* Tel: 206-382-4832.

Hispanic Ministry—MARIA ESTHER BAZAN, Dir., *910 Marion St., Seattle, 98104.* Tel: 206-382-4825; Fax: 206-382-2069.

Formation and Training—Dr. MARY CROSS, *910 Marion St., Seattle, 98104.* Tel: 206-382-4835. Mr. JOHN REID, *910 Marion St., Seattle, 98104.* Tel: 206-382-4096.

Holy Childhood, Pontifical Association of the—J.L. DROUHARD, Interim Dir., *910 Marion St., Seattle, 98104.* Tel: 206-382-4583.

Human Resources—COLLEEN BRANAGAN, *910 Marion St., Seattle, 98104.* Tel: 206-382-3920.

Inclusion Ministry—KATHY SMALLEY, Dir., *910 Marion St., Seattle, 98104.* Tel: 206-382-2014.

Justice and Peace Office—Mr. J. L. DROUHARD, Interim Dir., *910 Marion St., Seattle, 98104.* Tel: 206-382-4869; Fax: 206-382-3487.

Koreans, Ministry to—Revs. IL MO KOO, *7912 Golden Given Rd. E., Tacoma, 98404.* Tel: 206-536-8660. MICHAEL AHN, *11700 1st. Ave., N.E., Seattle, 98125.* Tel: 206-362-2492; 362-2278.

Marriage Encounter—Rev. JOHN D. MCCLUSKEY, S.J., Spiritual Dir., *9460 N.E. 14th, Bellevue, 98004.* Tel: 206-454-9536.

Ministry to Priests, Program of—Sr JOYCE COX, B.V.M., *910 Marion St., Seattle, 98104.* Tel: 206-382-4829.

Native American Ministry—Rev. PATRICK TWOHY, S.J.; Sr. JULIE CODD, C.S.J.P., *P.O. Box A, LaConner, 98257.* Tel: 206-466-4680.

Newspaper "The Catholic Northwest Progress"—Ms. KAY LAGRIED, Exec. Editor; DAN MADDEN, Mng. Editor, *910 Marion St., Seattle, 98104.* Tel: 206-382-4827.

Permanent Diaconate Program—Vacant, *910 Marion St., Seattle, 98104.* Tel: 206-382-3482.

Personnel Director for Priests—Rev. PAUL MAGNANO, *910 Marion St., Seattle, 98104.* Tel: 206-382-7317.

Polish Speaking, Ministry to—Revs. PIOTR DZIKOWSKI, S.Ch., *3422 Portland Ave., Tacoma, 98404.* Tel: 206-272-5232. JOZEF CALIK, S.Ch., *3221 14th Ave., W., Seattle, 98119.* Tel: 206-282-1804.

Presbyteral Council—Most Rev. THOMAS J. MURPHY, D.D., S.T.D., Pres.

Priests' Eucharistic League—Rev. DESMOND MCMAHON, Dir., *910 Marion St., Seattle, 98104.* Tel: 206-382-4886.

Priests' Health Plan—Most Rev. THOMAS J. MURPHY, D.D., S.T.D., Pres.; Rev. SEAN FOX, Chm.

Priests' Pension Plan—Most Rev. THOMAS J. MURPHY, D.D., S.T.D.; Rev. SEAN FOX, Chm.

Prison and Jail Ministry—Vacant, *910 Marion St., Seattle, 98104.* Tel: 206-382-1477.

Propagation of the Faith, Society for the—J.L. DROUHARD, Interim Dir., *910 Marion St., Seattle, Wa, 98104.* Tel: 206-382-4583.

Public Affairs Office—Mr. JAMES F. BRITT, Dir., *910 Marion St., Seattle, 98104.* Tel: 206-382-4862; Fax: 206-382-3487.

Resettlement Dir.—Mr. DENNY HUNTHAUSEN, *5410 N. 44th, Tacoma, 98407.* Tel: 206-752-2455.

Sacramental Resources—Ms. CAROLYN LASSEK, *910 Marion St., Seattle, 98104.* Tel: 206-382-4838.

Seminarians, Vocation Discernment and Formation—Rev. CLAYTON MEYER, Ph.D., *910 Marion St., Seattle, 98104.* Tel: 206-382-4880.

Sisters' Council—Sr. SHARON PARK, O.P., *22010 S.E. 35th St., Issaquah, 98027.* Tel: 206-391-4493.

Special Ministries: Blessed Margaret Guild for the Blind—Rev. ANTHONY HAYCOCK, *10240 12th Ave. S., Seattle, 98168.* Tel: 206-762-3343. *International Catholic Deaf Assoc.*, Seattle Chapter No. 62, Rev. RICHARD HAYATSU, Chap., *406 S. 4th, Renton, 98055.* Tel: 206-255-3132. *Ministry to Mentally Retarded*, Rev. JAMES BOYLE, *204 6th Ave. S.W., Puyallup, 98371.* Tel: 206-841-3923.

Theological Resources—Revs. PETER CHIRICO, S.S., S.T.D., *804 9th Ave., Seattle, 98104.* Tel: 206-628-3920. JAMES EBLEN, S.T.L., Ph.D., *408 Bellevue Ave. E., Seattle, 98102.* Tel: 206-329-5692. CLAYTON MEYER, Ph.D., *P.O. Box 1763, Bellevue, 98009.* Tel: 206-382-4880. MICHAEL RASCHKO, Ph.D., *910 Marion St., Seattle, 98104.* Tel: 206-382-4276.

Telecommunication—Ms. KATHRYN JOHNSON, *910 Marion St., Seattle, 98104.* Tel: 206-382-4827.

Vietnamese, Representative for—Rev. PHUONG DUC TRAN (Vietnam), *1230 E. Fir, Seattle, 98122.* Tel: 206-325-5626.

Vocations Office—Mr. RICHARD SHIVELY, *910 Marion St., Seattle, 98104.* Tel: 206-382-4595.

Worship, Resources—Ms. CAROLYN LASSEK, *910 Marion St., Seattle, 98104.* Tel: 206-382-4838.

CLERGY, PARISHES, MISSIONS AND PAROCHIAL SCHOOLS

CITY OF SEATTLE
(King County)

1—ST. JAMES CATHEDRAL, Very Rev. Michael G. Ryan; Rev. Richard Ward. In res., Most Rev. Raymond Hunthausen; Rev. Peter F. Chirico, S.S.
Res., 804 Ninth Ave., 98104. Tel: 206-622-3559; Fax: 206-622-5303.
Convent—907 Columbia St., 98104. Tel: 206-682-1308.
Sisters 7.

2—ST. ALPHONSUS, Rev. James Gandrau. In res., Revs. Timothy Moynihan; George Limbani (Malawi, Africa).
Res., 5816 15th Ave., N.W., 98107. Tel: 206-784-6464; Fax: 206-789-5709.
School—Kathryn Palmquist-Keck, Prin. Lay Teachers 15; Students 200.

3—ST. ANNE, Rev. Robert Camuso.
Res., 1411 1st Ave. W., 98119. Tel: 206-282-0223; Fax: 206-217-9541.
School—101 W. Lee St., 98119. Tel: 206-282-3538; Fax: 206-284-4191. Mrs. Pat Durand, Prin.
Sisters of the Holy Names of Jesus and Mary 1; Lay Teachers 13; Students 214.

4—ST. BENEDICT, Rev. Paul Waldie, O.M.I. In res., Revs. Gerard Clenaghan, O.M.I.; Edward T. McHugh, O.M.I.; Denis Pringle, S.A.
Res., 1805 N. 49th St., 98103. Tel: 206-632-1475; Fax: 206-632-2167.
School—4811 Wallingford N., 98103. Tel: 206-633-3375. Charles Secrest, Prin.
Sisters 2; Lay Teachers 12; Students 247.

5—ST. BERNADETTE, Rev. Fabian MacDonald, Admin.
Res., 861 S.W. 126th St., 98146. Tel: 206-242-7370; Fax: 206-242-7371.
School—1028 S.W. 128th St., 98146. Tel: 206-244-4934; Fax: 206-243-6010. Sr. Marie Colarossi, Prin.
Sisters 2; Lay Teachers 12; Students 240.

6—ST. BRIDGET, Rev. Harold Quigg.
Res., 4900 N.E. 50th, 98105. Tel: 206-523-8787; Fax: 206-528-7511.

7—ST. CATHERINE, Rev. David White, Admin.
Res., 8610 8th Ave. N.E., 98115. Tel: 206-523-9132.
School—8524 8th Ave., N.E., 98115. Tel: 206-525-0581. Ms. Noel Mishler, Prin.
Lay Teachers 13; Students 242.

8—ST. EDWARD, Rev. Joseph Tyson.
Res., 4213 S. Orcas St., 98118. Tel: 206-722-7888; Fax: 206-722-7895.
School—4212 S. Mead St., 98118. Tel: 206-725-1774. Sr. Nancy Anderson, S.N.J.M., Co-Prin.; Ms. Patty Mitchell, Co-Prin.
Lay Teachers 10; Students 128.

9—ST. GEORGE, Rev. William Heric, Pastor.
Res., 5306 13th Ave. S., 98108. Tel: 206-762-7744; Fax: 206-762-4207.
School—5117 13th Ave. S., 98108. Tel: 206-762-0656; Fax: 206-763-3220. Bernadette Mahoney, Prin.
Sisters 1; Lay Teachers 12; Students 251.

10—ST. JOHN, Rev. William A. McKee.
Office: 121 N. 80th St., 98103 Tel: 206-782-2810; Fax: 206-782-0242.
School—Tel: 206-783-0337. Dan Sherman, Prin.
Lay Teachers 26; Students 437.

11—ST. JOSEPH, Revs. Craig Boly, S.J.; Lee Kapfer, S.J.
Res., 732 18th Ave., E., 98112 Tel: 206-324-2522; Fax: 206-329-5698.
School—700 18 Ave. E., Tel: 206-329-3260; Fax: 206-324-7773. George Hofbauer, Prin.
Lay Teachers 39; Students 620.

12—ST. LUKE, Rev. Roger O'Brien.
Res., 322 N. 175th St., 98133 Tel: 206-546-2451; Fax: 206-546-0328.
School—17533 St. Luke Pl. N., 98133. Tel: 206-542-1133. Mr. George Stein, Prin.
Sisters of St. Dominic 1; Lay Teachers 23; Students 431.

13—ST. MARGARET OF SCOTLAND, Rev. Robert Camuso. In res., Rev. Joseph Calik, S.Ch., Polish Ministry.
Res., 3221 14th Ave., W., 98119. Tel: 206-282-1804; Fax: 206-282-6461.

14—ST. MARK, Rev. Dennis Kemp.
Res., 18033 15th Pl., N.E., 98155. Tel: 206-364-7900; Fax: 206-367-3919.
School—Tel: 206-364-1633; Fax: 206-364-1633. Ruth Foisy, Prin.
Lay Teachers 13; Students 235.

15—ST. MARY, Rev. Anthony J. Haycock, Admin.
Res., 611 20th Ave., S., 98144. Tel: 206-324-7100; Fax: 206-329-4596.
Convent—2021 S. Weller St., 98144. Tel: 206-324-1535. Religious of the Sacred Heart of Jesus.

16—ST. MATTHEW, Rev. Gordon Douglas; Very Rev. John McMullan; Sr. Kathleen Buzard, S.N.J.M., Pastoral Life Dir.
Res., 1240 N.E. 127th St., 98125. Tel: 206-363-6767; Fax: 206-362-4863.
School—1230 N.E. 127th, 98125. Tel: 206-362-2785. Sr. Monica Moffat, S.N.J.M., Prin.
Lay Teachers 12; Students 260.

17—ST. PATRICK, Very Rev. Lester J. McCloskey; Rev. James Eblen; Ms. Victoria Ries, Pastoral Life Dir.
Res., 2702 Broadway E., 98102. Tel: 206-329-2960; Fax & TTY: 206-329-2961.

18—ST. PAUL, Rev. William Heric, Co-Pastor; Very Rev. Lester J. McCloskey, Pastor.
Res., 5600 S. Ryan St., 98178. Tel: 206-725-2050; Fax: 206-725-7476.
School—10001 57th Ave. S., 98178. Tel: 206-725-0780. Mary Buza-Sims, Prin.

Lay Teachers 11; Students 214.

19—ST. PETER, Rev. Clay Meyer, Admin.
Res., 2807 15th Ave., S., 98144. Tel: 206-324-2290.

20—ST. THERESE, Very Rev. Lester J. McCloskey; Ms. Patricia Repikoff, Pastoral Life Dir.; Rev. Joseph McGowan, S.J.
Res., 3416 E. Marion St., 98122. Tel: 206-325-2711; Fax: 206-329-8373.
School—900-35th Ave., 98122. Tel: 206-324-0460; Fax: 206-324-8464. Mrs. Eileen Gray, Prin.
Sisters of Providence 1; Lay Teachers 13; Students 212.

21—ASSUMPTION, Sr. Kay Lewis, O.P., Pastoral Life Dir.; Revs. Michael Angelovic; John McMullan.
Res., 3214 N.E. 62nd St., 98115. Tel: 206-522-7674; Fax: 206-522-7675.
School—Tel: 206-524-7452; Fax: 206-524-6757. Michael Foy, Prin.
Sisters 1; Lay Teachers 24; Students 522.

22—BLESSED SACRAMENT, Revs. Michael B. Sweeney, O.P.; Joseph Bradshaw, O.P. In res., Revs. Leo Thomas, O.P.; Joseph Fulton, O.P.
Res., 5041 Ninth Ave., N.E., 98105. Tel: 206-547-3020; Fax: 206-547-6371.

23—CHRIST THE KING, Revs. W. Andrew Bullwinkel; Joseph Stocking, S.J., Parochial Vicar.
Res., 405 N. 117th St., 98133. Tel: 206-362-1545; Fax: 206-364-8325.
School—415 N. 117th, 98133. Tel: 206-364-6890.
Lay Teachers 15; Students 224.

24—HOLY FAMILY, Revs. Phillip Bloom, Admin.; C. Vincent Peterson.
Res., 9622 20th Ave., S.W., 98106. Tel: 206-767-6220; Fax: 206-767-0374.
School—Tel: 206-767-6640. Dr. Robert Scripko, Prin.
Sisters 1; Lay Teachers 13; Students 241.

25—HOLY ROSARY, Rev. Jeffery L. Sarkies.
Res., 4139 42nd Ave., S.W., 98116. Tel: 206-935-8353; Fax: 206-935-4303.
School—Tel: 206-937-7255. Kristi Brown, Prin.
Sisters 1; Lay Teachers 23; Students 407.

26—IMMACULATE CONCEPTION, Rev. John Nwanze, O.P.; Ms. Sharon Petre-Williams, Admin. In res., Rev. Jamie Tolang.
Res., 820 18th Ave., 98122. Tel: 206-322-5970; Fax: 206-322-9417.

27—OUR LADY OF FATIMA, Rev. Thomas Quinn. In res., Rev. Joseph Doogan.
Res., 3218 W. Barrett, 98199. Tel: 206-283-1456; Fax: 206-283-5788.
School—3301 W. Dravus St., 98199. Tel: 206-283-7031; Fax: 206-283-7696. Susan Burdett, Prin.
Sisters 1; Lay Teachers 19; Students 277.

28—OUR LADY OF GUADALUPE, Rev. William Hallahan, O.M.I.
Res., 7000-35th Ave. S.W., 98126. Tel: 206-935-0358; Fax: 206-935-1230.
School—3401 S.W. Myrtle, 98126. Tel: 206-935-0651; Fax: 206-938-3695. Barbara Heneghan, Ed.D., Prin.
Lay Teachers 12; Students 225.

29—OUR LADY OF THE LAKE, Very Rev. John E. McMullan.
Res., 8900 35th Ave., N.E., 98115. Tel: 206-523-6776; Fax: 206-524-0848.
School—3520 N.E. 89th St., 98115. Tel: 206-525-9980; Fax: 206-523-2858. Mrs. Maureen Blum, Prin.
Lay Teachers 16; Students 237.

30—OUR LADY OF LOURDES, Rev. Gerald L. Mayovsky.
Res., 10240 12th Ave. S., 98168. Tel: 206-762-3343; Fax: 206-768-1507.

31—OUR LADY OF MOUNT VIRGIN (Italian), Very Rev. Lester J. McCloskey; Rev. Pasquale M. Spoletini, S.J. In res., Rev. Msgr. John Chi (Taipei).
Res., 1531 Bradner Pl. S., 98144. Tel: 206-324-8521.

32—SACRED HEART OF JESUS, Revs. M. Durkin Fitzgerald, C.SS.R.; Joseph Curalli, C.SS.R.; Lyle Konen, C.SS.R. In res., Revs. Bernard Mulligan, C.SS.R.; Anthony Slane, C.SS.R.; Bernard Vanhoomissen, C.SS.R.
Res., 205 2nd Ave. N., P.O. Box 9040, Queen Anne Sta., 98109. Tel: 206-284-4680; Fax: 206-284-3161.

OUTSIDE THE CITY OF SEATTLE

Aberdeen, Grays Harbor Co., St. Mary's, Sr. Deanna Carr, B.V.M., Pastoral Life Dir.; Revs. Patrick McDermott; Scott Connolly; Stephen Roman; Very Rev. James Picton.
Res., 306 E. Third St., 98520. Tel: 360-532-8300; Fax: 360-538-9987.
School—518 N. H St., 98520. Tel: 360-532-1230; Fax: 360-532-1209. Sr. Angela McCarthy, C.S.J.P., Prin.
Lay Teachers 11; Students 187.
Mission—Westport, St. Paul, P.O. Box 332, Westport 98585. Tel: 206-268-0665. In res., Rev. Stephen Roman.
SS. Peter and Paul (Polish), Sr. Deanna Carr, B.V.M., Pastoral Life Dir.; Revs. Patrick McDermott; Scott Connolly; Stephen Roman; Very Rev. James Picton; Rev. Joseph A. Dominic, Pastor Emeritus.
Res., 306 E. Third St., 98520. Tel: 360-532-8300; Fax: 360-538-9987.

Anacortes, Skagit Co., St. Mary's, Rev. William R. Harris.
Res., 4001 St. Mary's Dr., 98221. Tel: 360-293-2101; Fax: 360-293-2102.

Arlington, Snohomish Co., Immaculate Conception, Rev. Richard J. Spicer.
Res., 1200 E. Fifth, P.O. Box 69, 98223. Tel: 360-435-8565; Fax: 360-435-3781.
Mission—Darrington, Snohomish Co., St. John Mary Vianney, 1150 Riddle St., Darrington, 98241.

Auburn, King Co., Holy Family, Rev. Phuong Hoang.
Res., 505 17th St. S.E., P.O. Box B, 98071. Tel: 206-833-5130; Fax: 206-833-3421.
School—(Grades K-6) 505 17th St., S.E., 98002. Tel: 206-833-8688. Kathleen Cowin, Prin.
Sisters 1; Lay Teachers 13; Students 230.

Bainbridge Island, Kitsap Co., St. Cecilia's, Rev. Patrick Godley.
Res., 1310 Madison Ave. N., 98110. Tel: 206-842-3594; Fax: 206-842-6988.

Battle Ground, Clark Co., Sacred Heart, Rev. Franklin Lott, Admin.
Mailing Address: P.O. Box 38, 23505 N.E. 132nd Ave., 98604. Tel: 360-687-4515; Fax: 360-687-3322.
Mission—Yacolt, Clark Co., St. Joseph the Workman, 33704 Ranck Ave., Yacolt, 98678.

Bellevue, King Co., Sacred Heart, Rev. Marlin Connole. In res., Rev. John D. McCluskey, S.J.
Res., 9460 N.E. 14th St., 98004. Tel: 206-454-9536; Fax: 206-450-3909.
School—9450 N.E. 14th, 98004. Tel: 206-451-1773; Fax: 206-454-9538. Dr. Karen Matthews, Prin.
Lay Teachers 30; Students 457.
St. Louise, Very Rev. Horacio V. Yanez; Rev. William Fenn.
Res., 141 156th Ave. S.E., 98007. Tel: 206-747-4450; Fax: 206-644-3678.
School—133 156th Ave., S.E., 98007. Tel: 206-746-4220. Dan Fitzpatrick, Prin.
Lay Teachers 23; Students 467.
St. Madeleine Sophie, Rev. George O. Rink; Deacon Eugene R. Vanderzanden.
Res., 4400 130th Pl., S.E., 98006-2014. Tel: 206-747-6770; Fax: 206-747-6349.

Bellingham, Whatcom Co., Assumption B.V.M., Rev. James Lee.
Res., 2116 Cornwall Ave., 98225. Tel: 360-733-1380; Fax: 360-733-5644.
School—Tel: 360-733-6133; Fax: 360-733-3601. Sr. Anne Brand, Prin.
Lay Teachers 14; Students 284.
Sacred Heart, Very Rev. Gary J. Morelli.
Res., 1111 14th St., 98225. Tel: 360-734-2850; Fax: 360-734-0947. [JC]

Black Diamond, King Co., St. Barbara, Rev. M. Charles Palluck.
Res., Sixth Ave. near Baker, P.O. Box 189, 98010. Tel: 360-886-2229.

Bothell, King Co., St. Brendan, Rev. Steven Sallis.
Res., 10051 N.E. 195th, 98011. Tel: 206-483-9400; Fax: 206-483-2839.
School—Tel: 206-483-8300. Arlene Sullivan, Prin.
Lay Teachers 15; Students 267.
Catechesis/Religious Programs—Students 530.
St. Elizabeth Ann Seton, Snohomish Co., Very Rev. Oliver F. Duggan.
Res., P.O. Box 12429, Mill Creek, 98082-0429. Tel: 206-481-0303; Fax: 206-485-8510.
Catechesis/Religious Programs—Mavis Kalbrener, D.R.E.
Students 534.

Bremerton, Kitsap Co., Our Lady, Star of the Sea, Very Rev. Joseph P. Mitchell; Deacon James Bemis.
Office: 1513-6th St., 98337. Tel: 360-479-3777; Fax: 360-479-3155.
School—511 Veneta Ave., 98337. Tel: 360-373-5162. Jill Metcalf, Prin.
Lay Teachers 9; Students 174.
Holy Trinity, Rev. Jack Buckalew.
Mailing Address: P.O. Box 910, Tracyton, 98393.
Res., 4215 Pine Rd., 98310. Tel: 360-377-7674; Fax: 360-377-3181.

Buckley, Pierce Co., St. Aloysius, Rev. Hervey Vanasse.
Res., 211 W. Mason St., P.O. Box H, 98321. Tel: 360-862-3014.
Mission—Wilkeson, Pierce Co., Our Lady of Lourdes.

Burlington, Skagit Co., St. Charles, Revs. Paul A. Magnano; J Michael Holland.
Res., 935 Peterson Rd., 98233. Tel: 360-757-0128; Fax: 360-757-0418.

Camas, Clark Co., St. Thomas, Rev. Ronald H. Belisle.
Res., 324 N.E. Oak, 98607. Tel: 360-834-2126; Fax: 360-834-5106. [CEM]
Mission—Stevenson, Skamania Co., Star of the Sea. P.O. Box 901.

Castle Rock, Cowlitz Co., St. Mary, Rev. Robert L. Evenson.
Res., 229 Front Ave., S.W., P.O. Box 960, 98611. Tel: 360-274-4911.

Centralia, Lewis Co., St. Mary's, Rev. Tuan Nguyen.
Res., 225 N. Washington Ave., 98531. Tel: 360-736-4356.

Chehalis, Lewis Co., St. Joseph's, Rev. Tuan Nguyen.
Mailing Address: 157 S.W. 6th St., 98532.
Res., 682 S.W. Cascade Ave., 98532. Tel: 360-748-4953; Fax: 360-748-3149.
School—123 S.W. 6th St., 98532. Tel: 360-748-0961; Fax: 360-748-3149. Laurie Heinz, Prin.
Sisters 1; Lay Teachers 8; Students 135.

Des Moines, King Co., St. Philomena, Rev. Dennis A. Wood.
Res., 1790 S. 222nd St., 98198. Tel: 206-878-8709; Fax: 206-824-3480.
School—1815 S. 220th, 98198. Tel: 206-824-4051; Fax: 206-878-4664. Karen Tarabochia, Prin.
Lay Teachers 14; Students 258.

Edmonds, Snohomish Co., Holy Rosary, Rev. Kenneth Haydock.
Res., 630 7th Ave., N., P.O. Box 206, 98020. Tel: 206-778-3122; Fax: 206-672-4909.
School—760 Aloha St., 98020. Tel: 206-778-3197; Fax: 206-672-4909. Barbara Polston, Prin.
Lay Teachers 16; Students 268.

Elma, Grays Harbor Co., St. Joseph's, Rev. John McLaughlin.
Res., 510 W. Waldrip St., P.O. Box AA, 98541. Tel: 206-482-3190. [CEM]
Mission—Montesano, Grays Harbor Co., St. John, Broadway and Church St., Montesano, 98563. Tel: 206-249-5766.

Enumclaw, King Co., Sacred Heart of Jesus, Rev. Gary M. Zender.
Res., 1614 Farrelly St., 98022. Tel: 360-825-3759; Fax: 360-825-6832.
Station—Crystal Springs, Crystal Mountain Chapel.

Everett, Snohomish Co., Immaculate Conception, Rev. Dennis E. Robb.
Mailing Address: 2619 Cedar St., 98201.
Res., 2430 Hoyt Ave., 98201. Tel: 206-259-2272; Fax: 206-252-6907. [JC]
School—2508 Hoyt Ave., 98201. Tel: 206-252-5175; Fax: 206-252-5176. Sr. Dolores Crosby, S.N.J.M., Prin.
Sisters 1; Lay Teachers 16; Students 426.
Our Lady of Perpetual Help, Rev. Dennis E. Robb.
Res., 2619 Cedar St., 98201. Tel: 206-259-2272; Fax: 206-252-6907. [JC]
St. Mary Magdalen, Revs. Joseph M. Marquart; Patrick Freitag.
Res., 8717 7th Ave. S.E., 98208. Tel: 206-353-1211; Fax: 206-348-0458.
School—8615 7th Ave. S.E., 98208. Tel: 206-353-7559; Fax: 206-356-2687. Sr. Joanne McCauley, O.P., Prin.
Sisters 3; Lay Teachers 20; Students 424.
Mission—Mukilteo, Snohomish Co., St. John Evangelist.

Federal Way, King & Pierce Cos., St. Theresa, Rev. Kevin Moran, Admin.
Res., 3939 S.W. 331st, 98023. Tel: 206-838-5924; Fax: 206-838-6825.
St. Vincent De Paul, King Co., Revs. Thomas L. Vandenberg; Anthony Lan Tran (Vietnam).
Res., 30525 8th Ave., S., 98003. Tel: 206-839-2320; Fax: 206-839-1819.
School—30527 8th Ave., S., 98003. Tel: 206-839-3532; Fax: 206-839-1819. Wanda Stewart, Prin.
Lay Teachers 19; Students 284.

Ferndale, Whatcom Co., St. Joseph, Rev. Timothy J. Sauer.
Res., 5781 Hendrickson Ave., 98248. Tel: 360-384-3651; Fax: 360-384-1879.
Missions—Blaine, Whatcom Co., St. Anne, 608 H. St., Blaine, 98230. Tel: 360-332-8048; Lummi, Whatcom Co., St. Joachim (Indian Reservation), Kwina & Lummi, Lummi, 98226. Tel: 360-734-2044.

Forks, Clallam Co., St. Anne Parish, Rev. Gerald O. Brunet, O.M.I.
Res., 553 Ackerly St., P.O. Box 2359, 98331. Tel: 360-374-9184.
Mission—Clallam Bay, Clallam Co., St. Thomas the Apostle.

Friday Harbor, San Juan Co., St. Francis, Rev. Thomas R. Garvin, S.J.
Res., 425 Price St., P.O. Box 1489, 98250. Tel: 360-378-2910 (Office); 378-6603 (Rectory).
Stations—Eastsound, St. Francis, Baker Rd. & N. Beach Rd., Eastsound, 98245. Tel: 360-376-6301;

378-2910; Lopez Island; San Juan Island, Roche Harbor.

Gig Harbor, Pierce Co., St. Nicholas, Rev. Gary Weisenberger.
Res., 3510 Rosedale St., P.O. Box 220, 98335. Tel: 206-851-8850.

Hoquiam, Grays Harbor Co., Our Lady of Good Help, Sr. Deanna Carr, B.V.M., Pastoral Life Dir.; Revs. Scott Connolly; Patrick McDermott; Stephen Roman; Very Rev. James Picton.
Res., 200 L St., 98550. Tel: 360-532-6103; Fax: 360-533-9012.
Mission—Quinault, Grays Harbor & Jefferson Cos., Our Lady of the Olympics, Box 165, Quinault, 98575. Tel: 360-288-2802.

Issaquah, King Co., Mary, Queen of Peace, Rev. J. Paul Dalton.
Res., 1121 228th Ave. S.E., 98029. Tel: 206-391-1178; 868-8251; Fax: 206-391-7979.
St. Joseph, Rev. Patrick S. Clark.
Res., 220 Mt. Park Blvd. S.W., P.O. Box 200, 98027. Tel: 206-392-5516; Fax: 206-392-2722.

Kelso, Cowlitz Co., St. Mary, Rev. Robert Evenson.
Res., 2200 Allen St., 98626. Tel: 360-423-3650; Fax: 360-423-4165.

Kent, King Co., Holy Spirit Parish, Very Rev. Peter J. Duggan.
Res., 310 3rd Ave. S., 98032. Tel: 206-859-0444; Fax: 206-859-5974. [CEM]
St. John the Baptist, Rev. Jack Walmesley.
Church—25810 156th Ave. S.E., 98042. Tel: 206-630-0701; Fax: 206-630-3174.

Kirkland, King Co., Holy Family, Revs. James L. Dalton; Emil Anderson.
Res., 7355 120th Ave. N.E., 98033. Tel: 206-822-0295; Fax: 206-827-0648.
School—Tel: 206-827-0444. Sue Ford Clausen, Prin.
Lay Teachers 17; Students 330.
St. John Mary Vianney, Rev. Joseph DeFolco; Deacon Edward F. White, Sr.
Res., 12600 84th Ave., N.E., 98034. Tel: 206-823-0787; Fax: 206-814-2115.

LaConner, Skagit Co., Sacred Heart, Rev. Paul Magnano; Deacon George Peterson, Pastoral Assoc.
Res., P.O. Box 757, 98257-0757. Tel: 206-466-3967.
St. Paul (Swinomish), Revs. Paul Magnano; Patrick Twohy, S.J., Parochial Vicar.
Mailing Address: P.O. Box 2100, 98257. Tel: 360-466-5737.
Church—1742 Pioneer Pky. Rd., 98257.

Lacey, Thurston Co., Sacred Heart of Jesus, Rev. Richard Parle.
Res., P.O. Box 3805, 98509-3805. Tel: 360-491-0890; Fax: 360-456-1028.

Langley, Island Co., St. Hubert, Rev. Gerald Moffat.
Mailing Address: P.O. Box 388, 98260.
Res., 815 Saratoga Ave., 98260. Tel: 360-221-5383.

Longview, Cowlitz Co., St. Rose de Viterbo, Rev. Lawrence Mender, O.S.B., Admin.
Mailing Address: 701-26th, 98632.
Res., 2571 Nichols Blvd., 98632. Tel: 360-425-4660; Fax: 360-577-5820.
School—Lay Teachers 14; Students 252.
Mission—Cathlamet, Wahkiakum Co., St. Catherine, 400 Columbia St., Cathlamet, 98612. Tel: 360-795-8725.

Lynden, Whatcom Co., St. Joseph's, Rev. Richard McCallister.
Res., 205 Twelfth St., 98264. Tel: 360-354-2334.
Mission—Deming, Whatcom Co., St. Peter, 6210 Mt. Baker Hwy., Deming, 98244. [CEM]

Lynnwood, Snohomish Co., St. Thomas More, Rev. John J. Renggli.
Res., 17414-64th W., Lynwood, 98037. Tel: 206-743-2929; Fax: 206-743-3652.
School—6511 176th S.W., 98037. Tel: 206-743-4242. Patrick White, Prin.
Sisters 1; Lay Teachers 12; Students 253.

Marysville, Snohomish Co., St. Mary's, Rev. John Bulger.
Res., 4200 88th St. N.E., 98270. Tel: 360-653-9400; Fax: 360-658-7439. [CEM]
Mission—Tulalip, Snohomish Co., Tulalip Indian Reservation, St. Anne, 7213 Totem Beach Rd., Tulalip, 98271.

Mercer Island, King Co., St. Monica, Rev. John Bowman; Deacon Jack Warfield. In res., Rev. John Horan.
Res., 4301 88th S.E., P.O. Box 730, 98040. Tel: 206-232-2900; Fax: 206-232-7875.
School—4320 87th S.E., 98040. Tel: 206-232-5432; Fax: 206-232-7875. Ken Dorsett, Prin.
Lay Teachers 19; Students 246.

Monroe, Snohomish Co., St. Mary of the Valley, Rev. Philip Fitzsimons.
Res., 601 W. Columbia, P.O. Box 279, 98272. Tel: 360-794-8945; Fax: 360-489-1409.

Morton, Lewis Co., Sacred Heart, Very Rev. Roger J. Smith.
Res., 7th and W. Adams Sts., P.O. Box 880, 98356. Tel: 360-496-5456; Fax: 360-496-5616.
Mission—Harmony, Lewis Co., St. Yves. [CEM]
Station—Packwood.

Mountlake Terrace, Snohomish Co., St. Pius X, Rev. Sean P. Fox.
Res., 22106 56th W., 98043. Tel: 206-775-7545; Fax: 206-775-8744.
School—22105 58th W., 98043. Tel: 206-778-9861. Mrs. Terri McDermott, Prin.
Sisters 2; Lay Teachers 10; Students 208.

Mount Vernon, Skagit Co., Immaculate Conception, Revs. Paul A. Magnano; John Schwartz, S.J., Parochial Vicar.
Res., 110 S. Fifth St., 98273. Tel: 360-336-6622; Fax: 360-336-5203.
School—1321 E. Division St., 98273. Tel: 360-428-3912; Fax: 360-424-8838. Mary Schau, Prin.
Lay Teachers 18; Students 285.

Oak Harbor, Island Co., St. Augustine, Rev. G. Barry Ashwell.
Res., 185 N. Oak Harbor St., 98277. Tel: 360-675-2303; Fax: 360-675-9490.
Mission—Coupeville, Island Co., St. Mary, 207 N. Main, 98239. Tel: 360-618-6536.

Ocean Shores, Grays Harbor Co., St. Jerome, Sr. Deanna Carr, B.V.M., Pastoral Life Dir.; Revs. Patrick McDermott; Scott Connolly; Stephen Roman; Very Rev. James Picton; Deacon Bruce MacPherson.
Res., P.O. Box 143, 98569. Tel: 360-289-2838; Fax: 360-289-0163.

Olympia, Thurston Co., St. Michael's, Revs. Michael J. Ryan; Robert Riler.
Res., 1021 S. Boundary, P.O. Box 766, 98507. Tel: 360-754-4666; Fax: 360-754-0628. [CEM]
School—1203 E. 10th, 98501. Tel: 360-754-5131. Thomas Ward, Prin.
Lay Teachers 13; Students 250.

Pe Ell, Lewis Co., St. Joseph's, Very Rev. Roger J. Smith; Sr. Virginia Miller, S.P., Pastoral Life Dir.; Rev. Richard Gallagher.
Res., Main and Pe Ell Ave., P.O. Box 235, 98572. Tel: 360-291-3434; 942-3207. [CEM]
Mission—Frances, Pacific Co., Holy Family.

Port Angeles, Clallam Co., Queen of Angels, Rev. John Wilkie.
Res., 209 W. 11th St., 98362. Tel: 360-452-2351; Fax: 360-452-1447.
School—1107 S. Oak, 98362. Tel: 360-457-6903; Fax: 360-457-6866. Mrs. Theresa Sekac, Prin.
Lay Teachers 16; Students 200.

Port Orchard, Kitsap Co., St. Gabriel's, Rev. Dennis C. Sevilla.
Res., 1150 Mitchell Ave., 98366-4499. Tel: 360-876-2762; Fax: 360-876-6085.
Mission—Belfair, Kitsap Co., Prince of Peace, N.E. 1171 Sand Hill Rd., P.O. Box 517, Belfair, 98528. Tel: 360-275-8760.

Port Townsend, Jefferson Co., St. Mary's, Star of the Sea, Rev. Raymond J. Heffernan.
Res., 1335 Blaine St., 98368. Tel: 360-385-3700. [CEM]

Poulsbo, Kitsap Co., St. Olaf, Rev. Hung Nguyen; Deacon Carl Moyer.
Res., 18943 Caldart Ave., N.E., P.O. Box 907, 98370. Tel: 360-779-4291; Fax: 360-598-5888.
Mission—Suquamish, Kitsap Co., St. Peter.

Puyallup, Pierce Co., All Saints, Revs. Alan Marshall; Ronald Knudsen; Deacon Michael McGillicuddy. In res., Revs. James Boyle Tel: 206-841-3923; Gary Southerton.
Res., 204 6th S.W., 98371. Tel: 206-845-7521; Fax: 206-845-3105.
Schools—504 2nd S.W., 98371. Tel: 206-845-5025; Fax: 206-845-3105. Alice Milam, Prin.
Lay Teachers 11; Students 151; St. Martin of Tours School (Satellite School), (Grades PreK-2) 2303 54th Ave. E., Fife, 98424. Tel: 206-922-5360. Alice Milam, Prin.
Lay Teachers 10; Students 178.
Holy Disciples, Rev. Gary Southerton.
Res., 15012 Meridian Ave. E., Ste. 4, 98373. Tel: 206-845-0828; Fax: 206-845-0930.
Mission—Eatonville, Pierce Co., Our Lady of Good Counsel, 229 Antonie Ave. N., Eatonville, 98328.

Raymond, Pacific Co., St. Lawrence, Very Rev. Roger J. Smith; Sr. Elizabeth Joyce, S.P., Pastoral Life Dir.; Rev. Richard Gallagher.
Res., 1112 Blake St. P.O. Box 31, 98577. Tel: 360-942-3000; Fax: 360-942-3000.

Redmond, King Co., St. Jude, Rev. Gerald F. Lovett.
Res., 10526 166th N.E., 98052. Tel: 206-883-7685; Fax: 206-881-2207.

Renton, King Co., St. Anthony's, Revs. Richard Hayatsu; Gerald Woodman; Deacon Richard Combs.
Res., 314 S. 4th St., 98055. Tel: 206-255-3132; Fax: 206-271-4729.
School—336 Shattuck Ave. S., 98055. Tel: 206-255-0059; Fax: 206-235-6555. Doug Arthur, Prin.
Sisters 2; Lay Teachers 25; Students 510.
St. Stephen the Martyr, Rev. John C. Madigan.
Res., 13055 S.E. 192nd St., 98058. Tel: 206-631-1940; Fax: 206-255-2943.

Seahurst, King Co., St. Francis of Assisi, Rev. Philip D. Wallace.
Res., 15236 21st Ave. S.W., P.O. Box 929, 98062. Tel: 206-242-4575; Fax: 206-242-1957.
School—P.O. Box 870, 98062. Tel: 206-243-5690. Sheila Keaton, Prin.
Lay Teachers 25; Students 376.

Seaview, Pacific Co., St. Mary, Rev. Richard J. Gallagher.
Res., P.O. Box 274, 98644. Tel: 360-642-2002.
Station—McGowan.

Sedro Woolley, Skagit Co., Immaculate Heart of Mary, Revs. Paul A. Magnano; Victor Olvida, Parochial Vicar.
Res., 719 Ferry St., 98284. Tel: 360-855-0077; 855-2282.
Mission—Concrete, Skagit Co., St. Catherine, 239 Limestone, Concrete, 98237. Tel: 360-853-8941.

Sequim, Clallam Co., St. Joseph, Rev. Thomas Beattie.
Res., 121 E. Maple, P.O. Box 1209, 98382. Tel: 360-683-6076; Fax: 360-683-4674.

Shelton, Mason Co., St. Edward's, Rev. Dominic Hahn, O.S.B.
Res., 321 N. 3rd St., P.O. Box 758, 98584. Tel: 360-426-6134; Fax: 360-426-6231. [CEM]

Snohomish, Snohomish Co., St. Michael's, Rev. Dennis V. Champagne.
Res., 1512 Pine Ave., 98290. Tel: 360-568-0821; Fax: 360-568-6426.
Mission—Granite Falls, Snohomish Co., Holy Cross, Tel: 360-691-5945.

Snoqualmie, King Co., Our Lady of Sorrows, Rev. Jan Larson.
Res., 39025 S.E. Alpha St., P.O. Box 909, 98065. Tel: 206-888-2974; Fax: 206-888-7098.
Missions—Carnation, King Co., St. Anthony, P.O. Box 175, Carnation, 98014. Tel: 206-333-4930; Duvall, King Co., Holy Innocents, P.O. Box 850, Duvall, 98109. Tel: 206-788-1400; 775-1477. Very Rev. George Thomas.
Station—Snoqualmie Summit, St. Bernard's Chapel, Tel: 206-454-6161.

Stanwood, Snohomish Co., St. Cecilia's, Rev. Matthew Williams, O.C.D. In res., Rev. Colm Stone, O.C.D.
Res., 26900 78th Ave., N.W., P.O. Box 1002, 98292. Tel: 360-629-3737.

Sumner, Pierce Co., St. Andrew, Rev. Thomas A. Belleque.
Res., 704 Kincaid Ave., 98390. Tel: 206-863-2253; Fax: 206-863-3567.
Mission—Orting, Pierce Co., SS. Cosmas and Damian, 213 W. Leber St., Orting, 98360.

Tacoma, Pierce Co.,

1—St. Ann, Revs. Vincent Pastro; Patrick O'Neill, Parochial Vicar; John Koehler.
Res., 7001 S. Park Ave., 98408. Tel: 206-472-1360.

2—St. Charles Borromeo, Revs. Patrick J. Ritter; Michael Wright.
Res., 7112 S. 12th St., 98465. Tel: 206-564-5185; Fax: 206-565-0936.
School—Tel: 206-581-2908. Patrick Feist, Prin.
Sisters of St. Francis of Philadelphia 3; Lay Teachers 23; Students 512.

3—St. Frances Cabrini, Very Rev. James P. Coyne.
Res., 5505 108th St., S.W., 98499. Tel: 206-588-2141; Fax: 206-582-5351.
School—Tel: 206-584-3850. Stephanie Van Leuven, Prin.
Sisters 1; Lay Teachers 12; Students 249.

4—St. John Bosco, Rev. Ralph Carney, O.F.M., Admin.
Res., 10508 112 St. S.W., 98498. Tel: 206-582-1028; Fax: 206-584-0633.
Mission—Steilacoom, Pierce Co., Immaculate Conception.

5—St. John of the Woods, Revs. Vincent Pastro; Patrick G. O'Neill, Parochial Vicar; John Koehler.
Res., 9903 24th Ave. E., 98445. Tel: 206-537-8551.

6—St. Joseph's, (Slovak), Rev. Richard Cebula, O.S.B., Admin.; Deacon Jack W. Buck.
Res., 608 S. 34th St., 98408. Tel: 206-472-2489.

7—St. Leo the Great, Rev. John D. Fuchs, S.J.; Deacon Thomas Horlander.
Res., 710 S. 13th St., 98405. Tel: 206-272-5136; Fax: 206-272-6285.

8—St. Martin of Tours, Rev. Patrick K. O'Brien.
Res., 2303-54th Ave. E., 98424. Tel: 206-922-7882.

9—St. Patrick's, Rev. Seamus Laverty.
Res., 1001 N. J St., 98403. Tel: 206-383-2783; Fax: 206-627-5396.
School—1112 N. G St., 98403. Tel: 206-272-2297. Frank McGowan, Prin.

Sisters 3; Lay Teachers 27; Students 457.

10—SS. PETER & PAUL, (Polish), Rev. Piotr Dzikowski, S.Ch.
Res., 3422 Portland Ave., 98404. Tel: 206-272-5232; Fax: 206-627-7848.

11—ST. RITA, Rev. Carmine J. Sacco, S.J.
Res., 1403 S. Ainsworth, 98405. Tel: 206-627-4851.

12—HOLY CROSS, Rev. Robert Rekofke, S.J.
Res., 5510 N. 44th St., 98407. Tel: 206-759-3368.

13—HOLY ROSARY, Revs. Richard S. Cebula, O.S.B.; Edward Receconi, O.S.B.
Res., 512 S. 30th St., 98402. Tel: 206-383-4549.
School—504 S. 30th, 98402. Tel: 206-272-7012. Sr. Catherine Lendosky, Prin.
Sisters 3; Lay Teachers 8; Students 227.
Convent—424 S. 30th, 98402.

14—OUR LADY, QUEEN OF HEAVEN, Rev. Michael McDermott; Deacon Robert R. Dardis.
Res., 14601 A St. S., 98444. Tel: 206-537-3252; Fax: 206-536-2662.

15—SACRED HEART, Revs. Vincent Pastro; Patrick O'Neill, Parochial Vicar; John Koehler.
Res., 4520 McKinley Ave., 98404. Tel: 206-472-7738.

16—VISITATION, Rev. David Gese.
Res., 3314 S. 58th St., 98409. Tel: 206-473-4960.
School—3306 S. 58th, 98409. Imelda Mead, Prin.
Lay Teachers 9; Students 222.

Toledo, Lewis Co., St. Francis Xavier, Rev. Timothy Berg, Admin.
Res., 139 Spencer Rd., 98591. Tel: 206-864-4126; 1-800-846-2374. [CEM]

Tukwila, King Co., St. Thomas, Rev. Gerald L. Mayovsky.
Res., 4415 S. 140th St., 98168. Tel: 206-242-5501; Fax: 206-244-9387.

Vancouver, Clark Co.,

1—OUR LADY OF LOURDES, Revs. Robert Dell, C.O., Admin.; Clarence Jones, C.O.; Deacon Robert Tomich.
Res., 4723 Franklin St., N.W., 98663. Tel: 360-695-1366; Fax: 360-695-7966.
School—Tel: 360-696-2301. Ms. Shirley Loesch, Prin.
Lay Teachers 14; Students 259.

2—ST. JAMES, Rev. Anthony Ton.
Res., 218 W. 12th St., 98660. Tel: 360-693-3052; Fax: 360-693-3077. [CEM]

3—ST. JOHN, Rev. Michael C. OBrien.
Res., 8701 N.E. 119 St., 98662. Tel: 360-573-3325; Fax: 360-573-3344. [CEM]
Station—Larch Mountain Corrections Center.

4—ST. JOSEPH, Revs. Hans Olson; Reynaldo Yu (Philippines).
Res., 6600 Highland Dr., 98661. Tel: 360-696-4407; Fax: 360-696-3959.
School—6500 Highland Dr., 98661. Tel: 360-696-2586; Fax: 360-696-3959. Teri Stegman, Prin.
Lay Teachers 21; Students 370.

Vashon, King Co., St. John Vianney, Revs. James Meehan, S.J.; David Giusti, Pastoral Life Dir.; Very Rev. Lester McCloskey.
Res., P.O. Box 308, 98070. Tel: 206-567-4149; Fax: 206-567-4198.
Mission—Dockton, King Co., St. Patrick, Tel: 206-463-3224.

Winlock, Lewis Co., Sacred Heart, Rev. Timothy Berg, Admin.
Res., P.O. Box 69, 98596. Tel: 360-864-4126.
Station—St. Urban.

Woodland, Cowlitz Co., St. Philip's, Rev. Joseph O'Shea.
Res., 430 Bozarth, Box 177, 98674. Tel: 360-225-8308.
Missions—Kalama, Cowlitz Co., St. Joseph; Ridgefield, Clark Co., St. Mary of Guadalupe.

Yelm, Thurston Co., St. Columban, Rev. Terence J. Wager, O.S.B.
Res., P.O. Box 956, 98597. Tel: 360-458-3031; Fax: 360-458-4094.
Mission—Tenino, Thurston Co., St. Peter, P.O. Box 744, Sussex & Keithan St., Tenino, 98589. Tel: 360-264-2124.

Chaplains of Public Institutions

SEATTLE. *U.S. Public Health Hospital.* Attended by St. Peter's Church.
Veterans Administration Medical Center. Rev. Thomas Park, O.S.B.
Youth Service Center. Sr. Anne Davis, C.S.J., Pastoral Min.

BUCKLEY. *Rainier School.* Rev. James Boyle.
Western State Custodial School. Attended from St. Aloysius Church.

CHEHALIS. *State Training School for Boys.* Rev. Tuan Nguyen.

GIG HARBOR. *Washington Corrections Center for Women.* Rev. John Haas.

MCNEIL ISLAND. *McNeil Island Correction Center.* Rev. Thomas Suss.

MONROE. *Washington State Reformatory.* Ms. Michael Traux, Pastoral Min.

ORTING. *U.S. Soldiers' Home.* Rev. Thomas Belleque.

RETSIL. *Washington Veterans Home Hospital.* Rev. Dennis Sevilla.

SHELTON. *Washington Corrections Center,* P.O. Box 900, 98584. Sr. Esperanza Cintron, Pastoral Min.

SNOQUALMIE. *Echo Glen School.* Rev. Jan Larson.

STEILACOOM. *Western State Hospital.* Rev. Robert Tino.

TACOMA. *Veterans Admin. Medical Center.* Rev. David Prebula, O.S.B.

VANCOUVER. *Veterans Administration Hospital.* Attended from St. James.
Washington State School for the Blind. Attended from St. James.
Washington State School for the Deaf. Attended from St. Joseph.

Special Assignment:
Reverend Fathers—
Ahn, Michael, Peace of Christ Korean Center, 11700 1st Ave., Seattle, WA 98125
Bawyn, Anthony, American College, University of Louvain, Naamestraat 100, 3000 Leuven, Belgium
Eblen, James, Theologian, 910 Marion St., Seattle, WA 98104. Tel: 206-382-4593
Hart, Brian, 13 Salisbury Ave., Antrin Rd., Belfast, 15 Ireland
Jaeger, David, AIDS Ministry, 910 Marion St., Seattle, WA 98104
Koo, Il Mo (Peter), Korean Ministry, 7912 Golden Given Rd. E., Tacoma, WA 98404
Meyer, Clayton, Coord. for Discernment & Formation of Seminarians, P.O. Box 1763, Bellevue, WA 98009
Picton, James, Episcopal Vicar, 910 Marion St., Seattle, WA 98104
Raschko, Michael, Theologian, 910 Marion St., Seattle, WA 98104
Rowan, Stephen, Seattle University, Res., P.O. Box 51029 Seattle, WA 98115
Thomas George, Episcopal Vicar, 910 Marion St., Seattle, WA 98104
Williams, James, Tribunal, 910 Marion St., Seattle, WA 98104. Tel: 206-382-4598

On Duty Outside the Archdiocese:
Reverend Fathers—
Larrivee, Leo J., S.S., 4210 N. Charles St. #3, Baltimore, MD 21218
Rogerson, Daniel, Mount Angel Abbey, St. Benedict, OR 97373

Military Chaplains:
Reverend Fathers—
Bailey, Lawrence, 15 ABG/HC, 180 Kuntz Ave., Hickam AFB, HI 96853-5112
McKenna, Timothy J., 435 Logistic SUPSQ AW/HC, PSC 5 Box 2311 APO, AE 09097

Unassigned:
Reverend Fathers—
Clark, John, 910 Marion St., Seattle, WA 98104
Gonzales, Emilio, 910 Marion St., Seattle, WA 98104
Jonientz, Bernard, 4231 S. Juneau, Seattle, WA 98118
Lesnick, Richard, 910 Marion St., Seattle, WA 98104
Pins, Herbert, 910 Marion St., Seattle, WA 98104
Salazar, Felipe, 910 Marion St., Seattle, WA 98104
Tucker, Michael, 910 Marion St., Seattle, WA 98104
Vega (Vega-Montalbo), Jose (Giuseppe), 910 Marion St., Seattle, WA 98104

Medical Leave:
Reverend Fathers—
McMahon, Desmond, 1115 North I St., #104, Tacoma, WA 98403
Naumes Matthew, 1100 University, 11J, Seattle, WA 98101
Sondergeld, Theodore, 2627 S. 310th, Federal Way, WA 98003

Retired:
Reverend Monsignors—
Doogan, John P., 500 Wall St. #314, Seattle, WA 98121
Mattie, John G., 4831 35th Ave., S.W., Seattle, WA 98126
Reverend Fathers—
Aspiras, Jose, Station Rita East, Agoo, La Union Philippines
Auer, Paul, 1208 7th St., Anacortes, WA 98221
Buck, James, 1701 18th Ave. S., Seattle, WA 98144
Byrne, Paul, 3023 - 14th W. #203, Seattle, WA 98119
Cloquet, Victor, P.O. Box 1232, Allyn, WA 98524-1232
Cody, Michael, 910 Marion St., Seattle, WA 98104
Crosse, Charles, 8539 Zircon Dr. S.W., Tacoma, WA 98498
Delahunty, Thomas, 7320C 142nd Ave., E., Summer, WA 98390
Domandich, Anthony, 2600 N.E. Minnehaha St., #105, Vancouver, WA 98665
Dominic, Joseph A., 3333 Ensign Rd., N.E., Olympia, WA 98506
Donohoe, John P., 2500 S. 370th St., #252, Federal Way, WA 98003
Doogan, Joseph H., 3218 W. Barrett, Seattle, WA 98199
Gallagher, William E., 6108 N. Park, Tacoma, WA 98407
Hamilton, James, 4831 35th Ave., S.W., Seattle, WA 98126
Harrington, Cornelius, 1156 Alki Ave. S.W., Seattle, WA 98116
Heneghan, Jorlath, 9460 N.E. 44th, Bellevue, WA 98004
Heneghan, Sean, 12450 20th Ave. S., Seattle, WA 98168
Horan, John, P.O. Box 730, Mercer Island, WA 98040
Jennings, John, 2430 S. 371st St., Federal Way, WA 98003
Knelleken, James, 215 N. 120th, Seattle, WA 98104
Kramis, Joseph, 2009 Walker Park Rd., Shelton, WA 98584
Lane, Thomas, 4831-35 Ave. S.W., Seattle, WA 98126
Lane, William, 20826 70th Ave. W., #6, Lynnwood, WA 98036
Linehan, David, 515 S. 136th St., Seattle, WA 98168
Lukas, Michael, 495 Toutle Rd., Apt. 4, Castle Rock, WA 98611
Lynch, Ibar, 1427 3rd Ave. W., #19, Seattle, WA 98119
Mallahan, James, 949 N. 35th St., #103, Seattle, WA 98103
McEnnis, Thomas, 9508 Bowdoin Way, Edmonds, WA 98020
McGreal, James, 910 Marion St., Seattle, WA 98104
Moore, Gerald T., 2810 W. Hayes, Seattle, WA 98199
Moynihan, Timothy, 5816 15th Ave. N.W., Seattle, WA 98107
Murray, Maximillian, P.O. Box 402, Bremerton, WA 98310
O'Callaghan, Thomas, P.O. Box 346, Suquamish, WA 98392
O'Neil, Michael, 910 Marion, Seattle, WA 98104
O'Neill, Patrick, 9903 24th Ave. E., Tacoma, WA 98445
Petosa, Joseph, 22404-59th Ave. W, Mountlake Terrace, WA 98403
Phelan, Thomas, 1601 S. Jackson, Tacoma, WA 98465
Rafalowski, Leonard, 2137 Washington, #4, Port Townsend, WA 98368
Rice, John A., 1208-6455 Willingdon Ave., Burnaby, B.C. V5H 4E4
Slate, William, P.O. Box 4258, Kent, WA 98032
Szeman, Stephen, 12611 S.E. 30th, #1, Bellvue, WA 98005
Tolang, Jaime, 820 18th Ave., Seattle, WA 98122
Treacy, William, 9460 N.E. 14th, Bellevue, WA 98004
van Gogh, James A., 17836 7th Pl. S.W., Normandy Park, WA 98166
Welch, Paul, S.S., St. Charles Villa, 603 Maiden Choice Ln., Baltimore, MD 21228

Permanent Deacons:
Alexander, Richard
Allen, Daniel
Anderson, Carl
Anderson, David
Bemis, James
Benedict, Nathan
Bentley, Ernest
Burkholder, Thomas, On Leave
Cavanaugh, Robert
Cliffton, Glenn
Crandall, Charles
Curtis, Joseph
Dardis, Robert
Denby, Marshall
Dodson, Arthur, On Leave
Dolan, Robert
Dorr, LuVerne
Duffell, Denny
Dunne, Joseph, Inactive

Edtl, Lee
Ellis, Rolland
Erskine, Thomas
Ficken, George
Frost, Harold
Hanika, Donald
Hartzell, Clay
Hawkins, Tom
Henn, Thomas, Richland
Ho, Bernard, San Jose, CA
Hoover, Delbert
Horlander, Tom
Huelett, William
Kim, Duk
Krempl, Joseph
La Russa, John
Lane, Loren
MacPherson, Bruce
Magnuson, John
Maher, Dean, Walla Walla
Majeau, Henrie, On Leave
Marcell, Terrance
Marshall, Norman, On Leave
McGary, Fred, On Leave
McGary, Robert, On Leave
McGillicuddy, Michael
Michalak, William, On Leave
Miller, Robert L., Jackson, WY
Minetti, Bernard, Tucson, AZ
Monuteaux, Lawrence
Moyer, Carlton
Moynihan, Patrick
Murdy, Don, Inactive
Myer, Philip
Nathe, Richard
O'Loane, Phil
O'Neill, Richard, Inactive
Olsen, Richard, S. San Francisco, CA
Origenes, Maurice
Parsons, Eamon D.
Pellegrino, Joseph
Peterson, George
Pioli, Albert, On Leave
Ricciardi, John
Ruiz, Nehemias, Thornton, CO
Rupno, Robert
Sarver, Richard, Las Vegas, NV
Shields, Walter J.
Snider, Lloyd
Stenson, Mark
Stromberg, Alton L., Seaside, OR
Tanasse, William
Taube, William
Tomich, Robert
Townsend, William
Vanderzanden, Gene
Warfield, Jack
Warmuth, David
Wiese, Ted
Wilson, Howard
Zipp, Frank
Zuanich, Matthew

INSTITUTIONS LOCATED IN THE ARCHDIOCESE

[A] COLLEGES AND UNIVERSITIES

SEATTLE. *Seattle University*, 900 Broadway, 98122. Tel: 206-296-6000.
For a complete listing, refer to the Colleges and Universities section.

LACEY. *St. Martin's College*, 5300 Pacific Ave., S.E., 98503. Tel: 360-491-4700.
For a complete listing, refer to the Colleges and Universities section.

[B] HIGH SCHOOLS, ARCHDIOCESAN

SEATTLE. *Blanchet High School*. (Coed), 8200 Wallingford Ave. N., 98103. Tel: 206-527-7711; Fax: 206-527-7712. Dr. Joseph R. Haggerty, Prin.; Rev. Gordon Douglas. Sisters 2; Lay Teachers 58; Students 967.

John F. Kennedy Memorial High School. (Coed), 140 S. 140th, 98168. Tel: 206-246-0500; Fax: 206-242-0831. Mr. John Schuster, Prin.; Rev. Michael J. Batterberry. Priests 1; Sisters 1; Lay Teachers 55; Students 760.

O'Dea High School. (Boys), 802 Terry Ave., 98104. Tel: 206-622-6596; Fax: 206-340-4110.
Conducted by the Congregation of Christian Brothers. Bro. Dominic Murray, C.F.C., Prin. Brothers 9; Lay Teachers 23; Students 465.

[C] HIGH SCHOOLS, PRIVATE

SEATTLE. *Holy Names Academy*. (Girls), 728 21st Ave. E., 98112. Tel: 206-323-4272. Sisters of the Congregation of the Holy Names of Jesus and Mary. Ms. Elizabeth Swift, Prin. Sisters 10; Lay Teachers 40; Students 435.

Seattle Preparatory School, 2400 11th E., 98102. Tel: 206-324-0400; Fax: 206-323-6509. Mr. Robert P. Graby, Ed.D., Pres.; Mr. Christopher P. Conroy, Prin. Priests 2; Lay Teachers 70; Students 645.

BELLEVUE. *Eastside Catholic High School*. (Coed), 11650 S.E. 60th, 98006. Tel: 206-644-7737. James E. Dean, Prin.; Rev. Richard Basso. Priests 1; Sisters 1; Lay Teachers 45; Students 574.

Forest Ridge School of the Sacred Heart. (Grades 5-12). (Girls), 4800 139th Ave. S.E., 98006. Tel: 206-641-0700. Sr. Suzanne Cooke, R.S.C.J., Prin. Religious of the Sacred Heart 5; Lay Teachers 40; Students 313.

EVERETT. *Holy Cross High School*. (Coed), 2617 Cedar St., 98201. Tel: 206-252-6203; Fax: 206-252-3581. Dr. Kristine Brynildsen-Smith, Prin. Students 159; Lay Teachers 16.

TACOMA. *Bellarmine Preparatory School*. (Coed), 2300 S. Washington, 98405. Tel: 206-752-7701; Fax: 206-756-3887.
Owned by the Jesuit Fathers. Board of Directors: 5 members of the Jesuit order and 12 others. Very Rev. Gerard E. Chapdelaine, S.J., Rector; Mr. Jack Peterson, Pres. In res., Revs. Frederick P. Mayovsky, S.J.; James Meehan, S.J.; James E. Poole, S.J.; Francis Walsh, S.J.; Daniel C. Weber, S.J.; Bros. Paul Cawthorne, S.J.; Patrick Flannigan, S.J.; Michael Richards, S.J.; William Yam, S.J., Ministry to Street People, 1419 1/2 G St., 98405. Tel: 206-627-4347. Priests 6; Brothers 4; Sisters 1; Lay Teachers 70; Students 950.

[D] ELEMENTARY SCHOOLS, PRIVATE

SEATTLE. *Villa Academy*. (Grades K-8). (Coed), 5001 N.E. 50th St., 98105. Tel: 206-524-8885. Mr. Thomas Lord, Headmaster. Lay Teachers 47; Students 488.

LACEY. *Holy Family School*. (Grades PreK-8), 2606 Carpenter Rd., S.E., P.O. Box 3700, 98503. Tel: 360-491-7060; Fax: 360-456-3725. Mr. John Oliver, Prin. Lay Teachers 11; Students 184.

[E] CATHOLIC SOCIAL SERVICES OF THE ARCHDIOCESE OF SEATTLE

SEATTLE. *Catholic Community Services of Western Washington*, 100 23rd Ave. S., 98144-2302. Tel: 206-328-5696; Fax: 206-328-5699. Mr. Michael Reichert, Pres.

Archdiocesan Housing Authority, 1902 2nd Ave., 98101. Tel: 206-448-3360.

St. Martin's Housing Institute, 1902 2nd Ave., 98101. Tel: 206-448-8500. Michael Reichert, Pres.

Catholic Community Services, King County, 100 23rd Ave. S., 98144-2302. Tel: 206-323-6336. Josephine Tamayo Murray, Agency Dir.

Catholic Community Services, Northwest (Bellingham), 1756 Iowa St., P.O. Box 5704, Bellingham, 98227-5704. Tel: 360-733-5804. Mr. Tom MacIntyre, Agency Dir.

Catholic Community Services, Snohomish (Everett), 1918 Everett Ave., Everett, 98201. Tel: 206-259-9188. Mr. Tom MacIntyre, Agency Dir.

Catholic Community Services - Southwest (Tacoma), 1323 S. Yakima, Tacoma, 98405. Tel: 206-383-3697. Ms. Pat Ditter, Agency Dir.

[F] DAY CARE CENTERS

SEATTLE. *Martin Luther King. Jr., Day Home Center*, 1855 S Ln., 98144. Tel: 206-328-5670. Mr. Michael L. Koetje, Dir.

Our Place Day Care, 717 20th Ave. S., 98144. Tel: 206-328-5724. Terri Yaffe, Dir.

EVERETT. *Child Space*, 10110 19th Ave. S.E., #R100, 98208. Tel: 206-316-0728; Fax: 206-337-6586. Sherrie Winicky, Dir.

OLYMPIA. *St. Mike's Tikes*, 1010 Eastside St., 98501. Tel: 360-943-3080. Marsha Brown, Dir.

POULSBO. *St. Olaf's Daycare*, P.O. Box 907, 98370. Tel: 360-779-5791; Fax: 360-598-5888. Doreen Valverde, Dir.

[G] GENERAL HOSPITALS

SEATTLE. *Providence Seattle Medical Center*, 500 17th Ave., Box 34008, 98124. Tel: 206-320-2000.
For a complete listing, refer to the Hospitals section.

BELLINGHAM. *St. Joseph Hospital*, 2901 Squalicum Pkwy., 98225. Tel: 360-734-5400; Fax: 360-738-6393.
For a complete listing, refer to the Hospitals section.

CENTRALIA. *Providence Centralia Hospital*, 1820 Cooks Hill Rd., 98531. Tel: 360-736-2803.
For a complete listing, refer to the Hospitals section.

EVERETT. *Providence General Medical Center*, 14th & Colby, P.O. Box 1147, 98206. Tel: 206-261-2000.
For a complete listing, refer to the Hospitals section.

FEDERAL WAY. *St. Francis Hospital of Federal Way*, 34515 9th Ave. S., 98003. Tel: 206-927-9700; 838-9700.
For a complete listing, refer to the Hospitals section.

LONGVIEW. *St. John Medical Center*, 1614 E. Kessler Blvd., 98632. Tel: 360-423-1530; Fax: 360-636-4952.
For a complete listing, refer to the Hospitals section.

OLYMPIA. *Providence St. Peter Hospital*, 413 Lilly Rd., N.E., 98506. Tel: 360-491-9480.
For a complete listing, refer to the Hospitals section.

TACOMA. *St. Clare Hospital*, 11315 Bridgeport Way S.W., 98499. Tel: 206-588-1711; Fax: 206-584-3001.
For a complete listing, refer to the Hospitals section.

St. Joseph Medical Center, 1717 S. J St., 98405. Tel: 206-627-4101.
For a complete listing, refer to the Hospitals section.

[H] HOMES FOR CHILDREN

BELLINGHAM. *The Martin Center*, 2806 Douglas, 98225. Tel: 206-733-5804.
For a complete listing, refer to the Special Care Facilities section.

[I] NURSING HOMES

SEATTLE. *Providence Mount St. Vincent*, 4831 35th Ave. S.W., 98126. Tel: 206-937-3700; Fax: 206-938-8999.
For a complete listing, refer to the Special Care Facilities section.

ISSAQUAH. *Marianwood*, 3725 Providence Point Dr., S.E., 98027. Tel: 206-391-2800; Fax: 206-391-5440.
For a complete listing, refer to the Special Care Facilities section.

[J] HOSPICES

SEATTLE. *Providence Home Services*, 425 Pontius Ave., N., Ste. 300, 98109. Tel: 206-320-4848.
For a complete listing, refer to the Special Care Facilities section.

EVERETT. *Providence Home Care and Hospice of Snohomis County*, 2731 Wetmore Ave., #520, 98201. Tel: 206-261-4800.
For a complete listing, refer to the Special Care Facilities section.

OLYMPIA. *Providence Mother Joseph Care Center*, 3333 Ensign Rd., N.E., 98506. Tel: 360-493-4900.
For a complete listing, refer to the Special Care Facilities section.

Providence SoundHomeCare and Hospice, 3706 Griffin Ln., S.E., 98501. Tel: 800-869-7062; 360-459-8311.
For a complete listing, refer to the Special Care Facilities section.

[K] RESIDENCES FOR ELDERLY OR DISABLED

SEATTLE. *Chancery Place*, 910 Marion, 98104. Tel: 206-343-9415.
For a complete listing, refer to the Special Care Facilities section.

The Franciscan, 15237 21st Ave. S.W., 98166. Tel: 206-431-8001.
For a complete listing, refer to the Special Care Facilities section.

The Josephinum, 1902 2nd Ave., 98101. Tel: 206-448-8500.
For a complete listing, refer to the Special Care Facilities section.

Providence Mount St. Vincent, 4831 35th Ave. S., 98126. Tel: 206-937-3700.
For a complete listing, refer to the Special Care Facilities section.

Vincent House, 1423 First Ave., 98101. Tel: 206-682-9307.
For a complete listing, refer to the Special Care Facilities section.

The Westlake, 2008 Westlake Ave., 98121. Tel: 206-340-0410.
For a complete listing, refer to the Special Care Facilities section.

BELLEVUE. *Champion House*, 1800 145th Pl. S.E., 98007. Tel: 206-644-4477.
For a complete listing, refer to the Special Care Facilities section.

Elbert House, 16000 N.E. 8th St., 98008. Tel: 206-747-5111.
For a complete listing, refer to the Special Care Facilities section.

Halcyon, 1200 134th Ave. N.E., 98005. Tel: 206-643-780; Fax: 206-746-0438.
For a complete listing, refer to the Special Care Facilities section.

BOTHELL. *The Franciscan Healthcare Center at Bothell*, 10909 N.E. 185th St., 98011. Tel: 206-486-7174; 483-9905; Fax: 206-487-1313.
For a complete listing, refer to the Special Care Facilities section.

CHEHALIS. *Providence Place*, 350 S.E. Washington Ave., 98532. Tel: 360-740-8389.
For a complete listing, refer to the Special Care Facilities section.

ENUMCLAW. *The Franciscan Healthcare Center at Enumclaw*, 2323 Jensen St., 98022. Tel: 360-825-2541;

825-9938; Fax: 360-825-7023.
For a complete listing, refer to the Special Care Facilities section.

REDMOND. *Emma McRedmond Manor*, 7960 169th N.E., 98052. Tel: 206-869-2424.
For a complete listing, refer to the Special Care Facilities section.

TACOMA. *The Franciscan Health Care Center at Tacoma*, 6220 S. Alaska, 98408. Tel: 206-473-2273.
For a complete listing, refer to the Special Care Facilities section.

The Franciscan Health Care Center at University Place, 2901 Bridgeport Way W., 98466. Tel: 206-564-1643; 564-1663; Fax: 206-565-5965.
For a complete listing, refer to the Special Care Facilities section.

Norm Fournier Court, 112 S. 127th, 98444. Tel: 206-531-5087.
For a complete listing, refer to the Special Care Facilities section.

TUMWATER. *Tumwater Apartments*, 5701 6th Ave., S.W., 98501. Tel: 206-352-4321.
For a complete listing, refer to the Special Care Facilities section.

[L] SOCIAL SERVICES

SEATTLE. *Association for Catholic Childhood*, 2360 43 Ave. E., 98112. Tel: 206-328-5222. Mrs. Agnes Davis.

Catholic Seamen's Club, 2330 1st Ave., 98121. Tel: 206-441-4773. Rev. Anthony Haycock, Chap., St. Mary Church, 611 20th Ave. S., 98144. Tel: 206-324-7100.

Providence Hospitality House, P.O. Box 22382, 98122. Tel: 206-322-2107. Sisters of Providence - Pariseau Association.

St. Francis House, 169 12th Ave., 98122. Tel: 206-621-0945. Third Order of St. Francis, Sponsor. Mary Lou Newman, Admin.

Sojourner Place, P.O. Box 95892, 98105. Tel: 206-545-4200. Sisters of Providence - Pariseau Association.

AUBURN. *Store and Workshop*, 926 Auburn Way N., 98002. Tel: 206-833-0400.

BELLEVUE. *Society of St. Vincent de Paul - Archdiocesan Council*, 10638 N.E. 13th, 98004. Tel: 206-454-2392. Mrs. Patricia A. Meehan, Pres.

Society of St. Vincent de Paul-Family Welfare Office, 5950 4th Ave. S., Seattle, 98108-3208. Tel: 206-767-6449. Mr. Harry Coveny, Exec. Sec./Dir.

Society of St. Vincent de Paul District - Council of Seattle Area, 5950 4th Ave. S., Seattle, 98108-3208. Tel: 206-767-6449. Mrs. Barbara Carver, Pres.

Society of St. Vincent de Paul - Stores. No. 1, 17712 15th Ave. N.E., Seattle, 98155. Tel: 206-364-1492. No. 2, 9835 16th Ave., S.W., Seattle, 98106. Tel: 206-763-2130. No. 3, 13445 1st Ave., S., Seattle, 98166. Tel: 206-243-6370. No. 4, 2825 Sunset Blvd., N.E., Seattle, 98056. Tel: 206-226-9426. No. 5, 5950 4th Ave. S., Seattle, 98108-3208. Tel: 206-767-3835. Mr. Donald Stephens, Gen. Mgr., No. 6, 4503 Tolt Ave., S., Carnation, 98014.

BREMERTON. *St. Vincent dePaul Assistance Office*, 1137 N. Callow, 98312. Tel: 360-479-7017. Thrift Store, 1117 N. Callow, 98312. Tel: 360-377-2929.

EVERETT. *Society of St. Vincent de Paul*, Council of Snohomish County, 5303 Evergreen Way, 98203. Tel: 206-355-3525; Fax: 206-513-6051. Mr. Chuck Seider, Pres.; Mr. William Cramer, Exec. Dir., Store, 6430 S. Broadway, 98203. Tel: 206-355-3504; 3505.

MANCHESTER. *Society of St. Vincent de Paul and Related Stores*, District Council of Olympic Peninsula, Box 24, 98353-0024. Tel: 360-871-3100. 803 Puget Dr. E., Port Orchard, 98366. Mr. Marvin R. Heuer.

OLYMPIA. *Sunshine House*, 413 N. Lilly Rd., 98506. Tel: 206-493-7900. Legal Title: *Sisters of Providence in Washington*.

TACOMA. *Society of St. Vincent de Paul - Particular Council of Tacoma*, 4009 S. 56th, 98409. Mr. Robert Z. Lowe, Pres.

Society of St. Vincent de Paul Stores and Workshop. No. 1, 4009 S. 56th St., 98409. Tel: 206-474-0519. No. 2, 3805-07 S. Yakima Ave., 98408. Tel: 206-472-7334. No. 3, 113 Meeker W., 98371. Tel: 206-848-5637. St. Vincent de Paul Emergency Office, 4009 S. 56th St., 98409. Tel: 206-472-1783.

[M] MONASTERIES AND RESIDENCES OF PRIESTS AND BROTHERS

SEATTLE. *Congregation of Christian Brothers*. (Irish Christian Brothers), 1021 Columbia St., 98104-2018. Tel: 206-622-2639. Bros. J. Hugh Greenan, C.F.C., Supr.; James R. McDonald, C.F.C.; Jerome A. Heustis, C.F.C.; Robert A. Koppes, C.F.C.; T. Kieran Lawler, C.F.C.; D. Clement Mahoney, C.F.C.; D. Peter Ryan, C.F.C.; Gregory G. Lindeman, C.F.C.; D Dominic Murray, C.F.C.; John A. Pettit, C.F.C.; D. Thomas LeJeune, C.F.C. Brothers 11.

Maryknoll Fathers, Catholic Foreign Mission Society of America, 958 16th Ave. E., 98112. Tel: 206-322-8831. Revs. Thomas J. Marti, M.M.; Richard T. Ouellette.

LACEY. *St. Martin's Abbey*. Order of St. Benedict, College, and Novitiate, 98503. Tel: 206-491-4700. Rt. Revs. Neal G. Roth, O.S.B., Abbot; Conrad R. Rausch, O.S.B., Resigned Abbot; Adrian J. Parcher, O.S.B., Resigned Abbot; Very Revs. Urban Feucht, O.S.B., Prior; Nicholas Rausch, O.S.B., Subprior; Rev. Sean R. Malvey, O.S.B., Formation Dir.; Rt. Rev. Neal G. Roth, O.S.B., Dir. of Vocations; Revs. Alfred J. Hulscher, O.S.B., Dir. of Fiscal Affairs; William A. Maat, O.S.B.; Arnold J. Fox, O.S.B.; Luke N. O'Donnell, O.S.B.; Killian Malvey, O.S.B.; Richard S. Cebula, O.S.B.; David W. Prebula, O.S.B.; Michael Feeney, O.S.B.; Clement H. Pangratz, O.S.B.; Timothy J. Lamm, O.S.B.; Placidus G. Reischman, O.S.B.; Thaddaeus R. Arledge, O.S.B.; George J. Seidel, O.S.B.; Alfred J. Hulscher, O.S.B.; Dominic D. Hahn, O.S.B.; Kieran P. Cunningham, O.S.B.; Thomas R. Park, O.S.B.; Terence Wagner, O.S.B.; Justin D. McCreedy, O.S.B.; Gerard D. Kirsch, O.S.B.; John Scott, O.S.B.; Edward R. Receconi; Harvey J. Wingfield, O.S.B.; Benedict L. Auer, O.S.B. Priests 29; Brothers 16.

[N] CONVENTS AND RESIDENCES FOR SISTERS

SEATTLE. *St. Joseph's Carmelite Monastery*. 2215 N.E. 147th, Shoreline, 98155. Sr. Marie Suzanne, O.C.D., Supr. Discalced Carmelites 8; In Formation 2.

St. Joseph's Residence, 4800 37th Ave. S.W., 98126. Tel: 206-937-4600. Sr. Shirley Smith, S.P., Supr.; Rev. John A. Jennings, Chap. Sisters of Providence 57; Dominican Sisters 7; Daughters of Mary 2; Benedictines 2.

Sisters of St. Joseph of Peace, 1104 21st Ave., E., 98112. Tel: 206-324-1529. Sisters 4.

Sisters of the Good Shepherd, 11544 Phinney Ave., N., 98133. Tel: 206-362-3832. Sr. Frances L. Groesbeck, R.G.S., Coord. Sisters 5.

BELLEVUE. *St. Mary's House of Studies*, 1663 Killarney Way, P.O. Box 1763, 98009. Tel: 206-451-1833; Fax: 206-462-9760. Sr. Helen Haigh, Admin. Sisters of St. Joseph of Peace 40.
Our Lady's Province.

St. Mary's Provincialate, 1663 Killarney Way, Box 248, 98009-0248. Tel: 206-451-1770. Sr. Sheila Lemieux, C.S.J.P., Prov. Sisters of St. Joseph of Peace, Our Lady Province.

EDMONDS. *Rosary Heights*. (Motherhouse of the Dominican Sisters Congregation of Holy Cross), 23120 Woodway Park Rd., P.O. Box 280, 98020. Tel: 206-542-7511. Sr. Judy Byron, O.P., Prioress.

LACEY. *St. Placid Priory*, 500 College St., N.E., 98516. Tel: 360-438-1771. Sr. Sharon McDonald, O.S.B., Prioress. Sisters of St. Benedict 31.

SHAW ISLAND. *Franciscan Sisters of the Eucharist*, P.O. Box 455, 98286. Mother Helen Jean Brinkman, F.S.E., Supr. Sisters 3.

Our Lady of the Rock Priory. (Cloistered), P.O. Box 425, 98286. Benedictine Nuns. Rev. Mother Therese Critchley, O.S.B., Supr. Professed Nuns 7; Postulants 1

TACOMA. *III Order of St. Dominic*, Tacoma Dominican Center, 935 Fawcett Ave., S., 98402. Tel: 206-272-9688. Sr. Agnes Huck, O.P., Pres.
(Congregation of St. Thomas Aquinas), Sisters of Saint Dominic of Tacoma Charitable Trust - Tacoma Dominican Center.

St. Charles Borromeo Convent, 7114 S. 12th St., 98465. Tel: 206-564-3880.

St. Marguerite Convent, 4019 S. Thompson, 98408. Tel: 206-472-9702.

Sister of St. Francis of Philadelphia, St. Ann Retirement Convent, 6602 S. Alaska St., 98408. Tel: 206-474-8319; 475-0791; Fax: 206-474-0734. Serra House, 6602 S. Alaska St., 98408. Tel: 206-474-8026. Evergreen House, 6602 S. Alaska St., 98408. Tel: 206-474-9803. Olympus House, 6602 S. Alaska St., 98408. Tel: 206-474-8573. Marian House, 6802 47th St. W., 98466. Tel: 206-564-1816. LaVerna, 701 North K St. #12, 98403. Tel: 206-272-2232.

[O] RETREAT HOUSES, CONFERENCE CENTERS AND CAMPS

SEATTLE. *Camp Don Bosco*, Contact C.Y.O., 910 Marion, 98104. Tel: 206-382-4562.

Still Point, 1111 Harvard Ave., 98122. Tel: 206-322-8006. Sr. Carol Deschane, Dir.

BOTHELL. *St. Thomas Center*, 14500 Juanita Dr., N.E., 98011. Tel: 206-823-1300. Mr. Donald A. Leak, Admin.

EDMONDS. *Dominican Reflection Center*, 23120 Woodway Park Rd., P.O. Box 280, 98020. Tel: 206-542-3740; 546-6561. Sr. Kathleen Logan, O.P., Dir.

FEDERAL WAY. *Palisades Retreat House*, P.O. Box 3739, 98063. Tel: 206-838-9583; 927-9621 (Tacoma); Fax: 206-927-9624. Rev. Richard Ochiltree, C.Ss.R., Dir.; Bro. William Roberts, C.Ss.R., Admin.; Rev. Raymond Maiser, C.S.Sp., Palisades Retreat Assoc.

MONROE-DUVALL. *Camp Hamilton*, 25405 Lake Frontal Rd., 98272. Contact C.Y.O., 910 Marion, Seattle, 98104. Tel: 206-382-4562.

TOLEDO. *St. Mary Conference Center*, 107 Spencer Rd., 98591. Tel: 360-864-6464; Fax: 360-864-6465.

[P] NEWMAN CENTERS

SEATTLE. *Office of Campus and Young Adult Ministry*, 910 Marion St., 98104. Tel: 206-527-5072. Rev. Thomas De Man, O.P., Dir., Seattle University, Campus Ministry, Broadway & E. Madison, 98122. Tel: 206-626-5900. Mary Romer Cline, Dir., University of Washington, Catholic Newman Center, 4502 20th Ave. N.E., 98105. Tel: 206-527-5072. Revs. Thomas De Man, O.P., Dir.; Jordan Bradshaw, O.P., Western Washington University (Bellingham). Campus Christian Ministry. 102 Highland Dr., Bellingham, 98225. Tel: 206-733-3400. Sr. Shirley Osterhaus, O.S.F, St. Martin's College (Lacey). Campus Ministry., Lacey, 98503. Tel: 206-491-4700. Rev. Jack Frerker.

[Q] MISCELLANEOUS

SEATTLE. *Catholic Hospital Ministries*, 910 Marion St., 98104. Revs. Brian Snyder; Mark Stehly; Ross Fewing. Hospitals served include: Harborview, Virginia Mason, Fred Hutchinson Cancer Center, Swedish Medical Center.

CHANNEL Program, 9641 20th Ave., S.W., 98106. Tel: 206-768-9250; Fax: 206-768-9253. Stephen Hueffed, Dir.

Cursillo Movement, P.O. Box 68803, 98168-0803. Tel: 206-536-4804. Mr. Ed Schaefer. Tel: 206-361-5579.

Intercommunity Housing, 150 12th Ave., #3, 98122. Tel: 206-223-1051. Sr. Charlotte Davenport, C.S.J.P., Contact Person.

Intercommunity Housing Ferndale, 150 12th Ave., 98122. Tel: 206-223-1051; Fax: 206-621-7046. Sr. Charlotte Davenport, C.S.J.P., Pres./Exec. Dir.

**Intercommunity Peace & Justice Center*, 150 12th Ave. #3, 98122. Tel: 206-223-1138; 328-5307. Sr. Linda Haydock, S.N.J.M., Exec. Dir.

Intercommunity Properties, 150 12th Ave., 98122. Tel: 206-223-1051. Sr. Charlotte Davenport, C.S.J.P., Exec. Dir.

The Rosary, P.O. Box 33762, 98133. Mrs. Pauline Coveny, Pres.

St. Mary's Food Bank, 611 20th Ave., S., 98144. Tel: 206-324-0050. Bonnie Baker, Dir.

Seattle, Vietnamese Catholic Center, 1230 E. Fir St., 98122. Tel: 206-325-5626. Rev. Phuong Duc Tran (Vietnam).

Sisters of Providence Health System, 520 Pike Tower, P.O. Box 11038, 98111-9038. Tel: 206-464-3355. Sisters of Providence in Oregon, Sisters of Providence in Washington, Sisters of Providence in California, Sisters of Providence Pariseau Association, and Provincial Offices for Sacred Heart Province. Sr. Judith Desmarais, S.P., Acting Prov. Supr.; Sr. Diana Bader, O.P., Vice Pres. Mission Leadership.
For detailed information on corporate holdings for the Sisters of Providence, please refer to Religious Institutes of Women in the back of the directory.

Washington State Catholic Conference, 419 Occidental Ave. S., Ste. 608, 98104. Tel: 206-382-4821. Mr. Edward E. Dolejsi, Exec. Dir.

BELLEVUE. *Sisters of St. Joseph of Peace, Our Lady Province, Charitable Trust*, 1663 Killarney Way, P.O. Box 248, 98009-0248. Tel: 206-451-1770. Sheila Lemieux, C.S.J.P., Prov. Leader.

Sisters of St. Joseph of Peace, PeaceHealth, Corporate Center, 15325 S.E. 30th Pl., Ste. 300, 98007. Tel: 206-747-1711; Fax: 206-649-3825. Sr. Monica F. Heeran, C.S.J.P., Pres.

EDMONDS. *Intercommunity Ministry Volunteer Program*, P.O. Box 280, 98020-0280. Tel: 206-542-3212. Sr. Judy Byron, O.P., Pres.

LACONNER. *Skagit Valley Regional Ministry*, P.O. Box 1260, 98257. Tel: 206-336-6622; Fax: 360-424-8838. Rev. Paul A. Magnano.

TACOMA. *Catholic Pastoral Care-Hospital Tacoma Ministry*, 911 S. Fifth St., 98405. Tel: 206-591-9474. Rev. Michael E. Walsh, S.J., Dir.

Pierce County Association of Catholic Educators (PACE), 2300 S. Washington, 98405. Tel: 206-756-7830. Mr. Justin Morrill.

Pierce County Deanery, 1001 N. J St., 98403. Tel: 206-383-3496. Deacon Del Hoover, Admin.

VANCOUVER. *Vancouver Oratorian Community*, 4723 N.W. Franklin St., 98663. Tel: 360-696-3725. Revs. Robert Dell, C.O.; Clarence Jones, C.O.

RELIGIOUS INSTITUTES OF MEN REPRESENTED IN THE ARCHDIOCESE

For further details refer to the corresponding bracketed number in the Religious Institutes of Men or Women section.

[0200]—*Benedictine Monks*. (Olympia, WA).—O.S.B.

[0310]—*Congregation of Christian Brothers*. (Western U.S.).—C.F.C.

[0260]—*Discalced Carmelites Friars*. (California Prov.).—O.C.D.

[0520]—*Franciscan Friars.* (Prov. of Santa Barabara).—O.F.M.

[0690]—*Jesuit Fathers and Brothers.* (Oregon Province).—S.J.

[0800]—*Maryknoll.*—M.M.

[0910]—*Oblates of Mary Immaculate.* (Western Province).—O.M.I.

[]—*Oratorian Community.*

[0430]—*Order of Preachers (Dominicans).* (San Francisco, CA).—O.P.

[1070]—*Redemptorist Fathers.* (Oakland Province).—C.SS.R.

[1250]—*Society of Christ.* (American-Canadian Prov.).—S.Ch.

[1290]—*Society of the Priests of Saint Sulpice.*—S.S.

RELIGIOUS INSTITUTES OF WOMEN REPRESENTED IN THE ARCHDIOCESE

[0180]—*Benedictine Nuns of the Primitive Observance.*—O.S.B.

[0230]—*Benedictine Sisters of Pontifical Jurisdiction.* (Lacey, WA; Duluth, MN).—O.S.B.

[]—*Carmelite.*—O.L.

[]—*Congregation of Divine Province.*—C.D.P.

[2100]—*Congregation of the Humility of Mary.*—C.H.M.

[1920]—*Congregation of the Sisters of the Holy Cross.*—C.S.C.

[1780]—*Congregation of the Sisters of the Third Order of St. Francis of Perpetual Adoration.* (Western Region).—F.S.P.A.

[0420]—*Discalced Carmelite Nuns.*—O.C.D.

[1070-03]—*Dominican Sisters.* (Edmonds).—O.P.

[1070-04]—*Dominican Sisters.* (Tacoma).—O.P.

[1070-13]—*Dominican Sisters.* (San Rafael).—O.P.

[1070-19]—*Dominican Sisters.* (Sinsinawa).—O.P.

[1070-20]—*Dominican Sisters.* (Adrian).—O.P.

[1070-21]—*Dominican Sisters.* (Houston).—O.P.

[]—*Franciscan Sisters of Rochester.*—O.S.F.

[]—*Franciscan Sisters of St. Mary of the Angels.*—F.S.M.A.

[1250]—*The Institute of the Franciscan Sisters of the Eucharist.*—F.S.E.

[2860]—*Missionary Sisters of the Sacred Heart.*—M.S.C.

[1830]—*Religious of the Good Shepherd.*—R.G.S.

[4070]—*Religious of the Sacred Heart.*—R.S.C.J.

[]—*Religious Sisters of Mercy.*—R.S.M.

[2970]—*School Sisters of Notre Dame.*—S.S.N.D.

[3500]—*Servants of the Blessed Sacrament.*—S.B.S.

[]—*Sisters for Christian Community.*—S.F.C.C.

[0480]—*Sisters of Charity of Leavenworth, Kansas.*—S.C.L.

[0430]—*Sisters of Charity of the Blessed Virgin Mary.*—B.V.M.

[3000]—*Sisters of Notre Dame De Namur.*—S.N.D.deN.

[3350]—*Sisters of Providence.*—S.P.

[]—*Sisters of Social Service.*—S.S.S.

[1705]—*The Sisters of St. Francis of Assissi.*—O.S.F.

[1630]—*Sisters of St. Francis of Penance and Christian Charity.*—O.S.F.

[1650]—*The Sisters of St. Francis of Philadelphia.*—O.S.F.

[3830-08]—*Sisters of St. Joseph at Cleveland.*—C.S.J.

[3840]—*Sisters of St. Joseph of Carondelet.* (California Prov.).—C.S.J.

[]—*Sisters of St. Joseph of Carondelet.* (St. Paul, MN Prov.).—C.S.J.

[3890]—*Sisters of St. Joseph of Peace.*—C.S.J.P.

[3960]—*Sisters of St. Mary of Oregon.*—S.S.M.O.

[1990]—*Sisters of the Holy Names of Jesus and Mary.*—S.N.J.M.

[]—*Sisters of the Holy Names of Jesus and Mary.* (Oregon Prov.).—S.N.J.M.

[]—*Sisters of the Holy Names of Jesus and Mary.* (California Prov.).—S.N.J.M.

ARCHDIOCESAN CEMETERIES

Central Office: 910 Marion, 98104. Tel:206-382-9281

SEATTLE. *Calvary*, 5041 35th Ave. N.E., 98105. Tel: 206-522-0996.

Holyrood, 205 N.E. 205th, 98155. Tel: 206-363-8404.

FEDERAL WAY. *Gethsemane*, 37600 Pacific Hwy. S., 98003. Tel: 206-838-2240.

NECROLOGY

† Conger, Donald W., (Retired). —Died June 7, 1996.

† Squier, Andrew J., (Retired). —Died Aug. 7, 1996.

Diocese of Shreveport

(Dioecesis Sreveportuensis in Louisiana)

Most Reverend

WILLIAM B. FRIEND, D.D.

Bishop of Shreveport; ordained May 7, 1959; appointed Titular Bishop of Pomaria and Auxiliary Bishop of Alexandria-Shreveport August 31, 1979; ordained Bishop October 30, 1979; appointed Bishop of Alexandria-Shreveport November 23, 1982; installed January 11, 1983; appointed Bishop of Shreveport June 16, 1986. *Address all communications to: Catholic Center, 2500 Line Ave., Shreveport, LA, 71104-3043.* Tel.: 318-222-2006; Fax: 318-222-2080.

Chancery Office: Catholic Center, 2500 Line Ave., Shreveport LA, 71104-3043. Tel.: 318-222-2006; Fax: 318-222-2080.

ESTABLISHED AND CREATED A DIOCESE JUNE 16, 1986.

Comprises the Counties (parishes) of Bienville, Bossier, Caddo, Claiborne, DeSoto, East Carroll, Jackson, Lincoln, Morehouse, Ouachita, Red River, Richland, Sabine, Union, Webster and West Carroll.

For legal titles of parishes and diocesan institutions, consult the Chancery Office.

STATISTICAL OVERVIEW

Personnel	
Bishop	1
Priests: Diocesan Active in Diocese	32
Priests: Active Outside Diocese	2
Priests: Retired, Sick or Absent	9
Number of Diocesan Priests	43
Religious Priests in Diocese	11
Extern Priests in Diocese	4
Ordinations:	
Diocesan Priests	2
Permanent Deacons in Diocese	7
Total Sisters	71
Parishes	
Parishes	31
With Resident Pastor:	
Resident Diocesan Priests	22
Resident Religious Priests	8
Without Resident Pastor:	
Administered by Priests	1
Missions	15
Pastoral Centers	2
Professional Ministry Personnel:	
Sisters	3
Lay Ministers	18
Welfare	
Catholic Hospitals	2
Total Assisted	191,527
Health Care Centers	1
Total Assisted	30,163
Homes for the Aged	1
Total Assisted	132
Day Care and Extended Day Care Centers	1
Total Assisted	100
Specialized Homes	2
Total Assisted	20
Special Centers for Social Services	15
Total Assisted	17,221
Residential Care of Disabled	1
Total Assisted	184
Other Institutions	2
Total Assisted	1,433
Educational	
Diocesan Students in Other Seminaries	4
Total Seminarians	4
High Schools, Diocesan and Parish	2
Total Students	811
Elementary Schools, Diocesan and Parish	11
Total Students	2,579
Catechesis/Religious Education:	
High School Students	725
Elementary Students	2,334
Total Students Under Catholic Instruction	6,453
Teachers in the Diocese:	
Sisters	9
Lay Teachers	215
Vital Statistics	
Receptions into the Church:	
Infant Baptism Totals	527
Adult Baptism Totals	118
Received into Full Communion	185
First Communions	634
Confirmations	613
Marriages:	
Catholic	118
Interfaith	109
Total Marriages	227
Deaths	340
Total Catholic Population	38,365
Total Population	785,635

Vicar General—Vacant.

Vicars Forane—Rev. Msgr. EARL V. PROVENZA, V.F., *Christ the King Church, 425 McCormick St., Bossier City, 71111-4692.* Tel: 318-221-0238. Rev. J. ROBERT INZINA, V.F., *Our Lady of Fatima Church, P.O. Box 4136, Monroe, 71211-4136.* Tel: 318-325-7595. Rev. WILLIAM H. CAREY, V.F., *St. John the Baptist Church, 1130 E. San Antonio Ave., Many, 71449-3226.* Tel: 318-256-5689.

Chancery Office—Catholic Center, 2500 Line Ave., Shreveport, 71104-3043. Tel: 318-222-2006; Fax: 318-222-2080.

Chancellor—Sr. MARGARET DAUES, C.S.J., Ph.D.

Archives—Mrs. CHRISTINE RIVERS.

Diocesan Tribunal—2500 Line Ave., Shreveport, 71104-3043. Tel: 318-222-2006; Fax: 318-222-2080.

Judicial Vicar—Rev. PETER B. MANGUM, J.C.L.

Secretary—Ms. PATTY S. WHEELER.

Defender of the Bond—Rev. PHILIP F. MICHIELS.

Promotor of Justice—Rev. Msgr. HARRY O. BARKER.

Judges—Rev. Msgr. FRANZ GRAEF, S.T.D.; Rev. PETER B. MANGUM, J.C.L., J.V.; Rev. Msgr. EDMUND J. MOORE; Rev. ROTHELL PRICE, J.C.L. Candidate.

Notaries—Rev. PHILIP F. MICHIELS; Ms. PATTY S. WHEELER.

Procurator-Advocate—Rev. Msgr. EDMUND J. MOORE; Rev. Msgr. FRANZ GRAEF, S.T.D.

Corporate Council—Most Rev. WILLIAM B. FRIEND, D.D.; Sr. MARGARET DAUES, C.S.J., Ph.D.

College of Consultors—Rev. Msgr. EARL V. PROVENZA, V.F.; Rev. J. ROBERT INZINA, V.F.; Rev. WILLIAM H. CAREY, V.F.; Rev. Msgr. EDMUND J. MOORE; Revs. TIMOTHY C. HURD; EDMUND A. "LARRY" NIEHOFF; ROTHELL PRICE; WILLIAM SPENCER, O.F.M.

Finance Council—Ms. MARY A. BROWN; Mr. DAVID CATTAR; Mrs. JOAN FISHER; Mr. JOHN HUSSEY; Dr. JAMES ROBERT MICHAEL; Rev. Msgr. WILLIAM O'HANLON; Mrs. LYNN ROOS; Mr. NICHOLAS ROPPOLO; Mr. LAWRENCE H. RUSSO, III; Mr. WILLIAM STAAB; Mr. EALIE THORNTON. Ex Officio: Most Rev. WILLIAM B. FRIEND; Sr. MARGARET DAUES, C.S.J.

Presbyteral Council—Revs. TIMOTHY C. HURD, Chm. WILLIAM SPENCER, O.F.M., Vice Chm. LAVERNE (PIKE) THOMAS, Sec.; Rev. Msgr. J. CARSON LACAZE; Revs. GOVIE MORAUS; EDMUND A. "LARRY" NIEHOFF; ROTHELL PRICE. Ex Officio: Rev. Msgr. EARL V. PROVENZA, V.F.; Revs. J. ROBERT INZINA, V.F.; WILLIAM H. CAREY, V.F.

Pastoral Council—Mrs. KATHRYN BARATTINI; Mrs. ROSE MARIE CLARKE; Mr. DAVID FOLEY; Mrs. LINDA HOLYFIELD; Ms. ROYLENE JONES; Mrs. KATHY ROWLAND; Mr. CHARLES SCOTT; Ms. BETH VALIULIS; Sr. MARGARET DAUES, C.S.J.,(Four more to be assigned).

Priests' Retirement Board—Rev. Msgr. J. CARSON LACAZE, Chm.; Rev. Msgr. EARL V. PROVENZA, V.F.; Revs. J. ROBERT INZINA, V.F.; EARL G. BEAULIEU; EDMUND A. "LARRY" NIEHOFF; DANIEL M. WALSH; Mr. WADE DUPUIS; Mr. NICHOLAS ROPPOLO.

The Catholic Foundation of North-Central Louisiana, Inc.—P.O. Box 8021, Alexandria, 71306-1021. Tel: 318-487-9222.

Diocesan Offices and Directors

Black Catholic Commission—Rev. ROTHELL PRICE, Chap., *Catholic Center, 2500 Line Ave., Shreveport, 71104-3043.* Tel: 318-222-2006.

Business Affairs—Mr. E. MICHAEL SCHOFIELD, C.P.A., *Catholic Center, 2500 Line Ave., Shreveport, 71104-3043.* Tel: 318-222-2006.

Campaign for Human Development—Address Communications to: Office of Community and Family Life Ministries: *Catholic Center, 2500 Line Ave., Shreveport, 71104-3043.* Tel: 318-222-2006.

Campus Ministry—Sr. EILEEN MCGRORY, S.C., Coord., *Catholic Center, 2500 Line Ave., Shreveport, 71104-3043.* Tel: 318-222-2006.

Catechetics and Worship—Mrs. MARY MCGILL, M.A., *Catholic Center, 2500 Line Ave., Shreveport, 71104-3043.* Tel: 318-222-2006.

Catholic Relief Services—Address Communications to: Office of the Vicar General, *Catholic Center, 2500 Line Ave., Shreveport, 71104-3043.* Tel: 318-222-2006.

Cemeteries—Mr. E. MICHAEL SCHOFIELD, C.P.A., *Catholic Center, 2500 Line Ave., Shreveport, 71104-3043.* Tel: 318-222-2006.

Censor of Books—Rev. Msgr. FRANZ GRAEF, S.T.D.

Charismatic Movement—Mr. JOHN J. GUERRIERO, JR., *2316 Sauvelle Dr., Monroe, 71201-2953.* Mr. THOMAS HARLAN, *9536 Pitch Pine, Shreveport, 71118-4527.*

Church Vocations—Revs. ROTHELL PRICE, Dir. TIMOTHY C. HURD, Assoc. Dir., *2500 Line Ave., Shreveport, 71104-3043.* Tel: 318-222-2006.

Church Vocations Board—Mr. LAWRENCE W. PETTIETTE, JR., Chm.; Revs. ROTHELL PRICE, Dir. TIMOTHY C. HURD, Assoc. Dir. CHARLES GLORIOSO; PHILIP F. MICHIELS; Sr. MAVIS CHAMPAGNE, O.L.S.; Sr. EILEEN MCGRORY, S.C.; Mrs. SHARON CHANEY; Mrs. ANNE JONES; Mr. DON ANZELMO; Mr. SAM GILLIAM;

Mr. BRIAN D. LANDRY; Mr. MACK MILES, JR. Ex-Officio Member: Most Rev. WILLIAM B. FRIEND.

Continuing Education for the Clergy—Rev. RICHARD NORSWORTHY, Dir., *St. Jude Church, 3800 Viking Dr. East, Bossier City, 71111-7403.* Tel: 318-746-2508.

Development and Public Relations—Mr. JOHN MARK WILLCOX, Dir., *Catholic Center, 2500 Line Ave., Shreveport, 71104-3043.* Tel: 318-222-2006.

Diocsan Publications—Ms. POLLY VOORHIES, Editor, *Catholic Center, 2500 Line Ave., Shreveport, 71104-3043.* Tel: 318-222-2006.

Ecumenism and Interreligious Affairs—Rev. Msgr. CARSON J. LACAZE, *Our Lady of the Holy Rosary Church, 1755 Corbitt St., Shreveport, 71108-3098.* Tel: 318-636-3530.

Evangelization—Vacant.

Community and Family Life Ministries—Vacant, *Catholic Center, 2500 Line Ave., Shreveport, 71104-3043.* Tel: 318-222-2006.

Greco Institute—Mr. DONALD R. EMGE, Ph.D., *Catholic Center, 2500 Line Ave., Shreveport, 71104-3043.* Tel: 318-222-2006.

Health Ministry—Rev. WILLIAM H. CAREY, V.F., Coord., *St. John the Baptist Church, 1130 E. San Antonio Ave., Many, 71449-3226.* Tel: 318-256-5689.

Hispanic Community—Mrs. ELISA MILAZZO, Coord., *Catholic Center, 2500 Line Ave., Shreveport, 71104-3043.* Tel: 318-222-2006. Rev. RIGOBERTO BETANCURT, O.S.M., Chap.

Holy Childhood—Mr. GARY GELO, M.E., Contact Person, *Catholic Center, 2500 Line Ave., Shreveport, 71104-3043.* Tel: 318-222-2006.

Information Systems Management—Ms. PATRICIA PILLORS, Dir., *Catholic Center, 2500 Line Ave., Shreveport, 71104-3043.* Tel: 318-222-2006.

Jail-Prison Ministry—Rev. DANIEL WALSH, Coord., *St. Clement Church, 819 N. Pine St., Vivian, 71082-3354.* Tel: 318-375-2789.

Liturgy Commission—Mrs. MARY CUNNINGHAM; Mrs. SUSAN GIBSON; Mrs. JO KAUFMAN; Mr. MICHAEL KENNEY; Mrs. TAMI KING; Mrs. CAROLE MOON; Mr. ARCHIE PERRY; Mr. JIM SPANN; Mrs. JODI TOLIVER; Revs. TIMOTHY C. HURD; PHILIP F. MICHIELS; ROTHELL PRICE; DAVID RICHTER; Mrs. MARY MCGILL, Ex-Officio.

Mission Director—Address Communications to: Office of the Vicar General, *Catholic Center, 2500 Line Ave., Shreveport, 71104-3043.* Tel: 318-222-2006.

Permanent Deacon Coordinator—Rev. PHILIP F. MICHIELS, *St. Mary of the Pines Church, 1050 Bert Kouns Industrial Loop, Shreveport, 71118-3499.* Tel: 318-687-5121. Deacon CLARY NASH, Dean Permanent Deacons, *St. John Berchmans Cathedral, 939 Jordan St., Shreveport, 71101-4391.* Tel: 318-221-5296.

Propagation of the Faith—Address Communications to: Office of the Vicar General, *Catholic Center, 2500 Line Ave., Shreveport, 71104-3043.* Tel: 318-222-2006.

Religious Education—Mrs. MARY MCGILL, M.A., Dir., *Catholic Center, 2500 Line Ave., Shreveport, 71104-3043.* Tel: 318-222-2006.

Religious-Advisory Council—Sr. ANNA MARIA IANNETTI, O.L.S.

Schools—Mr. GARY GELO, M.E., Supt., *Catholic Center, 2500 Line Ave., Shreveport, 71104-3043.* Tel: 318-222-2006.

Child Nutrition Program—Mrs. LAVON G. PRUITT, M.S., R.D., *2500 Line Ave., Shreveport, 71104-3043.* Tel: 318-222-2055.

Scouting—Rev. DAVID RICHTER, Coord., *St. Joseph Church, P.O. Box 8, Zwolle, 71486-0008.* Tel: 318-645-9852; 645-6155.

Spanish-Speaking Ministers—Rev. Msgr. C. MURRAY CLAYTON, *Catholic Center, 2500 Line Ave., Shreveport, 71104-3043.* Revs. RIGOBERTO BETANCURT, O.S.M., *St. Joseph Church, P.O. Box 1203, Monroe, 71210-1203.* JUAN GARCIA, *Cathedral of St. John Berchmans, 939 Jordan St., Shreveport, 71101-4391.*

St. Catherine Community Center—Mr. ROBERT ALFORD, Dir., *331 E. 71st St., Shreveport, 71106-4305.* Tel: 318-865-9817.

St. Vincent de Paul Society—Mrs. SHEILA FRITZ, Contact Person, *Catholic Center, 2500 Line Ave., Shreveport, 71104-3043.* Tel: 318-222-2006.

The Beginning Experience—Mrs. CONNIE CRAWFORD, *266 Settlers Ln., Shreveport, 71115-3197.*

Young and Young Adult Ministry—Sr. EILEEN MCGRORY, S.C., Dir., *Catholic Center, 2500 Line Ave., Shreveport, 71104-3043.* Tel: 318-222-2006; Fax: 318-222-2080.

CLERGY, PARISHES, MISSIONS AND PAROCHIAL SCHOOLS

CITY OF SHREVEPORT
(Caddo Parish)

1—ST. JOHN BERCHMANS CATHEDRAL (1902), Revs. Juan F. Garcia R.; Charles Glorioso; Deacon Clary Nash. In res., Rev. Rothell Price.
Res., 939 Jordan St., 71101-4391. Tel: 318-221-5296; Fax: 318-221-8076.
School—Tel: 316-221-6005. Miss Marie R. Rinaudo, Prin.
Sisters 1; Lay Teachers 23; Students 308.
Catechesis/Religious Programs—947 Jordan St., 1101. Tel: 318-424-2317; Fax: 318-221-8076.

2—HOLY TRINITY (1856), Rev. Msgr. William O'Hanlon.
Res., 315 Marshall St., P.O. Box 144, 71161-0144. Tel: 318-221-5990.

3—OUR LADY OF THE BLESSED SACRAMENT (1923), Rev. Richard K. Pusch.
Res., 1558 Buena Vista St., 71101-2448. Tel: 318-222-3790.
School—2932 Murphy St., 71103-2241. Tel: 318-222-5051. Dr. Thomas Archey, Prin.
Sisters of the Holy Spirit and Mary Immaculate 2; Lay Teachers 14; Students 325.

4—OUR LADY OF THE HOLY ROSARY (1952), Rev. Msgr. J. Carson LaCaze.
Res., 1755 Corbitt St., 71108-3098. Tel: 318-636-3530; Fax: 318-636-9123.
School—1730 Cox St., 71108. Tel: 318-636-3826; Fax: 318-636-9123. Sr. Sandra Norsworthy, O.L.S., Prin.
Sisters of Our Lady of Sorrows 3; Lay Teachers 13; Students 187.

5—SACRED HEART OF JESUS (1966), Rev. Msgr. Harry O. Barker; Rev. Msgr. C. Murray Clayton.
Res., 4736 Lyba St., P.O. Box 19467, 71149-0467. Tel: 318-635-2121.

6—ST. CATHERINE OF SIENA (1938), Rev. William Spencer, O.F.M.
Res., 331 E. 71st St., 71106-4305. Tel: 318-868-6506; Fax: 318-861-6177.

7—ST. ELIZABETH ANN SETON (1984), Revs. LaVerne Thomas, III; Mark A. Watson; Deacon William Long.
Res., 522 E. Flournoy-Lucas Rd., 71115-2073. Tel: 318-798-1887; Fax: 318-797-7302.

8—ST. JOSEPH (1949), Revs. Richard J. Lombard; Curtis Woods.
Res., 228 Patton Ave., P.O. Box 5188, 71135-5188. Tel: 318-865-3581; Fax: 318-865-5125.
School—1210 Anniston Ave., 71135. Tel: 318-865-3585; Fax: 318-868-1859. Mrs. Carmen Heflin, Prin.
Lay Teachers 38; Students 562.

9—ST. MARY OF THE PINES (1973), Revs. Philip F. Michiels; Joseph Howard.
Res., 1050 Bert Kouns Industrial Loop, 71118-3499. Tel: 318-687-5121; Fax: 318-687-5124. [CEM]
Mission—Stonewall, DeSoto Parish, St. Ann, Tel: 318-925-0591.

10—ST. PIUS X (1955), Rev. John D. Pardue.
Res., 4300 N. Market St., 71107-2953. Tel: 318-222-2165.

11—ST. THERESA. Consolidated with St. John Berchmans Cathedral.

OUTSIDE THE CITY OF SHREVEPORT

Bastrop, Morehouse Parish, St. Joseph (1943), Rev. Joseph A. Martina, Jr.
Res., 217 Harrington Ave., 71220-3025. Tel: 318-281-4327. [CEM]
School—Tel: 318-281-5890. Angie Druhan, Prin.
Lay Teachers 11; Students 178.
Our Lady Help of Christians. Consolidated with St. Joseph, Bastrop.

Bossier City, Bossier Parish, Christ the King (1939), Rev. Msgr. Earl V. Provenza; Rev. Msgr. Norman Buvens; Rev. Ron Matthews (ALX); Deacon David Ludke.
Res., 425 McCormick St., 71111-4692. Tel: 318-221-0238; Fax: 318-425-0011.
School—1000 Ogilvie St., 71111. Tel: 318-222-8934; Fax: 318-424-7002. Dr. Julia Johnson, Prin.
Lay Teachers 14; Students 203.
Missions—Caplis, Bossier Parish, Mary, Queen of Peace; Doyline, Webster Parish, Mary, Queen of the Holy Rosary, Tel: 318-747-9496.
St. Jude (1964), Rev. Richard Norsworthy; Deacon John J. Finnom, Jr.; Mrs. Twyla Saterthwaite, Parish Life Coord.
Res., 3800 Viking Dr., E., 71111-7403. Tel: 318-746-2508; Fax: 318-742-4526.
Mission—Benton, Mary, Queen of Heaven.

Grambling, Lincoln Parish, St. Benedict the Black (1966), Rev. Adrian Fischer, O.F.M.
Res., 471 Main St., 71245-3088. Tel: 318-247-6734.

Hodge, Jackson Parish, St. Lucy (1935), Rev. Joseph B. Hagen, O.F.M.
Res., Second St., P.O. Drawer 100, 71247-0100. Tel: 318-259-2326. [CEM]

Lake Providence, East Carroll Parish, St. Patrick (1870), Rev. John Scanlan.
Res., P.O. Box 351, 71254-0351. Tel: 318-559-1276. [CEM]
School—Rte. 2, Box 313, Tel: 318-559-1644. Nancy Gates, Prin.
Lay Teachers 8; Students 119.

Mansfield, DeSoto Parish, St. Joseph (1907), Rev. Edmund A. Niehoff.
Res., 305 Jefferson St., P.O. Box 760, 71052-0760. Tel: 318-872-1158; Fax: 318-872-1161. [CEM]
Mission—Coushatta, Red River Parish, St. George, 1811 Ashland Rd., P.O. Box 937, 71019-0937. Tel: 318-932-3733.

Many, Sabine Parish, St. John the Baptist (1871), Rev. William H. Carey.
Res., 1130 E. San Antonio Ave., 71449-3226. Tel: 318-256-5680; 256-5689; Fax: 318-256-9177. [CEM]
Mission—Many, Sabine Parish, St. Terence, Hwy. 191 & 476, 1130 E. San Antonio Ave., 71449. Tel: 318-586-7444.

Minden, Webster Parish, St. Paul (1942), Rev. Peter Mangum.
Res., 414 Fincher Rd., P.O. Box 799, 71058-0799. Tel: 318-377-5364; Fax: 318-377-5119.
Missions—Ringgold, Bienville Parish, Blessed Sacrament, Hwy. 7 at Hwy. 4, Ringgold, 71068.; Haynesville, Claiborne Parish, St. Michael, Hwy. 79 at Roland St., Haynesville, 71038.; Homer, Claiborne Parish, St. Margaret, 600 E. 2nd St., Homer, 71040. Tel: 316-927-2865; Springhill, Webster Parish, Sacred Heart, 304 Gaisser St., Springhill, 71075. Tel: 318-539-4919.

Monroe, Ouachita Parish,

1—JESUS THE GOOD SHEPHERD, (1958), Rev. Msgr. Edmund J. Moore; Rev. Timothy C. Hurd; Deacon John Cummings.
Res., 2510 Emerson St., 71201-2699. Tel: 318-325-7549.
School—900 Good Shepherd Ln., 71201. Tel: 318-325-8569.
Daughters of the Cross 2; Lay Teachers 10; Students 257.

2—LITTLE FLOWER OF JESUS, (1940), Rev. Carroll Mizicko, O.F.M.
Res., 600 S. 16th St., 71201. Tel: 318-322-1224.
School—610 S. 16th St., 71201. Tel: 318-322-7379. Mr. Sammy Goldsmith, Prin.
Lay Teachers 8; Students 100.

3—OUR LADY OF FATIMA, (1952), Revs. Joseph Robert Inzina; Thomas Kizito Nwachukwu (Nigeria).
Res., 3205 Concordia, P.O. Box 4136, 71211-4136. Tel: 318-325-7595.
School—3202 Franklin St., 71211. Tel: 318-387-1851. Nancy Williams, Prin.
Lay Teachers 13; Students 206.
Mission—Swartz, St. Lawrence, 203 School Rd., P.O. Box 554, 71281.

4—ST. JOSEPH, (1956), Rev. Rigoberto Betancurt, O.S.M. (Colombia).
Res., 506 Benton Ave., P.O. Box 1203, 71210-1203. Tel: 318-325-4527.

5—ST. MATTHEW, (1856), Rev. John D. Kennedy. In res., Rev. Msgr. George W. Martinez, (Retired), Tel: 318-361-3880; Rev. Joseph Puthuppally (India).
Res., 121 Jackson St., P.O. Box 33, 71210-0033. Tel: 318-323-8878; 323-8879; Fax: 318-323-8878. [CEM]

Noble, Sabine Parish, St. Ann (1955), Rev. Kenneth Williams.
Res., 5272 Hwy. 482, 71462. Tel: 318-645-9419. [CEM]
Mission—Noble, St. Catherine, Tel: 318-645-2711. [CEM]

Oak Grove, West Carroll Parish, Sacred Heart (1947), Rev. Joseph A. Martina, Jr.
Church—203 Purvis St., P.O. Box 419, 71263-0419. Tel: 318-428-2683.

Rambin, DeSoto Parish, St. Mary. Consolidated with St. Joseph, Mansfield.

Rayville, Richland Parish, Sacred Heart (1920), Rev. Thomas J. Flynn, C.S.Sp.
Res., 716 Francis St., P.O. Box 717, 71269-0717. Tel: 318-728-2445.
Mission—Delhi, St. Theresa, 705 Main St., P.O. Box 363, 71232-0363. Tel: 318-878-3484.

Ruston, Lincoln Parish, St. Thomas Aquinas (1941), Rev. Jerome Thelen, O.F.M.; Deacon John J. Serio.
Res., 810 Carey Ave., 71270-4915. Tel: 318-255-2870; Fax: 318-254-8319.

Vivian, Caddo Parish, St. Clement (1945), Rev. Daniel M. Walsh.
Office: 819 N. Pine, 71082-3354. Tel: 318-375-2789.

West Monroe, Ouachita Parish, St. Paschal (1940), Rev.

Robert Leonhardt, O.F.M. In res., Rev. Donatus Grunloh, O.F.M.
Res., 711 N. Seventh St., 71291-4211. Tel: 318-323-1631; Fax: 318-361-0527. [CEM]
School—102 Wilson St., 71291. Tel: 318-322-8246. Catherine Letendre, Prin.
Lay Teachers 11; Students 134.
Missions—Calhoun, St. Francis of Assisi, Tel: 318-644-5440; 323-1631; Farmerville, Our Lady of Perpetual Help, Tel: 318-368-9239. Rev. Adrian Fischer, O.F.M., Admin.
Res., 471 Main St., Grambling, 71245-3088. Tel: 318-247-6734.

Zwolle, Sabine Parish, St. Joseph (1881), Rev. David T. Richter; Mr. Ronald J. Morris, Pastoral Assoc.
Res., P.O. Box 8, 71486-0008. Tel: 318-645-9852. [CEM]

Chaplains of Public Institutions

SHREVEPORT. *Louisiana State University Medical Center.* Pastoral Care Office P.O. Box 33932, 71130-3932. Tel: 318-675-6930. Rev. Patrick A. Scully.
Overton Brooks Veteran's Administration Medical Center 510 E. Stoner Ave., 71101. Rev. Philip Michiels, Chap. Emergencies, Res., St. Mary of the Pines Church, 1050 Bert Kouns Industrial Loop, 71118-3499. Tel: 318-687-5121; 687-1818.

MONROE. *E.A. Conway Memorial Hospital.* Rev. J. Robert Inzina, Chap., Res., Our Lady of Fatima Church, P.O. Box 4136, 71211-4136. Tel: 318-325-7595.
Louisiana Training Institute 4701 S. Grand, 71202-6499. Tel: 318-323-4406. Rev. Joseph Robert Inzina.

On Duty Outside the Diocese:
Reverend Monsignors—
Graef, Franz, Notre Dame Seminary, New Orleans, LA
Reverend Fathers—
Madden, Patrick, St. Mary Seminary and University, Baltimore, MD

On Leave:
Reverend Fathers—
Ebarb, Walter E.

Retired:
Reverend Monsignors—
Martinez, George W.
Reverend Fathers—
Albert, J. W. (HT)
Armando, Fuoco
Beaulieu, Earl
Binh, John Phan Cong
Germain, Jean
McMullen, Roger
Pierce, William J.
Tremblay, Leger

Permanent Deacons:
Cummings, John
Finnorn, John J., Jr.
Long, William R.
Ludke, David
Nash, Clary
Serio, John J.
Wisdom, Clarence, Inactive

INSTITUTIONS LOCATED IN THE DIOCESE

[A] HIGH SCHOOLS, DIOCESAN

SHREVEPORT. *Loyola College Prep,* 921 Jordan St., 71101-4390. Tel: 318-221-2675. Mrs. Mary Ann Whited, Prin.; Rev. Joseph C. Howard, Jr., Chap. Priests 1; Sisters 1; Lay Teachers 26; Students 402.

MONROE. *St. Frederick High School,* 3300 Westminster, 71201-3299. Tel: 318-323-9636. Franciscan Sisters of Our Lady of Perpetual Help. Mr. Grady Jones, Prin.; Rev. John D. Kennedy, Chap. Sisters 1; Lay Teachers 26; Students 409.

[B] GENERAL HOSPITALS

SHREVEPORT. *Schumpert Medical Center,* (1907) One St. Mary Pl., P.O. Box 21976, 71120-1976. Tel: 318-681-4500.
For a complete listing, refer to the Hospitals section.

MONROE. *St. Francis Medical Center,* P.O. Box 1901, 71210-1901. Tel: 318-327-4000; Fax: 318-327-4142.
For a complete listing, refer to the Hospitals section.
**St. Francis Specialty Hospital,* (1995) 309 Jackson St., P.O. Box 1532, 71210. Tel: 318-327-4600.
For a complete listing, refer to the Hospitals section.

[C] PROTECTIVE INSTITUTIONS

SHREVEPORT. *Holy Angels Residential Facility,* 10450 Ellerbe Rd., 71106-7712. Tel: 318-797-8500; 797-9070.
For a complete listing, refer to the Special Care Facilities section.

[D] HOMES FOR AGED

MONROE. *St. Joseph Home,* 2301 Sterlington Rd., P.O. Box 6057, 71211-6057. Tel: 318-323-3426.
For a complete listing, refer to the Special Care Facilities section.

[E] SPECIAL CENTERS FOR SOCIAL SERVICES & ASSISTANCE

SHREVEPORT. *St. Catherine Community Center,* 331 E. 71st St., 71106-4305. Tel: 318-865-9817. Mr. Robert Alford, Dir.

[F] CONVENTS AND RESIDENCES FOR SISTERS

SHREVEPORT. *Motherhouse of the Daughters of the Cross in America,* 1000 Fairview St., 71104-4182. Tel: 318-869-3482. Sr. Marietta Welsh, Supr.; Rev. Govie Moraus, Chap. Sisters 16.
Religious House of Formation and Retirement-Our Lady of Sorrows, 9894 Norris Ferry Rd., 71106-7724. Tel: 318-797-0213; Fax: 318-797-7003. Sr. Anita Bianchini, O.L.S., Supr. Sisters 8.

[G] NEWMAN CENTERS

GRAMBLING. *Student Center,* 471 S. Main St., 71245-3088. Tel: 318-247-6288; 247-6734 (Office). Rev. Adrian Fischer, O.F.M., Campus Min.

MONROE. *Catholic Campus Ministry at Northeast Louisiana University,* 911 University Ave., P.O. Box 7250, 71211-7250. Tel: 318-343-4897. Revs. Joseph Robert Inzina, Chap.; John D. Kennedy, Assoc. Chap.

RUSTON. *E. Donn Piatt Catholic Student Center at Louisiana Tech University,* 600 S. Thornton St., 71270-4946. Tel: 318-251-0793. Rev. Jerome Thelen, O.F.M.; Sr. Edith Schnell, O.P.

RELIGIOUS INSTITUTES OF MEN REPRESENTED IN THE DIOCESE

For further details refer to the corresponding bracketed number in the Religious Institutes of Men or Women section.

[0275]—*Carmelites of Mary Immaculate (India).*—C.M.I.

[0520]—*Franciscan Friars.* (Sacred Heart Prov.).—O.F.M.

[0650]—*Holy Ghost Fathers of Ireland.* (Louisiana Prov.).—C.S.Sp.

[1240]—*Order of Friar Servants of Mary.*—O.S.M.

[0560]—*Third Order Regular of St. Francis (Spanish Province of Immaculate Conception).*—T.O.R.

RELIGIOUS INSTITUTES OF WOMEN REPRESENTED IN THE DIOCESE

[0470]—*Congregation of the Sisters of Charity of the Incarnate Word, Houston, Texas.*—C.C.V.I.

[0770]—*Daughters of the Cross.*—D.C.

[1070-14]—*Dominican Sisters.*—O.P.

[1380]—*Franciscan Missionaries of Our Lady.*—O.S.F.

[1180]—*Franciscan Sisters of Allegany.* New York.—O.S.F.

[1430]—*Franciscan Sisters of Our Lady of Perpetual Help.*—O.S.F.

[1530]—*Franciscan Sisters of Sylvania.* Ohio.—O.S.F.

[2420]—*Marist Missionary Sisters (Missionary Sisters of the Society of Mary Inc.).*—S.M.S.M.

[2970]—*School Sisters of Notre Dame, St. Louis Province.*—S.S.N.D.

[0650]—*Sisters of Charity of St. Vincent de Paul of New York.*—S.C.

[1010]—*Sisters of Divine Providence of San Antonio, Texas.*—C.D.P.

[3120]—*Sisters of Our Lady of Sorrows.*—O.L.S.

[3840]—*Sisters of St. Joseph of Carondelet.*—C.S.J.

[2050]—*Sisters of the Holy Spirit and Mary Immaculate.*—S.H.Sp.

NECROLOGY

† Kwaaitaal, Rev. Msgr. William, (Retired). —Died Jan. 16, 1996.

† Maguire, Bernard F., (Retired). —Died April 10, 1996.

Diocese of Sioux City

(Dioecesis Siopolitana)

Most Reverend

LAWRENCE D. SOENS, D.D.

Bishop of Sioux City; ordained May 6, 1950; appointed Bishop of Sioux City June 15, 1983; consecrated and installed August 17, 1983. *Address all correspondence to: P.O. Box 3379, Sioux City, IA, 51102-3379; Fax: 712-233-7598.*

Corporate Title: *"The Diocese of Sioux City."*

ESTABLISHED JANUARY 15, 1902.

Square Miles 14,518.

Comprises 24 Counties in the northwest part of Iowa, west of Winnebago, Hancock, Wright, Hamilton and Story Counties, and north of Harrison, Shelby, Audubon, Guthrie and Dallas Counties.

For legal titles of parishes and diocesan institutions, consult the Chancery.

Chancery: Administrative Offices, 1821 Jackson St., P.O. Box 3379, Sioux City, IA, 51102-3379. Tel.: 712-255-7933; 233-7512; Fax: 712-233-7598.

STATISTICAL OVERVIEW

Personnel	
Bishop	1
Priests: Diocesan Active in Diocese	121
Priests: Active Outside Diocese	10
Priests: Diocesan in Foreign Missions	1
Priests: Retired, Sick or Absent	47
Number of Diocesan Priests	179
Ordinations:	
Diocesan Priests	2
Transitional Deacons	2
Permanent Deacons in Diocese	35
Total Sisters	128
Parishes	
Parishes	118
With Resident Pastor:	
Resident Diocesan Priests	95
Without Resident Pastor:	
Administered by Priests	24
Administered by Pastoral Teams, etc.	4
Missions	10
Professional Ministry Personnel:	
Sisters	19
Lay Ministers	5
Welfare	
Catholic Hospitals	3
Total Assisted	318,297
Homes for the Aged	3
Total Assisted	270
Residential Care of Children	4
Total Assisted	7
Specialized Homes	1
Total Assisted	30
Special Centers for Social Services	4
Total Assisted	6,280
Educational	
Diocesan Students in Other Seminaries	5
Total Seminarians	5
Colleges and Universities	1
Total Students	1,116
High Schools, Diocesan and Parish	8
Total Students	2,380
Elementary Schools, Diocesan and Parish	28
Total Students	6,540
Catechesis/Religious Education:	
High School Students	4,086
Elementary Students	8,764
Total Students Under Catholic Instruction	22,891
Teachers in the Diocese:	
Priests	7
Sisters	26
Lay Teachers	518
Vital Statistics	
Receptions into the Church:	
Infant Baptism Totals	1,784
Adult Baptism Totals	80
Received into Full Communion	480
First Communions	1,689
Confirmations	1,529
Marriages:	
Catholic	379
Interfaith	324
Total Marriages	703
Deaths	1,206
Total Catholic Population	99,377
Total Population	472,136

Former Bishops—Most Rev. PHILIP J. GARRIGAN, D.D., ord. June 11, 1870; appt. March 21, 1902; cons. May 25, 1902; died Oct. 14, 1919.—Most Rev. EDMOND HEELAN, D.D., ord. June 24, 1890; cons. April 8, 1919; died Sept. 20, 1948.—Most Rev. JOSEPH M. MUELLER, D.D., ord. June 14, 1919; cons. Oct. 16, 1947; died Aug. 9, 1981.—Most Rev. FRANK H. GRETEMAN, D.D., ord. Dec. 8, 1932; appt. Titular Bishop of Vissalsa April 14, 1965; cons. May 26, 1965; appt. Bishop of Sioux City Oct. 20, 1970; installed Dec. 9, 1970; retired Aug. 17, 1983; died March 21, 1987.

Vicar-General—Rev. Msgr. ROGER J. AUGUSTINE, V.G., *Immaculate Conception Church, 419 Jones St., P.O. Box C, Moville, 51039-0802.* Tel: 712-873-3745.

Chancery—Administrative Offices, 1821 Jackson St., P.O. Box 3379, Sioux City, 51102-3379. Tel: 712-255-7933; 233-7512; Fax: 712-233-7598.

Chancellor—Rev. KEVIN C. MCCOY, S.T.D., *Res., 2514 Leech Ave., Sioux City, 51107-1244.* Tel: 712-276-7368.

Vice Chancellor—Rev. R. MARK DUCHAINE, J.C.L., *Res., Our Lady of Good Counsel Church, 513 Mueller St., Holstein, 51025-9802.* Tel: 712-368-4755.

Diocesan Tribunal—Address all marriage related materials to: *Diocesan Tribunal, P.O. Box 3379, Sioux City, 51102-3379.* Tel: 712-233-7533.

Judicial Vicar—Rev. R. MARK DUCHAINE, J.C.L., *1821 Jackson St., P.O. Box 3379, Sioux City, 51102-3379., Res., Our Lady of Good Counsel Church, 513 Mueller St., Holstein, 51025-9802.* Tel: 712-368-4755.

Associate Judicial Vicar—Rev. EUGENE J. ULSES, J.C.L., *1821 Jackson St., P.O. Box 3379, Sioux City, 51102-3379., Res., St. Joseph Church, 408 S. Main St., P.O. Box 457, Schaller, 51053-0457.* Tel: 712-378-2722.

Promotor of Justice—Rev. KEVIN C. MCCOY, S.T.D.; Rev. Msgr. RICHARD E. ZENK, J.C.D.

Defender of the Bond—Revs. ROBERT P. BROWN, S.T.L.; KEVIN C. MCCOY, S.T.D.; Rev. Msgr. RICHARD E. ZENK, J.C.D.

Judges—Rev. Msgrs. MICHAEL D. SERNETT, J.C.D.; ROGER AUGUSTINE, V.G.; Revs. PAUL-LOUIS ARTS; JEROME COSGROVE.

Notary—JUDY E. PUETZ.

Diocesan Corporate Board—Most Rev. LAWRENCE D. SOENS, D.D., Pres.; Rev. Msgr. ROGER J. AUGUSTINE, V.G., Vice Pres.; Rev. KEVIN C. MCCOY, Sec. Directors: Revs. THOMAS E. GEELAN; ROGER J. LINNAN; Mr. WILLIAM C. METZ; Mr. MICHAEL J. MOELLER; Mr. JEFFREY R. MOHRHAUSER; Mrs. SUSAN H. PIERCE; Dr. DANIEL J. SHEY; Sr. MARGARET WICK.

Diocesan Legal Counsel—Mr. JAMES M. COSGROVE-,(Shull, Cosgrove, Hellige & Lundberg Law Firm, Sioux City). Refer all legal matters to The Chancery.

Priests' Senate—Rev. Msgr. ROGER J. AUGUSTINE, V.G.; Revs. PAUL-LOUIS ARTS; STEVEN W. BRODERSEN; R. MARK DUCHAINE; PAUL F. EISELE; THOMAS E. GEELAN; TIMOTHY A. JOHNSON; JAMES C. MCALPIN; HARRY D. MCALPINE; KEVIN C. MCCOY; ALFRED E. MCCOY; VICTOR R. RAMAEKER; ROBERT J. SCHIMMER; MERLIN J. SCHRAD; JAMES TIGGES.

Diocesan Consultors—Rev. Msgr. ROGER J. AUGUSTINE, V.G.; Revs. PAUL-LOUIS ARTS; JEROME COSGROVE; THOMAS E. GEELAN; LAWRENCE MCCARTY; A. E. MCCOY.

Deans—Very Revs. ROBERT J. SCHIMMER, V.F., Southwestern Deanery; MERVIN J. HOOD, V.F., Central Deanery; THOMAS J. HART, V.F., South Central Deanery; DONALD C. RIES, V.F., Southeastern Deanery; ALBERT O. GRENDLER, V.F., Northeastern Deanery; Rev. TIMOTHY J. HOGAN, V.F., Northwestern Deanery.

Diocesan Offices and Directors

Board of Education—Most Rev. LAWRENCE D. SOENS, D.D., Ex Officio Chm.; Mr. EUGENE MEISTER, Pres.; Revs. THOMAS E. GEELAN, Vice Pres. PATRICK J. O'KANE; WILLIAM A. SCHREIBER; CRAIG A. COLLISON; GERALD F. FEIERFEIL; Sr. MARGE FELDNER, O.S.F.; Sr. M. EUGENE GOSS, P.B.V.M.; Dr. KEITH GUY; Mrs. KATHLEEN HANSEN; Sr. MARY ANN HELLE, O.S.F.; Mrs. MARGARET MOIR; Mrs. SHERRY NILLES; Mr. JOHN PERKINS; Mr. PATRICK RINKER; Sr. JOAN STOFFEL, O.S.F.

Building Commission—Most Rev. LAWRENCE D. SOENS, D.D., Chm.; Revs. CLAIR L. BOES; JEROME DEGEN; BRIAN C. HUGHES.

Catholic School Foundation of the Diocese of Sioux City—Most Rev. LAWRENCE D. SOENS, D.D., Pres., *1821 Jackson St., P.O. Box 3379, Sioux City, 51102.*

Archives—Sr. KEVIN CUMMINGS, P.B.V.M., *1821 Jackson St., P.O. Box 3379, Sioux City, 51102-3379.* Tel: 712-233-7525.

Catholic Youth Organization—Rev. CRAIG A. COLLISON, Dir., *St. Mary Church, R.R.1, Box 57A, Carroll, 51401-9726.* Tel: 712-792-4516.

Office of Religious Education and Youth Ministry—Mr. PATRICK RINKER, Dir., *1821 Jackson St., P.O. Box 3379, Sioux City, 51102-3379.*

Censor Librorum—Rev. Msgr. JAMES K. LAFFERTY, Ph.D., *St. John Church, P.O. Box 23, Arcadia, 51430-0023.* Tel: 712-689-2595.

Catholic Charities—Mr. BRUNO FINOCCHARIO, M.S.W., Dir., *1601 Military Rd., Sioux City, 51103.* Tel: 712-252-4547. Fort Dodge Office: *3 N. 16th, Fort*

Dodge, 50501. Tel: 515-576-4156. Carroll Office: *409 1/2 W. 7th St., P.O. Box 13, Carroll, 51401.* Tel: 712-792-9597.

Office of Youth Ministry and Catechesis—Directors: Mr. PATRICK RINKER; Sr. ELENA HOYE, *1821 Jackson St., P.O. Box 3379, Sioux City, 51102-3379.* Tel: 712-233-7520.

Continuing Education for Priests—Rev. ROGER J. LINNAN, Ph.D., Dir., *St. Francis of Assisi Church, 744 Main St., Rockwell City, 50579-1399.* Tel: 712-297-8263.

Council of Catholic Women—Rev. EUGENE T. SCHUMACHER, Moderator, *Holy Name Church, R.R. 2, Box 71, Rock Rapids, 51246-9529.* Tel: 712-472-3248.

Ecumenical Commission—Rev. Msgr. FRANK J. BRADY, Chm.; Revs. ROBERT W. GRALAPP; JOSEPH KERWIN; JAMES C. MCALPIN; ALFRED E. MCCOY.

Episcopal Representative for Religious—Sr. ROSALIE ERDMANN, S.L.W., *1812 Jackson St., Sioux City, 51105-1054.* Tel: 712-258-2579.

Episcopal Representative for Hospitals and Health Care—Rev. KEVIN C. MCCOY, S.T.D., *1821 Jackson St., P.O. Box 3379, Sioux City, 51102-3379.*

Family Life Office And Adult Ministries—Mrs. KAY MORRISSEY, Dir., *1821 Jackson St., P.O. Box 3379, Sioux City, 51102-3379.* Tel: 712-233-7530.

Holy Childhood Association—Rev. Msgr. RICHARD E. ZENK, J.C.D., Dir., *P.O. Box 3379, Sioux City, 51102-3379.*

Liturgy Commission—Mrs. MARJORIE KRAFT, Chm.; Revs. STEVE BRODERSEN; TIM FITZGERALD; BRUCE LAWLER; HARRY MCALPINE; Sr. JULIE MARSH, P.B.V.M.; Sr. M. ARNOLD STAUDT, O.S.F.; Sr. RUTH ANN TAKES, P.B.V.M.; Mr. RICHARD CAREY; Mrs. MARLENE FITZPATRICK; Mr. BERNARD KENINGER; Ms. KRIS MUELLER; Mrs. MONICA PEARSON.

Office Of Communications—"The Globe"—Deacon JOSEPH F. MAHER, Mgr., *1825 Jackson St., P.O. Box 5079, Sioux City, 51102-5079.* Tel: 712-255-2550. Editorial Office; Circulation.

Office of Catholic Education—Revs. PATRICK J. O'KANE, Supt. of Secondary Education, *1821 Jackson St., P.O. Box 3379, Sioux City, 51102-3379.* Tel: 712-233-7527. Sr. JOAN STOFFEL, Supt. of Elementary Education.

Permanent Diaconate—Rev. ARMAND J. BERTRAND, Co-Dir., *Our Lady of Good Counsel Church, P.O. Box 306, Fonda, 50540-0306.* Tel: 712-288-6480. Deacon RONALD M. FORREST, Co-Dir., *1821 Jackson St., P.O. Box 3379, Sioux City, 51102-3379.*

Priests' Eucharistic League—Rev. MERVIN J. HOOD, Dir., *Early, 50535.*

Priests' Personnel Board—Rev. Msgr. ROGER J. AUGUSTINE, V.G., Bishop's Liaison; Revs. LAURENCE J. BURNS; ANDREW W. HOFFMAN; JOHN J. MCGUIRK; PATRICK J. O'KANE.

Priests' Pension Plan - Board of Trustees—Most Rev. LAWRENCE D. SOENS, D.D.; Rev. KEVIN C. MCCOY; Rev. Msgr. FRANK J. BRADY; Mr. WILLIAM C. METZ; Mr. RICHARD L. BILLINGS; Mr. PATRICK D. KUEHL; Mr. MICHAEL J. MOELLER; Mr. JEFFREY R. MOHRHAUSER; Mr. ROBERT V. WILLIAMS.

Priests' Provident Society—Most Rev. LAWRENCE D. SOENS, D.D., Pres.

Propagation of the Faith, Association of the Holy Childhood, Catholic Students' Mission Crusade—Rev. Msgr. RICHARD E. ZENK, J.C.D., Dir., *1821 Jackson St., P.O. Box 3379, Sioux City, 51102-3379.*

Radio and Television—Deacon JOSEPH F. MAHER, Dir., *P.O. Box 5079, Sioux City, 51102-5079.*

Rural Life Conference—MARILYN MURPHY, Dir., *1601 Military Rd., Sioux City, 51103.* Tel: 712-252-4547.

St. Joseph Student Aid Society—(Diocesan Seminarian Board). Most Rev. LAWRENCE D. SOENS, D.D., Honorary Pres.; Rev. PAUL-LOUIS ARTS, Exec. Sec., *P.O. Box 2817, Sioux City, 51106-2817.* Tel: 712-276-4821.

Vocations—Rev. BRIAN C. HUGHES, *3303 Rebecca St., Sioux City, 51104-2340.* Tel: 712-233-7523; 279-5461.

CLERGY, PARISHES, MISSIONS AND PAROCHIAL SCHOOLS

CITY OF SIOUX CITY
(Woodbury County)

1—CATHEDRAL OF THE EPIPHANY (1867), Revs. Edward M. Girres; Randy J. Guerdet; Hieu Nguyen (Vietnam); Verne P. Stapenhorst; Eriberto Costa (Brazil).
Res., 1011 Douglas St., 51105-1399. Tel: 712-255-1637.
School—Holy Family Epiphany Center. (Grades 6-8) 1000 Douglas St., 51105. Tel: 712-252-3181.
Sisters 1; Lay Teachers 9; Students 130.
Catechesis/Religious Programs—Students 56.

2—BLESSED SACRAMENT (1922), Revs. Thomas E. Geelan; Joseph Andrew Dillinger; Deacons John Hefferman; James Sands; Fred Karpuk; George Spellman.
Res., 3012 Jackson St., 51104-2799. Tel: 712-277-2949; Fax: 712-277-2963.
School—3030 Jackson St., 51104. Tel: 712-277-4739; Fax: 712-277-8592.
Priests 1; Lay Teachers 28; Students 435.
Catechesis/Religious Programs—Patricia Walsh, D.R.E.
Students 143.

3—ST. BONIFACE (1906), Rev. Marvin J. Boes. In res., Rev. Richard A. Sitzmann.
Res., 703 W. Fifth St., 51103-3799. Tel: 712-255-3577. [JC]
School—Holy Family, (Grades K-5) 700 W. Sixth St., 51103. Tel: 712-258-9464.
Sisters of the Living Word 1; Lay Teachers 5; Students 101.
Catechesis/Religious Programs—Students 122.

4—ST. CASIMIR (1915) (Lithuanian), Revs. Paul-Louis Arts; Christian Van Oosbree; Deacon Ron Forrest.
Mailing Address: P.O. Box 2817, 51107. Tel: 712-276-4821.
Res., Clustered with Immaculate Conception, Sioux City. 1212 Morningside Ave., P.O. Box 2817, 51106. Tel: 712-276-4821. [JC]

5—ST. FRANCIS OF ASSISI (1907) (Polish), Revs. Paul-Louis Arts; Christian Van Oosbree; Deacon Ron Forrest.
Mailing Address: P.O. Box 2817, 51106. Tel: 712-276-4821.
Res., Clustered with Immaculate Conception, Sioux City. 1212 Morningside Ave., P.O. Box 2817, 51106. Tel: 712-276-4821. [JC]

6—IMMACULATE CONCEPTION (1905), Revs. Paul-Louis Arts; Christian Van Oosbree; Deacon Ron Forrest.
Res., P.O. Box 2817, 51106-2817. Tel: 712-276-4821. [JC]
School—3719 Ridge Ave., 51106. Tel: 712-276-6216.
Priests 2; Lay Teachers 15; Students 314.
Catechesis/Religious Programs—Students 213.

7—ST. JOSEPH (1887), Rev. Robert J. Schimmer; Deacons Jerome Reicks; Ronald Pietz; Patrick McCruden.
Res., 1112 Eighth St., 51105-1899. Tel: 712-258-3813. [JC]
School—Holy Family, (Grades K-5). Consolidated with St. Francis, Cathedral of the Epiphany and St. Boniface. 709 Iowa St., 51105. Tel: 712-258-4962.
Lay Teachers 6; Students 92.
Catechesis/Religious Programs—Students 58.

8—ST. MICHAEL (1907), Rev. Lawrence L. McCarty; Deacons Larry Sitzman; William Berger; Sr. Sally Mitchell, O.S.F., Pastoral Min.
Res., 2223 Indian Hills Dr., 51104-1605. Tel: 712-239-2411; Fax: 712-239-4910. [JC]
School—4106 Van Buren St., 51104. Tel: 712-239-1090.
Sisters of the Blessed Virgin Mary 2; Lay Teachers 15; Students 258.
Catechesis/Religious Programs—Students 90.

9—NATIVITY OF OUR LORD JESUS CHRIST (1966), Rev. Msgr. Michael D. Sernett.
Res., 4242 Natalia Way, 51106-4099. Tel: 712-276-3022.
School—Mater Dei School, (Grades 6-8). Consolidated with Immaculate Conception Parish. Tel: 712-274-0268; Fax: 712-274-0377.
Catechesis/Religious Programs—Tel: 712-274-0497.
Students 358.

10—SACRED HEART (1907), Rev. James A. Bruch.
Res., 5000 Military Rd., 51103-1564. Tel: 712-233-1652. [JC]
School—5010 Military Rd., 51103. Tel: 712-233-1624.
Sisters 1; Lay Teachers 11; Students 204.
Catechesis/Religious Programs—Students 117.

OUTSIDE SIOUX CITY

Akron, Plymouth Co., St. Patrick's (1988), Rev. Richard E. Zenk.
Res., P.O. Box 317, 51001-0317. Tel: 712-568-3292. [CEM]
Catechesis/Religious Programs—Students 95.

Algona, Kossuth Co., St. Cecelia (1892), Rev. Steven W. Brodersen; Deacon Joseph Straub.
Res., P.O. Box 633, 50511-0633. Tel: 515-295-3435; Fax: 515-295-9290. [CEM]
School—Seton Elementary. Consolidation of St. Cecelia, Algona, St. Benedict, St. Joseph, Wesley, St. Joseph, Bode. Tel: 515-295-3509; Fax: 515-295-7739.
Presentation Sisters 6; Lay Teachers 19; Students 253.
Catechesis/Religious Programs—Students 186.

Alton, Sioux Co., St. Mary's (1870), Rev. James Tigges.
Res., 609 10th St., 51003-0181. Tel: 712-756-4224. [CEM]
School—Spalding Elementary, (Grades 3-6). Consolidation of Alton, Hospers and Granville. Tel: 712-756-4532.
Lay Teachers 9; Students 88.
Catechesis/Religious Programs—Students 60.

Anthon, Woodbury Co., St. Joseph's (1890), Rev. David Hogan; Sr. Mary Clare Walling, Pastoral Min.
Res., P.O. Box 285, 51004-0285. Tel: 712-373-5573. [CEM]
Catechesis/Religious Programs—Tel: 712-373-5011.
Students 128.

Arcadia, Carroll Co., St. John the Baptist (1875), Rev. Msgr. James K. Lafferty.
Res., P.O. Box 23, 51430-0023. Tel: 712-689-2595. [CEM]
School—Holy Cross Elementary. Consolidaion of Arcadia and Vail. Tel: 712-689-2589.
Lay Teachers 3; Students 44.
Catechesis/Religious Programs—Students 68.

Armstrong Emmet Co., St. Mary's (1892), Rev. Thomas C. Nash.
Res., 404 Fifth Ave., 50514-9301. Tel: 712-864-3160. [CEM][JC]
Catechesis/Religious Programs—Students 92.

Ashton, Osceola Co., Our Lady of Perpetual Help (1880), Rev. Timothy J. Hogan.
Res., P.O. Box 157, 51232-0157. Tel: 712-724-6411. [CEM]
Catechesis/Religious Programs—2191 Nettle Ave., 51232. Tel: 712-724-6297. Mrs. Nancy Marnach, D.R.E.
Students 55.

Auburn, Sac Co., St. Mary's (1893) (German), Rev. Merlin J. Schrad.
Res., P.O. Box H, 51433. Tel: 712-688-2845. [CEM][JC]
Catechesis/Religious Programs—Students 51.

Bancroft, Kossuth Co., St. John the Baptist's (1891), Rev. John M. Thomas; Deacon Philip Doocy.
Res., P.O. Box 195, 50517-0195. Tel: 515-885-2462; Fax: 515-885-2462. [CEM]
School—St. John's Elementary School, Tel: 515-885-2580.
Lay Teachers 7; Students 57.
Catechesis/Religious Programs—Students 199.

Barnum, Webster Co., St. Joseph's (1891), Rev. Dale E. Reiff.
Res., P.O. Box 105, Clare, 50524-0105. Tel: 515-546-4505. [CEM]
Catechesis/Religious Programs—Students 53.

Boone, Boone Co., Sacred Heart (1868), Rev. Gerald Feierfeil.
Res., 921 12th St., 50036-2295. Tel: 515-432-1971. [CEM]
School—Sacred Heart Elementary, Tel: 515-432-4124; Fax: 515-432-4124.
Lay Teachers 13; Students 220.
Catechesis/Religious Programs—Tel: 515-432-2884.
Students 208.

Breda, Carroll Co., St. Bernard's, Very Rev. Thomas J. Hart, V.F.
Res., P.O. Box 31, 51436-0031. Tel: 712-673-2351. [CEM]
School—Christ the King Elementary. Consolidation of Breda, Lidderdale, Maple River and Mt. Carmel. Tel: 712-673-2582.
Lay Teachers 12; Students 206.

Carroll, Carroll Co., St. Lawrence (1916), Revs. Lawrence J. Burns; Douglas Michael Klein; Deacon Robert Bruner.
Res., 1607 N. West St., 51401-4198. Tel: 712-792-9244; Fax: 712-792-9245. [JC]
School—1519 N. West St., 51401. Tel: 712-792-2123; Fax: 712-792-8072.
Franciscan Sisters of Perpetual Adoration 1; Lay Teachers 45; Students 321.
Catechesis/Religious Programs—Tel: 712-792-4386. John Crosheck, D.R.E.
Students 467.

Holy Spirit (1964), Revs. James D. McCormick; Steven J. McLoud; Deacon Anthony Reuter.
Res., 421 E. Bluff St., 51401-3099. Tel: 712-792-4386; Fax: 712-792-8072. [JC]
School—Kuemper Catholic Grade Schools, Tel: 712-792-3610.
Franciscan Sisters of Perpetual Adoration 1; Lay Teachers 46; Students 240.
Catechesis/Religious Programs—John Crosheck, D.R.E.
Students 107.

Charter Oak, Crawford Co., St. Boniface (1883) (German-Irish), Rev. Benjamin E. Jensen.

Res., P.O. Box 317, Dow City, 51528. Tel: 712-678-3449. [CEM]
Mission—Ute, Monona Co., St. Mary's, c/o Box 317, 51439. [CEM]
Catechesis/Religious Programs—Students 66.

Cherokee, Cherokee Co., Immaculate Conception (1870), Rev. James R. Smith; Deacon Leroy Rupp.
Res., 709 W. Cedar St., P.O. Box 658, 51012-0658. Tel: 712-225-4606. [CEM]
Catechesis/Religious Programs—7th & Willow, 51012. Tel: 712-225-4466.
Students 399.

St. Dymphna (1960). (Mental Health Institute, Chapel for Patients). Rev. Eugene E. Sitzmann.
Res., 1200 W. Cedar St., 51012. Tel: 712-225-6929; Fax: 712-225-6925.

Churdan, Greene Co., St. Columbkille's (1886), Rev. Dennis W. Meinen.
Res., P.O. Box 128, 50050-0128. Tel: 515-389-3625; Fax: 515-389-3795. [JC]
Catechesis/Religious Programs—Students 84.

Clare, Webster Co., St. Matthew's (1886), Rev. Dale E. Reiff.
Res., P.O. Box 105, 50524-0105. Tel: 515-546-4505. [CEM]
Catechesis/Religious Programs—Students 70.

Coon Rapids, Carroll Co., Annunciation (1891), Rev. Robert M. Fangman.
Res., P.O. Box 76, 50058-0076. Tel: 712-684-2823.
Catechesis/Religious Programs—Students 139.

Danbury, Woodbury Co., St. Mary's (1897), Rev. David Hogan.
Res., P.O. Box 318, 51019-0318. Tel: 712-883-2406. [CEM]
School—Danbury Elementary, Tel: 712-883-2244.
Priests 1; Sisters 1; Lay Teachers 5; Students 68.
Catechesis/Religious Programs—Students 56.

Dayton, Webster Co., Christ the King (1950), Rev. Thomas J. Munn. Pastoral Ministers: Sr. Mary Lois Lehmann, P.B.V.M.; Sr. Mary Bernard Mauss, P.B.V.M.
Res., P.O. Box 528, Ogden, 50530-0528. Tel: 712-275-2580. [CEM]
Catechesis/Religious Programs—Tel: 515-547-2743.
Students 61.

Dedham, Carroll Co., St. Joseph's (1892), Rev. Terry A. Roder.
Res., P.O. Box 47, 51440-0047. Tel: 712-683-5744. [CEM]
School—Kuemper Catholic Grade Schools. Consolidation of Dedham, Willey Elementary, Holy Spirit and St. Lawrence.

Denison, Crawford Co., St. Rose of Lima (1872), Rev. Andrew W. Hoffmann.
Res., 1008 2nd Ave. S., P.O. Box 280, 51442-0280. Tel: 712-263-2152. [CEM]
School—Tel: 712-263-5408.
Lay Teachers 8; Students 112.
Catechesis/Religious Programs—Students 272.

Dow City, Crawford Co., St. Mary's (1947) (German-Irish), Rev. Benjamin E. Jensen.
Res., 215 Clark St., P.O. Box 317, 51528-0317. Tel: 712-674-3329.
Catechesis/Religious Programs—Students 71.

Duncombe, Webster Co., St. Joseph's (1880), Rev. Richard Adam.
Res., P.O. Box 140, 50532-0140. Tel: 515-543-4332. [CEM]

Early, Sac Co., Sacred Heart (1882), Very Rev. Mervin J. Hood.
Res., P.O. Box 378, 50535-0378. Tel: 712-273-5482; Fax: 712-273-5798. [CEM]
Catechesis/Religious Programs—Tel: 712-273-5577.
Students 69.

Emmetsburg, Palo Alto Co., Holy Family (1870) (Irish), Rev. Eugene L. Murray.
Res., 2001 S. Broadway, P.O. Box 322, 50536-0322. Tel: 712-852-3187. [CEM]
School—Emmetsburgh Catholic School, (Grades 1-8). Tel: 712-852-3464. Sr. Lucille Hass, O.S.F., Prin.
Lay Teachers 12; Students 141.
Catechesis/Religious Programs—Mary Freeman, D.R.E.
Students 190.

St. Thomas. Closed. For sacramental records contact Holy Family, Emmetsburg.

Estherville, Emmet Co., St. Patrick's (1891), Rev. Thomas C. Nash.
Res., P.O. Box 383, 51334-0383. Tel: 712-362-5851. [CEM]
Catechesis/Religious Programs—Duhigg Center, 902 Central Ave., 51334. Tel: 712-362-4172.
Students 376.

Fonda, Pocahontas Co., Our Lady of Good Counsel (1884), Rev. Armand J. Bertrand; Deacon J. R. Hogan; Sr. Ruth Ann Takes, Pastoral Min.
Res., P.O. Box 306, 50540-0306. Tel: 712-288-6480. [CEM]
School—Tel: 712-288-4465.
Sisters 1; Lay Teachers 6; Students 77.
Catechesis/Religious Programs—Students 60.

Fort Dodge, Webster Co., Corpus Christi (1856), Very Rev. Donald C. Ries, V.F.; Rev. Brian Danner.
Res., 430 N. 8th St., P.O. Box 994, 50501-0994. Tel: 515-573-3616. [JC]
School—Tel: 515-576-0522.
Lay Teachers 20; Students 308.
Catechesis/Religious Programs—Students 144.

Holy Rosary (1946), Rev. Thomas J. Topf.
Res., 2401 9th Ave. S., 50501-6246. Tel: 515-573-3162 (Res.); 573-2018 (Church). [CEM]
School—2406 9 1/2 Ave. S., 50501. Tel: 515-576-0574.
Lay Teachers 6; Students 121.
Catechesis/Religious Programs—Students 58.

Sacred Heart (1897), Rev. Harry D. McAlpine.
Res., 1321 Second Ave. S., 50501-4925. Tel: 515-573-7617. [JC]
School—214 S. 13th St., 50501. Tel: 515-576-0563.
Lay Teachers 15; Students 135.
Catechesis/Religious Programs—Students 117.

Gilmore City, Pocahontas Co., St. John's (1889), Rev. Timothy J. Fitzgerald.
Res., P.O. Box 262, 50541-0262. Tel: 515-373-6016. [CEM]
Catechesis/Religious Programs—Students 55.

Graettinger, Palo Alto Co., Immaculate Conception, Rev. Msgr. Thomas M. Donahoe.
Res., P.O. Box 448, 51342-0448. Tel: 712-859-3327. [CEM]
Catechesis/Religious Programs—Tel: 712-859-3990.
Students 96.

Grand Junction, Greene Co., St. Brigid's (1873) (Irish), Rev. Daniel C. Guenther.
Res., 50107. Tel: 515-738-2684. [CEM]
Catechesis/Religious Programs—St. Brigid Parish Center, 602 Hager St. E., 50107. Tel: 515-738-2254.
Students 60.

Granville, Sioux Co., St. Joseph (1886), Rev. Clem W. Currans.
Res., P.O. Box 127, 51022-0127. Tel: 712-727-3551; Fax: 712-727-3455. [CEM]
School—Spalding Catholic School, (Grades 7-8). Consolidation of Alton, Hospers and Granville. Tel: 712-727-3451.
Lay Teachers 2; Students 46.
High School—Spalding Catholic High School.
Lay Teachers 16; Students 104

Halbur, Carroll Co., St. Augustine's (1904), Rev. Paul J. Kelly.
Res., P.O. Box 13, 51444-0013. Tel: 712-658-2464. [CEM]
School—Holy Trinity Elementary. Consolidation of Halbur, Templeton and Roselle. Tel: 712-669-3346.
Lay Teachers 4; Students 65.
Catechesis/Religious Programs—Students 123.

Hawarden, Sioux Co., St. Mary's (1887), Rev. Msgr. Kevin M. Richter; Deacon Joseph Maher.
Res., P.O. Box 271, 51023-0271. Tel: 712-552-1501. [JC]
Catechesis/Religious Programs—Students 137.

Holstein, Ida Co., Our Lady of Good Counsel (1884), Rev. R. Mark Duchaine.
Res., 513 Mueller St., 51025-9802. Tel: 712-368-4755. [CEM]
Catechesis/Religious Programs—Tel: 712-368-2504.
Students 120.
Mission—Quimby, Cherokee Co., St. John the Baptist, 208 E. Railway, Quimby, 51049. Tel: 712-445-2256.

Hornick, Woodbury Co., St. Philip's (1900). Closed. For inquiries for parish records contact the Chancery.

Hospers, Sioux Co., St. Anthony's (1877), Rev. James Tigges.
Res., 506 Elm, P.O. Box 86, 51238-0086. Tel: 712-752-8784. [CEM]
School—Spalding Elementary, (Grades K-2). Consolidation of Alton, Hospers and Granville. Tel: 712-752-8286.
Lay Teachers 5; Students 70.

Humboldt, Humboldt Co., St. Mary's (1878), Rev. Michael T. Larkin.
Res., 311 Fourth St. N., 50548-1647. Tel: 515-332-2856. [CEM]
School—Tel: 515-332-2134.
Sisters 1; Lay Teachers 11; Students 208.
Catechesis/Religious Programs—Students 131.

Ida Grove, Ida Co., Sacred Heart (1878), Rev. Gerald M. Fisch.
Res., 800 N. Main, P.O. Box 244, 51445-1297. Tel: 712-364-2718. [CEM]
Catechesis/Religious Programs—Tel: 712-364-3628.
Students 183.

Jefferson, Greene Co., St. Joseph's (1875), Rev. Daniel C. Guenther.
Res., 503 N. Chestnut St., 50129-1507. Tel: 515-386-2638; Fax: 515-386-3672. [CEM]
Catechesis/Religious Programs—501 N. Locust, 50129. Tel: 515-386-4010.
Students 200.

Kingsley, Plymouth Co., St. Michael's (1888), Rev. James E. Fangman.
Res., P.O. Box 486, 51028-0486. Tel: 712-378-2722. [CEM]
Catechesis/Religious Programs—Tel: 712-378-2021.
Students 167.

Lake City, Calhoun Co., St. Mary's (1894), Rev. Robert A. Thiele; Deacon Don Kunecke.
Res., P.O. Box 131, 51449-0131. Tel: 712-464-3395. [CEM]
Catechesis/Religious Programs—Students 131.

Larchwood, Lyon Co., St. Mary (1898) (German-Dutch), Rev. Francis J. Nemmers; Deacon Jeffrey F. Gallagher.
Res., P.O. Box 37, 51241-0037. Tel: 712-477-2273. [JC]
Catechesis/Religious Programs—Students 175.

Laurens, Pocahontas Co., Sacred Heart (1893), Rev. Msgr. Leonard M. Ziegmann.
Res., P.O. Box 171, 50554-0171. Tel: 712-845-4596. [CEM]
Catechesis/Religious Programs—Tel: 712-845-4760.
Students 122.

Ledyard, Kossuth Co., Sacred Heart (1887), Rev. John M. Thomas.
Mailing Address: P.O. Box 67, 50556-0067. Tel: 515-646-2525.
Res., 204 S. Summit Ave., P.O. Box 195, Bancroft, 50517. Tel: 515-885-2462. [CEM]

Le Mars, Plymouth Co., St. Joseph's (1875) (German), Revs. Jerome P. Cosgrove; William A. Schreiber; Rev. Msgr. Gerald Lyon, (Retired).
Res., 20 Sixth Ave. N.E., 51031-3714. Tel: 712-546-5223. [JC]
Catechesis/Religious Programs—Tel: 712-546-6038.
Students 135.

St. James (1883), Rev. Richard S. Ries; Deacon Donald Kunkel.
Res., 109 Sixth Ave. S.W., 51031-3434. Tel: 712-546-5201. [JC]
School—Gehlen Catholic Elementary, Tel: 712-546-5126.
Lay Teachers 22; Students 434.
High School—Gehlen Catholic High School, Tel: 712-546-4181.
Lay Teachers 24; Students 199.
Catechesis/Religious Programs—20 Sixth Ave. N.E., 51031. Tel: 712-546-5223.
Students 216.

Lidderdale, Carroll Co., Holy Family (1914) (German), Rev. Richard A. Kielbasa.
Res., P.O. Box 160, 51452-0160. Tel: 712-822-5522. [CEM]
School—Christ the King Elementary. Consolidation of Breda, Lidderdale, Maple River and Mt. Carmel. Tel: 712-673-2582.
Catechesis/Religious Programs—Glidden, 51443. Tel: 712-655-3051.
Students 178.
Mission—Glidden, Carroll Co., St. Elizabeth Seton, Montana St., Glidden, 51443. Tel: 712-659-3051.

Livermore, Humboldt Co., Sacred Heart (1881), Rev. Michael T. Larkin.
Res., 311 Fourth St. N., Humboldt, 50548-1647. Tel: 515-332-2856. [CEM]
Catechesis/Religious Programs—Tel: 515-379-2508.
Students 71.

Lohrville, Calhoun Co., St. Joseph's (1885), Rev. Dennis L. Sefcik.
Res., 305 Ash St., 51453-1002. Tel: 712-465-2085. [CEM]
Catechesis/Religious Programs—Students 78.

Madrid, Boone Co., St. Malachy's (1923), Rev. Msgr. Louis H. Kollasch; Deacon Frank Milani.
Res., 207 Gerald St., 50156-1464. Tel: 515-795-2731.
Church—405 Gerald St., 50156. Tel: 515-795-2613.
Catechesis/Religious Programs—Students 181.

Mallard, Palo Alto Co., St. Mary's (1889), Rev. Peter J. Fransco.
Res., P.O. Box 236, 50562-0236. Tel: 712-425-3359. [CEM]
Catechesis/Religious Programs—Students 43.

Manilla, Crawford Co., Sacred Heart (1887), Rev. Robert W. Gralapp.
Res., 269 6th St., P.O. Box 339, 51454-0339. Tel: 712-654-9511. [CEM]

Catechesis/Religious Programs—Students 139.

Manning, Carroll Co., Sacred Heart (1916) (German), Rev. Ralph W. Reinhart.
Res., 203 Sue St., 51455-1399. Tel: 712-653-3804. [CEM]
Catechesis/Religious Programs—Tel: 712-653-2933.
Students 259.

Manson, Calhoun Co., St. Thomas (1885), Rev. Jerome A. Degen.
Res., P.O. Box G, 50563-9998. Tel: 712-469-3743. [CEM]
Catechesis/Religious Programs—Students 116.

Maple River, Carroll Co., St. Francis of Assisi (1907) (German), Rev. Robert Brown.
Res., R.R. 2, Carroll, 51401-9499. Tel: 712-792-3934. [CEM]
School—Christ the King Elementary. Consolidation of Breda, Lidderdale, Maple River and Mt. Carmel.
Lay Teachers 6.
Catechesis/Religious Programs—Tel: 712-792-9422.
Students 56.

Mapleton, Monona Co., St. Mary's (1894), Rev. Edmund Tiedeman. In res., Rev. Gerald Zensen.
Res., 703 Heisler St., 51034-1222. Tel: 712-827-4467. [CEM]
Catechesis/Religious Programs—Students 106.
Mission—Oto, Woodbury Co., St. Mary's, 620 State St., Box 67, 51044-6007. Tel: 712-827-4467.

Marcus, Cherokee Co., Holy Name (1877), Rev. Richard R. Remmes.
Res., 110 N. Elm St., P.O. Box 366, 51035-0366. Tel: 712-376-2628. [CEM]
Catechesis/Religious Programs—Tel: 712-376-2625.
Students 180.

Maryhill, Cherokee Co., Visitation of the B.V.M. (1895), Rev. Eugene E. Sitzmann.
Res., 975-540th St., Cherokee, 51012-7151. Tel: 712-225-2131. [CEM]
Catechesis/Religious Programs—Students 75.

Merrill, Plymouth Co., Assumption Church (1893), Rev. Richard D. Ball.
Res., P.O. Box 175, 51038-0175. Tel: 712-938-2236. [CEM]
Catechesis/Religious Programs—Tel: 712-239-2845. Cindy Palmer, D.R.E.
Students 113.
Mission—Ellendale, Plymouth Co., St. Joseph's.

Milford, Dickinson Co., St. Joseph's (1884), Rev. John A. Vakulskas, Jr.; Deacon M. Peter Hart.
Res., 1413 Okoboji Ave., 51351-1232. Tel: 712-338-2172 (Res.); 338-2274 (Office); Fax: 712-338-2191. [CEM]
Catechesis/Religious Programs—Ruthanne Muller, D.R.E.
Students 250.

Moorland, Webster Co., Our Lady of Good Counsel (1902), Rev. Eugene F. Ceperley.
Res., P.O. Box 135, 50566-0135. Tel: 515-549-3556. [CEM]
Catechesis/Religious Programs—Students 84.

Mount Carmel, Carroll Co., Our Lady of Mt. Carmel (1869) (German), Rev. Robert Brown.
Res., 19481 140th St., Carroll, 51401-9499. Tel: 712-792-3934. [CEM]
School—Christ the King Elementary. Consolidation of Breda, Lidderdale, Maple River and Mt. Carmel. Tel: 712-792-3977.
Lay Teachers 6; Students 207.

Moville, Woodbury Co., Immaculate Conception (1892), Rev. Msgr. Roger J. Augustine, V.G.
Res., P.O. Box C, 51039-0802. Tel: 712-873-3745. [CEM]
Catechesis/Religious Programs—Tel: 712-873-3644.
Students 190.

Neptune, Plymouth, St. Joseph's (Hinton) (1900), Rev. Timothy J. Boekelman.
Res., 28172 Nature Ave., Hinton, 51024-8553. Tel: 712-546-8228. [CEM]
Catechesis/Religious Programs—St. Joseph Church, 20 6th Ave. NE, LeMars, 51031. Tel: 712-546-5223.
Students 113.

Odebolt, Sac Co., St. Martin's (1877), Rev. Walter L. Bruch.
Res., P.O. Box 500, 51458-0500. Tel: 712-668-2690. [CEM]
Catechesis/Religious Programs—Students 136.

Ogden, Boone Co., St. John's (1896), Rev. Thomas J. Munn. Pastoral Ministers: Sr. Mary Lois Lehman, P.B.V.M.; Sr. Mary Bernard Mauss, P.B.V.M.
Res., P.O. Box J, 50212-0810. Tel: 515-275-2580. [CEM]
Catechesis/Religious Programs—Tel: 800-796-2722.
Students 78.
Mission—Dayton, Christ the King.

Onawa, Monona Co., St. John's (1900), Rev. Alfred E. McCoy.
Res., 1009 13th St., 51040-0417. Tel: 712-423-2656.
Catechesis/Religious Programs—Students 136.
Mission—Blencoe, Monona Co., St. Bernard's.

Oyens, Plymouth Co., St. Catherine's (1900), Rev. Randy L. Schon.
Res., P.O. Box 538, 51045-0538. Tel: 712-546-4588. [CEM]
School—St. Catherine-St. Mary's Elementary. (Oyens, Remsen). Tel: 712-786-2764.
Lay Teachers 16; Students 234.

Pocahontas, Pocahontas Co., Church of the Resurrection, Rev. Merle F. Kollasch.
Res., 21 3rd St. S.W., 50574-0157. Tel: 712-335-3242; Fax: 712-335-3242. [CEM]
School—Pocahontas Catholic Elementary, Tel: 712-335-3603.
Sisters 1; Lay Teachers 7; Students 104.
Catechesis/Religious Programs—Students 98.

Pomeroy, Calhoun Co., St. Mary's (1881), Rev. Richard J. Macke; Deacon Robert Lenz.
Res., P.O. Box 57, 50575-0057. Tel: 712-468-2473. [CEM]
Catechesis/Religious Programs—Tel: 712-468-2248.
Students 69.
Mission—Palmer, Pocahontas Co., St. Joseph's.

Remsen, Plymouth Co., St. Mary's (1889), Rev. John J. McGuirk; Deacon Allan Wieler.
Res., Box Section A, #509, 51050. Tel: 712-786-1437. [CEM]
School—St. Catherine-St. Mary's. (Oyens-Remsen). Tel: 712-786-1160.
Sisters 1; Lay Teachers 18; Students 234.
High School—Tel: 712-786-1433; Fax: 712-786-2499.
Priests 1; Sisters 1; Lay Teachers 16; Students 116.
Catechesis/Religious Programs—Tel: 712-786-2376; Fax: 712-786-1167.
Students 350.

Rock Rapids, Lyon Co., Holy Name (1871) (Irish), Rev. Eugene T. Schumacher.
Res., 1108 S. Carroll St., 51246-9529. Tel: 712-472-3248. [CEM]
Catechesis/Religious Programs—Students 94.

Rock Valley, Sioux Co., St. Mary's (1895), Rev. Dale George.
Res., 1821 14th St., 51247-0098. Tel: 712-476-2060. [CEM]
Catechesis/Religious Programs—Tel: 712-476-2007.
Students 64.
Mission—Alvord, Lyon Co., Sacred Heart, Tel: 712-473-2215. [CEM]

Rockwell City, Calhoun Co., St. Francis of Assisi (1899), Rev. Roger J. Linnan.
Res., 744 Main St., 50579-1399. Tel: 712-297-8263. [CEM]
Catechesis/Religious Programs—Tel: 712-297-7183.
Students 105.

Rolfe, Pocahontas Co., St. Margaret's (1895), Rev. Timothy J. Fitzgerald.
Res., St John's Rectory, P.O. Box 262, Gilmore City, 50541-0262. Tel: 515-373-6016. [CEM]
Catechesis/Religious Programs—Students 51.

Roselle, Carroll Co., Holy Angels (1874), Rev. Paul J. Kelly.
Res., Box 13, Halbur, 51444-0013. Tel: 712-658-2464. [CEM]
School—Holy Trinity Elementary, Tel: 712-669-3346.
Catechesis/Religious Programs—Students 55.

Royal, Clay Co., St. Louis (1923) (French-German), Rev. Anthony P. Pick.
Res., P.O. Box 49, 51357-0049. Tel: 712-933-2667; Fax: 712-933-2356.
Catechesis/Religious Programs—Tel: 712-933-2604.
Students 110.
Mission—Everly, Clay Co., St. Mary's, P.O. Box 49, 51357. Tel: 712-834-2681.

Ruthven, Palo Alto Co., Sacred Heart (1888), Rev. Allen Reicks.
Church—P.O. Box 400, 51358-0400. Tel: 712-837-5240. [CEM]
Catechesis/Religious Programs—Students 33.
Mission—Ayrshire, Palo Alto Co., Sacred Heart, Ayrshire, 50515. Tel: 515-426-3260.

Sac City, Sac Co., St. Mary's (1892) (German-Irish), Rev. Mark E. Harrington.
Res., P.O. Box 324, 50583-0324. Tel: 712-662-7240. [CEM]
Catechesis/Religious Programs—Tel: 712-662-7240.
Students 138.

St. Benedict, Kossuth Co., St. Benedict's (1877), Rev. Lynn Bruch.
Res., 2003 190th St., Algona, 50511-9801. Tel: 515-679-4165. [CEM]
School—Seton Elementary. Consolidation of St. Cecelia, Algona, St. Benedict and St. Joseph, Wesley. Tel: 515-295-3509; Fax: 515-295-7739.
Catechesis/Religious Programs—St. Cecelia, 715 E. North St., Algona, 50511.
Students 50.

St. Joseph, Kossuth Co., St. Joseph's (1876), Rev. Paul F. Eisele.
Res., 1023 Hwy. 169, Bode, 50519. Tel: 515-379-1470. [CEM]
Catechesis/Religious Programs—Students 103.

Salix, Woodbury Co., St. Joseph's (1869), Rev. Bruce A. Lawler.
Res., P.O. Box 270, 51052-0270. Tel: 712-946-5635. [CEM][JC]
Catechesis/Religious Programs—Students 186.

Sanborn, O'Brien Co., St. Cecilia's (1882), Rev. David A. Hemann.
Res., P.O. Box 326, 51248-0326. Tel: 712-729-3423. [CEM]
Catechesis/Religious Programs—Students 141.
Mission—Hartley, O'Brien Co., St. Joseph's, Tel: 712-728-2626.

Schaller, Sac Co., St. Joseph's (1891), Rev. Eugene Ulses.
Res., P.O. Box 457, 51053-0457. Tel: 712-275-4238. [CEM]
Catechesis/Religious Programs—Students 70.

Scranton, Greene Co., St. Paul's (1926) (German-Irish), Rev. Dennis W. Meinen.
Res., P.O. Box 215, 51462-0215. Tel: 712-652-3448; Fax: 712-652-3795. [JC]
Catechesis/Religious Programs—Tel: 515-389-3625.
Students 51.

Sheldon, O'Brien Co., St. Patrick's (1873), Rev. James C. McAlpin.
Res., 310 10th St., 51201-1530. Tel: 712-324-3220. [CEM]
School—Tel: 712-324-3181.
Sisters 2; Lay Teachers 10; Students 121.
Catechesis/Religious Programs—Tel: 712-324-4588.
Students 139.

Sibley, Osceola Co., St. Andrew's (1896), Rev. Timothy Hogan.
Res., 716 Eighth St., P.O. Box 130, 51249-0130. Tel: 712-754-3311. [CEM]
Catechesis/Religious Programs—Tel: 712-754-2739.
Students 183.

Sioux Rapids, Buena Vista Co., St. Joseph's (1886), Rev. J. Charles Yetmar.
Res., P.O. Box 450, 50585-0450. Tel: 712-283-2765. [CEM]
Catechesis/Religious Programs—Students 45.

Spencer, Clay Co., Sacred Heart (1883), Rev. Timothy R. Schott.
Res., 1111 4th Ave. W., P.O. Box 817, 51301-0817. Tel: 712-262-3047.
School—Tel: 712-262-6428.
Lay Teachers 11; Students 152.
Catechesis/Religious Programs—Students 276.

Spirit Lake, Dickinson Co., St. Mary's (1914), Rev. Albert O. Grendler.
Res., P.O. Box 354, 51360-0354. Tel: 712-336-1742. [CEM]
Catechesis/Religious Programs—Students 223.

Storm Lake, Buena Vista Co., St. Mary's (1872), Revs. Clair L. Boes; Michael J. Erpelding.
Res., Third & Seneca Sts., P.O. Box 1106, 50588-1106. Tel: 712-732-3110. [CEM]
School—Elementary & High School, Tel: 712-732-1856 (Elem.); 732-4166 (High); Fax: 712-732-4590.
Sisters of the Presentation 3; Lay Teachers 22; Students 385.
Catechesis/Religious Programs—Students 238.

Struble, Plymouth Co., St. Joseph's (1903), Rev. Timothy J. Boekelman.
Res., 28174 Nature Ave., Hinton, 51024. Tel: 712-546-8228. [CEM]
Catechesis/Religious Programs—Students 59.

Sutherland, O'Brien Co., Sacred Heart (1883), Rev. Gerald L. Zeman.
Res., P.O. Box 70, 51058-0070. Tel: 712-446-3742. [CEM]
Catechesis/Religious Programs—Students 43.
Mission—Primghar, O'Brien Co., St. Anthony of Padua, 375 S. Green St., Primghar, 51245. Tel: 712-757-3735. [CEM]

Templeton, Carroll Co., Sacred Heart (1882), Rev. Gary B. Snyder.
Res., P.O. Box 104, 51463-0104. Tel: 712-669-3345. [CEM]

School—Holy Trinity Elementary. Consolidation of Halbur, Templeton and Roselle. Tel: 712-669-3341. Students 141.
Catechesis/Religious Programs—Students 23.

Vail, Crawford Co., St. Ann's (1878), Rev. Victor F. Ramaeker.
Res., P.O. Box 158, 51465-0158. Tel: 712-677-5556. [CEM]
School—Holy Cross Elementary, Tel: 712-677-5555.
High School—Interparochial Catholic High School, Tel: 712-792-3596.
Students 17.
Sisters of St. Francis of Clinton: Tel: 712-689-2589.
Lay Teachers 4; Students 40.
Catechesis/Religious Programs—Tel: 712-677-5514.
Students 99.

Varina, Pocahontas Co., St. Columbkille's (1882), Rev. Armand J. Bertrand; Sr. Mary Ruth Ann Takes, P.B.V.M., Pastoral Min.
Res., 50593. Tel: 712-288-6446. [CEM]

Wall Lake, Sac Co., St. Joseph's (1878), Rev. Leo L. Riesberg.
Res., P.O. Box L, 51466-0607. Tel: 712-664-2915.
Catechesis/Religious Programs—Tel: 712-664-2910.
Students 158.

Wesley, Kossuth Co., St. Joseph's (1891), Rev. Paul D. Bormann.
Res., P.O. Box 38, 50483-0038. Tel: 515-679-4279; 679-4135. [CEM]
School—Seton Elementary. Consolidation of St. Cecelia, Algona, St. Benedict and St. Joseph, Wesley. Tel: 515-295-3509.
Students 92.

West Bend, Palo Alto Co., SS. Peter and Paul (1888), Rev. Bruce A. Lefebvre; Deacon Gerald Streit.
Res., P.O. Box 316, 50597-0316. Tel: 515-887-3333; Fax: 515-887-3333. [CEM]
School—Tel: 515-887-4542.
Lay Teachers 8; Students 81.
Catechesis/Religious Programs—Tel: 515-887-4058.
Students 79.

Whittemore, Kossuth Co., St. Michael's (1889), Rev. Edward G. Murray; Deacon Joseph Straub.
Res., P.O. Box 337, 50598-0337. Tel: 515-884-2669. [CEM]

Willey, Carroll Co., St. Mary's, Rev. Craig A. Collison.
Res., 201 Olympic Ave., Carroll, 51401-9726. Tel: 712-792-4516. [CEM]
School—Consolidation of Holy Spirit, Dedham, Willey and St. Lawrence Elementary. Tel: 712-792-3610.
Catechesis/Religious Programs—Tel: 712-792-4386.
Students 9.

Woodward, Boone Co., St. John of God (1965). (State Hospital and School). Rev. Msgr. Louis H. Kollasch; Deacon Frank Milani.
Res., 207 Gerald St., Madrid, 50156-1464. Tel: 515-795-2731.

Chaplains of Public Institutions

SIOUX CITY. *Marian Health Center*. Rev. Richard A. Sitzmann.
CARROLL. *St. Anthony Regional Hospital*. Rev. Robert L. Leiting.
CHEROKEE. *State Mental Health Institute*. Rev. Eugene E. Sitzmann.
FORT DODGE. *Trinity Regional Hospital*. Revs. P. Joseph Nooney; Eugene F. Walding.
ROCKWELL CITY. *Calhoun County State Reformatory, Minimum Security for Men*. Rev. Roger J. Linnan, Chap.
WOODWARD. *Woodward State Hospital and School*. Rev. Msgr. Louis H. Kollasch.

Special Assignment:
Reverend Fathers—
Friedrichsen, Timothy A., Briar Cliff College, 3303 Rebecca St., Sioux City, IA 51104-2340. Tel: 712-279-1704; 712-562-6401 (Res.)
Guredet, Randy J., Co-Dir., Minorities & Human Development, 1011 Douglas St., Sioux City, IA 51105-1399
Seuntjens, LeRoy L., Chap., Holy Spirit Retirement Home, 1701 W. 25th St., Sioux City, IA 51103-1799. Tel: 712-252-2726
Stone, Stanley R., Chap., Sioux City Nursing Homes, 1122 Grandview Blvd., Apt. 7, Sioux City, IA 51103-4398. Tel: 712-258-5202

On Duty Outside the Diocese:
Reverend Monsignors—
Schnurr, Dennis M., General Secretary, National Conference of Catholic Bishops, St. John's Hall, 4001 14th St. N.E., Washington, DC 20017
Reverend Fathers—
Barrett, Miles J., USS Kitty Hawk (CV-63), Chaplain's Office, FPO AP, 96634-2770
Dandurand, Douglas E., Archdiocese of St. Paul and Minneapolis, MN
Devine, William B., 210 Harris Dr., Apt. 5, Norfolk, NE 68701
Farrell, Emmet L., 2020 Alaquinas Dr., San Ysidro, CA 92173
Flanagan, Thomas J., Pfarrer-Bendel-Weg 2, D-61462 Koenigstein-Mammolshain, Germany. Tel: 011-496-1734-169
Higgins, Francis E., 2746 E. Hwy. 86, Castle Rock, CO 80104. Tel: 303-688-3057
Holland, Thomas D., U.S. Air Force, 4050 Harbors Dr., Apt. 244, Las Vegas, NV 89121
Kurzak, John, U.S. Air Force, 2685 S. Dayton Way #205, Denver, CO 80231. Tel: 303-676-6480
Seifried, Kenneth A., 6 W. Staff Row, Atlanta, GA 30310. Tel: 404-755-1487

Graduate Studies:
Reverend Fathers—
Slaven, Donald J., 1025 Michigan Ave., NE, Washington, D.C., 20017-1895. Tel: 202-529-7937; FAX: 202-529-4489
Stoll, Mark J., Divine Word College, 1025 Michigan Ave., NE, Washington, DC, 20017-1895. Tel: 202-529-6446

Absent on Leave:
Reverend Fathers—
Waters, Robert J.

Retired:
Reverend Monsignors—
Behrens, A.W., P.O. Box 94, Marcus, IA 51035-0094. Tel: 712-376-4788
Brady, Frank J., 1703 W. 25th St., Apt. B208, Sioux City, IA 51103-1799. Tel: 712-255-9343
Kevane, Eugene, 1701 W. 25th St., Sioux City, IA 51103-3935
Lilly, E. C., 1701 W. 25th St., Bldg B, Apt. 205, Sioux City, IA 51103-1799. Tel: 712-255-5423
Lyon, Gerald F., 20-6th Ave., NE, LeMars, IA 51031. Tel: 712-546-3714
Morkunas, Simon, 1701 W. 25th St., Sioux City, IA 51103-1799
Quinn, Robert J., P.O. Box 1346, Imperial Beach, CA 91933-1346. Tel: 619-437-0180
Ruba, Nicholas J., 403 Cleveland Ct., Remsen, IA 51050. Tel: 712-786-2719
Walker, Dean P., P.O. Box 2142, Sioux City, IA 51104-2142
Reverend Fathers—
Adams, Edmond F., Sacred Heart Church, 1321 2nd Ave. S., Fort Dodge, IA 50501-4925. Tel: 515-573-7617
Alvey, J. Paul, May thru October, 27 First Ave., NE, Pocahontas, IA 50594; 712-335-3705, 7791 E. Via Del Futuro, Scottsdale, AZ 85258
Beacom, Vincent L., R.R. 3, Arnolds Park, IA 51331-9803
Becker, Nicholas J., January thru March: 10360 N. 76th Dr., Peoria, AZ., P.O. Box 633, Algona, IA 50511-0633
Birdsall, Richard W., Bayview Ter., Box 128, Forestville, WI 51401-0128. Tel: 414-856-6998
Brennan, C. John, 1703 W. 25th, Apt. 204, Sioux City, IA 51103-1799. Tel: 712-277-8981
Bruch, Walter L., 110 Peeble Ln., Apt. 16, Carroll, IA 51401. Tel: 712-792-6251
Cain, John F., P.O. Box 34, Larchwood, IA 51241-0034. Tel: 605-338-9329
Calkins, Raymond J., 326 Green Chase Cir., Montgomery, AL 36117. Tel: 334-215-1813
Carel, William L., October 1st thru April 1st: Rod & Reel Ct., 1059 S. Indiana, Brownsville, TX 78521; Tele: 512-831-2601, 28170 Nature Ave., Hinton, IA 51024-8553. Tel: 712-546-8677
Carpenter, Edward V., 1122 Grandview Blvd., Apt. #5, Sioux City, IA 51105-4398. Tel: 712-252-2338
Cooper, Harold V., 2507-33rd. St., Sioux City, IA 51105. Tel: 712-239-2880
Friedman, Cecil H., 1021 E. Call St., Algona, IA 50511
Greving, Louis H., Grotto of the Redemption, P.O. Box 376, West Bend, IA 50597-0376. Tel: 515-887-2371
Hoffmann, Edward D., 1122 Grandview Blvd., Apt. 8, Sioux City, IA 51105-4398. Tel: 712-277-8480
Kerwin, Joseph A., 229 Courtyard Blvd., Apt. 104, Sun City Center, FL 33573-5768. Tel: 813-634-4813
Koster, Dale F., P.O. Box 264 W. 1st St., Apt. 8, Auburn, IA 51433
Lisowski, Jan, 1122 Grandview Blvd., Apt. 3, Sioux City, IA 51103-4398. Tel: 716-549-0372
Lynch, Daniel C., 407 S. 13th St., Sac City, IA 50583. Tel: 712-662-4801
McFadden, George B., 1122 Grandview Blvd., Apt. 2, Sioux City, IA 51105-4398. Tel: 712-255-0827
Meyer, Henry H., 1414 N. West St., Carroll, IA 51401-1442. Tel: 712-792-2368
Montag, Bernard J., P.O. Box 73, West Bend, IA 50597-0073. Tel: 515-887-6874
Nemmers, Reinhard E., Plymouth Manor, 954 7th Ave., S.E., LeMars, IA 51031
Nooney, Patrick J., Trinity Regional Hospital, S. Kenyond Rd., Fort Dodge, IA 50501-5795
O'Rourke, Gabriel A., Holy Spirit Retirement Home, 1701 W. 25th St., Sioux City, IA 51103-1798
Phillips, Robert W., Lakeside Lutheran Home, 705 Lake St., Emmetsburg, IA 50536-2468
Schissel, John G., 605 N. 11th St., Cherokee, IA 51012-1526
Schumacher, Leo C., Apt. A-2, 2320 6th Ave. N., Fort Dodge, IA 50501-3561. Tel: 515-955-2275
Smith, Donald R., 3929 Winona Way, Apt. 4, Sioux City, IA 51104-4447. Tel: 712-239-5865
Staber, Francis H., 1122 Grandview Blvd., Apt. 6, Sioux City, IA 51103-4398. Tel: 712-255-5668
Thom, Elmer D., 1122 Grandview Blvd., Apt. 9, Sioux City, IA 51103-4398. Tel: 712-277-3954
Waite, Patrick J., 5682 Tulane St., San Diego, CA 92122-3244
Weimer, Henry V., 1122 Grandview Blvd., Apt. 3, Sioux City, IA 51103-4398. Tel: 712-233-1358
White, LLoyd W., 130 Peeble Ln., Apt. 6, Carroll, IA 51401-3020. Tel: 712-792-5633
Wieling, Raymond P., 3015 Chicago Ave., Sioux City, IA 51106-1259. Tel: 762-276-7065
Wingert, D. William, 4014 Yellow Ave., Hartley, IA 51346-7606
Wingert, Gerald R., 216 W. Nebraska, Algona, IA 50511-2608. Tel: 515-295-3123
Young, Edward J., 1122 Grandview Blvd., Apt. 1, Sioux City, IA 51103-4398. Tel: 712-277-4638
Zensen, Gerald F., P.O. Box 67, Oto, IA 51044-0067

Permanent Deacons:
Berger, William J., St. Michael's, Sioux City
Bertrand, Gerald L., Holy Name, Marcus
Bruner, Robert S., St. Lawrence, Carroll
Doocy, Philip F., St. John the Baptist, Bancroft
Dunn, Francis M., Immaculate Conception Church, Graettinger
Easter, Jack L., Sacred Heart, Spencer
Forrest, Ronald M., Associate Dir., Permanent Diaconate, Sioux City
Gallagher, Jeffrey F., St. Mary Church, Larchwood
Hand, Michael J., Church of the Nativity, Sioux City
Hart, M. Peter, St. Joseph, Milford
Heffernan, John J., Blessed Sacrament Church, Sioux City
Hogan, Joseph R., Our Lady of Good Counsel Church, Fonda
Karpuk, Fred P., Blessed Sacrament Church, Sioux City
Kelley, Richard C.
Kunecke, Donald L., St. Mary's Church, Lake City
Kunkel, Donald M., St. Joseph Church, LeMars
Lenz, Robert D., St. Mary's Church, Pomeroy
Lester, Jary
MacDonald, W. B., St. Cecelia Church, Algona
Maher, F. Joseph, St. Mary's Church, Hawarden
McCruden, Patrick J., St. Joseph Church, Sioux City, IA
Milani, Frank J., St. Malachy's Church, Madrid
Pietz, Ronald C., St. Joseph Church, Sioux City
Portz, Ray, St. Patrick, Sheldon
Reicks, Jerome A., St. Joseph Church, Sioux City
Reuter, Anthony C., Holy Spirit Church, Carroll
Rupp, J. LeRoy, Immaculate Conception Church, Cherokee
Sands, James H.
Sitzman, Larry K., St. Michael's Church, Sioux City
Spellman, George G., Ph.D., Marian Health Center and Blessed Sacrament Church, Sioux City
Straub, Joseph J., St. Michael's Church, Whittmore
Streit, Gerald B., Sts. Peter & Paul Church, West Bend
Weiler, Allan A., St. Mary's Church, Remsen
Westendorf, Louis B., M.D., St. Lawrence Church, Carroll
Wiskus, Robert A., Sacred Heart Church, Sioux City

INSTITUTIONS LOCATED IN THE DIOCESE

[A] COLLEGES AND UNIVERSITIES

SIOUX CITY. *Briar Cliff College*, 3303 Rebecca St., P.O. Box 2100, 51104-2100. Tel: 712-279-5321; Fax: 712-279-5410.
For a complete listing, refer to the Colleges and Universities section.

[B] HIGH SCHOOLS, INTER-PAROCHIAL

SIOUX CITY. *Bishop Heelan Catholic High School*, 1021 Douglas St., 51105. Tel: 712-252-0573.
Serving the parishes of the Siouxland area. Rev. Alfred E. McLoy, Pres. Pro Tem; Dr. Michael J. Avise, Prin.; Revs. Edward M. Girres; Verne P. Stapenhorst. Priests 3; Sisters 2; Lay Teachers 45; Students 773.

ALGONA. *Bishop Garrigan Catholic High School*, 1224 N. McCoy St., 50511. Tel: 515-295-3521.
Serving the parishes at Algona, St. Benedict, Bode, Wesley, and Whittemore. Rev. Gerald F. Feierfeil, Pres.; Mr. Eugene Meister, Pres. Priests 1; Sisters 2; Lay Teachers 23; Students 240.

CARROLL. *Kuemper Catholic High School*, 109 S. Clark St., 51401. Tel: 712-792-3596.
Serving the thirteen parishes of Carroll-Holy Spirit and St. Lawrence Parishes; Arcadia; Dedham; Halbur; Lidderdale-Glidden; Maple River; Mount Carmel; Roselle; Templeton; Vail; Willey and Breda. Rev. Merlin J. Schrad, Pres.; Dr. Keith Guy, Prin.; Revs. Craig A. Collison; Terry A. Roder, Spiritual Dir. Priests 3; Sisters 1; Lay Teachers 36; Students 529.

FORT DODGE. *St. Edmond High School*, 501 N. 22nd St., 50501. Tel: 515-955-5850; Fax: 515-955-8473. Rev. Patrick R. Walsh, Pres.; Mr. Michael G. Kavars, Prin.; Mr. Thomas Mikio, Dir. Devel.; Rev. Richard A. Adam; Sr. Dominic Church, P.B.V.M. Priests 2; Sisters 1; Lay Teachers 28; Students 321.

GRANVILLE. *Spalding Catholic High School*, 51022. Tel: 712-727-3451.
Serving the parishes of Granville; Alton and Hospers. Revs. Clem Currans, Pres.; Tim Johnson, Religion Teacher. Priests 3; Sisters 1; Lay Teachers 15; Students 96.

LE MARS. *Gehlen Catholic School*, 709 Plymouth St. N.E., 51031. Tel: 712-546-4181.
Serving the two parishes of LeMars; Assumption, Merrill; St. Joseph's, Ellendale; St. Joseph's, Neptune; St. Joseph's, Struble. Revs. William A. Schreiber, Admin.; Timothy J. Boekelman; Richard D. Ball. Priests 3; Sisters 2; Lay Teachers 51; Students 673.

REMSEN. *St. Mary's High School*, 523 Madison, 51050. Sr. Elaine Tworek, S.L.W., Prin. Priests 1; Sisters 1; Lay Teachers 14; Students 116.

STORM LAKE. *St. Mary's High School*, 50588.
Serving St. Mary's. Priests 1; Lay Teachers 17; Students 89.

[C] ORPHANAGES

SIOUX CITY. *St. Anthony's Orphanage*. Mailing Address: Catholic Charities of the Diocese of Sioux City, 1601 Military Rd., P.O. Box 2025, 51104. Tel: 712-252-4547.
For a complete listing, refer to the Special Care Facilities section.

[D] GENERAL HOSPITALS

SIOUX CITY. *Marian Health Center*, 801 Fifth St., 51101. Tel: 712-279-2010; Fax: 712-279-2034.
For a complete listing, refer to the Hospitals section.

CARROLL. *St. Anthony Regional Hospital*, 51401. Tel: 712-792-3581.
For a complete listing, refer to the Hospitals section.

ESTHERVILLE. *Holy Family Hospital*, 826 N. Eighth St., 51334. Tel: 712-362-2631.
For a complete listing, refer to the Hospitals section.

[E] HOMES FOR THE AGED

SIOUX CITY. *Holy Spirit Retirement Home*, 1701 W. 25th St., 51103. Tel: 712-252-2726.
For a complete listing, refer to the Special Care Facilities section.

CARROLL. *St. Anthony Nursing Home*, 406 E. Anthony St., 51401. Tel: 712-792-3581.
For a complete listing, refer to the Special Care Facilities section.

FORT DODGE. *The Marian Home*, 2400 Sixth Ave. N., 50501.
For a complete listing, refer to the Special Care Facilities section.

[F] CONVENTS AND RESIDENCES FOR SISTERS

SIOUX CITY. *Monastery of the Discalced Carmelite Nuns*, 2901 S. Cecelia St., 51106-3299. Tel: 712-276-1680. Mother Therese of the Spirit of Love, O.C.D., Prioress. Chaplains: Revs. Gerald Hartz; Patrick J. O'Kane. Solemn Professed 12; First Profession 1.

[G] SECULAR INSTITUTES

POCAHONTAS. *Opus Spiritus Sancti*, 21 SW 3rd St., 50574. Tel: 712-335-3242. Rev. Merlee Kollasch, Regl. Coord.
A federation of communities of priests, sisters, and lay people having in common their dedication to the Holy Spirit and life according to the evangelical counsels.

[H] MISCELLANEOUS

SIOUX CITY. *The Catholic Schools Foundation of the Diocese of Sioux City*, 1821 Jackson St., 51105.
Diocese of Sioux City Priests' Welfare Foundation, 1821 Jackson St., 51102-3379. Rev. Kevin C. McCoy, Contact Person.
Holy Spirit Retirement Home Foundation, Inc., 1701 W. 25th St., 51103. Tel: 712-252-2726. Lawrence D. Soens, Pres. Directors: Roger J. Augustine; Patrick J. Tomscha.

CARROLL. *Orchard View, Inc.*, S. Clark St., 51401. Tel: 712-792-3581. Franciscan Sisters of Perpetual Adoration. Gary P. Riedmann, Admin. Total in Residence 54.
St. Anthony Foundation, S. Clark St., 51401. Tel: 712-792-3581. Rev. Gary P. Reidmann.

WEST BEND. *Grotto of the Redemption*. Mailing Address: P.O. Box 376, 50597. Tel: 515-887-2371. Gerald Streit, Dir.

RELIGIOUS INSTITUTES OF WOMEN REPRESENTED IN THE DIOCESE

For further details refer to the corresponding bracketed number in the Religious Institutes of Women section.

[0230]—*Benedictine Sisters of the Pontifical Jurisdiction.*—O.S.B.
[2100]—*Congregation of the Humility of Mary.* (Davenport, Iowa).—C.H.M.
[1780]—*Congregation of the Sisters of the Third Order of St. Francis of Perpetual Adoration.* (Central Prov.).—F.S.P.A.
[0420]—*Discalced Carmelite Nuns.*—O.C.D.
[3270]—*Opus Spiritus Sancti.*—O.S.S.
[055]—*Sacramentine Nuns.*
[2970]—*School Sisters of Notre Dame.* (Mankato Province).—S.S.N.D.
[2970]—*School Sisters of Notre Dame.* (St. Louis Province).—S.S.N.D.
[1680]—*School Sisters of St. Francis.*—S.S.S.F.
[3580]—*Servants of Mary.*—O.S.M.
[]—*Sisters For Christian Community.*—S.F.C.C.
[0430]—*Sisters of Charity of the Blessed Virgin Mary.*—B.V.M.
[2575]—*Sisters of Mercy of the Americas.*—R.S.M.
[1570]—*Sisters of St. Francis of the Holy Family.*—O.S.F.
[2350]—*Sisters of the Living Word.*—S.L.W.
[3320]—*Sisters of the Presentation of the B.V.M.*—P.B.V.M.
[4100]—*Sisters of the Sorrowful Mother (Third Order of St. Francis).*—S.S.M.

DIOCESAN CEMETERIES

SIOUX CITY. *Calvary*, Office, 1821 Jackson St., P.O. Box 3379, 51102-3379. Tel: 712-233-7511.

NECROLOGY

† Bauer, Rev. Msgr. W. B., (Retired). —Died Jan. 24, 1996.
† Doherty, Rev. Msgr. John C., (Retired). —Died May 24, 1996.
† Terpstra, John R., (On Leave). —Died Oct. 10, 1996.
† Weimer, Henry V., (Retired). —Died Nov. 20, 1995.

Diocese of Sioux Falls

(Dioecesis Siouxormensis)

Most Reverend

ROBERT J. CARLSON

Bishop of Sioux Falls; ordained May 22, 1970; appointed Titular Bishop of Aviocala and Auxiliary Bishop of Saint Paul and Minneapolis November 22, 1983; consecrated January 11, 1984; appointed Coadjutor Bishop of Sioux Falls, 1994; succeeded to the See, March 21, 1995.

Most Reverend

PAUL V. DUDLEY, D.D.

Retired Bishop of Sioux Falls; ordained June 2, 1951; appointed Titular Bishop of Ursona and Auxiliary Bishop of St. Paul and Minneapolis November 16, 1976; Episcopal ordination January 25, 1977; appointed Bishop of Sioux Falls September 26, 1978; installed December 13, 1978; retired March 21, 1995. *Res., 116 Linden St., N., Northfield, MN, 55057.* Tel.: 507-663-1145.

"Jesus is Lord"

ESTABLISHED NOVEMBER 12, 1889.

Square Miles 35,091.

Comprises that part of the State of South Dakota East of the Missouri River.

For legal titles of parishes and diocesan institutions, consult the Chancery Office.

Chancery Office: 3100 W. 41st St., Sioux Falls, SD, 57105. Tel.: 605-334-9861; Fax: 605-333-3346.

E-mail address: sfcath@iw.com

STATISTICAL OVERVIEW

Personnel	
Bishop	1
Retired Bishops	1
Abbots	1
Retired Abbots	2
Priests: Diocesan Active in Diocese	79
Priests: Active Outside Diocese	6
Priests: Retired, Sick or Absent	43
Number of Diocesan Priests	128
Religious Priests in Diocese	44
Extern Priests in Diocese	10
Ordinations:	
Diocesan Priests	1
Permanent Deacons in Diocese	24
Total Brothers	13
Total Sisters	461
Parishes	
Parishes	156
With Resident Pastor:	
Resident Diocesan Priests	69
Resident Religious Priests	16
Without Resident Pastor:	
Administered by Priests	53
Administered by Permanent Deacons	4
Administered by Women Religious	4
Administered by Pastoral Teams, etc.	10
New Parishes Created	1
Closed Parishes	1
Professional Ministry Personnel:	
Brothers	4
Sisters	36
Lay Ministers	20
Welfare	
Catholic Hospitals	9
Total Assisted	485,000
Homes for the Aged	9
Total Assisted	1,500
Specialized Homes	2
Total Assisted	145
Special Centers for Social Services	5
Total Assisted	112,000
Residential Care of Disabled	1
Total Assisted	15
Educational	
Diocesan Students in Other Seminaries	22
Total Seminarians	22
Colleges and Universities	2
Total Students	2,350
High Schools, Diocesan and Parish	3
Total Students	1,120
Elementary Schools, Diocesan and Parish	23
Total Students	4,352
Catechesis/Religious Education:	
High School Students	8,283
Elementary Students	12,047
Total Students Under Catholic Instruction	28,174
Teachers in the Diocese:	
Priests	2
Sisters	11
Lay Teachers	259
Vital Statistics	
Receptions into the Church:	
Infant Baptism Totals	1,925
Adult Baptism Totals	64
Received into Full Communion	269
First Communions	2,111
Confirmations	1,885
Marriages:	
Catholic	364
Interfaith	382
Total Marriages	746
Deaths	1,129
Total Catholic Population	118,596
Total Population	500,000

Former Bishops—Rt. Rev. MARTIN MARTY, O.S.B., D.D., appt. Bishop of Tiberias, Aug. 8, 1879; appt. Vicar Apostolic of Dakota, Aug. 12, 1879; cons. Feb. 1, 1880; Bishop of Sioux Falls, 1889; transferred to St. Cloud, MN, 1894; died Sept. 19, 1896.—Rt. Rev. THOMAS O'GORMAN, D.D., appt. Jan. 24, 1896; cons. April 19, 1896; died Sept. 18, 1921.—Most Rev. BERNARD J. MAHONEY, D.D., appt. May 22, 1922; cons. June 29, 1922; died March 20, 1939.—Most Rev. WILLIAM O. BRADY, S.T.D., D.D., appt. Bishop of Sioux Falls, June 10, 1939; cons. Aug. 24, 1939; appt. Coadjutor of St. Paul, June 21, 1956; succeeded to the See, Oct. 11, 1956; died Oct. 1, 1961.—Most Rev. LAMBERT A. HOCH, D.D., Former Bishop of Sioux Falls; ord. May 30, 1928; Bishop of Bismarck; appt. Jan. 23, 1952; cons. March 25, 1952; transferred to Sioux Falls, Nov. 27, 1956; retired June 13, 1978; died June 27, 1990.—Most Rev. PAUL V. DUDLEY, D.D., Bishop of Sioux Falls; ord. June 2, 1951; appt. Sept. 26, 1978; installed Dec. 13, 1978; retired March 21, 1995.

Vicar General—Rev. Msgr. RICHARD MAHOWALD, P.A., V.G., *3100 W. 41st St., Sioux Falls, 57105.*

Chancery Office—3100 W. 41st St., Sioux Falls, 57105. Tel: 605-334-9861; Fax: 605-333-3346. Refer all official business to this address.

Chancellor—JEROME KLEIN, *3100 W. 41st St., Sioux Falls, 57105.* Tel: 605-333-3345.

Vice Chancellor—JAY CONZEMIUS, *3100 W. 41st St., Sioux Falls, 57105.*

Diocesan Theologian—STEPHEN A. HIPP, *3100 W. 41st St., Sioux Falls, 57105.*

Diocesan Tribunal—3100 W. 41st St., Sioux Falls, 57105. Tel: 605-333-3357. (Address all rogatory commissions to this address).

Tribunal Judges—Revs. AL KRZYZOPOLSKI; RODNEY FARKE; LEONARD FOX; DONALD IMMING; THOMAS RYAN, Presiding Judge; GARY TERNES; Sr. LYNN MARIE WELBIG, P.B.V.M., J.C.L.

Defenders of the Matrimonial Bond—Revs. DONALD KETTLER, J.C.L.; JAMES ENGLERT; GREGORY TSCHAKERT, J.C.L.

Promoters of Justice—Rev. GREGORY TSCHAKERT, J.C.L.

Judges of the Appellate Court—Revs. JIM FRIEDRICH; JEROME KOPEL; KENNETH KOSTER; JOHN LANTSBERGER; JOSEPH MARDIAN; PIUS MARDIAN; CHARLES CIMPL; JEROME RANEK.

Defender of the Bond-Appellate Tribunal—Rev. CHARLES MANGAN, J.C.L.

Judicial Vicar—Rev. DONALD KETTLER, J.C.L.

Executive Coordinator of Matrimonial Tribunal—Mrs. VICKIE BEACH.

Director—Sr. LYNN MARIE WELBIG, P.B.V.M., J.C.L.

Diocesan Consultors—Rev. Msgr. RICHARD MAHOWALD, V.G.; Revs. TERRY ANDERSON; DENIS MEIER; RICHARD CASHEL; DANIEL MANNING; JOSEPH SHORT; DARRELL LAMBERTY; GREGORY TSCHAKERT; JOSEPH RIPP.

Consilium Administrationis—Most Rev. Bishop, Vicar General, Chancellor.

Deans—Revs. TERRY ANDERSON; DENIS MEIER; RICHARD CASHEL; DANIEL MANNING; JOSEPH SHORT; DARRELL LAMBERTY; GREGORY TSCHAKERT; JOSEPH RIPP.

Presbyteral Council—Most Rev. ROBERT J. CARLSON; Rev. Msgr. RICHARD MAHOWALD, V.G.; Revs. TERRY ANDERSON; DENIS MEIER; RICHARD CASHEL; DANIEL MANNING; DARRELL LAMBERTY; THOMAS HILLENBRAND, O.S.B.; MICHAEL KELLY; JOSEPH SHORT;

CHESTER MURTHA; GREGORY TSCHAKERT; JOSEPH RIPP.

Diocesan Offices and Directors

Apostleship of Prayer—Rev. CHARLES M. MANGAN, Dir., *P.O. Box 166, Kranzburg, 57245.*

Pastoral Ministry with Disabled Persons—VICKI KERKVLIET, Dir., *Catholic Pastoral Center, 3100 W. 41st St., Sioux Falls, 57105.* Tel: 605-333-3365.

Bishop's Bulletin—Rev. MICHAEL GRIFFIN, Exec. Editor; BERNIE HUNHOFF, JR., Editor, *Box 175, Yankton, 57078.* Tel: 605-665-3365; Fax: 605-665-6659.

Building Commission—JEROME KLEIN, Chancellor, *Catholic Chancery Office, 3100 W. 41st St., Sioux Falls, 57105.*

Campaign For Human Development—JAMES MASON, *3100 W. 41st St., Sioux Falls, 57105.*

Catholic Charities—JAMES MASON, Dir., *3100 W. 41st St., Sioux Falls, 57105.* Tel: 605-333-3351; Fax: 605-333-3346.

Catholic Foundation for Eastern South Dakota—MARK CONZEMIUS, Exec. Dir., *3100 W. 41st St., Sioux Falls, 57105.*

Catholic Relief Services—JEROME KLEIN, Chancellor, *3100 W. 41st St., Sioux Falls, 57105.*

Catholic Family Services—Sr. MARY CAROLE CURRAN, O.S.B., Exec. Dir., *3100 W. 41st St., Sioux Falls, 57105.* Tel: 605-333-3375.

Catholic Family Sharing Appeal—TIM BENZ, Dir., *3100 W. 41st St., Sioux Falls, 57105.* Tel: 605-333-3387.

Censor Librorum—Rev. CHARLES MANGAN, *3100 W. 41st St., Sioux Falls, 57105.*

Communications Office—DARYL THURINGER, *3100 W. 41st St. Sioux Falls, 57105.* Tel: 605-333-3390.

Cursillo—Rev. ROD FARKE, *P.O. Box 689, Yankton, 57078.*

Development Office—MARK CONZEMIUS, Dir., *3100 W. 41st St., Sioux Falls, 57105.* Tel: 605-333-3384.

Diocesan Archivist—JEROME KLEIN, Chancellor, *3100 W. 41st St., Sioux Falls, 57105.* Tel: 605-334-9861.

Diocesan Liturgical Commission—Rev. MICHAEL KELLY, Coord., *133 5th St. S.E., Huron, 57350.*

Diocesan Office of Education—Sr. NATHALIE MEYER, O.P., Ph.D., Supt. of Schools; KEITH BORCHERS, Dir. Education, *3100 W. 41st St., Sioux Falls, 57105.* Tel: 605-333-3366.

Ecumenical Commission—Rev. JAMES ANDRASCHKO, *3601 E. Dudley Ln., Sioux Falls, 57103.*

Family Life Ministry—SHANNON MILES, *3100 W. 41st St., Sioux Falls, 57105.*

Finance Officer—MICHAEL BANNWARTH, *3100 W. 41st St., Sioux Falls, 57105.* Tel: 605-333-3359; Fax: 605-333-3346.

Kateri Indian Center—MARLENE WORTH, *300 N. Main, Sioux Falls, 57102.* Tel: 605-335-3321.

Worldwide Marriage Encounter—Rev. JAMES M. JOYCE, *P.O. Box 80, Brandon, 57005.* Tel: 605-582-6902.

Newman Apostolate—Rev. JOSEPH VOGEL, Coord., *310 15th Ave. S.E., Aberdeen, 57401.*

Permanent Diaconate Council—Deacon RALPH COUNTER, *601 Edward Dr., Sioux Falls, 57103.* Tel: 605-332-4495.

Personnel Board—Most Rev. ROBERT J. CARLSON, Chm.

Propagation of the Faith—Rev. JOSEPH HOLZHAUSER, Dir., *St. Margaret, Box 137, Kimball, 57355.*

Respect Life Office—MARCELLA EFFERTZ, Dir., *3100 W. 41st St., Sioux Falls, 57105.* Tel: 605-335-3321.

Search—Sr. FRANCELLE CLARKE, P.B.V.M., Coord., *Presentation Heights, Aberdeen, 57401.* KEVIN MILES, *Yankton Search, 3100 W. 41st St., Sioux Falls, 57405.*

Spanish-Speaking Apostolate—Rev. JOHN RADER, *1220 E. 8th St., Sioux Falls, 57103.*

Teens Encounter Christ—*Youth Office, 3100 W. 41st St., Sioux Falls, 57105.*

Vocations—KEVIN MILES, Exec. Dir., *3100 W. 41st St., Sioux Falls, 57105.* Tel: 605-333-3372.

Youth Ministry—NANCY WERNER, *3100 W. 41st St., Sioux Falls, 57105.* Tel: 605-333-3385.

CLERGY, PARISHES, MISSIONS AND PAROCHIAL SCHOOLS

CITY OF SIOUX FALLS
(Minnehaha County)

1—ST. JOSEPH CATHEDRAL, Rev. Msgr. Stephen T. Barnett; Rev. James Zimmer; Deacon Mike Huntington. In res., Rev. Nathaiel Ndiokwere.
Res., 504 N. Summit Ave., 57104. Tel: 605-336-7390; Fax: 605-330-0416. [JC]
School—See separate listing under Inter-Parochial Schools in the Institution section. Tel: 605-338-3159; Fax: 605-338-2647.
Catechesis/Religious Programs—Students 529.

2—CHRIST THE KING (1949), Rev. Msgr. Richard Mahowald, P.A.; Rev. Brian Simon; Deacon James J. Walden.
Res., 1501 W. 26th St., 57105. Tel: 605-332-5477; Fax: 605-332-0552.
School—See separate listing under Inter-Parochial Schools in the Institution section. Tel: 605-338-5103; Fax: 605-335-1231.
Catechesis/Religious Programs—Students 215.

3—HOLY SPIRIT (1988), Rev. Msgr. James F. Andraschko; Deacon John Cole.
Res., 3601 E. Dudley Ln., 57103. Tel: 605-371-2320; Fax: 605-371-1957.
Catechesis/Religious Programs—Students 804.

4—OUR LADY OF GUADALUPE (1996), Rev. John S. Rader.
Res., 1220 E. 8th St., 57103-1702. Tel: 605-338-8126. [JC]
Catechesis/Religious Programs—Students 100.

5—ST. LAMBERT (1957), Rev. Msgr. Donald Kettler; Rev. Joseph Forcelle; Deacons Ralph C. Counter; Jerome F. Wathen.
Res., 1000 S. Bahnson Ave., 57103. Tel: 605-336-8808; Fax: 605-339-4389.
School—See separate listing under Inter-Parochial Schools in the Institution section. Tel: 605-338-7042; Fax: 605-336-8727.
Catechesis/Religious Programs—Students 461.

6—ST. MARY (1947), Rev. James Michael Doyle.
Res., 2109 S. Fifth Ave., 57105. Tel: 605-332-6391; Fax: 605-338-2953.
School—See separate listing under Inter-Parochial Schools in the Institution section. Tel: 605-334-9881; Fax: 605-334-9224.
Catechesis/Religious Programs—Students 187.

7—ST. MICHAEL (1979), Revs. Michael G. Wensing; Chester Murtha.
Res., 1600 S. Marion Rd., 57106. Tel: 605-361-1600; Fax: 605-361-4350. [JC]
School—See separate listing under Inter-Parochial Schools in the Institution section. Tel: 605-361-0021; Fax: 605-361-0094.
Catechesis/Religious Programs—Tel: 605-361-1317.
Students 1,185.

8—ST. THERESE (1917), Rev. Charles L. Cimpl. In res., Rev. Gary Ternes.
Res., 1301 N. Dubuque Ave., 57110-6450. Tel: 605-338-2433.
School—See separate listing under Inter-Parochial Schools in the Institution section.
Catechesis/Religious Programs—Students 164.

OUTSIDE THE CITY OF SIOUX FALLS

Aberdeen, Brown Co., Sacred Heart (1882), Revs. John R. Lantsberger; Thomas Clement.
Res., 409 3rd Ave., S.E., 57401. Tel: 605-225-7065. [CEM]
Catechesis/Religious Programs—Students 360.
St. Mary, Revs. Robert Vinslauski; Mark Lichter.
Res., 215 N. Arch St., 57401. Tel: 605-229-4422; Fax: 605-226-4908. [CEM]

Alexandria, Hanson Co., St. Mary of Mercy (1880) (German), Rev. Robert J. Fox.
Res., P.O. Box 158, 57331. Tel: 605-239-4532; Fax: 605-239-4532. [CEM]
Catechesis/Religious Programs—Students 126.

Andover, Day Co., All Saints (1880). Attended by Groton.
Mailing Address: Box 407, Groton, 57445. Tel: 605-397-8448.

Arlington, Kingsbury Co., St. John the Evangelist. Attended by Ramona.
Mailing Address: Box 128, Ramona, 57054.
Catechesis/Religious Programs—Students 68.

Armour, Douglas Co., St. Paul the Apostle (1886), Rev. Simon M. Engler, T.O.R.
Res., Box 400, 57313. Tel: 605-724-2191.
Catechesis/Religious Programs—Tel: 605-724-2121.
Students 80.

Artesian, Sanborn Co., St. Charles. Attended by St. Wilfrid, Woonsocket.
Mailing Address: Box 266, Woonsocket, 57385. [JC]
Catechesis/Religious Programs—Students 60.

Athol, Spink Co., St. Mary (1885). Closed. For inquiries for parish records contact All Saints, Mellette.

Aurora, Brookings Co., St. William (1881). Attended by Elkton.
Mailing Address: Box E, Elkton, 57026. [CEM]
Catechesis/Religious Programs—Students 36.

Beresford, Union Co., St. Teresa of Avila (1885), Rev. Denis Meier.
Res., 903 S. Third, 57004. Tel: 605-763-2028; 763-5159 (Church Res.). [CEM]
Catechesis/Religious Programs—Students 150.

Big Bend, Hughes Co., St. Catherine (1950). Attended by Fort Thompson.
Box 47, Fort Thompson, 57339. Tel: 605-245-2350. [CEM]

Big Stone City, Grant Co., St. Charles (1882), Rev. Ray Otto, O.S.B.
Res., P.O. Box 68, 57216. Tel: 605-862-8485. [CEM]
Catechesis/Religious Programs—Students 56.

Blunt, Hughes Co., Holy Spirit. Closed. For inquiries for parish records contact the Chancery.

Bowdle, Edmunds Co., St. Augustine (1894), Rev. Paul T. Josten. Also serves: Holy Trinity, Hosmer; St. Thomas, Roscoe. Box 310, 57428. Tel: 605-285-6466. [CEM]

Brandon, Minnehaha Co., Risen Savior (1979), Rev. James M. Joyce; Deacon Edwin Gruhot.
Res., 309 N. Needles, P.O. Box 80, 57005-0080. Tel: 605-582-6902. [JC]
Catechesis/Religious Programs—Tel: 605-582-2292.
Students 407.

Bridgewater, McCook Co., St. Stephen (1880), Rev. Paul Offerman
Res., Box 49, 57319. Tel: 605-729-2505. [CEM]
Catechesis/Religious Programs—Students 71.

Bristol, Day Co., St. Anthony (1885), Sr. Karen La Follette, P.B.V.M., Admin.
Res., Box 336, 57219. Tel: 605-492-3135. [CEM]

Britton, Marshall Co., St. John de Britto (1888), Rev. Daniel J. Manning.
Res., Box 108, 57430. Tel: 605-448-5379. [JC]
Catechesis/Religious Programs—Students 59.

Brookings, Brookings Co., St. Thomas More (1904), Rev. Thomas A. Heck.
Res., 924 Fourth St., 57006. Tel: 605-692-4361; Fax: 605-692-6176. [CEM]
Catechesis/Religious Programs—Tel: 605-692-6941.
Students 536.

Bryant, Hamlin Co., St. Mary (1881). Attended by St. Thomas, De Smet.
Res., Box 15, De Smet, 57231. Tel: 605-854-3564. [CEM]

Canton, Lincoln Co., St. Dominic, Rev. Larry Jonas, S.J.; Deacon Edward B. Oliver.
Res., 800 E. Walnut, 57013. Tel: 605-987-5640.

Castlewood, Hamlin Co., St. John (1885). Attended by Kranzburg.
Mailing Address: Box 166, Kranzburg, 57245. [JC]
Catechesis/Religious Programs—Students 72.

Cavour, Beadle Co., St. Patrick (1883). Attended by Church of the Resurrection, Huron.
Mailing Address: 400 20th St. S.W., Huron, 57350. Tel: 605-352-3403. [CEM]

Centerville, Turner Co., Good Shepherd (1888). Attended by Beresford.
207 S. First, Beresford, 57004. Tel: 605-763-2028. [JC]
Catechesis/Religious Programs—Students 84.

Chamberlain, Brule Co., St. James (1891), Rev. Anthony Kelly, S.C.J.
Res., 400 S. Main, 57325. Tel: 605-734-6122; Fax: 605-734-6729. [JC]
Catechesis/Religious Programs—Tel: 605-734-6122; Fax: 605-734-6729.
Students 225.

Chelsea, Faulk Co., Sacred Heart. Attended by Mellette.
Mailing Address: P.O. Box 46, Millette, 57461. Tel: 605-887-3414; Fax: 605-887-3414.

Clark, Clark Co., St. Michael (1887), Rev. Ken Bain.
Res., 110 N. Idaho St., 57225. Tel: 605-532-3855. [CEM]
Catechesis/Religious Programs—112 N. Idaho St., 57225. Tel: 605-532-3776.
Students 109.

Clear Lake, Deuel Co., St. Mary (1900), Rev. Joseph Short.
Res., 408 Third St. W., Box 589, 57226. Tel: 605-874-2080.
Catechesis/Religious Programs—Students 126.

Colman, Moody Co., St. Peter (1905), Rev. David Roehrich; Deacon Robert Cross.
Res., Box J, 57017. Tel: 605-534-3612. [CEM]
Catechesis/Religious Programs—Students 133.

Conde, Spink Co., St. John the Baptist (1906) (German), Rev. Mathew Vazhappily, C.M.I. (India).
Res., P.O. Box 228, 57434. Tel: 605-382-5902. [CEM]

Dante, Charles Mix Co., Assumption B.V.M. (1909). Attended by T.O.R. Team Ministry.
P.O. Box 36, 57329-0036. Tel: 605-384-5155. [CEM]
Catechesis/Religious Programs—Students 125.

Dell Rapids, Minnehaha Co., St. Mary's (1898), Rev. Hal L. Barber.

Res., 608 8th St., 57022. Tel: 605-428-3390. [CEM][JC]
School—Tel: 605-428-3459.
Sisters of the Presentation B.V.M. 2; Lay Teachers 9; Students 191.
High School—Tel: 605-428-5591; Fax: 605-428-5377.
Priests 1; Sisters 1; Lay Teachers 9; Students 68.
Catechesis/Religious Programs—Tel: 605-428-3597.
Students 178.

De Smet, Kingsbury Co., St. Thomas Aquinas, Rev. David A. Janes.
Res., Box 15, 57231. Tel: 605-854-3564. [CEM]
Catechesis/Religious Programs—Students 85.

Dimock, Hutchinson Co., SS. Peter and Paul (1885) (German), Rev. Richard Cashel.
Res., R.R. 1, Box 14 A, 57331. Tel: 605-928-3883. [CEM]
Catechesis/Religious Programs—Students 97.

Doland, Spink Co., St. Joseph of Doland (1909). Attended by Conde.
P.O. Box 393, 57436-0393. Tel: 605-635-6301; Fax: 605-635-6411.
Catechesis/Religious Programs—Students 53.

Duncan, Buffalo Co., St. Placidus (1887). Wessington Springs.
510 N. Wallace, P.O. Box N, Wessington Springs, 57382-0348. [CEM]

Eden, Marshall Co., Sacred Heart (1917), Rev. William L. Hamak.
Res., Box 15, 57232. Tel: 605-486-4702. [CEM]
Catechesis/Religious Programs—Students 82.

Elk Point, Union Co., St. Joseph (1901), Rev. John C. Rasmussen.
Res., Box 340, 605 E. Main St., 57025. Tel: 605-356-2693. [CEM]
Catechesis/Religious Programs—Students 149.

Elkton, Brookings Co., Our Lady of Good Counsel (1879), Rev. Susainathan Michael (India); Sr. Marlene Konrady, O.S.B., Admin.
Res., Box E, 57026. Tel: 605-542-8221. [CEM]
Catechesis/Religious Programs—P.O. Box 192, 57026. Tel: 605-542-3121. Diane Baker, D.R.E. Students 114.

Emery, Hanson Co., St. Martin (1884), Rev. Joseph Thalanamy.
Res., Box 312, 57332. Tel: 605-449-4374. [CEM]
Catechesis/Religious Programs—Students 81.

Epiphany, Hanson Co., Church of the Epiphany (1896) (German), Rev. Leo C. Pospichal.
Res., R.R. 1, Box 107, Canova, 57321. Tel: 605-523-2640. [CEM]
Catechesis/Religious Programs—Students 81.

Estelline, Hamlin Co., St. Francis de Sales (1884). Attended by Clear Lake.
Res., Box B, 57234. Tel: 605-873-2254. [CEM]
Catechesis/Religious Programs—Students 56.

Ethan, Davison Co., Holy Trinity (1889). Attended by Dimock.
R.R. 1, Box 14A, Dimock, 57331. Tel: 605-928-3883. [CEM]
Catechesis/Religious Programs—Tel: 605-227-4666. Mrs. Glen Erpenback, D.R.E.
Students 77.

Eureka, McPherson Co., St. Joseph (1896) (German). Attended by Herreid.
Mailing Address: P.O. Box 37, Herreid, 57632. Tel: 605-437-2614.
Catechesis/Religious Programs—Students 50.

Farmer, Hanson Co., St. Peter (1889). Attended by Epiphany.
Mailing Address: Rte. 1, Canova, 57321-9417.
Church—57336. Tel: 605-523-2640.

Faulkton, Faulk Co., St. Thomas the Apostle (1903), Rev. Terence Anderson; Deacon Arvid Holsing.
Res., P.O. Box 394, 57438. Tel: 605-598-6590. [CEM]
Catechesis/Religious Programs—Tracy Beidler, D.R.E.
Students 86.

Flandreau, Moody Co., SS. Simon and Jude (1882), Rev. David Roehrich.
Res., 105 S. Bates, 57028. Tel: 605-997-2610. [CEM]
Catechesis/Religious Programs—Students 180.

Florence, Codington Co., Blessed Sacrament, Rev. Gregory Frankman.
Res., Box 6, 57235. Tel: 605-758-2271. [CEM]
Catechesis/Religious Programs—Students 62.

Fort Thompson, Buffalo Co., St. Joseph (1889), Rev. Yvon Sheehy, S.C.J., Moderator.
Mailing Address: Box 47, 57339. Tel: 605-245-2350. [CEM]
Catechesis/Religious Programs—Students 130.

Frankfort, Spink Co., St. Ann (1884). Attended by Redfield.
Mailing Address: 213 E. 6th Ave., Redfield, 57469. Tel: 605-472-2500.

Garretson, Minnehaha Co., St. Rose of Lima (1898), Rev. John Riedman.
Res., Drawer O, 57030. Tel: 605-594-3750. [CEM]
Catechesis/Religious Programs—Students 115.

Garryowen, Union Co., St. Mary. Closed. For sacramental records contact St. Joseph, Elk Point.

Gary, Deuel Co., St. Peter (1900). Attended by Clear Lake.
408 3rd St. W., Box 589, Clear Lake, 57226. Tel: 605-874-2080.

Geddes, Charles Mix Co., St. Ann (1902). Attended by Platte.
Mailing Address: P.O. Box 335, Platte, 57369-0335. Tel: 605-337-2465; 337-3710. [CEM][JC]
Catechesis/Religious Programs—Students 57.

Gettysburg, Potter Co., Sacred Heart (1905), Rev. Michael R. Schneider.
Res., Box 285, 57442. Tel: 605-765-2161. [CEM]
Catechesis/Religious Programs—Students 138.

Grenville, Day Co., St. Joseph. Attended by Immaculate Conception, Waubay. Rev. Donald Marohn.
Res., Box 759, 57239. Tel: 605-947-4540. [CEM]
Catechesis/Religious Programs—Students 71.

Groton, Brown Co., St. John Baptist (1883), Rev. Marvin E. McPhee.
Res., 603 N. Main, 57445. Tel: 605-397-8448. [CEM]
Catechesis/Religious Programs—Students 97.

Grover, Codington Co., St. Peter. Attended by Blessed Sacrament, Florence.
Mailing Address: P.O. Box 6, Florence, 57235. Tel: 605-758-2271.

Harrold, Hughes Co., St. John the Evangelist. Attended by Highmore.
Box 457, Highmore, 57345. Tel: 605-852-2733. [CEM]

Hartford, Minnehaha Co., St. George (1882), Rev. Gregory Tschakert; Sr. Muriel Spartz, O.S.B., Pastoral Assoc.
Res., 102 N. Mundt, Box 377, 57033. Tel: 605-528-3426. [CEM]
Catechesis/Religious Programs—St. George Center, 207 S. Main Ave., 57033. Tel: 605-528-3902. Students 231.

Hecla, Brown Co., St. Anthony (1904). Attended by St. John, Britton.
Box 108, Britton, 57430. Tel: 605-448-5379. [JC]

Henry, Codington Co., St. Henry. Florence.
Mailing Address: P.O. Box 6, Florence, 57235. Tel: 605-758-2271.
Catechesis/Religious Programs—Students 57.

Herreid, Campbell Co., St. Michael (1895), Rev. Jim D. Friedrich.
Res., Box 37, 57632. Tel: 605-437-2614. [CEM]
Catechesis/Religious Programs—Students 79.

Highmore, Hyde Co., St. Mary, Rev. Ivo Martini, Admin.
Res., Box 457, 57345. Tel: 605-852-2733. [CEM]
Catechesis/Religious Programs—Students 115.

Hosmer, Edmunds Co., Holy Trinity. Attended by Bowdle.
Res., P.O. Box 46, 57448. Tel: 605-283-2275. [CEM]

Hoven, Potter Co., St. Anthony of Padua (1887), Rev. William A. Osborn.
Res., Box 98, 57450. Tel: 605-948-2451. [CEM]
School—Tel: 605-948-2245.
Lay Teachers 6; Students 75
Catechesis/Religious Programs—Students 168.

Howard, Miner Co., St. Agatha (1882), Rev. John R. Kasch.
Res., Box H, 57349. Tel: 605-772-5564. [CEM]
Catechesis/Religious Programs—Students 178.

Humboldt, Minnehaha Co., St. Ann (1912) (German), Rev. Terry Weber; Deacon Francis Graff; Sr. Mildred Nikolas, O.S.B.
Res., 204 S. Jefferson, 57035. Tel: 605-363-3330. [CEM]
Catechesis/Religious Programs—Tel: 605-363-5068.
Students 116.

Huntimer, Minnehaha Co., St. Joseph the Workman (1889). Unassigned.
Mailing Address: 3100 W. 41st St., Sioux Falls, 57105. Tel: 605-334-9861. [CEM]
Catechesis/Religious Programs—Students 135.

Huron, Beadle Co., Church of the Resurrection (1969), Rev. J. E. Murphy.
Res., 400 20th St., S.W., 57350. Tel: 605-352-3403. [JC]
Catechesis/Religious Programs—Tel: 605-352-2237.
Students 230.

St. Martin (1881), Rev. Michael D. Kelly.
Res., 133 5th St., S.E., 57350. Tel: 605-352-2203; Fax: 605-352-2203. [CEM]
School—Tel: 605-352-9344.
Lay Teachers 10; Students 198.
Catechesis/Religious Programs—Students 251.

Idylwilde, Turner Co., St. Boniface (1885). Attended by Parker.
Box 610, Parker, 57053. Tel: 605-297-4983. [CEM]
Catechesis/Religious Programs—Students 57.

Ipswich, Edmunds Co., Holy Cross (1886), Rev. Edward P. Burian. In res., Rev. Raymond Mowry.
Res., Box 67, 57451. Tel: 605-426-6967. [CEM]
School—Tel: 605-426-6222.
Lay Teachers 4; Students 57.
Catechesis/Religious Programs—Students 208.

Iroquois, Kingsbury Co., St. Paul. St. Thomas Aquinas, De Smet.
Box 15, De Smet, 57231. Tel: 605-854-3564. [CEM]

Jefferson, Union Co., St. Peter (1867), Rev. Andrew K. Swietochowski.
Res., P.O. Box 188, 57038-0188. Tel: 605-966-5716; Fax: 605-966-5492. [CEM]
School—P.O. Box 98, 57038-0098. Tel: 605-966-5529.
Lay Teachers 7; Students 64.
Catechesis/Religious Programs—Students 148.

Kimball, Brule Co., St. Margaret (1884), Rev. Joseph Holzhauser.
Res., Box 137, 57355. Tel: 605-778-6420. [CEM]
Catechesis/Religious Programs—Tel: 605-778-6487.
Students 200.

Kranzburg, Codington Co., Holy Rosary (1879), Rev. Charles Mangan.
Res., Box 166, 57245. Tel: 605-886-9166. [CEM]
School—(Grades K-6). Tel: 605-886-8114.
Lay Teachers 3; Students 41.
Catechesis/Religious Programs—Students 112.

Lake Andes, Charles Mix Co., St. Mark (1904), Rev. Gary Lantz, S.C.J.
Res., Box 250, 57356. Tel: 605-487-7300. [CEM]
Catechesis/Religious Programs—Students 38.

Lake City, Marshall Co., St. Joseph (1919). Attended by Eden.
Box 15, Eden, 57232. Tel: 605-486-4702. [CEM]

Lennox, Lincoln Co., St. Magdalen. Attended by St. Nicholas, Tea.
Mailing Address: Box 136, 57039. Tel: 605-647-2187. [CEM]
Catechesis/Religious Programs—Students 126.

Leola, McPherson Co., Our Lady of Perpetual Help (1891), Rev. Edward P. Burian.
Res., P.O. Box 67, Ipswich, 57451. Tel: 605-426-6967. [CEM]
Catechesis/Religious Programs—Students 58.

Lesterville, Yankton Co., St. John the Baptist (1904). Attended by St. Wenceslaus, Tabor. Rev. Msgr. Carlton P. Hermann.
Mailing Address: Box 168, 57040. Tel: 605-364-7581. [CEM]
Catechesis/Religious Programs—Students 58.

Letcher, Sanborn Co., St. Scholastica. Closed. For inquiries for parish records contact the Chancery.

Lily, Day Co., St. Joseph. Closed. For sacramental records contact St. Anthony, Bristol.

Madison, Lake Co., St. Thomas Aquinas (1881), Rev. Anthony Opem.
Res., 217 N.W. Fourth St., 57042. Tel: 605-256-2304. [CEM]
School—Tel: 605-256-4419.
Lay Teachers 9; Students 123.
Catechesis/Religious Programs—Students 317.

Marion, Turner Co., Our Lady of Perpetual Help (1880),
Res., Box 610, Parker, 57053. Tel: 605-297-4983. [CEM]
Catechesis/Religious Programs—Students 68.

Marty, Charles Mix Co., St. Paul's Church (1913). Attended by T.O.R. Team Ministry, Lake Andes. Sr. Miriam Shindelar, O.S.B.S., Admin.; Deacon Edward P. Zephier.
Res., 57361. Tel: 605-384-3234; 487-7300. [CEM]
Catechesis/Religious Programs—Tel: 605-384-3234.
Students 75.

Mayfield, Yankton Co., St. Columba (1884) (Irish), Rev. Leonard Kayser.
1105 W. Eighth St., Yankton, 57078. Tel: 605-267-2676. [CEM]
Catechesis/Religious Programs—Tel: 605-668-1236.
Students 51.

Mellette, Spink Co., All Saints, Rev. Antonio W. Ramos.
Box 46, 57461. Tel: 605-887-3414. [CEM]
Catechesis/Religious Programs—Students 77.

Milbank, Grant Co., St. Lawrence (1882), Rev. Thomas Roznowski, O.S.B.

Res., 101 6th St., S., 57252. Tel: 605-432-5353. [CEM]
School—Tel: 605-432-5673.
Sisters 1; Lay Teachers 7; Students 130.
Catechesis/Religious Programs—Tel: 605-432-5353.
Students 264.

Miller, Hand Co., St. Ann (1884), Rev. Donald J. Molumby.
Res., 709 E. 4th, 57362. Tel: 605-853-2207. [CEM]
Catechesis/Religious Programs—Students 169.

Mitchell, Davison Co., Holy Family (1880), Rev. Edward J. Pierce.
Res., 321 E. 3rd Ave., 57301. Tel: 605-996-3639; Fax: 605-996-9257. [CEM]
School—Holy Family/Holy Spirit-Mitchell Catholic Schools, Tel: 605-996-2365.
Lay Teachers 15; Students 266.
Catechesis/Religious Programs—200 N. Kimball St., 57301. Tel: 605-996-3842.
Students 353.

Holy Spirit (1962), Rev. Richard Fox.
Res., 1412 W. Cedar Ave., 57301. Tel: 605-996-7424.
School—Holy Family/Holy Spirit-Mitchel Catholic Schools. See Holy Family for details. Tel: 605-996-2365.
Catechesis/Religious Programs—Tel: 605-996-3842.
Students 491.

Mobridge, Walworth Co., St. Joseph (1912), Rev. Jerome M. Ranek.
Res., 514 W. Second Ave., 57601. Tel: 605-845-2100. [JC]
Catechesis/Religious Programs—614 W. Second Ave., 57601. Tel: 605-845-2646.
Students 201.

Montrose, McCook Co., St. Patrick (1904), Rev. Terry Weber.
211 S. Church, 57048. Tel: 605-363-5068; Fax: 605-363-5068. [CEM]
Catechesis/Religious Programs—Students 131.

Mount Vernon, Davison Co., St. Michael. Attended by Plankinton.
Box 430, Plankinton, 57368.

New Effington, Roberts Co., Sacred Heart (1913). Attended by Rosholt.
P.O. Box 45, Rosholt, 57260. Tel: 605-537-4583.

Oldham, Kingsbury Co., St. Catherine of Sienna. Attended by Ramona.
P.O. Box 128, Ramona, 57054.

Onaka, Faulk Co., St. John the Baptist (1906). Attended by St. Anthony of Padua, Hoven.
P.O. Box 98, Hoven, 57450. Tel: 605-948-2451. [CEM]

Onida, Sully Co., St. Pius X (1959). Attended by Sacred Heart, Gettysburg. Rev. Michael R. Schneider; Sr. Veronica Haag, O.S.B., Pastoral Min.
P.O. Box 13, 57564. Tel: 605-258-2336. [CEM]
Catechesis/Religious Programs—Students 78.

Orient, Faulk Co., St. Joseph (1884). Attended by Polo.
H.C.1 Box 82, 57467.

Parker, Turner Co., St. Christina (1887), Deacon William Frankman, Admin.
Res., P.O. Box 610, 57053. Tel: 605-297-4983. [CEM]
Catechesis/Religious Programs—Students 55.

Parkston, Hutchinson Co., Sacred Heart (1887), Rev. Robert V. Krantz; Deacon Barry Wagner.
Res., Box 460, 57366. Tel: 605-928-3676. [CEM]
Catechesis/Religious Programs—Students 204.

Pierre, Hughes Co., SS. Peter and Paul (1882), Revs. Darrell V. Lamberty; Gary Lantz, S.C.J.
Res., 304 N. Euclid, 57501. Tel: 605-224-2483; Fax: 605-224-1483. [CEM]
School—Tel: 605-224-7185.
Benedictine Sisters 3; Lay Teachers 8; Students 158.
Catechesis/Religious Programs—Students 509.

Plankinton, Aurora Co., St. John, Rev. Alex Bombera, T.O.R.
Res., Box 430, 57368. Tel: 605-942-7125.

Platte, Charles Mix Co., St. Peter the Apostle (1904), Rev. Donald R. Imming.
Res., Box 335, 57369. Tel: 605-337-3710, 337-2465. [CEM]
Catechesis/Religious Programs—Students 84.

Polo, Hand Co., St. Liborius (1904), Sr. Mary Myles Schwahn, S.S.N.D., Admin.
Res., H.C. 1, Box 82, Orient, 57467. Tel: 605-392-2440. [CEM]
Catechesis/Religious Programs—Students 45.

Pukwana, Brule Co., St. Anthony. Attended by Chamberlain.
400 S. Main, Chamberlin, 57325. Tel: 605-734-6122; Fax: 605-734-6729.

Ramona, Lake Co., St. William of Vercelli, Rev. Richard Baumberger.
Res., Box 128, 57054. Tel: 605-482-8214. [CEM]
Catechesis/Religious Programs—Students 52.

Redfield, Spink Co., St. Bernard (1884), Rev. John Fischer.
Res., 213 E. 6th Ave., 57469-1249. Tel: 605-472-2500. [CEM]
Catechesis/Religious Programs—Tel: 605-472-1482.
Students 240.

Revillo, Grant Co., Annunciation, Rev. Ray Oho, O.S.B.
Res., Box 128, 57259. Tel: 605-623-4541; 432-5528. [CEM]
Catechesis/Religious Programs—Students 54.

Roscoe, Edmunds Co., St. Thomas Apostle. Attended by Bowdle. Rev. Paul T. Josten.
Res., P.O. Box 257, 57471. Tel: 605-287-4378. [JC]
Catechesis/Religious Programs—Students 59.

Rosholt, Roberts Co., St. John the Baptist (1911), Rev. Ronald Harrer, O.M.I.
Res., Box 45, 57260. Tel: 605-537-4583. [CEM]
Catechesis/Religious Programs—Students 60.

Salem, McCook Co., St. Mary (1885) (German), Rev. Joseph Ripp. In res., Rev. Ladislaus Dudek, (Retired).
Res., Box 308, 340 N. Idaho, 57058. Tel: 605-425-2600; Fax: 605-425-2600. [CEM]
School—Lay Teachers 10; Students 108.
Catechesis/Religious Programs—Students 124.

Scotland, Bon Homme Co., St. George, Rev. John Maliyekal (India).
Res., Box 449, 57059. Tel: 605-583-4318.
Catechesis/Religious Programs—Tel: 605-583-4696.
Students 88.

Selby, Walworth Co., St. Anthony. Attended by Herreid.

Seneca, Faulk Co., St. Boniface (1903). Attended by St. Thomas the Apostle, Faulkton.

Sigel, Yankton Co., St. Agnes (1885) (German), Rev. Leonard Kayser.
R.R. 1 Box 26, Utica, 57067. Tel: 605-665-5358. [CEM]

Sisseton, Roberts Co., St. Catherine (1962), Revs. Mietek Bajek, O.M.I.; Gari Ruthenberg, O.M.I.
Office: 120 E. Chestnut, 57262. Tel: 605-698-7414; Fax: 605-698-7236. [CEM]
Mission—Veblen, Marshall Co., St. Matthew.

St. Peter (1899), Revs. Mietek Bajek, O.M.I.; Gari Ruthenberg, O.M.I.
Office: 120 E. Chestnut, 57262. Tel: 605-698-7414; Fax: 605-698-7236. [CEM]
Catechesis/Religious Programs—Students 161.

Spencer, McCook Co., St. Mary (1906). Attended by Bridgewater.
Box 49, Bridgewater, 57319. Tel: 615-729-2505.

Springfield, Bon Homme Co., St. Vincent. Attended by Tyndall.

Stephan, Hyde Co., Immaculate Conception (1886), Revs. Yvon Sheehy, S.C.J., Moderator; James Walters, S.C.J.
Res., 57346. Tel: 605-852-2216. [CEM][JC]

Stickney, Aurora Co., St. Mary (1908). Attended by Armour.
Box 400, Armour, 57313. Tel: 605-724-2191. [CEM]

Tabor, Bon Homme Co., St. Wenceslaus (1872), Rev. Msgr. Carlton P. Hermann.
Res., 205 N. Lidice St., 57063-2005. Tel: 605-463-2336. [CEM]
Catechesis/Religious Programs—Students 116.

Tea, Lincoln Co., St. Nicholas (1905), Rev. Kenneth Koster.
Res., 510 W. Maple, P.O. Box 116, 57064. Tel: 605-368-5449; 333-3348. [JC]
Church—200 Maple St., 57064. Tel: 605-368-5449.
Catechesis/Religious Programs—Students 140.

Tripp, Hutchinson Co., Holy Rosary. Attended by Parkston.

Turton, Spink Co., St. Joseph (1888). Attended by Conde.
Mailing Address: P.O. Box 127, 57477. Tel: 605-382-5902. [CEM][JC]

Tyndall, Bon Homme Co., St. Leo (1890), Rev. Jerry Kopel.
Res., Box 47, 57066. Tel: 605-589-3504. [CEM]
Catechesis/Religious Programs—Students 149.
Station—Springfield Correctional Facility, Tel: 605-369-2201. Bro. Placid Hellman, O.S.B., Chap.

Veblen, Marshall Co., St. John Nepomucene. Attended by Catholic Community, Sisseton.

Vermillion, Clay Co., St. Agnes (1860), Rev. Leonard D. Fox; Deacon Thomas Vogel.
Res., 505 Catalina, 57069. Tel: 605-624-4479. [CEM 2][JC 3]
School—909 E. Lewis St., 57069. Tel: 605-624-4144.
Lay Teachers 7; Students 141.
Catechesis/Religious Programs—Students 184.

Vodnany, Bon Homme Co., SS. Cyril and Methodius (1886). Attended by Scotland.
Mailing Address: R.R. 2, Kaylor, 57354. [CEM]

Wagner, Charles Mix Co., St. John the Baptist (1903), Pastoral Team: Revs. Joseph Glancy, T.O.R.; Jordan Hite, T.O.R.; David Tickerhoof, T.O.R.; Bro. Martin Zatsick, T.O.R.; Deacon Albert J. Kocer.
Res., Box 637, 57380. Tel: 605-384-5518; Fax: 605-384-5518. [CEM]
Catechesis/Religious Programs—Tel: 605-384-5314.
Students 120.

Wakonda, Clay Co., St. Patrick (1904) (Irish), Rev. James O.J. Englert.
Res., Box 386, 57073. Tel: 605-267-2676. [CEM 2]
Catechesis/Religious Programs—Tel: 605-267-2676.
Students 70.

Watertown, Codington Co., Holy Name (1955), Rev. Jerome J. Holtzman.
Res., 1009 Skyline Dr., 57201. Tel: 605-886-2628; Fax: 605-886-2142. [JC]
Catechesis/Religious Programs—Tel: 605-886-3368; Fax: 605-886-2141.
Students 468.

Immaculate Conception (1887), Revs. Roger Geditz; Paul Pathiyamoola (India).
Res., 309 Second Ave. S.E., 57201. Tel: 605-886-4049. [CEM]
School—Tel: 605-886-3883.
Lay Teachers 11; Students 183.
Catechesis/Religious Programs—103 Third St. S.E., 57201. Tel: 605-886-2772.
Students 673.

Waubay, Day Co., Immaculate Conception (1894), Rev. Donald Marohn.
Res., Box 77, 57273. Tel: 605-947-4540. [CEM]
Catechesis/Religious Programs—Students 88.

Waverly, Codington Co., St. Joseph (1889). Attended by Kranzburg.
Box 166, Kranzburg, 57245. Tel: 605-886-9166. [CEM]

Webster, Day Co., Christ the King, Rev. John M. Garvey.
Res., 1101 E. 1st St., 57274. Tel: 605-345-3447; Fax: 605-345-4871. [CEM]
Catechesis/Religious Programs—Students 255.

Wellington, Minnehaha Co., St. Joseph. Closed. For sacramental records contact St. Ann, Humboldt.

Wessington, Beadle Co., St. Joseph. Attended by Miller.

Wessington Springs, Jerauld Co., St. Joseph (1906). Unassigned.
Mailing Address: P.O. Box N, 510 N. Wallace, 57382. Tel: 605-539-9569. [JC]
Catechesis/Religious Programs—Students 99.

Westport, Brown Co., Sacred Heart of Westport (1889), Rev. Joseph Vogel.
Mailing Address: Box 85, 57481. Tel: 605-229-1011. [CEM]
Catechesis/Religious Programs—Students 64.

White, Brookings Co., St. Paul Attended (1898). Brookings Student Center. Rev. Michael Griffin.
Box 7019, University Sta., Brookings, 57007. Tel: 605-692—9461. [JC]
Catechesis/Religious Programs—Students 50.

White Lake, Aurora Co., St. Peter (1883), Rev. Arnold Petrosky, T.O.R.
Res., Box 277, 57383. Tel: 605-249-2700. [CEM]
Catechesis/Religious Programs—Students 110.

Willow Lake, Clark Co., St. James (1895). Attended by St. Michael, Clark.
110 N. Idaho St., Clark, 57225.

Wilmot, Roberts Co., St. Mary (1886), Rev. John McMullen, O.S.B.
Res., Box 204, 57279. Tel: 605-938-4289; Fax: 605-432-4754. [CEM]
Catechesis/Religious Programs—Students 60.

Woonsocket, Sanborn Co., St. Wilfrid (1884), Rev. Gerald Thury.
Res., Box 266, 57385. Tel: 605-796-4666. [CEM]
Catechesis/Religious Programs—Students 112.

Worthing, Lincoln Co., St. Edward (1908). Attended by St. Dominic, Canton.
800 E. Walnut, Canton, 57013. Tel: 605-987-5640. [CEM]

Yankton, Yankton Co., St. Benedict (1993), Rev. Rodney Farke.
Res., 1500 St. Benedict Dr., 57078. Tel: 605-665-6214. [JC]
Catechesis/Religious Programs—1500 St. Benedict Dr., 57078. Tel: 605-665-6214.
Students 300.

Sacred Heart (1871), Revs. James I. Bream; Lawrence Regynski; Deacon Thomas Healy.
Res., 509 Capitol St., 57078. Tel: 605-665-3655. [CEM]

School—Tel: 605-665-5841.
Sisters 1; Lay Teachers 12; Students 211.
Catechesis/Religious Programs—Students 359.

Zell, Hand Co., St. Mary. Attended by Mellette.
Catechesis/Religious Programs—Students 65.

Chaplains of Public Institutions

SIOUX FALLS. *South Dakota State Penitentiary & Minnehaha County Jail*. Rev. Bernard Ashfeld.
State School for the Deaf. Vacant. 3100 W. 41st St., 57105.

FLANDREAU. *Government Indian School*. Attended by SS. Simon & Jude, Flandreau.

PLANKINTON. *State Training School*. Attended by St. John Church, Plankinton. Rev. Alex Bombera, T.O.R.

REDFIELD. *State Hospital and State School, SD*. Attended by St. Bernard Church, Redfield.

SPRINGFIELD. *State Prison*. Attended by Tyndall. Bro. Placid Hellman, O.S.B.

YANKTON. *State Hospital*. Rev. Leonard Kayser, Federal Prison Camp, Rev. Denis Quinkert, O.S.B.

On Duty Outside the Diocese:
Reverend Monsignors—
Gullickson, Thomas E., Apostolic Delegation, P.O. Box 19-199, Jerusalem, Israel

Military Chaplains:
Reverend Fathers—
Imberi, Anthony, Chap., 311-B Lovell Ave., Carlisle Barracks, PA 17013
Krogman, David L., PSC 45, Box 128, APO, AE 09468
Wagner, Joseph, PSC 94, Box 2051, APO, AE 09824

Graduate Studies:
Reverend Fathers—
Sieverding, Dale, San Anselmo, Rome, Italy

On Leave of Absence:
Reverend Fathers—
Benda, Dennis
Dobitz, Roger
Johnson, Douglas
McCormick, James
McNeil, Frank J.

Retired:
Reverend Monsignors—
Duraczynski, Jerome A., 1041 Singer Ln., Norristown, PA 19403
Foley, Andrew E., 1265 4th St. NW, Watertown, SD 57201-1128
Martin, Myron F., St. William Home, 901 E. Virgil, Milbank, SD 57252
McEneaney, John P.A., 423 N. Duluth, Sioux Falls, SD 57104
Zwinger, Leonard, 500 S. 4th Ave., #101, Sioux Falls, SD 57104

Reverend Fathers—
Althoff, Gaudentius, Aberdeen Living Center, 1700 N. Hwy 281, Aberdeen, SD 57401
Anderson, Joseph R., R.R. 1 Box 75-A, Corona, SD 57227
Bachman, Paul B., Oakwood Apts. #10, 4504 S. Prince of Peace Pl., Sioux Falls, SD 57103-5830
Brady, John, 509 Broadway, Yankton, SD 57078
Burns, Thomas, 411 Vander Horck, P.O. Box 297, Britton, SD 57430
Carroll, Howard, 4701 S. Oxbow Ave., #320, Sioux Falls, SD 57106
Connolly, Thomas, 3109 Corona Dr., Holiday, FL 34690
Dudek, Ladislaus, 330 N. Idaho, Salem, SD 57058. Tel: 605-425-2031
Duman, Charles J., P.O. Box 841, Yankton, SD 57078-0841
Duraczynski, Walter, 2007 New Hope St., Norristown, PA 19401
Fox, Leo, P.O. Box 1441, Watertown, SD 57201
Friedrich, Lawrence, 4510 S. Prince of Peace Pl., Apt. #213, Sioux Falls, SD 57103. Tel: 605-371-4537
Keating, David, 4500 S. Prince of Peace Pl., Sioux Falls, SD 57103
Krzyzopolski, Al, 4700 S. Cliff Ave., #210, Sioux Falls, SD 57103
Latterell, Glenn, 4504 S. Prince of Peace Pl., #26, Sioux Falls, SD 57103
Liepold, Donald F., 500 W. 16th, Sioux Falls, SD 57104. Tel: 605-336-3674
MacArthur, Bruce, P.O. Box 416, Clint, TX 79836
Marbach, Lawrence J., 617 Maple St., Yankton, SD 57078-3823
Mardian, Joseph P., 4510 S. Prince of Peace Pl., #205, Sioux Falls, SD 57103
Mardian, Pius, 4510 S. Prince of Peace Pl. #120, Sioux Falls, SD 57103
McMahon, Marvin J., 509 Broadway Ave., Yankton, SD 57078
McPhillips, Thomas J., Bishop Hoch Villa, 500 S. Ohlman, Box 430, Mitchell, SD 57301
Mociun, Casimir T., 1320 Cedar Ave., Scranton, PA 18505
Morgen, Paul, 4510 S. Prince of Peace Pl. #210, Sioux Falls, SD 57103
Mowry, Raymond G., Holy Cross Rectory, P.O. Box 67, Ipswich, SD 57451-0067
Murray, John I., 912 Missoula Ave., Helena, MT 59601
Ortmeier, Richard J., 1300 N. Harrison Ave., #303, Pierre, SD 57501-2830
Patrick, Maurice, 2345 W. 86th St., Indianapolis, IN 46260
Petrucci, Dominic, 1417 W. Ash Ave., Mitchell, SD 57301
Presinell, Joseph C., St. William Home, 901 E. Virgil, #219, Milbank, SD 57252
Ryan, Thomas J., 609 W 5th St., Sioux Falls, SD 57104-2734
Stanton, Leonard F., Benet Place, 100 28th Ave. S.E., Watertown, SD 57201
Wolf, James, 215 N. Arch, Aberdeen, SD 57401

Permanent Deacons:
Beaubien, Steven, St. Nicholas, Tea
Bierer, Richard B., St. Mary, Sioux Falls
Cheskie, Pete, St. Rose, Garretson
Cole, John M., Holy Spirit, Sioux Falls
Conrads, Michael
Counter, Ralph, St. Lambert, Sioux Falls
Cross, Robert, St. Peter, Colman
Frankman, William, Holy Spirit, Sioux Falls
Graff, Francis, St. Ann, Humboldt
Gruhot, Edward, Risen Savior, Brandon
Healy, Thomas, Sacred Heart, Yankton
Holsing, Arvid, St. Thomas the Apostle, Faulkton
Huntington, Michael, St. Joseph Cathedral, Sioux Falls
Knapp, Henry J., St. Mary's, Sioux Falls
Kocer, Albert, St. John the Baptist, Wagner
Kostel, David, SS. Peter and Paul, Pierre
Oliver, Edward B., St. Dominic, Canton
Stevens, Truman, St. Mary, Aberdeen
Vogel, Thomas, St. Patrick, Wakonda
Wagner, Barry, Sacred Heart, Parkston
Walden, James I., Christ the King Parish, Sioux Falls
Wathen, Jerome F., St. Lambert, Sioux Falls
Zephier, Edward P., Jr., St. Paul Indian Mission

INSTITUTIONS LOCATED IN THE DIOCESE

[A] COLLEGES AND UNIVERSITIES

ABERDEEN. *Presentation College*, 57401. Tel: 605-225-1634; Fax: 605-229-8430.
For a complete listing, refer to the Colleges and Universities section.

YANKTON. *Mount Marty College*, 1105 W. 8th St., 57078 Fax: 605-668-1357.
For a complete listing, refer to the Colleges and Universities section.

[B] EDUCATION CENTERS, PRIVATE

CHAMBERLAIN. *St. Joseph Indian School*, N. Main, 57326. Tel: 605-734-3300; Fax: 605-734-3480. Revs. Joseph Haselbauer, S.C.J.; T. Anthony Kluckman, S.C.J.; Bro. David Nagel, S.C.J., Exec. Dir. Brothers 1; Lay Teachers 24; Students 224.

WATERTOWN. *Harmony Hill Center-Mt. Morty Branch Campus*, 57201. Tel: 605-886-6777; Fax: 605-886-2108. Conducted by Benedictine Sisters (Mother of God Monastery, Watertown). Sr. Ramona Fallon, O.S.B., Admin. Sisters 2; Lay Teachers 25; Students 300.

[C] INTER-PAROCHIAL SCHOOLS

SIOUX FALLS. *Sioux Falls Catholic School System*, 3201 S. Kiwanis Ave., 57105. Tel: 605-336-6241. Dr. Thomas Lorang, Supt.
O'Gorman High School, 3201 S. Kiwanis Ave., 57105. Tel: 605-336-3644; Fax: 605-336-9272. Brett Bradfield, Prin.; Rev. Greg Tschakert, Chap. Priests 1; Sisters 2; Lay Teachers 47; Students 705.
St. Joseph Cathedral Elementary & Junior High School, 601 W. 4th St., 57104. Tel: 605-338-1359; Fax: 605-338-2647. Nancy Kramer, Prin. Lay Teachers 20; Students 358.
St. Mary Elementary & Junior High School, 2001 S. 5th Ave., 57105. Tel: 605-334-9881; Fax: 605-334-9224. Collette Broveleit, Prin. Sisters 1; Lay Teachers 24; Students 471.
Christ the King Elementary School, 1801 S. Lake Ave., 57105. Tel: 605-338-5103; Fax: 605-335-1231. Courtney Tielke, Prin. Benedictine Sisters 1; Lay Teachers 18; Students 353.
St. Lambert Elementary School, 1000 S. Bahnson Ave., 57103. Tel: 605-338-7042; Fax: 605-336-8727. Elsie Baye, Prin. Lay Teachers 15; Students 263.
St. Michael Elementary School, 1600 S. Marion Rd., 57106. Tel: 605-361-0021. Lisa Huemoeller, Prin. Lay Teachers 4; Students 90.

ABERDEEN. *Aberdeen Catholic Schools Education Office*, 1400 N. Dakota St., S.E., 57401. Tel: 605-226-2100; Fax: 605-226-0616. Mr. Don Meyer, Supt.
Roncalli Elementary School. (Grades PreK-2), 424 Second Ave. N.E., 57401. Tel: 605-225-3460. Nancy A. Zenk, Prin. Sisters 1; Lay Teachers 8; Students 189.
Roncalli High School, 1400 N. Dakota St., 57401. Tel: 605-225-7440; Fax: 605-226-0616. (Junior and Senior High School). Lay Teachers 23; Students 347.
Roncalli Middle School. (Grades 3-6), 505 Third Ave. S.E., 57401. Tel: 605-229-4100. Nancy A. Zenk, Prin. Lay Teachers 10; Students 181.

[D] GENERAL HOSPITALS

SIOUX FALLS. *McKennan Hospital*, 57117-5045. Tel: 605-339-8000.
For a complete listing, refer to the Hospitals section.

ABERDEEN. *St. Luke's Midland Regional Medical Center*, 57401. Tel: 605-622-5000.
For a complete listing, refer to the Hospitals section.

GETTYSBURG. *Gettysburg Medical Center*, 57442. Tel: 605-765-2488.
For a complete listing, refer to the Hospitals section.

MILBANK. *St. Bernard Providence Hospital*, 57252. Tel: 605-432-4538.
For a complete listing, refer to the Hospitals section.

MITCHELL. *Queen of Peace Hospital*, 525 N. Foster, 57301. Tel: 605-995-2000; Fax: 605-995-2441.
For a complete listing, refer to the Hospitals section.

PARKSTON. *St. Benedict Health Care Center; Borman Manor; Parkston Supervised Living*, 57366. Tel: 605-928-3311.
For a complete listing, refer to the Hospitals section.

PIERRE. *St. Mary's Foundation*, 800 E. Dakota, 57501. Tel: 605-224-3451.
For a complete listing, refer to the Hospitals section.
St. Mary's Healthcare Center of Pierre, South Dakota, 800 E. Dakota, 57501. Tel: 605-224-3100.
For a complete listing, refer to the Hospitals section.

TYNDALL. *St. Michael's Hospital*, 57066. Tel: 605-589-3341.
For a complete listing, refer to the Hospitals section.

YANKTON. *Sacred Heart Health Services*, 501 Summit, 57078. Tel: 605-668-8000.
For a complete listing, refer to the Hospitals section.

[E] HOMES FOR AGED

SIOUX FALLS. *Prince of Peace Retirement Community, Inc.*, 4500 Prince of Peace Pl., 57103. Tel: 605-371-0700.
For a complete listing, refer to the Special Care Facilities section.

ABERDEEN. *Aberdeen Living Center*. 1700 N. Hwy. 281, 57401. Tel: 605-225-7315.
For a complete listing, refer to the Special Care Facilities section.
Mother Joseph Manor, Nursing Care Facility, 1002 N. Jay St., 57401. Tel: 605-229-0550.
For a complete listing, refer to the Special Care Facilities section.

MILBANK. *St. William Home for the Aged*, 57252. Tel: 605-432-4538; Fax: 605-432-5412.
For a complete listing, refer to the Special Care Facilities section.

MITCHELL. *Brady Memorial Home*, 500 S. Ohlman, P.O. Box 430, 57301. Tel: 605-966-7701; Fax: 605-996-5726.
For a complete listing, refer to the Special Care Facilities section.

SISSETON. *Tekakwitha Nursing Center, Inc.*, 6 E. Chestnut, 57262. Tel: 605-693-7693; Fax: 605-698-3091.
For a complete listing, refer to the Special Care Facilities section.

[F] MONASTERIES AND RESIDENCES OF PRIESTS AND BROTHERS

CHAMBERLAIN. *Priests of the Sacred Heart*. P.O. Box 89, 57325. Tel: 605-734-3300; 734-3325. Rev. Joseph Haselbauer, S.C.J.; Bro. David Nagel, S.C.J., Admin. Priests 1; Brothers 2.
St. Joseph Indian School.

MARVIN. *Blue Cloud Abbey*. P.O. Box 98, 57251. Tel: 605-432-5528; Fax: 605-432-4754. Rt. Revs. Thomas Hillenbrand, O.S.B.; Alan Berndt, O.S.B., Retired Abbot; Denis Quinkert, O.S.B., Retired Abbot; Revs. George Lyon, O.S.B., Prior; Daniel Madlon, O.S.B.; Stanislaus Maudlin, O.S.B.; Julius Armbruster, O.S.B.; Thomas Roznowski, O.S.B.; Odo

Gogel, O.S.B.; Lawrence Kratz, O.S.B.; Guy Gau, O.S.B.; Peter Schwartz, O.S.B.; Bede Roman, O.S.B.; John McMullen, O.S.B.; Raymond Otto, O.S.B.; Basil Dilger, O.S.B.; Cletus Miller, O.S.B.; Odilo Burkhardt, O.S.B.; Bernardine Ness, O.S.B.; Paul McHarness, O.S.B.; Theophane Gonnelly, O.S.B.; Larry Barnett, O.S.B.; Christopher Uehlein, O.S.B.; Wilfrid Lambertz, O.S.B.; Pedro Choc, O.S.B.; Francisco Arrivillaga Lemus, O.S.B. Priests 26; Brothers 16.

[G] CONVENTS AND RESIDENCES FOR SISTERS

ABERDEEN. *Presentation Convent*, 57401. Tel: 605-225-0420; Fax: 605-229-8412. Motherhouse and Novitiate of the Sisters of the Presentation of the B.V.M. Sr. Joyce Meyer, P.B.V.M., Pres. Final Professed Sisters 173.

MARTY. *Motherhouse Oblate Sisters of the Blessed Sacrament*. St. Sylvester's Convent, Box 217, 57361-0217. Tel: 605-384-3305. Sr. Patricia Mylott, O.S.B.S. Professed Sisters 7.

MITCHELL. *Sisters of St. Francis of Our Lady of Guadulupe*, 1417 W. Ash, 57301. Private Association of the Faithful. Sr. Marita Pfau, Sister Leader. Professed Sisters 6.

WATERTOWN. *Mother of God Monastery*, 110 28th Ave. S.E., 57201-8418. Motherhouse and Novitiate of Benedictine Sisters. Sr. Sandra Meek, O.S.B., Prioress. Sisters 85.

YANKTON. *Sacred Heart Monastery*, 1005 W. Eighth St., 57078. Tel: 605-668-1011; Fax: 605-668-1511. Motherhouse and Novitiate of the Benedictine Sisters. Sr. Kathryn Easley, O.S.B., Prioress. Chaplains: Revs. Mel Patton, O.S.B.; Denis Quinkert, O.S.B. Sisters 173.

[H] NEWMAN CENTERS

ABERDEEN. *Aquinas Student Center*. Northern State University, 310 15th Ave., S.E., 57401. Tel: 605-229-1011. Rev. Joseph Vogel, Chap.; Michala Heller, Campus Min.

Diocesan Newman Apostolate, 310 15th Ave., S.E., 57401-7505. Rev. Joseph Vogel, Coord.

BROOKINGS. *Pius XII Student Center*. Our Lady of Wisdom Chapel. South Dakota State University, Box 7019 University Station, 57007. Tel: 605-692-9461. Rev. Michael Griffin. Mission. St. Paul, White, 57276.

MADISON. *Dakota State University Newman Center*. Attended by St. Thomas Parish, Madison. 217 N.W. 4th St., 57042. Tel: 605-256-2304.

VERMILLION. *St. Thomas More Catholic Newman Center*. University of South Dakota, 320 Cherry St., 57069. Tel: 605-624-2697. Rev. James Englert, Dir.; Sr. Rosemarie Maly, O.S.B., Assoc. Dir.; Brian Begley, Activities Coord.

[I] MISCELLANEOUS LISTINGS

SIOUX FALLS. *The Banquet*, 300 N. Main Ave., 57102. Tel: 605-335-7066. Carolyn Downs, Dir.

The Berakkah House, 400 Western Ave. N., 57104. Tel: 605-332-4017. Rev. Howard Carroll, Dir.

The Catholic Foundation for Eastern South Dakota, 3100 W 41st St., 57105. Mark Conzemius, Exec. Dir.

Community Outreach, 431 N. Cliff Ave., 57103. Jerry Bohnhoff, Dir.

Good Shepherd Center, 300 N. Main Ave., 57102. Deacon Jim Welden, Dir.

Kateri Indian Center, 300 N. Main Ave., 57104. Tel: 605-335-3321. Marlene Worth, Dir.

Little Flower of Jesus School Foundation, Inc., 1301 N. Dubuque Ave., 57110-6450.

Our Lady of Guadalupe, 1220 E. 8th St., 57103.

St. Francis House, 1301 E. Austin St., 57103. Tel: 605-334-3879. Sr. Bernadette McGowen, O.S.B., Dir.

St. Joseph Catholic Housing, Inc., Catholic Chancery Office, 3100 W. 41st St., 57105. Tel: 605-334-9861. Mr. James Mason, Dir., Catholic Charities.

St. Joseph Catholic Housing - Rolling Hills, Inc.

St. Joseph Catholic Housing - West Creek Woods, Inc.

St. Joseph Catholic Housing - Northridge, Inc.

St. Joseph Catholic Housing - Heritage, Inc.

St. Vincent de Paul Store, 431 N. Cliff Ave., 57103. Tel: 605-335-5823. Nick Feyerisen, Mgr.

Sioux Falls Catholic School Corporation, 3201 S. Kiwanis, 57105; Fax: 605-336-6241.

ALEXANDRIA *Fatima Family Apostolate*, St. Mary of Mercy Church, P.O. Box 158, 57311. Tel: 605-239-4532. Rev. Robert J. Fox, Dir.

MARVIN. *Blue Cloud Abbey Retirement Trust*, P.O. Box 98, 57251-0098. Tel: 605-432-5528. Rev. John McMullen, O.S.B., Treas.

SISSETON. *Tekakwitha Adolescent Treatment Center*, R.R. 2, Box 187, 57262. Tel: 605-698-3935; 800-658-4727. Clayton R. Houff, Exec. Dir.

Tekakwitha Housing Corp, 711 Veteran's Ave., 57262.

Tekakwitha Indian Mission, Inc., 120 E. Chestnut, 57262. Tel: 605-698-7414.

Tekekwitha Fine Arts Center, 401 S. 8th Ave. W., P.O. Box 208, 57262. Tel: 605-698-7058. Harold D. Moore, Curator. Staff 3.

WATERTOWN *Immaculate Conception School Foundation, Inc.*, 309 2nd Ave. S.E., 57201.

Retirement Trust, Mother of God Monastery, 110 28th Ave. S.E., 57201.

St. Ann's Corporation, Mother of God Monastery, 110 28th Ave. S.E., 57201. Tel: 605-886-6799. Sr. Amanda Wolf, Exec. Dir.

Benet Place. Independent Living. 100 28th Ave., S.E. Tel: 605-886-9177. Units 39; Staff 4.

YANKTON. *Benedictine Center, Inc.*, 1005 W. 8th, 57078.

Benedictine Health Foundation, Inc., 1017 W. Fifth, 57078. Kelly Kathol, Exec. Dir.

Benedictine Health System, 1005 W. 8th St., 57078. Tel: 605-668-1503; Fax: 605-668-1559.

The House of Mary Shrine, Inc., Box 455, Lewis & Clark Lake, 57078-0455. Russell Weller, Pres. Bd. Dirs.; Rev. Rodney Farke, Spiritual Dir.

RELIGIOUS INSTITUTES OF MEN REPRESENTED IN THE DIOCESE

For further details refer to the corresponding bracketed number in the Religious Institutes of Men or Women section.

[0200]—*Benedictine Monks*. (Aurora, IL; Marvin, SD).—O.S.B.

[]—*Carmelite*. (India).

[1130]—*Congregation of the Priests of the Sacred Heart*. (Hales Corners, WI).—S.C.J.

[0690]—*Jesuit Fathers and Brothers*. (Wisconsin Prov.).—S.J.

[0910]—*Oblates of Mary Immaculate*. (Central Prov.).—O.M.I.

[0560]—*Third Order Regular of Saint Francis*. (Loretto, PA).—T.O.R.

[]—*Vincentian*. (India).

RELIGIOUS INSTITUTES OF WOMEN REPRESENTED IN THE DIOCESE

[0230]—*Benedictine Sisters of Pontifical Jurisdiction*. (Yankton, Watertown, SD).—O.S.B.

[0940]—*Daughters of St. Mary of Providence*.—D.S.M.P.

[]—*Dominican*. Grand Rapids.

[3010]—*Oblate Sisters of the Blessed Sacrament*.—O.S.B.S.

[3320]—*Sisters of the Presentation of the B.V.M.*—P.B.V.M.

[1720]—*Sisters of the Third Order Regular of St. Francis of the Congregation of Our Lady of Lourdes*.—O.S.F.

INTER-PAROCHIAL CEMETERIES

SIOUX FALLS. *St. Michael*, 3001 N. Cliff, 57104. Tel: 605-338-3376.

NECROLOGY

† Sampson, Rev. Msgr. Francis, (Retired). —Died Jan. 28, 1996.

Diocese of Spokane

(Dioecesis Spokanensis)

Most Reverend

WILLIAM S. SKYLSTAD, D.D.

Bishop of Spokane; ordained May 21, 1960; appointed Bishop of Yakima February 22, 1977; consecrated and installed May 12, 1977; transferred to Spokane April 17, 1990; succeeded to the See April 27, 1990. *Office: W. 1023 Riverside Ave., P.O. Box 1453, Spokane, WA, 99210-1453. Res., W. 1025 Cleveland, Spokane, WA, 99205-3320.*

Catholic Pastoral Center: W. 1023 Riverside Ave., P.O. Box 1453, Spokane, WA, 99210-1453. Tel.: 509-358-7300.

Solemnly consecrated to the Immaculate Heart of Mary on December 8, 1948.

ESTABLISHED DECEMBER 17, 1913.

Square Miles 24,356.

Corporate Title: *"The Catholic Bishop of Spokane, a Corporation Sole."*

Comprises the following Counties in the State of Washington: Okanogan, Ferry, Stevens, Pend Oreille, Lincoln, Spokane, Adams, Whitman, Franklin, Walla Walla, Columbia, Garfield and Asotin.

For legal titles of parishes and diocesan institutions, consult the Chancery Office.

STATISTICAL OVERVIEW

Personnel	
Bishop	1
Retired Abbots	1
Priests: Diocesan Active in Diocese	47
Priests: Active Outside Diocese	5
Priests: Diocesan in Foreign Missions	1
Priests: Retired, Sick or Absent	31
Number of Diocesan Priests	84
Religious Priests in Diocese	97
Extern Priests in Diocese	4
Ordinations:	
Diocesan Priests	2
Permanent Deacons in Diocese	37
Total Brothers	13
Total Sisters	299
Parishes	
Parishes	78
With Resident Pastor:	
Resident Diocesan Priests	42
Resident Religious Priests	7
Without Resident Pastor:	
Administered by Priests	29
Administered by Women Religious	1
Administered by Lay People	1
Missions	5
Pastoral Centers	1
Professional Ministry Personnel:	
Brothers	1
Sisters	2
Lay Ministers	5

Welfare	
Catholic Hospitals	7
Total Assisted	323,693
Health Care Centers	2
Total Assisted	17,008
Homes for the Aged	11
Total Assisted	1,521
Residential Care of Children	14
Total Assisted	896
Day Care and Extended Day Care Centers	14
Total Assisted	811
Specialized Homes	2
Total Assisted	212
Special Centers for Social Services	4
Total Assisted	14,032
Other Institutions	1
Total Assisted	693
Educational	
Seminaries, Diocesan	1
Students from This Diocese	12
Students from Other Diocese	5
Diocesan Students in Other Seminaries	8
Seminaries, Religious	1
Students Religious	17
Total Seminarians	37
Colleges and Universities	1
Total Students	4,416
High Schools, Diocesan and Parish	1
Total Students	881

High Schools, Private	1
Total Students	434
Elementary Schools, Diocesan and Parish	16
Total Students	3,206
Catechesis/Religious Education:	
High School Students	1,846
Elementary Students	4,536
Total Students Under Catholic Instruction	15,356
Teachers in the Diocese:	
Priests	17
Scholastics	3
Brothers	13
Sisters	4
Lay Teachers	81
Vital Statistics	
Receptions into the Church:	
Infant Baptism Totals	1,323
Adult Baptism Totals	321
Received into Full Communion	117
First Communions	787
Confirmations	384
Marriages:	
Catholic	291
Interfaith	159
Total Marriages	450
Deaths	1,631
Total Catholic Population	80,102
Total Population	708,891

Former Bishops—Most Rev. A. F. SCHINNER, D.D., cons. Bishop of Superior, July 25, 1905; resigned from that See, Jan. 15, 1913; appt. first Bishop of Spokane, March 18, 1914; resigned Dec. 17, 1925, and made Titular Bishop of Sala; died Feb. 7, 1937.—Most Rev. CHARLES D. WHITE, D.D., ord. Sept. 24, 1910; appt. Dec. 20, 1926; cons. Feb. 24, 1927; died Sept. 25, 1955.—Most Rev. BERNARD J. TOPEL, D.D., Ph.D., appt. coadjutor Bishop Aug. 9, 1955; cons. Sept. 21, 1955; succeeded to to the See Sept. 25, 1955; retired April 11, 1978; died Oct. 22, 1986.—Most Rev. LAWRENCE H. WELSH, D.D., ord. May 26, 1962; appt. Bishop of Spokane Nov. 7, 1978; cons. and installed Dec. 14, 1978; resigned April 17, 1990; appt. Auxiliary of St. Paul-Minneapolis, Nov. 5, 1991.

Vicar General—Rev. JOHN M. STEINER, *P.O. Box 1453, Spokane, 99210-1453.* Tel: 509-358-7303; 466-0220; 326-8748.

Catholic Pastoral Center—W. 1023 Riverside Ave., P.O. Box 1453, Spokane, 99210-1453. Tel: 509-358-7300; Fax: 509-358-7302. Office Hours: Mon.-Fri. 9-5.

Moderator of the Curia—Rev. JOHN M. STEINER, *P.O. Box 1453, Spokane, 99210-1453.* Tel: 509-358-7303.

Chancellor—Rev. MARK PAUTLER, *P.O. Box 1453, Spokane, 99210.* Tel: 509-358-7336.

Archivists—Revs. EDWARD J. KOWRACH; THEODORE BRADLEY, *P.O. Box 1453, Spokane, 99210-1453.* Tel: 509-358-7300.

Diocesan Tribunal—W. 1023 Riverside Ave., P.O. Box 1453, Spokane, 99210. Tel: 509-358-7336.

Judicial Vicar—Rev. MARK PAUTLER, J.C.L.

Defensor Vinculi—Rev. JOHN M. STEINER; JUDY ELLIFRITT, Sec.

Diocesan Consultors/Presbyteral Council—Revs. JOHN M. STEINER; DARRIN CONNALL; THOMAS KHUE; OTTO KOLTZENBURG; JAMES MANGAN; JAMES KUHNS; ROBERT LYONS, S.J.; JAMES MCGREEVY; MARK PAUTLER; RICHARD ROOT; JOHN SAND; EUGENE TRACY; JAKE MORTON, S.J.; PAUL VEVIK.

Pastoral Council—Revs. JOHN M. STEINER; MARTY MARKARIAN; Sr. ANNE BOSSERMAN, S.N.J.M.; MIKE CAREY; JUDY DAVIS; ERNEST DOROW; Sr. MAUREEN HEALY, O.P.; JUANITA CONTRERAS; MARTY MARKARIAN; KENNETH DUNLAP; ANN FIGENSHOW; GERALD MOSMAN; PAUL KIENBAUM; JULIE KIENBAUM; JON MCFARLAND; LUISA ORELLENA-WESTBROOK; EILEEN PERKINS; LORETTA MOSMAN; SHIRLEY PANTALEO; GEORGE VASIL; JOHN VLAHOVICH; JAMES WYNNE; Rev. TERENCE TULLY; PATTI VAN HEEL.

Diocesan Offices and Directors

Administrative Division: Diocesan Business Affairs—Sr. BERNADETTE BOTCH, S.P., Bishop Sec., *W. 1023 Riverside Ave., P.O. Box 1453, Spokane, 99210.* Tel: 509-358-7300; Fax: 509-358-7302.

Director of Fiscal Services—MERRILIN FULTON, *P.O. Box 1453, Spokane, 99210-1453.* Tel: 509-358-7320.

Catholic Foundation-Development Office—STEVEN C. KOCHARHOOK, Ph.D, *P.O. Box 1453, Spokane, 99210.* Tel: 509-358-4280.

Computer Office—JERRY M. DUFRESNE, *P.O. Box 1453, Spokane, 99210-1453.* Tel: 509-358-7346.

Administrative Division: Catholic Schools—Bishop's Secretary: Mr. DUANE SCHAFER, Supt., *Office of Education, P.O. Box 1453, Spokane, 99210.* Tel: 509-358-7330.

Administrative Division: Evangelization and Ministries Formation—BETTY NEWSTROM, Bishop's Sec., *P.O. Box 1453: Spokane, 99210-1453.* Tel: 509-358-7311.

Parish Services Office—BETTY NEWSTROM, Dir., *P.O. Box 1453, Spokane, 99210.* Tel: 409-358-7311.

Communications Office—ERIC MEISFJORD, Dir. & Editor, *Inland Register, P.O. Box 1453, Spokane, 99210-1453.* Tel: 509-358-7340. NANCY LOBERG, Advertising Mgr. Tel: 509-358-7343.

Charismatic Renewal—Rev. DANIEL WETZLER, *St. Paschal Parish, 7404 E. Marietta Ave., Spokane, 99212.* Tel: 509-924-4871.

Ecumenical Relations—Rev. THOMAS CASWELL, *Sacred Heart Parish, N.E. 440 Ash St., Pullman, 99163.* Tel: 509-332-5312.

Spanish Speaking Apostolates—Rev. HELIODORO LUCATERO, *Sacred Heart Parish, P.O. Box 548, Brewster, 98812.* Tel: 509-689-2931.

Vietnamese Apostolate—Vietnamese Catholic Community of the Diocese of Spokane, Revs. JOACHIM L. HEIN; TOM KHUE, *St. Anthony, P.O. Box C, Newport, 99156.* Tel: 509-447-4231.

Vocation Director—Rev. RICHARD ROOT, *Bishop White Seminary, 429 E. Sharp, Spokane, 99202.* Tel: 509-487-6363.

Diocesan Liturgical Commission—Rev. STEVE DUBLINSKI, St. Charles Parish: *4515 N. Alberta, Spokane, 99205.* Tel: 509-327-9573.

Permanent Deaconate Formation—Dr. JOHN BYRNE, Ph.D., Dir., *E. 502 Boone Ave., Spokane, 99258.* Tel: 509-328-4220.

Deacon Council—Deacon JOHN SICILIA, *8112 N. Howard Dr., Spokane, 99208.* Tel: 509-466-0220.

Catholic Committee on Scouting—Rev. TERENCE TULLY, Chap., *221 E. Rockwood Blvd., Apt.308, Spokane, 99202-1200.* Tel: 509-458-7674.

Bishop White Seminary—Rev. RICHARD ROOT, Dir. Seminarians & Rector, *E. 429 Sharp Ave., Spokane, 99202.* Tel: 509-326-3255.

Administrative Division: Social Ministries—Mrs. DONNA HANSON, Bishop's Sec., *W. 1023 Riverside, P.O. Box 1453, Spokane, 99210-1453.* Tel: 509-358-4250.

Catholic Family Services—MICHAEL T. RYAN, Dir., *W. 1023 Riverside, P.O. Box 1453, Spokane, 99210-1453.* Tel: 509-358-4260.

St. Vincent de Paul Society—*E. 2901 Trent Ave., Spokane, 99202.* Tel: 509-535-2491.

Censor Liborum—Rev. MICHAEL SAVELESKY, Ph.D., *P.O. Box 1453, Spokane, 99210-1453.* Tel: 509-456-7140.

Continuing Education of Priests—Rev. JAMES KUHNS, Chm., *Our Lady of Fatima Parish, 1517 E. 33rd, Spokane, 99203.* Tel: 509-747-7213.

Detention Ministry—Sr. MYRTA ITURRIAGA, S.P., *P.O. Box 1453, Spokane, 99210.* Tel: 509-358-7315.

Director of Cemeteries—DENNIS FAIRBANK, *Catholic Cemeteries of Spokane, P.O. Box 18006, Spokane, 99208-0006.* Tel: 509-467-5496.

Holy Childhood, Pontifical Association—Rev. MARK PAUTLER, *W. 1023 Riverside Ave., P.O. Box 1453, Spokane, 99210.* Tel: 509-358-7336.

Immaculate Heart Retreat Center—Sr. K.C. YOUNG, O.P., Dir., *S. 6910 Ben Burr Rd., Spokane, 99223.* Tel: 509-448-1224.

Priests' Personnel Board—Revs. THOMAS CASWELL, Chm. MARK PAUTLER, Sec. JOHN ROMPA; JOSEPH PASH; PAUL VEVIK; TOM MELE, *P.O. Box 1453, Spokane, 99210-1453.* Tel: 509-358-7336.

Propagation of the Faith—Rev. MARK PAUTLER, *W. 1023 Riverside Ave., P.O. Box 1453, Spokane, 99210.* Tel: 509-358-7336.

CLERGY, PARISHES, MISSIONS AND PAROCHIAL SCHOOLS

CITY OF SPOKANE
(Spokane County)

1—CATHEDRAL OF OUR LADY OF LOURDES, Rev. James M. Ribble, Ph.D.; Deacons J. Andrew Phelps, M.D.; Charles W. Fosmire.
Res., 1115 W. Riverside Ave., 99201. Tel: 509-358-4292; Fax: 509-358-4277.

2—ASSUMPTION OF THE BLESSED VIRGIN MARY, Rev. Joseph W. Bell.
Office: 3624 W. Indian Trail Rd., 99208. Tel: 509-326-0144; 326-6951.
School—Tel: 509-328-1115; Fax: 509-328-1449. Sally Merriwether, Prin.
Lay Teachers 14; Students 320.
Station—Tum Tum, Our Lady of the Lake, Tel: 509-276-6165.

3—MARY QUEEN, Rt. Rev. Adrian Parcher, O.S.B.
Res., E. 3423 Carlisle Ave., 99207. Tel: 509-483-4384.

4—OUR LADY OF FATIMA, Rev. James Kuhns; Deacons John Byrne; Walter Weid.
Res., E. 1517-33rd Ave., 99203. Tel: 509-747-7213; Fax: 509-747-7217.
School—All Saints Interparochial, (Grades 5-8). Tel: 509-624-5712; Fax: 509-624-7752. Ms. Kathy Hicks, Prin.
Lay Teachers 12; Students 180.

5—SACRED HEART, Rev. George Haspedis; Deacon Dan Ritchie.
Res., E. 219 Rockwood Blvd., 99202. Tel: 509-747-5810.

6—ST. ALOYSIUS, Mr. Donald Weber, Parochial Admin.; Revs. L. Patrick Carroll, S.J.; Thomas Williams, S.J.; Deacons Jack Back; James E. Murphy.
Res., 330 E. Boone Ave., 99202. Tel: 509-484-6496.
School—E. 611 Mission, 99202. Tel: 509-489-7825. Richard Shea, Prin.
Montessori Education Center—Susan Boughton, Dir.
Lay Teachers 14; Students 266.

7—ST. ANN, Linda Kobe-Smith, Admin.; Rev. James Dallen.
Res., W. 1104 Heroy Ave., 99205. Tel: 509-325-9756.
Church—E. 2120 First Ave., 99202. Tel: 509-535-3031.

8—ST. ANTHONY, Rev. Msgr. John Donnelly.
Res., N. 2320 Cedar St., 99205. Tel: 509-327-1162; Fax: 509-328-8728.
School—Trinity Interparochial School. Serving St. Anthony and St. Joseph. Tel: 509-327-9369. Mike Trudeau, Prin.
Lay Teachers 8; Students 144.
Educare Center—.
Lay Teachers 6; Students 28.

9—ST. AUGUSTINE, Rev. Robert A. Pearson; Deacons Kenneth Dunlap; Gary Cooper, Pastoral Assoc.
Res., 428 W. 19th Ave., 99203. Tel: 509-747-4421.
School—Cataldo Catholic Interparochial, Tel: 509-624-8759; Fax: 509-747-9086.
Lay Teachers 21; Students 384.

10—ST. CHARLES, Rev. Steven L. Dublinski.
Res., N. 4515 Alberta St., 99205. Tel: 509-327-9573.
School—Tel: 509-327-9575; Fax: 509-328-4575. Marquita Yriarte, Prin.
Lay Teachers 18; Students 311.

11—ST. FRANCIS OF ASSISI, FRIARS, Revs. Stephen C. Barnufsky, O.F.M.; Sebastian Drake, O.F.M.; Bro. Franklin Fong, O.F.M.; Deacons Stephen Barnufsky, Sr.; Donald Bentley. In res., Rev. William Sisk, O.F.M.
Res., W. 1104 Heroy Ave., 99205. Tel: 509-325-1321.

12—ST. FRANCIS XAVIER, Rev. Paul Vevik.
Res., 545 E. Providence Ave., 99207. Tel: 509-487-6363.
School—Tel: 509-487-1571. Mr. Richard Winkler, Prin.
Lay Teachers 5; Students 92.

13—ST. JOHN VIANNEY, Rev. Tyrone J. Schaff; Deacon Derwood Braungardt. In res., Rev. Charles D. Skok.
Office: 503 N. Walnut Rd., 99206. Tel: 509-926-5428; Fax: 509-922-5282.
School—(Grades Prek-8) N. 501 Walnut Rd., 99206. Tel: 509-926-7987. Dr. Judith Morbeck, Prin.
Lay Teachers 14; Students 228.

14—ST. JOSEPH, Sr. Ann Pizelo, S.N.J.M., Parish Admin.; Rev. Mark Pautler.
Res., W. 1503 Dean Ave., 99201. Tel: 509-328-4841.
School—Trinity Interparochial School. (See listing under St. Anthony).

15—ST. MARY, Revs. Frank J. Bach; Edward Borchardt; Deacons Richard Malone; James Blaine.
Res., S. 304 Adams Rd., 99216. Tel: 509-928-3210; Fax: 509-926-9550.
School—14601 E. 4th Ave., 99216. Tel: 509-924-4300. Mrs. Carol Speltz, Prin.
Lay Teachers 14; Students 236.

16—ST. PASCHAL, Rev. Daniel E. Wetzler; Deacon John Crandall.
Res., 7404 E. Marietta Ave., 99212. Tel: 509-924-4871; Fax: 509-924-8731.
School—N. 2521 Park Rd., 99212. Tel: 509-924-5090; Fax: 509-924-6106. Sr. Loretta Giampietri, F.S.P.A., Prin.
Sisters 1; Lay Teachers 5; Students 73.
Educare Center—Tel: 509-922-7616. Dawn Davis, Dir. & Prog. Supr.
Lay Teachers 5; Students 73.

17—ST. PATRICK, Rev. Joseph Weitensteiner.
Res., N. 5021 Nelson St., 99207. Tel: 509-487-1325.
School—Tel: 509-487-2830. Ms. Joanne Duffy, Prin.
Sisters 1; Lay Teachers 8; Students 200.
Convent—N. 5008 Lacey St., 99207. Tel: 509-487-1166.

18—ST. PETER, Rev. Eugene Tracy.
Res., 3520 E. 18th Ave., 99223-3814. Tel: 509-534-2227; Fax: 509-534-5522.
School—All Saints Interparochial, (Grades K-4). Tel: 509-534-1098; Fax: 509-534-1529. Ms. Kathy Hicks, Prin.
Lay Teachers 10; Students 211.

19—ST. THOMAS MORE, Rev. John M. Steiner; Deacon John F. Sicilia.
Res., N. 8112 Howard Dr., 99208. Tel: 509-466-0220; Fax: 509-466-7738.
School—Tel: 509-466-3811; Fax: 509-466-3316. Ann Doherty, Prin.
Lay Teachers 11; Students 247.

OUTSIDE THE CITY OF SPOKANE

Brewster, Okanogan Co., Sacred Heart, Rev. Pat Kerst.
Res., Box 548, 98812. Tel: 509-689-2931.

Cheney, Spokane Co., St. Rose of Lima, Rev. James Severyn Westbrook.
Res., N. 460 Fifth St., 99004. Tel: 509-235-6229.

Chewelah, Stevens Co., St. Mary of the Rosary, Rev. Albert Grasher, Jr.
Res., P.O. Box 26, 99109. Tel: 509-937-2452.
Church—E. 504 Main St., Box 26, 99109. Tel: 509-935-3028. [CEM]

Clarkston, Asotin Co., Holy Family, Rev. Leonard Forsmann.
Res., 917 Chestnut St., 99403. Tel: 509-758-6102; Fax: 509-758-4997. [CEM]
School—(Grades PreK-6). Tel: 509-758-6621. Mrs. Sharon Clizer, Prin.
Lay Teachers 8; Students 136.
Educare Preschool—.
Students 55.

Clayton, Stevens Co., St. Joseph, Rev. Edward F. Caffrey.
Mailing Address: N. 316 Main St., P.O. Box 749, Deer Park, 99006. Tel: 509-276-2948.

Colbert, Spokane Co., St. Joseph, Rev. Michael Kwiatkowski.
Res., 3720 E. Colbert Rd., 99005. Tel: 509-466-4991.

Colfax, Whitman Co., St. Patrick, Rev. Felix P. Lorge.
Res., S. 1108 Main St., 99111. Tel: 509-397-3921.

Colton, Whitman Co., St. Gall, Rev. Patrick MacMahon.
Res., P.O. Box 108, 99113. Tel: 509-229-3548. [CEM]
School—Guardian Angel-St. Boniface Interparochial, Tel: 509-299-3579.
Lay Teachers 5; Students 58.

Colville, Stevens Co., Immaculate Conception, Rev. Darrin Connall.
Res., 320 N. Maple St., 99114. Tel: 509-684-6223; Fax: 509-684-8084.

Connell, Franklin Co., St. Vincent, Rev. Richard Poole.
Res., Box 1030, 99326. Tel: 509-234-2262; Fax: 509-234-0295.

Coulee Dam, Okanogan Co., St. Benedict. Closed. Sacramental records maintained at St. Henry's, Grand Coulee (Diocese of Yakima).
Mailing Address: 509 Grand Ave. W., Box 108, Grand Coulee, 99133. Tel: 509-633-1180.

Curlew, Ferry Co., St. Patrick, Rev. George Morbeck.
Res., Box 333, Republic, 99166. Tel: 509-775-3935.

Cusick, Kalispel Indian Reservation, Our Lady of Sorrows, Rev. Thomas L.T. Khue.
Res., W. 612 First St., Box C, Newport, 99156. Tel: 509-447-4231.

Davenport, Lincoln Co., Immaculate Conception, Rev. John P. Krier (GF); Deacon David Schutt.
Res., 1310 Adams, P.O. Box 910, 99122. Tel: 509-725-1761. [CEM]

Dayton, Columbia Co., St. Joseph, Rev. John P. Sand.
Res., 112 S. First St., 99328-1307. Tel: 509-382-2311.

Deer Park, Spokane Co., St. Mary's Presentation, Rev. Edward F. Caffrey.
Res., N. 316 Main St., P.O. Box 749, 99006. Tel: 509-276-2948. [CEM]

Eltopia, Franklin Co., St. Paul, Rev. Richard Poole.
Res., 14181 Glade North Rd., 99330. Tel: 509-297-4371.

Ford, Stevens Co., St. Philip Benizi, Rev. Jake Morton, S.J.
Res., Indian-Spokane Reservation, Box 214, Wellpinit, 99040. Tel: 509-258-7233.

Harrington, Lincoln Co., St. Francis of Assisi, Rev. John P. Krier (GF); Deacon David Schutt.
Res., P.O. Box 166, 99134. Tel: 509-253-4310.

Inchelium, Ferry Co., St. Michael's Mission, Rev. Jake Morton, S.J.; Jenny-Ann Edgen, Admin.
Res., Box 122, 99138. Tel: 509-722-4592.

Ione, Pend Oreille Co., St. Bernard, Rev. Thomas L.T. Khue.
Mailing Address: Box 731, 99139. Tel: 509-447-4231.
Res., W. 612 First St., Box C, Newport, 99156. Tel: 509-447-4231.

Keller, Ferry Co., St. Rose of Lima, Rev. Robert Erickson, S.J.; Deacon Archie Arnold.
Res., Box 70, Nespelem, 99155. Tel: 509-634-4249.

Kettle Falls, Stevens Co., Sacred Heart, Rev. Darrin Connall.
Mailing Address: Box 303, 99141. Tel: 509-738-2356.

Lacrosse, Whitman Co., St. Joseph, Rev. Felix P. Lorge.
Res., St. Patrick Parish, S. 1018 Main St., Colfax, 99111. Tel: 509-397-3921.

Lind, Adams Co., St. Ambrose, Rev. James McGreevy.
Res., E. 404 Fifth Ave., Ritzville, 99169. Tel: 509-659-0437.

Medical Lake, Spokane Co., St. Anne, Rev. Tom Mele; Deacon Robert King.
Res., E. 708 Lake St., Box 125, 99022. Tel: 509-299-3585.

Metaline Falls, Pend Oreille Co., St. Joseph, Rev. Thomas L.T. Khue.
Mailing Address: P.O. Box 417, 99153. Tel: 509-446-2651.
Res., W. 612 First St., Box C, Newport, 99156. Tel: 509-447-4231.

Nespelem, Okanogan Co., Sacred Heart Mission, Rev. Robert Erickson, S.J.
Res., Box 70, 99155. Tel: 509-634-4249. [CEM]

Newport, Pend Oreille Co., St. Anthony, Rev. Thomas L.T. Khue; Deacon William Sando.
Res., W. 612 First St., Box C, 99156. Tel: 509-447-4231.

Northport, Stevens Co., Pure Heart of Mary, Rev. Darrin Connall.
Res., Box 29, 99157. Tel: 509-732-4552.

Oakesdale, Whitman Co., St. Catherine of Alexandria, Rev. Eugene Glatt.
Res., Box 8, Rosalia, 99170. Tel: 509-523-4011.

Odessa, Lincoln Co., St. Joseph, Rev. Edward Marier.
Mailing Address & Res.—P.O. Box 106, Wilbur, 99185. Tel: 509-647-2380.

Okanogan-Omak, Okanogan Co., Our Lady of the Valley, Rev. Robert D. Turner.
Res., Rte. 2, N. 2511 Elmway, Okanogan, 98840. Tel: 509-422-5049.

Omak, Okanogan Co., St. Mary Mission, Rev. Robert Erickson, S.J.; Sr. Suzanne Moynihan, Pastoral Assoc.
Res., Rte. 2, Box 66A, 98841. Tel: 509-826-6401. [CEM]

St. Joseph, Rev. Robert Erickson, S.J.
Mailing Address: 6th & Jackson, Rte. 2, P.O. Box 12, 98841.
Res., 323 Edmonds, 98841. Tel: 509-826-6401.

Oroville, Okanogan Co., Immaculate Conception, Rev. Kevin Codd.
Res., 1715 Main St., Box 340, 98844. Tel: 509-476-2110.

Othello, Adams Co., Sacred Heart, Rev. Heliodoro Lucatero; Deacons Antonio Beraza; Joel Pruneda.
Res., E. 616 Juniper St., 99344. Tel: 509-488-5653.

Otis Orchards, Spokane Co., St. Joseph, Rev. James Mangan.
Res., 4521 N. Arden Rd., 99027-9358. Tel: 509-926-7133.

Pasco, Franklin Co., St. Patrick, Revs. Pedro Ramirez-Alejos; Rory Pitstick; Deacons Andres Espinoza; Robert Kalinowski; Gary Franz; Juanita Contreras, Pastoral Assoc.
Res., 1320 W. Henry, 99301. Tel: 509-547-8841.
School—1016 N. 14th Ave., 99301. Tel: 509-547-7261. Patricia Wilson, Prin.
Lay Teachers 9; Students 220.

Pomeroy, Garfield Co., Holy Rosary, Rev. John P. Sand.
Mailing Address: Rte. 1, Box 4, 99347-9702.
Res., 634 High St., 99347. Tel: 509-843-3801. [CEM]

Pullman, Whitman Co., Sacred Heart, Rev. Thomas C. Caswell.
Office: N.E. 440 Ash St., 99163. Tel: 509-332-5312.

Reardan, Lincoln Co., St. Michael, Rev. John P. Krier (GF); Deacon David Schutt.
Mailing Address: P.O. Box 451, Rearden, 99029. Tel: 509-725-1761.
Res., 455 Cottonwood, 99029.

Republic, Ferry Co., Immaculate Conception, Rev. George H. Morbeck.
Res., 756 S. Portland, 99166. Tel: 509-775-3935.

Ritzville, Adams Co., St. Agnes, Rev. James V. McGreevy.
Res., E. 404 Fifth Ave., 99169. Tel: 509-659-0437.

Rockford, Spokane Co., St. Joseph,
Res., Box 54, 99030. Tel: 509-291-3481.

Rosalia, Whitman Co., Holy Rosary, Rev. Eugene Glatt.
Res., P.O. Box 8, N. 600 Whitman Ave., 99170. Tel: 509-523-4011.

St. John, Whitman Co., Our Lady of Perpetual Help, Rev. Eugene Glatt.
Mailing Address: P.O. Box 325, 99171.
Res., P.O. Box 8, Rosalia, 99170. Tel: 509-523-4011.

Sprague, Lincoln Co., Mary Queen of Heaven, Rev. James V. McGreevy.
Res., E. 404 Fifth Ave., Ritzville, 99160. Tel: 509-659-0437. [CEM]

Springdale, Stevens Co., Sacred Heart, Rev. Albert Grasher, Jr.
Res., P.O. Box 188, Valley, 99181. Tel: 509-937-2452.

Tekoa, Whitman Co., Sacred Heart, Rev. Eugene Glatt.
Res., P.O.Box 8, Rosalia, 99170. Tel: 509-523-4011. [CEM]

Tonasket, Okanogan Co., Holy Rosary, Rev. Kevin Codd.
Res., 1715 Main St., Box 340, Oroville, 98844. Tel: 509-476-2110.

Twisp, Okanogan Co., St. Genevieve, Rev. Pat Kerst; Deacon Charles Breslin.
Res., P.O. Box 6, 98856. Tel: 509-997-4201.

Uniontown, Whitman Co., St. Boniface, Rev. Patrick MacMahon.
Res., P.O. Box 108, Colton, 99113. Tel: 509-229-3548. [CEM]
School—Guardian Angel-St. Boniface Interparochial. See St. Gall, Colton.

Usk, Pend Oreille Co., St. Jude, Rev. Thomas L.T. Khue.
Res., W. 612 First St., Box C, Newport, 99156. Tel: 509-447-4231.

Valley, Stevens Co., Holy Ghost, Rev. Albert Grasher, Jr.
Res., P.O. Box 188, 99181. Tel: 509-937-2452.
Station—Jump-off Joe, Stevens Co., St. Joseph.

Waitsburg, Walla Walla Co., St. Mark, Rev. John P. Sand.
Res., 112 S. First St., Dayton, 99328-1307. Tel: 509-382-2311.

Walla Walla, Walla Walla Co., Assumption of the Blessed Virgin Mary, Rev. Otto Koltzenburg.
Res., 2098 E. Alder St., 99362. Tel: 509-525-8163.
School—Assumption Interparochial, Tel: 509-525-9283. Mrs. Michele Acock, Prin.
Lay Teachers 13; Students 204.

St. Francis of Assisi, Revs. Michael Savelesky, Ph.D.; Timothy Hayes; Sr. Sharon Bongiorno, F.S.P.A., Pastoral Min.
Res., 722 W. Alder St., 99362. Tel: 509-525-1663; Fax: 509-529-7849.
Sisters 2.

St. Patrick, Revs. Michael Savelesky, Ph.D.; Timothy Hayes. Pastoral Assocs.: Sr. Karen Dunham; Deacons Olegario Reyes; Bob Dalecki.
Office: 425 W. Alder St., 99362-2811.
Res., 408 W. Poplar St., 99362. Tel: 509-525-1602.

Washtunca, Adams Co., Holy Trinity, Rev. James V. McGreevy.
Res., E. 404 Fifth St., Ritzville, 99169. Tel: 509-659-0437.

Wellpinit, Stevens Co., Sacred Heart, Rev. Jake Morton, S.J.
Res., Indian-Spokane Reservation, Box 214, 99040. Tel: 509-258-7233. [CEM]

Westend, Stevens Co., Our Lady of Lourdes, Rev. Jake Morton, S.J.
Res., Indian-Spokane Reservation, P.O. Box 214, Wellpinit, 99040. Tel: 509-258-7233.

Wilbur, Lincoln Co., Sacred Heart, Rev. Edward Marier.
Res., P.O. Box 106, 99185. Tel: 509-647-2380.

Chaplains of Public Institutions

SPOKANE. *U.S. Veterans Hospital*. Rev. George McCabe.
WALLA WALLA. *U.S. Veterans Hospital*. Vacant.
Washington State Penitentiary. Served by priests of Walla Walla.

Special Ministry:
Reverend Fathers—
Birk, John, Our Lady of Lourdes Health Center, Pasco
Venneri, Michael D., Sacred Heart Medical Center, Spokane

On Duty Outside the Diocese:
Reverend Fathers—
Baronti, David
Hein, Joachim Le Quang
McGrann, John

Military Chaplains:
Reverend Fathers—
Eis, Charles, U.S. Navy
Floch, W. Roy, U.S. Army

Absent on Leave:
Reverend Fathers—
Boulden, Garry
Hemenway, Richard

Retired:
Reverend Monsignors—
Mertens, Arthur, E. 221 Rockwood Blvd., No. 320, Spokane, WA 99202
Rosage, David E., 221 Rockwood Blvd., No. 222, Spokane, WA 99202
Reverend Fathers—
Barry, Bernard J., E221 Rockwood Blvd., #318, Spokane, WA 99202
Beaver, Reinard W., 1101 Powell St., Steilacoon, WA 98388
Bradley, Theodore F.X., 700 W. 7th Ave., Apt. 801, Spokane, WA 99204
Brennan, William J., 2030 Delaware, Walla Walla, WA 99362
Breznikar, Victor, 1018 Whitman St., #111, Walla Walla, WA 99362-3475
Donnelly, Sean, 1 Parkview, Freshford Rd., Kilkenny, Ireland
Dugan, William M., 272 Kennedy St., No. 48, Chula Vista, CA 92011
Flour, Anton, 14819 E. Mission, Spokane, WA 99216-1960
Grant, James, W. 217 Spokane Falls, No. 1802, Spokane, WA 99201
Hanley, William, Killula, Newmarket-on-Fergus, Claire Co., Ireland
Helfenstein, Maurice R., 14819 E. Mission, Spokane, WA 99216-1960
Hullings, Clifford, 3110 E. Chattaroy Rd. #43, Chattaroy, WA 99003
Kelley, Joseph, 221 E. Rockford Blvd., Apt. 104, Spokane, WA 99202-1200
Kelley, N. F., 629 S. Main St., #7, Fond du Lac, WI 54935
Kowrach, Edward, 530 Flora Rd., Veradale, WA 99037
McCabe, George, W. 1224 Riverside Ave., Apt. 603, Spokane, WA 99201
O'Brien, John P., P.O. Box 1808, Santa Rosa, CA 95402
O'Dea, John W., Ballingaddyworth, Kilmallock, Limerick Co., Ireland
O'Malley, James J., Kilsallagh, Westport, Mayo Co., Ireland
Pash, Joseph, E. 221 Rockwood Blvd., No. 204, Spokane, WA 99202
Rompa, John, 4423 S. Sunny Creek Dr., Spokane, WA 99204-8460
Schoffelmeer, Arnold L., Box 36123, N. Findlay Rd., Deer Park, WA 99006
Schwemin, Ralph H., N. 3915 Washington St., Spokane, WA 99205
Tully, Terence, 021 E. Rockwood Blvd., #308, Spokane, WA 99202
Verdoon, Cornelius, St. Joseph, Odessa, WA
Wenning, Paul A., N. 7423 Laurelhurst Dr., Spokane, WA 99208

Permanent Deacons:
Arnold, Archie, St. Rose of Lima, Keller
Arnoux, Richard
Back, Jack, St. Aloysius, Spokane
Barnufsky, Stephen, St. Francis of Assisi, Spokane
Bentley, Donald, St. Francis Assisi, Spokane
Beraza, Antonio, Sacred Heart, Othello
Braungardt, Derwood, St. John Vianney, Spokane
Buckman, Thomas, Kateri Institute
Byrne, John, Our Lady of Fatima, Spokane
Cooper, Gary, St. Augustine, Spokane
Crandall, John, St. Paschal, Spokane
Crow, John, Assumption Parish, Spokane
Dalecki, Robert
Dunlap, Kenneth, St. Augustine, Spokane
Espinoza, Andres, St. Patrick, Pasco
Farrell, Daniel, St. Henry, Grand Coulee
Fosmire, Charles, Our Lady of Lourdes Cathedral, Spokane
Franz, Gary, St. Patrick, Pasco
Gress, John, St. Patrick's Parish, Spokane
Kalinowski, Robert, St. Patrick, Pasco
King, Robert, St. Anne, Medical Lake
Mackin, Francis, Sitka, AL
Maher, Dean, Washington State Penitentiary, Walla Walla
Malone, Richard, St. Mary, Spokane
Martinez, Gonzalo, St. Mary's, Spokane
Murphy, James E., Sacred Heart Medical Center, Spokane
Phelps, J. Andrew, Our Lady of Lourdes, Spokane
Polensky, Hugh, Sacred Heart Medical Center, Spokane
Pruneda, Joel, Sacred Heart, Othello
Reyes, Olegario, St. Patrick, Walla Walla
Ritchie, Dan, Sacred Heart, Spokane
Samuel, Mike, St. Patrick's, Spokane
Sando, William, St. Anthony, Newport
Schuster, Donald, St. Peter's, Spokane
Schutt, David, Immaculate Conception, Davenport
Shaeffer, Dale, St. Joseph, Dayton
Sicilia, John F., St. Thomas More, Spokane
Weid, Walter, Our Lady of Fatima, Spokane
Wilson, Charles, Port Angeles
Yenko, David, Our Lady of the Valley, Okanogan

INSTITUTIONS LOCATED IN THE DIOCESE

[A] SEMINARIES, DIOCESAN

SPOKANE. *Bishop White Seminary*, E. 429 Sharp Ave., 99202. Tel: 509-326-3255. Rev. Richard Root, Rector. Students 12.

[B] SEMINARIES, RELIGIOUS, OR SCHOLASTICATES

SPOKANE. *Mater Dei Institute*, E. 405 Sinto Ave., 99202. Tel: 509-328-8332; Fax: 509-325-4011. Revs. Richard Troman, Ph.D., Dir.; Armond Nigro, S.J., Devel. Dir.; Mrs. Diane Imes, Bus. Mgr.

St. Michael's Institute, Gonzaga University, N. 1107 Astor St., 99202. Tel: 509-328-4220; Fax: 509-324-5820. Very Rev. Joseph E. LIngan, S.J. (Maryland), Rector; Revs. Kevin P. McGinley, S.J., Dean; Richard J. Comboy, S.J. (Missouri), Min. Scholastics; Sr. Bridget McNamara, O.S.F., Dir. Ministries. Fathers 5; Scholastics 26; Brothers 1.

[C] COLLEGES AND UNIVERSITIES

SPOKANE. *Gonzaga University*, 99258. Tel: 509-328-4220.
For a complete listing, refer to the Colleges and Universities section.

[D] HIGH SCHOOLS, INTERPAROCHIAL

WALLA WALLA. *Walla Walla Catholic School System*. (Grades Educare-12), E. 919 Sumach, 99362. Tel: 509-525-3030. Mrs. Michele Acock, Prin. (Grades K-5); Mr. Robert R. Wehde, Admin & Prin. (Grades 6-12). Lay Teachers 29; Students: Elementary 205; High 205.

[E] HIGH SCHOOLS, PRIVATE

SPOKANE. *Gonzaga Preparatory School*, E. 1224 Euclid Ave., 99207. Tel: 509-483-7737. Mr. John Traynor, Pres.; Mr. Al Falkner, Prin.; Revs. Robert Mike Tyrrell, S.J., Rector; J.K. Adams; Thomas A. Colgan, S.J.; Paul Kane, S.J., Scholastic; Steven Dillard, S.J.; Robert A. Goebel, S.J.; Kevin P. McGinley, S.J.; Richard R. Mercy, S.J.; William Vogel, S.J.; Deacon Tom Lamanna, S.J. Priests 8; Lay Teachers 60; Students 950; Scholastics 2.

[F] INTERPAROCHIAL GRADE SCHOOLS

SPOKANE. *All Saints School*. (Grades 5-8), E. 1428 33rd Ave., 99203. Tel: 509-624-5712. Kathy Hicks, Prin.

All Saints Primary. (Grades K-4), E. 3406 18th Ave., 99223. Tel: 509-534-1098. Kathy Hicks, Prin. Serving St. Peter, St. Ann, and Our Lady of Fatima Parishes. Lay Teachers 23; Students 392.

Cataldo Catholic School. (Grades K-8), W. 455-18th Ave., 99203. Tel: 509-624-8759. Mr. Dick Pelkie, Prin. Serving St. Augustine, Sacred Heart, and Our Lady of Lourdes Parishes. Lay Teachers 22; Students 383.

St. Francis School. (Grades K-8), E. 544 Providence, 99207. Tel: 509-487-1571. Mr. Richard Winkler, Prin. Serving St. Francis of Assisi and St. Francis Xavier Parishes. Lay Teachers 6; Students 92.

Trinity School. (Grades K-8), W. 1306 Montgomery Ave., 99205. Tel: 509-327-9369. Mr. Michael S. Trudeau, Prin.
Serving St. Anthony and St. Joseph Parishes. Lay Teachers 8; Students 144.

COLTON. *Guardian Angel-St. Boniface School*, P.O. Box 48, 99113. Tel: 509-229-3579. Mr. Walt O'Neill, Prin.
Serving St. Gall and St. Boniface Parishes. Lay Teachers 5; Students 58.

WALLA WALLA. *Assumption Elementary School*. (Grades K-5), E. 2066 Alder St., 99362. Tel: 509-525-9283. Mrs. Michele Acock, Prin. & Bldg. Admin.
Serving Assumption, St. Francis of Assisi, and St. Patrick Parishes. Lay Teachers 12; Students 204.

Walla Walla Catholic School System. See listing under High Schools, Interparochial.

[G] GENERAL HOSPITALS

SPOKANE. *Holy Family Hospital*, N. 5633 Lidgerwood St., 99207. Tel: 509-482-0111.
For a complete listing, refer to the Hospitals section.

Holy Family Hospital Adult Day Health. c/o Dominican Network, N. 5633 Lidgerwood, 99207. Tel: 509-482-2475.
For a complete listing, refer to the Hospitals section.

Sacred Heart Medical Center, W. 101 Eighth Ave., TAF-C9, 99220. Tel: 509-455-3131.
For a complete listing, refer to the Hospitals section.

CHEWELAH. *St. Joseph's Hospital of Chewelah*, E. 500 Webster, 99109. Tel: 509-935-8211.
For a complete listing, refer to the Hospitals section.

COLVILLE. *Mount Carmel Hospital*, 982 E. Columbia, Box 351, 99114. Tel: 509-684-2561.
For a complete listing, refer to the Hospitals section.

DEER PARK. *Deer Park Health Center and Hospital*, P.O. Box 742, 99006.
For a complete listing, refer to the Hospitals section.

PASCO. *Our Lady of Lourdes Health Center*, 520 N. Fourth Ave., P.O. Box 2568, 99302. Tel: 509-547-7704.
For a complete listing, refer to the Hospitals section.

WALLA WALLA. *St. Mary Medical Center*, 401 W. Poplar St., 99362. Tel: 509-525-3320.
For a complete listing, refer to the Hospitals section.

[H] PROTECTIVE INSTITUTIONS
(Catholic Social Service)

SPOKANE. *Catholic Charities, Inc.*, W. 1023 Riverside Ave., P.O. Box 1453, 99210-1453. Tel: 509-358-4250.
For a complete listing, refer to the Special Care Facilities section.

Catholic Family Service, W. 1023 Riverside Ave., P.O. Box 1453, 99210-1453. Tel: 509-358-4260.
For a complete listing, refer to the Special Care Facilities section.

Guse Summit View, 820 N. Summit Blvd., 99201.
For a complete listing, refer to the Special Care Facilities section.

House of Charity, W. 9 Main Ave., P.O. Box 1453, 99210-1453. Tel: 509-624-7821.
For a complete listing, refer to the Special Care Facilities section.

Miryam's House, W. 1805 Ninth St., 99204.
For a complete listing, refer to the Special Care Facilities section.

St. Anne's Children's Home, N. 707 Cedar St., 99201-1999. Tel: 509-325-7672.
For a complete listing, refer to the Special Care Facilities section.

St. Joseph's Counseling Center, N. 1016 Superior St., 99202. Tel: 509-483-6495.
For a complete listing, refer to the Special Care Facilities section.

St. Margaret's Shelter, P.O. Box 1453, 99210. Tel: 509-624-7624.
For a complete listing, refer to the Special Care Facilities section.

St. Vincent de Paul Parish Conference, 4207 N. Jefferson, 99205. Tel: 509-327-9149.
For a complete listing, refer to the Special Care Facilities section.

St. Vincent de Paul Social Service Office, E. 2901 Trent Ave., 99202. Tel: 509-534-2824 (Social Svc.); 535-2491 (Main Store & Office).
For a complete listing, refer to the Special Care Facilities section.

St. Vincent de Paul Society, E. 2901 Trent Ave., 99202. Tel: 509-534-2824.
For a complete listing, refer to the Special Care Facilities section.

Transitional Living Center, 3128 N. Hemlock, 92204.
For a complete listing, refer to the Special Care Facilities section.

Women's Drop In Center, 218 S. Howard, 92204-1419.
For a complete listing, refer to the Special Care Facilities section.

CHEWELAH. *Dominicare*, 303 E. King St., P.O. Box 1070, 99109.
For a complete listing, refer to the Special Care Facilities section.

CLARKSTON. *Lewis and Clark District Council of St. Vincent de Paul*. Office:, 604 Second St., 99403. Tel: 509-758-7061; Fax: 509-758-9545.
For a complete listing, refer to the Special Care Facilities section.

COLVILLE. *The Rhodena, A Washington Non-profit Organization*, 2305 Wynne St., 99114.
For a complete listing, refer to the Special Care Facilities section.

DAYTON. *St. Vincent de Paul Store*, 257 E. Main St., 99328. Tel: 509-382-4146.
For a complete listing, refer to the Special Care Facilities section.

MANITO STATION. *Spokane Boys' Ranch, Inc.*, P.O. Box 8087, 99203. Tel: 509-448-1411.
For a complete listing, refer to the Special Care Facilities section.

PASCO. *St. Vincent de Paul Store*, 1120 W. Sylvester, 99301. Tel: 509-547-2341; Fax: 509-547-7804.
For a complete listing, refer to the Special Care Facilities section.

WALLA WALLA. *Catholic Children and Family Services*, 5 W. Alder St., Ste. 333, 99362. Tel: 509-525-0572; Fax: 509-525-0576.
For a complete listing, refer to the Special Care Facilities section.

St. Vincent de Paul Store, 308 W. Main St., 99362. Tel: 509-525-3903 (Store); 529-6778 (Office).
For a complete listing, refer to the Special Care Facilities section.

[I] SENIOR CITIZEN HOUSING

SPOKANE. *Cathedral Plaza Apartments*, W. 1120 Sprague Ave., 99204.
For a complete listing, refer to the Special Care Facilities section.

The Delaney, W. 242 Riverside Ave., 99201.
For a complete listing, refer to the Special Care Facilities section.

Fahy Garden Apartments, W. 1403 Dean Ave., 99201.
For a complete listing, refer to the Special Care Facilities section.

Fahy West Apartments, W. 1523 Dean Ave., 99201.
For a complete listing, refer to the Special Care Facilities section.

The O'Malley, E. 707 Mission Ave., 99202.
For a complete listing, refer to the Special Care Facilities section.

Rockwood Lane/Court, E. 221 Rockwood Blvd., 99202.
For a complete listing, refer to the Special Care Facilities section.

Senior Citizen Housing, W. 242 Riverside Ave., 99201. Tel: 509-624-6060.
For a complete listing, refer to the Special Care Facilities section.

CLARKSTON. *Austen Manor*, 1222 Chestnut St., 99403.
For a complete listing, refer to the Special Care Facilities section.

PULLMAN. *Pioneer Square*, S.E. 220 Kamiaken, 99163.
For a complete listing, refer to the Special Care Facilities section.

WALLA WALLA. *Garden Court Apartments*, Sixth & Alder Sts., 99362.
For a complete listing, refer to the Special Care Facilities section.

Mike Foye Apartments, Sixth & Alder Sts., 99362.
For a complete listing, refer to the Special Care Facilities section.

[J] HOMES FOR AGED

SPOKANE. *St. Joseph Care Center*, W. 20 Ninth Ave., 99204. Tel: 509-838-6437.
For a complete listing, refer to the Special Care Facilities section.

St. Joseph dba St. Brendan Continuing Care Center, E. 17 Eighth Ave., 99202. Tel: 509-624-1161.
For a complete listing, refer to the Special Care Facilities section.

[K] MONASTERIES AND RESIDENCES OF PRIESTS AND BROTHERS

SPOKANE. *Regis Community*, N. 1107 Astor St., 99202. Tel: 509-328-4220; Fax: 509-484-2818. Most Rev. Robert L. Whelan, S.J. (Fairbanks), (Retired); Revs. Thomas G. Williams, S.J.; James P. Goodwin, S.J.; James P. Hurley, S.J.; John F. Hurley, S.J.; Anton P. Jahner, S.J.; Leo B. Kaufmann, S.J.; Paul P. Luger, S.J.; James McCready, S.J.; Howard L. Moran, S.J.; James D. Nelson, S.J.; Joseph D. Ringwood, S.J.; Edmund J. Robinson, S.J.; Robert J. Schlim, S.J.; Michael T. Shannon, S.J.; Richard J. Sisk, S.J.; John R. Thatcher, S.J.; John K. Wood, S.J.; Bros. Stephen Karfinski, S.J.; James J. Lee, S.J.; M. John Miller, S.J.

[L] CONVENTS AND RESIDENCES FOR SISTERS

SPOKANE. *Convent of the Holy Names*, 2911 W. Fort George Wright Dr., 99224. Tel: 509-328-4310; Fax: 509-328-9824. Sisters of the Holy Names of Jesus and Mary. Sr. Shirley Roberg, S.N.J.M., Prov. Dir. Professed Sisters 213.

Dominican Center, Sinsinawa Dominican Sisters, 3102 W. Fort George Wright Dr., 99224-5297. Tel: 509-328-8033.

Dominican House, N. 5621 Lacey St., 99207. Tel: 509-489-9112. Dominican Sisters 2.

Dominican Sisters, E. 427 Augusta, 99207. Tel: 509-487-9280.

Holy Names Foundation, 2911 W. Fort George Wright Dr., 99224. Tel: 509-328-7470; Fax: 509-328-9824. Sr. Shirley Roberg, S.N.J.M., Prov. Dir. Support for educational activities of Sisters of the Holy Names of Jesus and Mary.

Holy Spirit Community, 2416 E. 46th Ave., 99223-6412. Tel: 509-448-6224. Elisabeth M. Pfeiffer, Pres.

Mary of the Angels Convent, E. 4624 Jamieson Rd., 99223-2028. Tel: 509-448-0674; Fax: 509-448-5192. Western Regional Admin. of Franciscan Sisters of Perpetual Adoration. Sr. Patricia Gordon, F.S.P.A., Reg. Admin. Sisters 5; Professed Sisters in Region 67.

Monastery of St. Clare, 4419 N. Hawthorne St., 99205-1399. Tel: 509-327-4479. Sr. Mary Rita Dolan, O.S.C., Abbess. Poor Clare Nuns, Solemn Vows.
Papal Enclosure Novitiate. Professed Cloistered Nuns 9.

Mount St. Joseph. Retirement residence and community. 12 W. Ninth Ave., 99204-2394. Tel: 509-838-2594; Fax: 509-838-3220. Sisters of Providence, St. Ignatius Province. Bob Vail, Gen. Mgr.; Sr. Ida Mae Marceau, Supr. Sisters 57.

Sisters of Providence, St. Ignatius Province, 9 E. Ninth Ave., 99202-1295. Tel: 509-455-4884; Fax: 509-455-4882. Sr. Eileen Croghan, S.P., Prov. Supr.

Sisters of Providence, St. Ignatius Province (a Washington non-profit corporation), Sisters of Providence of Montana, Sisters of Providence Institutions, Members of Providence Services (a Washington non-profit corporation). Sisters 5.

NEWPORT. *Carmelite Sisters of Mary*, 2892 Hwy. 211, 99156. Sr. Leslie L. Lund, Prioress. Sisters 2; Hermitages 4.

[M] RETREAT HOUSES

SPOKANE. *Immaculate Heart Retreat Center*, 6910 S. Ben Burr Rd., 99223. Tel: 509-448-1224; Fax: 509-448-1623. Sr. K.C. Young, O.P., Dir.; Rev. Msgr. William Van Ommeren.

KAIROS House of Prayer, 1714 W. Stearns Rd., 99208. Tel: 509-466-2187. Sr. M. Florence Leone, Poch, O.S.F., Coord. Provides a place called to a prayerful, reflective environment. Spiritual direction is available.

TUM TUM. *House of the Lord Retreat Center, Inc.*, P.O. Box 1034, 99034. Tel: 509-276-2219. Ramona Salvatore, Dir.

[N] NEWMAN CENTERS

CHENEY. *Catholic Newman Center at Eastern Washington University*, 837 Elm St., 99004. Tel: 509-235-8402. Rev. James Severyn Westbrook, Chap.; Maria Wallander, Campus Min.

PULLMAN. *Washington State University - St. Thomas More Chapel, Newman Center*, N.E. 820 B St., P.O. Box 2070, College Station, 99165. Tel: 509-332-6311. Rev. Michael Krieg, Chap.; Sr. Rosalie Locati, S.P., Campus Min.

[O] MISCELLANEOUS

SPOKANE. *BECOMING*. Mailing Address: 1832 E. South Riverton #304, 99207. Sr. Maureen O'Sullivan, R.S.M., Exec. Dir. Regional Centre of Self-Esteem Processes for Women in Transition.

The Catholic Foundation of the Spokane Diocese, W. 1023 Riverside Ave., P.O. Box 1453, 99210-1453. Tel: 509-358-4280; Fax: 509-358-7302. Steven C. Kocharhook, Ph.D., Exec. Dir.

Dominican Health Services, N. 5633 Lidgerwood, 99207. Tel: 509-482-2576. Ronald J. Schurra, Pres.; Mr. Ronald DeArth, Vice Pres. Finance; Ms. Barbara Savage, Vice Pres. Mission Svcs. Serves as a multi-hospital system which includes Holy Family Hospital in Spokane, Mount Carmel Hospital in Colville, and St. Joseph's Hospital of Chewelah in Chewelah.

Dominican Network, N. 5633 Lidgerwood St., 99207. Tel: 509-482-2576. Ronald J. Schurra, Pres.; Ronald DeArth, Vice Pres. Finance; Bob Wellmon, Treas.; Earl Davenport, Sec. Serves as a member of Dominican Health Services, a multi-health care system which includes Dominican Health Services, Holy Family Hospital, Spokane; Mount Carmel Hospital, Colville; St. Joseph's Hospital of Chewelah, Chewelah; and Holy Family Hospital Adult Day Health, Spokane; Deer Park Health Center & Hospital, Deer Park; Domini Care, Chewelah.

Dominican Outreach Foundation c/o Dominican Center, W. 3102 Fort George Wright Dr., 99224. Tel: 509-328-8033. James G. Falkner, Pres. Supports the Sisters educational, religious, and charitable ministries.

Holy Names Music Center, 3910 W. Custer Dr., 99224. Dr. Judith L. Myers, Exec. Dir. Sisters 5; Lay Teachers 31; Students 560.
Sponsored by Sisters of the Holy Names, Washington Province.

Immaculate Heart Retreat Center Foundation, S. 6910 Ben Burr Rd., 99223-1819.

Kateri Northwest Ministry Institute, 330 E. Boone, 99202-1778. Tel: 509-484-2646; 484-2414; 324-6305 (Office). Directors: Revs. Richard R. Mercy, S.J.; Thomas A. Colgan, S.J. Purpose: Evangelization and training of Native Americans in the four Northwestern states and one Canadian province for all ministries in the Catholic Church and service in the native community, with attention to recovery ministries from Alcoholism and Dysfunctional Families. Goal: The development of fully indigenous Catholic churches in Urban centers and on Reservations.

Providence Services, 9 E. Ninth Ave., 99202-1295. Tel: 509-455-4884.

Serra Club of Spokane, P.O. Box 414, 99220-0414.

Sisters of Providence, St. Ignatius Province Reserve Fund Trust, 9 E. Ninth Ave., 99202-1295. Tel: 509-455-4884; Fax: 509-455-4882.

SPOKANE CATHOLIC INVESTMENT TRUST, P.O. Box 1453, 99210-1453. Most Rev. William S. Skylstad, Pres. A Washington Non-Profit Corporation established to invest funds on behalf of the charitable organizations organized within the Catholic Diocese of Spokane.

Transitional Program for Women dba Transitions, c/o Dominican Center, W. 3102 Fort George Wright Dr., 99224. Tel: 509-328-6702. Monica Walters, Pres.
Transitions.
Miryam's House of Transition.
Transitional Living Center.
Women's Drop In Center.

DAYTON. *Project Timothy: Christian Service Center*, 238 E. Main St., 99328. Tel: 509-382-2943. Mailing Address: 112 S. First St., 99328-1307.
Sponsored by St. Joseph's & St. Mark's Churches. Sophie J. Arebalos, Interim Dir.

PASCO. *Tri-Cities Preparatory School*. (A Development Committee), c/o Gerald F. Roach, 428 W. Shoshone, 99301. A proposed high school located in the Diocese of Spokane.

RELIGIOUS INSTITUTES OF MEN REPRESENTED IN THE DIOCESE

For further details refer to the corresponding bracketed number in the Religious Institutes of Men or Women section.

[0520]—*Franciscan Friars*. (Santa Barbara Prov.).—O.F.M.

[0690]—*Jesuit Fathers and Brothers*.—S.J.

RELIGIOUS INSTITUTES OF WOMEN REPRESENTED IN THE DIOCESE

[1780]—*Congregation of the Sisters of the Third Order of St. Francis of Perpetual Adoration*.—F.S.P.A.

[1070-03]—*Dominican Sisters*.—O.P.

[3760]—*Order of St. Clare*.—O.S.C.

[2970]—*School Sisters of Notre Dame*.—S.S.N.D.

[3350]—*Sisters of Providence*.—S.P.

[1650]—*The Sisters of St. Francis of Philadelphia*.—O.S.F.

[3840]—*Sisters of St. Joseph of Carondelet*.—C.S.J.

[1990]—*Sisters of the Holy Names of Jesus and Mary*.—S.N.J.M.

DIOCESAN CEMETERIES

SPOKANE. *Catholic Cemeteries of Spokane*, 7200 N. Wall St., 99208. Dennis Fairbank, Dir.

Holy Cross, 7200 N. Wall St., 99208. Tel: 509-328-1070.

St. Joseph, 17825 Trent, 99216. Tel: 509-891-6240.

NECROLOGY

† Gerhart, Rudolph, (Retired). —Died April 28, 1996.

† Mulligan, Eugene, (Retired). —Died Sept. 20, 1996.

Diocese of Springfield-Cape Girardeau

(Dioecesis Campifontis-Capitis Girardeauensis)

Most Reverend

JOHN J. LEIBRECHT, D.D., PH.D.

Bishop of Springfield-Cape Girardeau; ordained March 17, 1956; appointed October 23, 1984; consecrated December 12, 1984. *Office: The Catholic Center, 601 S. Jefferson Ave., Springfield, MO, 65806-3143.*

ESTABLISHED AUGUST 24, 1956.

Square Miles 25,719.

Comprises the following Counties in the State of Missouri: Barry, Barton, Bollinger, Butler, Cape Girardeau, Carter, Cedar, Christian, Dade, Dallas, Dent, Douglas, Dunklin, Greene, Howell, Iron, Jasper, Laclede, Lawrence, McDonald, Madison, Mississippi, New Madrid, Newton, Oregon, Ozark, Pemiscot, Polk, Reynolds, Ripley, Scott, Shannon, Stoddard, Stone, Taney, Texas, Wayne, Webster and Wright.

For legal titles of parishes and diocesan institutions, consult The Catholic Center.

Chancery Office: The Catholic Center, 601 S. Jefferson Ave., Springfield, MO, 65806-3143. Tel.: 417-866-0841; Fax: 417-866-1140.

STATISTICAL OVERVIEW

Personnel	
Bishop	1
Abbots	1
Retired Abbots	2
Priests: Diocesan Active in Diocese	60
Priests: Active Outside Diocese	4
Priests: Retired, Sick or Absent	12
Number of Diocesan Priests	76
Religious Priests in Diocese	64
Extern Priests in Diocese	3
Ordinations:	
Religious Priests	3
Transitional Deacons	1
Permanent Deacons in Diocese	5
Total Brothers	74
Total Sisters	135
Parishes	
Parishes	64
With Resident Pastor:	
Resident Diocesan Priests	51
Resident Religious Priests	13
Without Resident Pastor:	
Administered by Priests	4
Missions	21
Professional Ministry Personnel:	
Sisters	16
Lay Ministers	26
Welfare	
Catholic Hospitals	5
Total Assisted	341,018
Homes for the Aged	2
Total Assisted	318
Specialized Homes	1
Total Assisted	294
Special Centers for Social Services	1
Total Assisted	1,666
Total Assisted	25,595
Educational	
Diocesan Students in Other Seminaries	4
Seminaries, Religious	2
Students Religious	20
Total Seminarians	24
High Schools, Diocesan and Parish	3
Total Students	788
Elementary Schools, Diocesan and Parish	23
Total Students	3,801
Catechesis/Religious Education:	
High School Students	1,784
Elementary Students	3,786
Total Students Under Catholic Instruction	10,183
Teachers in the Diocese:	
Sisters	15
Lay Teachers	224
Vital Statistics	
Receptions into the Church:	
Infant Baptism Totals	692
Adult Baptism Totals	234
Received into Full Communion	429
First Communions	1,263
Confirmations	841
Marriages:	
Catholic	177
Interfaith	258
Total Marriages	435
Deaths	542
Total Catholic Population	54,525
Total Population	1,050,206

Former Bishops—Most Rev. CHARLES H. HELMSING, D.D., cons. as Titular Bishop of Axomis and Auxiliary Bishop of Archdiocese of St. Louis, April 19, 1949; appt. Bishop of Springfield-Cape Girardeau, Aug. 24, 1956; transferred to Diocese of Kansas City-St. Joseph, Jan. 27, 1962; died Dec. 20, 1993.—Most Rev. IGNATIUS J. STRECKER, D.D., appt. April 7, 1962; cons. June 20, 1962; transferred to Archdiocese of Kansas City in Kansas, Sept. 10, 1969.—His Eminence WILLIAM CARDINAL BAUM, S.T.D., appt. Feb. 18, 1970; cons. April 6, 1970; transferred to Archdiocese of Washington, May 9, 1973; elevated to Cardinal, May 24, 1976 appointed to the Prefect of the Sacred Congregation Seminaries and Catholic Institutes, Jan. 15, 1980.—His Eminence BERNARD CARDINAL LAW, D.D., ord. May 21, 1961; appt. Bishop of Springfield-Cape Girardeau, Oct. 22, 1973; cons. Dec. 5, 1973; appt. Archbishop of Boston, Jan. 23, 1984; elevated to Cardinal, May 25, 1985.

Vicars General—Rev. Msgr. PHILIP A. BUCHER, V.G.; Rev. Msgr. THOMAS E. REIDY, V.G.; Rev. Msgr. RICHARD C. ROLWING, V.G.

Chancery Office—The Catholic Center, 601 S. Jefferson Ave., Springfield, 65806-3143. Tel: 417-866-0841; Fax: 417-866-1140.

Chancellor—Rev. Msgr. THOMAS E. REIDY, V.G.

Vice Chancellor—Rev. THOMAS P. KIEFER, J.C.L.

Regional Priest Moderators—Region I: Rev. THOMAS E. ALLEN,Region II: Rev. JOHN S. BRAUN,Region III: Rev. GREGORY E.J. ZATINA,Region IV: Rev. MARK C. ERNSTMANN,Region V: Rev. SHERMAN B. WALL, O.M.I.,Region VI: Rev. JAMES J. UNTERREINER,Region VII: Rev. J. PATRICK WISSMAN,Region VIII: Rev. Msgr. WILLIAM J. STANTON,Region IX: Rev. MICHAEL V. MCDEVITT.

Office of Administration

Catholic Foundation Of The Diocese Of Springfield-Cape Girardeau—Most Rev. JOHN J. LEIBRECHT, D.D., Ph.D., Pres.; Rev. Msgr. THOMAS E. REIDY, V.G., Vice Pres.; Mrs. JANET L. SMITH, Sec. Treas.

Development and Properties—Mr. THOMAS B. WALMSLEY.

Diocesan Development Fund—Mr. THOMAS B. WALMSLEY, Dir. Development and Properties; Mr. RICHARD G. BATH; Rev. MARK J. BINDER; Rev. LEONARD J. CHAMBERS; Mrs. JEANETTE A. CURTISS.

Finance—Mrs. JANET L. SMITH.

Financial Council—Mrs. JANET L. SMITH, Director of Finance; Mr. THOMAS B. WALMSLEY, Diocesan Dir. of Devel. & Properties; Mr. PETER CHARLES; Mrs. PATRICIA HOPKINS; Mr. GEORGE MARINO; Mr. JAMES MOORE; Mr. PETER RAMSOUR; Mr. JAMES P. REINAGEL; Mr. O. J. TAYLOR; Mrs. KAY A. VAN PELT.

Office Of Education

Catholic Schools—Sr. LUCILLE KALINOWSKI, S.S.N.D., Supt.

Communications (Public Relations)—Mrs. MARILYN VYDRA, Dir

Ecumenism—Vacant.

Media Library—Mrs. MARILYN VYDRA, Supvr.

"The Mirror", Official Newspaper, Diocese of Springfield-Cape Girardeau—Rev. MARK G. BOYER, M.A., M.Div., Editor; Mrs. MARILYN VYDRA, Staff Asst.; Mrs. ANN ELWELL, Staff Asst.; Mrs. KARLA ESSNER, Staff Asst.

Religious Education—Sr. ROSALIE DIGENAN, D.C., M.Ed., Dir.

Office Of Ministry

Campus Ministries—Rev. EDDIE DELEON, C.M.F., Southwest Missouri State Univ. Campus Min. Tel: 417-865-0802. Rev. J. FRIEDEL, Southeast Missouri State Univ. Campus Min. Tel: 573-335-3899; 334-0088.

Diocesan Spiritual Director—Rev. ANTHONY J. FALANGA, C.M. Tel: 573-335-4056.

Family Ministries—Mr. TROY CASTEEL, M.S., Dir.

Diocesan Council on Family Ministry—Region I, JIM & MARGE NEWTON,Region II, DIANE WHITNEY,Region III and IV, MARGARET SCHATZ; SHIRLEY WIRTH,Region V, Rev. ERNEST J. MARQUART,Region VI, Rev. JAMES J. UNTERREINER,Region VII, Rev. J. PATRICK WISSMAN; RON ROTH,Region VIII, Rev. MARK J. BINDER; JACK JACKOVIC; PAT JACKOVIC,Region IX, MAGGIE SANDERS.

Natural Family Planning—Mr. TROY CASTEEL, M.S., L.P.C., Dir.

Rite Of Christian Initiation Of Adults—Rev. PAUL J. MCLOUGHLIN, Co-Dir.; Sr. ROSALIE DIGENAN, D.C., M.Ed., Co-Dir.

Hispanic Ministries—Sr. SANDRA STRAUB, Dir.

Social Ministry-Resettlement—Sr. FRAN STEIN, R.S.M., Dir.; Sr. PATRICIA SULLIVAN, D.C., Volunteer.

Regional Catholic Leadership—Rev. DAVID F. HULSHOF,

Dir.

Regional Leaders—Region I, Sr. MARY NORBERT FLESCH, R.S.M.; Mr. RICHARD SNOWBERGER,Region II, Mr. MICHAEL HAMMOND; Mr. KENT BOURSHESKI; Mrs. STACIE DURKIN,Region III-A, Mr. GENE CONFALONE; Mrs. PHYLLIS CONFALONE,Region III-B, Mrs. DOROTHY MEZZACAPPA; Mrs. CARYN WULLNER-,Region IV-A, Mrs. SUE FREY; Mrs. KAY CHARLES-,Region V-A, Mr. HARRY CLARK; Mrs. CONNIE CLARK; Ms. BERNICE GIBSON,Region V-B, Mr. PATRICK STEPHENS; Mrs. LYNN LEWIS; Mr. ED PRATT,Region V-C, Rev. CHARLES COSTELLO; Mrs. JEAN HORST,Region VI, Dr. RAYMOND DRONEY; Rev. JAMES UNTERREINER,Region VII-A, Mrs. DONNA ESSNER; Mrs. BARB MCKEON,Region VII-B, Mrs. PAT MOORE,Region VIII, Rev. ROGER LEVEILLEE; Mrs. KATHY MITCHELL; Ms. JAN STEPHENS,Region IX, Ms. BARBARA BATH; Mr. ROBERT SMITH.

Tribunal—

Judicial Vicar—Rev. Msgr. THOMAS E. REIDY, V.G.

Adjutant Judicial Vicar—Rev. THOMAS P. KIEFER, J.C.L.

Judge—Rev. Msgr. MICHAEL F. SWALINA, S.T.D.; Rev. VINCENT BERTRAND, J.C.L.

Auditor—Sr. INEZ HALLINAN, C.S.J.

Promoter of Justice—Rev. Msgr. PHILIP A. BUCHER, V.G.

Advocate—Rev. Msgr. EDWARD M. EFTINK, Ph.D.; Revs. MICHAEL V. MCDEVITT, M.A.; DAVID F. HULSHOF.

Defenders of the Bond—Rev. Msgr. PHILIP A. BUCHER, V.G.; Rev. MARK E. ERNSTMANN, M.A.

Notary—Mrs. LINDA MURPHY; Mrs. MARIE MEYER.

Vicars For The Religious—Rev. Msgr. THOMAS E. REIDY, V.G.; Rev. ROBERT A. SCHUMACHER.

Vocations-Seminarians—Rev. DAVID F. HULSHOF, Dir.

Associate Director of Vocations / Seminarians—Rev. THOMAS P. KIEFER, J.C.L.

Youth Ministry—Ms. LEIGH STERTEN, Dir.

Catholic Scouting—Rev. JOSEPH A. ORTHEL, Diocesan Chap. Tel: 417-887-0600. Rev. GLENN A. EFTINK, Assoc. Diocesan Chap. Tel: 573-335-9347.

Camp Re-NEW-All—Miss VIRGINIA SANDER, Camp Dir.; Ms. MARY KELSO, Sec.

Office Of Worship

Office of Worship—Rev. PAUL J. MCLOUGHLIN, Dir. & Coord.

Liturgical Commission—Rev. RICK L. JONES. Tel: 417-673-2044. Rev. PAUL J. MCLOUGHLIN, Exec. Sec.

Priests' Eucharistic League Confraternity Of The Most Blessed Sacrament—Rev. MICHAEL V. MCDEVITT, Dir.

Officials And Committees

Catholic Relief Services—Rev. Msgr. THOMAS E. REIDY, V.G.

Cemeteries—Rev. Msgr. THOMAS E. REIDY, V.G.

Censor Of Books—Rev. MARK C. ERNSTMANN, S.T.L., M.Ed. Tel: 417-546-5208.

Health Affairs—Mr. TROY CASTEEL, M.S., L.P.C., Dir.

Holy Childhood Association—Rev. Msgr. MICHAEL F. SWALINA, S.T.D. Tel: 573-748-5183.

Missionary Apostolate—Society for the Propagation of the Faith, Rev. Msgr. MICHAEL F. SWALINA, S.T.D. Tel: 573-748-5183.

Mission of the Laity—Apostleship of Prayer, Rev. Msgr. MICHAEL F. SWALINA, S.T.D. Tel: 573-748-5183.

National Shrine Of The Immaculate Conception—Rev. Msgr. THOMAS E. REIDY, Dir.

Priests' Mutual Benefit Society—Rev. LEONARD CHAMBERS, Pres.; Rev. STEPHEN SCHNEIDER, Vice Pres.; Rev. Msgr. THOMAS E. REIDY, V.G., Exec. Sec.; Rev. Msgr. MICHAEL F. SWALINA, S.T.D.; Rev. MICHAEL J. CASTEEL; Rev. WILLIAM C. KRUDWIG; Rev. NORMAND G. VARONE.

Priests' Purgatorial Society—Revs. MARK C. ERNSTMANN, S.T.L., M.Ed., Dir. Tel: 417-546-5208. BENEDICT W. HARTER, Sec.

Pro-Life Director—Sr. FRAN STEIN R.S.M., Dir.

Rural Life Movement—Rev. SYLVESTER W. BAUER. Tel: 573-744-5913.

Diocesan Consultative Groups

Diocesan Consultors—Rev. JOHN A. BRATH; Rev. Msgr. PHILIP A. BUCHER, V.G.; Revs. THOMAS P. KIEFER, J.C.L.; ERNEST J. MARQUART; Rev. Msgr. THOMAS E. REIDY, V.G.; Rev. JAMES L. REYNOLDS; Rev. Msgr. WILLIAM J. STANTON; Rev. Msgr. JOHN H. WESTHUES, Pres. of the Presbyteral Council (Ex Officio).

Presbyteral Council—Revs. ALLEN L. SAUNDERS, Pres. ROBERT A. LANDEWE; RICK L. JONES, Sec. GERARD FULLER, O.M.I.; JOHN M. HARTH; FRANCIS BRENNAN, S.J.; Rev. Msgr. RAYMOND V. ORF; Rev. Msgr. MICHAEL F. SWALINA, S.T.D.; Rev. GREGORY E.J. ZATINA, Sec. Appointed Members: Rev. Msgr. PHILIP A. BUCHER, V.G.; Rev. Msgr. RICHARD C. ROLWING; Rev. Msgr. THOMAS E. REIDY, V.G.

Diocesan Pastoral Council—Rev. LEONARD CHAMBERS, Exec. Sec.; Mr. TOM RANKIN, Chm.

Diocesan School Board—Sr. LUCILLE KALINOWSKI, S.S.N.D., Supt.

Diocesan Communications Advisory Board—Rev. MARK BOYER, Co-Chm.; Mrs. MARILYN VYDRA, Co-Chm.

Diocesan Lay Endowment Board—Rev. DAVID F. HULSHOF, Chm.

Catholic Organizations And Movements

Cursillo Movement—

Secretariat for Cursillo—Rev. ROGER L. LEVEILLEE, Diocesan Chap.; Rev. Msgr. PHILIP A. BUCHER, V.G., Asst. Diocesan Chap.

Daughters of Isabella—Rev. JAMES W. BAKER.

Daughters of St. Francis de Sales—Rev. Msgr. JOSEPH E. GOSCHE, Diocesan Chap. Chaplains: Revs. THOMAS P. KIEFER, J.C.L.

Diocesan Council Of Catholic Women (DCCW)—Revs. JAMES J. UNTERREINER, Diocesan Spiritual Moderator; DAVID F. HULSHOF, Assoc. Spiritual Moderator; ELIZABETH ESTHER, Pres. Tel: 417-588-3520.

Charismatic Prayer Groups—Mr. KLAUS TAMME. Tel: 417-887-8070. Rev. ROGER L. LEVEILLEE. Tel: 573-264-4500.

Legion of Mary—Annunciation Comitium: Rev. Msgr. JOHN J. RYNISH, Chap. Cape Girardeau Curia:

St. Vincent De Paul Society—Rev. Msgr. THOMAS E. REIDY, V.G., Diocesan Chap.

Apostolates And Commissions

Apostolate to the Deaf—Rev. DAVID L. MILLER, Dir. Tel: 417-476-2463.

Diocesan Peace and Justice Commission—Sr. FRAN STEIN, R.S.M.; Mr. MICK GILLIAM, Chm. Tel: 417-277-5802. Rev. SYLVESTER BAUER. Tel: 573-744-5913.

State Office

Diocesan Delegates To The Missouri Catholic Conference—

Public Policy Committee—Sr. ROSALIE DIGENAN, D.C., M.Ed.; Mr. MICK GILLIAM.

CLERGY, PARISHES, MISSIONS AND PAROCHIAL SCHOOLS

CITY OF SPRINGFIELD
(Greene County)

1—CATHEDRAL OF ST. AGNES (1908), Rev. Thomas P. Kiefer. In res., Rev. David F. Hulshof.
Res., 533 S. Jefferson Ave., 65806. Tel: 417-831-3565. [CEM][JC]
School—531 S. Jefferson Ave., 65806. Tel: 417-866-5038; Fax: 417-866-2906. Ms. Jeanne Skahan, Prin.
Lay Teachers 11; Students 234.
Catechesis / Religious Programs—Students 141.

2—HOLY TRINITY (1966), Rev. Msgr. Thomas E. Reidy, V.G. In res., Rev. Frank C. Palermo.
Res., 2818 E. Bennett, 65804. Tel: 417-883-3440. [JC]
Catechesis / Religious Programs—Students 157.

3—IMMACULATE CONCEPTION (1868), Revs. Stephen A. Schneider; David N. Coon; Joseph A. Orthel; Deacon William McNamee.
Res., 3535 S. Fremont, 65804. Tel: 417-887-9769. [JC]
Church—3555 S. Fremont, 65804. Tel: 417-887-0600; Fax: 417-881-7087.
School—3555A S. Fremont, 65804. Tel: 417-881-7000; Fax: 417-881-7087. Mrs. Ann Meese, Prin.
Lay Teachers 23; Students 595.
Catechesis / Religious Programs—Mrs. Kathy Lukavich, D.R.E.
Students 220.

4—SACRED HEART (1882), Rev. Joseph Peplansky, C.M.F.
Mailing Address: 1609 N. Summit Ave., 65803. Tel: 417-869-3646.
Res., Villa Claret, 1530 N. Summit, 65803. Tel: 417-869-0075. [JC]
Catechesis / Religious Programs—Students 81.

5—ST. ELIZABETH ANN SETON (1981), Revs. Fergus Monaghan; Patrick A. Teter.
Church—2200 W. Republic Rd., 65807. Tel: 417-887-6472; Fax: 417-887-7027. [CEM]
Catechesis / Religious Programs—Tel: 417-887-6088. Sr. Helen Therese Nienhaus, D.R.E.
Students 353.

6—ST. JOSEPH'S (1892), Revs. Joel Derks, O.S.B.; Anthony Shidler, O.S.B., Chap., St. John's Medical Center.
Res., 1115 N. Campbell Ave., 65802. Tel: 417-865-1112. [JC]
School—515 W. Scott, 65802. Tel: 417-866-0667. Leon Witt, Prin.
Lay Teachers 8; Students 145.
Catechesis / Religious Programs—Students 61.

CITY OF CAPE GIRARDEAU
(Cape Girardeau County)

1—CATHEDRAL OF ST. MARY (1868), Rev. Msgr. Richard C. Rolwing, V.G.; Rev. Glenn A. Eftink.
Res., 629 William St., 63703. Tel: 573-335-9347; Fax: 573-335-4142. [CEM][JC]
School—210 S. Sprigg, 63703. Tel: 573-335-3840; Fax: 573-335-4142.
Lay Teachers 13; Students 212.
Catechesis / Religious Programs—Students 28.
Old St. Vincent's—(Chapel of Ease).

2—ST. VINCENT DE PAUL (1838), Revs. Milton Fleming Ryan, C.M.; Joseph Williams, C.M.; Bro. Joe Sebek, C.M.
Res., 741 Forest, 63701. Tel: 573-335-7667; Fax: 573-335-0034.
School—1919 Ritter Dr., 63701. Tel: 573-334-9594.
Lay Teachers 20; Students 468.
Catechesis / Religious Programs—Students 201.

OUTSIDE THE CITIES OF SPRINGFIELD AND CAPE GIRARDEAU

Advance, Stoddard Co., St. Joseph (1905), Rev. Frederick J. Lutz.
Res., P.O. Box 640, 63730. Tel: 573-722-3504. [CEM]
Catechesis / Religious Programs—Students 56.
Mission—Glennon, Bollinger Co., St. Anthony. [CEM]

Aurora, Lawrence Co., Holy Trinity (1906), Rev. Peter J. Morciniec.
Res., Hwy. 60 & Carnation Rd., P.O. Box 533, 65605. Tel: 417-678-2403. [CEM]
Catechesis / Religious Programs—Students 80.

Benton, Scott Co., St. Denis (1840), Rev. Normand G. Varone.
Res., P.O. Box 127, 63736. Tel: 573-545-3864; Fax: 573-545-3017. [CEM]
School—P.O. Box 189, 63736. Tel: 314-545-3017. Mrs. Deborah McCann, Prin.
Lay Teachers 6; Students 87.
Catechesis / Religious Programs—Students 28.

Billings, Christian Co., St. Joseph (1879), Rev. James L. Reynolds.
Res., P.O. Box 100, 65610. Tel: 417-744-2112. [CEM]
Catechesis / Religious Programs—Students 155.

Bolivar, Polk Co., Sacred Heart (1946), Rev. Gregory E.J. Zatina.
Res., 1405 W. Fair Play St., P.O. Box 146, 65613. Tel: 417-326-5596. [CEM]
Catechesis / Religious Programs—Students 102.
Mission—Humansville, Polk Co., St. Catherine, P.O. Box 42, Humansville, 65674. Tel: 417-754-8825.

Branson, Taney Co., Our Lady of the Lake (1951), Rev. Msgr. Philip A. Bucher, V.G.
Res., 202 Vaughn Dr., 65616. Tel: 417-334-2928; Fax: 417-334-6883.
Catechesis / Religious Programs—Mrs. Shirley Wirth, D.R.E.
Students 168.

Buffalo, Dallas Co., St. William (1946), Rev. Bruce Swift, O.S.B.
Res., c/o Sacred Heart Parish, P.O. Box 8, Conway, 65632. Tel: 417-589-6782.

Carthage, Jasper Co., St. Ann (1872), Rev. Timothy Mai Vinh Loc, C.M.C.
Res., 908 S. Clinton St., 64836. Tel: 417-358-1841.
School—1156 Grand, 64836. Tel: 417-358-2674.
Lay Teachers 7; Students 95.
Catechesis / Religious Programs—Students 80.

Caruthersville, Pemiscot Co., Sacred Heart (1900), Rev. William M. Hodgson.
Res., 605 Ward Ave., 63830. Tel: 573-333-4301.
Catechesis / Religious Programs—Students 41.

Chaffee, Scott Co., St. Ambrose (1907), Rev. Allan L. Saunders.
Res., 419 S. Third St., 63740. Tel: 573-887-3953. [CEM]
School—Tel: 573-887-6711. Sr. Jacklyn Pritchard, C.D.P., Prin.
Sisters 1; Lay Teachers 8; Students 102.
Catechesis / Religious Programs—Students 54.

Charleston, Mississippi Co., St. Henry (1874), Rev. Richard Lause, C.M.
Res., 304 Court St., 63834. Tel: 573-683-4737; Fax: 573-683-4737.
School—306 Court St., 63834. Tel: 573-683-6218. Mrs. Kay Glastetter, Prin.
Lay Teachers 7; Students 80.
Catechesis / Religious Programs—Students 30.

Conway, Laclede Co., Sacred Heart (1908), Rev. Bruce Swift.
Res., Box 8, 65632. Tel: 417-589-6782. [CEM]

Dexter, Stoddard Co., Sacred Heart (1889), Rev. John Sheley.
Res., 103 E. Market St., 63841. Tel: 573-624-8888.
Church—102 E. Castor, 63841. Tel: 573-624-7333.
Catechesis/Religious Programs—Students 115.
Convent—115 E. Market St., 63841. Tel: 573-624-3306.

Doniphan, Ripley Co., St. Benedict (1859), Rev. David J. Dohogne.
Res., 306 Kegler, 63935. Tel: 573-996-3301. [CEM]
Mission—Grandin, Carter Co., St. Anne.

El Dorado Springs, Cedar Co., St. Elizabeth (1946), Rev. William C. Krudwig.
Res., 609 S. Main, 64744. Tel: 417-876-3216. [CEM]
Mission—Stockton, Cedar Co., St. Peter the Apostle, 308 E. Oak St., P.O. Box 583, Stockton, 65785. Tel: 417-276-5588.

Forsyth, Taney Co., Our Lady of the Ozarks (1980), Rev. Mark C. Ernstmann.
Res., 355 Shadowrock Dr., P.O. Box 639, 65653. Tel: 417-546-5208.

Fredericktown, Madison Co., St. Michael (1827), Rev. Msgr. Joseph E. Gosche.
Res., 304 W. Main St., P.O. Box 618, 63645. Tel: 573-783-2182; Fax: 573-783-5230. [CEM]
Catechesis/Religious Programs—Students 70.

Glennonville, Dunklin Co., St. Teresa, Deacon Fred Hirtz.
Res., Rte. No. 1, Box 371, Campbell, 63933. Tel: 573-328-4544. [CEM]
School—Rte. No. 1, Box 369, Campbell, 63933. Tel: 573-328-4197. Sr. Michael Ann Monaghan, O.S.U., Prin.
Sisters 1; Lay Teachers 6; Students 95.

Houston, Texas Co., St. Mark (1975), Rev. Gary M. Carr.
Res., 117 S. Oak Crest, 65483. Tel: 417-967-3589.
Missions—Roby, Texas Co., St. Vincent de Paul; Licking, Texas Co., St. John The Baptist.

Ironton, Iron Co., Ste. Marie Du Lac (1878), Rev. James J. Unterreiner. In res., Rev. Anthony M. Gaydos, O.S.M., Senior Priest.
Res., 350 S. Main St., 63650. Tel: 573-546-2611. [CEM]
Catechesis/Religious Programs—Students 130.
Missions—Lesterville, Reynolds Co., Our Lady of Sorrows; Viburnum, Iron Co., St. Philip Benizi.
Chapel—Pilot Knob, Arcadia Valley Hospital.

Jackson, Cape Girardeau Co., Immaculate Conception (1874), Rev. Msgr. Edward M. Eftink.
Res., 208 S. Hope St., Ste. 101, 63755. Tel: 573-243-3182; Fax: 573-243-6833. [CEM]
School—308 S. Hope St., 63755. Tel: 314-243-5013.
Sisters 1; Lay Teachers 10; Students 240.
Catechesis/Religious Programs—Students 280.

Joplin, Jasper Co., St. Mary (1938), Rev. Raymond W. Kunkel.
Res., 2415 Moffet Ave., 64804. Tel: 417-623-3333; Fax: 417-623-4015. [JC]
School—505 W. 25th St., 64804. Tel: 417-623-1465. Mrs. Jeanette Stengel, Prin.
Lay Teachers 13; Students 270.
Catechesis/Religious Programs—Students 103.

St. Peter (1877), Rev. Leonard R. Chambers.
Res., 812 Pearl Ave., 64801-4396. Tel: 417-623-8643; Fax: 417-623-0866. [JC]
School—802 Byers, 64801-4396. Tel: 417-624-5605. Mr. Clay Kubicek, Prin.
Lay Teachers 8; Students 99.

Kelso, Scott Co., St. Augustine (1878), Rev. M. Oliver Clavin.
Res., 201 S. Messmer, Box 26, 63758. Tel: 573-264-4724.
School—230 S. Messmer, P.O. Box 97, 63758-0097. Tel: 573-264-4644; Fax: 573-264-1475. Mr. Thomas Howard, Prin.
Lay Teachers 8; Students 148.

Kennett, Dunklin Co., St. Cecilia (1923), Rev. Mark J. Binder.
Res., College & North Bypass, P.O. Box 306, 63857. Tel: 573-888-2412; Fax: 573-888-0613.

Kimberling City, Stone Co., Our Lady of the Cove (1979), Rev. John A. Brath.
Res., Lake Rd. 13-50, Box 548, 65686. Tel: 417-739-4700.
Catechesis/Religious Programs—Students 104.

Lamar, Barton Co., St. Mary (1904), Rev. Thomas E. Allen.
Res., 200 E. 17th St., 64759. Tel: 417-682-2492. [CEM]
Catechesis/Religious Programs—Students 103.
Mission—Golden City, Barton Co., St. Joseph.

Lebanon, Laclede Co., St. Francis De Sales (1870), Rev. Msgr. Raymond V. Orf.
Res., 345 Grand St., 65536. Tel: 417-532-4811; Fax: 417-532-8847. [CEM]
Catechesis/Religious Programs—Students 166.
Chapel—Bennett Springs, Sportman's Chapel.

Leopold, Bollinger Co., St. John (1856), Rev. Williams A. Huggins.
Res., P.O. Box 83, 63760. Tel: 573-238-3300. [CEM]
Catechesis/Religious Programs—Students 161.

Malden, Dunklin Co., St. Ann (1890), Deacon Fred Hirtz.
Res., 304 N. Douglas St., 63863. Tel: 573-328-4544.

Mansfield, Wright Co., Immaculate Heart of Mary (1943), Revs. Leonard M. Baldus, O.M.I.; Robert J. Olson, O.M.I.
Res., Rte. 1, Box 232, Ava, 65608. Tel: 417-924-3779; 683-5249.
Catechesis/Religious Programs—Students 132.
Missions—Ava, Douglas Co., St. Leo the Great, Rte. 1, Box 232, Ava, 65608. Tel: 417-683-5249; Gainesville, Ozark Co., St. William, P.O. Box 367, Gainesville, 65655. Tel: 417-679-4804. Rev. Gerald Fuller, O.M.I.

Marshfield, Webster Co., Holy Trinity (1892), Rev. Vincent E. Bertrand.
Res., 515 E. Washington, 65706-1865. Tel: 417-468-2228.
Catechesis/Religious Programs—Students 63.

Monett, Barry Co., St. Lawrence (1891), Rev. John S. Braun.
Res., 405 Seventh St., 65708. Tel: 417-235-3286. [CEM]
School—407 Seventh St., 65708. Tel: 417-235-3721. Sr. Dominic Rechtorik, V.S.C., Prin.
Sisters 1; Lay Teachers 2; Students 71.
Catechesis/Religious Programs—Students 133.

Mountain Grove, Wright Co., Sacred Heart (1893), Rev. Justin Huelsing, O.M.I.
Res., 302 E. State St., 65711. Tel: 417-926-3803.
Mission—Cabool, Texas Co., St. Michael.

Mountain View, Howell Co., St. John Vianney (1951), Rev. Ernest J. Marquart; Deacon Charles Costello.
Res., 808 State Rd. Y, P.O. Box 38, 65548. Tel: 417-934-2649.
Mission—Eminence, Shannon Co., St. Sylvester.

Mount Vernon, Lawrence Co., St. Susanne (1939), Rev. Msgr. John H. Westhues.
Res., P.O. Box 126, 65712. Tel: 417-466-4190.
Catechesis/Religious Programs—Students 119.
Mission—Greenfield, Dade Co., St. Patrick.

Neosho, Newton Co., St. Canera (1871), Revs. John M. Harth; Joseph Tran Van Lism, C.M.C.
Res., 504 S. Washington St., 64850. Tel: 417-451-3411. [JC]
Catechesis/Religious Programs—Students 112.
Mission—Noel, McDonald Co., Nativity of Our Lord, P.O. Box 555, Noel, 64854.

New Hamburg, Scott Co., St. Lawrence (1847), Rev. Ralph J. Duffner.
Res., R.R. 1 (New Hamburg), Box 540, Benton, 63736. Tel: 573-545-3317. [CEM]
Catechesis/Religious Programs—Students 161.

New Madrid, New Madrid Co., Immaculate Conception (1789), Rev. Msgr. Michael F. Swalina.
Res., 605 Davis St., 63869. Tel: 573-748-5183.
School—560 Powell, 63839. Tel: 314-748-5123. Ms. Agnes J. Harrington, Prin.
Lay Teachers 5; Students 64.

Oran, Scott Co., Guardian Angel (1892), Rev. Frederick J. Lutz.
Res., P.O. Box 158, 63771. Tel: 573-262-3210. [CEM 2]
School—610 Church St., 63771. Tel: 573-262-3583. Mrs. Barbara Tyler, Prin.
Sisters 2; Lay Teachers 5; Students 90.

Ozark, Christian Co., St. Joseph the Worker (1961), Rev. Paul J. McLoughlin.
Res., 1796 N. State Hwy. NN, 65721. Tel: 417-581-6328; Fax: 417-581-4957.
Catechesis/Religious Programs—Students 230.

Piedmont, Wayne Co., St. Catherine of Siena (1873), Rev. Matthew J. Rehrauer.
Res., 109 Piedmont Ave., 63957. Tel: 573-223-4924.
Catechesis/Religious Programs—Students 61.
Missions—Van Buren, Carter Co., St. George; Williamsville, Wayne Co., Our Lady of Sorrows.

Pierce City, Lawrence Co., St. Mary (1883), Rev. Daniel J. Hirtz.
Res., 200 Front St., 65723. Tel: 417-476-2827; Fax: 417-476-3025. [CEM 2]
School—202 Front St., 65723. Tel: 417-476-2824; Fax: 417-476-3025. Mr. Jay Bierorette, Prin.
Lay Teachers 7; Students 120.
Catechesis/Religious Programs—Students 47.

Poplar Bluff, Butler Co., Sacred Heart (1891), Revs. Michael V. McDevitt; Joseph Campbell.
Res., 123 N. Eighth St., 63901. Tel: 573-785-9635; Fax: 573-785-5836. [CEM]
School—Eighth Ave. and Vine, 63901-5034. Tel: 573-785-5836. Sr. Carol Shively, O.S.V., Prin.
Lay Teachers 8; Students 137.
Catechesis/Religious Programs—Students 146.
Station—Poplar Bluff, V.A. Hospital.

Portageville, New Madrid Co., St. Eustachius (1902), Rev. Roger L. Leveille.
Res., 200 W. Fourth St., 63873. Tel: 573-379-3401.
School—214 W. Fourth St., 63873. Tel: 573-379-3525. Mrs. Sue Ellen Flynn, Prin.
Sisters 1; Lay Teachers 5; Students 77.

Pulaskifield, Barry Co., SS. Peter and Paul (1892), Rev. David L. Miller.
Res., P.O. Drawer L, Pierce City, 65723. Tel: 417-476-2463. [CEM]
Catechesis/Religious Programs—Students 114.
Mission—Cassville, Barry Co., St. Edward, 107 W. 17th St., Box 492, Cassville, 65625.

Salem, Dent Co., Sacred Heart (1880), Rev. Robert A. Landewe.
Res., 602 W. Butler, 65560. Tel: 573-729-4291.
Catechesis/Religious Programs—Mr. Patrick J. Keefe, D.R.E.
Students 65.
Mission—Bunker, Reynolds Co., Christ the King.
Chapel—Montauk, St. Jude.

Sarcoxie, Newton Co., St. Agnes (1870), Rev. Jacob S. Biernacki.
Res., 26952 Cherry Rd., 64862. Tel: 417-548-3540. [CEM]

Scott City, Scott Co., St. Joseph (1911), Rev. J. Patrick Wissman.
Res., 604 Sycamore, 63780. Tel: 573-264-4500. [CEM]
School—606 Sycamore, 63780. Tel: 573-264-2600. Mrs. Darlene Leonard, Prin.
Lay Teachers 6; Students 82.

Seneca, Newton Co., St. Mary (1884), Revs. John M. Harth; Joseph Than Van Liem, C.M.C.
Res., P.O. Drawer N, 64865. Tel: 417-776-3786. [CEM]

Shell Knob, Barry Co., Holy Family (1978), Rev. Thomas Thro, S.J.
Res., Lake Rd. 39-30, P.O. Box 229, 65747. Tel: 417-858-3678.

Sikeston, Scott Co., St. Francis Xavier's (1893), Rev. Msgr. William J. Stanton; Rev. Robert A. Schumacher.
Res., 217 W. Center St., 63801. Tel: 573-471-2447.
School—106 N. Stoddard, 63801. Tel: 573-471-0841. Sr. Agnes Therese Aydt, S.S.N.D., Prin.
Sisters 3; Lay Teachers 4; Students 90.
Catechesis/Religious Programs—Students 125.

Verona, Lawrence Co., Sacred Heart (1874), Rev. Peter J. Morciniec.
Res., P.O. Box 37, 65769. Tel: 417-498-6754. [CEM]
Catechesis/Religious Programs—Students 55.

Webb City, Jasper Co., Sacred Heart (1908), Rev. Rick L. Jones.
Res., 909 N. Madison, 64870. Tel: 417-673-4249.
Catechesis/Religious Programs—Students 134.

West Plains, Howell Co., St. Mary (1902), Rev. Justin Monaghan.
Res., 965 Thayer Ave., 65775. Tel: 417-256-2556.
School—957 Thayer Ave., 65775. Tel: 417-256-8634.
Sisters 3; Lay Teachers 4; Students 90.
Catechesis/Religious Programs—Students 54.
Mission—Thayer, Oregon Co., Sacred Heart.

Willow Springs, Howell Co., Sacred Heart (1897), Rev. Sherman B. Wall, O.M.I.
Res., 1050 W. Bus Hwy. 60-63, 65793. Tel: 417-469-2447. [CEM]
Mission—White Church, Howell Co., St. Joseph, Rte. 1, Pamona, 65789.

Chaplains of Public Institutions

SPRINGFIELD. *Diocesan Hospital Ministry,* 2818 E. Bennett, 65804. Tel: 417-883-3440. Rev. Frank C. Palermo.
U.S. Medical Center, 1900 W. Sunshine, 65802. Tel: 417-862-7041, Ext. 255. Rev. Antonio R. Rigonan, Chap.; Sr. Pauline Grady, A.S.C.

FORDLAND. *Ozark Correctional Center,* Rte. 1, P.O.Box 1-P, 65652. Tel: 417-767-4491. Reverend Father Bruce Swift, O.S.B.

JOPLIN. *Joplin Hospital Ministry,* 2727 McClelland Blvd., 64801. Tel: 417-781-2727. Rev. Benedict W. Harter.

Special Assignment:
Reverend Fathers—
Boyer, Mark G., Editor of "The Mirror", 1703 S. National, Springfield, MO 65804-1123. Tel: 417-887-4811

Friedel, John (J.) F., Chap., Southeast Missouri State University, 512 N. Pacific, Cape Girardeau, MO 63701. Tel: 573-335-3899
Hulshof, David F., Vocation Dir., Dir. Regional Catholic Leadership, 533 S. Jefferson Ave., Springfield, MO 65806. Tel: 417-863-9211

On Duty Outside the Diocese:
Reverend Fathers—
Drewelow, David C., 5308 W. 99th Ter., Overland Park, KS 66207. Tel: 1-800-901-3629
Gregovich, Lawrence E., 918 Winged Foot Dr. #103, O'Fallon, MO 63366. Tel: 314-272-4725

Military Chaplains:
Reverend Fathers—
Wilk, Mitchell S., Chap., U.S.A., Offices of the Chaplain, HH, 2D, FSB 2D LD, Unit #15057, APO, AP 96224-0318

Sabbatical:
Reverend Fathers—
Morey, Charles W., P.O. Box 11172, Springfield, MO 65708. Tel: 417-887-8245

Leave of Absence:
Reverend Fathers—
Casteel, Michael J., 3840 S. Virginia Pl., Springfield, MO 65807. Tel: 417-887-5287

Retired:
Reverend Monsignors—
Rynish, John F., 620 W. Scott, Springfield, MO 65802
Reverend Fathers—
Baker, John W., Franciscan Villa, 620 W. Scott, Springfield, MO 65802
Bauer, Sylvester W., Rte. 1, P.O. Box 24B, Freeburg, MO 65035
Boeding, Damian, 725 Ohio Ave., Joplin, MO 64801-4925
Brownfield, Frowin, 526 S. Jefferson #2, Springfield, MO 65806. Tel: 417-865-6761
Edwards, Byron H., 35 Air Rd., P.O. Box 422, Higden, AR 72067
Eschbacher, Jerome J., 620 W. Scott, Springfield, MO 65802
Holterman, Herbert J., Green Meadow Retirement Home, Room 113, Linn, MO 65051
Ilmberger, Clement F., 3601 W. Silver Springs Rd., Ocala, FL 34475. Tel: 904-840-0620
Seyer, James A., 150 S. Silver Springs Rd., #4, Cape Girardeau, MO 63701
Shibley, Amel A., 704 Hedgegrove Dr., Memphis, TN 38117. Tel: 901-374-9684

INSTITUTIONS LOCATED IN THE DIOCESE

[A] SEMINARIES, RELIGIOUS, OR SCHOLASTICATES

AVA. *Assumption Novitiate (Trappists)*, Mailing Address: Rte. 5, Box 1056, 65608. Tel: 417-683-5110. Rt. Rev. James Conner, O.C.S.O., Abbot; Rev. Cyprian Harrison, O.C.S.O., Novice Master.

CARTHAGE. *Congregation of the Mother Co-Redemptrix*, 1900 Grand Ave., 64836. Tel: 417-358-7787; Fax: 417-358-9508. Very Rev. Joseph M. Tran Ngoc Diep, C.M.C., Prov.

[B] HIGH SCHOOLS, DIOCESAN

SPRINGFIELD. *Springfield Catholic High School*. Coed. 2340 S. Eastgate, 65804-2832. Tel: 417-887-8817; Fax: 417-885-1165. Mr. Dean O. Crayton, Prin.; Mr. Christopher Stecklein, Asst. Prin. Lay Teachers 29; Students 304.

Springfield Catholic School System, 1763 E. Elm, 65802-3227. Tel: 417-865-5567; Fax: 417-865-5278.

CAPE GIRARDEAU. *Notre Dame Regional High School*, 1912 Ritter Dr., 63701. Tel: 314-335-6772.
Co-Instructional Regional High School. School Sisters of Notre Dame. Sr. Mary Ann Fischer, S.S.N.D., Prin. Priests 1; Sisters 2; Lay Teachers 26; Students 348.

JOPLIN. *McAuley Regional High School*, 930 Pearl Ave., 64801. Tel: 417-624-9320. Principals: Jeanette Stengel; Clay Kubicek. Lay Teachers 15; Students 142.

St. Mary. (Grades PreK-5), 505 W. 25th St., 64804. Tel: 417-623-1465. Mrs. Jeanette Stengel, Prin. Lay Teachers 13; Students 270.

St. Peter's Junior High School. (Grades 6-8), 802 Byers, 64801. Tel: 417-624-5605. Mr. Clay Kubicek, Prin. Lay Teachers 8; Students 99.

[C] GENERAL HOSPITALS

SPRINGFIELD. *St. John's Regional Health Center*, 1235 E. Cherokee St., 65804. Tel: 417-885-2000.
For a complete listing, refer to the Hospitals section.

*CAPE GIRARDEAU. *St. Francis' Medical Center*, 211 St. Francis Dr., 63703. Tel: 573-335-1251.
For a complete listing, refer to the Hospitals section.

JOPLIN. *St. John's Regional Medical Center; Mercy Lifecare Systems, Inc.*, 2727 McClelland Blvd., 64804. Tel: 417-781-2727.
For a complete listing, refer to the Hospitals section.

MOUNTAIN VIEW. *St. Francis Hospital*, P.O. Box 82, 65548. Tel: 417-934-2246.
For a complete listing, refer to the Hospitals section.

PILOT KNOB. *Arcadia Valley Hospital*, P.O. Box 548, 63663. Tel: 573-546-3924.
For a complete listing, refer to the Hospitals section.

[D] SPECIAL HOSPITALS

SPRINGFIELD. *St. John's Mercy Villa*, 1100 E. Montclair, 65807. Tel: 417-888-8500; Fax: 417-888-8532.
For a complete listing, refer to the Special Care Facilities section.

[E] MONASTERIES AND RESIDENCES OF PRIESTS AND BROTHERS

SPRINGFIELD. *Claretians Missionaries' Residence-Villa Claret*, 1530 N. Summit, 65803. Tel: 417-869-0075. Revs. Wayne J. Barron, C.M.F.; Eddie DeLeon, C.M.F.; Joseph Peplansky; Bro. Thomas Haerle, C.M.F.

Congregation of Mother Co-Redemptrix, Our Lady of the Rosary House, 418 S. Kimbrough, 65806. Tel: 417-869-3822. Rev. Francis M. Luong Mihn Tuat, C.M.C., Dir. Priests 1; Brothers 5.

AVA. *Assumption Abbey (Trappist)*, Rte. 5, Box 1056, 65608. Tel: 417-683-5110; Fax: 417-683-5658. Rt. Revs. James Conner, O.C.S.O., Abbot; Robert Matter, Abbot Emeritus; Cyprian Harrison, O.C.S.O., Abbot Emeritus; Revs. David Blackburn, O.C.S.O., (Mercy Villa); Leon Brockman, O.C.S.O.; Richard Fox, O.C.S.O.; Donald Joseph Hamilton, O.C.S.O.; Theodore Koster, O.C.S.O.; Anthony Menz, O.C.S.O., (Manhattan, KS). Priests 6; Brothers 9.

CARTHAGE. *Congregation of the Mother Co-Redemptrix, United States Assumption Province*, 1900 Grand Ave., 64836. Tel: 417-358-7787; Fax: 417-358-9508. Very Rev. Joseph M. Tran Ngoc Diep, C.M.C., Prov.; Revs. Francis Xavier M. Do Cao Tung, C.M.C., Asst. I; Anselm M. Dinh Vuong Can, C.M.C., Asst. II; Polycarp M. Nguyen Duc Thuan, C.M.C., Treas.; Athanasius M. Nguyen Linh Uy, C.M.C., Sec.; Paul M. Nguyen Mang Cach, C.M.C.; Joseph M. Cao Xuan Canh, C.M.C.; Michael M. Do Quang Chinh, C.M.C.; Pius M. Nguyen Quang Dan, C.M.C.; Raymond M. Nguyen Chau Dien, C.M.C.; John Bosco M. Pham Tien Duc, C.M.C.; Ignatius Antioch M. Nguyen Hai Duong, C.M.C.; John Eudes M. Vu Quang Huy, C.M.C.; Joseph M. Than Nhu Huu, C.M.C.; Leo M. Vu Dinh Huyen, C.M.C.; Barnabas M. Nguyen Duc Kien, C.M.C.; Felix M. Dinh Viet Luan; Peter M. Ngo Chau Minh, C.M.C.; Bartholomew M. Pham An Su, C.M.C.; Cyril M. Vu Thanh Thien, C.M.C.; John Bosco M. Pham Trung Thuc, C.M.C.; Bartholomew Pham Minh Van, C.M.C. Priests 21; Brothers 69. Mater Dei Building. (Home for retired priests). In res., (Not members of the Congregation of the Mother Co-Redemptrix). Revs. Peter Tran Dien; Dominic Luong Kim Dinh; Joseph Dinh Tuan Ngan; Joseph Cao Phuong Ky, S.S.; John M. Phan Cong Binh; Simon Huynh Tan Cong.

MARIONVILLE. *The Society of Our Mother of Peace, Sons of Our Mother of Peace*, Queen of Heaven Solitude, Rte. 1, Box 107A, 65705. Tel: 417-744-2011. Revs. Placid Guste, S.M.P., Supr.; John R. Hansen, S.M.P. Legal Title: *The Society of Our Mother of Peace, Sons of Our Mother of Peace - Queen of Heaven Solitude.*

[F] CONVENTS AND RESIDENCES FOR SISTERS

SPRINGFIELD. *Congregation of Mary Queen*, 625 S. Jefferson Ave., 65806. Tel: 417-869-9842. Sisters 7.

St. Anne Monastery, 424 E. Monastery St., 65807-6099. Tel: 417-881-2115. Mother Mary Charles Nelson, O.C.D., Prioress. Discalced Carmelite Nuns 6.

Sisters of Mercy of the Americas. (St. Louis), 1260 E. Sunshine, 65804. Tel: 417-882-1297. Sisters 10.

AVA. *Nazareth Hermitage*, Rte. 5, Box 1122, 65608. Sisters 6.

MARIONVILLE. *The Society of Our Mother of Peace, Daughters of Our Mothers of Peace*, Rte. 1, Box 107A, 65705. Tel: 417-744-2011. Legal Title: *The Society of Our Mother of Peace, Daughters of Our Mother of Peace, Queen of Heaven Solitude*. Sisters 5.

PILOT KNOB. *Our Lady of the Valley*, Box 548, 63663. Tel: 314-546-2590. Franciscan Sisters of Mary 4.

REPUBLIC. *Little Portion Franciscans*, 645 Assisi Way, 65738. Tel: 417-732-6684. Sisters 4.

[G] RETREAT HOUSES

AVA. *Assumption Abbey*. (Trappist), Rte. 5, Box 1056, 65608. Tel: 417-683-5110. Rt. Rev. James Connor, O.C.S.O., Abbot.

MARIONVILLE. *The Society of Our Mother of Peace, Daughters of Our Mother of Peace*, Rte. 1, Box 107A, 65705. Tel: 417-744-2011. Legal Title: *The Society of Our Mother of Peace, Daughters of Our Mother of Peace, Queen of Heaven Solitude.*

REPUBLIC. *Cordis House*, 648 S. Assisi Way, 65738. Tel: 417-732-8602. Rev. Eric Kahn, O.F.M.; Sr. Coletta Wrasman, P.H.J.C.

Little Portion Retreat Center, 645 S. Assisi Way, 65738. Tel: 417-732-6684. Sr. Roberta Cusack, O.S.F., Co-ord.

[H] SHRINES

CARTHAGE. *Shrine of Immaculate Heart of Mary*, 1900 Grand Ave., 64836. Tel: 417-358-8580. Rt. Rev. Joseph Calasanz Tran Ngoc Diep, C.M.C., Prov.

[I] NEWMAN CENTERS

SPRINGFIELD. *The Nancy McGregor House, Southwest MO State University, Drury College, Ozark Technical College*, Catholic Campus Ministry, 847 S. Holland, 65806. Tel: 417-865-0802. Rev. Eddie DeLeon, C.M.F., Dir.

CAPE GIRARDEAU. *Southeast Missouri State University, Newman Center*, 512 N. Pacific, 63701. Tel: 573-334-0088; 335-3899. Rev. John J. Freidel, Chap.

BRANSON. *Catholic Christian Newman Association*. (College of the Ozarks), 202 Vaughn, 65616. Tel: 417-334-3378. Sr. Cynthia Hruby, N.D., Campus Min.

WEBB CITY. *Newman Club, Missouri Southern College*, 909 N. Madison, 64870. Newman Club, Missouri Southern State College, Joplin. Tel: 417-673-2044.

[J] MISCELLANEOUS

SPRINGFIELD. *Franciscan Villa*, 620 W. Scott, 65802. Tel: 417-869-5417. Gene Vestal, Admin.

Hope House, 1635 N. Summit, 65803. Tel: 417-864-8399. Sr. M. Rachel Lawler, A.S.C., Co-Dir.; Sr. Martha Wachtel, A.S.C., Co-Dir. Sisters 2.

The Kitchen, 420 E. Commercial St., 65803. Tel: 417-831-6452. Sr. Lorraine Biebel, O.S.F., Coord.

Queen of Angels DayCare Center, 625 S. Jefferson, 65806. Tel: 417-869-9842.

**St. John's Health System, Inc.*, 1235 E. Cherokee, 65804. Tel: 417-885-2000.

CARTHAGE. *Office of the Immaculate Heart of Mary Shrine*, 1749 Grand Ave., 64836. Tel: 417-358-8580.

ELLINGTON. *Casa Guadalupe, Family Growth Center*, Rte. 2, Box 302, 63638. Sr. Cynthia Brinkman, S.S.N.D.

RELIGIOUS INSTITUTES OF MEN REPRESENTED IN THE DIOCESE

For further details refer to the corresponding bracketed number in the Religious Institutes of Men or Women section.

[1330]—*Congregation of the Missions (Vincentians)*.—C.M.
[]—*Congregation of the Mother Coredemptrix*.—C.M.C.
[0520]—*Franciscan Friars*.—O.F.M.
[0360]—*Missionary Sons of the Immaculate Heart of Mary (Claretians)*.—C.M.F.
[0910]—*Oblates of Mary Immaculate (Oblates)*. (Central Prov.).—O.M.I.
[0350]—*Order of Cistercians of the Strict Observance (Trappist)*.—O.C.S.O.
[0200]—*Order of St. Benedict (Benedictines)*.—O.S.B.
[1240]—*Order of the Servants of Mary (Servites)*. (Chicago Prov.).—O.S.M.
[1030]—*Paulist Fathers*.—C.S.P.
[0690]—*Society of Jesus (Jesuits)*. (Missouri Prov.).—S.J.
[]—*The Society of Our Mother of Peace*.—S.M.P.

RELIGIOUS INSTITUTES OF WOMEN REPRESENTED IN THE DIOCESE

[0100]—*Adorers of the Blood of Christ*. (Ruma).—A.S.C.
[0230]—*Benedictine Sisters of the Pontifical Jurisdiction*. (Columbia).—O.S.B.
[0230]—*Benedictine Sisters of the Pontifical Jurisdiction*. (Eau Claire, WI).—O.S.B.
[]—*Congregation of Mary, Queen*.—C.M.R.
[0460]—*Congregation of the Sisters of Charity of the Incarnate Word*. (San Antonio).—C.C.V.I.
[0760]—*Daughters of Charity of St. Vincent de Paul*. (St. Louis).—D.C.
[0920]—*Daughters of St. Francis of Assisi*. (Lacon, Illinois).—D.S.F.
[0420]—*Discalced Carmelite Nuns*.—O.C.D.
[1415]—*Franciscan Sisters of Mary*.—F.S.M.
[1780]—*Franciscan Sisters of Perpetual Adoration*.—F.S.P.A.

[1240]—*Franciscan Sisters, Daughters of the Sacred Hearts of Jesus and Mary*. (Wheaton).—O.S.F.
[]—*Little Portion Franciscans*.—O.S.F.
[]—*Nazareth Hermitage*.
[2960]—*Notre Dame Sisters*. (Omaha).—N.D.
[3230]—*Poor Handmaids of Jesus Christ*. (Donaldson, IN).—P.H.J.C.
[2970]—*School Sisters of Notre Dame*. (St. Louis).—S.S.N.D.
[2970]—*School Sisters of Notre Dame*. (Dallas).—S.S.N.D.
[0430]—*Sisters of Charity of the Blessed Virgin Mary*. (Dubuque).—B.V.M.
[0990]—*Sisters of Divine Providence*. (St. Louis Prov.).—C.D.P.
[1010]—*Sisters of Divine Providence of San Antonio, TX*.—C.D.P.
[2575]—*Sisters of Mercy of the Americas*. (Cedar Rapids, IA Region).—R.S.M.
[2575]—*Sisters of Mercy of the Americas*. (Dallas, PA Region).—R.S.M.
[2575]—*Sisters of Mercy of the Americas*. (St. Louis, MO Region).—R.S.M.
[2575]—*Sisters of Mercy of the Americas*. (Omaha, NE Region).—R.S.M.
[2990]—*Sisters of Notre Dame*. (Chardon, OH).—S.N.D.
[1530]—*Sisters of St. Francis*. (Sylvania, OH).—O.S.F.
[1570]—*Sisters of St. Francis of the Holy Family*. (Dubuque).—O.S.F.
[3840]—*Sisters of St. Joseph of Carondelet*. (St. Louis).—C.S.J.
[3830]—*Sisters of St. Joseph of LaGrange, IL*.—C.S.J.
[3270]—*Sisters of the Most Precious Blood*. (O'Fallon, MO).—C.PP.S.
[3320]—*Sisters of the Presentation of the B.V.M.* (Fargo).—P.B.V.M.
[1720]—*Sisters of the Third Order Regular of St. Francis of Our Lady of Lourdes*. (Rochester, MN).—O.S.F.
[]—*The Society of Our Mother of Peace*.—S.M.P.
[4110]—*Ursuline Nuns (Roman Union)*. (Crystal City, MO).—O.S.U.
[4120]—*Ursuline Nuns of the Congregation of Paris*. (Maple Mount, Kentucky).—O.S.U.
[4160]—*Vincentian Sisters of Charity*. (Pittsburg, PA).—V.S.C.

NECROLOGY

† Ingoldsby, Gervase W., (Retired). —Died June 9, 1996.
† Parrott, Thomas W., (Retired). —Died Jan. 31, 1996.

Diocese of Springfield in Illinois

(Dioecesis Campifontis in Illinois)

Most Reverend

DANIEL L. RYAN, D.D., J.C.L.

Bishop of Springfield in Illinois; ordained May 3, 1956; ordained Titular Bishop of Surista in Mauritania and auxiliary to the Bishop of Joliet in Illinois September 30, 1981; appointed Bishop of Springfield in Illinois November 22, 1983; installed January 18, 1984. *Res., P.O. Box 1667, Springfield, IL, 62705-1667. Office: Catholic Pastoral Center, 1615 W. Washington St., P.O. Box 3187, Springfield, IL, 62708-3187.* Tel.: 217-698-8500; Fax: 217-698-0802.

FORMERLY DIOCESE OF QUINCY.

ERECTED JULY 29, 1853.

SEE TRANSFERRED TO ALTON, JANUARY 9, 1857. TO SPRINGFIELD, OCTOBER 26, 1923.

Square Miles 15,139.

Comprises the following Counties of Illinois: Adams, Bond, Brown, Calhoun, Cass, Christian, Clark, Coles, Crawford, Cumberland, Douglas, Edgar, Effingham, Fayette, Greene, Jasper, Jersey, Macon, Macoupin, Madison, Menard, Montgomery, Morgan, Moultrie, Pike, Sangamon, Scott and Shelby.

For legal titles of parishes and diocesan institutions, consult the Chancery Office.

Catholic Pastoral Center: 1615 W. Washington St., P.O. Box 3187, Springfield, IL, 62708-3187. Tel.: 217-698-8500; Fax: 217-698-8602.

STATISTICAL OVERVIEW

Personnel	
Bishop	1
Priests: Diocesan Active in Diocese	101
Priests: Active Outside Diocese	8
Priests: Diocesan in Foreign Missions	1
Priests: Retired, Sick or Absent	39
Number of Diocesan Priests	149
Religious Priests in Diocese	69
Extern Priests in Diocese	4
Ordinations:	
Diocesan Priests	1
Permanent Deacons in Diocese	2
Total Brothers	19
Total Sisters	717
Parishes	
Parishes	166
With Resident Pastor:	
Resident Diocesan Priests	85
Resident Religious Priests	17
Without Resident Pastor:	
Administered by Priests	59
Administered by Women Religious	5
New Parishes Created	1
Closed Parishes	1
Professional Ministry Personnel:	
Brothers	3
Sisters	40
Lay Ministers	46
Welfare	
Catholic Hospitals	8
Total Assisted	870,661
Homes for the Aged	3
Total Assisted	400
Residential Care of Children	1
Total Assisted	130
Day Care and Extended Day Care Centers	1
Total Assisted	126
Specialized Homes	1
Total Assisted	135
Residential Care of Disabled	1
Total Assisted	93
Educational	
Diocesan Students in Other Seminaries	13
Seminaries, Religious	1
Students Religious	5
Total Seminarians	18
Colleges and Universities	2
Total Students	1,677
High Schools, Diocesan and Parish	3
Total Students	742
High Schools, Private	4
Total Students	1,949
Elementary Schools, Diocesan and Parish	54
Total Students	12,692
Catechesis/Religious Education:	
High School Students	2,777
Elementary Students	11,464
Total Students Under Catholic Instruction	31,319
Teachers in the Diocese:	
Priests	9
Brothers	4
Sisters	54
Lay Teachers	924
Vital Statistics	
Receptions into the Church:	
Infant Baptism Totals	2,588
Adult Baptism Totals	387
Received into Full Communion	462
First Communions	2,906
Confirmations	2,596
Marriages:	
Catholic	585
Interfaith	605
Total Marriages	1,190
Deaths	1,745
Total Catholic Population	170,478
Total Population	1,106,124

Former Bishops—Rt. Rev. HENRY DAMIAN JUNCKER, D.D., cons. April 28, 1857; died Oct. 2, 1868.—Rt. Rev. PETER JOSEPH BALTES, D.D., cons. Jan. 23, 1870; died Feb. 15, 1886.—Rt. Rev. JAMES RYAN, D.D., cons. May 1, 1888; died July 2, 1923.—Most Rev. JAMES A. GRIFFIN, D.D., cons. Feb. 25, 1924; died Aug. 5, 1948.—Most Rev. WILLIAM A. O'CONNOR, D.D., cons. March 7, 1949; installed March 17, 1949; retired July 22, 1975; died Nov. 14, 1983.—Most Rev. JOSEPH A. MCNICHOLAS, D.D., cons. March 25, 1969; installed Sept. 3, 1975; died April 17, 1983.

Diocesan Curia—

All diocesan agencies and councils are located at the Catholic Pastoral Center, unless the contrary is indicated. *Catholic Pastoral Center, 1615 W. Washington, P.O. Box 3187, Springfield, 62708-3187.* Tel: 217-698-8500; Fax: 217-698-0802.

Central Pastoral Administration

Office of the Bishop—Most Rev. DANIEL L. RYAN, D.D., J.C.L.; Sr. JULIA SHEA, S.P., M.A., Admin. Asst.

Office of the Vicar General/Moderator of the Curia—Very Rev. JOHN A. RENKEN, V.G., S.T.D., J.C.D., M.A. (Civil Law). Tel: 217-629-9109 (evenings & weekends). Bro. PATRICK SHEA, O.F.M., J.C.D., J.D., Exec. Asst. to Vicar General; Legal Counsel; Mrs. DORIS RAY, Assoc. to Vicar General - Records Mgmt./Office Mgr./Notary; Mrs. CAROL MULLER, Exec. Sec. & Notary; Mrs. JOAN REED, Special Projects Coord. & Notary; Mrs. NANCY GILLITUK, Receptionist, Catholic Pastoral Center.

Vicar General/Director for Clergy Personnel—Very Rev. THOMAS P. HOLINGA, V.G., *711 S. Sixth St., P.O. Box 234, Petersburg, 62675-0234.* Tel: 217-632-2561 (Rectory); 217-632-7118 (Office); Fax: 217-632-7154.

Commission for the Care of Infirm and Retired Priests—Revs. T. J. DAVENPORT; PETER DONOHOE; THOMAS P. HOLINGA; MICHAEL KUSE; CHARLES MULCRONE; JAMES NEUMAN; MARTIN O'HARA; DAVID SCHAUER; ROGER SIMPSON; TERENCE TRACEY.

Office of the Chancellor/Planning Coordinator—Very Rev. EUGENE E. COSTA, S.T.L.; Miss PATRICIA BOLT, Sec.

Curial Agencies

Office for Campus Ministry—Mr. ROY LANHAM, Dir., *909 E. Lincoln Ave., Charleston, 61920.* Tel: 217-348-0188.

Office for Catholic Charities (Central Administration)—Mr. LAWRENCE DRURY, Exec. Dir., *800 S. Fifth St., Springfield, 62703.* Tel: 217-523-9201; Fax: 217-523-5624.

Office for Catholic Education—Sr. MARILYN JEAN RUNKEL, O.P., Dir.; Mrs. ROSE MERSINGER, Assoc. Dir., Elementary Education; Mr. TIM PFAU, Assoc. Dir., Youth Ministry; Mrs. CHRIS MALMEVICK, Assoc. Dir., Adult Education/Cathechist Formation; Ms. BARB BURRIS, Assoc. Dir., Planning; Mrs. JO BUCKLEY, Exec. Sec.; Mrs. JACQUELINE ARMSTRONG, Elementary & Secondary School/Planning & Devel. Sec.; Mrs. ALICE BULINSKI, Adult Educ., Catechist Formation/Youth Ministry Sec.; Ms. SUSAN DONNELLY, Statistics/Data Specialist.

Board of Catholic Education—Mr. BOB BERGMAN; Sr. JUDITH HILBING, O.P.; Ms. HELEN KLOSTERMANN; Bro. JAMES LEWNARD, C.S.V.; Mr. RICHARD LUCIDO; Sr. THERESE MACKINNON, D.C.; Mr. EDWARD MCCARTHY; Mr. LEE W. MARTEN; Mrs. JAN MULROONEY-KUHN; Rev. DAVID PETERS; Mr. JOHN R. PHILLIPS; Ms. GINA S. PINTO; Rev. DAVID SCHAUER; Mr. PETER MICHAEL VOELZ; Sr. JOANN VOLK, S.S.N.D.

Media Resource Center (Library)—Sr. MATTHIAS CLARK, O.P., Resource Contact; Mrs. JOAN REED, Sec.

Office for Catholic Times—Mr. DAVID BAKKE, Dir. & Editor; Mrs. LAURIE WEAKLEY, Office Mgr.; Mr. KEVIN HECKER, Layout & Design Coord.; Mrs. CATHERINE LOCHER, Reporter; Mrs. BELINDA MULSHINE, Advertising; Mrs. MARIAN GREENAN, Bookkeeper; Mrs. BARBARA DAVIS, Sec. & Receptionist. Fax: 217-698-0619.

Office for Communications—Ms. KATHLEEN SASS, Dir. Tel: 217-467-5535 (Pager); Fax: 217-698-0619.

Office for Family Life—Mrs. DONNA DAUSMAN, Dir.; Mrs. LANA BASDEN, Sec.

Office for Finances—Mr. JOHN J. MAXWELL, Dir.; Mr. THOMAS REISER, Assoc. Dir. Property, Buildings and Cemeteries/Coord. of Lay Employee Health Insurance; Mrs. EDNA MAE BROWN, Assoc. Dir. Insurance (Fire, Extended Coverage, Vandalism, Multi-peril Liability, Workers' Compensation, Boiler, Unemployment, Lay Employee Pension Plan, Priests' Personal Property, Seminarians' Medical Care).; Mr. DAN GAUWITZ, Programmer & Analyst. Accountants: Mr. BRIAN CONLON; Mr. TIM BARNHART; Mrs.

CHERYL KANNALL, Coord., Annual Catholic Svcs. Appeal; Mrs. KAREN REGAN, Clerk, Annual Catholic Svcs. Appeal; Mrs. SANDY KOVSKI, Sec.

Lay Employees' Health Insurance Committee—Mrs. EDNA MAE BROWN; Ms. JUDY KOHLRUS; Mr. LEO LENN; Mr. JOHN J. MAXWELL; Mrs. JOAN MCKINNEY; Mr. HENRY PETRILLI; Rev. MAURICE QUILLIGAN; Mr. THOMAS REISER; Very Rev. JOHN A. RENKEN, V.G.; Sr. MARILYN JEAN RUNKEL, O.P.; Mr. ROBERT TEREBA; Ms. SUSAN VASQUEZ.

Lay Employees' Pension Plan Administrative Committee—Mrs. EDNA MAE BROWN; Mr. LEO LENN; Mr. JOHN J. MAXWELL; Mrs. ROSE MERSINGER; Mr. HENRY PETRILLI; Very Rev. JOHN A. RENKEN, V.G.; Mr. THOMAS REISER; Bro. PATRICK SHEA, O.F.M.; Rev. Msgr. PAUL SHERIDAN; Mr. GARY STREMSTERFER; Rev. DONALD L. WOLFORD.

Commission for Buildings and Property—Rev. DANIEL BERGBOWER; Mr. H. F. BOYLE; Mr. ROBERT BUDNIK, Chm.; Sr. CHAMINADE KELLY, O.S.F.; Very Rev. VIRGIL MANK; Mr. JOHN J. MAXWELL; Rev. DAVID PETERS; Very Rev. JOHN A. RENKEN, V.G.; Mr. THOMAS REISER, Consultant.

Office for Lay Ministry—Rev. DAVID S. LANTZ, Dir.; Mrs. JOAN REED, Sec.

Advisory Board—Sr. JANE BOOS, S.S.N.D.; Sr. KATHLEEN COUR, O.P.; Mrs. DONNA DAUSMAN; Dr. BRENT DELAND; Mrs. MARY HANDLEY; Mr. ELIOT KAPITAN; Mrs. SUE MORRIS; Mr. TIM PFAU; Very Rev. JOHN A. RENKEN, V.G.; Sr. MARILYN JEAN RUNKEL, O.P.; Very Rev. KENNETH STEFFEN.

Track "A" (Area Specialization) Coordinators—Catechetical Leadership Ministry, Mrs. CHRIS MALMEVICK,*Clinical Pastoral Care Ministry,* Mrs. MARY HANDLEY,*Family Life Ministry,* Very Rev. KENNETH STEFFEN; Mrs. DONNA DAUSMAN,*Liturgical Ministry: Christian Initiation of Adult Leadership Skills;* Mr. ELIOT KAPITAN,*Liturgical Ministry: Liturgical Leadership Skills,* Sr. KATHLEEN COUR, O.P.,*Social Concerns Ministry,* Sr. JANE BOOS, S.S.N.D.,*Tribunal Advocacy Ministry,* Very Rev. JOHN A. RENKEN, V.G.,*Youth Ministry,* Mr. TIM PFAU.

Track "B" (Parish Life Ministry) Coordinators—Very Rev. JOHN A. RENKEN, V.G.

Office for Lay Organizations—Rev. JOHN R. OSSOLA, Dir.; Ms. SHARON MASTERSON, Sec.

Office for Ministry to Priests—Rev. HENRY SCHMIDT, Dir., *800 Stevenson Dr., Springfield, 62703.* Tel: 217-529-1606.

Office for the Missions—Rev. JOHN BURNETT, Dir.; Mrs. RITA GREENWALD, Prog. Coord.; Mr. BRUCE COMPTON, Admin. Asst.

Office for Rural Life—Mr. JOSEPH BERGSCHNEIDER, Dir.; Mrs. MAYME BERGSCHNEIDER, Assoc. Dir., *31 Westfair Dr., Jacksonville, 62650.* Tel: 217-243-2832.

Office for Social Concerns—Sr. JANE BOOS, S.S.N.D., Dir.; Mrs. SUE MORRIS, Assoc. Dir.; Mrs. NANCY HARPER Assoc. Dir. Tel: 217-245-4299 (v/tty); Mrs. MARTHA MAYFIELD, Admin. Asst. Tel: 217-698-9581 (tty); Mrs. ELAINE VONDERHEIDE, Assoc. Dir. Tel: 217-342-2718.

Diocesan Task Force Against Racial Injustice—RENEE SAUNCHES, Co-Chm. Tel: 217-875-7251. MARY CLUNEY JOHN, Co-Chm. Tel: 217-429-1452.

Campaign for Human Development Advisory Board and Allocation Committee—Sr. JANE BOOS, S.S.N.D., Chm.; Mr. LARRY DRURY. Deanery Representatives: Mr. HERB REISINGER, Alton Deanery: Mr. WILLIAM JOYNER, Decatur Deanery: Mr. KEN HANDLEY, Decatur Deanery: Mr. FRED FASIG, Effingham Deanery: Ms. RUTH ANN STEWART, Jacksonville Deanery: Mr. EUGENE ESSELMAN, Quincy Deanery: Mrs. NICOLE WELCH, Quincy Deanery: Mrs. MARGUERITE SCHNEIDER, Quincy Deanery: Mr. LLOYD MOSLEY, Springfield Deanery: Mr. LEROY JORDAN, Springfield Deanery: Members At Large: Rev. JOHN SPREEN; Mr. KEN STEINER.

Office for Stewardship and Development—Mrs. MARLENE MULFORD, Acting Dir.; Mrs. CATHY FURKIN, Sec.

Steering Committee—Ms. BARBARA BURRIS; Rev. THOMAS DENNIS; Mr. JOHN J. MAXWELL; Very Rev. JOHN A. RENKEN, V.G.; Ms. KATHIE SASS; Very Rev. KENNETH STEFFEN, J.C.L.(cand.), M.A., D. Min.

Office for the Tribunal—Very Rev. JOHN A. RENKEN, S.T.D., J.C.D., M.A. (Civil Law), Judicial Vicar & Dir.; Very Rev. KENNETH STEFFEN, J.C.L.(Cand.), M.A., D. Min., Adjutant Judicial Vicar & Assoc. Dir.; Sr. ESTHER REDMANN, O.S.U., J.C.L., Judge; Bro. PATRICK SHEA, O.F.M., J.C.D., J.D., Defender of the Bond; Mrs. JEAN KIRK, Office Mgr. & Notary; Mrs. LANA BASDEN, Sec. & Notary.

Office for Vocations—Rev. MICHAEL KUSE, V.F., Dir., *1119 S. 7th St., Quincy, 62301.* Tel: 217-222-2759; Fax: 217-222-6463.

Office for Worship—Sr. KATHLEEN COUR, O.P., Dir.; Mr. ELIOT KAPITAN, Assoc. Dir., RCIA; Mrs. JAN GIGGS, Sec.

Commission for the Liturgy—Mr. JERRY BAUMAN; Mr. RICH BYERS; Sr. KATHLEEN COUR, O.P.; Mrs. SHARRY GOETZ; Revs. BARRY HARMON; ROBERT JALLAS Mr. PAUL JOHNSON; Mr. ELIOT KAPITAN; Mrs. MARY KELDERMANS; Rev. JOSEPH RING, Chm.; Mrs. CAROL SEIFERT.

Deans

Alton Deanery—Very Rev. VIRGIL W. MANK, V.F.
Decatur Deanery—Very Rev. KEVIN W. VANN, V.F.
Effingham Deanery—Very Rev. LEO J. ENLOW, V.F.
Jacksonville Deanery—Very Rev. JOHN W. SPREEN, V.F.
Litchfield Deanery—Very Rev. LAWRENCE AUDA, V.F.
Quincy Deanery—Very Rev. JOHN P. BEVERIDGE, V.F.
Springfield Deanery—Very Rev. PATRICK J. WRIGHT, V.F.

Councils

Diocesan Finance Council—Sr. CHRISTINE BRAMLET, O.S.U.; Sr. LINDA HAYES, O.P.; Mr. WILFRED KALTENBACH; Mr. WILLIAM KESSLER; Mr. LEO LENN, Chm.; Dr. ROBERT MANDEVILLE; Rev. JAMES NEUMAN. Consultants: Very Rev. JOHN A. RENKEN, V.G.; Mr. JOHN J. MAXWELL; Mr. THOMAS REISER.

Presbyteral Council—Most Rev. DANIEL L. RYAN, Pres.; Revs. MICHAEL BARRETT, O.F.M.; GERALD BUNSE; JOHN CARBERRY; EUGENE E. COSTA; JEFFREY GRANT; THOMAS HAGSTROM, Vice Chm. THOMAS HENSELER; THOMAS HOLINGA; CARL KEMME; DANIEL LACOUNT; KEVIN LAUGHERY; LAMBERT LEYKAM, O.F.M.; VIRGIL MANK; WILLIAM MAUL, Chm. CHARLES NELSON; DAVID PETERS; JOHN A. RENKEN, V.G., Sec. & STreas. KENNETH STEFFEN; EUGENE WEITZEL, C.S.V.; DONALD L. WOLFORD.

Catholic Charities Institutions

Area Offices—

Alton. Catholic Charities of Alton and Wood River—RICK FACCIN, Area Dir., *735 Park Dr., Alton, 62002.* Tel: 618-462-0634; Fax: 618-462-3209.

Carlinville. Catholic Charities—PATRICIA A. POPE, Area Dir., *525 W. Second South St., Carlinville, 62626.* Tel: 217-854-4511; Fax: 217-854-8049.

Decatur. Catholic Charities—MARIE RADEMACHER, Area Dir., *247 W. Prairie, Decatur, 62523.* Tel: 217-428-3458.

Effingham. Catholic Charities—Sr. BETH MARIE RUDER, D.C., Area Dir., *601 W. Fayette, Effingham, 62401.* Tel: 217-342-9800; Fax: 217-342-3873.

Granite City. Catholic Charities—MARY ALYCE BEARDSLEE, Area Dir., *2105 State St., Granite City, 62040.* Tel: 618-877-1184; Fax: 618-877-1890.

Quincy. Catholic Social Services—Sr. MARY SHAW, A.S.C., Area Dir., *926 State St., Quincy, 62301.* Tel: 217-222-0958; Fax: 217-222-8737.

Springfield. Catholic Charities—MARY STONE, Area Dir., *120 S. 11th St., Springfield, 62703.* Tel: 217-525-0500; Fax: 217-525-0554.

Institutions—

Alton. Catholic Children's Home—Mr. LAWRENCE DRURY, Dir. STEVEN ROACH, Admin., *1400 State St., Alton, 62002.* Tel: 618-465-3594; Fax: 618-465-4023.

Springfield. St. Monica's Center—Mr. LAWRENCE DRURY, Dir. JUDITH A. COMERIO, Admin., *109 E. Lawrence Ave., Springfield, 62704.* Tel: 217-523-7922; Fax: 217-525-8241.

Springfield. St. John's Breadline—*430 N. Fifth St., Springfield, 62701.* Tel: 217-528-6098.

CLERGY, PARISHES, MISSIONS AND PAROCHIAL SCHOOLS

CITY OF SPRINGFIELD
(Sangamon County)

1—CATHEDRAL OF THE IMMACULATE CONCEPTION (1928), Revs. John R. Ossola; Thomas J. Dennis; Paschal LoBianco, S.V.D.
Res., 524 E. Lawrence Ave., P.O. Box 1667, 62705. Tel: 217-522-3342; Fax: 217-522-1151. [JC]
School—Tel: 217-523-2652; Fax: 217-523-2750.
Springfield Dominican Sisters 4; Lay Teachers 17; Students 217; Preschool 19.

2—BLESSED SACRAMENT (1924), Revs. John C. Burnett; Christopher Comerford. In res., Rev. Chester Fabisiak, S.J.
Res., 1725 S. Walnut Ave., 62704. Tel: 217-528-7521; Fax: 217-528-3137.
School—Lay Teachers 25; Students 490.
Catechesis/Religious Programs—Students 95.

3—CHRIST THE KING (1963), Revs. David S. Lantz; M. Brendan Keane; Barry Harmon.
Res., 1930 Barberry Dr., 62704. Tel: 217-546-3527; Fax: 217-793-6393.
School—Tel: 217-546-2159.
Lay Teachers 24; Students 506.
Catechesis/Religious Programs—Elementary, 1920 Barberry Dr., 62704.
Students 65.

4—LITTLE FLOWER (1947), Revs. Henry C. Schmidt; Rodney A. Schwartz.
800 Stevenson Dr., 62703. Tel: 217-529-1606. [JC]
School—Tel: 217-529-4511; Fax: 217-529-3622.
Sisters 3; Lay Teachers 26; Students 391.
Catechesis/Religious Programs—Students 108.

5—ST. AGNES (1889), Very Rev. Patrick J. Wright, V.F.; Revs. Thomas J. Hagstrom; Robert T. Becker.
Res., 245 N. Amos Ave., 62702. Tel: 217-793-1330; Fax: 217-793-3212.
School—Tel: 217-793-1370; Fax: 217-793-1238.
Springfield Dominican Sisters 2; Lay Teachers 21; Students 520.
Catechesis/Religious Programs—Students 210.

6—ST. ALOYSIUS (1928), Revs. John Titus; Donald Meehling.
Res., 2119 N. 20th St., 62702. Tel: 217-544-4554.
School—Tel: 217-544-4553.
Lay Teachers 23; Students 423.
Catechesis/Religious Programs—Students 69.

7—ST. FRANCES CABRINI (1948), Rev. David V. Schauer.
Res., 1020 N. Milton Ave., 62702. Tel: 217-522-8555; Fax: 217-522-8555.
School—Tel: 217-528-8302.
Lay Teachers 8; Students 122.

8—ST. JOSEPH (1875), Rev. Patrick W. Render, C.S.V.
Res., 1345 N. Sixth St., 62702. Tel: 217-544-7426; Fax: 217-544-7467.
School—Tel: 217-523-6597.
Ursuline Sisters 1; Lay Teachers 13; Students 208.
Catechesis/Religious Programs—Students 57.

9—ST. PATRICK, Rev. John Eck, C.S.V.
Res., 1720 S. Grand Ave., E., P.O. Box 4302, 62708. Tel: 217-528-0436. [JC]
School—Springfield Dominican Sisters 1; Lay Teachers 7; Students 62.

10—SS. PETER AND PAUL (1859) (German), Rev. Frank J. O'Hara.
Res., 426 N. Sixth St., 62702. Tel: 217-523-3681. [JC]

11—SACRED HEART OF JESUS (1884) (German), Rev. John E. Eck, C.S.V. In res., Rev. Eugene Cieslik (Poland).
Res., 725 S. 12th St., 62703. Tel: 217-523-1861. [JC]

OUTSIDE THE CITY OF SPRINGFIELD

Alexander, Morgan Co., Visitation B.V.M., Rev. Joseph P. Kerber.
Mailing Address: P.O. Box 20, New Berlin, 62670. Tel: 217-488-2410; Fax: 217-488-2410.
Church—Old U.S. 36, 62601.

Altamont, Effingham Co., St. Clare (1874), Rev. T. Vincent Worland.
Res., 216 N. Ninth St., 62411. Tel: 618-483-5346. [CEM]
Catechesis/Religious Programs—Students 144.

Alton, Madison Co.,

1—SS. PETER AND PAUL, (1855), Revs. Thomas G. Meyer, O.M.I.; James P. Brobst, O.M.I.
Res., 717 State St., 62002. Tel: 618-465-4221; Fax: 618-465-0346. [JC]
School—Tel: 618-465-8711.
Lay Teachers 9; Students 200.

2—IMMACULATE CONCEPTION-ST. MARY'S, (1858), Revs. John Paul Klein, O.M.V.; Daniel Barron, O.M.V.; Craig MacMahon, O.M.V.; William Brown, O.M.V.; Bros. Philip Chisholm; John Wykes.
Res., 525 E. Fourth St., 62002. Tel: 618-465-4284; Fax: 618-463-4637. [CEM]
School—Tel: 618-465-8523.
Sisters of St. Francis of the Martyr of St. George 4; Lay Teachers 10; Students 222.
Catechesis/Religious Programs—Students 150.

3—ST. PATRICK, (1883), Revs. Daniel Barron, O.M.V.; Craig MacMahon, O.M.V.; John Paul Klein, O.M.V.; William Brown, O.M.V.; Bros. Phil Chisholm; John Wykes.
Res., 525 E. Fourth St., 62002.
Church—918 E. Fifth St., 62002. Fax: 618-463-4637. [JC]

4—ST. MATTHEW, (1947), Rev. Robert J. Jallas.
Res., 1015 Milton Rd., 62002-3167. Tel: 618-465-8582; Fax: 618-465-5994.
School—Tel: 618-462-6032.
Lay Teachers 10; Students 162.

Arcola, Douglas Co., St. John the Baptist (1865), Rev. Michael D. Mullink; Sr. Phyllis Schenk, O.P.
Res., 205 S. Locus St., Box 133, 61910. Tel: 217-268-3545;268-3766. [JC]
Catechesis/Religious Programs—210 S. Pine St., 61910.
Students 110.

Arenzville, Cass Co., St. Fidelis (1859) (German), Rev. Eugene J. Weitzel, C.S.V.

Res., 215 W. Fifth St., Beardstown, 62618. Tel: 217-323-4345. [JC]

Ashland, Cass Co., St. Augustine (1875), Rev. John W. Spreen.
Res., 320 N. Saratoga, P.O. Box 438, 62612. Tel: 217-476-8856. [CEM]
Catechesis/Religious Programs—Students 59.

Assumption, Christian Co., Assumption B.V.M. (1870), Rev. Alan Hunter.
Res., 301 St. Peter St., 62510. Tel: 217-226-3536; Fax: 217-226-3538. [CEM]
Catechesis/Religious Programs—Tel: 217-226-3205.
Students 111.

Athens, Menard Co., Holy Family (1903), Rev. Eugene E. Costa.
Res., 129 Stardust Dr., Sherman, 62684. Tel: 217-523-3816; Fax: 217-523-3954.
Church—Springfield Rd., 62613. Tel: 217-636-8238.
Catechesis/Religious Programs—Students 87.

Auburn, Sangamon Co., St. Benedict (1903), Rev. Daniel E. LaCount.
Res., 126 E. Washington St., P.O. Box 168, 62615. Tel: 217-438-6222. [CEM][JC]
Catechesis/Religious Programs—Students 72.

Barry, Pike Co., Holy Redeemer (1954), Rev. Donald F. Sederwall.
Res., 226 E. Adams, Pittsfield, 62363. Tel: 217-285-4321; Fax: 217-285-9400.

Batchtown, Calhoun Co., St. Barbara (1910), Rev. John Sullivan, O.F.M.
Office: P.O. Box 38, Brussels, 62013. Tel: 618-883-2400; Fax: 618-883-2511.
Res., Meppen Ln., Meppen, 62013. Tel: 618-883-2309. [CEM]

Beardstown, Cass Co., St. Alexius (1838), Rev. Eugene J. Weitzel, C.S.V.
Res., 215 W. 5th St., 62618. Tel: 217-323-4345. [CEM]
Catechesis/Religious Programs—Students 86.
Mission—Arenzville, St. Fidelis.

Belleview, Calhoun Co., St. Agnes (1900), Revs. James E. Wheeler, O.F.M.; Sylvano Pera, O.F.M.
Res., 404 Main St., P.O. Box C, Hardin, 62047. Tel: 618-576-2517. [CEM]

Beltrees, Jersey Co., St. Michael (1877), Rev. Charles F. Hurkes, O.M.I.
Res., 11 N. Evans St., P.O. Box 218, Grafton, 62037. Tel: 618-786-3512. [CEM]
Church—Beltrees Rd., 62022.

Benld, Macoupin Co., St. Joseph (1915), Rev. Lawrence Auda.
Res., 304 N. Macoupin, Gillespie, 62033. Tel: 217-839-3456.
Church—310 W. Central Ave., 62009. Tel: 217-835-4701.

Bethalto, Madison Co., Our Lady Queen of Peace (1945), Rev. James A. Flach, Admin.
Res., 132 Butcher St., P.O. Box 100, 62010. Tel: 618-377-6519.
School—Tel: 618-377-6401.
Lay Teachers 11; Students 165.
Catechesis/Religious Programs—Students 88.

Bethany, Moultrie Co., St. Isidore (1865), Rev. Kevin W. Vann.
Res., 3850 Lourdes Dr., Decatur, 62526. Tel: 217-877-4404; Fax: 217-877-5257. [CEM]

Bishop Creek, Effingham Co., St. Aloysius (1865), Rev. Edwin O. Albers, O.F.M.
Res., R.R. 2, Box 125, Dieterich, 62424. Tel: 217-925-5579. [CEM]
Catechesis/Religious Programs—Students 233.

Black Jack, Madison Co., St. John the Baptist. Closed. For inquiries for parish records contact the Chancery.

Bluffs, Scott Co., St. Patrick (1871), Rev. Charles T. Nelson.
Res., 108 Pearl St., Winchester, 62694. Tel: 217-742-5224.

Brighton, Macoupin Co., St. Alphonsus (1868) (German), Rev. Peter J. Donohoe.
Res., 918 N. Main St., 62012. Tel: 618-372-3352.
Catechesis/Religious Programs—Students 85.

Brocton, Edgar Co., St. Thomas Aquinas (1899). Closed. For inquiries for parish records contact the Chancery.

Brussels, Calhoun Co., St. Mary (1851), Rev. John Sullivan, O.F.M.
Office: P.O. Box 38, 62013. Tel: 618-883-2400; Fax: 618-883-2511.
Res., Meppen Ln., Meppen, 62013. Tel: 618-883-2309. [CEM]
School—Tel: 618-883-2124. Mrs. Jo Ann Nolte, Prin.
Lay Teachers 6; Students 105.

Buffalo, Sangamon Co., St. Joseph (1882), Parish Life Coordinators: Sr. Lois Kikkert, O.P.; Sr. Bridget Maier, O.P.
Res., 410 Anne St., P.O. Box 47, Illiopolis, 62539. Tel: 217-486-3851.
Catechesis/Religious Programs—Students 35.

Bunker Hill, Macoupin Co., St. Mary (1926), Rev. Robert N. Porter.
Res., 300 S. Putnam, P.O. Box A-H, 62014-9512. Tel: 618-585-4700; Fax: 618-585-3449. [CEM]
Catechesis/Religious Programs—Students 62.

Camp Point, Adams Co., St. Thomas (1860), Rev. Anthony J. Thieman.
Res., #6 Paradise Ave., P.O. Box 228, Liberty, 62347-0228. Tel: 217-645-3444; 647-3055; Fax: 217-645-3444.
Church—Spring St. & Ohio St., 62320.
Catechesis/Religious Programs—Sr. Joan Schnorbus, C.PP.S., D.R.E.
Students 72.

Carlinville, Macoupin Co., St. Mary's of the Immaculate Conception. Closed. For inquiries for parish records contact St. Joseph.

SS. Mary & Joseph. SS. Mary & Joseph was formed by the merger of St. Mary's of the Immaculate Conception & St. Joseph. Rev. R. Dean Probst.
Res., 535 S. West St., P.O. Box 647, 62626-0647. Tel: 217-854-7151; Fax: 217-854-9228. [JC]
Church—State Rt. 108 E., 62626.
Catechesis/Religious Programs—Holy Family School of Religion, Tel: 217-854-9220; Fax: 217-854-9228.
Students 331.

Carrollton, Greene Co., St. John the Evangelist (1858), Rev. Charles A. Edwards.
Res., 414 Third St., 62016-1319. Tel: 217-942-3551; Fax: 217-942-3551. [CEM]
School—426 Third St., 62016-1319. Tel: 217-942-6814. Mr. Gary E. Miller, Prin.
Lay Teachers 9; Students 135.
Catechesis/Religious Programs—Students 50.

Casey, Clark Co., St. Charles Borromeo (1878), Rev. Jeffery A. Grant.
Church—300 E. Jefferson, P.O. Box 72, 62420.
Res., 110 Lincoln Dr., P.O. Box 156, Greenup, 62428. Tel: 217-923-3523.

Chandlerville, Cass Co., St. Basil. Merged with St. Luke, Virginia.

Charleston, Coles Co., St. Charles Borromeo (1873), Revs. Robert L. Meyer; Joseph G. Ring.
Res., 921 E. Madison St., 61920. Tel: 217-345-3332; Fax: 217-345-4252.
Catechesis/Religious Programs—Students 248.

Chatham, Sangamon Co., St. Joseph (1920), Rev. Robert B. Franzen.
Res., 700 E. Spruce, 62629. Tel: 217-483-3772.
Catechesis/Religious Programs—62629. Tel: 217-483-4514.
Students 518.

Coffeen, Montgomery Co., St. John the Baptist (1898), Rev. Carl Schmidt.
Res., 400 Jefferson, P.O. Box 278, 62017. Tel: 217-534-2220. [CEM][JC]

Collinsville, Madison Co., SS. Peter and Paul (1855) (Italian), Revs. Robert Morris; J. Michael Jenkins; Sr. Mary Magdelen Fearon, O.S.U., Pastoral Assoc.
Res., 207 Vandalia St., 62234. Tel: 618-345-4343. [CEM]
School—Tel: 618-344-5450; Fax: 618-344-5536.
Lay Teachers 23; Students 402.
Catechesis/Religious Programs—Students 127.

Dalton City, Moultrie Co., Sacred Heart (1891). Closed. For inquiries for parish records contact the Chancery.

Decatur, Macon Co.,

1—Holy Family, (1959), Revs. Carl Kemme; James O'Shea.
Res., 2400 S. Franklin St., 62521. Tel: 217-423-6223; Fax: 217-423-6237. [JC]
School—Tel: 217-423-7049.
Springfield Dominican Sisters 4; Lay Teachers 13; Students 257.
Catechesis/Religious Programs—Students 63.

2—Our Lady of Lourdes, (1958), Rev. Kevin W. Vann. In res., Revs. Donald E. Knuffman; Jeffrey W. Goeckner.
Res., 3850 Lourdes Dr., 62526. Tel: 217-877-4404; Fax: 217-877-5257. [JC]
School—3950 Lourdes Dr., 62526-1799. Tel: 217-877-4408.
Springfield Dominican Sisters 1; Lay Teachers 15; Students 350.
Catechesis/Religious Programs—Students 171.

3—St. Patrick, (1853), Rev. Donald L. Wolford.
Res., 407 E. Eldorado St., 62523. Tel: 217-429-5363; Fax: 217-429-8206. [JC]
School—Tel: 217-423-4351.
Lay Teachers 14; Students 193.
Catechesis/Religious Programs—Students 66.

4—St. James, (1877), Very Rev. Martin Mangan, V.F.
Res., 742 E. Clay St., 62521. Tel: 217-428-7733; Fax: 217-428-7426. [JC]
School—Tel: 217-422-7031.
Lay Teachers 10; Students 100.
Catechesis/Religious Programs—Students 70.

5—St. Thomas the Apostle, (1925), Rev. Dennis D. Kollross.
Res., 2160 N. Edward St., P.O. Box 2697, 62524-2697. Tel: 217-877-4146; Fax: 217-877-4147.
Catechesis/Religious Programs—62524-2697.
Students 51.

Dieterich, Effingham Co., Immaculate Conception (1905), Rev. Edwin O. Albers, O.F.M.
Res., R.R. 2, P.O. Box 125, 62424. Tel: 217-925-5579. [CEM]
Catechesis/Religious Programs—Students 96.

Divernon, Sangamon Co., Sacred Heart (1905), Rev. Msgr. Aloysius B. Schwarz, Admin.; Rev. Dan LaCount, Admin.
Res., 126 E. Washington St., Auburn, 62530. Tel: 217-438-6222. [CEM]
Church—230 S. Lincoln, 62530. Tel: 217-628-3629.

East Alton, Madison Co., St. Kevin (1959), Rev. Delix Michel, Admin.
Res., 108 Airwood Dr., E., 62024. Tel: 618-259-3363.
School—Tel: 618-259-6040.
Lay Teachers 8; Students 122.
Catechesis/Religious Programs—Students 115.

Edgewood, Effingham Co., St. Anne (1865), Rev. T. Vincent Worland.
Res., 216 N. Ninth, Altamont, 62411. Tel: 618-483-5346. [CEM]

Edwardsville, Madison Co., St. Boniface (1869) (German), Rev. John Corredato, C.S.V.
Res., 110 N. Buchanan St., P.O. Box 423, 62025. Tel: 618-656-6450; Fax: 618-656-7669. [CEM]
School—Tel: 618-656-6917.
Lay Teachers 9; Students 227.
Catechesis/Religious Programs—Students 205.

St. Mary (1842), Rev. Gerald L. Bunse.
Res., 1802 Madison, 62025. Tel: 618-656-4857; Fax: 618-656-1715. [JC]
School—Tel: 618-656-1230.
Priests 1; Lay Teachers 14; Students 236.
Catechesis/Religious Programs—Students 155.

Effingham, Effingham Co., Sacred Heart (1892), Rev. Daniel J. Bergbower.
Res., 405 S. Henrietta, P.O. Box 870, 62401. Tel: 217-347-7177; Fax: 217-347-0728. [JC]
School—Tel: 217-342-4060; Fax: 217-342-9251.
Lay Teachers 14; Students 210.
Catechesis/Religious Programs—Students 125.

St. Anthony of Padua (1858), Very Rev. Leo J. Enlow; Rev. Mark E. Lewis.
Res., 417 N. Third, P.O. Box 764, 62401. Tel: 217-347-7129; Fax: 217-342-6980. [CEM]
School—Tel: 217-347-0419; Fax: 217-347-2749.
Sisters 3; Lay Teachers 28; Students 486.
High School—Tel: 217-342-6969; Fax: 217-342-6997.
Priests 1; Lay Teachers 17; Students 234.
Catechesis/Religious Programs—Students 58.

Farmersville, Montgomery Co., St. Mary (1876), Rev. Kevin M. Laughery.
Res., 310 Nobbe St., P.O. Box 80, 62533-0080. Tel: 217-227-3349; Fax: 217-698-8620. [CEM]
School—St. Isidore, Tel: 217-227-3359.
Lay Teachers 5; Students 81.

Fieldon, Jersey Co., St. Mary, Rev. William Hembrow.
Res., 306 N. Washington, Jerseyville, 62052. Tel: 618-498-3416. [CEM]

Franklin, Morgan Co., Sacred Heart of Jesus (1886), Rev. Joseph P. Kerber.
Mailing Address: P.O. Box 20, New Berlin, 62670. Tel: 217-488-2410; Fax: 217-488-2410. [CEM]
Office & Res.—P.O. Box 20, New Berlin, 62670.
Church—62638.
Parish Center—Tel: 217-675-2631.

Gillespie, Macoupin Co., SS. Simon and Jude (1879), Rev. Lawrence Auda.
Res., 304 N. Macoupin St., 62033. Tel: 217-839-3456. [CEM]
School—Tel: 217-839-2888.
Lay Teachers 3; Students 51.
Catechesis/Religious Programs—Students 56.

Girard, Macoupin Co., St. Patrick (1887), Rev. Kevin M. Laughery.
Res., 310 Nobbe St., P.O. Box 80, Farmersville, 62533-0080. Tel: 217-227-3349; Fax: 217-698-8620.
Catechesis/Religious Programs—Tel: 217-627-3575.
Students 86.

Glen Carbon, Madison Co., St. Cecilia (1928), Rev. Stephen J. Pohlman.
Res., 155 N. Main St., 62034. Tel: 618-288-3200; Fax: 618-288-3292.
Catechesis/Religious Programs—St. Cecilia Family Life Center, Tel: 618-288-5523.
Students 147.

Godfrey, Madison Co., St. Ambrose (1947), Very Rev.

Virgil Mank, V.F.; Mr. Les Himstedt, Pastoral Assoc.; Mr. Patrick Fitzgerald, Pastoral Min.
Church—820 W. Homer Adams Pkwy., 62035. Tel: 618-466-2921; Fax: 618-466-2959.
Res., 3307 Morkel Dr., 62035. Tel: 618-466-6408.
School—Tel: 618-466-4216. Mary Jo Jacobs, Prin.
Lay Teachers 24; Students 417.
Catechesis/Religious Programs—Students 173.

Grafton, Jersey Co., St. Patrick (1871), Rev. Charles F. Hurkes, O.M.I.
Res., 11 N. Evans, P.O. Box 218, 62037. Tel: 618-786-3512. [CEM]

Granite City, Madison Co., Holy Family (1988), Revs. William P. Fisherkeller, C.S.V.; Thomas F. Wise, C.S.V.
Res., 2606 Washington Ave., 62040-4810. Tel: 618-877-7158. [JC]
School—Tel: 618-877-5500.
Springfield Dominican Sisters 2; Lay Teachers 16; Students 318.
Catechesis/Religious Programs—Tel: 618-452-8244.
Students 168.

St. Elizabeth (1871), Rev. Thomas Liebler. In res., Rev. Francis Tebangura (Uganda).
Res., 2301 Pontoon Rd., 62040. Tel: 618-931-2916; Fax: 618-931-2928. [JC]
School—Tel: 618-931-0125.
Lay Teachers 13; Students 216.
St. Elizabeth Preschool—2300 Pontoon Rd., 62040. Tel: 618-931-0127.
Catechesis/Religious Programs—Students 87.

Grantfork, Madison Co., St. Gertrude (1972), Rev. James A. Flach.
Res., 120 N. Windmill, P.O. Box 457, Marine, 62061. Tel: 618-887-4535. [CEM]
Catechesis/Religious Programs—12514 Frey Rd., Highland, 62249. Tel: 618-675-2883. Shirley Schwarz, D.R.E.
Students 62.

Green Creek, Effingham Co., St. Mary Help of Christians (1860) (German), Rev. Emil G. Helfrich, O.M.I.
Res., R.R. 3, Box 162, Effingham, 62401. Tel: 217-844-2062. [CEM]
Catechesis/Religious Programs—Tel: 217-895-2166.
Students 92.

Greenfield, Greene Co., St. Michael (1880), Rev. Edward Groesch.
Res., 411 Sheffield, 62044. Tel: 217-368-2176. [CEM]

Greenup, Cumberland Co., Christ the King (1937), Rev. Jeffery A. Grant.
Res., 110 Lincoln Dr., P.O. Box 156, 62428. Tel: 217-923-3523.
Catechesis/Religious Programs—Students 70.

Greenville, Bond Co., St. Lawrence (1868), Rev. Victor J. Kaltenbach.
Res., 512 S. Prairie St., 62246. Tel: 618-664-3169. [CEM]
Catechesis/Religious Programs—Students 170.

Griggsville, Pike Co., Holy Family. Closed. For details for parish records see St. Mary, Pittsfield.

Hagaman, Macoupin Co., St. Catherine (1905), Rev. Edward Groesch.
Res., 411 Sheffield, Greenfield, 62044. Tel: 217-368-2176.

Hardin, Calhoun Co., St. Norbert (1872), Revs. James E. Wheeler, O.F.M.; Sylvano Pera, O.F.M.
Res., 404 Main St., P.O. Box C, 62047. Tel: 618-576-2517. [CEM]
School—(Grades 1-5). Tel: 618-576-2514.
Lay Teachers 3; Students 51.
Catechesis/Religious Programs—Tel: 618-576-2628.
Students 66.

Highland, Madison Co., St. Paul (1846), Revs. David L. Peters; Robert W. Spriggs.
Res., 1412 Ninth St., 62249. Tel: 618-654-2339; Fax: 618-654-2330. [CEM]
School—(Grades PreK-8). Tel: 618-654-7525.
Sisters 1; Lay Teachers 25; Students 392.
Catechesis/Religious Programs—1420 Ninth St., 62249. Tel: 618-654-4313.
Students 368.

Hillsboro, Montgomery Co., St. Agnes (1840), Rev. George Morelock.
Res., 216 E. Tremont, P.O. Box 98, 62049. Tel: 217-532-5288. [CEM]
Catechesis/Religious Programs—Tel: 217-532-2631.
Students 208.

Hume, Edgar Co., St. Michael (1876), Rev. Paul H. Skelton.
Res., 208 N. Pine, Box 17, Villa Grove, 61956. Tel: 217-832-8352.

Illiopolis, Sangamon Co., Visitation B.V.M. (1866), Parish Life Coordinators: Sr. Lois Kikkert, O.P.; Sr. Bridget Maier, O.P.
Res., 410 Anne St., P.O. Box 47, 62539. Tel: 217-486-3851. [CEM][JC]

Island Grove, Jasper Co., St. Joseph (1874), Rev. Edwin O. Albers, O.F.M.
Res., R.R. 2, Box 125, Dieterich, 62424. Tel: 217-925-5579. [CEM]
Catechesis/Religious Programs—Students 96.

Jacksonville, Morgan Co., Our Saviour (1851), Revs. Ken J. Venvertloh; Allen Kemme.
Mailing Address: 453 E. State St., 62650. Tel: 217-245-6184; Fax: 217-245-6185. [CEM]
School—62650. Tel: 217-243-8621. Mrs. Peggy Goodwin, Prin.
Lay Teachers 20; Students 350.
High School—Routt High School, 500 E. College St., 62650. Tel: 217-243-8563; Fax: 217-243-3138. Dr. Robert Clancy, Prin.
Springfield Dominican Sisters 1; Lay Teachers 13; Students 140.
Catechesis/Religious Programs—Tel: 217-245-7633.
Students 182.

Jerseyville, Jersey Co., Holy Ghost (German), Rev. William Hembrow.
Res., 306 N. Washington St., 62052. Tel: 618-498-3416. [JC]
School—St. Francis/Holy Ghost School. See St. Francis. Tel: 618-498-4916.
Catechesis/Religious Programs—Students 367.

St. Francis Xavier (1857), Rev. William E. Kekeisen.
Res., 506 S. State St., P.O. Box 260, 62052-0260. Tel: 618-498-3518. [CEM][JC]
School—St. Francis/Holy Ghost School, Tel: 618-498-4823.
St. Francis: (Grades K & 5-8) 412 S. State St., 62052. Tel: 618-498-4823.; Holy Ghost: (Grades 1-4) 309 N. Washington St., 62052. Tel: 618-498-4910. Sr. Zita Telkamp, C.D.P., Prin.
Sisters 1; Lay Teachers 20; Students 368.
Catechesis/Religious Programs—Tel: 618-498-5497.
Students 103.

Kampsville, Calhoun Co., St. Anselm (1877), Revs. James E. Wheeler, O.F.M.; Sylvano Pera, O.F.M.
Res., 404 Main St., P.O. Box C, Hardin, 62047. Tel: 618-576-2517. [CEM]

Kincaid, Christian Co., St. Rita (1920), Rev. Charles Dahlby.
Res., P.O. Box 439, 62540. Tel: 217-237-4339.
Catechesis/Religious Programs—Students 59.

Liberty, Adams Co., St. Brigid (1860), Rev. Anthony J. Thieman.
Church—P.O. Box 228, 62347. Tel: 217-645-3444; Fax: 217-645-3444. [CEM]
Res., #6 Paradise Ave., P.O. Box 228, 62347-0228.
Catechesis/Religious Programs—Sr. Joan Schorbus, C.PP.S., D.R.E.
Students 117.

Lillyville, Cumberland Co., Sacred Heart of Jesus (1877) (German), Rev. Emil Helfrich, O.M.I.
Mailing Address: R.R. 1, Sigel, 62462.
Res., R.R. 3, Box 162, Effingham, 62401. Tel: 217-844-2062. [CEM]
Catechesis/Religious Programs—Tel: 217-844-2221.
Students 80.

Litchfield, Montgomery Co., Holy Family (1988). Former St. Mary, founded in 1857. Rev. David L. Schmidt.
Res., 410 S. State St., 62056. Tel: 217-324-2776; Fax: 217-324-2868. [CEM]
Catechesis/Religious Programs—211 E. Columbia St., 62056. Tel: 217-324-2336.
Students 106.

Livingston, Madison Co., Sacred Heart (1913), Rev. George Radosevich Tel: 618-635-8490.
Res., 188 Livingston Ave., P.O. Box 458, 62058. Tel: 618-637-2211. [CEM]
Mission—New Douglas, Madison Co., St. Ubaldus, 1st St., New Douglas, 62074.

Lovington, Moultrie Co., St. Mary. Closed. Sacramental records are located at Our Lady of the Holy Spirit.

Macon, Macon Co., St. Stanislaus (1866), Rev. Alan Hunter.
Res., 301 St. Peter St., Assumption, 62510. Tel: 217-226-3536.

Madison, Madison Co., Our Lady of Czestochowa (1912). (St. Mary). Rev. James Keefner, O.F.M., Admin.
Res., 1621 10th St., 62060. Tel: 618-452-5180. [JC]

Marine, Madison Co., St. Elizabeth (1856), Rev. James A. Flach.
Res., 120 N. Windmill St., P.O. Box 457, 62061. Tel: 618-887-4535. [CEM]
Catechesis/Religious Programs—4500 State Rt. 4, Alhambra, 62001. Tel: 618-887-4614. Evelyn Duffin, D.R.E.
Students 85.

Marshall, Clark Co., St. Mary (1847), Rev. Jeffery Grant, Admin.
Mailing Address: 414 S. Sixth St., 62441.
Res., 110 Lincoln Dr., P.O. Box 156, Greenup, 62428. Tel: 217-923-3523; 826-2845. [CEM]
Catechesis/Religious Programs—Students 106.

Maryville, Madison Co., Mother of Perpetual Help, Rev. Maurice Quilligan.
Res., 200 N. Lange, 62062. Tel: 618-344-6464.
School—St. John Neumann School, Tel: 618-345-7230; Fax: 618-345-4350.
Springfield Dominican Sisters 1; Lay Teachers 15; Students 300.
Catechesis/Religious Programs—Tel: 618-344-9666.
Students 132.

Mattoon, Coles Co., Immaculate Conception (1856), Rev. Herman J. Niebrugge.
Res., 320 N. 21st St., P.O. Box 468, 61938-0468. Tel: 217-235-0539. [CEM]
School—Tel: 217-235-0431.
Lay Teachers 9; Students 164.
Catechesis/Religious Programs—Tel: 217-234-6648.
Students 113.

Medora, Macoupin Co., St. John the Evangelist (1914), Rev. Raphael Paul, Admin.
Res., c/o St. Alphonsus Church, 918 N. Main St., Brighton, 62012. Tel: 217-372-3352; Fax: 618-372-8133.

Mendon, Adams Co., St. Edward (1890). Vacant.
Res., R.R. 1, Box 36, 62351. Tel: 217-936-2289. [CEM]
Catechesis/Religious Programs—Students 105.

Meppen, Calhoun Co., St. Joseph (1864), Rev. John Sullivan, O.F.M.
Office: P.O. Box 38, Brussels, 62013. Tel: 618-883-2400; Fax: 618-883-2511. [CEM]
Res., Meppen Ln., 62013. Tel: 618-883-2309.

Michael, Calhoun Co., St. Michael (1864), Revs. James E. Wheeler, O.F.M.; Sylvano Pera, O.F.M.
Res., 404 Main St., P.O. Box C, Hardin, 62047. Tel: 618-576-2517. [CEM 2][JC]

Montrose, Effingham Co., St. Rose of Lima (1879), Rev. Lambert Leykem, O.F.M., Admin.
Mailing Address: P.O. Box 68, 62445. Tel: 217-924-4337. [CEM]
Catechesis/Religious Programs—Students 132.

Morrisonville, Christian Co., St. Maurice (1870), Rev. John T. Hannigan (CHI) Admin.
Res., 706 E. Fourth St., P.O. Box 45, 62546-0045. Tel: 217-526-3363. [CEM]
School—(Grades 1-8). Tel: 217-526-3534.
Lay Teachers 4; Students 51.
Catechesis/Religious Programs—Students 58.

Mount Olive, Macoupin Co., Ascension (1886) (Croatian), Rev. Larry Anschutz, Admin.
Res., 705 E. Main St., 62069. Tel: 217-999-4981. [CEM]
Catechesis/Religious Programs—Students 67.

Holy Trinity (1912) (Slovak), Rev. Larry Anschutz, Admin.
Res., 705 E. Main St., 62069. Tel: 217-999-4981. [CEM]

Mount Sterling, Brown Co., Holy Family (1864), Rev. Thomas Henseler.
Res., 401 W. North St., P.O. Box 252, 62353. Tel: 217-773-3233.
School—Tel: 217-773-2825.
Lay Teachers 11; Students 161.
Catechesis/Religious Programs—Students 105.

Mt. Zion, Macon Co., Our Lady of the Holy Spirit (1976), Revs. Carl A. Kemme, Admin.; James D. O'Shea.
Res., 400 Woodland, 62549. Tel: 217-864-3467.
Catechesis/Religious Programs—Tel: 217-864-4941.
Students 108.

Moweaqua, Shelby Co., St. Frances de Sales (1895), Rev. Alan Hunter.
Res., 301 St. Peter St., Assumption, 62510. Tel: 217-226-3536; Fax: 217-226-3538.

Murrayville, Morgan Co., St. Bartholomew (1883), Rev. Charles T. Nelson.
Res., P.O. Box 47, 62668. Tel: 217-882-3781. [CEM]

Neoga, Cumberland Co., St. Mary of the Assumption (1897), Rev. W. Jeffrey Holtman.
Res., Church St., P.O. Box 68, Sigel, 62462. Tel: 217-844-3371. [CEM]
Church—690 N. Walnut St., 62447. Tel: 217-895-2166.
Catechesis/Religious Programs—Students 95.

New Berlin, Sangamon Co., Sacred Heart of Mary (1858), Rev. Joseph P. Kerber.
Res., 404 E. Birch, P.O. Box 20, 62670. Tel: 217-488-2410; Fax: 217-488-2410. [CEM]
School—Tel: 217-488-3545.

Sisters of Notre Dame 1; Lay Teachers 4; Students 65.
Catechesis/Religious Programs—Students 68.

Newton, Jasper Co., St. Thomas (1873), Rev. Joseph Molloy.
Res., 402 W. Jourdan St., P.O. Box 225, 62448. Tel: 618-783-8741. [CEM 3]
School—Tel: 618-783-3517.
Lay Teachers 8; Students 123.
Catechesis/Religious Programs—Students 250.

Niantic, Macon Co., St. Ann (1889), Parish Life Coordinators: Sr. Lois Kikkert, O.P.; Sr. Bridget Maier, O.P.
Res., 410 Anne St., Illiopolis, 62539. Tel: 217-486-3851. [JC]

Nokomis, Montgomery Co., St. Louis (1870), Rev. Pat G. Jakel.
Res., 311 S. Elm St., 62075. Tel: 217-563-7146; 563-7808 (Personal); Fax: 217-563-8671. [CEM]
School—509 E. Union, 62075. Tel: 217-563-7445.
Lay Teachers 7; Students 130.
Catechesis/Religious Programs—Students 69.

North Arm, Edgar Co., St. Aloysius (1817), Rev. William J. Overmann.
Res., P.O. Box 577, Paris, 61944. Tel: 217-466-3355. [CEM]

Oblong, Crawford Co., Our Lady of Lourdes (1954), Rev. Richard W. Weltin.
Res., 207 E. Walnut St., P.O. Box 428, Robinson, 62454. Tel: 618-544-7526.

Oconee, Shelby Co., Sacred Heart of Jesus (1872) (German), Rev. Don J. Roberts, Admin.
Res., P.O. Box 45, 62553. Tel: 217-539-4325. [CEM]

Palmyra, Macoupin Co., Holy Rosary (1954), Rev. August Spell.
c/o Sacred Heart Church: 721 N. Springfield St., Virden, 62690.

Pana, Christian Co., St. Patrick (1858), Rev. Robert A. Porter. In res., Rev. Zvonimir Damjanov, (Retired).
Res., 6 E. Fifth St., P.O. Box 440, 62557. Tel: 217-562-5396; Fax: 217-562-2308. [CEM]
School—Sacred Heart, Tel: 217-562-2425. Mr. David L. Jones, Prin.
Lay Teachers 10; Students 151.
Catechesis/Religious Programs—Tel: 217-824-6120.
Students 100.

Panama, Bond Co., Sacred Heart (1916), Rev. Carl Schmidt.
Res., 400 Jefferson, P.O. Box 278, Coffeen, 62017. Tel: 217-534-2220. [JC]

Paris, Edgar Co., St. Mary (1849), Rev. William J. Overmann.
Res., P.O. Box 577, 528 N. Main St., 61944. Tel: 217-466-3355. [CEM]
School—Tel: 217-463-3005; Fax: 217-463-3005.
Lay Teachers 7; Students 89.
Catechesis/Religious Programs—Students 99.

Pawnee, Sangamon Co., St. Mary (1899) (Irish-German), Revs. Charles G. Dahlby; John M. Savores.
Res., 509 Carroll St., P.O. Box 1010, 62558. Tel: 217-625-7540. [CEM]
Catechesis/Religious Programs—Students 85.

Petersburg, Menard Co., St. Peter (1868), Very Rev. Thomas P. Holinga, V.G.
Res., 711 S. Sixth St., 62675. Tel: 217-632-7118; Fax: 217-632-2561. [CEM]
Catechesis/Religious Programs—Students 226.

Pierron, Madison and Bond Cos., Immaculate Conception (1892), Rev. Msgr. Paul W. Sheridan.
Res., P.O. Box 25, 62273. Tel: 618-654-3604. [CEM]
Catechesis/Religious Programs—Students 94.

Pittsfield, Pike Co., Immaculate Conception (1870), Rev. Donald F. Sederwall.
Res., 226 E. Adams, 62363. Tel: 217-285-4321; Fax: 217-285-9400. [CEM]
Catechesis/Religious Programs—Tel: 217-285-4774.
Students 103.

Pocahontas, Bond Co., St. Nicholas, Rev. Msgr. Paul W. Sheridan.
Res., P.O. Box 25, Pierron, 62273. Tel: 618-654-3604.

Quincy, Adams Co.,

1—St. Anthony of Padua, (1859), Rev. Richard Bendorf, O.F.M.
Res., Quincy University, 1800 College Ave., 62301. Tel: 217-222-8020. [CEM]
Church—St. Anthony Rd., 62301. Tel: 217-222-5996.
School—Tel: 217-224-6477.
School Sisters of Notre Dame 1; Lay Teachers 5; Students 86.
Catechesis/Religious Programs—Students 104.

2—St. Boniface, (1837) (German), Rev. John Carberry.
Res., 117 N. Seventh St., 62301. Tel: 217-222-3000. [JC]
School—Tel: 217-223-6999.
Lay Teachers 6; Students 92.

3—St. Dominic, (1977). Unassigned.
Res., 3800 Columbus Rd., P.O. Box 3364, 62301. Tel: 217-224-9102. [JC]
Church—4100 Columbus Rd., 62301. Tel: 217-224-9102.
School—Tel: 217-224-0041.
Lay Teachers 12; Students 215.

4—St. Francis Solanus, (1860), Revs. Austin Albers, O.F.M.; Eugene Middendorf, O.F.M.; Michael Barrett, O.F.M.; Bro. Claver Boerner, O.F.M.
Res., 1721 College Ave., 62301. Tel: 217-222-2898. [JC]
School—Lay Teachers 11; Students 295.
Catechesis/Religious Programs—1721 College Ave., 62301. Tel: 217-222-4077.
Students 106.

5—St. John the Baptist, (1880) (German), Rev. John P. Beveridge.
Res., 1019 Cedar St., P.O. Box 3505, 62305-3505. Tel: 217-222-4622; Fax: 217-222-5554. [JC]
School—Tel: 217-228-1477.
Lay Teachers 9; Students 221.
Catechesis/Religious Programs—Students 222.

6—St. Joseph, (1868), Revs. Richard Bendorf, O.F.M.; Irenaeus Kimminau, O.F.M.; Sr. Pat Heidenry, C.H.M., Pastoral Assoc.
Res., Quincy University, 1800 College Ave., 62301. Tel: 217-228-5429.
Church—R.R. 1, 62301. Tel: 217-434-8442. [CEM]

7—St. Mary, (1867). (Immaculate Conception). Rev. Michael Kuse.
Res., 1119 S. Seventh St., 62301. Tel: 217-222-2759; Fax: 217-222-6463. [JC]
School—Tel: 217-223-3388.
Lay Teachers 11; Students 223.
Catechesis/Religious Programs—Students 104.

8—St. Peter, (1839) (Irish), Rev. Roy R. Bauer.
Res., 2600 Maine St., 62301. Tel: 217-222-3155; Fax: 217-222-3584. [JC]
School—Tel: 217-223-1120.
Lay Teachers 26; Students 589.
Catechesis/Religious Programs—Students 116.

9—St. Rose of Lima, (1892) (Irish), Rev. Francis D. Lee, Admin.
Res., 1009 N. Eighth St., 62301. Tel: 217-222-2511. [JC]

Ramsey, Fayette Co., St. Joseph (1870) (German-Irish), Rev. Don J. Roberts.
Res., 118 E. Main, P.O. Box 455, 62080. Tel: 618-423-2424. [CEM]
Catechesis/Religious Programs—Students 55.

Raymond, Montgomery Co., St Raymond (1881), Rev. William Maul.
Res., 306 S. McElroy, 62560. Tel: 217-229-4435. [CEM]
Catechesis/Religious Programs—Students 70.

Riverton, Sangamon Co., St. James (1871), Co-Pastors: Very Revs. John A. Renken, V.G.; Kenneth C. Steffen.
Res., 112 N. Sixth St., P.O. Box 590, 62561-0590. Tel: 217-629-9109 (Rectory); 629-7717 (Office).
Catechesis/Religious Programs—Tel: 217-629-7717. Mrs. Karen Buckman, D.R.E.
Students 161.

Robinson, Crawford Co., St. Elizabeth (1908), Rev. Richard W. Weltin.
Res., 207 E. Walnut St., 62454. Tel: 618-544-7526.
Catechesis/Religious Programs—Tel: 618-544-9327.
Students 202.

Rochester, Sangamon Co., Church of St. Jude (1976), Rev. Patrick Cahill, C.S.V.
Res., 633 S. Walnut St., 62563. Tel: 217-498-9197; Fax: 217-498-7180.
Parish Center: 635 S. Walnut St., 62563. Tel: 217-498-9524.
Catechesis/Religious Programs—Students 220.

St. Elmo, Fayette Co., St. Bonaventure (1843), Rev. T. Vincent Worland.
Res., 216 N. Ninth, Altamont, 62411. Tel: 618-483-5346. [JC]
St. Mary (1904), Rev. T. Vincent Worland.
Res., 216 N. Ninth, Altamont, 62411. Tel: 618-483-6464. [JC]

St. Jacob, Madison Co., St. James (1894), Rev. James A. Flach.
Res., 120 N. Windmill St., Box 457, Marine, 62061. Tel: 618-887-4535.
Catechesis/Religious Programs—111 Bethel Mine Rd., Caseyville, 62232. Tel: 618-345-4779. Lori Nicholas, D.R.E.
Students 67.

Ste. Marie, Jasper Co., St. Mary of the Assumption (1837), Sr. Ancilla Caulfied, O.P., Parish Life Coordinator.
Res., P.O. Box 68, 62459. Tel: 618-455-3155. [CEM]
Catechesis/Religious Programs—P.O. Box 68, 112 W. Embarras St., 62459.
Students 110.
Mission—Oblong, Crawford Co., St. Valentine's Chapel, Oblong, 62449.

Shelbyville, Shelby Co., Immaculate Conception (1879), Res., N. First at Washington St., P.O. Box 233, 62565. Tel: 217-774-3434.
Catechesis/Religious Programs—Students 75.

Sherman, Sangamon Co., St. John Vianney (1934), Rev. Eugene E. Costa.
Res., 129 Stardust Dr., P.O. Box 229, 62684. Tel: 217-523-3816; Fax: 217-523-3954.
Catechesis/Religious Programs—Students 97.

Shipman, Macoupin Co., St. Denis (1876), Rev. Robert N. Porter.
Res., P.O. Box A H, Bunker Hill, 62014-9512. Tel: 618-585-4700; Fax: 618-585-3449. [CEM]

Shumway, Effingham Co., Church of the Annunciation (1879), Rev. Alexis Pruemer, O.F.M.
Res., P.O. Box 96, 62461. Tel: 217-857-6404. [CEM]
Catechesis/Religious Programs—Students 92.

Sigel, Shelby Co., St. Michael the Archangel (1867), Rev. W. Jeffrey Holtman.
Res., Box 68, 62462. Tel: 217-844-3371. [CEM]
School—Tel: 217-844-2231.
Sisters 1; Lay Teachers 8; Students 164.
Catechesis/Religious Programs—Students 227.

Staunton, Macoupin Co., St. Michael (1875), Rev. George Radosevich.
Office: P.O. Box 240, 62088. Tel: 618-635-3140; Fax: 618-635-3140.
Res., 322 E. Main, 62088. Tel: 618-635-8490. [CEM]
School—419 E. Main, 62088. Tel: 618-635-3210.
Religious 1; Lay Teachers 6; Students 80.
Catechesis/Religious Programs—Students 159.

Stonington, Christian Co., Holy Trinity (1879) (Irish-German), Rev. Martin O'Hara.
Mailing Address: P.O. Box 257, 62567. Tel: 217-325-3697.
Res., 116 W. Adams, Taylorville, 62568. Tel: 217-824-8178.
Church—108 N. Elm St., 62567.
Catechesis/Religious Programs—Students 66.

Sullivan, Moultrie Co., St. Columcille (1905), Rev. John E. Sohm.
Res., 516 W. Jackson, P.O. Box 464, 61951. Tel: 217-728-4040.
Catechesis/Religious Programs—Students 73.

Taylorville, Christian Co., St. Mary (1845), Rev. John O'Connell.
Res., 116 W. Adams St., P.O. Box 470, 62568. Tel: 217-824-8178.
School—(Grades PreK-6). Tel: 217-824-6501.
Lay Teachers 11; Students 187.
Catechesis/Religious Programs—Students 185.

Teutopolis, Effingham Co., St. Francis of Assisi (1839), Very Rev. Lambert Leykam, O.F.M.; Revs. Vitus J. Duschinsky, O.F.M.; Patrick Curtis, O.F.M.
Res., 203 E. Main St., P.O. Box 730, 62467. Tel: 217-857-6404. [CEM]
Catechesis/Religious Programs—Tel: 217-857-6477; 857-1500. D.R.E.: Sr. Ann Vincent Siemer, S.S.N.D., (Grade School); Mrs. Maureen Brocker, (High School).
Students 816.

Troy, Madison Co., St. Jerome (1881), Rev. Steven A. Janoski.
Res., 511 S. Main, P.O. Box 94, 62294. Tel: 618-667-3397; Fax: 618-667-2697. [CEM 2]
School—St. John Neumann, Maryville, Tel: 618-345-7200.
Catechesis/Religious Programs—107 Wayland, 62294. Tel: 667-6571; Fax: 618-667-2697. Judy Werp, D.R.E.
Students 315.

Tuscola, Douglas Co., Forty Martyrs (1865), Rev. Michael Mullink; Sr. Pyllis Schenk, O.P.
Res., 201 E. Van Allen St., P.O. Box 352, 61953. Tel: 217-253-4412; Fax: 217-253-5010.
Catechesis/Religious Programs—Students 202.

Vandalia, Fayette Co., Mother of Dolors (1850), Rev. Stephen T. Sotiroff.
Res., 322 N. Seventh St., P.O. Box 377, 62471. Tel: 618-283-0214; Fax: 618-283-0751. [CEM]
Catechesis/Religious Programs—Students 73.

Venice, Madison Co., St. Mark (1871), Rev. Delix Michel.
Res., Sixth and Broadway, 62090. Tel: 618-451-1411. [JC]

Villa Grove, Douglas Co., Sacred Heart (1906), Rev. Paul H. Skelton.

Res., 208 N. Pine, Box 17, 61956. Tel: 217-832-8352.
Catechesis/Religious Programs—Students 105.
Mission—Hume, Edgar Co., St. Michael's, Hume, 61932. Tel: 217-385-2482.

Virden, Macoupin Co., Sacred Heart (1914) (Slovak). St. Catherine's (1866)- Merged in 1978. Rev. August J. Sperl.
Res., 721 N. Springfield, 62690. Tel: 217-965-4545.
Catechesis/Religious Programs—Students 124.

Virginia, Cass Co., St. Luke (1840), Rev. Ken Venvertloh.
Res., 240 E. Myrtle St., 62691. Tel: 217-452-7529.
Catechesis/Religious Programs—Students 58.

Waverly, Morgan Co., St. Sebastian (1856), Rev. Dan LaCount.
Office and Residence: 125 E. Washington St., Auburn, 62615. Tel: 217-438-6222. [CEM]

White Hall, Greene Co., All Saints (1883), Rev. Charles A. Edwards, Admin.
Res., c/o St. John, 414 Third St., Carrollton, 62016. Tel: 217-942-3551.
Church—S. Main St., 62092.

Wilsonville, Macoupin Co., Holy Cross (1854), Rev. Robert N. Porter.
Res., 300 S. Putnam, P.O. Box A-H, Bunker Hill, 62014-9512. Tel: 618-585-4700; Fax: 618-585-3449.

Winchester, Scott Co., St. Mark (1860), Rev. Charles T. Nelson.
Res., 108 Pearl St., 62694. Tel: 217-742-5224. [CEM]

Witt, Montgomery Co., St. Barbara (1905), Rev. Pat G. Jakel.
Res., 311 S. Elm St., Nokomis, 62075. Tel: 217-563-7146; 563-7808 (Personal); Fax: 217-563-8671. [CEM]

Wood River, Madison Co., St. Bernard (1919), Rev. James L. Neuman; Sr. Brendan Jacoby, O.S.U., Pastoral Assoc.
845 Danforth St., Alton, 62002. Tel: 618-462-4771.
Res., 345 Acton Ave., 62095. Tel: 618-254-0679 (Office); Fax: 618-254-2690.
School—Tel: 618-254-2697.
Lay Teachers 10; Students 140.
Catechesis/Religious Programs—Students 63.

Chaplains of Public Institutions

ALTON. *Alton State Hospital*. Vacant. St. Matthew Parish, 1015 Milton Rd., 62002. Tel: 618-465-8582.

HILLSBORO. *Graham Correctional Center*. 306 S. McElroy, P.O. Box 349, Raymond, 62560. Tel: 217-229-4435. Rev. George L. Morelock, Chap.

JACKSONVILLE. *Illinois State Hospital*. Attended by Our Savior Parish. 462 E. State St., 62650. Tel: 217-245-6184.
School for the Blind. Attended by Our Savior Parish. 462 E. State St., 62650. Tel: 217-245-6184.
School for the Deaf. Attended by Our Savior Parish. 462 E. State St., 62650. Tel: 217-245-6184.

MOUNT STERLING. *Western Illinois Correctional Center*. Attended by Holy Family Parish. 401 W. North St., 62353. Tel: 217-773-3233.

QUINCY. *Illinois Veterans' Home*, 1901 N. 18th, 62301. Tel: 217-224-0591. Rev. Richard M. Jeske, O.F.M.

TAYLORVILLE. *Taylorville Correctional Center*. Attended by St. Mary Parish. 116 W. Adams St., P.O. Box 248, 62658. Tel: 217-824-8178.

VANDALIA. *Vandalia Correctional Center*. Attended by Mother of Dolors Parish. 322 N. Seventh, 62471. Tel: 618-283-0214.

On Duty Outside the Diocese:
Reverend Fathers—
Habing, Paul, Prelatura, Apt. 102, Ayaviri-Puno, Peru
Meyer, Bernard A., 2425 Sage Rd., Apt. 45, Houston, TX 77056. Tel: 713-629-4822
Trojcak, Ronald, 59 Orkney Crescent, London, Ontario N5X 3R7 Canada
Westhoff, Frank D., P.O. Box 715, Columbia, MO 65205. Tel: 314-445-5335

Military Chaplains:
Reverend Fathers—
Blickhan, Donald, Chap., U.S. Army.
Gallenbach, Thomas, Chap., U.S. Air Force
Nolan, John, Chap., U.S. Air Force
Simburger, R. Joseph, Chap., U.S. Navy

Absent on Leave:
Reverend Fathers—
Cernich, Joseph
Poterucha, Michael
Schwellenbach, Aloysius

Retired:
Reverend Monsignors—
Bretz, John W., St. Joseph's Home, 3306 S. Sixth St., Springfield, IL 62703. Tel: 217-529-4883
Heinen, Paul, P.O. Box 363, Jerseyville, IL 62052. Tel: 618-498-2208
Plocki, Robert, 191 Steward Dr., Tiburnon, CA 94920. Tel: 415-435-2731
Suddes, James A., Marian Heights Apartments, 20 Oak St., Alton, IL 62002. Tel: 618-465-9209
Toliusis, Casimir, 624 Sumner St., Carlinville, IL 62626. Tel: 217-854-7314
Will, Irvin R., 100 Marian Pkwy., Sherman, IL 62684

Reverend Fathers—
Campbell, John, 295 Mellody Rd., Lake Forest, IL 60045. Tel: 708-295-1875
Colavecchio, John A., Villa Health Care Center, 100 Stardust Dr., P.O. Box 349, Room #27, Sherman, IL 62684. Tel: 217-544-5918
Corrigan, F. J., 1625 W. Washington, Springfield, IL 62702. Tel: 217-793-0515
Damjanov, Zvonimir, St. Patrick Church, P.O. Box 440, Pana, IL 62557. Tel: 217-562-5396
Davenport, Thomas J., 1625 W. Washington, Springfield, IL 62702. Tel: 217-793-0515
Gierut, Casimir, P.O. Box 156, Westmont, IL 60559
Heintz, Robert L., 422 Foulds Ave., Alton, IL 62002. Tel: 618-462-9747
Higgins, Patrick O., 76 Centre Dr., Manhasset, NY 11030
Houran, J. William, 3233 N.E. 32nd Ave., Apt. 902, Fort Lauderdale, FL 33308. Tel: 305-566-9802
Hughes, James J., Illinois Veterans Home, 1707 N. 12th, Springfield, IL 62301. Tel: 217-222-8641
Kennedy, John, 60 Spring Lake Estates, Quincy, IL 62301. Tel: 217-224-5288
Kondrath, James A., 9412 Francisco, Evergreen Park, IL 60642. Tel: 708-425-7164
Mack, Henry J., 38742 N. Drexel Blvd., Antioch, IL 60002. Tel: 312-395-1949
Mascari, Peter, 115 Stardust Dr., Sherman, IL 62684. Tel: 217-789-0611
McCarthy, Joseph F., 130 Curtis Ave., Burlington, VT 05401
Miller, Joseph, 127 Stardust Dr., Sherman, IL 62684. Tel: 217-523-5803
Mulcrone, Charles, 520 S. Second St., #704, Springfield, IL 62702
O'Reilly, Joseph, 1319 Tendick St., #3, Jacksonville, IL 62650-3120
Rieck, Raymond, 632 Sheridan Dr., Venice, FL 34292
Schmidt, Anthony, 520 S. Second St., #906, Lincoln Tower Suites, Springfield, IL 62701
Sheahan, John F., 513 Park Ave., Gillespie, IL 62033. Tel: 217-839-3650
Simpson, Roger, 271 E. Myrtle St., Virginia, IL 62691. Tel: 217-452-3168
Sullivan, James, 10311 Mason Ave., Oak Lawn, IL 60453-4335
Tamulis, Anthony J., 412 W. Fourth St., Mount Olive, IL 62069
Tracey, Terence, St. Francis Convent, Sangamon Ave., Springfield, IL 62794-9431

INSTITUTIONS LOCATED IN THE DIOCESE

[A] SEMINARIES, RELIGIOUS OR SCHOLASTICATES

GODFREY. *Immaculate Heart of Mary Novitiate*, 4563 Levis Ln., 62035. Tel: 618-466-2233; Fax: 618-466-2430. Revs. Joseph Paris, O.M.I.; Stephen Conserva, O.M.I.; Darrell Rupiper, O.M.I.; Bro. Herbert Beimert, O.M.I. Priests 3; Brothers 1; Clerical Novices 5.

[B] COLLEGES AND UNIVERSITIES

QUINCY. *Quincy University*, (1860) 1800 College Ave., 62301. Tel: 217-222-8020; 228-5318.
For a complete listing, refer to the Colleges and Universities section.

[C] JUNIOR COLLEGES

SPRINGFIELD. *Springfield College in Illinois*, 1500 N. Fifth St., 62702. Tel: 217-525-1420.
For a complete listing, refer to the Colleges and Universities section.

[D] HIGH SCHOOLS, PRIVATE

SPRINGFIELD. *Sacred Heart-Griffin*, 1200 W. Washington St., 62702. Tel: 217-787-1595; Fax: 217-787-9856. Springfield Dominican Sisters. Sr. Kathleen Anne Tait, O.P., Prin.; Sr. Margaret Joanne Grueter, Vice Prin. Sisters 15; Priests 3; Brothers 1; Lay Teachers 56; Students 846.
St. Joseph's Ursuline Academy, 1400 N. Fifth St., 62702. Tel: 217-523-5169; Fax: 217-523-2131. Dr. Karen Hunter Anderson. Ursuline Sisters 2; Priests 1; Lay Teachers 20; Students 260.

ALTON. *Marquette Catholic High School*, 219 E. Fourth St., 62002. Tel: 618-463-0580. John L. Rogers, Prin. Brothers 2; Sisters 1; Lay Teachers 25; Students 371.

DECATUR. *St. Teresa High School*, 2710 N. Water St., 62526. Tel: 217-875-2431. Mr. Lowell Brosamer, Prin. Ursuline Sisters 1; Lay Teachers 25; Students 309.

EFFINGHAM. *St. Anthony High School*, Roadway Ave., P.O. Box 545, 62401. Tel: 217-342-6969.

JACKSONVILLE. *Routt High School*, 500 E. College, 62650. Tel: 217-243-8563.

QUINCY. *Quincy Notre Dame High School*, 10th & Jackson Sts., 62301. Tel: 217-223-2479; Fax: 217-223-0023. Ray E. Heilmann, Prin. School Sisters of Notre Dame 1; Lay Teachers 28; Students 534.

[E] HIGH SCHOOLS, PAROCHIAL

SPRINGFIELD. High Schools are maintained in the following parishes (for particulars refer to the individual parish listing): St. Anthony, Effingham; Our Saviour, Jacksonville.

[F] THE CATHOLIC CHARITIES OF THE DIOCESE OF SPRINGFIELD IN ILLINOIS

SPRINGFIELD. *Catholic Charities of Springfield*, 120 S. 11th St., 62704. Tel: 217-525-0500. Mr. Lawrence Drury, Exec. Dir.
St. John's Breadline, 430 N. Fifth St., 62702. Tel: 217-528-6098. Meals Served Annually 160,000.
Society of St. Vincent de Paul (Diocesan Central Council), 800 S. Fifth St., 62703. Tel: 217-523-9201.

ALTON. *Catholic Charities of Alton and Wood River*, 735 Park Dr., 62002. Tel: 618-462-0634; Fax: 217-462-3209. Rick J. Faccin, Area Dir.

DECATUR. *Catholic Charities Community Services*, 401 N. Martin Luther King Jr. Dr., 62523. Tel: 217-428-5724. Judy Rogers, On Site Supvr.; Marie Rademacher, Area Dir.
Decatur Catholic Charities, 247 W. Prairie Ave., 62523. Tel: 217-428-3458. Mailing Address: Office for Catholic Charities, Diocese of Springfield, IL, Administration, 800 S. Fifth St., Springfield, 62703. Mrs. Marie Rademacher, Area Dir. Total Assisted 14,825.

EFFINGHAM. *Catholic Charities of Effingham*, 601 W. Fayette, 62401. Tel: 217-342-9800. Sr. Beth Marie Ruder, D.C., Area Dir.

GRANITE CITY. *Catholic Charities of Quad Cities*, 2105 State St., 62040. Tel: 618-877-1184; Fax: 618-877-1890. Mrs. Mary Alyce Beardslee, Area Dir.

QUINCY. *Catholic Social Services*, 926 State St., 62301. Tel: 217-222-0958. Sr. Mary Shaw, A.S.C., Area Dir.

[G] CHILDREN'S HOMES

ALTON. *Catholic Children's Home*, 1400 State St., 62002. Tel: 618-465-3594; Fax: 618-465-4023.
For a complete listing, refer to the Special Care Facilities section.

[H] GENERAL HOSPITALS

SPRINGFIELD. *St. John's Hospital*, 800 E. Carpenter St., 62769. Tel: 217-544-6464.
For a complete listing, refer to the Hospitals section.

ALTON. *Saint Anthony's Health Center*, Saint Anthony's Way, P.O. Box 340, 62002-0340. Tel: 618-465-2571.
For a complete listing, refer to the Hospitals section.

DECATUR. *St. Mary's Hospital*, 1800 E. Lake Shore Dr., 62521. Tel: 217-464-2966; Fax: 217-464-1616.
For a complete listing, refer to the Hospitals section.

EFFINGHAM. *St. Anthony's Memorial Hospital*, 503 N. Maple St., 62401. Tel: 217-342-2121.
For a complete listing, refer to the Hospitals section.

GRANITE CITY. *St. Elizabeth Medical Center*, 2100 Madison Ave., 62040. Tel: 618-798-3000; Fax: 618-798-3508.
For a complete listing, refer to the Hospitals section.

HIGHLAND. *St. Joseph's Hospital*, 1515 Main St., 62249. Tel: 618-654-7421; Fax: 618-654-2012.
For a complete listing, refer to the Hospitals section.

LITCHFIELD. *St. Francis Hospital*, 1215 E. Union, P.O. Box 1215, 62056. Tel: 217-324-2191.
For a complete listing, refer to the Hospitals section.

TAYLORVILLE. *St. Vincent Memorial Hospital*, 201 E. Pleasant St., 62568. Tel: 217-824-3331; Fax: 217-824-2099.
For a complete listing, refer to the Hospitals section.

[I] SPECIAL CARE INSTITUTIONS

SPRINGFIELD. *Brother James Court*, 2500 St. James Rd., 62707. Tel: 217-544-4876.
For a complete listing, refer to the Special Care Facilities section.
St. Monica's Center, 109 E. Lawrence Ave., 62704. Tel: 217-523-7922; Fax: 217-525-8241.
For a complete listing, refer to the Special Care Facilities section.

[J] HOMES FOR AGED

SPRINGFIELD. *Pope John Paul Apartments*, 1 Pope John

Paul Plaza, 62703. Tel: 217-528-1771; Fax: 217-528-5110.
For a complete listing, refer to the Special Care Facilities section.
St. Joseph's Home, 3306 S. Sixth St. Rd., 62703. Tel: 217-529-5596.
For a complete listing, refer to the Special Care Facilities section.
ALTON. *Marian Heights Apartments*, 20 Marian Heights Dr., 62002. Tel: 618-462-0363.
For a complete listing, refer to the Special Care Facilities section.

[K] MONASTERIES AND RESIDENCES OF PRIESTS AND BROTHERS

SPRINGFIELD. *Franciscan Brothers of the Holy Cross*, 2500 St. James Rd., 62707. Tel: 217-544-4876. Bro. Raphael Kreikemeier, F.F.S.C., Supr.
Priests' Purgatorial Society, Catholic Pastoral Center, 1615 W. Washington, P.O. Box 3187, 62708-3187. Tel: 217-698-8500.
Priests' Retirement Facility, Catholic Pastoral Center, 1625 W. Washington, 62702. Tel: 217-793-0515.
QUINCY. *St. Francis Solanus Friary*, 1721 College Ave., 62301. Tel: 217-222-2898. Revs. Austin Albers, O.F.M., Supr. and Pastor; Eugene Middendorf, O.F.M.; Michael Barrett, O.F.M.; Bro. Claver Boerner, O.F.M. Priests 3; Brothers 1.
SHERMAN. *Our Lady of Angels Friary*, 59 Woodsmill Dr., 62684. Tel: 217-496-2803; 496-2066. Retirement Community of Our Lady of Friars Minor (Sacred Heart Province). Bro. Joseph Sandlin, Guardian; Revs. Ralph Zetzl, Vicar; Owen Blum, O.F.M.; William Barnickel, O.F.M.; Roy Hassett, O.F.M.; Roger Niemeyer, O.F.M.; Cloud Billig, O.F.M.; Laurin Buzynski, O.F.M.; Hugolinus Kiener, O.F.M.; Walfrid Boesche, O.F.M.; Fabiano Merz, O.F.M.; Ralph Scherrer, O.F.M.; Ianatius Eckelkamp, O.F.M.; Warren Peternel, O.F.M.; Apollinaris Wackenheim, O.F.M.; Donulus Wunderlich, O.F.M.; Bros. Eugene Besand, O.F.M.; Justin Deken, O.F.M.; Kevin O'Connell, O.F.M.; Patrick Shea, O.F.M.; Denis Snelling, O.F.M.; Francis Stein, O.F.M.; Joseph Weithman, O.F.M.
TEUTOPOLIS. *St. Francis Assisi Friary*, 203 E. Main St., P.O. Box 730, 62467-0730. Tel: 217-857-6404. Revs. Lambert Leykam, O.F.M.; Vitus J. Duschinsky, O.F.M.; Patrick Curtis, O.F.M.; Gabriel Brinkman, O.F.M., Chap.; Alexis Pruemer, O.F.M.; Theodore Bracco, O.F.M.; Edwin Albers, O.F.M. Priests 7.

[L] CONVENTS AND RESIDENCES FOR SISTERS

SPRINGFIELD. *Convent of Our Lady of the Sacred Heart*, 1237 W. Monroe St., 62704. Tel: 217-787-0481. Legal Title: *Dominican Sisters of Springfield in Illinois.* Motherhouse of the Springfield Dominican Sisters. Motherhouse and Novitiate of the Dominican Sisters of Springfield in Illinois. Sr. Rose Miriam Schulte, O.P., Prioress Gen.; Sr. Norma Somers, O.P., Vicaress Gen.; Sr. M Regina Graham, O.P.; Rev. John H. Gerlach, O.P., Chap. Sisters in the Congregation 340; in Motherhouse 117; Novices 6.
St. Francis Convent, 4849 LaVerna Rd., P.O. Box 19431, 62794-9431. Tel: 217-522-3386. Motherhouse of the Hospitals Sisters of the Third Order of St. Francis. Mailing Address: P.O. Box 19431, 62794-9431. Sr. Bernadine Gutowski, O.S.F., Prov. Supr.; Sr. Mary Kelly, O.S.F., Religious Coord.; Rev. Terence Tracey, Chap. Sisters 167.
Other Locations: 2101 Shabbona, 62702. Tel: 217-789-4936. Sisters 4. 2405 Shabbona, 62702. Tel: 217-525-2137. Sisters 3. 2501 Sherborn Rd., 62702. Tel: 217-528-6492. Sisters 2. 4145 Sunderland Dr., Decatur, 62526. Tel: 217-877-2278. Sisters 3. 4309 Leslie Ln., Decatur, 62526. Tel: 217-875-2147. Sisters 3. 710 St. Anthony Ave., Effingham, 62401. Tel: 217-342-2873. Sisters 4. 1635 Main St., Highland, 62249. Tel: 618-654-9759. Sisters 5. 52 Fairview, 62704. Tel: 217-529-3050. Professed Sisters 218.
Ursuline Convent, 1400 N. Fifth St., 62702. Tel: 217-789-7910. Ursuline Nuns of the Roman Union in Community 30.
ALTON. *St. Francis Convent*, 2120 Central Ave., P.O. Box 9020, 62002-9020. Tel: 618-463-2750. Headquarters of the Province St. Elizabeth and Novitiate of the Sisters of St. Francis of the Martyr St. George. Mother M. Ingeborg, O.S.F., Prov. Final Professed 72(in US + 36 in Brazil); Junior Professed 25 (in US + 5 in Brazil); Novices 6 (in US + 7 in Brazil); Postulants 3 (in US + 7 in Brazil.).
Ursuline Convent of the Holy Family of the Ursuline Nuns of the Roman Union, 845 Danforth St., 62002. Tel: 618-465-9112. Sr. Theresa Davey, O.S.U., Prioress. Sisters 24. Ursuline Infirmary, 845 Danforth St., 62002. Tel: 618-465-0791. Sr. Colette Jokerst, Delegate Supr. Sisters 32.

[M] NEWMAN CENTERS

CARLINVILLE. *Blackburn College*, State Route 108 East, P.O. Box 647, 62626. Tel: 217-854-7151.
CHARLESTON. *Eastern Illinois University Newman Center*, 909 E. Lincoln Ave., 61920. Tel: 217-348-0188. Rev. Robert L. Meyer, Chap.; Mr. Roy Lanham, Dir.; Mrs. Lynn O'Dell, Vol. Coord.
DECATUR. *Millikin University Newman Catholic Community*, P.O. Box 2697, 62524-2697. Tel: 217-877-4146. Rev. Dennis Kollross, Chap.
EDWARDSVILLE. *Southern Illinois University Catholic Newman Center*, P.O. Box 1059, 62026. Tel: 618-692-3246. Mr. Ron Knapp, Campus Min.
GODFREY. *Lewis and Clark Junior College Newman Center.* P.O. Box 1059, Edwardsville, 62026. Tel: 618-692-3246. Mr. Ron Knapp, Campus Min.
JACKSONVILLE. *Illinois College Newman Center*, 462 E. State St., 62650. Tel: 217-245-6184. Rev. Allen Kemme, Chap.
MacMurray College Newman Center, 462 E. State St., 62650. Tel: 217-245-6184. Rev. Allan Kemme, Chap.

[N] MISCELLANEOUS LISTINGS

SPRINGFIELD. *Catholic Care Center, Inc.*, One Pope John Paul Plaza, 62703. Tel: 217-528-1771; Fax: 217-528-5110. Mr. Willard Bunn, Jr., Pres. Directors: Leo A. Lenn; John Maxwell, Treas.
Diocesan Care Management, Inc., 1 Pope John Paul Plaza, 62703. Tel: 217-528-1771; Fax: 217-528-5110. Most Rev. Daniel L. Ryan, J.C.L., D.D., Pres.; Mr. Leo Lenn, Dir.
Fields-Wright Medical Facility, Inc., 4936 La Verna Rd., P.O. Box 19431, 62794-9431. Tel: 217-523-4747. Sponsored by Hospital Sisters of St. Francis. Keith L. Callahan, Pres.; Sr. Jomary Trstensky, O.S.F., Contact Person.
Foundation for the People of the Diocese of Springfield in Illinois, Catholic Pastoral Center, 1615 W. Washington, 62702. Legal Title: *The Foundation for the People of the Roman Catholic Diocese of Springfield in Illinois.*
Hospital Sisters Health System, 4936 LaVerna Rd., P.O. Box 19431, 62794-9431. Tel: 217-523-4747. Sr. Jomary Trstensky, O.S.F., Pres.
Hospital Sisters of St. Francis Foundation, Inc., 4936 LaVerna Rd., P.O. Box 19431, 62794-9431. Tel: 217-523-4747. Jerry Gladu, Pres.; Sr. Jomary Trstensky, O.S.F., Contact Person.
Hospital Sisters Services, Inc., 4936 LaVerna Rd., P.O. Box 19431, 62794-9431. Tel: 217-523-4747. Sr. Jomary Trstensky, O.S.F., Pres.
Hunger, Inc., 800 S. Fifth St., 62703. Tel: 217-253-9201. Most Rev. Daniel L. Ryan, Chm.
Legion of Mary, 2109 Claremont Dr. Plaza, 62703. Tel: 217-529-0392. Elsie Venvertloh, Comitium Pres.; Marie T. Henebry, Comitium Pres.
**Springfield Developmental Center Ltd.*, 2500 St. James Rd., 62707. Tel: 217-525-8271. Developmental Training Program for Developmentally Disabled Adults. Cathy S. Barnett, Dir. Lay Staff 19; Clients 73.
Villa Maria - Catholic Life Center, 1903 E. Lake Dr., 62707. Tel: 217-529-2213. Mrs. Martina Kocher, Activities Coord.
Weber House - Weber Care Corporation, 2520 St. James Rd., 62707. Tel: 217-522-8406. Bros. Raphael Kreikemeier, Pres.; Gerald Voycheck, Vice Pres.; Luke Morin, Asst. Bed capacity 6; Residence capacity 6.
ALTON. *Saint Anthony's Foundation, Inc.*, Saint Anthony's Way, P.O. Box 340, 62002-0340. Tel: 618-465-2571.
Affiliates: Saint Anthony's Health System and Saint Anthony's Health Center. William E. Kessler, Pres.
Saint Anthony's Health System, Inc., St. Anthony's Way, P.O. Box 340, 62002-0340. Tel: 618-465-2571. Affiliates: Saint Anthony's Health Center and Saint Anthony's Foundation, Inc. William E. Kessler, Pres.; Rev. Craig MacMahon, O.M.V., Chap. Sisters of St. Francis of the Martyr St. George 19.
Saint Clare's Hospital, 915 E. Fifth St., 62002. Tel: 618-463-5150.
A Division of Saint Anthony's Health Center. William E. Kessler, Pres.; Rev. Craig MacMahon, O.M.V., Chap. Sisters of St. Francis of the Martyr St. George 19.
St. Francis Day Care Center, 710 College Ave., P.O. Box 9020, 62002-9020. Kindergarten & Day Care Center. Sisters of St. Francis of the Martyr St. George 2.
RIVERTON. *Benincasa-Dominican Renewal Center*, 7th and Adams Sts., P.O. Box 679, 62561-0679. Tel: 217-629-8469. Sr. Melanie Roetker, O.P., Dir.

RELIGIOUS INSTITUTES OF MEN REPRESENTED IN THE DIOCESE

For further details refer to the corresponding bracketed number in the Religious Institutes of Men or Women section.

[1320]—*Clerics of St. Viator.* (Chicago Prov.).—C.S.V.
[0510]—*Franciscan Brothers of the Holy Cross.*—F.F.S.C.
[0520]—*Franciscan Friars.* (Sacred Heart Province).—O.F.M.
[0690]—*Jesuit Fathers and Brothers.* (Missouri Province).—S.J.
[0910]—*Oblates of Mary Immaculate.* (Central Province).—O.M.I.
[0940]—*Oblates of the Virgin Mary.*—O.M.V.
[0430]—*Order of Preachers (Dominicans).*—O.P.
[]—*Society of Jesus*
[0420]—*Society of the Divine Word.*—S.V.D.

RELIGIOUS INSTITUTES OF WOMEN REPRESENTED IN THE DIOCESE

[0100]—*Adorers of the Blood of Christ.* (Ruma, IL; Wichita, KS).—A.S.C.
[0230]—*Benedictine Sisters of Pontifical Jurisdiction.* (Nauvoo, IL).—O.S.B.
[2100]—*Congregation of the Humility of Mary.*—C.H.M.
[1710]—*Congregation of the Third Order of St. Francis of Mary Immaculate, Joliet, IL.*—O.S.F.
[0760]—*Daughters of Charity of St. Vincent De Paul.* (East Central Prov.).—D.C.
[1070-10]—*Dominican Sisters.*—O.P.
[1070-13]—*Dominican Sisters.*—O.P.
[1440]—*Franciscan Sisters of the Poor.*—S.F.P.
[1820]—*Hospital Sisters of Third Order of St. Francis.*—O.S.F.
[2575]—*Institute of the Sisters of Mercy of the Union of the Americas.* (Chicago, IL).—R.S.M.
[3230]—*Poor Handmaids of Jesus Christ.*—P.H.J.C.
[2970]—*School Sisters of Notre Dame.* (St. Louis, MO).—S.S.N.D.
[1680]—*School Sisters of St. Francis.*—O.S.F.
[3520]—*Servants of the Holy Heart of Mary.*—S.S.C.M.
[0430]—*Sisters of Charity of the Blessed Virgin Mary.*—B.V.M.
[0990]—*Sisters of Divine Providence.* (St. Louis Prov.).—C.D.P.
[3360]—*Sisters of Providence of Saint Mary-of-the-Woods, Indiana.*—S.P.
[1570]—*Sisters of St. Francis of the Holy Family.*—O.S.F.
[1580]—*Sisters of St. Francis of the Immaculate Conception.*—O.S.F.
[1600]—*Sisters of St. Francis of the Martyr St. George.*—O.S.F.
[]—*Sisters of St. Joseph.* (India).
[3270]—*Sisters of the Most Precious Blood (O'Fallon, MO).*—C.PP.S.
[4110]—*Ursuline Nuns (Roman Union).* (Central Prov.).—O.S.U.

DIOCESAN CEMETERIES

SPRINGFIELD. *Calvary Cemetery Association.*
CARLINVILLE. *Calvary Cemetery Association.*
DECATUR. *Calvary Cemetery Association.*
EDWARDSVILLE. *Calvary Cemetery Association.*
LITCHFIELD. *Holy Cross Cemetery Association.*
MOUNT STERLING. *Catholic Cemetery Association.*
QUINCY. *Catholic Cemetery Association.*

NECROLOGY

† Dunn, Edward J., (On Duty Outside the Diocese). —Died Aug. 28, 1996.
† Huag, Rev. Msgr. William, Springfield, IL, Sacred Heart Convent. —Died April 17, 1996.
† Moore, John D., Macon, IL, St. Stanislaus Church. —Died May 15, 1996.
† Peradotto, Richard, Carlinville, IL, SS. Mary & Joseph Church. —Died Dec. 28, 1995.
† Shea, Louis C., Quincy, IL, St. Dominic Church. —Died Nov. 15, 1996.

Diocese of Springfield in Massachusetts

(Dioecesis Campifontis)

Most Reverend

THOMAS LUDGER DUPRE, D.D., J.C.D.

Bishop of Springfield; ordained May 23, 1959; appointed Auxiliary Bishop of Springfield and Titular Bishop of Hodelm April 19, 1990; consecrated May 31, 1990; appointed Bishop of Springfield March 14, 1995; installed May 8, 1995. *Res., 68 Elliot St., Springfield, MA, 01101. Mailing Address: P.O. Box 1730, Springfield, MA, 01101.*

Most Reverend

JOSEPH F. MAGUIRE, D.D.

Retired Bishop of Springfield; ordained June 29, 1945; appointed Auxiliary Bishop of Boston and Titular Bishop of Mactaris December 1, 1971; consecrated February 2, 1972; appointed Coadjutor Bishop of Springfield with right of succession April 3, 1976; officially installed as Bishop of Springfield on November 4, 1977; resigned December 27, 1991. *Res., 76 Elliot St., P.O. Box 1730, Springfield, MA, 01101.*

Chancery Office: P.O. Box 1730, Springfield, MA, 01101. Tel.: 413-732-3175; Fax: 413-737-2337.

ESTABLISHED JUNE 14, 1870.

Square Miles 2,822.

Comprises the Counties of Berkshire, Franklin, Hampden and Hampshire in the State of Massachusetts.

For legal titles of parishes and diocesan institutions, consult the Chancery Office.

STATISTICAL OVERVIEW

Personnel	
Bishop	1
Retired Bishops	1
Priests: Diocesan Active in Diocese	157
Priests: Active Outside Diocese	13
Priests: Diocesan in Foreign Missions	1
Priests: Retired, Sick or Absent	50
Number of Diocesan Priests	221
Religious Priests in Diocese	58
Extern Priests in Diocese	2
Ordinations:	
Diocesan Priests	2
Permanent Deacons in Diocese	35
Total Brothers	10
Total Sisters	644
Parishes	
Parishes	135
With Resident Pastor:	
Resident Diocesan Priests	122
Resident Religious Priests	13
Without Resident Pastor:	
Administered by Priests	8
Administered by Permanent Deacons	1
Missions	14
Pastoral Centers	1
Professional Ministry Personnel:	
Brothers	2
Sisters	53
Lay Ministers	68
Welfare	
Catholic Hospitals	2
Total Assisted	92,000
Health Care Centers	1
Total Assisted	140
Homes for the Aged	5
Total Assisted	441
Residential Care of Children	1
Total Assisted	125
Day Care and Extended Day Care Centers	1
Total Assisted	85
Specialized Homes	1
Total Assisted	155
Special Centers for Social Services	2
Total Assisted	52,198
Residential Care of Disabled	1
Total Assisted	325
Other Institutions	6
Educational	
Diocesan Students in Other Seminaries	10
Seminaries, Religious	1
Students Religious	5
Total Seminarians	15
Colleges and Universities	1
Total Students	1,187
High Schools, Diocesan and Parish	4
Total Students	1,945
Elementary Schools, Diocesan and Parish	30
Total Students	8,288
Non-residential Schools for the Disabled	1
Total Students	1,200
Catechesis/Religious Education:	
High School Students	9,230
Elementary Students	23,345
Total Students Under Catholic Instruction	45,210
Teachers in the Diocese:	
Priests	4
Sisters	82
Lay Teachers	574
Vital Statistics	
Receptions into the Church:	
Infant Baptism Totals	4,465
Adult Baptism Totals	156
Received into Full Communion	233
First Communions	4,118
Confirmations	3,112
Marriages:	
Catholic	1,283
Interfaith	327
Total Marriages	1,610
Deaths	4,189
Total Catholic Population	294,269
Total Population	802,611

Former Bishops—Most Rev. PATRICK THOMAS O'REILLY, D.D., cons. Sept. 25, 1870; died May 28, 1892.—Most Rev. THOMAS DANIEL BEAVEN, cons. Oct. 18, 1892; died Oct. 5, 1920.—Most Rev. THOMAS M. O'LEARY, D.D., cons. Sept. 8, 1921; died Oct. 10, 1949.—Most Rev. CHRISTOPHER J. WELDON, D.D., cons. March 24, 1950; retired Oct. 15, 1977; died March 19, 1982.—Most Rev. JOHN A. MARSHALL, D.D., cons. Bishop of Burlington, Jan. 25, 1972; installed Bishop of Springfield, Feb. 18, 1992; died July 3, 1994.—Most Rev. JOSEPH F. MAGUIRE, D.D., cons. Auxiliary Bishop of Boston, Feb. 2, 1972; installed Bishop of Springfield, Nov. 4, 1977; retired Dec. 27, 1991.

Vicar General—Rev. RICHARD S. SNIEZYK, Vicar General and Moderator of the Curia, *65 Elliot St., P.O. Box 1730, Springfield, 01101.* Rev. LEO A. LECLERC, *St. Rose de Lima Rectory, 600 Grattan St., Chicopee, 01020.*

Episcopal Vicars—Vicars for the Clergy: Revs. DAVID JOYCE; GEORGE FARLAND, Vicar for Finance: Rev. KARL HULLER, Vicar for Religious: Sr. JUDITH O'CONNELL, S.S.J., *65 Elliot St., P.O. Box 1730, Springfield, 01101.* Berkshire Vicariate: Rev. JOHN J. VARLEY, Franklin-Hampshire Vicariate: Rev. MICHAEL J. TWARDZIK, Hampden East Vicariate: Rev. HUGH CREAN, Hampden Central and Hampden West Vicariate: Rev. HOWARD MCCORMICK.

Chancery Office—*76 Elliot St., Springfield, 01105., Mailing Address: P.O. Box 1730, Springfield, 01101.* Tel: 413-732-3175; Fax: 413-737-2337.

Chancellor—Rev. DANIEL P. LISTON, J.C.L.

Vice-Chancellors—Rev. ROBERT W. THRASHER, J.C.D.; Sr. CAROL CIFATTE, C.S.J., J.C.L.

Vicar for Canonical Affairs—Rev. DANIEL P. LISTON, J.C.L.

Secretary to the Bishop—Rev. WILLIAM J. HAMILTON.

Judicial Vicar—Rev. JOHN L. SULLIVAN, J.C.L.

Adjutant Judicial Vicars—Rev. Msgr. ROGER VIAU, J.C.D.; Rev. JOHN P. MCDONAGH, J.C.L.

Director of the Tribunal—Sr. CLAIRE LAPOINTE, S.A.S.V., J.C.L.

Judges—Rev. DANIEL R. FOLEY, J.C.D.; Rev. Msgr. JOHN F. HARRINGTON, J.C.L.; Rev. Msgr. JOSEPH I. JOHNSON, J.C.D.; Revs. HENRY KARWEL, O.F.M.Conv., J.C.L.; DANIEL P. LISTON, J.C.L.; JOHN J. SHEA, J.C.D.; ROBERT W. THRASHER, J.C.D.

Promotor of Justice—Rev. JOHN R. BOURQUE, J.C.D.

Defenders of the Bond—Sr. CAROL CIFATTE, C.S.J., J.C.L.; Sr. CLAIRE LAPOINTE, S.A.S.V., J.C.L.; Rev. JOHN P. MCDONAGH, J.C.L.

Tribunal Instructor—Rev. EDWARD KENNEDY.

Procurators-Advocate—Revs. JEDDIE P. BROOKS; JUAN GARCIA, C.R.I.C.; Rev. DANIEL B. BRUNTON.

Psychotherapeutic Counselor—Rev. J. DONALD R. LAPOINTE, L.I.C.S.W.

Psychological Experts—MARTIN J. MARKEY, Ph.D.; ALFRED MILLETTE, L.I.C.S.W.; ROBERT SAISI, Ph.D., Ed.D.

Notaries—Mrs. CAROL MENDREK; Mrs. GERALDINE OLSON; Mrs. ELLEN RIVERS; Mrs. LORRAINE MCCORMICK.

Diocesan Tribunal—65 Elliot St., P.O. Box 1730, Springfield, 01101. Tel: 413-732-3175.

Bishop's Commission for Clergy—Revs. DAVID JOYCE, Chm. RICHARD S. SNIEZYK; CHRISTOPHER CONNELLY; EUGENE HONAN; JAMES JOYCE; GERARD LAFLEUR; LEO A. LECLERC; HOWARD W. MCCORMICK; KENNETH J. TATRO.

Diocesan Commission for Ecumenism—Rev. BRUCE N. TEAGUE, Chm., *76 Elliot St., P.O. Box 1730, Springfield, 01101.* Tel: 413-732-3175.

Diocesan Commission for the Liturgy—Rev. WILLIAM HAMILTON, Chm., *Christian Education Center, 625 Carew St., Springfield, 01104.* Tel: 413-732-3175.

Diocesan Director of Ceremonies—Rev. WILLIAM J. HAMILTON, *76 Elliot St., P.O. Box 1730, Springfield, 01101.* Tel: 413-732-3175; Fax: 413-737-2337.

Diocesan Consultors—Rev. Msgr. THOMAS F. DEVINE; Rev. Msgr. JOHN F. HARRINGTON, J.C.L.; Revs. HUGH F. CREAN; LEO A. LECLERC, V.G.; KARL HULLER; DAVID J. JOYCE; GERARD A. LAFLEUR; RICHARD S. SNIEZYK; DANIEL P. LISTON, J.C.L.

Deans—Franklin Deanery: Rev. TIMOTHY J. CAMPOLI, Greater Holyoke Deanery: Rev. ROLAND J. GALIPEAU, Greater Springfield I Deanery: Rev. THOMAS M. SHEA, Greater Springfield II Deanery: Rev. GEORGE A. FARLAND, Hampden Central Deanery: Rev. GERARD A. LAFLEUR, Hampden East Deanery: CHARLES KUZMESKI, Hampden West Deanery: Rev. KENNETH J. TATRO, Hampshire Deanery: ROBERT J. COONAN, Northern Berkshire Deanery: WARREN SAVAGE, Southern Berkshire Deanery: Rev. JOHN A. KOONZ.

Presbyteral Council—Rev. Msgr. THOMAS F. DEVINE; Rev. Msgr. JOHN F. HARRINGTON, J.C.L.; Revs. HUGH F. CREAN; VERNON P. DECOTEAU; CHRISTOPHER CONNELLY; RICHARD SCIOLI, C.S.S.; KARL HULLER; DAVID J. JOYCE; LEO A. LECLERC, V.G.; JAMES K. JOYCE; GERARD A. LAFLEUR; DANIEL P. LISTON, J.C.L.; RICHARD S. SNIEZYK; PAUL E. MANSHIP; JAMES P. MENGE; RICHARD M. RUNTE.

Vicar For Clergy—Rev. RICHARD S. SNIEZYK, *65 Elliot St., P.O. Box 1730, Springfield, 01101.* Tel: 413-732-3175.

Vicar for Finance—Rev. KARL HULLER, *65 Elliot St., P.O. Box 1730, Springfield, 01101.* Tel: 413-732-3175.

Vicar for Religious—Sr. JUDITH O'CONNELL, S.S.J., Vicar, *65 Elliot St., P.O. Box 1730, Springfield, 01101.*

Diocesan Offices and Directors

Apostolate to the Handicapped—Rev. ROBERT F. WAGNER, Dir., *Bureau for Exceptional Children and Adults, 537 Northampton St., P.O. Box 1039, Holyoke, 01041.* Tel: 413-538-7450 (voice and TTY); Fax: 413-536-5691.

Apostolate for Southeast Asian Catholics—Rev. JOHN H. PHAM, Dir., *Blessed Sacrament Rectory, 1945 Northhampton St., Holyoke, 01040.* Tel: 413-532-0713.

Apostolate of the Suffering—ROBERT J. LETASZ, Dir., *P.O. Box 535, Chicopee, 01021.* Rev. ADRIEN T. REMY, Chap., *Mont Marie, Holyoke, 01040.*

Blue Army—Rev. ALBERT E. BRETON, *St. Theresa's Rectory, 74 Bridge St., Agawam, 01001.* Tel: 413-786-4451.

Building Commission—Rev. JOHN J. SHEA, J.C.D., *Immaculate Heart of Mary Rectory, 256 State St., Granby, 01033.* Tel: 467-9821.

Building Consultant—Mr. FREDERICK R. PIQUETTE, *65 Elliot St., P.O. Box 1730, Springfield, 01101.* Tel: 413-732-3175.

Campaign for Human Development—Rev. MICHAEL J. DOYLE, Cabinet Sec.; Sr. ANNETTE M. MCDERMOTT, S.S.J., Dir., *65 Elliot St., P.O. Box 1730, Springfield, 01101.* Tel: 413-732-3175.

The Catholic Charismatic Renewal of Springfield, Inc.—Rev. GERALD BRADY, *Holy Trinity Rectory, Main St., Hatfield, 01038.* Tel: 413-247-3133. Sr. MARGARET WALSH, S.S.J., Coord., *P.O. Box 4668, Springfield, 01101-4668.* Tel: 413-247-9001; Fax: 413-247-5605.

Catholic Charities—Rev. MICHAEL J. DOYLE, M.S.W., *65 Elliot St., P.O. Box 1730, Springfield, 01103.* Tel: 413-732-3175.

Annual Catholic Appeal—Revs. KARL HULLER, Exec. Dir. MICHAEL J. DOYLE, Coord. of Allocations; PATRICIA EVANS, Coord. of Admin., *65 Elliot St., P.O. Box 1730, Springfield, 01101., Mailing Address: P.O. Box 1730, Springfield, 01101.* Tel: 413-732-3175.

Catholic Nurses Council—Rev. LAWRENCE J. BERNIER, Chap., St. Michael's Rectory, *128 Maple St., East Longmeadow, 01023.* Tel: 413-525-4253.

Catholic Relief Services—Rev. MICHAEL J. DOYLE, *65 Elliot St., P.O. Box 1730, Springfield, 01101.* Tel: 413-732-3175.

Cemeteries—Rev. FRANCIS P. LAVELLE, Diocesan Dir., *St. Michael's Cemetery, 1601 State St., Springfield, 01109.* Tel: 413-733-0659.

Censor of Books—Rev. Msgr. THOMAS F. DEVINE, *519 Longmeadow St., Longmeadow, 01106.* Tel: 413-567-3124.

Clergy Counseling Service—Rev. GEORGE A. FARLAND, *Sacred Heart Rectory, 395 Chestnut St., Springfield, 01104.* Tel: 413-732-3721.

Commission on Church Music—Rev. WILLIAM HAMILTON, Chm., *Christian Education Center, 625 Carew St., Springfield, 01104.* Tel: 413-732-3175; Fax: 413-732-1944.

Communications Committee—Mr. MICHAEL GRAZIANO, Chm., *65 Elliot St., P.O. Box 1730, Springfield, 01101.* Tel: 413-732-3175.

Continuing Education for Priests—Rev. JOHN T. SMEGAL, *North American Martyrs Rectory, 17 Juleann Dr., R.R. 01, Box 37, Lanesboro, 01237-9518.* Tel: 413-442-2063.

Office of Religious Education-CCD—Sr. PAULA ROBILLARD, S.S.J., Dir. JOAN SMOLA, Consultant for R.C.I.A. VIRGINIA WEBB, Consultant, *Christian Education Center, 625 Carew St., Springfield, 01104.* Tel: 413-732-3175. THERESA O'KEEFE, Berkshire Consultant, *100 Briggs Ave., Pittsfield, 01201.* Tel: 413-443-3187.

Cursillo Movement—Rev. JOHN J. BRENNAN, Dir. English-Speaking Cursillo Movement, *22 State St., Westfield, 01085.* Tel: 413-568-5421. Rev. REGIS J. GIROUX, Dir. Spanish-Speaking Cursillo Movement, *445 Plainfield St., Springfield, 01107.* Tel: 413-736-0076.

Diocesan Board of Christian Education—Rev. Msgr. THOMAS F. DEVINE, Chm., *625 Carew St., Springfield, 01104.* Tel: 413-732-3175.

Diocesan Office of Black Catholic Ministry—Mr. MICHAEL JONES, Coord., *255 King St., P.O. Box 81036, Springfield, 01138.* Tel: 413-732-0772.

Diocesan Office for Communications—Mr. MICHAEL A. GRAZIANO, Coord., *65 Elliot St., P.O. Box 1730, Springfield, 01101.* Tel: 413-732-3175; Fax: 413-747-0273.

Director of Personnel—Sr. CAROL CIFATTE, C.S.J., J.C.L.

Education—Sr. BETTE GOULD, S.S.J., Supt. of Schools; Sr. JANICE CARMEN, S.N.D., Coord. Student Svcs.; Sr. MAUREEN TOOMEY, S.N.D., Dir. Personnel; Sr. CONSTANCE ROY, S.S.J., Coord. of Curriculum, *Christian Education Center, 625 Carew St., Springfield, 01104.* Tel: 413-732-3175; Fax: 413-732-1944.

Director of Pittsfield Catholic Schools—Rev. JOHN J. BONZAGNI, *22 Maplewood Ave., Pittsfield, 01201.* Tel: 413-443-9686.

Family Life Bureau—625 Carew St., Springfield, 01104. Tel: 413-732-3175.

Fiscal Affairs—WILLIAM F. LABROAD, JR., Finance Officer; Miss JEANNE M. DESROSIERS, Controller, *65 Elliot St., P.O. Box 1730, Springfield, 01101.* Tel: 413-732-3175.

Holy Childhood Association—Rev. Msgr. JOHN F. HARRINGTON, J.C.L., Dir., *65 Elliot St., P.O. Box 1730, Springfield, 01101.* Tel: 413-732-3175.

Holy Family League of Charity—c/o Office of Catholic Charities, P.O. Box 1730, Springfield, 01101. Tel: 413-732-3175.

Marriage Counseling—Rev. JOHN J. JOHNSON, Dir. Counselors: Mr. ALFRED A. D'AMATO; Mrs. ROSEMARY CASTONGUAY, *65 Elliot St., P.O. Box 1730, Springfield, 01101.* Tel: 413-732-3175.

Massachusetts Catholic Conference—Rev. LEO A.J. LECLERC, V.G., *65 Elliot St., P.O. Box 1730, Springfield, 01101.* Tel: 413-732-3175. Rev. MICHAEL J. DOYLE, *65 Elliot St., P.O. Box 1730, Springfield, 01101.* Tel: 413-732-3175. Rev. RICHARD S. SNIEZYK, *65 Elliot St., P.O. Box 1730, Springfield, 01101.* Tel: 413-732-3175.

Ministry to the Deaf—Sr. CAROL LAREAU, S.S.J., *34 Nye St., Springfield, 01104.* Tel: 413-736-0020.

Ministry to the Divorced and Separated—Pastoral Ministry Office, Christian Education Center, 625 Carew St., Springfield, 01104. Tel: 413-732-3175.

Ministry to Priests—Rev. JOHN T. SMEGAL, *North American Martyrs Rectory, 17 Juleann Dr., R.R. 01, Box 37, Lanesboro, 01237.* Tel: 413-442-2063.

Newman Apostolate and Campus Ministry—Sr. BETTE GOULD, S.S.J., Dir., *Diocesan Schools Office, Christian Education Center, 625 Carew St., Springfield, 01104.* Tel: 413-732-3175; Fax: 413-732-1944.

Parish Councils—Sr. MARY LOU GILLON, S.S.J., *625 Carew St., Springfield, 01104.* Tel: 413-732-3175; Fax: 413-732-1944.

Pastoral Development—Rev. LEO A. LECLERC, V.G., *65 Elliot St., P.O. Box 1730, Springfield, 01101.* Tel: 413-732-3175.

Pastoral Ministry—Sr. MARY LOU GILLON, S.S.J., *Christian Education Center, 625 Carew St., Springfield, 01104.* Tel: 413-732-3175; Fax: 413-732-1944.

Peace and Justice—Rev. RICHARD S. SNIEZYK, Chm., *65 Elliot St., P.O. Box 1730, Springfield, 01101.* Tel: 413-732-3175.

Permanent Diaconate—Rev. TIMOTHY J. MURPHY, Dir.; Deacon JOSEPH GARDE, Co-Dir., *65 Elliot St., P.O. Box 1730, Springfield, 01101.* Tel: 413-732-3175.

Planned Giving—Rev. GEORGE G. GREENWAY, Dir., *65 Elliot St., P.O. Box 1730, Springfield, 01101.* Tel: 413-732-3175.

Press—"The Catholic Observer"; Mrs. SHARON ROULIER, Editor, *65 Elliot St., P.O. Box 1730, Springfield, 01101.* Tel: 413-732-3175; Fax: 413-747-0273.

Priests' Retirement Program—Rev. RICHARD SNIEZYK, V.G., Chm., *65 Elliot St., P.O. Box 1730, Springfield, 01101.*

Pro-Life Commission—Rev. JOHN L. SULLIVAN, J.C.L., *65 Elliot St., P.O. Box 1730, Springfield, 01101-1730.* Tel: 413-732-3175.

Propagation of the Faith—Rev. Msgr. JOHN F. HARRINGTON, J.C.L., *65 Elliot St., P.O. Box 1730, Springfield, 01101.* Tel: 413-732-3175.

Radio and Television—MICHAEL GRAZIANO, Coord. of Communications; Bro. TERRENCE SCANLON, C.P., Dir., *Catholic Communications Office, 65 Elliot St., P.O. Box 1730, Springfield, 01101.* Tel: 413-732-3175; Fax: 413-747-0273.

Refugee Resettlement Program/Immigration Services—Rev. MICHAEL J. DOYLE, Dir.; TUNG T. PHAM; Ms. ANNA BARANOVSKI, *65 Elliot St., P.O. Box 1730, Springfield, 01101.* Tel: 413-632-3175.

Representative of the Bishop at—Mercy Hospital, Springfield: Rev. KARL HULLER, Mont Marie Health Care Center: Rev. DANIEL P. LISTON, J.C.L., Providence Hospital, Holyoke: Rev. KARL HULLER, Sisters of Providence Care Centers, Inc.: Rev. JOHN L. SULLIVAN, J.C.L., Our Lady of Providence Children's Center, West Springfield: Rev. J. DONALD R. LAPOINTE, L.I.C.S.W., Sisters of Providence Health System: Mr. WILLIAM COLLINS.

Retired Priests' Service—Rev. EDWARD M. CALLAHAN, *Sacred Heart Rectory, 395 Chestnut St., Springfield, 01104.*

Saint Vincent de Paul Societies—65 Elliot St., P.O. Box 1730, Springfield, 01101. Tel: 413-732-3175.

Spanish Apostolate—Revs. MICHAEL J. DOYLE, Dir., *Blessed Sacrament Rectory, 1777 Dwight St., Springfield, 01107.* Tel: 413-736-8208. FRANCIS E. REILLY, Dir., *Casa Maria, 51 Hamilton St., Holyoke, 01040.* Tel: 413-533-6016. PAUL E. MANSHIP, *Holy Family Rectory, P.O. Box 91333, Springfield, 01139-1333.* Tel: 413-732-1422.

Springfield Diocesan Council of Catholic Women—Mrs. KATHERINE KUBERA, Pres., *11 Orchard Rd., East Longmeadow, 01028.*

Vigilance, Council of—The Deans.

Vocations—Rev. CHRISTOPHER MALATESTA, *65 Elliot St., P.O. Box 1730, Springfield, 01101.* Tel: 413-732-3175.

Office of Youth Ministry—Vacant, *Christian Education Center, 625 Carew St., Springfield, 01104.* Tel: 413-732-3175; Fax: 413-732-1944.

CLERGY, PARISHES, MISSIONS AND PAROCHIAL SCHOOLS

CITY OF SPRINGFIELD
(Hampden County)

1—ST. MICHAEL'S CATHEDRAL (1847), Rev. Karl Huller, Rector. In res., Rev. John P. McDonagh.
Res., 260 State St., 01103. Tel: 413-781-3656.

2—ALL SOULS (1908) (Spanish), Rev. Regis J. Giroux, Admin. In res., Rev. Steven McGuigan.
Res., 445 Plainfield St., 01107. Tel: 413-736-0076.
[CEM]
Catechesis/Religious Programs—Students 70.

3—BLESSED SACRAMENT (1953) (Hispanic), Revs. Michael J. Doyle; Juan F. Garcia, C.R.I.C. (Peru); Sr. Jane Morrissey, S.S.J., Pastoral Min.; Deacon Genaro Medina.
Res., 1777 Dwight St., 01107. Tel: 413-736-8208; Fax: 413-731-0962.
Catechesis/Religious Programs—Sr. Mary Cronin, D.M., D.R.E.
Students 334.

4—HOLY CROSS (1949), Revs. Thomas M. Shea; Daniel S. Pacholec. In res., Rev. Msgr. Robert E. Foudy, Pastor Emeritus.
Res., 221 Plumtree Rd., 01118. Tel: 413-783-4111; Fax: 413-783-4112.

School—153 Eddywood St., 01118. Tel: 413-782-5246. Sr. Patricia Rumse, S.S.J., Prin.
Sisters of St. Joseph 5; Lay Teachers 22; Students 503.
Catechesis/Religious Programs—175 Eddywood St., 01118. Tel: 413-782-8284.
Students 293.

5—HOLY FAMILY (1901) (African American-Hispanic), Rev. Paul E. Manship; Deacon Raphael Velazquez.
Res., 235 Eastern Ave., 01109. Tel: 413-732-1422.
Catechesis/Religious Programs—Tel: 413-732-0767.
Students 85.

6—HOLY NAME (1909), Revs. Hugh F. Crean, S.T.D.; Christopher D. Connelly; Sr. Catherine Leary, S.S.J., Pastoral Min.
Res., 323 Dickinson St., 01108. Tel: 413-733-5823.
School—37 Alderman St., 01108. Tel: 413-736-4235. Martha Kelliher, Prin.
Sisters of St. Joseph 2; Lay Teachers 24; Students 413.
Catechesis/Religious Programs—Tel: 413-736-4145.
Students 240.
Center—57 Alderman St., 01108. Tel: 413-734-7113.

7—IMMACULATE CONCEPTION (1905) (Polish), Revs. Adrian J. Benoit; Stefan J. Niemczyk.
Res., 25 Parker St. (Indian Orchard), 01151. Tel: 413-543-3627; Fax: 413-543-4301.
School—34 Kopernick St., 01151. Tel: 413-543-2897.
Felician Sisters 2; Lay Teachers 8; Students 170.

8—OUR LADY OF HOPE (1906), Revs. David J. Joyce; John V. Corbett, C.Ss.R. In res., Revs. Matthew J. O'Connor; George V. Joyce (WDC).
Res., 577 Carew St., 01104. Tel: 413-739-7369. [CEM]
School—474 Armory St., 01104. Tel: 413-734-4125.
Lay Teachers 25; Students 449.
Catechesis/Religious Programs—Students 224.

9—OUR LADY OF MT. CARMEL (1907) (Italian), Rev. Richard A. Scioli, C.S.S.; Sr. Elizabeth A. Matuszek, S.S.J., Pastoral Assoc.
Res., 123 William St., 01105. Tel: 413-734-5433; Fax: 413-731-0680.
School—36 Margaret St., 01105. Tel: 413-739-3616.
Daughters of Mercy 1; Lay Teachers 12; Students 155.
Catechesis/Religious Programs—Students 546.
Convent—56 Margaret St., 01105. Tel: 413-733-7410.
Mission—West Springfield, Hampden Co., St. Ann, 576 Memorial Ave., West Springfield, 01089. Tel: 413-736-3101. Revs. James E. Flanagan, C.S.S.; Joseph Massaro, C.S.S. In res., Rev. George Ecker, C.S.S.

10—OUR LADY OF THE ROSARY (1917) (Polish), Rev. John P. Skowronski; Deacon Rodney Szymczyk.
Res., 28 Underwood St., 01104. Tel: 413-733-0508.
Catechesis/Religious Programs—Students 104.

11—OUR LADY OF THE SACRED HEART (1929), Revs. Gerald J. Lapean; Richard A. Bondi.
Office: 51 Rosewell Ave., 01109. Tel: 413-782-8041; Fax: 413-783-9150.
Res., 417 Boston Rd., 01109.
School—52 Rosewell Ave., 01109. Tel: 413-782-8021.
Sisters of St. Joseph 2; Lay Teachers 17; Students 600.
Catechesis/Religious Programs—Students 261.

12—SACRED HEART (1872), Rev. George A. Farland. In res., Revs. Edward M. Callahan Tel: 413-372-3721; Mark S. Stelzer.
Res., 395 Chestnut St., 01104. Tel: 413-732-3721; Fax: 413-733-5731.
Catechesis/Religious Programs—Students 181.

13—ST. ALOYSIUS (1873) (French), Rev. Merle L. Lavoie.
Res., 1326 Worcester St., (Indian Orchard), 01151. Tel: 413-543-3739. [CEM]

14—ST. CATHERINE OF SIENA (1961), Revs. Charles F. Gonet; John G. Lessard-Thibodeau; Deacon Joseph Garde.
Res., 1023 Parker St., 01129. Tel: 413-783-8619; Fax: 413-783-2344.
Catechesis/Religious Programs—Tel: 413-783-8691.
Students 370.

15—ST. JOSEPH'S (1873) (French), Rev. William A. Tourigny.
Res., 82 Howard St., 01105. Tel: 413-733-3527; 733-3745.
School—1259 Columbus Ave., 01105. Tel: 413-733-8125.
Lay Teachers 11; Students 140.

16—ST. MARY'S (1948), Rev. James J. Scahill. In res., Rev. Richard S. Sniezyk.
Res., 840 Page Blvd., 01104. Tel: 413-739-0456.
Catechesis/Religious Programs—Tel: 413-736-1622.
Students 246.

17—ST. MATTHEW'S (1878), Rev. Merle L. Lavoie.
Res., 1326 Worcester St. (Indian Orchard), 01151. Tel: 413-543-3634.
School—90 Berkshire St., 01151. Tel: 413-543-1066.
Sisters of St. Joseph 1; Lay Teachers 18; Students 170.

18—ST. PATRICK'S (1961), Rev. Thomas M. Courtney; Deacon Donald E. Moore.
Res., 1900 Allen St., 01118-1820. Tel: 413-783-6201.
Catechesis/Religious Programs—Alan E. O'Dell, D.R.E.
Students 276.

19—ST. PAUL (1960), Rev. Francis H. Crombie; Deacon Robert Morrissey.
Res., 51 Fenimore Blvd., 01108. Tel: 413-737-4422.
Catechesis/Religious Programs—Students 238.
Mission—East Longmeadow, Hampden Co., St. Joseph's, 146 Vineland Ave., East Longmeadow, 01028. Tel: 413-737-8650.

20—ST. THOMAS AQUINAS (1908), Rev. William A. Pomerleau.
Res., 35 Harriet St., 01107-1898. Tel: 413-732-7525.
Mission—Springfield, Center for South East Asian Apostolate, Tel: 413-538-9875. Rev. John Pham, Dir.

OUTSIDE THE CITY OF SPRINGFIELD

Adams, Berkshire Co., Notre Dame des Sept Douleurs (1882) (French), Rev. Daniel J. Boyle.
Res., 21 Maple St., P.O. Box 231, 01220-0231. Tel: 413-743-0577; Fax: 413-743-4665.
St. Stanislaus Kostka (1902) (Polish), Rev. John C. Chwalek.
Res., 25 Hoosac St., 01220. Tel: 413-743-0041. [CEM]
School—108 Summer St., 01220. Tel: 413-743-1091.
Felician Sisters 2; Lay Teachers 9; Students 173.
Catechesis/Religious Programs—Students 186.
Convent—23 Hoosac St., 01220. Tel: 413-743-1221.
St. Thomas Aquinas (1875), Rev. Daniel J. Boyle.
Res., 2 Columbia St., P.O. Box 231, 01220-0231. Tel: 413-743-0577; Fax: 413-743-4665.
Catechesis/Religious Programs—Students 404.

Agawam, Hampden Co., St. John the Evangelist (1946), Revs. Howard W. McCormick; John K. Sheaffer.
Res., 833 Main St., 01001. Tel: 413-786-8105; Fax: 413-789-6266.
Catechesis/Religious Programs—Students 546.
St. Theresa of the Child Jesus (1883), Rev. Albert E. Breton.
Res., 74 Bridge St., 01001. Tel: 413-786-4451.
Catechesis/Religious Programs—Students 163.
Mission—Agawam, Hampden Co., St. Anthony, 108 Bridge St., 01001. Tel: 413-786-3724. Rev. John L. Sullivan, Admin.

Amherst, Hampshire Co., St. Brigid's (1872), Rev. Bruce N. Teague.
Res., 122 N. Pleasant St., P.O. Box 424, 01004. Tel: 413-253-2829; 256-6181. [CEM]
Catechesis/Religious Programs—Tel: 413-253-9873. Lucia Brown, D.R.E.
Students 227.
Students 227.

Belchertown, Hampshire Co., St. Francis of Assisi (1926), Rev. Vernon Decoteau; Deacon Louis Pancotti.
Res., 10 Park St., 01007. Tel: 413-323-6272.
Catechesis/Religious Programs—D.R.E. Mrs. Shelly Rose; Patrick Hegarty.
Students 775.

Bondsville, Hampden Co., St. Bartholomew's (1878), Rev. Eugene J. Plasse.
Res., 76 Thorndike St., Palmer, 01069. Tel: 413-283-5091; 283-8841 (Church). [JC]
Catechesis/Religious Programs—Students 71.
St. Adalbert's (1910), Rev. Normand F. Mailloux, M.S.
Res., 13 Depot St., P.O. Box 1083, 01009. Tel: 413-283-6749.

Brimfield, Hampden Co., St. Christopher's (1953), Rev. Walter A. Swift.
Res., Sturbridge Rd., Rte. 20, P.O. Box 387, 01010. Tel: 413-245-7274; Fax: 413-245-7274.
Catechesis/Religious Programs—Students 235.
Mission—Wales, Hampden Co., St. Monica.
Station—Holland, St. Bernadette's.

Cheshire, Berkshire Co., St. Mary of the Assumption (1926), Rev. Thomas B. Begley.
Res., 159 Church St., 01225. Tel: 413-743-2110.
Catechesis/Religious Programs—Students 255.

Chicopee, Hampden Co.,

1—ASSUMPTION, (1885) (French), Rev. Gerard A. LaFleur, V.F. In res., Rev. Michael H. Devlin.
Res., 104 Springfield St., 01013. Tel: 413-592-1597.
Catechesis/Religious Programs—Tel: 413-592-9344.
Students 120.

2—HOLY NAME OF JESUS, (1838), Rev. James J. Flahive.
Res., 33 South St., 01013. Tel: 413-592-0122. [CEM]
School—63 South St., 01013. Tel: 413-592-6857.
Sisters of Notre Dame 3; Lay Teachers 11; Students 230.
Catechesis/Religious Programs—Tel: 413-592-7813.
Students 120.

3—NATIVITY OF THE BLESSED VIRGIN MARY, (1897) (French), Rev. Robert H. Riel; Deacon George Kozach.
Res., 780 Chicopee St., 01013-2747. Tel: 413-532-9421; Fax: 413-532-1410.
School—Mount Carmel, 35 Mount Carmel Ave., 01013. Tel: 413-536-7293.
Lay Teachers 9; Students 163.

4—ST. ANNE'S, (1912), Rev. J. Victor Carrier; Deacons Edward J. Finnie, (Retired); Frederick J. Pelletier.
Res., 30 College St., 01020. Tel: 413-532-7503.
Catechesis/Religious Programs—Tel: 413-533-8038.
Students 367.

5—ST. ANTHONY'S, (1926) (Polish), Revs. Michael Lewandowski, O.F.M.Conv.; Michael Slonecki, O.F.M.Conv.
Res., 56 St. Anthony St., 01013. Tel: 413-538-9475; Fax: 413-538-9859.
Catechesis/Religious Programs—Students 82.

6—ST. GEORGE'S, (1893) (French), Rev. Ronald P. Lussier.
Res., 202 E. Main St., 01020. Tel: 413-598-8622.
School—Consolidated to form St. Joan of Arc/St. George School. 587 Grattan St., 01020.
Catechesis/Religious Programs—Students 225.

7—ST. MARY'S, (1939), Rev. Francis M. Kennedy.
Res., 840 Chicopee St., 01013. Tel: 413-532-1854.
Catechesis/Religious Programs—Students 100.

8—ST. PATRICK'S, (1872) (Irish), Revs. James Paul Menge; William C. Rousseau.
Res., 319 Broadway, 01020. Tel: 413-592-4178. [CEM]
School—125 Montgomery St., 01020. Tel: 413-594-8166.
Sisters of Saint Joseph 3; Lay Teachers 10; Students 302.
Catechesis/Religious Programs—Tel: 413-592-4344.
Students 337.

9—ST. ROSE DE LIMA, (1909) (French), Revs. Leo A. Leclerc; Christopher Waitekus; Deacon Leon Mireault.
Res., 600 Grattan St., 01020. Tel: 413-536-4558. [CEM][JC]
School—St. Joan of Arc/St. George School, 587 Grattan St., 01020. Tel: 413-533-1475.
Sisters of the Presentation of Mary 4; Lay Teachers 12; Students 213.
Catechesis/Religious Programs—Tel: 413-536-6038.
Students 329.

10—ST. STANISLAUS BASILICA, (1891) (Polish), Revs. Michael Kolodziej, O.F.M.Conv.; Steven Frenier, O.F.M.Conv.; Albert Scherer, O.F.M.Conv.; Anthony Francis Spilka, O.F.M.Conv.; Adalbert Piatkowski, O.F.M.Conv.; Bros. William Sudyka, O.F.M.Conv.; Frank Grimaldi, O.F.M.Conv. In res., Revs. Placid Kaczorek, O.F.M.Conv.; Herbert Baloga, O.F.M.Conv.
Res., 566 Front St., 01013. Tel: 413-594-6669; Fax: 413-594-5259. [CEM]
School—Tel: 413-592-5135. Sr. Deborah Ciolek, F.S.S.J., Prin.
Franciscan Sisters of St. Joseph 5; Lay Teachers 23; Students 465.
Catechesis/Religious Programs—Students 223.

Dalton, Berkshire Co., St. Agnes (1907), Rev. John A. Koonz; Deacon Pasqual Baldasaro.
Res., 489 Main St., 01226. Tel: 413-684-0125.
School—30 Carson St., 01226. Tel: 413-684-3143.
Sisters of St. Joseph 1; Lay Teachers 16; Students 330.
Catechesis/Religious Programs—33 Apple Tree Ln., 01226. Tel: 413-684-1745.
Students 460.

Easthampton, Hampshire Co., Immaculate Conception (1871), Revs. Richard M. Runte; Christopher A. Malatesta.
Res., 33 Adams St., 01027. Tel: 413-527-9778. [CEM]
School—Notre Dame-Immaculate Conception School, Tel: 413-527-6133. Miss Wendy E. Woods, Prin.
Lay Teachers 12; Students 252.
Catechesis/Religious Programs—11 Clifford St., 01027. Tel: 413-527-1588.
Students 650.
Our Lady of Good Counsel (1906) (French), Rev. Thomas R. Champigny.
Res., 35 Pleasant St., 01027. Tel: 413-527-9588.

School—Notre Dame-Immaculate Conception, Tel: 413-527-6133.
Lay Teachers 11; Students 245.
Catechesis/Religious Programs—Students 250.
Sacred Heart (1909) (Polish), Rev. Ronald F. Sadlowski.
Res., 33 Knipfer Ave., 01027. Tel: 413-527-9036; Fax: 413-527-9036. [CEM]
Catechesis/Religious Programs—Students 158.

East Longmeadow, Hampden Co., St. Michael's (1894), Revs. Lawrence J. Bernier, V.F.; John D. Betit.
Mailing Address: 128 Maple St., 01028.
Res., 49 Somers Rd., 01028. Tel: 413-525-4253.
Catechesis/Religious Programs—Tel: 413-252-0371. Mrs. Shirley Skiffington, D.R.E.
Students 794.

Feeding Hills, Hampden Co., Sacred Heart (1946), Rev. Kenneth J. Tatro; Sr. Eileen Sullivan, S.S.J., Pastoral Min.; Deacon James Martone.
Res., 1103 Springfield St., 01030. Tel: 413-786-8200.
Catechesis/Religious Programs—Tel: 413-789-6705. Kathryn Patterson, D.R.E.
Students 941.

Granby, Hampshire Co., Immaculate Heart of Mary (1951), Rev. John J. Shea.
Res., 256 State St., 01033. Tel: 413-467-9821.
Catechesis/Religious Programs—Tel: 413-467-3566.
Students 499.

Great Barrington, Berkshire Co., St. Peter's (1864), Rev. William H. Wallis.
Res., 16 Russell St., 01230. Tel: 413-528-1157. [CEM]
Catechesis/Religious Programs—Students 213.

Greenfield, Franklin Co., Blessed Sacrament (1960), Rev. Timothy J. Campoli, V.F.
Res., 182 High St., 01301. Tel: 413-773-3311; Fax: 413-773-5785. [CEM]
School—Holy Trinity School, 10 Beacon St., 01301. Tel: 413-773-3831. Sr. Christine Lavoie, S.S.J., Prin.
Lay Teachers 15; Students 189.
Catechesis/Religious Programs—Tel: 413-774-2918.
Students 200.
Holy Trinity (1868), Rev. Franklin A. Darling; Deacon Donald Chabot.
Res., 133 Main St., 01301. Tel: 413-774-2884.
Catechesis/Religious Programs—Students 160.
Sacred Heart (1912) (Polish), Team Ministry: Revs. Stanley J. Aksamit; Daivd M. Darcy.
Res., St. Mary's, 90 Seventh St., Turners Falls, 01376. Tel: 413-863-2585. [CEM]
Catechesis/Religious Programs—Students 79.

Hadley, Hampshire Co., Holy Rosary (1916) (Polish), Rev. William P. Murphy.
Res., 120 Russell St., P.O. Box 375, 01035. Tel: 413-584-1326. [CEM]
Catechesis/Religious Programs—Students 170.
St. John's (1915), Rev. Joseph Quigley, Admin.
Mailing Address: P.O. Box 597, 01035.
Res., 49 Middle St., 01035. Tel: 413-584-4185.
Catechesis/Religious Programs—Students 60.

Hampden, Hampden Co., St. Mary's (1951), Rev. Timothy J. Murphy.
Res., 27 Somers Rd., 01036. Tel: 413-566-8843. [CEM]
Catechesis/Religious Programs—Students 331.

Hatfield, Hampshire Co., St. Joseph's (1899), Rev. Robert J. Coonan.
Mailing Address: P.O. Box 34, 01038.
Res., 11 School St., 01038. Tel: 413-247-9079.
Catechesis/Religious Programs—Students 167.
Holy Trinity (1916) (Polish), Rev. Gerald Brady.
Res., 73 Main St., P.O. Box 110, 01038. Tel: 413-247-3133. [CEM]

Haydenville, Hampshire Co., St. Mary's (1889), Rev. Ronald G. Yargeau.
Res., 173 Main St., P.O. Box 277, 01039-0277. Tel: 413-268-7212. [CEM]
Catechesis/Religious Programs—Students 142.

Hinsdale, Berkshire Co., St. Patrick's (1868), Rev. R. Joseph LeVay.
Res., 43 Church St., P.O. Box 428, 01235. Tel: 413-655-2208. [CEM]
Catechesis/Religious Programs—78 Washington St., Becket, 01223.
Students 135.
Mission—Becket, St. Matthew.

Holyoke, Hampden Co.,

1—Blessed Sacrament, (1913), Revs. Peter G. Loughran; John Pham (Vietnam); C. Lee Gilbertson. In res., Rev. James D. McKenna.
Res., 1945 Northampton St., 01040. Tel: 413-532-0713.
School—21 Westfield Rd., 01040. Tel: 413-536-2236.
Sisters of St. Joseph 2; Lay Teachers 28; Students 441.
Catechesis/Religious Programs—15 Westfield Rd., 01040. Tel: 413-532-8647.
Students 190.
Mission—Holyoke, Hampden Co., Holyoke Soldier's Home Chapel, 110 Cherry St., 01040. Tel: 413-532-9475.

2—Holy Cross, (1905), Rev. Roland J. Galipeau; Rev. Msgr. John F. Harrington. In res., Rev. William J. Hamilton.
Res., 23 Sycamore St., 01040. Tel: 413-532-5661.
Catechesis/Religious Programs—Tel: 413-533-1665.
Students 201.

3—Holy Family, (1949), Rev. Robert W. Thrasher; Deacon Joseph A. Badame.
Res., 15 Holy Family Rd., 01040. Tel: 413-536-6777.
Catechesis/Religious Programs—Students 131.

4—Immaculate Conception, (1905), Revs. William D. LaFosse, M.S.; Henri Durand, M.S.; Bro. Bonaventure Russell, M.S; Deacon Lincoln Rael. In res., Rev. William J. Doherty, M.S.
Res., 54 N. Summer St., 01040. Tel: 413-532-5784. [JC]
Catechesis/Religious Programs—Students 72.

5—Mater Dolorosa, (1896) (Polish), Revs. Raphael Zwolenkiewicz, O.F.M.Conv.; Stanley Sobiech, O.F.M.Conv.; Andrew Skiba, O.F.M.Conv.; Adam Ziolkowski, O.F.M.Conv.; Bro. Stephen Murphy, O.F.M.Conv., Pastoral Assoc.
Res., 71 Maple St., 01040. Tel: 413-536-5271; Fax: 413-538-6754. [CEM]
School—25 Maple St., 01040. Tel: 413-532-2831.
Franciscan Sisters of St. Joseph 2; Lay Teachers 18; Students 341.
Catechesis/Religious Programs—Students 120.

6—Our Lady of Perpetual Help, (1890) (French-Canadian), Rev. Roland A. Renaud, Admin.
Res., 271 Chestnut St., 01040. Tel: 413-534-4407; 532-9751; Fax: 413-552-3779. [CEM][JC 2]
School—Tel: 413-536-5703.
Lay Teachers 12; Students 157.

7—Our Lady of the Rosary, (1886). Closed. For inquiries for parish records contact the Chancery.

8—Precious Blood, (1869). Closed. Parish records at Our Lady of Perpetual Help.

9—Sacred Heart, (1876), Revs. Francis E. Reilly; William H. Lunney.
Res., 435 Maple St., 01040 Tel: 413-532-4282. [JC]
Catechesis/Religious Programs—Students 300.

10—St. Jerome's, (1856), Rev. Daniel R. Foley, V.F.; Sr. Joan Ryzewicz, S.S.J., Pastoral Min.
Res., 169 Hampden St., 01040. Tel: 413-532-6381. [CEM]

Housatonic, Berkshire Co., Corpus Christi (1899), Rev. Anthony J. Jutt.
Res., 520 Main St., Box 569, 01236. Tel: 413-274-3443. [CEM]
Catechesis/Religious Programs—Students 76.
All Saints (1913) (Polish), Rev. Anthony J. Jutt.
Res., 204 Highland St., 01236. Tel: 413-274-6517.
Catechesis/Religious Programs—Students 62.

Huntington, Hampshire Co., St. Thomas (1886), Rev. Donald A. Noiseux.
Res., 8 E. Main St., P.O. Box 547, 01050. Tel: 413-667-3350; Fax: 413-667-5367. [CEM]
Mission—Chester, Hampden Co., St. John, Middlefield St., Chester, 01011.

Lanesboro, Berkshire Co., North American Martyrs (1969), Rev. John T. Smegal, Admin.; Deacon William C. Moesley.
Res., 17 Juleann Dr., 01237. Tel: 413-442-2063.
Catechesis/Religious Programs—Students 145.

Lee, Berkshire Co., St. Mary's (1857), Revs. Gary M. Dailey, Admin.; Brian F. McGrath.
Res., 40 Academy St., 01238. Tel: 413-243-0275; Fax: 413-243-1926. [CEM]
School—115 Orchard St., 01238. Tel: 413-243-1079.
Sisters of St. Joseph 3; Lay Teachers 9; Students 215.
Catechesis/Religious Programs—Students 270.
Missions—Otis, Berkshire Co., St. Mary of the Lakes, Tel: 413-269-4200; South Lee, Berkshire Co., St. Francis of Assisi.

Leeds, Hampshire Co., St. Catherine's (1911), Rev. Vincent M. O'Connor.
Res., 195 Main St., 01053. Tel: 413-584-1726.
Catechesis/Religious Programs—Students 170.

Lenox, Berkshire Co., St. Ann's (1891), Revs. Daniel B. Brunton; Donald L. Barron; Deacon George Keator.
Res., 134 Main St., 01240. Tel: 413-637-0157. [CEM]
Catechesis/Religious Programs—Tel: 413-637-4027. Mrs. Helen Stuart, D.R.E.
Students 218.

Lenox Dale, Berkshire Co., St. Vincent de Paul's (1904), Rev. Daniel B. Brunton. In res., Rev. John J. Bonzagni Tel: 413-637-1085.
Mailing Address: P.O. Box 259, 01242-0259.
Res., 29 Crystal St., 01242. Tel: 413-637-3525.

Longmeadow, Hampden Co., St. Mary's (1936), Rev. Msgr. Thomas F. Devine; Revs. William P. Murphy; Dariusz Wudarski.
Res., 519 Longmeadow St., 01106. Tel: 413-567-3124.
School—56 Hopkins Pl., 01106. Tel: 413-567-0907.
Sisters of St. Joseph 2; Lay Teachers 12; Students 257.
Catechesis/Religious Programs—Tel: 413-567-3420.
Students 850.

Ludlow, Hampden Co.,

1—Christ the King, (1948) (Polish), Rev. Raymond A. Soltys.
Res., 41 Warsaw Ave., 01056. Tel: 413-583-2630.
Catechesis/Religious Programs—Students 387.

2—Our Lady of Fatima, (1948) (Portugese), Rev. Vitor Oliveira, Admin.
Res., 438 Winsor St., 01056. Tel: 413-583-2312; Fax: 413-547-0207.
Catechesis/Religious Programs—Students 571.

3—St. John the Baptist, (1904) (French), Rev. Homer P. Gosselin; Deacon Edward Faber. In res., Rev. Lionel E. Bonneville.
Res., 181 Hubbard St., 01056. Tel: 413-583-3467; Fax: 413-583-2036.
School—217 Hubbard St., 01056. Tel: 413-583-8550.
Sisters of St. Ann 3; Lay Teachers 15; Students 265.
Catechesis/Religious Programs—Tel: 413-583-4258.
Students 308.

4—St. Mary, (1968), Revs. Francis J. Manning; Gerald L. Malboeuf; Deacon Robert L. Duval.
Res., 12 Cedar St., 01056. Tel: 413-583-2691.
Catechesis/Religious Programs—Students 539.

Millers Falls, Franklin Co., St. John's (1898), Rev. Dennis P. Bombardier.
Res., 5 Church St., 01349. Tel: 413-659-3435.
Mission—Erving, Franklin Co., St. Blanche, 16 East Prospect, Millers Falls 01344.

Monson, Hampden Co., St. Patrick's (1878), Rev. Jeddie P. Brooks; Deacon Bernard Pellissier.
Res., 22 Green St., P.O. Box 473, 01057. Tel: 413-267-3622. [CEM]
Catechesis/Religious Programs—Students 320.

North Adams, Berkshire Co.,

1—Holy Family, (1919), Rev. Warren J. Savage, Admin.; Deacon Robert R. Moulton.
Parish Center: 635 State Rd., 01247. Tel: 413-663-3976.
Res., Notre Dame Rectory, 228 E. Main St., 01247. Tel: 413-663-7131; Fax: 413-663-4940.
Catechesis/Religious Programs—Students 81.

2—Notre Dame, (1875), Rev. Warren J. Savage, Admin.; Deacon Robert R. Moulton; Bro. Edward Hall, C.P.
Res., 228 E. Main St., 01247. Tel: 413-663-7131.
Catechesis/Religious Programs—Students 125.

3—Our Lady of the Incarnation, (1955), Rev. Warren Savage, Admin.
Res., 228 E. Main St., 01247. Tel: 413-663-7131; Fax: 413-664-4940.
Catechesis/Religious Programs—Jackie Gould, D.R.E.
Students 94.

4—St. Anthony of Padua, (1903) (Italian), Rev. Daniel J. O'Hear.
Res., 70 Marshall St., 01247. Tel: 413-663-3112.
Catechesis/Religious Programs—Tel: 413-663-7331.
Students 162.

5—St. Francis, (1863), Rev. Philippe D. Roux.
Res., 12 Union St., 01247. Tel: 413-663-5316. [CEM]
Catechesis/Religious Programs—Tel: 413-662-2038.
Students 343.

Northampton, Hampshire Co.,

1—Annunciation, (1878), Revs. Roy H. Duquette; John S. Lis, Parochial Vicar; Thomas E. Cuff, Admin.
Res., 42 Beacon St., P.O. Box 60055, 01060-0055. Tel: 413-584-1520.
Catechesis/Religious Programs—87 Beacon St., Florence, 01060. Tel: 413-548-2041.
Students 305.

2—Blessed Sacrament, (1899), Rev. Francis P. Lavelle; Deacon Francis J. McCarthy.
Res., 336 Elm St., 01060. Tel: 413-584-1280.
Catechesis/Religious Programs—Tel: 413-586-1111.
Students 195.

3—Sacred Heart, (1886) (French), Rev. J. Donald R. Lapointe.
Res., 101 King St., 01060. Tel: 413-584-7422.
Catechesis/Religious Programs—Tel: 413-584-4339. Mrs. Helen Lucey, D.R.E.

Students 64.

4—ST. JOHN CANTIUS, (1904) (Polish), Rev. J. Donald R. Lapointe.
Res., 10 Hawley St., 01060. Tel: 413-584-1510.

5—ST. MARY OF THE ASSUMPTION, (1866), Rev. Eugene D. Honan; Deacon Bernard J. Fleury. In res., Rev. Leo J. Hoar.
Res., 3 Elm St., P.O. Box 180, 01061. Tel: 413-584-7310. [CEM]
Catechesis/Religious Programs—Tel: 413-586-1111. Students 150.

Northfield, Franklin Co., St. Patrick (1973), Rev. John J. Ayers; Deacon Arthur E. Ratte.
Res., 80 Main St., 01360. Tel: 413-498-2728. [CEM]
Catechesis/Religious Programs—Students 150.

Orange, Franklin Co., St. Mary (1903), Rev. James E. Diemand; Deacon James F. Donelan.
Res., 19 Congress St., 01364. Tel: 508-544-2900.
Catechesis/Religious Programs—Tel: 508-544-8105.
Students 256.

Palmer, Hampden Co., St. Thomas the Apostle (1864), Rev. Eugene J. Plasse,.; Deacon Edward J. Tenczar.
Res., 76 Thorndike St., 01069. Tel: 413-283-5091. [CEM]
Catechesis/Religious Programs—Tel: 413-283-5651.
Students 355.

Pittsfield, Berkshire Co.,

1—HOLY FAMILY, (1912) (Polish), Rev. Alexander Szymborski, C.R.L., Admin.
Res., 133 Seymour St., 01201. Tel: 413-442-2036.

2—NOTRE DAME, (1868) (French), Rev. Earl Hebert; Deacon Ralph R. Cyr.
Res., 50 Melville St., 01201. Tel: 413-499-2736.

3—OUR LADY OF MT. CARMEL, (1903) (Italian), Revs. Geoffrey J. Deeker, C.S.S.; Rinaldo A. Ribezzi, C.S.S.
Res., 359 Fenn St., 01201. Tel: 413-442-4458.
Catechesis/Religious Programs—Tel: 413-445-4856.
Students 102.
Mission—Pittsfield, Berkshire Co., All Souls, 51 Pembroke Ave., 01201. Tel: 413-442-5090.

4—SACRED HEART, (1919), Revs. James K. Joyce; Royal J. Gardner; Deacon James A. Hager; Mrs. Teresa Giardina, Pastoral Min.
Res., 191 Elm St., 01201. Tel: 413-443-6960.
School—Regional School, (Grades K-5) One Meadow Lane, 01201. Tel: 413-443-6379.
Sisters of St. Joseph 1; Lay Teachers 18; Students 338.
Catechesis/Religious Programs—Tel: 413-442-5564. D.R.E.: Mr. Robert Esposito; Mrs. Margaret Dextradeur.
Students 691.

5—ST. CHARLES, (1893), Rev. Peter A. Gregory; Sr. Barbara C. Faille, S.S.J., Pastoral Assoc.; Deacon William G. Moesley.
Res., 89 Briggs Ave., 01201. Tel: 413-442-7470; Fax: 413-445-5267.
Catechesis/Religious Programs—100 Briggs Ave., 01201. Tel: 413-442-0591.
Students 286.

6—ST. FRANCIS, (1960), Rev. John J. Mara.
Res., 80 Morningview Dr., 01201. Tel: 413-499-1955.
Catechesis/Religious Programs—Tel: 413-448-2987.
Students 152.

7—ST. JOSEPH'S, (1849), Rev. Michael Shershanovich; Deacon Eugene C. Momnie.
Res., 414 North St., 01201. Tel: 413-445-5789. [CEM]

8—ST. MARK'S, (1913), Rev. Henry L. Dorsch. In res., Rev. Msgr. Joseph I. Johnson, P.A., V.F., Pastor Emeritus.
Res., 27 Onota St., 01201. Tel: 413-447-7510.
Catechesis/Religious Programs—400 Columbus Ave. Ext., 01201. Tel: 413-442-8444.
Students 486.

9—ST. MARY THE MORNING STAR, (1915), Rev. Ralph A. Pollone.
Res., 665 Tyler St., 01201. Tel: 413-445-5008.
Convent—75 Plunkett St., 01201. Tel: 413-447-7533.

10—ST. TERESA, (1926), Rev. John J. Varley.
Res., 290 South St., 01201. Tel: 413-442-2202.
Catechesis/Religious Programs—Tel: 413-443-5366.
Students 176.

Russell, Hampden Co., Our Lady of the Rosary (1969), Rev. Armando C. Russo.
Res., Huntington Rd., 01071. Tel: 413-862-4418.
Catechesis/Religious Programs—Students 165.

Sheffield, Berkshire Co., Our Lady of the Valley (1901), Revs. Frederick L. Heberle; Stanley Sokol, Admin.; Deacon Herbert L. Cary.
Res., 99 Maple Ave., 01257. Tel: 413-229-3028. [CEM]
Catechesis/Religious Programs—Students 150.
Missions—Mill River, Berkshire Co., Immaculate Conception; Monterey, Berkshire Co., Our Lady of the Hills.

Shelburne Falls, Franklin Co., St. Joseph's (1883), Rev. John A. Roach.
Res., 34 Monroe Ave., 01370. Tel: 413-625-6405.
Missions—Colrain, Franklin Co., St. John the Baptist, Church St., Colrain, 01346.; Charlemont, Franklin Co., St. Christopher, Rte. 2, Charlemont, 01339.

South Deerfield, Franklin Co., St. James (1895), Rev. Julius A. Jutt.
Res., 85 Main St., 01373. Tel: 413-665-4535.
Catechesis/Religious Programs—Students 258.
Mission—Conway, St. Mark.

St. Stanislaus B. and M. (1908) (Polish), Rev. Michael W. Twardzik.
Mailing Address: 29 Sugarloaf St., 01373.
Res., 27 Sugarloaf St., 01373. Tel: 413-665-2417. [CEM]
Catechesis/Religious Programs—33 Sugarloaf St., 01373. Tel: 413-665-4656.
Students 185.

South Hadley, Hampshire Co., St. Theresa of the Infant Jesus (1946), Revs. Cyril J. Burns; Richard Riendeau; Deacon Thomas A. Callahan.
Res., 9E Parkview Dr., P.O. Box 159, 01075. Tel: 413-532-3228.
Catechesis/Religious Programs—Tel: 413-538-6276. Sandra M. Turban, D.R.E.
Students 1,197.

St. Patrick's (1877), Rev. Richard M. Turner; Deacon John Bledsoe. In res., Rev. David R. Raymond.
Res., 30 Main St., 01075. Tel: 413-532-2850. [CEM]
Catechesis/Religious Programs—Students 460.

Southwick, Hampden Co., Our Lady of the Lake (1951), Rev. Timothy J. Hallahan.
Res., 224 Sheep Pasture Rd., P.O. Box 1148, 01077. Tel: 413-569-0161.
Catechesis/Religious Programs—Rose M. Salzer, D.R.E.
Students 590.

Stockbridge, Berkshire Co., St. Joseph's (1922), Rev. Leonard J. Perreault.
Mailing Address: 143 Elm St., 01262.
Res., 30 Albany Rd., West Stockbridge, 01266. Tel: 413-232-4427. [CEM]

Thorndike, Hampden Co., St. Mary's (1876), Deacon Edward J. Tenczar, Admin.
Mailing Address: 80 Main St., 01079. Tel: 413-283-3501.
Res., 25 Cheney St., Three Rivers, 01080. Tel: 413-283-5776.

Three Rivers, Hampden Co., St. Anne's (1882) (French), Rev. Sylvio E. Levesque.
Res., 2230 Main St., 01080. Tel: 413-283-5041. [CEM]
Catechesis/Religious Programs—Students 155.

SS. Peter and Paul (1903) (Polish), Rev. Robert J. Ceckowski.
Res., 2267 Main St., 01080. Tel: 413-283-6030. [CEM]
Catechesis/Religious Programs—Students 240.
Convent—358 Main St., 01080. Tel: 413-283-7402.
The Sisters Minor of Mary Immaculate 4.

Turners Falls, Franklin Co., St. Mary's (1872), Revs. Stanley J. Aksamit; David M. Darcy.
Res., 90 Seventh St., 01376. Tel: 413-863-2585; Fax: 413-863-8978. [CEM]
Catechesis/Religious Programs—Students 185.

Our Lady of Czestochowa (1909) (Polish), Rev. Charles J. DiMascola.
Res., 84 K St., 01376. Tel: 413-863-4748. [CEM]
Catechesis/Religious Programs—Students 162.

St. Anne (1884) (French), Revs. Stanley Aksamit; David M. Darcy.
Mailing Address: 90 Seventh St., 01376. Tel: 413-863-2585. [CEM]
Church—J St., 01376. Fax: 413-863-4678.

Ware, Hampshire Co., All Saints (1860), Rev. Edward T. Fitzgerald.
Res., 17 North St., 01082. Tel: 413-967-4963. [CEM]
Catechesis/Religious Programs—Students 120.

Our Lady of Mt. Carmel (1871) (French), Rev. Paul A. Bombardier.
Res., 17 Convent Hill Rd., 01082. Tel: 413-967-5704. [CEM]
Catechesis/Religious Programs—Students 127.

St. Mary's (1905) (Polish), Revs. Charles H. Kuzmeski; Henry Karwel, O.F.M.Conv.
Res., 60 South St., 01082. Tel: 413-967-5913; Fax: 413-967-4679. [CEM]
School—59 South St., 01082. Tel: 413-967-9936; Fax: 413-967-8217.
Sisters of Immaculate Conception 3; Lay Teachers 9; Students 245.
Catechesis/Religious Programs—Tel: 413-967-5914.
Students 244.

Westfield, Hampden Co.,

1—HOLY TRINITY, (1903) (Polish), Revs. Gerald R. Biron, M.S.; Rene J. Butler, M.S.
Res., 335 Elm St., 01085. Tel: 413-568-1506.
School—(Grades K-8) 331 Elm St., 01085. Tel: 413-568-4352. Mrs. Janet Snow, Prin.
Lay Teachers 13; Students 161.
Catechesis/Religious Programs—Students 245.

2—OUR LADY OF THE BLESSED SACRAMENT, (1910), Rev. Francis X. Sullivan.
Res., 6 Union St., 01085. Tel: 413-562-3450.
Catechesis/Religious Programs—Tel: 413-562-3615. D.R.E.: Sr. M. Barbara Ebbe; Mrs. Deborah Lanoue.
Students 552.

3—ST. CASIMIR'S, (1915) (Lithuanian), Rev. John J. Brennan.
Res., 22 State St., 01085. Tel: 413-568-5421; Fax: 413-562-3879.
Catechesis/Religious Programs—Students 63.

4—ST. MARY'S, (1862), Revs. Anthony J. Creane; John C. Salatino; Deacon Francis D. Rogers.
Res., 30 Bartlett St., 01085. Tel: 413-562-5477; Fax: 413-562-5478. [CEM]
School—Tel: 413-568-2388.
Sisters 4; Lay Teachers 14; Students 245.
High School—Tel: 413-568-5692.
Sisters 2; Lay Teachers 16; Students 151.
Catechesis/Religious Programs—Tel: 413-568-1127. D.R.E.: Mrs. Kay Mowatt, Elementary; Mrs. Elizabeth Cassin, Elementary; Mr. Paul McKenna, High School.
Students 787.
Convent—86 Mechanic St., 01085. Tel: 413-568-8077.
Sisters of St. Joseph 3.

5—ST. PETER'S, (1913) (Slovak), Rev. John J. Brennan; Sr. Ann Marie Yenca, O.S.F., Pastoral Min. In res., Rev. John T. Dean.
Res., 22 State St., 01085. Tel: 413-568-5421; Fax: 413-562-3879.
Catechesis/Religious Programs—32 State St., 01085. Tel: 413-568-6261. Sr. Marcella Meluch, O.S.F., D.R.E.
Students 211.

West Springfield, Hampden Co., Immaculate Conception (1877), Rev. Michael J. Twohig. In res., Rev. John J. Johnson.
Res., 475 Main St., 01089-3998. Tel: 413-736-4071.

St. Louis de France (1895) (French), Rev. Daniel P. Liston.
Res., 817 Main St., 01089. Tel: 413-733-8026.

St. Thomas the Apostle (1904) (Irish), Revs. John T. Cain; Mark DiFabio; Steven Amo.
Res., 47 Pine St., 01089. Tel: 413-739-4779; Fax: 413-739-1608. [CEM]
School—89 Pine St., 01089. Tel: 413-739-4131.
Sisters of St. Joseph 2; Lay Teachers 26; Students 483.
Catechesis/Religious Programs—75 Pine St., 01089. Tel: 413-737-8267; Fax: 413-739-1608. D.R.E.: Mrs. Maxine Stawaz; Mrs. Diana Fontana.
Students 1,128.

West Stockbridge, Berkshire Co., St. Patrick's (1871), Rev. Leonard M. Perreault.
Res., Albany Rd., 01266. Tel: 413-232-4427. [CEM]

Wilbraham, Hampden Co., St. Cecilia's (1951), Rev. Joseph M. Soranno; Sr. Mary McCue, S.N.D., Pastoral Ministry.
Res., 7 Maple St., 01095. Tel: 413-596-4232; Fax: 413-596-9937.
Catechesis/Religious Programs—64 Main St., 01095. Tel: 413-596-9937. Sr. Mary Patrice Mahoney, S.N.D., D.R.E.
Students 1,001.

Williamstown, Berkshire Co., St. Patrick's (1887), Rev. William F. Cyr.
Res., 54 Southworth St., 01267. Tel: 413-458-4946; Fax: 413-458-4954.
Catechesis/Religious Programs—53 Southworth St., 01267. Tel: 413-458-5443.
Students 150.

St. Raphael's (1891), Rev. William F. Cyr.
Res., 54 Southworth St., 01267. Tel: 413-458-4946; Fax: 413-458-4954.
Catechesis/Religious Programs—Students 76.

Chaplains of Public Institutions

SPRINGFIELD. *Baystate Medical Center, Springfield Hospital Unit.* Rev. Michael H. Devlin, Assumption Rectory, 104 Springfield St., Chicopee, 01013. Tel: 413-592-1597. Rev. Steven McGuigan, All Souls, 445 Plainfield, 01107. Tel: 413-736-0076.

Municipal Hospital, Sacred Heart Rectory, 395 Chestnut St., 01104. Tel: 413-732-3721. Rev. Edward M. Callahan.

Wesson Memorial Hospital Unit, Sacred Heart Rectory, 395 Chestnut St., 01104. Tel: 413-732-3721. Rev. Edward M. Callahan.

Wesson-Women's Hospital Unit. Tel: 413-736-8773. Revs. Michael H. Devlin; Philip G. Gallerani.

HOLYOKE. *Soldiers' Home.* Served by Blessed Sacrament Parish. Tel: 413-532-0713.

MONSON. *State Hospital.* Bureau for Exceptional Children and Adults. 537 Northampton St., Box 1039, Holyoke, 01041. Tel: 413-538-7450. Rev. Robert F. Wagner; Deacon Rodney Szymczk.

NORTHAMPTON. *Veterans Administration Hospital,* 421 N. Main St., 01060. Tel: 413-584-4040. Rev. Sigmund Brambilla, O.F.M., Chap.

PITTSFIELD. *Berkshire Medical Center.* Tel: 413-447-2000. Rev. Leroy Smith, One County Rte. 13, Chatham Center, N.Y 12184-9639.

WESTFIELD. *Western Massachusetts Hospital.* Served by Our Lady of the Blessed Sacrament Parish. Tel: 413-562-3450.

Special Assignment:
Reverend Fathers—
Greenway, George G., 65 Elliot St., P.O. Box 1730, Springfield, MA 01105

On Duty Outside the Diocese:
Reverend Fathers—
Bermudez, Jose, 11801 Claridge Rd., Wheaton, MD 20902-2220
Cournoyer, Alfred, Parraquia San Ramon, Villanueva, Cortes, Honduras
DesRosiers, Denis, 300 Vernon St., #2, Oakland, CA 94610
Devino, Terrence P., Arrupe House, 35 Creighton St., Jamaica Plain, MA 02130
Marchese, Joseph P., Chap., Boston College, Chestnut Hill, MA 02167
Pham, Pierre, San Jose, CA
Potvin, Raymond H., Professor Emeritas, Catholic University, Box 1264, Washington, DC 20064
Tuohey, John F., Mercy Health Systems Oklahoma, 4300 West Memorial Rd., Oklahoma City, OK 73120-8362

Military Chaplains:
Reverend Fathers—
Walsh, Francis E., Office of the Chap., PSC 476, Box 61, FPO, AP 96322-1102

Graduate Studies:
Reverend Fathers—
Caron, David, Catholic Theological Union, 5401 S. Cornell, Chicago, ILL 60615
Schmitt, Thomas, Gregorian University, Rome, Italy
Stelzer, Mark, Sacred Heart Rectory, 395 Chestnut St., Springfield, MA 01104
Suszek, Eugene, Rome, Italy

Absent on Leave:
Reverend Fathers—
Cuff, Thomas E.
Dube, Donald V.
Farland, David
Gallerani, Philip G.
Graham, James
Graves, Alfred C.
Lavigne, Richard R.
Meehan, Richard
Sousa, Kevin
Sullivan, Charles J.

Retired:
Reverend Monsignors—
Foudy, Robert E., Holy Cross Rectory, 221 Plumtree Rd., Springfield, MA 01118
Guerin, Eugene E., Mont Marie Health Care Center, Holyoke, MA 01040
Harrington, John F., Holy Cross Rectory, 23 Sycamore St., Holyoke, MA 01040
Johnson, Joseph I., St. Mark Rectory, 27 Onota St., Pittsfield, MA 01201
Montcalm, Rosario L.U., 47 Pine Grove Dr., South Hadley, MA 01075-2196
Viau, Roger, St. Michael's Residence, 86 Wendover Rd, Springfield, MA 01118

Reverend Fathers—
Allen, William F., 18 Casino Ave., Chicopee, MA 01013
Anoia, John, 820 Jasmine Way, Clearwater, FL 34616
Baranowski, Xavier S., 13 Griswold Rd., G.N.B., P.O. Box 322, Niantic, CT 06357
Bernard, Paul J., 56 Sutton Rd., Millbury, MA 01527
Bourque, John R., 79 Clover Ln., P.O. Box 561, Mashpee, MA 02649
Cronin, James E., 14 Fairlawn Dr., Worcester, MA 01602
Delehanty, Thomas F., 2C Stonypoint Dr., P.O. Box 425, Ware, MA 01082
Desilets, Donald A., 35 Raymond Rd., Guildrod, CT 06437
Fennessey, Luke T., St. Michael's Residence, 86 Wendover Rd., Springfield, MA 01118
Forand, Clarence W., #293, 281 Chauncey Walker St., Belchertown, MA 01007
Fournier, W. Donald, 474 Grattan St., Chicopee, MA 01020
Gauvreau, Thomas H., 32 Richards St., North Adams, MA 01247
Greene, Thomas S., St. Michael's Residence, 86 Wendover Rd., Springfield, MA 01118
Lucey, John P., P.O. Box 636, Norwell, MA 02061
Lynes, Thomas E., P.O. Box 212, Old Saybrook, CT 06475
Malboeuf, Gerald L., 12 Cedar St., Ludlow, MA 01056
McCarthy, Thomas J., Holyoke Geriatric Center, 45 Lower Westfield Rd., Holyoke, MA 01040
McKenna, James, 1945 Northhampton St., Holyoke, MA 01040
Moreau, Ernest P., 4851 Gandy Blvd., 15-31, Tampa, FL 01104
Nadeau, Leon C., Chapin Terrace, 200 Kendall St., Springfield, MA 01104
O'Connor, Francis A., 22 Fiske St., Worcester, MA 01602
Ozimek, Eugene F., Mount St. Vincent Nursing Home, 35 Holy Family Rd., Holyoke, MA 01040
Pagano, Peter E., 1215 Massachusetts Ave., North Adams, MA 01247
Posco, Raphael A., Charlene Manor, 130 Colrain Rd., Greenfield, MA 01301
Quigley, J. Joseph, Newman Center, 472 N. Pleasant St., Amherst, MA 1002
Remy, Adrien T., Mont Marie Motherhouse, Holyoke, MA 01040
Riedl, Paul D., Mount St. Vincent Nursing Home, 35 Holy Family Rd., Holyoke, MA 01040
Rocha, Manuel, St. Michael's Residence, 86 Wendover Rd., Springfield, MA 01118
Sexton, John J., St. Michael's Residence, 86 Wendover Rd., Springfield, MA 01118
Sgueglia, Charles J.M., 44 Dexter St., Methuen, MA 01844
Sullivan, Francis J., St. Michael's Residence, 86 Wendover Rd., Springfield, MA 01118
Switalksi, Casimir S., Mount St. Vincent Nursing Home, 35 Holy Family Rd., Holyoke, MA 01040
Tokarz, John, St. Michael's Residence, 86 Wendover Rd., Springfield, MA 01118

Permanent Deacons:
Badame, Joseph, Holy Family, Holyoke
Baldasaro, Pasqual, St. Agnes, Dalton
Bledsoe, John, St. Patrick, South Hadley
Callahan, Thomas A., St. Theresa, South Hadley
Cary, Herbert L., Our Lady of the Valley, Sheffield
Chabot, Donald P., Holy Trinity, Greenfield
Chapdelaine, Roland G., Springfield Municipal Hospital
Cyr, Ralph R., Notre Dame, Pittsfield
Diaz, Celso B., On Duty Outside the Diocese
Donelan, James, St. Mary, Orange
Duval, Robert L., St. Mary of the Assumption, Ludlow
Faber, Edward H., St. John the Baptist, Ludlow
Finnie, Edward J., (Retired)
Fleury, Bernard J., St. Mary of the Assumption, Northampton
Garde, Joseph, St. Catherine, Springfield
Geary, Coleman P., On Duty Outside the Diocese
Hager, James A., Sacred Heart, Pittsfield
Herrick, Eugene, Burlington, VT
Keator, George, St. Ann, Lenox
Kozach, George, Nativity of the Blessed Virgin Mary, Chicopee
Martone, James A., Sacred Heart, Feeding Hills
McCarthy, Francis J., Blessed Sacrament, Northampton
Medina, Genaro, Sr., Spanish Apostolate at Blessed Sacrament, Springfield
Miller, Lucien M., Campus Ministry, Univ. of Massachusetts, Amherst
Mireault, Leon, St. Rose de Lima, Chicopee
Moesley, William C., St. Charles, Pittsfield
Momnie, Eugene C., St. Joseph, Pittsfield
Moore, Donald E., St. Patrick, Springfield
Morrissey, Robert J., St. Paul, Springfield
Moulton, Robert R., Notre Dame, Holy Family & Our Lady of Incarnation, North Adams
O'Brien, John P., On Duty Outside the Diocese
Pancotti, Louis
Pelletier, Frederick J., St. Ann, Chicopee
Pellissier, Bernard, St. Patrick, Monson
Rael, C. Lincoln, Immaculate Conception, Holyoke
Ratte, Arthur E., St. Patrick, Northfield
Rivera, Jose, On Duty Outside the Diocese
Rogers, Francis, St. Mary, Westfield
Szymzyk, Rodney J., Our Lady of the Rosary, Springfield
Tenczar, Edward J., St. Thomas the Apostle, Palmer
Velazquez, Raphael, Holy Family, Springfield
Wallen, Paul

INSTITUTIONS LOCATED IN THE DIOCESE

[A] SEMINARIES, RELIGIOUS, OR SCHOLASTICATES

GRANBY. *St. Hyacinth College and Seminary,* 01033. Faculty Residence: Tel: 413-467-7180. Student Residence: Tel: 413-467-7157. College: Tel: 413-467-7191. Friars Minor Conventual; Liberal Arts and Sciences. Certificates in Lay Ministry, Biblical Studies, and Catholic Spirituality. Revs. Jude Surowiec, O.F.M.Conv., Chief Academic Officer (Pres.) and Registrar; Gregory Moore, O.F.M.Conv., Guardian and Dir. Lay Min. Program; Claude Jarmak, O.F.M.Conv.; James E. McCurry, O.F.M.Conv., Dir. Marian Apostolate Knight of the Immaculata. Tel: 413-467-9190; Zeno Wierzbinski, O.F.M.Conv., (Retired); Jeremy Chodacki, O.F.M.Conv., (Retired); Cyprian Sondej, O.F.M.Conv., (Retired). Priests 7; Lay Professors 3; Non-Resident Students 34.

[B] COLLEGES AND UNIVERSITIES

CHICOPEE. *College of Our Lady of the Elms,* 01013. Tel: 413-594-2761; Fax: 413-592-4871.
For a complete listing, refer to the Colleges and Universities section.

[C] HIGH SCHOOLS, DIOCESAN

SPRINGFIELD. *Cathedral High School,* 260 Surrey Rd., 01118. Tel: 413-782-5285. Sr. Denise Granger, S.S.J., Prin.; Revs. Matthew J. O'Connor; David R. Raymond, Spiritual Dir. Priests 2; Sisters 11; Lay Teachers 76; Students 1,143.

HOLYOKE. *Holyoke Catholic High School,* 91 Chestnut St., 01040. Tel: 413-533-0347. Sisters of St. Joseph. Rev. David R. Raymond, Spiritual Dir.; Mr. William Fitzgerald, Prin. Priests 2; Sisters 7; Lay Teachers 25; Students 382.

PITTSFIELD. *St. Joseph Central High School,* 22 Maplewood Ave., 01201. Sisters of St. Joseph. Rev. John J. Bonzagni, Prin. & Dir. Pittsfield Catholic Schools. Priests 1; Sisters 2; Lay Teachers 26; Students 287.

[D] ELEMENTARY SCHOOLS, DIOCESAN

SPRINGFIELD. *Catholic Schools of Chicopee.* Diocesan School Department, Christian Education Center. 625 Carew St., 01104. Tel: 413-732-3175. Students 1,480; Total Staff 67.

Sacred Heart School, 370 Stafford St., 01104. Tel: 413-733-3630. Ms. Carol Brown, Prin. Sisters 2; Lay Teachers 11; Students 139.

[E] ORPHANAGES

WEST SPRINGFIELD. *The Brightside for Families & Children.* 2112 Riverdale St. Springfield, 01089. Tel: 413-788-7366.
For a complete listing, refer to the Special Care Facilities section.

[F] GENERAL HOSPITALS

SPRINGFIELD. *Mercy Hospital,* 271 Carew St., Box 9012, 01102-9012. Tel: 413-748-9000.
For a complete listing, refer to the Hospitals section.

HOLYOKE. *Providence Hospital, Inc.,* 1233 Main St., 01040. Tel: 413-536-5111; Fax: 413-539-0429.
For a complete listing, refer to the Hospitals section.

TURNERS FALLS. *Farren Care Center, Inc.,* 340 Montague City Rd., 01376. Tel: 413-774-3111.
For a complete listing, refer to the Hospitals section.

[G] FAMILY SERVICES

SPRINGFIELD. *Marriage Counseling Service*, 65 Elliot St., P.O. Box 1730, 01101-1730. Tel: 413-732-3175; 732-2909; Fax: 413-747-0273. Rev. John J. Johnson, Dir. Counselors: Mr. Alfred A. D'Amato; Mrs. Rosemary Castonguay. Total Staff 3; Total Assisted 539.

HOLYOKE. *Mont Marie Child Care Center, Inc.*, Mont Marie, 01040. Tel: 413-536-2964. Sr. Eleanor T. Harrington, S.S.J., Dir. Sisters of St. Joseph 1; Total Staff 16; Children 85.

Providence Ministries for the Needy, Inc., 476 Appleton St., P.O. Box 6269, 01041. Tel: 413-536-9109. Sponsored by the Sisters of Providence of Holyoke, MA. Mr. Robin L. Goshea, Admin. Total Staff 18; Total Assisted 51,659.

Broderick House. An around-the-clock family shelter. 56 Cabot St., P.O. Box 6269, 01041. Tel: 413-534-7610. Capacity 35.

Margaret's Pantry. Provides emergency food to families and individuals.

St. Jude's Center. Distributes clothing, furniture, and household items to the poor.

St. Joseph of Arimathia Guild. Provides advocacy to assure a dignified funeral and burial of the dead poor.

Loreto House. An around-the-clock shelter for homeless men. 264 Elm St., P.O. Box 6269, 01041. Tel: 413-532-7859. Capacity 18.

Kate's Kitchen. A soup kitchen which provides one meal daily to anyone in need - no questions asked. 264 Elm St., P.O. Box 6269, 01041. Tel: 413-532-0233. Capacity 99.

NORTHAMPTON. *Christian Life Center*, 95 King St., 01060. Tel: 413-584-7422.

PITTSFIELD. *Catholic Charities Counseling Office*, 467 North St., Rm. 15, P.O. Box 1372, 01202. Tel: 413-443-3169. Thomas A. Duane, L.I.C.S.W., Supr. Counselors: Robert T. Sykes; Janet M. O'Brien. Total Staff 3; Total Assisted 720.

TURNERS FALLS. *Montague Catholic Social Ministries, Inc.*, 25 Sixth St., 01376. Tel: 413-863-4805. Sr. Kathleen Hinga, S.S.J., Contact Person.
Purpose: To assist in providing information and referral, adult education, leadership and neighborhood development, partnership, coalition building and participation, facilitate parish concerns and social justice efforts. Total Staff 2; Total Assisted 400.

[H] HOMES FOR AGED

SPRINGFIELD. *St. Michael's Residence*, 86 Wendover Rd., 01118. Tel: 413-783-6773.
For a complete listing, refer to the Special Care Facilities section.

HOLYOKE. *Mont Marie Health Care Center, Inc.*, 34 Lower Westfield Rd., 01040. Tel: 413-536-0853; Fax: 413-533-3275.
For a complete listing, refer to the Special Care Facilities section.

Sisters of Providence Care Centers, Inc., 35 Holy Family Rd., 01040-2758.
For a complete listing, refer to the Special Care Facilities section.

[I] MONASTERIES AND RESIDENCES OF PRIESTS AND BROTHERS

STOCKBRIDGE. *Congregation of Marians*, Eden Hill, 01262. Tel: 413-298-3931; Fax: 413-298-1147.
Province: Tel: 413-298-1101; Fax: 413-298-1147. Revs. Walter Dziordz, M.I.C., Prov. Supr.; Kazimierz Chwakek, M.I.C., Prov. Econome; Bro. Kenneth Galisa, M.I.C., Prov. Sec.
The National Shrine of Divine Mercy: Tel: 413-298-3931; Fax: 413-298-3910. Rev. Joseph Roesch, M.I.C., Local Supr./Shrine Rector.
Marian Helpers Center: Bro. Andrew Maczynski, M.I.C., Dir., Marian Helpers Center.
Divine Mercy International: Revs. Seraphim Michalenko, M.I.C., Dir.; George Kosicki, C.S.B., Asst. Dir.
John Paul II Institute of Divine Mercy: Revs. Seraphim Michalenko, Dir.; George Kosiki, Asst. Dir. In res., Revs. Kazimierz Chalek, M.I.C., Local Supr.; Joseph Roesch, M.I.C.; Fidelis Grabowski, M.I.C.; Walter Dziordz, M.I.C.; Walter Pelczynski, M.I.C.; Seraphim Michalenko, M.I.C.; Bros. John Bryda, M.I.C., House Econome; Alphie Gagne, M.I.C.; Fred Wells, M.I.C.; Ken Galisa, M.I.C.; Andrew Maczynski, M.I.C.; Andrew Kwasnica, M.I.C. (Divine Providence Province, Poland. Priests 13; Felician Sisters 3; Brothers 6.
On Duty Outside Of House: Revs. Bernard Backiel, M.I.C.; Richard J. Drabik, M.I.C.; John J. Gayton, M.I.C.; Francis Duda, M.I.C.; Martin Rzeszutek, M.I.C.
On Duty Outside The U.S.A.: Revs. Mark Garrow, M.I.C., Third Gen. Councillor, Gen. Dir. Formation; Casimir Krzyzanowski, M.I.C., Sec. Gen., Postulator Gen., Procurator Gen.

[J] CONVENTS AND RESIDENCES FOR SISTERS

SPRINGFIELD. *Convent of the Good Shepherd*, 280 Tinkham Rd., 01129. Tel: 413-783-1251. Sr. Clare Marie Klein. Contemplative Sisters of the Good Shepherd 18; Total Staff 2.

HOLYOKE. *Daughters of the Heart of Mary Provincial Residence*, 1339 Northampton St., 01040-1913. Tel: 413-532-7406; Fax: 413-533-4217. Sr. Miriam Najimy, D.H.M., Prov. Total in Residence 38; Total Staff 3.

Marian Residence, 1365 Northampton St., 01040. Tel: 413-534-4502; Fax: 413-534-7353. Sr. Margaret E. Linehan, D.H.M., Supr. Daughters of the Heart of Mary 26.

Mont Marie, 01040. Tel: 413-536-0853. Motherhouse of the Sisters of St. Joseph of Springfield. Sr. Constance Quinlan, S.S.J., Pres.; Sr. Mary Quinn, S.S.J., Vice Pres.; Rev. Adrien T. Remy, Chap. Sisters 409; Total Assisted 85; Total Staff 16.

Providence Motherhouse - Sisters of Providence, 5 Gramlin St., 01040-4080. Tel: 413-536-7511; Fax: 413-536-7917. Motherhouse of the Sisters of Providence. Sr. Ruth McGoldrick, S.P., Pres. of Congregation; Rev. John L. Sullivan, Chap. In Residence. Sisters 132.

Sisters of Providence Health System, Inc. Includes an array of Health and Social Service Institutions in the Diocese. 1233 Main St., 01040-4080. Sr. Kathleen Popko, S.P., Pres., CEO.

Providence Ministries for the Needy, Inc., P.O. Box 6269, 01041-6269. Tel: 413-536-9109.

Genesis Spiritual Life Center, 53 Mill St., Westfield, 01085-4253. Tel: 413-562-3627.

Queen of Peace Centennial House, 64 North St., Greenfield, 01301. Tel: 413-772-2000.

Provincial House and Formation House, 1039 Northampton St., 01040. Tel: 413-532-8156. Franciscan Missionary Sisters of Assisi. Sr. Norbert Petrucci, S.J.M.A., Vice Prov. Sisters 8.

TYRINGHAM. *Order of the Visitation of Holy Mary*, Monastery of the Visitation, P.O. Box 432, 01264. Tel: 413-243-3995. Sr. Mary Francis de Sales. Order of the Visitation of Holy Mary 16.

WEST SPRINGFIELD. *Cana*, 686 Elm St., 01089. Tel: 413-732-9311. Sisters of Providence 3.

Monastery of the Mother of God, Dominican Nuns (Contemplative), 1430 Riverdale St., 01089-4698. Tel: 413-736-3639. Perpetual Adoration of the Most Blessed Sacrament. Sr. Mary St. John, O.P., Prioress; Rev. John T. Carrigan, O.P., Chap. Solemnly Professed Nuns 24; Professed Extern Sisters 1; Novices 4.

[K] RETREAT HOUSES AND CHRISTIAN LIFE CENTERS

SPRINGFIELD. *Center for Spiritual Direction*. Memorial House, Mercy Hospital. P.O. Box 9012, 01102-9012. Tel: 413-734-8843; 788-0195. Sr. Catherine Griffiths, S.N.D., Coord. Sisters 4; Total Staff 5; Laystaff 1.

WESTFIELD. *Genesis Spiritual Life Center*, 53 Mill St., 01085. Tel: 413-562-3627. Sr. Elizabeth Oleksak, S.P., Admin.; Sr. Ann Horgan, S.P., Asst. Admin; Ms. Ann McGaharn, Program Coord.; Sr. Vivian Pyne, S.S.J., Registrar. Total Staff 10; Total in Residence 2.

WILLIAMSTOWN. *Mount Carmel Retreat Center*, Oblong Rd., P.O. Box 613, 01267. Tel: 413-458-3164; Fax: 413-458-9420. Revs. Richard Champigny, O.Carm.; Maurice Cummings, O.Carm. Priests 2.

[L] INFORMATION CENTERS

SPRINGFIELD. *St. Francis of Assisi Chapel and Catholic Information Center*, 254 Bridge St., 01103-1410. Tel: 413-733-3101, 733-9298; Fax: 413-731-0691.
E-mail address: padrepio@wca.com
Revs. Barnabas J. Keck, O.F.M.Cap., Rector & Guardian; Andrew Drew, O.F.M.Cap.; Zachary Grant, O.F.M.Cap., Vicar; Raymond Hand, O.F.M.Cap.; Walter O'Brien, O.F.M.Cap., (Retired); John Schug, O.F.M.Cap.; Dominic Silvestro; Bro. Andrew Duclos, O.F.M.Cap. Priests 7.

CHICOPEE. *Open Window Book and Gift Shop of the Diocese of Springfield, Inc.*, 12-14 Center St., 01013. Tel: 413-594-5111. Mrs. Ann M. Kotfila, Mgr.

[M] SPANISH APOSTOLATES

SPRINGFIELD. *Casa Cristo Rey*, 1777 Dwight St., 01107. Tel: 413-736-2167. Revs. Michael J. Doyle; Juan F. Garcia, C.R.I.C. (Peru); Deacon Genaro Medina.

HOLYOKE. *Casa Maria*, 51 Hamilton St., 01040. Tel: 413-533-6016. Revs. Francis E. Reilly, Dir.; William H. Lunney, Assoc. Pastoral Associates: Sr. Ninfa Arellano, S.P.; Sr. M. Immaculate Conception, S.P.

NORTHAMPTON. *Spanish Apostolate*, Blessed Sacrament Rectory, 336 Elm St., 01060. Tel: 413-584-1280. Rev. Francis Lavelle, 336 Elm St., 01060.

[N] BUREAU FOR EXCEPTIONAL CHILDREN AND ADULTS

HOLYOKE. *Bureau for Exceptional Children and Adults Inc.*, 537 Northampton St., Box 1039, 01041. Tel: 413-538-7450; Fax: 413-536-5691. Rev. Robert F. Wagner, Dir.; Sr. Joan Magnani, S.S.J., Assoc. Dir. Sisters 2; Deacons 1; Lay Staff 3.

PITTSFIELD. *Bureau for Exceptional Children and Adults*, 414 North St., 01201. Tel: 413-538-7450; Fax: 413-536-5691. Rev. Robert F. Wagner; Sr. Joan Magnani, S.S.J., Assoc. Dir. Sisters 2; Deacons 1; Lay Staff 3.

[O] YOUTH SERVICES

GOSHEN. *Holy Cross Camp Grounds*, Cape St., P.O. Box 501, 01032-0501. Tel: 413-268-7819. Rev. Matthew J. O'Connor. Total Staff 3.

PITTSFIELD. *Catholic Youth Center*, 26 Melville St., 01201. Tel: 413-445-5496. Mr. Vincent P. Marinaro, Exec. Dir.

[P] NEWMAN APOSTOLATES AND CAMPUS MINISTRIES

AMHERST. *University of Massachusetts and Amherst College, Newman Center*, 472 N. Pleasant St., 01002-1739. Tel: 413-549-0300. Revs. Francis P. Lavelle; J. Joseph Quigley; Norman B. Bolton; Sr. Kathleen Keough, S.S.J.; Sr. Christine Methe, S.S.J.; Deacon Lucien Miller.

College of Our Lady of the Elms College (Chicopee), 291 Springfield St., Chicopee, 01013. Tel: 413-594-2761.

Bay Path College (Longmeadow), St. Mary's Rectory, 519 Longmeadow St., Longmeadow, 01106-2299. Tel: 413-567-3124.

Berkshire Community College (Pittsfield), St. Mark's Rectory, 27 Onota St., Pittsfield, 01201-3194. Tel: 413-447-7510.
Served through the priests at St. Mark's Rectory, Pittsfield.

North Adams State College (North Adams), North American Martyrs Rectory, 17 Juleann Dr., R.R.1, Box 37, Lanesboro, 01237. Tel: 413-442-2063. Rev. John T. Smegel.

Smith College (Northampton), Helen Hills, Hills Chapel, Northampton, 01063. Tel: 413-585-2750; 585-2752. Elizabeth E. Carr, Ph.D., Chap.

Mount Holyoke College (South Hadley), Office of the Chaplains, Eliot House, South Hadley, 01075. Tel: 413-538-2054. Mary Sue Calan-Fanley, Chap.

American International College; Springfield College; Springfield Tech Comm. College. (Springfield). Rev. Leo James Hoar, Campus Min.

St. Mary Rectory, 3 Elm St., P.O. Box 180, Northampton, 01061-0180. Tel: 413-748-3210.

Springfield College Campus Ministry Center, Beveridge Center, 263 Alden St., Springfield, 01109-3797. Tel: 413-748-3208; 3209.

Western New England College (Springfield), 1215 Wilbraham Rd., Springfield, 01119-2684. Tel: 413-782-1628; 549-0300 (Home); 782-1207 (Emergency).

Westfield State College (Westfield). Rev. John T. Dean.

St. Peter's Rectory, 22 State St., Westfield, 01085-3814. Tel: 413-568-5421.

Williams College (Williamstown), Baxter Hall, 39 Chapin Hall Drive, Williamstown, 01267-2569. Tel: 413-597-2483.

Holyoke Community College (Holyoke), 303 Homestead Ave., Holyoke, 01040. Tel: 413-538-7000, Ext. 511. Rev. Lee Gilbertson, Chap.

[Q] MISCELLANEOUS

SPRINGFIELD. *Good Shepherd Association of Springfield Mass.*, 280 Tinkham Rd., 01129. Tel: 413-783-1251. Sisters 18; Total Staff 2.

GRANBY. *Knights of the Immaculata Movement (Militia Immaculatae, M.I.).* (established 1931), St. Hyacinth College-Seminary, 66 School St., 01033. Tel: 413-467-9190. Rev. James E. McCurry, O.F.M.Conv., Dir.

HOLYOKE. *Mont Marie Conference Center*, 34 Lower Westfield Rd., 01040. Tel: 413-536-0853. Agnes Fleming, Dir.

RELIGIOUS INSTITUTES OF MEN REPRESENTED IN THE DIOCESE

For further details refer to the corresponding bracketed number in the Religious Institutes of Men or Women section.

[]—*The Association of Marian Helpers of Stockbridge, MA.*

[0470]—*The Capuchin Fathers.* (St. Mary's Prov.).—O.F.M.Cap.

[0270]—*Carmelite Fathers and Brothers.* (St. Elias Prov.).—O.Carm.

[0740]—*Congregation of Marians of the Immaculate Conception.*—M.I.C.

[1000]—*Congregation of the Passion.* (West Hoboken, NJ).—C.P.

[0480]—*Conventual Franciscans.*—O.F.M.Conv.

[0720]—*The Missionaries of Our Lady of La Salette.*—M.S.

[1280]—*Stigmatine Fathers and Brothers.*—C.S.S.

RELIGIOUS INSTITUTES OF WOMEN REPRESENTED IN THE DIOCESE

[1830]—*Contemplative Sisters of the Good Shepherd.*—C.G.S.
[0860]—*Daughters of Mary of the Immaculate Conception.*—D.M.
[0890]—*Daughters of Our Lady of Mercy.*—D.M.
[0810]—*Daughters of the Heart of Mary.*—D.H.M.
[0820]—*Daughters of the Holy Spirit.*—D.H.S.
[1050]—*Dominican Contemplative Nuns.*—O.P.
[1170]—*Felician Sisters.*—C.S.S.F.
[1330]—*Franciscan Missionary Sisters of Assisi.*—S.F.M.A.
[1470]—*Franciscan Sisters of St. Joseph.*—F.S.S.J.
[1180]—*Franciscan Sisters of the Allegany, New York.*—O.S.F.
[]—*Schonestatt Sisters of Mary.*
[1700]—*School Sisters of St. Francis.*—O.S.F.
[]—*Sister of the Most Holy Soul of Christ.*—S.S.Ch.
[]—*Sisters Minor of Mary Immaculate.*—S.M.M.I.
[3000]—*Sisters of Notre Dame de Namur.*—S.N.D.deN.
[3340]—*Sisters of Providence.*—S.P.
[3718]—*Sisters of St. Ann.*—S.S.A.
[3750]—*Sisters of St. Chretienne.*—S.S.Ch.
[3830-16]—*Sisters of St. Joseph.*—S.S.J.
[3850]—*Sisters of St. Joseph of Chambery.*—C.S.J.
[0150]—*Sisters of the Assumption.*—S.A.S.V.
[3320]—*Sisters of the Presentation of the B.V.M.*—P.B.V.M.
[3310]—*Sisters of the Presentation of Mary.*—P.M.
[4190]—*Visitation Nuns.*—V.H.M.

DIOCESAN CEMETERIES

SPRINGFIELD. *Gate of Heaven*, 421 Tinkham Rd., 01129. Tel: 413-782-4731.
St. Michael's, 1601 State St., 01109. Tel: 413-733-0659.

HOLYOKE. *Calvary*, Northampton St., 01040. Tel: 413-733-0659.

NECROLOGY

† Carberry, Paul A., (Retired). —Died Jan. 1, 1996.
† Daugiello, Conrad, (Retired). —Died Oct. 12, 1996.
† Joyce, Walter Joseph, (Retired). —Died July 16, 1996.
† Menard, Anthony J., (Retired). —Died Jan. 22, 1996.
† Nadeau, Leon, (Retired). —Died Nov. 14, 1996.

Diocese of Steubenville

(Dioecesis Steubenvicensis)

Most Reverend

GILBERT I. SHELDON, D.D., D.MIN.

Bishop of Steubenville; ordained February 28, 1953; appointed Auxiliary and Titular Bishop of Taparura April 20, 1976; consecrated June 11, 1976; appointed to Steubenville January 28, 1992; installed April 2, 1992. *Mailing Address: P.O. Box 969, Steubenville, OH, 43952.*

Most Reverend

ALBERT H. OTTENWELLER, D.D., S.T.L.

Bishop of Steubenville; ordained June 19, 1943; appointed Titular Bishop of Perdices and Auxiliary of Toledo April 17, 1974; consecrated May 29, 1974; appointed to Steubenville October 11, 1977; installed November 22, 1977; retired April 2, 1992. *Res., 609 N. Seventh St., Steubenville, OH, 43952.*

ESTABLISHED 1944.

Square Miles 5,913.

Comprises these thirteen Counties in the State of Ohio: Athens, Belmont, Carroll, Gallia, Guernsey, Harrison, Jefferson, Lawrence, Meigs, Morgan, Monroe, Noble and Washington.

For legal titles of parishes and diocesan institutions, consult the Chancery Office.

Chancery Office: 422 Washington St., P.O. Box 969, Steubenville, OH, 43952. Tel.: 614-282-3631; Fax: 614-282-3327.

STATISTICAL OVERVIEW

Personnel	
Bishop	1
Retired Bishops	1
Priests: Diocesan Active in Diocese	65
Priests: Active Outside Diocese	15
Priests: Diocesan in Foreign Missions	1
Priests: Retired, Sick or Absent	44
Number of Diocesan Priests	125
Religious Priests in Diocese	20
Extern Priests in Diocese	4
Ordinations:	
Religious Priests	2
Permanent Deacons in Diocese	5
Total Brothers	11
Total Sisters	89
Parishes	
Parishes	74
With Resident Pastor:	
Resident Diocesan Priests	73
Resident Religious Priests	1
Without Resident Pastor:	
Administered by Priests	1
Missions	3
Professional Ministry Personnel:	
Brothers	2
Sisters	5
Lay Ministers	13
Welfare	
Catholic Hospitals	2
Total Assisted	237,074
Homes for the Aged	1
Total Assisted	87
Special Centers for Social Services	1
Total Assisted	11,057
Residential Care of Disabled	1
Total Assisted	62
Educational	
Diocesan Students in Other Seminaries	6
Total Seminarians	6
Colleges and Universities	1
Total Students	1,936
High Schools, Diocesan and Parish	3
Total Students	728
Elementary Schools, Diocesan and Parish	16
Total Students	2,899
Catechesis/Religious Education:	
High School Students	1,056
Elementary Students	2,809
Total Students Under Catholic Instruction	9,434
Teachers in the Diocese:	
Priests	1
Sisters	10
Lay Teachers	242
Vital Statistics	
Receptions into the Church:	
Infant Baptism Totals	785
Adult Baptism Totals	350
First Communions	1,622
Confirmations	1,383
Marriages:	
Catholic	194
Interfaith	172
Total Marriages	366
Deaths	729
Total Catholic Population	46,015
Total Population	506,136

Former Bishops—Most Rev. JOHN KING MUSSIO, D.D., J.C.D., named First Bishop of Steubenville. Ordained for Diocese of Cincinnati Aug. 15, 1935; appt. First Bishop of Steubenville, March 16, 1945; cons. May 1, 1945; retired Oct. 11, 1977; died April 15, 1978.

Vicar General—Rev. Msgr. ROGER J. FOYS, V.G., *Res., 422 Washington St., P.O. Box 969, Steubenville, 43952.* Tel: 614-282-3631.

Moderator of the Curia—Rev. Msgr. ROGER J. FOYS, V.G., *Res., 422 Washington St., P.O. Box 969, Steubenville, 43952.* Tel: 614-282-3631.

Chancellor—Mrs. LINDA A. NICHOLS.

Chancery Office—*422 Washington St., P.O. Box 969, Steubenville, 43952.* Tel: 614-282-3631; Fax: 614-282-3327.

Diocesan Finance Office—Rev. Msgr. ROGER J. FOYS, V.G., Dir.; Mr. DAVID FRANKLIN, Comptroller, *P.O. Box 969, Steubenville, 43952.* Tel: 614-282-3631.

Diocesan/Parish Share Campaign—Rev Msgr. ROGER J. FOYS, V.G., Dir. MARTIN THOMPSON, Assoc. Dir. Tel: 614-282-3631.

Diocesan Tribunal—*422 Washington St., P.O. Box 969, Steubenville, 43952.* Tel: 614-282-3631.

Judicial Vicar—Very Rev. KURT H. KEMO, J.C.L.

Adjutant Judicial Vicar—Rev. Msgr. ROGER J. FOYS, V.G.

Defender of the Bond—Rev. Msgr. GERALD E. CALOVINI.

Auditors/Defenders of the Bond—Revs. THOMAS A. CHILLOG; WILLIAM D. CROSS.

Secretary to the Tribunal & Notary—COLLEEN BAHEN.

Judges—Rev. Msgr. ROGER J. FOYS, V.G.; Rev. Msgr. TERRENCE A. TRAVIS, V.F.; Rev. Msgr. MARK J. FROEHLICH; Rev. Msgr. ROBERT H. PUNKE, V.F.; Rev. Msgr. GENE W. MULLETT, V.F.; Revs. VINCENT J. HUBER; JAMES DUNFEE.

Diocesan Data Processing—Rev. Msgr. ROGER J. FOYS, V.G., Dir.; Mr. ANTHONY TARGOSS, Mgr.; MARTIN B. THOMPSON, Assoc. Manager, *422 Washington St., P.O. Box 969, Steubenville, 43952.* Tel: 614-282-3631.

Diocesan Deaneries and Deans

Deans—Annunciation Deanery: Rev. Msgr. GEORGE W. YONTZ, V.F., Immaculate Heart of Mary Deanery: Rev. Msgr. GERALD E. CALOVINI, V.F., Mother of God Deanery: Rev. Msgr. JOHN C. KOLESAR, V.F., Nativity of Mary Deanery: Rev. Msgr. PATRICK GAUGHAN, V.F., Presentation Deanery: Rev. Msgr. ROBERT H. PUNKE, V.F., Visitation Deanery: Rev. Msgr. WILLIAM C. YONTZ, V.F., Assumption Deanery: Rev. Msgr. CHARLES HIGHLAND, V.F., Coronation Deanery: Rev. Msgr. J. MICHAEL CAMPBELL, V.F., Immaculate Conception Deanery: Rev. Msgr. WILLIAM MYERS, V.F., Queen of Peace Deanery: Rev. Msgr. GENE W. MULLETT, V.F.

Continuing Education/Alliance of Priests—Rev. Msgr. ROGER J. FOYS, V.G., Dir.; Rev. Msgr. LEWIS F. GAETANO; Rev. Msgr. GERALD E. CALOVINI, V.F.; Very Rev. KURT H. KEMO, J.C.L.; Revs. WILLIAM D. CROSS; THOMAS A. CHILLOG.

Pastoral Staff—Most Rev. GILBERT I. SHELDON, D.D., D.Min.; Rev. Msgr. ROGER J. FOYS, V.G.; Rev. Msgr. JAMES A. BOEHM; Mrs. LINDA A. NICHOLS; Very Rev. KURT H. KEMO, J.C.L.; Rev. THOMAS A. CHILLOG; Rev. Msgr. GERALD E. CALOVINI, V.F.; Sr. ANNE FLYNN, S.C.; Sr. MARY ANN CORR, S.C.; Rev. KEVIN L. GREENWOOD; Dr. PETER CHILA; Rev. WILLIAM D. CROSS; Mr. BRIAN HARVEY.

Presbyteral Council—Most Rev. GILBERT I. SHELDON, D.D., D.Min., Pres.; Rev. Msgr. GERALD E. CALOVINI, V.F.; Rev. Msgr. WILLIAM R. CORNELIUS; Revs. TIMOTHY MCGUIRE; VINCENT J. HUBER; Rev. Msgr. JOSEPH A. NEALON; Revs. THOMAS A. MAGARY; DAVID GAYDOSIK; SAMUEL SAPRANO; WILLIAM D. CROSS, Exec. Sec. WALTER HEINZ; Very Rev. KURT H. KEMO, J.C.L., Vice Chm.; Revs. LEONARD T. CENCULA;

THOMAS NAU; RICHARD DAVIS, T.O.R.; CHESTER PABIN; Rev. Msgr. ROGER J. FOYS, V.G., Chm.; Mrs. LINDA NICHOLS, Recording Sec.

College of Consultors—Rev. Msgr. GERALD D. CALOVINI, V.F.; Rev. Msgr. WILLIAM R. CORNELIUS; Rev. WALTER HEINZ; Very Rev. KURT H. KEMO, J.C.L.; Rev. RONALD MOHNICKEY, T.O.R.; Rev. Msgr. ROGER J. FOYS, V.G.

Priests Personnel Board—Rev. MARTIN HOLLER, Southern Area; Rev. Msgr. WILLIAM R. CORNELIUS, Senior Clergy; Rev. Msgr. PATRICK GAUGHAN, V.F., Middle Age Clergy; Rev. Msgr. ROBERT KAWA, Northern Area; Rev. Msgr. VICTOR CINSON, Younger Clergy; Rev. JAMES DUNFEE, Central Area; Rev. Msgr. ROGER J. FOYS, V.G., Ex-Officio.

Diocesan Offices and Directors

Building Commission—Mr. BRIAN HARVEY, Chm., *P.O. Box 969, Steubenville, 43952.* Tel: 614-282-3631; Fax: 614-282-3327.

Building & Property Supervisor—Mr. BRIAN HARVEY, *P.O. Box 969, Steubenville, 43952.* Tel: 614-282-3631; Fax: 614-282-3327.

Campus Ministry—Rev. MARTIN J. HOLLER, *75 Stewart St., Athens, 45701.* Tel: 614-592-2711.

Office of Christian Formation—Sr. MARY ANN CORR, S.C., Dir., *P.O. Box 969, Steubenville, 43952.* Tel: 614-282-3631; Fax: 614-282-3327.

Diocesan Communications—Rev. Msgr. GERALD E. CALOVINI, V.F., *P.O. 969, Steubenville, 43952.* Tel: 614-282-3631; Fax: 614-282-3327.

Continuing Education of Priests—Very Rev. KURT H. KEMO, J.C.L., Dir., *P.O. Box 969, Steubenville, 43952.* Tel: 614-282-3631; Fax: 614-282-3327.

Diocesan Financial Advisory Committee—Rev. Msgr. ROGER J. FOYS, V.G., Chm., *422 Washington St., P.O. Box 969, Steubenville, 43952.* Tel: 614-282-3631; Fax: 614-282-3327.

Diocesan Director of Cemeteries—Rev. Msgr. JOHN C. KOLESAR, V.F., *P.O. Box 597, Adena, 43901.* Tel: 614-546-3463.

Diocesan Director of Ecumenism—Rev. Msgr. DONAL O'CARROLL, *St. Mary Church, P.O. Box 188, Lafferty, 43951.* Tel: 614-968-3200.

Diocesan Office of Worship—Very Rev. KURT H. KEMO, J.C.L., Dir., *P.O. Box 969, Steubenville, 43952.* Tel: 614-282-3631; Fax: 614-282-3327.

Education Board—Sr. MARY ANN CORR, S.C., Supt., Schools, *P.O. Box 1196, Steubenville, 43952.* Tel: 614-282-3631; Fax: 614-282-3327.

Health Panel of the Clergy—Rev. Msgr. DONAL O'CARROLL, Contact Person, *St. Mary Church, P.O. Box 188, Lafferty, 43951.* Tel: 614-968-3200.

Holy Childhood Association—Vacant.

Hospitals—Trinity Health System, *Trinity Medical Center, West, 4000 Johnson Rd., Steubenville, 43952.* Tel: 614-264-8000; Fax: 614-264-8620., *Trinity Medical Center, East, 380 Summit Ave., Steubenville, 43952.* Tel: 614-283-7000. FRED B. BROWER, Pres. Tel: 614-283-7390. ANGELO G. CALBONE, Vice Pres. Tel: 614-264-8303. Rev. JOHN MCCOY, Chap. Tel: 614-264-8133; 8000.

National Catholic Rural Life Conference—Rev. Msgr. CHARLES HIGHLAND, V.F., Dir., *Res., R.F.D. 2, Marietta, 45750.* Tel: 614-896-2060.

Central Office of Catholic Charities—Rev. Msgr. GERALD E. CALOVINI, V.F., Dir., *P.O. Box 969, Steubenville, 43952.* Tel: 614-282-3631; 1-800-339-7890; Fax: 614-282-3327. Services: Campaign for Human Development; Respect Life; Child Welfare & Family Life; Information & Referral; Substance Abuse & AIDS Ministry, Jefferson County RSVP: Tel: 614-282-9232., St. Steubenville, Housing for Elderly: Tel: 614-282-9232., Samaritan House: Tel: 614-282-0563.

Priest Retirement Committee—Rev. Msgr. JAMES C. MARSHALL, *Holy Rosary Church, 200 Rosemont Ave., Steubenville, 43952.* Tel: 614-264-4880.

Propagation of the Faith—Most Rev. GILBERT I. SHELDON, *P.O. Box 969, Steubenville, 43952.* Tel: 614-282-3631.

Publication, "Steubenville Register"—Most Rev. GILBERT I. SHELDON, D.D., D.Min., Pres.; Rev. Msgr. JAMES A. BOEHM, Editor/Publisher, *422 Washington St., P.O. Box 160, Steubenville, 43952.* Tel: 614-282-3631; Fax: 614-282-3327., *Res., Blessed Sacrament, 852 Main St., Wintersville, 43952.* Tel: 614-264-0868.

RCIA—Very Rev. KURT H. KEMO, J.C.L., Dir., *P.O. Box 969, Steubenville, 43952.* Tel: 614-282-3631; Fax: 614-282-3327.

St. Vincent de Paul Society—Rev. Msgr. GERALD E. CALOVINI, V.F., Dir., *422 Washington St., P.O. Box 969, Steubenville, 43952.* Tel: 614-282-3631.

Schools—Sr. MARY ANN CORR, S.C., Supt., *P.O. Box 1196, Steubenville, 43952.* Tel: 614-282-3631; Fax: 614-282-3327.

Seminary Review Board—Rev. KEVIN L. GREENWOOD, Chm., *Pontifical College Josephinum, 7625 N. High St., Columbus, 43235-1498.* Tel: 614-885-5585.

Vicar for Religious—Rev. Msgr. J. MICHAEL CAMPBELL, V.F., *St. Gabriel, P.O. Box 275, Minerva, 44657.* Tel: 614-868-4498.

Vicar for Retired Priests—Rev. VINCENT J. HUBER, *1225 N. River Ave., Toronto, 43964.* Tel: 614-537-4433.

Vocations—Rev. KEVIN L. GREENWOOD, Dir., *Pontifical College Josephinum, 7625 N. High St., Columbus, 43235-1498.* Tel: 614-885-5585.

Woman's Club—Rev. Msgr. ROGER J. FOYS, V.G., Moderator; Mrs. JOANN RAHA, Pres., *600 Wilson Ave., Mingo Jct., 43938.* Tel: 614-282-1612.

CLERGY, PARISHES, MISSIONS AND PAROCHIAL SCHOOLS

CITY OF STEUBENVILLE (Jefferson County)

1—HOLY NAME CATHEDRAL, Very Rev. Timothy Shannon, Rector.
Rectory: 411 S. Fifth St., 43952. Tel: 614-282-7322. [JC]

2—HOLY FAMILY, Rev. Richard Tuttle.
Res., 2608 Hollywood Blvd., 43952. Tel: 614-264-2825. [JC]

3—HOLY ROSARY, Rev. Msgr. James C. Marshall; Rev. John McCoy.
Res., 200 Rosemont Ave., 43952. Tel: 614-264-4880. [JC]
School—Central Grade School.
Sisters of St. Dominic 1; Lay Teachers 22; Students 402.

4—IMMACULATE HEART OF MARY CHAPEL. Closed. For inquiries for parish records contact the Chancery.

5—OUR LADY OF NORTH AMERICA MARTYRS, Rev. John Galea.
Res., R.D. 1, Lee Ridge Rd., 43952. Tel: 614-283-2983; Fax: 614-283-2107. [JC]

6—ST. ANTHONY OF PADUA, Very Rev. Timothy Shannon.
Res., 415 S. 5th St., 43952. Tel: 614-282-7322. [JC]
School—All Saints, Tel: 614-282-4201.

7—ST. PETER'S, Rev. Msgr. George W. Yontz; Rev. Richard Battocletti; Bro. Patrick Geary, I.H.M., Pastoral Assoc.; Deacon Dominic Cerrato.
Res., 425 N. Fourth St., 43952. Tel: 614-282-7612; 282-9263. [JC]
School—All Saints Central School, Tel: 614-282-4201.
Lay Teachers 10; Students 148.

8—ST. PIUS X, Rev. Msgr. William R. Cornelius. In res., Rev. Msgr. Frederick A. Pasquinelli, (Retired).
Res., 700 Lovers Ln., 43952. Tel: 614-264-7681. [JC]
School—Aquinas Central, R.D. 3, Lovers Ln., 43952.
Lay Teachers 16; Students 306.

9—ST. STANISLAUS, Rev. Msgr. George W. Yontz; Rev. Richard Battocletti.
Mailing Address: 425 N. 4th St., 43952. Tel: 614-282-7612. [JC]

OUTSIDE THE CITY OF STEUBENVILLE

Adena, Jefferson Co., St. Casimir's, Rev. Msgr. John C. Kolesar.
Res., 221 Hanna Ave., P.O. Box 594, 43901. Tel: 614-546-3463. [CEM]

Amsterdam, Jefferson Co., St. Joseph, Rev. Virgil Reischman.
Res., P.O. Box 35, 43903. Tel: 614-543-3652. [CEM]

Athens, Athens Co., Christ the King University Parish, Rev. Msgr. Donald Horak; Rev. Martin J. Holler, Dir. Campus Ministry.
Res., 75 Stewart St., 45701. Tel: 614-592-2711.
St. Paul's, Rev. Msgr. Patrick E. Gaughan, V.F.
Res., 38 N. College St., 45701. Tel: 614-593-7822. [CEM]
Chapel—Guysville, St. John.

Barnesville, Belmont Co., Assumption, Rev. Charles E. Mascolino.
Res., 306 W. Main St., 43713. Tel: 614-425-2181. [CEM]

Barton, Belmont Co., Our Lady of Angels, Rev. Michael Rotolo.
Res., P.O. Box 768, 43905. Tel: 614-695-3039.

Bellaire, Belmont Co., St. John, Rev. Msgr. Gene W. Mullett; Rev. Ralph Salciccia (Italy).
Res., 3745 Tallman Ave., 43906. Tel: 614-676-0051. [JC]
School—Central Grade School.
Lay Teachers 12; Students 226.
St. Michael's, Rev. Msgr. Gene W. Mullett.
Res., c/o St. John Church, 415 37th St., 43906. Tel: 614-676-0051. [CEM][JC]

Belle Valley, Noble Co., Corpus Christi, Rev. Dale Tornes.
Res., c/o St. Stephen Church, P.O. Box 186, Caldwell, 43724. Tel: 614-732-4129.
Church—Main St., 43717. Tel: 614-732-7202. [CEM]

Belpre, Washington Co., St. Ambrose, Rev. David L. Huffman.
Res., 120 Maple St., P.O. Box 426, 45714. Tel: 614-423-7422; Fax: 614-423-7422. [CEM]

Beverly, Washington Co., St. Bernard, Rev. Msgr. Robert J. Kawa.
Res., 307 Seventh St., 45715. Tel: 614-984-2555. [CEM]

Blaine, Belmont Co., All Saints, Rev. Michael Rotolo.
Res., 53839 National Rd., P.O. Box 337, 43909. Tel: 614-635-0642.

Bridgeport, Belmont Co., St. Anthony of Padua, Rev. Msgr. Francis Manieri.
Res., 630 Main St., 43912. Tel: 614-635-0283. [JC]
St. Joseph, Rev. Msgr. Mark J. Froehlich.
Res., 68210 Neola Ave., 43912. Tel: 614-635-0408; Fax: 614-635-1166. [JC]
School—Lay Teachers 12; Students 189.

Brilliant, Jefferson Co., Our Lady of Fatima. Closed. Sacramental records are located at St. Agnes, Mingo Junction.

Buchtel, Athens Co., St. Patrick. Consolidated with St. Andrew to form St. Mary of the Hills, Nelsonville.

Burkhart, Monroe Co., St. Joseph's, Revs. James M. Dunfee; Frederick C. Kihm.
Mailing Address: c/o St. Sylvester Church, 330 S. Main St., Woodsfield, 43793.

Byesville, Guernsey Co., Holy Trinity, Rev. Msgr. William C. Yontz.
Res., 222 S. Fifth St., Box 26, 43723. Tel: 614-685-2184. [CEM]
School—Central Grade School, Tel: 614-685-2573.
Lay Teachers 6; Students 82.

Cadiz, Harrison Co., St. Teresa, Rev. Thomas A. Vennitti.
Res., 143 E. South St., 43907. Tel: 614-942-2211.

Caldwell, Noble Co., St. Stephen, Rev. Dale F. Tornes.
Res., 1036 Belford St., Box 186, 43724. Tel: 614-732-4129. [CEM]

Cambridge, Guernsey Co., St. Benedict, Rev. Robert D. Borer.
Res., 714 Gomber Ave., 43725. Tel: 614-432-7609.
School—Tel: 614-432-6751.
Franciscan Sisters of Christian Charity 6; Lay Teachers 9; Students 145.

Carlisle, Noble Co., St. Michael, Rev. Samuel Saprano.
Res., R.D. 1, Caldwell, 43724. Tel: 614-838-4842. [CEM]

Carrollton, Carroll Co., Our Lady of Mercy, Rev. David L. Gaydosik.
Res., 616 Roswell Rd., N.W., P.O. Box 155, 44615. Tel: 216-627-4664; Fax: 216-627-6341.

Chesapeake, Lawrence Co., St. Ann, Rev. James M. Bryant.
Res., 310 Third Ave., Box 428, 45619-0428. Tel: 614-867-4434.

Churchtown, Washington Co., St. John the Baptist, Rev. Msgr. Charles F. Highland, V.F.
Res., R.F.D. 2, Marietta, 45750. Tel: 614-896-2060. [CEM]
School—Central Grade School, Tel: 614-896-2697.
Lay Teachers 11; Students 138.

Colerain, Belmont Co., St. Frances Cabrini, Rev. Msgr. David E. Reasbeck.
Res., Rte. 250, Box 38, 43916. Tel: 614-635-9933.

Dillonvale, Jefferson Co., St. Adalbert, Rev. Leonard Cencula.
Res., P.O. Box 577, 43917. Tel: 614-769-2186. [CEM]
School—Central Grade School, Tel: 614-769-2710.
Lay Teachers 4; Students 36.

Fairpoint, Belmont Co., St. Joseph, Rev. Thomas J. Graven.
Mailing Address: 71793 Church St., P.O. Box 308, Maynard, 43937.
Church—46982 Columbia St., Box 98, 43927. Tel: 614-695-0840; 695-2618.

Flushing, Belmont Co., St. Paul's, Rev. Msgr. John A. Cymbor.
Res., 115 Morristown Rd., Box 45, 43977. Tel: 614-968-4159. [CEM]

Fulda, Noble Co., Immaculate Conception, Rev. Samuel Saprano.
Res., Caldwell R.F.D. 4, 43700 Fulda Rd., Caldwell, 43724. Tel: 614-732-4576. [CEM]

Gallipolis, Gallia Co., St. Louis, Rev. Msgr. William R. Myers, V.F.

Res., 85 State St., 45631. Tel: 614-446-0669. [CEM]

Glouster, Athens Co., Holy Cross, Rev. John Mucha.
Rectory: 31 Republic Ave., 45732. Tel: 614-767-3068.
Res., 110 E. Washington St., Nelsonville, 45764. Tel: 614-753-1770; Fax: 614-753-4199. [CEM]
Church—Corner of Madison & Republic Avenues, 45732.

Harriettsville, Noble Co., St. Henry, Rev. Victor Cinson, Jr., Admin.
Mailing Address: R.D. 1, Box 90-B, Lowell, 45744. Tel: 614-896-2207.
Church—Rte. 1, 34575 Church St., CR 47, Lower Salem, 45745. Tel: 614-585-2383. [CEM]

Hopedale, Harrison Co., Sacred Heart, Rev. Edmondo Stabene, Parochial Admin.
Res., 205 Cross St., P.O. Box 445, 43976-0445. Tel: 614-937-2301. [JC]

Ironton, Lawrence Co., St. Joseph, Rev. Thomas R. Nau.
Res., 905 S. Fifth St., P.O. Box 499, 45638. Tel: 614-532-0561; 532-0712. [JC]
St. Lawrence, Rev. Thomas R. Nau.
Res., 905 S. Fifth St., P.O.Box 499, 45638-0499. Tel: 614-532-0561. [JC]
School—St. Lawrence Central Grade School, (Grades K-6). Tel: 614-532-5052.
Lay Teachers 10; Students 136.
High School—St. Joseph Central High School, (Grades 7-12). Tel: 614-532-0485.
Lay Teachers 15; Students 94.

Lafferty, Belmont Co., St. Mary, Rev. Msgr. Donal O'Carroll.
Res., P.O. Box 188, 43951. Tel: 614-968-3200. [CEM]

Lore City, Guernsey Co., SS. Peter and Paul, Rev. Thomas A. Chillog.
Res., P.O. Box 175, 43755. Tel: 614-685-5582. [CEM]

Lowell, Washington Co., Our Lady of Mercy, Rev. Victor Cinson, Jr.
Res., R.D. 1, Box 90-B, 45744. Tel: 614-896-2207. [CEM]

McConnelsville, Morgan Co., St. James, Rev. Paul Walker.
Res., 257 Bell Ave., P.O. Box 539, 43756. Tel: 614-962-2856.

Malvern, Carroll Co., St. Francis Xavier, Rev. Thomas Marut.
Res., 125 Carrollton St., P.O. Box 486, 44644. Tel: 216-863-0305. [CEM]

Marietta, Washington Co., St. Mary's, Rev. Msgr. Edward Kakascik; Rev. Chester Pabin.
Res., 506 Fourth St., 45750. Tel: 614-373-3643. [CEM]
School—320 Marion St., 45750. Tel: 614-374-8181; Fax: 614-374-8602.
Lay Teachers 12; Students 286.

Martins Ferry, Belmont Co., St. Mary, Revs. Thomas A. Magary; Norbert Connelly.
Res., 20 N. Fourth St., 43935. Tel: 614-633-1416. [CEM]
School—St. Mary Central, 24 N. Fourth St., 43935. Tel: 614-633-5424. Sr. Louise Smith, S.C.N., Prin.
Sisters 1; Lay Teachers 9; Students 244.

Maynard, Belmont Co., St. Stanislaus, Rev. Thomas J. Graven.
Res., 71793 Church St., P.O. Box 308, 43937. Tel: 614-695-2618.

Miltonsburg, Monroe Co., St. John the Baptist, Revs. James M. Dunfee; Chester Pabin.
Res., 35560 Miltonsburg-Calais Rd., Woodsfield, 43793. Tel: 614-472-1019. [CEM]

Minerva, Stark Co., St. Gabriel the Archangel, Rev. Msgr. John Michael Campbell. In res., Rev. Msgr. Cronan T. Molloy, (Retired).
Res., 400 West High, P.O. Box 275, 44657. Tel: 216-868-4498.

Mingo Junction, Jefferson Co., Annunciation, Rev. Msgr. Lewis F. Gaetano; Sr. June Smith, O.S.F., Pastoral Assoc.; Deacon Al Iafrate.
Church—110 Valley Rd., 43938. Tel: 614-535-1491; Fax: 614-535-0039.
St. Agnes, Rev. Msgr. Lewis F. Gaetano; Sr. June Smith, O.S.F., Pastoral Assoc.; Deacon Al Iafrate.
Mailing Address: 204 St. Clair St., 43938. Tel: 614-535-1491. [CEM]
School—Central Grade School, Tel: 614-535-1012; Fax: 614-535-0039.
Franciscan Sisters of Christian Charity 3; Lay Teachers 11; Students 188.
St. Bernadette. Closed. Sacramental records are located at St. Agnes, Mingo Junction.

Morges, Carroll Co., St. Mary, Rev. Msgr. David L. Gaydosik.
Res., 8012 Bachelor Rd. N.W., P.O. Box 690, Waynesburg, 44688. Tel: 330-866-2023; Fax: 330-627-6341. [CEM]

Neffs, Belmont Co., Sacred Heart, Rev. Timothy McGuire.
Res., 54038 St. Mary Ave., P.O. Box 425, 43940-0425. Tel: 614-676-3277; Fax: 614-676-3400.

Nelsonville, Athens Co., St. Mary of the Hills. Consolidated St. Andrew, Nelsonville consolidated with St. Patrick, Buchtel to form St. Mary of the Hills. Rev. John Mucha.
Res., 110 E. Washington St., 45764. Tel: 614-753-1770; Fax: 614-753-4199.

Pine Grove, Lawrence Co., St. Mary, Rev. Francis L. Kinney, C.PP.S.
Res., Box 639, Ironton, 45638. Tel: 614-532-2420. [CEM]

Piney Fork, Jefferson Co., St. Therese, Rev. A. Donald Mantica, Admin.
Res., Box 25, 43941. Tel: 614-733-7820; 733-7595.

Pomeroy, Meigs Co., Sacred Heart, Rev. Walter E. Heinz.
Res., 161 Mulberry Ave., P.O. Box 592, 45769. Tel: 614-992-5898. [CEM]

Powhatan Point, Belmont Co., St. John Vianney, Rev. Timothy P. McGuire.
295 Hwy. 7, N., 43942. Tel: 614-795-4804; Fax: 614-676-3400.

Richmond, Jefferson Co., St. John Fisher, Rev. Msgr. Kenneth Uram.
Res., R.D. 1, 43944. Tel: 614-765-4142.

St. Clairsville, Belmont Co., St. Mary's, Rev. Msgr. Robert H. Punke.
Res., 230 W. Main St., 43950. Tel: 614-695-9993.
School—Central Grade School, 226 W. Main St., 43950. Tel: 614-695-3189; Fax: 614-695-3851.
Lay Teachers 12; Students 235.

Shadyside, Belmont Co., St. Mary, Rev. Paul D. Welton.
350 E. 40th St., P.O. Box 68, 43947. Tel: 614-676-3282.

Smithfield, Jefferson Co., Our Lady, Queen of Peace, Rev. A. Donald Mantica.
Res., P.O. Box 453, 43948. Tel: 614-733-7595. [JC]

Temperanceville, Belmont Co., St. Mary's, Rev. Charles Mascolino.
Res., R.D. 1, Barnesville, 43713. Tel: 614-679-2912; 425-2181 [CEM]

Tiltonsville, Jefferson Co., St. Joseph, Rev. Msgr. George R. Coyne; Sr. Luke Boiarski, S.C.N., Pastoral Assoc
Res., 204 Mound St., 43963. Tel: 614-859-4018; Fax: 614-859-6041.

Toronto, Jefferson Co., St. Francis of Assisi, Rev. Msgr. Roger J. Foys, V.G.; Very Rev. Kurt H. Kemo; Rev. Vincent J. Huber; Bro. Anthony Motto, I.H.M., Pastoral Assoc.
Res., 1225 N. River Ave., 43964. Tel: 614-537-4433; Fax: 614-537-9305. [JC]
School—Tel: 614-537-2151; Fax: 614-537-9380.
Vincentian Sisters of Charity 1; Lay Teachers 8; Students 155.
St. Joseph's, Rev. Msgr. Roger J. Foys, V.G.; Very Rev. Kurt H. Kemo; Rev. Vincent J. Huber; Bro. Anthony Motto, I.H.M., Pastoral Assoc.
Res., 1225 N. River Ave., 43964. Tel: 614-537-4433; Fax: 614-537-9305. [JC]

Vincent, Washington Co., St. Ambrose. Consolidated with St. Ambrose, Belpre.

Wintersville, Jefferson Co., Blessed Sacrament, Rev. Msgr. Gerald E. Calovini; Rev. William D. Cross. In res., Rev. Msgr. James A. Boehm.
Res., 852 Main St., 43952. Tel: 614-264-0868; Fax: 614-264-5449. [JC]
School—Aquinas Elementary, (Grades K-8) R.D. No. 3, Lovers Ln., Steubenville, 43952. Tel: 614-264-3651.
Our Lady of Lourdes, Rev. Msgr. Gerald E. Calovini; Rev. William D. Cross.
Res., P.O. Box 2612, 43952. Tel: 614-264-2798; 282-3631 (Office); Fax: 614-264-5449.

Woodsfield, Monroe Co., St. Sylvester, Revs. James M. Dunfee; Frederick C. Kihm.
Res., 330 S. Main St., 43793. Tel: 614-472-0187; Fax: 614-472-1994. [CEM]
School—Central Grade School.
Franciscan Sisters of Christian Charity 4; Lay Teachers 6; Students 162.

Yorkville, Jefferson Co., St. Lucy's, Rev. Bernard Krajcovic.
Res., 107 St. Lucy Ave., 43971. Tel: 614-859-2274.

DIOCESAN MISSIONS

Bloomingdale, Jefferson Co., St. Thomas More Mission. Closed. Sacramental records are located at St. John Fisher, Richmond.

Chauncey, Athens Co., St. Jude Mission. Closed. Sacramental records are located at St. Paul Church, Athens.

Crescent, Belmont Co., St. Elizabeth Mission. Closed. Sacramental records are located at St. Stanislaus Church, Maynard.

Freeport, Harrison Co., St. Matthias Mission, Rev. Thomas Vennitti.
Res., 143 E. South St., Cadiz, 43907. Tel: 614-942-2211.
Church—Main St., Box 195, 43973. Tel: 614-658-3300.

Hammondsville, Jefferson Co., Nativity of Our Lord Mission. Closed. Sacramental records are located at St. Joseph Church, Toronto.

Jewett, Harrison Co., Our Lady of Perpetual Help Mission, Rev. Thomas Vennitti, Admin.
Mailing Address: & Res.—143 E. South St., Cadiz, 43907. Tel: 614-942-2211.

Sardis, Monroe Co., St. John Bosco Mission, Rev. James Dunfee.
Res., c/o St. Sylvester Church, 330 S. Main St., Woodsfield, 43793. Tel: 614-795-4804.

Tappan Lake, Harrison Co., Christ the King Summer Mission. Closed. Sacramental records are located at: 143 E. South St., Cadiz 43907. Tel: 614-942-2211.

Toronto, Jefferson Co., Servants of Christ the King, Rev. Msgr. Roger J. Foys.
Res., 1225 N. River Ave., 43964. Tel: 614-537-4433; Fax: 614-537-9305.

Tupper Plains, Meigs Co., Our Lady of Loretto Church. Closed. Sacramental records are located at Sacred Heart Church, Pomeroy.

On Duty Outside the Diocese:
Reverend Monsignors—
Petronek, Thomas, Maryknoll Fathers, P.O. Box 43058, Nairobi, Kenya
Wippel, John E., 10105 Portland Pl., Silver Springs, MD 20901. Tel: 301-593-9345; 816-942-8400
Reverend Fathers—
Calabrese, Charles L., University Ministries Office, P.O. Box 32898, TCU Station, Ft. Worth, TX 76129-0001. Tel: 817-923-2176; 921-7830
Cronin, Frank C., Ohio University, Ellis Hall, Athens, OH 45701. Tel: 614-592-6147; 593-2812
Dinger, Clair M., Immaculate Conception Church, 420 North St., Milan, MI 48160. Tel: 313-439-2667
Direnzo, Michael J., Chap., 21 Titan Dr., San Pedro, CA 90732. Tel: 310-831-5857; 363-1956
Gallagher, Robert A., 5539 Lucky Ln., Wichita Falls, TX 76306. Tel: 817-885-3676
Goodbout, George E., Our Lady of the Lake Regional Medical Center, 5000 Hennessy Blvd., Baton Rouge, LA 70809. Tel: 504-765-8896
Greenwood, Kevin L., Pontifical College Josephinum, 7625 N. High St., Columbus, OH 43235-1498. Tel: 614-885-5585
Massucci, Joseph D., University of Dayton, 330 Chaminade Hall, Dayton, OH 45469. Tel: 513-299-3730
McCarthy, John R., St. Philomena Church, 13824 Euclid Ave., Cleveland, OH 44114. Tel: 216-541-3540
Mellott, David, 5400 Roland Ave., Baltimore, MD 21210. Tel: 410-433-8622; 323-3200
Peltz, Carl, St. Alban, 2001 Shepard Rd., Glencoe, MO 63038. Tel: 314-458-2977
Pliauplis, Christopher, St. Joseph Church, 45 Church St., Ronkonkoma, NY 11779. Tel: 516-223-0723
Safraniec, Joseph, Chap., Chaplain's Office (125), Dept. of VAMC, 1 Veteran's Dr., Minneapolis, MN 55417
Smith, Martin D., 4616 Mitchell Ave., Cincinnati, OH 45232. Tel: 513-681-5310

Absent on Leave:
Reverend Fathers—
Bernas, Elwood S., 30675 Park St., #106, Lindstrom, MN 55045-9618. Tel: 612-257-5605
Bielanski, Joseph J., 246 Dorland #4, San Francisco, CA 94114
Gadzinski, Mark, 363 W. 2nd Ave., Columbus, OH 43201
Holmes, John, 464 S. Powell, Columbus, OH 43204. Tel: 614-276-5161
Huffman, Timothy, P.O. Box 182, Victoria, VA 23974
McLaughlin, Eugene
Moran, Charles
Travis, Terrence A., 849 Pine Cone Oval, Sagamore Hills, OH 44067-2232
Zalenski, Gary, 419 N. 9th St., Martins Ferry, OH 43935

Retired:
Reverend Monsignors—
Adams, George J., 785 Broad St., Brockway, PA 15824. Tel: 814-265-8371
Cappelli, Angelo J., 19241 Edgefield, Apt. 101, Harperswoods, MI 48225. Tel: 313-882-6683

Giannamore, Anthony J., 8110 Clyo Rd., Centerville, OH 45458. Tel: 513-435-3626; 433-7224
Luciana, Lawrence, c/o St. Stephen Church, 2491 James River Tpke., Ona, WV 25545-9722. Tel: 304-743-3234
Maher, Patrick K., Corville, Roscrea Co., Tipperary, Ireland. Tel: 0505-22600
Metzger, Paul E., 67800 Graham Rd., St. Clairsville, OH 43950. Tel: 614-695-4912
Molloy, Cronan T., St. Gabriel Church, 400 W. High St., P.O. Box 275, Minerva, OH 44657. Tel: 216-868-4498
Nealon, Joseph A., P.O. Box 158, Carrollton, OH 44615-0158. Tel: 216-627-7083; 627-7647
Nugent, James B., 97D Georgetown Dr., Columbus, OH 43214
Pasquinelli, Frederick A., St. Pius X Church, 700 Lovers Ln., Steubenville, OH 43952. Tel: 614-264-7681
Pollack, Joseph, The Colony House, Apt. 124, 941 Pocahontas Dr., Fort Walton Beach, FL 32547. Tel: 904-863-9887
Wadowicz, Joseph M., 106 Via Estrada #A, Laguna Hills, CA 92653-4077. Tel: 714-770-6691
Zekas, Stanley, 4409 Country Club Dr., Apt. 46, Steubenville, OH 43952. Tel: 614-266-6947

Reverend Fathers—
Belfield, John, P.O. Box 119, Avon Park, FL 33825. Tel: 813-386-0631
Bober, Bernard, 1711 S. Jefferson, New Castle, PA 16102-1524. Tel: 412-652-4127
Borosh, Carl, Box 587, Barton, OH 43905. Tel: 614-695-0827
Brown, Francis, Box 4242, 403 N. 4th, Apt. 11, Steubenville, OH 43952. Tel: 614-282-5729
Connor, Francis J., 10248 Snead Circle N., Sun City, AZ 85351. Tel: 602-977-7141
Deasio, August J., 915 Yellow Mills Rd., Shortsville, NY 14548. Tel: 716-289-4431
Gallagher, Cornelius F., 10520 Oakmont Ave., Sun City, AZ 85351. Tel: 602-974-5902
Lyden, Dennis P., St. Joseph Church, P.O. Box 98, Fairpoint, OH 43927. Tel: 614-695-0840
Maciejewski, Richard J., 1497 Beckwith Ave., N.E., Grand Rapids, MI 49505-5811. Tel: 616-454-4565
Marr, James G., St. Patrick's Church, 215 Court St., Elizabeth, NJ 07206
Martinosky, Joseph A., 603 Franklin Ave., Apt. #1, Columbus, OH 43215. Tel: 614-258-3043
Mascolino, Robert A., P.O. Box 4032, Steubenville, OH 43952-8032. Tel: 614-282-7675
Nadzam, John B., 258 Schwab Ave., Munhall, PA 15120-2239. Tel: 412-461-0623
Pandolfo, Anthony, River Bridge-The Island, 1063 Island Manor Dr., West Palm Beach, FL 33413. Tel: 407-439-5685
Patala, William S., Lancia Country Club Manor, 575 Lovers Ln., Steubenville, OH 43952
Raab, Alexander, Caritas Altenh, St. Antonius Filchner Str. 42, 81476, Munich 7, Germany. Tel: 4989-759-4464
Reardon, John J., P.O. Box 68, Shadyside, OH 43947-0068
Rothbauer, Francis J., 3515 Steubenville Rd., S.E., Amsterdam, OH 43903. Tel: 216-739-4564
Sartori, Peter V., 416 Buena Vista, Columbus, OH 43228. Tel: 614-878-4066
Stromski, Adam F.X., 17530 S.W. 90th Ave., Miami, FL 33157. Tel: 305-251-9948
Voytko, Geo., 2341 Shelva Dr., Akron, OH 44321. Tel: 216-745-8424
Zahorchak, Michael, Holy Rosary Church, P.O. Box 151, Seeleyville, IN 47878. Tel: 812-877-1279

Permanent Deacons:
Cerrato, Dominic, Rd. #2, Box 129A, Bloomingdale, OH 43910. Tel: 614-944-1846
Helgeson, Ray (SAC), 1205 Maryland Ave., Steubenville, OH 43952. Tel: 614-282-7925
Hickey, Gerald, 1803 Williams Pl., Steubenville, OH 43952. Tel: 614-283-1585
Iafrate, Albert (WH), c/o St. Agnes Church, 204 St. Clair St., Mingo Junction, OH 43938. Tel: 614-535-1491
Meagher, Lawrence, Steubenville, 4620 Lexington Dr., Steubenville, OH 43952. Tel: 614-264-3122

INSTITUTIONS LOCATED IN THE DIOCESE

[A] COLLEGES AND UNIVERSITIES

STEUBENVILLE. *Franciscan University of Steubenville*, University Blvd., 43952. Tel: 614-283-3771.
For a complete listing, refer to the Colleges and Universities section.

[B] HIGH SCHOOLS, CENTRAL

STEUBENVILLE. *Catholic Central High School*, 320 West View, 43952. Tel: 614-264-5538. Mr. Kenneth Voss, Prin.; Rev. Msgr. Roger J. Foys, Pastoral Admin. Lay Teachers 26; Students 403.

BELLAIRE. *St. John Central High School*, 3625 Guernsey St., 43906. Tel: 614-676-4932. Lay Teachers 15; Students 232.

[C] JUNIOR-SENIOR CENTRAL HIGH SCHOOLS

IRONTON. *St. Joseph Central*. (Grades 7-12), 45638. Tel: 614-532-0485. Edward Noll, Prin. Lay Teachers 12; Students 93.

[D] PRIVATE SCHOOLS

CARROLLTON. *St. John Villa*, P.O. Box 457, 44615. Tel: 612-627-9789; Fax: 612-627-4826. Residential facility for persons with developmental disabilities. Sr. Elaine Weber, O.S.F., Exec. Dir. Faculty Staff 72; Students 62.

[E] GENERAL HOSPITALS

STEUBENVILLE. *Trinity Health System*.
For a complete listing, refer to the Hospitals section.

[F] MONASTERIES AND RESIDENCES OF PRIESTS AND BROTHERS

STEUBENVILLE. *Diocesan Brotherhood of Immaculate Heart of Mary*. Villa Maria Motherhouse. Villa Maria Motherhouse, 609 N. Seventh St., 43952. Tel: 614-283-2462. Bro. Dominic Carroll, I.H.M., Supr. Gen. Brothers 5.
Holy Spirit Monastery, Franciscan Way, 43952. Tel: 614-283-3771. Revs. James Angert, T.O.R.; Brian Cavanaugh, T.O.R.; Richard Davis, T.O.R.; Jose Del Toro, T.O.R.; Augustine Donegan, T.O.R.; Robert Hilz, T.O.R.; Stanley Holland, T.O.R.; Ronald Mohnickey, T.O.R., Local Min.; Aidan Mullaney, T.O.R.; Daniel Pattee, T.O.R.; David Pivonka, T.O.R.; Michael Scanlan, T.O.R.; Daniel Sinisi, T.O.R.; Laurence Uhlman, T.O.R.; Bros. Joseph Johnsson, T.O.R.; Mark Klaus, T.O.R.; Michael Tripka, T.O.R. In res., Revs. Giles Dimock, O.P.; Conrad Harkins, O.F.M.; David Testa (ALB). Priests 17; Brothers 3.

BLOOMINGDALE. *Hermits of Mt. Carmel*, Rte. 2, Box 41A, 43910. Sisters 2.
Holy Family Hermitage, Rd. #2, Box 36, 43910. Tel: 614-765-4511. Revs. Basil Corriere, e.c., Prior; Paul Vankeirsbilck, e.c.; Mauro Ventura, Regular Oblate. Hermits 4; Priests 2; Regular Oblate Priest 1; Temporary Vows 1.

[G] CONVENTS AND RESIDENCES FOR SISTERS

STEUBENVILLE. *Sacred Heart Villa*, Sunshine Park, R.D. 3, 43952. Tel: 614-282-3801. Sr. Rosalba Putrino, Supr. Handmaids of Reparation of the Sacred Heart of Jesus, Motherhouse of America Foundation. Engaged in Kindergarten, Pre-Kindergarten and Parish work.

CARROLLTON. *Motherhouse and Novitiate of Sisters of Our Lady of Charity*, 44615-9399. Tel: 216-627-7647. Sr. Kevin Crain, Supr. Professed Sisters 17; Novices 1.

TORONTO. *Franciscan Sisters Third Order Regular of Penance of the Sorrowful Mother*, 170 Little Church Rd., 43964. Tel: 614-544-5542. Sr. Jean Daugherty, T.O.R., Supr. Sisters 14; Novices 2; Postulants 3.

[H] SHRINES

FATIMA. *Our Lady of Fatima Shrine*. Mailing Address: Parish Offices, P.O. Box 499, Ironton, 45638-0499. Old Rte. 52, Franklin Furnace, 45629. Mr. Lawrence Holtzapfel. Tel: 614-532-2696.

[I] NEWMAN CENTERS

STEUBENVILLE. *Jefferson County Technical Institute*, c/o Christ the King Chapel, Franciscan Univ. of Steubenville, Franciscan Way, 43952. Tel: 614-283-6277. Rev. Ronald H. Mohnickey, Contact Person.

ATHENS. *Christ the King University Parish - Ohio University*, 75 Stewart St., 45701. Tel: 614-592-2711. Rev. Msgr. Donald E. Horak; Rev. Martin J. Holler, Dir. Campus Ministry.

BEVERLY. *Washington Technical College*, R.F.D. #2, 45750. Tel: 614-896-2060. Rev. Charles Highland.

MARIETTA. *Marietta College*, c/o St. Mary Church, 506 Fourth St., 45750. Tel: 614-373-3643. Rev. Msgr. Edward Kakascik, Dir.

NELSONVILLE. *Hocking Technical College*, 45764. Rev. John Mucha, Dir., Res., 110 E. Washington St., 45764. Tel: 614-753-1770.

RIO GRANDE. *Rio Grande University*, 91 State St., 45674. Tel: 614-446-0669. Rev. Msgr. William R. Myers, Contact Person.

ST. CLAIRSVILLE. *Ohio University - Eastern*, c/o St. Mary's Church, 230 W. Main St., 43950. Tel: 614-695-9993. Rev. Msgr. Robert H. Punke, Contact Person.
Ohio University - Ironton Branch, c/o St. Joseph Church, P.O. Box 112, Ironton, 45638. Tel: 614-532-0712. Rev. Msgr. Thomas Nay, Contact Person.

[J] MISCELLANEOUS LISTINGS

STEUBENVILLE. *Campaign for Human Development*, P.O. Box 969, 43952. Tel: 614-282-3631; Fax: 614-282-3327. Rev. Msgr. Gerald E. Calovini, Diocesan Dir.
Catholic Community Center, P.O. Box 521, 148 S. Fourth St., 43952. Tel: 614-282-7566. Mr. Roger Bertoia, Exec. Dir.; Mr. John Serafini, Business Mgr.
**Catholics United for the Faith, Inc.*, 827 N. Fourth St., 43952. Tel: 614-28-FAITH; Fax: 614-283-4011. Curtis A. Martin, Pres.
Diocesan Committee of Administrative Review, P.O. Box 969, 43952. Tel: 614-282-3631. Rev. Msgr. Roger J. Foys, V.G.
F.I.R.E., Franciscan University, University Blvd., 43952. Tel: 614-283-6318. Mr. Jack Rook, Admin. A Catholic Alliance for Faith, Intercession, Repentance, and Evangelism.
Holy Name Society. St. Joseph Church, 68210 Neola Ave., Bridgeport, 43912. Tel: 614-635-0408. Rev. Msgr. Mark J. Froehlich, Dir.
Information & Referral, P.O. Box 969, 43952. Tel: 614-282-6880; 800-339-7890. Ms. Diana Jackson, Dir.
Lay Employees Pension Plan, P.O. Box 969, 43952. Tel: 614-282-3631. Rev. Msgr. Roger J. Foys.
Marian Manor, Inc., 180 N. Fourth St., 43952. Tel: 614-282-9232. Mr. Anthony Satkowski, A.H.M., Mgr.
Merciful Mother Association, P.O. Box 4505, 43952. Tel: 614-282-2335; Fax: 614-282-0561. Sr. Isabel Bettwy, Dir.
Natural Family Planning, P.O. Box 969, 43952. Tel: 614-282-3631; 800-339-7890.
Office of Substance Abuse and AIDS Ministry, P.O. Box 969, 43952. Tel: 614-282-3631; 800-339-7890.
Ohio Conference Advisory Council, P.O. Box 969, 43952. Tel: 614-282-3631. Mrs. Eileen Carpino, Lay Womens' Rep.; Rev. David L. Huffman, Priest Rep.; Mr. John Sissler, Laymen Rep.
Propagation of the Faith Holy Childhood Association, c/o Diocese of Steubenville, P.O. Box 969, 43952. Tel: 614-282-3631.
RCIA, P.O. Box 969, 43952. Tel: 614-282-3631; Fax: 614-282-3327. Very Rev. Kurt H. Kemo, J.C.L., Dir.
Synod Committee, 422 Washington St., P.O. Box 969, 43952. Tel: 614-282-3631. Rev. Msgr. Roger J. Foys, V.G., Contact Person.
**The Fraternity of Priests, Inc.*, 100 Belleview Blvd., 43952. Tel: 614-283-4400. Revs. Forrest Rouelle, International Coord. & Chm., Board of Directors; Daniel Cook, Guest Master of Visitation House.

BELPRE. *Boy Scouts*, P.O. Box 426, 45714. Tel: 614-423-7422. Rev. David L. Huffman, Dir.

BEVERLY. *Marriage Encounter*. Mailing Address: St. Bernard Church, 307 Seventh St., 45715. Rev. Msgr. Robert J. Kawa, Dir.

BLOOMINGDALE. *Apostolate for Family Consecration*, John Paul II Holy Family Center, 3375 County Rd. 36, 43910-7903. Tel: 614-765-4301.

BRIDGEPORT. *Cursillo Moderator*, St. Anthony Church, 630 Main St., 43912. Rev. Msgr. Frank Manieri; Mrs. Peggy Cotton, Lay Dir.

MARIETTA. *Search*, St. John's Church, Churchtown, R.D. 2, 45750. Tel: 614-896-2060. Rev. Msgr. Charles F. Highland, Diocesan Dir.

MARTINS FERRY. *Catholic Daughters of the America*, 626 Columbus Ave., 43935. Mrs. Elaine Kiss, State Regent & Contact Person.

TORONTO. *Charismatic Renewal*, 1225 N. River Ave., 43964. Rev. Msgr. Roger J. Foys.

WORTHINGTON. *Seminary Reivew Board Vocations*, P.O. Box 537, 43085.

RELIGIOUS INSTITUTES OF MEN REPRESENTED IN THE DIOCESE

For further details refer to the corresponding bracketed number in the Religious Institutes of Men or Women section.

[0680]—*Brothers of the Immaculate Heart of Mary.*—I.H.M.

[0230]—*Camaldolese Hermits of the Congregation of Monte Corona.*—Er.Cam.

[0560]—*Third Order of Saint Francis. (Sacred Heart Prov.).*—T.O.R.

RELIGIOUS INSTITUTES OF WOMEN REPRESENTED IN THE DIOCESE

[]—*Carmelite Hermits of Reparation.*—E.C.R.

[]—*Congregation of St. Joseph, Cleveland, OH.*—C.S.J.

[1070-02]—*Dominican Sisters, Columbus.*—O.P.

[1230]—*Franciscan Sisters of Christian Charity, Manitowac, WI.*—O.S.F.

[]—*Franciscan Third Order Regular Sisters of the Sorrowful Mother.*—T.O.R.

[1870]—*Handmaids of the Sacred Heart of Jesus.*—A.C.J.
[1880]—*Handmaids of the Sacred Heart of Jesus for Reparation.*—A.R.
[0500]—*Sisters of Charity of Nazareth.*—S.C.N.
[0570]—*Sisters of Charity of Seton Hill, Greensburg, PA.*—S.C.
[]—*Sisters of Holy Family of Nazareth.*—C.S.F.N.
[]—*Sisters of Notre Dame de Namur, Cincinnati, OH.*
[3073]—*Sisters of Our Lady of Charity.*
[]—*Sisters of St. Francis of Assisi, Milwaukee, WI.*
[1530]—*Sisters of St. Francis of the Congregation of Our Lady of Lourdes, Sylvania, Ohio.*—O.S.F.
[3840]—*Sisters of St. Joseph of Carondelet.*—C.S.J.
[2110]—*Sisters of the Humility of Mary.*—H.M.
[4160]—*Vincentian Sisters of Charity.*—V.S.C.

NECROLOGY

† Baudo, Rev. Msgr. Francis J., (Retired). —Died June 21, 1996.

† Hellmer, Rev. Msgr. Michael D., (Absent on Leave). —Died Aug. 11, 1996.

Diocese of Stockton

(Dioecesis Stocktoniensis)

Most Reverend

DONALD W. MONTROSE, D.D.

Bishop of Stockton; ordained May 7, 1949; appointed Titular Bishop of Vescovio and Auxiliary of Los Angeles on March 25, 1983; consecrated May 12, 1983; translated Bishop of Stockton December 19, 1985; installed February 20, 1986. *Office: 1105 N. Lincoln St., Stockton, CA, 95203. Mailing Address: P.O. Box 4237, Stockton, CA, 95204.* Tel.: 209-466-0636.

ESTABLISHED JANUARY 13, 1962.

Square Miles 10,023.

Legal Title: The Roman Catholic Bishop of Stockton, a Corporation Sole.

Comprises six Counties in the State of California-viz., Alpine, Calaveras, Mono, San Joaquin, Stanislaus and Tuolumne.

For legal titles of parishes and diocesan institutions, consult the Chancery Office.

Chancery Office: P.O. Box 4237, Stockton, CA, 95204-0237. Tel.: 209-466-0636; Fax: 209-941-9722.

STATISTICAL OVERVIEW

Personnel	
Bishop	1
Priests: Diocesan Active in Diocese	46
Priests: Active Outside Diocese	2
Priests: Retired, Sick or Absent	16
Number of Diocesan Priests	64
Religious Priests in Diocese	20
Extern Priests in Diocese	17
Ordinations:	
Diocesan Priests	1
Permanent Deacons in Diocese	27
Total Brothers	4
Total Sisters	69
Parishes	
Parishes	32
With Resident Pastor:	
Resident Diocesan Priests	22
Resident Religious Priests	5
Without Resident Pastor:	
Administered by Priests	5
Missions	16
Pastoral Centers	2
Professional Ministry Personnel:	
Brothers	1
Sisters	24
Lay Ministers	13
Welfare	
Catholic Hospitals	3
Total Assisted	325,164
Homes for the Aged	2
Total Assisted	448
Special Centers for Social Services	1
Total Assisted	25,000
Educational	
Diocesan Students in Other Seminaries	7
Total Seminarians	7
High Schools, Diocesan and Parish	2
Total Students	1,324
Elementary Schools, Diocesan and Parish	12
Total Students	3,439
Catechesis/Religious Education:	
High School Students	1,927
Elementary Students	9,909
Total Students Under Catholic Instruction	16,606
Teachers in the Diocese:	
Priests	4
Brothers	2
Sisters	28
Lay Teachers	195
Vital Statistics	
Receptions into the Church:	
Infant Baptism Totals	5,124
Adult Baptism Totals	315
Received into Full Communion	438
First Communions	3,268
Confirmations	2,345
Marriages:	
Catholic	648
Interfaith	152
Total Marriages	800
Deaths	1,396
Total Catholic Population	161,437
Total Population	1,035,972

Former Bishops—Most Rev. HUGH A. DONOHOE, D.D., ord. June 14, 1930; appt. Titular Bishop of Taium and Auxiliary of San Francisco Aug. 2, 1947; cons. Oct. 7, 1947; appt. to Stockton Feb. 21, 1962; transferred to Fresno Aug. 27, 1969; died Oct. 26, 1987.—Most Rev. MERLIN J. GUILFOYLE, D.D., J.C.D., ord. June 10, 1933; appt. Titular Bishop of Bulla and Auxiliary of San Francisco Aug. 15, 1950; cons. Sept. 21, 1950; translated to Bishop of Stockton Nov. 19, 1969; retired Feb. 26, 1980; died Nov. 20, 1981.—Most Rev. ROGER M. MAHONY, D.D., ord. May 1, 1962; appt. Titular Bishop of Tamascani and Auxiliary of Fresno, Jan. 7, 1975; cons. March 19, 1975; translated Bishop of Stockton Feb. 26, 1980; elevated to Archbishop of Los Angeles July 16, 1985; elevated to Cardinal, June 28, 1991.

Chancery Office—1105 N. Lincoln St., Stockton, 95203., Mailing Address: P.O. Box 4237, Stockton, 95204-0237. Tel: 209-466-0636; Fax: 209-941-9722.

Vicar General—Rev. Msgr. JAMES E. CAIN.

Episcopal Vicar for Judicial Affairs—Rev. Msgr. RICHARD J. RYAN, J.C.D.

Episcopal Vicar for Religious Vocations—Rev. MATTHEW O'DONNELL.

Chancellor—Rev. Msgr. RICHARD J. RYAN, J.C.D.

Business Manager—JAN YTURRI.

Special Assistant for Administrative Affairs—Rev. ROBERT J. PEREIRA.

Diocesan Tribunal—1105 N. Lincoln St., Stockton, 95203., Mailing Address: P.O. Box 4237, Stockton, 95204-0237. Tel: 209-466-0636; Fax: 209-941-9722.

Officialis—Rev. Msgr. RICHARD J. RYAN, J.C.D.

Vice-Officialis—Revs. GEORGE F. LACEY; JOHN J.M. FOSTER, J.C.L.

Judges—Revs. HARMON SKILLEN, J.C.D.; DAVID DEIBEL, J.C.L; Mrs. DEBORAH A. BARTON, J.C.L.

Tribunal Personnel—LENORE SYPNIESKI; Mrs. DIANE TARICCO, Notary.

Diocesan Consultors—Revs. EDWARD DONOHOE; EUGENE TRAINER; KHOI PHAM; ROBERT J. PEREIRA; JOHN C. SILVA; LEO SUAREZ; BOB SILVA; LAWRENCE MCGOVERN, S.T.L. Ex-Officio Members: Rev. Msgr. JAMES E. CAIN, V.G.; Rev. ARMANDO VERGARA; Rev. Msgr. RICHARD RYAN, J.C.D.; Rev. JOHN P. FALLON, O.S.F.S.

Deans—Deanery I: Rev. WILLIAM C. MOORE, Deanery II: Rev. JOHN ARMISTEAD, S.T.L., Deanery III: Rev. BERNARD J. MANNION, M.A., M.C.F., V.F., Deanery IV: Rev. JOHN P. O'NEILL, O.S.F.S.

Examiners and Parochial Consultors—Revs. ALOYS CONRAD GRUBER; JOSEPH P. O'HARE; IVO D. ROCHA; JOHN M. PRUETT.

The Roman Catholic Welfare Corporation of Stockton—Mailing Address: P.O. Box 4237, Stockton, 95204. 1105 N. Lincoln St., Stockton, 95203-0237. Tel: 209-466-0636; Fax: 209-941-9722.

Diocesan Offices and Directors

Apostleship of Prayer—Rev. GEORGE LACEY, *P.O. Box 4237, Stockton, 95204-0237.* Tel: 209-466-0636.

Building Committee—Rev. Msgr. JAMES E. CAIN, V.G., Chm.; Rev. Msgr. RICHARD J. RYAN J.C.D.; Rev. FRANCIS PRENDERGAST, Sec. LEONARD M. ABBOTT.

Catholic Charities—MARGE VERNER, *1106 N. El Dorado, Stockton, 95202.* Tel: 209-948-1501.

Catholic Youth Organization—MICHAEL SCRIVEN, Sports Dir., *1618 W. Longview, Stockton, 95207.* Tel: 209-477-1107.

Cemeteries—Rev. Msgr. JAMES E. CAIN, V.G., Dir., *Mailing Address: P.O. Box 4237, Stockton, 95204-0237.* Tel: 209-466-0636. *1105 N. Lincoln St., Stockton, 95203.*

Censor Librorum—Vacant.

Centro Catolico de Pastoral Hispana—Mrs. DIGNA RAMIREZ-LOPEZ, Office: *1125 N. Lincoln St., Stockton, 95203.* Tel: 209-464-1976.

Communications Department—PATRICK JOYCE, Office: *1125 N. Lincoln St., P.O. Box 4237, Stockton, 95204-0237.* Tel: 209-466-5811.

Newspaper—"The Catholic Lantern".

Community of Caring—NANCY BONNET; MARGO KOZINA, *1125 N. Lincoln St., Stockton, 95204.* Tel: 209-465-5433.

Continuing Education of Clergy—Rev. EUGENE TRAINER, *505 West Granger Ave., Modesto, 95350-4299.* Tel: 209-524-7421.

Cursillo Movement-English and Spanish—Rev. ARMANDO VERGARA, Dir.

Stewardship Office—JAN YTURRI.

Development Department—GEORGE REINERT, Dir., *1125 N. Lincoln St., P.O. Box 4237, Stockton, 95204-0237.* Tel: 209-466-5812.

Diocesan Pastoral Council—Rev. HARMON D. SKILLIN, J.C.D., Chm., *P.O. Box 4237, Stockton, 95204-0237.* Tel: 209-948-3450.

Ecumenism—Rev. PATRICK WALKER, Dir., *650 Rose St., Turlock, 95380-4186.* Tel: 209-634-8578.

Education, Religious—Sr. DIANE SMITH, C.S.J., Dir. School of Ministry; Sr. GLORIA DEJESUS SANCHEZ, E.F.M.S., Diocesan Dir. of Religious Education, Central Office: *1125 N. Lincoln St., Stockton, 95203.* Tel: 209-466-6796. Contact this office for various CCD Centers.

Education, Special—YVONNE HARROLD, Dir., *1125 N. Lincoln St., Stockton, 95203.* Tel: 209-466-9374. Programs for physically & mentally impaired.

Engaged Encounter—CAROL HAGAN; LEE HAGAN, *P.O. Box 576107, Modesto, 95355.* Tel: 209-521-1252.

English Language School of Ministries Program—Sr. DIANE SMITH, *1105 N. Lincoln St., P.O. Box 4237, Stockton, 95204-0237.* Tel: 209-466-0636.

Spanish School of Ministries Program—GLORIA MAGDELANO.

Episcopal Liaison of Catholic Charismatic Renewal—

WILLIAM BRENNAN, Ph.D., *13 Pardee Ln., Stockton, 95207.* Tel: 209-474-0571.

Family Life Commission—Rev. MARK WAGNER, *2728 Topeka St., River Bank, 95367-2252.* Tel: 209-869-2996.

Legion of Mary—Stockton Curia: Rev. WILLIAM J. RYAN, M.A., Spiritual Dir., *425 West Magnolia, Stockton, 95203.* Tel: 209-463-1305. Stanislaus and Tuolumne Curia: Vacant.

Liturgical Commission—Rev. JOHN J.M. FOSTER, J.C.L., Chm., *1105 N. Lincoln St., P.O. Box 4237, Stockton, 95204-0237.* Tel: 209-466-0636.

Natural Family Planning—Rev. MARK WAGNER, *2827 Topeka St., Riverbank, 95367-2252.* Tel: 209-869-2996.

Newman Apostolate—The Newman House, Rev. DAVID FONTAINE, O.Carm., Dir., *4101 N. Manchester, Stockton, 95207.* Tel: 209-951-0881. Rev. LONACHAN W. AROUJE, *Catholic Campus Community, 1560 Geer Rd., Suite 1, Box 33, Turlock, 95380.* Tel: 209-632-2415.

Order of Christian Initiation of Adults—Rev. Msgr. RICHARD J. RYAN, J.C.D., *1105 North Lincoln St., Stockton, 95203.* Tel: 204-466-0636.

Permanent Diaconate Program—Deacon JOHN RYAN, Dir., *163 W. Eaton Ave., Tracy, 95376.* Tel: 209-835-4560.

Pontifical Association of Holy Childhood—Rev. ROBERT J. PEREIRA, *1105 N. Lincoln St., P.O. Box 4237, Stockton, 95204-0237.* Tel: 209-466-0636.

Priests, Health and Retirement Board—Rev. Msgr. JAMES E. CAIN, V.G.; Revs. EDWARD DONOHOE; GEORGE F. LACEY; JOHN P. GLEESON; WILLIAM C. HUGHES, *1105 N. Lincoln St., P.O. Box 4237, Stockton, 95204-0237.* Tel: 209-466-0636.

Propagation of the Faith—Rev. ROBERT J. PEREIRA, Dir., *P.O. Box 4237, Stockton, 95204.* Tel: 209-466-0636.

Respect Life Board—MICHAEL FIELDS, Chm., *1125 N. Lincoln St., Stockton, 95203.* Tel: 209-463-1118.

Vicar for Religious Women—Sr. ANN VENITA BRITTO, F.C., *St. Joseph Convent, 1168 S. Country Club Dr., Stockon, 95204.*

Schools—Sr. MAUREEN O'BRIEN, F.C., Supt.; Rev. Msgr. JAMES E. CAIN, V.G., Fiscal Advisor, *P.O. Box 4237, Stockton, 95204-0237.* Tel: 209-464-3775.

Child Help - Our Investment - Catholic Education - Scholarship—(CHOICES) A division of the Roman Catholic Welfare Corporation of Stockton; Sr. MARY ANN BISAILLON, D.H.S., Coord., *Mailing Address: P.O. Box 4237, Stockton, 95204-0237.* Tel: 209-464-3775.

Vocations—Revs. MATTHEW O'DONNELL, Dir., *Mailing Address: P.O. Box 4237, Stockton, 95204.* Tel: 209-835-4560.

Youth Ministry—CHRISTIANE ROCELI, English Dir. JOSE LOPEZ CEJA, Spanish Coord., *1125 N. Lincoln St., Stockton, 95203.* Tel: 209-463-1118.

Catholic Committee on Scouting—Mr. PAT DODD, Chm.; Rev. JOHN J.M. FOSTER, J.C.L., Chap., *1105 N. Lincoln St., P.O. Box 4237, Stockton, 95204-0237.* Tel: 209-466-0636.

CLERGY, PARISHES, MISSIONS AND PAROCHIAL SCHOOLS

CITY OF STOCKTON
(San Joaquin County)

1—CATHEDRAL OF THE ANNUNCIATION (1955), Revs. William J. Ryan, M.A.; Raymond D. Devlin, S.J.
Res., 425 W. Magnolia St., 95203-2412. Tel: 209-463-1305; Fax: 209-463-0807.
School—1110 N. Lincoln St., 95203. Tel: 209-465-0205; Fax: 209-465-1274. Mrs. Carla Donaldson, Prin.
Lay Teachers 14; Students 290.
Catechesis/Religious Programs—Students 292.

2—ST. BERNADETTE (1955), Rev. William C. Moore.
Res., 2544 Plymouth Rd., 95204. Tel: 209-465-3081; Fax: 209-547-1327.
Catechesis/Religious Programs—Students 181.

3—ST. EDWARD (1967) (Hispanic),
Res., 731 S. Cardinal Ave., 95215. Tel: 209-466-3020.
Catechesis/Religious Programs—Tel: 209-466-0719.
Students 230.

4—ST. GEORGE (1951), Revs. John M. Armistead; Leonardo Suarez; Editho Mascardo; Deacons Jim Janukites; Don Rodgers; Arturo Sanchez; Sr. Gladys Guenter, S.H.F., Pastoral Admin.
Res., 120 W. Fifth St., 95206. Tel: 209-463-3413.
School—144 W. Fifth St., 95206. Tel: 209-463-1540. Mr. Alan Cook, Prin.
Sisters 2; Lay Teachers 12; Students 261.
St. George REALMS Foundation—.
Catechesis/Religious Programs—Students 347.
Missions—French Camp, San Joaquin Co., Good Shepherd, P.O. Box 354, French Camp, 95231. Tel: 209-982-0578; Lathrop, San Joaquin Co., Our Lady of Guadalupe, 16019 Cambridge Dr., Lathrop, 95330. Tel: 209-858-4834.

5—ST. GERTRUDE (1913) (Mexican), Revs. Charles G. Countie, O.Carm.; Jeffry L. Fairfield, O.Carm.; Thomas J. Alkire, O.Carm.; Deacon Jorge Torres.
Res., 1663 E. Main St., 95205. Tel: 209-466-0278.
School—1701 E. Main St., 95205. Tel: 209-941-0301. Mrs. Olga Rodriguez, Prin.
Religious 2; Lay Teachers 8; Students 217.
Catechesis/Religious Programs—Tel: 209-941-0501.
Students 345.

6—ST. LINUS (1965), Rev. Lawrence M. Guerrero, Admin. In res., Rev. Jose Domingo Ruiz.
Res., 2620 S. B St., 95206. Tel: 209-465-1430; Fax: 209-465-5240.
Catechesis/Religious Programs—Students 350.
Convent—2600 S. B St., 95206. Tel: 209-465-0416.

7—ST. LUKE (1951) (Vietnamese), Revs. Harmon D. Skillin, J.C.D.; Dean McFalls; Tuan Nguyen, S.D.B. (Vietnam); Titian A. Miani, (Retired); George Lacey, (Retired); Deacon Joseph Artesi.
Res., 3847 N. Sutter St., 95204. Tel: 209-948-3450; Fax: 209-948-2841.
School—4005 N. Sutter St., 95204. Tel: 209-464-0801; Fax: 209-466-1150. Mrs. Mary Lou Curtis, Prin.
Lay Teachers 11; Students 375.
Catechesis/Religious Programs—Tel: 209-462-0410.
Students 125.
Convent—230 E. Atlee St., 95204. Tel: 209-463-6533.

8—ST. MARY OF THE ASSUMPTION (1851), Revs. Alvaro U. Araque; Jairo H. Ramirez; Deacon Julian Sepulveda.
Res., 203 E. Washington St., 95202. Tel: 209-948-0661; Fax: 209-948-0673.
Catechesis/Religious Programs—Tel: 209-946-9536.
Students 154.

9—ST. MICHAEL (1921) (Italian), Rev. Michael Pintacura, Admin. In res., Rev. Msgr. Richard Ryan.
Res., 5882 N. Ashley Ln., 95215-9308. Tel: 209-931-0639; Fax: 209-931-3621.
Catechesis/Religious Programs—Tel: 209-931-2696.
Students 220.

10—PRESENTATION OF B.V.M. (1952), Rev. Robert J. Silva. In res., Rev. Hung Joseph Nguyen.
Res., 1521 McClellan Way, 95207. Tel: 209-472-2150; Fax: 209-472-0541.
Ministry Center—6715 Leesburg Pl., 95207. Tel: 209-472-2150; Fax: 209-472-0541.
School—1635 W. Benjamin Holt Dr., 95207. Tel: 209-472-2140. Mrs. Linda Boragno-Dopp, Prin.
Lay Teachers 10; Students 310.
Catechesis/Religious Programs—Students 570.

OUTSIDE CITY OF STOCKTON

Angels Camp, Calaveras Co., St. Patrick (1856) (Italian), Rev. Henry P. Johnston.
Res., P.O. Box 576, 95222. Tel: 209-736-4575. [CEM][JC]
Catechesis/Religious Programs—820 S. Main, 95222. Tel: 209-736-4458.
Students 100.
Missions—Murphys, Murphys Co., St. Patrick, 619 Sheepranch Rd., Murphys, 95247. Tel: 209-728-2854; Arnold, Arnold Co., Our Lady of the Sierra, 1301 Linebaugh Rd., Arnold, 95223. Tel: 209-795-7625.

Ceres, Stanislaus Co., St. Jude (1962), Revs. Mark Wagner; Octavio Escobar.
Res., 3824 Mitchell Rd., 95307-9422. Tel: 209-537-0516; Fax: 209-537-3412. [CEM]

Escalon, San Joaquin Co., St. Patrick (1878), Rev. James F O'Dwyer.
Res., 19399 E St., Rte. 120 Hwy., Ripon, 95366. Tel: 209-838-2133.
Catechesis/Religious Programs—Tel: 209-838-3101.
Students 400.

Hughson, Stanislaus Co., St. Anthony (1921) (Hispanic), Revs. Ernesto Arbelaez, Admin.; Joseph Illo; Deacon Raymond Flanders.
Mailing Address: P.O. Box 909, 95256. Tel: 209-883-4310; Fax: 209-883-2531.
Res., 2020 Euclid Rd., 95256.
Catechesis/Religious Programs—Tel: 209-883-2280.
Students 1,176.
Mission—La Grange, Stanislaus Co., St. Louis, Floto St., La Grange, 95329.

Linden, San Joaquin Co., Holy Cross (1963), Rev. Armando Vergara.
Res., 18633 E. Front St., P.O. Box 52, 95236. Tel: 209-887-3341.
Catechesis/Religious Programs—Students 130.

Lockeford, San Joaquin Co., St. Joachim (1991). (Quasi-Parish). Rev. Enda J. Maguire.
Mailing Address: P.O. Box 232, 95237. Tel: 209-727-3912.
Catechesis/Religious Programs—Students 65.

Lodi, San Joaquin Co., St. Anne (1904), Revs. Thomas P. Hayes; Gustavo Quintero; Murty M. Fahy, O.S.F.S.; Robert O'Neill; Deacons Juan Mendez; Porfirio Cisneros; Don Bo.
Mailing Address: P.O. Box 480, 95241. Tel: 209-369-1907; Fax: 209-369-1971.
Office: 215 W. Walnut St., 95240.
Res., 150 S. Pleasant St., 95241. [CEM]
School—200 S. Pleasant St., 95241. Tel: 209-333-7580. Mr. Dennis Taricco, Prin.
Lay Teachers 10; Students 291.
Catechesis/Religious Programs—D.R.E.: Sr. Mary Ruth Faisca; Sr. Ancila De La O.
Students 690.
St. Anne's Endowment—Tel: 209-334-1935; Fax: 209-334-0178.
Mission—Thornton, San Joaquin Co., Mater Ecclesiae, 95241.

Mammoth Lakes, Mono Co., St. Joseph (1939), Rev. Andrew C. Dachauer, S.J.; Bro. Daniel C. Corona, S.J.; Deacon Eliseo Gutierrez.
Res., P.O. Box 372, 93546. Tel: 619-934-6276; Fax: 619-934-6276.
Missions—Bridgeport, Mono Co., Infant of Prague, Hwy. 395, Bridgeport, 93517; Lee Vining, Mono Co., Our Savior of the Mountains, 2nd & Mono, Lee Vining, 93541; Walker, Mono Co., Our Lady of the Valley. Walker Community Center.
Catechesis/Religious Programs—Students 125.

Manteca, San Joaquin Co., St. Anthony (1917), Revs. Lawrence J. McGovern, V.F.; Francisco Naranjo; Deacon Alfredo Maestas. In res., Revs. Theodore Lambert; John Foster.
Res., 525 E. North St., 95336. Tel: 209-823-7197; Fax: 209-823-5238.
School—Tel: 209-823-4513. Stephanie Papas, Prin.
Lay Teachers 9; Students 249.
Catechesis/Religious Programs—Tel: 209-239-4302.
Students 740.
St. Vincent de Paul Society—Tel: 209-823-8099.
St. Anthony School Educational Foundation—.

Modesto, Stanislaus Co., St. Joseph (1967), Revs. Joseph P. O'Hare; Neville Jansze.
Res., 1813 Oakdale Rd., 95355. Tel: 209-551-4973; Fax: 209-551-3213.
Catechesis/Religious Programs—Tel: 209-551-0593.
Students 654.

Our Lady of Fatima (1951), Rev. John M. Pruett; Rev. Msgr. William P. Kennedy, V.F., (Retired); Revs. Eugene Trainer; Khoi Pham; Francisco Javier Campechano; Deacon Stanley Gumerlock.
Res., 505 W. Granger Ave., 95350. Tel: 209-524-7421; Fax: 209-524-7713.
School—501 W. Granger Ave., 95350. Tel: 209-524-4170; Fax: 209-524-3960. Linda Partlow, Prin.
Lay Teachers 14; Students 305; Extended Day Care 100.
Catechesis/Religious Programs—Tel: 209-529-0843.
Students 943.
The Monsignor William P. Kennedy Education Foundation—.

St. Stanislaus (1881), Revs. Gilbert L. Arango (Colombia); George Nimal (Sri Lanka); Alvaro Lopez (Colombia).
Res., 709 J St., P.O. Box 292, 95353. Tel: 209-524-4381; Fax: 209-524-1910.
School—1416 Maze Blvd., 95351. Tel: 209-524-9036; Fax: 209-524-4344. Mr. John D. Hendrickson, Prin.
Sisters 1; Lay Teachers 12; Students 315.
Catechesis/Religious Programs—Tel: 209-522-6534.
Students 650.

Newman, Stanislaus Co., St. Joachim (1909), Revs. Louis L. Sweeny; Nicolas Garcia.
Res., 1121 O St., 95360. Tel: 209-862-3528.
Catechesis/Religious Programs—Tel: 209-862-2878.
Students 160.

Oakdale, Stanislaus Co., St. Mary of the Annunciation (1902), Revs. Aloys Conrad Gruber, Pastor; Bernard J. Mannion, V.F., Pastor Emeritus; Deacon Roberto Magdaleno.
Res., 1225 Olive Ave., 95361. Tel: 209-847-2715.

Catechesis/Religious Programs—Tel: 209-847-3498.
Students 220.

Patterson, Stanislaus Co., Sacred Heart (1917), Revs. Andrew E. Bellisario, C.M.; James V. Connors, C.M.; Minh J. Pham, C.M.
Res., 529 I St., 95363. Tel: 209-892-9321; Fax: 209-892-2102.
School—505 M St., 95363. Tel: 209-892-3544. Marian De Groot, Prin.
Students 205.
Catechesis/Religious Programs—Tel: 209-892-6381.
Students 423.
Mission—Crows Landing, Stanislaus Co., Immaculate Heart of Mary, H St., Crows Landing, 95313.
Station—Westley, Guadalupe Center.

Riverbank, Stanislaus Co., St. Frances of Rome (1953), Revs. Thomas M. Rajanayagam (Sri Lanka); Juan de la Cruz Zape (Columbia); Deacon Felipe Vallejo.
Res., 2827 Topeka St., 95367. Tel: 209-869-2996.
Catechesis/Religious Programs—Tel: 209-869-5830.
Students 341.

San Andreas, Calaveras Co., St. Andrew (1963) (Caucasian), Revs. William L. Kraft; Martin Starc, Pastor Emeritus.
Res., 162 Church Hill Rd., P.O. Box 550, 95249. Tel: 209-754-3815.
Catechesis/Religious Programs—Students 128.
Missions—Mokelumne Hill, Calaveras Co., St. Thomas Aquinas, 8398 Lafayette St., Mokelumne Hill, 95245; West Point, Calaveras Co., Our Lady of Fatima, 22581 Hwy. 26, West Point, 95255.

Sonora, Tuolumne Co., St. Patrick (1851), Revs. Michael E. Kelly; John Foley, O.S.F.S.; Sr. Nancy P. O'Shea, S.N.D., Pastoral Assoc.
Res., 116 W. Bradford Ave., 95370. Tel: 209-532-7139; Fax: 209-532-6152. [CEM 5][JC]
Catechesis/Religious Programs—Fax: 209-532-4389.
Students 250.
Missions—Big Oak Flat, Tuolumne Co., Our Lady of Mt. Carmel, Cemetery Rd., Big Oak Flat, 95321. Tel: 209-962-2156; Columbia, Tuolumne Co., St. Anne, 22518 Church Ln., Columbia, 95310.

Tracy, San Joaquin Co., St. Bernard's (1908), Revs. Ivo D. Rocha; Mario Castaneda; Matthew O'Donnell; Deacon John Ryan.
Res., 163 W. Eaton Ave., 95376. Tel: 209-835-4560, Ext. 110; Fax: 209-835-4588.
School—165 W. Eaton Ave., 95376. Tel: 209-835-4560, Ext. 130. Mrs. Diane Rothschild, Prin.
Sisters 1; Lay Teachers 12; Students 312.
Catechesis/Religious Programs—Tel: 209-835-4560, Ext. 116.
Students 779.
Convent—165 W. Eaton Ave., 95376. Tel: 209-835-7391. Daughters of the Cross

Turlock, Stanislaus Co., Sacred Heart (1910), Revs. Francis Prendergast; J. Patrick Walker; Alexandre Pacheco (India); Oscar A. Pelaez.
Res., 650 Rose St., 95380. Tel: 209-634-8578; 8579; Fax: 209-634-7124.
School—1225 Cooper Ave., 95380. Tel: 209-634-7787; Fax: 209-634-0156. Mrs. Donna Noceti, Prin.
Sisters 2; Lay Teachers 12; Students 307.
Preschool—Tel: 209-667-5512. Debra Cannella, Prin.
Lay Teachers 9; Students 69.
Catechesis/Religious Programs—Sacred Heart Religious Education, 1250 Cooper # 1, 95380. Tel: 209-634-5111.
Students 653.
Convent—1301 Cooper Ave., 95380. Tel: 209-634-7708.

Our Lady of the Assumption of the Portuguese (1973), Rev. Manuel F. Sousa.
Mailing Address: P.O. Box 2030, 95381. Tel: 209-634-2222; 634-3140; Fax: 209-634-2366.
Res., 2602 S. Walnut Rd., 95380.
Catechesis/Religious Programs—Tel: 209-874-5739.
Students 275.

Twain Harte, Tuolumne Co., All Saints (1962), Rev. John Fitzgerald; Deacon Edward Zoma.
Res., 18674 Cherokee Dr., P.O. Box 642, 95383. Tel: 209-586-3161. [JC]
Catechesis/Religious Programs—Students 100.
Mission—Tuolumne, Tuolumne Co., St. Joseph, Tuolumne, 95379.
Stations—Pinecrest. (Summer); Strawberry. (Winter).

Chaplains of Public Institutions

STOCKTON. *DeWitt Nelson Training Center,* 7650 Newcastle Rd., P.O. Box 213003, 95213-9003. Tel: 209-944-6187. Rev. William Linakis, S.A., Chap.
Karl Holton School, 7650 Newcastle Rd., P.O. Box 213002, 95213-9002. Tel: 209-944-6364. Rev. Theodore Lambert, Chap.
Northern California Women's Facility, 7150 Arch Rd., P.O. Box 213006, 95213-9006. Tel: 209-943-1600. Mr. Randy Rainwater, Chap.
O.H. Close School, 7650 Newcastle Rd., P.O. Box 213001, 95213-9001. Tel: 209-944-6135; 944-6349. Rev. Pius Kurera, Chap.
Stockton Developmental Center. Vacant. 510 E. Magnolia St., 95202-3288. Tel: 209-948-7111.

FRENCH CAMP. *San Joaquin County Jail.* Vacant. 999 W. Matthews Rd., 95231. Tel: 209-468-4562.
San Joaquin General Hospital. Vacant. 500 W. Hospital Rd., 95231. Tel: 209-468-6000.

JAMESTOWN. *Sierra Conservation Center.* Mailing Address: P.O. Box 497, 95327-1213. Tel: 209-984-5291. Rev. Ray Abella, O.S.F.S., Chap.

TRACY. *Deuel Vocational Institution.* Mailing Address: P.O. Box 400, 95376-3593. Tel: 209-466-8055. Rev. Ron Rissling, O.M.I., Chap.

On Duty Outside the Diocese:
Reverend Fathers—
Sullivan, George D., 197 Collingwood, San Francisco, CA 94114

Absent on Leave:
Reverend Fathers—
Gabino, Pedro
Garcia, Louis
Myers, William S.

Retired:
Reverend Monsignors—
Doyle, Walter H., Pastor Emeritus, Mailing Address: P.O. Box 1618, Diamond Springs, CA 95619
Kennedy, William P., Pastor Emeritus, Our Lady of Fatima Church, 1635 Sherwood Ave., Modesto, CA 95350-4299
Reverend Fathers—
Coghlan, John A., Pastor Emeritus, 1152 De Haro, San Francisco, CA 94107
Donohoe, Edward, 5835 Cherokee Rd., #69, Stockton, CA 95215
Ford, William A., St. Mary Star of the Sea, 888 Blvd. of the Arts, #1508, Sarasota, FL 34236
Gleeson, John P., Mailing Address: Cathedral of the Annunciation, P.O. Box 899, Stockton, CA 95201-0899
Hughes, William C., Casa Manana, 3700 N. Sutter St., #272, Stockton, CA 95204
Lacey, George F., Pastor Emeritus, 3700 N. Sutter St., Stockton, CA 95204
McCaffrey, James Leo, 27 Miramonte Dr., Moraga, CA 94556
Miani, Titian, Casa Manana, 3700 N. Sutter St., #207, Stockton, CA 95204

Permanent Deacons:
Artesi, Joseph, St. Luke's, Stockton
Brennan, William, Stockton
Broderick, Thomas, St. Anthony, Hughson
Cisneros, Porfirio, St. Anne, Lodi
Flanders, Raymond, St. Anthony, Hughson
Garza, Hector, St. George, Stockton
Griego, Nick, St. Patrick, Sonora
Gumerlock, Francis, Our Lady of Fatima, Modesto
Hernandez, Arnold, Sacred Heart, Patterson
Isobaker, Joseph, St. Joseph's Medical Center, Stockton
Janukites, James, St. George, Stockton
Maestas, Alfredo, St. Anthony, Manteca
Magdaleno, Roberto, St. Mary, Oakdale
Mendez, Juan, St. Anne, Lodi
Neumann, Stanley, St. Patrick, Sonora
Reyes, Domingo, St. Linus, Stockton
Rippey, William, Leave of Absence
Rodgers, Donald, St. George, Stockton
Ryan, John G., St. Bernard, Tracy
Sanchez, Arturo, St. Anthony, Manteca
Schepcoff, Jacques, Annunciation, Stockton
Sepulveda, Julian R., St. Mary of the Assumption, Stockton
Torres, Jorge, St. Gertrude, Stockton
Vallejo, Felipe, St. Frances of Rome, Riverbank
Vargo, John, St. Jude, Ceres
Warren, William E., St. Joachim, Lockeford
Zoma, Edward T., St. Patrick, Sonora

INSTITUTIONS LOCATED IN THE DIOCESE

[A] HIGH SCHOOLS, DIOCESAN

STOCKTON. *St. Mary's High School,* 5648 N. El Dorado St., P.O. Box 7247, 95267-0247. Tel: 209-957-3340; Fax: 209-957-0861. Non-resident students. Rev. John P. Fallon, O.S.F.S., Pres.; Mr. Peter Morelli, Prin.; Revs. John A. Lindsay, O.S.F.S.; Clark T. Kelley, O.S.F.S.; Bros. James Dorazio, O.S.F.S.; Neil McMenamin, O.S.F.S. Priests 3; Brothers 2; Sisters 1; Lay Teachers 56; Students 914.
St. Mary's High School Foundation.

MODESTO. *Central Catholic High School,* 200 S. Carpenter Rd., 95351. Tel: 209-524-9611; Fax: 209-524-4913. Non-resident students. Mr. Jim Pecchenino, Pres.; Dr. Rex Wetzel, Prin. Priests 1; Lay Teachers 23; Administrators 5; Students 400.
Central Catholic High School Foundation. Tel: 209-524-6818; 524-9611.

[B] CATHOLIC CHARITIES

STOCKTON. *The Catholic Charities of the Diocese of Stockton,* 1106 N. El Dorado St., 95202. Tel: 209-948-1501. Marge M. Verner, Exec. Dir.; Mr. Woody Bagley, Chm. Corp. Bd.
The following services and programs are listed according to counties:
SAN JOAQUIN COUNTY:
Homemaker-Companion Program, 1106 N. El Dorado, 95202. Julie Homan, Prog. Mgr. Homemakers 20; Clients Served 135. (See separate listing for Modesto).
Refugee Resettlement (U.S.C.C.), 1106 N. El Dorado, 95202. Mr. Kham O. Baccam, Resettlement Dir. Case Managers 1; Refugees Resettled 350.
Respite Care Program, 1106 N. El Dorado, 95202. Tel: 209-948-1582. Julie Homan, Prog. Mgr. Caretakers 15; Clients Served 50.
Making the Right Connections, 1106 N. El Dorado, 95202. Tel: 209-948-1501. Marge Verner, Dir. Students per year 700.
Senior Home Repair, 1106 N. El Dorado, 95202. Tel: 209-948-1582. Julie Homan, Prog. Mgr. Part-time Repairman; Seniors Served 162.
STANISLAUS COUNTY: Homemaker Program (Modesto), 400 12th St., Modesto, 95354. Tel: 209-529-3784. Jane Weinheimer, Prog. Mgr. Homemakers 14; Clients 207.
Long Term Care Ombudsman Program, 400 12th St., Ste. 4, Modesto, 95354. Tel: 209-529-3784. Jane Weinheimer, Prog. Mgr. Ombudsman 18; Facilities Monitored 257; Clients served 6,000.
Senior Transportation, 400 12th St., Ste. 4, Modesto, 95354. Tel: 209-529-3784. Collette Pepelis, Coord. Part-time Staff 1; Seniors Served 120.
Elder Abuse Program, 400 12th St., Ste. 4, Modesto, 95354. Tel: 209-529-3784. Jane Weinheimer, Prog. Mgr. Community-wide education.
Eldercare Management, 400 12th St., Ste. 4, Modesto, 95354. Tel: 209-529-3784. Nancy Brookshire, Prog. Mgr. Part-time Staff 2; Seniors Served 125.
Laura's House, 400 12th St., Ste. 4, Modesto, 95354. Residential substance abuse program. Jane Weinheimer, Prog. Mgr. Full-time Staff 3; Part-time Staff 5; Maximum Occupancy 25.
MOTHER LODE:
Long Term Care Ombudsman Program, 171 N. Washington St., Sonora, 95370. Tel: 209-532-6272. Tom McHenry, Coord. Ombudsmen 12; Facilities Monitored 14; Clients Served 650.
Elder Abuse Program, 171 N. Washington St., Sonora, 95370. Tel: 209-532-6272. Tom McHenry, Coord. Community-wide education.
Legal Advocacy Program, 171 N. Washington St., Sonora, 95370. Tel: 209-532-6262. Celia Gainer, Coord. Part-time Staff 1; Legal Advisor 1; Clients Served 100.

[C] GENERAL HOSPITALS

STOCKTON. *St. Joseph's Behavioral Health Center,* 2510 N. California St., 95204. Tel: 209-948-2100.
For a complete listing, refer to the Hospitals section.
St. Joseph's Medical Center of Stockton, 1800 N. California St., P.O. Box 213008, 95213-9008. Tel: 209-943-2000.
For a complete listing, refer to the Hospitals section.
St. Joseph's Regional Health System of Northern San Joaquin Valley, 1800 N. California St., P.O. Box 213008, 95213-9008. Tel: 209-943-2000.
For a complete listing, refer to the Hospitals section.

MANTECA. *St. Dominic's Hospital,* 1777 W. Yosemite Ave., P.O. Box 1307, 95337. Tel: 209-825-3500.
For a complete listing, refer to the Hospitals section.

[D] HOMES FOR AGED

STOCKTON. *Casa Manana Inn,* 3700 N. Sutter St., 95204. Tel: 209-466-4046.
For a complete listing, refer to the Special Care Facilities section.
Garden Oaks, 3334 Wagner Heights Rd., 95209. Tel: 209-956-3401.
For a complete listing, refer to the Special Care Facilities section.
St. Joseph's Regional Housing Corp., 1805 N. California St., Ste. 407, 95204. Tel: 209-467-6312.
For a complete listing, refer to the Special Care Facilities section.

[E] CONVENTS AND RESIDENCES FOR SISTERS

STOCKTON. *The Daughters of the Cross*, St. Joseph Convent, 1168 S. Country Club Blvd., 95204. Tel: 209-944-9781. Sisters 3.

Daughters of the Holy Spirit, St. Gertrude Convent, 1655 E. Main St., 95205. Tel: 209-462-9445. Sisters 5.

Dominican Sisters of San Rafael, California, St. Joseph's Convent, 407 E. Walnut St., 95204. Tel: 209-462-8486. Sisters 10.

Eucharistic Franciscan Missionary Sisters, Blessed Sacrament Convent, 1205 N. San Joaquin St., 95202. Tel: 209-462-3906. Sisters 6.

Holy Cross Sisters, Casita Esperanza, P.O. Box 9, 95201. Tel: 209-467-8042.

Holy Family Sisters, 4900 N. Hwy. 99, #146, 95212. Tel: 209-931-2949. 187 San Marcos Dr., Lodi, 95240. Tel: 209-931-2949.

Maryknoll Sisters, 25 S. Commerce St., No. 237, 95202. Tel: 209-462-9394.

Sacro Costato Missionary Sisters, St. Luke's Convent, 230 E. Atlee St., 95204. Tel: 209-462-6533. Sisters 4.

Sisters of Charity of the Blessed Virgin Mary, Presentation Convent, 1626 McClellan Way, 95207. Tel: 209-472-2144. Sisters 3.

Sisters of St. Joseph of Carondelet, 1639 W. Swain, 95207. Tel: 209-957-7090.

MODESTO. *Sisters of the Cross of the Sacred Heart of Jesus*, Cloistered Convent, 1320 Maze Blvd., 95351. Tel: 209-526-3525. Sisters 7; Postulants 1; Novices 3.

Sisters of the Holy Cross, 601 W. Granger Ave., Apt. 116, 95350. Tel: 209-529-0401. Sr. Mary Mulvaney, C.S.C.

PATTERSON. *Daughters of the Holy Spirit*, Sacred Heart Convent, 505 M St., 95363. Tel: 209-892-3410. Sisters 4.

SONORA. *Sisters of Notre Dame De Namur*. Mailing Address: c/o St. Patrick Church, 116 W. Bradford Ave., 95370-4924. Interfaith Retreat Center, P.O. Box 1994, Murphys, 95247-1994. St. Stanislaus Parish, 1416 Maze Blvd., Modesto, 95351.

TRACY. *The Daughters of the Cross*, St. Bernard Convent, 165 W. Eaton Ave., 95376. Tel: 209-835-7391. Sisters 3.

TURLOCK. *Sisters of the Sacred Hearts of Jesus and Mary*, Sacred Heart Convent, 1301 Cooper Ave., 95380. Tel: 209-634-7708. Sisters 5.

[F] RETREAT CENTERS

COPPEROPOLIS. *Madonna of Peace Renewal Center*. (Youth Facility), 2010 Hunt Rd., P.O. Box 71, 95228. Tel: 209-785-9909; 785-2157 (Office). Total in Residence 2

[G] MISCELLANEOUS

STOCKTON. *The Bishop's Educational Foundation, Diocese of Stockton*, 1105 N. Lincoln St., 95203.

Instituto Fe y Vida, 1737 W. Benjamin Holt Dr., 95207. Total Staff 3.

St. Mary's High School Foundation, Box 7247, 95267-0247. Tel: 209-957-3340.

San Lorenzo Ruiz De Manila, 2079 Del Rio Dr., 95204.

LODI. *St. Anne's Endowment*, 215 W. Walnut St., 95240. Tel: 209-369-1907.

MANTECA. *St. Vincent de Paul Society*, 525 E. North St., 95336. Tel: 209-823-8099. Total Staff 25; Total Assisted 13,000.

MODESTO. *Central Catholic High School Foundation*, 200 Carpenter Rd., 95351. Tel: 209-524-6822. Volunteer Board Members 25.

Father John C. Silva Education Foundation, P.O. Box 292, 95353.

The Monsignor William P. Kennedy Education Foundation, 501 W. Granger Ave., 95350. Tel: 209-524-4170.

TURLOCK. *The McElligott Sacred Heart School Foundation*, 650 Rose St., 95380. Tel: 209-634-8578. Rev. Francis Prendergast, Dir. Total Staff 3; Total Students 50.

RELIGIOUS INSTITUTES OF MEN REPRESENTED IN THE DIOCESE

For further details refer to the corresponding bracketed number in the Religious Institutes of Men or Women section.

[0270]—*Carmelite Fathers and Brothers*.—O.Carm.

[0530]—*Franciscan Friars of the Atonement*.—S.A.

[0690]—*Jesuit Fathers and Brothers*. (California, Columbia Prov.).—S.J.

[0910]—*Oblates of Mary Immaculate*.—O.M.I.

[0920]—*Oblates of St. Francis De Sales*. (Toledo-Detroit Prov.).—O.S.F.S.

[1190]—*Salesians of St. John Bosco*.—S.D.B.

[]—*Vincentian Fathers*.

RELIGIOUS INSTITUTES OF WOMEN REPRESENTED IN THE DIOCESE

[1920]—*Congregation of the Sisters of the Holy Cross*. (Notre Dame, IN).—C.S.C.

[0880]—*Daughter of Mary and Joseph*.—D.M.J.

[0780]—*Daughters of the Cross of Liege*.—F.C.

[0820]—*Daughters of the Holy Spirit*. (Putnam, CT).—D.H.S.

[1070-04]—*Dominican Sisters*. (San Rafael).—O.P.

[1150]—*Eucharistic Franciscan Missionary Sisters*.—E.F.M.S.

[1190]—*Franciscan Sisters of the Atonement*.—S.A.

[2470]—*Maryknoll Sisters of St. Dominic*.—M.M.

[]—*Missionary Sisters of the Sacred Side of Jesus and the Sorrowful Mother*. (Italy).

[2519]—*Religious Sisters of Mercy*.—R.S.M.

[0430]—*Sisters of Charity of the Blessed Virgin Mary*. (Dubuque, IA).—B.V.M.

[3000]—*Sisters of Notre Dame de Namur*.—S.N.D.deN.

[3840]—*Sisters of St. Joseph of Carondelet*.—C.S.J.

[]—*Sisters of the Cross of the Sacred Heart of Jesus*. (Tijuana, Mexico).—R.C.S.C.J.

[1960]—*Sisters of the Holy Family*. (San Francisco).—S.H.F.

[3320]—*Sisters of the Presentation of the B.V.M.*. (San Francisco).—P.B.V.M.

[3680]—*Sisters of the Sacred Hearts of Jesus and Mary*.—S.H.J.M.

DIOCESAN CEMETERIES AND MAUSOLEUMS

STOCKTON. *San Joaquin Cemetery and Mausoleum*. Mr. Al Vigil, Supt.

ESCALON. *St. John Cemetery*. Evelyn Swass, Supt.

MODESTO. *St. Stanislaus Cemetery and Chapel Crypts*. Mrs. Irene Silva, Supt.

NECROLOGY

† Silva, John C., Modesto, CA, St. Stanislaus Church. —Died Feb. 25, 1996.

Diocese of Superior

(Dioecesis Superiorensis)

Most Reverend

RAPHAEL M. FLISS, D.D.

Bishop of Superior; ordained May 26, 1956; appointed Coadjutor Bishop of Superior with right of succession November 6, 1979; ordained December 20, 1979; succeeded to See, June 27, 1985. *Res., Gitchinadji Dr., Superior, WI, 54880. Office: 1201 Hughitt, Superior, WI, 54880. Mailing Address: Box 969, Superior, WI, 54880.*

ESTABLISHED MAY 3, 1905.

Square Miles 15,715.

Comprises the Counties of Ashland, Barron, Bayfield, Burnett, Douglas, Iron, Lincoln, Oneida, Polk, Price, Rusk, Sawyer, St. Croix, Taylor, Vilas and Washburn in the State of Wisconsin.

Incorporated under the laws of the State of Wisconsin as the *Diocese of Superior.*

For legal titles of parishes and diocesan institutions, consult the Chancery.

Chancery Office: 1201 Hughitt Ave., Box 969, Superior, WI, 54880. Tel.: 715-392-2937; Fax: 715-392-2015.

STATISTICAL OVERVIEW

Personnel	
Bishop	1
Priests: Diocesan Active in Diocese	53
Priests: Active Outside Diocese	3
Priests: Retired, Sick or Absent	23
Number of Diocesan Priests	79
Religious Priests in Diocese	16
Ordinations:	
Diocesan Priests	1
Transitional Deacons	2
Permanent Deacons	2
Permanent Deacons in Diocese	42
Total Brothers	2
Total Sisters	133
Parishes	
Parishes	115
With Resident Pastor:	
Resident Diocesan Priests	49
Resident Religious Priests	10
Without Resident Pastor:	
Administered by Priests	49
Administered by Women Religious	2
Administered by Lay People	5
Pastoral Centers	2
Closed Parishes	1
Professional Ministry Personnel:	
Sisters	9
Lay Ministers	15
Welfare	
Catholic Hospitals	4
Total Assisted	97,629
Homes for the Aged	2
Total Assisted	357
Day Care and Extended Day Care Centers	5
Total Assisted	275
Special Centers for Social Services	4
Total Assisted	4,482
Residential Care of Disabled	16
Total Assisted	2,500
Other Institutions	10
Total Assisted	2,300
Educational	
Diocesan Students in Other Seminaries	11
Total Seminarians	11
Elementary Schools, Diocesan and Parish	18
Total Students	3,069
Catechesis/Religious Education:	
High School Students	3,977
Elementary Students	8,879
Total Students Under Catholic Instruction	15,936
Teachers in the Diocese:	
Sisters	11
Lay Teachers	196
Vital Statistics	
Receptions into the Church:	
Infant Baptism Totals	1,183
Adult Baptism Totals	1,455
Received into Full Communion	125
First Communions	1,530
Confirmations	1,207
Marriages:	
Catholic	338
Interfaith	249
Total Marriages	587
Deaths	1,256
Total Catholic Population	87,546
Total Population	381,350

Former Bishops—Rt. Rev. AUGUSTIN FRANCIS SCHINNER, D.D., ord. March 7, 1886; cons. July 25, 1905; resigned Jan. 15, 1913; appt. Bishop of Spokane, WA, March 18, 1914; died Feb. 7, 1937.—Rt. Rev. JOSEPH M. KOUDELKA, D.D., ord. Oct. 8, 1875; cons. Auxiliary Bishop of Cleveland and Titular Bishop of Germanicopolis, Feb. 25, 1908; transferred to Milwaukee as Auxiliary Bishop, Sept. 4, 1911; appt. to the See of Superior, Aug. 6, 1913; died June 24, 1921.—Rt. Rev. JOSEPH G. PINTEN, D.D., ord. Nov. 1, 1890 elected Dec. 3, 1921; cons. May 3, 1922; transferred to the See of Grand Rapids, June 25, 1926; retired Nov. 1, 1940; died Nov. 6, 1945.—Most Rev. THEODORE H. REVERMAN, D.D., ord. July 26, 1901; cons. Nov. 30, 1926; died July 18, 1941.—Most Rev. WILLIAM PATRICK O'CONNOR, D.D., Ph.D., ord. March 10, 1912; cons. March 7, 1942; transferred to the See of Madison, Jan. 15, 1946.—His Eminence ALBERT GREGORY MEYER, D.D., S.S.L., ord. July 11, 1926; appt. Feb. 18, 1946; cons. April 11, 1946; promoted to Archbishop of Milwaukee, July 21, 1953; transferred to Archbishop of Chicago, Sept. 19, 1958; created Cardinal, Dec. 14, 1959; died April 9, 1965.—Most Rev. JOSEPH JOHN ANNABRING, D.D., ord. May 3, 1927; appt. Jan. 27, 1954; cons. March 25, 1954; died Aug. 27, 1959.—Most Rev. GEORGE A. HAMMES, D.D., Bishop Emeritus of Superior; appt. March 28, 1960; cons. May 24, 1960; retired June 27, 1985; died April 11, 1993.

Chancery—1201 Hughitt Ave., Box 969, Superior, 54880. Tel: 715-392-2937; Fax: 715-392-2015.

Vicar General—Very Rev. EDWARD G. MEULEMANS, *Res., 1410 Baxter Ave., Superior, 54880.* Tel: 715-392-8511.

Moderator of the Curia—Very Rev. PHILIP J. HESLIN, Ph.D., *1201 Hughitt Ave., P.O. Box 969, Superior, 54880.* Tel: 715-392-2937.

Chancellor—Sr. EILEEN LANG, F.S.P.A., D.Min.

Secretary to Bishop—Mrs. SHERYL PETREY.

Diocesan Tribunal—1201 Hughitt Ave., Box 969, Superior, 54880. Tel: 715-392-2937.

Judicial Vicar—Very Rev. JAMES F. TOBOLSKI, J.C.L.

Promotor of Justice—Very Rev. EDWARD G. MEULEMANS.

Defender of the Bond—Rev. WILLIAM G. HORATH.

Advocate—Sr. RITA MARIE SCHNEIDER, S.S.N.D.

Notary—Mrs. PATTI J. HOLT.

Vicar for Canonical Affairs—Very Rev. JAMES F. TOBOLSKI, J.C.L.

Vicar for Religious—Sr. EILEEN LANG, F.S.P.A.

Diocesan Pastoral Council—Most Rev. RAPHAEL M. FLISS, D.D., Pres.; South Central Deanery: WARREN WAGNER; PATRICIA PARKER; JEROME THIER, Eastern Deanery: RAYMOND BROZ; JOSEPH BENBENEK; ALAN ZYHOWSKI, Northwest Deanery: MARY GIESEN, Vice Chm. PETER MORAN; ROBERT ULBRICH, North Central Deanery: MIKE BARK; DAVID HNATH; MARY JO HOLZHAEUSER, Southwest Deanery: SAMUEL CARI; LARRY WOJCHIK, Chm. WILLIAM HANSEN. Ex Officio Members: Very Revs. EDWARD G. MEULEMANS; PHILIP J. HESLIN; Sr. MARY ANTHONY MENTING, S.C.S.C.; Sr. ANITA SWANSEN, O.S.M.; Sr. MARIE KYLE, F.S.P.A.; Sr. EILEEN LANG, F.S.P.A., Liaison.

Deaneries and Deans—Northwest Deanery: Very Rev. JAMES F. TOBOLSKI, Southwest Deanery: Very Rev. PETER F. SZLESZINSKI, North Central Deanery: Very Rev. VERNON J. OLMER, O.F.M., South Central Deanery: Very Rev. DENNIS T. MEULEMANS, East Deanery: Very Rev. JAMES R. HORATH.

Pastoral Consultors—Revs. LEONARD FRAHER; WILLIAM H. GREEN; PHILIP DAN STACK.

Presbyteral Council & Diocesan Consultors—Most Rev. RAPHAEL M. FLISS, Pres.; Very Revs. PHILIP J. HESLIN; EDWARD G. MEULEMANS, Chm. DENNIS T. MEULEMANS; PETER F. SZLESZINSKI; JAMES F. TOBOLSKI, Sec.; Revs. JOHN A. DRUMMY; ALOYS EBACH, C.PP.S.; WILLIAM H. GREEN, Treas. GERALD A. HAGEN; BRENDAN J. KUNDA; BRENNAN SCHMIEG, O.F.M.

Personnel Placement Board—Very Rev. EDWARD MEULEMANS; Revs. DAVID P. OBERTS; ALBERT L. VERDEGAN; KEVIN GORDON, Sec. GERALD HARRIS; GREGORY HOPEFL; JAMES P. POWERS.

Conciliation and Arbitration Board—THOMAS DUFFY, Chm. REBECCA JEAN ECK; Rev. DAVID P. OBERTS; RAYMOND RYNDA; Sr. RITA MARIE SCHNEIDER, S.S.N.D., Sec.

Diocesan Offices and Directors

Apostleship of Prayer—Contact Chancery.

Apostolate of the Sea—Contact Chancery.

Bureau of Information—Mr. SAM LUCERO, Dir., *1512 N. 12th St., Superior, 54880.* Tel: 715-392-8268.

Catholic Charities Bureau—Mr. BRIAN SOLAND, M.A., Exec. Dir., Office: *1416 Cummings Ave., Box 219, Superior, 54880.* Tel: 715-394-6617; Fax: 715-394-5951.

Hudson District Office—Box 222, Hudson, 54016. Tel: 715-386-3701.

Rhinelander District Office—Box 566, Rhinelander, 54501. Tel: 715-362-3329.

Catholic Boy and Girl Scout—Rev. THOMAS E. THOMPSON, *P.O. Box 295, Rib Lake, 54470.* Tel: 715-427-5259.

Catholic Women, Council of—Rev. JAMES S. DABRUZZI, Chap., *206 Wisconsin St., N. #202, Hudson, 54016.* Tel: 715-381-2815. Mrs. HALCYON KASMAREK, Pres.,

9248 Cty. Hwy. J, Minocqua, 54548. Tel: 715-356-3994.

Censor Librorum—Appointed in each case by the Most Rev. Ordinary.

Charismatic Renewal Liaison—Vacant; Sr. CASIMIRA BENBENEK, O.S.M., Assoc. Liaison.

Christian Formation—Sr. GENEVIEVE SCHILLO, C.S.J., Ph.D., *1201 Hughitt Ave., P.O. Box 969, Superior, 54880.* Tel: 715-392-1042., *Res., 404 24th Ave., E., Superior.* Tel: 715-398-3002.

Cursillo Movement—Rev. BRENNAN SCHMIEG, O.F.M., Spiritual Dir. Secretaries: Mrs. MARY JIRELE; Mr. AL JIRELE, *27607 Thompson Bay Rd., Webster, 54893.* Tel: 715-866-8732.

Diocesan Coordinator of Health Affairs—Rev. KEVIN GORDON, *111 West Marshall St., Rice Lake, 54868.* Tel: 715-234-2032.

Ecumenical Commission—Very Rev. JAMES F. TOBOLSKI, *P.O. Box 969, Superior, 54880.* Tel: 715-392-2937.

Evangelization, Office of—Sr. EILEEN LANG, F.S.P.A., *P.O. Box 969, Superior, 54880.* Tel: 715-392-2937.

Family Life Apostolate—Rev. WILLIAM H. GREEN, Dir., *417 Dakota Ave., P.O. Box 32, Hayward, 54893.* Tel: 715-634-2867.

Holy Childhood Association—Rev. JOHN J. SPANJERS, Dir., *P.O. Box 118, Turtle Lake, 54889.* Tel: 715-986-4651.

Liturgical Commission—Mrs. GINNY HENNINGER; Deacon ARTHUR E. GILDE LAMADRID, Chm, *P.O. Box 969, Superior, 54880.* Tel: 715-392-2937.

Newman Apostolate—Superior: Newman Student Center, University of Wisconsin, Mr. MATTHEW CETNAR, *P.O. Box 969, Superior, 54880.* Tel: 715-394-7710. River Falls: Newman Center—WSU, *423 E. Cascade, River Falls, 54022.* Rev. NORMAN VOLK, O.M.I., Chap., *Res., 423 E. Cascade, River Falls, 54022.* Tel: 715-425-7600.

Newspaper—"Catholic Herald", Superior Edition; Mr. SAM LUCERO, Editor, *1512 N. 12th St., P.O. Box 969, Superior, 54880.* Tel: 715-392-8268., *Res., 1413 E. 3rd St., Superior, 54880.* Tel: 715-398-5027. Rev. ROBERT M. URBAN, Contributing Editor, *Res., R.R. 2, Box 62A, Glenwood City, 54013.* Tel: 715-265-7133.

Permanent Diaconate Program—Deacon TIMOTHY J. KUEHN, Dir., *P.O. Box 969, Superior, 54880.* Tel: 715-392-2937. Rev. DENNIS M. MULLEN, Consultant-Instructor. Tel: 715-822-2948.

Pro-Life Concerns—VINCENT ACKERET; KATHRYN ACKERET, *1068 W. Cedar St., Medford, 54451.* Tel: 715-748-4769.

Propagation of the Faith—Rev. JOHN J. SPANJERS, *St. Ann Church, P.O. Box 118, Turtle Lake, 54889.* Tel: 715-986-4651.

Radio and Television—Mr. SAM LUCERO, Dir., *1512 N. 12 St., Superior, 54880.* Tel: 715-392-8268., *Res.* Tel: 715-398-5027.

The Bishop George A. Hammes Center for Religious Education and Youth Ministry—Deacon ROGER CADOTTE, Dir., *315 W. Fifth St., P.O. Box 280, Haugen, 54841.* Tel: 715-234-5044; Fax: 715-234-5241.

Branch Office of Religious Education—1201 Hughitt Ave., P.O. Box 969, Superior, 54880. Tel: 715-392-1042.

Sisters Council—Sr. CASIMIRA BENBENEK, O.S.M., *715 S. Tomahawk Ave., Tomahawk, 54487.* Tel: 715-453-8090.

St. Pius Priest Fund—Bd. of Dirs.: Most Rev. RAPHAEL M. FLISS, Pres.; Very Revs. JAMES R. HORATH, Treas. PETER F. SZLESZINSKI; Revs. WILLIAM H. GREEN; WILLIAM G. HORATH; Very Rev. DENNIS MEULEMANS; Rev. DAVID P. OBERTS; Very Rev. JAMES F. TOBOLSKI, Sec.; Revs. DENNIS MULLEN, Vice Pres. JOHN J. SPANJERS; GEORGE L. VOTRUBA; JAMES P. POWERS.

St. Vincent De Paul Society—Very Rev. EDWARD G. MEULEMANS, Moderator, *1918 N. 21st St., Superior, 54880.* Tel: 715-394-6453. Mr. MATTHEW CETNAR, *1217 Ogden Ave., Superior, 54880.* Tel: 715-394-3538. Deacon STAN MERCIER, *38 S. Main St., Rice Lake, 54868.* Tel: 715-234-7003.

Superintendent of Schools—Mrs. PHYLLIS SCHLAGEL, Office: *1201 Hughitt Ave., Box 969, Superior, 54880.* Tel: 715-392-1042.

Vocation—Rev. KEVIN M. GORDON, Dir., *111 W. Marshall St., Rice Lake, 54868.* Tel: 715-234-2032. Asst. Dirs.: Sr. BONNIE ALHO, O.S.M.; Rev. JOHN R. GERRITTS.

Office of Worship—Mrs. GINNY HENNINGER, Dir., *1201 Hughitt Ave., P.O. Box 969, Superior, 54880.* Tel: 715-392-2937.

CLERGY, PARISHES, MISSIONS AND PAROCHIAL SCHOOLS

CITY OF SUPERIOR
(Douglas County)

1—CATHEDRAL OF CHRIST THE KING (1886), Very Rev. Edward G. Meulemans, V.G., Rector; Revs. John C. Anderson; Arthur Gilde Lamadrid.
Res., 1410 Baxter Ave., 54880. Tel: 715-392-8511. [CEM]
School—Cathedral School, 1419 Baxter Ave., 54880. Tel: 715-392-2976. Roy Hamlin, Prin.
Lay Teachers 28; Students 447.

2—ASSUMPTION OF THE B.V.M. (1891), Rev. George L. Votruba, Also serves at St. William, Pattison Park.
Res., 5617 Tower Ave., 54880. Tel: 715-394-4883.

3—ST. ANTHONY (1870), Rev. Dean T. Buttrick; Deacon Timothy J. Kuehn.
Res., 4315 E. 3rd St., 54880. Tel: 715-398-7774.

4—SS. CYRIL AND METHODIUS (Slovak). Closed. For sacramental records contact Cathedral of Christ the King.

5—ST. FRANCIS XAVIER (1853), Very Rev. James F. Tobolski; Deacon Philip Martineau.
Res., 710 16th Ave., E., 54880. Tel: 715-398-3033. [CEM]
Church—2316 E. 4th St., 54880. Tel: 715-398-7174.

6—ST. LOUIS. Closed. For sacramental records contact Cathedral of Christ the King.

7—ST. PATRICK. Closed. For sacramental records contact Cathedral of Christ the King.

8—ST. STANISLAUS (Polish). Closed. For sacramental records contact Cathedral of Christ the King.

OUTSIDE THE CITY OF SUPERIOR

Almena, Barron Co., Sacred Heart of Jesus Church of Almena (1890), Rev. John J. Spanjers; Deacon Timothy J. Byrnes.
Res., Box 118, Turtle Lake, 54889. Tel: 715-986-4651. [CEM]

Amery, Polk Co., St. Joseph (1890). Also serves Our Lady of the Holy Rosary, Georgetown. Rev. John A. Drummy; Deacon Florian Heiser.
Res., 404 Wisconsin Ave., 54001. Tel: 715-268-7717.

Ashland, Ashland Co., Our Lady of the Lake Catholic Community (1872), Revs. Vernon J. Olmer, O.F.M.; Conan Mitchell, O.F.M.
Res., 106 2nd Ave. E., 54880. Tel: 715-682-7620. [CEM]
School—215 E. Lake Shore Dr., 54806. Tel: 715-682-7622. Bro. Joseph Rogenski, Prin.
Sisters 1; Lay Teachers 14; Students 170.
Holy Family (Polish). Closed. Inquiries should be directed to Our Lady of the Lake Parish.

Balsam Lake, Polk Co., Our Lady of the Pines (1875), Rev. Daniel J. Dahlberg; Deacon Fred E. Johnson.
Res., P.O. Box 220, Centuria, 54824-0220. Tel: 715-646-2253.

Barron, Barron Co., St. Joseph (1907). Also serves St. Peter, Cameron and St. Boniface, Chetek. Rev. Girard I. Willger, Pastoral Supr.
Res., 827 E. LaSalle Ave., 54812. Tel: 715-537-3255.

Bayfield, Bayfield Co., Holy Family (1878). Also serves St. Joseph, LaPointe, St. Ann, Cornucopia and St. Francis, Red Cliff. Rev. Glenn Phillips, O.F.M.
Res., P.O. Box 1290, 54814. Tel: 715-779-3316.
Church—P.O. Box 1290, 54814. Tel: 715-779-3316. [CEM 2]
School—Holy Family/St. Francis School, 232 N. 1st St., P.O. Box 1290, 54814. Tel: 715-779-3342. Sr. Phyllis Wilhelm, O.S.F., Prin.
Lay Teachers 4; Students 41.

Birchwood, Washburn Co., St. John Evangelist (1908), Rev. James L. Imse, Admin.; Deacons Stanley J. Mercier; Harvey G. Drost.
Res., 2411 23rd St., Rice Lake, 54868. Tel: 715-234-2917.

Bloomville, Lincoln Co., St. John the Baptist (1908), Rev. Michael J. Tupa, Pastoral Supr.; Michele Rein, Parish Dir.; Deacons Bernard J. Lyngdal; Darrell P. Smerz; C. Dan Towle.
Res., N10090 County B., Tomahawk, 54487. Tel: 715-453-2561. [CEM]

Boulder Junction, Vilas Co., St. Anne (1938). Also serves St. Mary, Sayner, and St. Rita, Presque Isle. Rev. Brendan J. Kunda.
Res., P.O. Box 110, 54512. Tel: 715-385-2390. [CEM]

Bruce, Rusk Co., St. Mary (1893), Rev. John R. Long; Deacon James E. Roberge.
Res., P.O. Box 207, Weyerhaeuser, 54895. Tel: 715-353-2400. [CEM]

Butternut, Ashland Co., Immaculate Conception (1880), Rev. Linus Evers, C.PP.S.
113 N. 4th St., P.O. Box 6, 54514-0006.
Res., 255 E. 2nd St., P.O. Box 182, Glidden, 54537-0182. Tel: 715-264-3471. [CEM]

Cable, Bayfield Co., St. Ann (1902), Rev. William H. Green, Pastoral Supr.; Sr. Virginia Schwartz, O.S.M., Parish Dir.; Deacon Joseph E. Reuter.
P.O. Box 37, 54821-0037. Tel: 715-798-3855.
Res., 417 Dakota Ave., P.O. Box 32, Hayward, 54843. Tel: 715-634-2867.

Cameron, Barron Co., St. Peter (1908), Rev. Gerard I. Willger.
Res., 827 E. LaSalle Ave., Barron, 54812. Tel: 715-537-3255.
Church—9th & Arlington, 54822.

Catawba, Price Co., St. Paul the Apostle (1907). Also serves St. John the Baptist, Prentice. Rev. Dismas Kalcic, O.S.B.
Res., W9485 Hwy. 8, 54515-0137. Tel: 715-474-2223. [CEM]

Centuria, Polk Co., St. Patrick (1856), Rev. Daniel J. Dahlberg; Deacon Fred E. Johnson.
Res., Hwy. 35 & Tenth Ave., Box 39, Osceola, 54020. Tel: 715-755-2300. [CEM]

Chelsea, Taylor Co., Assumption of the Blessed Virgin Mary (1887), Revs. Thomas E. Thompson, Pastoral Supr.; Michael D. Cullen, Parish Dir.; Deacon Paul M. Ochodnicky.
Mailing Address: P.O. Box 186, Westboro, 54490. Tel: 715-427-5266.

Chetek, Barron Co., St. Boniface (1880), Rev. Gerard I. Willger, Pastoral Supr.; Sr. Rosine Kaminski, O.S.F., Parish Dir.
Res., 419 S. Third St., 54728. Tel: 715-924-3514. [CEM]

Clam Lake, Ashland Co., St. George (1890), Rev. Linus Evers, C.PP.S.
Res., St. George, P.O. Box 182, Glidden, 54527. Tel: 715-264-3471.

Clear Lake, Polk Co., St. John (1890). Also serves St. Bridget, Stanton. Rev. Joseph C. Trinka.
Res., Box 337, 54005. Tel: 715-263-2032.

Cornucopia, Bayfield Co., St. Ann (1914), Rev. Glenn Phillips, O.F.M.
Res., P.O. Box 1290, Bayfield, 54814. Tel: 715-779-3316.

Crescent Lake, Burnett Co., Sacred Hearts of Jesus and Mary (1857), Rev. Ronald Olson, O.F.M.Conv.
Res., P.O. Box 7, Webster, 54893. Tel: 715-866-7321. [CEM]

Cumberland, Barron Co., St. Anthony The Abbot (1893), Rev. Dennis M. Mullen.
Res., 900 Anthony St., 54829. Tel: 715-822-2984. [CEM 2]

Danbury, Burnett Co., Our Lady of Perpetual Help (1920), Rev. Ronald Olson, O.F.M.Conv.
Res., P.O. Box 7, Webster, 54893. Tel: 715-866-7321. [CEM]

Dauby, Bayfield Co., St. Peter (1918), Rev. Barry Schneider, O.F.M.
Res., P.O. Box 97, Iron River, 54847. Tel: 715-372-4756.

Dobie, Barron Co., Our Lady of Lourdes (1875). Also serves Holy Trinity, Haugen, and St. John the Evangelist, Birchwood. Rev. James L. Imse, Admin.; Deacons Stanley J. Mercier; Harvey Drost.
Res., 2411 W. 23rd St., Rice Lake, 54868. Tel: 715-234-2917. [CEM]

Eagle River, Vilas Co., St. Peter the Fisherman (1894), Rev. Robert J. Koszarek; Deacons Albert A. Goodrich; John "Skip" McCaughn; Sr. Marla Clercx, O.S.M., Pastoral Assoc.
Res., 509 Wall St., Box 728, 54521. Tel: 715-479-8704. [CEM]
School—115 S. 3rd St., P.O. Box 729, 54521. Tel: 715-479-4332. Dr. Helene Machac, Prin.
Lay Teachers 6; Students 92.

Erin, St. Croix Co., St. Patrick (1857), Rev. James J. Kraker; Deacon Joseph F. Paron.
Res., P.O. Box 18, Hammond, 54015. Tel: 715-796-2244. [CEM]

Farmington, St. Croix Co., Assumption of the Blessed Virgin Mary (1869), Rev. James J. Brinkman; Deacon A. Maurice Baillargeon.
Res., 140 Church Hill, P.O. Box 9, Somerset, 54025. Tel: 715-247-3310. [CEM]

Fifield, Price Co., St. Francis of Assisi (1888), Rev. Aloys Ebach, C.PP.S.; Deacon Chester E. Ball, Jr.
Res., 142 5th Ave. S., Park Falls, 54552. Tel: 715-762-4494.

Flambeau, Rusk Co., St. Francis of Assisi (1866), Rev. Philip J. Juza, Admin.
Res., Rte. 1, Box 7B, Sheldon, 54766. Tel: 715-868-3475. [CEM]

Frederic, Polk Co., St. Dominic (1904). Also serves Immaculate Conception, Grantsburg. Rev. James A. Dluge; Deacon Stanley Marczak.
Res., 107 W. Birch St., Box 606, 54837. Tel: 715-327-8119. [CEM]

Georgetown, Polk Co., Our Lady of the Holy Rosary

(1906), Rev. John A. Drummy; Deacon Florian H. Heiser.
Res., 404 Wisconsin Ave., Amery, 54001. Tel: 715-268-7717. [CEM]

Gilman, Taylor Co., SS. Peter and Paul (1910). Also serves St. Stanislaus, Lublin. Rev. James P. Bartelme.
Res., Box 100, 54433. Tel: 715-447-8510. [CEM]

Glenwood City, St. Croix Co., St. John the Baptist (1886). Also serves St. Bridget, Wilson. Rev. Robert M. Urban; Deacon Wesley G. Tuttle.
Res., 753 First St., 54013. Tel: 715-265-7133. [CEM]

Glidden, Ashland Co., Most Precious Blood (1884). Also serves Immaculate Conception, Butternut and St. George, Clam Lake. Rev. Linus Evers, C.PP.S.
Res., Box 182, 54527. Tel: 715-264-3471. [CEM]

Gordon, Douglas Co., St. Anthony of Padua (1878), Rev. Vincent M. Bromley; Deacons Stanley J. Marczak; Peter R. Huntowski.
Res., P.O. Box 303, Solon Springs, 54873. Tel: 715-378-4431.

Grantsburg, Burnett Co., Immaculate Conception (1909), Rev. James A. Dluge.
Res., 107 W. Birch St., P.O. Box 606, Frederic, 54837. Tel: 715-327-8119.

Hammond, St. Croix Co., Immaculate Conception (1877). Also serves St. Patrick, Erin. Rev. James J. Kraker; Deacon Joseph F. Paron.
Res., P.O. Box 18, 54015. Tel: 715-796-2244. [CEM]

Harrison, Lincoln Co., St. Augustine (1905), Rev. Michael J. Tupa, Pastoral Supr.; Deacons Clarence D. Towle; Bernard J. Lyngdal; Darrell P. Smerz; Michele Rein, Dir.
Res., Tomahawk N10090 Hwy. B, Tomahawk, 54487. Tel: 715-453-2561. [CEM]

Haugen, Barron Co., Holy Trinity (1896), Rev. James L. Imse, Admin.; Deacons Harvey G. Drost; Stanley J. Mercier.
Res., 2411 W. 23rd St., Rice Lake, 54868. Tel: 715-234-2917. [CEM]

Hawkins, Rusk Co., St. Mary Czestowchowa (1913), Rev. David Oberts; Deacons Richard J. Brockbank; Jerome J. Drahos; Richard D. Leonhard.
Res., 611 S. 1st St., Ladysmith, 54848. Tel: 715-532-3051.

Hayward, Sawyer Co., St. Joseph's (1882). Also serves St. Ann, Cable. Rev. William H. Green, Pastoral Supr.
Res., P.O. Box 32, 54843. Tel: 715-634-2867.

Highbridge, Ashland Co., St. Anthony (1880), Rev. Gerald Hagen.
Res., P.O. Box 17, Mellen, 54546. Tel: 715-274-3701.

Hudson, St. Croix Co., St. Patrick (1840), Very Rev. Peter F. Szleszinski; Rev. William J. Murphy; Deacons Peter Braum; Bernard Drevnick.
Res., 1500 Vine St., 54016. Tel: 715-381-5120.
School—403 St. Croix St., 54016. Tel: 715-386-3941. Rita Bibeau, Prin.
Lay Teachers 20; Students 344.

Hurley, Iron Co., St. Mary of the Seven Dolors (1885). Also serves Sacred Heart, Montreal; Holy Redeemer, Pence; and St. Ann, Saxon. Rev. Robert E. O'Connell; Deacon Russell J. Lundgren.
Res., 404 Iron St., 54534. Tel: 715-561-2606. [CEM]

Ino, Bayfield Co., St. Florian (1913), Rev. Gabriel C. Zepczyk, Admin.
Res., P.O. Box 97, Iron River, 54847. Tel: 715-372-4756. [CEM]

Iron River, Bayfield Co., St. Michael (1892). Also serves St. Peter, Dauby. Rev. Barry Schneider, O.F.M.
Res., P.O. Box 97, 54847. Tel: 715-372-4756. [CEM]

Jump River, Taylor Co., St. Michael (1915), Rev. Philip J. Juza, Admin.
Res., Rte. 1, Box 7B, Sheldon, 54766. Tel: 715-452-5374.

Lac du Flambeau, Vilas Co., St. Anthony Catholic Church (1862), Rev. John P. Stremski; Sr. Corinne Kabara, R.S.M., Pastoral Assoc.
Mailing Address: Box 38, 54538. Tel: 715-588-3148.
Res., 650 Old Abe Rd., 54538. [CEM]

Ladysmith, Rusk Co., Our Lady of Sorrows (1906). Also serves St. Mary, Hawkins, and St. Anthony, Tony. Rev. David P. Oberts; Deacons Richard J. Brockbank; Jerome J. Drahos.
Res., 611 S. 1st St., 54848. Tel: 715-532-3051.
School—105 E. Washington Ave., 54848. Tel: 715-532-3232.
Lay Teachers 11; Students 140.

Lake Nebagamon, Douglas Co., St. Anthony (1899), Rev. Dean T. Buttrick; Deacon Timothy J. Kuehn.
Res., 4315 E. 3rd St., Superior, 54880. Tel: 715-398-3261.

Lake Tomahawk, Oneida Co., St. John Vianney (1859), Rev. Virgil O. Heinen, Admin.
Res., P.O. Box 237, 54539. Tel: 715-277-2461.

Land-O'-Lakes, Vilas Co., St. Albert (1894). Also serves St. Mary, Phelps. Rev. William F. Speerstra.
Res., Box 237, 54540. Tel: 715-547-3558.

LaPointe, Bayfield Co., St. Joseph (1669), Rev. Glenn Phillips, O.F.M.
Res., Box 1290, Bayfield, 54814. Tel: 715-779-5467. [CEM]

Lublin, Taylor Co., St. Stanislaus (1907) (Polish), Rev. James P. Bartelme.
Res., P.O. Box 100, Gilman, 54433. Tel: 715-447-8510. [CEM]

Manitowish Waters, Vilas Co., Our Lady Queen of Peace (1858), Rev. Joseph L. Kleinheinz.
Res., 3136 Lakeview Ave., P.O. Box 575, Mercer, 54547. Tel: 715-476-2697.

Medford, Taylor Co., Our Lady of the Holy Rosary (1870), Very Rev. Dennis T. Meulemans; Sr. Shirley Wagner, F.S.P.A., Pastoral Assoc.
Res., 424 W. Cedar St., 54451. Tel: 715-748-3288. [CEM]
School—215 S. Washington Ave., 54451. Tel: 715-748-3336. Patricia Dougherty, Prin.
Sisters of Mary 1; Lay Teachers 10; Students 125.

Mellen, Ashland Co., Holy Rosary (1886). Also serves St. Anthony, Highbridge. Rev. Gerald Hagen, Admin.
Res., P.O. Box 17, 54546. Tel: 715-274-3701.

Mercer, Iron Co., St. Isaac Jogues and Companions (1912). Also serves Our Lady, Queen of Peace, Manitowish Waters. Rev. Joseph Kleinheinz.
Res., P.O. Box 575, 54547. Tel: 715-476-2697.

Merrill, Lincoln Co., St. Francis Xavier (1875), Very Rev. James R. Horath; Deacons Howard Zuch; Richard G. Heckman.
Res., 500 W. 8th St., 54452. Tel: 715-536-4645. [CEM]
Schools—St. Francis Elementary, 1708 E. 10th St, 54452. Tel: 715-536-2803; St. Francis Middle School, 500 W. 8th St., 54452. Tel: 715-536-4954. Karen Barrett-Evjue, Prin.
Lay Teachers 6; Students 169.

St. Robert Bellarmine (1886). Closed. For inquiries for parish records contact the Chancery.

Minocqua, Oneida Co., St. Patrick (1893), Rev. Joseph N. Miller.
Res., P.O. Box 107, 54548. Tel: 715-356-3440. [CEM]

Minong, Washburn Co., St. Mary (1904), Rev. Vincent M. Bromley; Deacon Peter R. Huntowski.
Res., P.O. Box 303, Solon Springs, 54873. Tel: 715-378-4431.

Montreal, Iron Co., Sacred Heart of Jesus (1904), Revs. Robert E. O'Connell; Russell J. Lundgren.
Res., 404 Iron St., Hurley, 54534. Tel: 715-561-2606.

Moquah, Bayfield Co., Ss. Peter and Paul (1912), Rev. Gabriel C. Zepczyk, Admin.
Res., P.O. Box 97, Iron Horse, 54847. Tel: 715-746-2549. [CEM 2]

New Post, Sawyer Co., St. Ignatius (1884), Rev. Gregory J. Hopefl.
Res., Rte. 2, Box 340, Stone Lake, 54876-9545. Tel: 715-865-3669.

New Richmond, St. Croix Co., Immaculate Conception (1884), Rev. Allan P. Bradley; Deacon Hugh C. Mayer.
Office: 151 S. Washington Ave., 54017. Tel: 715-246-4652.
Res., 140 Pershing Ave., 54017. Tel: 715-246-2294. [CEM]
School—257 S. Washington Ave., 54017. Tel: 715-246-2469.
Lay Teachers 10; Students 135.

Odanah, Ashland Co., St. Mary (1855), Rev. Michael Lange, O.F.M.
Res., Box 182, 54861. Tel: 715-682-8350.

Osceola, Polk Co., St. Joseph (1915). Also serves Our Lady of the Pines, Balsam Lake, and St. Patrick, Centuria. Rev. Daniel J. Dahlberg; Deacon Fred E. Johnson.
Res., Hwy. 35 & 10th Ave., Box 399, 54020. Tel: 715-755-2300.

Park Falls, Price Co., St. Anthony (1881). Also serves St. Francis of Assisi, Fifield. Rev. Aloys Ebach, C.PP.S.; Deacon Chester Ball.
Res., 276 S. 5th St., 54552. Tel: 715-762-4494.
School—200 S. 5th Ave., 54552. Tel: 715-762-4494. Beatrice Weiland, Prin.
Priests 1; Lay Teachers 12; Students 165.

Pattison Park, Douglas Co., St. William (1908), Rev. George L. Votruba; Deacon Jack McKenna.
Res., 3095 E. County Rd. B, Foxboro, 54836. Tel: 715-399-2450. [CEM]

Pelican Lake, Oneida Co., St. John (1905), Rev. Michael T. Hayden; Deacons Matthew C. Porten; Michael O. Harvey.
Res., 110 S. Conro St., Rhinelander, 54501. Tel: 715-362-4012. [CEM]

Pence, Iron Co., Holy Redeemer (1908), Rev. Robert E. O'Connell; Deacon Russell J. Lundgren.
Res., 404 Iron St., Hurley, 54534. Tel: 715-561-2606.

Phelps, Vilas Co., Holy Redeemer (1908), Rev. William F. Speerstra.
Res., P.O. Box 237, Land O'Lakes, 54540. Tel: 715-547-3558.

Phillips, Price Co., Our Lady of the North (1876), Rev. Terence Fitzmaurice, O.S.B.
Res., 125 N. Argyle Ave., 54555. Tel: 715-339-2222. [CEM]

Pier-Willow, Oneida Co., St. Francis of Assisi (1887), Rev. Michael J. Tupa; Deacons Bernard J. Lyngdal; Darrell P. Smerz; C. Dan Towle.
Res., 320 E. Washington Ave., Tomahawk, 54487. Tel: 715-453-2878. [CEM]

Prentice, Price Co., St. John (1886), Rev. Dismas B. Kalcic, O.S.B.
Res., W9485 Hwy. 8, Catawba, 54515-0137. Tel: 715-474-2223.

Presque Isle, Vilas Co., St. Rita (1950), Rev. Brendan J. Kunda.
Res., P.O. Box 110, Boulder Junction, 54512. Tel: 715-385-2390.

Radisson, Sawyer Co., Sacred Heart (1919), Rev. Albert L. Verdegan.
Res., P.O. Box 216, Winter, 54896. Tel: 715-266-3441.

Red Cliff, Bayfield Co., St. Francis (1861), Rev. Glenn Phillips, O.F.M.
Res., P.O. Box 1290, Bayfield, 54814. Tel: 715-779-3316.

Reserve, Sawyer Co., St. Francis of Solanus (1889) (Indian). Also serves St. Ignatius, New Post, and St. Philip, Stone Lake. Rev. Gregory Hopefl.
Rte. 2, Box 340, 54876-9545. Tel: 715-865-3669. [CEM]
School—St. Francis Solanus, P.O. Box 341, Reserve Stone Lake, 54876. Tel: 715-865-3662. Sr. M. Felissa Zander, O.S.F., Prin.
Sisters of St. Francis 2; Lay Teachers 3; Students 108.

Rhinelander, Oneida Co., Immaculate Conception (1883). Also serves St. John, Pelican Lake. Rev. Michael T. Hayden; Deacons Michael O. Harvey; Mathew C. Porten.
Res., 110 S. Conro St., 54501. Tel: 715-362-4012. [CEM]

St. Joseph's (1909), Rev. John R. Gerritts; Deacon Ronald J. Bosi.
Res., 1350 N. Stevens St., 54501. Tel: 715-362-3169. [CEM]
Schools—St. Joseph's, 1340 N. Stevens St., 54501. Tel: 715-362-5588. Yvonne VandenBerg, Prin.; St. Mary's, 103 E. King, 54501. Tel: 715-362-5588.; Rhinelander Catholic Central.
Franciscan Sisters of Christian Charity 2; Lay Teachers 17; Students 286.

Rib Lake, Taylor Co., St. John the Baptist (1896), Rev. Thomas E. Thompson, Pastoral Supr.; Deacon Paul M. Ochodnicky.
Res., P.O. Box 295, 54470. Tel: 715-427-5259. [CEM]

Rice Lake, Barron Co., St. Joseph (1878), Rev. Kevin M. Gordon; Sr. Bonnie Alho, O.S.M., Pastoral Assoc.
Res., 111 W. Marshall St., 54868. Tel: 715-234-2032. [CEM]
School—St. Joseph School, 128 Humbird St., 54868. Tel: 715-234-7721. Tamara Sharp, Prin.
Sisters of St. Joseph of the Third Order of St. Francis 1; Lay Teachers 12; Students 232.

River Falls, St. Croix Co., St. Bridget (1854), Rev. Gerald P. Harris; Deacon Lawrence P. Hennemann.
Res., 547 N. Dallas St., P.O. Box 86, 54022. Tel: 715-425-1876. [CEM]
School—135 E. Division St., 54022. Tel: 715-425-1872; Fax: 715-425-1873. Catherine Burke, Prin.
Lay Teachers 13; Students 174.

Sanborn, Ashland Co., St. Anne (1895), Rev. Brennan Schmieg, O.F.M.
Res., St. Louis Church, P.O. Box 070, Washburn, 54891. Tel: 715-373-2132.

Sarona, Washburn Co., St. Catherine (1917), Rev. Edward R. Senn.
Res., P.O. Box 490, Shell Lake, 54871. Tel: 715-468-7850.

Saxon, Iron Co., St. Ann's (1886), Rev. Robert O'Connell; Deacon Russell J. Lundgren; Sr. Caroline Pfeiffer, C.S.J., Pastoral Assoc.
Res., 404 Iron St., Hurley, 54534. Tel: 715-561-2606. [CEM]

Sayner, Vilas Co., St. Mary (1912), Rev. Brendan J. Kunda.
Res., P.O. Box 110, Boulder Junction, 54512. Tel:

715-542-3480.

Sheldon, Rusk Co., St. John the Apostle (1955). Also serves St. Michael, Jump River, and St. Francis of Assisi, Flambeau. Rev. Philip J. Juza, Admin.
Res., Rte. 1, P.O. Box 7B, 54766. Tel: 715-452-5374.

Shell Lake, Washburn Co., St. Joseph (1880). Also serves St. Catherine, Sarona. Rev. Edward R. Senn.
Res., P.O. Box 490, 54871. Tel: 715-468-7850. [CEM]

Solon Springs, Douglas Co., St. Pius X (1878). Also serves St. Anthony of Padua, Gordon; St. Mary, Minong. Rev. Vincent Bromley.
Res., Box 303, 54873. Tel: 715-378-4431. [CEM]

Somerset, St. Croix Co., St. Anne (1851). Also serves Assumption of the Blessed Virgin Mary, East Farmington. Rev. James J. Brinkman; Deacon A. Maurice Baillargeon.
Res., P.O. Box 9, 54025. Tel: 715-247-3310.
School—140 Church Hill Rd., 54025. Tel: 715-247-3762.
Sisters of St. Joseph of Medaille, Crookston 1; Lay Teachers 6; Students 129.

Spooner, Washburn Co., St. Francis De Sales (1886), Rev. James J. Jackson.
Res., 409 Summit St., 54801. Tel: 715-635-3105. [CEM 2]
School—300 Oak St., 54801. Tel: 715-635-2774.
Servants of Mary 1; Lay Teachers 10; Students 105.

Stanton, St. Croix Co., St. Bridget (1875), Rev. Joseph C. Trinka.
Res., P.O. Box 337, Clear Lake, 54005. Tel: 715-263-2032. [CEM]

Stetsonville, Taylor Co., Sacred Heart of Jesus (1884), Rev. Frederick Brost.
Res., 322 W. CTH A, 54480. Tel: 715-678-2395. [CEM]

Stone Lake, Sawyer Co., St. Philip (1905), Rev. Gregory Hopefl.
Res., Rte. 2, Box 340, 54876. Tel: 715-865-3669.

Strickland, Rusk Co., Assumption of the Blessed Virgin Mary (1897), Rev. John R. Long.
Res., 251 1st St., P.O. Box 207, Weyerhauser, 54895. Tel: 715-353-2400. [CEM]

Sugar Camp, Oneida Co., St. Kunegunda (1892), Rev. Philip Dan Stack; Deacon Albert A. Goodrich.
Res., 6895 Hwy. 17 N., Rhinelander, 54501. Tel: 715-272-1191. [CEM]

Three Lakes, Oneida Co., St. Theresa (1892), Rev. William G. Horath.
Res., 1701 Superior St., P.O. Box 8, 54562. Tel: 715-546-2159.

Tomahawk, Lincoln Co., St. Mary (1887). Also serving: St. Francis of Assisi, Pier-Willow; St. Augustine, Harris; St. John the Baptist, Bloomville. Rev. Michael J. Tupa; Deacons Bernard J. Lyngdal; Darryl P. Smerz; C. Dan Towle.
Res., 320 E. Washington St., 54487. Tel: 715-453-2878. [CEM]
School—110 N. 7th St., 54487. Tel: 715-453-3542. Mary A. Cherf, Prin.
Lay Teachers 6; Students 112.

Tony, Rusk Co., St. Anthony de Padua (1901), Rev. David P. Oberts; Deacons Jerome J. Drahos; Richard J. Brockbank; Richard D. Leonhard.
Res., 611 S. 1st St., Ladysmith, 54848. Tel: 715-532-3051. [CEM]

Turtle Lake, Barron Co., St. Ann (1882). Also serves Sacred Heart of Jesus, Almena. Rev. John J. Spanjers; Deacon Timothy Byrnes.
Res., P.O. Box 118, 54889. Tel: 715-986-4651. [CEM]

Washburn, Bayfield Co., St. Louis (1882). Also serves St. Anne, Sanborn. Rev. Brennan Schmieg, O.F.M. In res., Rev. Humbert Korgie, O.F.M.; Bro. Crispin Koeppl, O.F.M.
Res., 217 W. 7th St., Box 070, 54891. Tel: 715-373-2132.
School—713 Washington Ave., P.O. Box 70, 54891. Tel: 715-373-5322. Loretta Bagby, Prin.
Lay Teachers 8; Students 95.

Webster, Burnett Co., St. John the Baptist (1880). Also serves Sacred Hearts of Jesus and Mary, Crescent Lake, and Our Lady of Perpetual Heart, Danbury. Rev. Ronald Olson, O.F.M.Conv.; Deacon Ralph Heffner.
Res., 26455 S. Muskey Ave., Box 7, 54893. Tel: 715-866-7321. [CEM]

Westboro, Taylor Co., St. Theresa (1904). Also serves Our Lady of Perpetual Help, Whittlesey, and Assumption of B.V.M., Chelsea. Rev. Thomas E. Thompson; Deacon Paul Ochodnicky; Michael D. Cullen, Dir.
Res., P.O. Box 186, 54490. Tel: 715-427-5266.

Weyerhauser, Rusk Co., SS. Peter and Paul (1891). Also serves Assumption B.V.M., Strickland, and St. Mary, Bruce. Rev. John R. Long.
Res., Box 207, Weyerhaueser, 54895. Tel: 715-353-2400. [CEM 2]

Wilson, St. Croix Co., St. Bridget (1886), Rev. Robert M. Urban; Deacon Wesley G. Tuttle.
Res., 753 1st St., Glenwood City, 54013. Tel: 715-265-7133. [CEM]

Whittlesey, Our Lady of Perpetual Help (1891), Rev. Thomas E. Thompson, Pastoral Supr.; Deacons Paul M. Ochodnicky; Michael D. Cullen, Dir.
Res., P.O. Box 186, Westboro, 54490. Tel: 715-427-5266. [CEM]

Winter, Sawyer Co., St. Peter (1908), Very Rev. Albert L. Verdegan.
Res., P.O. Box 216, 54896. Tel: 715-266-3441. [JC]

Woodruff, Oneida Co., Our Lady Queen of the Universe (1955), Rev. James A. Hoffman; Sr. Jolynn Brehm, F.S.P.A., Pastoral Assoc.
Res., Box 30, 54568. Tel: 715-356-6284.

Chaplains of Public Institutions

SUPERIOR. *Middle River Center,* 54880. Rev. Vincent Bromley.

On Special or Other (Arch)Diocesan Assignment:
Reverend Fathers—
Heslin, Philip J., Moderator of the Curia, Chancery, Box 969, Superior, WI 54880

On Duty Outside the Diocese:
Reverend Monsignors—
Durst, Gerald F., Pontificial College Josephinum, Worthington, OH
Reverend Fathers—
Briody, Hugh J., Emmanual House of Providence, Clonfert, Ballinasole, Co. Galway, Ireland

Military Chaplains:
Reverend Fathers—
Gonia, Raymond L.

Graduate Studies:
Reverend Fathers—
Powers, James P., Edifice Deschatets, 175 Main St., Canada, K1S IC3

On Leave:
Reverend Fathers—
Beutner, Edward F.
Lusson, David R.
Murphy, Charles J.

Retired:
Reverend Fathers—
Anctil, Leo, 645 Knotty Oak Rd., Coventry, RI 02816
Canfield, Joseph, 163 Schoolcraft St., Lake Linden, MI 49943. Tel: 906-296-1068
Cary, William J., 113 Tilltag Dr., #64, Balsam Lake, WI 54810. Tel: 715-485-3305
Corrigan, Austin B., 1900 New York Ave., Room 208 S, Superior, WI 54550
Dabruzzi, James S., Lake Mallalieu Apartments, 206 Wisconsin St., N. #202, Hudson, WI 54016. Tel: 715-381-2815
Fraher, Leonard W., 804 Woodland Ln., New Richmond, WI 54017. Tel: 715-246-7855
Haefner, Charles, 2525 E. First St., Apt. 408, Fort Meyers, FL 33901
Kelchak, Joseph M., 4165 Oakmont Ct., Crown Point, IN 46307
Kowalski, Wladyslaw J., St. John the Baptist Parish (Peplin), 3308 Hwy. 153, Mosinee, WI 54455
Krynski, Leo, 1240 Easthill Dr., Wausau, WI 54401
Meyett, Irving C., 2528 E. 3rd St., Superior, WI 54880. Tel: 715-398-7196
Nesbitt, James B., 3157 South 66th St., Milwaukee, WI 53219. Tel: 414-545-1651
Niggemann, Bernard, 991 Meadow Ln., Chetek, WI 54728. Tel: 715-859-2867
Pakosta, Francis, 13207 Hwy. G, Caledonia, WI 53108. Tel: 414-835-9020
Powell, Edward F., W6771 Branch Rd., Tomahawk, MI 54487-9230. Tel: 715-453-1357
Regh, John, N4102 Noll Rd., Keenan, WI 54537. Tel: 715-474-3461
Slowey, John P., 184 N. Eyder Ave., Phillips, WI 54555. Tel: 715-339-4068
Wenninger, William, 1918 N. 21st St., Apt. 7, Superior, WI 54880. Tel: 715-394-6453
West, Norbert, House of Loreto, 2812 Harvard Ave., N.W., Canton, OH 44709. Tel: 216-492-1240
Very Rev.—
Schoone, Raymond L., 1900 New York Ave., Apt. E410, Superior, WI 54880. Tel: 715-395-0178

Permanent Deacons:
Baillargeon, Maurice, St. Anne, Somerset
Ball, Chester, St. Anthony, Park Falls
Bosi, Ronald, St. Joseph, Rhinelander
Braum, Peter, St. Patrick, Hudson
Brockbank, Richard J., Our Lady of Sorrows, Ladysmith
Byrnes, Timothy J., St. Ann, Turtle Lake
Cadotte, Roger, Bishop Hammes Center, Haugen
Drahos, Jerome J., St. Anthony, Tony
Drevnick, Bernard, St. Patrick, Hudson
Drost, Harvey, Holy Trinity, Haugen
Gil de Lamadrid, Arthur, Cathedral of Christ the King, Superior
Goodrich, Albert A., St. Peter, Eagle River
Harvey, Michael O., Immaculate Conception, Rhinelander
Heckman, Richard G., St. Robert Bellarmine, Merrill
Heffner, Ralph W., St. Dominic, Frederic
Heiser, Florian H., St. Joseph, Amery
Hennemann, Lawrence P., St. Bridget, River Falls
Hinks, Gerald J.
Huntowski, Peter R., St. Mary, Minong
Johnson, Fred, St. Joseph, Osceola
Koach, Allen
Kuehn, Timothy J., St. Anthony, Superior
Leonhard, Richard D., St. Anthony, Tony
Lundgren, Russell J., St. Mary, Hurley
Lyngdal, Bernard J., St. Mary, Tomahawk
Maier, Louis A., St. Theresa, Three Lakes
Marczak, Stanley, Immaculate Conception, Grantsburg
Martineau, Philip, St. Francis Xavier, Superior
Mayer, Hugh C., Immaculate Conception, New Richmond
McCaughn, John "Skip", St. Peter the Fisherman, Eagle River
McKenna, Jack, St. William, Pattison Park
Mercier, Stanley J., Our Lady of Lourdes, Dobie
Ochodnicky, Paul, St. Theresa, Westboro
Paron, Joseph F., Immaculate Conception, Hammond
Porten, Matthew C., Immaculate Conception, Rhinelander
Reuter, Joseph, St. Joseph, Hayward
Roberge, James, Ss. Peter & Paul, Weyerhaueser
Smerz, Darrell, St. Mary, Tomahawk
Stefancin, Joseph
Towle, C. Dan, St. Augustine, Harrison
Tuttle, Wesley G., St. John the Baptist, Glenwood City
Zuch, Howard, St. Francis Xavier, Merrill

INSTITUTIONS LOCATED IN THE DIOCESE

[A] GENERAL HOSPITALS

SUPERIOR. *St. Mary's Hospital of Superior,* 3500 Tower Ave., 54880. Tel: 715-392-8281.
For a complete listing, refer to the Hospitals section.

MERRILL. *Good Samaritan Health Center of Merrill, Wisconsin, Inc.,* 601 S. Center Ave., 54452. Tel: 715-536-5511.
For a complete listing, refer to the Hospitals section.

NEW RICHMOND. *Holy Family Hospital,* 535 Hospital Rd., 54017. Tel: 715-246-2101.
For a complete listing, refer to the Hospitals section.

RHINELANDER. *Sacred Heart-St. Mary's Hospitals, Inc.,* 1044 Kabel Ave., 54501. Tel: 715-369-6600.
For a complete listing, refer to the Hospitals section.

TOMAHAWK. *Sacred Heart-St. Mary's Hospitals, Inc.,* 216 N. 7th St., 54487. Tel: 715-453-7700.
For a complete listing, refer to the Hospitals section.

[B] HOMES FOR AGED

SUPERIOR. *St. Francis Home, Inc.,* 1800 New York Ave., 54880. Tel: 715-394-5591.
For a complete listing, refer to the Special Care Facilities section.

[C] MONASTERIES

FIFIELD. *King of Martyrs Priory,* 54524. Tel: 715-339-2447. Rev. Clement Sobr, O.S.B.

[D] CONVENTS AND RESIDENCES FOR SISTERS

ARBOR VITAE. *Marywood Eastern Region Center,* AV 3560 Hwy. 51 N., 54568-9540. Tel: 715-385-2732; 385-3243; Fax: 715-385-9118. Franciscan Sisters of Perpetual Adoration. Sr. Michon Desmond, F.S.P.A., Reg. Leader. Professed 287.

HUDSON. *Carmel of the Sacred Heart,* 430 Laurel Ave., 54016. Tel: 715-386-2156. Sr. Gemma Angelo, Prioress. Sisters 6.

LADYSMITH. *Servants of Mary,* 1000 College Ave., 54848. Tel: 715-532-3364; 532-3365. Sr. Anita Swansen, O.S.M., Pres. Tel: 612-778-9344. Sisters 103.

MERRILL. *Holy Cross Provincial Office,* 700 E. Riverside

Ave., 54452. Tel: 715-536-5445. Sr. Mary Anthony Menting, Prov.
Bell Tower Residence, Inc., 1500 O'Day St., 54452. Tel: 715-536-5575. Residence for the Elderly. Sisters 11; Lay Residents 62.
Sisters of Mercy of the Holy Cross Community Support Charitable Trust, 700 E. Riverside Ave., 54452-3358.

[E] CATHOLIC CHARITIES BUREAU

SUPERIOR. *Catholic Charities Bureau, Inc.*, 1416 Cummings Ave., P.O. Box 219, 54880. Tel: 715-394-6617. Brian Soland, M.A., Exec. Dir.; William Anderson, Dir. Finance; Anthony Coletta, Dir. Housing and Community Svcs. for the Elderly; David Bilden, Dir. Special Svcs.; Terry Hendrick, Dir. Resources & Planning; Marilyn Christopherson, Coord. Diocesan Rels.; Jennifer LeMone, Admin. Coord.
Alpha House I, 2416 Hill Ave., 54880. Tel: 715-394-2771. Residence for Handicapped. Richard Klun, Dir.
Alpha House II, 2406 Hill Ave., 54880. Tel: 715-394-2771. Residence for Handicapped. Richard Klun, Dir.
Challenge Center, Inc., 39 N. 25th St. E., 54880. Tel: 715-394-2771. Rehabilitation Center for Disabled. Richard Klun, Dir.
Harborview Group Home-Handicapped, 910 E. 5th St., 54880. Tel: 715-394-2771. Richard Klun, Dir.
Cypress House, 1415 Cypress, 54880. Tel: 715-394-2771. Richard Klun, Dir.
Elmwood Apartments, 1020 Weeks Ave., 54880. Tel: 715-394-3447. Housing for Handicapped. Bruce Todd, Mgr.
Foster Grandparent Program, 1100 Weeks Ave., Ste. C, 54880. Tel: 715-394-5382. Margaret Hogg, Dir.
Challenge Center Day Care, 39 N. 25th St. E., 54880. Tel: 715-394-2771. Richard Klun, Dir.
North Country Independent Living, Inc., 2231 Catlin Ave., Box 1245, 54880. Tel: 715-392-9118. John Nousaine, Dir.
Phoenix Villa, 1100 Weeks Ave., 54880. Tel: 715-392-3447. Housing for the Elderly. Bruce Todd, Mgr.
Retired Senior Volunteer Program, 1100 Weeks Ave., Ste. A, 54880. Tel: 715-394-4425. Helen Mikrot-Mattila, Dir.
Royalton Manor, Inc., 1900 New York Ave., 54880. Tel: 715-392-1014. Housing for the Elderly. Gregg Arseneau, Mgr.
St. Francis Home Inc., 1800 New York Ave., 54880. Tel: 715-394-5591. Kurt Graves, CEO.
St. Francis Home South, 1500 N. 34th St., 54880. Tel: 715-392-1177. Tom Wondolkowski, Admin.
Woodview Group Home, 6001 E. Third St., 54880. Tel: 715-394-2771. Residence for the Handicapped. Richard Klun, Dir.
Apple River, Inc. (Amery), Minneapolis & Broadway, Amery, 54001. Tel: 715-234-8299. Housing for Mentally Disabled. Robert Heinze, Mgr.
Evergreen Apartments (Chetek), 707 Tainter Ave., Chetek, 54728. Tel: 715-234-8299. Housing for Elderly. Robert Heinze, Mgr.
Acorn Apartments (Crandon), 508 W. Washington, Crandon, 54520. Tel: 715-369-2550. Housing for Elderly. Carol Pederson, Mgr.
Phoenix Villa North (Cumberland), 1490 Arcade, Cumberland, 54829. Tel: 715-234-8299. Housing for Mentally Ill. Robert Heinze, Mgr.
Phoenix Villa of Hayward (Hayward), Rte. 10, 436 Muriel St., Hayward, 54843. Tel: 715-234-8299. Robert Heinze, Mgr.
Hudson Day Care Center (Hudson), 816 Fourth St., Hudson, 54016. Tel: 715-386-5912. Linda Groom, Dir.
Phoenix Villa of Iron River (Iron River), Hwy. H, Iron River, 54847. Tel: 715-392-3447. Housing for Elderly. Bruce Todd, Mgr.
Phoenix Villa of Lake Nebagamon (Lake Nebagamon), Main St., Lake Nebagamon, 54849. Tel: 715-392-3447. Housing for the Elderly. Bruce Todd, Mgr.
Black River Industries, Inc. (Medford), 639 S. 2nd St., Medford, 54451. Tel: 715-748-2950. Rehabilitation Center for Disabled. Bill Hrabe, Dir.
Maywood Apartments, 521 Lemke Ave., Medford, 54451. Tel: 715-369-2550. Housing for Handicapped. Carol Pederson, Mgr.
Acorn Apartments (Minong), P.O. Box 438, Minong, 54859. Residence for Elderly. Robert Heinze, Mgr. Tel: 715-234-8299.
Maywood Apartments (Plover), 2601 Madison Ave., Plover, 54467. Tel: 715-369-2550. Housing for Elderly. Carol Pederson, Mgr.
Headwaters. Inc. (Rhinelander), 1441 E. Timber Dr., Box 618, Rhinelander, 54501. Tel: 715-369-1337. Rehabilitation Center for Disabled. Elio Pascutti, Dir.
Phoenix Villa of Rhinelander, 1011 Mason St., Rhinelander, 54501. Tel: 715-369-2550. Carol Pederson, Mgr. Housing for Elderly.
Retired Senior Volunteer Program, P.O. Box 284, Rhinelander, 54501. Tel: 715-369-1919. Lori Stroede, Dir.
Timberlane Apartments, 880 E. Timber Dr., Rhinelander, 54501. Tel: 715-369-2550. Housing for Elderly. Carol Pederson, Mgr.
Blue Valley, Inc (Rice Lake), 301 N. Wisconsin Ave., Rice Lake, 54868. Tel: 715-234-8299. Housing for Mentally Disabled. Robert Heinze, Mgr.
Phoenix Villa North, 1305 N. Wisconsin St., Rice Lake, 54868. Tel: 715-234-8299. Housing for Mentally Ill. Robert Heinze, Mgr.
Kids N' Company Day Care Center (River Falls), 410 S. 3rd St., River Falls, 54022. Tel: 715-425-9512. Linda Groom, Dir.
Evergreen Apartments (Shell Lake), 801 N. Lake Dr., Shell Lake, 54871. Tel: 715-234-8299. Housing for Elderly. Robert Heinze, Mgr.
Birchview Group Home (Siren), 7754 Rasmussen St., Siren, 54872. Tel: 715-349-5724. Residence for Disabled. Jim Auchue, Dir.
Diversified Services, Inc., Box 501, Siren, 54872. Tel: 715-349-5724. Rehabilitation Center for Disabled. James Auchue, Dir.
Lakewoods Apartments, Fourth Ave., Siren, 54872. Tel: 715-234-8299. Housing for Handicapped. Robert Heinze, Mgr.
Oakwood Apartments (Superior), 1112 John Ave., 54880. Tel: 715-392-3447. Housing for Chronically Mentally Ill. Bruce Todd, Mgr.
Acorn Apartments (Wisconsin Rapids), 2721 Tenth St. S., Wisconsin Rapids, 54494. Tel: 715-369-2550. Housing for Handicapped. Carol Pederson, Mgr. The Dove Agency, Inc., 1820 Hammond Ave., 54880. Tel: 715-392-3133. Beth Carlson, Dir.
The Dove, Inc., 1820 Hammond Ave., 54880. Tel: 715-394-6617. Beth Carlson, Dir.
United Day Care, Inc., 1416 Cumming Ave., 54880. Tel: 715-386-5912. Linda Groom, Dir. Westbay, Inc. (Washburn), 1416 Cumming Ave., 54880. Tel: 715-394-6617. Housing for the Mentally Ill. Anthony Coletta, Mgr.

[F] RETREAT HOUSES

AMERY. *Mount Carmel Hermitage*, 897 U.S. Hwy. 8, 54001-2541. Tel: 715-268-9313. Sr. Kristine Haugen, H.M.C., Coord.

ARBOR VITAE. *Marywood Franciscan Spirituality Center*, 3560 Hwy. 51, N., 54568-9540. Tel: 715-385-3750. Sr. Pauline Wittry, F.S.P.A.; Sr. Ronalda Hophan, F.S.P.A.; Sr. Jolynn Brehm, F.S.P.A.

RICE LAKE. *St. Francis Center*, 1111 E. Orchard Beach Ln., 54868. Tel: 715-234-4811.

[G] NEWMAN CENTERS

SUPERIOR. *University of Wisconsin, Superior, Newman Community*, 823 N. 16th Ave., 54880. Tel: 715-394-7710. Mr. Matthew Cetnar, Dir.

RIVER FALLS. *St. Thomas More Newman Center*, 423 E. Cascade, 54022. Rev. Norman Volk, O.M.I.

[H] ASSOCIATION OF THE FAITHFUL

AMERY. *Hermits of Mt. Carmel*, 897 Hwy. 8, 54001. Tel: 715-268-5111. Sr. Kristine Haugen, H.M.C., Coord.

[I] MISCELLANEOUS

MERRILL. *Good Samaritan Health Center Foundation of Merrill, Wisconsin, Inc.*, 601 S. Center Ave., 54452. Tel: 715-536-5511. Michael Hammer, Pres.
Sisters of Mercy of the Holy Cross Community Support Charitable Trust, 700 E. Riverside Ave., 54452-3358. Tel: 715-536-5445. Sr. Mary Anthony Menting, S.C.S.C., Pres.

NEW RICHMOND. *Holy Family Hospital Foundation, Inc.*, 535 Hospital Rd., 54017. Tel: 715-246-2101; Fax: 715-243-7222. Jean Needham, Pres.

WEBSTER. *Thomas More Center for Preaching and Prayer, Inc.*, 27781 Leef Rd., 54893. Tel: 715-866-7436. Revs. Michael A. Champlin, O.P., Pres.; Nicholas W. Punch, O.P.; Sr. Joan Bakrey, O.S.F., Vice Pres.

WINTER. *Camp We-Ha-Kee.* (Girls), N. 8104 Barker Lake Rd., 54896. Sr. Arturo Cranston, O.P., Dir.

RELIGIOUS INSTITUTES OF MEN REPRESENTED IN THE DIOCESE

For further details refer to the corresponding bracketed number in the Religious Institutes of Men or Women section.

[0200]—*Benedictine Monks.* (Lisle, IL).—O.S.B.
[0480]—*Conventual Franciscans-Province of St. Joseph of Cupertino.* Arroyo Grande, CA.—OFM Conv.
[0520]—*Franciscan Friars.* (Sacred Heart Province).—O.F.M.
[0910]—*Oblates of Mary Immaculate Central Province.* St. Paul, MN.—OMI.
[0430]—*Order of Preachers-Province of St. Albert the Great.* Chicago.—OP.
[1060]—*Society of the Precious Blood.* (Kansas City.—C.PP.S.

RELIGIOUS INSTITUTES OF WOMEN REPRESENTED IN THE DIOCESE

[0320]—*Carmelite Nuns of the Ancient Observance.*—O.Carm.
[1780]—*Congregation of Sister of the Third Order of St. Francis of Perpetual Adoration.*—F.S.P.A.
[3710]—*Congregation of the Sisters of Saint Agnes.*—C.S.A.
[1710]—*Congregation of the Third Order of St. Francis of Mary Immaculate.* (Joilet, IL).—O.S.F.
[1230]—*Franciscan Sisters of Christian Charity.*—O.S.F.
[2970]—*School Sisters of Notre Dame (Mankato/Milwaukee).*—S.S.N.D.
[1680]—*School Sisters of St. Francis.*—S.S.F.
[3590]—*Servants of Mary (Servite Sisters).*—O.S.M.
[1070-03]—*Sinsinawa Dominican Congregation of the Most Holy Rosary.*—O.P.
[2575]—*Sisters of Mercy of the Americas.*—R.S.M.
[2630]—*Sisters of Mercy of the Holy Cross.*—S.C.S.C.
[1705]—*Sisters of St. Francis of Assisi, Milawaukee.*—OSF.
[3840]—*Sisters of St. Joseph of Carondelet.* (Prov. of St. Paul).—C.S.J.
[3880]—*Sisters of St. Joseph of Medaille.*—C.S.J.
[3930]—*Sisters of St. Joseph of the Third Order of St. Francis.* (Prov. of Immaculate Conception; St. Joseph Prov.).—S.S.J.-T.O.S.F.
[4100]—*Sisters of the Sorrowful Mother.* (Third Order of St. Francis).—S.S.M.
[1760]—*Sisters of the Third Order of St. Francis of Penance and Charity.*—O.S.F.
[1720]—*Sisters of the Third Order Regular of St. Francis of the Congregation of Our Lady of Lourdes.*—O.S.F.

NECROLOGY

† Riedmueller, Robert F., (Retired). —Died Oct. 2, 1996.

Diocese of Syracuse

(Dioecesis Syracusensis)

Most Reverend

JAMES M. MOYNIHAN, D.D.

Bishop of Syracuse; ordained December 15, 1957; appointed Bishop of Syracuse April 4, 1995; consecrated and installed in See of Syracuse May 29, 1995. *Office: 240 E. Onondaga St., P.O. Box 511, Syracuse, NY, 13201-0511. Res., Cathedral of the Immaculate Conception, 295 E. Onondaga St., Syracuse, NY, 13202.*

Most Reverend

FRANK J. HARRISON, D.D.

Retired Bishop of Syracuse; ordained June 4, 1937; appointed Titular Bishop of Aquae and Auxiliary Bishop of Syracuse March 1, 1971; consecrated April 22, 1971; appointed Bishop of Syracuse November 16, 1976; installed February 6, 1977; retired June 16, 1987. *Res., Bishop Grimes Faculty House, 6655 Kirkville Rd., East Syracuse, NY, 13057.*

Most Reverend

JOSEPH T. O'KEEFE, D.D.

Retired Bishop of Syracuse; ordained April 17, 1948; appointed Titular Bishop of Tre Taverne and Auxiliary Bishop of New York July 3, 1982; consecrated September 8, 1982; appointed Bishop of Syracuse June 16, 1987; installed in See of Syracuse August 3, 1987; retired April 4, 1995. *Res., St. John the Evangelist, 214 N. State St., Syracuse, NY, 13203.*

Most Reverend

THOMAS J. COSTELLO, D.D., V.G.

Auxiliary Bishop of Syracuse and Titular Bishop of Perdices; ordained June 5, 1954; appointed January 10, 1978; consecrated March 13, 1978. *Res., 1515 Midland Ave., Syracuse, NY, 13205.*

ESTABLISHED NOVEMBER 26, 1886.

Square Miles 5,749.

Corporate Title: The Roman Catholic Diocese of Syracuse NY.

Comprises the Counties of Broome, Chenango, Cortland, Madison, Oneida, Onondaga and Oswego.

For legal titles of parishes and diocesan institutions, consult the Chancery Office.

Chancery Office: P.O. Box 511, Syracuse, NY, 13201. Tel.: 315-422-7203; Fax: 315-478-4619.

STATISTICAL OVERVIEW

Personnel	
Bishop	1
Auxiliary Bishops	1
Retired Bishops	2
Priests: Diocesan Active in Diocese	227
Priests: Active Outside Diocese	20
Priests: Retired, Sick or Absent	53
Number of Diocesan Priests	300
Religious Priests in Diocese	44
Ordinations:	
Permanent Deacons	5
Permanent Deacons in Diocese	69
Total Brothers	18
Total Sisters	514
Parishes	
Parishes	172
With Resident Pastor:	
Resident Diocesan Priests	165
Resident Religious Priests	7
Without Resident Pastor:	
Administered by Priests	3
Missions	18
Pastoral Centers	10
Welfare	
Catholic Hospitals	3
Total Assisted	650,000
Day Care and Extended Day Care Centers	1
Total Assisted	99
Specialized Homes	7
Total Assisted	401
Special Centers for Social Services	8
Total Assisted	56,616
Residential Care of Disabled	16
Total Assisted	562
Other Institutions	2
Total Assisted	344
Educational	
Diocesan Students in Other Seminaries	12
Seminaries, Religious	1
Students Religious	14
Total Seminarians	26
Colleges and Universities	1
Total Students	2,800
High Schools, Diocesan and Parish	5
Total Students	2,618
High Schools, Private	1
Total Students	726
Elementary Schools, Diocesan and Parish	39
Total Students	9,024
Catechesis/Religious Education:	
High School Students	7,544
Elementary Students	38,967
Total Students Under Catholic Instruction	61,705
Teachers in the Diocese:	
Priests	12
Brothers	7
Sisters	100
Lay Teachers	825
Vital Statistics	
Receptions into the Church:	
Infant Baptism Totals	6,160
Adult Baptism Totals	374
Received into Full Communion	504
First Communions	6,029
Confirmations	4,129
Marriages:	
Catholic	1,667
Interfaith	744
Total Marriages	2,411
Deaths	4,609
Total Catholic Population	372,665
Total Population	1,223,591

Former Bishops—Rt. Rev. PATRICK ANTHONY LUDDEN, D.D., ord. June 21, 1864; cons. May 1, 1887; died Aug. 6, 1912.—Rt. Rev. JOHN GRIMES, D.D., ord. Feb. 19, 1882; cons. May 16, 1909; Coadjutor Bishop, 1909-1912; succeeded to the See, Aug. 6, 1912; died July 26, 1922.—Most Rev. DANIEL JOSEPH CURLEY, D.D., ord. May 19, 1894; cons. May 1, 1923; died Aug. 3, 1932.—Most Rev. JOHN ALOYSIUS DUFFY, D.D., ord. June 13, 1908; cons. June 29, 1933; installed July 11, 1933; appt. Bishop of Buffalo, Jan. 9, 1937; installed in See of Buffalo, April 14, 1937; died Sept. 27, 1944.—Most Rev. WALTER A. FOERY, D.D., Ph.D., ord. June 10, 1916; appt. May 26, 1937; cons. Aug. 18, 1937; appt. assistant at the Pontifical Throne, Dec. 11, 1961; retired and named Titular Bishop of Miseno-Cape, Aug. 4, 1970; died May 10, 1978.—Most Rev. DAVID F. CUNNINGHAM, D.D., ord. June 12, 1926; appt. Titular Bishop of Lampsacus and Auxiliary Bishop of Syracuse, April 5, 1950; cons. June 8, 1950; appt. Coadjutor Bishop "Cum jure successiones," June 19, 1967; succeeded to the See, Aug. 4, 1970; died Feb. 22, 1979.—Most Rev. FRANK J. HARRISON, D.D., ord. June 4, 1937; appt. Titular Bishop of Aquae and Auxiliary Bishop of Syracuse, March 1, 1971; cons. April 22, 1971; appt. Bishop of Syracuse, Nov. 16, 1976; retired June 16, 1987.—Most Rev. JOSEPH T. O'KEEFE, D.D., Bishop of Syracuse; ord. April 17, 1948; appt. Titular Bishop of Tre Taverne and Auxiliary Bishop of New York, July 3, 1982; cons. Sept. 8, 1982; appt. Bishop of Syracuse, June 16, 1987; installed in See of Syracuse, Aug. 3, 1987; retired April 4, 1995.

Vicar General / Vicar for Parishes—Most Rev. THOMAS J. COSTELLO, D.D., *1515 Midland Ave., Syracuse, 13205.*

Vicars Forane—Northern Area Vicar: Rev. Msgr. FRANCIS J. FURFARO, *182 W. 2nd St., Oswego, 13126.* Southern Area Vicar: Rev. Msgr. PETER J. OWENS, *9 Leroy St., Binghamton, 13905.* Eastern Area Vicars: Rev. Msgr. WILLIAM M. KELLY, *1807 Bedford St., Rome, 13440.* Rev. DONALD H. KARLEN, *702 Columbia St., Utica, 13502.* Western Area Vicars: Rev. MICHAEL J. CARMOLA, *500 Brookford Rd., Syracuse, 13224.* Rev. GEORGE F. SHEEHAN, *6651 Kirkville Rd., East Syracuse, 13057.*

Chancery Office—240 E. Onondaga St., Syracuse, 13202., Mailing Address: P.O. Box 511, Syracuse, 13201. Tel: 315-422-7203; Fax: 315-478-4619. Office Hours: Mon.-Fri. 8:30-4:30 Send official mail, including marriage dispensations, to Chancery.

Chancellor—Rev. MICHAEL P. MINEHAN, *6104 Cherry Valley Rd., LaFayette, 13084.*

Assistant Chancellor / Secretary to Bishop Moynihan—Rev. AMEDEO G. GUIDA, *500 Brookford Rd., Syracuse, 13224.*

Board of Diocesan Consultors—Most Rev. THOMAS J. COSTELLO, D.D.; Rev. Msgr. FRANK J. FURFARO; Rev. Msgr. WILLIAM M. KELLY; Rev. Msgr. PETER J. OWENS; Revs. MICHAEL J. CARMOLA; ROBERT D. CHRYST; DONALD H. KARLEN; RICHARD M. KOPP; JAMES P. LANG; THOMAS J. MCGRATH; GEORGE F. SHEEHAN.

Management Team—Most Rev. JAMES M. MOYNIHAN; Most Rev. THOMAS J. COSTELLO, D.D.; Revs. TIMOTHY S. ELMER; AMEDEO G. GUIDA; MICHAEL P. MINEHAN; JOSEPH H. PHILLIPS; ROBERT P. STEPHENSON; J. ROBERT YEAZEL; Sr. FRANCINE BAUSER, C.S.J.; Sr. NORA GATTO, D.C.; Sr. MARY ANNE HEENAN, C.S.J.; Mrs. GERRIE KALUZNY; Ms. DANIELLE MOEN-CUMMINGS; Ms. EILEEN MCCANN.

Pastoral Council—Most Rev. JAMES M. MOYNIHAN, Pres.; Ms. KATHLEEN M. DYER, Exec. Sec., *101 Ridge Rd.,*

Fulton, 13069. Tel: 315-592-5566.

Pastoral Examiners—Revs. JOHN P. FENLON; MORITZ FUCHS; THOMAS KEATING; JAMES KENNEDY; RICHARD V. O'NEILL; DANIEL G. MURPHY; JOHN F. ROSE; JOSEPH SALERNO; JOSEPH S. ZARESKI.

Priests' Senate—Most Rev. JAMES M. MOYNIHAN, Pres.; Rev. JAMES P. LANG, Chm. Ex Officio: Most Rev. THOMAS J. COSTELLO; Rev. Msgr. FRANCIS J. FURFARO; Rev. Msgr. WILLIAM M. KELLY; Rev. Msgr. PETER J. OWENS; Revs. MICHAEL J. CARMOLA; DONALD H. KARLEN; MICHAEL P. MINEHAN; GEORGE F. SHEEHAN.

Senators—Revs. ROBERT AMRHEIN, O.F.M.Conv.; DONALD J. BAUER; JOHN A. BOLAND, S.J.; PAUL A. BRIGANDI; DANIEL M. CARUSO; FRANCIS J. CASE; ROBERT D. CHRYST; EDMUND J. DURR; ROBERT D. DWYER; CHARLES H. ECKERMANN; TIMOTHY S. ELMER; WILFRED F. EVANS; GARY M. FUKES; LAWRENCE E. GIBLIN; PHILLIP A. HEARN; THOMAS F. HOBBES; THOMAS P. KOBUSZEWSKI; GREGORY C. LESTRANGE; JOHN R. MADDEN; JAMES L. RILEY; JOHN C. SCHOPFER; CARLO C. STIRPE; RICHARD R. THOMPSON.

Diocesan Tribunal—

Judicial Vicar—Rev. TIMOTHY S. ELMER.

Judges—Rev. Msgr. WILLIAM J. DONOVAN; Revs. ROBERT P. HYDE, J.C.L.; LAURENCE W. KENNEDY.

Associate Judges—Revs. DAVID J. BAEHR; JOHN J. MULRANEN; DANIEL G. MURPHY; ROBERT G. TIERNEY; DONALD C. VANAMBURGH; WILBUR J. VOTRAW; LEO J. WIMETT.

Defender of the Bond—Rev. MICHAEL P. MINEHAN, J.C.L.

Promotor of Justice—Rev. Msgr. JAMES A. MCCLOSKEY.

Notary of the Tribunal—KATHLEEN CUSHING.

Advocates—Sr. ANNA WALTER MOSSDORF, O.S.F.; MARGARET EDGECOMB.

Auditors—Revs. JOHN P. DONOVAN; MARK J. GANTLEY.

Case Coordinators/Staff—MARY BEALL; KATHLEEN CUSHING.

Vicar for Administration—Rev. MICHAEL P. MINEHAN, *240 E. Onondaga St., P.O. Box 511, Syracuse, 13201.* Tel: 315-422-7203.

Vicar for Community Services—Rev. ROBERT S. STEPHENSON, *240 E. Onondaga St., P.O. Box 511, Syracuse, 13201.* Tel: 315-424-1830.

Vicar for Parishes—Most Rev. THOMAS J. COSTELLO, D.D., *240 E. Onondaga St., P.O. Box 511, Syracuse, 13201.* Tel: 315-422-7203.

Vicar for Ministerial Formation—Sr. NORA GATTO, D.C., *240 E. Onondaga St., P.O. Box 511, Syracuse, 13201.* Tel: 315-470-1421.

Vicar for Priests—Rev. J. ROBERT YEAZEL, *240 E. Onondaga St., P.O. Box 511, Syracuse, 13201.* Tel: 315-470-1460.

Vicar for Religious—Sr. FRANCINE BAUSER, C.S.J., *240 E. Onondaga St., P.O. Box 511, Syracuse, 13201.* Tel: 315-422-7203; 470-1468.

Diocesan Offices

Accounting—Ms. DEBRA SOCHAN, CFO, *P.O. Box 511, Syracuse, 13201.* Tel: 315-470-9045; Fax: 315-422-9139.

Adminstration—Rev. MICHAEL P. MINEHAN, Vicar, *P.O. Box 511, Syracuse, 13201.* Tel: 315-422-7203.

Archives—Mr. CARL ROESCH, Archivist, *P.O. Box 511, Syracuse, 13201.* Tel: 315-470-1493.

Asian Apostolate—Rev. MICHAEL MAI TRAN, C.M.C.; Sr. JUDITH HOWLEY, C.S.J., *215 N. State St., Syracuse, 13203.* Tel: 315-472-7043.

Benefits—Ms. CAROLYN CAIN, Dir., *P.O. Box 511, Syracuse, 13201.* Tel: 315-422-9091.

Black Catholic Ministry—Bro. DOUGLAS MCMILLAN, O.F.M.Conv., Dir., *P.O. Box 511, Syracuse, 13201.* Tel: 315-470-1463.

Boy Scouts/Girl Scouts—Rev. JAMES P. LANG, Chap., *St. Thomas More Chapel, 110 Walnut Pl., Syracuse, 13210.* Tel: 315-478-5959.

Building Commission—Most Rev. JAMES M. MOYNIHAN; Most Rev. THOMAS J. COSTELLO, D.D.; Revs. MICHAEL P. MINEHAN; JOSEPH E. SCARDELLA; Mr. THOMAS V. DADEY, Esq.; Mr. EDWARD T. KING; Mr. J. DOUGLAS ROSS; Ms. DEBRA J. SOCHAN.

Catholic Cemeteries—Rev. JAMES C. FRITZEN, Dir.; Mr. MARK LAZAROSKI, Exec. Dir., *2315 South Ave., Syracuse, 13207.* Tel: 315-475-4639; Fax: 315-422-0363.

Catholic Charities—Rev. ROBERT B. STEPHENSON, *P.O. Box 511, Syracuse, 13202.* Tel: 315-424-1830; Fax: 315-478-4619.

Onondaga County Director—Mr. BRIAN WALTON, *1654 W. Onondaga St., Syracuse, 13204.* Tel: 315-424-1806.

Downtown Emergency Assistance Office—SANDY SMITH, *264 E. Onondaga St., Syracuse, 13202.* Tel: 315-424-1876.

Broome County Director—Mr. JOSEPH G. SLAVIK, *232 Main St., Binghamton, 13905.* Tel: 607-729-9166.

Chenango County Director—JANE CODDINGTON, Dir., *3 O'Hara Dr., Norwich, 13815.* Tel: 607-334-8244.

Cortland County Director—PAULA CURRIE, *33-35 Central Ave., Cortland, 13045.* Tel: 607-756-5992.

Oneida and Madison Counties Director—Mr. DENNIS MANNING, *1408 Genesee St., Utica, 13502.* Tel: 315-724-2150.

Oswego County Director—ANDREA MCCABE, *365 First St., Fulton, 13069.* Tel: 315-598-3980.

Catholic Deaf Community—Rev. PETER T. WILLIAMS, Dir., *1119 Elm St., Utica, 13501.* Tel: 315-735-8184 (TTY/Voice).

Catholic Relief Services—Rev. ROBERT B. STEPHENSON, Dir., *P.O. Box 511, Syracuse, 13201.* Tel: 315-424-1830.

Catholic Schools—Sr. MARY ANNE HEENAN, C.S.J., Supt., *P.O. Box 511, Syracuse, 13201.* Tel: 315-470-1450. Rev. CHARLES S. VAVONESE, Assoc. Supt.; Mrs. SHEILA LIEGEL, Dir. Curriculum.

Northern & Western Regions—Sr. MARY ELLEN SHIRTZ, C.S.J., Area Supt., *P.O. Box 511, Syracuse, 13201.* Tel: 315-470-1450; Fax: 315-478-4619.

Southern Region—Dr. JOHN J. COLLIGAN, Area Supt., *206 Madison Ave., P.O. Box 7158, Endicott, 13761.* Tel: 607-748-1541; Fax: 607-748-0083.

Eastern Region—Ms. KATHLEEN COYE, Area Supt., *17 Herkimer Rd., Utica, 13502.* Tel: 315-735-2111; Fax: 315-735-3603.

Catholic Sun—Ms. ANNE CHECKOSKY, Editor in Chief & Gen. Mgr., *421 S. Warren St., Syracuse, 13202.* Tel: 315-422-8153; 800-333-0571; Fax: 315-422-7549.

Catholic Television—Mr. JAMES FUNSON, Dir., *1342 Lancaster Ave., Syracuse, 13210.* Tel: 315-472-3584.

Christopher Community—Mr. PETER WHITE, Exec. Dir., *1654 W. Onondaga St., Syracuse, 13204.* Tel: 315-414-1821.

Clerical Fund Society of the Roman Catholic Diocese of Syracuse—Most Rev. JAMES M. MOYNIHAN, Pres.; Most Rev. THOMAS J. COSTELLO, D.D., Vice Pres.; Rev. MICHAEL P. MINEHAN, Sec. & Treas.

Office of Communications—Ms. DANIELLE MOEN-CUMMINGS, Dir., *P.O. Box 511, Syracuse, 13201.* Tel: 315-471-1476; Fax: 315-478-4619.

Council of Religious—Sr. ROSE GARFAMONE, O.S.F., Pres., *P.O. Box 511, Syracuse, 13201.*

Development Office—Ms. JENNIFER E. TURCK, *1342 Lancaster Ave., Syracuse, 13210.* Tel: 315-472-0203; 472-7902; Fax: 315-472-8409.

Disabilities Office—Mr. THOMAS CUNNINGHAM, JR., Dir., *P.O. Box 511, Syracuse, 13201.* Tel: 315-424-1830; Fax: 315-478-4619.

Ecumenical Commission—Rev. Msgr. RONALD C. BILL, Dir., *8229 S. Main St., Cicero, 13039.* Tel: 315-699-2752.

Family Life Education—Rev. JOSEPH H. PHILLIPS, Dir., *1342 Lancaster Ave., Syracuse, 13210.* Tel: 315-472-6754; Fax: 315-472-8409.

Finance Committee—Most Rev. JAMES M. MOYNIHAN; Revs. MICHAEL P. MINEHAN; J. ROBERT YEAZEL; Mr. JOHN D. BURKE, SR.; Mr. JOHN KIRSCH; Mr. JOSEPH MCGLYNN; Mr. JAMES MURPHY; Ms. CAROL PIEKLIK; Mr. ROGER W. SHAVER; Ms. DOREEN SIMMONS, Esq.; Ms. DEBRA SOCHAN.

Formation for Ministry—Sr. NORA GATTO, D.C., Dir., *P.O. Box 511, Syracuse, 13202.* Tel: 315-470-1421; Fax: 315-478-4619.

Health Care—Rev. ROBERT B. STEPHENSON, Dir., *P.O. Box 511, Syracuse, 13201.* Tel: 315-424-1830; Fax: 315-478-4619.

HOPE Appeal—Ms. LOUANN CHRISTO, Assoc. Dir., *1342 Lancaster Ave., Syracuse, 13210.* Tel: 315-472-0203; 800-295-4776; Fax: 315-472-8409.

Human Life Office—Mrs. CINDY FALISE, Dir., *P.O. Box 511, Syracuse, 13201.* Tel: 315-424-1830; Fax: 315-478-4619.

Liturgy—Sr. LAURA BUFANO, C.S.J., Dir., *P.O. Box 511, Syracuse, 13201.* Tel: 315-470-1425.

Parish Services/Purchasing—Mr. ROBERT GILL, Dir., *P.O. Box 511, Syracuse, 13201.* Tel: 315-470-9101; Fax: 315-422-9139.

Permanent Diaconate—Deacon LESLIE F. DISTIN, Dir., *P.O. Box 511, Syracuse, 13201.* Tel: 315-470-1466.

Priest Personnel—Rev. J. ROBERT YEAZEL, Dir., *P.O. Box 511, Syracuse, 13201.* Tel: 315-470-1460; Fax: 315-478-4619.

Priests' Personnel Committee—Most Rev. JAMES M. MOYNIHAN; Most Rev. THOMAS J. COSTELLO, D.D.; Revs. DAVID J. BAEHR; GERALD J. BUCKLEY; MICHAEL J. CARMOLA; JOHN P. FLANAGAN; ROBERT L. KELLY; MICHAEL P. MINEHAN; JAMES T. O'BRIEN; JAMES T. QUEEN; CLARENCE F. RUMBLE; THOMAS J. RYAN; J. ROBERT YEAZEL.

Project Rachel—Mrs. CINDY FALISE, Dir., *P.O. Box 511, Syracuse, 13201.* Tel: 315-424-3737.

Personal Resource Center—Rev. NEAL QUARTIER, Dir., *420 Montgomery St., Syracuse, 13202.* Tel: 315-470-1462.

Propagation of the Faith—Rev. JOSEPH H. PHILLIPS, Dir., *1342 Lancaster Ave., Syracuse, 13210.* Tel: 315-472-3442; Fax: 315-472-8409.

Religious Education—Mrs. GERRIE KALUZNY, Dir., *P.O. Box 511, Syracuse, 13202.* Tel: 315-470-1431; Fax: 315-478-4619.

Eastern Region—Sr. KATHLEEN EIFFE, Dir., *One Sherman St., New Hartford, 13413.* Tel: 315-797-4030.

East (Rome)—JOAN LEAHY, *Resource Center, 212 W. Liberty St., Rome, 13440.* Tel: 315-336-2900.

Northern Region—Sr. GERMANE HILSTON, Dir., *108 E. 6th St., Oswego, 13126.* Tel: 315-343-5557.

Southern Region—Sr. BERNICE ANN CARROLL, Dir., *1031 Chenango St., Binghamton, 13901.* Tel: 607-772-0071.

South (Norwich)—ANGIE DIAMOND, *Resource Center, 20 Randall Ave., Norwich, 13815.* Tel: 607-334-2883.

Western Region—MARY STANLEY, Dir., *1342 Lancaster Ave., Syracuse, 13210.* Tel: 315-472-6751. JEAN LOVAS, Resource Center. Tel: 315-472-6752.

West (Cortland)—Vacant, *44 N. Main St., Cortland, 13045.* Tel: 607-756-2532.

Religious—Sr. FRANCINE BAUSER, Dir., *P.O. Box 511, Syracuse, 13201.* Tel: 315-470-1426; Fax: 315-478-4619.

Respect for Life—Mrs. CINDY FALISE, Dir., *P.O. Box 511, Syracuse, 13201.* Tel: 315-424-1859.

Laymen & Laywomen Retreat Movements—Rev. MICHAEL J. CARMOLA, Dir., *Christ the King Retreat House, 500 Brookford Rd., Syracuse, 13224.* Tel: 315-446-2680.

Spanish Apostolate—Rev. ROBERT D. CHRYST, Dir., *170 Seymour St., Syracuse, 13204.* Tel: 315-442-9390.

Syracuse Catholic Press Association, Inc.—"The Catholic Sun", ANNE CHECKOSKY, Editor in Chief & Gen. Mgr.; Most Rev. JAMES M. MOYNIHAN, Pres., *421 S. Warren St., Syracuse, 13202.* Tel: 315-422-2153; 1-800-333-0571; Fax: 315-422-7549.

Teen Seminar—Rev. THOMAS CATUCCI, Dir., *25 Doubleday St., Binghamton, 13901.* Tel: 607-724-3047.

Vocation Formation—Rev. NEAL E. QUARTIER, Dir., *P.O. Box 511, Syracuse, 13201.* Tel: 315-470-1452; Fax: 315-478-4619.

Vocation Promotion—Rev. JAMES F. QUINN, Dir., *P.O. Box 511, Syracuse, 13201.* Tel: 800-471-1468; Fax: 315-478-4619.

Youth Ministry—EILEEN MCCANN, Dir., *P.O. Box 511, Syracuse, 13201.* Tel: 315-424-1830; Fax: 315-478-4619.

CLERGY, PARISHES, MISSIONS AND PAROCHIAL SCHOOLS

CITY OF SYRACUSE
(Onondaga County)

1—THE CATHEDRAL OF THE IMMACULATE CONCEPTION (1841), Rev. Msgr. Joseph M. Champlin, Rector; Most Rev. James M. Moynihan; Revs. Jon K. Werner; John C. Schopfer; Neal E. Quartier; Jerome Amachei; Deacon Pio Peter Carranti.

Res., 259 E. Onondaga St., 13202. Tel: 315-422-4177.

School—420 Montgomery St., 13202. Tel: 315-422-7217. Sr. Mary Jane Wilcox, D.C., Prin.

Daughters of Charity of St. Vincent de Paul 3; Lay Teachers 8; Students 147.

Stations—The Burt Street Housing; Castle Rest Nursing Home; Clinton St. Plaza; McCarthy Manor; Plaza Nursing Home.

2—ASSUMPTION B.V.M. (1844) (German), Revs. Raynald E. Yudin, O.F.M.Conv.; Robert Amrhein, O.F.M.Conv.; Firmin Finn, O.F.M.Conv.; Bartholomew Gaske, O.F.M.Conv.; Charles Nelipowitz, O.F.M.Conv.; Herman Seibert, O.F.M.Conv.; Jeffrey Keefe, O.F.M.Conv., Ph.D., Prov. Psychologist, Franciscan Counseling; Regis Rodda, O.F.M.Conv.; Michael Taylor, O.F.M.Conv.; Bros. John Douglas McMillan, O.F.M.Conv.; Thomas Connelly, O.F.M.Conv.

Res., St. Francis Friary, 812 N. Salina St., 13208. Tel: 315-422-4833; Fax: 315-475-4363. [CEM]

Assumption Cemetery Corporation—2401 Court St., 13208.

3—BLESSED SACRAMENT (1921), Revs. James T. O'Brien; Kevin Corcoran; Rev. Msgr. Robert E. Dillon.

Res., 3127 James St., 13206. Tel: 315-437-3394; Fax: 315-463-1628.

School—(Grades PreK-6) 3129 James St., 13206. Tel: 315-437-1261. Mrs. Andrea Polcaro, Prin.

Sisters of St. Joseph of Carondelet 2; Lay Teachers 11; Students 257.

4—HOLY TRINITY (1891) (German), Rev. Edmund J. Durr; Sr. Mary Margaret Singer, C.S.J., Pastoral Assoc.

Res., 501 Park St., 13203. Tel: 315-474-8681; Fax:

315-474-3154.

5—Most Holy Rosary (1913), Rev. Peter M. Creed. In res., Revs. Thomas E. Neary, (Retired); James F. Quinn.
Res., 111 Roberts Ave., 13207-1397. Tel: 315-478-5749; Fax: 315-478-8629.
School—1031 Bellevue Ave., 13207. Tel: 315-476-6035. Eamon O'Neill, I.H.M., Prin.
Sisters Servants of the Immaculate Heart of Mary 3; Lay Teachers 18; Students 268.

6—Our Lady of Lourdes (1947), Rev. Thomas P. Fitzpatrick; Deacon Leo Needham.
Res., 300 Valley Dr., 13207. Tel: 315-476-9576.
School—301 Valley Dr., 13207. Ms. Joan T. Smith, Prin.
Lay Teachers 8; Students 130.

7—Our Lady of Pompei (1924) (Italian), Rev. Joseph E. Scardella. In res., Revs. John R. Cramer; Frederick Pompei; Michael Mai; Deacon Kenneth Money.
Res., 301 Ash St., 13208. Tel: 315-422-7163; Fax: 315-422-7164.
School—(Grades PreK-6) 915-917 N. McBride St., 13208. Tel: 315-422-8548.
Lay Teachers 12; Students 164.
Convent—920 N. McBride St., 13208. Tel: 315-422-7922. Franciscan Missionary Sisters of the Immaculate Conception

8—Our Lady of Solace (1926), Rev. William R. Jones. In res., Rev. Alfred J. Bebel.
Res., 516 Salt Springs Rd., 13224. Tel: 315-446-2060.

9—Sacred Heart (1892) (Polish), Revs. Peter W. Gleba; Stanley Dudkiewicz (Poland); Stanley Matula; Deacons James L. Morse; Joseph Daniszewski.
Res., 927 Park Ave., 13204. Tel: 315-422-2343. [CEM 2]
School—1001 Park Ave., 13204. Tel: 315-422-7372. Sr. Melanie Jaworski, C.S.S.F., Supr. & Prin.
Felician Sisters 2; Lay Teachers 12; Students 179.

10—St. Andrew the Apostle (1953), Rev. Joseph F. Kane. In res., Rev. Wilfred F. Evans; Sr. Patricia Bergan, O.S.F., Pastoral Assoc.
Res., 124 Alden St., 13210. Tel: 315-476-8656.

11—St. Ann (1955), Rev. John L. Roark. In res., Rev. Joseph H. Phillips.
Res., 4461 Onondaga Blvd., 13219. Tel: 315-468-1803.
School—Mrs. Nancy Toscano, Prin. Lay Teachers 7; Students 130.

12—St. Anthony of Padua (1891), Rev. Robert D. Chryst. In res., Most Rev. Thomas J. Costello.
Res., 1515 Midland Ave., 13205. Tel: 315-475-4114.

13—St. Brigid and St. Joseph (1926 and 1869), Rev. Laurence W. Kennedy; Deacon Leonard S. Monnat.
Res., 318 Herkimer St., 13204. Tel: 315-488-7122.

14—St. Charles (1929), Rev. James H. Carey; Deacon Peter Vanelli; Sr. Paula Jude Egan, C.S.J., Parish Min.
Res., 417 S. Orchard Rd., 13219. Tel: 315-468-4122.
School—200 W. High Ter., 13219. Tel: 315-488-7631; Fax: 315-488-0617. Sr. Donna Driscoll, Prin.
Sisters 3; Lay Teachers 14; Students 249.
Convent—401 E. Corey Rd., 13219. Tel: 315-468-6041. Missionary Franciscan Sisters of the Immaculate Conception

15—St. Daniel (1932), Rev. Msgr. Eugene M. Yennock; Rev. Mark J. Gantley.
Res., 3004 Court St., 13208. Tel: 315-454-4946.
School—Tel: 315-455-7021. Sr. Ancilla Yim, Prin.
Sisters of the Third Franciscan Order 3; Lay Teachers 12; students (K-6) 192; Students (PreK-K) 27.

16—St. James (1925), Revs. Michael T. Meagher; Daniel J. O'Hara.
Res., 4845 S. Salina St., 13205. Tel: 315-469-7789.
School—(Grades PreK-6) 4837 S. Salina St., 13205. Tel: 315-492-1054. Sr. David Agnes De Forest, Prin.
Sisters 2; Lay Teachers 11; Students 206.
Convent—111 Munson Dr., 13205. Tel: 315-492-3654. Sisters of the Third Franciscan Order M.C.
Station—Brighton Towers.

17—St. John the Baptist (1827), Rev. John R. DeLorenzo. In res., Revs. Robert E. Brennan; Michael A. Dietrich.
Res., 406 Court St., 13208. Tel: 315-478-0916.
School—1406 Park St., 13208. Tel: 315-422-6982. Mrs. Sally Lisi, Prin.
Sisters of St. Joseph of Carondelet 2; Lay Teachers 12; Students 190.

18—St. John the Evangelist (1851), Rev. Robert B. Stephenson; Deacon John H. Collins. In res., Most Rev. Joseph T. O'Keefe; Rev. Daniel C. Muscalino.
Res., 214 N. State St., 13203. Tel: 315-422-0786.

19—St. Lucy (1872), Rev. James D. Mathews. In res., Rev. Msgr. Charles J. Fahey.
Res., 432 Gifford St., 13204. Tel: 315-475-7273; Fax: 315-475-7273.
School—(Grades K-5) 422 Gifford St., 13204. Tel: 315-478-6312. Ms. Karen McCann, Prin.
Lay Teachers 6; Students 90.

20—St. Patrick (1870), Rev. E. Peter Reddick.
Res., 216 N. Lowell Ave., 13204. Tel: 315-475-2185.
School—(Grades PreK-6) 210 Schuyler St., 13204. Tel: 315-476-4076. Sr. Catherine Anthony O.S.F., Prin.
Sisters of St. Joseph of Carondelet 1; Lay Teachers 9; Students 163.

21—St. Peter (1890) (Italian), Rev. Tarcisio Bagatin, C.S.
Res., 709 James St., 13203. Tel: 315-472-4451; Fax: 315-422-3441.

22—St. Stephen (1915) (Slovak), Revs. Peter W. Gleba; Tadeusz Rudnik (Canada).
Res., 305 N. Geddes St., 13204. Tel: 315-422-5224.

23—St. Therese the Little Flower of Jesus (1926), Rev. Edward J. Reimer.
Res., 112 Lancaster Pl., 13210. Tel: 315-472-9934.
Parish Helpers—1226 Lancaster Ave., 13210. Tel: 315-472-2685.
Sisters of St. Joseph of Carondelet 5.

24—St. Vincent de Paul (1893), Rev. Alfred E. Nortz. In res., Rev. Wilbur J. Votraw.
Res., 342 Vine St., 13203. Tel: 315-479-6689; Fax: 315-479-6689.
Convent—1101 Burnet Ave., 13203. Tel: 315-479-8012. Sisters of St. Joseph of Carondelet

25—Transfiguration (1911) (Polish), Rev. Stanley M. Szewczyk.
Res., 740 Teall Ave., 13206. Tel: 315-479-6129; Fax: 315-479-6336.

OUTSIDE THE CITY OF SYRACUSE

Bainbridge, Chenango Co., St. John the Evangelist (1914), Rev. Donald E. Bourgeois.
Res., 34 S. Main St., 13733. Tel: 607-967-4481.
Mission—Afton, St. Agnes, Tel: 607-639-1200.

Baldwinsville, Onondaga Co., St. Augustine (1966), Rev. John Rose.
Res., 7333 O'Brien Rd., 13027. Tel: 315-638-0585.
St. Elizabeth Ann Seton (1985), Rev. John P. Wagner; Deacon William A. Dotterer.
Res., 3494 NY State Rte. 31, 13027. Tel: 315-652-4300; Fax: 315-622-1761.
St. Mary (1852), Rev. Richard M. Kopp.
Res., 47 Syracuse St., 13027. Tel: 315-635-5762. [CEM]
School—49 Syracuse St., 13027. Tel: 315-635-3977. Sr. Rose Marie, Prin.
Sisters of the Third Franciscan Order M.C. 1; Lay Teachers 8; Students 200.

Binghamton, Broome Co.,

1—St. Andrew, (1955), Rev. Gerald J. Buckley.
Res., 356 Conklin Ave., 13903. Tel: 607-722-4049.
Parish Center—356 Conklin Ave., 13903. Tel: 607-722-9474.

2—St. Ann, (1925) (Slovak), Revs. Paul J. Keebler; Kevin J. Bunger, Spanish Apostolate. In res., Rev. John J. Mulranen, (Retired).
Res., 346 Prospect St., 13905. Tel: 607-797-1856.

3—St. Catherine of Siena, (1929), Rev. Laurence J. Lord; Sr. Karen Gaube, C.S.J., Pastoral Assoc.; Deacon Raymond Goskowski.
Res., 1031 Chenango St., 13901. Tel: 607-722-4388; Fax: 607-722-1336.

4—St. Christopher, (1940), Rev. Edward J. Zandy.
Res., 103 Castle Creek Rd., 13901. Tel: 607-723-0677.

5—SS. Cyril and Method, (1904) (Slovak), Revs. Brennan-Joseph Farleo, O.F.M.Conv.; George Sandor, O.F.M.Conv. In res., Revs. Kenan McGowan, O.F.M.Conv.; Hilary Miketinac.
Res., 148 Clinton St., 13905. Tel: 607-724-1372; Fax: 607-724-1468.

6—St. John the Evangelist, (1907), Revs. Paul J. Alciati; C. Patrick Keating.
Res., 1263 Vestal Ave., 13903. Tel: 607-722-0493; Fax: 607-722-0493.

7—St. Joseph, (1914) (Lithuanian), Rev. John E. Mikalajunas.
Res., 1 Judson Ave., 13905. Tel: 607-797-5264; Fax: 607-797-5264.

8—St. Mary of the Assumption, (1887; 1913), Rev. Msgr. Paul A. Brigandi; Rev. Clarence J. Cerwonka; Sr. Linda Gaige, C.S.J.
Res., 37 Fayette St., 13901. Tel: 607-723-5383.

9—St. Patrick, (1838), Rev. Msgr. Peter J. Owens; Deacon Edward M. Blaine. In res., Revs. Gerald F. McMahon, C.S.C.; Christopher Boretto.
Res., 9 Leroy St., 13905. Tel: 607-722-1060.
Convent—46 Oak St., 13905. Tel: 607-722-4745. Sisters of St. Joseph of Carondelet

10—St. Paul, (1896), Rev. Corey S. Van Kuren.
Res., 15 Doubleday St., 13901. Tel: 607-722-6492.

11—St. Stanislaus Kostka, (1914) (Polish), Rev. Matthew S. Wieczorek.
Res., 368 Prospect St., 13905-1810. Tel: 607-797-3564.
School—(Grades PreK-3) 372 Prospect St., 13905. Tel: 607-797-3793. Sr. M. Virginita Tarnacki, C.S.S.F., Prin.
Felician Sisters 3; Lay Teachers 4; Students 17.
Convent—376 Prospect St., 13905. Tel: 607-797-5732.

12—St. Thomas Aquinas, (1927), Rev. James D. Tormey. In res., Rev. Msgr. Lawrence E. Giblin.
Res., 1 Aquinas St., 13905. Tel: 607-797-4015.

Boonville, Oneida Co., St. Joseph (1875), Rev. David J. Orzel.
Res., 110 Charles St., 13309. Tel: 315-942-4618. [CEM]
Convent—108 Charles St., 13309. Tel: 315-942-2019.
Sisters 2.

Brewerton, Onondaga Co., St. Agnes (1958), Rev. William T. Guckert.
Res., 5472 Miller Rd., 13209. Tel: 315-676-7050.

Bridgeport, Onondaga Co., St. Francis of Assisi (1952), Rev. Ralph White, O.F.M.Conv.
Res., P.O. Box 550, 13030-0550. Tel: 315-633-2561.
Parish Center—13030-0550. Tel: 315-633-9682.

Camden, Oneida Co., St. John (1852), Rev. Joseph P. Kennedy.
Res., 22 Church St., 13316. Tel: 315-245-1603. [CEM]

Camillus, Onondaga Co., St. Joseph (1852), Revs. John S. Finnegan; Robert Hyde; Joseph Egbule.
Res., 5600 W. Genesee St., 13031. Tel: 315-488-8490.

Canastota, Madison Co., St. Agatha (1883), Rev. Anthony F. Tosti. Pastoral Ministers: Sr. Florence Joseph Flaherty, D.C.; Sr. Loretta Genter, D.C.; Sr. Ellen Hensberry, D.C.
Res., 329 N. Peterboro St., 13032. Tel: 315-697-7104; Fax: 315-697-7108. [CEM]
Convent—406 Spencer St., 13032. Tel: 315-697-7210.

Cazenovia, Madison Co., St. James (1847), Rev. Henry J. Pedzich.
Res., 6 Green St., 13035. Tel: 315-655-3441; Fax: 315-655-3442. [CEM]

Central Square, Oswego Co., St. Michael (1928), Rev. John J. Smegelsky; Deacon Leo Matzke.
Res., 598 S. Main St., P.O. Box 514, 13036. Tel: 315-676-2898.

Chadwicks, Oneida Co., St. Anthony of Padua (1907), Rev. Edward J. Hayes.
Res., 3364 Oneida St., P.O. Box 310, 13319. Tel: 315-737-8066.

Chenango Forks, Broome Co., St. Rita (1946), Rev. Stanley J. Gerlock.
Res., 2530 NY State Rte. 12, 13746. Tel: 607-648-8816.

Chittenango, Madison Co., St. Patrick (1853), Rev. Timothy Elmer.
Res., 1341 Murray Dr., 13037. Tel: 315-687-6105; Fax: 315-687-0046. [CEM]

Cicero, Onondaga Co., Sacred Heart (1888), Rev. Msgr. Ronald Bill; Rev. David J. James.
Res., 8229 S. Main St., 13039. Tel: 315-699-2752; Fax: 315-699-3775.

Clark Mills, Oneida Co., Church of the Annunciation (1908), Rev. J. Michael Carney.
Mailing Address: 7616 E. South St., Clinton, 13323.
Res., 25 South St., 13321. Tel: 315-853-6138.

Clayville, Oneida Co., St. Patrick (1864), Rev. William S. Baker.
Res., 8 Church St., Box 285, 13322. Tel: 315-839-5483. [CEM]

Cleveland, Oswego Co., St. Mary of the Assumption (1854), Rev. William C. Esposito.
Res., 148 State Rte. 49, 13042. Tel: 315-675-3542. [CEM]
Mission—Constantia, Oswego Co., St. Bernadette, State Rte. 49, Constantia 13044.

Clinton, Oneida Co., St. Mary (1850), Rev. John P. Croghan.
Res., 13 Marvin St., 13323. Tel: 315-853-2935. [CEM]
School—(Grades K-6) Prospect St., 13323. Tel: 315-853-6196. Ms. Martha Powers, Prin.
Lay Teachers 12; Students 177.

Cortland, Cortland Co., St. Anthony (1917) (Italian), Rev. Jerome A. Katz.
Res., 45 Crandall St., 13045. Tel: 607-756-7533.
St. Mary (1855), Rev. John P. Fenlon; Deacon Richard J. Dwyer.
Res., 44 N. Main St., 13045. Tel: 607-756-9967; Fax: 607-756-9968.
School—61 N. Main St., 13045. Sr. Harriet Hamilton, O.S.F., Prin.

Franciscan Sisters of Allegany 1; Lay Teachers 27; Students 345.

Deposit, Broome Co., St. Joseph (1851), Rev. John A. Booth.
Res., 98 Second St., 13754. Tel: 607-467-2291. [CEM]
Parish Center—74 Second St., 13754. Tel: 607-467-2226.

Dewitt, Onondaga Co., Holy Cross (1943), Revs. James E. Gehl; Gary M. Fukes. In res., Rev. Msgr. Daniel B. O'Brien, (Retired).
Res., 4112 E. Genesee St., 13214. Tel: 315-446-0473; Fax: 315-446-0482.
School—Tel: 315-446-4890. Sr. Rose Alice Carbery, O.S.F., Prin.
Sisters of the Third Franciscan Order M.C. 2; Lay Teachers 11; Students 194.

Durhamville, Oneida Co., St. Francis (1860) (German), Rev. Joseph F. Kehoe.
Res., 5334 Foster St., 13054. Tel: 315-363-1572. [CEM]
Mission—Irish Ridge, St. Mary. [CEM]

East Syracuse, Onondaga Co., St. Matthew (1880), Revs. John J. Heagerty; Leo J. Heizman. In res., Rev. Msgr. Robert F. Lavin; Deacon John Nelson.
Res., 229 W. Yates St., 13057. Tel: 315-437-8318; Fax: 315-463-6399.
School—214 Kinne St., 13057. Tel: 315-437-1339. Sr. Julienne Brandt, O.S.F., Prin.
Sisters of the Third Franciscan Order M.C. 4; Lay Teachers 16; Students 292.

Endicott, Broome Co.,

1—Our Lady of Good Counsel, (1941), Rev. Richard J. Giblin; Deacon Thomas M. Harley. In res., Rev. Robert A. Ours.
Res., 701 W. Main St., 13760. Tel: 607-748-7417.

2—St. Ambrose, (1908), Rev. Robert G. Tierney. In res., Revs. James J. O'Hanlon; Joseph Mattath, C.M.I. (India).
Res., 203 Washington Ave., 13760. Tel: 607-754-2330; Fax: 607-785-6947.

3—St. Anthony of Padua, (1917) (Italian), Rev. Clarence F. Rumble; Deacons Dominick Rossi; Frank Longo.
Res., 306 Odell Ave., 13760. Tel: 607-754-4333.
School—Consolidated. See separate listing under Institutions Located in the Diocese.

4—St. Casimir, (1928) (Polish), Rev. Mark A. Pasik.
Res., 212 N. McKinley Ave., 13760. Tel: 607-785-3262.

5—St. Joseph, (1923) (Slovak), Revs. Adam Keltos, O.F.M.Conv.; Odoric Foley, O.F.M.Conv.
Res., 207 Hayes Ave., 13760. Tel: 607-748-0442; Fax: 607-748-7725.
School—210 N. Jackson Ave., 13760. Tel: 607-748-8631; Fax: 607-748-7745. Sr. Denise Marie, S.S.C.M., Prin.
Sisters 2; Lay Teachers 11; Students 199.

Endwell, Broome Co., Christ the King (1949), Rev. Thomas F. Hobbes.
Res., 1501 Davis Ave., 13760. Tel: 607-785-3180.
Our Lady of Angels (1964), Rev. John D. Roock; Deacon George Phillips.
Res., 3600 Phyllis St., 13760. Tel: 607-754-1266.

Fairmount, Onondaga Co., Holy Family (1935), Revs. Paul F. Angelicchio; Edmund Wolak; Deacon John P. Brody.
Res., 119 Chapel Dr., Syracuse, 13219. Tel: 315-488-3139; Fax: 315-487-1112.
School—123 Chapel Dr., 13219. Tel: 315-487-8515. Linda Shulkin, Prin.

Fayetteville, Onondaga Co., Immaculate Conception (1869), Rev. Gregory C. LeStrange. Pastoral Ministers: Sr. Marcia Barry, O.S.F.; Sr. Monica Zmolek, O.S.F. In res., Rev. Msgr. Edward J. Ryan; Rev. Msgr. James A. McKloskey.
Res., 400 Salt Springs St., 13066. Tel: 315-637-9846. [CEM]
School—Tel: 315-637-3961. Sr. Elizabeth John, O.S.F., Prin.
Sisters of the Third Franciscan Order M.C. 2; Lay Teachers 16; Students 205.

Florence, Oneida Co., St. Mary (1845), Rev. James T. Queen.
Res., c/o 1807 Bedford St., Rome, 13440. Tel: 315-336-3082; Fax: 315-336-3083. [CEM]
Mission—Redfield, Oswego Co., St. Paul, Redfield, 13437.

Forestport, Oneida Co., St. Patrick (1848), Rev. John E. Phelan.
Mailing Address: P.O. Box 1, 13338. Tel: 315-392-2341; Fax: 315-392-2341. [CEM]
Mission—Otter Lake, St. Mary of the Snows.

Fulton, Oswego Co., Holy Family (1930), Rev. Richard R. Thompson. In res., Rev. John J. Daley. Pastoral Assocs.: Sr. Dorothy A. Bunal, C.S.J.; Sr. Eleanor Grace Spiridilozzi, O.S.F.
Res., 45 W. Fourth St., 13069. Tel: 315-592-4159.
Immaculate Conception (1854), Rev. William J. Brown.
Res., 57 S. Third St., 13069. Tel: 315-598-2118. [CEM]
St. Michael (1924) (Polish), Rev. Edmund S. Pilat.
Res., 301 Beech St., 13069. Tel: 315-592-7632.

Greene, Chenango Co., Immaculate Conception (1889), Rev. Richard Dellos.
Res., 20 Coventry Rd., 13778. Tel: 607-656-9546; Fax: 607-656-9546.

Hamilton, Madison Co., St. Mary (1869), Rev. Msgr. John R. Madden.
Res., 16 Wylie St., 13346. Tel: 315-824-2164. [CEM]

Hannibal, Oswego Co., Our Lady of the Rosary (1954), Rev. Moritz A. Fuchs.
Office: 923 Cayuga St., 13074-0185. Tel: 315-564-5201.
Mission—Southwest Oswego, St. Joseph.

Hinckley, Oneida Co., St. Ann (1895), Rev. Joseph E. Moskal.
Res., 13352. Tel: 315-896-2540. [CEM]

Holland Patent, Oneida Co., St. Leo (1882), Rev. Robert J. Kloster; Deacon Donald E. Joslin.
Res., Elm St., 13354. Tel: 315-865-5371.

Homer, Cortland Co., St. Margaret (1908), Rev. R. Daniel DeLorme.
Res., 14 Copeland Ave., P.O. Box 356, 13077. Tel: 607-749-2542.

Jamesville, Onondaga Co., St. Mary (1899), Rev. Raymond B. Wood.
Res., 6437 E. Seneca Tpke., P.O. Box 368, 13078-0368. Tel: 315-469-6949.

Johnson City, Broome Co., Blessed Sacrament (1945), Rev. Msgr. James D. Kane.
Res., Cenacle Plaza, 13790. Tel: 607-797-5151.
St. James (1900), Revs. Thomas J. Ryan; Daniel M. Caruso. Pastoral Assocs.: Sr. Rose Margaret Noonan, C.S.J.; Sr. Catherine Joseph McDonough, D.C.; Mr. William P. Gallagher. In res., Rev. James J. Fallon.
Res., 155 Main St., 13790. Tel: 607-729-6147.
Convent—147 Main St., 13790. Tel: 607-797-5181.

Jordan, Onondaga Co., St. Patrick (1858), Rev. Albert J. Proud.
Res., 28 N. Main St., 13080. Tel: 315-689-9051. [CEM]

Kirkwood, Broome Co., St. Mary (1888), Rev. Thomas F. Catucci.
Res., 975 NY Rte. 11, 13795. Tel: 607-775-0086.

Lacona, Oswego Co., St. Frances Xavier Cabrini (1946), Rev. John F. Hogan, Jr.
Mailing Address: c/o St. John the Evangelist, 23 Niagara St., Pulaski, 13142-4425. Tel: 315-387-3016; Fax: 315-298-3749.

Lafayette, Onondaga Co., St. Joseph (1866), Rev. Michael P. Minehan.
Res., 6104 Cherry Valley Rd., Box 169, 13084. Tel: 315-677-3439.

Lakeland, Onondaga Co., Our Lady of Peace (1935), Rev. John E. Fetcho.
Res., 203 Halcomb St., Syracuse, 13209. Tel: 315-487-6832.

Lee Center, Oneida Co., St. Joseph (1923), Rev. R. Paul Mathis. In res., Rev. Msgr. Francis J. Culkin.
Res., 13363. Tel: 315-336-2661.
Parish Center—Tel: 315-339-1890.

Liverpool, Onondaga Co.,

1—Christ the King, (1964), Rev. Patrick C. O'Leary.
Res., 26 Cherry Tree Cir., 13090. Tel: 315-652-3233; 315-652-9266 (Parish Center).

2—Immaculate Heart of Mary, (1950), Revs. John V. Ahern; Thomas P. Kobuszewski.
Res., 425 Beechwood Ave., 13088. Tel: 315-457-8060.

3—St. John, (1971), Rev. Gaetano T. Baccaro; Deacons George Maynard; Kenneth Money. In res., Rev. Leonard F. Kotzbauer.
Res., 8290 Soule Rd., 13090. Tel: 315-652-6591; Fax: 315-652-6631.

4—St. Joseph the Worker, (1890), Rev. Charles M. Major. In res., Rev. Michael J. Breen.
Res., 1001 Tulip St., 13088. Tel: 315-457-6060; Fax: 315-457-4119.

Maine, Broome Co., Holy Rosary (1944), Rev. Thomas F. Keating.
Res., 2596 Main St., Box 248, 13802. Tel: 607-862-3216.

Manlius, Onondaga Co., St. Ann (1920), Rev. Msgr. Charles H. Eckermann; Deacons John R. Murray; Gerard T. Pittman. In res., Rev. John H. Hill.
Res., 104 Academy St., 13104. Tel: 315-682-5181; Fax: 315-682-5248.

Marathon, Cortland Co., St. Stephen (1870), Rev. Lester E. Smith.
Res., 12 Academy St., P.O. Box 475, 13803. Tel: 607-849-3480.
Mission—Cincinnatus, Our Lady of Perpetual Help.

Marcellus, Onondaga Co., St. Francis Xavier (1873), Rev. J. Michael Donovan.
Res., P.O. Box 177, 1 W. Main St., 13108. Tel: 315-673-2531. [CEM]

Mattydale, Onondaga Co., St. Margaret (1926), Revs. Kevin E. Hannon; Edward F. McNally. In res., Rev. George F. Hartnett; Deacon Donald R. Whiting.
Res., 203 Roxboro Rd., Syracuse, 13211. Tel: 315-455-5534; Fax: 315-454-4102.
School—Sr. Miriam Anthony, Prin. Sisters of the Third Franciscan Order M.C. 3; Lay Teachers 12; Students 355.

Mexico, Oswego Co., St. Mary, Star of the Sea (1914), Rev. Stephen E. Wirkes.
Res., 5785 Main St., P.O. Box 487, 13114. Tel: 315-963-7182.

Minetto, Oswego Co., Our Lady of Perpetual Help (1932), Rev. Joseph M. Larkin.
Res., West River Rd., P.O. Box 236, 13115. Tel: 315-343-7922.

Minoa, Onondaga Co., St. Mary (1838), Revs. Henry F. Madigan, O.F.M.Conv.; Timothy Mulligan, O.F.M.Conv. In res., Rev. Nevin Hammon, O.F.M.Conv.
Res., 401 N. Main St., 13116. Tel: 315-656-2257; Fax: 315-633-0672. [CEM]
Office: Tel: 315-656-3441.

Morrisville, Madison Co., St. Joan of Arc (1931), Rev. Thomas P. Durant.
Parish Office: P.O. Box 1087, 13408. Tel: 315-684-9551.
Res., St. Therese Rectory, Main St., Munnsville, 13409. Tel: 315-495-2424.

Munnsville, Madison Co., St. Therese of the Infant Jesus (1926), Rev. Thomas P. Durant.
Res., St. Therese Rectory, Main St., 13409. Tel: 315-495-2424; 684-9551 (Office).

New Berlin, Chenango Co., St. Theresa of the Infant Jesus (1955), Rev. Francis J. Case, Admin.
Res., 24 N. Main St., P.O. Box 780, 13411-0780. Tel: 607-847-6851.
Mission—Leonardsville, Our Lady of the Valley.

New Hartford, Oneida Co., Our Lady of the Rosary (1949), Rev. James L. Riley.
Res., 1736 Burrstone Rd., 13413. Tel: 315-724-0402.
St. John the Evangelist (1883), Revs. Paul J. Drobin; Frederick R. Mannara; Sr. Rose Benedict Troy, C.S.J., Pastoral Assoc. In res., Rev. Msgr. Thomas J. Hayes.
Res., 66 Oxford Rd., 13413. Tel: 315-732-8521; Fax: 315-735-1569.
St. Thomas (1957), Rev. Robert Conrad. In res., Rev. John M. Quinn.
Res., 150 Clinton Rd., 13413. Tel: 315-735-8381.

New London, Oneida Co., Holy Cross (1968), Rev. Joseph F. Kehoe.
Res., 5334 Foster St., Durhamville, 13054. Tel: 315-363-1572.

New York Mills, Oneida Co., St. Mary (1909), Rev. Valentine C. Krul.
Res., 201 Main St., 13417. Tel: 315-736-4432; Fax: 315-736-8079. [CEM]
School—Consolidated. See separate listing under Institutions Located in the Diocese.

North Bay, Oneida Co., St. John (1843), Rev. Leo J. Wimett.
Res., P.O. Box A, 13123. Tel: 315-245-0853. [CEM]
Mission—Verona Beach, Oneida Co., St. Mary, Verona Beach, 13162.

North Syracuse, Onondaga Co., St. Rose of Lima (1926), Revs. James M. Kennedy; Frank Young; Sr. Corinne Mullen, O.S.F., Pastoral Min.
Parish Office: 409 S. Main St., 13212. Tel: 315-458-0283.
Res., 407 S. Main St., 13212. Tel: 315-458-0283.
School—411 S. Main St., 13212. Tel: 315-458-6036. Sr. Catherine Laboure, Prin.
Sisters of the Third Franciscan Order M.C. 8; Lay Teachers 25; Students 642.

Norwich, Chenango Co., St. Bartholomew the Apostle (1923), Rev. Joseph S. Zareski. Pastoral Ministers: Sr. Julie Eigo, C.S.J.; Helen M. Markham.
Office: 8 Silver St., 13815. Tel: 607-336-2222.
Convent—79 E. Main St., 13815. Tel: 607-334-2527.
St. Paul (1851), Rev. Douglas Cunningham.
Res., 30 Pleasant St., 13815. Tel: 607-334-4931; Fax: 607-334-6521. [CEM]

Oneida, Madison Co., St. Joseph (1893), Rev. Stanley M. Szewczyk; Rev. Msgr. Matthew C. Luczycki.
Res., 121 St. Joseph Pl., 13421. Tel: 315-363-3280.
Parish Center—111 St. Joseph Pl., 13421. Tel: 315-363-5061.
St. Patrick (1843), Rev. William A. Mesmer.
Res., 347 Main St., 13421. Tel: 315-363-7570. [CEM]
School—354 Elizabeth St., 13421. Tel: 315-363-3620.

Lay Teachers 10; Students 165.

Onondaga Hill, Onondaga Co., St. Michael (1874), Rev. Richard P. Morisette. In res., Rev. James C. Hayes. Res., 4782 W. Seneca Tpke., Syracuse, 13215. Tel: 315-469-6995.
Mission—Onondaga, St. Peter.

Oriskany, Oneida Co., St. Stephen, Protomartyr, Rev. Walter F. Cannan.
Res., 106 Dexter Ave., P.O. Box 780, 13424. Tel: 315-736-9033.

Oriskany Falls, Oneida Co., St. Joseph (1870), Rev. Vincent J. Kelly.
Res., 229 Main St., 13425. Tel: 315-821-6122. [CEM]

Oswego, Oswego Co.,

1—St. John the Evangelist, (1869), Rev. Chester A. Misercola; Deacon Peter F. Benz, Pastoral Assoc., Bus. Mgr.
Res., 38 Erie St., 13126. Tel: 315-343-4961.

2—St. Joseph, (1915) (Italian), Rev. James M. Cesta; Deacon Joseph Chillemi.
Res., 178 W. Second St., 13126. Tel: 315-343-2160.

3—St. Louis, (1870) (French), Rev. George E. Wurz, Admin.
Res., 81 E. Fourth St., 13126. Tel: 315-343-8912.

4—St. Mary, (1850), Rev. David J. Baehr.
Res., 103 W. Seventh St., P.O. Box 118, 13126. Tel: 315-343-3953.
School—76 W. Sixth St., 13126. Tel: 315-343-0700.
Lay Teachers 11; Students 165.

5—St. Paul, (1830), Rev. Eric K. Harer.
Res., 50 E. Mohawk St., 13126. Tel: 315-343-2333.
Church—134 E. Fifth St., 13126.
School—115 E. Fifth St., 13126. Tel: 315-343-6700. Mrs. Baiba Pierce, Prin.
Lay Teachers 12; Students 235.
Convent—42 E. Albany St., 13126. Tel: 315-343-9551. Sisters of St. Francis of Williamsville

6—St. Peter, (1862) (German), Rev. George E. Wurz, Admin.
Res., 83 E. Albany St., 13126. Tel: 315-343-1352.
Mission—Scriba, Sacred Heart.

7—St. Stephen the King, (1908) (Polish), Rev. Anthony Pepel.
Res., 138 Niagara St., Box 417, 13126. Tel: 315-343-0350; Fax: 315-343-0350.

Oxford, Chenango Co., St. Joseph (1849), Rev. Joseph S. Zareski.
Res., 3 Scott St., 13830. Tel: 607-843-7021. [CEM]
Station—New York State Veterans' Home, 13830.

Parish, Oswego Co., St. Ann (1950), Rev. Msgr. John M. Zeder.
Res., P.O. Box 27, 13131. Tel: 315-625-7093. [CEM]
Mailing Address: P.O. Box 33, Williamstown, 13493. Tel: 315-964-2400.
Mission—Williamstown, St. Patrick.

Phoenix, Oswego Co., St. Stephen (1880), Rev. James C. Fritzen; Deacon Frank Forish.
Res., 721 Main St., 13135. Tel: 315-695-4531; 695-4608.

Pompey, Onondaga Co., Immaculate Conception (1850), Rev. Paul V. Carey.
Res., 7386 Academy St., 13138. Tel: 315-677-3061. [CEM]
Mission—Fabius, Onondaga Co., St. Paul, Fabius, 13063.

Pulaski, Oswego Co., St. John the Evangelist (1888), Rev. John F. Hogan, Jr.; Deacon Richard E. Jenkins.
23 Niagara St., 13142-4425.
Res., 68 Park St., 13142. Tel: 315-298-5350; Fax: 315-298-3749.

Rome, Oneida Co.,

1—St. John the Baptist, (1909) (Italian), Revs. Joseph J. Clemente; John M. Wood.
Res., 210 E. Dominick St., 13440. Tel: 315-337-0990. [CEM]

2—St. Mary of the Assumption, (1848), Rev. Vincent P. Long. In res., Rev. Robert C. Weber.
Res., 210 W. Liberty St., 13440. Tel: 315-336-4832. [CEM]
Station—Rome, Betsy Ross HRF.

3—St. Paul, (1954), Rev. Msgr. William M. Kelly; Rev. James T. Queen; Deacon Nicholas A. Rosher.
Res., 1807 Bedford St., 13440-2199. Tel: 315-336-3082; Fax: 315-336-3083.

4—St. Peter, (1837), Rev. Philip A. Hearn. Pastoral Assocs.: Sr. Ellen John Emmons, C.S.J.; Sr. Ursula Marie Murphy, C.S.J.; Sr. Phyllis Wulforst, C.S.J. In res., Rev. James A. Culver.
Res., 105 E. Liberty St., 13440. Tel: 315-336-5072; 337-8307. [CEM]

5—Transfiguration, (1909) (Polish), Rev. William P. Gleba. In res., Revs. William C. Cahill; Eugene Rosielski.
Res., 111 Ridge St., 13440. Tel: 315-336-1152; Fax: 315-339-5931.
School—(Grades K-6) 400 S. James St., 13440. Tel: 315-336-3430. Mrs. Cheryl Canfield, Prin.
Lay Teachers 7; Students 116.

Sanitaria Springs, Broome Co., St. Joseph (1914), Rev. Kevin J. Bunger, Admin.
Res., 659 New York Rte. 7, P.O. Box 429, Port Crane, 13833. Tel: 607-648-5209.

Sherburne, Chenango Co., St. Malachy (1858), Rev. Edmund A. Castronovo.
Res., 31 E. State St., 13460. Tel: 607-674-2791. [CEM]

Sherrill, Oneida Co., St. Helena (1917), Rev. John J. Costello.
Res., 210 Primo Ave., 13461. Tel: 315-363-3882. [CEM]

Skaneateles, Onondaga Co., St. Mary of the Lake (1855), Rev. Thomas J. McGrath; Deacon Robert Borchert.
Res., 81 Jordan St., 13152. Tel: 315-685-5083. [CEM]

Solvay, Onondaga Co., St. Cecilia (1903), Revs. Angelo L. Morbito; Robert J. Birchmeyer; Deacon Julius Kulak.
Res., 1001 Woods Rd., 13209. Tel: 315-488-3221.
Convent—502 Gertrude Ave., 13209. Tel: 315-468-1273. Sr. Anne Rutledge, O.S.F., Supr.

South Onondaga, Onondaga Co., Corpus Christi (1938), Rev. Dennis J. Hayes.
Res., 4466 S. Onondaga Rd., Nedrow, 13120. Tel: 315-492-0814.
Church—3126 Cedarvale Rd., R.D. 1, Nedrow, 13120. Tel: 315-492-0814.
Apostolate—Onondaga Indian Reservation. [CEM]

Taberg, Oneida Co., St. Patrick (1876), Rev. Francis A. Wapen.
Res., 9170 Main St., 13471. Tel: 315-336-4079. [CEM]
Mission—Glenmore, St. Anne, (1846).

Truxton, Cortland Co., St. Patrick (1854), Rev. David J. Jutton.
Res., 3656 Rte. 13, Box 15, 13158. Tel: 607-842-6326. [CEM]
Mission—DeRuyter, St. Lawrence.

Tully, Onondaga Co., St. Leo (1891), Rev. Louis F. Aiello.
Res., 10 Onondaga St., 13159. Tel: 315-696-5092.
Mission—Otisco, St. Patrick.

Utica, Oneida Co.,

1—Blessed Sacrament, (1924), Rev. Robert L. Kelly; Sr. Teresa Waldron, O.S.F., Pastoral Min.
Res., 1603 St. Agnes Ave., 13501. Tel: 315-724-8131.
School—Consolidated. See separate listing under Institutions Located in the Diocese.

2—Holy Trinity, (1896) (Polish), Revs. Arthur R. Hapanowicz; Richard J. Wilczynski (Poland); Deacon Wilbur H. Hazard.
Res., 1206 Lincoln Ave., 13502. Tel: 315-724-7238; Fax: 315-797-2130. [CEM]
School—(Grades PreK-6) 1214 Lincoln Ave., 13502. Tel: 315-724-0540. Sr. Mary Beatrice, C.S.F.N., Prin. & Supr.
Religious 7; Lay Teachers 12; Students 232.
Convent—1218 Lincoln Ave., 13502. Tel: 315-733-5492.

3—Our Lady of Lourdes, (1919), Rev. Msgr. William J. Donovan; Revs. Sean P. O'Brien; Patrick Kanja Washira (Kenya); Deacon Paul M. Mullin; Sr. Julia Coyle, S.A. In res., Rev. Jerome F. Weber.
Res., 2 Barton Ave., 13502. Tel: 315-724-3155; Fax: 315-732-3346.
School—Consolidated. See separate listing under Institutions Located in the Diocese.

4—Sacred Heart, (1926), Rev. John Flanagan; Sr. Joan Blanch, C.S.J., Pastoral Assoc. In res., Rev. Hyacinth Seremet; Deacon John Kopec.
Res., 2115 Caroline St., 13502. Tel: 315-735-6105; Fax: 315-735-0216.
School—(Grades PreK-6) 1109 Ney Ave., 13502. Tel: 315-724-3612. Sr. Roseann Klosterman, C.S.J., Prin.
Religious 1; Lay Teachers 9; Students 195.

5—St. Agnes, (1887), Rev. Msgr. Francis J. Willenburg.
Res., 700 Kossuth Ave., 13501. Tel: 315-735-5273; Fax: 315-735-5274.
Convent—783 Blandina St., 13501. Tel: 315-732-1078.

6—St. Anthony of Padua, (1911) (Italian), Revs. Felix R. Colosimo; Anthony LaFache; Deacon William Dischiavo.
Res., 422 Tilden Ave., 13501. Tel: 315-732-1177.

7—St. Francis de Sales, (1876), Rev. Frederick D. Daley.
Res., 1119 Elm St., 13501. Tel: 315-732-6171; Fax: 315-735-3503.

8—St. George, (1911) (Lithuanian), Rev. Donald H. Karlen.
Res., 702 Columbia St., 13502. Tel: 315-735-4429. [CEM]

9—St. John, (1819), Rev. John A. Buehler. Pastoral Assocs.: Sr. Catherine Joseph Croghan, C.S.J.; Sr. Mary Theresa Kobosinski, D.C.; Deacon William R. Dischiavo.
Res., 240 Bleecker St., 13501. Tel: 315-724-6159.
Parish Apostolate Center—520 John St., 13501. Tel: 315-732-2417. Sr. Mary Theresa Kobosinski, D.C.

10—St. Joseph and St. Patrick, (1841 and 1849), Rev. Donald H. Karlen. In res., Revs. Joseph E. Moskal; Donald J. Bauer; James Q. Quinn; Theodore Sash, O.F.M.Conv.
Res., 702 Columbia St., 13502. Tel: 315-735-4429; Fax: 315-735-1691.

11—St. Mark, (1963), Rev. Lucian Urbaniak.
Res., 440 Keyes Rd., 13502. Tel: 315-724-1645.

12—St. Mary, (1870), Rev. Richard V. O'Neill.
Res., 421 South St., 13501. Tel: 315-724-0083.

13—St. Mary of Mt. Carmel, (1896) (Italian), Revs. Joseph Salerno; Luis Olguin; Peter Williams; Deacon Robert Riggalls.
Res., 648 Jay St., 13501. Tel: 315-735-1482; Fax: 315-735-9806.

14—St. Peter, (1872), Rev. Msgr. H. Charles Sewall; Rev. Edward Kwoka.
Res., 422 Coventry Ave., 13502. Tel: 315-724-6310; Fax: 315-724-4942. [CEM]
School—(Grades PreK-6) 19 Herkimer Rd., 13502. Tel: 315-724-4708. Mrs. Maria Pilla, Prin.
Religious 1; Lay Teachers 13; Students 200.

15—St. Stanislaus, (1911) (Polish), Rev. Casimir J. Krzysiak.
Res., 607 Nichols St., 13501. Tel: 315-732-5919. [CEM]

Vernon, Oneida Co., Holy Family (1926; 1976), Rev. Edwin T. Comeskey.
Res., 4343 Peterboro St., P.O. Box 988, 13476. Tel: 315-829-3295.

Verona, Oneida Co., Our Lady of Good Counsel (1913), Rev. Edmund J. Morelle.
Res., 5259 Beacon Rd., P.O. Box 135, 13478. Tel: 315-363-7696.

Vestal, Broome Co., Our Lady of Sorrows (1941), Revs. Donald C. VanAmburgh; John Broderick. In res., Rev. Mathew F. Brown.
Res., 157 Clark St., P.O. Box 408, 13850. Tel: 607-748-8287.
St. Vincent de Paul (1965), Rev. C. Vincent Lane; Deacon James P. Crowley. In res., Rev. Richard Hunt, S.J.
Res., 165 Clifton Blvd., 13850. Tel: 607-722-3988.

Warners, Onondaga Co., Our Lady of Good Counsel (1913), Rev. Vincent J. Kilpatrick.
Res., Newport Rd., Box 69, 13164. Tel: 315-672-3725.
Parish Hall—Tel: 315-672-3750.

Waterville, Oneida Co., St. Bernard (1850), Rev. Richard J. Kapral.
Res., 199 Stafford Ave., 13480. Tel: 315-841-4481. [CEM]
Mission—North Brookfield, St. Mary.

Whitesboro, Oneida Co., St. Anne (1965), Rev. Frederick J. Prevost. In res., Rev. Msgr. Thomas M. Doran.
Res., 8539 Clark Mills Rd., 13492-2754. Tel: 315-736-7672.
St. Paul (1883), Rev. Abraham L. Esper.
Res., 16 Park Ave., 13492. Tel: 315-736-1124; Fax: 315-768-7915.

Whitney Point, Broome Co., St. Patrick (1869), Rev. James P. Serowik.
Res., Box 711, 13862. Tel: 607-692-3911. [CEM]

Windsor, Broome Co., Our Lady of Lourdes (1947), Rev. Daniel G. Murphy.
Res., P.O. Box 361, 13865. Tel: 607-655-2116.

Chaplains of Public Institutions

Hospitals

Syracuse. *Community General Hospital,* Broad Rd., 13215. Tel: 315-492-5011. Rev. James Hayes; Sr. Mary Ann Kane, O.S.F.

Crouse Irving Memorial Hospital, 736 Irving Ave., 13210. Tel: 315-470-7615. Rev. George Hartnett; Sr. Carmel Rose Nicita; Sr. Antonella Giba, C.S.J.

James Square Nursing Home. Attended from Blessed Sacrament Parish.

Loretto Geriatric Center, 700 E. Brighton Ave., 13205. Tel: 315-469-5570. Rev. Wilbur Votraw.

Plaza Extended Care Facility. Tel: 315-474-4431. Sr. Monica Hogan, C.S.J.

St. Camillus Health & Rehab Center, 813 Fay Rd., 13219. Tel: 315-488-2951. Ms. Mary Grace McGuire, Chap.

St. Joseph's Hospital Health Center, 301 Prospect

Ave., 13203. Tel: 315-448-5116. Revs. Robert Amrhein, O.F.M.Conv.; Firmin Finn, O.F.M.Conv.; Sr. Marie Therese Nicholson, O.S.F.; Sr. Patrice Ward, O.S.F.; Sr. Mary Louise Williams, O.S.F.; Sr. Jacqueline Spiridlozzi, Dir.; Sr. Frances Agnes Ryan; Sr. Mary Daniel Golmbieski.

University Hospital, 750 E. Adams St., 13210. Tel: 315-464-5540. Rev. Alfred J. Bebel; Sr. Mary Francellette.

Van Duyn Home & Hospital, Tel: 315-469-5511. Rev. Msgr. Robert B. Davern; Susan Marcoccia.

Veterans Administration Hospital. Res: 800 Irving Ave., 13210. Tel: 315-476-7461. Rev. Wilfred F. Evans.

BINGHAMTON. *Binghamton General Hospital.* Tel: 607-762-2200. Rev. John Mikalajunas; Sr. Joan Thomas Mcherney, C.S.J.

Binghamton Psychiatric Hospital. Revs. John Booth; Gerald J. Buckley.

Broome Developmental Center. Tel: 607-770-0211. Rev. Paul Keebler.

Our Lady of Lourdes Memorial Hospital, 179 Riverside Dr., 13905. Tel: 607-798-5111. Sr. Ann Molesevick, D.C., Dir.; Rev. Chris Boretto; Bro. Daniel Gallucci; Sr. Mary Roark; Sr. Catherine Marie McGranary.

JOHNSON CITY. *Wilson Memorial Hospital,* 33 Harrison St., 13790. Tel: 607-763-6000. Rev. Timothy Taugher.

LIVERPOOL. *Developmental Center,* 36 Grampian Rd. #5, 13090. Rev. Charles A. Aho.

ROME. *Central New York Developmental Services Office.* Vacant. P.O. Box 550, Lower South James, 13442-0550. Tel: 315-336-2300, Ext. 251.

UTICA. *Faxton Hospital,* 1676 Sunset Ave., 13502. Tel: 315-738-6545. Sr. Maureen Denn, C.S.J.

St. Elizabeth Hospital, 2209 Genesee St., 13501. Tel: 315-798-8100. Rev. Matthew Thelly; Sr. Irene Zegarelli, O.S.F.; Sr. Mary Nicholas Amodio, O.S.F.; Sr. Margaret Woods, O.S.F.

St. Luke, Champlin Ave., 13503. Tel: 315-798-6000. Sr. Genevieve Ciscek, C.S.J.; Sr. Susanne Bonville, C.S.J.; Rev. Donald Hebert.

VESTAL. *Binghamton Nursing Homes,* Our Lady of Sorrows, 157 Clark St., 13850. Tel: 607-748-8287. Rev. Matthew F. Brown, Pastoral Care Chap.

Psychiatric Facilities

SYRACUSE. *Hutchings Psychiatric Center,* 406 Court St., 13208. Tel: 315-473-4980. Rev. Michael A. Dietrich.

BINGHAMTON. *Binghamton Psychiatric Hospital.* Tel: 607-724-1391. Revs. John Booth; Gerald J. Buckley.

MARCY. *Central New York Psychiatric Center,* Old River Rd., Box 330, 13403. Tel: 315-736-8271. Rev. Richard O'Neill.

UTICA. *Mohawk Valley Psychiatric Center,* 1400 Noyes at York, 13502. Rev. Frederick Daley.

Jails

SYRACUSE. *Elmcrest Children's Center.* Vacant. Salt Springs Rd., 13224.

Hillbrook Detention Center, 4949 Velasko Rd., 13215. Tel: 315-492-1721. Sr. Judith Falk.

Jail Ministry Office. Vacant. 208 Slocum Ave., 13204. Tel: 315-424-1877.

Public Safety Building, 342 Vine St., 13203. Tel: 315-424-1877. William M. Cuddy.

BINGHAMTON. *Broome County Jail.* Vacant. Rev. Stanley Gerlock.

CORTLAND. *Cortland County Jail.* Vacant.

GEORGETOWN. *Camp Georgetown,* 31 E. State St., Sheburne, 13346. Tel: 315-837-4446. Rev. Edmund A. Castronovo.

JAMESVILLE. *Jamesville Penitentiary,* P.O. Box 143, 13078. Tel: 315-469-5581. Rev. Edward Reimer; Sr. Maura Rhode.

MARCY. *Mid-State Correctional Facility,* 210 W. Liberty St., 13403. Tel: 315-768-8581. Rev. Robert C. Weber.

MOHAWK. *Oneida Correctional Facility I,* P.O. Box 8450, Rome, 13440. Tel: 315-339-6880. Rev. William C. Cahill.

Oneida Correctional Facility II, 578 Main St., P.O. Box 8450, Oneida, 13421. Deacon James Chappell.

NORWICH. *Norwich County Jail.* Vacant.

ORISKANY. *Oneida County Jail,* 120 Dexter Ave., 13424. Tel: 315-736-9033. Rev. Richard J. Stuczko.

OSWEGO. *Oswego County Jail,* 178 W. Second St., 13126. Tel: 315-343-2160. Rev. Msgr. Francis J. Furfaro.

ROME. *Walsh Facility.* Tel: 315-339-5232. Rev. Luis Olguin.

SOUTH PLYMOUTH. *Camp Pharsalia.* Rev. Edmund A. Castronovo.

UTICA. *Marcy Correctional Facility,* 15-8 Rox Pl., 13502. Tel: 315-768-1400. Deacon William Hotaling.

Special Assignment:
Reverend Fathers—
Aho, Charles A.
Bebel, Alfred J.
Brown, Matthew F.
Cahill, William C.
Carmola, Michael J.
Casey, Robert A.
Catucci, Thomas F.
Chryst, Robert D.
Costello, Thomas J.
Croghan, John P.
Davern, Robert B.
Dietrich, Michael A.
Donovan, John P.
Evans, Wilfred F.
Hartnett, George F.
Hayes, James C.
Hebert, Donald J.
Kopp, Richard M.
Lang, James P.
Lauducci, V. James
Mattice, George F.
Minehan, Michael P.
Moynihan, James M.
Muscalino, Daniel C.
O'Heron, Edward J.
Olguin, Luis
Ours, Robert A.
Philips, Joseph H.
Pompei, Frederick A.
Quartier, Neal E.
Quinn, James F.
Sambor, David R.
Schopfer, John C.
Seremet, Hyacinth
Slater, Dennis W.
Sullivan, Robert J.
Taugher, Timothy J.
Vavonese, Charles S.
Votraw, William J.
Weber, Jerome F.
Weber, Robert C.
Williams, Peter A.
Worn, G. Peter
Yeazel, J. Robert

On Duty Outside the Diocese:
Reverend Monsignors—
Fahey, Charles J., Fordham University, New York, NY
Sewall, Charles H.
Reverend Fathers—
Bassano, Michael
Cincotta, Anthony
Harrold, John
Heintz, Daniel W.
Keane, Philip S.
Nichols, Louis J.
Pelkey, Richard
Rossetti, Stephen
Schoenhofen, Darr, North American College, Rome, Italy
Sears, G. David, Staten Island, NY
Wagner, John P.
Wallace, Harry C.
Walsh, Vincent
Woolever, James

Military Chaplains:
Reverend Fathers—
Dunn, Richard, U.S. Air Force
Elkin, Fredic F., U.S. Navy
Gryga, Theodore, U.S. Navy
Madej, Paul D., U.S. Navy

Graduate Studies:
Reverend Fathers—
Baraski, Andrew, The Catholic University of America, Washington, D.C.

Absent on Leave:
Reverend Fathers—
Lupa, Gerard
Pichette, David
Quinn, James A.

Absent on Sick Leave:
Reverend Fathers—
Fallon, James J.
Florczyk, Walter
Moskal, Joseph

Sabbatical:
Reverend Fathers—
Keefe, Anthony J.
Mannara, Frederick R.

Retired:
Reverend Monsignors—
Borgognoni, Charles L.
Casey, Robert A.
Culkin, Francis J.
Denti, Carl J.
Dillon, Robert E.
Doran, Thomas M.
Dwyer, M. Shields
Furfaro, Francis J.
Giblin, Lawrence E.
Hayes, Thomas J.
Kantor, Adolph A.
Lavin, Robert F.
Luczycki, Matthew
McCloskey, James A.
O'Brien, Daniel B.
Ryan, Edward J.
Sammons, Francis L.
Reverend Fathers—
Bauer, Donald J.
Brennan, Robert E.
Cummings, Frederick F.
D'Alessandro, Salvatore
Daley, John J.
Doran, Matthew J.
Dwyer, William M.
Guyder, Thomas F.
Hall, Robert E.
Hearn, Edward C.
Hill, John H.
Jakubik, Emil
Kent, Joseph E.
Kiernan, Thomas
Libera, Angelo
Majdanik, Albin J.
Manning, Thomas J.
McCabe, William J.
McKay, Robert J.
Mulranen, John J.
Neary, Thomas E.
Nold, Joseph K.
O'Hanlon, James J.
Pilla, P. Carl
Ploeckl, Joseph M.
Prozny, Leopold V.
Regan, William P.
Segrue, Joseph D.
Shanahan, William J.
Sizing, Theodore
Stuczko, Richard J.
Tucker, Richard
Walsh, Bernard
Wright, Robert

Permanent Deacons:
Altmeter, Robert (ROC), Norwich
Ashley, John, Binghamton
Benz, Peter F., Baldwinsville
Blaine, Edward, Endicott
Borchert, Robert, Skaneateles
Brody, John P., Camillus
Brush, Wesley J., Madison, WI, (On Leave)
Busch, Robert L., Syracuse
Carranti, Pio Peter, Syracuse
Castro, Joseph, North Syracuse
Chappell, James C., Oneida
Chiesa, Richard J., Camillus
Chillemi, Joseph, Oswego
Collins, John H., Pennellville
Cretaro, John T., Oswego
Crosby, James P., Syracuse (On Leave)
Crossett, Thomas F., Johnson City (On Leave)
Crowley, James, Vestal
Dischiavo, William R., Utica
Distin, Leslie, Johnson City
Dotterer, William A., Liverpool
Droz, John J., Sr., (Retired), New Hartford
Dwyer, Richard J., Cortland
Forish, Frank M., Baldwinsville
Gallagher, James T., Binghamton (On Leave)
Goskowski, Raymond, Binghamton
Hachey, Thomas, North Syracuse
Harley, Thomas, Sanitaria Springs
Hazard, Wilbur, Utica
Hotaling, William P., Utica
Joslin, Donald E., Holland Patent
Kopec, John
Kotch, Myron, (Eastern Rite), Syracuse
Kulak, Julius F., Solvay
Longo, Frank A., Endicott
Mailloux, William, Baldwinsville
Manzene, Stephen, Liverpool
Matzke, Leo P., Central Square
Maynard, George E., Clay
McGrath, Michael B., Syracuse
Money, Kenneth, Liverpool
Monnat, Leonard S., Syracuse
Morse, James L., Syracuse
Mulvey, John, Syracuse
Murray, John, Manlius
Needham, Leo I., Syracuse
Nelson, John J., Kirkville
O'Connor, Charles, Syracuse
Phillips, George, Endwell
Pittman, Gerard, Fayetteville
Powers, Paul F., Afton

Riggalls, Robert, Sr., Waterville
Rossi, Dominic L., Endicott
Sims, John E., Endwell (On Leave from Diocese)
Sweenie, David, Oswego
Trepa, John, Greene
Vanelli, Peter P., Syracuse
Vinciguerra, Ralph S., Syracuse
Warren, Franklin, Oswego
Whiting, Donald R., North Syracuse
Wilber, Richard, Chesire, CT, (On Leave)
Winslow, Frank L., Utica
Woeste, James (NOR), Syracuse

INSTITUTIONS LOCATED IN THE DIOCESE

[A] SEMINARIES, RELIGIOUS, OR SCHOLASTICATES

SYRACUSE. *Saint Andrew Hall*, 420 Demong Dr., 13214-1499. Tel: 315-446-0142. Novitiate for the New York and Maryland Provinces, Society of Jesus. Revs. Gerald R. Blaszczak, S.J., Rector & Dir. Novices; Bruce A. Maivelett, S.J., Assoc. Dir.; James F. Smith, S.J., Min. & Treas. Priests 3; Novices 16.

SKANEATELES. *Roosevelt Hall*, 1 Tallcot Ln., 13152. Tel: 315-685-6417. Novitiate for the United States/ Toronto Brothers of the Christian Schools. Bro. Timothy Wentworth, F.S.C., Dir. Novices. Brothers 8.

[B] COLLEGES AND UNIVERSITIES

SYRACUSE. *Le Moyne College*, 13214.
For a complete listing, refer to the Colleges and Universities section.

[C] HIGH SCHOOLS, DIOCESAN

SYRACUSE. *Bishop Ludden Junior/Senior High School*, 815 Fay Rd., 13219. Tel: 315-468-2591. Mr. Dennis J. Meehan, Prin. Priests 1; Sisters 5; Lay Teachers 42; Students 684.

BINGHAMTON. *Seton Catholic Central High School of Broome County*, 70 Seminary Ave., 13905. Tel: 607-723-5307. Ms. Kathleen M. Dwyer, Prin.; Mr. Max Deus, Asst. Prin.; Rev. Robert A. Ours. Priests 1; Sisters 3; Lay Teachers 42; Students 483.

EAST SYRACUSE. *Bishop Grimes Jr./Sr. High School*, 6653 Kirkville Rd., 13057. Tel: 315-437-0356. Rev. George F. Sheehan, Prin. Priests 2; Sisters 4; Lay Teachers 27; Students 451.

ROME. *Rome Catholic Junior-Senior High School*, 800 Cypress St., 13440. Tel: 315-336-6190. Sr. de Paul Juliano, O.S.F., Prin.; Rev. James T. Queen. Priests 1; Sisters 2; Lay Teachers 25; Students 300.

UTICA. *Notre Dame Jr./Sr. High School*, 2 Notre Dame Lane, 13502. Tel: 315-724-5118. Mrs. Kathleen Donovan. Sisters 4; Lay Teachers 48; Students 596.

[D] HIGH SCHOOLS, PRIVATE

SYRACUSE. *Christian Brothers Academy*. (Grades 9-12), 6245 Randall Rd., 13214. Tel: 315-446-5960. Bro. Michael Shubnell, F.S.C., Prin. Brothers of the Christian Schools 3; Sisters 1; Lay Teachers 45; Students 482.

[E] JUNIOR HIGH SCHOOLS, DIOCESAN

SYRACUSE. *All Saints Junior High School*, 301 Valley Dr., 13207. Tel: 315-472-7488. Joan Theresa Smith, Prin. Lay Teachers 3; Students 34.

[F] JUNIOR HIGH SCHOOLS, PRIVATE

SYRACUSE. *Christian Brothers Academy*. (Grades 7-8), 6245 Randall Rd., 13214. Tel: 315-446-5960. Students 244.

[G] CONSOLIDATED SCHOOLS

BINGHAMTON. *St. Catherine*. (Grades PreK-3), 1051 Chenango St., 13901. Tel: 607-722-2028. Ms. Mary Ellen Meskell, Prin. Lay Teachers 9; Students 141.
St. John the Evangelist. (Grades K-8), 9 Livingston St., 13903. Tel: 607-723-0703. Sr. Albert J. Guzzi, Prin. Religious 10; Lay Teachers 18; Students 370.
St. Patrick Academy. (Grades 4-8), 58 Oak St., 13905. Tel: 607-723-4601. Mr. Curt Czarniak, Prin. Lay Teachers 9; Students 105.
St. Thomas Aquinas. (Grades PreK-3), 3 Aquinas St., 13905. Tel: 607-797-6528. Sr. Katharine Earley, C.S.J., Prin. Religious 1; Lay Teachers 10; Students 138.

ENDICOTT. *St. Anthony*. (Grades Nursery-4), 906 Jenkins St., 13760. Tel: 607-754-0875. Sr. Paul Kathryn Barno, C.S.J., Prin. Religious 1; Lay Teachers 8; Students 194.
Seton Catholic Middle School. (Grades 5-8), 1112 Broad St., 13760. Tel: 607-748-7423. Ms. Anne Cowling, Prin. Lay Teachers 7; Students 120.

FULTON. *Fulton Catholic*, 309 Buffalo St., 13069. Tel: 315-593-2049. Serves the parishes of Fulton, Phoenix, Mexico & Hannibal. Margaret Donnelly, Prin. Lay Teachers 12; Students 101; Pre-K 19.

JOHNSON CITY. *Blessed Sacrament*. (Grades PreK-3), Cenacle Plaza, 13790. Tel: 607-729-3302. Mary Ellen Kelley, Prin. Lay Teachers 12; Students 226.
St. James Middle School, 143 Main St., 13790. Tel: 607-797-5444. Mrs. Maria Carucci, Prin. Sisters 2; Lay Teachers 11; Students 218.

NORWICH. *Holy Family School*. (Grades PreK-6), 17 Prospect St., 13815. Tel: 607-334-6934. Sr. Marie Denise Monser, C.S.J., Prin. Sisters 1; Lay Teachers 11; Students 120.

ROME. *St. Peter*. (Grades K-6), 400 Floyd Ave., 13440. Tel: 315-336-2360. Sr. Cheryl Canfield, C.S.S.F., Prin. Religious 1; Lay Teachers 12; Students 166.

UTICA. *Our Lady of Lourdes*. (Grades PreK-6), 10 Barton Ave , 13502. Tel: 315-732-4374. Mrs. Carol Polito, Prin. Lay Teachers 26; Students 543.

VESTAL. *Our Lady of Sorrows*. (Grades PreK-4), 801 Main St., 13850. Tel: 607-785-3214. Barbara Vanston, Prin. Lay Teachers 5; Students 187.

[H] CATHOLIC CHARITIES OF SYRACUSE

SYRACUSE. *Catholic Charities of the Roman Catholic Diocese of Syracuse*, 240 E. Onondaga St., 13202. Tel: 315-424-1830. Rev. Robert B. Stephenson, Exec. Vice Pres.; Mr. Brian Walton, Area Dir., 1654 W. Onondaga St., 13204. Tel: 315-424-1800. Mr. Paul Welch, Assoc. Dir., 1654 W. Onondaga St., 13204. Tel: 315-424-1800. Kevin Domanico, Chief Financial Officer, 1654 W. Onondaga St., 13204. Tel: 315-424-1800. Kay Muller, Dir. Human Resources; Patricia Walton, Exec. Dir., Toomey Residential Svcs.; Mark Clary, Assoc. Dir.; Joseph O'Hara, Dir. Devel.
Jail Ministry, Slocum House, 208 Slocum Ave., 13204. Mary Czelusniak, Coordinator.
Keener Seniors, 1654 W. Onondaga St., 13204. Tel: 315-424-1804. Nutrition Program for the Elderly. Mr. Jack Haney, Dir.

BINGHAMTON. *Associated Catholic Charities*, 232 Main St., 13905. Tel: 607-729-9166. Mr. Joseph G. Slavik, Exec. Admin.
Catholic Charities Adolescent Group Home, 57 Chestnut St., 13905. Tel: 607-723-6355. Ms. Karen Cerasaro, Dir.
The Catholic Foundation of Broome County, 232 Main St., 13905. Tel: 607-729-9166; Fax: 607-729-2062. Mr. Robert W. Aber, Pres. Legal Title: *The Bishops Catholic Education and Charities Foundation, Inc.*
Catholic Social Services of Broome County, 232 Main St., 13905. Tel: 607-729-9166. Mr. Daniel L. Yeager, M.A., Exec. Dir.; Grazia Tonelli, C.S.W., Supervisor of Clinical Services.

CORTLAND. *Catholic Charities of Cortland County*, 33-35 Central Ave., 13045. Tel: 607-756-5992. Paula Currie, Dir.
Case Management Services.
Residential Services. (Lawrence House Community Residence). Supported Housing; Supportive Apartments. Alcohol Halfway House & Recovery Apartments.
Food Pantry. Emergency Assistance Program, Foster Care.
Catholic Charities-STEPS-TASA, 33-35 Central Ave., 13045. Tel: 607-756-5992; Fax: 607-756-5999. (Supportive Teen Education-Parents Services), TASA; Case Management; Men's Support Group.

FULTON. *Catholic Charities of Oswego County*, 365 W. First St., 13069. Tel: 315-598-3980. 108 E. Sixth St., Oswego, 13126. Tel: 315-343-9540. Andrea McCabe, Area Dir.

NORWICH. *Chenango County Catholic Charities*, 3 O'Hara Dr., 13815. Tel: 607-334-8244.
The Counseling Program. See separate listing.
Chenango House, 49 Fair St., 13815. Tel: 607-336-8939. Supervised by Community Residence Program.
Intensive Supportive Apartment Program. 49 Fair St., 13815. Tel: 607-336-4359.
Supported Housing Program. 49 Fair St., 13815. Tel: 607-336-4492.
Crossbridge Adolescent Home. Granville Hill Rd., 13460. Tel: 607-674-9422.
Community Residence Program. Catholic Charities of Chenango County, 3 O'Hara Dr., 13815. Tel: 607-334-8244; Fax: 607-336-5779. Provides housing for mentally ill adults and adolescent boys.
The Counseling Program. Catholic Charities of Chenango County, 3 O'Hara Dr., 13815. Tel: 607-334-8244; Fax: 607-336-5779. Jane Coddington, Dir. Provides comprehensive counseling for children/ adults and specialized counseling for abused children.
Crime Victims-Witness Assistance Program. Catholic Charities of Chenango County, 3 O'Hara Dr., 13815. Tel: 607-336-1528. Provides 24 hour Hotline at 607-336-1101, Crisis Intervention, Safe Dwelling, Safe Housing; Court accompaniment; filing affidavits and claims with Crime Victims Board; advocacy with law enforcement agencies; information and referrals.

ONEIDA. *Madison County Catholic Charities*, 119 E. Walnut St., 13421. Tel: 315-363-5274. Dennis Manning, Exec. Dir.; Sue Panetta, Assoc. Dir.

ROME. *Catholic Charities of Rome*, 212 W. Liberty St., 13440. Tel: 315-337-8600. Kathleen O. Mahoney, Dir.

UTICA. *Catholic Charities, Eastern Region*, 1408 Genesee St., 13502. Tel: 315-724-2150. Mr. Dennis Manning, Area Dir.; Kathleen C. Eichenlaub, Dir. of Admin.; Anthony J. Conestabile, Dir. of Finance; Nanette Conney, Dir. of Residential Support; Kathleen O. Mahoney, Dir. of Family & Community Support.
Catholic Social Services of Utica, 1408 Genesee St., 13502. Tel: 315-724-3167. Leslee Kovel, Assoc. Dir.

[I] OFFICES OF HUMAN DEVELOPMENT

SYRACUSE. *Bishop Foery Foundation*, 401 South Ave., 13204. Tel: 315-474-6823. Socio-Educational instruction center for racial minorities.
Childcare Center. Larry King, Dir.

BINGHAMTON. *Broome County Human Development*, 232 Main St., 13905. Tel: 607-729-9166; Fax: 607-729-2062. Mrs. Frances C. Scoville, Dir.

[J] ST. VINCENT DE PAUL SOCIETY

SYRACUSE. *St. Vincent de Paul Furniture and Clothing Inc.*, 500 Seymour St., 13204. Tel: 315-476-4797. 755 N. Salina, 13208. Tel: 315-476-4659; 476-4686; 475-1717. 2849 S. Salina, 13205. Tel: 315-478-0809. Mr. John Graham, Dir.; Mr. David Suchewski, Mgr.
St. Vincent de Paul Society, 500 Seymour St., 13204. Tel: 315-476-4797. Mr. John Graham, Dir.

FULTON. *St. Vincent de Paul Thrift Shop*, 365 W. First St., 13069. Tel: 315-598-3980.

[K] CATHOLIC YOUTH ORGANIZATIONS

SYRACUSE. *Alliance Division, Catholic Charities*, 1654 W. Onondaga St., 13204. Tel: 315-424-1880; Fax: 315-424-6045. Mark Clary, Assoc. Dir.
Brighton Family Center, 100 Edmund Ave., 13205. Tel: 315-424-9378. Ms. Patricia Campany, Dir.
Catholic Charities, 1654 W. Onondaga St., 13204. Tel: 315-424-1800. Brian Walton, Area Dir.
Family Division, Catholic Charities, 1654 W. Onondaga St., 13204. Tel: 315-424-1840. Mr. Hugh Gratz, Assoc. Dir.
Hawley Youth Organization, 716 Hawley Ave., 13203. Tel: 315-472-6343. Dotti Barraco Hetnar, Dir.
Near East Side Adventures Program, 1085 E. Genesee St., 13210. Tel: 315-472-6362. Richard Kline, Dir.
Neighborhood Division, Catholic Charities, 1654 W. Onondaga St., 13204. Tel: 315-424-1804. Mr. Paul Welch, Assoc. Dir.
Northside CYO, 527 N. Salina St., 13208. Tel: 315-474-7428.
Salina Civic Center, 2826 Lemoyne Ave., Mattydale, 13211. Tel: 315-455-7096. Sandra Diefendorf, Dir.
Toomey Residential and Community Services Corp., 1654 W. Onondaga St., 13204. Tel: 315-424-1845; Fax: 315-424-7567. Patricia M. Walton, Exec. Dir.
Vincent House, 514 Seymour St., 13204. Tel: 315-475-9844. Mr. John Graham, Branch Dir.

BINGHAMTON. *Broome County CYO*, 232 Main St., 13905. Tel: 607-729-5190. Kevin McGoff, Exec. Dir.

FULTON. *CYO Fulton*, 365 W. First St., 13069. Tel: 315-598-3980. Mr. James Smiley, Dir.

UTICA. *Catholic Charities, Youth Services Division*, 1408 Genesee St., 13502. Tel: 315-724-6118. Mr. James T. Carroll, Dir.

[L] CHILDREN'S INSTITUTIONS AND DAY CARE CENTERS

SYRACUSE. *DePaul Day Care Corporation*, 1654 W. Onondaga St., 13204. Tel: 315-424-8129. Mrs. Sharon Coulter, Dir.
House of Providence, 1654 W. Onondaga St., 13204. Tel: 315-424-1800. Mr. Brian Walton. Records only.
Sister Patricia Ann's Preschool dba Gingerbread House Preschool, 2500 Grant Blvd., 13208. Tel: 315-471-4198.
Dorn Day Care Center (dba Gingerbread House Day Care Center), 2500 Grant Blvd., 13208. Tel: 315-471-4198. Sr. Suzanne Dunn, O.S.F., Dir.

[M] DIOCESAN SUMMER CAMPS

SYRACUSE. *Camp Nazareth*, Office: 1408 Genesee St., 13502. Tel: 315-724-6118. Woodgate, 13494. Tel: 315-392-3791. James T. Carroll, Dir.
Lourdes Camp, Office: 1654 W. Onondaga St., 13204. Tel: 315-424-1812. Camp Address: 10 Mile Point, Skaneateles, 13152. Michael Preston, Dir.

[N] FAMILY LIFE BUREAUS

SYRACUSE. *Eastern Region*, Brimfield St., Box 843, Clinton, 13323. Tel: 315-853-4281. Donna Blehar, Dir.

Family Life Education, 1342 Lancaster Ave., 13210. Tel: 315-472-6754. Rev. Joseph H. Phillips, Dir.; Margaret Dupee, Coord., Family & Marriage Enrichment; Mary Ann Davis, Sec.; Karen Bandoblu, Coord., Marriage Prep. & Speakers Bureau; Patricia Ennis, Coord., Separated/Divorced, The Third Option, and Parenting; Nancy Devine, Coord. Northern Region; Sue & Ronald Kielar, Coordinators Eastern Region; Kathy Colligan, Coord. Southern Region.

Northern Region, 108 E. Sixth St., Oswego, 13126. Tel: 315-342-1463. Nancy Devine, Regional Dir., Office of Family Life Education.

Northern Region Religious Education Office & Special Education for Catholics, 108 E. Sixth St., Oswego, 13126. Tel: 315-343-5557. Sr. Germaine Hilston, C.S.J., Dir.; Mary Jackson, Resource Center Staff.

Southern Region Family Life Education, 400 Corey Ave., Endicott, 13760. Tel: 607-786-0828. Kathleen Colligan, Dir.

[O] GENERAL HOSPITALS

SYRACUSE. *St. Joseph's Hospital Health Center*, 301 Prospect Ave., 13203. Tel: 315-448-5111; Fax: 315-448-6161.
For a complete listing, refer to the Hospitals section.

BINGHAMTON. *Our Lady of Lourdes Memorial Hospital*, 169 Riverside Dr., 13905. Tel: 607-798-5111.
For a complete listing, refer to the Hospitals section.

UTICA. *St. Elizabeth Hospital*, 2209 Genesee St., 13501. Tel: 315-798-8100.
For a complete listing, refer to the Hospitals section.

[P] FACILITIES FOR THE AGED

SYRACUSE. *Bernardine Apartments, Inc.*, 417 Churchill Ave., 13205. Tel: 315-469-7786.
For a complete listing, refer to the Special Care Facilities section.

Loretto, 700 E. Brighton Ave., 13205. Tel: 315-469-5561.
For a complete listing, refer to the Special Care Facilities section.

Loretto Geriatric Community Residences, Inc., 5018 S. Salina St., 13205. Tel: 315-492-0896.
For a complete listing, refer to the Special Care Facilities section.

Loretto Rest, Inc., 750 E. Brighton Ave., 13205. Tel: 315-469-5061.
For a complete listing, refer to the Special Care Facilities section.

St. Camillus Health & Rehabilitation Center, 813 Fay Rd., 13219. Tel: 315-488-2951.
For a complete listing, refer to the Special Care Facilities section.

OSWEGO. *Saint Luke's Residential Health Care Facility Co., Inc.*, 299 E. First St., 13126. Tel: 315-342-3166.
For a complete listing, refer to the Special Care Facilities section.

UTICA. *St. Joseph Nursing Home*, 2535 Genesee St., 13501. Tel: 315-797-1230.
For a complete listing, refer to the Special Care Facilities section.

[Q] SPECIALTY HOUSING

SYRACUSE. *Christopher Community, Inc.*, 1654 W. Onondaga St., 13204. Tel: 315-424-1821.
For a complete listing, refer to the Special Care Facilities section.

Churchill Manor, Inc., 750 E. Brighton Ave., 13205. Tel: 315-424-1821.
For a complete listing, refer to the Special Care Facilities section.

Hawley Winton Housing Development Fund, Inc., Walter Ludovico Apts., 340 Winton St., 13203. Tel: 315-422-0475.
For a complete listing, refer to the Special Care Facilities section.

Ludden Housing Development Fund Company, Inc., 1654 W. Onondaga St., 13204. Tel: 315-424-1821.
For a complete listing, refer to the Special Care Facilities section.

Marcellus Apartments Housing Development Fund Company, Inc. Mailing Address: 1654 W. Onondaga St., 13204. Tel: 315-424-1821.
For a complete listing, refer to the Special Care Facilities section.

Miller Road Housing Development Co., Inc., (Brewerton). Mailing Address: 1654 W. Onondaga St., 13204. Tel: 315-424-1821.
For a complete listing, refer to the Special Care Facilities section.

Mother Marianne Cope Housing Development Fund Co., Inc., 1654 W. Onondaga St., 13204. Tel: 315-424-1821.
For a complete listing, refer to the Special Care Facilities section.

Mount St. James Corporation, 1654 W. Onondaga St., 13204. Tel: 315-424-1821.
For a complete listing, refer to the Special Care Facilities section.

Pompei Housing Development Fund Company, Inc. c/o Christopher Community, Inc., 1654 W. Onondaga St., 13204. Tel: 315-424-1821.
For a complete listing, refer to the Special Care Facilities section.

Pond St. Housing Development Fund Co., Inc., Bishop Harrison Apartments, Pond St., 13208.
For a complete listing, refer to the Special Care Facilities section.

Providence House Apartments, 1700 W. Onondaga St., 13204. Tel: 315-471-8427.
For a complete listing, refer to the Special Care Facilities section.

St. Peter's Italian Church Housing Development Fund Co., Inc. Villa Scalabrini Apts., 709 James St., 13203.
For a complete listing, refer to the Special Care Facilities section.

Stoneleigh Housing Development Fund Co., Inc., Stoneleigh Apartments, 400 Lamb Ave., Canastota, 13032.
For a complete listing, refer to the Special Care Facilities section.

Tyson Place Housing Development Fund Company, Inc. Mailing Address: Blessed Sacrament Apartments, 16544 W. Onondaga St., 13204. Tel: 315-424-1821.
For a complete listing, refer to the Special Care Facilities section.

AUBURN. *Mercy Housing Development Fund Co., Inc.*, Mercy Apartments, 1 Thornton Ave., 13021. Tel: 315-253-2015.
For a complete listing, refer to the Special Care Facilities section.

BALDWINSVILLE. *Smokey Hollow Housing Development Fund Company, Inc.* Mailing Address: St. Mary's Apartments, Baldwinsville, 1654 W. Onondaga St. Syracuse, 13204. Tel: 315-424-1821.
For a complete listing, refer to the Special Care Facilities section.

BREWERTON. *Bartell Road Housing Development Fund Co., Inc.*, Bartell Rd., 13029.
For a complete listing, refer to the Special Care Facilities section.

CICERO. *Cicero Housing Development Fund Company Inc.* Mailing Address: 1654 W. Onondaga St. Syracuse, 13204. Tel: 315-424-1821.
For a complete listing, refer to the Special Care Facilities section.

FAYETTEVILLE. *Redfield South Housing Development Fund Co., Inc.*, Redfield Village Apartments, 380 Salt Springs Rd., 13066. Tel: 315-637-8280.
For a complete listing, refer to the Special Care Facilities section.

NORTH SYRACUSE. *Pitcher Hill-Christopher Housing Development Fund Co., Inc.*, 114 Elbow Rd., 13212.
For a complete listing, refer to the Special Care Facilities section.

OSWEGO. *St. Luke's Housing Development Fund Co., Inc.*, St. Luke's Apartments, W. First St., 13126.
For a complete listing, refer to the Special Care Facilities section.

ROME. *C.N.C. Inc.*, W. Thomas St., 13440. Tel: 315-735-7545.
For a complete listing, refer to the Special Care Facilities section.

Rome Mall Housing Development Fund Company, Inc. Mailing Address: 1654 W. Onondaga St. Syracuse, 13204. Tel: 315-424-1821.
For a complete listing, refer to the Special Care Facilities section.

TOWN OF GATES. *Steger Housing Development Fund Co., Inc.*, 4100 Lydell Rd. 1654 W. Onondaga St. Syracuse, 13204. Tel: 315-424-1821.
For a complete listing, refer to the Special Care Facilities section.

UTICA. *Catherine St. Housing Development Fund Company, Inc.* Mailing Address: Mt. Carmel Apartments, 1654 W. Onondaga St. Syracuse, 13201-0511. Tel: 315-424-1821.
For a complete listing, refer to the Special Care Facilities section.

[R] PROGRAMS FOR THE HANDICAPPED

SYRACUSE. *L'Arche*, Office: 1232 Teall Ave., 13206. Tel: 315-479-8088; 479-8118. Robert Sackel, Dir. A Christian Community concerned with life sharing between persons with a developmental disability and persons who assist them. Homes at 1701 James St., 1226 Butternut St., & 1240-42 Teall Ave., Syracuse.

UTICA. *St. John and St. Joseph Home, Inc.*, 1408 Genesee St., 13502. Tel: 315-724-2150. Mr. Dennis J. Manning, Exec. Dir.

YORKVILLE. *The Heenan Spiritual Program for the Handicapped, Inc.*, 17 Sixth St., 13495. Tel: 315-736-4858. Mr. Stanley Zima, Dir.

[S] MONASTERIES AND RESIDENCES OF PRIESTS AND BROTHERS

SYRACUSE. *Jesuits at LeMoyne, Inc.*, 1419 Salt Springs Rd., 13214. Revs. John B. Breslin, S.J., Rector; John A. Boland, S.J., Min.; Thomas J. Kent, S.J., Treas.; Robert A. Mitchell, S.J., Pres.; William J. Bosch, S.J.; Raymond A. Bucko, S.J.; Paul B. Campbell, S.J. (Ireland); J. Donald Clark, S.J.; Theodore J. Clarkson, S.J.; William S. Dolan, S.J.; James J. Hennessey, S.J.; Paul S. Naumann, S.J.; Vincent W. Hevern, S.J.; Donald J. Kirby, S.J.; William J. McBrearty, S.J.; Thomas R. Marciniak, S.J.; Joseph B. Neville, S.J.; Edmund G. Ryan, S.J.; Vincent B. Ryan, S.J.; Robert E. Scully, S.J.; Andrew L. Szebenyi, S.J. (Hungary); M. Donald Zewe, S.J. Priests 23.

St. Pius X Home, Inc., 714 E. Brighton Ave., 13205. Tel: 315-492-1711. Diocesan home for priests. In res., Rev. Msgr. Robert B. Davern; Rev. Msgr. John R. Duffy; Revs. Robert J. McKay; Thomas F. Guyder; Robert Barett; P. Carl Pilla; Robert P. Wright; John T. McGraw.

EAST SYRACUSE. *Bishop Grimes Priests Residence*, 6655 Kirkville Rd., 13057. Tel: 315-437-8385. Most Rev. Frank J. Harrison; Rev. Msgr. A. Robert Casey; Rev. Msgr. Frank L. Sammons; Revs. William P. Regan; David R. Sambor; Charles S. Vavonese, Vianney House, 6651 Kirkville Rd., 13057. Revs. George F. Sheehan; J. Robert Yeazel.

UTICA. *St. Vincent's Mission House*, 10475 Cosby Manor Rd., 13502. Tel: 315-724-9237. Congregation of the Mission, Province of New England Vincentian Fathers. Bro. Richard Glinski, C.M., Dir.; Revs. Casimir Kiczuk, C.M.; John Kowalski, C.M.; Henry Czekala, C.M.; Edmund Kowalski, C.M.; Bros. Francis Andrzejewski, C.M., St. Joseph's Nursing Home, Utica; Richard Glinski, C.M.

[T] CONVENTS AND RESIDENCES FOR SISTERS

SYRACUSE. *Aquinas House*, 702 Danforth St., 13208. Tel: 315-424-8952.

Convent of St. Anthony and Motherhouse of the Third Franciscan Order, 1024 Court St., 13208. Sr. Verna Barboza, Ministerial Service, Generalate Offices, 2500 Grant Blvd., 13208. Sr. Grace Anne Dillenschneider, O.S.F., Gen. Supr. Total Sisters in Diocese 232; Total in Community 360.

Dominican Monastery of the Perpetual Rosary, 802 Court St., 13208. Tel: 315-471-6762. Sr. Mary Augustine, O.P., Prioress. Cloistered Nuns 10; Extern Sisters 1.

Franciscan Formation House, 112 Michaels Ave., 13208-1718. Tel: 315-471-7893. Sisters of the Third Franciscan Order. Sisters 4.

St. Clare Convent, 1001 Court St., 13208.

WINDSOR. *Transfiguration Monastery*, 701 NY Rte. 79, 13865-9230. Tel: 607-655-2366. Camaldolese Benedictine Nuns. Sisters 4; Novices 1.

[U] RETREAT HOUSES

SYRACUSE. *Christ the King Retreat House*, 500 Brookford Rd., 13224. Tel: 315-446-2680. Rev. Michael J. Carmola, Dir.; Sr. Rose Raymond, O.S.F., Asst. Dir.; Maureen Gallivan, Business Mgr. General retreat house for priests, nuns, laity, and youth of Upstate New York. Priests 1; Sisters 1.

SKANEATELES. *Stella Maris Retreat Center*, 13152. Tel: 315-685-6836. Sisters of the Third Franciscan Order, M.C. Sr. John Olivia, O.S.F., Admin. & Dir. Retreat Ministry. Team oriented center for renewal.

[V] NEWMAN CENTERS

SYRACUSE. *LeMoyne College Newman Center*, 13214. Tel: 315-445-4110.

Onondaga Community College Newman Center, 111 Roberts Ave., 13207. Tel: 315-478-5749.

Syracuse University, St. Thomas More Foundation, Inc., Alibrandi Catholic Center, 110 Walnut Pl., P.O. Box 0038, 13210-0038. Tel: 315-478-5959. Rev. James P. Lang, Chap.

BINGHAMTON. *Broome Community College Newman Center*, 157 Clark St., P.O. Box 408, 13850. Tel: 607-748-8287.

CAZENOVIA. *Cazenovia College Newman Center*, 10 Seminary St., 13035. Steven R. Young, Chap.

CLINTON. *Hamilton College Newman Center*, 13323. Tel: 315-859-4129. Rev. John P. Croghan, Chap.

CORTLAND. *Newman Foundation of Cortland, Inc. at the State University College of New York*, 8 Calvert St., 13045. Tel: 607-753-6737. Rev. Edward J. O'Heron, Chap.

HAMILTON. *Catholic Newman Community of Colgate University*, 13 Oak Dr., 13346. Tel: 315-824-7680. Rev. John P. Donovan.

MORRISVILLE. *Newman Association at SUNY Morrisville*, 210 Lab Classroom, 13408. Legal Title: *St. Joan of Arc Newman Association at the State University of New York (SUNY) Morrisville Agricultural and Technical College.*

OSWEGO. *Newman Foundation, Inc., State University of New York*, Hall Newman Center, New St., P.O. Box 207, 13126. Tel: 315-341-7562. Rev. G. Peter Worn.

UTICA. *Mohawk Valley Community College*. Newman Apostolate, 1204 Sherman Dr., 13501. Tel: 315-797-3419.
SUNY Institute of Technology at Utica/Rome Newman Center, 1433 Burrstone Rd., 13502. Tel: 315-792-3284. Rev. V. James Lauducci, Chap. Legal Title: *State University of New York (SUNY) Institute of technology at Utica/Rome Newman Center*.
Utica College of Syracuse University Newman Center, 1433 Burrstone Rd., 13502. Tel: 315-792-3284. Rev. V. James Lauducci, Chap., Res., 1433 Burrstone Rd., 13502. Tel: 315-792-3284.

VESTAL. *Binghamton University Newman Center*, 400 Murray Hill Rd., 13850. Tel: 607-798-7202. Rev. Robert J. Sullivan, Chap.

[W] MISCELLANEOUS LISTINGS

SYRACUSE.
**David W. Barry Foundation*, 240 E. Onondaga St., P.O. Box 511, 13201-0511. Tel: 315-422-7203; Fax: 315-478-4619. Most Revs. James M. Moynihan, Pres.; Thomas J. Costello, Vice Pres.; Rev. Michael P. Minehan, Sec. & Treas.
Grimes Foundation. (Incorporated by special act of the New York State Legislature, May 1, 1916), 240 E. Onondaga St., 13202. Corporation created to establish and maintain charitable, religious and educational facilities within the Roman Catholic Diocese of Syracuse, New York. Most Rev. James M. Moynihan, D.D., Pres. Ex-Officio.
Lasalle Syracuse, Inc., 6245 Randall Rd., 13214.
Loretto Apartments Housing Development Fund Co., Inc., 700 E. Brighton Ave., 13205.
ONE (Opportunity Network in Economics), 1101 Burnet Ave., 13203. Tel: 315-479-6301. Kenneth Leeb, Dir.
Onondaga County Catholic School Foundation (Western Region Catholic School Foundation), 240 E. Onondaga St., P.O. Box 511, 13201-0511. Tel: 315-470-1450; Fax: 315-478-4619. Sr. Mary Ellen Shirtz, Area Supt. Western Region Schools.
St. Francis Social Adult Day Service, 1108 Court St., 13208. Tel: 315-424-1003; 1004. Sr. Christopher Dixon, O.S.F., Admin. A non-residential adult day-service providing holistic care for the frail elderly. Operated by the Sisters of the Third Franciscan Order.
Saint Thomas Preparatory Seminary Fund, P.O. Box 511, 13201. Incorporated under the Laws of the State of New York, 1963, as a Membership Corporation to solicit funds for the construction of a diocesan seminary.
Sisters of the Third Franciscan Order-Retirement Trust Fund, 2500 Grant Blvd., 13208. Tel: 315-425-0132; Fax: 315-425-0610.
Spiritual Renewal Center, 1118 Court St., 13208.

BINGHAMTON. *Ladies of Charity*, 232 Main St., 13905. Tel: 607-729-9166.

ENDICOTT. *Bishop Harrison Education Foundation*. Mailing Address: P.O. Box 7158, 13760.

MAINE. *Mount St. Francis Hermitage*. Mailing Address: P.O. Box 276, 13802. Tel: 607-754-9813.

UTICA. *The Good News Foundation of Central New York*, 2306 Genesee St., 13502. Tel: 315-735-9730. Deacon John Droz, Exec. Dir.

RELIGIOUS INSTITUTES OF MEN REPRESENTED IN THE DIOCESE

For further details refer to the corresponding bracketed number in the Religious Institutes of Men or Women section.

[1350]—*Brothers of St. Francis Xavier*. (St. Joseph Prov., Milton, MA).—C.F.X.
[0330]—*Brothers of the Christian Schools*. (New York Prov.).—F.S.C.
[1330]—*Congregation of the Mission (Vincentian Fathers)*.—C.M.
[1210]—*Congregation of the Missionaries of St. Charles*. (St. Charles Borromeo Prov.).—C.S.
[0480]—*Conventual Franciscans*.—O.F.M.Conv.
[0690]—*Jesuit Fathers and Brothers*. (New York Prov.).—S.J.

RELIGIOUS INSTITUTES OF WOMEN REPRESENTED IN THE DIOCESE

[0230]—*Benedictine Sisters of Pontifical Jurisdiction*. (Erie, PA).—O.S.B.
[]—*Camaldolese Benedictine Sisters*.—O.S.B.Cam.
[0330]—*Carmelite Sisters for the Aged and Infirm*.—O.Carm.
[0760]—*Daughters of Charity of St. Vincent de Paul*.—D.C.
[1050]—*Dominican Contemplative Nuns*.—O.P.
[1070-01]—*Dominican Sisters*.—O.P.
[1170]—*Felician Sisters*.—C.S.S.F.
[1180]—*Franciscan Sisters of Allegany, New York*.—O.S.F.
[1410]—*Franciscan Sisters of St. Joseph (Mill Hill)*.—F.M.S.J.
[2575]—*Institute of the Sisters of Mercy of the Americas*. (New York, NY; Omaha, NE).—R.S.M.
[1360]—*Missionary Franciscan Sisters of the Immaculate Conception*.—O.S.F.
[3160]—*Parish Visitors of Mary Immaculate*.—P.V.M.I.
[0590]—*Sisters of Charity of Saint Elizabeth, Convent Station*.—S.C.
[3340]—*Sisters of Providence (Holyoke)*.—S.P.
[3950]—*Sisters of Saint Mary of Namur*.—S.S.M.N.
[3780]—*Sisters of Saints Cyril and Methodius*.—SS.C.M.
[1800]—*Sisters of St. Francis of the Third Order Regular*. (Williamsville, New York).—O.S.F.
[3830-14]—*Sisters of St. Joseph*. (Rochester, NY).—S.S.J.
[3840]—*Sisters of St. Joseph of Carondelet*.—C.S.J.
[1970]—*Sisters of the Holy Family of Nazareth*.—C.S.F.N.
[1490]—*Sisters of the Third Franciscan Order*.—O.S.F.
[2160]—*Sisters, Servants of the Immaculate Heart of Mary*.—I.H.M.
[4110]—*Ursuline Nuns (Roman Union)*.—O.S.U.

DIOCESAN CEMETERIES

SYRACUSE. *St. Mary-St. Agnes*, 2315 South Ave., 13207. Tel: 315-475-4639. Rev. James C. Fritzen, Dir.; Richard Dadey, Supt.; Daniel Moorhead, Asst. Supt.

CORTLAND. *St. Mary*, 4101 West Road, 13045. Tel: 607-756-8838. Rev. John Fenlon, Dir.; Russell Teeter, Supt.

JOHNSON CITY. *Calvary-St. Patrick*, 501 Fairview St., 13790. Tel: 607-797-2906. Daniel Vuille, Supt.; Ann Tesar, Sec.

OSWEGO. *St. Peter & St. Paul*, R.R. 04 Box 4B, Rte. 481, E. River Rd., 13126. Tel: 315-343-5002. Rev. Msgr. Paul Brigandi, Dir.; John Taber, Supt.

UTICA. *Calvary*, 2407 Oneida St., 13501. Tel: 315-735-2727. Rev. Msgr. William Donovan, Dir.; Donald Deck, Supt.
Holy Trinity, Chaplain Ave., 13502. Tel: 315-724-0616. Rev. Arthur Hapanowicz, Dir.; Daniel Williams, Supt.
St. Agnes, 601 Arthur St., 13501. Tel: 315-732-8588. Lawrence F. Hagan, Coord.; John McCarthy, Supt.
St. Mary, Webster St., 13501. Tel: 315-735-2727. Donald Deck, Supt.

WHITESBORO. *Mount Olivet*, 70 Wood Rd., 13492. Tel: 315-736-4446. Rev. Donald H. Karlen, Dir.; Joseph Usyk, Supt.

NECROLOGY

† Cummings, Frederick F., (Retired). —Died Oct. 16, 1996.
† Hill, John H., (Retired). —Died Nov. 11, 1996.
† Powell, Thomas M., Corpus Christi, TX, Most Precious Blood. —Died June 7, 1996.
† Shanahan, William J., (Retired). —Died Sept. 20, 1996.
† Sullivan, Robert J., Binghamton, NY, St. Paul. —Died June 8, 1996.

Diocese of Toledo

(Dioecesis Toletana in America)

Most Reverend

JAMES R. HOFFMAN, D.D., J.C.L.

Bishop of Toledo; ordained July 28, 1957; appointed Titular Bishop of Italica and Auxiliary Bishop of Toledo April 18, 1978; ordained Bishop June 23, 1978; appointed to Toledo December 16, 1980. *Res., 2544 Parkwood Ave., Toledo, OH, 43610.*

Most Reverend

ROBERT W. DONNELLY, D.D.

Auxiliary Bishop of Toledo; ordained May 25, 1957; appointed Titular Bishop of Garba and Auxiliary Bishop of Toledo March 20, 1984; ordained Bishop May 3, 1984. *Res., 2544 Parkwood Ave., Toledo, OH, 43610.*

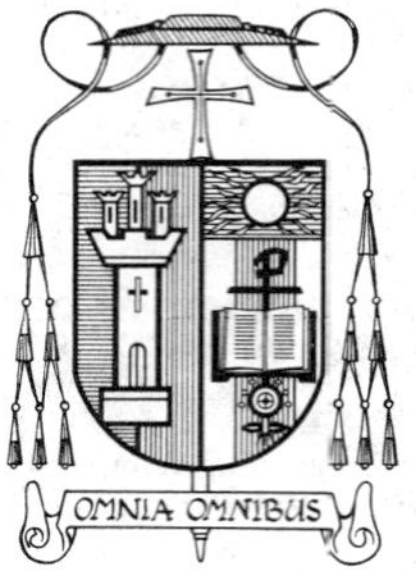

ESTABLISHED APRIL 15, 1910.

Square Miles 8,222.

Comprises the following Counties of northwest Ohio: Williams, Fulton, Lucas, Ottawa, Defiance, Henry, Wood, Sandusky, Erie, Paulding, Putnam, Hancock, Seneca, Huron, Van Wert, Allen, Wyandot, Crawford and Richland.

For legal titles of parishes and diocesan institutions, consult the Chancery.

Chancery: P.O. Box 985, Toledo, OH, 43697-0985. Tel.: 419-244-6711; Fax: 419-244-4791.

STATISTICAL OVERVIEW

Personnel	
Bishop	1
Auxiliary Bishops	1
Retired Bishops	1
Priests: Diocesan Active in Diocese	153
Priests: Active Outside Diocese	8
Priests: Diocesan in Foreign Missions	2
Priests: Retired, Sick or Absent	54
Number of Diocesan Priests	217
Religious Priests in Diocese	66
Extern Priests in Diocese	6
Ordinations:	
Diocesan Priests	6
Transitional Deacons	8
Permanent Deacons	4
Permanent Deacons in Diocese	190
Total Brothers	10
Total Sisters	877
Parishes	
Parishes	163
With Resident Pastor:	
Resident Diocesan Priests	103
Resident Religious Priests	12
Without Resident Pastor:	
Administered by Priests	34
Administered by Permanent Deacons	4
Administered by Women Religious	7
Welfare	
Catholic Hospitals	8
Total Assisted	820,465
Homes for the Aged	3
Total Assisted	459
Residential Care of Children	1
Total Assisted	75
Special Centers for Social Services	13
Total Assisted	5,502
Other Institutions	19
Total Assisted	79
Educational	
Diocesan Students in Other Seminaries	14
Students Religious	5
Total Seminarians	19
Colleges and Universities	2
Total Students	1,838
High Schools, Diocesan and Parish	10
Total Students	4,100
High Schools, Private	4
Total Students	2,824
Elementary Schools, Diocesan and Parish	83
Total Students	22,231
Elementary Schools, Private	4
Total Students	803
Catechesis/Religious Education:	
High School Students	3,041
Elementary Students	15,555
Total Students Under Catholic Instruction	50,411
Teachers in the Diocese:	
Priests	24
Sisters	145
Lay Teachers	1,761
Vital Statistics	
Receptions into the Church:	
Infant Baptism Totals	4,292
Adult Baptism Totals	467
Received into Full Communion	653
First Communions	5,667
Confirmations	5,106
Marriages:	
Catholic	1,172
Interfaith	928
Total Marriages	2,100
Deaths	3,045
Total Catholic Population	328,623
Total Population	1,479,041

Former Bishops—Most Rev. JOSEPH SCHREMBS, D.D., appt. auxiliary of Grand Rapids, MI Jan. 8, 1911; cons. Feb. 22, 1911; transferred to Toledo, Aug. 11, 1911; transferred to Cleveland, OH, May 11, 1921; died Nov. 2, 1945.—His Eminence Cardinal SAMUEL A. STRITCH, D.D., cons. Bishop of Toledo, Nov. 30, 1921; appt. Archbishop of Milwaukee, Aug. 30, 1930; appt. Archbishop of Chicago, Dec. 27, 1939; created Cardinal, Feb. 18, 1946; named Pro-Prefect of the Sacred Congregation of the Propagation of the Faith, March 1, 1958; died in Rome, May 27, 1968.—Most Rev. KARL J. ALTER, D.D., LL.D., appt. Bishop of Toledo, April 17, 1931; cons. June 17, 1931; promoted to Archbishop of Cincinnati, June 14, 1950; died Aug. 23, 1977.—Most Rev. GEORGE REHRING, D.D., cons. Oct. 7, 1937; appt. Bishop of Toledo, July 18, 1950; retired Feb. 25, 1967; died Feb. 29, 1976.—Most Rev. JOHN A. DONOVAN, D.D., ord. Dec. 8, 1935; Titular Bishop of Rhasus and Auxiliary of Detroit, Sept. 6, 1954; ord. Bishop, Oct. 26, 1954; transferred Toledo, Feb. 25, 1967; retired July 29, 1980; died Sept. 18, 1991.

Chancery—Mailing Address: P.O. Box 985, Toledo, 43697-0985. 1933 Spielbusch, Toledo, 43624. Tel: 419-244-6711; Fax: 419-244-4791. Office Hours: Mon.-Fri. 8:30-5.

Vicar General—Most Rev. ROBERT W. DONNELLY, V.G., *1933 Spielbusch, Toledo, 43624. Mailing Address: P.O. Box 985, Toledo, 43697-0985.* Tel: 419-244-6711.

Cabinet—Most Rev. ROBERT W. DONNELLY, V.G., Sec. Personnel & Admin. Svcs. MICHAEL WASSERMAN, Secretariat of Ministerial Leadership Formation; Sr. JANET DOYLE, O.P., Sec. of Catholic Youth & School Svcs.; Rev. Msgr. DONALD E. HEINTSHEL, Sec. Communications & Public Rels. DONALD L. WISLER, L.I.S.W., Sec. Catholic Charities; SALLY MALHOIT, Admin. Aide, *1933 Spielbusch, Toledo, 43624.* Tel: 419-244-6711.

Advisory To Bishop

All Diocesan Offices and Secretaries are located at 1933 Spielbusch, Toledo, OH 43624. Address all mail to: P.O. Box 985, Toledo, OH 43697-0985. Tel: 419-244-6711.

Bishop's Education Council—JOHN STOEPLER, Pres.; Mrs. CAROL COLLINS, Vice Pres.; Dr. HARRY BASH; WILLIAM BOYLE; ROBERT DANIEL; DAVID WALROD; JOHN GILWEE; Mr. JAMES HAUDAN; Rev. JAMES HOLMER; Sr. MARY SUZANNE KENNEDY; Rev. KEITH J. MCCORMACK; JOHN C. MOORE; TOM NOE; DANIEL J. RING; Mrs. DEBRA SCHAEFER; Mrs. SALLY KOPPINGER; Mr. ROMAN ACE; Rev. ROBERT YEAGER.

Building Commission—Dr. GEORGE MURNEN, Chm.; Revs. GERALD J. CHMIEL; RICHARD T. WURZEL; Mr. DAVID BAGGETT; Mr. JAMES CIHAK; Dr. MARK PICKETT.

Consultors—Revs. MARVIN G. BORGER; GERALD L. CERANOWSKI; THOMAS LEYLAND; GREGORY L. PEATEE; J. MICHAEL RICKER; RICHARD WURZEL.

Deans—Defiance Deanery: Very Rev. EDWARD J. SCHLETER, V.F., Defiance, Henry and Paulding Counties; Fremont Deanery: Very Rev. RONALD LEJEUNE, V.F., Ottawa and Sandusky Counties; Lima Deanery: Very Rev. DAVID M. ROSS, V.F., S.T.L., J.C.D., Ph.D., Allen, Van Wert and Putnam Counties; Mansfield Deanery: Very Rev. HERBERT F. WEBER, V.F., Richland and Crawford Counties; Tiffin Deanery: Very Rev. FRANCIS A. MURD, V.F., Seneca, Wyandot and Hancock Counties; Toledo Central: Very Rev. RONALD R. WARNIMONT, V.F., Toledo Northwest: Very Rev. ROBERT REINHART, Toledo Southwest: Very Rev. DENNIS METZGER, To-Lu-Wo Deanery: Very Rev. JOSEPH STEINBAUER, Acting Dean for East Lucas and Wood Counties; Sandusky Deanery: Very Rev.

FRANKLIN P. KEHRES, V.F., Erie and Huron Counties; Will-Ful-L Deanery: Very Rev. STEPHEN P. CAIRNS, V.F., Williams, Fulton and West Lucas Counties.

Diocesan Pastoral Council—CAROL HENS, Pres., *271 Chorus Ln., Toledo, 43615.* NANCY YOUNG, Sec. & Gen. Coord., *1933 Eastgate, Toledo, 43614.*

Finance Committee—Most Rev. JAMES R. HOFFMAN; Most Rev. ROBERT W. DONNELLY, V.G.; Mr. RICHARD FAIST; Mr. ROBERT J. KIRK; Mr. THOMAS KRESS.

Priests' Council—Revs. THOMAS J. LEYLAND, Chm. Tel: 419-352-4195. RICHARD T. WURZEL, Vice Chm. Tel: 419-885-5791. GREGORY L. PEATEE, Sec. & Treas. Tel: 419-475-4348.

Sisters' Council—Sr. MYRA CIESIELSKI, O.S.F.S., *530 Regina Pkwy., Toledo, 43612.* Tel: 419-476-9750.

Secretariat Of Administrative Services

Secretary-Vicar General—Most Rev. ROBERT W. DONNELLY, V.G., *P.O. Box 985, Toledo, 43697-0985.* Tel: 419-244-6711.

Diocesan Department Of Development—RICHARD WARING, Ph.D., Dir. DOROTHY LANGENDERFER, Assoc. Dir.

Financial Services—JOHN HEINZE, Dir.

Internal Auditor—Ms. SARA G. MARTIN, C.P.A.

Associate Auditor—Mr. ROBERT MASON.

MIS (Management Information Systems)—SHARON LANDIS, Coord.

Affiliated:

Cemeteries Office—JOHN E. CARPENTER, Dir., *5725 Hill Ave., Toledo, 43615-5852.* Tel: 419-531-5747; Fax: 419-531-0946.

Cemeteries—Calvary: *2424 Dorr St., Toledo, 43607.* Tel: 419-536-3751., Mount Carmel: *15 E. Manhattan Blvd., Toledo, 43608.* Tel: 419-536-3751., Resurrection: *5725 Hill Ave., Toledo, 43615.* Tel: 419-531-5747.

Catholic Office Building Services—Ms. PATRICIA STEIN, Mgr.

Court of Equity—Mrs. JUDITH GAJDOSTIK, Clerk; Ms. PAULA MINZING, Presiding Judge, *3250 Hazelton Dr., Oregon, 43616.* Tel: 419-691-7436.

Judges—FRANCIS LANDRY; Sr. EMILY LECHLAK, O.S.F.S.; FRANK LINK; COLIN MCQUADE; Rev. DANIEL RING; Sr. DOROTHY THUM, R.S.M.; HARRY WELSH; BRUCE WINTERS; Rev. RICHARD T. WURZEL.

Conciliators—JAMES CARUSO; RICHARD HANUSZ; JUDE SUTTER; JOHN F. WETLI.

Intake Officers—Mrs. JOHN HILLER; ROBERT J. SUTTER; CLARA WESOLEK; ELIZABETH ZEPF.

Synod Implementation Office—RITA BAUR, Coord. Sec.

DCCW (Diocesan Council of Catholic Women)—Mrs. CHRIS YOUNG, Pres., *1542 Ralston Cir., Ste. 207, Toledo, 43615.* Tel: 419-534-2252.

Secretariat Of Personnel

Secretary—Most Rev. ROBERT W. DONNELLY, V.G.

Vicar for Priests and Director of Ministry to Priests Program—Rev. RAYMOND C. SHEPERD, Vicar.

Vicar for Deacons—Rev. RAYMOND C. SHEPERD.

Vicar For Religious—Sr. MARY SUE KENNEDY, O.P., A.D.

Diocesan Case Manager—Mr. WILLIAM JENKS.

Vicar for Seminarians—Rev. WILLIAM KUBACKI.

Priests' Personnel Board—Rev. KENNETH G. MORMAN, Chm. Members: Revs. FRANKLIN P. KEHRES, V.F.; KENNETH LILL; JOSEPH R. STEINBAUER; ROBERT J. WILHELM, V.F.; HERBERT J. WILLMAN, *2544 Parkwood Ave., Toledo, 43610-1317.* Tel: 419-255-1890; Fax: 419-244-0471.

Office of Personnel Services—Mr. JOHN LECHMAN, Dir.

Tribunal—

Director—Sr. MARCIA MARIE DESTATTE, S.N.D., J.C.L.

Judicial Vicar—Very Rev. JOHN A. MCCLURE, V.J., J.C.L., M.C.L.

Associate Judicial Vicar—Rev. JOHN C. REED, S.J.

Defenders of the Bond—Revs. THOMAS BEAUREGARD; STANLEY SZYBKA; Sr. MARCIA MARIE DESTATTE, S.N.D., J.C.L.; Rev. CHRISTOPHER VASKO, J.C.L.

Presiding Judges—Revs. JOSEPH O'BRIEN; JOHN THOMAS; JOHN C. REED; RONALD R. WARNIMONT, V.F.; JOHN A. MCCLURE, V.J., J.C.L., M.C.L.

Associate Judges—Revs. RAYMOND ETZEL; JAMES SAY; JAMES WALSH; Sr. MARCIA MARIE DESTATT, S.N.D., J.C.L.

Notaries—CHARLOTTE LAMMERS; ANGELA WALKER; Mrs. PAULA BUTLER.

Interdiocesan Appeals Court: Northwest Section—

Judicial Vicar—Very Rev. DAVID M. ROSSV.F., S.T.L., J.C.D., Ph.D.

Defenders of the Bond—Revs. ROBERT TUCCERI; JOSEPH VAMOS.

Judges—Most Rev. JAMES R. HOFFMAN; Rev. Msgr. DONALD E. HEINTSCHEL; Revs. JAMES AUTH; JAMES CRYAN, O.S.F.S.; FREDERICK HUG; JOSEPH JAROS; WILLIAM PARKER; DENNIS SCHROEDER; JOHN A. THOMAS; RICHARD WURZEL.

Notary—Mrs. MARIAN KRASNIEWSKI,

Affiliated:

Retirement Plan for Lay Employees—Mrs. MARY C. DEPINET, Admin.

Employee Benefit Fund—Mrs. MARY C. DEPINET, Admin.

Secretariat of Ministerial Leadership Formation

Secretary—Mr. MICHAEL WASSERMAN.

Ministry and Adult Formation—Team Members: Sr. JOYCE MARIE BATES, S.N.D.; Mr. ALFREDO DIAZ; Mrs. JEANNINE BURCH; Sr. MARGARET MCGUINESS, O.P./Ad; Mr. MICHAEL NACHMAN; Mr. LEO BISTAK; Sr. CATHERINE EDGAR, S.H.C.J.

Coordinator for Liturgy—Sr. GEORGETTE ZALEWSKA, R.S.M.,Affiliated Committees: RCIA Committee; Liturgical Commission.

Department of Global Concerns—Rev. BERNARD J. BOFF, Dir.

Mission of Accompaniment Pastoral Team—Rev. TIMOTHY M. KUMMERER, *All Souls Catholic Mission, Box 37 Binga, Zimbabwe, Africa.*

Ecumenical & Interreligious Affairs Commission—Rev. DAVID BRUNING, Chm., *6230 W. Tiffin St., Bascom, 44809.* Tel: 419-937-2715.

Shared Parish Ministry Group Co-Conveners—Sr. JOY BARKER, O.S.F.S.; Ms. PAMELA MESSEROLL.

Secretariat of Catholic Youth & School Services

Secretary—Sr. JANET DOYLE, O.P. Team Members: Sr. JULIA MARIE HUTCHISON, S.N.D.; Sr. MIRIAM EBLE, S.N.D.; Sr. MARY BURKE, S.N.J.M.; Ms. DONNA THERKELSEN; Sr. JOAN FRANCES FURLONG, S.N.D.; Sr. NADINE KASCHALK, C.P.P.S.; Mrs. SHARI BEIER; Sr. MARY JO SZPILA, S.N.D.; Mr. MICHAEL BEIER, Govt. Prog. Coord.

Catholic Club—PAUL SZYMANSKI, *1601 Jefferson Ave., Toledo.* Tel: 419-243-7255; Fax: 419-243-6337.

Chaplain for Youth—Rev. MELVIN VERHOFF.

Youth Ministry—Rev. MELVIN VERHOFF, Dir. JEFF MIELCAREK, CYO Dir. THOMAS MURNEN, Board Pres. Area Coordinators: SARAH NYE, Back to Earth, Mansfield Deanery. Tel: 419-492-2270. DIANE VERHOFF, Hearthstone, Lima Deanery. Tel: 419-523-5410. MARY KRYSTOWSKI, Heartland, Sandusky Deanery. Tel: 419-929-8722. CINDY MOLNAR, Prism, Toledo. Tel: 419-693-9293. MARY SLATTERY, Crossroads, Defiance & Will-Ful-L Deaneries. Tel: 419-542-7327. MARY ORTON, Two Rivers & Tiffin Deanery. Tel 419-422-7774. LORI KAMELESKI, Beacon, Fremont Deanery. Tel: 419-542-7327. JOYCE MEYER, Kaleidoscope, Toledo. Tel: 419-478-5846. Affiliated Boards: Bishop's Education Council; Catholic Club; Mr. ERIC STOCKARD, Pres.

Resource Center—Mr. DAVID VROOMAN, Interim Dir.

Campus Ministry—Rev. DANIEL ZAK, Dir., *2086 Brookdale Rd., Toledo, 43606.* Tel: 419-531-4992.

Secretariat of Catholic Charities

Catholic Charities—Mr. DONALD L. WISLER, L.I.S.W., Sec. & Exec. Dir.

Direct Services Division:

Adoption Services—PEG GEHRING, Dir.

Counseling Department—ALAN WILLCOX, Dir. Serving Lucas, Wood, eastern Fulton & western Ottawa Counties.

Regional Offices:

Eastern—MORGAN ROGERS, Dir., *249 W. Main St., Norwalk, 44857.* Tel: 419-668-3073; Fax: 419-663-5070. Serving Crawford, Erie, Huron, eastern Ottawa, Richland, Sandusky, Seneca and Wyandot Counties.

Western—SANDRA HERMAN, Dir., *1012 Ralston Ave., Defiance, 43512.* Tel: 419-782-4933; Fax: 419-784-4760. Serving Allen, Defiance, western Fulton, Hancock, Henry, Paulding, Van Wert and Williams Counties.

Social Ministry and Advocacy Division:

Parish and Community Outreach Department—LOUIS COCCHIARELLA, Dir. Tel: 419-244-6711.

English as a Second Language—Sr. MARCIA BUCHAED, F.M.I.

Hispanic Ministry—Sr. ESTELLA IBARRA, F.M.I.

Ministry to Aging—DONNA POSLUSZNY.

Parish Outreach/CCMT—MARGARET BOWMAN.

Project Mustard Seed—MSIMBI SHUMAN.

Social Action/Campaign for Human Development—Sr. JOAN MICHALIK, I.H.M., Dir.

Family Life/Respect Life—LUCY ABU-ABSI, Dir.

Rural Life Ministries—Sr. MARY CHRISTINE PRATT, O.S.U., Dir., *301 S. Main St., Fostoria, 44830.* Tel: 419-435-1543.

Ministry to Persons with Disabilities—JUDY DALTON; Dir., *Kateri Center, 443 Sixth St., Toledo, 43605.* Tel: 419-698-9696; 698-9914 (TTD).

Black Catholic Ministry—GAIL FRANKLIN, Dir.

Migrant Ministry—ALVINA COSTELLA. Tel: 419-244-6711.

Affiliated:

Mareda, Inc. (Vistula Management Co.)—JOHN KIELY, Dir., *P.O. Box 4719, Toledo, 43620.* Tel: 419-242-2300.

Madonna Homes—JEANETTE VANOVER, Mgr., *722 Huron St., Toledo, 43604.* Tel: 419-244-3758.

Regina Manor—JODY DOWNEY, Mgr., *3731 N. Erie St., Toledo, 43611.* Tel: 419-246-4731.

Delaware Acres—MELAINIE PARKS-BAYNARD, Mgr., *725 Buchanan, Fremont, 43420.* Tel: 419-334-9558.

Moody Manor—KATHY KEANE, Mgr., *2293-1/2 Kent St., Toledo, 43620.* Tel: 419-246-4737.

Hope Manor—CATHY CROSSEN, Mgr., *4702 Violet Rd., Toledo, 43623.* Tel: 419-246-4733.

Michaelmas Manor—HALLEY DOWNEY, Mgr., *3260 Schneider Rd., Toledo, 43614.* Tel: 419-246-4735.

St. Anthony Villa—GARY Q. TESTER, Dir., *2740 W. Central Ave., Toledo, 43606.* Tel: 419-473-1353.

St. Vincent De Paul Society—CHARLES NEUSER, Pres. SANDRA BLOOMQUIST, Vice Pres., *1001 Washington St., Toledo, 43624.* Tel: 419-243-6963.

Secretariat of Communications and Public Relations

Secretary—Rev. Msgr. DONALD E. HEINTSCHEL, *6832 Convent Blvd., Sylvania, 43560.* Tel: 419-882-1530.

Diocesan Archives—Vacant, *c/o 2544 Parkwood Ave., Toledo, 43610.* Tel: 419-255-1890.

"Catholic Chronicle"—PATRICIA L. MORRISON, Mng. Editor, *2130 Madison Ave., P.O. Box 1866, Toledo, 43624.* Tel: 419-243-4178.

Affiliated:

Diocesan Directory—Mrs. RITA BAUR, Editor.

Other Organizations

CCMT (Central City Ministries of Toledo)—Cochairpersons: Sr. VIRGINIA WELSH, O.S.F.T.; Ms. CANDICE RENNER; Miss SUZANNE STAPLETON; SHARON RAPPAPORT, Dir. Devel. & Public Rels. DENNIS PAKULSKI, Business Mgr., *1119 W. Bancroft St., Toledo, 43606.* Tel: 419-244-9516.

Corda Club—Co-Chm.: BECKY CRABTREE; MARY GUSTWILLER.

Cursillo Movement—Spiritual Directors: Rev. EDWARD J. LITTELMANN, *430 Main St., Huron, 44839.* Tel: 419-433-5725. Rev. JAMES E. BROWN, *821 N. Wheeling St., Toledo, 43605.* Tel: 419-693-2198. Deacon JOSE BAUTISTA, *10917 Nelson Rd., Bowling Green, 43402.* Tel: 419-352-6477. Sr. EDNA MICHEL, O.S.F.T., *200 St. Francis Ave., Tiffin, 44883.* Tel: 419-447-0435. Lay Directors: PAT MILLER; GUS MILLER, *4254 Co. Rd. 27, Helena, 43435.* Tel: 419-638-3790.

Diocesan Attorneys—JOHN HAYWARD; TOM PLETZ, *1000 Jackson St., Toledo, 43624.* Tel: 419-241-4201.

Diocesan Insurance Program—JOSEPH SPENTHOFF, Branch Mgr., *Gallagher-Bassett Insurance Services, 5640 Southwyck Blvd, Toledo, 43614.* Tel: 419-865-8821.

MCCR (Ministry To Catholic Charismatic Renewal)—Mr. ROY HANDY, *550 Clark St., Toledo, 43605-2296.*

Serra International—Dr. AL VOEGELE, District Governor, *126 Redwood, Mansfield, 44907.*

Lima Serra Club—Mr. EDWARD ODENWELLER, Pres., *11065 Dutch Rd., Delphos, 45833.*

Mansfield Serra Club—Mr. PAUL WEITZEL, Pres., *132 Betzstone Dr., Mansfield, 44907.*

Tiffin Serra Club—Mrs. JANET DELL, Pres., *95 Gibbon Ct., Tiffin, 44883.*

Toledo Serra Club—Mr. DAVID LINCOLN, *3310 Craigmoor Ave., Toledo, 43614.*

Secular Order of Discalced Carmelites—KENNETH KRASNIEWSKI, Contact Person, *Our Lady of the Holy Rosary Fraternity, 5631 304th St., Toledo, 43611.*

Secular Franciscans—(Formerly Third Order), Contact: Our Lady of Consolation Province Minister. Tel: 216-839-2023. Deacon JOHN KINDER, S.F.O.

St. Paschal Fraternity—*1933 Spielbusch, Toledo, 43624.* MARGARET L. SHANTEAU, *2929 131st St., Toledo, 43611.*

Worldwide Marriage Encounter—Registration Couple: JOE NOONAN; CHERYL NOONAN, *P.O. Box 871, Toledo, 44883.*

National Marriage Encounter, Northwest Ohio, Inc.—Registration Couple: DENNIS ALT; GAY ALT, *1448 State Rte. 4, Bellevue, 44811.* Tel: 419-483-5129.

Retrouvaille—Coordinating Couple: JEFF RUSSELL; TERRY RUSSELL. Tel: 419-868-6447. Registration Couple: STEVE KYLE; JANET KYLE. Tel: 419-882-2558.

Vision Time, Inc.—*200 St. Francis Ave., Tiffin, 44883.* Tel: 419-243-6723. Sr. NANCY WESTMEYER, O.S.F., Contact Person.

St. Francis de Sales High School Endowment Fund, Inc.—*2323 W. Bancroft St., Toledo, 43607.*

CLERGY, PARISHES, MISSIONS AND PAROCHIAL SCHOOLS

CITY OF TOLEDO
(Lucas County)

1—QUEEN OF THE MOST HOLY ROSARY CATHEDRAL (1915), Very Rev. Ronald R. Warnimont, Rector; Deacons Lawrence Adams; Hugh Murray; Jesus Villagomez. In res., Most Revs. James R. Hoffman; Robert W. Donnelly; Albert Ottenweller; Revs. Bernard J. Boff; Kenneth G. Morman.
Office: 2535 Collingwood Blvd., 43610. Tel: 419-244-9575; Fax: 419-244-0471.
Res., 2544 Parkwood Ave., 43610-1300. Tel: 419-255-1890.
Church—2561 Collingwood Blvd. and Islington St., 43610. [JC]
School—Tel: 419-243-4396.
Sisters 2; Lay Teachers 12; Students 212.

2—BLESSED SACRAMENT (1924), Revs. Robert Reinhart; Patrick J. Rohen; Deacons Robert Gillen; Ronald Ludwikowski; Norman Maciejewski; Harold Welch.
Res., 4227 Bellevue Rd., 43613-3999. Tel: 419-472-2288. [JC]
School—2216 Castlewood Dr., 43613. Tel: 419-472-1121; Fax: 419-472-1679.
Catechesis/Religious Programs—Students 582.

3—CHRIST THE KING (1953), Revs. Neil Lucas; Greg Peatee; Deacons Edward Frazier; Lawrence Trotter; Gerald Sortman; Mrs. Suzanne Marciniak, Pastoral Assoc.
Res., 4100 Harvest Ln., 43623-4399. Tel: 419-475-4348; Fax: 419-475-4050. [JC]
School—Tel: 419-475-0909.
Sisters 2; Lay Teachers 19; Students 597.
Catechesis/Religious Programs—Students 200.

4—COMMUNITY OF THE RISEN CHRIST (1972), Rev. Michael G. Madden.
Res., P.O. Box 544, Perrysburg, 43552-0544. Tel: 419-243-7255.

5—CORPUS CHRISTI, UNIVERSITY OF TOLEDO (1970), Rev. James J. Bacik; Ms. Pam Meseroll, Admin. In res., Rev. Earl Loeffer.
Res., 2080 Brookdale Rd., 43606. Tel: 419-536-7796; 531-4992 (Office); Fax: 419-531-1775.

6—GESU (1920), Revs. Clement Metzger, S.J.; Paul A. Woefl, S.J.; Deacons Larry Petersen; Ed Kelley; Richard Warren.
Res., 2049 Parkside Blvd., 43607. Tel: 419-531-1421; Fax: 419-531-0270. [JC]
School—Tel: 419-536-5634; Fax: 419-531-8932.
Sisters of Notre Dame 1; Lay Teachers 25; Students 430.
Catechesis/Religious Programs—Students 110.

7—GOOD SHEPHERD (1873), Rev. Jerome Nowakowski; Deacon Leon Holmer. In res., Rev. Gerald Knueven.
Res., 550 Clark St., 43605. Tel: 419-691-5815. [JC]
Catechesis/Religious Programs—Students 62.

8—HOLY ROSARY (1906) (Slovak), Rev. Kenneth G. Morman; Deacon Richard Fazekas.
Res., 821 N. Wheeling St., 43605. Tel: 419-693-2198. [JC]
School—Tel: 419-691-1653.
Religious 3; Lay Teachers 10; Students 179.

9—IMMACULATE CONCEPTION (1868), Rev. Paul M. Kwiatkowski.
Res., 434 Western Ave., 43609. Tel: 419-243-1829.
School—Queen of Apostles Consolidated, 235 Courtland St., 43609. Tel: 419-241-7829. Sr. Brenda Haynes, S.N.D., Prin.
Students 153.
Catechesis/Religious Programs—Students 115.

10—LITTLE FLOWER OF JESUS (1928), Rev. T. Patrick Scharf.
Res., 5522 Dorr St., 43615. Tel: 419-537-6997; Fax: 419-537-1469. [JC]
School—Tel: 419-536-1194.
Lay Teachers 17; Students 369.
Catechesis/Religious Programs—Students 141.

11—OUR LADY OF LOURDES (1926) (Polish), Rev. Thomas Wehinger; Deacons Clifford Kujawa; Robert Pacholski; Steve Veselka.
Res., 6149 Hill Ave., 43615. Tel: 419-865-2345; Fax: 419-865-2545.
School—Tel: 419-866-0736.
Lay Teachers 9; Students 242.
Catechesis/Religious Programs—P.R.E.P. Sr. Dorothy Forman, O.S.F.S., Pastoral Assoc. & Christian Form. Dir.
Students 70.

12—OUR LADY OF PERPETUAL HELP (1918), Rev. Francis J. Speier; Deacons Victor DeCrane; Daniel Quinn; Philip Skeldon; Robert Lesinski; Diego Perez; Ben Cooley, (Retired); Michael Learned.
2255 Central Grove Ave., 43614.
Res., 3464 Glynn Dr., 43614. Tel: 419-382-4992.
Church—2255 Central Grove, 43614. Tel: 419-382-5511; Fax: 419-382-7360. [JC]
School—(Grades PreK-8). Tel: 419-382-5696.
Lay Teachers 27; Students 552.
Catechesis/Religious Programs—Students 112.

13—REGINA COELI (1954), Rev. James E. Auth; Deacons James Dudley; George Mitchell; Larry Schaupp; John Wiciak. In res., Rev. Raymond C. Sheperd.
Res., 530 Regina Pkwy., 43612. Tel: 419-476-0922 (Office); 476-2281 (Home).
School—Tel: 419-476-0920.
Lay Teachers 20; Students 367.
Catechesis/Religious Programs—Students 130.

14—SACRED HEART OF JESUS (1883) (German), Rev. Frank E. Eckart; Deacon Howard Narges; Sr. Mary Maxine, S.N.D., Pastoral Assoc. In res., Revs. William J. Kubacki; Joel Buchman.
Res., 509 Oswald St., 43605. Tel: 419-698-1664. [JC]
School—Tel: 419-691-0869.
Sisters of Notre Dame 1; Lay Teachers 8; Students 229.

15—ST. ADALBERT (1907) (Polish), Rev. Gerald R. Grupczynski, S.Ch.
Res., 3233 Lagrange St., 43608. Tel: 419-241-4179; Fax: 419-241-1136.
School—Tel: 419-243-5257.
Felician Sisters 2; Lay Teachers 9; Students 199.

16—ST. AGNES (1910), Rev. Richard G. Miller; Deacons John C. Vogel; Clarence Fisher.
Res., 3854 Berkeley Dr., 43612. Tel: 419-478-2384; Fax: 419-478-6556. [JC]
School—Tel: 419-478-7778.
Franciscan Sisters 1; Lay Teachers 11; Students 199.
Catechesis/Religious Programs—Students 60.

17—ST. ANN. Consolidated with St. Teresa to form St. Martin de Porres. See separate listing.

18—ST. ANTHONY (1882) (Polish), Rev. Gerald E. Knueven, Admin.
Res., 1416 Nebraska Ave., 43607. Tel: 419-241-6465.

19—ST. CATHERINE OF SIENA (1930), Rev. Michael G. Hohenbrink; Sr. Nancy Ferguson, O.S.F., Pastoral Assoc. In res., Rev. Melvin Verhoff.
Res., 4555 N. Haven Ave., 43612. Tel: 419-478-9558; Fax: 419-478-9434. [JC]
School—1155 Corbin Rd., 43612. Tel: 419-478-9900.
Lay Teachers 19; Students 390.
Catechesis/Religious Programs—Students 70.

20—ST. CHARLES BORROMEO (1904), Rev. Thomas J. Extejt. In res., Rev. Bruce L. Farmer.
Res., 1842 Airport Hwy., 43609-2069. Tel: 419-385-7431; Fax: 419-385-9152. [JC]
School—Tel: 419-382-7271.
Lay Teachers 11; Students 231.
Catechesis/Religious Programs—Students 62.

21—ST. CLEMENT (1947), Revs. Gary R. Miller; Raymond A. Fisher; Deacons Wilbur Moore; Ronald Peeps; Ray Burzynski.
Res., 3030 Tremainsville Rd., 43613. Tel: 419-472-2111; Fax: 419-479-3215. [JC]
School—Tel: 419-474-9657.
Lay Teachers 16; Students 357.
Catechesis/Religious Programs—Tel: 419-472-1259.
Students 450.

22—ST. FRANCIS DE SALES (1841), Sr. Kathleen Scott, L.C.M., Pastoral Admin.; Rev. Theodore Miller; Sr. Angelita Abair, O.S.U., Pastoral Assoc.
Office: 501 Cherry St., 43604. Tel: 419-243-4242.

23—ST. HEDWIG (1875) (Polish), Rev. Joseph J. Przybysz; Deacons Michael Pence; Thomas Bland.
Res., 2916 Lagrange St., 43608. Tel: 419-729-3148. [JC]
School—Tel: 419-729-3658.
Franciscan Sisters 4; Lay Teachers 12; Students 256.

24—ST. HYACINTH (1927) (Polish), Rev. Jonathan C. Wight; Deacon Irvin Gonsiorowski; Sr. M. Pius, O.S.F.S., Parish Min.
Res., 719 Evesham Ave., 43607. Tel: 419-535-7077. [JC]
School—Tel: 419-535-7078.
Sisters of St. Francis 1; Lay Teachers 8; Students 197.
Catechesis/Religious Programs—Students 197.

25—ST. JAMES (1913), Rev. Paul M. Kwiatkowski; Deacon Bernabe Romo.
Res., 914 Colburn St., 43609. Tel: 419-243-2640.
School—Queen of Apostles, Tel: 419-241-7829.
Lay Teachers 14; Students 150.

26—ST. JOAN OF ARC (1978), Rev. Gerald L. Ceranowski; Deacons Stan Przybylek; Larry Lottier.
Res., 5856 Heatherdowns Blvd., 43614. Tel: 419-866-6181.
School—5850 Heatherdowns Blvd., 43614. Tel: 419-866-6177; Fax: 419-866-4107.
Lay Teachers 22; Students 606.
Catechesis/Religious Programs—Fax: 419-866-6142.
Students 135.

27—ST. JOHN THE BAPTIST (1918), Revs. Robert J. Wilhelm; Kent R. Kaufman.
Res., 5153 Summit St., 43611. Tel: 419-726-2034; Fax: 419-726-1447. [JC]
School—Tel: 419-726-7761.
Sisters 2; Lay Teachers 20; Students 495.
Catechesis/Religious Programs—Tel: 419-726-9141.
Students 150.

28—ST. JOSEPH (1854) (French), Rev. Stephen Majoros.
Mailing Address: P.O. Box 790, 43697. Tel: 419-248-4378.
Res., 626 Locust St., 43604.
Church—Erie & Locust Sts., 43604. [JC]

29—ST. JUDE (1955), Rev. Bernard A. Kokocinski. In res., Rev. Gerald J. Robinson.
Res., 3650 Victory Ave., 43607. Tel: 419-531-1294.
School—Tel: 419-531-4951.
Lay Teachers 10; Students 152.

30—ST. LOUIS (1872) (French), Rev. Kenneth G. Morman, Admin.
Res., 459 6th St., 43605. Tel: 419-691-0422; Fax: 419-691-0422. [JC]
Outreach—Helping Hands Soup Kitchen. Sr. Barbara Vano, O.S.F., Program Dir.

31—ST. MARTIN DE PORRES (1990), Rev. P. Martin Donnelly; Deacons John Algee; Tom Carone; Timothy Etue.
Res., 1119 W. Bancroft, 43606. Tel: 419-241-4544; Fax: 419-244-3676.
Schools—(Grades PreK-3). Tel: 419-241-2892.; (Grades 4-8) 1462 Woodland Ave., 43606. Tel: 419-244-7141. Sr. Mary Lynda Snyder, S.N.D., Prin.; Sr. Barbara Marie Sloan, S.N.D., Asst. Prin.
Sisters of Notre Dame 3; Lay Teachers 11; Students 230.

32—ST. MARY OF THE ASSUMPTION (1854), Sr. Virgina Welsh, O.S.F., Pastoral Admin.; Rev. Theodore Miller, Chap.; Deacons Stanley Gogol; James Hendricks; Mark Bussemeier.
Res., 219 Page St., 43620. Tel: 419-243-9213; Fax: 419-243-5405. [JC]
School—Tel: 419-241-3361; Fax: 419-243-5405.
Sisters 2; Lay Teachers 10; Students 220.
Convent—217 Page St., 43620. Tel: 419-241-2349.

33—ST. MICHAEL (1900), Rev. Robert J. Fisher; Deacons John Grandowicz; Harry Yeackel.
Res., 420 Sandusky St., 43611. Tel: 419-726-1947.
School—St. Elizabeth Seton School, 1030 Clay St., 43608. Tel: 419-726-4471.
Sisters 3; Lay Teachers 6; Students 218.

34—ST. PATRICK HISTORIC (1863) (Irish), Rev. Richard J. Saelzler.
Res., 130 Avondale Ave., 43602. Tel: 419-243-6452; Fax: 419-243-7032.

35—ST. PATRICK OF HEATHERDOWNS (1956), Revs. Dennis M. Metzger; Keith A. Stripe; George J. Wagner; Mrs. Marla Overholt, Pastoral Assoc.; Deacons Carl Braham; Joe Kest; Albert Righi; Joe Windham.
Res., 4201 Heatherdowns Blvd., 43614. Tel: 419-381-1540; Fax: 419-381-2727. [JC]
School—Tel: 419-381-1775; Fax: 419-389-1161.
Sisters 3; Lay Teachers 34; Students 745.
Catechesis/Religious Programs—Tel: 419-381-0240. Ms. Kathy Juhasz, D.R.E.
Students 200.

36—SS. PETER AND PAUL (1866) (Hispanic), Rev. Richard E. Notter.
Office: 728 S. St. Clair St., 43609. Tel: 419-241-5822.
School—Queen of Apostles. (Also serves Immaculate Conception Parish and St. James Parish). 235 Courtland, 43609. Tel: 419-241-7829.
Lay Teachers 9; Students 165.

37—ST. PIUS X (1953), Rev. Dennis J. Kelsch, O.S.F.S. In res., Revs. James R. Sanford, O.S.F.S.; John Graden, O.S.F.S.
Res., 2929 Ilger Ave., 43606. Tel: 419-535-7672; Fax: 419-535-7810.
School—Tel: 419-535-7688.
Lay Teachers 12; Students 229.

38—ST. STANISLAUS (1912) (Polish), Rev. Gerald E. Knueven.
Mailing Address: 1416 Nebraska Ave., 43607. Tel: 419-241-6465.
Church—421 N. Detroit Ave., 43607. Tel: 419-255-6245.

39—ST. STEPHEN (1898) (Hungarian), Rev. Joseph L. Vamos.
Res., 1880 Genesee St., 43605. Tel: 419-691-1673. [JC]
School—2018 Consaul, 43605. Tel: 419-691-8760.
Lay Teachers 13; Students 195.

40—ST. TERESA. Consolidated with St. Ann to form St. Martin de Porres. See separate listing.

41—St. Thomas Aquinas (1915), Rev. John R. Blaser.
Res., 729 White St., 43605-2719. Tel: 419-698-1519.
School—Tel: 419-691-4328; Fax: 419-691-4365.
Lay Teachers 10; Students 243.
Catechesis/Religious Programs—Students 234.

42—St. Vincent de Paul (1928), Rev. Gerald Robinson, Admin.; Deacon Gerald Ignatowski.
Res., 1035 Woodward Ave., 43608. Tel: 419-726-1448. [JC]
School—St. Elizabeth Seton School, 1030 Clay St., 43608. Tel: 419-726-4471.
Sisters 4; Lay Teachers 8; Students 222.

OUTSIDE THE CITY OF TOLEDO

Alvada, Seneca Co., St. Peter (1854), Rev. Leonard A. Kistler, C.PP.S.; Deacon Lewis E. Reinhart.
Mailing Address: 41 N. Perry St., P.O. Box89, New Riegel, 44853. Tel: 419-595-2567. [CEM]
Catechesis/Religious Programs—Students 66.

Antwerp, Paulding Co., St. Mary (1868), Rev. Herman F. Scherger; Deacon Robert L. Nighswander, Admin.
Res., 303 S. Monroe St., P.O. Box G, 45813. Tel: 419-258-8335. [JC]
Catechesis/Religious Programs—Students 131.

Archbold, Fulton Co., St. Peter (1846), Rev. Gary M. Ferguson.
Res., 614 N. Defiance St., 43502. Tel: 419-446-9288. [CEM]
Catechesis/Religious Programs—Tel: 419-446-2150.
Students 170.

Assumption, Fulton Co., St. Mary of Assumption (1877), Rev. Lawrence F. Varney; Deacon Joseph Repka.
Residence and Mailing—2649 U.S. 20, Swanton, NY 43558. Tel: 419-644-4014.
School—Holy Trinity, 2639 U.S. 20, Swanton, 43558. Tel: 419-644-3971; Fax: 419-644-5018.
Lay Teachers 9; Students 140; Preschool 29.

Attica, Seneca Co., SS. Peter and Paul (1882), Rev. Joseph P. Szybka.
Res., P.O. Box 461, 44807. Tel: 419-426-3043; Fax: 419-426-3043. [CEM]
Church—14204 E. County Rd. 56, 44807.
Catechesis/Religious Programs—Students 106.

Bascom, Seneca Co., St. Patrick (1864), Rev. David R. Bruning.
Res., 6230 W. Tiffin, Box 226, 44809. Tel: 419-937-2715. [CEM]
Parish Hall: Tel: 419-937-2713.
Catechesis/Religious Programs—Students 138.

Bellevue, Huron Co., Immaculate Conception (1859), Rev. Robert A. Tucceri; Sr. Mary Susanna Weaver, S.N.D.; Deacons Robert Swartz; Frank Klein.
Res., 231 E. Center St., 44811. Tel: 419-483-3417; Fax: 419-483-2585. [CEM]
School—Immaculate Conception School, Tel: 419-483-6066; Fax: 419-483-5059.
Sisters 2; Lay Teachers 19; Students 360.
Catechesis/Religious Programs—Students 210.

Bethlehem, Richland Co., Sacred Heart of Jesus (1833), Rev. Gary R. Walters; Deacons Leo Hartings; Stephen R. Keller.
Res., 5746 State Rte. 61 S., Shelby, 44875. Tel: 419-342-2797. [CEM]
School—Tel: 419-683-1697.
Lay Teachers 6; Students 32.

Bismark, Huron Co., St. Sebastian (1846) (German), Rev. William Hoyng, C.PP.S.
Res., 16209 E. C. Rd. #46, Bellevue, 44811. Tel: 419-483-3231. [CEM]
Church—5582 Bismark Rd., Bellevue, 44811.
Catechesis/Religious Programs—Students 90.

Blakeslee, Williams Co., St. Joseph (1865) (German), Rev. Frederick J. Duschl.
Res., P.O. Box 196, 43505. Tel: 419-272-2214. [CEM]
School—Tel: 419-272-2914.
Lay Teachers 6; Students 70.
Catechesis/Religious Programs—Students 70.

Bluffton, Allen Co., St. Mary (1866), Sr. Yvonne Fischer, O.S.F., Pastoral Leader; Rev. David Beck, Chap.; Deacon Jack Stahl.
Mailing Address: P.O. Box 92, 45817. Tel: 419-358-8631.
Catechesis/Religious Programs—Students 220.

Bono, Lucas Co., Our Lady of Mt. Carmel (1917), Rev. Charles Denny, Chap.; Sr. Marilyn Gottemoeller, R.S.M., Pastoral Leader.
Res., 1105 Elliston Rd., Martin, 43445. Tel: 419-836-7681; Fax: 419-836-7681.
Catechesis/Religious Programs—Students 89.

Bowling Green, Wood Co., St. Aloysius (1862), Rev. Thomas Leyland; Deacons Jose Bautista; Ramon Llanas.
Res., 150 S. Enterprise, P.O. Box 485, 43402. Tel: 419-352-4195; Fax: 419-352-4738.
School—Tel: 419-352-8614. Mrs. Mary Goodenow, Prin.
Lay Teachers 12; Students 265.
Catechesis/Religious Programs—Tel: 419-352-1139.
Students 265.

St. Thomas More University Parish (1967), Sr. Mary Kuhlman, O.S.F., Pastoral Leader; Rev. Daniel Zak, Chap. In res., Revs. Paul Mueller; Joseph Weigman.
Res., 425 Thurstin, P.O. Box 677, 43402. Tel: 419-352-7555; 255-3609; Fax: 419-352-7557.

Bryan, Williams Co., St. Patrick (1857), Rev. Charles F. Ritter; Deacons Dennis Jackson; Ignacio Garza; Tom Dominique.
Res., 704 S. Portland, 43506. Tel: 419-636-1044.
School—Tel: 419-636-3592.
Lay Teachers 10; Students 154.
Catechesis/Religious Programs—Tel: 419-636-8771.
Students 180.

Bucyrus, Crawford Co., Holy Trinity (1865) (German), Rev. Dennis A. Schroeder.
Res., 760 Tiffin Rd., 44820. Tel: 419-562-1346; Fax: 419-562-2784. [CEM]
School—Tel: 419-562-2741.
Lay Teachers 13; Students 230.
Catechesis/Religious Programs—Tel: 419-562-2645.
Students 194.

Carey, Wyandot Co., Our Lady of Consolation, Basilica-National Shrine (1867), Revs. Pius Poff, O.F.M.Conv.; Peter Gough, O.F.M.Conv.; George Schroeder, O.F.M.Conv.; Edmund Goldback, O.F.M.Conv.; Alfred Sartor, O.F.M.Conv.; Bros. Andrew Bramanti, O.F.M.Conv.; Bryan Hoban, O.F.M.Conv.; Joseph Candel, O.F.M.Conv.; Deacons Arden Harold Nye; Floyd Derr.
Res., 315 W. Clay St., 43316. Tel: 419-396-7107; Fax: 419-396-3355. [CEM]
School—Tel: 419-396-6166.
Lay Teachers 10; Students 178.
Catechesis/Religious Programs—Students 105.
Mission—Salem Township, Wyandot Co., St. Joseph. [CEM]

Cecil, Paulding Co., Immaculate Conception (1879), Rev. Herman Scherger; Deacon David Laker Tel: 419-899-2479.
Res., Rte. 2, 21706 State Rte. 114, Cloverdale, 45827. Tel: 419-488-3563. [CEM]
Church—Stratford St., 45821. Tel: 419-399-5644.

Cloverdale, Putnam Co., St. Barbara (1898) (German), Rev. Albert C. Miorin.
Res., 160 Main St., P.O. Box 8, 45827. Tel: 419-488-2391.

Clyde, Sandusky Co., St. Mary (1890), Rev. George H. Losiewicz; Deacon Tito Ollervides.
Res., 609 Vine St., 43410. Tel: 419-547-9610. [CEM]
School—615 Vine St., 43410. Tel: 419-547-9687. Sr. Rita Rogier, Prin.
Sisters 2; Lay Teachers 8; Students 171.
Catechesis/Religious Programs—Sr. Bonnie Smith, D.R.E.
Students 100.

Columbus Grove, Putnam Co., St. Anthony of Padua (1912) (German), Rev. Keith J. McCormack.
Res., 512 W. Sycamore St., 45830. Tel: 419-659-2263. [CEM]
School—Tel: 419-659-2103.
Sisters of the Most Precious Blood 3; Lay Teachers 12; Students 226.
Catechesis/Religious Programs—Students 148.

Continental, Putnam Co., St. John the Baptist (1907), Rev. Albert C. Miorin; Deacon Joseph Heeter.
203 E. Elm St., P.O. Box 368, 45831. Tel: 419-596-3419. [JC]

Crestline, Crawford Co., St. Joseph (1861) (German), Rev. Gary R. Walters; Deacons Joseph Burkhart; William Horning; William Rall.
Res., 331 N. Thoman St., 44827. Tel: 419-683-2015. [CEM]
School—333 N. Thoman St., 44827. Tel: 419-683-1284.
Lay Teachers 9; Students 140.
Catechesis/Religious Programs—Students 65.

Cuba, Putnam Co., St. Isidore (1917), Rev. John Hoying, C.PP.S.; Deacon Robert Klausing.
Res., 312 N. Broad St., Kalida, 45853. Tel: 419-532-3431; Fax: 419-532-3437.

Custar, Wood Co., St. Louis (1864), Rev. Paul Fahrbach; Sr. Dionne Sartor, O.S.F., Pastoral Assoc., Tel: 419-669-3920.
Res., 22792 Defiance Pike, 43511. Tel: 419-669-2845. [CEM][JC]
School—Tel: 419-669-2878.
Sisters of St. Francis 1; Lay Teachers 5; Students 53.

Cygnet, Wood Co., Sacred Heart (1890), Sr. Betty Glemboski, O.S.F.S., Pastoral Leader.
Mailing Address: 115 E. Cherry St., North Baltimore, 45872-1134. Tel: 419-257-2319.
Church—Bradford St., 43413.

Defiance, Defiance Co., St. John the Evangelist (1850), Rev. George E. Wenzinger; Deacons Chris Mendez; Randall Redington; Donald Meyer.
Res., 510 Jackson St., 43512. Tel: 419-782-7121. [CEM]
School—Tel: 419-782-2136.
Lay Teachers 8; Students 168.
Catechesis/Religious Programs—Students 260.

St. Mary (1873), Very Rev. Edward J. Schleter; Deacon George Newton, Pastoral Assoc.
Res., 707 Jefferson Ave., 43512. Tel: 419-782-2776.
School—(Grades PreK-6). Tel: 419-782-2751.
Lay Teachers 11; Students 218.
Catechesis/Religious Programs—Tel: 419-782-2776.
Students 501.

Delphos, Allen Co., St. John the Evangelist (1844) (German), Revs. Thomas Gorman; Todd Dominique. Pastoral Assocs.: Sr. M. Dean Pfahler; Charles Honigford.
Res., 331 E. Second St., 45833. Tel: 419-695-4050; Fax: 419-695-4060. [CEM]
School—Tel: 419-692-8561.
Sisters of Notre Dame 5; Lay Teachers 34; Students 721.
High School—Tel: 419-692-5371; Fax: 419-692-5371.
Sisters 2; Lay Teachers 20; Students 322.
Catechesis/Religious Programs—Tel: 419-692-1286.
Students 207.

Deshler, Henry Co., Immaculate Conception (1871), Rev. Paul Fahrbach; Sr. Dionne Sartor, O.S.F.T., Pastoral Assoc., Tel: 419-669-3920.
Mailing Address: 230 Allendale Ave., 43516. Tel: 419-278-3686.
Res., 22767 Defiance Pike, Custar, 43511. Tel: 419-669-3920.
Catechesis/Religious Programs—Students 70.

Edgerton, Williams Co., St. Mary (1865), Rev. Thomas E. Oedy; Deacon Roy Sanders.
Res., 133 Bement St., P.O. Box 355, 43517. Tel: 419-298-2932. [CEM]
School—Tel: 419-298-2531.
Sisters of St. Francis 1; Lay Teachers 6; Students 111.
Catechesis/Religious Programs—Students 100.

Fayette, Fulton Co., Our Lady of Mercy (1943), Rev. James J. Holmer.
Res., Box 429, 43521. Tel: 419-237-2441.
Church—409 E. Main St., 43521. Tel: 419-237-2441.
Catechesis/Religious Programs—14691 E. Camden Rd., Waldron, MI 49288. Tel: 517-286-6496.
Students 120.

Findlay, Hancock Co., St. Michael (1834), Revs. Martin Nassr; Jose Corral; Ronald A. Schock; Deacons Robert Billmaier; Dorsey Hazelton; David Sadler; John Zoll. Pastoral Assocs.: Felix Goebel-Komala; Thomas J. Leddy.
Mailing Address: 422 Western Ave., 45840. Tel: 419-422-2646. [CEM]
School—Tel: 419-422-2512.
Lay Teachers 32; Students 605.
Catechesis/Religious Programs—Tel: 419-423-2123.
Students 441.

Fort Jennings, Putnam Co., St. Joseph (1848) (German), Rev. Michael Schelling.
Res., 135 Water St., P.O. Box 68, 45844-0068. Tel: 419-286-2132. [CEM]
Catechesis/Religious Programs—Tel: 419-286-2019.
Students 406.

Fostoria, Seneca Co., St. Wendelin (1858), Revs. Daniel J. Ring; Joseph P. Cardone; Deacon Joseph Hulderman.
Res., 222 N. Wood St., P.O. Box 836, 44830. Tel: 419-435-1875; Fax: 419-435-7826. [CEM]
School—Tel: 419-435-1809.
Sisters of Notre Dame 3; Lay Teachers 25; Students 441.
High School—Tel: 419-435-8144.
Priests 1; Sisters 1; Lay Teachers 21; Students 245.
Catechesis/Religious Programs—Tel: 419-435-6681. Sr. Madeleva, O.S.F.S.
Students 249.

Fremont, Sandusky Co.,

1—Sacred Heart, (1956), Rev. Mark J. Herzog; Sr. M. Francein, S.N.D., Pastoral Assoc.; Deacon Jose Sanchez. In res., Rev. Donald R. Mueller.
Res., 550 Smith Rd., 43420. Tel: 419-332-7339; Fax: 419-332-9808. [JC]
School—(Grades K-8). Tel: 419-332-7102.
Sisters 4; Lay Teachers 17; Students 289.

2—ST. ANN, (1843), Rev. Gerald J. Chmiel; Deacons Alfredo Diaz; Norbert Wethington.
Res., 1021 W. State St., 43420. Tel: 419-332-7472. [JC]
School—Tel: 419-332-2461.
Lay Teachers 15; Students 185.
Catechesis/Religious Programs—Students 150.

3—ST. CASIMIR, (1915) (Polish), Rev. Robert Weithman; Deacon Tom Ackerman.
Res., 537 Lime St., 43420. Tel: 419-332-1157. [JC]

4—ST. JOSEPH, (1857) (German), Very Rev. Ronald J. LeJeune; Revs. Daniel E. Borgelt; Dennis Hartigan; Deacons William Snyder; James Hammer.
Res., 709 Croghan St., 43420. Tel: 419-334-2638; Fax: 419-334-6929. [CEM][JC]
School—Tel: 419-332-5161; Fax: 419-332-7299.
Sisters of Notre Dame 2; Lay Teachers 18; Students Grades (K-8) 336; Preschool 34.
Catechesis/Religious Programs—120 N. Clover St., 43420. Tel: 419-332-7367.
Students 190.

Frenchtown, Seneca Co., St. Nicholas (1857) (German-French), Rev. Alfred J. Sartor, O.F.M.Conv.
Res., 315 W. Clay St., Carey, 43316. Tel: 419-396-7107; Fax: 419-396-3355. [CEM]
Catechesis/Religious Programs—Students 151.

Galion, Crawford Co., St. Joseph (1853), Rev. Anthony A. Borgia; Deacons Kevin Wintersteller; Alfred Sisson; Gregory Kirk; Raymond Lyons, Jr.
Res., 135 N. Liberty St., 44833. Tel: 419-468-2884. [CEM]
School—(Grades PreK-8). Tel: 419-468-5436; Fax: 419-468-3611.
Sisters 3; Lay Teachers 8; Students 230.
Catechesis/Religious Programs—Students 140.

Genoa, Ottawa Co., Our Lady of Lourdes (1856), Rev. Thomas S. Quinn; Deacons William Perez; Phillip Dazley.
Church—204 Main St., 43430. Tel: 419-855-8501.
Catechesis/Religious Programs—Tel: 419-855-7181.
Students 305.

Gibsonburg, Sandusky Co., St. Michael Church (1892), Rev. Frederick J. Schill; Deacon Rene Gonzalez.
Res., 317 E. Madison St., 43431. Tel: 419-637-2255. [CEM]
Catechesis/Religious Programs—Students 210.

Glandorf, Putnam Co., St. John the Baptist (1834), Rev. Harold C. Brown, C.PP.S.; Sr. Carol Pothast, Pastoral Assoc.; Deacon Robert M. Burwell.
Res., 109 Main St., Box 48, 45848. Tel: 419-538-6928; Fax: 419-538-6147. [CEM][JC]
Catechesis/Religious Programs—Tel: 419-538-6335.
Students 781.

Hamler, Henry Co., St. Paul (1886), Rev. Robert J. Kill; Deacon Donald Badenhop.
Res., 316 Chicago Ave., Holgate, 43527. Tel: 419-264-3321. [CEM]
Catechesis/Religious Programs—Students 66.

Hicksville, Defiance Co., St. Michael (1878). Attended by Edgerton. Rev. Thomas E. Oedy; Deacon Walter Conkle.
Mailing Address: P.O. Box 52, 43526. Tel: 419-542-8202.
Res., 133 W. Bement St., P.O. Box 355, Edgerton, 43517. Tel: 419-298-2932.
Catechesis/Religious Programs—Students 179.

Holgate, Henry Co., St. Mary (1886), Rev. Robert J. Kill; Deacon LaVon Mack.
Res., 316 Chicago Ave., 43527. Tel: 419-264-3321. [CEM]
Catechesis/Religious Programs—Students 80.

Huron, Erie Co., St. Peter (1888), Rev. Edward J. Littelmann; Deacons John Barrett; Jack Busam.
Res., 430 Main St., 44839. Tel: 419-433-5725; Fax: 419-433-7225. [JC]
School—Tel: 419-433-4640; Fax: 419-433-2118.
Lay Teachers 11; Students 190.
Catechesis/Religious Programs—Students 324.

Junction, Paulding Co., St. Mary (1846), Rev. David D. Tscherne; Deacon Richard Carnahan.
Mailing Address: 05480 Moser Rd., Rte. 3, Defiance, 43512. Tel: 419-393-2890.
Catechesis/Religious Programs—Students 55.

Kalida, Putnam Co., St. Michael (1878), Rev. John Hoying, C.PP.S.; Deacon Robert Klausing.
Office: 312 N. Broad St., 45853. Tel: 419-532-3474; Fax: 419-532-3474.
Res., 206 N. Broad St., 45853. Tel: 419-532-3431. [CEM]
Catechesis/Religious Programs—Tel: 419-532-3494. Sr. Mary Louisa Heinl, S.N.D., D.R.E.
Students 643.
Mission—Cuba, Putnam Co., St. Isidore. [CEM]

Kansas, Seneca Co., St. James (1890), Rev. Omer Rethinger.
Res., c/o 875 State Rte. 635, Helena, 43435. Tel: 419-638-3041.
Parish Office—Tel: 419-638-3042.

Kelley's Island, Erie Co., St. Michael (1861), Rev. Nicholas J. Cunningham.
Mailing Address: P.O. Box 490, 43438-0490. Tel: 419-746-2481.

Kirby, Wyandot Co., St. Mary (1861), Rev. William Bodart; Sr. Barbara Jean Miller, Pastoral Assoc.
Res., 225 N. Eighth St., Upper Sandusky, 43351. Tel: 419-294-1268. [CEM]
Catechesis/Religious Programs—Students 101.

Landeck, Allen Co., St. John Baptist (1866), Rev. John W. Fleck.
Res., 14755 Landeck Rd., Rte. 1, Delphos, 45833. Tel: 419-692-0636. [CEM]
Catechesis/Religious Programs—Tel: 419-695-2141.
Students 110.
Mission—Spencerville, Allen Co., St. Patrick, 500 S. Canal, Spencerville, 45887 Tel: 419-695-4138.

Leipsic, Putnam Co., St. Mary (1873), Rev. John K. Joseph, C.M.I. (India).
Res., 318 State St., 45856. Tel: 419-943-2952. [CEM]
School—Tel: 419-943-2801.
Sisters of Notre Dame 3; Lay Teachers 8; Students 175.
Catechesis/Religious Programs—Students 267.

Lexington, Richland Co., Resurrection (1969), Rev. Stanley S. Szybka; Deacon James Hostutler.
Res., 2600 Lexington Ave., 44904. Tel: 419-884-0060; Fax: 419-884-0261.
Catechesis/Religious Programs—Students 372.

Liberty, Seneca Co., St. Andrew (1834), Rev. David R. Bruning.
Church—State Rte. 635 N., P.O. Box 226, Bascom, 44809. Tel: 419-937-2613.
Res., 6230 W. Tiffin St., Bascom, 44809. Tel: 419-937-2715. [CEM]
Catechesis/Religious Programs—Students 58.

Lima, Allen Co.,

1—ST. CHARLES BORROMEO, (1953), Very Rev. David M. Ross; Rev. Arthur Niewiadomski.
Res., 2200 W. Elm, 45805. Tel: 419-228-7635; Fax: 419-229-2835. [JC]
School—Tel: 419-222-2536; Fax: 419-222-8720.
Lay Teachers 38; Students 741.
Catechesis/Religious Programs—Students 311.

2—ST. GERARD, (1916), Very Rev. Denis J. Sweeney, C.SS.R.; Revs. Stephen S. Haynes, C.Ss.R.; Louis A. Olive, C.Ss.R.; Deacon Elias Pina. In res., Revs. Thomas J. Barrett, C.Ss.R.; Andrew Costello, C.Ss.R.
Res., 240 W. Robb Ave., 45801. Tel: 419-224-3080; Fax: 419-225-2231.
School—(Grades PreK-8). Tel: 419-222-0431; Fax: 419-224-6580.
Ursuline Sisters 1; Lay Teachers 21; Students 381.
Catechesis/Religious Programs—Students 304.
Stations—Allen Inn, Tel: 419-221-1346; Lima Manor, Tel: 419-227-2611; Allen Correctional Institute, Tel: 419-224-8000; Lima Correctional Institute, Tel: 419-225-8060; Oakwood Correctional Institute, Tel: 419-225-8052.

3—ST. JOHN THE EVANGELIST, (1901), Rev. David J. Beck; Deacon Richard Gleason.
Res., 781 S. Main St., 45804. Tel: 419-223-4476. [JC]

4—ST. ROSE, (1856), Rev. J. Norbert Howe. In res., Rev. Christopher Vasko.
Res., 479 N. West St., 45801-4294. Tel: 419-222-5521; Fax: 419-228-8439. [JC]
School—Tel: 419-223-6361. Mrs. Janet A. Swallow, Prin.
Lay Teachers 11; Students 125.

Lyons, Fulton Co., Our Lady of Fatima (1946), Rev. James J. Holmer; Deacon Gene Betz.
Mailing Address: & Church—P.O. Box 112, 43533. Tel: 419-923-3170.
Res., P.O. Box 429, Fayette, 43521. Tel: 419-237-2441. [CEM]
Catechesis/Religious Programs—1-8645-S, 43533. Helen Blanchong, D.R.E.
Students 98.

Mansfield, Richland Co., St. Mary (1949), Rev. Gregory R. Hite; Deacons Allan D. Kopp; Russell Shoemaker.
Res., 1630 Ashland Rd., 44905. Tel: 419-589-5464; Fax: 419-589-7085. [JC]
School—Tel: 419-589-2114.
Lay Teachers 9; Students 114.
Catechesis/Religious Programs—Students 91.

St. Peter (1844), Revs. Herbert F. Weber; Stephen G. Rogers; Richard Kennedy.
Res., 54 S. Mulberry St., 44902. Tel: 419-524-2572; Fax: 419-522-2553. [CEM]
School—63 S. Mulberry St., 44902. Tel: 419-524-3351.
Sisters of St. Francis of Mary Immaculate (Joliet, IL) 1; Lay Teachers 21; Students 445.
High School—104 W. First St., 44903. Tel: 419-524-0979.
Sisters of St. Francis of Mary Immaculate (Joliet, IL) 2; Lay Teachers 25; Students 218.
Catechesis/Religious Programs—Students 165.

Marblehead, Ottawa Co., St. Joseph (1867), Rev. James E. Brown.
Res., 802 Barclay, 43440-2101. Tel: 419-798-4177; Fax: 419-798-4260. [CEM]
Catechesis/Religious Programs—113 James St., 43440. Tel: 419-798-5543.
Students 114.

Marygrove, Lucas Co., Immaculate Conception (1840), Rev. Bruce Farmer, Chap.; Deacon David Vrooman, Pastoral Leader.
Res., 1750 Raab Rd., Swanton, 43558. Tel: 419-829-3451. [CEM]
Parish Office: 11383 Sylvania, Berkey, 43504. Tel: 419-825-5421.
Catechesis/Religious Programs—Holy Trinity School (Consolidated), 2639 U.S. Rte. 20, Swanton, 43558. Tel: 419-644-3971.
Students 250.

Marysdale, Defiance Co., Immaculate Conception (1873), Rev. William J. Martin.
Res., 16166 Speaker Rd., Rte. 1, Sherwood, 43556. Tel: 419-899-2549. [CEM]
Catechesis/Religious Programs—Students 70.

Marywood, Seneca Co., St. Michael's (1839) (German), Rev. William Hoyng, C.PP.S.
Res., 16209 E.County Rd. 46, Bellevue, 44811. Tel: 419-483-3231. [CEM]
Catechesis/Religious Programs—Students 88.
Shrine—Sorrowful Mother. For further details see listing under Retreat Houses. Rev. Robert Kunisch, C.PP.S., Dir.

Maumee, Lucas Co., St. Joseph (1841), Rev. Jeffery P. Sikorski; Deacons Kenneth Dickey; Richard Heban; Edward Irelan; Terry McCauley; Paul Morris; Sr. Adrian Walsh, O.S.F., Pastoral Assoc.
Res., 104 W. Broadway, 43537. Tel: 419-893-4848; Fax: 419-891-6969. [CEM]
School—Tel: 419-893-3304.
Notre Dame Sisters 1; Lay Teachers 20; Students 361.
Catechesis/Religious Programs—Tel: 419-893-7025.
Students 365.

Milan, Erie Co., St. Anthony (1862), Rev. James A. Walsh.
Res., 145 Center St., P.O. Box 1200, 44846-1200. Tel: 419-499-4274. [CEM]
Catechesis/Religious Programs—Tel: 419-499-4300.
Students 170.

Miller City, Putnam Co., St. Nicholas (1888), Rev. A. Robert DeSloover.
Mailing Address: Box 36, 45864. Tel: 419-876-3481. [CEM]
Catechesis/Religious Programs—Kathy Degler, D.R.E.
Students 279.
Sister Parish—Holy Family, New Cleveland, Tel: 419-876-3155.

Millersville, Sandusky Co., St. Mary (1859), Rev. Omer Rethinger; Deacon George P. Miller.
Res., 875 State Rte. 635, Helena, 43435. Tel: 419-638-3041. [CEM]
Parish Office—Tel: 419-638-3042.
School—Tel: 419-638-3631.
Lay Teachers 6; Students 74.
Catechesis/Religious Programs—Students 59.
Mission—Kansas, Seneca Co., St. James, 875 SR635 Helena, 43435.

Monroeville, Huron Co., St. Joseph (1861), Rev. Lawrence C. Scharf.
Res., 66 Chapel St., P.O. Box 338, 44847. Tel: 419-465-4142; Fax: 419-465-2319. [CEM]
School—Tel: 419-465-2625.
Sisters of Notre Dame 3; Lay Teachers 10; Students 202.

Montpelier, Williams Co., Sacred Heart (1911), Rev. Frederick J. Duschl; Deacon Ralph Dominique.
Mailing Address: P.O. Box 196, Blakeslee, 43505. Tel: 419-485-5914.
Res., 220 S. East Ave., 43543.
Catechesis/Religious Programs—Students 120.

Napoleon, Henry Co., St. Augustine (1856), Rev. Robert L. Dendinger; Deacons Peter Calvillo; Louis Recker; Robert Bost; Bruce Buckmaster.
Office: 210 E. Clinton St., 43545. Tel: 419-592-7656; 592-6316. [CEM]
School—722 Monroe St., 43545. Tel: 419-592-3641.
Lay Teachers 11; Students 158.
Catechesis/Religious Programs—Students 174.

New Bavaria, Henry Co., Sacred Heart of Jesus (1893) (German), Rev. Stephen Stanbery; Deacon Kenneth Klear.
Res., 13-779 Road Y, Rte. 1, 43548. Tel: 419-653-4157. [CEM]

Catechesis/Religious Programs—Students 135.
Mission—North Creek, Putnam Co., St. Joseph, 13-779 Rd. Y, Rte. 1, 43548.

New Cleveland, Putnam Co., Holy Family, Rev. A. Robert DeSloover.
Res., c/o Box 36, Miller City, 45864. Tel: 419-876-3481. [CEM]
Sister Parish—St. Nicholas, Miller City.
Catechesis/Religious Programs—Students 157.

New London, Huron Co., Our Lady of Lourdes (1853), Rev. Robert Haas.
Res., 18 Park Ave., 44851. Tel: 419-929-4401. [CEM]
Catechesis/Religious Programs—Students 147.

New Riegel, Seneca Co., St. Boniface (1834), Rev. Leonard A. Kistler, C.PP.S.; Deacon Lewis E. Reinhart.
Res., 41 N. Perry St., P.O. Box 89, 44853. Tel: 419-595-2567. [CEM]
Catechesis/Religious Programs—Students 233.

New Washington, Crawford Co., St. Bernard (1844), Rev. Thomas W. Kuhn.
Res., 412 W. Mansfield, 44854. Tel: 419-492-2295. [CEM]
School—Tel: 419-492-2693.
Sisters 1; Lay Teachers 8; Students 164.
Catechesis/Religious Programs—Students 87.

North Auburn, Crawford Co., Mother of Sorrows (1879), Rev. Thomas W. Kuhn.
Mailing Address: 412 W. Mansfield, New Washington, 44854. Tel: 419-492-2295. [CEM]

North Baltimore, Wood Co., Our Lady of the Miraculous Medal (1891), Sr. Betty Glemboski, O.S.F.S., Pastoral Leader.
Res., 115 E. Cherry St., 45872-1134. Tel: 419-257-2319.
Catechesis/Religious Programs—Students 84.
Mission—Cygnet, Wood Co., Sacred Heart, Bradford St., Cygnet, 43413.

North Creek, Putnam Co., St. Joseph (1887) (German), Rev. Stephen Stanbery; Deacon Kenneth Klear.
Res., c/o 13-779 Road Y, Rte. 1, New Bavaria, 43548. Tel: 419-653-4157. [CEM]

Norwalk, Huron Co., St. Mary, Mother of the Redeemer (1860) (Irish), Rev. Nelson Beaver; Deacon Jack Bleile.
Res., 38 W. League St., 44857. Tel: 419-668-2005; Fax: 419-668-3269. [CEM]
School—Tel: 419-668-8780.
Sisters of Notre Dame 2; Lay Teachers 11; Students 282.

St. Paul (1876) (German), Revs. Herbert Willman; Thomas McQuillen; Krzysztof Kardzis (Poland). In res., Rev. Harvey M. Keller, (Retired).
Res., 91 E. Main St., 44857. Tel: 419-668-6044; Fax: 419-663-5770. [CEM]
School—Tel: 419-668-6091.
Sisters of Notre Dame 1; Lay Teachers 22; Students 546.
High School—Tel: 419-668-3005; Fax: 419-668-6417.
Priests 1; Sisters 1; Lay Teachers 20; Students 296.
Catechesis/Religious Programs—Julie Wise, D.R.E. Students 138.

Oak Harbor, Ottawa Co., St. Boniface (1866), Rev. James E. Peiffer, Admin.
Res., 215 Church St., 43449. Tel: 419-898-1389.
School—Tel: 419-898-1340.
Lay Teachers 7; Students 84.
Catechesis/Religious Programs—Students 208.

Oregon, Lucas Co., St. Ignatius (1883) (Territorial), Rev. Albert B. Ceranowski.
Res., 212 N. Stadium Rd., 43616. Tel: 419-693-1150. [CEM]
Catechesis/Religious Programs—Tel: 419-693-7662.
Students 435.

Ottawa, Putnam Co., SS. Peter and Paul (1868), Revs. Thomas Hemm, C.PP.S.; Ralph Schneider, C.PP.S.; Deacon Jim Rump.
Res., 307 N. Locust St., 45875. Tel: 419-523-5216. [CEM]
School—Tel: 419-523-3697.
Lay Teachers 18; Students 339.
Catechesis/Religious Programs—320 N. Locust St., Tel: 419-523-5078.
Students 260.

Ottoville, Putnam Co., Immaculate Conception (1848), Rev. Sylvan W. Obergefell; Deacons Leon Turnwald; Jose Flores; Walter Miller. In res., Rev. Roger D. Bonifas.
Res., 189 Church St., Box 296, 45876. Tel: 419-453-3513; Fax: 419-453-3513. [CEM]
Catechesis/Religious Programs—Tel: 419-453-3702.
Students 540.

Paulding, Paulding Co., St. Joseph (1894), Rev. Cleo Schmenk; Deacon Francis Koenn.
Res., 314 N. Main St., 45879. Tel: 419-399-2576.
Catechesis/Religious Programs—Tel: 419-399-5668.
Students 179.

Payne, Paulding Co., St. John the Baptist (1892), Rev. Joseph M. Schmelzer; Deacons Donald Coughlin; David Jordan.
Res., P.O. Box 38, 203 W. Townline, 45880. Tel: 419-263-2469. [CEM]
School—Tel: 419-263-2114.
Sisters of St. Francis 2; Lay Teachers 4; Students 114.

Perrysburg, Wood Co., St. Rose (1861), Revs. John A. Thomas; Robert B. Kirtland; Charles E. Singler; Deacons Lawrence Tiefenbach; Ken Cappelletty; Ray Kemer.
Res., 71 Elm St., 43551-2254. Tel: 419-874-2217; Fax: 419-874-7462. [CEM][JC]
School—217 E. Front St., 43551-2254. Tel: 419-874-5631; Fax: 419-874-1002.
Lay Teachers 23; Students 447.
Catechesis/Religious Programs—Tel: 419-874-9474. Sr. Jeanne Marie Holtz, O.S.U, D.R.E.
Students 501.

Peru, Huron Co., St. Alphonsus Liguori (1828) (German), Rev. Nelson Beaver; Deacon George Stepanic.
Res., 38 W. League St., Norwalk, 44857. Tel: 419-668-2005. [CEM]
Catechesis/Religious Programs—1360 Settlement Dr., Norwalk, 44857. Tel: 419-668-5030.
Students 71.

Plymouth, Huron Co., St. Joseph (1864), Sr. Joann Brodman, O.S.F., Pastoral Leader; Rev. Paul E. Perry, Chap.
Res., 117 Sandusky St., 44865. Tel: 419-687-4611.

Port Clinton, Ottawa Co., Immaculate Conception (1861), Rev. Raymond Ensman; Sr. Mary Jane Fisher, R.S.M., Pastoral Assoc.
414 Madison St., 43452-1922. Tel: 419-734-4004; Fax: 419-734-3477.
Res., 1800 Fulton St., 43452-9616. Tel: 419-734-6264; Fax: 419-734-3477.
School—109 W. Fourth St., 43452. Tel: 419-734-3315.
Sisters of Notre Dame 2; Lay Teachers 15; Students 170.
Catechesis/Religious Programs—Tel: 419-734-2421.
Students 191.

Providence, Lucas Co., St. Patrick (1842) (Irish), Rev. F. Anthony Gallagher; Brenda Krukowski, Vol. Pastoral Min.
Mailing Address: 14010 U.S. 24, Grand Rapids, 43522-9678. Tel: 419-832-5215. [CEM]

Put-In-Bay, Ottawa Co., Mother of Sorrows, Rev. Nicholas J. Cunningham, Chap.
Mailing Address: Box 179, 43456. Tel: 419-285-2741.

Reed, Seneca Co., Assumption (1867) (German), Rev. William Hoyng, C.PP.S.
Res., 16209 E. County Rd. 46, Bellevue, 44811. Tel: 419-483-3231. [CEM]
Church—15030 E. Twp. Rd. 126, Bellevue, 44811.
Catechesis/Religious Programs—Students 68.

Republic, Seneca Co., St. Aloysius (1879), Rev. Joseph P. Szybka; Deacon Urban Arbogast.
Res., 211 East St., Box 250, 44867. Tel: 419-585-4411; Fax: 419-585-4411.
Catechesis/Religious Programs—Students 103.

Richfield Center, Lucas Co., St. Elizabeth of Hungary (1914), Rev. Bruce L. Farmer, Chap.; Deacon David S. Vrooman, Pastoral Leader.
Offices: 11383 Sylvania Ave., Berkey, 43504. Tel: 419-829-5421.
Res., 1750 N. Raab Rd., Swanton, 43558. Tel: 419-829-3451. [CEM]
Catechesis/Religious Programs—Holy Trinity School (Consolidated). See Immaculate Conception, Marygrove for details.

Rossford, Wood Co., All Saints (1990). Consolidated of SS. Cyril and Methodius and St. Mary Magdalene. Rev. Joseph Steinbauer; Deacons Jerry Nellett; Rick Vascik; Susan VanHersett, Pastoral Assoc.
Church—721 Dixie Hwy., 43460. Tel: 419-666-1393.
Res., 124 Maple St., 43460. Tel: 419-666-5633.
School—134 Maple St., 43460. Tel: 419-666-0717.
Sisters 1; Lay Teachers 14; Students 238.
Catechesis/Religious Programs—Tel: 419-661-2070.
Students 230.

St. Michael's Ridge, Defiance Co., St. Michael (1861), Rev. David D. Tscherne; Sr. Margie Verhoff, C.D.P., Pastoral Assoc. & D.R.E.
Res., 05480 Moser Rd., Rte. 3, Defiance, 43512. Tel: 419-497-2161. [CEM]
Catechesis/Religious Programs—Tel: 419-497-3122.
Students 147.

St. Stephen, Seneca Co., St. Stephen (1844), Rev. Joseph Szybka; Deacon Robert Felter.
Res., 12087 E. Township Rd. 44, Attica, 44807. Tel: 419-426-1145; Fax: 419-426-1145. [CEM]

Salem Twp., Wyandot Co., St. Joseph (1849) (English), Revs. Pius Poff, O.F.M.Conv.; George Schroeder, O.F.M.Conv.; Deacon Floyd Derr.
Res., 315 Clay St., Carey, 43316. Tel: 419-396-7107. [CEM]
Mission—Carey, Wyandot Co., O.L.C., 43316.

Sandusky, Erie Co., Holy Angels (1840), Rev. Nicholas Weibl.
Res., 1605 W. Jefferson Ave., 44870. Tel: 419-625-3698. [JC]
School—Tel: 419-626-3075.
Lay Teachers 12; Students 166.
Catechesis/Religious Programs—Students 145.

St. Mary (German), Revs. Philip S. Feltman; David W. Nuss; Thomas Landgraff, O.S.F.S.; Deacon Joseph A. Singler.
Res., 429 Central Ave., 44870. Tel: 419-625-7465; Fax: 419-626-2834. [CEM][JC 3]
School—530 Decatur St., 44870. Tel: 419-626-1648.
Sisters of Notre Dame 4; Lay Teachers 20; Students 473.
High School—410 W. Jefferson St., 44870. Tel: 419-626-1892; Fax: 419-621-2252.
Sisters of Notre Dame 4; Priests 4; Lay Teachers 24; Students 308.
Catechesis/Religious Programs—Tel: 419-626-0614.
Students 237.

SS. Peter and Paul (1866), Revs. Franklin P. Kehres; Mark E. Davis; Deacons Milton Opper; Raymond Middaugh; John Downey; Sr. Martha Bertke, C.PP.S., Pastoral Assoc.
Res., 510 Columbus Ave., 44870. Tel: 419-625-6655; Fax: 419-625-6576. [CEM][JC]
School—Tel: 419-625-1017.
Sisters of St. Francis of the Congregation of Our Lady of Lourdes 2; Lay Teachers 17; Students 290.
Catechesis/Religious Programs—J. Michael Tynan, D.R.E.
Students 253.

Shelby, Richland Co., Most Pure Heart of Mary (1866) (German), Rev. John C. Missler; Deacons Harry L. Turner; Dennis Burkett.
Res., 29 West St., 44875. Tel: 419-347-2381. [CEM]
School—Tel: 419-342-2626; Fax: 419-347-2072.
Sisters 1; Lay Teachers 11; Students 250.
Catechesis/Religious Programs—Sr. Karen Elliott, C.PP.S., D.R.E.
Students 250.

Spencerville, Allen Co., St. Patrick (1858), Rev. John Fleck.
Res., 14755 Landeck Rd., Rte. 1, Delphos, 45833. Tel: 419-692-0636. [JC]
Catechesis/Religious Programs—Students 127.

Stryker, William Co., St. John the Evangelist (1861) (German-Hispanic), Rev. Gary M. Ferguson.
Res., c/o 614 N. Defiance St., Archbold, 43502. Tel: 419-682-1372.

Swanton, Fulton Co., St. Richard (1893), Rev. Stephen P. Cairns; Sr. Marguerite Lamberjack, O.S.F., Pastoral Assoc.; Deacon Timothy Worline.
Res., 333 Brookside Dr., 43558. Tel: 419-826-2791. [CEM]
School—Tel: 419-826-5041. Deacon Thomas Carone.
Lay Teachers 10; Students 185.
Catechesis/Religious Programs—Students 221.

Sycamore, Wyandot Co., St. Pius X (1951), Revs. Frank A. Murd; William J. Rose; Deacon John Daniel.
Res., 85 S. Sandusky St., Tiffin, 44883-3098. Tel: 419-447-2087; Fax: 419-447-9940.

Sylvania, Lucas Co., St. Joseph (1873), Revs. Richard T. Wurzel; Kenneth J. Lill; Sr. Susan Mahalik, I.H.M., Pastoral Assoc.; Deacons Robert Bodette; William Ulmer.
Res., 5373 S. Main St., 43560. Tel: 419-885-5791; Fax: 419-882-5235. [CEM]
School—5411 S. Main St., 43560. Tel: 419-882-6670.
Sisters 1; Lay Teachers 38; Students 767.
Catechesis/Religious Programs—Tel: 419-885-2181.
Students 862.

The Bend, Defiance Co., St. Stephen (1855), Rev. William J. Martin.
Res., 16166 Speaker Rd., Rte. 1, Sherwood, 43556. Tel: 419-899-2549. [CEM]
Catechesis/Religious Programs—Students 86.
Mission—Marysdale, Defiance Co., Immaculate Conception, 16166 Speaker Rd., Rte. 1, 43556.

Tiffin, Seneca Co., St. Joseph (1845), Rev. James K. Say; Deacon Daniel Scherger. In res., Rev. Msgr. Edward C. Dunn.
Res., 36 Melmore St., 44883-3098. Tel: 419-447-5848; Fax: 419-447-7580. [CEM]
School—357 S. Washington St., 44883. Tel: 419-447-5790.

Sisters 1; Lay Teachers 17; Students 400.
Catechesis/Religious Programs—Students 235.

St. Mary (1831), Very Rev. Francis A. Murd; Rev. William J. Rose; Deacons Walter Beat; Robert Hartzell; George Huffman; Donald Worland. In res., Rev. G. Allan Fillman.
Res., 85 S. Sandusky St., 44883. Tel: 419-447-2087; Fax: 419-447-9940. [CEM]
School—75 S. Sandusky St., 44883. Tel: 419-447-5202.
Lay Teachers 23; Students 278.
Catechesis/Religious Programs—Tel: 419-448-9341.
Students 294.

Upper Sandusky, Wyandot Co., St. Peter (1857), Rev. William D. Bodart.
Res., 225 N. 8th St., 43351. Tel: 419-294-1268. [CEM][JC]
School—Tel: 419-294-1395.
Sisters of Mercy 2; Lay Teachers 5; Students 208.
Catechesis/Religious Programs—Students 120.

Van Wert, Van Wert Co., St. Mary (1876), Rev. J. M. Schmelzer; Deacons Norbert Reinhart; Andrew McMahon.
Res., 601 Jennings Rd., 45891. Tel: 419-238-3979.
School—Tel: 419-238-5186.
Lay Teachers 7; Students 120.
Catechesis/Religious Programs—611 Jennings Rd., 45891. Tel: 419-238-3079. Mrs. Cherie Freewalt, D.R.E.
Students 185.

Vermilion, Erie Co., St. Mary (1851), Rev. Stephen J. Blum; Deacon John Hartman; Sr. Regina Smith, O.S.U., Pastoral Assoc.
Res., 731 Exchange St., P.O. Box 397, 44089. Tel: 216-967-8711; Fax: 216-967-8712. [JC]
School—5450 Ohio St., 44089. Tel: 216-967-7911.
Sisters 1; Lay Teachers 8; Students 190.
Catechesis/Religious Programs—Students 325.

Wakeman, Huron Co., St. Mary (1852) (Irish), Deacon John M. Kinder, Pastoral Admin.
Mailing Address: P.O. Box 276, 44889. Tel: 216-839-2023. [CEM]
Church—46 E. Main St., 44889. Tel: 216-839-2023.

Walbridge, Wood Co., St. Jerome (1962), Rev. William C. Parker.
Res., 300 Warner St., 43465. Tel: 419-666-2857; Fax: 419-661-2281.
School—(Grades PreK-8). Tel: 419-666-2855.
Sisters of St. Francis 1; Lay Teachers 13; Students 319.
Catechesis/Religious Programs—Students 113.

Wauseon, Fulton Co., St. Caspar (1850), Rev. Robert A. Holden; Deacons Juan Rodriguez; James Dominique; James Schmidt.
Res., 1205 N. Shoop Ave., 43567. Tel: 419-335-3656. [CEM]
Catechesis/Religious Programs—Tel: 419-337-2322.
Students 370.

Willard, Huron Co., St. Francis Xavier (1875), Rev. Paul E. Perry; Deacons Vincent Foos; Russell Niedermeier; Paul Jones.
Res., 21 W. Perry St., 44890. Tel: 419-935-1149; Fax: 419-933-6000. [CEM]
School—Tel: 419-935-4744.
Lay Teachers 7; Students 165.
Catechesis/Religious Programs—Students 165.

Chaplains of Public Institutions

TOLEDO. *St. Vincent Medical Center,* 2213 Cherry St., 43608-2691. Tel: 419-321-3232. Rev. Joel Buchman.

LIMA. *St. Rita Hospital and Medical Center,* 730 W. Market St., 45801. Rev. John Stites.

MANSFIELD. *Mercy Hospital*. Vacant.
Ohio State Reformatory. Rev. David K. Foxen, M.S.C.
St. Charles Hospital, 2600 Navarre, 43616. Rev. Charles Denny.

SANDUSKY. *Soldiers and Sailors Home*. Rev. Bertrand J. Shenk, Res., 11911 Thomas Rd., Monroeville, 44847. Tel: 419-499-4395.

Special Assignment:
Reverend Fathers—
Morman, Kenneth, Scripture Scholar, Chancery
Sheperd, Raymond C., Toledo Diocesan Vicar for Priests

On Duty Outside the Diocese:
Reverend Fathers—
Brickner, Ronald J.
Hiltz, John T., 19767 Yorba Linda Blvd., Yorba Linda, CA 92686
Kummerer, Timmothy, All Souls Catholic Mission, P.O. Box 37, Binga, Zimbabwe, Africa
McCullen, John L., St. Ambrose Church, Box 999, Deerfield Beach, FL 33441
Thomas, Robert R., P.O. Box 483, Green Valley, AZ 85614

Military Chaplains:
Kirk, David R., Chap., US Army
Reverend Fathers—
Brown, Michael, Chap., U.S. Navy.
Nordhaus, Jeffrey J., Lt. Chap., U.S. Navy.

Absent on Leave:
Reverend Fathers—
Hemstreet, John G.
Henning, David K.
Maag, Timothy J.
McLaughlin, Michael P.
Tremmel, Michael B.

Awaiting Assignment:
Reverend Fathers—
Lautermilch, David J.

Absent on Sick Leave:
Reverend Fathers—
Nieset, Frank
Nigro, Dominick
Richey, Herbert

Retired:
Reverend Monsignors—
Dunn, Edward C., 36 Melmore St., Tiffin, OH 44883
Mossing, Lawrence A., 2-11676-L, Wauseon, OH 43567
Schmit, Jerome, 6539 Ravine Dr., Sylvania, OH 43560
Smith, Bernard E., 3837 Secor Rd., Toledo, OH 43623
Yates, Robert J., 19100 N. Miami Ave., Miami, FL 33169

Reverend Fathers—
Ankenbrandt, Thomas W., 75 Tomb St., tiffin, OH 44883
Badger, Arthur, 3607 Naples Dr., Toledo, OH 43615
Beauregard, Thomas, 4100 Harvest Ln., Toledo, OH 43623
Bonifas, Roger D., P.O. Box 296, Ottoville, OH 45876
Caballero, Francisco, P.O. Box 985, Toledo, OH 43697-0985
Crowley, Charles, 4845 Lake-to-Lake Rd., Greenbush, MI 48738
Curtis, Robert J., P.O. Box 1977, Monterey, CA 93940. Tel: 408-373-1216
Downey, Timothy M., 1125 S. East St., Bucyrus, OH 44820
Dunn, Richard C., 190 St. Francis Ave., #207, Tiffin, OH 44883
Etzel, Raymond A., 5679 Monroe St., #1015, Sylvania, OH 43560
Gillig, Russell F., 182 St. Francis Ave., Apt. 110, Tiffin, OH 44883
Hanacsek, John, 05971 Lubica Okres, Poprad, Slovakia
Hernady, Martin, H-1016, Budapest, Derek U, 4, Hungary
Hoshock, Richard, 26869 Ayersville Rd., Defiance, OH 43512
Hug, Frederick I., 20410 Rt. 65, Grand Rapids, OH 43522
Keller, Harvey M., 91 E. Main St., Norwalk, OH 44857
Klaus, Donald R., 15537 S.W. 110 Ter., Miami, FL 33196
Koerber, George, 2930 W. Lincolnshire, Toledo, OH 43606
Lamantia, A. Robert, 247 Meadowwood, Perrsburg, OH 42551
Lammers, William F., Calvary Manor Nursing Home, R. 4, Ottawa, OH 45875
Lehmkuhl, John, 921 Mulberry, Fremont, OH 43420
Lester, John E., 1001 N. Byrne Rd., Apt. 321, Toledo, OH 43607
Lovisa, Eugene L., P.O. Box 677, Sylvania, OH 43560
Mueller, Paul, P.O. Box 677, Bowling Green, OH 43402-0677
Niedermier, Jerome G., 5341 Glendale Dr., Harrison, MI 48625
Nieset, Frank E., 1876 E. Lynwood Dr., Concord, CA 94519
Nietfeld, Fred J., 10852 N. Kendall Dr., Miami, FL 33176
O'Brien, Joseph L., 2596 Sun Valley #202, Port Clinton, OH 43452
O'Grady, James W., 3508 Douglas Rd., Apt. 1, Toledo, OH 43606
Ollivier, John, 2585 Sand Rd., Port Clinton, OH 43452
Pfeifer, William A., 1550 Lehigh Acres, Lehigh Acres, FL 33936
Pitula, Zygmunt J., ul. 22 Lipca 8, 86050 Solec Kujawski, woj. Bydgoszcz, Poland
Przybyla, Raymond C., 5906 Hill Ave., Toledo, OH 43615
Radecki, Albin A., 4312 Holland-Sylvania Rd., #323, Toledo, OH 43623
Reichert, Ralph, 3230 Centennial Rd. #31, Sylvania, OH 43560
Richter, William, 1035 Woodward, Toledo, OH 43608
Ringholz, Benedict E., 117 Leisure Ln., Norwalk, OH 44857
Rinkowski, George M., 3409 W. Alexis, Toledo, OH 43623
Risacher, James E., 308 Knollwood Village, Southern Pines, NC 28387
Ruess, Charles W., 507 Park Ave., Defiance, OH 43512
Shanahan, John, 512 W. Sycamore St., Columbus Grove, OH 45830-1020
Shenk, Bertrand J., 11911 Thomas Rd., Monroeville, OH 44847
Shenk, Joseph D., c/o 11911 Thomas Rd., Rte. 1, Monroeville, OH 44847
Sherbno, John, c/o R.J. Bradner, 2854 Sylvania Ave., Toledo, OH 43613
Steinle, James, 312 Greenfield St., Tiffin, OH 44883-2427

Permanent Deacons:
Ackerman, Tom
Adams, Lawrence
Algee, John
Andrzejewski, Walter
Arbogast, Urban
Badenhop, Donald
Barrett, John
Bautista, Jose
Beat, Walter
Betz, Eugene
Billmaier, Robert
Bistak, Leo T.
Bland, Thomas
Bleile, Jack
Bodette, Robert
Bost, Robert
Braham, Carl
Buckmaster, Bruce
Burkett, Dennis
Burkhart, Joseph
Burwell, Robert M.
Burzynski, Raymond
Busam, Jack
Bussemeier, Mark
Calvillo, Pedro
Cappelletty, Ken
Carnahan, Richard
Carone, Thomas
Cleary, Edward
Conkle, Walter
Contreras, Ignacio
Cooley, Benjamin
Coughlin, Donald
Cousino, Wesley
Daniel, John
Dazley, Phil
DeCrane, Victor
Derr, Floyd
Diaz, Alfredo
Dickey, Kenneth
Dominique, James
Dominique, Ralph
Dominique, Tom
Downey, John F.
Dudley, James
Dunn, James
Etue, Tim
Fazekas, Richard
Feick, Michael
Felter, Robert
Flores, Jose
Foos, Vincent
Fox, Edward
Frazier, Edward
Fritz, Julius
Garza, Ignacio
Gillen, Robert
Gleason, Richard
Gogol, Stanley
Gonsiorowski, Irvin
Gonzalez, Rene
Grandowicz, John
Gryczewski, Edward
Hammer, James
Hartings, Leo
Hartman, John
Hartzell, Robert
Hazelton, Dorsey
Heban, Richard
Heeter, Joseph
Hellrung, Edward
Hendricks, James

Holmer, Leon
Horning, William
Hostutler, James
Huffman, George
Hulderman, Joseph
Ignatowski, Gerald
Irelan, Ed
Jackson, Dennis
Jones, Paul
Jordan, David
Karpanty, David
Keller, Steve
Kelley, Edward L.
Kemer, Ray
Kest, Joseph, Jr.
Kinder, John
Klausing, Robert R.
Klear, Kenneth
Klein, Frank
Koenn, Francis
Kopp, Allan D.
Kozek, Richard
Kujawa, Clifford
Laker, David
Lesinski, Robert
Lira, Rudy
Llanos, Ramon
Lochotzki, William
Lopez, Valentin
Lottier, Larry
Ludwikowski, Ronald
Maciejewski, Norm
Mack, La Von
Marshall, James
Martinez, Rosalio
McCabe, Patrick
McCauley, Terry
McMahon, Andy
Mendez, Chris
Meyer, Donald
Middaugh, Raymond
Miller, George
Miller, Walter
Mitchell, George
Moncher, James
Moore, Wilbur
Morris, Paul
Mumford, Robert
Murray, Hugh
Narges, Howard
Nellett, Gerald
Newton, George
Niedermeier, Russell
Niese, Thomas
Nighswander, Robert
Nye, Harold
Ollervides, Tito
Opper, Milton
Pacholski, Robert
Peeps, Ronald
Pence, Michael
Perez, Diego
Perez, William
Petersen, Laurence
Philpott Terry
Pina, Elias
Przybylek, Stanley
Quinn, Daniel
Rall, William
Recker, Louis
Redington, Randall
Reinhart, Lewis E.
Reinhart, Norbert
Repka, Joseph
Righi, Al
Rodriguez, Juan
Romo, Bernabe
Romo, Jose
Rump, James
Sadler, David
Sanchez, Jose
Sanchez, Salvador
Sanders, Roy
Scherger, Daniel
Schmidt, James
Segura, Alfredo
Selmek, Zenon
Shoemaker, Russell
Singler, Joseph
Sisson, Alfred
Skeldon, Philip
Snyder, William
Sortman, Jerry
Stahl, John
Stepanic, George C.
Swartz, Robert
Tiefenbach, Lawrence
Trotter, Lawrence
Turner, Harry
Turnwald, Leon
Ulmer, William
Vascik, Rick
Veselka, Stephen
Villagomez, Jesus
Vogel, Curt
Vrooman, David
Warren, Richard
Welch, Harold
Westrick, Eugene
Wethington, Norbert
Wiciak, John
Windham, Joe
Winterstellar, Kevin
Wolf, Rudolph
Worland, Donald
Worline, Timothy
Wurm, Eugene
Yakir, Michael
Yeackel, Harry
Young, James
Zalewski, Stan
Zoll, Jack

INSTITUTIONS LOCATED IN THE DIOCESE

[A] COLLEGES AND UNIVERSITIES

SYLVANIA. *Lourdes College*, 6832 Convent Blvd., 43560. Tel: 419-885-3211.
For a complete listing, refer to the Colleges and Universities section.

[B] HIGH SCHOOLS, DIOCESAN

TOLEDO. *Central Catholic High School*, 2550 Cherry St., 43608. Tel: 419-255-2280; Fax: 419-259-2848. Conducted by Diocesan Priests and Sisters. Mr. Jack J. Altenburger, Prin.; Revs. Michael R. Billian, Pastor & Pres.; Richard J. Saelzler; Mr. William G. Axe, Asst. Prin. Priests 2; Teaching Sisters 3; Lay Teachers 69; Students 1,315.

FREMONT. *St. Joseph Central Catholic High School*. Consolidated from St. Joseph, Fremont, St. Ann, Fremont, Sacred Heart, Fremont, St. Casimir, Fremont, St. Mary, Clyde, St. Mary, Millersville, & Immaculate Conception, Bellevue. 702 Croghan St., 43420. Tel: 419-332-9947; Fax: 419-332-4945. Rev. Dennis P. Hartigan. Priests 1; Lay Teachers 23; Students 344.

LIMA. *Central Catholic High School*, 720 S. Cable Rd., 45805. Mr. Dan Rupert, Prin. Lay Teachers 29; Students 438.

OREGON. *Cardinal Stritch High School*, 3225 Pickle Rd., 43616. Tel: 419-693-0465; Fax: 419-693-0465. Serves parishes in Greater Toledo, including Oregon, Rossford, Perrysburg, Bono, Walbridge and Genoa. Rev. Robert J. Yeager, Prin.; Mr. Timothy Mahoney, Assoc. Prin. Priests 1; Sisters 2; Lay Teachers 21; Students 351.

TIFFIN. *Calvert High School*, 152 Madison St., 44883. Mr. James V. Wright, Prin.; Michael Kaucher, Asst. Prin.; Rev. G. Allan Fillman. Priests 1; Sisters 1; Lay Teachers 24; Students 284.

[C] HIGH SCHOOLS, PRIVATE

TOLEDO. *Notre Dame Academy*, 3535 Sylvania Ave., 43623. Tel: 419-475-9359; Fax: 419-475-2558. School for girls. Sisters of Notre Dame. Sr. Mary Carol Gregory, S.N.D., Pres & Prin. Sisters 20; Lay Teachers 43; Students 742.

St. Francis de Sales High School, 2323 W. Bancroft St., 43607. Tel: 419-531-1618. School for boys. Oblates of St. Francis de Sales. Revs. Ronald Olszewski, O.S.F.S., Pres.; Martin C. Lukas, O.S.F.S., Prin.; Daniel J. Earley, O.S.F.S., (Retired); John I. Extejt, O.S.F.S.; Bro. Leonard J. Juras, O.S.F.S., (Retired). Faculty: Revs. Thomas P. O'Neill, O.S.F.S.; James R. Sanford, O.S.F.S.; James Roth, O.S.F.S.; John Ebenhoeh, O.S.F.S.; Thomas L. McNamara, O.S.F.S., (Retired); Paul Gillespie, O.S.F.S., (Retired); Richard Morse, O.S.F.S., Prov. Govt.; Bro. Paul Spader, O.S.F.S., (Retired). Priests 8; Lay Teachers 38; Students 729; Total Staff 46.

St. John's Jesuit High School, 5901 Airport Hwy., 43615. Tel: 419-865-5743. School for boys. Jesuits of the Detroit Province. Revs. Donald Vettese, S.J., Pres.; Thomas J. Pipp, S.J.; Charles J. Sweeney, S.J.; Ronald F. Torina, S.J.; Francis E. Canfield, S.J., Rector; David Watson, S.J.; Bros. John Sebian, S.J.; John Moriconi, S.J. Priests 5; Brothers 2; Lay Teachers 50; Students 810; Total Staff 81.

St. Ursula Academy, 4025 Indian Rd., 43606. Tel: 419-531-1693. Ursuline Sisters of the Sacred Heart. Sr. Kathleen Padden, O.S.U., Pres.; Mrs. Jane Charette, Prin. Sisters 2; Lay Teachers 34; Students 543; Total Staff 34.

[D] CONSOLIDATED ELEMENTARY SCHOOLS

TOLEDO. *Queen of Apostles*. Consolidated from Immaculate Conception, St. James, and SS. Peter & Paul. 235 Courtland, 43609. Tel: 419-241-7829. Sr. Mary Brenda Haynes, Prin. Sisters 2; Lay Teachers 9; Total Staff 11; Students 151.

ROSSFORD. *All Saints Catholic School*, 134 Maple, 43460. Tel: 419-666-0717. Sr. Diana Lynn Eckel, Prin. Sisters 3; Lay Teachers 7; Total Staff 10; Students 268.

SWANTON. *Holy Trinity*. Consolidated from St. Elizabeth & Immaculate Conception. 2639 U.S. 20, 43558. Tel: 419-644-3971. Mary K. Williams, Prin. Lay Teachers 8; Students 140.

[E] ELEMENTARY SCHOOLS, PRIVATE

TOLEDO. *Ladyfield School*, 3837 Secor Rd., 43623. Tel: 419-475-5451. Sisters of Notre Dame. Sr. Mary Jo Szpila, S.N.D. Sisters 7; Lay Teachers 8; Students 276.

WHITEHOUSE. *Lial Elementary School*, 5900 Davis Rd., 43571. Tel: 419-877-5167. Sisters of Notre Dame. Sr. Margaret Mary Faist, S.N.D., Prin. Sisters 2; Lay Teachers 13; Students 197.

[F] ELEMENTARY SCHOOLS

TOLEDO. *Mary Immaculate School*, 3837 Secor Rd., 43623. Tel: 419-474-1688. Day School for children with learning disabilities. Sr. Mary Alan Miller, S.N.D., Prin. Sisters of Notre Dame 18; Students 80; Lay Teachers 3; Total Staff 21.

SYLVANIA. *St. Francis Education Center*, 6832 Convent Blvd., 43560. Tel: 419-885-3273. Preschool & Elementary Extended Care. Sisters of St. Francis 2; Lay Teachers 26; Students 250.

[G] CHILD CARE INSTITUTIONS

TOLEDO. *St. Anthony Villa/Boysville of Michigan, Inc.*, 2740 W. Central Ave., 43606. Tel: 419-473-1353; Fax: 419-473-2963.
For a complete listing, refer to the Special Care Facilities section.

[H] GENERAL HOSPITALS

TOLEDO. *Mercy Hospital*, 2200 Jefferson Ave., 43624-9988. Tel: 419-259-1500.
For a complete listing, refer to the Hospitals section.

St. Vincent Medical Center, 2213 Cherry St., 43608. Tel: 419-321-3232; Fax: 419-321-3810.
For a complete listing, refer to the Hospitals section.

LIMA. *St. Rita's Medical Center*, 730 W. Market St., 45801. Tel: 419-227-3361.
For a complete listing, refer to the Hospitals section.

OREGON. *St. Charles Hospital*, 2600 Navarre Ave., 43616. Tel: 419-698-7200; Fax: 419-698-7328.
For a complete listing, refer to the Hospitals section.

SANDUSKY. *Providence Hospital Inc.*, 1912 Hayes Ave., 44870. Tel: 419-621-7000.
For a complete listing, refer to the Hospitals section.

TIFFIN. *Mercy Hospital*, Sr. Janet Hay, 44883. Tel: 419-447-3130.
For a complete listing, refer to the Hospitals section.

WILLARD. *Mercy Hospital, Willard*, 110 E. Howard St., 44890. Tel: 419-933-2931.
For a complete listing, refer to the Hospitals section.

[I] SPECIAL HOSPITALS AND SANITORIA FOR INVALIDS

GREEN SPRINGS. *St. Francis Health Care Center, Rehab Hospital Section*, 401 N. Broadway St., 44836. Tel: 419-639-2626; Fax: 419-639-3559.
For a complete listing, refer to the Special Care Facilities section.

[J] HOMES FOR AGED

GREEN SPRINGS. *St. Francis Health Care Centre (ICF & Skilled)*, 401 N. Broadway St., 44836. Tel: 419-639-2626; Fax: 419-639-3559.
For a complete listing, refer to the Special Care Facilities section.

OREGON. *Sacred Heart Home*, 4900 Navarre Ave., 43616-3599. Tel: 419-698-4331; Fax: 419-698-1109.
For a complete listing, refer to the Special Care Facilities section.

TIFFIN. *St. Francis Home Inc.*, 182 St. Francis Ave., 44883.
For a complete listing, refer to the Special Care Facilities section.

[K] MONASTERIES AND RESIDENCES OF PRIESTS AND BROTHERS

TOLEDO. *Oblates of St. Francis de Sales*. Provincial Residence, 2056 Parkwood Ave., 43620-1616. Tel: 419-243-5105; Fax: 419-243-8827. Very Rev. James F. Cryan, O.S.F.S., Prov.; Revs. Martin C. Lukas, O.S.F.S., Prin., St. Francis de Sales H.S.; John I. Extejt, O.S.F.S.; James H. Roth, O.S.F.S., Teacher, St. Francis de Sales H.S.

Priests serving elsewhere: Rev. Ray G. Abella, O.S.F.S., 12651 Yankee Hill Rd., P.O. Box 1315, Columbia, CA, 95310. Tel: 209-532-7423. Rev. James F. Bradley, O.S.F.S., 15581 Northline Rd.,

Southgate, MI, 48195. Tel: 313-283-0610. Rev. Fernan Brennan, O.S.F.S., (Retired), Sacred Heart Home for Aged/Little Sisters of the Poor, 4900 Navarre Ave., Oregon, 43616. Rev. G. Wm. Fischer, O.S.F.S., 10018 Seeley St., Lake City, PA, 16423. Tel: 814-774-9655. Rev. John L. Graden, O.S.F.S., 2929 Ilger, 43606. Tel: 419-535-7672. Rev. Thomas Helfrich, O.S.F.S., 1512 W. Washington St., Jackson, MI, 49203. Tel: 517-789-8169. Rev. Edward A. Kuefer, O.S.F.S., (Retired), 408 W. Front St., Monroe, MI, 48161. Tel: 313-457-1989. Rev. Stewart M. Lindsay, O.S.F.S., 2671 Lower Mountain Rd., Ransomville, NY, 14131-9754. Tel: 716-731-9694. Rev. John J. Loughran, O.S.F.S., 36109 Martin, Livonia, MI, 48154. Tel: 313-953-8846. Rev. Thomas A. Ribits, O.S.F.S., 152 Plymouth Ave., Buffalo, NY, 14201. Tel: 716-886-6597. Rev. James J. Sottek, O.S.F.S., (Retired), 408 W. Front St., Monroe, MI, 48161. Tel: 313-241-1476. Revs. Anthony R. Ceresko, O.S.F.S., Foreign Missions; William G. Auth, O.S.F.S., Mexican Missions; Charles A. LaPenta, O.S.F.S., Assumption Rectory, 711 Hickory St., Duncan, OK, 73533. Tel: 405-255-0590. Rev. David A. Kenehan, O.S.F.S., 3812 Vermont Ct., Alexandria, VA, 22304. Tel: 703-370-2040.

St. Francis de Sales High School Faculty House. 2323 W. Bancroft, 43607. Tel: 419-531-1619. Revs. Ronald W. Olszewski, O.S.F.S., Pres.; Richard E. Morse, O.S.F.S.; Paul G. Gillespie, O.S.F.S.; Thomas L. McNamara, O.S.F.S., (Retired); Bro. Paul V. Spaeder, O.S.F.S.; Revs. Daniel J. Earley, O.S.F.S.; John O. Ebenhoeh; Thomas P. O'Neill, O.S.F.S.; Bros. Leonard J. Juras, O.S.F.S.; Alfred D. Durant, O.S.F.S., 722 N. Huron St., 43604-1754.

St. Francis de Sale High School Endowment Fund, Inc. Rev. Ronald Olszewski, O.S.F.S., Pres. Priests 14; Brothers 3.

St. Mary's Jesuit Community, 56 Birckhead Pl., 43608-2321. Tel: 419-244-9817. Revs. J. Peter Deane, S.J.; Patrick F. Hussey, S.J.; Thomas J. Powers, S.J.; John C. Reed, S.J.

CAREY. *Franciscan Mission Association*, 322 West St., 43316. Tel: 419-396-6455; Fax: 419-396-6455. Bro. Bryan Hoban, O.F.M.Conv., Dir.

[L] CONVENTS AND RESIDENCES FOR SISTERS

TOLEDO. *Kateri Catholic Center*, 443 Sixth St., 43605. Co-Directors: Judy Dalton.

Monastery of the Visitation. (Contemplative), 1745 Parkside Blvd., 43607-1599. Tel: 419-536-1343. Sr. Jane Frances Rohen, V.H.M., Supr.; Sr. sharon Elizabeth Gworek, V.H.M., Supr. Sisters 19; Perpetual Vows 15; In Formation 4.

Notre Dame Convent, 3535 Sylvania Ave., 43623. Sisters of Notre Dame. Sr. Marie Julie Reineke, S.N.D., Supr. Sisters 30.

Notre Dame Provincialate, 3837 Secor Rd., 43623-4484. Tel: 419-474-5485; Fax: 419-474-1336. Sisters of Notre Dame. Sr. Joan Marie Recker, S.N.D., Prov.; Sr. Diane Marie Pfahler, Local Supr.; Rev. Msgr. Bernard E. Smith, Chap. Sisters 308; Total Assisted 92; Total Staff 19.

Ursuline Convent of the Sacred Heart. Congregational Offices & Novitiate, 4045 Indian Rd., 43606. Tel: 419-536-9587. Sr. Nancy Mathias, O.S.U., Gen. Supr.; Rev. Bernard J. Boff, Chap. Professed Sisters 107; Associates 122.

CAREY. *Franciscan Renewal Center / Pilgrim House*, 321 Clay St., 43316. Tel: 419-396-7970. Diocese of Toledo, auspices of Shrine of Our Lady of Consolation, Carey, OH. Lucy Pahl, Admin.

FREMONT. *Our Lady of the Pines Convent*, 1250 Tiffin St., 43420. Tel: 419-332-6522. Sr. Pauline Marie Swint, R.S.M.

St. Bernardine Home, 1220 Tiffin St., 43420. Tel: 419-332-8208. Sisters of Mercy of the Americas, Cincinnati Regional Community. Sr. Joan Marie Warnement, R.S.M., Admin.; Sr. Rose Olivieri, R.S.M., Coord.; Mrs. Carolyn Sue Hartenstein, Health Coord. Sisters 30.

SYLVANIA. *Sisters of St. Francis of the Congregation of Our Lady of Lourdes*, 6832 Convent Blvd., 43560-2897. Tel: 419-882-2016; Fax: 419-885-8643. Sr. Ruth Marie Kachelek, O.S.F., Min. Gen.; Rev. Msgr. Donald Heintschel; Very Rev. John A. McClure, Chap. Legal Title: *Sisters of St. Francis of the Congregation of Our Lady of Lourdes, Motherhouse and Novitiate.* Professed Sisters 310; Novices 1.

TIFFIN. *St. Francis Convent*, 200 St. Francis Ave., 44883. Motherhouse and Novitiate, Sisters of St. Francis of Tiffin. Sr. Jacquelyn Doepker, Community Min.; Rev. G. Allan Fillman, Chap. Sisters 153; Total Staff 25.

WHITEHOUSE. *Lial Residence, Sisters of Notre Dame*, 5900 Davis Rd., 43571. Tel: 419-877-0431. Sr. Mary Alma Rose Langenderfer, S.N.D., Supr. Sisters 34.

[M] RETREAT HOUSES AND CENTERS OF SPIRITUALITY

BELLEVUE. *Sorrowful Mother Shrine*, 4106 State Rte. 269, 44811. Tel: 419-483-3435. Revs. Robert Kunisch, C.PP.S., Dir.; Norbert Adelman, C.PP.S.; Donald Shea, C.PP.S.; Vincent Schuster, C.PP.S., (Retired); John Nagele, C.PP.S.; Rocco Consentine, C.PP.S.; Bro. Norbert Hoying, C.PP.S.

FREMONT. *Our Lady of the Pines Retreat Center*, 1250 Tiffin St., 43420. Tel: 419-332-6522. Sisters of Mercy. Sr. Marianne Longo, R.S.M., Dir. Total in Residence 5; Total Staff 12.

SYLVANIA. *Chiara Center*, 6832 Convent Blvd., 43560. Tel: 419-885-7612. Sr. Mary Ann Szydlowski, O.S.F.S., R.N., Dir. Licensed Message Therapist, Registered Polarit Practioner

Trinity House of Prayer.

Sophia Counseling Center. Sr. Rachel Marie Nijakowski, O.S.F.S., Psychologist (Ohio 4699); Sr. Sharon Pollnow, C.S.A., Lic. Social Worker; Bonnie Schrock, Licensed Social Worker.

TIFFIN. *St. Joseph Renewal Center*, 200 St. Francis Ave., 44883. Tel: 419-447-0435; Fax: 419-447-1612. Sisters of St. Francis, Tiffin. Sr. Barbara Westrick, O.S.F., Dir.

[N] CAMPUS MINISTRY

TOLEDO. *University of Toledo Campus Ministry.* Attended by Corpus Christi Parish. 2086 Brookdale Rd., 43606. Tel: 419-531-4992. Rev. James Bacik.

BLUFFTON. *Bluffton College Campus Ministry*, College Ave., 45817. Tel: 419-358-3000. Deacon John Stahl, Campus Min.

BOWLING GREEN. *Bowling Green State University Campus Ministry.* Attended by St. Thomas More University Parish. 425 Thurstin Ave., P.O. Box 677, 43402. Tel: 419-352-7555. Revs. Joseph Weigman; Daniel Zak; Sr. Mary Kuhlman, O.S.F., Pastoral Leader. Total in Residence 47; Total Staff 6.

DEFIANCE. *Defiance College Newman Campus Ministry*, 701 N. Clinton, 43512. Tel: 419-784-4010, Ext. 444. Sr. Rita Marie Schroeder, Newman Minister.

FINDLAY. *University of Findlay Campus Ministry*, 422 Western Ave., 45840. Tel: 419-423-2123. Donna Brown, Campus Min.

TIFFIN. *Heidelberg College Campus Ministry*, 310 E. Market St., 44883. Tel: 419-448-2058. Sr. Margaret Slowick, O.S.F., Campus Min.

[O] MISCELLANEOUS LISTINGS

TOLEDO. *Catherine's Early Childhood Center*, 2211B Jefferson Ave., 43624. Patricia L. Majer, Dir. Sisters of Mercy of the Americas, Cincinnati Regional Community.

Catholic Club, The, 1601 Jefferson Ave., 43624. Tel: 419-243-7255. Mr. Paul Szymanski, Dir.

Catholic Foundation of the Diocese of Toledo, P.O. Box 985, 43697-0985. Mr. John Heinze, Contact Person.

The Catholic Migrant Farmworker Network, P.O. Box 985, 43697-0985. Rev. Richard Notter, Agent.

Christ Child Society of Toledo, P.O. Box 23022, 43623. Tel: 419-535-6633. Sue Savage, Pres.; Kathryn Wetli, Vice Pres.; Karen Landes, Treas.; Sheila Johnson, Sec.

Farley Health Care Corp., 1001 Madison St., 43608. Sisters of Mercy. Affiliated with Mercy Health System. Mr. Steven L. Mickus, Pres. & CEO.

Hope Manor, 4702 Violet Rd., 43623. Cathy Crossen, Mgr.

Kateri Catholic Center, Ministry with Hearing-Vision Disabled Persons, 443 Sixth St., 43605. Tel: 419-698-9914 (TDD); 698-9696 (Voice). Co-Directors: Judy Dalton.

Madonna Homes, Inc., 722 N. Huron St., 43604. Jeannette Vanover, Assoc. Mgr. Units 196.

Mareda, Inc., 1931 Scottwood Ave., Ste. 700, P.O. Box 4719, 43620. Tel: 419-242-2300; Fax: 419-246-4703. Housing Agency of the Diocese of Toledo. John Kiely, Dir.

Michaelmas Manor, Inc., 3250-3260 Schneider Rd., 46314. Halley Downey, Mgr. A corporation organized and operated for the purpose of providing housing facilities and services to elderly persons and handicapped persons. Units for the Elderly 70; Units for the Physically Handicapped 24.

Moody Manor, 2293 1/2 Kent St., 43620. Tel: 419-241-6985. Cathy Keane, Mgr. Family & Elderly Units 119.

Oblate Residences. Mailing Address: c/o 2056 Parkwood Ave., 43620-1616. 1225 Flaire Dr., 43615. Apartments 100.

Office of Global Concerns, 1933 Spielbusch Ave., 43624. Tel: 419-244-6711; Fax: 419-244-4791. Rev. Bernard J. Boff, Dir. Society for the Propagation of the Faith; Holy Childhood Association; Catholic Relief Services; Mission of Accompaniment. Mission of Accompaniment Pastoral Team: Rev. Timothy Kummerer, All Souls Catholic Mission Africa, P.O. Box 37, Binga, Zimbabwe.

Regina Manor, Inc., 3731 N. Erie St., 43611. Jody Downey, Mgr. Family & Elderly Units 180.

Sisters of Mercy Health Foundation, 222 N. 23rd St., 43624. Sr. Robert Maxwell, Foundation Pres.; Cathleen Nelson, CEO & Pres. Mercy and St. Charles Hospitals.

Sisters of Mercy Health System, North, 222 N. 23rd St., 43624. Randall D. Kordash, Pres. Total Staff 41.

Toledo Catholic Charities Corporation, 1933 Spielbusch Ave., 43624. John F. Heinze, Dir., Financial Svcs. The Catholic Charities Corporation is the Diocesan vehicle to collect and distribute endowment funds and bequests for charitable purposes.

BELLEVUE.

**Mary Lay Center*, 4500 State Rte. 269, 44811. Tel: 419-483-0762. Residence for staff of Sorrowful Mother Shrine. Rev. Robert Kunisch, C.PP.S., Mgr.

DELPHOS. *St. John Parish Foundation, Inc.* St. John the Evangelist Church, 331 E. Second St., 45833. Tel: 419-695-4050.

FINDLAY. *St. Michael Schools Educational Foundation*, 422 Western Ave., 45840. Michael J. Langevin, Pres.

FREMONT. *Delaware Acres, Inc.*, 725 S. Buchanan St., 43420. Tel: 334-9558. Melanie Parks-Baynard, Mgr. Family Units 68.

GREEN SPRINGS. *St. Francis Hospital Foundation*, 401 N. Broadway, 44836. Tel: 419-321-1347. Judith Leb Udell, Contact Person.

LIMA. *Lima Central Catholic Educational Foundation*, 720 S. Cable Rd., 45805. George T. Scheid, Jr., Chm.

S.R.H.C. Foundation, 730 W. Market St., 45801-4667; Fax: 419-226-9750. Mr. James P. Reber, Pres.; Mr. Kenneth G. Payne, Sec.-Treas.

OREGON. *RSM Creative Services, Inc.*, 2600 Navarre Ave., 43616. Tel: 419-698-7341. Randall Kordash, Pres.

SANDUSKY. *The Providence Fund*, 1912 Hayes Ave., 44870. Tel: 419-621-7234; Fax: 419-621-7077. Hospital Foundation. Sr. Nancy Linenkugel, O.S.F., Chm.; Sandra E. Cairelli, B.A., Dir.

SWANTON. *St. Richard's School Endowment Foundation*, 333 Brookside Dr., 43558-1097.

SYLVANIA. *Franciscan Center*, 6832 Convent Blvd., 43560. Tel: 419-885-1547. Sr. Sheila Shea, O.S.F., Exec. Dir. Total Staff 14.

Franciscan Properties, Inc., 6832 Convent Blvd., 43560. Sr. Jeanne Stack, O.S.F., Pres. Total in Residence 109; Total Staff 3; Apartments 98.

Franciscan Services Corporation, 6832 Convent Blvd., 43560; Fax: 419-882-7360. Mr. John W. O'Connell, Pres.

Franciscan Shelters-Bethany House, 6832 Convent Blvd., 43560. Tel: 419-729-2017. Sr. Faith Cosky, O.S.F., Contact Person.

Lourdes College Foundation, 6832 Convent Blvd., 43560. Tel: 419-885-3211. G. Patrick Williams, M.S., A.C.F.R.E., Pres. & CEO.

TIFFIN. *Mercy Tiffin Health Foundation*, 485 W. Market St., P.O. Box 727, 44883. Tel: 419-447-3130. Walter A. Daniel, M.D., Chm.

St. Francis Home Memorial Foundation, Inc., 182 St. Francis Ave., 44883. Tel: 419-447-2723. Sr. Jane Schimmoeller, O.S.F., Chm.

St. Francis Villas, Inc., 182 St. Francis Ave., 44883. Tel: 419-447-2723. Sr. Jacquelyn Doepker, O.S.F., Chm.

Tiffin Calvert Foundation, P.O. Box 45, 44883. Robert Warnement, Pres.

Vision Time, Inc., 200 St. Francis Ave., 44883. Mailing Address: P.O. Box 4887, Toledo, 43620. Sr. Nancy Westmeyer, O.S.F.

VERMILION. *St. Mary's Church Educational Endowment Foundation*, Box 397, 44089. Mr. David Nocjar, Pres.

RELIGIOUS INSTITUTES OF MEN REPRESENTED IN THE DIOCESE

For further details refer to the corresponding bracketed number in the Religious Institutes of Men or Women section.

[0275]—*Carmelites of Mary Immaculate.*—C.M.I.

[0480]—*Conventual Franciscans.* (Mt. St. Francis, IN).—O.F.M.Conv.

[0520]—*Franciscan Friars.*—O.F.M.

[0690]—*Jesuit Fathers and Brothers.*—S.J.

[1110]—*Missionaries of the Sacred Heart of Jesus.* (Geneva, IL).—M.S.C.

[]—*Missionary Society of St. Thomas the Apostle.*—S.S.T.

[0910]—*Oblates of St. Francis de Sales.*—O.S.F.S.

[1070]—*Redemptorist Fathers.* (Baltimore Prov.).—C.SS.R.

[1260]—*Society of Christ.*—S.Ch.

[0420]—*Society of Divine Word.*—S.V.D.

[1060]—*Society of the Precious Blood.* (Cincinnati Prov.).—C.PP.S.

RELIGIOUS INSTITUTES OF WOMEN REPRESENTED IN THE DIOCESE

[3710]—*Congregation of the Sisters of Saint Agnes.*—C.S.A.

[1710]—*Congregation of the Third Order of St. Francis of Mary Immaculate, Joliet, IL.*—O.S.F.
[0790]—*Daughters of Divine Charity.*—F.D.C.
[1070-13]—*Dominican Sisters.*—O.P.
[1070-14]—*Dominican Sisters.*—O.P.
[1070-28]—*Dominican Sisters.*—O.P.
[1170]—*Felician Sisters.*—C.S.S.F.
[1430]—*Franciscan Sisters of Our Lady of Perpetual Help.*—O.S.F.
[2575]—*Institute of the Sisters of Mercy of the Americas.* (Cincinnati, OH).—R.S.M.
[2340]—*Little Sisters of the Poor.* (Baltimore Prov.).—L.S.P.
[3040]—*Oblate Sisters of Providence.* (Baltimore, MD).—O.S.P.
[3560]—*Servants of Jesus.*—S.J.
[0440]—*Sisters of Charity of Cincinnati, Ohio.*—S.C.
[0490]—*Sisters of Charity of Montreal (Grey Nuns).*—S.G.M.
[0580]—*Sisters of Charity of St. Augustine.*—C.S.A.
[1000]—*Sisters of Divine Providence of Kentucky.*—C.D.P.
[]—*Sisters of Mercy.* (Brooklyn Regional Community).—R.S.M.
[2990]—*Sisters of Notre Dame.*—S.N.D.
[1530]—*Sisters of St. Francis of the Congregation of Our Lady of Lourdes, Sylvania, Ohio.*—O.S.F.
[3830-11]—*Sisters of St. Joseph.*—S.S.J.
[2270]—*Sisters of the Little Company of Mary.*—L.C.M.
[3260]—*Sisters of the Precious Blood.* (Dayton, OH).—C.PP.S.
[1760]—*Sisters of the Third Order of St. Francis of Penance and Charity.*—O.S.F.
[2150]—*Sisters, Servants of the Immaculate Heart of Mary.*—I.H.M.
[4120-03]—*Ursuline Nuns of the Congregation of Paris.*—O.S.U.
[4120-06]—*Ursuline Nuns of the Congregation of Paris.*—O.S.U.
[4120]—*Ursuline Sisters of the Congregation of Paris.*—O.S.U.-B.C.
[4190]—*Visitation Nuns.*—V.H.M.

DIOCESAN CEMETERIES

TOLEDO. *Calvary*, 2224 Dorr St., 43607. Tel: 419-536-3751. Mr. John O'Connell, Mgr.
Mount Carmel, 15 E. Manhattan Blvd., 43608. Tel: 419-241-2015.
Resurrection, 5725 Hill Ave., 43615.
FREMONT. *St. Joseph*.
LIMA. *Gethsemane*.
SANDUSKY. *Calvary*.

NECROLOGY

† Flynn, John, (Retired). —Died Aug. 21, 1996.
† Hug, Edward O., (Retired). —Died Aug. 21, 1996.
† Sudock, Joseph, (Retired). —Died Dec. 30, 1995.
† Swiatecki, Jerome, (Retired). —Died Jan. 5, 1996.

Diocese of Trenton

(Dioecesis Trentonensis)

Most Reverend

JOHN C. REISS, D.D., J.C.D.

Bishop of Trenton; ordained May 31, 1947; appointed Titular Bishop of Simidicca and Auxiliary of Trenton October 21, 1967; consecrated December 12, 1967; appointed Bishop of Trenton March 4, 1980; installed April 22, 1980. *Res., 901 W. State St., Trenton, NJ, 08618.*

Most Reverend

JOHN M. SMITH, J.C.D., D.D.

Coadjutor Bishop of Trenton; ordained May 27, 1961; appointed Titular Bishop of Tre Taverne and Auxiliary Bishop of Newark December 1, 1987; consecrated January 25, 1988; appointed Bishop of Pensacola-Tallahassee June 25, 1991; installed July 31, 1991; appointed Coadjutor Bishop of Trenton November 21, 1995.

Legal Corporate Title: "The Diocese of Trenton."

ESTABLISHED AUGUST 11, 1881.

Square Miles 2,155.56.

Comprises four Counties in the State of New Jersey: Burlington, Mercer, Monmouth and Ocean.

For legal titles of parishes and diocesan institutions, consult the Chancery Office.

Chancery Office: 701 Lawrenceville Rd., P.O. Box 5309, Trenton, NJ, 08638. Tel.: 609-882-7125; Fax: 609-771-6793.

STATISTICAL OVERVIEW

Personnel	
Bishop	1
Retired Bishops	1
Priests: Diocesan Active in Diocese	166
Priests: Active Outside Diocese	18
Priests: Retired, Sick or Absent	59
Number of Diocesan Priests	243
Religious Priests in Diocese	94
Extern Priests in Diocese	41
Ordinations:	
Diocesan Priests	3
Transitional Deacons	2
Permanent Deacons	17
Permanent Deacons in Diocese	215
Total Brothers	57
Total Sisters	509
Parishes	
Parishes	126
With Resident Pastor:	
Resident Diocesan Priests	107
Resident Religious Priests	16
Without Resident Pastor:	
Administered by Priests	3
Missions	15
Welfare	
Catholic Hospitals	1
Total Assisted	142,153
Health Care Centers	1
Total Assisted	3,687
Homes for the Aged	1
Total Assisted	180
Residential Care of Children	9
Total Assisted	14
Day Care and Extended Day Care Centers	2
Total Assisted	230
Specialized Homes	9
Total Assisted	7,010
Special Centers for Social Services	13
Total Assisted	20,000
Other Institutions	1
Total Assisted	5,395
Educational	
Diocesan Students in Other Seminaries	13
Total Seminarians	13
Colleges and Universities	1
Total Students	2,422
High Schools, Diocesan and Parish	8
Total Students	6,362
High Schools, Private	3
Total Students	1,116
Elementary Schools, Diocesan and Parish	54
Total Students	21,105
Elementary Schools, Private	2
Total Students	452
Non-residential Schools for the Disabled	7
Total Students	200
Catechesis/Religious Education:	
High School Students	788
Elementary Students	52,073
Total Students Under Catholic Instruction	84,531
Teachers in the Diocese:	
Brothers	23
Sisters	202
Lay Teachers	1,317
Vital Statistics	
Receptions into the Church:	
Infant Baptism Totals	10,724
Adult Baptism Totals	390
Received into Full Communion	862
First Communions	10,589
Confirmations	8,462
Marriages:	
Catholic	2,355
Interfaith	755
Total Marriages	3,110
Deaths	6,404
Total Catholic Population	695,575
Total Population	1,763,149

Former Bishops—Rt. Rev. MICHAEL J. O'FARRELL, D.D., cons. Nov. 1, 1881; died April 2, 1894.—Rt. Rev. JAMES A. MCFAUL, D.D., LL.D., cons. Oct. 18, 1894; died June 16, 1917.—Most Rev. THOMAS J. WALSH, S.T.D., J.C.D., cons. July 25, 1918; transferred to Newark, NJ, March 2, 1928.—Most Rev. JOHN J. MCMAHON, D.D., cons. April 26, 1928; died Dec. 31, 1932.—Most Rev. MOSES E. KILEY, S.T.D., cons. March 17, 1934; appt. Archbishop of Milwaukee, Jan. 1, 1940.—Most Rev. WILLIAM A. GRIFFIN, D.D., appt. Bishop of Trenton, May 22, 1940; cons. May 1, 1938; died Jan 1, 1950.—Most Rev. GEORGE W. AHR, S.T.D., appt. Bishop of Trenton, Jan. 28, 1950; cons. March 20, 1950; retired June 23, 1979; died May 5, 1993.

Vicar-General—Rev. Msgr. CASIMIR H. LADZINSKI, V.G., *St. Aloysius Church, 935 Bennetts Mill Rd., P.O. Box 1285, Jackson, 08527.*

Episcopal Vicars—Burlington County: Rev. Msgr. JAMES H. DUBELL, Mercer County: Rev. Msgr. HUGH F. RONAN, Monmouth County: Rev. Msgr. ALFRED D. SMITH, Ocean County: Rev. Msgr. FREDERICK A. VALENTINO.

Chancery Office—701 Lawrenceville Rd., P.O. Box 5309, Trenton, 08638. Tel: 609-882-7125; Fax: 609-771-6793.

Moderator of the Curia—Most Rev. JOHN M. SMITH, V.G., J.C.D., D.D.

Chancellor—Rev. Msgr. WILLIAM F. FITZGERALD, P.A., S.T.L., J.C.D.

Vice Chancellor and Secretary to the Bishop—Rev. Msgr. EDWARD J. ARNISTER, J.C.L.

Assistant Chancellors—Rev. Msgr. JOHN K. DERMOND, J.C.L.; Rev. JAMES G. INNOCENZI.

Diocesan Tribunal—701 Lawrenceville Rd., Trenton, 08648. Tel: 609-883-8284; Fax: 609-771-6793.

Judicial Vicar—Rev. Msgr. JOHN K. DERMOND, J.C.L.

Associate Judicial Vicars—Revs. JAMES G. INNOCENZI; ROBERT J. PARENTI.

Defenders of the Bond—Rev. Msgr. ANTHONY L. CAPITANI, J.C.L.; Rev. CARLOS DAVANTES, J.C.L.; Sr. ANNE FULWILER, I.H.M., J.C.L.

Tribunal Judges—Rev. Msgr. EDWARD J. ARNISTER, J.C.L.; Rev. Msgr. SAMUEL CONSTANCE; Rev. Msgr. JOHN GIBBONS; Rev. Msgr. JOSEPH C. SHENROCK, S.T.L.; Rev. Msgr. WILLIAM E. MAGUIRE, S.T.D.; Rev. Msgr. AMEDEO L. MORELLO; Rev. Msgr. WALTER E. NOLAN, M.Div., M.S.; Rev. Msgr. ARMAND A. PEDATA, J.C.D.; Rev. Msgr. ALFRED D. SMITH; Rev. Msgr. EDWARD D. STRANO; Rev. Msgr. LEONARD R. TOOMEY; Rev. Msgr. THADDEUS J. WOJCIEHOWSKI; Revs. RALPH W. STANSLEY, M.Div.; RONALD BECKER, M.Div.; THOMAS BRENNAN; EMMETT CARROLL, O.F.M.Conv.; LOUIS W. KRALOVICH, Th.M; EUGENE M. REBECK; JOHN SCULLY; CHARLES B. WEISER, Th.M.; Deacon JOSEPH HANNAWACKER.

Promotor of Justice—Rev. Msgr. LEONARD R. TOOMEY.

Notaries—PATRICIA ADAMO; JUDITH MCLAUGHLIN.

Diocesan Consultors—Rev. Msgr. CASIMIR H. LADZINSKI, V.G.; Rev. Msgr. WILLIAM F. FITZGERALD, P.A., S.T.L., J.C.D.; Rev. Msgr. LEONARD R. TOOMEY; Rev. Msgr. JOSEPH A. O'CONNOR; Rev. Msgr. THADDEUS J. WOJCIEHOWSKI; Rev. Msgr. ALFRED D. SMITH; Rev.

Msgr. HUGH F. RONAN; Rev. Msgr. JAMES H. DUBELL.
Parish Priest Consultors—Rev. Msgr. CASIMIR H. LADZINSKI, V.G.; Rev. Msgr. ALFRED D. SMITH; Rev. Msgr. SAMUEL C. CONSTANCE.
Diocesan Council of Priests—Most Rev. JOHN C. REISS, Pres.; Revs. DANIEL GOWAN, Chm. BRIAN BUTCH, Vice Chm. EDWARD M. JAWIDZIK, Sec.; Rev. Msgr. JOHN K. DERMOND, J.C.L., Parliamentarian; Rev. Msgr. THOMAS LUEBKING, At-Large; Rev. JACK DWYER, At-Large.
Council of Deacons—Mr. JOSEPH HEPP, Pres.
Vicariate Representatives—Burlington Co.: Mr. RONALD KERR; Mr. BARRY TARZY, Mercer Co.: Mr. FRANK PRIHODA, Monmouth Co.: Mr. RALPH IMHOLE; Mr. JOHN KLINCEWICZ, Ocean Co.: Mr. PAUL GALLAGHER; Mr. JOHN GILCHRIST.
Diocesan Pastoral Council—Most Rev. JOHN C. REISS, D.D., J.C.D.; Mr. GASTON SCHMIDT, Pres. GLORIA ANTRIM, Vice Pres. JOANNE D'APOLITO, Sec.
Finance Council—Rev. Msgr. WILLIAM F. FITZGERALD, P.A., S.T.L., J.C.D., Chm.; Mr. BERNARD MCGLONE; Hon. DANIEL O'DONNELL; Mr. EDWARD PIESLAK.
Censor Librorum—Rev. Msgr. WILLIAM E. MAGUIRE, S.T.D.
Synod Implementation Office—Rev. Msgr. EDWARD J. ARNISTER, J.C.L., Interim Contact.
Office of Planning—Rev. LEONARD F. TROIANO, *Chancery Office, 701 Lawrenceville Rd., P.O. Box 5309, Trenton, 08638.* Tel: 609-882-7125; Fax: 609-771-6793.

Vicariate For Organizational Services

Vicar—Rev. Msgr. WILLIAM F. FITZGERALD, P.A., S.T.L., J.C.D.
Chancery Office—701 Lawrenceville Rd., P.O. Box 5309, Trenton, 08638-0309. Tel: 609-882-7125; Fax: 609-771-6793.
Chancellor—Rev. Msgr. WILLIAM F. FITZGERALD, P.A., S.T.L., J.C.D.
Office of Finance—Rev. Msgr. WILLIAM F. FITZGERALD, P.A., S.T.L., J.C.D.
Finance Director—Ms. DARYL ROWE.
Building Commission—Rev. Msgr. FREDERICK A. VALENTINO, Chm.
Expansion and Development—Rev. Msgr. FREDERICK A. VALENTINO, Chm.
Budget Committee—Rev. Msgr. WILLIAM F. FITZGERALD, P.A., S.T.L., J.C.D., Chm.
Insurance and Pension—Rev. Msgr. WILLIAM F. FITZGERALD, P.A., S.T.L., J.C.D.
Office of Data Processing—Ms. KATHLEEN A. MOORE, Mgr., *1931 Brunswick Ave., Trenton, 08648.* Tel: 609-394-8989; Fax: 609-396-6008.
Office of Human Resources—Mr. NORMAN E. LEAVER, Dir., *701 Lawrenceville Rd., P.O. Box 5309, Trenton, 08638-0309.* Tel: 609-882-7125; Fax: 609-771-6793.

Vicariate For Personnel Services

Vicar—Rev. Msgr. JOHN J. GIBBONS, *St. Dominic Church, 250 Old Squan Rd., Brick, 08724.* Tel: 908-840-1410; Fax: 908-840-0522.
Office of Priest Personnel—Rev. Msgr. WALTER E. NOLAN, M.Div., M.S., Dir., *199 Hendrickson Dr., Princeton Junction, 08550.* Tel: 609-799-1567; Fax: 609-799-0538.
Director of Religious—Sr. ANNE FULWILER, I.H.M., Dir., *1931 Brunswick Ave., Trenton, 08648.* Tel: 609-599-3545; Fax: 609-396-6008.
Office of Permanent Deacons—Rev. RALPH W. STANSLEY, Dir., *1 Centre St., Trenton, 08611.* Tel: 609-394-3080; Fax: 609-394-0493.
Vocations Office—Rev. ROBERT M. TYNSKI, Dir., Vocation, *701 Lawrenceville Rd., P.O. Box 5309, Trenton, 08638-0309.* Tel: 609-882-7125; Fax: 609-771-6793.

Vicariate For Social Services

Vicar—Rev. Msgr. JOSEPH C. SHENROCK, P.A., *St. Elizabeth Ann Seton, 30 Schoolhouse Rd., Whiting, 08759.* Tel: 908-350-5001; Fax: 908-350-4618.
Catholic Charities—Mr. FRANCIS E. DOLAN, Dir., *47 N. Clinton Ave., P.O. Box 1423, Trenton, 08607-1423.* Tel: 609-394-5181; Fax: 609-695-6978.
Peace and Justice—Rev. RONALD J. CIOFFI, Dir., *St. Joseph Church, 376 Maple Pl., Keyport, 07735.* Tel: 908-264-0322; Fax: 908-888-3280.
Catholic Relief Services and Campaign for Human Development—Rev. BRIAN T. BUTCH, *St. Paul's Church, 214 Nassau St., Princeton, 08540.* Tel: 609-924-1743.
Mount Carmel Guild—Sr. MARIAN IMMACULATE GILLEN, S.C., Exec. Sec., *73 N. Clinton Ave., Trenton, 08609.* Tel: 609-392-5159.
St. Vincent de Paul Society—Rev. ARTHUR F. CONLON, Dir., *St. Vincent de Paul Church, 555 Allentown Rd., Yardville, 08620.* Tel: 609-585-6470.
Health Care Facilities and Lay Ministry—Rev. Msgr. GEORGE A. ARDOS, *St. George Church, 1370 River Rd., Titusville, 08560.* Tel: 609-737-2015; Fax: 609-737-7863.
Holy Innocents Society—Mr. ANGELO ROMANELLO, Pres., *5 Shelburne Dr., Trenton, 08638.* Tel: 609-882-4567.
Office of Ecumenism—Rev. JEFFREY E. LEE, Dir., *St. Charles Borromeo, 2226 Riverton Rd., P.O. Box 2220, Cinnaminson, 08077.* Tel: 609-829-3322; Fax: 609-829-3411.
Cemeteries—Rev. Msgr. JAMES H. DUBELL, *St. Paul Church, 223 E. Union St., Burlington, 08016.* Tel: 609-386-0163; Fax: 609-386-1345.
Office of Catholic Persons with Disabilities—Sr. HELEN KLINE, S.S.J., Dir., *60 Randall Ave., Trenton, 08611.* Tel: 609-278-6657 (TTY); 278-6656 (Voice).

Vicariate For Catholic Education Services

Vicar—Rev. GREGORY VAUGHAN, *St. Mary Church, P.O. Box 624, New Monmouth, 07748.* Tel: 908-671-0071; Fax: 908-671-0079.
Catholic Education Office—Dr. LARRY A. THOMPSON, Supt., *Sacred Heart Convent, 327 S. Broad St., Trenton, 08608.* Tel: 609-396-0500; Fax: 609-396-1789.
Elementary Education—Sr. MARY HELEN BEIRNE, S.S.J., Assoc. Supt. Tel: 609-396-0500.
Consultant for Curriculum and Special Program—Mrs. MARGARET BOLAND.
Office of Religious Education—Mrs. ROSEMARIE MCGINTY, M.A., Dir., *315 Lowell Ave., Trenton, 08619.* Tel: 609-586-7300; Fax: 609-586-7817.
Elementary Religious Education—Sr. SHAUN KATHLEEN WILSON, C.S.B., M.A., Assoc. Dir.
Secondary Religious Education—Sr. SHAUN KATHLEEN WILSON, C.S.B., M.A., Assoc. Dir. Tel: 609-586-7300; Fax: 609-586-7817.
Office of Family Life—Rev. THOMAS N. GERVASIO, Dir., *16 Beechwood Ave., P.O. Box 7, W. Long Branch, 07764.* Tel: 908-229-0403.
Campus Ministry—Rev. GEORGE VAUGHAN, Dir., *St. Mary Church, P.O. Box 624, New Monmouth, 07748.* Tel: 908-671-0071; Fax: 908-671-0079.
Office of Youth Ministry—Sr. DONNA D'ALIA, R.S.M., Dir., *50 Hurleys Ln., Lincroft, 07738.* Tel: 908-219-5944; Fax: 908-219-5791.
Office of Adult Ministry—Sr. DONNA D'ALIA, R.S.M., Dir., *50 Hurleys Ln., Lincroft, 07738.* Tel: 908-219-5944; Fax: 908-219-5791.
Catholic Youth Organization—Mr. THOMAS MLADENETZ, Exec. Dir., *920 S. Broad St., Trenton, 08611-2097.* Tel: 609-396-8383.
Monitor-Communications—Mr. JOSEPH M. DONADIEU, Editor-in-Chief, *315 Lowell Ave., P.O. Box 3095, Trenton, 08619.* Tel: 609-586-7400; Fax: 609-586-7688.
"The Monitor" (Diocesan Newspaper)—Mr. JOSEPH M. DONADIEU, Exec. Dir. & Mng. Editor, *315 Lowell Ave., P.O. Box 3095, Trenton, 08619.* Tel: 609-586-7400; Fax: 609-586-7688.

Vicariate For Christian Life Services

Vicar—Rev. Msgr. WILLIAM J. DAILEY, *St. Joseph Church, 540 N. Olden Ave., Trenton, 08638.* Tel: 609-394-5757; Fax: 609-599-4402.
Pontifical Mission Aid Societies—Rev. RICHARD L. TOFANI, Dir., *1194 Parkway Ave., P.O. Box 5452, Trenton, 08628.* Tel: 609-771-3614; Fax: 609-538-0468.
Office of Parish Life and Evangelization—Sr. MARGARET MACKEY, O.S.F., Dir., *1 Centre St., Trenton, 08611.* Tel: 609-394-5666; Fax: 609-394-0493.
Diocesan Office of Worship—Rev. SAM A. SIRIANNI, Dir., *1931 Brunswick Ave., Trenton, 08648.* Tel: 609-599-3406; Fax: 609-396-6008.
Cursillo—Rev. JOHN VINCENT BOWDEN, Spiritual Dir., *Church of Epiphany, 615 Thiele Rd., Brick, 08724.* Tel: 908-458-0220; Fax: 908-458-6921.
Legion of Mary—Rev. MICHAEL L. BURNS, Dir., *St. Mary's Church, 45 Crosswicks St., Bordentown, 08505.* Tel: 609-298-0261; Fax: 609-298-7178.
Martin House—Rev. BRIAN MCCORMICK, *Mailing Address: P.O. Box 1025, Trenton, 08606. 802 E. State St., Trenton, 08609.* Tel: 609-989-8143.
Migration and Refugee Services—Sr. JOANNE COMPANINI, I.H.M., Dir., *33 W. Front St., Trenton, 08608.* Tel: 609-394-8299.
Black Apostolate—Sr. M. LORETTO EVANS, O.S.B., *P.O. Box 22120, Trenton, 08618.* Tel: 609-695-8216.
Haitian Ministry—Sr. RUTH PODESTA, Dir., *33 Front St., Trenton, 08608.* Tel: 609-394-5693.
Hispanic Apostolate—Rev. MANUEL FERNANDEZ, *St. John the Baptist Church, 272 Willow Ave., Long Branch, 07740.* Tel: 908-229-8527; Fax: 908-571-0280.
Korean Apostolate—Vacant.
Scouting—Rev. MICHAEL A. SANTANGELO,Catholic Committees on Scouting, *St. Joan of Arc, 100 Willowbend Rd., Marlton, 08053.*
Charismatic Renewal—Rev. H. BRENDAN WILLIAMS, *St. Veronica, 4215 Hwy. No. 9 N., Howell, 07731.* Tel: 908-363-4200; Fax: 908-370-3891.
Francis House of Prayer—*Mailing Address: P.O. Box 392, Rancocas, 08073.* Tel: 609-877-0509; Fax: 609-877-5810. Location: *39 Springside Rd., Mt. Holly, 08060.* Sr. MARCELLA SPRINGER, S.S.J.
Upper Room Spiritual Center—Sr. MAUREEN CONROY; Sr. MAUREEN CHRISTENSEN, *W. Bangs Ave. and Rte. 33, P.O. Box 1104, Neptune, 07753-1104.* Tel: 908-922-0550; Fax: 908-922-3904.

CLERGY, PARISHES, MISSIONS AND PAROCHIAL SCHOOLS

CITY OF TRENTON
(Mercer County)

1—ST. MARY CATHEDRAL (1868) (Hispanic), Revs. Raymond S. Bianchi, Rector; Roman A. Modino; George A. Medina; Deacons Emiliano Vazquez; Jose Beauchamps; Juan E. Valentin; Juan A. Rivera, Jr.
Res., 151 N. Warren St., 08608. Tel: 609-396-8447; Fax: 609-396-5624. [CEM]
Catechesis/Religious Programs—D.R.E.: Sr. Pilar Socorro Garcia; Sr. Susana Islas.
Students 265.
Convent—211 N. Warren St., 08608. Tel: 609-393-4356.
Sisters 2.

2—BLESSED SACRAMENT (1912), Rev. Richard L. Tofani; Deacons Joseph A. Hannawacker; Louis F. Slee. In res., Rev. Joy T. Chacko.
Res., 716 Bellevue Ave., 08618. Tel: 609-396-9231; Fax: 609-396-6432.
School—720 Bellevue Ave., 08618. Tel: 609-393-8036; Fax: 609-394-8757.
Lay Teachers 16; Students 211.
Station—Mercer Hospital, Tel: 609-394-4000.

3—HOLY ANGELS (1921), Revs. Sam A. Sirianni; Stanley W. Kryzston. In res., Rev. James P. McManimon; Deacons Robert Tharp; Daniel Chase; Salvatore Marcello; Dennis Slavin.
Res., 1733 S. Broad St., 08610. Tel: 609-396-8316; Fax: 609-393-3747.
School—10 New Cedar Ln., 08610. Tel: 609-396-8916.
Lay Teachers 12; Students 222.
Catechesis/Religious Programs—Sr. Jane Urban, R.S.M., D.R.E.
Students 206.
Convent—1701 S. Broad St., 08610. Tel: 609-393-2337.

4—HOLY CROSS (1891) (Polish), Rev. Msgr. Edward A. Arnister; Rev. Henry T. Krajewski, O.F.M.Cap.; Deacon John R. Grussler.
Res., 201 Adeline St., 08611. Tel: 609-393-4826; Fax: 609-278-1192. [CEM]
School—22 Grand St., 08611. Tel: 609-393-8407; Fax: 609-393-5313.
Lay Teachers 15; Students 252.
Convent—233 Adeline St., 08611. Tel: 609-392-3786.

5—IMMACULATE CONCEPTION (1874), Revs. Dominic McGee, O.F.M.Conv.; Angelus Kissam, O.F.M.Conv. In res., Rev. Vincent Rinaldi, O.F.M.Conv.
Res., 540 Chestnut Ave., 08611. Tel: 609-392-5193; Fax: 609-989-1913.
School—Tel: 609-396-8347.
Sisters of St. Francis of Philadelphia 3; Lay Teachers 15; Students 265.
Catechesis/Religious Programs—Students 110.

6—INCARNATION (1947), Rev. Msgr. Hugh F. Ronan. In res., Rev. Msgr. Henry S. Bogdan.
Res., 1545 Pennington Rd., 08618. Tel: 609-882-2860; Fax: 609-637-0460.
School—1555 Pennington Rd., 08618. Tel: 609-882-3228.
Sisters, Servants of the Immaculate Heart of Mary (West Chester) 5; Lay Teachers 13; Students 299.
Catechesis/Religious Programs—Students 225.

7—OUR LADY OF THE DIVINE SHEPHERD (1941) (African American), Rev. Timothy M. Donnelly, S.V.D.
Res., 72 Pennington Ave., 08618. Tel: 609-393-4493; Fax: 609-989-7510.
School—34 Pennington Ave., 08618. Tel: 609-599-1341.
Sisters 3; Lay Teachers 7; Students 156.

8—OUR LADY OF GOOD COUNSEL (1942), Rev. Msgr. William F. Fitzgerald; Rev. Harry E. Cenefeldt; Deacon Robert Brady.
Res., 137 W. Upper Ferry Rd., 08628. Tel: 609-882-3277; Fax: 609-882-4375.
Catechesis/Religious Programs—Students 161.

9—OUR LADY OF MOUNT CARMEL. Closed. For Sacramental records please contact St. Mary Cathedral, Trenton.

10—OUR LADY OF SORROWS (1939), Revs. Paul S. Rimassa; Joseph Gnarackatt; Joseph Xavier Infantini; Deacons Joseph Malloy; Anthony J. D'Agostino; Jeffery Pierfy.
Res., 3816 E. State St., 08619. Tel: 609-587-4372; Fax: 609-587-7998.
School—3800 E. State St. Ext., 08619. Tel: 609-587-4140; Fax: 609-584-8853.
Lay Teachers 26; Students 425.
Catechesis/Religious Programs—3800 E. State St. Ext., 08619. Tel: 609-587-2555. Mrs. Rita Lynn Everist, D.R.E.
Lay Teachers 61; Students 916.
Station—Mercer County Geriatric, Tel: 609-588-5859.

11—SACRED HEART (1814), Rev. Dennis A. Apoldite.
Res., 343 S. Broad St., 08608. Tel: 609-393-2801; Fax: 609-396-4757. [CEM]
School—Lay Teachers 9; Students 220.

12—ST. ANTHONY (1921), Rev. Msgr. Joseph L. Ferrante; Revs. Daniel F. Gowen; Charles R. Kandula. In res., Rev. Robert M. Tynski.
Res., 626 S. Olden Ave., 08629. Tel: 609-586-4181; Fax: 609-586-7206.
School—St. Anthony Grammar School, 530 S. Olden Ave., 08629. Tel: 609-586-5888; Fax: 609-631-9295.
Sisters 3; Lay Teachers 20; Students 401.
High School—McCorristin High School, 175 Leonard Ave., 08610. Tel: 609-586-3705; Fax: 609-586-6584.
Priests 2; Sisters 5; Lay Teachers 39; Students 576.
Catechesis/Religious Programs—530 South Olden Ave., 08629. Tel: 609-586-4330.
Students 200.

13—ST. FRANCIS OF ASSISIUM (1864) (German), Rev. Msgr. John K. Dermond; Rev. Castor G. Sanchez (Philippines). In res., Rev. Ronald Becker.
Res., 31 W. Front St., 08608. Tel: 609-393-4851; Fax: 609-393-4555. [CEM 2]

14—ST. GREGORY THE GREAT (1953), Revs. Richard D. LaVerghetta; Michael P. Lang; Stephen Szmutko, S.V.D.; Deacons Richard D'Angelo; Joseph Glukowski; John Groffie; Allan Parr; Neil Pirozzi; William A. Wilson; Ralph LaMachia.
Res., 4620 Nottingham Way, 08690. Tel: 609-587-4877; Fax: 609-588-0192.
School—4680 Nottingham Way, 08690. Tel: 609-587-1131; Fax: 609-587-7704.
Sisters 1; Lay Teachers 49; Students 647.
Catechesis/Religious Programs—Sr. Patricia Bove, O.S.F., D.R.E.
Students 1,150.
Convent—13 Stanley Dr., Robbinsville, 08691. Tel: 609-259-3384.

15—ST. HEDWIG (1904) (Polish), Revs. Henry F. Schabowski; Arcadius Klejnowski.
Res., 872 Brunswick Ave., 08638. Tel: 609-396-9068; Fax: 609-396-9068. [CEM 2]
School—641 Indiana Ave., 08638. Tel: 609-396-3960.
Felician Sisters 2; Lay Teachers 11; Students 286.
Catechesis/Religious Programs—Tel: 609-394-1534.
Students 133.

16—ST. JAMES (1919) (Italian), Revs. Boniface Ruzich, O.SS.T.; Raphael Malcom-Hollis, O.SS.T.
Res., 29 E. Paul Ave., 08638. Tel: 609-393-4403; Fax: 609-393-6078.
Convent—1016 Princeton Ave., 08638. Tel: 609-695-4088.

17—ST. JOACHIM (1901) (Italian), Revs. Thomas N. Gervasio; Charles B. Davantes; Deacon Guido Mattozzi.
Res., 19 Bayard St., 08611. Tel: 609-695-6089; Fax: 609-695-4376.
School—25 Bayard St., 08611. Tel: 609-394-1445.
Sisters 5; Lay Teachers 8; Students 189.

18—ST. JOSEPH (1891), Rev. Msgr. William J. Dailey.
Res., 540 N. Olden Ave., 08638. Tel: 609-394-5757; Fax: 609-599-4402.
Catechesis/Religious Programs—Students 322.
Station—Helene Fuld Hospital, Tel: 609-394-6000.

19—ST. MICHAEL (1921) (Slovak), Rev. James G. Innocenzi.
Res., 1130 Brunswick Ave., 08638. Tel: 609-393-4050; Fax: 609-393-7335.
Catechesis/Religious Programs—Students 67.

20—SS. PETER AND PAUL (1899) (Slovak), Rev. Francis Zalewski.
Res., 480 Centre St., 08611. Tel: 609-396-2214. [CEM]
Church—480 Second St., 08611.
Catechesis/Religious Programs—Students 70.

21—ST. RAPHAEL (1943) (White Horse), Revs. Ernest J. Siska; John Dwyer. In res., Rev. Leonard Troiano.
Res., 3500 S. Broad St., 08610. Tel: 609-585-7049; Fax: 609-585-5876.
School—151 Gropp Ave., 08610. Tel: 609-585-7733.
Sisters 6; Lay Teachers 13; Students 298.
Catechesis/Religious Programs—151 Gropp Ave., 08610. Tel: 609-585-3848.
Students 496.
Convents—3472 Broad St., 08610. Tel: 609-585-8203.
Contemplative Sisters of the Good Shepherd 11; 68 Lakeview Ct., 08620. Tel: 609-585-7041.
Sisters 4.
Station—Robert Wood Johnson University Hospital at Hamilton, Tel: 609-585-7900.

22—ST. STANISLAUS (1890) (Polish), Rev. Christian Wojciechowski, O.F.M.Conv.; Bro. Gerry Seipp, O.F.M.Conv. In res., Rev. Eugene Kole, O.F.M.Conv.
Res., 60 Randall Ave., 08611. Tel: 609-396-9366; Fax: 609-396-3346. [CEM]
Catechesis/Religious Programs—Students 20.

23—ST. STEPHEN (1903) (Hungarian), Rev. Francis Zalewski.
Mailing Address: P.O. Box 4563, 08611. Tel: 609-394-5965. [CEM]

24—ST. VINCENT DE PAUL (1954), Rev. Arthur F. Conlon.
Res., 555 Allentown Rd., Yardville, 08620. Tel: 609-585-6470; Fax: 609-585-0137.
Catechesis/Religious Programs—Students 57.

OUTSIDE THE CITY OF TRENTON

Allentown, Monmouth Co., St. John (1878), Rev. Joseph J. Procaccini; Rev. Msgr. Leonard R. Toomey, (Retired); Sr. Anastasia Marie Haughey, R.S.M., Pastoral Assoc., Tel: 609-259-2151.
Res., 1282 Yardville-Allentown Rd., 08501. Tel: 609-259-3391; Fax: 609-259-3586. [CEM]
Catechesis/Religious Programs—Students 443.

Asbury Park, Monmouth Co., Holy Spirit (1879), Rev. Leonard P. Lang; Deacons Joseph D. Caroll; Edner Andre.
Res., 705 2nd Ave., Box 617, 07712. Tel: 908-775-0030; Fax: 908-775-7358. [CEM]
Mt. Calvary Cemetery—Rte. 66 and Neptune Blvd., Box 362, Neptune, 07754. Tel: 908-775-3320.

Our Lady of Mt. Carmel (1905) (Italian), Revs. Gerard F. Lynch, O.SS.T.; Joseph K. Mitko, O.SS.T.; Joseph J. Gross, O.SS.T.; Deacon Alfred E. Caponigro, Jr.
Res., 805 Pine St., 07712. Tel: 908-775-1056; Fax: 908-775-8767.
School—First Ave. & Pine St., 07712. Tel: 908-775-8989.
Sisters 4; Lay Teachers 13; Students 209.

St. Peter Claver (1943) (African American), Rev. Gerhard Vogel, S.V.D.; Deacon John Cook.
Res., 108 Ridge Ave., 07712. Tel: 908-775-4157; Fax: 908-774-4531.

Atlantic Highlands, Monmouth Co., St. Agnes (1890), Revs. Leon J Inverso; Bernardino C. Esguerra; Deacon James G. Crowley.
Res., 103 Center Ave., 07716. Tel: 908-291-0272; Fax: 908-291-4982.
School—Tel: 908-291-1050; Fax: 908-291-2035.
Lay Teachers 27; Students 405.
Catechesis/Religious Programs—Students 517.

Avon, Monmouth Co., St. Elizabeth (1907), Rev. Joseph A. Radomski. In res., Rev. Msgr. John J. Endebrock; Rev. Douglas V. Hermansen.
Res., 424 Lincoln Ave., 07717. Tel: 908-774-4089.
Catechesis/Religious Programs—Students 118.

Barnegat, Ocean Co., St. Mary (1942), Rev. Kenard J. Tuzeneu.
Res., 747 West Bay Ave., P.O. Box 609, 08005. Tel: 609-698-5531; Fax: 609-698-6255. [CEM]
Catechesis/Religious Programs—Dolores Kirkpatrick, D.R.E.
Students 1,242.

Bay Head, Ocean Co., Sacred Heart (1913), Revs. Thomas Brennan; Dominic A. Marchese, S.S.J.; Deacon John Czarnecki.
Res., 751 Main Ave., 08742. Tel: 908-899-1398.
Catechesis/Religious Programs—Students 72.

Bayville, Ocean Co., St. Barnabas (1966), Revs. Rocco A. Cuomo; Michael D. Sullivan; Sr. Patricia McNiff, O.S.F., Pastoral Assoc.; Sr. Patricia Lally, O.P., Pastoral Assoc.; Deacons Nick Amatelli, Pastoral Assoc.; James H. Cummings; Peter M. Clausen.
Res., 33 Woodland Rd., Box I, 08721. Tel: 908-269-2208; Fax: 908-269-2557.
Catechesis/Religious Programs—Tel: 908-269-3590.
Students 1,200.

Belmar, Monmouth Co., St. Rose (1888), Rev. Msgr. Alfred D. Smith; Rev. Edward M. Jawidzik; Deacons Normand C. Bailey; Eugene G. Malhame.
Res., 603 Seventh Ave., 07719. Tel: 908-681-0512; Fax: 908-681-1693.
School—Tel: 908-681-5555; Fax: 908-681-5890.
Sisters 4; Lay Teachers 18; Students 537.
High School—Tel: 908-681-2858; Fax: 908-280-2745.
Sisters 6; Lay Teachers 47; Students 541.

Beverly, Burlington Co., St. Joseph (1864), Rev. G. William Evans; Deacons Herman J. Mosteller; Matthew J. Stap; Ronald J. Ulmer; Charles A. Perkins.
Res., 524 Warren St., 08010. Tel: 609-387-0172; Fax: 609-386-8535.
School—805 Warren St., 08010. Tel: 609-387-0991.
Lay Teachers 14; Students 135.
Catechesis/Religious Programs—805 Warren St., 08010. Tel: 609-387-2928.
Students 140.

Bordentown, Burlington Co., St. Mary (1845), Rev. Michael J. Burns; Deacons James Magee; David Harris; Harry Putnam. In res., Rev. Msgr. James S. Foley; Deacon Gary T. Richardson.
Res., 45 Crosswicks St., 08505. Tel: 609-298-0261; Fax: 609-298-7178. [CEM]
School—30 Elizabeth St., 08505. Tel: 609-298-1448. Sr. Joyce Marie Riley, Prin.
Sisters 2; Lay Teachers 10; Students 178.
Convent—49 Crosswicks St., 08505. Tel: 609-298-0220; Fax: 609-298-7178.
Catechesis/Religious Programs—Tel: 609-291-8281.
Students 425.

Bradley Beach, Monmouth Co., Ascension (1907), Rev. James J. Brady; Deacons John Gerard; James McNulty.
Res., 501 Brinley Ave., 07720. Tel: 908-774-0456; Fax: 908-775-9335.
Catechesis/Religious Programs—Students 146.

Brant Beach, Ocean Co., St. Francis of Assisi (1971), Revs. Andrew J. Reitl; Raymond E. Hirt, O.F.M.; William Bried; Francis DiSpigno, O.F.M.; Deacons Albert J. Schwind; James Dougherty.
Office: 4700 Long Beach Blvd., 08008. Tel: 609-494-8813; Fax: 609-494-1466.
Res., 100 3rd St., Beach Haven, 08008. Tel: 609-492-2893.
Catechesis/Religious Programs—Sr. Margaret Magee, O.S.F., D.R.E.
Students 610.
Missions—Beach Haven, Ocean Co., St. Thomas Aquinas, 2nd & Atlantic, 08008; Loveladies, Ocean Co., St. Clare, 56th & Long Beach Blvd., 08008; Surf City, Ocean Co., St. Thomas of Villanova, 13th & Long Beach Blvd., 08008.

Brick Town, Ocean Co., Epiphany (1973), Revs. John V. Bowden; John F. Wake; Deacons Joseph McCormack; Ron Nowak; Michael Mullarkey; William Cortright.
Res., 615 Thiele Rd., 08724. Tel: 908-458-0220; Fax: 908-458-6921.
Catechesis/Religious Programs—Tel: 908-785-0576; 785-0872; Fax: 908-458-6921. Sr. Maria James Riedel, O.S.F., D.R.E.
Students 1,059.

Visitation (1942), Revs. William M. Dunlap; John A. Sullivan (PAT); Deacon Edward Fischer, III. In res., Rev. Edito Amora (Philippines); Deacons Salvadore Vicari; Leonard Kruk.
Res., 730 Lynnwood Ave., 08723-5302. Tel: 908-477-0028; Fax: 908-477-1274.
Catechesis/Religious Programs—Tel: 908-477-5217. Mrs. Nancy Grodberg, D.R.E.
Students 1,222.

St. Dominic (1962), Rev. Msgr. John J. Gibbons; Revs. Richard Basznianin; M. Jones Jayaraj (India); Deacon Damian Ayers; Sr. Margaret Mary Foley, R.S.M., Pastoral Min.
Res., 250 Old Squan Rd., 08724. Tel: 908-840-1410; Fax: 908-840-0522.
School—Tel: 908-840-1412.
Sisters 6; Lay Teachers 26; Students 695.
Catechesis/Religious Programs—Tel: 908-840-1414. Mrs. Margaret Ferrara, D.R.E.
Students 665.

Browns Mills, Burlington Co., St. Ann (1906), Revs. Edwin J. Mathias; James P. Quinn.
Church & Res.—22 Trenton Rd., 08015. Tel: 609-893-3246; Fax: 609-893-8056.
Catechesis/Religious Programs—Students 411.
Stations—Burlington Co. Minimum Security Jail; Burlington Co. Juvenile Detention Center; Deborah Heart & Lung Center; Buttonwood Hall, Evergreen Park.

The Church of the Korean Martyrs (Korean), Rev. Peter Choi, Admin.
Res., 3311 Town Court South, Lawrenceville, 08648. Tel: 609-716-9144; Fax: 609-899-9094.

Burlington, Burlington Co., St. Paul (1864), Rev. Msgr. James H. Dubell; Deacons George Carlin; Francis A. Jones.
Res., 223 E. Union St., 08016. Tel: 609-386-0163; Fax: 609-386-0085.
School—6th & James Sts., 08016. Tel: 609-386-1645.

Sisters of Mercy 1; Lay Teachers 21; Students 400.
Catechesis/Religious Programs—Students 280.

All Saints (1910) (Polish), Rev. Msgr. Martin M. Komosinski; Rev. Casimir Milewski.
Res., 502 High St., 08016. Tel: 609-386-0152; Fax: 609-387-1358.
School—510 High St., 08016. Tel: 609-387-9207.
Lay Teachers 13; Students 207.
Catechesis/Religious Programs—Students 24.

Cinnaminson, Burlington Co., St. Charles Borromeo (1961), Revs. Thomas J. Triggs; Jeffrey E. Lee; Deacons William S. Sepich; William Burke; William Gallagher.
Res., 2226 Riverton Rd., P.O. Box 2220, 08077. Tel: 609-829-3322; Fax: 609-829-3411.
School—2500 Branch Pike, 08077. Tel: 609-829-2778.
Sisters of Mercy 2; Lay Teachers 24; Students 446.
Catechesis/Religious Programs—Mrs. Marie Serfling, D.R.E.
Students 723.

Colts Neck, Monmouth Co., St. Mary (1887), Rev. Edward J. Griswold.
Res., Hwy. 34 and Phalanx Rd., Box H, 07722. Tel: 908-780-2666; Fax: 908-780-0394.
Catechesis/Religious Programs—Tel: 908-294-8841.
Students 779.

Deal, Monmouth Co., St. Mary of the Assumption (1901), Rev. John G. DeSanre; Deacons Kenneth M. McKenna; John McCabe.
Res., 46 Richmond Ave., 07723. Tel: 908-531-1409.
School—73 Wickapecko Dr., Ocean, 07712. Tel: 908-531-4433; Fax: 908-531-4054.
Lay Teachers 16; Students 255.
Catechesis/Religious Programs—Tel: 908-531-1889.
Students 254.

Delran, Burlington Co., Holy Name, Revs. Michael J. O'Connor; Robert A. Stefanotti, O.Carm.; Mr. Tony Pancamo; Mr. Jim Manaloris.
Res., 260 Conrow Rd., Box 1038, 08075. Tel: 609-461-6555; Fax: 609-461-1293.
Catechesis/Religious Programs—Students 450.

Eatontown, Monmouth Co., St. Dorothea (1905), Revs. Vincent E. Keane; Antonio G. Lanuza (Phillipines); Deacons Stephen W. Andrews; Edward R. Herr.
Res., 240 Broad St., 07724. Tel: 908-542-0148; Fax: 908-542-1531.
Catechesis/Religious Programs—Tel: 908-542-0303.
Students 532.

Immaculate Conception (1984) (Korean), Rev. Michael Lee.
Res., 64 Broad St., 07724. Tel: 908-389-3830; Fax: 908-389-2705.
Catechesis/Religious Programs—Students 53.

Englishtown, Monmouth Co., Our Lady of Mercy (1948), Rev. Charles R. Valentine.
Res., 58 Main St., 07726. Tel: 908-446-6324.
Catechesis/Religious Programs—Students 1,060.
Mission—Perrineville, Monmouth Co., St. Joseph, 58 Main St., 07726. Tel: 908-446-6324. [CEM]

Evesham Township, Burlington Co., St. Isaac Jogues (1995), Rev. Phillip C. Pfleger.
P.O. Box 1268, Marlton, 08053. Tel: 609-797-0999; Fax: 609-797-0463.
Catechesis/Religious Programs—St. Joan of Arc Church, 100 WillowBend Rd., Marlton, 08053. Tel: 609-983-7575.
Students 988.

Fair Haven, Monmouth Co., Nativity (1954), Revs. Jerome M. Nolan; Richard R. Sweeny; Deacon John A. Cole.
Res., Ridge and Hance Rds., P.O. Box 66, 07704. Tel: 908-741-1714; Fax: 908-741-6837.
Catechesis/Religious Programs—Tel: 908-741-4543. Mrs. Merrie Brambilla, D.R.E.
Students 721.

Farmingdale, Monmouth Co., St. Catherine of Siena (1912), Rev. Michael S. Vona; Deacon Michael J. Principato.
Res., 15 N. Main St., 07727. Tel: 908-938-5375; Fax: 908-938-3260.
Catechesis/Religious Programs—Tel: 908-938-4129.
Students 355.

Florence, Burlington Co., St. Clare (1874) (Irish/Italian), Rev. Felix F. Venza.
Res., 232 E. Front St., 08518. Tel: 609-499-0122. [CEM]
Catechesis/Religious Programs—Duffy House, 306 E. Front St., 08518. Tel: 609-499-0122.
Students 175.

Forked River, Ocean Co., St. Pius X (1961), Revs. George E. Deutsch; Robert T. Leahy; Deacon James Heller; Sr. Theresa Gillespie, S.S.J., Pastoral Min.
Res., 203 W. Lacey Rd., 08731-3598. Tel: 609-693-5107; Fax: 609-693-6829.
Catechesis/Religious Programs—Tel: 609-693-2379.
Students 1,165.

Freehold, Monmouth Co., St. Rose of Lima (1871), Revs. Gerard J. McCarron; Joseph Rosie. In res., Rev. William T. Schneider; Deacon John Wanat.
Res., 16 McLean St., 07728. Tel: 908-462-0859; Fax: 908-462-8173. [CEM]
School—51 Lincoln Pl., 07728. Tel: 908-462-2646; Fax: 908-462-0331.
Sisters 2 Lay Teachers 31; Students 636.
Catechesis/Religious Programs—Tel: 908-308-0215. Mrs. Michele Rizzo, D.R.E.
Students 685.

St. Robert Bellarmine (1971), Revs. Thomas J. O'Connor; Matthew Adackapara; Brendan Duggan, C.S.S.P.
61 Georgia Rd., 07728. Tel: 908-462-7429; Fax: 908-409-3496.
Catechesis/Religious Programs—Tel: 908-431-3404. Mrs. Margo Weber, D.R.E.
Students 1,015.

Hainesport, Burlington Co., Our Lady Queen of Peace (1944), Rev. Daniel Sullivan; Sr. Pat McGinley, S.S.J., Pastoral Assoc.; Sr. Grata Seidenburg, Parish Min.; Sr. Laurene Tracey, S.S.J, Pastoral Assoc.
Res., 1603 Marne Hwy., P.O. Box 188, 08036. Tel: 609-267-0230; Fax: 609-267-0372.
Catechesis/Religious Programs—Tel: 609-267-3641.
Students 360.

Highlands, Monmouth Co., Our Lady of Perpetual Help (1883), Rev. John M. Dobrosky.
Res., 141 Navesink Ave., 07732. Tel: 908-872-1290; Fax: 908-872-2796.
School—121 Miller St., 07732. Tel: 908-872-0281; Fax: 908-291-7907.
Franciscan Missionary Sisters of the Infant Jesus 4; Lay Teachers 8; Students 214.
Convent—159 Navesink Ave., 07732. Tel: 908-872-1420.
Sisters 4

Hightstown, Mercer Co., St. Anthony of Padua (1885), Revs. Patrick J. Castles; Jacek Labinski; Marco Caceres, C.SS.R., Hispanic Min.; Deacons Thomas Garvey; Thomas Gregory; Joseph Hepp; Frank Prihoda; Stephen Rasi; Patrick Kennedy.
Res., 251 Franklin St., 08520. Tel: 609-448-0141.
Catechesis/Religious Programs—Tel: 609-443-3318. Sr. Anne McCambley, S.S.J., D.R.E.
Students 788.

Holmdel, Monmouth Co., St. Benedict (1959), Revs. William C. Anderson; Paul Varga, O.F.M.Conv.; Deacons Herbert J. Schwarz; Raymond R. Pelkowski.
Res., 165 Bethany Rd., 07733-1699. Tel: 908-264-4712; Fax: 908-264-9080.
School—Tel: 908-264-5578; Fax: 908-264-9080.
Lay Teachers 24; Students 434.
Catechesis/Religious Programs—Tel: 908-264-4714.
Students 771.

St. Catharine (1879), Rev. Eugene M. Rebeck; Deacons John P. Flanagan; James G. McGrath; Sr. Ann Murtha, O.P., Pastoral Assoc.; Karen Sanders, Coord. Pastoral Care. In res., Rev. Joseph McGroarty, O.P.
Res., P.O. Box 655, 07733. Tel: 908-842-3963; Fax: 908-842-9283.
Catechesis/Religious Programs—Tel: 908-842-9253; Fax: 908-842-9283. Sr. Patricia Schladebeck, M.S.C., D.R.E.
Students 1,018.

Hopewell, Mercer Co., St. Alphonsus (1877), Rev. Ralph W. Stansley.
Res., 54 E. Prospect St., 08525. Tel: 609-466-0332; Fax: 609-466-2023. [CEM]
Catechesis/Religious Programs—Tel: 609-466-2694. Sr. Rosemary Hendry, O.S.F., D.R.E.
Students 280.

Howell Township, Monmouth Co., St. Veronica (1962), Revs. H. Brendan Williams; Norman St.John, S.V.D.; Donald J. O'Brien.
Res., 4215 Hwy. 9 N., Howell, 07731. Tel: 908-363-4200; Fax: 908-370-3891.
School—Tel: 908-364-4130; Fax: 908-363-4932.
Sisters 4; Lay Teachers 36; Students 709.
Catechesis/Religious Programs—Tel: 908-364-4137. Sr. Valerie Paccone, C.R., D.R.E.
Students 2,212.
Mission—Freewood Acres, Monmouth Co., St. Mary of the Assumption, Tel: 908-363-4200.

St. William the Abbot (1985), Rev. Msgr. Leo A. Kelty; Deacon Thomas Noone.
Mailing Address: P.O. Box 500, Allenwood, 08720. Tel: 908-840-3535; Fax: 908-840-3663.
Res., 2400 Lakewood-Allenwood Rd., Wall, 07719.
Catechesis/Religious Programs—Students 425.
Stations—Geraldine Thompson Nursing Home, Tel: 908-938-5250; Brisbane Child Treatment Center.

Jackson, Ocean Co., St. Aloysius Gonzaga (1964), Rev. Msgr. Casimir H. Ladzinski, V.G.
Res., 935 Bennetts Mills Rd., P.O. Box 1285, 08527. Tel: 908-370-0500; Fax: 908-370-3555.
School—Saint Aloysius Grammar School, Tel: 908-370-1515. Mrs. Julia Hungerford, Prin.
Catechesis/Religious Programs—Students 680.

Keansburg, Monmouth Co., St. Ann (1924), Revs. Daniel Cahill; Pablo Gadenz; Deacons Edwin Cook; Robert Vlcej.
Res., 311 Carr Ave., 07734. Tel: 908-787-0315.
School—285 Carr Ave., 07734. Tel: 908-787-1027; Fax: 908-495-3338. Sr. Mary Dora McGrath, R.S.M., Prin.
Sisters 2; Lay Teachers 15; Students 310.
Catechesis/Religious Programs—Tel: 908-787-5744.
Students 590.
St. Ann Child Care Center—121 Main St., 07734. Tel: 908-787-7220.
Sisters 2; Students 80.
Bayshore Senior Day Center—100 Main St., 07734. Tel: 908-495-2454.
Sisters 1; Seniors Serviced 1,500.
Hansel and Gretel Preschool—267 Carr Ave., 07734. Tel: 908-787-9237.
Sisters 1; Children 95.
Project Paul—211 Carr Ave., 07734. Tel: 908-787-4887.

Keyport, Monmouth Co., St. Joseph (1854), Revs. Ronald J. Cioffi; James A. Conover; Ms. Jean Potter, Pastoral Assoc.; Deacon Christopher O'Brien. In res., Rev. Daniel J. Ryan.
Res., 376 Maple Pl., 07735. Tel: 908-264-0322; Fax: 908-888-3280. [CEM]
School—St. Joseph School, Maple Pl., 07735. Tel: 908-264-9459; Fax: 908-264-8696. Sr. Constance Gleason, R.S.M., D.R.E. & Prin.
Sisters 2; Lay Teachers 20; Students 436.
Convent—301 Ryan St., 07747. Tel: 908-583-0578.

Jesus the Lord (1978), Rev. Raniero C. Marincioni, S.J.S., Admin.
Res., 123 Broad St., 07735-0673. Tel: 908-739-0323; Fax: 908-264-8276.
Church—120 Broad St., 07735. Tel: 908-264-9672.
Catechesis/Religious Programs—Students 92.

Lakehurst, Ocean Co., St. John (1969), Rev. Ronald Bacovin; Deacons Gabriel Gregory; John Gilchrist; Anthony Tarala.
Res., 619 Chestnut St., 08733. Tel: 908-657-6347; Fax: 908-657-8690.
Catechesis/Religious Programs—Tel: 908-657-2348.
Students 420.

Lakewood, Ocean Co., St. Anthony Claret (1977). (Hispanic Parish for Ocean Co.). Revs. Pedro L. Bou, S.V.D.; Manuel Myvett, S.V.D.; Miguel A. Virella, S.V.D.; Sr. Augustine Serrano, O.S.F.
Res., 780 Ocean Ave., 08701-3644. Tel: 908-367-8486; Fax: 908-367-0460.
Catechesis/Religious Programs—Susana Hulbert, D.R.E.
Students 180.

St. Mary of the Lake (1890), Rev. Msgr. Michael J. Walsh; Revs. Eugene Vavrick; Leon Buni; Deacons Thomas Cater; Silverius Galvan; John Cullinane; Anthony Martucci; Sr. Mary Franey, R.S.M., Pastoral Min.; Mrs. Terry Ginther, Pastoral Assoc.
Res., 43 Madison Ave., 08701. Tel: 908-363-0139; Fax: 908-905-1410. [CEM]
School—Holy Family School, E. County Line Rd., 08701. Tel: 908-363-4771; Fax: 908-363-2914. Sr. Laura M. Longo, M.P.S., Prin.; Sr. Gloria J. Barone, M.P.F., Asst. Prin.
Sisters 2; Lay Teachers 36; Students 822.
Catechesis/Religious Programs—Students 564.
Mission—Lakewood, Ocean Co., Holy Family Church. Fax: 908-905-1410.

Lavallette, Ocean Co., St. Bonaventure (1921), Rev. Msgr. Frederick A. Valentino. In res., Rev. Eugene T. Keenan.
Res., 103 Washington Ave., 08735. Tel: 908-793-7291; Fax: 908-793-8204.

Lawrenceville, Mercer Co., St. Ann (1937), Revs. R. Vincent Gartland; Scott Shaffer; Deacon Gerald De Mauro.
Res., 1253 Lawrence Rd., 08648. Tel: 609-882-6491; Fax: 609-882-4366.
School—34 Rossa Ave., 08648. Tel: 609-882-8077. Mrs. Claire Hamm, M.A., Prin.
Lay Teachers 23; Students 272.
Catechesis/Religious Programs—Tel: 609-882-1212.
Students 460.

Lincroft, Monmouth Co., St. Leo the Great (1958), Rev. James M. Clark; Deacon Robert R. Nimon. Pastoral Associates: Sr. Ann Barry, S.S.J.; Sr. Joan Dreisbach, O.S.F.
Res., 50 Hurley's Ln., 07738. Tel: 908-747-5466; Fax: 908-219-5181.

School—Tel: 908-741-3133; Fax: 908-741-2241.
Lay Teachers 25; Students 564.
Catechesis/Religious Programs—Tel: 908-530-0717.
Students 800.

Long Branch, Monmouth Co.,

1—OUR LADY STAR OF THE SEA, (1878), Rev. M. Joseph Mokrzycki; Deacon John G. Klincewicz; Sr. Diane Matera, R.S.M., Hospital Pastoral Min.
Res., 101 Chelsea Ave., 07740. Tel: 908-229-0526; Fax: 908-229-2886. [CEM]
Catechesis/Religious Programs—Students 87.
Station—Long Branch, Long Branch City.

2—HOLY TRINITY, (1906) (Italian), Rev. Albert Ricciardelli; Deacons Albert M. Pacitti; James A. Kelly; John A. Yaccarine.
Res., 408 Prospect St., 07740. Tel: 908-222-3216; Fax: 908-222-4313.
School—375 Exchange Pl., 07740. Tel: 908-222-8878; Fax: 908-222-8854.
Religious Teachers Filippni 4; Lay Teachers 12; Students 205.
Catechesis/Religious Programs—Tel: 908-870-1778.
Students 168.
Convent—380 Division St., 07740. Tel: 908-222-8535.

3—ST. JOHN THE BAPTIST, (1984) (Spanish), Rev. Manuel Fernandez.
Res., 272 Willow Ave., 07740. Tel: 908-229-8527; 229-8905; Fax: 908-571-0280.
Catechesis/Religious Programs—Tel: 908-571-1003.
Students 281.
Missions—Hightstown-Princeton, Mercer Co., Our Lady of Fatima; Freehold-Red Bank, Monmouth Co., Our Lady of Guadalupe.

4—ST. MICHAEL, (1885), Rev. Charles B. Weiser.
Res., 800 Ocean Ave., West End, 07740. Tel: 908-222-8080; Fax: 908-870-1174.
Catechesis/Religious Programs—Students 403.

Manalapan, Monmouth Co., St. Thomas More (1974), Revs. Paul A. Scaglione; John P. Bambrick; Deacons Keith J. Casey; James Mark Micali; John J. Zebrowski; John J. Walsh.
Res., 186 Gordon's Corner Rd., 07726. Tel: 908-446-6661; Fax: 908-446-6507.
Catechesis/Religious Programs—Tel: 908-446-3232.
Students 1,251.

Manasquan, Monmouth Co., St. Denis (1909), Revs. Robert J. Parenti; Dominic Dellaporte; Charles F.X. Dolan.
Res., 90 Union Ave., Box 340, 08736. Tel: 908-223-0287; Fax: 908-528-1901.
School—119 Virginia Ave., 08736. Tel: 908-223-4928.
Sisters 2; Lay Teachers 14; Students 301.
Catechesis/Religious Programs—Tel: 908-223-1161.
Students 609.
Chapel—Manasquan Beach, Our Lady Star of the Sea. (Summer).

Maple Shade, Burlington Co., Our Lady of Perpetual Help (1920), Revs. Bernard J. Keigher; Kenneth W. Ekdahl; Deacons Joseph McHugh; Ronald J. Kerr; Joseph A. Card; Michael P. Boehm.
Res., 236 E. Main St., 08052. Tel: 609-667-8850; Fax: 609-667-3083.
School—Tel: 609-779-7526.
Sisters 5; Lay Teachers 14; Students 346.
Catechesis/Religious Programs—Students 469.

Marlboro, Monmouth Co., St. Gabriel (1885), Revs. Eugene J. Roberts; Michael J. Lynch; William Weider, T.O.R.; Deacons James C. Russo; Gerald Henwood; James McKeon; Donald Lydick; Lester Owens.
Res., 100 N. Main St., 07746. Tel: 908-946-4487; Fax: 908-946-7276.
Catechesis/Religious Programs—Tel: 908-946-2696; Fax: 908-946-2080. Maureen P. Kelly, D.R.E.
Students 1,233.

Marlton, Burlington Co., St. Joan of Arc (1961), Rev. Msgr. Armand A. Pedata; Revs. Michael A. Santangelo; Adam Kearns; Deacon Barry Tarzy.
Church & Res.—100 Willow Bend Rd., 08053. Tel: 609-983-0077; Fax: 609-983-7716.
School—101 Evans Rd., 08053. Tel: 609-983-0774.
Sisters of St. Joseph 2; Lay Teachers 23; Students 497.
Catechesis/Religious Programs—Tel: 609-983-7575. Sr. Mary Elizabeth Maier, S.S.J., D.R.E.
Students 1,988.
Convent—99 Evans Rd., 08053. Tel: 609-983-0258.

Matawan, Monmouth Co., St. Clement (1965), Rev. John J. Scully; Deacon Donald C. Miller.
Res., 172 Freneau Ave., 07747. Tel: 908-566-3616; Fax: 908-566-9275.
Catechesis/Religious Programs—Tel: 908-591-8090.
Students 803.

Medford, Burlington Co., St. Mary of the Lakes (1943), Revs. Joseph A. Tedesco; A. Edward Siecienski; Cesar R. Anson (Philippines); Vicente Magdaraog; Deacons John M. Iadanza; Norbert J. Klimaszewski; Lawrence J. MacDonald; Joseph R. Patton; W. Norman Talbot; Donald P. Doyle; Ronald Little.
Res., 40 Jackson Rd., 08055. Tel: 609-654-8208; Fax: 609-654-1734.
School—196 Rte. 70, 08055. Tel: 609-654-2546; Fax: 609-654-8125.
Sisters of St. Francis of Philadelphia 3; Sisters of St. Joseph 2; Lay Teachers 23; Students 474.
Catechesis/Religious Programs—196 Rte. 70, 08055. Tel: 609-654-8243.
Students 1,278.
Convents—27 Schoolhouse Dr., 08055. Tel: 609-654-5896. Sisters of St. Francis; 24 Summerhill Lane, 08055. Tel: 609-654-1941. Sisters of St. Joseph.
St. Vincent DePaul Society-Medford: P.O. Box 1131, 08055. Tel: 609-953-0021; Fax: 609-953-2432. Mr. Paul V. Cannon, Treas.

Monmouth Beach, Monmouth Co., Church of the Precious Blood (1947), Rev. John T. Kielb; Deacon William Murray.
Res., 72 Riverdale Ave., 07750. Tel: 908-222-4756; Fax: 908-229-6448.
Catechesis/Religious Programs—Tel: 908-870-1293.
Students 238.

Moorestown, Burlington Co., Our Lady of Good Counsel (1879), Rev. Msgr. James J. McGovern; Rev. John J. Quinn; Deacons Frank Giglio; Francis P. McGann.
Res., 42 W. Main St., 08057. Tel: 609-235-0181; Fax: 609-235-4987. [CEM]
School—Tel: 609-235-7885; Fax: 609-235-4987. Sr. Michael Vincent Dailey, O.P., Prin.
Dominic Sisters of Hope 1; Lay Teachers 29; Students 497.
Catechesis/Religious Programs—Tel: 609-235-7136. Mrs. Linda M. Dix, D.R.E.
Students 744.

Mount Holly, Burlington Co., Sacred Heart (1848), Revs. Robert J.W. Schecker; David A. Adams.
Res., 260 High St., 08060-1404. Tel: 609-267-0209; Fax: 609-267-9293. [CEM]
School—250 High St., 08060. Tel: 609-267-1728; Fax: 609-267-1728.
Lay Teachers 24; Students 440.
Catechesis/Religious Programs—Students 436.
Mission—Jobstown, Burlington Co., St. Andrew, 2489 Monmouth Rd., Jobstown, 08041. Tel: 609-324-0806. Deacon John F. Hoefling.
Stations—County Jail, Tel: 609-267-3300; Burlington County Hospital Extended Care Center, Tel: 609-367-0700.

Christ the Redeemer (1976) (Hispanic), Rev. Victoriano F. Sandoval, O.S.A.
Res., 35 South Ave., 08060. Tel: 609-261-0181; Fax: 609-261-0017.
Catechesis/Religious Programs—250 High St., Mt. Holly, 08060. Tel: 609-267-1728.
Students 64.

Mount Laurel, Burlington Co., St. John Neumann (1978), Revs. Lino S. Parente, O.Cist. (Italy); Anselmo M. Florio, O.Cist. (Italy); Maurizio Nicoletti, O.Cist (Italy); Deacon John Hughes.
Res., 560 Walton Ave., 08054. Tel: 609-235-1330; Fax: 609-235-9632.
Catechesis/Religious Programs—Students 738.

Neptune, Monmouth Co., Holy Innocents (1959), Deacon Michael Auleta. In res., Revs. Lawrence Kunnel; Charles F. Moore.
Res., 3455 W. Bangs Ave., P.O. Box 806, 07753. Tel: 908-922-4242; Fax: 908-922-2848.
School—Tel: 908-922-3141; Fax: 908-922-6531.
Religious Teachers Filippini 2; Lay Teachers 14; Students 303.
Catechesis/Religious Programs—Students 216.
Stations—Convacenter Nursing Home; Green Grove Nursing Home; Heritage Hall Nursing Home; Medicenter Nursing Home; The Lodge, Kings Manor.

Our Lady of Providence (1981) (Spanish), Rev. James Vorwerk, S.V.D.; Sr. Grace Forker, S.S.J., Pastoral Assoc.; Deacons Felix L. Rodriguez; Victor L. Gomez. In res., Rev. Adam Midor, S.V.D.
Res., 1228 Fifth Ave., 07753. Tel: 908-776-7164.
Catechesis/Religious Programs—Tel: 908-776-7164.
Students 140.

New Egypt, Ocean Co., Assumption (1853), Rev. Anthony M. Carotenuto; Deacon Martin Ervin.
Res., 76 Evergreen Rd., 08533. Tel: 609-758-2153; Fax: 609-758-6240. [CEM]
Catechesis/Religious Programs—Students 672.
Mission—Jackson, Ocean Co., Church of St. Monica, 679 W. Veteran's Hwy., Jackson, 08527. Tel: 908-928-0279.

New Monmouth, Monmouth Co., St. Mary (1878), Revs. Gregory D. Vaughan; Jeffrey J. Kegley; Gerald E. McBride; James D. Keating, O.P.; Deacon Henry Ernst; Sr. Laura Garges, O.S.F., Pastoral Assoc.
Res., 26 Leonardville Rd., 07748. Tel: 908-671-0071; Fax: 908-671-0079.
School—538 Church St., 07748. Tel: 908-671-0129; Fax: 908-671-2653. Mrs. Victoria Quinn, Prin.
Sisters 6; Lay Teachers 26; Aides 12; Students 720.
High School—Mater Dei High School, Tel: 908-671-9100; Fax: 908-671-9214. Mr. Frank Poleski, Jr., Prin.; Mr. William V. Smith, Asst. Prin.
Lay Teachers 27; Students 397.
Catechesis/Religious Programs—Tel: 908-671-0124. Mrs. Alex Margaret Krasutsky, D.R.E.
Students 1,504.

Normandy Beach, Ocean Co., Our Lady of Peace (1979), Rev. Laszlo F. Rauch.
Residence and Mailing: P.O. Box 728, 7th Ave. & Rte. 35 S., 08739. Tel: 908-793-7803; Fax: 908-793-1808.
Catechesis/Religious Programs—Students 25.

Middletown, Monmouth Co., St. Catherine (1948), Rev. L. Jacqueline Callahan, Pastoral Assoc. & D.R.E.
Res., 5 Shore Acres Ave., 07748. Tel: 908-787-1318; Fax: 908-787-6139.
Catechesis/Religious Programs—Tel: 908-495-7779.
Students 503.

Pennington, Mercer Co., St. James (1897), Revs. James J. McConnell; Benedict Worry, O.S.B.; Deacons James W. Palsir; Samuel Sciarrotta.
Res., 115 E. Delaware Ave., 08534. Tel: 609-737-0122; Fax: 609-737-6912.
Catechesis/Religious Programs—Tel: 609-737-2717.
Students 734.

Point Pleasant, Ocean Co., St. Martha (1972), Revs. Patrick F. Magee; Vincent J. Donadio; Deacons Edward Maier; John Haney.
Mailing Address: 3800 Herbertsville Rd., 08742. Tel: 908-295-3630; Fax: 908-295-9315.
Res., 3800 Herbertsville Rd., 08742. Tel: 908-899-7269; 295-3630.
Catechesis/Religious Programs—Tel: 908-295-8252.
Students 617.

Point Pleasant Beach, Ocean Co., St. Peter (1882), Revs. Joseph Angelini, O.F.M.Conv.; Richard Rossell, O.F.M.Conv.; William D'Arcy, O.F.M.Conv.; Deacon Edwin H. Brookes, Jr.
Res., 406 Forman Ave., 08742. Tel: 908-892-0049; Fax: 908-295-9782.
School—Tel: 908-892-1260.
Sisters 4; Lay Teachers 12; Students 306.
Catechesis/Religious Programs—Students 590.
Convent—401 Atlantic Ave., 08742. Tel: 908-899-2390.

Princeton, Mercer Co., St. Paul (1864), Revs. Evasio De Marcellis; Brian Butch; Deacons Maurice Benedetti; Paul LaChance; Michael Ross.
Res., 214 Nassau St., 08540. Tel: 609-924-1743; Fax: 609-924-7980. [CEM]
School—216 Nassau St., 08540. Tel: 609-921-7587; Fax: 609-921-0164.
Sisters 4; Lay Teachers 25; Students 388.
Catechesis/Religious Programs—Tel: 609-924-2681.
Students 350.

Red Bank, Monmouth Co., St. James (1864), Revs. Philip A. Lowery; Alex Enriquez; Michael G. Lankford.
Res., 94 Broad St., 07701. Tel: 908-741-0500; Fax: 908-747-1936. [CEM]
(Grades Preschool).
Lay Teachers 2; Students 45.
School—St. James Grammar School, Tel: 908-741-3363.
Lay Teachers 27; Students 493.
High School—Red Bank Catholic High School, Tel: 908-747-1774.
Sisters 2; Lay Teachers 56; Students 774.
Station—Riverview Hospital, Tel: 908-530-2231; Fax: 908-530-2394.

St. Anthony (1920) (Italian), Rev. Joseph J. Miele.
Res., 121 Bridge Ave., 07701. Tel: 908-747-0813; Fax: 908-224-0059.
Catechesis/Religious Programs—16 Herbert St., 07701. Tel: 908-741-0261. Mrs. Patricia H. Foley, D.R.E.
Students 205.

Riverside, Burlington Co., St. Peter (1878), Revs. Julius Toth, O.F.M.Conv.; Justin Biase, O.F.M.Conv., Pastoral Assoc.; Deacon Joseph Fuoco. In res., Rev. Crispin Fuino, O.F.M.Conv.
Res., 102 Middleton St., Box 248, 08075. Tel: 609-461-0100; Fax: 609-764-6133.
School—St. Peter, Middleton and Hancock Sts., 08075. Tel: 609-461-1087.
Sisters 2; Lay Teachers 18; Students 415.

Catechesis/Religious Programs—Tel: 609-461-9343.
Students 304.
St. Casimir (1913) (Polish), Revs. Dennis Mason, O.F.M.Conv.; Stephen King, O.F.M.Conv. In res., Rev. Jude Michael Krill, O.F.M.Conv.
Res., 502 New Jersey Ave., 08075. Tel: 609-461-0532; Fax: 609-461-2590.
School & Preschool—500 New Jersey Ave., 08075. Tel: 609-461-7410.
Sisters 3; Lay Teachers 13; Students 240.
Catechesis/Religious Programs—Students 240.

Riverton, Burlington Co., Sacred Heart (1878), Rev. John P. Czahur; Deacons Joseph Knipp; Joseph Donadieu.
Res., 101-03 Fourth St., 08077. Tel: 609-829-0090; Fax: 609-829-2087.
Catechesis/Religious Programs—Tel: 609-829-1848.
Students 526.

Roebling, Burlington Co., Holy Assumption (1914), Revs. Francis Walter, O.F.M.; Januarius Izzo, O.F.M.; Deacon Robert D. Machion. In res., Revs. Maximus J. Mandl, O.F.M.; Alexander Krupa, O.F.M.
Res., 1290 Hornberger Ave., 08554. Tel: 609-499-0161; Fax: 609-499-3074.
School—Tel: 609-499-0045.
Lay Teachers 9; Students 230.
Catechesis/Religious Programs—Students 141.

Rumson, Monmouth Co., Holy Cross (1884), Rev. Joseph W. Hughes; Deacon Jay C. Harbeck; Sr. Rosamond Blanchet, R.S.H.M., Pastoral Assoc.
Res., 30 Ward Ave., 07760. Tel: 908-842-0348; Fax: 908-842-3226.
School—(Grades PreK-8) Ward Ave. and Rumson Rd., 07760. Tel: 908-842-0348; Fax: 908-842-3226.
Lay Teachers 23; Students 330.
Mission—Rumson, Monmouth Co., Holy Rosary.

Sea Girt, Monmouth Co., St. Mark (1953), Rev. William J. Carton. In res., Rev. Msgr. Robert T. Bulman.
Res., 215 Crescent Pkwy., 08750. Tel: 908-449-6364; Fax: 908-449-1646.
Catechesis/Religious Programs—Tel: 908-449-8360.
Students 445.

Seaside Heights, Ocean Co., Our Lady of Perpetual Help (1946), Rev. Jude De Angelo, O.F.M. Conv.
Res., 100 Grant Ave., 08751. Tel: 908-793-6881; Fax: 908-793-7632.

Seaside Park, Ocean Co., St. Catharine of Siena (1906), Revs. Emmett Carroll, O.F.M.Conv.; Timothy Lyons, O.F.M.Conv., Supr.; Armand Sorento, O.F.M.Conv.; Eugene Zwahl, O.F.M.Conv.; Eric Fenner, O.F.M.Conv.; Reginald Sweeney, O.F.M.Conv.; Justin Grabovsky, O.F.M.Conv.
Res., 50 E. St., 08752. Tel: 908-793-0041; Fax: 908-793-5483.
Catechesis/Religious Programs—Students 298.

Spring Lake, Monmouth Co., St. Catharine (1901), Rev. Msgr. Thomas A. Luebking; Rev. K. Michael Lambeth; Deacons John P. O'Connor; David Fursman; Edward Jennings.
Res., 215 Essex Ave., 07762. Tel: 908-449-5765; Fax: 908-449-0916. [CEM 2]
School—Tel: 908-449-4424; Fax: 908-449-7876.
Sisters 4; Lay Teachers 30; Students 577.
Catechesis/Religious Programs—Students 592.
Convent—211 Essex Ave., 07762. Tel: 908-449-6199.
Mission—Spring Lake, Monmouth Co., St. Margaret.

Tabernacle, Burlington Co., Holy Eucharist (1982), Revs. Richard Milewski; Joseph Farrell; Deacons Joseph Lambarski; Stanley Orkis; John Zimmerle.
Office: 520 Medford Lakes Rd., 08088. Tel: 609-268-8383; Fax: 609-268-3294.
Catechesis/Religious Programs—Tel: 609-268-7742. Dolores Wright, D.R.E.
Students 760.
Station—New Lisbon Developmental Center, Tel: 609-726-1000.

Toms River, Ocean Co.,

1—St. Joseph, (Dover Township) (1883), Rev. Msgr. Sean P. Flynn; Revs. William P. Gardner; Roberto Ignacio; Daniel F. Swift; Deacons John E. Gormley; Francis J. Babuschak; Edwin L. Voll, Jr.; Frank J. McKenna.
Mailing Address: P.O. Box 387, 509 Hooper Ave., 08754. Tel: 908-349-0018; Fax: 908-286-7064. [CEM]
School—Tel: 908-349-2355; Fax: 908-349-1064.
Sisters 5; Lay Teachers 40; Students 922.
High School—Monsignor Donovan High School, Tel: 908-349-8801; Fax: 908-349-8956.
Sisters 7; Lay Teachers 73; Students 910.
Catechesis/Religious Programs—Tel: 908-914-2420.
Students 1,150.
Mission—Island Heights, Ocean Co., St. Gertrude, Ocean & Central Aves., 08732.

2—St. Justin, (Dover Township) (1972), Revs. William J. Nolan; Alejandro A. Gronifillo; Joseph Halpin; Deacons Gregory Wallack; Richard Hauenstein; David L. Shapiro; Brent McNally; Louis Cartnick; Michael Fullen.
Res., 975 Fischer Blvd., 08753. Tel: 908-270-3980; Fax: 908-929-9411.
Catechesis/Religious Programs—Tel: 908-270-3797. Mrs. Michele Williams, D.R.E.
Students 1,465.

3—St. Luke, (Dover Township) (1982), Rev. Louis W. Kralovich; Deacons Donald G. MacCarrick; Charles J. Cederroth; Ronald R. Wicks.
Res., 1674 Old Freehold Rd., Box 1686, 08755. Tel: 908-286-2222.
Catechesis/Religious Programs—Tel: 908-505-0108. Mrs. Mary Goss, D.R.E.
Students 1,077.

4—St. Maximilian Kolbe, (Dover Township) (1985), Rev. Francis E. Santitoro.
Residence and Mailing Address: 130 Vare St., 08756. Tel: 908-914-0300; 914-8550 (Res.); Fax: 908-240-9517.

Tuckerton, Ocean Co., St. Teresa (1944), Revs. Terence O. McAlinden; Ben Amora, Assoc.; Deacons George Seaton; Dean James Petrauskas.
Res., 128 Cedar St., 08087. Tel: 609-296-2504; Fax: 609-296-4530.
Catechesis/Religious Programs—Tel: 609-296-1940. Miss Susan Eggert, D.R.E.
Students 725.
Mission—Little Egg Harbor, Ocean Co., St. Michael. 64 W. Calabreie Way.

Union Beach, Monmouth Co., Holy Family (1942), Revs. Patrick G. Fitzpatrick; Stanislaus T. Polczyk; Francis Cheruparambil; Deacons George Hooker; John Clymore. Pastoral Ministers: Sr. Rose Mary Malague, R.S.M.; Sr. Gloria Jean Bateman.
Res., Hwy. 36, P.O. Box 56, Keyport, 07735. Tel: 908-264-1484; Fax: 908-264-8369.
School—Tel: 908-264-9549; Fax: 908-335-9605.
Sisters 2; Lay Teachers 20; Students 417.
Catechesis/Religious Programs—Tel: 908-264-7043; Fax: 908-335-9605. Sr. Denise O'Boyle, R.S.M., D.R.E.
Students 812.
Convents—Mercy Convent, 440 Sullivan Pl., 07735. Tel: 908-739-3065; Holy Family Convent, 41 Hemlock St., Hazlet, 07730. Tel: 908-264-5353.

Washington Crossing, Mercer Co., St. George (1924), Rev. Msgr. George A. Ardos; Rev. James Coley; Rev. Msgr. Walter E. Nolan; Rev. Edward Dougherty; Sr. Dorothy Jancola, R.S.M., Pastoral Assoc.; Deacons James Toolan; Thomas Daily.
Res., 1370 River Rd., P.O. Box 324, Titusville, 08560. Tel: 609-737-2015; Fax: 609-737-7863.
Catechesis/Religious Programs—Tel: 609-730-1703.
Students 185.
Station—Mercer County Correction Center.

Wayside, Monmouth Co., St. Anselm (1972), Rev. Robert F. Kaeding.
Res., 1028 Wayside Rd., 07712. Tel: 908-493-4411; Fax: 908-493-4272.
Catechesis/Religious Programs—Students 767.

West Long Branch, Monmouth Co., St. Jerome (1956), Rev. Frederick W. Jackiewicz.
Res., 254 Wall St., 07764. Tel: 908-222-1424; Fax: 908-222-2291.
School—250 Wall St., 07764. Tel: 908-222-8686; Fax: 908-222-3064.
Sisters 3; Lay Teachers 14; Students 254.
Catechesis/Religious Programs—250 Wall St., 07764.
Students 157.
Convent—250A Wall St., 07764. Tel: 908-222-2016.

West Windsor, Mercer Co., Church of St. David the King (1988), Rev. Timothy J. Capewell; Deacons Thomas Baker; Roger Dinella.
Res., 517 W. Village Rd., Princeton Jct., 08550. Tel: 609-275-7111; Fax: 609-799-1984.
Church—One New Village Rd., Princeton Jct., 08550-2003. Tel: 609-275-7111.
Catechesis/Religious Programs—Students 780.

Whiting, Ocean Co., St. Elizabeth Ann Seton (1976), Rev. Msgr. Joseph C. Shenrock, P.A.; Rev. Antony P. Poovakulam; Deacons Kyron J. Purcell; Joseph Rider; Robert Wolfe; David McComb; Russell Alexander.
Res., 30 Schoolhouse Rd., 08759. Tel: 908-350-5001; Fax: 908-350-0912.
Catechesis/Religious Programs—Tel: 908-350-7391.
Students 169.

Willingboro, Burlington Co., Corpus Christi (1959), Revs. Stanley P. Lukaszewski; Michael T. Babalya; Deacons James E. Ayrer; Stanley R. Olshevski; John F. Vassallo, Jr.; Joseph Billbrough. In res., Rev. Richard C. Brietske.
Res., 63 Sylvan Ln., 08046. Tel: 609-877-5322; Fax: 609-877-1695.
School—Charleston & Sunset Rds., 08046. Tel: 609-877-2144; Fax: 609-877-3153.
Sisters 1; Lay Teachers 18; Students 365.
Catechesis/Religious Programs—Charleston & Sunset Rds., 08046. Tel: 609-871-4680.
Students 240.

Chaplains of Public Institutions

Trenton. *Catholic Persons with Disabilities, New Jersey School for Deaf.* Sr. Helen Kline, S.S.J.
Donnelly Memorial Hospital of City of Trenton. Rev. Paul S. Rimassa.
Helene Fuld Hospital, St. Joseph Church, 08638. Rev. Msgr. William J. Dailey.
Mercer County Correction Center, St. George Rectory, Titusville, 08560. Rev. Msgr. George A. Ardos.
New Jersey State Prison, CN 861, 08629.
St. Francis Medical Center. Revs. Joel Szydlowski, O.F.M.; Linus E. Kopczewski, O.F.M.; Rudolph Wieszczck, O.F.M.

Bordentown. *Bordentown Correction Center, Burlington County.* Vacant.
Edward R. Johnstone Training and Research Center. Attended from St. Mary's Church.

Burlington. *Burlington County Hospital & Extended Care Center.* 311 High St., Mount Holly, 08060. Rev. Robert J. Schecker.
Burlington County Jail. 311 High St., Mount Holly, 08060. Rev. Robert J. Schecker.

Marlboro. *New Jersey State Hospital,* St. Rose of Lima, Freehold, 07728. Rev. William T. Schneider.

Monmouth. *Monmouth County Jail.* Rev. Robert F. Kaeding.

Neptune. *Jersey Shore Medical Center,* Holy Innocents, 07753. Rev. Douglas Hermansen, St. Elizabeth Church, 424 Lincoln Ave., Avon, 07717.

New Lisbon. *New Jersey State Colony,* Holy Eucharist, Tabernacle, 08088. Tel: 609-726-1000. Rev. Richard Milewski.
Ocean County Jail. Attended by St. Joseph, Toms River.

Yardville. *Garden State Correctional Center.* Rev. Andrew Hadalski, S.V.D.

Military Installations

Colts Neck. *Naval Weapons Station Earle.* Rev. Robert Paner.

Fort Dix. *Fort Dix.* Vacant.

Lakehurst. *U.S. Naval Air Warfare Center.* Rev. James F. Finley.

Little Silver. *Fort Monmouth.* Rev. Joseph D'Silva.

McGuire Air Force Base. *McGuire Air Force Base.* Rev. David Gaeta.

Sandy Hook. *Fort Hancock.* Vacant.

On Duty Outside the Diocese:
Reverend Monsignors—
Punderson, Joseph R., Villa Stritch, Via Della Nocetta 63, Rome, 00164 Italy
Reverend Fathers—
Barile, Ralph E.
Bicomong, Sergio, U.S. Penitentiary, Lewisburg, PA
Campoli, John F., His Love Ministry, P.O. Box 433, Allenhurst, NJ 07711
Chester, Thomas, 130 Michigan Ave., N.E., Apt. 0-42, Washington, D.C. 20017
Hendricks, John J., Society of St. James the Apostle, 24 Clark St., Boston, MA 02109
Krisak, Anthony F., S.S., 618 East St., NE, #B, Washington, DC 20002
Kselman, John J., S.S., Weston School of Theology, Three Phillips Pl., Cambridge, MA 02138
Laforge, Joseph M., Our Lady of Pepetual Help, 331 Hammond St., Rocky Mount, N.C. 27804
Loffredo, Peter J., 1610 Milvia St., Apt. 6, Berkeley, CA 94709
McKeone, William
Sloyan, Gerard S., 6216 41st Ave., Hyattsville, MD 20782
Thelly, Matthew, 2205 Genesee St., Utica, NY 13501
Zec, John J., Mount St. Mary Seminary, Plangborn Hall 366, Emmitsburg, MD 21727

Military Chaplains:
Reverend Fathers—
Flood, Peter J., 2603 Dow Dr., Omaha, NE 68123-1736
Inghilterra, Vincent J., Office Post Chap., Fort Leonard Wood, MO 65473
Liguori, Henry A., 7216 Enterprise Dr., Las Vegas, NV 89117

Leave of Absence:
Reverend Fathers—

Brown, Gerard J.
Christian, John S.
Fahey, Edward J.
Gallagher, Richard
Hillier, David A.
Iazzetta, Frank J.
McGrath, Francis
McHugh, Joseph F.
McManimon, James P.
Pienciak, Daniel B.
Rittenhouse, Thomas R.
Russo, John W.
Sauchelli, James J.

Retired:
Reverend Monsignors—
Bogdan, Henry S., Incarnation Church, 1545 Pennington Rd., Trenton, NJ 08618
Bradley, Paul F., 14 Mark Dr., Long Branch, NJ 07740
Bulman, Robert T., St. Mark's Church, 215 Crescent Pkwy., Sea Girt, NJ 08750
Capitani, Anthony L., 1305 Chambers St., Trenton, NJ 08610
Coffey, Thomas A., Villa Neumann, 2301 Lawrenceville Rd., P.O. Box 6589, Lawrenceville, NJ 08648
Constance, Samuel C., 521 Walden Cir., Robbinsville, NJ 08691
Endebrock, John J., St. Elizabeth's Church, 424 Lincoln Ave., Avon, NJ 07717
Foley, James S., St. Mary's Church, 45 Crosswicks St., Bordentown, NJ 08505
Frain, Thomas J., 600 Chelsea Pl., Ocean City, NJ 08232
Henry, Edward C., 3 Colonial Club Dr., No. 305, Boynton Beach, FL 33435
Maguire, William E., 9-C Lafayette Dr., Whiting, NJ 08759
Morello, Amedeo L., 232 Chelsea Ave., Box 422, Pine Beach, NJ 08741
O'Connor, Joseph A., Villa Neumann, 2301 Lawrenceville Rd., P.O. Box 6589, Lawrenceville, NJ 08648
Toomey, Leonard R., St. John Church, 1282 Yardville-Allentown Rd., Allentown, NJ 08501
Wilus, John M., 225 Walnut St., South Amboy, NJ 08879
Wojciehowski, Thaddeus, Villa Neumann, 2301 Lawrenceville Rd., P.O. Box 6589, Lawrenceville, NJ 08648
Reverend Fathers—
Albano, George M., St. Maximillian Kolbe Church, P.O. Box 4144, Toms River, NJ 08756-4144
Atzert, Edward P., Morries Hall, 2361, Lawrenceville, NJ 08648
Bausch, William, Box 1068, Point Pleasant Beach, NJ 08742
Byrnes, John P., 339 Holiday Lake Dr., E., Holiday, FL 33589
Cammisa, James N., 15 Hastings Pl., Monmouth Beach, NJ 07750
Campbell, William J., 92 Beattle St., Worcester, MA 01606
Cervenak, Andrew, Janosikova 21, 08001 Presov, Slovak Republic
Clancy, Frederick J., 52 New Haven Way, Rossmoor, Jamesburg, NJ 08831
Coley, James E., Versaille Apt., 224 Sullivan Way, A5B, Trenton, NJ 08628
Cook, John B., 7777 46th Ave., N., Lot 12, St. Petersburg, FL 33709
Davis, Eugene V., Villa Neumann, 2301 Lawrenceville Rd., P.O. Box 6589, Lawrenceville, NJ 08648
Delzell, David G., Tower of David, P.O. Box 292, Uniondale, PA 18470
Dougherty, Edward J., Villa Neumann, 2301 Lawrenceville Rd., P.O. Box 6589, Lawrenceville, NJ 08648
Eelman, William C., 171 Lakeshore Dr., Southampton, NJ 08088
Farre, Raymond P., Spain
Gannon, Earl A., Morris Hall, 1 Bishop Dr., Lawrenceville, NJ 08648
Getlik, Stephen J., 485 Fayette St., Perth Amboy, NJ 08861
Horvath, Stephen G., P.O. Box 112, Bushkill, PA 18324
Lloyd, Vincent A., 713 Egret Ct., Edgewater, FL 32032
Matera, Philip T., 750 Estates Blvd., Apt. 254, Mercerville, NJ 08619
Miller, Joseph B., Marcella Nursing & Rehab, 2305 Rancocas Rd., Burlington Twp., NJ 08916
Murray, Robert P., Morris Hall, 1 Bishop's Dr., Lawrenceville, NJ 08648
Petri, John C., 259 Squirrel Ridge Rd., Leasburg, NC 27291
Porazzo, Francis J., 61 Foxglove Rd., Pleasant Plains, Toms River, NJ 08753
Ridge, Thomas P., 47 Spruce St., Watertown, MA 02172
Rittenhouse, Thomas R., St. Clement's Church, 172 Freneau Ave., Matawan, NJ 07747
Rucinski, Joseph S., 181 N.E. 14th Ave., Hallandale, FL 33009
Sullivan, John E., Villa Neumann, 2301 Lawrenceville Rd., P.O. Box 6589, Lawrenceville, NJ 08648
Thompson, James A., 49A Cambridge Cir., Leisure Village West, Lakehurst, NJ 08733

Permanent Deacons:
Alexander, Russell, (Retired), St. Elizabeth Ann Seton, Whiting
Amatelli, Nicholas W., St. Barnabas, Bayville
Andre, Edner, Holy Spirit, Asbury Park
Andrews, Stephen W., St. Dorothea, Eatontown
Armstrong, Robert B., St. Mary, Barnegat
Auleta, Michael A., Holy Innocents, Neptune
Ayers, Damian, St. Dominic's, Brick
Ayrer, James E., Corpus Christi, Willingboro
Babuschak, Francis J., St. Joseph, Toms River
Bailey, Normand C., St. Rose, Belmar
Baker, Thomas, St. David the King, Princeton Junction
Beauchamps, Jose, St. Mary Cathedral, Trenton
Benedetti, Maurice T., St. Paul, Princeton
Billbrough, Joseph C., (Retired), Corpus Christi, Willingboro
Blackwell, M. Darrell, Sacred Heart, Mt. Holly
Boehm, Michael P., Our Lady of Perpetual Help, Maple Shade
Brady, Robert F., Our Lady of Good Council, West Trenton
Brookes, Edwin H., Jr., St. Peter, Point Pleasant
Burke, William F., St. Charles Borromeo, Cinnaminson
Caponigro, Alfred E., Our Lady of Mount Carmel, Asbury Park
Card, Joseph A., Our Lady of Perpetual Help, Maple Shade
Carlin, George M., St. Paul, Burlington
Carroll, Joseph D., Holy Spirit, Asbury Park
Cartnick, Louis C., St. Justin's, Toms River
Casey, Keith J., St. Thomas More, Manalapan
Cater, Thomas H., St. Mary of the Lake, Lakewood
Cederroth, Charles, (Retired), St. Luke's, Toms River
Chase, Daniel A., Holy Angels, Trenton
Clausen, Peter M., St. Barnabas, Bayville
Clymore, John L., Holy Family, Union Beach
Cole, John A., (Retired), Nativity, Fair Haven
Cook, Edwin, St. Ann, Keansburg
Cook, John, Sr., St. Peter Claver, Asbury Park
Cortright, William L., Marlboro Psychiatric Hospital, Marlboro
Crowley, James, St. Agnes Church, Atlantic Highlands
Cullinane, John F., St. Mary of the Lake, Lakewood
Cummings, James H., St. Barnabas, Bayville
Czarnecki, John W., Sacred Heart, Bay Head
D'Agostino, Anthony J., Our Lady of Sorrows, Mercerville
D'Angelo, Richard V., St. Gregory the Great, Trenton
Daily, Thomas P., St. George, Titusville
DeLuca, Peter J., Our Lady of Good Counsel, Moorestown
DeMauro, Gerald E., St. Ann's, Trenton
Dinella, Roger P., St. David the King, Princeton Junction
Donadieu, Joseph M., Diocesan Office of Communications
Dougherty, James, St. Francis of Assisi, Brant Beach
Doyle, Donald P., St. Mary, Medford
Earley, Daniel C., St. Ann, Browns Mills
Eby, Richard, St. Veronica, Howell
Ernst, Henry J., St. Mary, New Monmouth
Ervin, Martin A., Assumption, New Egypt
Fischer, Edward, III, Visitation, Brick
Flanagan, John P., St. Catharine, Holmdel
Fullen, Michael P., Sr., St. Justin, Toms River
Fuoco, Joseph R., St. Peter, Riverside
Fursman, James David, St. Catherine, Spring Lake
Gallagher, Paul A., St. Mary of the Lake, Lakewood
Gallagher, William J., St. Charles Borromeo, Cinnaminson
Galvan, Silverius F., St. Mary of the Lake, Lakewood
Garvey, Thomas J., St. Anthony of Padua, Hightstown
Gerard, John J., (Retired), Ascension, Bradley Beach
Giglio, Frank E., Our Lady of Good Counsel, Moorestown
Gilchrist, John A., St. John Church, Lakehurst
Glukowsky, Joseph A., St. Gregory the Great, Trenton
Gomez, Victor L., Our Lady of Providence, Neptune
Gormley, John E., St. Joseph, Toms River
Gregory, Gabriel, St. John, Lakehurst
Gregory, Thomas J., St. Anthony of Padua, Hightstown
Groffie, John F., St. Gregory the Great, Trenton
Grussler, John R., Holy Cross, Trenton
Gularek, Theodore V., St. Veronica, Howell
Hambleton, Richard N., St. Mary, Barnegat
Haney, John J., St. Martha, Point Pleasant
Hannawacker, Joseph A., Blessed Sacrament, Trenton
Harbeck, Jay C., Holy Cross, Rumson
Harris, David M., St. Mary, Bordentown
Hauenstein, Richard A., St. Justin, Toms River
Heller, James T., St. Pius X, Forked River
Henwood, Gerald V., St. Gabriel, Marlboro
Hepp, Joseph L., St. Anthony of Padua, Hightstown
Herr, Edward R., St. Dorothea, Eatontown
Hoefling, John F., Sacred Heart, Mount Holly
Hooker, George C., Holy Family, Keyport
Huether, Vincent E., Retired, Freehold
Hughes, John P., St. John Neumann, Mount Laurel
Iadanza, John M., St. Mary of the Lakes, Medford
Imholte, Ralph, St. Mary, Colts Neck
Jennings, Edward F., St. Catharine, Spring Lake
Johnson, James G., St. Mary, Barnegat
Jones, Francis A., St. Paul, Burlington
Katzer, Alfred W., St. Veronica, Howell
Kelly, James A., Holy Trinity, Long Branch
Kennedy, Patrick W., St. Anthony of Padua, Hightstown
Kerr, Ronald J., Sr., Our Lady of Perpetual Help, Maple Shade
Klimaszewski, Norbert J., St. Mary of the Lakes, Medford
Klincewicz, John G., Our Lady, Star of the Sea, Long Branch
Knipp, Joseph P., Sacred Heart, Riverton
Kruk, Leonard B., Visitation, Brick
Lachance, Paul A., St. Paul, Princeton
LaManchia, Ralph A., St. Gregory the Great, Hamilton Square
Lambarski, Joseph A., Holy Eucharist, Vincentown
Little, Ronald J., St. Mary of the Lake, Medford
Littlefield, James J., St. Veronica, Howell
Lombardo, Earl H., St. Mary, Barnegat
Lydick, Donald E., St. Gabriel, Marlboro
MacCarrick, Donald G., St. Luke, Toms River
MacDonald, Lawrence, (Retired)
Machion, Robert D., Holy Assumption, Roebling
Magee, James D., St. Mary, Bordentown
Maier, Edward, (Retired)
Malhame, Eugene G., Jr., St. Rose, Belmar
Malloy, Joseph J., Our Lady of Sorrows, Trenton
Manaloris, James A., Holy Name, Delran
Marcello, Salvatore, Holy Angels, Trenton
Martin, Patrick J., St. Mary, Barnegat
Martucci, Anthony R., St. Mary of the Lake, Lakewood
Mattozzi, Guido J., St. Joachim, Trenton
McCabe, John, St. Mary, Deal
McComb, David M., St. Elizabeth Ann Seton, Whiting
McCormack, Joseph, Epiphany, Bricktown
McGann, Francis P., Jr., Our Lady of Good Counsel, Moorestown
McGrath, James, St. Catherine, Holmdel
McHugh, Joseph, Our Lady of Perpetual Help, Maple Shade
McKenna, Frank, St. Joseph, Toms River
McKenna, Kenneth M., St. Mary, Deal
McKeon, James, St. Gabriel, Marlboro
McNally, Brent G., St. Justin, Toms River
McNulty, James, (Retired), Ascension, Bradley Beach
Micali, James Mark, St. Thomas More, Manalapan
Miller, Donald C., St. Clement, Matawan
Moir, Gene F., St. Veronica, Howell
Mosteller, Herman, St. Joseph, Beverly
Mullarkey, Michael F., Epiphany, Brick
Murray, William, Precious Blood Church, Monmouth Beach
Mustillo, Anthony D., St. Catharine, Holmdel
Mylod, Philip J., (Retired)
Nimon, Robert, St. Leo the Great, Lincroft
Noone, Thomas, St. William the Abbot, Allenwood
Nowak, Ronald, Epiphany, Bricktown
O'Brien, Christopher D., St. Joseph, Keyport
O'Brien, John, Office of Diaconate, Trenton
O'Connor, John P., (Retired), St. Catharine, Spring Lake
O'Donnell, John J., Our Lady Queen of Peace, Hainesport
Olshevski, Stanley R., Corpus Christi, Willingboro
Orkis, Stanley, Holy Eucharist, Vincentown
Owens, Lester J., St. Gabriel's, Marlboro
Pacitti, Albert, Holy Trinity, Long Branch
Palsir, James W., St. James, Pennington
Pancamo, Anthony, Holy Name, Delran
Parr, Allan T., Sr., St. Gregory the Great, Trenton
Patton, Joseph R., St. Mary of the Lakes, Medford
Pelkowski, Raymond R., St. Benedict, Holmdel

Perkins, Charles A., St. Joseph, Beverly
Petrauskas, James J., St. Theresa's, Tuckerton
Pierfy, Jeffery, Our Lady of Sorrows, Mercerville
Pirozzi, Neil, St. Gregory the Great, Trenton
Price, Walter L., St. Ann, Browns Mills
Prihoda, Frank J., St. Anthony of Padua, Hightstown
Principato, Michael, St. Catherine, Farmingdale
Purcell, Kyron J., St. Elizabeth Ann Seton, Whiting
Putnam, Harry A., St. Mary, Bordentown
Rasi, Stephen P., St. Anthony, Hightstown
Restivo, Louis C., Sacred Heart, Mount Holly
Richardson, Gary T., St. Mary, Bordentown
Rider, Joseph H., St. Elizabeth Ann Seton, Whiting
Rivera, Juan A., St. Mary Cathedral, Trenton
Rodriguez, Felix L., Our Lady of Providence, Neptune
Ross, Michael D., St. Paul's, Princeton
Rowley, William R., Sacred Heart, Mt. Holly
Russo, James C., St. Gabriel, Marlboro
Saake, Dennis J., St. Mark, Sea Girt
Schwarz, Herbert, St. Benedict, Holmdel
Schwind, Albert, St. Francis of Assisi, Brant Beach
Sciarrotta, Samuel P., St. James Church, Pennington
Seaton, George L., St. Theresa, Tuckerton
Sepich, William S., St. Charles Borromeo, Cinnaminson
Shapiro, David L., St. Justin, Toms River
Shea, Raymond A., St. Maximillian Kolbe, Toms River
Sherpensky, Frank, St. Ann, Browns Mills
Slavin, Dennis E., Office of Family Life, West Long Branch
Slee, Louis, Blessed Sacrament, Trenton
Sowa, Frank J., (Retired)
Stap, Matthew J., (Retired), St. Joseph, Beverly
Staub, Raymond W., Jr., St. Raphael, Trenton
Talbot, Norman, St. Mary of the Lakes, Medford
Tarala, Anthony M., (Retired), St. John's, Lakehurst
Tarzy, Barry R., St. Joan of Arc, Marlton
Tharp, Robert, Holy Angels, Trenton
Tobin, James R., Sacred Heart, Bay Head
Toolan, James W., St. George, Titusville
Ulmer, Ronald J., St. Joseph, Beverly
Valentin, Juan E., St. Mary Cathedral, Trenton
Vassallo, John F., Corpus Christi, Willingboro
Vazquez, Emiliano, St. Mary Cathedral, Trenton
Vicari, Salvatore J., Jr., Visitation, Brick Town
Vlcej, Robert J., St. Ann's, Keansburg
Vogel, Anthony D., St. Hedwig, Trenton
Voll, Edwin L., Jr., St. Joseph, Toms River
Wallack, Gregory B., St. Justin, Toms River
Walsh, John J., St. Thomas More, Manalapan
Wanat, John A., St. Rose of Lima, Freehold
White, Thomas, C. Wagner Youth Correctional Facility, Bordentown
Wicks, Ronald, St. Luke, Toms River
Wilson, William A., St. Gregory the Great, Hamilton Square
Wolfe, Robert A., (Retired)
Yaccarine, John A., Holy Trinity, Long Branch
Young, Donald A., St. Mary, New Monmouth
Zebrowski, John J., St. Thomas More, Manalapan
Zimmerle, John O., Holy Eucharist, Vincentown

INSTITUTIONS LOCATED IN THE DIOCESE

[A] COLLEGES AND UNIVERSITIES

LAKEWOOD. *Georgian Court College*, 900 Lakewood Ave., 08701-2697. Tel: 908-364-2200; Fax: 908-367-3920.
For a complete listing, refer to the Colleges and Universities section.

[B] HIGH SCHOOLS, DIOCESAN

TRENTON. *McCorristin High School*, 175 Leonard Ave., 08610. Tel: 609-586-3705; Fax: 609-586-6584. Mr. Joseph Lemme, Prin. Priests 1; Sisters 3; Lay Teachers 37; Students 576.

Notre Dame High School, 601 Lawrence Rd., 08648. Tel: 609-882-7900; Fax: 609-882-5723. Mr. Barry Edward Breen, Prin.; Mrs. Mary Liz Ivins, Asst. Prin.; Mr. David M. Milinowicz, Asst. Prin.; Rev. Scott Shaffer, Chap. Sisters of Mercy 1; Lay Teachers 69; Students 1,069.

BELMAR. *Saint Rose High School*, 605 Seventh Ave., 07719. Tel: 908-681-2858; Fax: 908-280-2745. Bro. Malcolm O'Sullivan, Prin. Students 540; Sisters 1; Lay Teachers 37.

DELRAN. *Holy Cross High School*, 5035 Rte. 130 S., 08075. Tel: 609-461-5400; Fax: 609-764-0806. Sisters of I.H.M., Scranton, PA. Mr. Jerome T. McGowan, Prin.; Rev. Kenneth Ekdahl. Sisters 8; Lay Teachers 64; Students 1,210.

HOLMDEL. *St. John Vianney High School*, Line Rd., 07733. Tel: 908-739-0800; Fax: 908-739-0824. Mr. Joseph F. Deroba, Prin.; Rev. Daniel J. Ryan, Chap. Sisters 1; Lay Teachers 56; Students 886.

NEW MONMOUTH. *Mater Dei High School*, 538 Church St., 07748. Tel: 908-671-9100; Fax: 908-671-9214. Mr. Frank Poleski, Prin. Students 397; Lay Teachers 27.

RED BANK. *Red Bank Catholic High School*, 10 Peters Pl., 07701. Tel: 908-747-1774; Fax: 908-741-1936. Mr. Robert Abatemarco, Prin. Sisters 2; Lay Teachers 56; Students 774.

TOMS RIVER. *Monsignor Donovan High School*, 711 Hooper Ave., 08753. Tel: 908-349-8801; Fax: 908-286-7064. Mr. Edward Gere, Prin. Sisters 7; Lay Teachers 66; Students 914; Priests 1.

[C] HIGH SCHOOLS, PRIVATE

TRENTON. *Villa Victoria Academy*, 376 W. Upper Ferry Rd., 08628. Tel: 609-882-1700. Upper School, Grades 7-8 (Coed); Grades 9-12 (Girls). Sr. Mary Ann Gecina, M.P.F., Prin.; Sr. Lillian Harrington, M.P.F., Pres. Sisters 4; Lay Teachers 14; Students 115.

LINCROFT. *Christian Brothers Academy*, 07738. Tel: 908-747-1959; Fax: 908-747-1643. Bros. Andrew O'Gara, F.S.C.; Ralph Montedoro, F.S.C. Priests 1; Brothers 21; Lay Teachers 46; Students 900.

PRINCETON. *Stuart Country Day School of the Sacred Heart.* (Grades PreK-8), 1200 Stuart Rd., 08540. Tel: 609-921-2330; Fax: 609-497-0784. Sisters 2; Lay Teachers 44; Students 350.

[D] ELEMENTARY SCHOOLS, DIOCESAN

TRENTON. *Cathedral Diocesan Elementary School*, 31 Chancery Ln., 08618. Tel: 609-394-5936; Fax: 609-394-7287. Ms. Mary Helen Ward, Prin. Sisters 2; Lay Teachers 11; Students 150.

[E] ELEMENTARY SCHOOLS, PRIVATE

TRENTON. *Villa Victoria Academy.* (Grades PreK-6). (Coed), 376 W. Upper Ferry Rd., 08628. Tel: 609-883-5760; Fax: 609-882-8421. Lower School. Sr. Joan DiRienzo, M.P.F., Prin. Sisters 3; Lay Teachers 6; Students 130.

PRINCETON. *Stuart County Day School of the Sacred Heart.* (Grades 9-12), 1200 Stuart Rd., 08540. Tel: 609-921-2330; Fax: 609-497-0784. Sisters 1; Lay Teachers 26; Students 105.

[F] CATHOLIC CHARITIES, DIOCESE OF TRENTON

TRENTON. *Catholic Charities*, 47 N. Clinton Ave., P.O. Box 1423, 08607. Tel: 609-394-5181; Fax: 609-695-6978. Mr. Francis E. Dolan, Exec. Dir.; George Bontcue, Assoc. Exec. Dir., Fiscal Affairs; Barry H. Cole, Ph.D., Assoc. Exec. Dir., Prog. Services; Michael R. Allen, Assoc. Exec. Dir., Community Affairs.

Burlington Behavioral Healthcare Division, 114 Delaware Ave., Burlington, 08016. Tel: 609-386-1746. Frank J. Helverson, Dir.

Mercer Behavioral Healthcare Division, 39 N. Clinton Ave., 08609. Tel: 609-394-9398. Jerome Lindauer, Dir.

Monmouth/Ocean Behavioral Healthcare Division, 36 W. Water St., Toms River, 08753. Tel: 908-505-3113. Roman Z. Mykyta, Dir.

Emergency Services Division, P.O. Box 2387, Cinnaminson, 08077. Tel: 609-786-1868. Nancy A. Milne, Dir.

Family Growth Division, 39 N. Clinton Ave., 08609. Tel: 609-394-5157. Services for victims and perpetuators of family violence. Ronald C. Gering, Dir.

Providence House Division, P.O. Box 496, Willingboro, 08046. Services to women and children in danger of physical abuse. Jean Metz, Dir.

Our Lady of Light Chapel, 47 N. Clinton Ave., Box 1423, 08607-1423. Tel: 609-386-6221; Fax: 609-394-5181.

St. Michael Children's Home, c/o Diocese of Trenton, 701 Lawrenceville Rd., 08648.

[G] DAY CARE CENTERS

LONG BRANCH. *St. John the Baptist Family Center*, 272 Willow Ave., 07740. Tel: 908-229-8905; 229-8527; 571-1003; Fax: 908-571-0280. Day Care and Child Development Center. Children 210.

[H] CARE INSTITUTIONS FOR CHILDREN

TRENTON. *Sister Georgine School*, 544 Chestnut Ave., 08611. Tel: 609-396-5444.
For a complete listing, refer to the Special Care Facilities section.

HOPEWELL. *St. Michael's Orphanage and Industrial School.* Mailing Address: c/o the Diocese of Trenton, 701 Lawrenceville Rd. Trenton, 08648.
For a complete listing, refer to the Special Care Facilities section.

[I] GENERAL HOSPITALS

TRENTON. *St. Francis Medical Center*, 601 Hamilton Ave., 08629. Tel: 609-599-5000.
For a complete listing, refer to the Hospitals section.

[J] SPECIAL HOSPITALS AND SANATORIA FOR INVALIDS

LAWRENCEVILLE. *Morris Hall/Saint Lawrence, Inc.*, 2381 Lawrenceville Rd., 08648. Tel: 609-896-9500.
For a complete listing, refer to the Special Care Facilities section.

Morris Hall/Saint Lawrence, Inc., 1 Bishop's Dr., 08648-0498. Tel: 609-896-0006.
For a complete listing, refer to the Special Care Facilities section.

[K] SPECIALIZED CHILD CARE AGENCIES

RED BANK. *Collier Group Home*, 180 Spring St., 07701. Tel: 908-842-8337.
For a complete listing, refer to the Special Care Facilities section.

WICKATUNK. *Collier Services*, Conover Rd., 07765. Tel: 908-946-4771.
For a complete listing, refer to the Special Care Facilities section.

[L] HOMES FOR AGED

TRENTON. *Cathedral Square Housing, Inc.*, 26 W. Hanover Pl., 08608. Tel: 609-392-1111.
For a complete listing, refer to the Special Care Facilities section.

LAWRENCEVILLE. *Morris Hall-Saint Lawrence, Inc.*, 1 Bishop's Dr., P.O. Box 6498, 08648-0498. Tel: 609-896-0006.
For a complete listing, refer to the Special Care Facilities section.

[M] MONASTERIES AND RESIDENCES FOR PRIESTS AND BROTHERS

TRENTON. *Villa Neumann* Lawrenceville, 2301 Lawrenceville Rd., P.O. Box 6589, 08648. Tel: 609-219-0177. In res., Rev. Msgr. Thomas A. Coffey; Rev. Msgr. Joseph A. O'Connor; Rev. Msgr. Thaddeus J. Wojciehowski; Revs. Eugene V. Davis; Edward Dougherty; John E. Sullivan.

BORDENTOWN. *Society of the Divine Word*, 101 Park St., 08505. Tel: 609-298-0549; Fax: 609-298-6014. Very Rev. Martin Padovani, S.V.D., Rector; Revs. Patrick Connor, S.V.D.; Francis Mahon, S.V.D.; Norman St. John, S.V.D.; Patrick Wenrick, S.V.D.; Joseph Fleishaker, S.V.D.; Victor Butler, S.V.D.; Jacques Nyssen, S.V.D.; Joseph Gunning, S.V.D.; Norbert Schuler, S.V.D.; Stephen Szmutko, S.V.D.; James Artzer, S.V.D.; Jerome Brzakowski, S.V.D.; Charles Erb, S.V.D.; William Kelly, S.V.D.; Peter Silvester, S.V.D.; Vance Thorne, S.V.D.; Aloysius Turbek, S.V.D.; Andrew Hadalski, S.V.D.; Paul McVinney, S.V.D.; Bros. Louis Gagnon, S.V.D.; Patrick Hegarty, S.V.D.; Thomas Granfield, S.V.D.; James Mullen, S.V.D.; Joseph Hornek, S.V.D.

LINCROFT. *Christian Brothers, St. La Salle Auxiliary*, 850 Newman Springs Rd., P.O. Box 238, 07738. Tel: 908-842-4359.

LaSalle Lincroft, Inc., 850 Newman Springs Rd., 07738. Tel: 908-842-7420. Bro. Michael Corry, F.S.C., Contact Person. Brothers 3.

De La Salle Hall, Inc., 810 Newman Springs Rd., 07738. Tel: 908-530-9470. Bro. Joseph Loewenstein, F.S.C., Dir. Brothers Retirement Home. Brothers 5; Lay Staff 35; Patients 25.

La Salle Provincialate, 800 Newman Springs Rd., 07738. Tel: 908-842-7420. Brothers of the Christian Schools. Bro. Michael Corry, F.S.C., Prov.

MOUNT LAUREL. *Cistercian Monastery of Our Lady of Fatima*, 564 Walton Ave., 08054-9582. Tel: 609-235-1330. Cistercian Fathers. Revs. Lino Parente, O.Cist., Prior, (Italy); Anselmo M. Florio, O.Cist.; Maurizio Nicoletti, O.Cist., (Italy).

[N] CONVENTS AND RESIDENCES FOR SISTERS

TRENTON. *Notre Dame Diocesan Convent* Lawrenceville. Intercongregational Living, 681 Lawrence Rd., 08648. Tel: 609-882-5982. Office for Religious. Tel: 609-559-3545; 800-552-5354. Sisters 10.

Sisters of St. Francis of Philadelphia, St. Clare Convent, 917 Melrose Ave., 08629. Tel: 609-695-7805. Sr. Doretta Egan.

Sisters of the Humility of Mary, 489 W. State St., Apt. 703, 08618.

BORDENTOWN. *Franciscan Monastery of Saint Clare*, 201 Crosswicks St., 08505. Tel: 609-298-0016. Sr. Mary McCourt, O.S.C., Abbess.

HAMILTON SQUARE. *Sisters of St. Francis of Philadelphia*, Franciscan Convent, 24 Shelley Ln., 08690. Tel: 609-588-9076. Sr. Mary Rita Barbernitz.

HARVEY CEDARS. *Maris Stella Retreat House.* (Summer Home), 7201 Long Beach Blvd., 08008. Tel: 609-494-0499. Sisters of Charity of St. Elizabeth, Convent Station. Sr. Audrey Boettcher, Admin.

HAZLET. *St. Benedict's Convent*, 31 Cresci Blvd., 07730. Tel: 908-264-3553.

PRINCETON. *Our Lady of Princeton*, Great and Drakes

Corner Rds., 08540. Tel: 609-924-1236. Congregation of Marianites of Holy Cross. Sr. Vincent Dornbush, Admin.; Rev. James T. Burtchaell, C.S.C., Chap. Sisters 15.

WICKATUNK. *Convent of the Sisters of Good Shepherd*, 160 Conover Rd., 07765. Tel: 908-946-7877; 946-7886. Sisters of Good Shepherd of New Jersey. Virginia Daniels, Coord. Sisters 9.

[O] CHAPELS

TRENTON. *Our Lady of Light Chapel*, 47 N. Clinton Ave., Box 1423, 08607-1423. Tel: 609-386-6221; 394-5181.

LAWRENCEVILLE. *Our Lady of the Rosary Chapel*, 1 Bishop's Dr., Box 6498, 08648. Tel: 609-896-0006. Located in Morris Hall. Rev. Justin J. Herbst, Chap.

[P] HOUSES OF PRAYER

TRENTON. *Morning Star House of Prayer*, 312 W. Upper Ferry Rd., 08628. Tel: 609-882-2766. Sr. Geraldine Calabrese, M.P.F. Religious Teachers Filippini 2.

MOUNT HOLLY. *Francis House of Prayer*, 39 Springside Rd., 08060. Mailing Address: P.O. Box 392, Rancocas, 08073. Tel: 609-877-0509; Fax: 609-877-5810. Sr. Marcella Springer, S.S.J.

NEPTUNE. *The Upper Room Spiritual Center*, P.O. Box 1104, 07754-1104. Tel: 908-922-0550; Fax: 908-922-3904. Sr. Maureen Christensen, Co-Dir.

[Q] RETREAT HOUSES

ELBERON. *Stella Maris Retreat House*, 981 Ocean Ave., 07740. Tel: 908-229-0602. Sr. Kathleen Connell, C.S.J.P., Dir. Sisters of St. Joseph of Peace 3.

HARVEY CEDARS. *Maris Stella*, Sisters Retreat and Vacation Center, 7201 Long Beach Blvd., 08008. Tel: 609-494-0499. Sisters of Charity of St. Elizabeth. Sr. Audrey Boettcher, Admin.

LONG BRANCH. *San Alfonso Retreat House*, 755 Ocean Ave., P.O. Box 3098, 07740. Tel: 908-222-2731. Revs. John F. Murray, C.SS.R., Rector Dir.; Andrew Skeabeck, C.SS.R.; John Ruef, C.SS.R.; William Collins, C.SS.R.; Dennis Foley, C.SS.R.; John McGowan, C.SS.R.; Bro. Bernard Colleran, C.SS.R.; Sr. Susan Dentz, O.S.F. Priests 6; Brothers 1; Sisters 1.

SOUTH MANTOLOKING. *St. Joseph by the Sea Retreat House*, 400 Rte. 35 N., 08738. Tel: 908-892-8494. Sr. Donna Gaglioti, M.P.F., Dir. Sisters 4.

[R] NEWMAN CENTERS

PRINCETON. *Campus Ministry for the Diocese of Trenton*, Aquinas Institute, Princeton University, 65 Stockton St., 08540. Tel: 609-924-1820. Rev. Thomas J. Mullelly, Dir. & Chap.

Emmaus House, Rider College, 2116 Lawrenceville Rd., Trenton, 08648. Tel: 609-896-0394. Rev. Benedict Michael Worry, O.S.B., Chap.

Mercer County Community College, 1200 Old Trenton Rd., Hamilton Township, 08690. Tel: 609-896-0394. Rev. Benedict Michael Worry, O.S.B., Chap.

Bede House, Trenton State College, 492 Ewingville Rd., Trenton, 08638. Tel: 609-771-9091. Rev. James Dever, O.F.S.F., Chap.

Georgian Court College, Lakewood Ave., Lakewood, 08701. Tel: 908-364-2200. Rev. Dennis Bajkowski, Campus Min.

Ocean County Community College. (Toms River). Rev. Louis W. Kralovich, Chap.

St. Luke Rectory, 1674 Old Freehold Rd., Toms River, 08753. Tel: 908-229-0403.

Monmouth University, Bethlehem House, 16 Beachwood Ave., West Long Branch, 07764. Tel: 908-229-0403. Rev. F. W. Jackiewicz, Chap.

[S] MISCELLANEOUS LISTINGS

TRENTON. *Martin House*, 802 E. State St., P.O. Box 1025, 08606. Tel: 609-989-1040. Revs. Brian McCormick; William J. McLaughlin; Sr. Marian Spearman, O.S.P.

ASBURY PARK. *Mercy Center, Inc.*, 1106 Main St., 07712. Tel: 908-774-9397. Carol Ann Henry, R.S.M., Dir.

BRICK. *Mid-Life Directions*, 4 Palm Ave., 08723. Tel: 908-255-1239. Sr. Anne Brennan, C.S.J., Contact Person. Purpose: Ministry for personal and spiritual growth specifically for people in midlife and later years.

ELBERON. *Emmaus House*, 80 Norwood Ave., 07740. Tel: 908-229-5834. Sr. Patricia Mary Walsh, O.P., Admin.

LAKEWOOD. *Health and Retirement Planning: Intercommunity Project*, 900 Lakewood Dr., 08701-2697. Tel: 908-364-2200, Ext. 212. Sr. Edwarda Barry, R.S.M., Project Coord. Purpose: to assist regional participating religious orders in meeting the health care and retirement needs of their members.

LAWRENCEVILLE. *Morris Hall/St. Lawrence, Inc.*, 2381 Lawrenceville Rd., 08648. Tel: 609-896-9500. Mr. Charles Brennan, Admin.; Rev. Justin J. Herbst, Chap.; Sr. Claire DeStefano, S.S.J., Dir. of Pastoral Care. Bed Capacity 116; Bed Licensure 116.

SWAINTON. *Holy Redeemer Visiting Nurse Agency, Inc.*, 1801 Rte. 9 N., 08210. Tel: 609-465-2082; 800-745-4693. Jerold S. Cohen, R.N., Pres. A subsidiary of Holy Redeemer Health System, Inc. Sponsor: Sisters of the Holy Redeemer, C.S.R. A Medicare Certified Home Health Agency serving patients in their own homes. A Medicare Certified Hospice Program providing services for terminally ill patients and their families. Outpatient Rehabiliation.

Atlantic County Office, 701 Rte. 50, Mays Landing, 08330. Tel: 609-625-2200; 800-788-3029. Jennifer Savon, R.N., Health Care Admin.

Ocean County Office, 2214 Rte. 37 E., Toms River, 08753. Tel: 908-288-0868; 800-488-2669.

Holy Redeemer Rehabilitation Center, 1261 Rte. 9 S., Ste. 1, Cape May Court House, 08210. Tel: 609-465-3866. Carol Frankenfield, PT, Chief Therapist.

RELIGIOUS INSTITUTES OF MEN REPRESENTED IN THE DIOCESE

For further details refer to the corresponding bracketed number in the Religious Institutes of Men or Women section.

[0200]—*Benedictine Monks*. (St. Mary's Abbey, Morristown, NJ).—O.S.B.
[0700]—*Saint Joseph's Society of the Sacred Heart*.—S.S.J.
[0030]—*Brothers of the Christian Schools*.—F.S.C.
[0270]—*Carmelite Fathers and Brothers*. (Prov. of the Most Pure Heart of Mary).—O.Carm.
[0340]—*Cistercian Fathers*.—O.Cist.
[0820]—*Congregation of the Fathers of Mercy*.—C.P.M.
[0390]—*Consolata Missionaries*.—I.M.C.
[0480]—*Conventual Franciscans*. (Provs. of the Immaculate Conception & St. Anthony of Padua).—O.F.M.Conv.
[0520]—*Franciscan Friars*. (Prov. of the Most Holy Name of Jesus).—O.F.M.
[0920]—*Oblates of Saint Francis de Sales*. (Wilmington-Philadelphia Prov.).—O.S.F.S.
[0430]—*Order of Preachers (Dominicans)*. (Prov. of St. Joseph).—O.P.
[1310]—*Order of the Holy Trinity*.—O.SS.T.
[1070]—*Redemptorist Fathers*. (Baltimore Prov.).—C.SS.R.
[0700]—*Saint Joseph's Society of the Sacred Heart (The Josephites)*.—S.S.J.
[0420]—*Society of the Divine Word*.—S.V.D.
[0560]—*Third Order Regular of Saint Francis*. (Prov. of the Most Sacred Heart of Jesus).—T.O.R.

RELIGIOUS INSTITUTES OF WOMEN REPRESENTED IN THE DIOCESE

[0233]—*Benedictine Sisters of Elizabeth, NJ*.—O.S.B.
[1810]—*Bernardine Sisters of Third Order of St. Francis*.—O.S.F.
[2410]—*Congregation of the Marianites of Holy Cross*.—M.S.C.
[1830]—*Contemplative Sisters of the Good Shepherd*.—R.G.S.
[1070-05]—*Dominican Sisters*. (Amityville, NY).—O.P.
[1070-15]—*Dominican Sisters*. (Blauvelt, NY).—O.P.
[1070-18]—*Dominican Sisters*. (Caldwell, NJ).—O.P.
[1070-06]—*Dominican Sisters*. (Newburgh, NY).—O.P.
[1070-11]—*Dominican Sisters*. (Sparkhill, NY).—O.P.
[1070-05]—*Dominican Sisters of Hope*. (Amityville, NY).—O.P.
[1170]—*Felician Sisters*.—C.S.S.F.
[1365]—*Franciscan Missionary Sisters of the Infant Jesus*.—F.M.I.J.
[1180]—*Franciscan Sisters of Allegany, NY*.—O.S.F.
[1425]—*Franciscan Sisters of Peace*.—F.S.P.
[1470]—*Franciscan Sisters of St. Joseph*.—F.S.S.J.
[]—*Franciscans Da Acao Pastoral of Sao Paolo, Brazil*.—F.A.P.
[1840]—*Grey Nuns of the Sacred Heart*.—G.N.S.H.
[2490]—*Medical Mission Sisters*.—S.C.M.M.
[2700]—*Missionary Catechists of the Sacred Hearts of Jesus & Mary*.—SS.CC.J.M.
[3040]—*Oblate Sisters of Providence*.—O.S.P.
[3760]—*Order of St. Clare*.—O.S.C.
[3465]—*Religious of the Sacred Heart of Mary*.—R.S.H.M.
[3430]—*Religious Teachers Filippini*.—M.P.F.
[]—*Sisters for Christian Community*.—S.F.C.C.
[0590]—*Sisters of Charity of Saint Elizabeth, Convent Station*.—S.C.
[0430]—*Sisters of Charity of the Blessed Virgin Mary*-(Dubuque, IA).—B.V.M.
[2575]—*Sisters of Mercy of the Americas*. (Dallas; Merion; New Jersey).—R.S.M.
[3000]—*Sisters of Notre Dame de Namur*. (Cincinnati).—S.N.D.deN.
[3730]—*Sisters of Order of St. Basil the Great*.—O.S.B.M.
[3360]—*Sisters of Providence of Saint Mary of the Woods, IN*.—S.P.
[3830]—*Sisters of Saint Joseph of Brentwood*. (New York).—C.S.J.
[]—*The Sisters of St. Francis of Baltimore*.
[1630]—*Sisters of St. Francis of Penance and Christian Charity*.—O.S.F.
[1650]—*The Sisters of St. Francis of Philadelphia*.—O.S.F.
[3840]—*Sisters of St. Joseph of Carondelet*.—C.S.J.
[3850]—*Sisters of St. Joseph of Chambery*.—C.S.J.
[3893]—*Sisters of St. Joseph of Chestnut Hill, Philadelphia*.—S.S.J.
[3890]—*Sisters of St. Joseph of Peace*.—C.S.J.P.
[1830]—*The Sisters of the Good Shepherd*.—R.G.S.
[2110]—*Sisters of the Humility of Mary*.—H.M.
[3480]—*Sisters of the Resurrection*.—C.R.
[1490]—*Sisters of the Third Franciscan Order*. (Syracuse).—O.S.F.
[2170]—*Sisters, Servants of the Immaculate Heart of Mary*. (Philadelphia).—I.H.M.
[2160]—*Sisters, Servants of the Immaculate Heart of Mary*. (Scranton).—I.H.M.
[4060]—*Society of the Holy Child Jesus*.—S.H.C.J.
[4070]—*Society of the Sacred Heart*.—R.S.C.J.

NECROLOGY

† Bulla, Charles A., (Retired). —Died Jan. 10, 1996.
† Kim, Joseph, Eatontown, NJ, Immaculate Conception. —Died Aug. 29, 1996.
† Kreger, Rev. Msgr. Edmund W., Normandy Beach, NJ, Our Lady of Peace. —Died Aug. 28, 1996.
† MacDonald, John H., (On Duty Outside the Diocese). —Died July 29, 1996.
† O'Toole, Eugene J., Bordentown, NJ, Bordentown Correction Center. —Died March 5, 1996.
† Opdenaker, Rev. Msgr. Theodore A., (Retired). —Died May 7, 1996.
† Remias, Joseph L., North Plainfield, NJ, St. Luke's. —Died Aug. 7, 1996.

Diocese of Tucson

(Dioecesis Tucsonensis)

Most Reverend

MANUEL D. MORENO, D.D.

Bishop of Tucson; ordained April 25, 1961; appointed Titular Bishop of Tanagra and Auxiliary of Los Angeles December 20, 1976; consecrated February 19, 1977; appointed Bishop of Tucson January 12, 1982. *Res., 192 S. Stone Ave., Box 31, Tucson, AZ, 85702.*

ESTABLISHED A VICARIATE-APOSTOLIC 1868.

ERECTED BY HIS HOLINESS POPE LEO XIII, MAY 8, 1897.

Square Miles 42,707.

Comprises the Counties of Cochise, Gila, Greenlee, Graham, La Paz, Pima, Pinal, Santa Cruz and Yuma in the State of Arizona.

For legal titles of parishes and diocesan institutions, consult the Chancery Office.

Chancery Office: 192 S. Stone Ave., Box 31, Tucson, AZ, 85702. Tel.: 520-792-3410.

Web site address: http://www.azstarnet.com/~rccdot

E-mail address: rccchan@azstarnet.com

E-mail address: rccdot@azstarnet.com

STATISTICAL OVERVIEW

Personnel	
Bishop	1
Priests: Diocesan Active in Diocese	76
Priests: Active Outside Diocese	6
Priests: Retired, Sick or Absent	29
Number of Diocesan Priests	111
Religious Priests in Diocese	76
Extern Priests in Diocese	33
Ordinations:	
Diocesan Priests	2
Transitional Deacons	1
Permanent Deacons	49
Permanent Deacons in Diocese	123
Total Brothers	8
Total Sisters	289
Parishes	
Parishes	64
With Resident Pastor:	
Resident Diocesan Priests	50
Resident Religious Priests	14
Without Resident Pastor:	
Missions	31
Pastoral Centers	15
Professional Ministry Personnel:	
Brothers	8
Sisters	268
Welfare	
Catholic Hospitals	3
Total Assisted	281,129
Health Care Centers	1
Total Assisted	23,000
Special Centers for Social Services	1
Total Assisted	385,000
Other Institutions	1
Total Assisted	2,369
Educational	
Diocesan Students in Other Seminaries	12
Total Seminarians	12
High Schools, Diocesan and Parish	1
Total Students	1,212
High Schools, Private	2
Total Students	371
Elementary Schools, Diocesan and Parish	18
Total Students	4,680
Elementary Schools, Private	2
Total Students	352
Catechesis/Religious Education:	
High School Students	3,212
Elementary Students	15,141
Total Students Under Catholic Instruction	24,980
Teachers in the Diocese:	
Priests	7
Brothers	2
Sisters	44
Lay Teachers	272
Vital Statistics	
Receptions into the Church:	
Infant Baptism Totals	7,203
Adult Baptism Totals	376
Received into Full Communion	721
First Communions	4,326
Confirmations	2,802
Marriages:	
Catholic	1,064
Interfaith	228
Total Marriages	1,292
Deaths	2,259
Total Catholic Population	291,230
Total Population	1,106,076

Former Bishops—Most Rev. JOHN BAPTIST SALPOINTE, D.D., ord. December 21, 1851; appt. Vicar Apostolic of Arizona and Titular Bishop of Doryla Sept. 25, 1868 and; ord. June 20, 1869; appt. Coadjutor Archbishop of Santa Fe with right of succession April 12, 1884 and Titular Archbishop of Anazarba Oct. 3, 1884; succeeded to the See of Santa Fe July 18, 1885; resigned and; appt. titular Archbishop of Tomi Jan. 27, 1894; died, Tucson, July 15, 1898.—Most Rev. PETER BOURGADE, D.D., ord. Nov. 30, 1869; appt. Vicar Apostolic of Arizona Jan. 23, 1885 and Titular Bishop of Thaumacum Feb. 7, 1885 and; ord. May 1, 1885; appt. first Bishop of Tucson May 10, 1897; appt. fourth Archbishop of Santa Fe Jan. 7, 1899; died Chicago, May 17, 1908.—Most Rev. HENRY REGIS GRANJON, D.D., ord. Dec. 17, 1887; appt. second Bishop of Tucson April 19, 1900, and; ord. June 17, 1900; died Brignais, France, Nov. 9, 1922.—Most Rev. DANIEL JAMES GERCKE, D.D., ord. June 1, 1901; appt. third Bishop of Tucson June 21, 1923; ord. Nov. 6, 1923; resigned and; appt. Titular Archbishop of Cotyaeum Oct. 26, 1960; died Tucson, March 19, 1964.—Most Rev. FRANCIS JOSEPH GREEN, D.D., ord. May 15, 1932; appt. Titular Bishop of Serra in Proconsulari and Auxiliary Bishop of Tucson May 29, 1953; cons. Sept. 17, 1953; appt. Coadjutor *"cum jure successionis"* May 11, 1960; succeeded to See to become fourth Bishop of Tucson Oct. 26, 1960; retired July 28, 1981; died May 11, 1995.

Vicar General—Rev. Msgr. ARSENIO S. CARRILLO, V.G.

Chancery Office—192 S. Stone Ave., P.O. Box 31, Tucson, 85702. Tel 520-792-3410.

Secretary and Chancellor—Rev. JOHN P. LYONS, J.D., J.C.L., Office: *192 S. Stone Ave., Tucson, 85701.* Tel: 520-792-3410., *Res., 8840 E. 22nd St., Tucson;* Rev. ALBERT E. VERBRUGGHE, Vice Chancellor.

Fiscal Manager Office—DEBBIE BAHRYCHUK, Mgr. CHARLES ASHLEY, Asst. Mgr.; Mr. CHARLES FOLEY, Parish Financial Svcs. Mgr., *P.O. Box 31, Tucson, 85702.* Tel: 520-792-3410.

Matrimonial Tribunal—Office: *192 S. Stone Ave., P.O. Box 31, Tucson, 85702.* Tel: 520-792-3410.

Judicial Vicar—Rev. ALBERT E. VERBRUGGHE, M.A., M.B.A., S.D.T., LL.D., J.C.D., Advocate of the Roman Rota.

Promoter of Justice—Rev. BRYAN SHERRY, J.C.L.

Judges—Rev Msgr. THOMAS CAHALANE; Revs. JOHN BRENT BARDON; RONALD GAGNON; JOSEPH KRAUSE; JOHN P. LYONS, J.C.L.; TODD O'LEARY.

Defenders of the Bond—Revs. MICHAEL BUCCIARELLI; ROBERT FOSTER; CHARLES KNAPP; MICHAEL STALLINGS.

Advocates and Auditors—Revs. JOSEPH BAKER; CHARLES CLOUD; JAMES HOBERT; CHARLES ASHLEY; Mrs. JEANNE PAIGE MESSERS; JOHN J. BRADY; RICHARD COSGROVE; THOMAS CURTI; FRED DARDIS; PETER GIANAS; LUIS KAME; VINCENT LACSAMANA; JOHN E. LINDBERG; LAWRENCE MCGRATH; THOMAS MCHUGH; JAMES MCNULTY, SR.; MICHAEL J. MURRAY; JOHN M. QUIGLEY; GERALD SWEENEY.

Auditors, Notaries, Secretaries—CLARA MORENO; HELEN EVANS.

Professional Consultant—STEPHEN J. SCHILTZ, M.S.W.

Finance Council—Most Rev. MANUEL D. MORENO, D.D., Chm. Bd. DEBBIE BAHRYCHUK, Chief Financial Officer; MATT ELLIS, Cash & Investment; Rev. JOHN P. LYONS, Chancellor; ROBERT E. HESLINGA, Dir. Devel. Members: JOHN T. GIRVIN; GARY GIESLER; HENRY AMADO; Mr. LAWRENCE MCDONOUGH; JOAN DONNELLY; Rev. FLOYD G. STROMBERG; Rev. Msgr. THOMAS P. CAHALANE; MARK MISTLER; HUMBERTO LOPEZ.

Investment Sub-Committee—HUMBERTO LOPEZ, Chm. DEBBIE BAHRYCHUK; CHARLES FOLEY; MATTHEW ELLIS; JOHN HALFEN; JOSEPH LADENBURG.

Audit Committee—JOHN GIRVIN, Chm. HENRY AMADO; Rev. Msgr. THOMAS P. CAHALANE; DEBBIE BAHRYCHUK; Rev. JOHN P. LYONS, J.D., J.C.L.

Catholic Foundation for the Diocese of Tucson—Most Rev. MANUEL D. MORENO, D.D., Chm. PHILIP J. SILVERS, Ph.D., Pres. JOHN M. NEIS, ESQ., Vice Pres. RANDY R. CASTELLINI, Treas.; Sr. BARBARA ANN STOWASSER, Sec. Members: Rev. GREGORY P. ADOLF; KATHLEEN B. COREY, ESQ.; FRED EMICH; DON EWING, M.D.; ANN B. FALLON; DENIS FITZGIBBONS, ESQ.; HUGH HEGARTY; MAURICE V. LATTARI; Mrs. CZARINA LOPEZ; Rev. THOMAS J. MILLANE; JAMES PFENNING; SONNY RODRIGUEZ; B. J. SULLIVAN, M.D.; JAMES M. SUSA. Honorary Members: Mrs. ORA DECONCINI-MARTIN; REG T. MORRISON; JAMES M. MURPHY, ESQ.; JAMES E. NEIHART; ALLAN NORVILLE; ELIZABETH ANN PARKMAN; ROBERT E.

HESLINGA, Exec. Dir.; Mrs. TERRY CARTER, Assoc. Dir. Past Members: CHARLES A. ALBANESE, A.I.A.; BRUCE D. BEACH; LARRY A. BROWN; JOSEPH R. CESARE; ARTHUR A. CHAPA, ESQ.; BERNARDT WM. COLLINS, C.P.A.; JOHN H. DAVIS; GARY L. GIESLER; MICHAEL J. HARRIS; BURTON J. KINERK, ESQ.; HUMBERTO S. LOPEZ; THOMAS M. MURPHY, ESQ.; MICHAEL J. NAIFEH, M.A.I.; FRANK J. NAUGHTON, SR.; JOSEPH E. NEVIN; Rev. Msgr. RICHARD O'KEEFFE; JAMES F. RONSTADT; Mrs. ANTOINETTE SANDERS; M. JAMES SOUTHARD.

Catholic Relief Services—JACK COTTER, Diocesan Dir., *155 W. Helen, Tucson, 85705.* Tel: 520-623-0344.

Diocesan Consultors—Rev. Msgr. ARSENIO S. CARRILLO, V.G.; Rev. Msgr. RICHARD O'KEEFFE; Rev. Msgr. THOMAS CAHALANE; Revs. KEVIN CLINCH; STEVEN G. STENCIL; JOHN P. LYONS, J.D., J.C.L.

Council of Priests—Most Rev. MANUEL D. MORENO, D.D.; Rev. Msgr. ARSENIO S. CARRILLO, V.G.; Rev. Msgr. ROBERT D. FULLER; Rev. Msgr. RICHARD W. O'KEEFFE; Revs. RAYMOND RATZENBERGER; CHARLES MALONEY; ROBERT G. TAMMINGA; RAUL TREVIZO; DOMENICO C. PINTI; JOHN BRENT BARDON; DANIEL P. MCLAUGHLIN, S.T.; MICHAEL R. BUCCIARELLI; MARCOS VELASQUEZ; PATRICK M. CRINO; EDWARD RYLE; JOHN P. LYONS, Chancellor; ALBERT E. VERBRUGGHE, Judicial Vicar & Vice Chancellor.

Vicar for Native Americans—Rev. DANIEL P. MCLAUGHLIN, S.T., *101 W. 31st St., Tuscon, 85713.* Tel: 520-791-7774.

Clergy Health—Rev. EDWARD C. CARSCALLEN.

Ministry to Priests Program—Rev. EDWARD C. CARSCALLEN, Spiritual Dir., *221 C. Paseo Tierra, Green Valley, 85614.* Tel: 520-625-4330. Members: Revs. PAUL H. ROSALES; JAMES M. HOBERT; FLOYD STROMBERG; PAUL LAROCQUE; JEFFREY THUERAUF.

Vicar for Religious—Rev. CYPRIAN KILLACKEY, O.C.D., *St. Margaret Parish, 801 N. Grande Ave., P.O. Box 2830, Tucson, 85745.* Tel: 520-622-0168.

Vicar for Priests—Rev. JAMES M. HOBERT, *St. Bernard, P.O. Box 3101, Pirtleville, 85626.* Tel: 520-364-2762.

Vicars Forane—Cochise Vicariate: Rev. RAYMOND RATZENBERGER, Gila-Pinal East Vicariate: Rev. MICHAEL R. BUCCIARELLI, Graham-Greenlee Vicariate: Rev. DOMENICO C. PINTI, Pima-Central Vicariate: Rev. Msgr. ROBERT D. FULLER, Pima-East Vicariate: Rev. ROBERT G. TAMMINGA, Pima-South Vicariate: Rev. RAUL TREVIZO, Pima-North Vicariate: Rev. JOHN BRENT BARDON, Pima West Vicariate: Rev. DANIEL P. MCLAUGHLIN, S.T., Pinal-West Vicariate: Rev. CHARLES MALONEY, Santa Cruz Vicariate: Rev. MARCOS VELASQUEZ, Yuma-La Paz Vicariate: Rev. Msgr. RICHARD W. O'KEEFFE.

Diocesan Offices and Directors

Archives—DAN BROSNAN, Archivist, *8800 E. 22nd St., Tucson, 85710.* Tel: 520-886-5202, Ext. 42.

Board of Education—Ex-Officio Members: Most Rev. MANUEL D. MORENO, D.D.; Sr. RUTHMARY POWERS, H.M., Supt. REGINA SASSEEN, Dir., Parish Life & Ministry; TERESA WELBORN, Pres. CYNTHIA RODRIQUEZ, Vice Pres. MOLLY HANSEN, Sec.

Building and Real Estate Committee—Most Rev. MANUEL D. MORENO, D.D., Honorary Chm. JAMES RONSTADT, Chm. BRIAN MCCARTHY, Vice Chm. DEBBIE BAHRYCHUK, Fiscal; LIZ AGUALLO, Sec. LARRY MCGRATH, Property Mgr.; Rev. TODD O'LEARY; ANDREW B. MARUM; HECTOR MARTINEZ; BOB SUAREZ; CAROL E. SCHRADER; DANIEL ROEBACH; Rev. ROBERT THOMAS.

Cash and Investments—MATT F. ELLIS, Mgr., *P.O. Box 31, Tucson, 85702.*

Cemeteries—Tucson: REGIS FLAHERTY, Dir., *Holy Hope Cemetery, 3555 N. Oracle Rd., P.O. Box 5158, Tucson, 85703.* Tel: 520-888-0860.

Our Lady of the Desert Cemetery—2151 S. Avenida Los Reyes, Tucson, 85703. Tel: 520-885-9173.

Desert Vista Cemetery—2151 S. Avenida Los Reyes, Tucson, 85748. Tel: 520-885-9173.

Censor Librorum—Vacant.

Campaign For Human Development—JOANNE WELTER, Dir., *4725 E. Pima St., Tuscon, 85712.* Tel: 520-795-1633.

Charismatic Movement Liaison Team—Rev. FRANK G. CADY, Spiritual Dir. English Speaking Liaisons: HELEN FORTUNO, *Regina Cleri Center, 8800 E. 22nd St., Tucson, 85710.* Tel: 520-886-4645. Voz en el Dieserto, Hispanic Speaking Liaisons: SALVADOR GONZALES, *1748 S. 4th Ave., Tucson, 85713.* Tel: 520-628-1692.

Community Relations—FRED ALLISON, Dir., *P.O. Box 31, Tucson, 85702.* Tel: 520-792-3410.

Cursillo Movement—Deacon GUILLERMO LUGO, Spiritual Dir., *St. Patrick Parish, P.O. Box 611, Bisbee, 85603.* Tel: 520-432-5753.

Detention Ministry—BARBARA MATTUS, Coord., *192 S. Stone Ave., P.O. Box 31, Tucson, 85702.* Tel: 520-792-3410, Ext. 333; 326.

Development Services (Annual Appeal, Parish Stewardship)—ROBERT E. HESLINGA, Dir., *192 S. Stone Ave., P.O. Box 31, Tucson, 85702.* Tel: 520-792-3410.

Ecumenical Commission—Rev. Msgr. THOMAS F. CAHALANE, *1800 S. Kolb Rd., Tucson, 85710.* Tel: 520-747-1321.

Fiscal Manager—DEBBIE BAHRYCHUKA, *P.O. Box 31, Tucson, 85702.* Tel: 520-792-3410.

Holy Childhood Association—Rev. Msgr. ARSENIO CARRILLO, Dir., *P.O. Box 31, Tucson, 85702.* Tel: 520-792-3410.

Interfaith Council—LAUVER EDIE. Tel: 520-745-9443.

Legion of Decency—Chancery Office, 192 S. Stone Ave., Tucson, 85702.

Diocesan Liturgical Commission—Rev. WILLIAM T. SHUPPERT, Coord., *Chancery Office, 192 S. Stone Ave., Tucson, 85701.* Tel: 520-792-3410.

Diocesan Parish Life and Ministry, Regina Cleri Center—REGINA SASSEEN, Dir. MICHAEL BERGER; RUBEN DAVALOS, Parish Svcs.; Sr. RUTHMARY POWERS, H.M., Supt., *Ministry of Catholic Schools, 8800 E. 22nd St., Tucson, 85710.* Tel: 520-886-5202.

Newspaper—"Catholic Vision", FRED ALLISON, *P.O. Box 31, Tucson, 85702.* Tel: 520-792-3410.

Office of Due Process—Chancery Office, P.O. Box 31, Tucson, 85702. Tel: 520-792-3410.

Permanent Diaconate Program—Deacon CHARLES GIRARD, Dir., *P.O. Box 31, Tucson, 85702.* Tel: 520-792-3410; 290-0873.

Deacon Formation—Rev. DANIEL TAYLOR, Dir., *201 S. Broad St., Globe, 85501.* Tel: 520-425-3137.

Priests' Assurance Association—Most Rev. MANUEL D. MORENO, D.D., Pres. ex-officio; Rev. JOHN P. LYONS, Sec. & Treas. Directors: Rev. Msgr. ROBERT D. FULLER; Rev. Msgr. GERALD BRYNDA; Revs. DOMENICO C. PINTI; JOHN F. ALT.

Priests' Placement Advisory Board—All Vicars Forane: Rev. Msgr. ROBERT D. FULLER; Revs. JAMES G. COLEMAN; MICHAEL R. BUCCIARELLI; RAYMOND RATZENBERGER; JOSEPH M. BAKER; ROBERT G. TAMMINGA; WILLIAM SHUPPERT; JOHN BRENT BARDON; DANIEL P. MCLAUGHLIN, S.T.; CHARLES MALONEY; MARCOS VELASQUEZ; FERNANDO MANZO.

Chancellor—Revs. JOHN P. LYONS; ALBERT E. VERBRUGGHE, Vice-Chancellor; PATRICK M. CRINO, Vocations Dir.

Propagation of the Faith—Rev. Msgr. ARSENIO CARRILLO, Dir. Pro. Tem., *P.O. Box 31, Tucson, 85702.* Tel: 520-792-3410.

Property Manager—LARRY MCGRATH, Mgr., Office: *192 S. Stone Ave., P.O. Box 31, Tucson, 85702.* Tel: 520-792-3410.

Rural Life Bureau—Box 31, Tucson, 85702. Tel: 520-792-3410.

Tuscon Council of Religious—Sr. JANET KUNKEL, O.S.F., Pres.; Sr. SCOLASTICA LAMMER, P.B.V.M., Treas. Pro. Tem., *5035 E. Cecilia, Tucson, 85711.* Tel: 520-327-3583.

Vocations—Rev. PATRICK M. CRINO, Dir., *Mailing Address: P.O. Box 31, Tucson, 85701.* Tel: 520-792-3410; 623-6351.

[*]Catholic Commission—JIM DOBRY, Pres., *231 W. Smoot Dr., Tucson, 85705.* Tel: 520-887-6803.

Vietnamese Catholic Community of Tucson—Rev. JOHN TRAN BICH, C.S.S.C., *Regina Cleri Center, 8800 E. 22nd St., Tuscon, 85710.* Tel: 520-888-5223.

Encuentros de Promocion Juvenile—Rev. JAVIER PEREZ, Spiritual Dir., *P.O. Box 1053, Tucson, 85702-1053.* Tel: 520-624-7409.

CLERGY, PARISHES, MISSIONS AND PAROCHIAL SCHOOLS

CITY OF TUCSON
(Pima County)

1—ST. AUGUSTINE'S CATHEDRAL (1863), Rev. William T. Shuppert, Rector; Rev. Msgr. Arsenio S. Carrillo, V.G.; Rev. Gonzalo J. Villegas.
Res., 192 S. Stone Ave., 85701. Tel: 520-623-6351; Fax: 520-623-5524.
Catechesis/Religious Programs—Tel: 520-624-8627. Miss Barbara Valenzuela, D.R.E., Tel: 520-624-8627.
Students 598.

2—BLESSED KATERI TEKAKWITHA (1984) (Native American), Rev. Daniel P. McLaughlin, S.T. Pastoral Assocs.: Sr. Yvonne M. Flores, I.H.M. In res., Revs. Raphael F. Toner, S.T.; Abram E. Dono; Bro. David T. Sommer, S.T.
Res., 101 W. 31st St., 85713. Tel: 520-791-7774.
Catechesis/Religious Programs—Tel: 520-622-5363.
Students 325.
Missions—South Tucson, Pima Co., St. Nicholas Indian Center, 349 W. 31st St., 85713; San Martin; Santa Rosa, Cristo Rey; San Ignacio; Marana, San Juan.

3—HOLY FAMILY (1915), Rev. Joseph M. Baker. In res., Revs. Edmund Benedett, S.J.; John M. Fahey.
Res., 338 W. University Blvd., 85705. Tel: 520-623-6773.
Catechesis/Religious Programs—Students 200.
Mission—Tucson, Pima Co., Santa Rosa, 2015 N. Calle, 85705. Tel: 520-622-3514.

4—MISSION SAN XAVIER DEL BAC (1692) (Native American), Revs. Michael Dallmeier, O.F.M.; John Gini, O.F.M.; Kieran McCarty, O.F.M.; Bro. Christian Rogan, O.F.M.; Deacon Thomas McGill. In res., Rev. Francis Guest, O.F.M.
Res., 1950 W. San Xavier Rd., 85746. Tel: 520-294-2624.
School—1980 W. San Xavier Rd., 85746. Tel: 520-294-0628. Sr. Carol Mathe, O.S.F., Prin.
Franciscan Sisters of Christian Charity 5; Students 140.
Catechesis/Religious Programs—Tel: 520-294-0628.
Students 291.
Convent—1996 W. San Xavier Rd., 85746.

5—MOST HOLY TRINITY (1975), Rev. Ronald P. Gagnon.
Res., 1300 N. Greasewood, 85745. Tel: 520-622-1300.
Catechesis/Religious Programs—Tel: 520-884-9021.
Students 186.

6—OUR LADY OF FATIMA (1972), Rev. Peter M. McGloin; Deacons Frank S. Lundgren, Jr.; Robert Negrette.
Res., 5969 S. Sorrel Ln., 85746. Tel: 520-883-1717.
Catechesis/Religious Programs—Tel: 520-883-1717.
Students 211.

7—OUR LADY, QUEEN OF ALL SAINTS (1987) (Hispanic), Rev. Floyd G. Stromberg; Deacons Oscar Magallanes; George Rodriguez.
Res., 2915 E. 36th St., 85713. Tel: 520-622-8602.
Catechesis/Religious Programs—Students 310.

8—OUR MOTHER OF SORROWS (1958), Rev. Msgr. Thomas P. Cahalane; Revs. Charles D. Knapp; Alfredo Silva; Deacons Robert Speers; Thomas Tighe; Paul J. Welsh.
Res., 1800 S. Kolb Rd., 85710. Tel: 520-747-1321; Fax: 520-790-3308.
School—Our Lady of Guadalupe Center for Children, 7041 E. Calle Denebola, 85710. Tel: 520-747-1027. Sr. Lauren Moss, O.S.F., Prin.
Lay Teachers 27; Students 501.
Catechesis/Religious Programs—Margaret E. Lordon, D.R.E.
Students 565.

9—SACRED HEART (1942), Rev. Joseph F. McGowan, O.Carm.; Deacon George Castelan. In res., Rev. John Fogarty, O.Carm.
Res., Priory, 601 E. Fort Lowell Rd., 85705. Tel: 520-888-1530; Fax: 520-888-1531.
Catechesis/Religious Programs—Students 270.

10—ST. AMBROSE (1946), Rev. Francisco Maldonado; Deacon Henry Gamboa.
Res., 300 S. Tucson Blvd., 85716. Tel: 520-622-6749.
School—Tel: 520-882-8678; Fax: 520-624-6853.
Lay Teachers 20; Students 360.
Catechesis/Religious Programs—Tel: 520-623-2925.
Students 350.

11—ST. CYRIL OF ALEXANDRIA (1948), Revs. William J. Dougherty, C.S.P.; Edward S. Pietrucha, C.S.P.; Robert J. Stulting, C.S.P., (Retired); Deacon Charles Pennington.
Res., 4725 E. Pima, 85712. Tel: 520-795-1633; Fax: 520-795-1639.
School—Tel: 520-881-4240; Fax: 520-795-0325. Mrs. JoAnn Sayre, Prin.
Lay Teachers 22; Students 398.
Catechesis/Religious Programs—Students 398.

12—ST. FRANCES CABRINI (1961), Rev. Msgr. Robert D. Fuller.
Res., 3201 E. Presidio Rd., 85716. Tel: 520-326-7670; Fax: 520-881-8480.
Catechesis/Religious Programs—Tel: 520-795-1110.
Students 153.

13—ST. FRANCIS DE SALES (1971), Revs. Robert G. Tamminga; Charles W. Cloud; Deacons Michael Ammerman; Frank J. Collura; Marvin Farmer; Charles Girard; Keith Pavlik; Dennis Scalpone; Leonard Fuller; Alvin Crockette; Russ Kingery; Hugh Montague; Robert Nevins; William Vigil.
Res., 1375 S. Camino Seco, 85710. Tel: 520-885-5908; Fax: 520-885-3109.

Catechesis/Religious Programs—Marian Gilbert, D.R.E.
Students 783.

14—ST. JOHN THE EVANGELIST (1934), Revs. Raul P. Trevizo; Javier Perez; Liam Leahy. In res., Deacons Ernesto Roche; Bernard Minetti; Jose Ojeda; Don Baker; Jose Duarte.
Res., 602 W. Ajo Way, 85713. Tel: 520-624-7409.
School—Dr. Ernestina Fuentes, Prin. Sisters 1; Lay Teachers 10; Students 289.
Catechesis/Religious Programs—Tel: 520-792-3366. Sr. Maria Emmanuel Martinez, D.R.E.
Students 747.

15—ST. JOSEPH (1953), Revs. John F. Allt; Frederic F. Curry, Pastor Emeritus; Deacons George Herrick; Leon Mazza; Philip Garcia; Paul Converse; John Broussard; Sr. Marie Chapla, Pastoral Assoc. In res., Rev. James Freeman.
Res., 215 S. Craycroft Rd., 85711. Tel: 520-747-3100; Fax: 520-745-4606.
Parish Center—Tel: 520-747-3100.
School—Tel: 520-747-3060. Mrs. Ellen S. Kwader, Prin.
Lay Teachers 21; Students 506.
Catechesis/Religious Programs—Sharon Takerer, D.R.E.
Students 206.

16—ST. MARGARET'S (1951), Revs. Gilbert Levario, O.C.D.; Bernard Perkins; Kevin McArdle, O.C.D.
Res., 801 N. Grande Ave., 85745. Tel: 520-622-0168; Fax: 520-882-8022. [CEM]
Catechesis/Religious Programs—Tel: 520-622-5982.
Students 376.

17—ST. MONICA (1964), Revs. Michael Martinez; Viliulfo Valderrama; Deacons John Garcia; Don Fisher; Tomas Morales; Eugene Fernandez.
Res., 212 W. Medina, 85706. Tel: 520-294-2694.
Catechesis/Religious Programs—Tel: 520-889-1944; Fax: 520-295-0335.
Students 950.

18—SAINT ODILIA (1965), Revs. John Brent Bardon; Richard E. Troutman; Deacon George Scherf.
Res. & Mailing Address—7570 Paseo del Norte, 85737-4499. Tel: 520-297-7271; 297-6361 (Office); Fax: 520-297-7271.
Catechesis/Religious Programs—Students 565.
Mission—Tucson, Pima Co., Santa Catalina, 14380 N. Oracle, 85739-9599. Tel: 520-825-9611. Sr. Carole Ruland, M.H.S.H., Admin.

19—ST. PIUS X (1969), Revs. Harry Ledwith; Richard Kingsley. In res., Rev. James G. Coleman.
Res., 1800 N. Caminoo Pio Decimo, 85715. Tel: 520-885-3573; Fax: 520-885-3573, Ext. 53.
Catechesis/Religious Programs—Karen Horton, D.R.E.
Students 600.

20—SAINTS PETER AND PAUL (1930), Revs. Van A. Wagner; Jay R. Luczak; Donald J. Fiedler; Arthur Devine, (Retired). In res., Rev. Patrick M. Crino.
Res., 1946 E. Lee St., 85719. Tel: 520-327-6015.
School—Tel: 520-325-2431; Fax: 520-881-4690. Sr. Ann Patrick Adams, S.C., Prin.
Sisters of Charity from Seton Hall 3; Lay Teachers 22; Students 530.
Catechesis/Religious Programs—Tel: 520-327-1229.
Students 191.
Convent—1947 E. Adams St., 85719. Tel: 520-325-2234.

21—SANTA CRUZ (1919), Revs. Cyprian Killackey, O.C.D.; Richard Claassen, O.C.D. In res., Bro. Christopher LaRocca, O.C.D.
Res., P.O. Box 2830, 85702. Tel: 520-623-3833.
School—Tel: 520-624-2093; Fax: 520-624-2833.
Sisters 2; Lay Teachers 9; Students 223.
Catechesis/Religious Programs—Tel: 520-882-9687.
Students 455.
Missions—Tucson, Pima Co., Our Lady of Guadalupe, 401 E. 31st St., 85713. Tel: 520-624-2066; Tucson, Pima Co., St. Anthony's Catholic Instruction Center and Capilla, 225 W. 34th St., 85713. Tel: 520-622-8972.

22—ST. ELIZABETH ANN SETON (1980), Revs. Thomas J. Millane; Remigio Tupaz Mariano, Jr.; Deacon James L. Burns.
8650 N. Shannon Rd., 85742. Tel: 520-297-7357; Fax: 520-797-8886.
Catechesis/Religious Programs—Tel: 520-297-8150. Roseanne Skapura, D.R.E.
Students 1,200.

23—ST. THOMAS THE APOSTLE (1984), Rev. Todd O'Leary (Ireland). In res., Rev. Timothy J. Howard, S.J.
Res., 5150 N. Valley View Rd., 85718. Tel: 520-577-8780.
Catechesis/Religious Programs—Tel: 520-577-8782; Fax: 520-577-0441.
Students 695.

OUTSIDE THE CITY OF TUCSON

Ajo, Pima Co., Immaculate Conception (1916), Rev. Richard J. Rego, Admin.
Office: 101 Rocalla, P.O. Drawer A F, 85321. Tel: 520-387-7049; 387-7900.
Catechesis/Religious Programs—Tel: 520-387-6300.
Students 97.

Apache Junction, Pinal Co., St. George (1968), Revs. Charles F. Maloney; Leo Spreitsma, O.F.M.Conv. In res., Rev. Willard Wiesler.
Res., 300 E. 16th Ave., 85219. Tel: 602-982-2929; Fax: 602-982-0036.
Catechesis/Religious Programs—Mrs. Therese E. Tirador, O.P., D.R.E.
Students 205.

Benson, Cochise Co., Our Lady of Lourdes (1895), Rev. Raymond Ratzenberger.
Mailing Address: 244 S. Gila, P.O. Box 2198, 85602. Tel: 520-586-3394; Fax: 520-686-3394.
Res., 210 Eighth St., 85602. Tel: 520-586-3394.
Catechesis/Religious Programs—Students 107.

Bisbee, Cochise Co., St. Patrick (1902), Rev. Stanley Nadolny. Deacons Guillermo Lugo; Robert Gonzales; Joseph L. Delgado.
Res., P.O. Box 164, 85603. Tel: 520-432-5753.
Catechesis/Religious Programs—Tel: 520-432-4012.
Students 329.
Mission—Naco, Cochise Co., St. Michael.

Casa Grande, Pinal Co., St. Anthony (1932), Rev. Steven G. Stencil; Deacons Bill Hughes; Joseph McGeeney; Bill Kinney.
Res., P.O. Drawer 12335, 85230-2335. Tel: 520-836-0601; Fax: 520-836-2985.
School—Tel: 520-836-7247; Fax: 520-836-2985. Ms. Rebecca Daley, Admin.
Lay Teachers 7; Students 130.
Catechesis/Religious Programs—Students 475.
Missions—Stanfield, Pinal Co., St. Mary, 85230-2335.; Maricopa, Pinal Co., St. Francis de Sales, P.O. Box 368, Maricopa, 85239-0368. Tel: 520-568-4605.

Clifton, Greenlee Co., Sacred Heart (1899), Rev. John F. Emanuel.
Mailing Address: P.O. Box 938, 85533.
Res., 329 Chase Creek, 85533. Tel: 520-865-2285; Fax: 520-865-3497.
Catechesis/Religious Programs—North Cornado Boulevard Parish Center.
Students 350.
Convent—Box 938, 85533. Tel: 520-865-3166.
Mission—Duncan, St. Mary, Third St., P.O. Box 554, 85534. Tel: 520-359-9212.
Convent—P.O. Box 554, Duncan, 85534.

Coolidge, Pinal Co., St. James (1947) (Hispanic), Rev. Jeffrey P. Thuerauf.
Parish Center—401 W. Wilson Ave., 85228. Tel: 520-723-3063.
Res., 437 W. Wilson Ave., 85228. Tel: 520-723-7870.
Catechesis/Religious Programs—Students 300.

Douglas, Cochise Co., Immaculate Conception (1907), Rev. Luis N. Chavez; Deacon Luciano Gonzales, Jr.
Res., 928 C Ave., P.O. Box 1176, 85607. Tel: 520-364-8494.
School—Lestonnac Kindergarten and Day Care Center, Tel: 520-364-3956. Sr. Amparo Herrera, O.D.N., Prin.
Sisters of the Company of Mary 4; Lay Teachers 4; Students 84.
Catechesis/Religious Programs—Students 400.
Convent—Tel: 520-364-7658; Fax: 520-364-3645. Sisters of the Company of Mary

St. Luke (1950), Revs. James M. Hobert, Jr.; Robert E. Carney; Deacons Armando Moulinet; Gabe Saspe.
Res., 1211 15th St., 85607. Tel: 520-364-4411; Fax: 520-364-4412.
School—Loretto Central Catholic, 1200 14th St., 85607. Tel: 520-364-5754. Sr. Antonia Teresa, O.C.D., Prin.
Sisters 6; Lay Teachers 6; Students 295.
Catechesis/Religious Programs—Tel: 520-364-7109. Toni Moulinet, D.R.E.
Students 523.
Convent—Tel: 520-364-7658; Fax: 520-364-3645. Carmelite Sisters of the Most Sacred Heart of Los Angeles, Loretto Convent

Eloy, Pinal Co., St. Helen (1952) (Hispanic), Rev. Joseph G. Gorsuch.
Res., 205 W. 8th St., 85231. Tel: 520-466-7258.
Catechesis/Religious Programs—Tel: 520-466-7934. D.R.E.: Sr. Mary Eulema Lyvers, S.S.N.D.; Sr. Mary Elwyn Brink, S.S.N.D.
Students 805.

Florence, Pinal Co., Assumption of the Blessed Virgin Mary (1870), Rev. Bryan W. Sherry, J.C.L. In res., Rev. Willard F. Wiesler.
Res., P.O. Box 550, 85232-0550. Tel: 520-868-5940.

Globe, Gila Co., Holy Angels (1905), Rev. Michael Bradly.
Res., 201 S. Broad St., 85501. Tel: 520-425-3137; Fax: 520-425-3136.
School—1300 E. Cedar St., 85501. Tel: 520-425-5703; Fax: 520-425-5703. Sr. Leonie Bracken, Prin. & Admin.
Presentation Sisters 2; Lay Teachers 5; Students 164.
Catechesis/Religious Programs—Tel: 520-425-3173.
Students 235.
Convent—Tel: 520-425-2034.

Green Valley, Pima Co., Our Lady of the Valley (1970), Revs. Joseph A. Lombardo; Robert Brazaskas; Deacons Francis E. Lambert; Pete Grimaldo; James Stotler.
Res., 505 N. La Canada Dr., 85614. Tel: 520-625-4536; Fax: 520-625-4536.
Catechesis/Religious Programs—Sahuarita, 85629. Tel: 520-625-4536; Fax: 520-625-4536.
160219.
Mission—Sahuarita, Pima Co., St. Martin de Porres.

Hayden, Gila Co., St. Joseph's (1913), Rev. William Taft; Deacon Arnold Moreno.
Res., P.O. Drawer C, 85235. Tel: 520-356-7223.
Catechesis/Religious Programs—Tel: 520-356-6462.
Students 100.

Kearny, Pinal Co., Infant Jesus of Prague (1961), Rev. Kevin D. Clinch, Admin.
Res., 501 Victoria Cir., P.O. Box 459, 85237. Tel: 520-363-7205.
Catechesis/Religious Programs—Students 70.

Mammoth, Pinal Co., Blessed Sacrament (1970) (Hispanic), Rev. Gilbert Padilla.
Res., 122 W. Church Dr., P.O. Box 20, 85618. Tel: 520-487-2451.
Catechesis/Religious Programs—Students 214.
Convent—Mammoth. Blessed Sacrament Convent

Marana, Pima Co., St. Christopher's (1954), Rev. L. Ignacio Gameros.
Res., 12101 Moore Rd., P.O. Box 188, 85653. Tel: 520-682-3375; Fax: 520-682-3928.
Education Center—Tel: 520-682-9011. Barbara Mattus, D.R.E.
Students 146.

Miami, Gila Co., Our Lady of the Blessed Sacrament (1915), Rev. Loren M. Gonzales, O.S.M.
Res., P.O. Drawer E, 85539. Tel: 520-473-3568; Fax: 520-473-3338.
Catechesis/Religious Programs—Students 215.
Convent—Tel: 520-473-2010. Sacred Heart
Missions—Claypool, Gila Co., St. Joseph; Roosevelt Lake, Gila Co., St. Theresa.

Morenci, Greenlee Co., Holy Cross (1913), Rev. Raul H. Rosales.
Mailing Address: P.O. Box 216, 85540.
Res., 205 Fairbanks Rd., 85540. Tel: 520-865-3183; Fax: 520-865-3183.
Catechesis/Religious Programs—Tel: 520-865-5226.
Students 405.

Nogales, Santa Cruz Co., Sacred Heart (1897), Revs. Marcos C. Velasquez; Antonio Felipe Martinez.
Res., P.O. Box 968, 85628. Tel: 520-287-9221; Fax: 520-287-9224.
School—Sacred Heart, Tel: 520-287-5484; Fax: 520-287-6065. Sr. Esther Hugues, C.F.M.M., Supr.
Minim Daughters of Mary Immaculate 3; Lay Teachers 12; Students 330.
Catechesis/Religious Programs—Tel: 520-287-9223; Fax: 520-287-9224.
Students 795.

San Felipe de Jesus (1987), Rev. Antonio A. Ruiz.
Mailing Address: P.O. Box 6600, 85628. Tel: 520-761-3100.
Res., 3272 Villa Hermosa, 85621. Tel: 520-761-3100.
Church—1901 Jose Gallego Ln., #1, 85621.
Catechesis/Religious Programs—Students 548.

Parker, La Paz Co., Sacred Heart (1950), Rev. Theodore Lobo.
Res., 916 11th St., 85344. Tel: 520-669-2502.
Catechesis/Religious Programs—Students 150.
Missions—Poston, Kateri Tekawitha Indian Mission; Wenden, St. John the Baptist; Quartzsite, Queen of Peace.

Patagonia, Santa Cruz Co., St. Theresa (1955), Rev. Anthony Jablonowski, C.M.M.I., Admin.
Res., Box 435, 85624. Tel: 520-394-2954; Fax: 520-394-2831.
Catechesis/Religious Programs—Students 68.
Mission—Sonoita, Santa Cruz Co., Our Lady of Angels, Fire Station, Sonoita, 85637.

Payson, Gila Co., Saint Philip the Apostle (1957), Rev. Joseph A. Krause; Sr. Marilita Michalski, O.S.F., Pastoral Min.
Res., 511 S. St. Philip, 85541-5144. Tel: 520-474-2392.

Catechesis/Religious Programs—Tel: 520-747-1269.
Students 107.

Pirtleville, Cochise Co., St. Bernard's (1914), Revs. James M. Hobert, Jr.; Robert E. Carney.
Res., P.O. Box 3101, 85626. Tel: 520-364-2762.
Catechesis/Religious Programs—Tel: 520-364-5994.
Students 180.
Chapels—Double Adobe, Our Lady of La Salette. Rev. Conrad Blanchett, M.S., (Retired), Tel: 520-364-5526; Douglas, Sacred Heart.

Rio Rico, Santa Cruz Co., Nativity of Our Lord Jesus Christ (1987), Rev. Frank G. Cady.
Mailing Address: P.O. Box 4024, 85648.
Res., 384 Cancun Corte, 85648. Tel: 520-281-8702; 281-7414.
Catechesis/Religious Programs—Students 183.

Safford, Graham Co., St. Rose of Lima (1937), In res., Revs. Domenico C. Pinti; Tadeusz Sypko.
Res., 311 Central Ave., 85546. Tel: 520-428-4920.
Catechesis/Religious Programs—Tel: 520-428-4922.
Students 555.
Missions—Pima, Graham Co., Pima Mission, Pima, 85543; Thatcher, Graham Co., Neuman Center, Thatcher, 85552.

San Carlos, Gila Co., San Carlos Catholic Mission (1950) (Apache), Rev. Walter J. Holly, O.F.M.
Res., P.O. Box 28, 85550. Tel: 520-475-2210.
School—Tel: 520-475-2449.
Sisters 5; Students 169.
Convent—P.O. Box 338, 85550. Tel: 520-475-2460. Sisters of the Blessed Sacrament
Mission—Bylas, Graham Co., Blessed Kateri Tekakwitha.

San Manuel, Pinal Co., St. Bartholomew (1954), Rev. Michael R. Bucciarelli. In res., Rev. Msgr. Loyola O'Dougherty, Pastor Emeritus.
Res., 609 Park Pl., Box 607, 85631. Tel: 520-385-4156.
Convent—313 Avenue A, P.O. Box 32, 85631. Tel: 520-385-4739. Sisters of Notre Dame de Namur
Mission—Oracle, Pinal Co., St. Helen, HCR 1, Box 2000, Oracle, 85623. Tel: 520-896-2708. Rev. Donald F. Jackson, Admin. In res., Rev. Paul J. Ranft, Pastor Emeritus.

Sierra Vista, Cochise Co., St. Andrew (1959), Revs. Gregory P. Adolf; Colman J. Nolan, S.T.
Res., 800 Taylor Dr., N.W., 85635. Tel: 520-458-2925; Fax: 520-452-0235.
Catechesis/Religious Programs—Tel: 520-458-4994.
Students 341.
Mission—Whetstone, Cochise Co., Good Shepherd.

Our Lady of the Mountains (1991), Rev. Robert R. Bryerton.
Res., 1425 Yaqui St., 85635. Tel: 520-378-2720; Fax: 520-378-6825.
Catechesis/Religious Programs—Tel: 520-378-7012.
Students 300.

Solomon, Graham Co., Our Lady of Guadalupe (1891), Rev. John J. Ancharski; Deacon Gilbert O. Martinez.
Res., P.O. Box 147, 85551. Tel: 520-428-0149.
Catechesis/Religious Programs—Students 63.
Mission—San Jose, Graham Co., San Jose.

Somerton, Yuma Co., Immaculate Heart of Mary (1954), Rev. Fernando L. Manzo.
Res., 310 W. Spring St., P.O. Box 597, 85350. Tel: 520-627-2918; Fax: 520-627-2918.
P.O. Box 2888, San Luis, 85349. Tel: 520-627-8011.
Mission—San Luis, Yuma Co., San Judas Tadeo, 22790 S. Hwy 95, 85349. Rev. Julian Sanz.
Catechesis/Religious Programs—Tel: 520-627-2244.
Students 950.

Sunsites, Cochise Co., St. Jude Thaddius (1983), In res., Rev. Msgr. John A. Oliver.
Res., P.O. Box 328, Pearce, 85625. Tel: 520-826-3869.
Catechesis/Religious Programs—Students 21.
Mission—Elfrida, Cochise Co., St. Francis of Assisi, P.O. Box 587, Elfrida, 85610. Tel: 520-642-3879.

Superior, Pinal Co., St. Francis of Assisi Parish (1930), Rev. Augustine Kattady; Deacon Jesus Yanez.
Res., 11 Church Ave., 85273. Tel: 520-689-2250.
Catechesis/Religious Programs—St. Mary's Center, 100 Sunset Dr., 85273. Tel: 520-689-2116.
Students 185.

Tombstone, Cochise Co., Sacred Heart (1880), Rev. William J. Parenteau.
Res., P.O. Box 547, 85638. Tel: 520-457-3364.
Catechesis/Religious Programs—Students 84.

Topawa, Pima Co., San Solano Missions - Tohono O'odham Indian Reservation (1908) (Native American). (For office and sacramental records pertaining to Tohono O'odham Indians and mission churches on the reservation, please refer to San Solano Missions at the P.O. Box 210, Topawa, AZ, 85639 address).
Mailing Address: P.O. Box 210, 85639. Tel: 520-383-2350. Revs. Maximilian Hottle, O.F.M., Admin.; Peter Verheggen, O.F.M.; Thomas Frost, O.F.M.

Tubac, Santa Cruz Co., St. Ann (1987), Revs. Clarke W. Moore; Robert A. Hyman.
Mailing Address: P.O. Box 2911, 85646-2911. Tel: 520-398-9711.
Missions—Amado, Santa Cruz Co., Assumption Chapel; Arivaca, Pima Co., St. Ferdinand.

Vail, Pima Co., Shrine of St. Rita in the Desert (1937), Rev. Robert Wicht, S.D.S. In res., Rev. Alan Wagner, S.D.S.
Res., P.O. Box 400, 85641. Tel: 520-762-5363.
Catechesis/Religious Programs—Students 74.

Willcox, Cochise Co., Sacred Heart (1936), Rev. Maurice O'Neil, S.S.
Res., P.O. Box 490, 85644. Tel: 520-384-2851.
Catechesis/Religious Programs—Students 114.
Mission—Cochise City, Cochise Co., San Simon-Cho, Cochise 85605.

Yuma, Yuma Co., Immaculate Conception (1866), Rev. Msgr. Richard W. O'Keeffe; Rev. Msgr. Gerald J. Brynda; Revs. Juan Guillen; Martin S. Martinez; Deacons Mark Vixen; Sampson; Fernando Mezquita.
Res., 509 Ave. B, 85364. Tel: 520-782-7516; Fax: 520-343-0172.
School—501 Ave. B, 85364. Tel: 520-783-5225. Sr. Carol Seidl, O.S.F., Prin.
Franciscan Sisters of Christian Charity 4; Lay Teachers 11; Students 216.
Catechesis/Religious Programs—Tel: 520-783-1324. D.R.E.: Mark Nixen; Mary Tellez.
Students 790.
Missions—Yuma, Yuma Co., Our Lady of Guadalupe, 417 15th Ave., 85364.; Wellton, Yuma Co., St. Joseph the Worker, P.O. Box 357, Wellton, 85356. Tel: 520-785-4275. Rev. Msgr. Richard W. O'Keeffe, Admin.; Rev. Tomas G. Munoz.
Convent—500 24th Ave., 85364. Tel: 520-783-5224. Franciscan Sisters of Christian Charity 10.

St. Francis of Assisi (1948), Revs. Daniel Taylor; Perry McCoy, O.S.M.; Gilberto Malu Musumbu, M.S.P.; Deacons Paul Muthart; E. Joseph Pozzi; Carlo Duarte; Donald L. Larson; Gary Pasquinelli; Rick Hernandez; Bill McDonald; Jerry Saladin; Rafael Vidal; Arnulfo Carbajal; Francisco Moreno.
Res., 1815 S. 8th Ave., 85364. Tel: 520-782-1875; Fax: 520-329-9479.
School—700 18th St., 85364. Tel: 520-782-1539. Dr. Diane Clark, Prin.
Franciscan Sisters of Christian Charity 3; Lay Teachers 8; Students 226.
Catechesis/Religious Programs—Tel: 520-783-7461. D.R.E.: Sherlyn Saladin, (English Apostolate); Lucy Quiroz, (Hispanic Apostolate).
Students 529.

St. John Neumann (1987), Rev. Damian M. Kobus, O.S.M.
Res Rev. Perry McCoy, O.S.M.; Res., 11750 S. Mesa Dr., 85367. Tel: 520-342-3544.

Chaplains of Public Institutions

TUCSON. *Arizona Correctional Training Center*. Vacant. Santa Rita Unit, 10000 S. Wilmot Rd., 85777. Detention Ministry, P.O. Box 31, 85702. Tel: 520-792-3410, Ext. 326; 333.
Arizona Western College. Attended from St. John Newmann Parish, Yuma. 11750 S. Mesa Dr., 85365. Tel: 520-342-3544.
Christ the King Chapel, 836 CSG/HC, Davis Monthan Air Force Base, 85707. Tel: 520-750-5411. Rev. Michael Weber, Chap.
Kino Community Hospital. Attended from Santa Cruz, Tucson. 1220 S. Sixth, 85707. Tel: 520-623-3833. 2800 E. Ajo Way, 85713.
Metropolitan Correctional Complex, 8901 S. Wilmont Rd., 85706. Tel: 520-741-3118. Rev. Patrick Dennis, Staff Chap., Detention Ministry, P.O. Box 31, 85702. Tel: 520-792-3410, Ext. 326; 333.
Tucson Medical Center, 5301 E. Grant Rd., 85712. Rev. William Koehler, C.SS.R., Chap.
U.S. Veterans Hospital, S. Sixth Ave., 85713. Tel: 520-792-1450. Chaplains: Revs. Roland Bedard, M.S.; Henry Dauphinais, M.S.
Villa Maria, 4310 E. Grant Rd., 85712. Tel: 520-323-9351. Rev. Alexander Mills, Chap.

CATALINA. *Arizona Youth Center*. Attended from St. Odilia Parish. Santa Catalina Mission, Catalina Rural Branch, P.O. Box 8601, 85738. Tel: 520-825-9611.

FLORENCE. *Arizona State Prison*, St. Dismas Chapel, P.O. Box 550, 85232. Tel: 520-868-5940. Rev. Lawrence Quilici, Chap.

FORT GRANT RURAL STATION. *Fort Grant Training Center*, 85632. Revs. Maurice O'Neil, S.S.; John J. Ancharski.

FORT HUCHUCA. *Fort Huchuca Army Post*, 85613. Rev. Arvids Bernans, Chap.

SAFFORD. *Conservation Center*. Tel: 520-428-0149. Rev. John J. Ancharski.

SOLOMON. *Our Lady of Guadalupe*, P.O. Box 147, 85551. Tel: 520-428-1049. Rev. John J. Ancharski.

WILLCOX. *Federal Prison Camp*, 85546. Tel: 520-428-6600. Rev. Maurice O'Neil, S.S.

YUMA. *MCAS Chapel*, Marine Corps Air Station, Davis Monthan Air Force Base, 85369. Tel: 520-341-2087. Rev. Ralph Sodano, Chap.
Yuma Regional Medical Center. Attended from St. Francis of Assisi. 1815 8th Ave., 85364. Tel: 520-782-1875.

Special Assignment:
Reverend Monsignors—
Carrillo, Arsenio S., Vicar General & Propagation of the Faith, Dir. Pro-Tem, P.O. Box 31, Tucson, AZ 85702. Tel: 520-792-3410
Reverend Fathers—
Carscallen, Eward C., Spiritual Dir. Ministry to Priests. Tel: 520-625-4330
Sherry, Bryan W., J.C.L., Canonical Consultant, P.O. Box 550, Florence, AZ 85232
Shuppert, William T., Coord. Diocesan Liturgy Comm. Tel: 520-792-3410

On Duty Outside the Diocese:
Reverend Fathers—
Bell, Brian T., U.S.A.F., 21-21st Space Wing/HQ, 455 Vincent St., Peterson AFB, CO 80914-1466
Gonzales, Robert A., Pontifical College Josephinum, 7625 N. High St., Columbus, OH 43085
McCarthy, Jeremiah J., Rector, St. John's Seminary, 5012 E. Seminary Rd., Camarillo, CA 93012
Ryle, Edward J., Exec. Dir., c/o Arizona Catholic Conference, 400 E. Monroe St., Phoenix, AZ 85004
Underwood, Gary E., U.S.A.F., 96 ABW/HC, 202 N. 8th St., Elgin AFB, FL 32542

Absent on Leave:
Reverend Monsignors—
Trupia, Robert C.
Reverend Fathers—
Cocio, Carlos
Garzon-Blanco, Armando
Noriega, Arnoldo
Rickson, Stephen E.
Rosensweig, Walter F.
Speers, David B.
Teta, Michael J.

Sabbatical Leave:
Reverend Fathers—
Thomas, Robert

Retired:
Reverend Monsignors—
O'Dougherty, Loyola A., P.O. Box 985, Mammoth, AZ 85618
Rosettie, Frederick D., 723 El Sol Cir., Benson, AZ 85602
Reverend Fathers—
Carscallen, Edward C., 221 S. Pas Tera C., Green Valley, AZ 85614
Connelly, George R., 826 N. Bellvedere, Tucson, AZ 85711
Costigan, Richard J., 3241 E. 23rd St., Tucson, AZ 85713
Cote, Gerald M., 5725 W. Box R St., Tucson, AZ 85713
Curry, Frederic F., 870 Natachee, Tucson, AZ 85710
Debski, John, 8800 E. 22nd St., Tucson, AZ 85710
Diehl, Michael C., 6333 Rancho Mission Rd., San Diego, CA 92109
Doyle, Thomas A., Holy Family Center, 1802 W. St. Mary's Rd., Tucson, AZ 85748
Fahey, John M., P.O. Box 938, Clifton, AZ 85333
Graff, Robert L., 5464 E. Boston St., Mesa, AZ 85205
LaRoque, Paul M., 392 W. Camino del Sonador, Green Valley, AZ 85614
McGrenra, Cornelius D., Laconnell, Aradra, Co. Donegal, Ireland
O'Flannigan, Thomas L., 409 W. Pontiac Dr. #6, Phoenix, AZ 85027
Phelan, Reginald L., Valley Health Care, 5545 E. Lee St., Tucson, AZ 85712
Ranft, Paul J., Box J, Oracle, AZ 85623
Rook, Paul, 4120 N. Flowing Wells Rd., Tucson, AZ 85705
Schlueter, Clemens M., P.O. Box 5886, Phoenix, AZ 85010
Whalen, Norman M., P.O. Box 911, San Marcos, TX 78666
Wiesler, Willard F., 300 E. 16th Ave., Apache Junction, AZ 85219

Permanent Deacons:
Ackerley, John K., St. Augustine Cathedral, Tucson
Adams, Thomas, Our Lady of Lourdes, Benson
Ammerman, Michael D., St. Francis de Sales, Tucson
Arbizo, Marcello A., St. Rose of Lima, Safford
Baker, Don, St. John the Evangelist, Tuscon
Bejarano, Thomas, St. Rose of Lima, Safford
Borquez, Henry S., St. Augustine Cathedral, Tucson
Broussard, John O., St. Joseph, Tucson
Bueno, Oscar L., St. Augustine's, Tucson
Burns, James, St. Elizabeth Ann Seton, Tucson
Carbajal, Arnulfo, St. Francis of Assisi, Yuma
Carmona, Salvador, St. Augustine Cathedral, Tuscon
Castelan, George P., Sacred Heart, Tucson
Castillo, Frank R., Our Lady of the Blessed Sacrament, Miami
Collura, Frank J., St. Francis de Sales, Tucson
Converse, Paul E., St. Joseph, Tucson
Crockette, Alvin, St. Francis de Sales, Tucson
Delgado, Joseph, St. Patrick, Tucson
Desmarais, Ronald, Our Lady of Lourdes, Benson
Duarte, Carlos V., St. Francis of Assisi, Yuma
Duarte, Jose, St. John the Evangelist, Tucson
Dugan, Patrick, St. Anthony of Padua, Casa Grande
Duran, Ralph, St. Rose of Lima, Safford
Farmer, Marvin F., (Retired), St. Francis de Sales, Tucson
Fernandez, Eugene, St. Monica, Tucson
Fisher, Donald, St. Monica, Tucson
Force, Richard C., Saints Peter & Paul, Tucson
Fullen, Samuel, Holy Cross, Morenci
Fuller, Leonard L., Development Office, Associate Director
Gallegos, Charles A., St. John the Evangelist, Tucson
Gamboa, Henry W.
Garcia, John A., St. Monica, Tucson
Garcia, Philip, St. Joseph, Tucson
Garcia, Ramon, St. Anthony of Padua, Casa Granade
Gaun, George, St. Andrew the Apostle, Sierra Vista
Gelabert, Carlos G., St. Margaret, Tucson
Gersitz, James M., Holy Angels, Globe
Girard, Charles, St. Francis de Sales, Tucson
Gonzales, David, Sacred Heart, Parker Dam, CA
Gonzales, Luciano, Jr., Immaculate Conception, Douglas
Gonzales, Richard A., Sacred Heart, Clifton
Gonzales, Robert J., St. Patrick, Bisbee & St. Michael Mission, Naco
Grijalva, Pilar, St. Anthony of Padua, Casa Grande
Grimaldo, Pedro, Our Lady of the Valley, Green Valley
Heames, Richard, Our Lady of the Mountains, Sierra Vista
Hernandez, Nieves, Office of Catholic Chaplain, Yuma
Hernandez, Richard R.
Herrick, George R., St. Joseph's, Tucson
Hughes, William G., St. Anthony, Casa Grande
Kingery, Russell, St. Francis de Sales, Tucson
Kinney, William, St. Anthony of Padua, Casa Grande
Lambert, Frank, Our Lady of the Valley, Green Valley
LaSalle, James F., St. Thomas More Newman Center, Tucson
Lee, Laurence
Leinfelder, Carl, St. Rita in the Desert, Vail
LeMieux, Richard, Holy Angels, Globe
Longoria, Leopoldo "Leo", St. Elizabeth Ann Seton, Tucson
Lopez, Jose, St. Jude Thaddeus Mission, San Luis
Lugo, Guillermo A. (Bill), St. Patrick's, Bisbee
Lundgren, Frank S., Jr., Our Lady of Fatima, Tucson
Magallanes, Oscar, Our Lady, Queen of All Saints, Tucson
Marion, Kenneth, (Retired)
Marshall, Russell L., Villa Maria Care Center, Tucson
Martinez, Carlos C., St. Augustine Cathedral, Tucson
Martinez, Frank B., St. Rose of Lima, Safford
Martinez, Gilbert O., Our Lady of Guadalupe, Solomon
Mazza, Leon S., St. Joseph, Tucson
McCandless, Charles, Our Lady of the Mountains, Sierra Vista
McDonald, William, St. Francis of Assisi, Yuma
McGeeney, Joseph, St. Francis de Sales Mission, Maricopa
McGill, Thomas M., Mission San Xavier del Bac, Tucson
Merritt, Willaim, Our Lady of the Mountains, Sierra Vista
Mezquita, Fernando, St. Francis of Assisi, Yuma
Milazzo, Mike, St. Andrew the Apostle, Sierra Vista
Miller, Anthony, St. Anthony of Padua, Casa Grande
Minetti, Bernard, St. John the Evangelist, Tucson
Montague, Hugh, St. Francis de Sales, Tucson
Morales, Tomas, St. Monica, Tucson
Moreno, Arnoldo L., St. Joseph, Hayden
Moreno, Francisco, St. Francis of Assisi, Yuma
Moulinet, Armando A., St. Luke's, Douglas
Murphy, J. James, Matrimonial Tribunal, Tucson
Muthart, Paul, St. Francis of Assisi, Yuma
Negrette, Robert, Our Lady of Fatima, Tucson
Nevins, Robert, St. Francis de Sales, Tucson
Nixen, Mark, Immaculate Conception, Yuma
Noriega, Rudy, Sacred Heart, Nogales
Ojeda, Jose, St. John the Evangelist, Tucson
Ornelas, Richard, Santa Cruz, Tucson
Pasquinelli, Gary, St. Francis of Assisi, Yuma
Paulus, Raymond V., Sacred Heart, Tucson
Pavlik, Keith F., St. Francis de Sales, Tucson
Pawloski, Chester E., Saints Peter and Paul, Tucson
Pennington, Charles H., St.Francis de Sales, Tucson
Pozzi, E. Joseph, St. Francis of Assisi, Yuma
Radke, Robert, St. Francis de Sales Mission, Maricopa
Roche, Ernest C., St. John the Evangelist, Tucson
Rodriguez, George M., Our Lady Queen of All Saints, Tucson
Rombach, Lionel E., St. Thomas More Chapel, Newman Center, Tucson
Sadorf, Robert G., St. Andrew the Apostle, Sierra Vista
Saladon, Jerry, St. Francis of Assisi, Yuma
Sampson, David, Immaculate Conception, Yuma
Sanchez, Falvio, St. Bartholomew, San Manuel
Saspe, Gabriel, St. Luke, Douglas
Scalpone, Dennis R., St. Francis de Sales, Tucson
Schaff, James, Our Lady of the Mountains, Sierra Vista
Scherf, George, St. Odilia, Tucson
Schneider, Paul L., Most Holy Trinity, Tucson
Silva, Alfredo A., Our Mother of Sorrows, Tucson
Speers, Robert M., Our Mother of Sorrows, Tucson
Stotler, Jim, Our Lady of the Valley, Green Valley
Tarango, Florentino, St. Anthony of Padua, Casa Grande
Tellez, Frank J., St. Rose of Lima, Safford
Terry, John, Holy Cross, Morenci
Tighe, Thomas P., Our Mother of Sorrows, Tucson
Valenzuela, Carlos, St. Augustine Cathedral, Tucson
Vega, Rodolfo, Sacred Heart, Nogales
Vidal, Rafael, St. Francis of Assisi, Yuma
Vigil, William, St. Francis de Sales, Tucson
Wagner, Thomas, St. Pius X, Tucson
Welsh, Paul J., Jr., Our Mother of Sorrows, Tucson, Diocesan Scout Chap.
Williams, Miguel, Immaculate Conception, Yuma
Yanez, Jesus L. "Chuy", St. Francis of Assisi, Superior

INSTITUTIONS LOCATED IN THE DIOCESE

[A] HIGH SCHOOLS

TUCSON. *Salpointe Catholic High School*, 1545 E. Copper St., 85719. Tel: 520-327-6581; Fax: 520-327-8477. Priory, 1540 E. Glenn St., 85719. Tel: 520-325-1537. Carmelite Order. Revs. Simon Kenny, O.Carm., Prin.; Roy Conry, O.Carm., Prior; Foster Hanley, O.Carm.; Brad Peterson, O.Carm. Brothers 2; Sisters 7; Lay Teachers 80; Students 1,392.

[B] HIGH SCHOOLS, PRIVATE

TUCSON. *Immaculate Heart High School*, 625 E. Magee Rd., 85704. Tel: 520-297-2851. Sr. Luisa Sanchez, I.H.M., Prin. Sisters of the Immaculate Heart of Mary 4; Lay Teachers 13; Students 108.

NOGALES. *Our Lady of Lourdes High School*, 555 Patagonia Rd., P.O. Box 1865, 85628. Tel: 520-287-5659; Fax: 520-287-2910. Sr. Barbara Monsequr, C.F.F.M., Prin.; Rev. Francis McCarthy, O.Carm., Chap. Priests 1; Minim Daughters of Mary Immaculate 5; Lay Teachers 12; Students 85.

[C] ELEMENTARY SCHOOLS, PRIVATE

TUCSON. *Immaculate Heart Academy*, 410 E. Magee Rd., 85704. Tel: 520-297-6672; Fax: 520-297-9152. Sr. M. Evelyn Soto, I.H.M., Prin. Sisters of the Immaculate Heart of Mary 4; Lay Teachers 16; Students 300.

[D] CATHOLIC COMMUNITY SERVICES

TUCSON. *Catholic Community Service of Southern Arizona, Inc.*, 155 S. Helen, 85703. Tel: 520-623-0344. Mailing Address: P.O. Box 5746, 85703. Rebecca Barnard, Corp. Board Pres.; Mr. John E. Cotter, M.S., CEO; John M. Schubert, Dir. Admin. Services.

Social Service Agencies: Pima County. (Including City of Tucson), 155 W. Helen St., Box 5746, 85703. Tel: 520-623-0344. Ronald A. Dankowski, Ph.D., Exec. Dir.

St. Nicholas of Myra Adoption Program, 899 N. Wilmot, No. C-4, 85711. Tel: 520-745-8791. Nancy Larison, C.I.S.W., Prog. Dir.

Catholic Community Services of Cochise County, 19 Howell Ave., Bisbee, 85603. Mr. Frank McDonough, M.S., Exec. Dir.

Migration and Refugee Services, 155 W. Helen, P.O. Box 5746, 85703. Tel: 520-623-0344. Loretta Tracy, M.S.W., Admin.

Santa Cruz Project, 2109 S. Sixth Ave., 85713. Tel: 520-623-0344. Sr. M. Teresa Apalategui, O.P., M.S.W., Admin.

Westside Nutrition Services, P.O. Box 5746, 85703. Tel: 520-623-0344. Ms. Linda Hutchings, M.S.R.D., Admin.

Merilac Lodge and Casa de Crianza, P.O. Box 5746, 85703. Tel: 520-623-0344. Sr. Mary Ann Bogosoff, C.S.A., Dir.

Immigration Counseling Service, 155 W. Helen St., 85703. Tel: 520-623-0344. Francisco Hoyos, Dir.

Field Offices:

Gila County Case Management, 175 E. Cedar St., Globe, 85501. Tel: 520-425-5130. Sherlyn Harris, M.A., C.O.G.

Catholic Community Services in Western Arizona, Yuma, 85364. Tel: 520-783-3308. Ms. Diana Murack, Exec. Dir.

Chaplaincy-Pastoral Ministry to Non-Denominational Nursing Homes, 155 W. Helen, 85703. Tel: 520-623-0344, Ext. 3058. Sr. Carolyn Nicolai, F.S.P., Coord.; Rev. Angelo Mastria, O.Carm., Chap.

Community Outreach Program for the Deaf, 268 W. Adams, 85705. Tel: 520-623-0344. Mrs. Marguerite Harmon, M.S.R., Exec. Dir.

St. Elizabeth of Hungary Out-Patient Clinic, 140 W. Speedway, 85705. Tel: 520-628-7871. Sr. Barbara Anne Stowasser, C.S.J., Exec. Dir.

Mobile Podiatry, Dentures and Eyeglasses Clinic, 140 W. Speedway Blvd., 85705. Tel: 520-628-7871.

Minority Liaison Agencies:

Pio Decimo Neighborhood Center, 848 S. 7th Ave., 85701. Tel: 520-622-2801. Margaret Kish, M.S.W., Exec. Dir

Project Ayuda, 155 W. Helen, Box 5746, 85703. Robert Cowles, M.S.W., Pro. Dir.

Independent Allied Community Agencies Mobile Meals of Tucson, 155 W. Helen, P.O. Box 5746, 85703. Kay Nixon, Prog. Dir.

[E] GENERAL HOSPITALS

TUCSON. *Carondelet Health Care Corporation of Arizona, Inc.*, 1601 W. St. Mary's Rd., 85745-2682.

For a complete listing, refer to the Hospitals section.

St. Elizabeth of Hungary Out-Patient Clinic, 140 W. Speedway Blvd., 85705. Tel: 520-628-7871.

For a complete listing, refer to the Hospitals section.

NOGALES. *Holy Cross Hospital, Inc.*, 1171 W. Target Range Rd., 85621. Tel: 520-287-2771; Fax: 520-287-7314.

For a complete listing, refer to the Hospitals section.

[F] MONASTERIES AND RESIDENCES OF PRIESTS AND BROTHERS

TUCSON. *Carmelite Priory*, 1540 E. Glenn St., 85719. Tel: 520-325-1537. Revs. Angelo Mastria, O. Carm., Prior; Simon Kenny, O.Carm., Prin.; Very Rev. Ronald Oakham, O. Carm., Western Commissary Provincial; Revs. Roy Conry, O.Carm.; Foster Hanley, O.Carm.; Vernon Malley; Bradley Peterson, O. Carm.; Bros. Thomas Schrader, O.Carm.; Gerald Willick, O.Carm.; Christopher Kulig, O.Carm. Fathers and Brothers at Salpointe Catholic High School. Priests 7; Brothers 3.

Discalced Carmelite Fathers of St. Margaret's, 801 N. Grande Ave., 85745. Tel: 520-622-0168. Revs. Gilbert Levario, O.C.D.; Bernard Perkins, O.C.D.; Kevin McArdle, O.C.D.

Jesuit Community of the Vatican Observatory, 2017 E. Lee St., 85719. Tel: 520-795-9866. Jesuit Residence. Revs. William Stoeger, S.J.; Joseph E. Henry, S.J., Vice Supr.; Richard P. Boyle, S.J.; George V. Coyne, S.J., Dir. Vatican Observatory; Martin F. McCarthy, S.J.; Bro. Guy Consolmagno, S.J.

**Vatican Observatory Foundation.*

Offices of The Vatican Observatory, Steward Observatory, The University of Arizona, 85721. Tel: 520-621-3225.

Kino House, 2844 E. 1st St., 85716. Tel: 520-327-7130. Jesuit Fathers residence. Rev. Charles W. Polzer, S.J., Supr., University of Arizona, Arizona State Museum, 85721. Tel: 520-621-6278. Rev. Christopher Corbally, S.J. (Vatican), Steward Observatory, University of Arizona. Tel: 520-621-3225.

Regina Cleri Center, 8800 E. 22nd St, 85710. Tel: 520-886-5223. Revs. Carlos Cocio; Armando Garzon-Blanco; John P. Lyons; James Modeen; Albert E. Verbrugghe; Rev. Msgr. Walter F. Rosensweig. In res., Most Rev. Francis A. Quinn, Bishop Emeritus of Sacramento, Domestic Department. Sisters of the Oblates of St. Martha 4.

Society of the Divine Word, 8 Tucson Ter., 85745. Tel: 520-791-2750.

CORTARO. *Desert House of Prayer*, 7350 W. Picture Rocks Rd., Box 574, 85652. Tel: 520-744-3825. Rev. John W. Kane, C.Ss.R.

ST. DAVID. *Holy Trinity Monastery*, P.O. Box 298, 85630. Tel: 520-720-4642; 720-4016. Benedictines. Revs. Louis B. Hasenfuss, O.S.B., Prior; Alcuin M. Almasy, O.S.B.; Lawrence M. Fedor, O.S.B.; Henri Capdeville, O.S.B.; Alexander Mills, O.S.B.; Bartolome Johnson, O.S.B. Professed 12; Novices 1; Postulants 2. Benedictine Sisters of Our Lady of Mount Olivet. Perpetually Professed 1.

SONOITA. *The Benedictine Monastery of Erlac in Sonoita*, P.O. Box 534, 85637. Tel: 520-394-2961. Rt. Rev. James R. Straif.

[G] CONVENTS AND RESIDENCES FOR SISTERS

TUCSON. *Benedictine Monastery*, 800 N. Country Club Rd., 85716. Tel: 520-325-6401. Sisters 22.

Carondelet Community, 6571 E. Carondelet Dr., 85710. Tel: 520-721-3832. Sisters 5.

Cathedral Convent, 435 S. 6th Ave., 85701. Sisters 4.

Guadalupe Community, 1833 W. St. Mary's Rd., 85745-2653. Tel: 520-620-4944. Sr. St. Charles Benton, C.S.J. Sisters 5.

Immaculate Heart Lodge Convent, 410 E. Magee Rd., 85704. Tel: 520-297-0704. Sr. Mary Evelyn Soto, I.H.M.; Sr. Barbara Ann Gamboa, I.H.M., Supr. Sisters of the Immaculate Heart of Mary 7.

Masmitja Hall Community, 410 E. Magee Rd., 85704. Tel: 520-297-8961. Sr. Wilhelmine Galle, Supr. Sisters of the Immaculate Heart of Mary 5.

Immaculate Heart Novititate, 4100 N. Sabino Canyon Rd., 85715. Tel: 520-885-4981. Sr. M. Dominic Pacheco, I.H.M., Novice Mistress. Sisters of the Immaculate Heart of Mary 2.

Immaculate Heart of Mary Provincial House, 4100 N. Sabino Canyon Rd., 85715. Tel: 520-886-4273. Sr. Alice Marie Martinez, I.H.M., Prov. Supr.; Sr. Evelyn Soto, I.H.M. Sisters of the Immaculate Heart of Mary 3.

Immaculate Heart Religious Center, 35 E. 15th St., 85701. Tel: 520-624-7221. Sr. Vivian Gallegos, I.H.M., Supr. Sisters of the Immaculate Heart of Mary 3.

Maria Community, 1835 W. St. Mary's Rd., 85745-2653. Tel: 520-620-4940. Sr. St. Joan Willert, C.S.J., Contact Person. Sisters 14.

Regina Cleri Convent, 8800 E. 22nd St., 85710. Tel: 520-296-9077. Sisters of the Oblates of St. Martha 4.

St. Ann Convent, 4100 Sabino Canyon Rd., 85715. Tel: 520-298-0064. Sr. M. Julian Valdez, Supr. Sisters of the Immaculate Heart of Mary 12.

St. Joseph Community, 6569 E. Carondelet Community, 85710. Tel: 520-721-3816.

Saints Peter and Paul Convent, 1947 E. Adams St., 85719. Tel: 520-325-2234.

San Xavier Mission, 1950 W. San Xavier Rd., 85746. Tel: 520-294-2624.

Sisters of the Holy Cross, 535 E. Drachman, 85705. Tel: 520-622-7902. 355 San Carlos Ave., San Carlos, 85550. Sisters 4.

DOUGLAS. *Loretto Convent*, 1200 - 14th St., 85607; Fax: 520-364-3645. Sr. Marina, O.C.D.

FLORENCE. *Chapel of the Gila*. (Historical Site), 255 E. 8th St., 85232. Mailing Address: P.O. Box 550, 85232-0550.

GLOBE. *Holy Angels Convent*, 1300 E. Cedar, 85501. Tel: 520-425-2034. Union of the Sisters of the P.B.V.M.

NOGALES. *Our Lady of Lourdes High School*, P.O. Box 1865, 85628-1865; Fax: 520-287-5659. Minim Daughters of Mary Immaculate C.F.M.M. 11.

St. Joseph Convent, 1175 W. Target Range Rd., 85621. Tel: 520-287-7139. Sr. Celia Ma. Ponce, C.F.M.M., Supr. Minim Daughters of Mary Immaculate C.F.M.M. 10.

SOMERTON. *Immaculate Heart of Mary Convent*, P.O. Box 2888, 85340.

SONOITA. *Santa Rita Abbey*, HC 1, Box 929, 85637-9705. Tel: 520-455-5595. Cistercian Nuns of the Strict Observance, O.C.S.O. Mother M. Beverly Aitken, O.C.S.O., Prioress. Solemn Professed 10; Simple Professed 3; Novices 1.

TOPAWA. *St. Catherine Convent*, P.O. Box 209, 85639. Sr. Karen Krahenbuhl, O.S.F., Contact Person, Village Ministry Services. Sisters 5.

YUMA. *Immaculate Conception Convent*, 500 - 24th Ave., 85364. Tel: 520-783-5224. Sisters 10.

[H] RETREAT HOUSES

TUCSON. *Redemptorist Picture Rocks Retreat*, 7101 W. Picture Rocks Rd., 85743. Tel: 520-744-3400. Mailing Address: P.O. Box 569, Cortaro, 85652. Revs. Patrick O'Brien, C.SS.R.; Thomas Danielsen, C.SS.R.

[I] NEWMAN CENTERS

TUCSON. *University of Arizona*, St. Thomas More Newman Student Center, 1615 E. 2nd St., 85719. Tel: 520-327-6662; Fax: 520-327-6559. Revs. Albert Felice-Pace, O.P., Supr.; Fred Lucci, O.P.; Bro. Bryan Kromholtz, O.P.; Sr. Kathleen Rose, O.P. In res., Rev. Robert A. Burns, O.P.; Sr. Carol Monzon, O.P.; Sr. Patricia Walsh, O.P.

CASA GRANDE. *Central Arizona College, Holy Family Newman Center*, P.O. Box 12335, 85230-2335. Tel: 520-836-0601. Rev. Steven G. Stencil, Chap.

DOUGLAS. *Cochise Community College*, St. Luke, 1211 15th St., 85607. Rev. James M. Hobert, Jr.; Janet Fullen, Admin.; Ray Nadolny, Dir.

THATCHER. *Eastern Arizona Junior College*, 85552. Rev. Antony Navarria, St. Rose of Lima, 311 Central Ave., Tucson. Tel: 520-428-4920. Cecilia Roudeluesh, Pres., Newman Sustaining Board; Linda Hedges, Dir., Newman Assoc.

[J] MISCELLANEOUS LISTINGS

TUCSON. *Carondelet Foundation*, 350 N. Wilmot, 85710. Tel: 520-513-0875. Jannie Fernandez, Exec.Dir. Tel: 520-721-3853.

Casa de los Ninos Crisis Center, 1101 N. 4th Ave., 85705. Tel: 520-624-5600; Fax: 520-623-2443. Jeanne Landdeck-Sisco, Exec. Dir.; Sr. Kathleen Clark, C.S.J., Founding Dir. Emeritus.

Casa Maria, 401 E. 26th St., 85713. Tel: 520-624-0312. Mr. Brian Flagg, Contact Person.

Christ Child Society of Tucson, P.O. Box 36212, 85740-6212. Tel: 520-297-8437. Joan Flaharty, Pres.; Pilar Fabula, Vice Pres.; Ann Marie Friend, Sec.; Kathryn Bossuyt, Treas.

Diocese of Tucson Catholic Cemeteries. (Sole Corporation), 3555 N. Oracle Rd., 85705. Tel: 520-888-0860; Fax: 520-887-7360. Regis J. Flaherty, Contact Person.

Integrated Auxiliaries The Friends of John Paul II Foundation. Dr. S.F. Poray-Tucholski, Pres., 10121 Prairie Hills Cir., Sun City, 85352. Dr. E.J. Bratkowsha-Kendall, Vice Pres./Treas., 5611 E. Rochridge Dr., Phoenix, 85018. Czeslaw A. Kozdroj, Esq., 10347 Campana Dr., Sun City, 85351. Mrs. Jacquelina M. Poray-Tucholski, 10121 Prairie Hills Cir., Sun City, 85351.

Knights of Columbus, 9019 E. Palms Park Dr., 85715. Tel: 520-886-7609. Mr. John H. Cardellina, Past State Deputy; Mr. John W. Tobin, State Deputy, 13621 N. 51st Pl., Scottsdale 85254. Tel: 602-996-6192; 870-1600.

Magnificat - Tucson Chapter, 2560 N. Via San Juanito, 85749. Tel: 520-749-0633. Mrs. L. J. Elizabeth Celenza, Pres. A ministry to Catholic women.

St. Nicholas Indian Center, 349 W. 31st St., 85713. Tel: 520-622-5363; 792-0230. Revs. Daniel P. McLaughlin, S.T.; Abram E. Dono, S.T.; Bro. David T. Sommer, S.T.

Society of St. Vincent de Paul, 829 S. 6th Ave., 85701. Tel: 520-628-7837.

ST. DAVID. *San Pedro Valley Center for the Arts*, Holy Trinity Monastery, Box 160, 85630. Tel: 520-720-4009. Patricia J. Don, Contact Person.

[K] DIOCESAN CEMETERIES

TUCSON. *Holy Hope Cemetery and Mausoleum*, Office, 3555 N. Oracle Rd., P.O. Box 5158, 85703. Tel: 520-888-0860. Mr. Regis Flaherty, Admin.

Our Lady of the Desert Cemetery and Mausoleum, Office, 2151 S. Avenida Los Reyes, P.O. Box 5158, 85703. Tel: 520-885-9173.

RELIGIOUS INSTITUTES OF MEN REPRESENTED IN THE DIOCESE

For further details refer to the corresponding bracketed number in the Religious Institutes of Men or Women sections.

[0200]—*Benedictine Monks*.—O.S.B.
[0470]—*The Capuchin Friars*. (Prov. of St. Joseph).—O.F.M.Cap.
[0270]—*Carmelite Fathers and Brothers*. (Prov. of Most Pure Heart of Mary).—O.Carm.
[0360]—*Claretian Missionaries*.—C.M.F.
[1320]—*Clerics of St. Viator*.—C.S.V.
[1330]—*Congregation of the Mission*.—C.M.
[0260]—*Discalced Carmelites*. (Angol-Irish Prov.).—O.C.D.
[0520]—*Franciscan Friars*.—O.F.M.
[0650]—*Holy Ghost Fathers*. (Western Prov.).—C.S.Sp.
[0690]—*Jesuit Fathers and Brothers*. (Western Prov.).—S.J.
[0720]—*The Missionaries of Our Lady La Salette*. (Immaculate Heart of Mary Prov.).—M.S.
[0840]—*Missionary Servants of the Most Holy Trinity*.—S.T.
[0910]—*Oblates of Mary Immaculate*.—O.M.I.
[0430]—*Order of Preachers (Dominicans)*.—O.P.
[1030]—*Paulist Fathers*.—C.S.P.
[1070]—*Redemptorist Fathers*. (Oakland Prov.).—C.SS.R.
[1240]—*Servites*.—O.S.M.
[1200]—*Society of the Divine Savior*.—S.D.S.
[0420]—*Society of the Divine Word*.—S.V.D.
[1060]—*Society of the Precious Blood*.—C.PP.S.

RELIGIOUS INSTITUTES OF WOMEN REPRESENTED IN THE DIOCESE

[0100]—*Adorers of the Blood of Christ*.—A.S.C.
[0233]—*Benedictine Nuns*.—O.S.B.
[0230]—*Benedictine Sisters of Pontifical Jurisdiction*.—O.S.B.
[0370]—*Carmelite Sisters of the Most Sacred Heart of Los Angeles*.—O.C.D.
[0670]—*Cistercian Nuns of the Strict Observance*.—O.C.S.O.
[0700]—*Company of Mary*.—O.D.N.
[0220]—*Congregation of the Benedictine Sisters of Perpetual Adoration of Pontifical Jurisdiction*.—O.S.B.
[0460]—*Congregation of the Sisters of Charity of the Incarnate Word*.—C.C.V.I.
[3710]—*Congregation of the Sisters of St. Agnes*.—C.S.A.
[1920]—*Congregation of the Sisters of the Holy Cross*.—C.S.C.
[1780]—*Congregation of the Sisters of the Third Order of St. Francis of Perpetual Adoration*.—F.S.P.A.
[1710]—*Congregation of the Third Order of St. Francis of Mary Immaculate, Joliet, IL*.—O.S.F.
[1070-03]—*Dominican Sisters*.—O.P.
[1070-09]—*Dominican Sisters*.—O.P.
[1070-12]—*Dominican Sisters*.—O.P.
[1070-13]—*Dominican Sisters*.—O.P.
[1070-30]—*Dominican Sisters*.—O.P.
[1140]—*Eucharistic Missionaries of St. Dominic*.—O.P.
[1230]—*Franciscan Sisters of Christian Charity*.—O.S.F.
[1310]—*Franciscan Sisters of Little Falls, Minnesota*.—O.S.F.
[1425]—*Franciscan Sisters of Peace*.—F.S.P.
[2575]—*Institute of the Sisters of Mercy of the Americas*.—R.S.M.
[2490]—*Medical Mission Sisters*.—S.C.M.M.
[2675]—*Minim Daughters of Mary Immaculate*.—C.F.M.M.
[2720]—*Mission Helpers of the Sacred Heart*.—M.H.S.H.
[]—*Missionary Sisters of the Immaculate Conception*. (Montreal, Canada).—M.I.C.
[]—*Oblates of St. Martha*.—O.S.M.
[3130]—*Our Lady of Victory Missionary Sisters*.—O.L.V.M.
[3300]—*Presentation Sisters of the Blessed Virgin*.—P.B.V.M.
[]—*Religious of St. Joseph of Australia*.—R.S.J.
[2970]—*School Sisters of Notre Dame*.—S.S.N.D.
[1680]—*School Sisters of St. Francis*.—S.S.S.F.-O.S.F.
[3580]—*Servants of Mary*.—O.S.M.
[3590]—*Servants of Mary (Servite Sisters)*.—O.S.M.
[3500]—*Servants of the Blessed Sacrament*.—S.S.S.
[]—*Seton Sisters of Our Lady of Guadalupe, Tucson*.—S.S.LOG.
[3620]—*Sister Servants of Mary Immaculate*.—S.S.M.I.
[0440]—*Sisters of Charity of Cincinnati, Ohio*.—S.C.
[480]—*Sisters of Charity of Leavenworth, Kansas*.—S.C.L.
[0570]—*Sisters of Charity of Seton Hill, Greensburg, Pennsylvania*.—S.C.
[3720]—*Sisters of Notre Dame de Namur*.—S.N.D.deN.
[3720]—*Sisters of St. Anne*.—S.S.A.
[1705]—*The Sisters of St. Francis of Assisi*.—O.S.F.
[1800]—*Sisters of St. Francis of the Third Order Regular (Williamsville, New York)*.—O.S.F.
[3830-06]—*Sisters of St. Joseph*.—S.S.J.
[3830-13]—*Sisters of St. Joseph*.—C.S.J.
[3840]—*Sisters of St. Joseph of Carondelet*.—C.S.J.
[0260]—*The Sisters of the Blessed Sacrament for Indians and Colored People*.—S.B.S.
[1030]—*Sisters of the Divine Savior*.—S.D.S.
[1990]—*Sisters of the Holy Names of Jesus and Mary*.—S.N.J.M.

[2110]—*Sisters of the Humility of Mary*.—H.M.

[3270]—*Sisters of the Most Precious Blood*.—C.PP.S.

[3260]—*Sisters of the Precious Blood*. (Dayton, Ohio).—C.PP.S.

[3320]—*Sisters of the Presentation of the Blesssed Virgin Mary*.—P.B.V.M.

[1720]—*Sisters of the Third Order Regular of St. Francis of the Congregation of Our Lady of Lourdes*.—O.S.F.

[2090]—*Sisters, Home Visitors fo Mary*.—H.V.M.

[2150]—*Sisters, Servants of the Immaculate Heart of Mary*. (Monroe).—I.H.M.

NECROLOGY

† Carr, Frank M., Yuma, AZ, St. Francis of Assisi. —Died Feb. 7, 1996.

† Debski, John, Solomon, AZ, Our Lady of Guadalupe. —Died Oct. 7, 1996.

† Doyle, Thomas A., Tombstone, AZ, Sacred Heart. —Died May 4, 1996.

Diocese of Tulsa

(Dioecesis Tulsensis)

Most Reverend

EDWARD J. SLATTERY

Bishop of Tulsa; ordained January 6, 1994 in Rome; installed January 12, 1994.

ESTABLISHED FEBRUARY 7, 1973.

Square Miles 26,417.

The Diocese of Tulsa comprises the following 31 Counties: Adair, Atoka, Bryan, Cherokee, Choctaw, Coal, Craig, Creek, Delaware, Haskell, Hughes, Latimer, LeFlore, McCurtain, McIntosh, Mayes, Muskogee, Nowata, Okfuskee, Okmulgee, Osage, Ottawa, Pawnee, Payne, Pittsburg, Pushmataha, Rogers, Sequoyah, Tulsa, Wagoner and Washington.

For legal titles of parishes and institutions, consult the Chancery Office.

Chancery Office: P.O. Box 2009, Tulsa, OK, 74101. Tel.: 918-587-3115; Fax: 918-587-6692.

Web site address: http:www.galstar.com/~rctulsa/int/

E-mail address: chantul@aol.com

STATISTICAL OVERVIEW

Personnel	
Bishop	1
Priests: Diocesan Active in Diocese	62
Priests: Active Outside Diocese	7
Priests: Retired, Sick or Absent	11
Number of Diocesan Priests	80
Religious Priests in Diocese	17
Extern Priests in Diocese	5
Ordinations:	
Diocesan Priests	3
Permanent Deacons	2
Permanent Deacons in Diocese	42
Total Brothers	5
Total Sisters	105
Parishes	
Parishes	80
With Resident Pastor:	
Resident Diocesan Priests	43
Resident Religious Priests	4
Without Resident Pastor:	
Administered by Priests	32
Administered by Permanent Deacons	1
Welfare	
Catholic Hospitals	2
Total Assisted	275,868
Homes for the Aged	1
Total Assisted	128
Specialized Homes	2
Total Assisted	87
Special Centers for Social Services	3
Total Assisted	36,232
Educational	
Diocesan Students in Other Seminaries	12
Total Seminarians	12
High Schools, Diocesan and Parish	1
Total Students	853
High Schools, Private	1
Total Students	567
Elementary Schools, Diocesan and Parish	10
Total Students	2,288
Elementary Schools, Private	1
Total Students	1,112
Catechesis/Religious Education:	
High School Students	1,538
Elementary Students	6,254
Total Students Under Catholic Instruction	12,624
Teachers in the Diocese:	
Priests	9
Brothers	3
Sisters	13
Lay Teachers	350
Vital Statistics	
Receptions into the Church:	
Infant Baptism Totals	1,005
Adult Baptism Totals	199
Received into Full Communion	298
First Communions	1,002
Confirmations	627
Marriages:	
Catholic	158
Interfaith	233
Total Marriages	391
Deaths	424
Total Catholic Population	52,255
Total Population	1,447,927

Former Bishops—Most Rev. BERNARD J. GANTER, D.D., ord. May 22, 1952; appt. Bishop of Tulsa, Dec. 19, 1972; ord. Feb. 7, 1973; transferred to Beaumont, Oct. 18, 1977.—Most Rev. EUSEBIUS J. BELTRAN, ord. May 14, 1960; appt. Bishop of Tulsa, Feb. 28, 1978; ord. April 20, 1978; transferred to Archdiocese of Oklahoma City, Nov. 24, 1992.

Vicar General—Rev. Msgr. DENNIS C. DORNEY.

Chancery Office—*111 W. Main, Ste. 400, Tulsa, 74103., Mailing Address: P.O. Box 2009, Tulsa, 74101.* Tel: 918-587-3115; Fax: 918-587-6692. Office Hours: Mon.-Fri. 9-5.

Chancellor—Dr. EDWARD L. MAILLET, D.S.W.

Vice Chancellor—Rev. PATRICK J. GAALAAS.

Financial Administrator—Mr. PHILIP J. CREIDER, *P.O. Box 2009, Tulsa, 74101.* Tel: 918-587-3115.

Diocesan Senators—Most Rev. EDWARD J. SLATTERY; Rev. Msgr. DENNIS C. DORNEY, V.G.; Revs. PATRICK J. GAALAAS; CHRISTOPHER DAIGLE; TIMOTHY J. DALEY; J. PAUL DONOVAN; PAUL E. EICHHOFF; GREGORY A. GIER; WILLIAM HAMILL, O.S.A.; BERNARD C. JEWITT; MARTIN J. MORGAN; DANIEL H. MUEGGENBORG; TAM N. NGUYEN; ROBERT T. SCHLITT; JOE C. TOWNSEND.

Ex Officio—Rev. Msgr. DENNIS C. DORNEY.

Diocesan Consultors—Revs. PAUL E. EICHHOFF; PATRICK J. GAALAAS; BERNARD C. JEWITT; ROBERT T. SCHLITT; Rev. Msgr. DENNIS C. DORNEY; Revs. DANIEL H. MUEGGENBORG; TAM N. NGUYEN.

Diocesan Marriage Tribunal—

Judicial Vicar—Rev. JOHN J. WADE.

Defender of the Bond—Rev. MICHAEL J. KNIPE, J.C.L.

Judges—Deacon KASPER E. WEIGANT; Rev. DANIEL H. MUEGGENBORG, S.T.L.

Accessory Auditor—Deacon GARY D. WALSH.

Interdiocesan Tribunal of Second Instance for Province of Oklahoma City—

Vice-Judicial Vicar—Rev. TAM N. NGUYEN, J.C.L.

Judges—Rev. Msgr. JAMES F. HALPINE; Rev. DANIEL A. PERLINSKI.

Defender of the Bond—Revs. THOMAS P. BILLER; WILLIAM J. SWIFT; JAMES D. WHITE.

Notary—Mrs. MARY JONES.

Priests' Personnel Committee—Rev. Msgr. DENNIS C. DORNEY, V.G.; Revs. J. RICHARD BRADLEY; PAUL E. EICHHOFF; PATRICK J. GAALAAS; GREGORY A. GIER.

Seminary Board—Rev. Msgr. DENNIS C. DORNEY, V.G.; Mr. ROBERT J. LAFORTUNE; Revs. TIMOTHY L. DAVISON; DANIEL H. MUEGGENBORG; JOE C. TOWNSEND.

Federation of Religious of the Diocese of Tulsa—Leadership Team: Sr. MARILYN NORWOOD, O.S.B.; Sr. EUGENIA BROWN, O.S.B., *P.O. Box 2009, Tulsa, 74101.* Tel: 918-587-3115.

Diocesan Offices

Archivist—Mrs. MARY JONES, *P.O. Box 2009, Tulsa, 74101.* Tel: 918-587-3115.

Campaign for Human Development—Dr. EDWARD L. MAILLET, *P.O. Box 2009, Tulsa, 74101.* Tel: 918-587-3115.

Campus Ministry—Rev. TIMOTHY L. DAVISON; Mrs. ELINOR HOAR, Sec. DEE BARLOW, *Campus Ministry, The University of Tulsa, 440 S. Florence, Tulsa, 74104.* Tel: 918-599-0204. Rev. JOE C. TOWNSEND, *201 N. Knoblock St., Stillwater, 74074.* Tel: 405-372-6408., *Oklahoma State University, 201 N. Knoblock St., Stillwater, 74075.* Tel: 405-372-6408.

Catholic Charities of the Diocese of Tulsa—Mrs. HAZEL LEITCH, Dir., *739 N. Denver, Tulsa, 74106.* Tel: 918-585-8167.

Cemetery—Mr. JACK CHARON, Dir., *P.O. Box 2009, Tulsa, 74101.* Tel: 918-587-3115. Mr. JAMES LIICHOW, Supvr., *Calvary Cemetery, 91st and Harvard, Tulsa, 74136.* Tel: 918-299-7348.

Clergy Education—Rev. DANIEL MUEGGENBORG, *P.O. Box 2009, Tulsa, 74101.* Tel: 918-587-3115.

Diocesan Catholic Committee on Scouting—Mr. JOHN D. KNECHT, Dir., *18144 E. 95th St., North Owasso, 74055.* Tel: 918-272-5483.

Diocesan Council of Catholic Women—Rev. Msgr. JAMES F. HALPINE, *P.O. Box 3204, Tulsa, 74101.* Tel: 918-582-6274.

Ecumenism—Rev. BERNARD C. JEWITT, Dir., *4001 E. 101st St. S., Tulsa, 74137.*

Education—Rev. DANIEL H. MUEGGENBORG, Vicar of Religious Education, *P.O. Box 2009, Tulsa, 74101.* Tel: 918-587-3115.

Family Life Office—Mr. TIMOTHY J. SULLIVAN, Dir., *739 N. Denver, Tulsa, 74106.* Tel: 918-585-8167., *P.O. Box 6429, Tulsa, 74148.*

Parochial Schools—Mrs. ARDEN GLENN, Supt. Catholic Schools, *P.O. Box 2009, Tulsa, 74101.* Tel: 918-587-3115.

Diocesan Pastoral Board—

Health Affairs—Rev. KENNETH HEBERLEIN, Dir. Pastoral Care & Health Affairs, *1923 S. Utica, Tulsa, 74104.* Tel: 918-744-2689.

Hispanic Ministry—Rev. PATRICK BRANKIN, Dir., *1541 E. Newton Pl., Tulsa, 74106.* Tel: 918-584-2424.

Historian—Rev. JAMES D. WHITE, *P.O. Box 2009, Tulsa, 74101.*

Holy Childhood Association—Rev. DANIEL C. KEOHANE, Dir., *Sacred Heart Church, 1777 E. Grayson St., Sapulpa, 74066.*

Pastoral Studies Institute—Ms. MONICA SKRZYPCZAK, Coord., *P.O. Box 2009, Tulsa, 74101.* Tel: 918-587-3115.

Office of Divine Worship—Rev. JAMES D. WHITE, Dir.

Newspaper "Eastern Oklahoma Catholic"—Mr. JAMES SELLARS, Editor, *P.O. Box 520, Tulsa, 74101.* Tel: 918-587-3115.

Office of Permanent Diaconate—Rev. J. RICHARD BRADLEY, Dir.; Sr. MARIE AMANDA ALLARD, O.P., Dir. Formation, *P.O. Box 2009, Tulsa, 74101.* Tel: 918-587-3115.

Propagation of Faith—Rev. MATTHEW J. GERLACH, Coord., *2200 W. Ithica, Broken Arrow, 74012.* Tel: 918-455-4451.

Guatemala Mission—Mikatokla, Santiago Atitlan, Dept. Solola, Guatemala, Central America.

Stewardship and Development—Mr. JON CALDER, Dir., *P.O. Box 2009, Tulsa, 74101.* Tel: 918-587-3115.

Vocations—Rev. TIMOTHY L. DAVIDSON, 440 S. Florence: *Tulsa, 74104.* Tel: 918-599-0204.

Catholic Student Ministries—440 South Florence, Tulsa, 74104. Tel: 918-599-0204.

Young Adult Ministry—Mr. CHARLES MICHIE, *P.O. Box 2009, Tulsa, 74101.* Tel: 918-587-3115.

Youth Ministry—Mr. CHARLES MICHIE, *P.O. Box 2009, Tulsa, 74101.* Tel: 918-587-3115.

CLERGY, PARISHES, MISSIONS AND PAROCHIAL SCHOOLS

CITY OF TULSA
(Tulsa County)

1—HOLY FAMILY CATHEDRAL (1899), Rev. Msgr. James F. Halpine; Revs. Gary Sherman; Khiet Nguyen; Sr. Eugenia Brown, O.S.B., Pastoral Assoc. & D.R.E. In res., Rev. Donald W. Brooks.
Res., 122 W. 8th St., P.O. Box 3204, 74101. Tel: 918-582-6247; Fax: 918-599-8334. [JC]
Catechesis/Religious Programs—Fax: 918-599-8334.
Students 240.

2—ST. AUGUSTINE'S (1955), Rev. Alex Kennedy; Sr. Phyllis Vaske, O.S.F., Pastoral Asst.; Deacon Theodore Prudhomme.
Res., 633 E. Marshall Pl., 74106. Tel: 918-587-2965.
Convent—Tel: 918-425-3642.

3—ST. BERNARD OF CLAIRVAUX (1978), Revs. Bernard C. Jewitt; Patrick W. Eastman; Sr. Diane Langford, C.D.P., Pastoral Min.; Deacons Richard Campbell; John Hancock; Alan Mikell.
Res., 4001 E. 101st St., 74137. Tel: 918-299-9406; Fax: 918-299-7796.
Catechesis/Religious Programs—Sharon Lechtenberg, D.R.E.
Students 757.

4—ST. CATHERINE (1925), Rev. Christopher P. Daigle; Deacons Bill Coburn; Sid Starr.
Res., 4532 S. 25th Ave., 74107. Tel: 918-446-8124; Fax: 918-446-4506. [JC]
School—2515 W. 46th St., 74107. Tel: 918-446-9756.
Sisters of St. Francis of the Martyr St. George 4; Lay Teachers 8; Students 140.

5—CHRIST THE KING (1917), Revs. Martin Morgan; Ken Harder; Sr. Connie Lennartz, O.P.; Sr. Joan Duerst, Pastoral Asst.; Deacon Loren Luschen.
Office: 1520 S. Rockford Ave., 74120. Tel: 918-584-4788; 4789; Fax: 918-584-0055.
Res., 1530 S. Rockford Ave., 74120. Tel: 918-584-6693. [JC]
Christ the King Board of Education Endowment Trust—.
School—Marquette School, 1519 S. Quincy, 74120. Tel: 918-584-4631; Fax: 918-584-0055. James J. Pohlman, Prin.
Lay Teachers 26; Students 381.
Catechesis/Religious Programs—Students 160.

6—ST. FRANCIS XAVIER-OUR LADY OF GUADALUPE (1926 (Hispanic), Revs. Timothy L. Davison; Steve Bonian, S.J.; Forrest O'Brien; Deacon Felix DeLeon.
Res., 2515 E. 1st St., 74104. Tel: 918-592-6770. [JC]
Church—2510 E. Admiral Blvd., 74150.
Catechesis/Religious Programs—Teresa Sotelo, D.R.E.
Students 90.

7—IMMACULATE CONCEPTION (1923). Unassigned.
Mailing Address: P.O. Box 2009, 74101.

8—ST. JOSEPH CHURCH (1977) (Vietnamese), Rev. Hoang Viet Le.
Res., 14905 E. 21st St., 74134. Tel: 918-438-1380; 437-9481.
Catechesis/Religious Programs—Students 74.

9—THE MADALENE (1946), Revs. Daniel H. Mueggenborg; Thomas P. Biller; Sr. Marie Pierre Fleming, O.S.B., Pastoral Assoc.; Deacon John Steward. In res., Rev. James D. White.
Res., 3188 E. 22nd St., 74114. Tel: 918-744-0023; Fax: 918-744-0024. [JC]
Catechesis/Religious Programs—Tel: 918-744-9417. Mrs. Kay Bashaw, D.R.E.
Students 105.

10—ST. MARY (1954), Rev. Msgr. Dennis C. Dorney, V.G.; Revs. William J. Swift; Jack A. Gleason.
Office: 1347 E. 49th Pl., 74105. Tel: 918-749-1423; Fax: 918-747-9532. [JC]
School—1365 E. 49th Pl., 74105. Tel: 918-749-9361. Francis Smith, Prin.
Lay Teachers 23; Students 348.
Catechesis/Religious Programs—Tel: 918-749-2561. Sr. Colleen Nolan, O.P., D.R.E.
Students 290.

11—ST. MONICA'S (1926) (African American), Rev. Alex Kennedy; Sr. Phyllis Vaske, O.S.F., Pastoral Asst.; Deacon Theodore Prudhomme.
Res., 633 E. Marshall, 74106. Tel: 918-587-2965.

12—OUR LADY OF GUADALUPE. Closed. For sacramental records contact St. Francis Xavier-Our Lady of Guadalupe, Tulsa.

13—SS. PETER AND PAUL (1950), Rev. Tam N. Nguyen; Deacon Tommy Young.
Res., 1436 N. 67th E. Ave., 74115. Tel: 918-836-2596; Fax: 918-836-2597. [JC]
School—1428 N. 67th E. Ave., 74115. Tel: 918-836-2165; Fax: 918-836-2596. Bonnie Jones, Prin.
Lay Teachers 16; Students 180.
Catechesis/Religious Programs—Karen Campbell, D.R.E.
Students 69.

14—ST. PIUS X (1955), Revs. Thomas M. Hildebrand; Robert M. Dye; Deacon Kasper Weigant.
Office: 1727 S. 75 E. Ave., 74112. Tel: 918-622-4488; Fax: 918-622-1239. [JC]
Res., 7628 E. 17th St., 74112. Tel: 918-664-9723.
School—1717 S. 75 E. Ave., 74112. Tel: 918-627-5367. Holly Goodwin, Prin.
Lay Teachers 25; Students 425.
Catechesis/Religious Programs—D.R.E.: Eileen Dolan; Anne Edwards.
Students 138.

15—RESURRECTION (1968), Rev. Michael J. Knipe.
Office: P.O. Box 33169, 74153. Tel: 918-663-1907; Fax: 918-663-2533.
Res., 4612 S. Granite, 74135. Tel: 918-664-8319.
Church—4804 S. Fulton, 74135. Tel: 918-663-1907.
Catechesis/Religious Programs—Linda Nicholson, D.R.E.
Students 146.

16—ST. THOMAS MORE (1972), Rev. Gerald J. Coleman; Deacons Noel Hollingshead; Ned Doty.
Res., Tel: 918-663-9238.
Church—2720 S. 129 E. Ave., 74134. Tel: 918-437-0168.
Catechesis/Religious Programs—Aline Harbison, D.R.E.
Students 273.

OUTSIDE CITY OF TULSA

Antlers, Pushmataha Co., St. Agnes (1897), Rev. John J. Marquardt; Sr. Teresa Twomey, S.M.G., Pastoral Min.
Res., 402 N.E. 2nd, P.O. Box 206, 74523. Tel: 405-298-6113.
Mission—Clayton, Pushmataha Co., Holy Trinity, 74523. Tel: 918-569-4767.
Station—Farris, McLeod Correctional Center.

Bartlesville, Washington Co., St. John's (1906), Revs. Gregory A. Gier; John Cunningham, (Retired); Robert K.C. Cain; Deacons Joseph Richard; Dan Willis.
Res., 715 S. Johnstone Ave., 74003. Tel: 918-336-4353; Fax: 918-336-4354. [CEM]
School—Tel: 918-336-0603. David Fox, Prin.
Lay Teachers 10; Students 122.
Catechesis/Religious Programs—Tonja Senn, D.R.E.
Students 104.

St. James (1965), Rev. William K. Skeehan.
Res., 5510 Douglas Ln., 74006. Tel: 918-333-5307. [JC]
Catechesis/Religious Programs—Tel: 918-335-0844. Jeanette Pearson, D.R.E.
Students 234.
Mission—Nowata, Nowata Co., St. Catherine, 217 W. Modoc, Nowata, 74048. Tel: 918-273-0737.

Bixby, Tulsa Co., St. Clement's (1958), Rev. Thomas K. Melton.
Res., 21 W. Stadium, 74008. Tel: 918-366-3164.
Catechesis/Religious Programs—Tel: 918-366-3166.
Students 140.

Broken Arrow, Tulsa Co., St. Anne (1936), Rev. Maurice J. O'Connell. In res., Deacon John Crescitelli.
Res., 301 S. 9th St., 74012. Tel: 918-251-4206; Fax: 918-251-8719. [JC]
Catechesis/Religious Programs—Tel: 918-251-5414. D.R.E.: Christian Jones; Dayna Cotter.
Students 169.

St. Benedict (1980), Revs. Patrick J. Gaalaas; Matthew J. Gerlach; Deacons John Donnelly; Lee Ellis.
Res., 2305 S. Chestnut, 74102. Tel: 918-455-7353.
Church—2200 W. Ithica St., 74012. Tel: 918-455-4451; Fax: 918-451-2199.
Catechesis/Religious Programs—Students 747.

Claremore, Roger Co., St. Cecilia (1911), Rev. Timothy J. Daley; Deacons Vincent Mrasek; Peter Schmidt.
Res., 1304 N. Dorothy, 74017. Tel: 918-341-2343.
Catechesis/Religious Programs—Tel: 918-341-4238.
Students 317.

Cleveland, Osage, St. Joseph (1905),
Mailing Address: 1314 Lynn Ave., Pawhuska, 74056. Tel: 918-287-1477.
Church—Osage and C Ave., 74020.

Coalgate, Coal Co., Blessed Sacrament (1889), Rev. Robert T. Wood (OKL).
Res., 1300 E. Beverly, Ada, 74820. Tel: 405-332-2450. [JC]

Collinsville, Tulsa Co., St. Therese (1906), Rev. Patrick Brankin; Deacon Donel Tucker.
Res., 1007 N. 19th St., Box 297, 74021. Tel: 918-371-2704.
Catechesis/Religious Programs—Jane Webb, D.R.E.
Students 126.

Coweta, Wagoner Co., St. Vincent de Paul (1981), Rev. Stephen A. MacAulay; Deacon James A. Pierret, Admin.
Res., 1100 S. G St., P.O. Box 771, 74429-0771. Tel: 918-486-4757.
Catechesis/Religious Programs—Students 39.

Cushing, Payne Co., SS. Peter and Paul (1894), Rev. Amalar Vima; Deacons Jack Berry; Alfonso A. Cardenas.
Res., 214 N. Steele St., Box 828, 74023. Tel: 918-225-0644. [CEM]
Catechesis/Religious Programs—Students 66.
Mission—Drumright, Creek Co., St. Mary, Cimarron & Wood, Drumright, 74030.

Dewey, Washington Co., Our Lady of Guadalupe (1955), Rev. Gregory A. Gier.
Res., 400 W. Ninth St., 74029. Tel: 918-534-3420.

Durant, Bryan Co., St. William, Rev. Norbert Karava; Deacon Albert Miller.
Res., 802 University Blvd., 74701. Tel: 405-924-1989.

Fairfax, Osage Co., Sacred Heart, Rev. Kenneth W. Lewis.
Mailing Address: 1314 Lynn Ave., Pawhuska, 74056. Tel: 918-287-1477.
Mission—Shidler, Osage Co., St. Ann.

Grove, Delaware Co., St. Elizabeth (1949), Rev. Kenneth A. King.
Res., 1653 113th St. N.W., 74344. Tel: 918-786-7343; 786-9312 (Church).

Hartshorne, Pittsburg Co., Holy Rosary (1895), Rev. Roger H. Blais; Deacon Clement W. Bradley.
Res., 912 Cherokee, 74547. Tel: 918-297-2453. [CEM][JC]
Catechesis/Religious Programs—D.R.E.: Tracy McMurtrey, (Holy Rosary); Debbie Cox, (St. Catherine); Gordon Bockus, (Sacred Heart).
Students 89.
Missions—Talihina, Leflore Co., St. Catherine of Siena, Second & Gann Sts., Talihina, 74571. Tel: 918-567-2587; Wilburton, Latimer Co., Sacred Heart, 102 Centerpoint Rd., Wilburton, 74578. Tel: 918-465-3996.

Henryetta, Okmulgee Co., St. Michael (1912), Rev. Neal E. Brogan.
Res., 1004 W. Gentry St., P.O. Box 148, 74437. Tel: 918-652-3445.

Holdenville, Hughes Co., St. Stephen's (1905), Rev. Matthew J. Brown, O.S.B.
Res., 515 E. Highway, P.O. Box 935, 74848. Tel: 405-379-2512.
Mission—Okemah, Okfuska Co., St. Teresa, (1927) 8th and Broadway, Okemah, 74859.

Hugo, Choctaw Co., Immaculate Conception, Rev. Robert Bond, Glmy.
Res., 403 N Broadway, Box 489, 74743. Tel: 405-326-7300.
Mission—Boswell, Choctaw Co., St. Jude, 511 11th St., Boswell, 74727.

Idabel, McCurtain Co., St. Francis De Sales (1945), Revs. John T. Brown, Glmy.; Joseph Dean, Glmy.

Res., 13 S.E. Jefferson, 74745. Tel: 405-286-3275.
Mission—Valiant, McCurtain Co., Good Shepherd, P.O. Box 1016, Valiant, 74764. Tel: 405-933-4742. In res., Rev. John Buzga, Glmy.
Mission—Plunketville, McCurtain Co., St. Henry, Star Rte., 74745. Tel: 405-286-3275. [CEM]

Krebs, Pittsburg Co., St. Joseph's (1886), Rev. Chi Peter Phung.
Res., P.O. Box 621, 74554. Tel: 918-423-6695. [CEM]
Catechesis/Religious Programs—Tel: 918-423-2661. Sharon Dunbar, D.R.E.
Students 110.
Mission—Eufaula, McIntosh Co., St. Paul's, 74554. Tel: 918-689-7345.
Stations—Jackie Brannon Correctional Center, Tel: 918-426-4470; Fax: 918-426-0004; Oklahoma State Penitentiary, McAlester, Tel: 918-423-4700; Fax: 918-423-3862.

Langley, Mayes Co., St. Frances of Rome. Unassigned.
Res., Hwy. 28, P.O. Box 267, 74350-0267. Tel: 918-782-2248. [CEM][JC]

McAlester, Pittsburg Co., St. John (1895), Rev. Stephen E. Austin.
Res., 300 E. Washington Ave., Box 220, 74502. Tel: 918-423-0810; Fax: 918-423-8824. [CEM]
Catechesis/Religious Programs—Tel: 918-423-1458. D.R.E.: Anne Frederick; Dolores Whitfield.
Students 170.
Mission—Pittsburg, Pittsburg Co., St. Edwards, 74502.

Miami, Ottawa Co., Sacred Heart (1900), Rev. Michael R. Rooney; Deacon Marvin Morris.
Res., 2515 N. Main, 74354. Tel: 918-542-5281; Fax: 918-542-1764.
Catechesis/Religious Programs—Tel: 918-542-5898. Karen Painter, D.R.E.
Students 130.

Muskogee, Muskogee Co., Assumption. Closed. For sacramental records contact Saint Joseph Church, Muskogee.
Sacred Heart. Closed. For sacramental records contact Saint Joseph Church, Muskogee.
Saint Joseph Church (1992), Rev. J. Richard Bradley; Deacons Edwin Falleur, Pastoral Assoc.; Ray Fabian. In res., Herman J. Foken.
Mailing Address: P.O. Box 189, 74402. Tel: 918-687-1351; Fax: 918-687-5541.
Church—321 N. Virginia, 74402. [CEM]
Parish Office and Residence—2310 W. Broadway, 74402. Tel: 918-687-1351.
School—(Grades PreK-8) 323 N. Virginia, 74403. Tel: 918-683-1291. Sharon McKee, Prin.
Lay Teachers 10; Students 184.
Catechesis/Religious Programs—Carleen Falleur, D.R.E.
Students 233.
Chapel—Sacred Heart, 2300 W. Broadway, 74402.

Okmulgee, Okmulgee Co., St. Anthony's (1910), Rev. Bryan V. Brooks. Pastoral Assocs.: Sr. Mary Fox, O.P.; Sr. Loretta McIluenna, O.P.
Res., 515 S. Morton Ave., P.O. Box 698, 74447. Tel: 918-756-4385; Fax: 918-756-3719. [JC]
School—Marian Academy, (Grades PreK-5). Tel: 918-756-9042. Sr. Loretta McIluenna, O.P., Prin.
Catechesis/Religious Programs—Students 50.
Mission—Okmulgee, Okmulgee Co., Uganda Martyrs Beach, 808 E. 3rd, 74447.

Owasso, Tulsa Co., St. Henry (1957), Rev. J. Paul Donovan; Deacon Vernon Foltz.
Mailing Address: P.O. Box 181, 74055-0181. Tel: 918-272-3710.
Res., 903 N. Elm, 74055. Tel: 918-272-7387.
Church—8500 Owasso Expy., 74055.
Catechesis/Religious Programs—Linda Hogan, D.R.E.
Students 303.

Pawhuska, Osage Co., Immaculate Conception (1887) (Osage Indian), Rev. Leonard H. Higgins.
Res., 1314 N. Lynn Ave., 74056. Tel: 918-287-1414. [JC]
Catechesis/Religious Programs—Students 54.
Mission—Barnsdall, Osage Co., St. Mary, 3rd and Chestnut, Barnsdall, 74002.

Pawnee, Pawnee Co., St. John (1907), Rev. Kenneth W. Lewis.
Church—8th St. and Oak, 74058.
Mailing Address: 1314 Lynn Ave., Pawhuska, 74056. Tel: 918-287-1477.

Poteau, Leflore Co., Immaculate Conception, Rev. Dovan Nguyen.
Church—410 Bagwell St., 74953. Tel: 918-647-3475.
Res., 502 N. Bagwell St., 74953.
Station—Hodgens, Ouachita Correctional Training Center.
Missions—Stigler, St. Joseph, 126 S Broadway, 74462.; Spiro, St. Elizabeth Seton, Hwy. 9, 74959.

Pryor, Mayes Co., St. Mark's (1942), Rev. Arthyr T. O'Hara.
Res., 1507 S. Vann, Box 576, 74361. Tel: 918-825-3753.
Catechesis/Religious Programs—Tel: 918-825-4186. Phyllis Buffo, D.R.E.
Students 105.

Sallisaw, Sequoyah Co., St. Francis Xavier (1952), Rev. Jeffrey S. Polasek; Deacons Tom Loney; Robert Barnes; Sr. Marie Grellinger, S.S.N.D.
Church—2110 N. Dogwood, 74955. Tel: 918-775-6217.
Catechesis/Religious Programs—Students 84.
Missions—Cookson, Cherokee Co., St. John the Evangelist; Webbers Falls, Muskogee Co., St. Joseph; Roland, Sequoyah Co., Blessed Kateri Tekakwitha.

Sand Springs, Tulsa Co., St. Patrick's (1919), Rev. Kenneth S. Fulton; Deacon Bob Garrett.
Res., 204 E. Fourth, 74063. Tel: 918-245-5254. [JC]
Catechesis/Religious Programs—Students 86.
Mission—Mannford, Creek Co., Our Lady of the Lake.

Sapulpa, Creek Co., Sacred Heart (1907), Rev. Jake A. Males; Deacon Francis Decker.
Church—1777 E. Grayson Ave., 74066. Tel: 918-224-0944. [JC]
Catechesis/Religious Programs—Raelyn McDonald, D.R.E.
Students 100.

Skiatook, Osage Co., Sacred Heart (1921). (Formerly St. William). Rev. Peter F. Dally, Admin.; Deacon Millard Kizzia.
Office: 3504 E. Independance, Tulsa, 74115.
Res., 109 W. 5th St., 74070. Tel: 918-396-1179.
Catechesis/Religious Programs—Students 73.
Mission—Hominy, Osage Co., St. Joseph, 4th Pettit, Hominy, 74035.

Skiatoon, Osage Co., St. Joseph's (1928). Closed. For inquiries for parish records contact the Chancery.

Stillwater, Payne Co., St. Francis Xavier (1895), Rev. Robert T. Schlitt.
Res., 623 S. West St., Box 909, 74076. Tel: 405-372-6886. [JC]
Catechesis/Religious Programs—Tel: 405-372-7987. D.R.E.: Cecilia Crane; Bobbi Bryson.
Students 110.
St. John University Parish and Catholic Student Center (1965), Rev. Joe C. Townsend; Deacon Bill Moler.
Res., 201 N. Knoblock, 74075. Tel: 405-372-6408; Fax: 405-372-6409.
Catechesis/Religious Programs—Tel: 405-372-7987. D.R.E.: CC Crane, (PreK-12); Bobbi Bryson, (Grades 7-12).
Students 204.

Tahlequah, Cherokee Co., St. Brigid (1966), Rev. Charles J. Swett.
Res., 807 Crafton St., 74464. Tel: 918-456-8388.
Catechesis/Religious Programs—Tel: 918-456-4204. Donna Ballew, D.R.E.
Students 70.

Vinita, Craig Co., Holy Ghost (1892), Rev. Paul E. Eichoff, Admin.
Res., 120 W. Sequoyah Ave., 74301. Tel: 918-256-2281.
Catechesis/Religious Programs—Tel: 918-256-3118. Sr. Mary Grace Sieben, D.R.E.
Students 80.
Mission—Welch, Craig Co., St. Ann, P.O. Box 25, Welch, 74369.
Stations—Eastern State Hospital.; Vinita, Northeastern Correctional Facility.

Wagoner, Wagoner Co., Holy Cross (1895), Rev. Stephen A. MacAulay; Deacon James A. Pierret.
Res., P.O. Box 710, 74477. Tel: 918-485-5145.
Church—S.W. 15th & Pierce, 74477.
Catechesis/Religious Programs—Tel: 918-485-8228. Sherry Ruyle, D.R.E.
Students 30.

Special Assignment:
Reverend Fathers—
Brooks, Donald W., Prison Ministry, P.O. Box 2009, Tulsa, OK 74101
White, James D., Historian and Dir. of Office of Divine Worship, P.O. Box 2009, Tulsa, OK 74101

On Duty Outside the Diocese:
Reverend Fathers—
Cashen, Michael, Chicago, IL
Lundberg, John W.
McSherry, Tom
Minh, Vu Duc, U.S. Air Force
O'Neil, Lee E.
Wells, Peter B., Rome

Retired:
Reverend Monsignors—
Finn, Cecil E., Franciscan Villa, 17110 E. 51st St., S., Broken Arrow, OK 74012
Maszkiewicz, Mark, 1426 S. Columbia Ave., Tulsa, OK 74104
Reverend Fathers—
Bartnik, Harry S., Franciscan Villa Apt. 2, 17110 E. 51st St. S., Broken Arrow, OK 74012
Cefai, John M., Franciscan Villa, 17110 E. 51st St., S., Broken Arrow, OK 74012
Foken, Herman J., P.O. Box 189, Muskogee, OK 74402-0189
Keohane, Daniel C., Franciscan Villa, 17110 E. 51st. St. S., Broken Arrow, OK 74012
Lange, Lawrence P., 13001 E. 40th St., No. 1011, Tulsa, OK 74134
Mazaika, Joseph J., 1710 Walnut, Grand Prairie, TX 75050
McCarthy, Jerry, Franciscan Villa, 17110 E. 51st St., S., Broken Arrow, OK 74012
McGlinchey, James J., 1767 S. Wheeling, Tulsa, OK 74104
Pickett, Robert T., 1414 E. 49th St., Tulsa, OK 74105-4798
Richard, Edward, 4112 Blue Ridge St., North Port, FL 34287

Permanent Deacons:
Barnes, Robert, Blessed Kateri Tekakwitha, Roland
Berry, Jack L., Sts. Peter & Paul, Cushing
Bradley, Clement W., Wilburton
Breazille, James E., Stillwater
Campbell, Richard, St. Bernard, Tulsa
Cardenas, Alfonso, SS. Peter & Paul, Cushing
Chamberlain, Richard, Bartlesville
Coburn, Wilfred C., St. Catherine, Tulsa
Crescitelli, John, St. Anne, Broken Arrow
Decker, Francis I., Sacred Heart, Sapulpa
DeLeon, Felix, St. Francis/OLOG, Tulsa
Donnelly, John E., St. Benedict, Broken Arrow
Doty, Edward, St. Thomas More, Tulsa
Ellis, Lee, St. Benedict, Broken Arrow
Fabian, Raymond F., St. Joseph, Muskogee
Falleur, Edwin E., St. Joseph, Muskogee
Foltz, Vernon, St. Henry, Owasso
Garrett, James R., St. Patrick, Sand Springs
Gerrior, Joseph A., On Medical Leave
Hancock, John, St. Bernard, Tulsa
Hollingshead, Noel, St. Thomas More, Tulsa
Kizzia, Millard H., Sacred Heart, Skiatook; St. Joseph, Hominy
Litwack, Stephen J., Immaculate Conception, Tulsa
Loney, Tom, St. Joseph, Webbers Falls
Luschen, Loren F., Christ the King, Tulsa
Mikell, Alan G., St. Bernard, Tulsa
Miller, Albert J., On Leave
Moler, William J., St. John University Parish, Stillwater
Morris, Marvin D., Sacred Heart, Miami
Mrasek, Vincent J., St. Cecilia, Claremore
Perez, Jose, Hispanic Ministries, Tulsa
Pierret, James A., St. Vincent de Paul, Coweta; Holy Cross, Wagoner, FL
Prudhomme, Theodore, Tulsa's Northside Ministries
Richard, Joseph N., St. John, Bartlesville
Schmidt, Peter, St. Cecilia, Claremore
Starr, Sid, St. Catherine, Tulsa
Steward, John N., Madalene, Tulsa
Toppins, Charles A., Unassigned
Tucker, Donel, St. Teresa, Collinsville
Walsh, Gary D., Our Lady of the Osage Hills Center, Tulsa
Weigant, Kasper E., St. Pius X, Tulsa
Willis, Daniel H., St. John, Bartlesville
Young, Thomas, SS. Peter & Paul, Tulsa

INSTITUTIONS LOCATED IN THE DIOCESE

[A] HIGH SCHOOLS, DIOCESAN

TULSA. *Bishop Kelley High School*, 3905 S. Hudson, 74135-5699. Tel: 918-627-3390. Alan V. Weyland, Academic Prin.; Bro. David Poos, F.S.C., Dir. Prin.; Marianne Stich, Campus Min. Brothers 4; Sisters 3; Lay Teachers 65; Students 854.

[B] HIGH SCHOOLS, PRIVATE

TULSA. *Cascia Hall Preparatory School*. (Grades 6-12), Mailing Address: Box 52247, 74152. Tel: 918-742-7373. 2520 S. Yorktown Ave., 74114. Augustinians (Order of St. Augustine). Coed College Preparatory School. Revs. James J. Sheridan, O.S.A.; John H. Gaffney, O.S.A.; William A. Hamill, O.S.A., Upper School Dir.; Henry V. Spielmann, O.S.A.; Theodore

E. Tack, O.S.A., Headmaster; Michael Schweifler, O.S.A., Prior; William A. Perez, O.S.A.; Bro. John M. Hibbard, O.S.A., Dean of Students Campus Min. Priests 7; Brothers 1; Sisters 1; Lay Teachers 41; Students 565.

[C] ELEMENTARY SCHOOLS, DIOCESAN

TULSA. *Holy Family School*, 820 S. Boulder St., 74119. Tel: 918-582-0422. Ms. Maureen Clements, Prin. Lay Teachers 12; Students 180.

BROKEN ARROW. *All Saints School*, 299 S. 9th St., 74012. Tel: 918-251-3000. Mrs. Fran Smith, Prin. Lay Teachers 15; Students 219.

[D] ELEMENTARY SCHOOLS, PRIVATE

TULSA. *Monte Cassino School*. (Grades PreK-8), 2206 S. Lewis, 74114. Tel: 918-743-4471. Sr. Mary Clare Buthod, O.S.B., Dir.-Prin. Sisters 5; Lay Teachers 70; Students 1,112.

[E] GENERAL HOSPITALS

TULSA. *Saint Francis Hospital, Inc.*, 6161 S. Yale Ave., 74136. Tel: 918-494-2200.
For a complete listing, refer to the Hospitals section.
St. John Medical Center, Inc., 1923 S. Utica Ave., 74104. Tel: 918-744-2345.
For a complete listing, refer to the Hospitals section.
Sisters of the Sorrowful Mother-St. John Ministry Corporation, 1923 S. Utica, 74104 Fax: 918-744-2716.
For a complete listing, refer to the Hospitals section.
Sisters of the Sorrowful Mother-US Health System, Inc., P.O. Box 4753, 74159-0753.
For a complete listing, refer to the Hospitals section.

[F] HOMES FOR THE AGED

BROKEN ARROW. *Franciscan Villa*, 17110 E. 51st St., S., 74012. Tel: 918-355-1596; Fax: 918-355-2954.
For a complete listing, refer to the Special Care Facilities section.

[G] MONASTERIES AND RESIDENCES OF PRIESTS AND BROTHERS

BROKEN ARROW. *St. Anne Church*, 301 S. 9th St., 74102-4409. Rev. Maurice J. O'Connell.

[H] CONVENTS AND RESIDENCES FOR SISTERS

TULSA. *St. Joseph Monastery*, 2200 S. Lewis, 74114-3100. Tel: 918-742-4989; Fax: 918-744-1374. Motherhouse of Benedictine Sisters (Federation of St. Scholastica). Sr. Barbara Austin, O.S.B., Prioress. Sisters in Community 37.
Sisters of Saint Joseph, 3942 S. Trenton, 74105. Sisters in Community 2.

BROKEN ARROW. *St. Clare Convent*, 17600 E. 51st St., S., 74012. Tel: 918-355-2740. Sr. Ida Nieberle, Coord. Sisters in Community 16.
Sisters of the Sorrowful Mother - Our Lady of Sorrows Convent, 17600 E. 51st St., S., 74012. Tel: 918-355-5581. Sr. M. Theresa Gil, Coord. Sisters 30.
Sisters of the Sorrowful Mother - U.S./Caribbean Province, Inc., 17600 E. 51st St., S., 74012. Tel: 918-355-1148. Sr. Catherine Marie Hanegan, U.S./Caribbean Prov. Sisters 231.

SAND SPRINGS. *Benedictine Sisters of Perpetual Adoration*, 18701 W. Monastery Rd., 74063. Tel: 918-245-2734. Osage Monastery, OM Forest of Peace Benedictine Convent of Perpetual Adoration in Oklahoma, Inc. Sr. M. Pascaline Coff, O.S.B., Supr. Sisters 5.

[I] NEWMAN CENTERS

TULSA. *University of Tulsa Newman Center*, 440 S. Florence, 74104. Tel: 918-599-0204. Rev. Timothy L. Davison, Chap.; Dee Barlow, Campus Min.; Elinor Hoar, Admin. Asst.

MIAMI. *Northeastern Oklahoma A & M College Newman Center*. Mailing Address: 2515 N. Main, 74354. 200 I N.E. St., 74354. Tel: 918-542-5281. Rev. Michael R. Rooney, Chap.

STILLWATER. *St. John's University Parish and Catholic Student Center*, 201 N. Knoblock, 74075. Tel: 405-372-6408. Rev. Joe C. Townsend; Sr. Sheila Carroll, Campus Min.

TAHLEQUAH. *Northeastern State University Catholic Student Organization*, 807 Crafton St., 74464. Tel: 918-456-8388. Rev. Charles J. Swett.

[J] MISCELLANEOUS

TULSA. *Bishop Kelley High School Endowment Trust*, P.O. Box 2009, 74101. Tel: 918-587-3115; Fax: 918-587-6692.
Catholic Foundation of Eastern Oklahoma, Inc., Mailing Address: P.O. Box 2009, 74101. 111 W. Main, Ste. 400, 74103. Tel: 918-587-3115. Mr. Jon Calder, Dir. Stewardship & Devel.
Our Lady of the Osage Hills Center, 5323 W. 31st St., N., 74127. Deacon Gary Walsh, Admin. Total Staff 7.
St. John Medical Center Foundation, Inc., 1923 S. Utica, 74104. Tel: 918-749-3553.
St. Joseph Residence, Inc., P.O. Box 6429, 74148. Total Assisted 37; Total Staff 6.

MUSKOGEE. *St. Joseph School Endowment Trust*, P.O. Box 189, 74402. Tel: 918-687-1351.

RELIGIOUS INSTITUTES OF MEN REPRESENTED IN THE DIOCESE

For further details refer to the corresponding bracketed number in the Religious Institutes of Men or Women section.

[0140]—*The Augustinians (Province of Our Mother of Good Counsel)*.—O.S.A.
[0200]—*Benedictine Monks*.
[0330]—*Brothers of the Christian Schools*. (Province of St. Louis).—F.S.C.
[0570]—*Glenmary Home Missioners*.—Glmy.
[0690]—*Jesuit Fathers and Brothers*. (Province of St. Louis).—S.J.

RELIGIOUS INSTITUTES OF WOMEN REPRESENTED IN THE DIOCESE

[0230]—*Benedictine Sisters of Pontifical Jurisdiction*. (Atchison, KS).—O.S.B.
[1010]—*Congregation of Divine Providence of San Antonio, Texas*.—C.D.P.
[0220]—*Congregation of the Benedictine Sisters of Perpetual Adoration of Pontifical Jurisdiction*.—O.S.B.
[]—*Congregation of the Benedictine Sisters of the Sacred Hearts*.—O.S.B.
[0470]—*Congregation of the Sisters of Charity of the Incarnate Word, Houston, TX*.—C.C.V.I.
[1070-03]—*Dominican Sisters*.—O.P.
[]—*Franciscan Sisters of Chicago*. (Lemont, IL).—O.S.F.
[3640]—*Poor Servants of the Mother of God*.—S.M.G.
[2970]—*School Sisters of Notre Dame*.—S.S.N.D.
[2150]—*Servants of the Immaculate Heart of Mary, Southwest Province*.—I.H.M.
[]—*Sisters for Christian Community*.—S.F.C.C.
[]—*Sisters of St. Benedict*.—O.S.B.
[]—*Sisters of St. Francis of Penance & Christian Charity*. (Denver, CO).—O.S.F.
[1570]—*Sisters of St. Francis of the Holy Family*.—O.S.F.
[1600]—*Sisters of St. Francis of the Martyr St. George*.—O.S.F.
[3830]—*Sisters of St. Joseph*.—S.S.J.
[]—*Sisters of the Blessed Sacrament*. (Bensalem, PA).—S.B.S.
[4100]—*Sisters of the Sorrowful Mother (Third Order of St. Francis)*.—S.S.M.
[]—*Ursuline Nuns*. (Paola, KS).—O.S.U.

CEMETERIES

TULSA. *Calvary*, 91st & Harvard, Rte. 2, 74136. Tel: 918-743-5571. Mailing Address: P.O. Box 2009, 74101. Tel: 918-587-3115. James S. Liichow, Suprv.; Mr. Jack Charon, Dir.

NECROLOGY

† Broyles, Henry J., Vinita, OK, Holy Ghost Church. —Died Oct. 16, 1996.
† Gavin, Justin H., Langley, OK, St. Frances of Rome Church. —Died Oct. 24, 1996.
† McGoldrick, Frances E., (Retired). —Died Aug. 20, 1996.

Diocese of Tyler

(Dioecesis Tylerensis)

Most Reverend

EDMOND CARMODY, D.D.

Bishop of Tyler; ordained to the priesthood June 8, 1957; appointed Auxiliary Bishop of San Antonio November 8, 1988; consecrated December 15, 1988; appointed Bishop of the Diocese of Tyler March 24, 1992; installed May 25, 1992. *Mailing Address: 1015 E.S.E. Loop 323, Tyler, TX, 75701-9663.* Tel.: 903-534-1077; Fax: 903-534-1370.

ESTABLISHED DIOCESE OF TYLER ON DECEMBER 12, 1986.

Square Miles 22,971.

Comprises the following Counties in the State of Texas: Anderson, Angelina, Bowie, Camp, Cass, Cherokee, Delta, Franklin, Freestone, Gregg, Harrison, Henderson, Hopkins, Houston, Lamar, Leon, Marion, Morris, Nacogdoches, Panola, Rains, Red River, Rusk, Sabine, San Augustine, Shelby, Smith, Titus, Trinity, Upshur, Van Zandt, and Wood.

For legal titles of parishes and diocesan institutions, consult the Chancery Office.

Chancery: 1015 E.S.E. Loop 323, Tyler, TX, 75701-9663. Tel.: 903-534-1077; Fax: 903-534-1370.

E-mail address: BpCarmody@aol.com

STATISTICAL OVERVIEW

Personnel	
Bishop	1
Priests: Diocesan Active in Diocese	19
Priests: Active Outside Diocese	1
Priests: Retired, Sick or Absent	5
Number of Diocesan Priests	25
Religious Priests in Diocese	21
Extern Priests in Diocese	20
Ordinations:	
Transitional Deacons	1
Permanent Deacons	26
Permanent Deacons in Diocese	29
Total Brothers	1
Total Sisters	61
Parishes	
Parishes	30
With Resident Pastor:	
Resident Diocesan Priests	20
Resident Religious Priests	10
Without Resident Pastor:	
Missions	20
Pastoral Centers	3
New Parishes Created	3
Professional Ministry Personnel	
Brothers	1
Sisters	7
Lay Ministers	26
Welfare	
Catholic Hospitals	3
Total Assisted	279,914
Health Care Centers	5
Total Assisted	8,313
Special Centers for Social Services	1
Total Assisted	100
Educational	
Diocesan Students in Other Seminaries	10
Total Seminarians	10
High Schools, Diocesan and Parish	1
Total Students	133
Elementary Schools, Diocesan and Parish	5
Total Students	963
Catechesis/Religious Education:	
High School Students	1,151
Elementary Students	4,779
Total Students Under Catholic Instruction	7,036
Teachers in the Diocese:	
Priests	1
Sisters	5
Lay Teachers	113
Vital Statistics	
Receptions into the Church:	
Infant Baptism Totals	1,387
Adult Baptism Totals	135
Received into Full Communion	170
First Communions	1,138
Confirmations	570
Marriages:	
Catholic	158
Interfaith	95
Total Marriages	253
Deaths	312
Total Catholic Population	42,796
Total Population	1,185,155

Former Bishop—Most Rev. CHARLES E. HERZIG, D.D., First Bishop of Tyler; ord. May 31, 1955; Bishop of Tyler; appt. Dec. 12, 1986; cons. Feb. 24, 1987; died Sept. 7, 1991.

Vicar General—Rev. JOHN A. BRENNAN, *Chancery, 1015 ESE Loop 323, Tyler, 75701-9663.* Tel: 903-534-1077; Fax: 903-534-1370.

Chancery—1015 ESE Loop 323, Tyler, 75701-9663. Tel: 903-534-1077; Fax: 903-534-1370. Office Hours: Mon.-Fri. 8:30a.m.-5p.m.

Chancellor—Rev. GAVIN N. VAVEREK, J.C.L., *1015 ESE Loop 323, Tyler, 75701-9663.* Tel: 903-534-1077.

Archivist—Mrs. MARY SEDBERRY. Tel: 903-534-1077.

College of Consultors—Rev. Msgr. JOHN A. BRENNAN, V.G.; Rev. Msgr. SAMUEL S. METZGER; Rev. Msgr. JAMES E. YOUNG; Revs. RONALD DIEGEL; BERNARD PUSTEJOVSKY; BENJAMIN SMYLIE; OCTAVIO SUAREZ; GAVIN N. VAVEREK; A. PETER WHITNEY.

Deans—East Central Deanery: Rev. RONALD DIEGEL, Northeast Deanery: Rev. Msgr. GERALD PRIEST, Northwest Deanery: Rev. ALPHONSE ANTHONY, Southeast Deanery: Rev. Msgr. JAMES E. YOUNG, Southwest Deanery: Rev. HAROLD P. PAULSEN, West Central Deanery: Rev. Msgr. SAMUEL S. METZGER.

Tribunal Office—1015 ESE Loop 323, Tyler, 75701-9663. Tel: 903-534-1077; Fax: 903-534-1370.

Judicial Vicar—Rev. Msgr. JOSEPH E. STRICKLAND, J.C.L.

Defender of the Bond—Rev. GAVIN N. VAVEREK, J.C.L.

Administrator/Notary—Mrs. MARGARET OPPENHEIMER.

Notary—Mrs. MARY SEDBERRY. Tel: 903-534-1077.

DIOCESAN ADMINISTRATION

Finance Officer—Mr. JAMES R. SMITH, *1015 ESE Loop 323, Tyler, 75701-9663.* Tel: 903-534-1077.

Diocesan Finance Council—Mr. BILL SULLIVAN, Chm.; Rev. Msgr. JOHN A. BRENNAN; Mr. JAMES CHIARIZIO; Mrs. JANET HUNT; Mr. JAMES KENNEDY; Mr. WESLEY RIVERS; JAMES R. SMITH; Mr. FRED WULF.

Diocesan Building Board—Mr. BILLY CORDOVA, Chm.; Mrs. P. ANNE HUGMAN, Vice-Chm.; Rev. DAN DAUGHERTY; Mrs. CHERYL FLOOD; Mr. JAMES R. SMITH; Rev. GAVIN N. VAVEREK.

East Texas Catholic Foundation—JAMES R. SMITH, *1015 ESE Loop 323, Tyler, 75701-9663.* Mr. DAVID CARLILE; Mrs. SUZIE HAIR; Mr. VINCE RICHBOURG; Mr. WALTER VOLZ; Mr. PAUL WALSH; Mr. TOM WOLF.

Priests' Pension Plan Board—Rev. Msgr. JOHN A. BRENNAN, Chm.; Mr. JAMES R. SMITH, Treas.; Rev. Msgr. JAMES E. YOUNG; Revs. GAVIN N. VAVEREK; A. PETER WHITNEY.

Campaign for Human Development—Mrs. MARY SEDBERRY. Tel: 903-534-1077.

Catholic School Superintendent—Sr. JOSEPH MARIE KASEL, S.S.N.D., *1015 ESE Loop 323, Tyler, 75701-9663.*

Diocesan School Board—Mr. PAUL WALKER, Chm.; Mrs. MARTHA ROBERTS, Sec.; Mr. WILLIAM BARTUSH; Mrs. BONNIE SHIVERS; Dr. JAMES STOCKS; Mrs. KATHIE WHITEHURST; Mr. GEORGE WING.

Director of Religious Education—Mrs. LINDA PORTER.

Pastoral Ministries—Rev. BERNARD PUSTEJOVSKY, Dir., *1015 ESE Loop 323, Tyler, 75701-9663.* Tel: 903-534-1077.

Family Life/Youth Ministry—Mr. EDDIE RUESEWALD, Dir., *1015 ESE Loop 323, Tyler, 75701-9663.* Tel: 903-534-1077.

Tyler Catholic Committee on Scouting—Rev. MICHAEL DOYLE, Chap., *1015 ESE Loop 323, Tyler, 75701-9663.* Tel: 903-534-1077. Mr. JERRY STOCK, Chm., *905 Happiness St., Longview, 75601.* Tel: 903-757-7524.

Campus Ministries—Rev. WM. JOHN DOMINIC LOGAN, O.P., *Stephen F. Austin State University, P.O. Box 7051 SFASU, Nacogdoches, 75962.* Tel: 409-564-0661.

Missions Office—Mrs. JOYCE CRAVENS. Tel: 903-534-1077.

Priests' Personnel Board—Rev. Msgr. JAMES E. YOUNG, Chm.; Rev. Msgr. SAMUEL S. METZGER; Rev. Msgr. JOSEPH E. STRICKLAND; Revs. RONALD DIEGEL; RUBEN FIGUEROA; HAROLD P. PAULSEN; BERNARD PUSTEJOVSKY.

Presbyteral Council—Rev. BERNIE PUSTEJOVSKY, Chm.; Rev. Msgr. JOHN A. BRENNAN; Rev. Msgr. SAMUEL S. METZGER; Rev. Msgr. JAMES E. YOUNG; Revs. BENJAMIN SMYLIE; OCTAVIO SUAREZ; GAVIN N. VAVEREK; A. PETER WHITNEY.

Office of Clergy Development/Continuing Education—Rev. Msgr. JAMES E. YOUNG, *504 North St., Nacogdoches, 75961.* Tel: 409-564-7807.

Permanent Diaconate Co-Directors—Rev. BEN COMISKY, *201 N. Vale St., Jefferson, 75657-2143.* Tel: 903-665-8778. Deacon JOHN K. SHAFFER, *2508 Appleby Sand Rd., Nacogdoches, 75961-4524.* Tel: 409-569-8544.

Vocations Director—Rev. GAVIN N. VAVEREK, *1015 ESE Loop 323, Tyler, 75701-9663.* Tel: 903-534-1077. Vocations Awareness Board Chm.: Mr. JIM FINEGAN.

Communications Director—Mr. JAMES H. D'AVIGNON, *1015 ESE Loop 323, Tyler, 75701-9663.* Tel: 903-534-1077.

Bishop's Annual Appeal—Mrs. JUDY GREEN, Dir., *1015 ESE Loop 323, Tyler, 75701-9663.* Tel: 903-534-1077.

Newspaper "Catholic East Texas"—Mr. JAMES H. D'AVIGNON, Editor. Reporters: Mrs. SUSAN DEMATTEO NECESSARY; Mrs. JOANNE FLORES EMBLETON, *1015 ESE Loop 323, Tyler, 75701-9663.* Tel: 903-534-1077; Fax: 903-534-1370.

Catholic Services for Immigrants—Deacon JOE MORENO, *1403 E. 1st St., Mt. Pleasant, 75456.* Tel: 903-572-5227.

DIOCESAN OFFICES

Diocesan Council of Catholic Women—Ms. BARBARA GARDINER, Pres., *502 Lansdown, Marshall, 75670.* Tel: 903-938-1051. Rev. GAVIN N. VAVEREK, Moderator, *2108 Ridgewood, Longview, 75605-1999.* Tel: 903-757-5855.

Respect Life Program—Rev. GAVIN N. VAVEREK, *2108 Ridgewood, Longview, 75605-1999.* Tel: 903-757-5855. Co-Directors: JOE DUDAS; MARGE DUDAS, *1605 H. G. Mosley Blvd., Longview, 75604.* Tel: 903-295-8608.

Disaster Relief Director—Mr. ROY SHEAR, *621 Bentley Ct., Tyler, 75703.* Tel: 903-561-0425.

CLERGY, PARISHES, MISSIONS AND PAROCHIAL SCHOOLS

CITY OF TYLER
(Smith County)

1—CATHEDRAL OF THE IMMACULATE CONCEPTION (1987), Rev. Msgr. Joseph E. Strickland, J.C.L.; Revs. Adam Ogorzaly (Poland); Augustine Tharappel (India); Deacons Anthony George; Dwight Hall; Ramiro Martinez; Ramon Noriega; William O'Sullivan. Pastoral Associate Ministries: Sr. Susan Seitz, O.S.F. Social Services: Deacon Ramon Noriega Tel: 903-592-0027.
Office: 423 S. Broadway, 75702. Tel: 903-592-1617; Fax: 903-593-7326.
Res., 114 W. Front St., 75702. Tel: 903-592-5462.
Schools—St. Gregory School, 500 S. College St., 75702. Tel: 903-595-4109; Fax: 903-592-8626. Kathy Shieldes Harry, Prin.
Lay Teachers 25; Students 341; Bishop T. K. Gorman Middle School, 1405 E.S.E. Loop 323, 75701. Tel: 903-561-2424; Fax: 903-561-2645. Dr. Rosemary Henry, Prin.
Students 157.
Bishop Gorman High School—Tel: 903-561-2424.
Priests 1; Lay Teachers 31; Students 133.
Catechesis/Religious Programs—Fax: 903-561-1645.
Lay Teachers 52; Students 646.
Missions—Lindale, Smith Co., Holy Family, P.O. Box 1071, Lindale, 75771-1078.; Tyler, Smith Co., Our Lady of Guadalupe, 922 Old Omen Rd., 75701-3709. Tel: 903-593-2006.
Chapel—St. Paul, 1015 E.S.E. Loop 323, 75702.

OUTSIDE THE CITY OF TYLER

Athens, Henderson Co., St. Edward Church (1947), Rev. Msgr. Samuel S. Metzger; Deacon William Flores.
Res., 800 E. Tyler, 75751-2140. Tel: 903-675-2509.
Catechesis/Religious Programs—Dennis Womack, D.R.E., Tel: 903-425-4342.
Students 264.
Mission—Canton, Van Zandt Co., St. Therese, Rte. 6, Box 138, Canton, 75103-9649. Tel: 903-567-4286.
Catechesis/Religious Programs—Students 58.

Atlanta, Cass Co., St. Catherine of Siena Church (1965), Rev. Abraham Mathews (India).
Res., 309 N. Louise St., P.O. Box 985, 75551. Tel: 903-796-4494; Fax: 903-796-9990.
Catechesis/Religious Programs—Tel: 903-796-3768. Kathleen O'Brien, D.R.E.
Students 49.

Carthage, Panola Co., St. William of Vercelli (1947), Rev. Benjamin Smylie.
Mailing Address: P.O. Drawer F, 75633.
Res., 202 West Loop 436, 75633-0240. Tel: 903-693-3766; Fax: 903-693-9006.
Catechesis/Religious Programs—Students 100.

Center, Shelby Co., St. Therese (1951), Rev. Arulappa Devaraj.
Res., Rte. 2, Box 1093, 75935-9269. Tel: 409-598-8458; Fax: 409-598-5599.
Catechesis/Religious Programs—Students 48.
Missions—Hemphill, Sabine Co., St. Pius I, P.O. Box 1925, Hemphill, 75948-1925. Rev. Basil Hoan; San Augustine, San Augustine Co., San Augustine. Rev. Basil Hoan; Timpson, Shelby Co., Epiphany. Rev. Devaraj Arulappa.

Clarksville, Red River Co., St. Joseph (1870), Rev. George Varakukala, H.G.N., (India) Admin.
Res., 500 E. Broadway, 75426-3110. Tel: 903-427-5044.

Crockett, Houston Co., St. Francis of the Tejas (1931), Revs. Tej Lal, I.M.S. (India); Sales T. (Ranjan) Cletus, I.M.S. (India).
Res., 609 N. Fourth, 75835-4001. Tel: 409-544-5338; Fax: 409-544-7914.
Catechesis/Religious Programs—Gerry Krenek, D.R.E.
Students 81.
Mission—Centerville, Leon Co., St. Leo the Great, P.O. Box 356, Centerville, 75833-0356. Tel: 903-536-5012.

Daingerfield, Morris Co., Our Lady of Fatima (1951) (Hispanic), Rev. Fidelis Levri, Glmy.
Mailing Address: Rte. 2, Box 4B, 75638-9704.
Res., Bert & Tiger Streets, 75638. Tel: 903-645-5637. [CEM]
Catechesis/Religious Programs—Students 59.

Diboll, Angelina Co., Our Lady of Guadalupe (1971) (Hispanic), Rev. Ruben Figueroa, O.F.M.
Mailing Address: P.O. Box 310, 75941-0310. [CEM]
Res., 100 Maynard St., 75941. Tel: 409-829-3650; 829-2416 (Res.); 829-2981 (Parish Hall).
Catechesis/Religious Programs—Mrs. Valerie Maynard, D.R.E.
Students 147.

Fairfield, Freestone Co., St. Bernard of Clarivaux (1976), Rev. A. Peter Whitney, Admin.
Res., 630 W. Main, 75840-1418. Tel: 903-389-4616.
Catechesis/Religious Programs—Tel: 903-389-2444.
Students 91.
Mission—Buffalo, Leon Co., Blessed Kateri Tekakwitha, (1979) 403 W. Commerce, Buffalo, 75831-0878. Tel: 903-322-3705. Rev. Theodore Rydelek, Admin.
Catechesis/Religious Programs—Bonnie Romeo, D.R.E.
Students 92.
Mission—Teague, Freestone Co., St. Mary, 609 Cedar, Teague, 75840-1617. Rev. Jesus Suarez (Colombia).
Station—Hilltop Lakes, Leon Co.

Gun Barrel City, Henderson Co., St. Jude (1975), Revs. Andrew Melel, O.I.C., (India) Admin.; Joseph Kallookalam, C.M.I. (India); Deacon A. Howard Palms.
Res., 103 Luther Ln., 75147-9358. Tel: 903-887-1452 (Office); 887-5803 (Res.).
Catechesis/Religious Programs—Mrs. Edna Beltz, D.R.E.
Students 109.
Mission—Malakoff, Henderson Co., Mary Queen of Heaven.

Henderson, Rusk Co., St. Jude (1934), Rev. Octavio Suarez, C.M.F., (Colombia) Admin.
Res., 200 Morningside, P.O. Box 128, 75652. Tel: 903-657-4398; Fax: 903-657-4472.
Catechesis/Religious Programs—Lucille Haag, D.R.E.
Students 145.
Mission—Tatum, San Pedro the Fisherman, 1835 Chapparral, Tatum, 75691.

Jacksonville, Cherokee Co., Our Lady of Sorrows (1954), Revs. Peter Revel (Sri Lanka) Admin.; Sebastian Kallarackal, C.M.I. Pastoral Associates: Sr. Joseph Ann Stull, O.S.B.; Sr. Emmanuel Cintron, O.S B.
Res., 1023 Corinth Rd., 75766-9801. Tel: 903-586-4538; Fax: 903-586-4996.
Catechesis/Religious Programs—Tel: 903-586-5016. James Gillard, D.R.E.
Students 245.
Mission—Rusk, Cherokee Co., Sacred Heart, Rusk. P.O. Box 947, Rusk, 75785. Tel: 903-589-1103.
Res., 351 E. 6th, Apt.7, Rusk, Tel: 903-683-2494.

Jefferson, Marion Co., Immaculate Conception, Rev. Ben Comsky, O.S.B.
Res., 201 N. Vale St., 75657-2143. Tel: 903-665-2869; Fax: 903-665-8778. [CEM]
Catechesis/Religious Programs—Students 31.
Mission—Waskom, Harrison Co., St. Lawrence Brindisi, P.O. Box 928, Waskom, 75292-0928. Tel: 903-687-2385.
Catechesis/Religious Programs—Students 51.

Kilgore, Gregg Co., Christ the King (1936), Rev. Mark Kusmirek (SFR); Deacons William H. Bridwell; Dennis Gilchrist; William Holda.
Res., 1407 Broadway, 75662-3209. Tel: 903-984-3716; Fax: 903-984-1426.
Catechesis/Religious Programs—Maxine Torres, D.R.E.
Students 195.
Mission—Overton, Rusk Co., Our Lady Queen of Angels.

Longview, Gregg Co., St. Anthony (1880), Rev. Thaddeus Markut (Poland) Admin.; Deacon Joseph Pipak.
Res., 908 E. Olive, 75601. Tel: 903-758-0116; Fax: 903-758-8303.
Catechesis/Religious Programs—Tel: 903-758-4684.
Students 431.

St. Mary (1982), Revs. Gavin Vaverek, J.C.L.; Bernard Boteju (India); Chris Gorski (Poland); Deacon John Borens.
Res., 2108 Ridgewood Dr., 75601-1999. Tel: 903-757-5855.
School—405 Hollybrook Dr., 75601-2464. Tel: 903-753-1657; Fax: 903-758-7347. Mrs. Janel Garner, Prin.
Lay Teachers 23; Students 310; Religious 1.
Catechesis/Religious Programs—Tel: 903-757-5891; Fax: 903-758-5074. Len Budai, D.R.E.
Students 368.

Lufkin, Angelina Co., St. Patrick (1928), Revs. Eduardo Nevares, M.S.; Maurice F. Linehan, M.S.; Alan McGuirk, M.S. In res., Bro. Fabian Fuemmeler, M.S.
Res., 2118 Lowry St., 75901-1316. Tel: 409-634-6833; Fax: 409-634-6891.
School—St. Patrick School, (Grades PreK-6). Tel: 409-634-6719. Maria Elena Cuchapin, Prin.
Religious 1; Lay Teachers 7; Students 90.
Catechesis/Religious Programs—Tel: 409-639-3676. D.R.E.: Della Vadnais, (PreK-6); Barbara Klimpt, (7-12).
Students 328.

Marshall, Harrison Co., St. Joseph (1874), Rev. Ron Diegel; Deacon Adrian Roden.
Res., 410 N. Alamo Blvd., 75670-3450. Tel: 903-935-2536; Fax: 903-938-1591. [CEM]
School—St. Joseph School, (Grades PreK-6) 2307 S. Garrett, 75670. Tel: 903-935-5502. Mrs. Dana Humphries, Prin.
Lay Teachers 11; Students 74.
Catechesis/Religious Programs—Students 250.

Mount Pleasant, Titus Co., St. Michael (1917), Rev. Gerald Haby, S.M.; Deacons Barry Beckman; Jose Moreno.
1403 E. First St., 75455-4715. Tel: 903-572-5227.
Res., 310 Denman Dr., 75455-4157. Tel: 903-572-5611.
Catechesis/Religious Programs—Thelma Longoria, D.R.E.
Students 255.

Nacogdoches, Nacogdoches Co., Sacred Heart (1716), Rev. Msgr. James E. Young; Revs. Said Duran (Ecuador); Darius Pawlowski (Poland); Deacon John K. Shaffer Tel: 409-569-8544.
2508 Appleby Sand Rd., 75961-4524. Tel: 409-564-7807; Fax: 409-564-7807.
Res., 504 North St., 75961. Tel: 409-564-7134.
Catechesis/Religious Programs—Tel: 409-564-5321. Sr. Mary Ann Aman, C.H.M., D.R.E.
Students 272.
Missions—Chireno, Nacogdoches Co., Our Lady of Lourdes, c/o St. Therese, Rte. 2, Box 1093, Center, 75935-9269. Tel: 409-598-3458; Fax: 409-598-5599. Rev. Devaraj Arulappa. [CEM]
Moral, Nacogdoches Co., Immaculate Conception, Hwy. 7 West, 75961. [CEM]
Chapel—Nacogdoches, St. Mary's Chapel, Stephen F. Austin State University, 211 E. College, 75961. Tel: 409-564-0661. Rev. Wm. John Dominic Logan, O.P.

New Boston, Bowie Co., St. Mary of the Cenacle (1918), Rev. Leo Schloemer, Glmy.
Mailing Address: P.O. Box 914, 75570-0914.
Res., 212 Magnolia St., 75570. Tel: 903-628-2323.
Catechesis/Religious Programs—Students 53.

Palestine, Anderson Co., Sacred Heart (1893), Revs. Harold P. Paulsen; Zacharias Kunnakkattuthara (India); Deacons Alex Kobar; Bryan Carey, Prison Chap.; Jesus H. Reyes.
Res., 503 N. Queen St., 75801-2718. Tel: 903-729-2463. [CEM]
Sacred Heart Preschool—503 N. Queen St., 75801-2718.
Catechesis/Religious Programs—Tel: 903-729-5375. David Bunch, D.R.E.
Students 258.

Paris, Lamar Co., Our Lady of Victory (1880), Rev. Anthony Alphonse (India).
Res., 3300 Clarksville St., 75460. Tel: 903-784-1000; Fax: 903-784-3946.
Catechesis/Religious Programs—Helen Ressler, D.R.E.
Students 154.

Pittsburg, Camp Co., Holy Cross (1987), Rev. Robert Poandl, Glmy.
Mailing Address: P.O. Box 846, 75686-0846.
413 Hill Ave., Pittsburgh, 75686. Tel: 903-856-6944.

Res., 100 Arch Davis Rd., 75686. Tel: 903-856-7609.
Catechesis/Religious Programs—Students 140.
Mission—Mount Vernon, Franklin Co., Sacred Heart, P.O. Box 918, Mount Vernon, 75457-0918.

Sulphur Springs, Hopkins Co., St. James (1880), Rev. Christopher Shackelford, Admin.; Deacons Donald R. Brown; Jose Hernandez; William O'Brien; Loren Seely.
Mailing Address: P.O. Box 93, 75483-0093.
297 Texas St., 75483. Tel: 903-885-1222; Fax: 903-885-5855.
Res., 303 Texas St., 75483.
Catechesis/Religious Programs—Tel: 903-885-0157. Laura Deckard, D.R.E.
Students 99.
Missions—Emory, St. John the Evangelist. Rev. Christopher Shackelford.; Gilmer, Upshur Co., St. Francis of Assisi, P.O. Box 704, Gilmer, 75644. Tel: 903-569-3665. Rev. Daniel Gonzalez.; Mineola, Wood Co., St. Peter the Apostle, P.O. Box 1022, Mineola, 75644. Rev. Daniel Gonzalez.; Winnsboro, Wood Co., St. Ann, P.O. Box 733, Winnsboro, 75494-0733. Tel: 903-629-7884. Rev. Eugeniusz Dobosz (Poland).

Texarkana, Bowie Co., Sacred Heart (1874), Rev. Msgr. Gerald Priest; Rev. Jerry Dobosz (Poland); Deacon Keith A. Woods.
Res., 4505 Elizabeth St., 75503-2998. Tel: 903-794-4444. [CEM 2]

Trinity, Trinity Co., Most Holy Trinity (1972), Rev. Felix Chirapurathel, O.Praem., (India) Admin.
Res., Rte. 1, Box 61-X, 75862-9801. Tel: 409-594-6664; Fax: 409-594-6664.

Union Grove-Gladewater, Upshur Co., St. Theresa of the Infant Jesus (1945), Rev. Henry J. Lenz, M.S.; Deacon Guy Blasingame.
Mailing Address: P.O. Box 967, Gladewater, 75647-0967.
Old Hwy. 271 & Point Pleasant Rd., Union Grove, Tel: 903-845-2306.
Catechesis/Religious Programs—Maureen Matson, D.R.E.
Students 70.

Whitehouse, Smith Co., Prince of Peace (1996), Rev. Daniel L. Daugherty.
Mailing Address: P.O. Box 456, 75771-1078.
Res., 14588 Hwy. 110 S., 75791. Tel: 903-581-9600; Fax: 903-561-4946.
Catechesis/Religious Programs—Students 113.

Chaplains of Public Institutions

FAIRFIELD. *Boyd Unit, Texas Department of Criminal Justice.* Rev. A. Peter Whitney. Mailing Address: 630 W. Main, 75840-1418.

LOVELADY. *Eastham Unit, Texas Department of Corrections,* Rte. 1, Box 93, 75851. Tel: 409-636-7147. Rev. Virginio Vazquez (CC) Chap. Mailing Address: P.O. Box 1974, Huntsville, 77342-1914.

NEW BOSTON. *Telford Unit.* Deacon Donald R. Brown Tel: 903-628-2706.

PALESTINE. *Beto I Unit and Louie C. Powledge Unit, Texas Department of Corrections.* Deacon Jesus H. Reyes, Chap. Mailing Address: Beto I Unit & Louie C. Powledge Unit, Texas Department of Corrections, Rte. 2, Box 2250, 75801-9612. Tel: 903-928-2217 (Beto I Unit); 723-5074 (Louie C. Powledge Unit).

RUSK. *Rusk State Hospital and Skyview Unit, Texas Dept. of Corrections.* Rev. Sebastian Kallarackal, C.M.I., Chap., Rte. 1, 1023 Corinth Rd., Jacksonville, 75766-3267. Tel: 903-586-4538.

TENNESSEE COLONY. *Michael Unit, Texas Department of Corrections.* Deacon T. Bryan Carey, Chap., Michael Unit, Box 4500, 75886-4500. Tel: 903-928-2311.

Special Assignment:
Reverend Monsignors—
Joseph, Milam, Pres., University of Dallas, 1845 E. Northgate, Irving, TX 75062. Tel: 214-721-4047

Retired:
Reverend Monsignors—
Szapka, Edward J., 123 S. Houston, Longview, TX 75602-1103
Reverend Fathers—
Knaresborough, Francis J., 1621 E. 42nd St., Rm. 404A, Texarkana, AR 75502
Przydacz, John, 800 E. Dawson, #6997, Tyler, TX 75701-2093
Weihrer, John A., Priest's Residence, 2407 E. Holcomb, Houston, TX 75773-0699

Absent on Sick Leave:
Reverend Fathers—
Zakshesky, Francis, c/o Mrs. Regina Zakshesky, 605 Miller St., Alpena, MI 49707

Permanent Deacons:
Beckman, Barry, St. Michael, Mt. Pleasant
Blasingame, Guylan, St. Theresa, Union Grove
Borens, John, St. Mary, Longview
Bridwell, William H., Christ the King, Kilgore
Brown, Donald R., Telford Unit, New Boston
Carey, Thomas B., Michael Unit, TDC, Tennessee Colony
Dunn, John E., Inactive, St. Joseph, Clarksville
Flores, William, St. Edward, Athens; St. Theresa, Canton
George, Anthony, (Retired), Cathedral of the Immaculate Conception, Tyler
Germann, Joseph, St. Ann, Winnsboro
Gilchrist, Dennis S., Christ the King, Kilgore
Hall, Dwight S., (Inactive), Cathedral of the Immaculate Conception, Tyler
Hernandez, Jose, St. James, Sulphur Springs
Holda, William M., Christ the King, Kilgore
Kobar, Alex, Sacred Heart, Palestine
Martinez, Ramiro, Cathedral of the Immaculate Conception, Tyler
Milton, John, Assignment Outside Diocese
Moreno, Joseph, St. Michael, Mt. Pleasant
Noriega, Ramon, Cathedral of the Immaculate Conception, Tyler
O'Brien, William E., St. James, Sulphur Springs
O'Sullivan, William H., (Retired), Cathedral of the Immaculate Conception, Tyler
Palms, Howard A., St. Jude, Gun Barrel City
Pipak, Joseph, St. Anthony, Longview
Reyes, Jesus, Our Lady of Guadalupe, Diboll
Reyes, Jesus H., Sacred Heart, Palestine
Roden, John Adrian, St. Joseph, Marshall
Seeley, Loren G., St. James, Sulphur Springs
Shaffer, John K., Sacred Heart, Nacogdoches
Woods, Keith A., Sacred Heart, Texarkana

INSTITUTIONS LOCATED IN THE DIOCESE

[A] GENERAL HOSPITALS

TYLER. *Trinity Mother Frances Health System,* 800 E. Dawson St., 75701. Tel: 903-593-8441.
For a complete listing, refer to the Hospitals section.

PARIS. *St. Joseph Hospital and Health Center,* 820 Clarksville St., P.O. Box 9070, 75461. Tel: 903-785-4521; Fax: 903-737-3848.
For a complete listing, refer to the Hospitals section.

TEXARKANA. *St. Michael Health Care Center,* 2600 St. Michael Dr., 75503.
For a complete listing, refer to the Hospitals section.
St. Michael Rehabilitation Hospital, 2400 St. Michael Dr., 75503.
For a complete listing, refer to the Hospitals section.

[B] MONASTERIES AND RESIDENCES OF PRIESTS

PALESTINE. *Hermitage,* Rte. 3, Box 3575, 75801. Rev. Denis Walsh. Other Institutions: Houses of Religious Men 1; Total in Residence 1; Total Staff 1.
Prayer Mountain Hermitage, Rte. 3, Box 3574, 75801. Sr. Mary Vogel, H.S.S.R.

[C] CONVENTS AND RESIDENCES FOR SISTERS

LUFKIN. *Monastery of the Infant Jesus,* 1501 Lotus Ln., 75904-2699. Tel: 409-634-4233. Cloistered Dominican Nuns. Sr. Mary John, O.P., Prioress. Professed Sisters 22.

[D] CAMPUS MINISTRY

TYLER. *Tyler Junior College and The University of Texas at Tyler Newman Center,* 423 S. Broadway, 75702. Tel: 903-592-1617. Attended from the Cathedral of the Immaculate Conception. Rev. Michael Doyle. Tel: 903-592-1617.

KILGORE. *Kilgore Junior College Newman Center,* 1407 Broadway, 75662. Tel: 903-984-2501. Kitty Wisener, Dir.

NACOGDOCHES. *Stephen F. Austin University Catholic Student Center,* P.O. Box 7051, SFASU, 75962. Tel: 409-564-0661. Rev. John D. Logan, O.P., Chap. Other Institutions: Newman Centers; Total in Residence 1; Total Staff 1.

[E] MISCELLANEOUS

TYLER. *Maternity Counseling and Adoption Services,* 922 Old Omen Rd., 75701. Tel: 903-596-7787; Fax: 903-596-7786. 24-Hour Maternity Line: 1-800-CARE-002. Mrs. Jody Westbrook, Dir.
**Tyler Catholic School Foundation,* 1015 E.S.E. Loop 323, 75701-9663. Mailing Address: P.O. Box 131175, 75713.

LONGVIEW.
**Longview Catholic School Endowment Fund,* 405 Hollybrook, 75605.

LUFKIN.
**Lufkin School Foundation,* 2118 Lowry, 75901.
**St. Patrick School Fund,* 2118 Lowry, 75901.

RELIGIOUS INSTITUTES OF MEN REPRESENTED IN THE DIOCESE

For further details refer to the corresponding bracketed number in the Religious Institutes of Men or Women section.

[0600]—*Brothers of the Congregation of the Holy Cross.*—C.S.C.
[]—*Carmelite of Mary Immaculate.*—C.M.I.
[0360]—*Claretian Missionaries.*—C.M.F.
[0570]—*Glenmary Home Missioners.*—Glmy.
[]—*Heralds of Good News.*
[]—*Indian Missionary Society.*—I.M.S.
[0720]—*The Missionaries of Our Lady of La Salette.*—M.S.
[]—*Missionaries of St. Francis de Sales.*—M.S.F.S.
[0430]—*Order of Preachers - Dominicans.*—O.P.
[]—*Order of the Imitation of Christ.*—O.I.C.
[]—*Religious Congregation of the Little Flower.*—C.S.T.
[0760]—*Society of Mary.*—S.M.

RELIGIOUS INSTITUTES OF WOMEN REPRESENTED IN THE DIOCESE

[0230]—*Benedictine Sisters of Pontifical Jurisdiction.*—O.S.B.
[2100]—*Congregation of the Humility of Mary.*—C.H.M.
[]—*Congregation of the Mother of Carmel.*—C.M.C.
[0470]—*Congregation of the Sisters of Charity of the Incarnate Word. Houston, Texas.* (San Antonio, TX).—C.C.V.I.
[1050]—*Dominican Contemplative Nuns.*—O.P.
[1070-19]—*Dominican Sisters of Houston, Texas (Congregation of the Sacred Heart).*—O.P.
[1310]—*Franciscan Sisters of Little Falls, MN.*—O.S.F.
[]—*Hermit Sisters of St. Romuald.*—H.S.S.R.
[2080]—*Home Mission Sisters of America (Glenmary).*
[2970]—*School Sisters of Notre Dame.*—S.S.N.D.
[1070-03]—*Sinsinawa Dominican Congregation of the Most Holy Rosary.*—O.P.
[4090]—*Sisters of Social Service.*—S.S.S.
[1570]—*Sisters of St. Francis of the Holy Family.*—O.S.F.
[1970]—*Sisters of the Holy Family of Nazareth.*—C.S.F.N.

NECROLOGY

† Novak, Emilian E., (Retired). —Died Aug. 27, 1996.

Diocese of Venice

(Diocesis Venetiae in Florida)

Most Reverend

JOHN J. NEVINS, D.D.

Bishop of Venice; ordained June 6, 1959; appointed Titular Bishop of Rusticiana and Auxiliary of Miami February 6, 1979; consecrated March 24, 1979; appointed First Bishop of Venice July 17, 1984; installed October 25, 1984. *Res., P.O. Box 2006, Venice, FL, 34284.*

ESTABLISHED OCTOBER 25, 1984.

Square Miles 9,035.

Comprises the Counties of Charlotte, Collier, DeSoto, Glades, Hardee, Hendry, Highlands, Lee, Manatee and Sarasota in the State of Florida.

For legal titles of parishes and diocesan institutions, consult the Chancellor.

To Serve with Mercy

Catholic Center: P.O. Box 2006, Venice, FL, 34284. Tel.: 941-484-9543; Fax: 941-484-1121.

STATISTICAL OVERVIEW

Personnel	
Bishop	1
Priests: Diocesan Active in Diocese	58
Priests: Active Outside Diocese	7
Priests: Retired, Sick or Absent	21
Number of Diocesan Priests	86
Religious Priests in Diocese	65
Extern Priests in Diocese	63
Ordinations:	
Diocesan Priests	2
Transitional Deacons	2
Permanent Deacons in Diocese	60
Total Brothers	20
Total Sisters	155
Parishes	
Parishes	50
With Resident Pastor:	
Resident Diocesan Priests	35
Resident Religious Priests	11
Without Resident Pastor:	
Administered by Priests	4
Missions	12
Professional Ministry Personnel:	
Brothers	4
Sisters	36
Lay Ministers	56
Welfare	
Catholic Hospitals	2
Total Assisted	198,083
Health Care Centers	6
Total Assisted	72,721
Homes for the Aged	5
Total Assisted	318
Specialized Homes	3
Total Assisted	3,340
Special Centers for Social Services	11
Total Assisted	18,922
Educational	
Diocesan Students in Other Seminaries	17
Total Seminarians	17
High Schools, Diocesan and Parish	3
Total Students	1,577
Elementary Schools, Diocesan and Parish	9
Total Students	3,999
Catechesis/Religious Education:	
High School Students	2,635
Elementary Students	8,618
Total Students Under Catholic Instruction	16,846
Teachers in the Diocese:	
Priests	3
Brothers	2
Sisters	16
Lay Teachers	274
Vital Statistics	
Receptions into the Church:	
Infant Baptism Totals	2,663
Adult Baptism Totals	204
Received into Full Communion	279
First Communions	2,483
Confirmations	2,067
Marriages:	
Catholic	465
Interfaith	313
Total Marriages	778
Deaths	2,266
Total Catholic Population	172,906
Total Population	1,367,235

Catholic Center—1000 Pinebrook Rd., Venice, 34292. Tel: 941-484-9543; Fax: 941-484-1121., *Mailing Address: P.O. Box 2006, Venice, 34284.*

Office of the Bishop—Sr. CARMELLA T. DECOSTY, S.N.J.M., Exec. Asst.; Ms. KATHRYN BLISS, Exec. Sec.; Mrs. MARY LYNN SERBIN, Sec. & Receptionist.

Vicar General—Very Rev. THOMAS G. ANGLIM, V.G.

Chancellor and Moderator of the Curia—Very Rev. JEROME A. CAROSELLA.

Administrative Assistant to the Chancellor/Notary—Miss JEANNE C. HICKEY.

College of Consultors—Rev. Msgr. ROBERT SCHIEFEN, J.C.D.; Very Revs. THOMAS G. ANGLIM, V.G.; JEROME A. CAROSELLA, Chancellor; EDWARD D. MORETTI, V.E.; ROBERT D. TABBERT, V.F.; ESTEBAN G. SOY, Treas.; Revs. GERARD FINEGAN; NICANOR LOBATO; VINCENT SHEEHY; JOSEPH STEARNS.

Episcopal Vicars and Deans—Northern and Eastern Deaneries: Very Rev. EDWARD D. MORETTI, V.E.; Southern and Central Deaneries: Vacant; Eastern Deanery: Very Rev. JOSE J. RUIZ, V.F.; Central Deanery: Very Rev. TIMOTHY MURPHY, V.F.; Southern Deanery: Very Rev. ROBERT D. TABBERT, V.F.; Northern Deanery: Vacant.

Presbyteral Council—Very Revs. THOMAS G. ANGLIM, V.G.; ROBERT R. CANNON, J.C.L., Moderator; JEROME A. CAROSELLA, Chancellor; EDWARD D. MORETTI, V.E.; JOSE J. RUIZ, V.F.; TIMOTHY MURPHY, V.F.; ESTEBAN SOY; ROBERT D. TABBERT, V.F.; Revs. NORMANDO FELIZ; GERALD P. GROGAN; JANUSZ JANCARZ; JEROME P. KAYWELL, Sec. THADDEUS KLOC; NICANOR LOBATO; CHARLES MALLEN, C.SS.R.; STEPHEN E. MCNAMARA; JOSEPH E. STEARNS.

Theologian to the Bishop—Rev. FAUSTO STAMPIGLIA, S.A.C.

Censor Librorum—Rev. JOEL SCHEVERS, O.Carm., M.A., Th.M.

Vicar for Clergy—Very Rev. EDWARD D. MORETTI, V.E.

Priest Personnel Board—Rev. STEPHEN E. MCNAMARA, Chm.

Continuing Education of Clergy—Rev. MARK HEUBERGER.

Official Archivist—Very Rev. JEROME A. CAROSELLA.

Historical Archivist—Mrs. GAIL M. MCGRATH.

Legal Counsel—Mr. STEPHEN W. BUCKLEY, ESQ., Goldberg, Goldstein, Buckley, P.A.

In-House Counsel—Ms. VICTORIA PFLUG, ESQ.

Delegate of the Bishop for Sexual Misconduct Cases—Dr. TERRY REILLY, D.Min., M.A., Case Mgr.

Diocesan Tribunal—All Pastoral Center searches for information prior to October 25, 1984, should be directed to the Diocese of St. Petersburg for Manatee, Hardee, Sarasota, DeSoto, Glades, Charlotte and Lee Counties; to the Diocese of Orlando for Highlands Co. and to the Archdiocese of Miami for Hendry, and Collier Counties.

Judicial Vicar—Very Rev. ROBERT R. CANNON, M.Th., J.C.L.

Assessor/Auditor Administrator—Dr. TERRY H. REILLY, M.A., D.Min.

Defender of the Bond—Rev. JOEL SCHEVERS, O.Carm., M.A., Th.M.

Promoter of Justice—Rev. Msgr. ROBERT SCHIEFEN, J.C.D.

Judges—Very Rev. ROBERT R. CANNON, M.Th., J.C.L.; Revs. DENNIS KLEMME, J.C.D.; JOHN V. DOLCIAMORE, S.T.L., J.C.L.; Rev. Msgr. JAMES MCGRATH, J.C.D.; Rev. Msgr. ELLSWORTH KNEAL, J.C.D.

Ecclesiastical Notaries—Mrs. JOHANNA MARONE; Miss JOANNE COYNE; Mrs. ANN MANRODT; Mrs. ZONIA HERRERA.

Consultant—Dr. WILLIAM I. STRYKER.

Vicar for Marriage Matters—Very Rev. ROBERT R. CANNON, M.Th., J.C.L.

Diocesan Offices and Directors

Building Department—Very Rev. ESTEBAN SOY, Dir.; Mr. RAYMOND HADDAD, Assoc. Dir.

Campaign for Human Development—Sr. MARY HEYSER, R.S.H.M., Dir.

Campus Ministry—Rev. JOHN H.R. ELLIS, D.Min., Dir., *The Newman House at the New College Campus, 528 58th St., Sarasota, 34243-2104.* Tel: 941-355-2099; 6415., *Mailing Address: Catholic Campus Ministries, 333 Somerset Ave., Sarasota, 34243-1926.*

Northern Deanery—Campus Ministers serving: New College, Manatee Community College (North Campus), Ringling School of Art & Design, University of South Florida; Miss ELEANOR CLUNE; Mrs. BURGESS ELLIS; Rev. JOHN H.R. ELLIS; Miss JENENE GARGUILO; Mrs. PAT GARGUILO; Mrs. TERRY MOSSLER; Ms. JUDY PARSONS; Mrs. SUE SOBZAK; Mrs. BABS WARREN; Mr. DENNIS WARREN-,Campus Minister serving: Manatee Community College (South Campus); Mr. GEOF KLEDZIK. Tel: 941-484-6397.

Eastern Deanery—Campus Ministers serving: South Florida Community College; Rev. GERALD P. GROGAN; Ms. PATRICIA A. WHITE. Tel: 941-453-4757.

Southern Deanery—Campus Minister serving: Florida Gulf Coast University, Edison Community College (Fort Myers and Naples), University of South Florida; Rev. RICK WOJNICKI, O.S.F.S. Tel: 941-275-8783.

Catholic Charities of the Diocese of Venice, Inc.—Mrs. ROSEMARY WINDER STRANGE, A.C.S.W., Exec. Dir.

Communications Department—Mrs. GAIL M. MCGRATH, Dir.; Mrs. SARA BRINN, Exec. Sec.

"The Florida Catholic, Venice Edition"—Most Rev.

JOHN J. NEVINS, D.D., Publisher; Miss JEAN A. PALOMBO, Editor/Reporter.

"The Florida Catholic of Venice, Inc."—Very Rev. JEROME A. CAROSELLA, Pres. & Dir.; Mrs. GAIL M. MCGRATH, Sec. & Dir.; Mr. JOHN G. BAUER, Treas. & Dir.

Catholic Mass on Television—Mrs. GAIL M. MCGRATH, Exec. Producer; Mrs. SARA BRINN, Production Coord. & Leaflet Missals; Mrs. CONSTANCE STENDARDO, Production Asst.

Community Information—Mrs. GAIL M. MCGRATH.

Media and Public Relations—Mrs. GAIL M. MCGRATH.

Venice Catholic Communications, Inc.—1000 Pinebrook Rd., Venice, 34292. Most Rev. JOHN J. NEVINS, D.D., Pres. & Dir.; Very Rev. JEROME A. CAROSELLA, Vice Pres. & Dir.; Mrs. GAIL M. MCGRATH, Sec. & Treas. & Dir.

Data Processing Office—Mr. WILLIAM TWOHIG, Mgr.

Development Office/Annual Bishop's Appeal—Mr. WILLIAM MCCARTHY, Dir.; Mrs. MARIAN DODSON, Asst. Dir. Devel. Oper.

Diaconate—Co-Directors: Revs. THADDEUS KLOC; FAUSTO STAMPIGLIA, S.A.C.

Ecumenical and Interreligious Affairs—Rev. WILLIAM ADAMS.

Education—Sr. ROBERTA SCHMIDT, C.S.J., Dir.; Sr. REGIS KRUSNIEWSKI, S.S.N.D., Dir., Catechetical Ministry; Vacant; Supt., Schools; Bros. PAUL HENNESSY, C.F.C., Pres., School for Pastoral Ministry; E. THOMAS HEWITT, C.F.C., Coord., Migrant Education Apostolate, Los Hermanos.

Finance Department—Very Rev. ESTEBAN SOY, Diocesan Treas.; Mr. JOHN BAUER, Dir.; Mrs. LEIGH MORROW, Controller.

Hispanic, Migrant and Spanish Speaking Apostolates/National Migration Week—Rev. NICANOR LOBATO, Dir.

Pastoral Ministries—Dr. MIMI REILLY, D.Min., Dir.

African-Caribbean American Ministry, Office of—Mr. TYRONE PETERS, Dir.

Charismatic Renewal—Very Rev. ROBERT R. CANNON, M.Th., J.C.L., Spiritual Dir.

Contemplative Prayer—Rev. ROBERT MATTINGLY, Spiritual Moderator.

Divorced and Separated Ministry—Rev. GERARD BENSON, O.Carm., Coord.

Family Life Office—(includes Parenting and all Marriage Enrichment and Marriage Preparation programs); Dr. MIMI REILLY, D.Min., Dir.; Mrs. PATRICIA HINES, Assoc. Dir. Natural Family Planning. Co-Directors: BRUCE CONROY; DIANE CONROY; Rev. ROBERT CANNON, Spiritual Moderator.

Lay Ministry Office—Dr. MIMI REILLY, D.Min., Dir.

Commission on Women—

Renew—Evangelization.

Older Catholics, Apostolate for—Dr. ANNE SWING, D.Min., Dir.

Parish Pastoral Ministers—Dr. MIMI REILLY, D.Min., Coord.

Peace and Social Justice—Mr. ROBERT HENNEMEYER.

Persons with Disabilities, Apostolate for—Mrs. OLIVIA BECKER, Dir.

Respect Life—Rev. NICHOLAS MCLOUGHLIN, Moderator; Very Rev. ROBERT R. CANNON, M.Th., J.C.L., Assoc. Moderator; Mrs. OLIVIA BECKER, Exec. Dir.

Project Rachel—Tel: 800-329-4787.

Youth Ministry Office—Mrs. DIANE KLEDZIK, Exec. Dir.

Teens Encounter Christ—Rev. JOSEPH CLIFFORD, Spiritual Moderator.

Scouting—Rev. TIMOTHY NAVIN, Spiritual Dir.

Prison Ministry—Priests of the Diocese; Deacon EDWARD D. LUNDY.

Religious, Vicar for—Sr. CHRYSTA LERHINAN, I.H.M.

Rural Life—Very Rev. JOSE J. RUIZ, V.F., Dir.

Vocations/Seminarian Formation—Revs. JOSEPH STEARNS, Dir. ROBB MONGIELLO, Assoc. Dir. EUGENE D. RYAN; MARK HEUBERGER.

Diocesan Apostolates and Other Offices

Aids, Ministry to People with—Sr. FRANCES NEVOLO, O.L.C.; Sr. MARY JOHN FRANEY, O.L.C.; Sr. JUDY SIMONIS, C.S.J.

Cursillo Movement—Rev. CHARLES MALLEN, C.SS.R., Spiritual Dir.; Mrs. IRENE BAUER, Lay Dir.

Secretariado Hispano de Cursillos—Rev. AURELIANO SANTA OLAYA, Dir. Espiritual; Mr. CARMELO ORTEGA, Dir. Laico.

Propagation of the Faith/Mission Cooperative Program—Rev. EDWARD PICK, Dir.

Miscellaneous

Campaign for Human Development—Sr. MARY HEYSER, R.S.H.M., Chm.

Catholic Relief Services—Sr. MARY HEYSER, R.S.H.M.

Equestrian Order of the Holy Sepulchre of Jerusalem—Mr. WILLIAM E. BALL, Diocesan Rep.

Holy Childhood Association—Rev. EUGENE MCCARTHY, Dir.

Knights of Columbus—Rev. DAVID CRONIN, Chap.

Legion of Mary—Revs. VINCENT CLEMENTE, Manasota Curia: RAFAEL PADILLA, Southwest Florida Curia:

St. Vincent DePaul Society—Mr. WILLIAM J. MARTYN, Diocesan Trustee.

Venice Diocesan Council of Catholic Women—Rev. CLAUDE BRUBAKER, Spiritual Dir.; Mrs. ROSLYN CORRIGAN, Pres.

Advisory Bodies

Bishop's Critical Concerns Commission—Dr. MIMI REILLY, D.Min., Exec. Dir.; Mr. JAMES HANKS, Chm.

Building Commission—Very Rev. ESTEBAN SOY, Chm./Dir.; Mr. RAYMOND HADDAD, Asst. Chm.

Campaign for Human Development Board—Sr. MARY HEYSER, R.S.H.M., Chm.; Rev. HOWARD ALLEN, SR., Vice Chm.

Catholic Charities Board of Directors—Most Rev. JOHN J. NEVINS, D.D.; Mrs. JUDY SULLIVAN, Chm.

Clergy Health Care Committee—THOMAS MCBRYAN, M.D., Chm.

Commission for Contemplative Prayer—Rev. ROBERT MATTINGLY, Spiritual Moderator; Dr. MIMI REILLY, D.Min., Chm.

Commission on Aging—Dr. ANNE SWING, D.Min., Dir.

Commission of Youth Ministry—Mrs. DIANE KLEDZIK, Exec. Dir.

Communications Committee—Mrs. GAIL M. MCGRATH, Chm.

Cursillo Secretariat—Rev. CHARLES MALLEN, C.SS.R., Spiritual Dir.; Mrs. IRENE BAUER, Lay Dir.

Finance Committee—Mr. THOMAS OWENS, Chm.; Mr. PATRICK GALLAGHER, C.P.A., Consultant.

Insurance Committee (Province of Miami)—Mr. JOHN BAUER, (Diocese of Venice).

Insurance Committee (Diocese of Venice)—Very Rev. THOMAS G. ANGLIM, V.G., Chm.

Investment Committee—Mr. THOMAS OWENS, Chm.; Mr. DONALD L. HAISMAN, Consultant.

Liturgy Commission—Rev. EUGENE RYAN, Chm.

Pension Plan Board of Trustees (Archdiocese of Miami/Dioceses of St. Petersburg and Venice)—Rev. Msgr. THOMAS NOEL FOGARTY, Chm. Co-Vice Chm.: Very Rev. THOMAS G. ANGLIM, V.G.; Rev. ROBERT GIBBONS.

Planning and Development Committee—Very Rev. THOMAS G. ANGLIM, V.G., Chm.

Priest Personnel Board—Rev. STEPHEN E. MCNAMARA, Chm.

Priestly Life Committee—Rev. JOSEPH STEARNS.

Real Estate Board—Rev. Msgr. JOHN O'DOWD, Co-Chm.; Rev. NEIL FLEMMING, Co-Chm.

Religious Education Advisory Council—Mrs. SUSAN MORUSIEWICZ, Pres.

Respect Life Consultants—Mr. EDWARD CUTHBERT; Mrs. PAT HINES; Ms. DIANE KLEDZIK; Miss KRISTA MARTIN; Sr. ROBERTA SCHMIDT, C.S.J.; Mrs. FLORENCE TULLY; Mr. STEPHEN WOOD.

School Board—Mrs. MARILYN PERCY, Chm.

Social Justice and World Peace Commission—Mr. ROBERT HENNEMEYER, Dir.

Vocations Committee—Rev. JOSEPH STEARNS, Chm.

Youth Council—Mrs. DIANE KLEDZIK, Exec. Dir.

Youth Ministry, Commission on—Mrs. DIANE KLEDZIK, Exec. Dir.

CLERGY, PARISHES, MISSIONS AND PAROCHIAL SCHOOLS

CITY OF VENICE
(Sarasota County)

1—EPIPHANY CATHEDRAL (1958), Very Rev. Esteban G. Soy, Rector; Revs. George Ratzmann; Chester Domaszewicz; Joel Schevers, O.Carm., (Retired); Peter F. Brudzynski, (Retired); Deacon John L. Blackburn, (Retired); Rev. Richard J. Mueller; Deacons Richard Nowak; Coleman Geary; Robert Tomasso; Francis Cole.
Res., 310 Sarasota St., 34285. Tel: 941-484-3505; Fax: 941-488-9333.
School—316 Sarasota St., 34285. Tel: 941-488-2215; Fax: 941-488-2216. Dewayne Byrnes, Prin.
School Sisters of Notre Dame 1; Lay Teachers 20; Students 366.
Catechesis/Religious Programs—Tel: 941-485-2325. Sr. Frances Lalor, R.S.M., D.R.E.
Students 395.
Convent—237 Nassau St., N., 34285. Tel: 941-484-4765.

2—OUR LADY OF LOURDES (1986), Rev. Vincent J. Sheehy; Deacon James Cooper. In res., Rev. Robert R. Cannon.
Res., 1301 Center Rd., 34292. Tel: 941-497-2931; Fax: 941-497-5849.
Catechesis/Religious Programs—Students 77.

OUTSIDE THE CITY OF VENICE

Arcadia, De Soto Co., St. Paul (1885), Revs. William Adams, S.T.L.; Juan Pascual de Miguel.
Res., 1208 N.E. Oak St., 34266. Tel: 941-494-2611; Fax: 941-494-6385.
Catechesis/Religious Programs—Tel: 941-494-2835.
Students 201.

Avon Park, Highlands Co., Our Lady of Grace (1956), Rev. Gerald P. Grogan.
Res., 595 E. Main St., 33825. Tel: 941-453-4757; Fax: 941-453-4757.
Catechesis/Religious Programs—Tel: 941-453-7537. Patricia A. White, D.R.E.
Students 149.

Boca Grande, Lee Co., Our Lady of Mercy (1988), Very Rev. Jerome A. Carosella.
Res., P.O. Box 181, 33921. Tel: 941-964-2254; Fax: 941-964-2254.

Bokeelia, Lee Co., Our Lady of the Miraculous Medal (1965), Revs. Vincent LeGere; Arthur Hannaway.
Res., 12175 H. Stringfellow Rd., 33922. Tel: 941-283-0456; Fax: 941-283-1118.
Catechesis/Religious Programs—Students 50.

Bonita Springs, Lee Co., St. Leo (1962), Revs. Thaddeus Kloc; Sofonias Ortez.
Res., 28290 Beaumont Rd., 34134. Tel: 941-992-0901; Fax: 941-992-0901.
Catechesis/Religious Programs—Cynoi Rypl, D.R.E.
Students 201.
Mission—Bonita Springs, Lee Co., Hispanic Mission, 33923.

Bradenton, Manatee Co., Sacred Heart (1969), Revs. Michael Mullen, I.C., Admin.; Michael O'Neill, I.C. In res., Rev. Daniel Sloan, I.C.
Res., 1220 15th St. W., 34205. Tel: 941-748-2221; Fax: 941-748-1744.
Catechesis/Religious Programs—Students 132.

St. Joseph (1927), Rev. Carmelo Cadarso (Spain).
Res., 2704 33rd Ave., W., 34205. Tel: 941-756-3732; Fax: 941-753-4095.
School—Tel: 941-755-2611; Fax: 941-755-2611. Sr. Christine Patrick, S.P., Prin
Sisters 2; Lay Teachers 26; Students 464.
Catechesis/Religious Programs—Tel: 941-755-4335. Sr. Carolyn Glynn, S.P., D.R.E.
Students 265.

SS. Peter and Paul the Apostles (1987), Very Rev. Edward D. Moretti, V.E.; Revs. Dennis Cooney; Anthony Pastucci.
Office: 2850 75th St., W., 34209. Tel: 941-795-1228; Fax: 941-794-0127. [CEM]
Catechesis/Religious Programs—Tel: 941-798-9705. Sonya Adkins, D.R.E.
Students 360.

Cape Coral, Lee Co., St. Andrew (1964), Very Rev. Timothy Murphy; Revs. Arnold Zebrowski; Jerome P. Kaywell; Rafael Padilla; Deacons Dennis Hedge; Lowell O'Grady.
Res., 2628 Del Prado Blvd., P.O. Box 845, 33910-0845. Tel: 941-574-4545.
School—(Grades K-8). Tel: 941-772-3922; Fax: 941-772-7182. Sr. Elizabeth Dunn, O.P., Prin.
Sinsinawa Dominicans 5; Lay Teachers 24; Students 494.
Catechesis/Religious Programs—Tel: 941-574-2411. Mr. Carmine Macedonio, D.R.E.
Students 885.

Blessed Katharine Drexel (1990), Revs. John F. Deary, O.S.A.; Tom Pohto, O.S.A.
Office: 1922S. 20th Ave., 33911. Tel: 941-285-9501; Fax: 941-283-9502.
Catechesis/Religious Programs—Colleen Spiro, D.R.E.
Students 240.

Clewiston, Hendry Co., St. Margaret (1932), Rev. Santo Cigolini, C.S.
Res., 208 N. Deane Duff Ave., 33440. Tel: 941-983-8585; Fax: 941-983-9673.
Catechesis/Religious Programs—Tel: 941-983-8844. Sr. Esther Gutierrez, D.R.E.
Students 280.

Englewood, Sarasota Co., St. Raphael (1957), Rev. Thomas J. Walsh, O.Carm.; Rev. Msgr. Ferdinand A. Evans (CIN) (Retired); Rev. Stanley S. Kromer, O.Carm.
Res., 770 Kilbourne Ave., 34223. Tel: 941-474-9595; Fax: 941-475-5697.
Catechesis/Religious Programs—Tel: 941-473-2359. Sr. Lorraine Soukup, S.S.N.D., D.R.E.
Students 50.

Fort Myers, Lee Co.,

1—ST. VINCENT DE PAUL, (1986), Rev. David Arle;

Deacon Joseph Jolin.
Church & Mailing Address—13031 State Rd. 80, 33905. Tel: 941-693-0818; Fax: 941-693-0818.
Catechesis/Religious Programs—Fax: 941-693-8459.
Students 107.

2—CHURCH OF THE RESURRECTION OF OUR LORD, (1974), Revs. Stephen E. McNamara; Adelbert Buscher, O.S.B.; Oliver Toner, O.Carm.
Mailing Address & Parish Center: 8121 Cypress Lake Dr., 33919. Tel: 941-481-7172; Fax: 941-481-8007.
Church—8051 Cypress Lake Dr., 33919.
Catechesis/Religious Programs—Tel: 941-481-6863. Joan Kamm, D.R.E.
Students 274.

3—ST. CECILIA, (1965), Revs. Thomas E. Murphy, O.S.F.S.; David J. Devlin, O.S.F.S.; Bro. Harry F. McGovern, O.S.F.S., Pastoral Assoc. In res., Revs. Richard J. Wojnicki, O.S.F.S., Campus Min.; John T. Doyle, O.S.F.S., (Retired); Deacons Steven P. Wetzel, O.S.F.S.; Bill Brodeur; Lorin Fortier.
Res., 5632 Sunrise Dr., 33919. Tel: 941-936-3635; Fax: 941-936-2108.
Catechesis/Religious Programs—Betty Crowell, D.R.E.
Students 172.

4—ST. COLUMBKILLE, (1993), Rev. Charles K. Sullivan.
Church—12171 Iona Rd., 33908. Tel: 941-489-3973; Fax: 941-432-0066.

5—ST. FRANCIS XAVIER, (1910), Very Rev. Thomas M. Anglim; Revs. Stanislaus Pierog (Poland); Marian Konobrocki; Jean-Ronald Joseph.
Res., P.O. Box 912, 2133 Heitman St., 33902. Tel: 941-334-2161; Fax: 941-332-4178.
School—Tel: 941-334-7707; Fax: 941-334-8605. Sr. Elaine Mahoney, O.S.F., Prin.
Franciscan Sisters of Allegany 2; Lay Teachers 27; Students 642.
Catechesis/Religious Programs—2048 Heitman St., 33902. Tel: 941-334-7636.
Students 257.
Missions—Fort Myers, Lee Co., Our Lady of Perpetual Help, 2063 Lafayette St., 33901. Tel: 941-334-2234; San Jose, Jesus the Worker, 4235 Figuera, 33905. Tel: 941-332-2829.

6—OUR LADY OF LIGHT, (1990), Revs. Angelo F. Maraldo, O.S.F.S.; Thomas J. Palko, O.S.F.S.
Office: 19680 Cypress View Dr., 33912. Tel: 941-267-7088; Fax: 941-267-5481.
Res., 9404 Windlake Dr., 33912. Tel: 941-267-2228.
Catechesis/Religious Programs—Students 312.

7—HISPANIC MISSIONS OF FORT MYERS, (Hispanic), Rev. Hector Gonzalez (Spain).
Res., 472 Figuera Ave., 33905. Tel: 941-693-5330; Fax: 941-693-5243. [JC]
Churches—Jesus the Worker. (Jesus Obrero). 4235 Michigan Link, 33916. Tel: 941-332-2829; San Jose, 10750 Gladiolus Dr., 33908. Tel: 941-481-1143.
Catechesis/Religious Programs—Tel: 941-693-6448.
Students 151.

Fort Myers Beach, Lee Co., Ascension (1962), Rev. Thomas J. Goggin; Deacon Charles Kiesel.
Res., 6025 Estero Blvd., 33931. Tel: 941-463-6754; Fax: 941-765-1923.
Catechesis/Religious Programs—Students 33.

Golden Gate, Collier Co., St. Elizabeth Seton (1975), Revs. Joseph A. Spinelli, O.S.A.; James V. Vitali, O.S.A.
Res., 2760 52 Ter., S.W., 34116. Tel: 941-455-3900; Fax: 941-455-6895.
School—Tel: 941-455-2262; Fax: 941-455-0549. Mrs. Judy Mankowski, Prin.
Lay Teachers 13; Students 290.
Catechesis/Religious Programs—Tel: 941-455-9598. Cecelia Andretta, D.R.E.
Students 357.

Grove City, Charlotte Co., St. Francis of Assisi (1978), Revs. Bartholomew Larkin, O.Carm.; Morris Wells, O.Carm.
Church—5265 Placida Rd., 34224. Tel: 941-697-4899; Fax: 941-697-0602.
Res., 80 Oakland Hills Pl., Rotonda West, 33947.
Catechesis/Religious Programs—Sr. Monica Hayes, D.R.E.
Students 120.

Holmes Beach, Manatee Co., St. Bernard's (1956), Revs. Patrick E. Farrell; Donald E. Baier.
Res., 248 S. Harbor Dr., 34217, P.O. Box 1036, 34218. Tel: 941-778-4769; Fax: 941-778-4644.
Catechesis/Religious Programs—Tel: 941-778-0277. Alice White, D.R.E.
Students 76.

Immokalee, Collier Co., Our Lady of Guadalupe (1957), Revs. Vilmar Orsolin, C.S.; Onorio Benacchio, C.S.; Jean Woady Louis.
Res., 207 South 9 St., 33934. Tel: 941-657-2666; Fax: 941-657-3431.
Catechesis/Religious Programs—Mrs. Maria Marquez, D.R.E.
Students 369.

LaBelle, Hendry Co., Our Lady Queen of Heaven (1975), Revs. Normando Feliz; Origenes Noboa, Pastoral Assoc.; Deacon Vincent Walsh.
Res., 355 S. Bridge St., P.O. Box 357, 33935. Tel: 941-675-0030; Fax: 941-675-0756. [JC]
Catechesis/Religious Programs—Tel: 941-675-7447; 3724. Sr. Muriel Cameron, D.R.E.
Students 166.

Lake Placid, Highland Co., St. James, Revs. Leo J. Culliton (BUF) (Retired); John J. Koros (OM) (Retired); Raymond Jones (DET) (Retired); Vincent Llaria (Spain).
120 Citrus Rd., N.E., 33852. Rev. Raymond Jones (DET) (Retired), 779 Hawk Ave., 33852.
Res., P.O. Box 1139, 33852. Tel: 941-465-3215. [JC]
Catechesis/Religious Programs—St. James Catholic Church, 3380 Placidview Dr., 33852. Tel: 941-465-3215 (Office); 465-5140 (Rectory).
Students 30.
Comunidad Catolica Hispana Santiago Apostol Mission, Highlands, Rev. Jose Gonzalez.
Mailing Address: P.O. Box 899, 33862. Tel: 941-385-6762.
Res., 685 CR 621 E., 33852.

Lehigh Acres, Lee Co., St. Raphael (1962), Revs. James Flemming; Walter Swietek (Poland); Deacons James Jacob; Lambert Kuhr; Armindo Guzman.
Res., 2514 Leigh Blvd., 33971. Tel: 941-369-1831; Fax: 941-369-1039. [JC]
Catechesis/Religious Programs—Tel: 941-369-6424. James C. Brantner, D.R.E.
Students 215.

Longboat Key, Manatee Co., St. Mary Star of the Sea (1973), Rev. Edward Pick.
Res., 4280 Gulf of Mexico Dr., Box 60, 34228. Tel: 941-383-1255; Fax: 941-383-8758.

Marco Island, Collier Co., San Marco (1971), Revs. Eugene J. McCarthy; J. Daniel Dymski.
Res., 851 San Marco Rd., 33937. Tel: 941-394-5181; Fax: 941-394-1385.
Catechesis/Religious Programs—Tel: 941-394-4068. David Swierczek, D.R.E.
Students 264.
Mission—Everglades City, Collier Co., Holy Family Church, Everglades City, 33929.

Moore Haven, Glades Co., St. Joseph the Worker (1960) (Spanish), Rev. Emilian Swiatecki.
Res., Hwy. 27 and St. Rd. 78, P.O. Box 1109, 33471. Tel: 941-946-0696; Fax: 941-946-3444. [JC]
Mission—Buckhead Ridge, Glades Co., St. Theresa of the Child Jesus, 33471. Tel: 941-946-0696.

Murdock, Charlotte Co., St. Maximilian Kolbe (1988), Rev. Robert Mattingly; Deacons Louis Cosentino; Edgar Cobett.
Office: 1441 Spear St., 33948. Tel: 941-743-6877; Fax: 941-743-9176.
Catechesis/Religious Programs—Barbara Sutton, Pastoral Assoc.
Students 199.

Naples, Collier Co.,

1—ST. ANN, (1935), Very Rev. Robert D. Tabbert, V.F.; Revs. Louis Massanet; Julius Lang; Sr. Judy Anne Baldino, S.S.J., Pastoral Assoc.
Res., 407-439 Ninth Ave., S., 33940. Tel: 941-262-4256; Fax: 941-262-4296.
School—542 Eighth Ave., S., 33940. Tel: 941-262-4110. Sr. George Francis Riseling, S.N.J.M., Acting Prin.
Sisters 1; Lay Teachers 22; Students 246.
Catechesis/Religious Programs—Christopher Wilkinson, D.R.E.
Students 246.

2—ST. JOHN THE EVANGELIST, (1988), Revs. Thomas J. Glackin; Donald H. Henry.
Res., 625 111th Ave., N., 34108. Tel: 941-566-8740; Fax: 941-566-9117. [CEM]
Catechesis/Religious Programs—Tel: 941-566-1678.
Students 493.

3—ST. PETER, (1974), Revs. Timothy M. Navin, Admin.; Robert M. Murphy; Deacons David Nolan; John J. O'Neill; Robert L. Tetrault.
Res., 5130 Rattlesnake Hammock Rd., 34113. Tel: 941-774-3337; Fax: 941-774-3077.
Mission—San Pedro, Collier Co., 5330 Caldwell St., 34113. Tel 941-774-3111.

4—ST. WILLIAM, (1973), Revs. Joseph E. Stearns; John F. Costello.
Mailing Address: P.O. Box 7188, 34101-7188. Tel: 941-261-4883; Fax: 941-261-8729.
Res., 750 Seagate Dr., 34103-2886. [JC]
Catechesis/Religious Programs—Tel: 941-263-5429. Debra Mahr, D.R.E.
Students 285.

North Port, Sarasota Co., San Pedro (1964), Rev. Patrick C. Organ.
Res., 14380 Tamiami Tr., 34287. Tel: 941-426-2500; 426-6810; Fax: 941-423-8710.
Catechesis/Religious Programs—Tel: 941-426-2893.
Students 195.

Palmetto, Manatee Co., Holy Cross (1956), Revs. Nicanor Lobato; Aureliano Santa-Olaya (Honduras); Robert J. Brague (SCR).
Res., 506-26th St. W., 34221. Tel: 941-729-3891; Fax: 941-722-1063. [JC]
Catechesis/Religious Programs—Tel: 941-729-1558.
Students 170.

Parrish, Manatee, St. Francis Xavier Cabrini (1992), Rev. Janusz Jancarz, S.Ch. (Poland).
Res., 12001 69th St., P.O. Box 220, 34219. Tel: 941-776-9790.

Port Charlotte, Charlotte Co., St. Charles Borromeo (1959), Revs. Nicholas McLoughlin; Thomas Murphy, (Retired); Thomas Wantland; John J. Mulvey.
Office: 21505 Augusta Ave., Ste. 4, 33952. Tel: 941-625-4754; Fax: 941-625-0256.
Church—2500 Easy St., P.O. Box 2545, 33949. [JC]
School—Tel: 941-625-5533; Fax: 941-625-7359. Sr. Susanne McCaslin, O.P., Prin.
Lay Teachers 14; Students 275.
Catechesis/Religious Programs—21505 Augusta Ave., Ste. 5, 33952. Tel: 941-625-5407. Susan Foster, D.R.E.
Students 450.
San Antonio (1993), Rev. Thomas J. Zedar.
24445 Rampart Blvd., 33980. Tel: 941-624-3799; Fax: 941-624-6184.
Catechesis/Religious Programs—Students 231.

Punta Gorda, Charlotte Co., Sacred Heart (1954), Rev. Robert Mongiello.
Res., 211 W. Charlotte Ave., 33950-5546. Tel: 941-639-3957; Fax: 941-639-2061.
Catechesis/Religious Programs—Tel: 941-639-9545. Sr. Josine Perez, D.R.E.
Students 137.

Sanibel, Lee Co., St. Isabel (1973), Rev. Msgr. Robert W. Schiefen; Rev. Carmen A. Caruso (JOL).
Res., 3559 Sanibel-Captiva Rd., 33957. Tel: 941-472-2763; Fax: 941-472-5351.
Catechesis/Religious Programs—Tel: 941-395-0070.
Students 71.

Sarasota, Sarasota Co.,

1—INCARNATION, (1958), Revs. Gerard Finegan; Joseph Clifford; Jeremiah Spillane; Deacon Joseph Cirieco.
Res., 2929 Bee Ridge Rd., P.O. Box 5516, 34277-5516. Tel: 941-921-6631; Fax: 941-927-2521.
School—Tel: 941-924-8588; Fax: 941-925-1248. Sr. Monica Paul Fraser, Prin.
Sisters 2; Lay Teachers 19; Students 310.
Catechesis/Religious Programs—Tel: 941-924-9566. John Garisto, D.R.E.
Students 624.

2—OUR LADY QUEEN OF MARTYRS, Manatee Co., (1959), Revs. Joseph Connolly, T.O.R.; Carl A. Birarelli; Louis McIntyre, T.O.R.
Res., 833 Magellan Dr., 34243. Tel: 941-755-1826; Fax: 941-753-1654. [CEM]
Catechesis/Religious Programs—34243. Tel: 941-755-3497. Nina Powell, D.R.E.
Students 355.

3—ST. MARTHA, (1912), Revs. Fausto Stampiglia, S.A.C.; Benedict Abraham, S.A.C.; Jose Poovakulath, S.A.C.; Vincent L. Clemente, Hospital Min.; Joseph S. Amato, J.C.L.; Celestino Gutierrez, Spanish Min.; Deacon John D. Wren, Jr.
Res., 235 Adelia St., P.O. Box 1706, 34230. Tel: 941-366-4210; Fax: 941-954-8434.
School—801 N. Orange Ave., 34236. Tel: 941-953-4181; Fax: 941-366-5580. Miss Carolyn Wheelock, Prin.
Lay Teachers 16; Students 325.
Catechesis/Religious Programs—Bro. R. Patrick Wilson, D.R.E.
Students 185.

4—ST. MICHAEL THE ARCHANGEL, (1958), Rev. Claude E. Brubaker.
Res., 5394 Midnight Pass Rd., 34242. Tel: 941-349-4174; Fax: 941-349-6388.
Catechesis/Religious Programs—Sr. Luke Crawford, S.P., D.R.E.
Students 120.

5—ST. PATRICK, (1988), Revs. Michael Hickey; George Brennan.
Res., 7900 Bee Ridge Rd., 34241. Tel: 941-378-1703; Fax: 941-378-2153.
Catechesis/Religious Programs—Tel: 941-378-1521.
Students 374.

6—ST. THOMAS MORE, (1979), Revs. Eugene D. Ryan; Jerome Callahan, O.Carm. Tel: 941-922-3273; Deacons Robert Horvath; Francis Cole.

Mailing Address: 2506 Gulf Gate Dr., 34231. Tel: 941-923-1691; Fax: 941-923-1692.
Res., 2612 Regatta Dr., 34231. [CEM]
Catechesis/Religious Programs—Students 95.

Sebring, Highlands Co., St. Catherine (1929), Very Rev. Jose H. Ruiz, V.F.
Res., 862 Bay St., P.O. Box 389, 33870. Tel: 941-385-0049. [CEM 2][JC]
Catechesis/Religious Programs—Tel: 941-385-3993. Sr. Joseph Louise Reichlin, O.S.F., D.R.E. Students 187.

Wauchula, Hardee Co., St. Michael (1969), Revs. Michael Koncik, C.SS.R.; Edmund Regensburger, C.SS.R.; George H. Bridge, C.SS.R.; James J. Burke, C.SS.R.
Res., 408 Heard Bridge Rd., Rte. 2. Box 8A, 33873. Tel: 941-773-4089; Fax: 941-773-5641.
Catechesis/Religious Programs—Tel: 941-773-4215.
Students 299.
Convent—409 Alice St., 33873. Tel: 941-773-4215. Vincentian Sisters of Charity
Sisters 3.
Missions—Bowling Green, Hardee Co., Holy Child, Chester Ave., Bowling Green, 33834.; Zolfo Springs, Hardee Co., San Alfonso Catholic Center, Schoolhouse Rd., Zolfo Springs, 33890.

On Duty Outside the Diocese:
Reverend Monsignors—
Mouch, Frank M., St. Leo College, P.O. Box 2187, St. Leo, FL 33574
Reverend Fathers—
Heuberger, Mark, Treas., St. Vincent de Paul Regional Seminary, 10701 S. Military Tr., Boynton Beach, FL 33436 Italy

Military Chaplains:
Reverend Fathers—
Kowalik, Jacek, Lackland AFB, TX 78236-1038
McLaughlin, Paul E., U.S. Navy, U.S. Marine Corps Air Station, Beaufort, SC 29904-5001

Absent on Leave:
Reverend Fathers—
Cikovic, Charles
Espin, Orlando O.
McGraw, John
McLoughlin, Edward

Absent on Sick Leave:
Reverend Monsignors—
LaFemina, Anthony A.
Reverend Fathers—
Morillo, Jose

Priests Released from Diocesan Assignment:
Reverend Fathers—
O'Connell, William
Walk, Donald J.

Graduate Studies:
Reverend Fathers—
Menzies, Scott

Sabbatical:
Reverend Fathers—
Rourke, John C.

Retired:
Reverend Monsignors—
O'Dowd, John
Reverend Fathers—
Beaumont, Joseph
Bentivoglio, Louis
Cronin, David
Dittman, Bernard
Duggan, Joseph P.
Gonzalez, Mario
Gorr, Benjamin
Loncar, Sebastian
Moran, Joseph P.
Romero, William

Permanent Deacons:
Attridge, James (NY)
Blackburn, John L.
Brodeur, Wilfred (CIN)
Cabrera, Crescencio (BO)
Camacho, Francis (FR)
Cirieco, Joseph
Cobett, Edgar
Cole, Francis (HRT)
Cook, James (TR)
Cooper, James
Cosentino, Louis A. (Y)
Crant, Ellis (PHX)
DiMeglio, Michael
DiSalvo, Aldo (HRT)
Dubay, Frank
Fathauer, Ronald (MIA)
Fortier, Lorin W.
Fox, Leonard (TOL)
Geary, Coleman (SFD)
Gilbert, John
Grant, Russ (WH)
Gratkowski, Daniel (PEO)
Groh, Al (TR)
Guze, John (PSC)
Guzman, Armindo (MIL)
Hanlon, William (CAM)
Harkin, John
Hedge, Dennis
Horvath, Robert (NY)
Jackson, Frank (TR)
Jacob, James (HRT)
Jolin, Joseph (NOR)
Kiesel, Charles
King, Lorin (WOR)
King, Robert (OG)
Kramer, Richard (NEW)
Kuhr, Lambert (SAG)
LaLone, Norman (DET)
Loafman, Frank (DET)
Lundy, Edward
McGreen, Michael (RVC)
Monat, Noe (SFD)
Nolan, David W.
Nowak, Richard (JOL)
O'Grady, Lowell
O'Neill, John
Pipher, Jessie (NY)
Rowland, James (TR)
Schaupp, Larry (TOL)
Tetrault, Robert (JOL)
Tholl, James (TOL)
Thoresen, Norman (MIL)
Tomasso, Robert (CHI)
Urrico, Francis (PRO)
Walsh, Vincent P. (FR)
Walton, Gilbert Jr. (HRT)
Wetzel, Stephen P.
Wren, John, Jr.
Zammett, Antony (HRT)

INSTITUTIONS LOCATED IN THE DIOCESE

[A] HIGH SCHOOLS

FORT MYERS. *Bishop Verot High School*, 5598 Sunrise Dr., 33919. Tel: 941-936-6700. Oblates of St. Francis de Sales. Revs. Christopher J. Hudgin, O.S.F.S., Prin. & Supr.; Joseph A. Beattie, O.S.F.S.; John A. Beattie, O.S.F.S. Priests 3; Lay Teachers 39; Students 683; Total Staff 61.

NAPLES. *St. John Neumann High School*, 3000 53rd St., S.W., 34116. Tel: 941-455-3044; Fax: 941-455-2966. Congregation of Christian Brothers. Bros. Damian D. Ryan, C.F.C., Prin.; John C. O'Neill, C.F.C.; Francis K. Fish, C.F.C.; Edward Sheehan, C.F.C.; Spencer Tafuri, C.F.C. Brothers 5; Lay Teachers 20; Students 287.

SARASOTA. *Cardinal Mooney High School*, 4171 Fruitville Rd., 34232. Tel: 941-371-4917; Fax: 941-371-6924. Sisters of Notre Dame of Chardon, OH. Sr. Mary Lucia Haas, S.N.D., Pres.; Mr. Robert Siccone, Prin. Sisters 2; Lay Teachers 36; Students 600; Total Staff 65.

[B] SCHOOLS FOR THEOLOGICAL, SPIRITUAL, PASTORAL, AND PERSONAL FORMATION

PORT CHARLOTTE. *School for Pastoral Ministry*, 2200 Kings Hwy., Bldg. 3L, Ste. 65, 33980-5760. Tel: 941-624-6339; Fax: 941-629-8555. Bro. Paul K. Hennessy, C.F.C., Pres. Priests 1; Sisters 1; Brothers 1; Students 98; Total Staff 6.

[C] MIGRANT EDUCATION

BONITA SPRINGS. *Migrant Education Apostolate, Los Hermanos*, P.O. Box 716, 34113. Tel: 941-947-9098. Brothers 3.

[D] GENERAL HOSPITALS

VENICE. *Bon Secours-Venice Healthcare Corp.*, 540 The Rialto, 34285. Tel: 941-483-7664.
For a complete listing, refer to the Hospitals section.

PORT CHARLOTTE. *Bon Secours-St. Joseph Hospital*, 2500 Harbor Blvd., 33952. Tel: 941-625-4122.
For a complete listing, refer to the Hospitals section.

[E] NURSING AND CONVALESCENT HOMES

PORT CHARLOTTE. *Bon Secours-St. Joseph Nursing Care Center, Inc.*, 2370 Harbor Blvd., 33952. Tel: 941-624-5966; Fax: 941-624-3963.
For a complete listing, refer to the Special Care Facilities section.

[F] RESIDENCES FOR THE AGED

FORT MYERS. *Villa Francisco*, 2140 Cottage St., 33901. Tel: 941-332-3229.
For a complete listing, refer to the Special Care Facilities section.

PORT CHARLOTTE. *St. Charles Housing I, Inc.*, 2550 Easy St., 33952. Tel: 941-624-2266.
For a complete listing, refer to the Special Care Facilities section.
St. Charles Housing II, Inc., 22250 Vick St., 33980. Tel: 941-624-4404; Fax: 941-624-5556.
For a complete listing, refer to the Special Care Facilities section.

SARASOTA. *St. Martha's Housing II, Inc.*, 800 N. Lemon Ave., 34236. Tel: 941-365-7913.
For a complete listing, refer to the Special Care Facilities section.
St. Martha's Housing, Inc., 1576 Eighth St., 34236. Tel: 941-366-4448.
For a complete listing, refer to the Special Care Facilities section.

[G] MONASTERIES AND RESIDENCES OF PRIESTS AND BROTHERS

VENICE. *Carmel in Venice*, 244 Harbor Dr., S., 34285. Tel: 941-485-0606. Revs. Gerard Benson, O.Carm.; Joel Schevers, O.Carm.
St. Alphonsus Residence, 1230 Schooner Ln., 34292. Tel: 941-485-3673. Rev. Charles Mallen, C.SS.R., Supr.
Xavieran Brothers, 609 Cornwell on the Gulf, 34285. Tel: 941-484-9641. Brothers of St. Francis Xavier - Retired.

ENGLEWOOD. *Society of St. Edmund Residence*, 611 W. Harvard St., 34223. Tel: 941-473-8214. Revs. Casimir Cichanowicz, S.S.E.; Edward Leary, S.S.E.; Francis Moriarty, S.S.E.; Maurice F. Ouellet, S.S.E.; Thomas D. Sullivan, S.S.E., Facilitator; Bro. George Francis Huyer, S.S.E.

FORT MYERS. *Oblates of St. Francis de Sales*, 5598 Sunrise Dr., 33919. Tel: 941-939-5334. Brothers 3.

NAPLES. *St. John Neumann High School Faculty Residence*, 3180 53rd St., S.W., 33999. Tel: 941-455-2255. Congregation of Christian Brothers. Brothers 5.

SARASOTA. *Congregation of the Holy Ghost*, 438-464 Golden Gate Pt., 34236. Tel: 941-955-1546; 941-957-3025; Fax: 941-953-4725. Revs. Raymond J. Kulwicki, C.S.Sp., Supr.; Stephen J. Lasko, C.S.Sp.; John R. Kanda, C.S.Sp.; Constantine J. Conan, C.S.Sp.; William J. Jackson, C.S.Sp.; Henry C. Schoming, C.S.Sp.; Henry C. Lemmens, C.S.Sp.; David C. Marshall, C.S.Sp.; Cornelius Van Der Poel, C.S.Sp.; Anthony A. Bacher, C.S.Sp.; Louis F. Dolan, C.S.Sp.; W. Robert Graves, C.S.Sp. Total in Residence 12.
Holy Cross Florida Regional Center, 1635 4th St., 34236. Tel: 941-365-0722. Holy Cross Brothers Residence.

[H] CONVENTS AND RESIDENCES FOR SISTERS

FORT MYERS BEACH. *San Damiano Monastery of St. Clare*. (Solemn Vows, Papal Enclosure), 6029 Estero Blvd., 33931-4325. Tel: 941-463-5599; Fax: 941-463-4993. Poor Clares. Sr. Mary Emmanuel Kilkenny, O.S.C., Abbess. Cloistered Sisters 4.

[I] RETREAT CENTERS

VENICE. *Our Lady of Perpetual Help Retreat and Spirituality Center*, 3989 S. Moon Dr., 34292. Tel: 941-486-0233. Rev. Charles Mallen, C.SS.R., Dir.

ALVA. *Mother of God House of Prayer*, 17880 Cypress Creek Rd., 33920. Tel: 941-728-3614; Fax: 941-728-3760. Sr. Sallie Latkovich, C.S.J., Dir. Total in Residence 2; Total Staff 4.

BRADENTON. *Zacchaeus Retreat House*, St. Joseph Parish, 2704 33rd Ave., W., 34205. Tel: 941-755-5812; Fax: 941-753-4095.

[J] CATHOLIC CHARITIES

VENICE. *Medical Supplies Project*, 1000 Pinebrook Rd., 34292. Tel: 941-488-5581.
Our Mother's House, 405 Manatee Ct., 34285. Tel: 941-485-6264. Catherine Christensen, Dir. Total Assisted 20. Social housing program for single mothers offering free child care. Adult residents must attend full-time educational or vocational training.

ARCADIA. *Catholic Charities of De Soto County*, 1210 E. Oak St., 34266. Tel: 941-494-1068; Fax: 941-494-1671.
Care-A-Van, 1210 E. Oak St., 34266. Tel: 941-494-1068. Total Assisted 2,291; Total Staff 5.

FORT MYERS. *Catholic Hispanic Social Services*, 4235 Michigan Ave. Link, P.O. Box 50301, 33994. Tel: 941-337-4193; Fax: 941-332-2799. Eileen M. Dhooghe, M.S.W., Dir. Total Assisted 2,704; Total Staff 7.

IMMOKALEE. *Guadalupe Social Services*, 211 S. Ninth St., P.O. Box 5034, 34143. Tel: 941-657-6242; Fax: 941-657-7761. Total Assisted 4,984; Total Staff 5.

NAPLES. *Catholic Charities in Collier County*, Counseling Services, 2210 Santa Barbara Blvd., 33999. Tel: 941-455-2655; Fax: 941-455-7235.

Emergency Assistance, Family Resource Center, 2408 Linwood Ave., Ste. #1, 33962. Tel: 941-793-0059.

PALMETTO. *Palmetto Catholic Charities*, 506 26 St., W., 34221. Tel: 941-723-1087 (Immigration); 721-0924 (Housing); Fax: 941-722-1063.

SARASOTA. *Catholic Charities District I*. Counseling Services. 1900 Main St., Ste. 204, 34236. Tel: 941-957-4496; Fax: 941-951-0223. Emergency Assistance. Tel: 941-955-6597.

Refugees Employed & Productive (REAP), 4029 N. Washington Blvd., Ste. K, 32434. Tel: 941-359-0352; Fax: 941-359-2244.

[K] FOUNDATIONS

VENICE. *Cardinal Mooney High School Foundation*, Catholic Center, 1000 Pinebrook Rd., 34292. Mailing Address: P.O. Box 2006, 34284. Tel: 941-484-9543.

Foundation for the Care of the Migrant Poor, 1000 Pinebrook Rd., 34292.

FORT MYERS. *The Bishop Verot High School Foundation*, 5598 Sunrise Dr., 33919. Tel: 941-936-6700. Rev. Christopher J. Hudgin, O.S.F.S.

St. Francis Xavier School Foundation, 2133 Heitman St., 33901. Tel: 941-334-2161; Fax: 941-332-4178. Very Rev. Thomas Anglim, V.G., Pres.; Dr. Michael Kyle, Chm.

NAPLES.

**St. Ann School Foundation, Inc.*, 407 Ninth Ave., S., 34102. Jean K. Clagett, Exec. Dir.

SARASOTA. *Incarnation School Foundation*, 2911 Bee Ridge Rd., 34239.

[L] MISCELLANEOUS LISTINGS

FORT MYERS. *Societies of St. Vincent de Paul*, 2200 First St., 33901. Tel: 941-334-2736. Mr. William J. Martyn, Diocesan Trustee.
District Council of Fort Myers, District Council of Manasota, District Council of Naples.

IMMOKALEE. *The Guadalupe Center*, 211 S. Ninth St., P.O. Box 1053, 33934. Tel: 941-657-4361; Fax: 941-657-6816. Sr. Judith A. Dohner, H.M., Dir. Total Assisted 150; Total Staff 11.

LAKE PLACID. *Comunidad Catolica Hispana Santiago Apostol Mission*, 685 CR 621 E., 33852. Mailing Address: P.O. Box 899, 33862. Tel: 941-385-6762. Rev. Jose Gonzalez, Priest-in-Charge of the Spanish speaking people of Highlands Co.

NAPLES. *Catholic Hispanic Center*, 5330 Caldwell St., 34113. Tel: 941-774-3111. Rev. Felix Alarcon (RVC), Priest-in-Charge.

PORT CHARLOTTE. *Pregnancy Crisis Careline, Inc.*, 2500 Harbor Blvd., P.O. Box 3028, 33949-3028. Olivia S. Becker, Dir. & Pres. Total Assisted 2,350; Total Staff 70.

SARASOTA. *Bethesda House*. (AIDS Ministry), P.O. Box 1706, 34230. Tel: 941-366-1886. Sr. Frances Nevolo, O.L.C.; Sr. Beverly Bobola, O.P. Total Assisted 3,320; Total Staff 2.

RELIGIOUS INSTITUTES OF MEN REPRESENTED IN THE DIOCESE

For further details refer to the corresponding bracketed number in the Religious Institutes of Men or Women section.

[0140]—*The Augustinians*.—O.S.A.
[0200]—*Benedictine Monks*.—O.S.B.
[1350]—*Brothers of St. Francis Xavier (Sacred Heart Province, St. Joseph Province)*.—C.F.X.
[0600]—*Brothers of the Congregation of Holy Cross*.—C.S.C.
[0270]—*Carmelite Fathers & Brothers*.—O.Carm.
[0310]—*Congregation of Christian Brothers*.—C.F.C.
[0480]—*Conventual Franciscans*.—O.F.M.Conv.
[0650]—*Holy Ghost Fathers*.—C.S.Sp.
[0300]—*Institute of Charity (Rosminians)*.—I.C.
[0730]—*Legionaries of Christ*.—L.C.
[1210]—*Missionaries of St. Charles Scalabrians*.—C.S.
[0590]—*Missionaries of the Holy Apostles*.—M.Ss.A.
[0920]—*Oblates of St. Francis de Sales*.—O.S.F.S.
[1070]—*Redemptorist Fathers*.—C.SS.R.
[0700]—*St. Joseph's Society of the Sacred Heart*.—S.S.J.
[0110]—*Society of African Missions*.—S.M.A.
[1260]—*Society of Christ*.—S.Ch.
[0440]—*Society of St. Edmund*.—S.S.E.
[0990]—*Society of the Catholic Apostolate*.—S.A.C.
[0560]—*Third Order Regular of St. Francis*.—T.O.R.

RELIGIOUS INSTITUTES OF WOMEN REPRESENTED IN THE DIOCESE

[0270]—*Congregation of Bon Secours*. (Marriotsville, MD).—C.B.S.
[1070-15]—*Congregation of St. Dominic (Sisters of St. Dominic of Blauvelt, NY)*.—O.P.
[1920]—*Congregation of the Sisters of the Holy Cross*.—C.S.C.
[1710]—*Congregation of the Third Order of St. Francis of Mary Immaculate*.—O.S.F.
[1070-06]—*Dominican Sisters of Hope*.—O.P.
[1070-13]—*Dominican Sisters / Congregation of the Most Holy Rosary (Adrian Dominicans)*.—O.P.
[1070-03]—*Dominican Sisters / Sinsinawa Dominican Congregation of the Most Holy Rosary*.—O.P.
[1170]—*Felician Sisters*.—C.S.S.F.
[1180]—*Franciscan Sisters of Allegheny, NY*.—O.S.F.
[2420]—*Marist Missionary Sisters*.—S.M.S.M.
[1845]—*Missionares Guadalupanas del Espiritu Santo*.—M.G.Sp.S.
[]—*Missionaries Daughters of Our Blessed Lady of the Light, Yucatan, Mexico*.—M.H.M.L.
[1360]—*Missionary Franciscan Sisters of the Immaculate Conception*. (Newton, MA).—O.S.F.
[2800]—*Missionary Sisters of the Most Sacred Heart of Jesus of Hilltrup*.—M.S.C.
[3070]—*North American Union of Sisters of Our Lady of Charity*.—O.L.C.
[3760]—*Order of St. Clare*.—O.S.C.
[3465]—*Religious of the Sacred Heart of Mary (Eastern North American Province)*.—R.S.H.M.
[2970]—*School Sisters of Notre Dame*.—S.S.N.D.
[1680]—*School Sisters of St. Francis*.—O.S.F.
[0590]—*Sisters of Charity of St. Elizabeth, Convent Station*.—S.C.
[0430]—*Sisters of Charity of the Blessed Virgin Mary*.—B.V.M.
[2575]—*Sisters of Mercy of the Americas*.—R.S.M.
[]—*Sisters of Mercy, Co. Longford, Ireland*.—R.S.M.
[2990]—*Sisters of Notre Dame*. (Chardon, OH).—S.N.D.
[3360]—*Sisters of Providence of St. Mary-of-the-Woods, IN*.—S.P.
[3720]—*Sisters of St. Ann*. (Marlboro, MA).—S.S.A.
[1630]—*Sisters of St. Francis of Pennance and Christian Charity*.—O.S.F.
[1650]—*Sisters of St. Francis of Philadelphia*.—O.S.F.
[3830-01]—*Sisters of St. Joseph of Boston*.—C.S.J.
[3840]—*Sisters of St. Joseph of Carondelet*.—C.S.J.
[3830-08]—*Sisters of St. Joseph of Cleveland*.—C.S.J.
[1990]—*Sisters of the Holy Name of Jesus and Mary*.—S.N.J.M.
[2110]—*Sisters of the Humility of Mary*.—H.M.
[2180]—*Sisters of the Immaculate Heart of Mary*. (Miami).—I.H.M.
[3730]—*Sisters of the Order of St. Basil the Great*.—O.S.B.M.
[1490]—*Sisters of the Third Franciscan Order*.—O.S.F.
[1710]—*Sisters of the Third Order of St. Francis*.—O.S.F.
[1760]—*Sisters of the Third Order of St. Francis of Penance and of Charity*. (Tiffin, OH).—O.S.F.
[2150]—*Sisters, Servants of the Immaculate Heart of Mary*. (Monroe, MI).—I.H.M.
[2160]—*Sisters, Servants of the Immaculate Heart of Mary*. (Scranton, PA).—I.H.M.
[4060]—*Society of the Holy Child Jesus*.—S.H.C.J.
[4070]—*Society of the Sacred Heart*.—R.S.C.J.
[4160]—*Vincentian Sisters of Charity*.—V.S.C.

NECROLOGY

(No Deaths)

Diocese of Victoria in Texas

(Dioecesis Victoriensis in Texia)

Most Reverend

DAVID E. FELLHAUER, PH.D., J.C.D.

Bishop of Victoria; ordained May 29, 1965; appointed Second Bishop of Victoria in Texas April 7, 1990; consecrated and installed May 28, 1990. *Res., 302 East Red River, Victoria, TX, 77901. Direct all official correspondence to: P.O. Box 4070, Victoria, TX, 77903.*

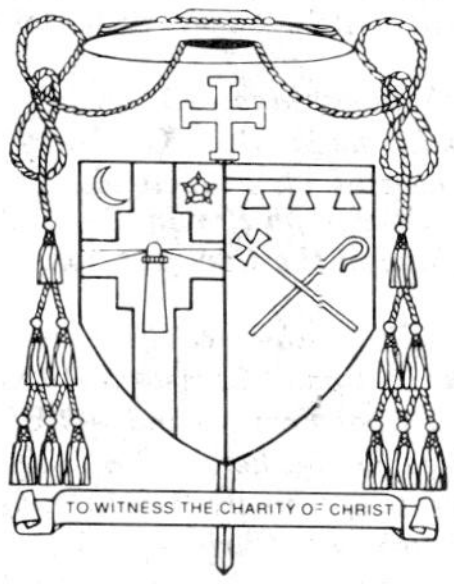

Legal Title: Diocese of Victoria in Texas.

ESTABLISHED AND CREATED A DIOCESE, MAY 29, 1982.

Square Miles Approximately 9,609.

Comprises the Counties of Calhoun, DeWitt, Goliad, Jackson, Lavaca, Matagorda, Victoria, Wharton and Colorado; also Fayette County west of the Colorado River in the State of Texas.

For legal titles of parishes and diocesan institutions, consult the Chancery Office.

Chancery Office: P.O. Box 4070, Victoria, TX, 77903. Tel.: 512-573-0828; Fax: 512-573-5725.

STATISTICAL OVERVIEW

Personnel	
Bishop	1
Priests: Diocesan Active in Diocese	44
Priests: Active Outside Diocese	3
Priests: Retired, Sick or Absent	8
Number of Diocesan Priests	55
Religious Priests in Diocese	13
Extern Priests in Diocese	10
Ordinations:	
Diocesan Priests	2
Permanent Deacons in Diocese	21
Total Brothers	1
Total Sisters	134
Parishes	
Parishes	50
With Resident Pastor:	
Resident Diocesan Priests	39
Resident Religious Priests	5
Without Resident Pastor:	
Administered by Priests	6
Missions	21
Professional Ministry Personnel:	
Brothers	1
Sisters	23
Lay Ministers	12
Welfare	
Homes for the Aged	1
Total Assisted	59
Educational	
Diocesan Students in Other Seminaries	7
Students Religious	2
Total Seminarians	9
High Schools, Diocesan and Parish	2
Total Students	174
High Schools, Private	1
Total Students	431
Elementary Schools, Diocesan and Parish	12
Total Students	2,294
Elementary Schools, Private	1
Total Students	510
Catechesis/Religious Education:	
High School Students	2,841
Elementary Students	7,294
Total Students Under Catholic Instruction	13,553
Teachers in the Diocese:	
Sisters	24
Lay Teachers	226
Vital Statistics	
Receptions into the Church:	
Infant Baptism Totals	1,642
Adult Baptism Totals	89
Received into Full Communion	127
First Communions	1,551
Confirmations	1,070
Marriages:	
Catholic	342
Interfaith	149
Total Marriages	491
Deaths	990
Total Catholic Population	108,573
Total Population	255,276

Former Bishops—Most Rev. CHARLES V. GRAHMANN, D.D., ord. March 17, 1956; appt. Titular Bishop of Equilio and Auxiliary of San Antonio, June 30, 1981; cons. Aug. 29, 1981; appt. First Bishop of Victoria, April 14, 1982; installed May 29, 1982; appt. Coadjutor of Dallas, Dec. 18, 1989; succeeded to See, July 14, 1990.

Chancery Office—1505 E. Mesquite Ln., Victoria, 77901., Mailing Address: P.O. Box 4070, Victoria, 77903. Tel: 512-573-0828; Fax: 512-573-5725. Office Hours: Mon.-Fri. 8:30-4:30.

Vicars General—Rev. Msgr. THOMAS C. MCLAUGHLIN, *P.O. Box 4070, Victoria, 77903.* Rev. Msgr. JAMES C. BRUNNER, *2001 Katy St., Bay City, 77414.*

Chancellor—Rev. Msgr. THOMAS C. MCLAUGHLIN, V.G., *P.O. Box 4070, Victoria, 77903.* Vice-Chancellor, Rev. GARY W. JANAK, J.C.L., *St. Joseph Church, P.O. Box 734, Yoakum, 77995.* Tel: 512-293-3518.

Diocesan Consultors—Rev. Msgr. THOMAS C. MCLAUGHLIN, V.G.; Rev. Msgr. JAMES C. BRUNNER, V.G.; Revs. JOHN C. BILY; GARY W. JANAK; CASIMIR JARZOMBEK, V.F.; TIMOTHY KOSLER, V.F.; LAWRENCE MATULA, V.F.; JOHN C. PETERS, V.F.; DONALD R. RUPPERT.

Vicars Forane—Victoria Deanery: Rev. MICHAEL HARROLD, V.F., *Our Lady of Victory Cathedral, 1309 E. Mesquite Ln., Victoria, 77901.* Tel: 512-575-4741. Cuero Deanery: Rev. WILLIAM DORAN, V.F., *SS. Peter & Paul, HC-01, P.O. Box 49B, Meyersville, 77974.* Tel: 512-275-3868. Edna Deanery: Rev. CASIMIR JARZOMBEK, V.F., *St. Anthony Church, P.O. Box 900, Palacios, 77465.* Tel: 512-972-2446. El Campo Deanery: Rev. LAWRENCE MATULA, V.F., *St. Robert Bellarmine Church, 512 Tegner, El Campo, 77437.* Tel: 409-543-4298. Hallettsville Deanery: Rev. JOHN C. PETERS, V.F., *Sacred Heart Church, P.O. Box H, Hallettsville, 77964.* Tel: 512-798-5888. Schulenburg Deanery: Rev. TIMOTHY KOSLER, V.F., *St. Rose of Lima Church, 1010 Lyons Ave., Schulenburg, 78956.* Tel: 409-743-3117.

Presbyteral Council—Rev. Msgr. THOMAS C. MCLAUGHLIN, V.G.; Rev. Msgr. JAMES C. BRUNNER, V.G.; Revs. JOHN C. PETERS, V.F.; CASIMIR JARZOMBEK, V.F.; LAWRENCE MATULA, V.F.; WILLIAM DORAN, V.F.; DANIEL GIORGI, O.SS.T.; JOHN BILY; MICHAEL HARROLD, V.F.; TIMOTHY KOSLER, V.F.; GARY W. JANAK; CHARLES SONNIER; MICHAEL LYONS; VICTOR SCOCCO, O.SS.T.; GABRIEL MAISON.

Diocesan Tribunal—1505 E. Mesquite Ln., Victoria, 77901. Tel: 512-573-0760.

Judicial Vicar—Rev. Msgr. THOMAS C. MCLAUGHLIN, V.G.

Judges—Revs. JOHN C. BILY; MICHAEL HARROLD, V.F.; GARY JANAK, J.C.L.; GABRIEL MAISON, J.C.D.; CELESTINO SAY.

Promoter of Justice—Appointed as needed.

Procurator Advocate—Revs. BENTON THURMOND; MICHAEL LYONS; CHARLES DWOMOH; MATTHEW HUEHLEFELD.

Defenders of the Bond—Revs. EUSTACE HERMES; DAN MORALES; TIMOTHY KOSLER, V.F.; DANIEL P. KAHLICH; THU VAN NGUYEN; FRANK LENZ; GREG KORENEK.

Notaries—Mrs. MINNIE BOCHAT; Mrs. MARY HAAS.

Priests' Personnel Board—Rev. Msgr. THOMAS C. MCLAUGHLIN, V.G., Chancellor; Rev. Msgr. JAMES C. BRUNNER, V.G.; Revs. JOHN C. PETERS, V.F.; MICHAEL HARROLD, V.F.; LAWRENCE MATULA, V.F.; TIMOTHY KOSLER, V.F.; WILLIAM DORAN, V.F.; CASIMIR JARZOMBEK, V.F.

Building Board—Deacon A. R. WEARDEN; Mr. AL HESSLER; Mr. HENRY SCHROEDER; Mr. CHARLES BLUNTZER; Mr. JAMES MIORI; Mr. ED MARTINKA.

Business Administration Office—Deacon A. R. WEARDEN, Mgr.; Mrs. JUNE OHRT; Mrs. SHARON JONES, *P.O. Box 4070, Victoria, 77903.* Tel: 512-573-0828.

Campaign For Human Development and Catholic Relief Services—Rev. GERARD CERNOCH, Dir., *SS. Cyril and Methodius Church, P.O. Box 66, Shiner, 77984.* Tel: 512-594-3836.

Catholic Youth and Family Life Ministry—Mrs. CAROLYN ADRIAN, Dir., *1505 E. Mesquite Ln., P.O. Box 4070, Victoria, 77901.* Tel: 512-573-0828.

Charismatic Renewal Movement—Sr. PERPETUA HAWES, I.W.B.S., *808 E. Nueces, Victoria, 77902.* Tel: 512-578-8456.

Council of Catholic Women (DCCW)—Rev. MICHAEL O'SHAUGHNESSEY, V.F., Moderator, *506 N. Allen, Edna, 77957.* Tel: 512-782-3588. Mrs. LILLIE MAE SCHERER, Chm., *1907 Locust Ave., Victoria, 77901.* Tel: 512-573-9547.

Diocesan Cemeteries—Rev. EUSTACE HERMES, Dir., *2303 E. Locust, P.O. Box 3098, Victoria, 77903.* Tel: 512-575-7337.

Diocesan Finance Board—Deacon A. R. WEARDEN; Mrs. BEATRICE GONZALEZ; Mrs. DOROTHY JORDAN; Mr. OTTO KALISHKO; Mr. ROMAN SHIMEK; Mr. GLEN VILLAFRANCA; Mr. JOHN STEVENSON; Rev. DONALD RUPPERT; Rev. Msgr. THOMAS C. MCLAUGHLIN, V.G.; Rev. Msgr. JAMES C. BRUNNER, V.G.

Diocesan Services Appeal—Mrs. DOROTHY JORDAN, Dir., *1505 E. Mesquite Ln., P.O. Box 4070, Victoria, 77901.* Tel: 512-573-0828.

Diocesan Office of Spiritual Renewal Center—Rev. THEODORE HAAG, O.F.M., *718A Gussie Schmidt Rd., Victoria, 77905-4303.* Tel: 512-572-0836.

Ecumenical Commission—Vacant.

Presidio of La Bahia—Mr. NEWTON WARZECHA, *P.O. Box 57, Goliad, 77963.* Tel: 512-645-3752.

Liturgical Commission—Rev. EDWARD J. WINKLER, *310 N. Stevenson, Eagle Lake, 77434.* Tel: 409-234-2842.

Permanent Diaconate Program—Rev. GABRIEL MAISON, J.C.D., Dir., *1505 E. Mesquite Ln., P.O. Box 4070, Victoria, 77903., P.O. Box 399, Moulton.*

Propagation of the Faith, Holy Childhood Association—Rev. Msgr. THOMAS C. MCLAUGHLIN, V.G., Dir.

Mission Cooperative Plan—Rev. Msgr. THOMAS C. MCLAUGHLIN, V.G., Dir., *Chancery Office, P.O. Box 4070, Victoria, 77903.*

Religious Education—Sr. DIGNA VELA, I.W.B.S., Dir., *1505 E. Mesquite Ln., P.O. Box 4070, Victoria, 77903.* Tel: 512-573-0828.

Respect Life-Pro Life—Vacant.

Rural Life Conference—Vacant.

Scouting—Vacant.

"The Catholic Lighthouse", Diocesan Newspaper—Ms. JACQUELINE SROUJI, Editor, *P.O. Box 4070, Victoria, 77903.* Tel: 512-573-0828.

Vietnamese American Apostolic Center—Rev. JOSEPH PHAM DUC TRIN, *St. Anthony Church, P.O. Box 900, Palacios, 77465.* Tel: 512-972-2685.

Vocations—Rev. GARY W. JANAK, *P.O. Box 4070, Victoria, 77903.* Tel: 512-573-0828.

CLERGY, PARISHES, MISSIONS AND PAROCHIAL SCHOOLS

CITY OF VICTORIA
(Victoria County)

1—OUR LADY OF VICTORY CATHEDRAL, Revs. Michael Harrold; Charles Dwomoh; Sr. Perpetua Hawes, I.W.B.S., Pastoral Asst.
Res., 1309 E. Mesquite Ln., 77901. Tel: 512-575-4741.
School—Tel: 512-575-5391; 578-5454. Sr. M. Leonita Barron, I.W.B.S., Prin.
Sisters 2; Lay Teachers 30; Students 519.
Catechesis/Religious Programs—Tel: 512-575-8132. Betty Mitchell, D.R.E.
Students 639.

2—HOLY FAMILY OF JOSEPH, MARY & JESUS, Revs. Peter Kaplinski; Gregory E. Korenek, Admin.; Deacon Steve Borowicz.
Office: 704 Mallette Dr., 77904. Tel: 512-573-5304.

3—OUR LADY OF LOURDES, Rev. Celestino Say, Admin.
Res., 105 N. William, 77901. Tel: 512-575-3813.

4—OUR LADY OF SORROWS, Revs. Raul P. Rendon, O.SS.T.; Wolfgang Mimms, O.SS.T.; Juan Antonio Perez, O.SS.T.; Victor Scocco, O.SS.T.; Matthew Maniamkerry, O.SS.T.; Deacons Edward Molina; Jesus Perez.
Res., 208 W. River St., P.O. Box 2548, 77901. Tel: 512-575-2293. [JC]
Catechesis/Religious Programs—Sr. Anna M. Lozano, M.C., D.R.E.
Students 1,234.
Convent—209 W. Murray St., 77901. Tel: 512-575-7654. Missionary Catechists of the Sacred Hearts of Jesus and Mary (Violetas)
Sisters 4.
Mission—Victoria, Victoria Co., Holy Trinity, 2511 Ozark, 77901.

5—ST. MARY'S, Revs. Joseph Hybner; Fred Krenek; Deacons Richard Wearden; James Koenig; Dudley Pagel.
Res., 402 S. Main, P.O. Box 2448, 77902. Tel: 512-573-4328. [JC]

OUTSIDE THE CITY OF VICTORIA

Ammannsville, Fayette Co., St. John The Baptist, Rev. Timothy Kosler, Admin. Pro-tem.
Mailing Address: 7745 Mensik Rd., Schulenburg, 78956. [CEM]
Mission—Holman, St. Wenceslaus. [CEM]

Bay City, Matagorda Co., Holy Cross, Rev. Msgr. James C. Brunner, V.G.
Res., 2001 Katy St., 77414. Tel: 409-245-6379. [CEM 2][JC]
School—Sr. M. Geraldine Pavlik, I.W.B.S., Prin.
Sisters 1; Lay Teachers 14; Students 204.
Convent—Tel: 409-245-3173.
Mission—Wadsworth, Sacred Heart.

Our Lady of Guadalupe, Rev. Edward Daniel Boren, O.F.M.; Bro. Camillus Smith, O.F.M.; Deacon Luan Van Tran.
Res., 1412 12th St., 77414. Tel: 409-245-2010.

Blessing, Matagorda Co., St. Peter's, Rev. Peter Higgins.
Res., Box 395, 77419. Tel: 512-588-6241. [CEM]
Mission—Markham, St. Robert.

Bloomington, Victoria Co., St. Patrick, Rev. Jacinto Olguin; Deacon Fred Soto.
Res., P.O. Box 217, 77951. Tel: 512-897-1155.

Cistern, Fayette Co., SS. Cyril and Methodius, Rev. Msgr. Stanley J. Petru.
Res., Holy Rosary Church, Hostyn 936 FM 2436, LaGrange, 78945. Tel: 409-247-4441.
Church—113 Manchester St., Flatonia, 78941. Tel: 512-865-2222. [CEM 2]

Columbus, Colorado Co., St. Anthony's, Rev. Daniel P. Kahlich.
Res., P.O. Box 669, 78934. Tel: 409-732-2562. [CEM]
School—635 Bonham, 78934. Tel: 409-732-5505. Mrs. Charlyne Spanihel, Prin.
Lay Teachers 13; Students 143.

Cuero, Dewitt Co., Our Lady of Guadalupe, Rev. Daniel Giorgi, O.SS.T., Admin.; Deacon Robert Ruiz.
Res., 705 W. Broadway, P.O. Box 547, 77954. Tel: 512-275-3135.

St. Michael, Rev. Johnson Owusu-Boateng.
Res., 302 E. Church St., 77954. Tel: 512-275-3554.
School—208 N. McLeod, 77954. Tel: 512-275-3854.
Sisters 2; Lay Teachers 10; Students 132.

Eagle Lake, Parish of the Nativity (1995), Rev. Edward J. Winkler.
Res., 310 N. Steveson, 77434. Tel: 409-234-2842.

East Bernard, Wharton Co., Holy Cross, Rev. Pavel Mikes.
Res., 839 Church St., P.O. Box 280, 77435. Tel: 409-335-7551. [CEM]
Convent—Tel: 409-335-4071.

Edna, Jackson Co., St. Agnes, Rev. Michael A. O'Shaughnessy; Deacon Manuel Hernandez.
Res., 506 N. Allen, 77957. Tel: 512-782-3588.

El Campo, Wharton Co., St. Philip's, Revs. Thu Van Nguyen; Michael Lyons; Deacon Jarrel Nohavitza.
Res., 304 W. Church St., 77437. Tel: 409-543-3770. [CEM]
School—Tel: 409-543-2901. Sr. Marjorie Vincik, S.S.C.J., Prin.
Lay Teachers 18; Students 272.
Catechesis/Religious Programs—D.R.E.: Sr. Carola Hajdik, Adult Spiritual Growth Program.
Students 379.

St. Robert Bellarmine, Rev. Lawrence Matula, V.F.; Sr. Elizabeth Riebschlaeger, C.C.V.I., Pastoral Assoc.; Deacon Margarito Cervantez, Jr.
Res., 512 Tegner St., 77437. Tel: 409-543-4298.

Flatonia, Fayette Co., Sacred Heart, Rev. Charles B. Carolan.
Res., P.O Box 186, 78941. Tel: 512-865-3568; Fax: 512-865-2518. [CEM]

Frelsburg, Colorado Co., SS. Peter and Paul (1836), Rev. Wayne N. Flagg; Deacon Charles Glynn.
Res., R.R. 2, Box 26, New Ulm, 78950. Tel: 409-732-3430. [CEM]

Ganado, Jackson Co., Assumption of the B.V.M., Rev. Arnold Anders.
Mailing Address: P.O. Box 369, 77962. Tel: 512-771-3425.
Res., 108 S. Sixth St., 77962. [CEM]

Goliad, Goliad Co., Immaculate Conception, Rev. Raphael Baidoo, O.SS.T.
Res., P.O. Box 49, 77963. Tel: 512-645-3095. [CEM 2]
Missions—Charco, Our Lady of Guadalupe; Fannin, Our Lady of Assumption; Berclair, Immaculate Heart of Mary.
Shrine—Our Lady of Loreto (Old Franciscan Mission).

Hallettsville, Lavaca Co., Sacred Heart, Rev. John C. Peters, V.F.; Deacons Joey Targac; W.S. (Sonny) Rogers.
Res., P.O. Box H, 77964. Tel: 512-798-5888. [CEM]
School—Tel: 512-798-4251. Mr. David Smolik, Prin. (Elementary & High School).
Sisters 2; Lay Teachers 15; Students 185.
High School—313 S. Texana, 77964.
Sisters 2; Lay Teachers 9; Students 116.

St. Mary, Rev. John C. Peters, Admin.
Church—Rte. 4, Box 369, 77964. Tel: 512-798-2128. [CEM 4]

High Hill, Fayette Co., Nativity of the Blessed Virgin Mary, Rev. Edward C. Bartsch, Admin.
Mailing Address: 2833 FM 2672, Schulenburg, 78956-5608. Tel: 409-561-8455. [CEM]
Res., 821 FM 1295, Flatonia, 78941. Tel: 512-865-3560.

Hillje, Wharton Co., St. Andrew, Rev. Clement Quainoo; Deacon Edward Wendel.
Mailing Address: Rte. 3, Box 39, El Campo, 77437. Tel: 409-648-2864. [CEM]
Mission—Louise, St. Procopius. [CEM]

Hostyn, Fayette Co., Holy Rosary, Rev. Msgr. Stanley J. Petru.
Res., 936 FM 2436, La Grange, 78945. Tel: 409-247-4441. [CEM]

Hungerford, Wharton Co., St. John the Baptist, Rev. Henry C. Rachunek.
Res., P.O. Box 121, 77448. Tel: 409-532-4747.

Inez, Victoria Co., St. Joseph's, Rev. Benton A. Thurmond.
Res., P.O. Box 337, 77968. Tel: 512-782-3181. [CEM]

Koerth, Lavaca Co., St. John the Baptist, Rev. Charles Sonnier.
Res., P.O. Box 201, Sweet Home, 77987. Tel: 512-741-3206. [CEM][JC]

Mentz, Colorado Co., St. Roch (1850), Rev. Wayne Flagg; Deacon Charles Glynn.
Mailing Address: Rte. 2, Box 191, Alleyton, 78935. Tel: 409-732-3460.

Meyersville, DeWitt Co., SS. Peter & Paul, Rev. William Doran.
Res., HC-01, Box 49B, 77974. Tel: 512-275-3868.
Mission—Westhoff, St. Aloysius.

Moulton, Lavaca Co., St. Joseph's, Rev. Gabriel Maison.
Res., P.O. Box 399, 77975. Tel: 512-596-4674; Fax: 512-596-4826. [CEM]

Nada, Colorado Co., Nativity of the Blessed Virgin Mary, Rev. Joseph A. Koebel.
Res., P.O. Box 97, 77460. Tel: 409-758-3218. [CEM]
School—St. Mary's, P.O. Box 128, 77460. Tel: 409-758-3267. Mr. Thomas Rohwer, Prin.
Lay Teachers 4; Students 65.

New Taiton, Wharton Co., St. John Nepomucene, Rev. Msgr. Julius A. Petru.
Res., Rte. 1, Box 250, El Campo, 77437. Tel: 409-543-6985. [CEM]

Palacios, Matagorda Co., St. Anthony's, Rev. Casey Jarzombek; Deacon Michael Vieira.
Res., 1004 Magnusson, Box 900, 77465. Tel: 512-972-2446.
Vietnamese Apostolate—100 Vietnam, 77465. Tel: 512-972-2685. Rev. Joseph Pham duc Trin.

Plum, Fayette Co., SS. Peter and Paul, Rev. Jerome J. Stryk.
Res., P.O. Box 97, 78952. Tel: 409-242-3600.

Port Lavaca, Calhoun Co., Our Lady of the Gulf, Revs. Dan Morales, O.M.I.; Matthew Huehlefeld; Deacon Alonzo F. Calzada.
Res., 415 W. Austin St., P.O. Box 87, 77979. Tel: 512-552-6140.
School—Our Lady of the Gulf School, Tel: 512-552-2774. Sr. Mary Clare Jones, O.S.F., Prin.
Sisters 1; Lay Teachers 2; Students 51.
Catechesis/Religious Programs—D.R.E.: Sr. Helen Rivas, C.D.P.; Sr. M Perpetua, I.W.B.S.
Students 600.
Missions—Point Comfort, St. Ann; Port O'Connor, St. Joseph; Seadrift, St. Patrick.
Vietnamese Apostolate—P.O. Box 934, Seadrift, 77983. Tel: 512-785-2515. Rev. Anthony Kiem (PT).

Praha, Fayette Co., St. Mary's, Rev. Edward C. Bartsch.
Res., 821 FM 1295, Flatonia, 78941. Tel: 512-865-3560. [CEM]

St. John, Fayette Co., St. John the Baptist, Rev. Brian Crookes.
Res., St. John Rd., Box 135, Schulenburg, 78956. Tel: 409-562-2222. [CEM]
Mission—Moravia, Lavaca Co., Ascension of Our Lord. [CEM]
In res., Rev. William Halata, (Retired).

Schulenburg, Fayette Co., St. Rose of Lima, Rev. Timothy Kosler, V.F.
Res., 1010 Lyons Ave., Box 310, 78956. Tel: 409-743-3117. [CEM]
School—400 Black, 78956. Tel: 409-743-3080. Mrs. Judy Roeber, Prin.
Sisters 1; Lay Teachers 11; Students 150.

Shiner, Lavaca Co., SS. Cyril and Methodius, Rev. Gerard Cernoch; Deacon Paul Patek. In res., Rev. Daniel O'Brien.
Res., Box 66, 77984. Tel: 512-594-3836. [CEM]
School—Mrs. Patricia Pesek, Prin. Sisters 1; Lay Teachers 13; Students 224.
High School—Mrs. Patricia Pesek, Prin. Sisters of the Incarnate Word and Blessed Sacrament 1; Lay Teachers 8; Students 58.

Sweet Home, Lavaca Co., Queen of Peace, Rev. Charles Sonnier.
Res., P.O. Box 201, 77987. Tel: 512-741-3206. [CEM][JC]

Vanderbilt, Jackson Co., St. John Bosco, Rev. James Deaconson.
Res., P.O. Box 337, 308 Garcitas St., 77991. Tel: 512-284-3361.
Mission—LaSalle, St. Theresa. [CEM]

Weimar, Colorado Co., St. Michael, Rev. John C. Bily.
Res., Box 36, 78962. Tel: 409-725-6714. [CEM]
School—Tel: 409-725-8461. Sr. M. Laura Toman, I.W.B.S., Prin.
Sisters of the Incarnate Word and Blessed Sacrament 2; Lay Teachers 7; Students 156.
Mission—Dubina, Fayette Co., SS. Cyril and Methodius.

Wharton, Wharton Co., Holy Family, Rev. Joseph L. Vrana; Deacon Alvin Matthys.
Res., 2011 Briar Ln., 77488. Tel: 409-532-3593.
Mission—Boling, St. Joseph.

Our Lady of Mt. Carmel, Revs. Raymond A. Jackson,

C.S.B.; James Blocher, C.S.B.
Res., 506 S. East Ave., 77488. Tel: 409-532-3492.

Yoakum, Lavaca Co., St. Joseph, Revs. Gary W. Janak, J.C.L.; William Lambe. In res., Rev. Charles Kram. Res., 210 Schrimscher St., Box 734, 77995. Tel: 512-293-3518. [CEM]
School—Sr. Isabel Estrada, I.W.B.S., Prin. Sisters of the Incarnate & Blessed Sacrament 2; Lay Teachers 13; Students 193.
Mission—Hochheim, St. Ann. [CEM]

Yorktown, Dewitt Co., Holy Cross, Rev. Frank B. Lenz. Res., Rte. 2, Box 152, 78164. Tel: 512-564-2893. [CEM]
Missions—Yorktown, San Luis; Nordheim, St. Ann's.

On Duty Outside the Diocese:
Reverend Fathers—
Euresti, Jesse, Austin, TX
Henninger, George, Indianapolis, IN
Mensah, Gabriel, Military Chap., U.S. Navy

On Sick Leave:
Reverend Fathers—
Ruppert, Donald R.

Retired:
Reverend Monsignors—
Schmidtzinsky, Victor
Reverend Fathers—
Bernasconi, Gino
Caponi, Jerome
Halata, William
Hermes, Eustace A.
Janson, Eugene
O'Brien, Daniel
Quiroz, Guido M.

Permanent Deacons:
Borowicz, Stephen James Michael
Calzada, Alonzo Farias
Cervantez, Margarito Candelario, Jr.
Glynn, Charles Jacky
Harper, Linard
Hernandez, Manuel
Koenig, James Nicholas
Matthys, Alvin
Molina, Edwardo Pina
Nohavitza, Jarrel Joseph
Pagel, Dudley Meryl
Patek, Paul, Sr.
Perez, Jesus Castillo
Rogers, Walter Smith, Jr.
Ruiz, Robert
Soto, Fred
Targac, Joseph
Tran, Luan Van
Vieira, Michael
Wearden, Arthur R.
Wendel, Edward

INSTITUTIONS LOCATED IN THE DIOCESE

[A] HIGH SCHOOLS, PRIVATE

VICTORIA. *St. Joseph High School*, 110 E. Red River, 77901. Tel: 512-573-2446. Sr. M. Emilie Eilers, I.W.B.S., Prin.; Sr. Michael Rose Stanzel, Vice Prin. Academics. Lay Teachers 35; Students 431.

[B] ELEMENTARY SCHOOLS, PRIVATE

VICTORIA. *Nazareth Academy*, 206 W. Convent, 77901. Tel: 512-573-6651. Sr. Kathleen Goike, I.W.B.S., Prin. Sisters of the Incarnate Word and Blessed Sacrament 6; Lay Teachers 23; Students 510. Attended from St. Mary's, Our Lady of Lourdes, Our Lady of Victory, Holy Family and Our Lady of Sorrows' Churches.

[C] HOMES FOR AGED

HILLJE. *Czech Catholic Home For The Aged*. Rte. 3, Box 40 El Campo, 77437. Tel: 409-648-2628.
For a complete listing, refer to the Special Care Facilities section.

[D] PERSONAL PRELATURES

SCHULENBURG. *Opus Dei*. Featherock Conference Center, 934 Holub Rd., 78956-5324. Tel: 409-743-3071.

[E] CONVENTS AND RESIDENCES FOR SISTERS

VICTORIA. *Franciscan Monastery of St. Clare*, 107 N. Depot St., 77901. Tel: 512-576-6347. Sr. Gabriel Zwiener, O.S.C., Supr.
Incarnate Word Convent, 1101 N.E. Water St., 77901-9298. Tel: 512-575-2266; Fax: 512-575-2165. Sr. Stephana Marbach, I.W.B.S., Supr. Gen.; Sr. M. Mildred Truchard, Local Supr. Sisters 58.
Missionary Catechists of the Sacred Hearts of Jesus and Mary, 209 W. Murray St., 77901. Sr. Antonieta Salazar, M.C.SS.CC.J.M., Supr. Sisters 4.

[F] MONASTERIES & RESIDENCES OF PRIESTS & BROTHERS

VICTORIA. *Trinity House*. Novitiate Holy Trinity Fathers. 1511 E. Commercial St., 77901. Tel: 512-573-7059. Revs. Thomas Dymowski, O.SS.T.; Victor Scocco, O.SS.T.

[G] CAMPUS MINISTRY

VICTORIA. *Catholic Student Center*, 2803 N. Ben Jordan, 77901. Tel: 512-578-1428.

WHARTON. *Wharton County Junior College Catholic Student Association*, 911 Boling Hwy., 77488.

[H] MISCELLANEOUS

VICTORIA. *Endowment Fund for the Catholic Diocese of Victoria in Texas*, P.O. Box 4070, 77903-4070. Mr. Arthur R. Wearden, Mailing Contact.
Sisters of the Incarnate Word and Blessed Sacrament of Victoria, 1101 N.E. Water St., 77901-9298. Sr. Stephana Marbach, I.W.B.S., Supr. Gen. & Mailing Contact. Legal Title: *Sisters of the Incarnate Word and Blessed Sacrament of Victoria, Texas Medical and Retirement Trust.*

RELIGIOUS INSTITUTES OF WOMEN REPRESENTED IN THE DIOCESE

For further details refer to the corresponding bracketed number in the Religious Institutes of Women section.

[2200]—*Congregation of the Incarnate Word and Blessed Sacrament.*—I.W.B.S.

[2700]—*Missionary Catechists of the Sacred Hearts of Jesus and Mary.*—M.C.SS.CC.J.M.

[3760]—*Order of St. Clare.*—O.S.C.

[]—*School Sisters of Notre Dame.*

[]—*School Sisters of St. Francis.*—S.S.S.F.

[0460]—*Sisters of Charity of Incarnate Word.*—C.C.V.I.

[0570]—*Sisters of Charity of Seton Hill, Greensburg, Pennsylvania.*—S.C.

[3950]—*Sisters of St. Mary of Namur.*—S.S.M.N.

[1010]—*Sisters of the Divine Providence of San Antonio, Texas.*—C.D.P.

[]—*Sisters of the Sacred Heart of Jesus.*—S.S.H.J.

NECROLOGY

(No Deaths)

Archdiocese of Washington

(Archidioecesis Washingtonensis)

His Eminence

JAMES CARDINAL HICKEY, S.T.D., J.C.D.

Archbishop of Washington; ordained June 15, 1946; ordained Auxiliary Bishop of Saginaw April 14, 1967; appointed Bishop of Cleveland June 5, 1974; appointed Archbishop of Washington June 17, 1980; installed August 5, 1980; created Cardinal June 28, 1988. *Office: Archdiocesan Pastoral Center, 5001 Eastern Ave., P.O. Box 29260, Washington, DC, 20017.* Tel.: 301-853-4540; Fax: 301-853-5359.

Archdiocesan Pastoral Center: 5001 Eastern Ave., P.O. Box 29260, Washington, DC, 20017. Tel.: 301-853-4500; Fax: 301-853-5346.

Most Reverend

ALVARO CORRADA, S.J., D.D., V.G.

Auxiliary Bishop of Washington, Regional Bishop of Montgomery County, Upper and Middle Prince George's County and Titular Bishop of Rusticiana; ordained July 6, 1974; consecrated August 4, 1985. *Res., 826 Wayne Ave., Silver Spring, MD, 20910.* Tel.: 301-589-3261; Fax: 301-589-2550.

Most Reverend

LEONARD J. OLIVIER, S.V.D., D.D., V.G.

Auxiliary Bishop of Washington, Regional Bishop for Northeast and Southeast Washington and Lower Prince George's County, Charles, Calvert and St. Mary's Counties and Titular Bishop of Leges; ordained June 29, 1951; consecrated December 20, 1988. *Res., 3340 St. Peter's Church Rd., Waldorf, MD, 20601.* Tel.: 301-843-1388; Fax: 301-843-1041.

Most Reverend

WILLIAM E. LORI, S.T.D., V.G.

Auxiliary Bishop of Washington, Vicar General in Curia, Regional Bishop for Northwest East and Northwest West Washington and Titular Bishop of Bulla; ordained May 14, 1977; consecrated April 20, 1995. *Res., 5001 Eastern Ave., P.O. Box 29260, Washington, DC, 20017.* Tel.: 301-853-4520; Fax: 301-853-5346.

ESTABLISHED ARCHDIOCESE JULY 22, 1939; SEPARATED FROM BALTIMORE NOVEMBER 15, 1947; BECAME A METROPOLITAN SEE OCTOBER 12, 1965

Square Miles 2,104.

Comprises the District of Columbia and Montgomery, Prince George's, St. Mary's, Calvert and Charles Counties in Maryland.

The Province of Washington has as a Suffragan, the Diocese of St. Thomas in the Virgin Islands.

For legal titles of parishes and archdiocesan institutions, consult the Chancery Office.

STATISTICAL OVERVIEW

Personnel	
Cardinal	1
Archbishop	1
Auxiliary Bishops	3
Abbots	1
Retired Abbots	2
Priests: Diocesan Active in Diocese	237
Priests: Active Outside Diocese	25
Priests: Diocesan in Foreign Missions	1
Priests: Retired, Sick or Absent	73
Number of Diocesan Priests	336
Religious Priests in Diocese	495
Extern Priests in Diocese	105
Ordinations:	
Diocesan Priests	5
Religious Priests	2
Transitional Deacons	5
Permanent Deacons	11
Permanent Deacons in Diocese	245
Total Brothers	125
Total Sisters	885
Parishes	
Parishes	139
With Resident Pastor:	
Resident Diocesan Priests	123
Resident Religious Priests	16
Without Resident Pastor:	
Missions	9
Pastoral Centers	1
Professional Ministry Personnel:	
Brothers	6
Sisters	30
Lay Ministers	172

Welfare	
Catholic Hospitals	3
Total Assisted	452,959
Health Care Centers	5
Total Assisted	92,143
Homes for the Aged	9
Total Assisted	773
Residential Care of Children	1
Total Assisted	447
Day Care and Extended Day Care Centers	5
Total Assisted	781
Specialized Homes	8
Total Assisted	1,168
Special Centers for Social Services	68
Total Assisted	109,220
Residential Care of Disabled	42
Total Assisted	203
Other Institutions	15
Total Assisted	14,302
Educational	
Seminaries, Diocesan	1
Students from This Diocese	9
Students from Other Diocese	51
Diocesan Students in Other Seminaries	22
Seminaries, Religious	33
Students Religious	190
Total Seminarians	221
Colleges and Universities	3
Total Students	20,958
High Schools, Diocesan and Parish	1
Total Students	704
High Schools, Private	16

Total Students	7,154
Elementary Schools, Diocesan and Parish	79
Total Students	22,665
Elementary Schools, Private	9
Total Students	1,418
Non-residential Schools for the Disabled	1
Total Students	71
Catechesis/Religious Education:	
High School Students	3,230
Elementary Students	24,150
Total Students Under Catholic Instruction	80,571
Teachers in the Diocese:	
Priests	29
Scholastics	3
Brothers	23
Sisters	124
Lay Teachers	2,329
Vital Statistics	
Receptions into the Church:	
Infant Baptism Totals	6,924
Adult Baptism Totals	568
Received into Full Communion	662
First Communions	6,998
Confirmations	4,609
Marriages:	
Catholic	1,314
Interfaith	853
Total Marriages	2,167
Deaths	2,646
Total Catholic Population	440,000
Total Population	2,388,506

Former Bishops—Most Rev. MICHAEL J. CURLEY, D.D., cons. Bishop of St. Augustine, June 30, 1914; promoted to the See of Baltimore, Aug. 10, 1921; named Archbishop of Baltimore and Washington, July 22, 1939; died May 16, 1947.—His Eminence PATRICK CARDINAL O'BOYLE, cons. Jan. 14, 1948; retired March 3, 1973; died Aug. 10, 1987.—His Eminence WILLIAM CARDINAL BAUM, installed May 8, 1973; appt. Prefect, Sacred Congregation for Catholic Education in the Vatican, Jan. 15, 1980; Major Penitentiary; appt. April 6, 1990.

Regional Offices—Most Rev. ALVARO CORRADA, S.J., D.D., V.G., Auxiliary Bishop of Washington; Regional Bishop of Montgomery Co., Upper and Middle Prince George's Co., Office: *826 Wayne Ave., Silver Spring, MD, 20910.* Tel: 301-589-3261; Fax: 301-589-2550. Most Rev. LEONARD J. OLIVIER, S.V.D., D.D., V.G., Auxiliary Bishop of Washington; Regional Bishop for Northeast and Southeast Washington, Lower Prince George's Co., Charles, Calver and St. Mary Counties, Office: *3340 St. Peter's Church Rd., Waldorf, MD, 20601.* Tel: 301-843-1388; Fax: 301-843-1041. Most Rev. WILLIAM E. LORI, S.T.D , V.G., Auxiliary Bishop of Washington; Vicar General in Curia; Regional Bishop for Northwest East and Northwest West Washington, *Res., 5001 Eastern Ave., P.O. Box 29260, Washington, 20017.* Tel: 301-853-4520; Fax: 301-853-5346.

Unless otherwise indicated, all Archdiocesan Offices, including the Chancery and the Tribunal, are located in the Archdiocesan Pastoral Center, *5001 Eastern Ave., P.O. Box 29260, Washington, 20017.* Tel: 301-853-4500; Fax: 301-853-5346. Office Hours: Mon.-Fri. 8:30-5.

Vicars General—Most Revs. ALVARO CORRADA, S.J., D.D.; LEONARD J. OLIVIER, S.V.D., D.D.; Most Rev. WILLIAM E. LORI, S.T.D.; Rev. Msgr. WILLIAM J. KANE, Ph.D.

Moderator of the Curia—Most Rev. WILLIAM E. LORI, V.G., S.T.D. Tel: 301-853-4520; Fax: 301-853-5346.

Chancellor—Rev. Msgr. BERNARD C. GERHARDT, S.T.L.,

J.C.D. Tel: 301-853-4520; Fax: 301-853-5346.

Canonical Consultant to the Cardinal—Sr. ELIZABETH MCDONOUGH, O.P., J.C.D.

Archivist—Deacon BERNARD A. BERNIER. Tel: 301-853-5316.

Secretary To The Archbishop—Rev. BARRY KNESTOUT. Tel: 301-853-4537; Fax: 301-853-5359.

Secretariats—Catholic Education: Mr. DANIEL CURTIN; Parish Life & Worship: Rev. ROBERT CARY HILL; Clergy: Rev. Msgr. WILLIAM ENGLISH; Women Religious: Sr. HELEN SCARRY, R.J.M.; Finance & Management: Rev. Msgr. KEVIN FARRELL; Social Concerns: Vacant; Communications: (See separate sections below).

Executive Directors—Office of Black Catholics: Mrs. JACQUELINE WILSON,Office of Hispanic Pastoral Affairs: Miss MARGARITA ROQUE, (See separate sections below).

The Tribunal

Judicial Vicar—Rev. Msgr. JOSEPH F. SADUSKY, M.Div., M.Ch.A., J.C.D. Tel: 301-853-4543; Fax: 301-853-7674.

Asst. Judicial Vicar—Rev. GODFREY T. MOSLEY, J.C.D.

Judges—Rev. Msgr. E. ROBERT ARTHUR, P.A., S.T.B., J.C.L.; Rev. Msgr. BERNARD C. GERHARDT, S.T.L., J.C.D.; Revs. G. PAUL HERBERT, J.C.L.; ROBERT J. BOZEK, J.C.L.; VINCENT J. RIGDON, M.A., J.C.L.; JAMES PROVOST, J.C.D.; GEORGE E. STUART, J.C.L.; PAUL J. BARRY, S.T.D.; Deacon JOSEPH B. MCGRATH, J.C.L.; Sr. ELIZABETH MCDONOUGH, O.P., J.C.D.

Promoter of Justice—Rev. DAVID F. O'CONNOR, S.T., J.C.D.

Defenders of the Bond—Revs. DAVID F. O'CONNOR, S.T., J.C.D.; KEVIN T. HART, J.C.D.; JOSEPH BUI TRANG NGHIEM, M.A., S.T.L., J.U.D.; MICHAEL J. KING, J.C.D.

Auditors—Rev. MICHAEL W. DOUGLAS; Deacons JOHN G. HAMILTON; ANTHONY J. MCMAHON.

Advocates—Rev. Msgr. THOMAS M. WELLS, M.A.; Revs. GEORGE E. GOLDEN, M.Div.; ROBERT G. AMEY; DONALD BRICE; MARK E. BRENNAN; JOHN T. DAKES, S.T.L.; PAUL D. LEE, S.T.D.; MICHAEL W. DOUGLAS.

Notaries—Sr. M. PAUL, O.P.; Mrs. PATRICIA K. DEBERNARDIS; Mrs. BARBARA MCGUIRE; Ms. PATRICIA A. PERKINSON; Mrs. STEPHANIE POTTS; Mrs. DENISE SMITH.

Consultative Groups

Archdiocesan College of Consultors—Most Rev. ALVARO CORRADA DEL RIO, S.J., D.D.; Most Rev. LEONARD J. OLIVIER, S.V.D., D.D.; Most Rev. WILLIAM E. LORI, S.T.D.; Rev. Msgr. THOMAS M. DUFFY; Rev. Msgr. RAYMOND G. EAST; Rev. Msgr. JOHN J. ENZLER; Rev. Msgr. DONALD S. ESSEX; Rev. Msgr. BERNARD C. GERHARDT; Rev. Msgr. W. RONALD JAMESON; Rev. Msgr. WILLIAM J. KANE, Ph.D.; Rev. Msgr. THOMAS A. KANE; Rev. GODFREY T. MOSLEY.

Archdiocesan Pastoral Council—His Eminence JAMES CARDINAL HICKEY, Pres.; Mrs. HARRIET HAYES, Sec.; Most Rev. WILLIAM E. LORI; Rev. ROBERT CARY HILL; Mr. EMMANUEL AKPAN; Mr. KENNETH J. AUBERGER; Mrs. CONCHITA BROWN; Mr. ROLAND CALDWELL; Mr. JOSEPH CAREY; Mr. JAMES CONNELL; Ms. LUISA DUARTE; Mr. ARMANDO GARCILAZO; Mrs. ALVINA LONG; Mr. ABELL LONGMORE, JR.; Mr. RANSFORD PALMER; Mr. MICHAEL S. STEELE; Ms. JANE TENNYSON; Ms. COLLEEN M. WALSH.

Archdiocesan Finance Council—His Eminence JAMES CARDINAL HICKEY, Pres.; Rev. Msgr. DONALD ESSEX; Most Rev. WILLIAM E. LORI; Rev. Msgr. KEVIN FARRELL; W. SHEPHERDSON ABELL; FRED J. BRINKMAN; DANIEL CALLAHAN; JEREMIAH C. COLLINS; RICHARD GRAVES; PAUL INTERDONATO; EUGENE I KANE; Sr. CAROL KEEHAN; ROBERT LIGHTHIZER; MICHAEL MCGARRY; B. FRANCIS SAUL, II.

Deans—Northwest West, D.C.: Rev. Msgr. RONALD JAMESON, Northwest East, D.C.: Rev. Msgr. PETER VAGHI, Southeast, D.C.: Rev. RAYMOND J. WADAS, Northeast, D.C.: Rev. EDDIE TOLENTINO, Upper Montgomery County: Rev. MILTON JORDAN, Middle Montgomery County: Rev. Msgr. THOMAS WELLS, Lower Montgomery County: Rev. JOHN PENNINGTON, Upper Prince George's County: Rev. Msgr. WILLIAM F.X. BERRY, Middle Prince George's County: Rev. MICHAEL J. KING, Lower Prince George's County: Rev. MARK HUGHES, Calvert County: Rev. PAUL M. DUDZIAK, Charles County: Rev. WILLIAM J. THOMPSON, St. Mary's County: Rev. JAMES P. MEYERS.

Council of Priests—His Eminence JAMES CARDINAL HICKEY, Pres.; Rev. Msgr. RAYMOND G. EAST, Moderator; Rev. PETER J. DALY, Vice Moderator; Rev. ROBERT CARY HILL, Sec.; Rev. Msgr. THOMAS M. WELLS, Treas.

Sisters' Senate—Sr. M. BERCHMANS HANNAN, V.H.M., Pres.; Sr. MARY LOUISE JENKINS, R.S.C.J., Vice Pres.; Sr. ELIZABETH PREMO, O.P., Sec.

Secretariat For Education

Secretary for Catholic Education—Mr. DANIEL F. CURTIN, B.S., M.Ed., M.A. Tel: 301-853-4519; Fax: 301-853-7670.

Assistant Secretary for Education—Rev. CHARLES PARRY. Tel: 301-853-5358.

Superintendent of Schools—Mr. LAWRENCE CALLAHAN. Tel: 301-853-4518.

Assistant Superintendent for Secondary Schools—Bro. WILLIAM GRIFFIN, C.F.X. Tel: 301-853-4597.

Assistant Superintendent for Elementary Schools—Mrs. TRUDY SAMPUGNARO. Tel: 301-853-4553.

Director of Curriculum Services—Sr. EILEEN CLINTON, I.H.M. Tel: 301-853-5353.

Director of Government Programs—Ms. SUZETTE CHAGNON. Tel: 301-853-4552.

Director of Instructional Services—Mrs. NOEL GESSNER. Tel: 301-853-4590.

Director of School Staff Services and Teacher Service Corps.—Sr. ROSE MARY COLLINS, S.S.J. Tel: 301-853-4549.

Financial Officer—Ms. ELIZABETH BRAWLEY. Tel: 301-853-5356.

School Marketing—VINCENT P. CLARK. Tel: 301-853-4589.

Board of Education—Mr. CARL E GIRTH, Pres.

Special Education Consultant—REBECCA S. SALON. Tel: 202-529-7600.

Office of Youth Ministry/CYO—Rev. LEROY FANGMEYER, Exec. Dir. Tel: 301-853-4591; Fax: 301-853-4501. Rev. Msgr. JOHN J. ENZLER, Coord., Devel. Tel: 301-365-1415. Rev. JOSEPH DEL VECCHIO, S.S.J., Assoc. Dir.

CYO Programs—THOMAS J. MANCO, Dir. Tel: 301-853-5382.

Ministry Development Facilitator—LYDIA CHANDLEE, (Hispanic). Tel: 301-853-5377.

Ministry Development Facilitator—DARREN FOSTER, (African American). Tel: 301-853-5375.

Scouting—Rev. Msgr. JOHN BRADY, Chap. Coord. Tel: 301-769-3332. FRANK ROSSOMONDO, Arch. Lay Co-ord., Cath. Comm. Boy Scouts & Camp Fire. Tel: 301-770-7450. ROBERT KAMMER, Arch. Lay Chm., Cath. Comm. Boy Scouting. Tel: 301-942-0882. Arch. Co-Chm., Girl Scouts: BARBARA ANN FOSTER. Tel: 301-972-2067. JOAN TREACY. Tel: 301-924-0394.

Our Lady of Mattaponi Youth Retreat and Conference Center—Tel: 301-952-9074; Fax: 301-952-0609.

Office for Religious Education—Mr. LAWRENCE RILLA, S.T.L., Dir. Tel: 301-853-4506; Fax: 301-853-7670.

Coordinator for Catechist Formation—ELIZABETH SIEGEL. Tel: 301-853-5386.

At-Large Field Representative—MICHAEL BERRY. Tel: 301-853-5385.

Hispanic Catholics Religious Education—Sr. JOAN MARY WILLIAMS, O.P. Tel: 301-853-4531.

Special Religious Education—DOLORES WILSON, Coord. Tel: 301-853-4560.

D.J. Corbett Media Center—Sr. GRACE MANLEY, R.J.M., Coord. Tel: 301-853-2200.

Campus Ministry, University of Maryland at College Park—Rev. ROBERT KEFFER, Dir. Tel: 301-864-6233; Fax: 301-864-8411.

Propagation of the Faith—Rev. VINCENT RIGDON, Archdiocesan Dir. Tel: 301-853-4527; Fax: 301-853-7670.

Mission Education Coordinator—Sr. BARBARA ANN GOODING, R.S.M. Tel: 301-853-4534.

Holy Childhood Association—Rev. VINCENT RIGDON, Dir. Tel: 301-853-4527.

Sacred Heart Basic Adult Education Center—Sr. MARIE LUCEK, O.P., Dir.; Sr. ELIZABETH PAWLICKI, O.P., Asst. Dir. Tel: 202-462-6499.

Secretariat For Parish Life and Worship

Secretary for Parish Life and Worship—Rev. ROBERT CARY HILL. Tel: 301-853-4557; Fax: 301-853-7670. Mrs. VI COLLINS, Admin. Asst., Notary Public. Tel: 301-853-4558.

Office for Adult Religious Formation—DOMINIC LOMBARDI, Dir. Tel: 301-853-5331.

Office for Ecumenical and Interreligious Affairs—Rev. PAUL LEE, Dir. Tel: 301-853-5378.

Office for Evangelization—Ms. Dir. Tel: 301-853-4596.

Office for Hispanic Liturgical Ministry - RCIA—Sr. FANCISCA MOTA, C.ach., Coord. Tel: 301-853-5334.

Office for Family Life Ministry—Mrs. JOAN O'BRIEN, Dir. Tel: 301-853-4546.

Office for Hispanic Family Life Ministry—Vacant. Tel: 301-853-5335.

Natural Family Planning—Mrs. ANNE LANCTOT, Dir. Tel: 301-853-4561.

Office for Persons with Disabilities—Ms. DOLORES WILSON, Dir. Tel: 301-853-4560.

Office of Worship—Rev. WALTER J. TAPPE, Dir. Tel: 301-853-4595. Sr. CONSTANCE WARD, S.S.J., Admin. Asst. Tel: 301-853-4594; Fax: 301-853-7684.

Alcoholism and Substance Abuse, Consultant on—Rev. JAMES J. POWDERLY, *520 Veirs Mill Rd., Rockville, MD, 20852.* Tel: 301-424-5550; Fax: 301-424-5579.

Charismatic Renewal Regional Service Committee—Rev. DONALD DEROZA; Mrs. DONALD DEROZA, *13103 Tamarack Rd., Silver Spring, MD, 20994.* Tel: 301-384-5568.

Cursillo Movement—Rev. PETER R. ALLIATA, Spiritual Dir., *St. James, 3628 Rhode Island Ave., Mt. Rainier, MD, 20712.* Tel: 301-927-0567. Lay Directors: LARRY JACKSON; SYLVIA JACKSON, *6002 40th Ave., Hyattsville, MD, 20782.* Tel: 301-864-9275.

St. Francis of Assisi Catholic Church and Center for the Deaf—Rev. EDWARD J. HELM, Dir., *7202 Buchanan St., Landover Hills, MD, 20784.* Tel: 301-459-7464; Fax: 301-459-8186.

Holy Name Society—Rev. Msgr. THOMAS A. KANE, *4101 Norbeck Rd., Rockville, MD, 20853.* Tel: 301-924-2284.

Ancient Order of Hibernians—Mr. JAMES CLARKE, *7108 Plantation Ln., Rockville, MD, 20852.* Tel: 301-881-4512.

Archdiocesan Council of Catholic Women—Rev. ROBERT G. AMEY, Spiritual Dir., *11801 Claridge Rd., Wheaton, MD, 20705.* Tel: 301-946-3636. Mrs. ANGELA WEEKS, Pres., *7501 Democracy Blvd., Bethesda, MD, 20817.* Tel: 301-365-1887.

Blue Army of our Lady of Fatima—Rev. Msgr. WILLIAM F. O'DONNELL, Spiritual Dir., *St. Thomas the Apostle, 2665 Woodley Rd. N.W., Washington, 20008-4199.* Tel: 202-234-1488. Mrs. ANNA ZACYNSKI, *14518 Perrywood Dr., Burtonsville, MD, 20866.* Tel: 301-236-4012.

Catholic Daughters of the Americas Court District of Columbia No. 212—Mrs. VIRGINIA BORKENHAGEN, Regent, *1805 19th St. N.W., Washington, 20009.* Tel: 202-667-1613.

Catholic Hospital Chaplains—Rev. JOSEPH O'BRIEN, *Cardinal O'Boyle Residence, 1150 Varnum St. N.E., Washington, 20017.* Tel: 202-219-7100.

Catholic Interracial Council of Washington, DC—Mrs. MADELINE FURTH, Pres., *3224 Northampton St. N.W., Washington, 20015.* Tel: 202-966-6794.

Catholic War Veterans of the United States—419 N. Lee St., Alexandria, VA, 22314. Tel: 703-549-3622.

Auxiliary to Post #180-(James T. Brady) Catholic War Veterans—Mrs. ADELAIDE KOWANSKY, Pres., *5900 Carlton Ln., Bethesda, MD, 20816.* Tel: 301-229-2420.

Society of St. Francis de Sales—Very Rev. JOHN CROSSIN, O.S.F.S., Chap., *721 Lawrence St. N.E., Washington, 20017.* Tel: 202-269-9412. Mrs. JOAN MCDERMOTT, Eastern U.S.A. Regional Dir., *17 Lakeview Trail, Fairfield, PA, 17320.* Tel: 717-642-6647.

First Friday Club—Rev. Msgr. JOSEPH JOSHUA MUNDELL, Spiritual Dir., *4000 Harewood Rd. N.E., Washington, 20017.* Tel: 202-332-8888.

International Federation of Catholic Alumnae—The Catholic University of America, 416 Administration Bldg., Washington, 20017. Tel: 202-526-5916.

John Carroll Society—Rev. Msgr. PETER VAGHI, Chap., *619 10th St. N.W., Washington, 20001.* Tel: 202-347-2713. Mrs. JANE GOLDEN BELFORD, Pres., *1503 N. Jefferson St., Arlington, VA, 22205.* Tel: 703-237-0704.

Knights of Columbus—Most Rev. WILLIAM E. LORI, S.T.D., Chap., *P.O. Box 29260, Washington, 20017.* Tel: 202-526-8300.

Knights of St. Jerome—Mr. VINCENT BISBOE, *St. Peter Claver, St. Inigoes, MD.* Tel: 301-872-5377.

Knights of St. John—Most Rev. LEONARD OLIVIER, *St. Peter's, P.O. Box 2352, Waldorf, MD, 20601.* Tel: 301-843-1388; Fax: 301-843-1041.

Womens Retreat League—Sr. FRANCES FLYNN, S.A., Dir., *4000 Harewood Rd. N.E., Washington, 20017.* Tel: 202-529-1111.

Engaged Encounter—Contact the Office of Family Life. Tel: 301-853-4561.

Marriage Encounter-Worldwide—Contact the Office of Family Life. Tel: 301-853-4561.

Sodality Union—Rev. GREGORY C. BUTTA, *St. Augustine Parish, 1419 V St., N.W., Washington, 20009-5810.* Tel: 202-265-1470. Mrs. GRACIELA STEVENS, Pres., *13103 Clarion Ct., Ft. Washington, MD, 20744.* Tel: 301-292-1055.

Secretariat For Social Concerns

Secretary—Vacant. Tel: 301-853-4556; Fax: 301-853-7671.

Associated Catholic Charities—EDWARD J. ORZECHOWSKI, M.S.W., Pres., *1438 Rhode Island Ave. N.E., Washington, 20018.* Tel: 202-526-4100.

A.C.C. Housing & Initiative Corp.—1438 Rhode Island Ave. N.E., Washington, 20018. Tel: 202-526-4100.

A.C.C. Model Cities Corp.—1125 Neal St. N.E., Washington, 20002. Tel: 202-396-8100.

A.C.C. Otis Street Corp.—1438 Rhode Island Ave. N.E., Washington, 20018. Tel: 202-526-4100.

SHARE, DC, Inc.—5170 Lawrence Pl., P.O. Box 768, Bladensburg, MD, 20710. Tel: 301-864-3115.

Anchor Mental Health Association, Inc.—Rev. Msgr. JOHN G. KUHN, Dir., *1001 Lawrence St. N.E., P.O. Box 29058, Washington, 20017-0058.* Tel: 202-635-5900.
Pro-Life Office—Mr. THOMAS GRENCHIK, Dir. Tel: 301-853-4555; Fax: 301-853-7671.
Campaign for Human Development—Ms. SANDY MATTINGLY-PAULEN. Tel: 301-853-5340.
Office of Social Development—Vacant. Tel: 301-853-5346; Fax: 301-853-7671.
St. Vincent de Paul Society—Mr. ARTHUR M. MCKNEW, Pres. Tel: 301-864-2106.
Ladies of Charity—Mrs. MARGARET HEDLEY, Pres., *1438 Rhode Island Ave. N.W., Washington, 20018.* Tel: 202-526-4100. Rev. CARL F. DIANDA, Spiritual Dir., *St. Francis de Sales Parish, Washington;* Sr. LETITIA, D.C., Moderator, *Providence Hospital, Washington.*
Lt. Joseph P. Kennedy Institute—Dr. RICHARD BIRKEL, Pres./CEO, *801 Buchanan St. N.E., Washington, 20017.* Tel: 202-529-7600.
St. Ann's Infant & Maternity Home—Sr. JOSEPHINE MURPHY, D.C., Admin., *4901 Eastern Ave., Hyattsville, MD, 20782.* Tel: 301-559-5500.
Christ Child Society—PAT SCANLON, Pres.; Rev. Msgr. W. LOUIS QUINN, Spiritual Dir., *5101 Wisconsin Ave. N.W., Washington, 20016.* Tel: 202-966-9250.
Community Center of the Missionaries of Charity—Sr. MARY ELIZABETH SETON, M.C., Supr., *3310 Wheeler Rd. S.E., Washington, 20032.* Tel: 202-562-6890.
Missionaries of Charity—Sr. PIETRA, M.C., Supr., *Gift of Peace Home, 2800 Otis St. N.E., Washington, 20017.* Tel: 202-269-3313. Sr. M. LIZEN, M.C., Supr., *Mother Teresa's Infant Home, 5649 Western Ave. N.W., Washington, 20015.* Tel: 202-237-6633.
Victory Housing, Inc.—Mr. JAMES A. BROWN, JR., Exec. Dir., *1515-17 Dunster Rd., Rockville, MD, 20854.* Tel: 301-279-9200.
Byron House, Inc.—1515 Dunster Rd., Rockville, MD, 20854. Tel: 301-279-9200.
Raphael, Inc.—Mr. JAMES A. BROWN, JR., Pres., *1515 Dunster Rd., Rockville, MD, 20854.* Tel: 301-279-9200.
Faith House—Sr. JOSEPHINE MURPHY, D.C., Admin., *4903 Eastern Ave., Hyattsville, MD, 20782.* Tel: 301-559-5500.
Malta House, Inc.—Mr. JAMES A. BROWN, JR., Pres., *1515 Dunster Rd., Rockville, MD, 20854.* Tel: 301-279-9200.
Bartholomew House, Inc.—Mr. JAMES BROWN, *1515 Dunster Rd., Rockville, MD, 20854.* Tel: 301-279-9200.
Manor Apartments, Inc.—Mr. JAMES A. BROWN, JR., Pres., *1515 Dunster Rd., Rockville, MD, 20854.* Tel: 301-279-9200.

Secretariat For The Clergy

Secretary for Services for Clergy, Religious Men and Secular Institutes—Rev. Msgr. WILLIAM J. ENGLISH. Tel: 301-853-4550; Fax: 301-853-7671.
Director of Priests Personnel—Rev. Msgr. WILLIAM J. ENGLISH. Tel: 301-853-4550.
Assistant to the Secretary for Clergy—Rev. PETER J. REYNIERSE. Tel: 301-853-4583.
Director, Vocations for Men—Rev. MARK BRENNAN. Tel: 301-853-4580.
Associate Director, Vocations for Men—Rev. JAMES M. STACK. Tel: 202-362-3323.
Continuing Education for Clergy—Rev. PAUL D. LEE. Tel: 301-853-5378.
St. John Vianney House—Rev. Msgr. WILLIAM ENGLISH, Dir., *4214 Saul Rd., Kensington, MD, 20895.* Tel: 301-942-1191.
Director, Permanent Diaconate—Deacon WILLIAM T. DITEWIG. Tel: 301-853-4582.
Associate Director, Permanent Diaconate—Rev. PETER J. REYNIERSE. Tel: 301-853-4583.
Priests Retirement Board—Rev. Msgr. THOMAS DUFFY, Chm. Tel: 202-966-6575.
Cardinal O'Boyle Residence for Priests—Rev. JOSEPH A. O'BRIEN, Rector, *P.O. Box 29206, Washington, 20017.* Tel: 202-269-7818.
Serra Club of Washington—Mrs. LORRAINE NOSACEK, *12306 Malin Ln., Bowie, MD, 20715.* Tel: 301-262-5755.
Serra Club of Downtown Washington—Mr. HERBERT HARMON, *5029 Domain Pl., Alexandria, VA, 22311.* Tel: 703-379-2799.
Serra Club of Prince George's Co.—Mr. ROBERT PRANGLEY, *6114 42nd Pl., Hyattsville, MD, 20781.* Tel: 301-927-3106.
Serra Club of Southern Maryland—Rev. WALTER ROURKE, Pres., *10548 Wicomico Ridge Rd., Charlotte Hall, MD, 20622.* Tel: 301-884-7464.
Liaison with Council of Priests—(see Consultative Bodies) Religious priests and brothers, Secular Institutes, Consultant on Alcoholism.

Secretary For Women Religious

Secretary for Services to Women Religious and Secular Institutes—Sr. HELEN SCARRY, R.J.M. Tel: 301-853-4576; Fax: 301-853-7671.
Liaison with Sisters' Senate—(see Consultative Bodies).

Secretariat For Finance and Management

Secretary For Finance and Management—Rev. Msgr. KEVIN FARRELL. Tel: 301-853-4523; Fax: 301-853-2787.
Accounting and Financial Management—Mr. RICHARD B. GRAVES, Controller. Tel: 301-853-4525.
Facilities Management—Mr. RICHARD DE STWOLINSKI. Tel: 301-853-4572; Fax: 301-853-7679.
Materials and Pastoral Center Management—Ms. ALESSANDRA STYLES. Tel: 301-853-4532; Fax: 301-853-7673.
Personnel and Benefits—DOROTHY MOORE, Dir. Tel: 301-853-4513; Fax: 301-853-7680.
Archdiocesan Building Committee—Rev. Msgr. JOSEPH A. RANIERI, Chm.
Paul VI Institute for the Arts—Rev. Msgr. MICHAEL DI TECCIA FARINA, Dir., *924 G St. N.W., Washington.* Tel: 202-347-1450.
Archdiocesan Finance Council—(see Consultative Bodies).
Carroll Publishing Company—(see Secretariat for Communications).
Archdiocesan Sacred Arts Committee—Rev. Msgr. W. RONALD JAMESON, *1725 Rhode Island Ave. N.W., Washington, 20036.* Tel: 202-347-3215; Fax: 202-347-7184.
Cornerstone for Tomorrow, Inc.—Rev. Msgr. KEVIN FARRELL, *P.O. Box 29260, Washington, 20017.* Tel: 301-853-4523.
Priest Retirement Fund of the Archdiocese of Washington, Inc.—Rev. Msgr. KEVIN FARRELL, *P.O. Box 29260, Washington, 20017.* Tel: 301-853-4523.
Parish Accounting—Mr. TERRENCE FARRELL.
Parish Audit Department—Ms. HEATHER HOLLAND.

Development Office

Office of Development—GREGORY F. GANNON, Dir. Tel: 301-853-4574; Fax: 301-853-7671.
Cardinal's Stewardship Appeal—Tel: 301-853-4575.
Office of Planned Giving—Ms. SUSAN LEAHY, Dir. Tel: 301-853-4573.

Office of Communications

Director—Mrs. DAWN CEOL. Tel: 301-853-4516; 853-4500 (Asst.). Tel: 301-853-4515; Fax: 301-853-7672.
Radio & TV Programming—Mr. JOHN CAPOBIANCO. Tel: 301-853-4515.
Carroll Publishing Company—His Eminence JAMES CARDINAL HICKEY, Publisher; Mr. THOMAS SCHMIDT, Pres. Tel: 301-853-4562; Fax: 301-853-3349.
Newspaper—"The Catholic Standard", MARK ZIMMERMAN, Editor. Tel: 301-853-4599; Fax: 301-853-3349., *"El Pregonero";* Mr. OSCAR REYES, Editor. Tel: 301-853-4504; Fax: 301-853-3349.

Office Of Black Catholics

Executive Director—Mrs. JACQUELINE E. WILSON. Tel: 301-853-4579; Fax: 301-853-7671. Coordinating Office for the Black Catholic History Center; Combating Racism; Black Catholic Congress; REJOICE! Conference on Black Catholic Liturgy; Archdiocesan Mass Choir; Other Programs & Resources for Leadership and Evangelization in the Black Community.
Council of Black Catholics—Mrs. RUBY TYNES, Contact Person.

Office Of Hispanic Pastoral Affairs

Executive Director—Ms. MARGARITA ROQUE. Tel: 301-853-4566; Fax: 301-853-7671.
Spanish Catholic Center—Rev. MARK POLETUNOW, O.F.M.Cap, Dir., *1618 Monroe St. N.W., Washington, 20010.* Tel: 202-483-5665.

CLERGY, PARISHES, MISSIONS AND PAROCHIAL SCHOOLS

DISTRICT OF COLUMBIA

1—ST. MATTHEW CATHEDRAL (1840), Rev. Msgr. W. Ronald Jameson; Revs. James D. Watkins; Jose Lobaton, O.F.M.; G. Paul Herbert; Vincent Peterson, O.F.M.Conv.; Deacons Ulysses Rice; Lawrence C. Gordon. In res., Rev. Msgr. Bernard C. Gerhardt.
Res., 1725 Rhode Island Ave., N.W., 20036. Tel: 202-347-3215; Fax: 202-347-7184.

2—ST. ALOYSIUS, Washington, (1859), Revs. Francis M. O'Connor; John A. Conlin, S.J.; Joseph M. McCloskey, S.J.; Deacons Jesse Dudley; Willis Daniels.
Res., 19 Eye St., N.W., 20001. Tel: 202-336-7200.
Father McKenna Center—Tel: 202-842-1112. Sr. Henrita Frost, S.S.N.D., Dir.

3—ST. ANN, Washington, (1869), Rev. Msgr. William J. Awalt; Revs. David W. Beaubien; Joseph B. Pierce; Deacon Robert W. Whitaker.
Res., 4001 Yuma St., 20016. Tel: 202-966-6288; Fax: 202-966-7722.
School—(Grades PreK-8). Tel: 202-363-4460. Mrs. Barbara Kelly, Prin.
Catechesis/Religious Programs—Students 212.

4—ANNUNCIATION, Washington, (1948), Rev. Msgr. James F. Montgomery; Revs. James M. Stack; Donald Brice. In res., Rev. Brien R. McCarthy.
Res., 3125 39th St., N.W., 20016. Tel: 202-362-3323; Fax: 202-363-4057.
School—3825 Klingle Pl., 20016. Tel: 202-362-1408. Sr. Joan Rigney, S.H.C.J., Prin.
Sisters of Holy Child Jesus 5; Lay Teachers 15; Students 207.
Catechesis/Religious Programs—Students 65.
Convent—3200 39th St., N.W., 20016. Tel: 202-362-1464.

5—ST. ANTHONY, Washington, (1892), Rev. Msgr. Richard Burton; Revs. Samuel L. Craig; Berard Marthaler, O.F.M.Conv.; Deacon John Kelly. In res., Revs. Barthasar Kim; Victor Wong (Nanking); John Rodney, S.V.D.
Res., 1029 Monroe St., N.E., 20017. Tel: 202-526-8822; Fax 202-526-1543.
School—Tel: 202-526-4657; Fax: 202-832-5567.
Lay Teachers 16; Students 266.
Catechesis/Religious Programs—Students 36.

6—ASSUMPTION, Washington, (1916), Rev. T. Ansgar Laczko.
Res., 3401 Martin Luther King Jr. Ave., S.E., 20032-1597. Tel: 202-561-4178; Fax: 202-561-0336.
School—Tel: 202-562-7070; Fax: 202-574-5829.
Lay Teachers 10; Students 194.

7—ST. AUGUSTINE, Washington, (1858) (African American), Rev. Msgr. Russell L. Dillard; Revs. George W. Wilson; John Payne, O.S.A.
Parish Office—1419 V St., N.W., 20009. Fax: 202-234-1787.
Res., 1425 V St., N.W., 20009. Tel: 202-265-1470.
School—1421 V St., N.W., 20009. Tel: 202-667-2608. Shelore C. Williams, Prin.
Oblate Sisters of Providence 2; Lay Teachers 13; Students 220.
Catechesis/Religious Programs—Students 180.

8—ST. BENEDICT THE MOOR, Washington, (1946) (African American), Revs. Roderick J.D. Coates, S.S.J.; Charles T. Coughlin, S.S.J.
Res., 320 21st St., N.E., 20002. Tel: 202-397-3895; Fax: 202-398-3415.
School—Tel: 202-397-3897; Fax: 202-398-3415. Sr. Brenda Cherry, O.S.P., Prin.
Oblate Sisters of Providence 2; Lay Teachers 16; Students 245.
Convent—Tel: 202-398-7696.

9—ST. BLAISE. (Croation Pastoral Mission). Rev. Gabriel Badurina, T.O.R.
Res., St. Jerome House of Study, 1359 Monroe St., N.E., 20017. Tel: 202-832-6364.

10—BLESSED SACRAMENT, SHRINE OF THE MOST, Washington, (1911), Rev. Msgr. Thomas M. Duffy; Revs. Philip A. O'Shea; Percival L. D'Silva; Raymond F. Schmidt; Deacons John M. Leonard; Joseph B. McGrath.
Res., 6001 Western Ave., N.W., 20015. Tel: 202-966-6575; Fax: 202-966-9255.
School—5841 Chevy Chase Pkwy., N.W., 20015. Tel: 202-966-6682; Fax: 202-966-4938. Mrs. Frances Scango, Prin.
Lay Teachers 30; Students 489.
Catechesis/Religious Programs—Tel: 202-363-8938. D.R.E.: Mrs. Kathleen Curtin; Mrs. Patricia Armelin, (Grades K-6); Ms. Susan Mitchell (Grades 7-12).
Students 375.

11—ST. DOMINIC CHURCH & PRIORY, Washington, (1856), Very Rev. Francis C. Duffy, O.P., Prior; Revs. William A. Newman, O.P., Subprior; Donald P. Thibault, O.P.; John A. McMahon, O.P.; Robert D. Riley, O.P.; Robert L. Walker, O.P.; Edmund J. Way, O.P.; Robert R. Haller, O.P.; Bros. Fabian Butler, O.P.; Peter Osbourne, O.P. In res., Revs. Cornelius T. Kane, O.P.; Guy B. Dupont, O.P; John J. Ryan, O.P.; Joseph J. Jurasko, O.P.; Joseph A. Cote, O.P.; Charles V. Lucier, O.P.; William B. Tarrier, O.P.; J. Aumann, O.P.; W. Becket Soule, O.P.; William M. O'Bierne, O.P.
Res., 630 E St., S.W., 20024. Tel: 202-554-7863; Fax: 202-554-0231.

12—EPIPHANY, Washington, (1925), Rev. Gabriel Duffy.
Res., 2712 Dumbarton Ave., N.W., 20007. Tel: 202-965-1610; Fax: 202-337-8377.

13—ST. FRANCIS DE SALES, Washington, Revs. Carl F. Dianda; Robert T. Guillen; Deacons Floyd H. Agostinelli; Harold Jackson. In res., Revs. John S. Wintermyer; Henry Slevin; Christian Nwaka Egbulem, O.P.
Res., 2021 Rhode Island Ave., N.E., 20018. Tel: 202-529-7451.
School—Sisters 2; Lay Teachers 9; Students 230.

14—ST. FRANCIS XAVIER (1924), Rev. Michael A. Salah; Deacons Anthony Smith; Henry Rauson. In res., Rev. Msgr. John L. Bailey.
Res., 2800 Pennsylvania Ave., S.E., 20020. Tel: 202-582-5021; Fax: 202-581-7224.
School—Tel: 202-581-2010. Mrs. Kathleen Pardue, Prin.
Sisters 2; Lay Teachers 9; Students 170.
Catechesis/Religious Programs—Students 79.
Convent—2812 Pennsylvania Ave., S.E., 20020. Tel: 202-584-5621. Sisters of St. Joseph Sr. M. Brigid S.S.J., Supr.; Sr. Miriam Naughton.

15—ST. GABRIEL, Washington, (1920), Revs. Patrick J. McCaffrey; Richard Scott; Deacon Robert L. Berry. In res., Rev. Tesfamariam Baraki.
Res., 26 Grant Cir., N.W., 20011. Tel: 202-726-9092; Fax: 202-291-0334.
School—Tel: 202-726-9212; Fax: 202-726-1881. Mrs. Mary Hawkins, Prin.
Lay Teachers 9; Students 250.

16—HOLY COMFORTER—ST. CYPRIAN, Washington, (1893), Revs. Eddie Tolentino; Charles Pope; Deacons Charles Edelin; Kevin Butler. In res., Rev. F. Michael Bryant.
Res., 1357 E. Capitol St., 20003. Tel: 202-546-1885; Fax: 202-544-1385.
School—Tel: 202-547-7556; Fax: 202-547-5686. Sr. Mary Charlotte Marshall, O.S.P., Prin.
Oblate Sisters of Providence 2; Lay Teachers 9; Students 190.
Catechesis/Religious Programs—Tel: 202-547-2510. Mrs. Dolores Gorham, D.R.E.
Students 300.

17—HOLY NAME, Washington, (1892) (African American), Rev. David P. Russell; Deacons James Ford; William Thomas.
Res., 920 11th St., N.E., 20002. Tel: 202-397-2525.
School—Tel: 202-397-1614. Sr. Owen Patricia Bonner, S.S.J., Prin.
Sisters of St. Joseph 3; Lay Teachers 15; Students 230.

18—HOLY REDEEMER, Washington, (1922) (African American), Rev. David Bava.
Res., 206 New York Ave., N.W., 20001. Tel: 202-347-7510; Fax: 202-628-0401.
School—Holy Redeemer School, (Grades PreK-8) 1135 New Jersey Ave., N.W., 20001. Tel: 202-638-5789. Dr. Angela King-Kittrell, Prin.
Priests 1; Sisters 3; Deacons 1; Lay Teachers 10; Students 250.
Catechesis/Religious Programs—Students 62.

19—HOLY ROSARY, Washington, (1913) (Italian), Rev. Charles Zanoni, C.S.
Res., 595 Third St., N.W., 20001-2703. Tel: 202-638-0165; Fax: 202-638-0793.

20—HOLY TRINITY, Washington, Revs. Lawrence J. Madden, S.J.; Richard P. McHugh, S.J.; Joseph P. Lacey, S.J.; Paul J. McCarren, S.J.; Gerard J. Campbell, S.J.; Douglas F. Peduti, S.J.
Church—36th St., N.W., between N and O Sts., 20007.
Parish Center Offices—3513 N St., N.W., 20007.
Res., 3514 O St., N.W., 20007. Tel: 202-337-2840; Fax: 202-337-9048.
School—Tel: 202-337-2339; Fax: 202-337-0368.
Sisters of St. Joseph (Chestnut Hill, PA) 2; Lay Teachers 30; Students 335.
Catechesis/Religious Programs—Students 660.

21—NATIONAL SHRINE OF THE IMMACULATE CONCEPTION, Washington.,

22—IMMACULATE CONCEPTION, Washington, (1864) (African American), Rev. Msgr. J. Joshua Mundell.
Res., 1315 8th St., N.W., 20001. Tel: 202-332-8888; Fax: 202-332-0173.
School—(Grades PreK-6) 711 N St., N.W., 20001. Tel: 202-234-1093. Sr. Carol Ann Knight, S.H.C.J., Prin.
Sisters 1; Lay Teachers 8; Students 125.

23—INCARNATION, Washington, Rev. Lowell D. Case, S.S.J.; Deacons Hiram Haywood; Harry Draper; Alfred Brokenborough; Thomas Forbes.
Res., 880 Eastern Ave., N.E., 20019. Tel: 202-396-0942; Fax: 202-396-6064.
Catechesis/Religious Programs—Students 119.

24—ST. JOSEPH ON CAPITOL HILL, Washington, (1869), Revs. Paul E. Lavin; Christopher Begg. In res., Rev. Eugene Henrick (JOL).
Res., 313 Second St., N.E., 20002. Tel: 202-547-1223; Fax: 202-547-4189.

25—KIDANE-MEHRET GE'EZ RITE CATHOLIC CHURCH, Washington, (Ethiopian-Eritrean), Rev. Tesfamariam Baraki.
Mailing Address: 1001 Lawrence St., N.E., P.O. Box 29616, 20017.
Res., 26 Grant Cir., N.W., 20011. Tel: 202-529-8420; Fax: 202-529-8523.
Catechesis/Religious Programs—Students 105.

26—CHURCH OF ST. LOUIS, Washington. (Eglise St. Louis). Rev. Andre Millot.
Res., 4125 Garrison St., N.W., 20016. Tel: 202-537-0709; Fax: 202-244-9649.
Catechesis/Religious Programs—Students 187.

27—ST. LUKE, Washington, (1957), Revs. Stephen F. Brett, S.S.J., J.D., Ph.D.; Joseph N. Begay, S.S.J.; Deacons Earle W. Coleman; Joseph M. Conrad.
Res., 4925 E. Capitol St., 20019-5202. Tel: 202-584-8322; Fax: 202-584-3421.
Catechesis/Religious Programs—Students 61.

28—ST. MARTIN OF TOURS, Washington, (1901), Rev. Michael J. Kelley.
Res., 1908 N. Capitol St., 20002. Tel: 202-232-1144; Fax: 202-832-6772.
Catechesis/Religious Programs—Students 60.

29—ST. MARY, MOTHER OF GOD, Washington, Rev. David Conway; Deacon Bernard Johnson.
Res., 727 Fifth St., N.W., 20001. Tel: 202-289-7771.

30—NATIVITY, Washington, (1901) (African American), Rev. Joseph R. Sileo; Deacon James A. Harley.
Res., 6000 Georgia Ave., N.W., 20011. Tel: 202-726-6262.
School—Tel: 202-723-3322; Fax: 202-291-0219. Valerie Smith, Prin.
Sisters 8; Lay Teachers 15; Students 240.
Catechesis/Religious Programs—Tel: 202-829-4051. Sr. Stephanie Romiti, S.P.C., D.R.E.
Students 150.

31—NIGERIAN CATHOLIC COMMUNITY, Rev. Aloysius Achonwa.
Res., Nativity Parish, 6000 Georgia Ave., N.W., 20011. Tel: 202-726-8363.

32—OUR LADY OF PERPETUAL HELP, Washington, (1920), Revs. Thomas R. Frank, S.S.J.; Anthony Okey Nwachukwu-Udaku, S.S.J.; Bro. Marx Tyree, S.S.J.; Deacons Samuel Johnson; Ira Chase; Reynaldo Thurston.
Res., 1600 Morris Rd., S.E., 20020. Tel: 202-678-4999; Fax: 202-610-3189.
School—Tel: 202-889-1662 (Grades PreK-4); 678-0211 (Grades 5-8). Principals: Sr. Mary Elizabeth Semmelmayer, S.S.N.D.; Mrs. Charlene Hursey.
Brothers 1; School Sisters of Notre Dame 4; Lay Teachers 11; Students 270.
Catechesis/Religious Programs—Students 130.

33—OUR LADY QUEEN OF THE AMERICAS, Washington, (1986) (Hispanic-Portuguese), Rev. Jose I. Somoza, O.F.M.; Deacons Bartolo Serafini; Jorge Vargas. In res., Rev. Ademir Guerini, S.C.
Church, Office and Residence—2200 California St., N.W., 20008. Tel: 202-332-8838; Fax: 202-332-2967.
Catechesis/Religious Programs—Sr. Felipa Blazquez, C.ach., D.R.E.
Students 235.

34—OUR LADY QUEEN OF PEACE, Washington, (1948) (African American), Revs. George W. Wilson; Joseph W. Somerville.
Res., 3800 Ely Pl., S.E., 20019. Tel: 202-582-8600; Fax: 202-575-3317.
School—Tel: 202-584-4278; Fax: 202-584-1922. Sr. Ellen Marie Hagar, D.C., Prin.
Daughters of Charity of St. Vincent de Paul 5; Lay Teachers 13; Students 200.
Convent—3740 Ely Pl., S.E., 20019. Tel: 202-581-4963.

35—OUR LADY OF VICTORY, Washington, (1906), Rev. William E. Foley; Deacons Edward Redding; Leo Flynn. In res., Rev. Msgr. Harry A. Echle; Revs. Kenneth Martin, S.S.; Emanuel Magro.
Res., 4835 MacArthur Blvd., N.W., 20007. Tel: 202-337-4835; Fax: 202-338-4759.
School—4755 Whitehaven Pkwy., N.W., 20007. Tel: 202-337-1421; Fax: 202-338-4759. Susan Milloy, Prin.
Lay Teachers 18; Students 141.

36—ST. PATRICK, Washington, (1794), Rev. Msgr. Peter J. Vaghi; Revs. Winthrop J. Brainerd; Paul F. Liston; Deacon John J. McGinness. In res., Rev. Msgr. Michael diTeccia Farina; Rev. Sebastian Mongo Behon (Cameroon).
Res., 619 Tenth St., N.W., 20001-4587. Tel: 202-347-2713; Fax: 202-347-1401.

37—ST. PETER, Washington, (1821), Rev. Michael J. O'Sullivan. In res., Rev. Msgr. Joseph F. Sadusky; Rev. Stuart Swetland (PEO).
Res., 313 Second St., S.E., 20003. Tel: 202-547-1430; Fax: 202-547-5732.
School—422 Third St., S.E., 20003. Tel: 202-544-1618; Fax: 202-547-5101. Mary M. Randolph, Prin.
Sisters 1; Lay Teachers 17; Students 231.
Catechesis/Religious Programs—Tel: 202-544-1618.
Students 50.

38—PORTUGUESE CATHOLIC COMMUNITY, Rev. Ademir Guerini, C.S.
Res., Our Lady Queen of the Americas, 2200 California St., N.W., 20008.

39—SHRINE OF THE SACRED HEART, Washington, (1899), Revs. Francis X. Russo, O.F.M.Cap.; Stephen Carter, O.F.M.Cap.; Moises Villalta, O.F.M.Cap.; Bro. Paul Zaborowski, O.F.M.Cap.; Deacons Sylvester Brown; James Quander, (Retired). In res., Revs. Joseph Mindling, O.F.M.Cap.; Thomas Weinandy, O.F.M.Cap.
Res., 3211 Pine St., 20010. Tel: 202-234-8000; Fax: 202-234-8001.
School—1625 Park Rd., N.W., 20010. Tel: 202-265-4828; Fax: 202-265-0595. Portia Boston, Prin.
Lay Teachers 17; Students 235.
Catechesis/Religious Programs—Tel: 202-667-2446.
Students 370.

40—ST. STEPHEN MARTYR, Washington, (1867), Revs. Thomas J. Sheehan; M. Valentine Keveny; Paul E. Murray; Deacon John W. Bobbitt. In res., Rev. Raymond B. Kemp.
Res., 2436 Pennsylvania Ave., N.W., 20037. Tel: 202-785-0982.

41—ST. TERESA OF AVILA, Washington, (1879), Rev. Msgr. Raymond East; Deacons Ralph Cyrus; Lawrence Miles.
Res., 1430 Minnesota Ave., S.E., 20020. Tel: 202-678-3709; Fax: 202-678-3325.
Catechesis/Religious Programs—Students 63.

42—ST. THOMAS APOSTLE, Washington, (1909), Rev. Thomas G. Morrow; Rev. Msgr. Henry Otero; Rev. Harry W. Jacobs; Deacon William C. Boesman. In res., Rev. Msgr. William F. O'Donnell.
Res., 2665 Woodley Rd., N.W., 20008. Tel: 202-234-1488; Fax: 202-234-1480.
Catechesis/Religious Programs—Students 54.

43—ST. THOMAS MORE, Washington, Revs. Raymond J. Wadas; John P. Kinter; Deacon Nerus O. Martin, Jr.
Res., 4275 4th St., S.E., 20032. Tel: 202-562-0431.
School—Mrs. Wilma Durham, Prin. Lay Teachers 10; Students 250.

44—ST. VINCENT DE PAUL, Washington, (1903) (African American), Revs. Joseph F. Del Vecchio; Frank Kramer.
Res., 14 M St., S.E., 20003-3511. Tel: 202-488-1354; Fax: 202-488-7899.
Catechesis/Religious Programs—Students 73.

CHURCHES IN MARYLAND

Avenue, St. Mary's Co., Holy Angels (1906), Rev. Msgr. John B. Brady; Rev. Msgr. Aloysius E. O'Connor, Pastor Emeritus.
Res., 21340 Colton Point Rd., 20609-2422. Tel: 301-769-3332; Fax: 301-769-2541. [JC]
School—Holy Angels-Sacred Heart, Tel: 301-769-3389; Fax: 301-769-4948.
Priests 2; Lay Teachers 8; Students 167.
Catechesis/Religious Programs—Students 60.

Baden, Prince Georges Co., St. Michael (1957), Rev. Louis J. Faust; Deacon Harvey Ballard.
Res. and Mailing Address—17510 Horsehead Rd., Brandywine, 20613. Tel: 301-888-1498; Fax: 301-888-9164.
Catechesis/Religious Programs—Tel: 301-579-6409; Fax: 301-579-0019.
Students 135.
Mission—St. Dominic's.

Barnesville, Montgomery Co., St. Mary Church and Shrine of Our Lady of Fatima, Rev. George B. Reid.
Res., 18230 Barnsville Rd., P.O. Box 67, 20838. Tel: 301-972-8660. [CEM]

Beltsville, Prince Georges Co., St. Joseph (1963), Rev. Roderick D. McKee; Deacon Andrew J. Betz. In res., Revs. Robert Cary Hill; Albert H. Ledoux (ALT).
Res., 11007 Montgomery Rd., 20705. Tel: 301-937-7183; Fax: 301-937-7780.
School—Tel: 301-937-7154.
Lay Teachers 10; Students 262.
Catechesis/Religious Programs—Tel: 301-937-7419.
Students 205.

Benedict, Charles Co., St. Francis de Sales (1903), Rev. Saverio T. Vitturino.
Res., 7185 Benedict Ave., P.O. Box 306, 20612-0306. Tel: 301-274-3416; 870-4991; Fax: 301-274-0689.
Catechesis/Religious Programs—7209 Benedict Ave., 20612.
Students 68.

Bethesda, Montgomery Co.,

1—ST. BARTHOLOMEW, (1960), Rev. Msgr. James T.

Beattie; Revs. Thomas J. Nelson; Luis Salcedo.
Res., 7212 Blacklock Rd., 20817. Tel: 301-229-7933; Fax: 301-229-7998.
School—6900 River Rd., 20817. Tel: 301-229-5586. Mr. Daniel Shaheen, Prin.
Sisters 1; Lay Teachers 17; Students 219.
Catechesis/Religious Programs—Tel: 301-229-3413; Fax: 301-229-7998.
Students 352.

2—ST. JANE FRANCES DE CHANTAL, (1950), Rev. Msgr. Donald S. Essex; Revs. Alan R. Helwig; Ronald A. Potts. In res., Rev. John Hotze (WCH).
Res., 9701 Old Georgetown Rd., 20814. Tel: 301-530-1550; Fax: 301-493-8953.
School—9525 Old Georgetown Rd., 20814. Tel: 301-530-1221; Fax: 301-530-1688. Mrs. Betsy Hamilton, Prin.
Lay Teachers 24; Students 507.
Catechesis/Religious Programs—Tel: 301-530-1640. Mr. Stephen Matuszak, D.R.E.
Students 220.

3—LITTLE FLOWER, Rev. Msgr. William J. Kane; Rev. Msgr. Joseph B. Coyne; Revs. Mark W. Chimiak; George Stuart.
Res., 5607 Massachusetts Ave., 20816. Tel: 301-320-4538; Fax: 301-320-4541.
School—Tel: 301-320-3273; Fax: 301-320-2867.
Sisters of the Immaculate Heart of Mary 5; Lay Teachers 18; Students 231.
Catechesis/Religious Programs—Tel: 301-320-5233.
Students 210.

4—OUR LADY OF LOURDES, (1926) (Spanish), Rev. Msgr. Thomas M. Wells; Rev. Carlos Roman; Deacon John Shewmaker. In res., Rev. William J. Silk, Senior Priest; Rev. Msgr. W. Louis Quinn.
Res., 7500 Pearl St., 20814. Tel: 301-654-1287; Fax: 301-986-8716.
School—Tel: 301-654-5376. Marcella Schraml, Prin.
Sisters 1; Lay Teachers 14; Students 165.
Catechesis/Religious Programs—Tel: 301-654-5954.
Students 110.

5—OUR LADY OF VIETNAM, (1990) (Vietnamese), Revs. Peter Nguyen-Thanh-Long; Hilary Tran-Khac Hy, (Retired); Deacon John Huong Nguyen.
Res., 11812 New Hampshire Ave., Silver Spring, 20904. Tel: 301-622-4895; Fax: 301-625-9384.

Bowie, Prince Georges Co.,

1—ASCENSION, (1893), Rev. James S. Betz; Deacons Finis Thompson; Raymond Barrett; Thomas Elliott.
Mailing Address: P.O. Box 96, 20719. Tel: 301-262-2227; Fax: 301-805-5053. [CEM]
Catechesis/Religious Programs—Tel: 301-262-4054. D.R.E.: Pam Rozanski; Christine Jolliffe.
Students 252.

2—SACRED HEART, (1892), Rev. Msgr. John F. Hogan; Deacon H. Jeffrey Raffensperger.
Res., 16501 Annapolis Rd., 20715. Tel: 301-262-0704; Fax: 301-805-4686. [CEM]
Catechesis/Religious Programs—Tel: 301-262-1221. Sr. M. John Helene Meskill, O.S.F., D.R.E.
Students 270.

3—ST. EDWARD, (1972), Rev. Thomas F. Kehoe.
Res., 16304 Pond Meadow Ln., 20716. Tel: 301-249-9199.
Catechesis/Religious Programs—Tel: 301-249-9599; Fax: 301-249-1303.
Students 310.

4—ST. PIUS X, (1962), Revs. W. Paul Hill; Raymond H. Moore; Deacons Robert J. Tracy; Thomas Knestout; Eugene Mastrangelo; Andrew Nosacek.
Res., 3300 Moreland Pl., 20715. Tel: 301-262-2141.
Church—14720 Annapolis Rd., 20715. Fax: 301-262-2142.
School—Tel: 301-262-0203; Fax: 301-805-8875.
Sisters of St. Joseph 3; Lay Teachers 28; Students 595.
Catechesis/Religious Programs—Cathy Gallagher, D.R.E.
Students 473.

Bryantown, Charles Co., St. Mary (1793), Rev. William J. Thompson; Deacons Eugene Burroughs; Henry Middleton.
Res., 13715 Notre Dame Pl., 20617-2224. Tel: 301-870-2220; 274-3187; Fax: 301-274-0253. [CEM]
School—Tel: 301-932-6883.
School Sisters of Notre Dame 2; Lay Teachers 9; Students 229.
Catechesis/Religious Programs—Tel: 301-274-4357.
Students 270.

Burtonsville, Montgomery Co., Resurrection Parish (1981), Revs. John R. Pennington, III; Charles E. Brown; Sr. Mary Louise Full, C.S.C., Pastoral Assoc.; Deacon Donald DeRoze.
Res., 3315 Greencastle Rd., 20866. Tel: 301-236-5200; Fax: 301-236-5204.
Catechesis/Religious Programs—Tel: 301-236-5200.
Students 731.

Bushwood, St. Mary's Co., Sacred Heart (1755), Rev. Francis J. Early.
Res., 20618. Tel: 301-769-3100. [JC]
Catechesis/Religious Programs—See Holy Angels-Sacred Heart School, Avenue, MD, for details.
Students 57.

Camp Springs, Prince Georges Co., St. Philip the Apostle, Revs. Charles McCann; Bernard R. Ihrie, Jr., Senior Priest; Deacon Frank D. Clarke.
Res., 5416 Henderson Way, 20746. Tel: 301-423-4244.
School—Lay Teachers 10; Students 196.

Chapel Point, Charles Co., St. Ignatius (1641), Rev. Salvador Jordan, S.J.
Res., St. Thomas Manor, 8855 Chapel Point Rd., Port Tobacco, 20677. Tel: 301-934-8245. [CEM]
Catechesis/Religious Programs—Christine Mais, D.R.E.
Students 194.

Chaptico, St. Mary's Co., Our Lady of the Wayside (1938), Rev. John P. Stack.
Res., Rte. 238, P.O. Box 97, 20621. Tel: 301-884-2502; Fax: 301-884-0381.
School—Mother Catherine Spalding Tri Parish School, Tel: 301-884-3165.
Lay Teachers 14; Students 290.
Mailing Address: Rte. 238, Helen, 20638. Tel: 301-884-3165; Fax: 301-884-3165.
Catechesis/Religious Programs—Students 111.

Cheverly, Prince Georges Co., St. Ambrose (1886), Rev. G. William Finch; Deacons John Vergot, (Retired); Edwin Beller. In res., Revs. Edward Evans; Francis Walsh.
Res., 3107 63rd Ave., 20785. Tel: 301-773-9300; Fax: 301-773-2611.
School—Tel: 301-773-0223; Fax: 301-773-9218. Mrs. Barbara Edmonson, Prin.
Lay Teachers 12; Students 265.
Catechesis/Religious Programs—Tel: 301-341-3284. Sr. Francene Van Eck, O.S.B., D.R.E.
Students 57.

Chillum, Prince Georges Co., St. John Baptist de la Salle (1951), Revs. Robert C. Richardson; James Holloway.
Res., 5706 Sargent Rd., 20782. Tel: 301-559-3636; Fax: 301-559-3062.
School—Tel: 301-559-3525; Fax: 301-559-2678. Mrs. Rosemarie Garten, Prin.
Lay Teachers 20; Students 175.
Catechesis/Religious Programs—Tel: 301-559-6232.
Students 73.

Clinton, Prince Georges Co., Church of St. John the Evangelist (1875), Revs. Thomas W. Pollard; L. James Downs; Robert P. Buchmeier; Deacons Anthony Mol; Carl Blaesing.
Res., 8908 Old Branch Ave., 20735. Tel: 301-868-1070; Fax: 301-868-7915. [CEM]
School—Tel: 301-868-2010; Fax: 301-856-8941. Sr. Jean Louise Bachetti, I.H.M., Prin.
Sisters of the Immaculate Heart of Mary 3; Lay Teachers 13; Students 261.
Catechesis/Religious Programs—Tel: 301-868-3026. Sr. Blanche Twigg, M.H.S.H., D.R.E.
Students 257.

College Park, Prince Georges Co., Holy Redeemer (1912), Revs. William F. Berry; Robert A. Finamore; Deacon Bartholomew Merella.
Res., 4902 Berwyn Rd., 20740. Tel: 301-474-3920; Fax: 301-441-4954.
School—Tel: 301-474-3993. Linda Cullinan, Prin.
Lay Teachers 15; Students 274.
Catechesis/Religious Programs—Tel: 301-474-4299. Mrs. Sandra Tucker, D.R.E.
Students 178.

St. Andrew Kim (1974) (Korean), Revs. Jung Soon (Benedict) Shin; Jun Gui (Michael) Choi.
Res., 8108 54th Ave., 20740. Tel: 301-474-0186; Fax: 301-474-6785. [CEM][JC]

Damascus, Montgomery Co., St. Paul (1957), Revs. Peter J. Sweeney; Walter J. Norris, Pastor Emeritus; Deacons Vince Moskaitis; John Finerty.
Res., 9240 Damascus Rd., 20872. Tel: 301-253-2027; Fax: 301-391-6755.
Catechesis/Religious Programs—Tel: 301-253-5941.
Students 816.

Darnestown, Montgomery Co., Our Lady of the Visitation (1991), Rev. Raymond L. Fecteau; Deacon Paul DiDuca.
Res., 14200 Darnestown Rd., 20874-3008. Tel: 301-948-5536; Fax: 301-948-7452.
Catechesis/Religious Programs—Students 183.

Mary of Nazareth Roman Catholic Elementary School (1994), Sr. Francis Stavalo, Prin.
Res., 14131 Seneca Rd., 20874. Tel: 301-869-0940; Fax: 301-869-0942.
Catechesis/Religious Programs—Students 141.

Derwood, Montgomery Co., St. Francis of Assisi (1972), Revs. Donald P. Worch; Charles H. Muzzey; Joseph Zalotay; Deacons Pascal Hong; Wilbur Pinder; Robert Whitfield.
Res., 6701 Muncaster Mill Rd., 20855. Tel: 301-840-1407; Fax: 301-258-5080.
Catechesis/Religious Programs—Tel: 301-258-9193.
Students 876.

Dunkirk, Calvert Co., Jesus the Good Shepherd (1985), Rev. Paul M. Dudziak.
Res., 1555 Mount Harmony Rd. W., Owings, 20736. Tel: 301-855-4400; Fax: 410-257-6334.
Catechesis/Religious Programs—Students 559.

Forestville, Prince George Co., Church of the Holy Spirit (1966), Rev. Michael J. Murray.
Res., 1717 Ritchie Rd., 20747. Tel: 301-336-3707; Fax: 301-324-1649.
Catechesis/Religious Programs—Students 65.

Mt. Calvary (1942), Revs. George E. Golden; Everett Pearson; Mrs. Dawn Woods, Pastoral Assoc.
Res., 6700 Marlboro Pike, 20747. Tel: 301-735-5532; Fax: 301-735-2005. [CEM]
School—Tel: 301-735-5262; Fax: 301-736-5044.
Brothers 1; Sisters 1; Lay Teachers 27; Students 476.
Catechesis/Religious Programs—6704 Marlboro Pike, 20747. Tel: 301-420-4499.
Students 135.

Fort Washington, Prince Georges Co., St. Ignatius (1849), Revs. Mark F. Hughes; Robert P. Wummer. In res., Rev. Salvatore A. Criscuolo.
Res., 2315 Brinkley Rd., Oxon Hill, 20744. Tel: 301-567-4740. [CEM]
School—2317 Brinkley Rd., Oxon Hill, 20744. Tel: 301-567-4090. Mrs. Patricia O'Brien Nolton, Prin.
Lay Teachers 11; Students 240.

Gaithersburg, Montgomery Co., St. John Neumann (1978), Rev. Ralph C. Torsiello.
Church—9000 Warfield Rd., 20882. Tel: 301-977-5492; Fax: 301-977-5451.
Res., 8900 Lockhaven Dr., 20882. Fax: 301-977-3559.
Catechesis/Religious Programs—Tel: 301-977-7990; Fax: 301-330-3235.
Students 431.

St. Martin (1920) (Spanish), Revs. Michael J. Mellone; Edward J. Filardi; William A. Ryan; Deacons Lawrence Bell; Eugene J. Cummins, Jr.; Stanley E. Weightman; Kenneth Barrett.
Res., 201 S. Frederick Ave., 20877. Tel: 301-840-1830; Fax: 301-990-7538.
School—Tel: 301-840-1748. Mrs. Shirley Wise, Prin.
Lay Teachers 16; Students 289.
Catechesis/Religious Programs—Tel: 301-840-1838. M. Patricia Dorney, D.R.E.
Students 1,095.

St. Rose of Lima (1972), Rev. Robert D. Duggan; Deacon James McCann.
Mailing Address: 11701 Clopper Rd., 20878-1024. Tel: 301-948-7545; Fax: 301-869-2170. [CEM]
Catechesis/Religious Programs—Mary Ann Deak, D.R.E.
Students 637.

Garrett Park, Montgomery Co., Holy Cross (1960), Rev. Msgr. Vincent S. Gatto; Deacon Jerome Donlon.
Res., 4900 Strathmore Ave., P.O. Box 249, 20896. Tel: 301-942-1020; Fax: 301-949-3543.
School—Tel: 301-949-0053; Fax: 301-949-5074. Sr. Miriam R. Brosnan, Prin.
Lay Teachers 22; Students 264.
Catechesis/Religious Programs—Tel: 301-942-8790.
Students 109.

Germantown, Montgomery Co., Mother Seton Parish (1974), Revs. Milton E. Jordan; Jeffrey M. Defayette; Deacons William Vita; Timothy Enright; Philip Cooper.
Res., 19951 Father Hurley Blvd., 20874. Tel: 301-924-3838; Fax: 301-428-4951.
Catechesis/Religious Programs—Students 602.

Great Mills, St. Mary's Co., Holy Face, Rev. John F. Myslinski.
Res., 20634. Tel: 301-994-0525; Fax: 301-994-1547. [CEM]
School—Little Flower, Tel: 301-994-0404.
Sisters 3; Lay Teachers 16; Students 300.
Catechesis/Religious Programs—Students 120.

Greenbelt, Prince Georges Co., St. Hugh (1947), Revs. Thomas F. Crowley; Walter J. Tappe.
Res., 135 Crescent Rd., 20770. Tel: 301-474-4322; Fax: 301-474-9263.
School—145 Crescent Rd., 20770. Tel: 301-474-4071; Fax: 301-474-3950. Mrs. Harriann Walker, Prin.
Lay Teachers 17; Students 264.

Catechesis/Religious Programs—Tel: 301-474-0239.
Students 80.

Hillcrest Heights, Prince Georges Co., Holy Family (1952), Rev. Michael W. Fisher.
Res., 2210 Callaway St., 20748. Tel: 301-894-2222.
School—2200 Callaway St., 20748. Tel: 301-894-2323.
Catechesis/Religious Programs—Students 218.

Hilltop, Charles Co., St. Ignatius Loyola (1851), Rev. Matthew E. Thompson; Deacon Frank L. Hopson.
Mailing Address: P.O. Box 278, Port Tobacco, 20677. Tel: 301-934-9630. [CEM]

Hollywood, St. Mary's Co., St. John (1690), Rev. Msgr. Martin P. Harris; Rev. Gary R. Studniewski.
Res., P.O. Box 69, 20636. Tel: 301-373-2281. [CEM]
School—Tel: 301-373-2142. Patricia T. Suit, Prin.
Students 245.
Catechesis/Religious Programs—Mrs. Johnita Jackson, D.R.E.
Students 290.

Huntingtown, Calvert Co., Jesus the Divine Word Parish (1994), Rev. Roger A. Soley.
Res., 710 Joy Lee Ct., 20639-9239. Tel: 301-855-1825; Fax: 410-535-9057.
Catechesis/Religious Programs—Students 198.

Hyattsville, Prince Georges Co., St. Jerome (1886), Rev. Msgr. Joseph A. Ranieri; Rev. Msgr. Joseph L. Teletchea, Pastor Emeritus; Deacons Jerome Tintle; David Duggin. In res., Rev. Jerome Plotkowski.
Res., 5205 43rd Ave., 20781. Tel: 301-927-6684.
School—Tel: 301-277-4568; Fax: 301-927-6684. Dr. Joyce Volpini, S.N.D., Prin.
Sisters of Notre Dame de Namur 3; Lay Teachers 23; Students 552.
Convent—5300 43rd Ave., 20781. Tel: 301-864-2016.
Child Center—Tel: 301-699-1314.
Catechesis/Religious Programs—Students 588.

St. Mark (1958), Revs. Julio Alvarez; Timothy K. Baer; Deacons Antonio Chaves; Edward Holson; Philip Ricker; Nathaniel D. Cordova; Mark Gallagher. In res., Rev. Charles Parry.
Res., 7501 Adelphi Rd., 20783. Tel: 301-422-8300; Fax: 301-422-2313.
School—Tel: 301-422-7440; Fax: 301-422-7710.
Lay Teachers 26; Students 571.
Catechesis/Religious Programs—Tel: 301-422-7822.
Students 296.

Indian Head, Charles Co., St. Mary Star of the Sea (1918), Rev. William F. Goode; Deacon Thomas O. Hill.
Res., 30 Mattingly Ave., 20640. Tel: 301-753-9177; Fax: 301-753-6995. [CEM]
School—Tel: 301-283-6151.
Lay Teachers 14; Students 198.
Catechesis/Religious Programs—Tel: 301-375-9466.
Students 180.

Issue, Charles Co., Holy Ghost (1880), Rev. Arnold W. DePorter.
Res., 15848 Rock Point Rd., Newburg, 20664. Tel: 301-259-2515; Fax: 301-259-2289. [CEM]
Catechesis/Religious Programs—Tel: 301-259-0237.
Students 110.
Mission—Rock Point, Charles Co., St. Francis de Sales, 13675 Furbush Rd., Newburg, 20664. Tel: 301-259-0254.

Kensington, Montgomery Co., Holy Redeemer (1948), Revs. Walter L. Lawrence; Kevin C. Kennedy; Deacons Frank A. Robey; William Ditewig. In res., Rev. Michael T. Jones.
Res., 9705 Summit Ave., 20895. Tel: 301-942-2333; Fax: 301-942-1020.
School—9715 Summit Ave., 20895. Tel: 301-942-3701; Fax: 301-942-4981. Trish Beeks, Prin.
Lay Teachers 34; Students 428.
Catechesis/Religious Programs—Tel: 301-942-3430. Miss Suzanne Shaffer, D.R.E.
Students 107.

Largo, Prince Georges Co., St. Joseph (1922) (African American), Rev. Michael J. King, J.C.D.; Deacon Leon Bechet.
Res., 2020 St. Joseph Dr., 20774. Tel: 301-773-4838; Fax: 301-773-6832.
Catechesis/Religious Programs—Tel: 301-773-2480.
Students 150.

Landover Hills, Prince Georges Co., St. Mary's Catholic Church (1948), Revs. Joseph P. Kennedy; Michael J. Blackwell; Deacons B. Paul Blaine; Michael J. Taylor; Stephen M. Robinson.
Res., 7401 Buchanan St., 20784-2394. Tel: 301-577-8844; Fax: 301-577-3996.
School—7207 Annapolis Rd., 20784. Tel: 301-577-0031. Mrs. Mary Anne Patchan, Prin.
Lay Teachers 16; Students 311.
Catechesis/Religious Programs—Tel: 301-577-2478; Fax: 301-459-1355.
Students 115.

Syro-Malankara Mission, Rev. Thomas Poovannal.
Res., 7401 Buchanan St., 20784-9998. Tel: 301-577-8844; Fax: 202-399-7953.

Lanham, Prince Georges Co., St. Matthias (1960), Rev. Msgr. John J. Scanlan; Rev. Eamon McManus; Deacons Jay A. Pyle; William E. Davis.
Res., 9475 Annapolis Rd., 20706. Tel: 301-459-4814; Fax: 301-577-2259.
School—Tel: 301-577-9412. Mr. Robert E. Love, Prin.
Lay Teachers 14; Students 311.
Catechesis/Religious Programs—Tel: 301-577-6567.
Students 178.

La Plata, Charles Co., Sacred Heart (1901), Revs. Matthew J. Siekierski; Keith A. Woods; Bernard C. O'Leary, S.J.; Deacon George V. Foster.
Res., 20646. Tel: 301-934-2261; Fax: 301-934-5435. [CEM]
School—Archbishop Neale School, Tel: 301-934-9595; Fax: 301-753-1717. Sr. Helene Fee, Prin.
Sisters of the Immaculate Heart of Mary 2; Lay Teachers 36; Students 509.
Catechesis/Religious Programs—Tel: 301-934-3386. Christian S. Wainwright, D.R.E.
Students 312.

Laurel, Prince Georges Co., St. Mary (1843), Revs. V. James Lockman; Kevin P. O'Reilly; Robert Keesler, Pastor Emeritus; Joseph G. Stankavage; Deacons John Ponzette; Douglas Sinchak.
Res., 114 St. Mary's Pl., 20707. Tel: 301-725-3080; 953-3255; Fax: 301-725-2409. [CEM]
School—Tel: 301-498-1433. Alberta Martino, Prin.
Lay Teachers 22; Students 330.
Catechesis/Religious Programs—Tel: 301-490-8770. Sr. Loretta Primus, S.F.C.C., D.R.E.
Students 729.

St. Nicholas (1967), Rev. John M. Barry; Deacon Francis Hannagan.
Res., 8603 Contee Rd., 20708. Tel: 301-490-5116; 5117; Fax: 301-490-1527.
Catechesis/Religious Programs—Tel: 301-776-8303. Rev. John M. Barry, D.R.E.
Students 280.

Leonardtown, St. Mary's Co., St. Aloysius (1710), Revs. James P. Meyers; John D. Vail; David A. Thompson.
Res., 120 Washington St., P.O. Box 310, 20650. Tel: 301-475-8064. [CEM]
School—The Father Andrew White, S.J., Tel: 301-475-9795.
Sisters 1; Lay Teachers 15; Students 253.
Catechesis/Religious Programs—Students 135.

Lexington Park, St. Mary's Co., Immaculate Heart of Mary (1947), Rev. Thomas A. Gude.
Mailing Address: P.O. Box 6, 20653. Tel: 301-863-8144; Fax: 301-863-8180. [CEM]
Catechesis/Religious Programs—Tel: 301-863-8793. Patricia DeCarlo, D.R.E.
Students 224.

McConchie, Charles Co., St. Catherine of Alexandria (1911), Rev. Matthew E. Thompson; Deacon Frank L. Hopson.
Mailing Address: P.O. Box 278, Port Tobacco, 20677. Tel: 301-934-9630. [CEM]

Mechanicsville, St. Mary's Co., Immaculate Conception (1876), Rev. Msgr. Paul J. Gozaloff.
Mailing Address: P.O. Box 166, 20659. Tel: 301-884-3123; Fax: 301-884-7437.
Catechesis/Religious Programs—Tel: 301-884-3016.
Students 280.

Medley's Neck, St. Mary's Co., Our Lady's (1776), Rev. Robert J. Kosty; Deacon Thomas C. Spalding, Sr.
Mailing Address: P.O. Box 111, Leonardtown, 20650. Tel: 301-475-8403. [CEM]
Catechesis/Religious Programs—Students 65.

Mitchellville, Prince Georges Co., Holy Family (1938), Revs. Michael C. Kidd; Desmond P. Murphy; Deacon Charles A. Mallon.
Mailing Address: P.O. Box 1599, 20717. Tel: 301-249-2266; Fax: 301-249-2524. [CEM]
Catechesis/Religious Programs—Tel: 301-249-1167.
Students 104.

Morganza, St. Mary's Co., St. Joseph, Rev. Neal A. Ward; Deacon James A. Somerville.
Res., 20660. Tel: 301-884-4229. [JC]

Mount Rainier, Prince Georges Co., St. James (1905) (Hispanic), Revs. Peter R. Alliata; Agustin Mateo Ayala; Deacons Rodney R. Forbes; John H. Turner. In res., Rev. Auxentius Panares.
Res., 3628 Rhode Island Ave., 20712. Tel: 301-927-0567; Fax: 301-927-5289.
Catechesis/Religious Programs—Tel: 301-922-0567.
Students 197.

Newport, Charles Co., St. Mary (1674), Rev. Frederick H. McIntyre.
Res., 11555 St. Mary's Church Rd., Charlotte Hall, 20622. Tel: 301-934-8825; Fax: 301-934-0245. [CEM]
Catechesis/Religious Programs—Students 92.

Newtowne, St. Mary's Co., St. Francis Xavier (1640), Rev. John S. Mattingly.
Res., 21370 Newtowne Neck Rd., Leonardtown, 20650. Tel: 301-475-9885; Fax: 301-475-5662. [CEM]
Catechesis/Religious Programs—Students 103.

Norbeck, Montgomery Co., St. Patrick (1966), Rev. Msgr. Thomas A. Kane; Revs. Paul A. Morel; Alfred J. Harris; Deacon Ronald Crowley.
Res., 4101 Norbeck Rd., Rockville, 20853. Tel: 301-924-2284; 2285; Fax: 301-929-3017.
Catechesis/Religious Programs—Tel: 301-929-9314.
Students 600.

North Beach, Calvert Co., St. Anthony (1905), Rev. Robert S. Grace; Deacons John F. Lynch; Michael L. Hoffman.
Res., 8820 Chesapeake Ave., 20714. Tel: 410-257-2368; 202-855-7756 (Washington).
Catechesis/Religious Programs—Tel: 202-855-0897. Sr. Anne Parker, D.R.E.
Students 237.

Olney, Montgomery Co., St. Peter (1898), Revs. Thomas M. Kalita; Damian Shadwell; Robert Panke. In res., Rev. Canice Treacy.
Res., 2900 Sandy Spring Rd., 20832. Tel: 301-924-3774; Fax: 301-774-5259.
School—Tel: 301-774-9112. Mrs. Carol Mikoni, Prin.
Lay Teachers 22; Students 312.
Catechesis/Religious Programs—Tel: 301-570-4952. D.R.E.: Mrs. Gloria Zapiain, (Grades PreK-5); Mr. Robert Bellows, (Grades 6-8).
Students 982.

Oxon Hill, Prince Georges Co., St. Columba (1960), Revs. Godfrey Mosley; Fidel de Ramos; Deacon Richard Fisher.
Res., 7804 Livingston Rd., 20745. Tel: 301-567-5506; Fax: 301-567-6546.
School—7800 Livingston Rd., 20745. Tel: 301-567-6212; Fax: 301-567-6907.
Lay Teachers 11; Students 269.
Catechesis/Religious Programs—Tel: 301-567-6113.
Students 250.

Piscataway, Prince Georges Co., St. Mary (1830), Revs. Kevin Hart; Mark W. Ervin.
Res., 13401 Piscataway Rd., Clinton, 20735. Tel: 301-292-0527; Fax: 301-292-8786.
School—Tel: 301-292-2522.
Lay Teachers 14; Students 267.
Catechesis/Religious Programs—Tel: 301-292-2486.
Students 147.

Pomfret, Charles Co., St. Joseph (1763), Rev. J. Michael Quill.
Mailing Address: P.O. Box 100, 20675. Tel: 301-870-3041; 934-8943. [CEM]
Catechesis/Religious Programs—Tel: 301-934-0775.
Students 235.

Poolesville, Montgomery Co., Our Lady of the Presentation (1992), Rev. Y. David Brault.
Mailing Address: P.O. Box 428, 20837. Tel: 301-349-2045; 972-7504; Fax: 301-349-5423.
Catechesis/Religious Programs—Students 247.

Potomac, Montgomery Co., Our Lady of Mercy (1959), Rev. Msgr. John J. Enzler; Revs. Joseph F. Byron; William C. Metzdorf; Deacons F. Ian Ravenscroft; James Yun. In res.,
Res., 9200 Kentsdale Dr., 20854. Tel: 301-365-1415; Fax: 301-365-3104. [CEM]
School—9222 Kentsdale Dr., 20854. Tel: 301-365-4477. Sr. Virginia Pfau, I.H.M., Prin.
Sisters 1; Lay Teachers 21; Students 270.
Catechesis/Religious Programs—Tel: 301-365-1318.
Students 260.

Prince Frederick, Calvert Co., St. John Vianney (1965), Rev. Peter J. Daly; Deacon Christopher E. Wallmark.
Res., 105 Vianney Ln., 20678-4123. Tel: 410-535-0223; 301-855-1928; Fax: 410-535-4422.
Catechesis/Religious Programs—Tel: 410-535-4395. Jeanette M. Pedone, D.R.E.
Students 282.

Ridge, St. Mary's Co., St. Michael (1824), Rev. Karl A. Chimiak.
Res., 20680. Tel: 301-872-4321. [CEM]
School—P.O. Box 429, 20680. Tel: 301-872-5454.
Sisters of St. Joseph of Chambery (Hartford, CT) 3; Lay Teachers 8; Students 220.

Catechesis/Religious Programs—Students 98.
Riverdale, Prince Georges Co., St. Bernard (1950), Revs. Maurice V. O'Connell; An Ngoc Vu; Deacons Ferd Meyer; John Waltz; Alfredo Hidalgo.
Res., 5700 St. Bernard Dr., 20737-2185. Tel: 301-277-1000; Fax: 301-277-3464.
School—Tel: 301-864-3801. Sr. Elizabeth Raffo, C.S.C., Prin.
Sisters of the Holy Cross 2; Lay Teachers 12; Students 254.
Catechesis/Religious Programs—Tel: 301-277-4220; Fax: 301-277-3464. Mr. Howell A. McConnell, D.R.E.
Students 172.
Convent—Tel: 301-864-3323.
Rockville, Montgomery Co.,
1—St. Elizabeth, (1964), Rev. John F. Macfarlane.
Res., 917 Montrose Rd., 20852. Tel: 301-881-1380; Fax: 301-881-3068.
School—Tel: 301-881-1824; Fax: 301-881-6035.
Lay Teachers 22; Students 410.
Catechesis/Religious Programs—Students 180.
2—Shrine of St. Jude, (1956), Revs. Oliver McGready; William D. Byrne; G. Ralph Duffy; Deacons John W. Locke; Nicholas E. Scholz. In res., Rev. Leroy Fangmeyer.
Res., 12701 Veirs Mill Rd., 20853. Tel: 301-946-8200; Fax: 301-946-4527.
School—Tel: 301-946-7888; Fax: 301-929-8927.
Lay Teachers 29; Students 515.
Catechesis/Religious Programs—Tel: 301-949-2336.
Students 230.
3—St. Mary, (1813), Rev. Msgr. Adam J. Kostick; Rev. Stephen M. Cocca. In res., Rev. James J. Powderly.
Res., 520 Veirs Mill Rd., 20852. Tel: 301-424-5550; Fax: 301-424-5579. [CEM]
School—Tel: 301-762-4179; Fax: 301-762-8507.
Lay Teachers 15; Students 293.
Catechesis/Religious Programs—Tel: 301-762-8750.
Students 413.
Mission—Rockville, Montgomery Co., Our Lady of China, 1001 Grandin Ave., 20851. Tel: 301-294-3574. Rev. Paul Tsau.
4—St. Raphael, (1966), Revs. Michael Wilson; Miguel Umana, (Hispanic Ministry); Deacons Daniel Thompson; Lawrence Gordon; James Roan; Charles Mangold; Richard Mattocks; Frank Salatto.
Res., 1590 Kimblewick Rd., 20854. Tel: 301-762-2143; Fax: 301-762-0719.
Catechesis/Religious Programs—Students 805.
Rosaryville, Prince George's Co., Church of the Most Holy Rosary (1966), Rev. J. Isidore Dixon; Deacon Donald Carroll.
Res., 11704 Duley Station Rd., Upper Marlboro, 20772. Tel: 301-856-3880; 3881; Fax: 301-856-3944. [CEM]
Catechesis/Religious Programs—Tel: 301-868-5475. Mary Farrimond, D.R.E.
Students 110.
St. Inigoes, St. Mary's Co., St. Peter Claver, Rev. Patrick A. Smith.
Res., P.O. Box 240, 20684. Tel: 301-872-5460. [CEM]
St. Mary's City, St. Mary's Co., St. Cecilia (1974), Rev. Francis W. Krastel.
Res., 47950 Mattapany Rd., P.O. Box 67, 20686-0067. Tel: 301-862-4600; Fax: 301-863-7780. [JC]
Seat Pleasant, Prince Georges Co., St. Margaret (1908) (African American), Rev. Martin Gomes, SS.CC.; Deacons John Hill; Sam Minor.
Res., 408 Addison Rd., S., 20743. Tel: 301-336-3344; Fax: 301-336-5501.
School—410 Addison Rd., S., 20743. Tel: 301-336-3113.
Catechesis/Religious Programs—Students 205.
Mission—St. Matthias.
Silver Spring, Montgomery Co.,
1—St. Andrew Apostle, (1959), Rev. Msgr. Thomas P. Kelley; Rev. Charles V. Antonicelli. In res., Revs. Joseph J. Kleinstuber; Vincent J. Rigdon.
Res., 11600 Kemp Mill Rd., 20902. Tel: 301-649-3700; Fax: 301-681-3527.
School—Tel: 301-649-3555; Fax: 301-649-2352. Mrs. Joan Hosmer, Prin.
Lay Teachers 24; Students 566.
Catechesis/Religious Programs—Tel: 301-649-4200.
Students 200.
2—St. Bernadette, (Four Corners), Revs. Bernard E. Martin; Samuel C. Giese; Deacons Bernard A. Bernier; Dennis J. O'Neill; Thomas E. Roszkowski.
Res., 70 University Blvd., E., 20901. Tel: 301-593-0357; Fax: 301-593-3088.
School—Tel: 301-593-5611; Fax: 301-593-9042.
Sisters 3; Lay Teachers 18; Students 450.
Catechesis/Religious Programs—Mrs. Jane Bailey, D.R.E.
Students 144.
3—St. Camillus, (1951), Revs. Michael Tyson, O.F.M.; Jud Weiksnar, O.F.M.; Alban Maguire, O.F.M.; Ambrose Donehue, O.F.M.; Deacon Peter Barbernitz. In res., Rev. Alban Maguire, O.F.M.
Res., 1600 St. Camillus Dr., 20903. Tel: 301-434-8400; Fax: 301-431-1442.
School—1500 St. Camillus Dr., 20903.
Sisters 1; Brothers 1; Lay Teachers 14; Students 289.
Catechesis/Religious Programs—Tel: 301-434-2111. Pauline Fournier, D.R.E.
Students 340.
Child Care—(Four Corners), Tel: 301-439-1640. Mary Beth Smedley, Dir.
Certified Child Care Workers 14.
4—St. Catherine Laboure, (Wheaton) (1951), Rev. Robert G. Amey; Rev. Msgr. W. Joyce Russell, Pastor Emeritus; Rev. Rory T. Conley; Deacons Carlos Contreras; Raymond L. Chaput. In res., Rev. Santos Rene Maldonado.
Res., 11801 Claridge Rd., 20902. Tel: 301-946-3636; Fax: 301-946-5064.
School—Tel: 301-946-1717; Fax: 301-946-9572.
Daughters of Charity 3; Lay Teachers 24; Students 511.
Catechesis/Religious Programs—Tel: 301-946-3010.
Students 851.
5—Christ the King, (Wheaton) (1961), Revs. Robert J. Bozek; Luis Antonio Marroquin, 86.
Res., 2300 East-West Hwy., 2301 Colston Dr., 20910. Tel: 301-589-8616; Fax: 301-587-1929.
Catechesis/Religious Programs—Tel: 301-589-8620. Sr. Dorothy A. Owen, R.S.C.J., D.R.E.
Students 230.
6—St. John the Baptist, (Spring Brook) (1960), Rev. Francis G. Kazista; Rev. Msgr. E. Carl Lyon; Rev. John J. Hurley; Deacons Norman Keller; Jack Hamilton.
Res., 12319 New Hampshire Ave., 20904. Tel: 301-622-1122; Fax: 301-625-9266.
School—Tel: 301-622-3076. Marianne Moore, Prin.
Servants of the Holy Heart of Mary 1; Lay Teachers 14; Students 267.
Catechesis/Religious Programs—Tel: 301-622-3933. Patricia Roberts, D.R.E.
Students 295.
7—St. John the Evangelist, (Wheaton) (1774), Revs. Oliver Mahedy; Thomas A. Meighan; Joseph F. Perkins; Deacon Dan P. Stallings.
Res., 10103 Georgia Ave., 20902. Tel: 301-681-7663; Fax: 301-681-8793. [CEM]
School—Tel: 301-681-7656. Sr. Kathleen Lannak, I.H.M., Prin.
Sisters-Servants of Immaculate Heart of Mary 2; Lay Teachers 20; Students 344.
Catechesis/Religious Programs—Tel: 301-681-7634.
Students 225.
8—St. Michael, (Wheaton) (1930), Rev. Peter C. Cronin; Rev. Msgr. Joseph W. Hartman, Pastor Emeritus; Rev. John R. Clark; Deacons Tom C. Newman; John A. Marinari; Roberto Salgado. In res., Rev. Michael W. Douglas.
Res., 824 Pershing Dr., 20910. Tel: 301-589-1155; Fax: 301-589-3470.
School—824 Wayne Ave., 20910. Tel: 301-585-6873; Fax: 301-587-1142. Sr. Mary Raymond, Prin.
Lay Teachers 15; Students 276.
Catechesis/Religious Programs—Students 253.
9—Our Lady of Grace, (Leisure World) (1983), Rev. Msgr. John J. Madigan; Deacon Paul Pernecky, (Retired).
Res., 3134 Adderley Ct., 20906. Tel: 301-598-4233; Fax: 301-598-0843.
10—Our Lady Queen of Poland and Saint Maximilian Kolbe, (Leisure World) (1983) (Polish), Rev. Krzysztof Oska, S.Ch. (Poland).
Res., 9700 Rosensteel Ave., 20910. Tel: 301-589-1857.
Catechesis/Religious Programs—Students 50.
Solomons, Calvert Co., Our Lady Star of the Sea (1888), Rev. Richard E. Gardiner; Deacons John G. Etzel; Robert L. Connelly; Thomas B. Ricker.
Mailing Address: Box 560, 20688. Tel: 410-326-3535; Fax: 410-326-3679. [CEM]
School—Tel: 410-326-3171; Fax: 410-326-9478. Sr. Rosella Summe, C.D.P., Prin.
Sisters 2; Lay Teachers 9; Students 199.
Catechesis/Religious Programs—David Spigler, D.R.E.
Students 289.
Suitland, Prince George's Co., St. Bernardine (1966), Rev. John T. Dakes; Deacon Reginald A. Thomas. In res., Rev. Peter G. Williams (Australia).
Res., 2400 Brooks Dr., 20746. Tel: 301-736-0707.
Takoma Park, Prince Georges Co., Our Lady of Sorrows (1932), Revs. Francisco Gonzalez, S.F.; James Suntum, S.F.; Henry Charles (Trinidad); Deacon James Wilson, Jr.
Res., 1006 Larch Ave., 20912. Tel: 301-891-3500; Fax: 301-891-1523.
School—1010 Larch Ave., 20912. Tel: 301-891-2555; Fax: 301-270-6919. Mrs. Gail Ruffin, Prin.
Lay Teachers 12; Students 232.
Catechesis/Religious Programs—Tel: 301-891-2033.
Students 105.
Upper Marlboro, Prince Georges Co., Saint Mary of the Assumption (1848), Rev. Msgr. Richard A. Hughes; Rev. Joseph A. Jenkins; Deacons Frank Klco; Anthony Barrasso.
Res., 14908 Main St., 20772. Tel: 301-627-3255; Fax: 301-627-5533. [CEM]
School—Tel: 301-627-4170; Fax: 301-627-6383. Mrs. Carol Marvin, Prin.
Sisters - Servants of the Immaculate Heart of Mary 3; Students 288.
Catechesis/Religious Programs—Tel: 301-627-4542. Mr. Charles Long, D.R.E.
Students 160.
Valley Lee, St. Mary's Co., St. George (1851), Rev. Robert B. Riedel; Deacons Grafton T. Keller; David R. Powell.
Mailing Address: P.O. Box 9, 20692. Tel: 301-994-0607; Fax: 301-994-1793. [CEM]
Chapel—St. George's Island, St. Francis Xavier.
Catechesis/Religious Programs—Tel: 301-994-0737.
Students 88.
Waldorf, Charles Co., St. Peter (1700), Rev. Msgr. Andrew J. Cassin; Revs. J. Wilfrid Parent; Prudencio Sanchez; Deacon Charles J. Wilson.
Res., 3320 St. Peter's Dr., 20601. Tel: 301-843-8916; Fax: 301-843-3163. [CEM]
School—Tel: 301-843-1955; Fax: 301-843-6371. Judith DeLucco, Prin.
Lay Teachers 27; Students 511.
Catechesis/Religious Programs—Tel: 301-843-9583. Sr. Josephine Fogarty, R.S.M., D.R.E.
Students 224.
Our Lady Help of Christians (1980), Rev. Eamon Dignan.
Mailing Address: 100 Village St., 20602-1837. Tel: 301-645-7112.
Res., 930 Barrington Dr., 20602-2838. Tel: 301-843-8823; Fax: 301-645-3635.
Catechesis/Religious Programs—Sr. Margery Rose, M.H.S.H., D.R.E.
Students 582.

Chaplains of Public Institutions

Washington. *General Hospital.* Rev. Thomas Poovanal, Chap.
St. Elizabeth's Hospital (Government Operated), National Rehabilitation Hospital and Children's Medical Center, 20032. Tel: 202-574-7018. Rev. Benedict Faneye, O.P., Chap.
Washington Hospital Center. Revs. John S. Wintermyer, Chap.; Auxentius Panares, Assoc. Chap.
Bethesda, MD. *National Institutes of Health, Clinical Center.* Rev. Eugene J. Linehan, S.J.
Lanham, MD. *P.G. Doctor's Hospital.* Vacant. St. Mathias Parish, 20706.

Special Ministries:
Reverend Monsignors—
McMain, Robert O., Special Delegate for the Preservation of Historic Documents & Artifacts
O'Donnell, William F., Dir., Catholic Cemeteries
Roensch, Roger C., Dir., Spiritual Programs and Pilgrimages, Basilica of the National Shrine of the Immaculate Conception
Reverend Fathers—
Adams, John E., Dir., S.O.M.E.
Begg, Christopher T., Catholic University of America
Bradley, Denis J.M., Georgetown University
Bryant, Michael, Chap., District of Columbia Jail
Criscuolo, Salvatore A., Chap., Police and Fire Dept.
Hargrove, Jerry E., Chap., Howard University
Helm, Edward J., Catholic Deaf Center
Jones, Michael T., Chap., Good Counsel High School
Keffer, Robert F., Newman Center, University of Maryland
Kemp, Raymond B., Fellow, Woodstock Theological Center, Georgetown University
Kleinstuber, Joseph J., Dir., Admissions, Public Rels. & Recruiting, St. John's College
Kuhn, John G., Dir., Anchor Mental Health Assoc.
McCarthy, Brien R., Chap., American University
Montgomery, William L., Teacher, Carroll High School
Mordino, Robert F., Dir., CYO Retreats
Mudd, John, Dir., Fundraising Carroll High School
O'Brien, Joseph A., Rector, Cardinal O'Boyle Residence

O'Brien, Raymond C., Asst. Dean, Catholic University
Powderly, James J., Substance Abuse Coord.
Rigdon, Vincent J., Dir., Propagation of the Faith
Stack, James, Assoc. Dir., Office of Vocations for Men
Trancone, Gerard A., Center for the Deaf

Pastoral Center Special Ministries:
Most Rev.—
Lori, William E., Vicar General in Curia
Reverend Monsignors—
English, William J., Sec., Clergy
Farrell, Kevin J., Sec., Finance & Mgmt.
Gerhardt, Bernard C., Chancellor
Kane, William J., Vicar General
Sadusky, Joseph, Judicial Vicar Tribunal
Reverend Fathers—
Bozek, Robert J., Tribunal
Brennan, Mark E., Dir., Vocations for Men
Douglas, Michael W., Tribunal
Fangmeyer, LeRoy J., Exec. Dir., Office of Youth Ministry
Herbert, G. Paul, Tribunal
Hill, R. Cary, Sec., Parish Life & Worship
Knestout, Barry, Sec., Archbishop
Lee, Paul D., Dir., Continuing Educ. of Clergy & Dir., Office for Interreligious & Ecumenical Affairs.
Parry, Charles, Asst. Sec. Catholic Educ.
Reynierse, Peter J., Asst. to the Sec. for Clergy and Asst. Dir. of the Permanent Diaconate
Tappe, Walter J., Dir., Office of Worship

Hospital & Nursing Home Ministries:
Reverend Monsignors—
Arthur, E. Robert
Reverend Fathers—
Hurley, Leonard F.
Panares, Auxentius
Samaha, Jeffrey F.
Tou, Louis A.
Walsh, Francis M.
Wintermyer, John S.

On Duty Outside the Archdiocese:
Reverend Monsignors—
Albacete, Lorenzo, Ponce, Puerto Rico
Bazan, Joaquin, Albuquerque, NM
Gillen, James G., Vatican City State, Europe
Langsfeld, Paul J., Mount St. Mary Seminary, Emmitsburg, MD
Roeltgen, Kenneth W., Mount St. Mary Seminary, Emmitsburg, MD
Reverend Fathers—
Bender, Lawrence, S.S., Baltimore, MD
Culkin, Michael, Lancaster, PA
Holt, Paul-Stephen, New York
Izac, Andre C.
Jacobs, Peter
Kuebler, A. Seamus, Massachusetts
Oberle, James
Sanz, Jose, Antonio, TX
Slevin, Henry
Twohig, Christopher T., Ireland
Ulshafer, Thomas, S.S., Baltimore, MD

Military Chaplains:
Reverend Fathers—
Cunningham, Gerard M.
Cusick, Kevin M.
Fitz-Patrick, David M.
Hines, J. William
Lee, Matthew (J.T.)
Mudd, David A.
Saltysiak, Paul M.
Siriani, Klaus-Werner J.

Absent On Leave:
Reverend Fathers—
Cook, Brian
Finan, James A.
Scott, James A.
Vaughan, Brian S.

On Sick Leave:
Reverend Monsignors—
Joy, James B.

Retired:
Reverend Monsignors—
Albert, Louis W., 1514 Perrel Ln., Bowie, MD 20716
Bailey, John L., St. Francis Xavier, Washington, DC
Benson, John D., Washington, DC
Coyne, Joseph B., Carroll Manor, 1150 Varnum St., N.E., Washington, DC 20017
DiNardo, Ramon A., The Westchester, 4000 Cathedral Ave., Apt. 854-B, Washington, DC 20016
Dooley, R. Joseph, (Outside the Diocese)
Echle, Harry, Our Lady of Victory, Washington, DC 20007
Farina, Michael F., St. Patrick, Washington, DC
Grodavent, Thomas J., 7 Scott Rd., Colorado Springs, CO 80906
Hartman, Joseph W., Cardinal O'Boyle Residence, P.O. Box 29206, Washington, DC 20017
Jimenez, Armando, Cardinal O'Boyle Residence, P.O. Box 29206, Hyattsville, MD 20017
Kuehner, Ralph J.
Lyon, E. Carl, St. John the Baptist, Silver Spring, MD
Mohan, Robert P.
Murphy, John J., St. Joseph Manor, 215 Thatcher St., Brockton, MA 02402
O'Connor, Aloysius, Holy Angels, Avenue, MD
Quinn, W. Louis, Our Lady of Lourdes, Bethesda, MD
Russell, W. Joyce, St. Catherine Laboure, Wheaton
Teletchea, Joseph L., St. Jerome, Hyattsville, MD
Reverend Fathers—
Barry, Paul, 5404 Bye St., Capitol Heights, MD 20743
Bloom, R. Frederick, 6304 Waverley Dr., Frederick, MD 21702
Bober, Francis J., 2475 Virginia Ave., N.W., #407, Washington, DC 20037
Bonfigilo, Anthony J., 12790 Griffing Blvd., North Miami, FL 33161
Branch, Leslie, Carroll Manor, 1150 Varnum St., N.E., Washington, DC 20017
Brogan, Hugh T., 678 Main St., Sugar Notch, PA 18706
Byron, Joseph F., Manor Care, 10714 Potomac Tennis Ln., Potomac, MD 20854
Caimi, Luke A., Rte. 11, Box 312, Hendersonville, NC 28739
Casey, James E., 3507 Farragut Ave., Kensington, MD 20895
Cole, J. Gerard, Cardinal O'Boyle Residence, P.O. Box 29206, Washington, DC 20017
Connor, John V., 137 Bayshore Dr., South Bethany, DE
DiNorcin, Americo
Evans, Edward, St. Ambrose, Cheverly, MD 20785
Flaherty, Francis T., P.O. Box 321, Deal, NJ 07723
Gallagher, Roger P., Cardinal O'Boyle Residence, P.O. Box 29206, Washington, DC 20017
Hartel, Edward T., Washington, DC
Higgins, John J., 300 Ocean Ave., Seabright, NJ 07760
Holden, Paul, Lot 72A, Massey's Landing, Millsboro, DE 19966
Januszkiewicz, Henry, 3860 Central Ave., #103, Fort Myers, FL 33901
Joyce, George V., 15 Orchard St., Holyoke, MA 01040
Keesler, Robert L., St. Mary, Laurel, MD
Kemp, Patrick W., 2900 Shipmaster Way, #301, Annapolis, MD 21401
Lubey, John A., Cardinal O'Boyle Residence, P.O. Box 29206, Washington, DC 20017
McCormack, Brendan, Bethesda, MD
McGuigan, Robert, Jeanne Jugan Residence, 4200 Harewood Rd., N.E., Washington, DC 20017
McMahon, John B., 575-B Turnberry Blvd., Newport News, VA 23602
Murphy, Desmond P., Holy Family, Mitchellville, MD
Newman, Aloysius T., 6260 Crain Hwy., P.O. Box 2225, LaPlata, MD 20646
Norris, Walter J., St. Paul's, 9240 Main St., Damascus, MD 02872
O'Shea, Philip, Blessed Sacrament, Washington, DC
Pagone, Joseph, Carroll Manor, 1150 Varnum St., N.E., Washington, DC 20017
Petrella, Robert
Pritchard, Edward, Washington, DC
Quinones, Miguel, Cardinal O'Boyle Residence, P.O. Box 29206, Washington, DC 20017
Roy, J. Jean, 15 Talmuth Ave., Haverhill, MA 01830
Salcedo, Luis G., St. Bartholomew, 7212 Blacklock Rd., Bethesda, MD 20817
Schaefer, Thomas, Washington, DC
Schellenberg, Milton A., 5914 Welborn Dr., Bethesda, MD 20816
Smith, Alphonsus M., Washington, DC
Studney, J. Edward, Cardinal O'Boyle Residence, P.O. Box 29206, Washington, DC 20017
Tran-Khac-Hy, Hilarius, Gaithersburg, MD
Trapold, John T., New Jersey
Treacy, Canice, St. Peter, 2900 Sandy Spring Rd., Olivey, MD 20832
Twiddy, Paul, Charlotte Hall Veteran's Home, Rte. 5, Charlotte Hall, MD 20622
Wharton, Robert H., Cardinal O'Boyle Residence, P.O. Box 29206, Washington, DC 20017
Winnenberg, John O., San Diego, CA
Znotinas, John, 2712 Fairlawn St., Temple Hills, MD 20748

Permanent Deacons:
Abbate, Paul J., St. Joseph, Archdiocese of Agana
Agostinelli, Floyd D., St. Francis de Sales, Washington, DC
Allen, David A., St. Elizabeth, Rockville, MD
Bailey, Aston A., (Unassigned)
Ballard, Harvey W., St. Michael, Baden, MD
Barnes, David J., St. Edward the Confessor, Bowie, MD
Barnes, John R., St. Joseph, Pomfret, MD
Barrasso, Anthony T., Mount Calvary, Forestville, MD
Barrett, Kenneth, St. Martin, Gaithersburg, MD
Barrett, Raymond J., Ascension, Bowie, MD
Barry, T. Kevin, St. Edward, Bowie, MD
Battaglia, Thomas D., St. John Vianney, Prince Frederick, MD
Bechet, Leon J., St. Joseph, Landover, MD
Begg, George B., Jr., St. Jane de Chantal, Bethesda, MD
Bell, Lawrence G., St. Martin, Gaithersburg, MD
Beller, Edwin J., (Retired)
Bernier, Bernard A., Jr., St. Bernadette, Silver Spring, MD
Berry, Robert L., St. Gabriel, Washington, DC
Betz, Andrew J., St. Joseph, Beltsville, MD
Black, Joseph L., Santa Fe, NM
Blaesing, Carl F., St. John the Evangelist, Clinton, MD
Blaine, B. Paul, Jr., St. Mary, Landover Hills, MD
Bobbitt, John W., St. Stephen Martyr, Washington, DC
Boesman, William C., St. Thomas the Apostle, Washington, DC
Brink, Edward J., St. Mary, Upper Marlboro, MD
Briscoe, John A., Assumption, Washington, DC
Brokenborough, Alfred T., Incarnation, Washington, DC
Brown, James H., Holy Redeemer, Washington, DC
Brown, Sylvester, Sacred Heart, Washington, DC
Brown, William J., III, Peacham, VT
Burroughs, Eugene, St. Mary, Bryantown, MD
Butler, Kevin A., Sr., Holy Comforter/St. Cyprian, Washington, DC
Cahoon, David L., Jr., St. Mary, Barnesville, MD
Cain, Leonard F., Wyomissing, PA
Carr, James, Resurrection, Burtonsville, MD
Carroll, Donald T., Holy Rosary, Upper Marlboro, MD
Chaput, Raymond L., St. Catherine Laboure, Silver Spring, MD
Chase, Ira E., Our Lady of Perpetual Help, Washington, DC
Chaves, Antonio, St. Mark's, Hyattsville, MD
Coates, Vincent J., St. Joseph, Capitol Hill, DC
Coleman, Earle W., St. Luke, Washington, DC
Connelly, Robert L., Our Lady Star of the Sea, Solomons, MD
Connor, James E., Salisbury, MD
Connors, John A., Washington Hospital Center, DC
Conrad, Joseph M., St. Luke, Washington, DC
Contreras, Carlos E., St. Catherine La Boure, Silver Spring, MD
Cooper, Philip J., Mother Seaton, Germantown, MD
Cordova-Ferrer, Nathaniel, St. Mark, Hyattsville, MD
Crowley, Ronald C., St. Patrick, Rockville, MD
Cummins, Don E., Tacoma, WA
Cummins, Eugene J., Jr., St. Martin, Gaithersburg, MD
Cyrus, Ralph W., St. Teresa of Avila, Washington, DC
Daniels, Willis, St. Aloysius, Washington, DC
Davies, Gary, Little Flower, Bethesda, MD
Davis, William E., St. Matthias, Lanham, MD
DeRoze, Donald G., Resurrection, Burtonsville, MD
DiDuca, Paul, Our Lady of the Visitation, Darnestown, MD
Ditewig, William, Holy Redeemer, Kensington, MD
Donlon, Jerome A., Holy Cross, Garrett Park, MD
Draper, Harry R., Incarnation, Washington, DC
Dudley, Jesse J., St. Aloysius, Washington, DC
Dunne, Joseph E., Leave of Absence
Ealey, Ronald R., Wichita, KS
Edelin, Charles E., Jr., Holy Comforter-St. Cyprian, Washington, DC
Elliott, Thomas B., Ascension, Bowie, MD
Emley, William P., Jr., St. Ignatius, Chapel Point, MD
Enderle, Francis X., Military Services Archdiocese
Enright, Timothy D., Mother Seton, Germantown, MD
Etzel, John G., Our Lady Star of the Sea, Solomons, MD
Feneis, Albert G.
Finerty, John F., St. Paul, Damascus, MD
Fisher, Richard A., St. Columba, Oxon Hill, MD
Flanagan, Michael W., Our Lady Help of Christians, Waldorf, MD
Flynn, Leo, Our Lady of Victory, Washington, DC

Forbes, Rodney R., St. James, Mt. Rainier, MD
Forbes, Thomas S., Incarnation, Washington, DC
Ford, James A., Holy Name, Washington, DC
Fortney, Charles R., St. Joseph, Morganza, MD
Foster, George, (Unassigned)
Garcia, David F., New Mexico
Garrah, Thomas, St. Ambrose, Cheverly, MD
Genis, Thomas P., Immaculate Conception, Washington, DC
Gignilliat, Robert L., St. Joseph, Pomfret, MD
Gordon, Lawrence C., St. Matthew's Cathedral, Washington, DC
Hamilton, John G., St. John Baptist, Silver Spring, MD
Hannagan, Francis L., St. Nicholas, Laurel, MD
Harley, James A., Nativity, Washington, DC
Haywood, Hiram H., Jr., Basilica of the Shrine of the Immaculate Conception, Washington, DC
Hidalgo, Alfredo, St. Bernard, Riverdale, MD
Hill, Charles, S.O.M.E., Washington, DC
Hill, Thomas O., Sr., St. Mary Star of the Sea, Indian Head, MD
Hoffman, Michael R., St. Anthony, North Beach, MD
Holson, Edward, St. Mark, Hyattsville, MD
Hong, Pascal, St. Francis of Assisi, Derwood, MD
Hopson, Frank, St. Ignatius, Hilltop, MD
Hume, W. Michael, Duluth, MN
Interlandi, Joseph S., St. Peter, Olney, MD
Jackson, Harold I., St. Francis de Sales, Washington, DC
Jardeleza, Jack, (Retired)
Johnson, Bernard C., St. Mary Mother of God, Washington, DC
Johnson, Samuel A., Our Lady of Perpetual Help, Washington, DC
Keller, Grafton T., St. George, Valley Lee, MD
Keller, Norman B., St. John Baptist, Silver Spring, MD
Kelly, John D., St. Anthony, Washington, DC
Klco, Frank, St. Mary, Upper Marlboro, MD
Knestout, Thomas, (Retired)
Kostka, Daniel S., Mother Seaton, Germantown, MD
Kraemer, Francis W., Sr., St. Peter, Washington, DC
Kronschnabel, Michael C., Archdiocese of Baltimore, MD
Kube, Carl B., Christ the King, Silver Spring, MD
Kunsemiller, John H., Archdiocese of Los Angeles, CA
L'Heureux, George G., Arlington, VA
Lacovaro, James G., Archbishop Carroll High School, Washington, DC
Lemon, John, St. Peter, Olney, MD
Lennon, Joseph M., St. Catherine Laboure, Silver Spring, MD
Leonard, John M., Blessed Sacrament, Washington, DC
Levy, Richard A., Jr., Archdiocese of San Francisco, CA
Locke, John W., Shrine of St. Jude, Rockville, MD
Luetjen, Palmer, St. Jane de Chantal, Bethesda, MD
Lynch, John F., St. Anthony, North Beach, MD
Mallon, Charles A., Holy Family, Mitchellville, MD
Mangold, Charles C., St. Raphael, Rockville, MD
Marinari, A. John, St. Michael, Silver Spring, MD
Martin, E. Chad, Jesus the Good Shephard, Dunkirk, MD
Martin, J. Murry, St. Mary, Upper Marlboro, MD
Martin, Nerus O., Jr., St. Thomas More, Washington, DC
Mastrangelo, Eugene K., St. Pius X, Bowie, MD
Mattocks, Richard E., St. Raphael, Rockville, MD
McAskill, Donald K., Fredericksburg, VA
McCann, James C., St. Rose of Lima, Gaithersburg, MD
McCartin, Matthew J., St. Mary, Rockville, MD
McGinness, John J., St. Patrick, Washington, DC
McGlade, H. Donald, National Naval Medical Center
McGrath, Joseph B., Blessed Sacrament, Washington, DC
McMahon, Anthony, National Naval Medical Center
Merella, Bartholomew J., Holy Redeemer, College Park, MD
Meyer, Ferdinand, St. Bernard, Riverdale, MD
Middleton, Henry D., III, St. Mary, Bryantown, MD
Migliorini, Louis, Sr., Retired, Ocean City, MD
Miles, Lawrence A., St. Teresa of Avila, Washington, DC
Miller, Lawrence L., Archdiocese for Military Services, U.S.A.
Minor, Samuel L., Jr., St. Margaret, Seat Pleasant, MD
Moll, Anthony W., St. John, Clinton, MD
Moskaitis, J. Vincent, St. Paul, Damascus, MD
Newman, C. Thomas, St. Michael, Silver Spring, MD
Nguyen, John H., Our Lady of Vietnam, Silver Spring, MD
Nosacek, Andrew J., St. Pius X, Bowie, MD
O'Neill, Dennis J., St. Bernadette, Silver Spring, MD
Oettinger, Frank F., Diocese of Orlando
Olivares, Jose, St. Raphael, Rockville, MD
Om, Michael W., Our Lady of Mercy, Potomac, MD
Paolucci, Robert J., St. Ambrose, Cheverly, MD
Parker, Charles J., Leave of Absence
Parker, Donald A., (Unassigned)
Pernecky, Paul, (Retired)
Picard, Adrien D., Columbia, MD
Pinder, Wilbur L., Jr., St. Francis of Assisi, Derwood, MD
Ponzette, John, St. Mary, Laurel, MD
Powell, David R., St. George, Valley Lee, MD
Pyle, Jay Allen, St. Matthias, Lanham, MD
Quander, James W., (Retired)
Raffensperger, Jeffrey, Sacred Heart, Bowie, MD
Ravenscroft, F. Ian, Our Lady of Mercy, Potomac, MD
Redding, Edward R., Our Lady of Victory, Washington, DC
Rice, Ulysses, St. Matthew Cathedral, Washington, DC
Ricker, Philip W., St. Mark, Hyattsville, MD
Ricker, Thomas B., Jr., Our Lady Star of the Sea, Solomons, MD
Roan, James A., Jr., St. Raphael, Rockville, MD
Robey, Frank A., Jr., Holy Redeemer, Kensington, MD
Robinson, Stephen M., St. Mary, Landover Hills, MD
Roszkowski, Thomas E., St. Bernadette, Silver Spring, MD
Rourke, Walter G., Holy Ghost, Issue, MD
Rouson, Henry E., (Retired)
Salgado, Roberto, Capilla Latina, Washington, DC
Scholz, Nicholas E., Shrine of St. Jude, Rockville, MD
Schopfer, Richard J., Little Flower, Bethesda, MD
Serafini, Bartolo, Capilla Latina, Washington, DC
Sferrella, Joseph J., York, PA
Shewmaker, John B., Our Lady of Lourdes, Bethesda, MD
Sinchak, J. Douglas, St. Mary of the Mills, Laurel, MD
Smith, Anthony S., St. Francis Xavier, Washington, DC
Somerville, James, St. Joseph, Morganza, MD
Somerville, John W., Bascilica of the Shrine of the Immaculate Conception, Washington, DC
Somerville, Joseph W., Our Lady Queen of Peace, Washington, DC
Spalding, Thomas C., Our Lady's Church, Medley's Neck, MD
Springer, James R., El Paso, TX
Stackpole, Terrell U., St. Nicholas, Laurel, MD
Stallings, Dan P., Sr., St. John Evangelist, Silver Spring, MD
Stewart, John P., St. Teresa of Avila, Washington, DC
Sweeney, Anthony J., III, Immaculate Heart of Mary, Lexington Park, MD
Taylor, Michael J., St. Mary, Landover Hills, MD
Testudine, Joseph, Airmen's & Soldier's Home, Washington, DC
Thomas, Reginald A., St. Bernardine of Siena, Suitland, MD
Thomas, William, Holy Name, Washington, DC
Thompson, Daniel R., St. Raphael, Rockville, MD
Thompson, Finis E., Ascension, Bowie, MD
Thurston, Reynaldo J., Our Lady of Perpetual Help, Washington, DC
Tintle, Jerome A., St. Jerome, Hyattsville, MD
Treacy, Robert J., Diocese of Wilmington
Trichel, Allen J., Our Lady of Help of Christians, Waldorf, MD
Vargas, Jorge W., Our Lady Queen of the Americas, Washington, DC
Vergot, John J., (Retired)
Vita, William A., Jr., Mother Seton, Germantown, MD
Wakefield, Walter W., III, Diocese of Cincinnati, OH
Wallmark, Christopher E., St. John Vianney, Prince Frederick, MD
Waltz, John F., St. Bernard, Riverdale, MD
Weightman, Stanley, St. Bernard, Riverdale, MD
Welch, Joseph, St. Edward, Bowie, MD
West, Richard A., (Retired)
Whitaker, Robert W., St. Ann, Washington, DC
Whitfield, Robert J., St. Francis of Assisi, Derwood, MD
Wilbur, Carl, N.I.H., Bethesda, MD
Wilkinson, Lawrence A., St. Anthony, Washington, DC
Wilson, Charles J., St. Martin, Washington, DC
Wilson, James, Our Lady of Sorrows, Takoma Park, MD
Yates, Paul F., (Retired)
Yun, James, Our Lady of Mercy, Potomac, MD
Ziemianski, Lawrence L., Arlington, VA
Zuluaga, Gustavo, Hispanic Catholic Center, Washington, DC
Zusi, J. Michael, Archdiocese of Baltimore, MD

INSTITUTIONS LOCATED IN THE ARCHDIOCESE

[A] SEMINARIES, ARCHDIOCESAN

WASHINGTON. *Theological College of the Catholic University of America*, 401 Michigan Ave., N.E., 20017. Tel: 202-319-5900; Fax: 202-319-5909. Sulpician Fathers. Legal Title: *The Sulpician Seminary of Washington*.
Faculty: Revs. Howard P. Bleichner, S.S., Ph.D., Rector; William J. Moorman, O.SS.T.; William R. Viola, S.S., M.S., S.T.M., S.T.L.; Albert C. Giaquinto, S.S., M.A., S.T.L.; Thomas Hurst, S.S., S.T.L., Ph.D., Vice Rector; Bro. Donald Boccardi, S.M. In res., Revs. Robert B. Eno, S.S., M.A., S.T.D.; Michel Oyama, S.S. Priests 8; Students 60.

[B] SEMINARIES, RELIGIOUS OR SCHOLASTICATES

WASHINGTON. *Atonement Seminary-Francisan Friars of the Atonement*, 145 Taylor St., N.E., 20017. Tel: 202-529-1114. Rev. Patrick Cogan, S.A., Admin. In res., Revs. Paul Ojibway, S.A.; Carmen Giuliano, S.A.; Dennis Murphy, S.A., (Retired); Clement St. Jacques, S.A., (Retired). Priests 5; Brothers 1; Students 1.

Augustinian College, Order of St. Augustine, 3700 Oakview Ter., N.E., 20017-2521. Tel: 202-635-5299; Fax: 202-635-5296. Revs. Martin L. Smith, O.S.A., Prior & Treas.; Francis J. Doyle, O.S.A., Dir., Professed Prog. & Prenovices. In res., Revs. Francis J. Horn, O.S.A.; Brian Frawley, O.S.A.; Ronald A. Hamaday O.S.A. Priests 5; Students 5.

Cluster of Independent Theological School, The (1970), 391 Michigan Ave., N.E., 20017. Tel: 202-269-3934. Cluster of Three Independent Schools of Theology. Oblate College, 391 Michigan Ave., N.E., 20017. De Sales School of Theology, 721 Lawrence St., N.E., 20017. Dominican House of Studies, 487 Michigan Ave., N.E., 20017. Revs. John Crossin, O.S.F.S., Chm.; Harry Winter, O.M.I., Treas.; Thomas McCreesh, O.P., Sec. Priests 26; Sisters 1; Lay Teachers 8; Students 118.

DeSales School of Theology, 721 Lawrence St., N.E., 20017. Tel: 202-269-9412; Fax: 202-526-2720. Rev. John W. Crossin, O.S.F.S., Pres. Priests 8; Brothers 1; Sisters 1; Lay Teachers 2; Total Enrollment 60.

Deshairs Community-Oblates of St. Francis de Sales Residence, 1621 Otis St., N.E., 20018-2321. Tel: 202-526-7403. Revs. John W. Crossin, O.S.F.S.; Thomas J. Erbrick, O.S.F.S.; William J. Ruhl, O.S.F.S.; Bros. Edward J. Ogden, O.S.F.S.; John M. Carroll, O.S.F.S. Priests 3; Brothers 1.

Diocesan Laborer Priests, House of Studies (1966), 3706 15th St., N.E., 20017. Tel: 202-832-4217; Fax: 202-526-5692. Revs. Rutilio J. del Riego, Dir.; Joseph M. Ambros; Thomas E. Murphy; Gabriel Calvo. Priests 4; Total Enrollment 4.

Dominican House of Studies, 487 Michigan Ave., N.E., 20017. Tel: 202-529-5300; Fax: 202-636-4460. Very Rev. John Vidmar, O.P., Prior; Revs. Vincent Wiseman, O.P., Student Master; Thomas P. McCreesh, O.P., Pres., Pontifical Faculty; John W. Burke, O.P., Dir. Word of God Institute; Bro. Michael Downey, O.P., Economic Admin.; Revs. Kurt Pritzl, O.P., Regent of Studies; Joseph Augustine DiNoia, O.P., Exec. Dir. Secretariate - Doctrine/Pastoral Practices NCCB; Peter M. Batts, O.P.; Steven C. Boguslawski, O.P.; Michael Ciccone, O.P.; Pierre H. Conway, O.P.; William J. Conlan, O.P.; Lawrence J. Donohoo, O.P.; John Martin Egan, O.P.; Norman H. Fenton, O.P.; Kenneth Harkins, O.P.; John Frederick Hinnebusch, O.P.; William J. Hill, O.P.; Mark Heath, O.P.; Augustine Judd, O.P.; John P. McGovern, O.P.; Matthew Rzeczkowski, O.P.; Brian Shanley, O.P.; Kevin McGrath, O.P.; Albert Raretsky, O.P.; J. Raymond Vandegrift, O.P.; Luke Tancrell, O.P.; Joseph Tortorici, O.P. In res., Revs. Daniel Dempski, O.S.B.; Jaroslaw Kupczak, O.P.; Philip Pan, O.P.; Paul O'Shea, O.P.; Liem Tran, O.P. Priests 32; Brothers 1; Clerical Students 23; Seminarians 23.

Franciscan Fathers, T.O.R., Tau Fraternity, 1359 Monroe St., N.W., 20017. Tel: 202-526-6324. Candidates 6.

Franciscan Mission Service of North America, 401 Michigan Ave., N.E., 20017. Tel: 202-832-1762; Fax: 202-832-1778. 650 Jackson N.E., 20017. Sr. Jean Amore, S.M.I.C., Coord., Overseas Lay Ministry Prog.; Rev. Joseph Nangle, O.F.M., Exec. Dir. Priests

1; Sisters 1; Lay Staff 2.

Josephite Pastoral Center, 1200 Varnum St., N.E., 20017. Tel: 202-526-9270; 9271. Rev. John G. Harfmann, S.S.J., Dir.; Maria M. Lannon, Assoc. Dir. Priests 1; Brothers 2; Deacons 1; Lay Women 5.

LaSalette Novitiate, 1243 Monroe St., N.E., 20017. Tel: 202-526-8070. Rev. Raymond G. Cadran, M.S., Dir. Priests 2; Scholastics 4; Novices 1.

Marian Fathers Scholasticate, 3885 Harewood Rd., N.E., 20017. Tel: 202-526-8884; Fax: 202-832-6551. Rev. Shaun O'Connor, M.I.C., Supr. & Rector; Dan Papineau, M.I.C., Seminarian, First Councillor; David Briggs, M.I.C., Seminarian, Second Councillor; Revs. Roger L. Wojcik, M.I.C., Third Councillor & Treasurer; Lawrence P. Dunn, M.I.C., Vocation Dir.; John Kobza, M.I.C.; Jaroslaw Gamrot, M.I.C. (Poland); Joseph Sielski, M.I.C. Tel: 410-778-7088. In res., Revs. Donald B. Conroy; Andrius Narbekovas (Lithuania). Priests 6; Students 7.

Marist College, The-Scholasticate, 220 Taylor St., N.E., 20017-1095. Tel: 202-529-2821. Revs. Edwin L. Keel, S.M., Rector & Supr.; James F. McGoldrick, S.M., Formation Team. Priests 2; Scholastics 5.

Maryknoll Fathers and Brothers, 4834 16th St., N.W., 20011. Tel: 202-726-4252; Fax: 202-726-0466. Revs. Peter C. Brien, M.M., Dir.; Richard Albertine, M.M.; Daniel Dolan, M.M.; Bros. John Blazo, M.M., Mission Educ. Dept.; Ronald Rinella, M.M., Office of Justice and Peace, P.O. Box 29132, 20017. Tel: 202-832-1780. Mr. Terence Miller, Dir.; Rev. Peter Ruggere, M.M.

Monastery of Our Lady of Mount Carmel, 2131 Lincoln Rd., N.E., 20002. Tel: 202-832-6622. Legal Title: *Monastery of Our Lady of Mount Carmel-House of Studies Order of Discalced Carmelite Friars*. Revs. Steven Payne, O.C.D., Prior; Valerian Noronha, O.C.D.; Theodore Centala, O.C.D.; Kieran Kavanaugh, O.C.D.; Francis Miller, O.C.D.; Patrick MacNamara, O.C.D., M.S.; Bros. Antonine DiSabella, O.C.D.; Bryan Paquette, O.C.D.; Edward O'Donnell, O.C.D.; Michael Stoegbauer, O.C.D. Priests 6; Brothers 4; Students 2.

Oblate College/Oblate Center for Mission Studies, 391 Michigan Ave., N.E., 20017-1586. Tel: 202-529-5244. Revs. Harry Winter, O.M.I., Ph.D., Pres.; Henry L. Lemoncelli, O.M.I., M.Ed., Dean; Raymond Prybis, O.M.I., Ph.D. Ed., Treas.; David N. Power, O.M.I., S.T.D.; Jerry Orsino, O.M.I.; Charles W. Gilles, O.M.I.; Donald Joyce, O.M.I., M.A.; John J. Leddy, O.M.I., M.A.; George F. McLean, O.M.I., Ph.D.; William M. O'Donnell, O.M.I., S.T.L., Supr.; Seamus Finm, O.M.I., Ph.D.; Richard McAlear, O.M.I., S.T.L., Vocations; Gode Iwele, O.M.I., S.T.L.; Paul Costello, O.M.I.; J. Wiliam Sheehan, O.M.I., M.A., Prov.; John Pallard, O.M.I., Ph.D.; James E. Sullivan, O.M.I.; William Antonio; Bros. Thomas Cruise, O.M.I.; Michael Holly, O.M.I. Priests 18; Brothers 2; Priests Foreign Countries 4; Lay Teachers 4; Total Enrollment 19.

Oblates of Mary Immaculate, De Mazenod Residence (1979), 391 Michigan Ave., N.E., 20017. Tel: 202-529-8882. Legal Title: *Missionary Oblates of Mary Immaculate, Eastern American Province*. Revs. Henry L. Lemoncelli, O.M.I., Dir. Formation; Philip Singarayar, O.M.I., Asst. Dir. Formation. In res., Rev. Armand Mathew, O.M.I. House of Formation for Oblate Religious Seminarians and Brothers. Priests 3; Students 6.

Oblates of St. Francis de Sales House of Studies, 721 Lawrence St., N.E., 20017. Tel: 202-269-9410. Revs. Donald Heet, O.S.F.S., Supr.; Michael Cavanaugh, O.S.F.S.; William F. Davis, O.S.F.S.; Peter Leonard. Priests 6; Scholastics 9; Candidates 2.

Queen of Pious Schools House of Studies-Piarist Fathers, 1339 Monroe St., N.E., 20017-2510. Tel: 202-529-7734. Revs. Andrew C. Buechele, Sch.P., Ph.D., Rector & Master of Clerics; Theodore E. Podson, Sch.P., M.E., San Antonio/Amarillo, TX; Mario Vizcaino, Sch.P., M.A., S.T.L., Miami, FL; Washington, DC. Priests 3.

St. Bonaventure Friary, 3514 15th St., N.E., 20017. Tel: 202-529-5324; 832-0953; Fax: 202-635-4871. Revs. Paul Liniger, O.F.M.Conv.; Adam E. Bunnell, O.F.M.Conv., Ph.D.; John D. Burkhard, O.F.M.Conv.; Berard L. Marthaler, O.F.M.Conv., S.T.D., Ph.D.; Vincent Petersen, O.F.M.Conv., M.Div.; Thomas Reist, O.F.M.Conv.; Marcelo DaLuz, O.F.M.Conv. In res., Bro. Philip Kelly, O.F.M.Conv. Priests 7; Students 12.

St. Francis Friary-Capuchin College, 4121 Harewood Rd., N.E., 20017-1593. Tel: 202-529-2188. Revs. John A. Pavlik, O.F.M.Cap., Supr., Formation Dir.; Francis Yacobi, O.F.M.Cap., Vicar; James Froehlich, O.F.M.Cap., Treas.; Christopher Rengers, O.F.M.Cap.; Thomas Russman, O.F.M.Cap.; Sebastian F. Miklas, O.F.M.Cap.; J. Daniel Mindling, O.F.M.Cap.; Peter Weisswange, O.F.M.Cap. (South Africa); Carroll L. Warner, O.F.M.Cap.; Mark Poletunow, O.F.M.Cap.; Benjamin Madden, O.F.M.Cap.; Vincent Fortunato, O.F.M.Cap.; Luis Pepeu, O.F.M.Cap. (Brazil); Alvadi Marmentini, O.F.M.Cap. (Brazil); Bros. Michael Letosak, O.F.M.Cap.; Alfred Vincent, O.F.M.Cap.; Charles McElroy, O.F.M.Cap. Priests 14; Scholastics 12; Brothers 3; Total Enrollment 14.

St. Joseph's Seminary, 1200 Varnum St., N.E., 20017. Tel: 202-526-4231; 526-4229 (Student). St. Joseph's Society of the Sacred Heart-Josephite Fathers & Brothers. Very Rev. John L.M. Filippelli, S.S.J., Rector; Revs. James A. Hayes, S.S.J., Vice Rector; John A. Carroll, S.S.J., Spiritual Dir.; John G. Harfmann, S.S.J., Dir. Josephite Pastoral Center; James E. McLinden, S.S.J., Vocation Dir.; Bros. Thomas Vincent, S.S.J.; Earl Kent, S.S.J. In res., Revs. Robert Kinel, S.S.J.; Howard Johnson; John Doerfler; J.T. Putnam; Rev. Msgr. Godwin Akpan, M.S.P. (Nigeria); Revs. Cosmas Nwosuh, M.S.P. (Nigeria); Stephen Achi, M.S.P. (Nigeria). Priests 12; Franciscan Sisters of St. Joseph 4.

St. Paul's College, 3015 Fourth St., N.E., 20017-1199. Tel: 202-832-6262; Fax: 202-269-2507. Paulist Fathers. Revs. Frank R. Desiderio, C.S.P., Supr. & Dir. Ministerial Formation; Ronald G. Roberson, C.S.P., S.E.O.D.; Paul D. Huesing, C.S.P., Ph.D., Assoc. Dir. of Formation & Treas.; Lawrence E. Boadt, C.S.P., S.S.D.; Kenneth G. Boyack, C.S.P., D.Min.; Thomas E. Comber, C.S.P.; John P. Donahue, C.S.P.; John J. Geaney, C.S.P.; John E. Lynch, C.S.P., Ph.D.; Neil J. McEleney, C.S.P., S.S.L.; Bruce Nieli, C.S.P.; Lawrence Rice, C.S.P.; Robert S. Rivers, C.S.P. Priests 13; Sisters 6; Laity 7; Students 14.

Washington Theological Union, 6896 Laurel St., N.W., 20012. Tel: 202-726-8800. Legal Title: *Washington Theological Union, Inc.* Established in 1968 as the Coalition of Religious Seminaries. The Union is a school of theology owned by seven religious communities: Carmelite Order, Provinces of the Most Pure Heart of Mary and St Elias; Congregation of the Sacred Hearts of Jesus and Mary; Order of Friars Minor, Province of the Most Holy Name of Jesus; Order of Friars Minor Conventual; Province of Our lady of Consolation; Order of St. Augustine, Province of St. Thomas; Redemptorist Fathers and Brothers. Revs. Vincent de P. Cushing, O.F.M., S.T.D., Pres.; Andrew Ciferni, O.Praem., Academic Dean. Priests 18; Sisters 3; Lay Teachers 1; Students 264.

Whitefriars Hall, 1600 Webster St., N.E., 20017. Tel: 202-526-1221; Fax: 202-526-9217. Rev. Lukas Schmidt, O.Carm., Prior & Formation Dir.; Sr. Angele Sadlier, O.Carm., Assoc. Dir. of Formation; Revs. David Blanchard, O.Carm.; Gregory Battafarano, O.Carm.; Donald W. Buggert, O.Carm.; Patrick McMahon, O.Carm.; Roland Murphy, O.Carm.; George Kennedy, O.Carm.; Andrew Skotnicki, O.Carm.; John Welch, O.Carm.; Lambert Yore, O.Carm.; Fergus Lickteig, O.Carm.; Craig Morrison, O.Carm.; Bros. Stephen Diekemper, O.Carm.; Raphael Sutherland, O.Carm. In res., Rev. Clifford Aniefuna, O.Carm. (Nigeria). Friars in Solemn Profession 4; Sisters in Final Profession 1; Brothers in First Profession 6; Pre-Novitate Students 10.

BELTSVILLE, MD. *Ammendale Normal Institute of Prince George's County-LaSalle Hall (1880)*, 6001 Ammendale Rd., 20705. Tel: 301-210-7443. Brothers of the Christian Schools. Bros. Kevin Erb, F.S.C., Dir.; Leo Quinn, F.S.C., Assoc. Dir. Residence for Retired and Convalescent Brothers. Brothers 20.

The Saint LaSalle Auxiliary, P.O. Box 1610-C, 20704-1610. Tel: 301-210-7444. Bro. Charles Lackes, F.S.C., Dir.

The Auxiliary is the Development Office for the Christian Brothers of the Baltimore Province. Brothers 2; Lay Staff 3.

BROOKEVILLE, MD. *Marian Novitiate*, 19101 Georgia Ave., Box 220, 20833. Tel: 301-774-2242. Bro. Leonard Konopka, M.I.C., Supr.; Rev. Gerald Ornowski, M.I.C., Novice Master; Bro. Michael Opalacz, M.I.C. Priests 1; Brothers 2; Novices 3.

Marian Spiritual Center, 19101 Georgia Ave., Box 50, 20833. Tel: 301-774-5454. Rev. Gerald Ornowski, M.I.C.; Bro. Michael Opalacz, M.I.C. Priests 1; Brothers 2.

CHEVERLY, MD. *Damien House*, 6013 Inwood St., 20785. Tel: 301-386-4840. Congregation of the Sacred Hearts. Rev. Ambrose R. Forgit, SS.CC.

SILVER SPRING, MD. *Austin Friars Hall, Order of St. Augustine*, 2123 Edgewater Pkwy., 20903-1210. Tel: 301-445-2583. Revs. Joseph F. Wimmer, O.S.A., Prior & Treas.; Robert P. Hickey, O.S.A.; Cedric M. Wilson, O.S.A.; William M. Cleary, O.S.A., Subprior; Joseph G. Ryan, O.S.A. Priests 5.

Holy Family Seminary, 401 Randolph Rd., P.O. Box 4138, 20904. Tel: 301-622-3582. Very Rev. Luis Picazo, S.F., Vice Prov. Supr.; Revs. Joseph Cubells, S.F.; Francis Gonzalez, S.F.; Jim Sunturn, S.F.; John A. Sierra, S.F.; Palmo Valente, S.F.; Marvin Archuleta, S.F.; Bro. Sebastian Lee, S.F. Priests 6; Brothers 1; Students 1.

Holy Name College, 1650 St. Camillus Dr., 20903. Tel: 301-434-3400. House of Studies for Holy Name Province of the Order of Friars Minor. Revs. Daniel McLellan, O.F.M., Ph.D., Supr. & Dir. Formation; James P. Scullion, O.F.M., Ph.D., Vicar & Asst. Dir. Formation; Daniel P. Grigassy, O.F.M., Ph.D.; Christopher B. Keenan, O.F.M., D.Min.; Joseph G. Rozansky, O.F.M.; Peter C. Sheridan, O.F.M. Solemnly Professed Friars 6; Simply Professed Friars 16.

Holy Trinity Mission Seminary (1926), 9001 New Hampshire Ave., 20903. Tel: 301-434-5400; Fax: 301-434-7206.

Central Administrative Offices: Revs. Leon Buggy, S.T., Supr.; Leonard Bachmann, S.T.; Ralph Frisch, S.T.; Joseph McDonough, S.T.; David F. O'Connor, S.T.; Thomas Stepanski, S.T.; Bros. Jordan Baxter, S.T.; Alexis Norton, S.T., Mission Procure Office: Tel: 301-434-6761. Vocation Department: Tel: 301-434-6764. Treasurer General Office: Tel: 301-439-0333.

Salvatorian Community, 14506 Dunsinane Ter., 20906. Tel: 301-598-1883. Society of the Divine Savior Salvatorians. Rev. John E. Gorman, S.D.S., Reg. Supr.; Bro. James Rieden, S.D.S., Vicar Supr.; Revs. Glen Willis, S.D.S.; Richard Maloney, S.D.S.; Eliot Nitz, S.D.S.; Roman Stadtmueller, S.D.S.; Robert Ross, S.D.S.; Philip Vogel, S.D.S.; Raul Gomez, S.D.S. Priests 8; Brothers 5; Lay Members 22.

WEST HYATTSVILLE, MD. *Pallottine Seminary at Green Hill*, 2009 Van Buren St., 20782. Tel: 301-422-3777. Society of the Catholic Apostolate. Rev. John G. Biermann, S.A.C., Rector, Dir. of Preparatory Formation. Priests 1; Students 1.

WHEATON, MD. *Holy Ghost Fathers Development Office*, 11411 Amherst Ave., 20902. Tel: 301-933-6130. Rev. Timothy T. McDonough, C.S.Sp., Dir.

St. Thomas More Friary, Third Order Regular of St. Francis, 2303 Patternbond Dr., 20902. Tel: 301-649-9000. Bros. Didacus R. Wilson, T.O.R., Local Min. & Dir. of Studies; Alexis Nagle, T.O.R., Admin. & Econome. In res., Revs. Columba J. Enright, T.O.R.; Ambrose K. Phillips, T.O.R., Vicar & Formation Dir. Priests 2; Student Friars 1; Solemnly Professed Brothers 2.

[C] COLLEGES AND UNIVERSITIES

WASHINGTON. *Catholic University of America, The*, (1887) Nugent Hall/Executive Offices, 20064. Tel: 202-319-5000.

For a complete listing, refer to the Colleges and Universities section.

**Georgetown University*, (1789) 37th and O Sts., N.W., 20057. Tel: 202-687-0100.

For a complete listing, refer to the Colleges and Universities section.

Trinity College, Michigan Ave. and Franklin St., N.E., 20017. Tel: 202-939-5000.

For a complete listing, refer to the Colleges and Universities section.

[D] HIGH SCHOOLS, ARCHDIOCESAN

WASHINGTON. *Archbishop Carroll High School*. (Coed), 4300 Harewood Rd., N.E., 20017. Tel: 202-529-0900; Fax: 202-529-5989. Mr. John T. Butler, Pres.; Revs. Leslie Branch; William Montgomery; John Mudd. Priests 3; Sisters 3; Lay Teachers 50; Students 710.

[E] HIGH SCHOOLS, PRIVATE

WASHINGTON. *Georgetown Visitation Preparatory School*, 1524 35th St., N.W., 20007. Tel: 202-337-3350. Sr. Mary Berchmans Hannan, V.H.M., Pres.; Mr. Dan Kerns, Headmaster. Sisters 3; Teachers 60; Students 424.

Gonzaga College High School, 19 Eye St., N.W., 20001. Tel: 202-336-7100. Society of Jesus. Rev. Allen P. Novotny, S.J., Pres.; Dr. Joseph J. Ciancaglini, Headmaster; Revs. Daniel K. Lahart, S.J., Vice Pres., Finance & Admin.; Edward T. Hogan, S.J., Chap.; Henry B. Haske, S.J., Rector. Jesuit Community. Revs. Lucien F. Longtin, S.J.; G. Harry Hock, S.J.; Thomas Clifford, S.J.; Kenneth E. Meehan, S.J.; Gerald V. O'Connor, S.J.; Bruce A. Steggert, S.J.; John B. Woodward, S.J. In res., Revs. Walter J. Burghardt, S.J.; John A. Conlin, S.J.; Henry G. Heffernan, S.J.; Joseph M. McCloskey, S.J.; Anthony I. McHale, S.J.; Francis X. Moan, S.J.; Francis M. O'Connor, S.J.; William P. Sampson, S.J.; Bro. Donald Dixon, S.J.; Deacon Edward F. Beckett, S.J.; Mr. Daniel Concha, S.J.; Mr. Thomas Flanagan, S.J. Priests 19; Brothers 1; Deacons 1; Lay Teachers 57; Scholastics 2; Students 818.

Oakcrest School. (Grades 7-12), 4101 Yuma St., N.W., 20016. Tel: 202-686-9736. College Preparatory for Girls. Ms. Barbara Falk, Dir. Priests 1; Lay Teachers 19; Students 150.

St. Anselm's Abbey School. (Grades 6-12), 4501 South Dakota Ave., N.E., 20017. Tel: 202-269-2350. Operated by the Benedictine Monks of St. Anselm's Abbey. Seven year college preparatory courses. Rev. Dom Peter Weigand, O.S.B., Headmaster. Priests 6; Brothers 3; Lay Teachers 41; Students 224.

St. John's College High School (1851). (Boys Grades 7-8, Coed Grades 9-12), 2607 Military Rd., N.W., 20015. Tel: 202-363-2316. Brothers of the Christian Schools. Legal Title: *St. John's College.* College Preparatory, Elective Army Junior ROTC. Bro. Edward Gallagher, F.S.C., Prin. Priests 1; Brothers 13; Sisters 1; Lay Teachers 32; Students 515.

BETHESDA, MD. *Mater Dei School, Inc.*, 9600 Seven Locks Rd., 20817. Tel: 301-365-2700; 301-365-2701; Fax: 301-365-2710. Mr. Christopher S. Abell, Prin.

Stone Ridge School of the Sacred Heart, 9101 Rockville Pike, 20814. Tel: 301-657-4322; Fax: 301-657-2381. Religious of the Sacred Heart. Sr. Anne Dyer, Headmistress. Sisters 5; Lay Teachers 67; Students 677.

BLADENSBURG, MD. *Elizabeth Seton High School*, 5715 Emerson St., 20710-1844. Tel: 301-864-4532. Sr. Vincentia Goeb, D.C., Pres.; Mrs. Geraldine Buckley, Prin. Daughters of Charity of St. Vincent de Paul 7; Lay Staff 72; Girls 563.

FORESTVILLE, MD. *Bishop McNamara High School.* (Coed), 6800 Marlboro Pike, 20747. Tel: 301-735-8401; Fax: 301-735-0934. Holy Cross Brothers. Ms. Heather Gossart, Pres.; Mr. Matthew Goyette, Prin.; Bro. Roger Croteau, C.S.C., Dir. Sisters 1; Brothers 8; Lay Teachers 52; Students 650.

GAITHERSBURG, MD. *Mother of God Community School*, P.O. Box 2418, 20886. Tel: 301-990-2088.

HYATTSVILLE, MD. *De Matha Catholic High School*, 20781. Tel: 301-864-3666. Conducted by the Trinitarian Fathers of the Province of the Immaculate Heart of Mary. Rev. William J. Sullivan, O.SS.T., Rector; Mr. John L. Moylan, Prin. Priests 4; Brothers 1; Lay Teachers 60; Students 925.

KENSINGTON, MD. *The Academy of the Holy Cross, Inc.*, 4920 Strathmore Ave., 20895. Tel: 301-942-2100; Fax: 301-929-6440. Legal Title: *The Academy of the Holy Cross, Inc.* Sr. Katherine Kase, C.S.C., Prin. Sisters 12; Lay Teachers 32; Students 425.

LAUREL, MD. *St. Vincent Pallotti High School*, 20707. Tel: 301-725-3228. Missionary Sisters of the Catholic Apostolate. Paul J. Leonarczyk, Prin. Priests 1; Sisters 2; Lay Teachers 36; Students 450.

LEONARDTOWN, MD. *St. Mary's Ryken High School*, Camp Calvert Rd., 20650. Tel: 301-475-2814; 932-4422; Fax: 301-475-7972. Sponsored by the Xaverian Brothers. Mr. Harry L. Swaney, Prin. Brothers 2; Lay Teachers 33; Students 500.

NORTH BETHESDA, MD. *Georgetown Preparatory School*, 20852. Tel: 301-493-5000; Fax: 301-530-9531. Jesuit Community. Society of Jesus. Dr. James P. Power, Headmaster; Revs. R. Bruce Bavinger, S.J., Supr.; Thomas E. Roach, S.J., Pres.; Richard C. Schmidt, S.J.; Aloysius C. Galvin, S.J.; James A.P. Byrne, S.J.; William J. Elliott, S.J.; Raymond M. Lelii, S.J. Tel: 301-881-1380 Ext. 24; Eugene J. Linehan, S.J.; Vincent M. O'Brien, S.J.; Garrett D. Orr, S.J. Priests 9; Brothers 1; Scholastics 1; Lay Teachers 38; Students 426.

POTOMAC, MD. *Connelly School of the Holy Child.* (Grades 6-12), 9029 Bradley Blvd., 20854. Tel: 301-365-0955. Sisters of the Holy Child Jesus. College Preparatory for Girls. Maureen K. Appel, Headmistress. Sisters 1; Lay Teachers 45; Students 384.

The Heights School. (Grades 3-12), 10400 Seven Locks Rd., 20854. Tel: 301-365-4300. College Preparatory for Boys. Mr. Joseph W. McPherson, Headmaster. Priests 2; Lay Teachers 28; Students 270.

WHEATON, MD. *Good Counsel High School*, 11601 Georgia Ave., 20902. Tel: 301-942-1155; Fax: 301-942-3656. Xaverian Brothers. Mr. Michael E. Murphy, Pres.; Mr. Charles P. Dusterhoff, Prin.; Revs. Michael T. Jones, Chap.; Barry R. Gross (LFT), Diocesan. Priests 2; Brothers 1; Sisters 2; Lay Teachers 74; Students 1,012.

[F] ELEMENTARY SCHOOLS, PRIVATE

BETHESDA, MD. *The Woods Academy*, 6801 Greentree Rd., 20817. Tel: 301-365-3080. Mary Worch, Head of School. Students 216; Lay Teachers 25.

[G] SPECIAL SCHOOLS

WASHINGTON. *Lt. Joseph P. Kennedy, Jr., Institute*, 801 Buchanan St., N.E., 20017. Tel: 202-529-7600. Rev. Richard C. Birkel, Ph.D., Pres. & CEO.

Nonprofit Organizations Serving Children and Adults With Developmental Disabilities: Adult Learning & Employment Services. Staff 56; Participants 116. Family & Personal Employment Services. Staff 23; Participants 39. Early Intervention & Preventive Services. Staff 29; Participants 45. Kennedy School & Youth Services. Staff 23; Students 73.

Outreach Program (Washington, DC; Prince George's & Montgomery Counties, MD and Southern MD): Staff 2; Students 50. Residential Division. Staff 68; Residents 65. Administration Division. Staff 20. The Lt. Joseph P. Kennedy, Jr., Institute of the Archdiocese of Washington is a private, nonprofit organization providing education, training and employment, therapeutic and residential services to children and adults with developmental disabilities.

ROCKVILLE, MD. *The Frost Center*, Society of the Divine Savior, 4915 Aspen Hill Rd., 20853. Tel: 301-933-3451. Bro. Sean McLaughlin, S.D.S., Dir.; Rev. Glen Willis, S.D.S., Business Mgr.; Bros. Roger Nelson, S.D.S.; Peter Farnesi, S.D.S., Plant Mgr. A School and Therapy Program for Emotionally Disturbed Teens and Families. Priests 1; Brothers 3; Staff 25; Students 45.

[H] CATHOLIC CHARITIES OF THE ARCHDIOCESE

WASHINGTON. *Catholic Charities of the Archdiocese of Washington, Inc.*, 1438 Rhode Island Ave., N.E., 20018. Tel: 202-526-4100. Mr. Edward Orzechowski, M.S.W., Pres.

Montgomery County Regional Office, 1500 St. Camillus Dr., Silver Spring, MD, 20903. Tel: 301-434-2550.

Prince George's County Regional Office, 4019 38th St., Brentwood, MD, 20722. Tel: 301-669-0587.

Calvert County Office, P.O. Box 779, Prince Frederick, MD, 20678. Tel: 410-35-0865.

Southern Maryland Regional Office, Rtes. 5 & 231, P.O. Box 613, Hughesville, MD, 20637. Tel: 301-870-5308.

Charles County Office, 115 LaGrange Ave., P.O. Box 487, LaPlata, MD, 20646. Tel: 301-934-2582; 870-3538 (Direct). Total Assisted 78,000; Total Staff 206.

[I] ARCHDIOCESAN VOLUNTEER ORGANIZATIONS

WASHINGTON. *Archdiocesan Association of Ladies of Charity*, P.O. Box 10038, 20018. Mary L. Linstrom, Pres. Purpose: individual charity work, usually of emergency nature and support various other agencies, foodbanks, child care centers and pregnancy aid centers.

RIVERDALE, MD. *Society of St. Vincent de Paul*, Archdiocese of Washington, 6028 Mustang Dr., 20737.

Office of Archdiocesan Council. Tel: 301-864-2106.

[J] ORPHANAGES AND INFANT HOMES

HYATTSVILLE, MD. *St. Ann's Infant and Maternity Home*, 4901 Eastern Ave., 20782. Tel: 301-559-5500; Fax: 301-853-6985.

For a complete listing, refer to the Special Care Facilities section.

[K] GENERAL HOSPITALS

WASHINGTON. *Center for Life of Providence Hospital*, 1150 Varnum St., N.E., 20017.

For a complete listing, refer to the Hospitals section.

De Paul Foundation, Inc., 1150 Varnum St., N.E., 20017.

For a complete listing, refer to the Hospitals section.

Georgetown University Hospital, 3800 Reservoir Rd., N.W., 20007. Tel: 202-784-3000.

For a complete listing, refer to the Hospitals section.

Providence Hospital.

For a complete listing, refer to the Hospitals section.

Providence Hospital, 1150 Varnum St., N.E., 20017. Tel: 202-269-7000; Fax: 202-269-7160.

For a complete listing, refer to the Hospitals section.

SILVER SPRING, MD. *Holy Cross Hospital of Silver Spring, Inc.*, 1500 Forest Glen Rd., 20910. Tel: 301-905-0100; Fax: 301-905-1011.

For a complete listing, refer to the Hospitals section.

[L] HOMES FOR AGED

WASHINGTON. *Cardinal O'Boyle Residence for Priests*, 1150 Varnum St., N.E., 20017.

For a complete listing, refer to the Special Care Facilities section.

Jeanne Jugan Residence-St. Joseph's Villa, 4200 Harewood Rd., N.E., 20017. Tel: 202-269-1831.

For a complete listing, refer to the Special Care Facilities section.

HYATTSVILLE, MD. *Sacred Heart Home Inc.*, 5805 Queens Chapel Rd., 20782. Tel: 301-277-6500.

For a complete listing, refer to the Special Care Facilities section.

MITCHELLVILLE, MD. *Villa Rosa Nursing Home, Inc.*, 3800 Lottsford Vista Rd., 20721-4026. Tel: 301-459-4700; Fax: 301-459-0754.

For a complete listing, refer to the Special Care Facilities section.

[M] MONASTERIES AND RESIDENCES OF PRIESTS AND BROTHERS

WASHINGTON. *Carmelite Community*, 1136 McKenna Walk, N.W., 20001. Tel: 630-971-0050. Bro. Leo McCarthy, O.Carm., Contact Person.

Carroll House, 1225 Otis St., N.E., 20017. Tel: 202-529-1252. Jesuit House of Studies at the Catholic University. Revs. James P. Bradley, S.J., Supr.; Christopher M. Cullen, S.J.; Francis T. Gignac, S.J.; Jerome M. Hall, S.J.; John B. Yong-woo Lee (Korea); Gabriel Mmassi (East Africa). Priests 6; Total Staff 1.

Commissariat of the Holy Land, Franciscan Monastery - Mount St. Sepulchre, 1400 Quincy St., N.E., 20017. Tel: 202-526-6800. Bro. Callistus Welch, O.F.M., Guardian, and Commissary of the Holy Land; Revs. Kevin Treston, O.F.M., Almanac Editor; Patrick Flannigan, O.F.M.; Sabin Plechta, O.F.M.; Stephen F. Sabbagh, O.F.M., Spiritual Asst. to Sec. Franciscan Order; Francis X. Sihuay, O.F.M. (Peru); Manuel Ybarra, O.F.M., Vicar & Vice Commissary, Procurator; Mark Hurst, O.F.M. Priests 9; Brothers 14; Solemnly Professed 25; Postulants 4; Novices 2; Missionaries in the Holy Land 24; Rome, Italy 1.

Divine Word College, 1025 Michigan Ave., N.E., 20017. Tel: 202-526-5047. Revs. Raymond T. Lennon, S.V.D., Rector; Henry Gaska, S.V.D. (Poland); John Rodney, S.V.D.; Raymond Sanders, S.V.D.; Peter De Ta Vo, S.V.D. (Vietnam); Robert Mertes, S.V.D.; Francisco Estepa, S.V.D. (Philippines); Jun Inoue, S.V.D. (Japan); Anumu Quaye-Foli, S.V.D. (Togo); Darius Piwowarczyk, S.V.D. (Poland); Xavier Thirukudumbam, S.V.D. (India); Bros. R. Zalikowski, S.V.D., Vice Rector; G. Raker, S.V.D., Treas.; Bernard Spitzley, S.V.D., Formation Dir. Divine Word College has 40 Priests and Brothers in Residence. Fifteen of these are members of the S.V.D.; the other 25 are from other religious communities or dioceses in the U.S.A., and are studying at the Catholic University. We offer them our House for the duration of their studies. Residents 40.

Glenmary House of Studies, 1323 Quincy St., N.E., 20017. Tel: 202-635-0163; 526-1339. Rev. Chet Artysiewicz, Dir. Students in Residence 3; Total in Residence 6; Total Staff 1.

Holy Redeemer College (1930), 3112 Seventh St., N.E., 20017. Tel: 202-529-4410; 529-4484; Fax: 202-832-1321. Opened in 1930. Redemptorist Theology Residence Since 1985. Legal Title: *Holy Redeemer College.* Very Rev. Philip Dabney, C.SS.R., Rector & Dir. Formation; Revs. Kevin O'Neil, C.SS.R., Asst. Dir. Formation; James Wallace, C.SS.R., Vicar; James Dowds, C.SS.R., Vocation Dir.; Dennis Billy, C.SS.R.; Mark Tucker, C.SS.R.; Bro. Jeffrey Rolle, C.SS.R.; Revs. James Coen, C.SS.R.; Thomas Forrest, C.SS.R. Owned and Operated by the Redemptorists of the Baltimore Province for their Own Religious Candidates. Students Attend Washington Theological Union. Priests 8; Brothers 1; Religious Students 10.

The Jesuit Community at Georgetown University, 37th and O Sts., N.W., 20057. Tel: 202-687-1770; Fax: 202-687-7679. Rev. William J. Byron, S.J., Rector; Bros. John B. Hollywood, S.J., Admin. & Treas.; Steven L. Alvey, S.J.; Rev. Edward W. Bodnar, S.J.; Bro. Francis J. Boyle, S.J.; Revs. Francis Alves, S.J. (India); Thomas J. Buckley, S.J.; Timothy J. Cadigan, S.J.; Martin J. Calkins, S.J. (Detroit); Martin J. Casey, S.J.; Paul L. Cioffi, S.J.; T. Byron Collins, S.J.; Walter A. Cook, S.J.; R. Emmett Curran, S.J.; Vincent P. DeCola, S.J. (New York); Robert F. Drinan, S.J. (New England); Joseph T. Durkin, S.J.; Stephen M. Fields, S.J.; Joseph A. Fitzmyer, S.J.; Gerald P. Fogarty, S.J.; William L. George, S.J.; Julio Giulietti, S.J. (New England); Joseph A. Haller, S.J.; Patrick A. Heelan, S.J. (Ireland); Otto H. Hentz, S.J.; Brendan Hurley, S.J.; Edward J. Ingebretsen, S.J. (California); Josef Kadlec, S.J.; William J. Kaifer, S.J.; Shinzo Kawamura, S.J. (Japan); John R. Keating, S.J. (New York); John T. Kelly, S.J.; Gustaaf M. Keppens, S.J.; Thomas M. King, S.J.; Robert B. Lawton, S.J.; James A. Martin, S.J.; John Martis, S.J. (Australia); William C. McFadden, S.J.; Dennis L. McNamara, S.J. (Wisconsin); Paul D. McNelis, S.J.; Richard T. McSorley, S.J.; Ralph E. Metts, S.J.; William H. Millerd, S.J.; Joseph M. Moffitt, S.J.; G. Ronald Murphy, S.J.; Richard J. O'Brien, S.J. (Chicago); Daniel C. O'Connell, S.J. (Missouri); Joseph F. O'Connell, S.J.; Leo J. O'Donovan, S.J.; Ladislas Orsy, S.J. (Hungary); Francis Parmar, S.J. (India); Scott Pilarz, S.J.; J. Eugene Poirier, S.J. (China); Kevin P. Quinn, S.J. (New York); Bro. George F. Reilly, S.J.; Revs. Alvaro Ribeiro, S.J. (China); Solomon I. Sara, S.J. (New England); James V. Schall, S.J. (California); Francis Schemel, S.J.; James M. Shea, S.J.; John Songster, S.J.; Peter Steele, S.J. (Australia); Joseph F. Sweeney, S.J.; Terrence Toland, S.J.; Joseph N. Tylenda, S.J.; Jeffrey von Arx, S.J. (New York); James P.M. Walsh, S.J.; William Watson, S.J. (Oregon); Kevin W. Wildes, S.J.; John W. Witek, S.J. (Chicago). Priests 69; Brothers 4.

K Street Jesuit Community, 320 K St., N.E., 20002. Tel: 202-546-1958. Revs. James E. Hug, S.J., Supr.; Fred Kammer, S.J. Residents 2.

La Salette Community, 1243 Monroe St., N.E., 20017. Legal Title: *Missionaries of La Salette Corporation.* Revs. Raymond G. Cadran, M.S., Dir.; Joseph Baxer, M.S.

Leonard Neale House, 1726 New Hampshire Ave., N.W., 20009. Tel: 202-387-5375; 387-5376. Revs. Thomas F. Gleeson, S.J.; William J. Hutchinson, S.J.; Thomas J. Massaro, S.J.; Daniel C. McDonald, S.J.; J. Donald Monan, S.J.; George T. Dennis, S.J.; Richard C. Burbach, S.J.; Thomas M. Rockford, S.J.; Gregory F. Lucey, S.J.; Richard J. Ryscavage, S.J.; Andrew J. Christiansen, S.J.; Theodore F. Zuern, S.J.; Robert W. McChesney, S.J. Priests 13; Total Staff 13.

Marist Provincial House, 815 Varnum St., N.E., 20017-2199. Tel: 202-529-4800. The Marists Provincial Headquarters of the Washington Province of the Society of Mary, Marist Fathers and Brothers. Very Rev. William F. Rowland, S.M., Prov.; Revs. Valentine A. Becker, S.M., Archivist; Thomas E. Dubay, S.M.; Joseph M. Fleury; Philip S. Gage, S.M.; Charles A. Girard; John H. Harhager, S.M.; Joseph C. Hurtuk, S.M.; Mark G. Kenney, S.M.; George M. Lepping, S.M.; Howard C. Smith, S.M.; Timothy F. Sugrue, S.M., Business Mgr.

Priests Not Listed Elsewhere: Rev. Joseph D. Fenton, S.M., P.O. Box 4702, London, UK, SW10 94G. Rev. Patrick D. Primeaux, S.M., 150 Burns St., #6-C, Forest Hills, NY, 11375. Rev. Edward Templeton, S.M., 6901 Chef Menteur Hwy., New Orleans, LA, 70126. Rev. Charles J. Barrett, S.M., (Retired), 8671 Limestone Ave., Tampa, FL, 33615. Rev. Leonard P. Kellermann, S.M., (Retired), Mary Joseph Residence, 4201 Woodland Dr., New Orleans, LA, 70131. Rev. George J. Meiluta, S.M., (Retired), St. Joseph Home for the Aged, 1182 Holland Rd., Holland, PA, 18966. Rev. Leonard J. Moran, S.M., (Retired), 1516 Council Dr., Sun City Center, FL, 33573. Rev. John A. Richmond, S.M., (Retired), 4200 Harewood Rd., N.E., 20017. Rev. John L. White, S.M., (Retired), 8200 S. Kildare Ave., Chicago, IL, 60652. Rev. John J. Moore, S.M., (Retired), Mary Joseph Residence, 4201 Woodland Dr., New Orleans, LA, 70131. Rev. Charles F. Brogley, S.M., (Retired), 6445 Germantown Ave., Philadelphia, PA, 19119. Rev. Timothy G. Keating, S.M., 120 Westway Rd. #102, Greenbelt, MD, 20770. Rev. Stanley W. Hosie, S.M., 2440 Virginia Ave., N.W., D-1301, 20037. Rev. Leo Foley, S.M., Carroll Manor, 1150 Varnum St, N.E., Rm. 436, 20017. Rev. John J. Martell, S.M., (Retired), Mary Joseph Residence, 4201 Woodland Dr., New Orleans, LA, 70131-7398. Rev. Thomas G. Carey, S.M., (Retired), Sts. Mary And Joseph Home, 4291 Rochmond Rd., Cleveland, OH, 44122-6199. Rev. Edward J. Corrigan, S.M., (Retired), Sts. Mary and Joseph Home, 4291 Richmond Rd., Cleveland, OH, 44122-6199.

Missionaries of Africa, 1624 21st St., N.W., 20009. Tel: 202-232-5154. Provincial House. Revs. William F. Moroney, M.Afr., Prov.; David J. Goergen, M.Afr., Prov. Treas.; Roger Bisson, M.Afr.; Albert Jamme, M.Afr. (Belgium); Sjef Donders, M.Afr. (Holland); William Dyer, M.Afr., Community Coord.; Pierre Benson, M.Afr. (Canada); Bro. Charles Feldmann, M.Afr. Priests 7; Brothers 1; Total Staff 6.

Missionaries of the Company of Mary-Montfort Missionaries, 1302 Quincy St., N.E., 20017. Tel: 202-832-8319. Rev. Donald G. LaSalle, S.M.M., Dir. Formation. Residents 1.

Missionary Oblates of Mary Immaculate, Provincial Office: 391 Michigan Ave., N.E., P.O. Box 29152, 20017. Tel: 202-529-5958. Very Rev. J. William Sheehan, O.M.I., Prov.; Rev. William M. O'Donnell, O.M.I., Vicar Prov.

St. Anselm's Abbey, 4501 South Dakota Ave., N.E., 20017. Tel: 202-269-2300; Fax: 202-269-2312. Benedictine Foundation at Washington, DC, Order of St. Benedict. Rt. Revs. Aidan Shea, O.S.B., Abbot; Alban Boultwood, O.S.B.; Revs. James A. Wiseman, O.S.B., Prior; Urban Schnaus, O.S.B.; Hugh Monmonier, O.S.B.; Daniel Kirk, O.S.B.; Joseph Jensen, O.S.B.; John Farrelly, O.S.B.; David Granfield, O.S.B.; Patrick Granfield, O.S.B.; Hilary Hayden, O.S.B.; Thomas Fahy, O.S.B.; Edmund Henkels, O.S.B.; Michael Hall, O.S.B.; Christopher Wyvill, O.S.B.; Mark Sheridan, O.S.B.; Peter Weigand, O.S.B.; Giles LeVasseur, O.S.B.; Isaac Borocz, O.S.B.; Benet Hill, O.S.B.; Paul McKane, O.S.B.; Boniface von Nell, O.S.B. Priests 21; Brothers 5.

St. Louis Friary, 831 Varnum St., N.E., 20017. Tel: 202-529-0171. House of Post-Novitiate Formation for Franciscan Friars, T.O.R., Province of the Most Sacred Heart of Jesus. Revs. Peter Lyons, T.O.R.; John Carroll, T.O.R.; Samuel Vaccarella, T.O.R. Friars in Post-Novitiate Formation 8; Total in Residence 11.

Woodstock Jesuit Community, 1419 35 St., N.W., 20007. Tel: 202-337-7750. Revs. James Connor, S.J., Supr.; Thomas J. Reese, S.J.; J. Leon Hooper, S.J.; Gasper F. LoBiondo, S.J.; William J. Walsh, S.J.; Rev. Msgr. Richard M. Liddy. Priests 6.

ADELPHI, MD. *Father Thomas O'Keeffe Missionary Cenacle*, 2717 Curry Dr., 20783. Tel: 301-422-8039. Rev. Stephen Ernst, S.T., Dir.

Missionary Servants of the Most Holy Trinity, 1733 Metzerott Rd., 20783. Senior Ministry Residence. Revs. Robert Shay, S.T., Dir.; Gabriel Hannan, S.T.; Lambert Stack, S.T.; Gerald Swift, S.T.; Charles Tague, S.T.; Paul Keenan, S.T.; Denis Fitzgerald, S.T.; Joseph Cornely, S.T.; Shaun McCarty, S.T.; Peter Holden, S.T.; Bros. Malachy Sofield, S.T.; Raymond Ise, S.T.; Robert Conway, S.T.; Jonathan Daneski, S.T.; Howard Piller, S.T., Asst. Dir.; David Koessler, S.T.; Daniel McCauley, S.T.; Loughlan Sofield, S.T.; Aaron LeBlanc, S.T.

HYATTSVILLE, MD. *St. John de Matha Monastery, Order of Most Holy Trinity*, 4310 Madison St., 20781. Tel: 301-927-6418; Fax: 301-927-0807. Revs. Thomas N. Cerulo, O.SS.T., Supr.; Albert M. Anuszewski, O.SS.T., Vicar; William J. Sullivan, O.SS.T.; Claude J. Gravel, O.SS.T.; Lawrence C. Hernandez, O.SS.T.; Thomas A. Morris, O.SS.T.; Bro. Patrick Wildgen, O.SS.T. Priests 3; Brothers 5; Scholastics 4; Affiliates 6; Total Staff 4.

POTOMAC, MD. *Legionaries of Christ*, 10211 Norton Rd., 20854. Tel: 301-299-0806; Fax: 301-299-0809. Revs. William Izguierdo, L.C., Supr.; Richard Gill, L.C.; Daniel Long, L.C.; Bros. Craig Early, L.C.; Armando Venegas, L.C.

RIVERDALE, MD. *Holy Spirit Missionary Cenacle* 1996, 5809 Riverdale Rd., 20737. Tel: 301-277-7442; Fax: 301-209-0355. Rev. Austin Walsh, S.T., Dir. Tel: 301-277-7476. In res., Rev. Sidney Griffith, S.T., Semantics/Early Christian Studies, Faculty, Catholic University of America. Tel: 301-927-4919; Bro. Richard McCann, S.T., Asst. Mission Procurator, Trinity Missions, Silver Spring, MD. Tel: 301-209-9638. Theological Students 3; Novices 2.

SILVER SPRING, MD. *Gemelli House*, Franciscan Friars-Holy Name Province, 10400 Lorain Ave., 20901. Tel: 301-681-9478; Fax: 301-681-7170. Revs. Kenneth R. Himes, O.F.M.; Vincent de Paul Cushing, O.F.M.; Dominic V. Monte, O.F.M.; Gene B. Pistacchio.

TAKOMA PARK, MD. *Society of African Missions (S.M.A.)*, 256 N. Manor Cir., 20912-4561. Tel: 301-270-2008. Revs. Eugene Riordan, S.M.A., Supr.; Daniel J. Lynch, S.M.A., Asst. Supr. & Dir. of Formation.

Lay Mission Program, 207 S. Manor Cir., 20912-4555. Tel: 301-891-2014 (Home); 301-891-2037 (Office). Theresa Hicks, Dir.

Vocations Office, 209 Lincoln Ave., 20912-5738. Tel: 301-270-8435. Rev. Brendan Darcy, S.M.A., Vocation Dir.

Justice, Peace & Environmental Care Office, 209 Lincoln Ave., 20912-5738. Tel: 301-270-4756. Dr. Stephen Price, Ph.D., Dir. Priests 3; Lay S.M.A. 1; Seminarians 1; Lay Candidates 3.

UNIVERSITY PARK, MD. *Holy Trinity Missionary Cenacle* 1995, 4001 Van Buren St., 20782. Tel: 301-779-0939; Fax: 301-699-1745. Bros. Jordan Baxter, S.T., Asst. Custodian; Alexis Norton, S.T. Tel: 301-699-1729; Revs. Leonard Bachmann, S.T. Tel: 301-277-2629; David O'Connor, S.T. Tel: 301-699-3508; Randall Woods, S.T. Tel: 301-277-1473.

[N] MINISTRY TO PRIESTS

KENSINGTON, MD. *St. John Vianney House*, 4214 Saul Rd., 20895. Tel: 301-942-1191. Rev. Msgr. William J. English.

[O] CONVENTS AND RESIDENCES FOR SISTERS

WASHINGTON. *Daughters of Wisdom*, 914 Perry Pl., N.E., 20017. Tel: 202-529-3343. Sisters 2.

Franciscan Sisters of Atonement, 4000 Harewood Rd., N.E., 20017. Tel: 202-529-1111. Sisters 5; Total Staff 8.

Georgetown Visitation Convent, 1500 35th St., N.W., 20007. Tel: 202-337-0350. Mother M. Philomena Tisinger, Supr. Professed Sisters 30.

Institute of Our Lady of Mount Carmel, 4415 Eighth St., N.E., 20017. Total Assisted 48; Total Staff 7.

Julie Billiart Residence, 1625 16th St., N.W., 20009. Tel: 202-232-3300. Inter-Community Residence for Sisters. Sisters 20.

Little Sisters of Jesus, 1740 Euclid St., N.W., Apt. 1, 20009. Sisters 2.

Little Sisters of the Poor, 4200 Harewood Rd., N.E., 20017. Tel: 202-269-1831. Sisters 20.

Missionaries of Charity, 3310 Wheeler Rd., S.E., 20032. Tel: 202-562-6890. Sisters 6; Total Assisted 16,181.

Missionaries of Charity, 1244 V St., S.E., 20020. Tel: 202-889-6100. Sr. M. Andrea, M.C., Supr.

Missionaries of Charity, Gift of Peace Convent, 2800 Otis St., N.E., 20018. Tel: 202-269-3313. Sr. M. Manorama, M.C., Supr. Total Assisted 50; Total in Residence 45; Total Staff 25.

Oblates Sisters of the Most Holy Eucharist, 2907 Ellicott Ter., N.W., 20008. Tel: 202-244-7714. Sisters 8.

Poor Clares of Perpetual Adoration, 3900 13th St., N.E., 20017-2699. Tel: 202-526-6808. Cloistered Monastery of Perpetual Adoration. Cloistered Nuns 10.

Religious of the Sacred Heart, 821 Varnum St., N.E., 20017. Tel: 202-635-7987. Sr. Catherine Collins, R.S.C.J., Dir. Center for Educational Design & Communication. Sisters 2.

Rosary House of Studies-Dominican Sisters of The Presentation, 1201 Monroe St., N.E., 20017. Tel: 202-529-1768. Sisters 5.

St. Dominic's Monastery, 4901 16th St., N.W., 20011. Tel: 202-726-2107. Dominican Nuns, a Contemplative Community with Solemn Vows and Papal Enclosure. Sr. Mary Paul, O.P., Prioress. Sisters 10.

Sisters of St. Mary of Washington, 5001 Eastern Ave., 20017.

Sisters of the Holy Child Jesus, 1033 Newton St., N.E., 20017. Tel: 202-526-6832. Novitiate Community. Sr. Karen Gosser, S.H.C.J., Novice Dir. Sisters 5.

Other Convents: 1244 Monroe St., N.E., 20017. Tel: 202-832-3237. Sisters 5.

Immaculate Conception School (1 Sister); St. Anthony's School (1 Sister).

Sisters of the Third Franciscan Order-Syracuse, NY, 1334 Perry St., N.E., 20017-2531. Tel: 202-526-8017. Sisters 2.

BALTIMORE, MD. *Comtemplative Sisters of the Good Shepherd*, 4100 Maple Ave., 21227-4099.

BROOKVILLE, MD. *Oblate Sisters of the Most Holy Eucharist*, 19101 Georgia Ave., P.O. Box 220, 20833. Tel: 301-774-4478. Sisters 9.

CHEVY CHASE, MD. *Missionary Sisters of Our Lady of Africa*, 3715 Williams Ln., 20815. Tel: 301-654-2047. Students 13.

FORT WASHINGTON, MD. *The Missionary Catechists of St. Therese of the Infant Jesus, Inc.*, 2400 Brinkley Rd., 20744. Tel: 301-839-7751. Sr. Catalina P. Superable, Pres.

HYATTSVILLE, MD. *DeMatha Convent*, 4310 Madison St., 20781. Oblates of St. Martha, Saltillo, Mexico. Sisters 3; Total Staff 3.

KENSINGTON, MD. *Sisters of the Holy Cross*, Saint Angela Hall, 5000 Strathmore Ave., 20895. Tel: 301-949-2244. Legal Title: *Sisters of the Holy Cross, Inc.* Retirement House for the Sisters of the Holy Cross. Sr. Marian Daniel, C.S.C., Supr. Sisters 35.

Academy of the Holy Cross Convent, 4920 Strathmore Ave., 20895. Tel: 301-942-2102. Sisters 13. Legal Title: *The Academy of the Holy Cross, Inc.*

Holy Cross Hospital Convent, 1523 Forest Glen Rd., 20910. Tel: 301-681-5596. Sisters 6.

Our Lady of the Woods, 9820 Dameron Dr., 20902. Tel: 301-681-5732.

Sisters of the Holy Cross, 4523 32nd St., Mount Rainier, 20712. Tel: 301-927-0712. Sisters 3. 12623 Laurie Dr., 20904. Tel: 301-236-4967. Sisters 2. Holy Cross Convent, 4900 Strathmore Ave., Garrett Park, 20896. Tel: 301-933-2213. Sisters 6.

Our Lady of Lourdes Convent, 4511 East-West Hwy., Bethesda, 20814. Tel: 301-986-5741. Sisters 3.

LANHAM-SEABROOK, MD. *Mission Helpers of the Sacred Heart*, 9471 Annapolis Rd., 20706. Tel: 301-459-8078. Sisters 6.

LAUREL, MD. *Pallotti Convent*, 404 Eighth St., 20707. Tel: 301-725-1717. Sr. M. Karen Lester, S.A.C., Local Supr. Professed Sisters 10; Total Assisted 124; Total Staff 3.

MOUNT RAINIER, MD. *Congregation of Jesus and Mary, Provincialate*, 3706 Rhode Island Ave., 20712. Tel: 301-277-3594; Fax: 301-277-8656. Sr. Rosemary Mangan, R.J.M., Prov. Administrative Team 4; Staff 2.

Other Residences: Religious of Jesus and Mary, 6709 41st Ave., University Park, 20782. Tel: 301-779-0662. Sisters 3. 6908 Wake Forest Dr., College Park, 20740. Tel: 301-699-3931. Sisters 3. 3521 13th St., N.W., Washington, DC, 20010. Tel: 202-265-8811. Sisters 3. Jesus Mary Provincialate, St. James Convent, 3706 Rhode Island Ave., 20712. Tel: 301-277-3334. Sisters 8.

PORT TOBACCO, MD. *Carmel of Port Tobacco*, 5678 Mount Carmel Rd., 20646-9611. Professed 11.

SILVER SPRING, MD. *Carmelite Sisters of Charity*, 701 Beacon Rd., 20903. Tel: 301-434-6344. Formation House. Sr. Maria-Pilar Chamorro, C.C.V., Reg. Supr.; Sr. Amaya Duralde, C.C.V., First Councilor & Formation Dir.; Sr. Maria Carmen De Juan, C.C.V., Second Councilor & Treas.

Good Shepherd Provincialate, 504 Hexton Hill Rd., 20904-3300. Tel: 301-384-1169; Fax: 301-384-8889. Legal Title: *Sisters of the Good Shepherd of the City of Washington, DC.* Sr. M. Brigid Lawlor, R.G.S., Prov. Sisters 5. Contemplative Sisters of the Good Shepherd, 3601 Reservoir Rd., Washington, DC, 20007-2339. Sisters 9; Total in Residence 9; Total Staff 2. Good Shepherd Corporation dba Shepherd's Dwelling. (Residence for women with AIDS), Washington, DC. Total Assisted 2; Total Staff 1.

Sister of Charity of St. Charles Borromeo, Inc., 11320 Classical Ln., 20901. Tel: 301-681-9665. Sr. Caecilia H. Hadiwijana, Pres.

Sisters of Mercy Convent, 10 Springvale Ln., 20910. Sisters 4.

Sisters of Mercy of the Americas Administrative Center, 8300 Colesville Rd., Ste. 300, 20910. Tel: 301-587-0423; Fax: 301-587-0533.
Legal Holdings; Mercy Action, Inc.; McAuley Institute, Inc.; Mercy Corps., Inc. Sr. Doris Gottemoeller, R.S.M., Pres. Administrative Team 5.

Sisters of the Holy Names (S.N.J.M.), 715 Pershing Dr., 20910. Tel: 301-587-1717; Fax: 301-587-1717.
Other Convents: 519 Varnum St., N.W., 20011. Tel: 202-829-8671. Sisters 3. 9212 Glenville Rd., 20901. Tel: 301-593-3385. 3122 Quartet Ln., 20904. Tel: 301-890-7159. Sisters 5.

[P] RETREAT HOUSES

WASHINGTON. *Washington Retreat House, Inc.* (1930), 4000 Harewood Rd., N.E., 20017. Tel: 202-529-1111. Franciscan Sisters of the Atonement. Sr. Frances B. Flynn, S.A., Dir. Sisters 5; Total in Residence 6; Total Staff 8.

FAULKNER, MD. *Loyola on the Potomac Retreat House*, P.O. Box 9, 20632. Tel: 301-934-8862; 870-3515; 870-3725. Rev. J. Donald Freeze, S.J., Supr. & Dir. Associate Directors: Revs. Francis J. Miles, S.J.; Stephen M. Garrity, S.J.; Joseph A. Kemme, S.J.; Sr. Patricia McDermott, I.H.M. Total in Residence 4; Total Staff 5.

UPPER MARLBORO, MD. *Our Lady of Mattaponi Youth Retreat and Conference Center*, 11000 Mattaponi Rd., 20772. Tel: 301-952-9074; Fax: 301-952-0609. Rev. Robert F. Mordino. Total in Residence 1; Total Staff 3.

[Q] NATIONAL SHRINE

WASHINGTON. *Basilica of the National Shrine of the Immaculate Conception*, 400 Michigan Ave., N.E., 20017. Tel: 202-526-8300; Fax: 202-526-8313. Rev. Msgr. Michael J. Bransfield (PH), Rector; Rev. Msgr. Walter R. Rossi (SCR), Dir. Pilgrimages; Revs. Daniel J. Maher (ARL), Assoc. Rector; John J. Leddy, O.M.I., Spiritual Counselor; Columba J. Enright, T.O.R., Spiritual Counselor.

[R] HOUSES OF PRAYER

WASHINGTON. *Madonna House*, 220 C St., N.E., 20002. Tel: 202-547-0177. Catherine A. Mitchell, Dir. Total in Residence 3; Total Staff 3.

[S] OFFICES OF CAMPUS MINISTRY

WASHINGTON. *Archdiocesan Campus Ministry.*

American University, Kay Spiritual Life Center, 4400 Massachusetts Ave., N.W., 20016-8010. Tel: 202-885-3327. Rev. Brien R. McCarthy; Dr. Karin Thornton, Assoc. Chap.

Gallaudet University Catholic Community, 20002. Rev. Gerard A. Trancone, 7202 Buchanan St., Landover Hills, MD, 20784. Tel: 202-651-5102.

George Washington Univ. Newman Center, 2210 F St., N.W., 20037. Tel: 202-676-6855. Rev. James J. Greenfield, O.S.F.S., Chap.

Howard Univ. Newman Center, 2417 First St. N.W., 20001. Tel: 202-529-0900. Rev. Gerard Hargrove, Chap.

Washington Hospital School of Nursing Newman Club. Rev. John S. Wintermeyer, Chap.

University of Maryland Catholic Student Center, 4141 Guilford Dr., College Park, MD, 20740. Tel: 301-864-6223; 6224. Rev. Robert F. Keffer, Chap. & Dir. of Campus Ministry for Archdiocese; Sr. Rita Ricker, R.J.M., Assoc.

St. Mary's College Campus Ministry, P.O. Box 67, St. Mary's City, MD, 20686. Tel: 301-862-4600. Rev. Francis W. Krastel.

[T] PERSONAL PRELATURES

WASHINGTON. *Opus Dei*, 2301 Wyoming Ave., N.W., 20008. Tel: 202-234-1567. Revs. Malcolm M. Kennedy; L. Michael Curtin; Lawrence A. Kutz.
Other Residence: 4300 Garrison St., N.W., 20016. Tel: 202-362-2419. Revs. William G. Shaughnessy; Ronald Gillis. Legal Title: *Opus Dei, Work of God.*

[U] SECULAR INSTITUTES

WASHINGTON. *Caritas Christi*, Bladensburg Rd., N.E., P.O. Box 41372, 20018. A Secular Institute of Pontifical Right.

Community of Christ, 1003 Kearney St., N.E., 20017. Tel: 202-832-9710; 797-8806. Rev. John Adams (RIC), Moderator. A Private Association Community of Archdiocesan Right for Priest, Lay Men and Lay Women. The Community of Christ Purpose is Simple Lifestyle, Poverty Ministry, Spiritual Growth and Prayer of Community Members.

WEST BETHESDA, MD. *Missionaries of the Kingship of Christ*, P.O. Box 34513, 20827-0513. Rev. Dominic V. Monti, O.F.M.

[V] MISCELLANEOUS

WASHINGTON. *"The Americas"*, Catholic University of America, Gibbons Hall, Room B 17, 20064. Tel: 202-319-5890; Fax: 202-319-5569.

American Catholic Philosophical Association, The Catholic University of America, 20064. Tel: 202-319-5518; Fax: 202-319-6408. Dr. Therese-Anne Druart, Sec.

Archbishop Carroll High School, 4300 Harewood Rd., N.E., 20017. Tel: 202-529-0900; Fax: 202-529-5989. Records Center for the Archdiocese of Washington.
Alumni Office. John Badaczewski, Dir. Tel: 202-529-0900 Ext. 32.

Archdiocese of Cotabato, 391 Michigan Ave., N.E., 20017. Tel: 202-529-5244. Most Rev. Philip F. Smith, O.M.I., D.D.; Mrs. Anne Weeks, Sec. to the Archbishop.

Black Leadership and Christ's Kingdom Society, P.O. Box 4579, 20017. Tel: 202-529-4860; 301-888-2566. Rev. Robert S. Pittman, S.S.S., Dir. Total in Residence 8; Total Staff 14.

CARA, Center for Applied Research in the Apostolate, Georgetown University, 20057-1033. Tel: 202-687-8080; Fax: 202-687-8083. Gerald H. Early, Exec. Dir.

Carmelite Institute, 1600 Webster St., N.E., 20017. Tel: 202-635-3534. Rev. John Welch, O.Carm., Pres. Tel: 202-526-1221 Ext. 118.

Carroll Manor Nursing & Rehabilitation Center, 1150 Varnum St., N.E., 20017-2180. Tel: 202-269-7100; Fax: 202-269-7816. Rev. Msgr. Leonard F. Hurley, Chap.; Rev. Brian J. O'Connell, C.M.

Catholic Biblical Association, Catholic University of America, 296 Leahy Hall, 20064. Tel: 202-319-5519. Rev. Joseph Jensen, O.S.B., Exec. Sec.

Catholic Historical Society of Washington, 2665 Woodley Rd., N.W., 20008. Tel: 202-234-1488. Rev. Msgr. Robert O. McMain.

Catholic Information Center, 825 15th St., N.W., 20005. Tel: 202-783-2062. Rev. L. Michael Curtin.

Center of Concern, 3700 13th St., N.E., 20017. Tel: 202-635-2757. Revs. Philip S. Land, S.J., Research Assoc.; James E. Hug, S.J., Exec. Dir.

Centro Maria, 650 Jackson St., N.E., 20017. Tel: 202-635-1697; Fax: 202-635-7542. Sr. Cristina Lopez, R.M.I., Dir.

Christ Child Society of Washington, DC, Inc., 5101 Wisconsin Ave., N.W., 20016. Tel: 202-966-9250. Mrs. Patricia S. Scanlon, Pres. A Non-Profit, Volunteer Organization with Membership of Approximately 1,000 Persons. Its Volunteers Actively Participate in the Operation of the Society's Programs Which are Directed by a Paid Staff Composed of Administrative Professionals and Clinical Social Workers. Total Assisted 7,760; Total staff 22.

Christian Life Communities, Washington Area Promoters: 5040 Nebraska Ave., N.W., 20008-2938. Tel: 202-363-4593. Ms. Margaret Fox, 201 E. Wayne Ave., Silver Spring, MD, 20901-3808. Tel: 301-495-2969; Fax 301-495-7318. Fred and Betty Leone.

Communio: International Catholic Review, 487 Michigan Ave., N.E., 20017. David L. Schindler, Contact Person.

The Community of St. John, 1215 Quincy St., N.E., 20017. Tel: 202-529-4253; Fax: 202-635-7656. David L. Schindler, Contact Person. Total in Residence 5.

Council for Research in Values and Philosophy, The Catholic University of America, 20064. Tel: 202-319-5636; 319-6089. Rev. George F. McLean, O.M.I., Sec.

District of Columbia Detention Facility, Office of Chaplain, 1901 D St., S.E., 20003. Tel: 202-547-1715. Rev. F. Michael Bryant, Ph.D., Chap. Total in Residence 2,000; Total Staff 20.

Dorothy Day Catholic Worker, 503 Rock Creek Church Rd., N.W., 20010. Tel: 202-882-9649. Total Assisted 200; Total Staff 8.

**Education for Parish Service Programs*, Trinity College, 125 Michigan Ave., N.E., 20017-1094. Tel: 202-884-9020; Fax: 202-483-0253.

Equestrian Order of the Holy Sepulchre of Jerusalem - Middle Atlantic Lieutenancy of the U.S., P.O. Box 9611, 20016-9611. Tel: 301-963-0459; Fax: 301-840-9880. Lt. Bernard J. Ficarra, M.D., K.G.C.H.S.

Ethiopian and Eritrean Catholic Mission, USA, 100 Lawrence St., N.E., 20017. Tel: 202-829-3934. Rev. Tesfamariam Baraki (Ethiopia), Dir.

Fellowship of Catholic Scholars, Catholic University, School of Philosophy, 20064. Tel: 202-319-5259. Dr. Jude P. Dougherty, Exec. Sec. Research and Scholarship.

Holy Childhood Association, 1720 Massachusetts Ave., N.W., 20036. Tel: 202-775-8637; Fax: 202-429-2987. Rev. Francis W. Wright, C.S.Sp., National Dir.

**Institute for Pastoral Renewal, Inc.*, c/o Jesuit Community, Georgetown University, 20057. Tel: 202-687-4164; Fax: 202-687-2045. Rev. Paul L. Cioffi, S.J., Dir. 645 Priests attend retreats, workshops, and seminars on liturgical renewal. None in residence. One staff member.

Institute of Carmelite Studies and ICS Publications, 2131 Lincoln Rd., N.E., 20002. Tel: 800-832-8489; Fax: 202-832-8967. Revs. Regis Jordan, O.C.D., Chm.; Kieran Kavanaugh, O.C.D., Publisher; Steven Payne, O.C.D., Editor, ICS Publications; Bro. Bryan Paquette, O.C.D., Business Mgr. & Promotion Dir.

ITP Paulist Communications, 3055 4th St., N.E., 20017-1102. Tel: 301-269-6064; Fax: 301-269-4304. Revs. John Geaney, C.S.P., Exec. Dir.; Lawrence Rice, C.S.P., Assoc. Dir.

Jesuit Conference, Inc., 1616 P St., N.W., Ste. 400, 20036-1405. Tel: 202-462-0400; Fax: 202-328-9212. P.O. Box 34513, Bethesda, MD, 20827. Revs. Gregory F. Lucey, S.J., Pres.; Daniel C. McDonald, S.J., Exec. Sec.

Jesuit Missions, Inc., 1616 P St., N.W., #400, 20036. Tel: 202-462-0400; Fax: 202-328-9212. Revs. Robert W. McChesney, S.J., Pres.; Richard J. Ryscavage, S.J.

Jesuit Refugee Service, 1616 P St., N.W., #400, 20036-2286. Tel: 202-462-5200; Fax: 202-328-9212.
E-mail:jesuitusa@igc.apc.org
Rev. Richard J. Ryscavage, S.J., Natl. Coord.

Jesuit Secondary Education Association, 1616 P St., N.W., Ste. 400, 20036-1405. Tel: 202-667-3888. Revs. Joseph F. O'Connell, S.J., Pres.; Ralph E. Metts, S.J., Vice Pres.; James F. Fox, S.J., Vice Pres.; Ms. Laurel Muro, Devel. Dir.; Shelly C. Frieden, Admin. Coord.; Silvia Bailey Gonzalez, Receptionist. Total Staff 6.

Jesuit Social Ministries-National Office, 1616 P St., N.W., 20036-1405. Tel: 202-462-7008; Fax: 202-462-7009. Rev. William Hutchinson, S.J., Acting Dir.

Jesuit Volunteers: International, P.O. Box 25478, 20007. Tel: 202-687-1132; Fax: 202-687-5082.
E-mail:jvi@gunet.georgetown.edu
Staff 4.

The John Carroll Society, P.O. Box 29260, 20017. Jane Golden Belford, Pres.; Rev. Peter J. Vaghi.

McKenna House, 1501 Park Rd., N.W., 20010. Tel: 202-332-7333. Hagos Weldegiorgis, Prog. Mgr.

**Missionary Vehicle Association, Inc.* MIVA America. 1400 Michigan Ave., N.E., 20017. Tel: 202-635-3444. Revs. Philip DeRea, M.S.C., National Dir.; Anthony F. Krisak, S.T.D.

Mount Carmel House, 471 G Pl., N.W., 20001. Tel: 202-289-6315. Sr. Ann Forrest, O.S.F., Dir. Transitional Rehabilitative Housing for Women with 26 beds.

National Black Sisters' Conference, 3027 Fourth St., N.E., 20017. Tel: 202-529-9250; Fax: 202-529-9370.

National Catholic Conference for Interracial Justice, 1200 Varnum St., N.E., 20017-2796. Tel: 202-529-6480; Fax: 202-526-1262. Deacon Joseph M. Conrad, Jr., Exec. Dir.

National Christ Child Society, 5101 Wisconsin Ave., N.W., Ste. 304, 20016. Tel: 202-363-9516; Fax: 202-966-2880. Mrs. Kathleen L. Gibbons, Pres., National Christ Child Society, Inc.

National Institute for the Family, Inc., 3019 Fourth St., N.E., 20017. Tel: 202-462-2591. Rev. Donald B. Conroy, S.T.L., Ph.D. (GBG), Exec. Dir.; Dr. Carolyn Gutowski, M.A.T., Ph.D., Research Dir. Research Program: Intergenerational Parish Ministry. Seminary and Lay Leadership Training in association with the Washington Theological Union.

Nativity of the Blessed Virgin (German Mission). Mailing Address: Archdiocese of Washington, P.O. Box 29260, 20017. Tel: 301-853-4520; Fax: 301-853-5346. Physical Location, 6330 Linway Ter., McLean, VA, 22101. Tel: 703-356-4473. Rev. Msgr. Bernd Kaut.

**Notre Dame Education Center*, 125 Michigan Ave., N.E., 20017.

Paul VI Institute for the Arts, 924 G St., N.W., 20001. Tel: 202-347-1450. Rev. Msgr. Michael diTeccia Farina.

Paulist National Catholic Evangelization Assoc., 3031 Fourth St., N.E., 20017-1102. Tel: 202-832-5022; Fax: 202-269-0209. Rev. Kenneth G. Boyack, C.S.P., Dir.; Sr. Susan Wolf, S.N.D., Assoc. Dir.; Rev. Robert S. Rivers, C.S.P., Dir. of Parish & Diocesan Svcs.; Mr. Denny Marcotte, Gen. Business Mgr.; Mr. Edward Maurer, Dir. Financial Devel.; Ms. Maria Luisa Gaston, Dir., Hispanic Ministry; Rev. Thomas E. Comber, C.S.P., Dir., PNCEA/Prison Ministries.

S.M.A. Social Concerns Department, 1242 Newton St., N.E., 20017. Rev. Edward Galvin, S.M.A., Dir.

S.N.D.B.C. Charitable Trust, 3037 Fourth St., N.E., 20017. Tel: 202-832-8770. Sr. Claire McCormick, S.N.D., Exec. Sec.

St. Vincent Pallotti Center for Apostolic Development, Inc., P.O. Box 893, Cardinal Sta., 20064. Tel: 202-529-3330; Fax: 202-529-0911.
E-mail: pallotti:01@aol.com
Dr. Andrew D. Thompson, Natl. Dir. Total Assisted 15,000; Total Staff 4.

Sisters of Notre Dame de Namur Base Communities, Inc., 3037 Fourth St., N.E., 20017. Sisters 17.

Sovereign Military Order of Malta-Federal Association of the U.S.A., 1730 M St., N.W., Ste. 403, 20036. Tel: 202-331-2494; Fax: 202-331-1149.
E-mail: smomfausa@aol.com
Milan C. Miskovsky, Pres.; Joseph J. Dempsey, Jr., Exec. Dir.

Spanish Catholic Center, P.O. Box 11450, 20008. Tel: 202-483-5665.

District of Columbia Health Center, 3055 Mt. Pleasant St., N.W., 20009. Tel: 202-332-6664.

Spanish Catholic Center Langley Office, 1015 University Blvd. E., Silver Spring, MD, 20903. Tel: 301-431-3773.

Maryland Health Center, 1015 University Blvd. E., Second Floor, Silver Spring, MD, 20903. Tel: 301-434-3999.

Spanish Catholic Center Gaithersburg Office, 402 E. Diamond Ave., Gaithersburg, MD, 20877. Tel: 301-417-9113.

District of Columbia Social Services, 3055 Mt. Pleasant St., N.W., 20009. Tel: 202-483-1520.

Administration, 1618 Monroe St., N.W., 20010. Tel: 202-483-5665.

Spiritual Life, 2131 Lincoln Rd., N.E., 20002. Tel: 202-832-8489; Fax: 202-832-8967. A Quarterly of Contemporary Spirituality. Bros. Bryan Paquette, O.C.D., Business Mgr.; Edward O'Donnell, O.C.D., Editor; Michael Stoegbaur, O.C.D., Promotion Mgr.

**The Morley Institute*, 1511 K St., N.W., 20005.

Theological Studies, Inc., Georgetown University, 37th and O St., N.W., 20057. Tel: 202-338-0754. Publisher of the Quarterly Theological Studies. Revs. Michael A. Fahey, S.J., Pres.; John R. Keating, S.J., Mgr.

Woodstock Theological Center, Georgetown University, 20057-1097. Tel: 202-687-3532. Revs. James L. Connor, S.J., Dir.; John P. Langan, S.J.; Walter J. Burghardt, S.J.; J. Leon Hooper, S.J.; Raymond B. Kemp; Gasper F. LoBiondo, S.J.; Thomas J. Reese, S.J.; Rev. Msgr. Richard M. Liddy; Revs. R. Randall Rainey, S.J.; Joseph N. Tylenda, S.J.; William J. Walsh, S.J.

BETHESDA, MD. *Alpha Omega, Inc. The Legion of Christ Inc.*, Our Lady of Bethesda Retreat Center, 7007 Bradley Blvd., 20817. Tel: 301-365-0612; Fax: 301-469-7522. Rev. Richard Gill, L.C.

Center for International Resources, Inc. (CIRIMEX), 4603 Cheltenham Dr., 20814. Tel: 301-652-2463; Fax: 301-652-2473. Spanish language and Latin cultural training center. Sr. Kathryn A. Bissell, Chm., Exec. Dir., U.S.A.; Sr. Caridad Inda, Chm., Exec. Dir., Mexico.

Lay Women's Assn., Villa Cortona, P.O. Box 34513, 20827. Tel: 301-469-7085. National Headquarters of the LWA.

Natural Family Planning Center of Washington, DC, Inc., P.O. Box 30239, 20824-0239. 8514 Bradmoor Dr., 20817-3810. Tel: 301-897-9323; Fax: 301-897-9323. Teen STAR Program and Billings Ovulation Method Association of the U.S. Total in Residence 2; Total Staff 3.

CAPITAL PLAZA, MD. *Archdiocese of Washington Division, The Blue Army, World Apostolate of Fatima*, P.O. Box 6702, 20789. Tel: 301-322-4978. Patricia B. Whiteman, Pres.; Rev. Msgr. William F. O'Donnell, Spiritual Dir.

FRONT ROYAL, VA. *Human Life International*, 4 Family Life, 22630. Tel: 540-635-7884. Rev. Paul B. Marx, O.S.B.

GAITHERSBURG, MD. *Emmanuel, Inc.*, Mother of God School, P.O. Box 2418, 20886-2418. Tel: 301-990-2088. Students 127; Total Staff 17.

HYATTSVILLE, MD. *Faith House, Inc.*, 4901 Eastern Ave., 20782. Tel: 301-559-5500. Sr. Josephine Murphy, CEO. Total Assisted 8.

Prison Outreach Ministry, P.O. Box 2173, 20784. Tel: 310-773-1926. Rev. Michael Bryant, Chap. Total in Residence 1,800.

KENSINGTON, MD. *Inter Mirifica*, P.O. Box 241, 20895. Tel: 301-942-9577; Fax: 301-942-9572. Rev. John Hardon, S.J.; Dolores O'Connell, Contact Person. Religious publications.

LANDOVER HILLS, MD. *Catholic Deaf Center*, 7202 Buchanan, 20784. Tel: 301-459-7464 (TDD); 459-7465 (Voice); Fax: 301-459-8186. Rev. Edward J. Helm, Dir. In res., Rev. Gerard A. Trancone. Total in Residence 2; Total Staff 3.

POMFRET, MD. *Ministr-O-Media, Inc.*, St. Joseph Church, 20675. Tel: 301-870-3990. Rev. Msgr. John B. Brady, Pres.

SEAT PLEASANT, MD. *Osmund Program*, 6407 Rolling Ridge Dr., 20743. Tel: 301-350-0566. Francis W. Kraemer, Jr., Pres.

SILVER SPRING, MD. *All Hallows Mission Fund, Inc.*, P.O. Box 3691, 20918.

Apostleship of Prayer, League of the Sacred Heart, 8611 Cedar St., 20910-4324. Tel: 301-589-3894. Rev. Gerard P. Bell, S.J., Archdiocesan Dir.

Camp St. Charles, Inc., 104 Bishop Dr., 20905. Tel: 301-384-5432. Rev. Glen Willis, S.D.S. Total Assisted 575; Total Staff 30.

Catholics Committed to Support the Pope, 9402 Stateside Ct., 20903. Tel: 301-434-3245; 434-7763; Fax: 301-277-4047. George P. Morse, K.G.C.S.G., Pres. & Publisher. Councilors: His Eminence James Cardinal Hickey; His Eminence John Cardinal O'Connor; His Eminence Mario Luigi Cardinal Ciappi; His Eminence Edouard Cardinal Gagnon; His Eminence Alfonso Cardinal Lopez Trujillo; Dr. William E. May. Theological Advisors: Most Rev. William E. Lori; Rev. Msgr. Peter J. Elliott. Prepares and Distributes World-Wide Eleven-Volume Series Precis of Official Catholic Teaching for Rectors, Seminarians, Nuncios, Bishops and Others with Particular Application to Seminaries and Teaching.

Friends of John Paul II Foundation, 9700 Rosensteel Ave., 20910. Tel: 301-589-1857. Rev. Stanislaw Hajkowski, S.Ch.

Leadership Conference of Women Religious in the U.S.A., 8808 Cameron St., 20910. Tel: 301-588-4955. Sr. Anne Munley, I.H.M., Pres.; Sr. Mary Waskowiak, R.S.M., Vice Pres.; Sr. Nancy Schreck, O.S.F., Past Pres.; Sr. Mary Ann Gschwind, F.S.P.A., Sec.; Sr. Judith Ann Karam, C.S.A.; Sr. Margaret Cafferty, P.B.V.M., Exec. Dir.

Lumen Catechetical Consultants, Inc., P.O. Box 1761, 20915. Tel: 301-593-1066; Fax: 301-593-1689. Mr. John M. Capobianco, Pres. Provides Consulting & Production Services to Catholic Organizations; Assist in Development and Production of Catechetical Materials in Various Media.

National Association for Treasurers of Religious Institutes, 8824 Cameron St., 20910-4113. Tel: 301-587-7776. Bro. Henry Sammon, F.M.S., Pres.; Sr. Carol Wester, O.P., Exec. Dir.

Oblate Conference, 8818 Cameron St., 20910. Tel: 301-565-0060; Fax: 301-587-4575. Rev. Seamus Finn, O.M.I., National Coord.

Saint Luke Institute, Inc., 8901 New Hampshire Ave., 20903. Tel: 301-445-7970; Fax: 301-422-5400. Rev. Stephen J. Rossetti, Ph.D., D. Min., CEO. Total Assisted 65; Total Staff 75.

SOAR, 1400 Spring St., Ste. 3200, 20910-2735. Tel: 301-589-9811; Fax: 301-589-2482. Rita A. Hofbauer, Pres.

Spanish Catholic Center, Office of the, 1015 University Blvd., E., 20903. Tel: 301-431-3773; Fax: 301-431-0886. Sr. Carmen Banegas, C.A.Ch., Coord.

TAKOMA PARK, MD. *Dominican Friar Residence - Southern Dominican Province*, 8019 Glenside Dr., 20912-7326. Tel: 301-439-4495. Total in Residence 2.

WALDORF, MD. *Body of Christ Farm Community, Inc.*, 3325 Martha Pl., 20601. Tel: 301-888-2566. Rev. Robert S. Pittman, S.S.S., Dir.

RELIGIOUS INSTITUTES OF MEN REPRESENTED IN THE ARCHDIOCESE

For further details refer to the corresponding bracketed number in the Religious Institutes for Men or Women section.

[0140]—*The Augustinians*.—O.S A.
[0200]—*Benedictine Monks*.—O.S.B.
[1350]—*Brothers of St. Francis Xavier*.—C.F.X.
[0330]—*Brothers of the Christian Schools*. (Baltimore Prov.).—F.S.C.
[0600]—*Brothers of the Congregation of Holy Cross*.—C.S.C.
[0400]—*Canons Regular of the Order of the Holy Cross*.—O.S.C.
[0470]—*The Capuchin Friars*. (Prov. of St. Augustine).—O.F.M.Cap.
[0270]—*Carmelite Fathers & Brothers*.—O.Carm.
[1140]—*Congregation of the Sacred Hearts of Jesus and Mary*.—SS.CC.
[0480]—*Conventual Franciscans*.—O.F.M.Conv.
[0260]—*Discalced Carmelite Fathers (Prov. of the Most Pure Heart of Mary)*.—O.C.D.
[0520]—*Franciscan Friars (Commissariat of the Holy Land)*.—O.F.M.
[0530]—*Franciscan Friars of the Atonement*.—S.A.
[0650]—*Holy Ghost Fathers (Eastern Prov.)*.—C.S.Sp.
[0690]—*Jesuit Fathers and Brothers (Prov. of Maryland)*.—S.J.
[0730]—*Legionaries of Christ*.—L.C.
[0740]—*Marian Fathers*.—M.I.C.
[0770]—*The Marist Brothers*.—F.M.S.
[0780]—*Marist Fathers*.—S.M.
[0800]—*Maryknoll*.—M.M.
[0850]—*Missionaries of Africa*.—M.Afr.
[0720]—*The Missionaries of Our Lady of La Salette*.—M.S.
[1210]—*Missionaries of St. Charles (Scalabrinians)*.—C.S.
[0590]—*Missionaries of the Holy Apostle*.—M.Ss.A.
[0840]—*Missionary Servants of the Most Holy Trinity*.—S.T.
[0870]—*Montfort Missionaries*.—S.M.M.
[0910]—*Oblates of Mary Immaculate (Eastern Prov.)*.—O.M.I.
[0920]—*Oblates of St. Francis de Sales*.—O.S.F.S.
[0430]—*Order of Preachers (Dominican) (Prov. of St. Joseph)*.—O.P.
[1310]—*Order of the Holy Trinity (American Prov.)*.—O.SS.T.
[1030]—*Paulist Fathers*.—C.S.P.
[1040]—*Piarist Fathers*.—Sch.P.
[0610]—*Priests of the Congregation of Holy Cross*. (Indiana Prov.).—C.S.C.
[1070]—*Redemptorist Fathers*. (Baltimore Prov.).—C.Ss.R.
[0700]—*St. Joseph Society of the Sacred Heart*.—S.S.J.
[0110]—*Society of African Missions*.—S.M.A.
[1260]—*Society of Christ*.—S.Ch.
[0990]—*Society of the Catholic Apostolate (Immaculate Conception Prov.)*.—S.A.C.
[1200]—*Society of the Divine Savior*. (Milwaukee, WI).—S.D.S.
[0420]—*Society of the Divine Word*.—S.V.D.
[1290]—*Society of the Priests of Saint Sulpice*.—S.S.
[0640]—*Sons of the Holy Family*.—S.F.
[0560]—*Third Order Regular of Saint Francis (Prov. of the Immaculate Conception)*.—T.O.R.

RELIGIOUS INSTITUTES OF WOMEN REPRESENTED IN THE ARCHDIOCESE

[0230]—*Benedictine Sisters of Pontifical Jurisdiction*. (Elizabeth, NJ; Duluth, MN).—O.S.B.
[1810]—*Bernardine Sisters of the Third Order of St. Francis*.—O.S.F.
[0340]—*Carmelite Sisters of Charity*.—C.Ch.
[1920]—*Congregation of the Sisters of the Holy Cross*.—C.S.C.
[0760]—*Daughters of Charity of St. Vincent de Paul*.—D.C.
[0960]—*Daughters of Wisdom*.—D.W.
[0420]—*Discalced Carmelite Nuns*.—O.C.D.
[1050]—*Dominican Contemplative Nuns*.—O.P.
[1070-03]—*Dominican Sisters*.—O.P.
[1100]—*Dominican Sisters of Charity of the Presentation of the Blessed Virgin*.—O.P.
[1470]—*Franciscan Sisters of St. Joseph*.—H.F.S.J.
[1190]—*Franciscan Sisters of the Atonement*.—S.A.
[0410]—*Institute of the Sisters of Our Lady of Mt. Carmel*.—O.Carm.
[2330]—*Little Sisters of Jesus*.—L.S.J.
[2320]—*Little Sisters of the Holy Family*.—P.S.S.F.
[2340]—*Little Sisters of the Poor*.—L.S.P.
[2345]—*Little Workers of the Sacred Hearts of Jesus and Mary*.—P.O.S.C.
[2490]—*Medical Mission Sisters*.—S.C.M.M.
[2720]—*Mission Helpers of the Sacred Heart*.—M.H.S.H.
[2710]—*Missionaries of Charity*.—M.C.
[2820]—*Missionary Sisters of Our Lady of Africa*.—M.S.O.L.A.
[2900]—*Missionary Sisters of St. Charles Borromeo*.—M.S.S.C.B.
[2865]—*Missionary Sisters of the Sacred Heart of Our Lady of Guadalupe*.—M.S.C.Gpe.
[3530]—*Missionary Sisters, Servants of the Holy Spirit*.—S.Sp.S.
[3040]—*Oblate Sisters of Providence*.—O.S.P.
[]—*Oblate Sisters of the Most Holy Eucharist*.—O.S.S.E.
[3210]—*Poor Clares of Perpetual Adoration*.—P.C.P.A.
[3450]—*Religious of Jesus and Mary*.—R.J.M.
[2970]—*School Sisters of Notre Dame*.—S.S.N.D.
[3520]—*Servants of the Holy Heart of Mary*.—S.S.C.M.
[3620]—*Sister Servants of Mary Immaculate*.—S.S.M.I.
[0500]—*Sisters of Charity of Nazareth*.—S.C.N.
[0570]—*Sisters of Charity of Seton Hill, Greensburg, Pennsylvania*.—S.C.
[1000]—*Sisters of Divine Providence of Kentucky*.—C.D.P.
[2575]—*Sisters of Mercy of the Americas*.—R.S.M.
[3000]—*Sisters of Notre Dame de Namur*. (Maryland, Chesapeake & Base Communities Prov.).—S.N.D.deN.
[3360]—*Sisters of Providence of St. Mary-of-the-Woods, IN*.—S.P.
[3893]—*Sisters of Saint Joseph of Chestnut Hill, Philadelphia*.—S.S.J.
[3718]—*Sisters of St. Ann*.—S.S.A.
[3740]—*Sisters of St. Casimir*.—S.S.C.
[1650]—*Sisters of St. Francis of Philadelphia*.—O.S.F.
[3830-13]—*Sisters of St. Joseph*.—C.S.J.
[3850]—*Sisters of St. Joseph of Chambery*.—C.S.J.
[3890]—*Sisters of St. Joseph of Peace*.—C.S.J.P.
[3980]—*Sisters of St. Paul of Chartres*.—S.P.C.
[3140]—*Sisters of the Catholic Apostolate (Pallotine)*.—S.A.C.
[1830]—*Sisters of the Good Shepherd*.—R.G.S.
[1950]—*Sisters of the Holy Family*.—S.S.F.
[1990]—*Sisters of the Holy Names of Jesus and Mary*.—S.N.J.M.
[1720]—*Sisters of the Third Order Regular of St. Francis of the Congregation of Our Lady of Lourdes*.—O.S.F.

[2160]—*Sisters, Servants of the Immaculate Heart of Mary.*—I.H.M.
[4060]—*Society of the Holy Child Jesus.*—S.H.C.J.
[4070]—*Society of the Sacred Heart.*—R.S.C.J.
[4190]—*Visitation Nuns.*—V.H.M.

ARCHDIOCESAN CEMETERIES

WASHINGTON. *The Catholic Cemeteries of the Archdiocese of Washington, Inc.* 13801 Georgia Ave., Silver Spring, MD, 20906. Tel: 301-871-1300. All offices 9-4:30 P.M. Mr. Frank Markowski, Dir.; Rev. Msgr. William F O'Donnell, Dir.

Mount Olivet, 1300 Bladensburg Rd., N.E., 20002. Tel: 202-399-3000. Warren A. Meny.

St. Mary's, 2121 Lincoln Rd., N.E., 20002. Tel: 202-635-7444. Warren A. Meny.

CLINTON, MD, 8000 Woodyard Rd., 20735. Tel: 301-868-5141. Harry S. Lancaster, Jr.

LEONARDTOWN, MD, Box 379, 20650. Tel: 301-475-5005. Mr. John A. Spalding.

SILVER SPRING, MD. *Gate of Heaven*, 13801 Georgia Ave., 20906. Tel: 301-871-6500. Samuel E. French, Jr., Mgr

St. John's Forest Glen, Rosensteel Ave., 20910. Tel: 301-871-6500. Samuel E. French, Jr.

NECROLOGY

† Dressel, Rev. Msgr. John J., Silver Spring, MD, Christ the King Church. —Died April 5, 1996.
† Gorman, Charles D., (Retired). —Died Nov. 20, 1995.
† McAllister, Rev. Msgr. Joseph B., Garrett Park, MD, Holy Cross Church. —Died Dec. 16, 1995.
† Naughton, Joseph J., (Retired). —Died Sept. 12, 1996.
† Norton, Paul P., (Retired). —Died Aug. 16, 1996.
† Troch, Louis G., (Retired). —Died June 22, 1996.

Diocese of Wheeling-Charleston

(Dioecesis Vhelingensis carolopolitanus)

Most Reverend

BERNARD W. SCHMITT, D.D.

Bishop of Wheeling-Charleston; ordained May 28, 1955; appointed Titular Bishop of Walla Walla and Auxiliary Bishop of Wheeling-Charleston May 31, 1988; ordained to the Episcopacy August 1, 1988; appointed Seventh Bishop of Wheeling-Charleston March 30, 1989; installed May 17, 1989. *Address all correspondence to: 1300 Byron St., P.O. Box 230, Wheeling, WV, 26003.*

ESTABLISHED AS DIOCESE OF WHEELING JULY 19, 1850.

REDESIGNATED DIOCESE OF WHEELING-CHARLESTON OCTOBER 4, 1974.

Square Miles 24,282.

Comprises the entire State of West Virginia.

For legal titles of parishes and diocesan institutions, consult the Chancery Office.

Chancery Office: 1300 Byron St., P.O. Box 230, Wheeling, WV, 26003. Tel.: 304-233-0880; Fax: 304-233-0890.

STATISTICAL OVERVIEW

Personnel	
Bishop	1
Priests: Diocesan Active in Diocese	77
Priests: Active Outside Diocese	4
Priests: Retired, Sick or Absent	42
Number of Diocesan Priests	123
Religious Priests in Diocese	64
Extern Priests in Diocese	12
Ordinations:	
Diocesan Priests	1
Permanent Deacons in Diocese	26
Total Brothers	8
Total Sisters	311
Parishes	
Parishes	115
With Resident Pastor:	
Resident Diocesan Priests	71
Resident Religious Priests	26
Without Resident Pastor:	
Administered by Priests	17
Administered by Women Religious	1
Missions	29
Pastoral Centers	18
New Parishes Created	1
Closed Parishes	2
Professional Ministry Personnel:	
Brothers	4
Sisters	31
Lay Ministers	24
Welfare	
Catholic Hospitals	3
Total Assisted	267,870
Health Care Centers	2
Homes for the Aged	5
Residential Care of Children	1
Special Centers for Social Services	5
Educational	
Diocesan Students in Other Seminaries	7
Total Seminarians	7
Colleges and Universities	1
Total Students	1,527
High Schools, Diocesan and Parish	7
Total Students	1,659
High Schools, Private	1
Total Students	58
Elementary Schools, Diocesan and Parish	27
Total Students	5,319
Elementary Schools, Private	2
Total Students	252
Catechesis/Religious Education:	
High School Students	1,912
Elementary Students	6,550
Total Students Under Catholic Instruction	17,284
Teachers in the Diocese:	
Priests	13
Brothers	1
Sisters	16
Lay Teachers	548
Vital Statistics	
Receptions into the Church:	
Infant Baptism Totals	1,291
Adult Baptism Totals	327
Received into Full Communion	303
First Communions	1,802
Confirmations	1,703
Marriages:	
Catholic	301
Interfaith	417
Total Marriages	718
Deaths	1,398
Total Catholic Population	103,678
Total Population	1,793,477

Former Bishops—Rt. Rev. RICHARD VINCENT WHELAN, D.D., cons. March 21, 1841; Bishop of Richmond; transferred to Wheeling in 1850; died July 7, 1874.—Rt. Rev. JOHN JOSEPH KAIN, D.D., cons. May 23, 1875; transferred June 15, 1893, to the Titular Archiepiscopal See of Oxyrynchia; appt. July 6, 1893; Coadjutor "cum jure successionis" to the Most Rev. Archbishop of St. Louis, MO; created Archbishop of St. Louis, May 21, 1895; died Oct. 13, 1903.—Rt. Rev. PATRICK JAMES DONAHUE, D.D., cons. April 8, 1894; died Oct. 4, 1922.—Most Rev. THOMAS J. MCDONNELL, D.D., LL.D., cons. Sept. 15, 1947; appt. Auxiliary Bishop of New York, June 21, 1947; appt. Coadjutor of Wheeling, March 7, 1951; died Feb. 25, 1961.—Most Rev. JOHN J. SWINT, D.D., LL.D., appt. Auxiliary Bishop of Wheeling Feb. 22, 1922; cons. May 11, 1922; appt. Bishop of Wheeling Dec. 11, 1922; promoted to rank of Archbishop "ad personam," March 12, 1954; died Nov. 23, 1962.—Most Rev. JOSEPH H. HODGES, D.D., ord. Dec. 8, 1935; appt. Titular Bishop of Rusadus and Auxiliary of Richmond Aug. 8, 1952; cons. Oct. 15, 1952; transferred to Wheeling See as Coadjutor, "cum jure successionis", May 24, 1961; succeeded to the See Nov. 23, 1962; died Jan. 27, 1985.—Most Rev. FRANCIS B. SCHULTE, D.D., ord. May 10, 1952; appt. Titular Bishop of Afufenia and Auxiliary Bishop of Philadelphia; cons. Bishop Aug. 12, 1981; transferred to Wheeling July 31, 1985; transferred to Archdiocese of New Orleans Feb. 14, 1989.

Vicar General—Rev. ROBERT C. NASH, V.G., *1300 Byron St., P.O. Box 230, Wheeling, 26003.* Tel: 304-233-0880.

Chancery Office—1300 Byron St., P.O. Box 230, Wheeling, 26003. Office Hours: Mon.-Fri. 8:30-4:30. Tel: 304-233-0880; Fax: 304-233-0890.

Chancellor—Rev. ROBERT C. NASH, V.G.

Vice Chancellor—Rev. JOHN R. GALLAGHER.

Diocesan Tribunal—All Rogatory Commissions should be addressed to the office of the Diocesan Tribunal., *P.O. Box 588, Wheeling, 26003.* Tel: 304-233-0880.

Judicial Vicar—Rev. RICHARD W. SHODA, J.C.L.

Associate Judicial Vicar—Rev. HILARION V. CANN, S.T.L., J.C.D.

Administrator of the Tribunal—Sr. MARY BYRON, S.S.J., J.C.L.

Promotor Justitiae—Very Rev. JOSEPH L. PETERSON, V.F.

Defensores Vinculi—Revs. EUGENE S. OSTROWSKI; ROBERT C. NASH, V.G.; Sr. MARY BYRON, S.S.J., J.C.L.

Judices Pro-Synodales—Revs. HILARION V. CANN, S.T.L., J.C.D.; FREDERICK P. ANNIE; Sr. MARY BYRON, S.S.J., J.C.L.; EMIL J. DOBOSZ; JOHN S. LEDFORD; WILLIAM J. NOLTE; EUGENE S. OSTROWSKI; EUGENE J. WEBER.

Diocesan Consultors—Rev. F. LEON ALEXANDER; Very Rev. JOSEPH L. PETERSON, V.F.; Revs. FREDERICK P. ANNIE; EDWARD M. BELL; ROBERT C. NASH, V.G.; P. EDWARD SADIE.

Vicar for Religious—Rev. ROBERT C. NASH, V.G., *1300 Byron St., P.O. Box 230, Wheeling, 26003.* Tel: 304-233-0880.

Associate Vicar—Sr. KATHLEEN DURKIN, S.S.J., *1300 Byron St., P.O. Box 230, Wheeling, 26003.* Tel: 304-233-0880.

Delegate for Clergy—Rev. ROBERT G. PARK, *7 13th St., P.O. Box 230, Wheeling, 26003.* Tel: 304-233-0880.

Rural Deans—Wheeling Deanery: Very Rev. A. JAMES MYLES, V.F., Beckley Deanery: Very Rev. SAMUEL S. SACUS, V.F., Bluefield Deanery: Very Rev. PATSY J. IAQUINTA, V.F., Charleston Deanery: Very Rev. PAUL J. WHARTON, V.F., Clarksburg Deanery: Very Rev. JOSEPH M. MASCIOLI, V.F., Elkins Deanery: Very Rev. WILLIAM A. ANDERSON, V.F., Fairmont Deanery: Very Rev. JAMES A. HALEY, C.S.P., V.F., Huntington Deanery: Very Rev. JOSEPH L. PETERSON, V.F., Keyser Deanery: Very Rev. IVAN M. LEBAR, T.O.R., V.F., Logan Deanery: Very Rev. DAVID J. SCHMITT, V.F., Martinsburg Deanery: Very Rev. JOHN V. DIBACCO, JR., V.F., Parkersburg Deanery: Very Rev. ANTHONY J. CONLON, V.F., Weirton Deanery: Very Rev. STEPHEN D. DUBE, V.F., Weston Deanery: Very Rev. ELMER NADICKSBERND, V.F., S.V.D.

Finance Council—P.O. Box 230, Wheeling, 26003.

Finance Officer—Rev. ROBERT C. NASH, V.G., *P.O. Box 230, Wheeling, 26003.* Tel: 304-233-0880.

Diocesan Seminary Committee—Rev. JOHN R. GALLAGHER, Exec. Sec.

Diocesan Offices and Directors

Adoration, Union of Daily—Vacant.

Apostleship of Prayer—Vacant, *P.O. Box 230, Wheeling, 26003.*

Archivist—Rev. ROBERT C. NASH, V.G., *P.O. Box 230, Wheeling, 26003.*

Behavioral Counseling and Ministry—Rev. ROBERT G. PARK, *7 13th St., P.O. Box 230, Wheeling, 26003.* Tel: 304-233-0880.

Blessed Sacrament, Confraternity of the—Vacant, *P.O. Box 230, Wheeling, 26003.*

Board of Education—Miss JUDITH MINEAR, Pres., *P.O. Box 230, Wheeling, 26003.* Tel: 304-233-0880.

Building Committee—Mr. DONALD P. MORRIS, Building & Property Supvr., *P.O. Box 230, Wheeling, 26003.* Tel: 304-233-0880.

Catholic Community Services, Inc.—Mr. GEORGE E. SMOULDER, Exec. Dir., *7 13th St., P.O. Box 230, Wheeling, 26003-0030.* Tel: 304-233-0880. Northern Regional Office: *7 13th St., P.O. Box 230, Wheeling, 26003-0030.* Tel: 304-233-0880., *3101 Main St., Weirton, 26062-4711.* Tel: 304-748-1081. Western Regional Office: *8024 Court Ave., Hamlin, 25523.* Tel: 304-824-5069. Central Regional Office: *235 High St., Ste. 210, Morgantown, 26505.* Tel: 304-292-6597. Southern Regional Office: *P.O. Box 386, 865 Mercer St., Princeton, 24740-2909.* Tel: 304-425-4306. Eastern Regional Office: *20 S. Marsham St., Romney, 26757.* Tel: 304-822-5414.

Catholic University, Friends of—Rev. ROBERT C. NASH, V.G., Dir., *P.O. Box 230, Wheeling, 26003.* Tel: 304-233-0880.

Cemeteries—Rev. CHARLES B. TEUFEL, Dir., *1300 Charles St., Wellsburg, 26070.* Tel: 304-737-0429.

Censor Librorum—Vacant.

D.C.C.W.—Rev. HARRY N. CRAMER, Moderator; Mrs. KELLY GEORGE, *2040 Weberwood Dr., Charleston, 25303.* Tel: 304-342-2964.

Stewardship and Development, Office of—Mr. BRYAN MINOR, Dir., *P.O. Box 230, Wheeling, 26003.* Tel: 233-0880.

Diaconal Council—Mr. JOHN J. LYNCH, Chm., *John XXIII Pastoral Center, 100 Hodges Rd., Charleston, 25314.* Tel: 304-342-0507.

Finance Office-Vicar for Administrative Services and Finance—Rev. ROBERT C. NASH, V.G.; Mr. JOHN L. HOFFMAN, Business Mgr., *1300 Byron St., P.O. Box 230, Wheeling, 26003.* Tel: 304-233-0880.

Health Affairs, Coordinator of—Sr. DIANE BUSHEE, S.A.C., *St. Mary's Hospital, 2900 First Ave., Huntington, 25702.* Tel: 304-526-1234., *P.O. Box 230, Wheeling, 26003.* Tel: 304-233-0880.

Hispanic Affairs—Rev. EUGENE J. WEBER, Dir., *407 Jackson St., Fairmont, 26554-2998.* Tel: 304-366-0948.

Holy Childhood Association—Mr. VICTOR A. BOERIO, *11 13th St., P.O. Box 230, Wheeling.* Tel: 304-233-0880.

Holy Name Society—Vacant, *97 14th St., P.O. Box 230, Wheeling, 26003.* Tel: 304-233-0880.

Home and Foreign Missions, Society for the Propagation of the Faith and Catholic Students' Mission Crusade—Very Rev. A. JAMES MYLES, V.F., Diocesan Dir., *P.O. Box 230, Wheeling, 26003.*

Hospitals, Representative for Catholic—Sr. DIANE BUSHEE, S.A.C., *St. Mary's Hospital, 2900 First Ave., Huntington, 25702.* Tel: 304-526-1234.

Human Resources, Office of—Mr. MICHAEL NAU, Dir., *P.O. Box 230, Wheeling, 26003.* Tel: 304-233-0880.

Infirm Priests Association—Most Rev. BERNARD W. SCHMITT, D.D., Pres.; Rev. ROBERT C. NASH, V.G., Sec. & Treas., *P.O. Box 230, Wheeling, 26003.* Tel: 304-233-0880.

Justice and Peace, Office of—Mr. GEORGE SMOULDER, Dir. Tel: 304-233-0880., *7 13th St., P.O. Box 230, Wheeling, 26003.*

Legion of Mary—Rev. RICHARD W. SHODA, J.C.L., Spiritual Dir., *201 Richardson St., P.O. Box W, Bethany, 26032.* Tel: 304-829-4622.

Migration and Refugee Services, Office of—Mrs. KIM KEENE, Dir., *1033 Quarrier St., Ste. 105, Charleston, 25301.* Tel: 304-343-1036.

Natural Family Planning—Mr. STEPHEN J. BOTOS, *7 13th St., Wheeling, 26003.* Tel: 304-233-0880.

Pastoral Council—*P.O. Box 230, Wheeling, 26003.* Tel: 304-233-0880.

Pastoral Ministry for Religious—*1300 Byron St., P.O. Box 230, Wheeling, 26003.* Tel: 304-233-0880.

Pastoral Planning, Office of—Rev. EUGENE S. OSTROWSKI, Dir., *1300 Byron St., P.O. Box 230, Wheeling, 26003.* Tel: 304-233-0880.

Presbyteral Council—Rev. FREDERICK P. ANNIE, Chm., *1304 6th Ave., P.O. Box 369, Huntington, 25708-0369.* Tel: 304-525-5202.

Priests Eucharistic League—Rev. THADDEUS J. GRONDALSKI, Dir., *1276 National Rd., Wheeling, 26003.*

Public Affairs Representative—G. NICHOLAS CASEY, JR., ESQ., *Ste. 700, One Valley Square, P.O. Box 1746, Charleston, 25326.* Tel: 304-345-2000.

Purchasing Agency, Diocesan—*1300 Byron St., P.O. Box 230, Wheeling, 26003.* Tel: 304-233-0880.

Religious Unity, Diocesan Commission for—Rev. JOHN H. MCDONNELL, Chm., *4807 Staunton Ave. S.E., Charleston, 25304-1951.* Tel: 304-925-2864.

Resettlement of Displaced Persons—Mr. GEORGE SMOULDER, Dir., *P.O. Box 230, Wheeling, 26003.* Tel: 304-233-0880.

Respect Life Office—Rev. D. BRIAN SHODA, *St. Leo Parish, Sulphur Spring Rd., P.O. Box 93, Inwood, 25428-0093.* Tel: 304-229-8945.

Rural Life Apostolate—Rev. DENNIS LOGUE, S.V.D., Dir., *Rte. 2, Box 25, Camden, 26338.* Tel: 304-269-1767.

Scholarship Association—Miss JUDITH MINEAR, Sec. & Treas., *P.O. Box 230, Wheeling, 26003.* Tel: 304-233-0880.

Scouting—Rev. STEPHEN D. DUBE, *229 California Ave., Weirton, 26062-3729.* Tel: 304-723-2054.

Social Ministries, Department of—Mr. GEORGE SMOULDER, Dir., *7 13th St., P.O. Box 230, Wheeling, 26003.* Tel: 304-233-0880.

Vocations, Office of—Rev. JOHN R. GALLAGHER, Dir., *1300 Byron St., P.O. Box 230, Wheeling, 26003.* Tel: 304-233-0880.

West Virginia State Catholic Conference—Rev. JOHN R. GALLAGHER, Dir., *1300 Byron St., P.O. Box 230, Wheeling, 26003.* Tel: 304-233-0880.

Women's Affairs, Office of—Sr. KATHLEEN DURKIN, S.S.J., *1300 Byron St., P.O. Box 230, Wheeling, 26003.* Tel: 304-233-0880.

Women's Counseling and Referral Center—Sr. MARY LOUISE LISOWSKI, S.C., *7 13th St., Wheeling, 26003.* Tel: 304-233-0880.

Catholic Education and Formation

Catholic Education and Formation, Dept. of—Vacant; Dir., *11 13th St., P.O. Box 230, Wheeling, 26003-0030.* Tel: 304-233-0880.

Adult Formation—Mr. JAMES J. RUPP, Coord., *11 13th St., P.O. Box 230, Wheeling, 26003-0030.* Tel: 304-233-0880.

Catholic Charismatic Renewal—Very Rev. PATSY J. IAQUINTA, V.F., Liaison, *P.O. Box 608, Bluefield, 24701.* Tel: 304-327-5623.

Cursillo—Mr. EDWARD A. MARN, Lay Dir.

Communications—Rev. LARRY W. DORSCH, Dir. Communications, *1213 Byron St., P.O. Box 230, Wheeling, 26003-0030.* Tel: 304-233-0880.

Audio-Visuals—Mrs. CONNIE GORDER, *1213 Byron St., P.O. Box 230, Wheeling, 26003-0030.* Tel: 304-233-0880.

"Catholic Spirit, The"—Mr. RICHARD W. CAIN, JR., Editor, *1213 Byron St., P.O. Box 230, Wheeling, 26003-0030.* Tel: 304-233-0880.

TV-Radio-Media Services—Mr. TED ROUSE, Exec. Producer, *1213 Byron St., P.O. Box 230, Wheeling, 26003-0030.* Tel: 304-233-0880.

Confraternity of Christian Doctrine—Mrs. ANNE COMEAUX, Coord., *11 13th St., P.O. Box 230, Wheeling, 26003-0030.* Tel: 304-233-0880.

Evangelization—Mr. BRYAN S. REISING, Coord., *1213 Byron St., P.O. Box 230, Wheeling, 26003-0030.* Tel: 304-233-0880.

Family Life—Mr. STEPHEN J. BOTOS, Coord., *11 13th St., P.O. Box 230, Wheeling, 26003-0030.* Tel: 304-233-0880.

Christian Family Movement—

Marriage Preparation—

Phoenix Group—

Liturgical Practices—Dr. PATRICIA BARTLE, Coord., *11 13th St., P.O. Box 230, Wheeling, 26003-0030.* Tel: 304-233-0880.

Liturgical Art and Architecture Commission—Very Rev. WILLIAM A. ANDERSON, V.F., Chm.

Liturgical Music—Sr. CAROL HANNIG, Coord.

Schools, Superintendent of—Miss JUDITH MINEAR, Supt.; Mr. JOHN F. ELCESSER, Asst. Supr. & Admin & Finance, *11 13th St., P.O. Box 230, Wheeling, 26003-0030.* Tel: 304-233-0880.

Curriculum—Sr. MARY LOU PALAS, S.C., Diocesan Coord.

Religious Education in Catholic Schools—Mr. VICTOR A. BOERIO, *11 13th St., P.O. Box 230, Wheeling, 26003-0030.* Tel: 304-233-0880.

Ministry with Persons who are Disabled—Ms. MICHELLE M. BOWE, *1213 Byron St., P.O. Box 230, Wheeling, 26003-0030.* Tel: 304-233-0880.

Youth Ministry—Mr. MICHAEL R. HALL, Diocesan Coord., *7 13th St., P.O. Box 230, Wheeling, 26003-0030.* Tel: 304-233-0880.

Campus Ministry—Mr. MICHAEL R. HALL, Diocesan Coord., *7 13th St., P.O. Box 230, Wheeling, 26003-0030.* Tel: 304-233-0880.

Teens Encounter Christ (TEC)—Mr. MICHAEL R. HALL.

Regional Coordinators for Catholic Education and Formation—

Region 1: Wheeling-Weirton—Mr. MARC LARRIVEE, Reg. Coord., *Paul VI Pastoral Center, 667 Stone and Shannon Rd., Wheeling, 26003.* Tel: 304-277-1897.

Region 2: Charleston-Huntington-Logan—Sr. JANE HARRINGTON, S.S.J., Reg. Coord., *John XXIII Pastoral Center, 100 Hodges Rd., Charleston, 25314-2281.* Tel: 304-342-5051.

Region 3: Beckley-Bluefield—Sr. MELISSA HESTER, I.H.M., Reg. Coord., *P.O. Box 7254, Sprague, 25926-0254.* Tel: 304-255-6531.

Region 4: Clarksburg-Fairmont-Parkersburg—Sr. MARIAN MILLS, C.S.J., Reg. Coord., *510 E. Pike St., Clarksburg, 26301.* Tel: 304-624-5701.

Region 5: Elkins-Weston—Mrs. CAROLYN SANTILLI, Reg. Coord., *P.O. Box 278, Buckhannon, 26201.* Tel: 304-472-5698.

Region 6: Keyser-Martinsburg—Sr. M. SHAWN SCANLAN, S.N.D.deN., Reg. Coord., *2 Lincoln St., P.O. Box 588, Fort Ashby, 26719-0588.* Tel: 304-298-4472.

CLERGY, PARISHES, MISSIONS AND PAROCHIAL SCHOOLS

CITY OF WHEELING
(Ohio County)

1—ST. JOSEPH'S CATHEDRAL (1828). Including former parishes: Blessed Trinity, St. Joan of Arc, and Sacred Heart. Rev. Larry W. Dorsch, Rector. In res., Revs. John R. Gallagher; Robert C. Nash; Eugene S. Ostrowski; Robert G. Park.
Res., 14 13th St., 26003-0051. Tel: 304-233-4121; Fax: 304-233-4129.
School—Wheeling Catholic Elementary School, 26003. Tel: 304-233-1515.

2—BLESSED TRINITY (1931). Closed. Merged with St. Joseph's Cathedral.

3—CORPUS CHRISTI (1916), Very Rev. A. James Myles, V.F.
Res., 1516 Warwood Ave., 26003-7197. Tel: 304-277-2911.
School—Sr. Johnette Dzuba, V.S.C., Prin. Sisters of St. Joseph 1; Lay Teachers 11; Students 252.
Station—West Liberty.

4—IMMACULATE CONCEPTION (ST. MARY) (1873). Closed. Merged with St. Alphonsus.

5—OUR LADY OF PEACE (1962), Rev. Raymond D. Jablinske.
Res., 2 Allendale Rd., Mt. Olivet, 26003-4601. Tel: 304-242-6575.
School—Tel: 304-242-1383. Mrs. C'Ann Reilly, Prin. Lay Teachers 11; Students 219.

6—SACRED HEART (1903). Closed. Merged with St. Joseph's Cathedral.

7—ST. ALPHONSUS (1856). Including former parishes St. Mary and St. Ladislaus. Revs. Ronald G. Prechtl; S. Brian Owens.
Res., 49-36th St., 26003-1997. Tel: 304-232-2005.
Church—2111 Market St., 26003-3827. Tel: 304-232-4353.
School—Wheeling Catholic Elementary School, 26003.

8—ST. JOAN OF ARC (1923). Closed. Merged with St. Joseph's Cathedral.

9—ST. LADISLAUS (1902). Closed. Merged with St. Alphonsus.

10—ST. MICHAEL'S (1897), Revs. James M. Sobus; Peter A. Giannamore.
Res., 1225 National Rd., 26003-5791. Tel: 304-242-1560; Fax: 304-243-5710.
School—1221 National Rd., 26003. Tel: 304-242-3966.
Lay Teachers 24; Students 521.

11—ST. VINCENT DE PAUL'S (1895), Revs. James LaCrosse, S.M.; H. Joseph Wilhelm, S.M.; Deacons Paul H. Bischof, Jr.; Ronald J. Wojcicki.
Res., 2244 Marshall Ave., 26003-7421. Tel: 304-242-0406; Fax: 304-243-0837.
School—Tel: 304-242-5844.
Sisters 2; Lay Teachers 18; Students 309.
Mission—Triadelphia, Ohio Co., Our Lady of Seven Dolors, Chapel Hill Rd., Triadelphia, 26059. Tel: 304-547-5342. [CEM]

CITY OF CHARLESTON
(Kanawha County)

1—SACRED HEART CO-CATHEDRAL (1866), Revs. P. Edward Sadie, Rector; John P. McDonough; Deacon John J. Lynch.
Res., 1032 Virginia St. E., 25301-2879. Tel: 304-342-8175; Fax: 304-344-3907. [CEM]
School—Tel: 304-346-5491. Mrs. Debra Sullivan, Prin.; Miss Lynn Nehoda, Asst. Prin.
Lay Teachers 27; Students 504.

2—ST. ANTHONY'S (1905), Rev. Richard J. Zelik, O.F.M.Cap.; Deacon David Wuletich. In res., Bro. Phillip Hainen, O.F.M.Cap.; Rev. Kieran Quinn, O.F.M.Cap.
Res., 1000 Sixth St., 25302. Tel: 304-342-2716.
School—Tel: 304-346-8441. Ms. Myrtolyn English. Capuchin Brother 1; Sister of Divine Providence 1; Lay Teachers 10; Students 138.

3—ST. AGNES (1922), Rev. John H. McDonnell.
Res., 4807 Staunton Ave., S.E., 25304. Tel: 304-925-2836; Fax: 304-925-4423.

School—4801 Staunton Ave., S.E., 25304. Tel: 304-925-4341; Fax: 304-925-4423. Sr. Judith Ann Teufel, S.S.J., Prin.
Sisters of St. Joseph 1; Lay Teachers 9; Students 203.
Convent—300 49th St., S.E., 25304. Tel: 304-925-2480.

OUTSIDE THE CITIES OF WHEELING AND CHARLESTON

Beckley, Raleigh Co., St. Francis De Sales (1907), Very Rev. Samuel S. Sacus, V.F.; Rev. William K. Matheny, Jr.; Deacons William D. Wise; John F. Ziolkowski.
Res., 614 S. Oakwood Ave., 25801. Tel: 304-253-3695; Fax: 304-253-3694. [CEM]
School—Tel: 304-252-4087.
Lay Teachers 10; Students 169.
Mission—Whitesville, Boone Co., St. Joseph the Worker, (1958) P.O. Box 444, Whitesville, 25209-0444. Tel: 304-854-2997; Fax: 304-854-2997. Sr. Ann Marie Liston, S.J.C., Pastoral Coord.

Beech Bottom, Brooke Co., Holy Family. Closed. See St. John, Wellsburg.

Belington, Barbour Co., Resurrection Mission (1978), Sr. Teresa Reddington, S.S.J., Dir.
Res., 701 Brown Ave., 26250. Tel: 304-823-1576.

Belle, Kanawha Co., St. John (1951), Rev. Albert Alexandrunas, O.F.M.Cap.
Res., 321 E. Tenth St., 25015. Tel: 304-949-3063.
Mission—Coalburg, Kanawha Co., Good Shepherd, Box 16, East Bank, 25067. Tel: 304-595-6002.

Benwood, Marshall Co., St. John's (1875), Rev. John C. Valentine.
Res., 622 Main St., 26031. Tel: 304-232-6455.
School—Sts. James and John Consolidated School, Tel: 304-232-1587.

Berkeley Springs, Morgan Co., St. Vincent de Paul (1931), Rev. John S. Ledford.
Res., 116 S. Washington St., 25411-1577. Tel: 304-258-1311. [CEM]

Bluefield, Mercer Co., Sacred Heart (1895), Very Rev. Patsy Iaquinta, V.F.
Res., 1017 Wyoming St., P.O. Box 608, 24701. Tel: 304-327-5623; Fax: 304-327-7769.

Bridgeport, Harrison Co., All Saints (1946), Rev. Harry N. Cramer.
Res., 317 E. Main St., 26330-1750. Tel: 304-842-2283.
School—Harrison Co. Catholic School System, Tel: 304-624-5129.

Buckhannon, Upshur Co., Holy Rosary (1921), Revs. James B. McCafferty, S.M.; Thomas B. Hogan, S.M.
Res., 35 Franklin St., 26201. Tel: 304-472-3414; Fax: 304-472-3414.
Missions—Century, Barbour Co., Our Lady of Sorrows, Century, 26214.; Pickens, Randolph Co., Sacred Heart, Pickens, 26230. [CEM]

Camden, Lewis Co., St. Boniface (Leading Creek) (1875), Rev. Dennis Logue, S.V.D.
Res., Rte. 2, Box 25, 26338-9737. Tel: 304-269-1767. [CEM]
Chapel—St. Clara, St. Clare. [CEM]

Cameron, Marshall Co., St. Martin (1871), Rev. Will Roger Malave.
Res., 1 Fitzgerald Ave., 26033. Tel: 304-686-3551. [CEM]

Charles Town, Jefferson Co., St. James (1889). Includes St. Peter, Harper's Ferry. Rev. Bert W. Valdes.
Res., 311 S. George St., P.O. Box 370, 25414-0370. Tel: 304-725-5558; Fax: 304-725-1685. [CEM]

Cheat Lake, Monongalia Co., St. Luke, Rev. Jeremiah F. McSweeney.
Res., Rte. 6, Box 145CC, Morgantown, 26505-9211. Tel: 304-594-2353; Fax: 304-594-2359.
School—St.Francis Central Catholic School, 375 Birch St., Morgantown, 26505. Tel: 304-598-0133.
Mission—Bruceton Mills, Preston Co., Mary Help of Christians, (1983) Bruceton Mills, 26525. Tel: 304-379-4220.

Chester, Hancock Co., Sacred Heart (1902), Rev. F. Rodger Hughes.
Res., 424 Fourth St., Box 313, 26034-0313. Tel: 304-387-0198.

Clarksburg, Harrison Co., Immaculate Conception (1864), Revs. Cesidio J. Federico; George J. Romage.
Res., 126 E. Pike St., 26301-2155. Tel: 304-622-8280. [CEM]
Parish Office: Tel: 304-622-8243.
School—Harrison Co. Catholic School System, Tel: 304-623-1026; 622-9831.

St. James (1924), Rev. Robert A. Perriello; Deacons Anthony P. Santilli; Donald F. Molinari.
Res., 2107 Pride Ave., 26301-1819. Tel: 304-622-1668.
School—Harrison County Catholic School System, Tel: 304-623-1026; 622-9831.

Coalton, Randolph Co., St. Patrick Church (1918), Rev. Albert J.B. Anselmi.
Res., P.O. Box 99, 26257-0099. Tel: 304-636-5754. [CEM 4]

Dunbar, Kanawha Co., Christ the King, Rev. Dean G. Borgmeyer.
Res., 2219 22nd St., P.O. Box 339, Nitro, 25143. Tel: 304-755-0791.
Church—1508 Grosscup Ave., 25064-2925. Tel: 304-768-2527.

Elkins, Randolph Co., St. Brendan (1897), Very Rev. William A. Anderson, V.F.
Res., 1 Park St., P.O. Box 2205, 26241. Tel: 304-636-0467; 636-0546. [CEM]

Elkview, Kanawha Co., Our Lady of the Hills, Rev. John C. Reich.
Res., 4084 Indian Creek Rd., 25071-9328. Tel: 304-965-7670; Fax: 304-965-7670.
Mission—Clendenin, Kanawha Co., Catholic Community of Clendenin, 63 Elk River Rd., S., Clendenin, 25045. Tel: 304-548-7147. Co-Directors: Sr. Jacqueline Le Boeuf, S.S.A.; Sr. Marguerite St. Amand, S.S.A.
Mission—Bancroft, Putnam Co., St. Patrick, 207 Jefferson St., P.O. Box 238, Bancroft, 25011. Tel: 304-586-3485; Fax: 304-586-3485.

Fairmont, Marion Co.,

1—St. Peter's, (1873), Rev. Eugene J. Weber.
Res., 407 Jackson St., 26554-2998. Tel: 304-366-0948; Fax: 304-367-0739. [CEM]
School—Fairmont Catholic Grade School, Tel: 304-363-5313.

2—Immaculate Conception, (1960), Rev. Casey B. Mahone.
Res., 413 Maryland Ave., P.O. Box 1726-E, 26554. Tel: 304-363-1840.
School—Fairmont Catholic Grade School, Tel: 304-363-5313.

3—St. Anthony, (1964), Rev. Gary P. Naegele.
Res., 1660 Mary Lou Retton Dr., 26554-2099. Tel: 304-363-1328.
School—Fairmont Catholic Grade School, Tel: 304-363-5313.

4—St. Joseph's, (1909), Rev. S. Brian Owens.
Res., 219 Robinson St., 26554-3045. Tel: 304-366-1967. [CEM]
School—Fairmont Catholic Grade School, Tel: 304-363-5313.
Mission—Barrackville, Marion Co., All Saints.

Farmington, Marion Co., St. Peters (1921), Rev. Donald X. Higgs.
Res., 1304 Mill St., P.O. Box 150, 26571-0150. Tel: 304-825-6651.

Follansbee, Brooke Co., St. Anthony's (1906), Revs. Anthony Cincinnati; Anthony Thurston.
Res., 1017 Jefferson St., 26037-1334. Tel: 304-527-2286.
School—Tel: 304-527-0990.
Lay Teachers 10; Students 65.

Fort Ashby, Mineral Co., Annunciation of the Lord, Rev. D. Kent Durig.
Res., P.O. Box 553, 26719-0553. Tel: 304-298-3392.

Franklin, Pendleton Co., St. Elizabeth Ann Seton, Rev. James J. Creedon, M.Ss.A. Co-Directors: Sr. Pauline Laurence, S.S.A.; Sr. Yvette Dargy, S.S.A.
Church & Res.—P.O. Box 890, 26807. Tel: 304-358-7012.

Gary, McDowell Co., Our Lady of Victory (1904), Rev. Nguyen Ngoc That Son; Sr. Mary Denise Thomas, I.H.M., Parochial Coord.
Church—P.O. Box 130, 24836. Tel: 304-448-2749.
Res., U.S. 52, P.O. Box 187, Fowhatan, 24877-0167. Tel: 304-862-3494. [CEM]

Gassaway, Braxton Co., St. Thomas, Very Rev. Elmer Nadicksbernd, S.V.D., V.F.; Sr. Mary Weatherly, C.D.P., Pastoral Assoc.
Res., 624 Kanawha St., 26624-1208. Tel: 304-364-5895.

Glen Dale, Marshall Co., St. Jude (1968), Rev. William J. Stenger, Sr.
Res., 710 Jefferson Ave., P.O. Box 147, 26038-0147. Tel: 304-845-8165 (Rectory); 845-2646 (Office).

Glenville, Gilmer Co., Good Shepherd (1958), Rev. Edwin Daschbach, S.V.D.
Res., 701 Mineral Rd., 26351-1310. Tel: 304-462-7130.

Grafton, Taylor Co., St. Augustine (1852), Very Rev. Joseph M. Mascioli, V.F.
Res., 17 W. Washington St., 26354-1398. Tel: 304-265-1848; 265-3861 (Office). [CEM 2]

Grant Town, Marion Co., St. Anthony's (1907), Rev. James H.T. Brady, S.O.L.T.
Res., 102 Church St., P.O. Box 219, 26574-0219. Tel: 304-278-5371.
Mission—Rivesville, Marion Co., Our Lady of the Assumption, 207 Clayton St., Rivesville, 26588.

Harpers Ferry, Jefferson Co., St. Peter (1830). Closed. Merged with St. James, Charles Town.

Harrisville, Ritchie Co., Christ Our Hope (1980), Rev. Thomas Karachira; Sr. Kathryn Holohan, O.S.F., Pastoral Assoc.; Deacon John F. Maher.
Res., Rte. 1, Box 44A, 26362. Tel: 304-643-4261.
Chapel—Pennsboro, St. Joseph. [CEM]

Hinton, Summers Co., St. Patrick (1874), Rev. John N. Duhaime.
Res., 309 Second Ave., P.O. Box 8, 25951. Tel: 304-466-3966. [CEM]
Mission—Alderson, Greenbrier Co., St. Mary of the Greenbrier, P.O. Box 441, Alderson, 24910. Tel: 304-445-7967.

Holden, Logan Co., St. Mary's (1961). Consolidated with Our Lady of Mount Carmel, Logan, to form St. Francis of Assisi, Logan.

Huntington, Cabell Co.,

1—St. Joseph's, (1872), Revs. Fredrick P. Annie; M. Julian Marneni.
Res., 1304 Sixth Ave., P.O. Box 369, 25708. Tel: 304-525-5202; Fax: 304-525-3972. [CEM]
School—520 Thirteenth St., 25701. Tel: 304-522-2644. Mrs. Georgeann Warfuel, Prin.
Lay Teachers 9; Students 134.

2—Our Lady of Fatima, Very Rev. Joseph L. Peterson, V.F.
Res., 545 Norway Ave., 25705. Tel: 304-525-0866; Fax: 304-525-0390.
School—535 Norway Ave., 25705. Tel: 304-523-2861; 523-2863. Mrs. Marcia McDonald, Prin.
Sisters 1; Lay Teachers 11; Students 182.

3—Sacred Heart, (1934), Rev. Andrew G. Kranyc; Sr. Mary Terence Wall, S.A.C., Pastoral Assoc.
Res., 2015 Adams Ave., 25704-1419. Tel: 304-429-5234.

4—St. Peter Claver, (1937) (African-American), Rev. Andrew G. Kranyc; Sr. Patricia Burke, S.M.S.M., Parochial Coord.
Res., 828 Fifteenth St., 25701. Tel: 304-523-7311.

Hurricane, Putnam Co., Catholic Church of the Ascension (1980), Very Rev. Paul J. Wharton, V.F.
Res., 905 Hickory Mill Rd., 25526. Tel: 304-562-5816; Fax: 304-562-3589.

Huttonsville, Randolph Co., St. John Bosco (1948), Rev. Albert Anselmi; Deacon Louis J. Belldina.
Res., Rte. 1, Box 9D, 26273-9737. Tel: 304-335-2165.
Station—Huttonsville Correctional Center, Tel: 304-338-6323.

Inwood, Berkeley Co., St. Leo (1982), Rev. D. Brian Shoda.
Res., Sulphur Spring Rd., P.O. Box 93, 25428-0093. Tel: 304-229-8945.

Keyser, Mineral Co., Assumption (1874), Very Rev. Ivan M. Lebar, T.O.R., V.F.; Bro. Luke D. Stone, T.O.R., Pastoral Assoc.
Res., 34 James St., 26726-2721. Tel: 304-788-2488. [CEM]

Kingwood, Preston Co., St. Sebastian's (1914), Revs. Jerome McKenna, C.P.; William Davin, C.P.; Deacon Truman A. Lipscomb.
Res., P.O. Box 519, 26537. Tel: 304-329-1519; Fax: 304-329-2546. [CEM 3]
Mission—Terra Alta, Preston Co., St. Edward.

Logan, Logan Co., St. Francis of Assisi (1996), Very Rev. David J. Schmitt, V.F.
Res., 561 Main St., 25601. Tel: 304-752-3017.

Lubeck, Wood Co., St. Monica's (1976), Rev. John H. Fahey.
Res., R.R. 1, Box 362, Washington, 26181-9615. Tel: 304-863-5580. [CEM]
Church—State Rt.68.

Madison, Boone Co., St. Mary, Queen of Heaven (1957), Rev. James E. O'Connor.
Res., P.O. Box 467, 25130-0467. Tel: 304-369-4538; Fax: 304-369-6268.
Church—51 Madison Ave., 25130.
Mission—Chapmanville, Logan Co., St. Barbara, (1979) H.C. 74, Box 3018, Chapmanville, 25508-9522. Tel: 304-855-7962. Sr. Carol Symon, S.N.D., Parochial Coord.

Man, Logan Co., St. Edmund (1961), Very Rev. David J. Schmitt, V.F.
Res., 561 Main St., Logan, 25601-3899. Tel: 304-752-3017.
Church—110 S. Bridge St., 25635-1002. Tel: 304-583-7729.

Mannington, Marion Co., St. Patrick's, Rev. Donald X. Higgs.
Res., 204 Furbee Ave., 26582-1399. Tel: 304-986-2321.
Mission—Littleton, Wetzel Co., Assumption of the Blessed Virgin Mary, (1859) Littleton, 26581. [CEM]

Marlinton, Pocahontas Co., St. John Neumann (1977), Rev. Arnold Lang, S.V.D.
Res., 714 10th Ave., 24954-1314. Tel: 304-799-6778.

Mission—Bartow, Pocahontas Co., St. Mark the Evangelist, (1977) Bartow, 24920.

Martinsburg, Berkeley Co., St. Joseph's (1803), Very Rev. John V. DiBacco, Jr., V.F.
Res., 219 S. Queen St., 25401-3213. Tel: 304-264-8947; Fax: 304-263-7357. [CEM]
School—Tel: 304-267-6447; Fax: 304-267-8057. Daughters of Charity of Vincent de Paul 1; Lay Teachers 13; Students 239.
Mission—Hedgesville, Berkeley Co., St. Bernadette, 205 W. Main St., P.O. Box 11, Hedgesville, 25427. Tel: 304-754-7830.

Masontown, Preston Co., St. Zita's (1962), Revs. Jerome McKenna, C.P.; William Davin, C.P.; Deacon Truman A. Lipscomb.
Res., P.O. Box 519, Kingwood, 26537. Tel: 304-329-1519; Fax: 304-329-2546.
Church—Tel: 304-864-5512.

Maysel, Clay Co., Church of The Risen Lord (1972), Very Rev. Elmer Nadicksbernd, S.V.D., V.F.
Res., HC 60, Box 7, 25133. Tel: 304-587-4740.

McMechen, Marshall Co., St. James (1900), Rev. John C. Valentine; Deacon Paul Smith.
Res., 326 Logan St., 26040. Tel: 304-232-1227.
School—Sts. James and John Consolidated Schools, Tel: 304-232-1587.

Monongah, Marion Co., Holy Spirit (1982), Rev. James J. Neville, S.J.
Res., 687 Maple Ter., 26554-116. Tel: 304-534-3020. [CEM]

Montgomery, Fayette Co., Immaculate Conception (1888), Rev. Thomas Joyce.
Res., P.O. Box 65, 25136. Tel: 304-442-2101.
Mission—Boomer, Fayette Co., St. Anthony Shrine, (1928).

Moorefield, Hardy Co., Epiphany of the Lord (1980), Rev. Gerard A. Petta, M.Ss.A. In res., Rev. Michael A. Nofi, M.Ss.A.
Res., Rte. 2, Box 400, 26836. Tel: 304-434-2547.

Morgantown, Monongalia Co., St. Theresa's, Rev. Mario R. Claro.
Res., 44 Beechurst Ave., 26505-4912. Tel: 304-296-5353.
School—St. Francis Central Catholic School, 375 Birch St., 26505. Tel: 304-598-0133.

St. John's University Parish, Newman Hall (1966), Very Rev. James A. Haley, C.S.P., V.F.; Revs. Michael E. Evernden, C.S.P.; Paul Reynolds, C.S.P.; Deacon Joseph Prentiss.
Res., 1481 University Ave., 26505-5598. Tel: 304-296-8231; Fax: 304-296-4650.
School—St. Francis Central Catholic School, 375 Birch St., 26505. Tel: 304-598-0133.

Moundsville, Marshall Co., St. Francis Xavier's (1857), Revs. Ronan J. Deegan, T.O.R.; Albert Driesch, T.O.R.
Res., 912 Seventh St., 26041. Tel: 304-845-1593.
School—(Grades K-8). Tel: 304-845-2562. Mr. Frank Giannamore.
Sisters 1; Lay Teachers 11; Students 131; Preschool 15.
Station—Northern Regional Jail and Correctional Facility, Tel: 304-843-4067.

Mullens, Wyoming Co., St. John the Evangelist (1923), Rev. Pericles P. Malacaman; Sr. Katherine O'Neil, I.H.M., Pastoral Assoc.
Res., 13 Terry St., 25882-1624. Tel: 304-294-8128.
Mission—Pineville, Wyoming Co., Holy Cross, Rte. 10, P.O. Box 927, Pineville, 24874. Tel: 304-732-9188.

New Cumberland, Hancock Co., Immaculate Conception (1904), Rev. Ronald A. Getsinger.
Res., 1016 Ridge Ave., P.O. Box 666, 26047-0666. Tel: 304-564-5068.

New Martinsville, Wetzel Co., St. Vincent de Paul (1901), Rev. Charles J. Schneider, V.F.; Sr. Catherine Mullooly, S.S.J., Pastoral Assoc.
Res., 21 Rosary Rd., 26155-1602. Tel: 304-455-4615.

Nitro, Kanawha Co., Holy Trinity (1962), Rev. Dean G. Borgmeyer.
Res., 2219 22nd St., P.O. Box 339, 25143-0339. Tel: 304-755-0791; Fax: 304-755-3473.

Oak Hill, Fayette Co., SS. Peter and Paul (1906), Rev. Harold W. Moore.
Res., Oyler Ave., P.O. Box 1247, 25901-1247. Tel: 304-465-5445. [CEM]
School—Tel: 304-465-5045. Mrs. Karen Willson, Prin.
Lay Teachers 6; Students 123.

Ona, Cabell Co., St. Stephen (1980), Rev. Msgr. Lawrence J. Luciana (STU) Admin.
Res., 2491 James River Tpke., 25545-9722. Tel: 304-743-3234.

Paden City, Tyler and Wetzel Cos., Mater Dolorosa (1921), Rev. Joseph Ezharath (India).
Res., 302 E. Main St., 26159-1736. Tel: 304-337-9837.
Mission—Middlebourne, Tyler Co., St. Lawrence, Box 267, Middlebourne, 26149. Tel: 304-758-4649.

Parkersburg, Wood Co., St. Francis Xavier's (1853), Rev. Michael P. O'Reilly. In res., Rev. Manuelpillai Soosaipillai.
Res., 532 Market St., 26101-5144. Tel: 304-422-3142; 422-3145; Fax: 304-422-3142. [CEM 3]

St. Margaret Mary (1923), Rev. Edward M. Bell; Deacons Gerald B. Goetemann; George B. Showalter.
Res., 2500 Dudley Ave., 26101-2695. Tel: 304-428-1262; Fax: 304-422-4905.

Petersburg, Grant Co., St. Mary's, Rev. James J. Creedon, M.Ss.A.
Res., 5 Pierpont St., 26847-1633. Tel: 304-257-1057.
Church—4 Grant St., 26847.

Philippi, Barbour Co., St. Elizabeth Parish and Newman Center (1953), Rev. Damian P. Drass, T.O.R.
Res., College Hill, Rte. 3, Box 257, 26416-9581. Tel: 304-457-2641. Deacon A. Ray Shaw, III.; Res., Rte. 3, Box 38-I, 26416-9581. Tel: 304-457-1408.

Point Pleasant, Mason Co., Sacred Heart (1948), Rev. Melvin E. Averman, O.F.M.Cap.
Res., 2222 Jackson Ave., 25550-2004. Tel: 304-675-4602.
Mission—Mason, Mason Co., St. Joseph, (1856) Mason, 25260. [CEM]

Powhatan, McDowell Co., Sacred Heart (1895), Rev. Nguyen Ngoc That Son.
Res., HC 76, Box 402, 24877-0167. Tel: 304-862-3494.

Princeton, Mercer Co., Sacred Heart (1915), Rev. Lawrence Wrenn; Sr. Theresa Metz, S.S.J., Pastoral Assoc.
Res., 507 Harrison St., 24740-3198. Tel: 304-425-3664.
Mission—Peterstown, Monroe Co., St. Peter, 203 Mill St., P.O. Box 644, Peterstown, 24963-0644. Tel: 304-753-4279. Sr. Molly Bauer, S.S.J., Parochial Coord.
Campus Ministry, Concord College—Athens, 24712. Tel: 304-384-9502.

Rainelle, Greenbrier Co., Sacred Heart, Rev. Harold F. Dunn, M Ss.A.
Res., 401-13th St., 25962-1703. Tel: 304-438-8687.
Chapel—Springdale, Sacred Heart. (1876). [CEM]
Station—Rainelle, Alderson Federal Prison.

Ravenswood, Jackson Co., St. Matthew (1957), Rev. John H. Fahey.
Res., 600 Crooks Ave., 26164-1312. Tel: 304-273-2175; Fax: 304-273-2175.

Richwood, Nicholas Co., Holy Family (1904), Revs. William F. Seli, S.M.; Jerome D. Rawa, S.M.; Bro. Richard McKenna, S.M.
Res., 4 Maple St., 26261-1318. Tel: 304-846-2873. [CEM]

Ridgeley, Mineral Co., St. Anthony (1916), Rev. D. Kent Durig.
Res., Box 553, Fort Ashby, 26719-0553. Tel: 304-298-3392.

Romney, Hampshire Co., Our Lady of Grace (1951), Rev. Joseph A. Salazar, M.Ss.A.
Res., 299 School St., P.O. Box 871, 26757-0871. Tel: 304-822-5561.

Ronceverte, Greenbrier Co., St. Catherine of Siena (1892), Rev. John C. McGinnity.
Res., 407 Walnut St., 24970-1233. Tel: 304-647-4515.
Missions—Lewisburg, Monroe Co., St. Louis, (1977) P.O. Box 1814, Lewisburg, 24901. Tel: 304-645-7544; Union, Monroe Co., St. Andrew, (1977) P.O. Box 347, Union, 24983. Tel: 304-772-5849. Sr. Molly Bauer, S.S.J., Parochial Coord.
Station—Williamsburg, Mary Immaculate, (1879). [CEM]
Chaplaincy—WV School of Osteopathic Medicine.

St. Albans, Kanawha Co., St. Francis of Assisi, Rev. Patrick M. McDonough; Deacon Robert B. Lilly.
Res., 1023 Sixth Ave., P.O. Box 1406, 25177-1406. Tel: 304-727-3033.
School—Priests 1; Lay Teachers 11; Students 200.

St. Joseph Settlement, Marshall Co., St. Joseph's, Rev. Will Roger Malave.
Res., R.F.D. 1, Box 203, Proctor, 26055-9705. Tel: 304-455-4303. [CEM]

St. Marys, Pleasants Co., St. John (1913), Rev. Thomas Karachira (India); Deacon John F. Maher.
Mailing Address: P.O. Box 338, 26170-0338.
Res., 310 Washington St., 26170-1313. Tel: 304-684-7669.

Salem, Harrison Co., Sacred Heart (1915), Rev. Donald E. Hile.
Res., Rtes. 23 S. & 50, P.O. Box 248, 26426-0248. Tel: 304-782-2277. [CEM]

Shepherdstown, Jefferson Co., St. Agnes (1794), Rev. T. Matthew Rowgh.
Res., 216 S. Duke, P.O. Box 1603, 25443-1603. Tel: 304-876-6436.

Shinnston, Harrison Co., St. Ann's, Rev. Karl R. Wohinc.
Res., 610 Pike St., 26431-1451. Tel: 304-592-2733.
Mission—Spelter, Harrison Co., Holy Family, Spelter, 26438.

Sistersville, Tyler Co., Holy Rosary (1898), Rev. Joseph Ezharath (India).
Church—519 Main St., 26175-1405. Tel: 304-652-6381.

South Charleston, Kanawha Co., Blessed Sacrament (1941), Rev. F. Leon Alexander; Deacon John J. Hanna.
Res., 305 E St., 25303-1597. Tel: 304-744-5523; Fax: 304-744-5669.

Spencer, Roane Co., Holy Redeemer (1957), Rev. Don Tranel, Glmy.
Res., 424 Parkersburg Rd., 25276-1024. Tel: 304-927-2013.
Missions—Elizabeth, Wirt Co., St. Elizabeth of Hungary, (1977) Hwy. 14, P.O. Box 191, Elizabeth, 26143. Tel: 304-275-4226. Sr. Nancy Fortkort, O.S.F., Pastoral Assoc.; Grantsville, Calhoun Co., Jesus Christ, Prince of Peace, (1977) Hwy. 16, P.O. Box 416, Grantsville, 26147. Tel: 304-354-7937.

Star City, Monongalia Co., St. Mary's (1952), Rev. Carl E. Bauer; Deacons John Shultz; George Nedeff; Jeanne Howell, Pastoral Assoc.
Res., 3344 University Ave., P.O. Box 4204, 26504-4204. Tel: 304-599-3747; Fax: 304-599-3769. [CEM]
School—St. Francis Central Catholic School, 375 Birch St., Morgantown, 26505. Tel: 304-598-0133.

Stonewood, Harrison Co., Our Lady of Perpetual Help (1955), Revs. Martin D. Brady, T.O.R.; Edward Sabo, T.O.R.
Res., 707 Third St., 26301-4896. Tel: 304-623-2334.

Summersville, Nicholas Co., St. John The Evangelist (1849), Revs. William Seli, S.M.; Jerome D. Rawa, S.M.
Res., 1704 Webster Rd., 26651-1049. Tel: 304-872-2554. [CEM]

Thomas, Tucker Co., St. Thomas Aquinas (1897), Rev. Lino P. Ebejer.
Res., P.O. Box 300, 26292-0300. Tel: 304-463-4488. [CEM]
Mission—Parsons, Tucker Co., Our Lady of Mercy, (1960) 221 Water St., P.O. Box 97, Parsons, 26287-0097. Tel: 304-478-4575. Sr. Patricia Marren, S.C., Parochial Coord.

Vienna, Wood Co., St. Michael's (1956), Very Rev. Anthony J. Conlon, V.F.; Deacon James R. Kelly.
Res., 5501 Fourth Ave., 26105-2007. Tel: 304-295-6109.

War, McDowell Co., Christ the King (1942), Rev. Donald L. Meuret, Jr.
Res., Box 728, 24892-0728. Tel: 304-875-3827.

Wayne, Wayne Co., Nativity of Our Lord (1980). Unassigned.
Res., Rte. 2, Box 2502, 25570-9738. Tel: 304-272-6176.
Station—Genoa Christian Center, P.O. Box 67, Genoa, 25517. Tel: 304-385-4583; Fax: 304-385-4583. Sr. Monica Schieber, C.P.P.S., Dir.

Webster Springs, Webster Co., St. Anne's (1920), Rev. Xavier Cooney, S.V.D.
Res., 160 McGraw, 26288-1134. Tel: 304-847-5512.

Weirton, Hancock Co., St. Paul's (1910), Revs. Thomas E. Schiffer; Francis A. O'Kruta; Deacon Edwin T. Mullavey.
Res., 140 Walnut St., 26062-4521. Tel: 304-748-4118. [CEM]
School—Tel: 304-748-5225. Ms. Bette Burns, Prin.
Lay Teachers 11; Students 208.

Sacred Heart of Mary (1916) (Polish), Rev. J. Stephen Vallelonga; Deacon Richard W. Mankowski.
Res., 175 Stroud Ave., 26062-3995. Tel: 304-723-0703; Fax: 304-723-0729.
School—Tel: 304-723-1560.
Lay Teachers 11; Students 107.

St. Joseph the Worker (1962), Very Rev. Stephen D. Dube, V.F.; Rev. James J. Chetock.
Res., 229 California Ave., 26062-3729. Tel: 304-723-2054; 723-2057; Fax: 304-723-3961.
School—Tel: 304-723-1970. Mr. Albert Boniti, Prin.
Sisters 1; Lay Teachers 12; Students 176.

Welch, McDowell Co., St. Peter, Rev. Donald L. Meuret, Jr.
Res., 111 Virginia Ave., 24801-2424. Tel: 304-436-2014.
Chapel—Kimball, Our Lady Queen of the Apostles. (1959).

Wellsburg, Brooke Co., St. John The Evangelist (1857), Rev. Charles B. Teufel.
Res., 1300 Charles St., 26070-1408. Tel: 304-737-0429. [CEM]
School—Tel: 304-737-0511. Mrs. Tonette Alward, Prin.

Lay Teachers 9; Students 98.
Mission—Beech Bottom, Brooke Co., Holy Family (Formerly Power), (1980) Box 7, Beech Bottom, 26030. Tel: 304-394-5929. Sr. Ellen Dunn, O.P., Parochial Coord.
Station—Bethany College Campus Ministry, 201 Richardson St., Bethany, 26032. Tel: 304-829-4622.

Weston, Lewis Co., St. Patrick's (1845), Rev. James J. Murphy.
Res., 222 Center Ave., 26452-2029. Tel: 304-269-3048. [CEM]
School—Tel: 304-269-5547. Sr. Eileen Marie Sinnott, S.S.J., Prin.
Lay Teachers 7; Students 107.
Chapels—Sandfork, St. Bernard. [CEM]
Roanoke, St. Bridget. [CEM]
Chaplaincy—Weston State Hospital, Tel: 304-269-3048.

Westover, Monogalia Co., St. Elizabeth Ann Seton (1977), Rev. Stanley T. Tuchalski.
Res., 213 Parkview, P.O. Box 2010, 26502-2010. Tel: 304-292-3819; Fax: 304-292-6257.
School—St. Francis Central Catholic School, 375 Birch St., Morgantown, 26502-2010. Tel: 304-598-0133.
Mission—Pursglove, Monongalia Co., St. Ursula, (1933). Tel: 304-599-7780.

West Union, Doddridge Co., St. Patrick's (1856), Rev. Donald E. Hile; Sr. Mary Clark, S.S.J., Parochial Coord.
Res., 503 W. Main St., 26456-1129. Tel: 304-873-2547.

White Sulphur Springs, Greenbrier Co., St. Charles Borromeo (1903), Rev. Joseph F. O'Reilly.
Res., P.O. Box 598, 24986. Tel: 304-536-1813. [CEM]
Chapel—Sweet Springs, St. John The Evangelist. (1859). [CEM 2]

Whitesville, Boone Co., St. Joseph the Worker (1958). Closed. See St. Francis De Sales, Beckley.

Williamson, Mingo Co., Sacred Heart (1911), Rev. Leonard A. Smith.
Res., 110 W. Fourth Ave., 25661. Tel: 304-235-2982.
School—126 W. Fourth Ave., 25661. Tel: 304-235-3027.
Sisters 1; Lay Teachers 4; Students 50.

On Duty Outside the Diocese:
Reverend Fathers—
Condron, Patrick A., c/o Divine Word College, 1025 Michigan Ave., N.E., Washington, DC 20017-1895
Cullinane, Jeremiah J., St. Francis College, 2701 Spring St., Fort Wayne, IN 46803. Tel: 219-434-3260; 434-3100
Fryer, Patrick L., CHC-USN, BUMED (CODE006), 23rd and East St., N.W., Washington, DC 20372-5120
Quirk, Kevin M., Casa Santa Maria, Viadell Umilta, 30, Rome, 00187 Italy

---

Absent on Sick Leave:
Reverend Fathers—
Cupp, Edwin
Finnell, John H.
Lee, Michael G.
McCallister, Charles E.
McCormick, Michael

Absent on Leave:
Reverend Fathers—
Wash, Pat J.

Retired:
Reverend Monsignors—
O'Reilly, John L., All Saints Parish, 317 E. Main St., Bridgeport, WV 26330
Staud, Sylvester W., Welty Apartments #411, 1276 National Rd., Wheeling, WV 26003-5743
Wanstreet, Joseph W., Good Shepherd Nursing Home, 159 Edgington Ln., Wheeling, WV 26003
Reverend Fathers—
Arnold, Andrew L., Welty Apartments #402, 1276 National Rd., Wheeling, WV 26003
Bandiera, Colombo F., 442 Ash St., Morgantown, WV 26505-6668
Bell, Milford C., Rte. 1, Box 171, Kearneysville, WV 25430-9727
Beyer, Leroy O., 889 Wess Rd., Mineral Point, PA 15942
Briggs, Everett F., Maple Terrace, P.O. Box 9066, Monongah, WV 26555-9066
Brunner, Frank J., Welty Apartments #404, 1276 National Rd., Wheeling, WV 26003
Campi, Vincent L., P.O. Box 856, Frederick, MD 21701
Cann, Hilarion V., All Saints Parish, 317 E. Main St., Bridgeport, WV 26330-1750
DeMeester, Peter, 1100 Willard Dr., Blacksburg, VA 24060
Dene, Joseph, 6 Cool View Ln., Bridgeport, WV 26330
Dobosz, Emil J., Good Shepherd Nursing Home, 159 Edgington Ln., Wheeling, WV 26003
Gillooly, Patrick J., 517 S. Green St., Berkeley Springs, WV 25411
Gornick, Thomas, 331 Third St., Trafford, PA 15085
Grondalski, Thaddeus J., Welty Apartments #409, 1276 National Rd., Wheeling, WV 26003-5743
Jacobs, Eugene S., Box 54, Loretto, PA 15940
Jamula, Joseph M., The Welty Home, 21 Washington Ave., Wheeling, WV 26003-6297
Lombard, Roy A., Welty Apartments, #405, 1276 National Rd., Wheeling, WV 26003-5743
Lukas, Andrew F., P.O. Box 201, Fairmont, WV 26555-0201
Lydon, Leo B., 236 Parkway Dr., Clarksburg, WV 26301
Maguire, Seamus J., Church of Our Lady of Perpetual Help, Harris Promenade, San Fernando, Trinidad, W.I.
Martis, Albin A., 5639 Midland Dr., Charleston, WV 25306
Nolte, William J., Jr., P.O. Box 2568, Martinsburg, WV 25401-2568
O'Donovan, Donal, Westwood, Chapel St., Dummanway, County Cork, Ireland
O'Loughlin, Eugene P., 362 Redford Ct., Wicklow, Greystone County, Ireland
Rafferty, Thomas A., Box 9066, Monongah, WV 26554
Ralph, John, 1757 State St., Biloxi, MS 39531
Savage, Charles H., 336 Maxwell Ave., Chester, WV 26034-1528
Schmitt, Eugene A., Welty Apartments, #406, 1276 National Rd., Wheeling, WV 26003-5720
Snincak, Stephen A., 2104 Hyde Park St., Sarasota, FL 33579
Werner, Leo E., 324 Kenna Dr., South Charleston, WV 25309
Wojtus, Anthony, P.O. Box 3803, Charleston, WV 24338-3803
Wolan, Stephen J., 1276 National Rd., Wheeling, WV 26003

Permanent Deacons:
Bartemes, David W., Christ the King, Dunbar
Belldina, Louis J., St. John Bosco, Huttonsville
Bischof, Paul H., Jr., St. Vincent de Paul, Wheeling
Goetemann, Gerald B., St. Margaret Mary, Parkersburg
Grant, Russell J.
Hanna, John J., Blessed Sacrament, South Charleston
Higgs, Henry F., St. Margaret Mary, Parkersburg
Iafrate, Albert L.
Kelly, James R., St. Michael, Vienna
Lilly, Robert B.
Lipscomb, Truman A., St. Sebastian, Kingwood
Lynch, John J., Sacred Heart, Charleston
Maher, John F., Christ Our Hope, Harrisville; St. John, St. Marys
Mankowski, Richard W., Sacred Heart of Mary, Weirton
Molinari, Donald F., St. James, Clarksburg
Moses, John T., St. Joseph Cathedral, Wheeling
Mullavey, Edwin T., St. Paul, Weirton
Nedeff, George A., St. Mary, Star City
Prentiss, Joseph J., St. John University, Morgantown
Runions, Cecil Glenn
Santilli, Anthony P., St. James, Clarksburg
Shaw, A. Ray, III, St. Elizabeth, Philippi
Showalter, George B., St. Margaret Mary, Parkersburg
Shultz, John A., St. Mary, Star City
Smith, Paul J., St. James, McMechen
Wise, William Donald, St. Frances de Sales, Beckley
Wojcicki, Ronald J., St. Vincent de Paul, Wheeling
Wuletich, David E., St. Anthony, Charleston
Ziolkowski, John F., St. Francis de Sales, Beckley

INSTITUTIONS LOCATED IN THE DIOCESE

[A] COLLEGES AND UNIVERSITIES

WHEELING. *Wheeling Jesuit University*, 316 Washington Ave., 26003-6295. Tel: 304-243-2000.
For a complete listing, refer to the Colleges and Universities section.

[B] HIGH SCHOOLS, CENTRAL

WHEELING. *Central Catholic High School*, 75-14th St., 26003. Tel: 304-233-1660; Fax: 304-233-3187. Dr. Joseph F. Viglietta, Ph.D., Prin. Sisters of St. Joseph 1; Lay Teachers 25; Students 326.

CHARLESTON. *Charleston Catholic High School*, 1033 Virginia St., E., 25301. Tel: 304-342-8415; Fax: 304-344-3907. Mrs. Debra K. Sullivan, Prin. Sisters 1; Lay Teachers 33; Students 455.

CLARKSBURG. *Harrison Co. Catholic School System. Notre Dame High School*. (Grades 7-12), 127 E. Pike St., 26301. Tel: 304-623-1026; Fax: 304-623-1026. Mr. Louie D. LeRoy, Prin. Lay Teachers 15; Students 181.

HUNTINGTON. *St. Joseph Central Catholic High School*, 600 13th St., 25701. Tel: 304-525-5096; Fax: 304-522-2512. Mr. Tod Faller, Prin.; Rev. Frederick Annie, Pastor. Lay Teachers 14; Students 166.

MCMECHEN. *Bishop Donahue Memorial High School*. (For Marshall Co.), 325 Logan St., 26040. Tel: 304-233-3850; Fax: 304-233-8677. Mr. Alan R. Jafrate, Prin. Lay Teachers 15; Students 129.

PARKERSBURG. *Parkersburg Catholic Junior-Senior High School*, 3201 Fairview Ave., 26104. Tel: 304-485-6341. Mr. Michael R. Hattman, Prin. Lay Teachers 21; Students 236.

WEIRTON. *Madonna High School*, 150 Michael Way, 26062. Tel: 304-723-0545; Fax: 304-723-0564. Mr. Robert Gill, Prin. Lay Teachers 11; Students 169.

[C] HIGH SCHOOLS, PRIVATE

WHEELING. *Mount de Chantal Visitation Academy, Inc.*, 410 Washington Ave., 26003. Tel: 304-233-3771. Day School. (Girls Grades PreK-12, Boys Grades PreK-4). Visitation Nuns. Sisters 6; Lay Teachers 29; Students 180.

[D] ELEMENTARY SCHOOLS, CENTRAL

WHEELING. *Wheeling Catholic Elementary School*, 14th and Byron St., 26003. Tel: 304-233-1515. Consolidation of the following parishes: St. Alphonsus; St. Ladislaus; St. Mary; St. Joseph; Sacred Heart. Sr. Mary Palmer, S.S.J., Prin. Sisters 1; Lay Teachers 8; Students 84.

BENWOOD. *SS. James and John Elementary School*, 52 Seventh St., 26031. Tel: 304-232-1587. Consolidation of the following parishes: St. John, Benwood; St. James, McMechen. Lay Teachers 8; Students 93.

CLARKSBURG. *Harrison County Catholic School System. St. Mary's Central Grade School*. (Grades K-6), 107 E. Pike St., 26301. Tel: 304-622-9831. Consolidation of the following parishes: All Saints, Bridgeport; Immaculate Conception, Clarksburg; St. James, Clarksburg; Our Lady of Perpetual Help, Stonewood; St. Ann, Shinnston; Sacred Heart, Salem. Lay Teachers 15; Students 154.

FAIRMONT. *Fairmont Catholic Grade School*. (Grades K-8), 416-A Madison St., 26554. Tel: 304-363-5313. Consolidation of the following parishes: St. Peter; Immaculate Conception; St. Anthony; St. Joseph. Sr. Mary DiDomenico, S.S.J., Prin. Sisters 1; Lay Teachers 13; Students 217.

MORGANTOWN. *St. Francis de Sales Central Elementary School*, 375 Birch St., 26505. Tel: 304-598-0133. Sr. Patricia Ann Foley, C.S.J. Sisters 2; Lay Teachers 26; Students 390.

PARKERSBURG. *Parkersburg Catholic Elementary School*, 810 Juliana St., 26101. Tel: 304-422-6694. Mr. Kevin Simonton, Prin. Lay Teachers 12; Students 226.

[E] ELEMENTARY SCHOOLS, PRIVATE

MONONGAH. *SS. Peter and Paul Catholic School*, 689 Maple Ter., P.O. Box 9086, 26555-9086. Tel: 304-534-3189. Sisters Auxiliaries of the Apostolate. Mrs. Rachel A. Merrifield, Prin. Sisters 1; Lay Teachers 13; Students 135.

[F] PASTORAL CENTERS

WHEELING. *Paul VI Pastoral Center*, 667 Stone & Shannon Rd., 26003. Tel: 304-277-3300. Miss Antoinette Oliver, Dir. In res., Rev. John H. Finnell. Capacity 72.

CHARLESTON. *John XXIII Pastoral Center*, 100 Hodges Rd., 25314. Tel: 304-342-0507. Deacon John J. Lynch, Dir. Capacity 166.

HUTTONSVILLE. *Bishop Hodges Pastoral Center*, Rte. 1, Box 9D, 26273. Tel: 304-335-2165. Deacon Louis J. Belldina, Dir. Capacity 72.

KEARNEYSVILLE. *Priest Field Pastoral Center*, State Rte. 51, Box 133, 25430. Tel: 304-725-1435. Very Rev. Theodore Midile, T.O.R., V.F., Dir. Capacity 110.

[G] ASSOCIATED SPIRITUAL AND PASTORAL LIFE CENTERS

WHEELING. *Maryhill Hermitage*, 2264 Marshall Ave., 26003.
St. Joseph Center-Mount St. Joseph, Pogue Run Rd., 26003. Tel: 304-232-8160. Sr. Teresa Fleckenstein, S.S.J., Dir. Overnight Capacity 8; Daytime Capacity 25.
St. Thomas More Center, Mailing Address: P.O. Box

230, 26003. 2264 Marshall Ave., 26003. Tel: 304-233-0880. Accommodations for youth retreats, cursillo and area retreats.

Sisters of the Visitation, 410 Washington Ave., 26003. Tel: 304-232-3771. Legal Title: *Sisters of the Visitation of Holy Mary of Mount de Chantal, Inc.*

CHARLESTON. *Cenacle Retreat House*, 1114 Virginia St., E., 25301. Tel: 304-345-0926; Fax: 304-345-8206. Conducted by the Congregation of Our Lady of the Retreat in the Cenacle. Sr. Mary Pellicane, Dir. Sisters 3; Overnight Capacity 28; Daytime Capacity 50.

MORGANTOWN. *Our Lady of Good Counsel Franciscan Friary*, Tyrone Rd., Rte. 7, Box 183, 26505-9199. Tel: 304-594-1714; Fax: 304-594-9247. Rev. Jude J. Mili, O.F.M., S.T.D., Dir. In res., Rev. John Agapito, C.P.M.; Deacon George J. Doerr.

OLD FIELDS. *Holy Spirit Hermitage*, H.C. 66, Box 20, 26845-9201. Rev. Richard B. Hite, M.Ss.A.

[H] GENERAL HOSPITALS

WHEELING. *Bishop Joseph H. Hodges Continuous Care Center*, Medical Park, 26003. Tel: 304-243-3800.
For a complete listing, refer to the Hospitals section.

Wheeling Hospital, Medical Park, 26003. Tel: 304-243-3000.
For a complete listing, refer to the Hospitals section.

BUCKHANNON. *St. Joseph's Hospital of Buckhannon, Inc.*, 1 Amalia Dr., 26201. Tel: 304-473-2000.
For a complete listing, refer to the Hospitals section.

HUNTINGTON. *St. Mary's Hospital of Huntington, Inc.*, 2900 First Ave., 25702. Tel: 304-526-1234.
For a complete listing, refer to the Hospitals section.

[I] NURSING HOMES

WHEELING. *Good Shepherd Nursing Home*, 159 Edgington Ln., 26003. Tel: 304-242-1093.
For a complete listing, refer to the Special Care Facilities section.

[J] HOMES FOR AGED

WHEELING. *Welty Home for the Aged, Inc.*, 21 Washington Ave., 26003-6261. Tel: 304-242-5233.
For a complete listing, refer to the Special Care Facilities section.

[K] HEALTH SERVICES

WHEELING. *Children's Health Care, Inc.*, 1300 Byron St., 26003.
For a complete listing, refer to the Hospitals section.

HUNTINGTON. *Pallottine Health Services, Inc.*, 2900 First Ave., 25702. Tel: 304-526-1028.
For a complete listing, refer to the Hospitals section.

PINEVILLE. *Children's Health Care, Inc.*, Pineville Children's Clinic, Box 1419, 24874. Tel: 304-732-7069.
For a complete listing, refer to the Hospitals section.

RHODELL. *Rhodell Health Clinic*, P.O. Box 158, 25915. Tel: 304-683-4318.
For a complete listing, refer to the Hospitals section.

[L] SOCIAL SERVICE INSTITUTIONS

WHEELING. *Catholic Charities Neighborhood Center*, 125-18th St., P.O. Box 6176, 26003-0713. Tel: 304-232-7157. Directors: Sr. Constance Dodd, S.M.; Bro. David Cooney, F.M.S.

Sisters of St. Joseph House of Hospitality, Inc., 110-15th St., 26003.

Society of St. Vincent de Paul, Society of St. Vincent de Paul Store, 23rd & Main Sts., 26003. Tel: 304-232-4230.

GHENT. *Catholic Center*, 478 Odd Rd., 25843. Tel: 304-787-3523.

HUTTONSVILLE. *Camp Tygart*, Rte. 1, Box 9D, 26273. Tel: 304-335-2130 (In Season); 335-2165 (Out of Season). Diocesan Children's Camp. Mr. Michael Hall, Admin.

NAUGATUCK. *A.B.L.E. Families, Inc.*, P.O. Box 272, 25685. Tel: 304-393-4987.

SALEM. *Nazareth Farm*, Rte. 2, Box 194-3, 26426. Tel: 304-782-2742.

[M] HOMES FOR DEPENDENT CHILDREN

WHEELING. *St. John's Home for Children*, 141 Key Ave., 26003-7412. Tel: 304-242-5633.
For a complete listing, refer to the Special Care Facilities section.

[N] MONASTERIES AND RESIDENCES OF PRIESTS AND BROTHERS

WHEELING. *Webb Farm Residence*, 667 Stone & Shannon Rd., 26003. Tel: 304-277-4670. Rev. Charles E. McCallister.

CHARLESTON. *Capuchins-St. Anthony Friary*, 1000 Sixth St., 25302. Tel: 304-342-2716. Revs. Richard J. Zelik, O.F.M.Cap., Guardian; Kieran Quinn, O.F.M.Cap., Vicar & Ch.; Albert Alexandrunas, O.F.M.Cap.; Melvin R. Averman, O.F.M.Cap.; Philip Hainen, O.F.M.Cap.

HINTON. *Monastery of Christ on the Mountain*, 25951-0429. Tel: 304-466-4782. Discalced Carmelite Hermits. Revs. Kevin Culligan, O.C.D., Dir.; Bonaventure Lussier, O.C.D.; Regis Jordan, O.C.D.; Bro. Gilbert Tovares, O.C.D.

[O] CONVENTS AND RESIDENCES FOR SISTERS

WHEELING. *Mt. St. Joseph*, Pogue Run Rd., 26003. Tel: 304-232-8160; Fax: 304-232-1404. Motherhouse of the Sisters of St. Joseph. Sr. Christine Riley, S.S.J., Pres. Professed Sisters 110.
Attended by Wheeling Jesuit University.

North America Union Sisters of Our Lady of Charity, Inc., 141 Edgington Ln., 26003. Tel: 304-242-7070. Legal Title: *North American Union Sisters of Our Lady of Charity, Inc.* Sr. Martha Teresa Gomez, Local Supr. Sisters 21.

St. Joseph's Convent, 1322 Eoff St., 26003. Tel: 304-232-1232. Sr. Rosina Bell, S.S.J., Coord. Sisters 5.

Sisters of the Visitation, Mount de Chantal, 410 Washington Ave., 26003. Tel: 304-232-1283. Legal Title: *Sisters of the Visitation of Holy Mary of Mount de Chantal, Inc.* Sr. Mary Grace Flynn, V.H.M., Supr. Professed Sisters 29.
Attended by Wheeling Jesuit College.

MONONGAH. *SS. Peter and Paul Convent*, 689 Maple Ter., P.O. Box 9086, 26555. Tel: 304-534-3081. General Motherhouse of the Sisters Auxiliaries of the Apostolate. Sr. Angela Marie Pastore, S.A.A., Supr. Professed Sisters 6.
Attended by Holy Spirit Church.

[P] FOUNDATIONS

WHEELING. *Carmelite Monastery of Wheeling*, P.O. Box 230, 26003-0030.

Central Catholic High School Educational Foundation, Inc., 75-14th St., 26003.

Common Fund for Schools, P.O. Box 230, 26003.

Medical Park Foundation, Inc., One Medical Park, 26003.

Sisters of St. Joseph Charitable Fund, Inc., Mount St. Joseph, Pogue Run Rd., 26003. Tel: 304-232-8160. Sr. Christine Riley, S.J.

Sisters of St. Joseph of Wheeling Foundation, Inc., Pogue Run Rd., 26003; Fax: 304-232-1404.

CLARKSBURG. *Harrison County Catholic Education Foundation, Inc.*, 126 E. Pike St., 26301-2720.

PARKERSBURG. *De Sales Heights Monastery of the Visitation.* c/o P.O. Box 230, Wheeling, 26003.

Parkersburg Catholic Schools Foundation, Inc., 3201 Fairview Ave., 26104-2111.

WEIRTON. *Society of Friends of Madonna High School, Inc.*, Park Ave., 26062.

[Q] NEWMAN CENTERS

CHARLESTON. *University of Charleston Newman Center*, 25364.

ATHENS. *Concord College Newman Center*, 301 Vermillion, P.O. Box 447, 24712. Tel: 304-425-3664. Rev. Lawrence Wrenn.

BETHANY. *St. John Fisher Catholic Chapel*, 201 Richardson St., Box W, 26032. Tel: 304-829-4622. Rev. Richard W. Shoda.

BUCKHANNON. *West Virginia Wesleyan College Newman Center*, 35 Franklin St., Box 848, 26201-0848. Tel: 304-473-8000. Rev. James McCafferty, S.M.

FAIRMONT. *Fairmont State College Newman Center*, 1101 Locust Ave., 26554. Tel: 304-363-2300. Rev. Jude Molnar, T.O.R.

HUNTINGTON. *Marshall Newman Center*, 1609 Fifth Ave., 25703. Tel: 304-525-4618. Rev. William J. Petro.

PHILIPPI. *Newman Center Alderson-Broaddus College*, College Hill, Rte. 3, Box 257, 26416. Tel: 304-457-2641. Rev. Damian P. Drass, T.O.R.

WEST LIBERTY. *West Liberty State College, St. Thomas Aquinas Campus Ministry.* Mailing Address: Box W, Bethany, 26032. 134 Chatham St., 26074. Tel: 304-336-7476;829-4622 (Bethany). Rev. Richard W. Shoda.

[R] MISCELLANEOUS

WHEELING. *Mid Ohio Valley - S.J. Health Service, Inc*, Mount St. Joseph, Poque Run Rd., 26003.

Saint Francis Health System, Inc., Mount Saint Joseph, Poque Run Rd., 26003.

Saint Francis Hospital, Inc., Mount Saint Joseph, Poque Run Rd., 26003.

St. Joseph's Hospital of Parkersburg, Inc., Mount St. Joseph, Poque Run Rd., 26003. Tel: 304-232-8160. Sr. Christine Riley, S.J.

WEBSTER SPRINGS. *The Catholic Committee of Appalachia*, P.O. Box 662, 26288. Tel: 304-847-7215.

[S] CHILD CARE CENTERS

WHEELING. *Holy Family Child Care Center*, 161 Edgington Ln., 26003. Tel: 304-242-5222.
For a complete listing, refer to the Special Care Facilities section.

CLARKSBURG. *Madonna Day Care Center*, 444 E. Pike St., 26031. Tel: 304-622-4453.
For a complete listing, refer to the Special Care Facilities section.

RELIGIOUS INSTITUTES OF MEN REPRESENTED IN THE DIOCESE

For further details refer to the corresponding bracketed number in the Religious Institutes of Men or Women section.

[0330]—*Brothers of the Christian Schools.*—F.S.C.
[0470]—*The Capuchin Friars.*—O.F.M.Cap.
[1000]—*Congregation of the Passion.*—C.P.
[0260]—*Discalced Carmelite Fathers.*—O.C.D.
[0520]—*Franciscan Friars.*—O.F.M.
[0570]—*Glenmary Home Missioners.*—Glmy.
[]—*Heralds of Good News Missionary Society.* (Eluru, India).—H.G.N.
[0690]—*Jesuit Fathers and Brothers.*—S.J.
[0780]—*Marist Fathers.*—S.M.
[0590]—*Missionaries of the Holy Apostles.*—M.Ss.A.
[1030]—*Paulist Fathers.*—C.S.P.
[0420]—*Society of the Divine Word.*—S.V.D.
[0560]—*Third Order Regular of St. Francis.*—T.O.R.

RELIGIOUS INSTITUTES OF WOMEN REPRESENTED IN THE DIOCESE

[2100]—*Congregation of Humility of Mary.*—C.H.M.
[3110]—*Congregation of Our Lady of the Retreat in the Cenacle (Eastern Province).*—R.C.
[1730]—*Congregation of the Sisters of the Third Order of St. Francis.*—O.S.F.
[0760]—*Daughters of the Charity of St. Vincent de Paul (Emmitsburg Province).*—D.C.
[0960]—*Daughters of Wisdom.*—D.W.
[1070-02]—*Dominican Sisters.*—O.P.
[1070-14]—*Dominican Sisters.*—O.P.
[1105]—*Dominican Sisters of Hope.*—O.P.
[1430]—*Franciscan Sisters of Our Lady of Perpetual Help.*—O.S.F.
[2420]—*Marist Missionary Sisters.*—S.M.S.M.
[2430]—*Marist Sisters.*—S.M.
[3070]—*North American Union Sisters of Our Lady of Charity.*—N.A.U.-O.L.C.
[3150]—*Pallottine Missionary Sisters.*—S.A.C.
[2970]—*School Sisters of Notre Dame.*—S.S.N.D.
[1680]—*School Sisters of St. Francis.*—O.S.F.
[3590]—*Servants of Mary (Servite Sisters).*—O.S.M.
[3830-08]—*Sister of St. Joseph.* (Cleveland).—C.S.J.
[0140]—*Sisters Auxiliaries of the Apostolate.*—S.A.A.
[0570]—*Sisters of Charity of Seton Hill, Greensburg, PA.*—S.C.
[0590]—*Sisters of Charity of St. Elizabeth, Convent Station.*—S.C.
[0990]—*Sisters of Divine Providence (St. Peter Province).*—C.D.P.
[1000]—*Sisters of Divine Providence of Kentucky.*—C.D.P.
[2360]—*Sisters of Loretto at the Foot of the Cross.*—S.L.
[2575]—*Sisters of Mercy of the Americas.*—R.S.M.
[3000]—*Sisters of Notre Dame de Namur (Chesapeake, Ohio, California Provs.).*—S.N.D.deN.
[3720]—*Sisters of St. Anne.*—S.S.A.
[1630]—*Sisters of St. Francis of Penance and Christian Charity.*—O.S.F.
[1650]—*Sisters of St. Francis of Philadelphia.*—O.S.F.
[1530]—*Sisters of St. Francis of the Congregation of Our Lady of Lourdes.*—O.S.F.
[3830-05]—*Sisters of St. Joseph.*—C.S.J.
[3830-13]—*Sisters of St. Joseph.*—C.S.J.
[3830-17]—*Sisters of St. Joseph.*—S.S.J.
[3860]—*Sisters of St. Joseph of Cluny.*—S.J.C.
[2980]—*Sisters of the Congregation de Notre Dame (Connecticut Province).*—C.N.D.
[2110]—*Sisters of the Humility of Mary.*—H.M.
[3270]—*Sisters of the Most Precious Blood, O'Fallon, MO.*—C.PP.S.
[3220]—*Sisters of the Poor Child Jesus.*—P.C.J.
[1760]—*Sisters of the Third Order of St. Francis of Penance and Charity.*—O.S.F.
[2160]—*Sisters, Servants of the Immaculate Heart of Mary.* (Scranton).—I.H.M.
[4060]—*Society of the Holy Child Jesus.*—S.H.C.J.
[4120-03]—*Ursuline Nuns of the Congregation of Paris.*—O.S.U.
[4160]—*Vincentian Sisters of Charity.*—V.S.C.
[4190]—*Visitation Nuns.* (Wheeling, WV).—V.H.M.

DIOCESAN CEMETERIES

WHEELING. *Mount Calvary* (1872), 1685 National Rd., 26003-5599. Tel: 304-242-0460. Rev. Charles B. Teufel, Dir.

NECROLOGY

† Arkle, Robert V., Wheeling, WV, St. Joseph's Cathedral. —Died May 24, 1996.

† Ballouz, Marcel A., Hutington, WV, Sacred Heart. —Died June 21, 1996.

† James, Gerard A., Buckhannon, WV, Holy Rosary. —Died Feb. 9, 1996.

† Schwarten, Paul J., (Retired). —Died Dec. 5, 1995.

Diocese of Wichita

(Dioecesis Wichitensis)

Most Reverend

EUGENE J. GERBER, D.D.

Bishop of Wichita; ordained May 19, 1959; appointed Bishop of Dodge City October 16, 1976; ordained December 14, 1976; installed December 15, 1976; appointed Bishop of Wichita November 23, 1982; installed February 9, 1983. *Res., 307 E. Central, Wichita, KS, 67202.*

ESTABLISHED AUGUST 2, 1887.

Square Miles 20,021.

New boundaries established by Apostolic Letters dated May 19, 1951. Bounded on the west by the west lines of Rice, Reno, Kingman and Harper counties, south by Oklahoma, east by Missouri, and north by the north lines of Bourbon, Allen, Woodson, Greenwood, Morris, Marion, McPherson and Rice Counties in Kansas.

For legal titles of parishes and diocesan institutions, consult the Chancery Office.

The Chancery: 424 N. Broadway, Wichita, KS, 67202. Tel : 316-269-3900; Fax: 316-269-3936.

STATISTICAL OVERVIEW

Personnel	
Bishop	1
Priests: Diocesan Active in Diocese	87
Priests: Active Outside Diocese	9
Priests: Diocesan in Foreign Missions	2
Priests: Retired, Sick or Absent	31
Number of Diocesan Priests	129
Religious Priests in Diocese	8
Ordinations:	
Diocesan Priests	1
Transitional Deacons	2
Permanent Deacons in Diocese	2
Total Sisters	414
Parishes	
Parishes	95
With Resident Pastor:	
Resident Diocesan Priests	66
Resident Religious Priests	1
Without Resident Pastor:	
Administered by Priests	28
Professional Ministry Personnel:	
Sisters	15
Lay Ministers	13
Welfare	
Catholic Hospitals	5
Total Assisted	477,751
Health Care Centers	2
Total Assisted	25,581
Homes for the Aged	2
Total Assisted	240
Specialized Homes	1
Total Assisted	54
Special Centers for Social Services	1
Total Assisted	14,022
Residential Care of Disabled	1
Total Assisted	5
Other Institutions	1
Total Assisted	3,787
Educational	
Diocesan Students in Other Seminaries	19
Total Seminarians	19
Colleges and Universities	1
Total Students	1,984
High Schools, Diocesan and Parish	4
Total Students	1,919
Elementary Schools, Diocesan and Parish	33
Total Students	7,524
Catechesis/Religious Education:	
High School Students	2,887
Elementary Students	8,311
Total Students Under Catholic Instruction	22,644
Teachers in the Diocese:	
Sisters	43
Lay Teachers	487
Vital Statistics	
Receptions into the Church:	
Infant Baptism Totals	2,447
Adult Baptism Totals	353
Received into Full Communion	381
First Communions	2,348
Confirmations	1,876
Marriages:	
Catholic	422
Interfaith	371
Total Marriages	793
Deaths	794
Total Catholic Population	105,172
Total Population	910,544

Former Bishops—Most Rev. JAMES O'REILLY, D.D., Bishop-Elect; died July 26, 1887.—Most Rev. JOHN JOSEPH HENNESSY, D.D., cons. Nov. 30, 1888; died July 13, 1920.—Most Rev. AUGUSTUS JOHN SCHWERTNER D.D., ord. June 12, 1897; cons. June 8, 1921; installed June 22, 1921; died Oct. 2, 1939.—Most Rev. CHRISTIAN HERMAN WINKELMANN, S.T.D., ord. June 11, 1907; cons. Auxiliary Bishop of St. Louis, Nov. 30, 1933; installed March 5, 1940; died Nov. 18, 1946.—Most Rev. MARK K. CARROLL, S.T.D., ord. June 10, 1922; appt. Feb. 15, 1947; cons. April 23, 1947; installed May 6, 1947; resigned Sept. 27, 1967; died Jan. 12, 1985.—Most Rev. LEO C. BYRNE, D.D., ord. June 10, 1933; appt. Titular Bishop of Sabidia and Auxiliary of St. Louis, May 21, 1954; cons. June 29, 1954; transferred to Wichita, "cum jure successionis" 1961; appt. Apostolic Administrator, Feb. 25, 1963; transferred to St. Paul and Minneapolis, Sept. 27, 1967; died Oct. 21, 1974.—Most Rev. DAVID M. MALONEY, S.S., S.T.L., J.C.D., former Bishop of Wichita; ord. Dec. 8, 1936; appt. Titular Bishop of Ruspae Auxiliary of Denver, Nov. 9, 1960; cons. Jan. 4, 1961; transferred to Wichita, Dec. 6, 1967; resigned July 16, 1982; died Feb. 15, 1995.

Vicars General—Rev. RONALD M. GILMORE, S.T.L., V.G., *424 N. Broadway, Wichita, 67202.*

Chancery Office—424 N. Broadway, Wichita, 67202. Tel: 316-269-3900; Fax: 316-269-3936.

Vicar for Priests—Rev. JOHN P. GILSEMAN, J.C.L.

Vicar General & Moderator of Diocesan Curia, Vicar for Pastoral Planning & Services—Rev. RONALD M. GILMORE, S.T.L., V.G.

Chancellor—Rev. ROBERT E. HEMBERGER, J.C.L.

Vice Chancellor—Rev. JOHN P. LANZRATH, S.T.L.; Sr. JACINTA LANGLOIS, A.S.C.

College of Consultors—Revs. DWIGHT BIRKET, Chm. JOHN P GILSENAN, J.C.L.; Rev. Msgr. CHARLES F. WALSH; Revs. SHERMAN ORR, Sec. DWIGHT BIRKET; Rev. Msgr. DENIS DOUGHERTY; Revs. TERRANCE MCCLOSKEY, C.S.S.R.; RONALD M. GILMORE, S.T.L., V.G.; ROBERT E. HEMBERGER, J.C.L.; THOMAS MCGREAD; THOMAS SCALETTY; DANIEL SPEXARTH; PAUL COAKLEY.

Parish Priests Consultors—Rev. Msgr. CHARLES F. WALSH; Revs. JOHN P. GILSENAN; CHARLES W. REGAN.

Tribunal—424 N. Broadway, Wichita, 67202. Tel: 316-269-3960.

Officialis—Rev. ROBERT E. HEMBERGER, J.C.L.

Vice Officialis—Rev. RICHARD F. STUCHLIK, S.T.L.

Judges—Revs. STEPHEN R. BAXTER, J.C.L.; JOHN P. GILSENAN, J.C.L.; MICHAEL E. NOLAN, J.C.L.; ROBERT E. HEMBERGER, S.T.L.

Defenders of the Bond—Revs. J. PATRICK MANNION, J.C.L.; RICHARD F. STUCHLIK, S.T.L.; DOUGLAS CAMPBELL, J.C.L.

Procurator-Advocates—Sr. JACINTA LANGLOIS, A.S.C.

Notaries—Mrs. ROBERTA RAU; Mrs. CLAUDINE WALD.

Deans—Coffeyville: Vacant; Kingman: Rev. IVAN C. ECK, V.F.; Newton: Rev. Msgr. CHARLES F. WALSH, V.F.; Parsons: Rev. Msgr. VINCENT HOGAN, V.F.; Pittsburg: Rev. THOMAS J. STROOT, V.F.; North Sedgwick: Rev. THOMAS MCGREAD; South Sedgwick: Rev. ARTHUR A. BUSCH.

Continuing Education of the Clergy Committee—Revs. BRIAN EGAN; JOSEPH GILE; JOHN P. GILSENAN, J.C.L., Dir. ROBERT E. HEMBERGER, J.C.L., Prog. Dir. TERRENCE MCCLOSKEY, C.SS.R.; SHAWN MCKNIGHT; MICHAEL E. NOLAN, J.C.L.; KENNETH J. SCHUCKMAN; KENNETH VAN HAVERBEKE.

Diocesan Offices and Directors

Catholic Diocese of Wichita—Most. Rev. EUGENE J. GERBER, D.D., Pres.

Apostleship of Prayer—6900 E.45th St., N., Wichita, 67226.

Catholic Charities—Ms. JANET VALENTE PAPE, Dir., *437 N. Topeka, Wichita, 67202.* Tel: 316-264-8344.

Catholic Life Center—424 N. Broadway, Wichita, 67202. Tel: 316-269-3900.

Cemeteries—Mr. JEROME GERBER, *424 N. Broadway, Wichita, 67202.* Tel: 316-269-3900.

Commission for Communications—Rev. ARTHUR A. BUSCH, *3205 Grand Ave., Wichita, 67218.* Tel: 316-682-1415.

Cursillo—Rev. JEROME A. BEAT, *2007 Arkansas, Wichita, 67203.* Tel: 316-262-4683.

Diocesan Apostolate for Previously Married Catholics—Rev. GERARD PECHT, C.SS.R., *Spiritual Life Center, 7100 E. 45th St., N., Wichita, 67226.* Tel: 316-744-0167.

Wichita Diocesan Charismatic Services—Rev. LEON J. KERSCHEN, Moderator, *314 S. Jefferson, Iola, 66749.* Tel: 316-365-3454. Rev. JAMES S. MAINZER, Assoc. Moderator, *St. James Church, 813 State St., Augusta, 67010.* Tel: 316-775-2155.

Diocesan Apostolate to Engaged Encounter—Rev. MICHAEL SCHEMM, *1807 Stevens, Parsons, 67357.*

Catholic Marriage Preparation-Evenings for Engaged—Rev. H. PATRICK MALONE, *1425 N. Chautauqua, Wichita, 67214.* Tel: 316-682-8712.

Diocesan Apostolate to Marriage Encounter—Rev. DANIEL J. SPEXARTH, *335 N. Annie St., R.R. #9, Wichita, 66861.* Tel: 316-522-4728.

Diocesan Apostolate to Widowed Catholics—Rev. GERALD PECHT, C.SS.R.

Diocesan Building Commission—Revs. DWIGHT BIRKET; PAUL COAKLEY; KENT HEMBERGER; ROBERT HEMBERGER; THOMAS SCALETTY; Mr. WILMER FREUND; Mr. FRED HERMES; Mr. DANIEL LOUGHMAN; Mr. KENT NOLLER; Mrs. THERESA WHITE.

Diocesan Commission on Christian Unity—Vacant.

Diocesan Council of Catholic Women—Rev. REINHARD C. ECK, Moderator, *424 N. Broadway, Wichita, 67202.*

Diocesan Director of Stewardship and Finance—Mr. DANIEL L. LOUGHMAN, *424 N. Broadway, Wichita, 67202.* Tel: 316-269-3900.

Diocesan Finance Committee—Most. Rev. EUGENE J. GERBER, D.D.; RONALD M. GILMORE, S.T.L., V.G.; Mr. DANIEL CARNEY; Mr. JOE DELLASEGA; Mr. RICHARD KERSCHEN; Mr. DANIEL L. LOUGHMAN; Mr. PATRICK E. O'SHAUGNESSY; Ms. MARILYN PAULY; Mr. DALE WIGGINS; Mr. PERRY WINTER.

Diocesan Liaison for Health Affairs—Rev. ROBERT E. HEMBERGER, J.C.L., *424 N. Broadway, Wichita, 67202.* Tel: 316-269-3962.

Diocesan Office for Ministry with Persons with Disabilities—Sr. M. VERONICE BORN, C.S.J., Dir., *Holy Family Center, 619 S. Maize Rd., Wichita, 67209.* Tel: 316-722-8159.

Education—Mr. ROBORT VOBORIL, Supt., *424 N. Broadway, Wichita, 67202.* Tel: 316-269-3950.

Office of Religious Education, C.C.D.—Ms. PATRICIA A. YATES, Dir., *424 N. Broadway, Wichita, 67202.* Tel: 316-269-3940.

Special C.C.D. Services—Vacant. Tel: 316-686-7171.

Latin America Missions and Volunteer Services—Sr. ANACLETA SCHUETTE, A.S.C., Dir., *424 N. Broadway, Wichita, 67202.* Tel: 316-269-3946.

Legion of Mary—Rev. JOHN C. REINKEMEYER, *638 Ave. D. W., Kingman, 67068.* Tel: 316-532-5440.

Liaison to Interfaith Rural Life Committee—Vacant.

Marriage and Family Life Services—Coordinated by Spiritual Life Center.

Natural Family Planning Office—Ms. MONIKA KING, Dir., *1148 S. Hillside, Ste. 10, Wichita, 67211.* Tel: 316-685-6776; Fax: 316-685-7540.

Newspaper: "The Catholic Advance" Diocesan Weekly—Mr. CHRISTOPHER M. RIGGS, Editor; Mr. DANIEL LOUGHMAN, Business Mgr., *424 N. Broadway, Wichita, 67202.* Tel: 316-269-3965.

Office of Development and Planned Giving—Mr. LOUIS N. BASSO, *424 N. Broadway, Wichita, 67202.* Tel: 316-269-3900.

Office of Pastoral Life and Ministry—*424 N. Broadway, Wichita, 67202.* Tel: 316-269-3947.

Office of Worship—RAWN HARBOR, Dir., *424 N. Broadway, Wichita, 67202.* Tel: 316-269-3945.

Presbyteral Council—Rev. Msgr. CHARLES F. WALSH, Chm.; Revs. ROBERT E. HEMBERGER, J.C.L., Vice Chm. SHERMAN ORR, Sec. DWIGHT BIRKET; DANIEL SPEXARTH; PAUL COAKLEY; THOMAS SCALETTY; JOHN P. GILSENAN, J.C.L.; RONALD M. GILMORE, S.T.L., V.G.; THOMAS MCGREAD; DENIS DOUGHERTY; TERRENCE MCCLOSKEY, C.SS.R.

Propagation of the Faith and Holy Childhood Assn.—Sr. ANACLETA SCHUETTE, A.S.C., Dir., *424 N. Broadway, Wichita, 67202.* Tel: 316-269-3946.

Respect Life Office—Vacant, *424 N. Broadway, Wichita, 67202.* Tel: 316-269-3948.

Retreats—Rev. TERRENCE MCCLOSKEY, C.SS.R., Dir., *Spiritual Life Center, 7100 E. 45th St. N., Wichita, 67226.* Tel: 316-744-0167.

Rural Life Conference—Vacant.

Social Service—Ms. JANET VALENTE PAPE, *437 N. Topeka, Wichita, 67202.* Tel: 316-264-8344.

Society of St. Vincent de Paul—Rev. KENT HEMBERGER.

Vocations—Rev. MATTHEW C. MCGINNESS, Dir., *424 N. Broadway, Wichita, 67202.*

Wichita Diocesan Hispanic Council—Rev. ROBERT PALACIOZ, *424 N. Broadway, Wichita, 67202.* Tel: 316-269-3900.

Youth and Young Adult Ministry—Ms. CHRISTINE SANTNER, Dir., *424 N. Broadway, Wichita, 67202.* Tel: 316-269-3930.

CLERGY, PARISHES, MISSIONS AND PAROCHIAL SCHOOLS

CITY OF WICHITA
(Sedgwick County)

1—CATHEDRAL OF THE IMMACULATE CONCEPTION (1887), Revs. William M. Carr, Rector; Harold W. McCormick; Sr. Renee Kirmer, A.S.C., Pastoral Assoc. & D.R.E. In res., Rev. Joseph M. Gile.
Res., 307 E. Central Ave., 67202. Tel: 316-263-6574. [JC]
Catechesis/Religious Programs—Students 94.

2—ALL SAINTS (1946), Revs. Arthur A. Busch; Bernard X. Gorges.
Res., 3205 Grand St., 67218. Tel: 316-682-1415. [JC]
School—Tel: 316-682-6021; Fax: 316-682-8734. Toni Bryant, Prin.
Lay Teachers 18; Students 333.
Catechesis/Religious Programs—Tel: 316-686-9736. Sr. Lorene Orth, A.S.C., D.R.E.
Students 85.

3—BLESSED SACRAMENT (1927), Revs. John P. Gilsenan; W. Shawn McKnight. In res., Rev. James Wilkinson.
Res., 124 N. Roosevelt Ave., 67208. Tel: 316-682-4557. [JC]
School—Tel: 316-684-3752; Fax: 316-687-1082. Cindy Honton, Prin.
Sisters of St. Joseph 5; Lay Teachers 23; Students 443.
Catechesis/Religious Programs—Cindy Honton, D.R.E.
Students 65.
Convent—138 N. Roosevelt, 67208. Tel: 316-684-3977.

4—CHRIST THE KING (1950), Rev. Charles W. Regan. In res., Revs. Sherman A. Orr; David W. Linnebur.
Res., 4411 Maple Ave., 67209. Tel: 316-943-4353. [JC]
School—4501 Maple Ave., 67209. Tel: 316-943-4353. Richard Sleefe, Prin.
Sisters, Adorers of the Blood of Christ 3; Lay Teachers 13; Students 244.

5—CHURCH OF THE MAGDALEN (1950), Revs. Daniel L. Vacca; Kenneth S. VanHaverbeke; Sr. Gael Gensler, O.S.F., Pastoral Assoc.
Res., 457 S. Woodlawn St., 67218. Tel: 316-683-6516.
School—Tel: 316-683-5181; Fax: 316-683-9245. Eva Williams, Prin.
Lay Teachers 22; Students 516.
Catechesis/Religious Programs—Students 215.

6—CHURCH OF THE RESURRECTION (1965), Rev. Paul S. Coakley.
Res., 4910 N. Woodlawn, 67220. Tel: 316-744-2776; Fax: 316-744-3027.
School—(Grades Prek-5). Tel: 316-744-3576. Sr. Marietta Conrardy, C.S.J., Prin.
Lay Teachers 7; Students 153.
Catechesis/Religious Programs—D.R.E.: Greg Davied; Kelly Davied.
Students 67.

7—HOLY SAVIOR (1948) (African American), Rev. H. Patrick Malone; Deacon Ronald Ealey.
Res., 1425 N. Chautauqua, 67214. Tel: 316-682-8712; Fax: 316-682-8712.
School—Tel: 316-684-2141; Fax: 316-682-4797. Gerald Fields, Prin.
Lay Teachers 11; Students 125.
Catechesis/Religious Programs—Students 57.

8—OUR LADY OF GUADALUPE. Closed. For sacramental records contact St. Margaret Mary, Wichita.

9—OUR LADY OF PERPETUAL HELP (1927), Revs. Floyd McKinney; Jerome A. Beat. Pastoral Assocs.: Sr. Clotilde Orduna; Sr. Virginia Alfaro; Sr. Guadalupe de la Rosa.
Res., 2351 N. Market St., 67219. Tel: 316-838-8373. [JC]
Catechesis/Religious Programs—Tel: 316-832-1670. D.R.E.: Sherri Ramirez; Johnny & Becky Palacioz.
Students 95.
Convent—2354 N. Market St., 67219. Tel: 316-838-3190.
Congregation of the Daughters of the Passion of Our Lord Jesus Christ and the Sorrows of Mary 3.
Parish Center—2409 N. Market St., 67219. Tel: 316-838-5750.

10—ST. ANNE (1955), Rev. Kent A. Hemberger; Mary Beth Steiner, Pastoral Assoc.; Vicki Albright, Business Mgr.
Office: 2801 S. Seneca, 67217-2399. Tel: 316-522-2383; Fax: 316-524-2370.
School—(Grades K-8). Tel: 316-522-6131.
Sisters 4; Lay Teachers 12; Students 255.
Catechesis/Religious Programs—Kevin Swinicki, D.R.E.
Students 224.

11—ST. ANTHONY (1887) (German), Rev. Hung Q. Pham.
Residence and Mailing: 325 Ohio, 67214. Tel: 316-269-4641.

12—ST. ELIZABETH ANN SETON (1982), Revs. James J. Billinger; Stuart M. Smeltzer.
Res., 645 N. 119th St. W., 67235. Tel: 316-721-1686; Fax: 316-721-1723. [CEM]
School—Tel: 316-721-5693. Mrs. Janet Eaton, Prin.
Lay Teachers 23; Students 514.
Catechesis/Religious Programs—Tel: 316-721-1686.
Students 377.

13—ST. FRANCIS OF ASSISI (1959), Revs. Thomas McGread, V.F.; Thomas Hoisington; Daryl Befort.
Res., 861 N. Socora, 67212. Tel: 316-722-4404; Fax: 316-722-4738.
School—Tel: 316-722-5171; Fax: 316-722-0492. Mr. Larry Conrardy, Prin.
Adorers of the Blood of Christ 4; Lay Teachers 34; Students 776.
Catechesis/Religious Programs—Barbara King, D.R.E.
Students 534.

14—ST. JOSEPH (1886), Revs. Daniel Andree, C.SS.R.; Walter Karrer, C.SS.R.; Edward Morgan, C.SS.R.
Res., 145 S. Millwood Ave., 67213. Tel: 316-262-1877; Fax: 316-262-5250. [JC]
School—Tel: 316-265-7962; Fax: 316-265-7963. Mrs. Sheila Shaw, Prin.
Sisters 2; Lay Teachers 12; Students 198.
Catechesis/Religious Programs—Mrs. Pat Pilens, D.R.E.
Students 140.
Convent—128 S. Vine Ave., 67213. Tel: 316-262-4419.

15—ST. JUDE (1958), Rev. Thomas F. Scaletty; Sr. Mary Francis Morriss, Pastoral Assoc.
Res., 3130 Amidon Ave., 67204. Tel: 316-838-1963.
School—Tel: 316-838-0800; Fax: 316-838-0866. Mrs. Candace Buser, Prin.
Lay Teachers 12; Students 235.
Catechesis/Religious Programs—Debby Dean, D.R.E.
Students 188.

16—ST. MARGARET MARY (1954), Rev. Dwight Birket.
Res., 2701 Pattie, 67216. Tel: 316-262-1821; Fax: 316-267-1707.
School—(Grades Pre K-8). Tel: 316-267-4911; Fax: 316-267-1707. Mary Samms, Prin.
Lay Teachers 12; Students 371.
Catechesis/Religious Programs—Tel: 316-267-0120. Anne Schock, D.R.E.
Students 77.

17—ST. PATRICK (1895), Rev. Jerome A. Beat.
Res., 2007 Arkansas Ave., 67203. Tel: 316-262-4683; Fax: 316-262-6217. [JC]
School—2023 Arkansas Ave., 67203. Tel: 316-262-4071. Mr. Donald C. Wilson, Prin.
Sisters of St. Joseph 1; Lay Teachers 13; Students 231.
Catechesis/Religious Programs—Linda F. Gosche, D.R.E.
Students 60.
Convent—2045 Arkansas Ave., 67203. Tel: 316-267-0021.

18—ST. PAUL PARISH (1970), Rev. Matthew C. McGinness.
Res., 1810 N. Roosevelt, 67208. Tel: 316-684-6896; Fax: 316-684-2679.

19—ST. THOMAS AQUINAS (1957), Revs. John J. O'Shea; John Sherlock; Ned Blick; Sr. Malachy Stockemer, O.P., Pastoral Assoc. & D.R.E.
Res., 1321 Stratford Ln., 67206. Tel: 316-683-6569; Fax: 316-683-1028.
School—Tel: 316-684-9201; Fax: 316-684-7421. Dr. Janyce Rooney, Prin.
Sisters 1; Lay Teachers 34; Students 644.
Catechesis/Religious Programs—Students 95.

20—ST. VINCENT DE PAUL (1955), Rev. Michael E. Baldwin.
Res., 123 N. Andover Rd., Andover, 67002. Tel: 316-733-1423; Fax: 316-733-1687.
Catechesis/Religious Programs—Ann Hughes, D.R.E.
Students 633.

OUTSIDE THE CITY OF WICHITA

Aleppo, Sedgwick Co., Immaculate Conception (1900), Revs. Philip J. Allen; John J. Curran.
Church—25741 W. 13th St., N., Garden Plain, 67050. Tel: 316-535-2210. [CEM]

Andale, Sedgwick Co., St. Joseph (1890) (German), Rev. Reinhard C. Eck.
Res., 318 Rush Ave., Box 8, 67001. Tel: 316-444-2196. [CEM]
Catechesis/Religious Programs—Mary Jo Hieger, D.R.E.
Students 255.

Anthony, Harper Co., Sacred Heart (1934), Rev. Robert J. Hartmann; Sr. Josephine O'Gorman, C.S.J., Pastoral Min.
Res., 1023 W. Main, P.O. Box 218, Harper, 67058. Tel: 316-896-7886.

Arkansas City, Cowley Co., Sacred Heart (1886), Rev. Francis Cox.
Res., 325 S. C St., P.O. Box 895, 67005. Tel:

316-442-0566.
School—308 S. B St., Tel: 316-442-6550. Mr. Dean McGrath, Prin.
Sisters of the Adorers of the Blood of Christ 1; Lay Teachers 6; Students 94.
Catechesis/Religious Programs—Becky Hewitt, D.R.E.
Students 94.

Arma, Crawford Co., St. Joseph (1934), Rev. Donald Thissen.
Res., 310 W. South St., P.O. Box 948, 66712. Tel: 316-347-4525.
Catechesis/Religious Programs—(Grades 1-5). Students 12.

Augusta, Butler Co., St. James (1879), Rev. James S. Mainzer.
Res., 813 State St., P.O. Box 250, 67010. Tel: 316-775-2155. [CEM]
School—Tel: 316-775-5721. Mrs. Sharon Dolan, Prin.
Sisters 1; Lay Teachers 5; Students 120.
Catechesis/Religious Programs—Tel: 316-775-3222. Tama Dutton, D.R.E.
Students 201.

Baxter Springs, Cherokee Co., St. Joseph (1868), Rev. Charles Middleton.
Res., 307 Galena, P.O. Box 296, Galena, 66739. Tel: 316-783-1693.

Burns, Marion Co., Immaculate Conception. Closed. For sacramental records contact Holy Family, Marion.

Bushton, Rice Co., Holy Name of Jesus (1878), Rev. James J. Roth.
Res., 67427. Tel: 316-562-3427. [CEM]
Catechesis/Religious Programs—Students 61.

Caldwell, Sumner Co., St. Martin of Tours (1888), Rev. Patrick Larkin.
Res., 428 N. Main, 67022. Tel: 316-845-6763. [JC]

Caney, Montgomery Co., Sacred Heart (1914), Rev. Edward J. Steinberger.
Res., P.O. Box 276, Moline, 67353-0276. Tel: 316-647-3577.

Capaldo, Crawford Co., St. Alice. Closed. For sacramental records contact Sacred Heart, Frontenac.

Castleton, Reno Co., St. Agnes, Rev. Gerald F. Rowan.
Res., 211 E. Fifth, Hutchinson, 67501. Tel: 316-665-0475.

Cedar Vale, Chautauqua Co., St. Joseph. Closed. For inquiries for parish records contact the Chancery.

Chanute, Neosho Co., St. Patrick (1873), Rev. Michael J. Maybrier; Sr. Connie Haug, O.P., Pastoral Min. & D.R.E.
Res., 315 S. Malcolm, 66720. Tel: 316-431-2921. [CEM]
School—(Grades PreK-5). Tel: 316-431-4020. Sr. Sylvana Schulte, Prin.
Sisters 2; Lay Teachers 5; Students 94.
Catechesis/Religious Programs—Tel: 316-431-3165.
Students 170.

Chase, Rice Co., St. Mary (1888) (German), Rev. Joseph P. Slomski, Admin.
Res., P.O. Box 306, 67524. Tel: 316-938-2382. [CEM][JC]

Cherokee, Crawford Co., St. Anastasia. Closed. For sacramental records contact Our Lady of Lourdes, Pittsburg.

Cherryvale, Montgomery Co., St. Francis Xavier's (1871), Rev. Kevin Trayers.
Res., 202 S. Liberty St., 67335. Tel: 316-336-2337. [CEM]

Chetopa, Labette Co., Sacred Heart (1873), Rev. John S. Zich.
Res., 1112 W. Third., Box 193, Oswego, 67356. Tel: 316-795-2262. [CEM]

Chicopee, Crawford Co., St. Barbara. Closed. For sacramental records contact Our Lady of Lourdes, Pittsburg.

Clonmel, Sedgwick Co., St. John (1879), Rev. Leroy Linnebur.
Res., 18630 W. 71st St., South Viola, 67149. Tel: 316-545-7171; 794-2784; Fax: 316-794-2784. [CEM]
Parish Hall: Tel: 316-545-7211.
Catechesis/Religious Programs—D.R.E.: Sylvia Kerschen; Art Gentry.
Students 93.

Coffeyville, Montgomery Co., Holy Name (1869), Rev. Leo A. Kerschen.
Res., 408 Willow St., 67337. Tel: 316-251-0475. [CEM]
School—409 Willow St., 67337. Tel: 316-251-0480. Sr. Janice Roberts, Prin.
Sisters of St. Joseph 2; Lay Teachers 7; Students 157.
Catechesis/Religious Programs—Evelyn Goad, D.R.E.
Students 96.

Columbus, Cherokee Co., St. Rose (1887), Rev. Chrysostom Ah Maung (Burma).
Res., 115 W. Walnut St., 66725. Tel: 316-429-2639.
Catechesis/Religious Programs—Tel: 316-674-8587.
Students 54.

Colwich, Sedgwick Co., Sacred Heart (1901), Rev. Msgr. Denis R. Dougherty.
Res., 310 S. Fifth St., P.O. Box 578, 67030. Tel: 316-796-1224. [CEM]
Catechesis/Religious Programs—Students 341.

Conway Springs, Sumner Co., St. Joseph (1886), Rev. Robert B. Wachter.
Res., 217 N. Sixth St., Box 157, 67031. Tel: 316-456-2276. [CEM]
School—Tel: 316-456-2270. Ms. Michaelita J. Wasinger, Prin.
Lay Teachers 7; Students 175.
Catechesis/Religious Programs—D.R.E.: Mike Ternes; Lillian Palsmeier.
Students 210.

Council Grove, Morris Co., St. Rose (1883), Rev. Paul J. Oborny.
Res., 316 Spencer St., 66846. Tel: 316-767-6412. [CEM]
Catechesis/Religious Programs—Tel: 316-767-6706. Rita Buchanan, D.R.E.
Students 150.

Cunningham, Kingman Co., Sacred Heart (1908) (German), Rev. John Miller.
Res., P.O. Box 216, 67035. Tel: 316-298-2601; Fax: 316-298-2926. [CEM]
Catechesis/Religious Programs—Tel: 316-298-4038. Linda Kerschen, D.R.E.
Students 94.

Danville, Harper Co., Immaculate Conception (1883), Rev. Robert J. Hartmann; Sr. Josephine O'Gorman, C.S.J., Pastoral Assoc.
Res., 1023 W. Main, P.O. Box 218, Harper, 67058. Tel: 316-896-7886.

Derby, Sedgwick Co., St. Mary's (1954), Rev. H. Jay Setter; Sr. Janice Grochowsky, C.S.J., Pastoral Assoc.
Res., P.O. Box 325, 722 N. Derby, 67037. Tel: 316-788-5525; Fax: 316-788-1577.
School—700 N. Derby, 67037. Tel: 316-788-3151. Mr. Charles Monckton, Prin.
Sisters of St. Joseph 2; Lay Teachers 12; Students 253.
Catechesis/Religious Programs—Tel: 316-788-1253.
Students 298.

El Dorado, Butler Co., St. John (1915), Rev. Msgr. Charles F. Walsh, V.F.
Res., 302 N. Denver Ave., 67042. Tel: 316-321-4796.
Catechesis/Religious Programs—Tel: 316-321-4933. Karen May, D.R.E.
Students 264.

Erie, Neosho Co., St. Ambrose (1915), Rev. Msgr. Vincent Hogan.
Res., 519 N. Main, 66733. Tel: 316-244-3216.

Eureka, Greenwood Co., Sacred Heart (1881) (German), Rev H. Michael Peltzer.
Res., 514 N. Elm St., 67045. Tel: 316-583-7100.
Catechesis/Religious Programs—Students 51.
Missions—Hamilton, Greenwood Co., St. John, Hamilton, 66853.; Madison, Greenwood Co., St. Teresa Of Avila, Madison, 66860. Tel: 316-437-2504.

Florence, Marion Co., St. Patrick. Closed. Merged with St. Mark, Marion; St. John Nepomucene, Pilsen; and Holy Redeemer, Tampa to form Holy Family, Marion.

Fort Scott, Bourbon Co., Mary Queen of Angels (1860), Rev. Brian Bebak.
Res., 716 S. Eddy St., P.O. Box 271, 66701. Tel: 316-223-4340. [CEM]
School—(Grades 1-5). Tel: 316-223-6060. Thomas M. Gorman, Prin.
Lay Teachers 6; Students 77.
Catechesis/Religious Programs—Tel: 316-223-0668. Debbie Martin, D.R.E.
Students 75.

Fredonia, Wilson Co., Sacred Heart (1906), Rev. Stephen R. Baxter.
Res., 428 N. 12th St., 66736. Tel: 316-378-2694. [CEM]
Catechesis/Religious Programs—Tel: 316-378-3565. Judy Puckett, D.R.E.
Students 70.

Frontenac, Crawford Co., Sacred Heart (1891) (Italian), Rev. Patrick G. York.
Res., 100 S. Cherokee St., 66763. Tel: 316-231-7747.
Parish Hall: 102 S. Cherokee St., 66763. Tel: 316-232-2354. [CEM]
Catechesis/Religious Programs—Students 96.

Fulton, Bourbon Co., St. Patrick. Closed. For sacramental records contact Mary Queen of Angels, Fort Scott.

Galena, Cherokee Co., St. Patrick (1879), Rev. Charles Middleton.
Res., 307 Galena, P.O. Box 296, 66739. Tel: 316-783-1693.

Garden Plain, Sedgwick Co., St. Anthony (1901), Revs. Philip J. Allen; John J. Curran.
Res., 615 N. Main, 67050. Tel: 316-535-2247; Fax: 316-531-8820. [CEM]
Catechesis/Religious Programs—Tel: 316-535-2593.
Students 269.

Girard, Crawford Co., St. Michael (1925), Rev. Donald R. Thissen.
Res., 106 N. Western, 66743. Tel: 316-724-8717.
Catechesis/Religious Programs—Joan Davied, D.R.E.
Students 132.

Greenbush, Crawford Co., St. Aloysius. Closed. For sacramental Records contact St. Michael, Girard.

Halstead, Harvey Co., Sacred Heart of Jesus (1874), Rev. James R. O'Shea.
Res., 419 Poplar, 67056. Tel: 316-835-2173. [JC]
Catechesis/Religious Programs—Tel: 316-835-2083. Louise Weber, D.R.E.
Students 156.

Hamilton, Greenwood Co., St. John (1888) (German), Rev. H. Michael Peltzer.
Res., 514 N. Elm St., Eureka, 67045. Tel: 316-583-7100.

Harper, Harper Co., St. Patrick (1882), Rev. Robert J. Hartmann; Sr. Josephine O'Gorman, C.S.J., Pastoral Assoc.
Res., 1023 W. Main, P.O. Box 218, 67058. Tel: 316-896-7886.
Catechesis/Religious Programs—Karen Dunkelberger, D.R.E.
Students 40.

Haysville, Sedgwick Co., St. Cecilia (1959), Rev. Andy Kuykendall.
Res., 1802 W. Grand, 67060. Tel: 316-524-7801; Fax: 316-524-6183.
School—(Grades K-6) 1912 W. Grand, 67060. Tel: 316-522-0461. Sr. Eloise Hertel, O.P., Prin.
Sisters 2; Lay Teachers 7; Students 153.
Catechesis/Religious Programs—D.R.E.: JoAnne Audley; Marsha Miller.
Students 140.

Humboldt, Allen Co., St. Joseph (1867), Rev. Michael Maybrier; Sr. Cecilia Leiker, A.S.C., Pastoral Min. & D.R.E.
Church—514 Central St., 66748. Tel: 316-473-2129. [CEM]
Res., 424 S. Central Ave., Chanute, 66720. Tel: 316-431-3165.
Catechesis/Religious Programs—Tel: 316-473-2739.
Students 90.

Hutchinson, Reno Co., Holy Cross (1957), Rev. Brian J. Egan.
Res., 2631 Independence Rd., 67502. Tel: 316-665-5163. [JC]
School—2633 Independence Rd., 67502. Tel: 316-665-6168. Mr. Harry Heppler, Prin.
Lay Teachers 7; Students 175.
Catechesis/Religious Programs—Students 243.

Our Lady of Guadalupe (1927), Rev. Colin J. Boor.
Res., 612 S. Maple, South Hutchinson, 67505-2099. Tel: 316-662-6443.
Catechesis/Religious Programs—Mr. & Mrs. Martin Vieyra, D.R.E.
Students 90.

St. Teresa (1897), Rev. Richard Stuchlik, S.T.L. In res., Rev. Gerald Rowan.
Res., 211 E. Fifth St., 67501. Tel: 316-662-7812. [CEM]
School—215 E. Fifth St., 67501. Tel: 316-662-5601. Mr. John Rodriguez, Prin.
Lay Teachers 8; Students 210.
Catechesis/Religious Programs—Students 140.

Independence, Montgomery Co., St. Andrew (1869), Rev. Kevin Trayers.
Res., 210 N. Fourth St., 67301. Tel: 316-331-1789. [CEM]
School—Tel: 316-331-2870. Kristie Blaes, Prin.
Lay Teachers 8; Students 112.
Catechesis/Religious Programs—Students 88.

Iola, Allen Co., St. John (1897), Rev. Leon J. Kerschen.
Office: 310 S. Jefferson Ave., 66749. Tel: 316-365-2277.
Res., 310 S. Jefferson Ave., 66749. Tel: 316-365-3454. [CEM][JC]
Catechesis/Religious Programs—Tel: 316-365-6041. Mrs. Charles A. Heffern (Bernita), D.R.E.
Students 177.

Kingman, Kingman Co., St. Patrick (1885) (Irish), Rev. John C. Reinkemeyer.

Res., 638 Ave. D W., 67068. Tel: 316-532-5440. [JC]
School—Tel: 316-532-5338. Mr. James Gales, Prin. Lay Teachers 10; Students 165.
Catechesis/Religious Programs—Helena Arnold, D.R.E.
Students 96.

Liberty, Montgomery Co., All Saints. Closed. For inquiries for parish records contact the Chancery.

Lindsborg, McPherson Co., St. Bridget of Sweden, Rev. Douglas Campbell.
Church—206 W. Swensson, P.O. Box 268, 67456. Tel: 913-227-3588.
Res., 520 E. Northview, McPherson, 67460. Tel: 316-241-0821.
Catechesis/Religious Programs—Mary Patrick, D.R.E.
Students 35.

Little River, Rice Co., Holy Trinity (1885), Rev. James N. Hoagland.
Res., 415 St. Francis St., Lyons, 67554. Tel: 316-257-3503.
Catechesis/Religious Programs—Tel: 316-489-6436. Cynthia Wright, D.R.E.
Students 46.

Lyons, Rice Co., St. Paul (1927), Rev. James N. Hoagland.
Res., 415 St. Francis St., 67554. Tel: 316-257-3503.
Catechesis/Religious Programs—Tel: 316-257-3314. Cheryl Steinert, D.R.E.
Students 108.

Madison, Greenwood Co., St. Teresa of Avila (1954) (German), Rev. H. Michael Peltzer.
Res., 514 N. Elm St., Eureka, 67045. Tel: 316-583-7100; 437-2504 (Church).

Marion, Marion Co., Holy Family 1992. Parish formed from merger of St. Mark, Marion; St. John Nepomucene, Pilsen; St. Patrick, Florence; and Holy Redeemer, Tampa. Rev. Stephen Gronert.
Residence and Mailing: 415 N. Cedar St., 66861. Tel: 316-382-3422. [CEM 4]
Catechesis/Religious Programs—Tel: 316-382-3369. Rose Davidson, D.R.E.
Students 230.
Mission—Tampa, Marion Co., Holy Redeemer, 66861.

McPherson, McPherson Co., St. Joseph (1880), Rev. Douglas Campbell.
Res., 520 E. Northview, 67460. Tel: 316-241-0821.
School—Tel: 316-241-3913. Richard Sleefe, Prin. Lay Teachers 6; Students 107.
Catechesis/Religious Programs—Linda Reese, D.R.E.
Students 180.

Moline, Elk Co., St. Mary's (1899), Rev. Edward J. Steinberger.
Res., Box 276, 67353-0276. Tel: 316-647-3577. [CEM]

Mount Vernon, Kingman Co., St. Rose (1911) (German-Irish), Rev. Ivan C. Eck.
Res., 13015 E. Maple Grove Rd., Mount Hope, 67108. Tel: 316-444-2210. [CEM]
Catechesis/Religious Programs—Tel: 316-542-3990.
Students 77.

Mulberry, Crawford Co., St. Gabriel. Closed. For sacramental records contact Sacred Heart, Frontenac.

Mulvane, Sumner Co., St. Michael the Archangel (1948), Rev. John P. Lanzrath.
Res., 545 E. Main, 67110. Tel: 316-777-4221.
Catechesis/Religious Programs—Tel: 316-777-0444. Karen Oblinger, D.R.E.
Students 190.

Neodesha, Wilson Co., St. Ignatius (1873), Rev. Stephen R. Baxter.
Res., P.O. Box 186, 66757. Tel: 316-378-2694. [CEM]
Catechesis/Religious Programs—Tel: 316-325-3244.
Students 40.

Newton, Harvey Co., St. Mary (1872), Rev. Kenneth J. Schuckman.
Res., 106 E. Eighth St., 67114. Tel: 316-283-0459. [CEM]
School—Tel: 316-283-1974. Mr. Richard Guy, Prin. Sisters of St. Joseph 3; Lay Teachers 8; Students 192.
Catechesis/Religious Programs—Tel: 316-283-4991. Mrs. Marie Morford, D.R.E.
Students 130.

Our Lady of Guadalupe (1919) (Hispanic), Rev. Robert Palacioz.
Res., 415 S. Ash St., 67114. Tel: 316-283-3499. [JC]
Catechesis/Religious Programs—D.R.E.: Sharon Lampman; Joe Ramirez.
Students 153.

Ost, Reno Co., St. Joseph (1880) (German), Rev. Ivan C. Eck.
Res., 13015 E. Maple Grove Rd., Mount Hope, 67108. Tel: 316-444-2210. [CEM]
Catechesis/Religious Programs—Tel: 316-444-2637.
Students 90.

Oswego, Labette Co., Mother of God (1878), Rev. John S. Zich.
Res., 1112 W. Third., Box 193, 67356. Tel: 316-795-2262. [JC]
Catechesis/Religious Programs—Students 65.

Oxford, Sumner Co., St. Mary (1872) (French), Rev. Michael E. Nolan.
Res., 412 E. Eighth St., Winfield, 67156. Tel: 316-221-3610. [JC]
Catechesis/Religious Programs—Myra Jacobs, D.R.E.
Students 40.

Parsons, Labette Co., Mary Queen of Peace (1909). Closed. For inquiries for parish records contact St. Patrick, Parsons.

St. Patrick (1876), Rev. Michael J. Schemm.
Res., 1807 Stevens Ave., 67357. Tel: 316-421-6762. [CEM 2][JC]
School—Parsons Catholic Elementary School. See Elementary School, Interparochial under Institutions Located in the Diocese. Tel: 316-421-0710.
Catechesis/Religious Programs—Students 265.

Pilsen, Marion Co., St. John Nepomucene. Closed. Merged with St. Mark, Marion; St. Patrick, Florence; and Holy Redeemer, Tampa to form Holy Family, Marion.

Piqua, Woodson Co., St. Martin (1884) (German), Rev. Ser Khu Wilson.
Res., Rte. 1, Box 83, 66761. Tel: 316-468-7441. [CEM]

Pittsburg, Crawford Co., Our Lady of Lourdes (1881), Revs. Thomas J. Stroot; Robert W. McElwee; Samuel J. Pinkerton.
Res., 916 N. Locust St., P.O. Box 214, 66762. Tel: 316-231-2135; Fax: 316-231-4804. [CEM]
School—St. Mary's Elementary, 213 E. Ninth, 66762. Tel: 316-231-6941. Mr. Frank Crespino, Prin.
Sisters of St. Joseph 1; Lay Teachers 23; Students 381.
High School—St. Mary-Colgan High School, 212 E. 9th, P.O. Box 266, Pittsburgh, 66762. Tel: 316-231-4690.
Sisters of St. Joseph 1; Priests 1; Lay Teachers 14; Students 158.
Catechesis/Religious Programs—Denise Loy, D.R.E.
Students 137.
Convent—821 N. Locust St., 66762. Tel: 316-231-6014.

St. Leo, Kingman Co., St. Leo the Great (1902) (German), Rev. John Miller.
Res., 8035 S.W. 160 Ave., Nashville, 67112. Tel: 316-246-5370. [CEM]
School—Tel: 316-246-5387. Sr. Dorothy Felder, Prin.
Sisters of St. Dominic 1; Lay Teachers 3; Students 31.

St. Mark's, Sedgwick Co., St. Mark (1876) (German), Rev. John Patrick Mannion.
Res., R.F.D. 1, Colwich, 67030. Tel: 316-796-1604. [CEM]
Catechesis/Religious Programs—Mary Ann Hensley, D.R.E.
Students 180.

St. Paul, Neosho Co., St. Francis (1847), Rev. Msgr. Vincent Hogan.
Res., 208 Washington St., P.O. Box 216, 66771-0216. Tel: 316-449-2224. [CEM 2]
Catechesis/Religious Programs—Tel: 316-449-2672. Mary Frances Casey, D.R.E.
Students 200.

Scammon, Cherokee Co., St. Bridget's (1868), Rev. Chrysostom Ah Maung.
Res., 155 W. Walnut, Columbus, 66725. Tel: 316-429-2639. [CEM]
Catechesis/Religious Programs—Students 55.

Schulte, Sedgwick Co., St. Peter's (1905), Rev. Daniel J. Spexarth.
Res., 335 N. Annie St., R.R. 24, Wichita, 67215. Tel: 316-522-4728. [CEM]
School—Tel: 316-524-6585. Sr. Mary Rose Engel, Prin.
Sisters of St. Dominic 2; Lay Teachers 15; Students 264.
Catechesis/Religious Programs—Helen Ruth Welsby, D.R.E.
Students 163.
Convent—134 W. Peter St., R.R. 24, Wichita, 67215. Tel: 316-524-4259.

Sedan, Chautauqa Co., St. Robert Bellarmine (1962), Rev. Edward J. Steinberger.
Res., P.O. Box 276, Moline, 67353-0276. Tel: 316-647-3577.

Strong City, Chase Co., St. Anthony of Padua (1880), Rev. Paul J. Oborny.
Res., 316 Spencer, Council Grove, 66846. Tel: 316-767-6412. [CEM]
Catechesis/Religious Programs—Jeanette Black, D.R.E.
Students 61.

Tampa, Marion Co., Holy Redeemer. Now an oratory of Holy Family, Marion.

Walnut, Crawford Co., St. Patrick. Closed. For sacramental records contact St. Francis Church, St. Paul.

Waterloo, Kingman Co., St. Louis (1881) (German-Irish), Rev. Ivan C. Eck.
Res., 13015 E. Maple Grove Rd., Mt. Hope, 67108. Tel: 316-444-2210. [CEM]

Weir, Cherokee Co., Sacred Heart. Closed. For sacramental records contact St. Rose of Lima, Columbus.

Wellington, Sumner Co., St. Anthony (1884). All info is for both St. Anthony and St. Rose. Rev. Andrew J. Seiler; Sr. Connie Beiriger, C.S.J., Pastoral Assoc. & D.R.E.
Mailing Address: 210 North B St., 67152. Tel: 316-326-2522.
Catechesis/Religious Programs—Tel: 316-326-3480.
Students 341.

St. Rose of Lima (1949) (Hispanic), Rev. Andrew J. Seiler; Sr. Connie Beiriger, C.S.J., Pastoral Assoc. & D.R.E.
Mailing Address: 210 N. B St., Wellingon, 67152. Tel: 316-326-2522.
Church—1205 E. Harvey, 67152. Tel: 316-326-3572.
Catechesis/Religious Programs—Tel: 316-326-3480.
Students 341.

West Mineral, Cherokee Co., Immaculate Conception. Closed. For sacramental records contact St. Rose of Lima, Columbus.

Willowdale, Kingman Co., St. Peter's (1884) (German), Rev. John P. Miller.
Res., P.O. Box 86, Zenda, 67159. Tel: 316-243-5451. [CEM]

Winfield, Cowley Co., Holy Name (1878), Rev. Michael E. Nolan.
Res., 412 E. Eighth St., 67156. Tel: 316-221-3610. [JC]
School—Tel: 316-221-0230. Mrs. Linda Gross, Prin. Lay Teachers 6; Students 81.
Catechesis/Religious Programs—Tel: 316-221-4053. Fran Parks, D.R.E.
Students 80.

Yates Center, Woodson Co., St. Joseph (1957), Rev. Ser Khu Wilson.
Res., 107 E. Bell St., 66783. Tel: 316-625-2103.
Catechesis/Religious Programs—Students 90.

Zenda, Kingman Co., St. John (1908) (German), Rev. John P. Miller.
Res., P.O. Box 86, 67159. Tel: 316-243-5451. [CEM]
Catechesis/Religious Programs—Anna Jane Goetz, D.R.E.
Students 62.

Chaplains of Public Institutions

WICHITA. *Sedgwick County Adult Local Detention Facility*. Rev. Daniel J. Spexarth.
Veterans Administration Hospital. Vacant.

HUTCHINSON. *Kansas State Industrial Reformatory*. 612 S. Maple, South Hutchinson, 67505. Tel: 316-662-6443. Rev. Colin J. Boor.

On Duty Outside the Diocese:
Reverend Fathers—
Conley, James, Ministry in Rome, Italy
Hotze, John, Graduate Studies, Washington, DC
Jackson, James
Joyce, Raymond
Kocour, Robert F., Apartado 407, Barquisimeto, Venezuela
Machado, Jose, Apartado 407, Barquisimeto
Nolan, Joseph T
O'Connor, Charles
Quach, Binh The
Spencer, Robert, Apartado 407, Barquisimeto

Military Chaplains:
Reverend Fathers—
Schmid, Wayne L., P.O. Box 729, Fort Knox, KY 40121

Leave of Absence:
Reverend Fathers—
Bradley, Randall

Retired:
Reverend Monsignors—

Gerstenkorn, Joseph J., 629 S. Vassar, Wichita, KS 67218
Hertel, Herbert N., 3214 Zimmerly, Wichita, KS 67218
Lampe, Irvin F., 13014 La Terraza Dr., Sun City West, AZ 85375
Malone, Quintin J., 6900 E. 45th St., N., Wichita, KS 67226
Schmidt, George N., 6900 E. 45th St., N., Wichita, KS 67226
Smith, Charles A., 914 Torrey Pines Dr., Pasa Robles, CA 93446
Tonne, Arthur, 520 N. Freeborn, Marion, KS 66861. Tel: 316-382-3166

Reverend Fathers—
Bieberle, Victor, 29 Tiburon Way, Hot Springs, AR 71909
Colbert, C. F., 6900 E. 45th St., N., Wichita, KS 67226
Dinan, John, 1915 N. Porter, Apt. A-78, Wichita, KS 67203
Downs, Leroy J., Catholic Care Center, 6700 E. 45th St. N., Wichita, KS 67226
Finnegan, Peter J., 6900 E. 45th St., N., Wichita, KS 67226
Freed, Robert, 3330 E. Bellaire St., Wichita, KS 67218
Garrahy, Michael, 6900 E. 45th St., N., Wichita, KS 67226
Harvey, Charles K., 6900 E. 45th St., N., Wichita, KS 67226
Hay, Francis J., 6900 E. 45th St., N., Wichita, KS 67226
Metcko, Leo E., 6900 E. 45th St., N., Wichita, KS 67226
Mullen, John, P.O. Box 246, Halstead, KS 67056
Mulvihill, Daniel R., RR 10, Box 14, Apt. 4, Joplin, MO 64804
O'Hare, Donal J. q, P.O. Box 3758 (Beach Station), Vera Beach, FL 32964
O'Leary, David A., 6900 E. 45th St., N., Wichita, KS 67226
O'Malley, Michael W.
Pepe, Robert F., 4 Circle Dr., Port Duncan, Afton, OK 74331
Rusteika, John B., 5 Carballo Pl., Hot Springs Village, AR 71909
Spexarth, James, R.R. 1, P.O. Box 30, Marion, KS 66861
Stremel, Adolph, c/o P.A. Sullivan, 801 Main St., Victoria, KS 67671
Walsh, Ulich
York, Edward, 46 Leicester Dr., Bella Vista, AR 72714

INSTITUTIONS LOCATED IN THE DIOCESE

[A] COLLEGES AND UNIVERSITIES

WICHITA. *Kansas Newman College*, 3100 McCormick Ave., 67213. Tel: 316-942-4291; Fax: 316-942-4483. *For a complete listing, refer to the Colleges and Universities section.*

[B] HIGH SCHOOLS, DIOCESAN

WICHITA. *Bishop Mark K. Carroll High School*, 8101 W. Central, 67212. Tel: 316-722-2390; Fax: 316-722-6670. Leticia C. Nielsen, Prin.; Rev. Sherman A. Orr. Tel: 316-943-4353. Priests 1; Sisters 7; Lay Teachers 42; Students 792.

Kapaun Mt. Carmel High School, 8506 E. Central, 67206. Tel: 316-634-0315. David Evans, Prin.; Rev. John Sherlock, Chap. Sisters 2; Priests 1; Lay Teachers 53; Students 779.

HUTCHINSON. *Trinity High School*, 1400 E. 17th, 67501. Tel: 316-662-5800. Dr. Richard Robl, Pres. of Hutchinson Catholic Schools; Mr. Brian Cordel, Prin.; Rev. Richard Stuchlik, Chap. Sisters 1; Lay Teachers 15; Students 190.

The Trinity High School Education Endowment Fund, 1400 E. 17th, 67501. c/o Eugene J. Gerber, 424 N. Broadway, Wichita, 67202.

PITTSBURG. *St. Mary-Colgan High School*, 212 E. 9th St., 66762. Tel: 316-231-4690. Rev. Thomas J. Stroot, Admin.; Mr. Patrick Forbes, Prin. Sisters of St. Joseph 1; Lay Teachers 14; Students 158.

[C] ELEMENTARY SCHOOLS, INTERPAROCHIAL

PARSONS. *Parsons Catholic Elementary School*, 1831 Stevens, 67357. Sr. Jacklyn Duncan, Prin. Consolidated from St. Mary's School and St. Patrick's School, Parsons. Sisters of St. Joseph 2; Lay Teachers 8; Students 118.

[D] SPECIAL EDUCATION

WICHITA. *Art of Learning Center*, 201 S. Millwood, 67213. Tel: 316-265-6853. Sr. Sibyllina Mueller, O.P., Dir. Speech, Language, Reading Therapy. Total Assisted 2,350; Total Staff 3.

[E] GENERAL HOSPITALS

WICHITA. *St. Joseph Health Corporation*, 929 N. St. Francis, 67214. Tel: 316-268-5000.
For a complete listing, refer to the Hospitals section.

Via Christi Regional Medical Center, Inc., 929 N. St. Francis, 67214. Tel: 316-268-5000.
For a complete listing, refer to the Hospitals section.

Via Christi Rehabilitation Hospital, Inc., Lourdes Campus, 1151 N. Rock Rd., 67206. Tel: 316-634-3400.
For a complete listing, refer to the Hospitals section.

FORT SCOTT. *Mercy Hospital*, 821 Burke St., 66701. Tel: 316-223-7057; Fax: 316-223-5327.
For a complete listing, refer to the Hospitals section.

INDEPENDENCE. *Mercy Hospitals of Kansas-Independence*, 800 W. Myrtle St., 67301. Tel: 316-331-2200.
For a complete listing, refer to the Hospitals section.

PITTSBURG. *Mount Carmel Medical Center; Mount Carmel Foundation*, Centennial and Rouse, 66762. Tel: 316-231-6100.
For a complete listing, refer to the Hospitals section.

[F] HOMES FOR AGED

WICHITA. *Catholic Care Center, Inc.*, 6700 E. 45th St., N., 67226. Tel: 316-744-2020.
For a complete listing, refer to the Special Care Facilities section.

Georgetown Village, Inc., 1655 Georgetown St., 67218.
For a complete listing, refer to the Special Care Facilities section.

MULVANE. *Villa Maria*, 116 S. Central, 67110. Tel: 316-777-1129; Fax: 316-777-4406.
For a complete listing, refer to the Special Care Facilities section.

[G] MONASTERIES AND RESIDENCES FOR PRIESTS AND BROTHERS

WICHITA. *Priests Retirement Center*, 6900 E. 45th St., N., 67226. Tel: 316-744-2020. Fred Hermes, CEO. Residents 14.

Redemptorist Community, 7100 E. 45th St., N., 67226. Tel: 316-744-0167; Fax: 316-744-8072. Revs. J. Terrence McCloskey, C.SS.R., Supr.; William J. Parker, C.SS.R.; Gerard J. Pecht, C.SS.R.; James W. White, C.SS.R. Residents 4; Staff 4.

Redemptorist Mission House, 145 S. Millwood Ave., 67213. Tel: 316-262-1877. Revs. Daniel Andree, C.SS.R., Supr.; Walter Karrer, C.SS.R.; Edward Morgan, C.SS.R. Residents 3; Staff 3.

[H] CONVENTS AND RESIDENCES FOR SISTERS

WICHITA. *Blessed Sacrament Sisters of Charity*, 6547 St. James Pl., 67226. Tel: 316-744-8768; Fax: 316-744-3447. Sr. Michaela Park. Sisters 4.

Dominican House of Studies, 201 S. Millwood, 67213. Tel: 316-267-4551. Sisters of the Third Order of St. Dominic (Congregation of the Immaculate Conception, Great Bend, KS). Residents 9.

Medical Sisters of St. Joseph-United States Foundation, 3435 E. Funston, 67218. Tel: 316-686-4746. Sr. Audrey, Supr. Professed Sisters 3.

Mt. St. Mary Convent, Motherhouse and Novitiate of the Sisters of St. Joseph, 3700 E. Lincoln, 67218-2099. Tel: 316-686-7171; Fax: 316-689-4056. Sr. Veronice Born, C.S.J., Pres.; Rev. Robert E. Hemberger, Chap. Professed Sisters 220; Sisters in Temporary Profession 2.
Other Residences: 1103 S. Yale, 67218. 1124 S. Yale, 67218. 1144 S. Yale, 67218. 3427 E. Funston, 67218. 3333 Bellaire Ct., 67218-4807. 619 S. Maize Rd., 67209-1399. 7627 E. 37th N. #3701, 67226. 3427 E. Funston, 67218. KS, 1144 S. Yale. 1206 Regal, 67217. 1742 S. Spruce, 67211-4622. 1103 S. Yale, 67218-3013. 2045 Arkansas, 67203-2568. 138 N. Roosevelt, 67208-3717.

Provincialate of the Sisters Adorers of the Blood of Christ, 1400 S. Sheridan, 67213. Tel: 316-943-1203; Fax: 316-943-1427. Sr. Charlotte Rohrbach, A.S.C., Supr.; Rev. Thomas Welk, C.PP.S., Chap. Professed Sisters 236; Postulants 1; Novices 1.

Sisters of the Immaculate Heart of Mary of Wichita, Inc. (I.H.M.), 605 N. Woodchuck, 67212. Tel: 316-722-9316 Sr. Giovanni Oliveri, I.H.M., Supr. Professed Sisters 9; Novices 4.

[I] RETREAT HOUSES

WICHITA. *Spiritual Life Center*, 7100 E. 45th St., N., 67226. Tel: 316-744-0167; Fax: 314-744-8072. Rev. J. Terrence McCloskey, C.SS.R., Dir. Associate Directors: Rev. Joseph Gile; Philip St. Romain; Rev. Gerard J Pecht, C.SS.R.; Sr. Carmen Echevarria, S.C.L.; Rev. James W. White, C.SS.R.; Rhonda Lohkamp, R.C.I.A.; Linda Sargent, Prog. Dir.; Rev. William Parker, C.SS.R. Residents 4; Staff 21.

[J] COMMUNITY CENTERS

WICHITA. *Catholic Charities*, 437 N. Topeka, 67202. Tel: 316-264-8344; Fax: 316-264-4442. Staff 67.

Counseling Services, 425 N. Topeka, 67202. Tel: 316-263-6941. Counseling 650; Adoption 112.

Harvest House, 437 N. Topeka, 67202. Tel: 316-264-8344. Staff 2; Centers 25; Members Assisted 1,600.

Anthony Family Shelter (and Emergency Services), 256 N. Ohio, 67214. Tel: 316-264-7233. Staff 10; Individuals Assisted 4,437.

Southeast Kansas Counseling, Pius X Catholic Center, 201 E. Cleveland, Pittsburgh, 66762. Tel: 316-231-3638. Staff 2; Families Assisted 135.

Adult Day Services, 1209 Indiana, 67214. Tel: 316-264-9723. Total Assisted 110.

St. Dismas Missioners, 437 N. Topeka, 67202. Tel: 316-264-8344. Volunteers visit jails and prisons.

Harbor House, P.O. Box 3759, 67201. Staff 12; Women & Children Assisted 363; Victims Advocate Program 3,984.

**Center of Hope*, 400 N. Emporia, 67202-2514. Tel: 316-267-0222; Fax: 316-267-7778. Sponsored by Adorers of the Blood of Christ. Sr. Stella Rosenhamer, A.S.C., Dir. Tel: 316-267-0222; 267-7778 (Fax). Staff 3; Total Assisted 3,787.

Foster Grandparent Program, 437 N. Topeka, 67202. Tel: 316-264-8344. Ms. Janet Valente-Pape, Exec. Dir. Provides 75,043 hours of service. Staff 1; Assisted 367.

Guadalupe Clinic, 940 S. St. Francis, 67211. Tel: 316-264-8974. Ms. Patricia Kastens, Dir. Staff 6; Total Assisted 24,102.

Refugee Services, 437 N. Topeka, 67202. Tel: 316-264-0197. Ms. Janet Valente-Pape, Exec. Dir. Staff 2; Total Assisted 1,007.

[K] NEWMAN CENTERS

WICHITA. *Wichita State University*, 1810 N. Roosevelt, 67208. Tel: 316-684-6896; Fax: 316-684-2679. Rev. Matthew C. McGinness, Chap.

PITTSBURG. *St. Pius X Center (Pittsburg State University)*, 301A E. Cleveland, 66762. Tel: 316-235-1138. Rev. Patrick York, Chap.

[L] CATHOLIC CHARITIES

WICHITA. *Catholic Charities, Inc.*, 437 N. Topeka, 67202. Tel: 316-264-8344; Fax: 316-264-4442.

Southeast Kansas Counseling, Piux X Catholic Center, 201 E. Cleveland, Pittsburg, 66762. Tel: 316-231-3638.

Adult Day Services, 1209 Indiana, 67214. Tel: 316-264-9723.

Anthony Family Shelter (and Emergency Services), 256 N. Ohio, 67214. Tel: 316-264-7233.

Harbor House, P.O. Box 3759, 67201.

[M] MISCELLANEOUS

WICHITA. *Adorers of the Blood of Christ Charitable Trust Fund*, 1400 S. Sheridan, 67213. Tel: 316-943-1203; Fax: 316-943-1427. Sr. Susan Reeves, Exec. Trustee.

Christina House, 856 N. Socora, 67212. Tel: 316-721-8159.

Diocesan Office, Ministry with Persons with Disabilities, 619 S. Maize Rd., 67209. Tel: 316-722-5381.

Gerard House, Inc., 3144 N. Hood, 67204. Tel: 316-832-0777; Fax: 316-832-1327. Lisa Egan, Dir. Shelter for Needy Pregnant Women.

Leaven International Corporation, 1400 S. Sheridan, 67213; Fax: 316-943-1427. Sr. Charlotte Rohrbach, Pres. A charitable organization of the Adorers of the Blood of Christ.

The Mary Magdalen Foundation, 457 S. Woodlawn, 67218. Tel: 316-683-6516.

Serra Club of Wichita - Downtown, 424 N. Broadway, 67202. Tel: 316-269-3900. Rev. Kenneth J. Schuckman, Chap.

Serra Club of Wichita - Metro, 424 N. Broadway, 67202. Tel: 316-269-3900. Rev. Thomas McGread, Chap.

Via Christi Foundation, Inc., 959 N. Emporia, Ste. 402, 67214. Tel: 316-268-5100. Mr. Robert Giroux, Pres. Owned by Congregation of the Sisters of St. Joseph of Wichita and the Sisters of Sorrowful Mother, sponsoring org. for 10 hospitals and logterm care facilities and their affiliated org. located in 3 states.

Via Christi Health Partners, 929 N. St. Francis, 67214.

Via Christi Health System, Inc., 929 N. St. Francis, 67214. Tel: 316-268-5000. Mr. LeRoy Rheault, Pres. & CEO. Owned by the Congregations of the Sisters of St. Joseph of Wichita and the Sisters of the Sorrowful Mother. Sponsoring organization for 8 hospitals and long-term care facilities and their affiliated organizations located in two states.

Via Christi Property Services, Inc., 929 N. St. Francis, 67214.

Via Christi Senior Services, Inc., 3720 E. Bayley, 67218. Tel: 316-689-4000.

RELIGIOUS INSTITUTES OF MEN REPRESENTED IN THE DIOCESE

For further details refer to the corresponding bracketed number in the Religious Institutes of Men or Women section.

[1070]—*Redemptorist Fathers.* (Province of St. Louis).—C.SS.R.

[1060]—*Society of the Precious Blood.* (Kansas City Prov.).—C.SS.R.

RELIGIOUS INSTITUTES OF WOMEN REPRESENTED IN THE DIOCESE

[0100]—*Adorers of the Blood of Christ.*—A.S.C.

[]—*Carmelite Sisters of St. Teresa.*—C.S.S.T.

[]—*Charity Sisters of the Blessed Sacrament.* (Korean Foundation).

[]—*Congregation of the Daughters of the Passion of Our Lord Jesus Christ and the Sorrows of Mary.*—C.F.P.

[1070-24]—*Dominican Sisters.*—O.P.

[1430]—*Franciscan Sisters of Our Lady of Perpetual Help.*—O.S.F.

[2575]—*Institute of the Sisters of Mercy of the Americas.*—R.S.M.

[2500]—*Medical Sisters of St. Joseph.*—M.S.J.

[0440]—*Sisters of Charity of Cincinnati, Ohio.*—S.C.

[0430]—*Sisters of Charity of the Blessed Virgin Mary.*—B.V.M.

[1540]—*Sisters of St. Francis, Clinton, Ohio.*—O.S.F.

[3830-18]—*Sisters of St. Joseph.*—C.S.J.

[2185]—*Sisters of the Immaculate Heart of Mary of Wichita.*—I.H.M.

[4100]—*Sisters of the Sorrowful Mother (Third Order of St. Francis).*—S.S.M.

[2150]—*Sisters, Servants of the Immaculate Heart of Mary.*—I.H.M.

NECROLOGY

† Blackledge, Michael R., (Retired). —Died Nov. 29, 1995.

† Matz, Leroy A., (Retired). —Died Dec. 12, 1995.

† Tockert, Joseph V., Yates Center, KS, St. Joseph Church. —Died Nov. 23, 1995.

Diocese of Wilmington

(Dioecesis Wilmingtoniensis)

Most Reverend

MICHAEL A. SALTARELLI, D.D.

Bishop of Wilmington; ordained May 28, 1960; appointed Titular Bishop of Mesarfelta and Auxiliary Bishop of Newark, June 12, 1990; episcopal ordination July 30, 1990; appointed Eighth Bishop of Wilmington November 21, 1995; installed January 23, 1996.

ESTABLISHED MARCH 3, 1868.

Square Miles Delaware 1,932; Maryland 3,375; Total 5,307.

Comprises the State of Delaware and the Counties of Caroline, Cecil, Dorchester, Kent, Queen Anne's, Somerset, Talbot, Wicomico and Worcester in Maryland.

For legal titles of parishes and diocesan institutions, consult the Chancery Office.

Chancery Office: 1925 Delaware Ave., Ste. 1A, Wilmington, DE. Tel.: 302-573-3100; Fax: 302-573-3128.

STATISTICAL OVERVIEW

Personnel	
Bishop	1
Priests: Diocesan Active in Diocese	95
Priests: Active Outside Diocese	11
Priests: Retired, Sick or Absent	23
Number of Diocesan Priests	129
Religious Priests in Diocese	86
Extern Priests in Diocese	15
Ordinations:	
Diocesan Priests	3
Religious Priests	1
Transitional Deacons	3
Permanent Deacons	1
Permanent Deacons in Diocese	45
Total Brothers	35
Total Sisters	297
Parishes	
Parishes	55
With Resident Pastor:	
Resident Diocesan Priests	49
Resident Religious Priests	3
Without Resident Pastor:	
Administered by Priests	1
Administered by Pastoral Teams, etc.	2
Missions	21
Pastoral Centers	10
Closed Parishes	1
Professional Ministry Personnel:	
Brothers	1
Sisters	38
Lay Ministers	61
Welfare	
Catholic Hospitals	1
Total Assisted	298,000
Health Care Centers	2
Total Assisted	200
Homes for the Aged	4
Total Assisted	360
Residential Care of Children	4
Total Assisted	113
Day Care and Extended Day Care Centers	1
Total Assisted	147
Specialized Homes	1
Total Assisted	425
Special Centers for Social Services	15
Total Assisted	321,546
Residential Care of Disabled	1
Total Assisted	140
Educational	
Diocesan Students in Other Seminaries	6
Total Seminarians	6
High Schools, Diocesan and Parish	4
Total Students	2,845
High Schools, Private	4
Total Students	1,867
Elementary Schools, Diocesan and Parish	25
Total Students	9,720
Elementary Schools, Private	5
Total Students	996
Non-residential Schools for the Disabled	1
Total Students	104
Catechesis/Religious Education:	
High School Students	910
Elementary Students	8,247
Total Students Under Catholic Instruction	24,695
Teachers in the Diocese:	
Priests	18
Brothers	6
Sisters	38
Lay Teachers	806
Vital Statistics	
Receptions into the Church:	
Infant Baptism Totals	2,886
Adult Baptism Totals	228
Received into Full Communion	311
First Communions	2,701
Confirmations	1,887
Marriages:	
Catholic	702
Interfaith	459
Total Marriages	1,161
Deaths	1,371
Total Catholic Population	164,973
Total Population	1,049,769

Former Bishops—Rt. Rev. THOMAS A. BECKER, D.D., cons. Aug. 16, 1868; transferred to Savannah, 1886; died July 29, 1899.—Rt. Rev. ALFRED A. CURTIS, D.D., cons. Nov. 1886; resigned 1896; named Titular Bishop of Echinus; died July 11, 1908.—Most Rev. JOHN J. MONAGHAN, D.D., cons. May 9, 1897; resigned and named Titular Bishop of Lydda, July 10, 1925; died Jan. 7, 1935.—Most Rev. EDMOND JOHN FITZMAURICE, D.D., cons. Nov. 30, 1925; resigned March 2, 1960 and named Titular Archbishop of Tomi; died July 25, 1962.—Most Rev. HUBERT J. CARTWRIGHT, D.D., cons. Coadjutor "with right of succession," Oct. 24, 1956; died March 6, 1958.—Most Rev. MICHAEL W. HYLE, D.D., cons. Sept. 24, 1958 as Titular Bishop of Christopolis and Coadjutor with right of succession; succeeded to See, March 2, 1960; died Dec. 26, 1967.—Most Rev. THOMAS J. MARDAGA, D.D., cons. Jan. 25, 1967; named Titular Bishop of Mutugenna; appt. Bishop of Wilmington, March 13, 1968; installed April 6, 1968; died May 28, 1984.—Most Rev. JAMES C. BURKE, O.P., cons. May 25, 1967; named Titular Bishop of Lamiggiga; Vicar Apostolic of Chimbote, Peru, 1962-1978 Served in Diocese of Wilmington, 1978-1994; died May 28, 1994.—Most Rev. ROBERT E. MULVEE, D.D., J.C.D., ord. June 30, 1957; Auxiliary Bishop of Manchester and Titular Bishop of Summa, Feb. 15, 1977; cons. April 14, 1977; appt. Bishop of Wilmington, Feb. 19, 1985; installed April 11, 1985; appt. to Diocese of Providence as Coadjutor Bishop of Providence, Feb. 7, 1995; installed March 27, 1995.

Vicar General for Administration and Moderator of the Curia—Rev. Msgr. J. THOMAS CINI, M.A., *1925 Delaware Ave., Ste. 2A, P.O. Box 2030, Wilmington, 19899.* Tel: 302-573-3118.

Vicar General for Pastoral Concerns and Chancellor—Rev. Msgr. JOSEPH F. REBMAN, S.T.L., J.C.L., *1925 Delaware Ave., Ste. 1A, P.O. Box 2030, Wilmington, 19899.* Tel: 302-573-3100.

Episcopal Vicar for Clergy—Rev. Msgr. CLEMENT P. LEMON, E.V.C., *1925 Delaware Ave., Ste. 3A, P.O. Box 2030, Wilmington, 19899.* Tel: 302-573-3144.

Pastoral Concerns Department

Secretary, Pastoral Concerns Department—Rev. Msgr. JOSEPH F. REBMAN, V.G., S.T.L., J.C.L.

Chancery Office—Rev. Msgr. JOSEPH F. REBMAN, V.G., S.T.L., J.C.L., Chancellor, *Mailing Address: P.O. Box 2030, Wilmington, 19899.* Office: *1925 Delaware Ave., Ste. 1A, Wilmington,* Office Hours: Mon.-Fri. 8:30-4:30. Tel: 302-573-3100; Fax: 302-573-3128. Send all marriage dispensation requests to Chancery Office.

Archives—Mr. DONN DEVINE, Archivist, *P.O. Box 4019, Greenville, 19807.* Tel: 302-655-0597.

Master of Ceremonies—Rev. Msgr. JOSEPH F. REBMAN, V.G., S.T.L., J.C.L., *P.O. Box 2030, Wilmington, 19899.* Tel: 302-573-3100.

Censor of Books—Rev. Msgr. JOHN H. DEWSON, S.T.L., *Immaculate Heart of Mary, Wilmington, 19803.* Tel: 302-764-0357.

Ecumenical and Interreligious Affairs—Rev. Msgr. JOSEPH F. REBMAN, V.G., S.T.L., J.C.L., Chancellor.

Diocesan Tribunal—Mailing Address: P.O. Box 2030, Wilmington, 19899. 1925 Delaware Ave., Ste. 2B, Wilmington. Tel: 302-573-3107; Fax: 302-573-3128.

Judicial Vicar—Very Rev. THEODORE E. OLSON, J.C.L.

Office Supervisor—Mrs. JOANN KUBASKO.

Court of First Instance Judges—Revs. GEORGE J. BRUBAKER, J.C.L.; Sr. MARY KATHLEEN KUENSTLER, P.H.J.C., J.C.D.; STANLEY R. DRUPIESKI, O.S.F.S.; Mr. ALBERT R. LANPHEAR.

Defenders of the Bond—JACK D. ANDERSON, J.C.D.; Rev. CYPRIAN ROSEN, O.F.M.Cap., J.C.L.

Secretaries/Notaries—Mrs. MARIE BRADLEY; Mrs. PATRICIA KILLEN; Mrs. LINDA SCHUMAN.

Serving on the Interdiocesan Tribunal of the Province of Baltimore (Court of Second Instance)—

Judges—Rev. Msgr. JOSEPH F. REBMAN, V.G., S.T.L., J.C.L.; Rev. Msgr. PAUL J. SCHIERSE, J.C.D.; Rev. RICHARD A. REISSMANN, J.C.L.

Defender of the Bond—Rev. CHARLES C. DILLINGHAM.

Notary—Mrs. JOANN KUBASKO.

Catholic Cemeteries—Rev. Msgr. JOSEPH F. REBMAN, V.G., S.T.L., J.C.L., Dir.; Mr. MARK A. CHRISTIAN, Exec. Dir., *Mailing Address: P.O. Box 2506, Wilmington, 19805.* Tel: 302-656-3323; Fax: 302-656-1069.

Supervisor of Institutional Chaplains—Rev. Msgr. CLEMENT P. LEMON, E.V.C., *1925 Delaware Ave., Ste. 3A, P.O. Box 2030, Wilmington, 19899.* Tel: 302-573-3144.

Vocation Office—Rev. CHARLES C. DILLINGHAM, Dir., *1925 Delaware Ave., Ste. 3A, P.O. Box 2030, Wilmington, 19899.* Tel: 302-573-3113.

Office for Deacons—Rev. CHARLES C. DILLINGHAM, Dir.; Deacon F. EDMUND LYNCH, Assoc. Dir.; Rev. PAUL MAST, Dir., Formation, *1925 Delaware Ave., Ste. 3A, P.O. Box 2030, Wilmington, 19899.* Tel: 302-573-3113.

Office for Clergy—Rev. Msgr. CLEMENT P. LEMON, E.V.C., Dir., *1925 Delaware Ave., Ste. 3A, P.O. Box 2030, Wilmington, 19899.* Tel: 302-573-3144.

Office for Parish Renewal & Evangelization—Rev. WILLIAM J. LAWLER, Dir., *1925 Delaware Ave., Ste. 3A, P.O. Box 2030, Wilmington, 19899.* Tel: 302-573-2390.

Office for Religious—Sr. ELIZABETH A. SWEENEY, S.S.J., Dir., *Ste. 3A, 1925 Delaware Ave., P.O. Box 2030, Wilmington, 19899.* Tel: 302-573-3124.

Mission Office—Propagation of the Faith and Holy Childhood Association, Rev. JOHN P. KLEVENCE, Dir., *1626 N. Union St., P.O. Box 2030, Wilmington, 19899.* Tel: 302-573-3104.

Marian Devotions Office—Rev. Msgr. JOSEPH F. REBMAN, V.G., S.T.L., J.C.L., Dir. Assoc. Directors: Rev. JOSEPH J. PIEKARSKI; Deacon EDWARD A. DUNNING, *1925 Delaware Ave., P.O. Box 2030, Wilmington, 19899.* Tel: 302-573-3100.

Latino and Migrant Ministry—Vacant, *135 Fourth St., Seaford, 19973.* Tel: 302-629-5705; Fax: 302-629-7403.

Christian Formation Department

Secretary, Christian Formation Department—Mr. EDMUND F. GORDON.

Catholic Schools—Sr. MARIE LOURDES VANSTON, I.H.M., Supt. Asst. Supts.: Sr. KATHLEEN CALLAGHAN, S.S.J.; Sr. PATRICIA CLUNE, C.S.J., *1626 N. Union St., Wilmington, 19806.* Tel: 302-573-3133; Fax: 302-573-2393.

Religious Education—Mr. EDMUND F. GORDON, Diocesan Dir. GLORIA REINHARDT, Asst. Dir., *1626 N. Union St., Wilmington, 19806.* Tel: 302-573-3130; Fax: 302-573-2393.

Ministry for Handicapped and Hearing Impaired—Mrs. JO ANN DORA, Coord. Special Religious Education; Mrs. MARGARET WYNN, Coord. Hearing Impaired, *1626 N. Union St., Wilmington, 19806.* Tel: 302-573-3130.

Office of Worship—Vacant, *1626 N. Union St., Wilmington, 19806.* Tel: 302-573-3137; Fax: 302-573-2393.

Educational Resource Center—Ms. ANTHEA SIBERT, *1626 N. Union St., Wilmington, 19806.* Tel: 302-573-3136.

Catholic Youth Organization—Rev. JOHN P. HOPKINS, Dir.; Mr. BRIAN M.P. MCGLINCHEY, Assoc. Dir., *803 N. Broom St., Wilmington, 19805.* Tel: 302-658-3800; 3801; Fax: 302-658-7617.

Newman Apostolate—Very Rev. MICHAEL F. SZUPPER, Ph.D., Dir.; Rev. ROBERT J. MALONE, C.S.C., Assoc. Dir., *University of Delaware, 45 Lovett Ave., Newark, 19711.* Tel: 302-368-4728.

Youth Ministry—Rev. JOHN P. HOPKINS, Dir., *803 N. Broom St., Wilmington, 19806.* Tel: 302-658-3800.

Catholic Scouting—

Boy Scouts—Bro. PATRICK PRESS, O.S.F.S., Chap., *1801 N. Broom St., Wilmington, 19802.* Tel: 302-655-1592.

Girl Scouts—Rev. JOHN P. HOPKINS, Chap., *803 N. Broom St., Wilmington, 19806.* Tel: 302-658-3800.

Communication Department

Secretary, Communication Department—Mr. F. EUGENE DONNELLY.

Office of Public Relations, Radio and T.V.—Mr. F. EUGENE DONNELLY, Dir., *1626 N. Union St., Wilmington, 19899.* Tel: 302-573-3116; Fax: 302-573-2393.

"The Dialog"—(Weekly Diocesan Newspaper), Most Rev. MICHAEL A. SALTARELLI, Publisher; Mr. GARY MORTON, Editor, *P.O. Box 2208, Wilmington, 19899.* Editorial Offices: *1925 Delaware Ave., Ste. 3B, Wilmington, 19806.* Tel: 302-573-3109; 573-3112 (Advertising Dept.); Fax: 302-573-3128.

Finance Department

Financial Officer and Secretary, Finance Department—Mr. JOSEPH P. CORSINI, *Mailing Address: P.O. Box 2030, Wilmington, 19899. 1925 Delaware Ave., Ste. 1B, Wilmington, 19806.* Tel: 302-573-3105; Fax: 302-573-3128.

Development Office—Mrs. DEBORAH FOLS, Dir., *Mailing Address: 1925 Delaware Ave., Ste. 2A, Wilmington, 19899.* Tel: 302-573-3120; Fax: 302-573-3128.

Annual Catholic Appeal—Mrs. DEBORAH FOLS, Dir., *Mailing Address: 1925 Delaware Ave., Ste. 2A, Wilmington, 19899.* Tel: 302-573-3120; Fax: 302-573-3128.

Catholic Charities Department

Catholic Charities—Mr. ALLAN J. DAUL, A.C.S.W., Diocesan Sec. & Exec. Dir., *Fourth St. and Greenhill Ave., P.O. Box 2610, Wilmington, 19805.* Tel: 302-655-9624; Fax: 302-655-9753. (Refer to separate listings in the Institutions for detailed information on Catholic Charities and related organizations.).

Advisory Groups to the Bishop

College of Consultors—Rev. Msgr. JOSEPH F. REBMAN, V.G., Sec.; Rev. Msgr. J. THOMAS CINI, V.G.; Rev. Msgr. PAUL J. TAGGART; Rev. Msgr. CLEMENT P. LEMON; Revs. MICHAEL A. ANGELONI; JOHN O. BARRES; JOHN P. HOPKINS; WILLIAM F. GRANEY, *P.O. Box 2030, Wilmington, 19899.*

Priests' Council—Rev. MICHAEL A. ANGELONI, Exec. Officer; Rev. Msgr. JOSEPH F. REBMAN, V.G., Sec., *P.O. Box 2030, Wilmington, 19899.* Tel: 302-573-3100.

Deans—Very Rev. JOHN F. O'BRIEN, V.F.; Very Rev. MICHAEL F. SZUPPER, V.F.; Very Rev. CHARLES L. BROWN, III, V.F.; Very Rev. JOHN MASTERSON, V.F.; Very Rev. STEPHEN J. CONNELL, V.F.; Very Rev. THOMAS J. PETERMAN, V.F.; Very Rev. CLEMENS D. MANISTA, V.F.; Very Rev. JOHN J. KAVANAUGH, V.F.

Finance Council—Rev. Msgr. J. THOMAS CINI, V.F., Chm., *P.O. Box 2030, Wilmington, 19899.* Tel: 302-573-3118.

Parish Priest Consultors—Rev. Msgr. PAUL J. SCHIERSE; Revs. RALPH L. MARTIN; THOMAS F. GARDOCKI; RICHARD A. REISSMANN; RAYMOND L. FORESTER; DANIEL W. GERRES.

Clergy Personnel Committee—Rev. Msgr. CLEMENT P. LEMON, E.V.C., Chm., *P.O. Box 2030, Wilmington, 19899.* Tel: 302-573-3144.

Priests' Continuing Formation Committee—Rev. JOHN P. HOPKINS, Chm., *P.O. Box 2030, Wilmington, 19899.* Tel: 302-658-3801.

Council of Religious—Mailing Address: P.O. Box 2030, Wilmington, 19899. Tel: 302-573-3124.

Diocesan Board of Catholic Education—Mr. EDMUND F. GORDON, Sec., *Mailing Address: 1626 N. Union St., Wilmington, 19806.* Tel: 302-573-3130.

Building Committee—Mr. PAUL S. ADAMS, JR., Chm., Diocese of Wilmington; Rev. Msgr. J. THOMAS CINI, V.G., Episcopal Liaison, *P.O. Box 2030, Wilmington, 19899.* Tel: 302-573-3118.

Liturgical Commission—Very Rev. CHARLES L. BROWN, III, V.F., Chm., *1626 N. Union St., Wilmington, 19806.* Tel: 302-573-3137.

Office for Pro Life Activities—Mr. THOMAS JEWETT, Chm., *P.O. Box 2610, Wilmington, 19805.* Tel: 302-655-9624.

Pastoral Council—Mr. ANTHONY G. FLYNN, Lay Chm.; Rev. Msgr. JOSEPH F. REBMAN, V.G., Recording Sec., *Mailing Address: P.O. Box 2030, Wilmington, 19899.* Tel: 302-573-3100.

Public Affairs Advisory Committee—Co-Chairs: Rev. Msgr. J. THOMAS CINI, V.G.; Rev. THOMAS E. HANLEY, *P.O. Box 2030, Wilmington, 19899.* Tel: 302-573-3118.

Real Estate Committee—Rev. Msgr. JOSEPH F. REBMAN, V.G., Chm., *P.O. Box 2030, Wilmington, 19899.* Tel: 302-573-3100.

Parish Social Ministry—Mrs. PEGGY HEINS, Dir., *Fourth St. & Greenville Ave., P.O. Box 2610, Wilmington, 19805.* Tel: 302-655-9624.

Respect Life Committee—Mr. THOMAS JEWETT, Chm., *Fourth St. & Greenhill Ave., Wilmington, 19805.* Tel: 302-655-9624.

Due Process Commission—Contact: Very Rev. THEODORE E. OLSON, Clerk, *P.O. Box 2030, Wilmington, 19899.* Tel: 302-573-3107.

Diocesan Corporations

Catholic Cemeteries, Inc.—Rev. Msgr. JOSEPH F. REBMAN, V.G., Treas., *P.O. Box 2506, Wilmington, 19805.* Tel: 302-737-2524.

Catholic Diocese of Wilmington, Inc.—A corporation sole under the laws of the State of Delaware. Rev. Msgr. J. THOMAS CINI, V.G., Sec. & Treas., *Mailing Address: P.O. Box 2030, Wilmington, 19899.* Tel: 302-573-3118. Office: *1925 Delaware Ave., Wilmington, 19899.*

Catholic Diocese Foundation—Rev. Msgr. J. THOMAS CINI, V.G., Treas., *P.O. Box 2030, Wilmington, 19899.* Tel: 302-573-3118.

Catholic Ministry to the Elderly, Inc.—Rev. Msgr. J. THOMAS CINI, V.G., Treas., *P.O. Box 2030, Wilmington, 19899.* Tel: 302-573-3118.

Catholic Press of Wilmington, Inc.—Rev. Msgr. J. THOMAS CINI, V.G., Vice Pres. & Treas., *P.O. Box 2208, Wilmington, 19899.* Tel: 302-573-3118.

Catholic Charities, Inc.—Mr. ALLAN J. DAUL, A.C.S.W., Sec., *Fourth St. & Greenhill Ave., P.O. Box 2610, Wilmington, 19806.* Tel: 302-655-9624.

Catholic Youth Organization, Inc.—Rev. JOHN P. HOPKINS, Sec., *Mailing Address: P.O. Box 2030, Wilmington, 19899.* Tel: 302-658-3801.

Children's Home, Inc.—Mr. ALLAN J. DAUL, A.C.S.W., Sec., *Fourth St. & Greenhill Ave., P.O. Box 2610, Wilmington, 19806.* Tel: 302-655-9624.

Diocese of Wilmington Schools, Inc.—Rev. Msgr. J. THOMAS CINI, V.G., Sec. & Treas., *1626 N. Union St., Wilmington, 19806.* Tel: 302-573-3118.

Seton Villa, Inc.—Mr. ALLAN J. DAUL, A.C.S.W., Sec., *Fourth St. & Greenhill Ave., P.O. Box 2610, Wilmington, 19806.* Tel: 302-655-9624.

Siena Hall, Inc.—Mr. ALLAN J. DAUL, A.C.S.W., Sec., *Fourth St. & Greenhill Ave., P.O. Box 2610, Wilmington, 19806.* Tel: 302-655-9624.

Society for the Propagation of the Faith—Rev. Msgr. JOSEPH F. REBMAN, V.G., Sec., *P.O. Box 2030, Wilmington, 19899.* Tel: 302-573-3100.

Activities

Apostleship of Prayer—Rev. JOSEPH R. MCMAHON, *P.O. Box 2030, Wilmington, 19899.* Tel: 302-654-5519.

Campaign for Human Development—Mr. ALLAN J. DAUL, A.C.S.W., Diocesan Dir., *Fourth St. & Greenhill Ave., P.O. Box 2610, Wilmington, 19806.* Tel: 302-655-9624.

Catholic Charismatic Renewal—Rev. STANLEY A. IANIERI, Chap., *St. John the Beloved, 907 Milltown Rd., Wilmington, 19808.* Tel: 302-999-0211.

Catholic Relief Services Inc.—Vacant, *P.O. Box 2030, Wilmington, 19899.* Tel: 302-573-3107.

Commission for the Catholic Missions Among the Colored People and the Indians—Rev. Msgr. JOSEPH F. REBMAN, S.T.L., J.C.L., Diocesan Dir., *P.O. Box 2030, Wilmington, 19899.* Tel: 302-573-3100.

Cursillo Movement—Deacons F. EDMUND LYNCH, *2008 N. Bancroft Pkwy., Wilmington, 19806.* Tel: 302-654-7471. ROBERT H. NORMOYLE, *7 Whaler Ln., 2726 Ocean Pines, Berlin, MD, 21811.* Tel: 410-641-7438. JANE H. LEITNER, Lay Dir., *1 Windflower Rd., Newark, 19711.*

Delmarva Catholic Network, Inc.—Mr. F. EUGENE DONNELLY, Contact Person, *P.O. Box 2030, Wilmington, 19899.* Tel: 302-573-3116.

Diocesan Healing Ministry—JEANNE CASEY, Lay Dir., *533 Waterford Dr., Hockessin, 19707.* Tel: 302-239-5982.

KAIROS Ministries, Inc.—Rev. GREGORY CORRIGAN, Contact Person, *P.O. Box 269, Claymont, 19703.* Tel: 302-798-2904.

Korean Catholic Community, Inc.—DANIEL YOON, Contact Person, *c/o Immaculate Heart of Mary Church, 4701 Weldin Rd., Wilmington, 19803.* Tel: 302-764-0357.

St. Thomas More Society—Rev. Msgr. PAUL J. TAGGART, Diocesan Liaison, *Mailing Address: P.O. Box 2030, Wilmington, 19899.* Tel: 302-655-3130.

St. Vincent dePaul Society—Mr. FRANK A. BUSH, Pres., *18 Vassar Ave., New Castle, 19720.* Tel: 302-328-9592.

Organizations With Which Diocese Has Liaison

**Birthright of Delaware, Inc.*—Mrs. MARY JO FROHLICH, Dir., *1311 N. Scott St., Wilmington, 19806.* Tel: 302-656-7080.

The Christian Council of DE & MD's Eastern Shore—Rev. PATRICIA MCCLURG, Pres., *E-62 Omega Dr., Newark, 19713.* Tel: 302-366-0595.

**Delaware Citizens for Life*—Mr. THOMAS JEWETT, Chm., *Fourth St. & Greenhill Ave., P.O. Box 2610, Wilmington, 19806.* Tel: 302-655-9624.

Delawareans United for Education—Rev. Msgr. J. THOMAS CINI, V.G., *P.O. Box 2030, Wilmington, 19899.* Tel: 302-573-3100.

**Jesus House*—Mr. CHRISTIAN MALMGREM, Dir. ANGELA MALMGREM, Assoc. Dir.; Deacon JOSEPH CONTE, Chap., *2500 Milltown Rd., Wilmington, 19808.* Tel: 302-995-6859.

Maryland Catholic Conference—(An agency of the Archdiocese of Baltimore, Washington and the Diocese of Wilmington); Mr. RICHARD J. DOWLING, Exec. Dir., *309 Cathedral St., Baltimore, MD, 21201.* Tel: 301-322-0901. Rev. Msgr. PAUL J. TAGGART, Diocesan Liaison, *P.O. Box 2030, Wilmington, 19899.* Tel: 302-655-3130.

National Catholic Ministry to the Bereaved—Sr. PATRICIA HAMILL, S.S.J., Contact Person, *1925 Delaware Ave., Wilmington, 19806.* Tel: 302-762-1229.

National Conference of Christians and Jews—Very Rev. CLEMENS D. MANISTA, V.F., *345 Bear-Christiana Rd., Bear, 19701.* Tel: 302-322-6430.

Operation Help, Inc.—Rev. PATRICK SHAULES, S.J., Pres. MARCINDA HAEDGE, Sec. & Treas., *P.O. Box 134, Hartly, 19953.* Tel: 302-492-8985; Fax: 302-492-8360.

Regina Coeli Society—Rev. JOHN F. HECKLE, O.S.F.S., Chap., *1801 N. Broom St., Wilmington, 19802.* Tel: 302-655-1592.

World Wide Marriage Encounter—Contact Persons: Rev. CHRIS LABARGE, *Immaculate Conception, Marydel, MD, 21649.* Tel: 410-482-8939. MIKE CAMPBELL; NANCY CAMPBELL, *218 S. Third St., Denton, MD, 21629.* Tel: 410-479-0154. MIKE GRANEY; MARIE GRANEY, *2305 Inwood Rd., Wilmington, 19810.* Tel: 302-475-0925.

CLERGY, PARISHES, MISSIONS AND PAROCHIAL SCHOOLS

DELAWARE, CITY OF WILMINGTON
(New Castle County)

1—CATHEDRAL OF ST. PETER, Rev. William B. Kauffman, Rector; Deacon George M. Taylor, Jr. In res., Rev. Msgr. Joseph F. Rebman, V.G.; Rev. Msgr. Paul J. Taggart, Dir. Development Office.
Res., 500 West St., 19801. Tel: 302-654-5920; Fax: 302-654-6850.
School—310 W. 6th St., 19801. Tel: 302-656-5234. Daughters of Charity of St. Vincent de Paul 3; Lay Teachers 13; Students 194.

2—ST. ANN, Revs. Joseph R. McMahon; William D. Melnick; Deacon James J. Lafferty, Jr. Pastoral Assts: Sr. John Regina Lang, M.S.B.T.; Sr. Marie Bernadette Lang, M.S.B.T.
Res., 2013 Gilpin Ave., 19806. Tel: 302-654-5519; 652-0152; Fax: 302-654-5527.
School—Tel: 302-652-6567. Mr. Ronald Bogia, Prin. Lay Teachers 10; Students 268.
Catechesis/Religious Programs—Tel: 302-654-8504. Kathy Hockmuth, D.R.E. Students 141.

3—ST. ANTHONY OF PADUA (Italian), Revs. Mark A. Hushen, O.S.F.S., Admin.; William J. Dougherty, O.S.F.S.; Charles C. Garst, O.S.F.S.; Bro. Michael J. Rosenello, O.S.F.S. In res., Revs. Roberto Balducelli, O.S.F.S.; Mario Bugliosi, O.S.F.S.; John J. Bradunas, O.S.F.S.
Res., 901 N. DuPont St., 19805. Tel: 302-421-3700; Fax: 302-421-3709.
School—9th & Scott Sts., 19805. Tel: 302-421-3743; Fax: 302-421-3796. Mr. Bernard J. Fisher, Prin. Sisters of St. Francis of Philadelphia 2; Lay Teachers 22; Students 527.
High School—Padua Academy, 905 N. Broom St., 19805. Sr. Ann Michele Zwosta, O.S.F., Prin. Sisters 4; Lay Teachers 48; Brothers 1; Students 569.
Convents—1710 W.9th St., 19805. Tel: 302-421-3754. Sisters 2; 1401 W. 10th St., 19806. Tel: 302-421-3749. Sisters 7.
St. Anthony's Education Fund, Inc.—901 N. DuPont St., 19805. Tel: 302-421-3700.

4—CHRIST OUR KING, Rev. Leonard J. Kempski; Deacon William J. Maloney, Jr.
Res., 2810 N. Monroe St., 19802. Tel: 302-762-4140; Fax: 302-762-8414.
School—28th & Madison Streets, 19802. Tel: 302-762-4031. Sisters of St. Joseph 2; Lay Teachers 9; Students 135.

5—ST. ELIZABETH, Very Rev. John F. O'Brien, V.F.; Revs. Edward J. Fahey, Jr.; Andrew Molewski. In res., Rev. Howard T. Clark.
Res., 809 S. Broom St., 19805-4296. Tel: 302-652-3626; Fax: 302-658-5957.
School—1500 Cedar St., 19805-4249. Tel: 302-655-8208. Sr. M. Gerard, O.S.B., Prin. Sisters of St. Benedict 3; Lay Teachers 24; Students 575.
High School—Sr. Mary Ellen, O.S.B., Prin. Sisters 7; Lay Teachers 29; Students 465.

6—ST. HEDWIG (Polish), Revs. Joseph J. Piekarski; Edward Glapiak; Norman P. Carroll.
Res., 408 S. Harrison St., 19805. Tel: 302-594-1400.
School—Linden & Harrison Sts., 19805. Tel: 302-594-1402; Fax: 302-594-1407. Felician Sisters 1; Lay Teachers 14; Students 286.

7—ST. JOSEPH'S R.C. CHURCH OF WILMINGTON, INC., Rev. Barry J. Langley, O.F.M.; Bros. David W. Schlatter, O.F.M.; Henry L. Fulmer, O.F.M.
Church—1012 French St., 19801. Tel: 302-658-4535.
Res., 1010 W. 4th St., 19805.

8—ST. MARY OF THE IMMACULATE CONCEPTION, Rev. James F. Trainor.
Res., 1414 King St., 19801. Tel: 302-652-0743.
Church—6th & Pine Sts., 19801.

9—ST. PATRICK, Rev. James F. Trainor.
Res., 1414 King St., 19801. Tel: 302-652-0743.

10—ST. PAUL'S, Revs. Lawrence J. Hayes, O.F.M.; William McIntyre, O.F.M. In res., Rev. Barry Langley, O.F.M.; Bros. David Schlatter, O.F.M.; Henry Fulmer, O.F.M.
Res., 1010 W. 4th St., 19805. Tel: 302-655-6596; Fax: 302-655-7684.
School—3rd & Van Buren Sts., 19805. Tel: 302-656-1372. Mr. Richard Adamo, Prin.; Sr. Nancy Donovan, R.S.M., Asst. Prin. Lay Teachers 12; Students 205.

11—SACRED HEART. Closed. For inquiries for sacramental records contact Cathedral of St. Peter. Tel: 302-654-5920; Fax: 302-654-6850.

12—ST. STANISLAUS KOSTKA (Polish), Rev. Edward J. Kaczorowski.
Mailing Address: P.O. Box 30110, 19805-7110.
Res., 901 E. 7th St., 19801. Tel: 302-571-0622; Fax: 302-571-1508.

13—ST. THOMAS, Rev. John L. Taggart. In res., Rev. Samu Irudayaraj.
Res., 301 N. Bancroft Pkwy., 19805. Tel: 302-658-5131.
School—201 Bayard Ave., 19805. Tel: 302-654-0746; Fax: 302-426-1738. Lay Teachers 21; Students 255.

DELAWARE
OUTSIDE THE CITY OF WILMINGTON

Bear, New Castle Co., St. Elizabeth Ann Seton, Revs. Clemens D. Manista; Joseph V. Bozzelli.
Res., 345 Bear-Christiana Rd., 19701. Tel: 302-322-6430.
Catechesis/Religious Programs—Sr. Paula Marie, O.S.F., D.R.E. Students 443.

Bellefonte, New Castle Co., St. Helena (Wilmington P.O.), Revs. Stanley J. Russell; John A. Sarro; Deacon Edward A. Dunning.
Res., 602 Philadelphia Pike, Wilmington, 19809. Tel: 302-764-0325.
School—210 Bellefonte Ave., Willmington, 19809. Tel: 302-762-5595; Fax: 302-762-5688. Sisters of St. Joseph 4; Lay Teachers 8; Students 204; Assistants 4.
Catechesis/Religious Programs—Sr. Mary Goodbody, S.S.J., D.R.E. Students 129.
Convent—610 Philadelphia Pike, Willmington, 19809.

Bethany Beach, Sussex Co., St. Ann, Very Rev. John J. Masterson; Deacons Edward Brink; Robert Tracy.
Res., 691 Garfield Ave., P.O. Box 149, 19930. Tel: 302-539-6449; Fax: 302-539-0657.

Brandywood, New Castle Co., Church of the Holy Child (Wilmington P.O.), Revs. James T. Kirk, Jr.; John P. Klevence; Deacon Samuel Torres. In res., Rev. Oscar H. Frundt.
Res., 2500 Naamans Rd., Wilmington, 19810. Tel: 302-475-6486.
Catechesis/Religious Programs—Marguerite Gomes, D.R.E. Students 209.

Claymont, New Castle Co., Holy Rosary, Revs. James M. Jackson; David F. Murphy; Deacons Richard J. Maichle; Allen Wolf. In res., Revs. Joseph Narimattam (India); Gregory M. Corrigan.
Res., 3200 Philadelphia Pike, 19703. Tel: 302-798-2904; 798-2987; Fax: 302-798-3609.
School—3110 Philadelphia Pike, 19703. Sisters of St. Joseph 4; Lay Teachers 22; Students 443.
Catechesis/Religious Programs—Sr. Ann Hughes, S.S.J., D.R.E. Students 211.

Delaware City, New Castle Co., St. Paul, Rev. Philip L. Siry.
Res., 209 Washington St., 19706. Tel: 302-834-4321; Fax: 302-834-1757.

Dover, Kent Co., Holy Cross, Revs. Thomas E. Hanley; Ralph T. Castelow; Roger DiBuo; Deacon Anthony Vinciguerra. In res., Rev. James D. Hreha.
Res., 631 S. State St., 19901. Tel: 302-674-5780; Fax: 302-674-5783. [CEM]
School—Tel: 302-674-5784. Ms. Marcia Bertino, Prin. Lay Teachers 30; Students 544.
Catechesis/Religious Programs—Carmella Jones, D.R.E. Students 758.

Elsmere, New Castle Co., Corpus Christi (Wilmington P.O.), Revs. Francis J. Rogers; Steven B. Giuliano; Deacon John G. Parisi. In res., Rev. Theodore E. Olson.
Res., 901 New Rd., Elsmere, Wilmington, 19805. Tel: 302-994-2922; Fax: 302-892-3315.
School—907 New Rd., Elsmere, Wilmington, 19805. Tel: 302-995-2231. Sr. Donna Desien, O.S.F., Prin. Sisters 5; Lay Teachers 21; Students 576.
Catechesis/Religious Programs—Sr. Maryanne Bemiller, S.S.J., D.R.E. Students 95.
Convent—905 New Rd., Elsmere, Wilmington, 19805. Tel: 302-994-5641.

Fairfax, New Castle Co., St. Mary Magdalen (Wilmington P.O.), Revs. William F. Graney; Michael T. Casari; Mark A. Kelleher; Deacons Richard Recce; Tony Catka. In res., Rev. Charles C. Dillingham.
Res., 7 Sharpley Rd., P.O. Box 7085, Wilmington, 19803. Tel: 302-652-6800; Fax: 302-652-6806.
School—9 Sharpley Rd., Wilmington, 19803. Tel: 302-656-2745. Barbara Wanner, Prin. Lay Teachers 34; Students 522.
Catechesis/Religious Programs—Tel: 302-652-7141. Barbara Rogers, D.R.E. Students 229.

Garfield Park, New Castle Co., Holy Spirit (New Castle P.O.), Rev. Frederick A. Kochan. In res., Rev. Stephen P. Breen.
Res., 12 Winder Rd., Garfield Park, New Castle, 19720. Tel: 302-658-1069.
School—Church Dr., New Castle, 19720. Tel: 302-658-5345. Sisters 4; Lay Teachers 10; Students 254.

Georgetown, Sussex Co., St. Michael the Archangel, Rev. Anthony F. Greco; Deacon Joseph Baker.
Res., 202 Edward St., 19947. Tel: 302-856-6451.
Mission—Millsboro, Sussex Co., Mary Mother of Peace.

Greenville, New Castle Co., St. Joseph on the Brandywine, Very Rev. Stephen J. Connell; Rev. Joseph E. Wharton; Deacon F. Edmund Lynch.
Res., 10 Old Church Rd., Wilmington, 19807. Tel: 302-658-7017; Fax: 302-428-0639. [CEM]
Catechesis/Religious Programs—Tel: 302-656-7185. Joan Kornacki, D.R.E. Students 223.

Hockessin, New Castle Co., St. Mary of the Assumption, Revs. Roy F. Pollard; Francis P. Kenney; Deacon John W. Freebery, Jr. In res., Rev. Msgr. Clement P. Lemon; Rev. Paul Mast.
Res., 7200 Lancaster Pike, P.O. Box 1240, 19707. Tel: 302-239-7100; Fax: 302-239-8219. [CEM]
Catechesis/Religious Programs—Mr. John D. Ryan, D.R.E. Students 634.

Liftwood, New Castle Co., Immaculate Heart of Mary (Wilmington P.O.), Revs. Daniel W. Gerres; David A. Baumgartel; Sr. Brigid Clarahan, Pastoral Min. In res., Rev. Msgr. J. Thomas Cini; Rev. Msgr. John H. Dewson.
Res., 4701 Weldin Rd., Liftwood, Wilmington, 19803. Tel: 302-764-0357; Fax: 302-762-1510.
School—1000 Shipley Rd., Liftwood, Wilmington, 19803. Karen Himelreich, Prin. Lay Teachers 29; Students 524.
Catechesis/Religious Programs—Sr. Natalie Dombrowski, D.R.E. Students 294.

Middletown, New Castle Co., St. Joseph, Revs. Thomas A. Flowers; Joseph M.P.R. Cocucci.
Res., 115 Cleaver Farm Rd., Box 196, 19709. Tel: 302-378-5800; Fax: 302-378-5808. [CEM]
Catechesis/Religious Programs—Tel: 302-378-5802. D.R.E.: Susan Long; Laurie McCarley. Students 650.
Mission—Chesapeake City, Cecil Co., St. Rose of Lima, Lock St., 21915. Tel: 410-885-5533.
Shrine—Warwick, St. Francis Xavier-Old Bohemia.

Milford, Kent and Sussex Cos., St. John the Apostle, Revs. Michael A. Angeloni; Christopher Kopec; Deacons James D. Malloy; Anthony Bianco.
Res., 506 Seabury Ave., 19963-2217. Tel: 302-422-5123.
Catechesis/Religious Programs—Students 343.
Mission—Harrington, Kent Co., St. Bernadette, 109 Dixon, Harrington, 19952. Tel: 302-398-8269.

New Castle, New Castle Co., St. Peter, Revs. Arthur B. Fiore; Vincent V. Iocco.
Res., 35 E. 5th St., 19720. Tel: 302-328-2335; Fax: 302-328-0519. [CEM]
School—6th & Harmony Sts., 19720. Lay Teachers 17; Students 282.

Newark, Newcastle Co., Parish of the Resurrection, Rev. Joseph J. Drobinski; Deacons Joseph J. Conte; Francis J. Huhn. Office: 3000 Videre Dr., Skyline Ridge, Wilmington, 19808. Tel: 302-368-0146; Fax: 302-368-3536.
Res., 119 Larkspur Rd., 19711. Tel: 302-737-3066.

St. John the Baptist-Holy Angels, New Castle Co., Revs. Richard A. Reissmann; Stephen C. Lonek; John A. Grasing; Robert W. Kunze; Deacon Hugh J. McCann.

Res., 82 Possum Park Rd., 19711. Tel: 302-731-2200; Fax: 302-731-2434. [CEM]
School—Tel: 302-731-2210.
Lay Teachers 25; Students 593.

St. Thomas More Oratory, New Castle Co. (Personal Parish for Students & Faculty of University of Delaware). Very Rev. Michael F. Szupper, V.F.; Rev. Robert J. Malone, C.S.C.
Res., 155 Haines St., 19711. Tel: 302-368-5020; Fax: 302-368-2548.
Church—45 Lovett Ave., 19711. Tel: 302-368-4728.

Ogletown, New Castle Co., Holy Family (Newark P.O.), Revs. William E. Irwin; Charles W. Wiggins; James Nash; Deacons William Murrian; John L. Seador.
Res., 15 Gender Rd., P.O. Box 8093, Newark, 19714. Tel: 302-368-4665; Fax: 302-368-4667.
Catechesis/Religious Programs—Melody Duffy, D.R.E.
Students 875.

Wilmington, New Castle Co., St. Catherine of Siena (Wilmington P.O.), Rev. John M. Hynes; Deacons John J. Falkowski, Jr.; Francis J. Staab.
Res., 2503 Centerville Rd., 19808. Tel: 302-633-4900; Fax: 302-633-4960.
School—Tel: 302-633-4901.
Lay Teachers 14; Students 312.
Catechesis/Religious Programs—2503 Centerville Rd., Tel: 302-633-4903. Sr. Theresa Cappelli, D.R.E.
Students 215.

Rehoboth, Sussex Co., St. Edmond, Rev. Philip P. Sheekey. In res., Rev. Patrick A. Brady; Deacon John A. Smith.
Office: 409 King Charles St., P.O. Box 646, Rehoboth Beach, 19971. Tel: 302-227-4550; Fax: 302-227-4557.
Res., 402 King Charles St., P.O. Box 646, Rehoboth Beach, 19771.
Catechesis/Religious Programs—Tel: 302-227-4553. Sr. Eileen Lally, M.H.S.H., D.R.E.
Students 257.
Mission—Lewes, Sussex Co., Shrine of St. Jude.

Seaford, Sussex Co., Our Lady of Lourdes, Revs. Patrick W. Gaffney, C.SS.R.; Gerard Smith, C.SS.R.
Res., 528 Stein Hwy., P.O. Box 719, 19973. Tel: 302-629-3591. [CEM]
Catechesis/Religious Programs—Mrs. Debra Depta, D.R.E.
Students 322.

Sherwood Park, New Castle Co., St. John the Beloved, Very Rev. John J. Kavanaugh; Revs. Stanley A. Ianieri; Joseph Kandathiparampil; Deacon James Haley. In res., Rev. Christopher H. Plokhooy.
Res., 907 Milltown Rd., Wilmington, 19808. Tel: 302-999-0211.
School—903 Milltown Rd., Wilmington, 19808. Tel: 302-998-5525.
Sisters of St. Francis of Philadelphia 2; Lay Teachers 30; Students 617.
Catechesis/Religious Programs—Tel: 302-994-7757. Pauline Berlingieri, D.R.E.
Students 425.

Smyrna, Kent Co., St. Polycarp, Rev. Ralph L. Martin.
Res., 135 Ransom Ln., 19977. Tel: 302-653-8279; Fax: 302-653-3509.
Catechesis/Religious Programs—Tel: 302-653-4101. Sr. Ellen Gerlach, D.R.E.
Students 192.

Wilmington Manor, New Castle Co., Our Lady of Fatima (New Castle P.O.), Revs. Michael J. McDermott; Edmund T. Coppinger; John J. Mink; Thomas J. Protack; Deacon Joseph C. Romans.
Res., 801 Dupont Blvd., New Castle, 19720. Tel: 302-328-3431; 328-5773; Fax: 302-328-6318.
School—Tel: 302-328-2803; Fax: 302-328-5427.
Lay Teachers 29; Students 595.
Catechesis/Religious Programs—Tel: 302-328-0307. D.R.E.: Nancy-Jo Stryker; Patricia Walker.
Teachers 23; Students 295.

Woodcrest, New Castle Co., St. Matthew, Revs. Michael J. Cook; William M. Hazzard; William J. Klapps, (Retired U.S.N.); Deacon Harold Chalfant.
Res., 3 Curtis Ave., Wilmington, 19804. Tel: 302-633-5850; Fax: 302-633-6022.
School—One Fallon Ave., 19804. Tel: 302-633-5860.
Sisters Servants of the Immaculate Heart of Mary 4; Lay Teachers 19; Students 550.

MARYLAND

Cambridge, Dorchester Co., St. Mary Refuge of Sinners, Rev. Bruce Byrolly.
Res., 1515 Glasgow St., Box 218, 21613. Tel: 410-228-4770. [CEM]
Catechesis/Religious Programs—Sr. Kathleen Winkleman, O.S.F., D.R.E.
Students 70.
Mission—Meekin's Neck, Dorchester Co., St. Mary, Star of the Sea. [CEM]

Centreville, Queen Anne Co., Mother of Sorrows, Revs. James P. Eckrich; William J. Lawler, Admin.
Res., 303 Chesterfield Ave., 21617. Tel: 410-758-0140.
Mission—Queenstown, Queen Anne Co., St. Peter.

Chester, Kent Island, Queen Anne Co., St. Christopher, Revs. Theodore Heyburn, C.SS.R.; Brendan Greany, C.SS.R.
Res., Box 660, Harbor Dr., Chester, 21619. Tel: 410-643-6220; Fax: 410-643-4055.
Catechesis/Religious Programs—Students 445.

Chestertown, Kent Co., Sacred Heart, Rev. Leonard J. Blakely.
Res., 508 High St., 21620. Tel: 410-778-3160; Fax: 410-810-0427. [CEM]
Catechesis/Religious Programs—Sr. Constance Davis, D.R.E.
Students 180.
Missions—Rock Hall, Kent Co., St. John; Betterton, Most Precious Blood.

Easton, Talbot Co., SS. Peter and Paul, Revs. Paul F. Jennings, Jr.; Mark W. Kopacz.
Res., 215 Goldsborough St., 21601. Tel: 410-822-2344.
School—900 High St., 21601. Tel: 410-822-2275; Fax: 410-820-0136.
Lay Teachers 27; Students 509.
High School—Lay Teachers 17; Students 226.
Catechesis/Religious Programs—Students 735.
Missions—Cordova, Talbot Co., St. Joseph; St. Michaels, St. Michael.

Elkton, Cecil Co., Immaculate Conception, Revs. Daniel J. McGlynn; Michael J. Carrier.
Res., 300 Maryland Ave., P.O. Box 345, 21922. Tel: 410-398-1100; Fax: 410-398-1175. [CEM]
School—455 Bow St., 21921. Tel: 410-398-2636; 398-4161.
Sisters of St. Francis of Philadelphia 2; Lay Teachers 18; Students 266.
Catechesis/Religious Programs—Tel: 410-392-3551. Sr. Grace Andrew, D.R.E.
Students 494.
Mission—North East, Cecil Co., St. Jude.

Galena, Kent Co., St. Dennis, Very Rev. Thomas J. Peterman, V.F.
Mailing Address: P.O. Box 249, 21635. Tel: 410-648-5145. [CEM]

Marydel, Caroline Co., Immaculate Conception, Rev. Christopher LaBarge.
Res., 522 Main St., Box 399, 21649. Tel: 410-482-7687; Fax: 410-482-7253.
Catechesis/Religious Programs—Students 115.

Ocean City, Worcester Co., St. Mary, Star of the Sea, Rev. Msgr. Paul J. Schierse; Rev. Bert Akers, S.J.; Deacons Robert Normoyle; Richard McCarthy.
Res., 208 S. Baltimore Ave., 21842. Tel: 410-289-9419; Fax: 410-289-5858.
Catechesis/Religious Programs—Tel: 410-289-7038. Mary Lou Jones, D.R.E.
Students 170.
Mission—Ocean City, Worcester Co., Holy Saviour, Philadelphia Ave. & 17th St., Ocean City, 21842. Tel: 410-289-3463.

St. Luke and St. Andrew, Revs. William J. Porter; Patrick J. O'Neil; Deacon Jack H. Campbell.
Office: 144th St. & Lighthouse Ave., P.O. Box 2117, 21842. Tel: 410-250-0300; 0301; Fax: 410-250-0417.
Res., 403 141st St., P.O. Box 2117, 21842. Tel: 410-250-0399.
Catechesis/Religious Programs—Tel: 410-250-0342. Mrs. Mary Anne Blatzheim, D.R.E.
Students 160.
Mission—Ocean Pines, St. John Neumann.

Perryville, Cecil Co., Church of the Good Shepherd, Rev. Raymond L. Forester. In res., Rev. Walter D. Power.
Res., 828 Aiken Ave., 21903. Tel: 410-642-6534; Fax: 410-642-2234.
School—810 Aiken Ave., 21903. Tel: 410-642-6265; Fax: 410-642-6522.
Sisters 1; Lay Teachers 10; Students 184.
Missions—Port Deposit, Cecil Co., St. Teresa; Rising Sun, Cecil Co., St. Agnes.

Pocomoke City, Worcester Co., Holy Name of Jesus, Rev. Raymond F. Weisman; Deacon John Costello.
Res., 1913 Old Virginia Rd., P.O. Box 179, 21851. Tel: 410-957-1215; Fax: 410-957-1214.
Catechesis/Religious Programs—Patrick Russo, D.R.E.
Students 115.
Mission—Westover, Somerset Co., St. Elizabeth.

Ridgely, Caroline Co., St. Benedict, Rev. Robert E. Coine; Deacon Harold D. Jopp, Jr.
Res., 406 Central Ave., P.O. Box 459, 21660. Tel: 410-634-2253; Fax: 410-634-1997.
Catechesis/Religious Programs—Students 130.
Mission—Denton, Caroline Co., St. Elizabeth. [CEM]

Salisbury, Wicomico Co., St. Francis De Sales, Very Rev. Charles L. Brown, III, V.F.; Revs. David F. Kelley; James B. Smith.
Res., 514 Camden Ave., 21801. Tel: 410-742-6443; Fax: 410-742-9410.
School—500 Camden Ave., 21801. Tel: 410-749-6662; Fax: 410-749-6924. Sr. Betty Pflieger, R.S.M., Prin.
Lay Teachers 19; Students 303.
Catechesis/Religious Programs—Tel: 410-546-2908. Mrs. Michele Harris, D.R.E.
Students 537.
Convent—417 Wicomico St., 21801. Tel: 410-742-9343.
Mission—Delmar, Holy Redeemer.

Secretary, Dorchester Co., Our Lady of Good Counsel, Rev. William P. Mathesius, D. Min.
Res., 109 Willow Street, P.O. Box 278, 21664. Tel: 410-943-4300. [CEM]
Catechesis/Religious Programs—Sr. Juliana Dischler, O.P., D.R.E.
Students 87.
Mission—Bethlehem, Caroline Co., Holy Child, Rte. 331, P.O. Box 70, Bethlehem, 21609. Tel: 410-673-2199.

Chaplains of Public Institutions

National Guard

WILMINGTON. *Delaware Army National Guard,* 4701 Weldin Rd., 19803. Chaplains: Revs. Daniel W. Gerres; John J. Mink; David F. Murphy.
Pennsylvania Air National Guard, 901 New Rd., 19805. Tel: 302-994-2922. Rev. Francis J. Rogers, Chap.

BALTIMORE, MD. *Delaware Air National Guard,* 209 W. Fayette St., 21201-3403. Tel: 302-762-4140. Rev. George J. Brubaker, Chap.

Health Care

WILMINGTON. *A.I. du Pont Institute.* Rev. David A. Baumgartel, Chap., Tel: 302-764-0357.
Bissell Hospital. Rev. Joseph Kandathiparampil, Chap, Tel: 302-999-0211.
St. Francis Hospital, 7th St. & Clayton St., 19805. Tel: 302-421-4577. Rev. Joseph Narimattam.

DELAWARE CITY. *Governor Bacon Health Center.* Rev. Philip L. Siry, Chap., Tel: 302-834-4321.

ELSMERE. *Veteran's Hospital,* 1601 Kirkwood Hwy., Tel: 302-994-2511. Chaplains: Revs. John P. Connery, O.S.F.S.; William J. Dougherty, O.S.F.S., Asst. Chap.

NEW CASTLE. *Delaware State Hospital.* Rev. Carlos R. Vazquez, Chap.

NEWARK. *Medical Center of Delaware,* 4755 Ogleton-Stanton Rds., Tel: 302-733-1900; 733-1280. Chaplains: Revs. John Finn, O.S.F.S.; Howard T. Clark; Joseph J. McKenna, O.S.F.S.; Savarimuthu Irudayaraj.

PERRY POINT, MD. *Veterans Admin.* Rev. John J. Abraham Tel: 410-642-2411.

SMYRNA, MD. *Delaware Home & Hospital for the Chronically Ill.* Rev. Ralph L. Martin, Chap., Tel: 302-653-8279.

Correctional Facilities

WILMINGTON. *Ferris School and Bridge House.* Deacon George M. Taylor, Jr., Chap., Tel: 302-995-2350.
Gander Hill Correctional Center. Rev. Daniel W. Gerres, Chap., Tel: 302-764-0357.

SMYRNA, MD. *Delaware Correctional Center.* Rev. James D. Hreha, Chap., Tel: 302-653-9261, Ext. 258; 674-5787 (Res.).

WESTOVER, MD. *Eastern Correctional Institution.* Rev. Edward M. Aigner, Jr., Chap., Tel: 410-651-9000; 651-2054 (Res.).

Campus Ministry

CHESTERTOWN, MD. *Washington College,* Sacred Heart, 508 High St., 21620. Tel: 410-778-3160. Rev. Leonard J. Blakely, Chap.

DOVER. *Wesley College.* Rev. Robert J. Malone, C.S.C., St. Thomas More Oratory, 45 Lovett Ave., Newark, 19711. Tel: 302-368-4728.

NEWARK. *University of Delaware,* St. Thomas More Oratory, 45 Lovett Ave., 19711. Tel: 302-368-4728. Chaplains: Very Rev. Michael F. Szupper, Ph.D., Dir. Campus Ministry; Rev. Robert J. Malone, C.S.C., Assoc. Dir.

PRINCESS ANNE, MD. *University of Maryland, Eastern Shore,* P.O. Box 490, 21853. Tel: 410-651-2054. Rev. Edward M. Aigner, Chap.

SALISBURY, MD. *Salisbury State College,* St. Francis de Sales, 514 Camden Ave., 21801. Tel: 410-742-6443. Rev. Christopher A. Kopec, Chap.

Apostleship of the Sea:
Reverend Fathers—
Kauffman, William B., Chap., Cathedral of St. Peter, 500 West St., Wilmington, De 19801. Tel: 302-654-5920

Nursing Homes:
Reverend Fathers—
Storck, Edward J., Chap., Victorian Sq., 1504-2 N. Broom St., #17, Wilmington, DE 19806-3048. Tel: 302-428-1415

Special Assignment:
Reverend Fathers—
Hopkins, John P., Dir. Catholic Youth Organizations & Youth Ministry, 803 N. Broom St., Wilmington, DE 19805. Tel: 302-658-3800
Richardson, James E., 2001 Eden Rd., Wilmington, DE 19810. Tel: 302-529-7280

On Duty Outside the Diocese:
Reverend Monsignors—
Koper, Francis B., SS. Cyril and Methodius Seminary, Orchard Lake, MI 48033
Reverend Fathers—
Barres, John O., Casa Santa Maria, Via Dell'Umilta, 30, Rome, 00187 Italy
Brubaker, George J., Catholic Relief Services, 209 W. Fayette St., Baltimore, MD 21201-3403
Delaney, James T., Mt. St. Mary's College, Emmitsburg, MD 21727
Gallagher, Michael J., Trinity College, Theology Dept., 125 Michigan Ave., Washington, DC 20017
Martin, Kenneth J., Our Lady of Victory Church, 4835 MacArthur Blvd. N.W., Washington, DC 20007
McMahon, Kevin T., St. Charles Borromeo Seminary, 1000 E. Wynnewood Rd. Overbrook, Philadelphia, PA 19096
Pagano, Bernard T., St. Mary of Mt. Virgin, 190 Sanford St., New Brunswick, NJ 08901
Turley, Sean F., SS. Michael and James, Haunton near Tamworth, Staffordshire, B799HL (1848), Great Britain

Military Chaplains:
Reverend Fathers—
Mullen, Owen J., 249A Lee Rd., West Point, NY 10996
Papp, Christopher, Chap., USAF, 11707 Andriana Maria, San Antonio, TX 78253
Volmi, Dennis G., 3197A Minuteman St., Hill AFB, UT 84056

Absent on Sick Leave:
Reverend Fathers—
Dudzinski, Edward F., Jr.
McCloskey, Daniel J.
McGovern, Joseph A.

Retired:
Reverend Monsignors—
Dewson, John H., Immaculate Heart of Mary, 4701 Weldin Rd., Wilmington, DE 19803
Taggart, Paul J., Cathedral of St. Peter, 500 N. West St., Wilmington, DE 19801

Reverend Fathers—
Brady, Patrick A., St. Edmond, P.O. Box 646, Rehoboth Beach, DE 19971
Breen, Stephen B., Holy Spirit, 12 Winder Rd., New Castle, De 19720
Carley, Edward B., 302 Condo Park Blvd., Laurel St., Santurce, PR 00913
Clarahan, Eugene F., 2282 Sea Air, Rehoboth Beach, DE 19971
DeLuca, Francis G., Fahey Court, 100 Pastime Dr., Apt. 307, Syracuse, NY 13208
Dempster, Douglas W., P.O. Box 370, Marydel, MD 21649
Frundt, Oscar H., Church of the Holy Child, 2500 Naamans Rd., Wilmington, DE 19810
Gardocki, Thomas F., 4620 Sylvanus Dr., Wilmington, DE 19803
Gomolski, Joseph T., 241 Balboa Dr., Poinciana, FL 34758
Gorski, Alex F., 1401 Pennsylvania Ave., Apt. 1205, Wilmington, DE 19806
Harney, Peter, 17 Sheffield Dr., Sussex East, Lewes, DE 19958
Horgan, Joseph C., 1005 N. Franklin St, Apt. 704., Wilmington, DE 19806-4549
Jennings, William E., 2303 Inglewood Dr., Wilmington, DE 19803
Klapps, William J., Caravel Farms, 260 Benjamin Blvd., Bear, DE 19701
McGann, L. Philip, 5541 Bay Ave., Ocean City, NJ 08226
Paris, Charles W., Box 752, Toms River, NJ 08754
Perkins, Russell H., P.O. Box 2437, Manteo, NC 27954
Plokhooy, Christopher, St. John the Beloved, 907 Milltown Rd., Wilmington, DE 19808
Power, Walter D., Church of the Good Shepherd, 828 Aiken Ave., Perryville, MD 21903
Rhodes, George V., Jeanne Jugan Residence, 185 Salem Church Rd., Newark, DE 19713

Permanent Deacons:
Baker, Joseph G., St. Michael the Archangel, Georgetown, DE
Becker, John J., St. Peter, New Castle, DE
Beers, Carl (NYC), St. Francis de Sales, Salisbury, MD
Bianco, Anthony A., St. John the Apostle, Milford, DE
Brink, Edward J., St. Ann, Bethany Beach, DE
Campbell, Jack H., St. Luke and St. Andrew, Ocean City, MD
Catka, Tony E., St. Mary Magdalen and Family Life Bureau, Wilmington, DE
Chalfant, Harold F., St. Matthew, Wilmington, DE
Conner, James, St. Frances de Sales, Salisbury, MD
Conte, Joseph J., Parish of the Resurrection, Newark, DE
Costello, John L., Holy Name of Jesus, Pocomoke City, MD
Dunning, Edward A., St. Helena and Marian Devotions, Wilmington, DE
Falkowski, John J., Jr., St. Catherine of Siena, Wilmington, DE
Freebery, John W., Jr., St. Mary of the Assumption, Hockessin, DE
Haley, James J., St. John the Beloved, Wilmington, DE
Handlir, James, St. Peter, New Castle, DE
Huhn, Francis J., Parish of the Resurrection, Newark, DE
Jopp, Harold D., Jr., St. Benedict's, Ridgely, MD
Lafferty, James J., Jr., St. Ann's, Wilmington, DE
Lynch, Edmund F., St. Joseph on the Brandywine, Greenville, DE
Maichle, Richard J., Sr., Holy Rosary, Claymont, DE
Malloy, James D., St. John the Apostle, Milford, DE
Maloney, William J., Jr., Christ Our King, Wilmington, DE
McCann, Hugh J., St. John's/Holy Angel's, Newark, DE
McCarthy, Richard, St. Mary Star of the Sea, Ocean City, MD
Murrian, William J., Holy Family, Ogletown, DE
Normoyle, Robert H., St. Mary Star of the Sea, Ocean City, MD
O'Connor, Howard J., Holy Family, Newark, DE
Parisi, John G., Corpus Christi, Wilmington, DE
Passwaters, Arcy A., Our Lady of Lourdes, Seaford, DE
Recce, Richard L., St. Mary Magdalen, Wilmington, DE
Romans, Joseph C., Our Lady of Fatima, New Castle and Christiana Div., Medical Center of Delaware, New Castle, DE
Rose, Albert F., Parish of the Resurrection, Seton Villa, Siena Hall, Newark, DE
Seador, John L., Holy Family, Newark, DE
Shearer, John David, St. Francis de Sales, Popular Hill Correctional Center, Salisbury, MD
Siers, Ronald (L), St. Francis de Sales, Salisbury, MD
Smith, John A., St. Edmund, Rehoboth Beach, DE
Snow, Austin M., Jr., Immaculate Heart of Mary, Wilmington, DE
Staab, Francis J., St. Catherine of Siena, Wilmington, DE
Taylor, George M., Jr., Cathedral of St. Peter & Ferris School, Wilmington, DE
Torres, Samuel, Church of the Holy Child, Wilmington, DE
Tracy, Robert, St. Ann, Bethany Beach, DE
VanBourgondien, Cornelius J., SS Peter and Paul, Easton, MD
Vinciguerra, Anthony P., Holy Cross, Dover, DE
Wolf, Allen S., Claymont, DE, Holy Rosary; Christiana Div., Medical Center of Delaware, New Castle, DE

INSTITUTIONS LOCATED IN THE DIOCESE

[A] HIGH SCHOOLS, DIOCESAN

WILMINGTON. *St. Mark's High School*, Pike Creek Rd., 19808. Tel: 302-738-3300. Dr. John C. Monnig, Prin.; Rev. Gregory M. Corrigan. Priests 1; Sisters 7; Lay Teachers 108; Students 1,585.

[B] HIGH SCHOOLS, PRIVATE

WILMINGTON. *Salesianum School*, 1801 N. Broom St., 19802. Tel: 302-654-2495; 655-1592; Fax: 302-654-7767. Revs. Robert D. Kenney, O.S.F.S., Pres.; Thomas J. McGee, O.S.F.S., Prin.; John J. Fisher, O.S.F.S., Asst. Prin & Supr.; Paul J. Campbell, O.S.F.S.; Charles M. Chamberlain, O.S.F.S.; Anthony A. Gilborges, O.S.F.S.; Stephen E. Shott, O.S.F.S.; R. Douglas Smith, O.S.F.S.; Thomas J. Tucker, O.S.F.S.; Mark J. Wrightson, O.S.F.S.; Paul E. Burke, O.S.F.S.; John P. Connery, O.S.F.S.; Francis D. Dougherty, O.S.F.S.; Stanley R. Drupieski, O.S.F.S.; John F. Heckel, O.S.F.S.; Joseph J. McKenna, O.S.F.S.; John P. Spellman, O.S.F.S.; Vincent de Paul Burke, O.S.F.S.; John M. Mokluk, O.S.F.S.; Bros. Joseph G. Schodowski, O.S.F.S.; Patrick Press, O.S.F.S. Priests 13; Brothers 2; Lay Teachers 59; Boys 1025.

Ursuline Academy of Wilmington, DE, Inc., 1106 Pennsylvania Ave., 19806. Tel: 302-658-7158; Fax: 302-658-4297. (Coed Grades Early Childhood-3, All Girls Grades 4-12). Ms. Angela M. Boyle, Pres. Lay Faculty 77; Ursuline Nuns 2; Students 700.

CLAYMONT. *Archmere Academy*, 3600 Philadelphia Pike, 19703. Tel: 302-798-6632; Fax: 302-798-7290. Coed College Preparatory High School. Very Rev. Timothy F. Mullen, O.Praem., Prior; Rev. Joseph P. McLaughlin, O.Praem., Headmaster; Rev. James D., Bagnato, O.Praem.; Revs. Jeffrey T. Cesarone, O.Praem.; Michael T. Collins, O.Praem.; Paul J. DeAntoniis, O.Praem.; Blaise P. Krautsack, O.Praem.; Brian A. Zielinski, O.Praem. Priests 8; Lay Teachers 47; Students 492.

RIDGELY, MD. *The Benedictine School Habilitation Center*, 21660. Tel: 410-634-2115. Dixie Hughlett, Coord. Sisters 3; Lay Personnel 32; Students 42. Open Community Program MD/DE. Ages 21 and older. Tel: 410-634-1990. Eleanor Sweeney, Coord. Students 62; Lay Teachers 17.

WYOMING.

**Thomas More Academy, Inc.*, P.O. Box 521, 19934. Dr. Ralph A. Leitner, Headmaster.

[C] ELEMENTARY SCHOOLS, PRIVATE

WILMINGTON. *Saint Edmond's Academy*. (Grades 4-8), 2120 Veale Rd., 19810. Tel: 302-475-5370; Fax: 302-475-2256. Bros. Michael A. Smith, C.S.C., Headmaster; Joseph Ash, C.S.C.; Edward Quintal, C.S.C.; James DeTemple, C.S.C.; David Parrish, C.S.C.; Thomas Meany, C.S.C.; Thomas Durney, C.S.C.; Stanislay Esposito, C.S.C. Brothers of Holy Cross 8; Lay Teachers 17; Boys 261.

CHILDS, MD. *Mount Aviat Academy*. (Grades 1-8), 21916. Oblate Sisters of St. Francis de Sales. Sr. John Marie, O.S.F.S., Prin. Sisters 7; Lay Teachers 11; Students 210.

Oblate Sisters' Kindergarten and Nursery, Villa Aviat, 399 Childs Rd., 21916-0085. Tel: 410-398-3699. Oblate Sisters of St. Francis de Sales 2; Lay Teachers 2; Students 50.

RIDGELY, MD. *The Benedictine School for Exceptional Children*, 21660. Tel: 410-634-2112. Sisters of St. Benedict. Sr. Jeanette Murray, O.S.B., Dir.; Rev. Francis J. Rinaldi, O.S.F.S., Chap. Sisters 9; Lay Personnel 128; Students 140.

Benedictine School for Exceptional Children Foundation, Inc., 21660. Sr. Jeannette Murray, O.S.B., Dir. Sisters 1; Lay Staff 3.

[D] DIOCESAN CATHOLIC CHARITIES PROGRAM

WILMINGTON. *Catholic Charities, Inc.*, 2601 W. 4th St., P.O. Box 2610, 19805-0610. Tel: 302-655-9624; Fax: 302-655-9753. Mr. Allan J. Daul, A.C.S.W., Diocesan Sec. & Exec. Dir.; Ms. Barbara Grieco, M.C., M.B.A., Deputy Dir. & Dir. Children's Services; Katrina Furlong, Div. Dir.; Mr. Albert F. Rose, Jr., M.B.A., Dir. Finance; Ms. Donna Connor, Dir. Devel. Staff 180; Individuals Served 91,230; Fuel Program 31,333. New Castle. Tel: 302-654-6474. Sussex. Tel: 302-856-6200. Kent. Tel: 302-674-1782.

Social Service Counseling Centers. 4th St. & Greenhill Ave., P.O. Box 2610, 19805-0610. Tel: 302-655-9624.

Dover Office. 442 S. New St., Dover, 19904. Tel: 302-674-1600.

Georgetown Office. 600 N. Dupont Hwy., Georgetown, 19947. Tel: 302-856-9578.

Salisbury Office. 1405 Wesley Dr., Salisbury, MD, 21801. Tel: 410-749-1121.

Children's Services (adoption and foster care). 4th St. & Greenhill Ave., P.O. Box 2610, 19805-0610. Tel: 302-655-9624. Ms. Neomi Litonjua, L.C.S.W., Supvr.

Family & Individual Services (including Family Life Bureau). 4th St. & Greenhill Ave., P.O. Box 2610, 19805-0610. Tel: 302-655-9624. Mr. Thomas R. Jewett, M.C., Admin.

Community and Family Support Services.

Crisis Alleviation. 4th St. & Greenhill Ave., P.O. Box 2610, 19805-0610. Tel: 302-654-6473. Sharon Truitt, Contact Person, 121 W. Loockerman St., Dover, 19904. Tel: 302-674-4016; Fax: 302-674-4018. Betty Fean, Contact Person; Katrina Furlong, Div. Dir., New Castle Co. Tel: 302-654-6474. Kent Co. Tel: 302-674-1782. Sussex Co. Tel: 302-856-6200.

Energy Assistance. New Castle Co. Tel: 302-654-9295. Kent Co. Tel: 302-674-1782. Sussex Co. Tel: 302-856-6310.

Immigration & Refugee Program. 4th St. and Greenhill Ave., P.O. Box 2610, 19805-0610. Tel: 302-654-6460. Mabel N. Sturgeon, Contact Person.

Catholic Charities Thrift Shop. 1320 E. 23rd St., 19802. Tel: 302-764-2717. Diane Kelly, Mgr.

Catholic Charities Thrift Shop. 2000 W. 4th St. (4th St. & Union Sts.), 19805. Tel: 302-655-9300. Lorraine Shannon, Mgr.

Child & Adult Care Food Program. 442 S. New St., P.O. Box 495, Dover, 19904. Tel: 302-674-1600; 1-800-239-2839. Donna Costilow, Contact Person, New Castle Co. Tel: 302-366-0392. Hanne Dawson-Holt, Contact Person, Sussex Co. Tel: 302-856-9578. Pat Miller, Contact Person.

Addiction Services.

Center for Pastoral Care. Fifth St. & Greenhill Ave., P.O. Box 2610, 19805-0610. Tel: 302-656-0651. Janet Barkowsky, M.S.A., D.A.C.A.C., N.C.A.C. Dir.

Residential Services. 2307 Kentmere Pkwy., 19806. Tel: 302-656-2183. Barbara Grieco, M.C., Deputy Dir. & Dir. of Children's Services.

Siena Hall, Inc. 2307 Kentmere Pkwy., 19806. Tel: 302-656-2183. Barbara Grieco, M.C., Deputy Dir. & Dir. of Children's Services.

Seton Villa, Inc. 800 Bellevue Rd., 19809. Tel: 302-762-2982. Barbara Grieco, Deputy Dir. & Dir. of Children's Services.

Children's Home. 2901 Green St., Claymont, 19703. Tel: 302-798-0601. Barbara Grieco, M.C., Deputy Dir. & Dir. of Children's Services.

Casa San Francisco. 127 Broad St., P.O. Box 38, Milton, 19968. Tel: 302-684-8694; Fax: 302-684-2808. Ms. Marion Bau, Mgr.; Pat Saez, Contact Person.

Delaware Day Treatment Center. 1156 W. Walker Rd., Dover, 19904. Tel: 302-674-8211. Valleree R. Roach, M.S.S.W., Program Dir., Georgetown Office, 231 S. Race St., Georgetown, 19947. Tel: 302-855-9520. Valleree R. Roach, M.S.S.W., Prog. Dir.

Seton Center. 30632 Hampden Ave., P.O. Box 401, Princess Anne, MD, 21853. Tel: 410-651-9608.

Office for Parish Social Ministry. 4th St. & Greenhill Ave., P.O. Box 2610, 19805-0610. Tel: 302-655-9624. Margaret P. Heins, Dir.

[E] RESIDENCES FOR CHILDREN

WILMINGTON. *Seton Villa, Inc.*, 800 Bellevue Rd., 19809. Tel: 302-762-2982.
For a complete listing, refer to the Special Care Facilities section.

Siena Hall, Inc., 2307 Kentmere Pkwy., 19806. Tel: 302-656-2183.
For a complete listing, refer to the Special Care Facilities section.

CLAYMONT. *Children's Home, Inc.*, 2901 Green St., 19702. Tel: 302-798-0601.
For a complete listing, refer to the Special Care Facilities section.

[F] OTHER WELFARE AGENCIES

(Not under jurisdiction of Department of Social Concerns)

WILMINGTON. *Home of Divine Providence, Inc.-Bayard House*, 300 Bayard Ave., 19805. Tel: 302-654-1184.
For a complete listing, refer to the Special Care Facilities section.

Ministry of Caring, Inc., 506 N. Church St., 19801-4812. Tel: 302-652-5523; Fax: 302-652-1919.
For a complete listing, refer to the Special Care Facilities section.

NEWARK. *Our Lady of Grace Home for Children, Inc.*, 487 E. Chestnut Hill Rd., 19713. Tel: 302-738-4658; 737-6650.
For a complete listing, refer to the Special Care Facilities section.

RIDGELY, MD. *St. Martin's Ministries*, 14259 Benedictine Ln., 21660. Tel: 410-634-2497.
For a complete listing, refer to the Special Care Facilities section.

[G] HOMES FOR AGED

WILMINGTON. *The Antonian*, 1701 W. 10th St., 19805. Tel: 302-421-3758.
For a complete listing, refer to the Special Care Facilities section.

Franciscan Health System/Care at Wilmington, 801 N. Broom St., 19806. Tel: 302-652-3861.
For a complete listing, refer to the Special Care Facilities section.

St. Patrick's House, Inc., 115 E. 14th St., 19801. Tel: 302-654-6908.
For a complete listing, refer to the Special Care Facilities section.

HOCKESSIN. *Franciscan Health System/Care at Brackenville*, 100 St. Clare Dr., 19707. Tel: 302-234-5420.
For a complete listing, refer to the Special Care Facilities section.

NEWARK. *Jeanne Jugan Residence*, 185 Salem Church Rd., 19713.
For a complete listing, refer to the Special Care Facilities section.

Marydale Retirement Village, 135 Jeandell Dr., 19713. Tel: 302-368-2784.
For a complete listing, refer to the Special Care Facilities section.

[H] GENERAL HOSPITALS

WILMINGTON. *St. Francis Hospital, Inc.*, 7th and Clayton Sts., P.O. Box 2500, 19805-0500. Tel: 302-575-8300.
For a complete listing, refer to the Hospitals section.

[I] MONASTERIES AND RESIDENCES OF PRIESTS AND BROTHERS

WILMINGTON. *Brothers of Holy Cross, St. Edmond's Academy*, 2120 Veale Rd., 19810. Bro. Joseph W. Ash, C.S.C., Dir. Religious. Brothers 8.

Capuchin Franciscan Friars, St. Francis Renewal Center, 1901 Prior Rd., 19809. Tel: 302-798-1454; Fax: 302-798-3360. Revs. Cyprian Rosen, O.F.M.Cap., Guardian, Dir.; Thomas Pietrantonio, O.F.M.Cap., Vicar.

DeSales House, 1600 Brinckle Ave., 19806. Tel: 302-656-4342. Revs. William R. Gore, O.S.F.S., Supr.; John A. Finn, O.S.F.S.; William A. Guerin, O.S.F.S.; John J. Hurley, O.S.F.S.; William H. Juergens, O.S.F.S.; Joseph D. Bowler, O.S.F.S.; William J. Keech, O.S.F.S.; Richard D. Leone, O.S.F.S. Priests 8.

Oblates of St. Francis De Sales. Residence of the Provincial, 2200 Kentmere Pkwy., P.O. Box 1452, 19899. Tel: 302-656-8529. Very Rev. Joseph G. Morrissey, O.S.F.S., Prov.; Revs. Edward T. Fitzpatrick, O.S.F.S., Dir. Personnel; Richard R. De Lillio, O.S.F.S., Dir. Devel.; Joseph P. Jocco, O.S.F.S., Dir. Vocations; Francis J. Hanlon, O.S.F.S., Dir. Senior Oblates; Joseph J. Chorpenning, O.S.F.S.; Walter R. Dean, O.S.F.S.; Anthony J. Pinizzotto, O.S.F.S.; George S. Salzmann, O.S.F.S.; William J. Hultberg, O.S.F.S. Military Chaplains: Revs. John F. Friel, O.S.F.S.; James J. MacNew, O.S.F.S.; Stanley J. Dombrowski, O.S.F.S. Priests 3.

St. Felix Friary, 119 N. Jackson St., 19805-3670. Tel: 302-652-7010; Fax: 302-652-8943. Rev. Ronald Giannone, O.F.M.Cap., Guardian; Bro. Kevin O'Loughlin, O.F.M.Cap., Vicar. Brothers 4.

CHILDS, MD. *Oblates of St. Francis De Sales*. Retirement and Retreat Center, 1120 Blue Ball Rd., 21916. Tel: 410-398-3040; Fax: 410-398-0116. Rev. John W. Brennan, O.S.F.S., Supr. In res., Revs. Joseph A. Baird, O.S.F.S.; George J. Brownholtz, O.S.F.S.; Francis T. Christof, O.S.F.S.; George W. Martyn, O.S.F.S.; John J. Conmy, O.S.F.S.; Hugh E. Duffy, O.S.F.S.; Joseph T. Dunn, O.S.F.S.; James E. Cassidy, O.S.F.S.; James V. O'Neill, O.S.F.S.; Thomas F. Malloy, O.S.F.S.; Vincent J. Kowalewski, O.S.F.S.; Joseph F. Lynn, O.S.F.S.; Louis R. McCartney, O.S.F.S.; James J. McGuire, O.S.F.S.; Michael B. Donovan, O.S.F.S.; Hugh J. McKenna, O.S.F.S.; Anthony T. Schelich, O.S.F.S.; Joseph E. Stafford, O.S.F.S.; Joseph E. Woods, O.S.F.S.; Thomas J. Walsh, O.S.F.S. Brothers 7.

CLAYMONT. *Immaculate Conception Priory of the Canons Regular of Premontre*, 19703-0103. Tel: 302-792-2791. Norbertine Fathers of Our Lady of Daylesford Abbey, Paoli, PA. Revs. Timothy F. Mullen, O.Praem, Supr.; Joseph A. McLaughlin, O.Praem., Headmaster; James D. Bagnato, O.Praem.; Jeffrey T. Cesarone, O.Praem.; Michael T. Collins, O.Praem.; Paul J. DeAntoniis, O.Praem.; Blaise Krautsack, O.Praem.; Brian A. Zielinski, O.Praem. Priests 8.

SEAFORD. *Missionary Fraternity of Mary, USA, Ltd.*, 340 Pine St., 19973. Tel: 302-629-5705; Fax: 302-629-7403. Revs. Ruben Albano Soto, F.M.M.; Juan Vincente Hidalgo, F.M.M.

[J] CONVENTS AND RESIDENCES FOR SISTERS

WILMINGTON. *Casa de San Jose - Franciscan Sisters of Our Lady of the Sacred Heart*, 601 N. Jackson St., 19805. Tel: 302-654-8200. Sr. Ann Marie Gonzales, F.S.S.H., Supr.

Monastery of St. Veronica Giuliani. (Strict Enclosure), 816 Jefferson St., 19801. Tel: 302-654-8727; Fax: 302-652-1919. Capuchin Poor Clare Nuns of Delaware, Inc. Mother Maria del Carmen Quiroz, O.S.C.Cap., Abbess; Rev. Ronald Giannone, O.F.M.Cap., Chap. Sisters 10; Postulants 1; Novices 2.

Our Lady of Peace Convent, 1801 W. 8th St., 19805. Tel: 302-426-1809. The Sisters of St. Francis of Philadelphia 3.

St. Francis Convent, 701 N. Rodney St., 19805. Tel: 302-652-8489. The Sisters of St. Francis of Philadelphia 9.

St. Mark's Faculty Residence, 2503 Pike Creek Rd., 19808-3615. Tel: 302-738-5440. Intercommunity Sisters 18.

Ursuline Academy Inc., The, 1104 Pennsylvania Ave., 19806. Tel: 302-656-5890. Sr. Julia Dennehy, O.S.U., Supr. Sisters 18.

CHILDS, MD. *Villa Aviat Convent*, 399 Childs Rd., 21916. Tel: 410-398-3699. Oblate Sisters of St. Francis de Sales. Sr. John Marie, O.S.F.S., Supr. Sisters 11.

EASTON, MD. *Eastern Shore Co-op*, 304 Prospect Ave., 21601. Tel: 410-820-7437. Sisters 3.

HOCKESSIN. *St. Benedict-at-Innisfail*, 3975 Millcreek Rd., 19707. Tel: 302-239-0973. Sisters of St. Benedict 4.

NEW CASTLE. *Our Lady of Fatima Convent*, 100 W. Grant Ave., 19720. Tel: 302-328-2752. Sr. Anna May Coll, Supr. The Sisters of St. Francis of Philadelphia (Semi-retired) 10.

PRINCESS ANNE, MD. *Seton Center, Sisters of Charity*. (Convent Station), 30255 Mount Vernon Rd., 21853. Tel: 410-651-9608. Sisters 4; Assisted 11,970.

RIDGELY, MD. *St. Gertrude's Monastery, Motherhouse and Novitiate of the Sisters of St. Benedict*, 14259 Benedictine Ln., 21660. Tel: 410-634-2497; Fax: 410-634-1410. Sr. Mary Paul McLaughlin, O.S.B., Prioress. In res., Rev. Francis J. Rinaldi, O.S.F.S., Chap. Sisters 44.

SALISBURY, MD. *Joseph House, Little Sisters of Jesus & Mary.*, P.O. Box 1755, 21802. Tel: 410-543-1645. Sr. Mary Elizabeth Gintling, Dir. Sisters 6; Postulants 1.

[K] SECULAR INSTITUTES

NEWARK. *St. Francis De Sales Secular Institute*, 62 Willow Creek Ln., 19711. Tel: 302-239-8616. Mary H. Robinson, Formation Dir. U.S.A. & Contact; Joan Bereswill, Dir. U.S.A. Tel: 703-591-5196.

[L] RETREAT HOUSES, GENERAL

WILMINGTON. *St. Francis Renewal Center*, 1901 Prior Rd., 19809. Tel: 302-798-1454; Fax: 302-798-3360. Revs. Cyprian Rosen, O.F.M.Cap., Guardian, Dir.; Thomas Pietrantonio, O.F.M.Cap., Vicar. Priests 2.

[M] RETREAT HOUSES, WOMEN

HOCKESSIN. *Benedictines-at-Innisfail Spirituality and Conference Center*, 3975 Millcreek Rd., 19707. Tel: 302-239-0973. Benedictine Sisters.

RIDGELY, MD. *Berg Retreat Center*, St. Gertrude's Monastery, 14259 Benedictine Ln., 21660. Tel: 410-634-2497. Benedictine Sisters.

[N] INFORMATION CENTERS

WILMINGTON. *The Franciscan Center*, 833 N. Market St., 19801-3078. Tel: 302-656-0711. Bro. David W. Schlatter, O.F.M., Dir. Asst. Directors: Rev. Barry J. Langley, O.F.M.; Bro. Henry L. Fulmer, O.F.M.

[O] NEWMAN CENTERS

CHESTERTOWN, MD. *Washington College Newman Center*, Sacred Heart, 508 High St., 21620. Tel: 410-778-3160. Rev. Leonard J. Blakely, Chap.

NEWARK. *Univ. of Delaware Newman Center*, St. Thomas More Oratory, 45 Lovett Ave., 19711. Tel: 302-368-4728. Very Rev. Michael F. Szupper, Ph.D., Chap. & Diocesan Dir. Campus Ministry; Rev. Robert J. Malone, C.S.C.

Delmar Organization of Catholic Students - DOCS. Kimberly S. Zitzner, B.A., Dir.

Salisbury State College, St. Francis de Sales, 514 Camden Ave., Salisbury, MD, 21801. Tel: 410-742-6443. University of Maryland Eastern Shore, P.O. Box 490, Princess Anne, MD, 21853. Tel: 410-651-2054. Rev. Edward M. Aigner, Chap.

Wesley College. Tel: 302-368-4728. Rev. Robert J. Malone, C.S.C., Chap.

Washington College, 508 High St., Chestertown, MD, 21260. Tel: 410-778-3160. Rev. Leonard J. Blakely, Chap.

Wesley College Newman Center, St. Thomas More Oratory, 45 Lovett Ave., 19711. Tel: 302-368-4728. Rev. Robert J. Malone, C.S.C., Chap.

RELIGIOUS INSTITUTES OF MEN REPRESENTED IN THE DIOCESE

For further details refer to the corresponding bracketed number in the Religious Institutes of Men or Women section.

[0600]—*Brothers of the Congregation of Holy Cross*. (Eastern Province).—C.S.C.

[0900]—*Canons Regular of Premontre*.—O.Praem.

[0470]—*The Capuchin Friars*. (Prov. of the Stigmata).—O.F.M.Cap.

[0520]—*Franciscan Friars*. (Holy Name Province).—O.F.M.

[0690]—*Jesuit Fathers and Brothers*.—S.J.

[0855]—*Missionary Fraternity of Mary*.—F.M.M.

[0853]—*Missionary Servants of Christ*.—M.S.C.

[0920]—*Oblates of St. Francis de Sales.*—O.S.F.S.
[1070]—*Redemptorist Fathers.* (Baltimore, MD).—C.SS.R.
[0700]—*St. Joseph's Society of the Sacred Heart.* (Baltimore, MD).—S.S.J.
[1240]—*Servites.*—O.S.M.
[0560]—*Third Order Regular of Saint Francis.*—T.O.R.

RELIGIOUS INSTITUTES OF WOMEN REPRESENTED IN THE DIOCESE

[0100]—*Adorers of the Blood of Christ.*—A.S.C.
[0230]—*Benedictine Sisters of Pontifical Jurisdiction.*—O.S.B.
[3765]—*Capuchin Poor Clare Sisters.*—O.S.C.Cap.
[]—*Carmelite Sisters of Charity of Vedruna.*—C.C.V.
[0760]—*Daughters of the Charity of St. Vincent de Paul.*—D.C.
[1070-09]—*Dominican Sisters.*—O.P.
[1070-11]—*Dominican Sisters.*—O.P.
[1170]—*Felician Sisters.*—C.S.S.F.
[1180]—*Franciscan Sisters of Allegheny, New York.*—O.S.F.
[]—*Franciscan Sisters of Our Lady of the Sacred Heart.*—O.S.F.
[2331]—*Little Sisters of Jesus and Mary.*—L.S.J.M.
[2340]—*Little Sisters of the Poor.*—L.S.P.
[2720]—*Mission Helpers of the Sacred Heart.* (Prov. of Baltimore).—M.H.S.H.
[2790]—*Missionary Servants of the Most Blessed Trinity.*—M.S.B.T.
[3060]—*Oblates Sisters of St. Francis de Sales.*—O.S.F.S.
[3230]—*Poor Handmaids of Jesus Christ.*—P.H.J.C.
[2575]—*Religious Sisters of Mercy of the Americas.* (Baltimore, MD; Merion, PA).—R.S.M.
[2970]—*School Sisters of Notre Dame.*—S.S.N.D.
[0590]—*Sisters of Charity of Saint Elizabeth, Convent Station.* (Southern, Western Provs.).—S.C.
[0570]—*Sisters of Charity of Seton Hill.*—S.C.
[0990]—*Sisters of Divine Providence.* (St. Peter Prov.).—C.D.P.
[2990]—*Sisters of Notre Dame.*—S.N.D.
[1650]—*Sisters of St. Francis of Philadelphia.*—O.S.F.
[3840]—*Sisters of St. Joseph of Carondelet.* (Prov. of St. Louis).—C.S.J.
[3893]—*Sisters of St. Joseph of Chestnut Hill, Philadelphia.*—S.S.J.
[3730]—*Sisters of the Order of St. Basil the Great.*—O.S.B.M.
[2160]—*Sisters, Servants of Immaculate Heart of Mary.*—I.H.M.
[4060]—*Society of the Holy Child Jesus.*—S.H.C.J.
[4110]—*Ursuline Nuns (Roman Union).* (Eastern Prov.).—O.S.U.

DIOCESAN CEMETERIES

WILMINGTON. *All Saints*, Box 2506, 19805. Tel: 302-737-2524; Fax: 302-737-4091. Office, Kirkwood Hwy., 19805. Mark A. Christian, Exec. Dir.; Thomas J. Kane, Supt.

Cathedral, Box 2506, 19805. Tel: 302-656-3323; Fax: 302-656-1069. Office, 2400 Lancaster Ave., 19805. Mark A. Christian, Exec. Dir. & Supt.

NECROLOGY

† Hammel, James T., (Retired). —Died Aug. 4, 1996.
† Montgomery, Leo F., (Retired). —Died Nov. 27, 1996.

Diocese of Winona

(Dioecesis Winonensis)

Most Reverend

JOHN G. VLAZNY, D.D.

Bishop of Winona; ordained December 20, 1961; appointed Auxiliary Bishop of Chicago and Titular Bishop of Stagno October 31, 1983; consecrated December 13, 1983; appointed Bishop of Winona May 19, 1987; installed July 29, 1987. *Mailing Address: 55 W. Sanborn St., P.O. Box 588, Winona., MN, 55987.* Tel.: 507-454-4643; Fax: 507-454-8106.

Most Reverend

LORAS J. WATTERS, D.D.

Retired Bishop of Winona; ordained June 7, 1941; appointed Titular Bishop of Fidoloma and Auxiliary Bishop of Dubuque June 23, 1965; consecrated August 26, 1965; transferred to Winona January 8, 1969; retired October 14, 1986; appointed Apostolic Administrator October 14, 1986. *Res., 618 Forest, Apt. D, Pacific Grove, CA, 93950.* Tel.: 408-373-3715.

ESTABLISHED NOVEMBER 26, 1889.

Square Miles 12,282.

Comprises the Counties of Winona, Wabasha, Olmsted, Dodge, Steele, Waseca, Blue Earth, Watonwan, Cottonwood, Murray, Pipestone, Rock, Nobles, Jackson, Faribault, Martin, Freeborn, Mower, Fillmore and Houston in the State of Minnesota.

For legal titles of parishes and diocesan institutions, consult the Pastoral Center.

Pastoral Center: 55 W. Sanborn St., P.O. Box 588, Winona., MN, 55987. Tel.: 507-454-4643; Fax: 507-454-8106.

STATISTICAL OVERVIEW

Personnel	
Bishop	1
Retired Bishops	1
Priests: Diocesan Active in Diocese	78
Priests: Active Outside Diocese	8
Priests: Retired, Sick or Absent	43
Number of Diocesan Priests	129
Religious Priests in Diocese	14
Extern Priests in Diocese	5
Ordinations:	
Diocesan Priests	1
Permanent Deacons in Diocese	2
Total Brothers	19
Total Sisters	518
Parishes	
Parishes	122
With Resident Pastor:	
Resident Diocesan Priests	66
Resident Religious Priests	5
Without Resident Pastor:	
Administered by Priests	45
Administered by Women Religious	5
Administered by Lay People	1
Missions	1
Pastoral Centers	2
Professional Ministry Personnel:	
Sisters	15
Lay Ministers	51
Welfare	
Catholic Hospitals	2
Total Assisted	113,761
Health Care Centers	1
Total Assisted	5,025
Homes for the Aged	7
Total Assisted	673
Day Care and Extended Day Care Centers	3
Total Assisted	9,017
Specialized Homes	3
Total Assisted	173
Special Centers for Social Services	5
Total Assisted	10,938
Residential Care of Disabled	1
Total Assisted	30
Other Institutions	1
Total Assisted	93
Educational	
Seminaries, Diocesan	1
Students from This Diocese	6
Students from Other Diocese	33
Diocesan Students in Other Seminaries	4
Total Seminarians	10
Colleges and Universities	1
Total Students	7,387
High Schools, Diocesan and Parish	4
Total Students	1,228
Elementary Schools, Diocesan and Parish	27
Total Students	5,511
Catechesis/Religious Education:	
High School Students	5,636
Elementary Students	12,921
Total Students Under Catholic Instruction	32,693
Teachers in the Diocese:	
Priests	3
Sisters	14
Lay Teachers	348
Vital Statistics	
Receptions into the Church:	
Infant Baptism Totals	2,004
Adult Baptism Totals	68
Received into Full Communion	280
First Communions	2,065
Confirmations	1,926
Marriages:	
Catholic	493
Interfaith	352
Total Marriages	845
Deaths	1,146
Total Catholic Population	148,445
Total Population	528,303

Former Bishops—Rt. Rev. JOSEPH B. COTTER, D.D., cons. Dec. 27, 1889; died June 28, 1909.—Rt. Rev. PATRICK R. HEFFRON, D.D., cons. May 19, 1910; died Nov. 23, 1927.—Most Rev. FRANCIS M. KELLY, D.D., cons. June 9, 1926; transferred to Diocese of Winona, Feb. 10, 1928; transferred to Titular See of Nasal, Oct. 17, 1949; died June 24, 1950.—Most Rev. EDWARD A. FITZGERALD, D.D., cons. Sept. 12, 1946; Auxiliary Bishop of Dubuque; transferred to Winona, Oct. 20, 1949; retired and transferred to the Titular See of Zerta, Jan. 8, 1969; died March 30, 1972.—Most Rev. LORAS J. WATTERS, D.D., ord. June 7, 1941; appt. Titular Bishop of Fidoloma and Auxiliary Bishop of Dubuque, June 23, 1965; cons. Aug. 26, 1965; transferred to Winona, Jan. 8, 1969; retired Oct. 14, 1986; appt. Apostolic Administrator, Oct. 14, 1986.

Vicar General—Rev. GERALD A. MAHON, *Church of St. John, 11 4th Ave S.W., Rochester, 55902-3098.* Tel: 507-288-7372; Fax: 507-288-7373.

Chancellor—Mr. JOHN M. VITEK, *55 W. Sanborn St., P.O. Box 588, Winona, 55987.* Tel: 507-454-4643; Fax: 507-454-8106.

Deans—Winona: Rev. EDWARD F. MCGRATH, Rochester: Rev. DALE E. TUPPER, Austin-Albert Lea: Rev. THOMAS J. JENNINGS, Mankato: Rev. JOHN M. KUNZ, Worthington: Rev. GERALD C. KOSSE.

Diocesan Consultors—Most Rev. JOHN G. VLAZNY; Rev. GERALD A. MAHON, V.G.; Rev. Msgr. ROY E. LITERSKI; Rev. Msgr. J. RICHARD FEITEN; Revs. DONALD W. GRUBISCH; THOMAS J. JENNINGS; JOSEPH L. KEEFE; JOHN M. KUNZ; JAMES A. MCCAULEY; DONALD P. SCHMITZ.

Finance Council—Most Rev. JOHN G. VLAZNY; Rev. GERALD A. MAHON, V.G.; Mr. JOHN M. VITEK, Chancellor; Mr. ROBERT HOODECHECK; Mrs. SHARON WAGNER; Mr. JOHN BROADWATER, Finance Officer; Rev. ROBERT G. MEYER; Sr. ANN MARIE MERTH; Mrs. KATE KELLY; Mr. ROCKY SIELER.

Diocesan Board of Administration—(Civil Corporation): Most Rev. JOHN G. VLAZNY; Rev. GERALD A. MAHON, V.G.; Mr. JOHN M. VITEK, Sec.; Mr. ROBERT HOODECHEK; Mrs. SHARON WAGNER.

Judicial Officers—Censors of Books and Periodicals: Revs. WILLIAM M. BECKER; PATRICK J. RUGEN; JACK L. KROUGH,Due Process Panel: Dr. MATT VETTER, *Saint Mary's University of MN, Winona, 55987.*

Marriage Tribunal—*55 W. Sanborn St., P.O. Box 588, Winona, 55987.* Tel: 507-454-4643.

Vicar Judicial—Rev. MICHAEL J. HOEPPNER.

Adjutant Vicar Judicial—Rev. EDWARD F. MCGRATH.

Regional Tribunal Judge—Rev. Msgr. FRANK W. KLEIN.

Regional Tribunal Defender of the Bond—Rev. DONALD J. SCHMITZ.

Defenders of the Bond—Revs. DONALD P. SCHMITZ; JACK KROUGH; DANIEL L. MURRAY.

Advocates—Revs. DONALD F. CONNELLY; GERALD C. KOSSE; Mr. JOHN FRUNDT; Mr. THOMAS HEALY.

Promoter of Justice—Rev. DONALD P. SCHMITZ.
Notaries—Ms. KAREN EICH; Mrs. CAROL NEPPL; Rev. WILLIAM M. BECKER; Mr. JOHN M. VITEK.

Diocesan Offices and Directors

All Diocesan Offices and Directors are located at the Pastoral Center (unless otherwise indicated), 55 W. Sanborn St., P.O. Box 588, Winona, 55987. Tel: 507-454-4643; Fax: 507-454-8106
Curia—
Vicar General—Rev. GERALD A. MAHON, V.G., *Church of St. John, 11 4th Ave. S.W., Rochester, 55902-3098.* Tel: 507-288-7372; Fax: 507-288-7373.
Chancellor and Pastoral Planning—Mr. JOHN M. VITEK.
Finances—Mr. JOHN BROADWATER.
Catholic Charities—Mr. LLOYD W. LENARZ, *111 Market St., P.O. Box 379, Winona, 55987.* Tel: 507-454-2270; Fax: 507-457-3027.
Communications - "The Courier"—Mr. IVAN KUBISTA.
Office of RCIA, Liturgy and Evangelization—Sr. JEAN ERSFELD, S.S.N.D.
Education, Human Resources and Schools—Mrs. P. J. THOMPSON.
Education, Religious Education—Sr. JOANNE LOECHER, O.S.F.
Social Action Programs—Mr. TODD GRAFF, *111 Market St., P.O. Box 379, Winona, 55987.* Tel: 507-454-2270; Fax: 507-457-3027.
Youth and Family Life—Mrs. ALMA RICHARD.
Additional Ministries—
Annual Diocesan Appeal—Mrs. DIANE M. ZITTEL, Dir.
Director of Clergy Education—Rev. WILLIAM M. BECKER, *IHM Seminary, St. Mary's University of MN, 700 Terrace Hgts., Winona, 55987.* Tel: 507-457-7373; Fax: 507-457-8601.
Ecumenism—Rev. WILLIAM M. BECKER.
Propogation of the Faith—Rev. DONALD P. SCHMITZ, *Church of the Resurrection, 1600 11th Ave. S.E., Rochester, 55904-5499.* Tel: 507-288-5528; Fax: 507-252-0763.
Vicar for Hispanic Ministry—Rev. HILARY R. BRIXIUS, *Church of St. James, 623 4th St., St. James, 56081.* Tel: 507-375-3542.
Coordinator of Diocesan Health Ministry—Rev. JAMES F. BURYSKA, Diocesan Dir. of Hospitals, *St. Mary's Hospital, 1216 2nd St. S.W., Rochester, 55902.* Tel: 507-255-5551; Fax: 507-255-3125.
Advisory Bodies—
Presbyteral Council—
Bishop—Most Rev. JOHN G. VLAZNY.
Ex Officio—Rev. GERALD A. MAHON, V.G.
Deans—Winona: Rev. EDWARD F. MCGRATH, Rochester: Rev. DALE E. TUPPER, Austin-Albert Lea: Rev. THOMAS J. JENNINGS, Mankato: Rev. JOHN M. KUNZ, Worthington: Rev. GERALD C. KOSSE.
Elected Members—Revs. RICHARD M. COLLETTI; GERALD W. CONWAY; JOHN W. OZBUN; CHARLES I. COLLINS; JAMES C. BERNING; DONALD W. ZENK; DONALD J. SCHMITZ; THEODORE J. HOTTINGER, S.J.; MARK C. MCNEA; GREGORY P. LEIF.
Executive Committee of the Presbyteral Council—Most Rev. JOHN G. VLAZNY, Pres.; Revs. DALE E. TUPPER, Vice Pres. RICHARD M. COLLETTI, Sec./Treas. WILLIAM M. BECKER.
Appointed Members—Rev. Msgr. ROY E. LITERSKI; Revs. DONALD P. SCHMITZ; JOSEPH P. PETE; DONALD W. GRUBISCH; WILLIAM M. BECKER.
Priestly Assignments Committee—Most Rev. JOHN G. VLAZNY; Revs. GERALD A. MAHON, V.G.; RICHARD M. COLLETTI; DONALD P. SCHMITZ.
Diocesan Pastoral Council—Most Rev. JOHN G. VLAZNY; Rev. GERALD A. MAHON, V.G.; Mr. JOHN M. VITEK, Chancellor/Dir., Pastoral Planning; Sr. JANET WERMERSKIRCHEN, S.S.N.D.; Mrs. MAUREEN ANDERSON; Mr. DANIEL BRODERICK; Mr. DAVE DUNN; Mrs. NANCY MCLOONE; Mrs. PATRICIA MCCORMICK; Sr. SHIRLEY SCHMITZ, O.S.F.; Bro. LAURENCE WALTHER; Mr. LARRY DOSE; Rev. JOSEPH P. PETE; Miss FRANCES JANOUS; Mrs. DEANN KAPLAN; Ms. SYDELLE MCCABE; Mr. SHAWN MCMAHON; Mrs. FRANCES GREBIN; Mr. MICHAEL ZEBEDEE.
Priests' Pension Board—Most Rev. JOHN G. VLAZNY; Rev. Msgr. ROY E. LITERSKI; Revs. GERALD W. CONWAY; PAUL E. NELSON; Bro. LOUIS DETHOMASIS; Mrs. CAROL ORLOWSKE; Mr. TIMOTHY GEISLER; Mr. JOHN BROADWATER, Treas.
Commission on Sacred Liturgy—Most Rev. JOHN G. VLAZNY, Pres.; Rev. JOHN M. SAUER, Exec. Chm.; Sr. JEAN ERSFELD, S.S.N.D., Dir. (Ex Officio); Mrs. STEPHANIE ALTFILLISCH; Mr. RICHARD BREITER; Rev. RICHARD M. COLLETTI; Sr. ROSEMARIE WHITEHEAD, O.S.F.; Mrs. PAM GERVAIS; Rev. GERALD C. KOSSE; Mrs. SUSAN SHEPHARD; Mr. MARK KIEFFER; Mr. JAMES STOLPA.

Winona Diocesan Organizations-Agencies-Programs

Archives—Mr. JOHN M. VITEK, *Pastoral Center, 55 W. Sanborn St., P.O. Box 588, Winona, 55987.* Tel: 507-454-4643; Fax: 507-454-8106.
Boy Scouts—Mrs. ALMA RICHARD, Coord.
Chaplin—Rev. JAMES C. BERNING. Tel: 507-288-5528.
Chairman-Catholic Committee on Scouting, Diocese of Winona—Mr. WILLIAM SMALL, *118 Main St., Fairmont, 56031.* Tel: 507-235-3874.
Catholic Charities—Mr. LLOYD W. LENARZ, Dir., *111 Market St., P.O. Box 379, Winona, 55987.* Tel: 507-454-2270; Fax: 507-457-3027.
Catholic Charities Board—Mrs. ANN MERCHLEWITZ, Chm.
Regional Offices—
Albert Lea—*315 E. Clark St., Box 890, Albert Lea, 56007.* Tel: 507-377-3664.
Austin—*2001 2nd Ave. N.W., Austin, 55912.* Tel: 507-433-3062.
Mankato—*423 W. 7th St., Mankato, 56001.* Tel: 507-387-5586.
Owatonna—*512 S. Elm St., Owatonna, 55060.* Tel: 507-455-2008.
Rochester—*903 W. Center, Rochester, 55902.* Tel: 507-287-2047.
Winona—*111 Market St., P.O. Box 379, Winona, 55987.* Tel: 507-454-2270.
Worthington—*1118 Oxford St., Worthington, 56187.* Tel: 507-376-9757.
AIDS Ministry—Mr. TOD GRAFF, *111 Market St., P.O. Box 379, Winona, 55987.* Tel: 507-454-2270; Fax: 507-457-3027.
Spiritual Director—Rev. JACK L. KROUGH. Tel: 507-433-1841.
Resource Advisor—Rev. RICHARD G. THOMSON, O.S.C. Tel: 507-533-8257.
Deaneries—
Austin/Albert Lea Deanery—Mrs. JUDY MEYER. Tel: 507-373-1294.
Mankato Deanery—Sr. MARY ANN SCHAENZER, S.S.N.D. Tel: 507-345-2989.
Rochester Deanery—Sr. JEAN KENIRY, O.S.F. Tel: 507-282-7441. JOHN LINDOW. Tel: 507-533-8631.
Winona Deanery—TOM STOLTMAN-HAMILTON. Tel: 507-452-6183.
Worthington Deanery—KATHY THURSON. Tel: 507-425-3278. BETTY BOWYER. Tel: 507-372-2201. LINDA HALBER. Tel: 507-348-4415.
Developmentally Challenged—Mr. LLOYD W. LENARZ.
Hispanic Ministry—Sr. ROSE ANN FICKER, *1051 Linn Ave., Owatonna, 55060.* Tel: 507-451-0516.
Refugee Resettlement—*903 W. Center, Rochester, 55902.* Tel: 507-287-2047.
Rural Life Committee—Mr. TODD GRAFF, Chm.
Rural Outreach Project—Mr. TODD GRAFF, Dir.
Winona—*111 Market St., P.O. Box 379, Winona, 55987.* Tel: 507-454-2270; Fax: 507-457-3027.
Worthington—*1118 Oxford St., Worthington, 56187.* Tel: 507-376-9757.
Disaster Relief Services—*111 Market St., P.O. Box 379, Winona, 55987.* Tel: 507-454-2270; Fax: 507-457-3027.
Works of Justice Committee—Mr. TODD GRAFF, Chm.
Campaign for Human Development—
Catholic Relief Services—
Social Concerns Commission—Most Rev. JOHN G. VLAZNY, Ex-Officio; Mr. LLOYD W. LENARZ, Ex-Officio; Mr. TODD GRAFF, Chm.
Cemeteries—Mr. JOHN M. VITEK.
Charismatic Renewal—Rev. JOSEPH L. KEEFE, *St. Mary Church, 1303 W. Broadway, Winona, 55987.* Tel: 507-452-5656.
Council of Catholic Women—Mrs. THERESE BREITER, Pres., *120 Tile St., Mankato, 56001.* Tel: 507-345-4065. Rev. THOMAS J. HARGESHEIMER, Diocesan Moderator. Tel: 507-451-4854.
Diocesan Self-Insurance Plan—*Gallagher-Bassett Insurance Service, 111 Riverfront, P.O. Box 30127, Winona, 55987.* Tel: 507-454-6452.
Hospitals—Rev. JAMES F. BURYSKA, *St. Marys Hospital, Rochester, 55901.* Tel: 507-282-4425.
Girl Scouts—Mrs. ALMA RICHARD, Coord., *55 W. Sanborn St., P.O. Box 588, Winona, 55987.* Tel: 507-454-4643; Fax: 507-454-8106.
Coordinator, Girl Scout Religious Recognition Program—Ms. SYDELLE MCCABE, *St. Thomas More Newman Center, Mankato State University, 1331 Warren St., Mankato, 56001.* Tel: 507-387-4154.
Legion of Mary—Rev. VERNON J. SCHAEFER, *Holy Redeemer Church, Eyota, 55934.* Tel: 507-234-5203.
Marriage Preparation/Enrichment—Mrs. ALMA RICHARD, *55 W. Sanborn St., P.O. Box 588, Winona, 55987.* Tel: 507-454-4643; Fax: 507-454-8106.
Respect Life—Mrs. ALMA RICHARD, *55 W. Sanborn St., P.O. Box 588, Winona, 55987.* Tel: 507-454-4643; Fax: 507-454-8106.
Sexual Misconduct Policy Issues—Mr. JOHN M. VITEK, *Pastoral Center, 55 W. Sanborn St., P.O. Box 588, Winona, 55987.* Tel: 507-454-4643; Fax: 507-454-8106.
Vocations Committee—Rev. JAMES P. STEFFES, Dir., *55 W. Sanborn St., P.O. Box 588, Winona, 55987.* Tel: 507-454-4643; Fax: 507-454-8106. Rev. JOSEPH P. PETE, Assoc. Dir., *St. Joseph the Worker Church, 816 Hubbel Ave., Mankato, 56001.* Tel: 507-388-3766. Rev. JAMES C. BERNING, Assoc. Dir., *Church of the Resurrection, 1600 11th Ave. S.E., Rochester, 55904.* Tel: 507-288-5528. Rev. GREGOY G. HAVEL, Assoc. Dir., *Nativity of the Blessed Virgin Church, 640 1st Ave. S.W., P.O. Box 596, Harmony, 55939.* Tel: 507-886-2323. Rev. MARTIN T. SHAEFER, Assoc. Dir., *St. Adrian Church, P.O. Box 475, Adrian, 56110.* Tel: 507-483-2317. Sr. JUDI ANGST, O.S.F., *Assisi Heights, P.O. Box 4900, Rochester, 55903.* Tel: 507-282-7441; Fax: 507-282-7762. Sr. DIANE PERRY, S.S.N.D., *561 Hamline Ave. S., St. Paul, 55116-1641.* Tel: 612-639-8421.

CLERGY, PARISHES, MISSIONS AND PAROCHIAL SCHOOLS

CITY OF WINONA
(Winona County)

1—CATHEDRAL OF THE SACRED HEART (1950), Revs. John M. Sauer, Rector; James P. Steffes. In res., Rev. Cyril Fabian, O.P.
Res., 360 Main St., 55987-3299. Tel: 507-452-4770; Fax: 507-454-1974. [JC]
School—See listings under Centralized Catholic Schools.
Catechesis/Religious Programs—Students 195.
Mission—Wilson, Immaculate Conception.

2—ST. CASIMIR'S (1906), Rev. Michael J. Hoeppner.
Res., 624 W. Broadway, 55987-2721. Tel: 507-452-3434. [JC]
Catechesis/Religious Programs—Students 92.

3—ST. JOHN NEPOMUCENE (1888) (Bohemian). Attended by St. Stanislaus, Winona.
625 E. Fourth St., 55987-4297. Tel: 507-452-5430.
Catechesis/Religious Programs—602 E. Fifth St., 55987.
Students 53.

4—ST. MARY'S (1911), Revs. Joseph L. Keefe; Patrick J. Rugen (CHI).
Res., 1303 W. Broadway, 55987-2395. Tel: 507-452-5656. [JC]
School—See listings under Centralized Catholic Schools.
Catechesis/Religious Programs—Tel: 507-452-4585.
Students 240.

5—ST. STANISLAUS (1871) (Polish), Rev. Robert G. Meyer.
Res., 625 E. Fourth St., 55987-4297. Tel: 507-452-5430.
School—See listings under Centralized Catholic Schools.
Catechesis/Religious Programs—602 E. Fifth St., 55987. Tel: 507-452-3766.
Students 113.
Mission—Winona, Winona Co., St. John Nepomucene.

OUTSIDE THE CITY OF WINONA

Adams, Mower Co., Sacred Heart (1886) (German), Rev. Gregory P. Leif.
Res., 412 Main St., P.O. Box 352, 55909-9998. Tel: 507-582-3321. [CEM]
School—Tel: 507-582-3120. Sr. Yvonne Elskamp, Prin.
Sisters 1; Lay Teachers 7; Students 140.
Catechesis/Religious Programs—Tel: 507-582-3321.
Students 75.
Convent—Tel: 507-582-3304.
Mission—Johnsburg, Mower Co., St. John's, 55909. Tel: 507-582-3321.

Adrian, Nobles Co., St. Adrian (1877), Revs. Gerald C. Kosse; Martin T. Schaefer.
Res., 512 Maine Ave., P.O. Box 475, 56110-0475. Tel: 507-483-2317. [CEM]
Catechesis/Religious Programs—108 E. Sixth St., 56110. Tel: 507-483-2480.
Students 312.
Mission—Wilmont, Nobles Co., Our Lady of Good Council.

Albert Lea, Freeborn Co., St. Theodore's (1882), Rev. Robert J. Schneider.
Res., 315 E. Clark St., Box 890, 56007. Tel: 507-373-0603. [CEM]
School—See listings under Centralized Catholic Schools. Patricia Lindeman, Prin.
Parish Center—323 E. Clark St., 56007. Tel: 507-373-9657; Fax: 507-373-9657.
Catechesis/Religious Programs—Tel: 507-373-2987; Fax: 507-373-9657.

Students 513.

Altura, Winona Co., St. Anthony's (1919). Attended by St. Rose of Lima.
180 S. Fremont, P.O. Box 727, Lewiston, 55952-0727. Tel: 507-523-2428. [JC]
Catechesis/Religious Programs—Students 91.

Austin, Mower Co., St. Augustine's (1857), Rev. Paul E. Nelson.
Res., 405 Fourth St., N.W., 55912-3091. Tel: 507-437-4537. [JC]
School—See listings under Centralized Catholic Schools.
Catechesis/Religious Programs—Students 192.
St. Edward's (1960), Rev. Jack L. Krough.
Res., 2000 Oakland Ave., W., 55912-1599. Tel: 507-433-1841; Fax: 507-433-9680. [JC]
School—See listings under Centralized Catholic Schools.
Catechesis/Religious Programs—Students 112.
Mission—Brownsdale, Mower Co., Our Lady of Loretto.
Queen of Angels (1936), Rev. Virgil S. Duellman.
Res., 1001 Oakland Ave., E., 55912. Tel: 507-433-1888. [JC]
School—See listings under Centralized Catholic Schools.
Catechesis/Religious Programs—912 First Ave., N.E., 55912. Tel: 507-433-8474.
Students 315.
Convent/Retreat House—1009 E. Oakland Ave., 55912. Tel: 507-437-4015; 437-6921 (Sisters' Res.).

Blooming Prairie, Steele Co., St. Columbanus (1878), Rev. Richard J. Dernek.
Res., 114 E. Main, 55917-1427. Tel: 507-583-2529; 583-2784. [CEM]
Catechesis/Religious Programs—Tel: 507-583-2784.
Students 236.
Mission—Geneva, Freeborn Co., St. Mary.

Blue Earth, Faribault Co., SS. Peter and Paul's (1866), Rev. Msgr. Emmett F. Tighe.
Res., 214 S. Holland, 56013. Tel: 507-526-5626.
Catechesis/Religious Programs—Students 260.
Mission—Guckeen, Faribault Co., Our Lady of Mercy.

Brewster, Nobles Co., Sacred Heart (1901). Attended by Sacred Heart, Heron Lake.
321 9th St., P.O. Box 377, Heron Lake, 56137-9998. Tel: 507-842-5584. [CEM]
Catechesis/Religious Programs—P.O. Box187, 56119. Tel: 507-842-5584. Loretta Smith, D.R.E.
Students 93.

Brownsdale, Mower Co., Our Lady of Loretto (1946). Attended by St. Edward, Austin.
2000 Oakland Ave., W., Austin, 55912-1599. Tel: 507-433-1841.
Catechesis/Religious Programs—Tel: 507-584-6476.
Students 58.

Brownsville, Houston Co., St. Patrick's (1871) (Irish). Attended by St. Peter.
P.O. Box 355, Hokah, 55941-0355. Tel: 507-894-4242. [CEM][JC 2]
Catechesis/Religious Programs—P.O. Box 155, 55919. Tel: 507-482-6769.
Students 72.

Byron, Olmsted Co., Christ the King (1965), Rev. Charles I. Collins.
Res., 202 Fourth St., N.W., P.O. Box 1000, 55920-1000. Tel: 507-775-6455.
Catechesis/Religious Programs—Tel: 507-775-0501.
Students 261.
Mission—Kasson, Dodge Co., Holy Family.

Caledonia, Houston Co., St. Mary (1975), Rev. Donald J. Schmitz.
Res., 513 S. Pine St., P.O. Box 406, 55921-0406. Tel: 507-724-3804; Fax: 507-724-2001. [CEM]
School—Tel: 507-724-3355. Sr. Cheryl Marie Wagner, S.S.N.D., Prin.
Priests 1; Sisters 2; Lay Teachers 13; Students 219.
Catechesis/Religious Programs—Students 164.
Convent—308 E. South, 55921. Tel: 507-724-2069.

Canton, Fillmore Co., The Assumption (1891). Attended by Nativity of B.V.M.
640 First Ave., S.W., P.O. Box 596, Harmony, 55939-0596. Tel: 507-886-2393. [CEM]

Chatfield, Fillmore Co., St. Mary's (1866), Rev. Donald P. Schmidt; Ronald Trombley, Dir.
Office: 405 S.W. Twiford, 55923-1352. Tel: 507867-3148. [CEM 2]
Catechesis/Religious Programs—405 Bench St., S.W., 55923. Tel: 507-867-3138.
Students 228.

Claremont, Dodge Co., St. Francis de Sales (1869). Attended by St. John Baptist de La Salle, Dodge Center.
20 Second St., N.E., P.O. Box 310, Dodge Center, 55927-0310. Tel: 507-374-6830. [CEM]
Catechesis/Religious Programs—Students 41.

Currie, Murray Co., Immaculate Heart of Mary (1883), Rev. Paul C. Evers.
Res., 501 Mill St., P.O. Box 174, 56123-0174. Tel: 507-763-3145.
Catechesis/Religious Programs—Students 114.
Mission—Westbrook, Cottonwood Co., St. Anthony.

Dakota, Winona Co., Holy Cross (1890), Rev. Joseph C. Frisch.
Res., Box 387, 55925. Tel: 507-643-6163.
Catechesis/Religious Programs—Students 49.
Mission—LaMoille, Winona Co., Precious Blood.

Deerfield, Steele Co., Corpus Christi (1869). Attended by Christ the King, Medford.
205 N.W. Second Ave.,P.O. Box 120, Medford, 55049-9508. Tel: 507-451-6353.

Delavan, Faribault Co., Mater Dolorosa (1889). Attended by St. Mary, Winnebago.
P.O. Box 308, Winnebago, 56098-0308. Tel: 507-893-4242. [CEM]

Dodge Center, Dodge Co., St. John Baptist de La Salle (1945), Rev. Milo L. Ernster.
Res., 20 Second St. N.E., P.O. Box 310, 55927. Tel: 507-374-6830.
Catechesis/Religious Programs—Tel: 507-374-6765.
Students 82.
Missions—Claremont, Dodge Co., St. Francis de Sales; West Concord, Dodge Co., St. Vincent de Paul.

Dundee, Nobles Co., St. Mary. Closed. For inquiries about sacramental records contact St. Gabriel, Fulda.

East Chain, Martin Co., Holy Family (1925) (Polish). Attended by St. John Vianney, Fairmont.
Res., 901 S. Prairie Ave., Fairmont, 56031-3098. Tel: 507-235-5535. [CEM]

Easton, Faribault Co., Our Lady of Mount Carmel (1866), Rev. John P. Wilmot, M.H.M., Admin.
Res., P.O. Box 8, 56025-0008. Tel: 507-787-2303. [CEM]
School—Tel: 507-787-2233. Janet Sklenicka, Prin.
Priests 1; Lay Teachers 9; Students 64.
Catechesis/Religious Programs—Students 57.
Mission—Minnesota Lake, Fairibault Co., St. John the Baptist.

Elba, Winona Co., St. Aloysius (1877) (German-Luxembourg). Attended by St. Charles Borromeo, St. Charles.
736 Church Ave., St. Charles, 55972-1426. Tel: 507-932-3294. [CEM]

Ellendale, Freeborn Co., St. Aidan (1857). Attended by Holy Trinity, Litomysl.
R.R. 2, Box 91, Owatonna, 55060-9202. Tel: 507-451-3482. [CEM]
Catechesis/Religious Programs—Students 95.

Ellsworth, Nobles Co., St. Mary's (1885). Attended by St. Catherine, Luverne.
203 E. Brown St., Luverne, 56156-1599. Tel: 507-283-8502. [CEM]
Catechesis/Religious Programs—Tel: (712) 479-2444.
Students 55.

Eyota, Olmsted Co., Holy Redeemer (1891), Rev. Vernon J. Schaefer.
Res., 22 E. Second St., Box 1010, 55934. Tel: 507-545-2161.
Catechesis/Religious Programs—Students 214.

Fairmont, Martin Co., St. John Vianney (1952) (Hispanic), Revs. Joseph B. Fogal; Richard P. Loomis.
Parish Office: 901 S. Prairie Ave., 56031-3098. Tel: 507-235-5535. [CEM]
School—911 S. Prairie Ave., 56031. Tel: 507-235-5304. Bruce Tepfer, Prin.
Priests 2; Lay Teachers 11; Students 175.
Catechesis/Religious Programs—Tel: 507-235-5903.
Students 381.
Mission—East Chain, Martin Co., Holy Family.

Fountain, Fillmore Co., St. Lawrence O'Toole (1872). Attended by St. Columban, Preston.
408 N.W. Preston St., R.R. 2, Box 11, Preston, 55965. Tel: 507-765-3886.

Fulda, Murray Co., St. Gabriel's (1882) (German), Rev. Eugene E. Egan.
Res., 307 W. Lake Ave., 56131-9402. Tel: 507-425-2595. [CEM]
Catechesis/Religious Programs—Tel: 507-425-2369.
Students 185.
Mission—Iona, Murray Co., St. Columba.

Geneva, St. Mary (1867) (Irish). Attended by St. Columbanus, Blooming Prairie. Rev. Richard Dernek.
114 E. Main St., Blooming Prairie, 55917-1427. Tel: 507-583-2529; 583-2784. [CEM]
Catechesis/Religious Programs—Tel: 507-583-7530.
Students 49.

Good Thunder, Blue Earth Co., St. Joseph (1879). Attended by St. Teresa, Mapleton.
104 Silver St., W., P.O. Box 305, Mapleton, 56065. Tel: 507-524-3127. [CEM]
Catechesis/Religious Programs—Tel: 507-278-3444.
Students 84.

Grand Meadow, Mower Co., St. Finbarr's (1878). Attended by St. Patrick's, LeRoy.
Box 310, LeRoy, 55951-0310. Tel: 507-324-5203. [CEM]
Catechesis/Religious Programs—Students 155.

Guckeen, Faribault Co., Our Lady of Mercy (1903). Attended by Sts. Peter and Paul, Blue Earth.
214 S. Holland, Blue Earth, 56013. Tel: 507-526-5626.

Hammond, Wabasha Co., St. Clement's. Closed. For inquires for parish records contact SS. Peter and Paul, Mazeppa.

Harmony, Fillmore Co., The Nativity of the Blessed Virgin, Rev. Gregory G. Havel.
Res., 640 First Ave., S.W., P.O. Box 596, 55939-0596. Tel: 507-886-2393.
Catechesis/Religious Programs—Students 88.
Missions—Canton, Fillmore Co., Church of the Assumption; Mabel, Fillmore Co., St. Olaf.

Hayfield, Dodge Co., Sacred Heart (1935), Rev. Douglas J. Gits.
Res., 150 2nd St., N.E., P.O. Box 27, 55940-0027. Tel: 507-477-2256.
Catechesis/Religious Programs—Tel: 507-477-2297.
Students 108.

Heron Lake, Jackson Co., Sacred Heart (1884) (German), Rev. Steven J. Peterson.
Res., 321 9th St., P.O. Box 377, 56137-9998. Tel: 507-793-2357. [CEM]
Catechesis/Religious Programs—Students 159.
Missions—Brewster, Nobles Co., Sacred Heart; Lakefield, Jackson Co., St. Joseph.

Hokah, Houston Co., St. Peter's (1876), Rev. Paul J. Breza.
Res., P.O. Box 355, 55941-0355. Tel: 507-894-4242. [CEM]
School—Tel: 507-894-4375; 894-4944.
Lay Teachers 8; Students 118.
Mission—Brownsville, Houston Co., St. Patrick.

Houston, Houston Co., St. Mary's (1873). Attended by St. Joseph, Rushford. For inquiries for parish records contact the Chancery.
101 Rushford Ave., W., P.O. Box 577, Rushford, 55971-0557. Tel: 507-864-2257. [CEM]

Iona, Murray Co., St. Columba's (1891) (Irish). Attended by St. Gabriel, Fulda.
307 W. Lake Ave., Fulda, 56131-9402. Tel: 507-425-2595. [CEM]
Catechesis/Religious Programs—Students 64.

Jackson, Jackson Co., Good Shepherd (1891) (Czech-Bohemian), Rev. Charles J. Sullivan, Admin.
Res., 311 N. Sverdrup Ave., P.O. Box 65, 56143-1329. Tel: 507-847-2504; Fax: 507-847-5322. [CEM]
Catechesis/Religious Programs—Tel: 507-847-2719.
Students 164.
Mission—Sherburn, Martin Co., St. Luke, Box 669, Sherburn, 56171. Tel: 507-764-7831.

Janesville, Waseca Co., St. Ann's (1876), Rev. Sylvester F. Brown.
307 W. Second St., P.O. Box 218, 56048-0218. Tel: 507-234-6244. [CEM]
Catechesis/Religious Programs—Tel: 507-234-5753.
Students 223.

Jasper, Pipestone Co., St. Joseph's (1890). Attended by St. Leo's, Pipestone.
106 4th St., S.E., P.O. Box 0036, Pipestone, 56154-0036. Tel: 507-825-3152; Fax: 507-825-4492. [CEM]
Catechesis/Religious Programs—Students 53.

Jeffers, Cottonwood Co., St. Augustine's (1912). Attended by St. Francis Xavier, Windom.
548 17th St., Windom, 56101-1217. Tel: 507-831-3300. [JC]

Johnsburg, Mower Co., St. John's (1859) (German). Attended by Sacred Heart, Adams.
412 Main St., P.O. Box 352, Adams, 55909-9998. Tel: 507-582-3321. [CEM]

Kasson, Dodge Co., Holy Family (1976). Attended by Christ the King, Byron. Rev. Charles I. Collins.
202 Fourth St., N.W., P.O. Box 1000, Byron, 55920-1000. Tel: 507-775-6455. [CEM]
Catechesis/Religious Programs—Tel: 507-634-7520.
Students 290.

Kellogg, Wabasha Co., St. Agnes (1900), Rev. Harold E. Gavin.

Res., P.O. Box 8, 55945-0008. Tel: 507-767-4965.
Catechesis/Religious Programs—Students 58.
Mission—Kellogg, Wabasha Co., Immaculate Conception.

Immaculate Conception (1881). Attended by St. Agnes, Kellogg.
P.O. Box 8, Kellog, 55945-0008. Tel: 507-767-4965.
Catechesis/Religious Programs—Students 83.

La Crescent, Houston Co., The Crucifixion (1856), Rev. Donald W. Grubisch.
Res., 407 S. Second St., 55947-1326. Tel: 507-895-4720. [CEM 2]
School—420 S. Second St., 55947. Tel: 507-895-4402. Robert Adams, Prin.
Lay Teachers 10; Students 152.
Catechesis/Religious Programs—1380 Lancer Blvd., 55947. Tel: 507-895-2700.
Students 325.
Convent—423 S. Second St., 55947. Tel: 507-895-6867.

Lake City, Wabasha Co., St. Mary's (1877), Rev. James S. McCauley.
Res., 419 Lyon Ave., 55041-1649. Tel: 612-345-4134.
Catechesis/Religious Programs—Students 396.
Mission—Theilman, Wabasha Co., St. Joseph.

Lake Crystal, Blue Earth Co., Holy Family (1900). Attended by St. Joseph the Worker, Mankato. Rev. Joseph P. Pete.
Res., 816 Hubbell Ave., Mankato, 56001-2197. Tel: 507-388-3766; Fax: 507-388-3766. [CEM]
Catechesis/Religious Programs—Tel: 507-726-2725.
Students 158.

Lakefield, Jackson Co., St. Joseph (1897). Attended by Sacred Heart, Heron Lake.
321 9th St., P.O. Box 377, Heron Lake, 56137. Tel: 507-793-2357. [CEM]
Catechesis/Religious Programs—410 Broadway Ave., Box 517, 56150. Tel: 507-662-5819.
Students 108.

Lake Wilson, Murray Co., St. Mary (1916). Attended by St. Ann, Slayton.
2747 29th St., Slayton, 56172-9998. Tel: 507-836-8030. [JC]
Catechesis/Religious Programs—Students 57.

Lamoille, Winona Co., Precious Blood (1900). Attended by Holy Cross, Dakota.
Mailing Address: P.O. Box 387, Dakota, 55925-0387. Tel: 507-643-6163. [CEM 2]

Lanesboro, Fillmore Co., St. Patrick (1871). Attended by St. Columban, Preston.
408 N.W. Preston St., R.R. 2, Box 11, Preston, 55965. Tel: 507-765-3886.

Le Roy, Mower Co., St. Patrick's (1878), Rev. Matthew Vanissery.
Church—Box 310, 55951-0310. Tel: 507-324-5203. [CEM]
Catechesis/Religious Programs—Tel: 507-324-5032.
Students 122.
Mission—Grand Meadow, Mower Co., St. Finbarr.

Lewiston, Winona Co., St. Rose of Lima (1876), Rev. James W. Hennessy.
Res., 180 S. Fremont, P.O. Box 727, 55952. Tel: 507-523-2428. [CEM]
Catechesis/Religious Programs—Students 187.
Mission—Altura, Winona Co., St. Anthony.

Lismore, Nobles Co., St. Anthony's (1887) (German-Irish), Rev. Gerald C. Kosse; Sr. Brenda Penning, S.N.D., Parish Dir.
Mailing Address: 310 Third Ave., S., P.O. Box 158, 56155-0158. Tel: 507-472-8262. [CEM]
Catechesis/Religious Programs—Tel: 507-472-8262.
Students 36.
Mission—St. Kilian, Nobles Co., St. Kilian.

Litomysl, Holy Trinity (1877), Rev. Daniel L. Murray.
Mailing Address: R.R. 2, Box 91, Owatonna, 55060. Tel: 507-451-3482. [CEM]
School—St. Isidore, Tel: 507-451-5876. Lynn Smith, Prin.
Priests 1; Lay Teachers 3; Students 37.
Mission—Ellendale, Steele Co., St. Aiden.

Luverne, Rock Co., St. Catherine's (1881), Rev. Paul Heiting.
203 E. Brown, 56156-1599. Tel: 507-283-8502. [CEM]
Catechesis/Religious Programs—Tel: 507-283-8071.
Students 291.
Mission—Ellsworth, Nobles Co., St. Mary.

Lyle, Mower Co., Queen of Peace (1946). Attended by St. Peter, Rose Creek.
R.R. 1, Box 1E, Rose Creek, 55970-9701. Tel: 507-433-1532.
Catechesis/Religious Programs—Students 69.

Mabel, Fillmore Co., St. Olaf (1954). Attended by Nativity of B.V.M., Harmony.
640 First Ave. S.W., P.O. Box 596, Harmony, 55939-0596. Tel: 507-886-2393.
Catechesis/Religious Programs—Students 155.

Madelia, Watonwan Co., St. Mary (1872), Rev. Peter J. Klein.
Res., 212 First St., N.E., 56062-1701. Tel: 507-642-8305.
School—Tel: 507-642-3324. Mrs. Robin Osland, Prin.
Priests 1 Lay Teachers 8; Students 96.
Convent—13 Crosby Ave., N.E., 56062. Tel: 507-642-3323.
Catechesis/Religious Programs—Students 86.
Mission—Truman, Martin Co., St. Katherine.

Madison Lake, Blue Earth Co., All Saints (1894), Rev. James D. Russell.
Parish Endowment Fund, Inc. of All Saints Church: P.O. Box 217, 56063-0217. Tel: 507-243-3319. [CEM]
School—Tel: 507-243-3819. Sr. Mary Kay Ash, S.S.N.D., Prin.
Priests 1; Sisters 3; Lay Teachers 3; Students 65 (K-6); Preschool 22.
Catechesis/Religious Programs—Students 162.
Convent—Tel: 507-243-3010.

Mankato, Blue Earth Co.,

1—SS. PETER AND PAUL'S, (1858) (German), Revs. Karl Voelker, S.J.; Ervin J. Czarnecki, S.J.; Theodore Hottinger, S.J.; Charles L. Kerr, S.J.; Bro. James Becwar, S.J.
Res., 105 N. Fifth St., 56001-4442. Tel: 507-388-2995.
School—See listings under Centralized Catholic Schools.
Pastoral Center—512 Mulberry St., 56001-4442. Tel: 507-388-1664.
Catechesis/Religious Programs—Tel: 507-387-6228; Fax: 507-388-7628.
Students 330.

2—ST. FRANCIS XAVIER MISSION CHAPEL. Attended by SS. Peter and Paul, Mankato. 105 N. Fifth St., 56001. Tel 507-388-2995.
Church—Fourth Ave., 56001.
Catechesis/Religious Programs—Students 144.

3—ST. JOHN THE BAPTIST'S, (1884), Rev. Richard M. Colletti.
Res., 632 S. Broad St., 56001-3890. Tel: 507-625-3131. [JC]
Catechesis/Religious Programs—Tel: 507-625-3389.
Students 454.

4—ST. JOSEPH THE WORKER, (1957), Revs. Joseph P. Pete; James J. Seitz.
Res., 816 Hubbell Ave., 56001. Tel: 507-388-3766. [JC]
School—See listings under Centralized Catholic Schools.
Catechesis/Religious Programs—423 W. 7th St., 56001. Tel: 507-625-3450.
Students 208.
Convent—Tel: 507-388-2515.
Mission—Lake Crystal, Blue Earth Co., Holy Family.

Mapleton, Blue Earth Co., St. Teresa's (1876), Rev. Joseph W. Mountain; Sr. Lalande Hennen, S.S.N.D., Dir.
Res., 104 Silver St., P.O. Box 305, 56065. Tel: 507-524-3127. [CEM]
Catechesis/Religious Programs—Tel: 507-524-4606.
Students 179.
Missions—Good Thunder, Blue Earth Co., St. Joseph; Vernon Center, Blue Earth Co., St. Matthew.

Mazeppa, Wabasha Co., SS. Peter and Paul (1860), Rev. Richard J. Engels, Admin.
Res., 1st St. S., P.O. Box 224, 55956-0224. Tel: 507-843-3885.
Catechesis/Religious Programs—Students 138.
Mission—West Albany, Stearns Co., St. Patrick.

Medford, Steele Co., Christ the King (1943), Rev. Robert D. Herman.
Res., 205 N.W. Second Ave., P.O. Box 120, 55049-9508. Tel: 507-451-6353.
Catechesis/Religious Programs—Students 132.
Mission—Deerfield, Steele Co., Corpus Christi.

Minneiska, Wabasha Co., St. Mary's (1867). Attended by Holy Trinity, Rollingstone.
83 Main St., Rollingstone, 55969-9759. Tel: 507-689-2351.

Minnesota City, Winona Co., St. Paul's (1924), Rev. Edward Cunningham, O.M.I.
Res., P.O. Box 26, 55959-0026. Tel: 507-689-2485. [CEM]
Catechesis/Religious Programs—Students 51.

Minnesota Lake, Faribault Co., St. John the Baptist (1865). Attended by Our Lady of Mount Carmel, Easton. Rev. John P. Wilmot.
Mailing Address: P.O. Box 8, Easton, 56025-0008. Tel: 507-787-2303.
Church—P.O. Box 158, 56068. Tel: 507-462-3636. [CEM]
Catechesis/Religious Programs—P.O. Box 1, 56068. Tel: 507-462-3791.
Students 116.

New Richland, Waseca Co., All Saints (1879), Rev. Thien Van Nguyen.
Res., P.O. Box 185, 56072-0185. Tel: 507-465-8217. [CEM]
Catechesis/Religious Programs—Students 104.
Mission—Waldorf, Waseca Co., St. Joseph.

Oak Ridge, Winona Co., Immaculate Conception (1875). Attended by Holy Trinity, Rollingstone.
83 Main St., Rollingstone, 55969-9759. Tel: 507-689-2351; Fax: 507-689-2351. [CEM]

Owatonna, Steele Co., St. Joseph's (1891), Rev. Thomas J. Hargesheimer; Deacon Paul Hillyer.
Res., 512 S. Elm St., 55060-3399. Tel: 507-451-4845.
Catechesis/Religious Programs—Students 430.

Sacred Heart (1866) (Czech), Rev. Thomas J. Jennings; Deacon George Anderberg.
Res., 810 S. Cedar Ave., 55060-3297. Tel: 507-451-1588.
School—See listings under Centralized Catholic Schools.
Catechesis/Religious Programs—Marian Dr., Owakonna, 55060. Tel: 507-451-2699.
Students 350.

Pipestone, Pipestone Co., St. Leo's (1887), Rev. Kevin Connolly.
Res., 106 Fourth Ave. S.E., P.O. Box 36, 56164-0036. Tel: 507-825-3152. [CEM]
Catechesis/Religious Programs—Students 283.
Missions—Woodstock, Pipestone Co., St. Martin; Jasper, Pipestone Co., St. Joseph.

Plainview, Wabasha Co., St. Joachim's (1858) (German-Irish), Rev. Donald F. Connelly.
Res., 900 W. Broadway, 55964-1039. Tel: 507-534-3321. [CEM]
Catechesis/Religious Programs—Tel: 507-534-2887.
Students 511.

Preston, Fillmore Co., St. Columban (1869), Rev. Msgr. Francis A. Galles.
Res., 408 N.W. Preston St., R.R. 2, Box 11, 55965. Tel: 507-765-3886.
Catechesis/Religious Programs—Students 60.
Missions—Lanesboro, Fillmore Co., St. Lawrence O'Toole; Lanesboro, Fillmore Co., St. Patrick.

Rochester, Olmsted Co.,

1—HOLY SPIRIT, (1990), Rev. Dale E. Tupper.
Office: 5455 50th Ave., N.W., 55901. Tel: 507-280-0638; Fax: 507-288-5155.
Res., Tel: 507-281-8323. [JC]
School—See listings under Centralized Catholic Schools.
Catechesis/Religious Programs—Students 179.

2—PAX CHRISTI, (1973), Revs. LaVern E. Trocinski; Thomas A. Loomis.
Res., 4135-18th Ave., N.W., 55901-0460. Tel: 507-282-8542; Fax: 507-289-8741. [JC]
Catechesis/Religious Programs—Tel: 507-282-8938; Fax: 507-289-8741.
Students 809.

3—RESURRECTION, (1967), Revs. Donald P. Schmitz; James C. Berning.
Res., 1600-11th Ave., S.E., 55904-5499. Tel: 507-288-5528; Fax: 507-252-0763. [JC]
Catechesis/Religious Programs—Students 624.

4—ST. BRIDGET'S, (1857), Rev. George B. Nintemann, O.P.
Res., 2123 County Rd. 16, S.E., 55904-9998. Tel: 507-282-9139. [CEM]
Catechesis/Religious Programs—Students 63.

5—ST. FRANCIS OF ASSISI, (1937) (German-Irish), Revs. Donald J. Lovas; James F. Callahan, S.M.A.
Res., 338 11th Ave., S.E., 55904. Tel: 507-288-7313; Fax: 507-281-5997. [JC]
School—See listings under Centralized Catholic Schools.
Catechesis/Religious Programs—Tel: 507-289-2427; Fax: 507-289-2427.
Students 150.

6—ST. JOHN'S, (1863), Revs. Gerald A. Mahon; Peter L. Schuster.
Res., 11 4th Ave., S.W., 55902-3098. Tel: 507-288-7372; Fax: 507-288-7373. [JC]
School—See listings under Centralized Catholic Schools.
Catechesis/Religious Programs—Students 286.

7—ST. PIUS X, (1954), Revs. Paul W. Surprenant; Michael J. Cronin.
Res., 1315-12th Ave., N.W., 55901-1744. Tel: 507-288-8238; Fax: 507-288-8248. [JC]
School—See listings under Centralized Catholic Schools.

Catechesis/Religious Programs—Tel: 507-289-6317; Fax: 507-286-8769.
Students 443.
Convent—1203 N.W. 13th Ave., 55901. Tel: 507-282-9200.

Rollingstone, Winona Co., Holy Trinity (1862), Rev. Edward F. McGrath.
Res., 83 Main St., 55969-9759. Tel: 507-689-2351; Fax: 507-689-2351. [CEM]
Missions—Oak Ridge, Winona Co., Immaculate Conception; Minneiska, Wabasha Co., St. Mary.

Rose Creek, Mower Co., St. Peter's (1885), Rev. Ruben C. Spinler.
Res., R.R. 1, Box 1E, 55970. Tel: 507-433-1532. [CEM]
Catechesis/Religious Programs—Students 88.
Mission—Lyle, Mower Co., Queen of Peace.

Rushford, Fillmore Co., St. Joseph's (1868), Rev. William J. Kulas.
Res., 101 Rushford Ave., W., P.O. Box 577, 55971-0577. Tel: 507-864-2257. [CEM]
Catechesis/Religious Programs—Students 87.
Mission—Houston, Houston Co., St. Mary.

St. Charles, Winona Co., St. Charles Borromeo (1867) (Irish-German), Rev. Louis G. Cook.
Res., 736 Church Ave., 55972-1426. Tel: 507-932-3294. [CEM]
Catechesis/Religious Programs—Tel: 507-932-3303.
Students 227.
Mission—Elba, Winona Co., St. Aloysius.

St. Clair, Blue Earth Co., Immaculate Conception (1874), Rev. Russell G. Scepaniak.
Res., 120 Church St., P.O. Box 100, 56080-0100. Tel: 507-245-3448. [CEM]
Catechesis/Religious Programs—Students 231.

St. James, Watonwan Co., St. James (1873), Rev. Hilary R. Brixius.
Res., 623 Fourth St., 56081-1824. Tel: 507-375-3542. [CEM]
Catechesis/Religious Programs—Marcia Hurley, D.R.E.
Students 215.

St. Kilian, Nobles Co., St. Kilian (1903) (German-Irish). Attended by St. Anthony, Lismore.
Mailing Address: 310 Third Ave., S., P.O. Box 158, Lismore, 56155-0158. Tel: 507-472-8262. [CEM]
Catechesis/Religious Programs—Students 21.

Sherburn, Martin Co., St. Luke's (1888). Attended by Good Shepherd, Jackson.
Res., 311 N.Sverdrup Ave., P.O. Box 65, Jackson, 56143-1329. Tel: 507-847-2504; Fax: 507-847-5322. [CEM]
Catechesis/Religious Programs—Tel: 507-764-5029.
Students 124.

Slayton, Murray Co., St. Ann's (1897), Rev. John W. Ozbun.
Res., 2747 29th St., 56172. Tel: 507-836-8030. [CEM]
Catechesis/Religious Programs—Tel: 507-836-6261.
Students 130.
Mission—Lake Wilson, Murray Co., St. Mary.

Spring Valley, Fillmore Co., St. Ignatius (1878), Rev. Edgar J. Schaefer.
Res., 213 Franklin St., 55975-1312. Tel: 507-346-7565. [CEM]
Catechesis/Religious Programs—Students 145.
Mission—Wykoff, Fillmore Co., St. Kilian.

Stewartville, Olmsted Co., St. Bernard's (1894), Rev. Dr. Richard G. Thomson, O.S.C.
Res., 116 Fourth Ave. S.E., 55976. Tel: 507-533-8257. [CEM]
Catechesis/Religious Programs—Tel: 507-533-8192.
Students 365.

Theilman, Wabasha Co., St. Joseph's (1903). Attended by St. Mary, Lake City.
419 Lyon Ave., Lake City, 55041. Tel: 612-345-4134.

Trimont, Martin Co., St. Joseph. Closed. For inquiries for parish records see Good Shepherd, Jackson.

Truman, Martin Co., St. Katherine (1954). Attended by St. Mary, Madelia.
212 First St., N.E., Madelia, 56062-1702. Tel: 507-642-8305.
Catechesis/Religious Programs—Students 67.

Twin Lakes, Freeborn Co., St. James (1876), Rev. Donald W. Zenk, Admin.
Res., 602 31st St., N.W., Austin, 55912. Tel: 507-437-3579.

Vernon Center, Blue Earth Co., St. Matthew (1911). Attended by St. Teresa, Mapleton.
Mailing Address: 104 Silver St., W., P.O. Box 305, Mapleton, 56065. Tel: 507-524-3127. [CEM]
Catechesis/Religious Programs—Students 92.

Wabasha, Wabasha Co., St. Felix (1858), Rev. Gerald W. Conway.
Res., 117 W. Third St., 55981-1201. Tel: 612-565-3931. [CEM]
School—(Grades K-6) 130 Third St., E., 55981. Tel: 612-564-4446. Sr. M. Joann McMahon, S.S.N.D., Prin.
Priests 1; Sisters 2; Lay Teachers 6; Students 168.
Catechesis/Religious Programs—Tel: 612-565-3718.
Students 180.
Convent—36 Bailey Ave., 55981. Tel: 612-565-4578.

Waldorf, Waseca Co., St. Joseph's (1878). Attended by All Saints, New Richland.
Box 185, New Richland, 56072-0185. Tel: 507-465-8217. [CEM]
Catechesis/Religious Programs—Students 56.

Waseca, Waseca Co., Sacred Heart (1869), Rev. John M. Kunz.
Res., 111 Fourth St., N.W., 56093-2413. Tel: 507-835-1222. [CEM][JC 2]
School—(Grades 1-4) 308 W. Elm Ave., 56093. Tel: 507-835-2780. Sandra Allaire, Prin.
Priests 1; Sisters 1; Lay Teachers 9; Students 139.
Catechesis/Religious Programs—Tel: 507-835-1500.
Students 513.
Convent—400 Second Ave., N.W., 56093. Tel: 507-835-4867.

Wells, Faribault Co., St. Casimir's (1880), Rev. Eugene F. Stenzel.
Res., 320 Second Ave., 56097-1399. Tel: 507-553-5391. [CEM]
School—(Grades K-8) 330 Second Ave., S.W., 56097. Tel: 507-553-5822. Katy Schmitz, Prin.
Sisters 1; Lay Teachers 8; Students 136.
Catechesis/Religious Programs—Students 210.

West Albany, Wabasha Co., St. Patrick's of West Albany (1865). Attended by SS. Peter and Paul.
Box 224, Mazeppa, 55956-0224. Tel: 507-843-3885. [CEM]
Catechesis/Religious Programs—Students 53.

Westbrook, Cottonwood Co., St. Anthony's (1909). Attended by Immaculate Heart of Mary, Currie.
501 Mill St., P.O. Box 174, Currie, 56123-0174. Tel: 507-763-3145. [CEM]

West Concord, Dodge Co., St. Vincent de Paul (1945). Attended by St. John Baptist de La Salle, Dodge Center.
20 Second St., N.E., Box 310, Dodge Center, 55927-0310. Tel: 507-374-6830. [CEM]
Catechesis/Religious Programs—P.O. Box 117, 55985. Tel: 507-527-2384.
Students 90.

Wilmont, Nobles Co., Our Lady of Good Counsel (1903). Attended by St. Adrian, Adrian.
512 Maine St., P.O. Box 475, Adrian, 56110-0475. Tel: 507-483-2317. [CEM]
Catechesis/Religious Programs—Tel: 507-926-5305.
Students 88.

Wilson, Winona Co., Immaculate Conception (1874). Attended by Cathedral of the Sacred Heart.
360 Main St., Winona, 55987-3299. Tel: 507-452-4770.

Windom, Cottonwood Co., St. Francis Xavier's (1898), Rev. Charles J. Quinn.
Res., 548 17th St., 56101-1217. Tel: 507-831-3300.
Catechesis/Religious Programs—532 17th St., 56101. Tel: 507-831-1985.
Students 254.
Mission—Jeffers, Cottonwood Co., St. Augustine.

Winnebago, Faribault Co., St. Mary's (1893), Rev. John F. Traufler.
Res., P.O. Box 308, 56098-0308. Tel: 507-893-4242. [CEM]
Catechesis/Religious Programs—Students 100.
Mission—Delavan, Faribault Co., Mater Dolorosa.

Woodstock, Pipestone Co., St. Martin's (1882). Attended by St. Leo, Pipestone.
Mailing Address: 106 Fourth St., S.E., Pipestone, 56164-0036. Tel: 507-825-3152; Fax: 507-825-4492. [CEM]

Worthington, Nobles Co., St. Mary's (1886), Rev. Andrew D. Olsem.
Res., 1215 Seventh Ave., 56187-2297. Tel: 507-376-6005; Fax: 507-376-9167. [CEM]
School—(Grades K-6) Twelfth St. & Eighth Ave., 56187. Tel: 507-376-5236. Matthew Schoen, Prin.
Sisters 1; Lay Teachers 6; Students 160.
Catechesis/Religious Programs—1206 Eighth Ave., 56187. Tel: 507-372-2090.
Students 383.
Convent—1221 Seventh Ave., 56187. Tel: 507-376-4035.

Wykoff, Fillmore Co., St. Kilian's (1887). Attended by St. Ignatius, Spring Valley.
213 W. Franklin St., Spring Valley, 55975-1312. Tel: 507-346-7565. [CEM]

Chaplains of Public Institutions

ROCHESTER. *Federal Medical Center*, Bureau of Prisons, 2110 Center St. E., 55904. Sr. Emile Bormann, Chap.

WASECA. *Federal Correctional Institution*. 920 St. Andrews Pl., Owatonna, 55060. Deacon George T. Anderberg.

On Duty Outside the Diocese:
Reverend Fathers—
Beerman, Andrew J., Post Graduate Studies, North American College, 00120 Vatican City State, Europe
Brandenhoff, Peter B., 8859 Spring Lane, Woodbury, MN 55125
Dernek, Daniel R., Chap., St. Peter Treatment Center, 100 Freeman Dr., St. Peter, MN 56082
Hodapp, Timothy L., St. Margaret Mary Church, 2301 Zenith Ave., N., Golden Valley, MN 55422-3899
Maher, Robert G., 591 Bandera Dr., Camarillo, CA 93010
Murtagh, Lawrence, Box 66, Stockholm, SD 57264
Reker, Timothy T., NCCB, 3211 4th St. NE, Washington, DC 20017-1194

Military Chaplains:
Reverend Fathers—
Arnoldt, David M., 205 Whitworth Dr., Martinez, GA 30907

Absent on Leave:
Reverend Fathers—
Cashman, Joseph C.
Gallagher, Chester G.
Moore, Jon H.
Taylor, Robert H.
Verdick, Jerome F.

Retired:
Reverend Monsignors—
Dittman, Harold J., 1920 S. First St., #203, Minneapolis, MN 55454
Habiger, James D., 2115 Summit Ave., Box 4174, St. Paul, MN 55105
Klein, Edward, St. Elizabeth Hospital, 1200 W. 5th Grant Blvd., Wabasha, MN 55981-1098
Klein, Frank W., 1855 Waas Valley Rd., Dresbach, MN 55947
Literski, Roy E., 1328 D. McNally Dr., Winona, MN 55987
McGinnis, Joseph R., 1200 W. 5th Grant Blvd., Wabasha, MN 55981-1098
Ploof, Thomas M., 220 S. Broadway, 1122 Center Plaza, Rochester, MN 55904
Speltz, Richard, 604 S. Third St., La Crescent, MN 55947-1234
Reverend Fathers—
Clasen, Leonard, St. Elizabeth Hospital, 1200 W. 5th Grant Blvd., Wabasha, MN 55981-1098
Clinton, Kenneth J., 801 N. West St., Apt. 8, Janesville, MN 56048-9721
Cody, John F., 2485 Canabury Dr., Apt. 105, St. Paul, MN 55117
Curtis, William D., 500 Troendle St., S.E., P.O. Box 404, Mapleton, MN 56065-0404
Dandelet, James D., P.O. Box 46, Easton, MN 56025
Eikens, Leroy F., 728 First Ave., S.W. #403, Rochester, MN 55902-3307
Enright, Frank, Sacred Heart Hospice, 1200 12th St., S.W., Austin, MN 55912-2699
Ginther, Lawrence P., 5125 W. Seventh St., Apt. 8, Winona, MN 55987-5616
Glynn, Francis M., Deaconess Towers, Room 401, 503 Division St. E., Faribault, MN 55021
Haberman, Clayton J., 5371 Elkton Tr., Faribault, MN 55021-8453
Halloran, Jerome D., 5653 B Lake Murray Blvd., La Mesa, CA 92041
Halloran, Paul F., R.R. 2, Box 69A, Akeley, MN 56433-9507
Jewison, Harry P., 1024 Ninth St., N.E., Rochester, MN 55906
Kellen, Elmer W., 104 Park St., Box 171, Minnesota Lake, MN 56068
Kerrigan, Bernard, 300 Bridge St., P.O. Box 37, Millville, MN 55957
Kulas, Robert A., 7510 Cahill Rd., #201B, Edina, MN 55439
Kunz, Francis P., 240 Hudson Ave., E., Mankato, MN 56001
LaPlante, Joseph A., 31 Robinson Dr., Wabasha, MN 55981-3016
Leary, Donald G., #1504, 220 S. Broadway, Rochester, MN 55902
Loosbrock, Donald L., 149 Pioneer Dr., Wabasha, MN 55981

Mountain, Edward C., 420 11th St., S.E., Owatonna, MN 55060
Mountain, Harold B., 50 Teton Ln., #124, Mankato, MN 56001
Mountain, Joseph W., 5371 Elkton Tr., Faribault, MN 55021-8453
Neudecker, Urban C., P.O. Box 904, Sherburn, MN 56171
Peterson, Cyril P., c/o Jack Peterson, Box 238, Missouri Valley, IA 51555
Riordan, Richard J., 920 S. 10th St., St. James, MN 56081
Schiltz, Roger J., 1532 Glenrosa Dr., N. Las Vegas, NV 89031-5548
Smith, Leland J., 468 Center St., Winona, MN 55987
Speck, James A., 528 Maceman St., Apt. 308, Winona, MN 55987-2486
Sullivan, Wilfred, 234 First St., N.W., Apt. 3, P.O. Box 486, Winnebago, MN 56098
Vincent, John F., 513 S. Seventh St., Apt. C, LaCrescent, MN 55947-1275
Zenk, Donald W., St. James Church, c/o 602 31st St., N.W., Austin, MN 55912

INSTITUTIONS LOCATED IN THE DIOCESE

[A] SEMINARIES, DIOCESAN

WINONA. *Immaculate Heart of Mary Seminary, Saint Mary's University of MN #43*, 700 Terrace Hts., 55987-1399. Tel: 507-457-7373; Fax: 507-457-8601. Affiliated with Saint Mary's University of MN. Revs. William M. Becker, Rector; Mark C. McNea, Spiritual Dir. of Worship; Joseph A. LaPlante, Spiritual Dir.; David C. Kunz, Spiritual Dir., Dir. of Apostolic Works. Students 38.

[B] COLLEGES AND UNIVERSITIES

WINONA. *Saint Mary's University of Minnesota*, 700 Terrace Hts., 55987-1399. Tel: 507-452-4430; Fax: 507-457-1566.
For a complete listing, refer to the Colleges and Universities section.

[C] CENTRALIZED CATHOLIC SCHOOLS

WINONA. *Cotter High School*, 1115 W. Broadway, 55987. Tel: 507-453-5002. Dr. Jeanne-Marie Faller, Prin., CEO; Rev. Mark C. McNea, Campus Min.; William Crozier, Campus Min. Priests 1; Lay Teachers 32; Students 417.
Winona Area Catholic Schools, 352 Center St., 55987. Mr. Randy P. Althoff, Supt.
St. Mary's Primary School. (Grades PreK-1), 1315 W. Broadway, 55987. Tel: 507-452-2890. Mr. Randy P. Althoff, Prin. Students 198.
Cathedral Elementary School. (Grades 2-4), 352 Center St., 55987. Tel: 507-452-4936. Mr. Randy P. Althoff, Prin. Students 235.
St. Stanislaus Middle School. (Grades 5-8), 602 E. Fifth St., 55987. Tel: 507-452-3766. Dr. Donna E. Harris, Prin. Students 374.
Winona Area Catholic Schools Foundation, 360 Main St., 55987.

ALBERT LEA. *St. Theodore School*, 323 E. Clark St., 56007. Tel: 507-373-9657. Patricia Lindeman, Prin. Lay Teachers 4; Students 58.

AUSTIN. *Austin Area Catholic Schools*, 511 N.W. Fourth Ave., 55912. Tel: 507-433-6630.
St. Augustine's - St. Edward. (Grades PreK-2), 511 N.W. Fourth Ave., 55912. Tel: 507-433-8859. Richard J. Cook, Prin. Lay Teachers 6; Students 105.
Queen of Angels. (Grades 3-6), 912 First Ave., N.E., 55912. Tel: 507-433-8745. Richard J. Cook, Prin. Lay Teachers 10; Students 147.
Pacelli Junior/Senior High School. (Grades 7-12), 311 Fourth St., N.W., 55912. Tel: 507-437-3278. Terry Nelsen, Prin.; Alice Reese, Campus Min. Lay Teachers 11; Students 153.
United Catholic Schools Foundation of Austin, MN, Inc., 511 N.W. Fourth Ave., 55912. Tel: 507-433-6630. Mrs. Alice Snater, Financial Sec.

MANKATO. *Mankato Area Catholic Schools*, 145 Good Counsel Dr., 56001-3146; Fax: 507-388-3081. Mr. James Rouse, Supt.
St. Joseph - St. John School. (Grades K-3), 820 Hubbell, 56001-2100. Tel: 507-388-2536. Ms. Nancy Hackenmiller, Prin. Lay Teachers 4; Students 77.
SS. Peter and Paul School. (Grades K-3), 110 N. Sixth St., 56001. Tel: 507-387-3316. Ms. Nancy Hackenmiller, Prin. Lay Teachers 10; Students 152.
Fitzgerald Middle School. (Grades 6-8), 110 N. Fifth St., 56001-4499. Tel: 507-388-9344. Sr. Mary Donald Miller, S.S.N.D., Prin. Sisters 2; Lay Teachers 11; Students 153.
Loyola High School. (Grades 9-12), 145 Good Counsel Dr., 56001-3146. Tel: 507-388-2997. Mr. James Rouse, Prin.; Rev. James J. Seitz, Campus Min. Priests 1; Lay Teachers 18; Students 247.
Holy Rosary School. (Grades 4-5), 546 Grant Ave., 56003. Sr. Mary Donald Miller, S.S.N.D., Prin. Lay Teachers 4; Students 96.

OWATONNA. *St. Mary's School.* (Grades PreK-8), Marian Dr., 55060. Tel: 507-451-2694. Mr. Gerald Kent, Prin. Sisters 1; Lay Teachers 24; Students 403.

ROCHESTER. *Rochester Catholic Schools*, 621 W. Center St., 55902. Tel: 507-280-0349. Norm Glismann, Supt.
St. Francis School. (Grades PreK-8), 318 11th Ave., S.E., 55904. Tel: 507-288-4816. Mrs. Diane Schwinghammer, Prin. Priests 4; Lay Teachers 25; Students 560.
St. John School. (Grades K-8), 424 W. Center St., 55902. Tel: 507-282-5248. Mr. Ronald Gaines, Prin. Priests 2; Sisters 1; Lay Teachers 25; Students 286.
St. Pius X School. (Grades K-8), 1205 12th Ave., 55901. Tel: 507-282-5161. Sr. Patricia Gehling, S.S.N.D., Prin. Priests 5; Sisters 2; Lay Teachers 32; Students 610.
Lourdes High School of Rochester, Inc. (Grades 9-12), 621 W. Center St., 55902. Tel: 507-289-3991. Mr. Dennis Nigon, Prin.; Sherri Broadhead, Campus Min Priests 1; Sisters 2; Lay Teachers 35; Students 477.
Holy Spirit School. (Grades K-4), 5455 50th Ave., N.W., 55901. Tel: 507-288-8818. Ronald Gaines, Prin. Lay Teachers 11; Students 214.

[D] GENERAL HOSPITALS

ROCHESTER. *Poverello Foundation*, St. Marys Hospital, 1216 S.W Second St., 55902. Tel: 507-255-5158.
For a complete listing, refer to the Hospitals section.
**Saint Marys Hospital*, 55902-1970. Tel: 507-255-5123; Fax: 507-255-3125.
For a complete listing, refer to the Hospitals section.

WABASHA. *St. Elizabeth's Hospital*, 1200 5th Grant Blvd., W., 55981. Tel: 612-565-4531.
For a complete listing, refer to the Hospitals section.

[E] SPECIAL HOSPITALS AND REHABILITATION FACILITIES

WINONA. *St. Francis Community Programs of Minnesota, Inc.*, 725 W. Broadway, 55987. Tel: 507-454-7711.
For a complete listing, refer to the Special Care Facilities section.

ROCHESTER. *Guest House*, 4800 48th St., N.E., P.O. Box 954, 55903. Tel: 800-634-4155; 507-288-4693.
For a complete listing, refer to the Special Care Facilities section.

[F] HOMES FOR AGED

WINONA. *St. Anne Hospice, Inc.*, 1347 W. Broadway, 55987. Tel 507-454-3621.
For a complete listing, refer to the Special Care Facilities section.

AUSTIN. *Sacred Heart Hospice, Inc.*, 1200 Twelfth St., S.W., 55912. Tel: 507-433-1808.
For a complete listing, refer to the Special Care Facilities section.

ROCHESTER. *Madonna Towers of Rochester, Inc.*, 4001 19th Ave., N.W., 55901. Tel: 507-288-3911; Fax: 507-288-0393.
For a complete listing, refer to the Special Care Facilities section.

WABASHA. *St. Elizabeth's Health Care Center*, 626 Shields Ave., 55981. Tel: 612-565-4581.
For a complete listing, refer to the Special Care Facilities section.

[G] CONVENTS AND RESIDENCES FOR SISTERS

HOUSTON. *Hermits of St. Mary of Carmel, H.S.M.C.*, RR 1, Box 143, 55943-9737. Sr. Rosemary Quinn, H.S.M.C., Supr.; Rev. David Wechter, O.C.S.O. (DUB).

JACKSON. *Convent of Religious Sisters of Mercy*, RR 3, Box 79, 56143. Tel: 507-847-5498; Fax: 507-847-5689. Sr. Marie Paul Lockerd, R.S.M., Local Supr.

MANKATO. *Provincial House of the School Sisters of Notre Dame*, Convent of Our Lady of Good Counsel, 170 Good Counsel Dr., 56001-3198. Tel: 507-389-4200. Religious in Province 492; Sisters in Motherhouse 154; Novices 7.
School Sisters of Notre Dame at Mankato, MN, Inc.
School Sisters of Notre Dame at Mankato, MN, Inc. Charitable Trust.
School Sisters of Notre Dame Cooperative Investment Fund

ROCHESTER. *General Motherhouse of the Sisters of the Third Order Regular of St. Francis of the Congregation of Our Lady of Lourdes*, Box 4900, 55903. Tel: 507-282-7441; Fax: 507-282-7762. Sr. Valerie Usher, O.S.F., Pres. & Community Min.; Revs. James Buryska; James Kunz. Legal Title: *Academy of Our Lady of Lourdes.* Sisters 420.

[H] RETREAT HOUSES AND CENTERS OF SPIRITUALITY

WINONA. *Tau Center*, 511 Hilbert St., 55987. Tel: 507-454-2993. Sr. Joan Blank, O.S.F., Facility Dir.

AUSTIN. *Queen of Angels Center*, 1009 Oakland Ave., E., 55912. Tel: 507-437-4015. Kathleen Finnegan, Dir.

MANKATO. *Good Counsel Education Center*, 151 Good Counsel Dr., P.O. Box 8968, 56002. Tel: 507-389-4287. Susan J. Ward, Dir.

ROCHESTER. *Assisi Community Center*, Assisi Hts., Box 4900, 55903. Tel: 507-280-2180; Fax: 507-280-2190. Joan Elkins, Dir.

[I] NEWMAN CENTERS

WINONA. *St. Thomas Aquinas Newman Center*, 475 Huff St., 55987. Tel: 507-452-2781. Mr. Thomas Parlin, Dir.

MANKATO. *Newman Center*, 1331 Warren St., 56001. Tel: 507-387-4154. Rev. Russell G. Scepaniak, Spiritual Dir.; Ms. Sydelle McCabe, Dir.

[J] MISCELLANEOUS LISTINGS

WINONA.
**Diocese of Winona Deposit & Loan*, 55 W. Sanborn St., Box 588, 55987. Tel: 507-454-4643; Fax: 507-454-8106.
Diocese of Winona Foundation, 55 W. Sanborn St., Box 588, 55987. Tel: 507-454-4643; Fax: 507-454-8106.
St. Mary's Parish of Winona Endowment Fund, Inc., 1303 W. Broadway, 55987. Tel: 507-452-5656. Rev. Joseph L. Keefe, Contact.
Saint Mary's Press, Christian Brothers Publications, 702 Terrace Hts., 55987. Tel: 507-457-7900. Rev. Robert P. Stamschror; Bro. Damian Steger, F.S.C., Pres.
Third Order Regular Common Franciscan Novitiate, Inc., Tau Center, 511 Hilbert St., 55987. Tel: 507-454-0184.

ALBERT LEA. *St. Theodore Catholic School Endowment*, 315 E. Clark St., Box 890, 56007-0890. Tel: 507-373-0603. Rev. Robert J. Schneider, Contact.

JACKSON. *Sacred Heart Mercy Health Care Center*, 803 Fourth St., 56143. Tel: 507-847-3571. Sr. Patricia Glowski, R.S.M., Admin. Patients assisted annually 5,025.

RELIGIOUS INSTITUTES OF MEN REPRESENTED IN THE DIOCESE

For further details refer to the corresponding bracketed number in the Religious Institutes of Men or Women section.

[0330]—*Brothers of the Christian Schools.*—F.S.C.
[0240]—*Camillian Fathers and Brothers.* (North American Province).—O.S.Cam.
[0400]—*Canons Regular of the Order of the Holy Cross.* (Province of St. Odilla).—O.S.C.
[0340]—*Cistercian Fathers.* (Abbey of Our Lady of New Malleray).—O.Cist.
[0350]—*Cistercians Order of the Strict Observance, (Trappists).*—O.C.S.O.
[0690]—*Jesuit Fathers and Brothers.* (Wisconsin Province).—S.J.
[0830]—*Mill Hill Missionaries.*—M.H.M.
[0910]—*Oblates of Mary Immaculate.* (Central Province).—O.M.I.
[0430]—*Order of Preachers (Dominicans).* (Chicago Province).—O.P.
[0110]—*Society of African Missions.*—S.M.A.
[0370]—*Society of St. Columban.*—S.S.C.

RELIGIOUS INSTITUTES OF WOMEN REPRESENTED IN THE DIOCESE

[0230]—*Benedictine Sisters of Pontifical Jurisdiction.*—O.S.B.
[1780]—*Congregation of the Sisters of the Third Order of St. Francis of Perpetual Adoration.* (Eastern, Central Regions).—F.S.P.A.
[1070-13]—*Dominican Sisters.*—O.P.
[1070-14]—*Dominican Sisters.*—O.P.
[1310]—*Franciscan Sisters of Little Falls.*—O.S.F.
[]—*Hermits of Mount Carmel (Contemplative Community).*—H.M.C.
[2470]—*Maryknoll Sisters of St. Dominic.*—M.M.
[2519]—*Religious Sisters of Mercy of Alma, Michigan.*—R.S.M.
[2970]—*School Sisters of Notre Dame.*—S.S.N.D.
[1680]—*School Sisters of St. Francis.*—O.S.F.
[0430]—*Sisters of Charity of the Blessed Virgin Mary.*—B.V.M.
[1705]—*The Sisters of St. Francis of Assisi.*—O.S.F.
[1570]—*Sisters of St. Francis of the Holy Family.*—O.S.F.
[3320]—*Sisters of the Presentation of the B.V.M.*—P.B.V.M.

[4100]—*Sisters of the Sorrowful Mother (Third Order of St. Francis).*—S.S.M.

[1720]—*Sisters of the Third Order Regular of St. Francis of the Congregation of Our Lady of Lourdes.*—O.S.F.

[4110]—*Ursuline Nuns (Roman Union).* (Central Prov.).—O.S.U.

DIOCESAN CEMETERIES

WINONA. *Catholic Cemeteries of Winona*, 55 W. Sanborn St., P.O. Box 588, 55987. Mr. John M. Vitek.

NECROLOGY

† Corcoran, Daniel J., (Retired). —Died Dec. 7, 1995.

† Fasnacht, James P., (Retired). —Died Jan. 16, 1996.

† Kreidermacher, Andrew L., (Retired). —Died Dec. 24, 1995.

† Olson, Donald J., (Retired). —Died Jan. 30, 1996.

† Sheehan, Robert L., (Retired). —Died Dec. 15, 1995.

† Timm, James D., Adrian, MN, St. Adrian Church. —Died Feb. 29, 1996.

Diocese of Worcester

(Dioecesis Wigorniensis)

Most Reverend

DANIEL P. REILLY, D.D.

Bishop of Worcester; ordained May 30, 1953; appointed Bishop of Norwich June 17, 1975; consecrated August 6, 1975; appointed Bishop of Worcester October 27, 1994; installed December 8, 1994. *Res., 2 High Ridge Rd., Worcester, MA, 01602.*

Most Reverend

GEORGE E. RUEGER, D.D., V.G.

Auxiliary Bishop of Worcester; ordained January 6, 1958; appointed Auxiliary Bishop of Worcester and Titular Bishop of Maronana January 19, 1987; consecrated February 25, 1987. *Res., 2 High Ridge Rd., Worcester, MA, 01602.*

Most Reverend

BERNARD J. FLANAGAN, D.D., J.C.D.

Former Bishop of Worcester; ordained December 8, 1931; appointed Bishop of Norwich September 1, 1953; consecrated November 30, 1953; transferred to See of Worcester August 12, 1959; installed September 24, 1959; resigned March 31, 1983. *Res., Vianney House, 222 June St., Worcester, MA, 01602.*

Chancery Office: 49 Elm St., Worcester, MA, 01609. Tel.: 508-791-7171; Fax: 508-753-7180.

Most Reverend

TIMOTHY J. HARRINGTON, D.D.

Retired Bishop of Worcester; ordained January 19, 1946; appointed Auxiliary Bishop of Worcester and Titular Bishop of Rusuca April 2, 1968; consecrated July 2, 1968; named Bishop of Worcester September 6, 1983; installed October 13, 1983; retired October 27, 1994. *Res., St. John's, 44 Temple St., Worcester, MA, 01604.*

ESTABLISHED JANUARY 14, 1950.

Square Miles 1,532.

Comprises the County of Worcester in the State of Massachusetts.

For legal titles of parishes and diocesan institutions, consult the Chancery Office.

STATISTICAL OVERVIEW

Personnel	
Bishop	1
Auxiliary Bishops	1
Retired Bishops	3
Abbots	2
Retired Abbots	1
Priests: Diocesan Active in Diocese	189
Priests: Active Outside Diocese	20
Priests: Retired, Sick or Absent	63
Number of Diocesan Priests	272
Religious Priests in Diocese	116
Ordinations:	
Religious Priests	2
Permanent Deacons in Diocese	67
Total Brothers	78
Total Sisters	550
Parishes	
Parishes	130
With Resident Pastor:	
Resident Diocesan Priests	123
Resident Religious Priests	4
Without Resident Pastor:	
Administered by Priests	3
Missions	3
Professional Ministry Personnel:	
Sisters	18
Lay Ministers	5
Welfare	
Catholic Hospitals	1
Total Assisted	80,000
Homes for the Aged	7
Total Assisted	25,000
Residential Care of Children	1
Total Assisted	16
Day Care and Extended Day Care Centers	3
Total Assisted	450
Specialized Homes	2
Total Assisted	280
Special Centers for Social Services	10
Total Assisted	31,000
Other Institutions	1
Total Assisted	177
Educational	
Seminaries, Diocesan	1
Students from This Diocese	9
Diocesan Students in Other Seminaries	8
Total Seminarians	17
Colleges and Universities	3
Total Students	7,243
High Schools, Diocesan and Parish	4
Total Students	2,422
High Schools, Private	3
Total Students	1,313
Elementary Schools, Diocesan and Parish	20
Total Students	5,065
Elementary Schools, Private	3
Total Students	600
Non-residential Schools for the Disabled	1
Total Students	73
Catechesis/Religious Education:	
High School Students	6,999
Elementary Students	21,432
Total Students Under Catholic Instruction	45,164
Teachers in the Diocese:	
Priests	8
Brothers	13
Sisters	37
Lay Teachers	530
Vital Statistics	
Receptions into the Church:	
Infant Baptism Totals	5,096
Adult Baptism Totals	146
Received into Full Communion	264
First Communions	4,462
Confirmations	3,005
Marriages:	
Catholic	1,150
Interfaith	317
Total Marriages	1,467
Deaths	3,960
Total Catholic Population	303,793
Total Population	709,705

Former Bishops—His Eminence JOHN CARDINAL WRIGHT, D.D., ord. Dec. 8, 1935; appt. Titular Bishop of Aegea and Auxiliary Bishop of Boston, May 10, 1947; cons. June 30, 1947; transferred to new See of Worcester, Jan. 28, 1950 enthroned March 7, 1950; appt. Bishop of Pittsburgh, Jan. 28, 1959; created Cardinal, April 28, 1969; transferred to the Roman Curia Prefect, Sacred Congregation for the Clergy; died Aug. 10, 1979.—Most Rev. BERNARD J. FLANAGAN, D.D., J.C.D., resigned March 31, 1983.—Most Rev. TIMOTHY J. HARRINGTON, D.D., retired Oct. 27, 1994.

Vicars General—Most Rev. GEORGE E. RUEGER, D.D., V.G., *2 High Ridge Rd., Worcester, 01602.* Tel: 508-755-3165.

Chancery Office—*49 Elm St., Worcester, 01609.* Tel: 508-791-7171; Fax: 508-753-7180.

Diocesan Director of Educational Services—Most Rev. GEORGE E. RUEGER, D.D., V.G., *49 Elm St., Worcester, 01608.* Tel: 508-791-7171.

Diocesan Director of Fiscal Affairs—Rev. Msgr. EDMOND T. TINSLEY, V.G., *49 Elm St., Worcester, 01609.* Tel: 508-791-7171.

Diocesan Director for Human Services (and Catholic Relief Services)—Rev. Msgr. EDMOND T. TINSLEY, V.G., *Res., 77 Mulberry St., Leicester, 01524.* Tel: 508-892-4886.

Diocesan Expansion Fund—Most Rev. GEORGE E. RUEGER, D.D.; Mr. KEVIN CONDRON, Chm., *49 Elm St., Worcester, 01609.* Tel: 508-791-7171.

Diocesan Finance Committee—Mr. RICHARD J. FLYNN, Chm., *49 Elm St., Worcester, 01609.*

Diocesan Tribunal—Address all communications to: *49 Elm St., Worcester, 01609.* Tel: 508-791-7171.

Vicar for Canonical Affairs and Judicial Vicar—Rev. F. STEPHEN PEDONE, J.C.L., *49 Elm St., Worcester, 01609.*

Associate Judicial Vicars—Rev. PAUL T. O'CONNELL, J.C.D., Assoc. Judicial Vicar; Most Rev. BERNARD J. FLANAGAN, D.D., J.C.D., Assoc. Judicial Vicar, Court of the Boston Province.

Judges—Rev HENRY G. BOWEN, J.C.D.; Rev. Msgr. JOHN J. KELLIHER; Revs. ROBERT J. KASLYN, S.J., J.C.D.; PAUL T. O'CONNELL, J.C.D.; F. STEPHEN PEDONE, J.C.L.

Promotor of Justice—Most Rev. BERNARD J. FLANAGAN, J.C.D.

Secretary and Defender of the Bond—Deacon GEORGE L. O'TOOLE.

Advocates—Revs. ROLAND L. GAMACHE; THOMAS E. MAHONEY; LEO BARRY; JAMES P. KERRIGAN.

Notary—JUDITH M. GAUTHIER.

Diocesan Consultors—Most Rev. GEORGE E. RUEGER, D.D., V.G.; Rev. Msgr. RICHARD J. CARELLI; Revs. CHARLES DUMPHY; ROLAND GAMACHE; JOSEPH NALLY; ARTHUR OUILLETTE; F. STEPHEN PEDONE; ROCCO M. PICCOLOMINI; Rev. Msgr. FRANCIS J. SCOLLEN; Rev. JOSEPH SZWACH; Rev. Msgr. EDMOND T. TINSLEY.

Deans—Area I: Rev. CHARLES F. MONROE; Area II: Rev. Msgr. FRANCIS J. SCOLLEN; Area III: Rev. JAMES B. O'SHEA; Area IV: Rev. ARTHUR A. OUILLETTE; Area V: Rev. RICHARD F. TRAINOR; Area VI: Rev. PAUL J. TOUGAS; Area VII: Rev. MICHAEL J. ROY; Area VIII:

Rev. DANIEL R. MULCAHY; Area IX: Rev. CHESTER J. MISIEWICZ; Area X: Rev. LAWRENCE J. ESPOSITO; Area XI: Rev. RICHARD P. LEWANDOWSKI; Area XII: Rev. ROLAND J. GAMACHE; Area XIII: Rev. JAMES J. CLIFFORD, (Retired).

Vicar for Clergy—Rev. ROCCO M. PICCOLOMINI, *Res., Our Lady of Mt. Carmel-St. Ann, 53 E. Central St., Worcester, 01605.*

Vicar for Religious—Sr. PAULA KELLEHER, *49 Elm St., Worcester, 01609.* Tel: 508-791-7171.

Diocesan Offices and Directors

Apostleship of Prayer and Eucharistic Crusade—Rev. THADDEUS X. STACHURA, *Our Lady of Czestochowa, 34 Ward St., Worcester, 01610.* Tel: 508-755-5959.

Apostolate of Healing—Rev. RALPH A. DIORIO, Dir., *761 Main St., Leicester, 01524.* Tel: 508-892-9397.

Archivist—Most Rev. GEORGE E. RUEGER, *49 Elm St., Worcester, 01609.* Tel: 508-791-7171.

Brazilian Pastoral Ministry—Sr. BARBARA CICCOLINI, *555 Plantation St., Worcester, 01605.* Tel: 508-791-7171, Ext. 153; Fax: 508-753-7180.

Building Commission Members—Rev. Msgr. GEORGE E. DENOMME; Most Rev. GEORGE E. RUEGER, D.D., V.G.; Rev. Msgr. EDMUND G. HADDAD; Rev. Msgr. JAMES A. MONGELLUZZO; Rev. Msgr. EDMOND T. TINSLEY; Revs. LEE BARTLETT, Chm. JOHN FOLEY; THADDEUS STACHURA; JOHN THOMAS; Mr. HENRY MILLER; Mrs. MARY SLOCUM, *49 Elm St., Worcester, 01609.* Tel: 508-791-7171.

Campus Ministry—Rev. PETER J. SCANLON, Vicar for College Communities, *Diocesan Office, P.O. Box 903, Worcester, 01613., Res., The Center, 19 Schussler Rd., Worcester, 01609.* Tel: 508-757-6097., Newman Center: *281 Highland Ave., Fitchburg, 01420.* Tel: 508-345-2688.

Catholic Charities—CATHERINE LOEFFLER, Dir., *10 Hammond St., Worcester, 01610-1513.* Tel: 508-798-0191. (Refer to separate listings for detailed information on Catholic Charities and related organizations).

Cemeteries—Mr. FRANCIS F. ELLIOTT, Dir.; Rev. JOHN CAHILL, Priest liaison, *260 Cambridge St., Worcester, 01610.* Tel: 508-757-7415.

Charismatic Renewal, Office of—Mr. MICHAEL FREED, Liaison, *St. Joseph, West St., P.O. Box 284, Berlin, 01503.* Tel: 508-365-6492.

Clergy Benefit Plan—Rev. JOHN J. FOLEY, *1052 Pleasant St., Worcester, 01602.*

Collaborative for Education and Ministry: Institute for Academic and Pastoral Development—Most Rev. DANIEL P. REILLY, D.D., Chancellor.

Communication Office—RAYMOND L. DELISLE, Dir., *49 Elm St., Worcester, 01609.* Tel: 508-791-5357.

Continuing Education of the Clergy—Rev. MICHAEL ROSE, Dir., *89 Main St., S. Grafton, 01560.* Tel: 508-839-5354.

Cursillo—Rev. ROBERT A. GRATTAROTI, Dir., *37 Worcester Rd., Charlton City, 01508.* Tel: 508-248-7862.

Development Office—Bishop's Fund, Good Sheperd Endowment Fund, Adopt-A-Student, Annual Catholic School Appeal, Project Share for Christ, The Adopt-A-Student Endowment Trust. Mr. OWEN C. COOGAN, Dir., *49 Elm St., Worcester, 01609.* Tel: 508-754-0574; Fax: 508-754-2768.

Diocesan Expansion Fund—Mr. KEVIN CONDRON, Chm. Members: JANET S. SIMONDS; Revs. FRANK J. LIISTRO; LOUIS J. GOULD; EUGENE F. BERTHIAUME; Most Rev. GEORGE E. RUEGER; Rev. Msgr. EDMOND T. TINSLEY; Mrs. PATRICIA JONES; Mrs. JOAN HOULE.

Diocesan Scouts—Boy Scout Office: *120 Hill St., Whitinsville, 01588.* Tel: 508-234-0346., Girl Scout Office:*120 Hill St., Whitinsville, 01588.* Tel: 508-234-0346. Rev. RICHARD REIDY, *19 Chatham St., Worchester, 01609.*

Ecumenical and Interreligious Affairs, Diocesan Office for—Sr. THERESE DION, S.S.A., *49 Elm St., Worcester, 01609.*

Elderly, Ministry to—Rev. THOMAS M. BARRY, *48 Vernon St., Worcester, 01610.*

Evangelization, Office of—Rev. LAWRENCE J. ESPOSITO, Chm., *49 Elm St., Worcester, 01609.*

Family Life Ministry—Co-Directors: Mr. RONALD V. ARCIERI; Mrs. JANET M. ARCIERI, *49 Elm St., Worcester, 01609.* Tel: 508-791-7171.

Finance Office—Rev. Msgr. EDMOND T. TINSLEY, V.G., Fiscal Affairs; JEROME D. JUSSAUME, Mgr., Finance, *49 Elm St., Worcester, 01609.* Tel: 508-791-7171. Rev. DENNIS J. O'BRIEN, Dir.; Rev. JAMES FITTON, House of Priestly Formation, *761 Main St., Leicester, 01524.*

Holy Childhood Association—Rev. Msgr. THOMAS J. NEEDHAM, Dir., *353 Grove St., Worcester, 01605.* Tel: 508-754-8419.

Meet-the-Father Ministry, Inc.—Mrs. EILEEN GEORGE, Contact Person, *363 Greenwood St., Millbury, 01527.*

Newspaper—"The Catholic Free Press", GERARD E. GOGGINS, Exec. Editor, *47 Elm St., Worcester, 01609.* Tel: 508-757-6387.

Office for Worship—Rev. ROBERT JOHNSON, Dir., *19 Chatham St., Worcester, 01609.* Tel: 508-798-0417.

Pastoral Associate Ministry Consultative Board—Sr. PAULA KELLEHER, S.S.J., Chm., *49 Elm St., Worcester, 01609.* Tel: 508-791-7171

Permanent Diaconate—Co-Directors: Revs. ROCCO M. PICCOLOMINI; JAMES AQUINO, *49 Elm St., Worcester, 01609.*

Presbyteral Council—Most Rev. DANIEL P. REILLY, Pres.; Most Rev. GEORGE E. RUEGER; Revs. F. STEPHEN PEDONE; JAMES J. AQUINO; Rev. Msgr. RICHARD J. CARELLI; Revs. JOSEPH M. NALLY, Chm. ROCCO PICCOLOMINI; JOSEPH F. SZWACH; Rev. Msgr. EDMOND T. TINSLEY, Sec.; Revs. PAUL J. TOUGAS, Treas. CHARLES F. MONROE, Vice Chm., *Chancery Bldg., 49 Elm St., Worcester, 01609.* Tel: 508-791-7171.

Priests' Personnel Board—Rev. ROCCO M. PICCOLOMINI, *Our Lady of Mt. Carmel-St. Ann, 53 E. Central St., Worcester, 01605.* Tel: 508-792-4574.

Priests' Retirement Residence—Rev. JOHN F. CAHILL, Admin., *222 June St., Worcester, 01602.* Tel: 508-791-0311.

Pro-Life—Rev. CHESTER J. DEVLIN, Dir./Educational Coord., *49 Elm St., Worcester, 01609.*

Propagation of the Faith—Rev. Msgr. THOMAS J. NEEDHAM, Dir., *353 Grove St., Worcester, 01605.* Tel: 508-754-8419.

Religious Education Office—Rev. Msgr. LOUIS R. PIERMARINI, Dir., *49 Elm St., Worcester, 01609.* Tel: 508-791-7171., *Res., St. Roch, 334 Main St., Oxford, 01540.*

North County Office Fitchburg—Mrs. MARY G. HOVENESIAN, Assoc. Dir./North Country Coord., *89 Sheridan St., Fitchburg, 01420.* Tel: 508-345-6636.

School Department—Mr. CHARLES E. MCMANUS, Supt. PATRICIA M. HALPIN; KATHLEEN M. KELLIHER, Assoc. Supt., Schools, *49 Elm St., Worcester, 01609.* Tel: 508-791-7171.

Social Justice, Peace and Integrity of Creation, Office of—RACHELLE COMTOIS, Chm., *49 Elm St., Worcester, 01609.* Tel: 508-791-7171.

Spanish Apostolate—Rev. JOSE A. RODRIGUEZ, Bishop's Liaison, *429 Main St., Worcester, 01610., 49 Elm St., Worchester, 01609.* Tel: 508-791-7171.

St. Vincent dePaul Society—Central and Greater Worcester District Council—FRANCES PIKE, Pres.; Rev. Msgr. EDMOND T. TINSLEY, Spiritual Dir., *Res., 77 Mulberry St., Leicester, 01524.* Tel: 508-892-4886.

Northern Worcester County District Council—JOHN YOVINO, Pres.; Rev. Msgr. LEO J. BATTISTA, Chap.

Southern Worcester County District Council—ALFRED E. BALLARD, Pres.; Rev. J. NORMAND TREMBLAY, Chap.

Tri-Conference Retirement Fund for Religious—Sr. PAULA KELLEHER, S.S.J., Diocesan Coord., *49 Elm St., Worcester, 01609.* Tel: 508-791-7171.

Vicar for Priests—Rev. ROCCO M. PICCOLOMINI, *53 E. Central St., Worcester, 01605.*

Vicar for Religious—Sr. PAULA KELLEHER, S.S.J., *49 Elm St., Worcester, 01609.* Tel: 508-791-7171.

Vietnamese Apostolate—Rev. PHUONG VAN NGUYEN, *1052 Pleasant St., Worcester, 01602., 44 Temple St., Worcester, 01605.* Tel: 508-756-7165.

Vocation Office—Rev. THOMAS SULLIVAN, Dir., *49 Elm St., Worcester, 01609.* Tel: 508-756-7165.

Worcester Diocesan Commission for Women—Mrs. MARY DONOVAN, Chm., *49 Elm St., Worcester, 01609.* Tel: 508-791-7171.

Youth Ministry—Mr. TIMOTHY J. SEMBER, Dir., Office: *Oakhurst, 120 Hill St., Whitinsville, 01588.* Tel: 508-234-0346.

CLERGY, PARISHES, MISSIONS AND PAROCHIAL SCHOOLS

CITY OF WORCESTER
(Worcester County)

1—ST. PAUL'S CATHEDRAL (1866), Revs. Richard F. Reidy, Rector; Joseph P. Mahoney; Deacons James P. Quinlivan, Sr.; Francisco Escobar; Daniel Becker. In res., Revs. David E. Doiron; Timothy M. Brewer; Robert K. Johnson.
Res., 38 High St., 01609. Tel: 508-799-4193; Fax: 508-752-6308.
Catechesis/Religious Programs—Tel: 508-755-1414.
Students 209.

2—ASCENSION (1911), Rev. Joseph A. Adamo; Sr. Ruth Dolores Quinn, S.S.J., Pastoral Assoc.
Res., 48 Vernon St., 01610. Tel: 508-752-4459; Fax: 508-752-8821.

3—BLESSED SACRAMENT (1912), Rev. Charles J. Dumphy. In res., Rev. Peter R. Beaulieu.
Res., 551 Pleasant St., 01602. Tel: 508-755-5291; Fax: 508-755-6891.
Catechesis/Religious Programs—Epiphany House, Tel: 508-752-4368. Sr. Mary M. Duffy, S.S.J., D.R.E. Students 233.

4—CHRIST THE KING (1936), Revs. John J. Foley; Phuong Van Nguyen; Sr. Bernadette Lavoie, S.S.A., Pastoral Assoc.; Deacon Joseph M. Banieukiewicz.
Res., 1052 Pleasant St., 01602. Tel: 508-754-5361; Fax: 508-753-0448.
Catechesis/Religious Programs—Tel: 508-752-5514. Susan J. Wenc, D.R.E.
Students 612.

5—HOLY NAME OF JESUS (1893) (French), Rev. Msgr. Joseph V. Sirois.
Res., 51 Illinois St., 01610. Tel: 508-799-2792; Fax: 508-799-2368.
Catechesis/Religious Programs—Students 123.

6—IMMACULATE CONCEPTION (1873), Rev. Msgr. Thomas J. Needham.
Res., 353 Grove St., 01605. Tel: 508-754-8419; Fax: 508-756-2192.
Catechesis/Religious Programs—Father Connor Center, Tel: 508-791-5887.
Students 208.

7—NOTRE DAME DES CANADIENS - ST. JOSEPH (1869) (French), Rev. Richard G. Roger; Mary G. Guerin, Pastoral Assoc.
Res., 5 Whitman Rd., 01609. Tel: 508-754-6722; Fax: 508-797-1191. [CEM]

8—OUR LADY OF THE ANGELS (1916), Revs. Charles F. Monroe; William E. Champlin. Pastoral Assocs. Sr. Barbara Collins, S.N.D.; Deacon Alphonse Desautels.
Res., 1222 Main St., 01603. Tel: 508-791-0951; Fax: 508-753-9531.
School—1220 Main St., Rear, 01603. Tel: 508-752-5609.
Lay Teachers 18; Students 338.
Catechesis/Religious Programs—Tel: 508-754-4165.
Students 444.

9—OUR LADY OF CZESTOCHOWA (1903) (Polish), Revs. Thaddeus X. Stachura; Anthony S. Kazarnowicz.
Res., 34 Ward St., 01610. Tel: 508-755-5959; Fax: 508-767-1644.
School—St. Mary's, 50 Richland St., Tel: 508-753-0484. Sr. M. Dorothea Prin. & D.R.E.
Sisters of the Holy Family of Nazareth 3; Lay Teachers 9; Students 224.
High School—St. Mary's, Tel: 508-753-1170; Fax: 508-795-0560. Mark Manzello, Prin.
Sisters 2; Lay Teachers 16; Students 194.
Catechesis/Religious Programs—Students 224.

10—OUR LADY OF FATIMA (1952), Rev. Louis J. Gould; Sr. Emanuela Bacci, X.M.M., Spanish Apostolate. In res., Rev. Edward M. Ryan.
Res., 7 Auburn St., 01605. Tel: 508-755-3820.
Catechesis/Religious Programs—Students 127.

11—OUR LADY OF LORETO (1966) (Italian), Rev. James J. Aquino; Deacon Nicholas CaraDonna.
Res., 33 Massasoit Rd., 01604. Tel: 508-753-5001; Fax: 508-754-1537.
Catechesis/Religious Programs—37 Massasoit Rd., 01604. Tel: 508-799-2445.
Students 336.

12—OUR LADY OF LOURDES (1949), Rev. James B. O'Shea. In res., Rev. Bernard J. Conlin, (Retired).
Res., 1290 Grafton St., 01604. Tel: 508-757-0789; Fax: 508-757-0048.
Catechesis/Religious Programs—Tel: 508-753-5773. Jo-Ann Bafaro, D.R.E.
Students 200.

13—OUR LADY OF MT. CARMEL AND ST. ANN (1872) (Italian), Rev. Michael P. Bafaro; Deacon Philip Divine. In res., Rev. Rocco Piccolomini.
Res., 53 E. Central St., 01605. Tel: 508-752-2964; Fax: 508-755-3506.
Catechesis/Religious Programs—Tel: 508-791-6139. Joan D'rgeni, D.R.E.
Students 203.

14—OUR LADY OF THE ROSARY (1911), Rev. Msgr. John J. Kelliher; Rev. James M. Shea.
Res., 23 Fales St., 01606. Tel: 508-853-1640. Sr. Irene Moran, M.P.V., D.R.E.
Catechesis/Religious Programs—Father Riley Center, 9 Emerson Rd., 01604. Tel: 508-852-5474; Fax: 508-853-2426.
Students 503.

15—OUR LADY OF VILNA (1925) (Lithuanian), Rev. Alphonse A. Volungis.
Res., 153 Sterling St., 01610. Tel: 508-752-1825.

16—SACRED HEART (1880) (Irish), Revs. Lee F. Bartlett; Cyril A. LeBeau. In res., Rev. Peter J. Scanlon.
Res., 596 Cambridge St., 01610. Tel: 508-752-1608; Fax: 508-757-2462.
Catechesis/Religious Programs—Students 150.

17—St. Andrew the Apostle (1954), Rev. James F. Carmody; Sr. Therese Gosselin, S.S.A., Pastoral Assoc. In res., Revs. Bernard F. Davenport; John C. Petruaksas, M.I.C.
Res., 16 Vineyard St., 01603. Tel: 508-754-6057; Fax: 508-754-0830.
Catechesis/Religious Programs—Tel: 508-752-4701.
Students 146.

18—St. Bernard (1916), Rev. Edmund F. Falvey.
Res., 236 Lincoln St., 01605. Tel: 508-791-3104.
Catechesis/Religious Programs—One Harlow St., 01605.
Students 51.

19—St. Casimir's (1894) (Lithuanian), Rev. Anthony N. Nockunas, M.I.C., Temporary Admin.; Helen Midgley, Pastoral Assoc. In res., Rev. John C. Petruaskas, M.I.C.
Res., 41 Providence St., 01604. Tel: 508-754-5142.

20—St. Catherine of Sweden (1952), Rev. George J. Ridick; Deacon Thomas Wagner; Sr. Kathleen McGurk, Pastoral Assoc.
Res., 3 Wiser Ave., 01607. Tel: 508-752-1624; Fax: 508-793-2187.
Catechesis/Religious Programs—Tel: 508-793-2187.
Students 89.

21—St. Charles Borromeo (1954), Revs. Henry G. Bowen; Quynh Dinh Tran. In res., Rev. Thomas B. Garlick.
Res., 341 June St., 01602. Tel: 508-799-4031; Fax: 508-792-6675.
Catechesis/Religious Programs—Sr. Elaine Potvin, S.S.A., D.R.E.
Students 220.

22—St. Christopher (1956), Rev. Martin P. Donahue; Deacon Henry Morrissey.
Res., 950 W. Boylston St., 01606. Tel: 508-853-1492; Fax: 508-853-4338.
Catechesis/Religious Programs—Tel: 508-853-3302.
Students 197.

23—St. George (1951), Revs. Henry A. Donoghue; Stephen G. Copper; Deacon John F. Cahill. In res., Rev. F. Stephen Pedone.
Res., 40 Brattle St., 01606. Tel: 508-853-0183; Fax: 508-854-0864.
Catechesis/Religious Programs—Tel: 508-852-1784. Mrs. Shirley M. Granlund, D.R.E.
Students 609.

24—St. Joan of Arc (1950), Revs. Joseph M. Nally; Dennis O. O'Malley; Emerito Ortiz; Sr. Soledad Chacon, R.O.D.A., Pastoral Assoc.
Res., 570 Lincoln St., 01605. Tel: 508-852-3232; Fax: 508-852-3223.
Catechesis/Religious Programs—Students 400.

25—St. John's (1834), Rev. Joseph A. Coonan; Deacon Richard O'Connor. In res., Rev. Joseph P. Mahoney.
Res., 44 Temple St., 01604. Tel: 508-756-7165; Fax: 508-754-5153.
Catechesis/Religious Programs—Mrs. Janet O'Connor, D.R.E.
Students 100.

26—St. Margaret Mary (1922), Rev. Patrick J. Hawthorne; Deacon Bruce Vidito.
Res., 77 Alvarado Ave., 01604. Tel: 508-753-5788; Fax: 508-797-1644.
Catechesis/Religious Programs—Students 91.

27—St. Peter (1884), Revs. Francis J. Scollen; Jose Andres Rodriguez. In res., Rev. John F. Madden.
Res., 929 Main St., 01610. Tel: 508-752-4674.
Catechesis/Religious Programs—Tel: 508-752-0797; Fax: 508-767-1511.
Students 281.

28—St. Stephen's (1887), Rev. William F. Sanders; Deacon James F. DiPadua, Jr. In res., Rev. Thomas M. Barry, D.
Res., 16 Hamilton St., 01604. Tel: 508-755-3165; Fax: 508-755-0937.
School—355 Grafton St., Tel: 508-755-3209. Sr. Constance Gosselin, S.S.A., Prin.
Sisters 5; Lay Teachers 13; Students 318.
Catechesis/Religious Programs—Ramona Kneeland, D.R.E.
Students 200.

OUTSIDE THE CITY OF WORCESTER
(In the County of Worcester)

Ashburnham, St. Denis (1951), Rev. Joseph J. Jurgelonis; Deacons Michael P. Connor; Richard Desjardins.
Res., 85 Main St., P.O. Box 418, 01430. Tel: 508-827-5806. [CEM]
Catechesis/Religious Programs—Tel: 508-827-4892.
Students 375.

Athol, Our Lady Immaculate (1882), Rev. Stephen D. Johnson; Deacons James L. Linderman; Robert Dio.
Res., 192 School St., 01331-2399. Tel: 508-249-2738; Fax: 508-249-0447. [CEM 2]
Catechesis/Religious Programs—Tel: 508-249-7690. Sharon Maher, D.R.E.
Students 274.
Mission—South Royalston, Athol Co., Our Lady Queen of Heaven, Rte. 68, South Royalston, 01368. Tel: 508-249-4103.

St. Francis (1912), Rev. Raymond P. Messier.
Res., 105 Main St., 01331. Tel: 508-249-3361.

Auburn, St Joseph's (1907), Revs. Richard F. Trainor; Thomas G. Landry.
Res., 194 Oxford St., 01501. Tel: 508-832-2074; Fax: 508-832-8894.
Catechesis/Religious Programs—Tel: 508-832-5975. Ms. Susan Landry, D.R.E.
Students 820.

North American Martyrs (1952), Rev. John F. Gee.
Res., 8 Wyoma Dr., 01501. Tel: 508-798-8779; Fax: 508-791-6614.
Catechesis/Religious Programs—Tel: 508-798-0612.
Students 150.

Baldwinville, St. Vincent De Paul (1955), Revs. John E. Kelley; George A. Charland.
Res., 18 Pleasant St., 01436. Tel: 508-939-8851; Fax: 508-939-2120.
Catechesis/Religious Programs—Students 142.

Barre, St. Joseph's (1896), Rev. Thomas H. Hultquist; Deacon Walter Doyle.
Res., 90 Common St., 01005. Tel: 508-355-4463; Fax: 508-355-0136.
Catechesis/Religious Programs—Tel: 508-355-6402.
Students 230.
Mission—Wheelwright, Hardwick Co., St. Augustine, 98 Church Ln., Wheelwright, 01094. Tel: 508-355-4463.

Berlin, St. Joseph the Good Provider (1973), Rev. Lawrence J. Esposito.
Res., 52 West St., Box 284, 01503-0284. Tel: 508-365-5492; 838-2915 (Office); Fax: 508-365-9133.

Blackstone, St. Paul's (1850), Rev. James D. Champion.
Res., 48 St. Paul St., 01504. Tel: 508-883-6726; Fax: 508-883-2079. [CEM]
Catechesis/Religious Programs—Tel: 508-883-3542; Fax: 508-883-2079.
Students 372.

St. Theresa (1929) (French), Rev. Richard H. Labonte.
Res., 630 Rathbun St., 01504. Tel: 508-883-7206; Fax: 508-883-5250.
Catechesis/Religious Programs—Tel: 508-883-7527.
Students 190.

Bolton, St. Francis Xavier (1953), Rev. Robert L. Killion.
Res., 808 Main St., 01740. Tel: 508-779-2750; Fax: 508-779-0337.
Catechesis/Religious Programs—Students 110.

Boylston, St. Mary of the Hills (1952), Rev. Paul J. Tougas; Deacon Raymond H. Bolduc.
Res., 630 Cross St., 01505. Tel: 508-869-6771; Fax: 508-869-3465.
Catechesis/Religious Programs—Tel: 508-869-6776.
Students 187.

Brookfield, St. Mary's (1885), Rev. Eugene F. Berthiaume.
Res., 4 Howard St., 01506. Tel: 508-867-3188; Fax: 508-867-4313.
Catechesis/Religious Programs—Students 130.

Charlton City, St. Joseph's (1900), Revs. Robert A. Grattaroti; J. Normand Tremblay; Deacons Lawrence F. Miskell; William S. Miller.
Res., Box 338, 01508. Tel: 508-248-7862; Fax: 508-248-5332.
Catechesis/Religious Programs—Tel: 508-248-7986. Joanne Powell, D.R.E.
Students 650.

Clinton, St. John the Evangelist (1849), Revs. Thomas V. Walsh; Robert D. Bruso. Pastoral Assocs.: Sr. Theresa Sullivan, P.B.V.M.; Sr. Sheila Finnegan, S.N.D., Pastoral Assoc.
Res., 149 Chestnut St., 01510. Tel: 508-368-0366; Fax: 508-368-4359. [CEM]
Catechesis/Religious Programs—Tel: 508-368-0052.
Students 625.

Our Lady of Jasna Gora (1913) (Polish), Rev. Richard J. Zuscak.
Res., 128 Franklin St., 01510. Tel: 508-365-2724; Fax: 508-365-5705.
School—St.Mary's, R128 Franklin St., 01510. Tel: 508-365-3137. Dale Gorski, Prin.
Lay Teachers 8; Students 190.

Our Lady of the Rosary (1909), Rev. J. Brendan Nally.
Res., One Cross St., 01510. Tel: 508-365-3621; Fax: 508-368-3082. [CEM]
Catechesis/Religious Programs—Students 89.

Dudley, St. Andrew Bobola (1963) (Polish), Revs. Joseph F. Szwach; Joseph Bielonko.
Res., 54 W. Main St., P.O. Box 98, 01571. Tel: 508-943-5633; Fax: 508-949-6701. [JC]
Catechesis/Religious Programs—Students 67.

St. Anthony's (1969), Rev. Paul F. Campbell.
Res., 22 Dudley Hill Rd., Box 277, 01571-0277. Tel: 508-943-0470. [CEM]
Catechesis/Religious Programs—Tel: 508-949-0335; Fax: 508-943-5663.
Students 318.

East Brookfield, St. John the Baptist (1952), Rev. Joseph G. Loiselle.
Res., 121 Blaine Ave., 01515. Tel: 508-867-3738; Fax: 508-867-3738.
Catechesis/Religious Programs—Students 65.

East Douglas, St. Denis (1870), Rev. H. Edward Chalmers; Deacon Clement E. Benvenuti.
Res., Manchaug Rd., 01516. Tel: 508-476-2002; Fax: 508-476-2002. [CEM]
Catechesis/Religious Programs—Students 420.

East Templeton, Holy Cross (1952), Rev. George L. O'Brien; Deacon Arthur J. Chartier.
Res., 25 Lake Ave., P.O. Box 418, 01438. Tel: 508-632-2121; Fax: 508-630-3890.
Catechesis/Religious Programs—Tel: 508-632-2194.
Students 202.

Fiskdale, St. Anne's and St. Patrick's (1886), Revs. Donald B. Espinosa, A.A.; Paul Vandreuil, A.A.; Aidan M. Furlong, A.A.; Oliver R. Blanchette, A.A.; Deacon Clarence H. Martel.
Res., 16 Church St., 01518. Tel: 508-347-7338; Fax: 508-347-2982. [CEM]
Catechesis/Religious Programs—Tel: 508-347-9353.
Students 467.

Fitchburg

1—St. Anthony of Padua (1908), Rev. John M. Siciliano, Temporary Admin.; Deacon John B. LeBlanc.
Res., 2 Beekman St., 01420. Tel: 508-342-4706; Fax: 508-342-8160.
School—(Grades PreK-8). Tel: 508-345-7785. Margaret Haneisen.
Sisters 1; Lay Teachers 11; Students 243.
Catechesis/Religious Programs—Students 97.

2—St. Bernard's (1847) (Irish), Rev. H. Edward Chalmers. In res., Revs. Thomas M. Tierney; Theodore R. Laperle.
Res., 240 Water St., 01420. Tel: 508-343-7459; Fax: 508-343-0193. [CEM]
School—254 Summer St., 01420. Tel: 508-342-1948.
Sisters of the Presentation of the Blessed Virgin Mary 2; Lay Teachers 10; Students 250.
Catechesis/Religious Programs—Tel: 508-345-2777.
Students 185.

3—St. Camillus de Lellis (1953), Rev. Richard P. Lewandowski; Deacon Benjamin A. Nogueira.
Res., 333 Mechanic St., 01420. Tel: 508-342-7921; Fax: 508-345-2688.
Catechesis/Religious Programs—Tel: 508-342-5991.
Students 176.

4—St. Francis of Assisi (1903), Rev. Gerald A. Dorais; Deacon William Colon.
Res., 63 Sheridan, 01420. Tel: 508-342-9651; Fax: 508-342-7936.
Catechesis/Religious Programs—Tel: 508-342-3521. Susan Hanno, D.R.E.
Students 111.

5—Immaculate Conception (1886) (French), Rev. Msgr. Richard E. Collette; Deacons Norman Prince; Raymond P. Dauphinais; John Aliskevicz.
Res., 59 Walnut St., 01420. Tel: 508-342-5851; Fax: 508-345-2491.
Catechesis/Religious Programs—Students 58.

6—St. Joseph's (1890), Rev. Thomas G. Sickler, M.S.; Deacon Andre W. Croteau. In res., Revs. John J. Nally, M.S.; John Hughes, M.S.
Res., 49 Woodland St., 01420. Tel: 508-345-7997; Fax: 508-345-7678. [CEM]
School—35 Columbus St., 01420. Tel: 508-343-3630. Thomas Hartigan, Prin.
Lay Teachers 10; Students 221.
Catechesis/Religious Programs—Tel: 508-345-7997. Bette Gilman, D.R.E.
Students 120.

7—Madonna of the Holy Rosary (1955), Rev. Frank J. Liistro.
Res., 118 Theresa St., 01420. Tel: 508-342-1290; Fax: 508-345-3032.
Catechesis/Religious Programs—Tel: 508-345-4906. Judy A. Alario, D.R.E.
Students 225.

8—Sacred Heart of Jesus (1867), Rev. John A. Dwyer; Deacon Edgar B. Blackwelder.
Res., 22 Cottage St., 01420. Tel: 508-342-9606.
Catechesis/Religious Programs—Students 72.

Gardner

1—Holy Spirit (1955), Rev. Andre M. Gariepy.
Res., 45 Metcalf St., 01440. Tel: 508-632-3333; Fax: 508-632-3630.
Catechesis/Religious Programs—Students 207.

2—St. Joseph's (1908) (Polish), Rev. Thomas M. Tokarz.
Res., 358 Pleasant St., 01440. Tel: 508-632-0375; Fax: 508-632-1282. [CEM]

3—Our Lady of the Holy Rosary (1884) (French), Revs. J. Andre Guenette; Gerard Bertin; Laurie Leger, M.S.; Deacon Arthur Giard.
Res., 135 Nichols St., 01440. Tel: 508-632-0253; Fax: 508-630-1773. [CEM]
School—99 Nichols St., 01440. Tel: 508-632-8656; Fax: 508-630-1433. Sr. Helen Bissonnette, Prin.
Sisters of the Presentation of Mary 4; Lay Teachers 16; Students 360.
Catechesis/Religious Programs—Students 172.

4—Sacred Heart of Jesus (1874), Rev. Donald H. Baker; Deacon Paul J. Carrier.
Res., 166 Cross St., 01440. Tel: 508-632-0237; Fax: 508-630-2459. [CEM]
Parish Center: 100 Central St., 01440. Tel: 508-632-0217.
School—Sacred Heart Elementary, Lynde St., 01440. Tel: 508-632-0950. Frank Peterlin, Prin.
Lay Teachers 8; Students 177.
Catechesis/Religious Programs—Tel: 508-632-0218.
Students 360.
Day Care—Tel: 508-632-5745. Mrs. Jane Pineo, Dir.

Gilbertville, St. Aloysius (1894), Rev. Chester J. Misiewicz.
Res., 58 Church St., P.O. Box 542, 01031-0542. Tel: 413-477-6493; Fax: 413-477-6493. [CEM]
Catechesis/Religious Programs—Students 94.

Grafton, St. Philip's (1869), Rev. Anthony T. Marteka.
Res., 12 West St., 01519. Tel: 508-839-3325; Fax: 508-839-1310. [CEM]
Catechesis/Religious Programs—Tel: 508-839-9130; Fax: 508-839-1310.
Students 215.

Harvard, St. Theresa's (1950), Rev. Normand R. Gaumond; Deacon John W. Lee.
Res., 15 Still River Rd., P.O. Box P, 01451. Tel: 508-456-3563.
Catechesis/Religious Programs—Tel: 508-456-8807.
Students 300.

Hopedale, Sacred Heart of Jesus (1935), Rev. Raymond M. Goodwin, Jr.; Deacon Joseph Manella.
Res., 187 Hopedale St., Box 16, 01747. Tel: 508-473-1900; Fax: 508-473-1745.
Catechesis/Religious Programs—Tel: 508-473-1701. Carol Pellegrino, D.R.E.
Students 530.

Jefferson, St. Mary's (1884), Rev. Arthur A. Ouillette; Most Rev. Winnibald J. Menezes, D.D., (India) (Retired); Deacon William J. Ladroga.
Res., 114 Princeton St., 01522. Tel: 508-829-4508; Fax: 508-829-0429. [CEM]
Catechesis/Religious Programs—Tel: 508-829-6758. Charlene Dahlin, D.R.E.
Students 607.

Lancaster, Immaculate Conception (1915), Rev. Edward P. Lettic.
Res., 28 Packard St., P.O. Box 95, 01523. Tel: 508-365-6582; Fax: 508-365-3097.
Catechesis/Religious Programs—Fax: 508-365-3097.
Students 231.

Leicester, St. Joseph's (1851), Rev. Michael A. DiGeronimo; Deacon Raymond Bosse; Carol Cornacchioli, Pastoral Assoc.
Res., 759 Main St., 01524. Tel: 508-892-7407. [CEM]
Catechesis/Religious Programs—Tel: 508-892-9081. Colleen A. Bernard, D.R.E.
Students 455.
Day Care, Caring Place—Tel: 508-892-3168.
Students 55.

St. Pius X (1956), Rev. Michael A. DiGeronimo; Deacon Raymond J. Bosse; Carol A. Cornacchioli, Pastoral Assoc.
Mailing Address: 759 Main St., 01524. Tel: 508-892-7407.
Church—1161 Main St., 01524.

Leominster

1—St. Anna's (1937), Revs. Thomas B. Fleming; Ronald G. Falco.
Res., 199 Lancaster St., 01453. Tel: 508-537-5293; Fax: 508-537-2950.
School—Tel: 508-534-4770. Joanne Ethier, Prin.
Priests 2; Sisters 1; Lay Teachers 12; Students 201.
Catechesis/Religious Programs—Tel: 508-534-4770.
Students 345.

2—Holy Family of Nazareth (1963), Rev. Thomas F. Egan.
Res., 800 Union St., 01453. Tel: 508-537-3016; Fax: 508-534-1119.
Catechesis/Religious Programs—Tel: 508-537-5660; Fax: 508-534-1119. Sr. Patricia Roddy, P.B.V.M., D.R.E.
Students 230.

3—St. Cecilia's (1900) (French), Rev. Francis T. Goguen; Rev. Msgr. George E. Denomme; Deacon Ronald J. Aubuchon.
Res., 170 Mechanic St., 01453. Tel: 508-537-6541; Fax: 508-840-1965. [CEM]
Catechesis/Religious Programs—Tel: 508-534-6907. Sr. Anne Arpin, D.H.S., D.R.E.
Students 310.
Convent—190 Mechanic St., 01453. Tel: 508-534-6907.
Daughters of the Holy Spirit 3.

4—St. Leo's (1872), Revs. John E. Doran; Joseph M. Dolan. In res., Rev. Leo J. O'Neil.
Res., 108 Main St., 01453. Tel: 508-537-7257; Fax: 508-840-6182. [CEM]
School—120 Main St., 01453. Tel: 508-537-1007. Sr. Brian Elizabeth Barnicle, Prin.
Sisters of the Presentation of the Blessed Virgin Mary 6; Lay Teachers 18; Students 330.
Catechesis/Religious Programs—Tel: 508-537-1194.
Students 540.

5—Our Lady of the Lake (1952), Rev. Msgr. James A. Mongelluzzo; Deacon Fred A. Harkins.
Res., 1400 Main St., 01453. Tel: 508-342-2978; Fax: 508-342-8738.
Catechesis/Religious Programs—Tel: 508-345-7469. Sr. Rosemary Fay, S.N.D., D.R.E.
Students 536.

Linwood, Good Shepherd (1904), Rev. Daniel R. Mulcahy, Jr.; Deborah R. Blichalz, Pastoral Assoc., D.R.E.
Res., 121 Linwood St., P.O. Box 517, 01525. Tel: 508-234-7726; Fax: 508-234-0964.
Catechesis/Religious Programs—Tel: 508-234-5340.
Students 200.

Lunenburg, St. Boniface (1950), Rev. Edward D. Niccolls; Sr. Mary E. LeBlanc, P.B.V.M., Pastoral Assoc.; Deacon Joseph M. Cieri. In res., Rev. Donald C. Ouellete.
Res., 817 Massachusetts Ave., 01462. Tel: 508-582-4008; Fax: 508-582-9302.
Catechesis/Religious Programs—Tel: 508-582-6650. Mr. Thomas J. Griffin, D.R.E.
Students 596.

Manchaug, St. Anne's (1900), Rev. Stanley F. Krutcik.
Res., 31 Main St., Box 311, 01526. Tel: 508-476-2405; Fax: 508-476-4443.
Catechesis/Religious Programs—Students 51.

Mendon, St. Michael's (1952), Rev. Thomas E. Mahoney; Deacon Ernest E. Desmarais.
Res., 29 North Ave., P.O. Box 33, 01756. Tel: 508-478-4456; Fax: 508-254-5655.
Catechesis/Religious Programs—Students 293.

Milford, St. Mary of the Assumption (1848), Revs. Michael G. Foley; David B. Galonek; Eusiquio Munoz; Sr. Theresa Lucier, S.P., Pastoral Assoc.
Res., 27 Pearl St., 01757. Tel: 508-473-2000; Fax: 508-473-6907. [CEM]
School—Tel: 508-473-7303.
Sisters 1; Lay Teachers 13; Students 274.
Catechesis/Religious Programs—St. Mary's Parish Center, 17 Winter St., 01757. Tel: 508-478-7440. Martha LaFreniere Harris, D.R.E.
Students 770.

Sacred Heart (1905), Revs. Paul D. Burns, C.S.S.; Samuel J. Fayad, C.S.S. Pastoral Ministers: Sr. Claire Belforti, S.S.J.; Sr. Estelle Santarpia, S.S.J.; Deacon Joseph R. Manella.
Res., 5 E. Main St., 01757. Tel: 508-473-0331; Fax: 508-478-4993. [CEM]
Catechesis/Religious Programs—Tel: 508-473-1036. Sr. Catherine Walsh, R.S.M., D.R.E.
Students 555.

Millbury, Assumption (1884) (French), Rev. Richard A. Fortin.
Res., 16 Waters St., 01527. Tel: 508-865-2657; Fax: 508-865-4866.
School—21 Grove St., 01527. Tel: 508-865-5404. Sr. Rita St. Onge, S.A.S.V., Prin.
Lay Teachers 8; Students 179.
Montessori School—Tel: 508-865-6872.
Sisters of the Assumption of the B.V.M. 1; Lay Teachers 1; Students 64.
Catechesis/Religious Programs—Students 69.

St. Brigid (1849), Revs. Thomas J. Markey; Robert E. Kelley.
Res., 59 Main St., 01527. Tel: 508-865-6624; Fax: 508-865-3101. [CEM]
Catechesis/Religious Programs—Tel: 508-865-2752. Mrs. Gloria Schimke, D.R.E.
Students 425.

Millville, St. Augustine's (1884), Rev. Jean Paul Gagnon; Deacon William Lucier.
Res., 17 Lincoln St., 01529. Tel: 508-883-6678; Fax: 508-883-5878.
Catechesis/Religious Programs—15 Lincoln St., 01529. Tel: 508-883-8794.
Students 196.

Northboro, St. Bernadette (1959), Rev. Chester J. Devlin; Deacon Vincent A. Librandi.
Res., 266 Main St., P.O. Box 743, 01532. Tel: 508-393-2838; Fax: 508-393-2718.
Catechesis/Religious Programs—Tel: 508-393-7445. Judi Winning, Pastoral Assoc.& D.R.E.
Students 165.

St. Rose of Lima (1883), Rev. James A. Houston; Sr. M. Cathleen Toomey, R.S.M.
Res., 244 W. Main St., P.O. Box 685, 01532. Tel: 508-393-2413; Fax: 508-393-4922.
Catechesis/Religious Programs—P.O. Box 387, Tel: 508-393-6444. Mrs. Laverne Bertin, D.R.E.
Students 714.

Northbridge, St. Peter (1903), Rev. John F. Connell.
Res., 39 Church Ave., 01534. Tel: 508-234-2156; Fax: 508-234-5123.
Catechesis/Religious Programs—Tel: 508-234-6355. Barbara Ramian, D.R.E.
Students 159.

North Brookfield, St. Joseph's (1867), Rev. Richard T. Carey.
Res., 28 Mt. Pleasant St., 01535. Tel: 508-867-6811; Fax: 508-867-7756. [CEM]
Catechesis/Religious Programs—27 Mt. Pleasant St., 01535. Tel: 508-867-9302.
Students 342.

North Grafton, St. Mary's (1952), Rev. John J. Bagley; Sr. Beatrice Monette, S.A.S.V., Pastoral Assoc.
Res., 17 Waterville St., 01536. Tel: 508-839-3993; Fax: 508-839-1330.
Catechesis/Religious Programs—Tel: 508-839-4236. Sharon Doane, D.R.E.
Students 398.

North Oxford, St. Ann's (1906), Rev. James M. Steuterman; Sr. Jeanne Rouillard, S.A.S.V., Pastoral Assoc.
Res., 652 Main St., P.O. Box 488, 01537. Tel: 508-987-8892; Fax: 508-987-1598.
Catechesis/Religious Programs—P.O. Box 488, N. Oxford, 01537.
Students 240.

Otter River, St. Martin's (1864), Revs. Cornelius F. O'Leary; William G. O'Brien, Temporary Admin.
Res., 248 State Rd., 01436. Tel: 508-939-5588.
Church—247 State Rd., 01436.
Catechesis/Religious Programs—Students 64.

Oxford, St. Roch's (1886), Rev. Gerald P. Walsh. In res., Rev. Msgr. Louis R. Piermarini.
Res., 334 Main St., 01540. Tel: 508-987-8987; Fax: 508-987-0107. [CEM]
Catechesis/Religious Programs—Tel: 508-987-2382.
Students 383.

Paxton, St. Columba's (1951), Rev. John D. Thomas.
Res., 10 Richards Ave., 01612. Tel: 508-755-0408; Fax: 508-767-0759.
Catechesis/Religious Programs—Tel: 508-753-4126. Sr. Catherine Guild, R.S.M., D.R.E.
Students 365.

Petersham, St. Peter (1968), Rev. Raymond P. Messier.
Mailing Address: Main St., 01366. Tel: 508-249-3361.
Res., St. Francis, 105 Main St., Athol, 01331.

Princeton, Prince of Peace (1967), Rev. James J. Caldarella; Sr. Teresa Rose Carchidi, Pastoral Assoc.
Res., 5 Worcester Rd., P.O. Box 305, 01541. Tel: 508-464-2871; Fax: 508-464-0449.
Catechesis/Religious Programs—Students 209.

Rochdale, St. Aloysius-St. Jude (1904), Rev. Peter H. White.
Res., 2 Church Pl., P.O. Box 296, 01542-0296. Tel: 508-892-8296.
Catechesis/Religious Programs—Mrs. Terri Smith, D.R.E.
Students 220.

Rutland, St. Patrick's (1938), Rev. James P. Kerrigan; Deacon William J. Vigliotti.
Res., 290 Main St., Box 163, 01543. Tel: 508-886-4309; Fax: 508-886-2897.
Church—258 Main St., 01543. Tel: 508-886-6131.
Catechesis/Religious Programs—Tel: 508-886-4984. Michele Curtis, D.R.E.
Students 312.

Shrewsbury, St. Anne's (1950), Revs. Edward J. Moran;

Robert Spellman; Sr. Charlene O'Leary, P.B.V.M., Pastoral Assoc.
Res., 130 Boston Tpke., 01545. Tel: 508-757-5154; Fax: 508-797-9520. [CEM]
Catechesis / Religious Programs—Tel: 508-752-5040. Karen Weigold, D.R.E.
Students 742.

St. Mary's (1922), Revs. Paul T. O'Connell; Brian O'Toole; Leo Lancaster.
Res., 18 Summer St., 01545. Tel: 508-845-0161; Fax: 508-842-9132.
School—Tel: 508-842-1601; Fax: 508-845-1535. Jeanne Marie Gocha, Prin.
Sisters 1; Lay Teachers 13; Students 238.
Catechesis / Religious Programs—Tel: 508-845-1154. Mary Jane Person, D.R.E.
Students 858.

South Ashburnham, St. Anne (1895), Rev. Joseph J. Jurgelonis; Deacons Michael P. Connor; Richard Desjardins.
Pastoral Office: 85 Main St., P.O. Box 418, Ashburnham, 01430-0418. Tel: 508-827-5806.

South Barre, St. Thomas-A-Becket (1923), Rev. Mark M. Szymcik.
Res., P.O. Box 186, Vernon Ave., 01074. Tel: 508-355-2228; Fax: 508-355-0042.
Catechesis / Religious Programs—Students 110.

Southborough, St. Anne (1886), Rev. Thirburse F. Millott.
Res., 20 Boston Rd., P.O. Box C, 01772. Tel: 508-485-0141; Fax: 508-481-9374.
Catechesis / Religious Programs—Tel: 508-481-3159.
Students 399.

St. Matthew (1956), Rev. James B. Flynn.
Res., 105 Southville Rd., 01772. Tel: 508-485-2285; Fax: 508-482-4437. [JC]
Catechesis / Religious Programs—Tel: 508-229-2429.
Students 204.

Southbridge

1—ST. HEDWIG'S (1916) (Polish), Revs. Richard T. Zuscak; Joseph J. Pijunowski.
Res., 29 Summer St., 01550. Tel: 508-764-6947; Fax: 508-764-7707. [CEM]

2—NOTRE DAME (1869), Revs. Maurice L. Gilbert; Edward J. Hanlon; Deacon Michael J. Corby.
Res., 61 Marcy St., 01550. Tel: 508-765-0601; Fax: 508-764-4148. [CEM 3]
Catechesis / Religious Programs—Religious Education Center, 20 Marcy St., 01550. Tel: 508-764-8018.
Students 303.

3—SACRED HEART (1908) (French), Rev. Charles R. Armey; Deacon Thomas Skonieczny.
Res., 40 Charlton St., 01550. Tel: 508-764-6964; Fax: 508-764-3320.
Catechesis / Religious Programs—Tel: 508-765-5597.
Students 83.

4—ST. MARY'S (1861), Revs. Peter J. Joyce; Paul W. Lemire; Deacon Richard Olson.
Res., 263 Hamilton St., 01550. Tel: 508-764-3226; Fax: 508-764-3209. [CEM]
Catechesis / Religious Programs—Saint Peter's Center, Hamilton St., 01550. Tel: 508-765-0245. D.R.E.: Mrs. Beth Tobin, Pastoral Asst.; Sr. Ines Calvo, R.O.D.A., Pastoral Asst.
Students 511.

South Grafton, St. James (1887), Rev. Michael F. Rose; Deacon Edward Richards.
Res., 89 Main St., 01560. Tel: 508-839-5354; Fax: 508-839-5430.
Catechesis / Religious Programs—Tel: 508-839-6800.
Students 297.

Spencer, Mary, Queen of the Rosary (1994). Merger of St. Mary and Our Lady of the Rosary. Revs. James F. Hoey; William Cormier; Deacon Harry M. Sweet.
Office: 60 Maple St., 01562. Tel: 508-885-3111; Fax: 508-885-4905.
Res., 46 Maple St., 01562. Tel: 508-885-3806. [CEM]
Catechesis / Religious Programs—Mrs. Helene K. Sullivan, D.R.E.
Students 464.

Our Lady of the Rosary (1854). Merged with St. Mary's to form Mary, Queen of the Rosary. Deacon Harry M. Sweet.
Office: 60 Maple St., 01562. Tel: 508-885-9758.
Res., 46 Maple St., 01562. Tel: 508-885-9071. [CEM]

Sterling, St. Richard of Chichester (1953), Rev. Andre N. Remillard; Sr. Anne Marie Wildenhain, S.S.J., Pastoral Assoc.
Res., 4 Bridge St., P.O. Box 657, 01564. Tel: 508-422-8881; Fax: 508-422-0291.
Catechesis / Religious Programs—Sr. Gertrude Lanouette, D.H.S., D.R.E.
Students 344.

Sutton, St. Mark (1966), Revs. John E. Horgan; Joseph W. McKiernan; Deacon Amos Green.
Res., 356 Boston Rd., 01590. Tel: 508-865-3860; Fax: 508-865-5095.
Catechesis / Religious Programs—Anne Licopoli, D.R.E.
Students 610.

Upton, Holy Angels (1874), Rev. Laurence V. Brault.
Res., 2 Nelson St., 01568. Tel: 508-529-6981; Fax: 508-529-6317.
Catechesis / Religious Programs—Tel: 508-529-3109. Simone Caron, D.R.E.
Students 263.

Uxbridge, St. Mary's (1853), Revs. Ernest P. Allega; Ronald Damian.
Res., 77 Mendon St., 01569. Tel: 508-278-2226; Fax: 508-278-7949. [CEM]
Catechesis / Religious Programs—Tel: 508-278-3777. Evelyn LaDuke, D.R.E.
Students 425.

Warren, St. Paul's (1872), Rev. Roland L. Lajoie.
Res., 1082 Main St., 01083-1027. Tel: 413-436-7327; Fax: 413-436-7324. [CEM]
Catechesis / Religious Programs—Combined with St. Thomas Aquinas, Warren.
Students 124.

Webster, St. Joseph's (1887) (Polish), Rev. Anthony Czarneck (Poland); Rev. Msgr. Chester Janczukowicz.
Res., 53 Whitcomb St., 01570. Tel: 508-943-0467; Fax: 508-943-0808. [CEM]
School—Tel: 508-943-0378. Sr. Mary Angelia Rzasa, Prin.
Felician Sisters 2; Lay Teachers 11; Students 297.
Catechesis / Religious Programs—Students 89.

Sacred Heart of Jesus (1870), Rev. Michael J. Roy; Deacon Roland R. Michaud.
Res., 18 E Main St., 01570. Tel: 508-943-3140; Fax: 508-943-2213. [CEM]
School—Tel: 508-943-2735. Sr. Constance Bayeur, S.S.A., Prin.
Sisters of St. Anne 2; Lay Teachers 11; Students 270.
Catechesis / Religious Programs—Students 151.

St. Louis (1353), Revs. Joseph A. Marcotte; Gerald Dion.
Res., 15 Lake St., 01570. Tel: 508-943-0240; Fax: 508-943-0801. [CEM]
School—Tel: 508-943-0257. Sr. Daniel Maria, Prin.
Sisters 2; Lay Teachers 9; Students 250.
Catechesis / Religious Programs—Tel: 508-943-0817.
Students 345.

Westborough, St. Luke the Evangelist (1870), Revs. George O. Lange; Steven M. LaBaire; Sr. Mary Martina Lively, Pastoral Assoc.
Res., 70 W. Main St., 01581. Tel: 508-366-5502; Fax: 508-366-6049. [CEM]
Catechesis / Religious Programs—1 Ruggles St., 01581. Tel: 508-366-8509. Patricia Najarian, D.R.E.
Students 800.

West Boylston, Our Lady of Good Counsel (1869), Rev. John F. Burke. In res., Rev. John J. Roy.
Res., 111 Worcester St., 01583. Tel: 508-835-3606. [CEM]
Catechesis / Religious Programs—Tel: 508-835-6336. Thomas Faucher, D.R.E.
Students 433.

West Brookfield, Sacred Heart of Jesus (1950), Rev. Peter D. Shea.
Res., 10 Milk St., 01585-0563. Tel: 508-867-6469; Fax: 508-867-3670. [CEM]
Parish Center: Tel: 508-867-4460.
Catechesis / Religious Programs—Students 225.

Westminster, St. Edward the Confessor (1951), Rev. Francis A. Roberge, Admin.
Res., 10 Church St., 01473. Tel: 508-874-2362.
Catechesis / Religious Programs—Students 170.

West Warren, St. Stanislaus (1913) (Polish), Rev. Charles E.J Borowski.
Res., 2270 Main St., P.O. Box 503, 01092-0503. Tel: 413-436-5110; Fax: 413-436-0556.

St. Thomas Aquinas (1893), Rev. Roland L. Lajoie; Deacon Raymond E. Aiken.
Res., St. Paul's Rectory, 1082 Main St., P.O. Box 1027, Warren, 01083. Tel: 413-436-7327; Fax: 413-436-7327. [CEM]
Catechesis / Religious Programs—Combined with St. Paul, Warren.
Students 150.

Whitinsville, St. Patrick's (1889), Revs. Michael Broderick; Paul Doherty; Sr. Margaret Walsh, S.S.J., Pastoral Assoc.; Deacon Anthony R. Surozenski.
Res., 7 East St., P.O. Box 60, 01588. Tel: 508-234-5656; Fax: 508-234-6845. [CEM]
Catechesis / Religious Programs—Tel: 508-234-6826. MaryAnn DiGregorio, D.R.E.
Students 569.

Winchendon, Immaculate Heart of Mary (1870), Rev. Roland L. Gamache. Pastoral Assistants: Sr. Anne O'Shea, P.M.; Mr. Mark J. Carrier.
Res., 52 Spruce St., 01475. Tel: 508-297-0280; Fax: 508-297-3577. [CEM]
Catechesis / Religious Programs—Tel: 508-297-2699. Sr. Pauline Grenier, P.M., D.R.E.
Students 240.
Convent—Our Lady of Sorrows, Tel: 508-297-0275. Sisters of the Presentation of Mary 3.

Chaplains of Public Institutions

WORCESTER. *ADCARE Hospital of Worcester*. Rev. Peter R. Beaulieu, Chap.
Air National Guard. Serviced by Catholic Charities priests.
Hahnemann Hospital. Serviced by Priests of St. Bernard, St. Joan of Arc, Immaculate Conception, Our Lady of the Rosary Churches.
Memorial Hospital. Catholic Pastoral Ministry: Revs. Peter R. Beaulieu; Louis Gould.
University of Mass Medical Center. Revs. Bernard F. Davenport, Chap.; Edward M. Ryan.
Worcester Belmont House. Serviced by St. Margaret Mary Church.
Worcester Detention Center. Serviced by Urban Ministry.
Worcester State Hospital. Rev. Francis J. Roach, Chap.

BOYLSTON. *Worcester County Jail and House of Correction*. Rev. Leo J. O'Neil, Chap.
Worcester County Sanitarium. Rev. Leo J. O'Neil, Chap.

GARDNER. *Massachusetts Correctional Institution*. Rev. Thomas M. Tierney, Chap.

LANCASTER. *Massachusetts Correctional Institution*. Rev. J. Brendan Nally, Chap.

OTTER RIVER. *Walter E. Fernald State School*. Revs. John E. Kelley; Richard G. Roger.

On Special or Other (Arch)Diocesan Assignment:
Reverend Fathers—
Banach, Michael, Vatican Diplomatic Corp.
Beaulieu, Peter R., Worcester Memorial Hospital
Ciambelli, Blase A., Westboro State Hospital
Davenport, Bernard, University Massachusetts Hospital
DiOrio, Ralph A., Apostolate of Healing
Doiron, David E., Pastoral Counseling
Garlick, Thomas B., Fairlawn Hospital
Gilgun, Bernard E.
Gothing, Donald B., Admin., Capilia de la Santisima Trinidad, 69 Lincoln Ter., Leominster, MA 01453. Tel: 508-534-5258
Hillier, John G., Studies
Kilcoyne, Terence T., St. Vincent Hospital

On Duty Outside the Diocese:
Reverend Monsignors—
Kelly, Francis D., Rector, Pope John XXIII Seminary
Reverend Fathers—
Carr, David W., 740 Palm Trail, Delray Beach, FL 33447
Gerardo, John A., 532 Lamont Ave., Staten Island, NY 10312
Hill, George H., Abbey of the Genesee, Piffard, NY 14533
Hokanson, Richard P., 1524 E. Moorehead St., Charlotte, NC 28203
Imse, James L., 425 Cedar St., Medford, WI 54451
Kelly, David F., Duquesne Univ., Theology Dept., Pittsburgh, PA 15219
Lascelle, Roger L., Holy Family Parish, Box 866, Meeker, CO 81641
Mattimore, William F., SS. Peter and Paul Rectory, 800 Kaleka St., Honolulu, HI 96814
Roy, F. Gilles, Apartado 46, Sicuani (Via Cuzco), Peru

Military Chaplains:
Reverend Fathers—
Bomba, Paul M.
Boucher, Roger R.
Grochowski, Bernard J.
Rocheford, Dennis J.

Absent on Leave:
Reverend Fathers—
Bernard, Andre
Blizard, David
Branconnier, Gerard
Dunkley, George, El Paso, TX
Gelineau, H. Raymond
Iannetti, Lawrence
Kane, Thomas
Kardas, Thaddeus
Kelly, Robert
Nicewicz, Edward
Ritacco, Richard

Szantyr, John
Teczar, Thomas
Wondolowski, Robert

Retired:
Reverend Monsignors—
Battista, Leo
Carelli, Richard J., 30 Julio Dr., Shrewsbury, MA 01545
Daley, Thomas J., Vianney House, 222 June St., Worcester, MA 01602
Haddad, Edmond G., Vianney House, 222 June St., Worcester, MA 01602
Martin, John P., 37 Ridgeway Cir., Springfield, MA 01118
O'Brien, John J., 264 Springfield St., Springfield, MA 01107
Page, Raymond J., Southgate of Shrewsbury, 30 Julio Dr., Apt. 612, Shrewsbury, MA 01545
Reverend Fathers—
Anger, Raymond G., 30 Julio Dr., Apt. 317, Shrewsbury, MA 01545
Archey, Eugene C., P.O. Box 2025, Central Berkshire Blvd., Pittsfield, MA 01202
Ash, Joseph H., 49 Elm St., Worcester, MA 01690
Banach, Henry S., 64 Oakwood Ln., Worcester, MA 01604
Barry, Leo, 15 Sandro Cir., Warwick, RI 02886
Bedard, J. Raymond, 7 Jenny Hill Rd., North Falmouth, MA 02556
Capuano, John J., St. Francis Nursing Home
Choquette, Paul A., Providence House
Clifford, James J., 35 Julio Dr., Shrewsbury, MA 01545
Conlin, Bernard J., Our Lady of Lourdes Rectory, 1290 Grafton St., Worcester, MA 01604
Debitetto, Ronald E., 66 Stetson St., Hyannis, MA 02601
Devaney, Roy J., 532 Grove St., Worcester, MA 01605
DiPucchio, Anthony F.X., 151 Loring Ave., Box 1024, West Dennis, MA 02670
Dutram, Charles J., 880 School St., Webster, MA 01570
Dyer, Edward J., 30 Apricot St., Worcester, MA 01603
Foley, John J., 186 Prospect St., Northampton, MA 01060
Foley, Paul T., Shrewsbury Nursing Home, 66 S. Shrewsbury, Shrewsbury, MA 01545
Fontaine, John-Paul, 68 Natal Ave., East Falmouth, MA 02536
Gallagher, William J., P.O. Box 351, Woodstock, VA 22664
Gariepy, Robert E., 320 Sprice Dr., Ashburnham, MA 01453
Gionet, Urbain J., Southgate of Shrewsbury, 30 Julio Dr., Apt. 112, Shrewsbury, MA 01545
Harrity, Francis P., 115 Prescott St., Clinton, MA 01510
Hebert, Raymond L., P.O. Box 2835, St. Petersburg, FL 33731-2835
Hebert, Roland G., Southgate of Shrewsbury, 30 Julio Dr., Apt. 109, Shrewsbury, MA 01545
Holland, George G., Box 488, North Oxford, MA 01537
Kurzawski, Casimir J., 220 Lakeview Ave., Syracuse, NY 13204
Lamothe, C. Romero, 51 Chapel St., Chicopee, MA 01020
Lange, Raymond L., Southgate of Shrewsbury, 30 Julio Dr., Apt. 219, Shrewsbury, MA 01545
Laperle, Theodore R., St. Bernard Rectory, 240 Water St., Fitchburg, MA 01420
Lenk, Charles E., Bruce St., Grafton, MA 01519
Manahan, Martin J., 865 Grove St., Worcester, MA 01605
McGovern, William W., Vianney House, 222 June St., Worcester, MA 01602
McKenna, John J., 88 Melba Ave., Springfield, MA 01104
McNamara, Philip D., 30 Julio Dr., Shrewsbury, MA 01545
Moynahan, Joseph A., Southgate of Shrewsbury, 30 Julio Dr., Apt. 338, Shrewsbury, MA 01545
O'Brien, Thomas F., 7 Woodland Dr., Paxton, MA 01612
O'Donoghue, Brendon W., 30 Julio Dr., Apt. 246, Shrewsbury, MA 01545
O'Flaherty, John P., St. Patrick, Framingham
Pelletier, Edgar A., 9504 Via Segovia, New Port Richey, FL 33552
Porrello, Joseph J., Southgate of Shrewsbury, 30 Julio Dr., Apt. 508, Shrewsbury, MA 01545
Poulin, Robert P., 153 Crown Dr., Naples, FL 33942
Prunier, Arthur J., 22 Thorne St., Worcester, MA 01604
Raftery, William J., Tara Knoll, Box 307, Manomet, MA 02345
Sullivan, Andrew J., 20 Birmingham Rd., Worcester, MA 01606
Yankauskas, Albin J., Shrewsbury Nursing Home, 66 South St., Shrewsbury, MA 01545

Permanent Deacons:
Aiken, Raymond E., St. Paul, Warren, St. Thomas Aquinas, West Warren
Aliskevicz, John J., St. Camillus De Lellis, Fitchburg
Arsenault, Roger D., Holy Family of Nazareth, Leominster
Aubuchon, Ronald J., St. Cecilia, Leominster
Baniukiewicz, Joseph M., Refugee Apostolate, Permanent Diaconate Program, Christ the King, Worcester
Belliveau, Robert J., On Duty Outside of Diocese
Benvenuti, Clement E., St. Denis, E. Douglas
Blackwelder, Edgar B., Sacred Heart of Jesus, Fitchburg
Bolduc, Raymond H., St. Mary of the Hills, Boylston
Bosse, Raymond J., St. Joseph & St. Pius X, Leicester
Burns, Robert J., St. John, Worcester
Cahill, John F., St. George, Worcester
CaraDonna, Nicholas M., Jr., Our Lady of Fatima, Worcester
Carbone, Francis A., (Retired)
Carrier, Paul J., Sacred Heart of Jesus, Gardner
Chartier, Arthur J., Holy Cross, Pastoral Care Dept., St. Vincent Hospital, East Templeton
Cieri, Joseph M., Formational Asst., Permanent Diaconate Program, Lunenburg
Colon, William B., Hispanic Community, St. Francis, Fitchburg
Connor, Michael P., St. Denis, Ashburnham, St. Anne, South Ashburnham
Corby, Michael P., Notre Dame, Southbridge
Croteau, Andre W., St. Joseph, Fitchburg
Dauphinais, Raymond P., Pope John XXIII Seminary, Weston
Desautels, Alphonse T., Our Lady of the Angels, Worcester
Desmarais, Ernest E., Refugee Apostolate, Permanent Diaconate Program, St. Michael, Mendon
Devine, Philip E., Admin. Asst., Permanent Diaconate Program
DeVito, Frederick A., Campus Ministry, Fitchburg State College
Dio, Robert F., Our Lady of the Holy Rosary, Gardner
DiPadua, James F., Jr., St. Stephen, Worcester
Doyle, Walter F., Refugee Apostolate, Permanent Diaconate Program, St. Catherine of Sweden, Worcester
DuVarney, Joseph T., St. Joseph, Worcester.
Escobar, Francisco, St. Paul Cathedral, Worcester
Fenner, Harry, St. Mary of the Assumption, Milford
Foster, Deane C., St. Leo, Leominster
Green, Amos H., Sr., St. Mark, Sutton
Guay, Gerald A., St. Anna, Leominster
Harkins, Frederick A., Our Lady of the Lake, Whalom
Ladroga, William J., St. Paul, Worcester
LeBlanc, John B., St. Anthony of Padua, Fitchburg
Lee, John W., St. Theresa, Harvard
Librandi, Vincent A., St. Joseph, Auburn
Linderman, James L., Our Lady Immaculate, Athol
Manella, Joseph R., Our Lady of Loreto, Worcester
Martel, Clarence H., St. Anne & St. Patrick, Fiskdale
McCaffrey, Joseph A., St. Luke the Evangelist, Westboro
Michaud, Roland R., Sacred Heart, Webster
Miskell, Lawrence F., St. Joseph, Charlton
Mongeau, Laurent M., St. Mary, Southbridge
Montiverdi, Gerald M., University of Massachusetts Medical Center, Worcester
Morrissey, Henry F., (Retired), Office of the Bishop, St. Christopher, Worcester
Nogueira, Benjamin A., Campus Ministry, Fitchburg State College, Fitchburg
O'Connor, Richard J., St. Paul, Worcester
O'Toole, George L., Diocesan Tribunal, St. Joseph Chapel, Holy Cross College
Pagano, Matteo A., St. Vincent Hospital, Worcester
Prince, Ernest F., Immaculate Conception, Fitchburg
Prince, Norman A., St. Joseph, Fitchburg
Quinlivan, James P., Sr., St. Paul, Worcester
Raymond, Bernard B., St. Leo & Leominster Hospital, Leominster
Skonieczny, Thomas A., Sacred Heart, Southbridge
Starr, Peter J., St. Camillus de Lellis, Fitchburg
Surozenski, Anthony R., St. Patrick, Whitinsville
Sweet, Harry M., Our Lady of the Rosary, St. Mary, Spencer
Tatro, Leo J., Immaculate Heart of Mary, Winchendon
Tremblay, Robert J., Sacred Heat, Worcester
Vigliotti, William J., Pastoral Care, St. Vincent Hospital

INSTITUTIONS LOCATED IN THE DIOCESE

[A] SEMINARIES, RELIGIOUS, OR SCHOLASTICATES

SPENCER. *St. Joseph's Abbey School of Theology and Institute of Monastic Studies*, 01562. Tel: 508-885-8700; Fax: 508-885-8701. Rt. Rev. Damian Carr, Abbot & Rector; Revs. Joseph Chu Cong, Prior; Dominic Whedbee, O.C.S.O., Novice Master; David Lavich, O.C.S.O., Vocation Dir.; Luke Truhan, O.C.S.O., Dean of Studies; Bros. Robert Robinson O.C.S.O., Subprior; Aelred Marrah, O.C.S.O., Dean of Juniors. Professors 6; Students 5.

[B] COLLEGES AND UNIVERSITIES

WORCESTER. *Assumption College*, 500 Salisbury St., 01615-0005. Tel: 508-767-7000; Fax: 508-799-5411. *For a complete listing, refer to the Colleges and Universities section.*

College of the Holy Cross, Inc, 01610. Tel: 508-793-2011. *For a complete listing, refer to the Colleges and Universities section.*

PAXTON. *Anna Maria College*, 01612. Tel: 508-849-3300. *For a complete listing, refer to the Colleges and Universities section.*

[C] HIGH SCHOOLS, CENTRAL

WORCESTER. *Holy Name Central Catholic High School*, 144 Granite St., 01604. Tel: 508-753-6371; Fax: 508-831-1287. Rev. John F. Madden, Headmaster; Mrs. Mary E. Riordan, Prin.; Rev. James B. Flynn. Priests 2; Sisters 4; Lay Teachers 47; Students 765.

St. Peter-Marian Central Catholic Junior-Senior High School, 781 Grove St., 01605-3196. Tel: 508-852-5555. Mr. Timothy M. Rioux, Headmaster; Mr. Matthew Sturgis, Prin.; Miss Patricia Aubertine, Asst. Prin.; Rev. John J. Roy. Priests 1; Sisters 3; Lay Teachers 54; Students 989.

FITCHBURG. *St. Bernard's Central Catholic High School*, 45 Harvard St., 01420. Tel: 508-342-3212. Mr. John A. Bierden, Headmaster; Mr. Patrick O'Shea, Prin. In res., Rev. Donald Ouellette. Priests 1; Sisters 4; Lay Teachers 30; Students 475.

SOUTHBRIDGE. *Trinity Catholic Academy*, 11 Pine St., 01550. Tel: 508-765-5991; Fax: 508-765-0237. Sr. Lucille Roy, S.A.S.V., Prin. Sisters 1; Lay Teachers 14; Students 166.

[D] HIGH SCHOOLS, PAROCHIAL

WORCESTER. *St. Mary's Junior/Senior High School*, 50 Richland St., 01610. Tel: 508-753-1170. Congregation of the Sisters of the Holy Family of Nazareth. Sr. Vincent Zachwieja, Prin. Sisters 2; Lay Teachers 15; Students 193.

[E] HIGH SCHOOLS, PRIVATE

WORCESTER. *Notre Dame Accdemy*, 425 Salisbury St., 01609. Tel: 508-757-6200; Fax: 508-757-7200. A Private Day School for Girls. Ann Morrison, S.N.D., Prin. Sisters of Notre Dame de Namur 4; Other Religious Orders 2; Lay Teachers 29; Girls 310.

FITCHBURG. *Notre Dame Preparatory School*. (Grades 7-12), 171 South St., 01420. Tel: 508-343-7635. Mr. Jeff Hammond, Headmaster. Lay Teachers 8; Students 60.

SHREWSBURY. *St. John's High School*, 378 Main St., 01545. Tel: 508-842-8934; Fax: 508-842-3670. Xaverian Brothers. Bro. J. Conal Owens, C.F.X., Headmaster. Brothers 13; Lay Teachers 50; Boys 943.

STILL RIVER. *St. Benedict High School*, 254 Still River Rd., P.O. Box 22, 01467. Tel: 508-456-8017. Sr. Ann Mary, M.I.C.M., Prin. Sisters 2; Students 1.

[F] ELEMENTARY SCHOOLS, CENTRAL

WORCESTER. *St. Peter's Central Catholic Elementary School*, 865 Main St., 01610. Tel: 508-791-6496. Sisters of St. Joseph. Mrs. Maryann Pour Previti, Head of School; Josephine Dansereau, Teaching Prin. Lay Teachers 24; Students 346; Preschool Students 32; Total Enrollment 378.

MILFORD. *Milford Catholic Elementary School*, 11 E. Main St., 01757. Tel: 508-473-7303. Sr. Patricia Murphy, S.S.J., Prin. Sisters of St. Joseph 1; Lay Teachers 15; Students 256.

UXBRIDGE. *Our Lady of Valley Regional Elementary School*, 75 Mendon St., 01569. Tel: 508-278-5851. Sr. Kathleen Duffy, S.S.J., Prin. Sisters 1; Lay Teachers 8; Students 198; Part-Time Teachers 3.

[G] ELEMENTARY SCHOOLS, PRIVATE

WORCESTER. *Venerini Academy*, 27 Edward St., 01605.

Tel: 508-753-3210; Fax: 508-754-6050. Mrs. Patricia Marmen, Prin. Sisters 5; Lay Teachers 21; Students 325.

LEOMINSTER. *Julie Country Day School*, 365 Lindell Ave., 01453. Tel: 508-537-4939. Sr. Marguerite Timothy, S.N.D., Prin. Sisters 10; Lay Teachers 28; Students 274.

[H] CATHOLIC CHARITIES

WORCESTER. *Catholic Charities*, 10 Hammond St., 01610-1513. Tel: 508-798-0191; Fax: 508-797-5659. Catherine Loeffler, Diocesan Dir.; Gerard E. LaFleche, Asst. Dir. Financial Mgmt.

Northern Worcester Co., 53 Highland Ave., Fitchburg, 01420. Tel: 508-343-4879; Fax: 508-345-4161. Jacqueline Hager, Area Admin.

Gardner Office, Mary Kane Bldg., 175 Connors St., Gardner, 01440. Tel: 508-630-3631. Jacqueline Hager, Area Admin.

Athol Office, 12 Riverbend St., Athol, 01331. Tel: 508-249-4563; Fax: 508-249-2545. Joanna Haspod, Area Admin.

Southbridge Office, 79 Elm St., Southbridge, 01550-2601. Tel: 508-765-5936; Fax: 508-764-4153. Eldelmira A. Spence, Area Admin.

Blackstone Valley/Greater Milford Area Office, 9 Spring St., Whitinsville, 01588. Tel: 508-234-3800; Fax: 508-234-2321. Noreen Landry, Area Admin.

Clinton Office, 208 Church St., Clinton, 01510-2502. Tel: 508-365-7391. Jacqueline Hager, Area Admin.

Life-Line, 126 Main St., Room 6, Milford, 01715. Tel: 508-478-9632.

Senior Employment Service, 10 Hammond St., 01610-1513. Tel: 508-798-0191; Fax: 508-797-5659. Edward P. Binnall, Admin.

Refugee Resettlement, 10 Hammond St., 01610-1513. Tel: 508-798-0191; Fax: 508-797-5659. Sr. Theresa Khen Doan, Admin.

Child & Family Services, 10 Hammond St., 01610-1513. Tel: 508-798-0191; Fax: 508-797-5659. Sara Glenn, Admin.

Home Care Services, 10 Hammond St., 01610-1513. Tel: 508-798-0191; Fax: 508-797-5659. Rachel T. Renaud, Admin.

Literacy Volunteers, 10 Hammond St., 01610-1513. Tel: 508-798-0191; Fax: 508-797-5659. Madelyn Morales, Admin.

Crozier House, 10 Hammond St., 01610-1513. Tel: 508-798-0191; Fax: 508-797-5659. A Half-Way House for Substance Abusing Men. J. David Mulrooney, Admin.

Mercy Centre (Developmental Disabilities). Special Education Day Program and Sheltered Workshop for Developmentally Disabled Youngsters and Adults, 25 W. Chester St., 01605-1136. Tel: 508-852-7165; Fax: 508-856-9755. Heather McDonald, Admin.

Youville House Shelter for Homeless Families, 133 Granite St., 01604-4500. Tel: 508-753-3084; Fax: 508-754-0139. Sara Glenn, Admin.

[I] CHILD CARE AGENCIES

WORCESTER. *Guild of St. Agnes*, 133 Granite St., 01604. Tel: 508-756-8371. Mr. Edward Madaus, Dir. Day Care Centers for Infants, Toddlers, Preschoolers & School-age Children. Children aged 8 weeks-9 years. Children 211. Family Day Care Program ages 2 months-5 years. Children 160. For all: Total Staff 135.

FITCHBURG. *Guild of St. Agnes*, 62 Dover St., 01420. Tel: 508-343-3042. Total Assisted 120; Total Staff 12.

LEICESTER. *McAuley Nazareth Home for Boys*, 01524. Tel: 508-892-4886. Sisters of Mercy. Sr. Mary T. Barry, R.S.M., Exec. Dir.; Rev. Msgr. Edmond T. Tinsley, Chap. Sisters 3; Boys 16; (Residents); Special Education School: Boys 16; Lay Teachers 4.

[J] GENERAL HOSPITALS

WORCESTER. *Saint Vincent Hospital, Inc.*, 25 Winthrop St., 01604. Tel: 508-798-1234; Fax: 508-798-1240. *For a complete listing, refer to the Hospitals section.*

[K] SPECIAL HOSPITALS AND SANATORIA

WORCESTER. *Notre Dame Long Term Care Center*, 559 Plantation St., 01605. Tel: 508-852-3011; Fax: 508-852-0397.
For a complete listing, refer to the Special Care Facilities section.

Providence Extended Care Center, 119 Providence St., 01604. Tel: 508-860-5000.
For a complete listing, refer to the Special Care Facilities section.

MILLBURY. *Providence House Nursing Home of Millbury*, 29 Main St., 01527. Tel: 508-865-6106.
For a complete listing, refer to the Special Care Facilities section.

SOUTHBRIDGE. *Providence House Nursing Home of Southbridge*, 84 Chapin St., 01550. Tel: 508-765-9133.
For a complete listing, refer to the Special Care Facilities section.

WHITINSVILLE. *St. Camillus Nursing Home Inc.*, 447 Hill St., 01588. Tel: 508-234-7306.
For a complete listing, refer to the Special Care Facilities section.

[L] HEALTH SERVICES

WORCESTER. *Our Lady of Mercy Health Care Center, Inc.*, 101 Barry Rd., 01609. Tel: 508-798-3727.
For a complete listing, refer to the Hospitals section.

Pernet Family Health Service, 237 Millbury St., 01610. Tel: 508-755-1228.
For a complete listing, refer to the Hospitals section.

[M] HOMES FOR AGED

WORCESTER. *Vianney House*, 222 June St., 01602. Tel: 508-791-0311.
For a complete listing, refer to the Special Care Facilities section.

LEOMINSTER. *Presentation Health Care Center*, 99 Church St., 01453-3147. Tel: 508-537-7108.
For a complete listing, refer to the Special Care Facilities section.

[N] MONASTERIES AND RESIDENCES OF PRIESTS AND BROTHERS

WORCESTER. *Assumptionists (Augustinians of the Assumption)*, 50 Old English Rd., 01609. Tel: 508-754-6276. Revs. Alexis A. Babineau, A.A.; Andre E. Dargis, A.A.; Louis F. Dion, A.A.; Roland O. Guilmain, A.A.; Leonard LaRocque, A.A.; Bros. Paul Maurice Gosselin, A.A., Treas.; Omer Gemme, A.A.; Armand Lemaire, A.A.; John-Thomas McHugh, A.A.; Odoric Roy, A.A. Priests 5; Brothers 5; Total Staff 2.

Assumptionists of Assumption College, Emmanuel House, 512 Salisbury St., 01609-1326. Tel: 508-767-7523; Fax: 508-793-9701. Revs. Roger R. Corriveau, A.A., Supr.; Donat R. Lamothe, A.A., Treas.; Barry Bercier, A.A.; Wilfrid Dufault, A.A.; David M. Gallo, A.A.; Richard L. Lamoureaux, A.A.; Bros. Robert Francis Beaulac, A.A.; D. Wade DeCoste, Novice. Total in Residence 8; Total Staff 1.

Jesuits of Holy Cross College, Inc., 01610. Tel: 508-793-2011. Revs. John J. Higgins, S.J., Rector; John E. Brooks, S.J.; Richard P. Burke, S.J.; Edmund K. Cheney, S.J.; Terrence W. Curry, S.J.; Alfred R. Desautels, S.J.; James J. Drohan, S.J.; Charles J. Dunn, S.J.; Frederick M. Enman, S.J.; William H. Fitzgerald, S.J.; Michael F. Ford, S.J.; J. Thomas Hamel, S.J.; Eugene J. Harrington, S.J.; James M. Hayes, S.J.; Lionel P. Honore, S.J.; Anthony J. Kuzniewski, S.J.; Joseph J. LaBran, S.J.; Vincent A. Lapomarda, S.J.; Brian F. Linnane, S.J.; John J. MacDonnell, S.J.; Earle L. Markey, S.J.; Charles R. McKenney, S.J.; Francis X. Miller, S.J.; James J. Miracky, S.J.; Paul J. Nelligan, S.J.; William J. O'Halloran, S.J.; Joseph B. Pomeroy, S.J.; John P. Reboli, S.J.; Gerard C. Reedy, S.J.; William E. Reiser, S.J.; Philip C. Rule, S.J.; Joseph S. Scannell, S.J.; William E. Stempsey, S.J.; Edward J. Vodoklys, S.J.; Thomas W. Worcester, S.J. Priests 35. Casa Santa Maria del Camino, Inc., 6 Claremont St., 01610. Tel: 508-798-0104. Rev. William E. Reiser, S.J., Pres.

LEICESTER. *Father James Fitton House of Priestly Formation*, 761 Main St., 01524. Tel: 508-892-8439. Rev. Dennis J. O'Brien, Dir.

PETERSHAM. *St. Mary's Monastery*, N. Main St., P.O. Box 345, 01366. Tel: 508-724-3350. Rev. Anselm Atkinson, O.S.B., Supr. Priests-Monks 2; Monks 3; Novices 3; Postulants 1.

SHREWSBURY. *Passionist Fathers of Shrewsbury, Inc., Calvary Retreat Center*, 59 South St., P.O. Box 219, 01545-0219. Tel: 508-842-8821. Revs. Francis Landry, C.P., Rector; Pierre Myrand, C.P.; Joseph Sedley, C.P., Dir. Novices; Christopher Cleary, C.P.; Edward Wolanski, C.P.; Xavier Hayes, C.P., Vice Rector; Bro. August Parlavechio, C.P., Econome. Priests 6; Brothers 1.

Xaverian Brothers, 378 Main St., 01545. Tel: 508-845-1878; Fax: 508-842-3670. Bro. Stephen Comeau, C.F.X., Dir. Brothers 11.

SPENCER. *St. Joseph's Abbey*, 01562-1233. Tel: 508-885-8700. The Cistercian Order of the Strict Observance (Trappists). Legal Title: *The Cistercian Abbey of Spencer, Inc.* Rt. Revs. Damian Carr, O.C.S.O.; Paschal Skutecky, O.C.S.O., Retired Abbot; Very Rev. Joseph Chu Cong, O.C.S.O., Prior; Revs. George Calhoun, O.C.S.O.; Laurence Bourget, O.C.S.O.; Peter Zemanick, O.C.S.O., (On Leave); Adrian Proback, O.C.S.O.; Raphael Simon, O.C.S.O.; Pius Rivera-Martinez, O.S.C.O.; Basil Byrne, O.C.S.O.; Eugene Lacasse, O.C.S.O.; Simon Sansone, O.C.S.O.; Edward Steriti, O.C.S.O.; M. Basil Pennington, O.C.S.O.; Matthew Flynn, O.C.S.O.; Gabriel Bertoniere, O.C.S.O.; Patrick Brown, O.C.S.O.; Kevin Hunt, O.C.S.O.; Placid McSweeney, O.S.C.O.; Robert Morhous, O.C.S.O.; Vincent Dwyer, O.C.S.O.; Henry Scarborough, O.C.S.O.; Gerald Sears, O.C.S.O.; Edward John Mullaney, O.C.S.O.; Kizito Thompson, O.C.S.O.; Marius Granato, O.C.S.O.; Aquinas Keane, O.C.S.O.; Luke Truhan, O.C.S.O.; Aidan Logan, O.C.S.O.; Francis Rodriguez, O.C.S.O.; Andrew Johnson, O.C.S.O., (On Leave); Isaac Keeley, O.C.S.O.; Dominic Whedbee, O.C.S.O.; David Lavitch, O.C.S.O.; James Palmigiano, O.C.S.O. Solemnly Professed 77; Simply Professed 2; Novices 5; Total Priests in Community 37; Total in Community 82.

STILL RIVER. *Benedictine Monks, St. Benedict Abbey* (Harvard), 252 Still River Rd., P.O. Box 67, 01467. Tel: 508-456-3221. Rt. Rev. Gabriel Gibbs, O.S.B., Abbot; Very Rev. Xavier Connelly, O.S.B., Prior; Revs. Basil Rechenburg, O.S.B.; Peter Connelly, O.S.B.; Anthony Kloss, O.S.B.; Marc Crilly, O.S.B. In res., Rev. Francis Xavier (Sri Lanka). Priests 7; Brothers 13; Oblates 1.

WHITINSVILLE. *St. Camillus Community*, 497 Hill St., 01588. Tel: 617-234-3648. Bros. Thomas Farrell, O.S.Carm., Supr.; John Wiejkus, O.S.Cam.; Rev. John Gallagher, O.S.Cam. Priests 1; Brothers 2.

[O] CONVENTS AND RESIDENCES FOR SISTERS

WORCESTER. *Convent of Notre Dame*, 555 Plantation St., 01605. Sisters of Notre Dame de Namur and Long Term Care Center. Coordinators: Sr. Catherine T. Connolly, S.N.D., 555 Plantation St. Sr. Mary Anderson; Sr. Catherine Louise Beauregard; Sr. Adelaide Bisol; Sr. Mathilde Callahan; Sr. Kathleen Therese Cassidy; Sr. Frances St. Mary Congdon; Sr. Catherine Thomas Connolly; Sr. Irene Cotreau; Sr. Claire Aloyse Doherty; Sr. Mary Raphael Doody; Sr. Ellen Christine Doran; Sr. Agnes Marie Dwyer; Sr. Constance Marie Ecker; Sr. Bernadette Joseph Flood; Sr. Charlotte Flynn; Sr. Margaret St. Joseph Flynn; Sr. Rosina Gallahue; Sr. Dorothy Ann Gill; Sr. Helena St. John Harrington; Sr. Alice Roberta Kelleher; Sr. Ellen Marie Kennedy; Sr. Rose Marguerite Keohan; Sr. Margaret Teresa Kirk; Sr. Lucy Leonard; Sr. Marie Gabriel Mahoney; Sr. Mary McCarthy; Sr. Patrice McCarthy; Sr. Helen McEleney; Sr. Rose Elizabeth Monahan; Sr. Margaret Dolores Mullen; Sr. Irene Frances Mullin; Sr. Marie Murphy; Sr. Sandra Maria Napier; Sr. Catherine Neylon; Sr. Teresa O'Brien; Sr. Ursula Marie O'Brien; Sr. Catherine Aloyse O'Donnell; Sr. Mary Ellen O'Donnell; Sr. Patricia O'Donnell; Sr. Julie Patricia O'Neill; Sr. Aloyse Otis; Sr. Catherine Miriam Ring; Sr. Anne St. George Satchell; Sr. Caroline Marie Smith; Sr. Barbara Winn. Sisters of Notre Dame 45; Sisters of the Visitation 7.

Harper Residence, Res., 11 Beechmont St., 01609. Tel: 508-792-1619. Sisters 6.

Little Franciscans of Mary, 2 Dupont St., 01604-3706. Tel: 508-755-0878. Sr. Rena Mae Gagnon, P.F.M., Reg. Supr. Tel: 508-755-0878. Sisters 2.

Little Franciscans of Mary, 101 Plantation St., 01604. Tel: 508-755-8605. Sr. Jacquelyn Alix, P.F.M., Supr. Sisters 21.

Little Sisters of the Assumption, Pernet Family Health Service, Inc., 237 Millbury St., 01610. Tel: 508-755-1228. Family Health Agency. Nursing and Family Development Services-Home Based.

Religious Venerini Sisters Provincial Office, 23 Edward St., 01605. Sr. Hilda Ponte, M.P.V., Prov. Coord. Sisters 36; Total in Residence 24.

St. Joseph's Home (Residence for Women), 52 High St., 01609. Tel: 508-755-7707. Sr. Leona Donahue, R.S.M., Dir. Sisters of Mercy 1; Women 62; Total Staff 6.

Sisters of Mercy, 101 Barry Rd., 01609. Tel: 508-798-3727. Sr. Marie Finneron, Admin. Sisters 45.

Sisters of St. Anne, Esther House, 1015 Pleasant St., 01602. Tel: 508-757-6053. Sisters 7; Total in Residence 4; Total Staff 7.

Sisters of St. Joseph, S.S.J., 783 Grove St., 01605. Tel: 508-852-1659. Sisters 3.

Sisters of the Assumption of the Blessed Virgin Provincial Administration, 316 Lincoln St., 01605. Tel: 508-856-9448; Fax: 508-853-0881. Sr. Muriel A. Lemoine, S.A.S.V., Prov. Supr. Tel: 508-856-9383; Estelle Dube, S.A.S.V., Prov. Sec. Tel: 508-724-3468; Sr. Lorraine Normand, S.A.S.V., Prov. Treas. Tel: 508-856-9450.

Sisters of the Holy Family of Nazareth, 119 Endicott St., 01610. Tel: 508-753-3835. Sr. M. Roberta, C.S.F.N., Supr. Sisters 4.

Xaverian Missionary Society of Mary, Headquarters: 242 Salisbury St., 01609-1639. Tel: 508-757-0514. Sr. Rita Davoli, X.M.M., Supr. Sisters 5.

LEOMINSTER. *Presentation Convent*, 99 Church St., 01453. Tel: 508-537-7108; Fax: 508-840-1564. Motherhouse of the Sisters of the Presentation of the Blessed Virgin Mary. Sr. Catherine Hannigan, P.B.V.M., Pres.; Sr. Eileen Shea, House Coord. Professed Sisters 81.

Sacred Heart Convent, 318 Lindell Ave., 01453. Sisters of Notre Dame de Namur 2.

St. Cecilia's Convent, 196 Mechanic St., 01453. Tel: 508-534-6907. Daughters of the Holy Spirit 4.

St. Julie Convent, 342 Lindell Ave., 01453. Sr. Marguerite Timothy, S.N.D., Prin. Sisters of Notre Dame de Namur 3.

PETERSHAM. *Assumption Residence of the Sisters of the Assumption of the Blessed Virgin*, N. Main St., Box 128, 01366. Tel: 508-724-3468. Co-Administrators: Sr. Estelle Dube, S.A.S.V.; Sr. Lucille Pleau, S.A.S.V. Professed Sisters 69.

St. Scholastica Priory, 271 N. Main St., Box 606, 01366. Tel: 508-724-3213; Fax: 508-724-3574. Benedictine Nuns (Cloistered). Very Rev. Mary Clare Vincent, O.S.B., Prioress; Sr. Mary Frances Wynn, O.S.B., Sub Prioress. Nuns in Solemn Vows 12; in Simple Vows 1; Claustral Oblates 1; Novices 1.

STILL RIVER. *Sisters of Saint Benedict Center, Slaves of the Immaculate Heart of Mary Inc.*, St. Ann House, 254 Still River Rd., P.O. Box 22, 01467. Tel: 508-456-8017. Mother Teresa Beneway, M.I.C.M. Professed Sisters 15; Novices 2; Postulants 4; Live-In Oblates 2.

WEBSTER. *St. Joseph Convent*, 5 Maynard St., 01570. Tel: 508-943-2228. Sr. Mary Angelia Rzasa, C.S.S.F., Supr. Felician Sisters 3.

[P] RETREAT HOUSES AND HOUSE OF PRAYER

WORCESTER. *Community of Teresian Carmelites* (1971), 30 Chrome St., P.O. Box 826, 01613-0826. Tel: 508-752-5734; 756-1086 (24-hour prayer line). Bro. Paul-Joseph Richard, C.T.C., Supr. Gen.; Sr. Debra-Therese Carroll, C.T.C., Prioress; Bro. Dennis-Anthony Wyrzykowski, C.T.C., Vicar; Sr. Donna-Bernadette Allen, C.T.C., Chapter Councilor. Dir. Vocations: Bro. Daniel-Francis Charpentier, C.T.C., Dir., Vocations for Men; Sr. Susan-Elizabeth Terkanian, C.T.C., Dir., Vocations for Women; Ms. Loretta M. Carroll, C.T.C.S., Community Sec.; Ms. Christine M. Chabot, C.T.C.S., Community Treas.; Rev. Francis A. Roberge, Chap. Solemly Professed Sisters 3; Solemnly Professed Brothers 3; Novices 1.

SHREWSBURY. *Calvary Retreat Center, Passionist Community*. (See separate listing under Monasteries and Residences for Men.), 59 South St., P.O. Box 219, 01545-0219. Tel: 508-842-8821. Very Rev. Francis Landry, C.P., Rector & Retreat Dir.; Revs. Pierre Myrand, C.P; Joseph Sedley, C.P., Dir. Novices; Edward Wolanski, C.P.; Christopher Cleary, C.P.; Xavier Hayes, C.P., Vice Rector; Bro. August Parlavechio, C.P., Econome. Total in Residence 7; Total Staff 40.

SPENCER. *Ecumenical Institute of Spirituality*, Saint Joseph's Abbey, 01562. Tel: 508-885-4760. Dr. Douglas Steere, Pres.; Rev. Robert Lechner, C.P.P.S., Vice Pres.

Mary House, Inc., 186 N. Spencer Rd. (Rte. 31), P.O. Box 20, 01562. Tel: 508-885-5450. House of Prayer and Contemplation. Ms. Joyce Thomasmeyer, Pres.

St. Joseph Abbey, N. Spencer Rd., 01562. Tel: 508-885-8710. Guest house and Retreat house. Revs. Aidan Logan, O.C.S.O., Guestmaster; Placid McSweeney, O.C.S.O., Asst. Guestmaster; Gerald Sears, O.C.S.O., Asst. Guestmaster.

STILL RIVER. *Benedictine Monks, St. Benedict Abbey* (Harvard). (See separate listing under Monasteries and Residences for Men.), 252 Still River Rd., P.O. Box 67, 01467. Tel: 508-456-3221. Rt. Rev. Gabriel Gibbs, O.S.B., Abbot.

[Q] NEWMAN CHAPLAINS AND CENTERS

WORCESTER. *Campus Ministry*, P.O. Box 903, 01613. Rev. Peter J. Scanlon, S.T.L., Vicar. Total Staff 23.

Assumption College, 500 Salisbury St., 01609. Rev. Claude L. Grenache, A.A.; Mr. Peter Hart; Mr. John Fleming; Sr. Cecilia Hervas, R.A.; Frank Corbin, Ph.D.

Becker College, 19 Schussler Rd., 01609. Tel: 508-757-6097. Rev. Peter J. Scanlon, S.T.L., Chap., Religious Center.

Clark University, Box A-62, 01610. Tel: 508-793-7737. Beth Duffy Schaper, M.Ed.

Holy Cross College, The Office of the College Chaplain. Ms. Katherine McElaney, Dir.; Revs. Joseph J. LaBran, S.J.; James M. Hayes, S.J.; Michael F. Ford, S.J.; Paul Covino; Marybeth Cearns-Barrett; Andrea Goodrich; Sr. Lucille Cormier, S.A.S.V.

Becker College at Leicester. Refer to Diocesan Office.

Quinsigamond Community College, 670 W. Boylston St., 01606. Tel: 508-853-2300, Ext. 300. Sr. Helen Egan, S.S.J.

University of Massachusetts Medical School. Refer to Diocesan Office.

Worcester State College, Campus Ministry Center, 486 Chandler St., 01602. Tel: 508-793-8017. Rev. Timothy M. Brewer.

Worcester Polytechnic Institute, Religious Center at WPI, 19 Schussler Rd., 01609. Tel: 508-757-6097. Rev. Peter J. Scanlon, S.T.L.

Collegiate Religious Center, 19 Schussler Rd., 01609. Tel: 508-757-6097. Rev. Peter J. Scanlon, S.T.L.

Nichols College (Dudley), 01570. Tel: 508-943-1560. Rev. Conrad S. Pecevich, D.Min.

Fitchburg State College (Fitchburg), Newman Center, 281 Highland Ave., 01420. Tel: 508-345-2688. Rev. Richard P. Lewandowski, M.A., M.Div.; Deacon Benjamin A. Nogueira; Lois I. Nogueira, Chap.

Mt. Wachusett Community College (Gardner), Campus Ministry at MW CC, 419 Green St., Gardner, 01440. Tel: 508-632-6600, Ext. 193. Rev. Gerald L. Berten; Ms. Maureen Andrews, M.Ed.

PAXTON. *Anna Maria College*, Office of Campus Ministry, 01612-1198. Tel: 508-849-3398; 3399. Sr. Sarah Landis, I.H.M. Total Staff 1.

[R] MISCELLANEOUS

WORCESTER. *Casa Santa Maria del Camino, Inc.*, 6 Claremont Sq., 01610. Tel: 508-798-0104. Rev. William E. Reiser, S.J., Pres. Total in Residence 4; Total Staff 1. Pastoral Outreach Center for the Hispanic Community.

The Charlton Charitable Corporation, Inc. Diocese of Worcester. 49 Elm St., 01609.

The Guild of Our Lady of Providence. Mailing Address: Chancery Office of the Diocese of Worcester, 49 Elm St., 01609. Tel: 508-791-5357; Fax: 508-753-7180.

Monsignor Thomas Griffin Foundation, 49 Elm St., 01609. Tel: 508-791-7171. Rev. Msgr. Edmond T. Tinsley, Contact Person.

PACE - Parents Alliance for Catholic Education, 781 Grove St., 01605. Tel: 508-852-2200; Fax: 508-856-0792. Stephen A. Perla, Exec. Dir.

GARDNER. *House of Peace & Education, Inc.*, 20 Barthel Ave., 01440. Tel: 508-630-4752. Maxyene D. Schneider, S.S.J., Pres. Purpose: Neighborhood educational center for disadvantaged women and children.

PETERSHAM. *St. Bede's Publications*, 271 N. Main St., P.O. Box 545, 01366. Tel: 508-724-3407; Fax: 508-724-3574. Mother Mary Clare Vincent, O.S.B.

St. Mary and St. Scholastica Church, Inc., 271 N. Main St., Box 606, 01366.

SPENCER. *Cistercian Publications, Inc.*, St. Joseph's Abbey, 01562. Tel: 508-885-8730. Dr. Ernst Breisach, Pres.; Dr. E. Rozanne Elder, Exec. Vice Pres. & Mng. Editor; Rev. M. Basil Pennington, O.C.S.O., Sec.

WHITINSVILLE. *St. Camillus Institute, Inc.*, 447 Hill St., 01588. Tel: 617-234-7306. Very Rev. William F. Cronin, O.S.Cam., Pres. Order of the Servants of the Sick (St. Camillus).

RELIGIOUS INSTITUTES OF MEN REPRESENTED IN THE DIOCESE

For further details refer to the corresponding bracketed number in the Religious Institutes of Men or Women section.

[0130]—*Assumptionists*.—A.A.
[0200]—*Benedictine Monks*. (Petersham; Still River).—O.S.B.
[1350]—*Brothers of St. Francis Xavier*.—C.F.X.
[0350]—*Cistercians Order of the Strict Observance (Trappists)*.—O.C.S.O.
[0790]—*Congregation of Maronite Monks*.—O.Mar.
[1000]—*Congregation of the Passion*.—C.P.
[0690]—*Jesuit Fathers and Brothers*.—S.J.
[0740]—*Marian Fathers*M.I.C.
[0720]—*Missionaries of Our Lady of LaSalette*. (Seven Dolors Prov.).—M.S.
[0240]—*Order of St. Camilus - Camillian Fathers and Brothers*.—O.S.Cam.
[1280]—*Stigmatine Fathers and Brothers*.—C.S.S.

RELIGIOUS INSTITUTES OF WOMEN REPRESENTED IN THE DIOCESE

[0230]—*Benedictine Sisters of Pontifical Jurisdiction*. (Petersham; Rutland; Eau Clare, WI).—O.S.B.
[0820]—*Daughters of the Holy Spirit*.—D.H.S.
[1070-06]—*Dominican Sisters*. (Newburgh, NY).—O.P.
[1170]—*Felician Sisters*.—C.S.S.F.
[2575]—*Institute of the Sisters of Mercy of the Americas*. (New York, NY).—R.S.M.
[2280]—*Little Franciscans of Mary*.—P.F.M.
[2310]—*Little Sisters of the Assumption*.—L.S.A.
[2790]—*Missionary Servants of the Most Blessed Trinity*.—M.S.B.T.
[2420]—*Missionary Sisters of the Society of Mary (Marist)*.—S.M.S.M.
[3390]—*Religious of the Assumption*.—R.A.
[2070]—*Religious of the Holy Union of the Sacred Hearts*.—S.U.S.C.
[4180]—*Religious Venerini Sisters*.—M.P.V.
[]—*Sisters Oblates to Divine Love*.—R.O.D.A.
[3000]—*Sisters of Notre Dame de Namur*. (Boston, Ipswich, Japan and Connecticut Provs.).—S.N.D.deN.
[3340]—*Sisters of Providence*.—S.P.
[3720]—*Sisters of Saint Anne*.—S.S.A.
[1650]—*The Sisters of St. Francis of Philadelphia*.—O.S.F.
[3830-01]—*Sisters of St. Joseph*. (Boston, Brighton).—C.S.J.
[3830-16]—*Sisters of St. Joseph*.—S.S.J.
[3815]—*Sisters of Ste. Jeanne D'Arc*.—S.J.A.
[0150]—*Sisters of the Assumption*.—S.A.S.V.
[1970]—*Sisters of the Holy Family of Nazareth*.—C.S.F.N.
[3310]—*Sisters of the Presentation of Mary*.—P.M.
[3320]—*Sisters of the Presentation of the B.V.M.*.—P.B.V.M.
[4230]—*Xaverian Missionary Society of Mary, Inc.*.—X.M.M.

DIOCESAN CEMETERIES

WORCESTER. *St. John's*.

NECROLOGY

† Biscardi, Pasquale D., Fitchburg, MA, Madonna of the Holy Rosary. —Died June 22, 1996.
† Carberry, Francis J., Sterling, MA, St. Richard of Chichester. —Died Feb. 6, 1996.
† Chenier, Roland J., Millville, MA, St. Augustine. —Died Jan. 11, 1996.
† Donega, Carl D., Worcester, MA, Our Lady of Mt. Carmel-St. Ann. —Died Dec. 31, 1995.
† Foley, John J., Worcester, MA, Sacred Heart of Jesus. —Died July 26, 1996.
† Kochanowski, John P., West Warren, MA, St. Stanislaus. —Died March 31, 1996.
† Lehane, James A., Fitchburg, MA, St. Bernard's. —Died Jan. 4, 1996.
† Szamocki, John A., Dudley, MA, St. Andrew Bobola. —Died Aug. 16, 1996.

Diocese of Yakima

(Dioecesis Yakimensis)

Most Reverend

CARLOS A. SEVILLA, S.J., D.D.

Bishop of Yakima; ordained June 3, 1966; appointed December 6, 1988; Episcopal ordination January 25, 1989. *Address all correspondence to: 5301-A Tieton Dr., Yakima, WA, 98908.*

Most Reverend

NICOLAS E. WALSH, D.D.

Bishop Emeritus of Yakima; ordained June 6, 1942; appointed September 5, 1974; consecrated October 28, 1974; installed October 30, 1974; transferred to Archdiocese of Seattle as Auxiliary to the Archbishop August 10, 1976; resigned September 6, 1983. *Mailing Address: P.O. Box 1050, Mammoth, AZ, 85618.*

ESTABLISHED JUNE 23, 1951.

Square Miles 17,787.

Legal Title: Corporation of the Catholic Bishop of Yakima.

Comprises the following Counties in the State of Washington: Benton, Chelan, Douglas, Grant, Kittitas, Klickitat and Yakima.

For legal titles of parishes and diocesan institutions, consult the Pastoral Office.

Pastoral Office (Chancery): 5301-A Tieton Dr., Yakima, WA, 98908 Tel.: 509-965-7117; Fax: 509-966-8334.

STATISTICAL OVERVIEW

Personnel	
Bishop	1
Priests: Diocesan Active in Diocese	40
Priests: Active Outside Diocese	8
Priests: Retired, Sick or Absent	8
Number of Diocesan Priests	56
Religious Priests in Diocese	10
Extern Priests in Diocese	7
Ordinations:	
Diocesan Priests	1
Transitional Deacons	3
Permanent Deacons	4
Permanent Deacons in Diocese	25
Total Sisters	53
Parishes	
Parishes	41
With Resident Pastor:	
Resident Diocesan Priests	30
Resident Religious Priests	4
Without Resident Pastor:	
Administered by Priests	7
Missions	5
Pastoral Centers	2
Professional Ministry Personnel:	
Sisters	20
Lay Ministers	9
Welfare	
Catholic Hospitals	3
Total Assisted	291,781
Day Care and Extended Day Care Centers	2
Total Assisted	234
Special Centers for Social Services	6
Total Assisted	14,998
Educational	
Diocesan Students in Other Seminaries	20
Total Seminarians	20
High Schools, Private	1
Elementary Schools, Diocesan and Parish	7
Total Students	1,928
Catechesis/Religious Education:	
High School Students	1,777
Elementary Students	5,255
Total Students Under Catholic Instruction	8,980
Teachers in the Diocese:	
Sisters	7
Lay Teachers	95
Vital Statistics	
Receptions into the Church:	
Infant Baptism Totals	2,776
Adult Baptism Totals	154
Received into Full Communion	83
First Communions	1,943
Confirmations	650
Marriages:	
Catholic	343
Interfaith	140
Total Marriages	483
Deaths	519
Total Catholic Population	69,978
Total Population	461,000

Former Bishops—Most Rev. JOSEPH P. DOUGHERTY, D.D., First Bishop of Yakima; ord. June 14, 1930; appt. July 9, 1951; cons. Sept. 26, 1951; resigned Feb. 5, 1969; died July 10, 1970.—Most Rev. CORNELIUS M. POWER, D.D., Second Bishop of Yakima; ord. June 3, 1939; appt. Feb. 5, 1969; cons. May 1, 1969; elevated to Metropolitan See of Portland in Oregon, Jan. 24, 1974.—Most Rev. NICOLAS E. WALSH, D.D., Third Bishop of Yakima; ord. June 6, 1942; appt. Sept. 5, 1974; cons. Oct. 28, 1974; installed Oct. 30, 1974; transferred to Archdiocese of Seattle as Auxiliary Bishop, Aug. 10, 1976; resigned Sept. 6, 1983.—Most Rev. WILLIAM S. SKYLSTAD, D.D., Fourth Bishop of Yakima; cons. May 12, 1977; transferred to Spokane as Bishop of Spokane, April 17, 1990.—Most Rev. FRANCIS E. GEORGE, O.M.I., Ph.D., S.T.D., Fifth Bishop of Yakima; appt. July 10, 1990; cons. Sept. 21, 1990; appt. Metropolitan See of Portland in Oregon, April 30, 1996.

Administrator of Diocese of Yakima—Rev. Msgr. PERRON J. AUVE, *5301-A Tieton Dr., Yakima, 98908-3493.*

Pastoral Office (Chancery)—5301-A Tieton Dr., Yakima, 98908. Tel: 509-965-7117; Fax: 509-966-8334.

Vicar General—Vacant.

Vicar for Priests—Vacant.

Cemeteries—Rev. ROBERT J. SHIELDS, *P.O. Box 108, Grand Coulee, 99133.* Tel: 509-633-1180.

Chancellor and Moderator of the Curia—Very Rev. RONALD W. METHA.

Vice-Chancellor—Mrs. GAYLE MILLER.

Diocesan Tribunal—*5301-D Tieton Dr., Yakima, 98908.* Tel: 509-965-7123.

Judicial Vicar—Very Rev. MICHAEL J. IBACH, J.C.L.

Adjutant Judicial Vicar—Very Rev. Sir JOHN F. HENEGHAN, J.C.L.

Administrator—Mrs. MATILDA M. SMITH.

Judges—Very Rev. MICHAEL J. IBACH, J.C.L.; Very Rev. Sir JOHN F. HENEGHAN, J.C.L.

Defenders of the Bond—Rev. THOMAS C. CHAMPOUX; Rev. Msgr. JOHN A. ECKER; Rev. RICHARD A. WUERTZ.

Advocates—All Clergy with diocesan assignments and pastoral ministers by appointment.

Notaries—Mrs. LESLIE KNOWLES; Mrs. ANGELITA T. SALDIVAR.

Diocesan Consultors—Rev. Msgr. PERRON J. AUVE; Rev. THOMAS C. CHAMPOUX; Rev. Msgr. JOHN A. ECKER; Revs. JOHN J. MURTAGH; ARGEMIRO OROZCO; JOSE DE JESUS RAMIREZ; LAWRENCE T. REILLY; RICHARD D. SEDLACEK; RICHARD A. WUERTZ.

Bishop's Administrative Cabinet—Rev. Msgr. PERRON J. AUVE, Diocesan Admin.; Mr. JOHN L. YOUNG, Exec. Dir., Catholic Charities; Mrs. CATHY COLVER, Supt., Catholic Schools; Rev. Msgr. JOHN A. ECKER, Dir., Vocations; Mr. PATRICK FLYNN, Dir., Youth Ministry; Mr. ROBERT FONTANA, Dir., Evangelization; Mrs. VIRGINIA SANTILLANES, Dir., Social Justice and Peace, Family Life; Rev. RICHARD M. HOUSE, Chm., Commission on Public Worship; Very Rev. MICHAEL J. IBACH, J.C.L., Judicial Vicar; Ms. ROSEMARIE KEARNS, Dir., Religious Education; Mr. DONALD M. KLIPPSTEIN, Dir., Devel.; Mr. JOE KIESEL-NIELD, Dir., Catholic Campus Ministry; Rev. KENNETH M. KRON, Chm., Commission for the Catechumenate; Mrs. GAYLE MILLER, Vice-Chancellor; Rev. VICTOR ALVAREZ, Dir., Hispanic Ministries; Deacon JOHN CORNELL, Deacon Dir.; Mrs. PEGGY ROY, Finance Officer; Sr. MARIA DE JESUS YBARRA, O.P., Dir., Hispanic Ministry Formation.

Diocesan Offices, Commissions, Committees

Campaign for Human Development—Mrs. VIRGINIA SANTILLANES, *5301-B Tieton Dr., Yakima, 98908.* Tel: 509-965-7117.

Catholic Charities—Mr. JOHN L. YOUNG, Exec. Dir., Office: *5301-C Tieton Dr., Yakima, 98908.* Tel: 509-965-7100.

Catholic Women, Council of—Rev. JOHN M. SHAW, *213 N. Beech, Toppenish, 98948.*

Charismatic Renewal—Rev. Msgr. PERRON J. AUVE, Liaison, *5301-A Tieton Dr., Yakima, 98908.* Tel: 509-965-7117.

Conciliation Board—Rev. THOMAS C. CHAMPOUX; Mr. PAT COCKRILL; Mrs. MARY KOWALSKI; Mrs. TRUDY LEDWICH; Mrs. SANDY SEWARD, *5301-C Tieton Dr., Yakima, 98908.* Tel: 509-965-7100.

Cursillo, English—Rev. JOHN G. O'SHEA, *7409 W. Clearwater, Kennewick, 99336.* Tel: 509-735-8558.

Spanish—Mr. RAMON MATA, *1706 S. Vancouver,*

Kennewick, 99336. Tel: 509-586-9995.

Development Office / Catholic Foundation—Mr. DONALD M. KLIPPSTEIN, Dir., *5301-A Tieton Dr., Yakima, 98908.* Tel: 509-965-7117.

Diocesan Coordinator for Health Affairs—Rev. THOMAS C. CHAMPOUX, *5301-C Tieton Dr., Yakima, 98908.* Tel: 509-965-7100.

Diocesan Commission for the Catechumenate—Rev. KENNETH M. KRON, Chm., *P.O. Box 308, Quincy, 98848.* Tel: 509-787-2622. Mr. PETE BRAUN; Mrs. LUCY GARCIA; Sr. MARY ANN HERRES, S.N.J.M.; Rev. THOMAS KUYKENDALL; Mrs. JACQUE LOYND; Mrs. MARY SMITH.

Diocesan Commission on Public Worship—Rev. RICHARD M. HOUSE, Chm.; Mrs. NANCY BARTLETT; Mrs. CHERIE HANSES; Mr. FELIP HOLBROOK; Deacon RAY MILLER; Rev. ARGEMIRO OROZCO; Sr. MARIA DE JESUS YBARRA, O.P.

Diocesan Pastoral Council—Vacant.

Diocesan Millenium Planning Committee—Rev. Msgr. PERRON J. AUVE, Chm.; Mr. RICHARD ACOSTA; Rev. OSMAR AGUIRRE; Mrs. SYLVIA BRULE; Mrs. SUE CONNOLLY; Mr. MARK EVEVARD; Mr. ROBERT FONTANA; Mr. JOHN HANSON; Rev. RICHARD KEOLKER; Mr. TOM MARAVILLA; Rev. KEVIN MINDER; Mrs. ELEANOR RICE; Mr. RICHARD SEVIGNY; Mrs. SHANNON SEVIGNY; Mr. MARIO VILLANUEVA; Mrs. JANE VILLANUEVA.

Ecumenical Liaison—Rev. Msgr. JOHN A. ECKER, *15 S. 12th Ave., Yakima, 98902.* Tel: 509-575-3713.

Engaged Encounter—Mr. RON MELTON; Mrs. CAROL GEIER, *2344 Benton, Richland, 99352.* Tel: 509-375-3023.

Engaged Encounter, Spanish—Sr. MARIA DE JESUS YBARRA, O.P., *5301-B Tieton Dr., Yakima, 98908.* Tel: 509-965-7110.

Diocesan Finance Council—Rev. Msgr. PERRON J. AUVE, *Pastoral Center, 5301-A Tieton Dr., Yakima, 98908.* Very Rev. RONALD W. METHA, *5301-A Tieton Dr., Yakima, 98908.* Dr. ROBERT CASH; Mr. WILLIAM FORSYTHE; Mr. RICHARD GASSELING; Mr. DONALD M. KLIPPSTEIN; Mr. BILL MCCURLEY; Mrs. PAT MYERS; Mrs. ALICE CONE NELSON; Mrs. PEGGY ROY; Mr. JIM TUTTLE; Mr. GLENN VALENZUELA; Mr. LARRY WRIGHT; Rev. RICHARD A. WUERTZ.

Marriage Encounter, English—Mr. RICH BRESHEARS; Mrs. MARY ANN BRESHEARS, *1840 W. 23rd, Kennewick, 99337.* Tel: 509-582-4804.

Spanish—Rev. JOSE DE JESUS RAMIREZ, *P.O. Box 308, Granger, 98932.*

Ministry & Education Center—Mrs. CATHY COLVER, Admin. & Supt. of Schools, *5301-B Tieton Dr., Yakima, 98908.* Tel: 509-965-7110.

Hispanic Religious Education and Ministry Formation—Sr. MARIA DE JESUS YBARRA, O.P., Dir.

Evangelization and Lay Formation—Mr. ROBERT FONTANA, Dir.

Missionary Formation of Lay Evangelizers—Sr. SUSANNE THIBAULT, M.S.B.T.; Sr. PATRICIA WINDER, M.S.B.T., *15880 Summitview Rd., Cowiche, 98923.* Tel: 509-678-5535.

Religious Education—Ms. REE KEARNS, Dir.

Youth / Young Adult Director—Mr. PATRICK FLYNN.

Youth / Young Adult Hispanic Ministry—Mr. CARLOS CARRILLO.

Deacon Director—Deacon JOHN CORNELL, *2504 W. Chestnut, Yakima, 98902.*

Family Life / Social Justice & Peace—Mrs. VIRGINIA SANTILLANES.

Northwest Regional Office for Hispanic Affairs—ILSE WEFERS, Admin., *5301-F Tieton Dr., Yakima, 98908.* Tel: 503-233-8324.

Personnel Board—Rev. THOMAS C. CHAMPOUX; Rev. Msgr. MARTIN O. SKEHAN; Rev. RICHARD D. SEDLACEK.

Press (Central Washington Catholic)—Very Rev. RONALD W. METHA, Editor, *5301-A Tieton Dr., Yakima, 98908.* Tel: 509-965-7117.

Presbyteral Council Executive Committee—Vacant.

Propagation of the Faith—Rev. ROBERT J. SHIELDS, Dir., *P.O. Box 108, Grand Coulee, 99133.* Tel: 509-633-1180.

Holy Childhood Association—Rev. ROBERT J. SHIELDS, Dir., *P.O. Box 108, Grand Coulee, 99133.* Tel: 509-633-1180.

Native American Ministries—Sr. MARGARET BALL, S.N.J.M., *109 N. E St., Toppenish, 98948.* Tel: 509-877-2751.

Natural Family Planning—Mrs. DOLORES LACOURSIERE, *422 S. 15th Ave., Yakima, 98902.* Tel: 509-452-9960.

Prison Ministry—Rev. GEORGE PURDY, S.J., *P.O. Box 128, Naches, 98937.* Tel: 509-653-2534.

Retreat Center—

St. Peter Retreat Center—Rev. LAWRENCE T. REILLY, Dir., *15880 Summitview Rd., Cowiche, 98923.* Tel: 509-678-4935.

Respect Life Committee—Mrs. VIRGINIA SANTILLANES, Dir.; Mr. RUBEN BEEDLE; Rev. THOMAS C. CHAMPOUX; Mr. BILL FROMHERZ; Mr. CHUCK GONSALEZ; Mrs. DEE GONSALEZ; Mrs. JAN JOHNSON; Dr. GEORGE HOTCHKO; Dr. ANNE NEALEN; Mrs. SUSAN SCHWAEGLER; Mrs. DEE SCHWAB; Mrs. CHERI VAUSE; Sr. MARIA DE JESUS YBARRA, O.P., *5301-B Tieton Dr., Yakima, 98908.* Tel: 509-965-7110.

Scouting—Rev. WILLIAM E. SHAW, Chap., *P.O. Box 567, Zillah, 98953.* Tel: 509-829-5433. Mr. CARLOS CARRILLO; Mr. MARC DESGROSEILLIER; Mrs. CINDY DESGROSEILLIER; Deacon BILL DRONEN; Mrs. CHARLENE DRONEN; Mr. PATRICK FLYNN; Mrs. ILIANA GARZA; Mr. JOHN WARREN.

Separated, Divorced and Widowed Catholics—Mrs. ROSALIE C. LOCKHART, *4802 Richey Rd., Yakima, 98908.* Tel: 509-966-9855.

Social Justice Commission—Mrs. VIRGINIA SANTILLANES; Revs. OSMAR AGUIRRE; THOMAS C. CHAMPOUX; Mrs. LINDA CONROY; Mr. CHRIS CASSIDY; Mrs. TERRI AGUILERA-FLEMMING; Ms. ROSALINDA GUILLEN; Mrs. PATTY HOUTS-HUSSEY; Mr. TOM MARAVILLA; Mr. FRANK MCGREE; Rev. KEVIN MINDER; Mr. VIC ROHRET; Sr. GRACIELA ROSAS; Mrs. YVONNE SMITH, *5301-B Tieton Dr., Yakima, 98908.* Tel: 509-965-7110.

Hispanic Ministries—Rev. VICTOR ALVAREZ, Dir., *210 N. Beech, Toppenish, 98948.* Tel: 509-865-4040.

St. Vincent de Paul Society—Rev. THOMAS C. CHAMPOUX, Spirtual Dir., Office: *5301-C Tieton Dr., Yakima, 98908.* Tel: 509-965-7100.

Vocations—Rev. Msgr. JOHN A. ECKER, Dir., *15 S. 12th Ave., Yakima, 98902.* Tel: 509-575-3713.

CLERGY, PARISHES, MISSIONS AND PAROCHIAL SCHOOLS

CITY OF YAKIMA
(Yakima County)

1—ST. PAUL CATHEDRAL, Rev. Msgr. John A. Ecker; Rev. William Gallagher; Deacon Ray Miller; Sr. Ann Regimbal, Pastoral Assoc.
Res., 15 S. 12th Ave., 98902. Tel: 509-575-3713; Fax: 509-453-7497. [JC]
School—(Grades K-8) 1214 W. Chestnut Ave., 98902. Tel: 509-575-5604.
Lay Teachers 18; Students 345.
Catechesis / Religious Programs—Tel: 509-453-3897.
Students 175.

2—HOLY FAMILY, Rev. John J. Murtagh; Rev. Msgr. John J. McDonnell; Deacons John Cornell; Jim Kramper.
Res., 5315 Tieton Dr., 98908. Tel: 509-966-0830.
Catechesis / Religious Programs—Tel: 509-966-0788.
Students 575.
Mission—Ahtanum, Yakima Co., Holy Cross, Tel: 509-966-0865.

3—HOLY REDEEMER, Revs. John L. Tholen; Roberto B. Saenz, S.J.; Deacon Duane Berger; Sr. Judeen Seeberger, O.S.B., Pastoral Assoc.
Res., 1609 Landon Ave., 98902. Tel: 509-248-2241. [JC]
Catechesis / Religious Programs—Tel: 509-457-3435.
Students 210.

4—ST. JOSEPH'S, Revs. Patrick C. Carroll, S.J.; Thomas R. Royce, S.J.; Neill R. Meany, S.J.; Mr. Edward Lopez, S.J. In res., Rev. John T. Rashford, S.J., Chap., Providence Yakima Medical Center; Mary Bishoff, Admin.
Res., 212 N. 4th St., 98901-2499. Tel: 509-248-1911.
School—St. Joseph/Marquette.
Sisters of Providence 1; Lay Teachers 20; Students 408.
Catechesis / Religious Programs—Students 268.

OUTSIDE THE CITY OF YAKIMA

Benton City, Benton Co., St. Frances Xavier Cabrini (1963), Rev. Richard D. Sedlacek.
Church—Horn Rd., 99320. Tel: 509-786-1783.

Bridgeport, Douglas Co., St. Anne's (1964), Revs. Donald Dietz, O.M.I.; Arturo Rodriguez.
215 W. Allen Ave., P.O. Box 1089, Chelan, 98816. Tel: 509-682-2433.
Catechesis / Religious Programs—Students 57.
Mission—Mansfield, Douglas Co., St. Mary, (1909).

Cashmere, Chelan Co., St. Francis Xavier, Rev. Maurice F. Peterson; Deacon Bill Dronen.
Res., 307 Angier, 98815. Tel: 509-782-2643.
Catechesis / Religious Programs—Tracy Franklin, D.R.E.
Students 52.

Chelan, Chelan Co., St. Francis de Sales, Revs. Donald Dietz, O.M.I.; Arturo Rodriquez.
Res., 215 W. Allen Ave., P.O. Box 1089, 98816. Tel: 509-682-2433; 682-2702.
Catechesis / Religious Programs—Students 166.

Cle Elum, Kittitas Co., St. John the Baptist, Rev. Msgr. John Marasciulo.
Res., 303 W. 2nd St., 98922. Tel: 509-674-2531.
Catechesis / Religious Programs—Mary Anderson, D.R.E.
Students 180.

Cowiche, Yakima Co., St. Peter's, Rev. Lawrence T. Reilly; Deacon Walter A. Burnham.
Res., 15880 Summitview Rd., 98923. Tel: 509-678-4164; Fax: 509-678-4936.
Catechesis / Religious Programs—Students 155.

East Wenatchee, Douglas Co., Holy Apostles, Revs. Seamus Kerr; Alvaro Diez; Deacon Bill Loranger.
Res., P.O. Box 7279, 98802. Tel: 509-884-5444.
Catechesis / Religious Programs—1315 N.E. 8th St., 98801. Tel: 509-884-5444. D.R.E.: Debbie Patterson; Kristie Tuttle.
Students 223.

Ellensburg, Kittitas Co., St. Andrew's, Rev. Msgr. Perron Joseph Auve; Deacon Jack Spence.
Res., 401 S. Willow St., 98926. Tel: 509-962-9819; Fax: 509-962-9846. [CEM]
Catechesis / Religious Programs—Students 160.

Ephrata, Grant Co., St. Rose of Lima, Rev. Richard Mel House.
Parish Office: 323 D St., S.W., 98823. Tel: 509-754-3640; Fax: 509-754-4064. [CEM]
School—(Grades PreK-8) 520 S.E. Blvd., 98823. Tel: 509-754-4901.
Lay Teachers 10; Students 140.
Catechesis / Religious Programs—Angela Stacy, D.R.E.
Students 157.
St. Rose Children's Center—560 S.E. Blvd., 98825. Tel: 509-754-2897.
Mission—Soap Lake, Grant Co., Our Most Sorrowful Mother.

Goldendale, Klickitat Co., Holy Trinity, Rev. Thomas V. Lane.
Res., 210 S. Schuster St., P.O. Box 186, 98620. Tel: 509-773-4516. [CEM]
Catechesis / Religious Programs—Cheryl Swear Ingen, D.R.E.
Students 82.

Grand Coulee, Grant Co., St. Henry's, Revs. Anthony S. King; Robert J. Shields; Deacon Dan Farrell.
Res., 590 Grand Coulee Ave., W., P.O. Box 108, 99133. Tel: 509-633-1180.
Catechesis / Religious Programs—Students 54.
Mission—Coulee City, Grant Co., Holy Angels.

Grandview, Yakima Co., Blessed Sacrament, Revs. Robert P. Himes; Mario A. Salazar.
Res., 1201 Missouri, 98930. Tel: 509-882-1657; Fax: 509-882-1107.
Catechesis / Religious Programs—Students 234.

Granger, Yakima Co., Our Lady of Guadalupe, Rev. J. Jesus Ramirez; Deacon Al Rizzo.
Res., 608 Ave., E., P.O. Box 308, 98932. Tel: 509-854-1558.
Catechesis / Religious Programs—Students 164.

Hartline, Grant Co., St. Patrick's (1955). Served from Grand Coulee. Rev. Anthony King.
P.O. Box 108, Grand Coulee, 99133. Tel: 509-633-1180.

Kennewick, Benton Co., Holy Spirit, Rev. John G. O'Shea; Deacons Thomas Henn; John E. Powers.
Office: 7409 W. Clearwater, 99336. Tel: 509-735-8558.
Catechesis / Religious Programs—Tel: 509-735-8558. D.R.E.: Lori Casey; Jason Pfau.
Students 300.

St. Joseph's, Revs. Richard D. Sedlacek; Daniel G. Dufner; Deacons Michael H. Breier; William Mich; Gilberto Garcia; Sr. Robert Joseph, C.S.J., Pastoral Assoc. In res., Rev. Msgr. Desmond P. Dillon.
Res., 520 S. Garfield, 99336. Tel: 509-586-3820; Fax: 509-586-3558.
School—901 W. 4th Ave., 99336. Tel: 509-586-0481.
Sisters of St. Joseph of Carondelet 5; Lay Teachers 10; Students 354.
Catechesis / Religious Programs—Tel: 509-582-8460. Robert L. Fitzsimmons, D.R.E.
Students 275.

Leavenworth, Chelan Co., Our Lady of the Snows, Rev. Maurice F. Peterson; Deacon Don Griek.
Res., 145 Wheeler St., 98826. Tel: 509-548-5119.
Catechesis / Religious Programs—Students 58.

Mabton, WA, Yakima Co., Immaculate Conception (1910),
Res., 1201 Missouri, Grandview, 98930.
Mailing Address: P.O. Box 275, Mabton, 98935. Tel: 509-882-1657; Fax: 509-882-1107.
Catechesis / Religious Programs—Students 61.

Mattawa, Grant Co., Our Lady of the Desert, Rev. Francisco Hernandez-Gonzalez.
Mailing Address: P.O. Box 1717, 99349. Tel: 509-932-5424.
Catechesis/Religious Programs—Students 112.

Moses Lake, Grant Co., Our Lady of Fatima, Revs. John Morse, S.J.; Argemiro Orozco. In res., Rev. Msgr. Martin O. Skehan, (Retired).
Res., 318 W. Northshore Dr., 98837. Tel: 509-765-6729; Fax: 509-765-0114.
Parish Center—300 N. White Dr., 98837. Tel: 509-765-6311.
Catechesis/Religious Programs—Vinci Halbrook-Paterson, D.R.E.
Students 350.

Moxee City, Yakima Co., Holy Rosary, Rev. Msgr. Edmond G. McGrath.
Res., 201 N. Iler, P.O. Box 279, Moxee, 98936. Tel: 509-453-4061. [CEM]
Catechesis/Religious Programs—Tel: 509-453-6754. Patricia Verhey, D.R.E.
Students 198.
Convent—Tel: 509-248-6723.
Sisters of Providence 1.

Naches, Yakima Co., St. John's, Rev. George Purdy, S.J., Admin.
Res., 211 Moxee Ave., P.O. Box 128, 98937. Tel: 509-653-2534.

Prosser, Benton Co., Sacred Heart, Revs. Donal P. Kennedy; Bulmaro Alvarado Martinez.
Res., 1905 Highland Dr., 99350. Tel: 509-786-1783.
Catechesis/Religious Programs—Tel: 509-973-2265. Cynthia O'Brien, D.R.E.
Students 146.

Quincy, Grant Co., St. Pius X, Revs. Kenneth M. Kron; Mario P. Salazar.
Res., 805 Central Ave., N., P.O. Box 308, 98848. Tel: 509-787-2622.
Catechesis/Religious Programs—Tel: 509-787-3116. Kathleen Horning, D.R.E.
Students 324.

Richland, Benton Co., Christ the King, Revs. Thomas C. Champoux, Admin.; Richard A. Wuertz; Thomas S. Kuykendall; Deacons Robert DaValle; LeRoi Rice; Alfred Rizzo.
Office: 1126 Long Ave., 99352. Tel: 509-946-1675; Fax: 509-946-9940.
School—1122 Long Ave., 99352. Tel: 509-946-6158.
Lay Teachers 18; Students 356.
Catechesis/Religious Programs—Tel: 509-946-1675. LeRoi Rice, D.R.E.
Students 720.

Roslyn, Kittitas Co., Immaculate Conception, Rev. William Byron.
Mailing Address: Idaho B, Box 611, 98941. Tel: 509-674-2531.

Royal City, Grant Co., St. Michael the Archangel, Rev. Salomon P. Covarrubias; Deacon Francisco Martinez.
Res., P.O. Box 340, 99357. Tel: 509-346-2730.
Catechesis/Religious Programs—Students 130.

Selah, Yakima Co., Our Lady of Lourdes, Very Rev. Michael J. Ibach.
Res., 1112 W. Fremont, 98942. Tel: 509-697-4633.
Catechesis/Religious Programs—Fax: 509-697-7189. Sandra Seward, D.R.E.
Students 160.

Sunnyside, Yakima Co., St. Joseph's, Rev. Philip M. Cioppa.
Res., 920 S. 6th St., 98944. Tel: 509-837-2243; Fax: 509-837-7063.
School—(Grades K-8). Tel: 509-839-2241.
Missionary Daughters of the Most Pure Virgin Mary 1; Lay Teachers 10; Students 160.
Catechesis/Religious Programs—Students 450.
Convent—Tel: 509-837-2242.
Missionary Daughters of the Most Pure Virgin Mary 5.

Toppenish, Yakima Co., St. Aloysius, Revs. John M. Shaw; Osmar R. Aguirre. In res., Rev. Victor Alvarez, S.S.P. (Mexico).
Res., 213 N. Beech St., 98948. Tel: 509-865-4725; 865-2380; Fax: 509-865-3077.
Religious Education Center—214 N. Beech St., 98948. Tel: 509-865-2565.
St. Vincent De Paul Center—11 S. B, 98948. Tel: 509-865-5311.
Catechesis/Religious Programs—Darlene Riojas, D.R.E.
Students 253.

Wapato, Yakima Co., St. Peter Claver, Revs. Kevin W. Minder; David J. Jimenez; Deacons John Kassinger; Antonio Osorio.
Res., 509 S. Satus Ave., 98951. Tel: 509-877-2813.
Catechesis/Religious Programs—Tel: 509-877-4881.
Students 337.

Warden, Grant Co., Queen of All Saints (1966), Revs. John Morse, S.J.; Argemiro Orozco.
318 W. Northshore Dr., Moses Lake, 98837. Tel: 509-765-6729; Fax: 509-765-0114.
Catechesis/Religious Programs—Tel: 509-349-0403.
Students 90.

Waterville, Douglas Co., St. Joseph's, Rev. Bonifacio Salvana.
Res., Poplar St., P.O. Box 519, 98858. Tel: 509-745-8205.
Catechesis/Religious Programs—Noreen Daling, D.R.E.
Students 60.

Wenatchee, Chelan Co., St. Joseph's, Revs. Ronald J. Patnode; Robert Sewvello; Deacon Bill Osborn.
Res., 504 S. Chelan, P.O. Box 2138, 98807. Tel: 509-662-4569; Fax: 509-663-8437.
School—(Grades PreK-5). Tel: 509-663-2644; Fax: 509-663-8474.
Lay Teachers 9; Students 165.

White Salmon, Klickitat Co., St. Joseph, Rev. Thomas S. Dahlquist.
Res., 240 N.W. Washington., P.O. Box 2049, 98672. Tel: 509-493-2828.
Catechesis/Religious Programs—Tel: 509-493-1255.
Students 60.

White Swan, Yakima Co., St. Mary's, Rev. David Jimenez.
Res., P.O. Box 417, 98952. Tel: 509-874-2436.
Catechesis/Religious Programs—Anita Griffin, D.R.E.
Students 32.

Zillah, Yakima Co., Resurrection, Rev. William E. Shaw.
Mailing Address: P.O. Box 567, 98953-0567. Tel: 509-829-5433.
Catechesis/Religious Programs—Tel: 509-829-6244. Betty Collins, D.R.E.
Students 105.

On Duty Outside the Diocese:
Reverend Fathers—
Cerezo, Alberto F., 11637 100th Ave., N.E., #C2W, Kirkland, WA 98034
Dorian, Brendan, 330 West Coral Gables Dr., Phoenix, AZ 85023
Gallagher Brian T., 745 Mt. Rose, Reno, NV 89509
Kenna, Joseph J., 929 Lakefront Dr., Bowie, MD 20785
Keolker, Richard F., Mount Angel Seminary, 119 Anselm, St. Benedict, OR 97373
Moore, Michael, 218 Ackerman, Clifton, NJ 07011
Norman, Gary R., P.O. Box 508, Petersburg, AK 99833

Military Chaplains:
Reverend Fathers—
Greene, Daniel P., V.A. Admin. Med. Ctr., Chaplain Serv., Bay Pines, FL 33504

Retired:
Reverend Monsignors—
Dillon, Desmond P., St. Joseph Parish, 520 S. Garfield, Kennewick, WA 99336
Skehan, Martin O., W. 318 Northshore Dr., Moses Lake, WA 98837
Reverend Fathers—
Byron, Patrick J., Our Lady's House, Pallashill, Pallasgreane, Limerick, Ireland
Camacho, Enrique, Apartado Postal 7 Cocula, Jalisco, CP 48500 Mexico
Hannick, Anthony S., 1600 Roosmoor Pkwy., Walnut Creek, CA 94553
Heneghan, John F., Waverly Collacoon, Mayo, Ireland
Schindler, John H., P.O. Box 356, Chelan, WA 98816
Wawrzynski, Edward A., U.S.A.F.R., 5856 106th Ter., N., Pinellas Park, FL 34666

Permanent Deacons:
Alvarado, Berney, 91 York Ln., Zillah, WA 98953
Berger, Duane, 1706 Lower Ahtanum, Yakima, WA 98903
Breier, Michael, 2409 S. Conway, Kennewick, WA 99337
Burnham, Walter, 300 S. 76th Ave., #67, Yakima, WA 98908
Chavez, Nestor, 706 S. 8th St., Yakima, WA 98901
Cornell, John, 2504 W. Chestnut, Yakima, WA 98902
DaValle, Robert, 1837 Marshall Ave., Richland, WA 99352
Dronen, Bill, 306 Railroad Ave., Cashmere, 98815
Gilberto, Garcia, 18 N. Mayfield, Kennewick, WA 99336
Griek, Don, Mailing Address: P.O. Box 1023, Leavenworth, WA 98826
Henn, Thomas W., 455 Carner Ct. W., Richland, WA 99352
Kassinger, John, 1314 N. Ave., #4, Sunnyside, WA 98944
Kramper, James, 111 N. 26th Ave., Yakima, WA 98902
Loranger, Bill, 1104 10th St., N.E., East Wenatchee, WA 98801
Martinez, Frank, 3790 Rd. 10.4 S.W., Royal City, WA 99357
Mich, William, 601 N. Reed, Kennewick, WA 99336
Miller, Ray, 2412 W. Chestnut, Yakima, WA 98902
Osborn, Bill, 410 Cottage Ave., Cashmere, WA 98815
Osorio, Antonio, 14 S. I St., Toppenish, WA 98948
Powers, John, 3103 S. Dayton, Kennewick, WA 98837
Reyna, Lupe, 1130 S. Grand, Moses Lake, WA 98837
Rice, LeRoi, 1845 Mahan Ave., Richland, WA 99352
Rizzo, Al, 135 MacArthur St., Richland, WA 99352
Spence, Jack, 351 Hanson Rd., Ellensburg, WA 98926

INSTITUTIONS LOCATED IN THE DIOCESE

[A] COLLEGES AND UNIVERSITIES

*TOPPENISH. *Heritage College*, 3240 Fort Rd., 98948. Tel: 509-865-2244.
For a complete listing, refer to the Colleges and Universities section.

[B] HOSPITALS

YAKIMA. *Providence Yakima Medical Center*, 110 S. 9th Ave., 98902. Tel: 509-575-5000.
For a complete listing, refer to the Hospitals section.

RICHLAND. *Carondelet Behavioral Health Center*, 1175 Carondelet Dr., 99352. Tel: 509-943-9104.
For a complete listing, refer to the Hospitals section.

TOPPENISH. *Providence Hospital*, 504 W. 4th Ave., P.O. Box 672, 98948. Tel: 509-865-3105.
For a complete listing, refer to the Hospitals section.

[C] CATHOLIC SOCIAL SERVICE CATHOLIC CHARITIES

YAKIMA. *Carroll Children's Center*, 5301-H Tieton Dr., 98908. Tel: 509-965-7104. Maureen Mould, Dir. Capacity 150.
Catholic Charities of the Diocese of Yakima, 5301-C Tieton Dr., 98908. Tel: 509-965-7100. Mr. John L. Young, Exec. Dir.
Catholic Family and Child Service, 5301-C Tieton Dr., 98908. Tel: 509-965-7100. Mrs. Darlene Darnell, M.S.W., Branch Dir.
Day Care Nutrition, 5301-C Tieton Dr., 98908. Tel: 509-965-7107.
St. Vincent de Paul Store, 2629 S. First St., 98903. Tel: 509-457-5111. Mr. Frank McGree, Mgr. (Of All Stores in Diocese).

CHELAN. *St. Vincent de Paul Store*, 404 E. Woodin, P.O. Box 2387, 98816. Tel: 509-682-3655.

ELLENSBURG. *St. Vincent de Paul Store*, 1200 Canyon St., 98926. Tel: 509-925-2167.

EPHRATA. *Catholic Family and Child Service*, P.O. Box 191, 98823. Tel: 509-754-2211.

GRANDVIEW. *Catholic Family and Child Service*, 322 Division, P.O. Box 22, 98930. Tel: 509-882-3050. Kathryn J. Wilson, Supvr.

KENNEWICK. *St. Vincent de Paul Store*, 1401 W. Kennewick Ave., 99336. Tel: 509-586-1053.

MOSES LAKE. *Catholic Family and Child Service*, 414 Burress St., P.O. Box 672, 98837. Tel: 509-765-1875.

RICHLAND. *Catholic Family and Child Service*, 2139 Van Giesen, P.O. Box 1504, 99352. Tel: 509-946-4645. Judith Dirks, Branch Dir.

SUNNYSIDE. *St. Vincent de Paul Store*, 305 North Ave., 98944. Tel: 509-837-2055.

WENATCHEE. *Catholic Family and Child Service*, Morris Bldg., No. 320, 23 S. Wenatchee Ave., 98801. Tel: 509-662-6761. Ray Kennedy, Branch Dir.
St. Vincent de Paul Store, 330 S. Wenatchee Ave., 98801. Tel: 509-662-6010.

[D] RETIREMENT HOMES

YAKIMA.
**The Gamelin Association-Providence House*, 314 N. 4th St., 98901-2459. Tel: 509-452-5017. Sr. Shaughn Gorman, Dir.

[E] VOLUNTEER SERVICES

YAKIMA. *Holy Family Parish Conference*, 5315 Tieton Dr., 98908. Tel: 509-966-0830.
Holy Redeemer Parish Conference, 1609 Landon Ave., 98902. Tel: 509-248-2241. Raymond Faith, Pres.
St. Joseph's Parish Conference, 212 N. 4th St., 98901. Tel: 509-248-1911. Mrs. O. Gress, Pres.

St. Paul's Parish Conference, 15 S. 12th Ave., 98902. Tel: 509-575-3713; Fax: 509-453-7497. Dave Uhlman, Pres.; Phil Salatino, Vice Pres.; Fred Schilling, Treas.

Society of St. Vincent de Paul, Particular Council of Yakima, 2629 S. First St., 98903. Tom Maravilla, Pres.

EAST WENATCHEE. *Holy Apostles Parish Conference*, P.O. Box 7279, 98801. Tel: 509-884-5444. Paul White, Pres.

KENNEWICK. *St. Joseph Parish Conference*, 520 S. Garfield, 99336. Tel: 509-586-7569; Fax: 509-586-3558. Ramon Cardova, Pres.

MOSES LAKE. *Our Lady of Fatima Parish Conference*, W. 318 Northshore Dr., 98837. Tel: 509-765-6729. Wayne Vadnais, Pres.

RICHLAND. *Christ the King Parish Conference*, 1126 Long Ave., 99352. Tel: 509-946-1675. Bob Morford, Pres.

TOPPENISH. *St. Aloysius Parish Conference*, 213 N. Beech St., 98948. Tel: 509-865-4725.

St. Vincent de Paul Center, 213 N. Beech St., 98948. 11 S. B St., 98948. Tel: 509-865-5311. Adriana Hede, Dir.

WENATCHEE. *St. Joseph Parish Conference, St Vincent de Paul*, 1125 Idaho St., 98801. Tel: 509-662-4569. V. E. Houck, Pres.

WHITE SALMON. *St. Joseph Parish Conference*, P.O. Box 1161, 98672. Tel: 509-493-1980. Leo Gauvin, Pres.

[F] RETREAT HOUSES

COWICHE. *St. Peter the Apostle Retreat Center*, 15880 Summitview Rd., 98923. Tel: 509-678-4164. Rev. Lawrence T. Reilly, Dir.

[G] CAMPUS MINISTRY

ELLENSBURG. *Catholic Campus Ministry at Central Washington University*, 706 N. Sprague, 98926. Tel: 509-925-3043. Mr. Joseph Kiesel-Nield, Dir. & Campus Min.

[H] MISCELLANEOUS LISTINGS

YAKIMA. *La Salle High School, Yakima, Inc.*, 105 S. Third St., 98902. Tel: 509-457-6835. Mr. Timothy Edwards, Chm. & Contact Person.

Reach Youth Ministry, Christ the King Center, 1704 Grant, 98902. Tel: 509-575-8754. Mark Evevard, Dir.

SUNNYSIDE. *Ministerio Nueva Vida*, P.O. Box 911, 98944. Tel: 509-839-4331.

TOPPENISH. *Association of Catholic Sisters for Educational Opportunities for the Poor*, 3240 Fort Rd., 98948. Sr. Kathleen Ross, S.N.J.M., Pres.

RELIGIOUS INSTITUTES OF MEN REPRESENTED IN THE DIOCESE

For further details refer to the corresponding bracketed number in the Religious Institutes of Men or Women section.

[0200]—*Benedictine Monks (American Cassinese Congregation)*.—O.S.B.

[0690]—*Jesuit Fathers and Brothers (Oregon Providence)*.—S.J.

[0910]—*Oblates of Mary Immaculate*.—O.M.I.

RELIGIOUS INSTITUTES OF WOMEN REPRESENTED IN THE DIOCESE

[0230]—*Benedictine Sisters of Pontifical Jurisdiction*.—O.S.B.

[1070-20]—*Dominican Sisters*.—O.P.

[]—*Missionary Daughters of the Most Pure Virgin Mary*.

[2790]—*Missionary Servants of the Most Blessed Trinity*.—M.S.B.T.

[3350]—*Sisters of Providence (Prov. of Sacred Heart)*.—S.P.

[3840]—*Sisters of St. Joseph of Carondelet*.—C.S.J.

[1990]—*Sisters of the Holy Names of Jesus and Mary*.—S.N.J.M.

[2160]—*Sisters, Servants of the Immaculate Heart of Mary*.—I.H.M.

NECROLOGY

† Quintana, Rev. Msgr. Eusebio, White Swan, WA, St. Mary's Church. —Died Sept. 24, 1996.

† Sweeney, Rev. Msgr. William J., (Retired). —Died Jan. 9, 1996.

Diocese of Youngstown

(Dioecesis Youngstoniensis)

Most Reverend

THOMAS J. TOBIN, D.D.

Bishop of Youngstown; ordained July 21, 1973; appointed Titular Bishop of Novica and Auxiliary Bishop of Pittsburgh, November 3, 1992; appointed Fourth Bishop of Youngstown; installed February 2, 1996.

Most Reverend

BENEDICT C. FRANZETTA, D.D.

Retired Auxiliary Bishop of Youngstown; ordained April 29, 1950; appointed Titular Bishop of Oderzo and Auxiliary July 29, 1980; consecrated September 4, 1980; retired September 4, 1996. *Res., St. Columba Rectory, 159 W. Rayen Ave., Youngstown, OH, 44503.*

Most Reverend

JAMES W. MALONE, D.D.

Retired Bishop of Youngstown; ordained May 26, 1945; appointed Titular Bishop of Alabanda and Auxiliary January 2, 1960; consecrated March 24, 1960; appointed Apostolic Administrator January 22, 1966; succeeded to the See May 2, 1968; retired December 4, 1995. *Res., 6796 Tanglewood Dr., Youngstown, OH, 44512.*

Chancery Office: 144 W. Wood St., Youngstown, OH, 44503. Tel.: 330-744-8451; Fax: 330-742-6448; 744-2848.

ESTABLISHED MAY 15, 1943.

CANONICALLY ERECTED JULY 22, 1943.

Square Miles 3,404.

Comprises six Counties in the northeastern part of the State of Ohio, namely, Ashtabula, Columbiana, Mahoning, Portage, Stark and Trumbull Counties.

For legal titles of parishes and diocesan institutions, consult the Chancery Office.

STATISTICAL OVERVIEW

Personnel	
Bishop	1
Retired Bishops	2
Priests: Diocesan Active in Diocese	121
Priests: Active Outside Diocese	7
Priests: Retired, Sick or Absent	75
Number of Diocesan Priests	203
Religious Priests in Diocese	31
Extern Priests in Diocese	1
Ordinations:	
Diocesan Priests	2
Transitional Deacons	1
Permanent Deacons	2
Permanent Deacons in Diocese	51
Total Brothers	23
Total Sisters	284
Parishes	
Parishes	115
With Resident Pastor:	
Resident Diocesan Priests	97
Resident Religious Priests	5
Without Resident Pastor:	
Administered by Priests	11
Administered by Women Religious	2
Missions	2
Professional Ministry Personnel:	
Brothers	5
Sisters	39
Lay Ministers	65
Welfare	
Catholic Hospitals	3
Total Assisted	587,465
Homes for the Aged	3
Total Assisted	390
Day Care and Extended Day Care Centers	2
Total Assisted	70
Specialized Homes	7
Total Assisted	288
Special Centers for Social Services	5
Total Assisted	37,560
Other Institutions	2
Total Assisted	370
Educational	
Diocesan Students in Other Seminaries	7
Total Seminarians	7
Colleges and Universities	1
Total Students	1,447
High Schools, Diocesan and Parish	5
Total Students	2,933
High Schools, Private	1
Total Students	92
Elementary Schools, Diocesan and Parish	47
Total Students	12,242
Catechesis/Religious Education:	
High School Students	4,547
Elementary Students	15,362
Total Students Under Catholic Instruction	36,630
Teachers in the Diocese:	
Priests	6
Brothers	5
Sisters	65
Lay Teachers	859
Vital Statistics	
Receptions into the Church:	
Infant Baptism Totals	3,377
Adult Baptism Totals	382
Received into Full Communion	671
First Communions	3,587
Confirmations	2,409
Marriages:	
Catholic	840
Interfaith	714
Total Marriages	1,554
Deaths	3,138
Total Catholic Population	260,541
Total Population	1,229,220

Former Bishops—Most Rev. JAMES A. MCFADDEN, S.T.D., LL.D., appt. Titular Bishop of Bida and Auxiliary of Cleveland, May 13, 1932; cons. Sept. 8, 1932; appt. Bishop of Youngstown, June 2, 1943; died Nov. 16, 1952.—Most Rev. EMMET M. WALSH, D.D., ord. Jan. 15, 1916; appt. Bishop of Charleston, June 20, 1927; appt. Titular Bishop of Rhaedestus and Coadjutor, Sept. 8, 1949; succeeded to See, Nov. 16, 1952; died March 16, 1968.—Most Rev. JAMES W. MALONE, D.D., ord. May 26, 1945; appt. Titular Bishop of Alabanda and Auxiliary, Jan. 2, 1960; appt. Apostolic Administrator, Jan. 22, 1966; succeeded to See, May 2, 1968; retired Dec. 4, 1995.—

All Diocesan offices and personnel can be reached at 144 W. Wood St., Youngstown, OH, 44503, Tel: 330-744-8451, Fax: 330-742-6448; 744-2848 unless otherwise indicated.

Chancery Office

Vicar General and Moderator of the Curia—Rev. ROBERT J. SIFFRIN.

Chancellor—Mrs. NANCY YUHASZ.

"The Catholic Exponent," Diocesan Newspaper—Most Rev. THOMAS J. TOBIN, Publisher; Mr. LOUIS JACQUET, Editor & Assoc. Publisher. Tel: 330-744-5251.

Catholic Women, Diocesan Council of—Rev. JAMES A. CLARKE, Moderator, *157 Ohio Ave., Salem, 44460.* Tel: 330-332-0336.

College of Consultors—Revs. MICHAEL CARIGLIO; GERALD DELUCIA; JOHN DEMARINIS; JOHN FINNIGAN; TERRENCE HAZEL; JAMES MCKARNS; JOHN MULQUEEN; ROBERT SIFFRIN; DANIEL VENGLARIK.

Communications—

Catholic Television Network of Youngstown (CTNY)—Revs. JAMES KORDA, Pastoral Dir. GERALD DELUCIA, Asst. Pastoral Dir., *P.O. Box 430, Canfield, 44406-0430.* Tel: 330-533-2243.

Public-Media Relations—NANCY YUHASZ.

Development / Stewardship—Mr. PAT PALOMBO, Dir., The Foundation of the Roman Catholic Diocese of Youngstown.

Ecumenism—Rev. JOSEPH WITMER, Dir., Ecumenical Commission, *342 S. Chillicothe, Aurora, 44202.* Tel: 216-562-8519.

Office of Missions / Evangelization—Rev. PAUL HILL, M.S.C., Dir.

Scouting, Diocesan Office—Rev. JAMES R. KOLP, Dir., *206 Cherry Rd. N.E., Massillon, 44646.* Tel: 330-833-8501.

Department of Canonical Services

Rev. WILLIAM J. CONNELL, J.C.L., Exec. Dir., *141 W. Rayen Ave., Youngstown, 44503.* Tel: 330-744-8451.

Office of Conciliation—

Matrimonial Dispensations—

Tribunal—

Judicial Vicar—Rev. WILLIAM J. CONNELL, J.C.L.

Adjutant Judicial Vicar—Rev. MICHAEL J. CARIGLIO, J.C.L.

Judges—Revs. LAWRENCE C. FYE; ROBERT A. SABATINO, Ph.D.; PETER M. POLANDO, J.C.L.

Defenders of the Bond—Revs. MARTIN SUSKO, J.C.L.; FREDERICK LUKEHART; RICHARD REIS.

Advocates—Sr. PAULINE DALPE, O.S.U.; Revs. BERNARD N. GAETA; J. PATRICK MANNING; KEVIN PETERS; JOHN A. ZURAW.

Promoter of Justice—Rev. MARTIN SUSKO, J.C.L.

Notaries—BARBARA ROGICH; PATRICIA BOGGS; JULIE TABAKA; COLLEEN HARRIS.

Department of Catholic Charities Services; Sr. CONSOLATA KLINE, H.M., Exec. Dir

Office of Social Action—Mr. BRIAN CORBIN, Dir., Environment, Hunger & Rural Life Committee; Housing & Community Devel. Committee; Minorities Commission; Respect Life Committee; Diocesan Commission on the Role of Women in the Church and in Society.

Office of Social Services—Mrs. MARY ELLEN ANDERSON, Dir., Health & Human Svcs. Commission, Antonine Sisters Adult DayCare Center; Sr. CONSOLATA KLINE, H.M., Liaison to St. Vincent DePaul Society.

St. Vincent DePaul Society—Mr. PETER ANANIA, Pres., *235 Wick Ave., Youngstown, 44503.* Tel: 330-746-5222.

Department of Clergy and Religious Services

Rev. JOHN ZURAW, Exec. Dir.

Office of Vocations—Rev. JOHN ZURAW, Dir.

Serra International, Serra Club of Youngstown—Rev. FREDERICK LUKEHART, Chap., *4545 New Road, Austintown, 44515.* Tel: 216-792-1919.

Office for Clergy Services—Rev. JOHN ZURAW, Dir.

Priests' Council—Rev. JAMES KORDA, Chm., *811 Oak St., Youngstown, 44506.* Tel: 330-747-3533.

Office of Continuing Education—Rev. STEPHEN POPOVICH, Dir., *4490 Norquest Blvd., Youngstown, 44515.* Tel: 330-793-9988.

Office of Priests' Personnel Advisor—Rev. THOMAS EISWEIRTH, *400 Lincoln Park Dr., Youngstown, 44506.* Tel: 330-747-6080.

Office of Permanent Diaconate—Rev. ROBERT SABATINO, Dir.

Office of Religious—Sr. ROSEMARY MURRAY, H.M., Dir.

Diocesan Conference of Religious—Sr. ROSEMARY MURRAY, H.M., Dir.

Department of Financial Services

Rev. JOHN H. DEMARINIS, Treasurer & Econome; Mr. ROBERT A. HOFFMAN, Exec. Dir., Finance & Oper. Directors of Finance: Mr. JOHN DIDEK, JR.; Mrs. MARGARET FISHER; Sr. M. GERTRUDE PARIS, O.S.U, Dir. Admin. Svcs. Accounting, Auditing, Payroll/ Benefits, Property, Insurance.

Office of Cemeteries—Rev. FRANK A. CARFAGNA, Dir.

Office of Data Processing—Mr. LOUIS ORBIN, Dir.

Department of Pastoral and Educational Services

Rev. KENNETH E. MILLER, Exec. Dir.

Office of Catholic Schools—Dr. NICHOLAS WOLSONOVICH, Supt.; Sr. MARY BRENDON ZAJACK, S.N.D., Asst. Supt. Curriculum; Mr. THOMAS WELCSH, Dir. Certificated Personnel; Mr. WALLACE DUNNE, Dir. Gov't Programs & Resource Devel.

Board of Education—Rev. THOMAS DYER, Pres. LINDA BURKEY, Vice Pres.

The Catholic Diocese of Youngstown Educational Fund, Inc.

Office of Religious Education—BARBARA WALKO, Diocesan Dir., *225 Elm St., Youngstown, 44503.* Tel: 330-744-8451. THOMAS SAULINE, Consultant; CARLETTE CHORDAS, Media Resources.

Board of Religious Education—Ms. JANE SPEAR, Pres.; Mr. JAMES NAEGLI, Vice Pres.

Office of Youth Ministry—Sr. DIANNE LIVINGSTONE, M.H.S.H., Dir.; Mr. JAMES MERHAUT, Assoc. Dir.

Office of Campus Ministry—Sr. PATRICIA SLATER, S.N.D., Diocesan Dir., *254 Madison Ave., Youngstown, 44503.* Tel: 330-747-9202.

Hiram College—Rev. RICHARD J. PENTELLO, *St. Ambrose Parish, 10692 Freedom St., Garrettsville, 44231.* Tel: 330-527-4105.

Immaculate Heart of Mary University Parish (Kent State Newman Center)—Rev. JOHN JEREK, Pastor; MARCIE BIRCHER, Campus Min.; Deacon JOE RUDJAK, *1424 Horning Rd., Kent, 44240.* Tel: 330-678-0240.

Stark State College of Technology-Kent State Stark—Sr. VIRGINIA COLDREN, C.S.J., *Interfaith Campus Ministry, 6200 Frank Ave. N.W., Canton, 44720.* Tel: 330-489-1000 ext. 1992; 494-6170 ext. 264.

Walsh University—Rev. DON MILLER, O.F.M.; Sr. CAROL HEBERT, S.S.J., *2020 Easton St., N.W., North Canton, 44720.* Tel: 330-499-7344.

Youngstown State University—Sr. PATRICIA SLATER, S.N.D., *254 Madison Ave., Youngstown, 44504.* Tel: 330-747-9202.

Office of Worship—FRAN AMER, Dir.

Liturgical Commission—

Office of Parish Life—Sr. ELIZABETH APEL, C.D.P., Dir.

Office of Lay Ministry Formation—EILEEN NOVOTNY, Dir.

Office of Marriage & Family Life—Mr. DAVID SCHMIDT, Dir.

Other Ministries

Catholic Alumni Club of Youngstown, Inc.—Rev. ANDREW TORMA, M.S.C., Chap., *3128 Logan Ave., Youngstown, 44505.* Tel: 330-759-9359.

Charismatic Prayer Group—Rev. ROBERT EDWARDS, Dir., *271 Chestnut St., Lisbon, 44432.* Tel: 330-442-7648.

Disabled Services—

Physically and Developmentally—Rev. TERRENCE HAZEL, Chap., *2121 Reno Dr., Louisville, 44641.* Tel: 330-875-1631.

Deaf and Hearing Impaired—Rev. ROBERT SIFFRIN, Chap., *144 W. Wood St., Youngstown, 44503.* Tel: 330-744-8451.

Spanish Speaking—Rev. JOHN DAILEY, *50 Struthers-Coitsville Rd., Youngstown, 44505.* Tel: 330-755-3633.

CLERGY, PARISHES, MISSIONS AND PAROCHIAL SCHOOLS

CITY OF YOUNGSTOWN (Mahoning County)

1—CATHEDRAL OF ST. COLUMBA (1845), Revs. Lawrence C. Fye, M.Ed., V.F.; William J. Connell, J.C.L., Vice Rector. In res., Most Rev. Benedict C. Franzetta, D.D., V.G., (Retired).
Res., 159 W. Rayen Ave., 44503. Tel: 330-744-5233. [JC]

2—HOLY NAME (1916) (Slovak), Rev. Michael E. Ronik.
Res., 613 N. Lakeview Ave., 44509. Tel: 330-799-8873.

3—IMMACULATE CONCEPTION (1882), Rev. J. James Korda; Sr. Mary Lee Nalley, O.S.U., Pastoral Min.
Res., 811 Oak St., 44506. Tel: 330-747-3533; Fax: 330-747-3533.
School—810 Oak St., 44506. Tel: 330-747-9471. Mrs. Pat Yacucci, Prin.
Lay Teachers 9; Students 216.
Convent—835 Oak St., 44506. Tel: 330-744-2214.

4—IMMACULATE HEART OF MARY, Mahoning Co., (1954), Rev. Stephen Popovich. In res., Rev. William Yurko.
Res., 4490 Norquest Blvd., 44515. Tel: 330-793-9988.
School—Tel: 330-799-1944; Fax: 330-799-0151.
Sisters 3; Lay Teachers 9; Students 253.
Catechesis/Religious Programs—Tel: 330-799-4202.
Students 200.

5—OUR LADY OF HUNGARY (1929) (Hungarian), Rev. John E. Reiss, O.F.M.
Res., 545 N. Belle Vista, 44509. Tel: 330-799-6829 (Office).

6—OUR LADY OF MT. CARMEL (1908) (Italian), Rev. Michael J. Cariglio, J.C.L.
Res., 343 Via Mt. Carmel, 44505. Tel: 330-743-4144; Fax: 330-743-1035.
Catechesis/Religious Programs—Tel: 216-743-3508.
Students 190.

7—SACRED HEART OF JESUS (1888), Rev. Thomas Eisweirth; Deacon Joseph Zamary.
Res., 400 Lincoln Park Dr., 44506. Tel: 330-747-6080; Fax: 330-747-7003.
School—Combined with Immaculate Conception. Tel: 330-747-9471.

8—ST. ANTHONY'S (1898) (Italian), Rev. John H. DeMarinis.
Res., 1125 Turin Ave., 44510. Tel: 330-744-5091.

9—ST. BRENDAN'S (1923), Rev. Richard A. Brobst. In res., Rev. Robert Siffrin.
Res., 2800 Oakwood Ave., 44509. Tel: 330-792-3875; 792-3876; Fax: 330-792-9080.
School—144 N. Schenley Ave., 44509. Tel: 216-799-9741.
Catechesis/Religious Programs—Tel: 216-792-9080.
Students 230.

10—ST. CASIMIR'S (1903), Rev. Sy Kaminski.
Office: 149 Jefferson St., 44510. Tel: 330-743-3951.
Res., 1115 Eveningstar Dr., Rome, 44085-9763. Tel: 330-563-5316.

11—ST. CHRISTINE'S (1953), Revs. David W. Rhodes; Patrick B. Ferraro.
Res., 3165 S. Schenley Ave., 44511. Tel: 330-792-3829; Fax: 330-792-3820. [CEM]
School—3125 S. Schenley Ave., 44511. Tel: 330-792-4545; Fax: 330-792-6888.
Lay Teachers 20; Students 538.
Catechesis/Religious Programs—Tel: 216-793-0544.
Students 899.

12—SS. CYRIL AND METHODIUS, Mahoning Co., (1896) (Slovak). Unassigned.
Res., 252 E. Wood St., 44503. Tel: 330-743-5291.
Catechesis/Religious Programs—Students 71.

13—ST. DOMINIC'S (1923), Revs. Jacob Restrick, O.P.; William J. Rock, O.P.; Ernest Kelly, O.P., Chap. South Side; Matthew Erickson, O.P.; Robert R. Heuschkel; Andre-Joseph Lacasse, O.P.
Res., 77 E. Lucius Ave., 44507. Tel: 216-783-1900; Fax: 216-783-2396.
School—3403 Southern Blvd., 44507. Tel: 330-782-1123; Fax: 330-782-4616. John R. Rozzo, Prin.
Lay Teachers 13; Students 239.
Catechesis/Religious Programs—Students 170.

14—ST. EDWARD'S (1917), Rev. Frank M. Lehnerd.
Res., 240 Tod Ln., 44504. Tel: 330-743-2308; Fax: 330-743-1882.
School—(Grades K-8). Tel: 330-746-0576; Fax: 330-743-8321.
Lay Teachers 14; Students 238.
Catechesis/Religious Programs—Students 64.

15—ST. ELIZABETH'S (1922) (Slovak), Rev. George Duritsa, Admin.
Res., 124 Keystone St., Campbell, 44405. Tel: 330-747-4085; Fax: 330-747-8647.

16—ST. JOSEPH (1966), Revs. Frederick Lukehart; Joseph James.
Res., 4545 New Rd., Austintown, 44515. Tel: 330-792-1919.
School—Tel: 330-793-1250.
Lay Teachers 12; Students 205.
Catechesis/Religious Programs—Tel: 216-792-1934. Mrs. Lori Pugh, D.R.E.
Students 851.

17—ST. MATTHIAS (1914) (Slovak), Rev. Peter M. Polando, J.C.L.; Deacon Salvatore DiFrancesco.
Res., 915 Cornell Ave., 44502-2765. Tel: 330-788-5082; Fax: 330-788-2383.
School—2800 Shady Run Rd., 44502-2700. Tel: 330-788-0241; Fax: 330-788-0534.
Vincentian Sisters of Charity 3; Lay Teachers 8; Students 199.
Convent—937 Cornell Ave., 44502-2765. Tel: 330-788-5732.
Catechesis/Religious Programs—Students 202.

18—ST. PATRICK'S (1911), Rev. Edward P. Noga.
Res., 1420 Oak Hill Ave., 44507. Tel: 330-743-1109.

19—SS. PETER AND PAUL'S, Mahoning Co., (1911) (Croatian), Rev. Branimir Radetic.
Res., 421 Covington St., 44510. Tel: 330-747-6762.

20—ST. ROSE OF LIMA (1961) (Hispanic), Deacon Felipe Colon.
Res., 50 Struthers-Coitsville Rd., 44505. Tel: 330-755-3633.

21—ST. STANISLAUS KOSTKA'S (1902) (Polish), Rev. Edward J. Neroda; Deacon Michael Schlais.
Res., 430 Williamson Ave., 44507. Tel: 330-747-8503.
Catechesis/Religious Programs—Tel: 330-747-3015.
Students 57.

22—ST. STEPHEN OF HUNGARY (1905) (Magyar), Rev. Melvin E. Rusnak.
Church—854 Wilson Ave., 44506. Tel: 330-743-1905.

OUTSIDE THE CITY OF YOUNGSTOWN

Alliance, Stark Co., St. Joseph's (1859), Rev. Donald L. Feicht.
Res., 427 E. Broadway, 44601. Tel: 330-821-5760; Fax: 330-821-5783. [CEM]
Catechesis/Religious Programs—Students 130.

Regina Coeli (1958), Rev. Frank D. Mintjal; Sr. Yvonne Horning, O.P., Pastoral Assoc.
Res., 663 Fernwood Blvd., 44601-2796. Tel: 330-821-5880.
School—733 Fernwood Blvd., 44601-2796. Tel: 330-829-9239.
Lay Teachers 9; Students 204.
Catechesis/Religious Programs—Yvonne Welch, D.R.E.
Students 160.

Andover, Ashtabula Co., Our Lady of Victory (1949), Rev. Lawrence Frient.
Res., 481 S. Main St., P.O. Box 669, 44003-9778. Tel: 216-293-6218.
Catechesis/Religious Programs—Students 51.

Ashtabula, Ashtabula Co., Mother of Sorrows (1890), Rev. Bernard N. Gaeta.
Res., 1514 W. 6th St., 44004. Tel: 216-964-3922.
Catechesis/Religious Programs—Tel: 216-964-8802.
Students 108.

Our Lady of Mt. Carmel (1902) (Italian), Rev. Michael D. Balash.
Res., 1200 E. 21st St., 44004. Tel: 216-998-4111.
Catechesis/Religious Programs—Students 225.

St. Joseph's (1862), Rev. Philip Miller; Deacons Alan Prasek; Richard Johnson.
Res., 3330 Lake Ave., 44004. Tel: 216-997-5666; Fax: 216-993-3579. [CEM]
Mission—Ashtabula, Ashtabula Co., Our Lady of Miracles (St. Joseph Mission), 44004. Tel: 216-997-7121.
Catechesis/Religious Programs—Students 210.

Aurora, Portage Co., Our Lady of Perpetual Help (1955), Rev. Joseph W. Witmer; Sr. Lu Haidnick, C.D.P., Pastoral Assoc.
Res., 342 S. Chillicothe Rd., 44202-7184. Tel: 216-562-8519; Fax: 216-562-2529.
Catechesis/Religious Programs—Ms. Beth Frank, D.R.E.
Students 499.

Boardman, Mahoning Co., St. Charles Borromeo's (1926), Revs. Daniel M. Venglarik; John Keehner; Deacons Michael A. Kocjancic; Thomas Soich; Peter Gross, Business Mgr.
Res., 7345 Westview Dr., Youngstown, 44512. Tel: 330-758-2325; Fax: 330-758-7404.
School—7325 Westview Dr., Youngstown, 44512. Tel: 330-758-6689; Fax: 330-758-7404.
Sisters 1; Lay Teachers 26; Students 622.
Catechesis/Religious Programs—Tel: 216-758-8063. Miss Hedwig Olesky, D.R.E.
Students 943.
Convent—7515 Oregon Tr., Youngstown, 44512. Tel: 330-758-2396.

St. Luke (1962), Rev. Joseph A. Fata; Deacon Richard Milanek. In res., Revs. Gregory Fedor; Kenneth Miller.
Res., 5235 South Ave., 44512. Tel: 330-782-9783; Fax: 330-782-1574.
School—Tel: 330-782-4060.
Lay Teachers 9; Students 200.
Catechesis/Religious Programs—Students 400.

Brewster, Stark Co., St. Therese (1928), Rev. Dacian Barrette.
Res., 456 Wabash Ave., S., 44613. Tel: 330-767-3622. [JC]

Campbell, Mahoning Co., St. John the Baptist (1919) (Slovak), Rev. John S. Trimbur; Deacon Ronald J. Bunofsky.
Res., 159 Reed Ave., 44405. Tel: 330-755-4141. [CEM]
Catechesis/Religious Programs—Tel: 330-755-5251.
Students 57.

St. Joseph the Provider (1919) (Polish), Rev. Leo J. Pleban.
Res., 633 Porter Ave., 44405. Tel: 330-755-0266.
School—Tel: 330-755-4747.
Lay Teachers 9; Students 215.

St. Lucy's (1937) (Italian), Rev. John P. Ashton, Ph.D.
Res., 394 Tenney Ave., 44405. Tel: 330-755-4132.
Catechesis/Religious Programs—Students 91.

Canal Fulton, Stark Co., SS. Philip and James (1845), Rev. John R. Lody.
Res., 412 High St., 44614. Tel: 216-854-2332. [CEM]
School—Tel: 330-854-2823; Fax: 330-854-1109. Ms. Mary Fiala, Prin.
Lay Teachers 13; Students 225.
Catechesis/Religious Programs—Students 241.

Canfield, Mahoning Co., St. Michael's (1965), Rev. James E. O'Brien. Pastoral Ministers: Sr. Margaret Duffy; Sr. ZoeAnn Reiter.
Res., 281 Glenview Dr., 44406. Tel: 330-533-6839; Fax: 330-533-6839.
Catechesis/Religious Programs—Tel: 330-533-5275.
Students 625.

Canton, Stark Co.,

1—All Saints, (1920) (Polish), Rev. John C. Finnigan.
Res., 1386 Henry Ave., S.W., 44706. Tel: 330-453-6429.

2—Our Lady of Peace, (1952), Revs. John Nentwick; John E. Zuzik.
Res., 833 39th St., N.W., 44709. Tel: 330-492-0757; Fax: 330-492-1214.
School—1001 39th St., N.W., 44709. Tel: 330-492-0622; Fax: 330-492-0959.
Sisters 1; Lay Teachers 22; Students 452.
Catechesis/Religious Programs—Tel: 330-492-0929.
Students 230.

3—Sacred Heart, (1922) (Slovak), Rev. William Shipe; Deacon Edward Briestensky.
Res., 1620 Clark Ave., S.W., 44706. Tel: 330-453-1028.

4—St. Anthony's, (1908) (Italian), Rev. Thomas G. Bishop.
Res., 1530 11th St., S.E., 44707. Tel: 330-452-9539; Fax: 330-452-4870.
Catechesis/Religious Programs—Students 150.

5—St. Benedict, (1923), Rev. Carl J. Forgach.
Res., 2207 Third St., S.E., 44707. Tel: 330-452-0751.
Benedict Center: Tel: 330-453-3642.
Church—E. Tuscarawas St. & Girard Ave., S.E., 44707.
Catechesis/Religious Programs—Students 63.

6—St. Joan of Arc, (1944), Revs. Thomas P. Dyer; Kevin Peters; Deacon David Conversino. In res., Rev. John J. Daum.
Res., 4940 Tuscarawas St., W., 44708. Tel: 330-477-6796; 477-6797.
School—120 Bordner Ave., S.W., 44710. Tel: 330-477-2972; Fax: 330-478-2606.
Lay Teachers 15; Students 401.
Catechesis/Religious Programs—166 Bordner Ave., S.W., 44710. G. David Weikart, D.R.E.
Students 333.

7—St. John the Baptist, (1823), Rev. Ronald M. Klingler; Deacon Carl Burkhardt.
Res., 627 McKinley Ave., N.W., 44703. Tel: 330-454-8044. [CEM]

8—St. Joseph's, (1902), Revs. Frank A. Carfagna; James Zanni; Deacon Wilbur J. Bagley.
Res., 2427 W. Tuscarawas St., 44708. Tel: 330-453-2526.
School—126 Columbus Ave., N.W., 44708. Tel: 330-454-9787.
Lay Teachers 13; Students 291.
Catechesis/Religious Programs—Tel: 330-454-2144.
Students 235.

9—St. Mary, (1899), Rev. Gerald J. Sommer, M.S.C.
Res., 1602 Market Ave., S., 44707. Tel: 330-453-2110.

10—St. Michael the Archangel, (1952), Revs. Bradford N. Helman; Charles T. Poore; Sr. Mary Cunningham, H.M., Pastoral Assoc.
Res., 3430 St. Michael's Blvd., N.W., 44718. Tel: 330-492-3119; Fax: 330-492-0339.
School—3505 St. Michael's Blvd., N.W., 44718. Tel: 330-492-2657. Mrs. Patricia Gembar, Prin.
Sisters 2; Lay Teachers 17; Students 526.
Catechesis/Religious Programs—Mr. Michael Ress, D.R.E.
Students 620.

11—St. Paul's, (1907), Rev. Joseph P. Martin; Sr. Darla J. Vogelsang, O.S.U., Pastoral Assoc.
Res., 1459 Superior Ave., N.E., 44705. Tel: 330-456-7555. [JC]
Catechesis/Religious Programs—Students 130.

12—St. Peter's, (1845), Rev. John C. Finnigan. In res., Rev. Robert Bruce.
Res., 726 Cleveland Ave., N.W., 44702. Tel: 330-453-8493; Fax: 330-453-8083. [CEM]
School—702 Cleveland Ave., N.W., 44702. Tel: 330-452-0125.
Sisters of Notre Dame 4; Lay Teachers 9; Students 200.
Catechesis/Religious Programs—Students 143.

Champion, Trumbull Co., St. William (1963), Rev. Michael J. Smar; Sr. Mary Cora Skrivan, S.N.D., D.R.E.
Res., 5411 Mahoning Ave., N.W., Warren, 44483. Tel: 330-847-8677.
Catechesis/Religious Programs—Tel: 330-847-7206.
Students 201.

Columbiana, Columbiana Co., St. Jude (1966), Rev. Thomas G. Ziegler.
Res., 180 7th St., 44408. Tel: 330-482-2351.
Catechesis/Religious Programs—Tel: 330-482-2888. Ms. Mary Glasser, D.R.E.
Students 255.

Conneaut, Ashtabula Co., St. Mary's (1888), Rev. Nathan Willis.
Res., 480 State St., 44030. Tel: 216-599-8855. [CEM][JC]
Catechesis/Religious Programs—Students 250.

St. Frances Cabrini (1954), Rev. Andrew Edward Gretchko.
Res., 744 Mill St., 44030. Tel: 216-599-8570; Fax: 216-593-3772.
School—Tel: 216-593-1677.
Oblate Sisters of the Sacred Heart 1; Lay Teachers 8; Students 160.
Catechesis/Religious Programs—Students 105.

Cortland, Trumbull Co., St. Robert Bellarmine Parish (1952), Rev. Carl Kish.
Res., 4659 Niles-Cortland Rd., N.E., 44410. Tel: 330-637-1886; Fax: 330-637-0608. [CEM]
Catechesis/Religious Programs—Students 463.

Dungannon, Columbiana Co., St. Philip Neri (1817), Rev. Paul L. Gubser.
Res., Hanoverton P.O., 44423. Tel: 330-223-1973. [CEM]

East Liverpool, Columbiana Co., St. Aloysius (1838) (Irish), Rev. John D. MulQueen.
Res., 235 W. 5th St., 43920. Tel: 330-385-7131. [CEM]
School—335 W. 5th St., 43920. Tel: 330-385-5963.
Sisters of Notre Dame 2; Lay Teachers 10; Students 222.
Catechesis/Religious Programs—Students 67.

St. Ann's (1915), Rev. George J. Balasko.
Res., 1506 Pennsylvania Ave., 43920. Tel: 330-385-5582.

East Palestine, Columbiana Co., Our Lady of Lourdes (1880), Revs. Daniel Cipar, M.S.C.; Delso Torok, Pastor Emeritus.
Res., 200 E. Main St., 44413. Tel: 330-426-9346. [CEM]
Catechesis/Religious Programs—20 N. James St., 44413. Tel: 330-426-2254.
Students 131.

Garrettsville, Portage Co., St. Ambrose (1944), Rev. Richard J. Pentello; Deacon Robert Rapp.
Res., 10692 Freedom St., 44231. Tel: 330-527-4105; Fax: 330-527-2500.

Geneva, Ashtabula Co., Assumption B.V.M. (1915), Rev. Paul R. Tobin.
Res., 594 W. Main St., 44041. Tel: 216-466-3427.
School—Tel: 216-466-2104. Sr. Mary Gloria Auer, R.S.M., Prin.
Lay Teachers 12; Students 166.
Catechesis/Religious Programs—Students 161.

Girard, Trumbull Co., St. Rose (1892), Revs. Martin S. Susko, V.F.; Frank Zanni; Richard M. Reis; Tony Augustine, Pastoral Min.; Sr. Lucille Conley, H.M., Pastoral Ministry; Deacons Joseph Rudjack, Dir. Parish Ministries Process (PMP); Kevin Lamar; Paul Milligan. In res., Rev. Orlando S. Rich.
Res., 48 E. Main St., 44420. Tel: 330-545-4351; Fax: 330-545-0119.
School—65 E. Main St., 44420. Tel: 330-545-1163. Sr. Carole Suhar, O.S.U., Prin.
Sisters 2; Lay Teachers 17; Students 338.
Catechesis/Religious Programs—Tel: 216-545-1216. Marjorie O'Malley, D.R.E.
Students 673.

Hubbard, Trumbull Co., St. Patrick's (1869), Revs. Timothy O'Neill; James Johnson, s.P.; John A. Murray, (Retired); Deacons Edward Heutsche; Robert Friedman.
Res., 315 N. Main St., 44425. Tel: 216-534-1928; Fax: 216-534-0305. [CEM]
School—38 E. Water St., 44425. Tel: 216-534-4532; Fax: 216-534-0305.
Lay Teachers 16; Students 295.
Catechesis/Religious Programs—225 N. Main St., 44425. Tel: 216-534-8304; 534-4111. Mrs. Teresa A. Yarger, D.R.E.
Students 484.

Jefferson, Ashtabula Co., St. Joseph Calasanctius (1858), Rev. Stephen M. Wassie.
Res., 32 E. Jefferson St., 44047. Tel: 216-576-3651.
Catechesis/Religious Programs—Tel: 216-576-3339.
Students 143.

Kent, Portage Co., St. Patrick's (1864), Revs. Timothy Kenney; Joseph Ruggieri.
Res., 313 N. Depeyster St., 44240. Tel: 330-673-5849; Fax: 330-673-5849. [CEM]
School—127 Portage St., 44240. Tel: 330-673-7232; Fax: 330-678-6612.
Lay Teachers 18; Students 336.
Catechesis/Religious Programs—Tel: 330-677-4433.
Students 402.

Immaculate Heart of Mary (1953), Rev. John M. Jerek.
Res., 1424 Horning Rd., 44240. Tel: 330-678-0240; Fax: 330-678-7780.
Catechesis/Religious Programs—Students 169.

Kingsville, Ashtabula Co., St. Andrew (1936), Rev. Nathan S. Willis.
Res., 480 State St., Conneaut, 44030. Tel: 216-599-8855.
Church—3700 Rte. 193, 44048. Tel: 216-224-0987.

Kinsman, Trumbull Co., St. Patrick (1957). Attended by Our Lady of Victory, Andover.
481 S. Main St., P.O. Box 669, Andover, 44003-9778. Tel: 216-293-6218.
Catechesis/Religious Programs—6397 State Rte. 87 N.E.
Students 65.

Lake Milton, Mahoning Co., St. Catherine (1956), Rev. David W. Merzweiler.
Res., 1254 Grandview Rd., 44429-9542. Tel: 330-654-4001.
Catechesis/Religious Programs—Students 91.

Leetonia, Columbiana Co., St. Patrick's (1861), Rev. Thomas J. Ungashick.
Res., 167 Main St., P.O. Box 67, 44431. Tel: 330-427-6577. [CEM]
Catechesis/Religious Programs—Students 92.

Lisbon, Columbiana Co., St. George (1820), Rev. Robert Edwards; Deacon David H. Arend.
Res., 271 W. Chestnut St., 44432. Tel: 330-424-7648.
Catechesis/Religious Programs—Students 87.
Mission—West Point, Columbiana Co., St. Agatha,

P.O. Box 462, West Point, 44492. Tel: 330-424-0155.

Louisville, Stark Co., St. Louis (1838) (French-German), Revs. Frederick Slaven; Homer G. Oliver.
Res., 300 N. Chapel St., 44641. Tel: 330-875-1658. [CEM]
School—Tel: 330-875-1467.
Lay Teachers 12; Students 227.
Catechesis/Religious Programs—Tel: 330-875-3777.
Students 404.

Sacred Heart of Mary (1833), Rev. William B. Kraynak.
Res., 8277 Nickelplate Ave., N.E., 44641. Tel: 330-875-2827; Fax: 330-875-2410. [CEM]
School—8267 Nickelplate Ave., N.E., 44641. Tel: 330-875-5167. Donna Shadle, Prin.
Lay Teachers 9; Students 110.
Catechesis/Religious Programs—Students 95.

Lowellville, Mahoning Co., Our Lady of the Holy Rosary (1867), Rev. Gerald M. DeLucia.
Res., 131 E. Wood St., 44436. Tel: 330-536-6436; Fax: 330-536-9188. [CEM]
Catechesis/Religious Programs—Students 195.

McDonald, Trumbull Co., Our Lady of Perpetual Help (1943), Rev. Daniel J. Kulesa.
Res., 618 Ohio Ave., 44437. Tel: 330-530-6929.
Catechesis/Religious Programs—601 Indiana Ave., 44437. Tel: 330-530-1111.
Students 217.

Mantua, Portage Co., St. Joseph's, Rev. Thomas J. McCarthy.
Res., 11045 St. Joseph Blvd., 44255. Tel: 330-274-2114.
Parish Center—Tel: 330-274-2253.
School—Tel: 330-274-2268; Fax: 330-274-2412.
Lay Teachers 9; Students 190.
Catechesis/Religious Programs—Tel: 330-274-2253.
Students 208.

Massillon, Stark Co.,

1—St. Barbara's, (1867) (German), Rev. Thomas Cebula; Mrs. Marcia Popovich, Pastoral Min.
Res., 2813 Lincoln Way, N.W., 44647. Tel: 330-833-6898; Fax: 330-833-5164. [CEM]
School—2825 Lincoln Way, N.W., 44647. Tel: 330-833-9510.
Sisters 1; Lay Teachers 11; Students 271; Preschool Children 25.
Catechesis/Religious Programs—Fax: 216-833-5164.
Students 124.

2—National Shrine of St. Dymphna, (1938). Located on grounds of Massilon Psychiatric Center. Rev. Matthew M. Herttna, Chap. & Dir.
Church—3000 Erie St., S., P.O. Box 4, 44648-0004. Tel: 330-833-8478.

3—St. Joseph's, (1863), Rev. Raymond L. Paul.
Res., 322 Third St., S.E., 44646. Tel: 330-833-2607. [CEM]
Parish Center and Office—330 Fourth St., S.E., 44646. Tel: 330-833-4907; 833-6088; Fax: 330-833-3907.
Catechesis/Religious Programs—Students 170.

4—St. Mary's, (1839), Revs. James R. Kolp; Edward R. Brienz; Robert E. Brengartner; Deacons Edwards Kurkas; Joseph Fries.
Res., 206 Cherry Rd., N.E., 44646. Tel: 330-833-8501; Fax: 330-833-3359. [CEM]
School—640 First St., N.E., 44646. Tel: 330-832-9355; Fax: 330-832-9030.
Sisters 6; Lay Teachers 18; Students 436.
Catechesis/Religious Programs—Tel: 216-832-5719.
Students 480.

Masury, Trumbull Co., St. Bernadette (1940), Rev. Robert J. Hannon.
Res., 7800 Locust St., 44438. Tel: 330-448-8015; Fax: 330-448-0432.
Catechesis/Religious Programs—Brookfield Junior High, Brookfield, Tel: 330-448-3003.
Students 160.

Maximo, Stark Co., St. Joseph (1850), Rev. William E. Bantz.
Res., 12055 Easton St., N.E., P.O. Box 219, 44650. Tel: 330-823-7809. [CEM]
Catechesis/Religious Programs—Students 147.

Middlebranch, Stark Co., St. Therese Little Flower (1929), Revs. Kevin L. Fete; Edward F. Varble, Pastor Emeritus.
Res., 2040 Diamond St., N.E., North Canton, 44720. Tel: 330-494-2759; Fax: 330-494-2536.
Catechesis/Religious Programs—Tel: 330-499-6783.
Students 322.

Mineral Ridge, Trumbull Co., St. Mary's (1870), Rev. Richard Murphy.
Res., 3504 Main St., 44440. Tel: 330-652-7761; Fax: 330-652-7765.
Catechesis/Religious Programs—Students 135.

Navarre, Stark Co., St. Clement's (1830), Rev. Robert G. Gibas.
Res., 216 Wooster St. E., 44662. Tel: 330-879-5900; Fax: 330-879-5138. [CEM]
School—Tel: 330-879-2645.
Lay Teachers 9; Students 189.
Catechesis/Religious Programs—Students 98.

New Middletown, Mahoning Co., St. Paul the Apostle (1952), Rev. Nicholas R. Shori.
Res., 10143 Main St., P.O. Box 515, 44442. Tel: 330-542-3466. [JC]
Catechesis/Religious Programs—Tel: 330-542-3824.
Students 332.

Newton Falls, Trumbull Co., St. Joseph (1846), Rev. Kenneth L. Strader.
Res., 131 W. Quarry St., 44444-1560. Tel: 330-872-5742; Fax: 330-872-5744. [CEM]
School—Tel: 330-872-7676.
Students 169.
Catechesis/Religious Programs—Tel: 330-872-9947.
Students 133.

St. Mary (1928), Rev. Kenneth L. Strader.
Res., 131 West Quarry St., 44444. Tel: 330-872-5742; Fax: 330-872-5744. [CEM]

Niles, Trumbull Co., Our Lady of Mt. Carmel (1907) (Italian), Revs. Peter Chiodo, C.PP.S.; Albert DePascale, C.PP.S.; Carol DellaVecchia, C.PP.S.
Res., 381 Robbins Ave., 44446. Tel: 330-652-5825; Fax: 330-544-1872.
School—Tel: 330-652-5547; Fax: 330-652-9646.
Sisters 3; Lay Teachers 13; Students 335.
Catechesis/Religious Programs—Students 222.

St. Stephen's (1853), Rev. John H. Gubser.
Res., 129 W. Park Ave., 44446. Tel: 330-652-4396. [CEM]
School—(Grades PreK-8) 45 S. Chestnut, 44446. Tel: 330-652-5511; Fax: 330-652-4264.
Preschool 48; Lay Teachers 10; Students 207.
Catechesis/Religious Programs—Students 200.

North Canton, Stark Co., St. Paul's (1845), Revs. James E. McKarns; John Warner.
Res., 241 S. Main St., 44720. Tel: 330-499-2201; Fax: 330-499-8106. [CEM]
School—303 S. Main St., 44720. Tel: 330-494-0223. Jackie Zufall, Prin.
Lay Teachers 21; Students 460.
Catechesis/Religious Programs—Tel: 330-494-4036.
Students 775.

North Jackson, Mahoning Co., St. James Parish Family (1945), Rev. David W. Merzweiler.
Res., 1254 Grandview Rd., Lake Milton, 44429. Tel: 330-654-4001.
Catechesis/Religious Programs—Students 110.

Orwell, Ashtabula Co., St. Mary's (1922) (Polish), Rev. Raymond J. Thomas.
Res., 103 N. Maple, Box 217, 44076. Tel: 216-437-6262. [CEM]

Poland, Mahoning Co., Holy Family (1956), Revs. Philip P. Conley; Michael Swierz.
Res., 2729 Center Rd., 44514. Tel: 330-757-1545; Fax: 330-757-4443.
School—Tel: 330-757-3753; Fax: 330-757-7648.
Sisters 2; Lay Teachers 24; Students 370.
Catechesis/Religious Programs—Students 731.

Randolph Township, Portage Co., St. Joseph (1831), Rev. Edward R. Wieczorek.
Res., 2643 Waterloo Rd., Mogadore, 44260. Tel: 330-628-9941; Fax: 330-628-9942. [CEM]
School—Tel: 330-628-9555.
Sisters of Notre Dame 2; Lay Teachers 11; Students 246.
Catechesis/Religious Programs—Tel: 330-628-4844.
Students 352.

Ravenna, Portage Co., Immaculate Conception (1854), Revs. Robert A. Sabatino; Leo J. Wehrlin; Deacon Russell J. Brode.
Res., 409 W. Main St., 44266. Tel: 330-296-6434. [CEM]
School—225 S. Sycamore St., 44266. Tel: 330-296-4817.
Lay Teachers 9; Students 213.
Catechesis/Religious Programs—Students 400.

Rock Creek, Ashtabula Co., Sacred Heart (1956), Rev. Edward Kowaleski; Deacons John D. Pallo; John Lueders.
Res., 3409 N. Main St., P.O. Box 305, 44084. Tel: 216-563-3010. [JC]
Catechesis/Religious Programs—Students 95.

Rootstown, Portage Co., St. Peter of the Fields (1868), Sr. Regina Zeleznik, S.N.D., Parish Coord.; Deacon Thomas Shay.
Res., 3487 Old Forge Rd., 44272. Tel: 330-325-7543. [CEM]
Catechesis/Religious Programs—Students 150.

Salem, Columbiana Co., St. Paul's (1881), Rev. James A. Clarke. Pastoral Ministers: Amanda Raymond; Donna Lynn.
Res., 157 Ohio Ave., 44460. Tel: 330-332-0336.
School—929 E. State St., 44460. Tel: 330-337-3451; Fax: 330-337-3452.
Lay Teachers 10; Students 167.
Catechesis/Religious Programs—Tel: 330-332-4373. D.R.E.: Sr. Kathleen McCarragher, O.S.U.; Donna Dermotta.
Students 465.

Salineville, Columbiana Co., St. Patrick's (1873), Rev. Paul L. Gubser.
Res., P.O. Box 66, Summitville, 43962. Tel: 330-223-1871; 679-2511. [CEM]
Church—611 Jefferson St., 43945. Tel: 216-223-1871.

Sebring, Mahoning Co., St. Ann (1903), Sr. Maureen Smith, H.M.
Res., 323 S. 15th St., 44672. Tel: 330-938-2033.
Catechesis/Religious Programs—Students 75.

Streetsboro, Portage Co., St. Joan of Arc (1965), Revs. Robert V. Flynn; James F. Stenson, Pastor Emeritus.
Res., 8894 State Rte. 14, 44241. Tel: 330-626-3424; Fax: 330-626-3422.
Catechesis/Religious Programs—Tel: 330-626-2050.
Students 278.

Struthers, Mahoning Co., Holy Trinity (1907) (Slovak), Rev. Stephen C. Karas.
Res., 250 N. Bridge St., 44471. Tel: 330-755-2115; Fax: 330-750-9431.

St. Nicholas (1865), Revs. Philip E. Rogers; John Madden.
Res., 775 5th St., 44471-1795. Tel: 330-750-2555.
Parish Office—764 5th St., 44471-1704. Tel: 330-755-9819; Fax: 330-755-9949.
School—762 5th St., 44471-1704. Tel: 330-755-2128.
Lay Teachers 11; Students 209.
Catechesis/Religious Programs—Tel: 330-755-6245.
Students 440.

Summitville, Columbiana Co., St. John's (1852), Rev. Paul L. Gubser.
Res., 16017 Smith Rd., 43962. Tel: 216-223-1871. [CEM]

Uniontown, Stark Co., Holy Spirit (1979), Rev. John Zapp.
Res., 2952 Edison St., N.W., 44685. Tel: 330-699-4500; 877-1695.
Catechesis/Religious Programs—Tel: 330-699-4500; 877-1695.
Students 330.

Vienna, Trumbull Co., St. Vincent de Paul (1934), Rev. Thomas F. Murphy.
Res., 4453 Warren-Sharon Rd., 44473. Tel: 330-394-2461; 1-800-645-6684.
Catechesis/Religious Programs—Tel: 330-394-2361.
Students 210.

Warren, Trumbull Co.,

1—Blessed Sacrament, (1959), Rev. Donald E. King. In res., Rev. John Zuraw.
Res., 3020 Reeves Rd., N.E., 44483. Tel: 330-372-2215; Fax: 330-372-6380.
School—St. Mary Middle School, (Grades 5-8) 3000 Reeves Rd., N.E., 44483. Tel: 330-372-2375. Mrs. JoAnn Kandrac, Prin.
Sisters of Divine Providence 1; Lay Teachers 11; Students 225.
Catechesis/Religious Programs—Tel: 330-372-6930.
Students 414.

2—Christ Our King, (1951), Rev. Thomas M. Spisak.
Res., 1000 Tod Ave., S.W., 44485. Tel: 330-395-3747.

3—SS. Cyril and Methodius, (1928) (Slovak), Rev. Thomas M. Spisak.
Res., 185 Laird Ave., N.E., 44483. Tel: 330-393-9766.
Catechesis/Religious Programs—Students 88.

4—St. James, (1947), Revs. Charles W. Crumbley Tel: 330-369-3518; James Walker; Sr. Mary Regien Kingsbury, S.N.D., Pastoral Assoc.
Res., 2533 Burton St., S.E., 44484. Tel: 330-369-3888.
Schools—St. James School, (Grades K-4) 2106 Arbor St., S.E., 44484. Tel: 330-369-4218.
Lay Teachers 10; Students 130; St. Mary Middle School, (Grades 5-8) 261 Elm Rd., 44483. Tel: 216-399-5154. Sr. Mary Judith Anne Sabau, S.N.D., Prin.
Catechesis/Religious Programs—2106 Arbor St., S.E., 44484. Sr. Mary Ann McFadden, S.N.D., D.R.E.
Students 70.

5—St. Joseph, (1928) (Polish), Rev. John P. Turk. In res., Rev. George Popovich.
Res., 1346 Vernon St., N.W., 44483. Tel: 330-393-0226. [CEM]

6—ST. MARY'S, (1835), Rev. Bernard R. Schmalzried.
Res., 232 Seneca St., N.E., 44481. Tel: 330-393-8721; 394-3426. [CEM]

7—ST. PIUS X, (1959), Rev. William J. Loveless.
Res., 1401 Moncrest Ave., N.W., 44485. Tel: 330-399-8881; 399-8882.
School—St. Mary Middle School, (Grades 5-8). Tel: 216-399-5411. Sr. Theresa Dolan-Dixon, Prin.
Lay Teachers 7; Students 143.

Waynesburg, Stark Co., St. James (1928), Rev. Michael D. Seifert.
Res., 400 W. Lisbon St., 44688. Tel: 330-866-9449.
School—Tel: 330-866-9556.
Lay Teachers 7; Students 88.
Catechesis/Religious Programs—Students 89.

Wellsville, Columbiana Co., Immaculate Conception (1842), Rev. George J. Balasko.
Res., 1021 Riverside Ave., 43968. Tel: 330-532-3445. [CEM]
Catechesis/Religious Programs—Students 116.

Windham, Portage Co., St. Michael's (1943), Rev. James Paul Lang.
Res., 9736 E. Center St., 44288. Tel: 330-326-3531.

On Duty Outside the Diocese:
Reverend Fathers—
Bonnot, Bernard R., New York, NY
Daprile, James, Cincinnati, OH
Deffenbaugh, Joseph T., Pensacola, FL

Military Chaplains:
Reverend Fathers—
Garvey, Michael, U.S. Navy
Mikstay, Michael, U.S. Marines
Reidy, Robert, U.S. Navy

Absent on Sick Leave:
Reverend Fathers—
Tecca, Felix

Absent on Leave:
Reverend Fathers—
Crum, Thomas
Esposito, Anthony
Fondriest, James
Grabowski, Dennis
McCarragher, Timothy
Nuzzi, Ronald
Ryan, John
Santucci, Louis
Tamburrini, Joseph
Trucksis, Frederick
Tully, John
Vazquez, Jose
Ziemba, Howard

Retired:
Reverend Monsignors—
Fannon, Robert C.
Gutman, Gordon G.
Krispinsky, Joseph A.
Prokop, Andrew A.
Reagan, Donald
Reverend Fathers—
Adamko, Cyril A.
Bakos, Stephen
Barrett, Robert P.
Barrette, Dacian
Beller, Joseph
Braun, Warren
Brengartner, Robert E.
Bruce, Robert J.
Cavanaugh, James K.
Chamberlain, Robert
Chonko, Michael J.
Curran, Gerald X.
Czaja, Joseph S.
Daum, John J.
Dempster, A. Patrick
Dobosiewciz, Leon W.
Duritsa, George M.
Fabrizio, Henry E.
Fasline, Anthony
Franko, George M.
Friedrich, Ralph
Herttna, Matthew
Hill, Robert
Horvath, Stephen
Hughes, Francis J.
Kelly, Thomas F.
Klein, Albert J.
Lettau, David
Lyons, John F.
Malik, Joseph
Marrokal, Donald
Matulik, Martin
McNally, Thomas C.
Murray, John
Nachtigal, Fred
Nist, Arthur
O'Leary, Patrick D.
O'Neil, William J.
Oliver, Homer
Oser, Donald
Pierce, Blaine F.
Platt, Stewart
Rath, John G.
Rich, Orlando S.
Sargent, John
Schmidt, John W.
Slipski, William P.
Snock, Francis
Spitale, John
Stenson, James F.
Summers, John
Torok, Dezso
Vacca, Bernard
Varble, Edward F.
Welsch, John
Winca, George F.
Witt, William
Yablonsky, Gabriel
Yurko, William

Permanent Deacons:
Arend, David H., St. George, Lisbon
Bagley, Wilbur J., St. Joseph, Canton
Basile, Eugene, St. Jude, Columniana
Beil, David C., St. Christine, Youngstown
Brechbill, Kenneth W., St. Joseph, Massillon
Briestensky, Edward L., Sacred Heart, Canton
Brode, Russell J., Immaculate Conception, Ravenna
Brown, James, St. Christine, Youngstown
Bunofsky, Ronald J., St. John, Campbell
Burkhardt, Carl R., St. John the Baptist, Canton
Colon, Felipe, St. Rose of Lima, Youngstown
Conversino, David, St. Joan of Arc, Canton
Cosentino, Louis A., St. Jude, Columbia
Cuttica, Robert J., St. Christine, Youngstown
DiFrancesco, Salvatore, St. Matthias, Youngstown
Friedman, Robert J., St. Patrick, Hubbard
Fries, Joseph K., St. Mary, Massillon
Harvey, James G., St. William, Warren
Hatala, Ray H., Office of Permanent Diaconate
Hawkins, Edward, Holy Family, Poland
Ivan, Ellis C., Holy Spirit, Uniontown
Jaskiewicz, Albert F., St. Pius X, Warren
Johnson, Richard M., St. Joseph, Ashtabula
Klein, Robert E., St. Peter, Canton
Kocjancic, Michael A., St. Charles, Boardman
Krause, Harold R., SS. Philip & James, Canal Fulton
Kurkas, Edward G., St. Mary, Massillon
Lamar, Kevin T., St. Rose, Girard
Lambert, William H., St. Paul, North Canton
Layko, Ronald J., St. Christine, Youngstown
Lueders, John E., Sacred Heart, Rock Creek
Medvez, Alvin A., St. Stephen, Youngstown; C.T.N.Y.
Milanek, Richard, St. Luke, Boardman
Milligan, Paul, St. Rose, Girard
Nohra, Joseph S., St. Maron & Mt. Carmel, Youngstown
Pallo, John D., Sacred Heart, Rock Creek
Pohl, Peter P., SS. Philip & James, Canal Fulton
Prasek, Alan, St. Joseph, Ashtabula
Rapp, Robert, St. Ambrose, Garrettsville
Roberts, Michael R., Jr., St. Joseph, Austintown
Rohr, Thomas J., SS. Philip & James, Canal Fulton
Rudjak, Joseph S., KSU-Newman Center, Kent
Scarletto, Frederick C., St. Mary, Canton
Schlais, Michael, St. Stanislaus, Youngstown
Shay, Thomas R., Sr., St. Peter of the Fields, Rootstown
Sherwood, Ronald D., Timken Merecy Medical Center, Canton
Soich, Thomas G., St. Charles, Boardman
Toth, Joseph P., Blessed Sacrament, Warren
Vaughan, John H., (Retired)
White, James A., St. Joseph, Randolph
Zamary, Joseph J., Sacred Heart, Youngstown

INSTITUTIONS LOCATED IN THE DIOCESE

[A] SEMINARIES, RELIGIOUS, OR SCHOLASTICATES

YOUNGSTOWN. *Sacred Heart Retreat House & Renewal Center*, 3128 Logan Ave., P.O. Box 6074, 44501. Tel: 330-759-9539; Fax: 330-759-8235. Very Rev. Walter Downs, M.S.C., Supr.; Revs. Paul J. Hill, M.S.C., Dir. Novices; Donovan Mulert, M.S.C.; Andrew Torma, M.S.C.; Gerald R.J. Sommer, M.S.C.; Daniel Cipar; Earl Henley, M.S.C. Priests 7; Brothers 4. Applications for missions, retreats, recollection days, novenas and Forty Hours to be made to the Rev. Father Superior.

CANFIELD. *Society of St. Paul*, P.O. Box 595, 44406. Tel: 330-533-5503; 533-1076. Very Rev. Matthew Roehrig, S.S.P., Supr.; Revs. Thomas Fogarty, S.S.P.; Anthony L. Chenevey, S.S.P. Priests 3; Brothers 8.

[B] COLLEGES AND UNIVERSITIES

NORTH CANTON. *Walsh University*, 2020 Easton St., N.W., 44720-3396. Tel: 330-499-7090.
For a complete listing, refer to the Colleges and Universities section.

[C] HIGH SCHOOLS, DIOCESAN

YOUNGSTOWN. *Cardinal Mooney High School*, 2545 Erie St., 44507. Tel: 330-788-5007; Fax: 330-788-4511. Sr. Jane Marie Kudlacz, H.M., Prin.; Rev. Gregory Fedor, Assoc. Prin. Priests 1; Sisters 1; Lay Teachers 42; Students 650.

Ursuline High School, 750 Wick Ave., 44505. Tel: 216-744-4563. Rev. Richard Murphy, Assoc. Prin. Priests 1; Sisters 5; Lay Teachers 33; Students 609.

ASHTABULA. *St. John High School*, 3320 Station Ave., 44004. Tel: 330-997-5531. Mr. Dennis A. Dobos, Prin. Lay Teachers 9; Students 92.

CANTON. *Central Catholic High*, 4824 Tuscarawas St., W., 44708-5198. Tel: 330-478-2131; Fax: 330-478-6086. Rev. Robert W. Kaylor, Prin.; Mr. John Korecki, Asst. Prin.; Mr. Leo DeMatteis, Dean of Students; Mr. James Naegeli, Campus Ministry Dir. Priests 1; Sisters 1; Lay Teachers 49; Students 734; Total Staff 52.

LOUISVILLE. *St. Thomas Aquinas High School*, 2121 Reno Dr., N.E., 44641. Tel: 330-875-1631; Fax: 330-875-8469. Rev. Terrence Hazel, Prin.; Mr. Alan Digianantonio, Asst. Prin.; Miss Cindi Eby, Dean. Priests 1; Lay Teachers 40; Total Staff 41; Students 574.

WARREN. *John F. Kennedy High School*, 2550 Central Pkwy., S.E., 44484. Tel: 330-369-1804; Fax: 330-369-1125. Girard-Niles-Youngstown. Tel: 330-539-5242. Rev. William Petrunak, Chap.; Mr. James N. Ruffing, Prin.; Mr. James Boyle, Asst. Prin. Lay Teachers 25; Students 374.

[D] ELEMETARY SCHOOLS, DIOCESAN

ASHTABULA. *Ashtabula Catholic Elementary School*, Central Office, 1464 W. Sixth St., 44004. Tel: 216-964-3277. Sr. Mary Laurel Smith, H.M., Dir.
Primary Building. (Grades K-4), 2150 Columbus Ave., 44004. Tel: 216-997-5821. Ms. Donna Timonere, Prin. Lay Teachers 9; Students 185.
Middle Building. (Grades 5-8), Central Office, 1464 W. Sixth St., 44004. Tel: 216-964-3277. Sr. Mary Laurel Smith, H.M., Prin. Teachers 6; Students 132.

[E] MIDDLE SCHOOLS, DIOCESAN

WARREN. *Warren Parochial School*, St. Mary Middle Building, 261 Elm Rd., N.E., 44483. Tel: 330-399-5154. Sr Judith Anne Sabau, S.N.D., Prin. Sisters 2; Lay Teachers 20; Students 303.

[F] PRIVATE SCHOOLS

CANFIELD. *Ursuline Preschool & Kindergarten*, 4300 Shields Rd., 44406. Tel: 330-792-4150. Sr. Jacquelyn Herpy, O.S.U., Dir.; Sr. Jan Gier, O.S.U., Asst. Dir. Ursuline Sisters 4; Lay Teachers 5; Students 219.

[G] GENERAL HOSPITALS

YOUNGSTOWN. *HM Health Services*, 4964 Belmont Ave., 44505-1046. Tel: 330-759-7484.
For a complete listing, refer to the Hospitals section.
HM Health Services, St. Elizabeth Health Center, 1044 Belmont Ave., Box 1790, 44501. Tel: 330-746-7211.
For a complete listing, refer to the Hospitals section.
St. Elizabeth Health Resources, Inc., 1044 Belmont Ave., Box 1790, 44501.
For a complete listing, refer to the Hospitals section.

WARREN. *St. Joseph Health Center*, 667 Eastland Ave., S.E., 44484. Tel: 330-841-4000; Fax: 330-841-4048.
For a complete listing, refer to the Hospitals section.

[H] SPECIAL CARE FACILITIES

NORTH LIMA. *The Assumption Village*, 9800 Market St., 44452. Tel: 330-549-0740; Fax: 330-549-0701.
For a complete listing, refer to the Special Care Facilities section.

[I] HOMES FOR AGED

CANTON. *House of Loreto*, 2812 Harvard Ave., N.W., 44709. Tel: 330-453-8137.
For a complete listing, refer to the Special Care Facilities section.

HUBBARD. *Villa Maria Teresa*, 50 Warner Rd., 44425. Tel: 330-759-9329 (Villa); 875-4635 (Emmaus House).
For a complete listing, refer to the Special Care Facilities section.

LOUISVILLE. *Emmaus House*, 1515 California Ave., 44641. Tel: 330-875-4635.

For a complete listing, refer to the Special Care Facilities section.

St. Joseph Care Center, 2308 Reno Dr., 44641. Tel: 330-875-5562.

For a complete listing, refer to the Special Care Facilities section.

NORTH LIMA. *The Assumption Village*, 9800 Market St., 44452. Tel: 330-549-0740; Fax: 330-549-0701.

For a complete listing, refer to the Special Care Facilities section.

[J] MONASTERIES AND RESIDENCES OF PRIESTS AND BROTHERS

YOUNGSTOWN. *Mt. Alvernia Friary*, 517. S. Belle Vista Ave., 44509. Tel: 330-799-1888. Franciscan Fathers. Revs. Matthew J. Kiss, O.F.M., Guardian; Nicholas Dengl, O.F.M.; John Reis, O.F.M., Vicar, Pastor of Our Lady of Hungary; Deacon Kenneth Ghastin, O.F.M.; Bros. Reginald Antal, O.F.M.; Emery Kish, O.F.M.

[K] CONVENTS AND RESIDENCES FOR SISTERS

CANFIELD. *Motherhouse and Educational Center of the Ursuline Sisters*, 4250 Shields Rd., 44406. Tel: 330-792-7636. Sr. Nancy Dawson, O.S.U., Gen. Supr. Total in Community 83; Total in Residence 48; Total Staff 5.

CANTON. *Sancta Clara Monastery*, 4200 N. Market Ave., 44714. Tel: 330-492-1171. Rev. Kieran M. Kay, O.F.M., Chap. Poor Clares of Perpetual Adoration. Cloistered Professed Nuns 11.

HUBBARD. *Villa Maria Teresa*, 50 Warner Rd., 44425. Tel: 330-759-9329. Sr. Joyce Candidi, O.S.H.J., Regl. Supr.; Sr. Augustina Cagnazzo, O.S.H.J., Convent Supr. Novitiate and American Headquarters of Oblate Sisters of the Sacred Heart of Jesus. Sisters 21.

[L] CATHOLIC CHARITIES SOCIAL SERVICE AGENCIES

ASHTABULA. *Catholic Service League*, 4200 Park Ave., 44004. Tel: 216-992-2121. Danita M. Eartly, Exec. Dir. Total Assisted 3,000; Total Staff 1,075.

CANTON. *Catholic Community Services of Stark County, Inc.*, 625 Cleveland Ave., N.W., 44702. Tel: 330-455-0374. 876 Amherst Rd., N.E., Massillon, 44646. Tel: 330-833-8516. Professional Counseling and Licensed Adoption Social Service Agency. Mr. Daniel J. Fuline, A.C.S.W., L.I.S.W., CEO. Patients assisted annually 17,579; Total Staff 50.

KENT. *Family and Community Services of Catholic Charities*, 302 N. DePeyster St., 44240. Tel: 330-678-3911; Fax: 330-678-1264. Rev. Thomas McCarthy, Priests' Rep. Total Assisted 5,254; Total Staff 45.

LISBON. *Family & Community Services, Inc. of Catholic Charities of Columbiana County*, 966 1/2 N. Market St., Box 413, 44432. Tel: 330-424-9509; Fax: 330-424-7999. Mr. William C. F. Vest, Exec. Dir. Family & Community in Columbiana Co.; Deborah Morrow, Interim Mgr. Total Assisted 600.

WARREN. *Catholic Community Services, Inc. of Trumbull County*, 175 Laird Ave., N.E., 3rd Floor, 44483. Tel: 216-393-4254. Ms. Kathleen McCulloh, M.A., L.S.W., Exec. Dir. Family and Child Welfare Work in Trumbull Co.

[M] HOMES FOR WOMEN

YOUNGSTOWN. *Beatitude House*, 1515 Fifth Ave., 44504. Transitional Housing, Job Preparation, Job Training, and Case Management for Economically Disadvantaged Women. Sr. Margaret Scheetz, O.S.U., Dir. Total Assisted 44; Total Staff 3.

[N] RETREAT HOUSES

YOUNGSTOWN. *Sacred Heart Retreat and Renewal Center*, Logan Ave., Box 6074, 44501. Tel: 330-759-9539; Fax: 330-759-8235. Society of the Missionaries of the Sacred Heart. Revs. Walter J. Downs, M.S.C., Dir.; Andrew Torma, M.S.C., Program Dir.; Bro. John Peralta, M.S.C., House Mgr.

CANTON. *Servants of the Paraclete*, 2812 Harvard Ave., N.W., 44709. Tel: 330-455-1703. Rev. Joseph J. Phillips, S.P., Chap., House of Loreto. Total in Residence 98; Total Staff 102

[O] NEWMAN CENTERS

YOUNGSTOWN. *Newman Center at Youngstown State University*, 254 Madison Ave., 44504-1627. Tel: 330-747-9202. Total Staff 6.

KENT. *Kent State University Newman Center*, 1424 Horning Rd., 44240. Rev. John M. Jerek; Ms. Barbara Kaluczky; Mr. Joseph Rudjak; Ms. Marcie Bircher; Ms. Jenn Berridge; Ms. Jeanne Michel. Total in Residence 1; Total Staff 4.

[P] MISCELLANEOUS LISTINGS

YOUNGSTOWN. *Caritas Communities*, 225 Elm St., 44503. Tel: 330-744-8451; 836-8660; Fax: 330-742-6448.
E-mail: ay787@yfn.ysu.edu
Sr. Denise Maher, H.M., Pres. & CEO; Brian Corbin, Chap.
As a member of Corporation of Catholic Charities Housing Opportunities and the Humility of Mary Housing Program, Caritas Communities will serve as Property Management Corporation for low income and special needs housing.

Catholic Charities Housing Opportunities Corporation, 225 Elm St., 44503. Tel: 330-744-8452, Ext. 275; Fax: 330-744-8448.
E-mail: doyccsocact@connective.com
Mr. Brian Corbin, Pres. & CEO. Purpose: Provides coordination, integration and leadership in the provision of housing services which promote affordable housing in the community. Total Families Assisted 370; Total Staff 2.

Declaration of Trust of Trumbull, Department of Education, 225 Elm St., 44503. County Catholic School Endowment Fund.

Humility of Mary Information Systems, Inc., 1343 Belmont Ave., 44504.

St. Elizabeth Development Foundation, 1044 Belmont Ave., P.O. Box 1790, 44501-1790. Tel: 330-480-3349. Edward R. Toth, Jr., Pres. & CEO.

CANFIELD. *The Ursuline Center*, 4280 Shields Rd., 44406. Tel: 216-799-4941.

LOUISVILLE. *St. Thomas Aquinas High School Endowment Fund*, 2121 Reno Drive, N.E., 44641. Tel: 330-875-1631. Rev. Terrence J. Hazel, Pres.; Douglas Haubert, Sec.

WARREN. *St. Joseph Development Foundation*, 667 Eastland Ave., S.E., 44484. Edward R. Toth, Jr., Pres. & CEO.

[Q] DIOCESAN CEMETERIES

YOUNGSTOWN. *Calvary*, 248 S. Belle Vista Ave., 44509.
Resurrection, 300 N. Racoon Rd , 44515. Tel: 216-799-1900.

MASSILLON. *Calvary*, 3469 Lincoln Way, E., 44647.

WARREN. *All Souls*, Rte. 3, Box 500, 44483.

RELIGIOUS INSTITUTES OF MEN REPRESENTED IN THE DIOCESE

For further details refer to the corresponding bracketed number in the Religious Institutes of Men or Women section.

[0320]—*Brothers of Christian Instruction*.—F.I.C.

[]—*Congregation of the Apostles of Jesus*.—A.J.

[0480]—*Conventual Franciscans*.—O.F.M.Conv.

[0520]—*Franciscan Friars*. (Immaculate Conception Prov. of New York).—O.F.M.

[]—*Franciscans-Province of St. John the Baptist*.—O.F.M.

[1110]—*Missionaries of the Sacred Heart*.—M.S.C.

[]—*Order of Franciscans Minor*. (Holy Name Prov.).—O.F.M.

[0430]—*Order of Preachers (Dominicans)*. (Prov. of St. Joseph).—O.P.

[1020]—*Pauline Fathers and Brothers*.—S.S.P.

[]—*Priestly Fraternity of St. Peter*.—F.S.S.P.

[1230]—*Servants of the Paraclete*.—s.P.

[1060]—*Society of the Precious Blood*. (Cincinnati Prov. & Italian).—C.PP.S.

RELIGIOUS INSTITUTES OF WOMEN REPRESENTED IN THE DIOCESE

[0100]—*Adorers of the Blood of Christ*.—A.S.C.

[]—*Antonine Sisters*.—A.S.

[]—*Benediction Sisters (Byzantine Sisters)*.—O.S.B.

[1040]—*Congregation of the Divine Spirit*.—C.D.S.

[1710]—*Congregation of the Third Order of St. Francis of Mary Immaculate, Joliet, IL*.—O.S.F.

[1070-28]—*Dominican Sisters*.—O.P.

[]—*Mission Helpers of the Sacred Heart*.—M.H.S.H.

[3050]—*Oblate Sisters of the Sacred Heart of Jesus*.—O.S.H.J.

[3210]—*Poor Clares of Perpetual Adoration*.—P.C.P.A.

[0580]—*Sisters of Charity of St. Augustine*.—C.S.A.

[0990]—*Sisters of Divine Providence*.—C.D.P.

[2575]—*Sisters of Mercy of the Americas*.—R.S.M.

[2990]—*Sisters of Notre Dame*.—S.N.D.

[1230]—*Sisters of St. Francis of Penance and Christian Charity*.—O.S.F.

[3830-08]—*Sisters of St. Joseph*.—C.S.J.

[]—*Sisters of St. Joseph of Springfield*.—S.S.J.

[3910]—*Sisters of St. Joseph of St. Mark*.—S.J.S.M.

[2040]—*Sisters of the Holy Spirit*.—S.H.S.

[2110]—*Sisters of the Humility of Mary*.—H.M.

[3730]—*Sisters of the Order of St. Basil the Great*.—O.S.B.M.

[]—*Ursiline Sisters of Cleveland*.—O.S.U.

[4120-07]—*Ursuline Nuns of the Congregation of Paris*.—O.S.U.

[4160]—*Vincentian Sisters of Charity*.—V.S.C.

NECROLOGY

† Aleckna, Conrad, (Retired). —Died Nov. 3, 1996.

† Andrecic, John, Boardman, OH, St. Charles Parish. —Died Jan. 21, 1996.

† Kosin, Wallace W., (Retired). —Died Oct. 6, 1996.

† Lettau, Rev. Msgr. John J., Youngstown, OH, St. Edward. —Died May 25, 1996.

† Lucas, Joseph R., (Retired). —Died Dec. 2, 1995.

† Malik, Joseph A., Jefferson, OH, St. Joseph Parish. —Died Jan. 2, 1996.

1847 **150 Years** 1997

Franz Mayer of Munich, Inc.

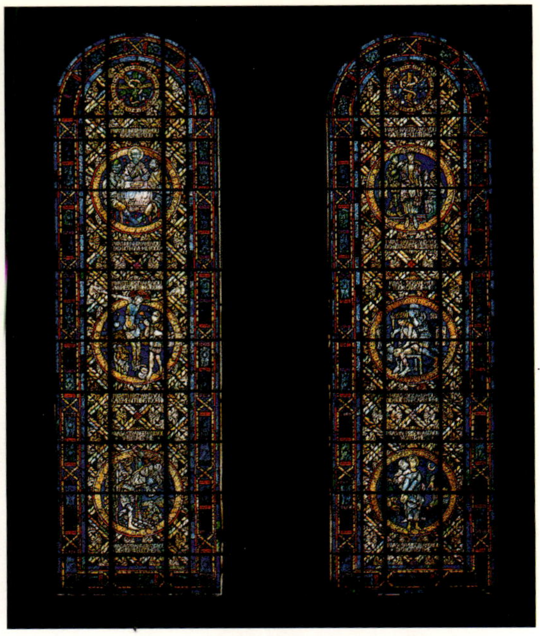

Examples of our Stained Glass work: Top left: Cathedral Basilica Covington, KY, 1909-22; right: St. James Cathedral, Seattle, WA, East Windows, 1994; bottom left: St. Joseph's University, Philadelphia, PA, 1992; center: St. Johannis Church, D-Neumarkt, 1995; right: CH-Romont, Cistercian Abbey, 1996.

150 years of excellence in stained glass and mosaic

Franz Mayer of Munich, Inc.
343 Passaic Avenue, Fairfield, NJ 07004
Phone 201-575-4777 Fax 201-575-5588

Franz Mayer of Munich, Inc.
25, Seidlstraße . D-80335 Munich,Germany
Phone 011-49-89-595484 Fax 011-49-89-593446

Apostolate to Hungarians

Most Reverend

ATTILA MIKLOSHAZY, S.J., S.T.D.

Titular Bishop of Castel Minore and Bishop for the spiritual assistance to the Hungarian emigrant people; ordained June 18, 1961; appointed August 12, 1989; consecrated November 4, 1989. *Res., St. Augustine's Seminary, 2661 Kingston Rd., Scarborough, Ontario, Canada, M1M 1M3.* Tel.: 416-261-7207; Fax: 416-261-2529.

ESTABLISHED MAY 20, 1983.

The Apostolate of the Bishop of Hungarians living outside of Hungary extends territorially to all the Hungarian communities existing outside of Hungary. The main purpose of the Apostolate is to give spiritual assistance to them through and in cooperation with the local ordinary and pastors.

Former Bishop—Most Rev. LADISLAUS A. IRANYI, Sch.P., ord. March 13, 1938; appt. May 20, 1983; cons. July 27, 1983; died March 6, 1987.

Bishop's Office—2661 Kingston Rd., Scarborough, Ontario, Canada, M1M 1M3. Tel: 416-261-7202; Fax: 416-261-2529.

Delegate of the Bishop in Europe—Rev. Dr. FERENC CSERHATI, *Ung.Kath.Mission, Oberfohringerstr.40, D-81925, Munchen, Germany.* Tel: 49-89-982-637; Fax: 49-89-985-419.

Delegate of the Bishop in the U.S.A.—Rev. STEPHEN N. MUSTOS, Sch.P., *223 Third St., Passaic, NJ, 07055.* Tel: 201-779-0332; Fax: 201-778-4263.

American Hungarian Catholic Priests' Association—East Coast Division: Rev. STEPHEN MUSTOS, Sch.P., *223 Third St., Passaic, NJ, 07055.* Tel: 201-779-0332; Fax: 201-778-4263.

Hungarian Catholic League of America, Inc.—Rev. Msgr. WILLIAM I. VARSANYI, P.A., Chm., *One Cathedral Sq., Providence, RI, 02903.* Tel: 401-278-4515; Fax: 401-831-1947.

Hungarian Priests' Association in Canada—Rev. ALEXANDER EROS, S.J., *337 Hellems Ave., Welland, Ontario, Canada, L3B 3C2.* Tel: 905-734-3772.

Newspapers & Magazines—"Eletunk" (Our Life); Rev. OTTO FEJOS, Editor, *Landwehrstrasse 66, D-80336, Munchen 2, Germany.* Tel: 89-532-8288; Fax: 89-532-8245.

"HIS- Press Service"—published by the Hungarian Institute for Sociology of Religion. Rev. EMERIC ANDRAS, S.J., Editor, *Gerlgasse 10/3, A-1030, Wien, Austria.* Tel: 43-222-80-233; Fax: 1-78-41-91.

"Tavlatok"—(Perspectives), Quarterly on Worldview, Spirituality and Culture, ed. by the Unio Cleri Hungarici. Revs. FERENC SZABO, S.J.; FERENC NAGY, S.J., *Sodras u. 13, H-1026, Budapest, Hungary.* Tel: 1-176-7062.

"A Sziv"—(Sacred Heart Messenger), monthly, published by the Hungarian Jesuit Fathers. Rev. NEMESHEGYI PETER, S.J., Editor, *Pf. 586, H-1398, Budapest, Hungary.* Tel: 1-176-7062; Fax: 1-275-0269., Address in Canada: *432 Sheppard Ave. E., Willowdale, Ontario, Canada, M2N 3B7.*

STATISTICS

Most personnel and institutions are under the jurisdiction of their local ordinaries.

NECROLOGY

Incorporated in diocesan and archdiocesan listings.

Lithuanian Apostolate For Lithuanian Catholics

Living Outside Lithuania

Most Reverend

PAUL A. BALTAKIS, O.F.M.

Titular Bishop of Egara and Bishop for Spiritual Assistance of Lithuanian Catholics Living Outside Lithuania; ordained August 24, 1952; appointed June 1, 1984; consecrated September 14, 1984. *Res., 361 Highland Blvd., Brooklyn, NY, 11207.* Tel.: 718-827-7932; Fax: 718-827-6696.

IN CARITATE SERVIAMUS DEO

ESTABLISHED JUNE 1, 1984.

The Apostolate of the Bishop for Lithuanian Catholics extends worldwide to all Lithuanian communities existing outside Lithuania, 75 percent of them in the U.S.A. The purpose of the apostolate is to give spiritual assistance to them, in cooperation with the local ordinaries and pastors. Specific faculties enabling the implementation of the Bishop's responsibilities were granted by the Holy See on July 21, 1986.

Former Lithuanian Bishops—Most Rev. VINCENTAS BRIZGYS, Ph.D., J.C.D., cons. May 19, 1940; Titular Bishop of Bosana; Auxiliary Bishop of Kaunas, Lithuania (Impeditus); died April 23, 1992.—Most Rev. ANTANAS DEKSNYS, Ph.D., cons. Jan. 15, 1969; Titular Bishop of Lavello, *Res., Villa Lithuania, Piazza Asti, 00182. Rome, Italy.*

Bishop's Office—361 Highland Blvd., Brooklyn, NY, 11207. Tel: 718-827-7932; Fax: 718-827-6696.

Secretary to the Bishop—Mr. PETRAS AZUOLAS.

"Bishop's Brief"—Quarterly information bulletin.

Bishop's Pastoral Council—Rev. ANTANAS SAULAITIS, S.J., Vice Pres.; Sr. IGNE MARIJOSIUS, Prog. Dir.; Mr. ALGIS SILBAJORIS, Information.

Lithuanian R. Catholic Religious Aid—Mrs. VIDA JANKAUSKAS, Exec. Dir., *351 Highland Blvd., Brooklyn, NY, 11207.* Tel: 718-647-2434; Fax: 718-827-6696.

Pontifical Lithuanian College of St. Casimir—Rev. Msgr. ALGIMANTAS BARTKUS, J.C.L., Rector, *via Casalmonferrato 20, 00182. Rome, Italy.* Tel: 06-70-24-908; Fax: 06-70-11-659.

Vocations and Public Relations Director—Rev. EDMUNDAS PUTRIMAS, *1011 College St., Toronto, Ontario, Canada, M6H-1A8.* Tel: 416-533-0621.

Publications—The Observer, Darbininkas, Draugas, Garsas, Journeys, Laiskai Lietuviams, Laivas, Moteru Dirva, Vytis, Musu Zinios, I Laisve.

World Lithuanian R. Catholic Priests' League—Rev. AGUSTINAS SIMANAVICIUS, O.F.M., Pres., *1011 College St., Toronto, Ontario, Canada, MGH 1A8.* Tel: 416-533-0621; Fax: 416-532-4816.

Lithuanian R. Catholic Priests' League of America—Rev. ALBERT CONTONS, Pres., *50 Orton-Marotta Way, Boston, MA, 02127.* Tel: 617-218-0353.

Lithuanian Franciscan Vice Province of St. Casimir—Very Rev. PLACIDAS BARIUS, O.F.M., Prov., *Kennebunkport, ME, 04046.* Tel: 207-967-2031; Fax: 207-967-5721.

Lithuanian Jesuit Province—Very Rev. ANTANAS SAULAITIS, S.J., Prov., *2345 W. 56th St., Chicago, IL, 60636.* Tel: 312-737-8400.

Lithuanian Marian Province of St. Casimir—Very Rev. DONALD PETRAITIS, M.I.C., Prov., *6336 Kilbourn Ave., Chicago, IL, 60636.* Tel: 312-582-1666.

Sisters of the Immaculate Conception of the Blessed Virgin Mary—Sr. PAULE SAVICKAITE, Prov., *Rte. 21, R.D. 2, Putnam, CT, 06260.* Tel: 203-928-7955; Fax: 203-928-1930.

Poor Sisters of Jesus Crucified and the Sorrowful Mother—Sr. CELESTINE STAKUTIS, Supr. Gen., *261 Thatcher St., Brockton, MA, 02402.* Tel: 617-588-5070.

Sisters of St. Casimir—Sr. MARILYN KUZMICKUS, Gen. Supr., *2601 W. Marquette Rd., Chicago, IL, 60609.* Tel: 312-776-1324.

Benedictine Sisters—Sr. RAPHAELA, Supr., *333 Wallace Rd., Bedford, NH, 03102.* Tel: 603-472-3339.

Sisters of St. Francis—Sr. JOAN BRAZINSKI, Dir., *Grove & Roberts Rd., Pittsburgh, PA, 15234.* Tel: 412-882-9911.

INSTITUTIONS LOCATED IN THE DIOCESE

[A] SCHOOLS

CHICAGO, IL. *Maria High School.*

THOMPSON, CT. *Marionapolis Prep School.*

[B] HOSPITALS

CHICAGO, IL. *Holy Cross Hospital.*

[C] NURSING HOMES AND HOMES FOR THE AGED

BROCKTON, MA. *St. Joseph Manor Nursing Home.*

ELMHURST, PA. *St. Mary's Villa.*

HOLLAND, PA. *St. Joseph Nursing Home.*

LEMONT, IL. *Holy Family Villa.*

PUTNAM, CT. *Maulaitis Nursing Home.*

[D] MISCELLANEOUS

BROOKLYN, NY. *Franciscan Cultural Center.*

CHICAGO, IL. *Catholic Action Fund.*

Jesuit Lithuanian Center.

Lithuanian Cultural Institution.

Matulaitis Institute.

MANCHESTER, MI. *Dainava Conference Center and Camp.*

PUTNAM, IL. *American Lithuanian Catholic Archives.*

WEST BRATTLEBORO, VT. *Camp Neringa.*

[E] CEMETERIES

CHICAGO, IL. *St. Casimir Lithuanian.*

RELIGIOUS INSTITUTES OF MEN REPRESENTED IN THE DIOCESE

For further details refer to the corresponding bracketed number in the Religious Institutes of Men or Women section.

[]—*Congregation of the Marians Province of St. Casimir.* (Chicago, IL).

[]—*Franciscan Fathers of the Lithuanian Vicariate of St. Casimir.* (Kennebunkport, ME).

[]—*Jesuit Fathers of Della Strada.* (Chicago, IL).

RELIGIOUS INSTITUTES OF WOMEN REPRESENTED IN THE DIOCESE

[0200]—*Benedictine Sisters.* (Bedford, NH).—O.S.B.

[3240]—*Poor Sisters of Jesus Crucified and the Sorrowful Mother.* (Brockton, MA).—C.J.C.

[2140]—*Sisters of Immaculate Conception of the Blessed Virgin Mary.* (Putnam, CT).

[3740]—*Sisters of St. Casimir.* (Chicago, IL).—S.S.C.

[1690]—*Sisters of St. Francis.* (Pittsburgh, PA).—O.S.F.

STATISTICS

Most personnel and institutions are under the jurisdiction of their local ordinaries.

NECROLOGY

(No Deaths)

Personal Prelatures

Personal prelatures are jurisdictional structures of a secular type which are established by the Holy See as an instrument within the hierarchical pastoral work of the Church to carry out special pastoral or missionary tasks. Personal prelatures are based on the principle of insertion into the local Church. In this they differ essentially from the personal dioceses, such as those constituted for the faithful of a particular rite, which are based on the principle of independence or autonomy in regard to local Churches.

Personal Prelatures

Vatican II provided for setting up personal prelatures (see Decree, *Presbyterorum ordinis*, no. 10). Additional norms were established in subsequent pontifical legislation (see Motu proprio *Ecclesiae Sanctae* no. 1, no. 4, August 6, 1966 and the Apostolic Constitution *Regimini Ecclesiae Universae*, no. 49, no. 1, Aug. 15, 1967). General legislation concerning personal prelatures is contained in canons 294 to 297 of the 1983 Code of Canon Law.

Personal prelatures are to be established by the Holy See after hearing the views of the respective Episcopal Conferences (can. 294). They are governed by a Prelate according to statutes given by the Holy See. The Prelate is their proper Ordinary, who may incardinate priests and must look after their spiritual and temporal welfare (can. 295). Lay people can dedicate themselves by means of a contractural agreement, to the apostolic activities of the prelature (can. 296). And the statutes are to determine the relations of the prelature with the Ordinaries of the places in which the prelature works, with the prior consent of the Ordinaries (can. 297).

OPUS DEI

(Praelatura Sanctae Crucis et Operis Dei)

Reverend Monsignor

JAVIER ECHEVARRIA, J.D., J.C.D.

Prelate of the Prelature of the Holy Cross and Opus Dei; ordained August 7, 1955; appointed April 20, 1994; episcopal ordination January 6, 1995. *Curia of the Prelature, Viale Bruno Buozzi 73, 00197, Rome, Italy. Tel: 6-808-961.*

Erected by the Apostolic Constitution, "Ut sit," on November 28, 1982 by Pope John Paul II.

Opus Dei was founded on October 2, 1928 by Blessed Josemaria Escriva, to spread in all sectors of society a profound awareness of the universal call to sanctity in ordinary life and, more specifically, in the exercise of one's work.

Curia of the Prelature—Viale Bruno Buozzi, 73, 00197. Rome, Italy. Tel: 6-808-961.

Vicar General—Rev. Msgr. Fernando Ocariz, Ph.D., S.T.D., *Viale Bruno Buozzi 73, 00197. Rome, Italy.* Rev. Frederick Dolan, residing at the Curia of the Prelature.

Regional Vicar for the United States—Rev. Msgr. James A. Kelly, Ph.D., *99 Overlook Circle, New Rochelle, NY 10804.* Tel: 914-235-1201.

Delegate Vicar for the Midwest—Very Rev. William H. Stetson, J.D., J.C.D., *5800 N. Keating Ave., Chicago, IL 60646.* Tel: 312-283-5800.

Delegate Vicar for California—Very Rev. George M. Rossman, Ph.D., *765 14th Ave., San Francisco, CA 94118.* Tel: 415-386-0431.

Delegate Vicar for Texas—Very Rev. Michael J. Barrett, S.T.D., *5505 Chaucer Dr., Houston, TX 77005.* Tel: 715-523-4351.

Represented in the Archdioceses of Boston, Chicago, Los Angeles, Milwaukee, Newark, New York, St. Louis, San Antonio, San Francisco, Washington and in the Dioceses of Burlington, Dallas, Fort Wayne-South Bend, Galveston-Houston, Gary, Oakland, Palm Beach, Peoria, Pittsburgh, Providence, Trenton and Victoria.

REGIONAL VICARIATE FOR THE UNITED STATES

State of New York

New Rochelle—Rev. Msgr. James A. Kelly, Ph.D. Reg. Vicar; Revs. Robert Brisson; Edward Maristany. *99 Overlook Cir., New Rochelle, NY 10804.* Tel: 914-235-0198. Revs. Bradley K. Arturi; Orestes Gonzalez. *117 Overlook Cir., New Rochelle, NY 10804.* Tel: 914-235-6128.

New York—Revs. Robert A. Connor; Martin J. Miller. *330 Riverside Dr., New York, NY 10025.* Tel: 212-222-3285.

District of Columbia

Washington—Revs. Malcolm M. Kennedy; L. Michael Curtin; Lawrence A. Kutz. *2301 Wyoming Ave. N.W., Washington, DC 20008.* Tel: 202-234-1567; Revs. Ronald S. Gillis. *4300 Garrison St. N.W., Washington, DC 20016.* Tel: 202-362-2419; William G. Shaughnessy, *4955 Linnean Ave., N.W., Washington, DC 20008.* Tel: 202-237-6894.

State of Massachusetts

Cambridge—Revs. Salvador M. Ferigle; John C. Agnew. *25 Follen St., Cambridge, MA 02138.* Tel: 617-354-3204.

Chestnut Hill—Revs. Raphael F. Caamano; Richard W. Rieman; Alvaro Silva; David J. Cavanagh. *481 Hammond St., Chestnust Hill, MA 02167.* Tel: 617-738-7348.

State of New Jersey

Princeton—Rev. C. John McCloskey. *34 Mercer St., Princeton, NJ 08540.* Tel: 609-497-9448.

South Orange—Revs. James W. Albrecht; Thomas J. Lamb. *170 Montrose Ave., South Orange, NJ 07079.* Tel: 201-763-8397.

State of Pennsylvania

Pittsburgh—Revs. Frank Hoffman; Joseph P. Landauer. *5090 Warwick Ter., Pittsburgh, PA 15213.* Tel: 412-683-8448.

State of Florida

Delray Beach—Revs. Christopher Schmitt; John J. Alvarez. *4409 Frances Dr., Delray Beach, FL 33445.* Tel: 305-498-1249.

State of Rhode Island

Providence—Rev. Michael J. Manz. *224 Bowen St., Providence, RI 02906.* Tel: 401-272-7834.

DELEGATE VICARIATE FOR THE MIDWEST

State of Illinois

Chicago—Very Rev. William H. Stetson, J.C.D. Delegate Vicar; Revs. Peter V. Armenio; John Meyer. *5800 N. Keating Ave., Chicago, IL 60646.* Tel: 312-283-5800; Revs. Fred Piegl; Claudio Urbano. *7225 N. Greenview Ave., Chicago, IL 60646.* Tel: 312-465-3468; Revs. John Debicki; Hilary Mahaney; Charles Ferrer. *1825 N. Wood St., Chicago, IL 60622.* Tel: 312-278-2644.

Oak Park—Revs. James Socias; Richard Schendt; Barry Cole. *829 S. Euclid, Oak Park, IL 60304.* Tel: 708-383-0928.

Urbana—Rev. Jerome L. Jung. , *715 W. Michigan, Urbana, IL 61801.* Tel: 217-367-6650.

State of Indiana

South Bend—Rev. Gerald Kolf, *1121 N. Notre Dame Ave., South Bend, IN 46617.* Tel: 219-232-0550.

State of Missouri

Kirkwood—Revs. Michael E. Giesler; Mark Mannion. *100 E. Essex Ave., Kirkwood, MO 63122.* Tel: 314-821-1608.

State of Wisconsin

Brookfield—Revs. Robert Bucciarelli; John Kubeck. *12900 W. North Ave., Brookfield, WI 53005.* Tel: 414-784-1523.

DELEGATE VICARIATE FOR THE STATE OF CALIFORNIA

San Francisco—Very Rev. George M. Rossman, Ph.D., Delegate Vicar; Revs. Torlach C. Delargy; Arne J. Panula. *765 14th Ave., San Francisco, CA 94118.* Tel: 415-386-0431.

Menlo Park—Rev. Salvador V. Serrano, *1835 Bay Laurel Dr., Menlo Park, CA 94025.* Tel: 415-327-1675.

Mill Valley—Rev. Paul A. Donlan. *108 Kipling Dr., Mill Valley, CA 94941.* Tel: 415-388-4531.

Los Angeles—Revs. Rene J. Schatteman; Jose P. Ruisanchez. *655 Levering Ave., Los Angeles, CA 90024.* Tel: 213-208-0941.

Berkeley—Rev. John R. Waiss. *2710 College Ave., Berkeley, CA 94705.* Tel: 510-548-2819.

DELEGATE VICARIATE FOR THE STATE OF TEXAS

Houston—Very Rev. Michael J. Barrett. S.T.D., Delegate Vicar; Revs. Jose Gomez; George W. Crafts. *5505 Chaucer Dr., Houston, TX 77005.* Tel: 713-523-4351.

Irving—Rev. John E. Solarski. *3610 Wingren, Irving, TX 75062.* Tel: 214-650-0064.

Eastern Church

Eastern Catholic Association (ECA)

The Eastern Catholic Associates is the association of all Eastern Catholic Bishops in the United States. All Eastern Catholic Bishops, diocesan bishops (and their equivalent in law) and auxiliaries are members. The Association represents the Armenian, Chaldean, Maronite Melkite, Romanian, Ruthenian and Ukrainian Churches. The Syriac, Syro-Malabar and Russian churches are also represented but without a bishop member since they presently have no established hierarchy in the United States. Officers of the Association are—*President:* Most Rev. NICHOLAS J. SAMRA, D.D., V.G., Auxiliary Bishop of Newton, 8525 Cole, Warren MI 48093-5239. Tel: 810-558-0143; Fax: 810-558-0144. *Vice President:* Most Rev. ROBERT M. MOSKAL, D.D., Bishop of the Ukrainian Diocese of St. Josaphat in Parma, 5720 State Rd., Parma, OH 44134-7180. Tel: 216-888-1522; Fax: 216-888-3477. *Secretary:* Most Rev. JOHN BOTEAN, Bishop of Romanian Catholic Diocese of St. George, Canton, 1121 44th St., N.E., Canton, OH 44714-1297. Tel: 330-492-4086; Fax: 330-493-1416.

Religious Education Department

The ECA has established the ECDD - The Eastern Catholic Conference of Diocesan Directors of Religious Education which oversees, through "God With Us Publications", all publications of catechetical materials published by it and used in Eastern Catholic Churches, mainly of Byzantine tradition. Rev. John S. Kachuba, M.A., Chm.-ECDD & Dir.-Religious Education, Eparchy of Parma, 532 Lloyd R., Euclid, OH 44132. Tel: 216-732-7292; Fax: 216-732-9434. Rev. Fred Saato, Asst. Chm./Dir.-Publications & Dir.-Education Services, Eparchy of Newton, 27 Lake Ave., Yonkers, NY 10703. Tel: 914-968-2428; Fax: 914-423-9239. Sr. Ann Laszok, O.S.B.M., Treas. & Bus. Mgr.-ECDD, 204 Olivia St., McKeesrocks, PA 15136. Tel: 412-481-9778; Fax: 412-331-8140. "God With Us Publications", P.O. Box 99203, Pittsburgh, PA 15233. Tel: 412-771-9119; Fax: 412-766-8244.

In addition to the Eastern Churches listed below there are other Eastern Churches in communion with Rome which do not have Ordinaries of their own in the United States. Consequently they are under the jurisdiction of the local Ordinary and the various parishes and institutions are incorporated in the Archdiocesan and Diocesan listings. Please consult these pages for full information regarding churches, personnel and statistics. For convenience, however, listed below are the Russian Eastern Churches and the cities in which they are located.

RUSSIAN

California

El Segundo (LA), St. Andrew

San Francisco (SFR), Our Lady of Fatima Center

New York

New York (NY), St. Michael Chapel (St. Patrick's Old Cathedral)

Armenian Catholic Exarchate of U.S.A. and Canada

Most Reverend

HOVHANNES TERTZAKIAN, O.M.VEN.

Apostolic Exarch for Armenian Catholics in the United States and Canada; ordained September 8, 1948; appointed Titular Bishop of Trebisonda and Apostolic Exarch for Armenian Catholics in the United States and Canada January 6, 1995; ordained April 29, 1995; installed May 7, 1995. *Office: 110 E. 12th, New York, NY, 10003-5395.*

Chancery & Vicar General Office: 110 E. 12th St., New York, NY, 10003-5395. Tel.: 212-477-2030; Fax: 212-477-2185.

Most Reverend

NERSES MIKAEL SETIAN, D.D., J.C.D.

Former Apostolic Exarch for the Armenian Catholics in the U.S.A. and Canada; born October 18, 1918; appointed Titular Bishop of Ancera and Apostolic Exarch for the Armenian Catholics in the U.S.A. and Canada July 3, 1981; ordained December 5, 1981; installed December 27, 1981; retired. *Res., c/o Our Lady Queen of Martyrs Church, 1327 Pleasant Ave., Los Angeles, CA, 90033.*

Legal Title: Apostolic Exarchate For Armenian Catholics In The United States of America.

STATISTICAL OVERVIEW

Personnel	
Bishop	1
Retired Bishops	1
Priests: Diocesan Active in Diocese	4
Number of Diocesan Priests	4
Religious Priests in Diocese	8
Ordinations:	
Total Sisters	14
Parishes	
Parishes	6
With Resident Pastor:	
Resident Diocesan Priests	4
Resident Religious Priests	2
Educational	
Elementary Schools, Diocesan and Parish	4
Total Students	977
Catechesis/Religious Education:	
Elementary Students	96
Total Students Under Catholic Instruction	1,073
Teachers in the Diocese:	
Priests	2
Sisters	14
Lay Teachers	91
Vital Statistics	
Receptions into the Church:	
Infant Baptism Totals	77
First Communions	49
Confirmations	81
Marriages:	
Catholic	15
Total Marriages	15
Deaths	28
Total Catholic Population	26,000

Chancery & Vicar General Office—*110 E. 12th St., New York, NY, 10003-5395.* Tel: 212-477-2030; Fax: 212-477-2185.

Vicar General—Rev. Msgr. SARKIS GABADIAN. Tel: 215-896-7789.

Chancellor—Rev. RAPHAEL ANDONIAN, O.M. Ven. Tel: 212-477-2030.

Newspaper Diocesan Bulletin—"The Eternal Flame," Office: *110 E. 12th St., New York, NY, 10003.* Tel: 212-477-2030.

Newspaper Diocesan Bulletin "VERELK"—Office: *1327 Pleasant Ave., Los Angeles, CA, 90033.* Tel: 213-267-1740.

Armenian Sacred Music—Rev. Msgr. JOSEPH KALAYJIAN.

CLERGY, PARISHES, MISSIONS AND PAROCHIAL SCHOOLS

STATE OF NEW YORK

Brooklyn, Kings Co., Visitation. Closed. For inquiries for parish records contact the Chancery.

New York, New York Co., St. Ann's Cathedral, Most Rev. Hovhannes Tertzakian, O.M.Ven.
Res., 110 E. 12th St., 10003. Tel: 212-477-2030; Fax: 212-477-2185.

STATE OF CALIFORNIA

Los Angeles, Los Angeles Co., Our Lady Queen of Martyrs, Revs. Raphael Minassian; Basil Ferhatian, C.M.Vd.
Res., 1327 Pleasant Ave., 90033. Tel: 213-261-9898; Fax: 213-261-0522.

STATE OF MASSACHUSETTS

Boston, Middlesex Co., Holy Cross, Rev. Raphael Andonian, O.M.Ven.
Res., 198 Lexington St., Belmont, 02178. Tel: 617-547-2122.

STATE OF MICHIGAN

Detroit, Wayne Co., St. Vartan's, Rev. Msgr. Joseph Kalajian, Ph.D.
Res., 8541 Greenfield Rd., 48228. Tel: 313-584-3345.

STATE OF NEW JERSEY

Paterson, Passaic Co., Sacred Heart (1927), Rev. Georges Kalousieh.

Res., 155 Long Hill Rd., Little Falls, 07424-2374. Tel: 201-890-0447; Fax: 201-890-0292.

STATE OF PENNSYLVANIA

Philadelphia, Philadelphia Co., St. Mark's Armenian Catholic (1924), Rev. Msgr. Sarkis Gabadian.

Res., 400 Haverford Rd., Wynnewood, 19096-2699. Tel: 610-896-7789; Fax: 610-896-0915.

INSTITUTIONS LOCATED IN THE DIOCESE

[A] SCHOOLS

STATE OF CALIFORNIA

LA CRESCENTA. *Mekhitarist School*, 4900 Maryland Ave., 91214. Tel: 818-249-6121; 6122; 6123; 6124; Fax: 818-249-0350. Revs. Augustin Szekula, Prin.; Mikael Akian.

MONTROSE. *Armenian Sisters of the Immaculate Conception*, 2361 Florencita Dr., 91020. Tel: 818-249-8783. Sr. Alphonsa Bedrossian, Supr. & Prin.

STATE OF MASSACHUSETTS

LEXINGTON. *Armenian Sisters Academy*, 6 Eliot Rd., 02173. Tel: 617-863-5962. Sr. Veronique Achikian, Supr. & Prin.

STATE OF PENNSYLVANIA

RADNOR. *Armenian Sisters Academy*, 440 Upper Gulph Rd., 19087. Tel: 215-687-4100; Fax: 610-687-2430. Sr. Louisa Kassarjian, Prin.

[B] RELIGIOUS INSTITUTES AND CONVENTS FOR WOMEN

STATE OF CALIFORNIA

MONTROSE. *Armenian Sisters of the Immaculate Conception*, 2361 Florencita Dr., 91020. Tel: 818-249-8783. Sr. Alphonsa Bedrossian, Supr. & Prin.

STATE OF MASSACHUSETTS

LEXINGTON. *Armenian Sisters of the Immaculate Conception*, 6 Eliot Rd., 02173. Tel: 617-863-5962. Sr. Veronique Achikian, Supr. & Prin.

STATE OF PENNSYLVANIA

RADNOR. *Armenian Sisters of the Immaculate Conception*, 440 Upper Gulph Rd., 19087. Tel: 215-688-9360; Fax: 610-687-2430. Sr. Louisa Kassarjian, Prin.

[C] EDUCATIONAL FOUNDATIONS

STATE OF CALIFORNIA

GLENDALE.

**Mekhitarian Educational Foundation*, 702 E. Glenoaks Blvd., 91207. Tel: 818-546-1967; Fax: 818-548-1166. Revs. Dadjad Yardemian, Exec. Dir.; Mesrop Sulahian.

NECROLOGY

(No Deaths)

Diocese of Newton (Melkite-Greek Catholic)

Most Reverend

JOHN A. ELYA, B.S.O., D.D.

Eparch of Newton; ordained February 17, 1952; appointed Auxiliary Bishop of Newton April 2, 1986; appointed Eparch of Newton November 25, 1993; installed January 25, 1994. *Res., 19 Dartmouth St., West Newton, MA, 02165.* Tel.: 617-969-8957; Fax: 617-969-4115.

Most Reverend

JOSEPH E. TAWIL, D.D., LL.D.

Eparch Emeritus of Newton; ordained July 20, 1936; consecrated January 1, 1960; appointed Apostolic Exarch October 29, 1969; appointed Eparch July 15, 1976; became emeritus December 12, 1989. *Res., 19 Dartmouth St., West Newton, MA, 02165.*

Most Reverend

NICHOLAS J. SAMRA, D.D.

Auxiliary Bishop of Newton and Protosyncellus; ordained May 10, 1970; appointed Auxiliary Bishop of Newton June 29, 1989. *Res., 8525 Cole St., Warren, MI, 48093.* Tel.: 810-558-0143; Fax: 810-558-0144.

ESTABLISHED AS AN APOSTOLIC EXARCHATE JANUARY 10, 1966.

ELEVATED TO EPARCHY, JULY 15, 1976; EMBRACES ALL MEMBERS OF THE MELKITE GREEK CATHOLIC CHURCH IN THE UNITED STATES.

For legal titles of parishes and institutions, consult the Chancery Office.

The Chancery: 19 Dartmouth St., West Newton, MA, 02165. Tel.: 617-969-8957; Fax: 617-969-4115.

Web site address: http://www.thenet.net/~melkite

E-mail address: Deakandy@aol.com

E-mail address: Rcgr71A@prodigy.com

STATISTICAL OVERVIEW

Personnel	
Retired Archbishops	1
Bishop	1
Auxiliary Bishops	1
Priests: Diocesan Active in Diocese	35
Priests: Active Outside Diocese	1
Priests: Retired, Sick or Absent	9
Number of Diocesan Priests	45
Religious Priests in Diocese	19
Extern Priests in Diocese	1
Ordinations:	
Religious Priests	1
Permanent Deacons	3
Permanent Deacons in Diocese	28
Total Brothers	1
Total Sisters	3
Parishes	
Parishes	35
With Resident Pastor:	
Resident Diocesan Priests	25
Resident Religious Priests	10
Without Resident Pastor:	
Missions	7
Welfare	
Specialized Homes	2
Total Assisted	5,700
Special Centers for Social Services	1
Total Assisted	5,400
Educational	
Seminaries, Diocesan	1
Students from This Diocese	2
Diocesan Students in Other Seminaries	1
Seminaries, Religious	1
Students Religious	1
Total Seminarians	4
Catechesis/Religious Education:	
High School Students	298
Elementary Students	1,306
Total Students Under Catholic Instruction	1,608
Teachers in the Diocese:	
Vital Statistics	
Receptions into the Church:	
Infant Baptism Totals	467
Adult Baptism Totals	21
Received into Full Communion	29
First Communions	527
Confirmations	594
Marriages:	
Catholic	135
Interfaith	28
Total Marriages	163
Deaths	182
Total Catholic Population	27,730

Former Bishops—Most Rev. JUSTIN A. NAJMY, B.A.O., D.D.,born April 23, 1898; ord. Dec. 25, 1926; cons. May 29, 1966; installed June 4, 1966; died June 11, 1968.—Most Rev. JOSEPH E. TAWIL, D.D., LL.D., ord. July 20, 1936; cons. Jan. 1, 1960; appt. Apostolic Exarch, Oct. 29, 1969; appt. Eparch, July 15, 1976 became emeritus Dec. 12, 1989.—Most Rev. IGNATIUS GHATTAS, B.S.O., D.D.,born Dec. 25, 1920; ord. July 7, 1946; appt. Dec. 12, 1989; cons. Feb. 23, 1990; died Oct. 11, 1992.

Diocesan Administration

Chancery Office—19 Dartmouth St., W. Newton, MA, 02165. Tel: 617-969-8957; Fax: 617-969-4115. Office Hours: Mon.-Fri. 9-5.

Protosyncellus—Most Rev. NICHOLAS J. SAMRA, D.D.

Chancellor—Deacon PAUL F. LAWLER, *19 Dartmouth St., W. Newton, MA, 02165.* Tel: 617-969-8957; Fax: 617-969-4115.

Diocesan Tribunal—18 New Dunstable Rd., Nashua, NH, 03060. Tel: 603-595-9815; Fax: 603-595-3452.

Judicial Vicar—Rt. Rev. GERASIMOS MURPHY, B.S.O., D.Min., J.C.D., *18 New Dunstable Rd., Nashua, NH, 03060.* Tel: 603-595-9815; Fax: 603-595-2389.

Defender of the Bond and Promoter of Justice—Rt. Rev. JOSEPH S. HAGGAR, M.A., J.C.L.; LOUISE TESSIER, J.C.L.

Judges—Revs. JOSEPH KOURY, J.C.D.; JOHN FARAJ, J.C.D.; HERBERT MAY, J.C.L.

Notaries—Deacons GEORGE YANY; PAUL LAWLER; LUCILLE LAROCHE.

Economos—Protodeacon ANDRE ST. GERMAIN.

Protopresbyters—Rt. Rev. JOSEPH HAGGAR, New England: Rt. Rev. PHILIP RACZKA, Mid-Atlantic: Rt. Rev. JOHN HADDAD, Southeast: Revs. IBRAHIM IBRAHIM, Mid-West: JAMES BABCOCK, West:

Consultative Bodies

College of Eparchial Consultors—Most Rev. NICHOLAS J. SAMRA; Rt. Rev. RONALD GOLINI, M.A., S.T.L.; Rt. Rev. WILLIAM HADDAD; Rt. Rev. JOSEPH S. HAGGAR, J.C.L.; Rt. Rev. GERASIMOS MURPHY, B.S.O., D.Min., J.C.D.; Rt. Rev. PHILIP RACZKA; Rt. Rev. ROMANOS V. RUSSO.

Presbyteral Council—Most Rev. JOHN A. ELYA, Pres.; Most Rev. NICHOLAS J. SAMRA; Rt. Rev. PHILIP RACZKA, Sec.; Rt. Rev. JOHN HADDAD, B.S.O.; Rt. Rev. JOSEPH S. HAGGAR; Rt. Rev. EDWARD KAKATY; Rt. Rev. ELIAS SKAFF; Revs. JOHN AZAR; JAMES BABCOCK; MARTIN HYATT, B.S.O.; FRANK MILIENEWICZ; BASIL SAMRA.

Diocese of Newton for the Melkites in the USA, Inc., a Massachusetts Corporation—Most Rev. JOHN A. ELYA; Most Rev. NICHOLAS J. SAMRA; Rt. Rev. JOSEPH FRANCAVILLA; Rt. Rev. JOHN HADDAD; Rev. GEORGE D. GALLARO; Protodeacon ANDRE ST. GERMAIN.

Finance Council—Protodeacon ANDRE ST. GERMAIN, Economos; Mr. JOSEPH GHOLL; Mr. STANLEY SABA; Mrs. KATHLEEN SABA RICHARDS; Dr. JOHN NAZARIAN; Deacon ROBERT SHALHOUB; GILBERT SHASHA; EDMUND NAHOM.

Priest's Sickness & Disability, and Retirement Plans—Most Rev. NICHOLAS J. SAMRA; Rt. Rev. JOSEPH FRANCAVILLA; Rt. Rev. RONALD GOLINI; Rt. Rev. JOSEPH S. HAGGAR; Rt. Rev. PHILIP RACZKA; Revs. JOHN FARAJ; GEORGE D. GALLARO; FRANK MILIENEWICZ; ALEXEI SMITH.

Canonical Consultant—Rt. Rev. Archimandrite VICTOR J. POSPISHIL, J.C.D.; Rev. JOHN FARAJ, B.S.O., J.C.D; Rt. Rev. JOHN D. FARIS, J.C.O.D.; Rev. GEORGE D. GALLARO, J.C.O.D.

Legal Consultant—CAMILLE F. SARROUF, ESQ., *95 Commercial Wharf, Boston, MA, 02110.* Tel: 617-227-5800.

Liturgical Consultants—Rev. ROBERT TAFT, S.J.; Archimandrite EUTHIMIOS SKAFF, B.S.O.

Pastoral Offices and Commissions

Continuing Education of Clergy Office—Revs. GEORGE D. GALLARO, Coord. PAUL FRECHETTE; GABRIEL GHANOUM; IGNATIUS HARRINGTON; FRED SAATO; ALEXEI SMITH.

National Association of Melkite Youth—Rev. SAMI BAROODY, *802 Rifle Camp Rd., W. Paterson, NJ, 07424.* Tel: 201-785-4144.

MAYA (Melkite Assoc. of Young Adults)—Rt. Rev. ROMANOS RUSSO, *228 91st St., Brooklyn, NY, 11209.* Tel: 718-836-7311.

Ambassadors—Rev. GABRIEL GHANOUM, B.S.O., *126 S.E. 15 Rd., Miami, FL, 33129.* Tel: 305-856-8666.

National Association of Melkite Women—Rev. EDWARD KAKATY, *7 V.F.W. Pkwy., Boston, MA, 02131.* Tel: 617-323-5242.

Liturgical Commission—Most Rev. NICHOLAS SAMRA, Chm.; Rt. Rev. JOSEPH HAGGAR; Rt. Rev. VICTOR SAMAHA; Rt. Rev. EDWARD KAKATY; Rt. Rev. ROMANOS RUSSO.

Educational Services—Rev. FRED SAATO, M.A., *27 Lake Ave., Yonkers, NY, 10703.* Tel: 914-968-2428.

Vocations Office—Rt. Rev. PHILIP RACZKA, Coord., *233 Grant Ave., Newton Centre, MA, 02179.* Tel: 617-965-9862; Fax: 617-527-5816. Rt. Rev. EDWARD KAKATY; Revs. SAMI BAROODY; IGNATIUS HARRINGTON; FRANK MILIENEWICZ; ALEXEI SMITH.

"Sophia" (A Journal)—Rev. JOHN T. AZAR, JR., *11245 Rye St., N. Hollywood, CA, 91602.*

Ecumenical & Interreligious Commission—Rev. GEORGE D. GALLARO, *8525 Cole Ave., Warren, MI, 48093.* Rt. Rev. EDWARD G. KAKATY.

Order of St. Nicholas—Most Rev. NICHOLAS J. SAMRA, Governor Gen.; Rev. GABRIEL GHANOUM, B.S.O., Exec. Dir. RAYMOND KAYAL, National Chm., *Mailing Address: 19 Dartmouth St., W. Newton, MA, 02165.*

Associated Melkite Charities—Rev. PHILARET LITTLEFIELD, *1617 W. State St., Milwaukee, WI, 53233.* Tel: 414-342-1543.

CLERGY, PARISHES, MISSIONS AND PAROCHIAL SCHOOLS

STATE OF MASSACHUSETTS

Boston, Suffolk Co., Annunciation Cathedral, Rt. Rev. Edward G. Kakaty; Deacon Paul Lawler.
Res., 7 V.F.W. Pkwy., 02131. Tel: 617-323-5242; Fax: 617-325-2662.

Lawrence, Essex Co., St. Joseph, Rev. Joseph Thomas, B.S.O.; Deacons Bryan McNeil; John MacMillan.
Res., 241 Hampshire St., 01841. Tel: 508-682-8152.

Worcester, Worcester Co., Our Lady of Perpetual Help, Rev. Paul G. Frechette.
Res., 256 Hamilton St., 01604. Tel: 508-752-4174.

STATE OF ALABAMA

Birmingham, Jefferson Co., St. George, Rev. Frank J. Milienewicz; Deacon Seraphim Ritchey.
Res., 425-Sixteenth Ave. S., 35205. Tel: 205-252-5788; Fax: 205-252-1085.

STATE OF ARIZONA

Phoenix, Maricopa Co., St. John of the Desert, Rev. Basil Samra.
Res., 2525 E. Osborn, 85016. Tel: 602-954-7258.

STATE OF CALIFORNIA

El Segundo, Los Angeles Co., St. Paul, Rev. Alexei R. Smith, Admin.
Res., 538 Concord, 90245. Tel: 310-322-1892.

Fremont, Alameda Co., St. Elias, Rev. James K. Graham.
Res., 45180 S. Grimmer Blvd., 94539. Tel: 510-656-5949.

Fullerton, Orange Co., Holy Cross, Rev. James K. Babcock; Deacon Luigi Merandi.
Res., 706 S. Lemon St., 92632. Tel: 714-992-0652; Fax: 714-992-6505.

North Hollywood, Los Angeles Co., St. Anne, Revs. John T. Azar, Jr.; George Said Bisharat; Deacons George Sayegh; Marion Rimmer.
Res., 11245 Rye St., 91602. Tel: 818-761-2034; Fax: 818-761-2922.

Oakland, Alameda Co., St. John The Theologian, Revs. Owen Carroll; Eugene M. Ludwig, O.F.M.Cap.
Res., 5 Gleneden Ave., 94611. Tel: 510-428-2234.

Sacramento, Sacramento Co., St. George, Rev. Mark E. Melone.
Church—1620 Bell St., 95825. Tel: 916-920-2900.

San Bernardino, San Bernardino Co., St. Philip. Attended by Fullerton. Rev. James K. Babcock, Admin.
Mailing Address: 706 S. Lemon St., Fullerton, 92632. Tel: 714-992-0652.

San Diego, San Diego Co., St. Jacob Mission. Services at Holy Angels Byzantine Catholic Church, 2235 Galahad Rd., San Diego. Rt. Rev. Nassir Matta, Admin.; Deacon Edward Bagdasar.
Mailing Address: 1317 Corto Ln., El Cajon, 92020.

Temecula, Riverside Co., Virgin Mary Mission, Rt. Rev. Nassir Matta, Admin.
Mailing Address: 24373 Saddlebag Ct., Murietta, 92362.
41770 Margarita Rd., #2109, 92591. Tel: 909-308-1060.
Church—Churchill Plaza, Front St., San Diego.

STATE OF CONNECTICUT

Danbury, Fairfield Co., St. Ann, Rev. Basil R. Parent.
Mailing Address: 181 Clapboard Ridge Rd., 06811. Tel: 203-743-5119.

Waterford, New London Co., St. Ann, Rev. Roderick McRae, B.S.O.
Res., 41 Cross Rd., 06385. Tel: 860-442-2211.

STATE OF FLORIDA

Miami, Dade Co., St. Jude, Rt. Rev. John W. Haddad, B.S.O.; Rev. Gabriel Ghanoum, B.S.O.
Res., 126 S.E. 15 Rd., 33129. Tel: 305-856-1500; Fax: 305-859-7982.

Delray Beach, Palm Beach Co., St. Nicholas. Served by Miami. Rev. Gabriel Ghanoum, B.S.O.
Res., 126 S.E. 15 Rd., Miami, 33129. Tel: 305-856-8666.

STATE OF GEORGIA

Atlanta, Fulton Co., St. John, Rt. Rev. William F. Haddad, B.S.O.
Res., 1428 Ponce de Leon Ave., N.E., 30307. Tel: 404-373-9522; Fax: 404-373-9522.

Augusta, Richmond Co., St. Ignatios of Antioch, Rev. Daniel Munn; Deacon Kent Plowman.
Church—1003 Merry St., 30914. Tel: 706-738-9388.
Mailing Address: P.O. Box 3351, 30904.
Res., 967 Meigs St., 30904. Tel: 706-738-5623.

STATE OF ILLINOIS

Northlake, Cook Co., St. John the Baptist, Rev. Albert Wehby, B.A.O.; Deacon Elias Sahyouni.
Res., 200 E. North Ave., 60164. Tel: 708-865-7050.

STATE OF INDIANA

Hammond, Lake Co., St. Michael the Archangel, Rev. Robert Rabbat, Admin.
Church—619 Sibley Blvd., 46320.
Mailing Address: 7113 Columbia Ave., 46324. Tel: 219-844-9027.

South Bend, St. Joseph Co., St. John of Damascus, Rev. Robert L. Kerby; Deacon Lawrence Farhat.
Church—839 Woodcliff Dr., 46615.
Res., 918 Simon Ct., 46615. Tel: 219-233-5338.

STATE OF MICHIGAN

Lansing, Ingham Co., St. Joseph, Rt. Rev. Victor M. Samaha, B.C.O.
Res., 1913 S. Rundel Ave., 48910. Tel: 517-485-4053.

Plymouth, Wayne Co., St. Michael, Rev. Edmond J. Ghazal, B.C.O., Admin.
Church—585 N. Mill St., 48170. Tel: 313-721-1562.
Res., 8525 Cole St., Warren, 48093. Tel: 810-751-6017; 558-0027.

Warren, Macomb Co., Our Lady of Redemption, Most Rev. Nicholas J. Samra; Revs. George D. Gallaro; Edmond J. Ghazal, B.C.O.; Deacons Joseph Daratony; James Soloman.
Res., 8525 Cole St., 48093. Tel: 810-751-6017.

STATE OF NEW HAMPSHIRE

Manchester, Hillsborough Co., Our Lady of the Cedars, Rev. Eugene Mitchell, B.S.O.; Deacons Andre St. Germain; Thomas P. Steinmetz.
Res., 161 S. Beech St., 03103. Tel: 603-623-8944.

STATE OF NEW JERSEY

Cliffside Park, Bergen Co., St. Demetrius, Rt. Rev. Philip G. Raczka, Admin.
Res., 802 Rifle Camp Rd., West Paterson, 07424. Tel: 201-890-4140.

West Paterson, Passaic Co., St. Ann's, Revs. Sami W. Baroody; Romanos V. Russo; Deacons Michael Jolly; Edward Bsarany; Roland Basinski; Robert Shalhoub.
Res., 802 Rifle Camp Rd., 07424. Tel: 201-785-4144; Fax: 201-890-9599.

STATE OF NEW YORK

Brooklyn, Kings Co., Church of the Virgin Mary, Rev. John Faraj, B.S.O.
Res., 216 Eighth Ave., 11215. Tel: 718-788-5454; Fax: 718-499-7702.

Rochester, Monroe Co., St. Nicholas, Rev. Kenneth Sherman; Deacon Edmond Elhilow.
Res., 1492 Spencerport Rd., 14606. Tel: 716-426-4218.

Utica, Oneida Co., St. Basil, Rt. Rev. Julien A. Eliane; Deacon Daniel Klockowski.
Res., 901 Sherman Dr., 13501. Tel: 315-732-4662.

Yonkers, Westchester Co., Christ the Savior Church, Rev. Fred Saato.
Res., 27 Lake Ave., 10703. Tel: 914-968-2428; Fax: 914-423-9239.

STATE OF OHIO

Akron, Summit Co., St. Joseph, Rev. Anthony Nachef, B.S.O.
Res., 600 W. Exchange St., 44302. Tel: 330-535-7364; Fax: 330-535-8037.

Brooklyn, Cuyahoga Co., St. Elias, Rev. Ibrahim Ibrahim, B.S.O.
Res., 8023 Memphis Ave., 44144. Tel: 216-661-1155; Fax: 216-661-3838.

Columbus, Franklin Co., Holy Resurrection, Rev. Ignatius Harrington.
Res., 284 E. 15th Ave., 43201. Tel: 614-421-1325.

Zanesville, Muskingum Co., Holy Trinity, Rev. Ignatius Harrington.
Res., 284 E. 15th Ave., Columbus, 43201. Tel: 614-421-1325.
Church—130 N. Fifth St., P.O. Box 2714, 43701.

STATE OF PENNSYLVANIA

Scranton, Lackawanna Co., St. Joseph, Rev. Philip Azoon.
Res., 130 N. Cabrini Ave., 18504. Tel: 717-343-6092.

STATE OF RHODE ISLAND

Central Falls, Providence Co., St. Basil the Great, Rt. Rev. Joseph S. Haggar; Archdeacon George M. Yany.
Church—445 Broad St., 02863.
Res., 111 Cross St., 02863. Tel: 401-722-1345; Fax: 401-722-2436.

Woonsocket, Providence Co., St. Elias, Rt. Rev. Joseph S. Haggar.
Church—80 Hamilton St., 02895.
Res., 111 Cross St., Central Falls, 02863. Tel: 401-722-1345.

STATE OF VIRGINIA

McLean, Fairfax Co., Holy Transfiguration, Rt. Rev. Joseph F. Francavilla; Deacon Paul Weyrich.
Res., 8501 Lewinsville Rd., 22102. Tel: 703-734-9198; Fax: 703-893-7248.

STATE OF WISCONSIN

Milwaukee, Milwaukee Co., St. George, Rev. Philaret Littlefield.
Res., 1617 W. State St., 53233. Tel: 414-342-1543.

On Special Projects:
Reverend Fathers—
Kirk, David, P.O. Box 1177, New York, NY 10035. Tel: 212-410-6006
McCarthy, Charles, 49 Burkeside Ave., Brockton, MA 02401. Tel: 508-588-1008

Military Chaplains:
Reverend Fathers—
Brown, Shaun
Gosselin, Lawrence

On Duty Outside the Eparchy:
Reverend Fathers—
Frey, Ross, B.S.O.

Leave of Absence:
Reverend Fathers—
Adcock, Basil W.
Golini, Ronald
Moloney, Patrick W.

Retired:
Reverend Fathers—
Hassey, Athanase
King, James E.
Rt. Rev. Archimandri—
Aboody, Charles
Chalhoub, Maximos
Dagher, George, B.S.O.
Hage, Simon
Jadaa, John
Mardelli, Maximos
Skaff, Elias B.

Deacons:
Basinski, Roland, West Paterson, NJ
Bsarany, Edward, West Paterson, NJ
Daratony, Joseph, Warren, MI

Elhilow, Edmond, Rochester, NY
Farhat, Lawrence, Southbend, IN
Jolly, Michael, Paterson, NJ
Klockkowski, Daniel, Utica, NY
Lawler, Paul, Boston, MA
MacMillan, John, Lawrence, MA
McNeil, Bryan, Lawrence, MA
Merandi, Luigi, Fullerton, CA
Plowman, Kent, Augusta, GA
Rimmer, Marion, N. Hollywood, CA
Ritchey, Seraphim, Birmingham, AL
Sahyouni, Elias, Northlake, IL
Sayegh, George, N. Hollywood, CA
Shalhoub, Robert, West Paterson, NJ
Soloman, James, Warren, MI
St. Germain, Andre, Manchester, NH
Steinmetz, Thomas, Manchester, NH
Weyrich, Paul, McLean, VA
Yany, George, Central Falls, RI

Deacons Serving Outside the Eparchy:
Boutros, Peter
Haddad, Gregory
Nasser, Andre P.
Richardson, David W.
Versage, Joseph V.

INSTITUTIONS LOCATED IN THE DIOCESE

[A] SEMINARIES

STATE OF MASSACHUSETTS

NEWTON. *Seminary of St. Gregory the Theologian*, 233 Grant Ave., 02159-2013. Tel: 617-965-9862; Fax: 617-527-5816. Rt. Rev. Philip Raczka. Priests 2; Students 3.

METHUEN. *Seminary of St. Basil the Great*, 30 East St., 01844. Tel: 508-683-2471. Rt. Rev. Gerasimos Murphy, B.S.O., J.C.D., Dean. Priests 1; Seminarians 1.

[B] MONASTERIES AND RESIDENCES FOR PRIESTS AND BROTHERS

STATE OF MASSACHUSETTS

METHUEN. *Basilian Salvatorian Order*, 30 East St., 01844. Tel: 508-683-2471; Fax: 508-794-3452. Rt. Rev. Gerasimos Murphy, B.S.O., J.C.D., Reg. Supr.; Revs. Eugene Mitchell, B.S.O., General Economos; Martin Hyatt, B.S.O., Local Supr.; Rt. Revs. George Dagher, B.S.O.; Joseph Dagher, B.S.O.; Simon Hage, B.S.O., (Retired); Yousef Aziz, B.S.O.; Lawrence Tumminelli, B.S.O.

[C] CONVENTS AND RESIDENCES FOR SISTERS

STATE OF CONNECTICUT

DANBURY. *Community of the Mother of God of Tenderness*, 79 Golden Hill Rd., 06811. Tel: 203-794-1486. Sr. Mary Ann Socha, C.M.G.T., Pres. Sisters 3.

[D] SOCIAL MINISTRY

STATE OF NEW YORK

Occupational training.

NEW YORK. *Emmaus East Harlem*, 2027 Lexington Ave., 10035. Tel: 212-410-6006. Healing community for 60 homeless persons.

Emmaus House/Harlem, 2027 Lexington, P.O. Box 1177, 10035. Tel: 212-410-6006. Rev. David Kirk, Pres. & Founder; Most Rev. John A. Elya, Chm. Community of homeless; men and women's shelter; community kitchen, and outreach.

Emmaus Inns, AIDS Ministry, 2027 Lexington, P.O. Box 1177, 10035. Tel: 212-410-6006. Homeless people with AIDS. Apartments 60.

STATE OF OHIO

STEUBENVILLE. *Ephrata House*, 711 North Ave., 43952. Home for Boys.

[E] MISCELLANEOUS

STATE OF ALABAMA

BIRMINGHAM. *National Shrine of St. George*, 16th Ave. and 10th Ct., S., 35205. Tel: 205-252-5788. Rev. Frank J. Milienewicz.

STATE OF MASSACHUSETTS

LAWRENCE. *St. Joseph's Plains Community Center*, 245 Hampshire St., 01841. Tel: 508-685-6001. Rev. Joseph Thomas, B.S.O.

METHUEN. *St. Basil's Salvatorian Center*, 30 East St., 01844. Tel: 508-683-2959. Deacon Allan Ramey, Dir.

STATE OF NEW YORK

YONKERS. *The Friends of the Holy Land, Inc.*, 347 Mile Square Rd., 10701. Tel: 914-969-0887; 949-2106. Ernest F. Russo, Governor Gen., Patriarchal Order of the Holy Cross of Jerusalem.

STATE OF VIRGINIA

ALEXANDRIA. *The Galilee Fund*, 6908 Columbia Drive, 22307. Tel: 703-765-7836; Fax: 703-765-7834. Saba L. Shami, Pres.

RELIGIOUS INSTITUTES OF MEN REPRESENTED IN THE EPARCHY

For further details refer to the corresponding bracketed number in the Religious Institutes of Men or Women section.

[]—*Basilian Aleppian Order*. (Deir-es-Chir, Lebanon).—B.A.O.

[]—*Basilian Chouerite Order*. (St. John Monastery, Khonchara, Lebanon).—B.C.O.

[0190]—*Basilian Salvatorian Order*. (Holy Saviour Monastery, Sidon, Lebanon).—B.S.O.

NECROLOGY

(No Deaths)

Diocese of Our Lady of Deliverance

For Syriac Catholics in the United States and Canada

Most Reverend

JOSEPH YOUNAN, D.D.

Bishop of Our Lady of Deliverance; ordained September 12, 1971; ordained Bishop January 7, 1996; installed February 10, 1996. *Chancery Office: 502 Palisade Ave., Union City, NJ, 07087-5213.*

DIOCESE ESTABLISHED NOVEMBER 18, 1996.

Chancery Office: 502 Palisade Ave., Union City, NJ, 07087-5213. Mailing Address: P.O. Box 8366, Union City, NJ, 07087-8262.

STATISTICAL OVERVIEW

Personnel	
Bishop	1
Priests: Diocesan Active in Diocese	9
Priests: Active Outside Diocese	1
Number of Diocesan Priests	10
Religious Priests in Diocese	1
Ordinations:	
Diocesan Priests	2
Permanent Deacons in Diocese	4
Parishes	
Parishes	6
With Resident Pastor:	
Resident Diocesan Priests	6
Without Resident Pastor:	
Missions	5
Vital Statistics	
Receptions into the Church:	
Infant Baptism Totals	74
Adult Baptism Totals	3
First Communions	73
Confirmations	77
Marriages:	
Catholic	23
Total Marriages	23
Deaths	16
Total Catholic Population	12,000

Chancery—502 Palisade Ave., Union City, NJ, 07087-5213. Tel: 201-617-7822; Fax: 201-583-0212., *P.O. Box 8366, Union City, NJ, 07087-8262.*

Vicar General—Chorbishop PIERRE MELKI.

Chancellor—Rev. ST. ANTOUN SUTTON. Tel: 201-583-1067.

Secretary—Rev. ST. ANTOUN SUTTON. Tel: 201-583-1067.

CLERGY, PARISHES, MISSIONS AND PAROCHIAL SCHOOLS

STATE OF NEW JERSEY

1—OUR LADY OF DELIVERANCE, Revs. Yousif Abdulmasih; ST Antoun Sutton.
Res., 502 Palisade Ave., Union City, 07087-5213. Tel: 201-617-5874.

STATE OF CALIFORNIA

North Hollywood, Los Angeles Co., Jesus Sacred Heart, Rev. Bernard Antoun, Admin.; Deacons Elias Azouz; George Qatto.
Res., 10837 Collins St., 91601-2009. Tel: 818-766-7001.

San Diego, San Diego Co., Our Mother of Perpetual Help, Deacon Emad Hanna Al-Shaikh, Pastoral Assoc.
Mailing Address: P.O. Box 152229, 92295. Tel: 619-660-1492.

STATE OF FLORIDA

Jacksonville, Duval Co., St. Ephrem, Rev. Mansour Mattosha, Admin.
Res., 9645 Baymeadows Rd., #733, 32256. Tel: 904-739-8941.

STATE OF ILLINOIS

Northbrook, Syriac Catholic Mission. Served by Chancery personnel.
Mailing Address: P.O. Box 8366, Union City, NJ 07087-8262. Tel: 201-617-7822.

STATE OF MICHIGAN

Farmington Hills, Oakland Co., St. Thomas, Rev. Thomas B. Azizo, Admin.
Res., 30465 Farmington Rd., 48334-1940. Tel: 810-569-3107.

CANADA

Toronto, St. Joseph, Rev. Yousif Abdulmasih, Admin.
Res., 222 Ridley Blvd., ON M5M 3M6. Tel: 416-485-7232.

Toronto, Syriac Catholic Mission, Rev. Yousef Hanna, Admin.
Res., 222 Ridley Blvd., ON M5M 3M6. Tel: 416-485-7232.

Laval, Eglise St. Ephrem, Chorbishop Pierre Melki; Rev. Georges Sakkal.
Res., 3000 Edouard Monpetit, PQ H7T 2T5. Tel: 514-682-7546.

Eparchy of Our Lady of Lebanon of Los Angeles

Most Reverend

JOHN GEORGE CHEDID, D.D.

Bishop of the Eparchy of Our Lady of Lebanon of Los Angeles; ordained December 21, 1951; appointed Titular Bishop of Callinicum and Auxiliary Bishop of St. Maron of Brooklyn October 28, 1980; consecrated January 25, 1981. *Res., Our Lady of Mt. Lebanon, 333 S. San Vicente Blvd., Los Angeles, CA, 90048.* Tel.: 310-275-6634.

Comprises the States of Ohio, West Virginia, Illinois, Alabama, Michigan, Minnesota, Missouri, Texas, Utah, Arizona, Nevada, Oregon, California, Alaska, Hawaii, Indiana, Kentucky, Tennessee, Mississippi, Wisconsin, Iowa, Arkansas, Louisiana, North Dakota, South Dakota, Kansas, Oklahoma, Nebraska, Montana, Wyoming, Colorado, New Mexico, Idaho and Washington.

Chancery Office: P.O. Box 16397, Beverly Hills, CA, 90209. Mailing Address: 331 S. San Vicente Blvd., Los Angeles, CA, 90048. Tel.: 310-247-8322; Fax: 310-247-9297.

STATISTICAL OVERVIEW

Personnel	
Bishop	1
Priests: Diocesan Active in Diocese	26
Priests: Active Outside Diocese	2
Priests: Diocesan in Foreign Missions	5
Number of Diocesan Priests	33
Religious Priests in Diocese	5
Ordinations:	
Diocesan Priests	2
Permanent Deacons	1
Permanent Deacons in Diocese	6
Parishes	
Parishes	25
With Resident Pastor:	
Resident Diocesan Priests	21
Resident Religious Priests	4
Without Resident Pastor:	
Missions	9
Educational	
Diocesan Students in Other Seminaries	6
Total Seminarians	6
Catechesis/Religious Education:	
Total Students Under Catholic Instruction	6
Vital Statistics	
Receptions into the Church:	
Infant Baptism Totals	376
Adult Baptism Totals	27
Received into Full Communion	25
First Communions	186
Confirmations	238
Marriages:	
Catholic	104
Interfaith	36
Total Marriages	140
Deaths	156
Total Catholic Population	21,790

Chancery—331 S. San Vicente Blvd., Los Angeles, CA, 90048. Tel: 310-247-8322; Fax: 310-247-9297., *P.O. Box 16397, Beverly Hills, CA, 90209.*

Advisor for Priests—Chorbishop ROBERT SHAHEEN.

College of Consulters—Chorbishop ROBERT SHAHEEN; Rev. Msgr. MICHAEL KAIL; Revs. ABDALLAH ZAIDAN, M.L.M.; DONALD SAWYER; FAOUZI ELIA; Chorbishop BERNARD KHACHAN; Chorbishop GREGORY J. MANSOUR.

Commission for Lebanon—Vacant.

Defender of the Bond—Rev. ROBERT BISHOP, C.F.M.

Eparchial Newsletter—"Maronites Today"; Rev. DONALD J. SAWYER, Editor, *P.O. Box 1891, Austin, TX, 78767.*

Judicial Vicar—Chorbishop WILLIAM LESER, S.T.B.

Moderator of the Tribunal—Bishop JOHN CHEDID, J.C.D., S.T.L.

Notary—Miss SIUIN MORRISSY.

Office for Immigration—Rev. FAOUZI ELIA.

Office for Missions—Revs. DONALD J. SAWYER; ANTHONY SPINOSA.

Office for Pastoral Leadership and Stewardship—Rev. Msgr. MICHAEL KAIL.

Office of Communications—Rev. Msgr. RICHARD SAAD.

Office of Inter-faith / Ecumenical Affairs—Rev. ANTHONY SPINOSA, Dir.

Office of Liturgy—Rev. PETER KARAM.

Office of Ministries—Rev. Msgr. RICHARD SAAD.

Office of Priestly Vocations—Rev. SHARBEL MAROUN.

Office of Religious Education—Rev. ANTHONY SALIM.

Office of Youth Ministries—Rev. Msgr. WILLIAM BONCZWESKI, Dir.

Presbyteral Council—Rev. Msgr. MICHAEL KAIL, Exec. Dir.; Chorbishop ROBERT SHAHEEN; Revs. ABDALLAH ZAIDAN, M.L.M.; DONALD SAWYER; Rev. Msgr. RICHARD SAAD; Revs. FAOUZI ELIA; SHARBEL MAROUN; Chorbishop JOSEPH FEGHALI; Chorbishop BERNARD KHACHAN; Chorbishop GREGORY J. MANSOUR, Ex-Officio.

Pro-Life Office—Rev. Msgr. WILLIAM BONCZWESKI; Rev. ANTOINE BAKH.

Procurator / Advocate—Rev. ABDALLAH E. ZAIDAN, M.L.M.; Chorbishop GERGORY J. MANSOUR, S.T.L.

Promoter of Justice—Chorbishop GREGORY J. MANSOUR, S.T.L.

Properties Owned—

St. Maron Office Building—Detroit, MI.

Father Toubia Retirement Home—North Jackson, OH.

Bishop's Residence—Bel Air, CA.

Priest's Retirement Home—El Monte, CA.

Protopresbyters—Chorbishop ROBERT SHAHEEN, Mid-America Region; Rev. Msgr. MICHAEL KAIL, Mid-west Region; Revs. ABDALLAH ZAIDAN, M.L.M., Southwest Region; DONALD SAWYER, Southern Region.

Protosyncellus and Chancellor—Chorbishop GREGORY J. MANSOUR.

Spiritual Director for the National Apostolate of Maronites—Rev. Msgr. MICHAEL KAIL.

Order of St. Sharbel—BEVERLY KIMES, Pres. NINA BEJANY, Vice Pres., *Eparchy of Our Lady of Lebanon of Los Angeles, P.O. Box 16397, Beverly Hills, CA, 90209.* Chorbishop ROBERT SHAHEEN, Spiritual Dir.

CLERGY, PARISHES, MISSIONS AND PAROCHIAL SCHOOLS

STATE OF CALIFORNIA

Los Angeles, Los Angeles Co., Our Lady of Mt. Lebanon-St. Peter Cathedral (1923) (Lebanese), Most Rev. John Chedid, D.D., S.T.L., J.C.D.; Rev. Abdallah E. Zaidan, M.L.M., Rector; Chorbishop Gregory J. Mansour, S.T.L., Chancellor.
Res., 333 S. San Vicente Blvd., 90048. Tel: 310-275-6634; Fax: 310-247-9297.

Fullerton, Orange Co., St. John Maron Mission (1988), Rev. Antoine Bakh; Subdeacon Alfred Harb.
Res., 601 N. Woods Ave., 92632. Tel: 714-525-4216.
Church—1546 E. LaPalma Ave., Anaheim, 92805. Tel: 714-520-5303.

Millbrae, San Mateo Co., Our Lady of Lebanon (1979), Rev. Peter Karam.
Res., 600 El Camino Real N.W., P.O. Box 896, 94030. Tel: 415-589-9653; Fax: 415-652-2422.

San Diego, San Diego Co., Saint Ephrem Mission (1989) (Lebanese), Rev. Nabil Mouannes, Admin.
Res., P.O. Box 130, Del Mar, 92014-0130. Tel: 619-285-9818; Fax: 619-285-9818.

Stockton, San Joaquin Co., Maronite Catholic Community, Rev. Peter Karam, Admin.

STATE OF ALABAMA

Birmingham, Jefferson Co., St. Elias (1910) (Lebanese), Rev. Msgr. Richard D. Saad; Subdeacons Joseph Stephens; Samuel Wehby.
Res., 836 Eighth St. S., 35205-4567. Tel: 205-251-5057; 252-3867; Fax: 205-251-5028.
Catechesis / Religious Programs—Students 110.

STATE OF ARIZONA

Phoenix, Maricopa Co., Maronite Catholic Community, Rev. Nabil Mouannes, Admin.

STATE OF COLORADO

Denver, Denver Co., Maronite Catholic Community, Rev. Abdallah Zaidan, M.L.M., Protopresbyter & Admin.

STATE OF ILLINOIS

Hillside, Cook Co., Our Lady of Lebanon Church (1952), Rev. Victor Kayrouz. In res., Rev. Msgr. John Naffah, (Retired).
Res., 425 N. Hillside Ave., 60162. Tel: 708-449-5558; Fax: 708-449-9813.
Mission—Michigan City, Maronite Catholic Community, Sacred Heart Church, Eigth St., Michigan City, IN 46360. Tel: 219-874-3491. Rev. Victor Kayrouz, Admin.

Peoria, Peoria Co., St. Sharbel (1973) (Lebanese), Rev. Faouzi Y. Elia; Deacon James Siedlecki.
Res., 2914 W. Scenic Dr., 61615. Tel: 309-688-5555; Fax: 309-688-0431. [JC]

STATE OF KENTUCKY

Louisville, Jefferson Co., Maronite Catholic Community (1953), Rev. Victor Kayrouz.
Mailing Address: 425 N. Hillside Ave., Hillside, IL 60162. Tel: 708-449-5558; Fax: 708-449-9813.

STATE OF LOUISIANA

Lafayette, Lafayette Parish, Maronite Catholic Community, Rev. Kenneth Morvant, Admin.

STATE OF MICHIGAN

Detroit, Wayne Co., St. Maron/St. Sharbel (1909), Chorbishop Joseph C. Feghali, Co-Pastor; Rev. Msgr. Kenneth A. Michael, Co-Pastor.
Res., 11466 Kercheval, 48215. Tel: 313-824-0196.; Res., 31601 Schoenherr Rd., Warren, 48093. Tel: 810-826-9688; Fax: 810-826-3521.
Catechesis/Religious Programs—Students 135.

Flint, Genesee Co., Our Lady of Lebanon (1973), Rev. Anthony S. Spinosa; Subdeacons Earl Matte; Charles Rossie; Martin Rachid.
Res., 4133 Calkins Rd., 48532. Tel: 810-733-1259; Fax: 810-732-2760.
Catechesis/Religious Programs—Students 62.

STATE OF MINNESOTA

Minneapolis, Hennepin Co., St. Maron (1948) (Lebanese), Rev. Sharbel G. Maroun.
Res., 219 Sixth Ave. N.E., 55413. Tel: 612-379-2758; Fax: 612-379-7647. [CEM]
Catechesis/Religious Programs—Students 80.

St. Paul, Ramsey Co., Holy Family Church (1918) (Maronite), Rev. Bakhos Chidiac.
Res., 203 E. Robie St., 55107. Tel: 612-291-1116; Fax: 612-291-7009.

STATE OF MISSOURI

St. Louis, St. Louis City Co., St. Raymond (1913) (Lebanese), Chorbishop Robert J. Shaheen; Subdeacons Louis Peters; George Simon.
Res., 931 Lebanon Dr., 63104. Tel: 314-621-0056; Fax: 314-231-9057.
Catechesis/Religious Programs—Students 85.

STATE OF NEVADA

Las Vegas, Clark Co., St. Sharbel Mission, Rev. Jean Pierre Barakat, Admin.

STATE OF OHIO

Cincinnati, Hamilton Co., St. Anthony of Padua (1910), Rev. Louis Baz; Subdeacons Joseph Mousie; Arthur Evans.
Res., 2530 Victory Pkwy., 45206. Tel: 513-961-0120; Fax: 513-961-6058.

Cleveland, Cuyahoga Co., St. Maron (1915), Chorbishop Bernard C. Khachan; Deacon George M. Khoury; Subdeacon James Peters.
Res., 1245 Carnegie Ave., 44115. Tel: 216-781-6161; Fax: 216-781-6162.
Catechesis/Religious Programs—Students 111.

Columbus, Franklin Co., Maronite Catholic Community, Rev. Msgr. Michael Kail, Protopresbyter & Admin.

Dayton, Montgomery Co., Saint Ignatius Mission (1993) (Lebanese), Rev. Alfred Al-Badwi, Admin.
Mailing Address: 727 Beckman St., 45410. Tel: 937-253-2525; Fax: 937-228-2227.

Fairlawn, Summit Co., Our Lady of the Cedars of Mt. Lebanon (1937) (Lebanese), Rev. Msgr. Michael J. Kail; Deacons Robert Foster; Fred Browne.
Res., 507 S. Cleveland-Massillon Rd., 44333-3019. Tel: 216-666-3598; Fax: 216-666-3897.
Catechesis/Religious Programs—Students 50.

Youngstown, Mahoning Co., St. Maron (1902) (Lebanese), Rev. Anthony J. Salim; Deacon Joseph Nohra; Subdeacon Thomas Craven.
Res., 1555 S. Meridian Rd., 44511-1199. Tel: 330-792-2371; 792-7671 (Center); Fax: 330-792-3026.
Catechesis/Religious Programs—Tel: 330-538-2567; Fax: 330-538-9820.
Students 148.

STATE OF OREGON

Portland, Multnomah Co., Saint Sharbel (1970), Rev. William Jonathan Decker.
Res., 1804 S.E. 16th Ave., 97214. Tel: 503-231-3853.
Mission—Seattle, Maronite Catholic Community. Rev. William Jonathan Decker, Admin.

STATE OF TEXAS

Austin, Travis Co., Our Lady's Maronite Parish (1982), Rev. Donald Sawyer, D.Min.; Deacon Joseph Crowley.
Mailing Address: (Church) 1320 E. 51st St., 78723. Tel: 512-458-3693; Fax: 512-451-9554.
Res., 5010 Caswell Ave., 78751. Tel: 512-454-6342.

El Paso, El Paso Co., Maronite Catholic Community, Rev. Donald Sawyer, Protopresbyter & Admin.

Houston, Harris Co., Our Lady of the Cedars Mission (1990), Revs. Milad T. Yaghi, M.L.M.; Fadi E. Tabet, M.L.M.
Res., P.O. Box 573002, 77257. Tel: 713-789-8539; Fax: 713-777-3950. [JC]

Lewisville, Denton Co., Our Lady of Lebanon Mission (1990) (Lebanese), Rev. Andre Estephan, M.L.M.
Res., 719 University Pl., 75067. Tel: 972-436-7617; Fax: 972-221-3430.

San Antonio, Bexar Co., St. George (1925) (Lebanese), Rev. Assad El-Bacha; Subdeacon Raymond E. Casillas. In res., Rev. Jean Al-Nahal, M.L.M. (Lebanon).
Res., 6070 Babcock, 78240. Tel: 210-690-9569; Fax: 210-690-5093.
Catechesis/Religious Programs—Students 23.

STATE OF UTAH

Murray, Salt Lake Co., Saint Jude Church (1975), Rev. Gebran Bou-Merhi; Subdeacon Roger Dannels.
Res., 4893 Wasatch St., 84107. Tel: 801-268-2820.
Church—4900 Wasatch St., 84107. Tel: 801-265-2195; Fax: 801-268-2820.

STATE OF WEST VIRGINIA

Wheeling, Ohio Co., Our Lady of Lebanon (1906) (Lebanese), Rev. Ghattas Khoury.
Res., 2216 Eoff St., 26003. Tel: 304-233-1688; Fax: 304-232-8303. [JC]

Graduate Studies:
Reverend Fathers—
Fisher, David, Rome, Italy

Awaiting Assignment:
Reverend Fathers—
Chaanine, George
Nasr, Toufic

Leave of Absence:
Reverend Fathers—
Coover, Thomas

Retired:
Chorbishop—
Trad, John
Reverend Monsignors—
Naffah, John
Reverend Fathers—
Hitti, Michael
Kleem, Ferris
Saad, Antoun

INSTITUTIONS LOCATED IN THE DIOCESE

[A] MONASTERIES AND RESIDENCES OF PRIESTS AND BROTHERS

SAN ANTONIO, TX. *The Congregation of Maronite Lebanese Missionaries*, Saint George Maronite Church, 6070 Babcock Rd., 78240. Tel: 210-690-9569; Fax: 210-690-5093. Revs. Marwan Tabet, M.L.M.; Abdallah E. Zaidan, M.L.M.; Milad Yaghi, M.L.M.; Fadi E. Tabet, M.L.M.; Andre S. Estephan, M.L.M.; John Al-Nahal, M.L.M.; Assaad El-Bacha, M.L.M.

[B] CONVENTS AND RESIDENCES FOR SISTERS

NORTH JACKSON, OH. *Antonine Maronite Sisters of Youngstown, Inc.*, 2691 N. Lipkey Rd., 44451. Tel: 330-538-2567. Sisters 7. Antonine Sisters Adult Day Care, Inc., 2675 N. Lipkey Rd., 44451. Tel: 330-538-9822; Fax: 330-538-9820. Total Staff 8; Total Assisted 40.

[C] NATIONAL SHRINES

NORTH JACKSON, OH. *National Shrine of Our Lady of Lebanon*, 2759 N. Lipkey Rd., 44451. Tel: 330-538-3351. Rev. Msgr. William D. Bonczewski.

[D] RELIGIOUS COMMUNITIES OF MEN

PHILIPPI, WV. *Our Lady of Solitude Hermitage*, 334 S. Main St., 26416. Tel: 304-457-3330. Rev. Bernard Grunewald, ER. O.L.S., Supr.

[E] RESIDENCES FOR CLERGY

NORTH JACKSON, OH. *Father Toubia Retirement Home*, 2759 N. Lipkey Rd., 44451. Tel: 330-538-3351.

[F] MISCELLANEOUS

LOS ANGELES. *Priest's Retirement Fund*, 333 S. San Vicente Blvd., 90048. Tel: 310-247-8322; Fax: 310-247-9297.

EL MONTE. *Priest's Retirement Home*. 333 S. San Vincente Blvd., Los Angeles, 90048.

RELIGIOUS INSTITUTES OF MEN REPRESENTED IN THE DIOCESE

For further details refer to the corresponding bracketed number in the Religious Institutes of Men section.

[0785]—*The Congregation of Maronite Lebanese Missionaries*. (San Antonio, TX).—M.L.M.

NECROLOGY

(No Deaths)

Byzantine Eparchy of Parma

Most Reverend

BASIL M. SCHOTT, O.F.M. D.D.

Bishop of Parma; ordained August 29, 1965; consecrated and installed July 11, 1996.

ESTABLISHED FEBRUARY 21, 1969.

Embraces all Byzantine Ruthenian Rite Catholics in the States of Illinois, Indiana, Iowa, Kansas, Michigan, Minnesota, Missouri, Nebraska, North Dakota, South Dakota and Wisconsin. Also the entire State of Ohio excluding the Counties of Ashtabula, Trumbull, Mahoning, Columbiana, Carroll, Harrison, Guernsey, Noble, Morgan, Athens, Meigs, Gallia and Lawrence.

For legal titles of parishes and diocesan institutions, consult the Chancery Office.

Chancery Office: 1900 Carlton Rd., Parma, OH, 44134. Tel.: 216-741-8773; Fax: 216-741-9356.

Web site address: http://www.parma.org

STATISTICAL OVERVIEW

Personnel	
Bishop	1
Priests: Diocesan Active in Diocese	32
Priests: Active Outside Diocese	1
Priests: Retired, Sick or Absent	8
Number of Diocesan Priests	41
Extern Priests in Diocese	1
Ordinations:	
Permanent Deacons	4
Total Sisters	12
Parishes	
Parishes	39
With Resident Pastor:	
Resident Diocesan Priests	27
Resident Religious Priests	1
Without Resident Pastor:	
Administered by Priests	10
Missions	2
Professional Ministry Personnel:	
Sisters	12
Welfare	
Day Care and Extended Day Care Centers	1
Total Assisted	106
Special Centers for Social Services	1
Total Assisted	9,100
Educational	
Diocesan Students in Other Seminaries	3
Total Seminarians	3
Elementary Schools, Diocesan and Parish	2
Total Students	342
Catechesis/Religious Education:	
High School Students	217
Elementary Students	1,104
Total Students Under Catholic Instruction	1,666
Teachers in the Diocese:	
Sisters	5
Lay Teachers	18
Vital Statistics	
Receptions into the Church:	
Infant Baptism Totals	140
Adult Baptism Totals	13
Received into Full Communion	20
First Communions	142
Confirmations	138
Marriages:	
Catholic	41
Interfaith	25
Total Marriages	66
Deaths	227
Total Catholic Population	12,714

Former Bishops—Most Rev. EMIL J. MIHALIK, D.D., ord. Sept. 21, 1945; appt. first Bishop of the Ruthenian Eparchy of Parma, March 22, 1969; installed June 12, 1969; died Jan. 27, 1984.—Most Rev. ANDREW PATAKI, D.D., appt. Titular Bishop of Tellmisus and Auxiliary of Passaic, NJ, May 30, 1983; installed Aug. 23, 1983; succeeded to See, June 19, 1984; transferred Parma See, Aug 16, 1984; transferred Byzantine Eparchy of Passaic, Nov. 21, 1995.

Chancery Office—1900 Carlton Rd., Parma, OH, 44134. Tel: 216-741-8773; Fax: 216-741-9356.

Chancellor—Rev. MICHAEL J. HUSZTI, J.C.L.

Eparchial Treasurer—Rev. EDWARD ZAVELL, Eparchial Finance Council: JERRY LUCAS; EDWARD MAHER; THOMAS PERCIAK; HELEN IRION, Sec.

Eparchial Consultors—Rev. Msgr. ROBERT V. YARNOVITZ; Revs. EDWARD ZAVELL; MICHAEL EVANICK; DAVID PETRAS, S.E.O.D.; DENNIS HRUBIAK; DAVID HANNES, J.C.L.; EMIL MASICH.

Protopresbyters—Ohio: Revs. EDWARD ZAVELL,Midwest: Rev. Msgr. FRANK KORBA,Great Lakes: Rev. JAMES KUBAJAK, M.Div.

Vicar Judicialis—Rev. DAVID HANNES, J.C.L.

Vicar Adjutant—Rev. MICHAEL J. HUSZTI, J.C.L.

Judge—Rev. NICHOLAS R.A. RACHFORD, J.C.L.

Secretary—Rev. NICHOLAS R.A. RACHFORD, J.C.L.

Defender of the Bond—Rev. JAMES KUBAJAK, M.Div.

Promoter of Justice—Rev. JAMES KUBAJAK, M.Div.

Notaries—Rev. JAMES BATCHA; HELEN IRION.

Eparchial Censors—Revs. DAVID PETRAS, S.E.O.D.; JOHN KACHUBA, M.A.

Eparchial Commissions

Sacred Liturgy—Rev. DAVID PETRAS, S.E.O.D., Chm.; Rev. Msgr. ROBERT V. YARNOVITZ; Revs. ROBERT BARTER; MICHAEL HAYDUK; VLADIMIR VANCIK, S.T.D.

Apostolate of St. Nicholas—Eparchial Director Cleveland West, Ohio: DAVID BASALLA, Spiritual Dir.; Rev. JAMES BATCHA, Chm. LORETTA NEMETH, Dir. Cleveland East: Rev. BRYAN R. EYMAN, (Chap.) Spiritual Dir. BRUCE ROYKO, Dir. Midwest: Chapter Dirs.: PAUL HOHRAN, St. Michael, Merrillville, IN; ANN MARIE ZIMA, St. Nicholas, Munster, IN; DON GRISHAM, St. Mary, Joliet, IL; HELEN TIMURA, St. Nicholas, Barberton, OH Great Lakes: Vacant.

Building Commission—Rev. Msgr. ROBERT V. YARNOVITZ, V.G., Chm.; Revs. DAVID PETRAS; BRYAN EYMAN; CHARLES LIZANICH.

Cantors' Institute—NICOLETTE BOROS, Dir. Cantors' Institute Faculty: Revs. DAVID PETRAS, S.E.O.D.; DENNIS HRUBIAK; MICHAEL HAYDUK; MICHAEL J. HUSZTI, J.C.L.; JAMES BATCHA; NICHOLAS RACHFORD, J.C.L., Cantors' Institute Advisory Board: EDWARD MAHER; VICTORIA BOROS; JERRY LUCAS; Revs. EDWARD ZAVELL; NICHOLAS RACHFORD.

Office of Religious Education—JOHN KACHUBA, M.A., Dir. Tel: 216-741-4102. Rev. BASIL HUTSKO, Great Lakes; Rev. Msgr. FRANK KORBA, Midwest.

Catechetical Board—Rev. Msgr. FRANK KORBA; Rev. JOHN KEBLESH; Sr. ELIZABETH JANE TEPLEY, O.S.B.M.; BETTY BARANKO; MELVIN CANNON; RENA FULKA; Deacon RICHARD GUIDEN; TIMOTHY LOYA; LISA STANICH.

Associate Religious Education Directors—Midwest: Rev. Msgr. FRANK KORBA, Great Lakes: Vacant.

Office of Youth Ministry—Revs. BRUCE RIEBE, Dir. BASIL HUTSKO, Great Lakes; JOHN KEBLESH, Ohio; Mr. THOMAS LOYA, Midwest.

Young Singles—Vacant; Dir.

Office of Family Life—FLORENCE BUKOVECKY, Dir.

Office of Lay Apostolate—ROBERT SHIRILLA, Dir.

Office of Evangelization and Missionary Activity—Rev. JAMES BATCHA, Dir.

Office of the Diaconate—Rev. DENNIS HRUBIAK, Dir.

Office of Vocations—Rev. DENNIS HRUBIAK, Dir.

Seminary Education and Priestly Formation Boad—Rev. DAVID PETRAS, S.E.O.D., Chm.; Rev. Msgr. ROBERT V. YARNOVITZ; Revs. MICHAEL HAYDUK; DENNIS HRUBIAK; JOHN KACHUBA, M.A.; NICHOLAS RACHFORD, J.C.L.; EDWARD ZAVELL.

Clergy Life Commission—Rev. DENNIS HRUBIAK, Chm.; Rev. Msgr. BASIL SMOCHKO; Rev. Msgr. ROBERT V. YARNOVITZ; Revs. MICHAEL EVANICK; DAVID HANNES, J.C.L.; MICHAEL J. HUSZTI, J.C.L.; JAMES KUBAJAK, M.Div.; DAVID PETRAS, S.E.O.D.; NICHOLAS RACHFORD, J.C.L.; EDWARD ZAVELL.

Office of Communication—Rev. NICHOLAS RACHFORD, J.C.L., Dir. Eparchial Newspaper, "Horizons." Tel: 216-741-3312; Fax: 216-741-9356.

Vicar for Religious—Vacant.

Delegates for Priests—Rev. Msgr. ROBERT V. YARNOVITZ, Chm.; Rev. MICHAEL EVANICK; Rev. DENNIS HRUBIAK.

Priest's Pension Board—Rev. Msgr. FRANK KORBA, Chm.; Rev. Msgr. ROBERT V. YARNOVITZ; Revs. ROBERT BARTER; JAMES BATCHA; BASIL HUTSKO; MICHAEL FELOCK; JOSEPH POHORLAK; JOSEPH RADVANSKY; EDWARD ZAVELL.

Office of Ecumenical Activity—Rev. DAVID PETRAS, S.E.O.D., Dir.

History and Research—Rev. MICHAEL J. HUSZTI, J.C.L., Dir.

Stewardship Office—MARY S. LIZANICH.

Scouting Office—Rev. NICHOLAS RACHFORD, J.C.L., Dir. & Chap., Boy Scouts.

Eparchial Shrine of the Weeping Madonna of Mariapoch—(Burton, OH): President, The Most Rev. Ordinary of the Parma Eparchy; Revs. MICHAEL J. HUSZTI, J.C.L., Dir. & Admin. JOHN KOVACH, Parochial Vicar. Tel: 216-834-8807. Assisted by the Social Mission Sisters. Sr. M. FLORA, S.M.S., Supr. Tel: 216-834-4078.

Respect Life Office—PATRICK PEROTTI.

Pre-Cana Office—Rev. MICHAEL HAYDUK.

CLERGY, PARISHES, MISSIONS AND PAROCHIAL SCHOOLS

STATE OF OHIO

Parma, Cuyahoga Co., Saint John the Baptist, Cathedral, Rev. Msgr. Robert Yarnovitz. In res., Revs. Edmund Jadwisiak; Nicholas Rachford.
Church—1900 Carlton Rd., 44134-3129. Tel: 216-661-8658; Fax: 216-741-9356.
Res., 1703 Carlton Rd., 44134.

Holy Spirit, Rev. Dennis M. Hrubiak.
Res., 5500 W. 54th St., 44129-2274. Tel: 216-884-8452; Fax: 216-884-8453.

Akron, Summit Co., St. Michael the Archangel, Rev. Bernard Danber, O.S.A.
Res., 847 Crouse St., 44306-1125. Tel: 330-376-6633; Fax: 330-376-4149.

Dormition of Virgin Mary Church, Rev. Bernard Danber, O.S.A.
Church—2321 17th St. S.W., 44314-2055.
Res., 847 Crouse St., 44306-1125. Tel: 330-376-6633; Fax: 330-376-4149.

Barberton, Summit Co., St. Nicholas, Rev. Michael Felock.
Res., 1051 E. Robinson St., 44203-3852. Tel: 216-753-0018.

Bedford, Cuyahoga Co., St. Eugene, Rev. Joseph Repko.
Res., 264 Warrensville-Center Rd., 44146-2741. Tel: 216-232-7302.

Brecksville, Cuyahoga Co., St. Joseph, Rev. Bruce Riebe.
Res., 8111 Brecksville, 44141-1204. Tel: 216-526-1818; Fax: 216-526-0016.

Brunswick, Medina Co., St. Emilian, Rev. John W. Keblesh.
Res., 1231 Substation Rd., 44212-1911. Tel: 330-225-9857.

Burton, Geauga Co., Church of Weeping Madonna, Revs. Michael J. Huszti, Shrine Dir.; John Kovach.
Res., 17486 Mumford Rd., 44021. Tel: 216-834-8807.
Shrine—Shrine of the Weeping Madonna of Mariapoch.
Social Mission Sisters of Hungary 2.

Cleveland, Cuyahoga Co., Holy Ghost, Rev. Quentin S. Koplinka, O.S.B.
Res., 2420 W. 14th St., 44113-4406. Tel: 216-861-2177.

St. Mary, Revs. Michael Hayduk; Ronald Timock.
Res., 4600 State Rd., 44109-5243. Tel: 216-741-7979; Fax: 216-749-7981.
School—Tel: 216-749-7980. Sr. Joanne Lickvar, Prin.
Sisters of St. Basil the Great 3; Lay Teachers 8; Students 209.

St. Nicholas (Croatian), Rev. Quentin S. Koplinka, O.S.B.
Res., 3431 Superior Ave., 44114-4160. Tel: 216-361-5069; Fax: 216-361-5069.

Columbus, Franklin Co., St. John Chrysostom, Rev. Eugene R. Linowski.
Res., 5858 Cleveland Ave., 43231-2862. Tel: 614-882-7578; Fax: 614-890-6048.

Dayton, Montgomery Co., St. Barbara, Revs. Eugene R. Linowski; Waldemar J. Kuchta.
Res., 5915 Springboro Pk., 45449-3249. Tel: 513-434-2051; Fax: 513-385-8559.

Euclid, Cuyahoga Co., St. Stephens, Rev. John S. Kachuba, M.A.
Res., 532 Lloyd Rd., 44132-1721. Tel: 216-732-7292; Fax: 216-732-9434.

Fairport Harbor, Lake Co., St. Michael, Rev. Bryan R. Eyman.
Res., 630 Plum St., 44077. Tel: 216-357-7896.

Fairview Park, Cuyahoga Co., St. Mary Magdalene, Rev. Edward Zavell, V.F.
Res., 5390 W. 220th St., 44126. Tel: 216-734-4644; Fax: 216-741-9365.

Lakewood, Cuyahoga Co., St. Gregory the Theologian, Rev. Msgr. Basil Smochko.
Res., 2035 Quail Ave., 44107. Tel: 216-521-1081; Fax: 216-521-1081.

Lorain, Lorain Co., St. Michael, Rev. James Batcha.
Res., 3056 Reeves Ave., 44052-4274. Tel: 216-282-3808.

St. Nicholas, Rev. James Batcha.
Res., 2711 W. 40th St., 44053-2252. Tel: 216-282-7525; Fax: 216-282-9185.
School—2707 W. 40th St., 44053-2252. Tel: 216-282-3289. Sr. Elizabeth Jane Templey, Prin.
Sisters of Saint Basil the Great 2; Lay Teachers 7; Students 132.

Marblehead, Ottawa Co., St. Marys, Rev. Joseph R. Radvansky.
Res., 506 E. Main St., 43440-2232. Tel: 419-798-4283.

Mentor-on-the-Lake, Lake Co., St. Andrew the Apostle, Rev. Bryan R. Eyman.
Res., 5768 Andrew Rd., 44060-2608. Tel: 216-257-3620; Fax: 216-257-3620.

Northwood, Lucas Co., St. Michael the Archangel, Rev. James Kubajak, V.F.
Res., 2526 Skagway Dr., 43619. Tel: 419-691-5656; Fax: 419-691-7669.
Church—4001 Navarre Ave., Oregon, 43616.

Solon, Cuyahoga Co., St. John the Baptist, Rev. Michael J. Huszti.
Res., 36125 Aurora Rd., 44139. Tel: 216-248-0417.

STATE OF ILLINOIS

Chicago, Cook Co., St. Mary, Rev. Thomas Loya.
Res., 60 W. 90th St., Oak Lawn, 60453. Tel: 815-726-6308.

Joliet, Will Co., St. Mary Assumption, Rev. Thomas Loya.
Res., 1004 Hacker Ave., 60432-1229. Tel: 815-726-6308.

STATE OF INDIANA

East Chicago, Lake Co., St. Basil's. Closed. For inquiries for parish records contact the Chancery.

Indiana Harbor Co., Holy Ghost. Closed. For inquiries for parish records contact the Chancery.

Indianapolis, Marion Co., St. Athanasius Church, Rev. Robert D. McElaney, O.S.B.
Res., 1117 Blaine Ave., 46221-1110. Tel: 317-632-4157.

Merrillville, Lake Co., St. Michael, Very Rev. Michael Evanick.
Res., 557 W. 57th Ave., 46410-2540. Tel: 219-980-0600.

Munster, Lake Co., Saint Nicholas, Rev. Msgr. Frank Korba, V.F.
Res., 8103 Columbia Ave., 46321-1802. Tel: 219-838-9380.

Whiting, Lake Co., Assumption of the Blessed Virgin, Rev. Joseph Pohorlak.
Res., 2011 Clark St., 46394-2023. Tel: 219-659-0277.

STATE OF MICHIGAN

Allen Park, Wayne Co., St. Stephen, Rev. Cyril Attak. In res., Rev. Msgr. John Kurty.
Res., 4141 Laurence Ave., 48101-3049. Tel: 313-382-5901.

Bay City, Bay Co., Saint George, Rev. Robert Stash.
Res., 204 N. Van Buren St., 48706-6519. Tel: 517-892-0763.

Detroit, Wayne Co., St. Nicholas, Rev. Robert J. Barter.
Church—19130 Beaconsfield St., 48224-1177. Tel: 313-521-6827.

St. John the Baptist. Closed. For inquiries for parish records contact the Chancery.

Flushing, Genesee Co., St. Michael, Rev. David A. Hannes.
Res., 2333 N. Elms Rd., 48433-9426. Tel: 810-659-4887; Fax: 810-659-8363.

Livonia, Wayne Co., Sacred Heart, Rev. Nicholas Ivan.
Res., 29125 W. Six-Mile Rd., 48152-3661. Tel: 313-522-3166.

Omer Co., St. John Mission, Rev. Robert Stash.
Mailing Address: P.O. Box 236, Omer, 48749-0236. Tel: 517-892-0763.
Res., 204 N. Van Buren St., Bay City, 48708-6519.

Sterling Heights, Macomb Co., St. Basils, Rev. Basil J. Hutsko.
Res., 4700 Metropolitan Pkwy., 48310-3905. Tel: 810-268-1082.

Taylor, Wayne Co., Christ the King. Closed. For inquiries for parish records contact the Chancery.

STATE OF MINNESOTA

Minneapolis, Hennepin Co., St. John the Baptist, Rev. Edward C. Wojciechowski.
Res., 2215 Third St., N.E., 55418-3422. Tel: 612-789-6252.

STATE OF MISSOURI

St. Louis, St. Louis Co., St. Louis Mission, Revs. Eugene Selzer; Paul Niemann; Joseph A. Weber.
Res., 9311 Stansberry Ave., 63134-3635. Tel: 314-428-7371; Fax: 314-428-1158.

Sugar Creek, Jackson Co., St. Luke, Byzantine Catholic Parish, Rev. Francis McGlynn.
Mailing Address: 700 E. 8th St., #910, Kansas City, 64106-1635.
Church—11411 Chicago, 64054. Tel: 816-842-3454; Fax: 816-842-3454.

STATE OF WISCONSIN

Bristol, Kenosha Co., St. Irene. Closed. For information regarding the Byzantine Catholic Community contact Rev. Gerald P. Schmitz, 4804 Seventh Ave., Kenosha, WI 53140-3397. Tel: 414-657-6875.

On Duty Outside the Diocese:
Reverend Fathers—
Petras, David, Byzantine Catholic Seminary, Pittsburgh

Absent on Leave:
Reverend Fathers—
Chelena, Thomas
Francisko, Gary
Rebovich, John
Ruglovsky, Robert
St. Germain, Brian

Retired:
Reverend Monsignors—
Kurty, John
Reverend Fathers—
Masich, Emil G., 3600 Biddulph Ave., Cleveland, OH 44109
Vancik, Vladimir, 18 Station St., Carnegie, PA 15106. Tel: 412-276-4093

Permanent Deacons:
Guiden, Richard
Hendricks, Lawrence
Kenes, Michael
O'Connell, Justin

INSTITUTIONS LOCATED IN THE DIOCESE

[A] CONVENTS AND RESIDENCES FOR SISTERS

NORTH ROYALTON. *Motherhouse and Novitiate*, 6688 Cady Rd., 44133. Tel: 216-237-6800. Byzantine Nuns of St. Clare. Sisters, Parma Eparchy, Byzantine Ruthenian Province, Monastery of the Holy Protection of the Mother of God. Sr. Mary Philomena Horkavi, B.N.S.C., Hegumena.

[B] RELIGIOUS SHRINES

BURTON. *Shrine of the Weeping Madonna of Mariapoch*, 17486 Mumford Rd., 44021. Tel: 216-834-8807. Revs. Michael J. Huszti, J.C.L., Shrine Dir.; John Kovach, Parochial Vicar; Sr. Flora, Supr. Tel: Convent Tel.: 216-834-4078.

[C] MISCELLANEOUS

CLEVELAND. *St. Mary Hospitality House*, 4600 State Rd., 44109. Tel: 216-749-7288. Dorothy Papke, Dir.

RELIGIOUS INSTITUTES OF WOMEN REPRESENTED IN THE DIOCESE

For further details refer to the corresponding bracketed number in the Religious Institutes of Women section.

[]—*Byzantine Nuns of St. Clare.* (Parma Eparchy).—B.N.S.C.

[3730]—*Sisters of the Order of St. Basil the Great.*—O.S.B.M.

[]—*Social Mission Sisters of Mariapoch.*—S.M.S.

NECROLOGY

(No Deaths)

Byzantine Catholic Diocese of Passaic

Most Reverend

ANDREW PATAKI, D.D.

Bishop of Passaic; appointed Titular Bishop of Tellmisus and Auxiliary Bishop of Passaic, May 30, 1983; consecrated August 23, 1983; appointed Bishop June 19, 1984; transferred to Parma See August 16, 1984; transferred to Passaic November 21, 1995.

Most Reverend

MICHAEL J. DUDICK, D.D.

Retired Bishop of Passaic; ordained November 13, 1945; appointed Bishop August 21, 1968; consecrated and installed October 24, 1968; retired November 21, 1995. *Res., 445 Lackawanna Ave., West Paterson, NJ, 07424.*

ESTABLISHED JULY 31, 1963.

Embraces all Catholics of the Byzantine-Ruthenian Rite in the States of New Jersey, Connecticut, Delaware, District of Columbia, Florida, Georgia, Maine, Maryland, Massachusetts, New Hampshire, New York, North Carolina, Rhode Island, South Carolina, Vermont, Virginia and all Eastern Pennsylvania within the western boundaries of the Counties of Franklin, Juniata, Lycoming, Mifflin, Union and Tioga.

For legal titles of parishes and diocesan institutions, consult the Chancery Office.

Chancery Office: 445 Lackawanna Ave., West Paterson, NJ, 07424. Tel.: 201-890-7777; Fax: 201-890-7175.

STATISTICAL OVERVIEW

Personnel	
Bishop	1
Retired Bishops	1
Priests: Diocesan Active in Diocese	71
Priests: Active Outside Diocese	4
Priests: Retired, Sick or Absent	18
Number of Diocesan Priests	93
Religious Priests in Diocese	20
Extern Priests in Diocese	5
Ordinations:	
Permanent Deacons	18
Permanent Deacons in Diocese	18
Total Sisters	13
Parishes	
Parishes	102
With Resident Pastor:	
Resident Diocesan Priests	69
Resident Religious Priests	5
Without Resident Pastor:	
Administered by Priests	27
Administered by Permanent Deacons	1
Missions	6
Pastoral Centers	4
Welfare	
Educational	
Diocesan Students in Other Seminaries	7
Total Seminarians	7
Elementary Schools, Diocesan and Parish	1
Total Students	1,055
Catechesis/Religious Education:	
High School Students	814
Elementary Students	2,676
Total Students Under Catholic Instruction	4,552
Teachers in the Diocese:	
Priests	1
Sisters	13
Lay Teachers	33
Vital Statistics	
Receptions into the Church:	
Infant Baptism Totals	395
Adult Baptism Totals	21
Received into Full Communion	109
First Communions	309
Confirmations	447
Marriages:	
Catholic	121
Interfaith	48
Total Marriages	169
Deaths	579
Total Catholic Population	66,965

Former Bishops—Most Rev. STEPHEN J. KOCISKO, D.D., ord. March 30, 1941; appt. Titular Bishop of Theveste and Auxiliary of Exarchate of Pittsburgh, July 20, 1956; appt. First Eparch of Passaic, July 31, 1963; appt. Eparch of Pittsburgh, Dec. 21, 1967; installed March 5, 1968; elevated to Metropolitan Archbishop of Pittsburgh, Feb. 21, 1969; retired June 12, 1991; died March 7, 1995.—Most Rev. MICHAEL J. DUDICK, D.D., ord. Nov. 13, 1945; appt. Bishop of Passaic, Aug. 21, 1968; installed Oct. 24, 1968; retired Nov. 21, 1995.

Vicar General—Very Rev. GERALD DINO, O.E.S.L.

Syncelli-Episcopal Vicars of the Eparchy—

Susquehanna—Very Rev. JOHN CIGAN, *Holy Spirit Church, 360 Clinton St., Binghamton, NY, 13905.* Tel: 607-797-2122.

Central PA—Very Rev. LEONARD M. HOLLICK, *Saint Michael Church, 17 E. Blaine St., McAdoo, PA, 18237.* Tel: 717-929-1062.

New Jersey—Very Rev. BASIL RAKACZKY, O.S.B.M., *Saint Michael Church, 401 Hall Ave., Perth Amboy, NJ, 08861.* Tel: 908-826-0792.

New York-New England—Rev. Msgr. ROBERT SENETSKY, J.C.D., *Saints Peter and Paul Church, 705 Shenandoah Ave., Peekskill, NY, 10566.* Tel: 914-737-8249.

Middle States—Very Rev. JOHN BASARAB, *Epiphany of Our Lord Church, 3410 Woodburn Rd., Annandale, VA, 22003.* Tel: 703-573-3986.

Southern States—Very Rev. PETER LICKMAN, *Saint Basil Church, 1475 N.E. 199th Street, Miami, FL, 33179.* Tel: 305-651-0991.

Chancery Office—Eparchial Center, 445 Lackawanna Ave., W. Paterson, NJ, 07424. Tel: 201-890-7777; Fax: 201-890-7175. Office Hours: Mon.-Fri. 9-12 & 1-4.

Chancellor—Very Rev. ROBERT J. HOSPODAR, J.C.L.

Eparchial Finance Officer—Rev. Msgr. ROBERT SENETSKY, J.C.D.

Administrative Assistant for Real Property and Insurance—Rev. Msgr. RAYMOND M. MISULICH, J.C.L.

Canonical Consultant to the Bishop—Rev. BENEDICT A. DESOCIO, J.C.L.

Eparchial College of Consultors—Very Rev. GERALD DINO, O.E.S.L.; Very Rev. JOHN CIGAN; Very Rev. LEONARD M. HOLLICK; Very Rev. BASIL RAKACZKY, O.S.B.M.; Rev. Msgr. ROBERT SENETSKY, J.C.D.; Very Rev. JOHN BASARAB; Very Rev. PETER LICKMAN; Very Rev. ROBERT J. HOSPODAR, J.C.L.

Presbyteral Council—Ex Officio Members: Very Rev. GERALD DINO, O.E.S.L.; Very Rev. JOHN CIGAN; Very Rev. LEONARD M. HOLLICK; Very Rev. BASIL RAKACZKY, O.S.B.M.; Rev. Msgr. ROBERT SENETSKY, J.C.D.; Very Rev. JOHN BASARAB; Very Rev. PETER LICKMAN; Rev. Msgr. RAYMOND M. MISULICH, J.C.L. Elected Memebers: Very Rev. EDWARD G. CIMBALA; Revs. NICHOLAS DEPROSPERO; JOHN ZEYACK; Very Rev. CONAN TIMONEY; Revs. BASIL KRAYNYAK; ANDOR RAKACZKI. Appointed Members: Rev. Msgr. ALAN BORSUK; Very Rev. ROBERT J. HOSPODAR, J.C.L.

Protopresbyters - Deans—Northern PA - Northern NY: Very Rev. EDWARD CIMBALA, Mid-PA: Very Rev. MICHAEL MONDIK, South PA: Very Rev. GREGORY J. NOGA, Northern NJ: Rev. Msgr. ROBERT G. MONETA, Central NJ: Very Rev. ROBERT RADVANSKY, New York - New England: Very Rev. ROBERT J. HOSPODAR, J.C.L., Middle States: Very Rev. CONAN TIMONEY, Southern States: Very Rev. ROBERT EVANCHO.

Eparchial Tribunal—445 Lackawanna Ave., West Paterson, NJ, 07424. Tel: 201-890-7777.

Judicial Vicar—Rev. Msgr. JOHN T. SEKELLICK, J.C.L.

Moderator of the Tribunal—Rev. BENEDICT A. DESOCIO, J.C.L.

Associate Judge—Very Rev. ROBERT J. HOSPODAR, J.C.L.

Defender of the Bond—Rev. ROBERT J. WOYTEK, J.C.L., Cand.

Notaries—Rev. BENEDICT A. DESOCIO, J.C.L.; Rev. ROBERT WOYTEK, J.C.L., Cand.

Commissions, Departments and Institutions

Altar Boys Retreat Camp—Rev. JAMES HAYER.

Boy Scouts—Vacant.

Eparchial Building and Properties Commission—Rev. Msgr. RAYMOND M. MISULICH, J.C.L., Chm.

Eparchial Insurance Commission—Rev. Msgr. RAYMOND M. MISULICH, J.C.L., Chm.

Clergy Continued Education—Rev. JOHN ZEYACK, S.T.L., Dir.

Commission for Ecumenism—Rev. Msgr. ALAN BORSUK, Chm.

Communications—Vacant.

Evangelization—Rev. EDWARD G. CIMBALA, Chm.

Respect Life—Very Rev. ROBERT J. HOSPODAR, J.C.L., Chm.

Family Life—Rev. Msgr. JOHN T. SEKELLICK, J.C.L., Chm.

Eparchial Historian—Very Rev. ROBERT J. HOSPODAR, J.C.L.
Holy Name Society—Rev. Msgr. ROBERT G. MONETA, Chm.
Eparchial Eparchial Liturgy and Art Commission—Rev. Msgr. ALAN BORSUK, Chm.
Eparchial Music Commission—Rev. ROBERT G. MONETA, Chm.
Eparchial Newspaper—The Eastern Catholic Life; Rev. JAMES HAYER, Mng. Editor; Rev. MATTHEW BUTRIE, Business Mgr.; Rev. GLENN DAVIDOWICH, Assoc. Editor.
Office of Religious Education—Dr. RICHARD NOVAK, Dir.
Retirement Plan Board—Under Review for Revision.
Saint Nicholas Shrine - Carpathian Village—Rev. MICHAEL SALNICKY, Dir., *P.O. Box 616, Canadensis, PA, 18325*. Tel: 717-595-3265.
Vocations—Revs. EDWARD G. CIMBALA, Chm.
Priesthood & Diaconate Formation Programs—Rev. EDWARD G. CIMBALA, Dir.
Vicar for Clergy—Vacant.
Vicar for Religious—Vacant.
Eastern Catholic Associates—Publication: God With Us; *445 Lackawanna Ave., W. Paterson, NJ, 07424.*

CLERGY, PARISHES, MISSIONS AND PAROCHIAL SCHOOLS

STATE OF NEW JERSEY

Passaic, Passaic Co., St. Michael Cathedral, Rev. Marcel Szabo.
Res., 96 First St., 07055. Tel: 201-777-2553. [CEM]
Catechesis/Religious Programs—Students 61.
Chapel—415 Lackawanna Ave., West Paterson, 07424. Tel: 201-256-0134.

Bayonne, Hudson Co., St. John the Baptist. Administered from Jersey City, NJ.
Res., 15 E. 26th St., 07002. Tel: 201-339-1840; Fax: 201-339-2640.

Carteret, Middlesex Co., St. Elias, Rev. Edward Semko.
Res., 42 Cooke Ave., 07008. Tel: 908-541-5213.

Dunellen, Middlesex Co., St. Nicholas, Rev. Leonard Kuberski.
Res., 121 Madison Ave., 08812. Tel: 908-968-3337.

East Brunswick, Middlesex Co., Nativity of Our Lord, Rev. James Hayer.
Res., 700 Old Bridge Tpke., 08816. Tel: 908-238-0865; Fax: 908-238-2950.

Elizabeth, Union Co., SS. Peter and Paul, Rev. Michael Chubirko, S.D.B.
Res., 316 First Ave., 07206. Tel: 908-353-7246.

Flanders, Morris Co., Holy Wisdom, Rev. Daniel Staniskis.
Res., 197 Emmans Rd., 07836. Tel: 201-584-1347.

Edison, Middlesex Co., St. Nicholas, Rev. John Onesko.
Res., 215 May St., 08837. Tel: 908-661-1160.

Jersey City, Hudson Co., St. Mary's, Rev. Robert J. Skurla.
Res., 231 Pacific Ave., 07304. Tel: 201-333-2975.

Linden, Union Co., St. George's, Very Rev. Gerald Dino, O.E.S.L.; Deacon William Tizio.
Res., 417 McCandless St., 07036. Tel: 908-486-6500.

Mahwah, Bergen Co., Holy Spirit, Rev. Marcel Szabo, Admin.
Res., Island Rd. at Church St., P.O. Box 825, 07430. Tel: 201-529-3269.

Hillsborough Township, Somerset Co., St. Mary's, Rev. Msgr. Alan J. Borsuk.
Res., 1900 Brook Blvd., 08876. Tel: 908-725-0615.
Catechesis/Religious Programs—Georgianna Kichura, D.R.E.
Students 110.

Newark, Essex Co., St. George, Rev. Msgr. Robert G. Moneta.
Res., 214 Warwick St., 07105. Tel: 201-589-7202.

New Brunswick, Middlesex Co., St. Joseph (Magyar), Rev. Joseph Homa.
Res., 30 High St., 08901. Tel: 201-545-1686.

Perth Amboy, Middlesex Co., St. Nicholas, Very Rev. Robert J. Radvansky.
Res., 320 Washington St., 08861. Tel: 908-442-0418. [CEM]
St. Michael (Magyar), Very Rev. Basil Rakaczky, O.S.B.M.
Res., 401 Hall Ave., 08861. Tel: 908-826-0792; Fax: 908-826-7993.

Phillipsburg, Warren Co., SS. Peter and Paul, Rev. Stephen Safko.
Res., 723 S. Main St., 08865. Tel: 908-454-5482.

Rahway, Union Co., St. Thomas the Apostle, Rev. John Zeyack, S.T.L.
Res., 1410 Church St., 07065. Tel: 908-382-5300.
Catechesis/Religious Programs—Mrs. Janet Gwiazda, D.R.E.
Students 141.

Roebling, Burlington Co., St. Nicholas. Unassigned.
Res., 191 Norman Ave., 08554. Tel: 609-499-0058. [CEM]
Mission—South Hampton Twp., Vincentown Co., St. Jude, 50 Burrs Mill Rd., South Hampton Twp., 08088.

Somerset, Somerset Co., SS. Peter and Paul, Rev. Pasquale Papalia.
Res., 285 Hamilton St., 08873. Tel: 908-545-5500.

Toms River, Ocean Co., Our Lady of Perpetual Help, Rev. Charles Yastishock.
Res., 1937 Church Rd., 08753. Tel: 908-255-6272.

Trenton, Mercer Co., St. Mary of the Assumption, Rev. Msgr. Nicholas I. Puhak, V.F.
Res., 411 Adeline St., 08611. Tel: 609-394-5004. [CEM]
School—Mrs. Carolyn Delvalle, Prin. Sisters of St. Basil the Great 2; Lay Teachers 12; Students 183.
Catechesis/Religious Programs—Deacon Thomas L. Vanisko, D.R.E.
Students 45.
Chapel—Hamilton Township, St. Mary Chapel.
St. Nicholas (Magyar), Rev. Lawrence Wolf, O.S.B.M.
Church—111 Adeline St., 08611. Tel: 609-695-5962. [CEM]
Res., 360 Monastery Ln., Matawan, 07747. Tel: 908-566-8445.

STATE OF CONNECTICUT

Bridgeport, Fairfield Co., Holy Trinity, Rev. Andor Rakaczki, S.T.D.
Res., 155 Scofield Ave., 06605. Tel: 203-334-7089; Fax: 203-334-5226.

Danbury, Fairfield Co., St. Nicholas, Rev. Michael George Popson.
Res., 13 Pembroke Rd., 06811. Tel: 203-743-1106.

Meriden, New Haven Co., St. Nicholas of Myra. Attended by Danbury.
Mailing Address: c/o 13 Pembroke Rd., Danbury, 06810.
89 Summer St., 06450.

New Britain, Hartford Co., Holy Trinity, Rev. Alan Kapron.
Res., 121 Beaver St., 06051. Tel: 203-229-2531. [CEM]

Trumbull, Fairfield Co., St. John the Baptist, Rev. Glenn M. Davidowich; Deacon William Sedlock.
Res., 100 St. John's Dr., 06611. Tel: 203-377-5967.

STATE OF FLORIDA

Coconut Creek, Broward Co., Our Lady of the Sign, Rev. Michael N. Kane.
Res., 7311 Lyons Rd., 33073. Tel: 954-429-0056.

Fort Pierce, Port St. Lucie Co., SS. Cyril and Methodius, Rev. Nicholas Kusevich.
Church—1002 Bahama Ave., P.O. Box 3525, 34948. Tel: 407-595-1021; Fax: 407-968-2021.

Jacksonville, Duval Co., Protection of the Mother of God. Attended by Ormond Beach. Rev. Michael Krulak, Admin.
Mailing Address: 14608 Stacey Rd., 32250. Tel: 904-223-0307.
Res., 17 Buckskin Ln., Ormond Beach, 32174. Tel: 904-677-8704.

Lake Worth, Duval Co., Holy Apostles, Rev. Nicholas Kusevich.
Res., 4788 Clock Rd., 33463. Tel: 305-968-8500; Fax: 407-968-2021.

Miami, Dade Co., St. Basil's, Very Rev. Peter Lickman; Deacon Ford Slagle.
Res., 1475 N.E. 199 St., 33179. Tel: 305-651-0991; Fax: 305-651-4902.

New Port Richey, Pasco Co., St. Anne's, Rev. Basil William Kraynyak; Deacon John Buga.
Church and Res.: 7120 Massachusetts Ave., 34653. Tel: 813-849-1190.

North Fort Myers, Lee Co., All Saints Byzantine Catholic, Rev. Ronald Barusefski.
Res., 10291 Bayshore Rd., 33917. Tel: 941-543-6363.
Mission—Naples.

Orlando, Orange Co., St. Nicholas of Myra, Rev. Salvatore A. Pignato; Deacon Robert Thanski.
Res., 5135 Sand Lake Rd., 32819. Tel: 407-351-0133.

Ormond Beach, Volusia Co., Holy Dormition, Rev. Michael Krulak; Deacon Frank Schaefer.
Res., 17 Buckskin Ln., 32174. Tel: 904-677-8704.

St. Petersburg, Pinellas Co., St. Therese, Very Rev. Robert Evancho. Pastoral Associates: Sr. Martha Moyta, O.S.B.M.; Sr. Victoria Puhak, O.S.B.M.; Sr. Susan Sisko, O.S.B.M.; Deacon Joseph Ciarciaglino.
Res., 4265 13th Ave., N., 33713. Tel: 813-323-4022.
Convent—4226 33rd Ave., N., 33713. Tel: 813-522-2260.

STATE OF GEORGIA

Roswell, Fulton Co., Epiphany Byzantine Church, Rev. Philip P. Scott; Deacon Charles Appel.
Res., 2030 Old Alabama Rd., 30076. Tel: 770-993-0973.

STATE OF MARYLAND

Baltimore, Baltimore Co., Patronage of the Mother of God, Very Rev. Conan Timoney.
Church—1260 Stevens Ave., 21227. Tel: 410-247-4936.
Missions—Abingdon, St. Francis; Hagerstown, St. Ann's.

Beltsville, Prince Georges Co., St. Gregory of Nyssa, Rev. Michael Kerestes.
Res., 12420 Old Gunpowder Rd., 20705. Tel: 301-953-9323; Fax: 301-953-1529.

STATE OF MASSACHUSETTS

South Hadley, Hampshire Co., St. Michael's, Rev. Alan Kapron.
Mailing Address: c/o 121 Beaver St., New Britain, CT 06051. Tel: 203-229-2531.
15 Lincoln Ave., 01075.

STATE OF NEW YORK

Amherst, Erie Co., St. Stephen's, Rev. Joseph Bertha; Deacon Chester Fortuna, M.D.
Res., 620 Ayer Rd., Williamsville, 14221. Tel: 716-688-9290.

Binghamton, Broome Co., Holy Spirit, Very Rev. John J. Cigan.
Res., 360 Clinton St., 13905. Tel: 607-797-2122. [CEM]

Brooklyn, Kings Co., St. Elias. Administered from St. Mary's, New York.
Saint Mary's Chapel. Attended by St. Mary's, New York.
Mailing Address: c/o St. Mary's: 246 E. 15th St., New York, 10003.
Church—197 34th St., 11232.

Endicott, Broome Co., SS. Peter and Paul's. Administered from Binghamton, NY.
Res., 106 N. Rogers Ave., 13760. Tel: 607-785-3132. [CEM]

Granville, Washington Co., SS. Peter and Paul, Rev. Harold Stockert.
Res., 2 Park Ave., 12832. Tel: 518-642-2884. [CEM]
Mission—Ballston Spa, Protection of Mother of God, Tel: 518-642-1556.

New York, New York Co., Exaltation of Holy Cross (Hungarian), Rev. Basil Vegvari, O.F.M.
Res., 229 E. 29th St., Apt. 4-L, 10016. Tel: 212-696-1709.
Church—323 E. 82nd St., 10028.
St. Mary's, Rev. Msgr. Raymond M. Misulich, J.C.L.; Rev. Matthew Peter Butrie.
Res., 246 E. 15th St., 10003. Tel: 212-677-0516; Fax: 212-260-6071.

Olean, Cattaragus Co., St. Mary's. Attended by Williamsville.

Peekskill, Westchester Co., SS. Peter and Paul, Rev. Msgr. Robert Senetsky, J.C.D.
Res., 705 Shenandoah Ave., 10566. Tel: 914-737-8249; Fax: 914-737-8438.

Smithtown, Suffolk Co., Resurrection, Rev. Daniel J. Bitsko.
Res., 37 Juniper Ave., 11787. Tel: 516-724-4979.

Westbury, Nassau Co., St. Andrew the Apostle, Deacon Nicholas Daddona, Admin.
Church—275 Ellison Ave., 11590. Tel: 516-333-3266.

White Plains, Westchester Co., St. Nicholas of Myra, Very Rev. Robert J. Hospodar, J.C.L.
Res., 768 North St., 10605. Tel: 914-681-0659.

Yonkers, Westchester Co., St. Nicholas of Myra. Attended by St. Nicholas of Myra, White Plains. Rev. Robert J. Hospodar.
Mailing Address: c/o St. Nicholas of Myra, 768 North St., White Plains, 10605. Tel: 914-681-0659.

STATE OF NORTH CAROLINA

Cary, Wake Co., SS. Cyril & Methodius Byzantine Catholic, Rev. Richard Rohrer.
Res., 2510 Piney Plains Rd., 27511. Tel: 919-851-9266; Fax: 919-233-3997.

STATE OF PENNSYLVANIA

Allentown, Lehigh Co., St. Andrew the Apostle. Attended by St. Michael, Allentown. Rev. Peter J. Hosak.

Church—518 N. Second St., 18102. Tel: 610-432-6773.
St. Michael, Rev. Peter J. Hosak.
Res., 156 Green St., 18102. Tel: 610-432-6773.

Beaver Meadows, Carbon Co., SS. Peter and Paul, Rev. Peter Donish; Deacon Michael Pataki.
Res., P.O. Box 206, 18216. Tel: 717-455-1442. [CEM]

Bethlehem, Northampton Co., SS. Peter and Paul, Rev. Robert Slesinski, Ph.D.
Res., 1140 Johnston Dr., 18017. Tel: 610-867-2322.

Brockton, Schuylkill Co., St. Mary's. Attended by St. Clair.
131 S. Morris St., St. Clair, 17970. Tel: 717-429-0520.

Clarks Summit, Lackawanna Co., Transfiguration. Attended by St. Mary, Scranton. Rev. Francis M. Twardzik, S.D.B.
Res., 1105 Gravel Pond Rd., 18411. Tel: 717-586-0100.

Coaldale, Schuylkill Co., St. John's. Attended by Lansford.
116 E. Bertsch St., Lansford, 18232. Tel: 717-645-2640.

Coatesville, Chester Co., St. Mary's, Very Rev. Gregory J. Noga.
Mailing Address: c/o St. Michael's, 203 Jacob St., Mont Clare, 19453. Tel: 610-933-2819; Fax: 610-935-9460.

Doylestown, Bucks Co., Christ the Saviour Byzantine Catholic Church at Our Lady of Czestochawa Shrine, Rev. Robert Lucas.
Ferry Rd., 18901. Tel: 215-862-9227.
Res., 310 Aquetong Rd., New Hope, 18938.

Dunmore, Lackawanna Co., St. Michael, Rev. Theodore Rudy.
Res., 511 E. Drinker St., 18512. Tel: 717-344-2521. [CEM]

Forest City, Susquehanna Co., St. John the Baptist, Rev. Edward Stanko.
Res., 306 Susquehanna St., 18421. Tel: 717-785-5296. [CEM]

Freeland, Luzerne Co., St. Mary's, Rev. James Demko.
Res., 643 Fern St., 18224. Tel: 717-636-0700. [CEM]

Harrisburg, Dauphin Co., St. Ann, Rev. Michael P. Shear; Deacon George Kashi.
4709 Rockledge Dr., 17110. Tel: 717-236-2053.
Res., 5408 Locust Lane, 17109. Tel: 717-652-1415; Fax: 717-652-5471.
Catechesis/Religious Programs—Students 117.

Hazleton, Luzerne Co., St. John the Baptist Church, Rev. Msgr. John Opalenick, V.F.
Res., 5 E. 20th St., 18201. Tel: 717-454-1142; Fax: 717-454-6120. [CEM 2]
School—201 N. Wyoming St., 18201. Tel: 717-454-5812. Sr. M. Leonora, O.S.B.M., Prin.
Sisters of St. Basil the Great 3; Students 93.
St. Mary's, Rev. Francis T. Gera.
Res., 227 E. Beech St., 18201. Tel: 717-455-3232. [CEM]

Jessup, Lackawanna Co., Holy Ghost, Very Rev. Edward G. Cimbala.
Res., 313 First St., 18434. Tel: 717-489-2353. [CEM]
School—LaSalle Academy, Tel: 717-489-2010. Sr. M. Christopher Godlewski, S.S.C.M., Prin.
Sisters 5; Lay Teachers 21; Students 580.

Kingston, Luzerne Co., St. Mary's, Rev. Theodore Krepp.
Res., 321 Chestnut Ave., 18704. Tel: 717-287-0282. [CEM]

Lansford, Carbon Co., St. John the Baptist, Rev. Emil Paulshock.
Res., 116 E. Bertsch St., 18232. Tel: 717-645-2640. [CEM]

Levittown, Bucks Co., Our Lady of Perpetual Help, Rev. Myron M. Badnerosky.
Res., 1787 Woodburne Rd., 19056. Tel: 215-945-5122.

Lopez, Sullivan Co., SS. Peter and Paul, Rev. Michael Mokris, Admin.
472 Church St., Swoyersville, 18704. Tel: 717-287-2306.

McAdoo, Schuylkill Co., St. Michael, Very Rev. Leonard Hollick.
Res., 17 E. Blaine St., 18237. Tel: 717-929-1062. [CEM]

Mahanoy City, Schuylkill Co., St. Mary's, Rev. Edward Higgins.
Res., 621 W. Mahanoy Ave., 17948. Tel: 717-773-2631. [CEM]

Minersville, Schuylkill Co., SS. Peter and Paul, Very Rev. Michael Mondik.
Res., 107 S. Fourth St., 17954. Tel: 717-544-2074. [CEM]

Mont Clare, Montgomery Co., St. Michael, Very Rev. Gregory J. Noga.
Res., 203 Jacob St., 19453. Tel: 610-933-2819; Fax: 610-935-9460.

Nanticoke, Luzerne Co., St. Mary's (Hanover). Attended by St. John's.
526 Church St., Wilkes-Barre, 18702.

Nesquehoning, Carbon Co., St. Mary's, Rev. George A. Bujnak.
Res., 141 W. High St., 18240. Tel: 717-669-6533. [CEM]

Old Forge, Lackawanna Co., St. Nicholas, Rev. Msgr. Stephen Zajac; Rev. Nicholas Kraynak.
Res., 140 Church St., 18518. Tel: 717-457-3042. [CEM]
Chapels—St. Nicholas, (1973), Rte. 940, Mount Pocono, 18344.; Saint Mary's, (1907), 700 Oak St., Taylor, 18517. [CEM]

Palmerton, Carbon Co., SS. Peter and Paul. Attended by St. Michael's, Allentown. Rev. Peter J. Hosak, Admin.
156 Green St., Allentown, 18102. Tel: 610-432-6773.

Philadelphia, Philadelphia Co., Holy Ghost, Rev. Eugene M. Hutter.
Res., 2310 S. 24th St., 19145. Tel: 215-334-5129.
Holy Trinity. Administered from Holy Ghost, Philadelphia.
Res., 6801 N. 10th St., 19126. Tel: 215-548-2837.

Pittston, Luzerne Co., St. Michael, Rev. Robert Kemeter.
Res., 205 N. Main St., 18640. Tel: 717-654-4564. [CEM]

Pottstown, Montgomery Co., St. John the Baptist, Very Rev. Nicholas DeProspero; Deacon Michael Erdek.
Res., 301 Cherry St., 19464. Tel: 215-326-1877. [CEM]

St. Clair, Schuylkill Co., St. Mary's, Rev. Christopher Petruska.
Res., 131 S. Morris St., 17970. Tel: 717-429-0520. [CEM]

Scranton, Lackawanna Co., St. John the Baptist, Rev. Robert W. Lozinski, C.S.C.
Res., 310 Broadway, 18505. Tel: 717-342-8930. [CEM]
St. Mary's Byzantine Catholic Church, Rev. Francis M. Twardzik, S.D.B.
Res., 310 Mifflin Ave., 18503. Tel: 717-342-8429. [CEM]

Sheppton, Schuylkill Co., St. Mary's. Attended by SS. Peter and Paul.
P.O. Box 206, Beaver Meadows, 18216. [CEM]

Swoyersville, Luzerne Co., St. Nicholas, Rev. James A. Mitchko.
Res., 271 Tripp St., 18704. Tel: 717-287-4418. [CEM]

Taylor, Lackawanna Co., St. Mary's. Attended by Old Forge.
Res., 700 Oak St., 18517. Tel: 717-457-3042. [CEM]

Wilkes-Barre, Luzerne Co., St. Mary's, Rev. Msgr. John T. Sekellick; Rev. Vincent Brady.
Res., 695 N. Main St., 18705. Tel: 717-822-6028; Fax: 717-823-8003. [CEM]
School—522 Madison St., 18705. Tel: 717-823-8003. Sr. Janet Decker, O.S.B.M., Prin.
Sisters of St. Basil the Great 3; Students 199.
Mission—Glen Lyon, Luzerne Co., St. Michael.
St. John's, Rev. John Balog.
Res., 526 Church St., 18702. Tel: 717-825-4338.

Williamstown, Dauphin Co., Holy Spirit. Attended by Minersville.
107 S. Fourth St., Minersville, 17954. Tel: 717-544-2074. [CEM]

STATE OF VIRGINIA

Annandale, Fairfax Co., Epiphany of Our Lord, Very Rev. John G. Basarab; Deacons Gerald McDonnell; Vincent Obsitnik. In res., Rev. Richard Kanar.
Res., 3410 Woodburn Rd., 22003. Tel: 703-573-3986.

Williamsburg, York Co., Ascension of Our Lord, Rev. Ronald Hatton.
Church—114 Palace Ln., 23185. Tel: 759-220-8098.
Res., 4528 Wimbledon Way, 23188. Tel: 759-253-5641.
Missions—Virginia Beach, Virginia Beach Co., Our Lady of Perpetual Help, 216 S. Parliament Dr., Virginia Beach, 23462. Tel: 759-456-0809; Richmond, Byzantine Catholic Mission.

On Duty Outside Diocese:
Reverend Fathers—
Custer, John, SS. Cyril & Methodius Seminary, 3605 Perrysville Ave., Pittsburgh, PA 15214. Tel: 412-321-8383; 321-9936 (Fax)
DeFronzo, Anthony R., 767 Elm St., Rocky Hill, CT 06064
Fulton, Eugene, Larchmont Trinity Retreat, One Pryer Manor Rd., Larchmont, NY 10538. Tel: 914-632-3743
Hamperzonian, Jerry, Chap., VA Medical Center, 3350 La Jolla Village Dr., San Diego, CA 92161

Leave of Absence:
Reverend Fathers—
Matrishion, Joseph
Siroki, David
Tutko, Michael

Absent on Sick Leave:
Reverend Fathers—
Baron, Jody
Czachor, Christopher
Kanar, Richard
Yurista, Michael

Retired:
Reverend Monsignors—
Jackanich, Joseph, 4036 Lockwood Blvd., Youngstown, OH 44511. Tel: 216-505-0302
Reverend Fathers—
Billy, George, 404 McCandless St., Linden, NJ 07036. Tel: 908-925-5211
Bovankovich, John, 8141 N. 16th St., Phoenix, AZ 85020. Tel: 602-944-2195
Boysak, Basil, Mt. Saint Macrina Manor, 520 W. Main St., Box 548, Uniontown, PA 15401. Tel: 412-437-1303
Brown, Charles, M.D.
Danilak, John, 2711 Veser Ln., Willow Grove, PA 19090
Eles, Joseph, 150 Horizons E., Apt. 305, Boynton Beach, FL 33435. Tel: 407-731-2682
Luzetsky, Stephen, Juniper Manor, 70 W. Juniper St., Hazleton, PA 18201
Moskva, Emil, 1801 W. Front St., Berwick, PA 18603. Tel: 717-752-3125
Musko, Andrew, Holy Family Manor, 1200 Spring St., Bethlehem, PA 18018. Tel: 610-865-5595
Tigyer, Paul, P.O. Box 658, Hamlin, PA 18427. Tel: 717-689-2153

Permanent Deacons:
Appel, Charles M.
Buga, John
Ciarciaglino, Joseph M.
Daddona, Nicholas
Erdek, Michael A.
Fortuna, Chester
Guze, John G.
Kashi, George
Kuntz, Edward E.
McDonnell, Gerald E.
Obsitnik, Vincent
Pataki, Michael
Schaefer, Frank
Sedlock, William
Slagle, Ford
Thanski, Robert
Tizio, William
Vanisko, Thomas L.

INSTITUTIONS LOCATED IN THE DIOCESE

[A] ELEMENTARY AND HIGH SCHOOLS, PRIVATE

MIAMI, FL.

Holy Cross Community and Academy. (Grades PreK-12), 12425 Sunset Dr., 33183. Tel: 305-598-0009; Fax: 305-598-8455. Rev. Anchim Gregory Wendt. Religious 6; Lay Teachers 43; Students 527.

[B] MONASTERIES

MATAWAN. *Basilian Fathers of Mariapoch,* 360 Monastery Ln., 07747. Tel: 908-566-8445. Very Rev. Joseph J. Erdei, O.S.B.M., Supr.; Revs. Basil M. Rakaczky, O.S.B.M. (Hungary), Prov. Supr.; Stephen J. Skinta, O.S.B.M., Novice Master for Basilian Fathers in Hungary; Lawrence Robert Wolf, O.S.B.M.

SYBERTSVILLE, PA. *Holy Dormition Monastery,* P.O. Box 270, 18251. Tel: 717-788-1212; Fax: 717-788-1212. Very Rev. James Carroll, O.F.M., Protohegumen; Revs. Paul Guthrie, O.F.M.; John Kapitan, O.F.M.; Marion Kawola; Bros. Augustine Paulik, O.F.M.;

Andrew Martino, O.F.M.; Douglas Shannon, O.F.M., Franciscan Friary, 50 Friars Ln., P.O. Box 4815, Stamford, CT, 06907. Tel: 203-322-0570. Rev. Anthony Skurla, O.F.M.

[C] CONVENTS AND RESIDENCES FOR SISTERS

SUGARLOAF, PA. *Holy Annunciation Monastery*, R.R. 1, Box 1336, 18249. Tel: 717-788-1205. Discalced Byzantine Carmelite Nuns. Mother Marija of the Holy Spirit, O.C.D., Prioress. Nuns with Solemn Vows 8; Nuns with Temporary Vows 3; Novices 2.

[D] MISCELLANEOUS

PASSAIC. *Eastern Catholic Associates*, 96 First St., 07055. God with Us Publications, 445 Lackawanna Ave., West Paterson, 07424. Most Revs. Nicholas Samra, Pres.; Robert Moskal, Vice Pres.; Rt. Rev. John M. Boean, Sec.; Most Rev. Andrew Pataki, J.C.L., Registered Agent.

RELIGIOUS INSTITUTES OF MEN REPRESENTED IN THE DIOCESE

For further details refer to the corresponding bracketed number in the Religious Institutes of Men or Women section.

[0520]—*Franciscan Friars*.—O.F.M.

[0180]—*Order of St. Basil the Great*.—O.S.B.M.

RELIGIOUS INSTITUTES OF WOMEN REPRESENTED IN THE DIOCESE

[0420]—*Discalced Carmelite Nuns (Byzantine Rite)*.—O.C.D.

[3730]—*Sisters of the Order of St. Basil the Great*.—O.S.B.M.

NECROLOGY

† Kranak, Donald, Minersville, PA, SS. Peter and Paul Church. —Died April 21, 1996.

† Powell, George C., (Retired). —Died March 13, 1996.

† Powell, Rev. Msgr. John K., (Retired). —Died Feb. 21, 1996.

† Scyocurka, Peter Joseph Dionysius, Trenton, NJ, St. Mary of the Assumption. —Died Oct. 29, 1996.

† Stim, Rev. Msgr. John A., (Retired). —Died Jan. 21, 1996.

Metropolitan Archdiocese of Philadelphia Ukrainian

Most Reverend

STEPHEN SULYK, D.D.

Archbishop of Archdiocese of Philadelphia for Ukrainians; appointed Archbishop of Philadelphia for Ukrainians and Metropolitan of the Ukrainian Catholic Church in the USA on December 29, 1980. *Res., 827 N. Franklin St., Philadelphia, PA, 19123.*

Most Reverend

WALTER PASKA

Auxiliary Bishop of Philadelphia Ukrainian; appointed February 4, 1992.

ESTABLISHED MAY 28, 1913.

The jurisdiction of the Metropolitan Archdiocese of Philadelphia includes the District of Columbia, the States of Virginia, Maryland, Delaware, New Jersey and eastern Pennsylvania to the eastern boundaries of the following Counties: Potter, Clinton, Center, Mifflin, Huntington and Fulton. With regard to persons, his subjects are all Catholics of the Byzantine Rite: 1. Who immigrated to this country from Galicia, Bucovina and other Ukrainian provinces; 2. Who descend from such persons (can. 755); 3. Women married to men referable to 1. and 2. if they comply with can. 98, n. 4; 4. Who in accordance with can. 98, n. 3 changed their Rite; 5. Converts to the Catholic Church of the Byzantine Rite; 6. And in fact all other Catholics of the Byzantine Rite who are attached to parishes subject to the jurisdiction of the Archbishop.

For legal titles of parishes and archdiocesan institutions, consult the Chancery Office.

Chancery Office: 827 N. Franklin St., Philadelphia, PA, 19123. Tel.: 215-627-0143; Fax: 215-627-0377.

STATISTICAL OVERVIEW

Personnel	
Archbishop	1
Auxiliary Bishops	1
Priests: Diocesan Active in Diocese	44
Priests: Active Outside Diocese	1
Priests: Retired, Sick or Absent	13
Number of Diocesan Priests	58
Religious Priests in Diocese	6
Extern Priests in Diocese	15
Ordinations:	
Permanent Deacons in Diocese	5
Total Brothers	3
Total Sisters	84
Parishes	
Parishes	77
With Resident Pastor:	
Resident Diocesan Priests	50
Resident Religious Priests	2
Without Resident Pastor:	
Administered by Priests	25
Closed Parishes	1
Professional Ministry Personnel:	
Sisters	2
Welfare	
Homes for the Aged	1
Total Assisted	45
Day Care and Extended Day Care Centers	2
Total Assisted	68
Other Institutions	1
Total Assisted	240
Educational	
Seminaries, Diocesan	1
Students from This Diocese	17
Total Seminarians	17
Colleges and Universities	1
Total Students	657
High Schools, Private	1
Total Students	350
Elementary Schools, Diocesan and Parish	7
Total Students	1,636
Catechesis/Religious Education:	
High School Students	400
Elementary Students	1,989
Total Students Under Catholic Instruction	5,049
Teachers in the Diocese:	
Priests	3
Sisters	25
Lay Teachers	300
Vital Statistics	
Receptions into the Church:	
Infant Baptism Totals	345
Adult Baptism Totals	2
Received into Full Communion	5
First Communions	379
Confirmations	347
Marriages:	
Catholic	188
Interfaith	7
Total Marriages	195
Deaths	596
Total Catholic Population	69,488

Former Bishops—Most Rev. STEPHEN SOTER ORTYNSKY, O.S.B.M., D.D., First Ukrainian Catholic Bishop of the United States; ord. July 18, 1891; cons. May 12, 1907; died March 24, 1916.—Most Rev. CONSTANTINE BOHACHEVSKY, D.D., S.T.D., appt. Bishop in the United States, May 20, 1924; appt. Metropolitan Archbishop of the Philadelphia Archeparchy, Byzantine Rite, Aug. 6, 1958; cons. June 15, 1924; died Jan. 6, 1961.—Most Rev. JOSEPH M. SCHMONDIUK, D.D., appt. Titular Bishop of Zeugma and Auxiliary of the Archeparchy of Philadelphia, July 20, 1956; transferred to the Diocese of Stamford See, Nov. 9, 1961; appt. Metropolitan Archbishop of Philadelphia, Oct. 1, 1977.—Most Rev. JOHN STOCK, D.D., appt. Titular Bishop of Pergamum and Auxiliary Bishop to the Archeparchy, Feb. 22, 1971; cons. May 25, 1971; died June 29, 1972.—Most Rev. AMBROSE SENYSHYN, O.S.B.M., D.D., appt. Auxiliary Bishop to the Philadelphia Bishop, July 6, 1942; appt. Exarch of Stamford, July 20, 1956; appt. Eparch of Stamford, Nov. 1, 1958; appt. Metropolitan Archbishop of Philadelphia, Aug. 14, 1961; died Sept. 11, 1976.—Most Rev. JOSEPH M. SCHMONDIUK, D.D., cons. Nov. 8, 1956; Archbishop of Archeparchy, Oct. 1, 1977; died Dec. 25, 1978.—His Eminence MYROSLAV CARDINAL LUBACHIVSKY, D.D., cons. Nov. 12, 1979; named Co-adjutor Major Archbishop of Lviw, March 24, 1980; transferred to Rome Assumed position of Major Archbishop of Lviw, Sept. 7, 1984. Created Cardinal, June 28, 1991.

Protosycellus—Most Rev. WALTER PASKA, J.C.D.

Chancellor—Sr. THOMAS HRYNEWICH, S.S.M.I. Tel: 215-627-0143.

Chancery Office—827 N. Franklin St., Philadelphia, PA, 19123-2097. Tel: 215-627-0143; Fax: 215-627-0377.

College of Archeparchial Counsultors—Most Rev. STEPHEN SULYK, D.D.; Most Rev. WALTER PASKA, J.C.D.; Rev. Msgr. JOHN BURA; Rev. Msgr. JOSEPH FEDOREK; Revs. ROMAN DUBITSKY; MARION KAWOLA, O.F.M.; JAMES MELNIC.

Presbyteral Council—Most Rev. STEPHEN SULYK, D.D.; Most Rev. WALTER PASKA, J.C.D.; Rev. Msgr. JOHN BURA; Rev. ROMAN DUBITSKY; Rev. Msgr. MICHAEL FEDOROWICH; Revs. JOHN FIELDS; MICHAEL HUTSKO; MARIAN KAWOLA, O.F.M.; NICK KOSTIUK; PAUL LABINSKY; JAMES MELNIC; Rev. Msgr. RAYMOND REVAK; Rev. JOHN SENIW.

Archeparchial Corporation—Most Rev. STEPHEN SULYK, D.D., Pres.; Most Rev. WALTER PASKA, J.C.D., Vice Pres.; Rev. JAMES MELNIC, Sec.; Revs. ROMAN DUBITSKY; JOHN FIELDS.

Archdiocesan Tribunal—827 N. Franklin St., Philadelphia, PA, 19123. Tel: 215-627-0143.

Judicial Vicar—Most Rev. WALTER PASKA, J.C.D.

Synodal Judges—Rev. Msgr. STEPHEN HRYNUCK, Ph.D.; Rev. Msgr. JOHN BILANYCH, J.U.D.; Rev. JAMES GRANT.

Defender of the Bond—Rev. DANIEL GUROVICH.

Promotor of Justice—Rev. Msgr. RONALD POPIVCHAK, Ph.D.

Notary—Sr. THOMAS HYRNEWICH, S.S.M.I.

Archeparchial Council for Economic Affairs—Most Rev. STEPHEN SULYK, D.D.; Revs. MICHAEL HUTSKO; JOHN FIELDS; ANDREW FYLYPOWYCH; RICHARD HANUSEY; JOSEPH REH; IHOR SHUST; MICHAEL SMYLIE.

Archeparchial Econom—Rev. MICHAEL HUTSKO; JOSEPH REH, Asst.

Protopresbyters (Deans)—Rev. Msgr. RONALD POPIVCHAK, Reading; Rev. Msgr. JAMES MELNIC, Philadelphia; Rev. Mitred Msgr. STEPHEN CHOMKO, Scranton Deanery; Rev. Msgr. JOSEPH FEDOREK; Rev. Msgr. MICHAEL FEDOROWICH, Shamokin.

Diocesan Offices and Directors

Acolyte Confraternity—Rev. MICHAEL HUTSKO.

Apostleship of Prayer—Rev. JOHN SENIW.

Apostolate—Most Rev. STEPHEN SULYK, D.D.; Revs. MICHAEL HUTSKO; JOHN FIELDS.

Cemeteries—Sr. THOMAS HRYNEWICH, S.S.M.I.

Censors—Rev. Msgr. Dr. RONALD POPIVCHAK; Rev. Msgr. JOHN BURA.

Holy Name Society—Rev. JOHN CIURPITA.

Insurance Commission—Rev. MICHAEL HUTSKO; JOSEPH REH.

League of Ukrainian Catholics—Sr. THOMAS HRYNEWICH, Archdiocesan Dir.

Press, The Way—Rev. JOHN M. FIELDS, English Editor; IVAN SKOCZYLAS, Ukrainian Editor.

Archdiocesan Bulletin—Office: *827 N. Franklin St., Philadelphia, PA, 19123.*

Priests Beneficial Fund—Most Rev. STEPHEN SULYK, D.D., Pres.; Rev. DANIEL GUROVICH, Sec. & Treas.

Board Members: Revs. MICHAEL HUTSKO; ROMAN DUBITSKY; Rev. Msgr. RAYMOND REVAK; Rev. Msgr. MICHAEL FEDOROWICH; Revs. JOHN SENIW; ANTHONY RADCHUK.

Office of Vocations—Rev. Msgr. RONALD POPIVCHAK.

Archdiocesan Radio Programs—"Christ Among Us", aired Sundays 9-9:30 am WTEL, 860 AM (Phila.); Rev. Msgr. JAMES MELNIC; Rev. JOHN SENIW.

CLERGY, PARISHES, MISSIONS AND PAROCHIAL SCHOOLS

CITY OF PHILADELPHIA (Philadelphia County)

1—IMMACULATE CONCEPTION OF BLESSED VIRGIN MARY, CATHEDRAL, Most Rev. Walter Paska, J.C.D.; Rev. Nestor Iwasiw.
Res., 833 N. Franklin St., 19123. Tel: 215-922-2222. [CEM]
Chapels—Immaculate Conception Cathedral Convent; Missionary Sisters of Mother God Convent; Chapel of St. Joseph of Arimathea and the Holy Myrrh-Bearing Women.

2—PROTECTION OF BLESSED VIRGIN MARY, Rev. T. Frank Patrylak.
Res., 100 S. Penn St., Clifton Heights, 19018. Tel: 610-626-9495.

3—ST. ANDREW. Attended by Cathedral of the Immaculate Conception, Philadelphia. In res., Rev. Ostap Oryshkewych.
427 Pine St., 19106. Tel: 215-925-7024.

4—ANNUNCIATION OF THE B.V.M., Rev. Msgr. James Melnic.
Res., 1204 Valley Rd., Melrose Park, 19127-3035. Tel: 215-635-1627.
Church—1206 Valley Rd., Melrose Park, 19127-3035.

5—ST. NICHOLAS. Attended by Rev. Wasyl Sivinsky, St. Basil Monastery, 710 Fox Chase Rd., Fox Chase Manor, PA 19046-4198. Rev. Wasyl Sivinsky (Ukraine).
Church—24th & Poplar Sts., 19123.

6—ST. JOSAPHAT'S, Rev. Msgr. James Melnic; Rev. Roman Pankiw (Ukraine).
Res., 2236 Orthodox St., 19137. Tel: 215-533-7968.
School—4521 Longshore Ave., 19135. Tel: 215-332-8008. Sr. Myron O.S.B.M., Prin.
Sisters 2; Lay Teachers 12; Students 404.
Convent—6932 Ditman St., 19135. Tel: 215-332-8488. Sisters of St. Basil the Great

7—SACRED HEART. Closed. For inquiries for parish records contact the Chancery.

8—CHRIST THE KING, Rev. Msgr. John Bilanych.
Res., 1629 W. Cayuga St., 19140. Tel: 215-455-2416.
Catechesis/Religious Programs—Students 77.

STATE OF DELAWARE

Wilmington, New Castle Co., St. Nicholas, Rev. William R. Gore, O.S.F.S.
Res., 801 Lea Blvd., 19802. Tel: 302-762-5511.

STATE OF MARYLAND

Baltimore, Baltimore Co., St. Michael's, Rev. Michael Michlik (Slovakia).
Res., 2401 Eastern Ave., 21224. Tel: 410-675-7557. [CEM]

Curtis Bay, Baltimore Co., SS. Peter and Paul. Attended by St. Michael's, Baltimore.
Church—1506 Church St., 21226-1440.

Chesapeake City, Cecil Co., St. Basil the Great. Attended by St. Nicholas, Wilmington.
Mailing Address: 801 Lea Blvd., Wilmington, DE 19802.
Catechesis/Religious Programs—Susan Hanchok, D.R.E.
Students 67.
Chapel—Chesapeake City, Sisters of St. Basil the Great.

Silver Spring, Montgomery Co., Holy Trinity, Rev. Taras R. Lonchyna, Admin.
Res., 16631 New Hampshire Ave., 20905-3919. Tel: 301-890-7730.

STATE OF NEW JERSEY

Bayonne, Hudson Co., Assumption B.V.M. Attended by SS. Peter and Paul, Jersey City.
Res., c/o SS. Peter and Paul, 30 Bentley Ave., Jersey City, 07304. Tel: 201-432-3122.
Church—30 E. 25th St., Box 260, 07002.

Carteret, Middlesex Co., St. Mary's, Rev. Orest Pidlypczak, O.S.B.M. (Poland).
Res., 719 Roosevelt Ave., 07008. Tel: 908-541-7678.

Cherry Hill, Camden Co., St. Michael's, Rev. Joseph Martyniuk.
Res., 675 Cooperlanding Rd., 08002. Tel: 609-482-0938.

Elizabeth, Union Co., St. Vladimir's, Rev. Msgr. Joseph J. Fedorek; Rev. Robert Hitchens; Deacon Arthur Dochych.
Res., 309 Grier Ave., 07202-3310. Tel: 201-352-8823. [CEM]
Catechesis/Religious Programs—Students 75.

Great Meadows, Warren Co., St. Nicholas. Attended by Holy Ghost, West Easton, PA. Rev. Bohdan Kin.
Mailing Address: c/o 315 Fourth St., West Easton, PA 18042.
Church—Rte. 46, P.O. Box 162, 07838. Tel: 908-637-4306.

Hillside, Union Co., Immaculate Conception. Attended by St. John the Baptist, Newark.
Res., 719 Sandford Ave., Newark, 07106. Tel: 201-371-1356.
Church—Bloy St. and Liberty Ave., 07205. Tel: 201-354-0472.

Jersey City, Hudson Co., SS. Peter and Paul, Rev. Marian Struc.
Res., 30 Bentley Ave., 07304. Tel: 201-432-3122.

Manville, Somerset Co., St. Michael's. Attended by New Brunswick. Rev. Paul Labinsky.
Church—1700 Brooks Blvd., 08835. Tel: 908-526-9195.

Marlboro, Monmouth Co., St. Volodymyr's. Attended by St. Mary's, Carteret. Deacon Michael Waak.
Mailing Address: c/o 684 Alta Vista Pl., Perth Amboy, 08861. Tel: 908-826-0767.
Church—Rte. 520, 07746.
Catechesis/Religious Programs—Students 65.

Millville, Cumberland Co., St. Nicholas, Most Rev. Walter Paska; Rev. Viktor Bek (Ukraine).
Res., 373 Carmel Rd., 08332. Tel: 609-825-4826. [CEM]

Newark, Essex Co., St. John the Baptist, Revs. Frank Szadiak, C.SS.R.; John Stuchlak, C.SS.R.; Volodymyr Baran, C.SS.R.; Leonid Malkov, C.SS.R.; Bro. John Kanski, C.SS.R.
Res., 719 Sandford Ave., 07106. Tel: 201-371-1356.
School—Tel: 201-373-9359. Sr. Chrysostom Lukiw, O.S.B.M., Prin.
Sisters of St. Basil the Great 2; Lay Teachers 15; Students 118.
Catechesis/Religious Programs—Students 26.

New Brunswick, Middlesex Co., Nativity of B.V.M., Rev. Paul Labinsky.
Res., 86 Livingston Ave., 08901. Tel: 908-246-8385.

Passaic, Passaic Co., St. Nicholas, Revs. Joseph Szupa; Vasyl Bunyk (Ukraine).
Res., 216 President St., 07055. Tel: 201-777-0230.
School—Tel: 201-779-0249. Sr. Albina S.S.M.I., Prin.
Sisters 2; Lay Teachers 7; Students 122.

Perth Amboy, Middlesex Co., Assumption of B.V.M., Revs. Roman Dubitsky; Augustine Molodowitz; Deacon Paul Makar.
Res., 684 Alta Vista Pl., 08861. Tel: 908-826-0767.
School—Tel: 908-826-8721. Sr. Vladymira M.S.M.G., Prin.
Missionary Sisters of Mother of God 2; Lay Teachers 11; Students 240.

Ramsey, Bergen Co., St. Paul. Attended by St. John the Baptist, Whippany.
Res., 7 S. Jefferson Rd., Whippany, 07981. Tel: 201-887-3616.

Rutherford, Bergen Co., Annunciation B.V.M. Attended by St. Nicholas, Passaic.
Res., c/o St. Nicholas, 216 President St., Passaic, 07055. Tel: 201-777-0230.
Church—70 Home Ave., 07070.

Toms River, Ocean Co., St. Stephen's. Attended by Assumption of B.V.M., Perth Amboy. Rev. Roman Dubitsky; Deacon Paul Makar.
Res., c/o Assumption of B.V.M., 684 Alta Vista Pl., Perth Amboy, 08861. Tel: 908-826-0767.
Church—1344 White Oak Bottom Rd., 08755. Tel: 908-505-6293.

Trenton, Mercer Co., St. Josaphat's, Rev. Wasyl Kharuk (Ukraine).
Res., 1195 Deutz Ave., 08611. Tel: 609-695-3771.

Whippany, Morris Co., St. John the Baptist, Rev. Archpriest Uriy Markewuch.
Res., 7 S. Jefferson Rd., 07981. Tel: 201-887-3616.
Church—Rte. 10, 07981.

Williamstown, Gloucester Co., SS. Peter and Paul. Attended by St. Michael's, Cherry Hill.
Mailing Address: 675 Cooperlanding Rd., Cherry Hill, 08002. Tel: 609-482-0938. [CEM]

Woodbine, Cape May Co., St. Nicholas. Attended by Millville.
Church—Lincoln Ave., 08270.

STATE OF PENNSYLVANIA

Alden Station, Luzerne Co., St. Vladimir. Attended by St. Nicholas, Glen Lyon. Rev. Msgr. Bohdan Olesh.
Res., c/o St. Nicholas, 194 E. Main St., Glen Lyon, 18617. Tel: 717-736-6382. [CEM]

Allentown, Lehigh Co., Immaculate Conception of B.V.M. Attended by St. Josaphat, Bethlehem.
Res., 1826 Kenmore Ave., Bethlehem, 18018.

Berwick, Columbia Co., SS. Cyril and Methodius, Rt. Rev. Mitred Msgr Stephen Chomko.
Res., 706 Warren St., 18603. Tel: 717-752-3172. [CEM]
Catechesis/Religious Programs—Students 66.

Bethlehem, Lehigh Co., St. Josaphat's, Rev. Daniel Gurovich.
Res., 1826 Kenmore Ave., 18018. Tel: 610-865-2521. [CEM]
Catechesis/Religious Programs—Students 169.

Bridgeport, Montgomery Co., SS. Peter and Paul, Rev. Msgr. Ronald P. Popivchak.
Res., 519 Union Ave., P.O. Box 126, 19405. Tel: 610-272-7035. [CEM]
Catechesis/Religious Programs—George Maxim, D.R.E.
Students 145.

Bristol, Bucks Co., St. Mary's, Rev. Msgr. Myron Grabowsky.
Res., 2026 Bath Rd., 19007. Tel: 215-788-7117.

Centralia, Columbia Co., Assumption of B.V.M. Attended by Mount Carmel. Rev. Daniel Troyan.
Res., 131 N. Beech St., Mount Carmel, 17851. Tel: 717-339-0650. [CEM]

Chester, Delaware Co., Holy Ghost, Rev. David Clooney.
Res., 3015 W. Third St., 19013. Tel: 610-494-7899; Fax: 610-494-2350.

Clifton Heights, Delaware Co., SS. Peter and Paul, Rev. T. Frank Patrylak.
Res., 104 S. Penn St., 19108.
Church—100 S. Penn St., 19018. Tel: 610-626-9495.

Edwardsville, Luzerne Co., St. Vladimir's, Rev. Alex Burak.
Res., 87 Zerbey Ave., 18704. Tel: 717-287-8471. [CEM]
Catechesis/Religious Programs—Tel: 717-822-1589. Mary Ann Mudrak, D.R.E.
Students 144.

Frackville, Schuylkill Co., St. Michael's, Rev. John Seniw.
Res., 45 S. Second St., 17931. Tel: 717-874-1101.
Catechesis/Religious Programs—Tel: 717-874-1101.
Students 50.

Glen Lyon, Luzerne Co., St. Nicholas, Rev. Msgr. Bohdan Olesh.
Res., 194 E. Main St., 18617. Tel: 717-736-6382.
Church—153 Main St., 18617.

Hazleton, Luzerne Co., St. Michael's. Attended by St. Michael, Shenandoah, PA. Rev. John Ciurpita.
Res., 74 N. Laurel St., 18201.

Lansdale, Montgomery Co., Presentation of Our Lord. Attended by Warrington. Rev. John Fields.
Mailing Address: 1545 Easton Rd., P.O. Box 417, Warrington, 18976.
Church—1564 Allentown Rd., 19446. Tel: 215-368-3993.

McAdoo, Schuylkill Co., St. Mary's. Attended by St. Michael, Shenandoah. Rev. John Ciurpita.
Church—210 W. Blaine St., 18237. Tel: 717-929-2804; Fax: 717-462-0517.

Mahanoy City, Schuylkill Co., St. Nicholas. Attended by St. Michael, Frackville.
Mailing Address: 45 S. Second St., Frackville, 17931. [CEM]

Maizeville, Schuylkill Co., St. John the Baptist. Attended by St. Michael, Frackville.
Mailing Address: 45 S. Second St., Frackville, 17931. Tel: 717-874-1821. [CEM]
Church—Main St., 17934.

Marion Heights, Northumberland Co., Patronage of the Mother of God. Attended by SS. Peter & Paul, Mount Carmel.

Middleport, Schuylkill Co., Nativity of B.V.M., Rev. Michael Hutsko.
Res., 415 N. Front St., Minersville, 17954. Tel: 717-544-4581. [CEM]
Church—Kaska St., 17953.

Minersville, Schuylkill Co., St. Nicholas, Rev. Michael Hutsko.
Res., 415 Front St., 17954. Tel: 717-544-4581; Fax: 717-544-9653. [CEM]
School—Tel: 717-544-2800.
Sisters 4; Lay Teachers 8; Students 150.

Catechesis/Religious Programs—Students 105.

Moscow, Lackawanna Co., Holy Ghost. Attended by Scranton.
Church—Aberdeen Rd., 18444.

Mount Carmel, Northumberland Co., SS. Peter and Paul, Rev. Daniel Troyan.
Res., 131 N. Beech St., 17851. Tel: 717-339-0650; Fax: 717-339-2715. [CEM]

Nanticoke, Luzerne Co., St. Nicholas, Rev. Jeffrey Paulish (SCR).
Res., 706 Warren St., Berwick, 18603. Tel: 717-752-3172.
Church—111 Green St., 18634.
Transfiguration of Our Lord, Rev. Nick Kostiuk.
Res., 240 Center St., 18634. Tel: 717-735-2262.

Northampton, Northampton Co., St. John the Baptist, Rev. Leonard Sinatra.
Res., 1343 Newport Ave., 18067. Tel: 610-262-4104. [CEM]
School—Tel: 610-262-2231. John Barner, Prin.
Lay Teachers 9; Students 130.

Olyphant, Lackawanna Co., SS. Cyril and Methodius, Very Rev. Msgr. Stephen Hrynuck.
Res., 135 River St., 18447. Tel: 717-489-2271. [CEM]
Catechesis/Religious Programs—Students 77.

Palmerton, Carbon Co., St. Vladimir's, Rev. Edward Levandusky.
Res., 101 Lehigh Ave., 18071. Tel: 610-826-2359.

Phoenixville, Chester Co., SS. Peter and Paul. Attended by SS. Peter and Paul, Bridgeport. Rev. Msgr. Ronald Popivchak.
Mailing Address: 519 Union Ave., P.O. Box 126, Bridgeport, 19405. Tel: 610-272-7035.

Plymouth, Luzerne Co., SS. Peter and Paul. Attended by Transfiguration of Our Lord, Nanticoke. Rev. Nick Kostiuk, Admin.
Mailing Address: 240 Center St., Nanticoke, 18634. Tel: 717-735-2262.

Pottstown, Montgomery Co., St. Michael's. Attended by Nativity B.V.M., Reading. Rev. Gregory Maslak.
Res., 1814 Philadelphia Ave., Reading, 19607. Tel: 610-376-0586. [CEM]

Reading, Berks Co., Nativity of Blessed Virgin Mary, Rev. Gregory Maslak.
Res., 1814 Philadelphia Ave., 19607. Tel: 610-376-0586. [CEM]

St. Clair, Schuylkill Co., St. Nicholas. Attended by Holy Trinity, St. Clair. Rev. John Wysochansky.
Res., c/o Holy Trinity, 254 N. Mill St., 17970. Tel: 717-429-2212. [CEM]
Church—N. Morris St., 17970.
Holy Trinity, Rev. John Wysochansky.
Res., 254 N. Mill St., 17970. Tel: 717-429-2212. [CEM]

Sayre, Bradford Co., Ascension of Our Lord. Attended by Elmira Heights, NY.
Res., 110 N. Higgins Ave., 18840. Tel: 717-888-2207. [CEM]

Scranton, Lackawanna Co., St. Vladimir's, Rev. Msgr. Raymond Revak.
Res., 430 N. Seventh St., 18503. Tel: 717-342-7023. [CEM]

Shamokin, Northumberland Co., Transfiguration of Our Lord, Rev. Msgr. Michael Fedorowich.
Res., 303 N. Shamokin St., 17872-5460. Tel: 717-648-5932. [CEM]
School—Tel: 717-648-6435. Sr. Anne Roman, S.S.M.I., Prin.
Sisters Servants of Mary Immaculate 3; Lay Teachers 9; Students 185.
Catechesis/Religious Programs—Students 100.

Shenandoah, Schuylkill Co., St. Michael's, Rev. John N. Ciurpita.
Res., 114 S. Chestnut St., 17976. Tel: 717-462-0809; Fax: 717-462-0517. [CEM]

Simpson, Lackawanna Co., SS. Peter and Paul, Rev. Theodore Boholnick.
Res., 43 Rittenhouse St., 18407. Tel: 717-282-0331. [CEM]

Warrington, Bucks Co., St. Anne's, Rev. John Fields.
Res., 1545 Easton Rd., Box 417, 18976. Tel: 215-343-0779; Fax: 215-343-8060.
Catechesis/Religious Programs—Students 58.

West Easton, Northampton Co., Holy Ghost, Rev. Bohdan Kin.
Res., 315 Fourth St., 18042. Tel: 610-252-4266; Fax: 610-252-8533. [CEM]

Wilkes-Barre, Luzerne Co., SS. Peter and Paul. Attended by St. Vladimir's, Edwardsville. Rev. Alex Burak, Admin.
Church—635 N. River St., 18701. Tel: 717-823-1821. [CEM]
Catechesis/Religious Programs—Mary Ann Mudrak, D.R.E.
Students 49.

STATE OF VIRGINIA

Manassas, Prince William Co., Annunciation of the Blessed Virgin Mary. Attended by Silver Spring, MD. Rev. Taras Lonchyna, Admin.
Mailing Address: P.O. Box 2735, 22111.
Res., 16631 New Hampshire Ave., Silver Spring, MD 20905-3919. Tel: 301-890-7730. [CEM]
Church—6719 Hoadly Rd., 22111. Tel: 703-791-6635.

Richmond, Henrico Co., St. John the Baptist. Attended by Silver Spring, MD. Rev. Taras Lonchyna, Admin.
Res., 16631 New Hampshire Ave., Silver Spring, MD 20905-3919. Tel: 301-890-7730.
Chapel—Sisters of Verona Chapel, Tel: 804-359-4934.

DISTRICT OF COLUMBIA

Washington, District of Columbia, Ukrainian Catholic National Shrine of the Holy Family, Rev. Petro Semenych (Ukraine) Admin. of Spiritualities; Deacon Theophil Staruch, Admin. of Temporalities.
Res., 4250 Harewood Rd., N.E., 20017. Tel: 202-526-3737; Fax: 202-526-1327.
Catechesis/Religious Programs—Students 152.

Absent on Leave:
Reverend Monsignors—
Canavan, Martin
Reverend Fathers—
Batcho, Michael
Korinchock, Joseph
Worschak, George D.

Retired:
Reverend Monsignors—
Batza, Joseph, Maria Joseph Manor, R.D. #4, Danville, PA 17815
Borsa, Anthony, 159 Wilson Ave., Aberdeen, NJ 07747
Pospishil, Victor J., 6 Michigan Dr., Matawan, NJ 07747
Stefaniuk, Dmytro, 911 N. Franklin St., #203, Philadelphia, PA 19123
Reverend Fathers—
Horoshko, Michael
Levytsky, Bohdan, R.D. No. 2, Box 431, Leighton, PA 18235
Oryshkewych, Ostap, 427 Pine St., Philadelphia, PA 19105

Permanent Deacons:
Dochych, Arthur J., Elizabeth, NJ
Latrick, Donald, Holy Family Ukrainian Catholic National Shrine, Washington, DC
Makar, Paul, Perth Amboy, NJ
Staruch, Theophil, Holy Family Ukrainian Catholic National Shrine, Washington, DC
Waak, Michael P., Perth Amboy, NJ

INSTITUTIONS LOCATED IN THE ARCHDIOCESE

[A] SEMINARIES, ARCHEPARCHY

WASHINGTON, DC. *St. Josaphat Seminary*, 201 Taylor St., N.E., 20017. Tel: 202-529-1177. Rev. Msgr. John Bura, Rector; Revs. Julian K. Anthony, Spiritual Dir.; Vasyl Repela (Ukraine), Prefect.

[B] COLLEGES AND UNIVERSITIES

JENKINTOWN. *Manor Junior College*, 700 Fox Chase Rd., 19046. Tel: 215-885-2360; Fax: 215-576-6564.
For a complete listing, refer to the Colleges and Universities section.

[C] HIGH SCHOOLS, PRIVATE

FOX CHASE MANOR. *St. Basil Academy*, 711 Fox Chase Rd., 19046. Tel: 215-745-5550; Fax: 215-885-4025. Sr. Carla Hernandez, O.S.B.M., Prin. Sisters 7; Lay Teachers 32; Students 350.

[D] HOMES FOR SENIOR CITIZENS

PHILADELPHIA. *Ascension Manor, Inc.*, 911 N. Franklin St., 19123. Tel: 215-922-1116.
For a complete listing, refer to the Special Care Facilities section.
Home of Divine Providence, 209 W. Chestnut Hill Ave., 19118. Tel: 215-247-7107.
For a complete listing, refer to the Special Care Facilities section.

[E] MONASTERIES AND RESIDENCES OF PRIESTS AND BROTHERS

SYBERTSVILLE. *Holy Dormition Monastery*. (Byzantine Slavonic Rite), P.O. Box 270, 18251. Tel: 717-788-1212. Very Rev. Anthony Skurla, O.F.M., Protohegumen.

[F] CONVENTS AND RESIDENCES FOR SISTERS

PHILADELPHIA. *Motherhouse of the Missionary Sisters of Mother of God*, 711 N. Franklin St., 19123. Sr. Josepha Kruchinsky, M.S.M.G., Supr. Gen.
Nursery School. Students 35. Professed Nuns 11.
Sisters Servants of Mary Immaculate, Home of Divine Providence, 209 W. Chestnut Hill Ave., 19118-3703. Sr. Cecelia Sworin, S.S.M.I. Sisters 11.

CHESAPEAKE CITY, MD. *St. Basil's Convent*, 415 Lock St., 21915. Sisters O.S.B.M. Sr. M. Augustine, Supr.

FOX CHASE MANOR. *Provincial Motherhouse of the Sisters of St. Basil the Great*, 710 Fox Chase Rd., 19046. Tel: 215-663-9153; Fax: 215-728-6129. Sr. Dorothy Ann Busowski, O.S.B.M., Prov. Supr.; Sr. Elizabeth Bertoldi, O.S.B.M., Asst. Prov. Councilors: Sr. Laura Palka, O.S.B.M.; Sr. Marie Francis Wolchansky, O.S.B.M.; Sr. Paula Jacynyk, O.S.B.M. Professed Sisters 75.

[G] MISCELLANEOUS

JENKINTOWN. *The Basileiad Library*, 700 Fox Chase Rd., 19046. Sisters of St. Basil the Great. Sr. Mary Anne Gorniowsky, O.S.B.M., Librarian.

RELIGIOUS INSTITUTES OF MEN REPRESENTED IN THE ARCHEPARCHY

For further details refer to the corresponding bracketed number in the Religious Institutes of Men or Women section.

[0520]—*Franciscan Friars*. (Slav-Byzantine Commissariat).—O.F.M.

[1070]—*Redemptorist Fathers*.—C.SS.R.

RELIGIOUS INSTITUTES OF WOMEN REPRESENTED IN THE ARCHEPARCHY

[2810]—*Missionary Sisters of Mother of God*.—M.S.M.G.

[3730]—*Sisters of the Order of St. Basil the Great*.—O.S.B.M.

[3610]—*Sisters Servants of Mary Immaculate*.—S.S.M.I.

ARCHDIOCESAN CEMETERIES

LANGHORNE. *Mother of Sorrows*, Langhorne & Yardley Rd., 19047. Tel: 215-627-0143.

NECROLOGY

† Stebelsky, Reverend Canons Basil, (Retired). —Died May 25, 1996.

Metropolitan Archdiocese of Pittsburgh, Byzantine

Most Reverend

JUDSON M. PROCYK, D.D.

Metropolitan Archbishop of Pittsburgh Byzantine; ordained May 19, 1957; appointed Archbishop of Pittsburgh Byzantine November 15, 1994; installed February 7, 1995. *Office: 66 Riverview Ave., Pittsburgh, PA, 15214. Res., 50 Riverview Ave., Pittsburgh, PA, 15214.*

ESTABLISHED FEBRUARY 25, 1924.

RAISED TO ARCHEPARCHY FEBRUARY 21, 1969.

Embraces all Byzantine Ruthenian Rite Catholics in that part of the State of Pennsylvania west of the western boundaries of the Counties of Tioga, Lycoming, Union, Mifflin, Juniata and Franklin. In the State of Ohio, the Counties of Ashtabula, Athens, Belmont, Carroll, Columbiana, Gallia, Guernsey, Harrison, Jefferson, Lawrence, Mahoning, Meigs, Morrow, Morgan, Noble, Trumbull and Washington and also the States of Alabama, Arkansas, Kentucky, Louisiana, Mississippi, Oklahoma, Tennessee, Texas and West Virginia.

For legal titles of parishes and diocesan institutions, consult the Chancery Office.

Chancery Office: 66 Riverview Ave., Pittsburgh, PA, 15214. Tel.: 412-231-4000; Fax: 412-231-1697.

STATISTICAL OVERVIEW

Personnel	
Archbishop	1
Abbots	1
Priests: Diocesan Active in Diocese	60
Priests: Active Outside Diocese	1
Priests: Retired, Sick or Absent	4
Number of Diocesan Priests	65
Religious Priests in Diocese	9
Ordinations:	
Transitional Deacons	1
Total Brothers	4
Total Sisters	108
Parishes	
Parishes	87
With Resident Pastor:	
Resident Diocesan Priests	56
Resident Religious Priests	6
Without Resident Pastor:	
Administered by Priests	25
Missions	3
Professional Ministry Personnel:	
Sisters	4
Welfare	
Homes for the Aged	3
Total Assisted	322
Day Care and Extended Day Care Centers	3
Total Assisted	90
Educational	
Seminaries, Diocesan	1
Students from This Diocese	3
Students from Other Diocese	8
Total Seminarians	3
Elementary Schools, Diocesan and Parish	3
Total Students	580
Catechesis/Religious Education:	
High School Students	605
Elementary Students	2,561
Total Students Under Catholic Instruction	3,749
Teachers in the Diocese:	
Sisters	8
Lay Teachers	37
Vital Statistics	
Receptions into the Church:	
Infant Baptism Totals	521
Adult Baptism Totals	55
Received into Full Communion	75
First Communions	367
Confirmations	639
Marriages:	
Catholic	230
Interfaith	78
Total Marriages	308
Deaths	718
Total Catholic Population	85,740

Former Bishops—Most Rev. BASIL TAKACH, ord. Dec. 12, 1902; appt. May 20, 1924; cons. June 15, 1924; died May 13, 1948.—Most Rev. DANIEL IVANCHO, D.D., Titular Bishop of Europus; ord. Sept. 30, 1934; appt. Coadjutor Bishop, August 29, 1946; cons. Nov. 5, 1946; succeeded to May 13, 1948; retired Dec. 2, 1954; died Aug. 2, 1972.—Most Rev. NICHOLAS T. ELKO, D.D., cons. March 6, 1955; transferred to Rome, Dec. 22, 1967; died May 18, 1991.—Most Rev. STEPHEN J. KOCISCKO, D.D., cons. July 20, 1956; retired June 12, 1991; died March 7, 1995.—Most Rev. THOMAS V. DOLINAY, ord. May 16, 1948; appt. Titular Bishop of Thyatira and Auxiliary of Passaic, Sept. 23, 1976; cons. Nov. 23, 1976; appt. First Ordinary of the Byzantine Catholic Diocese of Van Nuys; installed March 1982; appt. Coadjutor Archbishop of Pittsburgh, March 13, 1990; installed May 29, 1990; succeeded to June 12, 1991; died April 13, 1993.—Most Rev. JOHN M. BILOCK, ord. Feb. 3, 1946; appt. Titular Bishop of Pergamo and Auxiliary Bishop to the Metropolitan Archbishop of Pittsburgh; installed March 1, 1973; cons. May 15, 1973; appt. Archdiocesan Administrator, April 20, 1993; died Sept. 8, 1994.

Chancery Office—66 Riverview Ave., Pittsburgh, 15214. Office Hours: Mon.-Fri. 9:30-12 and 1-4. Tel: 412-231-4000; Fax: 412-231-1697.

Vicar General—Rev. Msgr. RUSSELL A. DUKER, S.E.O.D.

Chancellor—Rev. Msgr. RUSSELL A. DUKER, S.E.O.D.

Vice-Chancellor—Rev. JOHN KUDRICK.

Treasurer—GREGORY S. POPIVCHAK, C.P.A.

Vicar for Clergy—Very Rev. JOHN G. PETRO, V.C.

Vicar for Religious—Rev. JAMES A. SPONTAK, V.R.

Vocations Director—Rev. DENNIS M. BOGDA.

Archdiocesan Tribunal—66 Riverview Ave., Pittsburgh, 15214.

Judicial Vicar—Very Rev. RICHARD J. WHETSTONE, J.C.O.L.

Pro-Synodal Judges—Revs. DANIEL A. MAGULICK, J.C.O.L.; ANSELM ORLOSKY, O.S.B.

Defender of the Bond—Rev. JOHN MIHALCO, S.E.O.L.

Promoter of Justice—Rev. Msgr. ALEXIS MIHALIK.

Notaries—Rev. GREGORY MICHALISIN; DONNA OBSINCS.

Secretary to the Tribunal—Sr. ELAINE KISINKO, O.S.B.M.

Archdiocesan Consultors—Rev. Msgr. RUSSELL A. DUKER, Vicar General; Revs. JOSEPH J. BORODACH; JOSEPH JUGAN; ROBERT J. KARL; Rev. Msgr. ANDREW D. PARVENSKY; Revs. JOHN G. PETRO; JOHN D. YCOBAK.

Deans—Clairton Deanery: Very Rev. JOHN BORODACH, V.F., Johnstown Deanery: Rev. Msgr. RAYMOND A. BALTA, V.F., Mon-Valley Deanery: Very Rev. JOHN SALKO, V.F., Greater Pittsburgh Deanery: Rev. Msgr. NICHOLAS X. SMICIKLAS, V.F., North Central Deanery: Very Rev. SIMEON B. SIBENIK, V.F., Tri-State Deanery: Very Rev. DANIEL MAGULICK, V.F., Youngstown: Rev. Msgr. SYLVESTER HLADKY, V.F., Southwest: Very Rev. RONALD LARKO, V.F.

Presbyteral Council—Most Rev. JUDSON M. PROCYK, D.D., Pres. Ex-Officio Members: Rev. Msgr. RUSSELL A. DUKER, Vicar General; Very Rev. JOHN G. PETRO, Exec. Dir. Elected Members: Revs. DENNIS BOGDA; JOSEPH J. BORODACH; JOHN KUDRICK; JAMES SPONTAK; MICHAEL J. WYTISH, Sec. EUGENE YACKANICH; JOHN YCOBAK.

Finance Council—Most Rev. JUDSON M. PROCYK, Metropolitan Archbishop; GREGORY S. POPIVCHAK, C.P.A., Archdiocesan Treas.; Very Rev. JOHN BORODACH; ANGELO F. MONACO; MICHAEL I. ROMAN.

Personnel Board—Most Rev. JUDSON M. PROCYK; Rev. Msgr. RUSSELL A. DUKER; Rev. JOHN M. KUDRICK; Very Rev. JOHN G. PETRO; Very Rev. ROBERT J. KARL; Very Rev. JOHN J. BORODACH, V.F.; Rev. GREGORY MULLANEY.

Archdiocesan Offices and Directors

Priests' Pension Board—Ex-Officio Members: Most Rev. JUDSON M. PROCYK, Metropolitan Archbishop/Chm.; Rev.Msgr. RUSSELL A. DUKER, Vicar General; GREGORY S. POPIVCHAK, Archdiocesan Treas.

Elected Deanery Representatives—Clairton: Rev. Msgr. WILLIAM LEVKULIC, Sec.; Johnstown Deanery: Rev. DANIEL LOYA, Mon-Valley Deanery: Rev. JOHN LOUIS MINA, Greater Pittsburgh Deanery: Rev. GEORGE EVANCHO, North Central Deanery: Rev. SIMEON SIBENIK, Tri-State Deanery: Rev. ANDREW CHURA, Youngstown Deanery: Rev. Msgr. VICTOR ROMZA.

Newspaper—The Byzantine Catholic World, Official Publication of the Archeparchy. Most Rev. JUDSON M. PROCYK, D.D., Pres.; Rev. MICHAEL J. WYTISH, Editor.

Office of Religious Education—Sr. MORION DOBOS, O.S.B., Communications, *3605 Perrysville Ave., Pittsburgh, 15214.* Tel: 412-322-8773.

Byzantine Catholic Seminary Press—Rev. JOHN OPALENICK, Business Mgr., *3605 Perrysville Ave., Pittsburgh, 15214.* Tel: 412-322-8307.

CLERGY, PARISHES, MISSIONS AND PAROCHIAL SCHOOLS

STATE OF PENNSYLVANIA

Munhall, Allegheny Co., St. John the Baptist Cathedral, Very Rev. Robert J. Karl, Rector.

Res., 210 Greentree Rd., 15120. Tel: 412-461-0944. [CEM]

St. Elias (Magyar), Rev. Eugene P. Yackanich.

Res., 4200 Homestead, Duquesne Rd., 15120. Tel: 412-461-1712. [CEM]

Aliquippa, Beaver Co., St. George, Rev. Msgr. Michael A. Simodejka, V.F.

Res., 1001 Clinton St., 15001. Tel: 412-375-2742.

Ambridge, Beaver Co., St. Mary's, Rev. Msgr. Edward V. Rosack.

Res., 624 Park Rd., 15003. Tel: 412-266-2030.

Arcadia, Indiana Co., Ascension. Attended by Barnesboro.

719 Chestnut Ave., Barnesboro, 15714. Tel: 814-948-8242. [CEM]

Avella, Washington Co., St. John the Baptist. Attended by Weirton, WV.
Res., P.O. Box 565, 15312. Tel: 412-587-5819. [CEM]

Barnesboro, Cambria Co., St. John the Baptist, Rev. Donald Valasek.
Res., 719 Chestnut Ave., 15714. Tel: 814-948-8242. [CEM]

Beaver, Beaver Co., Saint Nicholas Chapel, Very Rev. John G. Petro, Admin.
Res., 5400 Tuscarawas Rd., 15009-9513. Tel: 412-495-3400.

Beaverdale, Cambria Co., St. Mary's, Rev. Stephen Kolcun.
Res., P.O. Box 610, 15921. Tel: 814-487-7458. [CEM]

Braddock, Allegheny Co., SS. Peter and Paul, Rev. Blaise Kovach.
Res., 431 George St., 15104. Tel: 412-271-1297.

Bradenville, Westmoreland Co., St. Mary's, Rev. Joseph Borodach.
Res., R.R. #1, Box 75, 15620-9711. Tel: 412-537-5839; Fax: 412-532-1499. [CEM]

Brownsville, Fayette Co., St. Nicholas, Rev. Jerome Botsko.
Res., 302 Third Ave., 15417. Tel: 412-785-7573. [CEM]

Canonsburg, Washington Co., St. Michael, Rev. Joseph Jugan.
Res., 143 E. College St., 15317. Tel: 412-745-7117.

Charleroi, Washington Co., Holy Ghost, Rev. Wesley M. Mash.
Res., 828 Meadow Ave., 15022. Tel: 412-483-8622.

Clairton, Allegheny Co., Ascension of Our Lord, Very Rev. John J. Borodach, V.F.
Res., 318 Park Ave., 15025. Tel: 412-233-7422. [CEM]

Clarence, Centre Co., St. Mary's. Attended by St. John the Baptist Church, Hawk Run. Rev. Donald J. Voss.
c/o St. John the Baptist Church, Hawk Run, 16840. Tel: 814-342-4315. [CEM]

Clymer, Indiana Co., St. Anne. Attended by Ernest.
P.O. Box 130, Ernest, 15739. Tel: 814-674-5552.

Coal Run, Indiana Co., Holy Cross. Attended by Homer City.
279 Yellow Creek St., Homer City, 15748. Tel: 412-479-2206.

Conemaugh, Cambria Co., Holy Trinity, Rev. Ronald W. Borsuk.
Res., 217 Fourth St., 15909. Tel: 814-535-5231.

Donora, Washington Co., St. Michael, Rev. David J. Shortt.
Res., 511 Murray Ave., 15033. Tel: 412-379-9751; Fax: 412-379-9752. [CEM]

Du Bois, Clearfield Co., Nativity of the Mother of God. Attended by Sykesville. Very Rev. Simeon Sibenik.
Res., 200 McCullough St., 15801. Tel: 814-371-4911.

Dunlo, Cambria Co., SS. Peter and Paul. Attended by Beaverdale.
P.O. Box 610, Beaverdale, 15921. Tel: 814-487-7458. [CEM]

Duquesne, Allegheny Co., SS. Peter and Paul, Rev. Msgr. William Levkulic.
Res., 701 Foster Ave., 15110. Tel: 412-466-3578. [CEM]

St. Mary's (Magyar), Rev. Edward Lucas.
Res., 1209 Kennedy Ave., 15110. Tel: 412-466-1914.

East Pittsburgh, Allegheny Co., St. Mary's, Rev. George Evancho.
Res., 317 Howard St., 15112. Tel: 412-824-1622.

Erie, Erie Co., SS. Peter and Paul, Rev. Julius Kubinyi.
Res., 3415 Wallace St., 16504. Tel: 814-866-7140.

Ernest, Indiana Co., St. Jude Thaddeus, Rev. Edward Pyo.
Res., Box 130, 15739. Tel: 412-463-3397.

Girard, Erie Co., SS. Cyril and Methodius, Rev. Francis Duchala, O.F.M.
Res., 1022 Tilden Ave., 16417. Tel: 814-774-3281.

Greensburg, Westmoreland Co., St. Nicholas of Myra, Rev. Regis Dusecina.
Res., 622 E. Pittsburgh St., 15601. Tel: 412-837-0295.

Hannastown, Westmoreland Co., St. Mary's. Attended by Greensburg.
622 E. Pittsburgh St., Greensburg, 15601. Tel: 412-837-0295.

Hawk Run, Clearfield Co., St. John the Baptist, Rev. Donald J. Voss.
Res., 16840. Tel: 814-342-4315.

Herminie, Westmoreland Co., St. Mary's. Attended by North Huntington.
Res., 7 Second St., 15637. Tel: 412-446-5570.

Hermitage, Mercer Co., St. Michael, Rev. Frank A. Firko, S.T.L.
Res., 2230 Highland Rd., 16148. Tel: 412-981-6680; Fax: 412-981-7422. [CEM]

Homer City, Indiana Co., Holy Protection of Mary, The Mother of God, Rev. John Cuccaro.
Res., 279 Yellow Creek St., 15748. Tel: 412-479-2206.

Jerome, Somerset Co., SS. Peter and Paul. Attended by Windber.
803 Somerset Ave., Windber, 15963. Tel: 814-467-8044; Fax: 814-467-8044. [CEM]

Johnstown, Cambria Co., St. Mary's, Rev. Msgr. Raymond A. Balta, V.F.
Res., 411 Power St., 15906. Tel: 814-535-4132. [CEM]

Leisenring, Fayette Co., St. Stephen, Rev. John Louis Mina, Ph.D.
Res., P.O. Box 128, 15455. Tel: 412-628-6611; Fax: 412-628-5009. [CEM]

Lyndora, Butler Co., St. John the Baptist, Rev. Dennis M.J. Bogda.
Res., 105 Kohler Ave., 16045. Tel: 412-287-5000; Fax: 412-287-6769. [CEM]

McKeesport, Allegheny Co., St. Nicholas, Rev. Stephen Veselenak, O.S.B.
Res., 410 Sixth Ave., 15132. Tel: 412-664-9131. [CEM]

Transfiguration of Our Lord (Magyar). Attended by St. Mary's, Duquesne.
Res., 121 Sixth Ave., 15132. Tel: 412-672-0728.

McKees Rocks, Allegheny Co., Holy Ghost, Rev. John Kudrick.
Res., 225 Olivia St., 15136. Tel: 412-771-3324; Fax: 412-331-1870.

Monessen, Westmoreland Co., Assumption of the Blessed Virgin, Rev. Msgr. Andrew D. Parvensky.
Res., 125 McKee Ave., 15062. Tel: 412-684-5662; Fax: 412-684-3301. [CEM]

Monongahela, Washington Co., St. Macrina. Attended by Charleroi.
Church—515 W. Main St., 15063.

Monroeville, Allegheny Co., Church of the Resurrection, Rev. Michael Jude Wytish.
Res., 455 Center Rd., 15146. Tel: 412-372-8650; Fax: 412-372-1442.

Nanty-Glo, Cambria Co., St. Nicholas. Attended by Connemaugh.
Res., 1191 Second St., 15943. Tel: 814-749-0421.

New Salem, Fayette Co., St. Mary's, Rev. Joseph Chornyak.
Res., P.O. Box 487, 15468. Tel: 412-245-7188. [CEM]

North Hills-Gibsonia, Allegheny Co., St. Andrew the Apostle, Rev. David M. Misbrener, Admin.
Res., 235 Logan Rd., 15044. Tel: 412-625-1160; 625-9904 (Hall).

North Huntingdon, Westmoreland Co., St. Stephen's, Rev. Gregory Michalisin.
Res., 90 Bethel Rd., 15642. Tel: 412-863-6776; Fax: 412-864-9685.

Patton, Cambria Co., SS. Peter and Paul, Rev. Donald Valasek.
Res., 516 Palmer Ave., 16668. Tel: 814-674-5552. [CEM]

Perryopolis, Fayette Co., St. Nicholas, Rev. John Louis Mina, Ph.D.
Res., R.D. No. 1, Box 88, 15473. Tel: 412-736-4344. [CEM]

Pittsburgh, Allegheny Co.,

1—HOLY SPIRIT, Rev. Msgr. Russell A. Duker, S.E.O.D.
Res., 4815 Fifth Ave., 15213. Tel: 412-687-1220.

2—HOLY GHOST, Rev. Msgr. Peter Tay.
Res., 1437 Superior Ave., 15212. Tel: 412-321-5072; Fax: 412-321-5072.

3—ST. JOHN THE BAPTIST. Attended by St. Pius X.
Res., 1720 Jane St., 15203. Tel: 412-431-1090. [CEM]

4—ST. JOHN CHRYSOSTOM, Rev. Richard Lambert.
Res., 506 Saline St., 15207. Tel: 412-421-0243; Fax: 412-421-0243.

5—NATIVITY OF B.V.M.. Attended by St. John Chrysostom, Pittsburgh.
Res., 4027 Beechwood Blvd., 15217. Tel: 412-421-5231.

6—ST. PIUS X, Rev. Msgr. Nicholas X. Smiciklas, V.F.
Res., 2336 Brownsville Rd., 15210. Tel: 412-881-8344.

Portage, Cambria Co., SS. Peter and Paul, Rev. Myron E. Kochaba, O.S.B.
Res., 605 Prospect St., 15946. Tel: 814-736-9780. [CEM]

Punxsutawney, Jefferson Co., SS. Peter and Paul, Rev. Theodore J. Seginak, O.S.B.
Res., 714 Second Ave., 15767. Tel: 814-938-6564. [CEM]

Rankin, Allegheny Co., St. John's. Attended by East Pittsburgh. Rev. George Evancho.
317 Howard St., East Pittsburgh, 15112. Tel: 412-824-1622.
Church—44 Miller Ave., 15104.

Sagamore, Armstrong Co., St. Mary's. Attended by Ernest.
Box 130, Ernest, 15739. Tel: 412-463-3397. [CEM]

Scottdale, Westmoreland Co., St. John the Baptist, Very Rev. John H. Salko, V.F.
Res., 525 Porter Ave., 15683. Tel: 412-887-5072; Fax: 412-887-3365. [CEM]

Sheffield, Warren Co., St. Michael, Rev. David A. Bosnich.
Res., 407 School St., 16347. Tel: 814-968-5478; Fax: 814-968-4445. [CEM]

South Fork, Cambria Co., St. Michael's. Attended by SS. Peter and Paul Church, Portage. Rev. Myron E. Kochaba, O.S.B., Admin.
605 Prospect St., Portage, 15946. Tel: 814-736-9780. [CEM]

Sykesville, Jefferson Co., Holy Trinity, Very Rev. Simeon B. Sibenik, V.F.
Res., 104 Shaffer St., 15865. Tel: 814-894-5440. [CEM]

Tarentum, Allegheny Co., Sts. Peter and Paul, Rev. Gregory C. Mullaney.
Res., 339 E. 10th Ave., 15084. Tel: 412-224-3026; Fax: 412-224-5242.

Trauger, Westmoreland Co., St. Mary's, Rev. Christopher R. Burke.
Res., R.D. 3, Box 373, Latrobe, 15650. Tel: 412-423-3673; Fax: 412-423-1808. [CEM]

Uniontown, Fayette Co., St. John the Baptist, Very Rev. Richard J. Whetstone, J.C.O.L.
Res., 185 E. Main St., 15401. Tel: 412-438-6027; Fax: 412-438-1382. [CEM]
School—Sr. Regina Adams, O.S.B.M., Prin. Sisters of St. Basil the Great 3; Lay Teachers 11; Students 110.

Upper St. Clair, Allegheny Co., St. Gregory Nazianzus, Rev. Bruno Asturi.
Res., 2005 Mohawk Rd., 15241.

Wall, Allegheny Co., Holy Trinity, Rev. Anselm Orlosky, O.S.B.
Res., 470 Wall Ave., 15148. Tel: 412-824-9803.

Windber, Somerset Co., St. Mary (Dormition) Church, Rev. Daniel Loya.
Res., 803 Somerset St., 15963. Tel: 814-467-8044; Fax: 814-467-8044. [CEM]

STATE OF OHIO

Ashtabula, Ashtabula Co., St. Nicholas, Rev. A. Edward Gretchko.
630 Plum St., 44004. Tel: 216-599-8570.

Boardman, Mahoning Co., Infant Jesus of Prague, Rev. Msgr. Alexis E. Mihalik.
Res., 7754 S. Ave. Extension, P.O. Box 7006, 44512. Tel: 330-758-6019.

Campbell, Mahoning Co., St. Michael, Rev. Msgr. Victor G. Romza.
Res., 463 Robinson Rd., Box 426, 44405. Tel: 330-755-4831. [CEM]

Mingo Junction, Jefferson Co., St. John the Baptist, Rev. John Kasarda.
Church—207 Standard St., 43938. Tel: 614-535-0271.

Newton Falls, Trumbull Co., St. Michael, Rev. John G. Pohorlak.
Res., 737 Ridge Rd., 44444. Tel: 330-872-5216. [CEM]

Pleasant City, Guernsey Co., St. Michael, Rev. Robert Halus.
Res., P.O. Box 226, 43772. Tel: 614-685-3292. [CEM]

Toronto, Jefferson Co., St. Joseph, Rev. Andrew Chura.
Res., 814 N. Fifth St., 43964. Tel: 614-537-1026.

Warren, Trumbull Co., SS. Peter and Paul's, Rt. Rev. Msgr. Sylvester Hladky, V.F.; Rev. John J. Koza, III.
Res., 180 Belvedere Ave., N.E., 44483. Tel: 330-372-1875; Fax: 330-372-5965. [CEM]
School—195 Belvedere Ave., N.E., 44483. Tel: 216-372-1312. Sr. Margaret Mary, O.S.B., Ph.D., Prin.
Sisters of the Order of St. Benedict 3; Lay Teachers 16; Students 250.

Youngstown, Mahoning Co.,

1—ASSUMPTION OF THE BLESSED VIRGIN, Rev. John D. Ycoback.
Res., 356 S. Belle Vista, 44509. Tel: 330-799-8163. [CEM]

2—ST. NICHOLAS, Rev. Joseph Kapusnak.
Res., 1898 Wilson Ave., 44506. Tel: 330-743-0419;

Fax: 330-743-6888. [CEM]
School—Byzantine Catholic Central, 5512 Youngstown-Poland Rd., 44514. Tel: 330-757-9185. Sisters 3; Lay Teachers 11; Students 220.

3—ST. GEORGE, (Magyar). Attended by St. Nicholas, Youngstown. Rev. Leo Schlosser, O.S.B., Admin.
1726 Canfield Rd., 44511. Tel: 330-782-2865.

4—ST. JOHN THE BAPTIST. Attended by St. Nicholas, Youngstown. Rev. Leo Schlosser, O.S.B., Admin.
319 Goldie Rd., 44505. Tel: 330-759-6910.

STATE OF TEXAS

Houston, Harris Co., St. John Chrysostom, Rev. John J. Mihalco.
Res., 5402 Acorn, 77092. Tel: 713-681-3580.
Mission—San Antonio, Bexar Co., Byzantine Catholic Church.

Irving, Dallas Co., St. Basil the Great, Very Rev. Ronald Larko, V.F.
Res., 1118 E. Union Bower Rd., 75061. Tel: 972-438-5644.

San Antonio, San Antonio Co., Byzantine Catholic Mission. Attended by St. John Chrysostom, Houston. Rev. John J. Mihalco.
Mailing Address: c/o St. George Maronite Church, 6070 Babcock Rd., 78240.
Res., 5402 Acorn, Houston, 77092. Tel: 713-681-3580.

STATE OF WEST VIRGINIA

Morgantown, Monongalia Co., St. Mary's Holy Protection, Rev. James Spontak.
Res., 2115 Listravia Ave., P.O. Box 3698, 26503-3698. Tel: 412-439-4475; Fax: 412-438-8660.
Church—Tel: 304-296-2455.
Mission—Clarksburg, Harrison Co., St. Nicholas Byzantine Catholic Mission, 315 Ohio Ave., P.O. Box 3080, Clarksburg, 26301.

Weirton, Hancock Co., St. Mary's, Rev. Daniel A. Magulick.
Res., 3116 Elm St., 26062. Tel: 304-748-2087.

Retired:
Reverend Monsignors—
Macko, John, P.O. Box 306, Lyndora, PA 16045
Reverend Fathers—
Gnall, Julian M., O.S.B., Chap., U.S. Navy, San Diego, CA
Gran, Thomas, 401 Cambria Ave., Windber, PA 15963
Mokris, Michael, 472 Church St., Swoyersville, PA 18704
Popovich, Josaphat, 5061 Stetson Dr., Prescott Valley, AZ 86314

INSTITUTIONS LOCATED IN THE ARCHDIOCESE

[A] SEMINARIES, ARCHDIOCESAN

PITTSBURGH. *Byzantine Catholic Seminary of SS. Cyril and Methodius*, 3605 Perrysville Ave., 15214-2297. Tel: 412-321-8383; Fax: 412-321-9936. Very Rev. John G. Petro, Rector. Tel: 412-321-7550; Revs. David M. Petras, Spiritual Dir. Tel: 412-321-5133; John S. Custer, Dean. Tel: 412-321-5993. Students for Priesthood 11.

[B] HOMES FOR AGED

UNIONTOWN. *Mount Macrina Manor Nursing Home*, 520 W. Main St., 15401. Tel: 412-437-1400; Fax: 412-430-1095.
For a complete listing, refer to the Special Care Facilities section.
St. Basil's Home, 530 W. Main St., Box 878, 15401. Tel: 412-437-7480; 437-5826.
For a complete listing, refer to the Special Care Facilities section.

WARREN, OH. *Infant of Prague Manor*, 169 Kenmore, N.E., 44483. Tel: 330-372-4700.
For a complete listing, refer to the Special Care Facilities section.

[C] CHILD CARE CENTERS

WARREN, OH. *Benedictine Early Learning Center*, 8628 Squires Ln., N.E., 44484. Tel: 330-856-5315. Mrs. Michelle Balzer, Admin. Early learning child care center/after school care. Sisters 1; Lay Teachers 1; Students 23.

[D] MONASTERIES AND RESIDENCES OF PRIESTS AND BROTHERS

BUTLER. *Holy Trinity Monastery*, P.O. Box 990, 16003. Rt. Rev. Leo R. Schlosser, O.S.B., Abbot/Hegumen; Very Rev. Anselm Orlosky, O.S.B., Prior; Bro. Michael Zetzer, O.S.B., Procurator. Priests 7; Brothers 4.

[E] CONVENTS AND RESIDENCES FOR SISTERS

MOUNT ST. MACRINA. *Motherhouse and Novitiate of the Sisters of St. Basil the Great.* Mailing Address: 500 W. Main St., P.O. Box 878, Uniontown, 15401. Sr. Ruth Plante, O.S.B.M., Prov. Supr.; Very Rev. James Spontak, S.T.L., Chap. Professed Sisters 96.

WARREN, OH. *Queen of Heaven Monastery*, 8640 Squires Ln., N.E., 44484. Sr. Barbara Pavlik, O.S.B., Prioress. Benedictine Sisters of the Byzantine Rite 12.

YOUNGSTOWN, OH. *Byzantine Convent*, 5512 Youngstown-Poland Rd., 44514. Sisters of St. Basil the Great 4.

RELIGIOUS INSTITUTES OF MEN REPRESENTED IN THE ARCHDIOCESE

For further details refer to the corresponding bracketed number in the Religious Institutes of Men or Women section.

[0200]—*Benedictine Monks.*—O.S.B.

RELIGIOUS INSTITUTES OF WOMEN REPRESENTED IN THE ARCHDIOCESE

[]—*Benedictine Sisters of the Byzantine Rite.*—O.S.B.
[3730]—*Sisters of the Order of St. Basil the Great.*—O.S.B.M.

NECROLOGY

† Sabo, William Robert, Johnstown, PA, St. Mary's Church. —Died Jan. 2, 1996.

Romanian Catholic Diocese of Saint George's in Canton

Most Reverend

JOHN MICHAEL BOTEAN, D.D.

Bishop for the Romanian Byzantine Faithful of the United States; ordained May 18, 1986; appointed July 15, 1993; Episcopal Ordination August 24, 1996. *Res., 1121 44th St., N.E., Canton, OH, 44714-1297.* Tel.: 330-492-4086 (Office); Fax: 330-493-1416.

Most Reverend

LOUIS PUSCAS, D.D.

Bishop Emeritus for the Romanian Byzantine Faithful of the United States; ordained May 14, 1942; appointed Exarch December 4, 1982; Episcopal ordination June 26, 1983; installed August 28, 1983; promoted first Eparch April 16, 1987; retired July 15, 1993. *Res., 609 N. Lincoln, Aurora, IL, 60505.* Tel.: 630-820-6414.

ESTABLISHED DECEMBER 4, 1982.

ELEVATED FROM APOSTOLIC EXARCHATE FOR ROMANIAN BYZANTINE TO THE RANK OF AN EPARCHY (DIOCESE) MARCH 26, 1987.

Legal Title: The Romanian Catholic Diocese of St. George in Canton.

The Jurisdiction of the Romanian Catholic Diocese of Canton extends territorially to all of the United States.

Diocesan Offices: 1121 44th St., N.E., Canton, OH, 44714-1297. Tel.: 330-492-4086; Fax: 330-493-1416.

E-mail address: 76672.1366@compuserve.com

STATISTICAL OVERVIEW

Personnel	
Bishop	1
Retired Bishops	1
Priests: Diocesan Active in Diocese	6
Priests: Active Outside Diocese	4
Priests: Retired, Sick or Absent	5
Number of Diocesan Priests	15
Religious Priests in Diocese	2
Extern Priests in Diocese	4
Ordinations:	
Permanent Deacons	2
Parishes	
Parishes	15
With Resident Pastor:	
Resident Diocesan Priests	9
Without Resident Pastor:	
Administered by Priests	6
Missions	3
Educational	
Diocesan Students in Other Seminaries	1
Total Seminarians	1
Catechesis/Religious Education:	
High School Students	5
Elementary Students	50
Total Students Under Catholic Instruction	56
Vital Statistics	
Receptions into the Church:	
Infant Baptism Totals	24
Adult Baptism Totals	1
Received into Full Communion	12
First Communions	12
Confirmations	25
Marriages:	
Catholic	7
Total Marriages	7
Deaths	39
Total Catholic Population	5,300

Former Bishop—Most Rev. LOUIS PUSCAS, ord. May 14, 1942; appt. Exarch, Dec. 4, 1982 Episcopal ordination, June 26, 1983; installed Aug. 28, 1983; promoted to to first Eparch, April 16, 1987; retired July 15, 1993.

Chancellor—Rev. Deacon JOHN J. SKALA.

Vice Chancellor—Vacant.

Finance Officer—Mr. JAMES P. DERSHAW, C.P.A.

Board of Consultors—Very Rev. GEORGE DAVID, V.G.; Revs. MICHAEL MOISIN; MICHAEL KIRILA; Very Rev. GREGORY DUMA.

Vicar General—Very Rev. GEORGE DAVID, V.G.

Director of Evangelization—Vacant.

Vicar for Theological Affaris—Sr. THERESA KOERNKE, I.H.M., Ph.D.

Director of Religious Education—Rev. Dr. ANDREI MATEI.

Pro-Life Commission—Mrs. ELIZABETH KIRILA, Chm.

Vicar Refugee/Migration Svcs.—Very Rev. GREGORY DUMA.

Director of Scouting Svcs.—Rev. Deacon GARY A. BOYCE, Dir.

Formation Council—Rev. RICHARD J. MUCOWSKI, O.F.M., Ph.D.; Sr. THERESA KOERNKE, I.H.M., Ph.D.; Rev. AUGUST J. DEASIO, M.A.; Very Rev. GREGORY DUMA.

CLERGY, PARISHES, MISSIONS AND PAROCHIAL SCHOOLS

STATE OF CALIFORNIA

Mission Hills, Los Angeles Co., St. Mary Romanian Catholic Mission, Rev. John Ciungu.
Res., 15519 Tuba St., 91345. Tel: 818-895-9275.

STATE OF ILLINOIS

Aurora, Du Page Co., St. George, Rev. Frederick Peterson, O.S.B.
Res., 850 Butterfield Rd., 60504. Tel: 630-897-7215, Ext. 346.
Church—720 Rural St., 60505. Tel: 630-851-4002; Fax: 630-851-4002.

St. Michael, Most Rev. Louis Puscas, D.D.
Res. & Church—609 N. Lincoln Ave., 60505. Tel: 630-897-8115; Fax: 630-897-5923.

Chicago, Cook Co., Ss. Peter and Paul Mission, Rev. Aurel Pater.
Res., 4309 Olcott Ave., East Chicago, IN 46312. Tel: 219-398-3760; Fax: 219-398-3760.
Mission—Chicago, 3107 Fullerton Ave., 60647.

STATE OF INDIANA

East Chicago, Lake Co., St. Nicholas, Rev. Aurel Pater.
Church & Res.: 4309 Olcott Ave., 46312. Tel: 219-398-3760; Fax: 219-398-3760.

STATE OF MICHIGAN

Dearborn, Wayne Co., St. Mary, Rt. Rev. Mircea Clinet.
Church—823 S. Military, 48124. Tel: 313-274-2347.

Detroit, Wayne Co., St. John the Baptist, Rev. Michael Kirila.
Res., 2371 Woodstock Dr., 48203. Tel: 313-386-1046; Fax: 313-368-5358.

STATE OF NEW JERSEY

Roebling, Burlington Co., St. Mary, Very Rev. George David, V.G.
Church—181 Norman Ave., 08554. Tel: 609-695-6093.

Trenton, Mercer Co., St. Basil, Very Rev. George David, V.G.
Res., 238 Adeline St., 08611. Tel: 609-695-6093.

STATE OF NEW YORK

Astoria, Queens Co., St. Mary Romanian Catholic Mission, Rev. Alois Isvanca.
Res., 104-05 49th Ave., Corona, 11368. Tel: 718-596-7569; Fax: 718-271-6726. Rev. Eugen Mihai.; Res., 23-30 33rd St., 11105. Tel: 718-721-9710.
Church—104-05 49th Ave., Corona, 11368.

STATE OF OHIO

Canton, Stark Co., St. Theodore, Very Rev. Gregory Duma.
Res., 1101 44th St. N.E., 44714-1297. Tel: 330-492-8413; Fax: 330-493-1416.

St. George Cathedral, Very Rev. Gregory Duma.
Res., 1101 44th St. N.E., 44714-1297. Tel: 330-492-8413; Fax: 330-493-1416. Most Rev. John Michael Botean, D.D.; Res., 1121 44th St. N.E., 44714-1297. Tel: 330-492-4086 (Chancery Office).

Chesterland, Geauga Co., Most Holy Trinity, Rev. Dr. Andrei Matei.
Res., St. Helena, 1367 W. 65th St., Cleveland, 44102. Tel: 216-651-0965; Fax: 216-631-3853.
Church—8549 Mayfield Rd., 44026. Tel: 216-729-7636.

Cleveland, Cuyahoga Co., St. Helena, Rev. Dr. Andrei Matei.
Res., 1367 W. 65th St., 44102. Tel: 216-651-0965; Fax: 216-631-3853.

Lorain, Lorain Co., St. Basil, Rev. Dr. Andrei Matei.
Res., St. Helena, 1367 W. 65th St., Cleveland, 44102. Tel: 216-651-0965.
Church—5255 French Creek Rd., 44054-2745. Tel: 216-277-5646; Fax: 216-631-3853.

Youngstown, Mahoning Co., St. Mary, Rev. George D. Gage.
Res., 7782 Glenwood Ave., Boardman, 44512. Tel: 330-726-8573; Fax: 330-726-4102.

STATE OF PENNSYLVANIA

McKeesport, Allegheny Co., St. Mary, Rev. John M. Elanjileth.
Res., 318 26th St., 15132. Tel: 412-673-5552. Rev. James E. Reiter.; Res., 1105 10th Ave., Irwin, 15642-3827. Tel: 412-863-6837; Fax: 412-863-6997.

Sharon, Mercer Co., St. John, Rev. George D. Gage.
Res., 7782 Glenwood Ave., Boardman, OH 44512. Tel: 330-726-8573; Fax: 330-726-4102.
Church—3056 Morefield Rd., Hermitage, 16148.

Special Assignment:
Reverend Fathers—
Brown, Konstantin K.
Kusevich, Nicholas
Moisin, Michael
Samayoa, Emmanuel G.
Yossa, Kenneth F.

Retired:
Reverend Fathers—
Ciungu, John
Filip, John T.
Streza, Charles V.

Permanent Deacons:
Buga, John
Skala, John

NECROLOGY

† Aron, Iuliu, Dearborn, MI, St. Mary Church. —Died June 2, 1994.
† Capros, Rev. Msgr. Carol, (Retired). —Died Dec. 28, 1995.
† Cornea, Very Rev. Teodor, Aurora, IL, St. Michael Church. —Died Feb. 20, 1995.
† Muresan, Very Rev. George, (Retired). —Died March 22, 1996.
† Pavel, John, (Retired). —Died May 5, 1994.
† Rusu, Rev. Dr. Gheorge, (Retired). —Died Feb. 25, 1996.

Ukrainian Catholic Diocese of St. Josaphat in Parma

Most Reverend

ROBERT M. MOSKAL, D.D.

Bishop of St. Josaphat in Parma; ordained March 25, 1963; appointed Titular Bishop of Agathopolis and Auxiliary Bishop of the Archeparchy of Philadelphia August 3, 1981; consecrated October 13, 1981; appointed First Bishop of St. Josaphat in Parma December 5, 1983. *Res., 5720 State Rd., P.O. Box 347180, Parma, OH, 44134.*

Chancery: 5720 State Rd., P.O. Box 347180, Parma, OH, 44134-7180. Tel.: 216-888-1522; Fax: 216-888-3477.

ESTABLISHED DECEMBER 3, 1983.

The jurisdiction of the Bishop of St. Josaphat in Parma extends territorially through all the States of Ohio, Mississippi, West Virginia, Kentucky, Tennessee, Alabama, Georgia, North Carolina, South Carolina, Florida and western Pennsylvania. With regards to persons, his subjects are Catholics of the Byzantine Ukrainian Rite: 1. Who immigrated to this country from Galicia, Bucovina and other Ukrainian provinces; 2. Who descend from such persons (Can. 755); 3. Women married to men referable to 1 and 2, if they comply with (Can. 98, n.4); 4. Who in accordance with (Can. 98, n.3) changed their Rite; 5. Converts to the Catholic Church of the Byzantine Ukrainian Rite; 6. And in fact, all other Catholics of the Byzantine Ukrainian Rite who are attached to parishes subject to the jurisdiction of the Bishop of St. Josaphat in Parma.

For legal titles of parishes and diocesan institutions, consult the Chancery.

STATISTICAL OVERVIEW

Personnel	
Bishop	1
Priests: Diocesan Active in Diocese	29
Priests: Active Outside Diocese	1
Priests: Retired, Sick or Absent	8
Number of Diocesan Priests	38
Religious Priests in Diocese	1
Extern Priests in Diocese	4
Ordinations:	
Permanent Deacons	1
Permanent Deacons in Diocese	9
Total Brothers	10
Total Sisters	10
Parishes	
Parishes	35
With Resident Pastor:	
Resident Diocesan Priests	27
Resident Religious Priests	1
Without Resident Pastor:	
Administered by Priests	7
Missions	2
Professional Ministry Personnel:	
Sisters	5
Welfare	
Homes for the Aged	2
Total Assisted	143
Educational	
Diocesan Students in Other Seminaries	1
Total Seminarians	1
Elementary Schools, Diocesan and Parish	2
Total Students	262
Catechesis/Religious Education:	
High School Students	105
Elementary Students	232
Total Students Under Catholic Instruction	600
Teachers in the Diocese:	
Sisters	2
Lay Teachers	26
Vital Statistics	
Receptions into the Church:	
Infant Baptism Totals	132
Adult Baptism Totals	4
Received into Full Communion	1
First Communions	110
Marriages:	
Catholic	44
Interfaith	21
Total Marriages	65
Deaths	267
Total Catholic Population	11,629

Vicar General—Rev. Msgr. LEO ADAMIAK.
Vicar General in Curia—Rev. Msgr. THOMAS A. SAYUK.
Chancellor—Rev. Msgr. THOMAS A. SAYUK.
Vice Chancellor—Rev. PETER WASLO.
Diocesan Treasurer—Rev. Msgr. THOMAS A. SAYUK.
Chancery—5720 State Rd., P.O. Box 347180, Parma, OH, 44134-7180. Tel: 216-888-1522; Fax: 216-888-3477. Office Hours: Mon.-Fri. 10-12 & 2-4.
Secretary—Sr. LAURENCE M. LALIK, O.S.B.M.
Diocesan Consultors—Rev. Msgr. LEO ADAMIAK; Rev. Msgr. MICHAEL POLOWAY; Rev. Msgr. MICHAEL REWTIUK; Rev. Msgr. GEORGE APPLEYARD; Rev. Msgr. RICHARD SEMINACK; Rev. Msgr. THOMAS A. SAYUK; Very Revs. JAROSLAW MYCHASLENKO; ROBERT HNATYSHYN; WALTER WYSOCHANSKY.
Diocesan Corporation—Most Rev. ROBERT M. MOSKAL, Pres.; Rev. Msgr. LEO TYMKIW, Vice Pres.; Rev. Msgr. THOMAS A. SAYUK, Sec. & Treas.
Diocesan Administrative Council—Most Rev. ROBERT M. MOSKAL; Rev. Msgr. LEO TYMKIW; Rev. Msgr. LEO ADAMIAK; Rev. PETER WASLO; Rev. Msgr. THOMAS SAYUK.
Protopresbyters-Deans—Western Deanery: Very Rev. JAROSLAW MYCHAJLENKO, Dean; Central Deanery: Rev. Msgr. MICHAEL POLOWAY, Dean; Rev. Msgr. GEORGE APPLEYARD, Vice Dean; Eastern Deanery: Very Rev. JAMES POORMAN, Dean; Southern Deanery: Rev. Msgr. JAROSLAV FEDYK, Dean; Rev. Msgr. JOHN STEVENSKY, Vice Dean.

Diocesan Offices and Directors

Acolyte Confraternity—Rev. STEVEN ZARICHNY.
Apostleship of Prayer—Rev. Msgr. LEO TYMKIW.
Catechetical Planning Committee—Sr. ANN LASZOK, O.S.B.M., Chm.; Rev. Msgr. RICHARD SEMINACK, D.R.E.; Rev. Msgr. GEORGE APPLEYARD; Sr. MARINA BOCHNEWICH, O.S.B.M.; Revs. XAVIER ELAMBASSERY; JAROSLAW MYCHAJLENKO; ANTHONY BALISTRERI.
Clergy Examiners—Rev. Msgr. LEO ADAMIAK; Rev. Dr. IVAN TYLAWSKYJ; Rev. Msgr. RICHARD SEMINACK; Very Rev. WALTER WYSOCHANSKY.
Department of Religious Education—Rev. Msgr. RICHARD SEMINACK, Dir.; Sr. ANN LASZOK, O.S.B.M., Asst. Dir., *726 Washington Ave., Carnegie, PA, 15106.* Tel: 412-279-4652.
Diocesan Ecumenical Office—Rev. Msgr. GEORGE APPLEYARD, Dir.
Diocesan Promoter for the Cause of Metropolitan Andrew Sheptytsky—MICHAEL BILON; ESTHER BILON; Rev. Msgr. THOMAS A. SAYUK.
Diocesan Resource Committee—Rev. Msgr. GEORGE APPLEYARD, Spiritual Dir. MICHAEL FEDORA, Chm. NICK C. KOTOW, Vice Chm. LILLIAN MISKO COURY, Recording Sec. GLORIA J. BARSHOWSKI, Corresponding Sec. PETER HLUTKOWSKY, Treas.
Director of Liturgical Chant—STEPHEN ZINSKI; LILLIAN MISKO COURY.
Director of Youth Ministries—Rev. ANTHONY BALISTRERI.
Lay Ministries—Sr. ANN LASZOK, O.S.B.M.; Sr. MARINA BOCHNEWICH, O.S.B.M.
League of Ukrainian Catholics (LUC)—Revs. STEVEN ZARICHNY, Spiritual Dir. of Ohio Council; MICHAEL POLOSKY, Spiritual Dir. of Western PA Council; Rev. Msgr. JOHN STEVENSKY, Organizer of Southern Deanery LUC.
League of Ukrainian Catholic Youth (LUCY)—Rev. ANTHONY BALISTRERI, Spiritual Dir.
Lector Training Team—Sr. ANN LASZOK, O.S.B.M., Dir.; Rev. JAROSLAW MYCHAJLENKO; Sr. MARINA BOCHNEWICH, O.S.B.M.; JOHN KOWICK; JOANNE KOWICK.
Marian Sodalities—Sr. LAURENCE M. LALIK, O.S.B.M.
Obnova—Rev. WOLODYMYR WOLOSZCZUK, Dir.
Office for Evangelization—Rev. MICHAEL POLOSKY, Liaison.
Pastoral Ministry Office—Sr. ANN LASZOK, O.S.B.M., Coord.; Sr. MARINA BOCHNEWICH, O.S.B.M., Adult Spiritual Formation; KATHY KRUTYHOLOWA, Adult Spiritual Formation. Adult Religious Education: Dr. VERA KROKONKO; Deacon JEFFREY SMOLILO, *727 E. Carson St., Pittsburgh, PA, 15203.* Tel: 412-481-9778.
Permanent Diaconate Program—Very Rev. JAROSLAW MYCHAJLENKO.
Prayer League for Canonization of Metropolitan Andrew Sheptytsky—Rev. Msgr. THOMAS SAYUK.
Presbyteral Council—Rev. Msgr. LEO ADAMIAK; Rev. Msgr. THOMAS A. SAYUK; Rev. Msgr. MICHAEL POLOWAY; Rev. Msgr. MICHAEL PEWTIUK; Rev. Msgr. RICHARD SEMINACK; Very Revs. JAMES POORMAN; WALTER WYSOCHANSKY; Rev. Msgr. GEORGE APPLEYARD; Revs. XAVIER ELAMBASSERY; PETER WASLO; STEVEN ZARICHNY; STEVEN PALIWODA; ANTHONY BALISTRERI; JOHN CHIROVSKY; JAROSLAW MYCHAJLENKO; MICHAEL POLOSKY.
Priests' Continuing Education—Rev. PETER WASLO.
Vocation Director—Very Rev. JAMES POORMAN.

CLERGY, PARISHES, MISSIONS AND PAROCHIAL SCHOOLS

STATE OF OHIO

1—ST. JOSAPHAT CATHEDRAL, Rev. Msgr. Michael Rewtiuk; Rev. Andrew Hanowsky.
Res., 5720 State Rd., 44134-2536. Tel: 216-886-2108.
School—Tel: 216-884-1812; Fax: 216-884-3435. Sisters of St. Basil the Great 2; Lay Teachers 13; Students 159.

2—ST. ANDREW, Rev. Msgr. Leo Tymkiw; Rev. Peter Waslo.
Res., 7700 Hoertz Rd., 44134-6404. Tel: 216-843-9149.

3—POKROVA UKRAINIAN CATHOLIC PARISH, Rev. John M. Freishyn-Chirovsky.
Office: 6812 Broadview Rd., 44134. Tel: 216-524-0918; Fax: 216-524-0919. [CEM]
Res., 6790 Broadview Rd., 44134-4804. Tel: 216-524-2505.

4—HOLY GHOST, Rev. Michael Krupka.
Res., 1859 Carter Ave., 44301. Tel: 216-724-8277.

5—ST. ANNE, Very Rev. Walter J. Wysochansky.
Res., 3055 S. Raccoon Rd., 44515-5351. Tel: 216-793-5436; 792-8555.
Church—4310 Kirk Rd., 44511-1899.
School—Lay Teachers 13; Students 97.

6—ST. NICHOLAS. Attended by Akron.
Church—1020 Lippert Rd., 44704.

7—SS. PETER AND PAUL, Rev. Steven Zarichny.
Res., 2280 W. 7th St., 44113. Tel: 216-861-2176. [CEM]

8—ST. JOHN THE BAPTIST, Rev. Steven Paliwoda, Admin.
Res., 3038 Charleston Ave., 44055-2121. Tel: 216-277-7114.
Church—2445 E. 31st St., 44055.

9—ST. MICHAEL, Rev. Anthony Balistreri, Admin.
Res., 133 Walnut St., 43460-1248. Tel: 419-666-5627.

10—PROTECTION B.V.M., Very Rev. Jaroslaw Mychajlenko.
Res., 27275 Aurora Rd., 44139-1804. Tel: 216-248-4549.

11—HOLY TRINITY, Rev. Msgr. Leo Adamiak, V.G.
Res., 526 W. Rayen Ave., 44502-1124. Tel: 216-744-5820.

STATE OF FLORIDA

Apopka, Orange Co., St. Mary's, Rev. Archpriest Matthew Berko.
Res., 20 E. Nightingale St., 32712. Tel: 407-880-1640.

Miami, Dade Co., Assumption of B.V.M., Rev. Msgr. John Stevensky.
Res., 39 N.W. 57th Ct., 33126. Tel: 305-262-4192.

North Port, Sarasota Co., Entrance of B.V.M. into the Temple, Rev. Archpriest Ivan Tylawskyj.
Res., 1078 N. Biscayne Dr., 34287. Tel: 813-426-7931.

St. Petersburg, Pinellas Co., Epiphany of Our Lord, Rev. Archpriest Matthew Berkov; Rev. Myroslaw Cisdyn.
Res., 434 90th Ave., N., 33702. Tel: 813-576-1001.

Spring Hill, Hernando Co., St. Andrew, Rev. Archpriest Matthew Berko.
Mailing Address: P.O. Box 5902, 34606. Tel: 813-577-0385.

STATE OF PENNSYLVANIA

Aliquippa, Beaver Co., Ss. Peter and Paul, Rev. Michael Derbish, O.F.M.
Res., 2001 Main St., 15001. Tel: 412-375-7016.

Altoona, Blair Co., Immaculate Conception. Attended by Barnesboro. Rev. Emanuel Rathapilly.
Res., 2020 20th St., 16601. Tel: 814-943-4553. [CEM]

Ambridge, Beaver Co., Ss. Peter and Paul, Revs. Michael Polosky; F. Alexander Ganzy.
Res., 404 6th St., 15003. Tel: 412-266-2262.

Barnesboro, Cambria Co., Immaculate Conception, Rev. Emanuel Rathapilly.
Res., 300 Campbell Ave., 15714. Tel: 814-948-9193.

Carnegie, Allegheny Co., Holy Trinity, Rev. Msgr. Richard Seminack.
Res., 730 Washington Ave., 15106. Tel: 412-279-4652. [CEM]

Ford City, Armstrong Co., St. Mary, Rev. Michael Sopp, Temp. Admin.
Res., 514 Ninth St., 16226. Tel: 412-763-1203. [CEM]

Jeannette, Westmoreland Co., St. Demetrius, Rev. Douglas Lorance.
Res., 1013 Gaskill Ave., 15644. Tel: 412-523-9389.

Johnstown, Cambria Co., St. John the Baptist, Rev. Anthony Kubacki, Admin.
Res., 606 Maple Ave., 15901. Tel: 814-535-2634. [CEM]

Latrobe, Westmoreland Co., Assumption of B.V.M., Rev. Xavier Elambassery.
Res., 526 Hillview Ave., 15650. Tel: 412-537-6450.

Lyndora, Butler Co., St. Michael, Very Rev. Archpriest Philip Bumbar.
Res., 25 Hansen Ave., 16045-1325. Tel: 412-283-6230; Fax: 412-283-0363.

McKeesport, Allegheny Co., St. John the Baptist, Very Rev. Robert Hnatyshyn.
Res., 1907 Eden Park Blvd., 15132. Tel: 412-672-0923.

McKees Rocks, Allegheny Co., St. John the Baptist. Attended by St. George, Pittsburgh. Rev. Msgr. George Appleyard.
Res., 3455 California Ave., Pittsburgh, 15212. Tel: 412-766-8801.
Church—204 Olivia St., 15136.

New Alexandria, Westmoreland Co., Nativity B.V.M. Attended by Latrobe.
526 Hillview Ave., Latrobe, 15650. Tel: 412-537-6450.
Church—Shersburg Rd., 15670. [CEM]

New Kensington, Westmoreland Co., St. Vladimir, Rev. John Ropke.
Res., 1601 Kenneth Ave., 15068. Tel: 412-339-9622.

Pittsburgh, Allegheny Co., St. George, Rev. Msgr. George Appleyard; Rev. Michael Bliszcz.
Res., 3455 California Ave., 15212. Tel: 412-766-8801; Fax: 412-766-8244.
St. John the Baptist, Rev. Msgr. Michael Poloway.
Res., 109 S. Seventh St., 15203. Tel: 412-431-2531. [CEM]

Ramey, Clearfield Co., Annunciation B.V.M., Very Rev. James E. Poorman.
Res., P.O. Box 205, 16671. Tel: 814-378-7688. [CEM]

Revloc, Cambria Co., Protection Blessed Virgin Mary. Attended by Johnstown.
606 Maple Ave., Johnstown, 15901. Tel: 814-535-2634.
Church—Cambria Ave., 15948.

West Leechburg, Armstrong Co., St. Michael. Attended by Ford City, PA.
Mailing Address: 514 Ninth St., Ford City, 16226. Tel: 412-763-1203.
Church—Main St., 15656.

Wilmerding, Allegheny Co., Ss. Peter and Paul. Attended by Jeannette, PA.
Mailing Address: 1013 Gaskill Ave., Jeannette, 15644. Tel: 412-523-9389.
Church—163 State St., 15148-1323.

STATE OF WEST VIRGINIA

Wheeling, Ohio Co., St. Mary, Rev. John Gribik, Temp. Admin.
Res., 4136 Jacob St., 26003. Tel: 304-232-2168.

Absent on Leave:
Reverend Fathers—
Zablotny, Carl

Graduate Studies:
Reverend Fathers—
Morozowich, Mark

Retired:
Reverend Monsignors—
Fedyk, Jaroslaw, Hollywood Trailer Park, 7230 4th St., N., Lot 1102, St. Petersburg, FL 33702
Kachmar, Walter, R.D. No. 5, Box 54, Blairsville, PA 15717-9139
Nestor, Michael, 867 N. Concord St., Gilbert, AZ 85234
Reverend Fathers—
Adamiak, Stephen, 5825 59th Way, N., St. Petersburg, FL 33709
Balaban, Oryst, 1532 Fourth Ave., Arnold, PA 15068-4402
Griffiths, James, 111 S. Cliff St., Apt. 6B6, Butler, PA 16001-6045
Nesevitch, Joseph, 167 Howard Ave., Ansonia, CT 06401
Woloszczuk, Wolodymyr, 4240 Timberline Blvd., Venice, FL 34293

Permanent Deacons:
Billy, Donald, 2515 McCollum Rd., Youngstown, OH 44509
Boyce, Gary, 240 Lindsey Rd., Munroe Falls, OH 44262
Dobosh, Michael, 7935 Carlyle Ave., Apt. 10, Miami Beach, FL 33141
Dukeley, Boris, 15008 S.W. 35th Cir., Ocala, FL 34473
Harwas, Roman, 300 S.W. 21st St., Okeechobee, FL 34974
Levy, Joseph M., 5216 Kerrington Dr., Gibsonia, PA 15044
Marko, Andrew, 33225 Electric Blvd., Avon Lake, OH 44012
Poklemba, Joseph, 1266 Signature Dr., Austintown, OH 44515
Smolilo, Jeffery, 7626 Keywest Dr., Parma, OH 44134

INSTITUTIONS LOCATED IN THE DIOCESE

[A] CONVENTS

PARMA. *St. Josaphat Convent*, 5720 State Rd., 44134-2536. Tel: 216-885-1245. Sisters of St. Basil the Great.

[B] HOMES FOR THE AGED

PARMA. *Shevchenko Manor*, 5620 W. 24th St., 44134. Tel: 216-459-1440. Judi Wick, Mgr.

PITTSBURGH, PA. *Sheptytsky Arms*, 3505 Mexico St., 15212. Tel: 412-766-8802; Fax: 412-766-0938. Sr. Dennys Polovischak, S.S.M.I., Mgr.; Sr. Consolata Trudik, S.S.M.I., Sec.

NECROLOGY

† Nakonechny, Emilian, (Retired). —Died Jan. 4, 1997.

Eparchy of St. Maron of Brooklyn

Most Reverend

FRANCIS M. ZAYEK, D.D., S.T.D., J.C.D.

Bishop, Eparchy of St. Maron of Brooklyn; born October 18, 1920; ordained March 17, 1946; appointed Titular Bishop of Callinicum May 30, 1962; consecrated August 5, 1962; appointed Eparch of the Diocese of Saint Maron November 11, 1971; installed June 4, 1972; elevated to Archbishop December 22, 1982. *Res., 8070 Harbor View Terrace, Brooklyn, New York, 11209.*

Established as an Apostolic Exarchate January 10, 1966; Elevated to a Diocese November 11, 1971.

The jurisdiction of the Diocese extends to all the Maronite Catholics in New York, New Jersey, Pennsylvania, Florida, Georgia, North Carolina, South Carolina, Delaware, Virginia, District of Columbia, Maine, New Hampshire, Vermont, Massachusetts, Rhode Island, Connecticut and Maryland.

For legal titles of parishes and diocesan institutions, consult the Chancery Office.

Chancery Office: The Pastoral Center, 294 Howard Ave., P.O. Box 360, Staten Island, NY, 10301. Tel.: 718-815-0436; Fax: 718-815-0536.

STATISTICAL OVERVIEW

Personnel	
Bishop	1
Priests: Diocesan Active in Diocese	45
Priests: Active Outside Diocese	4
Priests: Retired, Sick or Absent	13
Number of Diocesan Priests	62
Religious Priests in Diocese	10
Ordinations:	
Diocesan Priests	2
Permanent Deacons	10
Permanent Deacons in Diocese	10
Total Brothers	1
Total Sisters	12
Parishes	
Parishes	33
With Resident Pastor:	
Resident Diocesan Priests	33
Without Resident Pastor:	
Missions	3
Welfare	
Educational	
Seminaries, Diocesan	1
Students from This Diocese	3
Students from Other Diocese	1
Total Seminarians	3
Catechesis/Religious Education:	
High School Students	131
Elementary Students	890
Total Students Under Catholic Instruction	1,024
Vital Statistics	
Receptions into the Church:	
Infant Baptism Totals	330
Adult Baptism Totals	9
Received into Full Communion	38
First Communions	184
Confirmations	269
Marriages:	
Catholic	82
Interfaith	26
Total Marriages	108
Deaths	171
Total Catholic Population	30,000

Protosyncellus (Vicar General)—Chorbishop John D. Faris, J.C.O.D.

Syncellus (Episcopal Vicar for Priests)—Rev. Msgr. Joseph F.Kaddo.

Chancellor—Chorbishop James B. Namie.

Vice Chancellor—Rev. Francis J. Marini, J.C.O.D.

Archbishop's Secretary—Chorbishop James B. Namie.

Pastoral Center—294 Howard Ave., P.O. 010-360, Staten Island, NY, 10301. Tel: 718-815-0436; Fax: 718-815-0536. Office Hours: Mon.-Fri. 9-12 & 1:30-4. Closed on Maronite holy days and national holidays.

Tribunal of the Eparchy of Saint Maron of Brooklyn—P.O. Box 010-360, Staten Island, NY, 10301. Tel: 718-815-0043; Fax: 718-815-0536.

Episcopal Moderator—Most Rev. Francis M. Zayek, J.C.D., S.T.D.

Judicial Vicar—Rev. Francis J. Marini, J.C.O.D.

Defender of the Bond—Rev. W. Becket Soule, O.P., J.C.D.; Rev. Francis J. Marini, J.C.O.D.; Rev. Archimandrite Victor J. Pospishil, J.C.D.

Promotor of Justice—Rev. W. Becket Soule, O.P., J.C.D.

Advocates—Rev. Msgr. Joseph F. Kaddo, M.A.; Rev. Fahed Azar; Chorbishop Hector Y. Doueihi, S.T.D.

Presbyteral Council-Ex Officio Members—Most Rev. Francis M. Zayek; Chorbishop John D. Faris, J.C.O.D.; Chorbishop Seely Beggiani; Chorbishop Joseph Lahoud, Northern District; Rev. Fahed Azar, Central District; Rev. Michael G. Thomas, Southern District; Chorbishop Hector Doueihi; Chorbishop James B. Namie.

Elected Members—Rev. Msgr. Joseph Kaddo; Rev. Fahed Azar; Rev. Msgr. David M. George.

Appointed Members—Rev. Msgr. Norman Ferris.

Protopresbyters—(I); Chorbishop Joseph Lahoud,(Northern); Rev. Fahed Azar,(Central); Rev. Michael G. Thomas,(Southern).

Lebanon Commission—Chorbishop Seely Beggiani, Chm., *7164 Alaska Ave., N.W., Washington, DC, 20012.* Tel: 202-723-8831.

National Apostolate of Maronites National Office—Mr. Al Saker, Pres. Ed Shiner, Exec. Sec., *P.O. 126, Dyker Heights Stn., Brooklyn, NY, 11228.* Tel: 718-232-7292.

Diocesan Offices and Directors

Communications—Rev. George Sebaali, *4611 Sadler Rd., Glen Allen, VA, 23060.*

(Diocesan Newspaper) "The Maronite Voice"—Rev. George Sebaali, Editor, *4611 Sadler Rd., Glen Allen, VA, 23060.* Tel: 804-270-7234; Fax: 804-273-9914.

Finance Council—Most Rev. Francis M. Zayek, Chm.; Chorbishop John D. Faris, J.C.O.D.; Chorbishop Joseph Lahoud; Rev. Msgr. James Khoury; Mr. Philip Barrood; Mr. Peter Tanous; Mr. Francois Letaconnoux; Mr. Scott Geiger; Mr. L. Paul Kassouf; Mr. Richard Girasole; Mr. Kevin Kearney.

Liturgy—Chorbishop Hector Doueihi, *113 Remsen St., Brooklyn, NY, 11201.* Tel: 718-624-7228.

Ministries (Permanent Deacons and Subdeacons)—Rev. Edward Nedder, *375 Island Pond Rd., Springfield, MA, 01118.* Tel: 413-732-0589.

Director of Music—Rev. Joseph Amar,University of Notre Dame-Modern & Classical Languages, *Notre Dame, IN, 46556.* Tel: 219-239-7310.

Episcopal Vicar for Priests—Rev. Msgr. Joseph F. Kaddo.

Order of Saint Sharbel—Mr. John Solomon, *National Office, 294 Howard Ave., P.O. Box 010-360, Staten Island, NY, 10301.*

Pro-Life Director—Rev. Kevin Beaton.

Religious Education—Chorbishop Dominic Ashkar, *7164 Alaska Ave., N.W., Washington, DC, 20012.* Tel: 202-826-5554.

Vocations—Rev. Msgr. David George, *P.O. Box 2567, Brockton, MA, 02405-2567.* Tel: 508-586-1428.

Youth Ministry Office—Rev. John Morrison, *182 4th St., Troy, NY, 12180.* Tel: 518-272-6073.

Parish Renewal—Rev. James Root, *600 Dunster St., Pittsburgh, PA, 15226.* Tel: 412-531-4234.

CLERGY, PARISHES, MISSIONS AND PAROCHIAL SCHOOLS

STATE OF NEW YORK

Brooklyn, Kings Co., Cathedral of Our Lady of Lebanon, Chorbishop Hector Y. Doueihi, Rector.
Res., 113 Remsen St., 11201. Tel: 718-624-7228; Fax: 718-624-8034.

Olean, Cattaraugus Co., St. Joseph, Rev. Donald N. Thomas.
Res., 331 N. Fourth St., 14760. Tel: 716-372-4311.

Troy, Rensselaer Co., St. Ann, Rev. John A. Morrison.
Res., 182 Fourth St., 12180. Tel: 518-272-6073.

Utica, Oneida Co., St. Louis Gonzaga, Rev. Bassam Saade.
Res., 520 Rutger St., 13501. Tel: 315-732-6019.

Williamsville, Erie Co., St. John Maron, Rev. Msgr. Georges El-Khalli.
Res., 2040 Wehrle Dr., 14221-7041. Tel: 716-634-0669.

STATE OF CONNECTICUT

Danbury, Fairfield Co., St. Anthony, Rev. Moussa Joseph.
Res., 17 Granville Ave., 06810. Tel: 203-744-3372; Fax: 203-794-0949.

Torrington, Litchfield Co., St. Maron, Rev. Lawrence P. Michael.
Res., 613 Main St., 06790. Tel: 203-489-9015; Fax: 203-482-1614.

Waterbury, New Haven Co., Our Lady of Lebanon, Rev. Msgr. Joseph F. Kaddo.
Res., 8 E. Mountain Rd., 06706. Tel: 203-753-6633; 753-9428.

STATE OF FLORIDA

Miami, Dade Co., Our Lady of Lebanon, Rev. Michael G. Thomas.
Church—2055 Coral Way, 33145. Tel: 305-856-7449.
Res., 420 Como Ave., Coral Gables, 33146. Tel: 305-663-1438.

Orlando, Orange Co., St. Jude Mission, Revs. George Zina; Joseph Akiki.
Res., 6282 Sandcrest Cir., 32819. Tel: 407-363-7405.

West Palm Beach, Palm Beach Co., Mary Mother of Light Maronite Mission, Rev. Msgr. Ronald N. Beshara.
Res., 2800 N. Ocean Dr. A22D, Singer Island, 33404. Tel: 407-881-5583.

STATE OF GEORGIA

Atlanta, Fulton Co., St. Joseph's Maronite Church, Rev. Peter Boulos.
Res., 502 Seminole Ave., N.E., 30307. Tel: 404-525-2504.

STATE OF MAINE

Waterville, Kennebec Co., St. Joseph, Rev. Samuel A. Najjar.
Res., 3 Appleton St., 04901. Tel: 207-872-8515.

STATE OF MASSACHUSETTS

Brockton, Plymouth Co., St. Theresa, Rev. Msgr. David M. George.
Mailing Address: P.O. Box 2567, 02405. Fax: 508-587-8139.
Res., 10 Lebanon St., 02401. Tel: 508-586-1428.

Fall River, Bristol Co., St. Anthony of the Desert, Rev. Msgr. Norman J. Ferris.
Res., 300 N. Eastern Ave., 02723. Tel: 617-672-7653.

Jamaica Plain, Suffolk Co., Our Lady of the Cedars of Lebanon, Rev. Msgr. Joseph F. Lahoud.
Res., 61 Rockwood St., 02130. Tel: 617-522-0225; Fax: 617-522-0194.

Lawrence, Essex Co., St. Anthony, Rev. Msgr. James T. Khoury; Rev. Peter Boulos.
Res., 145 Amesbury St., 01841. Tel: 617-685-7233. [CEM]

New Bedford, Bristol Co., Our Lady of Purgatory, Rev. Charbel T. Semaan.
Res., 11 Franklin St., 02740. Tel: 508-996-8934; Fax: 508-996-2744.

Springfield, Hampden Co., St. Anthony, Rev. Edward T. Nedder; Deacon Terrence O'Connell.
Res., 419 Island Pond Rd., 01118-1002. Tel: 413-732-0589.
Church—375 Island Pond Rd., 01118-1002.

Worcester, Worcester Co., Our Lady of Mercy, Chorbishop Joseph Saidi.
Res., 70 Mulberry St., 01605. Tel: 617-752-4287.

STATE OF NEW HAMPSHIRE

Dover, Strafford Co., St. George, Rev. H. Paul Boackle.
Res., 66 Portland Ave., 03820. Tel: 603-742-1149.

STATE OF NEW JERSEY

Somerset, Somerset Co., St. Sharbel, Rev. Maroun Asmar.
Res., 12 Reeve St., 08873. Tel: 908-828-2055; Fax: 908-828-5488.

STATE OF NORTH CAROLINA

Fayetteville, Cumberland Co., Archangel Michael, Rev. Larry Jensen.
Res., 806 Arsenal Ave., 28305. Tel: 919-484-1531.

STATE OF PENNSYLVANIA

Easton, Northampton Co., Our Lady of Lebanon, Rev. Msgr. Sami Hayek.
Res., 54 S. Fourth St., 18042. Tel: 215-252-5275.

New Castle, Lawrence Co., St. John the Baptist, Rev. Joseph David.
Res., 2 W. Reynolds St., 16101. Tel: 412-658-0787.

Newtown Square, Delaware Co., St. Sharbel Mission, Rev. Paul Mooradd.
Res., 201 S. Newtown Square Rd., Newton Square, 19073. Tel: 610-353-5952.

Philadelphia, Philadelphia Co., St. Maron, Rev. Msgr. Sharbel Lischaa; Deacon Joseph Regan.
Res., 1010 Ellsworth St., 19147. Tel: 215-389-1300.

Pittsburgh, Allegheny Co., Our Lady of Victory, Rev. James A. Root.
Res., 600 Dunster St., 15226. Tel: 412-531-4234; Fax: 412-531-9184.

Scranton, Lackawanna Co., St. Ann, Rev. Fahed F. Azar.
Res., 1320 Price St., 18504-3336. Tel: 717-344-2129.

Uniontown, Fayette Co., St. George, Rev. Christopher J. Henderson.
Res., Lebanon Ter., 15401. Tel: 412-437-5589.

Wilkes-Barre, Luzerne Co., St. George, Rev. Kevin Beaton.
Res., 79 Loomis St., 18702. Tel: 717-824-3599.
St. Anthony, Rev. Ignace Sadek.
Res., 253 Dana St., 18702. Tel: 717-824-4448.

STATE OF RHODE ISLAND

Pawtucket, Providence Co., Holy Trinity-St. George, Rev. Paul Mouawad.
Res., 50 Main St., 02860. Tel: 401-723-8444.

STATE OF VIRGINIA

Richmond, Richmond City Co., St. Anthony, Rev. George M. Sebaali.
Res., 4611 Sadler Rd., Glen Allen, 23060. Tel: 804-270-7234; Fax: 804-273-9914.

Roanoke, Roanoke City Co., St. Elias, Rev. Msgr. Assad Awad.
Res., P.O. Box 822, 24004. Tel: 703-342-9872; 344-9493.

DISTRICT OF COLUMBIA

Washington, District of Columbia, Our Lady of Lebanon Church, Chorbishop Dominic F. Ashkar.
Res., 7164 Alaska Ave., N.W., 20012. Tel: 202-829-5554.

On Duty Outside the Diocese:
Reverend Fathers—
Amar, Joseph P.
Bartoul, William
El-Hayek, Nehmatallah
Thomas, Joseph

Unassigned:
Reverend Fathers—
Abi-Sarkis, Elias
Shaheen, Joseph

Retired:
Chorbishop—
Abi-Nader, Joseph
Trad, John
Reverend Monsignors—
Antoun, Elie
Bistany, Joseph
Joseph, Joseph D.
Naffah, John
Reverend Fathers—
Abi-Nadar, Maron
Akekee, Wlademer
Andary, John S.
Hitti, Michael
Kleem, Ferris
Mahfoud, Peter
Saad, Antoun
Zogheib, Hares

Permanent Deacons:
Calabrese, Robert, Danbury, CT
Joseph, Peter, Waterville, ME
Koury, Anthony, Easton, PA
Massoud, Donald, Fall River, MA
Nashawaty, Nicholas, MA
Nasser, Andre, Fall River, MA
Ramey, Al, Lawrence, MA
Regan, Joseph W., Sewell, NJ

INSTITUTIONS LOCATED IN THE DIOCESE

[A] SEMINARIES, DIOCESAN

WASHINGTON, DC. *Our Lady of Lebanon Maronite Seminary*, 7164 Alaska Ave., N.W., 20012. Tel: 202-723-8831. Chorbishop Seely Beggiani, S.T.D., Rector; Revs. David F. Michael; Rodolphe W. Wakim. Priests 1; Students 8.

[B] CONVENTS AND RESIDENCES FOR SISTERS

NORTH BROOKFIELD, MA. *Hermits of Jesus The Eternal Priest*, P.O. Box 421, 01535. Tel: 508-867-0134. Mother Elias, Supr.

RUTLAND, MA. *Mother of Light Community, Our Lady of Guadalupe Convent*, 374 Main St., P.O. Box 335, 01543-0335. Tel: 508-886-6745. Marionite Benedictine Sisters. Sr. Helen LaBud, O.S.B., Supr. Professed Sisters 5.

[C] RELIGIOUS COMMUNITIES OF MEN

BETHLEHEM, SD. *Holy Nativity Monastery*, 57708. Tel: 605-787-4606. Rev. Louis Marie Dauphinais, O.M.A.R. Priests 3.

PETERSHAM, MA. *Most Holy Trinity Monastery*, Dugway Rd., P.O. Box 605, 01366. Tel: 508-724-3347. Revs. William J. Driscoll, O.Mar., Supr.; Giles R. Goyette, O.Mar., Vicar. Priests 7; Brothers 1.

[D] RESIDENCES FOR CLERGY

BROOKLYN. *Archbishop's Residence*, 8070 Harbor View Ter., 11209. Chorbishop James B. Namie.

STATEN ISLAND. *Pastoral Center*, 294 Howard Ave., 10301. Chorbishop John D. Faris, J.C.O.D.; Rev. Francis J. Marini, J.C.O.D.

[E] MISCELLANEOUS

NEW BEDFORD, MA. *Cedar Holdings, Inc.*, P.O. Box 51021, 02745-0035. Tel: 508-996-8934; Fax: 508-996-2744. Rev. Charbel Semaan, Pres.

STATEN ISLAND. *Bishops Retirement Trust Fund*, 294 Howard Ave., 10301.
Order of St. Sharbel Trust Fund, 294 Howard Ave., 10301.
Priest Retirement Trust Fund, 294 Howard Ave., 10301.

WILLISTON, VT. *Blessed Rafka Retreat Center*, c/o Emmaus House, R.D. 2, Box 305A, 05495. Tel: 802-660-2528. Rev. Joseph Akiki.

NECROLOGY

(No Deaths)

Diocese of St. Nicholas in Chicago for Ukrainians

Most Reverend

MICHAEL WIWCHAR, C.SS.R., D.D.

Bishop of Chicago; ordained June 28, 1959; appointed Third Bishop of the St. Nicholas Diocese; installed September 28, 1993. *Mailing Address: 2245 W. Rice St., Chicago, IL, 60622.*

Most Reverend

INNOCENT LOTOCKY, O.S.B.M., D.D., PH.D.

Retired Bishop of Chicago; ordained November 24, 1940; appointed Second Bishop of Chicago January 29, 1981; consecrated March 1, 1981; installed April 2, 1981; retired September 28, 1993. *Mailing Address: 2245 W. Rice St., Chicago, IL, 60622.*

Comprises all of the United States west of the western borders of Ohio, Kentucky, Tennessee and Mississippi.

For legal titles of parishes and diocesan institutions, consult the Chancery Office.

Chancery Office: 2245 W. Rice St., Chicago, IL, 60622. Tel.: 312-276-5080; 276-4537; Fax: 312-276-6799.

STATISTICAL OVERVIEW

Personnel	
Bishop	1
Auxiliary Bishops	1
Retired Bishops	1
Abbots	1
Priests: Diocesan Active in Diocese	25
Priests: Active Outside Diocese	1
Priests: Retired, Sick or Absent	11
Number of Diocesan Priests	37
Religious Priests in Diocese	15
Extern Priests in Diocese	12
Ordinations:	
Diocesan Priests	2
Permanent Deacons in Diocese	14
Parishes	
Parishes	33
With Resident Pastor:	
Resident Diocesan Priests	20
Resident Religious Priests	4
Without Resident Pastor:	
Administered by Priests	7
Administered by Permanent Deacons	2
Missions	4
Welfare	
Educational	
High Schools, Diocesan and Parish	1
Total Students	80
Elementary Schools, Diocesan and Parish	2
Total Students	465
Catechesis/Religious Education:	
High School Students	50
Elementary Students	180
Total Students Under Catholic Instruction	725
Teachers in the Diocese:	
Priests	1
Sisters	3
Lay Teachers	48
Vital Statistics	
Receptions into the Church:	
Infant Baptism Totals	120
Adult Baptism Totals	3
First Communions	158
Marriages:	
Catholic	58
Interfaith	4
Total Marriages	62
Deaths	138
Total Catholic Population	10,000

Former Bishops—Most Rev. JAROSLAV GABRO, D.D., appt. First Bishop of Chicago, July 12, 1961; cons. Oct. 26, 1961; died March 28, 1980.—Most Rev. INNOCENT LOTOCKY, O.S.B.M., D.D., Ph.D., ord. Nov. 24, 1940; appt. Second Bishop of Chicago, Jan. 29, 1981; cons. March 1, 1981; installed April 2, 1981; retired Sept. 28, 1993.

Syncellus—Rev. Msgr. Canon WILLIAM M. BILINSKY.

Econome—Rev. ABRAHAM MILLER.

Chancery Office—2245 W. Rice St., Chicago, IL, 60622. Tel: 773-276-5080. If no answer. Tel: 773-276-4537; Fax: 773-276-6799. Office Hours: 9-4.

Diocesan Consultors—Rt. Rev. Mitred Archpriest JOHN LAZAR; Rev. WAYNE RUCHGY; Revs. MYRON PANCHUK; MICHAEL STELMACH.

Presbyteral Council—Very Rev. Canon WAYNE RUCHGY; Revs. MYRON PANCHUK; MYKHAILO KUZMA; PAVLO HAYDA; Very Rev. Canon IVAN KROTEC; Very Rev. Canon MICHAEL STELMACH; Rt. Rev. Mitred Archpriest JOHN LAZAR.

Personnel Board—Revs. RICHARD JANOWICZ; MYRON PANCHUK; Very Rev. Canon WAYNE RUCHGY.

Tribunal—Through Special Permission of the Holy See, Local Latin Rite Tribunals Handle the Cases Within the Diocese.

Diocesan Deans—Very Rev. Canon IVAN KROTEC; Rev. MICHAEL STELMACH; Rt. Rev. Mitred Archpriest JOHN LAZAR.

Diocesan Censor—Rev. SEBASTIAN SABOL, O.S.B.M.

Diocesan Bi-Monthly—"The New Star", IWANNA GORCHYNSKA, Editor, *2208 W. Chicago Ave., Chicago, IL, 60622.* Tel: 773-772-1919.

CLERGY, PARISHES, MISSIONS AND PAROCHIAL SCHOOLS

STATE OF ILLINOIS

1—ST. NICHOLAS UKRAINIAN CATHOLIC CATHEDRAL (1906), Most Rev. Michael Wiwchar, C.SS.R.; Revs. Jeffrey Kassian; Alexander Averamenko; David Fitzhugh; Bohoan Nalysnyk; Deacon Mychajlo Horodysky. In res., Rt. Rev. Mitred Arch Andrew Mykyta, (Retired); Revs. Richard Kirouac; Alexander Avramenko.
Res., 2238 W. Rice St., 60622. Tel: 773-276-4537; Fax: 312-276-5558. [CEM]
School—2200 W. Rice St., 60622. Tel: 773-384-7243. Sr. Maria Rozmarynowicz, O.S.B.M., Prin. Sisters 2; Lay Teachers 14; Students 204.
Convent—2230 W. Rice St., 60622. Tel: 312-486-6820. Sisters of St. Basil the Great Sr. Irenea Hankewych, O.S.B.M., Supr.

2—ST. JOSEPH (N.W. Chicago) (1956) (Ukrainian), Revs. Pavlo Hayda; Thomas L. Glynn.
Res., 5000 N. Cumberland Ave., 60656. Tel: 773-625-4833; 625-4805 (Office).
Catechesis/Religious Programs—Students 60.

3—SS. VOLODYMYR AND OLHA (1968), Very Rev. Canon Ivan Krotec Tel: 312-455-0178; Revs. Myron Panchuk Tel: 773-666-6051; Mykola Kosarchyn Tel: 312-486-1655; Deacon Michael Szyjan.
Parish Office: 2245 W. Superior St., 60612. Tel: 773-829-5209. [JC]

4—ST. MICHAEL'S, Very Rev. Canon John Kmech.
Res., 12211 S. Parnell Ave., 60628. Tel: 312-785-7443. [JC]

5—ST. MARY'S, Madison Co., Rev. Robert S. Piorkowski.
Res., 1312 Iowa St., 62060. Tel: 616-452-9118. [JC]

6—IMMACULATE CONCEPTION (1963) (Ukrainian), Very Rev. Canon Leo Bilos, Pastor Emeritus; Rev. Mykhailo Kuzma.
Res., 745 S. Benton, 60067. Tel: 847-991-0820; Fax: 847-991-7873.

7—NATIVITY OF B. V. M., Cook Co., (1911), Revs. Walter Rybicky, O.S.B.M.; Demetrius Wysochansky, O.S.B.M.
Res., 8530 W. 131 St., 60464. Tel: 708-361-8876; 361-8820.

STATE OF ARIZONA

Phoenix, Maricopa Co., Assumption of B.V.M. (1959), Rev. Hugo Soutus.
Church—3720 W. Maryland Ave., 85019.
Res., 3650 W. Maryland Ave., 85019. Tel: 602-973-3667.

Tucson, Pima Co., St. Michael (1978). Attended by Phoenix. Rev. Yaroslaw Dowbush.
Res., P.O. Box 12745, 1557 N. Brown Way, 85732. Tel: 602-298-4967.

STATE OF CALIFORNIA

Los Angeles, Los Angeles Co., Nativity of B.V.M., Rev. Oleh Romanenko.
Res., 5154 De Longpre Ave., Hollywood, 90027. Tel: 213-663-6307.

San Diego, San Diego Co., Our Lady of Perpetual Help, Rev. David Fitzhugh; Very Rev. Canon Michael Kurylo, Pastor Emeritus.
Res., 4061 Winona Ave., 92105. Tel: 619-282-9538.

San Francisco, San Francisco Co., Immaculate Conception (1957), Rev. Alexander Avramenko, Admin.

Res., 215 Silliman, 94134. Tel: 415-468-2601.
Mission—Sacramento, Sacramento Co., St. Andrew the Apostle, 1324 La Sierra Dr., Sacramento, 95864. Tel: 916-489-6373. Rev. John Lucas; Deacon Theodore Wroblicky, Admin.

Santa Clara, Santa Clara Co., St. Vladimir. Attended by San Francisco. Rev. Alexander Avramenko.

STATE OF COLORADO

Denver, Denver Co., Transfiguration of Our Lord (1954), Rev. Wasyl Prokopiw.
Res., 4118 Shoshone St., 80211. Tel: 303-433-2347.

STATE OF INDIANA

Mishawaka, St. Joseph Co., St. Michael (1916), Rev. John Hritzko.
Res., 712 E. Lawrence St., 46544. Tel: 219-259-7173.

Munster, Lake Co., St. Josaphat (1958) (Ukrainian), Rev. John Hritzko.
Res., 8624 White Oak Ave., 46321. Tel: 219-923-0984.

STATE OF MICHIGAN

Dearborn, Wayne Co., St. Michael's (1962), Very Rev. Canon Wayne J. Ruchgy.
Res., 6340 Chase Rd., 48126. Tel: 313-582-1424; Fax: 313-582-8157.

Dearborn Heights, Wayne Co., Our Lady of Perpetual Help (1963), Very Rev. Archpriest John Lazar.
Res., 26606 Ann Arbor Trail, 48127. Tel: 313-278-0470.

Detroit, Wayne Co., St. John the Baptist (1918) (Ukrainian), Revs. Prechasniuk, O.S.B.M.; Mario Dacechen, O.S.B.M.
Res., 3877 Clippert Ave., 48210. Tel: 313-897-7300; Fax: 313-897-7304. [JC]

Hamtramck, Wayne Co., Immaculate Conception of B.V.M. (1914) (Ukrainian), Very Rev. Tarcisio Lucavei, O.S.B.M., Pastor & Supr.; Revs. Constantine Wysochansky, O.S.B.M.; Sergio Saplak, O.S.B.M.
Res., 11700 McDougall St., 48212. Tel: 313-893-1710; Fax: 313-893-0770.
School—29500 Westbrook, Warren, 48093. Tel: 810-574-2480. Doris Jurek, Prin.
Priests 1; Sisters 1; Lay Teachers 20; Students 261.
High School—29400 Westbrook, Warren, 48092. Tel: 810-574-2723; Fax: 810-574-0510. Michalene Weigle, Prin.
Priests 1; Sisters 1; Lay Teachers 17; Students 81.
Catechesis / Religious Programs—Students 342.
Convent—11745 Gallagher, 48212. Tel: 313-366-2061. Sisters of St. Basil the Great Sr. Frances O.S.B.M., Supr.
Sisters 2.

Flint, Genesee Co., St. Vladimir's (1950), Rt. Rev. Mitred Arch John Lazar, Admin., Dearbornheights, MI.
Res., 3464 W. Pasadena Ave., 48504.

Grand Rapids, Kent Co., St. Michael's. Attended by Mishawaka, IN. Deacon Jaroslau Bohatch, Admin.
Mailing Address: 4390 Woodside Oaks Dr., S.E., 49504. Tel: 616-456-1967.

Warren, Macomb Co., St. Josaphat (1961), Revs. Basil Salkovski, O.S.B.M.; Sebastian Sabol, O.S.B.M.; Roman Hykawy, O.S.B.M.
Res., 26401 St. Josaphat Dr., 48091. Tel: 810-755-1740; Fax: 810-755-1399. [CEM]

STATE OF MINNESOTA

Minneapolis, Hennepin Co., St. Constantine (1913) (Ukrainian), Rev. Michael Stelmach.
Res., 515 University Ave., N.E., 55413-1944. Tel: 612-379-2394; Fax: 612-379-2470.

St. Paul, Ramsey Co., St. Stephen (1951) (Ukrainian). Attended by St. Constantine Church, Minneapolis.
Church—1260 Greenbrier St., 55106. Tel: 612-379-2394; Fax: 612-379-2470.

STATE OF MISSOURI

St. Joseph, Buchanan Co., St. Joseph's. Attended by Omaha, NE.
Church—526 Virginia, 64504. Tel: 816-238-1187.

St. Louis, St. Louis Co., Assumption B.V.M. (1894) (Ukrainian), Rev. Robert B. Piorkowski, Admin.
Church—11363 Oak Branch Dr., P.O. Box 10763, 63129.

STATE OF NEBRASKA

Lincoln, Lancaster Co., St. George's (1950), Rev. Thomas Dobrowolski, Admin.
Church—3330 N. 13th St., 68521. Tel: 402-435-5882; 345-1552.
Res., 1513 Martha St., Omaha, 68108.

Omaha, Douglas Co., Assumption of B.V.M. (1950), Rev. Thomas Dobrowolski, Admin.
Res., 1513 Martha St., 68108. Tel: 402-345-1552.
Mission—Lincoln, Lancaster Co., St. George Byzantine-Ukrainian Rite Catholic Church, 3330 N. 13th St., Lincoln, 68521.

STATE OF NORTH DAKOTA

Belfield, Stark Co., St. John the Baptist (1946) (Ukrainian), Rev. James G. Scharinger (Canada).
Res., P.O. Box 428, 58622-0428. Tel: 701-575-4281. [CEM]

Fairfield, Billings Co., St. Demetrius (1905) (Ukrainian), Rev. James Scharinger, Admin.
Res., P.O. Box 428, Belfield, 58622-0428. Tel: 701-575-4281. [CEM]

Wilton, McLean Co., SS. Peter and Paul (1890) (Ukrainian). Attended by Belfield.
Res., 100 Seventh St. N., P.O. Box 392, 58579. Tel: 701-734-6464. [CEM]

STATE OF OREGON

Springfield, Lane Co., Nativity of the Mother of God (1981) (Ukrainian), Rev. Richard Janowicz.
Res., 704 Aspen St., 97477. Tel: 541-726-7309; Fax: 541-726-7309.

STATE OF TEXAS

Houston, Harris Co., Protection of the Mother of God (1957) (Ukrainian), Rev. Andrij Taras Dwulit, Admin.
Res., 9102 Meadowshire St., 77037. Tel: 713-447-2749. [JC]

STATE OF WISCONSIN

Milwaukee, Milwaukee Co., St. Michaels (1950) (Ukrainian), Rev. George L. Pruys.
Res., 1025 S. 11th St., P.O. Box 64012, 53204. Tel: 414-672-5616.

Chaplains of Public Institutions

Hospitals

CHICAGO, IL. *Resurrection and Our Lady of Resurrection*. Rev. Msgr. William M. Bilinsky, Chap.
St. Mary of Nazareth Hospital Center. Rev. Abraham Miller, Chap.

Absent on Sick Leave:
Reverend Fathers—
Pedelesky, Nestor
Prodywus, Alexander

Retired:
Reverend Monsignors—
Knapp, Stephen V.
Leskiw, Peter
Reverend Fathers—
Mykyta, Andrew
Skaskiw, Bohdan, 24257 Greenhill Rd., Warren, MI 48091
Rt. Rev. Mitred Arch—
Bilos, Leo, 116 Brentwood Ave., Elk Grove Village, IL 60007
Oleshko, Myroslaw, 10398 Deanne Dr., Sun City, AZ 85351. Tel: 602-974-3089
Very Rev. Canon—
Bobersky, Michael, 6209 E. McKellips, Mesa, AZ 85205. Tel: 602-985-7620
Kurylo, Michael, 3821-49th St., San Diego, CA 92105. Tel: 619-282-7958

Permanent Deacons:
Bohatch, Jaroslav, St. Michael, Grand Rapids, MI
Bozio, Michael, Transfiguration of Our Lord, Denver, CO
Horodysky, Mychajlo, St. Nicholas Cathedral, Chicago, IL
Hrycyniak, Stephen
Kordonowy, Leonard, St. John the Baptist, Belfield, ND; St. Demetrius, Fairfield, ND
MacKinnon, William, (Solt)(Ukraine)
Marick, Thomas D., Honolulu, Hawaii
May, Andrew, Downers Grove, IL
Mykyta, Myron, Phoenix, AZ
Plishka, Andrew, St. Joseph, Chicago, IL
Shyan, Michael, Ss. Volodymyr & Olha, Chicago, IL
Wasylyna, E., Phoenix, AZ
Wroblicky, Theodore Peter, Sacramento, CA
Zientek, Theodore, Holy Transfiguration Monastery, Redwood Valley, CA

INSTITUTIONS LOCATED IN THE DIOCESE

[A] MONASTERIES

REDWOOD VALLEY, CA. *Holy Transfiguration Monastery*, 17001 Tomki Rd., P.O. Box 217, 95470. Tel: 707-485-8959; Fax: 707-485-1122. Monks of Mount Tabor. Rt. Rev. Archimandri Boniface Luykx. Priests 4; Deacons 1; Novices 3; Professed Monks 8; Aggregates 12; Postulants 1.

RELIGIOUS INSTITUTES OF MEN REPRESENTED IN THE DIOCESE

For further details refer to the corresponding bracketed number in the Religious Institutes of Men or Women section.

[0180]—*Order of St. Basil the Great.*—O.S.B.M.

RELIGIOUS INSTITUTES OF WOMEN REPRESENTED IN THE DIOCESE

[3730]—*Sisters of the Order of St. Basil the Great.*—O.S.B.M.

NECROLOGY

† Kosarchyn, Mykola, Chicago, IL, SS. Volodymyr and Olha Parish. —Died Oct. 23, 1996.

Eparchy of Saint Thomas the Apostle

Most Reverend

IBRAHIM N. IBRAHIM, D.D.

First Bishop-Eparch of the Eparchy of Saint Thomas the Apostle-Chaldean Catholic Diocese of America; ordained December 30, 1962; appointed Chaldean Apostolic Exarch and Titular Bishop of Anbar January 26, 1982; consecrated Bishop March 7, 1982 in Baghdad, Iraq; installed April 18, 1982 in Detroit; appointed First Bishop Eparch to the Eparchy of Saint Thomas the Apostle-Chaldean Catholic Diocese of America September 14, 1985. *Res., Chaldean Catholic Diocese of U.S.A., 25603 Berg Rd., Southfield, MI, 48034.*

EXARCHATE ERECTED JANUARY 26, 1982. ELEVATED TO THE RANK OF EPARCHY SEPTEMBER 14, 1985.

The Jurisdiction of the Eparchy extends territorially to all of the United States of America inclusive. With regard to persons, its subjects are all Catholics of the Chaldean or Assyrian-Chaldean Church: (1) Who immigrated to this country from the Middle East, especially from Iraq and Iran; (2) Who descends from such persons (can. 755); (3) Women married to men referable to (1) & (2) if they comply with can. 98, n. 4; (4) Who in accordance with can. 98, n. 3., changed their Rite; (5) Converts to the Catholic Church of the Chaldean Rite; (6) And in fact, all other Catholics of the Chaldean Rite who are attached to the parishes subject to the jurisdiction of the Eparch.

For legal titles of parishes and diocesan institutions, consult the Chancery Office.

Chancery Office: 25603 Berg Rd., Southfield, MI, 48034. Tel.: 810-351-0440; Fax: 810-351-0443.

STATISTICAL OVERVIEW

Personnel	
Bishop	1
Priests: Diocesan Active in Diocese	15
Priests: Active Outside Diocese	1
Priests: Retired, Sick or Absent	2
Number of Diocesan Priests	18
Parishes	
Parishes	12
With Resident Pastor:	
Resident Diocesan Priests	11
Without Resident Pastor:	
Administered by Priests	1
Welfare	
Homes for the Aged	1
Day Care and Extended Day Care Centers	1
Educational	
Students from This Diocese	1
Diocesan Students in Other Seminaries	1
Total Seminarians	2
Catechesis/Religious Education:	
Total Students Under Catholic Instruction	2
Vital Statistics	
Receptions into the Church:	
Infant Baptism Totals	1,052
Adult Baptism Totals	17
First Communions	865
Confirmations	1,069
Marriages:	
Catholic	309
Interfaith	13
Total Marriages	322
Deaths	126
Total Catholic Population	63,150

Chancery Office—25603 Berg Rd., Southfield, MI, 48034. Tel: 810-351-0440; Fax: 810-351-0443.

Vicar General—Rt. Rev. SARHAD Y. JAMMO, *2442 E. Big Beaver Rd., Troy, MI, 48083.* Tel: 810-528-3676; Fax: 810-524-1957.

Presbyteral Council and College of Consultors—Rt. Rev. SARHAD Y. JAMMO, Vicar General; Revs. YOSHIA SANA, Reg. Rep. EMMANUEL RAYES; JOHN HANNA CHEIKHO; MANUEL Y. BOJI.

Diocesan Corporation-The Chaldean Catholic Church of U.S.A.—Most Rev. IBRAHIM IBRAHIM, Pres.; Revs. MANUEL Y. BOJI, Sec. SARHAD Y. JAMMO, Treas.

Diocesan Bulletin—"The Star of Chaldeans", 25603 Berg Rd., Southfield, MI, 48034. Tel: 810-351-0440.

Eparchial Tribunal—Rev. STEPHEN H. KALLABAT, *Court of the First Instance, Chancery Office, 25603 Berg Rd., Southfield, MI, 48034.*

CLERGY, PARISHES, MISSIONS AND PAROCHIAL SCHOOLS

STATE OF MICHIGAN

Detroit, Wayne Co., Sacred Heart Chaldean Parish (1973), Rev. Jacob Yasso.
Res., 310 W. Seven Mile Rd., 48203. Tel: 313-368-6214 (Church); Fax: 313-891-0132.
Convent—19138 Danbury, 48203. Tel: 313-368-7999. Chaldean Sisters

Oak Park, Oakland Co., Mar Addai Chaldean Parish (1979) (Chaldean), Revs. Stephen Kallabat; Suleiman Denha.
Res., 24010 Coolidge Hwy., 48237. Tel: 810-547-4648.

Southfield, Oakland Co., Our Lady of Chaldeans Cathedral, Mother of God Chaldean Parish, Most Rev. Ibrahim Ibrahim; Revs. Manuel Y. Boji, Rector; Thomas Simon Nofaley; Frank Y. Kalabat; Sabin Iskandar.
Res., 25585 Berg Rd., 48034. Tel: 810-356-0565; 356-0569; 356-9809 (Hall); Fax: 810-356-5235.
Catechesis/Religious Programs—Ann Antoon, D.R.E.
Students 410.
Convent—23754 Clarkson, 48034. Tel: 810-355-1318. Chaldean Sisters

Troy, Oakland Co., St. Joseph Chaldean Parish (1981), Rt. Rev. Sarhad Jammo; Rev. Emanuel Rayes.
Res., 2442 E. Big Beaver Rd., 48083. Tel: 810-528-3676; 524-1144 (Church); Fax: 810-524-1957.
Convent—2554 Parasol, 48083. Tel: 810-740-2741. Chaldean Sisters
Mission—Flint, Genesee Co., (1993).

West Bloomfield, Oakland Co., St. Thomas Chaldean Catholic Parish (1992) (Chaldean), Rev. John Hanna Cheikho.
Mailing Address: 6900 Maple Rd., 48322. Tel: 810-788-2460; Fax: 810-788-2153.
Res., 3535 Indian Tr., Orchard Lake, 48324. Tel: 810-683-0333. [JC]
Catechesis/Religious Programs—Students 240.

STATE OF ILLINOIS

Chicago, Cook Co., St. Ephrem's Church (1904) (Chaldean-Assyrian), Rev. Msgr. Edward J. Bikoma.
Res., 2537 W. Bryn Mawr Ave., 60659. Tel: 312-271-8899. [JC]
Catechesis/Religious Programs—Students 76.
Mart Mariam Parish (1986) (Chaldean-Assyrian), Rev. Msgr. Edward J. Bikoma.
Mailing Address: 2537 W. Bryn Mawr, 60659.
Res., 2847 W. Chase Ave., 60645. Tel: 312-761-9401. [JC]

STATE OF CALIFORNIA

El Cajon, San Diego Co., St. Peter Chaldean Parish (1973) (Chaldean), Rev. Michael J. Bazzi; Najib Konja, Admin.
Res., 1627 Jamacha Way, 92019. Tel: 619-579-7913; 588-9921; Fax: 619-588-8281.
Catechesis/Religious Programs—Tel: 619-447-8876. Khelood Allos, D.R.E.
Students 525.
Convent—1710 E. Madison, 92021. Tel: 619-588-6391. Chaldean Sisters

North Hollywood, Los Angeles Co., St. Paul Assyrian-Chaldean Catholic Parish (1980), Rev. Emanuel Hana Isho.
Res., 13050 Vanowen St., 91605. Tel: 818-765-3665; Fax: 818-765-0493.
Mission—Fullerton, Orange Co., St. George, 706 S. Lemon St., Fullerton, 92632.

San Jose, Santa Clara Co., St. Mary Assyrian-Caldean Parish (1987), Rev. Yoshia Sana.
Rectory: 6348 Mayo Dr., 95123. Tel: 408-224-1136. [JC]
Church—109 First St., Compbell, 95008. Tel: 408-224-1136.
Catechesis/Religious Programs—Students 65.

Turlock, Stanislaus Co., St. Thomas Assyrian-Chaldean Parish, Rev. Kamal Warda Bidawid, Admin.
Res., 2901 N. Berkeley Ave., P.O. Box 219, 95380. Tel: 209-668-4500.
Convent—2937 N. Berkeley Ave., 95380. Tel: 209-634-2043. Chaldean Sisters
St. Thomas Retirement Center—Tel: 209-634-7252.

STATE OF ARIZONA

Scottsdale, Maricopa Co., Mar Auraha Chaldean Catholic Parish, Rev. Noel Gorgis, Admin.
Res., 6816 E. Cactus Rd., 85254. Tel: 602-596-6798; Fax: 602-596-9067.

On Assignment Outside the Diocese:
Reverend Fathers—
Buffington, Jon

Retired:
Reverend Fathers—
Ablahad, Najor, 28454 Red Leaf, Southfield, MI 48076. Tel: 810-569-5736

INSTITUTIONS LOCATED IN THE DIOCESE

RELIGIOUS INSTITUTE OF WOMEN IN THE EPARCHY

Institute of Sisters: Daughters of Mary Immaculate, founded in 1922 in Baghdad, Iraq. Convents in Detroit, Troy and Southfield, MI; Turlock, and San Diego, CA.

NECROLOGY

(No Deaths)

Ukrainian Catholic Diocese of Stamford

Most Reverend

BASIL H. LOSTEN, D.D., S.T.L., LL.D. (HON.)

Bishop of Stamford; ordained June 10, 1957; appointed Titular Bishop of Arcadiopolis and Auxiliary of Ukrainian Catholic Archeparchy of Philadelphia March 15, 1971; consecrated May 25, 1971; appointed Apostolic Administrator of Archeparchy of Philadelphia June 8, 1976; transferred to the Stamford See September 20, 1977. *Res., 161 Glenbrook Rd., Stamford, CT, 06902.*

ESTABLISHED AUGUST 8, 1956.

The jurisdiction of the Bishop of Stamford extends territorially throughout all of New York State and the New England States. With regard to persons, his subjects are all members of the Ukrainian Catholic Church (Byzantine Rite), irrespective of where they received Baptism.

For legal titles of parishes and diocesan institutions, consult the Chancery Office.

Chancery Office: 14 Peveril Rd., Stamford, CT, 06902-3019. Tel.: 203-324-7698; Fax: 203-967-9948.

E-mail address: BASILEOS@aol.com

STATISTICAL OVERVIEW

Personnel	
Bishop	1
Priests: Diocesan Active in Diocese	24
Priests: Retired, Sick or Absent	14
Number of Diocesan Priests	38
Religious Priests in Diocese	18
Extern Priests in Diocese	28
Ordinations:	
Diocesan Priests	1
Transitional Deacons	3
Permanent Deacons in Diocese	5
Total Brothers	3
Total Sisters	42
Parishes	
Parishes	49
With Resident Pastor:	
Resident Diocesan Priests	40
Resident Religious Priests	5
Without Resident Pastor:	
Administered by Priests	4
Missions	5
Pastoral Centers	2
Welfare	
Homes for the Aged	1
Total Assisted	30
Day Care and Extended Day Care Centers	1
Total Assisted	44
Special Centers for Social Services	1
Total Assisted	100
Educational	
Seminaries, Diocesan	1
Students from This Diocese	48
Diocesan Students in Other Seminaries	1
Total Seminarians	49
High Schools, Diocesan and Parish	1
Total Students	140
Elementary Schools, Diocesan and Parish	4
Total Students	463
Catechesis/Religious Education:	
High School Students	23
Elementary Students	848
Total Students Under Catholic Instruction	1,523
Teachers in the Diocese:	
Sisters	6
Lay Teachers	28
Vital Statistics	
Receptions into the Church:	
Infant Baptism Totals	188
Adult Baptism Totals	18
Received into Full Communion	7
First Communions	184
Confirmations	196
Marriages:	
Catholic	87
Interfaith	18
Total Marriages	105
Deaths	385
Total Catholic Population	32,117

Former Bishops—Most Rev. AMBROSE SENYSHYN, O.S.B.M., D.D., installed as first Bishop of Stamford, Dec. 15, 1956; transferred to the Archeparchy of Philadelphia, Oct. 26, 1961; died Sept. 11, 1976.—Most Rev. JOSEPH M. SCHMONDIUK, D.D., Bishop of Stamford, Nov. 9, 1961; transferred to the Archeparchy of Philadelphia, Sept. 20, 1977; died Dec. 25, 1978.

Chancery Office—14 Peveril Rd., Stamford, CT, 06902-3019. Tel: 203-324-7698; Fax: 203-967-9948. Office Hours: 9-5.

Vicar General—Very Rev. PATRICK PASCHAK, O.S.B.M., V.G.

Econome—Rt. Rev. Mitred Msgr. JOHN TERLECKY.

Chancellor & Archivist—Rev. Msgr. LEON A. MOSKO.

Secretary—OKSANA DRAGAN.

Notary Public—OLGA KROHLEY.

Diocesan Consultors—Very Rev. PATRICK PASCHAK, O.S.B.M., V.G.; Rt. Rev. Mitred Msgr. JOHN TERLECKY; Rev. Msgr. LEON MOSKO; Rev. JAROSLAW NALYSNYK; Rev. VLADIMIR MARUSCLEAC; Rev. IHOR MIDZAK.

Diocesan Tribunal—14 Peveril Rd., Stamford, CT, 06902-3019. Tel: 203-324-7698.

Vicar Judicial—Rt. Rev. Archimandrite Msgr. VICTOR POSPISHIL, J.C.D., S.E.O.D.

Judges—Rev. Msgr. GEORGE BINKOWSKI, B.S., M.S., B.D.; Rev. ROMAN CHOLIJ, J.C.D.

Defender of the Bond—"Ad Hoc" Appointment.

Notaries—Rev. MIROSLAV TROJANOWSKI; Rev. Deacon MARK HIRNIAK.

Diocesan Protopresbyters (Deans)—Albany: Rev. VLADIMIR MARUSCEAC, Acting Dean; Boston: Rev. ZBIGNIEW BRZEZICKI, Acting Dean; Brooklyn: Rev. Msgr. GEORGE BINKOWSKI, B.S., M.S., B.D., Buffalo: Very Rev. MARIJAN PROCYK, Hartford: Rev. IHOR MIDZAK, Acting Dean; New York: Rev. Msgr. JOHN SQUILLER, S.T.L., Syracuse: Rev. Msgr. ROMAN GOLEMBA.

Presbyteral Council—Most Rev. BASIL LOSTEN; Very Rev. PATRICK PASCHAK, O.S.B.M., V.G.; Rev. Msgr. LEON MOSKO; Very Rev. MARIJAN PROCYK; Rev. IHOR MIDZAK; Very Revs. EDWARD YOUNG, B.A., S.T.B.; PETER OHIRKO, B.A.; Revs. PETER DUDIAK, B.A.; Rev. Msgr. LEON MOSKO, B.A., M.A.; Rev. Canon LUBOMYR MUDRY; Rt. Rev. Mitred Msgr. JOHN TERLECKY, B.A., M.A., M.L.S.

Diocesan Offices and Directors

All offices are located at the following address unless otherwise noted., *14 Peveril Rd., Stamford, CT, 06902-3019.* Tel: 203-325-2116; Fax: 203-967-9948.

Administrative Council—Most Rev. BASIL H. LOSTEN; Very Rev. PATRICK PASCHAK, O.S.B.M., V.G.; Rev. Msgr. LEON MOSKO; Rt. Rev. Mitred Msgr. JOHN TERLECKY; Revs. IVAN KASZCZAK; ZBIGNIEW BREZICKI.

Apostolate—Vacant.

Apostleship of Prayer—Rev. MARIJAN PROCYK.

Catechetics (Heritage Schools)—Rev. IHOR MIDZAK, S.T.B.

Cemeteries—Directors: Most Rev. BASIL H. LOSTEN, Pres. & Chm.; Rev. Msgr. JOHN SQUILLER, S.T.L., Vice Pres.; Mr. JOHN O. FLIS, Esq., Sec.; Very Rev. PATRICK PASCHAK, O.S.B.M., V.G.; Rt. Rev. Mitred Msgr. JOHN TERLECKY; Rev. Msgr. LEON MOSKO; Mr. LOUIS NIGRO; Mr. JOHN SENKO, *Holy Spirit Ukrainian Catholic Cemetery, Rte. 1, Box 698, Sarah Wells Trail, Campbell Hall, NY, 10916.* Tel: 914-496-5506.

Censors—Revs. EDWARD YOUNG; JONATHAN MORSE; Very Rev. Archpriest CHARLES MEZZOMO.

Communications—Rev. Msgr. LEON MOSKO.

Diaconate, Permanent—Deacon WILLIS HOMICK.

Diocesan Charities and Missions—Most Rev. BASIL H. LOSTEN.

Ecumenical Commission—Most Rev. BASIL H. LOSTEN; Rev. ROMAN CHOLIJ; Rev. IVAN KASZCZAK; Very Rev. Archpriest CHARLES MEZZOMO; Very Rev. EDWARD YOUNG.

Educational Institutions—Most Rev. BASIL H. LOSTEN; Rev. JAMES MORRIS; Rev. JEFFREY A.G. RODEGHERO; Sr. MICHELE YAKYMOVITCH, S.S.M.I.; Rev. Msgr. GEORGE BINKOWSKI, B.S., B.D., M.S., Supt. of Diocesan Schools.

Family Life—Rev. JONATHAN MORSE.

Holy Name Societies—Rev. PHILIP WEINER.

League of Ukrainian Catholics—Rev. ROBERT BATCHO, Spiritual Dir. (New England); Very Rev. MARIJAN PROCYK, Spiritual Dir. (New York).

Liturgical Commission—Rev. Msgr. LEON MOSKO; Rev. Msgr. PETER SKRINCOSKY; Rev. PHILIP WEINER; Very Rev. Archpriest CHARLES MEZZOMO.

Missionaries, Diocesan—Revs. PHILIP SANDRICK, O.S.B.M.; BERNARD PANCZUK, O.S.B.M.

Museum, Heritage—WASYL LENCYK, Ph.D., Dir. LUBOW WOLYNEC, Curator.

Press, Diocesan: "The Sower"—Rev. Msgr. LEON MOSKO, English Editor; Mr. OSYP ROSZKA; Rev. Deacon MARK HIRNIAK, Ukrainian Editor; Dr. WASYL LENCYK, Ph.D., Contributing Editor.

Priests' Benevolent Association—Rt. Rev. Mitred Msgr. JOHN TERLECKY.

Religious Communities, Vicar—Very Rev. PATRICK PASCHAK, O.S.B.M., V.G.

Religious Education—Rev. JONATHAN MORSE.

Sodalities, B.V.M.—Rev. GEORGE LUKACZYK.

Ukrainian Catholic Relief, Inc.—Rev. JONATHAN MORSE.

Ukrainian Library & Research Center—Ms. LUBOW WOLYNEC, Dir., *39 Clovelly Rd., Stamford, CT, 06902.* Tel: 203-324-7698; Fax: 203-967-9948.

Vocations—Rev. IVAN KASZCZAK.

Youth Apostolate—Rev. JONATHAN MORSE.

Youth-For-Christ Association—KATHERINE FELOCK.

CLERGY, PARISHES, MISSIONS AND PAROCHIAL SCHOOLS

STATE OF CONNECTICUT

1—St. Vladimir Cathedral, Fairfield Co., (1916) (Ukrainian), Rt. Rev. Mitred Msgr John Terlecky.
Res., 24 Wenzel Ter., 06902. Tel: 203-324-0242.
Catechesis/Religious Programs—Priests 1; Sisters 1; Lay Teachers 2; Students 22.

2—SS. Peter and Paul, New Haven Co., (1897) (Ukrainian), Rev. Robert J. Batcho.
Res., 105 Clifton Ave., 06401. Tel: 203-734-3895. [CEM]

3—Protection of B.V.M., Fairfield Co., (1950) (Ukrainian), Rev. Christopher Rogalski.
Church—Holy Protection of B.V.M. Ukrainian Catholic Church, 457 Noble Ave., 06608. Tel: 203-367-5054.
Res., 255 Barnum Ave., 06608. Tel: 203-367-5054.

4—St. Mary Dormition, New London Co., (1948) (Ukrainian), Rev. Marijan Kostyk.
Res., 178 Linwood Ave., 06415. Tel: 203-537-2069. [CEM]

5—St. John the Baptist, Hartford Co., (1925) (Ukrainian). Attended by St. Michael's Ukrainian Church, Hartford. Rev. Paul Wolensky, Admin.
Church—26 New London Tpke., 06033.
Res., 135 Wethersfield Ave., Hartford, 06114. Tel: 203-525-7823.

6—St. Michael, Hartford Co., (1907) (Ukrainian), Revs. Ihor Midzak; Bohdan Danylo.
Church—125 Wethersfield Ave., 06114.
Res., 135 Wethersfield Ave., 06114. Tel: 203-525-7823. [CEM]
Saturday Ukrainian School—Tel: 203-728-8792.
Priests 2; Lay Teachers 11; Students 120.
Mission—Glastonbury, Hartford Co., St. John's, London Turnpike, 06114.

7—St. Josaphat, Hartford Co., (1951) (Ukrainian), Rev. Stepan Bereza.
Res., 303 Eddy Glover Blvd., 06053. Tel: 203-225-7340.
Catechesis/Religious Programs—Priests 1; Lay Teachers 3; Students 25.

8—St. Michael (1909) (Ukrainian), Rev. Paul Luniw.
Res., 569 George St., 06511. Tel: 203-865-0388.
St. Michaels Ukrainian Heritage School—(Saturdays).
Saturday Nursery School—Myron Melnyk, Prin.
Priests 1; Lay Teachers 5; Students 25.

9—St. Michael, Litchfield Co., (1910) (Ukrainian), Rev. George Lukaczyk; Deacon Paul Arena.
Res., 35 Allen St., 06786. Tel: 203-583-7588. [CEM]
Catechesis/Religious Programs—Donna Tuttle, D.R.E.
Priests 1; Lay Teachers 4; Students 25.

10—Protection of B.V.M., Windham Co., (1950) (Ukrainian), Rev. Pawlo Martyniuk, Admin.
Res., 69 Oak St., 06226. Tel: 203-423-5031.

STATE OF MASSACHUSETTS

Boston, Suffolk Co., Christ the King (1968), Rev. Jaroslaw Nalysnyk, Admin.
Res., 146 Forest Hills St., Jamaica Plain, 02130. Tel: 617-522-9720. [CEM]
Saturday Ukrainian School—.
Priests 1; Lay Teachers 3; Students 20.
Catechesis/Religious Programs—Priests 1; Lay Teachers 2; Students 20.

Fall River, Bristol Co., St. John-the-Baptist (1913). Attended by Woonsocket, RI. Rev. Zbigniew Brzezicki.
Church—339 Center St., 02724. Tel: 508-673-2353.
Res., 394 Blackstone St., Woonsocket, RI 02895. Tel: 401-762-2733. [JC]

Ludlow, Hampden Co., SS. Peter and Paul (1912)(1924) (Ukrainian), Rev. Kiril Angelov.
Res., 45 Newbury St., 01056. Tel: 413-583-2140.
Catechesis/Religious Programs—Priests 1; Students 14.

Pittsfield, Berkshire Co., St. John the Baptist (1921) (Ukrainian), Rev. Jeffery A.G. Rodeghero.
Res., 18 Watson St., 01201. Tel: 413-443-6798.

Salem, Essex Co., St. John the Baptist (1918) (Ukrainian), Rev. James Morris, Admin.
Mailing Address: P.O. Box 206, 01970-0206. Tel: 508-745-3151.
Church—124 Bridge St., 01970.
Catechesis/Religious Programs—Tel: 617-599-8138.
Students 12.

South Deerfield, Franklin Co., Holy Ghost (1920) (Ukrainian), Rev. Kiril Angelov.
Res., 44 Sugarloaf St., 01373. Tel: 413-665-3880.
Catechesis/Religious Programs—Priests 1; Lay Teachers 2; Students 15.

STATE OF NEW HAMPSHIRE

Manchester, Hillsboro Co., Protection of B.V.M. (1908) (Ukrainian), Rev. Joseph Lazor.
Church—54 Walnut St., 03104. Tel: 603-622-0034.
Res., 2 Partridge Ln., East Kingston, 03827. Tel: 603-642-5865.
Catechesis/Religious Programs—Sarah B. Lazor, D.R.E.
Priests 1; Lay Teachers 3; Students 20.

STATE OF NEW YORK

Amsterdam, Montgomery Co., St. Nicholas (1909) (Ukrainian), Rev. Stepan Yanovski, Admin.
Res., 24 Pulaski St., 12010. Tel: 518-842-8731. [CEM]

Auburn, Cayuga Co., SS. Peter and Paul (1901) (Ukrainian), Rev. Mihail Dubovici, Admin.
Res., 132 Washington St., 13021. Tel: 315-252-5573.
School—(Grades K-8). Tel: 315-252-5567. Sr. M. Boniface, O.S.B.M., Prin.
Sisters of St. Basil the Great 2; Lay Teachers 7; Students 138.
Catechesis/Religious Programs—Sisters 1; Lay Teachers 3; Students 35.

Bath, Steuben Co., Christ the King. Closed. For inquiries for parish records contact the Chancery.

Bronx, Bronx Co., St. Mary Protectress (1943) (Ukrainian), Rev. Maurice Popadiuk, O.S.B.M.
Church—1745 Washington Ave., 10457.
Res., East Beach Dr., Glen Cove, 11542. Tel: 516-671-0545; Fax: 516-676-7465. [JC]

Brooklyn, Kings Co., Holy Ghost (1913) (Ukrainian), Rev. Msgr. George Binkowski.
Church—162-168 N. Fifth St., 11211. Tel: 718-782-9592.
Mailing Address: 161 N. Fifth St., 11211.
Res., 159 N. Fifth St., 11211.
School—Tel: 718-782-0664. Lynda Larsen, Prin.
Priests 1; Lay Teachers 7; Students 84.
St. Nicholas (1916) (Ukrainian). Administered from St. Michael Parish, 21 Shonnard Place, Yongers, NY 10703, 914-963-0209.

Buffalo, Erie Co., St. Nicholas (1894) (Ukrainian), Very Rev. Marijan Procyk.
Res., 308 Fillmore Ave., 14206 Tel: 716-852-7566; Fax: 716-855-1319.
Catechesis/Religious Programs—Elaine P. Nowadly, D.R.E.
Priests 2; Students 50.

Cohoes, Albany Co., SS. Peter and Paul (1907) (Ukrainian), Rev. Vladimir Marusceac.
Res., 198 Ontario St., 12047. Tel: 518-237-0535.

Elmira Heights, Chemung Co., St. Nicholas (1895) (Ukrainian), Rev. Philip Weiner.
Res., 410 E. McCanns Blvd., 14903. Tel: 607-734-1221.
Catechesis/Religious Programs—Irene Moffe, D.R.E.
Priests 1; Lay Teachers 6; Students 39.

Fresh Meadows, Queens Co., Annunciation of the B.V.M. (1957) (Ukrainian), Rev. Roman Cholij.
Res., 48-26 171st St., 11365. Tel: 718-939-4116.
Catechesis/Religious Programs—Priests 1; Students 1.

Glen Spey, Sullivan Co., St. Volodymyr (1961) (Ukrainian), Rev. Ivan Tykohovytch.
Res., 2105 Rte. 41, 12737-5618. Tel: 914-856-5500. [JC]

Hamptonburgh, Orange Co., St. Andrew's Chapel (1983) (Ukrainian), Rev. Msgr. John Squiller.
Res., Rte. 1, Box 698, Sarah Wells Tr., Campbell Hall, 10916. Tel: 914-496-5506.
Catechesis/Religious Programs—Priests 1; Lay Teachers 1; Students 14.

Hempstead, Nassau Co., St. Vladimir (1944), Very Rev. Archpriest Charles Mezzomo, Admin.
Res., 709 Front St., 11550. Tel: 516-481-7717.
Parish Center: 226 Uniondale Ave., Uniondale, 11553. Tel: 516-485-0775.
Saturday Ukrainian School—.
Priests 1; Lay Teachers 8; Students 36.
Catechesis/Religious Programs—Priests 1; Lay Teachers 7; Students 38.

Hudson, Columbia Co., St. Nicholas (1923) (Ukrainian), Rev. Jeffery A.G. Rodeghero.
Res., 29 S. Second St., 12534. Tel: 518-828-5226.

Hunter, Greene Co., St. John the Baptist (1962) (Ukrainian). Administered from Holy Trinity Parish, R.R. 1, Box 129 Foordmore Rd., Kerhonkson, NY 12446, 914-626-2864.

Johnson City, Broome Co., Sacred Heart Ukrainian Catholic Church (1944) (Ukrainian), Rev. Ihor Stets.
Res., 230 Ukrainian Hill Rd., 13790. Tel: 607-797-6293. [CEM]
Saturday Ukrainian School—Tel: 607-798-9148.
Lay Teachers 3; Students 25.
Catechesis/Religious Programs—Tel: 607-723-7660. Christina Litwak, D.R.E.
Lay Teachers 5; Students 49.

Kenmore, Erie Co., St. John the Baptist (1904) (Ukrainian), Rev. Masim Kobasuk, O.S.B.M.
Res., 3275 Elmwood Ave., 14217. Tel: 716-873-5011.

Kerhonkson, Ulster Co., Holy Trinity (1965) (Ukrainian), Rev. Volodymyr Zaiats, Admin.
Mailing Address: R.R. 1, Box 129, Foordmore Rd., 12446.
Church—R.R. I-129, 12446. Tel: 914-626-2864.
Saturday Ukrainian School—.
Priests 1; Lay Teachers 2; Students 12.

Lackawanna, Erie Co., Our Lady of Perpetual Help (1925) (Ukrainian), Rev. Wasyl Hrynkiw.
Res., 1182 Ridge Rd., 14218. Tel: 716-823-6182.
Catechesis/Religious Programs—D.R.E.: Annette M. Nayda; Maria Slabyk.
Priests 1; Lay Teachers 2; Students 8.

Lancaster, Erie Co., St. Basil (1921) (Ukrainian). Attended by Lackawanna. Rev. Robert Moreno.
Res., 12 Embry Pl., 14086. Tel: 716-683-6018.
Church—3657 Walden Ave., 14086.

Little Falls, Herkimer Co., St. Nicholas (1912). Attended by Amsterdam. Rev. Stepan Yanovski.
Res., 150 Furnace St., 13365. Tel: 315-823-4474.

Long Island City, Queens Co., Holy Cross (1944) (Ukrainian), Revs. Philip Sandrick, O.S.B.M.; Gregory Chmylar, O.S.B.M.; Cyril Iszczuk, O.S.B.M. In res., Very Rev. Chistopher Woytyna, O.S.B.M., Prov.
Res., 31-12 30th St., 11106. Tel: 718-932-4060.
Catechesis/Religious Programs—Priests 1; Religious 2; Lay Teachers 2; Students 30.

New York, New York Co., St. George (1905) (Ukrainian), Very Rev. Patrick Paschak, O.S.B.M.; Revs. Lawrence Lawryniuk, O.S.B.M.; Taras Prokopiw, O.S.B.M.; Bernard Panczuk.
Res., 30 E. Seventh St., 10003. Tel: 212-674-1615; Fax: 212-475-7017.
School—215 E. Sixth St., 10003. Tel: 212-473-3130. Sr. Gabriel O.S.B.M., Prin.
Sisters of St. Basil the Great 1; Lay Teachers 8; Students 100.
High School—Tel: 212-473-3323.
Sisters 1; Lay Teachers 10; Students 140.

Niagara Falls, Niagara Co., Protection of B.V.M. (1920) (Ukrainian), Rev. Demetrius Laptuta, C.SS.R.
Res., 2713 Ferry Ave., 14301. Tel: 716-284-7066.

Ozone Park, Queens Co., St. Mary Protectress (Ukrainian), Very Rev. Peter Ohirko.
Res., 97-06 87th St., NY 11416. Tel: 718-845-5366.
Saturday Ukrainian School—.
Priests 1; Lay Teachers 2; Students 12.

Riverhead, Suffolk Co., St. John the Baptist (1924) (Ukrainian), Rev. Ihor Tarasiw.
Res., 820 Pond View Rd., 11901. Tel: 516-727-2766. [CEM]
Church—Franklin St., 11901.

Rochester, Monroe Co., St. Josaphat (1909) (Ukrainian), Rev. Msgr. Roman Golemba; Rev. Janus Jedrychowski.
Res., 940 Ridge Road E., 14621. Tel: 716-467-6457.
School—95 Stanton Ln., 14621. Tel: 716-266-8700. Sr. Bernitta Dub, S.S.M.I., Prin.
Priests 2; Sisters Servants of Mary Immaculate 2; Lay Teachers 10; Students 141.
Catechesis/Religious Programs—Lay Teachers 6; Students 141.
Convent—910 Ridge Rd., E., 14621. Tel: 716-266-1540.
Epiphany of Our Lord (1958) (Ukrainian), Rev. Vasile Godenciuc.
Res., 202 Carter St., 14621. Tel: 716-266-4036. [JC]

Rome, Oneida Co., St. Michael (1914) (Ukrainian). Attended by St. Vladimir, Utica. Rev. Michael Bundz.
Res., 296 Genessee St., Utica, 13502. Tel: 315-735-5138.
Church—133 River St., 13440. [CEM]

Spring Valley, Rockland Co., SS. Peter and Paul (1913) (Ukrainian), Rev. Oleksa Chouter.
Res., 41 Collins Ave., 10977. Tel: 914-356-1634.
Catechesis/Religious Programs—Tel: 201-529-4208. Irene Gojdycz, D.R.E.
Lay Teachers 4; Students 20.

Staten Island, Richmond Co., Holy Trinity (1949) (Ukrainian), Very Rev. Canon Lubomyr Mudry.
Res., 288 Vanderbilt Ave., 10304. Tel: 718-442-2555.

Syracuse, Onondaga Co., St. John the Baptist (1900), Revs. Ivan Mazuryk; James Karepin, O.P.; Bohdan Danylo; Deacon Myron Kotch.
Res., 207 Tompkins St., 13204. Tel: 315-478-5109.
Catechesis/Religious Programs—Priests 1; Lay Teachers 5; Students 36.

Troy, Rensselaer Co., Protection of B.V.M. (1952) (Ukrainian). Attended by SS. Peter and Paul, Cohoes. Rev. Vladimir Marusceac.
Res., 198 Ontario St., Cohoes, 12047. Tel: 518-237-0535. [JC]
Church—459 Second St., 12180. Tel: 518-274-5318.

Utica, Oneida Co., St. Volodymyr the Great (1950) (Ukrainian), Rev. Michael Bundz, Admin.
Res., 296 Genessee St., 13502. Tel: 315-735-5138. [CEM]
Saturday Ukrainian School—.
Priests 1; Lay Teachers 1; Students 15.

Watervliet, Albany Co., St. Nicholas (1905) (Ukrainian), Rev. Mikhail Myshchuk.
Res., 2410-4th Ave., 12189. Tel: 518-273-6752. [CEM][JC]
Saturday Ukrainian School & C.C.D.—.
Lay Teachers 6; Students 31.

West Islip, Suffolk Co., Holy Family (1924) (Ukrainian), Rev. Myroslav Jatsiv.
Res., 471 Montauk Hwy., 11795-4475. Tel: 516-661-0031.

Yonkers, Westchester Co., St. Michael (1899) (Ukrainian), Revs. Myroslav Trojanowski; Peter Gronski.
Res., 21 Shonnard Pl., 10703. Tel: 914-963-0209.
Catechesis/Religious Programs—Priests 1; Students 93.

STATE OF RHODE ISLAND

Woonsocket, Providence Co., St. Michael (1908), Rev. Zbigniew Brzezicki.
Res., 394 Blackstone St., 02895. Tel: 401-762-2733. [CEM][JC]
Church—396 Blackstone St., 02895.

Special Assignment:
Reverend Monsignors—
Mosko, Leon A., Chancellor
Reverend Fathers—
Morse, Jonathan, Ukrainian Catholic Relief, Inc.
Shubiak, Stephen, U.S. Chap. Corps

Retired:
Mitred Archpriest—
Andrushkiw, Vladimir, 195 Glenbrook Rd., Stamford, CT 06902
Rev. Archpriest—
Pelensky, Thor, P.O. Box 533, Westmoreland, NY 13490
Reverend Monsignors—
Chrepta, Stephen J., 16134 Veronica St., East Detroit, MI 48021
Feddish, Basil, 83 Sylvester Ave., Hawthorne, NJ 07506
Reverend Canons—
Sharanevych, Emile, 332 Foordmore Rd., Kerhonkson, NY 12446. Tel: 914-626-4947
Shust, Yaroslav, Gloria dei Towers, Apt. 307, 770 Welsh Rd., Huntingdon Valley, PA 19006. Tel: 215-947-1111
Reverend Fathers—
Graskow, Paul, 3415 La Fayette Ave., S., Seattle, WA 98144
Humanitzki, Theodore, 11416 Pine Forest Dr., New Port Richey, FL 34654. Tel: 813-856-4432
Karas, Boudau, 261 19th St., Brooklyn, NY 11215
Rt. Rev. Mitred Msgr—
Chomko, Stephen, 706 Warren St., Berwick, PA 18603
Very Rev.—
Figol, Volodymyr, St. Basil Seminary, 195 Glenbrook Rd., Stanford, CT 06902

Permanent Deacons:
Cybulski, Marius, Christ the King, Boston, MA
Hirniak, Mark, St. Vladimir, Stamford, CT
Homick, Willis, SS. Peter & Paul, Auburn, NY
Kotch, Myron, St. John the Baptist, Syracuse, NY
Malachowsky, Yourij, Holy Cross, Long Island City, NY

INSTITUTIONS LOCATED IN THE DIOCESE

[A] SEMINARIES, DIOCESAN

STAMFORD. *St. Basil College*, 195 Glenbrook Rd., 06902-3099. Tel: 203-324-4578; Fax: 203-357-7681. Most Rev. Basil H. Losten, D.D., S.T.L., LL.D., Pres.; Revs. Edward Young, B.A., S.T.B., Rector; Paul Wolensky, Vice Rector; Rev. Msgr. Peter Skrincosky, B.A., M.S., S.E.O.D., Dir. of Spiritual Formation; Rt. Rev. Mitred Msgr John Terlecky, B.A., M.A., M.L.S., Bursar; Rev. Robert Smolley, B.S., M.Div., Prefect for Students; Dr. Edward Bordeau, Ph.D., Dean and Registrar; Ms. Lubow Wolynetz, B.A., M.L.S., Librarian. Household Dept. in charge of the Institute of Catechists of the Heart of Jesus.

[B] SEMINARIES, RELIGIOUS

GLEN COVE, NY. *Basilian Fathers Novitiate of the Order of St. Basil the Great*, E. Beach Dr., 11542. Tel: 516-671-0545; Fax: 516-676-7465. Very Rev. Maurice Popadiuk, O.S.B.M., Supr. & Master of Novices; Revs. Theodosius Ilicki, O.S.B.M., Asst. Master of Novices; Julian Katrij, O.S.B.M., Prov. Consultant; Hilarion Benedik, O.S.B.M.; Athanasius B. Pekar, O.S.B.M. Priests 5; Brothers 2; Novices 2; Scholastics 5.

[C] NURSERY SCHOOLS

STAMFORD. *St. Ann's Nursery School*, 111 W. North St., 06902. Tel: 203-323-1237; 348-5675. Missionary Sisters of Mother of God 6; Nursery 44; Staff 3.

[D] ADULT FACILITIES

SLOATSBURG, NY. *St. Joseph's Home*, 125 Sisters Servants Ln., Box 25, 10974-0025. Tel: 914-753-2555.

For a complete listing, refer to the Special Care Facilities section.

[E] MONASTERIES AND RESIDENCES OF PRIESTS AND BROTHERS

NEW YORK, NY. *Provincialate of Basilian Fathers*. Res., 31-12 30th St., Long Island City, 11106. Tel: 718-278-6622. Very Rev. Chistopher Woytyna, O.S.B.M., Protohegumen. Priests 24; Scholastics 8; Brothers 3; Novices 2.

WEST BURKE, VT. *Mary Theotokos Centre*, P.O. Box 88, 05871-0088. Tel: 802-467-1132. Rev. Stephen C. von Fauer, Supr.

[F] MONASTERIES OF NUNS

STAMFORD. *Missionary Sisters of Mother of God*, 111 W. North St., 06902. Tel: 203-323-1237. Sr. Josepha Kruchinsky, M.S.M.G., Supr.; Rev. Jonathan Morse, Chap.

MIDDLETOWN, NY. *Nuns of St. Basil the Great*, Sacred Heart Monastery, 33 Keasel Rd., 10940. Tel: 914-343-1308. Mother M. Georgianna Snihur, O.S.B.M., Supr. Sisters 6.

SLOATSBURG, NY. *Immaculate Conception Provincialate*, Sisters Servants Ln., 9 Emmanuel Dr., P.O. Box 6, 10974-0006. Tel: 914-753-2840. Sisters Servants of Mary Immaculate Conception Province. Sr. Michele Yakymovitch, S.S.M.I., Prov. Supr.; Rev. Stephen Shubiak, Chap. Sisters 20.

[G] MISCELLANEOUS

STAMFORD. *Institute of Catechists of the Heart of Jesus*, 161 Glenbrook Rd., 06902. Tel: 203-327-6374. Cecilia Daciuk, Supr. Total Members 5.

**Ukrainian Catholic Relief, Inc.*, 14 Peveril Rd., 06902.

SLOATSBURG, NY. *St. Mary's Villa Spiritual, Cultural & Educational Center*, 150 Sisters Servants Ln., P.O. Box 6, 10974-0006. Tel: 914-753-5100. Sr. Bernardine Symionow, S.S.M.I., Coord.

RELIGIOUS INSTITUTES OF MEN REPRESENTED IN THE DIOCESE

For further details refer to the corresponding bracketed number in the Religious Institutes of Men or Women section.

[0180]—*Order of St. Basil the Great.*—O.S.B.M.
[1070]—*Redemptorists.*—C.Ss.R.

RELIGIOUS INSTITUTES OF WOMEN REPRESENTED IN THE DIOCESE

[]—*Institute of Catechists of the Heart of Jesus.*
[2810]—*Missionary Sisters of Mother of God.*—M.S.M.G.
[3730]—*Sisters of the Order of St. Basil the Great.*—O.S.B.M.
[3610]—*Sisters Servants of Mary Immaculate.*—S.S.M.I.

NECROLOGY

† Bryda, Richard, Staten Island, NY, Holy Trinity. —Died March 5, 1996.
† Fedorchuck, Rev. Msgr. Peter, (Retired). —Died April 27, 1996.

Byzantine Eparchy of Van Nuys

Most Reverend

GEORGE M. KUZMA, D.D.

Bishop of Van Nuys; ordained May 29, 1955; appointed Auxiliary Bishop of the Byzantine Eparchy of Passaic November 11, 1986; consecrated February 4, 1987; appointed Bishop of Eparchy of Van Nuys October 23, 1990; installed as Second Bishop of Van Nuys January 15, 1991. *Res., 8141 N. 16 St., Phoenix, AZ, 85020.*

ESTABLISHED DECEMBER 3, 1981.

Embraces all Catholics of the Byzantine-Ruthenian Church in the States of California, Oregon, Washington, Idaho, Nevada, Arizona, Utah, Wyoming, Montana, Colorado, New Mexico, Alaska and Hawaii.

For legal titles of parishes and diocesan institutions, consult the Chancery Office.

Legal Title: The Byzantine Catholic Bishop of Van Nuys, a Corporation Sole.

Principal Patron-Patronage of the Mother of God (Pokrov).

Chancery Office: 8131 N. 16 St., Phoenix, AZ, 85020. Tel.: 602-861-9778; Fax: 602-861-9796.

E-mail address: EVNizer@aol.com

STATISTICAL OVERVIEW

Personnel	
Bishop	1
Priests: Diocesan Active in Diocese	12
Priests: Active Outside Diocese	2
Priests: Retired, Sick or Absent	4
Number of Diocesan Priests	18
Religious Priests in Diocese	4
Extern Priests in Diocese	3
Ordinations:	
Permanent Deacons in Diocese	3
Total Brothers	4
Total Sisters	4
Parishes	
Parishes	16
With Resident Pastor:	
Resident Diocesan Priests	13
Resident Religious Priests	3
Without Resident Pastor:	
Pastoral Centers	4
Professional Ministry Personnel:	
Brothers	4
Sisters	4
Welfare	
Educational	
Diocesan Students in Other Seminaries	1
Total Seminarians	1
Catechesis/Religious Education:	
High School Students	76
Elementary Students	336
Total Students Under Catholic Instruction	413
Vital Statistics	
Receptions into the Church:	
Infant Baptism Totals	65
Adult Baptism Totals	7
Received into Full Communion	22
First Communions	128
Confirmations	140
Marriages:	
Catholic	12
Interfaith	5
Total Marriages	17
Deaths	28
Total Catholic Population	2,951

Former Bishop—Most Rev. THOMAS V. DOLINAY, D.D., ord. May 16, 1948; cons. Nov. 23, 1976; appt. Tutular Bishop of Thyatira and Auxiliary of Passiac, Sept. 23, 1976 First Ordinary of the Byzantine Catholic Diocese of Van Nuys, CA. Installed March 9, 1982; appt. Coadjutor Archbishop of Pittsburgh Byzantine Rite, March 13, 1990; succeeded to June 12, 1991; died April 13, 1993.

Chancery Office—Byzantine Catholic Eparchy of Van Nuys, Pastoral Center, 8131 N. 16th St., Phoenix, AZ, 85020. Tel: 602-861-9778; Fax: 602-861-9796. Office Hours: Mon.-Thurs. 10-3; Fri. 10-1.

Protosyncellus and Chancellor—Very Rev. WESLEY IZER, S.D.B.

Syncelli—Pacific Northwest Vicariate: Very Rev. STEPHEN GRESKOWIAK, Italo-Greeks Vicariate: Rt. Rev. FRANCIS M. VIVONA, S.T.M., J.C.L., Western Vicariate: Vacant; Southwest Vicariate: Very Rev. STEPHEN WASHKO.

Treasurer—Sr. CELESTINE PETRUSKA, O.S.B.M.

Eparchial Consultors - Presbyteral Council—Very Revs. STEPHEN GRESKOWIAK; WESLEY IZER, S.D.B.; Rev. JOSEPH STANICHAR, V.F.; Very Rev. STEPHEN WASHKO; Rt. Rev. FRANCIS M. VIVONA, S.T.M., J.C.L.

Diocesan Matrimonial Tribunal—Office of the Tribunal Eparcy of Van Nuys, 336 E. Desert Inn Rd., P.O. Box 18316, Las Vegas, NV, 89114-8316. Tel: 702-735-1210; Fax: 702-735-5146.

Judicial Vicar—Rt. Rev. FRANCIS M. VIVONA, S.T.M., J.C.L.

Promoter of Justice—Very Rev. Archpriest MICHAEL MORAN, J.C.D.

Secretary—Ms. SIDNEY MARSH.

Defender—Rev. PHILIP ACQUARO, C.S.B., J.C.D.

Judge—Very Rev. STEPHEN WASHKO.

Notary—Ms. SIDNEY MARSH.

Building Commission—Most Rev. GEORGE M. KUZMA; Very Rev. WESLEY IZER, S.D.B.; Deacon RICHARD WORTMAN.

Director of Religious Education and Evangelization—Sr. BARBARA SWINDELLS, O.S.B.M.

Eparchial Finance Commission—Most Rev. GEORGE M. KUZMA, Chm.; Very Rev. WESLEY IZER, S.D.B.; Sr. CELESTINE PETRUSKA, O.S.B.M.; Mrs. JOSEFINA DANOVICH; Mr. WILLIAM GOMBAR.

Vocation Director—Rev. ROBERT M. PIPTA.

Ecclesiatical Notary—Rev. ROBERT M. PIPTA.

Liturgy & Music Commission—Very Rev. STEPHEN WASHKO, Chm.; Revs. JOSEPH HUTSKO; ROBERT M. PIPTA; Sr. CHRISTOPHER MALCOVSKY, O.S.B.M.; Mr. BASIL RABAYDA, JR.

"Eparchial Newsletter"—Very Rev. WESLEY IZER, S.D.B., Editor.

Director of Development & Stewardship—Sr. CHRISTOPHER MALCOVSKY, O.S.B.M.

CLERGY, PARISHES, MISSIONS AND PAROCHIAL SCHOOLS

STATE OF ARIZONA

Gilbert, Maricopa Co., St. Thomas the Apostle, Rev. Philip A. Acquaro, C.S.B., Admin.; Deacon John Miller.
Mailing Address: P.O. Box 667, 85299-0667.
19 W. Bruce Ave., 85233. Tel: 602-497-5799.

Phoenix, Maricopa Co., St. Stephen. (Byzantine Catholic Pro-Cathedral). Revs. Wesley W. Izer, S.D.B., Rector; Robert M. Pipta; Sr. Christopher Malcovsky, O.S.B.M., Pastoral Assoc.; Deacon Michael Durka. In res., Revs. John Bovankovich (PSC) (Retired); John Dorich.
Res., 8141 N. 16th St., 85020-3999. Tel: 602-943-5379.
Convent—St. Stephen Convent, 8141 N. 16th St. #27, 85020. Tel: 602-944-5121; Fax: 602-861-9796. Sisters 2.

Tucson, Pima Co., St. Melany, Rev. William Skurla.
Church—1212 N. Sahuara, 85712-5018. Tel: 520-886-4225; Fax: 520-751-4574.

STATE OF ALASKA

Anchorage, Anchorage Co., Saint Nicholas of Myra, Rev. Stephen Greskowiak.
Res., 2200 Arctic Blvd., 99503. Tel: 907-277-6731; Fax: 907-277-6731.

STATE OF CALIFORNIA

Van Nuys, Los Angeles Co., Cathedral of St. Mary, Very Rev. Archpriest Michael Moran, Rector; Sr. Barbara Swindells, O.S.B.M., Pastoral Assoc.; Deacon Michael Hladky, (Retired).
Res., 5329 Sepulveda Blvd., 91411-3441. Tel: 818-907-5511.
Convent—5335 Sepulveda Blvd., 91411-3441. Tel: 818-907-1261.

Anaheim, Orange Co., Annunciation, Rev. Msgr. George N. Vida (PBR).
Res., 319 N. Harbor Blvd., 92805-2599. Tel: 714-533-6292.

Fontana, San Bernardino Co., St. Nicholas, Rev. Kurt Burnette, Admin.
Res., 9112 Oleander Ave., 92335-5599. Tel: 909-822-9917.

Fresno, Fresno Co., Byzantine Catholic Community of Fresno, CA. Closed. For inquiries for parish records contact the Chancery.

Palm Springs, Riverside Co., Byzantine Catholic Community of Palm Springs, CA. Closed. For inquiries for parish records contact the Chancery.

Sacramento, Sacramento Co., St. Philip the Apostle, Rev. William O'Brien, Admin.; Deacon Richard Wortman.
Mailing Address: 7001 Florin Rd., 95828-3015. Tel: 916-383-1552.

San Diego, San Diego Co., Holy Angels, Rev. Melvin Rybarczyk, C.R., Admin.
Mailing Address: 2235 Galahad Rd., 92123-3931. Tel: 619-277-2511; Fax: 619-277-5792.

San Jose-Palo Alto, Santa Clara Co., St. Basil the Great, Rev. William O'Brien, Admin.
Res., 923 Trophy Dr., Mountain View, 94040-2994. Tel: 415-965-1699.

San Luis Obispo, San Luis Obispo Co., Saint Anne, Rev. Edmund M. Idranyi, Admin.; Mr. Julius Dicky, Financial Admin.
Mailing Address: 222 Foothill Blvd., 93405-1540. Tel: 805-543-8883.

San Mateo, San Mateo Co., St. Macrina. Closed. All

records at the Chancery Office.

Stockton, San Joaquin Co., Byzantine Catholic Community of Stockton. Closed. For inquiries for parish records contact the Chancery.

STATE OF COLORADO

Colorado Springs, El Paso Co., Byzantine Catholic Mission. Attended by Holy Protection of the Mother of God, Denver.
1201 S. Elizabeth St., Denver, 80210. Tel: 303-778-8283.

Denver, Denver Co., Holy Protection of the Mother of God, Rev. Joseph Hutsko.
Res., 1074 S. Cook St., 80209-4923.
Church—1201 S. Elizabeth St., 80210. Tel: 303-778-8283.

STATE OF NEVADA

Las Vegas, Clark Co., Our Lady of Wisdom Italo-Greek Mission,
P.O. Box 18316, 89114-8316. Tel: 602-735-1210; Fax: 702-735-5146. Rev. Archimandrite Francis Vivona, Syncellus; Deacon Joshua Alves.
St. Gabriel the Archangel, Rev. Stephen G. Washko.
Res., 6904 Wood Bark Dr., 89119.
Church—2250 E. Maule Ave., 89119-4607. Tel: 702-361-2431; Fax: 702-361-2431#1.

STATE OF NEW MEXICO

Albuquerque, Bernalillo Co., Our Lady of Perpetual Help, Rev. Christopher L. Zugger; Deacon Frank Lucero.
Res., 1840 Palomas Dr. N.E., 87110-5113.
Church—1837 Alvarado N.E., 87110. Tel: 505-256-1539; Fax: 505-256-1278.

Las Cruces, Dona Ana Co., Byzantine Catholic Mission. Closed. Records are located at Albuquerque Parish.

STATE OF OREGON

Portland, Multnomah Co., Byzantine Catholic Community of Portland, OR. Attended by St. John Chrysostom, Seattle, WA. Rev. Joseph Stanichar.
Mailing Address: St. John Chrysostom Church, 1305 S. Lander St., Seattle, WA 98144.
Chapel—8261 S.E. Clatsop, 97266.

STATE OF UTAH

Salt Lake City, Salt Lake Co., Byzantine Catholic Mission. Closed. For inquiries for parish records contact the Chancery.

STATE OF WASHINGTON

Lacy, Thurston Co., Byzantine Catholic Community Attended from St. John Chrysostom, Seattle, WA, Rev. Joseph Stanichar.
Res., S. 1305 Lander St., Seattle, 98144-5038. Tel: 206-329-9219.

Seattle, King Co., St. John Chrysostom, Rev. Joseph Stanichar.
Res., S. 1305 Lander St., 98144-5038. Tel: 206-329-9219.

Spokane, Spokane Co., SS. Cyril & Methodius, Rev. David Logan.
Res., N. 4315 Evergreen Rd., 99216-1298. Tel: 509-922-4527.

Walla Walla, Walla Walla Co., Byzantine Catholic Mission. Closed. For inquiries for parish records contact the Spokane parish.

On Special Assignment:
Reverend Fathers—
Kovach, John, Shrine of the Weeping Madonna, 17486 Mumford Rd., Burton, OH 44021-9640
Michalenko, Alexei, Chap., Georgetown Law Center, 600 New Jersey Ave., N.W., Washington, DC 20001

On Leave:
Reverend Fathers—
Barrand, James

Retired:
Reverend Fathers—
Ridella, Joseph, 66285 Hacienda Ave., Desert Hot Springs, CA 92240
Rt. Rev. Mitred Arch—
Artim, Michael, 13211 Venus Way, Anchorage, AK 99515

Permanent Deacons:
Alves, Joshua (CHI), Las Vegas, NV
Hladky, Michael, Van Nuys, CA
Miller, John (PHX), Gilber, AZ
Wortman, Richard, Sacramento, CA

INSTITUTIONS LOCATED IN THE DIOCESE

[A] RELIGIOUS COMMUNITIES

PHOENIX. *Congregation of Saint Basil*, 8141 N. 16th St., #22, 85020-3901. Tel: 602-395-0457. Rev. Philip Acquaro, C.S.B.
St. Stephen Convent, 8141 N. 16th St. #27, 85020. Tel: 602-944-5121; Fax: 602-861-9796. Sr. Christopher, O.S.B.M.; Sr. Celestine, O.S.B.M.
Salesians of Don Bosco, 8141 N. 16th St., #19, 85020-3999. Tel: 602-943-5379. Very Rev. Wesley Izer, S.D.B.

NEWBERRY SPRINGS, CA. *Holy Resurrection Monastery*. (Monastic Community of Men est. Aug. 4, 1995), 45704 Valley Center Rd., 92365. Tel: 619-257-4008. Rev. Nicholas Zachariadis, Hegumen; Bros. Luke Bell, Guest Master; Maximos Davies, Protos.

REDLANDS, CA. *Byzantine Brothers of St. Francis*, 9458 Buckeye St., 92374. Tel: 909-793-1127. Bros. Michael Sullivan, B.B.S.F., Supr.; John Gray, B.B.S.F., Treas.

VAN NUYS, CA. *Saint Mary Convent*, 5335 Sepulveda Blvd., 91411-3441. Tel: 818-907-1261. Order of Sisters of St. Basil the Great. Sr. Barbara, O.S.B.M.; Sr. Fabiola, O.S.B.M.

RELIGIOUS INSTITUTES OF MEN REPRESENTED IN THE DIOCESE

For further details refer to the corresponding bracketed number in the Religious Institutes of Men or Women section.

[0170]—*Basilian Fathers.*—C.S.B.

[]—*Byzantine Brothers of St. Francis.*—B.B.S.F.

[0520]—*Franciscan Friars.*—O.F.M.

[1190]—*Salesians of Don Bosco.*—S.D.B.

RELIGIOUS INSTITUTES OF WOMEN REPRESENTED IN THE DIOCESE

[3730]—*Sisters of the Order of St. Basil the Great.*—O.S.B.M.

NECROLOGY

(No Deaths)

U.S. TERRITORIAL SEES
Archdiocese of Agana

Most Reverend

ANTHONY SABLAN APURON, O.F.M.CAP., D.D.

Archbishop of Agana; ordained August 26, 1972; appointed Auxiliary Bishop December 8, 1983; ordained Titular Bishop of Muzuca February 19, 1984; appointed Apostolic Administrator to the Archdiocese October 27, 1985; succeeded to Metropolitan See May 11, 1986. *Res., Archbishop's Residence Cuesta San Ramon, Agana, GU, 96910.* Tel.: 671-472-6116; 472-6573.

ERECTED BY POPE PIUS X, MARCH 1, 1911 AND COMMITTED TO THE ORDER OF FRIARS MINOR CAPUCHIN. EXTENDED TO ALL THE MARIANAS ISLANDS, JULY 4, 1946, WAKE ISLAND, JUNE 14, 1948. ELEVATED TO A DIOCESE, OCTOBER 14, 1965, AS A SUFFRAGAN OF SAN FRANCISCO. ELEVATED TO METROPOLITAN ARCHDIOCESE, MAY 20, 1984 WITH A SUFFRAGAN SEE, DIOCESE OF CAROLINE-MARSHALLS AND DIOCESE OF CHALAN KANOA (SUBSEQUENTLY ADDED JANUARY 13, 1985). MEMBER OF CEPAC CONFERENCE. MEMBER OF FEDERATION OF CATHOLIC BISHOPS CONFERENCE OF OCEANIA. OBSERVER TO NCCB-USCC CONFERENCE.

GUAM IS A TERRITORY OF THE U.S.A. BY ACT OF THE U.S. CONGRESS JULY 21, 1949.

Legal Title: *Archbishop of Guam, a Corporation Sole.*

STATISTICAL OVERVIEW

Personnel	
Archbishop	1
Priests: Diocesan Active in Diocese	27
Priests: Active Outside Diocese	2
Number of Diocesan Priests	29
Religious Priests in Diocese	19
Ordinations:	
Permanent Deacons in Diocese	9
Total Brothers	1
Total Sisters	120
Parishes	
Parishes	24
With Resident Pastor:	
Resident Diocesan Priests	13
Resident Religious Priests	11
Without Resident Pastor:	
Missions	2
Welfare	
Homes for the Aged	1
Total Assisted	65
Day Care and Extended Day Care Centers	4
Total Assisted	525
Specialized Homes	1
Total Assisted	175
Special Centers for Social Services	1
Total Assisted	120
Educational	
Diocesan Students in Other Seminaries	4
Students Religious	1
Total Seminarians	5
High Schools, Diocesan and Parish	3
Total Students	1,058
Elementary Schools, Diocesan and Parish	7
Total Students	2,699
Catechesis/Religious Education:	
High School Students	2,250
Elementary Students	4,589
Total Students Under Catholic Instruction	10,601
Teachers in the Diocese:	
Priests	2
Sisters	28
Lay Teachers	191
Vital Statistics	
Receptions into the Church:	
Infant Baptism Totals	2,289
Adult Baptism Totals	35
Received into Full Communion	54
First Communions	1,223
Confirmations	785
Marriages:	
Catholic	233
Interfaith	8
Total Marriages	241
Deaths	474
Total Catholic Population	114,906
Total Population	136,421

Former Vicars-Apostolic—Most Rev. FRANCIS X. VILLA Y MATEU, O.F.M.Cap., D.D., cons. Titular Bishop of Adraha, Oct. 1, 1911; died at Agana, Jan. 1, 1913.—Most Rev. AUGUSTIN BERNAUS Y SERRA, O.F.M.Cap., D.D., cons. Titular Bishop of Milopotamo, May 9, 1913; transferred to Vicariate-Apostolic of Bluefields, Nicaragua, 1914.—Most Rev. JOAQUIN FELIPE OLAIZ Y ZABALZA, O.F.M.Cap., D.D., cons. Titular Bishop of Docimeo, Nov. 30, 1914; died at Pamplona, Spain, Dec. 8, 1945.—Most Rev. MIGUEL ANGEL OLAND Y URTEAGA, O.F.M.Cap., D.D., cons. Titular Bishop of Lagina, May 5, 1935; resigned and made Asst. at Pontifical Throne Aug. 20, 1945; died at Agana, Guam May 21, 1970.—Most Rev. APOLLINARIS W. BAUMGARTNER, O.F.M.Cap., D.D., cons. Sept. 18, 1945; appt. First Bishop of Agana, Oct. 14, 1965; died at Agana, Guam Dec. 18, 1970.—Most Rev. FELIXBERTO CAMACHO FLORES, ord. April 30, 1949; appt. Apostolic Admin., Diocese of Agana, May 2, 1969; appt. Titular Bishop of Stonj, March 19, 1970; cons. May 17, 1970; succeeded to See, May 15, 1971; died Oct. 25, 1985.

Archdiocesan College of Consultors—Revs. DAVID C. QUITUGUA; ADRIAN CRISTOBAL; MICHAEL DALTON, O.F.M.Cap.; JOSE ANTONIO ABAD; JUAN CAMACHO; JAMES BENAVENTE; KENNETH HEZEL, S.J.; JOSE VILLAGOMEZ, O.F.M.Cap.

Vicar General—Rev. DAVID C. QUITUGUA.

Chancellor—Rev. ADRIAN CRISTOBAL.

Chancery Office—

Finance Officer and Business Mgr.—Mr. DOMINIC KIM. Assistants: Mrs. MARIA GUIAO; Mrs. ANITA DIZON.

Records Office—Mrs. JUNE UNGACTA.

Computers—Mr. MANNY CRUZ.

Receptionist—Ms. CHRISTINE OFTANA, Chancery Office: *196-B Cuesta San Ramon, Agana, 96910.* Tel: 671-472-6116; 472-8024; 472-6573; Fax: 671-477-3519. Office Hours: Mon.-Fri. 8-12 & 1-4.

Finance Council—Rev. JUAN CAMACHO. Tel: 671-646-5649; 472-6116. Sr. MARY STEPHEN TORRES, R.S.M. Tel: 671-646-7246. Mr. T. ROY SULLIVAN. Tel: 617-472-8891.

Archdiocesan Offices and Directors

Alee Shelter Program for Spousal Abuse—Sr. EILEEN MEARNS, R.G.S., Dir., *c/o Catholic Social Services, P.O. Box EJ, Agana, 96910.* Tel: 671-646-1924.

Campaign For Human Development—Sr. MARIA THECLA CAMACHO, R.S.M., Dir., *P.O. Box 17211, Inarajan, 96916.* Tel: 671-828-8285.

Campus Ministry—Rev. KENNETH HEZEL, S.J., Dir. Tel: 671-734-3507; Fax: 671-734-2943.

Catholic Charismatic Movement—Vacant.

Catholic Charities-Guam—Rev. ADRIAN M. CRISTOBAL, Chm., *196-B Cuesta San Ramon, Agana, 96910.* Tel: 671-472-6116.

Catholic Daughters of the Americas—Mrs. JOSEPHINE MCDONALD, Regent; Rev. DAVID I.A. QUITUGUA, Chap. Tel: 671-477-5632.

Catholic Education Office—Rev. JOSE ANTONIO ABAD, Vicar Catholic Educ.; Dr. KENNETH CARRIVEAU, Supt. Catholic Schools; Sr. JEAN ANN CRISOSTOMO, S.S.N.D., Curriculum Coord. Tel: 671-472-6116; Fax: 671-477-3519.

Catholic Educational Radio—Mr. JOHN DUNGCA, Program Mgr., *P.O. Box DZ, Agana, 96910.* Tel: 671-477-1875; Fax: 671-477-5656.

Catholic Social Services - Guam—Mrs. CERILA RAPADAS, Dir., *P.O. Box EJ, Agana, 96910.* Tel: 671-649-5717; Fax: 671-649-9224.

Cemetery Council—Rev. Msgr. ZOILO L.G. CAMACHO, Pres.

Chaplains—See separate listing.

Communications—Rev. BRIGIDO ARROYO, Dir., *P.O. Box 2553, Agana, 96910.* Tel: 671-472-6427.

Confraternity of Christian Mothers—Rev. ADRIAN CRISTOBAL, Spiritual Dir.; Mrs. PATRICIA GUERRERO, Pres.

Cursillo in Christianity Movement—Rev. JOEL DE LOS REYES, Spiritual Dir. Tel: 671-472-6116.

Office of Family and Youth Ministry—Coordinators: Mr. JOSE CALUAG; Mrs. JOSIE CALUAG, *196-B Cuesta San Ramon, Agana, 96910.* Tel: 671-472-6116; Fax: 671-472-4406.

Interfaith Volunteer Caregivers, Inc.—Mrs. LEONILA HERRERO, Dir. Tel: 671-472-2944; Fax: 671-477-2273.

Guma San Francisco—Mr. JOHN LIZAMA, *P.O. Box 306, Agana, 96910.* Tel: 671-472-6068.

Knights of Columbus—Hon. VIC CHIONG, District Deputy; Rev. BRIGIDO ARROYO, Chap. Knights of Columbus No. 5666, *P.O. Box BP, Agana, 96910.* Pale San Vitores Council, JOSE M. QUICHOCHO, Grand Knight Archbishop Felixberto Flores Council, Mr. EDWIN CARBONEL, Grand Knight, *P.O. Box 1252, Tamuning, 96911.*

Knights of Saint Sylvester—Knight Sir CRISTOBAL DUENAS. Tel: 671-472-6201.

Korean Catholic Community—Rev. PETER KANG, *P.O. Box 155, Agana, 96910.* Tel: 671-472-3330; Fax: 671-472-3340.

Legion of Mary—Mrs. JUANITA ULLOA, Pres.

Liturgical Commission—Rev. PATRICK GARCIA, Chm., *Cuesta San Ramon, Agana, 96910.*

Marriage Preparation Programs—

Pre-Cana Classes (Agana)—*Cuesta San Ramon, Agana, 96910.*

Pre-Cana Classes (Dededo)—*Santa Barbara, 48 Iglesia Circle, Dededo, 96912.*

Evenings for the Engaged—FRANCIS & CONNIE GUERRERO, Contact Couple, *c/o Barrigada Church, 229 San Roke St., Barrigada, 96913.*

Catholic Engaged Encounter—Rev. JOSE ANTONIO ABAD; Vicar Catholic Educ. Tel: 671-472-6116.

Marriage Encounter—Vacant.

Ministry with Persons with Disabilities—Ms. CATHERINE LEON GUERRERO, Dir. Tel: 671-472-3141.

Office of Religious Education—Rev. EFREN ADVERSARIO, Assoc. Dir.; Mrs. HELEN A.Q. FLORES, Sec. Tel: 671-472-6116; Fax: 671-472-3519.

Pontifical Holy Childhood Association & Pontifical Society for the Propagation of the Faith—Rev. Msgr. ZOILO L.G. CAMACHO. Tel: 671-632-5659.

Secular Franciscans—Rev. DANIEL CRISTOBAL, O.F.M.Cap., Spiritual Dir.
Tribunal—
Judicial Vicar—Rev. DAVID C. QUITUGUA, J.C.D.
Promoter of Justice—Rev. JOSE VILLAGOMEZ, O.F.M.Cap.
Defender of the Bond—Rev. ADRIAN CRISTOBAL.
Associate Judges—Rev. Msgr. ZOILO CAMACHO; Rev. ROBERT MAHER, O.F.M.Cap.; Sr. MARIA ANA LEE, O.P., J.C.L.; Rev. RAYMOND CEPEDA.
Advocates—Revs. EFREN ADVERSARIO; JAMES BENAVENTE.
Notary—Rev. FELIXBERTO LEON GUERRERO, O.F.M.Cap.
Office of Vocations—Revs. ADRIAN CRISTOBAL, Co-Dir. JAMES BENAVENTE, Co-Dir., *196-B Cuesta San Ramon, Agana, 96910.* Tel: 671-472-6116; 472-8024; 472-6201; Fax: 671-472-3519; 472-1729.

CLERGY, PARISHES, MISSIONS AND PAROCHIAL SCHOOLS

CITY OF AGANA
ISLAND OF GUAM

1—DULCE NOMBRE DE MARIA CATHEDRAL - BASILICA (1669), Most Rev. Anthony Sablan Apuron, O.F.M.Cap., D.D.; Revs. James L.G. Benavente; David C. Quitugua; Deacons Michael McCarthy; John Dierking.
Res., 207 Archbishop Felixberto C. Flores St., 96910. Tel: 671-472-6201; 477-1842; Fax: 671-472-1729.
Catechesis/Religious Programs—Students 110.

OUTSIDE THE CITY OF AGANA

Agana Heights, Our Lady of the Blessed Sacrament (1948), Rev. Michel W. Dalton, O.F.M.Cap.
Res., 135 Gunut Cir., 96919. Tel: 671-472-6246; Fax: 671-472-3335.
Catechesis/Religious Programs—Eleanor Cruz, D.R.E.
Students 269.

Agat, Our Lady of Mount Carmel (1957), Rev. Augustin Gumataotao, O.F.M.Cap.; Deacon Frank Tenorio.
Res., 135 Gunut Cir., Agana Heights, 96919. Tel: 671-565-2136. [CEM]
School—P.O. Box 7830, 96928. Tel: 671-565-5128; Fax: 671-565-3539. Sr. Bernadette Quintanilla, S.S.N.D., Prin.
School Sisters of Notre Dame 1; Lay Teachers 18; Students 221.
Catechesis/Religious Programs—Tel: 671-565-9676.
Students 253.

Asan, Holy Family, Nino Perdido, Rev. Rodolfo Arejola.
Res., P.O. Box 45, Agana, 96910. Tel: 671-477-2211.

Barrigada, San Vicente Ferrer (1947), Revs. Adrian F. Cristobal; Joel de los Reyes; Deacon Pedro S. Guerrero.
Res., 229 San Roke St., 96913. Tel: 671-734-4573; 734-4586; Fax: 671-734-5858.
School—San Vicente School, San Vicente Dr., 96913. Tel: 671-734-4242; 734-4562; Fax: 671-734-8718. Sr. Tarcisia Sablan, S.S.N.D., Prin.
Priests 1; School Sisters of Notre Dame 3; Lay Teachers 27; Students 449.
Catechesis/Religious Programs—Tel: 671-734-4586. Mr. Vincent Reyes Untalan, D.R.E.
Students 458.

Chalan Pago, Nuestra Senora de la Paz y Buen Viaje, Rev. Daniel Cristobal, O.F.M.Cap.
Res., 135 Gunut Cir., Agana Heights, 96919. Tel: 671-734-3723.
Catechesis/Religious Programs—Students 391.

Dededo, Santa Barbara (1947), Rev. Msgr. Zoilo L.G. Camacho; Revs. Tomasito Tibudan; James McDonough; Manuel Jerus; Deacon Ramon Diaz.
Res., 315 W. Sta., Barbara Ave., 96912. Tel: 671-632-5659; 632-9534.
Catechesis/Religious Programs—D.R.E.: Ann Tydingco; Virginia Avaricio; Cristeta Deliquina; Terry Cruz.
Students 1,062.

Inarajan, St. Joseph (1680) (Chamorro), Rev. Efren F. Adversario.
Res., P.O. Box 17002, 96917. Tel: 671-828-8102; Fax: 671-477-3519.
Catechesis/Religious Programs—Students 172.

Maina, Our Lady of the Purification (1949) (Filipino), Rev. Simeon Balmeo.
Res., P.O. Box 4477, Agana, 96910. Tel: 671-477-7256.
Catechesis/Religious Programs—Students 73.

Malojlo, San Isidro (1977), Rev. Manuel Trenchera.
Res., HCR Box 17083, Inarajan, 96917. Tel: 671-828-8454; Fax: 671-828-0001. [JC]
Catechesis/Religious Programs—Students 71.

Mangilao, Santa Teresita (1951), Rev. Joseph English, O.F.M.Cap.
Res., 192 Rte. 10, P.O. Box 306, Agana, 96910. Tel: 671-734-2100; Fax: 671-734-2171.
Catechesis/Religious Programs—Students 386.

Merizo, San Dimas and Our Lady of the Rosary (1800) (Chamorro), Rev. Jose Villagomez, O.F.M.Cap.
Res., P.O. Box 6099, 96916. Tel: 671-828-8056; Fax: 671-828-3100. [CEM]
Catechesis/Religious Programs—Students 528.

Mongmong, Nuestra Senora de Las Aquas (1969), Rev. Patrick Kenny Q. Garcia.
Res., P.O. Box 163, Agana, 96910. Tel: 671-477-6754; Fax: 671-477-1510.
Catechesis/Religious Programs—Tel: 671-477-3563. Mrs. Therese Mallari, D.R.E.
Students 150.

Ordot, San Juan Bautista (1947) (Chamorro), Rev. David I.A. Quitugua.
Res., P.O. Box 49, Agana, 96910. Tel: 671-472-8341; Fax: 671-472-2324.
Catechesis/Religious Programs—Students 96.

Piti, Assumption of Our Lady (1930), Rev. Wilfredo Lorilla.
Mailing Address: 314 Assumption Dr., 96925.
Res., 96910. Tel: 671-472-2272; Fax: 671-477-1955.
Catechesis/Religious Programs—Students 152.

Santa Rita, Our Lady of Guadalupe (1944), Rev. Jack Niland, O.F.M.Cap.
Res., P.O. Box 4632, Agana, 96910. Tel: 671-565-2160; Fax: 671-565-7078.
Catechesis/Religious Programs—Mrs. Cecilia Cruz, D.R.E.
Students 450.

Sinajana, Saint Jude Thaddeus (1962), Rev. Felixberto Leon Guerrero, O.F.M.Cap.; Deacon Anthony C. Leon Guerrero.
Church & St. Jude Rectory—122 Avenida Bien Venida, 96926. Tel: 671-475-6530; 6531; Fax: 671-477-5353.
Catechesis/Religious Programs—Sr. Gloria Aquon, F.S.P.A., D.R.E.
Students 290.

Talofofo, San Miguel (1945) (Chamorro), Rev. Robert L. Maher, O.F.M.Cap.
Res., 71 San Miguel St., 96930. Tel: 671-789-1069; Fax: 671-789-7665.
Catechesis/Religious Programs—Tel: 671-789-0130. Marie E. Meno, D.R.E.
Students 400.

Tamuning, St. Anthony and St. Victor (1946), Revs. Brigido U. Arroyo; James Ch'e; Jose Antonio P. Abad; Deacon Mario L. Celis. In res., Revs. Manuel Ombao; Hermogenes Quiambo.
Res., P.O. Box 7707, 96911. Tel: 671-646-7181; 646-8044; Fax: 671-646-1039.

Toto, Immaculate Heart of Mary (1975) (Chamorro), Rev. Alfonso Asis; Deacon Jose Santos.
Res., P.O. Box 2552, Agana, 96910. Tel: 671-477-9118.
Catechesis/Religious Programs—Students 165.

Tumon Bay, Blessed Diego Luis de San Vitores Church (1970), Rev. Juan L.G. Camacho.
Res., P.O. Box 24363, GMF, 96921. Tel: 671-646-5649; Fax: 671-649-6887.
Catechesis/Religious Programs—Students 52.

Umatac, San Dionisio (1800) (Chamorro), Rev. Jose Villagomez, O.F.M.Cap.
Res., P.O. Box 6099, Merizo, 96916. Tel: 671-828-8056; Fax: 671-828-3100. [CEM]
Catechesis/Religious Programs—Students 105.

Yigo, Our Lady of Lourdes (1947), Revs. Vito B. San Andres; Michael C. Crisostomo.
Res., P.O. Box 11001, 96929. Tel: 671-653-2584; Fax: 671-477-3519.
Catechesis/Religious Programs—Tel: 671-653-1102; Fax: 671-653-1102. D.R.E.: Femy Castro; Trinie Cruz; Elaine Gogue; Thelma Lumbre; Toni Nartia.
Students 752.
Mission—Machananao, Santa Bernadita, 96929. Tel: 671-653-2584.

Yona, San Francisco d'Assisi, Rev. Patrick Castro, O.F.M.Cap.
Res., San Fidelis Friary, 135 Gunut Cir., Agana Heights, 96919. Tel: 671-789-1491; Fax: 671-789-2845. [CEM]
Catechesis/Religious Programs—Josephine Santos, D.R.E.
Students 491.

On Duty Outside the Archdiocese:
Reverend Fathers—
Cepeda, Ray, St. Paul Univ., Quebec
D'Arcy, William, Armed Forces
Mintegui, Marc, Armed Forces
Perez, Antonio, St. Joseph College, San Jose, CA

Retired:
Reverend Monsignors—
Calvo, Oscar, P.O. Box 518, Agana, GU 96910. Tel: 671-477-8544
Reverend Fathers—
Brouillard, Louis A., 525 9th St., Pine City, MN 55063

INSTITUTIONS LOCATED IN THE ARCHDIOCESE

[A] SEMINARIES

AGANA. *Father Duenas Minor Seminary*, 196-B Cuesta San Ramon, 96910. Tel: 671-734-2883. Preparatory Seminary of the Archdiocese. Co-Directors: Revs. James L.G. Benavente; Adrian L.F. Cristobal.

[B] HIGH SCHOOLS

AGANA. *Academy of Our Lady of Guam*, 233 W. Archbishop Felixberto C. Flores St., 96910. Tel: 671-477-8203; Fax: 671-477-8555. Sisters of Mercy. Sr. Francis Jerome Cruz, R.S.M., Prin. Sisters 5; Lay Teachers 28; Staff 6; Students 427.

The Father Duenas Memorial School, P.O. Box FD, 96910. Tel: 671-734-2261; 734-2263; Fax: 671-734-5738. Mr. William Roth, Prin. Priests 1; Sisters 2; Lay Teachers 23; Students 383.

TALOFOFO. *Notre Dame High School*, 480 San Miguel St., 96930. Tel: 671-789-1745; 789-1675; Fax: 671-789-4847. Sr. Regina Paulino, S.S.N.D., Prin. Priests 1; Sisters 3; Lay Teachers 18; Students 248.

[C] ELEMENTARY & JUNIOR HIGH SCHOOLS

AGAT. *Our Lady of Mt. Carmel School*, P.O. Box 7830, 96928. Tel: 671-565-5128; Fax: 671-565-3539. Sr. Bernadette Quintanilla, S.S.N.D., Prin. Students 220.

DEDEDO. *Santa Barbara School*, 274-A W. Santa Barbara Ave., 96912. Tel: 671-632-5578. Mailing Address: 274-B W. Santa Barbara Ave., 96912. Sr. Bernadette Marie Leon Guerrero, R.S.M., Prin. Sisters 6; Lay Teachers 39; Students 476.

GMF. *San Vicente School*, San Vincente School Dr., P.O. Box 21335, 96921. Tel: 671-734-4242; 734-4562; Fax: 671-734-8718. Sr. Tarcisia Sablan, S.S.N.D., Prin. Students 465.

SINAJANA. *Bishop Baumgartner Memorial School*, 281 Calle Angel Flores St., 96926. Tel: 671-472-6670. Sr. Mary Charles Cameron, R.S.M., Pres. Cathedral Grade School merged with Bishop Baumgartner Middle School to form Bishop Baumgartner Memorial School. Sisters 3; Lay Teachers 29; Students 504.

TAMUNING. *Saint Anthony School*, 529 Chalan San Antonio, 96910. Tel: 671-646-9464; 649-0602; 649-0614; Fax: 671-649-7130. Sr. Doris San Agustin, R.S.M., Prin. Sisters 5; Lay Teachers 30; Students 588.

YIGO. *Dominican School*, 114 Chalan Pale Roman - Lagu, 96929. Tel: 671-653-3021; Fax: 671-653-3090. Sr. Zenaida Ancheta, O.P., Prin. Students 103.

YONA. *St. Francis School*, P.O. Box 8795, 96914. Tel: 671-789-1270; 789-3900; Fax: 671-789-5052. Sr. Vincent Marie Balajadia, S.S.N.D., Prin. Sisters 4; Lay Teachers 24; Students 343.

[D] KINDERGARTEN AND NURSERY SCHOOLS

AGANA HEIGHTS. *Maria Artero Nursery*, 161 A Sunset Dr., 96919. Tel: 671-472-8777. Sr. Mary Ann Becmer, M.M.B., Prin. Sisters 2; Lay Teachers 5; Students 65.

ORDOT. *Dominican Child Development Center*. P.O. Box 10342, Sinajana, 96926. Tel: 671-477-7228. Sr. Veronica Diaz, O.P., Prin. Sisters 5; Lay Teachers 4; Aides 5; Students 130.

PEREZVILLE-TAMUNING. *Mercy Heights Nursery and Kindergarten*, 211 San Vitores St., 96911. Tel: 671-646-1185. Sr. Mary Roberta Taitano, R.S.M., Admin. Students 179.

TAI. *Infant of Prague Nursery School*. P.O. Box 22865, GMF, 96921. Tel: 671-734-2785. Sisters of Mercy. Sr. Lucy Barazan, R.S.M., Admin. Students 166.

[E] CATHOLIC CHARITIES

AGANA. *Catholic Social Services of Guam*, P.O. Box EJ, 96910. Tel: 671-649-1224; 646-4974; Fax: 671-646-4974. Mrs. Cerila Rapadas, Dir.; Sr. Callista Camacho, R.S.M., Deputy Dir. Total Assisted 1,649; Total Staff 132.

Alee Shelter Program for Spouse Abuse, P.O. Box EJ,

96910. Tel: 472-6729; 472-6709. Sr. Eileen Mearns, R.G.S., Dir.

[F] MONASTERIES & RESIDENCES OF PRIESTS

AGANA HEIGHTS. *St. Fidelis Friary*. Mailing Address: 135 Gunut Cir., 96910-4128. Tel: 671-472-6339. Headquarters of Capuchin Friars (Vice Province, Star of the Sea). Very Rev. Michel W. Dalton, O.F.M.Cap., Vice Prov.; Revs. Ferdinand Pangelinan, O.F.M.Cap.; George Maddock, O.F.M.Cap., Post Novitiate Formation Dir., Hawaii; Eric Forbes, O.F.M.Cap., Initial Formation/Vocation Dir.; Bro. Brian Champoux, O.F.M.Cap.; Revs. Michael Cruz, O.F.M.Cap., Hawaii; Soke Maluafiti, O.F.M.Cap., Hawaii; Andre Eduvala, O.F.M.Cap.; Douglas Antipas, O.F.M.Cap.
Priests Retired: Revs. Marcian Pellett, O.F.M.Cap.; Eymard McKinnon, O.F.M.Cap.; Lee Friel, O.F.M.Cap.; Randolph Nowak, O.F.M.Cap., Hawaii.
Priests Abroad: Revs. Paul Minchak, O.F.M.Cap., Hawaii; Gordon Combs, O.F.M.Cap., Hawaii; Robert Phelps, O.F.M.Cap., Hawaii; William Shannon, O.F.M.Cap., Hawaii; Andrew Mannetta, O.F.M.Cap., Hawaii; Paulo Kosaka, O.F.M.Cap., Hawaii.

[G] CONVENTS & RESIDENCES FOR SISTERS

AGANA. *Cathedral Mercy Convent*, P.O. Box 3070, 96910. Tel: 671-477-9291. Sisters of Mercy 7.

AGANA HEIGHTS. *Mercedarian Missionaries of Berriz*, 161 A Sunset Dr., 96919. Mailing Address: P.O. Box 3487, Agana, 96910. Tel: 671-477-8303; Fax: 671-472-2326. Sr. MaryAnn Becmer, M.M.B., Regional Coord. Sisters 8.

AGAT. *Mt. Carmel Community*, P.O. Box 7705, 96928. Tel: 671-565-2369. Sr. Mary Juan Camacho, S.S.N.D.; Sr. Bernadette Quintanilla, S.S.N.D. Sisters 4. Sisters teach at Mt. Carmel Elementary & Jr. High.

BARRIGADA. *San Vicente Community*, St. Vicente School Dr., 96913. Tel: 671-734-3010. Mailing Address: c/o Notre Dame Regional Center, 480 San Miguel St., Talofofo, 96930. Tel: 671-734-3010. Sisters 4. Sisters teach at San Vicente Elementary & Jr. High.

DEDEDO. *Santa Barbara Convent*, 274 B. W. Santa Barbara St., 96912. Tel: 671-632-2384; Fax: 671-632-1414. Institute of the Sisters of Mercy of the Americas, North Carolina Region. Sisters 5.

INARAJAN. *Convent of Mercy Sisters*, P.O. Box 17211, 96916. Tel: 671-828-8285. Institute of Sisters of Mercy of the Americas, North Carolina Region 2.

MALOJLO. *Discalced Order Of Carmelites Monastery*. HCR Box 17084, Inarajan, 96917. Tel: 671-828-8280; Fax: 671-828-0001. Order of Discalced Carmelites. Mother Conception de Carlos, O.C.D., Prioress. Sisters 13.

ORDOT. *Religious Missionaries of St. Dominic*, P.O. Box 10342, 96926. Tel: 671-477-7228; 472-1524. Total in Residence 6; Total Staff 6.

Sisters of the Good Shepherd Convent. P.O. Box 3596, 96932. Tel: 671-472-3393; Fax: 671-472-8486. Sr. Helena Kusack, R.G.S., Supr.; Sr. Eileen Mearns, R.G.S.; Sr. Carol McClenon, R.G.S. Sisters work at abuse shelters under Catholic Social Services.

PEREZVILLE-TAMUNING. *Mercy Heights Convent*, 211 San Vitores St., 96911. Tel: 671-646-7246; Fax: 671-649-1822. Sr. Mary Angela Perez, R.S.M., Guam Region Pres. Administrative Residence and Offices of the Institute of the Sisters of Mercy of the Americas, North Carolina Region. Sisters in residence teaching and working in Tamuning, Sinajana, and Agana. Sisters 16.

SINAJANA. *St. Jude Thaddeus Convent*. P.O. Box 394, Agana, 96910. Tel: 671-472-6041. Franciscan Sisters of Perpetual Adoration.

TAI. *Mercy Convent and Formation House*. P.O. Box 22865, Barrigada, 96921. Tel: 671-734-3312. Institute of the Sisters of Mercy of the Americas, North Carolina Region. Professed Sisters in various Apostolates and Sisters in basic formation. Sisters 12.

TALOFOFO. *Notre Dame Community*, 480 San Miguel St., 96930. Tel: 671-789-1629; Fax: 671-789-3810.

S.S.N.D. Regional House, 480 San Miguel St., 96930. Tel: 671-789-1629; 789-5965; Fax: 671-789-3810.

St. Augustine Community, 480 San Miguel St., 96930. Tel: 671-789-5965.

Mother Theresa, 480 San Miguel St., 96930. Tel: 671-789-1629. Mother Theresa Community of Prayer and Presence. School Sisters of Notre Dame (Talofofo, Guam). Regional Councilors: Sr. M. Francine Perez, S.S.N.D., Regl. Leader; Sr. Maria Regina Paulino, S.S.N.D., Regl. Councilor; Sr. Joseph Ann Quinene, S.S.N.D., Regl. Councilor, Vicar. Sisters 30.

[H] MISCELLANEOUS LISTINGS

AGANA. *Our Lady of the Waters House of Prayer*. (Retreat Center), P.O. Box 163, 96932. Tel: 671-472-8385; Fax: 671-477-1510.

Saint Vincent de Paul Society, c/o Santa Teresita Parish, P.O. Box 306, 96910. Tel: 671-734-2100. Mr. John Lizama, Pres. Tel: 671-472-6068.

Secular Franciscans, P.O. Box CF, 96910. Tel: 671-472-6023; 472-6339. Rev. Daniel Cristobal, O.F.M.Cap., Spiritual Dir.; Mrs. Carmen Manibusan, Pres.

BARRIGADA. *Saint Dominics Senior Care Home*. 350 N. Sabana Barrigada Dr., Barrigada Heights, 96913. Tel: 671-632-9370; 632-9378; 9379; Fax: 671-637-1679. Sr. Fe Dural, O.P., Admin.

MANGILAO. *Campus Ministry, Newman Center, University of Guam*. 196 B Cuesta San Ramon, Agana, 96910. Tel: 671-734-3507; Fax: 671-734-2943. Rev. Kenneth J. Hezel, S.J.

RELIGIOUS INSTITUTES OF MEN REPRESENTED IN THE ARCHDIOCESE

For further details refer to the corresponding bracketed number in the Religious Institutes of Men or Women section.

[0470]—*The Capuchin Friars*. (Vice Prov. of Mary, Star of the Sea).—O.F.M.Cap.

[0690]—*Jesuit Fathers and Brothers*. (N.Y. Prov.).—S.J.

RELIGIOUS INSTITUTES OF WOMEN REPRESENTED IN THE ARCHDIOCESE

[1780]—*Congregation of the Sisters of the Third Order of St. Francis of Perpetual Adoration*. (La Crosse, WI).—F.S.P.A.

[0420]—*Discalced Carmelite Nuns*.—O.C.D.

[2510]—*Mercedarian Missionaries of Berriz*.—M.M.B.

[]—*Order of Saint Benedict*.—O.S.B.

[]—*Religious Missionaries of St. Dominic*.—O.P.

[2970]—*School Sisters of Notre Dame*. (Mequon, WI).—S.S.N.D.

[2575]—*Sisters of Mercy of the Americas*. (Belmont, NC).—R.S.M.

[1830]—*Sisters of the Good Shepherd*.—R.G.S.

NECROLOGY

(No Deaths)

Diocese of Arecibo, Puerto Rico

(Dioecesis Arecibensis)

Most Reverend

INAKI MALLONA TXERTUDI, C.P.

Bishop of Arecibo; ordained March 27, 1956; appointed December 14, 1991; consecrated January 6, 1992; installed January 25, 1992. *Res., 206 Dr. Salas St., P.O. Box 616, Arecibo, PR, 00613-0616.*

Most Reverend

MIGUEL RODRIGUEZ, C.SS.R., D.D.

Retired Bishop of Arecibo; ordained June 22, 1958; appointed January 21, 1974; consecrated March 23, 1974; retired March 1990. *Res., Apartado 238, Aguadilla, PR, 00605-0238.*

ESTABLISHED APRIL 30, 1960.

Square Miles 833.08.

Comprises the mid-northern part of the Island.

The Chancery: 206 Dr. Salas St., P.O. Box 616, Arecibo, PR, 00613. Tel.: 787-878-3180; Fax: 787-880-2661.

STATISTICAL OVERVIEW

Personnel	
Bishop	1
Retired Bishops	1
Priests: Diocesan Active in Diocese	56
Priests: Active Outside Diocese	19
Priests: Retired, Sick or Absent	10
Number of Diocesan Priests	85
Religious Priests in Diocese	43
Ordinations:	
Diocesan Priests	2
Religious Priests	2
Permanent Deacons in Diocese	7
Total Brothers	7
Total Sisters	116
Parishes	
Parishes	59
With Resident Pastor:	
Resident Diocesan Priests	44
Resident Religious Priests	15
Without Resident Pastor:	
Missions	228
Pastoral Centers	1
Welfare	
Homes for the Aged	3
Total Assisted	375
Residential Care of Children	2
Total Assisted	45
Specialized Homes	1
Total Assisted	380
Special Centers for Social Services	1
Total Assisted	3,165
Educational	
Seminaries, Diocesan	1
Students from This Diocese	9
Diocesan Students in Other Seminaries	9
Seminaries, Religious	4
Students Religious	10
Total Seminarians	28
Colleges and Universities	1
Total Students	768
High Schools, Diocesan and Parish	14
Total Students	2,839
Elementary Schools, Diocesan and Parish	14
Total Students	4,210
Catechesis/Religious Education:	
High School Students	3,950
Elementary Students	13,910
Total Students Under Catholic Instruction	25,705
Teachers in the Diocese:	
Priests	19
Brothers	5
Sisters	43
Lay Teachers	429
Vital Statistics	
Receptions into the Church:	
Infant Baptism Totals	4,780
Adult Baptism Totals	355
Received into Full Communion	839
First Communions	3,702
Confirmations	2,881
Marriages:	
Catholic	1,028
Interfaith	66
Total Marriages	1,094
Deaths	1,816
Total Catholic Population	379,366
Total Population	550,678

Former Bishops—Most. Rev. ALFRED F. MENDEZ, C.S.C., ord. 1935; cons. Oct. 28, 1960; retired Jan., 1974; died Jan. 28, 1995.—Most. Rev. MIGUEL RODRIQUEZ, C.S.S.R., D.D., ord. June 22, 1958; appt. Jan. 21, 1974; cons. March 23, 1974; retired March, 1990.

Secretary to the Bishop—SOR MARIA J. FONTANEZ, O.P.

Chancery Office—206 Dr. Salas St., P.O. Box 616, Arecibo, 00613. Tel: 787-878-3180; Fax: 787-880-2661.

Vicar General—Rev. SERAPIO FERNANDEZ, P.H., *P.O. Box 616, Arecibo, 00613.* Tel: 787-878-3180; 878-3110.

Chancellor—Rev. JOSEPH D. SCHRECK, O.F.M.Cap., *P.O. Box 616, Arecibo, 00613.* Tel: 787-878-3180.

Vice Chancellor—Miss SYLVIA VARGAS.

Secretary—Miss SYLVIA VARGAS.

Vicar of Diocesan Pastor Affairs—Rev. MIGUEL MERCADO.

Diocesan Consultors—Rev. Msgr. BUENAVENTURA BALLESTER, P.H.; Revs. SERAPIO FERNANDEZ; MIGUEL MERCADO; JOSEPH SCHRECK, O.F.M.Cap.; ELIAS FERNANDEZ, O.SS.T.; CARMELO URARTE; FRANCISCO CONCEPCION.

Diocesan Pastoral Council—Revs. SERAPIO FERNANDEZ; MIGUEL MERCADO; ELIAS FERNANDEZ; BENJAMIN QUINONES; MELQUIADES ROJAS; SOR ROSA DE FATIMA.

Dean of Arecibo Zone—Rev. Msgr. BUENAVENTURA BALLESTER, P.H., *P.O. Box 140637, Arecibo, 00614-0637.* Tel: 787-878-4910.

Dean of El Calvario Zone—Rev. ELIAS FERNANDEZ, O.SS.T., *P.O. Box 525, Isabela, 00662.* Tel: 787-872-2563.

Dean of Vega Baja Zone—Rev. FRANCISCO CONCEPCION, *P.O. Box 775, Vega Alta, 00692.* Tel: 787-883-4875.

Diocesan Offices and Directors

Confraternity of Christian Doctrine—Sr. ROSA DE FATIMA, O.P., *Calle Mariano Abril, Box 1151, Arecibo, 00612.* Tel: 787-878-8401.

Cursillos de Cristiandad—Rev. P. ELIAS FERNANDEZ, O.SS.T., *P.O. Box 1826, Arecibo, 00613.* Tel: 787-872-2563.

Diocesan Council of Catholic Women—Vacant.

Propagation of Faith—Rev. MANUEL P. CARDENAS, M.N.M.

Holy Childhood—Rev. MANUEL P. CARDENAS, M.N.M.

Director of Youth—Rev. MIGUEL MERCADO, *Box 2164, Arecibo, 00613.* Tel: 787-878-1528.

Legion of Mary—Vacant.

Movimiento Familiar Cristiano (CFM)—Vacant.

Prison Services—Vacant, *Box 673, Arecibo, 00613.* Tel: 787-878-4910.

Seminario Jesus Maestro College Seminary—Rev. MIGUEL MERCADO, Dir., *Box 2164, Arecibo, 00613.* Tel: 787-878-1528.

Seminary Board—Rev. MIGUEL MERCADO.

Pastoral Vocational Program—Revs. MIGUEL MERCADO; VICTOR SANCHEZ; FELIPE NUNEZ.

Superintendent of Schools—Miss LYDIA HERNANDEZ, *P.O. Box 1683, Arecibo, 00613.* Tel: 787-878-1095; Fax: 787-878-1095.

Catholic Charities—Sr. ROBERTA GRZELAK, *Box 616, Arecibo, 00613.* Tel: 787-878-6580.

Retreat House, Centro Diocesano Mons. Mendez—Vacant, *Apdo. 2164, Arecibo, 00613.* Tel: 787-878-4796.

Boy Scouts—Vacant.

Hospital Chaplains—

Regional—Miss ESTHER COSTA.

Municipal—Sr. MARIA ESTELA RESTREPO, C.B.P. Tel: 787-878-7272.

Buen Pastor—Vacant.

Cathedral of San Felipe Apostol Priests—Revs. ROBERTO VEGA; CESAR RAMIREZ.

Susoni—Vacant.

Vocations—Rev. MIGUEL MERCADO, *Apdo. 2164, Arecibo, 00613*. Tel: 787-878-1528.
Police Chaplain—Rev. FRANCISCO CONCEPCION.

Promotion and Human Development Office—Sr. ROBERTA GZELACK, C.D.P., *P.O. Box 616, Arecibo, 00613*. Tel: 787-878-6580.

Sociedad San Vincente de Paul (Vincentinos)—Mr. ANGEL GINES, Pres. Consejo Diocesano. Tel: 787-884-5087; 854-2562.

CLERGY, PARISHES, MISSIONS AND PAROCHIAL SCHOOLS

CITY OF ARECIBO

1—CATHEDRAL OF SAN FELIPE APOSTOL (1616), Revs. Roberto Vega, Rector; Cesar Ramirez. In res., Rev. Ricardo San Llorente.
Res., De Diego St., Box 577, 00613. Tel: 809-878-1149.
Convent—251 Magallanes St., 00613. Tel: 787-878-7179.
Dominican Sisters of Fatima 5.
Chapels—Islote II, Sagrada Familia; Islote III (Sector Vibora), San Juan Evangelista; Sector Boam, Maria Reina; Islote I (Vigia), N.S. del Carmen.

2—CHURCH OF SAGRADO CORAZON DE JESUS (1961), Rev. Msgr. Buenaventura Ballester, P.H.; Rev. Juan R. Mora.
Res., Box 140637, 00614. Tel: 787-878-4910; Fax: 787-879-2124. [JC]
School—Colegio San Felipe, Box 673, 00613. Tel: 809-878-3532. Judith Colon, Prin. (Elem./High). Lay Teachers 37; Students 419.
Catechesis / Religious Programs—Students 150.

3—NUESTRA SENORA DEL CARMEN (1961), Revs. Alberto Diaz; Delfin Rodriguez.
Res., Bo. Cotto No. 985, P.O. Box 9949, Cotto Sta., 00613. Tel: 787-878-1268. [JC]
School—Hogar-Colegio La Milagrosa, Ave., Cotto, 00613. Tel: 809-878-0341.
Sisters of Charity 7; Lay Teachers 26; Students 467.
Catechesis / Religious Programs—Students 268.
Chapels—Abra S. Francisco, San Antonio; Rodriguez Olmo, San Francisco.

4—SANTA ANA (1961), Rev. Luis Rios Cappiello. In res., Rev. Jose M. Lopez.
Res., Bo. Santana, Box 318, 00613. Tel: 787-881-6005. [JC]
Catechesis / Religious Programs—Students 333.
Chapels—Factor II, N.S. del Carmen; Santuario Cristo de los Milagros.

5—CHURCH OF CHRIST THE KING (1967), Rev. Serapio Fernandez.
Res., Box 1932, 00613. Tel: 809-878-9214.
Catechesis / Religious Programs—Students 155.
Chapel—Bo. Hato Arriba, Maria Auxiliadora.

6—OUR LADY OF HOPE (1986), Rev. Edwin Mercado.
Res., Box 489, 00613. Tel: 787-880-1943. [JC]
Catechesis / Religious Programs—Students 37.
Chapels—Cantagallo, Sgdo. Corazon de Jesus; Plan Bonito, San Rafael.

7—NUESTRA SENORA DE FATIMA (1967), Rev. Enrique A. Perez-Santiago.
Res., Box 667, Sabana Hoyos, 00688. Tel: 787-881-8274. [JC]
Catechesis / Religious Programs—Students 145.
Chapels—Garrochales, S. Fco. de Asis; Ballaja, N.S. del Carmen; Garrochales, La Milagrosa, San Luis; Espino, Immaculada Concepcion.

8—INMACULADO CORAZON DE MARIA (1987), Rev. Jose M. Lopez.
Res., Box 1282, Sabana Hoyos, 00688. [JC]
Chapels—Bo. Asomante, San Isidro.; Bo. Carolina, Sagrado Corazon de Jesus; Bo. Arrozal, San Jose; Los Muertos, San Francisco.

9—LA MILAGROSA (1973), Rev. Angel M. Santos.
Res., Box 204, Bajadero, 00616. Tel: 787-881-0295. [JC]
Catechesis / Religious Programs—Students 227.
Chapels—Bajadero, Immaculada Concepcion; Domingo Ruiz, N.S. La Providencia; Carreras, San Judas; Biafara, N.S. La Virgen del Carmen.

10—SAN JUAN BOSCO (1971), Rev. Melquiades Rojas.
Res., Urb. Jardines de Arecibo, Calle R-Y-26, 00613. Tel: 787-879-1070.
School—Tel: 809-879-2069.
Lay Teachers 15; Students 345.
Catechesis / Religious Programs—Students 140.
Chapel—Las Canelas, N.S. La Dolorosa, San Daniel. Sisters of Mercy 3.

11—CHURCH OF SAN MARTIN DE PORRES (1973), Rev. Carmelo Urarte.
Res., Calle 6 F-12, Box 14-2142, Urb. Univ. Gardens, 00613. Tel: 787-878-1822.
Catechesis / Religious Programs—Students 300.
Chapels—Victor Rojas II, San Jose Obrero; Bo. Obrero, Immaculada Concepcion.

12—CHURCH OF SANTA TERESITA (1980), Rev. Gabriel Maduro.
Res., Road 492, KM 1.9, P.O. Box 9242, Cotto Station, 00613. Tel: 787-878-7015. [JC]
Catechesis / Religious Programs—Students 50.
Chapels—Hato Arriba, N.S. La Providencia; Barrancas, La Milagrosa.

13—CHURCH OF SANTA CECILIA (1981), Rev. Jose M. Casco.
Res., HC-02 Box 13674, 00612. Tel: 787-879-3364. [JC]
Catechesis / Religious Programs—Students 120.
Chapels—Calichosa, San Jose; Los Canos, San Martin de Porres; La Guinea, La Milagrosa.

14—SANTISIMO SACRAMENTO (1990), Rev. Antonio Portalatin.
Res., Ste. 109, Call Box 4015, 00613. Tel: 809-878-9238. [JC]
Catechesis / Religious Programs—Students 65.
Chapels—Del Valle, La Milagrosa; Jobos, San Pascual.

OUTSIDE OF ARECIBO

Barceloneta, Church of Our Lady of Mt. Carmel (1882), Revs. Thomas Sharkey, C.S.Sp., Pastor; Gerard Siegfried, C.S.Sp.
Res., P.O. Box 187, 00617. Tel: 809-846-5625. [JC]
Catechesis / Religious Programs—Students 148.
Chapels—Garrochales I, N.S. de Fatima; Palmas Altas, San Antonio; Punta Palma, N.S. del Mar.

Our Lady of Victory (1963), Rev. Leon Perez, Admin.
Res., Ste. 125, Call Box 2020, 00617. Tel: 809-846-6120.
Catechesis / Religious Programs—Students 85.
Chapels—Parcelas Imberry, San Jose Obrero; Quebrada, Immaculate Heart of Mary; Tiburones, N.S. de Fatima.

Camuy

1—ST. JOSEPH (1827), Revs. Adrian Jimenez; David Rivas.
Res., P.O. Box 414, 00627. Tel: 809-898-3620. [JC]
Catechesis / Religious Programs—Students 377.
Convent—.San Jose Hermanas Terciarias Capuchinas 4.
Chapels—Membrillo, N.S. La Monserrate; Puente (Zarzas), Sagrado Corazon; Puente (Zarza Parcelas), N.S. La Milagrosa; Puente (Sector Pica), N.S. del Rosario; Abra Honda, Espiritu Santo; Zanjas, Immaculada Concepcion.

2—OUR LADY OF THE MIRACULOUS MEDAL (1962). (El Calvario). Revs. Florentino Flores; Zenaido Martin.
Res., HC-01 Buzon 5240, 00627. Tel: 809-898-5825. [JC]
Catechesis / Religious Programs—Students 322.
Chapels—Planas II, Santiago Apostol; Puertos, Sagrado Corazon; Cienaga, Cristo Rey; Camuy Arriba, N.S. del Carmen; Sector Riego, Santa Clara; Sector Mani, Sagrado Corazon.

3—OUR LADY OF ASUMPTION (1984), Rev. Rafael Munoz.
Res., HC-02 Box 8047, 00627. Tel: 809-898-8038. [JC]
Catechesis / Religious Programs—Students 372.
Chapels—Cibao Ocasio, N.S. del Perpetuo Socorro; Callejones, Sagrado Corazon; Callejones II, San Pablo de la Cruz; Cibao Lugo, Maria Auxiliadora.

4—OUR LADY OF MONSERRATE (1961), Rev. Antonio J. Vazquez.
Res., HC-03 Box 16512, Quebradillas, 00678-9820. Tel: 787-898-6784. [JC]
Catechesis / Religious Programs—Students 200.
Convent—Tel: 787-896-6176.
Hermanes Angeles Custodios 2.
Chapels—Piletas (Lares), N.S. del Carmen; Guajataca (Queb.), N.S. de Fatima; Aibonito Beltran, San Antonio; Cibao (S. Sebastian), Santa Ana; Planas I (Isabela), Santa Cruz, Planas II, N.S. del Rosario.

Ciales, Holy Rosary (1820), Revs. Salvador Rodrigo, O.Carm.; Luis Miranda, O.Carm.; Gabriel M. Torres.
Res., P.O. Box 26, 00638. Tel: 787-871-2205; 871-3485. [JC]
School—P.O. Box 1334, 00638 Tel: 787-871-1318. Mrs. Juanita Natal, Prin.
Lay Teachers 21; Students 349.
Catechesis / Religious Programs—Students 739.
Chapels—Pozas, San Elias; Cialitos, Buen Pastor; Hato Viejo, Corazon de Jesus; Hato Viejo, San Antonio; Jaguas, Santa Clara; Pesa, San Ignacio; Cialitos-Cruces, Corazon de Maria; Toro Negro, N.S.; Bo. Marias, Maternidad de la Virgen.

N.S. Madre del Redentor (1988), Rev. Wiktor Tarnawski.
Res., P.O. Box 1181, 00638. Tel: 787-871-2404. [JC]
Catechesis / Religious Programs—Students 200.
Chapels—Yunes, San Jose; Fronton (Sabana), Perpetuo Socorro; Cordillera 5, N.S. La Providencia; Limon, Smo. Rosario; Cordillera 7, Sagrada Familia.

Corozal, Holy Family (1804), Revs. Eugenio Gayarre; Pedro Hernandez.
Res., P.O. Box 474, 00783. Tel: 787-859-2595. [JC]
School—Tel: 809-859-2420.
Sisters of St. Joseph 9; Lay Teachers 35; Students 976.
Catechesis / Religious Programs—Students 926.
Chapels—Guarico Palmarejo I, San Judas Tadeo; Palmarejo II, San Vicente; Palmarejo II, San Francisco de Asis; Dos Bocas II, Santa Teresita; Cibuco, N.S. del Carmen; Abras, San Jose; Urb. Sylvia, Perpetuo Socorro.

Corozal-Padilla, Our Lady of the Seven Sorrows (1984), Revs. Luis A. Vazquez, Admin.; Miguel Rivera.
Res., P.O. Box 740, 00783. Tel: 787-859-1900.
Catechesis / Religious Programs—Students 700.
Chapels—Padilla Hermita, San Rafael; Padilla Hormiga, San Martin; Cieneguita (V.A.), N.S. del Perpetuo Socorro.

Corozal-Palmarito, La Milagrosa, Revs. Francisco J. Anduaga, C.R.L., Pastor; Domingo Figueroa, C.R.L.
Res., HC-03 Box 13976, 00783. Tel: 787-859-5306.
Catechesis / Religious Programs—Students 514.
Convent—HC-03 Box 14048, 00783. Tel: 787-859-8151.
Hnas. de San Francisco (Secular Institute) 3.
Chapels—Maguelles, Cristo Rey; Mana, N.S. de Fatima; Radio Oro, Nuestra Senora del Carmen.

Corozal-Palos Blancos, Christ the King (1968), Revs. Benjamin Quinones, C.R.L., Admin.; Rafael Gonzalez, C.R.L.
Res., P.O. Box 1091, Corozal, 00783. Tel: 787-859-7313. [JC]
Catechesis / Religious Programs—Students 725.
Chapels—Cuchillas, N.S. del Perpetuo Socorro; Negros, N.S. del Rosario; Palos Blancos, Santa Teresita; Palos Blancos, San Antonio.

Florida, Our Lady of Mercy (1887), Rev. Casimiro Domeck.
Res., P.O. Box 437, 00650. Tel: 787-822-2670. [JC]
Catechesis / Religious Programs—Students 120.
Chapels—Monte Bello, N.S. del Carmen; Pajornal (Bta.), Santa Rosa de Lima.

Hatillo, Our Lady of Mt. Carmel (1830), Revs. Fernando Morell, Pastor; Carlos E. Granados.
Res., P.O. Box 2, 00659. Tel: 809-898-5300. [JC]
School—Tel: 787-898-2800.
Sisters de la Caridad del Cardenal Sancha 6; Lay Teachers 51; Students 800.
Catechesis / Religious Programs—Students 610.
Chapels—Carrizales, Sagrado Corazon; Corcovados, Immaculada Concepcion; Capaez, N.S. Perpetuo Socorro; Carrizales, San Jose; Santa Rosa, Santa Rosa de Lima; Lechuga: San Pio X; Palma Gordo: Sagrada Familia.

Our Lady of Guadalupe (1961), Revs. Luis Maria de la Cruz, S.E.M.V., Prior; Rene A. Maria del Nino Jesus, S.E.M.V.; Victor R. Borrero, S.E.M.V.; Anibal Jesus Hostia de la Purisima, S.E.M.V.; David A. Maria Alabanza de la Trin, S.E.M.V.; Alberto Jesus Gloria de la Inmaculada, S.E.M.V.; Sr. Teresa Maria V. de la Eucaristia.
Res., Carr. Ins. 129, Arecibo to Lares, P.O. Box 1131, Arecibo, 00613. Tel: 787-898-8035.
Catechesis / Religious Programs—Students 348.
Chapels—Pajuil, Santa Rosa de Lima; Buena Vista, Inmaculada Concepcion; Bda Colon, N.S. La Providencia; Sector Naranjito, San Jose.

Perpetual Help (1961), Rev. Jose Estensoro.
Res., Ste. 119, Call Box 69001, 00659. Tel: 809-898-7771. [JC]
Catechesis / Religious Programs—Students 291.
Chapels—Aibonito, Cristo Rey; Berrocal, Sagrado Corazon de Jesus; Sonadora, La Milagrosa; Mariposa, N.S. del Carmen; Cantera, Ntra. Sra. de la Paz.

Isabela, St. Anthony (1835), Revs. Pedro Bustinza, O.SS.T.; Wilfredo Echevarria, O.SS.T.; Jorge I. Mantilla, O.SS.T.
Res., Box 525, 00662. Tel: 787-872-2563. [JC]
School—Sisters of St. Dominic 5; Lay Teachers 31; Students 557.
Catechesis / Religious Programs—Students 792.
Chapels—Medina, Sma. Trinidad; Curva, Santa Rosa de Lima; Cotto, San Martin de Porres; Arenales Bajo, N.S. La Monserrate; Vendrel, N.S. La Providencia; Jobos, Buen Pastor; Guayabos, Espiritu Santo; Arenales A., El Salvador; Arenales Alto, Sagrado Corazon, Tel: 787-872-0015.
Sister of Trinity (Valencia) 4.; Hogar Infantil/Jesus Nazareno, Isabella.

Our Lady of Mount Carmel (1983), Rev. Elias Fernandez, C.SS.T.
Res., Box 1555, 00662. Tel: 787-872-5550. [JC]
Catechesis / Religious Programs—Students 300.
Chapels—Poncito, Santos Inocentes; Planas, La

Encarnacion; La Tuna, San Juan de Mata; Galateo Bajo, La Milagrosa.

Lares, St. Joseph (1827), Revs. Manuel Elejalde, C.P.; Ignacio Goiburu, C.P.; Mariano Arrien, C.P.
Res., P.O. Box 103, 00669. Tel: 787-897-2067. [JC]
School—Tel: 809-897-2640.
Hermanas Pasionistas 4; Lay Teachers 14; Students 292.
Catechesis/Religious Programs—Students 640.
Chapels—Piletas II, San Carlos; Sebruguillo, La Resurreccion; Piletas Arece, La Milagrosa; Tabonuco, La Providencia.
Hermanas Josefinas de Mexico 6.

St. Judas Tadeos (1986), Rev. Angel R. Diaz, Admin.
Res., P.O. Box 1109, 00669. Tel: 809-897-3540. [JC]
Catechesis/Religious Programs—Students 225.
Chapels—Palmar Llano, Perpetuo Socorro; Vega de los Acevedo, La Dolorosa; Buenos Aires, Sgda. Familia de Nazaret; Matilde, San Antonio.

Manati

1—La Candelaria (1738), Revs. Emilio Tovar, C.M.; Santiago Arribas, C.M.
Res., Betances y Padial Streets, 00674. Tel: 809-854-2013. [JC]
School—Sisters of Charity 10; Lay Teachers 35; Students 823.
Catechesis/Religious Programs—Students 30.
Chapels—Pugnado, N.S. del Perpetuo Socorro; Villa Amalia, La Milagrosa; Cortes, Sagrado Corazon; Polvorin, La Monserrate; Ceiba, Espiritu Santo.

2—Our Savior, Rev. Angel Pagan.
Res., P.O. Box 465, 00674. Tel: 787-884-3664.
School—Colegio Marista, P.O. Box 462, 00764. Tel: 809-854-1075.
Marist Brothers 5; Lay Teachers 25; Students 509.
Catechesis/Religious Programs—Students 100.
Chapels—San Jose, San Jose; Lagunas Tierra Nueva, N.S. de Lourdes; Guayaney, San Martin de Porres.

3—Sagrada Familia (1972), Revs. Francisco J. Marredan, C.M.; Jose Abreu, C.M.
Res., P.O. Box 704, 00674. Tel: 787-854-2858. [JC]
Catechesis/Religious Programs—Students 216.
Chapels—Parcelas Marquez, San Judas Tadeo; Palo Alto, N.S. La Monserrate; Polvorin, La Milagrosa.

4—Nuestra Senora del Mar (1978), Rev. Jesus A. Rodriguez.
Res., Apdo. 1183, 00674. Tel: 787-854-5388. [JC]
Catechesis/Religious Programs—Students 200.
Chapels—Tierras Nuevas, Santa Rosa de Lima; Sector Cantito, La Milagrosa; Boquillas, Nuestra Senora del Carmen.

Morovis, Nuestra Senora del Carmen (1820), Revs. Antonio Rodriguez, O.Carm.; Elias Pascual, O.Carm.; Jose Oliveras, O.Carm.; Jesus Monreal, O.Carm.
Res., Box 428, 00687. Tel: 787-862-2620. [JC]
Catechesis/Religious Programs—Students 2,169.
Chapels—San Lorenzo, N.S. del Rosario; Perchas, N.S. del Carmen; Pastos, N.S. del Carmen; Rio Grande, La Milagrosa; Morovis Sur, San Jose; Unibon, San Miguel; Vaga III, La Milagrosa; MPatron I, Sagrada Familia; Cuchillas, Segrado Corazon; Morovis Sur, Inmaculada Concepcion.

St. Paul Apostle (1985), Rev. Tomas Pagan.
Res., P.O. Box 537, 00687. Tel: 787-862-4684. [JC]
Catechesis/Religious Programs—Students 690.
Chapels—Franquez, Nino de Praga; Franquez Carretera, La Providencia; Torrecillas, Senor de los Milagros.

Orocovis, San Juan Bautista (1838), Revs. Jose L. Gomez, S.D.B.; Julian San Nicasio, S.D.B.; Luis Dalbon, S.D.B.; Jorge Santiago, S.D.B.
Res., P.O. Box 2114, 00720. Tel: 787-867-2210. [JC]
School—Tel: 787-867-2295.
Salesians Sisters 6; Lay Teachers 15; Students 248.
Catechesis/Religious Programs—Students 1,350.
Chapels—Sabana, Angeles Custodios; Botijas I, Cristo Resucitado; Botijas II, Santa Clara; El Puente, San Pablo; Mata de Cana, Sagrado Corazon; Damian Arriba, Espiritu Santo; Montebello, N.S. del Carmen; Guadalupe, N.S. La Guadalupe; Gato Bajura, N.S. La Providencia; Gato, San Judas Tadeo.

Our Lady of Fatima (1975), Rev. Tosello Giangiacomo, C.S.Sp.
Res., Box 2118, 00720. Tel: 787-867-3277. [JC]
Catechesis/Religious Programs—Students 383.
Chapels—Bermejales, Cristo de la Salud; Bauta, N.S. La Dolorosa; Damian Arriba, N.S. del Perpetuo Socorro; Pellejas I, Espiritu Santo; Miraflores, San Martin.

Quebradillas, San Raphael (1828), Revs. Victor Sanchez, Admin.; Tomas Santos. In res., Rev. Msgr. Ernesto Munoz.
Res., Box 57, 00678. Tel: 787-895-2035. [JC]
School—Tel: 809-895-2280.
Sisters 4; Lay Teachers 13; Students 348.
Catechesis/Religious Programs—Students 450.
Chapels—San Jose, San Jose; Quebrada, N.S. del Carmen; Chivos, Santa Cruz; Cacao, La Milagrosa; Parcelas San Antonio, N.S. La Monserrate; San Antonio, San Antonio; Charcas, N.S. del Perpetuo Socorro; Las Talas, La Guadalupe.
Hermanes Dominicas Presentacion 5.

Sacred Heart (1977), Rev. Antonio Caraballo.
Res., Box 1569, 00678. Tel: 787-895-3033. [JC]
Catechesis/Religious Programs—Students 245.
Chapels—San Antonio, San Miguel; Yeguada, N.S. del Perpetuo Socorro; El Verde, Madre Dolorosa.

Utuado

1—San Miquel (1746), Revs. Roy Martinez, O.F.M.Cap.; Jose A. Carrion, O.F.M.Cap.; Alberto Figueroa, O.F.M.,Cap.; Joseph Schreck, O.F.M.Cap.; Jose McCarthy, O.F.M.Cap. In res., Bros. Bernardo Ayala, O.F.M.Cap.; Jose E. Sanchez, O.F.M.Cap.
Res., 8 Barcelo St., P.O. Box 10, 00641. Tel: 787-894-2696. [JC]
Schools—Elementary School, Progreso St., Box 10, 00641. Sr. Aracelia Cruz, C.D.P., Prin.
Sisters 1; Lay Teachers 22; Students 251; Intermediate and High School, San Miguel Ave., Box 10, 00641. Tel: 809-894-9386. Mrs. Maria F. Pagan, Prin.
Lay Teachers 22; Students 251.
Catechesis/Religious Programs—Students 536.
Chapels—Puente Blanco, San Fidel; Arenas, San Martin; Sabana Grande, N.S. del Perpetuo Socorro.

2—San Pedro y San Pablo (1988), Rev. Rafael Nuno.
Res., Box 679, 00641. Tel: 787-894-0696. [JC]
Catechesis/Religious Programs—Students 146.
Chapels—Las Palmas, San Francisco; Vivi Arriba, Immalculada Concepcion; La Pica, La Milagrosa; Consejo, San Jose; Vivi Abajo, Nuestra Senora de la Divina Providencia.
Monastery Mother of God Cloistered 30.

3—Our Lady of Angels (1967), Rev. Hector Zayas.
Res., Box 98, Angeles, 00611. Tel: 809-894-7722. [JC]
Catechesis/Religious Programs—Students 134.
Chapels—Corcho, San Jose.; Santa Isabela, N.S. La Monserrate.; Las Vegas, Sagrada Familia.

4—Nuestra Senora del Monte Carmelo (1981), Rev. Alan Irizarry.
Res., P.O. Box 299, Caonillas-Utuado, 00641. Tel: 787-894-9141. [JC]
Catechesis/Religious Programs—Students 35.
Chapels—Mameyes, San Antonio; Tetuan III, Sagrado Corazon; Tetuan II, Cristo Salvador; Don Alonso, La Milagrosa.

5—Our Lady of Sorrows (1983), Rev. Jose Cortez.
Res., Box 161, Angeles, 00611. Tel: 787-894-7722. [JC]
Catechesis/Religious Programs—Students 54.
Chapels—Roncador, San Martin de Porres; Cayuco, Cristo Rey; Jacanas, N.S. la Monserrate.

Vega-Alta, Immaculate Conception of Blessed Virgin Mary (1805), Revs. Francisco Concepcion; Cesar Santos.
Res., P.O. Box 775, 00692. Tel: 787-883-4875.
Catechetical Center—Calle Colon 17, 00692.
Sisters of Charity 4; Students 464.
Chapels—Maricao IV, Sagrado Corazon; Bajura II, San Vicente; Bajura I, Santa Ana; Candelaria, Inmaculado Corazon de Maria; Maricao II, N.S. La Guadalupe.

Santa Ana (1967), Rev. Jesus Diaz.
Res., Urb. Santa Ana, Apartado 2105, Calle 3H9, 00692. Tel: 787-883-2502.
Catechesis/Religious Programs—Students 146.
Chapel—Espinosa, N.S. del Carmen.

Perpetuo Socorro (1975), Rev. Felipe Nunez, Admin.
Res., Box 9018, Sabana Branch, Vega-Baja, 00694. Tel: 787-883-5776. [JC]
Catechesis/Religious Programs—Students 85.
Chapels—Sabana (V.B.), San Vicente; Cerro Gordo, N.S. del Carmen.

Vega-Baja

1—Holy Rosary (1794), Revs. Jose A. Rodriguez, Admin.; Edgardo Nunez.
Res., P.O. Box 1388, 00694. Tel: 787-858-2969. [JC]
School—Sisters 2; Lay Teachers 41; Students 698.
Catechesis/Religious Programs—Students 415.
Chapels—Arenales, San Jose; Almirante, N.S. de Fatima; Alto de Cuba, La Santa Cruz.

2—N.S. de la Providencia (1970), Rev. Angel Diaz.
Res., Guarico Rd. 14 Urb. Box 4056, Jardines de Vega Baja, 00694. Tel: 809-858-2171. [JC]
Catechesis/Religious Programs—Students 300.
Chapels—Brisas de Tortuguero, San Jose; Vega Baja Lakes, San Pedro.

3—The Blessed Trinity (1971), Rev. Ricardo Majan, Admin.
Res., P.O. Box 58, Almirante Sur Station, 00694. Tel: 809-858-8743.
Catechesis/Religious Programs—Students 310.
Chapels—Almirante Norte, Sagrada Familia; Patron II, N.S. La Providencia.

4—Our Lady of Carmen-Playa (1976), Rev. Bertulfo Acevedo, Admin.
Res., Apdo. 4095, 00694. Tel: 809-858-4275. [JC]
Catechesis/Religious Programs—Students 40.
Chapels—Naranjos, San Judas Tadeo; San Demetrio, Divino Nino Jesus.

5—Parroquia de San Martin de Porres (1967), Rev. Efrain Montesino.
Res., P.O. Box 254, Vega Baja, 00694. Tel: 809-858-1485. [JC]
Catechesis/Religious Programs—Students 229.
Chapels—Panaini, Del Carmen; Pugnado Adentro, San Jose; Vila Colombo, St. Anthony.
Maria Reparadora 4.

6—Our Lady of Lourdes (1984), Rev. Msgr. Victorino Cobeaga.
Res., P.O. Box 4414, 00694. Tel: 809-855-4942. [JC]
Catechesis/Religious Programs—Students 515.
Convent—Tel: 809-855-0341.
Hermanas Terciarias Capuchinas 3.
Chapels—Rio Abajo, Santa Rosa de Lima; Quebrada Arenas, San Juan Bautista; Las Granjas, S. Francisco de Asis.

7—Our Lady of Mt. Carmel (1968), Rev. Francisco Jimenez.
Res., P.O. Box 1417, 00694. Tel: 809-855-0159. [JC]
Catechesis/Religious Programs—Students 490.
Chapels—Pueblo Nuevo, La Milagrosa; Sabana Hoyos, San Judas; Santa Rosa, La Guadalupe.

Special Assignment:
Reverend Fathers—
Guzman, Alfredo S.J. (Colombia), Pontifical Catholic University of Puerto Rico
Lopez, Jose M., Chap., Interamerican University of Arecibo
Mercado, Edwin, Interdiocesan Tribunal of Ponce, Judicial Ministry of Arecibo
Mercado, Miguel, Jesus Maestro Seminary, Arecibo
Soberal, Jose, Dimas Catholic Education for Universities Svcs., Bayamon

---

On Duty Outside the Diocese:
Reverend Fathers—
Alvarez, Antonio, Estados Unidos
Ariza, Campo E., Diocese of Caguas
Davila, Andres, Estados Unidos
Fernandez, Daniel, Studying in Rome
Flores, Jose A., Diocese of Caguas
Garcia, Jose L., Spain
Gomez, Walter, Estados Unidos
Guerrero, Jose Ma., Espana
Hernandez, Jimmy, New Mexico
Irizarry, Rafael, Diocese of Ponce
Jiminez, P. Victorino, Espana
Leiva, Emilio
Morales, Luis Angel, Archdiocese of San Juan
Morales, Salomon, Archdiocese of San Juan
Rodriguez, Salvador, Diocese of Caguas
Rojas, Victor, Studying in Rome
Santiago, Angelo, Archdiocese of Boston
Sendra, Jesus, Espana
Velazquez, Luis

Retired:
Reverend Fathers—
Betti, Jose, Spain
Esparza, Luis, O.F.M.Cap., Bo. Almirante Sur Vega Baja, Box 4196, PR 99763. Tel: 809-885-8122
Lizarraga, Joaquin, Spain
Martinez, Francisco, Spain
San Llorente, Faustino, P.O. Box 4196, Vega Baja, 00694 Puerto Rico

INSTITUTIONS LOCATED IN THE DIOCESE

[A] EDUCATIONAL

Arecibo. *Pontificia Universidad Catholica de Puerto Rico, Recinto de Arecibo*, Mailing Address: P.O. Box 4045, 00613. Tel: 809-881-1212. Rev. Alfredo Guzman, S.J., Chap. Priests 6; Lay Teachers 43; Students 768.

Seminario de Jesus Maestro, Mailing Address: P.O. Box 2164, 00613. Tel: 809-878-1528. Rev. Miguel Mercado. Total Enrollment 18.

[B] HOMES FOR AGED AND ORPHANS

ARECIBO. *Hogar de Ancianos San Vicente*. Mailing Address: P.O. Box 4196 Vega Baja, P.R., 00694.
For a complete listing, refer to the Special Care Facilities section.

Hogar Sta. Maria Eufrasia, Calle Andres Garcia, No. 10, 00612. Tel: 809-878-5166.
For a complete listing, refer to the Special Care Facilities section.

La Milagrosa Home for Orphan Girls, Cotto Ave., No. 987, 00612. Tel: 809-878-6231.
For a complete listing, refer to the Special Care Facilities section.

San Rafael Home for Aged, 00612.
For a complete listing, refer to the Special Care Facilities section.

ISABELA, P.R. *Hogar Infantil Jesus Nazareno, Inc.*, P.O. Box 1671, 00662.
For a complete listing, refer to the Special Care Facilities section.

LARES. *Fundacion Irma Fe*, Calle Comerio No. 52, 00669. Tel: 787-897-6090.
For a complete listing, refer to the Special Care Facilities section.

RELIGIOUS INSTITUTES OF MEN REPRESENTED IN THE DIOCESE

For further details refer to the corresponding bracketed number in the Religious Institutes of Men or Women section.

[]—*Canonigos Regulares Lateranenses de San Agustin*. (Bronx, NY).—C.R.L.

[0470]—*Capuchin Friars*. (Province of Pittsburgh) .—O.F.M.Cap.

[0270]—*Carmelite Fathers and Brothers*. (Province de Aragon, Valencia, Espana).—O.Carm.

[1330]—*Congregation of the Mission*. (Vice-Province of Puerto Rico).—C.M.

[1000]—*Congregation of the Passion*. (Bilbao, Spain).—C.P.

[]—*Esclavos de la Eucaristia y Maria Virgen*.—E.E.M.V.

[0650]—*Holy Ghost Fathers*. (Eastern Province).—C.S.Sp.

[0770]—*Marist Brothers*.—F.M.S.

[]—*Misioneros Natividad de Maria*.—M.N.M.

[1310]—*Order of the Holy Trinity*. (Viscaya, Spain Province).—O.SS.T.

[1190]—*Salesians of Don Bosco*. (Province of Madrid).—S.D.B.

RELIGIOUS INSTITUTES OF WOMEN REPRESENTED IN THE DIOCESE

[]—*Congregation of Sisters of Passion*. (Mexico).

[0760]—*Daughters of Charity of St. Vincent de Paul*.—D.C.

[1070-05]—*Dominican Sisters*.—O.P.

[1100]—*Dominican Sisters of Charity of the Presentation of the Blessed Virgin*.—O.P.

[]—*Dominican Sisters of Fatima*. (Yauco PR).

[]—*Hermanas de San Jose de Corozal*. (Corozal).

[]—*Hermanas del Buen Pastor*.

[]—*Hermanas Esclaves del Santisimo y la Inmaculada*.

[]—*Hermanas Josefinas*. (Mexico).

[]—*Hermanas San Francisco*. (Instituto Religioso).

[]—*Misioneras de la Sagrada Familia*. (Instituto Secular).

[]—*Misioneras Sagrado Corazon*. (Santo Domingo).

[]—*Monasterio Madre de Dios - Cloistered Dominican Nuns*.

[]—*Salesian Sisters*. (Cuba).

[]—*Siervas de Maria*.

[]—*Sisters of Charity of Cardinal Sancha*. (Santo Domingo).

[0990]—*Sisters of Divine Providence*. (Pittsburgh).—C.D.P.

[]—*Sisters of Mercy*. (Spain).

[3930]—*Sisters of St. Joseph of the Third Order of St. Francis*. (South Bend, IN).—S.S.J.-T.O.S.F.

[2460]—*Society of Mary Reparatrix*.—S.M.R.

NECROLOGY

† Rodriquez, Victor J., Hatillo, Perpetual Help Church. —Died Dec. 30, 1995.

Diocese of Caguas, Puerto Rico

(Dioecesis Caguana)

Most Reverend

ENRIQUE HERNANDEZ RIVERA D.D.

Bishop of Caguas; ordained June 8, 1968; appointed Titular Bishop of Vanalla, North Africa and Auxiliary Bishop of San Juan June 11, 1979; consecrated August 17, 1979; appointed Bishop of Caguas February 13, 1981; officially installed March 8, 1981. *Res., Bishop's House, Box 8698, Caguas, PR, 00626.* Tel.: 787-747-5885; 747-5787; Fax: 787-747-5616; 747-5767.

ESTABLISHED NOVEMBER 1964.

Square Miles 737.

Comprises east and southeast portion of Puerto Rico and the Islands of Culebra and Vieques.

Patroness of the Diocese: Maria, Madre de la Iglesia - November 12, 1988.

STATISTICAL OVERVIEW

Personnel	
Bishop	1
Abbots	1
Priests: Diocesan Active in Diocese	65
Priests: Retired, Sick or Absent	2
Number of Diocesan Priests	67
Religious Priests in Diocese	53
Extern Priests in Diocese	1
Ordinations:	
Diocesan Priests	3
Transitional Deacons	6
Permanent Deacons	57
Permanent Deacons in Diocese	63
Total Brothers	1
Total Sisters	130
Parishes	
Parishes	43
With Resident Pastor:	
Resident Diocesan Priests	34
Resident Religious Priests	9
Without Resident Pastor:	
Welfare	
Health Care Centers	1
Total Assisted	100
Educational	
Seminaries, Diocesan	1
Students from This Diocese	20
High Schools, Diocesan and Parish	1
Total Students	110
High Schools, Private	6
Total Students	2,851
Elementary Schools, Diocesan and Parish	4
Total Students	650
Elementary Schools, Private	13
Total Students	4,248
Catechesis/Religious Education:	
High School Students	4,794
Elementary Students	7,288
Total Students Under Catholic Instruction	12,082
Teachers in the Diocese:	
Priests	19
Scholastics	4
Brothers	4
Sisters	17
Lay Teachers	365
Vital Statistics	
Receptions into the Church:	
Infant Baptism Totals	7,670
Adult Baptism Totals	490
Received into Full Communion	8,160
First Communions	5,630
Confirmations	3,350
Marriages:	
Catholic	1,180
Interfaith	24
Total Marriages	1,204
Deaths	1,680
Total Catholic Population	515,000
Total Population	653,012

Former Bishop—Most Rev. RAFAEL GROVAS, D.D., S.T.D., Ph.D., J.C.L., Retired Bishop of Caguas; retired Feb. 13, 1981; appt. Jan. 19, 1965; ord. April 7, 1928; cons. March 28, 1965; died Sept. 9, 1991.

Vicar General—Rev. AURELIO ADAN.

Sec. Chancellor—Rev. CARLOS N. COTTO.

Sec. Vice Chancellor—Rev. DANIEL P. CRONIN.

Diocesan Consultors—Rev. Msgr. MIGUEL A. MENDOZA; Revs. ANTONIO MATA; HIPOLITO RIVERA; AURELIO ADAN; JOSE M. CALVO; EUSEBIO RAMOS; EDWARD SANTANA.

Diocesan Tribunal of Caguas—Rev. EDWARD SANTANA, J.C.D., Judicial Vicar, *Box 8698, Caguas, 00626.* Tel: 787-747-5885; 747-5787.

Board of Diocesan Government—Revs. AURELIO ADAN; CARLOS N. COTTO; Mr. FRANCISCO HERNANDEZ; Deacon JOSE RODRIGUEZ.

Priests Senate—Rev. Msgr. MIGUEL A. MENDOZA; Revs. ANTONIO MATA; HIPOLITO RIVERA; JOSE M. CALVO; JOSE A. OQUENDO PABON; ORLANDO DE JESUS; JAVIER HERNANDEZ; AURELIO ADAN; EDWARD SANTANA; ANTONIO CARTAGENA; ANGEL CUADRADO, O.deM.; FELICIANO RODRIGUEZ.

Diocesan Offices and Directors

Economic Administrator—Mr. FRANCISCO HERNANDEZ, *Box 8698, Caguas, 00726.* Tel: 787-747-5885; 747-5787.

Planning Vicar—Vacant, *Box 8698, Caguas, 00726.* Tel: 787-747-5885; 747-5787.

Cursillos de Cristiandad—Rev. LORENZO JOVELLAR, S.J., *Box 6318, Caguas, 00726.* Tel: 787-746-4698.

Catholic Youth—Rev. JORGE CARDONA, *Box 8698, Caguas, 00726.* Tel: 787-744-6738.

Catholic Social Action—Rev. OSCAR RIVERA, *Caguas, 00726.* Tel: 787-747-5885; 747-5787.

Catholic School Consultors—DOMICIANO GARCIA, *Box 8699, Caguas, 00726.* Tel: 787-743-1171.

Catechetical Delegate—Deacon JOSE RODRIGUEZ, *Box 8698, Caguas, 00726.* Tel: 787-747-5885.

Building Commission—Revs. AURELIO ADAN; D. JOSE RODRIGUEZ, *Box 8698, Caguas, 00726.* Tel: 787-747-5885; 747-5787.

Liturgical Consultor—Rev. DANIEL CRONIN, *Box 8698, Caguas, 00626.* Tel: 787-747-5885.

Communication Office—Rev. PEDRO ORTIZ, *Box 8698, Caguas, 00726.* Tel: 809-746-3783.

Guerra Contra el Hambre (War on Hunger)—Rev. ROBERTO SOTO, *Box 8698, Caguas, 00726.* Tel: 787-747-5767.

Vicentian Society—Rev. D. PERFECTO RIVERA, *Box 8698, Caguas, 00726.*

Consejo de Laicos—JOSE RODRIGUEZ, *Parr. San Pedro Hotel, Calle 1. A. 11, Caguas, 00725.*

Hospitals—Revs. LORENZO JOVELLAR, S.J.; JOSE FLORES, *Box 8698, 00726.*

Legion of Mary—Rev. CLEMENTE CAHILL, *Box 967, Caguas, 00726.* PETRA FLORES, *Box 5215, Caguas, 00726.*

Master of Ceremonies—Rev. DANIEL CRONIN, *Box 8698, Caguas, 00726.* Tel: 809-747-5885. Rev. JOSE ANTONIO ORTIZ, *Parr. San Jose, Box 2038, Aibonito, 00705.*

Pastoral Vicar—Rev. FELICIANO RODRIGUEZ, *Box 8698, Caguas, 00726.* Tel: 787-286-0075.

Schools—*Box 8699, Caguas, 00726.* Tel: 787-743-1171.

Education Vicar—Rev. VICTOR R. ORTIZ.

Pastoral of Education—Sr. MARIA EUGENIA ORTIZ, S.S.N.D.

School Superintendent—Mr. DOMICIANO GARCIA.

Vocations—Rev. JORGE CARDONA, *Urb. Santa Elvira, Calle Santa Rita H-13, Caguas, 00725.*

CLERGY, PARISHES, MISSIONS AND PAROCHIAL SCHOOLS

CITY OF CAGUAS

1—CATHEDRAL DULCE NOMBRE DE JESUS (1730). Redemptorist Fathers. Revs. Gerardo Campbell, C.SS.R., Rector; Clemente Cahill, C.SS.R.; Juan Ramon Hernandez, C.SS.R.; Jose Orlando Serrano; Bro. Pedro Hernandez. In res., Rev. Damian Wall.

Res., 3 Corchado St., Box 967, 00726. Tel: 787-743-4311; 2927; Fax: 787-743-7567.

School—Colegio Catolico de Caguas, Acosta St., Box 967, 00726. Tel: 787-743-2385. School Sisters of Notre Dame. Sr. Bernardine Marie, S.S.N.D. Sisters 2; Lay Teachers 43; Students 1,031; Aids 10.

High School—Notre Dame, Urb. Borinquen, Box 541, 00726. Tel: 787-743-3693; 5501; Fax: 787-258-9648. School Sisters of Notre Dame. Mr. Jose G. Grillo.

Priests 2; Sisters 4; Lay Teachers 68; Students 1,200.

Chapels—Nuestra S. Perpetuo Socorro, (1929), 24 Aguayo St., 00726; San Gerardo, (1940), 221 B St., B-14, Jardines de Caguas, 00726; San Vicente de Paul, 221 B St., Brooklyn; La Sagrada Familia, (1978), 1004 P St., Bda. Morales.

2—SAN JOSE (1960). (Discalced Carmelites from Spain). Revs. Antonio Mata, O.C.D., Rector; Jesus H. Barrientos, O.C.D.; Alejandro Moral, O.C.D.; Luis Cestero.

Res., Carol St., Villa Blanca, Box 1101, 00726. Tel: 787-743-2032.

School—(Spanish Discalced Carmelite Sisters) Box 806, 00625. Fax: 787-258-0683. Sr. Soledad Diaz, C.M., Prin.

Priests 2; Sisters 5; Lay Teachers 32; Students 578.

High School—Mrs. Brenda Figueroa de Soler, Prin.

Priests 1; Lay Teachers 22; Students 442.

Chapel—Bairoa, Nuestra Senora del Rosario, (1981).

3—SAGRADO CORAZON DE JESUS (1963), Rev. Juan Alonso Ordonez.

Res., HC 04, Box 45078, Bo. Beatriz, 00726. Tel: 787-747-5170.
Chapel—Bo. Beatriz, Cristo Rey, (1960).

4—Nuestra Senora de la Providencia (1967), Rev. Hilario Rivera.
Res., Urb. Villa del Carmen, Box 6318, 00626. Tel: 787-743-8200.
Stations—Urb. Mariolga.; Caserio Publico.; Los Flamboyanes.; Rio Verde.

5—Santisimo Sacramento (1967). Blessed Sacrament Fathers. Revs. Martin Navarro, S.S.S.; Jesus Maria Maiza, S.S.S.; Adrian Alicea, S.S.S.; Domingo Gayarre, S.S.S.
Res., Reparto Caguax Calle 1 A-11, 00725. Tel: 787-743-8444.
Chapels—Urb. Caguas Norte, San Antonio de Padua.; Nuestra S. de Guadalupe, 5th St., Urb. Jose Delgado.

6—Nuestra Senora del Perpetuo Socorro (1968), Revs. Oscar Rivera; Nelson Lopez Aponte.
Res., Calle 2, A-13, Villa Nueva, 00725. Tel: 787-744-1420.
Stations—Bo. Canaboncito, San Patricio, (1926); Villa Esperanza, San Judas Tadeo, (1960); Bo. Canaboncito (Las Parcelas), Sagrado Corazon; Urb. Turabo Gardens, Nuestra S. del Carmen, (1988).

7—El Salvador (1970), Rev. Orlando De Jesus Gomez.
Res., Parcelas Bo. Boringuen, HC 03, Buzon 38888, 00625-9723. Tel: 787-747-3426.
Catechesis/Religious Programs—Students 300.
Chapels—Bo. San Salvador, Cristo Rey, (1922); Sector Anon, San Alfonso, (1929); Bo. San Salvador, Sector Hato, Nuestra S. del Carmen, (1911).

8—Immaculado Corozon de Maria (1971), Revs. Vincente Penalba, C.M.; Severiano Garcia, C.M.; Humberto Evangelista, C.M.F.
Mailing Address: HC 05, Box 57564, Caguas, 00725-9233. Tel: 787-747-6336.
Catechesis/Religious Programs—Students 230.
Chapels—Bo. La Barra, Cristo Rey, (1971); San Antonio, (1950); Bo. La Mesa, N.S. Providencia, (1982); Bo. La Mesa, Nuestra S. del Carmen; Bo. Quebra da Arenas, San Felipe; Guasabara, Sta. Teresa del Nino Jesus, (1995).

9—San Pablo Apostol (1982), Rev. Roberto Solivan Gonzales.
Res., Kennedy U-32 Urb. Jose Mercado, Caguas, 00625. Tel: 787-743-3546.
Chapels—Bo. Tomas de Castro I, Nuestra S. de Guadalupe, (1928); Bo. Tomas de Castro II, Santa Rose de Lima; Sector Ramal, San Martin, (1969).

10—San Pedro Apostol (1982), Rev. Antonio Munoz.
Res., Urb. Bonneville, Box 7112, Caguas, 00726. Tel: 787-746-0031.

11—San Juan Apostol y Evangelista (1982), Rev. Antonio Cartagena.
Res., Urb. Residencial Bairoa, Calle 27, Cagey, 00633-9522. Tel: 787-744-6359; Fax: 787-743-8266.
Catechesis/Religious Programs—Students 200.

12—Santisima Trinidad (1986), Rev. Efrain Zabala.
Res., Bo. Hormigas, Box 9630, Caguas, 00725. Tel: 787-747-6967.

13—Maria Madre de la Iglesia, Rev. Alberto Martinez.
Calle #3, Esq. 6, Urb Valle Tolima, Caguas, 00726. Tel: 787-258-4481.

14—Divino Nino, Rev. Campo Emilio Ariza.
Mailing Address: P.O. Box 9416, Caguas, 00726. Tel: 787-746-1450.

OUTSIDE THE CITY OF CAGUAS FROM LAS AMERICAS EXPRESS WAY TOWARD THE WEST

Aibonito, Aibonito Co., Church of St. Joseph (1897), Revs. Jose Antonio Ortiz; Angel Luis Cintron.
Res., Box 2038, 00705. Tel: 787-735-3741.
Chapels—Bo. Asomante (Cuadritos), Nuestra S. del Carmen, (1959); Bo. Asomante (Abejas), Inmaculada Concepcion (1965); Bo. Pasto, Nuestra S. de Guadalupe, (1970); Nuestra S. de la Providencia, (1982), Palestina St.; Bo. Rabanal (Parcelas), Nuestra S. de Fatima, (1972); Ext. San Luis, Nuestra S. del Carmen, (1986); La Plata, La Milagrosa, (1986).
Mission—Llanos, Sector El Juicio.

Aguas Buenas, Aguas Buenas Co., Church of Tres Santos Reyes (1838). Redemptorist Fathers. Revs. Andres Spacht, C.Ss.R.; John V. Caskey, C.Ss.R.; Carlos Corbett, C.Ss.R.; Carlos Valles, C.Ss.R.
Res., 5 Munoz Rivera St., Box 1, 00703. Tel: 787-732-2741.
School—Academia San Alfonso, Tel: 787-732-8288. Sr. Myrtha E. Arroyo de Lopez, Prin.
Lay Teachers 5; Students 275.
Chapels—Bo. Sumidero, Nuestra S. del Perpetuo Socorro, (1933); Sector Corujas del Barrio Sumidero, Sta. Juliana, (1984); Bo. Sonadora, Sagrado Corazon, (1937); Bo. Jagueyes Abajo, San Jose, (1939); Bo. Jagueyes Quinta, Divino Redentor, (1947); Bo. Caguitas, Madre del Perpetuo Socorro, (1941); Bo. Caguitas, Sector La Brusca; Parcelas Santa Clara, Santa Clara, (1974).

Espiritu Santo, Rev. Encarnacion Nieves.
Res., Box 1250, 00703. Tel: 787-732-1270.
Chapels—Carr. 156, Santa Teresita, (1929); Bo. Mulitas Alvelo, De Todos los Santos, (1974); Bo. Mulitas Tiza, San Gerardo Mayela, (1974).

Barranquitas, Barranquitas Co., Church of St. Anthony of Padua (1808; 1988), Rev. Msgr. Miguel A. Mendoza; Rev. John Alicea Velazquez.
Res., Box 1099, 00794. Tel: 787-857-3585.
Catechesis/Religious Programs—Students 1,800.
Chapels—San Francisco de Asis, (1960); Bo. Mana, Virgen del Carmen, (1963); Bo. Canabon, Virgen de la Providencia, (1968); Bo. Helechal, San Jose Obrero, (1968); Bo. Quebrada Grande, Nuestra Sra. de la Monserrate, (1968); Bo. Palo Hincado, Virgen del Perpetuo Socorro, (1975); Bo. Lajitas, Nuestra S. del Pilar, (1970); Sector La Torre, Santa Cruz, (1975); Bo. Helechal, San Martin de Porres, (1950).

San Andres Apostol (1986), Revs. Victor Raul Ortiz, Ph.D.; Raul Santos; Luis Manuel Ruiz.
Res., Bo. Quebradillas, Box 490, 00794. Tel: 787-875-5424; Fax: 787-875-5424.
Catechesis/Religious Programs—Students 226.
Chapels—Bo. Palomas, Comerio, San Jose, (1925); Bo. Quebradillas, Barranquitas, Corazon de Jesus, (1940; 1987); Bo. Cedro Arriba, Naranjito, San Antonio de Padua, (1955); Bo. Quebradillas, Barranquitas, Inmaculada Concepcion, (1957); Bo. Cedro Arriba, Naranjito, Santuario Maria Auxiliadora, (1992).

Cayey, Cayey Co., Nuestra Senora de la Asuncion (1787). Mercedarian Fathers. Revs. Fidel Fernandez, O.M., Supr.; Pedro J. Silva Bisbal, O.M.; Jose L. Garcia, O.M.; Pedro Ruiz Valero, O.M.
Res., Casa Parroquial, P.O. Box 37 2887, 00737-2887. Tel: 787-738-2763.
Catechesis/Religious Programs—Students 133.
Chapels—Bo. Jajome, Sagrado Corazon de Jesus, (1935); Bo. Pasto Viejo, Nuestra S. del Carmen, (1937; 1988); Bo. Toita, Nuestra S. de la Merced, (1946); Res. Brisas de Cayey, San Ramon Nonato, (1978); Bo. Maton Arriba, Santa Teresita del Nino Jesus, (1987).

Nuestra Senora de la Merced (1968), Revs. Angel Cuadrado, O.de.M.; Jesus Saez Castrillo, O.de.M.; Elias Lorenzana, O.de.M.; Gregorio Dafonte.
Res., Reparto Montellano, Box 1840, 00737. Tel: 787-738-3872.
Chapels—Bo. Vegas, San Ramon Nonato, (1961); Bo. Culebras, Nuestra S. del Carmen, (1973); Bo. Farallon, San Pedro Nolasco, (1980); San Pedro Armengol (La Plata), (1994).

San Esteban Protomartir (1985), Rev. Rafael A. Rodriguez; Deacons Anibal Gonzalez; Genaro Estrella; Felix Montanez; Silvestre Rodriguez.
Res., Bo. Borinquen Atravesada, HC 72, Box 8085, 00736-9522. Tel: 787-747-4555.
Chapels—Bo. Borinquen Pradera, Nuestra Senora del Carmen, (1910); Bo. Guavate, San Jose de la Montana, (1951; 1990).

Cidra, Cidra Co., Nuestra Senora del Carmen (1818), Revs. Baltazar Nunez Henandez; Edwin Rafael Hernandez Ortiz; Miguel Gil Diaz; Deacons Diego Reyes; Alfonso Delgado; Carlos A. Sola.
Res., Centro Plaza Municipal, Box 359, 00739. Tel: 787-739-2406.
Chapels—Bo. Rio Abajo, Madre del Salvador; Urb. Treasure Valley, La Milagrosa; Bo. Bayamon-Centenejas I, La Inmaculada; Bo. Montellano, Santa Teresa del Nino Jesus; Bo. Bayamon-Certenejas II, Perpetuo Socorro; Bo. Bayamon-Juan del Valle, Nuestra Senora del Rosario; Bo. Arena-Santa Clara, San Joaquin; Bo. Ceiba-Hevia, Nuestra Senora del Rosario; Bo. Arenas, Nuestra Senora de la Providencia; Bo. Ceiba, Cristo Rey; Bo. Bayamon-San Jose, San Jose; Bo. Rincon, San Francisco de Asis; Bo. Sud, La Milagrosa; Bo. Sud, San Pablo.

Nuestra Senora de Fatima (1963), Rev. Isidro Nazabal.
Res., Bo. Rabanal, Box 214, 00739. Tel: 787-739-0633.
Catechesis/Religious Programs—Students 596.
Chapels—Bo. Toita, Sagrado Corazon de Jesus, (1960); Bo. Salto, San Vicente, (1965); Bo. Honduras, Perpetuo Socorro, (1970); Bo. Rabanal, Bo. Salvador, (1970); Bo. Parcelas, La Milagrosa, (1978); Bo. Salto, Nuestra Senora de la Providencia; Bo. Salto, Santa Teresita, (1982); Santo Cristo de Los Milagros, (1987).

Comerio, Comerio Co., Santo Cristo de la Salud (1832), Revs. Raul Morales Berrios-Parroco; Roberto Angel Soto.
Box 1139, 00762. Tel: 787-875-4525.
Res., Calle Santiago R Palmer #12, 00782.
Chapels—Bo. Sabana, Nuestra Senora del Santisimo Rosario, (1966); Bo. Rio Hondo, Nuestra Senora de Fatima, (1953); Bo. Palomas, Santa Ceceilia, (1954); Bo. Cedrito, Virgen de la Providencia, (1958); Bo. Rio Hondo-Sector Las Parcelas, San Pablo, (1965); Bo. Pinas Arriba, Nuestra Senora del Carmen, (1973); Bo. Naranjo-Sector Las Parcelas, San Antonio de Padua, (1977); Bo. Vega Redonda, San Francisco de Asis, (1977); Bo. Cejas, Santa Rose de Lima, (1980); Bo. Dona Elena, San Martin de Porres, (1950); Rio Hondo II, Maria Madre de la Iglesia.

Naranjito, Naranjito Co., San Miguel Arcangel (1831), Revs. Hipolito Torres; Angel Molina Colon; Freddy Celano.
Res., Centro Parroquial, Box 68, 00719. Tel: 787-869-2840; Fax: 787-869-3050.
Chapels—Bo. Nuevo, Santa Rosa de Lima, (1953); Bo. Lomas Centro, Virgen del Carmen, (1954); Bo. Anones, La Milagrosa, (1962); Bo. Lomas Valles, San Judas Tadeo, (1963); Bo. Guadiana, La Monserrate, (1967); Bo. Achiote, Sagrado Corazon, (1978); Bo. Nuevo Parcelas, San Francisco de Asis, (1981); Bo. Cedro Abajo, San Jose, (1981).

OUTSIDE THE CITY OF CAGUAS FROM LAS AMERICAS EXPRESS WAY TOWARD THE EAST COAST

Ceiba, Ceiba Co., San Antonio de Padua (1840), Rev. Jose R. Oquendo Pabon, S.T.L.
Res., Plaza St., Box 77, 00735. Tel: 787-885-2530.
Missions—Ceiba, Sagrado Corazon de Jesus, Bo. Saco, 00735; Ceiba, Ceiba Co., Parcelas de Aguas Claras, H.S. del Carmen, 00735; Naguabo, Naguabo Co., Bo. Daguao, Naguabo, 00718; Bo. Rio Abajo, Ceiba Co., H.S. del Perpetuo Socorro Bo. Rio Abajo, Ceiba, 00735.
Chapel—Bo. Daguao, Nuestra Senora de Fatima, (1968).
Catechesis/Religious Programs—Students 110.

Fajardo, Fajardo Co., Santiago Apostol (1766). Redemptorist Fathers. Revs. Alfonso Amador, C.Ss.R.; Hector Garcia, C.Ss.R.; Julio Delgado, C.Ss.R.
Res., 16 Garrido Morales St., Box 806, 00738. Tel: 787-863-2365.
Chapels—Bo. Florencio, Santa Elena, (1962); Bo. Quebrada Vueltas, Perpetuo Socorro, (1965); La Milagrosa, (1978); Santa Isidra, Santiago Apostol.

Santisimo Redentor (1993), Rev. Kharlosg Lopez.
Res., Urb. Monte Brisas, Calle C-V-19, 00738. Tel: 787-863-5227; Fax: 787-860-0560.
Catechesis/Religious Programs—Students 165.

Gurabo, Gurabo Co., San Jose (1822), Rev. Hermenegildo Alayon; Deacon Clemente Guzman Cardona.
Res., 7 Santiago Iglesias St., Box 733, 00778. Tel: 787-737-2656.
Chapels—Bo. Jagual, Sagrado Corazon de Jesus, (1951); Bo. Jaguas Llano, Virgen del Carmen, (1967); Bo. Navarro, San Francisco Javier, (1968); Bo. Santa Rita, Santa Rita, (1968); La Milagrosa, (1973), Bo. Hato Nuevo; Bo. Celada, Santa Francisca Javier Cabrini, (1967); Bo. Santa Barbara, Santa Maria del Camino, (1987); Bo. Hato Nuevo, La Milagrosa, (1982); Bo. Jaguas Loma, San Miguel, (1989); Bo. Mamey II, Ntra. Sra. del Carmen.
Catechesis/Religious Programs—Students 377.

Humacao, Humacao Co., Dulce Nombre de Jesus (Pueblo) (1763), Revs. Eusebio Ramos Morales; Luis Antonio Alicea; Felix Oliveras Villanueva; David Diaz Matos; Deacon Angel Cruz Cruz.
Res., 3 Font Martelo St., Box 546, 00791. Tel: 787-852-0868.
Chapels—San Agustin, (1955), Parcela No. 44; Nuestra Senora de la Candelaria, (1956), Parcela No. 30, Candelero Arriba; Candelero Arriba San Jose, (1957), Carr. 922 Cotto Mabu; Bo. Junquito, Nuestra Senora de Fatima, (1962); Bo. Candelero Abajo, Santa Teresita, (1965); Caserio Roig, San Pedro y San Pablo, (1986); Bo. Parcelas Catano, Nuestra Senora de la Providencia; Bo. Buena Vista, Perpetuo Socorro, (1944).
Centers—Centro Comunal Palmas del Mar; Urbanizacion Villa Humacao.

Maria Reina de la Paz (Pueblo) (1989), Revs. Rafael Perez, O.S.B.; Eric R. Buermann, O.S.B.; Mauro Simpson, O.S.B.; Ignacio Aguirre, O.S.B.; Deacon Rafael Ulfret.
Mailing Address: Villa Universitaria, Box 10160 CUH Sta., 00792.
Res., Villa Universitaria, Calle 4 A20, 00792. Tel: 787-850-3081; Fax: 787-850-3080.
Catechesis/Religious Programs—Students 120.
Chapels—Sagrado Corazon de Jesus, (1940); San Martin de Porres, (1962); Bo. Mariana IV; Buen Pastor, (1970); Bo. Tejas, Cristo Rey, (1976); Bo. Mariana II, Santa Rosa de Lima, (1978); Comunidad Vista Hemosa.

Humacao Playa, Humacao Co., Nuestra Senora del Carmen (Punta Santiago) (1970), Rev. Pedro Oyarbide.
Res., Box 91, Punta Santiago, 00741. Tel: 787-850-2125.

Catechesis/Religious Programs—Calle 5 #103 Verde Mar, P.O. Box 91, Punta Santiago, 00741. Students 215.
Chapel—Bo. Pasto Viejo, Sector El batey, Nuestra Senora del Perpetuo Socorro, (1937; 1986).

Juncos, Juncos Co., Inmaculada Concepcion (1797), Revs. Jose M. Calvo Muniain; Miguel Arregui Moso.
Res., Almodovar St. #18, Box 1728, 00777. Tel: 787-724-2431.
Catechesis/Religious Programs—Students 81.
Chapels—Bo. Canta Gallo, Cristo Redentor, (1975); Bo. Ceiba Sur, Sagrado Corazon, (1976); Bo. Valenciano Sector Amigo, Espiritu Santo, (1976); Bo. Ceiba Norte, Cristo Rey, (1978); Bo. Valenciano Arriba, San Juan Bautista, (1979); Bo. Ceiba Norte Sector Chinos, Buen Pastor, (1979); Bo. Pinas, Santa Cruz, (1981); Bo. Lirios, San Jose, (1978); Bo. Canta Gallo Secto Reparto Valenciano, Maria Reina De La Paz, (1993).
Mission—Bo. Placita.

Las Piedras, Las Piedras Co., Inmaculada Concepcion (1801), Revs. Jose A. De Leon; Heriberto Mejias Castrillon.
Res., Box 324, 00771. Tel: 787-733-2381.
Catechesis/Religious Programs—Tel: 787-733-8325. Hna. Monica Mantilla, D.R.E. Students 186.
Chapels—Bo. Montones I, Perpetuo Socorro, (1935); Bo. Tejas Asomonte, Nuestra Senora de la Providencia, (1955); Bo. La Fermina, Jesus de Nazaret, (1979); Bo. Montones IV, Santa Teresa del Nino Jesus, (1980); Bo. Montones II, San Juan Bautista, (1982).
Mission—Salon Usos Multiples-April Gardens, Las Piedras.

San Juan Bautista (Bo. Pueblito del Rio) (1971), Rev. Tomas Galarza.
Res., Bo. Pueblito del Rio, HC 02, Buzon 4467, 00771. Tel: 787-733-6444.
Chapels—Finca Roig, San Juan Bautista, (1911; 1940); Bo. Boqueron, La Sagrada Familia, (1957); Bo. Pena Pobre, Santo Tomas de Aquino, (1964); Bo. Rio Blanco, La Milagrosa, (1972); Bo. Mango, San Francisco Javier.
Mission—Bo. Pasto Seco.

Maunabo, Maunabo Co., San Isidor Labrador (1799), Rev. Boris Espinosa.
Res., Box 248, 00707. Tel: 787-861-2595.
Chapels—Nuestra Senora del Carmen, (1962); Bo. La Playa, Nuestra Senora de la Providencia, (1971); Bo. Mattuyas, Nuestra Senora de la Candelaria, (1974); Bo. Palo Seco, San Judas Tadeo, (1975); Bo. Emajaguas, San Antonio de Padua, (1977).
Missions—Bo. Quebrada Arenas; Bo. Lizas; Bo. Talante; Bo. Tumbao; Bo. La Pica; Bo. California.

Naguabo, Naguabo Co., Nuestra Senora del Rosario (1798), Revs. P. Jose A. Rivera Maldonado; Juan Jose Colon.
Res., Box 665, 00718. Tel: 787-874-2235; Fax: 787-874-0150.
Chapels—Nuestra Senora del Perpetuo Socorro, (1942); Bo. Maizales, Nuestra Senora de la Altagracia, (1963); Bo. Duque, Nuestra Senora de Fatima, (1965); Bo. Florida, Nuestra Senora del Perpetuo Socorro, (1942); Nuestra Senora del Carmen Playa Hucares, (1920); Bo. Mariana, Nuestra Senora de la Providencia, (1965); Bo. Santiago y Lima (Botija), Santa Rosa de Lima, (1975).
Missions—Barrio Rio, Sector Brazo Seco; Barrio Cecilia, Sector La Fe.

San Lorenzo, San Lorenzo Co., Nuestra Senora de la Mercedes (1810), Revs. Samuel Santiago, C.Ss.R.; Federico J. Consla, C.Ss.R.; Dennis Demko, C.Ss.R.; Santiago Mallen, C.Ss.R.
Res., Munoz Rivera 55, Apartado 1280, 00754-1280. Tel: 787-736-2571.
Chapels—Bo. Quebrada Honda, Santa Teresita de Jesus, (1948); Bo. Jagual, Nuestra Senora del Carmen, (1952); Bo. Quemados, Nuestra Senora del Perpetuo Socorro, (1957); Bo. Cerro Gordo Abajo, Santisimo Redentor, (1965); Bo. Quebrada, Jesus Maestro; Bo. Florida, Santa Monica; Bda. Roosevelt, Nuestra Senora del Carmen, (1968); Bo. Hato Km. 6, Nuestra Senora del Perpetuo Socorro, (1968); Bo. Cayaguas, San Alfonso Maria de Ligorio, (1972); Bo. Cerro Gordo Arriba, Nuestra Senora del Perpetuo Socorro, (1977); Bo. Lorenzo del Valle, Inmaculado Corazon de Maria, (1978); Bo. Santa Clara, San Gerardo, (1986); Urb. Los Flamboyanes, Bo. Florida, Nuestra Senora de Lourdes, (1988).
Catechesis/Religious Programs—Students 708.

Sagrado Corazon de Jesus y 12 Apostoles (Bo. Espino), Rev. Luis Antonio Rivera.
Res., Bo. Espino, HC 81, Box 8141, 00754. Tel: 787-736-9090.
Chapels—San Francisco de Asis, (1988), Carr. 181; Santa Rosa de Lima, (1989), Carr. 181; San Jose, (1989), Carr. 181.

Yabucoa, Yabucoa Co., Santos Angeles Cutodios (1793), Revs. Javier Hernandez; Jose A. Arocho; Ramon Santana; Deacons Rafael Medina; Juan Ramon Delgado.
Res., Box 7, 00767. Tel: 787-893-2250; 3347.
Catechesis/Religious Programs—Students 335.
Chapels—Bo. Rosa Sanchez, Santa Rosa de Lima; Bo. Pueblo, Parroquia Santos Angeles Custodios; Bo. Jacanas Granjas, San Juan Evangelista; Bo. Jac. Piedra Blanca, Sagrado Corazon, (1976); Bo. Tejas Piedra Azul, Sta. Maria Reina Paz; Bo. Martorell, Santa Teresita del Nino Jesus; Bo. Tejas, Ntra. Sra. de la Divina Providencia; Bo. Playita Cuesta, San Bernardo; Bo. Playita Arriba, S. Antonio de Padua, (1947); Bo. Playita Parcelas, Virgen Milagrosa; Bo. Quebradillas, Ntra. Sra. del Carmen; Bo. Guayabota, La Sagrada Familia, (1948); Bo. Calabazas Arriba, San Jose, (1942); Bo. Quebrada Grande, San Benito; Bo. Playa Guayanes, Ntra. Sra. del Carmen; Bo. Aguacate, Ntra. Sra. del Perpetuo Socorro, (1937); Bo. Jagueyes, Inmaculada Concepcion, (1910); Bo. Ingenio, Santisima Trinidad; Bo. Camino Nuevo, San Jeronimo.

OUTSIDE THE MAIN ISLAND OF PUERTO RICO, THE SMALL ISLANDS

Culebra, Culebra Co., Nuestra Senora del Carmen (1889; 1990), Rev. Renelmo Ramirez.
Mailing Address: P.O. Box 236, 00775. Tel: 787-742-0133.

Vieques, Vieques Co., Inmaculada Concepcion (1840), Rev. Enrique Gomez; Deacons Justino Lopez Ortiz; Pedro Ramos.
Res., 442 Lebruon St., 00765. Tel: 787-741-2241.
Chapels—Bo. Puerto Real, Sagrado Corazon de Jesus, (1949); Bo. Esperanza, San Gerardo, (1952); Bo. Monte Santo, Nuestra Senora del Perpetuo Socorro, (1945); Bo. Santa Maria, Virgen del Carmen, (1942); Bo. Destino, Nuestra Senora de Fatima, (1950).

Chaplains of Public Institutions

CAGUAS. *Government Regional Hospital*. Rev. Lorenzo Jovellar, S.J.; Sr. Asuncion Ma. Vargas, M.B.P.
Hospital Hima. Rev. Jose Flores.

Retired:
Reverend Fathers—
Gutierrez, Julio
Martinez, Alfredo

INSTITUTIONS LOCATED IN THE DIOCESE

[A] PAROCHIAL SCHOOLS

CAGUAS. *Academia Cristo de los Milagros*, Box 7618, 00726-7618. Tel: 787-743-4855; 743-3131; 743-4242; Fax: 787-746-1428. Students 1,508; Priests 2; Lay Teachers 57.
Colegio Catolico Notre Dame Elemental, Box 967, 00726. Tel: 787-743-2385; 743-2524; Fax: 787-743-7567. Students 1,031; Priests 4; Brothers 1; Sisters 2; Lay Teachers 43; Aids 10.
Colegio Catolico Notre Dame Superior, Box 541, 00726. Tel: 787-743-3693; 743-5501; Fax: 787-258-9648. Students 1,200; Priests 2; Sisters 4; Lay Teachers 68.
Colegio San Jose Elemental, Box 806, 00726. Tel: 787-743-2032; Fax: 787-258-0683. Students 578; Priests 2; Sisters 5.
Colegio San Jose Superior, Box 1101, 00726. Tel: 787-744-8993; Fax: 787-744-4111. Priests 1; Lay Teachers 22; Students 442.
Colegio San Juan Apostol y Evangelista, P.O. Box 459, 00726-0459; Fax: 787-743-8266. Students 324.
Escuela Nuestra Sra. de la Providencia, P.O. Box 1723, 00726. Tel: 787-747-8866. Students 80.

AGUAS BUENAS. *Academia San Alfonso*. (Grades PreK-9), Pio Rechani St., Box 1, 00703. Tel: 787-732-8288. Students 249; Lay Teachers 15.

AIBONITO. *Colegio Parroquial San Jose*, Box 812, 00705. Tel: 787-735-7235. Students 107; Priests 1; Lay Teachers 12.

BARRANQUITAS. *Colegio San Francisco de Asis Elemental y Superior*, Box 789, 00794. Tel: 787-857-2123. Students 290.

CAYEY. *Colegio Nuestra Senora de la Merced*, Lucia Vazquez St., 00736. Tel: 787-738-3438; Fax: 787-263-5837. (Nuestra Senora de la Asuncion Parish). Students 550.

FAJARDO. *Colegio Santiago Apostol*. (Grades K-12), Box 907, 00738. Tel: 787-863-0524; 863-0445; Fax: 787-860-6655. Students 655; Priests 2; Sisters 1; Lay Teachers 33.

GURABO. *Colegio Ntra. Sra. De Pilar*, P.O. Box 733, 00778. Tel: 787-737-1400. Mrs. Lydia Acevedo. Students 75.

HUMACAO. *Colegio Nuestra Senora del Perpetuo Socorro de Humacao, Inc.*, P.O. Box 910, 00792. Tel: 787-852-0845; 850-0025; Fax: 787-852-8706. Students 444.
Colegio San Antonio Abad. (Benedictines), Box 729, 00792. Tel: 787-852-1616. Sra. Zenaida Aponte, Prin. Students 419; Priests 3; Brothers 3; Lay Teachers 28.
Collegio San Benito, Box 728, 00792. Tel: 787-852-1365; 850-7075. Students 826; Sisters 1; Lay Teachers 42.

JUNCOS. *Colegio Corazon de Maria*, Box 500, 00777. Tel: 787-734-5551; 734-5565; Fax: 787-734-2724. Priests 1; Sisters 2; Lay Teachers 19; Students 156.

NARANJITO. *Academia Santa Teresita*, Box 244, 00719. Tel: 787-869-5101; 869-6054. Students 573.

SAN LORENZO. *Colegio Catolico de San Lorenzo*, Box 52, 00754. Tel: 787-736-2619. Lay Teachers 20; Students 120.

[B] RETREAT HOUSES

AGUAS BUENAS. *Casa Cristo Redentor* (1967), Box 492, 00703-0492. Tel: 787-732-5161. Revs. Marcos Wise, C.SS.R.; Terry Tull, C.SS.R.; Bro. Mateo Perez, C.SS.R.

AIBONITO. *Casa Manresa*, Box 1319, 00705. Tel: 787-735-8016; 8017; Fax: 787-735-2421. Revs. Aurelio Adan, Dir.; Efrain Lopez.

JUNCOS. *Casa Cursillos de Cristiandad of Caguas*. (Lay Corp. of Cursillistas), Salida de Juncos Carretera 919, 00666. Tel: 787-734-7068. Rev. Lorenzo Jovellar, S.J., Spiritual Dir.

SAN LORENZO, P.R. *Casa Charlie Rodriguez*, P.O. Box 1190, 00754. Tel: 787-736-5750. Rev. Edward Santana, J.C.D.

[C] MONASTERIES AND RESIDENCES OF PRIESTS

CAGUAS. *Misioneros Hijos del Immaculado Corazon de Maria (Claretianos)*, Bo. Rio Canas HC-05 Box 57564, 00725-9233.

AIBONITO. *Casa Salesiana de Retiros*, P.O. Box 2019, 00705. Tel: 787-735-2486. Revs. Antonio Robles; Julian San Nicasio, 6; Isidro Fernandez; Bros. Santiago Arroyo; Jose Cabo.

HUMACAO. *San Antonio Abad Abbey of the Order of St. Benedict*, Box 729, 00792. Tel: 787-852-1616. Rt. Rev. Jose Rodriguez, O.S.B., Abbot; Very Rev. Eduardo Torrelas, Prior; Revs. Oscar Rivera, O.S.B.; Bernardo Watrin, O.S.B.; Julian Simon, O.S.B. Brothers 6.

[D] CLOISTER SISTERS

AGUAS BUENAS. *Reina de la Paz Convent*, Box 1183, 00703. Tel: 787-732-5339.

NARANJITO. *Visitation Nuns*, Box 302, 00719. Tel: 787-869-0861.

[E] SHRINES

SAN LORENZO, P.R. *Diocesan Shrine Our Lady of Mount Carmel*, P.O. Box 1190, 00754. Tel: 787-736-5750. Rev. Edward Santana, J.C.D., Rector.

[F] MISCELLANEOUS

CAGUAS, P.R. *Diocesan Tribunal of Caguas*, Box 8698, 00626. Tel: 787-747-5885;747-5787. Rev. Edward Santana, J.C.D., Judicial Vicar.
Instituto Secular de Ntra. Sra. de la Altagracia, Calle 13, L23. Urb. Delgado, 00725. Tel: 787-744-3628. Isabel Vazquez Rivera; Casilda Noboa Noboa; Maria Melendez Rivera; Ramonita Lopez Diaz; Zoraida Santos; Judith Colon; Olga Rodriguez Bennios; Maria Isabel Colon; Prixda Santos Agosto.
Movimiento Juan XXIII. 787-747-3748, P.O. Box 7229, 00726. Rev. Jose Flores.
Pastoral de Ecuadores. Association of Catholic Teachers. P.O. Box 1723, 00726.
Voluntarios en Accion, Contra el Sida, P.O. Box 656, 00726.

RELIGIOUS INSTITUTES OF MEN REPRESENTED IN THE DIOCESE

For further details refer to the corresponding bracketed number in the Religious Institutes of Men or Women section.

[0200]—*Benedictine Monks*. (Collegeville, MN).—O.S.B.
[]—*Claretian Fathers*.—C.M.F.
[0220]—*Congregation of the Blessed Sacrament*. (N. Spain Prov.).—S.S.S.
[0650]—*Holy Ghost Fathers*. (Eastern Prov.).—C.S.Sp.
[0690]—*Jesuit Fathers and Brothers*. (New York Prov.).—S.J.
[]—*Mercedarian Fathers*. (Spain).
[0840]—*Missionary Servants of the Most Holy Trinity*.—S.T.
[0910]—*Oblates of Mary Immaculate*. (Eastern Prov.).—O.M.I.
[1070]—*Redemptorist Fathers*. (San Juan Prov.).—C.SS.R.

[1190]—*Salesians of Don Bosco.* (Cuba).—S.D.B.

RELIGIOUS INSTITUTES OF WOMEN REPRESENTED IN THE DIOCESE

[0230]—*Benedictine Sisters of Pontifical Jurisdiction.* (St. Joseph, MN).—O.S.B.

[0420]—*Discalced Carmelite Nuns.* (Spain).—O.C.C.

[]—*Franciscan Nuns (Cloistered).*

[2790]—*Missionary Servants of the Most Holy Trinity.* (Spain).—M.S.B.T.

[3760]—*Order of St. Clare.*—P.C.C.

[]—*Sacred Heart Sisters.*

[]—*Salesian Sisters.*

[2970]—*School Sisters of Notre Dame.* (Wilton, CT).—S.S.N.D.

[]—*Siervas de Maria.* (Spain).

[0640]—*Sisters of Charity of St. Vincent de Paul.* (Puerto Rico Prov.).—S.C.

[]—*Sisters of Fatima.* (Diocesan).

[1650]—*The Sisters of St. Francis of Philadelphia.*—O.S.F.

[2150]—*Sisters Servants of the Immaculate Heart of Mary.*—I.H.M.

[4190]—*Visitation Nuns.* (Cloistered).—V.H.M.

NECROLOGY

† Rosario, Jorge del Valle, Caguas, Movimiento Juan XX111. —Died Oct. 24, 1995.

Diocese of The Caroline Islands

Most Reverend

AMANDO SAMO, D.D.

Bishop of the Caroline Islands; ordained Priest December 10, 1977; appointed Titular Bishop of Libertina and Auxiliary Bishop of the Caroline and Marshalls May 10, 1987; ordained Bishop August 15, 1987; named Coadjutor February 3, 1994; named Bishop of the Diocese March 25, 1995; installed June 6, 1995. *Res., P.O. Box 202, Chuuk, Caroline Islands, FM, 96942.* Tel.: 691-330-2399; Fax: 691-330-4585.

Most Reverend

MARTIN J. NEYLON, S.J., D.D.

Retired Bishop of the Caroline Islands; ordained June 18, 1950; appointed Titular Bishop of Libertina October 2, 1969, *"cum jure successionis"*; consecrated February 2, 1970; succeeded as Vicar Apostolic September 20, 1971; appointed First Bishop of Carolines-Marshalls May 3, 1979; installed February 3, 1980; retired June 6, 1995. *Res., Vicariate Residence, P.O. Box 250, Chuuk, Caroline Islands, FM, 96942.* Tel.: 691-330-2313; Fax: 691-330-4394.

Square Miles Ocean 1,800,000.

Total Population of 123,812.

Vicariate of the Caroline Islands erected December 10, 1905 and committed to the Order of Friars Minor Capuchin, extended to the Mariana Islands March 1, 1911.

Vicariate of the Marianas and Caroline and Marshall Islands erected May 4, 1923 and committed to the Society of Jesus. Marianas Islands separated July 4, 1946. Diocese of the Caroline-Marshalls created February 3, 1980. The Marshalls made a separate Prefecture Apostolic August 15, 1993, and the Diocese renamed "Diocese of the Caroline Islands."

Civilly it includes the four Federated States of Micronesia (Chuuk, Kosrae, Pohnpei and Yap) and the Republic of Palau.

E-mail address: 103651.1075@compuserve.com:

STATISTICAL OVERVIEW

Personnel	
Bishop	1
Retired Bishops	1
Priests: Diocesan Active in Diocese	11
Priests: Active Outside Diocese	1
Number of Diocesan Priests	12
Religious Priests in Diocese	16
Ordinations:	
Permanent Deacons	3
Permanent Deacons in Diocese	42
Total Brothers	2
Total Sisters	33
Parishes	
Parishes	21
With Resident Pastor:	
Resident Diocesan Priests	8
Resident Religious Priests	3
Without Resident Pastor:	
Administered by Permanent Deacons	8
Administered by Lay People	2
Missions	18
New Parishes Created	2
Professional Ministry Personnel:	
Sisters	4
Lay Ministers	4
Educational	
Diocesan Students in Other Seminaries	11
Total Seminarians	11
High Schools, Diocesan and Parish	3
Total Students	380
High Schools, Private	2
Total Students	321
Elementary Schools, Diocesan and Parish	5
Total Students	1,644
Catechesis/Religious Education:	
High School Students	450
Elementary Students	3,250
Total Students Under Catholic Instruction	6,056
Teachers in the Diocese:	
Priests	8
Scholastics	5
Brothers	1
Sisters	26
Lay Teachers	129
Vital Statistics	
Receptions into the Church:	
Infant Baptism Totals	1,895
Adult Baptism Totals	98
Received into Full Communion	71
First Communions	1,501
Confirmations	656
Marriages:	
Catholic	255
Interfaith	18
Total Marriages	273
Total Catholic Population	64,089
Total Population	122,027

Former Bishops—Most Rev. SALVADOR WALLAESER, O.F.M.Cap., cons. Titular Bishop of Tanagra, Aug. 21, 1912; resigned June 23, 1919; died Jan. 1, 1946; Most Rev. SANTIAGO LOPEZ DE REGO, S.J., Titular Bishop of Dionisiopolis; cons. Aug. 26, 1923; resigned June 2, 1939; died Aug. 5, 1940; Most Rev. THOMAS J. FEENEY, S.J., cons. Titular Bishop of Agno, Sept. 8, 1951; died Sept. 9, 1955; Most Rev. VINCENT I. KENNALLY, S.J., cons. Titular Bishop of Sassura, March 25, 1957; resigned Sept. 20, 1971; died April 12, 1977; Most Rev. MARTIN J. NEYLON, S.J., ord. Bishop, Feb. 2, 1970; succeeded to as Vicar Apostolic, Sept. 20, 1970; named to be Bishop of the new diocese, May 3, 1979; installed as first Bishop of the Diocese of the Carolines-Marshalls, Feb. 3, 1980; retired June 6, 1995.

Chancery Office—Nepukos, Chuuk: P.O. Box 202, Chuuk, FM, 96942. Tel: 691-330-2399; Fax: 691-330-4585.

Vicar General and Chancellor—Rev. JOHN F. CURRAN, S.J., J.C.L.

Diocesan Consultors—Revs. JULIO ANGKEL; JOHN F. CURRAN, S.J.; WILLIAM J. MCGARRY, S.J.; APOLLINARIS THALL, S.J.; FELIX YAOCH, S.J.

Finance Committee—Rev. JOHN F. CURRAN, S.J.; Mr. SANTI ASANUMA; Mr. ERHARD ATEN; Mr. TONY GANNGIYAN; Mr. WILLIAM IRIARTE; Mr. T. ROY SULLIVAN.

Episcopal Vicars—

Chuuk—Rev. JULIO ANGKEL, *P.O. Box 250, Chuuk, FM, 96942.* Tel: 691-330-4525; Fax: 691-330-4394.

Palau—Rev. FELIX YAOCH, S.J., *P.O. Box 128, Palau, PW, 96940.* Tel: 680-488-2226; Fax: 680-488-1725.

Pohnpei-Kosrae—Rev. WILLIAM J. MCGARRY, S.J., *P.O. Box 160, Pohnpei, FM, 96941.* Tel: 691-320-4661; Fax: 691-320-5876.

Yap—Rev. APOLLINARIS THALL, S.J., *P.O. Box "A", Yap, FM, 96943.* Tel: 691-350-2265/2547; Fax: 691-350-2784.

Diocesan Tribunal—

Judical Vicar—Rev. WILLIAM J. RAKOWICZ, S.J.

Defenders of the Bond—Most Rev. MARTIN J. NEYLON, S.J., D.D.; Revs. FLORENTINUS AKKIN; NEIL POULIN, S.J.; RUSK SABURO.

Notaries—Rev. PATRICK J. SULLIVAN, S.J.; Miss ELSA VELOSO.

Director, Pontifical Missions Societies—Rev. JOHN F. CURRAN, S.J.

Director, Apostleship of Prayer—Rev. KENNETH J. HEZEL, S.J.

Vocations—Most Rev. AMANDO SAMO.

CLERGY, PARISHES, MISSIONS AND PAROCHIAL SCHOOLS

CHUUK (TRUK) STATE, CAROLINE ISLANDS
Mailing Address: for Chuuk State: P.O. Box 250, Chuuk, Caroline Islands, FM 96942 unless otherwise noted.

Moen, Immaculate Heart of Mary Cathedral (Weno) (Tunnuk), Rev. Julio Angkel.
School—St. Cecilia's. Mrs. Dolores Rosokow, Prin. Mercedarian Missionaries of Berriz 3; Lay Teachers 31; Students 726.

Holy Family Church (Weno) (Nepukos), Rev. David Lewis; Deacon Eliot Cholymay.

Fefan, Sacred Heart, Rev. Kirino B. Halley.
Missions—Parem,; Tsis,; Magur, Marie Chapel; Ono, Sacred Heart; Onari, St. Cecilia; Pisarach, St. Catherine of Siena. Rev. Kirino B. Halley.

Ulul, Sacred Heart,
Missions—Magur, Marie Chapel; Ono, Sacred Heart; Onari, St. Cecilia; Pisarach, St. Catherine of Siena. Rev. Kirino Halley.

Udot, St. Francis Assisi, Deacons John Fritz; Eichy Karsom.
Missions—Romanum, St. Joseph; Uman, St. Michael. Deacon Iakim Sos.

Tol, Assumption of the Blessed Virgin Mary, Rev. Florentinus Akkin; Deacon Angkel Rapun.
School—St. Julia. Sr. Yolanda Delgadillo, M.M.B., Prin.
Mercedarian Missionaries of Berriz 5; Lay Teachers 7; Students 104.
Missions—Puluwat; Santiago; Pulusuk, Our Lady of Fatima; Tamatam, Maria Lourdes; Punlap, Sacred Heart. Rev. Florantinus Akhein.

Puluwat, Santiago Church, Rev. Florentinus Akkin.

Missions—Pulusuk, Our Lady of Fatima; Tamatam, Maria Lourdes; Punlop, Sacred Heart.

Dublon, St. Anthony's (Toloas), Rev. Basilio Dilipy; Deacon Tobias Soram.
Mission—Hall Islands. Rev. Basilio Dilipy.

Lukunor, Sacred Heart, Rev. Adalbert Umwech.
Missions—Satawan; Kutu; Moch; Ettal; Namoluk; Oneap; Ta; Nama; Piis; Losap.

POHNPEI STATE, CAROLINE ISLANDS
Mailing Address: for Pohnpei State: P.O. Box 160, Pohnpei, Caroline Islands, FM 96941. Tel: 691-320-2557, unless otherwise noted.

Kolonia, Our Lady of Mercy, Deacons Geronimo Victor; Martiniano Rodriguez.
School—Pohnpei Catholic School.
Sisters 2; Lay Teachers 10; Students 266.
Missions—Kapingmarangi; Ngatik.

Eni-mwahn, St. Augustine, Deacon Alius Dorres, Admin.
Tel: 691-320-3970.

Kitii, Christ the King, Deacon Koropin Kermen, Admin.

Palikir, St. Paul, Deacon Salus Olpet, Admin.

Seinwar, Most Pure Heart of Mary, Rev. Rex Edwin.

Sokens, St. Peter's, Rev. Etwel Pelep.

Tamoroi, FM, Sacred Heart, Deacon Peter Silbanuz, Admin.
Mission—Metip.

Uh, St. Joseph, Deacon Manuel Amor, Admin.

YAP STATE, CAROLINE ISLANDS
Mailing Address: for Yap State: P.O. Box A, Yap, Caroline Islands, FM 96943. Tel: 691-350-2265; 350-2547 Fax: 691-350-2784.

Nemar, St. Mary, Rev. Apollinaris I. Thall, S.J.
School—St. Mary's. Sr. Walter Marie Ray, S.S.N.D., Prin.
Sisters 2; Lay Teachers 14; Students 308.

Gagil, St. Joseph, Rev. Neil C. Poulin, S.J.

Tomil, St. Peter Chanel, Rev. Neil C. Poulin, S.J.

Ulithi & Neighboring Islands, Queen of Heaven, Rev. Nicholas Rahoy; Deacon John Rulmal.
Missions—Euripik; Fais; Faraulep; Lamotrek; Ngulu; Satawal; Asor; Fassarai.

Woleai & Neighboring Islands, St. Ignatius, Rev. Nicholas Rahoy.

REPUBLIC OF PALAU, CAROLINE ISLANDS
Mailing Address: for Palau: P.O. Box 128, Koror, Palau PW 96940. Tel: 680-488-2226; Fax: 680-488-1819.

Koror, Sacred Heart, Rev. Felix K. Yaoch, S.J.
School—Maris Stella. Mr. Felix Okabe, Prin.
Mercedarian Missionaries of Berriz 5; Lay Teachers 16; Students 236.
Missions—Ngcheangl; Sonsorol.
Convent— Our Lady of Lourdes
Mercedarian Missionaries of Berriz 8.
Manresa Jesuit Novitiate—Rev. Daniel J. Mulhauser, S.J., Dir.
Novices 1.

Angaur, Holy Rosary, Rev. Juan Bizkarra, S.J.

Babeldaob, Catholic Churches, Revs. Rusk R. Saburo; John Paul Ililau.

Permanent Deacons:
Albert, Joseph, Uman, Chuuk
Amor, Manuel, Awak, Pohnpei
Cholymay, Eliot, Moen, Chuuk
Dorres, Aluis, Enimwahn, Pohnpei
Else, Pelsiano, Sopwahfik, Pohnpei
Elukan, Augustine, Gagil-Tomil, Yap
Felichoo, Francisco, Gagil-Tomil, Yap
Fichibman, Donald, Gagil-Tomil, Yap
Fritz, John, Udot, Chuuk
Hartman, Marcello, (Retired), Udot, Chuuk
Ikuta, Francisco, Pwene, Chuuk
Ioanis, Lorens, Seinwar, Pohnpei
Itiraw, Bername, Moen, Chuuk
John, Sandy, Romanum, Chuuk
Karsom, Eichy, Udot, Chuuk
Kermen, Koropin, Kiti, Pohnpei
Lawrence, Adelino, Uh, Pohnpei
Mailos, Salvador, Uman, Chuuk
Meisa, Akiuo, Uman, Chuuk
Nimas, Andreas, Uman, Chuuk
Noporu, Yostaro, Fono, Chuuk
Olbet, Saulus, Palikir, Pohnpei
Oneitam, Nory, Uman, Chuuk
Paulus, Lucas, Fanapanges, Chuuk
Pelep, Etwel, Kolonia, Pohnpei
Pelep, Misael, (Retired), Kolonia, Pohnpei
Rapun, Angken, Tol, Chuuk
Rawit, Kintin, Wonei, Chuuk
Rodriguez, Martiniano, Kolonia, Pohupei
Rokop, Roke, Tol, Chuuk
Rulmal, John B., Ulithi, Yap
Ruta, Itol, Tol, Chuuk
Sam, Karlos, Uman, Chuuk
Santos, Thomas, Wene, Pohnpei
Sewell, Misa, Tol, Chuuk
Shuru, Edwin, Moen, Chuuk
Silbanuz, Peter, Tamworoi, Pohnpei
Soram, Tobias, Tolowas, Chuuk
Sos, Iakim, Uman, Chuuk
Victor, Geronimo, Kolonia, Pohnpei
Victus, Oiken, Pwene, Chuuk
William, Chitaro, Moen, Chuuk

INSTITUTIONS LOCATED IN THE DIOCESE

[A] PASTORAL RESEARCH INSTITUTE

POHNPEI. *Micronesia Seminar*, P.O. Box 160, 96941. Tel: 691-320-4067; Fax: 691-320-5876. Rev. Francis X. Hezel, S.J., Dir. Lay assistants 2.

[B] HIGH SCHOOLS

CHUUK. *Saramen Chuuk Academy*, P.O. Box 662, 96942. Tel: 691-330-4442; Fax: 691-330-4452. Mr. Patrick Blank, Prin.; Rev. Cuthbert Yifthog; Deacon Eliot Cholymay. Sisters 5; Lay Teachers 11; Students 226.
Xavier High School, P.O. Box 220, 96942. Tel: 691-330-4266; Fax: 691-330-4753. Rev. Patrick J. Sullivan, S.J., Dir.; Mr. Mike Toolan, Prin. Priests 2; Lay Teachers 12; Scholastics 5; Students 172.

PALAU, PW. *Mindszenty High School*, P.O. Box 69, 96940. Tel: 680-488-2437. Mr. Ben Imperial, Prin. Priests 1; Mercedarian Sisters 1.

POHNPEI. *Our Lady of Mercy Vocational Training School*, P.O. Box 73, 96941. Tel: 691-320-3168. Sr. Maria Perez-Caballero, M.M.S., Prin. Mercedarian Sisters 2; Lay Teachers 6; Students 38.
PATS (Pohnpei Agriculture and Trade School), P.O. Box 39, 96941. Tel: 691-320-2991; Fax: 691-320-6046. Revs. Joseph E. Billotti, S.J., Dir.; Paul L. Horgan, S.J., Chap.; Edward A. Soucie, S.J., Asst. Dir.; Bro. Terence N. Todd, S.J., Asst. Dir. Priests 3; Brother teaching 1; Lay Teachers 32; Students 148.

[C] RESIDENCES OF PRIESTS AND BROTHERS

KOLONIA, POHNPEI. *Jesuit House*, P.O. Box 160, 96941. Tel: 691-320-2317; Fax: 691-320-5876. In res., Very Rev. Francis X. Hezel, S.J., Regional Supr.; Revs. Gregory F. Muckenhaupt, S.J., Supt.; William J. McGarry, Vicar; Bro. Juan Ngiraibiruch, S.J.

KOROR, PALAU, PW. *Manresa Jesuit House*, P.O. Box 128, 96940. Tel: 680-488-2226; Fax: 680-488-1819; 488-1725. Revs. Felix Yaoch, S.J., Supr.; Daniel J. Mulhauser, S.J., Master of Novices. Priests 3; Novices 3.

TUNNUK, CHUUK. *Vicariate Residence*, P.O. Box 250, 96942. Tel: 691-330-2313; Fax: 691-330-4394. In res., Most Rev. Martin J. Neylon, S.J., D.D.; Revs. Julio Angkel; John F. Curran, S.J.; David Lewis; William E. Rively, S.J.; William T. Suchan, S.J.

[D] RESIDENCES OF SISTERS

AWAK, POHNPEI. *Sisters of Marie Auxiliatrice*, P.O. Box 1375, 96942. Tel: 691-320-2626. Sr. Hikari Saito, M.A., Supr. Sisters 6; Novices 2; Postulants 1.

COLONIA, YAP. *Maryknoll Sisters*, P.O. Box 26, 96943. Tel: 691-350-2148 (Colonia); 350-2420 (Tomil). Sr. Joanne McMahon, M.M., Contact Person. Sisters 3.
School Sisters of Notre Dame, P.O. Box 111, 96943. Tel: 691-350-2345. Sr. Walter Marie Ray, S.S.N.D., Contact Person. Sisters 2.

KOLONIA, POHNPEI. *Mercedarian Missionaries of Berriz*, P.O. Box 73, 96941. Tel: 691-320-2558. Sr. Justina Udui, M.M.B., Coord. Sisters 4.

KOROR, PALAU, PW. *Mercedarian Missionaries of Berriz*, P.O. Box 56, 96940. Tel: 680-488-2272. Sr. Antonia Malsol, M.M.B., Coord. Sisters 8.

NEEPWUKOS, CHUUK. *Religious Sisters of Mercy*, 96942. Sr. Cabrini Taitano, R.S.M., Coord. Sisters 2.
School Sisters of Notre Dame, P.O. Box 824, 96942. Tel: 691-330-2900. Sr. Bernard Umpingco, S.S.N.D., Coord. Sisters 2.

TOL, CHUUK. *Mercedarian Missionaries of Berriz*, P.O. Box 190, 96942. Sr. Yolanda Delgadillo, M.M.B., Coord. Sisters 6.

WEENO, CHUUK. *Mercedarian Missionaries of Berriz*, P.O. Box 67, 96942. Tel: 691-330-4587. Sr. Christina Imeong, M.M.B., Coord. Sisters 4.

RELIGIOUS INSTITUTES OF MEN REPRESENTED IN THE DIOCESE

For further details refer to the corresponding bracketed number in the Religious Institutes of Men or Women section.

[0690]—*Jesuit Fathers and Brothers*. (New York Prov.)—S.J.

RELIGIOUS INSTITUTES OF WOMEN REPRESENTED IN THE DIOCESE

[2470]—*Maryknoll Sisters of St. Dominic*.—M.M.

[2510]—*Mercedarian Missionaries of Berriz*.—M.M.B.

[2970]—*School Sisters of Notre Dame*.—S.S.N.D.

[2575]—*Sisters of Mercy of the Americas*.—R.S.M.

[]—*Sisters of Marie Auxiliatrice*.—M.A.

NECROLOGY

(No Deaths)

Diocese of Chalan Kanoa

(Dioecesis Vialembensis)

Most Reverend

TOMAS A. CAMACHO, D.D.

Bishop of Chalan Kanoa; ordained June 14, 1961; appointed Prelate of Honor by Pope Paul VI in 1974; appointed Bishop of Chalan Kanoa November 8, 1984; consecrated and installed January 13, 1985. *Res., Mount Carmel Rectory, P.O. Box 745, Saipan, MP, 96950.* Tel.: 670-234-3000.

ESTABLISHED NOVEMBER 8, 1984.

Square Miles 183.61.

Corporate Title: "Bishop of Chalan Kanoa, a Corporation Sole."

Comprises the Mariana Island chain except for Guam, known legally as the Commonwealth of the Northern Mariana Islands.

For legal titles of parishes and diocesan institutions, consult the Chancery Office.

E-mail address: richard.shewman@saipan.com

STATISTICAL OVERVIEW

Personnel	
Bishop	1
Number of Diocesan Priests	6
Religious Priests in Diocese	1
Extern Priests in Diocese	6
Ordinations:	
Diocesan Priests	1
Permanent Deacons in Diocese	3
Total Sisters	35
Parishes	
Parishes	9
With Resident Pastor:	
Resident Diocesan Priests	6
Resident Religious Priests	1
Without Resident Pastor:	
Administered by Priests	2
Missions	2
New Parishes Created	1
Professional Ministry Personnel:	
Sisters	2
Lay Ministers	99
Welfare	
Special Centers for Social Services	1
Total Assisted	2,284
Educational	
High Schools, Diocesan and Parish	1
Total Students	192
Elementary Schools, Diocesan and Parish	2
Total Students	509
Catechesis/Religious Education:	
High School Students	431
Elementary Students	1,021
Total Students Under Catholic Instruction	2,153
Teachers in the Diocese:	
Sisters	5
Lay Teachers	42
Vital Statistics	
Receptions into the Church:	
Infant Baptism Totals	850
Adult Baptism Totals	15
Received into Full Communion	1
First Communions	207
Confirmations	182
Marriages:	
Catholic	47
Interfaith	2
Total Marriages	49
Deaths	125
Total Catholic Population	47,322
Total Population	56,189

Chancery Office—P.O. Box 745, Saipan, MP, 96950. Tel: 670-234-3000; Fax: 670-235-3002.

Vicar General—Rev. GARY BRADLEY, S.J.

Diocesan Consultors—Revs. MANUEL CORCUERA; SALVADOR DUMAS; ROGER P.T. TENORIO; GARY BRADLEY, S.J.; MICHAEL MARTIN.

Chancellor—Deacon RICHARD SHEWMAN.

Diocesan Business Office—Mrs. LOLITA MAFNAS BABAUTA, Exec. Sec.; Sr. ASCENSION ZAMBARA, O.P., Archivist and Librarian, *Address all communications to: Chancery Office, P.O.Box 745, Saipan, MP, 96950.* Tel: 670-234-3000.

Diocesan Services and Associations

Superintendent of Catholic Schools—Deacon RICHARD SHEWMAN, *P.O. Box 745, Saipan, MP, 96950.* Tel: 670-234-3000; 234-8888.

Office of Religious Education—Sr. BRIGID PEREZ, R.S.M., Dir., *P.O. Box 745, Saipan, MP, 96950.* Tel: 670-234-3000.

Catholic Daughters of America—Mrs. FELICIDAD OGUMORO, Regent.

Karidat—Ms. LORI OGUMORO, Chm.; Ms. ANGIE GUERRERO, Exec. Dir.

Catholic Cemetery—Mr. MARLON CARLOS; CRIS SABLAN, Consultant.

Catholic Charismatic Renewal—Sr. ANTONETTA ADA, M.M.B.

Christian Mothers Association—Mrs. MALUA PETER, Island Board Pres.; Vacant, Vice Pres.; Vacant, Sec. & Treas.

Oran Katolico (Catholic T.V. Hour)—Rev. ISAAC AYUYU.

Diocesan Publications Office—Deacon RICHARD SHEWMAN, Dir.; Mr. RUY V. POLISTICO, Editor *"North Star" (Diocesan Newspaper)* "Umanidat" (A Journal) and Chamorro Language Devotional Materials.

Diocesan Tribunal—Deacon RICHARD SHEWMAN, J.C.L., Judge & Instructor; Mrs. DEBORAH BARTON, J.C.L., Defender of the Bond, *P.O.Box 745, Saipan, MP, 96950.*

Eucharistic Adoration Society—Most Rev. TOMAS A. CAMACHO; ELIZABETH CHO; FRANCISCO PALACIOS.

Holy Name Society—Mr. SANTIAGO C. TENORIO, Pres.

Hospital Chaplain—Rev. MATTHEW BLOCKLEY, *Commonwealth Health Center, Navy Hill, Saipan.*

Korean Catholic Community—Rev. MYUNG KIM SUNG, Spiritual Dir., *P.O. Box 693, Saipan, MP, 96950.* Tel: 670-234-7878; 234-7177.

Commission for Worship—Mrs. MARGARITA OLAPAI-TAITOUO, Chm.

Saipan Marriage Preparation—Rev. ROGER P.T. TENORIO, Coord.

Vocations—Rev. ROGER P.T. TENORIO, Dir.

Office for Worship—Rev. ISAAC AYUYU.

Youth Ministry—Rev. ROGER P.T. TENORIO, Dir.

Commission on Justice and Development—Ms. MARGARITA OLOPAI-TAITANO, Chm.; Mr. DAVID SABLAN; Mr. JOHN GONZALEZ; Mr. ERIC GREGORIE, Staff.

Diocesan Human Rights Advocate—Mr. ERIC GREGORIE.

Mount Carmel School, Inc.—Mr. DANIEL NIELSEN, Chm.; Sr. KATHLEEN SARMIENTO, R.S.M., Pres.

San Francisco de Borja School, Inc.—Ms. BENITA MANGLONA, Pres.; Sr. BENEDICT SAN NICOLAS, R.S.M., Pres.

Prison Chaplain—Rev. MATTHEW BLOCKLEY.

Police and Fire Chaplain—Rev. MICHAEL MARTIN.

CLERGY, PARISHES, MISSIONS AND PAROCHIAL SCHOOLS

ISLAND OF SAIPAN

Chalan Kanoa Village, Cathedral of Our Lady of Mt. Carmel, Most Rev. Tomas A. Camacho; Rev. Isaac Ayoyu; Deacon Richard D. Shewman.
P.O. Box 745, Saipan, 96950. Tel: 670-234-3000.
School—Mt. Carmel Elementary and High School, P.O. Box 8, 96950. Tel: 670-234-6184; 234-7188. Sr. Kathleen Sarmiento, R.S.M., Pres.
Shrines—Chalan Kanoa, Sacred Heart, District 1; Chalan Kanoa, Our Lady of Fatima, District 3.
Oratory—Mercedarian Missionary Sisters of Berriz. Formation House and Little House.

Garapan Village, District 11, Kristo Rai Parish, Rev. Gary Bradley, S.J.
Oratories—Maturana House of Prayer; Navy Hill, Commonwealth Health Center Chapel.

San Antonio Village, District 6, San Antonio De Padua Parish, Revs. Michael Martin; J. Rudolpho Colendrino.
Res., Mt. Carmel Rectory, P.O. Box 745, Saipan, 96950. Tel: 670-234-3000.

San Jose Village, District 7, San Jose Parish, Rev. Matthew Blockley.
Res., P.O. Box 745, Saipan, 96950. Tel: 670-234-3000.
Church—Tel: 670-234-6991.
Shrine—Chalan Laulau, Immaculate Heart of Mary.

Tanapag Village, District 8, Santa Remedios, Rev. Narcisco Sampana.
Res., Cathedral Rectory, P.O. Box 745, Saipan, 96950. Tel: 670-234-6960.

San Roque Village, District 9, San Roque Parish, Rev. Narcisco Sampana (Philippines).
Res., Cathedral Rectory, P.O. Box 745, Saipan, 96950. Tel: 670-234-6960.

San Vicente Village, District 10, San Vicente Ferrer Parish, Revs. Roger P.T. Tenorio; Vincente Vera.
Res., Mt. Carmel Rectory, P.O. Box 745, Saipan, 96950. Tel: 670-234-3000.
Mission—Saipan, Santa Soledad Mission, (1995). Revs. Roger P.T. Tenorio; Vincente Vera.
Shrine—As Teo, Our Lady of Lourdes.

Saipan, San Jude Parish, Revs. Michael Martin; Jose Rudolpho Colendrino.

Mailing Address: P.O. Box 745, 96950. Tel: 670-234-3000; Fax: 670-235-3002.

ISLAND OF ROTA

Songsong Village, San Francisco de Borja Parish, Rev. Manuel R. Corcuera (Philippines).
Res., Catholic Rectory, Songsong Village, P.O. Box 542, Rota, 96951. Tel: 670-532-3000.
School—San Francisco de Borja School, Inc., Tel: 670-532-5000. Sr. Benedict San Nicolas, R.S.M., Admin.
Shrines—Teneto, Our Lady of Fatima; New Village, Liyo, San Jude Tadeo; Patten Gogue, Santa Lourdes; District #1, Sacred Heart; Our Lady of Perpetual Help.

San Isidro Mission Parish (Sinapalo), Rev. Msgr. Louis Antonelli.
Res., Songsong Village, P.O. Box 542, Rota, 96951. Tel: 670-532-3000.

ISLAND OF TINIAN

San Jose Village, San Jose, Rev. Salvador Dumas (Philippines); Deacon Segundo Castro.
Res., Catholic Rectory, San Jose Village, Tinian, 96952. Tel: 670-433-3000.
Shrine—San Isidro.

DIOCESAN MISSIONS

1—San Jose Chapel.
2—Santa Cruz Chapel. (Alamagan).
3—San Ignacio Chapel. (Pagan).
4—Santa Cruz Chapel. (Agrihan).

INSTITUTIONS LOCATED IN THE DIOCESE

[A] RESIDENCES OF SISTERS

Saipan. *Formation House*, P.O. Box 136, 96950. Tel: 670-234-6127. Sr. Martha Ramarui, M.M.B., Local Coord. Sisters 3; Novices 4; Postulants 4.
Little House, P.O. Box 245, 96950. Tel: 670-234-6127. Sr. Antonieta Ada, M.M.B., Local Coord. Sisters 6.
Maturana House of Prayer, P.O. Box 1178, 96950. Tel: 670-322-9713; 322-6373. Sr. Mary Ann Hartman, M.M.B., Local Coord. Mercedarian Missionaries of Berriz 3.
San Antonio Parish Convent, P.O. Box 745. Tel: 670-234-1752. Sisters 4.

Rota. *Rota Mercy Convent*, P.O. Box 542, 96951. Tel: 670-532-3522. Sr. Benedict San Nicolas, R.S.M., Local Supr. Religious Sisters of Mercy 3.

RELIGIOUS INSTITUTES OF MEN REPRESENTED IN THE DIOCESE

For further details refer to the corresponding bracketed number in the Religious Institutes of Men or Women section.

[0690]—*The Society of Jesus*.—S.J.

[0420]—*Society of the Divine Word*.—S.V.D.

RELIGIOUS INSTITUTES OF WOMEN REPRESENTED IN THE DIOCESE

[]—*Dominican Sisters of the Holy Rosary*.—O.P.

[2510]—*Mercedarian Missionaries of Berriz*.—M.M.B.

[2519]—*Sisters of Mercy, Religious*.—R.S.M.

NECROLOGY

(No Deaths)

Prefecture Apostolic of the Marshall Islands

Very Reverend

JAMES C. GOULD, S.J.

First Prefect Apostolic of the Marshall Islands; appointed First Prefect Apostolic of the Marshall Islands April 23, 1993; installed August 15, 1993. *Res., Cathedral of the Assumption, P.O. Box 8, Majuro, MH, 96960.* Tel.: 011-692-625-6657; Fax: 011-692-625-5520.

Square Miles 500,000.

Total Population (est.) 50,000.

Prefecture Apostolic of the Marshall Islands divided from the Diocese of the Carolines-Marshalls and erected on August 15, 1993 and committed to the Society of Jesus, New York Province. Area is that of the Republic of the Marshall Islands which is civilly under a Compact of Free Association with the United States.

P.O. Box 8:, Majuro, MH, 96960. Tel.: 011-692-625-6657; Fax: 011-692-625-5520.

STATISTICAL OVERVIEW

Personnel	
Priests: Active Outside Diocese	1
Number of Diocesan Priests	1
Religious Priests in Diocese	5
Ordinations:	
Permanent Deacons in Diocese	2
Total Brothers	2
Total Sisters	15
Parishes	
Parishes	4
With Resident Pastor:	
Resident Religious Priests	2
Without Resident Pastor:	
Administered by Priests	2
Missions	9
Pastoral Centers	1
Professional Ministry Personnel:	
Brothers	2
Sisters	15
Lay Ministers	2
Educational	
Diocesan Students in Other Seminaries	1
Total Seminarians	1
High Schools, Diocesan and Parish	2
Total Students	289
Elementary Schools, Diocesan and Parish	6
Total Students	1,248
Catechesis/Religious Education:	
High School Students	55
Elementary Students	357
Total Students Under Catholic Instruction	1,950
Teachers in the Diocese:	
Brothers	2
Sisters	10
Lay Teachers	76
Vital Statistics	
Receptions into the Church:	
Infant Baptism Totals	95
Adult Baptism Totals	15
Received into Full Communion	21
First Communions	142
Confirmations	8
Marriages:	
Catholic	10
Interfaith	1
Total Marriages	11
Deaths	13
Total Catholic Population	4,000
Total Population	50,000

Prefecture Consultors—Rev. R. RICHARD MCAULIFF, S.J.; Sr. JOAN CREVCOURE, M.M.; Mrs. NEIMAT REIMERS; Mr. OSCAR DE BRUM.

Finance Committee—Mr. ALEX BING; Mr. ALAN FOWLER.

Judicial Vicar—Rev. WILLIAM J. RAKOWICZ, S.J., *P.O. Box 250, Chuuk, FM, 96942.*

Defenders of the Bond—Most Rev. MARTIN J. NEYLON, S.J.; Rev. R. RICHARD MCAULIFF, S.J.

Notary—Mrs. VERONICA KILUWE.

Vocations—Rev. Msgr. JAMES C. GOULD, S.J., *P.O. Box 8, Majuro, MH, 96960.*

CLERGY, PARISHES, MISSIONS AND PAROCHIAL SCHOOLS

MARSHALL ISLANDS

Mailing Address: for the Marshalls: P.O. Box 8, Majuro, MH 96960. Tel: (011) 692-625-6675; Fax: (011) 692-625-5520, unless otherwise noted.

Majuro, Cathedral of the Assumption, Rev. Msgr. James C. Gould, S.J.; Rev. R. Richard McAuliff, S.J.; Deacon Alfred Capelle.
Tel: 692-625-3307; Fax: 692-625-6507.
School—Sisters 2; Lay Teachers 22; Students 345.
High School—Sisters 2; Lay Teachers 9; Students 100.
Mission—Majuro Atoll, Laura.

Ebeye, Queen of Peace, Rev. Msgr. James C. Gould, S.J.; Revs. James P. Croghan, S.J.; Leonard G. Hacker, S.J.; Joseph Kanono, M.S.C.
Mailing Address: P.O. Box 5065, Marshall Islands, 96960. Tel: 692-329-3400; Fax: 692-625-3689.
School—School Sisters of Notre Dame 1; Lay Teachers 24; Students 535.
High School—Missionaries of the Sacred Heart (Brothers) 2; School Sisters of Notre Dame 1; Lay Teachers 8; Students 181.
Mission—Kwajalein, Santo.

Kwajalein, Blessed Sacrament, Rev. William Sullivan, S.J.
Mailing Address: P.O. Box 1711, APO AP, 96555. Tel: 805-355-2116;355-4535; Fax: 805-355-1787.

Outer Island Parish, Rev. Msgr. James C. Gould, S.J.
Schools—Arno.
Lay Teachers 4; Students 74; Jaluit.
Lay Teachers 5; Students 90; Wotje.
Lay Teachers 4; Students 75.
Missions—Arno; Ailinglaplap; Jaluit; Likiep; Namorik; Wotje.

Special Assignment:
Reverend Fathers—
Young, David, Military Chap.

INSTITUTIONS LOCATED IN THE DIOCESE

[A] MISCELLANEOUS

MAJURO. *Catholic Apostolic Center: Ajeltake*, P.O. Box 8, 96960. Tel: 011-692-247-7797; Fax: 011-692-625-5520. Sr. Damiana Kauea, O.L.S.H.

NECROLOGY

(No Deaths)

Diocese of Mayaguez, Puerto Rico

(Dioecesis Maiaguezensis)

Most Reverend

ULISES AURELIO CASIANO VARGAS, D.D.

Bishop of Mayaguez; ordained May 30, 1967; appointed Bishop March 4, 1976; ordained April 30, 1976. *Res., P.O. Box 2272, Mayaguez, PR, 00709.* Tel.: 809-833-2475; 833-5411 (Office).

Erected by the Bull *"Qui arcano Dei"* on March 1, 1976, by Pope Paul VI.

Comprises a portion of the southwest of the Island.

STATISTICAL OVERVIEW

Personnel	
Bishop	1
Retired Bishops	1
Priests: Diocesan Active in Diocese	31
Priests: Active Outside Diocese	1
Priests: Retired, Sick or Absent	5
Number of Diocesan Priests	37
Religious Priests in Diocese	32
Extern Priests in Diocese	3
Ordinations:	
Transitional Deacons	2
Permanent Deacons in Diocese	3
Total Brothers	5
Total Sisters	148
Parishes	
Parishes	29
With Resident Pastor:	
Resident Diocesan Priests	20
Resident Religious Priests	9
Without Resident Pastor:	
Pastoral Centers	152
Professional Ministry Personnel:	
Brothers	5
Sisters	148
Lay Ministers	500
Welfare	
Catholic Hospitals	1
Total Assisted	112,300
Homes for the Aged	1
Total Assisted	150
Special Centers for Social Services	1
Total Assisted	1,200
Educational	
Diocesan Students in Other Seminaries	9
Total Seminarians	9
Colleges and Universities	1
Total Students	2,509
High Schools, Diocesan and Parish	3
Total Students	392
High Schools, Private	4
Total Students	896
Elementary Schools, Diocesan and Parish	5
Total Students	1,697
Elementary Schools, Private	7
Total Students	2,731
Catechesis/Religious Education:	
High School Students	1,288
Elementary Students	8,345
Total Students Under Catholic Instruction	17,867
Teachers in the Diocese:	
Priests	9
Brothers	3
Sisters	9
Lay Teachers	301
Vital Statistics	
Receptions into the Church:	
Infant Baptism Totals	5,022
Adult Baptism Totals	148
Received into Full Communion	213
First Communions	3,067
Confirmations	3,152
Marriages:	
Catholic	1,017
Interfaith	32
Total Marriages	1,049
Deaths	2,187
Total Catholic Population	360,000
Total Population	451,000

Vicar General—Rev. Msgr. GONZALO DIAZ.

Episcopal Vicars—
For Pastoral—Rev. ROGELIO MUR, O.Carm.
For Diocesan Administration—Rev. Msgr. GONZALO DIAZ.

Chancery Office—*P.O. Box 2272, Mayaguez, 00681.* Tel: 787-833-5411.

Chancellor—Rev. Msgr. GONZALO DIAZ.

Diocesan Consultors—Rev. Msgr. FRANCIS R. LOPEZ; Rev. Msgr. ROMUALDO M. ORTIZ; Rev. Msgr. GONZALO DIAZ; Rev. Msgr. ANGEL LATRE; Rev. RAFAEL SASTRE.

Diocesan Board of Administration—Rev. Msgr. FRANCIS R. LOPEZ; Rev. Msgr. HECTOR ORTIZ; Rev. ANGEL LATRE.

Administrator—Mr. EFRAIN MOTTA FERRER.

Censor Librorum—Rev. JOSE MORENO.

Diocesan Offices and Directors

Youth Apostolate—Rev. ANGEL LUIS RIOS.

Communications Media—Rev. NOMAR J. CALERO; Sr. MARIA SOCORRO BONILLA, O.P.

Cursillos de Cristiandad—Revs. EDGARDO LOPEZ, Dir. PASCUAL DIEZ, O.S.B., Asst.

Holy Childhood—Most Rev. HERMIN NEGRON.

Legion of Mary—Rev. Msgr. ANGEL LATRE.

Supt. of Schools—Sr. VIVINA GRACIA, C.S.J.

Religious Consultor—JOSE MORENO.

Catechetics—Sr. CARLETA MUNOZ, C.S.J.

Christian Family Movement—Rev. ROBERTO SOLER.

Religious Coordinators—Vacant.

Development and Planification—Vacant.

Vocations—Rev. NOMAR J. CALERO.

Lay Pastoral Development—Rev. Msgr. FRANCIS R. LOPEZ, Rector, *Instituto de la Fe, Box 2272, Mayaguez, 00709.*

Catholic Social Services—Sr. SILVIA ARIAS, M.S.B.T., Dir., *Ramos Antonini No. 25 Oeste, Box 2272, Mayaguez, 00681.*

CLERGY, PARISHES, MISSIONS AND PAROCHIAL SCHOOLS

CITY OF MAYAGUEZ

1—CATHEDRAL OF OUR LADY OF PURIFICATION (1763), Rev. Msgr. Angel Latre, Vicar; Revs. Angel Leonides Soto; Vicente Perez.
Res., P.O. Box 220, Mayaguez, 00681-0220. Tel: 787-831-2444.
Schools—Academy of the Immaculate Conception, Tel: 809-265-7860. Mr. Monico Sanabria, Elementary Prin.; Mr. Donny Ramos, High School Prin.
Lay Teachers 36; Students: Elementary 463; High School 533; Colegio La Milagrosa, Tel: 809-834-0350. Sr. Trinidad Irizarry, Prin.
Sisters of Charity 4; Lay Teachers 28; Students: Elementary 246; High 140.
Missions—Mayaguez, Maria Socorro de los Cristianos Barrio Leguisamo; Mayaguez, Santa Ana. Quebrada Grande.

2—OUR LADY OF MT. CARMEL, Revs. Felix E. Catala, C.SS.R.; Andres Pacheco, C.SS.R.; John McKenna, C.SS.R. Pastoral Ministers: Sr. Elisa Doherty, O.P.
Res., Box 3166, Mayaguez, 00681. Tel: 787-831-6544; 832-2036 (Office).
Missions—Mani, Infant of Prague; Mani, Capilla de la Mora.
School—Mrs. Ester Rivera Santaliz, Prin. Sisters 1; Lay Teachers 19; Students 288.
Catechesis/Religious Programs—Students 347.

3—ASCENSION, Rev. Jose Fco. Baez Camacho.
Res., Box 4361, Salud Sta., Mayaguez, PR 00681-4361. Tel: 787-832-0766.
Missions—Bo. Limon, St. Teresita; Bo. Las Vegas, Our Lady of Perpetual Help; Bo. El Porvenir, Ntra. Sra. de la Providencia (Rep. Masias).
Catechesis/Religious Programs—Students 130.

4—CHURCH DE EL BUEN PASTOR (1986), Rev. Thomas R. Mitchell.
Res., San Gerardo St., No. A-1-A, Mayaguez Ter., Mayaguez, 00680. Tel: 809-833-8800.
Catechesis/Religious Programs—Students 187.
Missions—Alturas de Mayaguez, El Senor de Los Milagros, Tel: 809-265-5936; Parcelas Soledad, Sta. Teresita.

5—NUESTRA SENORA DE FATIMA (1986), Rev. Edwin Lugo Silva, Admin.
Res., Parcelas Castillo C-2, Mayaguez, 00680. Tel: 787-833-0794. [JC]
Catechesis/Religious Programs—Students 110.
Missions—Mayaguez, Cristo Rey, Andalucia St., Sultana, 00680; Mayaguez, Espiritu Santo, Sagitario St., Villa del Oeste, Sabalos, 00680; Mayaguez, Corpus Christi, Urb. Vista Verde, 00680.

6—SACRED HEART (1959), Revs. Toribio Pascual Diez, O.S.B.; Paulino Mazuelas, O.S.B.; Antonio M. Galban, O.S.B.
Res., R.F.D. 348 Buzon 400, Mayaguez, 00680. Tel: 787-832-1464.
School—St. Benedict College. (for boys), Tel: 809-832-9626. Rev. Paulino Mazuelas, O.S.B., Prin.
Lay Teachers 28; Students: Elementary 424; High School 148.
Missions—Rosario, San Jose; Rio Hondo, San Carlos y San Antonio; Bo. Malezas, La Milagrosa.

7—SANTA TERESITA (1970), Rev. Fernando Palacio.

Res., Principe St., 203 Bo. Colombia, Mayaguez, 00680. Tel: 787-832-2872.

8—SAN VICENTE (1965), Revs. Juan Lamela, C.M.; Manuel Araujo, C.M.; Jeronimo Sola, C.M.

Res., Ave. Guanajibo, No. 401, Mayaguez, 00680. Tel: 787-832-8874. [JC]

Catechesis/Religious Programs—Students 200.

9—CHURCH OF THE RESURRECTION (1988), Rev. Angel Mendez.

Res., Balboa 285, Mayaguez, 00680. Tel: 787-831-6180.

Catechesis/Religious Programs—Students 165.

Chapels—Consumo, Jesus Redentor; Rio Canas, Nuestra Senora del Perpetuo Socorro; Barrio Quemado, Nuestra Senor del Carmen.

OUTSIDE THE CITY OF MAYAGUEZ

Aguada, St. Francis of Assisi (1692), Revs. Felipe Fernandez Gutierrez, O.S.A. (Spain); Lesmes Bernabe Lazaro, O.S.A. (Spain); German Lombo, O.S.A. (Spain); Isaias Revilla, O.S.A. (Spain).

Res., P.O. Box 608, 00602. Tel: 787-868-2630.

Missions—Sabana, San Jose; Laguna, Santa Rita; Cruces, Santa Monica; Galicia-Columbani, Santo Tomas de Villanueva; Jaguey Chiquito, San Augustin; Rio Grande, Perpetuo Socorro; Naranjo Militar, Ntra. Sra. de Monserrate; Atalaya, Ntra. Sra. de Altagracia; Naranjo-Guanabanas, San Pablo; Marias, Asuncion de Maria; Cerro Gordo, Buen Consejo; Mamey, Perpetuo Socorro; Guaniquilla, Ntra. Sra. del Carmen; Carrizales, Ntra. Sra. de las Mercedes; Malpaso-Cesar Ruiz, Immaculada Concepcion; Bajio, Sagrada Familia; Quebrada Larga, Sgdo. Corazon de Jesus; Rio Grande-Playa, Ntra. Sra. del Carmen; Guayabo, El Buen Pastor; Piedras Blancas, Ntra. Sra. Reina de la Paz.

Convent—Calle Jose Hernandez, Box 1136, 00602. Hermanas de la Caridad del Cardenal Sancha

Santuario Protomartires de la Concepcion (1524), Rev. Roberto Soler.

Res., Bo. Espinar, Buzon 1162, 00602. Tel: 787-891-2889.

Chapels—Bo. Palmar, El Buen Pastor; Bo. Tablonar, El Nino Jesus.

Aguadilla, St. Charles Borromeo, Revs. Felipe Santiago, C.SS.R.; Cesar Jaramillo, C.SS.R.; Angelo G. Sanchez, C.SS.R.; Juan Edgardo Rosario, C.SS.R.

Res., P.O. Box 238, 00605. Tel: 809-891-0575. [CEM]

School—Tel: 787-891-1445. Mrs. Nydia E. Ugarte, Prin.

Lay Teachers 46; Students: Elementary 396; High School 328.

Convent—Tel: 787-882-3629. Sr. Nilsa Gonzalez, Supr.

Salesian Sisters 4.

Chapels—Bo. Corrales, Our Lady of Perpetual Help; Caimital Alto, St. John Baptist; Victoria-Nuestra, Senora de la Victoria; Esteves, N. S. del Rosario; Bda. Caban, Ntra. Sra. de la Sagrada Familia.

La Milagrosa (1920), Rev. Ramon E. Albino.

Res., Urb. Marbella, Calle 1 Num. 379, 00605. Tel: 809-891-7014.

Missions—Borinquen, Our Lady of Victory; Camaseyes, Our Lady of Fatima; San Judas Tadeo, Playuelas.

San Jose Obrero (1975), Revs. Franklin Santana, M.C.; Hiran Santiago; Mario Borgonovo.

Res., Poblado San Antonio, Box 425, San Antonio, 00690. Tel: 787-890-2449; Fax: 787-826-2494.

Missions—Bo. Guerrero, La Providencia; Ramey-Maleza, Los Santos Reyes.

Anasco, St. Anthony Abbot, Revs. Rogelio Mur Aguilar, O.Carm.; Juan Maria Amoros, O.Carm.; Jorge Rivera Maldonado, O.Carm.

Res., Box 392, 00610. Tel: 809-826-2215.

Missions—Miraflores, Chapel of Our Lady of Perpetual Help; La Playa, Our Lady of Carmel; Bo. Espino, St. Lawrence Martyr; Bo. Pinales, La Immaculade; Bo. Carreras, La Providencia; Bo. Cerro Gordo, Our Lady of Monserrat; Bo. Marias, St. Rita; Bo. Oveja, Cristo Redentor; Bo. Pozo Hondo, Santa Rosa de Lima.

Jesus Maestro Casa de Formaction—.

Cabo Rojo, St. Michael (1783), Revs. Jose A. Acaba; Angel Ortiz; Jose R. Linares.

Res., Box 625, 00623. Tel: 787-851-1283.

School—Miss Elba I. Santana Colon, Prin. Sisters 1; Lay Teachers 57; Students: High School 400; Elementary 343.

Missions—Puerto Real, Our Lady of Mt. Carmel; Joyuda, St. John the Baptist; Boqueron, St. Joseph; Llanos Tunas, Our Lady of Good Counsel; Las Palmas, St. Rita; Monte Grande, St. Jude Thaddeus; El Corozo, Cristo Rey; Betances, Our Lady of Fatima; Conde Avila, St. Martin de Porres; Bo. Miradero, Ntro. Sra. de la Providencia.

Hormigueros, Shrine of Our Lady of Monserrate (1874), Rev. Msgr. Gonzalo Diaz Hernandez; Rev. Angel Roman Ramos.

Res., Box 24, 00660. Tel: 787-849-2260.

Convent—Box 185, 00660. Tel: 787-849-2055. Sr. Maria Encarnacion, O.P., Supr.

Sisters of Fatima for Social Work 4.

Missions—Bo. Lavadero, Sagrado Corazon de Jesus; Bo. Jaquitas, Ntra. Sra. de la Paz; Bo. Carretera Nueva, La Asuncion; Bo. Guanajibo, San Martin de Porres; Bo. El Hoyo, Santa Rosa de Lima.

El Salvador (1969), Rev. Raphael Sastre.

Res., Box 567, 00660. Tel: 787-834-1993.

Chapels—Valle Hermoso Arriba, San Judas Tadeo; Parcelas S. Romualdo, Sta. Teresita.

Lajas, Our Lady of the Purification (1883), Revs. Angel Sanchez, Admin.; Rene Javier Hernandez.

Res., Box 425, 00667. Tel: 809-899-1911.

School—St. Louis Academy Sisters of St. Joseph. (Brooklyn). Tel: 787-899-4080. Sr. Teresita Alicea, C.S.J., Prin.

Sisters 2; Lay Teachers 24; Students: Elementary 140; High 152.

Catechesis/Religious Programs—Students 110.

Convent— La Providencia

Missions—Bo. La Plata, Sagrado Corazon de Jesus, Parcelas #201, 00667; Bo. Lajas Arriba (La Tea), Ntra. Sra. del Perpetuo Socorro, Carretera 118 Km 0, 00667; Bo. Lajas Arriba (Parcelas), San Pablo, Parcelas #48, 00667; Bo. Parcelas Santa Rosa, Santa Rosa de Lima, Comunidad Sta. Rosa #35, 00667; Bo. Parcelas Palmarejo, San Judas Tadeo, Parcelas #172, 00667; Bo. Palmarejo II, San Juan Bautista, Parcela #80, 00667.

De la Merced Parish (1971), Rev. Jorge Caro; Deacon Ramon Cardona.

Res., P.O. Box 1023, 00667-1063. Tel: 787-899-1910.

Missions—Bo. Maguayo, Ntra. Sra. de la Monserrate, Carr. 101 Ramal 303 K.2.4, Bo. Maguayo, 00667; Bo. Parguera, San Pedro, Carr. 304 Calle Principal, Bo. Parguera, 00667; Bo. Cuesta Blanca, Ntra. Sra. de Monserrate, Carr. 116 Parcellas Cuesta Blanca #264, Bo. Cuesta Blanca, 00667; Bo. Salinas, Ntra. Sra. del Carmen, Carr. 324 K. 5.6, Bo. Salinas, 00667; Bo. Paris, Ntra Sra. del Perpetuo Socorro, Carr. 306, Bo. Paris, 00667.

Las Marias, Immaculate Heart of Mary (1868), Rev. Delroy Thomas Scott.

Res., Box 126, 00670. Tel: 787-827-3300.

Missions—Anones, San Jose, Carr. 406, Km. 3.9, 00607; Buena Vista, La Milagrosa, Carr. 124, R. 370, Km. 6.8 Int Buena Vista, 00670; Palma Escrita, N.S. de Fatima.

Maricao, St. John the Baptist (1864), Rev. Angel L. Rios, M.C.

Res., Box 453, 00606. Tel: 787-838-2014.

Missions—Bucarabones, Sagrado Corazon; Indiera Fria, Santa Rosa.

Chapel—Montoso, Immaculado Corazon de Maria, Tel: 787-838-2272. Sr. Inocencia Olmeda, O.P., Supr.

Dominican Sisters of Our Lady of Fatima 6.

Moca, Our Lady of Monserrate (1772), Revs. Santiago Rivera Allende; David Perez Mendez; Nomar Calero Gomez; Juan Bautista Morales; Rev. Msgr. Hector Ortiz.

Res., P.O. Box 435, 00716. Tel: 787-877-2765.

Catechesis/Religious Programs—Emilia Hidalgo, D.R.E.

Students 1,914.

Missions—Bo. Cerro Gordo, San Judas; Bo. Voladoras Lomas, Espiritu Santo; Bo. Voladoras Parcelas, Sagrada Familia; Bo. Naranjo, Corazon de Jesus; Bo. Cuchillas La Salle, Santos Guillermo y Mateo; Bo. Chucillas Sabana, Corazon de Jesus; Bo. Limon, Virgen del Rosario; Bo. Cuchillas Loperena, Virgen del Carmen; Bo. Cordero, Virgen Monserrate; Bo. Rocha Magueyes, La Providencia; Bo. Punta Brava, San Pedro; Bo. Capa Barreto, Virgen del Rosario; Bo. Capa Bosque, Cristo Salvador; Bo. Cerro Gordo, La Inmaculada; Bo. Aceituna, San Martin de Porres.

Rincon, St. Rose of Lima (1789), Revs. Edgardo Acosta; Jose N. Marin; Deacon Fausto Duran.

Res., Box 128, 00677. Tel: 787-823-2650.

Missions—Bo. Calvache, Santa Rosa; Bo. Atalaya, El Cristo de la Reconciliacion; Bo. Corcega, La Milagrosa; Bo. Cruces, Sagrado Corazon de Jesus; Bo. Puntas, Nuestra Senora del Carmen; Bo. Jaguey, San Jose.

Rosario, Rosary, Rev. Edgardo Lopez, Admin.

Res., Box 692, 00636. Tel: 787-832-3533.

Missions—Rosario, Nuestra Senora del Rosario; Bo. Rosario Penon, La Monserrate, Bo. Rosario Penon, 00680.

Sabana Grande, Church of San Isidro, Revs. Hector E. Rivera; Harry Lopez Vazquez.

Res., Box 817, 00637. Tel: 787-873-4475.

Convent—Tel: 809-873-2750. Sr. Barbara Duran, O.P., Supr.

Sisters 4.

Missions—El Papayo, Cristo Rey, Carr.368 R.367 KM.2.0, 00637; Susua, La Resurreccion, Carr.121 Calle Agucena, 00637. Tel: 809-873-0382; Bo. Maginas, Sagrado Corazon de Jesus, Calle Rable #44-Carr.121 K. 5.0, 00637. Tel: 809-873-1368; Bo. La Pica, San Jose, Carr. 121 Km. 4.1, 00637. Tel: 809-873-4231; Bo. Cerro Gordo, San Francisco de Asis, Carr.369 Km.1.4, 00637. Tel: 809-873-8048; Bo. Molinas, Ntra. Sra. de Monserrate, Carr.2 R.365 Km.2.8 Int., 00637. Tel: 809-873-2656; Bo. Guaras, Ntra. Sra. de Fatima, Carr.328 Km.3.6, 00637. Tel: 809-873-0886; Bo. Latorre, Santa Catalina de Siena, Carr.388 Km.5.9 Int., 00637. Tel: 809-873-7591; Bo. La Maquina, Santa Ana, Carr.114 R.363 Km.2.4, 00637; Bo. Santana Pichel, Ntra. Sra. del Rosario, Carr.120 Km.6, 00637. Tel: 809-873-3707; Bo. El Hoyo, La Virgen Milagrosa, Carr.364 Km.7 Interior, 00637; Bo. Rayo Plata, San Judas Tadeo, Carr.117 Km.10.7, 00637; Bo. Sta. Ana Moreno, Sta Lucia, Carr.120 Km.3.1, 00637. Tel: 809-873-7962.

San German, San German de Auxerre, Rev. Humberto Lopez; Rev. Msgr. Romualdo M. Ortiz; Rev. Marcelino Arocho; Rev. Msgr. Francis R. Lopez; Rev. Rafael Mendez.

Res., Box 305, 00683. Tel: 787-892-1027.

School—Tel: 809-892-1009. Sr. Maria Ines Martin, C.S.J., Prin.

Sisters of St. Joseph (Brooklyn) 2; Lay Teachers 39; Students: Elementary 537; High 217.

Catechesis/Religious Programs—Students 250.

Missions—Duey, Chapel of St. Augustin; Hoconuco, Chapel of St. Joseph; Maresua, Gruta de Lourdes; Cotuy, Our Lady of Fatima; Sabana Eneas, San Judas Tadeo.

St. Rose of Lima (1967), Revs. Jose L. Diez, O.S.A.; Roberto Garcia, O.S.A.

Res., Box 364, 00683. Tel: 787-892-1276.

Missions—Bo. Guama, N. Sra. de la Consolacion; Bo. Minillas Carretera, Perpetuo Socorro; Bo. Retiro Tea, Santa Rita; Bo. Minillas Valle, Santa Monica; Bo. Cain, St. Martin de Porres.

San Sebastian, San Sebastian Martir (1752), Revs. Miguel Angel San Martin, C.P.; Jose Almendariz; Bernardo Onaindia, C.P.; Lino Muzquiz, C.P.

Res., P.O. Box 801, 00685. Tel: 787-896-1028.

School—Tel: 809-896-5728. Julio Arocho, Prin.

Lay Teachers 24; Students 334.

Catechesis/Religious Programs—Students 1,010.

Missions—Bo. Perchas 1, Cristo Rey; Bo. Perchas 11, La Pasion; Bo. Calabazas, San Gabriel de la Dolorosa; Bo. La Lechuza, La Asuncion; Bo. Juncal, Santa Teresita; Bo. Aibonito Guerrero, Ntra. Sra. del Carmen; Bo. Saltos, San Judas Tadeo; Bo. Hato Arriba, San Patricio; Bo. Hato Arriba (Parcelas), San Pablo de la Cruz; Bo. Altozano, Ntra. Sra. de Fatima; Bo. Robles, Sagrado Corazon; Bo. Hoyamala, San Jose Obrero; Bo. Parcelas Guacio (Parcelas), Santa Cruz.

On Special Assignment:

Reverend Fathers—

Diaz, Gonzalo, Chancellor, Box 24, Hormingueros, PR

INSTITUTIONS LOCATED IN THE DIOCESE

[A] HOSPITALS

SAN GERMAN. *Hospital of the Immaculate Conception*, Box 285, 00683.

For a complete listing, refer to the Hospitals section.

[B] INSTITUTIONS

MAYAGUEZ. *Asylum for the Poor and Aged*, Calle Post 62, 00680. Sisters of Charity (Spanish). Sr. Cruz M. Fontan, Supr. Sisters 6; Beds 113; Residents 102.

Convent of the Servants of Mary, Hostos Ave. 401, 00708. Tel: 787-832-0391. Sisters care for the sick in their homes and hospital. Sr. Prudencia Lopez de Arroyave, Supr. Sisters 17.

HORMIGUEROS. *Residence for the Aged, San Jose*, Valle Hermoso, 00660. Tel: 787-832-4243. Sr. Celsa Vazquez, Supr. Sisters 13; Residents 150.

[C] PERSONAL PRELATURES

MAYAGUEZ. *Opus Dei (Prelature of the Holy Cross and Opus Dei)*, 69 Orquidea St., Ensanche Martinez, 00680. Tel: 787-833-6461. Rev. Ramon Alvarez Infiesta.

RELIGIOUS INSTITUTES OF MEN REPRESENTED IN THE DIOCESE

For further details refer to the corresponding bracketed number in the Religious Institutes of Men or Women section.

[]—*Acies Christi*. (Spain).
[0140]—*Augustinians*.—O.S.A.
[0200]—*Benedictine Monks*. Spain.—O.S.B.
[0270]—*Carmelite Fathers and Brothers*. (Spain).—O.Carm.
[1330]—*Congregation of the Mission*. (Vice Province of Puerto Rico).—C.M.
[1000]—*Congregation of the Passion*.—C.P.
[1070]—*Redemptorist Fathers*.—C.SS.R.
[]—*Salesian Fathers*.

RELIGIOUS INSTITUTES OF WOMEN REPRESENTED IN THE DIOCESE

[]—*Acies Christi*. (Spain).
[]—*Carmelitas de Clausura*. (Spain).
[1070-13]—*Dominican Sisters*.—O.P.
[]—*Hermanas de la Caridad*.
[]—*Hermanas MM. del Buen Pastor*. (Puerto Rico).
[]—*Hermanas Salesianas*. (Spain).
[]—*Hermanas Teatinas*. (Spain).
[2340]—*Little Sisters of the Poor*.—L.S.P.
[]—*Madames of the Sacred Heart*.
[2790]—*Missionary Servants of the Most Blessed Trinity*.—M.S.B.T.
[]—*Monasterio Santa Maria del Monte Carmelo*.
[3580]—*Servants of Mary*. (Spain).—O.S.M.
[0650]—*Sisters of Charity of St. Vincent de Paul*. (Spanish).—S.C.
[]—*Sisters of Fatima*. (Puerto Rico).
[]—*Sisters of Schoenstatt*. (Germany).
[]—*Sisters of St. Joseph*. (Brooklyn).

NECROLOGY

(No Deaths)

Diocese of Ponce, Puerto Rico

(Dioecesis Poncensis)

Most Reverend

JUAN FREMIOT TORRES, D.D.

Bishop of Ponce; ordained April 10, 1950; appointed Bishop November 4, 1964; consecrated December 21, 1964. *Res., Bishop's House, P.O. Box 205, Sta. 6, CUPR, Ponce, PR, 00732.* Tel.: 809-848-5265; Fax: 809-841-1778.

Most Reverend

RICARDO SURINACH CARRERAS, D.D.

Titular Bishop of Aquae Albae in Mauretania and Auxiliary Bishop of Ponce; ordained April 13, 1957; appointed May 26, 1975; consecrated July 25, 1975. *Res., P.O. Box 205, Sta. 6, Ponce, PR, 00732.* Tel.: 809-848-5265; Fax: 809-841-1778.

ESTABLISHED NOVEMBER 21, 1924.

Square Miles 830.

Comprises the south portion of the Island of Puerto Rico and is in the Ecclesiastical Province of Puerto Rico.

STATISTICAL OVERVIEW

Personnel	
Bishop	1
Auxiliary Bishops	1
Priests: Diocesan Active in Diocese	42
Priests: Active Outside Diocese	34
Priests: Retired, Sick or Absent	7
Number of Diocesan Priests	83
Religious Priests in Diocese	55
Extern Priests in Diocese	11
Ordinations:	
Diocesan Priests	1
Religious Priests	1
Transitional Deacons	2
Permanent Deacons in Diocese	59
Total Brothers	2
Total Sisters	229
Parishes	
Parishes	40
With Resident Pastor:	
Resident Diocesan Priests	27
Resident Religious Priests	13
Without Resident Pastor:	
Missions	2
Pastoral Centers	228
Welfare	
Homes for the Aged	2
Total Assisted	252
Specialized Homes	1
Total Assisted	98
Special Centers for Social Services	1
Total Assisted	3,538
Other Institutions	1
Total Assisted	1,632
Educational	
Seminaries, Diocesan	1
Students from This Diocese	7
Students from Other Diocese	4
Diocesan Students in Other Seminaries	5
Seminaries, Religious	2
Students Religious	9
Total Seminarians	21
Colleges and Universities	1
Total Students	11,462
High Schools, Diocesan and Parish	20
Total Students	2,424
Elementary Schools, Diocesan and Parish	22
Total Students	7,674
Catechesis/Religious Education:	
Total Students Under Catholic Instruction	21,581
Teachers in the Diocese:	
Priests	16
Sisters	47
Lay Teachers	1,155
Vital Statistics	
Receptions into the Church:	
Infant Baptism Totals	4,660
Adult Baptism Totals	3,585
Received into Full Communion	812
First Communions	5,574
Confirmations	5,175
Marriages:	
Catholic	1,641
Interfaith	52
Total Marriages	1,693
Total Catholic Population	442,000
Total Population	551,525

Former Bishops—Most Rev. EDWIN V. BYRNE, D.D., cons. in Philadelphia, Nov. 30, 1925; transferred to San Juan, PR; promoted to Archbishop of Santa Fe, NM, June 15, 1943; died July 25, 1963.—Most Rev. ALOYSIUS J. WILLINGER, C.Ss.R., D.D., ord. July 2, 1911; appt. Bishop of Ponce March 8, 1929; cons. Oct. 28, 1929; appt. Titular Bishop of Bida and Coadjutor of Monterey-Fresno (cum jure successionis), Dec. 12, 1946; installed Bishop of Monterey-Fresno, Jan. 3, 1953; resigned Oct. 25, 1967; died July 25, 1973.—Most Rev. JAMES E. MCMANUS, C.SS.R., D.D., J.C.D., transferred to the Archdiocese of New York, Nov. 27, 1963.—His Eminence LUIS CARDINAL APONTE, D.D., ord. April 10, 1950; appt. Titular Bishop of Lares and Auxiliary of Ponce, July 23, 1960; cons. Oct. 12, 1960; appt. Coadjutor Bishop of Ponce, April 16, 1963; appt. Bishop of Ponce, Nov. 18, 1963; installed Feb. 20, 1964; promoted to Archbishop of San Juan, Nov. 4, 1964; installed Jan. 15, 1965; created Cardinal, March 5, 1973.

Vicar General—Most Rev. RICARDO SURINACH, D.D.

Pro-Vicar General—Rev. Msgr. PEDRO J. BALLESTER.

Chancellor—Rev. Msgr. HERMINIO DE JESUS.

Vice Chancellor—Rev. Msgr. JUAN ESPONA.

Bishop's Secretary—Rev. Msgr. JUAN ESPONA.

Episcopal Vicar for Diocesan Administration—Rev. Msgr. HERMINIO DE JESUS.

Episcopal Vicar for Pastoral Coordination—Rev. Msgr. ANDRES GUERRERO.

Episcopal Vicar for Clergy Affairs—Rev. Msgr. ROBERTO GARCIA-BLAY.

Tribunal Interdiocesano de Puerto Rico—Most Rev. JUAN FREMIOT TORRES, D.D., Moderator, *P.O. Box 229, Station 6, Calle Isabel No. 31, Ponce, 00732.* Tel: 787-843-4902; Fax: 787-841-7483. First instance for the Dioceses of Mayaguez and Ponce. Second Instance for the Archdiocese of San Juan.

Judicial Vicar—Rev. MANUEL SANTIAGO.

Associate Judicial Vicars—Rev. Msgr. HERMINIO DE JESUS; Rev. ELIAS MORALES; Mr. ABRAHAM MORALES.

Judges—Mayaguez: Rev. GONZALO DIAZ, Ponce: Rev. Msgr. RAFAEL SANTIAGO.

Diocesan Consultors—Most Rev. RICARDO SURINACH, D.D.; Rev. Msgr. PEDRO J. BALLESTER; Rev. Msgr. HERMINIO DE JESUS; Rev. Msgr. MARCOS A. PANCORBO; Rev. Msgr. FRANCISCO VELEZ; Rev. Msgr. RAFAEL SANTIAGO; Rev Msgr. JUAN ESPONA; Rev. JOSE LOZANO.

Diocesan Board of Administration—Most Rev. RICARDO SURINACH, D.D.; Rev. Msgr. MARCOS PANCORBO; Rev. Msgr. PEDRO J. BALLESTER; Mr. FERNANDO ROSADO; Deacon ALBERTO CASTRO; Mr. SANTIAGO RAMOS.

Parish Priests Consultors—Rev. Msgr. MARCOS PANCORBO; Rev. Msgr. ANDRES GUERRERO; Rev. Msgr. RAFAEL SANTIAGO.

Notaries—Rev. Msgr. JUAN ESPONA; Mrs. CONCEPCION MORA; Mrs. LUZ DELIA MEDINA; Mrs. MARIA V. RODRIGUEZ; Mrs. IRIS YOLANDA PAGAN, M.J.

Censores Librorum—Revs. PERFECTO ALVAREZ, O.S.A.; FELIX LAZARO, Sch.P.; BRIAN HARRISON, O.S.

Administrator—Rev. Msgr. JUAN ESPONA.

Diocesan Offices and Directors

Catechesis—Sr. FATIMA RIVERA, O.P., *P.O. Box 1064, Ponce, 00733.* Tel: 787-842-9178; Fax: 787-259-1718.

Catholic Youth Organization—Rev. GERARDO RAMIREZ.

Children of Mary—Rev. Msgr. ANDRES GUERRERO.

Committee for Community Planning—Rev. Msgr. HERMINIO DE JESUS; Mr. CHARLES CUPRILL, LL.B.

Communications—Sr. LOURDES MERCADO, O.P., *P.O. Box 986, Ponce, 00733.* Tel: 809-843-1548.

Cursillos de Cristiandad—Deacon LADISLAO LABOY; Mr. BENJAMIN PAGAN, *Marvesa, La Rambla, Ponce, 00731.*

Ecumenism—Rev. Msgr. ANDRES GUERRERO, *Box 205, Sta. 6, Ponce, 00732.*

Legion of Mary—Rev. Msgr. ANDRES GUERRERO, *P.O. Box 205, Sta 6, Ponce, 00732.*

Liturgical Commission—Most Rev. RICARDO SURINACH, D.D.; Rev. Msgr. JUAN ESPONA, *P.O. Box 205, Sta. 6, Ponce, 00732.*

Sacred Music Commission—Rev. ABEL DI MARCO; Miss FALINA RIVERA.

St. Vincent de Paul Conferences—Dr. RAFAEL BLASINI, *Cristo Rey Parish, 7W Ext. La Rambla, Ponce, 00731.*

Superintendent of Schools—Sr. MARIA UNA, R.A.D., *Sta. 6, P.O. Box 557, Ponce, 00732.* Tel: 787-848-4020; Fax: 787-844-5987.

Vigilance for the Faith—Most Rev. RICARDO SURINACH, D.D.

Vocations—Rev Msgr. JESUS R. DIEZ ANTONANZAS; Rev. ALFREDO ALVAREZ LACRUZ, *P.O. Box 110, Sta. 6, Ponce, 00732.* Tel: 787-848-5265.

Institute of Family Orientation—Deacon JESUS M. PAGAN, *Sta. 6, Ponce, 00732.* Tel: 787-840-6018.

CLERGY, PARISHES, MISSIONS AND PAROCHIAL SCHOOLS

CITY OF PONCE

1—CATHEDRAL OF OUR LADY OF GUADALUPE (1692), Rev. Msgr. Marcos A. Pancorbo; Revs. Carlos Roman; Jesus Pacho; Deacon Jose Mercado.
Res., 28 Cristina St., Box 210 Sta. 6, 00732. Tel: 787-842-0134; Fax: 787-848-9104.

2—CHRIST THE KING (1964), Revs. Juan Rodriguez Orengo; Demetrio Santana Guerrero; Deacon Anibal Rosario.
Res., 7 W. Ext., La Rambla, 00731. Tel: 809-843-3028; Fax: 809-840-7398.
School—Tel: 787-843-0766; Fax: 787-843-6443. Mrs. Imelda Rivera Martines, Prin.
Students 369.
Missions—Urb. Santa Teresita, Ponce Co., Santa Teresita Calle 33, Parque Central,; Rio Chiquito, Ponce Co., Nino Jesus de Praga Bo. Los Claves,; Ponce, La Dolorosa. Villa Ponce - Rambla #4st.

3—CHURCH OF THE RESURRECTION (1967), Revs. Roberto Garcia Blay; Esteban Santaella; Jose M. Herrero; Deacon Rafael Castro.
Res., Glenview Gardens, A-Q 8 W. 22nd St., 00731. Tel: 787-842-7167.
Missions—Bo. La Yuca, Ponce Co., Immaculate Heart of Mary; Bo. Collado, Ponce Co., Our Lady of Monserrate; Bo. Las Vallas, Ponce Co., San Lucas; Ponce, Saint Joseph Bo. La Yuca,; Ponce, Our Lady of Carmel. Bo. Carmelita.

4—OUR LADY OF MT. CARMEL (1883), Revs. Miguel Alvarez, Sch.P.; Jose Mateo, Sch.P.; Agustin Lopez, Sch.P., Prin.; Deacon Jose Rivera.
Res., P.O. Box 118, Playa de Ponce, 00734. Tel: 787-842-1333; Fax: 787-841-6861.
School—Tel: 787-842-5018. Mrs. Paquita Alvarado, Prin.
Students 202.
Missions—Villa del Carmen, Ponce Co., San Martin de Porres, Constancia Ave., 00734. Tel: 809-848-4355; Bo. Salistral, Ponce Co., Santa Marta.

5—SANTA TERESITA (1930), Revs. Edward Maldonado, O.F.M.Cap.; Roberto Martinez, O.F.M.Cap.; Francisco Garcia, O.F.M.Cap.; Bro. Reinaldo Saliva, O.F.M.Cap.; Deacons Casildo Rodriquez; Juan Rios.
Res., Box 7244, 342 Victoria St., 00732. Tel: 787-842-3137; 842-5055 (Friary); Fax: 787-844-7267.
School—344 Victoria St., 00732. Tel: 787-842-4110. Mrs. Mildred Reyes, Prin.
Students 337.
Catechesis / Religious Programs—Students 337.

6—SAN CONRADO (1948), Rev. Msgr. Pedro J. Ballester; Deacon Emerito Lopez.
Res., Box 7362, 00732. Tel: 809-843-0560.
School—P.O.Box 7111, 00732. Tel: 787-843-1405; 842-2293; Fax: 787-841-7303. Sr. Nildred Rodriguez, C.S.J., Prin.
Students 806.
Catechesis / Religious Programs—Students 806.

7—SANTA MARIA (1952), Revs. Romeo Salcido, M.J.; Thomas Cahill, M.J.; Christopher Foeckler, M.J.
Res., Box 101, Sta. 6, 00732. Tel: 787-848-5370; Fax: 787-843-6755.
School—Tel: 787-842-1164. Mrs. Aida C. de Reyes, Prin.
Students 960.

8—LA MILAGROSA (1928), Revs. Ignacio Alonso, C.M.; Javier Inigo, C.M.; Tomas de la Puebla, C.M.; Deacons Ramon L. Vazquez; Carlos Burgos.
Res., Guadalupe No. 2, 00731. Tel: 787-842-3188; Fax: 787-284-1100. [CEM]
School—Tel: 787-842-1164. Mr. Jorge Almodovar, Prin.
Students 515.
Catechesis / Religious Programs—Students 551.

9—LA MERCED (1928), Revs. Modesto Vaca, O.de.M.; Antonio Garcia, O.deM.; Silvino Gonzalez, O.de.M.; Luis Prieto, O.de.M.; Jose Luis Iturraran, O.de.M.; Deacons Carlos M. Rodriguez-Guilbe; Jose D. Ruiz.
Res., Luna St., No. 9, 00731. Tel: 787-842-0069; Fax: 787-842-0603.

10—LA SANTISIMA TRINIDAD (1971), Revs. Alejandro Nistal, O.SS.T.; Jose Luis Fernandez, O.SS.T.; Alfonso Rementeria, O.SS.T.; Deacon Francisco Lugo.
Res., Las Delicias, Box 8226, 00732. Tel: 787-842-6073; Fax: 787-842-6073.
Missions—Bo. Magueyes, Ponce Co., San Juan de Mata, Box 8226, 00732; Bo. Guaragoa, Ponce Co., San Andres, 00732; Bo. Guaragoa, Arriba, Ponce Co., Santa Ana, 00732; Bo. Marueno, Arriba, Ponce Co., N.S. Fatima, 00732; Parcelas de Marueno, Ponce Co., San Antonio de Padua, 00732; Bo. Madrigal, Ponce Co., N.S. del Rosario, 00732; Bo. Pastillo, Ponce Co., Inmaculada, 00732; Bo. Corral Viejo, Ponce Co., Cristo Rey, 00732; Bo. Santas Pascuas, Ponce Co., Resurreccion, 00732.
Catechesis / Religious Programs—Students 100.

11—SAN JOSE OBRERO (1979), Revs. Eduardo Garcia, O.S.; Brian Harrison, O.S.; Anthony Tyrrell, O.S.; Deacon Nestor Rentas.
Res., El Tuque, Calle 1 No. 3, Box 8027, 00732. Tel: 787-843-9072.
Mission—Punto Oro, Ponce Co., Ntra. Sra. del Pilar.

12—SAN JOSE (1965), Revs. Santiago Soria, O.C.D.; Mariano Fraile, O.C.D.; Alexio de Armas, O.C.D.; Bro. Fray Jorge Llorentes, O.C.D.; Deacon David Rodriguez.
Res., Urb. San Jose, Calle 6, Box 8414, 00732. Tel: 787-843-3910.

13—SANTUARIO SAN JUDAS TADEO (1964), Revs. Benigno Lopez, O.de.M.; Ramon Conde Ocampo, O.de.M.; Pedro Ruiz, O.de.M.; Javier Errecalde, O.de.M.; Vicente Salas Avello, O.de.M.; William Rabelo, O. de.M.
Res., P.O. Box 7046, 00732. Tel: 787-843-0572.
School—Oblates to the Divine Love, Tel: 787-844-2610. Mrs. Zaida Toro, Prin.
Students 597.
Kindergarten—Urb. Constancia H-467, 00731. Tel: 787-843-5378. Sisters of the Love of God (Spain). Sr. Paz Martinez, R.A.D., Prin.
Students 276.
Mission—Bo. Cuatro Calles, Ponce Co., St. Anthony.

14—SAN VICENTE-CANTERA, Revs. Jose Cummings, C.M.; Eugenio Villafranca, C.M.; Santiago Sanllorente, C.M.
Res., Mayor Cantera No. 67, 00731. Tel: 809-843-1976.
Mission—Rio Chiquito, Ponce Co., San Vicente.

15—CHURCH OF THE SACRED HEART (1969), Rev. Jose M. Galan; Deacon Reinaldo Rivera.
Res., Alta Vista C 21-S-6, 00731. Tel: 787-843-4891.
Mission—Bo. La Cuarta, Ponce Co., San Pedro Nolasco.

16—CHURCH OF THE GOOD SHEPHERD (1968), Rev. Msgr. Rafael Santiago; Deacons David Ramos; Rafael D. Ruiz; Andres Maldonado.
Res., Calle 35, H.H. 14, Jardines del Caribe, 00731. Tel: 787-843-6202.
Mission—Bo. Quebrado del Agua, Ponce Co., La Milagrosa, 00731.

17—OUR LADY OF MT. CARMEL (1973), Revs. Antonio Ferre; Manuel Santiago; Deacons Ladislao Laboy; Jose M. Vazquez.
Res., Box 187, Coto Laurel, 00780. Tel: 787-848-2030.
Missions—Bo. Hoyos, Ponce Co., Santa Maria Virgen, 00780; Bo. Las Raices, Ponce Co., Sagrado Corazon de Jesus, Carr. 511 K. 15, 00780; Bo. Real Anon Abajo, Ponce Co., San Mateo, 00780; Bo. Real Anon Arriba, Ponce Co., San Martin de Porres, 00780.

18—CHURCH SANTISIMO SACRAMENTO (1984), Revs. Gustavo Mardones, L.D.; Wilberto Reyes, L.D.; Angel Oscar Alvez, L.D.
P.O. Box 212, Sta. 6, 00732.
Res., Urb. Lirios del Sur, Calle 15-I #1, 00731. Tel: 787-843-0245.

Parishes in Formation

1—CHURCH OUR LADY OF MIRACULOUS MEDAL, Rev. Msgr. Marcos A. Pancorbo, Admin.
Res., P.O. Box 210, Sta. 6, 00732. Tel: 787-842-0134.

2—CHURCH SAN PATRICIO, Rev. Jose Lozano, Admin.
Res., La Pica, Cr. Buzon 234-B, 00730. Tel: 787-828-6350.

OUTSIDE THE CITY OF PONCE

Adjuntas, Adjuntas Co., St. Joachim (1815), Revs. Alfonso Amezcua, O.R.C.; Manuel C. Martinez, O.R.C.; Deacons Samuel Sepulveda; Radames Marcucci.
Res., 14 Rius Rivera St., 00601. Tel: 787-829-3145; Fax: 787-829-3145.
School—San Joaquin Elementary and Intermediate, 12 Primo Delgado St., 00601. Tel: 787-829-3040. Mr. Ernesto L. Santiago, Prin.
Students 184.
Missions—Garzas, San Francisco; Vegas Arriba, Sta. Ana; Tres de Jayuya, Santa Teresita; Pellejas, Santa Rosa; Yahuecas, Virgen del Carmen; Tanama, Sagrado Corazon; Guilarte, San Antonio; Vegas Abajo, La Milagrosa; Limani, Inm. Corazon de Maria.

Aguirre, Guayama Co., Sacred Heart (1946), Rev. Felix E. Alvarado.
Res., Box 260, Aquirre, 00704. Tel: 787-853-3620.
School—Perpetuo Socorro, Barrio/Coqui, 00704. Tel: 787-853-2270. Sr. Isabel Cruz, R.A., Prin.
Students 647.
Missions—Las Mareas, St. Judas; Coqui, Our Lady of Perpetual Help; San Felipe, St. Martin de Porres; Aguirre, La Milagrosa.

Arroyo, Arroyo Co., Our Lady of Mt. Carmel (1855), Revs. Carlos Nieves; Jose Antonio Lopez Vega.
Res., Box 388, 00714. Tel: 787-839-3465.
Catechesis / Religious Programs—P.O. Box 25, 00714. Students 170.
Missions—Bo. Pitahaya, Ntra Sra. del Carmen; Bda. Marin, La Milagrosa; Bo. Yaurel Palmarejo, San Jose; Bo. Palmas, Ntra Sra. de Fatima; Bo. Yaurel Santa Clara, San Martin.

Castaner, Our Lady of the Miraculous Medal (1969), Rev. Alfonso Amezcua, O.R.C.; Deacon William Ramos.
Res., Box 1006, 00631. Tel: 787-897-5843.
Missions—Bartolo, Immaculate Conception; Mirasol, La Virgen; Rio Prieto, Milagrosa.

Coamo, Coamo Co., St. Blase (1616), Rev. Msgr. Andres Guerrero; Revs. Jose Carlos Vargas; Cristobal Reilly, S.T.; Deacon Angel A. Negron.
Res., Box 196, 00769. Tel: 787-825-1122.
School—Ntra. Sra. de Valvanera, Box 1903, 00769. Tel: 787-825-1145. Mr. Emiliano Guzman, Prin.
Students 425.
Catechesis / Religious Programs—Students 450.
Missions—Coamo Arriba, Coamo Co., Sacred Heart, Box 196, 00769; Los Llanos, Coamo Co., St. Anthony, 00769; Palmarejo, Coamo Co., Sacred Heart of Mary, 00769; Pulguillas, Coamo Co., Christ the King, 00769; Hayales, Coamo Co., Our Lady of Mt. Carmel, 00769; Santa Catalina, Coamo Co., Miraculous Virgin, 00769; Santa Catalina, Coama Co., Sacred Heart Sector Descalabrado; Coamo, Coamo Co., Saint James Sector Cilantro; Pedro Garcia, Coamo Co., Miraculous Virgin, 00769; Santa Ana, Coamo Co., Santa Ana, 00769; Rio Jueyes, Coamo Co., Our Lady of Lourdes, 00769; San Diego, Coamo Co., San Diego, 00769; Emanueli, Coamo Co., Holy Family, 00769; Las Flores, Coamo Co., San Martin, 00769; Melendez, Coamo Co., Our Lady of Fatima, 00769.

Ensenada, Sacred Heart (1963), Revs. Gerardo Ramirez; Elias Morales; Deacon Wallis S. Sanchez.
Res., Box 179, 00647. Tel: 787-821-2857.
Missions—Salinas-Providencia, Divina Providencia; Bo. Fuig., Monserrate.

Guanica, Guanica Co., St. Anthony Abbot (1888), Revs. Gerardo Ramirez; Elias Morales; Deacon Reinaldo Galarza.
Res., Box 804, 00653. Tel: 787-821-2147.
School—Blessed Imelda, Tel: 787-821-2714; Fax: 787-821-2714. Mrs. Lissette M. Ortiz, Prin.
Students 183.
Missions—Bo. Belgica, Guanica Co., Cristo Rey; Bo. Santa Juanita, Guanica Co., N. Sra. Rosario; Bo. Luna, Guanica Co., San Judas; Bo. La Luna, Guanica Co., N. Sra Fatima; Bda. Esperanza, Guanica co., La Providencia.

Guayama, Guayama Co., St. Anthony of Padua (1736), Revs. Antonio Hernandez, C.Ss.R.; Thomas J. Gavigan, C.Ss.R.; J. Joseph Dtonne, C.Ss.R.; Hector Colon, C.Ss.R.; William Spillane, C.Ss.R.; Deacon Alberto Montanez.
Res., Box 2820, 00785. Tel: 787-864-4100; Fax: 787-864-5494.
School—Box 777, 00784. Tel: 787-864-2062; Fax: 787-864-1450. Mrs. Evelyn Adams, Prin.
Students 615.
Missions—Caimital, Our Lady of Perpetual Help; Bo. Puente Jobos, SS. Peter and Paul; Palmas, St. Gerard; Carmen, Our Lady of Mt. Carmel; Bo. Olimpo, Cristo Rey; Bo. Corazon, La Candelaria; Colonia Villodos, Perpetuo Socorro; Bo. Puerto Jobos, San Francisco de Asis; Bo. Guamani, Sgdo. Corazon; Bo. Carite, San Martin; Bo. Barrancas, La Monserrate.

Guayanilla, Guayanilla Co., Immaculate Conception (1841), Revs. Raymond L. Rivera; Orlando Rivera; Deacon Miguel Sepulveda.

Res., P.O. Box 560383, 00656-0383. Tel: 787-835-3035.
School—Tel: 787-835-2230. Sr. Alejandrina Torres, H.C.C.S., Prin.
Students 283.
Missions—Barrio Sierra Baja, Our Lady of Mt. Carmel; Magas Arriba, Perpetuo Socorro; Quebradas, San Francisco de Asis; Barrio Indios, San Juan Bosco; Consejo Alto, La Monserrate; Macana Rio, Virgen de Fatima; Quebrada Honda, Nuestra Senora; Macana Parcelas, San Martin de Porres.

Jayuya, Jayuya Co., Our Lady of Monserrate (1883), Revs. Jose Lozano; Fernando Gil Munoz; Jose Luis Larreategui, Sch.P.; Felix Lazaro, Sch.P.; Esteban Santaella; Deacons Luis Rosario; Carlos Orama; Jose A. Perez.
Res., Calle Figueras 13, 00664. Tel: 787-828-6350; Fax: 787-828-5062.
Missions—Collares, Jayuya Co., Cristo Rey, Figueras #13, 00664; Coabbey, Jayuya Co., San Jorge, 00664; Canalizo, Jayuya Co., La Milagrosa, 00664; Gripinas, Jayuya Co., Buen Pastor, 00664; Zama, Jayuya Co., Santa Cecila, 00664; Hoyo Planas, Jayuya Co., Esp. Santo, 00664; Mameyes, Jayuya Co., S. Antonio, 00664; Salto, Jayuya Co., Santos Reyes, 00664; Saliente, Jayuya Co., San Francisco, 00664; Puerto Plata, Jayuya Co., San Juan, 00664; La Pica, San Patricio Co.; Hogares Seguros, San Antonio Co.

Juana Diaz, Juana Diaz Co., St. Raymond Nonato (1798), Rev. Msgr. Francisco Velez; Rev. Santiago Solla; Deacons Hector L. Santiago; Narciso Ortiz.
Res., Box 1426, 00795. Tel: 787-837-2390.
Missions—Pastillo, Cotopaso Co., Santiago Apostol; Rio Canas, Rio Canas Abajo, San Judas; Jacaquas, Bo. Jacaguas, N.S. de Fatima; Collores, Bo. Jacaguas, La Milagrosa; Las Margaritas, Bo. Collores Arriba, Santiago, Ap.; Corral, P. Socorro; Guayabal, Bo. Guayabal, Our Lady of the Rosary; Callabo, Bo. Callabo, San Ramon; Bo. Rio Cana Arriba, La Merced.

Santa Teresita (Arus) (1984), Rev. Adalin Rivera; Deacons Pedro Garcia-Malavet; Secundino Torres.
Res., P.O. Box 131, Sta. 6, Ponce, 00732. Tel: 787-844-6670.
Missions—San Martin de Porres. (Singapur); Divine Mercy. (Piedra Aguza); Pastillito, Manzanilla, Our Lady of Carmel. (Galicia).

Nuestra Senora de Lourdes (Aguilita) (1984), Rev. Msgr. Herminio de Jesus; Deacons Jose Mendez; Cirilo Carmona; Ruperto Reyes; Jaime Velez.
Res., P.O. Box 1824, 00795. Tel: 787-837-1097.
Catechesis/Religious Programs—P.O. Box 1824, 00795. Tel: 787-260-2144.
Students 232.

Patillas, Inmaculado Corazon de Maria (1811), Revs. Alberto Muniz; Rafael Alvarado de Jesus; Deacon Francisco Vega.
Res., Box 635, 00723. Tel: 787-839-5333.
Missions—Bo. Marin Alto, Pastillas, Pastillas Co., Perpetuo Socorro; Bo. Guarderraya, Pastillas, Pastillas Co., Madre Cabrini; Bo. Recio, Pastillas, Pastillas Co., Sto. Cristo de Los Milagros; Bo. Jacaboa, Pastillas, Pastillas Co., Carmen; Bo. El Bajo, Pastillas, Pastillas Co., Cristo Rey; Bo. Providencia, Pastillas, Pastillas Co., Providencia; Bo. Los Pollos, Pastillas, Pastillas Co., Santa Rosa de Lima; Bo. Los Barros, Pastillas, Pastillas Co., S. Juan Evangelista; Bo. El Real, Pastillas, Pastillas Co., San Guillermo; Bo. Jagual, Pastillas, Pastillas Co., Carmen.

Penuelas, Penuelas Co., St. Joseph (1793), Revs. Segismundo Cintron; Francisco Sirvent-Dominguez; Deacons Carmelo Vazquez; Jose E. Gelpi; Glidden R. Perez; Joaquin Masoller.
Res., Box 25, 00624. Tel: 787-836-1038.
Missions—El Rucio, Penuelas Co., La Milagrosa, Carr. #391, 00624; El Alto, San Antonio Carr. #132; Macana, Fatima Carr. #131; Tallaboa Alta, Santa Ana St. Domingo, Carmen Carr. #132; Bo Barreal, Cristo de la Salud Carr. #386; Quebrada Ceiba, Milagrosa Carr. #387; Corozal, San Antonio. Carr. #387.

Sacred Heart (Tallaboa) (1928), Rev. Agustin Grinena.
Res., HC 01, Box 13063, 00624. Tel: 787-836-1164.
Mission—Bo. Buena Vista, Holy Family.

Salinas, Our Lady of Monserrat (1854), Revs. Angel Sanchez; Edwin Vazquez-Vega; Deacon Pablo F. Miranti.
Res., Box 1172, 00751. Tel: 787-824-2215.
Missions—Plena, San Jose; Coco, Santa Ana; Parcelas Vazquez, Esp. Santo; Bo. Las Palmas, Virg. del Carmen; Naranjo, Santa Marta; Las Ochenta, Inmaculada Concepcion; Bo. Playita, Virgen Milagrosa; Bo. Playa, Carmen; Sabana Llana, Perpetuo Socorro.

Santa Isabel, St. James (1854), Revs. Ismael Larena; Moises Navascues, Sch.P.; Deacon Jaime Martinez.
Res., Box 137, 00757. Tel: 809-845-2450; Fax: 809-845-2450.
Catechesis/Religious Programs—Students 300.
Missions—Playita Cortada, San Patricio; Bo. Penuelas, Virgen del Rosario; Bo. Paso Secos, Virgen del Rosario; Bo. Ollas, Monserrate; Jauca, San Ignacio de Loyola.

Villalba, Our Lady of Mt. Carmel (1917), Revs. Jose Diego Rodriguez; Emiliano Alamo; Fausto Ramos; Deacons Javier Gonzalez; Ramon A. Resto.
Res., Box 432, 00766. Tel: 787-847-0695.
School—Box 1066, 00766. Tel: 787-847-2875. Sisters of the Love of God.
Tel: 809-847-2874; 847-2391. Sr. Ana M. Santamarta, R.A.D., Prin.
Students 270.
Missions—Romero, Sagrado Corazon, HC01 Box 5081, 00766. Tel: 787-847-1591; Bo. Vista Alegre, Jesus Crucificado, 00766; Bo. Mogote, Santisima Tinidad, 00766; Bo. Cerro Gordo, Espiritu Santo, 00766; Bo. Jagueyes Arriba, La Milagrosa, 00766; Bo. Corillo, San Pedro, 00766; Bo. Palmarejo, San Jose, 00766; Bo. Higuero, Santisimo Sacramento, 00766; Bo. Camarones, Jesus Crucificado, 00766; Bo. Canonilla Abajo, Maria Madre de la Iglesia, 00766; Bo. Sierrita Caonillas, Cristo de la Salud, 00766; Barrio Jaguey, Madre Cabrini, 00766; Barrio Semil, Santa Cecilia, 00766; Barrio Apeadero, San Alfonso, 00766; Barrio Hatillo, Sagrada Familia, 00766; Bo. Camarones-Los Robles, San Antonio, 00766; Bo. Hatillo Viejo, La Milagrosa, 00766; Bo. Cuchilla del Limon, La Asuncion, 00766; Bo. Limon, Virgen de la Amargura, 00766; Bo. Dajas, N.S. del Carmen, 00766.

Our Lady Mother of Divine Providence (Mission Noell) (1962), Revs. Raymond D. Middendorf, S.M.; James A. Imhof, S.M., Pastoral Assoc.
Res., Box 1556, 00766. Tel: 787-867-2052.
Missions—Bo. Alturita, Cacao Co., Our Lady of Mt. Carmel; Bo. Cacao, Cacao Co., Imm. Concepcion; Bo. El Frio, Ala de La Piedra Co., Nino de Praga; Bo. Guineo, Ala de La Piedra Co., Santa Ana; Bo. Bauta, Bauta Abajo Co., N.S. del Rosario; Bo. Damian Abajo, Damian Abajo Co., N.S. del Pilar; Bo. Pozas, Damian Abajo Co., N.S. Monserrate; La Piedra, Ala de La Piedra Co., O.L. of Perp. Help; Matrullas, Cacao Co., Sacred Heart of Jesus; Ortiga, Bauta Abajo Co., San Mateo.

Yauco, Holy Rossary (1756), Revs. Jose Luis Alonso, O.P.; Alfredo Vallina, O.P.; Jozef de Vlamm, O.P.; Fortunato Bodero, O.P.; Felix Martinez del Cura, O.P.
Res., Box 46, 00698. Tel: 809-856-1222; Fax: 809-856-6845.
School—Box 26, 00698. Tel: 787-856-1001. Mrs. Judith Negron, Prin.
Students 610.
Convent—Tel: 787-856-1573. Sisters Of Fatima for Social Work Sr. Luisa Caraballo, O.P., Supr.
Sisters 16.
Missions—Collores, Sacred Heart; Duey, Virgin of Mt. Carmel; Barinas, St. James; Las Vegas, Sta. Teresita; Lluberas, St. Joseph; Cambalaches, Our Lady of Perpetual Help; Carrizales, Our Lady of Montserrat; Algarrobos, Our Lady of Fatima; Sierra Alta, St. Lucy; Almacigo Bajo, St. Martin de Porres; Naranjo, St. Anthony; Diego Hdez, St. Anthony; Quebradas, Sacred Heart; Aguas, St. Martin; Almacigo Alto, S. Juan Macias.

St. Martin de Porres (1969), Rev. Juan J. Saliva; Deacon Saba Gonzalez.
Res., Las Palomas, Box 2005, 00698. Tel: 787-856-3617.
Convent—Box 62, Santa Rita, 00698. Tel: 787-856-1476. Sisters of Fatima-Motherhouse Sr. Virgenmina Morell, O.P., Mother Gen.
Sisters 37; Novices 2; Postulants 4.
Missions—Bo. Susa, Guanica Co., Santa Rita; Bo. Susa, Guanica Co., N.S. de La Providencia; Bo. Arenas de Guancia, Guancia Co., S. Martin de Porres; Bo. Susa, Yauco Co., S. Francisco de Asis; Bo. Susa, Yauco Co., N.S. de La Monserrate.

Special Assignment:
Reverend Monsignors—
Bellester, Pedro J., Pro-Vicar Gen.
Espona, Juan, Admin. & Vice Chancellor

On Duty Outside the Diocese:
Reverend Monsignors—
Abad, Federico, Paseo de los Cubos 1, Burgos, 09003 Spain
Reverend Fathers—
Alvarez, Pablo D., 110 W. 35th St., Apt. 3, Hialeah, FL 33012
Aponte, Eliud, Calle 4 #239, Tallaboa Enc., Penuelas, PR 00624
Arguinzoniz, Francisco, Apartado 70, Durango, Vizcaya, Spain
Barret, Kevin S., Chap., Apostolate of Family Consecration, P.O. Box 151, Bloomingdale, OH 43910-0151
Cahill, Thomas, M.J, P.O. Box 348097, Chicago, IL 60634
Colon, Jose E., Colinas Montecarlo, Bldg. d-35, San Juan, PR 00927
DuChez, Daniel B., O.S., Carmel of the Holy Family, P.O. Box 1720, Georgetown, CA 95634
Duran, Alfonso M., M.J., Via Lorenzo il Magnifico 47, Int 7, Rome, 00162 Italy
Ewald, Daniel M.J., P.O. Box 348097, Chicago, IL 60634
Fernandez Cartagena, Elias, Jard. Arroyo, Calle D-D-13, Arroyo, PR 00714
Fletcher, Patrick, CMR 402 Box 1104, APO, AE 09180
Garcia, E. Roberto, B. Real Abajo KM 4, Ponce, PR 00731
Garcia, Salvador, Villafruela, Burgos, Spain
Gelis, Mark, M.J., Via Lorenzo il Magnifico 47, Int 7, Rome, 00162 Italy
Gusiora, Alphonsus, P.O. Box 61, Enugwu-Ukwu (Anambra State), Nigeria
Kelty, Edward, O.S., Via Concordia 1, Rome, 00183 Italy
Kuffel, Thomas, O.S., Via Concordia 1, Rome, 00183 Italy
MacIssac, Charles S., O.S., 8828 Murphy Gulch Rd., Littleton, CO 80127
Malachowski, Christopher, O.S., Corpus Christi Institute, 703 Pinon Dr., Santa Fe, NM 87501
Margola, Joseph F., 1831 N. Cambridge Ave., Milwaukee, WI 53202-1001
Medina, George, P.O. Box 286, East Boston, MA 02128
Mezquida, Ramon, San Jose 4, Alqueria Condesa 46715, Valencia, Spain
Munoz, Rafael, P.O. Box 187, Barceloneta, PR 00657
Nicoletti, Robert, M.J., Via Lorenzo il Magnifico 47, Int 7, Rome, 00162 Italy
Nischan, James R., 1625 Mayo Ave., Owensboro, KY 42301
Porada, Casey, O.S., St. Mary's Rectory, 580 I St., David City, NE 68632
Quinones, Leoncio, Urb. Apolo, Guaynabo, PR 00657
Rodriguez, Plinio, Apartado 1918, Santo Domingo, Dominican Rep.
Sancho Piquer, Enrique, Calvario 49, 2, 4, Pafelbunoli, Valencia, Spain
Vota, Paul, M.J., P.O. Box 256528, Chicago, IL 60625
Weslin, Norman U., O.S., 151 Harvard St., Colorado Springs, CO 80911
Zayas, Antonio, Naranjito, PR 00767

Retired:
Reverend Monsignors—
Colon, Jose, Box 242, Merceditas, PR 00715
Irizarry, Raul, Marginal 11 Urb. Mercedita, Ponce, PR 00731
Reverend Fathers—
Cano, Emilio, Box 21012, Rio Piedras, PR 00928
Oria, Manuel, Box 242, Merceditas, 00715 PR
Ramos, Fausto, Box 5081 HC-01, Villalba, PR 00766

INSTITUTIONS LOCATED IN THE DIOCESE

[A] SEMINARIES

PONCE. *Diocesan Seminary*. (Major Interdiocesan), Sta. 6, P.O. Box 110, 00732-2110. Tel: 787-848-4380. Rev. Msgr. Jesus R. Diez Antonanzas, Rector; Rev. Alfredo Alvarez Lacruz, Spiritual Dir. Priests 2; Lay Staff 2; Seminarians 11.

[B] COLLEGES & UNIVERSITIES

PONCE. *The Pontifical Catholic University of Puerto Rico*, 2250 Avenida de las Americas, 00731-6382. Tel: 787-841-2000.
For a complete listing, refer to the Colleges and Universities section.

[C] SCHOOLS - INSTITUTES OF EDUCATION

PONCE. *Centro San Francisco*. Mailing Address: Box 10479, 00732. Tel: 787-844-2434; Fax: 787-842-2776. Sisters of St. Joseph. Sr. Anita Moseley, C.S.J., Prin. Sisters 3; Lay Teachers 22; Librarians 2; Social Workers 2; Counselor 1; Students 334.

Colegio El Ave Maria, Dr. Luis Bartolomei 6, Rep. Valle Alegre, 00731. Tel: 787-284-2453. Operarias del Divino Maestro. Sr. Milagros Pizarro, O.D.M., Prin. Sisters 4; Lay Teachers 9; Students 360.

Colegio Sagrado Corazon, Calle Obispado Final, 00731. Tel: 787-842-0339; Fax: 787-843-0250. Religious of the Sacred Heart. Sr. Nancy McCloskey, Prin. 1; Lay Teachers 44; Students 602.

Holy Family School, Avenida Hostos 7, 00731. Tel: 787-842-3208. Sisters of Charity. Sr. Elena Cintron, H.C., Prin. Sisters 5; Lay Teachers 20; Students 422.

COTO LAUREL. *Colegio Ponceno*. (Day School). Mailing Address: Colegio Ponceno, HC 06, Box 4701, 00780-9508. Tel: 787-848-2525; Fax: 787-259-4282. Piarists Fathers. Revs. Julio Torralba, Sch.P.; Juan L. Cabrerizo, Sch.P.; Benito Forcano, Sch.P.; Fernado Torres, Sch.P. Priests 4; Lay Teachers 64; Students 1,121.

PLAYA PONCE. *Centros Sor Isolina Ferre, Inc.*, P.O. Box 213, 00734. Tel: 787-843-1910. Missionary Servants of the Most Blessed Trinity. Sr. M. Isolina Ferre, M.S.B.T., CEO; Sr. Rosita M. Bauza, M.S.B.T., Exec. Dir. Center for social services, health and technical education, artistic, cultural, economic, domestic and spiritual formation. Priests 1; Sisters 5; Lay Teachers 40; Councilors 8; Coordinators 26; Community Lay Leaders 128; Students 3,040.

[D] HOMES FOR THE AGED

PONCE. *Home for Aged and Infirm*, Barrio Sabenetas, P.O. Box 2127, 00731. Tel: 787-840-7575.

For a complete listing, refer to the Special Care Facilities section.

[E] MONASTERIES AND RESIDENCES OF PRIESTS AND BROTHERS

PONCE. *Residencia Asis*. (Postulantado), 342 Victoria St., Box 7244, 00732. Tel: 787-842-5055; Fax: 787-844-7267. Revs. Edward Maldonado, O.F.M.Cap., Guardian & Postulant Dir.; Roberto Martinez, O.F.M.Cap.; Francisco Garcia, O.F.M.Cap.; Bro. Reinaldo Saliva, O.F.M.Cap., Vicar. Postulants 2.

[F] CONVENTS & RESIDENCES OF SISTERS

PONCE. *Convent Apostolate*. Mailing Address: Box 8300, 00732. Tel: 787-842-4340. Mother Rufina Nagore, R.A., Supr. Sisters Apostolate of the Sacred Heart of Jesus 17.

Convent of Servants of Mary, Ext. La Rambla, Calle Siervas de Maria 500, 00731. Tel: 787-842-2336. Mother Ana Gil, S.M., Supr. Religious 27; Postulants 6; Novices 6; Administered in the home 1,100.

PLAYA DE PONCE. *Blessed Trinity Missionary Cenacle*, Box 213, 00734. Tel: 787-844-1627. Sr. Isolina Ferre, M.S.B.T., Custodian; Sr. Rosita Maria Bauza, M.S.B.T., Coord. Sisters 5.

[G] PERSONAL PRELATURES

ALHAMBRA, PONCE. *Prelature of the Holy Cross and Opus Dei*, 8 Alcazar, 00731. Tel: 787-844-2661. Revs. Luis F. Montoya; Andres Eiroa.

[H] MISCELLANEOUS

PONCE. *Albergue La Providencia, Inc.*, P.O. Box 10142, 00732. Tel: 787-841-2119. Rev. Francisco Garcia, O.F.M.Cap., Dir. Refuge Center for AIDS patients. Total Assisted 100; Total Staff 32.

Apostolate for Family Consecration. Mailing Address: International Spanish Center, Box 205, Sta. 6, 00732. Tel: 787-848-5265.

Miles Jesu, Ladies House, P.O. Box 165, Station 6, 00732. Tel: 787-840-9436. Men's House, Parroquia Santa Maria Reina, P.O. Box 166, Sta. 6, 00732. Tel: 787-848-5370.

Oblates of Wisdom. Mailing Address: Box 205, Sta. 6, 00732. Rev. Brian W. Harrison, O.S., Reg. Dir.

Pastoral Care of the Sick. Mailing Address: P.O. Box 205 Sta. 6, 00732. Tel: 787-844-2080 Ext. 1208, 787-848-7157. Sr. Teresa Jensen, C.S.J., Dir.

Shelter for the Homeless. Mailing Address: Misioneras De La Caridad, P.O. Box 177 Sta. 6, 00732. Tel: 787-841-5443. Sr. Mary Selma Thomas, M.C., Supr. Missionaries of Charity (Mother Theresa of Calcutta). Sisters 6; Residents 46; Total Assisted 72.

PENUELAS. *Training School for the Lay Apostolate (Hermanos Cheos)*. Mailing Address: P.O. Box 118, 00624. Rev. Msgr. Marcos Pancorbo, Dir.; Bro. William Perez Ramos, Pres. Brothers 91.

RELIGIOUS INSTITUTES OF MEN REPRESENTED IN THE DIOCESE

For further details refer to the corresponding bracketed number in the Religious Institutes of Men or Women section.

[0140]—*The Augustinians*.—O.S.A.

[0470]—*The Capuchin Friars (Vice Province of Puerto Rico)*.—O.F.M.Cap.

[0270]—*Carmelite Fathers & Brothers*.—O.Carm.

[1330]—*Congregation of the Mission*.—C.M.

[0650]—*Holy Ghost Fathers*. (Eastern Prov.).—C.S.Sp.

[0430]—*Order of Preachers-Dominicans*. (Holland Prov.).—O.P.

[1310]—*Order of the Holy Trinity*. (Spain).—O.SS.T.

[1040]—*Piarist Fathers*. (Spain).—Sch.P.

[1070]—*Redemptorist Fathers*. (San Juan Prov.).—C.SS.R.

RELIGIOUS INSTITUTES OF WOMEN REPRESENTED IN THE DIOCESE

[0130]—*Apostles of the Sacred Heart of Jesus*.—A.S.C.J.

[0340]—*Carmelite Sisters of Charity*.—C.a.Ch.

[]—*Congrecacion Hermanas de N.S. del Perpetuo Socorro*.—N.S.P.S.

[1070-05]—*Dominican Sisters*.—O.P.

[]—*Hermanas Del-Amor De Dios*.

[]—*Hermanas Dominicas de Fatima*.—O.P.

[]—*Hermanas Terciarias Capuchinas de la Sagrada Familia (Coamo, Ponce)*.—T.C.

[]—*Hijas de la Caridad del Card. Sancha*.—H.C.C.S.

[2340]—*Little Sisters of the Poor*.—L.S.P.

[2710]—*Missionaries of Charity*.—M.C.

[2790]—*Missionary Servants of the Most Blessed Trinity*.—M.S.B.T.

[]—*Religious de los Santos Angeles Custodios (Adjuntas, Ponce)*.—R.A.C.

[3580]—*Servants of Mary*.—O.S.M.

[3020]—*Sisters Oblates to Divine Love*. (Coamo, Ponce).—R.O.D.A.

[]—*Sisters of Charity of St. Vincent de Paul*.—H.C.

[]—*Sisters of St. Joseph*.—S.S.J.

[2150]—*Sisters, Servants of the Immaculate Heart of Mary*.—I.H.M.

NECROLOGY

† Martell, Ceferino, (Retired). —Died Aug. 25, 1996.

Diocese of Samoa-Pago Pago

Most Reverend

JOHN QUINN WEITZEL, M.M.

Bishop of Samoa-Pago Pago; ordained June 11, 1955; appointed First Bishop of Samoa-Pago Pago October 29, 1986. *Fatuoaiga: P.O. Box 596, Pago Pago, American Samoa, 96799.* Tel.: 684-699-1402; Fax: 684-699-1459.

CREATED A DIOCESE NOVEMBER, 1982.

The Diocese of Samoa-Pago Pago includes the islands of Tutuila; Swains; Manu'a Is., Ofu, Olosega & Ta'u; Aunu'u and Rose Island.

STATISTICAL OVERVIEW

Personnel	
Bishop	1
Priests: Diocesan Active in Diocese	10
Number of Diocesan Priests	10
Religious Priests in Diocese	1
Ordinations:	
Permanent Deacons	18
Permanent Deacons in Diocese	19
Total Sisters	16
Parishes	
Parishes	8
With Resident Pastor:	
Resident Diocesan Priests	8
Without Resident Pastor:	
Missions	1
Welfare	
Homes for the Aged	1
Total Assisted	31
Day Care and Extended Day Care Centers	1
Total Assisted	120
Special Centers for Social Services	1
Total Assisted	663
Educational	
Diocesan Students in Other Seminaries	6
Total Seminarians	6
High Schools, Diocesan and Parish	2
Total Students	320
Elementary Schools, Diocesan and Parish	2
Total Students	454
Catechesis/Religious Education:	
High School Students	360
Elementary Students	1,686
Total Students Under Catholic Instruction	2,826
Teachers in the Diocese:	
Priests	1
Sisters	7
Lay Teachers	44
Vital Statistics	
Receptions into the Church:	
Infant Baptism Totals	310
Adult Baptism Totals	47
Received into Full Communion	19
First Communions	248
Confirmations	205
Marriages:	
Catholic	46
Interfaith	8
Total Marriages	54
Deaths	56
Total Catholic Population	6,676
Total Population	58,070

Vicar General of Diocese—Rev. MIKAELE FALANIKO.

Chancellor—IVONA T. MAUGA.

Diocesan Consultors—Revs. VAN CAMP TAVAI; MASELINO PAULO; MIKAELE FALANIKO.

Bishop's Pastoral Council—Rev. MIKAELE FALANIKO, Chm.; Mrs. MARILYN ANESI, Sec.

Fatu-O-Aiga Multipurpose Cultural and Pastoral Center—Pastoral Team: Rev. VAN CAMP TAVAI, Dir. Faculty Members: EMANI TEVAGA; Sr. MARY NAAB, M.M.

Sagata Ana Society—Mrs. NIVE REED.

Sacred Heart Society—AGNES GABBARD.

Vicar for Youth—TAGATAESE MAUGAOTEGA, F.K., Dir. of Youth.

Director of Vocations—Rev. MIKAELE FALANIKO.

Port Chaplain—Rev. SEBASTIAN CHACKO.

Hospital Chaplain—Deacon FELISE TOILOLO, F.K.

Prison Chaplain—Deacon TOETOFI TAVALE, F.K.

Director of Propagation of the Faith—Rev. PETELO SILIAKO.

CLERGY, PARISHES, MISSIONS AND PAROCHIAL SCHOOLS

SAMOA-PAGO PAGO

1—CATHEDRAL OF THE HOLY FAMILY (1986), Most Rev. John Quinn Weitzel, M.M.; Revs. Setefano Tuisea; Viane Etuale; Deacons Anetele'a Puletasi; Lito Roque; Francis Leasiolagi; Toetofi Tavale; Edward Simon.
Mailing Address: Fatuoaiga, P.O. Box 3594, 96799-3594. Tel: 684-699-1446; Fax: 684-699-1459.
Catechesis/Religious Programs—Tel: 684-699-2209; Fax: 684-699-1459. D.R.E.: Deacons Lito Roque; Anitele's Puletasi; Iacinta Muliagatele. Students 340.
Mission—Manu'a Island, Mary, Star of the Sea.

2—CO-CATHEDRAL OF ST. JOSEPH THE WORKER (Fagatogo) (1974), Rev. Sebastian Chacko, Admin.; Deacons Felise Toilolo; Lutia Timoteo; Nikolao Pula; Tavita Pereira.
Mailing Address: Fagatogo, P.O. Box AA, 96799. Tel: 684-633-1458; Fax: 684-633-1483.
Catechesis/Religious Programs—Students 185.
Missions—Utulei; Fagasa; Pago Pago; Faga'alu.

3—CHURCH OF ST. PAUL (Ili'ili) (1974), Rev. Van Camp Tavai. Pastoral Assocs.: Deacons Sagapolutele Malaeola; Naisina Ma'ileoli; To'oto'oali'i Filisi; Deacons Anitele'a Iese; Silivelio Tufele.
Mailing Address: Ili'ili, P.O. Box 2004, 96799. Tel: 684-688-7671; Fax: 684-699-1459.
Office: Fatuoaiga—P.O. Box 596, 96799. Tel: 684-699-5710.
Catechesis/Religious Programs—Deacon Naisina Ma'ileoi, D.R.E.
Students 315.
Missions—Malaeloa; Futiga; Pava'ia'i; Aasu/Aoloau.

4—CHURCH OF ST. PETER AND PAUL (1969), Rev. Msgr. Etuale Lealofi; Deacons Setefano Lesa; Fred Pele.
Mailing Address: P.O. Box 985, Pago Pago, 96799. Tel: 684-644-5581; Fax: 684-644-2582.
Catechesis/Religious Programs—Tel: 684-644-4697. D.R.E.: Alefosio Bartley; Lafaele Mageo. Students 112.
Missions—Masefau; Faga'itua; Sa'ilele.

5—CHURCH OF THE HOLY CROSS (1861), Revs. Mikaele Falaniko; Falniko Atonio. Pastoral Assocs.: Deacons Lafaele Aunoa; Aukuso Gabriel.
Mailing Address: Leone, P.O. Box 1206, Pago Pago, 96799. Tel: 684-688-7663; Fax: 684-699-1459.
Missions—Amaluia; Asili; Amanave; Vailoatai.
Catechesis/Religious Programs—D.R.E.: Asalemo Taulamano; Iosefo Tarangi; Siliako Auva'a. Students 545.

6—CHURCH OF THE IMMACULATE CONCEPTION (1867), Rev. Emani Tevaga.
Mailing Address: Lepua, P.O. Box 398, Pago Pago, 96799. Tel: 684-644-5512; Fax: 684-699-1459. [CEM]
Catechesis/Religious Programs—Tel: 684-644-2411. D.R.E.: Paulo Luamanu; Lolesio Iosefo. Students 238.
Missions—Afono; Aua.

7—CHURCH OF CHRIST THE KING (Nuuuli) (1983), Rev. Maselino Paulo.
Mailing Address: Fatuoaiga, P.O. Box 596, 96799-0596. Tel: 684-699-9847; Fax: 684-699-1459.
Catechesis/Religious Programs—Deacon Tagataese Maugaotega, D.R.E.
Students 148.

8—CHURCH OF SACRED HEART (Alao) (1989), Rev. Petelo Siliako; Deacons Uikirifi Auelua; Sogimaletavai Leo.
Mailing Address: Alao, P.O. Box 985, 96799. Tel: 684-622-7516; Fax: 684-699-1459.
Catechesis/Religious Programs—Timoteo Tatino, D.R.E.
Students 163.
Missions—Aoa; Amouli.

Permanent Deacons:
Auelua, Ukirifi
Aunoa, Lafaele
Folau, Kalini
Gabriel, August
Lafaele, Setefano
Leasiolagi, Francis
Leo, Herman Sogimaletavai
Ma'ileoi, Naisina
Maugaotega, Tagataese
Pele, Tupuaga Fred
Pereira, Tavita
Pula, Taafulisia Nikolao
Puletasi, Niuatoa Andy
Roque, Rolito
Sagapolutele, Anthony Malaeola
Simon, Edward
Tavale, Toetofi
Timoteo, Lutia Laupapa
Toilolo, Felise

INSTITUTIONS LOCATED IN THE DIOCESE

[A] PRESCHOOLS

PAGO PAGO, AMERICAN SAMOA. *Mary The Mother Montesorri Pre-School*, c/o Diocese of Samoa-Pago Pago, Fatuoaiga-P.O. Box 596, 96799. Tel: 684-699-1402; Fax: 684-699-1459.

[B] ELEMENTARY SCHOOLS, PAROCHIAL

LEONE. *St. Theresa*, P.O. Box 883, 96799-0596; Fax: 684-688-1114. Missionary Sisters of the Society of Mary. Sr. Palepa Ioane, S.M.S.M., Prin. & Supr. Sisters 4; Lay Teachers 10; Students 240.

LEPUA. *St. Francis/Marist*, Fatuoaiga, P.O. Box 429, 96799-0429; Fax: 684-699-1459. Missionary Sisters of the Society of Mary. Sr. Akanesi Liongi, S.M.S.M., Prin. & Supr. Sisters 3; Lay Teachers 1; Students 214.

[C] HIGH SCHOOLS, PAROCHIAL

LEPUAPUA. *Fa'asao High School*, P.O. Box 729, 96799; Fax: 684-688-2055. Mrs. Veronika Mortenson Mata'utia, Prin.; Catherine Satele, Co-Admin. Lay Teachers 9; Volunteer Lay Missionaries 1; Students 193.

MALAELOA. *Marist High School*, Fatuoaiga, P.O. Box K, 96799; Fax: 684-688-2336. Mrs. Lina Galea'i-Scanlan, Prin.; Rev. Emani Tevaga, Vice Prin. Lay Teachers 8; Students 127.

[D] HOMES FOR AGED & SPECIAL CARE FOR CHILDREN

PAGO PAGO, AMERICAN SAMOA. *Nazareth House*, P.O. Box 1510, 96799. Tel: 684-699-2101; Fax: 684-699-1459.

For a complete listing, refer to the Special Care Facilities section.

[E] MISCELLANEOUS

PAGO PAGO. *Catholic Social Services, Inc.*, P.O. Box 596, 96799. Tel: 684-699-5683; Fax: 684-699-1459. Sr. Mary Naab, M.S.W., Dir.

RELIGIOUS INSTITUTES OF MEN REPRESENTED IN THE DIOCESE

For further details refer to the corresponding bracketed number in the Religious Institutes of Men or Women section.

[0800]—*Maryknoll.*—M.M.

RELIGIOUS INSTITUTES OF WOMEN REPRESENTED IN THE DIOCESE

[2420]—*Marist Missionary Sisters, Inc. (Missionary Sisters of the Society of Mary).*—S.M.S.M.

[2470]—*Maryknoll Sisters of St. Dominic.*—M.M.

[3242]—*Poor Sisters of Nazareth.*—P.S.O.N.

[]—*Religious Sisters of the Virgin Mary.*—R.V.M.

NECROLOGY

(No Deaths)

Archdiocese of San Juan, Puerto Rico

(Sancti Joannis Portoricensis)

His Eminence

LUIS CARDINAL APONTE MARTINEZ, D.D.

Archbishop of San Juan; ordained April 10, 1950; appointed Titular Bishop of Lares and Auxiliary of Ponce July 23, 1960; consecrated October 12, 1960; appointed Coadjutor Bishop of Ponce April 16, 1963; appointed Bishop of Ponce November 18, 1963; installed February 20, 1964; promoted to Archbishop of San Juan November 4, 1964; installed January 15, 1965; Created Cardinal March 5, 1973. *Res., 50 Cristo St., P.O. Box S-1967, San Juan PR, 00903.* Tel.: 809-725-4975; 727-7373 (Office).

(Editor's note: 1997 information not received)

Most Reverend

FRANCOIS BACQUE

Apostolic Delegate for Puerto Rico. *Office: Ponce de Leon Ave. #256, San Juan, PR, 00907. Mailing Address: P.O. Box 191771, San Juan, PR, 00919-1771.* Tel.: 809-723-1280; Fax: 809-723-1280.

Most Reverend

HECTOR M. RIVERA, D.D.

Titular Bishop of Tubune in Numidia and Auxiliary Bishop of San Juan PR; ordained June 12, 1966; appointed June 11, 1979; consecrated August 17, 1979. *Res., Lomas de Carolina, Calle Yunquecito UU #18, Carolina, PR, 00987.* Tel.: 727-7373. *Mailing Address: P.O. Box 1967, San Juan, PR, 00902-1967.*

Most Reverend

HERMIN NEGRON SANTANA, D.D.

Titular Bishop of Gegi, North Africa and Auxiliary Bishop of San Juan, PR; ordained May 30, 1969; appointed June 30, 1981; consecrated September 7, 1981. *Res., Calle 6, D-9 Urb. Royal Town, Bayamon, PR, 00956.* Tel.: 809-730-4310. *Archbishop's Office: San Jorge St., No. 201, Santurce, P.P. Mailing Address: P.O. Box S-1967, San Juan, PR, 00903.* Tel.: 809-727-7373.

ERECTED AUGUST 8, 1511.

ERECTED AN ARCHDIOCESE APRIL 30, 1960.

Square Miles 353.

Comprises the northeast portion of the Island of Puerto Rico, with a Total Population of 1,260,000.

Chancery Office: P.O. Box S-1967, San Juan, PR, 00902.

STATISTICAL OVERVIEW

Personnel	
Cardinal	1
Archbishop	1
Auxiliary Bishops	2
Priests: Diocesan Active in Diocese	142
Priests: Active Outside Diocese	1
Priests: Retired, Sick or Absent	11
Number of Diocesan Priests	154
Religious Priests in Diocese	145
Ordinations:	
Religious Priests	2
Transitional Deacons	1
Permanent Deacons	16
Permanent Deacons in Diocese	260
Total Brothers	36
Total Sisters	433
Parishes	
Parishes	152
With Resident Pastor:	
Resident Diocesan Priests	102
Resident Religious Priests	50
Without Resident Pastor:	
Pastoral Centers	150
Welfare	
Catholic Hospitals	2
Total Assisted	19,325
Health Care Centers	2
Total Assisted	381
Homes for the Aged	5
Total Assisted	954
Residential Care of Children	3
Total Assisted	110
Day Care and Extended Day Care Centers	37
Total Assisted	1,295
Specialized Homes	2
Total Assisted	60
Educational	
Seminaries, Diocesan	2
Students from This Diocese	25
Diocesan Students in Other Seminaries	9
Seminaries, Religious	6
Students Religious	22
Total Seminarians	56
Colleges and Universities	2
Total Students	9,620
High Schools, Diocesan and Parish	20
Total Students	5,411
High Schools, Private	30
Total Students	6,780
Elementary Schools, Diocesan and Parish	27
Total Students	10,806
Elementary Schools, Private	42
Total Students	14,136
Catechesis/Religious Education:	
High School Students	4,902
Elementary Students	19,711
Total Students Under Catholic Instruction	71,422
Teachers in the Diocese:	
Priests	34
Scholastics	2
Brothers	20
Sisters	130
Lay Teachers	2,210
Vital Statistics	
Receptions into the Church:	
Infant Baptism Totals	12,642
Adult Baptism Totals	1,172
First Communions	7,716
Confirmations	5,557
Marriages:	
Catholic	2,404
Interfaith	142
Total Marriages	2,546
Total Catholic Population	886,994
Total Population	1,233,743

Former Bishops—Rev. ALONSO MANSO, D.D., appt. May 1513.—Most Rev. JAMES H. BLENK, S.M.D.D., appt. Bishop of Puerto Rico, June 12, 1899; died April 20, 1917.—Most Rev. WILLIAM A. JONES, O.S.A., cons. Feb. 24, 1907; died Jan. 1921.—Most Rev. GEORGE J. CARUANA, D.D., promoted to the Apostolic Delegation of Mexico, 1925; promoted to Nunciature Apostolic of Cuba, 1927.—Most Rev. EDWIN VINCENT BRYNE, D.D., former Bishop of Ponce, Puerto Rico; cons. Nov. 30, 1925; appt. March 1929; promoted to Archdiocese of Santa Fe, June 15, 1943; died July 25, 1963.—Most Rev. JAMES PETER DAVIS, cons. Oct. 9, 1943; transferred to Archdiocese of Santa Fe, June, 1943; installed Feb. 25, 1964; retired Oct. 1974.

Vicars General—Most Rev. HECTOR RIVERA, D.D.; Most Rev. HERMIN NEGRON SANTANA, D.D.; Rev. Msgr. CELESTINO LINERA.

Episcopal Vicars—

for Administration of Temporalities—Rev. Msgr. BAUDILIO MERINO.

for Religious Women for Education—Rev. Msgr. BAUDILIO MERINO.

for Pastoral Affairs—Most Rev. HECTOR RIVERA.

for Geographic-Pastoral Zones—San Juan-Santurce: Rev. JUAN MARTINEZ, S.D.B., Bayamon: Rev. DANIEL TRUJILLO, Carolina: Rev. JOAQUIN RIVERA, Rio Piedras: Rev. REINALDO SAGARDIA, Rio Grande: Rev. EMILIO TORO FRANCO, Guaynabo-Puerto Nuevo: Rev. MARIO A. GUIJARRO.

Chancery Office—P.O. Box S-1967, San Juan, 00902.

Chancery Affairs—Rev. Msgr. C. LINERA.

Metropolitan Tribunal—

Moderator—His Eminence LUIS CARDINAL APONTE.

Judicial Vicar—Rev. Msgr. JAIME CAPO.

Adjunt Judicial Vicars—Revs. REINALDO SAGARDIA; SALVADOR RODRIGO, O.C.

Judges—Revs. LUIS O. CAPACETTI; REINALDO SAGARDIA; Rev. Msgr. FERNANDO FELICES.

Defenders of the Bond—Rev. FLORENTINO SANZ.

Instructors—Vacant.

Diocesan Consultors—Most Rev. HERMIN NEGRON SANTANA, D.D.; Most Rev. HECTOR RIVERA; Rev. Msgr. CELESTINO LINERA; Rev. Msgr. RAFAEL FONTANEZ; Rev. Msgr. JAMIE CAPO; Rev. Msgr. BAUDILIO MERINO; Rev. Msgr. FERNANDO FELICES.

Censor Librorum—Vacant.

Examinatores Cleri—Vacant.

Pro-Synodal Examiner—Vacant.

Archdiocesan Offices and Directors

Boy Scouts—Rev. LORENZO RUIZ, S.D.B., *Calle Lutz 370, Santurce.*

Catechetics—Most Rev. HECTOR RIVERA, Archdiocesan Coord., *Calle San Jorge 201, Santurce, 00914.*

Catechetics Center—San Juan-Santurce: Sr. ROSA MA. REYES; Sr. MARTA TOBON, Bayamon: Sr. IMELDA

MORALES, Rio Piedras: Sr. AILEEN BARDEN, Guaynabo-Ptonuevo: Sr. ROSE MORALES, Rio Grande: Sr. MARTHA L. GIL, Carolina: Sr. MARIA EUGENIA MORENO.

Catholic Social Action—Sr. CLOTILDE ARCE, H.C., Dir.

Children of Mary—Vacant.

Christian Family Movement—Rev. DAMIAN ARTIAGA, Dir., *Pastoral Office, Ave. Americo Miranda No. 1161, Reparto Metropolitano, Rio Piedras, 00921.* Tel: 809-783-4952.

Commission for Commun—Vacant.

"El Visitante"—Weekly Catholic Paper for All Dioceses (Interdiocesan). Published By The P.R., Episcopal Conference. Most Rev. INAKI MALLONA, C.P., Pres.; Rev. EFRAIN ZABALA, Editor; Dr. ANIBAL COLON ROSADO, Dir., *Mailing Address: P.O. Box 41305, Minillas Sta., Santurce, 00940-1305.* Tel: 809-728-3710; 728-3656. Offices: *Pumarada St. 1704, Santurce, 00914.*

Radio Stations—WORO and WKVM, *c/o Box 1967, San Juan, 00903.*

Television Station—WPRV-TV CHANNEL 13, *Carolina.*

Commission for Sacred Art—Dr. ARTURO DAVILA, *Univ. of Puerto Rico, Rio Piedras, 00921.*

Commission for Sacred Liturgy—Vacant.

Commission for Sacred Music—Rev. Msgr. FRANCISCO ARENAS, Chm., *Calle Encarnacion, No. 1564, Caparra Heights, 00920.*

Clergy Social Security (Prevision Social del Clero)—Revs. ARMANDO ALVAREZ, Pres. VIRGILIO MARTINEZ, Treas. PEDRO CAMPANA, Sec., *San Jose, Bloque ZM-215, Urb. Villa Caparra, Guaynabo, 00657.*

Cursillos De Cristiandad—Rev. Msgr. JAIME CAPO; Rev. VINCENTE FERNANDEZ-MARINO, *G.P.O. Box 1809, San Juan, 00936.*

Emigrant Aid—Sr. CLOTILDE ARCE, H.C.

Holy Childhood Association—Rev. PRISCILO MANUEL CARDENAS, D.D., *106 Ruiz Belvis St.66, Floral Park, P.O. Box 1882, Hato Rey, 00917.* Tel: 809-754-0995.

Holy Name Society—Rev. TEODORO VEERKAMP, O.P., *P.O. Box 1968, Bayamon, 00619.*

Hospitals—925 Isaura Arnau St., Country Club, Rio Piedras, 00924.

Istepa—Instituto Superior de Teologia y Pastoral, Apartado 11, 714 Caparra Heights Sta., Rio Piedras, 00920. Tel: 809-792-5320; 792-5324.

Labor Relations—Vacant.

Legion of Mary—Deacon JOSE LUIS PORRATA, *P.O. Box 5037, Puerta de Tierra Sta., San Juan, 00906.*

Marriage Encounter—1161 Americo Miranda Ave., Rio Piedras, 00921. Tel: 809-752-3163.

Master of Ceremonies to the Cardinal—Deacon PEDRO AREVALO.

Movimiento "Por Un Mundo Mejor"—Rev. JUAN J. GENOVARD, M.SS.CC., *Calle Duke 211, University Gardens, Rio Piedras, 00927.* Tel: 809-765-2255; 765-8042.

Nocturnal Adoration—Vacant.

Operation Head Start—862 Carmen Hernandez St., El Comandante, Rio Piedras, 00924. Tel: 809-752-5762; 752-3040.

Head Start-Municipality of San Juan—Rev. FRANCISCO RUBALCABA, Dir., *900 Eider St., Country Club, Rio Peidras, 00924.* Tel: 809-768-0580; 757-1913.

Our Lady of Providence Association—Vacant.

Perpetual Adoration—Rev. FRANCISCO QUINONES, Dir.; Mrs. VIRGINIA ALVAREZ, Asst., *Mailing Address: Box S-763, San Juan, 00902.* Tel: 809-725-7734.

Pius Union of the Clergy—Rev. Msgr. CELESTINO LINERA, *Mailing Address: P.O. Box 1967, San Juan, 00903.*

Propagation of the Faith—Rev. PRISCILO MANUEL CARDENAS, *100 Ruiz Belvis St., Floral Park, P.O. Box 1882, Hato Rey, 00917.*

Santa Maria de los Angeles Seminary—Rev. Msgr. FERNANDO FELICES, Rector & Promoter of Vocations; Rev. IVAN HUERTAS COLON, *Mailing Address: P.O. Box 11, 714, Caparra Heights Sta., Rio Piedras, 00922.* Tel: 809-781-6166; 783-1919. *Ave. De Diego 930, Urb. La Riviera, Rio Piedras, 00921.*

San Jose Minor Seminary—Rev. FREDDY ALECIO, Rector, *Demetrio O'Dally St. 1000, Country Club, Rio Piedras, 00924.* Tel: 809-768-3157.

Serra Clubs—Calle Encarnacion 1564, Caparra Heights, Rio Piedras, 00922., Mailing Address: P.O. Box 11, 238 Caparra Heights, Sta., Rio Piedras, 00920. Tel: 809-783-1919.

Society For The Protection of Children—His Eminence LUIS CARDINAL APONTE MARTINEZ, Dir. Admin., *Mailing Address: P.O. Box S-1967, San Juan, 00903.* Tel: 809-727-7373.

Superintendent of Schools—Mr. RAFAEL MORALES, Supt.; Mrs. BLANCA MARQUEZ, Asst.; Rev. EDDIE RIVERA, Religion Program Dir., Mailing Address: *Pumarada 1708, Santurce, 00912.* Tel: 809-268-6700; 268-6980.

War Against Hunger—Mrs. BERTA ALVIRA DE RODRIQUEZ, *San Jorge St., No. 201, Santurce, 00914., Mailing Address: P.O. Box 8812, Santurce, 00910.* Tel: 809-767-3348; 727-7373.

Young Catholic Action—Vacant, *c/o P.O. Box S-1967, San Juan, 00903.*

Young Christian Students—Bro. BENJAMIN, F.S.C., *40 Betances St., Bayamon, 00619.*

Young Catholic University Students—Rev. BAUDILIO GUZMAN, S.J., *Mariana Bracetti 10, Rio Piedras, 00925.* Tel: 809-767-3348.

Young Christian Workers—Vacant.

CLERGY, PARISHES, MISSIONS AND PAROCHIAL SCHOOLS

CITY OF SAN JUAN

1—CATEDRAL DE SAN JUAN BAUTISTA (1522). (Nuestra Sra. de los Remedios). Rev. Raul Saez Munoz, Rector.
Res., 151 Cristo St., Box S-2145, 00903. Tel: 809-722-0861.
Chapels—Santo Cristo; Santa Ana.

2—SAN AGUSTIN (1889), Revs. Tomas Gavigan, C.SS.R.; Kevin Moley, C.SS.R., Prov. Supr.; Robert Gaugler, C.SS.R.; Alfonso Amador, C.SS.R.; Juan Rosario, C.SS.R.
Res., 265 Ponce de Leon Ave., Pta. de Tierra, 00902. Tel: 809-722-4289.
School—Mailing Address, P.O. Box 5037, 00902-5037.
225 Ponce de Leon Ave., Box 5007, 00902. Tel: 809-722-4544. Sr. Marie Benitez, S.S.N.D., Supr. & Prin.
Sisters 2; Lay Teachers 15; Students 292.

3—NUESTRA SENORA DE LA ALTAGRACIA (1968), Rev. Franco Gutierrez (Spain); Deacon Ildefonso Lugo.
Mailing Address: Apartado 29493, 65 Inf. Sta., Rio Piedras, 00924-9493.
Res., Calle Felipe Gutierrez 672, Urb. Villa Prades, Rio Piedras, 00924. Tel: 809-765-0281.
School—Tel: 809-763-7755; Fax: 809-756-5195. Mrs. Zaida Silva, Prin.
Priests 1; Sisters 2; Lay Teachers 3; Students 433.

4—SAN ANTONIO (1908), Revs. Paul S. Brodie, O.F.M.Cap., Vice Prov.; Regis Schlick, O.F.M.Cap.; Ramon Lopez, O.F.M.Cap.; Claire Noll, O.F.M.Cap.
Res., Arzuaga Esq. Padres Capuchinos, Box 21350, Rio Piedras, 00928-1422. Tel: 809-765-0606; 765-1180; Fax: 809-764-4070.
School—Tel: 809-764-0090. Principals: Fe Villafane; Miguel Rosa.
Priests 3; Sisters 1; Lay Teachers 65; Students 1,071.
Mission—Nuestra Senora del Buen Consejo.

5—ASUNCION DE LA VIRGEN, Rev. Manuel Gamarra.
Res., Calle Calve No. 1483, Urb. Antonsanti, Rio Piedras, 00928. Tel: 809-250-6771.
Mission—State Penitentiary.

6—NUESTRA SENORA DE BELEN (1960), Rev. Joaquin Mansilla.
Mailing Address: P.O. Box 10,845, Caparra Heights, 00922. Tel: 809-792-3014; 792-3115; 793-2485.
Res., Ave., San Patricio Calle 6 (Final), Guaynabo.
School—Principals: Lilia Rivera; Rosa B. Pintor.
Priests 1; Lay Teachers 73; Students 1,128.

7—NTR. SRA. DE LA CARIDAD DEL COBRE (1969), Revs. Pablo Hughes, O.M.I.; Juan Curran, O.M.I., Chap.
Mailing Address: Box 4023, 00936-4023.
Res., Urb. Buena Vista, Calle 5, No. 124, Hato Rey, 00917. Tel: 809-753-0108.
Mission—Hato Rey, Sma. Trinidad, Calle Buenos Aires, No. 25, Parada 27, Hato Rey 00919.

8—NUESTRA SENORA DEL CARMEN (1923), Rev. Francisco Medina.
Mailing Address: P.O. Box 7275, Bo. Obrero Sta., Santurce, 00916-7275. Tel: 809-727-0737.
Res., Ave., Borinquen, Esq., Calle 8, Num. 609, Barrio Obrero, Santurce, 00916.
School—Father Berrios, Tel: 809-726-4851. Sr. Carmen Herrera Acevedo, H.C.C.S., Prin.
Sisters 4; Lay Teachers 9; Students 278.
Mission—San Martin de Porres.

9—SANTA CATALINA LABOURE (1977), Rev. Hilario Rivera Gonzalez.
Mailing Address: Ruta RFD 6, Box 9972, Rio Piedras, 00928. Tel: 809-720-0303.
Res., Barrio Caimito, Rio Piedras, 00928.
Missions—Medalla Milagrosa; San Pablo.

10—SANTA CECILIA (1969), Rev. Jose Ma. Lopez Mairal; Deacon Victor Merced de la Paz.
Mailing Address: P.O. Box 415, El Senorial Sta., Rio Piedras, 00926-0415.
Res., Carr Cupey Km. 3 Hm. 8, Rio Piedras, 00926. Tel: 809-755-8670.
Chapels—Asilo Santa Teresa Jornet; Capilla San Augustin.

11—CORPUS CHRISTI, Rev. Pablo Valenzuela; Deacons Francisco Gierbolini; Miguel Mendez; Luis R. Perez; Juan Figueroa; Rene Morales; Reinaldo Del Valle; Jose Perez.
Res., Calle Jose Abad, 1224 Urb. Club Manor, Rio Piedras, 00924. Tel: 809-757-5821.
Mission—Santo Domingo.

12—CRISTO REDENTOR, Rev. Damian Carvajal.
Res., Calle Ganges 140, Urb. El Paraiso, Rio Piedras, 00926. Tel: 809-764-1583.

13—CRISTO REY (1965), Rev. Msgr. Antonio Gomez; Deacon Victor Reyes.
Mailing Address: P.O. Box 29695, 65 Inf., Rio Piedras, 00929-0695.
Res., Calle Jaime Drew, No. 789, Urb. Los Maestros, Rio Piedras, 00929. Tel: 809-767-3289.
School—Tel: 809-767-0922. Sr. Jacinta Gutierrez, H.T.F., Prin.
Sisters 2; Lay Teachers 15.

14—NUESTRA SENORA DE LA ESPERANZA (1962), Rev. Carlos Dionisio Cruz.
Res., Calle Republica No. 864, Urb. Hipodromo, Parada 20, Box, Santurce, 00910. Tel: 809-723-5998.
Mission—Ntra. Sra. de la Providencia.
Chapel—Doctors Hospital.

15—ESPIRITU SANTO (1941), Rev. Valeriano Miguelez.
Res., 74 Ruiz Belvis St., Floral Park, Box 259, Hato Rey, 00919. Tel: 809-754-0570.
School—75 Ruiz Belvis Ave., Box 1715, Tel: 809-754-0490; 754-0555. Sr. Enedina Santos, Prin.
Priests 1; Lay Teachers 36; Students 713.
Chapel—Hospital Ntra. Sra. de Guadalupe.

16—NTRA. SRA. DE FATIMA (1967), Revs. Julio Fernandez Dominguez, O.M.; Martin Garamendi, O.M.; Jose M. Gallego, O.M.; Javier Gutierrez, O.M.
Mailing Address: P.O. Box 190396, 00919-0396.
Res., 608 Munoz Rivera Ave., Stop 34, Urb. Baldrich. Hato Rey, Box 396, Hato Rey, 00919.
School—La Merced, (1949), Box 606, 00919. Tel: 809-765-2388; 765-7342; 754-1162. Mrs. Rita Saveedra de Bravo, Prin., Tel: 809-766-3181.
Lay Teachers 36; Students 754.
Mission—Egida del Maestro.

17—FRANCISCA JAVIERA CABRINI (1967). (Santa Madre Cabrini). Rev. Msgr. Francisco Arenas; Rev. Rogelio Carod; Deacon Francisco Huertas.
Res., 1564 Encarnacion St., Caparra Heights, 00920. Tel: 809-783-7447; 782-0517 (College).
School—Colegio Madre Cabrini, Tel: 809-792-6180; 792-8745. Sr. M. Sacred Heart, O.S.F., Prin. Elementary. High School Principals: Sr. Ann Marie Gavin; Mrs. Mayra Mendez.
Sisters 3; Lay Teachers 36; Students 411.

18—SAN FRANCISCO DE ASIS (1858), Rev. Juan Bednarik, O.F.M.Cap.
Res., 301 San Francisco St., Box 4231, 00902. Tel: 809-724-1131.
Mission—Capilla San Conrado.

19—SAN FRANCISCO DE MONTE ALVERNIA, Rev. David Arrieta.
Res., Calle 10 #15 Ext. San Augustin, Rio Piedras, 00926. Tel: 809-765-8824.

20—SAN FRANCISCO JAVIER, Rev. Perfecto Fondevila; Deacons Elidio Aldarondo; Abel De varona; Jose Hernandez.
Res., Calle 19, G46. Urb. Fair View, Barrio Cupey Bajo, Rio Piedras, 00926. Tel: 809-761-2115.

21—NUESTRA SRA. DE GUADALUPE (1951), Rev. Juan Miranda; Deacon Andres Figueroa.
Mailing Address: G.P.O. Box 4125, 00936. Tel: 809-782-0016.
Res., 19th St., N.E. No. 1, Puerto Nuevo, 00920.
School—Tel: 809-782-0330; Fax: 809-781-3139. Mrs. Teresita Hernandez, Prin.
Lay Teachers 35; Students 860.

22—SAN IGNACIO DE LOYOLA (1958), Revs. Fabian Rodriguez, S.J.; Jorge Ferrer, S.J.; Jorge Ambert, S.J.; Guillermo Arias, S.J.
Res., Calle Narciso 1904, Rio Piedras, 00927-6706. Tel: 809-751-7680.
Jesuit Community—Revs. Juan J. Santiago, S.J.; Carlos J. Lavergne, S.J.; William J. Hendricks, S.J.; Juan Lopez Pedraz, S.J.; Francisco Marrero, S.J.; Jose Angel Borges, S.J.; Francisco Santiago, S.J.; Arthur A. Clarke, S.J.; Alberto Villaverde, S.J.; Baudilio Guzman, S.J.; Frank Golden, S.J.; Donald Vega, S.J.; Alfredo Guzman, S.J.; Walter Janer, S.J.; Bro. Jose Feliz, S.J.
Res., Calle Sauco 1940, Rio Piedras, 00927-6728. Tel: 809-765-3814.
School—Tel: 809-765-8190. Rev. Juan J. Santiago, S.J., Prin.
Sisters 2; Lay Teachers 18; Students 862.
Chapel—Hospital Psiquiatria.

23—INMACULADO CORAZON DE MARIA (1961), Rev. Jose Rivas; Deacon Benjamin Totti.

Mailing Address: Rio Piedras a Guaynabo Km. 4, Hm.3, P.O. Box 10932, Caparra Heights Sta., 00922.
Res., Ferrer y Ferrer St., Urb. Santiago Iglesias, 00922. Tel: 809-782-4176.
School—Tel: 809-783-5003. Mrs. Candida Quintero, Prin.
Priests 2; Sisters 2; Lay Teachers 18; Students 296.
Missions—Monacillos, San Fernando; San Fernando.
Chapels—Colegio Ntra. Sra. de la Providencia; Metropolitan Hospital.

24—JESUS MAESTRO (1968), Revs. Julian Martinez, C.M.; Javier Marrodon, C.M.; Deacons Miguel De la Sota; William Gomez; Rafael Velazquez.
Res., Segre, 1725 Urb. San Ferando, Rio Piedras, 00926. Tel: 809-763-8291.
Mission—Jesus de Nazaret.

25—SAN JORGE (1965), Revs. Jesus Santoalla; Luis Ricardo Gerena; Deacon Enrique Alvarez.
Res., Calle San Jorge 157, Box 6427, Santurce, 00914-0427. Tel: 809-724-7780.
School—1701-03 Colon St., 00911. Tel: 809-722-3182; 723-5182. Mrs. Maria T. Ambrusso, Prin.
Brothers 1; Lay Teachers 70; Students 812.

26—SAN JOSE (Villa Caparra), Rev. Msgr. Rafael Fontanez; Rev. James Tirado; Deacons Luis Colon; Carlos Ralat; Ramon Rodriguez.
Res., 1948 Urb. Villa Caparra, Bloque ZM 215, Guaynabo, 00966. Tel: 809-781-1155.
School—Calle A. 32, (Villa Caparra), Tel: 809-783-1995; 792-7538. Sr. Catherine Ortiz, O.P., Prin.; Sr. John Christian, Supr.
Priests 4; Sisters 5; Lay Teachers 76; Students 1,286.

27—SAN JOSE OBRERO (1956), Revs. Ruben Gonzalez, C.M.F.; Humberto Evangelista, C.M.F.; Jose Munoz, C.M.; Bro. Zacarias Pichardo, C.M.F.; Deacon Eugenio Rivera.
Mailing Address: Box 3753, San Jose Branch, Rio Piedras, 00930. Tel: 809-767-1448.
Res., Urb. San Jose, Calle 11 17, Urb. San Jose, Rio Piedras, 00923.
Missions—Bo. Plebiscito, San Antonio Ma. Claret; San Martin de Porres-Sierra Maestra.

28—SAN JUAN BOSCO (1945), Revs. Juan Martinez, S.D.B.; Antonio Polo, S.D.B., Supr.; Enrique Mendez, S.D.B.; Lorenzo Ruiz; Bros. Victorino Cayado, S.D.B.; Jose Artiagas, S.D.B.
Res., 370 Lutz St., P.O. Box 14, 125 Barrio Obrero Sta., Santurce, 00916. Tel: 809-726-1420; 726-0232.
Missions—La Milagrosa; Ntra. Sra. del Rosario; San Martin de Porres.

29—SAN JUAN DE LA CRUZ, Rev. Mario Mesa, O.F.M.Cap.; Deacon Martin Nieves.
Res., Ste. 216 Ave. Emiliano Pol 497 Urb. La Cumbre, Rio Piedras, 00926. Tel: 809-731-2016.

30—SAN JUAN EVANGELISTA (1962), Rev. Nicanor Valdes; Deacon Miguel De la Sota.
Res., Calle Church Hill, J-5, Urb. Torrimar, Guaynabo, 00922-0151. Tel: 809-783-3522.
Prescolar "LAURA"—Tel: 809-781-5325. Rev. Nicanor Valdes, Dir.
Priests 1; Sisters 1; Lay Teachers 13; Students 85.
Mission—San Francisco de Asis.

31—NUESTRA SENORA DE LOURDES (1969), Rev. Msgr. Efranin Rodriguez; Deacons Dionilo Torres; Enemias Garcia.
Res., Puerto Rico Ave., Cr. of Colton St., P.O. Box 14452, Bo. Obrero Sta., Santurce, 00916. Tel: 809-726-4643.

32—SAN LUCAS, Rev. Reinaldo Sagardia; Deacons Jose Rodriguez; Miguel Colon; Hactor Cruz D'Choudens.
Res., Pio Baroja St., No. 380, Urb. El Senorial, Rio Piedras, 00926. Tel: 809-761-5476.

33—SANTA LUISA DE MARILLAC (1962), Rev. Victoriano Ramos; Deacon Jose Lopez.
Res., Ave. Emiliano Pol, Urb. La Cumbre, Rio Piedras, 00926. Tel: 809-720-3150.
School—Nuestra Senora del Pilar.
R.R. #3, Box 3120, Rio Piedras, 00928.; Carretera #839, Km. 4 Hm. 4, Rio Piedras, 00928. Tel: 809-767-6962. Jose Marlasca, Prin.
Priests 1; Sisters 5; Lay Teachers 21; Students 591.

34—SAN LUIS GONZAGA (1965), Rev. Jose Antonio Landrau; Deacon Silverio Rubio.
Res., Calle Ronda A-17, Urb. Villa Andalucia, Rio Piedras, 00926. Tel: 809-761-9438.

35—SAN LUIS REY (1967), Rev. Virgilio Martinez; Deacon Vicente Ruiz.
Res., Calle 43 S.E. Final Urb. Reparto Metropolitano, Rio Piedras, 00921. Tel: 809-767-6235.
School—Calle 43 S.E. #469, Reparto Metropolitano, Rio Piedras, 00921. Tel: 809-767-4006. Mrs. Laura Genero, Prin.
Sisters 1; Lay Teachers 10; Students 209.

36—MARIA MADRE DE LA IGLESIA (1967), Rev. Gregorio Bravo; Deacons George Gonzalez; Eugenio Torres.
Res., 1123 Calle 3, Urb. Villa Nevarez, Rio Piedras, 00927. Tel: 809-765-0600.

37—MARIA AUXILIADORA (1962), Revs. Nicolas Parroco Navarro; Hiram Santiago, S.D.B.; Francisco Juan, S.D.B.; Nicanor Sta. Maria, S.D.B., (Apostolate of the Sea); Rogelio Barrango, S.D.B.; Andres Rivera, S.D.B.; Antonio Polo, S.D.B.; Bro. Leocadio Ramos, S.D.B.
Res., Carpenter Rd., Box 14367, Bo. Oberero Sta., Santurce, 00916. Tel: 809-726-1995.
School—Colegio San Juan Bosco, 00916. Tel: 809-726-0054.
Priests 2; Religious 15; Lay Teachers 2; Students 312.
Missions—Sagrado Corazon; Nra. Sra. del Altagracia; Ntra. Sra. de Fatima; Santisima Trinidad.

38—SANTA MARIA DE LOS ANGELES (1954), Rev. Leonardo Rodriguez Jimenez.
Mailing Address: Box 10716, Caparra Heights, 00922. Tel: 809-792-2640.
Res., De Diego Ave., No. 930, Urb. La Rivera, Rio Piedras.
Mission—Ntra. Senora de la Caridad del Cobre.

39—SAN MATEO (1773), Rev. Msgr. Manuel Rivera.
Res., Calle San Mateo, Esq. San Jorge, Stop 25, Santurce, 00912. Tel: 809-722-4158.

40—NUESTRA SENORA DE LA MERCED (1940), Revs. Jose Maria Reyes, O.de.M.; Fidel Fernandez, O.de.M.; Manuel Cid, O.de.M.
Res., Calle Antolinin, Corner to Espada St., Urb. Roosevelt, G.P.O. Box 4133, Hato Rey, 00936. Tel: 809-763-3657.

41—NTRA. SRA. DE LA MEDALLA MILAGROSA (1957), Rev. Ovidio Ortega Lemus.
Res., 209 Mayaguez St., Hato Rey, 00919. Tel: 809-751-2335.

42—NTRA. SRA. DE LA MONSERRATE (1913), Revs. Vidal Ortega, O.S.A.; Herber Nazario, O.S.A.; Urbano Saenz, O.S.A.
Res., 1058 Fernandez Juncos Ave., Box 13, 726, Santurce, 00908. Tel: 809-722-3134.
School—Santa Monica, Tel: 809-723-2573; 723-3845. Ms. Eva Luz Torres Perez, Prin. Elementary.
Sisters 1; Lay Teachers 42; Students 670.
Mission—Santa Ana.

43—SAN PABLO (1965), Rev. Jose Guillermo Hernandez; Deacons Jose Alicea; Tomas Ramirez; Orlando Sanchez.
Res., Duero St., No. 370, Urb. Villa Borinquen, Puerto Nuevo, 00920. Tel: 809-783-1790.
Mission—Ntra. Sra. de la Caridad.

44—SANTOS PEDRO Y PABLO LOS APOSTOLES, Rev. James Marin.
Res., Jardines Berwind, 65 de Inf., Rio Piedras, P.O. Box 29231, 00929. Tel: 809-750-2715.

45—NTRA. SRA. DEL PERPETUO SOCORRO (1941), Revs. Armando Alvarez; Jesus Gomez Hernandez; Deacons Latino Merino; Jose L. Porrata.
Res., 656 Union St., Miramar, Santurce, 00907. Tel: 809-721-1015; 721-1016.
School—Marti St., 00903. Tel: 809-724-1447; 721-4540. Principals: Mrs. Laura F. de Vega; Sr. Armand Marie, S.S.N.D.
Priests 1; Lay Teachers 102; Students 1,305.

46—NUESTRA SENORA DE LA PIEDAD (1956), Revs. Inmanol Alberdi, C.P.; Juan Bautista Benguria; Esteban Barruetabena, C.P., Supr.; Bro. Juan Landia, C.P.
Res., 13 Marginal St., Urb. Extension, Villamar, Isla Verde, Box 6277, Loiza Sta., Santurce, 00914. Tel: 809-726-2880.
School—Tel: 809-727-7585. Principals: Sr. Shelia O'Brien, S.S.J.; Dr. Juan B. Benguria.
Priests 1; Sisters 4; Lay Teachers 77; Students 829.

47—NUESTRA SENORA DEL PILAR (1714), Revs. Juan Maria Zurutuza, C.M.; Higinio Madrazo, C.M.; Manuel Vila, C.M.; Ramon Orlando Tirado, C.M.; Deacon Cesar Guiven.
Res., Plaza de Recreo, Rio Piedras, Box 21134, Rio Piedras, 00928. Tel: 809-764-5088.
Mission—Santa Teresita de Nino Jesus.
Chapels—Colegio La Milagrosa, De Diego St., Rio Piedras; San Jose, Hogar, Lasalle, Rio Piedras.

48—SAN PIO X, Rev. Manuel Otero; Deacons Julio Sanchez; Eduardo Carmona; Juan B. Perez.
Res., Carretera 848, K-1.2, P.O. Box 631, Urb. St. Just, Trujillo Alto, 00978. Tel: 809-761-5040.

49—NUESTRA SENORA DE LA PROVIDENCIA (1959), Rev. Msgr. Baudilio Merino; Deacons Nelson Figueroa; Pedro Rivera; Luis Vazquez.
Res., Santa Agueda St., No. 1731, Urb. Sagrado Corazon, Rio Piedras, 00927. Tel: 809-765-6240.
School—Carretera #176, Km. 2.7-C/Sta. Agueda 1733-Urb. San Gerardo, Rio Piedras, 00926. Tel: 809-767-6552; 767-6755. Maria M. Lee de Cobo, Prin.
Lay Teachers 63; Students 891.

50—NUESTRA SENORA DE LA PROVIDENCIA (1973), Rev. Eddie Rivera.
Res., 219 Aponte St., Santurce, 00912. Tel: 809-727-1878.

51—MARIA REINA DEL MUNDO (1971), Rev. Felix Varas.
Mailing Address: G.P.O. Box 3828, 00936-3828. Tel: 809-767-1372.
Res., Caserio Nemesio Canales, Roosevelt Ave. Puerto Nuevo, Rio Piedras.

52—RESURRECCION DEL SENOR (1968), Revs. Cruz Ajuria, O.F.M.; Luis Zabala, O.F.M.; Victorio Beain, O.F.M.; Tomas Gondra.
Res., Calle 31, S.O. 797, Urb. Las Lomas, Rio Piedras, 00921. Tel: 809-792-1416; 792-5939.

53—SANTA ROSA DE LIMA (1971), Rev. Jose D'Artiaga; Deacons Pedro Costa; Vicente Rio.
Res., Calle Lesbos No. 1765, Urb. Venus Gardens, Rio Piedras, 00926. Tel: 809-761-6586.

54—SAGRADA FAMILIA (1971), Rev. Msgr. Tomas Su; Deacon Vivente Colon.
Res., Ave. 65 de Inf., Esquina Calle 7, No. 112, Hills Brothers, Sabana Llana, P.O. Box 29, 311, 65 Infantry Sta., Rio Piedras, 00929. Tel: 809-767-1723.

55—SAGRADO CORAZON DE JESUS (1971), Revs. Basilio Roldan; Pablo Torres, C.M.; Jose Yanez, C.M.
Res., Calle Oxford 251, Esq. Howard Urb. University Gardens, Rio Piedras, 00927. Tel: 809-765-4798; 765-5267.
School—Iteramericana y Palma Real: Urb. University Gardens, Rio Piedras, 00927. Tel: 809-765-9430. Sr. Rose Colette, O.S.F., Prin. Sup.; Sr. Maria Kivick, O.S.F., Prin. Elm.

56—SAGRADO CORAZON DE JESUS (1909), Rev. Rafael Candelas.
Res., Ponce de Leon Ave., 1308, Stop 19, Box 8312, F.J. Sta., Santurce, 00910. Tel: 809-722-0235.

57—SANTISMO SACRAMENTO (1967), Rev. Jose Francisco Quiceno.
Res., 500 Jerusalem St., Urb. Matienzo Cintron, Rio Piedras, 00923. Tel: 809-764-3448.
Chapel—Hnas. Santos Angeles Custodios.

58—SANTISIMO SALVADOR (1965), Revs. Leopoldo Laredo, Sch.P.; Javier Goicoechea, Sch.P. (Spain); Francisco Javier Lopez, Sch.P.; Jose Andres Basols, Sch.P., Supr.; Cecilio Lacruz, Sch.P.; Angel Millan Lazaro, Sch.P. (Spain); Deacons Prudencio Rivera; Julio Alvarez; Rafael Colon; Luis O. del Rio; Gregorio Ayala.
Res., Niza St., 575, Urb. Villa Capri, Rio Piedras, 00924. Tel: 809-761-3314.
School—Calasanz, (1968), Ave. Montecarlo, P.O. Box 29067, 65 Inf. Sta., Rio Piedras, 00929. Tel: 809-750-2500; Fax: 809-257-0450. Iris Santos, Prin.
Priests 5; Lay Teachers 40; Students 491.
Missions—Rio Piedras, N. Sra. de la Paz C/1 Esq. C/8 Urb. Berwid States; Rio Piedras, San Jose. Calle #23 408 Parc. Hills Brothers.
Chapel—Ntr. Sra. del Carmen.

59—STELLA MARIS (1965), Rev. Teodoro Gray.
Res., 69 Cervantes St., Condado, Santurce, 00907. Tel: 809-723-2240.

60—SANTA TERESA JORNET, Rev. German Vargas; Deacon Vicente Lasanta.
Res., Carr. 176 Camino el Mundo, Km. 5.3 Cupey Alto Aptdo. 415, El Senorial Sta., Rio Piedras, 00926. Tel: 809-748-0185.
Missions—Cupey, San Martin de Porres Carrt. 176 H. 10.0; Cupey, Virgen de la Salud. Camino Los Guayabos Carr. 176.

61—SANTA TERESITA DEL NINO JESUS (1930), Revs. Tomas Ciscar, O.C., Sup. Regional; Franco Barreneche, O.C.; Tarcisio Gotay, O.C.; Francisco Armell, O.C.; Enrique Oria, O.C.
Res., 2059 Loiza St., Santurce, 00911. Tel: 809-727-0181; 727-0030; Fax: 809-728-0056.
Schools—Tel: 809-727-4260; 727-4317; 727-4358. Flor M. Caraballo, Prin.
Priests 1; Sisters 1; Lay Teachers 47; Students 577; Colegio Sagrada Familia, Urb. Llorens Torres, Santurce, Tel: 809-726-0570. Ana Rita Castro, Prin. Lay Teachers 6; Students 178.
Mission—Sagrada Familia, Tel: 809-726-0570.

62—SAN VICENTE DE PAUL (1940), Revs. Pascual Sota, C.M., Prov. Supr.; Evaristo Oliveras, C.M.; Bernardo Hernandez; Eugenio Sadaba, C.M.; Victor Santos; Bro. Wilfredo Acevedo, C.M.
Res., 1651 Los Angeles, Corner to Fernandez Juncos Ave., 19118, Fernandez Juncos Sta., Santurce, 00910. Tel: 809-727-3963.
School—709 Bolivar St., Box 8699, Tel: 809-727-4273; Fax: 809-728-2263. Mrs. Isabel Casana, Prin.
Sisters 3; Lay Teachers 17; Students 386.
Missions—Santa Catalina; San Jose; La Inmaculada.

OUTSIDE THE CITY OF SAN JUAN

Bayamon

1—SAN AGUSTIN (1964), Revs. Benigno Palomo Casares, O.S.A.; Eliseo Garcia, O.S.A.; Gonzalo Gonzalez, O.S.A.; Deacons Ignacio Perez; Cristobal Rivera; Pedro Miranda.

Res., Lomas Verdes Calle Duende 2E-21, Box 4263, Urb. Bayamon Gardens Branch, 00956. Tel: 809-785-8611.
School—(1964), Tel: 809-786-8055. Mr. Catalino Munoz Flores, Prin.
Sisters 3; Lay Teachers 23; Students 769.
Missions—Bayamon, San Martin de Porres, c/1 Barrio Juan Sanchez, 00959; Bayamon, Casa San Agustin; Bayamon, Villas de San Agustin.

2—San Antonio Maria Claret (1966), Revs. Rafael Beltran, C.M.F.; Francisco Verdia, C.M.F.; Deacon Jose Dolores Rivera. In res., Rev. Camilo Riano.
Res., D-24 Castiglioni Ave., Box 3292, Urb. Bayamon Gardens, 00958. Tel: 809-797-3337.

3—Catalina de Siena, Revs. Marcos Luis Espinel, O.P.; Felix Martinez del Cura; Deacons Francisco Cruz; Victor Lopez; Antonio Santiago.
Res., Santa, Urb. Hermanas Davila, Calle 10, Q-3, P.O. Box 4188, 00959. Tel: 809-785-2381; Fax: 809-269-5065.

4—Cristo Salvador, Rev. Enrique Vazquez (Spain).
Mailing Address: P.O. Box 459, 00960-0459.
Church—Carr. 177, Los Filtros; Casa Linda del Sur #N-205, 00959. Tel: 809-720-2348.

5—Nuestra Sra. de los Dolores (1976), Rev. Joaquin Suarez, S.M.; Deacons Francisco Hernandez; Noel A. Vazquez.
Res., Bloque DD-25, 18th St., Urb. Alturas de Flamboyan, 00959. Tel: 809-786-7494.

6—Santo Domingo de Guzman (1976), Rev. Juan Burgos, O.P.; Deacons Angel Davila; Louis J. Marin; Hector Negron; Jose A. Rodriguez; William Rodriguez.
Res., Ext. La Milagrosa Calle 2, P.O. Box 1968, 00960. Tel: 809-786-8592; 785-6542.

7—Santa Elena, Rev. Daniel Trujillo, Admin.; Deacons Luis A. Rodriguez; Jose Falcon; Jose Rios.
Res., Calle 6, H-14, P.O. Box 366, Gardens Sta., 00957. Tel: 809-785-6604.

8—Invencion de la Santa Cruz (1750), Revs. Natividad Acevedo, O.P.; Beltran Idsert; Victor Aviles; Deacon Jose A. Bermudez.
Res., 12 Degetau St., 00619. Tel: 809-785-2134.

9—San Jose (1964), Revs. Jose Nieto, C.M.F.; Norberto Padilla, C.M.F.; Javier Rivera, C.M.F.; Deacons Jose Rosado; Jose Torres.
Res., Daker St., F-169, Magnolia Ave., Ext., Forest View, 00620. Tel: 809-785-6675; Fax: 809-785-0670.
School—Academia Claret, Tel: 809-785-6685. Sr. Maria Huertas, Prin.
Priests 1; Sisters 2; Lay Teachers 24; Students 610.

10—San Juan Bautista de la Salle (1979), Revs. Jose M. Garcia Bazton, M.SS.CC.; Manuel Soler Pala, M.SS.CC.; Deacons Francisco Ortiz; Jose Vega; Jorge Rivera.
Res., 19 Rio Cialitos St., 1ra. Secc. Estancias Rio Hondo, 00961. Tel: 809-787-9567.

11—San Miguel Arcangel (1962), Rev. William Torres; Deacons Jose Pena; Santiago Latorre.
Mailing Address: G.P.O. Box 1714, San Juan, 00936. Tel: 809-787-4459.
Res., Urban. Jardines de Caparra, Calle 12A-AB., No. 32, 00619.

12—Nuestra Senora de la Milagrosa (1968), Rev. Hernan Adarve; Deacon Angel Rondon.
Res., Carr. 864, No. 82, Bo. Hato Tejas, P.O Box 2104, 00960. Tel: 809-785-6620.

13—Ascension Del Senor (1984), Revs. Epifanio Fernandez, O.SS.T.; Javier Elorriaga, O.SS.T.; Deacons Aureliz Garcia; Juan Perez del Valle. In res., Rev. Pedro Gorena.
Mailing Address: P.O. Box 3367, 00958-3367. Tel: 809-799-6120.
Res., Calle 34, BI No. 18, Urb. Rexville, 00958.

14—Espiritu Santo. (Parish in Formation). Rev. Pedro Corena, O.SS.T.
Mailing Address: Box 3367, 00958-3367. Tel: 809-799-6120.
Res., Calle 1, E #18, Bella Vista Gardens, 00957. Tel: 809-799-8604.

15—Ntra. Sra. Monserrate, Revs. Isaias Alvarez, O.S.A.; Domingo Aller, O.S.A.; Deacons Francisco Colon; Jesus Lopez.
Res., Carr. 167, Km. 5.6, Bo. Santa Olaya, P.O. Box 3948, Bayamon Gardens, 00958. Tel: 809-797-0708; 799-7340.
Missions—Cristo Rey; Bayamon, Ntra. Sra. de la Esperanza; Bayamon, Santa Monica.

16—Nuestra Senora del Perpetuo Socorro (1976), Rev. Victor Perez, O.P.; Deacons Felix Calderon; Anastacio Del Rio; Ramon L. Roman; Miguel Velez.
Res., Comerio St. No. 192, 00956. Tel: 809-785-0381; 780-4367.
Convent—Tel: 809-785-6542.

17—La Resurreccion del Senor, Most Rev. Hermin Negron, D.D.; Deacons Luis A. Gonzalez; Feliciano Ortiz.
Res., E-45 10th St., Repto. El Cortijo, 00956. Tel: 809-730-4310.

18—Santa Rita de Casia (1967), Revs. Mario Gonzalez, O.S.A., Supr.; Felix Moratiel, O.S.A.; Bro. Agustin Sanchez, O.S.A; Deacons Jose Perez; Eliezer Toro; Gregorio Velez (MIA); Ramon Luis Rivera (PCE).
Res., Ave. Hostos NS-8, Urb. Santa Juanita, 00956. Tel: 809-786-3971.
Retired House—Ntra. Sra. del Buen Consejo.
Missions—Bayamon, San Jose; Bayamon, Sagrado Corazon de Jesus; Bayamon, Ntra. Sra. del Carmen.

19—Santa Rosa de Lima (1978), Rev. Pedro Campana; Deacons Cesar Almodovar; Fernando Baez; Ricardo D'Auria; Ricardo Longueira; Juan R. Santos.
Res., Calle 12, Bloque No. 28; Casa No. 9, Urb. Santa Rosa, 00959. Tel: 809-798-2300; 787-1676; 798-2829; Fax: 809-780-3680.
School—Calle Main. Sr. Doris M. Lopez, O.P., Prin.
Sisters 1; Lay Teachers 28; Students 968.

20—Nuestra Senora del Rosario (1971), Rev. Jaime Vazquez Rojas; Deacons Luis Echegaray; Luis A. Navedo.
Res., Calle Zaragoza, Bloque, B No. 35, Esq. Calle Vizcaya, Urb. Villa Espana, 00961. Tel: 809-787-0418.

21—Nuestra Sra. del Rosario (1993), Rev. Dario Martinez.
Mailing Address: Box 3917, 00958.
Res., Carr. 816 Km. 2.2, Barrio Nuevo, Tel: 809-730-6000.

22—Sagrada Familia (1976), Rev. Alvaro Silva; Deacons Americo Arroyo; Gumercindo Colon; Ramon L. Ortiz.
Res., Calle Caracas and Valparaiso, Urb. Ext. Forest Hills, P.O. Box 4229, Bayamon Gardens Sta., 00959. Tel: 809-798-2010.
School—Tel: 809-785-2792. Mrs. Idalia Molina Rolon, Prin.
Lay Teachers 19; Students 405.

23—Santa Maria (1984), Revs. Juan J. Sepulveda, C.M.F.; Carlos Verdia, C.M.F.; Romualdo Fernandez, C.M.F., Prov. Supr.; Deacons Angel Oyola; Rafael Araya.
Res., Calle 24, II No. 21, Carr 167, Res. Cana, 00957. Tel: 809-797-7248; 797-8230.
Missions—San Gerardo de Mayella; Sagrado Corazon.

24—Santa Teresa de Avila (1983), Rev. Juan Curran, O.M.I.
Res., Calle Repto. Teresita, P.O. Box 9404, 00960. Tel: 809-787-8758; Fax: 809-780-3680.
Mission—San Martin de Porres.

25—Santiago Apostol (1966), Revs. Antonio Picornell, M.SS.CC.; Pedro Arturo Rondon, M.SS.C.; Deacons Luis F. Cordero; Felix Lopez; Juan Melendez; Angel Pabon.
Res., Urb. Sierra Bayamon, Calle 23, Bloque 23, Num. 17, 00961. Tel: 809-786-9179; Fax: 809-269-3965.
School—Mrs. Zoraida N. de Alonso, Prin. Priests 1; Lay Teachers 11; Students 284.

26—Santo Domingo De Guzman (1984), Rev. Nestor Yulfo; Deacons Virgilio Andino; Ramon Ramos.
Res., Parcelas Van Scoy-Bella Vista, Calle Principal Esq., Calle, 00958. Tel: 809-797-5510; 799-0148.

Canovanas

1—Nuestra Senora del Pilar (1937), Rev. Carmelo Soto; Deacon Jose Rivera.
Res., 77 Luis Hernaiz St., P.O. Box 1615, 00729. Tel: 809-876-2655.
School—3 Luis Hernaiz St., 00729. Tel: 809-876-3020. Mr. Samuel Rey Saldana, Dir.
Sisters 5; Lay Teachers 19; Students 563.
Mission—San Francisco Javier.

2—Resurreccion del Senior, Revs. Ratmond Riding, S.T.; Francisco Valdovinos; Deacon Pedro Florez.
Res., La, Parcelas de San Isidro, Carret. Bo. Mediania a Loiza, P.O. Box 896, 00729. Tel: 809-876-3917.
Mission—Ntra. Sra. de la Providencia.

3—Sagrado Corazon de Jesus, Rev. Orlando Londono, Admin.; Deacon Julio Ortiz.
Mailing Address: P.O. Box 1637, 00679-1637. Tel: 809-876-1355.

4—Santa Maria Madre de Dios (1971), Revs. Vicente Pasqualetto, S.T.; Thomas Norton, S.T.; Deacon Bartolo Burgos.
Res., E-189 Girasol St., Loiza Valley, 00729. Tel: 809-876-0827.

5—San Jose, Rev. Francisco Quintero; Deacon Raul Figueroa.
Res., Bo. Campo Rico Box 807, 00729. Tel: 809-876-4941.
Missions—Palma Sola, Ntra. Sra. de la Asuncion Carrt. 957 Km. 6.8; Alturas de Campo Rico., Ntra. Sra. Del Carmen. Carrt. 185 Km. 5.3.

Carolina

1—San Andres (1982), Rev. Raul A. Quesada; Deacons Marino Hernandez; Gilberto Mejias.
Res., Calle 401, Esq. Calle 482, Cuarta Extension, Urb. Country Club, Rio Piedras, 00982. Tel: 809-769-7076.

2—Santa Bernardita Soubirous (1982), Rev. Wilfredo Pena Moredo; Deacons Ismael Colon; Eladio Figueroa; Angel Rivera; Rafael Zanabria; Ramon Santiago.
Mailing Address: P.O. Box 29826, Rio Piedras, 00929-0826. Tel: 809-762-0375.
Res., Calle Espioncela, Esquina Calle Torcaza, Country Club, Rio Piedras, 00982. Tel: 809-762-5740; 257-7643.

3—Santa Clara de Asis (1966), Revs. Fernando Hortiguela, O.F.M.; Leandro Abarrategui, O.F.M.; Jose Francisco Labaka, O.F.M.; Deacons Luis Del Rio Pitre; Jose A. Morales; Luis Montes; Juan Ubarri.
Res., Via 14-2JL No. 456 Urb. Villa Fontana, 00983. Tel: 809-768-1708; Fax: 809-757-5044.
School—(1968), Tel: 809-768-7110. Mrs. Elsie Mujica, Prin.; Rev. Leanardo Abarratelegui, Dir.
Lay Teachers 21; Students 403.
Missions—San Francisco de Asis; Carolina, Parque Bolivariano 5-JL. Villa Fonta Park.

4—Santo Cristo de la Agonia, Rev. Jorge Castilejos; Deacon Samuel Sanchez.
Res., Santo, Calle Robles 39, Urb. Eduardo J. Saldana, P.O. Box 5108, 00984. Tel: 809-768-0374.

5—Santo Cristo de los Milagros (1971), Rev. Celso Martinez.
Res., Ave. Sanchez Castano, Urb. Villa Carolina, P.O. Box 834, 00985. Tel: 809-768-3810.
School—Colegio Maria Auxiliadora, Box 797, Tel: 809-762-0350; 768-6924. Lelis R. Iglesias, Prin.
Sisters 5; Lay Teachers 23; Students 1,639.

6—Epifania Del Senor, Rev. Frank De la Rosa; Deacons Roberto Mendia; Ibrahim Mestre.
Res., 246 Ave. San Marcos; Ext. El Comandante, 00982. Tel: 809-752-1149.

7—San Felipe Apostol (1971), Rev. Rafael Suazo; Deacons Eugenio Balastequi; Eduardo Gonzalez; Jose Vazquez.
Res., Calle 419, Bloque 165, No. 3, Ext. Villa Carolina, P.O. Box 1494, 00964. Tel: 809-762-6520.

8—San Fernando (1851), Rev. Joaquin Rivera; Deacons Jose Birriel; Enrique Colon; Santiago Diaz Rosa; Presbitero Rivera; Jose Torres.
Res., Calle Munoz Rivera, No. 65, P.O. Box 128, 00986. Tel: 809-769-0170.

9—Santa Gema Galgani (1971), Revs. Atanasio Amundarain, C.P.; Anselmo Andicoechea, C.P.; Felix Barruetabena, C.P.
Res., Marina Ave. No. 1454, Urb. Bahia Vistamar, P.O. Box 2789, 00984. Tel: 809-769-5663.
School—Mrs. Lilia Luna de Anaya, Prin. Sisters 1; Lay Teachers 26; Students 579.

10—Inmaculata Concepcion (1966), Rev. Leonardo Rodriguez-Ochoa, Admin.
Mailing Address: Apartado 3562, 00984-3562.
Res., Urb. Valle Arriba Heights, Calle 145-C-D-Num. 10, 00984. Tel: 809-276-1527.

11—Jesus Mediador, Rev. Freddy Alecio (Guatemala); Deacons Candido Martinez; Edwin Rivera.
Res., Calle Demetrio O'Dally 1000, Country Club, Rio Piedras, 00982. Tel: 809-768-3157.

12—San Juan de Dios (1971), Rev. Silverio Rueda; Deacon Luis R. O'Neill.
Res., R-19-A Canaria St., Jardines de Borinquen, P.O. Box 3179, 00984. Tel: 809-757-5060.
Mission—La Sagrada Familia.

13—Nuestra Senora de Lourdes (1956), Rev. Francisco Rubalcaba; Deacons Emilio Caceres; Alejandro Hernandez; Edwin Perez; Nelson Soto.
Mailing Address: P.O. Box 29793, Rio Piedras, 00929-0793.
Res., Calle Antonio Luciano, Esq. Calle Cruzado, Ext. El Comandante, 00630. Tel: 809-769-5740; 752-3716.

14—Ntra. Sra. Del Carmen (1984), Rev. Antonio Garcia (Spain); Deacons Ernie Diaz; Cesar Avila; Martin Morales.
Res., K-8 Monte Membrillo St., Lomas-Mansiones Carolina, P.O. Box 299, 00987. Tel: 809-757-4454; 752-6562.
School—Sr. Mary Ellen, C.S.F.N., Prin. Priests 1; Sisters 2; Lay Teachers 16; Students 262.

15—Ntra. Sra. Reina de la Paz (1969), Rev. Miguel Ferrer; Deacons Euripidez Lugo; Miguel Marrero; Manuel Reyes; Efigenio Rivera.
Res., Calle 6, Final, Urb. Sabana Gardens, P.O. Box 3688, 00983. Tel: 809-752-5607.

16—Ntra. Sra. Reina de los Angeles (1971), Rev. Msgr. Rafael Matienzo; Deacon Ildefonso Berrios. In res., Rev. Msgr. Tomas Maisonet.
Res., Bloque W. No. 17-A, Urb. Los Angeles, 00630. Tel: 809-791-2594.

17—SANTISIMA TRINIDAD (1982), Rev. Luis Angel Torres; Deacons Luis Colon; Esteban Valle; Bienvenido Domenech.
Res., Ave. Campo Rico PA-16, Tercera Extension, Urb. Country Club, Rio Piedras, 00982. Tel: 809-769-5665.

18—CRISTO REY (1971), Rev. Eduardo Toscano; Deacon Pedro E. Velez.
Res., Barrio Canovanillas, Carret. No. 857, K-2, 00987. Tel: 809-757-8712.
Missions—Parque Encuestra, S. Francisco de Asis Calle 23 N-25 Urb.; Bo. Canovanas, Maria Auxiliadora Carrt. 857 Km. 3.6; Bo. Cambute, Santa Cruz. Urb. Los Caobos Park.

19—NTRA. SRA. DE FATIMA. (Parish in Formation). Rev. Eduardo Gallego; Deacon Domingo Ocasio.
Res., Bo. Cedros, Carr 853, Km 13, P.O. Box 12076 Bo. Cedras, 00985. Tel: 809-750-8562.

20—SAN VALENTIN (1971), Rev. Salvador Rodriguez; Deacons Miguel Diaz; Antonio Quintana; Jose A. Pappeterra.
Res., Calle San Luis 128, Urb. Rolling Hills, P.O. Box 9382, 00988-9382. Tel: 809-750-5277.
Missions—Santa Rosa; San Antonio.

21—SAN FRANCISCO DE ASIS, Rev. Salomon Morales (Colombia); Deacons Justo Montanez; Marcos Santos.
Res., Calle 26, T-36 Urb. Metropolis, 00630. Tel: 809-768-8860.

Catano, San Francisco de Sales (1969), Revs. Demetrio Coello, S.D.B.; Abraham Cepeda, S.D.B.; Homero Berancourt, S.D.B.
Res., Ave., Flor del Valle Bloque BB-No. 108, Urb. Las Vegas, P.O. Box 567, 00963. Tel: 809-788-5036; Fax: 809-788-8163.
Missions—Santo Domingo; Maria Auxiliadora; San Judas Tadeo (Santuario).

Santa Rosa de Lima (1973), Rev. Julio Victor Garcia Padron (Cuba); Deacon Filiberty De Jesus.
Res., 16 Parque St., Barrio Amelia, Guaynabo, 00965. Tel: 809-781-5855; 783-9731.
Mission—Barriada Vietnam, La Milagrosa.

Nuestra Senora del Carmen (1893), Revs. Alberto Pagan, O.P.; Felix Struik, O.P.; Deacons Pedro Flores; Angel Oquendo; Enrique Rivera. In res., Rev. Malaky Clune, O.P.
Res., Calle Tren Num. 42, P.O. Box 427, 00963. Tel: 809-788-1098; Fax: 809-788-5905.
Missions—San Martin de Porres; San Jose Obrero.

Dorado, San Antonio de Padua (1842), Revs. Carlos Jimenez Van Derdys; Luis Eduardo Villada; Deacons Benito Lugo; Jose Marrero; Bernardino Medina; Arcadio Nunez; Luis Marcial Rivera; Romulo Rodriguez.
Res., P.O. Box 602, 00646. Tel: 809-796-1143.

Ntra. Sra. de La Salud (1982), Rev. Manuel Garcia; Deacons Hilario De Leon; Cresencio Rosario.
Res., Parcela 202, Buzon 210, Urb. San Antonio, Bo. Higuillar, P.O. Box 470, 00646. Tel: 809-796-3418.

Guaynabo

1—CORAZON DE JESUS (1992), Rev. Jesus Vieites, SS.CC.; Deacon Jacinto Ortiz.
Mailing Address: Carr. 834 Km. 2.2, Bo. Sonadora, Apartado 225, 00970-0225. Tel: 809-789-2014.

2—EL BUEN PASTOR (1970), Rev. Francisco Jimenez; Deacon Manuel Andino.
Res., Avenida Apolo, Urb. Apolo, Box 1848, 00970-1848. Tel: 809-789-2653.
Chapel—Colegio El Buen Pastor.

3—MARIA MADRE DE MI SENOR, Rev. Alberto Lopez; Deacon Julio H. Ortiz.
Res., P.O. Box 2150, 00970-2150. Tel: 809-789-1837.
Mission—Guaynabo, Ntra. Sra. del Carmen. Bo. Frailes Llanos Sector Los Baez.

4—SAN JUAN M. VIANNEY (1972). (Santo Cura de Ars). Rev. Florentino Sanz.
Res., Calle-2-F-14, Urb. Hillside, Rio Piedras, 00926. Tel: 809-790-2014.
Missions—La Milagrosa; Cristo del Perdon; Dulce Nombre de Maria; Ntra. Sra. del Carmen.

5—MARIA MADRE DE LA MISERICORDIA, Rev. Msgr. Jaime Capo; Revs. Luis O. Capacetti; Vincente Fernandez.
Res., Avenue Santa Ana Km. 13.2 La Villa de Torrimar, 00969. Tel: 809-789-0090.

6—SAN PEDRO MARTIR DE VERONA (1769), Rev. Mario A. Guijarro de Corzo; Deacons Carlos Rivera Martinez; Gumersindo Negron Morales; Humberto Reyes Anciano; Angel Loyola Zayas.
Res., Calle Tapia No. 5, P.O. Box 32, 00970. Tel: 809-720-2361; Fax: 809-272-8770.
School—Alpierre St., Urb. Colimar, P.O. Box 2560, 00970. Sr. Alicia Velazquez, R.A., Prin.
Priests 2; Sisters 9; Lay Teachers 45; Students 740.

7—DIVINO NINO JESUS (1992), Rev. Rodolfo Lamas (Cuba); Deacon Gerardo Comulada.
Res., PBM 143, HC-01, Box 29030, Caguas, 00725-8900. Tel: 809-720-0203.
Missions—San Rafael Arcangel; Jesus Nazareno; El Buen Pastor.

8—NUESTRA SENORA DE LA PAZ (1992), Revs. Javier Esparza, SS.CC.; Esteban Beltran, SS.CC.; Francisco Martinez, SS.CC.
Bo. Guaraguao, Apartado 225, 00970-0225. Tel: 809-789-2014.

9—SAGRADOS CORAZONES (1968), Revs. Mateo Mateo, SS.CC.; Millan Ramirez, SS.CC.; Jose Ma. Garcia, SS.CC.; Deacons Ivan E. Dominguez; Ulpiano H. Rivera; Israel Suarez.
Res., Urb. Ponce de Leon, Ave., A.P-2 No. 51, 00970-0225. Tel: 809-720-6151.
School—Avenue A. Ana Arce de Marrero, Prin.
Sisters 3; Lay Teachers 25; Students 793.
Mission—Virgen de la Paz.

Loiza, San Patricio (1719), Rev. Antonio Hernandez, S.T.; Deacons Santiago Acosta; Marcos Penaloza; Pastor Perez; Angel Pizarro.
Res., Calle Espiritu, Santo Box 504, 00772-0504. Tel: 809-876-2229.
Missions—Santa Rosa; Ntra. Sra. del Perpetuo Socorro; Santisima Trinidad; San Antonio; Ntra. Sra. de Fatima; San Rafael-Villa Nevarez.

Santiago Apostol, El Mayor (1971), Revs. Manuel Prado, C.M.; Luis Renier Brioso, C.M.
Res., Apdo. 118, Barrio Mediania, 00772-0118. Tel: 809-876-1879.
Missions—Ntra. Sra. Perpetuo Socorro; La Milagrosa; La Providencia; Nino de Praga.

Luquillo, Madre del Redentor, Rev. Msgr. Hernan Piedahita (Colombia).
Church—Barrio Pitaya, Sector Casablanca, Carr. 983, Km. 1.5, 00773.
Res., Apartado 591, 00773. Tel: 809-889-8137; Fax: 809-889-0733.

San Jose (1797), Rev. Emilio Toro; Deacons Raul Figueroa; Felipe Rivera.
Res., Calle Soledad No. 15, P.O. Box 493, 00773-0493. Tel: 809-889-2590; Fax: 809-889-6180.
Missions—San Judas; Ntra. Sra. del Cobre.

Palmer, Cristo Rey (1970), Rev. Calixto Soto.
Res., Calle Principal, P.O. Box 382, 00721-0382. Tel: 809-887-3552.
Missions—La Milagrosa; Ntra. Sra. de la Providencia.

Rio Grande, Nuestra Senora del Carmen (1840), Revs. Jesus M. Ciriza; Antonio Romero, M.SS.CC.; Juan Pocovi, M.SS.CC.
Res., No. 9 del Carmen St., Box 845, 00745-0845. Tel: 809-887-2365.
School—Calle 14 Urb. Alturas de Rio Grande, P.O. Box 818, 00745. Mrs. Elsa Quinones Santiago, Prin.
Missions—Rio Grande, Nuestra Senora de Fatima Bo. El Verde; Jardines de Rio Grande, Ntra. Sra. de Guadalupe; Rio Grande, San Pedro Bo. Bartolo; Alturas de Rio Grande, La Milagrosa. Calle 14.

San Francisco de Asis, Rev. Hernan Berdugo; Deacon Manuel Llanos.
Res., Barrio Malpica, P.O. Box 1449, 00745. Tel: 809-888-5302.

Toa Alta

1—SAN ESTEBAN, PROTOMARTIR, Rev. Jose Antonio Carrion-Parroco.
Res., Urb. La Providencia, Calle 7 IL-8.

2—SAN FERNANDO (1751), Revs. Angel Figueroa; Jesus Alberto Garcia; Deacons Jose Diaz; Jose Narvaez; Felipe Collazo; Luis Rivera.
Res., P.O. Box 63, Calle Jose de Diego, 00954. Tel: 809-870-2585.
Missions—San Antonio; San Judas Tadeo.

3—SAN JOSE, Rev. Jairo Salazar (Colombia); Deacons Francisco Villamil; Pablo Irene; Enrique Laureano.
Mailing Address: P.O. Box 777, 00954-0777.
Church—Barrio Rio Lajas, 00953.
Res., R.R. 2 Buzon 5929, 00953-0063. Tel: 809-870-6415.
Missions—Ntra. Sra. del Camino; Virgen del Carmen; Cristo de los Milagros; Santa Teresita; Sagrada Familia; Sagrado Corazon.

4—NUESTRA SENORA DE LA MEDALLA MILAGROSA, Rev. Luis Alberto Sierra; Deacons German Hernandez; Santos Nieves.
Res., Bo. Quebrada Cruz, P.O. Box 335, 00954-0335. Tel: 809-870-4090.
Missions—Nuestra Senora del Carmen; Sagrado Corazon de Jesus; Santa Teresa.

5—N. SRA. DE LA PROVIDENCIA, Revs. Luis Zabala; Carlos Verdia; Deacons Gregorio Cuevas; Jose C. Pacheco.
Res., P.O. Box 3836, Bayamon Gardens Sta. Bo. Pinas, Bayamon, 00958. Tel: 809-797-1618.
Missions—Cristo Rey; N. Sra. de Fatima; Sant. Trinidad; La Resurreccion.

Toa Baja

1—NUESTRA SENORA DE COVADONGA, Rev. Francisco Arana; Deacon Efrain Narvaez.
Mailing Address: Box 9076, Bayamon, 00960-8039. Tel: 809-251-6466.
Res., Calle 13 Esq. Calle 14, Urb. Covadonga, 00940.
Missions—Ntra. Sra. de Lourdes; San Martin de Porres.

2—NTRA. SRA. DE LA CANDELARIA, Rev. Heriberto Londono; Deacons Anselmo Miranda; Roberto Ortiz; Camildo Ortiz.
Res., Carret. No. 863, Km. 0.6, P.O. Box 892, 00951-0892. Tel: 809-251-0503.
Missions—Cristo Rey; Santa Maria; Santisima Trinidad.

3—ESPIRITU SANTO (1965), Revs. Luis Gonzalez-Chao; Roberto Garcia; Deacons Pablo Maldonado; Jose Miranda; Miguel Torres; Guillermo Vaello.
Res., Paseo Damisela No. 1453, Urb. Levittown, P.O. Box 50272, Levittown Sta., 00950. Tel: 809-784-4805.
School—Paseo Damiseala 1453, 00632. Tel: 809-784-0905. Rosa I. Perez, Prin.
Lay Teachers 16; Students 793.
Mission—Toa Baja, N. Sra. del Carmen, Calle Carmen, Bo. Palo Seco, 00759.

4—JOSE OBRERO, Revs. Luis Lizarralde, O.F.M.; Dario Carrero, O.F.M., Supr.; Alfonso Guzman, O.F.M.
Res., San, Barrio Sabana Seca, Box 173, 00952-0173. Tel: 809-784-1400.
Missions—Ntra. Sra. del Carmen; San Martin de Porres.

5—SAN PEDRO APOSTOL (1745), Rev. Juan Patron (Peru); Deacon Gerardo Trujillo.
Res., 47, Las Flores St., P.O. Box 513, 00951. Tel: 809-794-1327.
School—Calle Basilio Milan #13, Apartado 513, 00759.
Chapels—St. Teresita; Ntra. Sra. de Guadalupe; San Jose; San Pablo.

6—SANTISIMA TRINIDAD (1978), Rev. Juan M. Beristain; Deacons Eusebio Jaca; Justo Diaz.
Mailing Address: Apartado 50378, Levittown, 00950.
Res., Casse 500 Levittown, 00950. Tel: 809-261-2716; 784-2889.

Trujillo Alto

1—SAN BARTOLOME, Revs. Jose M. Alcocer, M.SS.CC.; Leoncio Mejia, M.SS.CC.; Deacons Alberto Gomez; Pablo Torres.
Res., 16-X-1, Ciudad Universitaria, 00760. Tel: 809-755-0120.

2—SANTA CRUZ (1801), Rev. Edgar Pinto (Peru); Deacons Alfredo Aponte; Domingo Vargas.
Res., J. Diaz St., Box 1808, 00977. Tel: 809-761-0507.
School—Dr. Fernandez St., 00977. Tel: 809-761-1100. Sr. Maria Ramon Santiago, O.S.F., Dir.; Mrs. Ana L. Monzon de Matos, Prin.
Sisters 3; Lay Teachers 25; Students 452.

3—SAN FRANCISCO DE ASIS (1992), Rev. Isidro Giber Valero; Deacon Hector Rivera.
Res., Bo. Quebrada Grande, Cdad. Colon P.O. Box 1316, 00977-1316. Tel: 809-748-5584.
Missions—La Milagrosa; San Jose de la Montana; La Inmaculada Concepcion.

4—BIENVETURADA VIRGEN MARIA DE LOURDES, Rev. Jose Ramon Fernandez; Deacons Vitelio Santiago; Oscar Sanchez.
Res., Santuario, Gruta de Lourdes, Barrio. Cuevas, P.O. 1081, 00977. Tel: 809-761-0571.

5—SAN JUDAS TADEO (1980), Rev. Miguel Pons; Deacon Jose Baez.
Mailing Address: Apartado 1535, 00977-1535.
Res., Calle 7, Urbanizacion El Conquistador, 00977-1535. Tel: 809-755-5993.
Missions—El Divino Pastor; Ntra. Sra. del Carmen.

Resident Chaplains:
Reverend Monsignors—
Valdes, Angel, Hospital del Maestro, Hato Rey
Reverend Fathers—
Mairal, Jose Ma. Lopez, Hogar de Sta. Teresa Jornet, Bo. Cupey, Rio Piedras, Trujillo Alto, PR
Ortega, Ovidio, Hogar de Ntra. Sra. de la Providencia, Ave. Ponce de Leon, Puerta de Tierra, Trujillo Alto, PR

On Duty Outside the Archdiocese:
Reverend Fathers—
Del Valle, Tomas
Esteve, Alfonso
Parello, Joseph J., St. Patrick Church, Smithtown, NY
Roldan, Juan
Sutil, Florencio
Torres, Ivan
Vicente, Julian

Graduate Studies:
Reverend Fathers—
Reyes, Pedro Luis, Rome

Retired:
Reverend Monsignors—
Cruz, Remberto
Oya, Eufrasio
Reverend Fathers—
Cruz, Gil (Spain)
Diaz, Alvaro
Egurrola, Vicente

Permanent Deacons:
Acosta, Santiago
Aldarondo, Elidio
Alicea, Angel L.
Alicea, Jose
Almodovar, Cesar
Alvarez, Enrique
Alvarez, Julio
Andino, Manuel
Andino, Virgilio
Aponte, Alfredo
Araya, Antonio
Araya, Rafael
Arevalo, Pedro Nel
Arroyo, Americo
Avila, Cesar
Ayala, Gregorio
Baez, Fernando
Baez, Jose
Balasquide, Eugenio
Bermudez, Jose A.
Berrios, Ildefonso
Birriel, Jose
Caban, Manuel
Caceres, Emilio
Calderon, Felix
Camacho, Manuel
Carmona, Eduardo
Carrasquillo, Jose
Casanova, Jorge
Castillo, Jose M.
Claudio, Pedro
Collazo, Felipe
Colon, Enrique
Colon, Francisco
Colon, Gumesindo
Colon, Ismael
Colon, Luis
Colon, Miguel
Colon, Rafael
Colon, Vicente
Comulada, Gerardo
Cordero, Luis
Cosme, Nicomedes
Costa, Pedro
Cotto, Bartolome
Cotto, Felix
Cruz, Francisco
Cruz, Hector
Cruz, Jose
Cuevas, Alfonso
Cuevas, Gregorio
D'Auria, Ricardo
Davila, Angel
De Jesus, Filiberty
De Jesus, Jose
De La Sota, Miguel
De Leon, Hilario
De Verona, Abel
Del Rio, Anastacio
Del Rio, Luis O.
Del Rio Pitre, Luis
Del Valle, Reinaldo
Delgado, Alfonso
Diaz, Agapito
Diaz, Ernie P.
Diaz, Jose
Diaz, Miguel
Diaz, Santiago
Diaz, Vidal
Domenech, Bienvenido
Dominguez, Ivan
Echegaray, Luis
Estrada, Martin
Falcon, Jose E.
Figueroa, Andres
Figueroa, Eladio
Figueroa, Juan
Figueroa, Nelson
Figueroa, Raul
Flores, Pedro
Franco, Porfirio
Garcia, Aureliz
Garcia, Enemias
Gierbolini, Francisco
Gomez, Alberto
Gomez, William
Gonzalez, Antonio
Gonzalez, Eduardo
Gonzalez, George
Gonzalez, Luis A.
Gonzalez, Pablo
Gonzalez, Pedro
Guiven, Cesar H.
Hernandez, Alejandro
Hernandez, Francisco
Hernandez, German
Hernandez, Jose
Hernandez, Marino
Huertas, Francisco
Irene, Pablo
Jaca, Eusebio
Lasanta, Vicente
Latorre, Santiago
Laureano, Enrique
Laureano, Juan
Llanos, Manuel
Longueira, Ricardo
Lopez, Felix
Lopez, Jesus
Lopez, Jose E.
Lopez, Victor
Loyola, Angel
Lugo, Benito
Lugo, Casiano
Lugo, Euripides
Lugo, Ildefonso
Maldonado, Eliezer
Maldonado, Pablo J.
Marin, Louis J.
Marini, Edwin
Marrero, Jose M.
Marrero, Miguel A.
Martinez, Candido
Martinez, Francisco
Martinez, Ricardo
Medina, Bernardino
Mejias, Gilberto
Melendez, Juan
Mendez, Miguel
Mendia, Roberto
Merced de la Paz, Victor
Merino, Latino
Mestre, Ibrahim
Miranda, Anselmo
Miranda, Jose
Miranda, Pedro
Montanez, Justo
Montes, Luis J.
Morales, Angel A.
Morales, Carlos R.
Morales, Jose
Morales, Martin
Morales, Rene
Narvaez, Efraim
Narvaez, Jose
Navedo, Luis A.
Negron, Gumersindo
Negron, Hector
Nerys, Jose A.
Nieves, Martin
Nieves, Santos
Nunez, Pedro
O'Neill, Luis R.
Ocasio, Domingo
Oliveras, Jose
Oquendo, Angel
Ortiz, Camildo
Ortiz, Enrique
Ortiz, Feliciano
Ortiz, Francisco
Ortiz, Jacinto
Ortiz, Julio
Ortiz, Julio H.
Ortiz, Justo
Ortiz, Pedro
Ortiz, Rafael
Ortiz, Ramon L.
Ortiz, Roberto
Oyola, Angel L.
Pabon, Angel
Pabon, Angel A.
Pacheco, Jose C.
Padilla, Isaias
Pappeterra, Jose
Pena, Jose
Penaloza, Marcos
Perez, Edwin
Perez, Ignacio
Perez, Jose
Perez, Jose R.
Perez, Juan
Perez, Juan B.
Perez, Luis R.
Perez, Pastor
Pineiro, Carlos
Pizarro, Angel M.
Porrata, Jose L.
Quintana, Antonio
Ralat, Carlos
Ramirez, Ferdinand
Ramirez, Tomas
Ramon, Ramon L.
Ramos, Ramon
Reyes, Humberto
Reyes, Manuel
Reyes, Rafael
Reyes, Victor
Rios, Jose M.
Rios, Vicente
Rios, William
Rivera, Angel
Rivera, Carlos
Rivera, Cristobal
Rivera, Edwin
Rivera, Efigenio
Rivera, Enrique
Rivera, Ernesto
Rivera, Eugenio
Rivera, Felipe
Rivera, Hector
Rivera, Jorge L.
Rivera, Jose
Rivera, Jose R.
Rivera, Jose A.
Rivera, Luis
Rivera, Luis Marcial
Rivera, Pedro
Rivera, Presbitero
Rivera, Prudencio
Rivera, Ramon L.
Rivera, Ulpiano
Robles, Jose L.
Rodriguez, Jose
Rodriguez, Jose A.
Rodriguez, Jose R.
Rodriguez, Juan
Rodriguez, Luis A.
Rodriguez, Orlando
Rodriguez, Ramon
Rodriguez, Romulo
Rodriguez, William
Rondon, Angel L.
Rosado, Jose
Rosario, Crescencio
Rubio, Silverio
Ruiz, Vicente
Sanabria, Rafael
Sanchez, Alejandro
Sanchez, Julio
Sanchez, Orlando
Sanchez, Oscar
Santiago, Antonio
Santiago, Ramon
Santiago, Vitelio
Santos, Juan Ramon
Santos, Marcos
Soto, Nelson
Suarez, Israel
Toro, Eliezer
Torres, Dionilo
Torres, Eugenio
Torres, Jose
Torres, Jose A.
Torres, Miguel A.
Torres, Pablo
Totti, Benjamin
Trujillo, Gerardo
Ubarri, Juan
Vaello, Guillermo
Valle, Esteban
Vargas, Domingo
Vazquez, Jose R.
Vazquez, Luis A.
Vazquez, Noel A.
Vega, Jose P.
Velazquez, Rafael
Velez, Gregorio
Velez, Miguel
Velez, Pedro
Villamil, Francisco

INSTITUTIONS LOCATED IN THE ARCHDIOCESE

[A] ELEMENTARY & HIGH SCHOOLS

SAN JUAN. *Colegio Parvulos Inmaculada Corazon de Maria*, 263 San Sebastian St., 00901. Tel: 809-722-1334. Sr. Ana I. Alvarado, Prin. Sisters 4; Lay Teachers 6; Students 158.

BAYAMON. *Colegio Ntra. Sra. del Rosario*, Calle 5, AA-7, Repto. Valencia, 00619. Tel: 809-798-5100. Sr. Ma. Ana Jimenez Maldonado, O.P., Prin. Students 338.

Colegio Santa Rosa, Calle Marti 15, P.O. Box 6032,

00619. Tel: 809-785-1195. Mrs. Esther Lopez, Prin. Lay Teachers 15.

Escuela Superior Catolica de Bayamon, Jazmin Esq. Millones, 2na. Ext. Lomas Verdes, P.O. Box 4225, 00956. Tel: 809-798-5260; 786-1615. Mrs. Maria C. de Marxuach, Dir. & Prin. Students 602.

Santo Domingo, 191 Comerio St., 00619. Tel: 809-785-0381. Ms. Carmen Ma. Ocasio Correa, Prin. Lay Teachers 12; Students 293.

Santo Tomas de Aquino. Mailing Address: P.O. Box 1557, 00960-1557. Tel: 809-785-3066; 780-8600. Mrs. Carmen J. Acosta, Elem. Prin.; Mrs. Micaela Hurtado, H.S. Prin. Lay Teachers 48; Students 1,183.

GUAYNABO. *Colegio Marista*, Alturas de Torrimar, 00657. Tel: 809-789-2186; 789-2187. Bro. Felipe Vegas, Prin. Brothers 13; Lay Teachers 57; Students 1,306.

Colegio Ntra. Sra. De La Caridad, Carretera Estatal #19, Ext. Villa Caparra., 00922. Tel: 809-781-8835; 783-3856. St. Joseph of the Mountain Sisters. Mother M. Covadonga Enriquez, S.J., Prin. Sisters 10; Lay Teachers 11; Students 275.

HATO REY. *Colegio Nuestra Senora De Lourdes*, 87 Mayaguez St., 00919. Tel: 809-769-6284. Mailing Address: P.O. Box 847, 00920. Sr. Maria Paz Asiain, O.P., Prin. Sisters 1; Lay Teachers 36; Students 551.

RIO PIEDRAS. *Colegio La Milagrosa*, 107 De Diego Ave., 00925. Tel: 809-765-6114. Sr. Maria Flores., H.C., Prin. Sisters 8; Lay Teachers 15; Students 557.

Colegio Nuestra Senora De La Providencia. (Girls), Ave. San Ignacio #1358, Urb. Altamesa, 00921. Tel: 809-781-7506. Spanish Mercedarian Sisters. Sr. Dolores Sanchez, Prin. Sisters 7; Lay Teachers 46; Students 978.

Colegio Nuestra Senora Del Carmen, R.R. 2, Box 15, 00928. Tel: 809-761-8010. Mr. Angel M. Castillo, Prin.; Mrs. Maria L. Defillo de Bernardo, Prin. Sisters 7; Lay Teachers 41; Students 780.

Colegio San Jose. Mailing Address: Box 21300, 00928. Bro. Joaquin Suarez, S.M., Prin. Brothers 8; Lay Teachers 35; Students 578.

SANTURCE. *Academia Sagrado Corazon*. Mailing Address: Box 11368, Fernandez Juncos Sta., 00910. Tel: 809-721-3300. Rev. Francisco Quinones, Spiritual Dir.; Mrs. Alma de la Vega, Prin. Lay Teachers 37; Students 564.

Colegio La Inmaculada, Stop 26, Ave. Ponce De Leon #1711, 00909. Tel: 809-727-6673. Sr. Mary Zuluaga, F.M., Prin. Sisters 10; Lay Teachers 24; Students 558.

Colegio Maria Auxiliadora, 2273 Eduardo Conde, 00915. Tel: 809-726-8288. Sr. Elia M. Rioseco, F.M.A., Prin. Sisters 16; Lay Teachers 15; Students 481.

[B] SPECIAL SCHOOLS AND SEMINARIES

SAN JUAN. *Instituto Psicopedagogico De P.R.*, Km. 8, Hm. 5, Carretera Bayamon Box 3949, 00904. Tel: 809-782-4680. Jesus Nazarene Sisters. Mother Avelina, Supr. Beds 64; Sisters 9; Patients assisted annually 122.

BAYAMON. *Seminario Misionero del Espiritu Santo*, Calle Zaya Verde #44, Bo. Hato Tejas, 00959. Tel: 809-786-8231; 780-1201. Rev. Cornelius T. McQuillan, C.S.Sp., M.Div., Prin. Supr.

Teologado Padre Liberman, Calle C#D 19, Urb. La Milagrosa, 00619-4892. Tel: 809-787-2398. Rev. Felix Abreu Montilla, C.S.Sp., Dir.

RIO PIEDRAS. *Fraternidad Santa Maria de los Angeles*, Expreso Trujillo Alto, Km. 1 Hm. 1. Tel: 809-761-8060. Revs. John Bednarik, O.F.M.Cap., Dir. Novices; Ramon J. Cosellas; Mario Mastrangelo, O.F.M.Cap., Mailing Address: Aptdo. 1864, 00760.

Jesuit Novitiate, Calle Jose Fidalgo Diaz, 2106, Barrio Caimito Abajo, R.F.D. 3, Buzon 5348, 00928. Tel: 809-790-3557. Revs. Orlando Torres, S.J., Master of Novices & Supr.; John Talbot, S.J. Seminarians 24.

Seminario Mayor Interdiocesano Santa Maria de los Angeles, Ave. De Diego No. 930, Urb. La Riviera, P.O. Box 10716, Caparra Heights, 00922. Tel: 809-782-2635. Revs. Fernando Felices, Rector; Ivan Huertas, Vice Rector.

Seminario Menor San Jose, Demetrio O'Dally St. 1000 Country Club, 00924. Tel: 809-768-3157. Rev. Freddy Alecio, Rector.

TOA ALTA. *Santo Domingo de Guzman Priory*, Ruta #2, Buzon 5905, Barrio Rio Lajas, 00953. Tel: 809-870-4540. Rev. Natividad Acevedo Fizcaya, O.P., Dir.

[C] SPECIAL CENTERS

SAN JUAN. *Santa Ana Chapel*. Perpetual Adoration, Calle Tetuan 203, Box 763, 00902. Tel: 809-725-7734. Rev. Raul Saez, Rector.

HATO REY. *Renovacion Conyugal*, Calle Sargento Medina 363, 00918. Tel: 809-751-6011; 766-1363. Rev. Jorge Ambert, S.J., Dir.

RIO PIEDRAS. *Centro Capuchino*, Expreso Trujillo Alto, Km. 1 Hm. 1. Tel: 809-761-8410. Mailing Address: Apto. 1865, 00760-1865. Rev. Ramon J. Casellas Rivera, O.F.M.Cap., Dir.

Centro Universitario Catolico, 10 Mariana Bracetti St., Box 22862, U.P.R. Sta., 00931. Tel: 809-767-3348. Revs. Baudilio Guzman, S.J., Dir.; Juan Lopez Pedraz, S.J., Coop.

[D] CLINICS, HEALTH CENTERS

SAN JUAN. *Centro Medico de P.R.*, Calle 10 #1030, Pto Nuevo, 00920. Apdo. 347, 00936. Tel: 809-763-7272.
For a complete listing, refer to the Hospitals section.

Our Lady Of Providence. Mailing Address: Box 614, 00903. Tel: 809-725-5358.
For a complete listing, refer to the Hospitals section.

VA Medical Center, One Veterans Plaza, 00927-5800. Tel: 809-758-7575, Ext. 3324.
For a complete listing, refer to the Hospitals section.

RIO PIEDRAS. *Hospital del Maestro*, Calle Flamboyanes #218, Hyde Park, 00929. Tel: 809-763-8383.
For a complete listing, refer to the Hospitals section.

SANTURCE. *Hospital de Diego*, Ave. de Diego #310, Pda. 22, 00908. Tel: 809-724-1700.
For a complete listing, refer to the Hospitals section.

[E] HOMES AND RESIDENCES

DORADO. *Santuario del Espiritu Santo*, Box 187, 00646-0187. Tel: 809-796-2798.
For a complete listing, refer to the Special Care Facilities section.

HATO REY. *Jesuit Community - Casa Claver*, 398 Francisca Sein, 00917.
For a complete listing, refer to the Special Care Facilities section.

PUERTA DE TIERRA. *Asylum For The Aged and Infirm*, Hogar de la Providencia, Stop 5, Box 5279, 00906. Tel: 809-722-1331.
For a complete listing, refer to the Special Care Facilities section.

RIO PIEDRAS. *Asylum For Orphan Girls*, 107 Jose de Diego St. S., 00925. Tel: 809-765-6114.
For a complete listing, refer to the Special Care Facilities section.

Centro N. Sra. de la Providencia, R.F.D. #2, Box 16T, 00928. Tel: 809-761-0273.
For a complete listing, refer to the Special Care Facilities section.

Hogar Carmelitano, Urb. San Martin, 00924. Tel: 809-769-6510.
For a complete listing, refer to the Special Care Facilities section.

Hogar Santa Teresa Jornet for the Aged, Cupey Alto, Km. 3, Hm. 8, Box 21012, 00928. Tel: 809-761-5805.
For a complete listing, refer to the Special Care Facilities section.

[F] PERSONAL PRELATURES

GUAYNABO. *Opus Dei*. (Prelature of the Holy Cross and Opus Dei), Region of Puerto Rico of the Prelature, A-35, Villa Caparra, 00657. Tel: 809-783-6206. Very Rev. Vicente Ariza, Reg. Vicar; Revs. Ramon Alvarez; Alfredo Gastalver; Gonzalo Diaz; Jorge L. Dominguez; Martin Llambias.

[G] MONASTERIES AND RESIDENCES FOR PRIESTS AND BROTHERS

RIO PIEDRAS. *The Viceprovince of Saint John the Baptist, Puerto Rico, of the Order Friars Minor Capuchins*, Calle Arzuaga, 218, Apartado Postal 21350, 00928-1350. Tel: 787-764-3090; Fax: 787-764-4070. Rev. John Bednarik, Vice Prov. Min.

RELIGIOUS INSTITUTES OF MEN REPRESENTED IN THE ARCHDIOCESE

For further details refer to the corresponding bracketed number in the Religious Institutes of Men or Women section.

[0470]—*The Capuchin Friars*. (Vice Prov. of Puerto Rico).—O.F.M.Cap.

[0270]—*Carmelite Fathers & Brothers*. (Prov. of Arago, Valentina, Spain).—O.Carm.

[0360]—*Claretian Missionaries*. (Spain).—C.M.F.

[0310]—*Congregation of Christian Brothers*. (Antilles Prov.).—C.F.C.

[0820]—*Congregation of the Fathers of Mercy*. (Madrid, Spain).—C.P.M.

[1330]—*Congregation of the Mission*. (Prov. of Puerto Rico).—C.M.

[1000]—*Congregation of the Passion*. (Bibao).—C.P.

[]—*Congregation of the Terciarios Capuchinos Ntra. Sra. de los Dolores*. (Spain).—T.C.

[0520]—*Franciscan Friars*. (Spain).—O.F.M.

[0650]—*Holy Ghost Fathers*. (American Prov.).—C.S.Sp.

[0690]—*Jesuit Fathers and Brothers*. (New York Prov.).—S.J.

[0740]—*Marian Fathers*.—M.I.C.

[0770]—*The Marist Brothers*.—F.M.S.

[1120]—*Missionaries of the Sacred Hearts of Jesus and Mary*. (Spain).—M.SS.CC.

[0840]—*Missionary Servants of the Most Holy Trinity*.—S.T.

[0430]—*Order of Preachers-Dominicans*. (Hollan Prov.).—O.P.

[1310]—*Order of the Holy Trinity*. (Spain).—O.SS.T.

[1040]—*Piarist Fathers*. (Spain).—Sch.P.

[1070]—*Redemptorist Fathers*. (San Juan Prov.).—C.SS.R.

[1190]—*Salesians of Don Bosco*. (Antilles Prov.).—S.D.B.

[0760]—*Society of Mary*. (New York Prov.).—S.M.

RELIGIOUS INSTITUTES OF WOMEN REPRESENTED IN THE ARCHDIOCESE

[0100]—*Adorers of the Blood of Christ*. (Red Bud, IL; San Juan).—A.S.C.

[]—*Apostolado del Sagrado Corazon de Jesus*. (Madrid, Spain).

[1810]—*Bernardine Sisters of the Third Order of St. Francis*. (Villanova, PA).—O.S.F.

[]—*Carmelitas Misioneras*. (Barcelona, Spain).

[]—*Compania de las Hijas de la Caridad de San Vicente de Paul*. (Paris, France).

[1070-02]—*Dominican Sisters*.—O.P.

[1070-05]—*Dominican Sisters*.—O.P.

[1070-06]—*Dominican Sisters*.—O.P.

[1070-13]—*Dominican Sisters*.—O.P.

[]—*Dominicanas Terciarieas del Santisimo Sacramento*. (Cadiz, Spain).

[]—*Hermanas Carmelitas de la Caridad*. (Barcelona, Spain).

[]—*Hermanas Carmelitas de Madre Candelaria (Venezuela)*.

[]—*Hermanas Carmelitas Teresas de San Jose (Barcelona, Spain)*.

[]—*Hermanas de la Amistad Misionera en Cristo Obrero*. (Spain).

[]—*Hermanas de la B.V. Maria del Monte Carmleo*. (Orihuela, Spain).

[]—*Hermanas de la Caridad del Cardenal Sancha*.

[]—*Hermanas de la Compania del Salvador*. (Spain).

[]—*Hermanas de Santos Angeles Custodios*. (Bilbao, Spain).

[]—*Hermanas Dominicas de la Presentacion*. (Tours, France; Colombia).

[]—*Hermanas Dominicas de Nuestra Senora de Fatima*. (Yauco).

[]—*Hermanas Dominicas de Nuestra Senora del Rosario de Fatima*.

[]—*Hermanas Hospitalarias de Jesus Nazareno*. (Cordoba, Spain).

[]—*Hermanas Mercedarias de la Caridad*. (Madrid, Spain).

[]—*Hermanas Misioneras de los Sagrados Corazones*. (Palma de Mallorca, Spain).

[]—*Hermanitas de los Ancianos Desamparados*. (Valencia, Spain).

[]—*Hijas de Maria Auxiliadora*. (Torino, Italy).

[]—*Instituto Misionero Hijas de San Pablo*. (Rome, Italy).

[]—*Instituto Santa Mariana de Jesus (Hermanas Marianitas)*. (Ecuador).—R.M.

[]—*Madres de Desamparados y San Jose de la Montana*. (Valencia, Spain).

[]—*Madres Escolapis*. (Rome).

[]—*Misioneras de Cristo Salvador*.

[]—*Misioneras del Buen Pastor*. (Caguas).

[]—*Misioneras del Santisimo Sacramento y Maria Inmaculada*. (Spain).

[]—*Misioneras Dominicas del Santisimo Rosario*. (Madrid, Spain).

[]—*Misioneras Guadalupanas del Espiritu Santo*. (Morelia, Mexico).

[2720]—*Mission Helpers of the Sacred Heart*.—M.H.S.H.

[2790]—*Missionary Servants of the Most Blessed Trinity*. (Philadelphia, PA).—M.S.B.T.

[]—*Monjas de la Orden de la Bienventurada Virgen Maria de Monte Carmelo*.

[]—*Oblates del Santisimo Redenteor*. (Madrid, Spain).

[]—*Religiosas del Amor de Dios*. (Spain).

[]—*Religiosas del Sagrado Corazon*. (Rome, Italy).

[]—*Religiosas Oblates del Divino Amor*.

[]—*Religiosas Teatinas de la Inmaculada Concepcion*. (Rome).

[]—*Religiosas Terciarias de San Francisco de Asie y de la Inmaculada Concepcion*. (Valencia, Spain).

[2970]—*School Sisters of Notre Dame.* (Wilton, CT).—S.S.N.D.

[]—*Siervas de Maria y Ministras de los Enfermos.* (Rome, Italy).

[2570]—*Sisters of Mercy.* (Pittsburgh, PA).—R.S.M.

[1620]—*Sisters of Saint Francis of Millvale, Pennsylvania.*—O.S.F.

[1650]—*Sisters of St. Francis of Philadelphia.*—O.S.F.

[1800]—*Sisters of St. Francis of the Third Order Regular.* (Williamsville, New York).—O.S.F.

[3830]—*Sisters of St. Joseph.* (Brentwood).—C.S.J.

[3930]—*Sisters of St. Joseph of the Third Order of St. Francis.*—S.S.J.-T.O.S.F.

[1970]—*Sisters of the Holy Family of Nazareth.*—C.S.F.N.

[1490]—*Sisters of the Third Franciscan Order.*—O.S.F.

[2150]—*Sisters, Servants of the Immaculate Heart of Mary.*—I.H.M.

[]—*Terciarias Franciscanas de la Purisima.* (Murcia, Spain).

NECROLOGY

(No Deaths)

Diocese of St. Thomas in the Virgin Islands

Most Reverend

ELLIOTT G. THOMAS, D.D.

Bishop of St. Thomas in the Virgin Islands; ordained June 6, 1986; consecrated and installed as Bishop December 12, 1993.

ESTABLISHED AS PRELATURE OF VI, JULY 23, 1960.

ESTABLISHED AS DIOCESE OF ST. THOMAS IN THE VIRGIN ISLANDS APRIL 20.1977

Comprises the Islands of St. Thomas, St. Croix and St. John.

Chancery Office: P.O. Box 301825, Charlotte Amalie, VI, 00803. Tel.: 809-774-3166; 776-1865; Fax: 809-774-5816.

E-mail address: ad728@VIRGIN.USVI.NET

STATISTICAL OVERVIEW

Personnel	
Bishop	1
Priests: Diocesan Active in Diocese	10
Priests: Active Outside Diocese	3
Number of Diocesan Priests	13
Religious Priests in Diocese	7
Ordinations:	
Permanent Deacons in Diocese	22
Total Brothers	2
Total Sisters	14
Parishes	
Parishes	8
With Resident Pastor:	
Resident Diocesan Priests	2
Resident Religious Priests	3
Without Resident Pastor:	
Administered by Priests	3
Missions	2
Welfare	
Day Care and Extended Day Care Centers	4
Total Assisted	76
Special Centers for Social Services	6
Total Assisted	716
Educational	
Diocesan Students in Other Seminaries	4
Total Seminarians	4
High Schools, Diocesan and Parish	2
Total Students	310
Elementary Schools, Diocesan and Parish	3
Total Students	642
Catechesis/Religious Education:	
High School Students	536
Elementary Students	543
Total Students Under Catholic Instruction	2,035
Teachers in the Diocese:	
Priests	2
Brothers	1
Sisters	2
Lay Teachers	71
Vital Statistics	
Receptions into the Church:	
Infant Baptism Totals	480
Adult Baptism Totals	24
Received into Full Communion	10
First Communions	273
Confirmations	196
Marriages:	
Catholic	60
Interfaith	26
Total Marriages	86
Deaths	146
Total Catholic Population	30,000
Total Population	101,809

Former Bishops—Most Rev. EDWARD J. HARPER, C.SS.R., D.D., ord. June 18, 1939; appt. July 23, 1960; cons. Oct. 6, 1960; named first residential bishop of Diocese of St. Thomas in the Virgin Islands, April 20, 1977; retired Oct. 15, 1985; died Dec. 2, 1990.—Most Rev. SEAN P. O'MALLEY, O.F.M.Cap., ord. Aug. 29, 1970; named coadjutor, May 30, 1984; ord. Bishop, Aug. 2, 1984; installed Oct. 16, 1985; transferred Fall River Aug. 11, 1992.

Chancery Office—P.O. Box 301825, Charlotte Amalie, 00803. Tel: 809-774-3166; 776-1865; Fax: 809-774-5816.

Chancellor—Sr. LOUIS MARIE BRYAN, S.C. Tel: 809-774-3166.

Fiscal Officer—CARL PENN.

Diocesan Consultors—Revs. GEORGE FRANKLIN; ALFRED BRADLEY, C.SS.R.; Rev. Msgr. MICHAEL KOSAK.

Religious Education Office—Vacant.

Youth Coordinator—Rev. KENNETH GADDY, *P.O. Box 547, Frederiksted, St. Croix, 00841.* Tel: 809-772-0138.

Hispanic Ministry—Revs. ALEJANDRO SANCHEZ; GERVASIO MALAVE, C.SS.R.; SERAPIO LOPEZ.

Historian—Rev. GEORGE FRANKLIN. Tel: 809-775-1650.

Catholic Charities of the Virgin Islands, Inc.—Sr. LOUIS MARIE BRYAN, S.C., Interim Dir., *P.O. Box 10736, Charlotte Amalie, 00801.* Tel: 809-777-8518; Fax: 809-777-4875.

Family Education Program—ALVIN HENLEY, *Charlotte Amalie.* Tel: 809-774-6418; 777-9322.

Projects for Assistance in the Transition from Homelessness (PATH)—Ms. AVILDA MATTHIAS, *P.O. Box 10736, Charlotte Amalie, 00801.* Tel: 809-777-8518.

Catholic Schools Office—Mrs. DIANA PARKER, Dir., *P.O. Box 301825, Charlotte Amalie, 00803.* Tel: 809-777-5583; Fax: 809-774-5816.

Vocations—Rev. GEORGE FRANKLIN, Dir., *P.O. Box 502218, St. Thomas, 00805.* Tel: 809-775-1650.

Charismatic Movement—Deacon HYACINTHE GEORGE, St. Croix; Rev. Msgr. MICHAEL KOSAK, St. Croix.

Diocesan Television Network—Mr. BERNARD GIBS, Dir. of Operations, *P.O. Box 301825, VDS, Charlotte Amalie, 00803.* Tel: 809-777-4828.

Caribbean Catholic Network—Channel 19, *P.O. Box 1860, Kingshill, St. Croix, 00851.* Tel: 809-779-3000.

Catholic Television Network (CTN)—Channel 16, *Charlotte Amalie, 00803.*

Diocesan Newspaper—"The Catholic Islander"; Ms. MARY CONWAY, Editor, *P.O. Box 301825, Charlotte Amalie, 00803.* Tel: 809-777-5583; Fax: 809-774-5816.

Communications Coordinator—Rev. Msgr. MICHAEL KOSAK.

Prison Ministry—Deacon ARNOLD HELENESE, St. Croix; Rev. JEROME FEUDJIO, St. Thomas.

Natural Family Planning Coordinator—Sr. LOUIS MARIE BRYAN, S.C. Tel: 809-774-3166.

Permanent Diaconate—Rev. Msgr. MICHAEL KOSAK, Dir. Tel: 809-778-0484.

Shelters for the Homeless—Sr. LOUIS MARIE BRYAN, S.C., Interim Dir., *Bethlehem House, P.O. Box 10736, Charlotte Amalie, 00801.* Tel: 809-774-4663., St. Croix: Tel: 809-778-1227., Administration: Tel: 809-777-8518; Fax: 809-777-4475.

Office of Evangelization—Sr. AMORA BINNOM, S.M.S.M., *P.O. Box 502218, Charlotte Amalie, 00805.* Tel: 809-775-1492.

ANSWER (Teenage Pregnancy Program)—Oswald Harris Ct., P.O. Box 10736, Charlotte Amalie, 00801. Tel: 809-774-6418. St. Croix: *P.O. Box 246, Christiansted, St. Croix, 00821.* Tel: 809-773-0132; Fax: 809-773-0302.

CLERGY, PARISHES, MISSIONS AND PAROCHIAL SCHOOLS

ISLAND OF ST. THOMAS

(Catholic Population, 12,500)

1—CATHEDRAL OF STS. PETER AND PAUL (1773), Revs. Gervasio Malave, C.SS.R.; Alejandro Sanchez; Jerome Feudjio; Deacons William Summer; Jose Vasquez; Frank Veraart; Arturo Watlington. In res., Rev. Cecil Corneille.

Mailing Address: P.O. Box 301767, Charlotte Amalie, 00803. Tel: 809-774-0201; Fax: 809-776-9586.

Res., 22A Kronprindsens Gade (Main St.), Charlotte Amalie, 00803.

Schools—Sts. Peter and Paul School, (Grades Jr.K-12) P.O. Box 301706, 00803. Tel: 809-774-5662; Fax: 809-777-5355. Mrs. Barbara Kenny, Asst. Prin.

Sisters 1; Lay Teachers 15; Grades Jr.K-6 Students 200; Tel: 809-774-2199. Mrs. Sara Connell, Prin.

Priests 2; Lay Teachers 18; Grades 7-12 Students 187.

Catechesis / Religious Programs—Students 258.

Convent—31 A Prindcesse Gade, P.O. Box 303785, Charlotte Amalie, 00803. Tel: 809-774-0248; Fax: 809-774-5816. Sisters of Charity of St. Elizabeth

Mission—Carenage, Chapel of St. Anne, Tel: 809-774-0201; Fax: 809-776-9586. Rev. Jerome Feudjio; Deacon Alberto Olive.

2—OUR LADY OF PERPETUAL HELP (1926), Rev. Cecil Corneille, Admin.; Deacon William Kenny.

Mailing Address: P.O. Box 304983, Charlotte Amalie, 00803. Tel: 809-774-0885; Fax: 809-774-0885.

[CEM]
Catechesis/Religious Programs—Students 65.

3—HOLY FAMILY PARISH (1969), Revs. George Franklin; Neil Scantlebury; Deacons Leonard Monsanto; Austin Medina.
Res., Cassi Hill, P.O. Box 502218, St. Thomas, 00805. Tel: 809-775-1650; Fax: 809-775-1750.
Catechesis/Religious Programs—Students 100.
Convent—Tel: 809-775-1492. Missionary Sisters of the Society of Mary

ISLAND OF ST. JOHN
(Catholic Population 300)

1—OUR LADY OF MT. CARMEL PARISH (1962). Unassigned.
Res., P.O. Box 241, St. John, 00831. Tel: 809-776-6339 (Res. & Office); Fax: 809-776-6339.

ISLAND OF ST. CROIX
(Catholic Population, approx. 17,200)

1—CHURCH ST. ANN (1823), Rev. Msgr. Michael F. Kosak; Revs. Simon Peter O'Pira; Bernard Campbell; Deacons Arnold Helenese; Joseph Mark; Ed Cave; Norbert Xavier; Neville Charles; Hyacinthe George, Pastoral Assoc.
Mailing Address: 42 Barrenspot Hill, Box 1160, Kingshill, St. Croix, 00851-1160. Tel: 809-778-0484; Fax: 809-779-3151.
Catechesis/Religious Programs—Students 281.
Chaplaincy—Herbert Grigg Home for the Aged.

2—CHURCH OF THE HOLY CROSS (1755), Revs. Alfred Bradley, C.SS.R.; James MacDonald, C.SS.R.; James R. Cascione, C.SS.R.; Bro. Leonard Samuel, C.SS.R.; Deacons Ulric Benjamin; Carlos Calderon; James Matthews.
Res., Box 1069, Christiansted, St. Croix, 00821-1069. Tel: 809-773-7564; Fax: 809-692-9997.
School—St. Mary's, P.O. Box 4090, Christiansted, St. Croix, 00822. Tel: 809-773-0117; Fax: 809-773-1166. Deacon Ulric Benjamin, Prin.
Lay Teachers 12; Students 162
Catechesis/Religious Programs—Mrs. Christina James, D.R.E.
Students 255.
Mission—LBJ Village, Sacred Heart Chapel. P.O. Box 1069, Christiansted.
Blessed Peter Donder's Formation Residence—P.O. Box 24839-Gallows Bay, Christiansted, St. Croix, 00824-0839. Tel: 809-692-9999; Fax: 809-692-9997.
Res., 20 Prince St., Christiansted, St. Croix, 00820.

3—CHURCH OF ST. PATRICK (1846), Revs. Michael Hopkins, C.SS.R.; Kenneth Gaddy, C.SS.R.; Deacons Felix Francis; Emith Fludd; Angel Maldonado.
Mailing Address: Box 547, Frederiksted, St. Croix, 00841. Tel: 809-772-0138; Fax: 809-772-4488.
School—P.O. Box 988, Frederiksted, St. Croix, 00841. Tel: 809-772-0138. Mary McIntosh, Prin.
Lay Teachers 14; Students 280.
Catechesis/Religious Programs—Students 120.
Convents—Caribbean Center, P.O. Box 95, Frederiksted, St. Croix, 00841. Tel: 809-772-0341. Missionary Sisters of the Immaculate Heart of Mary; P.O. Box 1756-Fredriksted, St. Croix, 00841. Tel: 809-772-3310. Missionaries of Charity
DeMeester Residence: P.O. Box 52, St. Croix, 00841. Tel: 809-772-0132.
Light of Christ Retreat Center—New St., P.O. Box 547, St. Croix, 00841. Tel: 809-772-4782.

4—CHURCH OF ST. JOSEPH (1947), Revs. Serapio Lopez; Michael Onyekwere; Deacons James Verhoff; Conrad Williams.
Mailing Address: P.O. Box 2150, Kingshill, St. Croix, 00851-2150. Tel: 809-772-2005; Fax: 809-772-2748.
Res., Mt. Pleasant, Frederiksted, St. Croix, 00841. Tel: 809-772-2005; Fax: 809-772-3748.
Catechesis/Religious Programs—Tel: 809-772-2005; Fax: 809-772-3748.
Students 300.
Convent—P.O. Box 1847, Kingshill, St. Croix, 00851. Tel: 809-778-5773; Fax: 809-778-5773. West Indian Franciscans

Chaplaincies

These chaplaincies only pertain to the Island of St. Thomas.

ST. THOMAS. *Lucinda Millin Home for the Aged.*
Queen Louise Home for the Aged.
St. Thomas Hospital and Community Health Center.

Permanent Deacons:
Benjamin, Ulric
Calderon, Carlos
Cave, Edward
Charles, Neville
Fludd, Emith
Francis, Felix
George, Hyacinthe
Helenese, Arnold
Kenny, William
Maldonado, Angel
Mark, Joseph T.
Matthew, James
Medina, Austin
Monsanto, Leonard
Olive, Alberto
Summer, William
Vazquez, Jose
Veraart, Frank
Verhoff, James
Watlington, Arturo
Williams, Conrad
Xavier, Norbert

INSTITUTIONS LOCATED IN THE DIOCESE

[A] INTERPAROCHIAL HIGH SCHOOLS

ST. CROIX. *St. Joseph High School*, 3 Mt. Pleasant, Rte. 2, Frederiksted, 00840. Tel: 809-692-2455; Fax: 809-692-2458. Gloria H.C. Waterman, Prin. Brothers 1; Sisters 1; Lay Teachers 12; Students 123.

[B] ORGANIZATIONS IN THE DIOCESE

ST. THOMAS. *Miscellaneous Organizations.* (For further information contact the Chancery Office.). Box 301825, Charlotte Amalie, 00803. Tel: 809-774-3166; Fax: 809-774-5816.
Catholic Daughters of the Americas. Mrs. Angelita Jennings, Regent. Tel: 809-774-7943.
COR (Christ in Others Retreat), Lawrence & Arsenta Sibilly. Tel: 809-776-7645. Rev. Kenneth Gaddy, C.SS.R. Tel: 809-772-0138.
Cursillo Movement, St. Croix. Rev. James R. Cascione, C.SS.R. Tel: 809-773-7564.
Knights of Columbus. Bertil MacGregor, Deputy. Tel: 809-773-7135.
Legion of Mary. Rev. James R. Cascione, C.SS.R. Tel: 809-773-7564.
Lumen 2000/Caribbean Region. Rev. Msgr. Michael F. Kosak.
Propagation of the Faith/Holy Childhood. Rev. Alfred Bradley, C.SS.R., Dir. Tel: 809-773-7564.
Secular Franciscans. Sr. Patricia Alexander, W.I.F., Spiritual Asst. Tel: 809-778-5773.
Fraternity Our Lady of the Angels. Deacon Conrad Williams, Min. Tel: 809-778-1733; Mrs. Cleo Hobson, Min. Tel: 809-775-0666.
St. Vincent de Paul Society. Christian Begraff. Tel: 809-773-0176.
Catholic Charities of the Virgin Islands. Sr. Louis Marie Bryan, S.C., Interim Dir. Tel: 809-777-8518.
Disciples of the Holy Spirit, Inc., P.O. Box 1160, Kingshill, St. Croix, 00851. Rev. Msgr. Michael F. Kosak, Dir. For all: Total Assisted 697; Total Staff 50.

RELIGIOUS INSTITUTES OF MEN REPRESENTED IN THE DIOCESE

For further details refer to the corresponding bracketed number in the Religious Institutes of Men or Women section.

[0920]—*Oblates of St. Francis De Sales.*—O.S.F.S.
[1070]—*Redemptorist Fathers.*—C.SS.R.

RELIGIOUS INSTITUTES OF WOMEN REPRESENTED IN THE DIOCESE

[]—*Association of West Indian Franciscans.*—W.I.F.
[2420]—*Marist Missionary Sisters.*—S.M.S.M.
[2710]—*Missionaries of Charity.*—M.C.
[2750]—*Missionary Sisters of the Immaculate Heart of Mary.*—I.C.M.
[0590]—*Sisters of Charity of Saint Elizabeth (Convent Station).*—S.C.

NECROLOGY
(No Deaths)

PART III
Canada and Mexico

APOSTOLIC NUNCIATURE

(For Canada)

Apostolic Pro-Nuncio:
Most Reverend Carlo Curis, Titular Archbishop of Medeli.
Counsellor—Rev. Msgr. Vito Rallo
Res., 724 Manor Ave., Rockcliffe Park, Ottawa, Ont., Canada, K1M OE3
Tel: 613-746-4914; Fax: 613-746-4786.

PROVINCE OF EDMONTON

Archdiocese of Edmonton; Dioceses of Calgary, and St. Paul.

PROVINCE OF GATINEAU-HULL

Archdiocese of Gatineau-Hull, Dioceses of Amos, Mont-Laurier and Rouyn-Noranda.

PROVINCE OF HALIFAX

Archdiocese of Halifax; Dioceses of Antigonish, Charlottetown, and Yarmouth.

PROVINCE OF KINGSTON

Archdiocese of Kingston; Dioceses of Alexandria-Cornwall, Peterborough, and Sault Ste. Marie.

PROVINCE OF MONTREAL

Archdiocese of Montreal; Dioceses of Joliette, Saint-Jean-Longueuil, St. Jerome, and Valleyfield.

PROVINCE OF MONCTON

Archdiocese of Moncton; Dioceses of Edmundston, Bathurst, and St. John.

PROVINCE OF OTTAWA

Archdiocese of Ottawa; Dioceses of Hearst, Pembroke, and Timmins.

PROVINCE OF QUEBEC

Archdiocese of Quebec; Dioceses of Chicoutimi, Ste. Anne-de-la-Pocatiere, and Trois-Rivieres.

PROVINCE OF RIMOUSKI

Archdiocese of Rimouski; Dioceses of Gaspe, and Baie Comeau.

PROVINCE OF REGINA

Archdiocese of Regina; Dioceses of Prince Albert, Gravelbourg, Saskatoon, and Muenster.

PROVINCE OF SHERBROOKE

Archdiocese of Sherbrooke; Dioceses of St. Hyacinthe, and Nicolet.

PROVINCE OF ST. BONIFACE

Archdiocese of St. Boniface.

PROVINCE OF ST. JOHN'S

Archdiocese of St. John's; Dioceses of Grand Falls, and St. George's.

PROVINCE OF TORONTO

Archdiocese of Toronto; Dioceses of Hamilton, London, St. Catharines, and Thunder Bay.

PROVINCE OF VANCOUVER

Archdiocese of Vancouver; Dioceses of Kamloops, Nelson, and Victoria.

PROVINCE OF KEEWATIN-LE PAS

Archdiocese of Keewatin-Le Pas; Dioceses of Churchill-Baie D'Hudson, Moosonee, and Labrador City-Schefferville.

PROVINCE OF GROUARD-MCLENNAN

Archdiocese of Grouard-McLennan; Dioceses of Mackenzie-Fort Smith, Prince George, and Whitehorse.

ARCHDIOCESE OF WINNIPEG

(Immediately subject to the Holy See)

PROVINCE OF UKRAINIAN BYZANTINE RITE

Metropolitan See of Winnipeg; Ukrainian Eparchates of Edmonton, New Westminster, Saskatoon, and Toronto.

MILITARY ORDINARIATE

CANADIAN CONFERENCE OF CATHOLIC BISHOPS

SECRETARIAT OF THE CANADIAN HIERARCHY
(Established October 12, 1943)

Address: 90 Parent Ave., Ottawa, Ont. K1N 7B1. Tel: 613-241-9461.

Rev. M. Emilius Goulet, P.S.S., General Secretary, (French Sector).
Rev. Douglas Crosby, General Secretary, (English Sector).
Mr. M.J. Fernand Tanguay, Asst. General Secretary, (French).
Mr. Bede M. Hubbard, Asst. General Secretary, (English).

MEMBERS AND OFFICERS C.C.C.B. PERMANENT COUNCIL

Executive Committee and Permanent Council: President: Most Rev. Francis J. Spence (Kingston). Vice-President: His Eminence Cardinal Jean-Claude Turcotte (Montreal). Co-Treasurers: Most Rev. Henri Goudreault (Grouard-McLennan); Most Rev. Gerald Wiesner (Prince George).

Programmes and Priorities Committee Representatives: Most Rev. Henri Goudreault (Grouard-McLennan); Most Rev. James H. MacDonald (St. John's).

Representants Des Regions-Regional Representatives: Most Rev. Austin E. Burke (Halifax); Most Rev. Martin Veillette (Trois-Rivieres); Most Rev. Anthony Tonnos (Hamilton); Most Rev. Gerald Wiesner (Prince George)

Representants Des Secteurs-Sector Representatives: Most Rev. Jacques Berthelet (Saint-Jean-Longueuil); Most Rev. Gerard Drainville (Amos); Most Rev. Raymond Saint-Gelais (Nicolet); Most Rev. Andre Richard (Bathurst); Most Rev. Blaise Morand (Prince Albert).

Membres De Droit-Ex Officio Members: His Eminence Cardinal Jean-Claude Turcotte (Montreal); Most Rev. Maurice Couture (Quebec); Most Rev. Aloysius Ambrozic (Toronto); Most Rev. Michael Bzdel, C.Ss.R., (Metropolitan, Winnipeg).

Programmes and Priorities Committee: His Eminence Cardinal Jean-Claude Turcotte (Montreal); Most Rev. Jean-Guy Couture (Chicoutimi); Most Rev. Henri Goudreault (Grouard-McLennan); Most Rev. J. Faber MacDonald (Grand Falls); Most Rev. James H. MacDonald (St. John's); Most Rev. Brendan O'Brien (Pembroke); Most Rev. Francois Thibodeau (Edmundston). General Secretaries.

EPISCOPAL COMMISSIONS

The CCCB's nine episcopal Commissions are appointed by the Permanent Council to undertake study and projects in specific areas of pastoral work. Six Commissions serve nationally and three Commissions relate to the French and English Sectors.

National Level

Social Affairs

Most Revs. Francois Thibodeau, Chm.; Bertrand Blanchet; Marcel A.J. Gervais; Nicola De Angelis; Pierre Morissette; Peter Sutton.

Canon Law - Inter Rite

Most Revs. Jean-Guy Couture, Chm.; Thomas B. Fulton; James M. Wingle; Severian Yakymyshyn.

Commission for Relations with Associations of Priests, Religious, and Laity

Most Revs. James H. MacDonald, Chm.; Jean-Guy Hamelin; Terrence Prendergast; Raymond Dumais.

Missions

Most Revs. J. Faber MacDonald, Chm.; Thomas J. Lobsinger; Andre Vallee; Andre Gaumond.

Ecumenism

Most Revs. Brendan O'Brien, Chm.; Vincent Cadieux; Vital Masse; Gilles Ouellet; Denis Croteau; Cornelius Pasichny.

Theology

Most Revs. Henri Goudreault, Chm.; Gerard Drainville; Adam Exner; Aloysius Ambrozic; Laurent Noel; Gerald Wiesner.

Sector Level

English Sector

Social Communications

Most Revs. Fred Colli, Chm.; Michael Bzdel, C.Ss.R.; Vernon Fougere; John Sherlock.

Christian Education

Most Revs. Anthony F. Tonnos, Chm.; Raymond J. Lahey; Peter Mallon; John M. O'Mara.

Liturgy

Most Revs. John S. Knight, Chm.; James M. Hayes; Peter Novecosky; Blaise Morand.

French Sector

Social Communications

Most Revs. Roger Ebacher, Chm.; Robert Lebel; Jean-Louis Plouffe; Andre Richard.

Christian Education

Most Revs. Gilles Cazabon, Chm.; Gerard Dionne; Gilles Lussier; Raymond Roussin.

Liturgy

Most Revs. Antoine Hacault, Chm.; Jacques Berthelet; Clement Fecteau; Jude Saint-Antoine.

ARCHDIOCESES

EDMONTON. *Archbishop*—Most Rev. Joseph Neil MacNeil, D.D.; *Chancellor*—Rev. C. Michael McCaffery; *Archdiocesan Office*—8421 101 Ave., Edmonton, Alberta T6A 0L1. Tel: 403-469-1010; Fax: 403-465-3003.

GATINEAU-HULL. *Archeveque*—Most Rev. Roger Ebacher; *Chancellor*—Mrs. Lucy Gorman McCoy; *Chancery Office*—180, boulevard Mont-Bleu, Hull, P.Q., J8Z 3J5. Tel: 819-771-8391; Fax: 819-778-8969.

GROUARD-MCLENNAN. *Archeveque*—Most Rev. Henri Goudreault, O.M.I., D.D.; *Chancellor*—Rev. Jean Marsan, O.M.I.; *Chancery Office*—Archbishop's Residence, P.O. Box 388, McLennan, Alberta T0H 2L0. Tel: 403-324-3002; Fax: 403-324-3952.

HALIFAX. *Archbishop*—Most Rev. Austin-E. Burke; *Vicars General*—Rev. Owen Connoly; Rev. Martin Currie; *Chancellor*—Rev. Martin Currie; *Chancery Office*—P.O. Box 1527, Halifax, N.S. B3J 2Y3. Tel: 902-429-9800; Fax: 902-423-5201.

KEEWATIN-LE PAS. *Archbishop*—Most Rev. Peter-Alfred Sutton, O.M.I., D.D.; *Chancellor*—Sr. Rose Arsenault, R.S.R.; *Chancery Office*—Archbishop's Residence, 108-1st St. West, P.O. Box 270, Le Pas, Manitoba, R9A 1K4. Tel: 204-623-2503; Fax: 204-623-6121.

KINGSTON. *Archbishop*—Most Rev. Francis Spence, D.D.; *Vicar General*—Rev. T. J. Raby; *Chancellor*—Rev. M.J. Lynch; *Chancery Office*—390 Palace Rd., Kingston, Ont., K7L 4T3. Tel: 613-548-4461; Fax: 613-548-4744.

MONCTON. *Archeveque*—Ernest Leger; *Chancellor*—Rev. Clarence Leger; *Chancery Office*—453, rue Amirault, Dieppe, P.O. Box 248, Moncton, N.B., E1C 8K9. Tel: 506-857-9531; Fax: 506-857-9533.

MONTREAL. *Archeveque*—His Eminence Cardinal Jean-Claude Turcotte; *Auxiliary Bishops*—Most Revs. Andre Cimichella; Jude Saint-Antoine; Andre Rivest; Leonard Crowley; Neil E. Willard. *Vicars General*—Canon Rev. Robert Beaupre, C.S.S.; *Chancellor*—Rev. Michel Parent, C.S.C., V.E., Chancery Office—2000 Sherbrooke St. W., Montreal, Quebec, H3H 1G4. Tel: 514-931-7311; Fax: 514-931-3432.

MONTREAL. *Archeparch*—Rev. Msgr. Michel Hakim; *Chancellor & Protosyncelle*—Rev. Msgr. Georges Coriaty, B.S. *Chancery Office*—34, Maplewood, Montreal, Quebec H2V 2M1. Tel: 514-272-6430; Fax: 514-272-2341.

MONTREAL. *Eparch*—Most Rev. Joseph Khoury; *Vicar General*—Rev. Msgr. Jean Slim, 12475 Grenet, Montreal, Quebec H4J 2K4. Tel: 514-331-2807; Fax: 514-334-5723.

OTTAWA. *Archbishop*—Most Rev. Marcel A.J. Gervais; *Auxiliary Bishops*—Most Revs. Paul Marchand; Fred Colli. *Vicars Generals*—Rev. Msgrs. Peter Schonenback; Paul Marachano; Roger Marin; *Most Rev.*— Fred Colli. *Chancellor*—Rev. Msgr. Roger Morin, P.A., V.E.; *Chancery Office*—1247 Kilborn Place, Ottawa, Ont., K1H 6K9. Tel: 613-738-5025; Fax: 613-738-0130.

QUEBEC. *Archeveque*—Most Rev. Maurice Couture, Primate of Canada; *Auxiliary Bishops*—Most Revs. Jean-Pierre Blais; Marc Leclerc; Eugene Tremblay. *Vicar General*—Rev. Msgr. Roger Boisvert; *Chancellor*—Mme. Lucienne Boisvert; *Chancery Office*—1073, boul. Rene Levesque Ouest, Quebec G1S 4R5. Tel: 418-688-1211. Residence: Archeveche de Quebec—2, Port Dauphin, C.P. 459, Haute-Ville, Quebec G1R 4R6. Tel: 1-418-692-1211; Fax: 418-688-1399.

REGINA. *Archbishop*—Most Rev. Peter Mallon, D.D.; *Chancellor*—Rev. J. Balzer. *Chancery Office*—445 Broad St. N., Regina, Sask. S4R 2X8. Tel: 306-352-1651; Fax: 306-545-0510.

RIMOUSKI. *Archeveque*—Most Rev. Bertrand Blanchet, P.M.E. *Chancellor*—Rev. Yves-Marie Melancon; *Chancery Office*—34 Rue de L'Eveche Ouest, P.O. Box 730, Rimouski, P.Q. G5L 7C7. Tel: 418-723-3320; Fax: 418-722-8978.

ST. BONIFACE. *Archeveque*—Most Rev. Antoine Hacault, D.D.; *Vicar Genereal* Rev. Msgr. Henri Perron, Ph.; —*Chancellor*—M. l'Abbe Roland Belanger. *Chancery Office*—151, Ave. de la Cathedrale, St. Boniface, Man., R2H 0H6. Tel: 204-237-9851; Fax: 204-231-2652.

ST. JOHN'S, NFLD. *Archbishop*—Most Rev. James H. MacDonald, D.D.; *Chancellor*—Rev. Douglas Stamp; *Chancery Office*—P.O. Box 1363, St. John's, Nfld. A1C 5N5. Tel: 709-726-3660; Fax: 709-753-5600.

SHERBROOKE. *Archeveque*—Most Rev. Andre Gaumond; *Chancellor*—Sr. Cecile Grenier, P.H.; *Archdiocesan Office*—130 rue de la Cathedrale, C.P. 430, Sherbrooke, Quebec, J1H 5K1. Tel: 819-563-9934; Fax: 819-562-0125.

TORONTO. *Archbishop*—Most Rev. Aloysius M. Ambrozic; *Auxiliary Bishops*—Most Revs. R. B. Clune, John Stephen Knight; Nicola De Angelis; Terrence Prendergast, S.J. *Chancellors*—Rev. John K. Murphy - Spiritual Affairs; Rev. Briant Cullinane, D.F.M. Conv. - Temporal Affairs. Catholic Pastoral Centre—1155 Yonge St., Toronto, Ontario, M4T 1W2. Tel: 416-934-0606; Fax: 416-934-3433. E-Mail: <spiritual@direct.com>

VANCOUVER. *Archbishop*—Most Rev. Adam Exner; *Vicar General*—Rev. Msgr. David Monroe. *Chancellor*—Rt. Rev. Gregory N. Smith; *Chancery Office*—150 Robson St., Vancouver, B.C., V6B 2A7. Tel: 604-683-0281; Fax: 604-683-4288.

WINNIPEG. *Archbishop*—Leonard J. Wall; *Chancellor and Episcopal Vicar*—Rev. D. Ward Jamieson. *Chancery Office*—1495 Pembina Hwy., Winnipeg, Manitoba, R3T 2C6. Tel: 204-452-2227; Fax: 204-475-4409.

DIOCESES

ALEXANDRIA-CORNWALL. *Eveque*—Most Rev. Eugene P. LaRocque, D.D.; *Chancellor*—Rev. Denis Vaillancourt; 220, Chemin Montreal, P.O. Box 1388, Cornwall, Ontario, K6H 5V4. Tel: 613-933-1138; Fax: 613-937-4931.

AMOS. *Eveque*—Most Rev. Gerard Drainville; *Chancellor*—Sr. Rejeanne Veuillette. *Chancery Office*—450 nord, rue Principale, Amos, P.Q., J9T 2M1. Tel: 819-732-6515; Fax: 819-732-7994.

ANTIGONISH. *Bishop*—Most Rev. Colin Campbell, D.D.; *Chancellor*—Sr. Florence Steele, C.S.M. *Chancery Office*—P.O. Box 1330, 155 Main St., Antigonish, Nova Scotia, B2G 2L7. Tel: 902-863-3335; Fax: 902-863-0037.

BAIE-COMEAU. *Eveque*—Most Rev. Pierre Morissette; *Vicar General*—Rev. Germain Gagnon; *Chancellor*—Sr. Jeanne-Mance Caron, S.C.I.M.; *Chancery Office*—639 rue de Bretagne, Baie-Comeau, Quebec, G5C 1X2. Tel: 418-589-5744; Fax: 418-295-3145.

BATHURST. *Eveque*—Most Rev. Andre Richard, C.S.C.; *Vicar General*—Rev. Zoel Saulnier; *Chancellor*—Rev. Lionel Comeau; *Chancery Office*—Bishop's Res., 645 Ave. Murray, P.O. Box 460, Bathurst, New Brunswick. E2A 3Z4. Tel: 506-546-1420; Fax: 506-546-1423.

CALGARY. *Bishop*—Most Rev. Paul J. O'Byrne, D.D.; *Chancellor*—Rev. Armand Lemire; Bishop's Office, Catholic Pastoral Centre, Room 290, 120, 17 Avenue, S.W., Calgary, Alberta, T2S 2T2. Tel: 403-264-4501; Fax: 403-264-0526.

CHARLOTTETOWN. *Bishop*—Most Rev. J. Vernon Fougere; *Vicar General*—Rev. Arthur O'Shea; *Chancellor*—Sr. Lauretta White, C.S.M., J.C.L.; *Chancery Office*—P.O. Box 907 - 350 North River Rd., Charlottetown, Prince Edward Island, CIA 7L9. Tel: 902-368-8005; Fax: 902-368-1644.

CHICOUTIMI. *Eveque*—Most Rev. Jean-Guy Couture, D.D.; *Auxiliary Bishop*—Most Rev. Roch Pedneault, D.D., V.G.; *Vicars Generals*—Most Rev. Roch Pedneault; Rev. Yvan Tremblay; *Chancellor*—Msgr. Jean-Roch Gaudin, C.S.S.; *Chancery Office*—602 rue Racine est. Chicoutimi, P.Q., G7H 6J6. Tel: 418-543-0783; Fax: 418-543-2141.

CHURCHILL-HUDSON BAY. *Eveque*—Mgr. Reynald Rouleau, O.M.I.; *Vicar Gen.*—R.P. Robert Lechat, O.M.I.; *Chancery Office*—P.O. Box 10, Churchill, Manitoba, R0B 0E0. Tel: 204-675-2541; Fax: 204-675-2140.

EDMUNDSTON. *Eveque*—Most Rev. Francois Thibodeau, C.J.M.; *Chancellor*—Sr. Ronilla Sirois, R.H.S.J.; *Chancery Office*—Centre diocesan, Edmundston, New Brunswick, E3V 3K1. Tel: 506-735-5578; Fax: 506-735-4271.

GASPE. *Eveque*—Most Rev. Raymond Dumais; *Chancellor*—Sr. Marie-Paule Couturier, F.M.A.; *Chancery Office*—P.O. Box 440, 172, rue Jacques-Cartier, Gaspe, Quebec, G0C 1R0. Tel: 418-368-2274; Fax: 418-368-3772.

GRAND FALLS. *Bishop*—Most Rev. Joseph Faber MacDonald, D.D.; *Vicar General*—Rt. Rev. E.T. Bromley; *Chancellor*—Sr. Sarah Moore, P.B.V.M.; *Chancery Office*—P.O. Box 397, Grand Falls, Windsor, Nfld., A2A 2J8. Tel: 709-489-4019. Fax: 709-489-6393.

GRAVELBOURG. *Eveque*—Most Rev. Raymond Roussin, S.M.; *Vicar General*—Lucien Rodrigue. *Chancery Office*—Bishop's Residence, P.O. Box 690, Gravelbourg, Sask., SOH IXO. Tel: 306-648-2615; Fax: 306-648-2477.

HAMILTON. *Bishop*—Most Rev. Anthony Tonnos; *Auxiliary Bishop*—Most Rev. Matthew Ustrzycki; *Vicar General*—Rev. Msgr. John Newstead. *Chancellor*—Rev. Gerard P. Bergie; *Chancery Office*—700 King St., W. Hamilton, Ont., L8P 1C7. Tel: 905-528-7988; Fax: 905-528-1088.

HEARST. *Eveque*—Most Rev. Pierre Fisette; *Vicars Generals*—Rev. Msgr. Rene Ferland; Rev. Pierre Gaudet; *Chancellor*—Rev. Rene Grandmont; *Chancery Office*—P.O. Box 1330, 76-7th St., Hearst, Ont., P0L IN0. Tel: 705-362-4903; Fax: 705-362-4421.

JOLIETTE. *Bishop*—Most Rev. Gilles Lussier; *Chancellor*—Sr. Jacynthe Ricard; *Chancery Office*—2, rue Saint-Charles-Borromee nord, C.P. 470, Joliette, P.Q., J6E 6H6. Tel: 514-753-7596; Fax: 514-759-0929.

KAMLOOPS. *Bishop*—Most Rev. Lawrence Sabatini, D.D.; *Vicar General*—Rt. Rev. John MacIntyre; *Chancellor*—Sr. Marie R. MacDonald, C.S.M.; *Chancery Office*—635A Tranquille Rd., Kamloops, B.C., V2B 3H5. Tel: 250-376-3351; Fax: 250-376-3363.

LABRADOR CITY-SCHEFFERVILLE. *Vacant.— Diocesan Admin.*—Rev. Joseph Baril, O.M.I.; *Chancellor*—Sr. Ann Adams. *Chancery*—318 Ave. Elizabeth, C.P. 545, Labrador City, Labrador (Terre-Neuve) A2V 2K7. Tel: 709-944-2046; Fax: 709-944-5798.

LONDON. *Bishop*—Most Rev. John M. Sherlock, D.D.; *Vicar General*—Rev. R. Anthony Daniels; *Chancellor*—Ms. Aurelia Hernandez. *Chancery Office*—1070 Waterloo St., London, Ont., N6A 3Y2. Tel: 519-433-0658; Fax: 519-433-0011.

MACKENZIE-FORT SMITH. *Bishop*—Most Rev. Denis Croteau, O.M.I. *Chancellor*—R. P. Gilles Mousseau, O.M.I., *Chancery Office*—5117, 52 St., Yellowknife, N. W. T., X1A 1T7. Tel: 403-920-2129; Fax: 403-873-9021.

MONT-LAURIER. *Eveque*—Most Rev. Jean Gratton, D.D.; *Vicar General*—Rev. Msgr. Jean Levert; *Chancellor*—Sr. Denise Savard, S.C.O.; *Chancery Office*—Bishop's House, 435, rue de la Madone, Mont-Laurier, P.Q., J9L 1S1. Tel: 819-623-5530; Fax: 819-623-9523.

MOOSONEE. *Eveque*—Most Rev. Vincent Cadieux, O.M.I.; *Vicar General*—Rev. Rodrigue Vezina, O.M.I.; *Chancellor*—Sr. Marie-Berthe Demers, O.S.U. *Chancery Office*—P.O. Box 40, Moosonee, Ont., PL0 IY0. Tel: 705-336-2908; Fax: 705-336-2759.

NELSON. *Bishop*—Most Rev. Eugene J. Conney; *Vicar General*—Rev. Charles Mulvihill; *Chancellor*—Rev. Michael E. Bannon. *Chancery Office*—813 Ward St., Nelson, B.C., V1L 1T4. Tel: 250-354-4740; Fax: 250-352-1737.

NICOLET. *Eveque*—Most Rev. Raymond Saint-Gelais, D.D.; *Vicar General*—Rev. Andre Genest; *Chancellor*—Rev. Msgr. Simon Heroux; *Chancery Office*—Bishop's House, 49 rue Mgr. Bruneault, Nicolet, P.Q., J3T 1X7. Tel: 819-293-4696; Fax: 819-293-6485.

PEMBROKE. *Bishop*—Most Rev. Brendan M. O'Brien, S.T.D., D.D.; *Vicars General*—Rev. Msgr. Michael J. Barry, P.A.; Mgr. Douglas N. Bridge, P.h.; *Chancellor*—Rev. Msgr. Robert L. Borne, P.H., J.C.D.; *Chancery Office*—188 Renfrew St., P.O. Box 7, Pembroke, Ont., K8A 6X1. Tel: 613-735-7652. Bishop's Tel: 613-732-1714.

PETERBOROUGH. *Bishop*—Most Rev. James L. Doyle; *Vicar General*—Rev. Msgr. Clayton O'Donoghue, P.A.; *Chancellor*—Sr. Gaudentia; *Chancery Office*—350 Hunter St. W., Box 175, Peterborough, Ont., K9J 6Y8. Tel: 705-745-5123; Fax: 705-745-2555.

PRINCE ALBERT. *Bishop*—Most Rev. Blaise Morand; *Chancellor*—Rev. Chislain Gaudet; *Chancery Office*—1415-4 Ave. W., Prince Albert, Sask., S6V 5H1. Tel: 306-922-4747; Fax: 306-922-4754

PRINCE GEORGE. *Bishop*—Gerald Wiesner, O.M.I., D.D.; *Vicar General*—Rev. Msgr. Lawrence Turgeon; *Chancellor*—Rev. James E. Larkin, O.M.I.; *Vice Chancellor*—Mme. Margaret Moore; *Chancery Office*—P.O. Box 7000, 2935 Highway 16 West, Prince George, B.C., V2N 3Z2. Tel: 250-964-4424; Fax: 250-964-2101.

ROUYN-NORANDA. *Eveque*—Most Rev. Jean-Guy Hamelin, D.D.; *Vicar General*—Rev. Robert Charron; *Chancellor*—Sr. Rosia Douaire, N.D.A.; *Chancery Office*—515 Cuddihy Ave., Rouyn-Noranda, Quebec, J9X 4C5. Tel: 819-764-4660; Fax: 819-764-3972.

ST. CATHARINES. *Bishop*—Most Rev. John A. O'Mara, D.D.; *Vicar General*—Rev. Richard Grecco, T.H.D.; *Chancellor*—Rev. Wayne Kirkpatrick, J.C.L.; *Chancery Office*—122 Riverdale Ave., St. Catharines, Ont., L2R 4C2. Tel: 905-684-0154; Fax: 905-684-2185.

ST. GEORGE'S. *Bishop*—Most Rev. Raymond J. Lahey; *Vicar General*—Rev. John Collins, P.P.; *Chancellor*—Rev. Msgr. William J. Boone, P.H.; *Chancery Office*—16 Hammond Dr., Corner Brook, Newfoundland, A2H 2W2. Tel: 709-647-3255; Fax: 709-639-8662.

ST. HYACINTHE. *Eveque*—Most Rev. Louis-de-Gonzague Langevin; *Vicar General*—Rev. Andre Vincent; *Chancellor*—Mgr. Jean-Roch Choiniere, P.H.; *Chancery Office*—C.P. 190, 1900 Ouest, Girouard, St. Hyacinthe, P.Q., J2S 7B4. Tel: 514-773-8581; Fax: 514-774-1895.

SAINT-JEAN-LONGUEUIL. *Vacant*—*Auxiliary Bishop & Vicar General*—Most Rev. Jacques Berthelet, C.S.W.; —Revs. Gustave Desourdy; Georges Milot; *Chancellor*—M. l'Abbe Jacques Leboeuf; *Chancery Office*—740 boul. Ste. Foy, Box 40, Longueuil, P.Q., J4K 4X8. Tel: 514-679-1100; Fax: 514-679-1102.

St. Jerome. *Eveque*—Most Rev. Charles Valois; *Chancellor*—M. L'Abbe Claude Massicotte, V.E.; *Chancery Office*—355 St. George St., C.P. 580, Saint. Jerome, P.Q., J7Z 5V3. Tel: 514-432-9742; Fax: 514-432-8155.

Saint John, N.B. *Bishop*—Most Rev. J. Edward Troy, D.D.; *Vicar General*—Rev. Msgr. Geroge W. Martin; *Chancellor*—Rev. John W. Keoughan; *Chancery Office*—1 Bayard Dr., St. John, N.B., E2L 3L5. Tel: 506-653-6800; Fax: 506-653-6812.

St. Paul in Alberta. *Eveque*—Most Rev. Raymond Roy; *Vicar General*—Rev. Rolland Bissonnette; *Chancellor*—Rev. Msgr. Jean-Luc Pigeon, P.H.; *Chancery Office*—4410, 51st Ave. Saint. Paul, Alberta, T0A 3A2. Tel: 403-645-3277; Fax: 403-645-6099.

Sainte-Anne-de-la-Pocatiere. *Bishop*—Most Rev. Clement Fecteau; *Chancellor*—Rev. Roland Picard, V.G.; *Chancery Office*—1200 4e Ave., C.P. 430, La Pocatiere, P.Q., G0R 1Z0. Tel: 418-856-1811; Fax: 418-856-5513.

Saskatoon. *Bishop*—Most Rev. V. James Weisgerber; *Chancellor*—Very Rev. Paul Donlevy. *Chancery Office*—106 5th Ave. N. Saskatoon, Saskatchewan, S7K 2N7. Tel: 306-242-1500; Fax: 306-244-6010.

Sault Ste. Marie. *Bishop*—Most Rev. Jean-Louis Plouffe; *Auxiliary Bishop*—Most Rev. Bernard F. Pappin; *Vicar General & Chancellor*—Rev. Msgr. N. F. Clement; *Chancery Office*—387 Algonquin, P.O. Box 510, North Bay, Ont., P1B 4W4. Tel: 705-476-1300; Fax: 705-476-9087; *Sudbury Office*—435 Ave. Notre Dame, Sudbury, Ont., P3C 5K6. Tel: 705-673-4566; Fax: 705-675-7593.

Thunder Bay. *Bishop*—Most Rev. Frederick B. Henry, D.D.; *Chancellor*—Sr. S. Grexton, C.S.J.; *Chancery Office*—P.O. Box 756, Thunder Bay, Ont., P7C 4W6. Tel: 807-343-9313; Fax: 807-343-9114.

Timmins. *Eveque*—Most Rev. Gilles Cazabon, O.M.I.; *Vicar General*—Rev. Maurice Magnan; *Chancellor*—Sr. Gisele Roy, C.N.D.; *Chancery Office*—65 E. Jubilee Ave., Timmins, Ont., P4N 5W4. Tel: 705-267-6224; Fax: 705-267-6226.

Trois-Rivieres. *Eveque*—Most Rev. Martin Veillette; *Vicar General*—Rev. Msgr. Louis Massicotte, P.H.; *Chancellor*—Rev. Guy Panneton; *Chancery Office*—362, rue Bonaventure, C.P. 879, Trois-Rivieres, P.Q., G9A 5J9. Tel: 819-374-9847; 374-9847; Fax: 819-375-6382.

Valleyfield. *Eveque*—Most Rev. Robert Lebel, D.D.; *Vicar General*—Rev. Gilles Bergeron; *Chancellor*—Mme. Monique Boisvert, i.j.r.; *Chancery Office*—11, rue de l'Eglise, Valleyfield, QC., J6T 1J5. Tel: 514-373-8122; Fax: 514-371-0000.

Victoria. *Bishop*—Most Rev. Remi J. De Roo, S.T.D.; *Vicar General*—Rev. Sigismono Lajoie, O.F.M.; *Chancellor*—Rt. Rev. Michael Lapierre; *Chancery Office*—1-4044 Nelthorpe St., Victoria, B.C., V8X 2A1. Tel: 250-479-1331; Fax: 250-479-5423.

Whitehorse. *Bishop*—Most Rev. Thomas Lobsinger, O.M.I.; *Chancellor*—Sr. Margaret Coyle, S.C.I.C.; *Chancery*—406 Steele St., Whitehorse, Yukon Y1A 2C8. Tel: 403-668-3826; Fax: 403-667-4713.

Yarmouth. *Bishop*—James M. Wingle; *Vicar General*—Rev. Gerald LeBlanc; *Chancellor*—Rev. Roland Soucie, C.S.C.; *Chancery Office*—P.O. Box 278, 53 Park St., Yarmouth, Nova Scotia, B5A 4B2. Tel: 902-742-7163; Fax: 902-742-2465.

ABBEY

Abbey Nullius of St. Peter. *Abbot-Ordinary*—Rt. Rev. Peter Novecosky, O.S.B.; *Vicar General*—Rev. Leo Hinz, O.S.B.; *Chancellor*—Rev. Roman Schneider, O.S.B.; *Chancery Office*—St. Peter's Abbey, Muenster, Saskatchewan, SOK 2YO. Tel: 306-682-1788; Fax: 306-682-1766.

UKRAINIAN CATHOLIC PROVINCE

Archeparchy and Metropolitan See of Winnipeg. *Archeparch Metropolitan*—Most Rev. Michael Bzdel, C.Ss.R., D.D.; *Chancellor*—Rev. Stephen Soroka; *Chancery Office—233 Scotia St., Winnipeg, Man., R2V 1V7. Tel: 204-338-7801; Fax: 204-339-4006.*

Eparchy of Toronto. *Eparch*—Most Rev. Isidore Borecky, D.D.; *Apostolic Administrator*—Most Rev. Roman Danylak, J.U.D.; *Chancery Office*—143 Franklin Ave., Toronto, Ont., M6P 3Y9. Tel: 416-538-1436. Fax: 416-538-1639.

Eparchy For Slovaks. *Eparch*—Most Rev. Michael Rusnak, C.SS.R., D.D.; *Chancery Office*—223 Carlton Rd., Unionville, Ont., L3R 3M2. Tel: 416-477-4867.

Eparchy of Edmonton. *Vacant*— *Chancellor*—Rev. Joseph Royer; *Chancery Office*—9645-108 Ave., Edmonton, Alta, T5H 1A3. Tel: 403-424-5496; Fax: 403-425-2330.

Eparchy of Saskatoon. *Eparch*—Most Rev. Cornelius Ivan Pasichny, O.S.B.M.; *Vicar General*—Rt. Rev. Msgr. Rudolph Luzney; *Chancellor*—Rt. Rev. V. Mudri; *Chancery Office*—866 Saskatchewan Crescent E., Saskatoon, Sask., S7N 0L4. Tel: 306-653-0138; Fax: 306-653-0138.

Eparchy of New Westminster. *Eparch*—Most Rev. Severian Yakymyshyn, O.S.B.M.; *Eparch's Residence*—502-5th Ave., New Westminster, B.C., V3L 1S2. Tel: 250-524-8824; 524-4158; Fax: 250-521-8015.

Information for the Apostolic Exarchate for Catholic Armenians for Canada and the United States; Our Lady of Deliverance for Syriac Catholics in the United States and Canada; and the Hungarian Emigrants can be found by referring to the table of contents found at the beginning of the Directory.

MILITARY ORDINARIATE OF CANADA

Military Ordinary—Vacant.*Chaplain General*—Brigadier General Rev. Jean Pelletier - Tel: 613-992-1261; *Dir. of Chaplaincy Administration*—Colonel Rev. Murray Farwell - Tel: 613-992-1412; *Dir. of Pastoral Services*—Lieutenant Colonel Rev. Ronald Bourque - Tel: 613-992-1399; *Chancellor*—Major Rev. Sylvain Maurais; *Curia Address*—Chaplain General (RC), National Defence Hq., Ottawa, Ont., Canada, K1A 0K2. Tel: 613-992-1400; Fax: 613-992-6025.

United States of Mexico

UNITED STATES OF MEXICO

The United States of Mexico (Estados Unidos Mexicanos) are ecclesiastically divided into 14 Provinces (14 Archdioceses, 56 Dioceses, 7 Prelacies, and 1 Vicariate Apostolic).

Apostolic Nuncio—Most Rev. Girolamo Prigione, D.D., Titular Archbishop of Lauriaco. Res. Juan Pablo II No. 118, Col. Guadalupe Inn, Deleg. Alvaro Obregon, 01020 Mexico, D.F. (Apartado Postal 19-106, 03910 Mexico, D.F.) Tel: 525-663-3999; 663-4115; 661-4527; Fax: 525-663-5308.

Secretaries—Rt. Rev. Msgr. Jose Spiteri.

PROVINCE OF ACAPULCO

ARCHDIOCESE OF ACAPULCO. Established March 18, 1958. Elevated to an archdiocese on February 10, 1983.
Archbishop—Most Rev. Rafael Bello Ruiz, D.D.; Apartado Postal 201, 39300 Acapulco, Guerrero. Tel: 5274-82-07-63; Fax: 5274-82-07-63.

DIOCESE OF CIUDAD LAZARO CARDENAS. Established in 1985.
Bishop—Most Rev. Salvador Flores Huerta, D.D.
Bishop Emeritus—Most Rev. Jesus Sahagun de la Parra, D.D.; Apartado Postal 500, 60950 Cd. Lazaro Cardenas, Michoacan. Tel: 52753-2-34-88; Fax: 52753-2-29-84.

DIOCESE OF CHILPANCINGO-CHILAPA. Established March 16, 1863. Chilapensis.
Bishop—Most Rev. Efren Ramos Salazar; Apartado Postal 185; 39000 Chilpancingo, Guerrero. Tel: 52747-1-05-92; 1-06-12; Fax: 52747-2-01-13.

DIOCESE OF CIUDAD ALTAMIRANO. Established October 27, 1964. Civitatis Altamirensis.
Bishop—Most Rev. Carlos Garfias Merlos, D.D. Apartado Postal 17, 40660 Ciudad Altamirano, Guerrero. Tel: 52-767-2-00-37; 2-17-74; Fax: 52767-2-19-12.

DIOCESE OF TLAPA. Established 1994.
Bishop—Most Rev. Alejo Zavala Castro, D.D.; Anexo Catedral, Centro, 41300 Tlapa de Comonfort, Guerrero. Tel: 52-747-6-08-35; 6-09-02; Fax: 52747-6-08-35.

PROVINCE OF CHIHUAHUA

ARCHDIOCESE OF CHIHUAHUA. Established June 23, 1891. Created Archbishopric November 22, 1958. Chihuahuensis.
Archbishop—Most Rev. Jose Fernandez Arteaga, D.D.; *Archbishop Emeritus*—Most Rev. Adalberto Almeida Merino, D.D.; Apartado Postal 7, 31000 Chihuahua, Chihuahua. Tel: 52-14-10-32-02; 10-32-03; Fax: 5214-10-56-21.

DIOCESE OF CIUDAD JUAREZ. Established April 10, 1957. Civitatis Juarezensis.
Bishop—Most Rev. Renato Ascencio Leon, D.D.; *Bishop Emeritus*—Most Rev. Manuel Talamas Camandari, D.D.; Apartado Postal 188, 32000 Cd. Juarez, Chihuahua. Tel: 52-16-15-09-22; 15-09-82; Fax: 5216-15-00-24.

DIOCESE OF CUAUHTEMOC-MADERA. Established April 25, 1966. Civitatis Materiensis.
Bishop—Most Rev. Juan Guillermo Lopez Soto, D.D.; Apartado Postal 4, 31940 Madera, Chihuahua. Tel: 52-157-2-04-28; Fax: 52-157-2-03-05.

PRELACY OF NUEVO CASAS GRANDES. Established April 13, 1977. Neograndicasensis.
Prelate—Most Rev. Hilario Chavez Joya, M.N.M., D.D., Bishop-Prelate of Nuevo Casas Grandes; Apartado Postal 198, 31700 Nuevo Casas Grandes, Chihuahua. Tel: 52-169-4-05-20; Fax: 52-169-4-36-15.

DIOCESE OF PARRAL.
Bishop—Most Rev. Jose Andres Corral Arredondo, D.D.; Apartado Postal 313, 33800 H. del Parral, Chihuahua. Tel: 52-152-2-03-71; Fax: 52-152-2-03-71.

DIOCESE OF TARAHUMARA.
Bishop—Most Rev. Jose Luis Dibildox Martinez, D.D.; Apartado Postal 11, 33180 Guachochi, Chihuahua. Tel: 52-154-3-02-07; Fax: 52-154-3-07-04.

PROVINCE OF DURANGO

ARCHDIOCESE OF DURANGO. Established September 17, 1620. Created Archbishopric June 23, 1891. Durangensis.
Archbishop—Most Rev. Jose Trinidad Medel Perez, D.D.; *Auxiliary Bishop*—Most Rev. Juan de Dios Caballero Reyes, D.D.; *Archbishop Emeritus*—Most Rev. Antonio Lopez Avina, D.D.; Apartado Postal 116, 34000 Durango, Durango. Tel: 52-18-11-42-42; 11-98-44; Fax: 52-18-12-88-81.

DIOCESE OF CULIACAN. Established May 24, 1883. Formerly Sinaloensis, as of February 16, 1959 became Culiacanensis.
Bishop—Most Rev. Benjamin Jimenez Hernandez, D.D.; *Bishop Emeritus*—Most Rev. Luis Rojas Mena, D.D.; Apartado Postal 666, 80220 Culiacan, Sinaloa. Tel: 52-67-12-32-72; 12-14-97; Fax: 52-67-12-14-97.

DIOCESE OF MAZATLAN. Established November 22, 1958. Mazatlanensis.
Bishop—Most Rev. Rafael Barraza Sanchez, D.D.; Apartado Postal 1, 82000 Mazatlan, Sinaloa. Tel: 52-69-81-33-52; Fax: 52-69-81-04-28.

DIOCESE OF TORREON. Established June 9, 1957. Torreonensis.
Bishop—Most Rev. Luis Morales Reyes, D.D.; *Bishop Emeritus*—Most Rev. Fernando Romo Gutierrez, D.D.; Apartado Postal 430, 27000 Torreon, Coahuila. Tel: 52-17-12-30-43; Fax: 52-17-12-57-81.

PRELACY OF EL SALTO. Established June 12, 1968. Saltensis in Mexico.
Bishop—Most Rev. Manuel Mireles Vaquera, D.D., Bishop-Prelate of El Salto; Apartado Postal 58, 34950, El Salto, Durango. Tel: 52-187-6-00-70 (Phone & Fax).

PROVINCE OF GUADALAJARA

ARCHDIOCESE OF GUADALAJARA. Established July 13, 1548. Created Archbishopric March 19, 1863. Formerly Compostellana now Guadalajarensis.
Archbishop—His Eminence Juan Cardinal Sandoval Iniguez, D.D.; *Auxiliary Bishops*—Most Rev. Adolfo Hernandez Hurtado, D.D.; Most Rev. Ramon Godinez Flores; Most Rev. Javier Navarro Rodriguez, D.D.; *Bishop Emeritus*—Most Rev. Antonio Sahagun Lopez; Apartado Postal 1-331, 44100 Guadalajara, Jalisco. Tel: 52-3-614-55-04; Fax: 52-3-658-23-00.

DIOCESE OF AGUASCALIENTES. Established August 27, 1899. De Aguas Calientes.
Bishop—Most Rev. Rafael Munoz Nunez, D.D.; Apartado Postal 628, 20000 Aguascalientes, Aguascalientes. Tel: 52-49-15-32-61; Fax: 52-49-16-33-12.

DIOCESE OF AUTLAN. Established January 28, 1961. Rivoriensis.
Bishop—Most Rev. Lazaro Perez Jimenez, D.D. Apartado Postal 8, 48900 Autlan, Jalisco. Tel: 52-338-2-12-28 (Phone & Fax).

DIOCESE OF COLIMA. Established December 11, 1881. Colimensis.
Bishop—Most Rev. Gilberto Valbuena Sanchez, D.D.; *Bishop Emeritus*—Most Rev. Rogelio Sanchez Gonzalez, D.D.; Apartado Postal 1, 28000 Colima, Colima. Tel: 52-331-2-02-62; Fax: 52-331-2-43-44.

DIOCESE OF TEPIC. Established June 22, 1891. Tepicensis.
Bishop—Most Rev. Alfonso Humberto Robles Cota, D.D.; *Auxiliary Bishop Emeritus*--Most Rev. Jose Manuel Pina Torres, D.D.; Apartado Postal 15, 63137 Tepic, Nayarit. Tel: 52-321-4-46-45;4-46-47; Fax: 52-321-3-20-23.

DIOCESE OF ZACATECAS. Established January 26, 1863. Zacatecensis.
Bishop—Most Rev. Javier Lozano Barragan, D.D.; Apartado Postal 1, 98000 Zacatecas, Zacatecas. Tel: 52-492-2-65-37; 2-12-74; Fax: 52-492-2-23-42.

PRELATURE OF JESUS MARIA OF NAYAR. Established May 24, 1962. Nayariana de Jesu et Maria.
Bishop—Most Rev. Antonio Perez Sanchez, O.F.M., D.D., Bishop-Prelate of Jesus Maria of Nayar; *Bishop Emeritus*—Most Rev. Manuel Romero Arvizu, D.D.; Apartado Postal 33-B, 63150 Tepic, Nayarit. Tel: 52-321-3-38-80; 2-14-21.

DIOCESE OF SAN JUAN DE LOS LAGOS. Established March 25, 1972. Sancti Ioannis a Lacubus.
Bishop—Most Rev. Jose Trinidad Sepulveda Ruiz-Velasco, D.D.; Apartado Postal 1, 47000 San Juan de los Lagos, Jalisco. Tel: 52-378-5-05-70; 5-06-57; 5-09-26; Fax: 52-378-5-29-71.

DIOCESE OF CIUDAD GUZMAN. Established March 25, 1972. Civitatis Gusmanopolitana.
Bishop—Most Rev. Serafin Vasquez Elizalde, D.D.; Apartado Postal 86, 49000 Cd. Guzman, Jalisco. Tel: 52-341-2-19-94; 2-05-28. Fax: 52-341-2-15-44.

PROVINCE OF HERMOSILLO

ARCHDIOCESE OF HERMOSILLO. Established May 7, 1779. Created Archbishopric September 4, 1963. Hermosillensis, formerly Sonorensis.
Archbishop—Most Rev. Jose Ulises Garcia Salcedo, D.D.; *Archbishop Emeritus*—Most Rev. Carlos Quintero Arce, D.D.; Apartado Postal 1, 83260 Hermosillo, Sonora. Tel: 52-62-13-21-38; Fax: 52-62-13-13-27.

DIOCESE OF CIUDAD OBREGON. Established June 20, 1959. Civitatis Obregonensis.
Bishop—Most Rev. Vicente Garcia Bernal, D.D.; Apartado Postal 402, 85000 Cd. Obregon, Sonora. Tel: 52-641-3-20-98; Fax: 52-641-4-99-94.

DIOCESE OF LA PAZ. Established March 30, 1988. Paciensis in California Inferiori Meridionali.
Bishop—Most Rev. Braulio Rafael Leon Villegas, D.D.; Apartado Postal 25, 23000 La Paz, Baja California Sur. Tel: 52-112-2-25-96; 2-02-08; Fax: 52-112-2-82-72.

DIOCESE OF MEXICALI. Established April 12, 1966. Mexicalensis.
Diocesan Administrator—Most Rev. Rafael Romo Munoz, D.D.; Apartado 3-547, 21100 Mexicali, Baja California Norte. Tel: 52-65-52-40-09; Fax: 52-65-52-45-96.

DIOCESE OF TIJUANA. Established June 13, 1963. Tigiuanaensis, formerly Vicariate Apostolic of Tijuana (July 13, 1957), formerly Californiae Inferioris (January 20, 1874).
Diocesan Administrator—Very Rev. Msgr. Sergio de la Cerda; Apartado Postal 226, 22000 Tijuana, Baja California Norte. Tel: 52-66-84-84-11; 84-84-12; Fax: 52-66-84-76-83.

PROVINCE OF MEXICO

ARCHDIOCESE OF MEXICO. Established Sept. 2, 1530. Created Archbishopric February 12, 1546. Mexicana.
Archbishop Primate—Most Rev. Norberto Rivera Carrera, D.D.; *Auxiliary Bishops*—Most Rev. Luis Mena Arroyo, D.D.; Most Rev. Francisco Maria Aguilera Gonzalez, D.D.; Most Rev. Abelardo Alvarado Alcantara; Most Rev. Jose Pablo Rovalo Azcue, D.D.; *Archbishop Emeritus*—His Eminence Ernesto Cardinal Corripio; Apartado Postal 24-433, 06700 Mexico, D.F. Tel: 52-5-525-1110; 208-3200; Fax: 52-5-208-5350.

DIOCESE OF ATLACOMULCO. Established December 27, 1984.
Diocesan Administrator—Very Rev. Rodrigo Guadarrama Rosas; Apartado Postal 22, 50450 Atlacomulco, Edo. de Mexico. Tel: 52-712-2-05-53 (Phone & Fax).

DIOCESE OF CUERNAVACA. Established June 23, 1891. Cuernavacensis.
Bishop—Most Rev. Luis Reynoso Cervantes, D.D.; Apartado Postal 13, 62000 Cuernavaca, Morelos. Tel: 52-73-18-45-90; 18-96-46; Fax: 52-73-18-63-18.

DIOCESE OF TOLUCA. Established June 4, 1950. Tolucensis.
Bishop—Most Rev. Francisco Robles Ortega, D.D.; Apartado Postal 82, 50000 Toluca, Edo. de Mexico. Tel: 52-72-15-25-35; 15-39-59; Fax: 52-72-14-69-55.

DIOCESE OF TULA. Established February 27, 1961. Tullanensis.
Bishop—Most Rev. Otavia Villegas Aguilar, D.D.; Apartado Postal 31, 42800 Tula de Allende, Hidalgo. Tel: 52-773-2-02-75 (Phone & Fax).

DIOCESE OF TULANCINGO. Established January 22, 1862. Tulancingensis.
Bishop—Most Rev. Pedro Aranda-Diaz Munoz, D.D.; Apartado Postal 14, 43600 Tulancingo, Hidalgo. Tel: 52-775-3-10-10 (Phone & Fax).

DIOCESE OF ECATEPEC. Established 1995.
Bishop—Most Rev. Onesimo Cepeda, D.D.; Apartado Postal 95, 55031 Ecatepec de Morelos, Edo de Mexico. Tel: 525-116-0976; Fax: 525-882-4019.

PROVINCE OF TLALNEPANTLA

ARCHDIOCESE OF TLALNEPANTLA. Established March 31, 1964. Tlalnepantlana. Established as Archdiocese June 28, 1989.
Archbishop—Most Rev. Ricardo Guizar Diaz, D.D.; Apartado Postal 268 y 270, 54000 Tlalnepantla, Edo. de Mexico. Tel: 52-5-565-39-44; 565-39-56; 565-82-90; Fax: 52-5-565-27-51.

DIOCESE OF TEXCOCO. Established April 30, 1960. Texcocensis.
Bishop—Most Rev. Magin C. Torreblanca Reyes, D.D.; Apartado 35, 56100 Texcoco, Edo. de Mexico. Tel: 52-595-4-02-82; 4-35-63. Fax: 52-595-4-08-69.

DIOCESE OF CUAUTITLAN. Established February 5, 1979.
Bishop—Most Rev. Manuel Samaniego Barriga, D.D.; Apartado Postal 14-21, 54800 Cuautitlan, Edo. de Mexico. Tel: 52-5-872-19-96; Fax: 52-5-872-3004.

DIOCESE OF NETZAHUALCOYOTL. Established May 1, 1979.
Bishop—Most Rev. Jose Maria Hernandez Gonzalez, D.D.; *Bishop Emeritus*—Most Rev. Jose Melgoza Osorio, D.D.; Apartado Postal 89, 57700 Cd. Netzahualcoyotl, Edo. de Mexico. Tel: 52-5-797-6132; 797-8301; Fax: 52-5-765-9804.

PROVINCE OF MONTERREY

ARCHDIOCESE OF MONTERREY. Established December 15, 1777. Created Archbishopric June 28, 1898. Monterreyensis formerly Linarensis.
Archbishop—His Eminence Adolfo Antonio Cardinal Suarez Rivera, D.D.; *Auxiliary Bishops*—Most Rev. Jose Lizares Estrada, D.D.; Most Rev. Alfonso Hinojosa Berrones, D.D.; *Chancery*—Apartado Postal 7, 64000 Monterrey, Nuevo Leon. Tel: 52-83-45-24-66; 45-24-18; Fax: 52-83-45-35-57.

DIOCESE OF CIUDAD VALLES. Established November 27, 1960. Vallipolitana.
Bishop—Most Rev. Jose Guadalupe Galvan Galindo, D.D.; *Chancery*—Apartado Postal 170, 79000 Ciudad Valles, San Luis Potosi. Tel: 52-138-2-25-97; Fax: 52-138-2-47-96.

DIOCESE OF CIUDAD VICTORIA. Established December 21, 1964. Civitatis Victoriensis.
Bishop—Most Rev. Antonio Gonzalez Sanchez, D.D.; *Bishop Emeritus*—Most Rev. Raimundo Lopez Mateas, O.F.M., D.D.; *Chancery*—Apartado Postal 335, 87000 Ciudad Victoria, Tamaulipas. Tel: 52-131-2-80-83; Fax: 52-131-6-48-11.

DIOCESE OF LINARES. Established April 30, 1962. Linarina.
Bishop—Most Rev. Ramon Calderon Batres, D.D.; Apartado Postal 70, 67700 Linares, Nuevo Leon. Tel: 52-821-2-00-54; Fax: 52-821-2-07-50.

DIOCESE OF MATAMOROS. Established February 16, 1958. Matamorensis.
Bishop—Most Rev. Francisco Javier Chavolla Ramos, D.D.; Apartado Postal 70, 87351 H. Matamoros, Tamaulipas. Tel: 52-88-13-36-58; Fax: 52-88-16-06-08.

DIOCESE OF NUEVO LAREDO. Established January 10, 1990. Nuevo Laredensis.
Bishop—Most Rev. Ricardo Watty Urquidi, M.Sp.S., D.D.; Apartado Postal 20-B, 88280 Nuevo Laredo, Tamaulipas. Tel: 52-871-5-29-28; 5-83-95; Fax: 52-871-5-57-99.

DIOCESE OF SALTILLO. Established June 23, 1891. Saltillensis.
Bishop—Most Rev. Francisco Raul Villalobos Padilla, D.D.; Apartado Postal 25, 25000 Saltillo, Coahuila. Tel: 52-84-12-37-84; Fax: 52-84-14-92-67.

DIOCESE OF TAMPICO. Established March 6, 1870. Tampicensis formerly Civitatis Victoriae or Tamaulipana.
Bishop—Most Rev. Rafael Gallardo Garcia, O.S.A., D.D.; Apartado Postal 545, 89000 Tampico, Tamaulipas. Tel: 52-12-12-28-10; 12-28-02; Fax: 52-12-12-67-81.

PROVINCE OF MORELIA

ARCHDIOCESE OF MORELIA. Established August 11, 1536. Created Archbishopric March 19, 1863. Moreliensis.
Archbishop—Most Rev. Alberto Suarez Inda, D.D.; *Archbishop Emeritus*—Most Rev. Estanislao Alcaraz Figueroa, D.D.; *Chancery*—Apartado Postal 17, 58000 Morelia, Michoacan. Tel: 52-43-12-05-23; 12-37-38; Fax: 52-43-12-37-44.

DIOCESE OF APATZINGAN. Established April 30, 1962. Apatzinganiensis.
Bishop—Most Rev. Miguel Patino Velazquez, M.S.F., D.D.; Apartado Postal 100, 60600 Apatzingan, Michoacan. Tel: 52-453-4-17-87; Fax: 52-453-4-22-26.

DIOCESE OF TACAMBARO. Established July 26, 1913. Tacambarensis.
Bishop—Most Rev. Rogelio Cabrera Lopez, D.D.; Apartado Postal 4, 61650 Tacambaro, Michoacan. Tel: 52-454-6-00-44; Fax: 52-454-6-07-30.

DIOCESE OF ZAMORA. Established January 26, 1862. Zamorensis.
Bishop—Most Rev. Carlos Suarez Cazarez, D.D.; *Chancery*—Apartado Postal 18, 59600 Zamora, Michoacan. Tel: 52-351-2-12-08; 2-04-82; Fax: 52-351-5-40-20.

PROVINCE OF OAXACA

ARCHDIOCESE OF OAXACA. Established 1535. Created Archbishopric June 23, 1981.
Archbishop—Most Rev. Hector Gonzalez Martinez, D.D.; *Auxiliary Bishop*—Most Rev. Miguel Angel Alba Diaz, D.D.; *Archbishop Emeritus*—Most Rev. Bartolome Carrasco Briseno, D.D.; Apartado Postal 31, 68000 Oaxaca, Oaxaca. Tel: 52-951-6-48-22; Fax: 52-951-4-13-48.

DIOCESE OF SAN CRISTOBAL DE LAS CASAS. Established March 19, 1539. S. Christophori de las Casas.
Bishop—Most Rev. Raul Vera Lopez, O.P., D.D; *Bishop Emeritus*—Most Rev. Samuel Ruiz Garcia, D.D.; *Chancery*—Av. 20 de Noviembre 1, Centro, 29200 San Cristobal de las Casas, Chiapas. Tel: 52-967-8-00-53; Fax: 52-967-8-31-36.

DIOCESE OF TAPACHULA. Established June 19, 1957. Tapacolensis.
Bishop—Most Rev. Felipe Arizmendi Esquivel, D.D.; Apartado Postal 70, 30700 Tapachula, Chiapas. Tel: 52-962-6-15-03; Fax: 52-962-6-50-24.

DIOCESE OF TEHUANTEPEC. Established June 23, 1891, in San Andres Tuxtla, State of Veracruz. Transferred May 23, 1959 to Tehuantepec, State of Oaxaca, Tehuantepecensis.
Bishop—Most Rev. Arturo Lona Reyes, D.D.; *Bishop Coadjutor*—Most Rev. Felipe Padilla Cardona, D.D.; *Bishop Emeritus*—Most Rev. Jesus Clemente Alba Palacios, D.D.; Apartado Postal 93, 70760 Tehuantepec, Oaxaca. Tel: 52-971-5-00-60; Fax: 52- 971-5-14-42.

DIOCESE OF TUXTLA GUTIERREZ. Established October 27, 1964. Tuxtlensis.
Bishop—Most Rev. Felipe Aguirre Franco, D.D.; *Chancery*—Anexo a St. Domingo, 1a Poniente Norte 232, 29000 Tuxtla Gutierrez, Chiapas. Tel: 52-961-2-21-54; Fax: 52-961-1-35-67.

DIOCESE OF TUXTEPEC. Established January 8, 1979.
Bishop—Most Rev. Jose de Jesus Castillo Renteria, M.N.M., D.D.; Apartado Postal 9, 68300 Tuxtepec, Oaxaca. Tel: 52-287-5-00-42.

PRELACY OF MIXES. Decreed on December 21, 1964. Mixepolitana.
Bishop-Prelate—Most Rev. Braulio Sanchez Fuentes, S.D.B., D.D., Bishop-Prelate of Mixes; Res., Ayutla-Mixes, Oaxaca; Mailing Address: Av. H. Colegio Militar No. 721, Colonia Reforma, 70283 Ayutla-Mixes, Oaxaca. Tel: 52-951-5-25-56 (Phone & Fax).

PRELACY OF HUAUTLA. Decreed October 7, 1972. Huautlensis.
Bishop-Prelate—Most Rev. Hermenegildo Ramirez Sanchez, M.J., D.D.; Apartado Postal 2, 68500 Huautla de Jimenez, Oaxaca. Tel: 52-237-8-00-19 (Phone & Fax).

PROVINCE OF SAN LUIS POTOSI

ARCHDIOCESE OF SAN LUIS POTOSI. Established August 31, 1854. S. Ludovici Potesiensis.
Archbishop—Most Rev. Arturo Antonio Szymanski Ramirez, D.D.; Apartado Postal 1, 78000 San Luis Potosi, S.L.P. Tel: 52-48-12-45-55; 12-22-50; Fax: 52-48-12-79-79.

DIOCESE OF CELAYA. Established October 13, 1973. Celayensis.
Bishop—Most Rev. Jesus Humberto Velazquez Garay, D.D.; Apartado Postal 207, 38000 Celaya, Guanajuato. Tel: 52-461-2-43-98 (Phone & Fax).

DIOCESE OF LEON. Established January 26, 1863. Leonensis.
Bishop—Most Rev. Jose Guadalupe Martin Rabago, D.D.; *Chancery*—Pedro Moreno 312, 37000 Leon, Guanajuato. Tel: 52-47-13-27-47; Fax: 52-47-13-27-47.

DIOCESE OF QUERETARO. Established January 26, 1882. Queretarensis.
Bishop—Most Rev. Mario de Gasperin Gasperin, D.D.; Apartado Postal 49, 76000 Queretaro, Queretaro. Tel: 52-42-12-10-33; Fax: 52-42-12-18-45.

PROVINCE OF PUEBLA DE LOS ANGELES

ARCHDIOCESE OF PUEBLA DE LOS ANGELES. Established October 13, 1525. Created Archbishopric August 11, 1903. Angelorum formerly Tlascalensis.
Archbishop—Most Rev. Rosendo Huesca Pacheco, D.D.; Apartado Postal 235, 72000 Puebla, Puebla. Tel: 52-22-32-62-12; Fax: 52-22-46-22-77.

DIOCESE OF HUAJUAPAN DE LEON. Established November 13, 1903. Huajuapanensis.
Diocesan Administrator—Rev. Msgr. Felipe Padilla Cardona, D.D.; *Bishop Emeritus*—Most Rev. Jose De Jesus Aguilera Rodriguez, D.D.; Apartado Postal 43, 69000 Huajuapan de Leon, Oaxaca. Tel: 52-953-2-07-97; Fax: 52-953-2-06-36.

DIOCESE OF HUEJUTLA. Established November 24, 1922. Huejutlensis.
Bishop—Most Rev. Salvador Martinez Perez, D.D.; *Chancery*—Apartado Postal 8, 43000 Huejutla, Hidalgo. Tel: 52-129-6-01-85 (Phone & Fax).

DIOCESE OF TEHUACAN. Established January 13, 1962. Tehuacaniensis.
Bishop—Most Rev. Mario Espinoza Contreras, D.D.; Apartado Postal 137, 75700 Tehuacan, Puebla. Tel: 52-238-3-20-00; Fax: 52-238-3-14-68.

DIOCESE OF TLAXCALA. Established May 23, 1959. Tlaxcalensis.
Bishop—Most Rev. Luis Munive Escobar, D.D.; *Coadjutor Bishop*—Most Rev. Jacinto Guerrero Torres, D.D.; Apartado Postal 84, 90000 Tlaxcala, Tlaxcala. Tel: 52-246-2-07-23; Fax: 52-246-2-0739.

PROVINCE OF XALAPA

ARCHDIOCESE OF XALAPA. Established March 19, 1863. Created Archbishopric June 29, 1951. Jalapensis, formerly Verae Crucis.
Archbishop—Most Rev. Sergio Obeso Rivera, D.D.; Apartado Postal 359, 91000 Xalapa, Veracruz. Tel: 52-28-17-29-35; Fax: 52-28-17-55-78.

DIOCESE OF PAPANTLA. Established November 24, 1922. Papantlensis.
Bishop—Most Rev. Lorenzo Cardenas Aregullin, D.D.; *Bishop Emeritus*—Most Rev. Genaro Alamilla Arteaga, D.D.; *Chancery*—Apartado Postal 27, 73800 Teziutlan, Puebla. Tel: 52-231-3-24-30.

DIOCESE OF SAN ANDRES TUXTLA. Established May 23, 1959. On March 14, 1984, the Diocese of San Andres Tuxtla was divided into two jurisdictions: San Andres Tuxtla and the New Diocese of Coatzacoalcos, as a suffragan diocese of Jalapa.
Bishop—Most Rev. Guillermo Ranzahuer Gonzalez, D.D.; Constitucion y Morelos s/n, 95700 San Andres Tuxtla, Veracruz. Tel: 52-294-2-12-45; Fax: 52-294-2-03-74.

DIOCESE OF COATZACOALCOS. Established March 14, 1984. Coatzacoalsensis.
Bishop—Most Rev. Carlos Talavera Ramirez, D.D.; Apartado Postal 513, 96400 Coatzacoalcos, Veracruz. Tel: 52-921-2-59-03; Fax: 52-921-2-73-23.

DIOCESE OF TUXPAN. Established June 9, 1962. Tuxpaniensis.
Bishop—Most Rev. Luis Gabriel Cuara Mendez, D.D.; *Bishop Emeritus*—Most Rev. Ignacio Lehonor Arroyo, D.D.; Juarez 30, Col. Centro, 92800 Tuxpan, Veracruz. Tel: 52-783-4-00-41; Fax: 52-783-4-16-36.

DIOCESE OF VERACRUZ. Established January 19, 1963. Verae Crucis.
Bishop—Most Rev. Jose Guadalupe Padilla Lozano, D.D.; Insurgentes Veracruzanos 470, Paseo del Malecon, 91700 Veracruz, Veracruz. Tel: 52-29-32-20-26; Fax: 52-29-31-24-13.

PROVINCE OF YUCATAN

ARCHDIOCESE OF YUCATANENSIS. Established December 16, 1561. Created Archbishopric November 11, 1906.
Archbishop—Most Rev. Emilio Carlos Berlie Belaunzaran, D.D.; *Archbishop Emeritus*—Most Rev. Manuel Castro Ruiz, D.D.; Calle 58, No. 501 Centro, 97000 Merida, Yucatan. Tel: 52-99-28-62-14; Fax: 52-99-25-46-07.

DIOCESE OF CAMPECHE. Established July 25, 1845. Campecorensis.
Bishop—Most Rev. Jose Luis Amezcua Mendoza, D.D.; *Bishop Emeritus*—Most Rev. Jesus Garcia Ayala, D.D.; Apartado Postal 127, 24000 Campeche, Campeche. Tel: 52-981-6-26-05; Fax: 52-981-6-03-39.

DIOCESE OF TABASCO. Established May 25, 1880. Tabasquensis.
Bishop—Most Rev. Florencio Olvera Ochoa, D.D.; Apartado Postal 97, 86000 Villahermosa, Tabasco. Tel: 52-93-12-13-97; Fax: 52-93-12--19-05.

PRELACY OF CHETUMAL. Established November 21, 1970. Chetumaliensis.
Bishop-Prelate—Most Rev. Jorge Bernal Vargas, L.C., D.D.; Apartado Postal 165, 77000 Chetumal, Quintana Roo. Tel: 52-983-2-06-38; Fax: 52-983-2-25-70.

EPARCHY OF NUESTRA SENORA DEL PARAISO (Melquite Greek Rite).
Administrator—Rev. Msgr. Antonio Mouhanna; Iglesia de Porta Coeli, Venustiano Carranza 107, 06060 Mexico, D.F. Tel: 52-5-542-0225; Fax: 52-5-575-1687.

EPARCHY OF THE MARONITES
Bishop—Most Rev. Pierre Wadih Tayah; Manzano 29, Col. Florida, 00130 Mexico, D.F. Tel: 525-661-9710.

VICARIATE APOSTOLIC OF TARAHUMARA. Established June 23, 1958.
Bishop—Most Rev. Jose Luis Dibildox Martinez, D.D; *Mailing Address*—Apartado Postal 11, 33180 Guachochi, Chihuahua. Tel: 52-154-3-02-07; Fax: 52-154-3-07-04.

MEXICAN BISHOPS' CONFERENCE—Most Rev. Sergio Obeso Rivera, Archbishop of Xalapa, Pres.; Most Rev. Luis Morales Reyes, Bishop of Torreon, Vice Pres.; Most Rev. Ramon Godinez Flores, Auxiliary Bishop of Guadalajara, Sec. Gral.; Most Rev. Gilberto Valbuena Sanchez, Bishop of Colima, Treas.; Most Rev. Jose Guadalupe Martin, Auxiliary Bishop of Guadalajara, First Vocal; Most Rev. Mario de Gasperin Gasperin, Second Vocal; Prolongacion Misterios 24-B, Col. Tepeyac Insurgentes, 07020 Mexico, D.F. Tel: 52-5-781-84-62; 577-54-01; 577-54-31. Fax: 52-5-577-5489.

SHRINE OF OUR LADY OF GUADALUPE. Abbot Rt. Rev. Msgr. Guillermo Schulenburg; Very Rev. Carlos Warnholtz Bustillos; Basilica de N.S. de Guadalupe, Apartado 14-120, 07050 Mexico, D.F. Tel: 52-5-577-6022; 577-6088; Fax: 52-5-577-5038.

CONFERENCIA DE INSTITUTOS RELIGIOSOS DE MEXICO. Rev. Jorge Ortiz Gonzalez, M.S.p.S., Pres.; Revs. Ismael Gomez-Gordillo Morales, Sec. Gral.; Sr. Raquel Hernandez G., H.J., Vice Pres.; Bro. Raul Valadez G., F.S.C., Vice Pres.; Vocals: Rev. Miguel Concha Malo, O.P.; Rev. Mario Lopez Barrio, S.J.; Rev. Aaron J. Cahuantzi Bello, Sch.P.; Rev. Enrique Sanchez G., M.C.C.J.; Sr. Delia Esther Peruyera, O.D.N.; Sr. Zelfa Jimenez Morales, D.P.; Sr. Maria del Rosario Llamas, C.S.C.; Sr. Teresa Mesa, R.J.M.; Sr. Maria Luisa Chapa, M.S.S.T.; Bro. Antonio Cavazos Bueno, F.M.S. Address: Av. Amores 1318, Col. del Valle, 03100 Mexico, D.F. Tel: 52-5-604-5414; Fax: 52-5-604-9555.

American Foreign Missions

Augustinian Missions (O.S.A.)

Foreign Missions of the American Provinces of the Order of St. Augustine (O.S.A.)

Foreign Missions

Provincial Headquarters

Province of Our Mother of Good Counsel (Midwestern): *Tolentine Center,* 20300 Governors Highway, Olympia Fields, IL 60461-1081. Tel: 708-748-5435; Fax: 708-481-2090. Very Rev. David L. Brecht, O.S.A., '65, Prov.; Bro. John J. Stobba, O.S.A., Mission Procurator.

Midwestern Augustinian Religious serving in foreign missions: Most Rev. John C. McNabb, O.S.A., D.D., ord. 52, *Peru;* Most Rev. Daniel T. Turley, O.S.A., ord. 68, *Peru;* Revs. Alfred M. Burke, O.S.A., '57, *Japan;* Charles J. Bodden, O.S.A., '78, *Peru;* David R. Klotz, O.S.A., '71, *Mexico;* Richard Palmer, O.S.A., '87, *Peru;* Robert F. Prevost, O.S.A., '82, *Peru;* John P. Tasto, O.S.A., '82, *Peru;* John A. Tyma, O.S.A., '59, *Peru;* Bro. John A. Sharp, O.S.A., *Peru.*

Augustinian Religious from other Provinces serving in our foreign missions: Revs. Joseph F. Girone, O.S.A., '81, *Peru (Villanova);* Steven M. Ochoa, O.S.A., *Peru (California);* Robert P. Terranova, O.S.A., '73, *Peru (Villanova).*

Province of St. Thomas of Villanova (Eastern): P.O. Box 338, Villanova, PA 19085-0338. Tel: 610-525-3330; Fax: 610-520-0618. Very Rev. John E. Deegan, O.S.A., '61, Prior Prov. Tel: 610-525-9962. Revs. Richard D. Appicci, O.S.A., '60, Dir. Missions; Anthony P. Burrascano, O.S.A., '79, Mission Procurator.

U.S. Religious serving in foreign missions: Revs. John J. Lydon, O.S.A., '84; Joseph F. Girone, O.S.A., '81, Peru; Patrick B. McStravog, O.S.A., '89, Japan; Richard G. Mullen, O.S.A., '81; Maurice J. Mahoney, O.S.A., '60; Thomas P. Dwyer, O.S.A., '53; Aquilino D. Gonzalez, O.S.A., '72; Robert P. Terranova, O.S.A., '73; Michael J. Hilden, O.S.A., '73; Michael H. Stanley, O.S.A., '81; Edward V. Hattrick, O.S.A., '56; Thomas P. Purcell, O.S.A., '43.

American Benedictine Foreign Missions (O.S.B.)

American - Cassinese Congregation Foreign Missions

St. Vincent Archabbey: 300 Fraser Purchase Rd., Latrobe, PA 15650-2686. Tel: 412-532-6600. Rt. Rev. Douglas R. Nowicki, O.S.B., ord. 72, Archabbot; Rev. Noel H. Rothrauff, O.S.B., '54, Mission Dir.

U.S. Religious serving Abroad: Bros. Anthony Kirsch, O.S.B., Subprior, *Brazil;* Nicholas Koss, O.S.B., Prior, *Taiwan;* Revs. Leo P. Rothrauff, O.S.B., '56, *Brazil;* Joseph J. Foote, O.S.B., '89, *Nicaragua;* Anthony St. Pierre, O.S.B., '78, *Papua, New Guinea.*

St. John's Abbey: Box 2015, Collegeville, MN 56321-2015; Fax: 612-363-3082.

U.S. Religious serving Abroad: Very Rev. Kieran Nolan, O.S.B., '59, Prior, *Japan;* Revs. Neal Henry Lawrence, O.S.B., '60, *Japan;* Very Rev. Mel Taylor, O.S.B., '67, Prior, *Nassau;* Revs. Fintan Bromenshenkel, O.S.B., '45, *Nassau;* Cletus Connors, O.S.B., '72; George Wolf, O.S.B., '44, *Nassau;* Thomas Wahl, O.S.B., '58, *Japan;* Cyprian Weaver, O.S.B., '72, *Taiwan;* William Skudlarek, O.S.B., '64, *Japan.*

St. Benedict's Abbey: Atchison, KS 66002. Tel: 913-367-5341; Fax: 913-367-6230. Rt. Rev. Barnabas Senecal, O.S.B., Abbot.

U.S. Religious serving in Brazil: Most Rev. Herbert Hermes; Very Rev. Kieran McInerey, O.S.B., '52; Revs. Eric Deitchman, O.S.B., '63; Duane Roy, O.S.B., '67.

St. Procopius Abbey: 5601 College Rd., Lisle, IL 60532. Tel: 630-969-6410; Fax: 630-969-6426.

U.S. Religious serving in China: Very Rev. Alban Hrebic, O.S.B., '52, Prior.

Assumption Abbey: P.O. Box A, Richardton, ND 58652. Tel: 701-974-3315.

U.S. Religious serving in South America: Very Rev. Philip Vanderlin, O.S.B., '80, Prior; Revs. Efraim Villegas, O.S.B., '88, Subprior; Sebastian Schmidt, O.S.B., '60; Carlos Suarez, O.S.B., '86; Francis Wehri, O.S.B., '61; Gonzalo Blanco, O.S.B., '92; Bros. Fabio Mejia; Nicolas Cano; Milton Martinez; Cesar Carreno.

Mount Angel Abbey: St. Benedict, OR 97373. Tel: 503-845-3030; Fax: 503-845-3594. Monks of Mount Angel Abbey (Benedictines).

U.S. Religious serving in Mexico: Very Rev Konrad Shaefer, O.S.B., '80; Revs. Louis Charvet, O.S.B., '45; Michael Mee, O.S.B., '78.

Marmion Abbey: 850 Butterfield Rd., Aurora, IL 60504.

U.S. Religious serving in Central America: Very Rev. John Brahill, O.S.B., '82, Prior; Revs. Matthias Zinkan, O.S.B., '40; Gerald Benkert, O.S.B., '34; Carlos Quintana, O.S.B., '49.

St. Benedict's Abbey: Benet Lake, WI 53102.

U.S. Religious serving in Mexico: Rt. Rev. Robert Schoofs, O.S.B., '58; Bro. George Koenigs, O.S.B.; Rev. Kevin John Murphy, O.S.B., '62.

Blue Cloud Abbey: Marvin, SD 57251. Tel: 605-432-5528; Fax: 605-432-4754. Rt. Rev. Thomas Hillenbrand, '65, Supr. & Mission Dir.

U.S. Religious serving in Guatemala: Revs. Basil Dilger, O.S.B., '61; Cletus Miller, O.S.B., '44; Bernardine Ness, O.S.B., '64.

New Subiaco Abbey: Subiaco, AR 72865; Fax: 501-934-4328. Rt. Rev. Jerome Kodell, O.S.B., Supr.

U.S. Religious serving in Central America: Revs. Richard Walz, O.S.B., '67, Prior; Bruno Fuhrmann, O.S.B., '54; Bros. Benedict Silva, O.S.B.; Omar Castillo, O.S.B.; Marcos Salam, O.S.B.; Maurus Glenn, O.S.B.; Sergio Coc, O.S.B.

St. Paul's Abbey: Newton, NJ 07860; Fax: 201-383-5782.

U.S. Religious serving Abroad: Revs. Damian Milliken, O.S.B., '58, *Tanzania;* Peter W. Blue, O.S.B., '70, *South Africa.*

American Capuchin Missions (O.F.M.Cap.)

Missions of the American Provinces of the Order of Friars Minor Capuchin (The Capuchin Friars) in the United States and other countries.

General Headquarters: *Via Piemonte,* 70, 00187, Rome, Italy; Most Rev. John Corriveau, O.F.M.Cap., Gen. Min.; Rev. Linus Faeh, O.F.M.Cap., Sec. Gen. for the Missions.

Provincial Headquarters

Capuchin Foreign Missions

Province of St. Joseph: 1740 Mt. Elliott Ave., Detroit, MI 48207; Fax: 313-922-0404. Revs. Daniel Fox, O.F.M.Cap., '75, Prov. Minister; Loran Miller, O.F.M.Cap., '64, Mission Sec.

U.S. Religious serving Abroad: Revs. Charles Bantle, O.F.M.Cap., '48, *Japan;* Evarist Bertrand, O.F.M.Cap., '63, *Nicaragua;* Phillip Casper, O.F.M.Cap., '43, *Panama;* Paul Craig, O.F.M.Cap., '66, *Middle East;* Camillus Doerfler, O.F.M.Cap., '45, *Nicaragua;* Francis Solanus Fary, O.F.M.Cap., '67, *Nicaragua;* Ralph Fellenz, O.F.M.Cap., '68, *Middle East;* Carmel Flora, O.F.M.Cap., '53, *Australia;* Bro. Patrick Forton, O.F.M.Cap., *Nicaragua;* Revs. Glenn Gessner, O.F.M.Cap., '60, *Nicaragua;* Kevin Heagerty, O.F.M.Cap., '61, *Panama;* Walter Kasuboski, O.F.M.Cap., '74, *Panama;* Wilbert Lanser, O.F.M.Cap., '59, *Nicaragua;* Theodore Niehaus, O.F.M.Cap., '65, *Nicaragua;* Marcian Pellett, O.F.M.Cap., '38, *Guam;* Florian Ruskamp, O.F.M.Cap., '45, *Nicaragua;* Most Rev. Paul Schmitz, O.F.M.Cap., Bishop-Vicar Apostolic of Bluefields; Revs. August Seubert, O.F.M.Cap., '57, *Nicaragua;* Wendelin Shafer, O.F.M.Cap., '46, *Nicaragua;* Joseph Smetana, O.F.M.Cap., '56, *Nicaragua;* Gregory Smutko, O.F.M.Cap., '58, *Costa Rica;* Bernard Wagner, O.F.M.Cap., '63, *Nicaragua;* Lawrence Webber, O.F.M.Cap., '80, *Costa Rica;* Andre Weller, O.F.M.Cap., '63, *Panama;* Nicholas Widhammer, O.F.M.Cap., '63, *Middle East;* Joseph Wolf, O.F.M.Cap., '64, *Nicaragua;* David Zywiec, O.F.M.Cap., '74, *Nicaragua.*

Province of St. Augustine: 220 37th St., Pittsburgh, PA 15201. Tel: 412-682-6011; Fax: 412-682-0506. Very Rev. Philip Fink, O.F.M.Cap., '77, Prov. Min.; Rev. Francis Fugini, O.F.M.Cap., '54, Coord. of Missions.

U.S. Religious serving in Puerto Rico (St. John the Baptist Vice Province): Revs. John Bednarik, O.F.M.Cap., '68, Vice-Prov.; Mario Mastrangelo, O.F.M.Cap., '58; Leo Morgan, O.F.M.Cap., '44; Claire Noll, O.F.M.Cap., '37; Joel Ostrowski, O.F.M.Cap., '51; Regis Schlick, O.F.M.Cap., '65.

U.S. Religious serving in Papua New Guinea (St. Michael the: Archangel Vice Province of Papua New Guinea and the Solomon Islands); Revs. Allan Wasiecko, O.F.M.Cap., '68, Vice-Prov.; Emilio Biosco, O.F.M.Cap., '94; Samuel Driscoll, O.F.M.Cap., '59; William Fey, O.F.M.Cap., '68; Dunstan Jones, O.F.M.Cap., '61; Benjamin Madden, O.F.M.Cap., '58; Brian Newman, O.F.M.Cap., '61; Cyril Repko, O.F.M.Cap., '62; Bro. Raymond Ronan, O.F.M.Cap.; Revs. Colman Studeny, O.F.M.Cap., '61; Roger White, O.F.M.Cap., '65; Jonathan Williams, O.F.M.Cap., '71.

Province of St. Mary: 30 Gedney Park Dr., White Plains, NY 10605. Tel: 914-761-3008. Very Rev. Bernard Smith, O.F.M.Cap., '64, Prov.; Rev. Peter Kaseta, O.F.M.Cap., '67, Mission Sec.

U.S. Religious serving Abroad: Revs. Peter Danaher, O.F.M.Cap., '84, *Honduras* , Most Rev.; Anthony Apuron, O.F.M.Cap., Archbishop of Agana; Revs. Wayne Berndt, O.F.M.Cap., '83, *Japan;* Jeremiah Cassidy, O.F.M.Cap., '56, *Japan;* Patrick Castro, O.F.M.Cap., '87, *Guam;* Louis Chiusano, O.F.M.Cap., '57, *Japan;* Gordon Combs, O.F.M.Cap., '64, *Guam;* Daniel Cristobal, O.F.M.Cap., '59, *Guam;* Roland Daigle, O.F.M.Cap., '84, *Japan;* Michel Dalton, O.F.M.Cap., '78, *Guam;* Joseph English, O.F.M.Cap., '90, *Guam;* Eric Forbes, O.F.M.Cap., '90, *Guam;* Lee G. Friel, O.F.M.Cap., '56, *Guam;* Earl Gallagher, O.F.M.Cap., '71, *Honduras;* Joseph Gurdak, O.F.M.Cap., '70, *Honduras;* Agustin Gumataotao, O.F.M.Cap., '73, *Guam;* Most Rev. Peter B. Ishigami, O.F.M.Cap., Bishop of Naha, *Japan;* Revs Paul Kosaka, O.F.M.Cap., '84, *Guam;* Felixberto Leon-Guerrero, O.F.M.Cap., '86, *Guam;* Robert L. Maher, O.F.M.Cap., '74, *Guam;* Andrew Mannetta, O.F.M.Cap., '83, *Guam;* Jose McCarthy, O.F.M.Cap., '60, *Puerto Rico;* Eymard McKinnon, O.F.M.Cap., '54, *Guam;* George Maddock, O.F.M.Cap., '64, *Guam;* Paul Minchak, O.F.M.Cap., '69, *Guam;* Bartholomew Minson, O.F.M.Cap., '64, *Japan;* John Niland, O.F.M.Cap., '76, *Guam;* Randolph Nowak, O.F.M.Cap., '52, *Guam;* Ferdinand Pangelinan, O.F.M.Cap., '81, *Guam;* LaSalle Parsons, O.F.M.Cap., '57, *Japan;* Robert Phelps, O.F.M.Cap., '66, *Guam;* Raymond Richard, O.F.M.Cap., '72, *Honduras;* Patrick Sullivan, O.F.M.Cap., '71, *Cuba;* Jose Villagomez, O.F.M.Cap., '74, *Guam;* Peter Von Essen, O.F.M.Cap., '56, *Japan;* William Shannon, O.F.M.Cap., '71, *Guam;* John Szamreta, O.F.M.Cap., '81, *Japan.*

The Seraphic Mass Association-Capuchin Mission Association , St. Mary's Province, 210 West 31st St., New York, NY 10001-2876.

This Association supports the Capuchin Foreign Mission.

Province of the Stigmata: *St. Francis Center,* 67 Lawrence Rd., Lafayette, NJ 07848. Tel: 201-383-6465. Brian Tomlinson, O.F.M.Cap., '65, Local Min.; Bro. Julius Tkaczyk, O.F.M.Cap., Assoc.

U.S. Religious serving in Zambia: Revs. Daniel Gomez, O.F.M.Cap., '61; Charles Hanley, O.F.M.Cap., '80; Bros. Rudolph Pieretti, O.F.M.Cap.; Crispin Valeri, O.F.M.Cap.

American Carmelite Missions (O.Carm)

Carmelite Foreign Missions

Foreign Missions of the American Province of the Most Pure Heart of Mary.

PROVINCIAL HEADQUARTERS: *Carmelite Fathers Provincial Office,* 1317 Frontage Rd., Darien, IL 60561; Fax: 630-971-0195. Very Rev. Leo McCarthy, O.Carm., '62, Prov.

MISSION OFFICE: *Carmelite Missions,* Darien, IL 60561. Rev. John Malley, O.Carm., '56, Mission Dir.

U.S. Religious serving in Peru: Revs. Herbert Jones, O.Carm., '60; Gerald Payea, O.Carm., '70, Formation Dir.; Joseph Lucchesi, O.Carm., '84; Michael Sgarioto, O.Carm., '85, Pastor; Kevin Lafey, O.Carm., '72; Rev. Msgr. Alban Quinn, O.Carm., '49; Revs. Joseph Cilia, O.Carm., '68; Salvador Bartolo, O.Carm., '52; Michael LaFay, O.Carm., '60; Ferdinand Lansang, O.Carm., '96; James Geaney, O.Carm., '59; Michael Brown, O.Carm., '93.

U.S. Religious serving in Mexico: Revs. John Hertel, O.Carm., '53; Thomas Jordan, O.Carm., '70; Joel Moelter, O.Carm., '51; William Smith, O.Carm., '54; Frank Sanchez, O.Carm., '.

Comboni Missionaries (Verona Fathers) (M.C.C.J.)

Comboni Foreign Missions

Legal Title: *Comboni Missionaries of the Heart of Jesus, Inc.*

U.S. HEADQUARTERS: *Comboni Mission Center,* 8108 Beechmont Ave., Cincinnati, OH 45255-3194. Tel: 513-474-4997; Fax: 513-474-0382. Revs. John Converset, M.C.C.J., '71, Prov. Supr.; Joseph Bragotti, M.C.C.J., '62, Mission Dir. & Vice Prov.

U.S. Religious serving Abroad: Revs. Albert Anichini, M.C.C.J., '62, *Uganda;* Manuel Baeza, M.C.C.J., '96, *South Africa;* Michael Barton, M.C.C.J., '75, *Kenya;* David Bohnsack, M.C.C.J., '94, *Kenya;* Angel Camorlinga, M.C.C.J., '96, *Ecuador;* Dennis Conway, M.C.C.J., '68, *Italy;* Paul Donohue, M.C.C.J., '75, *Kenya;* Patrick Duffy, M.C.C.J., ', *Sao Paulo;* James Francez, M.C.C.J., '57, *Mexico;* Louis Gasparini, M.C.C.J., '65, *Peru;* William Jansen, M.C.C.J., '66, *Guatemala;* Jon Jensen, M.C.C.J., ', *Mexico;* Luis Monzon-Tapia, M.C.C.J., '95, *Zambia;* Paul O'Donnell, M.C.C.J., '93, *Philippines;* Raymond Pax, M.C.C.J., '65, *Kenya;* Brian Quigley, M.C.C.J., '77, *Malawi.*

American Conventual Franciscan Missions (O.F.M.Conv.)

Conventual Franciscan Foreign Missions

GENERAL HEADQUARTERS: *Convento SS. XII Apostoli Piazza SS. Apostoli,* 51, 00187, Roma, Italia. Most Rev. Enrique Montero, O.F.M.Conv., Sec. Gen. for the Missions.

Provincial Headquarters

PROVINCE OF THE IMMACULATE CONCEPTION: P.O. Box 629, 517 Washington Ave., Rensselaer, NY 12144. Very Rev. Giles Van Wormer, O.F.M.Conv., '65, Prov. & Mission Dir. Tel: 518-472-1000.

U.S. Religious serving Abroad: Revs. Bertrand Hodes, O.F.M.Conv., '39; Maury Marhafer, O.F.M.Conv., '54; Andre Lambert, O.F.M.Conv., '57, Assoc. Pastor; Martin de Porres Ward, O.F.M.Conv., '55, Spiritual Dir. (Seminary); Most Rev. Elias Manning, O.F.M.Conv., Bishop of Valenca, Brazil.

PROVINCE OF SAINT ANTHONY OF PADUA: *Provincial House & Office of Mission Procurator,* 12300 Folly Quarter Rd., Ellicott City, MD 21042-1419. Tel: 410-531-9200; Fax: 410-531-4881. Very Rev. Mark L. Curesky, O.F.M.Conv., '75, Minister Prov.; Rev. Martin Kobos, O.F.M.Conv., '76, Mission Procurator.

Franciscan Mission Association 66 School St., Granby, MA 01033. Tel: 413-467-9196. Rev. Placid Kaczorek, O.F.M.Conv., '64, Mission Dir.

U.S. Religious serving Abroad: Revs. Vincent Lachendro, O.F.M.Conv., '63, *Philippines;* Jerome Lukaszewski, O.F.M.Conv., '48, *Japan;* Paul Marut, O.F.M.Conv., '72, *Ghana;* Ron Roll, O.F.M.Conv., '80, *Honduras;* Bro. Mitchell Sawicki, O.F.M.Conv., *Ghana;* Revs. Dominic Slemba, O.F.M.Conv., '51, *Ghana;* Nicholas Swiatek, O.F.M.Conv., '68, *Japan;* Giles Zakowicz, O.F.M.Conv., '75, *Ghana.*

PROVINCE OF OUR LADY OF CONSOLATION: *Provincial Office,* Mt. St. Francis, IN 47146. Rev. Kent Biergans, O.F.M.Conv., Min. Prov.

Religious serving Abroad: Revs. Gerard Scioscia, O.F.M.Conv., Pastor; Juniper Cummings, O.F.M.Conv., Custos; Bros. Aloysius Wagener, O.F.M.Conv.; Bryan Hoban, O.F.M.Conv.; Kamil Wenzel, O.F.M.Conv., Pastor & Guardian; John Doyle, O.F.M.Conv.; Aloysius Jacoby, O.F.M.Conv., Guardian and Pastor; Gerhard Wenzel, O.F.M.Conv.; Efisio Steri, O.F.M.Conv., Guardian; Joseph Scoma, O.F.M.Conv.; Werner Iten, O.F.M.Conv., Pastor; Joseph Weissling, O.F.M.Conv., Guardian; Hugo Lamm, O.F.M.Conv., *Kitwe, Zambia;* Revs. Lawrence Mattingly, O.F.M.Conv., *Costa Rica;* Emil Cook, O.F.M.Conv., *Honduras;* Ronald Roll, O.F.M.Conv., *Honduras;* Ivan Rohloff, O.F.M.Conv., *Honduras;* Pius Uitendaal, O.F.M.Conv., Pastor, Zambia; Terence Tobin, O.F.M.Conv., Guardian, Zambia; Jude Rochford, O.F.M.Conv., Zambia; Mark Weaver, O.F.M.Conv., Custos, *Honduras;* Bro. Anthony Droll, O.F.M.Conv., *Zambia;* Revs. Thomas Merrill, O.F.M.Conv., *Costa Rica;* Raymond Mallett, O.F.M.Conv., *Costa Rica;* Fritz O'Kelly, O.F.M.Conv.,

PROVINCE OF SAINT BONAVENTURE: *Provincial Office,* 6107 N. Kenmore Ave., Chicago, IL 60660-2797. Tel: 312-274-7681; Fax: 312-274-9751. Very Rev. Anthony Labedis, O.F.M.Conv., '60, Minister Prov. & Supr.; Rev. James Henning, O.F.M.Conv., '82, Mission Dir.

U.S. Religious serving Abroad: Rev. John Calgaro, O.F.M.Conv., '74, *Mexico;* Bros. Paschal Metzger, O.F.M.Conv., *Mexico;* Stanislaus Zabkiewicz, O.F.M.Conv., Zambia.

Crosier Fathers Missions (O.S.C.)

Crosier Foreign Missions

Crosier Fathers and Brothers (Canons Regular of the Order of the Holy Cross).

U.S. ADDRESS: *Crosier Missions-Province of St. Odilia,* 3510 Vivian Ave., Shoreview, MN 55126-3852. Tel: 612-486-7456; Fax: 612-486-7589. Very Rev. John Neville, O.S.C., '61, Prov.; Rev. David E. Gallus, O.S.C., '66, Mission Dir.

U.S. Religious serving Abroad: Very Rev. Glen Lewandowski, O.S.C., '74, *Indonesia;* Rev. Ernest Martello, O.S.C., '70, *Zaire;* Bro. Clarence Neuner, O.S.C., *Indonesia;* Rev. Virgil Petermeier, O.S.C., '77, *Indonesia;* Robert Rossi, O.S.C, '70, *Zaire;* Bro. James Scher, O.S.C., *Indonesia;* Most Rev. Alphonse Sowada, O.S.C., *Indonesia;* Revs. Frank Trenkenschuh, O.S.C., '66, *Indonesia;* Gregory Poser, O.S.C., '75, *Indonesia.*

American Divine Word Missionaries (S.V.D.)

Society of the Divine Word Foreign Missions

Missions of the American Provinces of the Society of the Divine Word (S.V.D.) commonly known as Divine Word Missionaries.

Latin: Societas Verbi Divini.

Provincial Headquarters in the U.S.A.

CHICAGO PROVINCE: *Society of the Divine Word-Province of Blessed Joseph Freinademetz, S.V.D.,* 1985 Waukegan Rd., P.O. Box 6038, Techny, IL 60082-6038. Tel: 847-272-2700; Fax: 847-272-2517. Very Rev. Stanley Uroda, S.V.D., '74, Prov. Supr.; Rev. Thomas A. Krosnicki, S.V.D., '66, Mission Dir. for all three Provinces.

Publication: *Divine Word Missionaries.*

SOUTHERN PROVINCE: *Society of the Divine Word-Province of St. Augustine,* 201 Ruella Ave., Bay St. Louis, MS 39520. Tel: 601-467-4322. Very Rev. Clifton Labbe, S.V.D., '69, Prov. Supr.

WESTERN PROVINCE: *Society of the Divine Word,* P.O. Box 77-F, Los Angeles, CA 90007. Tel: 213-483-3013. Very Rev. Eamonn Donnelly, S.V.D., '70, Prov. Supr.

American Divine Word Missionaries in Overseas Missions: Most Rev. Leo Arkfeld, S.V.D., *Papua New Guinea;* Revs. Thomas Ascheman, S.V.D., '82, *Italy;* Daniel Bauer, S.V.D., '74, *Taiwan;* Francis Beemsterboer, S.V.D., '51, *Ghana;* Andrew Biller, S.V.D., '61, *Philippines;* Joseph Bisson, S.V.D., '63, *Papua New Guinea;* Michael Blume, S.V.D., '72, *Rome;* Bro. William Brennan, S.V.D., *Philippines.* Revs. Francis Budenholzer, S.V.D., '72, *Taiwan;* Joseph Bugner, S.V.D., '63, *Papua New Guinea;* Most Rev. John Bukovsky, S.V.D., *Russia;* Revs. Francis Bures, S.V.D., '53, *Japan;* Vincent Burke, S.V.D., '61, *Ghana;* Dennis Callan, S.V.D., '87, *Taiwan;* Jack Cannuli, S.V.D., '85, *Taiwan;* Thomas Cassidy, S.V.D., '45, *Philippines;* Emil Cernaj, S.V.D., '51, *Australia;* David Cornett, S.V.D., '87, *Zaire;* Richard Daschbach, S.V.D., '64, *Indonesia;* Bro. Ignatius DiSanto, S.V.D., *Papua New Guinea;* Revs. Anthony Dugay, S.V.D., '62, *Ghana;* Felix Eckerman, S.V.D., '47, *India;* Elmer Elsbernd, S.V.D., '65, *Papua New Guinea;* Bro. Xavier Eshman, S.V.D., *Paraguay;* Revs. Kenneth Feehan, S.V.D., '59, *Papua New Guinea;* Lloyd Fiedler, S.V.D., '70, *Philippines;* Patrick Fincutter, S.V.D., '55, *Papua New Guinea;* Frederick Fox, S.V.D., '50, *England;* Bro. Ronald Fratzke, S.V.D., *Australia;* Revs. Paul Gootee, S.V.D., '55, *Indonesia;* Robert Grochowski, S.V.D., '96, *Japan;* Eric Groner, S.V.D., '96, *Colombia;* Edward Grzenia, S.V.D., '47, *Japan;* Lawrence Hambach, S.V.D., '61, *Indonesia;* John Healy, S.V.D., '43, *Philippines;* Bro. John Heckel, S.V.D., *Ghana;* Revs. James Heisig, S.V.D., '69, *Japan;* Edward Herberger, S.V.D., '60, *Jamaica;* Raymond Hober, S.V.D., '60, *Philippines;* Bros. Patrick Hogan, S.V.D., *Taiwan;* Andre Hotchkiss, S.V.D., *Kenya;* Revs. Clement Hotze, S.V.D., '47, *Ghana;* Alan Jenkins, S.V.D., '73, *Mexico;* Robert Johnson, S.V.D., '92, *Montserrat (Caribbean;* Most Rev. Raymond Kalisz, S.V.D., *Papua New Guinea;* Revs. Michael Keefe, S.V.D., '81, *Argentina;* Bros. Stephen Kerekes, S.V.D., *Papua New Guinea;* Lawrence Kieffer, S.V.D., *Papua New Guinea;* Revs. Jon Kirby, S.V.D., '71, *Ghana;* Robert Kisala, S.V.D., '85, *Japan;* Richard Kraft, S.V.D., '55, *Philippines;* Albert Kretschmer, S.V.D., '47, *Ghana;* Ronald Lange, S.V.D., '71, *Ghana;* Paul LaForge, S.V.D., '58, *Japan;* Lawrence LaPlante, S.V.D., '67, *Philippines;* Bernard LeFrois, S.V.D., '34, *Philippines;* William Liebert, S.V.D., '57, *Papua New Guinea;* James Liebner, S.V.D., '85, *Taiwan;* Michael Lindstrom, S.V.D., '82, *Japan;* Bro. Damien Lunders, S.V.D., *Papua New Guinea;* Revs. Matthew Lunzer, S.V.D., '45, *Papua New Guinea;* John Khien Luu, S.V.D., '92, *Australia;* David Mayer, S.V.D., '66, *Japan;* Dennis McKillip, S.V.D., '47, *Philippines;* John McSherry, S.V.D., '61, *Philippines;* Peter Michael, S.V.D., '40, *Philippines;* Francis Mihalic, S.V.D., '44, *Papua New Guinea;* Bro. Henry Miller, S.V.D., *Antigua/Caribbean;* Revs. Hilarion Morin, S.V.D., '37, *Papua New Guinea;* Theodore Murnane, S.V.D., '59, *Philippines;* John Musinsky, S.V.D., '44, *Rome;* Paul Nadolny, S.V.D., '89, *Mexico;* Lawrence Nemer, S.V.D., '60, *Australia;* Joseph Trong Nguyen, S.V.D., '91, *Philippines;* Peter Sam Cao Nguyen, S.V.D., '86, *Korea;* Joseph Nguyen Minh Vu, S.V.D., '96, *Australia;* Donald O'Connor, S.V.D., '64, *Papua New Guinea;* Vincent Ohlinger, S.V.D., '68, *Papua New Guinea;* Anthony Patik, S.V.D., '42, *Papua New Guinea;* Stanley Plutz, S.V.D., '53, *Philippines;* Jefferson Pool, S.V.D., '92, *Philippines;* William Popp, S.V.D., '49, *Indonesia;* Thomas Potts, S.V.D., '61, *Ghana;* Robert Pung, S.V.D., '44, *Rome;* Bro. Mark Rastall, S.V.D., *Australia;* Revs. Andrew Rentko, S.V.D., '49, *Mexico;* Robert Riemer, S.V.D., '60, *Japan;* Roger Risse, S.V.D., '54, *Indonesia;* James Risse, S.V.D., '61, *Philippines;* Eugene Rochford, S.V.D., '74, *Rome;* Charles Scanlon, S.V.D., '54, *Philippines;* Bartley Schmitz, S.V.D., '44, *Taiwan;* Eugene Schmitz, S.V.D., '67, *Indonesia;* Charles Schneider, S.V.D., '46, *Ghana;* Mark Schramm, S.V.D., '75, *Ghana;* William Seifert, S.V.D., '67, *Papua New Guinea;* John Seland, S.V.D., '68, *Japan;* Werner Shadeg, S.V.D., '45, *Papua New Guinea;* Norbert Shadeg, S.V.D., '49, *Indonesia;* Otto Shelly, S.V.D., '42, *Australia;* Arnold Steffen, S.V.D., '57, *Papua New Guinea;* Victor Stevko, S.V.D., '57, *Australia;* Nicholas Strawn, S.V.D., '62,

Indonesia; David Streit, S.V.D., '69, *Rome;* Richard Szippl, S.V.D., '81, *Japan;* Gerald Theis, S.V.D., '80, *Papua New Guinea;* Richard Thibeau, S.V.D., '57, *Mexico;* Bro. Wayne Till, S.V.D., *Papua New Guinea;* Revs. Frederick Timp, S.V.D., '71, *Ghana;* Joseph Huynh Tran, S.V.D., '93, *Taiwan;* Thomas Umbras, S.V.D., '81, *Mexico;* Edward Vargo, S.V.D., '63, *Thailand;* Joseph Vu Dao, S.V.D., '88, *Philippines;* Lawrence Wagner, S.V.D., '44, *Mexico;* Wilbert Wagner, S.V.D., '40, *Mexico;* John Wald, S.V.D., '43, *Papua New Guinea;* Hilbert Wiesen, S.V.D., '46, *Japan;* Bro. Daniel Yunck, S.V.D., *Paraguay;* Rev. Jerome Ziliak, S.V.D., '47, *India;* Bro. James Zabransky, S.V.D., *St. Kitts.*

American Dominican Missions (O.P.)

Dominican - Order of Preachers Foreign Missions

Foreign Missions of the American Provinces of the Order of Preachers.

Provincial Headquarters

PROVINCE OF ST. JOSEPH (EASTERN): 141 E. 65th St., New York, NY 10021. Tel: 212-734-4784. Very Rev. Urban Voll, O.P., '49, Prov.; Bro. Thomas-Aquinas Dolan, O.P., Mission Dir.

U.S. Religious serving in Pakistan: Revs. J. M. Connors, O.P., '51; J. F. Arnold, O.P., '56; T. C. McVey, O.P., '60; J. A. Breen, O.P., '63; J. Nuttall, O.P., '69; L. L. Turon, O.P., '55; G. L. Sukovaty, O.P., '51; Bro. M. Schratz, O.P.

Priests 7; Brothers 1.

U.S. Religious serving in Peru: Revs. J. L. Dolan, O.P., '60; Thomas K. Kraft, O.P., '86; T. B. Smith, O.P., '58; Ralph E. Cahouet, S.V.D., '62.

U.S. Religious serving in Kenya: Very Rev. W. T. Sinkele, O.P., '73, Vicar Prov. & Supr.; Revs. M. B. Schepers, O.P., '56; L. M. Shea, O.P., '52; Edward Gorman, O.P., '92; T. R. Heath, O.P., '50; David D. Izzo, O.P., '94; Kieran J. Healy, O.P., '61.

U.S. Religious serving elsewhere: Revs. D. G. Doherty, O.P., '57, *Philippines;* Frank I.Sutman, O.P., '85, *Russia;* Christopher Cardone, O.P., '86, *Solomon Islands;* Stanley Azaro, O.P., '75, *Lithuania.*

PROVINCE OF ST. ALBERT THE GREAT (CENTRAL): 1909 S. Ashland Ave., Chicago, IL 60608-2994; Fax: 312-829-8471. Very Rev. Edward M. Ruane, O.P., '69, Prov.; Rev. Bede Jagde, O.P., '60, Dir., *-St. Dominic Mission Society.*

U.S. Religious serving in Bolivia: Very Rev. Patrick Reardon, O.P., '60, Vicar Prov.; Revs. Thomas Lynch, O.P., '86; Chrysostom Geraets, O.P., '56; Mark Paraday, O.P., '83; Daniel Roach, O.P., '56; James Spahn, O.P., '81.

U.S. Religious serving in Honduras: Rev. James Q. Barnett, O.P., '65; Bro. Kevin Carroll, O.P.

U.S. Religious serving in Kenya: Rev. Lewis M. Shea, O.P., '52.

U.S. Religious serving in Nigeria: Very Rev. Peter Otillio, O.P., '57; Revs. Joseph H. Kenny, O.P., '50; Thomas K. McDermott, O.P., '83; Justus Pokrezewinski, O.P., '60; Edward H. Riley, O.P., '60; Gilbert Thesing, O.P., '75; Ambrose Windbacher, O.P., '54; Bro. Stephen Lucas, O.P.

PROVINCE OF THE HOLY NAME: *(Western Dominican Province),* 5877 Birch Court, Oakland, CA 94618. Very Rev. Daniel Syverstad, O.P., '82, Prov.; Very Rev. Reginald E. Martin, O.P., '74, Socius-Vicar Prov. & Dir. Devel.; Revs. Luke D. Buckles, O.P., '78, Corporate Sec. & Regent of Studies; Anthony G. Cordeiro, O.P., '67, Treas. & Dir. St. Dominic Cemetery; Basil B. Cole, O.P., '66, Western Regional Dir. of the Holy Name Society; Martin Walsh, O.P., '69; Fred Lucci, O.P., '93, Promoter of Social Justice; Vincent Serpa, O.P., '68, Master of Novices; Joseph Asturias, O.P., '37, Dir. Mission Foudation; Thomas Hayes, O.P., '59, Dir. Shrine of St. Jude; Sergius Propst, O.P., '73, Dir. Western Dominican Preaching Band; Michael J. Dodds, O.P., '77, Master of Students.

SOUTHERN DOMINICAN PROVINCE: *Province of St. Martin de Porres,* 1421 N. Causeway Blvd., Metairie, LA 70001-4144. Tel: 504-837-2129; Fax: 504-837-6604. Very Rev. Alberto Rodriguez, O.P., '71, Prov.; Rev. James A McDonough, O.P., '62, Dir. Southern Dominican Global Missions.

U.S. Religious serving abroad: Revs. Brian Pierce, O.P., '88, *Honduras;* James L. Dolan, O.P., '60, *Peru;* Carmen Mele, O.P., '80, *Costa Rica;* Jesus Guerra, O.P., '57, *Venezuela;* Edward Gregory Fay, O.P., '53, *British Columbia, Canada;* G. Brian Donovan, O.P., '64, *British Columbia, Canada;* Vincent Huu Du Nguyen, O.P., '46, *Calgary, Alberta, Canada.*

American Franciscan Missions (O.F.M.)

Franciscan Foreign Missions

Missions of the American Provinces of the Order of Friars Minor (Franciscans) in the United States and other countries.

HOLY NAME PROVINCE: 135 W. 31st St., New York, NY 10001-3439. Bro. Gordon Clark, O.F.M., Prov. Promoter of the Missions, Sec. Missionary Evangelization; Rev. Joachim A. Mahler, O.F.M., '49.

U.S. Religious serving in Japan: Revs. Jerome A. Donnelly, O.F.M., '39; Bede Fitzpatrick, O.F.M., '55; Campion Lally, O.F.M., '53; Bartholomew McMahon, O.F.M., '62; Lucian A. Mulhern, O.F.M., '62; Donnan P. Murray, O.F.M., '56; Callistus Sweeney, O.F.M., '; Stanislaus Widomski, '62.

U.S. Religious serving Brazil: Most Revs. John Burke O.F.M.; Benedict D. Coscia, O.F.M.; Capistran F. Heim, O.F.M.; Revs. David J. Babcock, O.F.M., '53; Donald J. Chin, O.F.M., '67; Alexander F. Eustace, O.F.M., '50; Thomas J. Fox, O.F.M., '46; Myles Glynn, O.F.M., '50; Berard J. Hanlon, O.F.M., '63; John J. Janson, O.F.M., '41; Juvenal F. Leahy, O.F.M., '58; Ignatius J. McGeady, O.F.M., '48; Aloysius Siracuse, O.F.M., '47; Joseph Sullivan, O.F.M., '55.

U.S. Religious serving in Peru: Revs. Pedro Barbero Fernandez, O.F.M., '62; Mariano Gagnon, O.F.M., '58; Mariano Guzman, O.F.M., '57; Christopher J. Dunn, O.F.M., '82; Bros. Declan McCabe, O.F.M.; Carlos Sarmiento, O.F.M.; Rev. Anthony Wilson, O.F.M., '87.

U.S. Religious serving in Taiwan: Rev. Pius Lui, O.F.M., '53.

U.S. Religious serving in Bolivia: Most Rev. Thomas R. Manning, O.F.M., ord. 47; Revs. Clement J. Comesky, O.F.M., '55; Gavin P. Hanlon, O.F.M., '56; Ignatius Harding, O.F.M., '65; William R. Keenan, O.F.M., '56; Thomas J. Kornacki, O.F.M., '88; Conor Mullaly, O.F.M., '51; Bernardine Ward, O.F.M., '42.

U.S. Religious serving in Israel: Revs. William DeBiase, O.F.M., '65; Edward J. Dillon, O.F.M., '55.

U.S. Religious serving in Africa: Revs. Roy Corrigan, O.F.M., '55; Joseph B. Ehrhardt, O.F.M., '76; Michael S. Joyce, O.F.M., '76; Finian A. Riley, O.F.M., '55; Charles A. Steen, O.F.M., '64; Bro. Paschal Gallagher, O.F.M.

U.S. Religious serving in Puerto Rico: Rev. Alfonso D. Guzman, O.F.M., '71.

FRANCISCAN PROVINCE OF THE IMMACULATE CONCEPTION: 147 Thompson St., New York, NY 10012. Rev. Alban V. Montella, O.F.M., '55, Sec./Missionary Evangelization & Franciscan Missionary Union.

Province-affiliated Religious serving in Honduras: Revs. Peter Paul Meilak, O.F.M., '49; Albert Gauci, O.F.M., '71; Bro. Guillermo Salgado, O.F.M.; Rev. Ubladimiro Rivera, O.F.M., '75; Most Revs. Maurice Muldoon, O.F.M.; Gerald Scarpone, O.F.M.; Revs. Roberto Camilleri, O.F.M., '75; Angelo Falzon, O.F.M., '84; Joseph Bonello, O.F.M., '85; Donald Salazar, O.F.M., '67.

Province-affiliated Religious serving in Guatemala: Revs. Athanasius Iazzetta, O.F.M., '54; Benedict Carrozza, O.F.M., '39; Miguel Blanco Guevera, O.F.M., '37; Rocco Famiglietti, O.F.M., '47; Ottaviano Battolini, O.F.M., '43; Robert Siguere, O.F.M., '73.

Province-affiliated Religious serving in El Salvador: Revs Flavian Mucci, O.F.M., '63; Guy Vellardita, O.F.M., '58, *San Pedro;* Rafael Fernandez, O.F.M., '87.

SACRED HEART PROVINCE: 3140 Meramec St., St. Louis, MO 63118. Tel: 314-353-3421. Revs. Kurt Hartrich, O.F.M., '66, Prov.; Thomas Gardner, O.F.M., '79, Promoter of the Missions, *Franciscan Missionary Union.* Tel: 314-353-7729.

U.S. Religious serving in Brazil: Revs. Michael Grawe, O.F.M., '70; Gregory Kemner, O.F.M., '55; Nestor Windolph, O.F.M., '55.

U.S. Religious serving in Alaska: Revs. William E. Cardy, O.F.M., '72; Joseph Hemmer, O.F.M., '59; Bro. Robert Ruzicka, O.F.M.

U.S. Religious serving Elsewhere: Revs. Louis B. Antl, O.F.M., '48, *Italy;* Bros. Thomas Courtney, O.F.M., *Israel;* Jeffrey Haller, O.F.M., *Taiwan;* Revs. Albert Haase, O.F.M., '83, *Taiwan;* Robert Karris, O.F.M., '65, *Italy;* James Perluzzi, O.F.M., '65, *Italy;* Michael Perry, O.F.M., '84, *England;* Basil Tsung, O.F.M., '53, *Taiwan.*

ST. BARBARA PROVINCE: 1500 34th Ave., Oakland, CA 94601; Fax: 510-536-3970.

U.S. Religious serving Overseas: Bro. Norbert Binder, O.F.M., *Philippines;* Revs. Melvin Stanley, O.F.M., '52, *Philippines;* Martin Gates, O.F.M., '63, *Mexico;* Camillus Cavagnaro, O.F.M., '46, *Mexico;* Elias Galvez, O.F.M., '56, *Mexico;* John Peterson, '63, *Mexico;* Bros. Miguel Lozano, O.F.M., *Mexico;* Ivo Toneck, O.F.M., *Mexico;* Leo Gonzalez, O.F.M., *Israel;* Gerard Saunders, O.F.M., *Peru;* Revs. Oscar Mendez, O.F.M., '89, *El Salvador;* Thomas King, O.F.M., '93, *Guatemala;* Bros. Elmer Yung. O.F.M., *Guatemala;* John Summers, O.F.M., *Thailand.*

ASSUMPTION B.V.M. PROVINCE: Pulaski, WI 54162. Tel: 414-383-7934; Fax: 414-383-0335. Revs. Paul Reczek, O.F.M., '72, Minister Prov.; Hugh Zurat, O.F.M., '62, *Franciscan Evangelization Center - Assumption Province,* Milwaukee, WI 53215. Tel: 414-389-0676; Fax: 414-389-0973.

Publication: *Mission Newsletter.*

U.S. Religious serving Abroad: Revs. Laurian Wegner, O.F.M., '78, *Japan;* Bro. Augustine Fraszczak, O.F.M., *Philippines;* Revs. Lyle Chrobak, O.F.M., '62, *Mexico;* Henry Howaniec, O.F.M., '56, *Kazakhstan;* Blase Karas, O.F.M., '59, *Russia.*

PROVINCE OF ST. JOHN THE BAPTIST: 1615 Vine St., Cincinnati, OH 45210-1222. Tel: 513-721-4700; Fax: 513-421-9672. Bro. Scott Obrecht, O.F.M., Dir.-Secretariat for Missionary Evangelization & Franciscan Missionary Union.

Publications: *Monthly newsletter, Friarworks.*

U.S. Religious serving Abroad: Revs. Malachy Brogan, O.F.M., '57, *Holy Land;* Harold Geers, O.F.M., '60, *Philippines;* Bede Clancy, O.F.M., '44, *Philippines;* Carl Kemphues, O.F.M., '56, *Philippines;* Elgar Nadon, O.F.M., '59, *Philippines;* Joseph Hund, O.F.M., '89, *Philippines;* Bro. Philip Wilhelm, O.F.M., *Philippines;* Revs. Bernardin Schneider, O.F.M., '44, *Japan;* David Turnbull, O.F.M., '57, *Phillipines;* Bertram Tiemeyer, O.F.M., '47, *Philippines;* Max Langenderfer, O.F.M., '73, *Kenya;* James Fehrenbach, O.F.M., '71, *Germany;* Bro. Ambrose Beam, O.F.M., *Greece;* Revs. Gil Wohler, O.F.M., '62, *South Africa;* Lawrence Landini, O.F.M., '61, *South Africa;* Bro. Roger Covero, O.F.M., *Philippines;* Rev. Daniel Kroger, O.F.M., '73, *Philippines.*

VI SLAV-BYZANTINE MISSIONS, U.S.A.

Custody of St. Mary of the Angels. Byzantine-Slavonic Rite (New Canaan, CT)

Established by decree of the Most Rev. Minister General of the Order of Friars Minor on November 7, 1947, with the approbation of the Sacred Congregation for the Oriental Church on October 28, 1947, among the peoples of the Byzantine Rite.

COMMISSARIATS OF THE HOLY LAND: 1400 Quincy St. N.E., Washington, DC 20017. Tel: 202-526-6800; Fax: 202-529-9889. Bros. Callistus Welch, O.F.M., Commissary; David Wathen, O.F.M.; James Paul Brabandt, O.F.M.; Revs. Pio Jackson, O.F.M., '91; Joshua Doyle, O.F.M., Brian McTommoney, O.F.M., '53.

ST. ANTHONY FRIARY: 3140 Meramec St., St. Louis, MO 63118. Rev. Thomas Gardner, O.F.M., '79, Commissary.

ST. JOSEPH'S FRIARY: 218 East 12th St., Los Angeles, CA 90015. Rev. Martial Luebke, O.F.M., '39, Commissary.

CUSTODY OF THE HOLY LAND: *Jordan, Israel, Lebanon, Syria, Cyprus, Egypt and Rhodes.*

U.S. Religious serving Abroad: Bro. Aloysius Florio, O.F.M., *Rome, Italy;* Rev. Xavier Geiser, O.F.M., '55, *Jerusalem, Israel;* Bros. Roger Petras, O.F.M., *Nicosia, Cyprus;* Michael Raum, O.F.M., *Jerusalem, Israel;* Ambrose Beam, O.F.M., *Rhodes;* Thomas Courtney, O.F.M., *Syria;* Revs. Peter Vasko, O.F.M., '87, *Jerusalem, Israel;* Raphael Bonanno, O.F.M., *Rome;* George Lewett, O.F.M., '88, *Bethlehem, Isreal;* Athanasius Macora, O.F.M., '92, *Jerusalem, Israel;* Matthias Rendon, O.F.M., '92, *Jerusalem, Israel;* Danielmose Shroeder, O.F.M., '91, *Jerusalem, Israel;* Guillermo Jaramillo, O.F.M., '94, *Jerusalem, Israel;* Bros. Leo Gonzales, O.F.M., *Mt. Tabor, Israel;* Angel Beda Ison, O.F.M., *Jerusalem, Israel.*

Franciscan Friars of the Atonement (S.A.)

GENERAL HEADQUARTERS: *St. James Friary,* P.O. Box 5, Garrison, NY 10524. Tel: 914-424-3038; Fax: 914-424-3978. Rev. Xavier Butler, S.A., '47, Mission Co-ord., Office, P.O. Box 300, Graymoor, Garrison, NY 10524-0300. Tel: 914-424-3671, Ext. 3412.

For detailed information on the U.S. Religious working in foreign: missions, please refer to the listings; under the Archdiocese of New York section entitled; "Monasteries and Residences of Priests and Brothers", Graymoor, Garrison, NY.

Holy Cross Mission Center (C.S.C.)

U.S. HEADQUARTERS AND PROCURE: *Holy Cross Mission Center for Cross-Cultural Ministries,* P.O. Box 543, Notre Dame, IN 46556. Tel: 219-631-5477. Rev. James T. Rahilly, C.S.C., '64, Dir.

Legal Title: *Holy Cross Foreign Mission Society, Inc.*

Holy Cross Foreign Missions

INDIANA PROVINCE: *Congregation of Holy Cross,* 1304 East Jefferson, South Bend, IN 46617.

MIDWEST PROVINCE: *Congregation of Holy Cross,* Box 460, Notre Dame, IN 46556.

EASTERN PROVINCE: *Congregation of Holy Cross,* 835 Clinton Ave., Bridgeport, CT 06604.

SOUTH-WEST PROVINCE: *Congregation of Holy Cross,* c/o St. Edward's University, Austin, TX 78704.

EASTERN PROVINCE OF BROTHERS: *Congregation of Holy Cross,* 85 Overlook Cir., New Rochelle, NY 10804.

SOUTHERN PROVINCE OF PRIESTS: *Congregation of Holy Cross,* 2111 Brackenridge St., Austin, TX 78704.

U.S. Religious serving in foreign missions: Bro. Ralph Baird, C.S.C., *Bangladesh;* Revs. Robert R. Baker, C.S.C., '70, *Peru;* Duane Balcerski, C.S.C., '71; James T. Banas, C.S.C., '57, *Bangladesh;* Bro. Kevin Barey, C.S.C., *Brazil;* Rev. Gerald R. Barmasse, C.S.C., '76, *Chile;* Bro. Donald Becker, C.S.C., *Bangladesh;* Rev. Thomas V. Bednar, C.S.C., '85, *Chile;* Bros. Thomas More Beere, C.S.C., *Bangladesh;* John Benesh, C.S.C., *Peru;* Rev. F. Frederick Bergmann, C.S.C., '39, *Bangladesh;* Bro. Richard Burgie, C.S.C., *Brazil;* Revs. Arthur J. Colgan, C.S.C., '73, *Peru;* Charles A. Delaney, C.S.C., '49, *Chile;* Philip T. Devlin, C.S.C., '56, *Peru;* Joseph M. Doherty, C.S.C., '41, *Chile;* Joseph A. Dorsey, C.S.C., '57, *Chile;* Bro. Ronald Drahozal, C.S.C., *Bangladesh;* Rev. David E. Farrell, C.S.C., ', *Chile;* Bros. John Flood, C.S.C., *Uganda;* Frederick Cosgrove, C.S.C., *Uganda;* Rev. Thomas Fotusky, C.S.C., '60, *Uganda;* Bro. William Gates, C.S.C., *Ghana;* Revs. Robert Gilbo, C.S.C., '67, *Chile;* Robert G. Gilmour, C.S.C., '68, *Ghana;* Bros. Vincent Gross, C.S.C., *Ghana;* Thomas Giumenta, C.S.C., *Chile;* Alan Gugel, C.S.C., *Uganda;* Alan Harrod, C.S.C., *Uganda;* John Harris, C.S.C., *Nepal;* Ronald Hein, C.S.C., *Brazil;* Alberic Houle, C.S.C., *Bangladesh;* Revs. Robert T. Hesse, C.S.C., '58, *Uganda;* Eugene E. Homrich, C.S.C., '55, *Bangladesh;* Charles Houser, C.S.C., '46, *Bangladesh;* James W. Irwin, C.S.C., ', *Mexico;* Christopher P. Johnson, C.S.C., ', *Chile;* Malcolm D. Johnson, C.S.C., '59, *Chile;* Bros. Richard F. Johnson, C.S.C., *Ghana;* Thomas Keefe, C.S.C., *Uganda;* Rev. T. Daniel Kennerk, C.S.C., '53, *Bangladesh;* Bros. Joseph Kinsman, C.S.C., *Brazil;* Bernard Klim, *Uganda;* Revs. Paul Kollman, C.S.C., ', *Uganda;* T. Daniel Kennerk, C.S.C., '53, *Bangladesh;* Bros. Jerome F. Kreotsch, C.S.C., *Ghana;* Donald Kuchenmeister, C.S.C., *Chile;* Tadeus Las, C.S.C., *Uganda;* Alfred Ledet, C.S.C., *Brazil;* Dismas Lenzi, C.S.C., *Brazil;* Rev. Joseph Lehane, C.S.C., '57, *Bangladesh;* Rev. T. Daniel Kennerk, C.S.C., '53, *Bangladesh;* Bro. Norbert Lengerich, C.S.C., *Brazil;* Revs. L. Peter Logsdon, C.S.C., '68, *Mexico;* George Lucas, C.S.C., '72, *Uganda;* Bros. Robert Ludwig, C.S.C., *Israel;* Peter Celestine Maranto, C.S.C., *Brazil;* Revs. H. Thomas McDermott, C.S.C., '79, *Uganda;* Russell McDougall, C.S.C., '91, *Italy;* Bro. Frederick McGlynn, C.S.C., *Ghana;* Most Rev. Mark G. McGrath, C.S.C., *Panama;* Rev. Joseph Moyer, C.S.C., *Mexico;* Bros. Harold Naudet, C.S.C., *Brazil;* James Nichols, C.S.C., *Uganda;* Revs. Bertram A. Nelson, C.S.C., ', *Bangladesh;* Daniel A. Panchot, C.S.C., '65, *Mexico;* Gerald T. Papen, C.S.C., '63, *Chile;* Leonard D. Paul, C.S.C., ', *Kenya;* Joseph S. Peixotto, C.S.C., '61, *Bangladesh;* William Persia, C.S.C., '62, *Peru;* James Phalen, C.S.C., ', *Peru;* George F. Pope, C.S.C., '58, *Bangladesh;* Richard L. Potthast, C.S.C., '67, *Uganda;* Francis Provenzano, C.S.C., '44, *Chile;* Francis Quinlivan, C.S.C., '70, *Bangladesh;* Bros. Leonard Reeson, C.S.C., *Brazil;* Frank Robinson, C.S.C., *Brazil;* Rev. Cornelius J. Ryan, C.S.C., '66, *Uganda;* Paul Schaefer, C.S.C., *Brazil;* Rev. David E. Schlaver, C.S.C., '71; Most Rev. Charles A. Schleck, C.S.C., ord. 51, *Italy;* Revs. Thomas Shea, C.S.C., '67, *Peru;* Robert G. Simon, C.S.C., '61, *Chile;* Thomas W. Smith, C.S.C., '72, *Kenya;* Bro. William St. Romain, C.S.C., *Brazil;* Rev. Frederick A. Schmidt, C.S.C., '37, *Mexico;* Bro. Sergio Stolf, C.S.C., *Brazil;* Rev. Richard E. Stout, C.S.C., '71, *Kenya;* Bros. J. Rodney Struble, C.S.C., *Bangladesh;* Gerald Suddick, C.S.C., *Uganda;* Nicholas Thielman, C.S.C., *Bangladesh;* Rev. Richard W. Timm, C.S.C., '49, *Bangladesh;* Bros. Ernest Turk, C.S.C., *Brazil;* Robert Weinmann, C.S.C., *Brazil;* Revs. Gerald J. Whelan, C.S.C., '55, *Chile;* Richard J. Wunsch, C.S.C., '66, *Uganda.*

Priests 55; Brothers 43.

Holy Ghost Fathers (C.S.Sp.)

Holy Ghost Foreign Missions

U.S.A. - EAST PROVINCE: *Holy Ghost Fathers,* 6230 Brush Run Rd., Bethel Park, PA 15102; Fax: 412-831-0970. Rev. Christopher P. Promis, C.S.Sp., '72, Prov.

U.S. Religious serving Abroad: Revs. Anthony A. Bacher, C.S.Sp., '46, *Republic of South Africa;* Remo J. Bonifazi, C.S.Sp., '45, *Republic of South Africa;* William H. Christy, C.S.Sp., '92, *Arusha, Tanzania;* Charles S. Giambrone, C.S.Sp., '60, *Arusha, Tanzania;* Francis A. Greff, C.S.Sp., '47, *Arusha, Tanzania;* Joseph M. Herzstein, C.S.Sp., '63, *Kilimanjaro;* Mortimer F. Kane, C.S.Sp., '56, *Arusha, Tanzania;* Joseph L. Kelly, C.S.Sp., '50, *Nairobi, Kenya;* Richard J. LeClair, C.S.Sp., '51, *Arusha, Tanzania;* Edward T. Marchessault, C.S.Sp., '64, *Arusha, Tanzania;* Josaphat Msongore, C.S.Sp., '63, *Arusha, Tanzania;* Patrick A. Patten, C.S.Sp., '78, *Arusha, Tanzania;* Edward J. Raszewski, C.S.Sp., '47, *Arusha, Tanzania;* Bro. Francis Sullivan, C.S.Sp., *Arusha, Tanzania;* Revs. Thomas P. Tunney, C.S.Sp., '60, *Nairobi, Kenya;* Vincent G. Stegman, C.S.Sp., '62, *Ethiopia.*

Jesuit Volunteers: International (S.J.)

U.S. HEADQUARTERS: *Jesuit International Volunteers,* P.O. Box 25478, Washington, DC 20007. Tel: 202-687-1132; Fax: 202-687-5082. Rev. Vincent DeCola, S.J., Dir.

A Christian service organization offering young College educated lay men and women an opportunity to volunteer in a developing country in collaboration with Jesuits. Volunteers serve for two years without returning to the U.S.

Jesuit Missions (S.J.)

Jesuit Foreign Missions

Jesuit Mission Inc. An official missionary organization of the Provinces of the United States Assistancy of the Society of Jesus.

NATIONAL HEADQUARTERS: *Jesuit Missions,* 1616 P St., N.W., #400, Washington, DC 20036. Tel: 202-462-0400; Fax: 202-328-9212. Revs. Richard J. Ryscavage, S.J., '77, Pres.; J. P. Horrigan, S.J., '69, Vice Pres.; Daniel C. McDonald, S.J., '81, Sec.-Treas.; Exec. Committee; Revs. William T. Wood, S.J., '48; Theodore T. Taheny, S.J., '56.

Provinces

SOCIETY OF JESUS: *California Province,* 284 Stanyan St., San Francisco, CA 94118. Tel: 415-221-1588.

Legal Title: *California Jesuit Missionaries;* Revs. John A. Privett, S.J., '72, Prov.; Theodore T. Taheny, S.J., '56, Mission Dir.

U.S. Religious serving in foreign missions: Revs. Louis G. Aldrich, S.J., '86, *Republic of China;* William A. Ameche, S.J., '81, *Mexico;* Ferdinand T. Azevedo, S.J., '70, *Brazil;* Robert Becka, S.J., '60, *Japan;* Walter Brennan, S.J., '60, *Japan;* James Chevedden, S.J., '78, *Republic of China;* Robert Chiesa, S.J., '68, *Japan;* Robert Cunningham, S.J., '55, *Philippines;* Bro. Richard Devine, S.J., *Japan;* Revs. John R. Donahue, S.J., '79, *Honduras;* John Donald, S.J., '72, *Honduras;* Rev. Msgr. Eugene Fahy, S.J., '45, *Republic of China;* Revs. Gustavo Fernandez, S.J., '67, *Honduras;* Thomas W. Franxman, S.J., '64, *Fiji Islands;* John Gordon, S.J., '45, *Philippines;* Fred Green, S.J., '58, *Peru;* Bro. Robert Griffin, S.J., *Philippines;* Mr. Thomas Griffin-Smolenski, S.J.; Revs. Robert B. Grimaldi, S.J., '68, *Honduras;* Russell Horton, S.J., '58, *Japan;* James E. Latham, S.J., '60, *France;* Keith Barry Martinson, S.J., '75, *Republic of China;* George G. Martinson, S.J., '73, *Republic of China;* Edward Murphy, S.J., '43, *Republic of China;* Paul O'Brien, S.J., '38, *Thailand;* John B. Palm, S.J., '41, *Republic of China;* Paul Pollock, S.J., *Thailand;* Stephen F. Pisano, S.J., '75, *Italy;* Bro. Donald Poetzl, S.J., *Mexico;* Revs. David Reed, S.J., '64, *Republic of China;* Robert Ronald, S.J., '65, *Republic of China;* Daniel Ross, S.J., '66, *Republic of China;* Richard Schneck, S.J., '72, *Ecuador;* Mr. Gregg D. Servis, *Brazil;* Revs. Robert J. Shinney, S.J., '68, *Uruguay;* Glen E. Smith, S.J., '63, *Japan;* William R. Stoeger, S.J., '72, *Vatican City;* Norman Walling, S.J., '61, *Hong Kong;* Charles Welsh, S.J., '72, *Republic of China.*

Priests 34; Brothers 3; Scholastics 2.

SOCIETY OF JESUS: *Chicago Province,* 2059 N. Sedgwick St., Chicago, IL 60614. Tel: 312-975-8181.

Legal title: *Jesuit International Missions, (Formerly, Jesuits in Peru, Chicago Province, and Patna Jesuit Mission Society);* Revs. Bradley M. Schaeffer, S.J., '77, Prov.; Gerald P. Grace, S.J., '54, Prov. Asst. Intl. Ministries.

U.S. Religious serving in foreign missions: Revs. Robert E. Beckman, S.J., '56, *Peru;* Fred F. Bergewisch, S.J., '55, *Peru;* Theodore B. Bowling, S.J., '53, *India;* Lawrence V. Brooks, S.J., '74, *Nepal;* Patrick M. Casey, S.J., '72, *Peru;* Francis M. Chamberlain, S.J., '68, *Peru;* Terrence P. Charlton, S.J., '76, *Kenya;* Martin P. Coyne, S.J., '66, *Nepal;* Cornelius L. Curtin, S.J., '56, *Nepal;* Edwin J. Daly, S.J., '59, *India;* Robert M. Deiters, S.J., '58, *Japan;* Robert L. Dolan, S.J., '73, *Peru;* James J. Donnelly, S.J., '59, *Nepal;* James J. Dressman, S.J., '61, *Nepal;* Jerome F. Durack, S.J., '60, *India;* William J. Everett, S.J., '53, *Japan;* Kevin H. Flaherty, S.J., '83, *Peru;* John P. Foley, S.J., '67, *Peru;* Charles J. Fox, S.J., '44, *India;* Kevin E. Gallagher, S.J., '61, *Peru;* Anthony J. Grollig, S.J., '55, *India;* Daniel F. Hartnett, S.J., '74, *Peru;* John J. Kenealy, S.J., '58, *India;* Jeffrey L. Klaiber, S.J., '74, *Peru;* Richard T. Lambert, S.J., '67, *India;* Charles A. Law, S.J., '64, *Nepal;* Roman B. Lewicki, S.J., '65, *India;* John K. Locke, S.J., '64, *Nepal;* Benjamin R. Morin, S.J., '56, *Peru;* Charles L. Murtaugh, S.J., '69, *Peru;* Joseph A. O'Brien, S.J., '43, *India;* James M. O'Leary, S.J., '91, *Peru;* John L. O'Malley, S.J., '63, *Japan;* Edward Schmidt, S.J., '71, *Peru;* John Sima, S.J., '76, *Peru;* Ludwig F. Stiller, S.J., '62, *Nepal;* Eugene L. Watrin, S.J., '52, *Nepal;* Joseph F. Willmes, S.J., '48, *India.*

Priests 44.

DETROIT PROVINCE: 7303 West Seven Mile Rd., Detroit, MI 48221. Tel: 313-861-7500.

Legal Title: *Jesuit International Missions, (Formerly Patna Jesuit Mission Society;* Revs. John F. Libens, S.J., '70, Prov.; Norman J. Dickson, S.J., '67, Mission Dir.

U.S. Religious serving in foreign missions: Revs. Paul H. Besanceney, S.J., '56, *Sudan;* Leo P. Cachat, S.J., '66, *Nepal;* Martin L. Chase, S.J., '91, *Denmark;* Richard W. Cherry, S.J., '69, *Uganda;* Bro. Richard L. Cure, S.J., *Japan;* Revs. Gerald A. Drinane, S.J., '62, *India;* Kevin L. Flannery, S.J., '87, *Rome;* Thomas E. Gafney, S.J., '65, *Nepal;* William G. Goudreau, S.J., '52, *India;* Eugene F. Hattie, S.J., '53, *Uganda;* Mark G. Henninger, S.J., '78, *Zimbabwe;* Paul S. Kehres, S.J., '51, *India;* James J. Kenney, S.J., '57, *India;* Joseph Knecht, S.J., '60, *India;* Kenneth M. Kunert, S.J., '57, *Uganda;* Bro. Joseph A. LaMielle, S.J., *India;* Revs. Norman Langenderfer, S.J., '54, *India;* Richard M. Mackowski, S.J., '61, *Rome;* Robert J. Mayer, S.J., '57,

India; Casper J. Miller, S.J., '64, *Nepal;* Joseph G. Mueller, S.J., '93, *France;* Joseph E. Mulligan, S.J., '73, *Nicaragua;* James J. Regan, S.J., '67, *Peru;* Robert H. Schmidt, S.J., '69, *India;* William A. Schock, S.J., ', *Philippines;* Bro. Joseph A. Shubitowski, S.J., *Tanzania;* Revs. John D. Smith, S.J., '59, *India;* Thomas F. Tobin, S.J., '65, *India;* Richard H. Twohig, S.J., '65, *Tanzania;* Theodore W. Walters, S.J., '56, *Tanzania;* W. Jared Wicks, S.J., '62, *Rome;* Raymond Zeitz, S.J., '51, *India;* George M. Ziebert, S.J., '41, *India.*

Priests 36; Brothers 4; Scholastics 1.

SOCIETY OF JESUS: *Maryland Province,* 5704 Roland Ave., Baltimore, MD 21210. Tel: 410-532-1400; Fax: 410-532-1419. Rev. James R. Stormes, S.J., '79, Prov. & Mission Dir.

Legal Title: *Jesuit Mission Bureau, Maryland Province, Inc., Jesuit Jamshedpur Mission Society, Inc.*

U.S. Religious serving in foreign missions: Revs. Eugene J. Barber, S.J., '63, *Chile;* Gerard S. Barry, S.J., '63, *Japan;* John K. Bingham, S.J., '58, *India;* Joseph H. Bittner, S.J., '39, *Philippines;* Bernard J. Boyle, S.J., '65, *Chile;* Edward J. Brady, S.J., '59, *Sudan;* Robert F. Currie, S.J., '71, *Nicaragua;* William J. Currie, S.J., '67, *Japan;* Angelo D'Agostino, S.J., '66, *Kenya;* Edgar J. Debany, S.J., '84, *Nigeria;* John J. Deeney, S.J., '52, *India;* James M. Desjardins, S.J., '77, *Russia;* Carl L. Dincher, S.J., '57, *India;* Edward C.A. Dougherty, S.J., '72, *South Africa;* Robert J. Dullahan, S.J., '57, *Nigeria;* Gerald J. Fitzpatrick, S.J., '71, *Chile;* Thomas M. Gavin, S.J., '75, *Chile;* Ralph B. Gehring, S.J., '46, *Philippines;* John F. Guidera, S.J., '56, *India;* Robert E. Hamm, S.J., '68, *Nigeria;* John F. Henry, S.J., '55, *Chile;* George A. Hess, S.J., '50, *India;* Brendan R. Horan, S.J., '93, *Nigeria;* F. Scott Howell, S.J., '77, *Japan;* Richard A. Kenna, S.J., '57, *India;* Simon C. Kirsch, S.J., '42, *India;* Sigmund J. Laschenski, S.J., '55, *Thailand;* Michael J. Lynch, S.J., '93, *Hong Kong;* John J. Mawhinney, S.J., '65, *El Salvador;* Edward H. McGrath, S.J., '53, *India;* Edward H. Nash, S.J., '46, *India;* John J. Nissel, S.J., '56, *Japan;* George W. Quickley, S.J., '80, *Nigeria;* James D. Redington, S.J., '78, *Zimbabwe;* William E. Rively, S.J., '46, *Micronesia;* Eugene M. Rooney, S.J., '57, *Chile;* A. Richard Sotelo, S.J., '87, *Jamaica;* John W. Swope, S.J., '86, *Chile;* Dominic J. Totaro, S.J., '67, *Nigeria;* David L. Ungerleider, S.J., '77, *Mexico;* Eugene A. Welch, S.J., '60, *India;* Charles E. Wolf, S.J., '49, *Philippines.*

Priests 42.

SOCIETY OF JESUS: *Missouri Province,* 4511 W. Pine Blvd., St. Louis, MO 63108. Tel: 314-361-7765; Fax: 314-758-7164.

Legal Title: *The Jesuits of the Missouri Province;* Revs. E. Edward Kinerk, S.J., '72, Prov.; Robert L. Sullivan, S.J., '67, Mission Dir.

U.S. Religious serving in foreign missions: Rev. Jeremiah L. Alberg, S.J., '87, *Japan;* Bro. Clyde C. Croy, S.J., *Belize;* Revs. Kevin L. Cullen, S.J., '86, *Uganda;* Leonard E. Dieckman, S.J., '62, *Belize;* Mauricio Gaborit, S.J., '78, *Spain;* Vernon R. Heinsz, S.J., '73, *Zimbabwe;* Carl J. Heumann, S.J., '92, *Belize;* John M. Hunthausen, S.J., '70, *Italy;* Daniel A. Kister, S.J., '66, *Korea;* John L. Maher, S.J., '74, *Belize;* Thomas F. Michel, S.J., '67, *Thailand;* Donald J. Murphy, S.J., '61, *Nicaragua;* Joseph A. Murphy, S.J., '73, *South Africa;* Maurice M. Murray, S.J., '66, *Belize;* Joe Tuoc T. Nguyen, S.J., '89, *Taiwan;* Bro. James O. O'Leary, S.J., *Honduras;* Rev. Robert F. O'Toole, S.J., '67, *Italy;* Bro. Lambert B. Otten, S.J.; Revs. Raymond A. Pease, S.J., '68, *Honduras;* Richard D. Perl, S.J., '78, *Belize;* Robert P. Raskowski, S.J., '46, *Belize;* Francis J. Ring, S.J., '47, *Belize;* Frank J. Schmitt, S.J., '83, *Belize;* James M. Short, S.J., '61, *Belize;* Robert A. Simms, S.J., '46, *Belize;* Carl F. Starkloff, S.J., '65, *Canada;* Ricardo Steinmetz, S.J., '55, *Mexico;* John J. Stochl, S.J., '54, *Belize;* Raymond L. Sullivant, S.J., '66, *Spain;* James H. Swetnam, S.J., '58, *Italy;* Bro. Harold A. Teel, S.J., *Belize;* Revs. J. Timothy Thompson, S.J., '70, *Belize;* Thomas M. Valiquette, S.J., '64, *South Africa;* Bro. N. Aloysius Vogt, S.J., *Belize;* Revs. Robert D. Voss, S.J., '72, *Honduras;* Jarrell D. Wade, S.J., '65, *Honduras;* Francis K. Wallace, S.J., '46, *Panama;* John B. Warner, S.J., '74, *Honduras;* Leo F. Weber, S.J., '56, *Belize;* John J. Welch, S.J., '55, *Italy;* Robert A. White, S.J., '62, *Italy;* John H. Willmering, S.J., '68, *Honduras;* John H. Zupez, S.J., '67, *Belize.*

Priests 34; Brothers 3.

SOCIETY OF JESUS: *New England Province,* 771 Harrison Ave., Boston, MA 02118. Tel: 617-266-7233; Fax: 617-536-8074.

Legal Title: *The Society of Jesus of New England;* Revs. William A. Barry, S.J., '62, Prov.; Martin P. MacDonnell, S.J., '66, Mission Dir.

U.S. Religious serving in foreign missions: Most Revs. Lawrence J. Burke, S.J., *Bahamas;* Samuel E. Carter, S.J., *Jamaica;* Revs. Dudley R.C. Adams, S.J., '92, *Jamaica;* Harry W. Ball, S.J., '42, *Jamaica;* John P. Banks, S.J., '51, *Jamaica;* Joseph F. Brennan, S.J., '56, *Jamaica;* Thomas J. Brodley, S.J., '72, *Jamaica;* John J. Bresnahan, S.J., '51, *Jamaica;* Clarence J. Burby, S.J., '67, *Jordan;* Robert B. Campbell, S.J., '57, *Lebanon;* John A. Carty, S.J., '59, *Egypt;* William A. Clark, S.J., '93, *Jamaica;* Bro. Calvin A. Clarke, S.J., *Jamaica;* Revs. Vincent F. Connolly, S.J., '70, *Jamaica;* William A. Connolly, S.J., '46, *Jamaica;* Richard A. Deshaies, S.J., '92, *Jamaica;* John J. Donohue, S.J., '59, *Lebanon;* Thomas J. Fitzpatrick, S.J., '68, *Jordan;* Louis L. Grenier, S.J., '49, *Jamaica,* Paul R. Hayes, S.J., '62, *Bahamas;* Alwyn C. Harry, S.J., '54, *Jamaica;* Vincent P. Kelliher, S.J., '55, *Alaska;* Donald L. Larkin, S.J., '66, *Jamaica;* Michael D. Linden, S.J., '80, *Jamaica;* Joseph A. MacWade, S.J., '61, *Jamaica;* Martin F. McDermott, S.J., '64, *Lebanon;* Andrew H. McFadden, S.J., '52, *Jamaica;* Gerard R. McKeon, S.J., '86, *Jamaica;* Gerald L. McLaughlin, S.J., '59, *Jamaica;* Oliver E. Nickerson, S.J., '54, *Jamaica;* Kevin G. O'Connell, S.J., '69, *Jordan;* Joseph V. Owens, S.J., '71, *Honduras;* Normand A. Pepin, S.J., '63, *Alaska;* Leo F. Quinlan, S.J., '45, *Jamaica;* Francis J. Ryan, S.J., '56, *Jamaica;* Stephen J. Sanford, S.J., '94, *Jamaica;* Thomas H. Schneider, S.J., '79, *Jamaica;* Martin J. Schade, S.J., '88, *Jamaica;* Paul A. Schweitzer, S.J., '70, *Brazil;* Gregory C. Sharkey, S.J., '88, *Nepal;* James F. Sheehan, S.J., '61, *Bahamas;* Lester O. Shields, S.J., '94, *Jamaica;* David A. Skelskey, S.J., '80, *Ethiopia;* John J. Sullivan, S.J., '44, *Jamaica;* Thomas Vallamattam, S.J., '64, *Jamaica;* Maurice B. Walsh, S.J., '46, *Jamaica.*

Bishop 2; Priests 42; Seminarians 1; Brothers 1.

SOCIETY OF JESUS: *New Orleans Province,* 211 Pere Marquette Bldg., New Orleans, LA 70112. Tel: 504-525-4043.

Legal Title: *Jesuit Mission Bureau;* Rev. Edward B. Arroyo, S.J., '75, Prov.

U.S. Religious serving in foreign missions: Revs. Donald G. Bahlinger, S.J., '59, *Paraguay;* Edward G. Benya, S.J., '84, *Brazil;* David C. Borbridge, S.J., '63, *Brazil;* Bro. Anthony S. Coco, S.J., *Brazil;* Revs. Fred Cooley, S.J., '54, *Sri Lanka;* Claude Daly, S.J., '43, *Sri Lanka;* Carlos E. de la Cruz, S.J., '75, *Paraguay;* Alfonso Del Marmol, S.J., '51, *Sri Lanka;* Edward J. Dougherty, S.J., '70, *Brazil;* A. Gerard Fineran, S.J., '50, *Brazil;* Bro. Robert E. Hollingsworth, S.J., *Brazil;* Revs. O. Kenneth Johnson, '92, *Zambia;* Leo V Leise, S.J., '94, *Paraguay;* Roland J. Lesseps, S.J., '65, *Zambia;* Lloyd Lorio, S.J., '56, *Sri Lanka;* Patrick S. Madigan, S.J., '83, *Zimbabwe;* Francis X. Mayer, S.J., '50, *Sri Lanka;* Joseph H. Meyer, S.J., '46, *Sri Lanka;* Harry Miller, S.J., '54, *Sri Lanka;* Harold J. Rahm, S.J., '50, *Brazil;* David H. Romero, S.J., '91, *Brazil;* Stephen C. Rowntree, S.J., '75, *Kenya;* John F. Schroder, S.J., '53, *Belize;* John Stacer, S.J., '63, *Zimbabwe;* Charles B. Thibodeaux, S.J., '59, *Paraguay;* Bro. Terence N. Todd, S.J., *Micronesia;* Rev. Harold J. Weber, S.J., '44, *Sri Lanka.*

Priests 27; Brothers 3; Scholastics 1.

SOCIETY OF JESUS: *New York Province,* 39 E. 83rd St., New York, NY 10028. Tel: 212-774-5500. Revs. Kenneth J. Gavin, S.J., '75, Prov.; William T. Wood, S.J., '48, Asst. Prov.-International Apostolates.

U.S. Religious serving in foreign missions: Revs. William M. Abbott, S.J., '72, *Philippines;* Gerald W. Aman, S.J., '73, *Nigeria;* Charles J. Beirne, S.J., '69, *El Salvador;* Henry J. Bertels, S.J., '62, *Rome;* Joseph E. Billotti, S.J., '63, *Micronesia;* Joseph H. Bittner, S.J., '39, *Philippines;* Kenneth C. Bogart, S.J., '56, *Philippines;* Robert A. Bomeisl, S.J., '52, *Philippines;* James J. Bowes, S.J., '66, *Micronesia;* J. Dean Brackley, S.J., '76, *El Salvador;* Gary J. Bradley, S.J., '75, *Micronesia;* Philip J. Calderone, S.J., '56, *Philippines;* John J. Carroll, S.J., '55, *Philippines;* Joseph A. Cavanagh, S.J., '62, *Micronesia;* John E. Chambers, S.J., '64, *Philippines;* Arthur A. Clarke, S.J., '47, *Puerto Rico;* Francis X. Clark, S.J., '43, *Philippines;* James P. Croghan, S.J., '85, *Micronesia;* John J. Curran, S.J., '59, *Micronesia;* Francis J. Cusimano, S.J., '68, *Nigeria;* Theodore E. Daigler, S.J., '36, *Philippines;* Vincent P. DeCola, S.J., '88, *Micronesia;* Francis C. Dolan, S.J., '60, *Philippines;* James F. Donelan, S.J., '53, *Philippines;* Martin Doyle, S.J., '91, *Micronesia;* Gaston Duchesneau, S.J., '44, *Philippines;* Robert J. Dullahan, S.J., '57, *Nigeria;* James P. Dunne, S.J., *Philippines;* Paul V. Finster, S.J., '45, *Philippines;* Robert J. Flynn, S.J., '50, *Japan;* Matthew N. Fullam, S.J., '42, *Philippines;* Joseph A. Galdon, S.J., '59, *Philippines;* Pasquale T. Giordano, S.J., '72, *Philippines;* Francis N. Glover, S.J., '58, *Philippines;* Very Rev. James C. Gould, S.J., '74, *Micronesia, Pref. Apostolic, Marshall Islands;* Revs. George R. Graziano, S.J., '59, *Japan;* Thomas H. Green, S.J., '63, *Philippines;* Leonard G. Hacker, S.J., '47, *Micronesia;* John J. Halligan, S.J., '61, *Ecuador;* Robert E. Hamm, S.J., '68, *Nigeria;* William L. Hayes, S.J., '44, *Philippines;* Gerald W. Healy, S.J., '46, *Philippines;* Victor J. Helly, S.J., '54, *Philippines;* William J. Hendricks, S.J., '64, *Puerto Rico;* Very Rev. Francis X. Hezel, S.J., '66, *Micronesia;* Revs. Kenneth J. Hezel, S.J., '66, *Micronesia;* Michael P. Hilbert, S.J., '83, *Rome;* Donald J. Hinfey, S.J., '63, *Ghana;* Robert C. Hogan, S.J., '64, *Philippines;* Raymond T. Holscher, S.J., '72, *Philippines;* Brendan R. Horan, S.J., '93, *Nigeria;* Paul J. Horgan, S.J., '68, *Micronesia;* Joseph A. Johnston, S.J., '52, *Australia;* William P. Klintworth, S.J., '61, *Philippines;* J. Gordon Koller, S.J., '42, *Philippines;* John G. Krebs, S.J., '65, *Philippines;* William H. Kreutz, S.J., '69, *Philippines;* Bartholomew P. Lahiff, S.J., '55, *Philippines;* Dennis M. Leder, S.J., '76, *Guatemala;* Francis C. Madigan, S.J., '49, *Philippines;* Paul J. Maher, S.J., '64, *Nigeria;* Donald C. Maldari, S.J., '85, *Haiti;* William J. Malley, S.J., '64, *Philippines;* John J. Madden, S.J., '69, *Nigeria;* Richard R. McAuliff, S.J., '92, *Micronesia;* Daniel F. McCoy, S.J., '45, *Japan;* James A. McDonough, S.J., '41, *Guam;* Francis X. McFarland, S.J., '50, *Ghana;* William J. McGarry, S.J., '58, *Micronesia;* Thomas B. McGrath, S.J., '64, *Tanzania;* Gerald J. McIntyre, S.J., '74, *Zimbabwe;* James A. McKeough, S.J., '54, *Philippines;* Daniel J. McNamara, S.J., '80, *Philippines;* James T. Meehan, S.J., '63, *Philippines;* Michael D. Moga, S.J., '64, *Philippines;* John F. Moran, S.J., '57, *Philippines;* Gregory F. Muckenhaupt, S.J., '88, *Micronesia;* Daniel J. Mulhauser, S.J., '60, *Micronesia;* Ugo R. Nacciarone, S.J., '64, *Zambia;* Most Rev. Martin J. Neylon, S.J., *Micronesia;* Revs. James J. O'Brien, S.J., '59, *Philippines;* Joseph F. O'Brien, S.J., '44, *Philippines;* James O'Donnell, S.J., '61, *Philippines;* Thomas H. O'Gorman, S.J., '63, *Philippines;* Thomas J. O'Shaughnessy, S.J., '44, *Philippines;* John J. Phelan, S.J., '58, *Philippines;* Calvin H. Poulin, S.J., '62, *Kenya;* Neil C. Poulin, S.J., '66, *Micronesia;* George W. Quickley, S.J., '80, *Nigeria;* William J. Rakowicz, S.J., '80, *Micronesia;* Francis E. Reilly, S.J., '53, *Philippines;* James B. Reuter, S.J., '46, *Philippines;* Robert A. Rice, S.J., '53, *Philippines;* Joseph L. Roche, S.J., '58, *Philippines;* Michael F. Rooney, S.J., '72, *Philippines;* Robert T. Rush, S.J., '59, *Japan;* John J. Ryan, S.J., '67, *Nigeria;* Patrick J. Ryan, S.J., '68, *Ghana;* Ramon A. Salomone, S.J., '65, *Nigeria;* Ronald W. Sams, S.J., '59, *Micronesia;* William J. Scanlon, S.J., '70, *Nigeria;* William J. Schmitt, S.J., '58, *Philippines;* Peter Schineller, S.J., '70, Supr., *Nigeria-Ghana Region;* Herbert Schneider, S.J., '70, *Philippines;* John N. Schumacher, S.J., '57, *Philippines;* Arthur F. Shea, S.J., '38, *Philippines;* John R. Sheehan, S.J., '92, *Nigeria;* Paul M. Sheehan, S.J., '52, *Philippines;* Joseph J. Smith, S.J., '57, *Philippines;* Thomas B. Steinbugler, S.J., '61, *Philippines;* James P. Stehr, S.J., '75, *Nigeria;* John A. St. George, S.J., '52, *Rome;* Robert J. Suchan, S.J., '56, *Philippines;* William T. Suchan, S.J., '58, *Micronesia;* Patrick J. Sullivan, '71, *Guam;* William M. Sullivan, S.J., '66, *Micronesia;* John F. Talbot, S.J., '59, *Puerto Rico;* Terence N. Todd, S.J., *Micronesia;* Dominic J. Totaro, S.J., '67, *Nigeria;* Donald M. Vega, S.J., '65, *Puerto Rico;* Juan C. Villegas, S.J., '75, *Colombia;* Robert P. Walsh, S.J., '60, *Philippines;* Charles E. Wolf, S.J., '46, *Philippines.*

Priests 91; Brothers 2; Scholastics 1.

SOCIETY OF JESUS: *Oregon Province,* 2222 N.W. Hoyt, Portland, OR 97210. Tel: 503-227-1174.

Legal Title: *American Jesuits in Africa;* Revs. Robert B. Grimm, S.J., '76, Prov.; Charles E. Schmitz, S.J., '72, Mission Dir.

U.S. Religious serving in foreign missions: Revs. Arnold R. Beezer, S.J., '64, *Honduras;* Thomas J. Bunnell, S.J., '74, *Peru;* Joseph B. Danel, S.J., '52, *Zambia;* John V. Hennessy, S.J., '72, *China;* Peter J. Henriot, S.J., '70, *Zambia;* Ronald E. Hidaka, S.J., '74, *Zambia;* William J. Loyens, S.J., '58, *Malawi;* James P. McGloin, S.J., '74, *Zambia;* Howard L. Morrison, S.J., '58, *Zambia;* Bartholomew J. Murphy, S.J., '72, *Kenya;* John J. O'Leary, S.J., '60, *Zambia;* Michael J. Schultheis, S.J., '65, *Brazil;* Joseph H. Small, S.J., '60, *Kenya;* Roy W. Thaden, S.J., '73, *Zambia;* Peter R. Titland, S.J., '70, *Zambia.*

Priests 15.

SOCIETY OF JESUS: *Wisconsin Province,* 3400 W. Wisconsin Ave., P.O. Box 08277, Milwaukee, WI 53208. Tel: 414-937-6949; Fax: 414-937-6950.

Legal Title: *Jesuit Mission Service, Inc.;* Revs. D. Edward Mathie, S.J., '68, Prov.; James E. Grummer, S.J., '82, Mission Dir.

U.S. Religious serving in foreign missions: Revs. Francis X. Buchmeier, S.J., '73, *Korea;* William J. Callahan, S.J., '72, *Uganda;* John V. Daly, S.J., '66, *Korea;* Emil J. Denemark, S.J., '81, *Korea;* Robert W. Dundon, S.J., '69, *Nigeria;* Jonathan Haschka, S.J., '75, *Kenya;* Francis E. Hogan, S.J., '47, *Honduras;* Daniel J. Kenney, S.J., '63, *Kenya;* Robert J. Kelly, S.J., '52, *Korea;* Eugene C. Kollasch, S.J., '59, *Korea;* John D. Mace, S.J., '68, *Philippines;* Peter E.

Marchetti, S.J., '77, *Nicaragua;* Francis H. Mathy, S.J., '58, *Japan;* Robert K. McIntosh, S.J., '72, *Korea;* Charles C. Murphy, S.J., '62, *Kenya;* Philip E. Pick, S.J., '50, *Honduras;* Basil M. Price, S.J., '54, *Korea;* Robert P. Raszkowski, S.J., '46, *Belize;* Francis J. Ring, S.J., '47, *Belize;* John R. Schak, S.J., '61, *Argentina;* Nicholas E. Schiel, S.J., '55, *Honduras;* Christopher A. Spalatin, S.J., '71, *Korea;* Norbert J. Tracy, S.J., '55, *Korea;* Anthony J. Wach, S.J., '72, *Uganda.*

Priests 23.

Maryknoll (M.M.)

A community of American secular priests and brothers. Established in 1911 by action of the United States Hierarchy. Authorized by Pope Pius X, with later approvals by Pope Benedict XV and Pope Pius XI.

U.S. Foundation: *Maryknoll Society Center & Administrative Offices,* Catholic Foreign Mission Society of America, P.O. Box 303, Maryknoll, NY 10545-0303. Tel: 914-941-7590; Fax: 914-762-0316. Revs. Raymond J. Finch, M.M., '76, Supr. Gen.; Jeremiah R. Burr, M.M., '67, Vicar Gen.; Thomas P. Henehan, M.M., '65, Asst. Gen.; Michael J. Snyder, M.M., '78, Asst. Gen.; Bro. Wayne J. Fitzpatrick, M.M., aSST. Gen.

The Society is incorporated in New York, under the legal title; *Catholic Foreign Mission Society of America, Incorporated.* It is also incorporated in California, Hawaii, Illinois, Massachusetts, Minnesota, Missouri, and New Jersey. Revs. Kenneth F. Thesing, M.M., '69, Pres.; Leo B. Shea, M.M., '66, Vice Pres.

For detailed information regarding statistics, activities in the Archdioceses and Dioceses in the United States, Properties owned or sponsored and Houses in the United States, and the placement of the Maryknollers in the various Archdioceses and Dioceses, please refer to the sections for Religious Institutes of Men and the designated Archdioceses and Dioceses.

Maryknoll Foreign Missions

Maryknollers serving overseas:

Religious serving in Tanzania: Revs. John C. Sivalon, M.M., '75, Regional Supr.; Louis I. Bayless, M.M., '46; J. Ernest Brunelle, M.M., '59; John P. Casey, M.M., '56; James A. Conard, M.M., '56; William F. Daley, M.M., '56; Marvin F. Deutsch, M.M., '57; James E. Eble, M.M., '88; John W. Eybel, M.M., '70; Paul E. Fagan, M.M., '60; J. Francis Flynn, M.M., '52; Herbert T. Gappa, M.M., '68; Joseph G. Healey, M.M., '66; Richard A. Hochwalt, M.M., '51; Robert A. Jalbert, M.M., '79; Leo R. Kennedy, M.M., '59; James W. Lehr, M.M., '53; Ramon J. McCabe, M.M., '56; Howard E. O'Brien, M.M., '55; Daniel F. Ohmann, M.M., '55; Edward J. Quinn, M.M., '51; Joseph A. Reinhart, M.M., '50; David J. Schwinghamer M.M., '73; Thomas J. Shea, M.M., '67; David A. Smith, M.M., '85; Michael J. Snyder, M.M., '79; William S. Stanley, M.M., '92; Kenneth J. Sullivan, M.M., '57; Donald F. Sybertz, M.M., '55; Thomas A. Tiscornia, M.M., '73; John W. Waldrep, M.M., '90.

Priests 31; Brothers 4.

Religious serving in Bangladesh: Revs. Robert T. McCahill, M.M., '64, Unit Coord.; William J. McIntire, M.M., '67; Douglas F. Venne, M.M., '59.

Priests 3.

Religious serving in Bolivia: Most Rev. Charles A. Brown, M.M. D.D., Auxiliary Bishop of Santa Cruz; Revs. Thomas A. McBride, M.M., '57, Regional Supr.; Donald Allen, M.M., '69; Denis P. Browne, M.M., '47; William J. Coy, M.M., '55; James W. Fitzgerald, M.M., '50; Gorden N. Fritz, M.M., '42; Bernard R. Garrity, M.M., '47; John F. Gorski, M.M., '63; Michael A. Gould, M.M., '54; Sigmund S. Jamroz, M.M., '66; Francis T. McGourn, M.M., '64; Paul A. O'Brien, M.M., '59; John J. Ogurchock, M.M., '54; Arthur J. Prall, M.M., '52; William Senger, M.M., '73.

Priests 15; Brothers 3.

Religious serving in Brazil: Revs. Daniel F. McLaughlin, '61; William F. Marley, M.M., '52; James L. Hilgeman, M.M., M.D., '65; Gerald M. Wickenhauser, M.M., '62, Unit Coord.

Priests 4; Brothers 1; Seminarians 1.

Religious serving in Chile: Revs. Dale F. Barron, M.M., '65; Jeremiah J. Brennan, M.M., '48; Richard L. Brooker, M.M., '55; Joseph H. Cappel, M.M., '35; Joseph R. English, M.M., '44; John J. Gallahue, M.M., '62; Thomas P. Golden, M.M., '51; Frederick J. Hegarty, M.M., '53; Thomas P. Henehan, M.M., '65; John A. Jensen, M.M., '44; Ernest C. Lukaschek, M.M., '64; Elmer J. Meyer, M.M., '54; George F. Painter, M.M., '44; Richard J. Sammon, M.M., '56; J. Lawrence Schanberger, M.M., '49; Eugene W. Toland, M.M., '64; James R. Weckesser, M.M., '55.

Priests 17; Brothers 2.

Religious serving in El Salvador: Revs. Thomas R. Amarillas, M.M., '68; William M. Boteler, M.M., '68; David C. Kelly, M.M., '57.

Priests 3.

Religious serving in Guatemala: Revs. Brian V. Allbright, M.M., '83; Paul D. Belliveau, M.M., '69; Leon L. Connolly (Iowa), '58; Robert F. Crohan, M.M., '62; Thomas P. Fox, M.M., '56; Francis J. Garvey, M.M., '43; Joseph W. Halpin, M.M., '52; Ronald W. Hennessey, M.M., '64, Reg. Supr.; James P. LaCoste, M.M., '56; Kevin A. Lynch, M.M., '61; John J. McGovern, M.M., '54; Joseph C. Nerino, M.M., '50; William J. Price, M.M., '56; John J. Ruessmann, M.M., '79.

Priests 13; Brothers 2; Lay Missionaries 1; Associate Priests 1.

Religious serving in Honduras: Revs. John M. Breen, M.M., '51; Robert F. Coyne, M.M., '83; Richard C. Frank, M.M., '53; Alfred C. Courneyer, '85; David E. LaBuda, M.M., '71; Ronald J. Potter, M.M., '61.

Priests 5; Associate Priests 1.

Religious serving in Hong Kong: Revs. John F. Ahearn, M.M., '73; Robert F. Astorino, M.M., '70; Peter J. Barry, M.M., '65; Robert C. Bayne, M.M., '63; Anthony V. Brennan, M.M., '61; Sean P. Burke, M.M., '78; John J. Casey, M.M., '56; John A. Cioppa, M.M., '59; Vincent F. Corbelli, M.M., '60; John P. Cuff, M.M., '69; Laurence A. Dugas, M.M., '54; Stephen B. Edmonds, M.M., '40; Lawrence W. Flynn, M.M., '87; John E. Geitner, M.M., '53; John P. Grady, M.M., '55; William J. Grimm, M.M., '77; Thomas F. Goekler, M.M., '67; Adam B. Gudalefsky, M.M., '59; Denis J. Hanly, M.M., '59; Matthew H. Kelleher, M.M., '67; Timothy Kilkelly, M.M., '90; Michael J. McKeirnan, M.M., '41; Edward F. Malone, M.M., '52; Thomas A. Peyton, M.M., '58, Reg. Supr.; Ronald R. Saucci, M.M., '65; Michael J. Sloboda, M.M., '85; John G. Sullivan, M.M., '60; C. Thomas Wilcox, M.M., '51; Elmer P. Wurth, M.M., '56.

Priests 28; Brothers 2.

Religious serving in Indonesia: Revs. Robert F. Baudhuin, M.M., '54; Vincent P. Cole, M.M., '71.

Priests 2.

Religious serving in Japan: Revs. Patrick F. O'Donoghue, M.M., '50, Reg. Supr.; Roy C. Assenheimer, M.M., '65; Richard A. Aylward, M.M., '53; Gerald L. Beausoleil, M.M., '52; Anthony B. Brodniak, M.M., '54; James P. Colligan, M.M., '55; Richard Czajkcwski, M.M., '61; William J. Eggleston, M.M., '47; Gregory J. Gilmartin, M.M., '48; Regis B. Ging, M.M., '66; James H. Gorman, M.M., '52; Kevin J. Hanlon, M.M., '89; Joseph H. Hermes, M.M., '62; James R. Jackson, M.M., '58; Walter T. Kelleher, M.M., '56; Joseph V. Maynard, M.M., '48; James J. Mylet, M.M., '75; Robert V. Nehrig, M.M., '54; Bryce T. Nishimura, M.M., '56; James K. Nishimuta, M.M., '54; James W. O'Neill, M.M., '55; Francis A. Riha, M.M., '68; Kenneth C. Sleyman, M.M., '90; Donald J. Vittengl, M.M., '56; Clarence J. Witte, M.M., '35; Louis J. Wolken, M.M., '46; Robert R. Zahn, M.M., '55.

Priests 26; Brothers 1; Seminarians 1.

Religious serving in Kenya: Revs. Richard M. Baker, M.M., '71; Lionel A. Bouffard, M.M., '63; Francis J. Breen, M.M., '70; Thomas J. Burke, M.M., '55; Donald F. Donovan, M.M., '55; Michael J. Duffy, M.M., '64; William Fryda, M.M., '88; Carroll B. Houle, M.M., '62, Reg. Supr.; William T. Knipe, M.M., '58; Michael C. Kirwen, M.M., '63; James J. Kuhn, M.M., '51; John J. Lange, M.M., '58; Philip F. McCue, M.M., '58; Edwin Metzer (Pennsylvania), '55; Edward J. Phillips, M.M., '74; Thomas C. Petronek (Ohio), '65; Richard J. Quinn, M.M., '54; James R. Roy, M.M., '61; Richard P. Smith, M.M., '76; Robert W. Vujs, M.M., '61; Maurice J. Zerr, M.M., '51.

Priests 19; Brothers 6; Associate Priests 2.

Religious serving in Korea: Most Rev. William J. McNaughton, M.M., D.D., Bishop of Inchon; Revs. Roman G. Theisen, M.M., '54, Reg. Supr.; Richard Agustin, M.M., '85; Francis H. Beninati, M.M., '55; Carl A. Costa, M.M., '71; Thomas R. Egan, M.M., '64; Gerald J. Farrell, M.M., '57; Russell J. Feldmeier, M.M., '80; Alfred J. Fleming, M.M., '60; James M. Gilligan, M.M., '55; Gerard E. Hammond, M.M., '60; Robert M. Lilly, M.M., '60; Philip W. Mares, M.M., '86; John P. Meehan, M.M., '59; James J. Najmowski, M.M., '76; Gerald P. O'Connor, M.M., '69; Fernand Paquet, M.M., '56; Robert R. Pellini, M.M., '59; David L. Pfeiffer, M.M., '66; Richard S. Rolewicz, M.M., '65; James P. Sinnott, M.M., '60; Joseph A. Slaby, M.M., '66; John F. Soltis, M.M., '62; Edward J. Whelan, M.M., '61; Michael O. Zunno, M.M., '53.

Priests 24.

Religious serving in Mexico: Revs. Richard L. Clifford, M.M., '53; Francis W. Collins, M.M., '49; Roman A. Kasprzak, M.M., '51; Martin P. Keegan, M.M., '65; Melvin E. Krumdick, M.M., '69; Thomas E. Lavelle, M.M., '55, Reg. Supr.; John P. Lomasney, M.M., '43; John P. Martin, M.M., '66, Reg. Supr.; John R. McGuire, M.M., '43; Charles A. Murray, M.M., '51; Peter J. Petrucci, M.M., '49; Thomas C. Saunders, M.M., '65; Eugene A. Theisen, M.M., '53; Robert E. Tobin, M.M., '57.

Priests 13; Brothers 1.

Religious serving in the Middle East Unit: Revs. John F. Felago, M.M., '68, Unit Coord.; Lance P. Nadeau, M.M., '90.

Priests 2; Brothers 3.

Religious serving in Nicaragua: Rev. John C. Moynihan, M.M., '67.

Priests 1.

Religious serving in Peru: Revs. Michael J. Briggs, M.M., '76; Thomas J. Burns, M.M., '69; Bernard P. Byrne, M.M., '56; Charles H. Cappel, M.M., '44; Edmund L. Cookson, M.M., '65; James L. Christiansen, M.M., '81; Patrick J. Donovan, M.M., '57; Philip N. Erbland, M.M., '66; Joseph L. Finan, M.M., '79; Raymond J. Finch, M.M., '76, Reg. Supr.; Joseph A. Farrell, M.M., '59; Thomas F. Garrity, M.M., '46; W. Robert Golish, M.M., '53; Joseph L. Hamel, M.M., '85; Robert E. Hoffman, M.M., '60; Robert A. Hurteau, M.M., '89; Joseph A. Kowalczyk, M.M., '61; Richard G. Laszewski, M.M., '51; James Lynch, M.M., '74; Gerard T. McCrane, M.M., '59; Martin F. Murphy, M.M., '51; James M. O'Brien, M.M., '49; James V. Roth, M.M., '54; James J. Stefaniak, M.M., '50.

Priests 24; Brothers 1.

Religious serving in the Philippine Islands: Revs. Jeremiah R. Burr, M.M., '67; Herman W. Cisek, M.M., '65; John F. Coholan, M.M., '46; Robert L. Depinet, M.M., '61; Francis J. Felter, M.M., '69; James T. Ferry, M.M., '56; William P. Heffernan, M.M., '55; James C. Kalchthaler, M.M., '56; Ralph S. Kroes, M.M., '58; William J. LaRousse, M.M., '80; James D. McAuley, M.M., '80; Donald P. McQuade, M.M., '65; Walter J. Maxcy, M.M., '47; John B. Northrop, M.M., '74; Roberto Rodriguez, M.M., '95; Clyde Philipps, M.M., '78, Reg. Supr.; Edward D. Shellito, M.M., '80; J. David Sullivan, M.M., '60; John D. Walsh, M.M., '56.

Priests 19; Brothers 2.

Religious serving in Taiwan: Revs. Alan T. Doyle, M.M., '64, Reg. Supr.; Kurt J. Anderson, M.M., '72; James V. Buttino, M.M., '47; Michael G. Collins, M.M., '59; Robert F. Crawford, M.M., '61; Richard M. Devoe, M.M., '56; Richard E. Downey, M.M., '44; Alan T. Doyle, M.M., '64; Clarence A. Engler, M.M., '59; Edward J. Flanigan, M.M., '56; Albert V. Fedders, M.M., '37; Donald F. Glover, M.M., '70; Delos A. Humphrey, M.M., '54; John B. Keaney, M.M., '55; Raymond H. Kelley, M.M., '58; John F. Kennedy, M.M., '55; Lawrence F. McCulloch, M.M., '70; J. Donald McGinnis, M.M., '53; John P. McKernan, M.M., '52; James T. Manning, M.M., '48; Leonard J. Marron, M.M., '57; John J. Moran, M.M., '66; Eugene M. Murray, M.M., '58; Nhuan D. Nguyen, M.M., '93; Brendan M. O'Connell, M.M., '63; Francis T. O'Donnell, M.M., '55; Norbert A. Pacheco, M.M., '79; Anthony V. Polyak, M.M., '62; Carroll I. Quinn, M.M., '45; Francis Rebol, M.M., '53; Louis B. Rost, M.M., '55; Francis F. Schexnayder, M.M., '64; R. Russell Sprinkle, M.M., '35; Peter A. Wu, M.M., '61; Richard E. Zeimet, M.M., '64.

Priests 34; Seminarians 1.

Religious serving in Thailand: Revs. John C. Barth, M.M., '91; Daniel A. Boyd, M.M., '82; Thomas J. Dunleavy, M.M., '75; Roberto T. Fuentes, M.M., '92; James W. Kofski, M.M., '91; James P. Noonan, M.M., '60, Unit Coord.; Thomas J. O'Brien, M.M., '74; William T. O'Leary, M.M., '61; Thomas E. Pesaresi, M.M., '85; Lawrence D. Radice, M.M., '85; Charles P. Robak, M.M., '70.

Priests 11; Brothers 2.

Religious serving in Samoa: Most Rev. J. Quinn Weitzel, M.M.

Priests 1; Brothers 2.

Religious serving in Venezuela: Revs. Thomas Ahearn, M.M., '68, Unit Coord.; Joseph A. Heim, M.M., '61; James L. Lenihan, M.M., '55; Donald P. McNamara, '61; Kenneth J. Moody, M.M., '70.

Priests 3; Priests Associates 1.

Religious serving in Italy: Revs. Joseph V. McCabe, M.M., '77; Robert F. Lefebvre, M.M., '57, Procurator, *Collegio Maryknoll,* Via Sardegna 83, Rome, Italy, 00187.

Priests 2.

Missionaries of Africa (M.Afr.)

Missionaries of Africa Foreign Missions

U.S. HEADQUARTERS: *Provincial House,* 1624-21 St. N.W., Washington, DC 20009-1055. Tel: 202-232-5154; Fax: 202-332-8640. Rev. William Moroney, M.Afr., '61, Prov.

U.S. Religious serving in Africa: Revs. Richard Archambault, M.Afr., '73; John J. Braun, M.Afr., '57; William Curran, M.Afr., '66; Rene Dionne, M.Afr. (Spain), '61; Melvin Doucette, M.Afr., '68; Maurice Gelinas, M.Afr., '41; John Heigl, M.Afr., '59; Roger A. LaBonte, M.Afr., '62; Michel J. Lavoie, M.Afr., '70; John Lynch, M.Afr., '62; J. Philip Reed, M.Afr., '88; Thomas Reilly, M.Afr., '78; Richard Roy, M.Afr., '71; Bros. Vernon Zachman, M.Afr.; Martin Chapper, M.Afr.; James Heintz, M.Afr.

Missionaries of the Sacred Heart (M.S.C.)

Missionaries of the Sacred Heart Foreign Missions

MISSIONARIES OF THE SACRED HEART: P.O. Box 270, 305 S. Lake St., Aurora, IL 60507. Tel: 630-892-2371; 892-8400 (Prov. Supr.); Fax: 630-892-1678. Very Rev. Mark McDonald, M.S.C., '68, Prov. Supr.; Revs. Gerald Paul, M.S.C., '60, Treas.; Raymond Diesbourg, M.S.C., '74, Sec. & Editor, *M.S.C. Spotlite.*

Publication: *M.S.C. Spotlite.*

Religious serving in Papua New Guinea: Revs. Steve Boland, M.S.C., '86; David DeLuca, M.S.C., '66; Henry Einhaus, M.S.C., '60; Bro. Anton Freitas, M.S.C.; Revs. Anthony Gendusa, M.S.C., '40; Joseph Gleixner, M.S.C., '65, Regional Supr.; Bernard Miller, M.S.C., '59; Bros. James Miller, M.S.C.; Patrick O'Hara, M.S.C.; Daniel Rakow, M.S.C.; Joseph Tesar, M.S.C.; Rev. Leon Weisenberger, M.S.C., '59.

Religious serving in Colombia, South America: Very Rev. Howard Fath, M.S.C., '61, Section Supr.; Rev. Wilson Tascon, M.S.C., '90; Joseph Jablonski, M.S.C., '76; Michael Miller, M.S.C., '85; German Barona Monsalve, M.S.C., '86; Tito Medina Mora, M.S.C., '92.

Religious serving in Namibia, Africa: Rev. Francis Westhoff, M.S.C., '35.

Religious serving in Slovakia: Rev. Hilary Fischer, M.S.C., '57.

Missionhurst (C.I.C.M.)

Missionhurst Foreign Missions

AMERICAN HEADQUARTERS (1946): *Congregation of the Immaculate Heart of Mary,* 4651 N. 25th St., Arlington, VA 22207. Tel: 703-528-3800; Fax: 703-528-5355. Rev. Joseph Lapauw, C.I.C.M., '73, Prov. Supr.

Publication: *Missionhurst.*

U.S. Religious serving Abroad: Revs. Vidal Ludan, C.I.C.M., '76, Prov. Supr., *Brazil;* Roy Shea, C.I.C.M., '86, *Brazil;* Bro. Robert Dixon, C.I.C.M., *Brazil;* Revs. Paul Bouchaert, C.I.C.M., '68, Prov. Supr., *Haiti;* Tim Atkins, C.I.C.M., '74, *Haiti;* Bro. Hubert Habets, C.I.C.M., *Haiti;* Revs. Joseph R. Guerrero, C.I.C.M., '85, Prov. Supr., *Guatemala;* Alphonse Rigouts, C.I.C.M., '48, *Guatemala;* Ramon Caluza, C.I.C.M., '79, Prov. Supr., *Dominican Republic;* Stan Szarwark, C.I.C.M., '64, *Dominican Republic;* Paul Delaere, C.I.C.M., '43, *Dominican Republic;* Camilo Boesmans, C.I.C.M., '47, *Dominican Republic;* David Curran, C.I.C.M., '71, *Dominican Republic;* Gerard Rogmans, C.I.C.M., '55, *Dominican Republic;* Bro. Leon Delanoy, C.I.C.M., *Dominican Republic;* Revs. Herman Louwagie, C.I.C.M., '58, Supr., *Mexico;* Thomas Matondo, C.I.C.M., '82, Prov. Supr., *Kinshasa, Zaire;* Bro. Jerry Galloway, C.I.C.M., *Kinshasa, Zaire;* Revs. Ward Van Haegenborgh, C.I.C.M., '55, Prov. Supr., *Belgium;* Jules Spriet, C.I.C.M., '44, *Belgium;* Albert Weyts, C.I.C.M., '44, *Belgium;* Paul Van Houtteghem, C.I.C.M., '48, *Belgium;* Paul VanMalderen, C.I.C.M., '40, *Belgium;* Joseph Verswyvel, C.I.C.M., '52, *Belgium;* Vincent VandeWeyer, C.I.C.M., *Belgium;* Paul Serruys, C.I.C.M., '36; Victor De Clercq, .C.I.C.M., '37, *Belgium;* Marcel Josson, C.I.C.M., '36, *Belgium;* William Missinne, C.I.C.M., '54, *Belgium;* Angel Luciano, C.I.C.M., '72, Prov. Supr., *Philippines;* Luke Moortgat, C.I.C.M., '65, *Philippines;* Ludo Goossens, C.I.C.M., '69, Prov. Supr., *Japan;* John Raymaker, C.I.C.M., '64, *Japan;* Michael Hann, C.I.C.M., '73, *Rome, Italy;* John B. Peters, C.I.C.M., '53, *Rome, Italy.*

American Oblate Missions (O.M.I.)

Home and Foreign Missions of the American Provinces of the Missionary Oblates of Mary Immaculate (Oblate Fathers).

Oblate Conference of the U.S., 8818 Cameron St., Silver Spring, MD 20910. Tel: 301-565-0060; Fax: 301-589-2897. Rev. Seamus Finn, O.M.I., '76, National Coord.

Oblates Foreign Missions

EASTERN PROVINCE: 391 Michigan Ave., N.E., P.O. Box 29152, Washington, DC 20017. Tel: 202-529-5958; Fax: 202-636-9444. Very Rev. William Sheehan, O.M.I., '58, Prov.

Publication: *The Oblate World.*

SOUTHERN PROVINCE: 7711 Madonna Dr., San Antonio, TX 78216. Tel: 210-349-1475; Fax: 210-349-7411. Very Rev. Eugene Canas, O.M.I., '64, Prov.

Publication: *Province Newsletter.*

NORTHERN U.S. PROVINCE: 61 Burns Hill Rd., Hudson, NH 03051. Tel: 603-883-3233; Fax: 603-883-6089. Very Rev. George G. Capen, O.M.I., '59, Prov.; Rev. Charles Breault, O.M.I., '59, Treas.

Publication: *Oblate World, Oblate Foreign Missions,* 46 Mt. Washington St., Lowell, MA 01854-3498. Tel: 508-458-4380; Fax: 508-454-5308. Bro. Augustin Cote, O.M.I., Dir.; Revs. Bernard Belley, O.M.I., '54; Real Bourque, O.M.I., '54; Adhemar Deveau, O.M.I., '52, Treas.; Henri Lavallee, O.M.I., '54.

CENTRAL PROVINCE: 267 E. 8th, St. Paul, MN 55101. Tel: 612-292-8622; Fax: 612-292-8769. Very Rev. David Kalert, O.M.I., '64, Prov.

Publications: *Oblates,* 15 S. 59th St., Belleville, IL 62222.

WESTERN PROVINCE: 14065 Nordhoff St., Arleta, CA 91331. Tel: 818-891-0579; Fax: 818-893-9819. Very Rev. David Ullrich, O.M.I., '71, Prov.; Rev. Edward J. Collins, O.M.I., '46, Mission Procurator, 1109 Coronel St., San Fernando, CA 91340.

U.S. Religious serving in the Philippines Islands: Most Rev. Philip Smith, O.M.I., Archbishop of Cotabato; Most Rev. George Dion, O.M.I., Bishop of Jolo (Retired); Revs. Armand Carignan, O.M.I., '53; Maurice Hemann, O.M.I., '50; Richard Pommier, O.M.I., '66; Charles Prass, O.M.I., '45; Robert Sullivan, O.M.I., '41; Cletus Ternes, O.M.I., '61; Richard Weixelman, O.M.I., '65.

U.S. Religious serving in Haiti: Revs. Richard Bolduc, O.M.I., '64; Alfred Charpentier, O.M.I., '71; Real Corriveau, O.M.I., '61; Omer Duplessis, O.M.I., '43; Roger Hallee, O.M.I., '63, Prov.; John Henault, O.M.I., '63; Roland Gagnon, O.M.I., '51; Charles Heon, O.M.I., '64; Leroy Landry, O.M.I., '61; Albert Lirette, O.M.I., '45; Raymond Marquis, O.M.I., '74; Francis Mitchell, O.M.I., '44; Roger Paradis, O.M.I., '48; Mauril Rancourt, O.M.I., '60; John St. Cyr, O.M.I., '61; Andre Tanguay, O.M.I., '53; Joseph Vaillancourt, O.M.I., '46.

U.S. Religious serving in Tahiti: Rev. Roger Roy, O.M.I., '49.

U.S. Religious serving in Indonesia: Rev. Lucien Bouchard, O.M.I., '55.

U.S. Religious serving in Brazil: Very Rev. James Gibbons, O.M.I., '69, Prov.; Revs. Roger Bergkamp, O.M.I., '64; Thomas Brown, O.M.I., '55; Peter Curran, O.M.I., '71; Thomas Delaney, O.M.I., '60; John Drexel, O.M.I., '62; Edward Figueroa, O.M.I., '60; Robert Fitzpatrick, O.M.I., '71; Bro. Daniel Hayes, O.M.I.; Very Rev. Bruce Heit, O.M.I., '64, Vicar Prov.; Revs. James Kohmetscher, O.M.I., '55; Edmund Leising, O.M.I., '46; William Lindkugel, O.M.I., '45; Louis Lougen, O.M.I., '79; Gerald McGovern, O.M.I., '57; Paul Medeiros, O.M.I., '64; Robert Mayer, O.M.I., '67; Daniel Meehan, O.M.I., '61; David O'Brien, O.M.I., '59; Thomas O'Brien, O.M.I., '55; Robert Reardon, O.M.I., '68; William Reinhard, O.M.I., '61; Anthony Rendon, O.M.I., '67; William Sheehan, O.M.I., '42; James Sullivan, O.M.I., '53; Charles Tierney, O.M.I., '73.

U.S. Religious serving in Canada: Revs. Richard G. Cote, O.M.I., '60; Normand Bonneau, O.M.I., '76.

U.S. Religious serving in Japan: Very Rev. John Mahoney, O.M.I., '54, Prov.; Revs. Raymond Bourgoin, O.M.I., '66; John Deely, O.M.I., '70; Francis Hahn, O.M.I., '72; Richard Harr, O.M.I., '52; Ronald Laframboise, O.M.I., '67; Thomas Maher, O.M.I., '57; William Maher, O.M.I., '66; Jerome Novotney, O.M.I., '68; Angelo Siani, O.M.I., '65, Prov.; Bertram Silver, O.M.I., '54; Edward Williams, O.M.I., '57.

U.S. Religious serving in Mexico: Revs. Carlos DeAnta, O.M.I., '50; Philip Ehrhardt, O.M.I., '27; Daniel Gagnon, O.M.I., '87; Robert Hickl, O.M.I., '79; Richard Junius, O.M.I., '56; Edwin Krzewinski, O.M.I., '52; Ernest Liekens, O.M.I., '61; Vincent Louwagie, O.M.I., '68; James Lyons, O.M.I.; Curtis Moffat, O.M.I.; Augustine Petru, O.M.I., '53; Francis Pfeifer, O.M.I.; Gilberto Pinon, O.M.I., '71; Gregorio Ramos, O.M.I., '50; Raymond Schoenstein, O.M.I.; John Schwider, O.M.I., '40; Jose Torres, O.M.I., '74; Robert Ward, O.M.I., '61; George Protopapas, O.M.I., '43; Gerald Kapustka, O.M.I., '65, *Guatemala.*

Religious in Scandinavian Missions: Bros. Olof Asblom, O.M.I.; Daniel Bozek, O.M.I.; Revs. Michael Bradley, O.M.I., '66; Allen Courteau, O.M.I., '76; Urban Figge, O.M.I., '67; Franz Hoyos, O.M.I., '86; Frank Jobst, O.M.I., '72; Leo Kertz, O.M.I., '63; Thomas M. Killeen, O.M.I., '58; Lon Konold, O.M.I., '77; Alex Kons, O.M.I., '55; Paul Marx, O.M.I., '65; Carroll Parker, O.M.I., '61; Clyde Rausch, O.M.I., '68; John Schoeberle, O.M.I., '61; Karl Smeenk, O.M.I., '50; Per Waago, O.M.I. Eric Westerberg, O.M.I., '86; Gerald Orsino, O.M.I., '66, *Bangkok, Thailand.*

U.S. Religious serving in Zambia: Revs. Paul Duffy, O.M.I., '62; Patrick Gizten, O.M.I., '75; Jack Joyce, O.M.I., '61; Edward R. Matthews, O.M.I., '84; John Staak, O.M.I., '95; Brian Walker, O.M.I., '; Ronald Walker, O.M.I., '61.

Oblates of St. Francis de Sales Missions (O.S.F.S.)

Oblates of St. Francis de Sales Foreign Missions

U.S. MISSION HEADQUARTERS: *Office of the Mission Procurator Oblates of St. Francis de Sales,* 1801 N. Broom St., Wilmington, DE 19802. Revs. Francis D. Dougherty, O.S.F.S., '38, Procurator. Tel: 302-652-3202. John J. Hurley, O.S.F.S., '68, Procurator. Tel: 302-654-2238. Francis J. Gross, O.S.F.S., Mission Procurator, Toledo-Detroit Prov., 69 O'Hara Rd., Tonawanda, NY 14150. Tel: 716-694-4950.

U.S. Religious serving in Africa & South America: Revs. Leon V. Bonikowski, O.S.F.S., '65; George J. Brownholtz, O.S.F.S., '69; Edward P. Canavan, O.S.F.S.; John J. Coyne, O.S.F.S., '71; Walter DeSa, O.S.F.S.; Walter J. Hartlove, O.S.F.S., '48; Peter J. Harvey, O.S.F.S., '60; Robert J. Hindley, O.S.F.S., '58; Most Rev. John B. Minder, O.S.F.S., D.D.; Revs. Michael Moore, O.S.F.S.; Edmund F. O'Rourke, O.S.F.S.; Harry J. Schlight, O.S.F.S., '44; Most Rev. Edward J. Schlotterback, O.S.F.S., D.D.; Revs. Alfred J. Smuda, O.S.F.S., '66; Joseph A. Travers, O.S.F.S.

American Passionist Missions (C.P.)

Passionist Foreign Missions

Home and Foreign Missions of the American Provinces of the Congregation of the Passion.

GENERAL MOTHERHOUSE: SS. Giovanni e Paolo 13, Rome, 00184. Italy. Most Rev. Jose Augustin Orbegozo, C.P., Supr. Gen.

Provincial Headquarters U.S.A.

ST. PAUL OF THE CROSS PROVINCE: *Province Pastoral Center,* 80 David St., South River, NJ 08882. Tel:

908-257-7177. Very Rev. Robert Joerger, C.P., '77, Prov. Supr.; Very Rev. Lucian Clark, C.P., '65, Dir. of Ministries.

U.S. Religious Serving Abroad: Rev. Richard Award, C.P., '81, *West Indies;* Bro. Louis Bouchard, C.P., *Philippines;* Revs. Thomas Brislin, C.P., '68, *Bahamas;* Bertram Chin, C.P., '91, *West Indies;* Herbert Eberly, C.P., '58, *Philippines;* Henry Free, C.P., '58, *Philippines;* Angelo Iacovone, C.P., '46, *Bahamas;* Aelred Lacomara, C.P., '57, *Africa;* Richard Leary, C.P., '46, *West Indies;* Bernard McEachern, C.P., '64, *Philippines;* Bro. Robert McKenna, C.P., *Philippines;* Revs. Bonaventure Moccia, C.P., '52, *Rome;* Peter O'Rourke, C.P., '64, *New Guinea;* David Roberts, C.P., '52, *Bahamas;* Bro. Michael Stomber, C.P., *West Indies;* Revs. Martin J. Tooker, C.P., '46, *West Indies;* Hilarion Walters, C.P., '47, *Philippines.*

Priests 16; Brothers 3.

Mission Procurators

EASTERN: Revs. Lucian Clark, C.P., '65, Dir., 80 David St., South River, NJ 08882; Sebastian Kolinovsky, C.P., '51, Passionist Missionaries, Monastery Pl., Union City, NJ 07087. Bro. Leo DiFiore, C.P., Passionist Overseas Missions, 148 Monastery Ave., Pittsburgh, PA 15203.

CANADA: 2102 Kipling Ave., Rexdale, ON M9W 4K5.

PHILIPPINES: Rev. Bernard McEachern, C.P., '64, Procurator, P.O. Box 1290 MCCPO, Metro Manila 1252, Makati.

CHINA: *Passionist Mission Procurator,* Maryknoll House, Stanley, Hong Kong.

HOLY CROSS PROVINCE (WESTERN): *Immaculate Conception Monastery,* 5700 N. Harlem Ave., Chicago, IL 60631. Tel: 773-631-6336; Fax: 773-631-8059. Very Rev. Michael Joseph Stengel, C.P., '57, Prov.; Rev. Luke Connolly, C.P., '52, Mission Appeals.

Mission Procurators

WESTERN: Mr. Edward Scholl, Dir.; Rev. Luke Connolly, C.P., '52, Mission Appeals, *Passionist Missions, Inc.,* 5700 N. Harlem Ave., Chicago, IL 60631. Tel: 773-631-1686; *Procuration Office of Holy Cross Province-Passionist, Missions, Inc.*

JAPAN: Rev. Francis Horack, C.P., '42, *Japan Passionist Missions,* Passionist Community 10-1, Yamatecho, Mefu Takarazuka-shi, Hyogo Prefecture 665. Japan. Tel: 0797 84-3111.

KOREA: Rev. Richard Thomson, C.P., '69, Passionist Vice Provincialate, Tobong P.O. Box 57, Seoul, 132-600. Korea.

INDIA: Rev. Walter Kaelin, C.P., '42, 1924 Newburg Rd., Louisville, KY 40205.

U.S. Religious serving in Japan: Revs. Ward Biddle, C.P., '51; Gabriel Brecheteau, C.P., '48; Francis Horack, C.P., '42; Leonard Kosatka, C.P., '59; Denis McGowan, C.P., '55; Ronan Newbold, C.P., '69; Clement Paynter, C.P., '52; Matthew Vetter, C.P., '38.

Also serving in Japan are the: *Cloistered Passionist Nuns;* Mother Marie Paul, C.P.; Supr.

Sisters 15.

U.S. Religious serving Elsewhere: Revs. Justin Bartoszek, C.P., '64, *Korea;* Richard Thomson, C.P., '69, *Korea;* Bro. Laurence Finn, C.P., *Korea;* Revs. Joseph Moons, C.P., '77, *India;* Joseph Vanleuwen, C.P., '64, *India;* Paul Placek, C.P., '45, *Philippines;* Warren Womack, C.P., '49, *Sweden.*

American Redemptorist Fathers (C.Ss.R.)

Mission of the Provinces and Vice-Provinces in the United States and other countries and lands.

Redemptorist Foreign Missions

BALTIMORE PROVINCE: *Redemptorist Fathers of New York,* 7509 Shore Rd., Brooklyn, NY 11209; Fax: 718-630-5666. Very Rev. George J. Keaveney, C.Ss.R., '66, Prov.

Publication: *Perpetual Help World,* 294 E. 150th St., New York, NY 10051.

U.S. Religious serving in Paraguay: Revs. Antonio Cannoles, C.Ss.R., '69; Robert Hopwood, C.Ss.R., '52; James Lacey, C.Ss.R., '43.

U.S. Religious serving in St. Lucia, W.I.: Revs. John M. Hamrogue, C.Ss.R., '63; John J. O'Toole, C.Ss.R., '53; Joseph E. Bertrand, C.Ss.R., '55; John P. Gallagher, C.Ss.R., '95.

U.S. Religious serving in Dominica, W.I.: Revs. Jerome Moody, C.Ss.R., '73; Rodney J. Olive, C.Ss.R., '86; Joseph F. Krastel, C.Ss.R., '64; John F. Murray, C.Ss.R., '94.

DENVER PROVINCE: P.O. Box 300399, Denver, CO 80203-0399. Tel: 303-370-0036; Fax: 303-370-0036. Very Rev. Richard Thibodeau, C.Ss.R., '76, Prov.; Rev. Gary Heinecke, C.Ss.R., '73, Dir.-Foreign Missions, P.O. Box 6, Glenview, IL 60025. Tel: 847-724-0425; Fax: 847-724-8953.

U.S. Religious serving in Brazil: Revs. Vince Aggeler, C.Ss.R., '58; Joseph Butz, C.Ss.R., '70; Willliam Fitzgerald, C.Ss.R., '43; John Gouger, C.Ss.R., '65; Donnell Kirchner, C.Ss.R., '66; Martin Laumann, C.Ss.R., '76; Patrick McBride, C.Ss.R., '85; John McCarthy, C.Ss.R., '62; Thomas McIntosh, C.Ss.R., '66; Most Rev. Alfred Novak, C.Ss.R., Bishop of Paranagua, Brazil; Most Rev. Gutemberg Regis, C.Ss.R., Bishop of Coari, Brazil; Bro. Leo Patin, C.Ss.R.; Revs. William Steiner, C.Ss.R., '54; Joseph Stenger, C.Ss.R., '57; Andrew Thompson, C.Ss.R., '81; Edward Vella, C.Ss.R., '85; Ronald Weninger, C.Ss.R., '49.

U.S. Religious serving in Thailand: Revs. Charles Beierwaltes, C.Ss.R., '67; Raymond Brennan, C.Ss.R., '59; Charles Cotant, C.Ss.R., '41; Most Rev. Clarence Duhart, C.Ss.R., Retired Bishop; Revs. Francis Gautreaux, C.Ss.R., '50; Joseph Maier, C.Ss.R., '65; Robert Martin, C.Ss.R., '50; Patrick Morrissy, C.Ss.R., '55; Lawrence Patin, C.Ss.R., '63; Most Rev. George Phimphisan, C.Ss.R., Bishop of Udon Thani; Revs. Michael Shea, C.Ss.R., '64; Harold J. Thiel, C.Ss.R., '56; Leo Travis, C.Ss.R., '54; William Wright, C.Ss.R., '60.

U.S. Religious serving in Nigeria: Rev. William M. Cleary, C.Ss.R., '62; Bro. Daniel L. Hall, C.Ss.R.; Revs. William A. Peterson, C.Ss.R., '67; Richard Thiele, C.Ss.R., '54; John Willett, C.Ss.R., '61; Robert Wirth, C.Ss.R., '64.

St. Columban's Foreign Mission Society (S.S.C.)

(THE COLUMBAN FATHERS)

Founded in 1918 with the approval of Pope Benedict XV. Placed under the patronage of St. Columban and made a Pontifical Society by Pope Pius XI.

GENERALATE: *St. Columban's,* Grange Rd., Donaghmede Dublin 13, Ireland. Very Rev. Nicholas Murray, S.S.C., '62, Supr. Gen.

U.S. FOUNDATION & ADMINISTRATION: *Columban Fathers,* St. Columbans, NE 68056. Tel: 402-291-1920. Very Rev. Brendan O'Sullivan, S.S.C., '70, Dir.; Rev. James J. Hastings, S.S.C., '72, Vice Dir.

Publication: *Columban Mission.*

Legal Title: St. Columban's Foreign Mission Society. The Society is incorporated in California, Illinois, Massachusetts, Nebraska, New York, Rhode Island, and Registered in Pennsylvania.

St. Columban's Foreign Mission

HOUSE OF POST-GRADUATE STUDIES: *Collegio Colombano,* Corso Trieste, 57, Roma, 00198. Italy. Very Rev. Padhraic O'Loughlin, S.S.C., '57, Procurator Gen.

U.S. Religious serving Overseas: Revs. Edward A. Allen, S.S.C., '30, *Philippines;* Clarence Beckley, S.S.C., '66, *Brazil;* William D. Bourke, S.S.C., '54, *Philippines;* Thomas Browning, S.S.C., '90, *Taiwan;* John A. Buckley, S.S.C., '68, *Brazil;* John Burger, S.S.C., '73, *Japan;* Vincent J. Busch, S.S.C., '74, *Philippines;* Richard W. Cannon, S.S.C., '54, *Philippines;* Salvatore S. Caputo, S.S.C., '76, *Korea;* Francis P. Carroll, S.S.C., '62, *Japan;* David J. Clay, S.S.C., '62, *Philippines;* John Comiskey, S.S.C., '68, *Philippines;* Thomas J. Daly, S.S.C., '54, *Fiji;* Martin R. Dubuc, S.S.C., '79, *Japan;* Charles Duster, S.S.C., '61, *Fiji;* William Hennessey, S.S.C., '35, *Philippines;* Michael Hoban, S.S.C., '70, *Chile;* Quentin F. Kalick, S.S.C., '42, *Philippines;* Francis J. Keaney, S.S.C., '65, *Philippines;* Ronald Kelso, S.S.C., '73, *Japan;* Donald Kill, S.S.C., '72, *Philippines;* Charles Lintz, S.S.C., '70, *Korea;* John Marley, S.S.C., '50, *Chile;* Vincent McCarthy, S.S.C., '64, *Brazil;* James J. McCaslin, S.S.C., '54, *Hong Kong;* Joseph McSweeny, S.S.C., '90, *Taiwan;* John P. Moran, S.S.C., '50, *Philippines;* Robert E. Mosher, S.S.C., '82, *Chile;* Richard L. Pankratz, S.S.C., '74, *Philippines;* Desmond Quinn, S.S.C., '54, *Philippines;* Edward I. Quinn, S.S.C., '55, *Fiji;* Francis A. Regan, S.S.C., '66, *Britain;* Paul Richardson, S.S.C., '54, *Philippines;* William Schmitt, S.S.C., '68, *Chile;* Thomas Shaughnessy, S.S.C., '66, *Philippines;* David M. Sheehan, S.S.C., '53, *Korea;* Robert P. Sweeney, S.S.C., '59, *Korea;* Albert Utzig, S.S.C., '83, *Korea;* Thomas Walsh, S.S.C., '57, *Chile;* Gerald P. Wilmsen, S.S.C., '59, *China;* Vincent J. Youngkamp, S.S.C., '59, *Japan.*

Priests 40.

Brothers of the Sacred Heart (S.C.)

Brothers of the Sacred Heart Foreign Missions

PROVINCIAL HOUSE: 685 Steere Farm Rd., Pascoag, RI 02859. Tel: 401-568-3361; Fax: 401-568-9810. Bros. Roland Ouellette, S.C., Prov. Supr.; Paul Hebert S.C., Mission Procurator. The Brothers of the Sacred Heart have mission schools and stations in Lesotho, Uganda, Zambia, and Zimbabwe.

Brothers 98; Brothers in Africa 55.

Salesians of Don Bosco (S.D.B.)

Salesians of Don Bosco Foreign Missions

SALESIAN PROVINCIAL HOUSE: 148 Main St., New Rochelle, NY 10801. Tel: 914-636-4225. Very Rev. Timothy C. Ploch, S.D.B., '76, Prov.; Rev. James Marra, S.D.B., '83.

U.S. Religious serving Abroad: Revs. Henry Bonetti, S.D.B., '73, *China;* Dominic DeBlase, S.D.B., '61, *Sierra Leone;* Robert Falk, S.D.B., '63, *Korea;* Lawrence Gilmore, S.D.B., '84, *Liberia;* Edward Liptak, S.D.B., '59, *Tanzania;* Harry Peterson, S.D.B., '61, *Chile;* John Thompson, S.D.B., '79, *Sierra Leone;* John Trisolini, S.D.B., '67, *Korea;* Bros. George Marquis, S.D.B., *Sierra Leone;* John Cosgrove, S.D.B., *Sierra Leone.*

SALESIAN PROVINCIAL HOUSE: 1100 Franklin St., San Francisco, CA 94109. Tel: 415-441-7144; Fax: 415-563-5394. Very Rev. William Schafer, S.D.B., '61, Prov.

U.S. Religious serving Abroad: Revs. Albert Mengon, S.D.B., '66, *Sierra Leone;* Christian Kot, S.D.B., '94, *Sierra Leone;* Bros. Joseph Reza, S.D.B., *Ethiopia;* Michael Touchstone, S.D.B., *Sierra Leone.*

Salvatorian Missions (S.D.S.)

Salvatorian Foreign Missions

U.S.A. PROVINCIAL HEADQUARTERS: *Salvatorian Provincial Residence,* 1735 Hi-Mount Blvd., Milwaukee, WI 53208-1720. Tel: 414-258-1735. Very Rev. Dennis D. Thiessen, S.D.S., '78, Prov.

U.S.A. PROCURATOR: 1735 Hi-Mount Blvd., Milwaukee, WI 53208-1720. Tel: 414-258-1735. Rev. Eric Midlecamp, S.D.S., '52, Mission Dir.

Publication: *The Salvatorian Newsletter.*

U.S. Religious serving in Tanzania: Revs. Carl Gleason, S.D.S., '56; James Weyker, S.D.S., '69; Bro. Donald Maurer, S.D.S.; Rev. David Brusky, S.D.S., '52.

Society of African Missions (S.M.A.)

Society of African Missions

U.S. PROVINCIAL HEADQUARTERS: *Society of African Missions,* 23 Bliss Ave., Tenafly, NJ 07670. Tel: 201-567-0450; 567-9085; Fax: 201-567-7156. Rev. Douglas B. Gilbert, S.M.A., '83, Prov. Supr.

U.S. Religious serving Abroad: Revs. Terrance Doherty, S.M.A., '70, *Liberia;* James Gessler, S.M.A., '63, *Liberia;* James Hayes, S.M.A., '55, *Cote d'Ivoire;* James C. Hickey, S.M.A., '46, *Liberia;*

Francis S. Hynes, S.M.A., '44, *Liberia;* Michael Moran, S.M.A., '81, *Liberia;* Austin Charles Ochu, S.M.A., '92, *Ghana;* Frank Allen Wright, S.M.A., '93, *Kenya.*

Society of St. Edmund (S.S.E.)

Edmundite Foreign Missions

U.S. Foundation: *Edmundite Generalate,* 270 Winooski Park, Colchester, VT 05439. Tel: 802-654-3400; Fax: 802-654-3409. Very Rev. Joseph L. Hart, S.S.E., '55, Supr. Gen.

U.S. Religious serving Abroad: Revs. Edward J. Dubriske, S.S.E., '64, *Venezuela;* Howard J. Muehlberger, S.S.E., '71, *Venezuela;* Philippe Simonnet, S.S.E., '52, *France.*

The Society of Mary (S.M.)

MARIST FATHERS

Marist Foreign Missions

General Motherhouse: Via Alesandro Poerio, 63, 00152, Rome, Italy. Very Revs. Joaquin Fernandez, S.M., '68, Supr. Gen.; Friedrich Arnold, S.M., '70, Vicar Gen.

U.S. Mission Promoter: *Marist Missions,* 29 Isabella St., Boston, MA 02116-5216. Tel: 617-482-0832; Fax: 617-482-1570. Rev. J. Armand Robichaud, S.M., '50, Dir.

Missions in Brazil, Burundi, Fiji, Japan, New Caledonia, Norway, Papua New Guinea, Peru, Philippine Islands, Samoa, Senegal, Solomon Islands, Tonga, Vanuatu, Venezuela, Wallis & Futuna, Republic of Cameroon.

U.S. Religious serving Abroad: Most Rev. Francis Lambert, S.M., *Vanuatu;* Revs. John P. Bolduc, S.M., '70, *Senegal;* Raymond Coolong, S.M., '71, *Peru;* Paul Frechette, S.M., '76, *Peru;* John Galvin, S.M., '63, *Solomon Islands;* Carlton Grenier, S.M., '54, *Papua New Guinea;* John Keady, S.M., '47, *Papua New Guinea;* Nicholas Kutulas, S.M., '55, *Papua New Guinea;* Louis Morosini, S.M., '56, *Solomon Islands;* Joseph Pusateri, S.M., '65, *Samoa;* Bertrand Soucy, S.M., '53, *Vanuatu;* Neil Soucy, S.M., '62, *New Caledonia.*

Society of St. James the Apostle

Society of St. James the Apostle, Inc.: 24 Clark St., Boston, MA 02109. Tel: 617-742-4715; Fax: 617-723-7389. Revs. Gabriel Troy (BO), '66, Dir.; Milton Eggerling (OAK), '54.

Founded by His Eminence Richard Cardinal Cushing, in 1958 to recruit Diocesan Priest volunteers for South America.

Serving in Peru: Revs. John E. Davis (FAR), '69; Frank Fairbairn (BO); George Flynn (BO), '56; Robert B. Gloisten (RIC); Donald Gorski (CHR); Eugene K. Kirke (BO), '62; Paul Madden (JKS), '70; Joseph I. Martin (BO), '56; Rudolph Masciarelli (BO), '49; J. Joseph McCarthy (BO), '66; Philip McKenna (MOB); John O'Leary (MIA), Gerard O'Meara (BO), '76; Hugh Joseph Shields (PH), '72; Raymond O'Sullivan (BO), '68; John J. Pashby (BO), '60; William Pearsall (BO); Jules Roos (PIT); Desmond Tynan (BO), '67.

Serving in Bolivia: Revs. William Baker (ALT), Donald J. Bowen (FR), '64; James Coleman (P), '73; Raymond Cowell (CHI), '56; Thomas Domurat (BO), '79; Bradley Killingsworth (P), '70; Paul M. Koch (DM), '61; Charles Stanley (BO), '71; John L. Sullivan (BO), '52.

Serving in Ecuador: Revs. James Cribbin (SD), John Hendricks (TR), '52; John Gordon (MET), '85; John Grimes (BO), '71; Cornelius Kiely (BAK), '67; Cornelois B. Lynch (PRO), John J. Moriarty (JOL), Paul McManus (BO), '87; Robert Thomas (BO),

Third Order Regular Missions

Third Order Regular of St. Francis

T.O.R. Foreign Missions

Provincial Residence: *Province of the Most Sacred Heart of Jesus,* 215 57th St., Pittsburgh, PA 15201. Tel: 412-781-1232. Very Rev. Edmund F. Carroll, T.O.R., '57, Minister Prov.; Bro. Mark McBride, T.O.R., Prov. Dir. of Foreign Missions.

U.S. Religious serving Abroad: Revs. Gerald J. King, T.O.R., '71, *Brazil;* Earl Jennings, T.O.R., '59, *South Africa;* Joseph A. Markalonis, T.O.R., '66, *Brazil;* Most Rev. Urban E. McGarry, T.O.R., D.D., (Retired), *India;* Rev. Paul R. Pavlik, T.O.R., '59, *Brazil;* Most Rev. Adrian J. Veigle, T.O.R., D.D., (Retired), *Brazil.*

Province of the Immaculate Conception: *Provincial Residence,* P.O. Box 29655, Brookland Station, Washington, DC 20017. Tel: 202-526-3332. Very Rev. Robert J. D'Aversa, T.O.R., Minister Prov.

U.S. Religious serving in Europe: Very Rev. Seraphin Conley, T.O.R., General Counselor Rome.

Missionary Servants of the Most Holy Trinity (S.T.)

Trinity Missions

International Headquarters

Generalate: 1215 N. Scott St., Arlington, VA 22209-3097. Tel: 703-276-8646; Fax: 703-522-2656. Rev. Domingo Rodriguez, S.T., '67, Supr. Gen.; Bro. Hilary Mettes, S.T., Sec. Gen.

U.S. Religious serving abroad: Revs. Francis Conkle, S.T., '78, *Costa Rica;* Stephen Giorno, S.T., '86, *Mexico;* Francisco Gomez, S.T., '83, *Mexico;* Charles Gordon, S.T., '67, *Costa Rica;* Eugene Mueller, S.T., '55, *Costa Rica;* Louis E. Murphy, S.T., '60, *Costa Rica;* Kevin Nugent, S.T., '51, *Costa Rica;* Victor Santiago Mateo, S.T., '82, *Mexico;* Harold Stone, S.T., '59, *Mexico;* Martin Van Trieste, S.T., '45, *Mexico;* Bruce Ward, S.T., '60, *Mexico.*

American Vincentian Missions (C.M.)

Vincentian Foreign Missions

Provincial Headquarters

Eastern Province: *St. Vincent's Seminary,* 500 East Chelten Ave., Philadelphia, PA 19144. Tel: 215-848-1985; Fax: 215-844-2085. Very Rev. Joseph L. Levesque, C.M., '67, Prov.

U.S. Religious serving abroad: Revs. Elmer Bauer, III, C.M., '93, *Concepcion, Panama;* John J. Buckley, C.M., '57, *Addis Ababa, Ethiopia;* Thomas M. Byrnes, C.M., '50, *Balboa, Panama;* John J. Carney, C.M., '82, *Puerto Armuelles, Panama;* Juan Chavarria, C.M., '95, *Puerto Armuelles, Panama;* Joseph V. Cummins, C.M., '72, *Balboa, Panama;* Robert P. Crawford, C.M., '47, *Philippines;* Joseph A. Elzi, C.M., '52, *Concepcion, Panama;* Edison Famania, C.M., '94, *Puerto Armuelles, Panama;* G. Gregory Gay, C.M., '80, *Boqueron, Panama;* Patrick J. Griffin, C.M., '79, *Rome;* Alcibiades Guerra, C.M., '90, *Concepcion, Panama;* Thomas Hynes, C.M., '59, *Solomon Islands;* Jose Pio Jimenez, C.M., '68, *Balboa, Panama;* Teodoro Justavino, C.M., '90, *Panama City, Panama;* John E. Kane, C.M., '70, *Balboa, Panama;* Arthur J. Kolinsky, C.M., '71, *Puerto Armuelles, Panama;* Alan J. McLellan, C.M., '65, *Colon, Panama;* John J. MacGillivray, C.M., '76, *Colon, Panama;* Robert P. Maloney, C.M., '66, *Rome;* Michael T. Mazurchuk, C.M., '86, *Colon, Panama;* Jose Angel Medina, C.M., '88, *Cuba;* Emmet J. Nolan, C.M., '92, *Concepcion, Panama;* John P. Prager, C.M., '82, *Concepcion, Panama;* Teodoro A. Rios, C.M., '76, *Panama City, Panama;* John D. Rutledge, C.M., '51, *Balboa, Panama;* Francisco Samudio, C.M., '92, *Panama City, Panama;* Charles G. Schuster, C.M., '55, *Soloy, Panama;* Thomas A. Sendlein, C.M., '72, *Taiwan;* Harold G. Skidmore, C.M., '50, *Balboa, Panama;* Juan Wardrope, C.M., '89, *Boqueron, Panama.*

Midwest Province: *Vincentian Fathers and Brothers,* 13663 Rider Trail N., Earth City, MO 63045-1512. Tel: 314-344-1184; Fax: 314-344-2989. Very Rev. William E. Hartenbach, C.M., '64, Prov.

U.S. Religious serving in foreign missions: Revs. Gerald Brown, C.M., '57; Stephen Gallegos, C.M., '88; Very Rev. Robert Wood, C.M., '56, Supr.; Revs. Francis A. Gaydos, C.M., '47; W. Barry Moriarty, C.M., '67; Thomas G. O'Hern, C.M., '77; C. William Stein, C.M., '39; Very Rev. Hugh F. O'Donnell, C.M., '61, Prov.; Revs. Edward Gallagher, C.M., '78; Jacob Johnson, C.M., '47; Robert W. Chap, C.M., '66; Richard Preuss, C.M., '73.

Southern Province: *Congregation of the Mission,* 3826 Gilbert Ave., Dallas, TX 75219-4346. Tel: 214-526-0234 or 526-2421; Fax: 214-526-3477. Very Rev. George J. Weber, C.M., '54, Prov.

Xaverian Missionary Fathers (S.X.)

Xaverian Foreign Missions

U.S. Foundation: *Xaverian Missionary Fathers,* 12 Helene Ct., Wayne, NJ 07470. Tel: 201-942-2975; Fax: 201-942-5012. Revs. Francis Signorelli, S.X., '59, Prov.; Herondi Fernandes, S.X., '76, Local Supr.; Frank B. Grappoli, S.X., '63, Treas. & Mission Dir.; Dario Maso, S.X., '82, Vocation Ministry.

Religious Serving Abroad: Most Rev. George Biguzzi, S.X., *Sierra Leone;* Revs. Danilo Boschetto, S.X., '70, *Mexico;* Carl Chudy, S.X., '86, *Philippines;* Oscar De LaTorre, S.X., '87, *Bangladesh;* Revs. Gerard Furlan, S.X., '58, *Sierra Leone;* Francis Gugliotta, S.X., '52, *Brazil;* Greg Holm, S.X., '87, *Japan;* Danilo Lago, S.X., '77, *Brazil;* Rene Lovat, S.X., '57, *Cameroun;* Mark Marangone, S.X., '84, *Colombia;* Joseph Matteucig, S.X., '84, *Taiwan;* Adolph Menendez, S.X., '68, *Mexico;* Victor Mosele, S.X., '60, *Sierra Leone;* Gino Nasini, S.X., '65, *Brazil;* Bruno Orru, S.X., '63, *Indonesia;* Julian Perozzi, '82, *Taiwan;* Luciano Peterlini, S.X., '63, *Sierra Leone;* Mario Pezzotti, S.X., '59, *Brazil;* Franco Qualizza, S.X., '71, *Indonesia;* Noel Tomasi, S.X., '60, *Zaire;* James Tully, S.X., '75, *Sierra Leone.*

Missionary Activities

RELIGIOUS SOCIETIES ENGAGED IN MISSIONARY WORK

Augustinian Recollect Fathers: *Province of St. Nicholas of Tolentine U.S. Delegation,* 2800 Scurz Ave., Bronx, NY 10465. Tel: 718-823-0460. Rev. Jose Luis Duenas, O.A.R., Supr. Delegate.

Engaged in missionary work among Spanish-speaking people. Sustains mission personnel in the Archdiocese of New York and in the Dioceses of Las Cruces and El Paso.

Augustinian Recollect Fathers and Brothers (1944): *Province of St. Augustine,* 29 Ridgeway Ave., West Orange, NJ 07052. Very Rev. Francis E. Peluso, O.A.R., Prov. Supr.

Missionary work among Spanish-speaking people established in colonies throughout a notable part of the U.S. and active in cursillo and retreat work in the Archdiocese of New York.

Blessed Sacrament Fathers And Brothers: *Province of St. Ann,* 5384 Wilson Mills Rd., Cleveland, OH 44143.

Brothers of the Christian Schools: *U.S.A. & Toronto Regional Office of the De La Salle Christian Brothers Conference,* 4351 Garden City Dr., Ste. 200, Landover, MD 20785. Tel: 301-459-9410; Fax: 301-459-8056.

The missionary activities administered by The Christian Brothers Conference include Bethlehem University, West Bank; East Africa; Eritrea/Ethiopia & St. Vincent Island, West Indies. Individual Province Mission responsibilities include San Francisco: Mexico, Tijuana; Toronto: The Grenadines & Nigeria. Christian Brothers also serve as missionaries in the Philippines & Central America.

* Christian Foundation for Children and Aging: One Elmwood Ave., Kansas City, KS 66103. Tel: 913-384-6500; 800-875-6564. Robert K. Hentzen, Pres.; Most Rev. Raymond A. Lucker, Member of the Board; Ed Stankard, Contact Person.

Christian Foundation for Children and Aging (CFCA) is an international Catholic mission organization dedicated to raising mission consciousness here at home and helping the poor at Catholic mission sites abroad. Founded by Catholic lay people in 1981, CFCA's develops suOpport through "sponsorship" — linking a child or aging friend in need with a sponsor in a mutually beneficial relationship. Sponsor assistance helps provide food, medical care, opportunity for education while at the same time permitting the sponsor to get to know the culture and life of their sponsored friend. CFCA currently works with over 40 missionary orders and the local church in 23 developing countries and also sponsors an extensive lay volunteer program.

Claretian Missionaries: *Headquarters of Western Province,* 1119 Westchester Pl., Los Angeles, CA 90019. Very Rev. Ralph Berg C.M.F., Prov. Tel: 213-734-1824; Fax: 213-737-0301.

Headquarters of Eastern Province, 400 N. Euclid Ave., Oak Park, IL 60302. Tel: 708-848-2076. Very Rev. Theodore Cirone, C.M.F., Prov.

Please refer to the Religious Institutes of Men section for activities and representation in the United States.

Publications: monthly magazine, *U.S. Catholic;* extensive line of Pamphlets and Paperback Books;, bi-monthly, *Newsletter; Fides-Claretian.*

Claret Center, 5536 S. Everett Ave., Chicago, IL Resources for Counseling and Spiritual Directions. Chicago, IL.

Missions outside the United States entrusted to the Claretians: Guatemala, Cameroons.

Columban Sisters (1922 Ireland): 73 Mapleton St., Brighton, MA 02135; Fax: 617-789-3569. Sr. Corona Colleary, S.S.C., Reg. Coord.

The Columban Sisters are religious women called to bring the good news of Christ to all in need, particularly the poor and the oppressed and those who have not yet had the Gospel proclaimed to them. The congregation strives to respond to the needs of the people by dedication to the work of evangelization through pastoral, educational, medical, and social ministries, and supporting the efforts of the local church where its members are sent. The congregation also endeavors, through programs of mission education and animation, to deepen an awareness of global vision and world justice.

Active in the U.S. in the Archdioceses of Boston, Chicago and Los Angeles, and in the Diocese of Buffalo.

Active outside the U.S. in Ireland, England, Scotland, Hong Kong, Korea, Philippines, Peru, Chile and Pakistan.

Comboni Missionaries of the Heart of Jesus, Inc. (Verona Fathers) Provincial Headquarters: *Comboni Mission Center,* 8108 Beechmont Ave., Cincinnati, OH 45255-3194. Tel: 513-474-4997. Revs. John Converset, M.C.C.J., Prov.; Joseph Bragotti M.C.C.J., Mission Dir., Foreign mission society, both priests and brothers, founded by Bishop Daniel Comboni, Vicar Apostolic of Central Africa.

Active in the Archdioceses of Chicago, Cincinnati, Los Angeles and Newark.

Comboni Missionaries work with local churches in: Africa—Benin, Central African Republic, Egypt, Eritrea, Ethiopia, Ghana, Kenya, Malawi, Mozambique, South Africa, Sudan, Chad, Togo, Uganda, Zambia and Zaire; Asia—Philippines, Macau; Latin America—Brazil, Chile, Colombia, Costa Rica, Ecuador, Guatemala, Mexico and Peru; North America—Canada and the United States.

Training Centers: Africa—Ethiopia, Kenya, Malawi, Mozambique, South Africa, Togo, Egypt, Sudan, Uganda, Zaire; Asia—Philippines; Europe— Austria, England, France, Germany, Italy, Poland, Portugal and Spain; Latin America—Brazil, Colombia, Costa Rica, Ecuador, Mexico and Peru; North America—United States.

Publications: *Comboni Press Network Newsletter; Comboni Press Feature Service;, Comboni Mission Newsletter.*

Comboni Missionary Sisters: *American Headquarters,* 1307 Lakeside Ave., Richmond, VA 23228. Tel: 804-262-8827; Fax: 804-264-2906. Sr. Ruth Ann Bryden, Prov. Supr.

An international congregation of 1,890 sisters founded by Bishop Daniel Comboni in 1872 in Verona, Italy. Engaged in pastoral and catechetical work; education; social services; health services; building Christian communities; training of local church leaders in Africa, Latin America and Middle East.

The American Province recruits and trains sisters for the foreign mission, mission education, fundraising for missions, pastoral ministry among the poor, and day care centers.

Congregation of Alexian Brothers: *Immaculate Conception Province,* U.S. Provincial Headquarters, 600 Alexian Way, Elk Grove Village, IL 60007. Tel: 847-640-7550. Bro. Edward Walsh, Provincial.

Missionary healthcare work in Davao City, Philippines directed by four Alexian Brothers. Please refer to the Religious Institutes of Men section for activities and representation in the United States.

Congregation of Christian Brothers: *Eastern American Province, United States Headquarters,* 21 Pryer Terr., New Rochelle, NY 10804. Bro. J. B. Moffett, C.F.C., Prov.; Bro. C. F. Miller, C.F.C., Mission Coord.

Missionary and educational work in Italy, Peru, West Indies.

Congregation of the Holy Ghost and of the Immaculate Heart of Mary (1872): 6230 Brush Run Rd., Bethel Park, PA 15102. Tel: 412-831-0302; Fax: 412-831-0970; *Holy Ghost Fathers and Brothers (C.S.Sp.), Eastern Province;* Very Rev. Christopher P. Promis, C.S.Sp., Prov., *Western Province,* (1963), 1700 W. Alabama St., Houston, TX 77098-2808. Tel: 713-522-2882; 713-522-2667; Fax: 713-522-8063. Very Rev. Donald S. Nesti, C.S.Sp., Prov.

Missionary work among the abandoned, including first evangelization, teaching, care of homeless children, and pastoral ministry.

Missionaries serve in 24 (arch)dioceses in the United States; the Archdiocese of San Juan and the Dioceses of Arecibo in Puerto Rico; the Diocese of Ciudad Valles and the Archdiocese of San Luis Potosi in Mexico; and the Diocese of Arusha, Mbulu and Zanzibar in Tanzania. Nairobi in Kenya; Bethlehem in South Africa; and Awasa in Ethiopia. Other establishments in North and South America, Europe, Africa and Australia.

Missionaries of Our Lady of La Salette: *Province of Our Lady of Seven Dolors,* 915 Maple Ave., Hartford, CT 06114-2330. Tel: 860-956-8870. Very Rev. Thomas A. Reilly, M.S., Prov. Supr.; Rev. Brian R. Sheridan, M.S., Procurator, 85 New Park Ave., Hartford, CT 06106-2184.

Active in Archdiocese of Buenos Aires, Dioceses of Santiago del Estero and Cordoba, Argentina; Cochabamba, Bolivia.

Please refer to the Religious Institutes of Men section for activities and representation in the United States.

Congregation of the Missionaries of Our Lady of La Salette: 947 Park St., P.O. Box 2965, Attleboro, MA 02703-0965. Tel: 508-222-7171; Fax: 508-222-6178; *Immaculate Heart of Mary Province La Salette Provincial House;* Very Rev. Gilles Genest, M.S., Prov. Supr.; Rev. William Slight, M.S., Procurator. Tel: 508-226-7747.

The southern portion of Isabela, Diocese of Ilagan is entrusted to the care of the Province Ina ng Pagasa, originating from the Immaculate Heart of Mary Province of the La Salette Missionaries. The La Salette Mission Seminary was established in 1962 in Santiago, Isabela, Philippines.

Please refer to the Religious Institutes of Men section for representation and statistics in the United States. Also active in the Archdiocese of Montreal and the Dioceses of London, Ontario and Gatineau-Hull, Quebec, Canada; Manila, Imus and Ilagan, Philippines; Bangalore, Trivandrum and Irinjalakuda, Kerala, S. India.

Congregation of the Missionaries of Our Lady of La Salette: *Province of Mary Queen,* 4650 S. Broadway, St. Louis, MO 63111-1303. Tel: 314-353-5000; Fax: 314-353-4582. Very Rev. Dennis J. Meyer, M.S., Prov.; Revs. John Nuelle, M.S., Procurator Missions of Morondava, Madagascar; Rev. Joseph Shea, M.S., Procurator Missions of Morondava, Madagascar.

Please refer to the Religious Institutes of Men section for activities and representation in the United States.

Publication: newsletter, *La Salette Ministries Development Center.*

Congregation of the Priests of the Sacred Heart, The: *U.S. Provincialate Offices,* P.O. Box 289, Hales Corners, WI 53130-0289. Tel: 414-425-6910. Very Rev. John Czyzynski, S.C.J., Prov. Supr.

Please refer to the Religious Institutes of Men section for other activities and representation in the United States.

Missionary work in the home and foreign missions; educational activities; welfare work, especially in industrial centers. Home Missions: Lower Brule and Cheyenne Indian Reservations, South Dakota; Black Missions, Diocese of Jackson, Mississippi; Spanish-speaking Apostolate, Dioceses of Brownsville, Galveston-Houston, and Archdiocese of San Antonio.

Foreign Missions: Zaire, Cameroon, Mozambique, South Africa, Brazil, Argentina, Uruguay, Chile, Venezuela, Indonesia and Finland.

Congregation of the Resurrection: *Resurrection Catholic Missions of the South, Inc.,* 2815 Forbes Dr., Montgomery, AL 36110. Tel: 334-263-4221; Fax: 334-263-4999.

The Resurrection Catholic Missions is a seven-building complex that includes a home for handicapped and severely mentally retarded children, an early childhood development facility for preschoolers, a church and elementary school, as well as an outreach program to homebound elders and an addictions counseling/prevention program; *Resurrection Catholic Nursing Home,* Marbury, AL 36051.

Please refer to the Religious Institutes of Men section for activities and representation in the United States. Active also in Australia, Brazil, Bolivia, Bulgaria, Canada and Poland.

Consolata Missionaries (1901): *Provincial Headquarters,* 2301 Hwy. 27, P.O. Box 5550, Somerset, NJ 08875. Tel: 908-297-9191; Fax: 908-940-3121. Rev. Anthony Bellagamba, I.M.C., Reg. Supr.

Legal Title: *Consolata Society for Foreign Missions.*

Serving in 20 countries around the world and in the United States.

Publication: *Consolata Missionaries.*

Consolata Missionary Sisters (1910): 6801 Belmont Ave., N.E., P.O. Box 371, Belmont, MI 49306. Tel: 616-361-2072; Fax: 616-361-2049. Sr. Felicia Bertaina, Supr.

The congregation is committed to all types of missionary apostolate, primarily in African and South American countries.

Corpus Christi Carmelites: 516 Broadway, Newport, RI 02840. Sr. Teresa Winefride, O.Carm., Supr.

Sisters work as catechists and social workers in America and abroad; own and/or operate homes for the aged, girls, and sick children; hostels; day nurseries; do ministry work in prisons and hospitals and educational work in kindergartens, primary and secondary schools.

CROSIER FATHERS AND BROTHERS: *Crosier Missions,* 3510 Vivian Ave., Shoreview, MN 55126-3852. Tel: 612-486-7456; Fax: 612-486-7589. Rev. DAVID E. GALLUS, O.S.C., Mission Dir.

Legal Title: *Canons Regular of the Order of the Holy Cross.*

Missionary work among the Asmat tribes of Irian Jaya Indonesia, since 1958.

Publications: quarterly by province, *Crossview,* irregular schedule anthropological study, *An Asmat Sketch Book.*

DAUGHTERS OF MARY HELP OF CHRISTIANS: *St. Philip Apostle Province,* 655 Belmont Ave., Haledon, NJ 07508. Mother THERESA KELLY, F.M.A., Prov.

Legal Title: *Missionary Society of the Salesian Sisters, Inc.*

Missionary work in home and foreign countries; catechetical, educational and training centers; social services; hostels, hospitals, clinics and dispensaries; mission centers, leper colonies and youth centers.

Active in U.S. within the Archdioceses of Newark and New York and in the Dioceses of Miami, Paterson, St. Petersburg, and Birmingham, Alabama.

EUCHARISTIC MISSIONARIES OF ST. DOMINIC: 3801 Canal Street, Suite 400, New Orleans, LA 70119. Tel: 504-486-1133; Fax: 504-486-6547. Sr. CATHERINE DRAWE, O.P., Pres.

Missionary work and ministry in religious education; diocesan offices; parish census; pastoral associates; social service; parish administrators; spirituality-retreat center; centers for the deaf; home & clinic nursing; hospital chaplaincy; counseling; pastoral care of the sick in homes; literacy ministry to Mayan immigrants.

FRANCISCAN FRIARS OF THE ATONEMENT-GENERALATE: *St. James Friary,* P.O. Box 5, Garrison, NY 10524-0005. Tel: 914-424-3038; Fax: 914-424-3978.

Mission activities outside of the U.S.: Japan. Also staff parishes in Western Canada, Ontario, England and the United States.

FRANCISCAN MISSIONARIES OF MARY, THE: *U.S. Provincial House,* 3305 Wallace Ave., Bronx, NY 10467; Fax: 718-547-4607. Sr. MARY PETROSKY, PROV.

Founded in India in 1877, for the work of evangelization and development in non-Christian and de-Christianized countries. Active mission apostolate is centered in daily adoration of the Blessed Sacrament exposed.

This international congregation serves 856 missions in 56 provinces.

Missionary work of evangelization and development, catechetics, social work, nursing, community development programs, educational and public health programs, pastoral activity and various forms of ministry and service.

FRANCISCAN MISSIONARY SISTERS FOR AFRICA: *American Headquarters Center for Promotion and Formation,* 172 Foster St., Box 35095, Brighton, MA 02135. Sr. MARY JORDAN, O.S.F., Supr. Gen.

Missions in Ethiopia, Kenya, Uganda, South Africa, Zambia and Zimbabwe.

Publication: *The Daystar.*

FRANCISCAN MISSION ASSOCIATION: *Franciscan Mission House,* Washington Ave., Rensselaer, NY 12144. Tel: 518-465-0062. Bro. JAMES AMRHEIN, O.F.M.Conv., Dir.

The American branch of the Franciscan Mission Crusade founded in 1924, approved by Pope Pius XI to further the work of the Conventual Franciscan Missionary Apostolate. The purpose is to aid the Mission of the Order in every possible way. The revenues of the Association accrue from the annual and perpetual enrollments in the Association, bequests, other free-will offerings and donations, membership in monthly mission club appeal.

FRANCISCAN MISSION ASSOCIATION (1953): *Province of Our Lady of Consolation, Franciscan Missions,* 322 West St., Carey, OH 43316. Tel: 419-396-6455. Bro. BRYAN HOBAN O.F.M.Conv., Dir.

The purpose of the association is to give financial and other material aid to the missionaries of Africa: the Dioceses of Ndola and Solwezi, Zambia; missionaries in the dioceses of Olancho, Tegucigalpa and Comayagua in Honduras and San Jose in Costa Rica; and missionaries of the Southwestern United States. Both living and deceased may be enrolled as members. Members of the laity have an active part in promoting the growth of the association as outlined in Vatican II.

FRANCISCAN MISSION ASSOCIATION, INC.: *Province of St. Anthony of Padua,* 66 School St., Granby, MA 01033. Tel: 413-467-9196; Fax: 413-467-7944. Rev. PLACID KACZOREK, O.F.M.Conv., Dir.

Founded to support the domestic and foreign missions of the Conventual Franciscans of St. Anthony Province.

FRANCISCAN SISTERS OF ALLEGANY: *St. Elizabeth Motherhouse,* Allegany, NY 14706. Sr. MARGARET MARY KIMMINS, O.S.F., Gen. Minister; Sr. MARIE DOLORES GIONTA, O.S.F., Mission Society Dir.

Sisters serve in areas of education; health-care; pastoral ministry; migrant ministry in the U.S; missionary work in the archdiocese of Kingston and dioceses of Montego Bay, Mandeville, Jamaica; the archdioceses of Brazilia and Goiania, and LaPaz; dioceses of Anapolis, Ipameri, Jatai, Ruy Barbosa, Goias, Cristalandia, Brazil and Pando, Bolivia.

Congregation 458; foreign missions 95.

Publication: *Zeal.*

FRANCISCAN SISTERS, DAUGHTERS OF THE SACRED HEARTS OF JESUS AND MARY: *Province of St. Clara,* P.O. Box 667, Wheaton, IL 60189-0667. Tel: 630-462-7422; Fax: 630-462-7148. Sr. MARY ELLEN MCALEESE, O.S.F., Prov. Dir.

Active in U.S.-institutional and home health care; housing; education; pastoral ministry; care of elderly; wellness; long-term care; social services; spiritual direction and retreats in archdioceses of Milwaukee, St. Louis, Dubuque, Denver and Chicago; in dioceses of Joliet, Green Bay, LaCrosse, Springfield-Cape Girardeau and Gary. Outside the U.S.-Santarem, Brazil, Nigeria.

FRANCISCAN SISTERS OF LITTLE FALLS, MN: *Motherhouse,* Little Falls, MN 56345. Tel: 612-632-2981. Sr. ROSE MARGARET SCHNEIDER, PRES.

Serving in Catholic and non-sectarian hospitals; Catholic and non- sectarian nursing homes; group homes; apartments for the elderly; home health nursing; public health nursing; Catholic high schools; Catholic elementary schools; special education; Spirituality Farm, Native Americans; community colleges; state colleges and universities; religious education; parish ministry; liturgical music ministry; music center; holistic growth center; health and recreation center; retreat ministry; counselling/spiritual direction; social service; ministry to the poor; ministry to the migrants; clinics; ministry to AIDS and chemical-dependency victims; Ministry to Native Americans; Education, health, social services in the Dioceses of Same, Tanzania, Africa; Kumbo, Cameroon, Africa; Managua, Nicaragua, C.A.; Guatemala, C.A.; and Quito, Ecuador, S.A.

FRANCISCAN SISTERS OF THE POOR: *Congregational Office,* 133 Remsen St., Brooklyn, NY 11201; Fax: 718-643-9710. Sr. BERNADETTE SULLIVAN, S.F.P., Pres.

Sisters serve in healing ministry; health care; social welfare; pastoral ministry in the U.S.; pastoral ministry and health care in the Dioceses of Rome, Padua and Messina in Italy. Mission ministry is represented in the Archdiocese of Goiania and in the Dioceses of Jatai and Ipameri in Brazil and in Kaolack and Dakar in Senegal, West Africa.

Number in Congregation 212; Mission ministry 20.

GLENMARY HOME MISSIONERS, THE (1939): *National Headquarters,* P.O. Box 465618, Cincinnati, OH 45246-5618. Rev. ROBERT DALTON, PRES.

Glenmary is a society of secular priests and lay brothers, and the only home mission society dedicated exclusively to establishing the Catholic Church in small towns and rural areas of the United States. Statistics show that there are more than 500 counties that do not have a resident priest. The Glenmary society employs every available technique in organizing viable and effective Catholic parishes in these areas. Priests and brothers are engaged in radio and television work, youth programs, systematic home visits, and a wide variety of projects designed to achieve better social conditions. When it is practical, these programs are conducted ecumenically; *Glenmary Research Center,* 750 Piedmont Ave., N.E., Atlanta, GA 30308. Sr. MARY PRINISKI, O.P., Interim Dir., *Glenmary Religious Education Center,* 1312 Fifth Ave., N., Nashville, TN 37208. Rev. DENNIS HOLLY, DIR.

Please refer to the Religious Institutes of Men section for activities and representation in the United States.

Publication: *The Glenmary Challenge.*

GLENMARY HOME MISSION SISTERS OF AMERICA (1941): *Glenmary Sisters,* P.O. Box 22264, Owensboro, KY 42302-2264; Fax: 502-686-8759. Sr. CHRISTINE BECKETT, PRES.

Glenmary is a community of women religious of diocesan right and the only home mission community dedicated to bringing mission presence and activity to the rural, small town areas of the United States. The sisters live and work among the poor, the sick, the oppressed and unchurched in Appalachia and the South in areas where less than 5% of the total population is Catholic. When possible the Sisters work in collaboration with the Glenmary Priests and Brothers and the Glenmary Co-Missioners. The Glenmary Sisters believe in a holistic approach to mission - the caring of the whole person - through their ministries of co-creating with local people a Catholic Christian faith community, ecumenism, evangelization, radio programs, pastoral outreach, religious education, home health, home visitations, and a wide variety of social services for the very poor.

Please refer to the Religious Institutes of Women section for activities in the United States.

Publication: *Kinship.*

INSTITUTE OF CHARITY (ROSMINIAN FATHERS): *Rosmini House,* 2327 W. Heading Ave., Peoria, IL 61604.

Active in the Dioceses of Peoria, St. Petersburg and Venice.

Missions and missionary work in Tanga, Tanzania; New Zealand; Venezuela; and Kerela, India.

JESUIT VOLUNTEERS:/INTERNATIONAL: P.O. Box 25478, Washington, DC 20007. Tel: 202-687-1132; Fax: 202-687-5082. Rev. VINCENT DECOLA, S.J., Dir.

A Christian service organization offering young college educated lay men and women an opportunity to volunteer in a developing country in collaboration with Jesuits. Volunteers serve for two years without returning to the U.S.

MARIANNHILL, CONGREGATION OF MISSIONARIES OF (1882): 23715 Ann Arbor Tr., Dearborn Hts., MI 48127. Rev. ALOYSIUS BLONIGEN, C.M.M., Provincial Supr.

The American-Canadian province recruits and trains young men as priests and lay brothers for foreign missions, secures funds for the foreign missions, and does a limited amount of pastoral work at home.

Active in the Archdiocese of Detroit.

Outside the U.S.: South Africa, Zimbabwe, Papua New Guinea, Zambia, Brazil, Germany, Switzerland, Spain, Austria, Netherlands and Poland.

Publication: *Leaves.*

Worldwide membership: Bishops 2; Priests 205; Brothers 113; Students Professed 49; Total Members 369.

MARIST BROTHERS OF THE SCHOOLS (ESOPUS PROVINCE): *Headquarters,* 1241 Kennedy Blvd., Bayonne, NJ 07002; Fax: 201-823-2232. Bro. JOHN KLEIN, F.M.S., Prov.

Missionary work in the educational field in Liberia.

MARIST MISSIONARY SISTERS: *North American Provincial Office,* 349 Grove St., Waltham, MA 02154. Tel: 617-893-0149. Sr. ROSALIE WARPEHA, S.M.S.M., Prov.; Sr. JEANETTE MISUIRA, S.M.S.M., Mission Promotor; Sr. CLAIRE RHEAUME, Vocation Directress.

We were founded in France in 1845 for mission in the South Pacific. Today, we are an International Missionary Congregation of 650 sisters (in seven provinces), serving the people of God in 28 countries around the world. The American Province has 126 sisters working in Massachusetts, Tennessee, Illinois, Iowa, Texas, Florida, Alaska, Arkansas, West Virginia, Louisiana, New York and Jamaica, W.I. Our mission is to bring the good news of God's love through spiritual and corporal works of mercy; catechetical, medical, educational and social services; pastoral ministry; formation of laity for leadership and a great concern for the poorest and most neglected. We work by preference among people of different cultures and languages, to bring about greater understanding, dignity and mutual respect.

Our formation is international with a French-speaking novitiate in New Caledonia, an English-speaking novitiate in New Zealand and a Spanish-speaking novitiate in Peru.

Province headquarters are in the United States, Italy, Australia, New Zealand, Peru, France and New Caledonia.

Legal Title: *Missionary Sisters of the Society of Mary, Inc.*

Please refer to the Religious Institutes of Women section for activities and representation in the United States.

MARYKNOLL SISTERS OF ST. DOMINIC, INC.: Maryknoll, NY 10545-0311. Sr. CLAUDETTE LAVERDIERE, M.M., Community Pres.; Sr. ROSE MARIE FRANKLIN, M.M., Gen. Sec.

A Pontifical Institute under the jurisdiction of the Congregation for the Institutes of Consecrated Life. The purpose of the Maryknoll Sisters Congregation is to participate in the mission presence and activity of the universal Church so that God's reign of peace, justice and love may be proclaimed and witnessed to throughout the world. The Maryknoll Sisters embrace a plurality of ministries while giving a clear sign of Christian community; faith-sharing; self-gift in service through pastoral and catechetical work; basic ecclesial communities; education; social services; medical and health promotion work; services through hostels; services to refugees; and ministries that promote human rights, social justice and the dignity and equality of women.

Please refer to the Religious Institutes of Women section for activities in the United States.

Active in Bangladesh, Bolivia, Brazil, Cambodia, Central Pacific, Chile, Ecuador, El Salvador, Guatemala, Hong Kong, Indonesia, Japan, Kenya, Korea,

Macau, Mexico, Nepal, Papua New Guinea, Namibia, Nicaragua, Panama, Peru, Philippines, Sudan, Taiwan, Tanzania, Thailand, USA and Zimbabwe.

MEDICAL MISSIONARIES OF MARY: *Regional Headquarters,* 563 Minneford Ave., City Island, NY 10464-1118. Tel: 718-885-0945; Fax: 718-885-0010. Sr. PHILOMENA SHEERIN, M.M.M., Supr. Gen.; Sr. ANNE MARIE HUBBARD, M.M.M., Regional Supr.

Missionary work in hospitals, clinics and leprosy treatment; public health and pastoral ministry centers in Africa, South America and Clinchco, VA.

Please refer to the Religious Institutes of Women section for activities and representation in the United States. Active also in Angola, Nigeria, Uganda, Tanzania, Liberia, Kenya, Malawi, Ethiopia, England, Ireland and Brazil.

Publication: quarterly, *The Mini MMM.*

MEDICAL MISSION SISTERS: *North American Headquarters,* 8400 Pine Rd., Philadelphia, PA 19111; Fax: 215-342-3948. Sr. RITA SYRON, M.M.S., Society Coord.; Sr. ESTELLE DEMERS, M.M.S., North American Sector Coord.; MONICA M. MCGINLEY, Pub. Rels. Dir.

Legal Title: *Society of Catholic Medical Missionaries, Inc., Society of Catholic Medical Missionaries Generalate, Inc.,* (effective 1991).

Medical Mission Sisters have the special call in the Church of "being a healing presence at the heart of a wounded world." Members commit themselves "to promote healing and wholeness in all aspects of life" in the spirit of Jesus. They share life with those who are sick and have been made poor, trying to help them to live fully as human beings. Medical Mission Sisters' healing presence today involves a full range of preventitive, curative and promotive health services; health training programs; and development and social justice activities in Ghana, Uganda, Kenya, Ethiopia, Malawi, Zaire, Pakistan, India, Belgium, Venezuela, Brazil, Peru, Indonesia, Philippines, Italy, Holland, Germany, England, and Mexico.

Medical Mission Houses in the United States are listed under the Religious Institutes of Women section.

Publication: *Medical Mission Sisters News.*

MILL HILL MISSIONARIES: *St. Joseph's Missionary Society,* 222 W. Hartsdale Ave., Hartsdale, NY 10530. Tel: 914-682-0645; Fax: 914-682-0862. Very Rev. TERENCE J. LEE, M.H.M., Regl. Rep.; Very Rev. THEO M. FELDBRUGGE, M.H.M., Admin. & Regl. Bursar, Los Angeles.

An international society of priests and brothers, founded in 1866, devoted entirely to the missionary needs of the Church.

Active in the U.S., in the Archdioceses of New York, Los Angeles, and Chicago, and the Dioceses of Corpus Christi, Fall River, Metuchen, Scranton and Winona.

Active outside the U.S. in the Diocese of Kingston, ON, Canada; the Archdiocese of Bamenda and the Dioceses of Buea, Kumbo and Ngoundere in Cameroon; the Diocese of Iskanderiya in Egypt; the Archdioce e Diocese of Basankusu in Zaire; the Diocese of Port Elizabeth in South Africa; Diocese of Hong Kong in China; the Archdioceses of Hyderabad and Bangalore, and the Dioceses of Jamma-Srinagar and Varan e Philippines; the Diocese of Geraldton in Australia; and the Dioceses of Aukland and Hamilton in New Zealand; the Archdiocese of Cochabamba in Bolivia; the Dioceses of Governador Valadares and Itaqua.

MISSION HELPERS OF THE SACRED HEART: 1001 W. Joppa Rd., Baltimore, MD 21204-3787. Tel: 410-823-8585; Fax: 410-825-6355. Sr. CATHARINE DAGAS, M.H.S.H., Pres.

A Pontifical, missionary congregation with principal work of evangelization and catechesis; adult religious education; instruction of youth and children; D.R.E. programs; pastoral ministers; pastoral associates; pastoral social ministers; special ministers of the Eucharist; ministry in homes and institutions; ministry to the elderly and infirm; catechesis of blind, deaf, retarded; campus ministry; hospital ministry; Hispanic pastoral ministry to adults and youth; spiritual direction and retreat work.

Please refer to the Religious Institutes of Women for activities and representation in the United States. Activities also in the Archdioceses of Caracas, Venezuela, and San Juan.

Publication: quarterly magazine, *The Mission Helper.*

MISSION INTERNATIONAL, INC.: 2301 Hwy. 27, Somerset, NJ 08873. Tel: 908-297-9191; Fax: 908-940-3121. Rev. ANTHONY BELLAGAMBA, Chm.

MISSIONARIES OF AFRICA M.AFR.: *U.S. Provincial Headquarters,* 1624 21st St., N.W., Washington, DC 20009-1055; Fax: 202-332-8640. Rev. WILLIAM MORONEY, M.Afr., Prov.

International and interracial missionary society of priests and brothers working in teams almost exclusively in Africa.

Active in the Archdioceses of Chicago and Washington and the Diocese of St. Petersburg and Los Angeles.

Training centers and mission promotion centers in Brazil, Canada, Belgium, France, Germany, Great Britain, Holland, India, Ireland, Italy, Mexico, Philippines, Poland, Spain and Switzerland.

Missionary work in Algeria, Burundi, Chad, Ethiopia, Ghana, Kenya, Malawi, Mali, Mozambique, Nigeria, Rwanda, Senegal, Sudan, Tanzania, Tunisia, Uganda, Burkina Faso, Zaire, Zambia, South Africa, Ivory Coast, and Niger. Totaling 99 dioceses and archdioceses in Africa; Jerusalem.

Publication: newsletter, *Missionaries of Africa Report.*

MISSIONARIES OF THE HOLY APOSTLES: 33 Prospect Hill Rd., Cromwell, CT 06416. Tel: 860-632-3039; Fax: 860-632-3035. Very Rev. BENEDICT KLUCINEC, M.S.A., Prov. Animator; Rev. MARTIN ROONEY, M.S.A., Sec. to the Prov.

Apostolic works consist in the promotion and training of adults for Christian leadership and for the diocesan or religious priesthood.

Please refer to the Religious Institutes of Men section for activities and representation in the United States. Activites also in Brazil, Venezuela, Colombia, Canada, and Peru.

MISSIONARY BENEDICTINE SISTERS: *Provincial Motherhouse & Novitiate-Immaculata Convent,* 300 N. 18th St., Norfolk, NE 68701. Tel: 402-371-3438; Fax: 402-379-2877. Sr. M. AGNES SALBER, O.S.B., Prioress.

Missionary work in elementary schools; catechetical programs; pastoral ministry; nursing homes; hospitals in the Archdiocese of Omaha and Diocese of New Ulm, Minnesota; Indian Mission, Northeast Nebraska; Hispanic ministry.

Missionary work outside the U.S. the Philippine Islands, Korea, Brazil, Australia, Tanzania, Namibia, Kenya, Angola, South Africa, Portugal, Germany, Italy, Spain, Switzerland, Bulgaria and Uganda.

MISSIONARY SERVANTS OF THE MOST BLESSED TRINITY: *Motherhouse, Novitiate and Generalate,* 3501 Solly Ave., Philadelphia, PA 19136; Fax: 215-335-7559. Sr. SIENA MARIE WAHL, M.S.B.T., Gen. Custodian.

The congregation's mission is the preservation of the faith. This involves nourishing the faithlife of those of the Roman Catholic tradition, cooperating in ecumenical endeavors, strengthening life-giving faith among all people, evangelization, actively promoting human development and social justice. The special apostolic intent is to advance and support the ministry of the laity in the mission of the Church, accomplished through the ministries of education, social work and health care on parish and diocesan levels.

Please refer to the Religious Institutes of Women section for activities and representation in the United States. Active also in the Archdiocese of San Juan and the Dioceses of Ponce, Caguas and Mayaguez in Puerto Rico as well as the Dioceses of Apatzingan and Texcoco in Mexico.

MISSIONARY SERVANTS OF THE MOST HOLY TRINITY (TRINITY MISSIONS): 1215 N. Scott St., Arlington, VA 22209-3097. Tel: 703-276-8646; Fax: 703-522-2656. Rev. DOMINGO RODRIGUEZ, S.T., Gen. Custodian; Bro. HILARY METTES, S.T., Sec. Gen.; Rev. RANDALL WOODS, S.T., Mission Procurator, P.O. Box 7130, Silver Spring, MD 20907-7130.

A clerical congregation of Pontifical Right founded for the preservation of the faith and missionary work wherever the Church directs. The major fields are the missionary areas of the southern United States and the Spanish-speaking people in the United States, Puerto Rico, Costa Rica and Mexico. The principal work is the development of Catholic lay leaders. There is also training for the missionary priesthood and brotherhood of the congregation.

Archdioceses of Boston, Milwaukee, Indianapolis, Los Angeles, Military Services-USA, Mobile, Newark, New Orleans, Philadelphia, St. Paul-Minneapolis, Washington DC, and San Juan and the Dioceses of Arlington, Biloxi, Boise, Birmingham, Cleveland, Jackson, Norwich, Ponce, PR, Orange, Paterson, San Diego, Savannah, Tucson and Wheeling-Charleston. Also in Mexico and Costa Rica.

Publication: *Trinity Missions.*

MISSIONARY SISTERS OF OUR LADY OF AFRICA: *American Headquarters,* 47 W. Spring St., Winooski, VT 05404. Sr. LUCILLE PILOTTE, District Supr.

Missionary activities in Africa and Yemen: catechetical, pastoral ministry, social work, education and health programs, and the founding and forming of African Religious Congregations.

MISSIONARY SISTERS OF ST. COLUMBAN (1922 IRELAND): 73 Mapleton St., Brighton, MA 02135; Fax: 617-789-3569. The Missionary Sisters of Saint Columban are also known as the Columban Sisters; Sr. CORONA COLLEARY, S.S.C., Reg. Coord.

The Missionary Sisters of St. Columban are religious women called to bring the good news of Christ to all in need, particularly the poor and the oppressed and those who have not yet had the Gospel proclaimed to them. The congregation strives to respond to the needs of the people by dedication to the work of evangelization through pastoral, educational, medical, and social ministries, and supporting the efforts of the local church where its members are sent. The congregation also endeavors, through programs of mission education and animation, to deepen an awareness of global vision and world justice.

Active in the U.S. in the Archdioceses of Boston, Chicago and Los Angeles, and in the Diocese of Buffalo.

Active outside the U.S. in Ireland, England, Scotland, Hong Kong, Korea, Philippines, Peru, Chile and Pakistan.

MISSIONARY SISTERS OF ST. PETER CLAVER (1894): *American Headquarters,* P.O. Box 401, 667 Woods Mill Rd., S. Chesterfield, MO 63006. Tel: 314-434-8084. Sr. M. AIDAN.

The congregation is of Pontifical Jurisdiction, fostering interest in and obtaining funds and requisites for the missions. Apostolate of the press in Africa.

Legal Title: *The Sodality of St. Peter Claver for the African Missions.*

Publications: monthly magazine, *Echo from Africa,* annual, *Claver Almanac.*

MISSIONARY SISTERS OF OUR LADY OF THE HOLY ROSARY: *American Regional House and Novitiate,* 205 Cricket Ave., Ardmore, PA 19003. Tel: 610-896-1786. Sr. MONICA DEVINE, Supr. Gen.; SR. PAULA MOLLOY, M.S.H.R., American Reg. Rep.

Founded for the evangelization of people in Africa and Latin America through educational, medical, social, pastoral and catechetical work.

Active in the U.S. in the Archdiocese of Philadelphia.

Active outside the U.S. in England, Ireland, Scotland, Nigeria, Sierra Leone, Cameroon, Ethiopia, Kenya, South Africa, Zambia, Ghana, Mexico and Brazil.

MISSIONARY SISTERS OF THE IMMACULATE CONCEPTION OF THE MOTHER OF GOD: *Generalate,* 48 Garden Ave., West Paterson, NJ 07424; Fax: 201-279-2991. Sr. LUCI CESAR FONTENELE, S.M.I.C., Coord. Gen.

Missionary work in homes for the aged, catechetical and social service centers, schools, dispensaries and hospitals.

Active in the U.S. in the Archdiocese of Newark and the Dioceses of Austin, Galveston-Houston, Paterson, Portland, San Antonio and San Bernardino.

Active outside the U.S. in Brazil, Germany, Namibia, Philippines and Taiwan.

MISSIONARY SISTERS OF THE IMMACULATE HEART OF MARY (1919): 238 E. 15th St., New York, NY 10003. Tel: 212-677-2959. Sr. ALENE GROTHUES, DIST. SUPR.; SR. ANNIE CLAES, COORD. Tel: 212-254-0658.

Please refer to the Religious Institutes of Women section for further details.

MISSIONARY SISTERS SERVANTS OF THE HOLY SPIRIT (1901): Techny, IL 60082-6026; Fax: 847-272-0113. Sr. PRISCILLA BURKE, Prov. Supr.; SR. DOLORES MARIE KUHL, Supr.

Home and foreign missions including teaching, nursing and social work.

Please refer to the Religious Institutes of Women section for activities and representation in the United States. Also active in the Philippine Islands, New Guinea, China, Indonesia, Japan, India, Africa, Australia, Europe, South America, Taiwan, Mexico, Cuba and Korea.

Publication: *SSpS Mission.*

OPAM-AMERICA (1984): *National Office,* 2301 Hwy. 27, P.O. Box 5657, Somerset, NJ 08875-5657. Tel: 908-297-9090; Fax: 908-297-6799. Rev. JOHN BERTELLO, I.M.C., Natl. Dir.

Charitable and educational organization established for the promotion of world literacy. It seeks to increase public awareness of the problem of illiteracy and its consequences, and encourage the American people to help eliminate it. The focus of the missionary and educational version of OPAM is to promote community development.

OPERATION HELP, INC.: P.O. Box 134, Hartly, DE 19953. Tel: 302-492-8985; Fax: 302-492-8360. Rev. PATRICK SHAULES, S.J., Pres.; MARCINDA HAEDGE, ADMIN., For Contributions: P.O. Box 566, Wilmington, DE 19899.

Operation Help, Inc., is an independently incorporated non-profit organization dedicated to helping Catholic priests and sisters bring spiritual and material salvation to the destitute poor. It offers advice and funding and places a special emphasis on Asian and African mission areas.

OUR LADY OF VICTORY MISSIONARY SISTERS: Victory-Noll, Box 109, Huntington, IN 46750. Tel: 219-356-

0628. Sr. Lucy Regalado, O.L.V.M., Pres.; Sr. Marjorie Curran, O.L.V.M., Gen. Sec.
Legal Title: *Our Lady of Victory Missionary Sisters, Inc.*
A Marian congregation proclaiming the Gospel in a personal, non-institutional way through pastoral ministry, religious education, social service and health- care programs in favor of the poor and oppressed.
Please refer to the Religious Institutes of Women section for activities and representation in the United States. Active also in foreign missions in Oruro, Bolivia.

Parish Visitors of Mary Immaculate: *Motherhouse Generalate and Novitiate-Marycrest,* P.O. Box 658, Monroe, NY 10950-0658. Tel: 914-783-2251. Sr. Carole Marie Troskowski, Gen. Supr.; Sr. Frances Walter, Gen. Sec.
Founded for the missionary visitation of families and individuals in the parish and for religious instruction of children and adults; assists parish priests in their ministry of evangelization, catechetical programs, spiritual surveys, census, informal visitation, follow-up religious counseling, religious social services, training laity.
Please refer to the Religious Institutes of Women section for activities and representation in the United States and Nigeria.
Publication: *The Parish Visitor.*

Passionist Sisters (1924): *Sisters of the Cross and Passion American Provincialate,* Holy Family Convent, One Wright Lane, North Kingstown, RI 02852. Sr. Ellen Downes, C.P., Prov. Supr.
Diversified apostolic works according to the needs of the Church; catechetical, pastoral and social work; educational functions; retreats; missionary in the United States and foreign countries.
Please refer to the Religious Institutes of Women section for activities and representation in the United States. Active also in Africa, Botswana, Europe, England, Ireland and Scotland, Latin America, Argentina, Chile, Peru, West Indies, Jamica and Papua New Guinea.

Pontifical Institute for Foreign Missions, P.I.M.E., Inc.: *U.S. Region,* 17330 Quincy Ave., Detroit, MI 48221. Tel: 313-342-4066; Fax: 313-342-6816. Very Rev. Bruno Piccolo P.I.M.E., Prov. Supr.
Legal Title: *Pontifical Institute for Foreign Missions (P.I.M.E.), Inc.*
American Province recruits and trains priests and brothers for foreign missionary work; secures funds for foreign mission work and mission education activities.
Active in the U.S. the Archdioceses of Detroit and the Dioceses of Columbus, Paterson and Palm Beach.
Outside the U.S. Brazil, Burma, Hong Kong, India, Japan, Bangladesh, Guinea-Bissau, Cameroon, Canada, Ivory Coast, Mexico, Papua New Guinea, Taiwan, Philippines, and Thailand.
Publication: national magazine, *PIME World.*

St. Joseph's Society of the Sacred Heart (Josephites): *Headquarters,* 1130 North Calvert St., Baltimore, MD 21202. Tel: 410-727-3386; Fax: 410-385-2231. Very Rev. Robert M. Kearns, S.S.J., Supr. Gen.. An organization of priests and brothers doing missionary work in the African American community of the United States.
Publication: *The Josephite Harvest.*

St. Patrick's Missionary Society: 70 Edgewater Rd., Cliffside Park, NJ 07010; Fax: 201-943-2946. Rev. James Barry, U.S. Supr.; Rev. Karl Langsdorf, Supr., Chicago, IL; Rev. Jeremiah Kiely, Supr., Saratoga, CA; Rev. James Barry, Supr., Cliffside Park, NJ.
A society of secular priests devoted entirely to the missionary needs of the Church.
Activities in the Archdioceses of Newark, Chicago, New Orleans, San Francisco and the Dioceses of San Jose, Paterson and Palm Beach. Outside the U.S. in Nigeria— Archdiocese of Lagos, Dioceses of Abakaliki, Calabar, Abuja, Minna, Ogoja, Warri, Port Harcourt and Missio Sui Juris Bomadi. Kenya— Archdiocese of Nairobi, Dioceses of Eldoret, Kitui, Lodwar and Nakuru. Sudan— Diocese of Torit. Malawi—Dioceses of Lilongwe, Chikwawa, Zomba and Mzuzu. Zambia—Archdiocese of Lusaka, Diocese of Chipata. Brazil—Archdioceses of Sao Paulo, Dioceses of Campo Limpo, Osasco, Santo Amaro, Sao Miguel Paulista and Campina Grande. Grenada—Diocese of St. George's. South Africa—Dioceses of Tzaneen and Witbank. Zimbabwe—Archdiocese of Harare and Diocese of Mutare. Cameroon—Archdiocese of Bamenda.
Publication: *Africa, St. Patrick's Mission.*

Salesian Missions: 2 Lefevre Ln., New Rochelle, NY 10801. Tel: 914-633-8344.
The Salesians were founded to help bring the Faith to all people, and contribute to their social and economic development through education, especially in trade and agricultural schools. The purpose of the society is the recruitment and preparation of vocations for the missions and the education of the American public on the needs of other people through lectures, mass media, direct mail and the magazine, *Salesian.* It is also the purpose of the society to educate the American public on the unique system of education developed by the society's founder, St. John Bosco, as well as to spread knowledge of his life and accomplishments. Funds are raised to implement the religious, educational and technical assistance projects of the society.
Please refer to the Religious Institutes of Men section for activities and representation in the United States. Represented in 120 countries throughout the world.
Publication: *Salesian.*

School Sisters of Notre Dame: *Milwaukee Province,* 13105 Watertown Plank Rd., Elm Grove, WI 53122-2291; Fax: 414-278-7085. Sr. Laura Jean Spaeth, Prov. Leader.
Missionary work outside the U.S.: Guam and Caroline-Marshall Islands; Africa: Ghana, Kenya; Nigeria; Central America: Guatemala, Honduras.
Baltimore Province, 6401 N. Charles St., Baltimore, MD 21212-1099. Sr. Jane Burke, Prov.
Missionary work outside the U.S.: Bolivia, El Salvador, Africa, Ghana and Nigeria.
St. Louis Province, 320 E. Ripa Ave., St. Louis, MO 63125-2897. Sr. Kathleen Wegman, S.S.N.D., Prov.
Missionary work outside the U.S.: The Gambia, Honduras, Japan, Nepal, Africa, Sierra Leone, Ghana, Kenya.
Mankato Province, Convent of Our Lady of Good Counsel, Mankato, MN 56001-3198. Sr. Katherine DuVal, Prov.
Missionary work outside the U.S.: Guatemala, Kenya, and Africa
Wilton Province, 345 Belden Hill Rd., Wilton, CT 06897. Sr. Marie Jeannette Blatz, Prov.
Missionary work outside the U.S.: Chile, Brazil, Ghana, Africa, Peru and Puerto Rico.
Dallas Province, 4500 W. Davis, Dallas, TX 75211. Sr. Elizabeth Newman, Prov.
Missionary work outside the U.S.: Ghana, Guatemala and Honduras.
Chicago Province, 1431 Euclid Ave., Berwyn, IL 60402. Sr. Catherine Sarther, Prov.
Missionary work outside the U.S.: Paraguay, Japan and Nepal.
Please refer to the Religious Institutes of Women section for activities and representations in the United States.

Sisters of the Blessed Sacrament for Indians and Colored People (1891): *St. Mary Generalate,* Bensalem, PA 19020-8502; Fax: 215-344-8174. Sr. Monica Loughlin, Pres.
Missionary work in the educational, catechetical and social services among Black and Native Americans as well as Haitians in the U.S. and Haiti.
Please refer to the Religious Institutes of Women section for activities and representation in the United States.
Publications: *Mission; The Peacemaker.*

Society of African Missions: *American Province,* 23 Bliss Ave., Tenafly, NJ 07670. Tel: 201-567-0450; Fax: 201-567-7156. Very Rev. Douglas B. Gilbert S.M.A., Prov.
Please refer to the Religious Institutes of Men section for activities and representation in the United States.
Active also in West Africa: Liberia—Diocese of Cape Palmas, Archdiocese of Monrovia, Diocese of Gbarnga; Ivory Coast—Archdiocese of Abidjan; Dioceses of Abengourou, Bondoukou, Bouake, Daloa, Gagnoa, Katiola, Grand-Bassam, Korhogo, Man, San Pedro and Yopougon; Ghana—Archdiocese of Cape Coast; Dioceses of Accra, Obvasi, Keta-Ho, Kumasi, Sekondi-Takoradi and Sunyani; Togo—Archdiocese of Lome; Dioceses of Atakpame and Sokode; Benin—Archdiocese of Cotonou; Dioceses of Abomey, Natitingou, Parakou and Porto-Novo; Nigeria—Archdioceses of Kaduna and Lagos; Dioceses of Benin City, Ibadan, Ijebu-Ode, Ilorin, Jos, Makurdi, Ondo and Warri; Niger—Diocese of Niamey; Cameroon—Archdiocese of Yaounde; Central African Republic—Archdiocese of Bangui; Dioceses of Bambari and Berberati. Central Africa: Zaire—Diocese of Kikwit. East Africa: Zambia—Diocese of Ndola. Egypt—Vicarate Apostolic of Alexandria. Tanzania—Dioceses of Geita and Shinyanga. Kenya—Archdiocese of Nairobi. Argentina—Archdiocese of Cordoba. Australia—Archdiocese of Perth. South Africa—Diocese of Rustenburg. Philippines—Archdiocese of Manila. South India: Tamil-Nadu. Poland—Warsaw.

Society of Mary: *Cincinnati Province, Marianist Provincialate,* 4435 E. Patterson Rd., Dayton, OH 45430-1095. Tel: 513-429-0794; Fax: 513-429-3195. Very Rev. James F. Fitz, S.M., Prov.
Missionary work in the following territories: Archdiocese of Nairobi, Kenya, Africa; Diocese of Mzuzu, Malawi, Africa; Diocese of Yokohama, Japan; Diocese of Lusaka, Zambia, Africa; Dhaka, Bangladesh.

Society of Mary: *St. Louis Province,* P.O. Box 23130, St. Louis, MO 63156. Tel: 314-367-0390; Fax: 314-361-3131. Rev. Timothy Dwyer S.M., Prov.
Educational, parish and development work in the following territories: Archdioceses of Arequipa and Trujillo, Peru; Archdiocese of Abidjan, Africa; Archdiocese of Ranchi, Bangalore in India; Diocese of Yokohama, Japan; Diocese of Muzaffarpur, India; Dioceses of Coatzacoalcos and Queretaro, Mexico; Diocese of Dhaka, Bangladesh.

Society of Mary: *Province of the Pacific (Marianists),* P.O. Box 1775, Cupertino, CA 95015-1775; Fax: 408-253-5280. Very Rev. Timothy Eden, S.M., Prov.
Educational, social and parish work in the following mission territories: Mokpo, Inchon, and Seoul, South Korea; Archdioceses of Seoul and Kwangju, South Korea; Dioceses of Inchon and Suwon, South Korea.

Society of Mary: *New York Province,* 4301 Roland Ave., Baltimore, MD 21210-2793. Bro. Stephen Glodek, S.M., Prov.
Educational, social and parish work in the following mission territories: Archdiocese of San Juan and Diocese of Ponce, Puerto Rico. Also in Africa in Karonga, Malawi; Nairobi, Kenya; and Lusaka, Zambia.

Society of St. Edmund: *Edmundite Generalate,* 270 Winooski Park, Colchester, VT 05439. Tel: 802-654-3400; Fax: 802-654-3409. Very Rev. Joseph L. Hart, S.S.E., Supr. Gen.
Legal Title: *Society of St. Edmund, Inc.*
Major missionary endeavors in the United States are in Selma, Alabama and surrounding areas, and in the inner city of New Orleans (LA).
See the Foreign Mission section for the list of priests serving abroad.
Publications: *Edmundite Missions.*

Society of the Precious Blood: *Cincinnati Province,* 431 E. Second St., Dayton, OH 45402; Fax: 513-228-6878. Very Rev. Kenneth F. Pleiman, C.PP.S., Prov. Dir.; Rev. James F. McCabe, C.PP.S., Prov. Sec.; Bro. Joseph J. Fisher, C.PP.S., Mission Procurator.
Mission activities outside the U.S. in Chile, Peru, South America, Guatemala, Central America; missions in La Tinta, Tucuru, Santiago, Purranque, Valdivia, LaOroya, Yauli, Lima, Guatemala City, Urutu, Guatemala.
Priests and brothers in foreign missions 38.
Publication: *C.PP.S. Today,* Provincial House, 431 E. Second St., Dayton, OH 45402-1764. Rev. James F. McCabe, C.PP.S., Editor.

Sons of Mary Missionary Society (1954): 567 Salem End Rd., Framingham, MA 01702. Bro. Kevin Courtney, Major Coord.; Revs. John Coss, Financial Coord.; Henry Cicale, Councilor.
Dedicated to the ministry of healing: medical, catechetical and social apostolates in the home and foreign missions.
Legal Title: *Sons of Mary, Health of the Sick, Inc.*

Third Order Regular of St. Francis: *Province of the Most Sacred Heart of Jesus, Franciscan T.O.R. Missions,* P.O. Box 188, Loretto, PA 15940. Tel: 814-472-3348. Bro. Mark McBride, T.O.R., Prov. Dir. of Foreign Missions; Very Rev. Edmund Carroll, T.O.R., Minister Prov. Tel: 412-781-1232.
Secures missionaries and material aid to missions.
Active in the Archdioceses of Manaus and Sao Paulo; the Prelacy of Borba, Brazil; the Diocese of Bhagalpur, Bihar, India; and Diocese of Vice Province of Saint Joseph, Republic of South Africa.

Xaverian Missionary Fathers: *Provincial Headquarters,* 12 Helene Ct., Wayne, NJ 07470-2813. Tel: 201-942-2975; Fax: 201-942-5012. Very Rev. Francis Signorelli, S.X.
A religious society of priests and brothers dedicated exclusively to foreign mission work and the training of candidates for missionary life.
Please refer to the Religious Institutes of Men section for activities and representation in the United States. Active also in Brazil, Zaire, Burundi, Chad, Cameroon, Bangladesh, Indonesia, Japan, Mexico, Sierra Leone, Colombia, Philippines, Taiwan, Italy, Spain and Great Britain.
Publication: *Xaverian Missions Newsletter.*

Pontifical Missionary Societies.

A. The Pontifical Society for the Propagation of the Faith (1822): *National Office,* 366 Fifth Ave., New York, NY 10001. Tel: 212-563-8700; Fax: 212-563-8725. Most Rev. William J. McCormack, National Dir.; Rev. Msgr. James A. Moloney, Vice Pres.; Rev. Msgr. Robert E. Duffy, Treas.; Rev. Msgr. Bernard H. Sandheinrich, Sec.; Rev. Msgr. Andrew F. Connell, Asst. Treas.
International Officers: Jozef Cardinal Tomko, Prefect of the Congregation for Evangelization of Peoples; Most Rev. Charles A. Schleck, C.S.C., Pres.;

Rev. Msgr. BERNARD A. PRINCE, Sec. Gen., Vatican City.

The Propagation of the Faith, under the direction of the Congregation for the Evangelization of Peoples, is established in every country where the Church is free to operate; it has a two-fold goal of promoting a universal missionary spirit and encouraging prayer and financial support for the local churches of the missions.

Each diocese in the United States has a director appointed by the Ordinary to promote the work of the Society through programs such as World Mission Sunday and Membership, presentations in seminaries, lesson plans and materials for mission animation in schools (grades 7-12) and parishes, news media and personal contact with parishes and diocesan organizations.

Offerings received by the Propagation of the Faith in the United States are joined with offerings from all other countries and distributed as equitably as possible to close to 1,000 mission dioceses and vicariates.

Publication: quarterly, *Mission;* Most Rev. WILLIAM J. McCORMACK, Publisher.

B. THE SOCIETY OF ST. PETER APOSTLE (1889): *National Office,* 366 Fifth Ave., New York, NY 10001. Tel: 212-563-8700. Most Rev. WILLIAM J. McCORMACK, National Dir.

International Officers: JOZEF CARDINAL TOMKO, Prefect of the Congregation for Evangelization of Peoples; Most Rev. CHARLES A. SCHLECK, C.S.C., Pres.; Rev. Msgr. BERNARD A. PRINCE, Sec.-Gen., Vatican City.

The Society of St. Peter Apostle, under the direction of the Congregation for the Evangelization of Peoples, is established for the support of seminarians and novices in the missions. During 1995, there were 26,414 major seminarians, 54,089 minor seminarians and 9,608 novices receiving assistance from the Society of St. Peter Apostle. The Society also helps support local religious communities and retired native clergy. Each diocese in the United States has a local director who is also the Director of the Propagation of the Faith.

C. THE PONTIFICAL MISSIONARY UNION (1916): *National Office,* 366 Fifth Ave., New York, NY 10001. Tel: 212-563-8700. Most Rev. WILLIAM J. McCORMACK, National Dir.

International Officers: JOZEF CARDINAL TOMKO, Prefect of the Congregation for Evangelization of Peoples; Most Rev. CHARLES A. SCHLECK, C.S.I., Pres.; Most Rev. ALESSANDRO STACCIOLI, O.M.I., Intl. Sec.; Rev. EUGENE LAVERDIERE, S.S.S., Natl. Sec.

The Missionary Union, under the direction of the Congregation for the Evangelization of Peoples, is established to inspire, deepen and sustain a mission spirit among priests, deacons, religious, seminarians, candidates for the religious life and others in the pastoral ministry of the Church. The director in each diocese is also the Director of the Propagation of the Faith.

D. HOLY CHILDHOOD ASSOCIATION–(HCA YOUNG CATHOLICS IN MISSION): *National Office,* 1720 Massachusetts Ave. N.W., Washington, DC 20036. Tel: 202-775-8637; Fax: 202-429-2987. Very Rev. FRANCIS W. WRIGHT, C.S.Sp., Natl. Dir., His Holiness Pope John Paul II, Supreme Head & Protector; Most Rev. GUISEPPE UHAC, Pres.; Rev. Msgr. JULIO D. BOTIA APONTE, Sec. Gen., Vatican City.

Founded in 1843 by Bishop Charles de Forbin Janson. It is the official agency of the Church by which Catholic children of the world contribute through their prayers and sacrifices to the welfare of other children in more than 100 mission countries. Since its beginning, it has become the personal favorite of every Pope. In 1926, Pope Pius XI elevated the society to Pontifical rank. Holy Childhood endeavors to attain its ends through the united efforts of all Catholic children who are taught to recognize that sensitivity to others is an essential dimension of Christianity. Funds raised through children's efforts are directed to the Association's two-fold mandate, the majority being distributed annually to every part of the mission world by a Ponitifical Commission and a portion being directed to education of children in the United States.

The Education and Promotion Fund solicits adult donations for the purpose of underwriting HCA educational efforts so that a greater portion of children's donations reach children in need.

All allocations sent to the missions through the agency of the Holy Childhood are used solely in the interests of the children of these missions. The Association is officially established in all archdioceses and dioceses of the United States.

Missionary Societies, Mission Boards and their Diocesan Branches.

AMERICAN BOARD OF CATHOLIC MISSIONS: 3211 Fourth St. N.E., Washington, DC 20017. Tel: 202-541-3010; Fax: 202-541-3322. Most Rev. VICTOR H. BALKE, Chm.; Dr. DAVID M. BYERS, Exec. Dir.

A committee of the National Conference of Catholic Bishops dedicated to support of the home missions. The ABCM makes grants to extend the Church's presence as a means of salvation where it is not now present and to strengthen the Church's presence where it is weak. Grantees include dioceses, religious institutes and national, regional and interdiocesan Catholic organizations in the United States and its dependencies. The ABCM funds a wide range of mission and evangelization activities; examples include parish support, seminary formation, lay ministry training, religious education, and Hispanic and Black ministry. Application materials are available September 1 of each year; the deadline for submission of completed applications is November 1. The ABCM makes grant decisions once a year in March, and grants are disbursed in quarterly payments July through June. The ABCM's funds come from two sources: a percentage of the receipts of the annual Mission Sunday Collection and a percentage of ordinary memberships in the Society for the Propagation of the Faith.

AMERICAN CONVENTUAL FRANCISCAN MISSIONS: Headquarters are at the following provinces.

Immaculate Conception Province, P.O. Box 629, Rensselaer, NY 12144. Tel: 518-465-3673. Rev. JAMES AMRCHIN O.F.M.Conv., Mission Procurator, *Missions:* Costa Rica, Brazil.

St. Anthony Province, 1300 Dundalk Ave., Baltimore, MD 21222. Tel: 301-633-8900. Rev. PLACID KACZOREK, O.F.M.Conv., Mission Procurator, Franciscan Mission Association, 66 School St., Granby, MA 01033. Tel: 413-467-7189. *Missions:* Japan, Ghana and Peru.

Our Lady of Consolation Province, Mount St. Francis, IN 47156. Tel: 812-923-8444. Rev. SEBASTIAN CUNNINGHAM, O.F.M.Conv., Mission Procurator, 322 West St., Carey, OH 43316. Tel: 419-396-7107. *Missions:* Zambia, Honduras, Costa Rica.

St. Bonaventure Province, 6107 N. Kenmore Ave., Chicago, IL 60660. Rev. VINCENT BRYLKA, O.F.M.Conv., Mission Procurator, Provincial Office, 6107 N. Kenmore Ave., Chicago, IL 60660. Tel: 312-274-7681. *Missions:* Mexico.

St. Joseph Cupertino Province, P.O. Box 820, Arroyo Grande, CA 93420. Tel: 805-489-1012. Rev. STEPHEN GROSS, O.F.M.Conv., Mission Procurator, St. Paul Friary, 1845 Church Ln., San Pablo, CA 94806. Tel: 415-232-5931.

BUREAU OF CATHOLIC INDIAN MISSIONS (1874): 2021 H St., N.W., Washington, DC 20006. Tel: 202-331-8542; Fax: 202-331-8544. His Eminence JOHN CARDINAL O'CONNOR, Pres.; His Eminence ANTHONY CARDINAL BEVILACQUA; His Eminence WILLIAM CARDINAL KEELER, D.D.; Rev. Msgr. PAUL A. LENZ, Exec. Dir.; Rev. TED ZUERN, S.J., Assoc. Dir.; PATRICIA L. O'ROURKE, Asst. Sec. & Treas.

Collecting and distribution of funds for the support of American Indian missions. The Bureau represents the missions in Government relations, specifically in Washington, DC. Active throughout the United States, where American Indian, Eskimo and Aleute missions are present.

Publication: monthly newsletter, *The Bureau of Catholic Indian Missions.*

CATHOLIC CHURCH EXTENSION SOCIETY OF THE UNITED STATES OF AMERICA, THE (1905): 35 East Wacker Dr., Rm. 400, Chicago, IL 60601-2105. Tel: 312-236-7240. Most Rev. OSCAR H. LIPSCOMB, Vice Chancellor; Rev. Msgr. KENNETH VELO, Pres.; RICHARD A. RITTER, Vice Pres. & Treas.; JAMES L. STOTT, Dir. Devel.

The Extension Society is a Papal fund-raiser that helps to support the Church in rural, remote and poor areas of the United States and its protectorates. The Society raises money through freewill donations, charitable gift annuities, trusts and will bequests.

Requests for funds are submitted by bishops in designated home mission dioceses. Funding is for religious purposes: construction of chapels and other home mission buildings; living expenses of priests, religious and lay people working for home missions; seminarian education; campus ministry; scholarships in religious education at Fordham University to those working in home mission catechetical programs; chapel furnishings; evangelization; religious education, including sponsorship of American Catholic radio show, parish calendars, videotapes on mission work in the U.S., and evangelization booklets.

Publications: *EXTENSION Magazine; Extension Parish Calendars.*

CATHOLIC MEDICAL MISSION BOARD, INC. (1928): 10 W. 17th St., New York, NY 10011-5765. Members of the Board: His Eminence JOHN CARDINAL O'CONNOR; Revs. FERDINANDO D. BERARDI; VINCENT M. COOK, S.J.; JOHN A. DONNELLY; DR. THEODORE J. DUBUQUE, Jr., M.D.; Rev. ROBERT J. FUHRMAN; Mr. VINCENT J. LEWIS; Dr. ANDREW J. McGOWAN, Jr., M.D.; THOMAS P. MELADY; THOMAS F. MURPHY; Rev. WILLIAM T. WOOD, S.J.

The Catholic Medical Mission Board, Inc. (CMMB) provides pharmaceuticals and health care supplies for clinical facilities which treat victims of poverty in developing and transitional countires. Funds are used to buy medications in USA and in foreign markets which offer easier access to cost-efficient, quality purchases. In addition to its schedule of shipments, CMMB responds to health care emergencies. For the past 68 years, over $350 million in medicines and related supplies have been shipped to 2,000 clinical facilites in 30 countries. Financial aid is also granted to students matriculated in accredited health care education programs. CMMB's placement program assists health providers interested in volunteering for short-term and long-term tours of service at selected clinical sites around the world. Over 1,600 volunteer personnel have been recruited since CMMB's founding. Catholic Medical Mission Board, Inc. publishes Medical Mission News, a quarterly magazine which offers information on its programs. Recipients of shipments and health care placement opportunities are featured.

CATHOLIC MISSIONARY UNION: 86-11 Midland Pkwy., Jamaica Estates, NY 11432. Tel: 718-291-5995. His Eminence JOHN CARDINAL O'CONNOR, Pres.; Rev. EDWARD WHITLEY, C.S.P., Sec. & Treas.

The corporation subsidizes missions to non-Catholics. Activities are in outlying districts of the South, particularly in those sections where there are few Catholics and facilities for practicing religion.

CATHOLIC NEAR EAST WELFARE ASSOCIATION (1926): 1011 First Ave., New York, NY 10022. His Eminence JOHN CARDINAL O'CONNOR, Pres. & Treas.; Most Rev. WILLIAM H. KEELER, Vice Pres.; Rev. Msgr. ROBERT L. STERN, Sec. Gen.; Rev. Msgr. JAMES M. MOYNIHAN, Assoc. Sec. Gen.

A papal agency for humanitarian and pastoral support established by Pope Pius XI in 1926. It promotes awareness of the condition and the needs of the churches, institutions and persons under the jurisdiction of the Congregation for the Eastern Churches and the Permanent Interdiscasterial Commission for the Church on Eastern Europe. It raises and distributes funds to help meet the material and spiritual needs of the people it serves.

The Association works for people in those lands in which from ancient times the majority of Christians have been members of the various eastern churches. Its mandate extends to the churches and peoples of the Middle East, Northeast Africa, India and Eastern Europe. It encourages and provides assistance to projects and programs of pastoral support, humanitarian assistance, interfaith communication and public awareness.

Publication: bimonthly magazine, *Catholic Near East.*

CATHOLIC NEGRO-AMERICAN MISSION BOARD (1907): 2021 H St., N.W., Washington, DC 20006. Tel: 202-331-8542. His Eminence JOHN CARDINAL O'CONNOR, Pres.; His Eminence ANTHONY CARDINAL BEVILACQUA; His Eminence WILLIAM CARDINAL KEELER; Rev. Msgr. PAUL A. LENZ, Exec. Dir.; PATRICIA L. O'ROURKE, Asst. Sec. & Treas.

Engaged in the support of priests and sisters throughout the states below Mason and Dixon Line, especially monthly support of sisters and lay teachers in poor black schools.

Active in the United States, particularly all states in the South.

COMMISSARIAT OF THE HOLY LAND: *Franciscan Monastery,* 14th and Quincy Sts., N.E., Washington, DC 20017. Tel: 202-526-6800; Fax: 202-529-9889. Bro. CALLISTUS WELCH, O.F.M.

Collecting funds for support of the sacred places, educational and charitable institutions in the Holy Land through the Good Friday collection, and educating young men for the Missions of the Custody of the Holy Land in Syria, Jordan, Lebanon, Cyprus, Rhodes, Israel and Egypt.

COMMISSARIAT OF THE HOLY LAND: 3140 Meramec St., St. Louis, MO 63118-4339. Tel: 314-353-7729; Fax: 314-353-2790. Rev. THOMAS GARDNER, O.F.M., Commissary.

Established for collecting and distributing funds for the support of the sacred places in the Holy Land. Regional Commissariat for the Ecclesiastical Provinces of Chicago, Cincinnati, Detroit, Dubuque, Indianapolis, Kansas City, Louisville, Milwaukee, Mobile, New Orleans, Oklahoma City, Omaha, St. Louis, St. Paul-Minneapolis and San Antonio.

COMMISSARIAT OF THE HOLY LAND: 218 E. 12th St., Los Angeles, CA 90015. Tel: 213-748-5394. Rev. MARTIAL LUEBKE, O.F.M., Commissary.

Established to collect and distribute funds for support of the Sacred Shrines and educational and charitable institutions in the Holy Land. Assigned Territory: Ecclesiastical Provinces of Denver, Los Angeles, Portland (OR), San Francisco, Santa Fe and Seattle.

COMMISSION FOR CATHOLIC MISSIONS AMONG THE COLORED PEOPLE AND THE INDIANS (BLACK AND INDIAN MISSION OFFICE) (1884): 2021 H St., N.W., Washington, DC 20006. Tel: 202-331-8542; Fax: 202-331-8544. Board of Directors: His Eminence JOHN CARDINAL O'CONNOR, Pres.; His Eminence ANTHONY CARDINAL BEVILACQUA; His Eminence WILLIAM CARDINAL KEELER; Rev. Msgr. PAUL A. LENZ, Exec. Dir.; PATRICIA L. O'ROURKE, Dir. Collection & Asst. Sec./Treas.

Organized by the Third Plenary Council as trustee of the funds collected in the churches for support of the Black and Indian mission work in the United States.

Publication: annual, *Annual Report.*

DOMINICAN MISSION SECRETARIATE: 141 E. 65th St., New York, NY 10021-6607. Tel: 212-861-3776; Fax: 212-639-9823. Bro. THOMAS AQUINAS DOLAN, O.P., Dir.

Founded by the Order of Preachers (Dominican Friars), Province of St. Joseph for the purpose of promoting American Dominican activity in the foreign missions throughout the world. Presently the Secretariate aids and supports work in the Archdioceses of Karachi and Lahore, the dioceses of Multan, Faisalabad and Islamabad-Rawalpindi in Pakistan. The Archdioceses of Lima and the diocese of Chimbote in Peru. Nairobi and Kisumu in Kenya. St. Petersburg, Russia; Vilnius, Lithuania; Calayan Island, Philippines, and the Solomon Islands.

Legal Title: *St. Jude Dominican Foreign Missions, Inc.* (formerly Rosary, Foreign Mission Society, Inc.); Special funds under the auspices of the Dominican Foreign Missions: *Handicapped Children Funds, Peru.*

FRANCISCAN CUSTODY OF ST. MARY OF THE ANGELS: *Holy Dormition Monastery,* P.O. Box 270, Sybertsville, PA 18251; Fax: 717-788-2431. Very Rev. ANTHONY SKURLA, O.F.M., Protohegumen.

Preparing missionaries to work among the people of Slav origin in the Byzantine Church.

GENERAL SECRETARIAT OF THE FRANCISCAN MISSIONS, INC.: P.O. Box 130, Waterford, WI 53185. Tel: 414-534-5470. Revs. SERENO BAIARDI, O.F.M., Dir.; SANTE DE ANGELIS, O.F.M., Assoc. Dir.

General American office for assistance to Franciscan Missions under the auspices of the General Minister of the Order of Friars Minor.

CATHOLIC NETWORK OF VOLUNTEER SERVICE: 4121 Harewood Rd., N.E., Washington, DC 20017. Tel: 202-529-1100; 800-543-5046; Fax: 202-526-1094. Most Rev. JOSEPH A. FRANCIS, S.V.D., Episcopal Advisor; JAMES G. LINDSAY, Exec. Dir.

National Office Team: PHYLLIS SCARINGE; MARY ELLEN MOORE; JEAN NEWELL; DEBORAH F. MCARDLE; JENNIFER L. SCHUMACHER; JACK DUNNE; KENT CHENG.

The Catholic Network of Volunteer Service promotes, recruits and refers volunteers to missions in the United States and overseas. We represent over 180 faith-based volunteer programs worldwide and work with the U.S. dioceses, religious communities and the private sector to determine their needs for help. The Catholic Network of Volunteer Service (CNVS) is committed to the goal that every Catholic man and woman be invited to consider a period of service in the missions, as a vital and important manifestation of the baptismal call of all Catholic people to missionary life. Currently, 5,500 men and women are serving in CNVS member mission programs offering their gifts and abilities in full-time service to people in need and living their Catholic faith more fully than many had imagined possible. These volunteers are serving domestically for a summer, six months, a year or more, and they are serving internationally for two or more years at a time. They are single and married, recent college graduates and early retirees, doctors and teachers, parish ministers and social workers, community organizers, computer operators, legal aides and more Gatherings: Annual Conference; Formation Workshops, Training Seminars.

Publications: annual, *The Response,* biweekly, *How Can I Help?,* quarterly, *Mission Handbook, Awards: The Father George Mader Award, given annually to honor organizations and individuals who promote the value of lay mission service.*

MISSIONARY ASSOCIATION OF CATHOLIC WOMEN (1916): *National Office,* 3501 S. Lake Dr., Milwaukee, WI 53235. Tel: 414-769-3406. Mr. DONALD J. MUELLER, Rep.

Pontifical Association providing material and financial aid to home and foreign missions.

MIVA-AMERICA MISSIONARY VEHICLE ASSOCIATION INC.: *National Office,* 1400 Michigan Ave., N.E., Washington, DC 20017. Tel: 202-526-3444; Fax: 202-526-0830. Revs. PHILIP DEREA, M.S.C., Natl. Dir.; ANTHONY F. KRISAK, Exec. Dir.; SR. FRANCIS ELIZABETH MCCARRON, S.N.D., Mission Appeal Coord.

The Missionary Vehicle Association raises funds to provide vehicles (cars, trucks, jeeps, boats) to American Missionaries in developing and undeveloped countries, whose work depends on safe, adequate transportation to provide health care and education and preaching the Gospel.

OBLATES OF ST. FRANCIS DE SALES (O.S.F.S.) (1906): *Wilmington-Philadelphia Province,* 2200 Kentmere Pkwy., Box 1452, Wilmington, DE 19899. Tel: 302-656-8529; Fax: 302-658-8052. Very Rev. JOSEPH G. MORRISSEY, O.S.F.S., Prov.

Toledo-Detroit Province, (1966), 2056 Parkwood Ave., Toledo, OH 43620. Tel: 419-243-5105. Very Rev. JAMES F. CRYAN, O.S.F.S., Prov.

American Mission Directors; Rev. JOHN J. HURLEY, O.S.F.S., 1600 Brinckle Ave., Wilmington, DE 19806. Rev. FRANCIS J. GROSS, O.S.F.S., 2056 Parkwood Ave., Toledo, OH 43620. Tel: 419-243-5105.

Missionary work in Republic of South Africa, Diocese of Keimeos; Nambia, Diocese of Keetmamshoop; South America—Uruguay, Archdiocese of Montevideo; Brazil, Archdioceses of Rio de Janeiro and Porto Alegre (Rio Grande de Sol), Dioceses of Bage (RGS), Cruz Alta (RGS), Frederico Westphalen (RGS), and Senhor do Bofim (Bahia); India, Archdiocese of Bangalore (province of Kerala); Haiti—Diocese of Les Gonaives; Mexico—Archdiocese of Merida.

Please refer to the Religious Institutes of Men section for activities and representation in the United States.

Provinces outside the United States: France, Germany, Austria, Switzerland, Italy, and Holland.

PONTIFICAL MISSION FOR PALESTINE (1949): 1011 First Ave., New York, NY 10022. Tel: 212-826-1480. Rev. Msgr. ROBERT L. STERN, Pres.; Rev. DENIS MADDEN, Vice Pres.; Rev. Msgr. JOHN F. MCCARTHY, Dir.-Vatican Office; Mr. ISSAM BISHARA, Dir.-Beirut Office; Rev. ROBERT REIDY, Dir.-Jerusalem Office.

A papal agency for humanitarian and charitable assistance established by Pope Pius XII in 1949. Its mission is to assist, without regard to nationality or religion, all who suffer as a result of the repeated conflicts which have devastated Palestine and neighboring regions of the Middle East.

It encourages and supports projects and programs of relief, rehabilitation, development; collaboration with other agencies; and education.

ST. PAUL'S GUILD, INC.: 1011 First Ave., Rm. 1940, New York, NY 10022. Rev. Msgr. Francis X. Duffy, Exec. Sec.

Formerly National Catholic Converts' League, now interested in assisting former Protestant clergymen and former Protestant religious.

TEKAKWITHA CONFERENCE NATIONAL CENTER, THE (1939): 1800 9th Ave., South No. 20, Great Falls, MT 59405. P.O. Box 6768, Great Falls, MT 59406. Tel: 406-727-0147; Fax: 406-452-9845.

Non-profit organization established for evangelization within the Catholic Church with American Indians, Eskimos and missionaries working together at the national level to develop a Native American voice and presence in the Catholic Church. Catechesis, liturgy, youth ministry, Incultration and related areas within the Catholic Church are goals of the Conference.

Publication: quarterly newsletter, Cross & Feather News.

United States Conference of Secular Institutes

U.S.C.S.I.: P.O. Box 4556, 12th St. N.E., Washington, DC 20017.

Members of the U.S.C.S.I. are Secular Institutes of Diocesan or Pontifical Right, canonically erected since 1947, following the promulgation of the Apostolic Constitution, "Provida Mater Ecclesia," by Pope Pius XII. The Institutes are listed on this page by the Congregation for the Institutes of Consecrated Life and for Societies of Apostolic Life. The purpose of the U.S.C.S.I., canonically erected by the Congregation as of its 1976 statutes, is to offer the Institutes an opportunity to exchange experiences, conduct research, and promote ways to make the vocation and Institutes known. The executive council includes: Dr. Helen St. Denis, Caritas Christi, President; Carol Winkler, Shoenstatt, Vice President; Rev. Frank Mawn, Institute of the Heart of Jesus, Secretary; Anita Plourde, Oblate Missionary of Mary Immaculate, Treasurer.

Caritas Christi: P.O. Box 5162, River Forest, IL 60305. Julia A. Lane, Natl. Sponsor. Forms and gives to the Church laywomen who according to their callings, talents and professional skills seek to respond to the love of Christ in their providential environment by following the demands of the Gospel.

Company of St. Paul: 52 Davis Ave., White Plains, NY 10605. Rev. Stuart Sandberg, Contact Person, (Lay People and Priests).

Founded in Milan, Italy November 17, 1920, under the auspices of Cardinal Andrew Ferrari; approved as a Secular Institute of Pontifical Right on June 30, 1950. Aim: The practice of evangelical counsels is the expression of consecration to God. Professional work becomes the main means of the apostolate.

Diocesan Laborer Priests: 3706 15th St. N.E., Washington, DC 20017. Tel: 202-832-4217; Fax: 202-526-5692. Rev. Rutilio J. del Riego, Delegate. A Secular Institute of Pontifical Right founded in Spain in 1886. The aim of the Institute is the promotion, sustenance and cultivation of apostolic, religious and priestly vocations.

St. Francis de Sales Secular Institute: 3503 Jean St., Fairfax, VA 22030. Tel: 703-591-5196. Joan Bereswill, Dir., (Laywomen).

Founded in Vienna, Austria; Pontifical Right 1964. Aim: Personal sanctification of its members living in the world according to the spirituality of St. Francis de Sales. Open to women: single, widowed and divorced who wish to embrace the consecrated life by the profession of vows.

Don Bosco Volunteers: 202 Union Ave., Paterson, NJ 07502. Rev. Paul P. Avallone, S.D.B., Contact Person.

Founded as a Secular Institute for Women by Blessed Philip Rinaldi, S.D.B., in Turin, Italy in 1917. Approved as an Institute of Pontifical Right in 1978. Existing in 35 countries, with over 1,200 members. Aim: To live in the spirit of St. John Bosco, in a wide variety of apostolates in one's own environment, and in the service of the local church, particularly on behalf of youth An Institute for Men was founded in Rome in November, 1994. For information, see address above.

Handmaids of Divine Mercy: 2410 Hughes Ave., Bronx, NY 10458.

A Secular Institute for women who, through the practice of the evangelical, counsel in a faithful imitation of Jesus Christ. The members commit themselves to the service of the Church by a parish- or diocesan- oriented apostolate under the leadership of and in collaboration with the clergy

Institute of Secular Missionaries: 2710 Ruberg, Cincinnati, OH 45211. Evelyn Dilger, Contact Person, (Women).

Founded in Vitoria, Spain in 1939, approved as Secular Institute in 1955. Working for the integral good of humankind, specifically for the poor who need and claim most of the Church's support at this time. This endeavor is taken within the spirit of the Beatitudes and in communion with the Church.

Missionaries of the Kingship of Christ: P.O. Box 34513, Bethesda, MD 20827. Under this title are included three distinct and juridically separate institutes following the spirituality of St. Francis of Assisi.

Women Missionaries of the Kingship of Christ.

Founded in Italy in 1919 and approved as an Institute of Papal Right in 1953. Existing in twenty-six countries, the American branch began in 1950 and has spread to 25 states. Through a consecrated life in the world they work individually in professions and apostolates for the reign of Christ in the world; Rev. Dominic Monti, O.F.M., Ecclesiastical Asst., Gemelli House, 10400 Lorain Ave., Silver Spring, MD 20901. Tel: 301-593-4479.

Men Missionaries of the Kingship of Christ.

Founded in Italy in 1928 as an institute of diocesan law and established in the United States in 1962. Their purpose is spreading the social reign of Christ through individual professions and occupations; Rev. Thomas Hartle, O.F.M., Ecclesiastical Asst., St. Mary Church, 17 Pompton Ave., Pompton Lakes, NJ 07442-1890. Tel: 201-831-6382.

Priest Missionaries of the Kingship of Christ.

Approved as an Institute of Pontifical Right, July 15, 1978; established in the United States, 1954.

Members are diocesan priests serving in the active ministry of their dioceses while promoting the social reign of Jesus Christ

Oblate Missionaries of Mary Immaculate: P.O. Box 303, Manville, RI 02838. P.O. Box 764, Lowell, MA 01853.

Founded in Canada in July 2, 1952. Approved of Pontifical Right March 24, 1984.

International Membership. The members profess the evangelical counsels. Unique spirituality based on five attitudes of life: presence of God, absence of criticism and complaints, service and peacemaking. Aim: Building and strengthening of the Kingdom of Christ in cooperation with the Church by bearing witness to the charity of Christ in the very midst of society

Opus Spiritus Sancti: 21 S.W. 3rd St., Pocahontas, IA 50574. Tel: 712-335-3242. Rev. Merle Kollasch, Regional Coord.. A federation of communities of priests, sisters, and lay people having in common their dedication to the Holy Spirit and life according to the evangelical counsels.

Pius X: Lynchville Park, Goffstown, NH 03045. Tel: 603-669-8614. (Men).

Founded in New Hampshire in 1940. Approved as a Secular Institute of Pontifical Right on Dec. 8, 1959. Aim: The general end is the perfection of its members. The members strive to achieve this aim through the effective practice in the world of the three evangelical counsels of perfection, and by making the promise to dedicate themselves totally to the particular apostolate of the Institute. The Institute also admits married or unmarried men as associate members.

Secular Institute of Schoenstatt Fathers: W. 284 N. 746 Cherry Ln., Waukesha, WI 53188. (Priests). Rev. Dieter A. Haas, Superior.

Founded by Father Joseph Kentenich in 1965, approved as a Secular Institute of Pontifical Right, June 24, 1988. Aim: To aid the moral and religious renewal of society and the realization of the post-Vatican II mission of the Church, especially through priestly service to the International Schoenstatt Movement. About 200 ordained members in 20 nations worldwide.

Secular Institute of Schoenstatt Sisters of Mary: HC 04, Box 100, Rockport, TX 78382-9606. (Women).

Founded in Germany in 1926 by Father Joseph Kentenich; approved as a Secular Institute of Pontifical Right in 1948. Aim: The moral and religious renewal of society. The members practice a Marian lay asceticism as a means of growing in love for God, and consecrating the world to Him. They are active within the Schoenstatt Movement and in a wide variety of professional spheres.

Servitum Christi (Women): Mailing Address, 1209 Greenwood Ave., Pueblo, CO 81003. 184 East 76th St., New York, NY 10021. Ms. Elaine Kozlowski, Contact Person.

Origin inspired by St. Peter Julian Eymard (1868), founder of the Congregation of the Blessed Sacrament. Founded in Holland, 1952; approved as a Secular Institute of Diocesan Right May 8, 1963. Aim: To live the mystery of the Eucharist fully as consecrated lay persons and to make known its meaning so that the reign of Christ may come and the glory of God be revealed to the world.

Society of Our Lady of the Way: 2339 N. Catalina St., Los Angeles, CA 90027. Additional Members in Cleveland, OH; San Francisco, CA; Stamford, CT; New Orleans, LA; and Casper, WY (Women).

Founded in Vienna, Austria in 1936; approved as a Secular Institute of Pontifical Right in 1953. To Christianize the secular order, members are consecrated to God through the vows of chastity, obedience and poverty. They pursue individual apostolates, seeking to manifest Christ in all the circumstances of their life and work. Spirituality is Marian and Ignatian.

Voluntas Dei Institute (1958): 4257 Tazewell Terr., Burtonsville, MD 20866. Deacon Michael Craig, Contact Person.

Approved as a Secular Institute of Pontifical Right in 1987.

The Institute unites in a common ideal—priests, laymen and married couples as associate members. Aim: To discover the will of God, adhere to, love and carry it out in the world. The Voluntas from the same region meet regularly to pray, celebrate, and share the Word of God. They enrich each other with their human, Christian and apostolic experiences. Through this team, life and personal spiritual attitudes including the evangelical counsels are prolonged. The members seek to bear witness in their milieu, where they work, or with their families.

U.S. Catholic Mission Association

United States Catholic Mission Association, 3029 Fourth St., N.E., Washington, DC 20017-1102. Tel: 202-832-3112. Fax: 202-832-3688. E-mail: uscma@igc.org. Rev. William J. Morton, S.S.C., Pres.; Sr. Rosanne Rustmeyer, S.S.N.D., Exec. Dir.; Rev. Eugene S. Pocernich, Assoc. Dir. The USCMA is a voluntary association of individuals and organizations for whom the missionary presence of the universal Church is of central importance. It is a nonprofit religious, educational and charitable organization which exists to promote global mission. Its primary emphasis is on cross-cultural evangelization and the promotion of international justice and peace. The Association is also responsible for continuosly updating U.S. Catholic Missionary Personnel statistics. Current information is published biannually by the Association.

(M—Indicates Men; W—Indicates Women)

COUNTRIES ABROAD SERVED BY U.S. CATHOLIC PERSONNEL

Alaska—63

M—31: 23 Jesuits, 2 Paulists, 2 Oblates of Mary Immaculate, 1 Lay, 1 Diocesan, 1 Brother of Christian Instruction, 1 Marian Father.
W—32: 9 Dominicans (Sinsinawa), 3 St. Anne, 3 Holy Cross (Notre Dame), 3 Holy Family, 2 St. Joseph of Peace, 2 St. Joseph of Chambery, 2 Precious Blood (O'Fallon), 1 Notre Dame de Namur, 1 Charity of St. Elizabeth, 1 Little Sister of Jesus, 1 St. Joseph of Lyons, 1 Marianite of the Holy Cross, 1 Marist, 1 School Sister of St. Francis, 1 Sister of St. Francis of Philadelphia.

Albania—1

W—1: 1 Missionary of Charity.

Algeria—2

M—1: 1 Holy Ghost Father.
W—1: 1 Little Sister of the Poor.

American Samoa—6

W—6: 2 Maryknoll, 2 Lay, 1 Little Sister of the Poor, 1 Marist.

Argentina—13

M—7: 3 Maryknoll, 2 Marian Fathers, 1 Lay, 1 Divine Word.
W—6: 4 Lay, 1 St. Casimir, 1 Sister of the Resurrection.

Australia—20

M—6: 6 Divine Word.
W—14: 5 Holy Family of Nazareth, 3 Marists, 2 Servants of the Holy Spirit, 2 Franciscan Missionaries of Mary, 1 Sacred Heart, 1 Little Sister of Jesus.

Austria—2

W—2: 2 Ursuline Nuns (Eastern).

Bahamas—20

M—14: 6 Benedictines (Collegeville), 3 Jesuits, 2 Salesians, 2 Passionists, 1 Congregation of the Sacred Hearts.
W—6: 3 Charity (New York), 2 Dominicans (Caldwell), 1 Franciscan (Clinton).

Bangladesh—35

M—20: 14 Holy Cross, 4 Maryknoll, 1 Marianist, 1 PIME Missionary.
W—15: 9 Holy Cross (Notre Dame), 6 Maryknoll.

Belize—53

M—32: 20 Jesuits, 7 Lay, 4 Benedictines (Subiaco), 1 Columban.
W—21: 10 Lay, 4 Pallottines, 3 Holy Family, 1 Mercy (Hartford), 1 Dominican (St. Catharine), 1 Charity of Nazareth, 1 Mercy (Merion).

Benin—1

W—1: 1 Religious Hospitaller of St. Joseph.

Bermuda—6

M—2: 2 Congregation of the Resurrection.
W—4: 4 Sisters of Charity of Halifax.

Bolivia—127

M—55: 32 Maryknoll, 8 Diocesan, 6 Dominican Friars, 5 Lay, 2 Oblates of Mary Immaculate, 1 Holy Cross Brother.
W—72: 25 Maryknoll, 11 Lay, 7 Most Precious Blood (O'Fallon), 6 Dominicans (Sinsinawa), 5 Presentation of the Blessed Virgin Mary, 5 Adorers of the Blood of Christ, 4 Our Lady of Victory, 3 Franciscans of Allegany, 2 Daughters of Charity (Albany), 1 Daughter of Charity (St. Louis), 1 School Sister of Notre Dame, 1 Dominican (Columbus), 1 Mercy (Merion).

Botswana—1

M—1: 1 Passionist.

Brazil—242

M—133: 26 Holy Cross, 25 Oblates of Mary Immaculate, 22 Redemptorists, 10 Jesuits, 6 Lay, 5 Conventuals, 5 Maryknoll, 4 Xaverian Fathers, 4 Benedictines (Atchison), 4 Columbans, 4 Benedictines (Latrobe), 3 Legionaries of Christ, 3 PIME Missionaries, 3 Franciscan Friars, 2 Diocesan, 2 Cistercians, 2 Missionhurst-CICM, 1 Comboni Missionary, 1 Holy Ghost Father.
W—109: 12 Holy Cross (Notre Dame), 10 Sisters of St. Joseph (Rochester), 9 Lay, 7 Third Order of St. Francis of Mary Immaculate, 5 Franciscans of Allegany, 5 Notre Dame de Namur, 5 Franciscans of the Sacred Heart, 4 Felicians, 4 St. Francis of the Providence of God, 4 St. Mary of Namur, 4 Franciscan Sisters of the Atonement, 3 Benedictines (Atchison), 3 Maryknoll, 3 Order of St. Clare, 3 Franciscan Sisters of Mary, 3 St. Joseph (Concordia), 3 Servants of the Immaculate Heart of Mary (Saco), 2 St. Francis of the Martyr St. George, 2 Benedictines (St. Joseph), 2 Filippini, 2 Servants of the Immaculate Heart of Mary (Monroe), 2 Immaculate Conception of the Mother of God, 1 Franciscan of the Poor, 1 St. Joseph of Lyons, 1 St. Francis of the Holy Eucharist, 1 Dominican (San Rafael), 1 Sister of the Divine Savior, 1 Sister of St. Joseph (Brentwood), 1 Cabrini Sister, 1 Ursuline Nun of the Roman Union, 1 Poor Handmaid of Jesus Christ, 1 Venerini, 1 Medical Mission Sister, 1 School Sister of Notre Dame.

Cambodia—10

M—4: 3 Maryknoll, 1 Lay.
W—6: 4 Maryknoll, 1 Our Lady of Lourdes, 1 Lay.

Cameroon—18

M—2: 1 Claretian, 1 Marist.
W—16: 3 Sisters of the Holy Union, 3 Servants of Mary, 2 Sisters of St. Mary of Namur, 2 Ursuline Nuns of the Roman Union, 1 Lay, 1 Sister of the Presentation of Mary, 1 Daughter of the Holy Spirit, 1 Sister of Charity of St. Joan Antida, 1 Daughter of Mary and Joseph, 1 Congregation of Notre Dame.

Canada—47

M—25: 9 Atonement Fathers, 5 Salesians, 3 Oblates of Mary Immaculate, 2 Diocesan, 2 Passionists, 2 Assumptionists, 1 Legionnaire of Christ, 1 Marianist.
W—22: 5 St. Joseph of Peace, 5 Little Sisters of the Poor, 4 Daughters of St. Mary of Providence, 2 Missionary Sisters of St. Charles Borromeo, 2 Servants of the Most Sacred Heart, 1 Franciscan Missionary of Mary, 1 Benedictine (Mt. Angel), 1 Religious of Jesus and Mary, 1 St. Joseph of Chambery.

Central African Republic—2

M—1: 1 Franciscan Friar.
W—1: 1 Missionary of Charity.

Chad—3

M—1: 1 Missionary of Africa.
W—2: 2 Holy Child Jesus.

Chile—121

M—68: 19 Maryknoll, 16 Holy Cross, 10 Lay, 9 Jesuits, 7 Precious Blood, 5 Columbans, 1 Divine Word, 1 Salesian.
W—53: 12 Maryknoll, 11 Lay, 6 School Sisters of Notre Dame, 5 Precious Blood (Dayton), 4 Sisters of the Holy Child Jesus, 4 St. Joseph of Carondelet, 3 Daughters of the Holy Spirit, 2 St. Columban, 1 Sister of St. Anne, 1 Mercy (Detroit), 1 Providence (Holyoke), 1 School Sister of St. Francis (Bethlehem), 1 School Sister of St. Francis (Pittsburgh), 1 Franciscan Sister of Allegany.

China—9

M—3: 1 Benedictine (Collegeville), 1 Columban, 1 Jesuit.
W—6: 3 Sacred Heart, 1 St. Columban, 1 Benedictine (Norfolk), 1 Benedictine of Pontifical Jurisdicition.

Colombia—29

M—11: 5 Lay, 4 Diocesan, 3 Missionaries of the Sacred Heart, 2 Consolata Missionaries, 1 Basilian Father, 1 Oblate of Mary Immaculate.
W—18: 6 Our Lady of Lourdes, 4 Marists, 2 Grey Nuns of Montreal, 1 Little Sister of the Poor.

Congo—2

W—2: 2 Little Sisters of the Poor.

Costa Rica—14

M—10: 4 Most Holy Trinity, 3 Capuchins, 2 Conventual Franciscans, 1 Lay.
W—4: 3 Oblates of Providence, 1 School Sisters of St. Francis.

Cuba—1

M—1: 1 Capuchin.

Cyprus—2

M—2: 2 Franciscan Friars.

Czechoslovakia—8

M—3: 3 Lay.
W—5: 5 Lay.

Denmark—5

M—5: 4 Oblates of Mary Immaculate, 1 Jesuit.

Dominica—3

M—3: 3 Redemptorists.

Dominican Republic—43

M—22: 8 Redemptorists, 5 Missionhurst-CICM, 4 Diocesan, 2 Lay, 1 Benedictine (Benet Lake).
W—21: 8 Dominicans (Adrian), 3 St. Joseph (Brentwood), 2 Religious Hospitallers of St. Joseph, 2 Sisters of St. Francis of Philadelphia, 2 Schoenstatt Sisters of Mary, 1 St. Mary of Namur, 1 Our Lady of Christian Doctrine, 1 Divine Providence, 1 Oblate Sister of Providence.

East Timor—3

W—3: 3 Maryknoll.

Ecuador—22

M—10: 5 Diocesan, 2 Lay, 1 Jesuit, 1 Comboni Missionary.
W—12: 4 Charity of the BVM, 2 Divine Providence (Melbourne), 2 Charity of Leavenworth, 2 Lay, 1 Charity of Cincinnati, 1 Franciscan of Little Falls.

Egypt—8

M—7: 4 Maryknoll, 1 Franciscan Friar, 1 Jesuit, 1 Comboni.
W—1: 1 Little Sister of the Assumption.

El Salvador—44

M—14: 10 Diocesan, 4 Maryknoll, 2 Franciscan Friars, 1 Jesuit.
W—30: 7 Maryknoll, 4 Lay, 3 St. Francis of the Holy Family, 2 Charity of the Incarnate Word (Houston), 2 Ursulines (Cleveland), 2 Humility of Mary (Villa Maria), 1 School Sister of Notre Dame, 1 Charity of St. Elizabeth, 1 Franciscan of Perpetual Adoration, 1 Society Helpers, 1 Congregation of Notre Dame, 1 Sister of St. Joseph (Orange), 1 Dominican (Sinsinawa).

Ethiopia—19

M—9: 6 Brothers of the Christian Schools, 1 Lay, 1 Diocesan, 1 Jesuit.
W—10: 2 Medical Mission Sisters, 2 Daughters of Charity, 1 Our Lady of Charity of the Good Shepherd, 1 Comboni Missionary, 1 Filippini, 1 Consolata, 1 Franciscan Missionary of Mary, 1 St. Francis of Philadelphia.

Fiji Islands—8

M—4: 3 Columbans, 1 Jesuit.
W—4: 4 Marist Sisters.

France—3

W—3: 1 Daughter of the Holy Spirit, 1 St. Joseph, 1 Religious of Jesus and Mary.

The Gambia—1

W—1: 1 Presentation of Mary.

Germany—7

M—4: 3 Legionaries of Christ, 1 Servite.
W—3: 2 Divine Savior, 1 Benedictine.

Ghana—82

M—33: 13 Divine Word Missionaries, 7 Holy Cross, 6 Conventuals, 4 Missionaries of Africa, 2 Lay, 1 Jesuit.
W—49: 15 School Sisters of Notre Dame, 7 Medical Mission Sisters, 6 Sisters of Divine Providence (Melbourne), 4 Missionary Sisters, Servants of the Holy Spirit, 4 Franciscan Missionaries of Mary, 4 Lay, 2 Sisters of Loretto, 2 Society of the Holy Child Jesus, 2 Sisters of the Immaculate Heart of Mary (Monroe), 2 Sisters of the Holy Cross (Notre Dame), 1 Presentation BVM.

Great Britain—9

M—7: 3 Franciscan Friars of the Atonement, 2 Divine Word, 1 Legionnaire of Christ, 1 Brother of Christian Schools.
W—2: 1 Medical Mission Sister, 1 St. Francis of Philadelphia.

Greece—1

M—1: 1 Franciscan Friar.

Greenland—1

M—1: 1 Oblate of Mary Immaculate.

Guam—16

M—12: 10 Capuchins, 2 Lay.
W—4: 2 Mercedarian Missionaries of Berriz, 1 School Sister of Notre Dame, 1 Third Order of St. Francis of Mary Immaculate.

Guatemala—172

M—70: 21 Maryknoll, 9 Diocesan, 7 Benedictines (Esquipulas), 6 Franciscan Friars, 6 Brothers of the Christian Schools, 6 Lay, 5 Benedictines (Aurora), 3 Oblates of Mary Immaculate, 2 Claretians, 2 Missionhurst-CICM, 2 Precious Blood, 1 Comboni.
W—102: 20 Maryknoll, 19 Lay, 7 School Sisters of Notre Dame, 6 School Sisters of St. Francis (Milwaukee), 6 Charity (New York), 4 Charity of the Incarnate Word (Houston), 4 Precious Blood (Dayton), 4 Daughters of Charity, 3 Presentation BVM, 3 Sisters of St. Francis of Philadelphia, 3 Benedictines (Ferdinand), 2 Congregation of Notre Dame, 2 Dominicans (Houston), 2 Adorers of the Blood of Christ, 2 Benedictines (Watertown), 2 Order of St. Clare, 2 Franciscan Sisters of Little Falls, 2 Charity of the BVM, 2 Franciscan Sisters of Peace, 1 Sister of Mercy (Dallas), 1 Sister of Mercy (Hartford), 1 Sister of Mercy (Pittsburgh), 1 Dominican (Akron), 1 St. Joseph (Holyoke), 1 Charity (Ohio), 1 Cabrini Sister.

Guyana—3

M—1: 1 Lay.
W—2: 1 Sister of Mercy (Dallas), 1 Ursuline Nun (Eastern).

Haiti—41

M—25: 17 Oblates of Mary Immaculate, 2 Lay, 2 Brothers of Christian Instruction, 2 Missionhurst-CICM, 1 Diocesan, 1 Montfort Missionary.
W—16: 3 Holy Cross (Manchester), 2 Sisters of St. Anne, 2 Hospital Sisters of the Third Order of St. Francis, 2 Immaculate Heart of Mary Missionaries, 2 Franciscan Missionaries of Our Lady, 1 Sister of Mercy (Hartford), 1 Little Sister of Jesus, 1 Lay, 1 Dominican (Edmonds), 1 Missionary of Charity.

Hawaii—115

M—45: 18 Marianists, 11 Maryknoll, 7 Marist Fathers, 7 Capuchins, 2 La Salette.
W—70: 28 Maryknoll, 23 St. Joseph of Carondelet, 8 Holy Family, 4 Franciscans of Christian Charity, 2 Our Lady of Charity of the Good Shepherd, 2 Notre Dame de Namur, 2 Charity of the Blessed Virgin Mary, 1 Sister of St. Francis of Philadelphia.

Honduras—59

M—35: 15 Jesuits, 6 Maryknoll, 4 Franciscan Friars, 3 Lay, 3 Capuchins, 2 Dominicans, 1 Conventual, 1 Passionist.
W—24: 7 School Sisters of Notre Dame, 4 Immaculate Heart of Mary (Monroe), 4 St. Francis of Perpetual Adoration, 2 Mercy (Chicago), 2 School Sisters of St. Francis (Milwaukee), 2 St. Agnes, 2 Lay, 1 Mercy (Dallas).

Hong Kong—75

M—36: 31 Maryknoll, 2 Jesuits, 1 Diocesan, 1 Franciscan Friar, 1 Oblate of Mary Immaculate.
W—39: 27 Maryknoll, 7 Franciscan Missionaries of Our Lady of Sorrows, 3 Our Lady of Charity of the Good Shepherd, 1 Notre Dame des Anges (Canada), 1 St. Columban.

Hungary—5

M—1: 1 Jesuit.
W—4: 3 Devoted to the Sacred Heart, 1 St. Joseph (Orange).

India—82

M—66: 54 Jesuits, 5 Marianists, 2 Divine Word Missionaries, 2 Congregation of the Sacred Hearts, 1 Passionist, 1 PIME Missionary, 1 Adorno Father.
W—16: 4 Sisters of Notre Dame, 4 Little Sisters of the Poor, 3 Charity of Nazareth, 1 Medical Mission Sister, 1 Missionary of Charity, 1 Franciscan Missionary of Mary, 1 Sister of Mary Immaculate (Leechburg), 1 Lay.

Indonesia—28

M—26: 9 Divine Word Missionaries, 8 Crosier Fathers, 3 Maryknoll, 2 Jesuits, 2 Sacred Heart Fathers and Brothers, 1 Xaverian Father, 1 Oblate of Mary Immaculate.
W—2: 1 Religious of the Sacred Heart, 1 St. Francis of Penance and Christian Charity.

Ireland—14

M—7: 5 Marianists, 2 Legionaries of Christ.
W—7: 5 Sisters of St. Francis of Philadelphia, 1 Servant of the Holy Spirit, 1 St. Joseph of Chambery.

Israel—30

M—22: 10 Franciscan Friars, 6 Brothers of Christian Schools, 3 Maryknoll, 1 Lay, 1 Jesuit, 1 Assumptionist.
W—8: 4 Holy Cross (Notre Dame), 1 Daughter of Charity, 1 St. Joseph (Orange), 1 Servant of the Immaculate Heart of Mary, 1 Lay.

Italy—51

M—24: 6 Divine Word, 5 Legionaries of Christ, 3 Christian Brothers, 3 Franciscan Friars of the Atonement, 3 Jesuits, 2 Brothers of Christian Schools, 1 Marianist, 1 Passionist.
W—27: 7 Servants of the Most Sacred Heart, 3 Notre Dame de Namur, 3 Divine Savior, 2 Franciscan Missionaries of Mary, 2 Servants of the Holy Spirit, 1 Charity of the Blessed Virgin Mary, 1 Comboni, 1 Daughter of Wisdom, 1 Holy Cross, 1 Holy Union Sister, 1 Religious of Jesus and Mary, 1 Missionary of Charity, 1 St. Charles Borromeo, 1 St. Joseph of Chambery, 1 Ursuline Nun (Eastern).

Ivory Coast—6

M—3: 2 Lay, 1 Christian Brother.
W—3: 2 Lay, 1 Franciscan Missionary of Mary.

Jamaica—68

M—35: 23 Jesuits, 5 Passionists, 3 Lay, 2 Columbans, 1 Franciscan Friar of the Atonement, 1 Resurrection (Canada).
W—33: 9 Franciscans of Allegany, 7 Mercy (Cincinnati), 3 Lay, 3 Dominicans (Blauvelt), 3 Servants of Mary (Omaha), 2 Marist Sisters, 2 St. Joseph (Pittsburgh), 1 Sister of Mercy (Merion), 1 Immaculate Heart of Mary Missionary, 1 Holy Child Jesus, 1 St. Francis of Penance and Christian Charity.

Japan—176

M—129: 28 Maryknoll, 14 Jesuits, 12 Divine Word Missionaries, 10 Oblates of Mary Immaculate, 8 Augustinians, 8 Marist Brothers, 7 Congregation of the Sacred Hearts, 7 Passionists, 5 Columbans, 4 Benedictines (Collegeville), 4 Atonement Fathers, 4 Marianists, 3 Conventuals, 3 Capuchins, 3 Franciscan Friars, 3 PIME Missionaries, 2 Lay, 1 Diocesan, 1 Brother of Christian Schools, 1 Missionhurst-CICM, 1 Xaverian Missionary Father.
W—47: 12 Maryknoll, 7 Notre Dame de Namur, 5 Daughters of Charity, 4 St. Joseph of Carondelet, 3 Passionist Nuns, 3 Sisters of St. Joseph (Wichita), 3 Lay, 2 Franciscan Missionaries of Mary, 2 Religious of the Sacred Heart, 1 Company of Mary, 1 School Sister of Notre Dame, 1 Order of St. Clare, 1 Presentation of Mary, 1 Sister of St. Francis of Millvale, 1 Sister of St. Francis of Assisi.

Jordan—3

M—3: 2 Jesuits, 1 Franciscan Friar.

Kazakhstan—1

M—1: 1 Franciscan Friar.

Kenya—200

M—124: 29 Maryknoll, 21 Jesuits, 15 Lay, 15 Brothers of Christian Schools, 10 Marianists, 6 Holy Cross, 5 Xaverian Brothers, 3 Vincentians, 3 Consolata Missionaries, 3 Society of African Missions, 2 Dominicans, 2 Brothers of the Sacred Heart, 2 Assumptionists, 2 Holy Ghost Fathers, 1 Mill Hill Missionary, 1 Comboni Missionary, 1 Divine Word Missionary, 1 Diocesan, 1 Franciscan Friar, 1 Passionist.
W—76: 11 School Sisters of Notre Dame, 10 Lay, 8 Notre Dame de Namur, 7 Consolata Missionaries, 7 Charity of the Incarnate Word, 5 Maryknoll, 4 Medical Mission Sisters, 4 St. Francis of Philadelphia, 3 Servants of the Sacred Heart of Jesus and the Poor, 2 Comboni Missionaries, 2 Sisters of the Incarnate Word and Blessed Sacrament (Corpus Christi), 2 Franciscan Missionaries of Mary, 2 Dominicans (Racine), 2 St. Joseph (Holyoke), 2 Franciscan Missionary Sisters for Africa, 1 Felician, 1 Servant of the Most Sacred Heart, 1 St. Anne, 1 Daughter of Charity, 1 St. Francis (Williamsville).

Korea—64

M—42: 26 Maryknoll, 6 Columbans, 3 Salesians, 2 Passionists, 1 Cistercian, 1 Assumptionist, 1 Jesuit, 1 Lay, 1 Divine Word.
W—22: 8 Maryknoll, 3 Charity (Seton Hill), 2 St. Columban, 2 Adorers of the Blood of Christ, 2 Order of St. Clare, 2 Little Sisters of the Poor, 1 Sister of St. Joseph (Orange), 1 Our Lady of Charity of the Good Shepherd, 1 Lay.

Latvia—1

M—1: 1 Lay.

Lebanon—6

M—3: 3 Jesuits.
W—3: 2 Religious of Jesus and Mary, 1 Daughter of Charity.

Lesotho—8

M—5: 5 Brothers of the Sacred Heart.
W—3: 2 Holy Child, 1 Servant of the Immaculate Heart of Mary.

Liberia—9

M—5: 2 Society of African Missions, 2 Salesians, 1 Lay.
W—4: 1 Lay, 1 Consolata Missionary, 1 Franciscan Missionary of Mary, 1 St. Joseph of Chambery.

Lithuania—7

M—3: 3 Lay.
W—4: 3 St. Francis of the Providence of God, 1 Lay.

Madagascar—6

M—3: 3 La Salette Fathers.
W—3: 2 Lay, 1 Franciscan Missionary of Mary.

Malawi—10

M—7: 3 Marianists, 2 Jesuits, 1 Franciscan Friar, 1 Missionary of Africa.
W—3: 2 Daughters of Wisdom, 1 Missionary of the Immaculate Conception (Canada).

Malaysia—2

M—1: 1 Jesuit.
W—1: 1 Little Sister of the Poor.

Mali—3

W—3: 3 Sisters of Holy Cross (Manchester).

Marshall Islands—19

M—3: 2 Lay, 1 Jesuit.
W—16: 6 Maryknoll, 6 Lay, 3 Franciscans of Perpetual Adoration, 1 School Sister of Notre Dame.

Mexico—221

M—127: 21 Maryknoll, 12 Oblates of Mary Immaculate, 12 Franciscan Friars, 10 Lay, 8 Divine Word, 8 Legionaries of Christ, 7 Marianists, 7 Missionary Servants of the Most Holy Trinity, 6 Diocesan, 4 Holy Cross, 4 Assumptionists, 4 Basilian Fathers, 3 Jesuits, 3 Conventuals, 2 Xaverian Fathers, 2 Congregation of the Resurrection, 2 Benedictines (Benet Lake), 1 Brother of Christian Schools, 1 Holy Ghost Father, 1 Missionhurst-CICM, 1 Comboni Missionary, 1 Dominican, 1 Sulpician, 1 Vincentian, 1 Redemptorist, 1 Norbertine.
W—94: 22 Lay, 7 Maryknoll, 5 Sisters of the Holy Spirit and Mary Immaculate, 4 Sisters of the Sacred Heart of Jesus (San Antonio), 4 Poor Handmaids of Jesus Christ, 4 School Sisters of Notre Dame, 3 Missionary Servants of the Most Blessed Trinity, 3 Presentation of the BVM, 3 Humility of Mary (Davenport), 3 Most Sacred Heart of Jesus, 3 St. Joseph of Orange, 2 Immaculate Heart of Mary (Monroe), 2 Servants of the Holy Spirit, 2 Holy Cross (Notre Dame), 2 Missionaries of Charity, 2 Sisters of Mercy (Omaha), 2 Ursulines of the Roman Union, 2 St. Francis of Penance and Christian Charity, 2 Xaverian Missionaries of Mary, 1 Religious of the Sacred Heart, 1 Holy Names, 1 Daughter of St. Mary of Providence, 1 Our Lady of Mount Carmel, 1 Franciscan Sister of Perpetual Adoration, 1 Third Order of St. Francis of Penance and Charity (Tiffin), 1 Poor Clare Missionary, 1 Charity of St. Elizabeth, 1 Mercedarian, 1 Marist Sister (Chicago), 1 Dominican (San Rafael), 1 Ursuline (Cleveland), 1 Ursuline (Eastern), 1 Franciscan Sister of Chicago, 1 Dominican (Edmonds), 1 Marianite of Holy Cross, 1 Missionary of St. Charles.

Micronesia—28

M—14: 11 Lay, 3 Jesuits.
W—14: 10 Lay, 3 Maryknoll, 1 Mercedarian.

Montserrat—1

W—1: 1 Immaculate Heart of Mary Missionary.

Morocco—1

M—1: 1 Franciscan Friar.

Mozambique—1

M—1: 1 Jesuit.

Namibia—5

M—1: 1 Sacred Heart Missionary.
W—4: 2 Missionary Benedictines, 2 Most Sacred Heart of Jesus.

Nepal—22

M—15: 10 Jesuits, 2 Maryknoll, 2 Lay, 1 Holy Cross Father.
W—7: 4 Lay, 3 Maryknoll.

Netherlands—1

M—1: 1 Legionnaire of Christ.

New Zealand—2

M—1: 1 Redemptorist.
W—1: 1 Marist Sister.

Nicaragua—74

M—33: 17 Capuchins, 4 Maryknoll, 3 Montfort Fathers, 3 Jesuits, 2 Lay, 1 Diocesan, 1 Brother of Christian Schools, 1 Blessed Sacrament Father, 1 Cabrini Mission Corps.
W—41: 11 Maryknoll, 9 St. Agnes, 4 Lay, 3 St. Francis of the Holy Cross, 3 Franciscans of Little Falls, 3 Notre Dame de Namur, 3 Holy Names of Jesus and Mary, 1 Marionite of the Holy Cross, 1 Servant of the Most Sacred Heart, 1 St. Teresa of Jesus, 1 St. Joseph of Carondelet, 1 St. Francis of Philadelphia.

Niger—1

M—1: 1 Missionary of Africa.

Nigeria—44

M—19: 8 Dominicans, 6 Jesuits, 4 Redemptorists, 1 Missionary of Africa.
W—25: 6 School Sisters of Notre Dame, 5 Dominicans (Great Bend), 4 Daughters of the Holy Spirit, 3 Notre Dame de Namur, 3 Society of the Holy Child Jesus, 2 Parish Visitors of Mary Immaculate, 1 Sister of the Holy Family, 1 St. Francis of Millvale.

Norway—1

M—1: 1 Oblate of Mary Immaculate.

Okinawa—7

M—7: 7 Capuchins.

Pakistan—12

M—2: 1 Brother of Christian Schools, 1 Mill Hill Missionary.
W—10: 5 Medical Mission Sisters, 3 Dominicans (Sparkill), 1 Religious of Jesus and Mary, 1 Franciscan Missionary of Mary.

Palau—3

M—3: 3 Lay.

Panama—33

M—23: 16 Vincentians, 5 Capuchins, 1 Jesuit, 1 Diocesan.
W—10: 8 Maryknoll, 1 Humility of Mary (Davenport), 1 St. Joseph of Chestnut Hill.

Papua New Guinea—86

M—69: 29 Divine Word, 20 Capuchins, 15 Missionaries of the Sacred Heart, 2 Marist Fathers, 1 PIME Missionary, 1 Jesuit, 1 Passionist.
W—17: 4 Servants of the Holy Spirit, 3 Maryknoll, 2 Lay, 2 Missionaries of the Sacred Heart (Reading), 2 Marist Sisters, 2 Sisters of the Sacred Heart (San Antonio), 1 Humility of Mary (Davenport), 1 Dominican (Grand Rapids).

Paraguay—17

M—15: 5 Divine Word, 5 Redemptorists, 4 Jesuits, 1 Diocesan.
W—2: 2 School Sisters of Notre Dame.

Peru—261

M—126: 25 Maryknoll, 23 Jesuits, 19 Diocesan, 14 Congregation of Christian Brothers, 9 Carmelites, 8 Precious Blood, 8 Holy Cross, 5 Norbertines, 4 Augustinians, 4 Franciscan Friars, 2 Lay, 2 Marianists, 2 Marist Fathers, 1 Comboni Missionary.
W—135: 18 Maryknoll, 10 Lay, 8 St. Joseph of Carondelet, 8 Charity of Leavenworth, 7 St. Joseph of Nazareth, 5 Dominicans (Springfield), 5 Sisters of Mercy (Merion), 5 Immaculate Heart of Mary (Scranton), 5 St. Columban, 5 Franciscans of Christian Charity, 4 Marist Sisters, 4 Notre Dame de Namur, 4 Dominicans (Columbus), 4 Sisters of Holy Cross (Notre Dame), 4 Benedictines (Ferdinand), 3 Charity of Halifax, 3 Medical Mission Sisters, 3 Sisters of Mercy (Burlingame), 3 Sisters of Third Franciscan Order, 3 Our Lady of Lourdes, 3 Sisters of Mercy (Pittsburgh), 2 Dominicans (Grand Rapids), 2 Sisters of the Sacred Heart of Jesus (San Antonio), 2 Sisters of Holy Cross (Manchester), 2 School Sisters of St. Francis (Milwaukee), 1 School Sister of Notre Dame, 1 Presentation BVM, 1 Dominican (Sparkill), 1 Ursuline Nun of the Roman Union, 1 Vincentian Sister of Charity (Pittsburgh), 1 Franciscan (Clinton), 1 St. Joseph (Chestnut Hill), 1 Daughter of the Holy Spirit, 1 Divine Providence (Allision Park), 1 Divine Providence (St. Louis), 1 Charity of Cincinnati, 1 Franciscan Missionary of Mary, 1 Notre Dame des Agnes (Canada).

Philippines—157

M—130: 22 Maryknoll, 22 Divine Word, 15 Columbans, 14 Franciscan Friars, 10 Brothers of Christian Schools, 8 Jesuits, 6 Passionists, 5 Blessed Sacrament, 4 Oblates of Mary Immaculate, 4 Discalced Carmelites, 3 Diocesan, 3 La Salette, 3 Sons of Mary, 2 Lay, 2 Alexian Brothers, 2 PIME Missionaries, 1 Missionhurst-CICM, 1 Stigmatine, 1 Vincentian, 1 Marist Brother, 1 Conventual Franciscan, 1 Comboni Missionary.
W—27: 8 Maryknoll, 4 St. Columban, 3 Sisters of Social Service, 3 Presentation of Mary, 2 Sacred Heart of Jesus, 1 Sister of Mercy (Buffalo), 1 Dominican Contemplative Nun, 1 Sister of Mercy (Omaha), 1 St. Joseph of Chestnut Hill, 1 Servant of the Holy Spirit, 1 St. Charles Borromeo.

Poland—2

W—2: 1 Dominican (Edmonds), 1 St. Francis of the Holy Family.

Puerto Rico—79

M—40: 21 Redemptorists, 9 Capuchins, 4 Holy Ghost Fathers, 3 Missionary Servants of the Most Holy Trinity, 3 Oblates of Mary Immaculate.
W—39: 9 St. Joseph (Brentwood), 6 School Sisters of Notre Dame, 4 St. Francis of Millvale, 4 St. Francis of Philadelphia, 3 Dominicans (Columbus), 3 Divine Providence (Allison Park), 3 St. Francis (Williamsville), 2 Dominicans (Adrian), 2 Immaculate Heart of Mary (Monroe), 1 Missionary Servant of the Most Blessed Trinity, 1 Social Service (Buffalo), 1 Charity (New York).

Romania—4

M—1: 1 Divine Word.
W—3: 1 Divine Providence, 1 Mercy (Burlingame), 1 School Sister of Notre Dame.

Russia—7

M—4: 1 Assumptionist Father, 1 Diocesan, 1 Jesuit, 1 Lay.
W—3: 3 St. Agnes.

Rwanda—1

W—1: 1 St. Mary of Namur.

St. Vincent—1

W—1: 1 Institute of the Blessed Virgin Mary.

Saipan—2

M—1: 1 Jesuit.
W—1: 1 Mercedarian Missionary of Berriz.

Scotland—1

M—1: 1 Missionary of Charity.

Senegal—3

M—1: 1 Marist.
W—2: 1 Marist, 1 St. Joseph of Lyons.

Seychelles—2

M—2: 2 Brothers of Christian Instruction.

Sierra Leone—25

M—8: 6 Xaverian Fathers, 1 Salesian, 1 Lay.
W—17: 10 School Sisters of Notre Dame, 4 Lay, 2 Xaverian Missionaries of Mary, 1 Poor Clare Missionary.

Singapore—1

W—1: 1 Little Sister of the Poor.

Slovenia—1

M—1: 1 Blessed Sacrament.

Solomon Islands—8

M—4: 3 Marist Fathers, 1 Vincentian.
W—4: 4 Marist Sisters.

South Africa—44

M—19: 6 Servites, 4 Sacred Heart Fathers and Brothers, 4 Jesuits, 3 Franciscan Friars, 1 Holy Ghost Father, 1 Diocesan.
W—25: 9 Immaculate Heart of Mary (Monroe), 4 Dominicans (Adrian), 4 Ursuline Nuns (Eastern), 2 School Sisters of St. Francis (Pittsburgh), 2 Missionary Benedictines, 1 Our Lady of Lourdes, 1 Lay, 1 Notre Dame de Namur.

South Korea—3

M—1: 1 Diocesan.
W—2: 1 Daughter of Charity, 1 Our Lady of Charity of the Good Shepherd.

Spain—3

M—1: 1 Legionnaire of Christ.
W—2: 1 Lay, 1 Sacred Heart.

Sri Lanka—13

M—10: 8 Jesuits, 1 Brother of the Christian Schools, 1 Lay.
W—3: 2 Franciscan Missionaries of Mary, 1 Little Sister of the Poor.

Sudan—7

M—2: 1 Jesuit, 1 Mill Hill Father.
W—5: 5 Maryknoll Sisters.

Swaziland—3

W—3: 3 Mantellate Sisters, Servants of Mary of Blue Island.

Sweden—5

M—4: 3 Oblates of Mary Immaculate, 1 Passionist.
W—1: 1 Sacred Heart.

Tahiti—2

M—2: 2 Oblates of Mary Immaculate.

Taiwan—112

M—63: 32 Maryknoll, 13 Jesuits, 8 Vincentians, 5 Divine Word Missionaries, 1 Benedictine (Lisle), 1 Columban, 1 Franciscan Friar, 1 Benedictine (Latrobe), 1 Lay.
W—49: 13 Daughters of Charity, 9 Maryknoll, 5 Franciscans of Our Lady of Sorrows, 4 Sisters of Providence (St. Mary-of-the-Woods), 4 Social Service (Los Angeles), 4 Society Devoted to the Sacred Heart, 4 Divine Savior, 1 Lay, 1 Servant of the Holy Spirit, 1 Ursuline Nun (Eastern), 1 Third Order of St. Francis (Milwaukee), 1 Missionary of the Sacred Heart (Rome), 1 Columban.

Tanzania—101

M—68: 36 Maryknoll, 12 Holy Ghost Fathers, 8 Lay, 5 Jesuits, 5 Salvatorians, 1 Missionary of Africa, 1 Salesian.
W—33: 20 Maryknoll, 6 Lay, 4 Franciscans of Little Falls, 1 St. Francis of Penance and Christian Charity, 1 Missionary Benedictine, 1 St. Francis of Our Lady of Lourdes (Sylvania).

Thailand—33

M—21: 7 Lay, 6 Maryknoll, 4 Jesuits, 2 Redemptorists, 2 Stigmatines.
W—12: 5 Ursuline Nuns (Eastern), 5 Lay, 1 Benedictine (St. Joseph), 1 Ursuline Nun of the Roman Union.

Tunisia—1

M—1: 1 Missionary of Africa.

Turkey—1

W—1: 1 Little Sister of the Poor.

Turks Islands—1

M—1: 1 Holy Ghost Father.

Uganda—60

M—37: 23 Holy Cross, 6 Jesuits, 3 Lay, 2 Sacred Heart Brothers, 2 Missionaries of Africa, 1 Xavieran Brother.
W—23: 10 Holy Cross Sisters (Notre Dame), 4 Medical Mission Sisters, 3 Lay, 3 Daughters of Mary and Joseph, 1 Comboni Missionary, 1 Franciscan Missionary for Africa, 1 Sister of Mary of the Presentation.

Uruguay—4

M—3: 3 Jesuits.
W—1: 1 Sister of Christian Charity.

Venezuela—28

M—17: 7 Diocesan, 5 Maryknoll, 3 Lay, 2 Edmundites.
W—11: 7 Lay, 3 Medical Mission Sisters, 1 Ursuline Nun (Eastern).

Vietnam—2

M—2: 2 Maryknoll.

Virgin Islands—14

M—7: 7 Redemptorist Fathers.
W—7: 3 Sisters of Charity of St. Elizabeth, 2 Marist Missionaries, 1 Sister of St. Francis of Millvale, 1 Dominican (Adrian).

West Indies—17

M—10: 3 Brothers of the Christian Schools, 3 Divine Word, 3 Diocesan, 1 Norbertine.
W—7: 3 Carmelites, 2 St. Francis of Philadelphia, 1 Dominican (Sinsinawa), 1 Ursuline Nun (Northeastern).

Western Samoa—4

M—4: 3 Maryknoll, 1 Marist.

Zaire—21

M—9: 2 Sacred Heart Fathers and Brothers, 2 Crosier Fathers, 1 Divine Word Missionary, 1 Missionhurst-CICM, 1 Adorno Father, 1 Franciscan Friar, 1 Xaverian Missionary Father.
W—12: 5 Daughters of Charity, 2 St. Mary of Namur, 1 Notre Dame de Namur, 1 Society of St. Ursula, 1 Ursuline Sister of Tildonk, 1 Immaculate Heart of Mary Missionary, 1 Religious of the Sacred Heart.

Zambia—55

M—44: 9 Conventual Franciscans, 9 Jesuits, 7 Oblates of Mary Immaculate, 5 Sulpician Fathers, 4 Sacred Heart Brothers, 4 Lay, 3 Missionaries of Africa, 1 Marianist, 1 Diocesan.
W—11: 6 Sisters of the Holy Spirit and Mary Immaculate, 2 Franciscan Missionaries for Africa, 2 Comboni Missionaries, 1 St. Joseph of Nazareth.

Zimbabwe—37

M—10: 5 Jesuits, 3 Lay, 1 Diocesan, 1 Marist Brother.
W—27: 8 Religious of the Sacred Heart of Mary, 8 Maryknoll Sisters, 3 Lay, 3 Notre Dame de Namur, 2 Servants of the Immaculate Heart of Mary (Monroe), 1 Franciscan of Perpetual Adoration, 1 Missionary Sister of the Precious Blood, 1 Franciscan Missionary for Africa.

Alphabetical Listing of Mission Churches in the United States

A

Aasu/Aoloau, AS, c/o [3] Pago Pago, AS, Church of St. Paul. (SPP)
Abernathy, TX, Hale Co., St. Isidore, c/o Petersburg, TX, Sacred Heart Church. (LUB)
Abeytas, NM, Socorro Co., San Antonio, c/o La Joya, NM, Our Lady of Sorrows Church. (SFE)
Abie, NE, Butler Co., SS. Peter and Paul, c/o Bruno, NE, St. Anthony Church. (LIN)
Abingdon, MD, St. Francis, c/o Baltimore, MD, Patronage of the Mother of God Church. (PSC)
Abo, NM, Torrance Co., c/o Mountainair, NM, St. Alice Church. (SFE)
Abram, TX, St. Mary Magdalene, c/o La Joya, TX, Our Lady, Queen of Angels Church. (BWN)
Absarokee, MT, St. Michael, c/o Columbus, MT, St. Mary's Church. (GF)
Acomita, NM, St. Anne, c/o Acoma, NM, San Esteban, Indian Mission Church. (GLP)
Acra, NY, St. Edmund, c/o Cairo, NY, Sacred Heart Church. (ALB)
Ada, MN, Norman Co., c/o [1] Crookston, MN, Cathedral of the Immaculate Conception. (CR)
Adel, GA, Cook Co., St. Margaret Mary, c/o Lakeland, GA, Queen of Peace Church. (SAV)
Adel, OR, St. Richard, c/o Lakeview, OR, St. Patrick's Church. (BAK)
Adona, AR, Conway Co., St. Elizabeth's, c/o Bigelow, AR, St. Boniface's Church. (LR)
Adrian, OR, Our Lady of Guadalupe, c/o Nyssa, OR, St. Bridget of Kildare Church. (BAK)
Afono, AS, c/o [6] (Lepua), AS, Church of the Immaculate Conception. (SPP)
Afton, NY, St. Agnes, c/o Bainbridge, NY, St. John the Evangelist Church. (SY)
Afton, WY, Lincoln Co., Holy Family, c/o Jackson, WY, Our Lady of the Mountains Church. (CHY)
Agawam, MA, Hampden Co., St. Anthony, c/o Agawam, MA, St. Theresa of the Child Jesus Church. (SPR)
Aguas, PR, St. Martin, c/o Yauco, PR, Holy Rossary Church. (PCE)
Aguila, AZ, Our Lady of Guadalupe, c/o Wickenburg, AZ, St. Anthony of Padua Church. (PHX)
Aguirre, PR, La Milagrosa, c/o Aguirre, PR, Sacred Heart Church. (PCE)
Ahmeek, MI, Our Lady of Peace, c/o Mohawk, MI, Keweenaw Catholic Missions Church. (MAR)
Ahtanum, WA, Yakima Co., Holy Cross, c/o [2] Yakima, WA, Holy Family Church. (YAK)
Ak Chin, AZ, St. Francis, c/o Bapchule, AZ, St. Peter's Church. (PHX)
Alameda, NM, Bernalillo Co., Our Lady of Mount Carmel, c/o Alameda, NM, Nativity of the Blessed Virgin Mary Church. (SFE)
Alamillo, NM, Socorro Co., c/o Socorro, NM, San Miguel Church. (SFE)
Alapaha, GA, Berrien Co., St. Ann, c/o Tifton, GA, Our Divine Saviour Church. (SAV)
Albany, IL, Whiteside Co., St. Patrick, c/o Fulton, IL, Immaculate Conception Church. (RCK)
Albany, NY, Albany Co., Albany Medical Center, c/o [16] Albany, NY, St. Teresa of Avila Church. (ALB)
Albany, NY, Albany Co., Child's Hospital & Eden Park Nursing Home, c/o [8] Albany, NY, St. James Church. (ALB)
Albany, WI, St. Patrick's, c/o Brodhead, WI, St. Rose Church. (MAD)
Alberton, MT, Mineral Co., St. Albert the Great, c/o Frenchtown, MT, St. John the Baptist Church. (HEL)
Albin, WY, Laramie Co., St. Joseph, c/o Pine Bluffs, WY, St. Paul's Church. (CHY)
Albuquerque, NM, Bernalillo Co., Prince of Peace, c/o [3] Albuquerque, NM, Community of the Risen Saviour Church. (SFE)
Albuquerque, NM, Bernalillo Co., San Jose de los Duranes, c/o [16] Albuquerque, NM, San Felipe de Neri Church. (SFE)
Alcalde, NM, Rio Arriba Co., c/o San Juan Pueblo, NM, St. John the Baptist Church. (SFE)
Alcoa, TN, Blount Co., St. Francis of Assisi, c/o Alcoa, TN, Our Lady of Fatima Church. (KNX)
Alderson, WV, Greenbrier Co., St. Mary of the Greenbrier, c/o Hinton, WV, St. Patrick Church. (WH)
Alexander, ND, McKenzie Co., Our Lady of Consolation, c/o Watford City, ND, Epiphany Church. (BIS)
Alexandria, NE, Thayer Co., St. Mary's, c/o Fairbury, NE, St. Michael's Church. (LIN)
Algarrobos, PR, Our Lady of Fatima, c/o Yauco, PR, Holy Rossary Church. (PCE)
Algodones, NM, Sandoval Co., c/o Bernalillo, NM, Our Lady of Sorrows Church. (SFE)
Alice, ND, St. Henry, c/o Enderlin, ND, St. Patrick's Church. (FAR)
Alice, TX, Jim Wells Co., Sacred Heart, c/o Alice, TX, St. Joseph Church. (CC)
Alice, TX, Jim Wells Co., Santo Nino De Atocha, c/o Alice, TX, Our Lady of Guadalupe Church. (CC)
Allaben, NY, Ulster Co., Our Lady of Lourdes, c/o Phoenicia, NY, St. Francis de Sales Church. (NY)
Allagash Plantation, ME, St. Paul, c/o St. Francis, ME, St. Charles Church. (PRT)
Allen, SD, Bennett Co., St. John of the Cross, c/o Kyle, SD, Our Lady of Sorrows Church. (RC)
Allendale, SC, Barnwell Co., St. Mary, c/o Orangeburg, SC, Holy Trinity Church. (CHR)
Alma, GA, Bacon Co., St. Raymond, c/o Waycross, GA, St. Joseph's Church. (SAV)
Alma, MN, c/o Argyle, MN, St. Rose Church. (CR)
Almacigo Alto, PR, S. Juan Macias, c/o Yauco, PR, Holy Rossary Church. (PCE)
Almacigo Bajo, PR, St. Martin de Porres, c/o Yauco, PR, Holy Rossary Church. (PCE)
Almont, ND, Morton Co., St. Mary, Queen of Peace, c/o New Salem, ND, St. Pius V Church. (BIS)
Alpine, CA, Viejas, c/o Lakeside, CA, Blessed Kateri Tekakwitha Church. (SD)
Alto, TN, Franklin Co., St. Margaret Mary, c/o Decherd, TN, Good Shepherd Church. (NSH)
Altona, NY, Jericho, St. Alexis, c/o Altona, NY, Holy Angels Church. (OG)
Altura, MN, Winona Co., St. Anthony, c/o Lewiston, MN, St. Rose of Lima Church. (WIN)
Alturar, CA, c/o Alturas, CA, Sacred Heart Church. (SAC)
Alturas de Campo Rico., PR, Ntra. Sra. Del Carmen, c/o [5] Canovanas, PR, San Jose Church. (SJN)
Alturas de Mayaguez, PR, El Senor de Los Milagros, c/o [4] Mayaquez, PR, Church De El Buen Pastor. (MGZ)
Alturas de Rio Grande, PR, La Milagrosa, c/o Rio Grande, PR, Nuestra Senora del Carmen Church. (SJN)
Alvord, IA, Lyon Co., Sacred Heart, c/o Rock Valley, IA, St. Mary's Church. (SC)
Alzada, MT, c/o Broadus, MT, St. David's Church. (GF)
Amado, AZ, Santa Cruz Co., Assumption Chapel, c/o Tubac, AZ, St. Ann Church. (TUC)
Amagansett, NY, Suffolk Co., St. Peter the Apostle, c/o East Hampton, NY, Most Holy Trinity Church. (RVC)
Amalia, NM, Taos Co., c/o Questa, NM, St. Anthony Church. (SFE)
Amaluia, AS, c/o [5] (Leone), AS, Church of the Holy Cross. (SPP)
Amanave, AS, c/o [5] (Leone), AS, Church of the Holy Cross. (SPP)
Amarillo, TX, Potter Co., Laotian Catholic Community, c/o [11] Amarillo, TX, St. Thomas the Apostle Church. (AMA)
Amelia, NE, Holt Co., St. Joseph, c/o O'Neill, NE, St. Patrick Church. (OM)
Amelia, VA, Good Samaritan, c/o [2] Richmond, VA, Church of the Epiphany. (RIC)
American Fork, UT, Utah Co., St. Peter's, c/o Provo, UT, St. Francis of Assisi Church. (SLC)
Amherst, NE, Buffalo Co., St. John Capistran, c/o Elm Creek, NE, Immaculate Conception Church. (GI)
Amherst, VA, Amherst Co., Catholic Community of Amherst, c/o Scottsville, VA, St. George Church. (RIC)
Amidon, ND, Slope Co., SS. Peter & Paul, c/o New England, ND, St. Mary Church. (BIS)
Amouli, AS, c/o [8] Pago Pago, AS, Church of Sacred Heart. (SPP)
Andes, NY, St. Ann, c/o Margaretville, NY, Sacred Heart Church. (ALB)
Andice, TX, Santa Rosa, c/o Georgetown, TX, St. Helen's Church. (AUS)
Andrews, SC, Georgetown Co., St. Leo the Great, c/o Georgetown, SC, St. Mary's Church. (CHR)
Andrus Cove, LA, Jefferson Davis Parish, St. Gertrude Chapel, c/o Lake Arthur, LA, Our Lady of the Lake Church. (LKC)
Aneta, ND, Nelson Co., Sacred Heart, c/o Cooperstown, ND, St. George's Church. (FAR)
Anguilla, MS, Our Mother of Mercy, c/o Belzoni, MS, All Saints Church. (JKS)
Anones, PR, San Jose, c/o Las Marias, PR, Immaculate Heart of Mary Church. (MGZ)
Ansley, NE, Custer Co., Sacred Heart, c/o Broken Bow, NE, St. Joseph's Church. (GI)
Antelope, OR, St. Mary's, c/o Wasco, OR, St. Mary's Church. (BAK)
Anton, TX, Hockley Co., St. Anthony, c/o Shallowater, TX, St. Phillip Benizi Church. (LUB)
Antonito, CO, Conejos Co., St. Augustine, c/o Conejos, CO, Our Lady of Guadalupe Church. (PBL)
Anza, CA, Cahuilla Indian Reservation, c/o Anza, CA, Sacred Heart Church. (SB)
Anza, CA, Riverside Co., Our Lady of the Snows, c/o Anza, CA, Sacred Heart Church. (SB)
Anza, CA, Riverside Co., Santa Rosa Indian Mission, c/o Anza, CA, Sacred Heart Church. (SB)
Anza, CA, Santa Rosa Reservation, c/o Anza, CA, Sacred Heart Church. (SB)
Aoa, AS, c/o [8] Pago Pago, AS, Church of Sacred Heart. (SPP)
Apache, OK, Caddo Co., Mother of Sorrows, c/o Sterling, OK, Our Lady of Perpetual Help Church. (OKL)
Arago, NE, Richardson Co., St. Mary's, c/o Rulo, NE, Immaculate Conception Church. (LIN)
Arapahoe, NE, Furnas Co., St. Germanus, c/o Cambridge, NE, St. John's Church. (LIN)
Arboles, CO, Archuleta Co., SS. Peter & Rose, c/o Ignacio, CO, St. Ignatius Parish Church. (PBL)
Arbuckle, CA, Colusa Co., Holy Cross, c/o Maxwell, CA, Sacred Heart Church. (SAC)
Arch Cape, OR, Clatsop Co., St. Peter the Fisherman, c/o Seaside, OR, Our Lady of Victory Church. (P)
Ardmore, SD, St. Aloysius, c/o Edgemont, SD, St. James Church. (RC)
Ardmore, SD, Fall River Co., St. Aloysius, c/o Hot Springs, SD, St. Anthony's Church. (RC)
Ardoch, ND, Walsh Co., St. John the Baptist, c/o Minto, ND, Sacred Heart Church. (FAR)
Arenzville, IL, St. Fidelis, c/o Beardstown, IL, St. Alexius Church. (SFD)
Argusville, ND, St. William, c/o [1] Fargo, ND, St. Mary's Cathedral Church. (FAR)
Arivaca, AZ, Pima Co., St. Ferdinand, c/o Tubac, AZ, St. Ann Church. (TUC)
Arkadelphia, AR, Clark Co., St. Mary's, c/o Malvern, AR, St. John the Baptist Church. (LR)
Arlee, MT, Lake Co., Sacred Heart, c/o St. Ignatius, MT, St. Ignatius Church. (HEL)
Armagh, MO, Franklin Co., St. Patrick, c/o Catawissa, MO, St. James Church. (STL)
Arnold, CA, Arnold Co., Our Lady of the Sierra, c/o Angels Camp, CA, St. Patrick Church. (STO)
Arnold, NE, St. Agnes, c/o Stapleton, NE, St. John the Evangelist Church. (GI)
Arnot, PA, Tioga Co., St. Stanislaus Kostka, c/o Blossburg, PA, St. Mary's Church. (SCR)
Arock, OR, Holy Family, c/o Jordan Valley, OR, St. Bernard's Church. (BAK)
Arroyo Hondo, NM, Taos Co., c/o Arroyo Seco, NM, Holy Trinity Church. (SFE)
Ashdown, AR, Little River Co., St. Elizabeth Ann Seton, c/o Hope, AR, Our Lady of Good Hope Church. (LR)
Ashfork, AZ, St. Anne, c/o Seligman, AZ, St. Francis Church. (PHX)
Ashland, NY, St. Joseph's Chapel, c/o Windham, NY, St. Theresa of Child Jesus Church. (ALB)
Ashley, ND, McIntosh Co., St. David, c/o Zeeland, ND, St. Andrew's Church. (FAR)
Ashtabula, OH, Ashtabula Co., Our Lady of Miracles (St. Joseph Mission), c/o Ashtabula, OH, St. Joseph's Church. (Y)
Ashuelot, NH, St. Michael, c/o Winchester, NH, St. Stanislaus Church. (MAN)
Asili, AS, c/o [5] (Leone), AS, Church of the Holy Cross. (SPP)
Asor, FM, c/o Ulithi & Neighboring Islands, FM, Queen of Heaven Church. (CI)
Aspen, CO, Snowmass in Snowmass Village, c/o Aspen, CO, St. Mary Church. (DEN)

Aspermont, TX, Stonewall Co., St. Mary, c/o Rotan, TX, St. Joseph Church. (LUB)
Asti, CA, Our Lady of Mt. Carmel, c/o Cloverdale, CA, St. Peter's Church. (SR)
Astor, FL, Lake Co., St. Hubert of the Forest, c/o [2] Ocala, FL, Our Lady of the Springs Church. (ORL)
Atalaya, PR, Ntra. Sra. de Altagracia, c/o Aguada, PR, St. Francis of Assisi Church. (MGZ)
Athena, OR, Sacred Heart, c/o Milton Freewater, OR, St. Francis of Assisi Church. (BAK)
Atlanta, GA, Fulton Co., San Felipe de Jesus Catholic Mission, c/o [12] Atlanta, GA, Shrine of the Immaculate Conception Church. (ATL)
Atlanta, IL, Logan Co., St. Mary, c/o Lincoln, IL, Holy Family Church. (PEO)
Atlantic Mine, MI, Houghton Co., St. Mary, c/o Houghton, MI, St. Ignatius Loyola Church. (MAR)
Atwood, CA, Orange Co., St. Therese, c/o Placentia, CA, St. Joseph Church. (ORG)
Aua, AS, c/o [6] (Lepua), AS, Church of the Immaculate Conception. (SPP)
Auburn, CA, Placer Co., St. Teresa of Avila, c/o Auburn, CA, St. Joseph Church. (SAC)
Auburn, PA, Susquehanna Co., St. Bonaventure, c/o Meshoppen, PA, St. Joachim's Church. (SCR)
Augusta, MT, Clark Co., St. Matthias, c/o Fairfield, MT, St. John Church. (HEL)
Ault, CO, Weld Co., St. Mary, c/o Greeley, CO, Our Lady of Peace Church. (DEN)
Aurora, NM, San Miguel Co., c/o Villanueva, NM, Our Lady of Guadalupe Church. (SFE)
Austin, NV, St. Augustine, c/o Battle Mountain, NV, St. John Bosco Church. (RNO)
Austin, PA, Potter Co., St. Augustine, c/o Coudersport, PA, St. Eulalia Church. (E)
Austwell, TX, Refugio Co., St. Anthony of Padua, c/o Tivoli, TX, Our Lady of Guadalupe Church. (CC)
Autrain, MI, Alger Co., St. Therese, c/o Trenary, MI, St. Rita Church. (MAR)
Ava, MO, Douglas Co., St. Leo the Great, c/o Mansfield, MO, Immaculate Heart of Mary Church. (SPC)
Avoca, NE, Cass Co., Holy Trinity, c/o Syracuse, NE, St. Paulinus Church. (LIN)
Avoca, WI, St. Joseph, c/o Muscoda, WI, St. John the Baptist Church. (MAD)
Avon, MT, Powell Co., St. Theodore, c/o Deer Lodge, MT, Immaculate Conception Church. (HEL)
Avondale, LA, Jefferson Civil Parish, Assumption of Mary, c/o [2] Marrero, LA, St. Agnes Le Thi Thanh Church. (NO)
Ayrshire, IA, Palo Alto Co., Sacred Heart, c/o Ruthven, IA, Sacred Heart Church. (SC)
Azle, TX, Tarrant Co., Holy Trinity, c/o [16] Fort Worth, TX, St. Thomas Church. (FWT)

B

Babb, MT, St. Mary, Queen of the World, c/o Browning, MT, Church of the Little Flower. (HEL)
Baden, MD, St. Dominic's, c/o Baden, MD, St. Michael Church. (WDC)
Badger, MN, Roseau Co., St. Mary's, c/o Roseau, MN, Sacred Heart Church. (CR)
Baggs, WY, Carbon Co., Our Lady of the Sage, c/o Rawlins, WY, St. Joseph's Church. (CHY)
Bahner, MO, Pettis Co., St. John, c/o Sedalia, MO, Sacred Heart Church. (JC)
Bailey Island, ME, Precious Blood, c/o Brunswick, ME, St. Charles Church. (PRT)
Bainville, MT, Sacred Heart, c/o Culbertson, MT, St. Anthony's Church. (GF)
Bajio, PR, Sagrada Familia, c/o Aguada, PR, St. Francis of Assisi Church. (MGZ)
Baker, CA, San Bernardino Co., Our Lady of the Desert, c/o Barstow, CA, St. Joseph Church. (SB)
Bakersfield, CA, Kern Co., Holy Spirit, c/o [1] Bakersfield, CA, Our Lady of Guadalupe Church. (FRS)
Bakersfield, CA, Kern Co., San Clemente, c/o [2] Bakersfield, CA, Our Lady of Perpetual Help Church. (FRS)
Bakersfield, CA, Kern Co., St. Jude, c/o [1] Bakersfield, CA, Our Lady of Guadalupe Church. (FRS)
Bald Knob, AR, White Co., St. Richard, c/o Searcy, AR, St. James Church. (LR)
Baldwin, IA, Holy Trinity, c/o Maquoketa, IA, Sacred Heart Church. (DUB)
Balfour, ND, St. Joseph, c/o Anamoose, ND, St. Francis Xavier Church. (FAR)
Ball Club, MN, Itasca Co., St. Joseph's, c/o Duluth, MN, Indian Missions Church. (DUL)
Ballantine, MT, Sts. Cyril & Methodius, c/o [4] Billings, MT, St. Bernard's Church. (GF)
Ballardvville, MA, St. Joseph's, c/o Andover, MA, St. Augustine Church. (BO)
Ballston Spa, NY, Protection of Mother of God, c/o Granville, NY, SS. Peter and Paul Church. (PSC)
Baltimore, MD, Baltimore Co., Holy Redeemer Chapel, c/o [85] Baltimore, MD, Sacred Heart of Jesus Church. (BAL)
Baltimore, MD, Baltimore Co., St. Gerard's Chapel, c/o [85] Baltimore, MD, Sacred Heart of Jesus Church. (BAL)
Bancroft, WV, Putnam Co., St. Patrick, c/o Elkview, WV, Our Lady of the Hills Church. (WH)
Banksville, CT, Fairfield Co., St. Timothy's, c/o [2] Greenwich, CT, St. Michael the Archangel Church. (BGP)
Banning, CA, Riverside Co., St. Mary, c/o Banning, CA, Precious Blood Church. (SB)
Banquete, TX, Nueces Co., St. Michael, c/o Agua Dulce, TX, St. Frances of Rome Church. (CC)
Barbeau, MI, Holy Family, c/o Rudyard, MI, St. Joseph Church. (MAR)
Barberville, FL, Volusia Co., San Jose Mission, c/o De Land, FL, St. Peter's Church. (ORL)
Bardstown, KY, Nelson Co., St. Mark, c/o Culvertown, KY, Immaculate Conception Church. (L)
Barinas, PR, St. James, c/o Yauco, PR, Holy Rossary Church. (PCE)
Barneston, NE, Gage Co., St. Joseph's, c/o Wymore, NE, St. Mary's Church. (LIN)
Barnesville, GA, Lamar Co., St. Ann, c/o Griffin, GA, Sacred Heart Church. (ATL)
Barneveld, WI, Immaculate Conception, c/o Ridgeway, WI, St. Bridget Church. (MAD)
Barnsdall, OK, Osage Co., St. Mary, c/o Pawhuska, OK, Immaculate Conception Church. (TLS)
Barnwell, SC, Barnwell Co., St. Andrew the Apostle, c/o Orangeburg, SC, Holy Trinity Church. (CHR)
Barrackville, WV, Marion Co., All Saints, c/o [4] Fairmont, WV, St. Joseph's Church. (WH)
Barriada Vietnam, Guaynabo, La Milagrosa, c/o Catano, PR, Santa Rosa de Lima Church. (SJN)
Barrineau Park, FL, Escambia Co., St. Elizabeth of Hungary, c/o Cantonment, FL, St. Jude Thaddeus Church. (PT)
Barrington, NH, Chapel of the Nativity, c/o Dover, NH, St. Joseph Church. (MAN)
Barrio Apeadero, PR, San Alfonso, c/o Villalba, PR, Our Lady of Mt. Carmel Church. (PCE)
Barrio Cecilia, Sector La Fe, PR, c/o Naguabo, PR, Nuestra Senora del Rosario Church. (CGS)
Barrio Hatillo, PR, Sagrada Familia, c/o Villalba, PR, Our Lady of Mt. Carmel Church. (PCE)
Barrio Indios, PR, San Juan Bosco, c/o Guayanilla, PR, Immaculate Conception Church. (PCE)
Barrio Jaguey, PR, Madre Cabrini, c/o Villalba, PR, Our Lady of Mt. Carmel Church. (PCE)
Barrio Rio, Sector Brazo Seco, PR, c/o Naguabo, PR, Nuestra Senora del Rosario Church. (CGS)
Barrio Semil, PR, Santa Cecilia, c/o Villalba, PR, Our Lady of Mt. Carmel Church. (PCE)
Barrio Sierra Baja, PR, Our Lady of Mt. Carmel, c/o Guayanilla, PR, Immaculate Conception Church. (PCE)
Barstow, TX, Our Lady of Refuge, c/o Pecos, TX, Santa Rosa Church. (ELP)
Bartlett, NH, Carroll, St. Joseph, c/o North Conway, NH, Our Lady of the Mountains Church. (MAN)
Bartolo, PR, Immaculate Conception, c/o Castaner, PR, Our Lady of the Miraculous Medal Church. (PCE)
Barton, MD, St. Gabriel, c/o Westernport, MD, St. Peter Church. (BAL)
Bartow, WV, Pocahontas Co., St. Mark the Evangelist, c/o Marlinton, WV, St. John Neumann Church. (WH)
Basile, LA, Assumption, c/o Basile, LA, St. Augustine Church. (LAF)
Basin, WY, Big Horn Co., St. Philip, c/o Greybull, WY, Sacred Heart Church. (CHY)
Bassett, NE, Rock Co., Holy Cross, c/o Ainsworth, NE, St. Pius X Church. (GI)
Basye, VA, Shenandoah Co., Our Lady of the Shenandoah, c/o Woodstock, VA, St. John Bosco Church. (ARL)
Batavia, NY, Genesee Co., St. Pius X, c/o [3] Batavia, NY, St. Mary Church. (BUF)
Batesville, TX, St. Patrick, c/o La Pryor, TX, St. Joseph Church. (SAT)
Bathgate, ND, Pembina Co., St. Anthony, c/o Walhalla, ND, St. Boniface's Church. (FAR)
Baxley, GA, Appling Co., St. Rose of Lima, c/o Hazlehurst, GA, Good Shepherd Church. (SAV)
Bayamon, PR, Casa San Agustin, c/o [1] Bayamon, PR, San Agustin Church. (SJN)
Bayamon, PR, Cristo Rey, c/o [15] Bayamon, PR, Ntra. Sra. Monserrate Church. (SJN)
Bayamon, PR, Ntra. Sra. de la Esperanza, c/o [15] Bayamon, PR, Ntra. Sra. Monserrate Church. (SJN)
Bayamon, PR, Ntra. Sra. del Carmen, c/o [18] Bayamon, PR, Santa Rita de Casia Church. (SJN)
Bayamon, PR, Sagrado Corazon, c/o [23] Bayamon, PR, Santa Maria Church. (SJN)
Bayamon, PR, Sagrado Corazon de Jesus, c/o [18] Bayamon, PR, Santa Rita de Casia Church. (SJN)
Bayamon, PR, San Gerardo de Mayella, c/o [23] Bayamon, PR, Santa Maria Church. (SJN)
Bayamon, PR, San Jose, c/o [18] Bayamon, PR, Santa Rita de Casia Church. (SJN)
Bayamon, PR, San Martin de Porres, c/o [1] Bayamon, PR, San Agustin Church. (SJN)
Bayamon, PR, San Martin de Porres, c/o [24] Bayamon, PR, Santa Teresa de Avila Church. (SJN)
Bayamon, PR, Santa Monica, c/o [15] Bayamon, PR, Ntra. Sra. Monserrate Church. (SJN)
Bayamon, PR, Villas de San Agustin, c/o [1] Bayamon, PR, San Agustin Church. (SJN)
Bayard, NE, Morrill Co., Sacred Heart, c/o Bridgeport, NE, All Souls Church. (GI)
Bayfield, CO, La Plata Co., St. Bartholemew, c/o Ignacio, CO, St. Ignatius Parish Church. (PBL)
Bayside, TX, Refugio Co., St. Mary, c/o Woodsboro, TX, St. Therese, The Little Flower Church. (CC)
Bda. Esperanza, PR, Guanica co., La Providencia, c/o Guanica, PR, St. Anthony Abbot Church. (PCE)
Bda. Marin, PR, La Milagrosa, c/o Arroyo, PR, Our Lady of Mt. Carmel Church. (PCE)
Beach Haven, NJ, Ocean Co., St. Thomas Aquinas, c/o Brant Beach, NJ, St. Francis of Assisi Church. (TR)
Beach Lake, PA, Wayne Co., St. Bernard, c/o White Mills, PA, St. Joseph's Church. (SCR)
Bear Creek Township, PA, Luzerne Co., St. Christopher, c/o [8] Wilkes-Barre, PA, Holy Saviour Church. (SCR)
Beardsley, KS, Rawlins Co., St. John's, c/o St. Francis, KS, St. Francis Church. (SAL)
Beaulieu, MN, Mahnomen Co., St. Joseph, c/o Mahnomen, MN, St. Michael's Church. (CR)
Beaver, OK, Beaver Co., St. Frances Cabrini, c/o Woodward, OK, St. Peter's Church. (OKL)
Beaver Creek, CO, Eagle Co., Beaver Creek Chapel, c/o Edwards, CO, St. Clare of Assisi Church. (DEN)
Bechyne, ND, Walsh Co., SS. Peter & Paul, c/o Michigan, ND, St. Lawrence O'Toole Church. (FAR)
Becket, MA, St. Matthew, c/o Hinsdale, MA, St. Patrick's Church. (SPR)
Bedford, KY, Trimble Co., St. Matthew, c/o LaGrange, KY, Immaculate Conception Church. (L)
Bedford Hills, NY, Westchester Co., St. Matthias, c/o Katonah, NY, St. Mary of the Assumption Church. (NY)
Bee, NE, Seward Co., St. Wenceslaus, c/o Dwight, NE, Assumption Church. (LIN)
Beech Bottom, WV, Brooke Co., Holy Family (Formerly Power), c/o Wellsburg, WV, St. John The Evangelist Church. (WH)
Bejou, MN, Mahnomen Co., Immaculate Conception, c/o Fertile, MN, St. Joseph Church. (CR)
Belaire Cove, LA, Sacred Heart, c/o Ville Platte, LA, Sacred Heart of Jesus Church. (LAF)
Belcourt, ND, St. Ann, c/o Turtle Mountain Reservation, ND, (Chippewa Indians) Church. (FAR)
Belcourt, ND, Rolette Co., St. Anthony Indian Mission, c/o Belcourt, ND, St. Ann Church. (FAR)
Belcourt, ND, Rolette Co., St. Benedict, c/o St. John, ND, St. John the Baptist Church. (FAR)
Belfair, WA, Kitsap Co., Prince of Peace, c/o Port Orchard, WA, St. Gabriel's Church. (SEA)
Belgrade, MT, Valley of Flowers, c/o Three Forks, MT, Holy Family Church. (HEL)
Belgrade Lakes, ME, St. Helena, c/o Oakland, ME, St. Theresa Church. (PRT)
Bellevue, LA, Christ the King, c/o Grand Coteau, LA, St. Charles Borromeo Church. (LAF)
Bellflower, IL, Mclean Co., St. John, c/o Farmer City, IL, Sacred Heart Church. (PEO)
Belltown, CA, Riverside Co., Our Lady of Guadalupe, c/o [8] Riverside, CA, St. John the Evangelist Church. (SB)
Bellwood, NE, Butler Co., St. Joseph's, c/o Bellwood, NE, St. Peter's Church. (LIN)
Bemidji, MN, Beltrami Co., Newman Center, c/o Bemidji, MN, St. Philip's Church. (CR)
Ben Bolt, TX, St. Peter's Church, c/o Alice, TX, St. Elizabeth Church. (CC)
Bena, MN, St. Anne's, c/o Ball Club, MN, St. Joseph's Church. (DUL)
Bennettsville, SC, Marlboro Co., St. Denis, c/o Cheraw, SC, St. Peter's Church. (CHR)
Bent, NM, Our Lady of Guadalupe, c/o Mescalero, NM, St. Joseph Church. (LSC)
Benton, LA, Mary, Queen of Heaven, c/o Bossier City, LA, St. Jude Church. (SHP)
Benton, PA, Columbia Co., Christ the King, c/o Bloomsburg, PA, St. Columba Church. (HBG)
Benwood, MN, Roseau Co., St. Joseph, The Worker, c/o Roseau, MN, Sacred Heart Church. (CR)
Berclair, TX, Immaculate Heart of Mary, c/o Goliad, TX, Immaculate Conception Church. (VIC)
Bergland, MI, Ontonagon Co., St. Ann, c/o White Pine, MI, St. Jude Church. (MAR)
Berino, NM, Immaculate Conception, c/o Anthony, NM, St. Anthony's Church. (LSC)
Bermuda, LA, St. Charles, c/o Isle Brevelle, LA, St. Augustine's Church. (ALX)
Bernal, NM, San Miguel Co., c/o Ribera, NM, San Miguel Del Vado Church. (SFE)
Berne, NY, Albany Co., St. Bernadette, c/o Altamont, NY, St. Lucy Church. (ALB)
Berrien Springs, MI, St. Gabriel, c/o Buchanan, MI, St. Anthony Church. (KAL)
Berryville, AR, Carroll Co., St. Anne's, c/o Eureka Springs, AR, St. Elizabeth's Church. (LR)

Berryville, VA, Clark Co., c/o Winchester, VA, Sacred Heart of Jesus Church. (ARL)
Berthold, ND, Ward Co., St. Ann, c/o Foxholm, ND, St. Mary Church. (BIS)
Bertram, TX, Burnet Co., Holy Cross, c/o Burnet, TX, Our Mother of Sorrows Church. (AUS)
Betances, PR, Our Lady of Fatima, c/o Cabo Rojo, PR, St. Michael Church. (MGZ)
Bethel, ME, Oxford Co., Our Lady of the Snows, c/o Norway, ME, St. Catherine of Sienna Church. (PRT)
Bethlehem, MD, Caroline Co., Holy Child, c/o Secretary, MD, Our Lady of Good Counsel Church. (WIL)
Bethlehem, NH, Grafton Co., Christ the King, c/o Littleton, NH, St. Rose of Lima Church. (MAN)
Bethlehem, NH, Grafton, Our Lady of the Snows, c/o Littleton, NH, St. Rose of Lima Church. (MAN)
Betterton, MD, Most Precious Blood, c/o Chestertown, MD, Sacred Heart Church. (WIL)
Beulah, CO, Pueblo Co., Our Lady of Lourdes, c/o [11] Pueblo, CO, St. Francis Xavier Church. (PBL)
Bevier, MO, Sacred Heart, c/o Macon, MO, Immaculate Conception Church. (JC)
Bibo, NM, Our Lady of Loretto, c/o Seboyeta, NM, Our Lady of Sorrows Church. (GLP)
Biddeford Pool, ME, York Co., St. Brendan, c/o Biddeford, ME, St. Mary's Church. (PRT)
Bieber, CA, Lassen Co., St. Stephen, c/o Burney, CA, St. Francis of Assisi Church. (SAC)
Big Bay, MI, Marquette Co., St. Mary, c/o [5] Marquette, MI, St. Michael Church. (MAR)
Big Bend, TX, Big Bend Mission, c/o Presidio, TX, Santa Teresa de Jesus Church. (ELP)
Big Elbow Lake, MN, Becker Co., St. Francis Cabrini, c/o Waubun, MN, St. Ann Church. (CR)
Big Lake, AK, Our Lady of the Lake, c/o Wasilla, AK, Sacred Heart Church. (ANC)
Big Oak Flat, CA, Tuolumne Co., Our Lady of Mt. Carmel, c/o Sonora, CA, St. Patrick Church. (STO)
Big Pine, CA, Inyo Co., St. Stephen, c/o Bishop, CA, Our Lady of Perpetual Help Church. (FRS)
Big Piney, WY, Sublette Co., St. Anne, c/o Pinedale, WY, Our Lady of Peace Church. (CHY)
Big Sky, MT, c/o Bozeman, MT, Resurrection Church. (HEL)
Big Sur, CA, Monterey Co., St. Francis of the Redwoods, c/o Carmel, CA, San Carlos Borromeo Basilica Church. (MRY)
Big Wells, TX, St. Michael, c/o Asherton, TX, Immaculate Conception Church. (SAT)
Bigfoot, TX, Our Lady of Mt. Carmel, c/o Von Ormy, TX, St. Peter the Fisherman Church. (SAT)
Billings, OK, Noble Co., Sacred Heart, c/o Perry, OK, St. Rose of Lima Church. (OKL)
Binger, OK, Binger Co., Our Lady of the Most Holy Rosary, c/o Anadarko, OK, St. Patrick's Church. (OKL)
Bird City, KS, Cheyenne Co., St. Joseph's, c/o St. Francis, KS, St. Francis Church. (SAL)
Bisbee, ND, Towner Co., c/o Rolette, ND, Sacred Heart Church. (FAR)
Biscoe, NC, Montgomery Co., Our Lady of the Americas, c/o Albemarle, NC, Our Lady of the Annunciation Church. (CHL)
Bismarck, MO, St. Francois Co., St. John, c/o Park Hills, MO, Immaculate Conception Church. (STL)
Black Canyon City, AZ, Yavapai Co., St. Philip Benizi, c/o Camp Verde, AZ, St. Frances Cabrini Church. (PHX)
Black Horse, PA, Montgomery Co., Our Lady of Mount Carmel, c/o [3] Norristown, PA, Holy Saviour Church. (PH)
Black Lake, LA, Our Lady of the Holy Rosary, c/o Campti, LA, Nativity of The Blessed Virgin Mary Church. (ALX)
Black Lake, NM, Colfax Co., St. Anthony, c/o Cimarron, NM, Immaculate Conception Church. (SFE)
Black Pipe-Corn Creek, SD, St. Joseph Hall, c/o Parmelee, SD, St. Agnes Church. (RC)
Blackville, SC, Barnwell Co., Sacred Heart, c/o Orangeburg, SC, Holy Trinity Church. (CHR)
Blackwater, AZ, Holy Family, c/o Bapchule, AZ, St. Peter's Church. (PHX)
Blackwell's Corner, CA, Kern Co., Nuestra Senora de la Paz, c/o Wasco, CA, St. John the Evangelist Church. (FRS)
Blaine, WA, Whatcom Co., St. Anne, c/o Ferndale, WA, St. Joseph Church. (SEA)
Blanca, CO, Costilla Co., St. James, c/o San Luis, CO, Sangre de Cristo Church. (PBL)
Blanchardville, WI, Immaculate Conception, c/o Hollandale, WI, St. Patrick Church. (MAD)
Blanconia, TX, Bee Co., St. Catherine, c/o Refugio, TX, Our Lady of Refuge Church. (CC)
Blencoe, IA, Monona Co., St. Bernard's, c/o Onawa, IA, St. John's Church. (SC)
Blooming Grove, PA, Good Shepherd, c/o Lords Valley, PA, St. John Neumann Church. (SCR)
Bloomingburgh, NY, Sullivan Co., Our Lady of the Assumption, c/o Middletown, NY, Our Lady of Mt. Carmel Church. (NY)
Bloomington, NE, Franklin Co., Sacred Heart, c/o Alma, NE, St. Joseph's Church. (LIN)
Blossburg, PA, Tioga Co., St. Andrew, c/o Blossburg, PA, St. Mary's Church. (SCR)
Blowing Rock, NC, Epiphany, c/o Boone, NC, St. Elizabeth Church. (CHL)
Blue Hill, NE, Webster Co., Holy Trinity, c/o Campbell, NE, St. Ann's Church. (LIN)
Blue Lake, CA, St. Joseph, c/o Arcata, CA, St. Mary's Church. (SR)
Blue Mountain Lake, NY, Hamilton Co., St. Paul, c/o Indian Lake, NY, St. Mary's Church. (OG)
Bluetown, TX, Cristo Rey, c/o Progreso, TX, Holy Spirit Church. (BWN)
Bluewater, NM, Risen Savior, c/o [4] Gallup, NM, St. John Vianney Church. (GLP)
Bly, OR, St. James the Apostle, c/o Chiloquin, OR, Our Lady of Mt. Carmel Church. (BAK)
Bo Barreal, PR, Cristo de la Salud, c/o Penuelas, PR, St. Joseph Church. (PCE)
Bo. Aceituna, PR, San Martin de Porres, c/o Moca, PR, Our Lady of Monserrate Church. (MGZ)
Bo. Aibonito Guerrero, PR, Ntra. Sra. del Carmen, c/o San Sebastian, PR, San Sebastian Martir Church. (MGZ)
Bo. Altozano, PR, Ntra. Sra. de Fatima, c/o San Sebastian, PR, San Sebastian Martir Church. (MGZ)
Bo. Alturita, PR, Cacao Co., Our Lady of Mt. Carmel, c/o Villalba, PR, Our Lady Mother of Divine Providence Church. (PCE)
Bo. Arenas de Guancia, PR, Guancia Co., S. Martin de Porres, c/o Yauco, PR, St. Martin de Porres Church. (PCE)
Bo. Atalaya, PR, El Cristo de la Reconciliacion, c/o Rincon, PR, St. Rose of Lima Church. (MGZ)
Bo. Barrancas, PR, La Monserrate, c/o Guayama, PR, St. Anthony of Padua Church. (PCE)
Bo. Bauta, PR, Bauta Abajo Co., N.S. del Rosario, c/o Villalba, PR, Our Lady Mother of Divine Providence Church. (PCE)
Bo. Belgica, PR, Guanica Co., Cristo Rey, c/o Guanica, PR, St. Anthony Abbot Church. (PCE)
Bo. Buena Vista, PR, Holy Family, c/o Penuelas, PR, Sacred Heart Church. (PCE)
Bo. Cacao, PR, Cacao Co., Imm. Concepcion, c/o Villalba, PR, Our Lady Mother of Divine Providence Church. (PCE)
Bo. Cain, PR, St. Martin de Porres, c/o San German, PR, St. Rose of Lima Church. (MGZ)
Bo. Calabazas, PR, San Gabriel de la Dolorosa, c/o San Sebastian, PR, San Sebastian Martir Church. (MGZ)
Bo. California, PR, c/o Maunabo, PR, San Isidor Labrador Church. (CGS)
Bo. Calvache, PR, Santa Rosa, c/o Rincon, PR, St. Rose of Lima Church. (MGZ)
Bo. Camarones, PR, Jesus Crucificado, c/o Villalba, PR, Our Lady of Mt. Carmel Church. (PCE)
Bo. Camarones-Los Robles, PR, San Antonio, c/o Villalba, PR, Our Lady of Mt. Carmel Church. (PCE)
Bo. Cambute, PR, Santa Cruz, c/o [18] Carolina, PR, Cristo Rey Church. (SJN)
Bo. Canonilla Abajo, PR, Maria Madre de la Iglesia, c/o Villalba, PR, Our Lady of Mt. Carmel Church. (PCE)
Bo. Canovanas, PR, Maria Auxiliadora, c/o [18] Carolina, PR, Cristo Rey Church. (SJN)
Bo. Capa Barreto, PR, Virgen del Rosario, c/o Moca, PR, Our Lady of Monserrate Church. (MGZ)
Bo. Capa Bosque, PR, Cristo Salvador, c/o Moca, PR, Our Lady of Monserrate Church. (MGZ)
Bo. Carreras, PR, La Providencia, c/o Anasco, PR, St. Anthony Abbot Church. (MGZ)
Bo. Carretera Nueva, PR, La Asuncion, c/o Hormigueros, PR, Shrine of Our Lady of Monserrate Church. (MGZ)
Bo. Cerro Gordo, PR, Espiritu Santo, c/o Villalba, PR, Our Lady of Mt. Carmel Church. (PCE)
Bo. Cerro Gordo, PR, La Inmaculada, c/o Moca, PR, Our Lady of Monserrate Church. (MGZ)
Bo. Cerro Gordo, PR, Our Lady of Monserrat, c/o Anasco, PR, St. Anthony Abbot Church. (MGZ)
Bo. Cerro Gordo, PR, San Francisco de Asis, c/o Sabana Grande, PR, Church of San Isidro. (MGZ)
Bo. Cerro Gordo, PR, San Judas, c/o Moca, PR, Our Lady of Monserrate Church. (MGZ)
Bo. Chucillas Sabana, PR, Corazon de Jesus, c/o Moca, PR, Our Lady of Monserrate Church. (MGZ)
Bo. Collado, PR, Ponce Co., Our Lady of Monserrate, c/o [3] Ponce, PR, Church of the Resurrection. (PCE)
Bo. Corazon, PR, La Candelaria, c/o Guayama, PR, St. Anthony of Padua Church. (PCE)
Bo. Corcega, PR, La Milagrosa, c/o Rincon, PR, St. Rose of Lima Church. (MGZ)
Bo. Cordero, PR, Virgen Monserrate, c/o Moca, PR, Our Lady of Monserrate Church. (MGZ)
Bo. Corillo, PR, San Pedro, c/o Villalba, PR, Our Lady of Mt. Carmel Church. (PCE)
Bo. Corral Viejo, PR, Ponce Co., Cristo Rey, c/o [10] Ponce, PR, La Santisima Trinidad Church. (PCE)
Bo. Cruces, PR, Sagrado Corazon de Jesus, c/o Rincon, PR, St. Rose of Lima Church. (MGZ)
Bo. Cuatro Calles, PR, Ponce Co., St. Anthony, c/o [13] Ponce, PR, Santuario San Judas Tadeo Church. (PCE)
Bo. Cuchilla del Limon, PR, La Asuncion, c/o Villalba, PR, Our Lady of Mt. Carmel Church. (PCE)
Bo. Cuchillas La Salle, PR, Santos Guillermo y Mateo, c/o Moca, PR, Our Lady of Monserrate Church. (MGZ)
Bo. Cuchillas Loperena, PR, Virgen del Carmen, c/o Moca, PR, Our Lady of Monserrate Church. (MGZ)
Bo. Cuesta Blanca, PR, Ntra. Sra. de Monserrate, c/o Lajas, PR, De la Merced Parish Church. (MGZ)
Bo. Dajas, PR, N.S. del Carmen, c/o Villalba, PR, Our Lady of Mt. Carmel Church. (PCE)
Bo. Damian Abajo, PR, Damian Abajo Co., N.S. del Pilar, c/o Villalba, PR, Our Lady Mother of Divine Providence Church. (PCE)
Bo. El Bajo, Pastillas, PR, Pastillas Co., Cristo Rey, c/o Patillas, PR, Inmaculado Corazon de Maria Church. (PCE)
Bo. El Frio, PR, Ala de La Piedra Co., Nino de Praga, c/o Villalba, PR, Our Lady Mother of Divine Providence Church. (PCE)
Bo. El Hoyo, PR, La Virgen Milagrosa, c/o Sabana Grande, PR, Church of San Isidro. (MGZ)
Bo. El Hoyo, PR, Santa Rosa de Lima, c/o Hormigueros, PR, Shrine of Our Lady of Monserrate Church. (MGZ)
Bo. El Porvenir, PR, Ntra. Sra. de la Providencia (Rep. Masias), c/o [3] Mayaquez, PR, Ascension Church. (MGZ)
Bo. El Real, Pastillas, PR, Pastillas Co., San Guillermo, c/o Patillas, PR, Inmaculado Corazon de Maria Church. (PCE)
Bo. Espino, PR, St. Lawrence Martyr, c/o Anasco, PR, St. Anthony Abbot Church. (MGZ)
Bo. Fuig., PR, Monserrate, c/o Ensenada, PR, Sacred Heart Church. (PCE)
Bo. Guama, PR, N. Sra. de la Consolacion, c/o San German, PR, St. Rose of Lima Church. (MGZ)
Bo. Guamani, PR, Sgdo. Corazon, c/o Guayama, PR, St. Anthony of Padua Church. (PCE)
Bo. Guanajibo, PR, San Martin de Porres, c/o Hormigueros, PR, Shrine of Our Lady of Monserrate Church. (MGZ)
Bo. Guaragoa, PR, Ponce Co., San Andres, c/o [10] Ponce, PR, La Santisima Trinidad Church. (PCE)
Bo. Guaragoa, Arriba, PR, Ponce Co., Santa Ana, c/o [10] Ponce, PR, La Santisima Trinidad Church. (PCE)
Bo. Guaras, PR, Ntra. Sra. de Fatima, c/o Sabana Grande, PR, Church of San Isidro. (MGZ)
Bo. Guarderraya, Pastillas, PR, Pastillas Co., Madre Cabrini, c/o Patillas, PR, Inmaculado Corazon de Maria Church. (PCE)
Bo. Guerrero, PR, La Providencia, c/o Aguadilla, PR, San Jose Obrero Church. (MGZ)
Bo. Guineo, PR, Ala de La Piedra Co., Santa Ana, c/o Villalba, PR, Our Lady Mother of Divine Providence Church. (PCE)
Bo. Hatillo Viejo, PR, La Milagrosa, c/o Villalba, PR, Our Lady of Mt. Carmel Church. (PCE)
Bo. Hato Arriba, PR, San Patricio, c/o San Sebastian, PR, San Sebastian Martir Church. (MGZ)
Bo. Hato Arriba (Parcelas), PR, San Pablo de la Cruz, c/o San Sebastian, PR, San Sebastian Martir Church. (MGZ)
Bo. Higuero, PR, Santisimo Sacramento, c/o Villalba, PR, Our Lady of Mt. Carmel Church. (PCE)
Bo. Hoyamala, PR, San Jose Obrero, c/o San Sebastian, PR, San Sebastian Martir Church. (MGZ)
Bo. Hoyos, PR, Ponce Co., Santa Maria Virgen, c/o [17] Ponce, PR, Our Lady of Mt. Carmel Church. (PCE)
Bo. Jacaboa, Pastillas, PR, Pastillas Co., Carmen, c/o Patillas, PR, Inmaculado Corazon de Maria Church. (PCE)
Bo. Jagual, Pastillas, PR, Pastillas Co., Carmen, c/o Patillas, PR, Inmaculado Corazon de Maria Church. (PCE)
Bo. Jaguey, PR, San Jose, c/o Rincon, PR, St. Rose of Lima Church. (MGZ)
Bo. Jagueyes Arriba, PR, La Milagrosa, c/o Villalba, PR, Our Lady of Mt. Carmel Church. (PCE)
Bo. Jaquitas, PR, Ntra. Sra. de la Paz, c/o Hormigueros, PR, Shrine of Our Lady of Monserrate Church. (MGZ)
Bo. Juncal, PR, Santa Teresita, c/o San Sebastian, PR, San Sebastian Martir Church. (MGZ)
Bo. La Cuarta, PR, Ponce Co., San Pedro Nolasco, c/o [15] Ponce, PR, Church of the Sacred Heart. (PCE)
Bo. La Lechuza, PR, La Asuncion, c/o San Sebastian, PR, San Sebastian Martir Church. (MGZ)
Bo. La Luna, PR, Guanica Co., N. Sra Fatima, c/o Guanica, PR, St. Anthony Abbot Church. (PCE)
Bo. La Maquina, PR, Santa Ana, c/o Sabana Grande, PR, Church of San Isidro. (MGZ)
Bo. La Pica, PR, c/o Maunabo, PR, San Isidor Labrador Church. (CGS)
Bo. La Pica, PR, San Jose, c/o Sabana Grande, PR,

Church of San Isidro. (MGZ)
Bo. La Plata, PR, Sagrado Corazon de Jesus, c/o Lajas, PR, Our Lady of the Purification Church. (MGZ)
Bo. La Yuca, PR, Ponce Co., Immaculate Heart of Mary, c/o [3] Ponce, PR, Church of the Resurrection. (PCE)
Bo. Lajas Arriba (La Tea), PR, Ntra. Sra. del Perpetuo Socorro, c/o Lajas, PR, Our Lady of the Purification Church. (MGZ)
Bo. Lajas Arriba (Parcelas), PR, San Pablo, c/o Lajas, PR, Our Lady of the Purification Church. (MGZ)
Bo. Las Palmas, PR, Virg. del Carmen, c/o Salinas, PR, Our Lady of Monserrat Church. (PCE)
Bo. Las Raices, PR, Ponce Co., Sagrado Corazon de Jesus, c/o [17] Ponce, PR, Our Lady of Mt. Carmel Church. (PCE)
Bo. Las Vallas, PR, Ponce Co., San Lucas, c/o [3] Ponce, PR, Church of the Resurrection. (PCE)
Bo. Las Vegas, PR, Our Lady of Perpetual Help, c/o [3] Mayaquez, Mayaguez, Ascension Church. (MGZ)
Bo. Latorre, PR, Santa Catalina de Siena, c/o Sabana Grande, PR, Church of San Isidro. (MGZ)
Bo. Lavadero, PR, Sagrado Corazon de Jesus, c/o Hormigueros, PR, Shrine of Our Lady of Monserrate Church. (MGZ)
Bo. Limon, PR, St. Teresita, c/o [3] Mayaquez, PR, Ascension Church. (MGZ)
Bo. Limon, PR, Virgen de la Amargura, c/o Villalba, PR, Our Lady of Mt. Carmel Church. (PCE)
Bo. Limon, PR, Virgen del Rosario, c/o Moca, PR, Our Lady of Monserrate Church. (MGZ)
Bo. Lizas, PR, c/o Maunabo, PR, San Isidor Labrador Church. (CGS)
Bo. Los Barros, Pastillas, PR, Pastillas Co., S. Juan Evangelista, c/o Patillas, PR, Inmaculado Corazon de Maria Church. (PCE)
Bo. Los Pollos, Pastillas, PR, Pastillas Co., Santa Rosa de Lima, c/o Patillas, PR, Inmaculado Corazon de Maria Church. (PCE)
Bo. Luna, PR, Guanica Co., San Judas, c/o Guanica, PR, St. Anthony Abbot Church. (PCE)
Bo. Madrigal, PR, Ponce Co., N.S. del Rosario, c/o [10] Ponce, PR, La Santisima Trinidad Church. (PCE)
Bo. Maginas, PR, Sagrado Corazon de Jesus, c/o Sabana Grande, PR, Church of San Isidro. (MGZ)
Bo. Maguayo, PR, Ntra. Sra. de la Monserrate, c/o Lajas, PR, De la Merced Parish Church. (MGZ)
Bo. Magueyes, PR, Ponce Co., San Juan de Mata, c/o [10] Ponce, PR, La Santisima Trinidad Church. (PCE)
Bo. Malezas, PR, La Milagrosa, c/o [6] Mayaquez, PR, Sacred Heart Church. (MGZ)
Bo. Marias, PR, St. Rita, c/o Anasco, PR, St. Anthony Abbot Church. (MGZ)
Bo. Marin Alto, Pastillas, PR, Pastillas Co., Perpetuo Socorro, c/o Patillas, PR, Inmaculado Corazon de Maria Church. (PCE)
Bo. Marueno, Arriba, PR, Ponce Co., N.S. Fatima, c/o [10] Ponce, PR, La Santisima Trinidad Church. (PCE)
Bo. Minillas Carretera, PR, Perpetuo Socorro, c/o San German, PR, St. Rose of Lima Church. (MGZ)
Bo. Minillas Valle, PR, Santa Monica, c/o San German, PR, St. Rose of Lima Church. (MGZ)
Bo. Miradero, PR, Ntro. Sra. de la Providencia, c/o Cabo Rojo, PR, St. Michael Church. (MGZ)
Bo. Mogote, PR, Santisima Tinidad, c/o Villalba, PR, Our Lady of Mt. Carmel Church. (PCE)
Bo. Molinas, PR, Ntra. Sra. de Monserrate, c/o Sabana Grande, PR, Church of San Isidro. (MGZ)
Bo. Naranjo, PR, Corazon de Jesus, c/o Moca, PR, Our Lady of Monserrate Church. (MGZ)
Bo. Olimpo, PR, Cristo Rey, c/o Guayama, PR, St. Anthony of Padua Church. (PCE)
Bo. Ollas, PR, Monserrate, c/o Santa Isabel, PR, St. James Church. (PCE)
Bo. Oveja, PR, Cristo Redentor, c/o Anasco, PR, St. Anthony Abbot Church. (MGZ)
Bo. Palmarejo, PR, San Jose, c/o Villalba, PR, Our Lady of Mt. Carmel Church. (PCE)
Bo. Palmarejo II, PR, San Juan Bautista, c/o Lajas, PR, Our Lady of the Purification Church. (MGZ)
Bo. Palmas, PR, Ntra Sra. de Fatima, c/o Arroyo, PR, Our Lady of Mt. Carmel Church. (PCE)
Bo. Parcelas Guacio (Parcelas), PR, Santa Cruz, c/o San Sebastian, PR, San Sebastian Martir Church. (MGZ)
Bo. Parcelas Palmarejo, PR, San Judas Tadeo, c/o Lajas, PR, Our Lady of the Purification Church. (MGZ)
Bo. Parcelas Santa Rosa, PR, Santa Rosa de Lima, c/o Lajas, PR, Our Lady of the Purification Church. (MGZ)
Bo. Parguera, PR, San Pedro, c/o Lajas, PR, De la Merced Parish Church. (MGZ)
Bo. Paris, PR, Ntra Sra. del Perpetuo Socorro, c/o Lajas, PR, De la Merced Parish Church. (MGZ)
Bo. Paso Secos, PR, Virgen del Rosario, c/o Santa Isabel, PR, St. James Church. (PCE)
Bo. Pastillo, PR, Ponce Co., Inmaculada, c/o [10] Ponce, PR, La Santisima Trinidad Church. (PCE)
Bo. Pasto Seco, PR, c/o Las Piedras, PR, San Juan Bautista Church. (CGS)
Bo. Penuelas, PR, Virgen del Rosario, c/o Santa Isabel, PR, St. James Church. (PCE)
Bo. Perchas 1, PR, Cristo Rey, c/o San Sebastian, PR, San Sebastian Martir Church. (MGZ)
Bo. Perchas 11, PR, La Pasion, c/o San Sebastian, PR, San Sebastian Martir Church. (MGZ)
Bo. Pinales, PR, La Immaculade, c/o Anasco, PR, St. Anthony Abbot Church. (MGZ)
Bo. Pitahaya, PR, Ntra Sra. del Carmen, c/o Arroyo, PR, Our Lady of Mt. Carmel Church. (PCE)
Bo. Placita, PR, c/o Juncos, PR, Inmaculada Concepcion Church. (CGS)
Bo. Playa, PR, Carmen, c/o Salinas, PR, Our Lady of Monserrat Church. (PCE)
Bo. Playita, PR, Virgen Milagrosa, c/o Salinas, PR, Our Lady of Monserrat Church. (PCE)
Bo. Plebiscito, PR, San Antonio Ma. Claret, c/o [27] San Juan, PR, San Jose Obrero Church. (SJN)
Bo. Pozas, PR, Damian Abajo Co., N.S. Monserrate, c/o Villalba, PR, Our Lady Mother of Divine Providence Church. (PCE)
Bo. Pozo Hondo, PR, Santa Rosa de Lima, c/o Anasco, PR, St. Anthony Abbot Church. (MGZ)
Bo. Providencia, Pastillas, PR, Pastillas Co., Providencia, c/o Patillas, PR, Inmaculado Corazon de Maria Church. (PCE)
Bo. Puente Jobos, PR, SS. Peter and Paul, c/o Guayama, PR, St. Anthony of Padua Church. (PCE)
Bo. Puerto Jobos, PR, San Francisco de Asis, c/o Guayama, PR, St. Anthony of Padua Church. (PCE)
Bo. Punta Brava, PR, San Pedro, c/o Moca, PR, Our Lady of Monserrate Church. (MGZ)
Bo. Puntas, PR, Nuestra Senora del Carmen, c/o Rincon, PR, St. Rose of Lima Church. (MGZ)
Bo. Quebrada Arenas, PR, c/o Maunabo, PR, San Isidor Labrador Church. (CGS)
Bo. Quebrado del Agua, PR, Ponce Co., La Milagrosa, c/o [16] Ponce, PR, Church of the Good Shepherd. (PCE)
Bo. Rayo Plata, PR, San Judas Tadeo, c/o Sabana Grande, PR, Church of San Isidro. (MGZ)
Bo. Real Anon Abajo, PR, Ponce Co., San Mateo, c/o [17] Ponce, PR, Our Lady of Mt. Carmel Church. (PCE)
Bo. Real Anon Arriba, PR, Ponce Co., San Martin de Porres, c/o [17] Ponce, PR, Our Lady of Mt. Carmel Church. (PCE)
Bo. Recio, Pastillas, PR, Pastillas Co., Sto. Cristo de Los Milagros, c/o Patillas, PR, Inmaculado Corazon de Maria Church. (PCE)
Bo. Retiro Tea, PR, Santa Rita, c/o San German, PR, St. Rose of Lima Church. (MGZ)
Bo. Rio Abajo, PR, Ceiba Co., H.S. del Perptro Socorro Bo. Rio Abajo, c/o Ceiba, PR, San Antonio de Padua Church. (CGS)
Bo. Robles, PR, Sagrado Corazon, c/o San Sebastian, PR, San Sebastian Martir Church. (MGZ)
Bo. Rocha Magueyes, PR, La Providencia, c/o Moca, PR, Our Lady of Monserrate Church. (MGZ)
Bo. Rosario Penon, PR, La Monserrate, c/o Rosario, PR, Rosary Church. (MGZ)
Bo. Salinas, PR, Ntra. Sra. del Carmen, c/o Lajas, PR, De la Merced Parish Church. (MGZ)
Bo. Salistral, PR, Ponce Co., Santa Marta, c/o [4] Ponce, PR, Our Lady of Mt. Carmel Church. (PCE)
Bo. Saltos, PR, San Judas Tadeo, c/o San Sebastian, PR, San Sebastian Martir Church. (MGZ)
Bo. Santa Juanita, PR, Guanica Co., N. Sra. Rosario, c/o Guanica, PR, St. Anthony Abbot Church. (PCE)
Bo. Santana Pichel, PR, Ntra. Sra. del Rosario, c/o Sabana Grande, PR, Church of San Isidro. (MGZ)
Bo. Santas Pascuas, PR, Ponce Co., Resurreccion, c/o [10] Ponce, PR, La Santisima Trinidad Church. (PCE)
Bo. Sierrita Caonillas, PR, Cristo de la Salud, c/o Villalba, PR, Our Lady of Mt. Carmel Church. (PCE)
Bo. Sta. Ana Moreno, PR, Sta Lucia, c/o Sabana Grande, PR, Church of San Isidro. (MGZ)
Bo. Susa, PR, Yauco Co., N.S. de La Monserrate, c/o Yauco, PR, St. Martin de Porres Church. (PCE)
Bo. Susa, PR, Guanica Co., N.S. de La Providencia, c/o Yauco, PR, St. Martin de Porres Church. (PCE)
Bo. Susa, PR, Yauco Co., S. Francisco de Asis, c/o Yauco, PR, St. Martin de Porres Church. (PCE)
Bo. Susa, PR, Guanica Co., Santa Rita, c/o Yauco, PR, St. Martin de Porres Church. (PCE)
Bo. Talante, PR, c/o Maunabo, PR, San Isidor Labrador Church. (CGS)
Bo. Tumbao, PR, c/o Maunabo, PR, San Isidor Labrador Church. (CGS)
Bo. Vista Alegre, PR, Jesus Crucificado, c/o Villalba, PR, Our Lady of Mt. Carmel Church. (PCE)
Bo. Voladoras Lomas, PR, Espiritu Santo, c/o Moca, PR, Our Lady of Monserrate Church. (MGZ)
Bo. Voladoras Parcelas, PR, Sagrada Familia, c/o Moca, PR, Our Lady of Monserrate Church. (MGZ)
Bo. Yaurel Palmarejo, PR, San Jose, c/o Arroyo, PR, Our Lady of Mt. Carmel Church. (PCE)
Bo. Yaurel Santa Clara, PR, San Martin, c/o Arroyo, PR, Our Lady of Mt. Carmel Church. (PCE)
Boardman, OR, Our Lady of Guadalupe, c/o Hermiston, OR, Our Lady of Angels Church. (BAK)
Bodega, CA, St. Teresa, c/o Occidental, CA, St. Philip Church. (SR)
Boiceville, NY, Ulster Co., Our Lady of La Salette, c/o Phoenicia, NY, St. Francis de Sales Church. (NY)
Boise City, OK, Cimarron Co., Good Shepherd, c/o Guymon, OK, St. Peter's Church. (OKL)
Boles Acres, NM, Our Lady of the Desert, c/o Alamogordo, NM, Immaculate Conception Church. (LSC)
Bolinas, CA, St. Mary Magdalen, c/o Olema, CA, Sacred Heart Church. (SFR)
Boling, TX, St. Joseph, c/o Wharton, TX, Holy Family Church. (VIC)
Bon Secour, AL, Our Lady of Bon Secour, c/o Magnolia Springs, AL, St. John the Baptist Church. (MOB)
Bonanza, OR, St. Frances Cabrini, c/o Merrill, OR, St. Augustine Church. (BAK)
Bongard, IL, Champaign Co., Immaculate Conception, c/o Philo, IL, St. Thomas Church. (PEO)
Bonhamtown, NJ, Middlesex Co., St. Margaret Mary Alacoque, c/o Edison, NJ, Guardian Angels Church. (MET)
Bonita Springs, FL, Lee Co., Hispanic Mission, c/o Bonita Springs, FL, St. Leo Church. (VEN)
Bonneau, SC, Berkeley Co., Our Lady of Peace, c/o Moncks Corner, SC, St. Philip Benizi Church. (CHR)
Booker, TX, St. Peter, c/o Perryton, TX, Immaculate Conception Church. (AMA)
Boomer, WV, Fayette Co., St. Anthony Shrine, c/o Montgomery, WV, Immaculate Conception Church. (WH)
Boone, CO, Pueblo Co., St. William, c/o Avondale, CO, Sacred Heart Church. (PBL)
Booneville, KY, Owsley Co., Booneville Catholic Church of the Holy Family, c/o Beattyville, KY, Queen of All Saints Church. (LEX)
Boonsboro, MD, Washington Co., St. James, c/o Hagerstown, MD, St. Mary Church. (BAL)
Boqueron, PR, St. Joseph, c/o Cabo Rojo, PR, St. Michael Church. (MGZ)
Borica, NM, Guadalupe Co., c/o Santa Rosa, NM, St. Rose of Lima Church. (SFE)
Borinquen, PR, Our Lady of Victory, c/o Aguadilla, PR, La Milagrosa Church. (MGZ)
Bosque, NM, Valencia Co., c/o Belen, NM, Our Lady of Belen Church. (SFE)
Boswell, OK, Choctaw Co., St. Jude, c/o Hugo, OK, Immaculate Conception Church. (TLS)
Boulder Valley, MT, Jefferson Co., St. John the Evangelist, c/o Boulder, MT, St. Catherine Church. (HEL)
Bowling Green, FL, Hardee Co., Holy Child, c/o Wauchula, FL, St. Michael Church. (VEN)
Bowmanstown, PA, Holy Cross, c/o Palmerton, PA, Sacred Heart Church. (ALN)
Box Elder, MT, St. Anthony, c/o Big Sandy, MT, St. Margaret Mary Church. (GF)
Braddock, ND, Emmons Co., St. Katherine, c/o Hazelton, ND, St. Paul Church. (BIS)
Bradley, CA, Monterey Co., Our Lady of Guadalupe, c/o San Miguel, CA, San Miguel Church. (MRY)
Brainardsville, NY, Franklin Co., St. Jude, c/o Chateaugay, NY, St. Patrick Church. (OG)
Braithwaite, LA, Plaquemines Parish, Assumption of the Blessed Virgin, c/o Pointe a la Hache, LA, St. Thomas Church. (NO)
Branch, LA, St. Edmund, c/o Robert's Cove, LA, St. Leo IV Church. (LAF)
Branson, CO, Las Animas Co., Blessed Sacrament, c/o Trinidad, CO, Most Holy Trinity, Trinidad Area Catholic Community (Trinidad Cluster) Church. (PBL)
Brant Lake, NY, Warren Co., St. Teresa, c/o Hague, NY, Blessed Sacrament Church. (ALB)
Bremen, ND, Wells Co., St. Joseph, c/o Fessenden, ND, St. Augustine's Church. (FAR)
Brewster, MN, Nobles Co., Sacred Heart, c/o Heron Lake, MN, Sacred Heart Church. (WIN)
Bridgeport, CA, Mono Co., Infant of Prague, c/o Mammoth Lakes, CA, St. Joseph Church. (STO)
Bridger, SD, Ziebach Co., Immaculate Conception, c/o Eagle Butte, SD, All Saints Church. (RC)
Bridger, SD, Ziebach Co., Immaculate Conception, c/o Eagle Butte, SD, Cheyenne River Reservation Church. (RC)
Bridport, VT, Addison Co., St. Bernadette, c/o Middlebury, VT, Assumption of the Blessed Virgin Mary Church. (BUR)
Brier Hill, NY, Our Lady of Grace, c/o Morristown, NY, St. John the Evangelist Church. (OG)
Brisbane, CA, Our Lady of Guadalupe, c/o [54] San Francisco, CA, Visitacion, Church of the. (SFR)
Bristol, CO, Prowers Co., St. Mary, c/o Holly, CO, St. Frances of Rome Church. (PBL)
Bristol, IL, Kendall Co., St. Patrick, c/o Plano, IL, St. Mary Church. (JOL)
Broadview, MT, Little Flower, c/o Roundup, MT, St. Benedict's Church. (GF)

Broadwater, NE, Cheyenne Co., St. Dominic, c/o Bridgeport, NE, All Souls Church. (GI)
Brocket, ND, Ramsey Co., St. Joseph, c/o Lakota, ND, St. Mary's Church. (FAR)
Brockton, MT, Roosevelt Co., St. Anthony, c/o Poplar, MT, Our Lady of Lourdes Church. (GF)
Brockton, MT, St. Thomas, c/o Poplar, MT, Our Lady of Lourdes Church. (GF)
Bromley, AL, St. John, c/o Daphne, AL, Shrine of the Holy Cross Church. (MOB)
Bronte, TX, Coke Co., St. James, c/o Ballinger, TX, St. Mary Star of the Sea Church. (SAN)
Brookline, NH, Hillsborough Co., Infant Jesus, c/o Milford, NH, St. Patrick Church. (MAN)
Brooklyn, NY, Queens Co., Our Lady of Mount Carmel, c/o [190] Queens, NY, St. Leo Church. (BRK)
Brooklyn, NY, Regina Pacis Votive Shrine, c/o [126] Brooklyn, NY, St. Rosalia-Regina Pacis Church. (BRK)
Brooks, MN, Red Lake Co., St. Joseph, c/o Oklee, MN, St. Francis Xavier's Church. (CR)
Brown City, MI, Sanilac Co., Sacred Heart, c/o North Branch, MI, St. Mary's Burnside Church. (DET)
Brownlee, NE, Cherry Co., St. Joan of Arc, c/o Mullen, NE, St. Mary's Church. (GI)
Brownsdale, MN, Mower Co., Our Lady of Loretto, c/o Austin, MN, St. Edward's Church. (WIN)
Brownstown, IN, Jackson Co., Our Lady of Providence, c/o Seymour, IN, St. Ambrose Church. (IND)
Brownsville, MN, Houston Co., St. Patrick, c/o Hokah, MN, St. Peter's Church. (WIN)
Brownsville, OR, Linn Co., Holy Trinity, c/o Sweet Home, OR, St. Helen Church. (P)
Brownsville, TN, Haywood Co., c/o Jackson, TN, St. Mary's Church. (MEM)
Brownsville, TX, Cameron Co., Sacred Heart, c/o [1] Brownsville, TX, Immaculate Conception Cathedral Church. (BWN)
Brownsville, TX, Cameron Co., St. Thomas, c/o [1] Brownsville, TX, Immaculate Conception Cathedral Church. (BWN)
Bruceton Mills, WV, Preston Co., Mary Help of Christians, c/o Cheat Lake, WV, St. Luke Church. (WH)
Bruni, TX, Webb Co., Sacred Heart, c/o Hebbronville, TX, Our Lady of Guadalupe Church. (CC)
Bruno, MN, Sacred Heart, c/o Sandstone, MN, St. Luke's Church. (DUL)
Brunswick, NE, Antelope Co., St. Ignatius, c/o Plainview, NE, St. Paul Church. (OM)
Bryce Canyon, UT, Garfield Co., St. Dominic, c/o Cedar City, UT, Christ the King Church. (SLC)
Bucarabones, PR, Sagrado Corazon, c/o Maricao, PR, St. John the Baptist Church. (MGZ)
Buchanan, ND, St. Margaret, c/o Jamestown, ND, The Basilica of St. James Church. (FAR)
Buck Run, PA, c/o Heckscherville, PA, St. Kieran Church. (ALN)
Buckhead Ridge, FL, Glades Co., St. Theresa of the Child Jesus, c/o Moore Haven, FL, St. Joseph the Worker Church. (VEN)
Buckhorn, CA, Amador Co., Our Lady of the Pines, c/o Jackson, CA, St. Patrick's Church. (SAC)
Buena Vista, GA, Marion Co., St. Mary Magdalen, c/o Americus, GA, St. Mary Church. (SAV)
Buena Vista, PR, La Milagrosa, c/o Las Marias, PR, Immaculate Heart of Mary Church. (MGZ)
Buenavista, NM, Mora Co., c/o Mora, NM, St. Gertrude Church. (SFE)
Bueyeros, NM, Harding Co., c/o Roy, NM, Holy Family-St. Joseph Church. (SFE)
Buffalo, ND, St. Thomas, c/o Casselton, ND, St. Leo Church. (FAR)
Buffalo, OK, Harper Co., St. Joseph, c/o Woodward, OK, St. Peter's Church. (OKL)
Buffalo, TX, Blessed Kateri Tekakwitha, c/o Fairfield, TX, St. Bernard of Clarivaux Church. (TYL)
Buffalo, WI, St. Andrew, c/o Pardeeville, WI, St. Mary Church. (MAD)
Buffalo Creek, CO, Jefferson Co., St. Elizabeth, c/o Conifer, CO, Our Lady of The Pines Church. (DEN)
Buhach, CA, Merced Co., Immaculate Conception, c/o Atwater, CA, St. Anthony Church. (FRS)
Buhl, MN, Our Lady of the Sacred Heart, c/o Chisholm, MN, St. Joseph's Church. (DUL)
Bullhead, SD, Corson Co., St. Aloysius, c/o McLaughlin, SD, St. Bernard Church. (RC)
Bullhead, SD, Corson Co., St. Aloysius, c/o Standing Rock, SD, Standing Rock Reservation Church. (RC)
Bullville, NY, Orange Co., St. Paul, c/o Middletown, NY, Our Lady of Mt. Carmel Church. (NY)
Buna, TX, Jasper Co., St. Francis of Assisi, c/o Silsbee, TX, St. Mark the Evangelist Church. (BEA)
Bunker, MO, Reynolds Co., Christ the King, c/o Salem, MO, Sacred Heart Church. (SPC)
Bunkerville, NV, Clark Co., La Virgen de Guadalupe, c/o Overton, NV, St. John, the Evangelist Church. (LAV)
Burchard, NE, Pawnee Co., Sacred Heart, c/o Steinauer, NE, St. Anthony Church. (LIN)
Bureau, IL, Bureau Co., St. Francis Xavier, c/o Granville, IL, Sacred Heart Of Jesus Church. (PEO)
Bureau, IL, Bureau Co., St. Francis Xavier, c/o Tiskilwa, IL, St. Mary's Church. (PEO)
Burkesville, KY, Cumberland Co , Holy Cross Catholic, c/o Albany, KY, Emmanuel Catholic Church. (L)
Burlington, TX, Milam Co., St. Michael's, c/o Rosebud, TX, St. Ann's Church. (AUS)
Burlington Junction, MO, Nodaway Co., St. Benedict Catholic Church, c/o Tarkio, MO, St. Paul the Apostle Church. (KC)
Burnham, PA, Mifflin Co., Mary Queen of All Saints, c/o Lewistown, PA, Sacred Heart of Jesus Church. (HBG)
Burnstad, ND, Logan Co., St. Clara, c/o Napoleon, ND, St. Philip Neri Church. (FAR)
Burnsville, NC, Yancey Co., Sacred Heart, c/o Mars Hill, NC, St. Andrew the Apostle Church. (CHL)
Busby, MT, Christ the King, c/o Lame Deer, MT, Blessed Sacrament Church. (GF)
Bush, LA, St. Tammany Civil Parish, St. Michael the Archangel, c/o Abita Springs, LA, St. Jane de Chantal Church. (NO)
Butner, NC, Granville Co., St. Bernadette, c/o [4] Durham, NC, St. Matthew Church. (R)
Butte La Rose, LA, Sacred Heart, c/o Henderson, LA, Our Lady of Mercy Church. (LAF)
Bylas, AZ, Graham Co., Blessed Kateri Tekakwitha, c/o San Carlos, AZ, San Carlos Catholic Mission Church. (TUC)

C

Cabezon, NM, San Jose, c/o Cuba, NM, Immaculate Conception Church. (GLP)
Cabool, MO, Texas Co., St. Michael, c/o Mountain Grove, MO, Sacred Heart Church. (SPC)
Cactus, TX, Our Lady of Guadalupe, c/o Dumas, TX, SS. Peter and Paul Church. (AMA)
Cade, LA, St. Anthony, c/o Broussard, LA, St. Joseph Church. (LAF)
Caimital, PR, Our Lady of Perpetual Help, c/o Guayama, PR, St. Anthony of Padua Church. (PCE)
Cainsville, MO, Harrison Co., St. Mary's, c/o Bethany, MO, Blessed Sacrament Church. (KC)
Cairo, GA, Grady Co., St. Elizabeth Ann Seton, c/o Thomasville, GA, St. Augustine's Church. (SAV)
Cairo, NY, Greene Co., Alphonsus Manor Rest, c/o Cairo, NY, Sacred Heart Church. (ALB)
Calamine, WI, St. Michael, c/o Belmont, WI, St. Philomena Church. (MAD)
Caldwell, TX, San Salvador, c/o Bryan, TX, St. Anthony's Church. (AUS)
Caledonia, OH, St. Lawrence O'Toole, c/o Marion, OH, St. Mary Church. (COL)
Calhoun, LA, St. Francis of Assisi, c/o West Monroe, LA, St. Paschal Church. (SHP)
Callabo, PR, Bo. Callabo, San Ramon, c/o Juana Diaz, PR, St. Raymond Nonato Church. (PCE)
Callaway, MN, c/o Lake Eunice Township, MN, St. Mary of the Lakes Church. (CR)
Callaway, NE, St. Boniface, c/o Stapleton, NE, St. John the Evangelist Church. (GI)
Calvert, TX, Robertson Co., St. Mary, c/o Hearne, TX, St. Mary's Church. (AUS)
Camarillo, CA, Ventura Co., Cabrillo Chapel, c/o Ventura, CA, Sacred Heart Church. (LA)
Camaseyes, PR, Our Lady of Fatima, c/o Aguadilla, PR, La Milagrosa Church. (MGZ)
Cambalaches, PR, Our Lady of Perpetual Help, c/o Yauco, PR, Holy Rossary Church. (PCE)
Cambridge, IL, Henry Co., St. John Vianney, c/o Kewanee, IL, St. Francis of Assisi Church. (PEO)
Camden, AL, Wilcox Co., St. Joseph, c/o Orrville, AL, Immaculate Conception Church. (MOB)
Cameron, LA, Cameron Parish St. Rose of Lima, c/o Creole, LA, Sacred Heart of Jesus Church. (LKC)
Cameron Corner, CA, St. Adelaide, c/o Jacumba, CA, St. Mary Magdalene Church. (SD)
Camilla, GA, Mitchell Co., St. John Vianney, c/o Moultrie, GA, Immaculate Conception Church. (SAV)
Camp Sacramento, CA, El Dorado Co., Our Lady of the Sierras, c/o South Lake Tahoe, CA, St. Theresa Church. (SAC)
Camp Summit, NY, N.Y.S. Correctional Facility, c/o Summit, NY, St. Anna Church. (ALB)
Camp Summit, NY, S.U.N.Y. Cobleskill College, c/o Summit, NY, St. Anna Church. (ALB)
Camp Wood, TX, St. Mary Magdalen, c/o Rocksprings, TX, Sacred Heart of Mary Church. (SAT)
Campbell, NY, Steuben Co., St. Joseph, c/o Bradford, NY, St. Stanislaus Church. (ROC)
Campbellton, TX, Sacred Heart, c/o Pleasanton, TX, St. Andrew Church. (SAT)
Campo Indian Reservation, CA, Our Lady of Mount Carmel, c/o Jacumba, CA, St. Mary Magdalene Church. (SD)
Campobello, ME, St. Timothy's, c/o Lubec, ME, Sacred Heart Church. (PRT)
Campton, KY, Wolfe Co., Catholic Church of the Good Shepherd, c/o Beattyville, KY, Queen of All Saints Church. (LEX)
Canaan, NH, Grafton Co., St. Mary, c/o Enfield, NH, St. Helena Church. (MAN)
Canaan, PA, Wayne Co., St. Patrick, c/o Waymart, PA, St. Mary's Church. (SCR)
Canada de Los Alamos, NM, Santa Fe Co., Our Lady of Guadalupe, c/o [3] Santa Fe, NM, Cristo Rey Church. (SFE)
Canadohta Lake, PA, Crawford Co., Our Lady of Fatima, c/o Union City, PA, St. Teresa of Avila Church. (E)
Canalizo, PR, Jayuya Co., La Milagrosa, c/o Jayuya, PR, Our Lady of Monserrate Church. (PCE)
Candelaria, TX, Our Lady of Peace, c/o Presidio, TX, Santa Teresa de Jesus Church. (ELP)
Canjilon, NM, St. Juan Nepumoceno, c/o Chama, NM, St. Patrick Church. (SFE)
Cannon Ball, ND, Sioux Co., St. Elizabeth, c/o Fort Yates, ND, St. Peter - Catholic Indian Mission Church. (BIS)
Canon de Vallecitos, NM, Rio Arriba Co., c/o El Rito, NM, San Juan Nepomuceno Church. (SFE)
Canoncito, NM, Santa Fe Co., c/o Pecos, NM, St. Anthony Church. (SFE)
Canoncito, NM, San Lorenzo, c/o Tijeras, NM, Holy Child Church. (SFE)
Canones, NM, c/o Abiquiu, NM, St. Thomas Apostle Church. (SFE)
Canovanas, PR, Ntra. Sra. de la Providencia, c/o [2] Canovanas, PR, Resurreccion del Senior Church. (SJN)
Canovanas, PR, San Francisco Javier, c/o [1] Canovanas, PR, Nuestra Senora del Pilar Church. (SJN)
Canton, MN, Fillmore Co., Church of the Assumption, c/o Harmony, MN, The Nativity of the Blessed Virgin Church. (WIN)
Canton, NC, Haywood Co., Immaculate Conception, c/o Waynesville, NC, St. John the Evangelist Church. (CHL)
Canton, TX, Van Zandt Co., St. Therese, c/o Athens, TX, St. Edward Church. (TYL)
Cantwell, AK, Denali National Park, c/o Healy, AK, Holy Mary of Guadalupe Church. (FBK)
Canyon, NM, Sandoval Co., c/o Jemez Pueblo, NM, San Diego Indian Missions Church. (SFE)
Canyon Ferry, MT, Our Lady of the Lake, c/o East Helena, MT, SS. Cyril and Methodius Church. (HEL)
Capitan, NM, Sacred Heart, c/o Carrizozo, NM, St. Rita Church. (LSC)
Caplis, LA, Bossier Parish, Mary, Queen of Peace, c/o Bossier City, LA, Christ the King Church. (SHP)
Capulin, NM, c/o Abiquiu, NM, St. Thomas Apostle Church. (SFE)
Carbondale, CO, Garfield Co., St. Mary of the Crown, c/o Basalt, CO, St. Vincent Church. (DEN)
Carenage, VI, Chapel of St. Anne, c/o [1] St. Thomas, VI, Cathedral of Sts. Peter and Paul. (STV)
Carey, OH, Wyandot Co., O.L.C., c/o Salem Twp., OH, St. Joseph Church. (TOL)
Carmen, PR, Our Lady of Mt. Carmel, c/o Guayama, PR, St. Anthony of Padua Church. (PCE)
Carnation, WA, King Co., St. Anthony, c/o Snoqualmie, WA, Our Lady of Sorrows Church. (SEA)
Carnegie, OK, Caddo Co., St. Richard, c/o Anadarko, OK, St. Patrick's Church. (OKL)
Carnuel, NM, Bernalillo Co., Holy Child, c/o Tijeras, NM, Holy Child Church. (SFE)
Caroga Lake, NY, St. Barbara, c/o Gloversville, NY, St. Mary of Mt. Carmel Church. (ALB)
Carolina, PR, La Sagrada Familia, c/o [12] Carolina, PR, San Juan de Dios Church. (SJN)
Carolina, PR, Parque Bolivariano 5-JL, c/o [3] Carolina, PR, Santa Clara de Asis Church. (SJN)
Carolina, PR, San Antonio, c/o [20] Carolina, PR, San Valentin Church. (SJN)
Carolina, PR, San Francisco de Asis, c/o [3] Carolina, PR, Santa Clara de Asis Church. (SJN)
Carolina, PR, Santa Rosa, c/o [20] Carolina, PR, San Valentin Church. (SJN)
Carpenter, WY, Laramie Co., St. Peter, c/o Pine Bluffs, WY, St. Paul's Church. (CHY)
Carrissa Plains, CA, San Luis Obispo Co., St. James Mission, c/o Santa Margarita, CA, Holy Angels Church. (MRY)
Carrizales, PR, Ntra. Sra. de las Mercedes, c/o Aguada, PR, St. Francis of Assisi Church. (MGZ)
Carrizales, PR, Our Lady of Montserrat, c/o Yauco, PR, Holy Rossary Church. (PCE)
Carroll, NH, St. Patrick, c/o Whitefield, NH, St. Matthew Church. (MAN)
Carroll Township, IA, St. Wenceslaus, c/o Clutier, IA, Immaculate Conception Church. (DUB)
Carroll Township, IA, St. Wenceslaus, c/o Traer, IA, St. Paul's Church. (DUB)
Carson, MS, Jefferson Davis Co., St. Elizabeth, c/o Bassfield, MS, St. Peter Church. (BLX)
Cartersville, IA, St. John, c/o Rockwell, IA, Sacred Heart Church. (DUB)
Cartersville, VA, St. Catherine, c/o Powhatan, VA, St. John Neumann Church. (RIC)

Caruthers, CA, Fresno Co., Our Lady of the Assumption, c/o Riverdale, CA, St. Ann Church. (FRS)
Casa Colorada, NM, Valencia Co., c/o Tome, NM, Immaculate Conception Church. (SFE)
Cascade, CO, El Paso Co., Holy Rosary, c/o [9] Colorado Springs, CO, Sacred Heart Church. (COS)
Cascade, MT, Sacred Heart, c/o Fort Shaw, MT, St. Ann Church. (GF)
Cascade, PA, Lycoming Co., Assumption of the B.V.M., c/o [6] Williamsport, PA, St. Ann's Church. (SCR)
Case, MO, Warren Co., St. Anthony, c/o Concord Hill, MO, St. Ignatius Church. (STL)
Cassville, MO, Barry Co., St. Edward, c/o Pulaskifield, MO, SS. Peter and Paul Church. (SPC)
Castine, ME, Hancock Co, Our Lady of Holy Hope, c/o Stonington, ME, St. Mary Star of the Sea Church. (PRT)
Castle Rock, WI, St. John Nepomucene, c/o Montfort, WI, St. Thomas Church. (MAD)
Catano, PR, Maria Auxiliadora, c/o Catano, PR, San Francisco de Sales Church. (SJN)
Catano, PR, San Jose Obrero, c/o Catano, PR, Nuestra Senora del Carmen Church. (SJN)
Catano, PR, San Judas Tadeo (Santuario), c/o Catano, PR, San Francisco de Sales Church. (SJN)
Catano, PR, San Martin de Porres, c/o Catano, PR, Nuestra Senora del Carmen Church. (SJN)
Catano, PR, Santo Domingo, c/o Catano, PR, San Francisco de Sales Church. (SJN)
Catarina, TX, St. Henry, c/o Asherton, TX, Immaculate Conception Church. (SAT)
Catatonk, NY, Tioga Co., St. Francis of Assisi, c/o Newark Valley, NY, St. John the Evangelist Church. (ROC)
Cathlamet, WA, Wahkiakum Co., St. Catherine, c/o Longview, WA, St. Rose de Viterbo Church. (SEA)
Cave Junction, OR, Josephine Co., St. Patrick, c/o Grants Pass, OR, St. Anne Church. (P)
Cayuga, ND, Sts. Peter & Paul, c/o Forman, ND, St. Mary's Church. (FAR)
Cazadero, CA, St. Colman, c/o Guerneville, CA, St. Elizabeth Church. (SR)
Cebolla, NM, Santo Nino, c/o Chama, NM, St. Patrick Church. (SFE)
Cedar Bluffs, NE, Saunders Co., St. Mary, c/o Colon, NE, St. Joseph's Church. (LIN)
Cedar Brook, NJ, Sacred Heart, c/o Blue Anchor, NJ, St. Lucy's Church. (CAM)
Cedar Creek, AZ, St. Anthony, c/o Cibecue, AZ, St. Catherine Church. (GLP)
Cedar Hill, NE, Saunders Co., Sacred Heart, c/o Morse Bluff, NE, St. George Church. (LIN)
Cedar Hill, TN, Robertson Co., St. Michael, c/o Springfield, TN, Our Lady of Lourdes Church. (NSH)
Cedaredge, CO, Delta Co., St. Philip Benizi, c/o Delta, CO, St. Michael Church. (PBL)
Cedarville, CA, c/o Alturas, CA, Sacred Heart Church. (SAC)
Cedarville, CA, Modoc Co., St. James, c/o Alturas, CA, Sacred Heart Church. (SAC)
Ceiba, PR, Sagrado Corazon de Jesus, Bo. Saco, c/o Ceiba, PR, San Antonio de Padua Church. (CGS)
Ceiba, PR, Ceiba Co., Parcelas de Aguas Claras, c/o Ceiba, PR, San Antonio de Padua Church. (CGS)
Celina, TN, Clay Co., Divine Savior, c/o Cookeville, TN, St. Thomas Aquinas Church. (NSH)
Center, MO, Ralls Co., St. Paul (Historic Church), c/o Perry, MO, St. William Church. (JC)
Center Barnstead, NH, St. Paul, c/o Alton, NH, St. Joan of Arc Church. (MAN)
Center Harbor, NH, Belknap Co., Our Lady of Victory, c/o Meredith, NH, St. Charles Church. (MAN)
Centermoreland, PA, Luzerne Co., Blessed Sacrament, c/o Carverton, PA, St. Frances Cabrini Church. (SCR)
Centerville, TX, Leon Co., St. Leo the Great, c/o Crockett, TX, St. Francis of the Tejas Church. (TYL)
Central City, CO, Gilpin Co., St. Mary of the Assumption, c/o Idaho Springs, CO, St. Paul's Church. (DEN)
Centreville, MI, St. Clare, c/o Three Rivers, MI, Immaculate Conception Church. (KAL)
Century, WV, Barbour Co., Our Lady of Sorrows, c/o Buckhannon, WV, Holy Rosary Church. (WH)
Cerrito, NM, San Miguel Co., c/o Villanueva, NM, Our Lady of Guadalupe Church. (SFE)
Cerro, NM, Taos Co., c/o Questa, NM, St. Anthony Church. (SFE)
Cerro Gordo, PR, Buen Consejo, c/o Aguada, PR, St. Francis of Assisi Church. (MGZ)
Chacon, NM, Mora Co., c/o Mora, NM, St. Gertrude Church. (SFE)
Chalan Kanoa Village, MP, Mercedarian Missionary Sisters of Berriz, c/o Chalan Kanoa Village, MP, Cathedral of Our Lady of Mt. Carmel. (CHK)
Challenge, CA, Yuba Co., St. Anthony, c/o Downieville, CA, Immaculate Conception Church. (SAC)
Chama, CO, Costilla Co., Immaculate Conception, c/o San Luis, CO, Sangre de Cristo Church. (PBL)
Chama, CO, Huerfano Co., Our Lady of Guadalupe, c/o Walsenburg, CO, St. Mary Church. (PBL)
Chamisal, NM, Taos Co., Santa Cruz Mission, c/o Penasco, NM, San Antonio de Padua Church. (SFE)
Chamita, NM, Rio Arriba Co., c/o San Juan Pueblo, NM, St. John the Baptist Church. (SFE)
Chaparral, NM, St. Thomas More, c/o Anthony, NM, St. Anthony's Church. (LSC)
Chapmanville, WV, Logan Co., St. Barbara, c/o Madison, WV, St. Mary, Queen of Heaven Church. (WH)
Charco, TX, Our Lady of Guadalupe, c/o Goliad, TX, Immaculate Conception Church. (VIC)
Charlemont, MA, Franklin Co., St. Christopher, c/o Shelburne Falls, MA, St. Joseph's Church. (SPR)
Charlestown, RI, Washington Co., St. James, c/o Carolina, RI, St. Mary's Church. (PRO)
Charley Creek, MT, St. Bernard's, c/o Sidney, MT, St. Matthew Church. (GF)
Charlo, MT, Mount Lake Co., St. Joseph's, c/o Ronan, MT, Sacred Heart Church. (HEL)
Chatom, AL, Washington Co., St. Paul, c/o Butler, AL, St. John Church. (MOB)
Cheek, TX, St. Martin de Porres, c/o Fannett, TX, St. Mary Church. (BEA)
Cherokee, NC, Our Lady of Guadalupe, c/o Bryson City, NC, St. Joseph Church. (CHL)
Cherry Creek, SD, Ziebach Co., St. Joseph, c/o Eagle Butte, SD, All Saints Church. (RC)
Cherry Creek, SD, Ziebach Co., St. Joseph, c/o Eagle Butte, SD, Cheyenne River Reservation Church. (RC)
Cherryfield, ME, St. Michael's, c/o Machias, ME, Holy Name of Jesus Church. (PRT)
Chesapeake City, MD, Cecil Co., St. Rose of Lima, c/o Middletown, DE, St. Joseph Church. (WIL)
Chester, CA, Plumas Co., Christ the King, c/o Westwood, CA, Our Lady of the Snows Church. (SAC)
Chester, MA, Hampden Co., St. John, c/o Huntington, MA, St. Thomas Church. (SPR)
Chester, PA, Delaware Co., Blessed Katharine Drexel Center for Evangelization, c/o [2] Chester, PA, Blessed Katharine Drexel Church. (PH)
Chester, PA, Delaware Co., St. Hedwig Chapel, c/o Clifton Heights, PA, Sacred Heart Church. (PH)
Chesterfield, NH, Cheshire, Our Lady of the Lake, c/o Hinsdale, NH, St. Joseph Church. (MAN)
Chicago, IL, c/o Chicago, IL, Ss. Peter and Paul Mission Church. (ROM)
Chicago, IL, Cook Co., Sacred Heart, c/o [83] Chicago, IL, Holy Name of Mary Church. (CHI)
Childersburg, AL, Talladega Co., Holy Name of Jesus, c/o Pell City, AL, Our Lady of the Lake Church. (BIR)
Chili, NM, Rio Arriba Co., c/o Espanola, NM, Sacred Heart Church. (SFE)
Chilili, NM, Bernalillo Co., San Juan de Nepumoceno, c/o Tijeras, NM, Holy Child Church. (SFE)
China Lake, ME, St. Peter, c/o North Vassalboro, ME, St. Bridget's Church. (PRT)
Chino Valley, AZ, Yavapai Co., St. Catherine Laboure, c/o Prescott, AZ, Sacred Heart Church. (PHX)
Chireno, TX, Nacogdoches Co., Our Lady of Lourdes, c/o Nacogdoches, TX, Sacred Heart Church. (TYL)
Chocorua, NH, Carroll Co., Our Lady of Perpetual Help, c/o Center Ossipee, NH, St. Joseph Church. (MAN)
Choctaw, LA, St. James, c/o Kraemer, LA, St. Lawrence the Martyr Church. (HT)
Christine, TX, St. Ignatius, c/o Jourdanton, TX, St. Matthew's Church. (SAT)
Christmas Valley, OR, Holy Family, c/o La Pine, OR, Holy Redeemer Church. (BAK)
Chugwater, WY, Platte Co., St. Theresa, c/o Wheatland, WY, St. Patrick's Church. (CHY)
Cincinnatus, NY, Our Lady of Perpetual Help, c/o Marathon, NY, St. Stephen Church. (SY)
Circle, MT, St Francis Xavier, c/o Glendive, MT, Sacred Heart Church. (GF)
Citra, FL, Marion Co., Christ the King, c/o [1] Ocala, FL, Blessed Trinity Church. (ORL)
Clallam Bay, WA, Clallam Co., St. Thomas the Apostle, c/o Forks, WA, St. Anne Parish Church. (SEA)
Clancy, MT, St. John's, c/o East Helena, MT, SS. Cyril and Methodius Church. (HEL)
Clanton, AL, Chilton Co., Church of the Resurrection, c/o Montevallo, AL, St. Thomas the Apostle Church. (BIR)
Claremont, MN, Dodge Co., St. Francis de Sales, c/o Dodge Center, MN, St. John Baptist de La Salle Church. (WIN)
Claremont, VA, St. Anne, c/o Hopewell, VA, St. James Church. (RIC)
Clark, WY, Park Co., Our Lady of the Valley, c/o Powell, WY, St. Barbara Church. (CHY)
Clarkdale, AZ, Yavapai Co., St. Cecilia, c/o Cottonwood, AZ, Immaculate Conception Church. (PHX)
Clarksburg, WV, Harrison Co., St. Nicholas Byzantine Catholic Mission, c/o Morgantown, WV, St. Mary's Holy Protection Church. (PBR)
Clarksville, MO, Pike Co., Mary Queen of Peace, c/o Louisiana, MO, St. Joseph Church. (JC)
Clatskanie, OR, Columbia Co., St. John the Baptist, c/o Rainier, OR, Nativity B.V.M. Church. (P)
Claudell, KS, Phillips Co., St. Francis, c/o Phillipsburg, KS, SS. Philip and James Church. (SAL)
Claybanks, MI, St. John, c/o Montague, MI, St. James Church. (GR)
Claypool, AZ, Gila Co., St. Joseph, c/o Miami, AZ, Our Lady of the Blessed Sacrament Church. (TUC)
Clayton, AL, Barbour Co., Ventress Correctional Facility, c/o Eufaula, AL, Holy Redeemer Church. (MOB)
Clayton, GA, Rabun Co., St. Helena's, c/o Clarkesville, GA, St. Mark's Church. (ATL)
Clayton, NM, St. Francis Xavier, c/o Roy, NM, Holy Family-St. Joseph Church. (SFE)
Clayton, OK, Pushmataha Co., Holy Trinity, c/o Antlers, OK, St. Agnes Church. (TLS)
Clear Lake, IN, Steuben Co., St. Paul Chapel, c/o Angola, IN, St. Anthony Church. (FTW)
Clear Spring, MD, St. Michael, c/o Williamsport, MD, St. Augustine Church. (BAL)
Clearmont, WY, Johnson Co., St. Mary, c/o Buffalo, WY, St. John the Baptist Church. (CHY)
Clendenin, WV, Kanawha Co., Catholic Community of Clendenin, c/o Elkview, WV, Our Lady of the Hills Church. (WH)
Cleveland, GA, Union Co., St. Paul the Apostle, c/o Blairsville, GA, St. Francis of Assisi Church. (ATL)
Cleveland, NM, Mora Co., c/o Mora, NM, St. Gertrude Church. (SFE)
Cleveland, OH, c/o [56] Cleveland, OH, Our Lady of Mount Carmel Church. (CLV)
Clifford, MI, St. Patrick's, c/o North Branch, MI, SS. Peter and Paul Church. (DET)
Climax Springs, MO, Our Lady of the Snows, c/o Hermitage, MO, St. Bernadette Church. (JC)
Clinton, AR, Van Buren Co., St. Jude, c/o St. Vincent, AR, St. Mary Church. (LR)
Clinton Corners, NY, Dutchess Co., St. Joseph, c/o Bangall, NY, Immaculate Conception Church. (NY)
Clintonville, NY, St. Catherine of Sienna, c/o Keeseville, NY, Church of the Immaculate Conception. (OG)
Cloquet, MN, Carlton Co., Holy Family Church, c/o Duluth, MN, Indian Missions Church. (DUL)
Cloudcroft, NM, Sacred Heart, c/o Alamogordo, NM, Immaculate Conception Church. (LSC)
Cloverdale, OR, Tillamook Co., St. Joseph, c/o Tillamook, OR, Sacred Heart Church. (P)
Clyde, TX, Callahan Co., Sts. Joachim and Ann, c/o [1] Abilene, TX, Sacred Heart Church. (SAN)
Clyde Park, MT, St. Margaret, c/o Livingston, MT, St. Mary's Church. (GF)
Coabbey, PR, Jayuya Co., San Jorge, c/o Jayuya, PR, Our Lady of Monserrate Church. (PCE)
Coal Mine, TX, Immaculate Conception, c/o Lytle, TX, St. Andrew Church. (SAT)
Coalburg, WV, Kanawha Co., Good Shepherd, c/o Belle, WV, St. John Church. (WH)
Coaldale, PA, Schuylkill Co., St. Patrick (Seek), c/o Tamaqua, PA, St. Jerome Church. (ALN)
Coamo, PR, Coamo Co., Saint James, c/o Coamo, PR, St. Blase Church. (PCE)
Coamo Arriba, PR, Coamo Co., Sacred Heart, c/o Coamo, PR, St. Blase Church. (PCE)
Cochise City, AZ, Cochise Co., San Simon-Cho, c/o Willcox, AZ, Sacred Heart Church. (TUC)
Cochiti, NM, Sandoval Co., Indian Pueblo, c/o Pena Blanca, NM, Nuestra Senora De Guadalupe Church. (SFE)
Cochranton, PA, Crawford Co., Our Lady of Lourdes, c/o Frenchtown, PA, St. Hippolyte Church. (E)
Coco, PR, Santa Ana, c/o Salinas, PR, Our Lady of Monserrat Church. (PCE)
Cocodrie, LA, Our Lady of the Gulf, c/o Chauvin, LA, St. Joseph Church. (HT)
Coeburn, VA, St. Mary, c/o Norton, VA, St. Anthony Church. (RIC)
Cogswell, ND, Our Lady of Mercy, c/o Forman, ND, St. Mary's Church. (FAR)
Cohasset, MN, St. Augustine's, c/o Grand Rapids, MN, St. Joseph's Church. (DUL)
Cohoes, NY, Sacred Heart of Jesus, c/o [6] Cohoes, NY, St. Rita-Sacred Heart Church. (ALB)
Cokedale, CO, Las Animas Co., Sacred Hearts of Jesus and Mary, c/o Trinidad, CO, Our Lady of Mt. Carmel, Trinidad Area Catholic Community (Trinidad Cluster) Church. (PBL)
Cokeville, WY, Lincoln Co., St. Dominic, c/o Kemmerer, WY, St. Patrick's Church. (CHY)
Cole Camp, MO, Benton Co., SS. Peter & Paul, c/o Warsaw, MO, St. Ann Church. (JC)
Collares, PR, Jayuya Co., Cristo Rey, c/o Jayuya, PR, Our Lady of Monserrate Church. (PCE)
Collegeville, AL, Jefferson Co., Sacred Heart, c/o [18] Birmingham, AL, Our Lady Queen of the Universe Church. (BIR)
Collores, PR, Bo. Jacaguas, La Milagrosa, c/o Juana Diaz, PR, St. Raymond Nonato Church. (PCE)
Collores, PR, Sacred Heart, c/o Yauco, PR, Holy Rossary Church. (PCE)
Colon, MI, St. Barbara, c/o Bronson, MI, St. Mary's Church. (KAL)
Colonia Nueva, TX, Christ the King, c/o Donna, TX, St. Joseph Church. (BWN)

Colonia Villodos, PR, Perpetuo Socorro, c/o Guayama, PR, St. Anthony of Padua Church. (PCE)
Colonias, NM, Guadalupe Co., c/o Santa Rosa, NM, St. Rose of Lima Church. (SFE)
Colrain, MA, Franklin Co., St. John the Baptist, c/o Shelburne Falls, MA, St. Joseph's Church. (SPR)
Columbia, AL, Houston,, Good Shepherd, c/o Dothan, AL, St. Columba Church. (MOB)
Columbia, CA, Tuolumne Co., St. Anne, c/o Sonora, CA, St. Patrick Church. (STO)
Columbia, KY, Adair Co., Good Shepherd, c/o Jamestown, KY, Holy Spirit Church. (L)
Columbia, LA, St. John, c/o Winnsboro, LA, St. Mary Church. (ALX)
Columbia, NC, All Souls, c/o Edenton, NC, St. Anne Church. (R)
Columbus, NM, Holy Family, c/o Deming, NM, St. Ann's Church. (LSC)
Comal, TX, St. Joseph, c/o New Braunfels, TX, SS. Peter and Paul Church. (SAT)
Commerce, GA, Jackson Co., St. Catherine Laboure, c/o Toccoa, GA, St. Mary's Church. (ATL)
Comstock, TX, Mary, Queen of the Universe, c/o Del Rio, TX, St. Joseph's Church. (SAT)
Concepcion, TX, Duval Co., Immaculate Conception, c/o Premont, TX, St. Theresa of the Infant Jesus Church. (CC)
Concrete, WA, Skagit Co., St. Catherine, c/o Sedro Woolley, WA, Immaculate Heart of Mary Church. (SEA)
Conde Avila, PR, St. Martin de Porres, c/o Cabo Rojo, PR, St. Michael Church. (MGZ)
Conehatta, MS, St. Catherine, c/o Philadelphia, MS, Holy Rosary Church. (JKS)
Conesus, NY, Livingston Co., St. William, c/o Livonia, NY, St. Joseph Church. (ROC)
Congress Junction, AZ, Yavapai Co., Good Shepherd of the Desert, c/o Prescott, AZ, Sacred Heart Church. (PHX)
Consejo Alto, PR, La Monserrate, c/o Guayanilla, PR, Immaculate Conception Church. (PCE)
Constantia, NY, Oswego Co., St. Bernadette, c/o Cleveland, NY, St. Mary of the Assumption Church. (SY)
Contoocook, NH, Merrimack, St. Mary, c/o Henniker, NH, St. Theresa Church. (MAN)
Contreras, NM, Socorro Co., San Jose, c/o La Joya, NM, Our Lady of Sorrows Church. (SFE)
Conway, MA, St. Mark, c/o South Deerfield, MA, St. James Church. (SPR)
Conway, ND, Walsh Co., St. Marks, c/o Pisek, ND, St. John Nepomucene Church. (FAR)
Cooke City, MT, St. John, c/o Livingston, MT, St. Mary's Church. (GF)
Cookson, OK, Cherokee Co., St. John the Evangelist, c/o Sallisaw, OK, St. Francis Xavier Church. (TLS)
Cooper Landing, AK, St. John Neumann Church, c/o Seward, AK, Sacred Heart Church. (ANC)
Copper Harbor, MI, Our Lady of the Pines, c/o Mohawk, MI, Keweenaw Catholic Missions Church. (MAR)
Coqui, PR, Our Lady of Perpetual Help, c/o Aguirre, PR, Sacred Heart Church. (PCE)
Coral, MI, St. Clara, c/o Sand Lake, MI, Mary Queen of Apostles Church. (GR)
Cordell, OK, Washita Co., St. Anne, c/o Clinton, OK, St. Mary's Church. (OKL)
Cordova, MD, Talbot Co., St. Joseph, c/o Easton, MD, SS. Peter and Paul Church. (WIL)
Cordova, NM, Rio Arriba Co., San Antonio, c/o Chimayo, NM, Holy Family Church. (SFE)
Corning, AR, Clay Co., St. Joseph, c/o Engelberg, AR, St. John the Baptist Church. (LR)
Corona, NM, St. Therese of the Little Flower, c/o Carrizozo, NM, St. Rita Church. (LSC)
Corozal, PR, San Antonio, c/o Penuelas, PR, St. Joseph Church. (PCE)
Corpus Christi, TX, Nueces, Mary, Mother of the Church, c/o [4] Corpus Christi, TX, Holy Family Church. (CC)
Corpus Christi, TX, Nueces Co., Our Lady of Mount Carmel, c/o [7] Corpus Christi, TX, Our Lady of the Rosary Church. (CC)
Corpus Christi, TX, Nueces Co., St. Mary, c/o [19] Corpus Christi, TX, St. Peter Prince of Apostles Church. (CC)
Corral, PR, P. Socorro, c/o Juana Diaz, PR, St. Raymond Nonato Church. (PCE)
Corrigan, TX, Polk Co., St. Martin de Porres, c/o Livingston, (1970), St. Joseph Church. (BEA)
Corsica, PA, Jefferson Co., St. Ann, c/o Brookville, PA, Immaculate Conception Church. (E)
Cossayuna Lake, NY, c/o Salem, NY, Holy Cross Church. (ALB)
Costilla, NM, Taos Co., c/o Questa, NM, St. Anthony Church. (SFE)
Cotton City, NM, St. Jude, c/o Lordsburg, NM, St. Joseph Church. (LSC)
Cottonwood, CA, Shasta Co., St. Anne, c/o Anderson, CA, Sacred Heart Church. (SAC)
Cottonwood, MT, St. John, c/o Havre, MT, St. Jude Thaddeus Church. (GF)
Cotuy, PR, Our Lady of Fatima, c/o San German, PR, San German de Auxerre Church. (MGZ)
Coulee City, WA, Grant Co., Holy Angels, c/o Grand Coulee, WA, St. Henry's Church. (YAK)
Coupeville, WA, Island Co., St. Mary, c/o Oak Harbor, WA, St. Augustine Church. (SEA)
Courtenay, ND, Stutsman Co., c/o Sanborn, ND, Sacred Heart Church. (FAR)
Coushatta, LA, Red River Parish, St. George, c/o Mansfield, LA, St. Joseph Church. (SHP)
Covelo, CA, Queen of Peace, c/o Willits, CA, St. Anthony Church. (SR)
Cox, SD, Harding Co., St. Agnes, c/o Bison, SD, Blessed Sacrament Church. (RC)
Cox, SD, Harding Co., St. Agnes, c/o Buffalo, SD, St. Anthony Church. (RC)
Coyanosa, TX, Pecos Co., St. Isidore, c/o Fort Stockton, TX, St. Agnes Church. (SAN)
Coyote, NM, c/o Abiquiu, NM, St. Thomas Apostle Church. (SFE)
Craftsbury, VT, Orleans Co., Our Lady of Fatima, c/o Greensboro Bend, VT, St. Michael Church. (BUR)
Crane, OR, St. Thomas, c/o Burns, OR, Holy Family Church. (BAK)
Cranfield, MS, St. John the Baptist, c/o Natchez, MS, Holy Family Church. (JKS)
Crates, PA, Clarion Co., St. Nicholas, c/o New Bethlehem, PA, St. Charles Church. (E)
Crawfordsville, AR, Crittenden Co., Sacred Heart, c/o West Memphis, AR, St. Michael's Church. (LR)
Creede, CO, Mineral Co., Immaculate Conception, c/o Del Norte, CO, Holy Name of Mary Church. (PBL)
Crescent, OK, Logan Co., St. Margaret Mary, c/o Guthrie, OK, St. Mary's Church. (OKL)
Crescent City, IL, St. Joseph, c/o Watseka, IL, St. Edmund Church. (JOL)
Creswell, OR, St. Philip Benizi, c/o Cottage Grove, OR, Our Lady of Perpetual Help Church. (P)
Cripple Creek, CO, Teller Co., St. Peter's, c/o Woodland Park, CO, Our Lady of the Woods Church. (COS)
Cristo Rey, TX, La Victoria, c/o Grulla, TX, Holy Family Church. (BWN)
Crittenden, NY, St. Patrick, c/o Corfu, NY, St. Francis of Assisi Church. (BUF)
Crockett Co., TN, c/o Humboldt, TN, Sacred Heart Church. (MEM)
Croghan, NY, Belfort, St. Vincent de Paul, c/o Croghan, NY, St. Stephen Church. (OG)
Croghan, NY, New Bremen, St. Peter, c/o Croghan, NY, St. Stephen Church. (OG)
Cromwell-Wright, MN, Immaculate Conception, c/o Carlton, MN, St. Francis Church. (DUL)
Crook, CO, Logan Co., St. Peters, c/o Julesburg, CO, St. Anthony Church. (DEN)
Crosbyton, TX, Crosby Co., St. Joseph, c/o Ralls, TX, St. Michael Church. (LUB)
Cross City, FL, Dixie Co., Holy Cross, c/o Chiefland, FL, St. John the Evangelist Church. (STA)
Crosstown, MO, Perry Co., St. James, c/o Perryville, MO, St. Vincent De Paul Church. (STL)
Crows Landing, CA, Stanislaus Co., Immaculate Heart of Mary, c/o Patterson, CA, Sacred Heart Church. (STO)
Cruces, PR, Santa Monica, c/o Aguada, PR, St. Francis of Assisi Church. (MGZ)
Crystal, ND, Pembina Co., St. Patrick, c/o Park River, ND, St. Mary's Church. (FAR)
Crystal Beach, TX, Galveston Co., St. Therese of Lisieux, c/o Port Bolivar, TX, Our Mother of Mercy Church. (GAL)
Crystal Lake, NY, c/o Greenville, NY, St. John the Baptist Church. (ALB)
Cuadrilla, TX, San Jose, c/o Fabens, TX, Our Lady of Guadalupe Church. (ELP)
Cuarteles, NM, c/o Santa Cruz, NM, Holy Cross Church. (SFE)
Cuba, OH, Putnam Co., St. Isidore, c/o Kalida, OH, St. Michael Church. (TOL)
Cubero, NM, Our Lady of Light, c/o San Fidel, NM, St. Joseph Church. (GLP)
Cuchillo, NM, St. Joseph, c/o Truth or Consequences, NM, Our Lady of Perpetual Help Church. (LSC)
Cuervo, NM, Guadalupe Co., c/o Santa Rosa, NM, St. Rose of Lima Church. (SFE)
Cummiskey, PA, Sullivan Co., St. Francis of Assisi, c/o Dushore, PA, St. Basil's Church. (SCR)
Cundiyo, NM, Rio Arriba Co., Santo Domingo, c/o Chimayo, NM, Holy Family Church. (SFE)
Cuny Table, SD, Shannon Co., St. Joseph, c/o Pine Ridge, SD, Holy Rosary Church. (RC)
Cupey, PR, San Martin de Porres, c/o [60] San Juan, PR, Santa Teresa Jornet Church. (SJN)
Cupey, PR, Virgen de la Salud, c/o [60] San Juan, PR, Santa Teresa Jornet Church. (SJN)
Curtis, MI, Mackinac Co., St. Timothy, c/o Grand Marais, MI, Holy Rosary Church. (MAR)
Custer, MT, St. Mary, c/o Hardin, MT, St. Joseph's Church. (GF)
Cuthbert, GA, Randolph Co., St. Luke, c/o Blakely, GA, Holy Family Church. (SAV)
Cygnet, OH, Wood Co., Sacred Heart, c/o North Baltimore, OH, Our Lady of the Miraculous Medal Church. (TOL)
Cypremort Point, LA, St. Francis, (Independent Mission), c/o Four Corners, LA, St. Peter the Apostle Church. (LAF)

D

Dahlia, NM, Guadalupe Co., c/o Anton Chico, NM, San Jose Church. (SFE)
Dallas, GA, Paulding Co., St. Vincent de Paul, c/o Lithia Springs, GA, St. John Vianney Church. (ATL)
Dallas City, IL, Hancock Co., Sacred Heart, c/o Nauvoo, IL, SS. Peter and Paul's Church. (PEO)
Dalton, NE, Cheyenne Co., St. Mary, c/o Bridgeport, NE, All Souls Church. (GI)
Danby, VT, Rutland Co., Holy Trinity, c/o East Dorset, VT, St. Jerome Church. (BUR)
Danforth, ME, St. Ann, c/o Lincoln, ME, St. Mary Church. (PRT)
Danville, VT, Calendonia Co., Our Lady Queen of Peace, c/o Marshfield, VT, North American Martyrs Church. (BUR)
Darby, MT, Mount Ravalli Co., St. Philip Benizi, c/o Hamilton, MT, St. Francis Church. (HEL)
Dardanelle, AR, Yell Co., St. Augustine's, c/o Russellville, AR, St. John's Church. (LR)
Darien, GA, McIntosh Co., Nativity of Our Lady, c/o Brunswick, GA, St. Francis Xavier Church. (SAV)
Darlington, SC, Darlington Co., St. Joseph the Worker, c/o Hartsville, SC, St. Mary the Virgin Mother Church. (CHR)
Darrington, WA, Snohomish Co., St. John Mary Vianney, c/o Arlington, WA, Immaculate Conception Church. (SEA)
Datil, NM, Nativity of the Blessed Virgin Mary, c/o Quemado, NM, Sacred Heart Church. (GLP)
Davenport Center, NY, Delaware Co., Chapel of St. Theresa the Little Flower, c/o South Kortright, NY, Church of the Most Precious Blood of Jesus. (ALB)
David City, NE, Butler Co., Assumption, c/o David City, NE, St. Mary's Church. (LIN)
Dawsonville, GA, Dawson Co., Christ Redeemer, c/o Dahlonega, GA, St. Luke Catholic Church. (ATL)
Dayton, IA, Christ the King, c/o Ogden, IA, St. John's Church. (SC)
Dayton, OR, Yamhill Co., St. Martin de Porres, c/o McMinnville, OR, St. James Church. (P)
Dayton, WI, St. James, c/o Belleville, WI, St. Mary of Lourdes Church. (MAD)
Dazey, ND, Barnes Co., St. Mary, c/o Sanborn, ND, Sacred Heart Church. (FAR)
De Bruce, NY, Sullivan Co., Sacred Heart, c/o Livingston Manor, NY, St. Aloysius Church. (NY)
De Ridder, LA, Beauregard Parish, St. Jude, c/o De Ridder, LA, St. Joseph's Church. (LKC)
Decatur, NE, Burt Co., Holy Family, c/o Tekamah, NE, St. Patrick Church. (OM)
Deerfield, KS, Kearny Co., Christ the King, c/o Garden City, KS, St. Mary Church. (DOD)
Deerfield, MN, Steele Co., Corpus Christi, c/o Medford, MN, Christ the King Church. (WIN)
Deerwood, MN, St. Joseph, c/o Crosby, MN, St. Joseph's Church. (DUL)
Del Rey, CA, St. Katherine's, c/o Sanger, CA, St. Mary Church. (FRS)
Delavan, MN, Faribault Co., Mater Dolorosa, c/o Winnebago, MN, St. Mary's Church. (WIN)
Delhi, LA, St. Theresa, c/o Rayville, LA, Sacred Heart Church. (SHP)
Dell City, TX, San Isidro, c/o Van Horn, TX, Our Lady of Fatima Church. (ELP)
Delmar, MD, Holy Redeemer, c/o Salisbury, MD, St. Francis De Sales Church. (WIL)
Delmas Dedeaux, MS, Harrison Co., Our Lady of Chartres, c/o [1] Gulfport, MS, St. Ann Church. (BLX)
Delta, UT, Millard Co., St. John Bosco, c/o Milford, UT, St. Bridget Church. (SLC)
Demarest, NJ, Bergen Co., St. Joseph Korean Catholic Community, c/o Demarest, NJ, St. Joseph's Church. (NEW)
Deming, WA, Whatcom Co., St. Peter, c/o Lynden, WA, St. Joseph's Church. (SEA)
Denmark, WI, New Denmark, Holy Trinity, c/o Denmark, WI, All Saints Church. (GB)
Dennis Port, MA, Barnstable Co., Our Lady of the Annunciation, c/o West Harwich, MA, Holy Trinity Church. (FR)
Denton, MD, Caroline Co., St. Elizabeth, c/o Ridgely, MD, St. Benedict Church. (WIL)
Denton, MT, St. Anthony, c/o Stanford, MT, St. Rose of Lima Church. (GF)
Denver, CO, Denver Co., St. Elizabeth of Hungary, c/o [12] Denver, CO, Holy Ghost Church. (DEN)
Denver, CO, Denver Co., St. Patrick, c/o [3] Denver, CO, Annunciation Church. (DEN)
Denver, NC, Lincoln Co., Holy Spirit, c/o Mooresville, NC, St. Therese Church. (CHL)
Dermott, AR, Chicot Co., Nativity of the Blessed Virgin Mary, c/o McGehee, AR, St. Mary Church. (LR)

DeRuyter, NY, St. Lawrence, c/o Truxton, NY, St. Patrick Church. (SY)
Des Moines, IA, Polk Co., Our Lady of Guadalupe, c/o [13] Des Moines, IA, Visitation Church. (DM)
Des Moines, NM, Union Co., Our Lady of Guadalupe, c/o Clayton, NM, St. Francis Xavier Church. (SFE)
Descanso, CA, Our Lady of the Pines, c/o Descanso, CA, Our Lady of Light Church. (SD)
Detroit, OR, Marion Co., St. Christopher, c/o Sublimity, OR, St. Boniface Church. (P)
Deweese, NE, Clay Co., Assumption, c/o Lawrence, NE, Sacred Heart Church. (LIN)
Dexter, NY, St. Elizabeth Seton, c/o Brownville, NY, Immaculate Conception of the B.V.M. Church. (OG)
Dexter, OR, Lane Co., St. Henry, c/o Oakridge, OR, St. Michael Church. (P)
Diamond, IN, Parke Co., St. Mary, c/o Brazil, IN, Annunciation of the Blessed Virgin Mary Church. (IND)
Dickey, ND, LaMoure Co., Assumption, c/o La Moure, ND, Holy Rosary Church. (FAR)
Dickson City, PA, Lackawanna Co., St. Thomas Apostle, c/o Dickson City, PA, Visitation of the Blessed Virgin Mary Church. (SCR)
Diego Hdez, PR, St. Anthony, c/o Yauco, PR, Holy Rossary Church. (PCE)
Diener Ranch At Five Points, CA, Fresno Co., Holy Family Chapel, c/o Riverdale, CA, St. Ann Church. (FRS)
Dilia, NM, Guadalupe Co., c/o Anton Chico, NM, San Jose Church. (SFE)
Dilley, TX, St. Mary, c/o Dilley, TX, St. Joseph's Church. (SAT)
Dillon Valley, CO, Summit Co., Our Lady of Peace, c/o Breckenridge, CO, St. Mary Church. (DEN)
Dimmick Township, IL, Sacred Heart, c/o [3] La Salle, IL, Resurrection Church. (PEO)
Diomede, AK, St. Jude, c/o Nome, AK, St. Joseph Church. (FBK)
Dividing Ridge, KY, Pendleton Co., St. John's, c/o Williamstown, KY, St. William Church. (COV)
Dixfield, ME, St. Joseph, c/o Mexico, ME, St. Theresa Church. (PRT)
Dixon, NE, Dixon Co., St. Anne, c/o Laurel, NE, St. Mary Church. (OM)
Dobbins, CA, Sacred Heart Church, c/o Marysville, CA, St. Joseph Church. (SAC)
Dobson, NC, Sacred Heart, c/o Mt. Airy, NC, Holy Angels Church. (CHL)
Dockton, WA, King Co., St. Patrick, c/o Vashon, WA, St. John Vianney Church. (SEA)
Dodson, MT, Sacred Heart, c/o Malta, MT, St. Mary's Church. (GF)
Doe Run, PA, Chester Co., St. Malachy, c/o Parkesburg, PA, Our Lady of Consolation Church. (PH)
Dolan Springs, AZ, Mohave Co., Our Lady of the Desert, c/o Kingman, AZ, St. Mary's Church. (PHX)
Dollar Bay, MI, Houghton Co., St. Francis of Assisi, c/o Hancock, MI, Resurrection Church. (MAR)
Dolores, CO, Montezuma Co., Our Lady of Victory Church, c/o Mancos, CO, St. Rita Church. (PBL)
Donalsonville, GA, Seminole Co., Church of the Incarnation, c/o Bainbridge, GA, St. Joseph's Church. (SAV)
Donken, MI, Houghton Co., Immaculate Heart of Mary, c/o Chassell, MI, St. Anne Church. (MAR)
Donna, TX, Hidalgo Co., Holy Cross Center, c/o Donna, TX, St. Joseph Church. (BWN)
Donnybrook, ND, Ward Co., St. Anthony, c/o Kenmare, ND, St. Agnes Church. (BIS)
Doraville, GA, Dekalb Co., Our Lady of the Americas, c/o [4] Atlanta, GA, Immaculate Heart of Mary Church. (ATL)
Dorothy, MN, Red Lake Co., St. Dorothy, c/o Red Lake Falls, MN, St. Joseph's Church. (CR)
Dorothy, NJ, St. Bernard, c/o Mays Landing, NJ, St. Vincent de Paul Church. (CAM)
Dorrance, KS, Russell Co., St. Joseph, c/o Wilson, KS, St. Wenceslaus Church. (SAL)
Dorris, CA, Siskiyou Co., Our Lady of Good Counsel, c/o Tulelake, CA, Holy Cross Church. (SAC)
Douglas, NE, Otoe Co., St. Martin's, c/o Palmyra, NE, St. Leo's Church. (LIN)
Dove Creek, CO, Dolores Co., St. Jude, c/o Cortez, CO, St. Margaret Mary Church. (PBL)
Dover, MO, Lafayette Co., St. John the Baptist, c/o Lexington, MO, Immaculate Conception Church. (KC)
Downey, CA, Los Padrinos Juvenile Hall, c/o Downey, CA, St. Raymond Church. (LA)
Downey, CA, Rancho Los Amigos Hospital, c/o Downey, CA, St. Raymond Church. (LA)
Downs, KS, Osborne Co., St. Mary's, c/o Osborne, KS, St. Aloysius Church. (SAL)
Downsville, NY, Delaware Co., Holy Family, c/o Walton, NY, St. John the Baptist Church. (ALB)
Doylesburg, PA, Franklin Co., Our Lady of Refuge, c/o Chambersburg, PA, Corpus Christi Church. (HBG)
Doyline, LA, Webster Parish, Mary, Queen of the Holy Rosary, c/o Bossier City, LA, Christ the King Church. (SHP)
Drain, OR, Douglas Co., St. John the Apostle, c/o Sutherlin, OR, St. Francis Xavier Church. (P)
Drake, ND, St. Margaret Mary, c/o Anamoose, ND, St. Francis Xavier Church. (FAR)
Draper, SD, Jones Co., St. Anthony of Padua, c/o Presho, SD, Christ the King Church. (RC)
Draper, UT, Salt Lake Co., St. John the Baptist, c/o [6] Sandy, UT, Blessed Sacrament Church. (SLC)
Drew, SD, Perkins Co., St. James, c/o Bison, SD, Blessed Sacrament Church. (RC)
Drewsey, OR, Our Lady of Loretto, c/o Burns, OR, Holy Family Church. (BAK)
Drifting, PA, Clearfield Co., St. Severin, c/o Frenchville, PA, St. Mary of the Assumption Church. (E)
Driftwood, PA, Cameron Co., St. James, c/o Emporium, PA, St. Mark Church. (E)
Driscoll, ND, Burleigh Co., St. Anthony, c/o Menoken, ND, St. Hildegard Church. (BIS)
Driscoll, TX, Nueces Co., St. James, c/o Bishop, TX, St. James Church. (CC)
Drummond Island, MI, Chippewa Co., St. Florence, c/o DeTour, MI, Sacred Heart Church. (MAR)
Drumright, OK, Creek Co., St. Mary, c/o Cushing, OK, SS. Peter and Paul Church. (TLS)
Dubina, TX, Fayette Co., SS. Cyril and Methodius, c/o Weimar, TX, St. Michael Church. (VIC)
Dublin, NH, Our Lady of the Snows, c/o Harrisville, NH, St. Denis Church. (MAN)
Dubois, WY, Fremont Co., Our Lady of the Woods, c/o Riverton, WY, St. Margaret's Church. (CHY)
Dubuisson, MS, Harrison Co., St. Ann, c/o DeLisle, MS, The Catholic Church in DeLisle. (BLX)
Duchesne, UT, Duchesne Co., Holy Spirit, c/o Roosevelt, UT, St. Helen's Church. (SLC)
Duey, PR, Chapel of St. Augustin, c/o San German, PR, San German de Auxerre Church. (MGZ)
Duey, PR, Virgin of Mt. Carmel, c/o Yauco, PR, Holy Rossary Church. (PCE)
Dulce, NM, St. Anthony, c/o Lumberton, NM, St. Francis of Assisi Church. (GLP)
Duluth, GA, Gwinnett Co., St. Monica, c/o Duluth, GA, St. Benedict Church. (ATL)
Dumas, AR, Desha Co., Holy Child Church, c/o McGehee, AR, St. Mary Church. (LR)
Duncan, AZ, St. Mary, c/o Clifton, AZ, Sacred Heart Church. (TUC)
Duncannon, PA, Perry Co., St. Bernadette, c/o Marysville, PA, Our Lady of Good Counsel Church. (HBG)
Dundee, NY, Yates Co., St. Andrew, c/o Penn Yan, NY, St. Michael Church. (ROC)
Dungannon, VA, St. Patrick, c/o Gate City, VA, St. Bernard Church. (RIC)
Dunmore, PA, Lackawanna Co., St. Casimir, c/o [5] Dunmore, PA, St. Mary of Mount Carmel Church. (SCR)
Dupree, SD, Ziebach Co., Sacred Heart, c/o Eagle Butte, SD, All Saints Church. (RC)
Dupree, SD, Ziebach Co., Sacred Heart, c/o Eagle Butte, SD, Cheyenne River Reservation Church. (RC)
Dupuyer, MT, Pondera Co., Holy Cross, c/o Valier, MT, St. Francis Church. (HEL)
Duran, NM, Torrance Co., c/o Vaughn, NM, St. Mary Church. (SFE)
Durham, CA, Butte Co., St. James, c/o Chico, CA, St. John the Baptist Church. (SAC)
Duryea, PA, Luzerne Co., St. Joseph's, c/o Duryea, PA, Sacred Heart of Jesus Church. (SCR)
Duvall, WA, King Co., Holy Innocents, c/o Snoqualmie, WA, Our Lady of Sorrows Church. (SEA)

E

Eagle, CO, Eagle Co., St. Mary, c/o Edwards, CO, St. Clare of Assisi Church. (DEN)
Eagle Harbor, MI, Holy Redeemer, c/o Mohawk, MI, Keweenaw Catholic Missions Church. (MAR)
Eagle Nest, NM, Colfax Co., St. Mel, c/o Cimarron, NM, Immaculate Conception Church. (SFE)
Eagles Mere, PA, Sullivan Co., St. Francis of Assisi, c/o Dushore, PA, St. Basil's Church. (SCR)
Eagles Mere, PA, Sullivan Co., St. Francis of Assisi, c/o Mildred, PA, St. Francis of Assisi Church. (SCR)
Eaglesville, CA, c/o Alturas, CA, Sacred Heart Church. (SAC)
Eagleville, CT, Tolland Co., St. Joseph, c/o Coventry, CT, St. Mary Church. (NOR)
Earth, TX, Lamb Co., St. Mary Magdalen, c/o Muleshoe, TX, Immaculate Conception Church. (LUB)
Easley, SC, Anderson Co., St. Luke, c/o Pickens, SC, Holy Cross Church. (CHR)
East Albany, VT, Orleans Co., St. John of the Cross, c/o Barton, VT, Conversion of St. Paul Church. (BUR)
East Barre, VT, Orange Co., Mother Cabrini, c/o Washington, VT, St. Cecilia Church. (BUR)
East Berkshire, VT, Franklin Co., Our Lady of Lourdes, c/o Richford, VT, All Saints Church. (BUR)
East Brewster, MA, Barnstable Co., Immaculate Conception, c/o Brewster, MA, Our Lady of the Cape Church. (FR)
East Chain, MN, Martin Co., Holy Family, c/o Fairmont, MN, St. John Vianney Church. (WIN)
East Durham, NY, St. Mary, c/o Cairo, NY, Sacred Heart Church. (ALB)
East Fairfield, VT, Franklin Co., St. Anthony-St. George, c/o Fairfield, VT, St. Patrick Church. (BUR)
East Glacier, MT, Church of the Ascension, c/o Browning, MT, Church of the Little Flower. (HEL)
East Highlands, CA, San Bernardino Co., St. John Bosco, c/o Highland, CA, St. Adelaide Church. (SB)
East Killingly, CT, Windham Co., Our Lady of Peace, c/o Danielson, CT, St. James Church. (NOR)
East Longmeadow, MA, Hampden Co., St. Joseph's, c/o [19] Springfield, MA, St. Paul Church. (SPR)
East Quogue, NY, c/o Hampton Bays, NY, St. Rosalie's Church. (RVC)
East Raymond, ME, St. Raymond, c/o Windham, ME, Our Lady of Perpetual Help Church. (PRT)
East Sebago, ME, Our Lady of Sebago, c/o Gorham, ME, St. Anne Church. (PRT)
Eastgate, TX, Liberty Co., St. Ann, c/o Dayton, TX, St. Joseph the Worker Church. (BEA)
Eastman, GA, Dodge Co., St. Mark, c/o McRae, GA, Holy Redeemer Church. (SAV)
Easton, CA, Fresno Co., St. Jude, c/o [6] Fresno, CA, St. Alphonsus Church. (FRS)
Eaton, CO, Weld Co., St. Michael, c/o Greeley, CO, Our Lady of Peace Church. (DEN)
Eatonton, GA, Christ Our Savior, c/o Greensboro, GA, Christ Our King Parish Church. (ATL)
Eatonville, WA, Pierce Co., Our Lady of Good Counsel, c/o Puyallup, WA, Holy Disciples Church. (SEA)
Eddyville, NE, St. Patrick, c/o Elm Creek, NE, Immaculate Conception Church. (GI)
Eden, VT, Lamoille Co., St. Gabriel, c/o Hyde Park, VT, St. Teresa Church. (BUR)
Eden, WY, Sweetwater Co., St. Christopher, c/o Pinedale, WY, Our Lady of Peace Church. (CHY)
Edenville, MI, Gladwin Co., St. Anne, c/o Coleman, MI, St. Philip Neri Church. (SAG)
Edgemont, SD, Fall River Co., St. James, c/o Hot Springs, SD, St. Anthony's Church. (RC)
Edgerly, LA, St. John Evangelist, c/o Vinton, LA, St. Joseph Church. (LKC)
Edgewater, FL, Volusia Co., c/o New Smyrna Beach, FL, Sacred Heart Church. (ORL)
Edgewood, NM, Santa Fe Co., c/o Moriarty, NM, Estancia Valley Catholic Parish Church. (SFE)
Edison, NJ, Middlesex Co., St. Therese of the Infant Jesus, c/o [7] New Brunswick, NJ, St. Mary of Mount Virgin Church. (MET)
Edisto Island, SC, Charleston Co., SS. Frederick & Stephen, c/o Yonges Island, SC, St. Mary Church. (CHR)
Edmeston, NY, Nativity of B.V.M., c/o Morris, NY, Holy Cross Church. (ALB)
Edroy, TX, San Patricio Co., Our Lady of Guadalupe, c/o Odem, TX, Sacred Heart Church. (CC)
Edwardsville, PA, Luzerne Co., SS. Cyril and Methodius, c/o Larksville, PA, St. Anthony of Padua Church. (SCR)
Effie, LA, St. Winifred, c/o Deville, LA, St. John the Baptist Church. (ALX)
Egan, LA, Acadia Parish, St. Michael, c/o Iota, LA, St. Joseph Church. (LAF)
Ekalaka, MT, St. Joan of Arc, c/o Baker, MT, St. John the Evangelist Church. (GF)
El Alto, PR, San Antonio, c/o Penuelas, PR, St. Joseph Church. (PCE)
El Cajon, CA, Sycuan, c/o Lakeside, CA, Blessed Kateri Tekakwitha Church. (SD)
El Carmen, NM, Mora Co., c/o Mora, NM, St. Gertrude Church. (SFE)
El Corozo, PR, Cristo Rey, c/o Cabo Rojo, PR, St. Michael Church. (MGZ)
El Duende, NM, Rio Arriba Co., c/o Espanola, NM, Sacred Heart Church. (SFE)
El Guache, NM, Rio Arriba Co., c/o Espanola, NM, Sacred Heart Church. (SFE)
El Guique, NM, Rio Arriba Co., c/o San Juan Pueblo, NM, St. John the Baptist Church. (SFE)
El Indio, TX, Our Lady of San Juan, c/o Eagle Pass, TX, Sacred Heart Church. (SAT)
El Macho, NM, San Miguel Co., c/o Pecos, NM, St. Anthony Church. (SFE)
El Papayo, PR, Cristo Rey, c/o Sabana Grande, PR, Church of San Isidro. (MGZ)
El Paso, TX, El Paso Co., Santa Teresita, c/o [38] El Paso, TX, San Judas Tadeo Church. (ELP)
El Pueblo, NM, San Miguel Co., c/o Ribera, NM, San Miguel Del Vado Church. (SFE)
El Rancho, NM, Santa Fe Co., c/o Pojoaque, NM, N.S. de Guadalupe del Valle de Pojoaque Church. (SFE)
El Rio, CA, Ventura Co., Santa Clara Chapel, c/o [2] Oxnard, CA, Santa Clara Church. (LA)
El Rucio, PR, Penuelas Co., La Milagrosa, c/o Penuelas, PR, St. Joseph Church. (PCE)
El Santuario, NM, Santa Fe Co., El Santuario Shrine, c/o Chimayo, NM, Holy Family Church. (SFE)
El Sauz, TX, Our Lady of Guadalupe, c/o Escobares, TX, Sacred Heart Church. (BWN)
El Valle, NM, Taos Co., San Miguel Archangel, c/o

Chimayo, NM, Holy Family Church. (SFE)
Elba, MN, Winona Co., St. Aloysius, c/o St. Charles, MN, St. Charles Borromeo Church. (WIN)
Elba, NE, St. Joseph, c/o Farwell, NE, St. Anthony of Padua Church. (GI)
Elberton, GA, Elbert Co., St. Mary's, c/o Washington, GA, St. Joseph's Church. (ATL)
Elbridge, MI, St. Joseph Church, c/o Hart, MI, St. Gregory's Church. (GR)
Eleele, HI, Kauai Co., Sacred Heart, c/o Kalaheo, HI, Holy Cross Church. (HON)
Elfrida, AZ, Cochise Co., St. Francis of Assisi, c/o Sunsites, AZ, St. Jude Thaddius Church. (TUC)
Elgin, OK, Comanche Co., St. Ann, c/o Sterling, OK, Our Lady of Perpetual Help Church. (OKL)
Elizabeth, IN, Harrison Co., St. Peter, c/o Corydon, IN, St. Joseph Church. (IND)
Elizabeth, LA, Allen Parish, St. Frances, c/o Oakdale, LA, Sacred Heart Church. (LKC)
Elizabeth, WV, Wirt Co., St. Elizabeth of Hungary, c/o Spencer, WV, Holy Redeemer Church. (WH)
Elizabethtown, NC, Bladen Co., Our Lady of Snows, c/o Riegelwood, NC, Christ the King Church. (R)
Elk, CA, Blessed Sacrament, c/o Point Arena, CA, St. Aloysius Church. (SR)
Elk, TX, McLennon Co., St. Joseph, c/o Tours, TX, St. Martin Church. (AUS)
Elk Grove, WI, St. Peter, c/o Seymour, WI, Our Lady of Hope Church. (MAD)
Elka Park, NY, Greene Co., St. Francis de Sales, c/o Haines Falls, NY, Immaculate Conception Church. (ALB)
Elkhorn City, KY, Pike Co., St. Joseph the Worker, c/o Pikeville, KY, St. Francis of Assisi Church. (LEX)
Elkin, NC, Surry Co., St. Stephen, c/o North Wilkesboro, NC, St. John Baptist de LaSalle Church. (CHL)
Ellendale, IA, Plymouth Co., St. Joseph's, c/o Merrill, IA, Assumption Church. (SC)
Ellendale, MN, Steele Co., St. Aiden, c/o Litomysl, MN, Holy Trinity Church. (WIN)
Ellijay, GA, Good Samaritan Mission, c/o Blue Ridge, GA, St. Anthony's Church. (ATL)
Ellsworth, MN, Nobles Co., St. Mary, c/o Luverne, MN, St. Catherine's Church. (WIN)
Elmer, LA, St. Peter, c/o Glenmora, LA, St. Louis Church. (ALX)
Elmwood, NE, Cass Co., St. Mary's, c/o Manley, NE, St. Patrick's Church. (LIN)
Elsie, NE, Perkins Co., Resurrection of Our Lord, c/o Wallace, NE, St. Mary's Church. (LIN)
Emanueli, PR, Coamo Co., Holy Family, c/o Coamo, PR, St. Blase Church. (PCE)
Eminence, KY, Henry Co., St. John Chrysostom, c/o Shelbyville, KY, Annunciation of the Blessed Virgin Mary Church. (L)
Eminence, MO, Shannon Co., St. Sylvester, c/o Mountain View, MO, St. John Vianney Church. (SPC)
Emmanuel, LA, Holy Rosary, c/o Cloutierville, LA, St. John the Baptist Church. (ALX)
Emory, TX, St. John the Evangelist, c/o Sulphur Springs, TX, St. James Church. (TYL)
Empire, LA, Plaquemines Parish, St. Ann, c/o Buras, LA, Our Lady of Good Harbor Church. (NO)
Empire, NV, St. Joseph the Worker, c/o Fernley, NV, St. Robert Bellarmine Church. (RNO)
Encinal, NM, Nativity of the Blessed Virgin Mary, c/o Laguna, NM, St. Joseph Church. (GLP)
Encino, NM, Torrance Co., c/o Vaughn, NM, St. Mary Church. (SFE)
Encino, TX, Brooks Co., St. Ann, c/o Falfurrias, TX, Sacred Heart Church. (CC)
England, AR, Lonoke Co., Holy Trinity Church, c/o Slovak, AR, SS. Cyril and Methodius Church. (LR)
Ensenada, NM, Rio Arriba Co., c/o Los Ojos, NM, San Jose Church. (SFE)
Eola, TX, Concho Co., St. Philip, c/o Eden, TX, St. Charles Church. (SAN)
Ephraim, UT, Sanpete Co., St. Jude, c/o Richfield/Monroe, UT, St. Elizabeth's Church. (SLC)
Ericson, NE, St. Theresa of the Child Jesus, c/o Burwell, NE, Sacred Heart Church. (GI)
Erie, IL, Whiteside Co., St. Ambrose, c/o Prophetstown, IL, St. Catherine Church. (RCK)
Errol, NH, Coos Co., St. Pius X, c/o Colebrook, NH, St. Brendan Church. (MAN)
Erving, MA, Franklin Co., St. Blanche, c/o Millers Falls, MA, St. John's Church. (SPR)
Escobosa, NM, Bernalillo Co., San Isidro, c/o Tijeras, NM, Holy Child Church. (SFE)
Esmond, ND, St. Boniface, c/o Anamoose, ND, St. Francis Xavier Church. (FAR)
Esopus, NY, Ulster Co., Sacred Heart, c/o Port Ewen, NY, Presentation of the Virgin Mary Church. (NY)
Esparto, CA, Yolo Co., St. Martin, c/o Winters, CA, St. Anthony Church. (SAC)
Essex, IL, Kankakee Co., St. Lawrence O'Toole, c/o South Wilmington, IL, St. Lawrence Church. (JOL)
Estaca, NM, Rio Arriba Co., c/o San Juan Pueblo, NM, St. John the Baptist Church. (SFE)
Estancia, NM, Torrance Co., c/o Moriarty, NM, Estancia Valley Catholic Parish Church. (SFE)
Esther, LA, St. James, c/o Henry, LA, St. John Church. (LAF)
Estherwood, LA, St. Margaret, c/o Mermentau, LA, St. John the Evangelist Church. (LAF)
Ethete, WY, Fremont Co., St. Joseph, c/o St. Stephens, WY, St. Stephen's Church. (CHY)
Etna, CA, Siskiyou Co., St. Mary, c/o Fort Jones, CA, Sacred Heart Church. (SAC)
Ettal, FM, c/o Lukunor, FM, Sacred Heart Church. (CI)
Euclid, MN, Polk Co., St. Mary, c/o [1] Crookston, MN, Cathedral of the Immaculate Conception. (CR)
Eufaula, OK, McIntosh Co., St. Paul's, c/o Krebs, OK, St. Joseph's Church. (TLS)
Eunice, NM, St. Clare, c/o Jal, NM, St. Cecilia Church. (LSC)
Eureka, CA, St. Joseph, c/o Eureka, CA, St. Bernard Church. (SR)
Eureka, UT, Utah Co., St. Patrick Parish, c/o Payson, UT, San Andres Church. (SLC)
Euripik, FM, c/o Ulithi & Neighboring Islands, FM, Queen of Heaven Church. (CI)
Europa, MS, Webster Co., St. John, c/o West Point, MS, Immaculate Conception Church. (JKS)
Everglades City, FL, Collier Co., Holy Family Church, c/o Marco Island, FL, San Marco Church. (VEN)
Everly, IA, Clay Co., St. Mary's, c/o Royal, IA, St. Louis Church. (SC)
Exeter, RI, Washington Co., Blessed Kateri Tekakwitha, c/o Wickford, RI, St. Bernard's Church. (PRO)
Expressway Heights, TX, Nuestra Senora de Guadalupe, c/o Weslaco, TX, San Martin de Porres Church. (BWN)
Eynon, PA, Lackawanna Co., St. Mary of Vilna, c/o Eynon, PA, St. Mary's Czestochowa Church. (SCR)

F

Fabius, NY, Onondaga Co., St. Paul, c/o Pompey, NY, Immaculate Conception Church. (SY)
Faga'alu, AS, c/o [2] Pago Pago, AS, Co-Cathedral of St. Joseph the Worker. (SPP)
Faga'itua, AS, c/o [4] (Lauli'i), AS, Church of St. Peter and Paul. (SPP)
Fagasa, AS, c/o [2] Pago Pago, AS, Co-Cathedral of St. Joseph the Worker. (SPP)
Fair Haven, NY, Cayuga Co., St. Jude Chapel, c/o Wolcott, NY, St. Thomas the Apostle Church. (ROC)
Fairfield, AL, Jefferson Co., St. Mary's, c/o [7] Birmingham, AL, Holy Family Church. (BIR)
Fairford, AL, Washington Co., Our Lady of Sorrows, c/o Chastang, AL, St. Peter the Apostle Church. (MOB)
Fairmount Springs, PA, Luzerne Co., St. Martha's, c/o Lake Silkworth, PA, Our Lady of Mount Carmel Church. (SCR)
Fairplay, CO, Park Co., St. Joseph, c/o Buena Vista, CO, St. Rose of Lima Church. (COS)
Fairview, MT, St. Catherine, c/o Sidney, MT, St. Matthew Church. (GF)
Fairview, OK, Major Co., St. Ann, c/o Bison, OK, St. Joseph's Church. (OKL)
Fais, FM, c/o Ulithi & Neighboring Islands, FM, Queen of Heaven Church. (CI)
Falcon, TX, Zapata Co., Santa Ana, c/o Zapata, TX, Our Lady of Lourdes Church. (CC)
Falcon Heights, TX, Holy Trinity, c/o Roma, TX, Our Lady of Refuge Church. (BWN)
Falls Village, CT, Litchfield Co., St. Patrick, c/o Canaan, CT, St. Joseph's Church. (HRT)
Falun, MN, Roseau Co., St. Philip, c/o Warroad, MN, St. Mary's Church. (CR)
Fannin, TX, Our Lady of Assumption, c/o Goliad, TX, Immaculate Conception Church. (VIC)
Faraulep, FM, c/o Ulithi & Neighboring Islands, FM, Queen of Heaven Church. (CI)
Farmersville, CA, Tulare Co., St. Anthony of Egypt, c/o Exeter, CA, Sacred Heart Church. (FRS)
Farmerville, LA, Our Lady of Perpetual Help, c/o West Monroe, LA, St. Paschal Church. (SHP)
Farnam, NE, Dawson Co., St. Joseph's, c/o Curtis, NE, St. James Church. (LIN)
Farrell, PA, Mercer Co., St. Paul, c/o [2] Farrell, PA, Our Lady of Fatima Church. (E)
Fashing, TX, St. Elizabeth, c/o Karnes City, TX, St. Cornelius Church. (SAT)
Fassarai, FM, c/o Ulithi & Neighboring Islands, FM, Queen of Heaven Church. (CI)
Fayette, AL, Fayette Co., Holy Family, c/o Winfield, AL, Holy Spirit Church. (BIR)
Faysville, TX, St. Theresa, c/o San Carlos, TX, St. Joseph the Worker Church. (BWN)
Faywood, NM, San Jose, c/o Hurley, NM, Infant Jesus Church. (LSC)
Federal Dam, MN, Sacred Heart, c/o Ball Club, MN, St. Joseph's Church. (DUL)
Federal Dam, MN, Sacred Heart, c/o Duluth, MN, Indian Missions Church. (DUL)
Fellsmere, FL, Indian River Co., c/o Fellsmere, FL, Our Lady of Guadalupe Mission Church. (PMB)
Fence Lake, NM, El Morro, c/o Tinaja, NM, San Lorenzo Church. (GLP)
Ferris, TX, Ellis Co., Corpus Christi, c/o Ennis, TX, St. John Nepomucene Church. (DAL)
Fierro, NM, St. Anthony, c/o Bayard, NM, Our Lady of Fatima Church. (LSC)
Fillmore, UT, Millard Co., Holy Family, c/o Milford, UT, St. Bridget Church. (SLC)
Fine, NY, St. Lawrence Co., St. Michael, c/o Star Lake, NY, St. Hubert Church. (OG)
Fingal, ND, Barnes Co., Holy Trinity, c/o Oriska, ND, St. Bernard's Church. (FAR)
Finlayson, MN, St. Joseph's, c/o Sandstone, MN, St. Luke's Church. (DUL)
Finley, ND, Steele Co., St. Olaf, c/o Hope, ND, St. Agatha's Church. (FAR)
Fish Creek, NY, SS. Peter & Paul, c/o West Leyden, NY, St. Mary's Nativity Church. (OG)
Fishville, LA, St. Edward, c/o Jena, LA, St. Mary Church. (ALX)
Fitchville, CT, New London Co., St. John, c/o [2] Norwich, CT, Sacred Heart Church. (NOR)
Fitzgerald, GA, Ben Hill Co., St. William, c/o Douglas, GA, St. Paul's Church. (SAV)
Fitzwilliam, NH, St. Joseph, c/o Troy, NH, Immaculate Conception Church. (MAN)
Flagler, CO, Kit Carson Co., St. Mary, c/o Limon, CO, Our Lady of Victory Church. (COS)
Flanagan, IL, Livingston Co., St. Joseph, c/o Minonk, IL, St. Patrick's Church. (PEO)
Flatwoods, LA, St. Cyril, c/o Boyce, LA, St. Margaret Church. (ALX)
Flaxville, MT, St. Louis, c/o Scobey, MT, St. Philip Bonitus Church. (GF)
Fleming, CO, Logan Co., St. Peter the Apostle, c/o Holyoke, CO, St. Patrick Church. (DEN)
Flint, MI, Genesee Co., c/o Troy, MI, St. Joseph Chaldean Parish Church. (EST)
Florence, MT, Ravalli Co., St. Joseph, c/o Stevensville, MT, St. Mary Church. (HEL)
Florian, MN, c/o Greenbush, MN, Blessed Sacrament Church. (CR)
Florida, NY, Orange Co., St. Edward, c/o Warwick, NY, St. Stephen Church. (NY)
Floyd, VA, Floyd Co., Church of All Saints, c/o Woodlawn, VA, St. Joseph's Church. (RIC)
Folkston, GA, Charlton Co., St. Francis of Assisi, c/o St. Marys, GA, Our Lady Star of the Sea Church. (SAV)
Folly Beach, SC, Charleston Co., Our Lady of Good Counsel, c/o [11] Charleston, SC, Church of the Nativity. (CHR)
Folsom, NM, Union Co., St. Joseph, c/o Clayton, NM, St. Francis Xavier Church. (SFE)
Ford City, MO, Gentry Co., St. Patrick's, c/o Stanberry, MO, St. Peter's Church. (KC)
Foreman, AR, Little River Co., Sacred Heart, c/o De Queen, AR, St. Barbara's Church. (LR)
Forest City, MO, Holt Co., St. Patrick, c/o Savannah, MO, St. Rose of Lima Church. (KC)
Forest City, PA, Susquehanna Co., St. Agnes, c/o Forest City, PA, Sacred Heart of Jesus Church. (SCR)
Forest City, PA, Susquehanna Co., St. Anthony, c/o Forest City, PA, Sacred Heart of Jesus Church. (SCR)
Forest City, PA, Susquehanna Co., St. Michael, c/o Forest City, PA, Sacred Heart of Jesus Church. (SCR)
Forest Park, GA, Fulton Co., Our Lady of Vietnam, c/o Hapeville, GA, St. John the Evangelist Church. (ATL)
Forestville, MI, Sanilac Co., St. John Chrysostom, c/o Port Sanilac, MI, St. Mary Church. (SAG)
Forestville, PA, Butler Co., St. Anthony, c/o Slippery Rock, PA, St. Peter Church. (PIT)
Forked Island, LA, Immaculate Conception, c/o Cow Island, LA, St. Anne Church. (LAF)
Forrest, IL, Livingston Co., St. James, c/o Fairbury, IL, St. John the Baptist Church. (PEO)
Fort Adams, MS, St. Patrick, c/o Woodville, MS, St. Joseph Church. (JKS)
Fort Belknap Agency, MT, Sacred Heart, c/o Hays, MT, St. Paul's Indian Mission Church. (GF)
Fort Bidwell, CA, c/o Alturas, CA, Sacred Heart Church. (SAC)
Fort Bridger, WY, Uinta Co., St. Helen, c/o Evanston, WY, St. Mary Magdalen Church. (CHY)
Fort Davis, TX, Jeff Davis Co., St. Joseph's, c/o Alpine, TX, Our Lady of Peace Church. (ELP)
Fort Duchesne, UT, Uintah Co., Blessed Kateri Tekakwitha, c/o Roosevelt, UT, St. Helen's Church. (SLC)
Fort Garland, CO, Costilla Co., Holy Family, c/o San Luis, CO, Sangre de Cristo Church. (PBL)
Fort Lauderdale, FL, Broward Co., Divine Mercy, c/o [10] Miami, FL, Notre Dame d'Haiti Church. (MIA)
Fort Meade, FL, Polk Co., St. Elizabeth Ann Seton, c/o Bartow, FL, St. Thomas Aquinas Church. (ORL)
Fort Mill, SC, York Co., St. Philip Neri, c/o Rock Hill, SC, St. Anne's Church. (CHR)
Fort Myers, FL, Lee Co., Our Lady of Perpetual Help, c/o [5] Fort Myers, FL, St. Francis Xavier Church.

(VEN)
Fort Payne, AL, DeKalb Co., Our Lady of the Valley, c/o Gadsden, AL, St. James Church. (BIR)
Fort Peck, MT, Our Lady of the Lake, c/o Glasgow, MT, St. Raphael's Church. (GF)
Fort Stanton, NM, Sacred Heart, c/o Ruidoso, NM, St. Eleanor Church. (LSC)
Fort Totten Reservation, ND, Benson Co., Seven Dolors Indian Mission, c/o Fort Totten Reservation, ND, (Sioux Indians) Church. (FAR)
Fort Valley, GA, Peach Co., St. Juliana, c/o Perry, GA, St. Patrick Church. (SAV)
Fort Washakie, WY, Fremont Co., Blessed Sacrament, c/o St. Stephens, WY, St. Stephen's Church. (CHY)
Fossil, OR, St. Catherine, c/o Condon, OR, St. John's Church. (BAK)
Foster City, MI, Dickinson Co., St. Joseph, c/o Channing, MI, St. Rose Church. (MAR)
Fountain, FL, Bay Co., Our Lady Queen of Peace, c/o Bayou George, FL, Our Lady of the Rosary Church. (PT)
Fowler, CO, Otero Co., Mary Queen of Heaven, c/o Rocky Ford, CO, St. Peter Church. (PBL)
Frances, CO, St. Francis, c/o Pagosa Springs, CO, Immaculate Heart of Mary Church. (PBL)
Frances, WA, Pacific Co., Holy Family, c/o Pe Ell, WA, St. Joseph's Church. (SEA)
Franconia, MN, Chisago Co., St. Francis Xavier, c/o Taylors Falls, MN, St. Joseph's Church. (STP)
Franklin, NY, Delaware Co., St. Paul, c/o Sidney, NY, Sacred Heart Church. (ALB)
Franklin, VT, Franklin Co., St. Mary, c/o Sheldon Springs, VT, St. Anthony Church. (BUR)
Frazer, MT, St. Joseph, c/o Wolf Point, MT, Immaculate Conception Church. (GF)
Frazier Park, CA, Our Lady of the Snows, c/o Lamont, CA, St. Augustine Church. (FRS)
Fredericksburg, TX, Our Lady of Guadalupe, c/o Fredericksburg, TX, St. Mary's Church. (SAT)
Freehold-Red Bank, NJ, Monmouth Co., Our Lady of Guadalupe, c/o [3] Long Branch, NJ, St. John the Baptist Church. (TR)
Freeland, PA, Luzerne Co., St. Anthony's, c/o [1] Freeland, PA, St. Ann's Church. (SCR)
Freeland, PA, Luzerne Co., St. Casimir's, c/o [1] Freeland, PA, St. Ann's Church. (SCR)
Freeland, PA, Luzerne Co., St. John Nepomucene, c/o [1] Freeland, PA, St. Ann's Church. (SCR)
Freeport, FL, Walton Co., Christ the King, c/o De Funiak Springs, FL, St. Margaret Church. (PT)
Freeport, ME, St. Jude's, c/o Yarmouth, ME, Sacred Heart Church. (PRT)
Freewood Acres, NJ, Monmouth Co., St. Mary of the Assumption, c/o Howell Township, NJ, St. Veronica Church. (TR)
Freiburg, MI, Sanilac Co., St. Ignatius, c/o Argyle, MI, St. Joseph Church. (SAG)
French Camp, CA, San Joaquin Co., Good Shepherd, c/o [4] Stockton, CA, St. George Church. (STO)
French Village, MO, St. Francois Co., St. Anne, c/o Bonne Terre, MO, St. Joseph's Church. (STL)
Frenchtown, IN, Crawford Co., St. Joseph, c/o Frenchtown, IN, St. Bernard Church. (IND)
Frenstat, TX, Burleson Co., Holy Rosary, c/o Somerville, TX, St. Ann's Church. (AUS)
Fresno, CA, St. Francis, c/o [1] Fresno, CA, St. John Cathedral Church. (FRS)
Fried, ND, Sacred Heart, c/o Jamestown, ND, The Basilica of St. James Church. (FAR)
Frilot Cove, LA, St. Ann, c/o Plaisance, LA, St. Joseph Church. (LAF)
Frisco, TX, Collin Co., St. Francis of Assisi, c/o McKinney, TX, St. Michael Church. (DAL)
Froid, MT, Immaculate Conception, c/o Culbertson, MT, St. Anthony's Church. (GF)
Fromberg, MT, St. Joseph, c/o Bridger, MT, Sacred Heart Church. (GF)
Fronton, TX, Lamb of God, c/o Roma, TX, Our Lady of Refuge Church. (BWN)
Fryeburg, ME, Oxford Co., St. Elizabeth Ann Seton, c/o Bridgton, ME, St. Joseph Church. (PRT)
Fulda, ND, McHenry Co., St. Anselm, c/o Balta, ND, Our Lady of Mount Carmel Church. (FAR)
Fullerton, CA, Orange Co., St. George, c/o [5] North Hollywood, CA, St. Paul Assyrian-Chaldean Church. (LA)
Fullerton, CA, Orange Co., St. George, c/o North Hollywood, CA, St. Paul Assyrian-Chaldean Catholic Parish Church. (EST)
Fullerton, ND, Dickey Co., St. Patrick, c/o Ellendale, ND, St. Helena's Church. (FAR)
Fulton, MS, Itawamba Co., Christ the King, c/o Amory, MS, St. Helen Church. (JKS)
Futiga, AS, c/o [3] Pago Pago, AS, Church of St. Paul. (SPP)

G

Gabbs, NV, St. Michael, c/o Hawthorne, NV, Our Lady of Perpetual Help Church. (RNO)
Gabriels, NY, Franklin Co., Assumption of the B.V.M., c/o Bloomingdale, NY, St. Paul Church. (OG)
Gackle, ND, Logan Co., St. Anne, c/o Windsor, ND, St. Mathias Church. (FAR)
Gainesville, MO, Ozark Co., St. William, c/o Mansfield, MO, Immaculate Heart of Mary Church. (SPC)
Galicia-Columbani, PR, Santo Tomas de Villanueva, c/o Aguada, PR, St. Francis of Assisi Church. (MGZ)
Galisteo, NM, Santa Fe Co., c/o Cerrillos, NM, St. Joseph Church. (SFE)
Gallatin, MO, Daviess Co., Mary Immaculate, c/o Hamilton, MO, Sacred Heart Church. (KC)
Gallegos, NM, Harding Co., c/o Roy, NM, Holy Family-St. Joseph Church. (SFE)
Gallina, NM, c/o Abiquiu, NM, St. Thomas Apostle Church. (SFE)
Gallinas, NM, San Miguel Co., Santo Nino, c/o Las Vegas, NM, Our Lady of Sorrows Church. (SFE)
Galveston, TX, Galveston Co., Queen of Peace Mission, c/o [4] Galveston, TX, St. Patrick Church. (GAL)
Galway, NY, St. Mary, c/o Broadalbin, NY, St. Joseph Church. (ALB)
Gamerco, NM, St. Joseph the Worker, c/o [2] Gallup, NM, St. Francis of Assisi Church. (GLP)
Garapan Village, District 11, MP, Maturana House of Prayer, c/o Garapan Village, District 11, MP, Kristo Rai Parish Church. (CHK)
Garapan Village, District 11, MP, Navy Hill, Commonwealth Health Center Chapel, c/o Garapan Village, District 11, MP, Kristo Rai Parish Church. (CHK)
Garcia, CO, Costilla Co., Sacred Heart of Jesus, c/o San Luis, CO, Sangre de Cristo Church. (PBL)
Gardiner, MT, St. William, c/o Livingston, MT, St. Mary's Church. (GF)
Gardner, CO, Huerfano Co., Sacred Heart, c/o Walsenburg, CO, St. Mary Church. (PBL)
Garrison, NY, Putnam Co., St. Joseph, c/o Cold Spring-on-Hudson, NY, Our Lady of Loretto Church. (NY)
Garzas, PR, San Francisco, c/o Adjuntas, PR, St. Joachim Church. (PCE)
Genesee, PA, Potter Co., Sacred Heart, c/o Shinglehouse, PA, St. Theresa Church. (E)
Geneseo, ND, Sargent Co., St. Martin, c/o Lidgerwood, ND, St. Boniface's Church. (FAR)
Geneva, AL, Geneva Co., St. Mary, c/o Enterprise, AL, St. John Church. (MOB)
Geneva, MN, Freeborn Co., St. Mary, c/o Blooming Prairie, MN, St. Columbanus Church. (WIN)
Gentilly, MN, Polk Co., St. Peter, c/o [1] Crookston, MN, Cathedral of the Immaculate Conception. (CR)
George West, TX, Live Oak Co., c/o George West, TX, St. George Church. (CC)
Georgetown, CA, El Dorado Co., St. James, c/o Placerville, CA, St. Patrick's Church. (SAC)
Georgetown, CO, Clear Creek Co., Our Lady of Lourdes, c/o Idaho Springs, CO, St. Paul's Church. (DEN)
Georgetown, MN, Clay Co., St. John, c/o Dilworth, MN, St. Elizabeth Church. (CR)
Georgia, VT, Franklin Co., Ascension, c/o Fairfax, VT, St. Luke Church. (BUR)
Gerald, MO, Franklin Co., St. Gerald, c/o Port Hudson, MO, Holy Family Church. (STL)
Geraldine, MT, St. Margaret, c/o Fort Benton, MT, Immaculate Conception Church. (GF)
Geranium, NE, St. Wenceslaus, c/o Farwell, NE, St. Anthony of Padua Church. (GI)
Germania, PA, Potter Co., St. Germain, c/o Galeton, PA, St. Bibiana Church. (E)
Germfask, MI, Schoolcraft Co., St. Therese, c/o Grand Marais, MI, Holy Rosary Church. (MAR)
Geyser, MT, St. Cyril, c/o Stanford, MT, St. Rose of Lima Church. (GF)
Gila, NM, St. Isidore, c/o Silver City, NM, St. Vincent de Paul Church. (LSC)
Gilbert, IL, Kane Co., St. Mary, c/o Dundee, IL, St. Catherine of Siena Church. (RCK)
Gilchrist, OR, Our Lady of the Snows, c/o La Pine, OR, Holy Redeemer Church. (BAK)
Gilcrest, CO, Weld Co., Sacred Heart, c/o Greeley, CO, Our Lady of Peace Church. (DEN)
Gildden, IA, Carroll Co., St. Elizabeth Seton, c/o Lidderdale, IA, Holy Family Church. (SC)
Gillett, AR, Arkansas Co., St. Henry's, c/o Stuttgart, AR, Holy Rosary Church. (LR)
Gilmer, TX, Upshur Co., St. Francis of Assisi, c/o Sulphur Springs, TX, St. James Church. (TYL)
Giltner, NE, Hamilton Co., St. Joseph's, c/o Aurora, NE, St. Mary's Church. (LIN)
Gladstone, ND, Dunn Co., St. Philip, c/o New Hradec, ND, SS. Peter and Paul Church. (BIS)
Gladstone, ND, Stark Co., St. Thomas the Apostle, c/o Lefor, ND, St. Elizabeth Church. (BIS)
Glasgo, CT, New London Co., St. Ann, c/o Voluntown, CT, St. Thomas Apostle Church. (NOR)
Glastonbury, CT, Hartford Co., St. John's, c/o [6] Hartford, CT, St. Michael Church. (STF)
Glen Haven, WI, St. Mary Help of Christians, c/o Cassville, WI, St. Charles Borromeo Church. (MAD)
Glen Lyon, PA, Luzerne Co., St. Denis, c/o Glen Lyon, PA, St. Adalbert's Church. (SCR)
Glen Lyon, PA, Luzerne Co., St. Michael, c/o Wilkes-Barre, PA, St. Mary's Church. (PSC)
Glen Lyon, PA, Luzerne Co., St. Michael's, c/o Glen Lyon, PA, St. Adalbert's Church. (SCR)
Glen Ullin, ND, Grant Co., St. Joseph, c/o Glen Ullin, ND, Sacred Heart of Jesus Church. (BIS)
Glencoe, LA, St. Joan of Arc, c/o Four Corners, LA, St. Peter the Apostle Church. (LAF)
Glendale, OR, Douglas Co., Holy Family, c/o Myrtle Creek, OR, All Souls Church. (P)
Glendale, RI, St. Louis Chapel, c/o Harrisville, RI, St. Patrick's Church. (PRO)
Glendo, WY, Platte Co., Our Lady of Lourdes, c/o Douglas, WY, St. James Church. (CHY)
Glenmont, OH, Holmes Co., SS. Peter and Paul, c/o Millersburg, OH, St. Peter Church. (COL)
Glenmore, NY, St. Anne, c/o Taberg, NY, St. Patrick Church. (SY)
Glennon, MO, Bollinger Co., St. Anthony, c/o Advance, MO, St. Joseph Church. (SPC)
Glennville, GA, Tattnall Co., St. Jude, c/o Claxton, GA, St. Christopher Church. (SAV)
Glentana, MT, Holy Family, c/o Scobey, MT, St. Philip Bonitus Church. (GF)
Glenwood, NM, Catron Co., Santo Nino, c/o Alpine, AZ, St. Helena Church. (GLP)
Glorieta, NM, Santa Fe Co., c/o Pecos, NM, St. Anthony Church. (SFE)
Gloster, MS, Amite Co., Holy Family, c/o Woodville, MS, St. Joseph Church. (JKS)
Gluckstadt, MS, St. Joseph, c/o Madison, MS, St. Francis of Assisi Church. (JKS)
Gnesen, MN, St. Joseph, c/o [9] Duluth, MN, St. John's Church. (DUL)
Gold Beach, OR, Curry Co., St. Charles Borromeo, c/o Brookings, OR, Star of the Sea Church. (P)
Goldcreek, MT, Powell Co., St. Mary, c/o Drummond, MT, St. Michael Church. (HEL)
Golden, NM, Santa Fe Co., c/o Cerrillos, NM, St. Joseph Church. (SFE)
Golden City, MO, Barton Co., St. Joseph, c/o Lamar, MO, St. Mary Church. (SPC)
Golden Meadow, LA, Our Lady of La Salette, c/o Golden Meadow, LA, Our Lady of Prompt Succor Church. (HT)
Goldens Bridge, NY, Westchester Co., St. Michael, c/o Croton Falls, NY, St. Joseph Church. (NY)
Golondrinas, NM, Mora Co., c/o Mora, NM, St. Gertrude Church. (SFE)
Goltry, OK, Alfalfa Co., St. Michael, c/o Enid, OK, St. Gregory the Great Church. (OKL)
Golva, ND, Golden Valley Co., St. Mary, c/o Beach, ND, St. John the Baptist Church. (BIS)
Gonzales, TX, Gonzales Co., Sacred Heart, c/o Gonzales, TX, St. James Church. (SAT)
Gonzales Ranch, NM, San Miguel Co., c/o Villanueva, NM, Our Lady of Guadalupe Church. (SFE)
Good Thunder, MN, Blue Earth Co., St. Joseph, c/o Mapleton, MN, St. Teresa's Church. (WIN)
Goodhue, MN, Goodhue Co., Holy Trinity, c/o Belle Creek, MN, St. Columbkill Church. (STP)
Goodridge, MN, Pennington Co., St. Ann, c/o Thief River Falls, MN, St. Bernards Church. (CR)
Gorum, LA, St. Margaret Mary, c/o Boyce, LA, St. Margaret Church. (ALX)
Goshen, NJ, St. Elizabeth, c/o Woodbine, NJ, St. Casimir's Church. (CAM)
Gothenburg, NE, Dawson Co., Our Lady of Good Counsel, c/o Cozad, NE, Christ the King Church. (GI)
Goudeau, LA, St. Charles, c/o Evergreen, LA, Little Flower Church. (ALX)
Grady, AR, Lincoln Co., Blessed Sacrament, c/o Star City, AR, St. Justin's Church. (LR)
Grafton, NY, Rensselaer Co., St. John Francis Regis, c/o Pittstown, NY, St. George Church. (ALB)
Granby, CO, Grand Co., Our Lady of the Snow, c/o Grand Lake, CO, St. Anne Church. (DEN)
Grand Chenier, LA, Cameron Parish, Immaculate Conception, c/o Grand Chenier, LA, St. Eugene Church. (LKC)
Grand Gorge, NY, Delaware Co., St. Philip Neri, c/o Stamford, NY, Sacred Heart Church. (ALB)
Grand Isle, VT, Grand Isle Co., St. Joseph, c/o South Hero, VT, St. Rose of Lima Church. (BUR)
Grand Meadow, MN, Mower Co., St. Finbarr, c/o Le Roy, MN, St. Patrick's Church. (WIN)
Grand Portage, MN, Holy Rosary, c/o Grand Marais, MN, St. John's Church. (DUL)
Grand Portage, MN, Holy Rosary, c/o Duluth, MN, Indian Missions Church. (DUL)
Grand Ridge, IL, LaSalle Co., St. Mary, c/o Ransom, IL, St. Patrick's Church. (PEO)
Grandfalls, TX, Ward Co., St. Gertrude, c/o Monahans, TX, St. John the Apostle and Evangelist Church. (ELP)
Grandfield, OK, Tillman Co., Our Lady of Perpetual Help, c/o Walters, OK, St. Patrick Church. (OKL)
Grandin, MO, Carter Co., St. Anne, c/o Doniphan, MO, St. Benedict Church. (SPC)
Granite Falls, WA, Snohomish Co., Holy Cross, c/o

Snohomish, WA, St. Michael's Church. (SEA)
Granjeno, TX, Our Lady of Fatima, c/o [2] Mission, TX, Our Lady of the Holy Rosary Church. (BWN)
Grant, MI, Our Lady of Guadalupe Church, c/o Newaygo, MI, St. Bartholomew's Church. (GR)
Grantsville, WV, Calhoun Co., Jesus Christ, Prince of Peace, c/o Spencer, WV, Holy Redeemer Church. (WH)
Granville, ND, McHenry Co., Our Lady of Perpetual Help, c/o Towner, ND, St. Cecilia's Church. (FAR)
Grass Flats, PA, Clearfield Co., SS. Peter & Paul, c/o Frenchville, PA, St. Mary of the Assumption Church. (E)
Grass Valley, OR, St. John the Baptist, c/o Wasco, OR, St. Mary's Church. (BAK)
Grassy Butte, ND, McKenzie Co., St. Peter Canisius, c/o Watford City, ND, Epiphany Church. (BIS)
Greasewood, AZ, Our Lady of the Rosary, c/o Ganado, AZ, All Saints Church. (GLP)
Great Falls, SC, Chester Co., St. Michael, c/o Lancaster, SC, St. Catherine's Church. (CHR)
Greeley, PA, Pike Co., Sacred Heart, c/o Shohola, PA, St. Ann's Church. (SCR)
Green Lake, ME, Our Lady of the Lake, c/o Ellsworth, ME, St. Joseph's Church. (PRT)
Green River, UT, Emery Co., St. Michael, c/o East Carbon, UT, Good Shepherd Church. (SLC)
Greene, ME, St. Francis, c/o Sabattus, ME, Our Lady of the Rosary Church. (PRT)
Greenfield, MO, Dade Co., St. Patrick, c/o Mount Vernon, MO, St. Susanne Church. (SPC)
Greensboro, AL, Hale Co., Our Lady of Lourdes, c/o Demopolis, AL, St. Leo Church. (BIR)
Greensboro, FL, Gadsden Co., Casa Guadalupana, Catholic Center for Evangelization, c/o Quincy, FL, St. Thomas the Apostle Church. (PT)
Greensboro, PA, Greene Co., Holy Family, c/o Bobtown, PA, St. Ignatius of Antioch Church. (PIT)
Greenup, KY, St. Lawrence, c/o Ashland, KY, Holy Family Church. (LEX)
Greenville, CA, Plumas Co., St. Anthony, c/o Quincy, CA, St. John Church. (SAC)
Greenwood, NE, Cass Co., St. Joseph's, c/o Ashland, NE, St. Mary's Church. (LIN)
Greig, NY, Lewis Co., St. Thomas, c/o Glenfield, NY, St. Mary Church. (OG)
Gripinas, PR, Jayuya Co., Buen Pastor, c/o Jayuya, PR, Our Lady of Monserrate Church. (PCE)
Grundy, SD, St. Joseph, c/o Richlands, VA, St. Mary Church. (RIC)
Grygla, MN, Marshall Co., St. Clement, c/o Thief River Falls, MN, St. Bernards Church. (CR)
Guachupanque, NM, Rio Arriba Co., c/o Espanola, NM, Sacred Heart Church. (SFE)
Guadalupe, NM, Sacred Heart of Mary, c/o Cuba, NM, Immaculate Conception Church. (GLP)
Guadalupita, NM, Mora Co., c/o Mora, NM, St. Gertrude Church. (SFE)
Gualala, CA, Mary, Star of the Sea, c/o Point Arena, CA, St. Aloysius Church. (SR)
Guaniquilla, PR, Ntra. Sra. del Carmen, c/o Aguada, PR, St. Francis of Assisi Church. (MGZ)
Guayabal, PR, Bo. Guayabal, Our Lady of the Rosary, c/o Juana Diaz, PR, St. Raymond Nonato Church. (PCE)
Guayabo, PR, El Buen Pastor, c/o Aguada, PR, St. Francis of Assisi Church. (MGZ)
Guayama, PR, Bo. Carite, San Martin, c/o Guayama, PR, St. Anthony of Padua Church. (PCE)
Guaynabo, PR, Cristo del Perdon, c/o [4] Guaynabo, PR, San Juan M. Vianney Church. (SJN)
Guaynabo, PR, Dulce Nombre de Maria, c/o [4] Guaynabo, PR, San Juan M. Vianney Church. (SJN)
Guaynabo, PR, El Buen Pastor, c/o [7] Guaynabo, PR, Divino Nino Jesus Church. (SJN)
Guaynabo, PR, Jesus Nazareno, c/o [7] Guaynabo, PR, Divino Nino Jesus Church. (SJN)
Guaynabo, PR, La Milagrosa, c/o [4] Guaynabo, PR, San Juan M. Vianney Church. (SJN)
Guaynabo, PR, Ntra. Sra. del Carmen, c/o [3] Guaynabo, PR, Maria Madre de Mi Senor Church. (SJN)
Guaynabo, PR, Ntra. Sra. del Carmen, c/o [4] Guaynabo, PR, San Juan M. Vianney Church. (SJN)
Guaynabo, PR, San Rafael Arcangel, c/o [7] Guaynabo, PR, Divino Nino Jesus Church. (SJN)
Guaynabo, PR, Virgen de la Paz, c/o [9] Guaynabo, PR, Sagrados Corazones Church. (SJN)
Guckeen, MN, Faribault Co., Our Lady of Mercy, c/o Blue Earth, MN, SS. Peter and Paul's Church. (WIN)
Guilarte, PR, San Antonio, c/o Adjuntas, PR, St. Joachim Church. (PCE)
Gulf Breeze, FL, Santa Rosa Co., Our Lady of the Assumption, c/o Gulf Breeze, FL, St. Ann Church. (PT)
Gulliver, MI, Schoolcraft Co., Divine Infant of Prague, c/o Engadine, MI, Our Lady of Lourdes Church. (MAR)
Gulnare, CO, Las Animas Co., San Jose, c/o Aguilar, CO, St. Anthony Church. (PBL)
Gussetville, TX, St. Joseph, c/o George West, TX, St. George Church. (CC)
Gwinner, ND, Sargent Co., St. Vincent, c/o Lisbon, ND, St. Aloysius Church. (FAR)

H

Hachita, NM, St. Catherine, c/o Lordsburg, NM, St. Joseph Church. (LSC)
Hackensack, MN, Sacred Heart, c/o Walker, MN, St. Agnes Church. (DUL)
Hagerman, NM, St. Catherine, c/o Dexter, NM, Immaculate Conception Church. (LSC)
Hagerstown, MD, St. Ann's, c/o Baltimore, MD, Patronage of the Mother of God Church. (PSC)
Hague, VA, Westmoreland Co., St. Paul, c/o Kilmarnock, VA, St. Francis de Sales Church. (ARL)
Haines Falls, NY, Greene Co., Wayside Shrine, c/o Haines Falls, NY, Immaculate Conception Church. (ALB)
Halaula, HI, Hawaii Co., Our Lady of Grace, c/o Hawi, HI, Sacred Heart Church. (HON)
Haleyville, AL, Winston Co., Our Lady of Guadalupe, c/o Jasper, AL, St. Cecilia Church. (BIR)
Halfway, OR, St. Therese, c/o [1] Baker, OR, Cathedral of St. Francis De Sales. (BAK)
Hall Islands, FM, c/o Dublon, FM, St. Anthony's Church. (CI)
Halstad, MN, Norman Co., c/o [1] Crookston, MN, Cathedral of the Immaculate Conception. (CR)
Halstad, MN, Norman Co., Holy Family, c/o Ada, MN, St. Joseph's Church. (CR)
Hamburg, AR, Ashley Co., c/o Crossett, AR, Holy Cross Church. (LR)
Hamilton, IL, Hancock Co., St. Mary, c/o Warsaw, IL, Sacred Heart Church. (PEO)
Hamilton, KS, Greenwood Co., St. John, c/o Eureka, KS, Sacred Heart Church. (WCH)
Hamilton City, CA, Glenn Co., St. Mary, c/o Orland, CA, St. Dominic Church. (SAC)
Hamlin, TX, Jones Co., Holy Trinity, c/o Anson, TX, St. Michael's Church. (LUB)
Hammond, OR, Clatsop Co., St. Francis de Sales, c/o Astoria, OR, St. Mary, Star of the Sea Church. (P)
Hampton, CT, Windham Co., Our Lady of Lourdes, c/o Brooklyn, CT, Our Lady of La Salette Church. (NOR)
Hampton, IL, Rock Island Co., St. Mary, c/o Rapids City, IL, St. John the Baptist Church. (PEO)
Hampton, SC, Hampton Co., St. Mary, c/o Ridgeland, SC, St. Anthony's Church. (CHR)
Hanalei, HI, Kauai Co., St. William, c/o Kapaa, HI, St. Catherine Church. (HON)
Hanceville, AL, Cullman Co., St. Boniface, c/o Cullman, AL, Sacred Heart Church. (BIR)
Hanna, WY, Carbon Co., St. Joseph, c/o Saratoga, WY, St. Ann's Church. (CHY)
Hanover, NM, Holy Family, c/o Bayard, NM, Our Lady of Fatima Church. (LSC)
Happy Camp, CA, Siskiyou Co., All Saints, c/o Fort Jones, CA, Sacred Heart Church. (SAC)
Hardeeville, SC, Jasper Co., St. Anthony's, c/o Bluffton, SC, St. Andrew's Church. (CHR)
Harding Lake, AK, North Star Borough, St. Mary's of the Lake, c/o [3] Fairbanks, AK, St. Mark University Parish Church. (FBK)
Hargill, TX, St. Frances Xavier Cabrini, c/o Raymondville, TX, Our Lady of Guadalupe Church. (BWN)
Harlem, MT, St. Thomas the Apostle, c/o Chinook, MT, St. Gabriel's Church. (GF)
Harlingen, TX, Le Moyne Chapel, c/o [4] Harlingen, TX, St. Anthony Church. (BWN)
Harmon, NY, Westchester Co., Church of the Good Shepherd, c/o Croton-on-Hudson, NY, Holy Name of Mary Church. (NY)
Harmony, WA, Lewis Co., St. Yves, c/o Morton, WA, Sacred Heart Church. (SEA)
Harquahala Valley, AZ, San Isidoro Labrador, c/o Buckeye, AZ, Saint Henry Church. (PHX)
Harrington, DE, Kent Co., St. Bernadette, c/o Milford, DE, St. John the Apostle Church. (WIL)
Harrison, NE, Sioux Co., Church of the Nativity of the Blessed Virgin Mary, c/o Crawford, NE, St. John the Baptist Church. (GI)
Hart, TX, St. John Nepomucene, c/o Dimmitt, TX, Immaculate Conception Church. (AMA)
Hartley, IA, O'Brien Co., St. Joseph's, c/o Sanborn, IA, St. Cecilia's Church. (SC)
Hartman, AR, Johnson Co., Sacred Heart, c/o Clarksville, AR, Holy Redeemer Church. (LR)
Hartselle, AL, Morgan Co., Holy Family, c/o Decatur, AL, St. Ann's Church. (BIR)
Harvard, MI, Kent Co., St. Margaret, c/o Greenville, MI, St. Charles Church. (GR)
Harwood, PA, Luzerne Co., St. Michael, c/o West Hazleton, PA, St. Francis of Assisi Church. (SCR)
Haskell, TX, Haskell Co., St. George, c/o Stamford, TX, St. Ann Church. (LUB)
Hato Rey, PR, Sma. Trinidad, c/o [7] San Juan, PR, Ntr. Sra. de la Caridad del Cobre Church. (SJN)
Hawk Run, PA, Clearfield Co., SS. Peter & Paul, c/o Morrisdale, PA, St. Agnes Church. (E)
Hawkinsville, CA, Siskiyou Co., Immaculate Conception, c/o Yreka, CA, St. Joseph Church. (SAC)
Hawley, MN, Clay Co., St. Andrew, c/o Lake Park, MN, St. Francis Xavier's Church. (CR)
Haxtun, CO, Phillips Co., Christ the King, c/o Holyoke, CO, St. Patrick Church. (DEN)
Hay Springs, NE, Sacred Heart, c/o Hemingford, NE, St. Bridget Church. (GI)
Hay Springs, NE, St. Columbkille, c/o Gordon, NE, St. Leo's Church. (GI)
Hayales, PR, Coamo Co., Our Lady of Mt. Carmel, c/o Coamo, PR, St. Blase Church. (PCE)
Hayden, NM, Quay Co., Holy Trinity, c/o Clayton, NM, St. Francis Xavier Church. (SFE)
Hayes, LA, Calcasieu Parish, St. Daniel Chapel, c/o Bell City, LA, St. John Vianney Church. (LKC)
Hayesville, NC, Clay Co., Immaculate Heart of Mary, c/o Murphy, NC, St. William Church. (CHL)
Hayfork, CA, Trinity Co., Holy Trinity, c/o Weaverville, CA, St. Patrick Church. (SAC)
Haymarsh, ND, Morton Co., St. Clement, c/o Hebron, ND, St. Ann Church. (BIS)
Haynesville, LA, Claiborne Parish, St. Michael, c/o Minden, LA, St. Paul Church. (SHP)
Hazard, NE, Sherman Co., St. Gabriel, c/o Pleasanton, NE, St. Mary's Church. (GI)
Hazlehurst, MS, St. Martin, c/o Crystal Springs, MS, St. John Church. (JKS)
Hazleton, PA, Luzerne Co., Our Lady of Mount Carmel, c/o [4] Hazleton, PA, Holy Trinity Church. (SCR)
Hazleton, PA, Luzerne Co., SS. Peter and Paul, c/o West Hazleton, PA, Transfiguration Church. (SCR)
Hazleton, PA, Luzerne Co., St. Ladislaus, c/o [6] Hazleton, PA, St. Joseph's Church. (SCR)
He Dog, SD, St. Patrick Hall, c/o Parmelee, SD, St. Agnes Church. (RC)
Healdton, OK, Carter Co., St. Cecilia, c/o Ardmore, OK, St. Mary Church. (OKL)
Heart Butte, MT, Mount Glacier Co., Holy Family Mission, c/o Heart Butte, MT, St. Anne Church. (HEL)
Heartwell, NE, Kearney Co., Holy Family, c/o Minden, NE, St. John's Church. (LIN)
Hebbronville, TX, Jim Hogg Co., Immaculate Conception, c/o Hebbronville, TX, Our Lady of Guadalupe Church. (CC)
Heber, CA, Sacred Heart, c/o Imperial, CA, St. Anthony of Padua Church. (SD)
Heber City, UT, Wasatch Co., St. Lawrence, c/o Park City, UT, St. Mary of the Assumption Church. (SLC)
Heber Springs, AR, Cleburne Co., St. Albert, c/o Searcy, AR, St. James Church. (LR)
Hedgesville, WV, Berkeley Co., St. Bernadette, c/o Martinsburg, WV, St. Joseph's Church. (WH)
Heidelberg, KY, Lee Co., St. Therese, c/o Beattyville, KY, Queen of All Saints Church. (LEX)
Helena, TX, St. Helena, c/o Panna Maria, TX, Immaculate Conception of the Blessed Virgin Mary Church. (SAT)
Hemphill, TX, Sabine Co., St. Pius I, c/o Center, TX, St. Therese Church. (TYL)
Henderson, NY, Jefferson Co., Queen of Heaven, c/o Sackets Harbor, NY, St. Andrew Church. (OG)
Henryville, IN, Clark Co., St. Francis Xavier, c/o Charlestown, IN, St. Michael Church. (IND)
Hermeleigh, TX, Scurry Co., St. John, c/o Snyder, TX, St. Elizabeth's Church. (LUB)
Hernandez, NM, Rio Arriba Co., c/o Espanola, NM, Sacred Heart Church. (SFE)
Hershey, NE, Our Lady of Guadalupe, c/o Sutherland, NE, Sacred Heart Church. (GI)
Hesperia, MI, Christ the King, c/o Brunswick, MI, St. Michael's Church. (GR)
Hessel, MI, Mackinac Co., Our Lady of the Snows, c/o Goetzville, MI, St. Stanislaus Kostka Church. (MAR)
Hickory Hill, LA, St. Richard, c/o Marksville, LA, Holy Ghost Church. (ALX)
High Falls, NY, Ulster Co., Our Lady Help of Christians, c/o Rosendale, NY, St. Peter Church. (NY)
Highland, MO, Perry Co., St. Joseph, c/o Perryville, MO, St. Vincent De Paul Church. (STL)
Highlands, NC, Macon Co., Our Lady of the Mountains, c/o Franklin, NC, St. Francis of Assisi Church. (CHL)
Hightstown-Princeton, NJ, Mercer Co., Our Lady of Fatima, c/o [3] Long Branch, NJ, St. John the Baptist Church. (TR)
Highwood, MT, St. Jane Frances, c/o Belt, MT, St. Mark the Evangelist Church. (GF)
Hill Top, PA, Wayne Co., St. Cecilia, c/o Pleasant Mount, PA, St. James Church. (SCR)
Hillsboro, NM, Our Lady of Guadalupe, c/o Garfield, NM, San Isidro Church. (LSC)
Hingham, MT, Our Lady of Ransom, c/o Chester, MT, St. Mary's Church. (GF)
Hinsdale, MT, St. Albert, c/o Glasgow, MT, St. Raphael's Church. (GF)
Hinton, OK, Caddo Co., Sacred Heart, c/o Weatherford, OK, St. Eugene's Church. (OKL)
Hitchcock, OK, Blaine Co., Sacred Heart, c/o Watonga,

OK, St. Rose of Lima Church. (OKL)
Hobart, AK, c/o Petersburg, AK, St. Catherine of Siena Church. (JUN)
Hobart, OK, Kiowa Co., Sts. Peter & Paul, c/o Mangum, OK, Sacred Heart Church. (OKL)
Hobson, MT, Sacred Heart, c/o Lewistown, MT, St. Leo's Church. (GF)
Hochheim, TX, St. Ann, c/o Yoakum, TX, St. Joseph Church. (VIC)
Hoconuco, PR, Chapel of St. Joseph, c/o San German, PR, San German de Auxerre Church. (MGZ)
Hode, KY, Martin Co., St. John Neumann, c/o Louisa, KY, St. Jude Church. (LEX)
Hoehne, CO, Las Animas Co., St. John Baptist, c/o Trinidad, CO, Most Holy Trinity, Trinidad Area Catholic Community (Trinidad Cluster) Church. (PBL)
Hogares Seguros, PR, San Antonio Co., c/o Jayuya, PR, Our Lady of Monserrate Church. (PCE)
Hogeland, MT, St. Thomas Aquinas, c/o Chinook, MT, St. Gabriel's Church. (GF)
Hollandale, MS, Immaculate Conception, c/o Leland, MS, St. James Church. (JKS)
Hollis, OK, Harmon Co., Our Lady of Guadalupe, c/o Altus, OK, Prince of Peace Church. (OKL)
Holly Beach, LA, Holy Trinity, c/o Hackberry, LA, St. Peter Apostle Church. (LKC)
Holly Hill, SC, Orangeburg Co., St. Ann, c/o Summerton, SC, St. Mary's Church. (CHR)
Holman, NM, Mora Co., c/o Mora, NM, St. Gertrude Church. (SFE)
Holman, NM, Mora Co., c/o Mora, NM, St. Gertrude Church. (SFE)
Holman, TX, St. Wenceslaus, c/o Ammannsville, TX, St. John The Baptist Church. (VIC)
Holualoa, HI, Hawaii Co., Immaculate Conception, c/o Holualoa, HI, St. Michael The Archangel Church. (HON)
Holyoke, MA, Hampden Co., Holyoke Soldier's Home Chapel, c/o [1] Holyoke, MA, Blessed Sacrament Church. (SPR)
Homer, IL, Champaign Co., St. Charles Borromeo, c/o Tolono, IL, St. Patrick's Church. (PEO)
Homer, LA, Claiborne Parish, St. Margaret, c/o Minden, LA, St. Paul Church. (SHP)
Homer, NE, Dakota Co., St. Cornelius, c/o South Sioux City, NE, St. Michael Church. (OM)
Hominy, OK, Osage Co., St. Joseph, c/o Skiatook, OK, Sacred Heart Church. (TLS)
Honokahua (Kapalua), HI, Maui Co., Sacred Hearts of Jesus and Mary, c/o Lahaina, HI, Maria Lanakila Church. (HON)
Honomu, HI, Good Shepherd, c/o Papaikou, HI, Immaculate Heart of Mary Church. (HON)
Hooker, OK, Texas Co., Sacred Heart, c/o Guymon, OK, St. Peter's Church. (OKL)
Hopedale, IL, Tazewell Co., St. Joseph's, c/o Delavan, IL, St. Mary's Church. (PEO)
Hopeton, CA, St. John the Baptist, c/o Merced, CA, Our Lady of Mercy/St. Patricks Church. (FRS)
Hopland, CA, St. Francis, c/o Ukiah, CA, St. Mary of the Angels Church. (SR)
Hornitos, CA, Mariposa Co., St. Catherine of Sienna, c/o Mariposa, CA, St. Joseph Church. (FRS)
Horse Cave, KY, Hart Co., Our Lady of the Caves Church, c/o Glasgow, KY, St. Helen Church. (L)
Horse Springs, NM, St. Anne, c/o Aragon, NM, Santo Nino Church. (GLP)
Horseshoe Lake, AR, Crittenden Co., St. Mary's of the Lake, c/o West Memphis, AR, St. Michael's Church. (LR)
Hostyn Hill, TX, Fayette Co., St. Mary's, c/o Fayetteville, TX, St. John's Church. (AUS)
Hot Springs, MT, Sacred Heart, c/o Plains, MT, St. James Church. (HEL)
Hot Springs, NC, Madison Co., Chapel of the Redeemer, c/o Mars Hill, NC, St. Andrew the Apostle Church. (CHL)
Hotchkiss, CO, Delta Co., St. Margaret Mary, c/o Paonia, CO, Sacred Heart Church. (PBL)
Houston, MN, Houston Co., St. Mary, c/o Rushford, MN, St. Joseph's Church. (WIN)
Houston, MS, Chickasaw Co., Immaculate Heart of Mary, c/o Aberdeen, MS, St. Francis of Assisi Church. (JKS)
Hoyo Planas, PR, Jayuya Co., Esp. Santo, c/o Jayuya, PR, Our Lady of Monserrate Church. (PCE)
Hubbard, NE, Dakota Co., St. Mary, c/o Jackson, NE, St. Patrick Church. (OM)
Hubbard, OR, Marion Co., St. Agnes, c/o Woodburn, OR, St. Luke Church. (P)
Hudson, WY, Ascension, c/o Lander, WY, Holy Rosary Church. (CHY)
Hugo, CO, Lincoln Co., St. Anthony of Padua, c/o Limon, CO, Our Lady of Victory Church. (COS)
Hulberton, NY, Orleans Co., St. Rocco, c/o Holley, NY, St. Mary Church. (BUF)
Hulett, WY, Crook Co., St. Matthew's, c/o Newcastle, WY, Corpus Christi Church. (CHY)
Humansville, MO, Polk Co., St. Catherine, c/o Bolivar, MO, Sacred Heart Church. (SPC)
Humarock, MA, St. Theresa's, c/o Marshfield, MA, St. Christine Church. (BO)
Humboldt, AZ, St. Lawrence, c/o Prescott Valley, AZ, St. Germaine Church. (PHX)
Hume, IL, Edgar Co., St. Michael's, c/o Villa Grove, IL, Sacred Heart Church. (SFD)
Hunnewell, MO, Shelby Co., St. John the Evangelist, c/o Indian Creek, MO, St. Stephen Church. (JC)
Hunter, ND, Cass Co., St. Agnes, c/o Mayville, ND, Our Lady of Peace Church. (FAR)
Hunter, NY, Greene Co., St. Mary of the Mountains, c/o Haines Falls, NY, Immaculate Conception Church. (ALB)
Hunter, TX, St. John, c/o New Braunfels, TX, Our Lady of Perpetual Help Church. (SAT)
Huntingdon, TN, Carroll Co., Holy Family Church, c/o Camden, TN, St. Mary Church. (MEM)
Huntington, OR, St. Joachim, c/o Ontario, OR, Blessed Sacrament Church. (BAK)
Huntington, UT, Emery Co., San Rafael, c/o Price, UT, Notre Dame de Lourdes Church. (SLC)
Huntsville, UT, Weber Co., St. Florence, c/o [3] Ogden, UT, St. Joseph's Church. (SLC)
Hurdsfield, ND, Wells Co., St. Patrick, c/o Sykeston, ND, St. Elizabeth's Church. (FAR)
Hurley, MS, Jackson Co., St. Ann, c/o Moss Point, MS, St. Joseph Church. (BLX)
Hurricane Branch, MO, Chariton Co., St. Joseph, c/o Marceline, MO, St. Bonaventure Church. (JC)
Hyannis, NE, Grant Co., All Saint's, c/o Mullen, NE, St. Mary's Church. (GI)
Hysham, MT, St. Joseph, c/o Forsyth, MT, Immaculate Conception Church. (GF)

I

Imperial, TX, Pecos Co., Our Lady of Lourdes, c/o Fort Stockton, TX, St. Agnes Church. (SAN)
Independence, CA, Inyo Co., St. Vivian, c/o Lone Pine, CA, Santa Rosa Church. (FRS)
Independencia, CA, Orange Co., Sacred Heart, c/o [3] Anaheim, CA, St. Justin Martyr Church. (ORG)
Indian, ND, Rolette Co., Immaculate Heart of Mary, c/o Dunseith, ND, St. Louis Church. (FAR)
Indian Township, ME, St. Theresa's Chapel, c/o Indian Township, ME, St. Ann Church. (PRT)
Indian Village, LA, Sacred Heart Parish, Sacred Heart, c/o Kinder, LA, St. Philip Neri Church. (LKC)
Indiera Fria, PR, Santa Rosa, c/o Maricao, PR, St. John the Baptist Church. (MGZ)
Industry, TX, Austin Co., Immaculate Conception, c/o Bellville, TX, SS. Peter & Paul Church. (GAL)
Inverness, MT, Sacred Heart, c/o Chester, MT, St. Mary's Church. (GF)
Iona, MN, Murray Co., St. Columba, c/o Fulda, MN, St. Gabriel's Church. (WIN)
Ione, CA, Amador Co., Mule Creek State Prison, c/o Ione, CA, Sacred Heart Church. (SAC)
Ione, CA, Preston School of Industry, California Youth Authority, c/o Ione, CA, Sacred Heart Church. (SAC)
Iowa, LA, Calcasieu Parish, St. Peter Claver, c/o Welsh, LA, St. Joseph Church. (LKC)
Iraan, TX, Pecos Co., St. Francis of Assisi, c/o McCamey, TX, Sacred Heart Church. (SAN)
Irasburg, VT, Orleans Co., St. John Vianney, c/o Orleans, VT, St. Theresa of Child Jesus Church. (BUR)
Irish Grove Rd., IL, Stephenson Co., St. Patrick, c/o Durand, IL, St. Mary Church. (RCK)
Irish Ridge, NY, St. Mary, c/o Durhamville, NY, St. Francis Church. (SY)
Irishtown, MI, Gratiot Co., St. Patrick, c/o St. Louis, MI, St. Joseph Church. (SAG)
Isabel, SD, Dewey Co., St. Mary, c/o Timber Lake, SD, Holy Cross Church. (RC)
Island Heights, NJ, Ocean Co., St. Gertrude, c/o [1] Toms River, NJ, St. Joseph Church. (TR)
Isle LaMotte, VT, Grand Isle Co., St. Joseph, c/o Alburg, VT, St. Amadeus Church. (BUR)
Isle of Hope, GA, Our Lady of Good Hope, c/o [8] Savannah, GA, St. James Church. (SAV)
Isleboro, ME, St. Mary of the Isles, c/o Belfast, ME, St. Francis of Assisi Church. (PRT)
Islesford, ME, Our Lady Star of the Sea, c/o Northeast Harbor, ME, St. Ignatius Church. (PRT)
Italy, TX, Ellis Co., Epiphany, c/o Waxahachie, TX, St. Joseph Church. (DAL)
Iuka, MS, Tishomingo Co., St. Mary, c/o Booneville, MS, St. Francis of Assisi Church. (JKS)

J

Jacaquas, PR, Bo. Jacaguas, N.S. de Fatima, c/o Juana Diaz, PR, St. Raymond Nonato Church. (PCE)
Jackpot, NV, Elko Co., Blessed Miguel Pro, c/o Elko, NV, St. Joseph's Church. (RNO)
Jackson, AL, Clarke Co., Visitation, c/o Grove Hill, AL, Sacred Heart Church. (MOB)
Jackson, GA, Butts Co., St. Mary's, c/o McDonough, GA, St. James The Apostle Church. (ATL)
Jackson, NJ, Ocean Co., Church of St. Monica, c/o New Egypt, NJ, Assumption Church. (TR)
Jacksonville, OR, Jackson Co., St. Joseph, c/o Medford, OR, Sacred Heart of Jesus Church. (P)
Jaguey Chiquito, PR, San Augustin, c/o Aguada, PR, St. Francis of Assisi Church. (MGZ)
Jamaica Beach, TX, Galveston Co., Mary, Star of the Sea, c/o [5] Galveston, TX, St. Peter the Apostle Church. (GAL)
James City, PA, Elk Co., SS. John and Stephen, c/o Kane, PA, St. Callistus Church. (E)
Jamestown, PA, Mercer Co., St. Margaret, c/o Greenville, PA, St. Michael Church. (E)
Jamestown, TN, Fentress Co., Fentress County Catholic Community, c/o Fairfield Glade, TN, St. Francis of Assisi Church. (KNX)
Jarales, NM, Valencia Co., c/o Belen, NM, Our Lady of Belen Church. (SFE)
Jardines de Rio Grande, PR, Ntra. Sra. de Guadalupe, c/o Rio Grande, PR, Nuestra Senora del Carmen Church. (SJN)
Jasper, GA, Pickens Co., Our Lady of the Mountains, c/o Canton, GA, Our Lady of LaSalette Church. (ATL)
Jasper, MN, Pipestone Co., St. Joseph, c/o Pipestone, MN, St. Leo's Church. (WIN)
Jauca, PR, San Ignacio de Loyola, c/o Santa Isabel, PR, St. James Church. (PCE)
Jayton, TX, Kent Co., Epiphany, c/o Spur, TX, St. Mary Church. (LUB)
Jeffers, MN, Cottonwood Co., St. Augustine, c/o Windom, MN, St. Francis Xavier's Church. (WIN)
Jefferson, NH, Coos, St. Agnes, c/o Lancaster, NH, All Saints Church. (MAN)
Jefferson, OR, Marion Co., St. Thomas, c/o Scio, OR, St. Bernard Church. (P)
Jeffrey City, WY, St. Brendan, c/o Lander, WY, Holy Rosary Church. (CHY)
Jenny Lind, AR, Sebastian Co., Sts. Sabina and Mary's Church, c/o Van Buren, AR, St. Michael's Church. (LR)
Jessie, ND, Griggs Co., St. Lawrence, c/o Cooperstown, ND, St. George's Church. (FAR)
Jessup, PA, Lackawanna Co., St. Michael, c/o Jessup, PA, St. James Church. (SCR)
Jessup, PA, Lackawanna Co., St. Stanislaus, c/o Jessup, PA, St. James Church. (SCR)
Jobstown, NJ, Burlington Co., St. Andrew, c/o Mount Holly, NJ, Sacred Heart Church. (TR)
Jocko, MT, Lake Co., St. John Berchman's, c/o St. Ignatius, MT, St. Ignatius Church. (HEL)
Johnsburg, MN, Mower Co., St. John's, c/o Adams, MN, Sacred Heart Church. (WIN)
Johnson, VT, Lamoille Co., St. John the Apostle, c/o Cambridge, VT, St. Mary Church. (BUR)
Johnson Bayou, LA, Our Lady of the Assumption, c/o Hackberry, LA, St. Peter Apostle Church. (LKC)
Johnson City, TX, Blanco Co., Good Shepherd, c/o Blanco, TX, St. Ferdinand's Church. (AUS)
Johnson Creek, WI, St. Mary Magdalene, c/o Lake Mills, WI, St. Francis Xavier Church. (MAD)
Johnsonville, SC, Florence Co., St. Patrick, c/o Lake City, SC, St. Philip's Church. (CHR)
Joliet, MT, St. John, c/o Bridger, MT, Sacred Heart Church. (GF)
Jonestown, PA, Lebanon Co., Our Lady of Fatima, c/o [1] Lebanon, PA, Assumption of the Blessed Virgin Mary Church. (HBG)
Jonesville, LA, St. Gerard, c/o Ferriday, LA, St. Patrick Church. (ALX)
Jordan, MT, St. John the Baptist, c/o Circle, MT, St. Francis Xavier Church. (GF)
Joyuda, PR, St. John the Baptist, c/o Cabo Rojo, PR, St. Michael Church. (MGZ)
Juana Diaz, PR, Divine Mercy, c/o Juana Diaz, PR, Santa Teresita Church. (PCE)
Juana Diaz, PR, Bo. Rio Cana Arriba, La Merced, c/o Juana Diaz, PR, St. Raymond Nonato Church. (PCE)
Juana Diaz, PR, San Martin de Porres, c/o Juana Diaz, PR, Santa Teresita Church. (PCE)
Judith Gap, MT, Wheatland Co., Immaculate Conception, c/o Harlowton, MT, St. Joseph Church. (HEL)
Julian, NE, Nemaha Co., St. Bernard's, c/o Paul, NE, St. Joseph's Church. (LIN)
Junction City, KY, Boyle Co., St. Patrick, c/o Danville, KY, SS. Peter & Paul Church. (LEX)
Juniata, NE, Adams Co., Assumption, c/o Roseland, NE, Sacred Heart Church. (LIN)
Juntura, OR, St. Charles, c/o Vale, OR, St. Patrick's Church. (BAK)

K

Kahakuloa, HI, Maui Co., St. Francis Xavier, c/o Waihee, HI, St. Ann Church. (HON)
Kahaluu, HI, Hawaii Co., St. Peter, c/o Holualoa, HI, St. Michael The Archangel Church. (HON)
Kalama, WA, Cowlitz Co., St. Joseph, c/o Woodland,

WA, St. Philip's Church. (SEA)
Kalaoa, HI, Hawaii Co., Holy Rosary, c/o Holualoa, HI, St. Michael The Archangel Church. (HON)
Kalawao, HI, Kalawao Co., St. Philomena, c/o Kalaupapa, HI, St. Francis Church. (HON)
Kalikonani, HI, Church of the Ascension, Puako, c/o Kamuela, HI, Church of the Annunciation. (HON)
Kalskag, AK, c/o Aniak, AK, St. Theresa Church. (FBK)
Kannapolis, NC, St. Joseph, c/o Concord, NC, St. James Church. (CHL)
Kansas, OH, Seneca Co., St. James, c/o Millersville, OH, St. Mary Church. (TOL)
Kapingmarangi, FM, c/o Kolonia, FM, Our Lady of Mercy Church. (CI)
Kaplan, LA, Vermilion Parish, St. Frances Xavier Cabrini, c/o Kaplan, LA, Our Lady of the Holy Rosary Church. (LAF)
Karlsruhe, ND, McHenry Co., Sts. Peter & Paul, c/o Velva, ND, St. Cecilia's Church. (FAR)
Karthaus, PA, Clearfield Co., SS. John & Paul, c/o Frenchville, PA, St. Mary of the Assumption Church. (E)
Kasson, MN, Dodge Co., Holy Family, c/o Byron, MN, Christ the King Church. (WIN)
Kaumakani, HI, St. Joseph, c/o Kekaha, HI, St. Theresa Church. (HON)
Kaupo, HI, Maui Co., St. Joseph, c/o Hana, HI, St. Mary Church. (HON)
Kawanui, HI, Hawaii Co., St. Paul, c/o Holualoa, HI, St. Michael The Archangel Church. (HON)
Kaycee, WY, Johnson Co., St. Hubert, c/o Buffalo, WY, St. John the Baptist Church. (CHY)
Keaau, HI, Holy Rosary, c/o Mountain View, HI, St. Theresa Church. (HON)
Kealakekua, HI, Hawaii Co., c/o Honaunau, HI, St. Benedict Church. (HON)
Keanae, HI, Maui Co., St. Gabriel, c/o Haiku, HI, St. Rita Church. (HON)
Keenesburg, CO, Weld Co., Holy Family, c/o Roggen, CO, Sacred Heart Church. (DEN)
Keithsburg, IL, Mercer Co., St. Mary's, c/o Aledo, IL, St. Catherine's Church. (PEO)
Kelliher, MN, Beltrami Co., St. Patrick, c/o Blackduck, MN, St. Ann's Church. (CR)
Kellogg, MN, Wabasha Co., Immaculate Conception, c/o Kellogg, MN, St. Agnes Church. (WIN)
Kelly, NM, Socorro Co., c/o Socorro, NM, San Miguel Church. (SFE)
Kelseyville, CA, St. Peter, c/o Lakeport, CA, St. Mary Church. (SR)
Kenel, SD, Corson Co., Assumption of the Blessed Virgin Mary Church, c/o Standing Rock, SD, Standing Rock Reservation Church. (RC)
Kenel, SD, Corson Co., Our Lady of the Assumption Parish, c/o McLaughlin, SD, St. Bernard Church. (RC)
Kennebunk, ME, St. Monica's, c/o Kennebunk, ME, St. Martha's Church. (PRT)
Kensal, ND, Stutsman Co., c/o Carrington, ND, Sacred Heart Church. (FAR)
Kenyon, MN, St. Michael, c/o Pine Island, MN, St. Michael Church. (STP)
Kerhonkson, NY, Ulster Co., Our Lady of Lourdes, c/o Ellenville, NY, St. Mary and St. Andrew Church. (NY)
Keshena, WI, Menominee Co., St. Joseph of the Lake, South Branch, c/o Keshena, WI, St. Michael Church. (GB)
Kettleman City, CA, St. Cecilia, c/o Avenal, CA, St. Joseph Church. (FRS)
Kewanna, IN, Fulton Co., St. Ann, c/o Rochester, IN, St. Joseph Church. (LFT)
Keyapaha, SD, St. Ann, c/o Winner, SD, Immaculate Conception Church. (RC)
Kilauea, HI, Kauai Co., St. Sylvester, c/o Kapaa, HI, St. Catherine Church. (HON)
Kindred, ND, St. Maurice, c/o [5] Fargo, ND, St. Anthony of Padua Church. (FAR)
King, NC, Stokes Co., Good Shepherd, c/o Winston-Salem, NC, St. Benedict the Moor Church. (CHL)
King George, VA, King George Co., St. Anthony's, c/o Colonial Beach, VA, St. Elizabeth Church. (ARL)
Kingman, ME, St. James, c/o Lincoln, ME, St. Mary Church. (PRT)
Kings Beach, CA, Placer Co., Our Lady of the Lake, c/o Truckee, CA, Assumption of the Blessed Virgin Mary Church. (SAC)
Kings Mountain, NC, Cleveland Co., Christ the King, c/o Shelby, NC, St. Mary's Church. (CHL)
Kingston, NH, Rockingham Co., St. Frederick, c/o Newton, NH, Mary, Mother of the Church. (MAN)
Kingston, WI, St. Mary, c/o Markesan, WI, St. Joseph Church. (MAD)
Kingsville, TX, Kleberg Co., Christ the King, c/o [2] Kingsville, TX, St. Gertrude Church. (CC)
Kinnear, WY, Fremont Co., St. Edward, c/o Riverton, WY, St. Margaret's Church. (CHY)
Kipahulu, HI, Maui Co., St. Paul, c/o Hana, HI, St. Mary Church. (HON)
Kirbyville, TX, Our Lady of La Salette, c/o Jasper, TX, St. Michael Church. (BEA)
Kirtland, NM, San Juan Catholic Center Ojo Amarillo Mission, c/o Waterflow, NM, Sacred Heart Church. (GLP)
Kissimmee, FL, Osceola Co., St. Catherine of Siena, c/o Kissimmee, FL, Holy Redeemer Church. (ORL)
Kit Carson, CO, Cheyenne Co., St. Augustine, c/o Cheyenne Wells, CO, Sacred Heart Church. (COS)
Kitzmiller, MD, Garrett Co., Immaculate Conception, c/o Oakland, MD, St. Peter the Apostle Church. (BAL)
Klagetoh, AZ, St. Anne, c/o Ganado, AZ, All Saints Church. (GLP)
Klamath, CA, St. Robert and Ann, c/o Crescent City, CA, St. Joseph Church. (SR)
Knickerbocker, TX, Tom Green Co., Immaculate Conception, c/o Eldorado, TX, Our Lady of Guadalupe Church. (SAN)
Knippa, TX, St. Joseph, c/o Sabinal, TX, St. Patrick's Church. (SAT)
Knox, ND, Benson Co., St. Mary, c/o Leeds, ND, St. Vincent de Paul Church. (FAR)
Koeltztown, MO, St. Boniface, c/o Argyle, MO, St. Aloysius Church. (JC)
Kolin, LA, Sts. Francis and Anne, c/o Deville, LA, St. John the Baptist Church. (ALX)
Koontz Lake, IN, Starke Co., St. Dominic, c/o Hamlet, IN, Holy Cross Church. (GRY)
Kress, TX, Swisher Co., St. Paul's, c/o Tulia, TX, Church of the Holy Spirit. (AMA)
Kukuihaele, HI, St. Theresa, c/o Honokaa, HI, Our Lady of Lourdes Church. (HON)
Kutu, FM, c/o Lukunor, FM, Sacred Heart Church. (CI)
Kwajalein, MH, Santo, c/o Ebeye, MH, Queen of Peace Church. (MI)

L

L'Erable, IL, Iroquois Co., St. John the Baptist, c/o Ashkum, IL, Assumption of the Blessed Virgin Mary Church. (JOL)
La Bajada, NM, Sandoval Co., c/o Pena Blanca, NM, Nuestra Senora De Guadalupe Church. (SFE)
La Barge, WY, Lincoln Co., La Barge Catholic Community, c/o Kemmerer, WY, St. Patrick's Church. (CHY)
La Cienega, NM, Santa Fe Co., c/o [6] Santa Fe, NM, San Isidro Church. (SFE)
La Cueva, NM, Mora Co., c/o Mora, NM, St. Gertrude Church. (SFE)
La Grange, CA, Stanislaus Co., St. Louis, c/o Hughson, CA, St. Anthony Church. (STO)
La Grange, MO, Lewis Co., Notre Dame, c/o Canton, MO, St. Joseph Church. (JC)
La Honda, CA, San Mateo Co., Our Lady of Refuge, c/o Half Moon Bay, CA, Our Lady of the Pillar Church. (SFR)
La Isla, TX, San Luis, c/o Fabens, TX, Our Lady of Guadalupe Church. (ELP)
La Jara, CO, Conejos Co., Our Lady of the Valley, c/o Capulin, CO, St. Joseph Church. (PBL)
La Jara, NM, Santo Nino, c/o Cuba, NM, Immaculate Conception Church. (GLP)
La Lagunita, NM, San Miguel Co., c/o Ribera, NM, San Miguel Del Vado Church. (SFE)
La Luz, NM, Our Lady of the Light, c/o Alamogordo, NM, Immaculate Conception Church. (LSC)
La Madera, NM, Rio Arriba Co., c/o El Rito, NM, San Juan Nepomuceno Church. (SFE)
La Mesilla, NM, c/o Santa Cruz, NM, Holy Cross Church. (SFE)
La Paloma, TX, Our Lady of Lourdes, c/o Ranchito, TX, St. Ignatius Church. (BWN)
La Pica, PR, San Patricio Co., c/o Jayuya, PR, Our Lady of Monserrate Church. (PCE)
La Piedra, PR, Ala de La Piedra Co., O.L. of Perp. Help, c/o Villalba, PR, Our Lady Mother of Divine Providence Church. (PCE)
La Playa, PR, Our Lady of Carmel, c/o Anasco, PR, St. Anthony Abbot Church. (MGZ)
La Puebla, NM, c/o Santa Cruz, NM, Holy Cross Church. (SFE)
La Puente, NM, Rio Arriba Co., c/o Los Ojos, NM, San Jose Church. (SFE)
La Puerta, TX, St. Paul, c/o Rio Grande City, TX, Immaculate Conception Church. (BWN)
La Rosita, TX, Duval Co., Holy Cross, c/o San Diego, TX, St. Francis de Paula Church. (CC)
La Sara, TX, St. Patrick, c/o Raymondville, TX, Our Lady of Guadalupe Church. (BWN)
La Union, NM, Our Lady of Refuge, c/o Anthony, NM, St. Anthony's Church. (LSC)
La Valle, WI, Holy Family, c/o Lime Ridge, WI, St. Boniface Church. (MAD)
La Veta, CO, Huerfano Co., Christ the King, c/o Walsenburg, CO, St. Mary Church. (PBL)
La Villa, TX, Our Lady of Guadalupe, c/o Edcouch, TX, St. Theresa of the Infant Jesus Church. (BWN)
Lacassine, LA, Jefferson Davis Parish, St. John the Evangelist, c/o Iowa, LA, St. Raphael Church. (LKC)
Lacey, MI, Our Lady of Great Oak, c/o Delton, MI, St. Ambrose Church. (KAL)
Lackawaxen, PA, Pike Co., St. Mary, c/o Shohola, PA, St. Ann's Church. (SCR)
LaCrosse, IN, LaPorte Co., St. Martin, c/o Wanatah, IN, Sacred Heart Church. (GRY)
Laddonia, MO, Audrain Co., St. John, c/o Vandalia, MO, Sacred Heart Church. (JC)
Lafayette, LA, Gift of Mary Chapel, c/o [11] Lafayette, LA, St. Genevieve Church. (LAF)
Lafayette, LA, Our Lady of Good Hope, c/o [2] Lafayette, LA, St. Paul The Apostle Church. (LAF)
Laguna, PR, Santa Rita, c/o Aguada, PR, St. Francis of Assisi Church. (MGZ)
Lajitas, TX, Big Bend National Park, c/o Alpine, TX, Our Lady of Peace Church. (ELP)
Lajitas, TX, Lajitas Mission, c/o Presidio, TX, Santa Teresa de Jesus Church. (ELP)
Lake Arthur, NM, Our Lady of Guadalupe, c/o Dexter, NM, Immaculate Conception Church. (LSC)
Lake Bonaparte, NY, St. Rita, c/o Harrisville, NY, St. Francis Solanus Church. (OG)
Lake Carmel, NY, Putnam Co., Our Lady of the Lake, c/o Carmel, NY, St. James the Apostle Church. (NY)
Lake Charles, LA, Calcasieu Parish, Christ the King, c/o [8] Lake Charles, LA, Our Lady Queen of Heaven Church. (LKC)
Lake Charles, LA, Calcasieu Parish, Our Lady of Fatima Chapel, c/o [2] Lake Charles, LA, Immaculate Heart of Mary Church. (LKC)
Lake Charles, LA, Calcasieu Parish, St. Martin de Porres, c/o [8] Lake Charles, LA, Our Lady Queen of Heaven Church. (LKC)
Lake City, CA, c/o Alturas, CA, Sacred Heart Church. (SAC)
Lake City, CO, Hinsdale Co., St. Rose of Lima, c/o Gunnison, CO, St. Peter Church. (PBL)
Lake Como, PA, Wayne Co., Assumption of the B.V.M., c/o Pleasant Mount, PA, St. James Church. (SCR)
Lake Crystal, MN, Blue Earth Co., Holy Family, c/o [4] Mankato, MN, St. Joseph the Worker Church. (WIN)
Lake Huntington, NY, Sullivan Co., Our Lady of the Lake, c/o Narrowsburg, NY, St. Francis Xavier Church. (NY)
Lake Itasca, MN, Clearwater Co., St. Catherine, c/o Bemidji, MN, St. Philip's Church. (CR)
Lake Itasca, MN, Clearwater Co., St. Catherine, c/o Callaway, MN, Assumption Church. (CR)
Lake Peekskill, NY, Putnam Co., North American Martyrs, c/o Cortlandt Manor, NY, St. Columbanus Church. (NY)
Lake Titus, NY, Franklin Co., St. Mary, c/o Chasm Falls, NY, St. Helen Church. (OG)
Lake Wallenpaupack, PA, Wayne Co., St. Veronica, c/o Hawley, PA, Blessed Virgin Mary, Queen of Peace Church. (SCR)
Lake Williams, ND, Kidder Co., Our Lady of the Lake, c/o Tappen, ND, St. Paul's Church. (FAR)
Lake Wilson, MN, Murray Co., St. Mary, c/o Slayton, MN, St. Ann's Church. (WIN)
Lake Wylie, SC, York Co., All Saints, c/o York, SC, Divine Saviour Church. (CHR)
Lakefield, MN, Jackson Co., St. Joseph, c/o Heron Lake, MN, Sacred Heart Church. (WIN)
Lakeshore, MS, Hancock Co., St. John, c/o Clermont Harbor, MS, St. Ann Church. (BLX)
Lakeside, CA, Barona, c/o Lakeside, CA, Blessed Kateri Tekakwitha Church. (SD)
Lakeside, SD, Meade Co., St. Margaret, c/o New Underwood, SD, St. John the Evangelist Church. (RC)
Lakeview, NY, Nassau Co., Chapel, c/o West Hempstead, NY, St. Thomas, the Apostle Church. (RVC)
Lakewood, NJ, Ocean Co., Holy Family Church, c/o Lakewood, NJ, St. Mary of the Lake Church. (TR)
Lambert, MT, St. Theresa, c/o Sidney, MT, St. Matthew Church. (GF)
Lamesa, TX, Dawson Co., Our Lady of Guadalupe, c/o Lamesa, TX, St. Margaret Mary Church. (LUB)
LaMoille, MN, Winona Co., Precious Blood, c/o Dakota, MN, Holy Cross Church. (WIN)
Lamotrek, FM, c/o Ulithi & Neighboring Islands, FM, Queen of Heaven Church. (CI)
Lancaster, MN, Kittson Co., Holy Rosary, c/o Hallock, MN, St. Patrick's Church. (CR)
Lanesboro, MN, Fillmore Co., St. Lawrence O'Toole, c/o Preston, MN, St. Columban Church. (WIN)
Lanesboro, MN, Fillmore Co., St. Patrick, c/o Preston, MN, St. Columban Church. (WIN)
Lankin, ND, Walsh Co., St. Joseph, c/o Pisek, ND, St. John Nepomucene Church. (FAR)
Lansford, ND, Bottineau Co., St. John, c/o Glenburn, ND, St. Philomena Church. (BIS)
Laporte, MN, Hubbard Co., St. Theodore, c/o Akeley, MN, St. John's Church. (CR)
Laporte, PA, Sullivan Co., Sacred Heart, c/o Dushore, PA, St. Basil's Church. (SCR)
Laporte, PA, Sullivan Co., Sacred Heart, c/o Mildred, PA, St. Francis of Assisi Church. (SCR)

Laredo, TX, Webb Co., San Francisco Javier, c/o [6] Laredo, TX, San Augustine Church. (CC)
Laredo, TX, Webb Co., Santa Cruz, c/o [4] Laredo, TX, Holy Redeemer Church. (CC)
Laredo, TX, Webb Co., Santo Nino Mission, c/o [6] Laredo, TX, San Augustine Church. (CC)
Las Colonias, NM, Taos Co., c/o Arroyo Seco, NM, Holy Trinity Church. (SFE)
Las Colonias, NM, San Miguel Co., c/o Pecos, NM, St. Anthony Church. (SFE)
Las Flores, PR, Coamo Co., San Martin, c/o Coamo, PR, St. Blase Church. (PCE)
Las Mareas, PR, St. Judas, c/o Aguirre, PR, Sacred Heart Church. (PCE)
Las Margaritas, PR, Bo. Collores Arriba, Santiago, Ap., c/o Juana Diaz, PR, St. Raymond Nonato Church. (PCE)
Las Milpas, TX, Nuestro Senor del Sagrado Corazon, c/o Pharr, TX, St. Jude Thaddeus Church. (BWN)
Las Nutrias, NM, Socorro Co., San Isidro, c/o La Joya, NM, Our Lady of Sorrows Church. (SFE)
Las Ochenta, PR, Inmaculada Concepcion, c/o Salinas, PR, Our Lady of Monserrat Church. (PCE)
Las Palmas, PR, St. Rita, c/o Cabo Rojo, PR, St. Michael Church. (MGZ)
Las Palomas, NM, San Ysidro, c/o Truth or Consequences, NM, Our Lady of Perpetual Help Church. (LSC)
Las Rucias, TX, Sacred Heart, c/o Ranchito, TX, St. Ignatius Church. (BWN)
Las Tablas, NM, Taos Co., c/o El Rito, NM, San Juan Nepomuceno Church. (SFE)
Las Vegas, PR, Sta. Teresita, c/o Yauco, PR, Holy Rossary Church. (PCE)
LaSal, UT, Grand Co., Sacred Heart, c/o Moab, UT, St. Pius X Church. (SLC)
LaSalle, TX, St. Theresa, c/o Vanderbilt, TX, St. John Bosco Church. (VIC)
Lathrop, CA, San Joaquin Co., Our Lady of Guadalupe, c/o [4] Stockton, CA, St. George Church. (STO)
Latimer, MS, Jackson Co., Christ the King, c/o Vancleave, MS, Catholic Church of the Holy Spirit. (BLX)
Lattimer Mines, PA, Luzerne Co., St. Mary, c/o Pardeesville, PA, St. Nazarius Church. (SCR)
Lattnerville, IA, Annunciation, c/o Peosta, IA, St. John the Baptist Church. (DUB)
Laurens, SC, Laurens Co., Holy Spirit, c/o Union, SC, St. Augustine's Church. (CHR)
Lavelle, PA, Schuylkill Co., St. Elizabeth, c/o Ashland, PA, St. Mauritius Church. (ALN)
Lavina, MT, St Joseph, c/o Roundup, MT, St. Benedict's Church. (GF)
Lawrence, NE, Nuckolls Co., St. Stephen's, c/o Lawrence, NE, Sacred Heart Church. (LIN)
Lawrenceville, VA, St. Bernard, c/o Emporia, VA, St. Richard Church. (RIC)
LBJ Village, VI, Sacred Heart Chapel, c/o [2] Christiansted, VI, Church of the Holy Cross. (STV)
Le Bleu Settlement, LA, Calcasieu Parish, St. Joseph, c/o Iowa, LA, St. Raphael Church. (LKC)
Le Doux, NM, Mora Co., c/o Mora, NM, St. Gertrude Church. (SFE)
Le Grand, CA, Merced Co., Our Lady of Lourdes, c/o Planada, CA, Sacred Heart Church. (FRS)
Leakesville, MS, Holy Trinity, c/o Waynesboro, MS, St. Bernadette Church. (BLX)
Leakey, TX, St. Raymond of Pennafort, c/o Rocksprings, TX, Sacred Heart of Mary Church. (SAT)
Leaton, MI, Isabella Co., St. Charles, c/o Rosebush, MI, St. Henry Church. (SAG)
Lebanon Junction, KY, St. Clare, c/o Lebanon Junction, KY, St. Benedict Church. (L)
Ledgedale, PA, Wayne Co., St. Mary, c/o Lake Ariel, PA, St. Thomas More Church. (SCR)
Lee Vining, CA, Mono Co., Our Savior of the Mountains, c/o Mammoth Lakes, CA, St. Joseph Church. (STO)
Leeds, NY, St. Bridget, c/o Catskill, NY, St. Patrick Church. (ALB)
Leggett, CA, St. Cecilia, c/o Garberville, CA, Our Lady of the Redwoods Church. (SR)
Lehi, AZ, St. Paschal Baylon, c/o [4] Tempe, AZ, St. Margaret Church. (PHX)
Leicester, VT, Addison Co., St. Agnes, c/o Brandon, VT, St. Mary's Church. (BUR)
Leming, TX, Our Lady of Guadalupe, c/o Pleasanton, TX, St. Luke-Loire Church. (SAT)
Lemitar, NM, Socorro Co., c/o Socorro, NM, San Miguel Church. (SFE)
Lenorah, TX, Martin Co., St. Isidore, c/o Stanton, TX, St. Joseph's Church. (SAN)
Leo, MN, Roseau Co., St. Aloysius, c/o Greenbush, MN, Blessed Sacrament Church. (CR)
Leonardsville, NY, Our Lady of the Valley, c/o New Berlin, NY, St. Theresa of the Infant Jesus Church. (SY)
Leroy, ND, Pembina Co., St. Joseph, c/o Walhalla, ND, St. Boniface's Church. (FAR)
Lesterville, MO, Reynolds Co., Our Lady of Sorrows, c/o Ironton, MO, Ste. Marie Du Lac Church. (SPC)
Lewes, DE, Sussex Co., Shrine of St. Jude, c/o Rehoboth, DE, St. Edmond Church. (WIL)
Lewisburg, WV, Monroe Co., St. Louis, c/o Ronceverte, WV, St. Catherine of Siena Church. (WH)
Lewiston, CA, Trinity Co., St. Gilbert, c/o Weaverville, CA, St. Patrick Church. (SAC)
Lexington, IL, McLean Co., St. Mary, c/o Chenoa, IL, St. Joseph's Church. (PEO)
Lexington, NY, St. Francis de Sales, c/o Haines Falls, NY, Immaculate Conception Church. (ALB)
Lexington, OK, Cleveland Co., St. John the Baptist, c/o Purcell, OK, Our Lady of Victory Church. (OKL)
Lexington, TX, Lee Co., Holy Family, c/o Rockdale, TX, St. Joseph's Church. (AUS)
Leyba, NM, San Miguel Co., c/o Villanueva, NM, Our Lady of Guadalupe Church. (SFE)
Liberty, KY, Casey Co., Sacred Heart, c/o Clementsville, KY, St. Bernard Church. (L)
Licking, MO, Texas Co., St. John The Baptist, c/o Houston, MO, St. Mark Church. (SPC)
Likely, CA, c/o Alturas, CA, Sacred Heart Church. (SAC)
Lilburn, GA, Gwinnet Co., St. Stephen the Martyr, c/o Lilburn, GA, St. John Neumann Church. (ATL)
Limani, PR, Inm. Corazon de Maria, c/o Adjuntas, PR, St. Joachim Church. (PCE)
Lime Rock, NY, Genesee Co., St. Anthony, c/o Le Roy, NY, St. Peter Church. (BUF)
Lincoln, MT, Lewis and Clark Co., St. Jude's, c/o Helmville, MT, St. Thomas Church. (HEL)
Lincoln, NE, Lancaster Co., St. George Byzantine-Ukrainian Rite Catholic Church, c/o Omaha, NE, Assumption of B.V.M. Church. (STN)
Lincoln, NM, San Juan, c/o Ruidoso, NM, St. Eleanor Church. (LSC)
Lindale, TX, Smith Co., Holy Family, c/o [1] Tyler, TX, Cathedral of the Immaculate Conception. (TYL)
Lindsay, OK, Garvin Co., St. Peter's, c/o Pauls Valley, OK, St. Catherine of Siena Church. (OKL)
Linlithgo, NY, Nativity of Our Lord, c/o Germantown, NY, Resurrection Church. (ALB)
Linville, NC, Avery Co., St. Bernadette, c/o Spruce Pine, NC, St. Lucien Church. (CHL)
Lisco, NE, St. Gall, c/o Chappell, NE, St. Joseph's Church. (GI)
Litchfield, ME, Kennebec Co., St. Leo, c/o Richmond, ME, St. Ambrose Church. (PRT)
Little Diomede, AK, St. Jude, c/o Teller, AK, St. Ann Church. (FBK)
Little Egg Harbor, NJ, Ocean Co., St. Michael, c/o Tuckerton, NJ, St. Teresa Church. (TR)
Little Italy, AR, Pulaski Co., St. Francis, c/o Bigelow, AR, St. Boniface's Church. (LR)
Little Meadows, PA, Susquehanna Co., St. Thomas the Apostle, c/o Friendsville, PA, St. Francis Xavier's Church. (SCR)
Little Orleans, MD, Allegany Co., St. Patrick's, c/o Hancock, MD, St. Peter's Church. (BAL)
Littleton, WV, Wetzel Co., Assumption of the Blessed Virgin Mary, c/o Mannington, WV, St. Patrick's Church. (WH)
Live Oak, CA, Sutter Co., Our Lady of Guadalupe, c/o Gridley, CA, Sacred Heart Church. (SAC)
Llano, TX, Holy Trinity Church, c/o Mason, TX, St. Joseph's Church. (AUS)
Llano Largo, NM, Taos Co., San Acacio Mission, c/o Penasco, NM, San Antonio de Padua Church. (SFE)
Llano Quemado, NM, Taos Co., N.S. del Carmel, c/o Ranchos De Taos, NM, San Francisco de Asis Church. (SFE)
Llano San Juan, NM, Taos Co., San Juan Nepomuceno Mission, c/o Penasco, NM, San Antonio de Padua Church. (SFE)
Llanos, PR, Sector El Juicio, c/o Aibonito, PR, Church of St. Joseph. (CGS)
Llanos Tunas, PR, Our Lady of Good Counsel, c/o Cabo Rojo, PR, St. Michael Church. (MGZ)
Lluberas, PR, St. Joseph, c/o Yauco, PR, Holy Rossary Church. (PCE)
Lobatos, CO, Sagrada Familia, c/o Conejos, CO, Our Lady of Guadalupe Church. (PBL)
Loch Lomond, CA, Our Lady of the Lake, c/o Middletown, CA, St. Joseph Church. (SR)
Lockney, TX, Floyd Co., San Jose, c/o Plainview, TX, St. Alice Church. (LUB)
Loda, IL, Iroquois Co., St. Joseph, c/o Paxton, IL, St. Mary Church. (JOL)
Lodge Pole, MT, St. Thomas, c/o Hays, MT, St. Paul's Indian Mission Church. (GF)
Lodgepole, NE, Sacred Heart, c/o Chappell, NE, St. Joseph's Church. (GI)
Logan, NM, Quay Co., c/o Tucumcari, NM, St. Anne Church. (SFE)
Loiza, PR, La Milagrosa, c/o Loiza, PR, Santiago Apostol, El Mayor Church. (SJN)
Loiza, PR, La Providencia, c/o Loiza, PR, Santiago Apostol, El Mayor Church. (SJN)
Loiza, PR, Nino de Praga, c/o Loiza, PR, Santiago Apostol, El Mayor Church. (SJN)
Loiza, PR, Ntra. Sra. de Fatima, c/o Loiza, PR, San Patricio Church. (SJN)
Loiza, PR, Ntra. Sra. del Perpetuo Socorro, c/o Loiza, PR, San Patricio Church. (SJN)
Loiza, PR, Ntra. Sra. Perpetuo Socorro, c/o Loiza, PR, Santiago Apostol, El Mayor Church. (SJN)
Loiza, PR, San Antonio, c/o Loiza, PR, San Patricio Church. (SJN)
Loiza, PR, San Rafael-Villa Nevarez, c/o Loiza, PR, San Patricio Church. (SJN)
Loiza, PR, Santa Rosa, c/o Loiza, PR, San Patricio Church. (SJN)
Loiza, PR, Santisima Trinidad, c/o Loiza, PR, San Patricio Church. (SJN)
Loleta, CA, St. Patrick, c/o Fortuna, CA, St. Joseph Church. (SR)
Lolo, MT, Missoula Co., Spirit of Christ, c/o [2] Missoula, MT, Holy Family Church. (HEL)
Lometa, TX, Lampasas Co., Good Shepherd Catholic Church, c/o Lampasas, TX, St. Mary's Church. (AUS)
Lomice, ND, Walsh Co., St. Catherine, c/o Michigan, ND, St. Lawrence O'Toole Church. (FAR)
London, CA, Tulare Co., Santa Cruz, c/o Kingsburg, CA, Holy Family Church. (FRS)
Long Beach, CA, Los Angeles Co., Our Lady of Mt. Carmel, c/o [1] Long Beach, CA, St. Anthony Church. (LA)
Long Eddy, NY, Sullivan Co., St. Patrick, c/o Callicoon, NY, Holy Cross Church. (NY)
Long Island, ME, Great Diamond Island, c/o [8] Portland, ME, St. Christopher's Church. (PRT)
Longcreek, OR, St. Katherine, c/o John Day, OR, St. Elizabeth's Church. (BAK)
Lopeno, TX, Zapata Co., San Pedro, c/o Zapata, TX, Our Lady of Lourdes Church. (CC)
Lopezville, TX, Immaculate Conception, c/o San Juan, TX, St. John the Baptist Church. (BWN)
Loraine, TX, Mitchell Co., San Jose, c/o Colorado City, TX, St. Ann's Church. (SAN)
Lorenzo, TX, San Lorenzo, c/o Idalou, TX, St. Philip Benizi Church. (LUB)
Loreto, WI, St. Patrick, c/o Plain, WI, St. Luke Church. (MAD)
Loris, SC, Horry Co., Church of the Resurrection, c/o Conway, SC, St. James Church. (CHR)
Los Alamos, CA, Santa Barbara Co., St. Anthony's Church, c/o Santa Maria, CA, St. Louis de Montfort Church. (LA)
Los Angeles, CA, Assumption, c/o [5] Los Angeles, CA, Assumption Church. (LA)
Los Angeles, CA, Los Angeles Co., La Purisima Chapel, c/o [29] Los Angeles, CA, Our Lady of the Rosary of Talpa Church. (LA)
Los Angeles, CA, Los Angeles Co., San Conrado, c/o [87] Los Angeles, CA, St. Peter Church. (LA)
Los Angeles, CA, Los Angeles Co., San Felipe, c/o [23] Los Angeles, CA, Our Lady of Guadalupe Church. (LA)
Los Angeles, CA, Los Angeles Co., St. John Bosco, c/o [83] Los Angeles, CA, St. Odilia Church. (LA)
Los Angeles, CA, St. Turibius, c/o [72] Los Angeles, CA, St. Joseph Church. (LA)
Los Chavez, NM, Valencia Co., c/o Belen, NM, Our Lady of Belen Church. (SFE)
Los Cordovas, NM, Taos Co., San Isidro, c/o Ranchos De Taos, NM, San Francisco de Asis Church. (SFE)
Los Coyotes Reservation, CA, St. Isadore, c/o Santa Ysabel, CA, Santa Ysabel Indian Mission Church. (SD)
Los Ebanos, TX, St. Michael, c/o La Joya, TX, Our Lady, Queen of Angels Church. (BWN)
Los Garcias Ranch, TX, Sacred Heart, c/o Rio Grande City, TX, Immaculate Conception Church. (BWN)
Los Hueros, NM, Mora Co., c/o Wagon Mound, NM, Santa Clara Church. (SFE)
Los Le Febres, NM, Mora Co., c/o Wagon Mound, NM, Santa Clara Church. (SFE)
Los Lentes, NM, Valencia Co., c/o Los Lunas, NM, St. Clement Church. (SFE)
Los Llanos, PR, Coamo Co., St. Anthony, c/o Coamo, PR, St. Blase Church. (PCE)
Los Martinez, NM, Our Lady of Guadalupe, c/o Blanco, NM, St. Rose Church. (GLP)
Los Saenz, TX, Holy Family, c/o Roma, TX, Our Lady of Refuge Church. (BWN)
Los Sauces, CO, St. Anthony, c/o Capulin, CO, St. Joseph Church. (PBL)
Los Valdeses, CO, St. Francis of Assisi, c/o Del Norte, CO, Holy Name of Mary Church. (PBL)
Losap, FM, c/o Lukunor, FM, Sacred Heart Church. (CI)
Louise, TX, St. Procopius, c/o Hillje, TX, St. Andrew Church. (VIC)
Louisville, GA, Jefferson Co., St. Joan of Arc, c/o Waynesboro, GA, Sacred Heart Church. (SAV)
Louisville, KY, c/o Louisville, KY, Maronite Catholic Community Church. (OLL)
Loveladies, NJ, Ocean Co., St. Clare, c/o Brant Beach, NJ, St. Francis of Assisi Church. (TR)
Lovingston, VA, St. Mary, c/o Scottsville, VA, St. George Church. (RIC)
Lowell, VT, Orleans Co., St. Ignatius Loyola, c/o Troy,

VT, Sacred Heart of Jesus Church. (BUR)
Lower San Francisco, NM, San Isidro, c/o Aragon, NM, Santo Nino Church. (GLP)
Loyal, OK, Kingfisher Co., St. Joseph, c/o Watonga, OK, St. Rose of Lima Church. (OKL)
Loyalton, CA, Sierra Co., Holy Rosary, c/o Portola, CA, Holy Family Church. (SAC)
Lozano, TX, St. Vincent de Paul, c/o Rio Hondo, TX, St. Helen Church. (BWN)
Lucedale, MS, St. Lucy, c/o Wiggins, MS, St. Francis Xavier Church. (BLX)
Lucerne, CA, Queen of the Rosary, c/o Lakeport, CA, St. Mary Church. (SR)
Lucero, NM, Mora Co., c/o Mora, NM, St. Gertrude Church. (SFE)
Ludlow, IL, Champaign Co., Sacred Heart, c/o Thomasboro, IL, St. Elizabeth's Church. (PEO)
Luis Lopez, NM, Socorro Co., c/o Socorro, NM, San Miguel Church. (SFE)
Lull, TX, Capilla de San Jose, c/o Edinburg, TX, Sacred Heart Church. (BWN)
Lummi, WA, Whatcom Co., St. Joachim (Indian Reservation), c/o Ferndale, WA, St. Joseph Church. (SEA)
Lunenburg, VT, Essex Co., St. Leo, c/o Gilman, VT, St. Theresa Church. (BUR)
Luquillo, PR, Ntra. Sra. del Cobre, c/o Luquillo, PR, San Jose Church. (SJN)
Luquillo, PR, San Judas, c/o Luquillo, PR, San Jose Church. (SJN)
Luther, MI, St. Ignatius, c/o Baldwin, MI, St. Ann's Church. (GR)
Luther, OK, Oklahoma Co., Saint Theresa of the Infant Jesus, c/o Jones, OK, St. Robert Bellarmine Church. (OKL)
Lyden, NM, Rio Arriba Co., San Jose, c/o Dixon, NM, St. Anthony Church. (SFE)
Lyle, MN, Mower Co., Queen of Peace, c/o Rose Creek, MN, St. Peter's Church. (WIN)
Lyman, NE, Sacred Heart, c/o Mitchell, NE, St. Theresa's Church. (GI)
Lyons, OR, Linn Co., St. Patrick, c/o Jordan, OR, Our Lady of Lourdes Church. (P)
Lyons Falls, NY, Lewis Co., St. John, c/o Port Leyden, NY, St. Martin Church. (OG)

M

Mabel, MN, Fillmore Co., St. Olaf, c/o Harmony, MN, The Nativity of the Blessed Virgin Church. (WIN)
Macana, PR, Fatima, c/o Penuelas, PR, St. Joseph Church. (PCE)
Macana Parcelas, PR, San Martin de Porres, c/o Guayanilla, PR, Immaculate Conception Church. (PCE)
Macana Rio, PR, Virgen de Fatima, c/o Guayanilla, PR, Immaculate Conception Church. (PCE)
MacDonaldton, PA, Somerset Co., St. Gregory, c/o Meyersdale, PA, SS. Philip and James Church. (ALT)
Machananao, GU, Santa Bernadita, c/o Yigo, GU, Our Lady of Lourdes Church. (AGN)
Macon, MS, Corpus Christi, c/o Starkville, MS, St. Joseph Church. (JKS)
Macy, NE, Thurston Co., Our Lady of Fatima, c/o Winnebago, NE, St. Augustine's Church. (OM)
Madawaska, ME, Aroostook Co., St. Michael's Chapel, c/o St. Agatha, ME, St. Agatha's Church. (PRT)
Maddock, ND, Benson Co., St. William, c/o Fessenden, ND, St. Augustine's Church. (FAR)
Madera, CA, Madera Co., St. Agnes, c/o Madera, CA, St. Joachim Church. (FRS)
Madera, PA, Clearfield Co., Immaculate Conception, c/o Houtzdale, PA, Christ the King Church. (E)
Madero, TX, Our Lady of Lourdes, c/o [2] Mission, TX, Our Lady of the Holy Rosary Church. (BWN)
Madill, OK, Marshall Co., Holy Cross, c/o Sulphur, OK, St. Francis Xavier Church. (OKL)
Madison, GA, Morgan Co., St. James, c/o Covington, GA, St. Augustine Church. (ATL)
Madison, KS, Greenwood Co., St. Teresa Of Avila, c/o Eureka, KS, Sacred Heart Church. (WCH)
Magas Arriba, PR, Perpetuo Socorro, c/o Guayanilla, PR, Immaculate Conception Church. (PCE)
Magdalena, NM, Socorro Co., c/o Socorro, NM, San Miguel Church. (SFE)
Mageetown, PA, Crawford Co., Immaculate Conception, c/o Titusville, PA, St. Titus Church. (E)
Magnolia, AR, Columbia Co., Immaculate Heart of Mary, c/o Camden, AR, St. Louis Church. (LR)
Magnolia, ID, St. Joseph's Chapel, c/o [1] Gloucester, MA, St. Ann Church. (BO)
Magnolia, MS, St. James, c/o Chatawa, MS, St. Teresa Church. (JKS)
Magur, FM, Marie Chapel, c/o Fefan, FM, Sacred Heart Church. (CI)
Magur, FM, Marie Chapel, c/o Ulul, FM, Sacred Heart Church. (CI)
Majuro Atoll, MH, Laura, c/o Majuro, MH, Cathedral of the Assumption. (MI)
Makoti, ND, Ward Co., St. Elizabeth, c/o Parshall, ND, St. Bridget Church. (BIS)
Malaeloa, AS, c/o [3] Pago Pago, AS, Church of St. Paul. (SPP)
Malaga, CA, Fresno, Christ the King, c/o [8] Fresno, CA, St. Anthony Claret Church (FRS)
Malaga, NM, Cristo Rey, c/o Loving, NM, Our Lady of Grace Church. (LSC)
Malakoff, TX, Henderson Co., Mary Queen of Heaven, c/o Gun Barrel City, TX, St. Jude Church. (TYL)
Malakoff Diggins, CA, Nevada Co., St. Columcille, c/o Downieville, CA, Immaculate Conception Church. (SAC)
Malpaso-Cesar Ruiz, PR, Immaculada Concepcion, c/o Aguada, PR, St. Francis of Assisi Church. (MGZ)
Mamey, PR, Perpetuo Socorro, c/o Aguada, PR, St. Francis of Assisi Church. (MGZ)
Mameyes, PR, Jayuya Co., S. Antonio, c/o Jayuya, PR, Our Lady of Monserrate Church. (PCE)
Manassa, CO, Conejos Co., St. Therese of the Child Jesus, c/o Capulin, CO, St. Joseph Church. (PBL)
Manderson, SD, Shannon Co., St. Agnes, c/o Porcupine, SD, Church of Christ the King. (RC)
Manderson, SD, Shannon Co., St. Peter's, c/o Porcupine, SD, Church of Christ the King. (RC)
Mani, PR, Capilla de la Mora, c/o [2] Mayaquez, PR, Our Lady of Mt. Carmel Church. (MGZ)
Mani, PR, Infant of Prague, c/o [2] Mayaquez, PR, Our Lady of Mt. Carmel Church. (MGZ)
Manito, IL, Mason Co., Immaculate Conception, c/o Havana, IL, St. Patrick's Church. (PEO)
Manitou Springs, CO, El Paso Co., Our Lady of Perpetual Help, c/o [9] Colorado Springs, CO, Sacred Heart Church. (COS)
Mannford, OK, Creek Co., Our Lady of the Lake, c/o Sand Springs, OK, St. Patrick's Church. (TLS)
Manset, ME, St. Peter's, c/o Northeast Harbor, ME, St. Ignatius Church. (PRT)
Mansfield, WA, Douglas Co., St. Mary, c/o Bridgeport, WA, St. Anne's Church. (YAK)
Mantador, ND, Richland Co., Sts. Peter & Paul, c/o Mooreton, ND, St. Anthony's Church. (FAR)
Manton, KY, Washington Co., Holy Rosary, c/o [3] Springfield, KY, Holy Trinity Church. (L)
Manu'a Island, AS, Mary, Star of the Sea, c/o [1] Pago Pago, AS, Cathedral of the Holy Family. (SPP)
Many, LA, Sabine Parish, St. Terence, c/o Many, LA, St. John the Baptist Church. (SHP)
Many Farms, AZ, St. Anthony, c/o Chinle, AZ, Our Lady of Fatima, Indian Mission Church. (GLP)
Manzano, NM, Torrance Co., c/o Mountainair, NM, St. Alice Church. (SFE)
Manzanola, CO, Otero Co., St. Joseph the Worker, c/o Rocky Ford, CO, St. Peter Church. (PBL)
Marak, TX, Milam Co., Ss. Cyril & Methodius, c/o Cyclone, TX, St. Joseph's Church. (AUS)
Marana, AZ, San Juan, c/o [2] Tucson, AZ, Blessed Kateri Tekakwitha Church. (TUC)
Marathon, TX, Brewster Co., St. Mary, c/o Alpine, TX, Our Lady of Peace Church. (ELP)
Marcellus, MI, Cass Co., St. Margaret Mary, c/o Mattawan, MI, St. John Bosco Church. (KAL)
Marenisco, MI, Gogebic Co., St. Catherine, c/o Wakefield, MI, Immaculate Conception of the Blessed Virgin Mary Church. (MAR)
Maresua, PR, Gruta de Lourdes, c/o San German, PR, San German de Auxerre Church. (MGZ)
Marian, TN, Marian Co., Virgin of the Poor Shrine, c/o South Pittsburg, TN, Our Lady of Lourdes Church. (KNX)
Marianna, AR, Lee Co., St. Andrew's, c/o Forrest City, AR, St. Francis of Assisi Church. (LR)
Marias, PR, Asuncion de Maria, c/o Aguada, PR, St. Francis of Assisi Church. (MGZ)
Maricopa, AZ, Pinal Co., St. Francis de Sales, c/o Casa Grande, AZ, St. Anthony Church. (TUC)
Marienville, PA, Forest Co., St. Anne, c/o Crown, PA, St. Mary Church. (E)
Marietta, OK, Love Co., Good Shepherd, c/o Ardmore, OK, St. Mary Church. (OKL)
Marion, NC, McDowell Co, Our Lady of the Angels, c/o Morganton, NC, St. Charles Borromeo Church. (CHL)
Marion, ND, LaMoure Co., St. Francis, c/o La Moure, ND, Holy Rosary Church. (FAR)
Marion, SC, Marion Co., Infant Jesus, c/o Dillon, SC, St. Louis Church. (CHR)
Marion, TX, Immaculate Conception, c/o Schertz, TX, Church of the Good Shepherd. (SAT)
Marked Tree, AR, Poinsett Co., St. Norbert's, c/o Weiner, AR, St. Anthony's Church. (LR)
Markham, TX, St. Robert, c/o Blessing, TX, St. Peter's Church. (VIC)
Marlin, TX, Falls Co., Sacred Heart, c/o Marlin, TX, St. Joseph's Church. (AUS)
Marlow, OK, Stephens Co., Immaculate Conception, c/o Duncan, OK, Assumption Church. (OKL)
Marmarth, ND, Slope Co., Immaculate Heart of Mary, c/o Bowman, ND, St. Charles Church. (BIS)
Marshall, AK, Our Lady of Guadalupe Russian Mission, c/o Marshall, AK, Immaculate Heart of Mary Church. (FBK)
Marshall, CA, Marin Co., St. Helen, c/o Tomales, CA, Church of the Assumption. (SFR)
Marshall, OK, Logan Co., St. Camillus, c/o Hennessey, OK, St. Joseph's Church. (OKL)
Martindale, TX, Caldwell Co., Immaculate Heart of Mary, c/o San Marcos, TX, St. John the Evangelist Church. (AUS)
Marysdale, OH, Defiance Co., Immaculate Conception, c/o The Bend, OH, St. Stephen Church. (TOL)
Marysville, MT, Lewis and Clark Co., Our Lady of Lourdes, c/o [3] Helena, MT, Our Lady of the Valley Church. (HEL)
Masefau, AS, c/o [4] (Lauli'i), AS, Church of St. Peter and Paul. (SPP)
Mason, TX, c/o Llano, TX, Holy Trinity Church. (AUS)
Mason, WV, Mason Co., St. Joseph, c/o Point Pleasant, WV, Sacred Heart Church. (WH)
Mason City, IL, Mason Co., St. Columba, c/o Lincoln, IL, Holy Family Church. (PEO)
Mason City, NE, Custer Co., St. Thomas, c/o Broken Bow, NE, St. Joseph's Church. (GI)
Matador, TX, Motley Co., Our Lady of Guadalupe, c/o Floydada, TX, St. Mary Magdalen Church. (LUB)
Matrullas, PR, Cacao Co., Sacred Heart of Jesus, c/o Villalba, PR, Our Lady Mother of Divine Providence Church. (PCE)
Mattingly Settlement, OH, Muskingum Co., St. Mary, c/o Dresden, OH, St. Ann's Church. (COL)
Mattituck, NY, Suffolk Co., Our Lady of Good Counsel, c/o Cutchogue, NY, Sacred Heart Church. (RVC)
Matunuck, RI, St. Romuald, c/o Wakefield, RI, St. Francis Church. (PRO)
Maud, OK, Seminole Co., St. Cecelia, c/o Seminole, OK, Immaculate Conception Church. (OKL)
Maupin, OR, St. Mary's, c/o Dufur, OR, St. Alphonsus Church. (BAK)
Max, ND, McClean Co., Immaculate Conception, c/o Garrison, ND, St. Nicholas Church. (BIS)
Maxwell, NM, Colfax Co., c/o Springer, NM, St. Joseph Church. (SFE)
Mayaguez, PR, Corpus Christi, c/o [5] Mayaquez, PR, Nuestra Senora De Fatima Church. (MGZ)
Mayaguez, PR, Cristo Rey, c/o [5] Mayaquez, PR, Nuestra Senora De Fatima Church. (MGZ)
Mayaguez, PR, Espiritu Santo, c/o [5] Mayaquez, PR, Nuestra Senora De Fatima Church. (MGZ)
Mayaguez, PR, Maria Socorro de los Cristianos, c/o [1] Mayaquez, PR, Cathedral of Our Lady of Purification. (MGZ)
Mayaguez, PR, Santa Ana, c/o [1] Mayaquez, PR, Cathedral of Our Lady of Purification. (MGZ)
Mayer, AZ, St. Joseph, c/o Prescott Valley, AZ, St. Germaine Church. (PHX)
Maysville, MO, DeKalb Co., St. Aloysius, c/o Cameron, MO, St. Munchin Church. (KC)
Mayville, ND, State University Newman Club, c/o Mayville, ND, Our Lady of Peace Church. (FAR)
McCartys, NM, Santa Maria de Acoma, c/o Acoma, NM, San Esteban, Indian Mission Church. (GLP)
McClellanville, SC, Charleston Co., McClellanville Mission, c/o Georgetown, SC, St. Mary's Church. (CHR)
McClusky, ND, Sheridan Co., Holy Family, c/o Sykeston, ND, St. Elizabeth's Church. (FAR)
McCook, NE, Red Willow Co., Sacred Heart, c/o McCook, NE, St. Patrick Church. (LIN)
McCook, NE, Red Willow Co., St. Ann's, c/o McCook, NE, St. Patrick Church. (LIN)
McCormick, SC, McCormick Co., Good Shepherd, c/o Abbeville, SC, Sacred Heart Church. (CHR)
McCrory, AR, Woodruff Co., St. Mary's, c/o Wynne, AR, St. Peter's Church. (LR)
McDermitt, NV, Humboldt Co., Sacred Heart, c/o Winnemucca, NV, St. Paul Church. (RNO)
McGill, NV, St, Michael's, c/o Ely, NV, Sacred Heart Church. (LAV)
McHenry, ND, Foster Co., SS. Peter & Paul, c/o New Rockford, ND, St. John's Church. (FAR)
McIntosh, SD, Corson Co., St. Bonaventure, c/o McLaughlin, SD, St. Bernard Church. (RC)
McKee, KY, Jackson Co., St. Paul, c/o Berea, KY, St. Clare Church. (LEX)
McRoberts, KY, Letcher Co., Holy Angels, c/o Jenkins, KY, St. George Church. (LEX)
Mead, CO, Weld Co., Guardian Angels, c/o Frederick, CO, St. Theresa Church. (DEN)
Meadowlands, MN, St. Mary's, c/o Floodwood, MN, St. Louis Church. (DUL)
Meadville, MS, St. Ann, c/o Natchez, MS, Assumption of the B.V.M. Church. (JKS)
Mechanic Falls, ME, Oxford Co., St. Mary, c/o Mechanic Falls, ME, Our Lady of Ransom Church. (PRT)
Medanales, NM, c/o Abiquiu, NM, St. Thomas Apostle Church. (SFE)
Medicine Bow, WY, Carbon Co., St. Malachy, c/o Saratoga, WY, St. Ann's Church. (CHY)
Medicine Lake, MT, St. Patrick, c/o Culbertson, MT, St. Anthony's Church. (GF)
Medicine Root, SD, Shannon, St. Stephens, c/o Kyle, SD, Our Lady of Sorrows Church. (RC)
Medina, ND, Stutsman Co., St. Mary, c/o Windsor, ND, St. Mathias Church. (FAR)
Medina Lake, TX, Bandera Co., St. Victor's Chapel, c/o

Bandera, TX, St. Stanislaus Church. (SAT)
Medora, ND, Billings Co., St. Mary, c/o Belfield, ND, St. Bernard Church. (BIS)
Meeker, OK, Lincoln Co., St.Michael, c/o Prague, OK, St. Wenceslaus, National Shrine of the Infant Jesus of Prague Church. (OKL)
Meekin's Neck, MD, Dorchester Co., St. Mary, Star of the Sea, c/o Cambridge, MD, St. Mary Refuge of Sinners Church. (WIL)
Meeteetsee, WY, Park Co., St. Theresa, c/o Cody, WY, St. Anthony Church. (CHY)
Meherrin, VA, Sacred Heart, c/o Crewe, VA, St. John the Baptist Church. (RIC)
Melendez, PR, Coamo Co., Our Lady of Fatima, c/o Coamo, PR, St. Blase Church. (PCE)
Melrose, MT, Silver Bow Co., St. John The Apostle, c/o Dillon, MT, St. Rose of Lima Church. (HEL)
Melrose, NM, Curry Co., c/o Clovis, NM, Sacred Heart Church. (SFE)
Melstone, MT, Our Lady of Mercy, c/o Roundup, MT, St. Benedict's Church. (GF)
Melvin, IL, St. George, c/o Gibson City, IL, Our Lady of Lourdes Church. (JOL)
Melvin, TX, McCullogh Co., St. Francis Xavier, c/o Brady, TX, St. Patrick's Church. (SAN)
Melvindale, MI, St. Thomas Indian Catholic Mission, c/o Melvindale, MI, St. Mary Magdalen Church. (DET)
Menlo Park, CA, St. Anthony, c/o [6] San Francisco, CA, St. Benedict Parish at St. Francis Xavier Church. (SFR)
Merced, CA, Merced Co., El Nido, c/o Merced, CA, Sacred Heart Church. (FRS)
Mercersburg, PA, St. Luke the Evangelist, c/o Greencastle, PA, St. Mark the Evangelist Church. (HBG)
Mereta, TX, Tom Green Co., Holy Family, c/o Wall, TX, St. Ambrose Church. (SAN)
Merkel, TX, Taylor Co., Our Mother of Mercy, c/o Sweetwater, TX, Holy Family Church. (SAN)
Merna, NE, Custer Co., St. Paul, c/o Anselmo, NE, St. Anselm's Church. (GI)
Merrimac, WI, Sauk Co., St. Mary, Health of the Sick, c/o Durward's Glen, WI, St. Camillus Church. (MAD)
Merriman, NE, St. Elizabeth, c/o Gordon, NE, St. Leo's Church. (GI)
Merryville, LA, Beauregard Parish, St. Bridget, c/o De Ridder, LA, St. Joseph's Church. (LKC)
Mertzon, TX, Irion Co., St. Peter's, c/o Eldorado, TX, Our Lady of Guadalupe Church. (SAN)
Mesa de Poleo, NM, c/o Abiquiu, NM, St. Thomas Apostle Church. (SFE)
Mesita, NM, Sacred Heart, c/o Laguna, NM, St. Joseph Church. (GLP)
Mesquite, NM, Our Lady of Perpetual Help, c/o San Miguel, NM, San Miguel Church. (LSC)
Metip, FM, c/o Tamoroi, FM, FM, Sacred Heart Church. (CI)
Metter, GA, Candler Co., Holy Family, c/o Swainsboro, GA, Holy Trinity Church. (SAV)
Mexico Beach, FL, Bay Co., Our Lady of Guadalupe, c/o Panama City, FL, St. Dominic Church. (PT)
Miami, FL, La Milagrosa, c/o [3] Miami, FL, Corpus Christi Church. (MIA)
Miami, FL, La Purisima, c/o [25] Miami, FL, St. Kieran Church. (MIA)
Miami, FL, Nuestra Senora de Altagracia, c/o [3] Miami, FL, Corpus Christi Church. (MIA)
Miami, FL, San Francisco y Santa Clara, c/o [3] Miami, FL, Corpus Christi Church. (MIA)
Miami, FL, San Juan Bautista, c/o [3] Miami, FL, Corpus Christi Church. (MIA)
Michigamme, MI, Marquette Co., St. Agnes, c/o Champion, MI, Sacred Heart Church. (MAR)
Michigan City, IN, c/o Louisville, KY, Maronite Catholic Community Church. (OLL)
Michigan City, IN, Maronite Catholic Community, c/o Hillside, IL, Our Lady of Lebanon Church. (OLL)
Mico, TX, St. Francis of Assisi (Medina Lake Chapel), c/o Castroville, TX, St. Louis Church. (SAT)
Middlebourne, WV, Tyler Co., St. Lawrence, c/o Paden City, WV, Mater Dolorosa Church. (WH)
Middleport, PA, Immaculate Heart of Mary Chapel, c/o New Philadelphia, PA, Sacred Heart Church. (ALN)
Middletown, IL, Logan Co., St. John the Baptist, c/o Elkhart, IL, St. Patrick Church. (PEO)
Middletown, PA, Susquehanna Co., St. Patrick, c/o Friendsville, PA, St. Francis Xavier's Church. (SCR)
Middleville, NY, St. Mary of the Assumption, c/o Newport, NY, St. John the Baptist Church. (ALB)
Midkiff, TX, Upton Co., St. Thomas, c/o St. Lawrence, TX, St. Lawrence Church. (SAN)
Midland, LA, St. Aloysius, c/o Morse, LA, Immaculate Conception Church. (LAF)
Midland, SD, Haakon Co., St. William, c/o Philip, SD, Sacred Heart Church. (RC)
Midwest, WY, Natrona Co., St. Francis Mission, c/o Casper, WY, St. Anthony of Padua Church. (CHY)
Milagro, NM, Guadalupe Co., c/o Santa Rosa, NM, St. Rose of Lima Church. (SFE)
Mildred, PA, Sullivan Co., St. Francis of Assisi, c/o Dushore, PA, St. Basil's Church. (SCR)
Milesville, SD, Haakon Co., St. Mary, c/o Philip, SD, Sacred Heart Church. (RC)
Milford Center, OH, Union Co., Sacred Heart, c/o Plain City, OH, St. Joseph Church. (COL)
Mill City, OR, Marion Co., St. Catherine of Siena, c/o Sublimity, OR, St. Boniface Church. (P)
Mill Creek, WI, St. John the Baptist, c/o Mazomanie, WI, St. Barnabas Church. (MAD)
Mill Rift, PA, Pike Co., Holy Family, c/o Matamoras, PA, St. Joseph's Church. (SCR)
Mill River, MA, Berkshire Co., Immaculate Conception, c/o Sheffield, MA, Our Lady of the Valley Church. (SPR)
Millen, GA, Jenkins Co., St. Bernadette, c/o Sylvania, GA, Our Lady of the Assumption Church. (SAV)
Millersview, TX, Concho Co., Our Lady of Guadalupe, c/o Eden, TX, St. Charles Church. (SAN)
Millerton, NY, Dutchess Co., St. Patrick, c/o Amenia, NY, Immaculate Conception Church. (NY)
Milligan, NE, Fillmore Co., St. Wenceslaus, c/o Friend, NE, St. Joseph's Church. (LIN)
Millington, MI, Tuscola Co., St. Bernard, c/o Vassar, MI, St. Frances Xavier Cabrini Church. (SAG)
Millsboro, DE, Sussex Co., Mary Mother of Peace, c/o Georgetown, DE, St. Michael the Archangel Church. (WIL)
Millwood, NY, Westchester Co., Our Lady of the Wayside, c/o Briarcliff Manor, NY, St. Theresa Church. (NY)
Milnor, ND, Sargent Co., St. Arnold, c/o Forman, ND, St. Mary's Church. (FAR)
Milo, ME, St. Paul, c/o Brownville Junction, ME, St. Francis Xavier Church. (PRT)
Milolii, HI, Hawaii Co., c/o Honaunau, HI, St. Benedict Church. (HON)
Milton, ND, Cavalier Co., St. Clothilde, c/o Wales, ND, St. Michael's Church. (FAR)
Milton, NH, Strafford Co., Sacred Heart, c/o Sanbornville, NH, St. Anthony Church. (MAN)
Minatare, NE, St. Mary, c/o Gering, NE, Christ the King Church. (GI)
Mineola, TX, Wood Co., St. Peter the Apostle, c/o Sulphur Springs, TX, St. James Church. (TYL)
Minerva, KY, Mason Co., St. James, c/o Brooksville, KY, St. James Church. (COV)
Minneiska, MN, Wabasha Co., St. Mary, c/o Rollingstone, MN, Holy Trinity Church. (WIN)
Minnesota Lake, MN, Fairibault Co., St. John the Baptist, c/o Easton, MN, Our Lady of Mount Carmel Church. (WIN)
Minnewauken, ND, Benson Co., St. James, c/o Leeds, ND, St. Vincent de Paul Church. (FAR)
Miraflores, PR, Chapel of Our Lady of Perpetual Help, c/o Anasco, PR, St. Anthony Abbot Church. (MGZ)
Mirando City, TX, Webb Co., St. Agnes, c/o Hebbronville, TX, Our Lady of Guadalupe Church. (CC)
Mirasol, PR, La Virgen, c/o Castaner, PR, Our Lady of the Miraculous Medal Church. (PCE)
Mission, SD, St. Thomas, c/o St. Francis, SD, Rosebud Reservation Church. (RC)
Mocanaqua, PA, Luzerne Co., Ascension, c/o Mocanaqua, PA, St. Mary, Our Lady of Perpetual Help Church. (SCR)
Moch, FM, c/o Lukunor, FM, Sacred Heart Church. (CI)
Mogollon, AZ, Our Lady, c/o Alpine, AZ, St. Helena Church. (GLP)
Mokelumne Hill, CA, Calaveras Co., St. Thomas Aquinas, c/o San Andreas, CA, St. Andrew Church. (STO)
Monacillos, PR, San Fernando, c/o [23] San Juan, PR, Inmaculado Corazon de Maria Church. (SJN)
Monarch, MT, St. Clement, c/o Belt, MT, St. Mark the Evangelist Church. (GF)
Moncla, LA, St. John the Baptist, c/o Fifth Ward, LA, Our Lady of Lourdes Church. (ALX)
Monet Ferry, LA, Holy Family, c/o Cloutierville, LA, St. John the Baptist Church. (ALX)
Monmouth, ME, Kennebec Co., St. Stanislaus, c/o Winthrop, ME, St. Francis Xavier Church. (PRT)
Mont Belvieu, TX, Chambers Co., Holy Trinity, c/o Anahuac, TX, Our Lady of Light Church. (BEA)
Monte Alto, TX, Hidalgo Co., Christ the King, c/o Elsa, TX, Sacred Heart Church. (BWN)
Monte Aplanado, NM, Mora Co., c/o Mora, NM, St. Gertrude Church. (SFE)
Monte Grande, PR, St. Jude Thaddeus, c/o Cabo Rojo, PR, St. Michael Church. (MGZ)
Monte Rio, CA, St. Catherine, c/o Guerneville, CA, St. Elizabeth Church. (SR)
Montecello, NM, St. Ignatius, c/o Truth or Consequences, NM, Our Lady of Perpetual Help Church. (LSC)
Monterey, MA, Berkshire Co., Our Lady of the Hills, c/o Sheffield, MA, Our Lady of the Valley Church. (SPR)
Montesano, WA, Grays Harbor Co., St. John, c/o Elma, WA, St. Joseph's Church. (SEA)
Montezuma, GA, Macon Co., St. Michael, c/o Americus, GA, St. Mary Church. (SAV)
Montezuma, IN, Parke Co., Immaculate Conception, c/o Rockville, IN, St. Joseph Church. (IND)
Montgomery, AL, Montgomery Co., Resurrection Catholic Mission, c/o [8] Montgomery, AL, Resurrection Catholic Church. (MOB)
Montgomery, LA, St. Patrick, c/o Colfax, LA, St. Joseph Church. (ALX)
Monticello, NY, Sullivan Co., St. Anne, c/o Monticello, NY, St. Peter Church. (NY)
Monticello, NY, Sullivan Co., St. Joseph, c/o Monticello, NY, St. Peter Church. (NY)
Monument, OR, St. Ann, c/o John Day, OR, St. Elizabeth's Church. (BAK)
Moody, TX, McLennan Co., Our Lady of San Juan, c/o McGregor, TX, St. Eugene Church. (AUS)
Moorcroft, WY, Crook Co., St. Patrick, c/o Gillette, WY, St. Matthew's Church. (CHY)
Moore, MT, St. Mathias, c/o Lewistown, MT, St. Leo's Church. (GF)
Moore, TX, St. Augustine, c/o Von Ormy, TX, St. Peter the Fisherman Church. (SAT)
Mooreland, OK, Woodward Co., Sacred Heart, c/o Woodward, OK, St. Peter's Church. (OKL)
Moorhead, MN, Clay Co., St. Thomas Newman Center, c/o Moorhead, MN, St. Joseph's Church. (CR)
Moquino, NM, Santa Rosalia, c/o Seboyeta, NM, Our Lady of Sorrows Church. (GLP)
Moral, TX, Nacogdoches Co., Immaculate Conception, c/o Nacogdoches, TX, Sacred Heart Church. (TYL)
Moravia, TX, Lavaca Co., Ascension of Our Lord, c/o St. John, TX, St. John the Baptist Church. (VIC)
Moretown, VT, Washington Co., St. Patrick, c/o Waitsfield, VT, Our Lady of the Snows Church. (BUR)
Morgan City, LA, St. Martin Parish, St. Rosalie, c/o Morgan City, LA, Holy Cross Church. (HT)
Morning View, KY, Kenton Co., Assumption of the Blessed Virgin, c/o Kenton, KY, St. Matthew Church. (COV)
Morongo Reservation, CA, Riverside Co., Indian Mission, c/o Banning, CA, Precious Blood Church. (SB)
Morrill, NE, St. Ann, c/o Mitchell, NE, St. Theresa's Church. (GI)
Morris, CT, Litchfield Co., Our Lady of Hope, c/o Bantam, CT, Our Lady of Grace Church. (HRT)
Morris, IN, Ripley Co., c/o Morris, IN, St. Anthony of Padua Church. (IND)
Morris, PA, Tioga Co., Sacred Heart, c/o Wellsboro, PA, St. Peter's Church. (SCR)
Morris Run, PA, Tioga Co., St. Joseph, c/o Blossburg, PA, St. Mary's Church. (SCR)
Morristown, SD, Corson Co., Sacred Heart, c/o Lemmon, SD, St. Mary's Church. (RC)
Moses, NM, Union Co., Sacred Heart, c/o Clayton, NM, St. Francis Xavier Church. (SFE)
Mosquero, NM, Harding Co., c/o Roy, NM, Holy Family-St. Joseph Church. (SFE)
Mount Carmel, ND, Cavalier Co., Our Lady of Mount Carmel, c/o Wales, ND, St. Michael's Church. (FAR)
Mount Holly, VT, Rutland Co., St. Mary, c/o Wallingford, VT, St. Patrick Church. (BUR)
Mount Hope, WI, St. Lawrence O'Toole, c/o Fennimore, WI, St. Mary Church. (MAD)
Mount Ida, AR, Montgomery Co., All Saints, c/o Mena, AR, St. Agnes Church. (LR)
Mount Olive, NC, Wayne Co., Posada Guadalupana, c/o Clinton, NC, Immaculate Conception Church. (R)
Mount Olive, NC, Wayne Co., St. Mary, c/o Clinton, NC, Immaculate Conception Church. (R)
Mount Palatine, IL, Putnam Co., Immaculate Conception, c/o Hennepin, IL, St. Patrick's Church. (PEO)
Mount Pulaski, IL, Logan Co., St. Thomas Aquinas, c/o Elkhart, IL, St. Patrick Church. (PEO)
Mount Vernon, TX, Franklin Co., Sacred Heart, c/o Pittsburg, TX, Holy Cross Church. (TYL)
Mount View, AR, Stone Co., St. Mary Mission, c/o Batesville, AR, St. Mary's Church. (LR)
Mountain Iron, MN, Sacred Heart, c/o Virginia, MN, Sacred Heart Church. (DUL)
Moxham, PA, Cambria Co., St. Anne's, c/o [17] Johnstown, PA, St. Therese of the Child Jesus Church. (ALT)
Mud Butte, SD, Meade Co., St. Joseph's Catholic Church, c/o Newell, SD, St. Mary Star of the Sea Church. (RC)
Mukilteo, WA, Snohomish Co., St. John Evangelist, c/o Everett, WA, St. Mary Magdalen Church. (SEA)
Mulvey, LA, St. David, c/o Gueydan, LA, St. Peter Church. (LAF)
Mumford, NY, Monroe Co., St. Patrick, c/o Caledonia, NY, St. Columba Church. (ROC)
Murdo, SD, Jones Co., St. Martin of Tours, c/o Presho, SD, Christ the King Church. (RC)
Murphys, CA, Murphys Co., St. Patrick, c/o Angels Camp, CA, St. Patrick Church. (STO)
Murray City, OH, Hocking/Athens, St. Philip Neri, c/o Logan, OH, St. John Church. (COL)
Musquiz, Mexico, Coahuila Co., Desert Apostolate Mission, c/o [6] Laredo, TX, San Augustine Church. (CC)
Musselshell, MT, St. Honorata, c/o Roundup, MT, St. Benedict's Church. (GF)

Myrtle Point, OR, Coos Co., Sts. Ann and Michael, c/o Coquille, OR, Holy Name Church. (P)

N

Naco, AZ, Cochise Co., St. Michael, c/o Bisbee, AZ, St. Patrick Church. (TUC)
Nags Head, NC, Holy Trinity, c/o Kill Devil Hills, NC, Holy Redeemer Church. (R)
Naguabo, PR, Naguabo Co., Bo. Daguao, c/o Ceiba, PR, San Antonio de Padua Church. (CGS)
Naknek, AK, St. Theresa, c/o Dillingham, AK, Holy Rosary Church. (ANC)
Nama, FM, c/o Lukunor, FM, Sacred Heart Church. (CI)
Nambe, NM, Santa Fe Co., Nambe Indian Pueblo, c/o Pojoaque, NM, N.S. de Guadalupe del Valle de Pojoaque Church. (SFE)
Namoluk, FM, c/o Lukunor, FM, Sacred Heart Church. (CI)
Nanticoke, PA, Luzerne Co., Holy Child, c/o [2] Nanticoke, PA, Holy Trinity Church. (SCR)
Nanticoke, PA, Luzerne Co., St. Joseph, c/o Wanamie, PA, St. Mary's Church. (SCR)
Naper, NE, Boyd Co., Sacred Heart, c/o Butte, NE, SS. Peter and Paul Church. (OM)
Naples, FL, c/o North Fort Myers, FL, All Saints Byzantine Catholic Church. (PSC)
Naponee, NE, Franklin Co., St. Mary, c/o Alma, NE, St. Joseph's Church. (LIN)
Nara Visa, NM, Quay Co., c/o Tucumcari, NM, St. Anne Church. (SFE)
Naranjo, PR, Santa Marta, c/o Salinas, PR, Our Lady of Monserrat Church. (PCE)
Naranjo, PR, St. Anthony, c/o Yauco, PR, Holy Rossary Church. (PCE)
Naranjo Militar, PR, Ntra. Sra. de Monserrate, c/o Aguada, PR, St. Francis of Assisi Church. (MGZ)
Naranjo-Guanabanas, PR, San Pablo, c/o Aguada, PR, St. Francis of Assisi Church. (MGZ)
Naschitti, NM, St. Anthony, c/o Tohatchi, NM, St. Mary Church. (GLP)
Nashua, MT, Queen of the Angels, c/o Glasgow, MT, St. Raphael's Church. (GF)
Nashville, AR, Howard Co., St. Martin's, c/o De Queen, AR, St. Barbara's Church. (LR)
Nashville, GA, Berrien Co., St. Mary, c/o Lakeland, GA, Queen of Peace Church. (SAV)
Nashville, MI, St. Cyril, c/o Hastings, MI, St. Rose of Lima Church. (KAL)
Natalia, TX, St. John Bosco, c/o Lytle, TX, St. Andrew Church. (SAT)
Natural Bridge, NY, St. Henry, c/o Carthage, NY, St. James Minor Church. (OG)
Naubinway, MI, Mackinac Co., St. Stephen, c/o Engadine, MI, Our Lady of Lourdes Church. (MAR)
Naytahwaush, MN, Mahnomen Co., St. Anne, c/o Waubun, MN, St. Ann Church. (CR)
Near Hamlin, TX, Fisher Co., Sacred Heart, c/o Rotan, TX, St. Joseph Church. (LUB)
Nebish, MN, Beltrami Co., St. John, c/o Red Lake, MN, St. Mary's Mission Church. (CR)
Neche, ND, Pembina Co., SS. Nereus and Achilleus, c/o Cavalier, ND, St. Bridget's Church. (FAR)
Nederland, CO, Boulder Co., St. Rita, c/o [1] Boulder, CO, Sacred Heart of Jesus Church. (DEN)
Nekoma, ND, Cavalier Co., St. Edwards, c/o Langdon, ND, St. Alphonsus Church. (FAR)
Neligh, NE, Antelope Co., St. Theresa, c/o Neligh, NE, St. Francis Church. (OM)
Nelson, NE, Nuckolls Co., Sacred Heart, c/o Superior, NE, St. Joseph's Church. (LIN)
Nenzel, NE, St. Mary, c/o Valentine, NE, St. Nicholas Church. (GI)
Nephi, UT, Utah Co., Our Lady of Victory Mission, c/o Payson, UT, San Andres Church. (SLC)
Nett Lake, MN, St. Louis Co., Immaculate Conception, c/o Duluth, MN, Indian Missions Church. (DUL)
Nevis, MN, Hubbard Co., Immaculate Conception, c/o Akeley, MN, St. John's Church. (CR)
New Almelo, KS, Norton Co., St. Joseph's Church, c/o Norton, KS, St. Francis of Assisi Church. (SAL)
New Boston, IL, Mercer Co., St. Theresa of the Little Flower, c/o Aledo, IL, St. Catherine's Church. (PEO)
New Boston, NY, Lewis Co., SS. Peter and Paul, c/o Copenhagen, NY, St. Mary Church. (OG)
New Deal, TX, Lubbock Co., Our Lady Queen of Apostles, c/o [7] Lubbock, TX, St. Patrick Church. (LUB)
New Dorp Beach, NY, Richmond Co., Our Lady of Lourdes, c/o [219] Staten Island, NY, Our Lady, Queen of Peace Church. (NY)
New Douglas, IL, Madison Co., St. Ubaldus, c/o Livingston, IL, Sacred Heart Church. (SFD)
New Galilee, PA, Beaver Co., St. Ann, c/o Darlington, PA, St. Rose of Lima Church. (PIT)
New Germany, PA, Cambria Co., Immaculate Conception, c/o Summerhill, PA, St. John Church. (ALT)
New Leipzig, ND, Grant Co., St. John the Baptist, c/o Mott, ND, St. Vincent de Paul Church. (BIS)
New Marion, IN, Ripley Co., St. Mary Magdalen, c/o Osgood, IN, St. John Church. (IND)
New Middletown, IN, Harrison Co., Most Precious Blood, c/o Corydon, IN, St. Joseph Church. (IND)
New Milford, PA, Susquehanna Co., St. John, c/o Great Bend, PA, St. Lawrence's Church. (SCR)
New Orleans, LA, Orleans Civil Parish, Our Lady of Guadalupe, c/o [1] New Orleans, LA, St. Louis Cathedral Church. (NO)
New Orleans, LA, Orleans Civil Parish, Our Lady of La Vang, c/o [14] New Orleans, LA, Mary, Queen of Vietnam Church. (NO)
New Orleans, LA, Jefferson Civil Parish, St. Joseph, c/o [2] Marrero, LA, St. Agnes Le Thi Thanh Church. (NO)
New River, AZ, Maricopa Co., Good Shepherd Mission, c/o [16] Phoenix, AZ, St. Luke Church. (PHX)
New Village, NJ, Warren Co., St. Christopher, c/o Phillipsburg, NJ, SS. Philip and James Church. (MET)
New York, NY, Richmond Co., Christ the King, c/o [214] Staten Island, NY, St. Mary of the Assumption Church. (NY)
New York, NY, New York Co., Gift of Love, c/o [120] New York, NY, St. Veronica Church. (NY)
Newald, WI, Argonne Co., St. Hubert, c/o Laona, WI, St. Leonard Church. (GB)
Newfields, NH, Rockingham Co., Sacred Heart, c/o Newmarket, NH, St. Mary Church. (MAN)
Newfound Lake, NH, Grafton Co., Our Lady of Grace, c/o Bristol, NH, St. Timothy Church. (MAN)
Newfoundland, PA, Wayne Co., St. Anthony of Padua, c/o Gouldsboro, PA, St. Rita Church. (SCR)
Newkirk, NM, Guadalupe Co., c/o Santa Rosa, NM, St. Rose of Lima Church. (SFE)
Newport, AR, Jackson Co., St. Cecilia, c/o Batesville, AR, St. Mary's Church. (LR)
Newton, MS, St. Anne, c/o Forest, MS, St. Michael Church. (JKS)
Newton, PA, Lackawanna Co., St. Benedict, c/o Clarks Summit, PA, Our Lady of the Snows Church. (SCR)
Newton Falls, NY, St. Lawrence Co., St. Anthony of Padua, c/o Star Lake, NY, St. Hubert Church. (OG)
Ngatik, FM, c/o Kolonia, FM, Our Lady of Mercy Church. (CI)
Ngcheangl, FM, c/o Koror, FM, Sacred Heart Church. (CI)
Ngulu, FM, c/o Ulithi & Neighboring Islands, FM, Queen of Heaven Church. (CI)
Nicasio, CA, St. Mary, c/o Lagunitas, CA, St. Cecilia Church. (SFR)
Nicolaus, CA, Sutter Co., St. Boniface, c/o Lincoln, CA, St. Joseph Church. (SAC)
Niland, CA, Imperial Co., Immaculate Heart of Mary, c/o Calipatria, CA, St. Patrick Church. (SD)
Ninilchik, AK, St. Peter, c/o Homer, AK, St. John the Baptist Church. (ANC)
Nisswa, MN, St. Christopher's, c/o Pequot Lakes, MN, St. Alice's Church. (DUL)
No Water, SD, Shannon Co., Our Lady of Good Counsel, c/o Pine Ridge, SD, Holy Rosary Church. (RC)
Noble, LA, St. Catherine, c/o Noble, LA, St. Ann Church. (SHP)
Noel, MO, McDonald Co., Nativity of Our Lord, c/o Neosho, MO, St. Canera Church. (SPC)
Noonan, ND, Divide Co., St. Luke, c/o Crosby, ND, St. Patrick Church. (BIS)
Norbone, MO, Carroll Co., Sacred Heart, c/o Richmond, MO, Immaculate Conception Church. (KC)
Norcross, GA, Gwinnett Co., Mary, Our Queen, c/o Dunwoody, GA, All Saints Catholic Church. (ATL)
Nordheim, TX, St. Ann's, c/o Yorktown, TX, Holy Cross Church. (VIC)
Norias Ranch, TX, Santa Elena, c/o Sarita, TX, Our Lady of Guadalupe Church. (CC)
Norris, SD, Sacred Heart, c/o St. Francis, SD, Rosebud Reservation Church. (RC)
North Brookfield, NY, St. Mary, c/o Waterville, NY, St. Bernard Church. (SY)
North Conway, NH, St. Charles Borromeo, c/o North Conway, NH, Our Lady of the Mountains Church. (MAN)
North Creek, OH, Putnam Co., St. Joseph, c/o New Bavaria, OH, Sacred Heart of Jesus Church. (TOL)
North East, MD, Cecil Co., St. Jude, c/o Elkton, MD, Immaculate Conception Church. (WIL)
North Eastham, MA, Barnstable Co., Church of the Visitation, c/o Orleans, MA, St. Joan of Arc Church. (FR)
North Fork, CA, Madera Co., St. Joseph the Worker, c/o Bass Lake, CA, St. Dominic Savio Church. (FRS)
North Greenbush, NY, Rensselaer Co., Van Rensselaer Manor, County Welfare Home, c/o [8] Troy, NY, St. Michael the Archangel Church. (ALB)
North Haven, ME, Our Lady of Peace, c/o Camden, ME, Our Lady of Good Hope Church. (PRT)
North Hero, VT, Grand Isle Co., St. Benedict Joseph Labre, c/o South Hero, VT, St. Rose of Lima Church. (BUR)
North Hollywood, CA, Los Angeles Co., Our Lady of Zapopan, c/o Sun Valley, CA, Our Lady of the Holy Rosary Church. (LA)
North Platte, NE, Lincoln Co., St. Elizabeth Ann Seton, c/o Curtis, NE, St. James Church. (LIN)
North Powder, OR, St. Anthony, c/o [1] Baker, OR, Cathedral of St. Francis De Sales. (BAK)
North Pownal, VT, Our Lady of Lourdes, c/o Bennington, VT, Sacred Heart-St. Francis de Sales Church. (BUR)
North Salem, NY, Westchester Co., St. John, c/o Croton Falls, NY, St. Joseph Church. (NY)
North San Juan, CA, Nevada Co., St. John, c/o Downieville, CA, Immaculate Conception Church. (SAC)
North Swanzey, NH, St. Stephen, c/o West Swanzey, NH, St. Anthony Church. (MAN)
North Truro, MA, Barnstable Co., Our Lady of Perpetual Help, c/o Wellfleet, MA, Our Lady of Lourdes Church. (FR)
Northland, MI, Marquette Co., St. Joseph, c/o Gwinn, MI, St. Anthony Church. (MAR)
Northome, MN, Koochiching Co., St. Michael, c/o Blackduck, MN, St. Ann's Church. (CR)
Northwood, NH, Rockingham Co., St. Joseph, c/o Pittsfield, NH, Our Lady of Lourdes Church. (MAN)
Norton, VT, Essex Co., St. Bernard, c/o Island Pond, VT, St. James the Greater Church. (BUR)
Nortonville, ND, LaMoure Co., Holy Spirit, c/o Edgeley, ND, Transfiguration Church. (FAR)
Norwich, VT, Windsor Co., St. Francis of Assisi, c/o Bradford, VT, Our Lady of Perpetual Help Church. (BUR)
Novinger, MO, Adair Co., St. Rose of Lima, c/o Kirksville, MO, Mary Immaculate Church. (JC)
Nowata, OK, Nowata Co., St. Catherine, c/o Bartlesville, OK, St. James Church. (TLS)
Noxon, MT, c/o Thompson Falls, MT, St. William Church. (HEL)
Nuangola, PA, Luzerne Co., St. Ann, c/o Mountaintop, PA, St. Jude's Church. (SCR)
Nucla, CO, Montrose Co., Our Lady of Sorrows, c/o Telluride, CO, St. Patrick Church. (PBL)
Nuremberg, PA, Luzerne Co., St. Joseph, c/o Weston, PA, Sacred Heart Church. (SCR)

O

O'Connor, NE, Our Lady of the Visitation, c/o Greeley, NE, Sacred Heart Church. (GI)
O'Connor Ranch, TX, Refugio Co., St. Dennis, c/o Tivoli, TX, Our Lady of Guadalupe Church. (CC)
Oak Beach, NY, Suffolk Co., c/o Babylon, NY, St. Joseph's Church. (RVC)
Oak Creek, CO, Routt Co., St. Martin Church, c/o Steamboat Springs, CO, Holy Name Church. (DEN)
Oak Forest, IN, Franklin Co., St. Cecilia of Rome, c/o St. Mary-of-the-Rock, IN, St. Mary-of-the-Rock Church. (IND)
Oak Grove, MO, Jackson Co., St. Jude the Apostle, c/o Odessa, MO, St. George Church. (KC)
Oak Ridge, MN, Winona Co., Immaculate Conception, c/o Rollingstone, MN, Holy Trinity Church. (WIN)
Oakland, CA, Alameda Co., Mary Help of Christians, c/o [9] Oakland, CA, St. Elizabeth's Church. (OAK)
Oblong, IL, Crawford Co., St. Valentine's Chapel, c/o Ste. Marie, IL, St. Mary of the Assumption Church. (SFD)
Ocala National Forest, FL, Marion Co., St. Joseph of the Forest, c/o [2] Ocala, FL, Our Lady of the Springs Church. (ORL)
Ocate, NM, Mora Co., c/o Wagon Mound, NM, Santa Clara Church. (SFE)
Ocean City, MD, Worcester Co., Holy Saviour, c/o Ocean City, MD, St. Mary, Star of the Sea Church. (WIL)
Ocean Pines, MD, St. John Neumann, c/o Ocean City, MD, St. Luke and St. Andrew Church. (WIL)
Oceano, CA, St. Francis of Assisi, c/o Arroyo Grande, CA, St. Patrick Church. (MRY)
Oconto, NE, St. Mary, c/o Stapleton, NE, St. John the Evangelist Church. (GI)
Odell, NE, Gage Co., St. Mary's, c/o Wymore, NE, St. Mary's Church. (LIN)
Odessa, TX, Our Lady of San Juan, c/o [3] Odessa, TX, St. Elizabeth Ann Seton Church. (SAN)
Odessa, TX, Ector Co., St. Martin de Porres, c/o [4] Odessa, TX, St. Joseph Church. (SAN)
Oelrichs, SD, Fall River Co., St. Martin, c/o Hot Springs, SD, St. Anthony's Church. (RC)
Ogema, MN, Becker Co., Most Holy Redeemer, c/o White Earth, MN, St. Benedict Church. (CR)
Ogilvie, MN, Kanabec Co., St. Kathryn, c/o Mora, MN, St. Mary's Church. (SCL)
Oglala, SD, Shannon Co., Our Lady of Sioux, c/o Pine Ridge, SD, Holy Rosary Church. (RC)
Ogunquit, ME, All Saints, c/o Wells, ME, St. Mary Church. (PRT)
Oilton, TX, Webb Co., St. Bridget, c/o Hebbronville, TX, Our Lady of Guadalupe Church. (CC)
Ojo Caliente, NM, Rio Arriba Co., c/o El Rito, NM, San Juan Nepomuceno Church. (SFE)
Ojo Feliz, NM, Mora Co., c/o Mora, NM, St. Gertrude Church. (SFE)
Ojo Sarco, NM, Rio Arriba Co., Santo Tomas, c/o

Chimayo, NM, Holy Family Church. (SFE)
Okemah, OK, Okfuska Co., St. Teresa, c/o Holdenville, OK, St. Stephen's Church. (TLS)
Okmulgee, OK, Okmulgee Co., Uganda Martyrs Beach, c/o Okmulgee, OK, St. Anthony's Church. (TLS)
Okolona, MS, Chickasaw Co., St. Theresa, c/o Aberdeen, MS, St. Francis of Assisi Church. (JKS)
Okreek, SD, St. Peter, c/o St. Francis, SD, Rosebud Reservation Church. (RC)
Okreek, SD, Todd Co., St. Peter's, c/o Mission, SD, St. Thomas the Apostle Church. (RC)
Olathe, CO, Montrose Co., Our Lady of Fatima, c/o Montrose, CO, St. Mary Church. (PBL)
Old River, LA, St. Anne, c/o Isle Brevelle, LA, St. Augustine's Church. (ALX)
Old Washington, TX, Washington Co., Blessed Virgin Mary, c/o Brenham, TX, St. Mary of the Immaculate Conception Church. (AUS)
Olga, ND, Cavalier Co., Our Lady of the Sacred Heart, c/o Walhalla, ND, St. Boniface's Church. (FAR)
Olivier, LA, St. Jude, c/o [4] New Iberia, LA, St. Edward Church. (LAF)
Olla, LA, St. William, c/o Winnfield, LA, Our Lady of Lourdes Church. (ALX)
Olmito, TX, Our Heavenly Father, c/o Los Fresnos, TX, St. Cecilia Church. (BWN)
Olton, TX, Lamb Co., St. Peter Apostle, c/o Hale Center, TX, St. Theresa's Church. (LUB)
Olympic Valley, CA, Placer Co., Queen of the Snows, c/o Tahoe City, CA, Corpus Christi Church. (SAC)
On the Creek, SD, Shannon Co., St. Paul, c/o Porcupine, SD, Church of Christ the King. (RC)
Onarga, IL, Iroquois Co., Our Lady of Guadalupe, c/o Gilman, IL, Immaculate Conception Church. (JOL)
Onari, FM, St. Cecilia, c/o Fefan, FM, Sacred Heart Church. (CI)
Onari, FM, St. Cecilia, c/o Ulul, FM, Sacred Heart Church. (CI)
Oneap, FM, c/o Lukunor, FM, Sacred Heart Church. (CI)
Oneida, PA, Schuykill, St. John the Baptist, c/o Sheppton, PA, St. Joseph Church. (ALN)
Ono, FM, Sacred Heart, c/o Fefan, FM, Sacred Heart Church. (CI)
Ono, FM, Sacred Heart, c/o Ulul, FM, Sacred Heart Church. (CI)
Onondaga, NY, St. Peter, c/o Onondaga Hill, NY, St. Michael Church. (SY)
Onset, MA, St. Mary Star of the Sea, c/o Buzzards Bay, MA, St. Margaret Church. (FR)
Ookala, HI, St. James, c/o Papaaloa, HI, St. Anthony Church. (HON)
Oquawka, IL, Henderson Co., St. Andrew, c/o Monmouth, IL, Immaculate Conception Church. (PEO)
Oracle, AZ, Pinal Co., St. Helen, c/o San Manuel, AZ, St. Bartholomew Church. (TUC)
Orange Grove, TX, Jim Wells, St. Pius X, c/o Orange Grove, TX, St. John of the Cross Church. (CC)
Orange Lake, NY, Orange Co., Our Lady of the Lake, c/o [1] Newburgh, NY, St. Patrick Church. (NY)
Ordway, CO, Crowley Co., St. Peter Church, c/o Rocky Ford, CO, St. Peter Church. (PBL)
Orick, CA, St. Thomas, c/o McKinleyville, CA, Christ the King Church. (SR)
Orlando, FL, Orange Co., St. Ignatius Kim Korean Mission, c/o [1] Orlando, FL, St. James Cathedral Church. (ORL)
Orrin, ND, Pierce Co., Sacred Heart, c/o Balta, ND, Our Lady of Mount Carmel Church. (FAR)
Orrville, AL, Dallas Co., Mission of Immaculate Conception, c/o Camden, AL, St. Joseph Church. (MOB)
Ortiga, PR, Bauta Abajo Co., San Mateo, c/o Villalba, PR, Our Lady Mother of Divine Providence Church. (PCE)
Orting, WA, Pierce Co., SS. Cosmas and Damian, c/o Sumner, WA, St. Andrew Church. (SEA)
Ortiz, CO, San Juan Nepomuceno y San Cayetano, c/o Conejos, CO, Our Lady of Guadalupe Church. (PBL)
Osceola, MO, St. Clair Co., St. Catherine's, c/o Clinton, MO, Holy Rosary Church. (KC)
Osceola, NE, Polk Co., St. Mary's, c/o Osceola, NE, St. Vincent's Church. (LIN)
Oshkosh, NE, St. Elizabeth, c/o Chappell, NE, St. Joseph's Church. (GI)
Oslo, MN, Marshall Co., St. Joseph, c/o Warren, MN, SS. Peter and Paul Church. (CR)
Osnabrock, ND, Cavalier Co., St. Joseph, c/o Wales, ND, St. Michael's Church. (FAR)
Otis, MA, Berkshire Co., St. Mary of the Lakes, c/o Lee, MA, St. Mary's Church. (SPR)
Otisco, NY, St. Patrick, c/o Tully, NY, St. Leo Church. (SY)
Oto, IA, Woodbury Co., St. Mary's, c/o Mapleton, IA, St. Mary's Church. (SC)
Otter Lake, NY, St. Mary of the Snows, c/o Forestport, NY, St. Patrick Church. (SY)
Outlook, MT, St. Boniface, c/o Plentywood, MT, St. Joseph's Church. (GF)
Overton, NE, Dawson Co., Holy Rosary, c/o Elm Creek, NE, Immaculate Conception Church. (GI)
Overton, PA, Sullivan Co., St. Francis Xavier, c/o Dushore, PA, St. Basil's Church. (SCR)
Overton, TX, Rusk/Smith Co., Our Lady Queen of Angels, c/o Kilgore, TX, Christ the King Church. (TYL)
Owasco, NY, Cayuga Co., St. Ann, c/o [2] Auburn, NY, Sacred Heart Church. (ROC)
Owenton, KY, Owen Co., St. Edward, c/o Warsaw, KY, St. Joseph Church. (COV)
Owingsville, KY, Bath Co., St. Julie Billiart, c/o West Liberty, KY, Prince of Peace Church. (LEX)
Owl's Head, NY, Franklin Co., St. Joseph, c/o Chasm Falls, NY, St. Helen Church. (OG)
Oxford, NE, Furnas Co., St. Michael's, c/o Orleans, NE, St. Mary's Church. (LIN)
Oxnard, CA, Ventura Co., Christ the King, c/o [3] Oxnard, CA, Our Lady of Guadalupe Parish Church. (LA)

P

Paauilo, HI, St. Joseph, c/o Honokaa, HI, Our Lady of Lourdes Church. (HON)
Packing Town, OK, Oklahoma Co., Our Lady of Guadalupe, c/o [14] Oklahoma City, OK, Our Lady of Mount Carmel and St. Therese Little Flower Church. (OKL)
Paducah, TX, Cottle Co., St. Elizabeth, c/o Floydada, TX, St. Mary Magdalen Church. (LUB)
Page, ND, Cass Co., St. James, c/o Hope, ND, St. Agatha's Church. (FAR)
Pageland, SC, Chesterfield Co., St. Ernest, c/o Cheraw, SC, St. Peter's Church. (CHR)
Pago Pago, AS, c/o [2] Pago Pago, AS, Co-Cathedral of St. Joseph the Worker. (SPP)
Pagosa Junction, CO, Archuleta Co., St. John Baptist, c/o Pagosa Springs, CO, Immaculate Heart of Mary Church. (PBL)
Paguate, NM, St. Elizabeth, c/o Laguna, NM, St. Joseph Church. (GLP)
Painesdale, MI, Houghton Co., Sacred Heart, c/o Chassell, MI, St. Anne Church. (MAR)
Paisley, OR, St. John the Apostle, c/o Lakeview, OR, St. Patrick's Church. (BAK)
Palisade, CO, Mesa Co., St. Ann, c/o Grand Junction, CO, Immaculate Heart of Mary Church. (PBL)
Palisade, NE, Hitchcock Co., Holy Family, c/o Trenton, NE, St. James Church. (LIN)
Palito Blanco, TX, Jim Wells Co., St. Joseph, c/o San Diego, TX, St. Francis de Paula Church. (CC)
Palma Escrita, PR, N.S. de Fatima, c/o Las Marias, PR, Immaculate Heart of Mary Church. (MGZ)
Palma Sola, PR, Ntra. Sra. de la Asuncion, c/o [5] Canovanas, PR, San Jose Church. (SJN)
Palmarejo, PR, Coamo Co., Sacred Heart of Mary, c/o Coamo, PR, St. Blase Church. (PCE)
Palmas, PR, St. Gerard, c/o Guayama, PR, St. Anthony of Padua Church. (PCE)
Palmer, IA, Pocahontas Co., St. Joseph's, c/o Pomeroy, IA, St. Mary's Church. (SC)
Palmer, MI, Marquette Co., Our Lady Perpetual Help, c/o Negaunee, MI, St. Paul Church. (MAR)
Palmer, PR, La Milagrosa, c/o Palmer, PR, Cristo Rey Church. (SJN)
Palmer, PR, Ntra. Sra. de la Providencia, c/o Palmer, PR, Cristo Rey Church. (SJN)
Palmetto, LA, St. Thomas, c/o Melville, LA, St. John the Evangelist Church. (LAF)
Palo Blanco, NM, Colfax Co., c/o Springer, NM, St. Joseph Church. (SFE)
Palolo, HI, Honolulu Co., St. James, c/o [11] Honolulu, HI, St. Patrick Church. (HON)
Panama, NY, Our Lady of the Snows, c/o French Creek, NY, St. Matthias Church. (BUF)
Panguitch, UT, Garfield Co., St. Gertrude, c/o Cedar City, UT, Christ the King Church. (SLC)
Paoli, IN, Orange Co., Our Lord Jesus Christ the King, c/o French Lick, IN, Our Lady of the Springs Church. (IND)
Paoli, WI, St. William, c/o Verona, WI, St. Andrew Church. (MAD)
Paplin, NE, Howard Co., Our Lady of Mt. Carmel, c/o Ashton, NE, St. Francis Church. (GI)
Parachute, CO, Garfield Co., St. Brendan, c/o Rifle, CO, St. Mary's Church. (DEN)
Paradise, MI, Chippewa Co., Our Lady of Victory, c/o Newberry, MI, St. Gregory Church. (MAR)
Paradise Valley, NV, Humboldt Co., St. Alphonsus, c/o Winnemucca, NV, St. Paul Church. (RNO)
Paraje, NM, St. Mary Margaret, c/o Laguna, NM, St. Joseph Church. (GLP)
Paramount, CA, Catholic Korean Community of St. Raphael (Downey & Alondra), c/o Paramount, CA, Our Lady of the Rosary Church. (LA)
Parcelas de Marueno, PR, Ponce Co., San Antonio de Padua, c/o [10] Ponce, PR, La Santisima Trinidad Church. (PCE)
Parcelas Soledad, PR, Sta. Teresita, c/o [4] Mayaquez, PR, Church De El Buen Pastor. (MGZ)
Parcelas Vazquez, PR, Esp. Santo, c/o Salinas, PR, Our Lady of Monserrat Church. (PCE)
Pardoe, PA, Mercer Co., St. Hermenegild, c/o Mercer, PA, Immaculate Heart Church. (E)
Parem, FM, c/o Fefan, FM, Sacred Heart Church. (CI)
Paris, MI, Mecosta Co., St. Anne, c/o Reed City, MI, St. Philip Neri Church. (GR)
Paris Creek, CA, c/o Alturas, CA, Sacred Heart Church. (SAC)
Parishville, NY, St. Lawrence Co., St. Michael, c/o Colton, NY, St. Patrick Church. (OG)
Parks, LA, St. Louis, c/o Parks, LA, St. Joseph Church. (LAF)
Parmelee, SD, St. Agnes, c/o St. Francis, SD, Rosebud Reservation Church. (RC)
Parque Encuestra, PR, S. Francisco de Asis, c/o [18] Carolina, PR, Cristo Rey Church. (SJN)
Parsons, TN, Decatur Co., St. Regina, c/o Lexington, TN, St. Andrew Church. (MEM)
Parsons, WV, Tucker Co., Our Lady of Mercy, c/o Thomas, WV, St. Thomas Aquinas Church. (WH)
Pastillito, Manzanilla, PR, Our Lady of Carmel, c/o Juana Diaz, PR, Santa Teresita Church. (PCE)
Pastillo, PR, Cotopaso Co., Santiago Apostol, c/o Juana Diaz, PR, St. Raymond Nonato Church. (PCE)
Pastura, NM, Guadalupe Co., c/o Vaughn, NM, St. Mary Church. (SFE)
Patch Grove, WI, St. John, c/o Bloomington, WI, St. Mary Church. (MAD)
Patrick Springs, VA, Church of the Risen Lord, c/o Woodlawn, VA, St. Joseph's Church. (RIC)
Patten, ME, St. Paul, c/o Island Falls, ME, St. Agnes Church. (PRT)
Paul Smiths, NY, Franklin Co., St. Gabriel, c/o Lake Clear, NY, St. John in the Wilderness Church. (OG)
Pava'ia'i, AS, c/o [3] Pago Pago, AS, Church of St. Paul. (SPP)
Pawnee, TX, Bee Co., Our Lady of Guadalupe, c/o Three Rivers, TX, Sacred Heart Church. (CC)
Paxton, NE, St. Patrick, c/o Sutherland, NE, Sacred Heart Church. (GI)
Peapack, NJ, Somerset Co., St. Brigid, c/o Far Hills, NJ, St. Elizabeth Church. (MET)
Pecan Island, LA, Sacred Heart, c/o Cow Island, LA, St. Anne Church. (LAF)
Peck, MI, Sanilac Co., St. John, c/o Croswell, MI, St. Patrick Church. (SAG)
Pedro Garcia, PR, Coamo Co., Miraculous Virgin, c/o Coamo, PR, St. Blase Church. (PCE)
Peerless, MT, St. Ann, c/o Scobey, MT, St. Philip Bonitus Church. (GF)
Pejepscot, ME, Topsham Co., St. Andrew, c/o Brunswick, ME, St. John the Baptist Church. (PRT)
Pelican, AK, c/o [1] Juneau, AK, Cathedral of the Nativity of The Blessed Virgin Mary. (JUN)
Pellejas, PR, Santa Rosa, c/o Adjuntas, PR, St. Joachim Church. (PCE)
Pellets Island (New Hampton), NY, Orange Co., St. Andrew Bobola, c/o Florida, NY, St. Joseph Church. (NY)
Pembroke, GA, Bryan Co., Holy Cross, c/o Claxton, GA, St. Christopher Church. (SAV)
Pembroke, ME, St. John the Evangelist, c/o Eastport, ME, St. Joseph Church. (PRT)
Pengilly, MN, St. Kevin, c/o Nashwauk, MN, St. Cecilia's Church. (DUL)
Penitas, TX, St. Anthony, c/o La Joya, TX, Our Lady, Queen of Angels Church. (BWN)
Pennington, MN, St. Charles, c/o Cass Lake, MN, St. Charles Church. (DUL)
Pensacola, FL, Escambia Co., Church of Our Savior, c/o [13] Pensacola, FL, St. Paul Church. (PT)
Pentwater, MI, St. Vincent, c/o Weare Twp., MI, St. Joseph's Church. (GR)
Pep, TX, Hockley Co., St. Philip Neri, c/o Morton, TX, St. Ann Church. (LUB)
Perkinsville, NY, Steuben Co., Sacred Heart of Jesus, c/o Cohocton, NY, St. Pius V Church. (ROC)
Perrineville, NJ, Monmouth Co., St. Joseph, c/o Englishtown, NJ, Our Lady of Mercy Church. (TR)
Perrinton, MI, Gratiot Co., St. Martin De Porres, c/o Ithaca, MI, St. Paul the Apostle Church. (SAG)
Perry, MO, Monroe Co., St. Frances Cabrini, c/o Perry, MO, St. William Church. (JC)
Perry, WI, Holy Redeemer, c/o Mount Horeb, WI, St. Ignatius Church. (MAD)
Perry Park, KY, Owen Co., Transfiguration, c/o Carrollton, KY, St. John the Evangelist Church. (COV)
Perryville, KY, Boyle Co., St. Mary, c/o Harrodsburg, KY, St. Andrew Church. (LEX)
Peru, NE, St. Clara, c/o Auburn, NE, St. Joseph's Church. (LIN)
Pescadero, CA, San Mateo Co., St. Anthony, c/o Half Moon Bay, CA, Our Lady of the Pillar Church. (SFR)
Petaca, NM, Taos Co., c/o El Rito, NM, San Juan Nepomuceno Church. (SFE)
Peterstown, WV, Monroe Co., St. Peter, c/o Princeton, WV, Sacred Heart Church. (WH)
Petersville, MD, Frederick Co., St. Mary's, c/o Brunswick, MD, St. Francis of Assisi Church. (BAL)
Petit Mamou, LA, St. Jules, c/o Evangeline, LA, St. Joseph Church. (LAF)
Petrolia, CA, St. Patrick, c/o Ferndale, CA, Church of

the Assumption. (SR)
Petronila, TX, Nueces Co., St. Vivian, c/o [7] Corpus Christi, TX, Our Lady of the Rosary Church. (CC)
Phelps, KY, Pike Co., Jesus of the Mountains Catholic Church, c/o Pikeville, KY, St. Francis of Assisi Church. (LEX)
Philadelphia, MS, St. Theresa, c/o Philadelphia, MS, Holy Rosary Church. (JKS)
Philadelphia, NY, Jefferson Co., St. Joseph, c/o Antwerp, NY, St. Michael Church. (OG)
Philadelphia, PA, c/o [47] Philadelphia, PA, St. Francis Xavier Church. (PH)
Philadelphia, PA, Philadelphia Co., Holy Redeemer Chinese Church, c/o [79] Philadelphia, PA, St. John the Evangelist Church. (PH)
Philadelphia, PA, Philadelphia Co., St. Roch Chapel, c/o [109] Philadelphia, PA, Mother of Divine Grace Church. (PH)
Phillipsburg, KY, Marion Co., Our Lady of Fatima, c/o Calvary, KY, Holy Name of Mary Church. (L)
Philmont, NY, Pine Haven Home, c/o Philmont, NY, Sacred Heart Church. (ALB)
Philo, OH, Muskingum Co., St. Ann, c/o Zanesville, OH, St. Thomas Aquinas Church. (COL)
Phoenix, AZ, Maricopa Co., c/o [7] Phoenix, AZ, SS. Anthony and Pius X Church. (PHX)
Phoenix, AZ, Maricopa Co., Our Lady of Fatima, c/o [7] Phoenix, AZ, SS. Anthony and Pius X Church. (PHX)
Phoenix, AZ, Maricopa Co., Santa Rosa Chapel, c/o [1] Phoenix, AZ, SS. Simon and Jude Cathedral Church. (PHX)
Phoenix, AZ, Maricopa Co., St. Philip the Deacon Catholic Center, c/o [17] Phoenix, AZ, St. Mark Church. (PHX)
Picacho, NM, St. Joseph, c/o Ruidoso, NM, St. Eleanor Church. (LSC)
Pickens, WV, Randolph Co., Sacred Heart, c/o Buckhannon, WV, Holy Rosary Church. (WH)
Pickerel, WI, St. Mary, c/o Elcho, WI, Holy Family Church. (GB)
Picuris Indian Pueblo, NM, Taos Co., San Lorenzo Mission, c/o Penasco, NM, San Antonio de Padua Church. (SFE)
Piedmont, AL, Calhoun Co., St. Joachim, c/o Jacksonville, AL, St. Charles Church. (BIR)
Piedras Blancas, PR, Ntra. Sra. Reina de la Paz, c/o Aguada, PR, St. Francis of Assisi Church. (MGZ)
Pigeon Forge, TN, Holy Cross, c/o Gatlinburg, TN, St. Mary Church. (KNX)
Piis, FM, c/o Lukunor, FM, Sacred Heart Church. (CI)
Pilar, NM, Taos Co., Nuestra Senora de los Dolores, c/o Dixon, NM, St. Anthony Church. (SFE)
Pima, AZ, Graham Co., Pima Mission, c/o Safford, AZ, St. Rose of Lima Church. (TUC)
Pin Oak, TX, Bastrop Co., St. Mary's, c/o Giddings, TX, St. Margaret Church. (AUS)
Pine Bluff, AR, Jefferson Co., St. Raphael's, c/o Pine Bluff, AR, St. Peter's Church. (LR)
Pine Mountain, GA, Harris Co., Christ the King, c/o [3] Columbus, GA, St. Anne Church. (SAV)
Pine Point, ME, Scarborough Co., St. Jude, c/o Scarborough, ME, St. Maximilian Kolbe Church. (PRT)
Pine Springs, AZ, St. Rose, c/o Houck, AZ, St. John Church. (GLP)
Pinedale, CA, Fresno Co., St. Agnes, c/o [2] Fresno, CA, Holy Spirit Church. (FRS)
Pineville, KY, Bell Co., St. Anthony, c/o Middlesboro, KY, St. Julian Church. (LEX)
Pineville, WV, Wyoming Co., Holy Cross, c/o Mullens, WV, St. John the Evangelist Church. (WH)
Pingree, ND, St. Michael, c/o Jamestown, ND, The Basilica of St. James Church. (FAR)
Pinon, AZ, Navajo Co., St. Mary of the Rosary, c/o Chinle, AZ, Our Lady of Fatima, Indian Mission Church. (GLP)
Pinos Altos, NM, Holy Cross, c/o Silver City, NM, St. Vincent de Paul Church. (LSC)
Pinos Wells, NM, Torrance Co., c/o Vaughn, NM, St. Mary Church. (SFE)
Pintada, NM, Guadalupe Co., c/o Santa Rosa, NM, St. Rose of Lima Church. (SFE)
Piru, CA, Ventura Co., San Salvador, c/o Fillmore, CA, St. Francis of Assisi Church. (LA)
Pisarach, FM, St. Catherine of Siena, c/o Fefan, FM, Sacred Heart Church. (CI)
Pisarach, FM, St. Catherine of Siena, c/o Ulul, FM, Sacred Heart Church. (CI)
Pittsburg, OK, Pittsburg Co., St. Edwards, c/o McAlester, OK, St. John Church. (TLS)
Pittsfield, MA, Berkshire Co., All Souls, c/o [3] Pittsfield, MA, Our Lady of Mt. Carmel Church. (SPR)
Pittsfield, VT, Rutland Co., St. Denis, c/o Bethel, VT, St. Anthony Church. (BUR)
Pittston, PA, Luzerne Co., St. Mary of the Assumption, c/o [6] Pittston, PA, St. Mary, Help of Christians Church. (SCR)
Pittstown, NJ, Hunterdon Co., St. Catherine of Siena, c/o Clinton, NJ, Immaculate Conception Church. (MET)
Placita, NM, Taos Co., Nuestra Senora de la Asuncion Mission, c/o Penasco, NM, San Antonio de Padua Church. (SFE)
Placitas, NM, Sandoval Co., c/o Bernalillo, NM, Our Lady of Sorrows Church. (SFE)
Placitas, NM, Rio Arriba Co., c/o El Rito, NM, San Juan Nepomuceno Church. (SFE)
Placitas, NM, San Lorenzo, c/o Truth or Consequences, NM, Our Lady of Perpetual Help Church. (LSC)
Plains, TX, Yoakum Co., Sacred Heart, c/o Denver City, TX, St. William Church. (LUB)
Plainview, SD, Meade Co., Our Lady of Victory, c/o Faith, SD, St. Joseph Church. (RC)
Plaisance, LA, St. Andrew, c/o Grand Prairie, LA, St. Peter Church. (LAF)
Plaquemine Point, LA, St. Agnes, c/o Lawtell, LA, Holy Family Church. (LAF)
Plasi, NE, Saunders Co., SS. Cyril and Methodius, c/o Prague, NE, St. John's Church. (LIN)
Platteville, CO, Weld Co., St. Nicholas, c/o Fort Lupton, CO, St. William Church. (DEN)
Playas, NM, St. Augustine, c/o Lordsburg, NM, St. Joseph Church. (LSC)
Playita Cortada, PR, San Patricio, c/o Santa Isabel, PR, St. James Church. (PCE)
Plaza, ND, Mountrail Co., Sacred Heart, c/o Parshall, ND, St. Bridget Church. (BIS)
Plaza Blanca, NM, Rio Arriba Co., c/o Los Ojos, NM, San Jose Church. (SFE)
Plaza de Arriba, NM, Guadalupe Co., c/o Anton Chico, NM, San Jose Church. (SFE)
Pleasant Hill, MO, Cass Co., St. Bridget, c/o Harrisonville, MO, Our Lady of Lourdes Church. (KC)
Pleasant Valley, PA, Blair Co., Our Lady of the Assumption, c/o [7] Altoona, PA, Our Lady of Mt. Carmel Church. (ALT)
Pleasanton, CA, Alameda Co., St. Elizabeth Seton, c/o Pleasanton, CA, St. Augustine Church. (OAK)
Pleasantville Park, NY, Westchester Co., Our Lady of Pompeii, c/o Pleasantville, NY, Holy Innocents Church. (NY)
Plena, PR, San Jose, c/o Salinas, PR, Our Lady of Monserrat Church. (PCE)
Plevna, MT, St. Anthony, c/o Baker, MT, St. John the Evangelist Church. (GF)
Plum Bayou, AR, Jefferson Co., St. Mary's, c/o Pine Bluff, AR, St. Joseph's Church. (LR)
Plum Island, MA, St. James, c/o Newburyport, MA, Immaculate Conception Church. (BO)
Plummer, MN, Red Lake Co., St. Vincent de Paul, c/o Oklee, MN, St. Francis Xavier's Church. (CR)
Plunketville, OK, McCurtain Co., St. Henry, c/o Idabel, OK, St. Francis De Sales Church. (TLS)
Plush, OR, St. Thomas, c/o Lakeview, OR, St. Patrick's Church. (BAK)
Plymouth, CA, Amador Co., St. Mary of the Mountains, c/o Sutter Creek, CA, Immaculate Conception Church. (SAC)
Pocahontas, PA, Somerset Co., St. Mary's, c/o West Salisbury, PA, St. Michael's Church. (ALT)
Pocono Summit, PA, Monroe Co., St. Joan of Arc, c/o Mount Pocono, PA, St. Mary of the Mount Church. (SCR)
Point Blank, TX, St. Stephen the Martyr, c/o New Waverly, TX, St. Joseph Church. (GAL)
Point Comfort, TX, St. Ann, c/o Port Lavaca, TX, Our Lady of the Gulf Church. (VIC)
Polvadera, NM, Socorro Co., c/o Socorro, NM, San Miguel Church. (SFE)
Pompano Beach, FL, Broward Co., St. Joseph, c/o [10] Miami, FL, Notre Dame d'Haiti Church. (MIA)
Ponce, P.R., La Dolorosa, c/o [2] Ponce, PR, Christ the King Church. (PCE)
Ponce, PR, Our Lady of Carmel, c/o [3] Ponce, PR, Church of the Resurrection. (PCE)
Ponce, PR, Saint Joseph, c/o [3] Ponce, PR, Church of the Resurrection. (PCE)
Pond Creek, OH, Scioto Co., Holy Trinity, c/o West Portsmouth, OH, Our Lady of Sorrows Church. (COL)
Pond Creek, OK, Grant Co., St. Joseph's, c/o Medford, OK, St. Mary's Church. (OKL)
Pond Eddy, NY, Sullivan Co., Sacred Heart, c/o Yulan, NY, St. Anthony of Padua Church. (NY)
Ponderosa, NM, Sandoval Co., c/o Jemez Pueblo, NM, San Diego Indian Missions Church. (SFE)
Ponsford, MN, Becker Co., St. Theodore, c/o White Earth, MN, St. Benedict Church. (CR)
Pontotoc, MS, Pontotoc Co., St. Christopher, c/o New Albany, MS, St. Francis of Assisi Church. (JKS)
Poplarville, MS, Pearl River Co., St. Joseph, c/o Lumberton, MS, Our Lady of Perpetual Help Church. (BLX)
Porcupine, ND, Sioux Co., St. James, c/o Fort Yates, ND, St. Peter - Catholic Indian Mission Church. (BIS)
Port Costa, CA, Contra Costa Co., St. Patrick, c/o Crockett, CA, St. Rose of Lima Church. (OAK)
Port Deposit, MD, Cecil Co., St. Teresa, c/o Perryville, MD, Church of the Good Shepherd. (WIL)
Port Norris, NJ, St. Anthony, c/o Cedarville, NJ, St. Michael's Church. (CAM)
Port O'Connor, TX, St. Joseph, c/o Port Lavaca, TX, Our Lady of the Gulf Church. (VIC)
Port Orford, OR, Curry Co., St. John the Baptist, c/o Bandon, OR, Holy Trinity Church. (P)
Port St. Joe, FL, Gulf Co., San Blas Catholic Mission, c/o Port St. Joe, FL, St. Joseph Church. (PT)
Portage, ME, Our Lady of the Lakes, c/o Ashland, ME, St. Mark's Church. (PRT)
Portal, ND, Burke Co., St. John the Baptist, c/o Bowbells, ND, St. Joseph Church. (BIS)
Portales, NM, Roosevelt Co., University Catholic Center, c/o Portales, NM, St. Helen Church. (SFE)
Porterville, CA, Our Lady of Guadalupe, c/o Porterville, CA, St. Anne Church. (FRS)
Portland, PA, Northampton Co., St. Vincent de Paul, c/o Bangor, PA, Our Lady of Good Counsel Church. (ALN)
Poston, AZ, Kateri Tekawitha Indian Mission, c/o Parker, AZ, Sacred Heart Church. (TUC)
Potash, LA, Plaquemines Parish, St. Joseph, c/o Port Sulphur, LA, St. Patrick Church. (NO)
Potatoe Creek, SD, Jackson Co., St. Henry, c/o Wanblee, SD, Ignatius Loyola Church. (RC)
Potter Place, NH, Merrimack Co., Immaculate Conception, c/o New London, NH, Our Lady of Fatima Church. (MAN)
Pottersville, NY, St. Pius X, c/o North Creek, NY, St. James Church. (ALB)
Power, MT, Guardian Angel, c/o Dutton, MT, St. William Church. (HEL)
Powers, OR, Coos Co., St. Bridget, c/o Coquille, OR, Holy Name Church. (P)
Powers Lake, ND, Burke Co., St. James, c/o Stanley, ND, Queen of the Most Holy Rosary Church. (BIS)
Prairie, IA, St. Joseph, c/o Peosta, IA, St. John the Baptist Church. (DUB)
Prairie Center, NE, Buffalo Co., St. Mary, c/o Pleasanton, NE, St. Mary's Church. (GI)
Prairie Laurent, LA, St. Jules, c/o Leonville, LA, St. Catherine Church. (LAF)
Prairie Ronde, LA, Sacred Heart, c/o Lawtell, LA, St. Bridget Church. (LAF)
Prairie View, AR, Logan Co., St. Meinrad, c/o Scranton, AR, St. Ignatius Church. (LR)
Prentiss, MS, Jefferson Davis Co., St. Mary's, c/o Bassfield, MS, St. Peter Church. (BLX)
Primghar, IA, O'Brien Co., St. Anthony of Padua, c/o Sutherland, IA, Sacred Heart Church. (SC)
Primrose, NE, Boone Co., St. Mary, c/o Cedar Rapids, NE, St. Anthony Church. (OM)
Princeton, CA, Colusa Co., St. Joseph, c/o Colusa, CA, Our Lady of Lourdes Church. (SAC)
Proctorsville, VT, Windsor Co., Holy Name of Mary, c/o Chester, VT, St. Joseph Church. (BUR)
Promise, SD, Dewey Co., St. Catherine, c/o Eagle Butte, SD, All Saints Church. (RC)
Promise, SD, Dewey Co., St. Catherine, c/o Eagle Butte, SD, Cheyenne River Reservation Church. (RC)
Promised Land, PA, Monroe Co., Our Lady of Fatima, c/o Canadensis, PA, St. Bernadette Church. (SCR)
Prudence Island, RI, Our Lady of Prudence, c/o Bristol, RI, St. Mary's Church. (PRO)
Pueblitos, NM, Valencia Co., c/o Belen, NM, Our Lady of Belen Church. (SFE)
Pueblo West, CO, Pueblo Co., St. Paul the Apostle, c/o [16] Pueblo, CO, St. Pius X Church. (PBL)
Puerto de Luna, NM, Guadalupe Co., c/o Santa Rosa, NM, St. Rose of Lima Church. (SFE)
Puerto Plata, PR, Jayuya Co., San Juan, c/o Jayuya, PR, Our Lady of Monserrate Church. (PCE)
Puerto Real, PR, Our Lady of Mt. Carmel, c/o Cabo Rojo, PR, St. Michael Church. (MGZ)
Pulaski, VA, St. Edward, c/o Wytheville, VA, St. Mary's Church. (RIC)
Pulguillas, PR, Coamo Co., Christ the King, c/o Coamo, PR, St. Blase Church. (PCE)
Pulusuk, FM, Our Lady of Fatima, c/o Tol, FM, Assumption of the Blessed Virgin Mary Church. (CI)
Pulusuk, FM, Our Lady of Fatima, c/o Puluwat, FM, Santiago Church. (CI)
Puluwat, FM, c/o Tol, FM, Assumption of the Blessed Virgin Mary Church. (CI)
Punaluu, HI, St. Joachim, c/o Kahuku, HI, St. Roch Church. (HON)
Punlap, FM, Sacred Heart, c/o Tol, FM, Assumption of the Blessed Virgin Mary Church. (CI)
Punlop, FM, Sacred Heart, c/o Puluwat, FM, Santiago Church. (CI)
Punta de Agua, NM, Torrance Co., c/o Mountainair, NM, St. Alice Church. (SFE)
Punto Oro, PR, Ponce Co., Ntra. Sra. del Pilar, c/o [11] Ponce, PR, San Jose Obrero Church. (PCE)
Pursglove, WV, Monongalia Co., St. Ursula, c/o Westover, WV, St. Elizabeth Ann Seton Church. (WH)
Puuiki, HI, Maui Co., St. Peter, c/o Hana, HI, St. Mary Church. (HON)

Q

Quartz Hill, CA, Los Angeles Co., St. Elizabeth, c/o

Lancaster, CA, Blessed Junipero Serra Church. (LA)
Quartzsite, AZ, Queen of Peace, c/o Parker, AZ, Sacred Heart Church. (TUC)
Quebrada Ceiba, PR, Milagrosa, c/o Penuelas, PR, St. Joseph Church. (PCE)
Quebrada Honda, PR, Nuestra Senora, c/o Guayanilla, PR, Immaculate Conception Church. (PCE)
Quebrada Larga, PR, Sgdo. Corazon de Jesus, c/o Aguada, PR, St. Francis of Assisi Church. (MGZ)
Quebradas, PR, Sacred Heart, c/o Yauco, PR, Holy Rossary Church. (PCE)
Quebradas, PR, San Francisco de Asis, c/o Guayanilla, PR, Immaculate Conception Church. (PCE)
Queen Creek, AZ, Maricopa Co., Our Lady of Guadalupe, c/o Gilbert, AZ, St. Anne Church. (PHX)
Queensbury, NY, Our Lady of the Assumption, c/o Lake George, NY, Sacred Heart Church. (ALB)
Queenstown, MD, Queen Anne Co., St. Peter, c/o Centreville, MD, Mother of Sorrows Church. (WIL)
Quemado, TX, Our Lady of Guadalupe, c/o Eagle Pass, TX, Our Lady of Refuge Church. (SAT)
Quimby, IA, Cherokee Co., St. John the Baptist, c/o Holstein, IA, Our Lady of Good Counsel Church. (SC)
Quinault, WA, Grays Harbor & Jefferson Cos., Our Lady of the Olympics, c/o Hoquiam, WA, Our Lady of Good Help Church. (SEA)
Quinlan, TX, Hunt Co., Our Lady of Fatima, c/o Greenville, TX, St. William Church. (DAL)
Quitman, MS, Good Shepherd, c/o Meridian, MS, St. Patrick Church. (JKS)

R

Raeville, NE, Boone Co., St. Bonaventure, c/o Petersburg, NE, St. John the Baptist Church. (OM)
Ragley, LA, Beauregard Parish, St. Pius X, c/o De Quincy, LA, Our Lady of La Salette Church. (LKC)
Rainsville, NM, Mora Co., c/o Mora, NM, St. Gertrude Church. (SFE)
Raleigh, MS, St. Paul, c/o Magee, MS, St. Stephen Church. (JKS)
Ralph, SD, Harding Co., St. Isidore, c/o Bison, SD, Blessed Sacrament Church. (RC)
Ralph, SD, Harding Co., St. Isidore, c/o Buffalo, SD, St. Anthony Church. (RC)
Ralston, PA, Lycoming Co., St. Aloysius, c/o Canton, PA, St. Michael Church. (SCR)
Ramey-Maleza, PR, Los Santos Reyes, c/o Aguadilla, PR, San Jose Obrero Church. (MGZ)
Ramirez, TX, Duval Co., Our Lady of Guadalupe, c/o Premont, TX, St. Theresa of the Infant Jesus Church. (CC)
Ranchester, WY, Sheridan Co., St. Edmund, c/o Sheridan, WY, Holy Name Church. (CHY)
Ranchitos, NM, Rio Arriba Co., c/o San Juan Pueblo, NM, St. John the Baptist Church. (SFE)
Rancho Murieta, CA, c/o Elk Grove, CA, St. Joseph Church. (SAC)
Randsburg, CA, Kern Co., Santa Barbara, c/o Ridgecrest, CA, St. Ann Church. (FRS)
Rangeley, ME, St. Luke, c/o Oquossoc, ME, Our Lady of the Lakes Church. (PRT)
Rangely, CO, Rio Blanco Co., St. Ignatius, c/o Meeker, CO, Holy Family Church. (DEN)
Rankin, IL, Vermilion Co., Holy Trinity, c/o Penfield, IL, St. Lawrence's Church. (PEO)
Rankin, TX, Upton Co., St. Thomas, c/o Big Lake, TX, St. Margaret of Cortona Church. (SAN)
Rapid City, SD, Pennington Co., Indian Health Service, Sioux San Hospital and Pennington County Jail, c/o [4] Rapid City, SD, St. Isaac Jogues Church. (RC)
Rasselas, PA, Elk Co., Holy Cross, c/o Wilcox, PA, St. Anne Church. (E)
Ray, ND, Williams Co., St. Michael, c/o Tioga, ND, St. Thomas Church. (BIS)
Rayburn, TX, St. Raymond, c/o Jasper, TX, St. Michael Church. (BEA)
Raymond, CA, Madera Co., St. Anne, c/o Madera, CA, St. Joachim Church. (FRS)
Raymond, MS, Immaculate Conception, c/o Clinton, MS, Holy Savior Church. (JKS)
Raynesford, MT, St. Mary, c/o Belt, MT, St. Mark the Evangelist Church. (GF)
Reading, PA, Berks Co., Holy Rosary Chapel, c/o [6] Reading, PA, Holy Rosary Church. (ALN)
Realitos, TX, Duval Co., Sacred Heart, c/o Hebbronville, TX, Our Lady of Guadalupe Church. (CC)
Rector, AR, Clay Co., St. Henry's, c/o Paragould, AR, St. Mary's Church. (LR)
Red Cliff, CO, Eagle Co., Our Lady of Mt. Carmel, c/o Minturn, CO, St. Patrick's Church. (DEN)
Red Feather Lakes, CO, Larimer Co., Our Lady of the Lakes, c/o [1] Fort Collins, CO, St. Joseph Church. (DEN)
Red Owl, SD, Meade Co., St. Anthony, c/o Faith, SD, St. Joseph Church. (RC)
Red River, NM, Taos Co., c/o Questa, NM, St. Anthony Church. (SFE)
Red Scaffold, SD, Ziebach Co., Sacred Heart, c/o Eagle Butte, SD, All Saints Church. (RC)
Red Scaffold, SD, Ziebach Co., Sacred Heart, c/o Eagle Butte, SD, Cheyenne River Reservation Church. (RC)
Red Shirt Table, SD, Shannon Co., St. Bernard, c/o Pine Ridge, SD, Holy Rosary Church. (RC)
Red Springs, NC, Robeson Co., St. Andrew, c/o Lumberton, NC, St. Francis De Sales Church. (R)
Reddick, IL, St. Mary, c/o Cabery, IL, St. Joseph Church. (JOL)
Redfield, NY, Oswego Co., St. Paul, c/o Florence, NY, St. Mary Church. (SY)
Redford, TX, San Jose, c/o Presidio, TX, Santa Teresa de Jesus Church. (ELP)
Redwood City, CA, San Mateo Co., St. Joseph the Workman, c/o [1] Menlo Park, CA, St. Anthony Church. (SFR)
Reeder, ND, Adams Co., Sacred Heart, c/o Hettinger, ND, Holy Trinity Church. (BIS)
Reeves, LA, Sacred Heart Parish, St. Maurice, c/o Kinder, LA, St. Philip Neri Church. (LKC)
Reform, AL, Dickens Co., St. Robert, c/o Tuscaloosa, AL, Holy Spirit Church. (BIR)
Reidsville, GA, Tattnall Co., St. Andrew the Apostle, c/o Vidalia, GA, Sacred Heart Church. (SAV)
Reilly Settlement, IA, Sacred Heart, c/o Little Turkey, IA, Assumption of the B. V. M. Church. (DUB)
Reilly Settlement, IA, Sacred Heart, c/o New Hampton, IA, St. Mary's Church. (DUB)
Remer, MN, St. Paul, c/o Longville, MN, St. Edward's Church. (DUL)
Reserve, NM, St. Francis, c/o Aragon, NM, Santo Nino Church. (GLP)
Retsof, NY, Livingston Co., St. Lucy, c/o Leicester, NY, St. Thomas Aquinas Church. (ROC)
Reva, SD, Harding Co., Our Lady of the Prairie, c/o Bison, SD, Blessed Sacrament Church. (RC)
Reva, SD, Harding Co., Our Lady of the Prairie, c/o Buffalo, SD, St. Anthony Church. (RC)
Rhame, ND, Bowman Co., St. Mel, c/o Bowman, ND, St. Charles Church. (BIS)
Rhinecliff, NY, Dutchess Co., St. Joseph, c/o Rhinebeck, NY, The Good Shepherd Church. (NY)
Ricardo, TX, Kleberg Co., Sacred Heart, c/o [2] Kingsville, TX, St. Gertrude Church. (CC)
Rich Hill, MO, Bates Co., St. Bridget's, c/o Butler, MO, St. Patrick's Church. (KC)
Richardton, ND, Stark Co., St. Stephen, c/o Richardton, ND, St. Mary Church. (BIS)
Richey, MT, St Francis de Sales, c/o Glendive, MT, Sacred Heart Church. (GF)
Richey, MT, St. Francis de Sales, c/o Circle, MT, St. Francis Xavier Church. (GF)
Richgrove, CA, Tulare Co., St. Vincent, c/o Delano, CA, St. Mary's of the Miraculous Medal Church. (FRS)
Richland, NJ, St. Joseph, c/o [5] Vineland, NJ, St. Mary's Church. (CAM)
Richmond, VA, Byzantine Catholic Mission,-c/o Williamsburg, VA, Ascension of Our Lord Church. (PSC)
Richmond, VA, St.Joseph Tridentine Community, c/o [7] Richmond, VA, St. Benedict Church. (RIC)
Rico, CO, Dolores Co., Immaculate Heart of Mary Chapel, c/o Mancos, CO, St. Rita Church. (PBL)
Rideau Settlement, LA, Sacred Heart, c/o Lebeau, LA, Immaculate Conception Church. (LAF)
Ridge Manor, FL, Hernando Co., St. Anne, c/o Brooksville, FL, St. Anthony Church. (SP)
Ridgebury, PA, Bradford Co., Our Lady of Perpetual Help, c/o Bentley Creek, PA, St. Ann's Church. (SCR)
Ridgefield, WA, Clark Co., St. Mary of Guadalupe, c/o Woodland, WA, St. Philip's Church. (SEA)
Ridgeview, SD, Dewey Co., St. Joseph, c/o Eagle Butte, SD, All Saints Church. (RC)
Ridgeview, SD, Dewey Co., St. Joseph, c/o Eagle Butte, SD, Cheyenne River Reservation Church. (RC)
Riley, NM, Socorro Co., c/o Socorro, NM, San Miguel Church. (SFE)
Rileyville, PA, Wayne Co., St. Joseph, c/o Honesdale, PA, St. John the Evangelist Church. (SCR)
Rimersburg, PA, Clarion Co., St. Richard, c/o East Brady, PA, St. Eusebius Church. (E)
Rincon, NM, Our Lady of All Nations, c/o Hatch, NM, Our Lord of Mercy Church. (LSC)
Ringgold, LA, Bienville Parish, Blessed Sacrament, c/o Minden, LA, St. Paul Church. (SHP)
Rio, WI, St. Joseph's, c/o Doylestown, WI, St. Patrick Church. (MAD)
Rio Canas, PR, Rio Canas Abajo, San Judas, c/o Juana Diaz, PR, St. Raymond Nonato Church. (PCE)
Rio Chiquito, NM, Rio Arriba Co., Sagrado Corazon, c/o Chimayo, NM, Holy Family Church. (SFE)
Rio Chiquito, PR, Ponce Co., Nino Jesus de Praga, c/o [2] Ponce, PR, Christ the King Church. (PCE)
Rio Chiquito, PR, Ponce Co., San Vicente, c/o [14] Ponce, PR, San Vicente-Cantera Church. (PCE)
Rio en Medio, NM, Sante Fe Co., Our Lady of Sorrows, c/o [2] Santa Fe, NM, Our Lady of Guadalupe Church. (SFE)
Rio Grande, PR, Nuestra Senora de Fatima, c/o Rio Grande, PR, Nuestra Senora del Carmen Church. (SJN)
Rio Grande, PR, Perpetuo Socorro, c/o Aguada, PR, St. Francis of Assisi Church. (MGZ)
Rio Grande, PR, San Pedro, c/o Rio Grande, PR, Nuestra Senora del Carmen Church. (SJN)
Rio Grande-Playa, PR, Ntra. Sra. del Carmen, c/o Aguada, PR, St. Francis of Assisi Church. (MGZ)
Rio Hondo, PR, San Carlos y San Antonio, c/o [6] Mayaquez, PR, Sacred Heart Church. (MGZ)
Rio Jueyes, PR, Coamo Co., Our Lady of Lourdes, c/o Coamo, PR, St. Blase Church. (PCE)
Rio Lucio, NM, Taos Co., Sagrado Corazon Mission, c/o Penasco, NM, San Antonio de Padua Church. (SFE)
Rio Piedras, PR, N. Sra. de la Paz, c/o [58] San Juan, PR, Santisimo Salvador Church. (SJN)
Rio Piedras, PR, San Jose, c/o [58] San Juan, PR, Santisimo Salvador Church. (SJN)
Rio Prieto, PR, Milagrosa, c/o Castaner, PR, Our Lady of the Miraculous Medal Church. (PCE)
Rio Verde, AZ, St. Dominic, c/o Fountain Hills, AZ, Ascension Church. (PHX)
Rios, TX, Duval Co., St. Francis of Assisi, c/o Premont, TX, St. Theresa of the Infant Jesus Church. (CC)
Ripley, NY, Chautauqua Co., St. Thomas More, c/o Westfield, NY, St. James Church. (BUF)
Ripley, TN, Lauderdale Co., Ave Maria, c/o Covington, TN, St. Alphonsus Church. (MEM)
Rising Sun, MD, Cecil Co., St. Agnes, c/o Perryville, MD, Church of the Good Shepherd. (WIL)
Ritter, SC, Colleton Co., St. James, c/o Walterboro, SC, St. Anthony's Church. (CHR)
Riverside, CA, Our Lady of Guadalupe, c/o [11] Riverside, CA, St. Thomas the Apostle Church. (SB)
Riverside, MT, Sacred Heart, c/o Wolf Point, MT, Immaculate Conception Church. (GF)
Riverton, NE, Franklin Co., St. Catherine's, c/o Red Cloud, NE, Sacred Heart Church. (LIN)
Rivesville, WV, Marion Co., Our Lady of the Assumption, c/o Grant Town, WV, St. Anthony's Church. (WH)
Riviera, TX, Kleberg Co., Our Lady of Guadalupe, c/o Vattman, TX, Our Lady of Consolation Church. (CC)
Roanoke, AL, Randolph Co., Immaculate Conception, c/o Lanett, AL, Holy Family Church. (BIR)
Roanoke, LA, Jefferson Davis Parish, St. Mary, c/o Welsh, LA, Our Lady of the Seven Dolors Church. (LKC)
Robbins, IL, Cook Co., St. Peter Claver, c/o Blue Island, IL, St. Benedict Church. (CHI)
Robbins, NC, Moore Co., Blessed Juan Diego, c/o Pinehurst, NC, Sacred Heart Church. (R)
Robbinsville, NC, Graham Co., Prince of Peace, c/o Andrews, NC, Holy Redeemer Church. (CHL)
Robert Lee, TX, Coke Co., Our Lady of Guadalupe, c/o [3] San Angelo, TX, St. Margaret Church. (SAN)
Roberts, IL, Immaculate Conception, c/o Piper City, IL, St. Peter Church. (JOL)
Roberts, MT, St. Thomas Aquinas, c/o Red Lodge, MT, St. Agnes Church. (GF)
Robinson Township, MI, St. Anthony, c/o Grand Haven, MI, St. Patrick's Church. (GR)
Roby, MO, Texas Co., St. Vincent de Paul, c/o Houston, MO, St. Mark Church. (SPC)
Rochester, VT, Windsor Co., St. Elizabeth, c/o Bethel, VT, St. Anthony Church. (BUR)
Rociada Abajo, NM, San Miguel Co., Santo Nino, c/o Las Vegas, NM, Our Lady of Sorrows Church. (SFE)
Rock City Falls, NY, St. Paul, c/o Greenfield Center, NY, St. Joseph Church. (ALB)
Rock Hall, MD, Kent Co., St. John, c/o Chestertown, MD, Sacred Heart Church. (WIL)
Rock Lake, ND, Towner Co., c/o Rolla, ND, St. Joachim's Church. (FAR)
Rock Lake, PA, Wayne Co., St. Juliana's, c/o Pleasant Mount, PA, St. James Church. (SCR)
Rock Point, MD, Charles Co., St. Francis de Sales, c/o Issue, MD, Holy Ghost Church. (WDC)
Rockvale, CO, Fremont Co., St. Patrick, c/o Florence, CO, St. Benedict Church. (PBL)
Rockville, MD, Montgomery Co., Our Lady of China, c/o [3] Rockville, MD, St. Mary Church. (WDC)
Rockville, NE, Sherman Co., St. Mary's, c/o Ravenna, NE, Our Lady of Lourdes Church. (GI)
Rockwood, ME, Somerset Co., St. Joseph's, c/o Greenville, ME, Holy Family Church. (PRT)
Rocky Boy Indian Reservation, MT, St. Mary, c/o Big Sandy, MT, St. Margaret Mary Church. (GF)
Rockyford, SD, Shannon Co., St. Peter's, c/o Manderson, SD, St. Agnes Church. (RC)
Rodarte, NM, Taos Co., Santa Barbara Mission, c/o Penasco, NM, San Antonio de Padua Church. (SFE)
Rodeo, NM, San Felipe, c/o Lordsburg, NM, St. Joseph Church. (LSC)
Roland, OK, Sequoyah Co., Blessed Kateri Tekakwitha, c/o Sallisaw, OK, St. Francis Xavier Church. (TLS)
Romanum, FM, St. Joseph, c/o Udot, FM, St. Francis Assisi Church. (CI)
Romeo, CO, Conejos Co., Our Lady of the Immaculate Conception, c/o Capulin, CO, St. Joseph Church. (PBL)

Romero, PR, Sagrado Corazon, c/o Villalba, PR, Our Lady of Mt. Carmel Church. (PCE)
Roosevelt Lake, AZ, Gila Co., St. Theresa, c/o Miami, AZ, Our Lady of the Blessed Sacrament Church. (TUC)
Ropesville, TX, Hockley Co., San Francisco de Asis, c/o Brownfield, TX, St. Anthony's Church. (LUB)
Rosamond, CA, St. Mary of the Desert, c/o Mojave, CA, St. Francis Church. (FRS)
Rosario, PR, Nuestra Senora del Rosario, c/o Rosario, PR, Rosary Church. (MGZ)
Rosario, PR, San Jose, c/o [6] Mayaquez, PR, Sacred Heart Church. (MGZ)
Roscoe, IL, Winnebago Co., Church of the Holy Spirit, c/o South Beloit, IL, St. Peter Church. (RCK)
Roscoe, NY, Sullivan Co., Gate of Heaven, c/o Livingston Manor, NY, St. Aloysius Church. (NY)
Roscoe, TX, Nolan Co., St. Albert the Great, c/o Sweetwater, TX, Immaculate Heart of Mary Church. (SAN)
Rosebud, SD, St. Bridget, c/o St. Francis, SD, Rosebud Reservation Church. (RC)
Roseton, NY, Orange Co., Our Lady of Mercy, c/o Marlboro, NY, St. Mary Church. (NY)
Rosita, TX, Santa Rosa de Lima, c/o Escobares, TX, Sacred Heart Church. (BWN)
Rossie, NY, St. Lawrence Co., St. Patrick, c/o Hammond, NY, St. Peter Church. (OG)
Rotten Bayou, MS, Harrison Co., St. William, c/o DeLisle, MS, The Catholic Church in DeLisle Church. (BLX)
Roulette, PA, Potter Co., St. Mary, c/o Port Allegany, PA, St. Gabriel the Archangel Church. (E)
Round Lake, MI, St. Joseph, c/o Custer, MI, St. Mary's Church. (GR)
Round Mountain & Fish Lake, NV, St. Barbara, c/o Tonopah, NV, St. Patrick Church. (LAV)
Round Rock, AZ, Our Lady of Guadalupe, c/o Lukachukai, AZ, St. Isabel Mission for Navajo Indians Church. (GLP)
Rouseville, PA, Venango Co., St. Venantius, c/o [1] Oil City, PA, Assumption of the Blessed Virgin Mary Church. (E)
Rowe, NM, San Miguel Co., c/o Pecos, NM, St. Anthony Church. (SFE)
Roxbury, CT, Litchfield Co., St. Patrick's, c/o Washington Depot, CT, Our Lady of Perpetual Help Church. (HRT)
Roxbury, NY, Our Lady of Good Counsel, c/o Margaretville, NY, Sacred Heart Church. (ALB)
Roxbury Pond, ME, St. Mary's Chapel, c/o Rumford, ME, St. Athanasius-St. John Church. (PRT)
Rudyard, MT, Holy Family Center, c/o Chester, MT, St. Mary's Church. (GF)
Rumson, NJ, Monmouth Co., Holy Rosary, c/o Rumson, NJ, Holy Cross Church. (TR)
Rural Linton, ND, Emmons Co., St. Michael's, c/o Strasburg, ND, Sts. Peter and Paul Church. (BIS)
Rush Springs, OK, Grady Co., St. Francis of Assisi, c/o Duncan, OK, Assumption Church. (OKL)
Rushville, NE, Immaculate Conception, c/o Gordon, NE, St. Leo's Church. (GI)
Rushville, NY, Ontario Co., St. Mary, c/o Stanley, NY, St. Theresa Church. (ROC)
Rusk, TX, Cherokee Co., Sacred Heart, c/o Jacksonville, TX, Our Lady of Sorrows Church. (TYL)
Russell, NY, St. Lawrence Co., St. Rene Goupil, c/o De Kalb Junction, NY, St. Henry Church. (OG)
Rutherford, CA, Holy Family, c/o Yountville, CA, St. Joan of Arc Church. (SR)
Rutten, ND, Ramsey Co., St. Benedict, c/o Devils Lake, ND, St. Joseph's Church. (FAR)
Ryan, OK, Jefferson Co., San Jose, c/o Duncan, OK, Assumption Church. (OKL)
Rye, CO, Pueblo Co., St. Aloysius, c/o [3] Pueblo, CO, Holy Family Church. (PBL)
Ryegate, MT, St Mathias, c/o Roundup, MT, St. Benedict's Church. (GF)

S

Sa'ilele, AS, c/o [4] (Lauli'i), AS, Church of St. Peter and Paul. (SPP)
Sabana, PR, San Jose, c/o Aguada, PR, St. Francis of Assisi Church. (MGZ)
Sabana Eneas, PR, San Judas Tadeo, c/o San German, PR, San German de Auxerre Church. (MGZ)
Sabana Llana, PR, Perpetuo Socorro, c/o Salinas, PR, Our Lady of Monserrat Church. (PCE)
Sabin, MN, Clay Co., St. Cecilia, c/o Barnesville, MN, Assumption Church. (CR)
Sabinal, NM, Socorro Co., San Antonio, c/o La Joya, NM, Our Lady of Sorrows Church. (SFE)
Sabine Pass, TX, St. Paul, c/o [5] Port Arthur, TX, St. James Church. (BEA)
Sabinoso, NM, San Miguel Co., c/o Roy, NM, Holy Family-St. Joseph Church. (SFE)
Sacaton, AZ, St. Anthony, c/o Bapchule, AZ, St. Peter's Church. (PHX)
Sacaton Flats, AZ, Our Lady of Victory, c/o Bapchule, AZ, St. Peter's Church. (PHX)
Saco, MT, St. Francis of Assisi, c/o Malta, MT, St. Mary's Church. (GF)
Sacramento, CA, Sacramento Co., St. Andrew the Apostle, c/o San Francisco, CA, Immaculate Conception Church. (STN)
Saegertown, PA, Crawford Co., St. Bernadette, c/o Meadville, PA, St. Agatha Church. (E)
Sagamore, MA, Barnstable Co., St. Theresa, c/o Sandwich, MA, Corpus Christi Church. (FR)
Saginaw, MN, St. Philip Neri, c/o Proctor, MN, St. Rose Catholic Church. (DUL)
Saguache, CO, St. Agnes, c/o Center, CO, St. Francis Jerome Church. (PBL)
Sahuarita, AZ, Pima Co., St. Martin de Porres, c/o Green Valley, AZ, Our Lady of the Valley Church. (TUC)
St. Anne, IN, Jennings Co., St. Anne, c/o St. Joseph, IN, St. Joseph Church. (IND)
St. Anthony, ND, Rolette Co., St. Anthony, c/o Turtle Mountain Reservation, ND, (Chippewa Indians) Church. (FAR)
St. Augustine, FL, St. Johns Co., Prince of Peace, c/o [1] St. Augustine, FL, Cathedral of St. Augustine. (STA)
St. Augustine, FL, St. Johns Co., St. Benedict the Moor, c/o [1] St. Augustine, FL, Cathedral of St. Augustine. (STA)
St. Boniface, PA, Cambria Co., St. Boniface Chapel, c/o Hastings, PA, St. Bernard Church. (ALT)
St. Bridget (Pinhook), IA, St. Bridget, c/o Sumner, IA, Immaculate Conception Church. (DUB)
St. Charles, IL, Kane Co., St. Patrick, c/o St. Charles, IL, St. Patrick Church. (RCK)
St. David, IL, Fulton Co., St. Michael, c/o Lewistown, IL, St. Mary's Church. (PEO)
St. Denis, IN, Jennings Co., St. Denis, c/o Millhousen, IN, Immaculate Conception Church. (IND)
St. Francis, SD, c/o St. Francis, SD, St. Charles Church. (RC)
St. Francis, SD, St. Charles, c/o St. Francis, SD, Rosebud Reservation Church. (RC)
Saint Helena Island, SC, Beaufort Co., Holy Cross, c/o Beaufort, SC, St. Peter's Church. (CHR)
St. Kilian, MN, Nobles Co., St. Kilian, c/o Lismore, MN, St. Anthony's Church. (WIN)
St. Landry, LA, St. Theresa, c/o Pine Prairie, LA, St. Peter Church. (LAF)
St. Mary, NE, Johnson Co., St. Mary's, c/o Tecumseh, NE, St. Andrew's Church. (LIN)
St. Michaels, AZ, St. Michael's Mission for Navajo Indians, c/o St. Michaels, AZ, St. Michael Church. (GLP)
St. Michaels, MD, St. Michael, c/o Easton, MD, SS. Peter and Paul Church. (WIL)
St. Paul, TX, St. Paul, c/o Sinton, TX, Sacred Heart Church. (CC)
St. Petersburg, FL, The Mercy of God Polish Mission, c/o [7] St. Petersburg, FL, St. Paul Church. (SP)
St. Petersburg, FL, Pinellas Co., Vietnamese Martyrs Mission, c/o [5] St. Petersburg, FL, St. Joseph Church. (SP)
St. Pius, IN, Ripley Co., St. Pius, c/o Milan, IN, St. Charles Borromeo Church. (IND)
St. Thomas, ND, Pembina Co., St. Thomas, c/o Drayton, ND, St. Edward's Church. (FAR)
St. Vincent de Paul, IN, c/o St. Vincent de Paul, IN, St. Vincent de Paul Church. (IND)
St. Xavier, MT, St. Francis Xavier, c/o Crow Agency, MT, St. Dennis Church. (GF)
Saipan, MP, Santa Soledad Mission, c/o San Vicente Village, District 10, MP, San Vicente Ferrer Parish Church. (CHK)
Salem, IN, Washington Co., St. Patrick, c/o Scottsburg, IN, American Martyrs Church. (IND)
Salem, OR, Marion Co., San Jose, c/o Salem, OR, St. Joseph Church. (P)
Salem Township, OH, Wyandot Co., St. Joseph, c/o Carey, OH, Our Lady of Consolation, Basilica-National Shrine Church. (TOL)
Saliente, PR, Jayuya Co., San Francisco, c/o Jayuya, PR, Our Lady of Monserrate Church. (PCE)
Salinas-Providencia, PR, Divina Providencia, c/o Ensenada, PR, Sacred Heart Church. (PCE)
Salineno, TX, St. Joseph, c/o Roma, TX, Our Lady of Refuge Church. (BWN)
Salon Usos Multiples-April Gardens, PR, Las Piedras, c/o Las Piedras, PR, Inmaculada Concepcion Church. (CGS)
Salt River Indian, AZ, St. Francis, c/o [4] Tempe, AZ, St. Margaret Church. (PHX)
Saltillo, MS, St. Thomas Aquinas, c/o Tupelo, MS, St. James Church. (JKS)
Salto, PR, Jayuya Co., Santos Reyes, c/o Jayuya, PR, Our Lady of Monserrate Church. (PCE)
Salyersville, KY, Magoffin Co., St. Luke's, c/o Prestonsburg, KY, St. Martha Church. (LEX)
San Acacio, CO, Costilla Co., San Acacio, c/o San Luis, CO, Sangre de Cristo Church. (PBL)
San Antonio, CO, San Antonio de Padua, c/o Conejos, CO, Our Lady of Guadalupe Church. (PBL)
San Antonio, NM, Socorro Co., c/o Socorro, NM, San Miguel Church. (SFE)
San Antonio, NM, Bernalillo Co., c/o Tijeras, NM, Holy Child Church. (SFE)
San Antonio, NM, San Miguel Co., Los Vigiles (Our Lady of Refuge), c/o Las Vegas, NM, Immaculate Conception Church. (SFE)
San Antonio, TX, Bexar Co., Byzantine Catholic Church, c/o Houston, TX, St. John Chrysostom Church. (PBR)
San Antonio, TX, Bexar Co., Purisima Concepcion, c/o [32] San Antonio, TX, St. Cecilia Church. (SAT)
San Antonio, TX, Bexar Co., San Francesco di Paola, c/o [1] San Antonio, TX, Cathedral of San Fernando. (SAT)
San Antonio, TX, Bexar Co., Santa Cruz, c/o [17] San Antonio, TX, Our Lady of Guadalupe Church. (SAT)
San Antonio, TX, Santa Maria Goretti, c/o [47] San Antonio, TX, St. Jude Church. (SAT)
San Antonio, TX, St. Catherine, c/o [52] San Antonio, TX, St. Margaret Mary Church. (SAT)
San Antonio, TX, St. Francis Cabrini, c/o [69] San Antonio, TX, San Francisco de la Espada Church. (SAT)
San Ardo, CA, Monterey Co., Our Lady of Ransom, c/o San Miguel, CA, San Miguel Church. (MRY)
San Augustine, TX, San Augustine Co., San Augustine, c/o Center, TX, St. Therese Church. (TYL)
San Benito, TX, St. Joseph, c/o San Benito, TX, Our Lady, Queen of the Universe Church. (BWN)
San Cristobal, NM, Taos Co., c/o Arroyo Seco, NM, Holy Trinity Church. (SFE)
San Diego, PR, Coamo Co., San Diego, c/o Coamo, PR, St. Blase Church. (PCE)
San Felipe, NM, Sandoval Co., Indian Pueblo, c/o Pena Blanca, NM, Nuestra Senora De Guadalupe Church. (SFE)
San Felipe, PR, St. Martin de Porres, c/o Aguirre, PR, Sacred Heart Church. (PCE)
San Felipe, TX, Austin Co., c/o [1] Harlingen, TX, Our Lady of the Assumption Church. (BWN)
San Francisco, CO, Costilla Co., St. Francis of Assisi, c/o San Luis, CO, Sangre de Cristo Church. (PBL)
San Ignacio, NM, Guadalupe Co., c/o Santa Rosa, NM, St. Rose of Lima Church. (SFE)
San Ignacio, TX, Zapata Co., St. Ignatius, c/o Zapata, TX, Our Lady of Lourdes Church. (CC)
San Ildefonso, NM, Sante Fe Co., Indian Pueblo, c/o [1] Santa Fe, NM, The Cathedral of San Francisco de Asis. (SFE)
San Isidro, CO, Costilla Co., St. Isidro, c/o San Luis, CO, Sangre de Cristo Church. (PBL)
San Isidro, NM, San Isidro, c/o Dona Ana, NM, Our Lady of the Purification Church. (LSC)
San Isidro Norte, NM, San Miguel Co., c/o Ribera, NM, San Miguel Del Vado Church. (SFE)
San Isidro Sur, NM, San Miguel Co., c/o Ribera, NM, San Miguel Del Vado Church. (SFE)
San Joaquin, CA, Fresno Co., St. Vincent de Paul, c/o Tranquillity, CA, St. Paul Church. (FRS)
San Jon, NM, Quay Co., c/o Tucumcari, NM, St. Anne Church. (SFE)
San Jose, AZ, Graham Co., San Jose, c/o Solomon, AZ, Our Lady of Guadalupe Church. (TUC)
San Jose, FL, Jesus the Worker, c/o [5] Fort Myers, FL, St. Francis Xavier Church. (VEN)
San Jose, NM, San Miguel Co., c/o Ribera, NM, San Miguel Del Vado Church. (SFE)
San Jose, NM, Arrey, c/o Garfield, NM, San Isidro Church. (LSC)
San Jose Ranch, TX, Duval Co., St. Joseph, c/o Benavides, TX, St. Rose of Lima Church. (CC)
San Juan, NM, San Miguel Co., c/o Ribera, NM, San Miguel Del Vado Church. (SFE)
San Juan, NM, San Juan, c/o Hurley, NM, Infant Jesus Church. (LSC)
San Juan, PR, Capilla San Conrado, c/o [18] San Juan, PR, San Francisco de Asis Church. (SJN)
San Juan, PR, Egida del Maestro, c/o [16] San Juan, PR, Ntra. Sra. de Fatima Church. (SJN)
San Juan, PR, Jesus de Nazaret, c/o [24] San Juan, PR, Jesus Maestro Church. (SJN)
San Juan, PR, La Inmaculada, c/o [62] San Juan, PR, San Vicente de Paul Church. (SJN)
San Juan, PR, La Milagrosa, c/o [28] San Juan, PR, San Juan Bosco Church. (SJN)
San Juan, PR, Medalla Milagrosa, c/o [9] San Juan, PR, Santa Catalina Laboure Church. (SJN)
San Juan, PR, Nra. Sra. del Altagracia, c/o [37] San Juan, PR, Maria Auxiliadora Church. (SJN)
San Juan, PR, Ntra. Senora de la Caridad del Cobre, c/o [38] San Juan, PR, Santa Maria de Los Angeles Church. (SJN)
San Juan, PR, Ntra. Sra. de Fatima, c/o [37] San Juan, PR, Maria Auxiliadora Church. (SJN)
San Juan, PR, Ntra. Sra. de la Caridad, c/o [43] San Juan, PR, San Pablo Church. (SJN)
San Juan, PR, Ntra. Sra. de la Providencia, c/o [14] San Juan, PR, Nuestra Senora de la Esperanza Church. (SJN)
San Juan, PR, Ntra. Sra. del Rosario, c/o [28] San Juan, PR, San Juan Bosco Church. (SJN)

San Juan, PR, Nuestra Senora del Buen Consejo, c/o [4] San Juan, PR, San Antonio Church. (SJN)
San Juan, PR, Sagrada Familia, c/o [61] San Juan, PR, Santa Teresita Del Nino Jesus Church. (SJN)
San Juan, PR, Sagrado Corazon, c/o [37] San Juan, PR, Maria Auxiliadora Church. (SJN)
San Juan, PR, San Fernando, c/o [23] San Juan, PR, Inmaculado Corazon de Maria Church. (SJN)
San Juan, PR, San Francisco de Asis, c/o [30] San Juan, PR, San Juan Evangelista Church. (SJN)
San Juan, PR, San Jose, c/o [62] San Juan, PR, San Vicente de Paul Church. (SJN)
San Juan, PR, San Martin de Porres, c/o [8] San Juan, PR, Nuestra Senora del Carmen Church. (SJN)
San Juan, PR, San Martin de Porres, c/o [28] San Juan, PR, San Juan Bosco Church. (SJN)
San Juan, PR, San Martin de Porres-Sierra Maestra, c/o [27] San Juan, PR, San Jose Obrero Church. (SJN)
San Juan, PR, San Pablo, c/o [9] San Juan, PR, Santa Catalina Laboure Church. (SJN)
San Juan, PR, Santa Ana, c/o [42] San Juan, PR, Ntra. Sra. de la Monserrate Church. (SJN)
San Juan, PR, Santa Catalina, c/o [62] San Juan, PR, San Vicente de Paul Church. (SJN)
San Juan, PR, Santa Teresita de Nino Jesus, c/o [47] San Juan, PR, Nuestra Senora del Pilar Church. (SJN)
San Juan, PR, Santisima Trinidad, c/o [37] San Juan, PR, Maria Auxiliadora Church. (SJN)
San Juan, PR, Santo Domingo, c/o [11] San Juan, PR, Corpus Christi Church. (SJN)
San Juan, PR, State Penitentiary, c/o [5] San Juan, PR, Asuncion de La Virgen Church. (SJN)
San Judas Tadeo, PR, Playuelas, c/o Aguadilla, PR, La Milagrosa Church. (MGZ)
San Lorenzo, NM, San Lorenzo, c/o Bayard, NM, Our Lady of Fatima Church. (LSC)
San Lucas, CA, Monterey Co., St. Luke, c/o King City, CA, St. John the Baptist Church. (MRY)
San Luis, AZ, Yuma Co., San Judas Tadeo, c/o Somerton, AZ, Immaculate Heart of Mary Church. (TUC)
San Luis, NM, Saint Aloysius Gonzaga, c/o Cuba, NM, Immaculate Conception Church. (GLP)
San Manuel, TX, St. Anne, c/o San Carlos, TX, St. Joseph the Worker Church. (BWN)
San Marcos, TX, Hays Co., Guadalupe Chapel, c/o San Marcos, TX, St. John the Evangelist Church. (AUS)
San Miguel, CO, San Miguel, c/o Conejos, CO, Our Lady of Guadalupe Church. (PBL)
San Patricio, NM, St. Jude Thaddeus, c/o Ruidoso, NM, St. Eleanor Church. (LSC)
San Patricio, TX, San Patricio Co., St. Patrick, c/o Mathis, TX, Sacred Heart Church. (CC)
San Pedro, CO, Costilla Co., SS. Peter and Paul, c/o San Luis, CO, Sangre de Cristo Church. (PBL)
San Pedro, FL, Collier Co., c/o [3] Naples, FL, St. Peter Church. (VEN)
San Pedro, NM, c/o Santa Cruz, NM, Holy Cross Church. (SFE)
San Pedro, TX, San Pedro, c/o [5] Brownsville, TX, Our Lady of Good Counsel Church. (BWN)
San Perlita, TX, Sacred Heart, c/o Raymondville, TX, St. Anthony Church. (BWN)
San Rafael, CO, San Pedro y San Rafael, c/o Conejos, CO, Our Lady of Guadalupe Church. (PBL)
San Saba, TX, Lampass Co., Izoro, c/o San Saba, TX, St. Mary's Church. (AUS)
San Ysidro, NM, Sandoval Co., c/o Jemez Pueblo, NM, San Diego Indian Missions Church. (SFE)
Sandersville, GA, Washington Co., St. William, c/o Dublin, GA, Immaculate Conception Church. (SAV)
Sandia Indian Pueblo, NM, Sandoval Co., c/o Bernalillo, NM, Our Lady of Sorrows Church. (SFE)
Sandy Valley, NV, St. Catherine of Siena, c/o [2] Las Vegas, NV, Christ the King Church. (LAV)
Sangerville, ME, Holy Family, c/o Dover-Foxcroft, ME, St. Thomas Church. (PRT)
Santa Ana, NM, Sandoval Co., c/o Jemez Pueblo, NM, San Diego Indian Missions Church. (SFE)
Santa Ana, PR, Coamo Co., Santa Ana, c/o Coamo, PR, St. Blase Church. (PCE)
Santa Catalina, PR, Coamo Co., Miraculous Virgin, c/o Coamo, PR, St. Blase Church. (PCE)
Santa Catalina, PR, Coama Co., Sacred Heart, c/o Coamo, PR, St. Blase Church. (PCE)
Santa Clara, NM, Rio Arriba Co., Indian Pueblo, c/o [1] Santa Fe, NM, The Cathedral of San Francisco de Asis. (SFE)
Santa Clara, NY, St. Peter, c/o Saint Regis Falls, NY, St. Ann Church. (OG)
Santa Cruz, AZ, St. Catherine, c/o Laveen, AZ, St. John The Baptist Church. (PHX)
Santa Maria, AZ, Our Lady of Guadalupe, c/o Cashion, AZ, St. William Church. (PHX)
Santa Maria, TX, St. Margaret Ann, c/o Progreso, TX, Holy Spirit Church. (BWN)
Santa Monica, TX, Santa Monica, c/o Lyford, TX, Prince of Peace Church. (BWN)
Santa Rosa, AZ, Cristo Rey, c/o [2] Tucson, AZ, Blessed Kateri Tekakwitha Church. (TUC)
Santan, AZ, St. Anne, c/o Bapchule, AZ, St. Peter's Church. (PHX)
Santiago, FM, c/o Tol, FM, Assumption of the Blessed Virgin Mary Church. (CI)
Santiago-Talco, NM, Mora Co., c/o Mora, NM, St. Gertrude Church. (SFE)
Santo Domingo, NM, Sandoval Co., Indian Pueblo, c/o Pena Blanca, NM, Nuestra Senora De Guadalupe Church. (SFE)
Santo Nino, NM, c/o Santa Cruz, NM, Holy Cross Church. (SFE)
Sapello, NM, San Miguel Co., Our Lady of Guadalupe, c/o Las Vegas, NM, Our Lady of Sorrows Church. (SFE)
Sapphire Valley, NC, Transylvania Co., St. Jude, c/o Brevard, NC, Sacred Heart Church. (CHL)
Saragosa, TX, Our Lady of Guadalupe, c/o Balmorhea, TX, Christ the King Church. (ELP)
Saratoga Lake, NY, Saratoga Co., St. Isaac Jogues, c/o Stillwater, NY, St. Peter the Apostle Church. (ALB)
Sardis, MS, St. John the Baptist, c/o Batesville, MS, St. Mary Church. (JKS)
Sargent, NE, Assumption of the Blessed Virgin Mary, c/o Burwell, NE, Sacred Heart Church. (GI)
Sartwell, PA, McKean Co., St. Mary, c/o Eldred, PA, St. Raphael Church. (E)
Saspamco, TX, Our Lady of Perpetual Help, c/o Elmendorf, TX, St. Anthony Church. (SAT)
Satawal, FM, c/o Ulithi & Neighboring Islands, FM, Queen of Heaven Church. (CI)
Satawan, FM, c/o Lukunor, FM, Sacred Heart Church. (CI)
Satin, TX, Satin Falls Co., Santa Rita, c/o [2] Waco, TX, St. Francis on the Brazos Church. (AUS)
Saugus, CA, Los Angeles Co., Blessed Kateri Tekakwitha Mission, c/o Canyon Country, CA, St. Clare Church. (LA)
Sault Ste. Marie,, MI, Chippewa Co., St. Isaac Jogues, c/o Brimley, MI, St. Francis Xavier Church. (MAR)
Savage, MT, St. Michael, c/o Glendive, MT, Sacred Heart Church. (GF)
Savannah, NY, Wayne Co., St. Patrick, c/o Clyde, NY, St. John the Evangelist Church. (ROC)
Savoy, LA, St. Thomas, c/o Richard, LA, St. Edward Church. (LAF)
Sawmill, AZ, Apache Co., St. Francis Mission, c/o Navajo, NM, St. Berard Church. (GLP)
Sawyer, MI, St. Agnes, c/o Three Oaks, MI, St. Mary of the Assumption Church. (KAL)
Sawyer, MN, SS. Mary & Joseph, c/o Cloquet, MN, Holy Family Church. (DUL)
Sawyer, MN, Carlton Co., SS. Mary and Joseph, c/o Duluth, MN, Indian Missions Church. (DUL)
Sawyer's Bar, CA, Siskiyou Co., St. Joseph, c/o Fort Jones, CA, Sacred Heart Church. (SAC)
Saxtons River, VT, Windham Co., St. Edmund of Canterbury, c/o Putney, VT, Our Lady of Mercy Church. (BUR)
Sayre, OK, Beckham Co., Queen of All Saints, c/o Elk City, OK, St. Matthew's Church. (OKL)
Schely, IA, Holy Cross, c/o Protivin, IA, Holy Trinity Church. (DUB)
Schenectady, NY, Schenectady Co., St. Teresa Carmelite Monastery, c/o [11] Schenectady, NY, St. Luke Church. (ALB)
Schenevus, NY, Otsego Co., St. Mary, c/o Worcester, NY, St. Joseph Church. (ALB)
Schodack Landing, NY, Assumption of B.V.M., c/o Castleton-on-Hudson, NY, Sacred Heart Church. (ALB)
Schodack Landing, NY, Shrine of St. Jude, c/o Castleton-on-Hudson, NY, Sacred Heart Church. (ALB)
Schoolcraft, NE, Madison Co., St. Francis de Sales, c/o Battle Creek, NE, St. Patrick's Church. (OM)
Scio, NY, Allegany Co., St. Joseph, c/o Belmont, NY, St. Mary Church. (BUF)
Scotia, NE, St. Patrick, c/o Greeley, NE, Sacred Heart Church. (GI)
Scotland, CT, Windham Co., St. Margaret, c/o Willimantic, CT, St. Joseph Church. (NOR)
Scotland Neck, NC, Halifax Co., St. Anne, c/o Ahoskie, NC, St. Charles Borromeo Church. (R)
Scotts Mills, OR, Marion Co., Holy Rosary, c/o Mt. Angel, OR, St. Mary Church. (P)
Scranton, ND, Bowman Co., Sacred Heart, c/o Hettinger, ND, Holy Trinity Church. (BIS)
Scranton, PA, Lackawanna Co., Holy Cross, c/o [21] Scranton, PA, St. Patrick's Church. (SCR)
Scranton, PA, Lackawanna Co., St. John the Baptist, c/o [21] Scranton, PA, St. Patrick's Church. (SCR)
Scranton, PA, Lackawanna Co., St. Stanislaus, c/o [9] Scranton, PA, Holy Rosary Church. (SCR)
Scranton, PA, St. Stephen's, c/o [9] Scranton, PA, Holy Rosary Church. (SCR)
Scriba, NY, Sacred Heart, c/o [6] Oswego, NY, St. Peter Church. (SY)
Scribner, NE, Dodge Co., St. Lawrence, c/o Hooper, NE, St. Rose of Lima Church. (OM)
Seabrook Beach, NH, Rockingham Co., St. Elizabeth's, c/o Hampton, NH, Our Lady of the Miraculous Medal Church. (MAN)
Seadrift, TX, St. Patrick, c/o Port Lavaca, TX, Our Lady of the Gulf Church. (VIC)
Seagraves, TX, Gaines Co., St. Paul's, c/o Seminole, TX, St. James Church. (LUB)
Seama, NM, St. Anne, c/o Laguna, NM, St. Joseph Church. (GLP)
Seat Pleasant, MD, St. Matthias, c/o Seat Pleasant, MD, St. Margaret Church. (WDC)
Seatonville, IL, Bureau Co., St. Gertrude, c/o Ladd, IL, St. Benedict's Church. (PEO)
Seattle, WA, Maronite Catholic Community, c/o Portland, OR, Saint Sharbel Church. (OLL)
Sebastian, TX, Willacy Co., St. Martin, c/o Lyford, TX, Prince of Peace Church. (BWN)
Seco Mines, TX, Our Lady of Lourdes, c/o Eagle Pass, TX, Our Lady of Refuge Church. (SAT)
Sedillo, NM, Bernalillo Co., San Isidro, c/o Tijeras, NM, Holy Child Church. (SFE)
Seeley, CA, Holy Spirit, c/o Imperial, CA, St. Anthony of Padua Church. (SD)
Seeley Lake, MT, Missoula Co., Living Water Mission, c/o Bonner, MT, St. Ann Church. (HEL)
Segundo, CO, Las Animas Co., St. Ignatius, c/o Trinidad, CO, Most Holy Trinity, Trinidad Area Catholic Community (Trinidad Cluster) Church. (PBL)
Seiling, OK, Dewey Co., St. Thomas, c/o Okeene, OK, St. Anthony's Church. (OKL)
Seldovia, AK, St. James the Apostle, c/o Homer, AK, St. John the Baptist Church. (ANC)
Selinsgrove, PA, Snyder Co., Selinsgrove Center, c/o Selinsgrove, PA, St. Pius X Church. (HBG)
Selz, ND, Pierce Co., c/o Harvey, ND, St. Cecilia's Church. (FAR)
Seminole, PA, Clarion Co., SS. Cosmas and Damian, c/o New Bethlehem, PA, St. Charles Church. (E)
Sena, NM, San Miguel Co., c/o Villanueva, NM, Our Lady of Guadalupe Church. (SFE)
Seneca, OR, St. Charles, c/o John Day, OR, St. Elizabeth's Church. (BAK)
Seneca, SC, Oconee Co., St. Paul the Apostle, c/o Clemson, SC, St. Andrew Church. (CHR)
Servilleta, NM, Taos Co., c/o El Rito, NM, San Juan Nepomuceno Church. (SFE)
Shafter, TX, Sgdo. Corazon de Jesus, c/o Presidio, TX, Santa Teresa de Jesus Church. (ELP)
Shamrock, TX, St. Patrick, c/o Wellington, TX, Our Mother of Mercy Church. (AMA)
Sharon, GA, Talifero Co., Purification, c/o Washington, GA, St. Joseph's Church. (ATL)
Sharon Springs, NY, St. Mary, c/o Cobleskill, NY, St. Vincent de Paul Church. (ALB)
Shasta Lake City, CA, Shasta Co., St. Michael, c/o Redding, CA, St. Joseph Church. (SAC)
Shattuck, OK, Ellis Co., Holy Name, c/o Woodward, OK, St. Peter's Church. (OKL)
Shawmut, MT, Wheatland Co., Blessed Sacrament, c/o Harlowton, MT, St. Joseph Church. (HEL)
Sheffield, TX, Crockett Co., Good Shepherd, c/o Ozona, TX, Our Lady of Perpetual Help Church. (SAN)
Shelby, IN, Lake Co., St. Theresa, c/o Lowell, IN, St. Edward Church. (GRY)
Sheldon, ND, St. Mary & Our Lady of the Scapular, c/o Enderlin, ND, St. Patrick's Church. (FAR)
Sheldon Point, AK, St. Peter's, c/o Alakanuk, AK, St. Ignatius Church. (FBK)
Shelton, NE, Sacred Heart, c/o Wood River, NE, St. Mary's Church. (GI)
Sherburn, MN, Martin Co., St. Luke, c/o Jackson, MN, Good Shepherd Church. (WIN)
Sheridan, AR, Grant Co., Holy Cross, c/o Fordyce, AR, Good Shepherd Church. (LR)
Sheridan, AR, Grant Co., Holy Cross, c/o Sheridan, AR, Holy Cross Church. (LR)
Sherman Station, ME, Penobscot Co., St. Joseph's Church, c/o Benedicta, ME, St. Benedict's Church. (PRT)
Sherwood, ND, Renville Co., St. James, c/o Mohall, ND, St. Jerome Church. (BIS)
Shevlin, MN, Clearwater Co., Our Lady of Victory, c/o Bagley, MN, St. Joseph Church. (CR)
Shickley, NE, Fillmore Co., St. Mary, c/o Geneva, NE, St. Joseph's Church. (LIN)
Shidler, OK, Osage Co., St. Ann, c/o Fairfax, OK, Sacred Heart Church. (TLS)
Shingletown, CA, Shasta Co., Mary Queen of Peace, c/o Anderson, CA, Sacred Heart Church. (SAC)
Shoreham, VT, Addison Co., St. Geneviere, c/o Orwell, VT, St. Paul Church. (BUR)
Shoshone-Tecopa, CA, Inyo Co., St. John the Baptist, c/o Lone Pine, CA, Santa Rosa Church. (FRS)
Shoshoni, WY, Fremont Co., St. Joseph, c/o Riverton, WY, St. Margaret's Church. (CHY)
Shubert, NE, Richardson Co., St. Ann's, c/o Dawson, NE, St. Mary's Church. (LIN)
Sidnaw, MI, Houghton Co., St. Francis Xavier, c/o Ewen, MI, Sacred Heart Church. (MAR)
Sieper, LA, St. Jude, c/o Glenmora, LA, St. Louis Church. (ALX)
Sierra Alta, PR, St. Lucy, c/o Yauco, PR, Holy Rossary Church. (PCE)
Sierra Blanca, TX, Our Lady of Miracles, c/o Van Horn,

TX, Our Lady of Fatima Church. (ELP)
Sierra City, CA, Sierra Co., St. Thomas, c/o Downieville, CA, Immaculate Conception Church. (SAC)
Sigel, PA, Jefferson Co., St. Dominic, c/o Brookville, PA, Immaculate Conception Church. (E)
Sile, NM, Sandoval Co., c/o Pena Blanca, NM, Nuestra Senora De Guadalupe Church. (SFE)
Siletz, OR, Lincoln Co., St. Mary, c/o Newport, OR, Sacred Heart Parish Church. (P)
Silt, CO, Garfield Co., Sacred Heart, c/o Rifle, CO, St. Mary's Church. (DEN)
Silver Lake, PA, Susquehanna Co., St. Augustine, c/o Friendsville, PA, St. Joseph's Church. (SCR)
Silver Springs, NV, Our Lady of the Blessed Sacrament, c/o Fernley, NV, St. Robert Bellarmine Church. (RNO)
Silverton, CO, San Juan Co., St. Patrick, c/o Ouray, CO, St. Daniel the Prophet Church. (PBL)
Silverton, TX, Briscoe Co., Our Lady of Loreto, c/o Tulia, TX, Church of the Holy Spirit. (AMA)
Simpson, PA, Lackawanna Co., Holy Trinity, c/o Simpson, PA, St. Michael's Church. (SCR)
Slim Butte, SD, Shannon Co., Our Lady of Lourdes, c/o Pine Ridge, SD, Holy Rosary Church. (RC)
Smith Valley, NV, Lyon Co., St. John the Baptist, c/o Yerington, NV, Holy Family Church. (RNO)
Smith's Landing, NY, St. Mary's, c/o Catskill, NY, St. Patrick Church. (ALB)
Smithfield, NE, Gosper Co., St. John's, c/o Holdrege, NE, All Saints Church. (LIN)
Smiths Corners, MI, Hurenco Co., Holy Trinity, c/o Rapson, MI, St. Joseph Church. (SAG)
Smiths Creek, MI, St. Clair Co., Holy Rosary, c/o Columbus, MI, St. Philip Neri Church. (DET)
Soap Lake, WA, Grant Co., Our Most Sorrowful Mother, c/o Ephrata, WA, St. Rose of Lima Church. (YAK)
Sodus Point, NY, Wayne Co., St. Rose, c/o Sodus, NY, Epiphany Church. (ROC)
Soileau, LA, Allen Parish, St. Joseph, c/o Oberlin, LA, St. Joan of Arc Church. (LKC)
Solana Beach, CA, San Diego Co., St. Leo, c/o Solana Beach, CA, St. James Church. (SD)
Soldier Creek, SD, St. Rose, c/o Rosebud, SD, St. Bridget Church. (RC)
Soldier Creek, SD, St. Rose, c/o St. Francis, SD, Rosebud Reservation Church. (RC)
Soledad, CA, Monterey Co., Nuestra Senora de la Soledad, c/o Soledad, CA, Our Lady of Solitude Church. (MRY)
Solen, ND, Sioux Co., Sacred Heart, c/o Selfridge, ND, St. Philomena Church. (BIS)
Solomon's Gap, PA, Luzerne Co., St. Catherine, c/o Mountaintop, PA, St. Jude's Church. (SCR)
Somers, MT, St. Ann, c/o Bigfork, MT, St. Catherine Church. (HEL)
Sonoita, AZ, Santa Cruz Co., Our Lady of Angels, c/o Patagonia, AZ, St. Theresa Church. (TUC)
Sonsorol, FM, c/o Koror, FM, Sacred Heart Church. (CI)
South Byron, NY, Genesee Co., St. Michael, c/o [2] Batavia, NY, St. Joseph Church. (BUF)
South Centerville, NY, Orange Co., Holy Cross, c/o Middletown, NY, Our Lady of Mt. Carmel Church. (NY)
South Chatham, MA, Barnstable Co., Our Lady of Grace, c/o Chatham, MA, Holy Redeemer Church. (FR)
South Colton, NY, St. Lawrence Co., St. Paul, c/o Colton, NY, St. Patrick Church. (OG)
South Fork, CO, Rio Grande Co., Holy Family, c/o Del Norte, CO, Holy Name of Mary Church. (PBL)
South Hampton Twp., NJ, Vincentown Co., St. Jude, c/o Roebling, NJ, St. Nicholas Church. (PSC)
South Harpswell, ME, St. Mary-by-the-Sea, c/o Brunswick, ME, St. Charles Church. (PRT)
South Hartford, NY, St. Philip, c/o Fort Ann, NY, St. Ann Church. (ALB)
South Lee, MA, Berkshire Co., St. Francis of Assisi, c/o Lee, MA, St. Mary's Church. (SPR)
South Royalston, MA, Athol Co., Our Lady Queen of Heaven, c/o Athol, MA, Our Lady Immaculate Church. (WOR)
South Royalton, VT, Windsor Co., St. Matthew, c/o Bethel, VT, St. Anthony Church. (BUR)
South Salem, NY, Westchester Co., S. Salem Presbyterian Church, c/o Katonah, NY, St. Mary of the Assumption Church. (NY)
South Sterling, PA, Wayne Co., St. Mary Magdalene, c/o Gouldsboro, PA, St. Rita Church. (SCR)
South Strafford, VT, Orange Co., Our Lady of Light, c/o Bradford, VT, Our Lady of Perpetual Help Church. (BUR)
South Tucson, AZ, Pima Co., St. Nicholas Indian Center, c/o [2] Tucson, AZ, Blessed Kateri Tekakwitha Church. (TUC)
South Vallejo, CA, Solano Co., St. Louis Bertrand, c/o Vallejo, CA, St. Vincent Ferrer Church. (SAC)
South Wayne, WI, St. John, c/o Gratiot, WI, St. Joseph Church. (MAD)
Southton, TX, St. Ann, c/o [71] San Antonio, TX, San Juan Capistrano Church. (SAT)
Southwest Oswego, NY, St. Joseph, c/o Hannibal, NY, Our Lady of the Rosary Church. (SY)
Spangler, PA, St. Jude Chapel, c/o Bakerton, PA, Sacred Heart Church. (ALT)
Spangler, PA, St. Jude Chapel, c/o Elmora, PA, St. Jude Church. (ALT)
Spanish Lake, LA, St. Anne, c/o Natchitoches, LA, Holy Cross Church. (ALX)
Sparta, NC, Alleghany Co., St. Frances of Rome, c/o Jefferson, NC, St. Francis of Assisi Church. (CHL)
Spartansburg, PA, Crawford Co., Our Lady of Victory, c/o Corry, PA, St. Elizabeth Church. (E)
Spearville, KS, Ford Co., St. John the Baptist, c/o Windthorst, KS, Immaculate Heart of Mary Church. (DOD)
Spelter, WV, Harrison Co., Holy Family, c/o Shinnston, WV, St. Ann's Church. (WH)
Spencer Mountain, NC, St. Helen, c/o Belmont, NC, Queen of the Apostles Church. (CHL)
Spencerville, OH, Allen Co., St. Patrick, c/o Landeck, OH, St. John Baptist Church. (TOL)
Spiro, OK, St. Elizabeth Seton, c/o Poteau, OK, Immaculate Conception Church. (TLS)
Spofford Junction, TX, St. Blaise, c/o Brackettville, TX, St. Mary Magdalen Church. (SAT)
Spotsylvania, VA, Spotsylvania Co., St. Matthew, c/o Chancellorsville, VA, St. Patrick's Church. (ARL)
Spring Creek, SD, St. Patrick, c/o St. Francis, SD, St. Charles Church. (RC)
Spring Creek, SD, St. Patrick, c/o St. Francis, SD, Rosebud Reservation Church. (RC)
Spring Lake, NJ, Monmouth Co., St. Margaret, c/o Spring Lake, NJ, St. Catharine Church. (TR)
Spring Lake Twp., MN, Scott Co., St. Catherine, c/o Cedar Lake, MN, St. Patrick Church. (STP)
Springfield, GA, St. Boniface, c/o Port Wentworth, GA, Our Lady of Lourdes Church. (SAV)
Springfield, MA, Hampden, Center for South East Asian Apostolate, c/o [20] Springfield, MA, St. Thomas Aquinas Church. (SPR)
Springfield, SC, Orangeburg Co., St. Theresa, c/o Orangeburg, SC, Holy Trinity Church. (CHR)
Springfield Center, NY, Blessed Sacrament, c/o Cherry Valley, NY, St. Thomas the Apostle Church. (ALB)
Springhill, LA, Webster Parish, Sacred Heart, c/o Minden, LA, St. Paul Church. (SHP)
Spurlington, KY, Taylor Co., St. Frances de Sales, c/o Calvary, KY, Holy Name of Mary Church. (L)
Squaw Valley, CA, Fresno Co., St. Rita, c/o Orange Cove, CA, St. Isidore the Farmer Church. (FRS)
Staatsburg, NY, Dutchess Co., St. Paul, c/o Hyde Park, NY, Regina Coeli Church. (NY)
Staffordville, CT, Tolland Co., St. Joseph, c/o Stafford Springs, CT, St. Edward Church. (NOR)
Stamford, VT, Bennington Co., St. John Bosco, c/o Readsboro, VT, St. Joachim Church. (BUR)
Standish, NY, Clinton Co., St. Michael, c/o Lyon Mountain, NY, St. Bernard Church. (OG)
Stanfield, AZ, Pinal Co., St. Mary, c/o Casa Grande, AZ, St. Anthony Church. (TUC)
Stanton, KY, Powell Co., Our Lady of the Mountains, c/o Ravenna, KY, St. Elizabeth Church. (LEX)
Star Lake, NM, San Ignacio, c/o Crownpoint, NM, St. Paul Church. (GLP)
Starks, LA, St. Michael, c/o Vinton, LA, St. Joseph Church. (LKC)
Starkweather, ND, Ramsey Co., Assumption of the Blessed Virgin Mary, c/o Devils Lake, ND, St. Joseph's Church. (FAR)
Starr School, MT, Sacred Heart, c/o Browning, MT, Church of the Little Flower. (HEL)
Starrucca, PA, Wayne Co., St. Paul, c/o Jackson, PA, St. Martin of Tours Church. (SCR)
Steele, ND, Kidder Co., St. Francis de Sales, c/o Tappen, ND, St. Paul's Church. (FAR)
Steilacoom, WA, Pierce Co., Immaculate Conception, c/o [4] Tacoma, WA, St. John Bosco Church. (SEA)
Stephentown, NY, St. Joseph, c/o Berlin, NY, Sacred Heart Church. (ALB)
Stepstone, KY, Pendleton Co., Immaculate Conception, c/o California, KY, Sts. Peter and Paul Church. (COV)
Sterling, CT, Windham Co., St. Joseph, c/o Moosup, CT, All-Hallows Church. (NOR)
Sterling City, TX, Sterling Co., St. Paschal Baylon, c/o Carlsbad, TX, St. Therese of the Child Jesus Church. (SAN)
Stevenson, WA, Skamania Co., Star of the Sea, c/o Camas, WA, St. Thomas Church. (SEA)
Stevinson, CA, Merced Co., St. Mary, c/o Hilmar, CA, Holy Rosary Church. (FRS)
Stigler, OK, St. Joseph, c/o Poteau, OK, Immaculate Conception Church. (TLS)
Stinnett, TX, St. Ann's, c/o Borger, TX, St. John the Evangelist Church. (AMA)
Stockton, MO, Cedar Co., St. Peter the Apostle, c/o El Dorado Springs, MO, St. Elizabeth Church. (SPC)
Stockton, NJ, Hunterdon Co., St. Agnes, c/o Lambertville, NJ, St. John the Evangelist Church. (MET)
Stone City, IA, St. Joseph, c/o Anamosa, IA, St. Patrick's Church. (DUB)
Stoneham, CO, Morgan Co., St. John, c/o Brush, CO, St. Mary Church. (DEN)
Stonewall, LA, DeSoto Parish, St. Ann, c/o [9] Shreveport, LA, St. Mary of the Pines Church. (SHP)
Stony Point, TX, Bastrop Co., c/o [24] Austin, TX, San Francisco Church. (AUS)
Stonyford, CA, Colusa Co., St. Mary of the Mountain, c/o Maxwell, CA, Sacred Heart Church. (SAC)
Story, WY, Sheridan Co., Our Lady of the Pines, c/o Sheridan, WY, Holy Name Church. (CHY)
Stowell, PA, Wyoming Co., St. Anthony, c/o Wyalusing, PA, St. Mary's Assumption Church. (SCR)
Strandquist, MN, Marshall Co., St. Edward, The Confessor, c/o Middle River, MN, St. Joseph, Husband of Mary Church. (CR)
Stratford, CA, Kings Co., St. Joseph, c/o Lemoore, CA, St. Peter Church. (FRS)
Stratton, ME, St. John, c/o Oquossoc, ME, Our Lady of the Lakes Church. (PRT)
Stratton, NE, Hitchcock Co., St. Joseph's, c/o Benkelman, NE, St. Joseph's Church. (LIN)
Stratton Mountain, VT, Windham Co., Chapel of the Snows, c/o Putney, VT, Our Lady of Mercy Church. (BUR)
Strawn, IL, Livingston Co., St. Rose, c/o Colfax, IL, St. Joseph's Church. (PEO)
String Praire, TX, Assumption of the Blessed Virgin Mary, c/o Rockne, TX, Sacred Heart Church. (AUS)
Stroud, OK, Lincoln Co., St.Louis, c/o Chandler, OK, Our Lady of Sorrows Church. (OKL)
Stuart, FL, Martin Co., St. Andrew, c/o Stuart, FL, St. Joseph Church. (PMB)
Sturgeon Lake, MN, St. Isidore's, c/o Willow River, MN, St. Mary's Church. (DUL)
Sugar Notch, PA, Luzerne Co., St. Charles Borromeo, c/o Sugar Notch, PA, Holy Family Church. (SCR)
Sugarloaf U.S.A., ME, Richard H. Bell Memorial Chapel, c/o Oquossoc, ME, Our Lady of the Lakes Church. (PRT)
Sugur Island, MI, Chippewa Co., Sacred Heart, c/o Brimley, MI, St. Francis Xavier Church. (MAR)
Sullivan City, TX, St. William, c/o La Joya, TX, Our Lady, Queen of Angels Church. (BWN)
Sulphur, LA, Calcasieu Parish, St. Peter Claver, c/o [3] Sulphur, LA, Our Lady of Prompt Succor Church. (LKC)
Sunapee, NH, Sullivan Co., St. Joachim, c/o Newport, NH, St. Patrick Church. (MAN)
Sunburst, MT, St. Thomas Aquinas, c/o Shelby, MT, St. William Church. (HEL)
Sundance, WY, Crook Co., St. Paul, c/o Newcastle, WY, Corpus Christi Church. (CHY)
Sundown, TX, Hockley Co., San Isidro, c/o Levelland, TX, St. Michael's Church. (LUB)
Sunray, TX, Christ the King, c/o Dumas, TX, SS. Peter and Paul Church. (AMA)
Sunrise Beach, TX, Burnet Co., Our Lady of the Lake, c/o Kingsland, TX, St. Charles Borromeo Church. (AUS)
Superior, MT, St. Mary Queen of Heaven, c/o Frenchtown, MT, St. John the Baptist Church. (HEL)
Superior, WY, Sweetwater Co., St. Vivian, c/o Rock Springs, WY, Our Lady of Sorrows Church. (CHY)
Suquamish, WA, Kitsap Co., St. Peter, c/o Poulsbo, WA, St. Olaf Church. (SEA)
Surf City, NJ, Ocean Co., St. Thomas of Villanova, c/o Brant Beach, NJ, St. Francis of Assisi Church. (TR)
Susquehanna, PA, Snyder Co., Susquehanna University, c/o Selinsgrove, PA, St. Pius X Church. (HBG)
Susua, PR, La Resurreccion, c/o Sabana Grande, PR, Church of San Isidro. (MGZ)
Swartz, LA, St. Lawrence, c/o [3] Monroe, LA, Our Lady of Fatima Church. (SHP)
Sweet Lake, LA, St. Patrick's, c/o Big Lake, LA, St. Mary of the Lake Church. (LKC)
Sweet Springs, MO, Holy Family, c/o Marshall, MO, St. Peter Church. (JC)

T

Ta, FM, c/o Lukunor, FM, Sacred Heart Church. (CI)
Table Rock, WY, Sweetwater Co., Catholic Community, c/o Rock Springs, WY, Our Lady of Sorrows Church. (CHY)
Tabor, MN, Polk Co., Holy Trinity Catholic, c/o Warren, MN, SS. Peter and Paul Church. (CR)
Tabor, NE, Colfax Co., St. Mary, c/o Heun, NE, Holy Trinity Church. (OM)
Tache Indian Reservation, CA, Kings Co., St. Rosa, c/o Lemoore, CA, St. Peter Church. (FRS)
Taconite, MN, St. Joseph's, c/o Marble, MN, St. Mary's Church. (DUL)
Tahoka, TX, Lynn Co., St. Jude, c/o O'Donnell, TX, St. Pius X Church. (LUB)
Tajique, NM, Torrance Co., c/o Moriarty, NM, Estancia Valley Catholic Parish Church. (SFE)
Talihina, OK, Leflore Co., St. Catherine of Siena, c/o Hartshorne, OK, Holy Rosary Church. (TLS)
Tallaboa Alta, PR, Santa Ana St. Domingo, Carmen, c/o

Penuelas, PR, St. Joseph Church. (PCE)
Talpa, NM, Taos Co., N.S. de San Juan de Los Lagos, c/o Ranchos De Taos, NM, San Francisco de Asis Church. (SFE)
Tamatam, FM, Maria Lourdes, c/o Tol, FM, Assumption of the Blessed Virgin Mary Church. (CI)
Tamatam, FM, Maria Lourdes, c/o Puluwat, FM, Santiago Church. (CI)
Tampa, FL, Hillsborough Co., St. Joseph Vietnamese Mission, c/o [3] Tampa, FL, Epiphany Church. (SP)
Tampa, KS, Marion Co., Holy Redeemer, c/o Marion, KS, Holy Family Church. (WCH)
Tanama, PR, Sagrado Corazon, c/o Adjuntas, PR, St. Joachim Church. (PCE)
Taos, NM, Taos Co., St. Jerome, c/o Taos, NM, Nuestra Senora De Guadalupe Church. (SFE)
Taos Pueblo, NM, c/o Taos, NM, Nuestra Senora De Guadalupe Church. (SFE)
Tapia, NM, San Miguel Co., c/o Moriarty, NM, Estancia Valley Catholic Parish Church. (SFE)
Tatum, NM, Our Lady of the Holy Rosary, c/o Lovington, NM, St. Thomas Aquinas Church. (LSC)
Tatum, TX, San Pedro the Fisherman, c/o Henderson, TX, St. Jude Church. (TYL)
Taylorsville, KY, Spencer Co., All Saints Church, c/o Fairfield, KY, St. Michael Church. (L)
Taylorsville, NC, Alexander Co., Holy Trinity, c/o Lenoir, NC, St. Francis of Assisi Church. (CHL)
Teague, TX, Freestone Co., St. Mary, c/o Fairfield, TX, St. Bernard of Clarivaux Church. (TYL)
Tecolotito, NM, San Miguel Co., c/o Anton Chico, NM, San Jose Church. (SFE)
Tehama, CA, Tehama Co., St. Stanislaus, c/o Corning, CA, Immaculate Conception Church. (SAC)
Teller, AK, St. Ann, c/o Nome, AK, St. Joseph Church. (FBK)
Temple, PA, Berks Co., St. Anthony, c/o [5] Reading, PA, Holy Guardian Angels Church. (ALN)
Tenino, WA, Thurston Co., St. Peter, c/o Yelm, WA, St. Columban Church. (SEA)
Tennessee, IL, McDonough Co., Sacred Heart, c/o Macomb, IL, St. Paul's Church. (PEO)
Terra Alta, WV, Preston Co., St. Edward, c/o Kingwood, WV, St. Sebastian's Church. (WH)
Terra Bella, CA, Blessed Miguel Agustin Pro, c/o Porterville, CA, St. Anne Church. (FRS)
Terrebonne, MN, Red Lake Co., St. Anthony, c/o Red Lake Falls, MN, St. Joseph's Church. (CR)
Terry, MT, Sacred Heart, c/o Miles City, MT, Sacred Heart Church. (GF)
Tesuque, NM, Sante Fe Co., Indian Pueblo, c/o [1] Santa Fe, NM, The Cathedral of San Francisco de Asis. (SFE)
Tesuque, NM, Santa Fe Co., San Ysidro, c/o [2] Santa Fe, NM, Our Lady of Guadalupe Church. (SFE)
Texico, NM, Curry Co., c/o Clovis, NM, Our Lady of Guadalupe Church. (SFE)
Texline, TX, St. Mary's, c/o Dalhart, TX, St. Anthony's Church. (AMA)
Thatcher, AZ, Graham Co., Neuman Center, c/o Safford, AZ, St. Rose of Lima Church. (TUC)
Thayer, MO, Oregon Co., Sacred Heart, c/o West Plains, MO, St. Mary Church. (SPC)
Thedford, NE, Thomas Co., St. Thomas of Canterbury, c/o Mullen, NE, St. Mary's Church. (GI)
Theilman, MN, Wabasha Co., St. Joseph, c/o Lake City, MN, St. Mary's Church. (WIN)
Theresa, NY, Jefferson Co., St. Theresa of Avila, c/o Evans Mills, NY, St. Mary Church. (OG)
Thomas, OK, Custer Co., Blessed Sacrament, c/o Weatherford, OK, St. Eugene's Church. (OKL)
Thomaston, GA, Upson Co., St. John the Baptist, c/o Griffin, GA, Sacred Heart Church. (ATL)
Thomaston, ME, Knox Co., St. James, c/o Rockland, ME, St. Bernard's Church. (PRT)
Thomasville, AL, Clarke Co., St. Joseph, c/o Grove Hill, AL, Sacred Heart Church. (MOB)
Thompson, ND, Grand Forks Co., St. Jude, c/o Reynolds, ND, Our Lady of Perpetual Help Church. (FAR)
Thorne Bay, AK, c/o Craig, AK, St. John by the Sea Church. (JUN)
Thornhurst, PA, Luzerne Co., St. Mark, c/o Bear Creek Township, PA, St. Elizabeth Church. (SCR)
Thornton, CA, San Joaquin Co., Mater Ecclesiae, c/o Lodi, CA, St. Anne Church. (STO)
Thornwell, LA, Jefferson Davis Parish, St. Francis of Assisi Chapel, c/o Lake Arthur, LA, Our Lady of the Lake Church. (LKC)
Three Rivers, CA, Tulare Co., St. Clair, c/o Woodlake, CA, St. Frances Cabrini Church. (FRS)
Three Rivers, NM, St. Patrick, c/o Mescalero, NM, St. Joseph Church. (LSC)
Three Rocks, CA, Fresno Co., Our Lady of Lourdes, c/o Mendota, CA, Our Lady of Guadalupe Church. (FRS)
Throop, PA, Lackawanna Co., St. Bridget, c/o Throop, PA, St. John the Baptist Church. (SCR)
Throop, PA, St. Mary, c/o Throop, PA, St. John the Baptist Church. (SCR)
Thunder Butte, SD, Ziebach Co., St. Luke, c/o Eagle Butte, SD, All Saints Church. (RC)
Thunder Butte, SD, Ziebach Co., St. Luke, c/o Eagle Butte, SD, Cheyenne River Reservation Church. (RC)
Tijeras, NM, San Antonito, c/o Tijeras, NM, Holy Child Church. (SFE)
Tilden, TX, St. Joseph, c/o Charlotte, TX, St. Rose of Lima Church. (SAT)
Timpson, TX, Shelby Co., Epiphany, c/o Center, TX, St. Therese Church. (TYL)
Tinaja, NM, Colfax Co., c/o Springer, NM, St. Joseph Church. (SFE)
Tioga, PA, Tioga Co., St. Mary, c/o Mansfield, PA, Holy Child Church. (SCR)
Tionesta, PA, Forest Co., St. Anthony, c/o Tidioute, PA, St. John Church. (E)
Tipton, OK, Tillman Co., Sacred Heart, c/o Frederick, OK, St. Helen Church. (OKL)
Tishomingo, OK, Johnston Co., St. Anthony, c/o Sulphur, OK, St. Francis Xavier Church. (OKL)
Toa Alta, PR, Cristo de los Milagros, c/o [3] Toa Alta, PR, San Jose Church. (SJN)
Toa Alta, PR, Cristo Rey, c/o [5] Toa Alta, PR, N. Sra. de la Providencia Church. (SJN)
Toa Alta, PR, La Resurreccion, c/o [5] Toa Alta, PR, N. Sra. de la Providencia Church. (SJN)
Toa Alta, PR, N. Sra. de Fatima, c/o [5] Toa Alta, PR, N. Sra. de la Providencia Church. (SJN)
Toa Alta, PR, Ntra. Sra. del Camino, c/o [3] Toa Alta, PR, San Jose Church. (SJN)
Toa Alta, PR, Nuestra Senora del Carmen, c/o [4] Toa Alta, PR, Nuestra Senora de la Medalla Milagrosa Church. (SJN)
Toa Alta, PR, Sagrada Familia, c/o [3] Toa Alta, PR, San Jose Church. (SJN)
Toa Alta, PR, Sagrado Corazon, c/o [3] Toa Alta, PR, San Jose Church. (SJN)
Toa Alta, PR, Sagrado Corazon de Jesus, c/o [4] Toa Alta, PR, Nuestra Senora de la Medalla Milagrosa Church. (SJN)
Toa Alta, PR, San Antonio, c/o [2] Toa Alta, PR, San Fernando Church. (SJN)
Toa Alta, PR, San Judas Tadeo, c/o [2] Toa Alta, PR, San Fernando Church. (SJN)
Toa Alta, PR, Sant. Trinidad, c/o [5] Toa Alta, PR, N. Sra. de la Providencia Church. (SJN)
Toa Alta, PR, Santa Teresa, c/o [4] Toa Alta, PR, Nuestra Senora de la Medalla Milagrosa Church. (SJN)
Toa Alta, PR, Santa Teresita, c/o [3] Toa Alta, PR, San Jose Church. (SJN)
Toa Alta, PR, Virgen del Carmen, c/o [3] Toa Alta, PR, San Jose Church. (SJN)
Toa Baja, PR, Cristo Rey, c/o [2] Toa Baja, PR, Ntra. Sra. de la Candelaria Church. (SJN)
Toa Baja, PR, N. Sra. del Carmen, c/o [3] Toa Baja, PR, Espiritu Santo Church. (SJN)
Toa Baja, PR, Ntra. Sra. de Lourdes, c/o [1] Toa Baja, PR, Nuestra Senora de Covadonga Church. (SJN)
Toa Baja, PR, Ntra. Sra. del Carmen, c/o [4] Toa Baja, PR, Jose Obrero Church. (SJN)
Toa Baja, PR, San Martin de Porres, c/o [1] Toa Baja, PR, Nuestra Senora de Covadonga Church. (SJN)
Toa Baja, PR, San Martin de Porres, c/o [4] Toa Baja, PR, Jose Obrero Church. (SJN)
Toa Baja, PR, Santa Maria, c/o [2] Toa Baja, PR, Ntra. Sra. de la Candelaria Church. (SJN)
Toa Baja, PR, Santisima Trinidad, c/o [2] Toa Baja, PR, Ntra. Sra. de la Candelaria Church. (SJN)
Tobias, NE, Saline Co., St. Joseph's, c/o Wilber, NE, St. Wenceslaus Church. (LIN)
Tohono O'Odham, AZ, St. Lucy, Paloma Ranch, c/o Gila Bend, AZ, St. Michael Church. (PHX)
Tok, AK, Holy Rosary, c/o Delta Junction, AK, Our Lady of Sorrows Church. (FBK)
Tokio, ND, Benson Co., Christ the King, c/o Fort Totten, ND, Seven Dolors Church. (FAR)
Tokio, ND, Christ the King, c/o Fort Totten Reservation, ND, (Sioux Indians) Church. (FAR)
Tolna, ND, Nelson Co., St. Joseph, c/o Lakota, ND, St. Mary's Church. (FAR)
Tompkinsville, KY, Monroe Co., Christ the King, c/o Edmonton, KY, Christ the Healer Church. (L)
Tonopah, NV, Our Lady of Guadalupe, c/o Tonopah, NV, St. Patrick Church. (LAV)
Tonyville, CA, St. Anthony, c/o Lindsay, CA, Sacred Heart Church. (FRS)
Tornillo, TX, Santa Rita, c/o Fabens, TX, Our Lady of Guadalupe Church. (ELP)
Torrance, CA, Los Angeles Co., St. Joseph, c/o Torrance, CA, Nativity Church. (LA)
Torreon, NM, Torrance Co., c/o Mountainair, NM, St. Alice Church. (SFE)
Torrey, UT, Wayne Co., St. Anthony of the Desert, c/o Richfield/Monroe, UT, St. Elizabeth's Church. (SLC)
Toston, MT, Broadwater Co., Immaculate Conception, c/o Townsend, MT, Holy Cross Church. (HEL)
Touhy, NE, Saunders Co., St. Vitus, c/o Weston, NE, St. John Nepomucene Church. (LIN)
Toulon, IL, Stark Co., St. John, c/o Wyoming, IL, St. Dominic's Church. (PEO)
Townshend, VT, Windham Co., Our Lady of the Valley, c/o Putney, VT, Our Lady of Mercy Church. (BUR)
Toyah, TX, St. Emily, c/o Pecos, TX, St. Catherine Church. (ELP)
Trail City, SD, Corson Co., Holy Rosary, c/o Timber Lake, SD, Holy Cross Church. (RC)
Trampas, NM, Taos Co., San Jose de Gracia, c/o Chimayo, NM, Holy Family Church. (SFE)
Trapper Creek, AK, St. Philip Benizi, c/o Talkeetna, AK, St. Bernard Church. (ANC)
Traver, CA, Tulare Co., St. John the Baptist Educational Center, c/o Kingsburg, CA, Holy Family Church. (FRS)
Tremonton, UT, Box Elder Co., Santa Ana, c/o Brigham City, UT, St. Henry Church. (SLC)
Trenton, MO, Mercer Co., Immaculate Heart of Mary Church, c/o Trenton, MO, St. Joseph's Church. (KC)
Trenton, ND, Williams Co., St. John the Baptist, c/o Williston, ND, St. Joseph Church. (BIS)
Tres de Jayuya, PR, Santa Teresita, c/o Adjuntas, PR, St. Joachim Church. (PCE)
Tres Piedras, NM, Taos Co., c/o El Rito, NM, San Juan Nepomuceno Church. (SFE)
Triadelphia, WV, Ohio Co., Our Lady of Seven Dolors, c/o [11] Wheeling, WV, St. Vincent de Paul's Church. (WH)
Trichel, LA, St. Joseph, c/o Campti, LA, Nativity of The Blessed Virgin Mary Church. (ALX)
Trinchera, CO, Las Animas Co., Sacred Heart, c/o Trinidad, CO, Most Holy Trinity, Trinidad Area Catholic Community (Trinidad Cluster) Church. (PBL)
Trinidad, CA, Holy Trinity, c/o McKinleyville, CA, Christ the King Church. (SR)
Trout Lake, MI, Chippewa Co., St. Mary, c/o Rudyard, MI, St. Joseph Church. (MAR)
Troy, MT, Immaculate Conception, c/o Libby, MT, St. Joseph Church. (HEL)
Troy, NY, Rensselaer Co., Hallmark Nursing Home, c/o [8] Troy, NY, St. Michael the Archangel Church. (ALB)
Troy, PA, Bradford Co., St. John Nepomucene, c/o Canton, PA, St. Michael Church. (SCR)
Truchas, NM, Rio Arriba Co., Holy Rosary, c/o Chimayo, NM, Holy Family Church. (SFE)
Trujillo, CO, St. James, c/o Pagosa Springs, CO, Immaculate Heart of Mary Church. (PBL)
Trujillo, NM, San Miguel Co., San Ignacio, c/o Las Vegas, NM, Our Lady of Sorrows Church. (SFE)
Trujillo Alto, PR, El Divino Pastor, c/o [5] Trujillo Alto, PR, San Judas Tadeo Church. (SJN)
Trujillo Alto, PR, La Inmaculada Concepcion, c/o [3] Trujillo Alto, PR, San Francisco de Asis Church. (SJN)
Trujillo Alto, PR, La Milagrosa, c/o [3] Trujillo Alto, PR, San Francisco de Asis Church. (SJN)
Trujillo Alto, PR, Ntra. Sra. del Carmen, c/o [5] Trujillo Alto, PR, San Judas Tadeo Church. (SJN)
Trujillo Alto, PR, San Jose de la Montana, c/o [3] Trujillo Alto, PR, San Francisco de Asis Church. (SJN)
Trujillo Creek, CO, Mount Carmel, c/o Aguilar, CO, St. Anthony Church. (PBL)
Truman, MN, Martin Co., St. Katherine, c/o Madelia, MN, St. Mary Church. (WIN)
Truman, WI, Immaculate Conception, c/o Belmont, WI, St. Philomena Church. (MAD)
Truro, MA, Barnstable Co., Sacred Heart, c/o Wellfleet, MA, Our Lady of Lourdes Church. (FR)
Tsaile, AZ, St. Ann, c/o Lukachukai, AZ, St. Isabel Mission for Navajo Indians Church. (GLP)
Tsis, FM, c/o Fefan, FM, Sacred Heart Church. (CI)
Tucson, AZ, Pima Co., Our Lady of Guadalupe, c/o [21] Tucson, AZ, Santa Cruz Church. (TUC)
Tucson, AZ, San Ignacio, c/o [2] Tucson, AZ, Blessed Kateri Tekakwitha Church. (TUC)
Tucson, AZ, San Martin, c/o [2] Tucson, AZ, Blessed Kateri Tekakwitha Church. (TUC)
Tucson, AZ, Pima Co., Santa Catalina, c/o [18] Tucson, AZ, Saint Odilia Church. (TUC)
Tucson, AZ, Pima Co., Santa Rosa, c/o [3] Tucson, AZ, Holy Family Church. (TUC)
Tucson, AZ, Pima Co., St. Anthony's Catholic Instruction Center and Capilla, c/o [21] Tucson, AZ, Santa Cruz Church. (TUC)
Tulalip, WA, Snohomish Co., Tulalip Indian Reservation, St. Anne, c/o Marysville, WA, St. Mary's Church. (SEA)
Tule Indian Reservation, CA, Tulare Co., Mater Dolorosa, c/o Porterville, CA, St. Anne Church. (FRS)
Tullytown, PA, Bucks Co., Sacred Heart of Jesus, c/o Bristol, PA, St. Ann Church. (PH)
Tunica, MS, Tunica Co., St. Anthony of Padua, c/o Walls, MS, Sacred Heart Church. (JKS)
Tuolumne, CA, Tuolumne Co., St. Joseph, c/o Twain Harte, CA, All Saints Church. (STO)
Turquillo, NM, Mora Co., c/o Mora, NM, St. Gertrude Church. (SFE)
Turtle Lake, ND, McLean Co., St. Catherine, c/o Underwood, ND, St. Bonaventure Church. (BIS)

Tuscaloosa, AL, Tuscaloosa Co., St. John, c/o Tuscaloosa, AL, Holy Spirit Church. (BIR)
Twin Bridges, MT, Jefferson Co., Notre Dame, c/o Whitehall, MT, St. Teresa Church. (HEL)
Twin Buttes, ND, Dunn Co., St. Joseph, c/o Mandaree, ND, St. Anthony Church. (BIS)
Twin Sisters, TX, Blanco Co., Our Lady Help of Christians, c/o Blanco, TX, St. Ferdinand's Church. (AUS)
Twin Valley, MN, Norman Co., c/o [1] Crookston, MN, Cathedral of the Immaculate Conception. (CR)
Twin Valley, MN, Norman Co., St.William, c/o Ada, MN, St. Joseph's Church. (CR)
Two Inlets, MN, c/o Park Rapids, MN, St. Peter's Church. (CR)
Two Strike, SD, Immaculate Conception, c/o St. Francis, SD, Rosebud Reservation Church. (RC)
Tyler, TX, Smith Co., Our Lady of Guadalupe, c/o [1] Tyler, TX, Cathedral of the Immaculate Conception. (TYL)
Tylertown, MS, Walthall Co., St. Paul the Apostle, c/o Columbia, MS, Most Holy Trinity Church. (BLX)
Tynan, TX, Bee Co., St. Francis Xavier, c/o Skidmore, TX, Immaculate Conception Church. (CC)

U

Uhland, TX, Hays Co., St. Michael's, c/o San Marcos, TX, St. John the Evangelist Church. (AUS)
Ulster, PA, Bradford Co., Immaculate Conception, c/o Towanda, PA, SS. Peter and Paul Church. (SCR)
Ulupalakua, HI, Maui Co., St. James the Less, c/o Kula, HI, Our Lady Queen of the Angels Church. (HON)
Uman, FM, St. Michael, c/o Udot, FM, St. Francis Assisi Church. (CI)
Unadilla, NY, Otsego Co., St. Ambrose, c/o Sidney, NY, Sacred Heart Church. (ALB)
Unalaska, AK, St. Christopher, c/o Dillingham, AK, Holy Rosary Church. (ANC)
Union, WV, Monroe Co., St. Andrew, c/o Ronceverte, WV, St. Catherine of Siena Church. (WH)
Union City, MI, Our Lady of Fatima, c/o Coldwater, MI, St. Charles Church. (KAL)
Union Springs, AL, Bullock Co., Bullock County Correctional Facility, c/o Eufaula, AL, Holy Redeemer Church. (MOB)
Union Springs, AL, Bullock Co., St. Piux X, c/o Eufaula, AL, Holy Redeemer Church. (MOB)
Unionville, MO, Putnam Co., St. Mary, c/o Milan, MO, St. Mary Church. (JC)
Unionville, NY, Orange Co., Our Lady of the Scapular, c/o Middletown, NY, Our Lady of Mt. Carmel Church. (NY)
Unity, OR, St. Joseph's, c/o [1] Baker, OR, Cathedral of St. Francis De Sales. (BAK)
Universal, IN, Vermillion Co., St. Joseph, c/o Clinton, IN, Sacred Heart Church. (IND)
Upper Black Eddy, PA, Bucks Co., St. Joseph, c/o Ottsville, PA, St. John the Baptist Church. (PH)
Upper Cutmeat, SD, Sacred Heart, c/o Parmelee, SD, St. Agnes Church. (RC)
Upper Cutmeat, SD, Sacred Heart, c/o St. Francis, SD, Rosebud Reservation Church. (RC)
Upper Little Caillou, LA, Our Lady of Prompt Succor, c/o Chauvin, LA, St. Joseph Church. (HT)
Upton, WY, Weston Co., St. Anthony, c/o Newcastle, WY, Corpus Christi Church. (CHY)
Urb. Santa Teresita, PR, Ponce Co., Santa Teresita, c/o [2] Ponce, PR, Christ the King Church. (PCE)
Uriah, AL, Monroe Co., Our Lady of Mount Carmel, c/o Monroeville, AL, Annunciation Church. (MOB)
Urich, MO, Henry Co., Holy Trinity, c/o Montrose, MO, Immaculate Conception Church. (KC)
Ute, IA, Monona Co., St. Mary's, c/o Charter Oak, IA, St. Boniface Church. (SC)
Utica, NE, Seward Co., St. Patrick's, c/o Beaver Crossing, NE, Sacred Heart Church. (LIN)
Utulei, AS, c/o [2] Pago Pago, AS, Co-Cathedral of St. Joseph the Worker. (SPP)

V

Vadito, NM, Taos Co., Nuestra Senora de los Dolores Mission, c/o Penasco, NM, San Antonio de Padua Church. (SFE)
Vado, NM, Dona Ana Co., San Pedro Del Cerro, c/o La Mesa, NM, San Jose Church. (LSC)
Vail, CO, Eagle Co., The Interfaith Chapel, c/o Minturn, CO, St. Patrick's Church. (DEN)
Vailoatai, AS, c/o [5] (Leone), AS, Church of the Holy Cross. (SPP)
Valdez, NM, Taos Co., c/o Arroyo Seco, NM, Holy Trinity Church. (SFE)
Valentine, TX, Sacred Heart, c/o Marfa, TX, St. Mary's Church. (ELP)
Valiant, OK, McCurtain Co., Good Shepherd, c/o Idabel, OK, St. Francis De Sales Church. (TLS)
Vallecitos, NM, Rio Arriba Co., c/o El Rito, NM, San Juan Nepomuceno Church. (SFE)
Valley Falls, NY, Our Lady of Good Counsel, c/o Schaghticoke, NY, St. John the Baptist Church. (ALB)
Van Alstyne, TX, Grayson Co., Holy Family, c/o McKinney, TX, St. Michael Church. (DAL)
Van Buren, ME, Aroostock Co., St. Rose Chapel, c/o Van Buren, ME, St. Bruno - St. Remi Church. (PRT)
Van Buren, MO, Carter Co., St. George, c/o Piedmont, MO, St. Catherine of Siena Church. (SPC)
Vanceboro, ME, Guardian Angel, c/o Lincoln, ME, St. Mary Church. (PRT)
Vandalia, NY, Cattaraugus Co., St. John the Baptist, c/o Allegany, NY, St. Bonaventure Church. (BUF)
Vanderpool, TX, St. Mary, c/o Sabinal, TX, St. Patrick's Church. (SAT)
Variadero, NM, San Miguel Co., Holy Family, c/o Las Vegas, NM, Our Lady of Sorrows Church. (SFE)
Veblen, SD, Marshall Co., St. Matthew, c/o Sisseton, SD, St. Catherine Church. (SFS)
Vegas Abajo, PR, La Milagrosa, c/o Adjuntas, PR, St. Joachim Church. (PCE)
Vegas Arriba, PR, Sta. Ana, c/o Adjuntas, PR, St. Joachim Church. (PCE)
Veguita, NM, Socorro Co., San Juan, c/o La Joya, NM, Our Lady of Sorrows Church. (SFE)
Velarde, NM, Rio Arriba Co., Nuestra Senora de Guadalupe, c/o Dixon, NM, St. Anthony Church. (SFE)
Venice, LA, Plaquemines Parish, St. Anthony, c/o Buras, LA, Our Lady of Good Harbor Church. (NO)
Verdigre, NE, Knox Co., St. William, c/o Verdigre, NE, St. Wenceslaus Church. (OM)
Verdunville, LA, Immaculate Conception, c/o Franklin, LA, St. Jules Church. (LAF)
Vernon Center, MN, Blue Earth Co., St. Matthew, c/o Mapleton, MN, St. Teresa's Church. (WIN)
Verona, ND, LaMoure Co., St. Raphael, c/o Oakes, ND, St. Charles Borromeo Church. (FAR)
Verona Beach, NY, Oneida Co., St. Mary, c/o North Bay, NY, St. John Church. (SY)
Versailles, MO, Morgan Co., St. Philip Benizi, c/o Laurie, MO, Shrine of St. Patrick Church. (JC)
Viburnum, MO, Iron Co., St. Philip Benizi, c/o Ironton, MO, Ste. Marie Du Lac Church. (SPC)
Victor, CO, Teller Co., St. Victor's, c/o Woodland Park, CO, Our Lady of the Woods Church. (COS)
Victoria, TX, Victoria Co., Holy Trinity, c/o [4] Victoria, TX, Our Lady of Sorrows Church. (VIC)
Vida, MT, St. Ann, c/o Wolf Point, MT, Immaculate Conception Church. (GF)
Vidrine, LA, Holy Spirit, c/o Mamou, LA, St. Ann Church. (LAF)
Vigil, CO, St. Isidore, c/o Trinidad, CO, Most Holy Trinity, Trinidad Area Catholic Community (Trinidad Cluster) Church. (PBL)
Villa del Carmen, PR, Ponce Co., San Martin de Porres, c/o [4] Ponce, PR, Our Lady of Mt. Carmel Church. (PCE)
Villard, MN, Pope Co., St. Bartholomew, c/o West Union, MN, St. Alexius Church. (SCL)
Vintondale, PA, Cambria Co., Immaculate Conception, c/o Twin Rocks, PA, St. Charles Church. (ALT)
Viola, IL, Mercer Co., St. John, c/o Matherville, IL, St. Anthony's Church. (PEO)
Virginia Beach, VA, Virginia Beach Co., Our Lady of Perpetual Help, c/o Williamsburg, VA, Ascension of Our Lord Church. (PSC)
Volcano, CA, Amador Co., St. Bernard, c/o Jackson, CA, St. Patrick's Church. (SAC)
Vredenburgh, AL, Monroe Co., St. Martin de Porres, c/o Monroeville, AL, Annunciation Church. (MOB)

W

Waco, TX, c/o [4] Waco, TX, St. John the Baptist Church. (AUS)
Wadena, IA, St. Joseph, c/o Elkader, IA, St. Joseph's Church. (DUB)
Wadesboro, NC, Anson Co., Sacred Heart, c/o Hamlet, NC, St. James Church. (CHL)
Wadsworth, TX, Sacred Heart, c/o Bay City, TX, Holy Cross Church. (VIC)
Waelder, TX, Gonzales Co., St. Patrick, c/o Gonzales, TX, St. James Church. (SAT)
Wahneta, FL, Polk Co., Our Lady of Guadalupe, c/o Bartow, FL, St. Thomas Aquinas Church. (ORL)
Waiakoa, HI, Maui Co., Holy Ghost, c/o Kula, HI, Our Lady Queen of the Angels Church. (HON)
Waikapu, HI, Maui Co., St. Joseph, c/o Waihee, HI, St. Ann Church. (HON)
Waimea, HI, Kauai Co., Sacred Hearts of Jesus & Mary, c/o Kekaha, HI, St. Theresa Church. (HON)
Waimea Bay, HI, SS. Peter and Paul, c/o Waialua, HI, St. Michael Church. (HON)
Wakefield, VA, Infant of Prague, c/o Franklin, VA, St. Jude Church. (RIC)
Wakita, OK, Grant Co., St. Mary's Assumption, c/o Medford, OK, St. Mary's Church. (OKL)
Wakpala, SD, Corson Co., St. Bede, c/o McLaughlin, SD, St. Bernard Church. (RC)
Wakpala, SD, Corson Co., St. Bede, c/o Standing Rock, SD, Standing Rock Reservation Church. (RC)
Walden, CO, Grand Co., St. Ignatius, c/o Kremmling, CO, St. Peter Church. (DEN)
Waldorf, MN, Waseca Co., St. Joseph, c/o New Richland, MN, All Saints Church. (WIN)
Waldron, AR, Scott Co., St. Jude Thaddeus, c/o Mena, AR, St. Agnes Church. (LR)
Wales, MA, Hampden Co., St. Monica, c/o Brimfield, MA, St. Christopher's Church. (SPR)
Walhalla, SC, Oconee Co., St. Francis of Assisi, c/o Clemson, SC, St. Andrew Church. (CHR)
Walker, CA, Mono Co., Our Lady of the Valley, c/o Mammoth Lakes, CA, St. Joseph Church. (STO)
Walker, MN, Ah-Gwah-Ching State Nursing Home, c/o Duluth, MN, Indian Missions Church. (DUL)
Walker Valley, NY, Ulster Co., Our Lady of the Valley, c/o Pine Bush, NY, The Infant Saviour Church. (NY)
Wallace, KS, Wallace Co., St. Peter, c/o Sharon Springs, KS, Holy Ghost Church. (SAL)
Wallace, NC, Transfiguration, c/o Burgaw, NC, St. Joseph Church. (R)
Wallkill, NY, Ulster Co., St. Benedict, c/o Walden, NY, Most Precious Blood Church. (NY)
Wallowa, OR, St. Pius X, c/o Enterprise, OR, St. Katherine's Church. (BAK)
Walnut Ridge, AR, Lawrence Co., Immaculate Heart of Mary, c/o Engelberg, AR, St. John the Baptist Church. (LR)
Walpole, NH, St. Joseph, c/o North Walpole, NH, St. Peter Church. (MAN)
Wanblee, SD, Bennett Co., St. Ignatius Loyola, c/o Kyle, SD, Our Lady of Sorrows Church. (RC)
Wanette, OK, Pottawatomie Co., St. Mary, c/o Konawa, OK, Sacred Heart Church. (OKL)
Warba, MN, St. Paul's, c/o Hill City, MN, St. John Church. (DUL)
Wardsboro, VT, Windham Co., Our Lady of Hope, c/o Putney, VT, Our Lady of Mercy Church. (BUR)
Warm Springs, GA, Meriwether Co., St. Elizabeth Seton, c/o LaGrange, GA, St. Peter's Church. (ATL)
Warm Springs, OR, Jefferson Co., Blessed Kateri Tekakwitha, c/o Madras, OR, St. Patrick's Church. (BAK)
Warner Springs, CA, San Diego Co., St. Francis, c/o Santa Ysabel, CA, Santa Ysabel Indian Mission Church. (SD)
Warren, AR, Bradley Co., St. Luke, c/o Monticello, AR, St. Mark Church. (LR)
Warren, NH, St. John Vianney, c/o Woodsville, NH, St. Joseph Church. (MAN)
Warrenton, NC, Warren Co., St. Joseph, c/o Henderson, NC, St. James the Greater Church. (R)
Warrenton, TX, Fayette Co., St. Martin's, c/o Fayetteville, TX, St. John's Church. (AUS)
Warrior, AL, Jefferson Co., St. Henry, c/o Gardendale, AL, St. Elizabeth Ann Seton Church. (BIR)
Washburn, ME, St. Catherine, c/o Caribou, ME, Holy Rosary Church. (PRT)
Washburn, ND, McLean Co., St. Edwin, c/o Wilton, ND, Sacred Heart Church. (BIS)
Washington, VA, Rappahannock Co., St. Peter, c/o Culpeper, VA, Precious Blood Church. (ARL)
Waskom, TX, Harrison Co., St. Lawrence Brindisi, c/o Jefferson, TX, Immaculate Conception Church. (TYL)
Wataga, IL, Knoxville Co., St. Aloysius, c/o Alexis, IL, St. Theresa's Church. (PEO)
Watauga, SD, Corson Co., St. Michael, c/o Lemmon, SD, St. Mary's Church. (RC)
Waterproof, LA, St. Francis of Assisi, c/o St. Joseph, LA, St. Joseph Church. (ALX)
Watrous, NM, Mora Co., c/o Wagon Mound, NM, Santa Clara Church. (SFE)
Watson, MI, Allegan Co., Sacred Heart, c/o Dorr, MI, St. Stanislaus Church. (KAL)
Wauneta, NE, Chase Co., St. John's, c/o Imperial, NE, St. Patrick's Church. (LIN)
Waurika, OK, Jefferson Co., St. Thomas Aquinas, c/o Walters, OK, St. Patrick Church. (OKL)
Wayland, MO, St. Martha, c/o Kahoka, MO, St. Michael the Archangel Church. (JC)
Waynoka, OK, Woods Co., Our Mother of Mercy, c/o Alva, OK, Sacred Heart Church. (OKL)
Webbers Falls, OK, Muskogee Co., St. Joseph, c/o Sallisaw, OK, St. Francis Xavier Church. (TLS)
Weirs Beach, NH, Belknap, St. Helena, c/o Lakeport, NH, Our Lady of the Lakes Church. (MAN)
Welch, OK, Craig Co., St. Ann, c/o Vinita, OK, Holy Ghost Church. (TLS)
Welches, OR, Clackamas Co., St. John, c/o Sandy, OR, St. Michael Church. (P)
Weldona, CO, Morgan Co., St. Francis of Assisi, c/o Fort Morgan, CO, St. Helena Church. (DEN)
Wellfleet, NE, Lincoln Co., St. William's, c/o Curtis, NE, St. James Church. (LIN)
Wells, NV, St. Thomas Aquinas, c/o Elko, NV, St. Joseph's Church. (RNO)
Wells, VT, Rutland Co., St. Paul, c/o Middletown Springs, VT, St. Anne Church. (BUR)
Wells River, VT, Orange Co., St. Eugene, c/o Bradford, VT, Our Lady of Perpetual Help Church. (BUR)

Wellton, AZ, Yuma Co., St. Joseph the Worker, c/o Yuma, AZ, Immaculate Conception Church. (TUC)
Wenden, AZ, St. John the Baptist, c/o Parker, AZ, Sacred Heart Church. (TUC)
Wendover, UT, Tooele Co., San Felipe, c/o Tooele, UT, St. Marguerite's Church. (SLC)
Wesby, MT, St. Elizabeth, c/o Plentywood, MT, St. Joseph's Church. (GF)
Weslaco, TX, St. Jude Chapel, c/o Weslaco, TX, San Martin de Porres Church. (BWN)
West Albany, MN, Stearns Co., St. Patrick, c/o Mazeppa, MN, SS. Peter and Paul Church. (WIN)
West Alton, MO, St. Charles Co., Immaculate Conception, c/o Portage Des Sioux, MO, St. Francis Church. (STL)
West Bangor, NY, Franklin Co., St. Edward, c/o North Bangor, NY, St. Augustine Church. (OG)
West Barnstable, MA, Barnstable Co., Our Lady of Hope, c/o Centerville, MA, Our Lady of Victory Church. (FR)
West Castleton, VT, Rutland Co., St. Matthew of Avalon, c/o Fair Haven, VT, Our Lady of Seven Dolors Church. (BUR)
West Charleston, VT, Orleans Co., St. Benedict Labre, c/o Derby Line, VT, St. Edward Church. (BUR)
West Columbia, TX, Brazoria Co., St. John the Apostle, c/o Sweeny, TX, Our Lady of Perpetual Help Church. (GAL)
West Concord, MN, Dodge Co., St. Vincent de Paul, c/o Dodge Center, MN, St. John Baptist de La Salle Church. (WIN)
West Forks, ME, SS. Philip & James, c/o Bingham, ME, St. Peter's Church. (PRT)
West Gilgo Beach, NY, Suffolk Co., c/o Babylon, NY, St. Joseph's Church. (RVC)
West Glacier, MT, Flathead Co., c/o Columbia Falls, MT, St. Richard Church. (HEL)
West Grove, PA, Chester Co., Santa Maria, Madra de Dios, c/o West Grove, PA, Assumption B.V.M. Church. (PH)
West Haven, CT, Our Lady of Mt. Carmel Chapel, c/o [5] West Haven, CT, St. Paul's Church. (HRT)
West Mount Vernon, AL, Mobile Co., St. Theresa, c/o Chastang, AL, St. Peter the Apostle Church. (MOB)
West Pawlet, VT, Rutland Co., St. Frances Cabrini, c/o Middletown Springs, VT, St. Anne Church. (BUR)
West Peru, NY, Clinton Co., St. Patrick, c/o Peru, NY, St. Augustine Church. (OG)
West Point, CA, Calaveras Co., Our Lady of Fatima, c/o San Andreas, CA, St. Andrew Church. (STO)
West Point, IL, Hancock Co., St. Mary, c/o Carthage, IL, Immaculate Conception Church. (PEO)
West Point, KY, Hardin Co., St. Patrick Church, c/o [2] Valley Station, KY, Our Lady Help of Christians Church. (L)
West Point, OH, Columbiana Co., St. Agatha, c/o Lisbon, OH, St. George Church. (Y)
West Ridge, IA, St. John the Baptist, c/o Waukon, IA, St. Patrick's Church. (DUB)
West Shokan, NY, Ulster Co., St. Augustine, c/o West Hurley-Woodstock, NY, St. John Church. (NY)
West Springfield, MA, Hampden Co., St. Ann, c/o [9] Springfield, MA, Our Lady of Mt. Carmel Church. (SPR)
West Thompson, CT, Windham Co., Sacred Heart, c/o North Grosvenordale, CT, St. Joseph Church. (NOR)
West Wareham, MA, Plymouth Co., St. Anthony, c/o Wareham, MA, St. Patrick's Church. (FR)
Westbrook, MN, Cottonwood Co., St. Anthony, c/o Currie, MN, Immaculate Heart of Mary Church. (WIN)
Westfield, IN, Hamilton Co., St. Maria Goretti, c/o Carmel, IN, Our Lady of Mount Carmel Church. (LFT)
Westfield, PA, Tioga Co., St. Catherine, c/o Elkland, PA, St. Thomas the Apostle Church. (SCR)
Westfield, WI, Marquette Co., Good Shepherd, c/o Montello, WI, St. John the Baptist Church. (MAD)
Westhoff, TX, St. Aloysius, c/o Meyersville, TX, SS. Peter & Paul Church. (VIC)
Westhope, ND, Bottineau Co., St. Andrew, c/o Bottineau, ND, St. Mark's Church. (FAR)
Westminster, CO, Adams Co., Our Lady of Visitation, c/o Westminster, CO, Holy Trinity Church. (DEN)
Weston, CO, Las Animas Co., Our Lord of Esquipula, c/o Trinidad, CO, Most Holy Trinity, Trinidad Area Catholic Community (Trinidad Cluster) Church. (PBL)
Westover, MD, Somerset Co., St. Elizabeth, c/o Pocomoke City, MD, Holy Name of Jesus Church. (WIL)
Westport, WA, St. Paul, c/o Aberdeen, WA, St. Mary's Church. (SEA)
Westville, NY, Franklin Co., Our Lady of Fatima, c/o Constable, NY, St. Francis of Assisi Church. (OG)
Westway, TX, El Paso Co., Immaculate Heart of Mary, c/o Canutillo, TX, St. Patrick Church. (ELP)
Wetumpka, AL, Elmore Co., St. Mark's, c/o Millbrook, AL, St. Elizabeth Ann Seton Church. (MOB)
Wewahitchka, FL, Gulf Co., St. Lawrence, c/o Blountstown, FL, St. Francis of Assisi Church. (PT)
Wheatfields, AZ, Our Lady of the Lake, c/o Lukachukai, AZ, St. Isabel Mission for Navajo Indians Church. (GLP)
Wheatland, CA, Yuba Co., St. Daniel, c/o Lincoln, CA, St. Joseph Church. (SAC)
Wheatville, TX, Genesee Co., St. Patrick, c/o Oakfield, NY, St. Cecilia Church. (BUF)
Wheelwright, MA, Hardwick Co., St. Augustine, c/o Barre, MA, St. Joseph's Church. (WOR)
Whetstone, AZ, Cochise Co., Good Shepherd, c/o Sierra Vista, AZ, St. Andrew Church. (TUC)
White Church, MO, Howell Co., St. Joseph, c/o Willow Springs, MO, Sacred Heart Church. (SPC)
White Horse, SD, Dewey Co., St. Therese, c/o Eagle Butte, SD, All Saints Church. (RC)
White Horse, SD, Ziebach Co., St. Therese, c/o Eagle Butte, SD, Cheyenne River Reservation Church. (RC)
White Horse Beach, MA, St. Catherine's Chapel, c/o [2] Plymouth, MA, St. Bonaventure Church. (BO)
White River, SD, St. Ignatius, c/o St. Francis, SD, Rosebud Reservation Church. (RC)
White Rock, NM, Los Alamos Co., c/o Los Alamos, NM, Immaculate Heart of Mary Church. (SFE)
White Shield, ND, McLean Co., Sacred Heart, c/o Mandaree, ND, St. Anthony Church. (BIS)
White Sulphur, KY, Scott Co., St. Francis de Sales, c/o Georgetown, KY, St. John's Church. (LEX)
Whitesboro, TX, Grayson Co., St. Francis of Assisi, c/o Sherman, TX, St. Mary Church. (DAL)
Whitesville, WV, Boone Co., St. Joseph the Worker, c/o Beckley, WV, St. Francis De Sales Church. (WH)
Whiteville, LA, Resurrection, c/o Morrow, LA, St. Peter Church. (LAF)
Whitewater, MT, St. John, c/o Malta, MT, St. Mary's Church. (GF)
Wibaux, MT, St. Peter, c/o Glendive, MT, Sacred Heart Church. (GF)
Wibaux, MT, St. Philip, c/o Glendive, MT, Sacred Heart Church. (GF)
Wichita Falls, TX, Wichita Co., The Assumption of Mary, c/o Wichita Falls, TX, Sacred Heart Church. (FWT)
Wiggins, CO, Morgan Co., Our Lady of Lourdes, c/o Roggen, CO, Sacred Heart Church. (DEN)
Wilburton, OK, Latimer Co., Sacred Heart, c/o Hartshorne, OK, Holy Rosary Church. (TLS)
Wildwood, FL, Sumter Co., St. Vincent de Paul Mission, c/o Bushnell, FL, St. Lawrence Church. (ORL)
Wilkes-Barre, PA, Luzerne Co., St. Francis of Assisi, c/o [2] Wilkes-Barre, PA, Blessed Sacrament Church. (SCR)
Wilkes-Barre, PA, Luzerne Co., St. John The Baptist, c/o [2] Wilkes-Barre, PA, Blessed Sacrament Church. (SCR)
Wilkes-Barre, PA, Luzerne Co., St. John the Evangelist, c/o [18] Wilkes-Barre, PA, Sacred Heart of Jesus Church. (SCR)
Wilkes-Barre, PA, Luzerne Co., St. Joseph, c/o [14] Wilkes-Barre, PA, St. Mary's Church of the Immaculate Conception. (SCR)
Wilkeson, WA, Pierce Co., Our Lady of Lourdes, c/o Buckley, WA, St. Aloysius Church. (SEA)
Willacoochee, GA, Atkinson Co., Holy Family, c/o Douglas, GA, St. Paul's Church. (SAV)
Willard, NM, Torrance Co., c/o Mountainair, NM, St. Alice Church. (SFE)
Williams, CA, Colusa Co., Annunciation, c/o Maxwell, CA, Sacred Heart Church. (SAC)
Williams, MN, Lake of the Woods Co., St. Joseph, c/o Baudette, MN, Sacred Heart Church. (CR)
Williamsfield, IL, Knox Co., St. James, c/o Brimfield, IL, St. Joseph's Church. (PEO)
Williamstown, NY, St. Patrick, c/o Parish, NY, St. Ann Church. (SY)
Williamstown, PA, Dauphin Co., Sacred Heart of Jesus, c/o Lykens, PA, Our Lady Help of Christians Church. (HBG)
Williamstown, VT, Orange Co., St. Edward, c/o Graniteville, VT, St. Sylvester Church. (BUR)
Williamsville, MO, Wayne Co., Our Lady of Sorrows, c/o Piedmont, MO, St. Catherine of Siena Church. (SPC)
Willow, AK, St. Christopher, c/o Talkeetna, AK, St. Bernard Church. (ANC)
Willow City, ND, Bottineau Co., Notre Dame, c/o Rolette, ND, Sacred Heart Church. (FAR)
Wills Creek, OH, Coshocton Co., Our Lady of Lourdes, c/o Coshocton, OH, Sacred Heart Church. (COL)
Wilmington, NY, Essex Co., St. Margaret, c/o Keene, NY, St. Brendan Church. (OG)
Wilmont, MN, Nobles Co., Our Lady of Good Council, c/o Adrian, MN, St. Adrian Church. (WIN)
Wilson, MN, Immaculate Conception, c/o [1] Winona, MN, Cathedral of the Sacred Heart. (WIN)
Wilson, TX, Blessed Sacrament Church, c/o Slaton, TX, St. Joseph's Church. (LUB)
Wilton, MN, Beltrami Co., Sacred Heart, c/o Bemidji, MN, St. Philip's Church. (CR)
Wimauma, FL, Hillsborough Co., Our Lady of Guadalupe Catholic Mission, c/o Sun City Center, FL, Prince of Peace Church. (SP)
Wimbledon, ND, Barnes Co., c/o Sanborn, ND, Sacred Heart Church. (FAR)
Wind Gap, PA, Northampton Co., St. Joseph, c/o Pen Argyl, PA, St. Elizabeth of Hungary Church. (ALN)
Winder, GA, Barrow Co., St. Matthew, c/o Snellville, GA, St. Oliver Plunkett Church. (ATL)
Windsor, CO, Weld Co., Our Lady of the Valley, c/o Johnstown, CO, St. John the Baptist Church. (DEN)
Windsor, MO, Henry Co., St. Bartholomew, c/o Clinton, MO, Holy Rosary Church. (KC)
Wing, ND, Burleigh Co., St. Ignatius, c/o Wilton, ND, Sacred Heart Church. (BIS)
Wingdale, NY, Dutchess Co., Our Lady of Solace Mission, c/o Dover Plains, NY, St. Charles Borromeo Church. (NY)
Winifred, MT, Holy Family, c/o Lewistown, MT, St. Leo's Church. (GF)
Winn, ME, Sacred Heart, c/o Lincoln, ME, St. Mary Church. (PRT)
Winn, MI, Isabella Co., St. Leo, c/o Shepherd, MI, St. Vincent De Paul Church. (SAG)
Winnett, MT, St. Aloysius, c/o Roundup, MT, St. Benedict's Church. (GF)
Winnsboro, SC, Fairfield Co., St. Theresa, c/o [2] Columbia, SC, St. Joseph Church. (CHR)
Winnsboro, TX, Wood Co., St. Ann, c/o Sulphur Springs, TX, St. James Church. (TYL)
Winona, MN, Winona Co., St. John Nepomucene, c/o [5] Winona, MN, St. Stanislaus Church. (WIN)
Winona, MS, Sacred Heart, c/o Lexington, MS, St. Thomas Church. (JKS)
Winston-Salem, NC, Forsyth Co., Our Lady of Fatima, c/o Winston-Salem, NC, Our Lady of Mercy Church. (CHL)
Winter Harbor, ME, St. Margaret, c/o Ellsworth, ME, St. Joseph's Church. (PRT)
Winter Park, CO, Grand Co., St. Bernard, c/o Grand Lake, CO, St. Anne Church. (DEN)
Winterhaven, CA, Imperial Co., St. Mary, c/o Winterhaven, CA, St. Thomas Church. (SD)
Wisdom, MT, Beaverhead Co., Our Lady of Wisdom, c/o Dillon, MT, St. Rose of Lima Church. (HEL)
Wishek, ND, McIntosh Co., St. Patrick, c/o Zeeland, ND, St. Andrew's Church. (FAR)
Wolbach, NE, St. Joseph, c/o St. Paul, NE, SS. Peter and Paul Church. (GI)
Wolf Creek, MT, Lewis and Clark Co., Sacred Heart, c/o [3] Helena, MT, Our Lady of the Valley Church. (HEL)
Wolfforth, TX, Lubbock Co., St. Francis of Assisi, c/o Woodrow, TX, San Ramon Church. (LUB)
Wood, SD, Melette Co., Our Lady of Good Counsel, c/o White River, SD, St. Ignatius Church. (RC)
Wood, SD, Our Lady of Good Counsel, c/o St. Francis, SD, Rosebud Reservation Church. (RC)
Woodstock, MN, Pipestone Co., St. Martin, c/o Pipestone, MN, St. Leo's Church. (WIN)
Woodville, CA, Tulare Co., St. Francis of Assisi, c/o Tipton, CA, St. John Church. (FRS)
Woodville, FL, Leon Co., St. Stephen the Protomartyr, c/o Medart, FL, St. Elizabeth Ann Seton Church. (PT)
Woodward, IA, Dallas Co., St. Ann, c/o Granger, IA, Assumption of the Blessed Virgin Mary Church. (DM)
Woodworth, LA, Mary, Mother of Jesus, c/o Lecompte, LA, St. Martin Church. (ALX)
Wounded Knee, SD, Shannon Co., Sacred Heart, c/o Manderson, SD, St. Agnes Church. (RC)
Wounded Knee, SD, Sacred Heart, c/o Porcupine, SD, Church of Christ the King. (RC)
Wright, WY, Campbell Co., Blessed Sacrament, c/o Gillette, WY, St. Matthew's Church. (CHY)
Wrightsville, PA, York Co., Mother of Holy Purity, c/o Columbia, PA, St. Peter Church. (HBG)
Wyanet, IL, Bureau Co., St. Margaret Mary, c/o Sheffield, IL, St. Patrick's Church. (PEO)
Wykoff, MN, Fillmore Co., St. Kilian, c/o Spring Valley, MN, St. Ignatius Church. (WIN)
Wyola, MT, Blessed Kateri Tekakwitha, c/o Lodge Grass, MT, Our Lady of Loretto Church. (GF)

Y

Yacolt, WA, Clark Co., St. Joseph the Workman, c/o Battle Ground, WA, Sacred Heart Church. (SEA)
Yadkinville, NC, Yadkin Co., Cristo Rey Catholic Hispanic Center of Yadkin Valley, c/o Clemmons, NC, Holy Family Church. (CHL)
Yahuecas, PR, Virgen del Carmen, c/o Adjuntas, PR, St. Joachim Church. (PCE)
Yancey, TX, Immaculate Heart of Mary, c/o Hondo, TX, St. John the Evangelist Church. (SAT)
Yarmouth Port, MA, Barnstable Co., Sacred Heart Chapel, c/o Hyannis, MA, St. Francis Xavier's Church. (FR)
Yarnell, AZ, Yavapai Co., St. Mary's, c/o Prescott, AZ, Sacred Heart Church. (PHX)
Yellowstone, WI, St. Michael, c/o Argyle, WI, St. Joseph

Church. (MAD)
Yellowstone National Park, WY, Park Co., c/o Cody, WY, St. Anthony Church. (CHY)
Yellville, AR, Marion Co., St. Andrew's, c/o Mountain Home, AR, St. Peter the Fisherman Church. (LR)
Yolo, CA, Yolo Co., Our Lady of Guadalupe, c/o Woodland, CA, Holy Rosary Church. (SAC)
York Beach, ME, St. Mary, Star of the Sea, c/o York Harbor, ME, St. Christopher-by-the-Sea Church. (PRT)
Yorktown, TX, San Luis, c/o Yorktown, TX, Holy Cross Church. (VIC)
Youngsville, NM, c/o Abiquiu, NM, St. Thomas Apostle Church. (SFE)
Yuma, AZ, Yuma Co., Our Lady of Guadalupe, c/o Yuma, AZ, Immaculate Conception Church. (TUC)

Z

Zama, PR, Jayuya Co., Santa Cecila, c/o Jayuya, PR, Our Lady of Monserrate Church. (PCE)
Zamora, CA, Yolo Co., St. Agnes, c/o Knights Landing, CA, St. Paul Church. (SAC)
Zia, NM, Sandoval Co., c/o Jemez Pueblo, NM, San Diego Indian Missions Church. (SFE)
Zolfo Springs, FL, Hardee Co., San Alfonso Catholic Center, c/o Wauchula, FL, St. Michael Church. (VEN)
Zortman, MT, St. Joseph, c/o Hays, MT, St. Paul's Indian Mission Church. (GF)

Index for Religious Institutes of Men

Religious Institutes of Men

The Conference of Major Religious Superiors of Men, U.S.A., 8808 Cameron St., Silver Springs, MD 20910. Tel: 301-558-4030. An association of the major Superiors of religious communities and institutes for the purpose of promoting the spiritual and apostolic welfare of Priests and Brothers. Rev. Gerald L. Brown, S.S., Pres.; Rev. Gregory Reisert, O.F.M.Cap., Exec. Dir.; Rev. Joseph Levesque, C.M., Pres.-Elect; Rev. James Fitz, S.M., Vice Pres.; Bro. Michael McKenery, F.S.C., Sec. & Treas.

[0100] (C.R.M.)—ADORNO FATHERS
(Clerics Regular Minor)

General Motherhouse: Via Alpi Apuane 1, Monte Sacro, Rome, Italy.

U.S. Foundation (1936): *St. Michael's Seminary,* 575 Darlington Ave., Ramsey, NJ 07446. Tel: 201-327-7375. Rev. Frank Palmieri, C.R.M., Supr.

Priests 10.

Represented in the Archdiocese of Newark and in the Diocese of Charleston.

[0110] (S.M.A.)—SOCIETY OF AFRICAN MISSIONS
(Societas Missionum ad Afros)

Founded Dec. 8, 1856 with the approval of Pope Pius IX. A clerical society of apostolic life.

General Motherhouse: Via della Nocetta 111, 00164, Rome, Italy. Very Rev. Daniel Cardot, S.M.A.; Revs. Kiernan O'Reilly, S.M.A., Vicar Gen.; Lorenzo Mandirola, S.M.A., Gen. Councillor.

American Province (1941): 23 Bliss Ave., Tenafly, NJ 07670. Tel: 201-567-0450; 567-9085; Fax: 201-567-7156. Very Rev. S. Douglas B. Gilbert, S.M.A., Prov. Supr.; Revs. Ulick Bourke, S.M.A., Vice Prov.; Brendan Darcy, S.M.A., Prov. Councillor; Ernest Magee, S.M.A., Prov. Treas.

Legal Title: *Society of African Missions, Inc. N.J.*

Priests 48; Lay Missionary in temporary commitment 9; Lay Missionary in permanent commitment 1; Priest Associates 1.

Represented in the Archdioceses of Boston, Newark and Washington.

[0120] (C.F.A.)—ALEXIAN BROTHERS
(Congregatio Fratrum Cellitarum seu Alexianorum)

Generalate: Signal Mountain, TN 37377. Tel: 423-886-2969. Bros. Dominic Walsh, Supr. Gen.; Warren Longo, Asst. Gen., 3910 Ohio, St. Louis, MO 63118; Kamillus Bonn, Gen. Councillor, 52001 Aachen, Germany; Dominick Champagne, Gen. Councillor, B-2530 Boechout, Belgium.

General Motherhouse: Congregation of Alexian Brothers, Aachen, Germany.

United States Province (1866): 600 Alexian Way, Elk Grove Village, IL 60007. Tel: 847-640-7550; Fax: 847-981-5561. Bro. Edward Walsh, Prov. Supr. Prov. Councillors: Bros. Thomas Keusenkothen; Philip Kennedy; Lawrence Krueger; Andrew Thome, Dir. Vocations; Bro. John Howard, Dir. of Novices. *Novitiate of Alexian Brothers,* 6007 North Kenmore Ave., Chicago, IL 60660.

Professed Brothers 45; Novice Brothers 7.

Properties owned or sponsored: General Hospitals 3; Life Care Centers 2; Novitiates 2; Nursing Homes 2; Residental AIDS Facility 1; Mobile Clinic (Davao, Philippines) 1.

Represented in the Archdioceses of Chicago, Milwaukee and St. Louis and in the Dioceses of Knoxville and San Jose. Also in Davao, Philippines.

[0130] (A.A.)—ASSUMPTIONISTS
(Augustinians of the Assumption)

General House: via San Pio V, 55, Rome, Italy, 00165. Very Rev. Claude Marechal, A.A., Supr. Gen.

Province of North America (1946): 330 Market St., Brighton, MA 02135. Tel: 617-783-0400. Very Rev. John L. Franck, A.A., Prov. Supr. Councillors: Revs. Donald Espinosa, A.A.; Richard Lamoureux, A.A.; Peter Precourt, A.A.; Stephen Goguen, A.A., Prov. Treas.

Priests 53; Brothers 22.

Parishes 3; Shrines 1; Colleges 1; Formation Centers 1; Novitiates 1; Residences 8.

Represented in the Archdioceses of Boston and New York, and in the Dioceses of Manchester, Nashville and Worcester. Also in Jerusalem, Kenya, Mexico, Russia and Canada.

[0140] (O.S.A.)—THE AUGUSTINIANS
(Ordo Fratrum Sancti Augustini)

Founded in 1244, first American foundation 1796.

Generalate: Via Paolo VI, 25, 00193, Rome, Italy. Most. Rev. Miguel Angel Orcasitas, O.S.A., Gen.

Province of St. Thomas of Villanova (1796): *Saint Augustine Friary,* 214 Ashwood Rd., P.O. Box 338, Villanova, PA 19085-0338. Tel: 610-527-3330. (The Brothers of the Order of Hermits of St. Augustine, a corporation in the state of Pennsylvania.) Very Rev. John E. Deegan, O.S.A., Prior Prov.; Revs. John E. Rotelle, O.S.A., Prov. Sec.; Anthony P. Burrascano, O.S.A., Prov. Treas. Prov. Councillors: Revs. Arthur D. Johnson, O.S.A.; Kail C. Ellis, O.S.A.; Bro. Robert M. Thornton, O.S.A.; Revs. Richard D. Appicci, O.S.A.; James R. Flynn, O.S.A.; Peter M. Donohue, O.S.A.; Mr. David Piazza, Dir. Devel. Office; Revs. Joseph A. Jordan, O.S.A., Dir. Augustinian Guild; Richard D. Appicci, O.S.A., Dir. Mission Office; John E. Rotelle, O.S.A., Dir. Communications & Augustinian Press; Alfred E. Murphy, O.S.A., Archivist.

Legal Title: *The Brothers of the Order of Hermits of Saint Augustine.*

Priests 253; Students in Theology 6; Brothers 16; Permanent Deacon 1.

Parishes 34; (USA 30; Japan 4); Major Seminary 1; Colleges 1; Universities 1; Preparatory Schools and High Schools 3; Foreign Missions 1.

Represented in the Archdioceses of Boston, Miami, New York, Philadelphia and Washington and in the Dioceses of Albany, Brooklyn, Camden, Ogdensburg, Orlando and Venice.

Province of Our Mother of Good Counsel (Order of St. Augustine) (1941): *Tolentine College & Center,* 20300 Governors Hwy., Olympia Fields, IL 60461-1081. Tel: 708-748-9500; Fax: 708-481-2090. Very Rev. David L. Brecht, O.S.A., Prior Prov.; Rev. G. Jerome Knies, O.S.A., Asst. Prov. & Personnel Dir.; Bros. Kenneth D. Mehn, O.S.A., Prov. Sec.; Bruce A. Jendraszak, O.S.A., Prov. Treas.; Rev. W. Timothy Cuny, O.S.A., Personnel Dir. & Vocation Dir.

Fathers 102; Bishops 2; Permanent Deacons 1; Professed Brothers 22; Professed Students 2.

Parishes 13; High Schools 4; Retreat Centers 1; Residences 9.

Represented in the Archdioceses of Chicago, Detroit, Milwaukee and St. Louis, and in the Dioceses of Fort Worth, Joliet, Kalamazoo, Lansing and Tulsa. Also in Hamilton, Ontario, Canada, Peru and Mexico.

Province of St. Augustine: 1605 28th St., San Diego, CA 92102-1417. Tel: 619-235-0247; 282-2028. Very Rev. James A. Mott, O.S.A., Prov. Counsillors: Revs. Patrick Keane, O.S.A.; James P. Clifford, O.S.A.; John D. Keller, O.S.A.; Gary E. Sanders, O.S.A.; Robert Gavotto, O.S.A., Sec.

Priests 30; Deacons 3; Brothers 4.

Parishes 7; High Schools 2; Retreat Centers 1; Low-Income Housing 2; Orphanages 1.

Legal Holdings or Titles: *St. Augustine High School,* San Diego, CA; *Villanova Preparatory School,* Ojai, CA; *Austin House - House of Formation,* San Diego, CA.

Represented in the Archdioceses of Los Angeles and Portland (OR) and in the Dioceses of Oakland and San Diego. Also in Peru.

Order of St. Augustine Province of St. Joseph: P.O. Box 333, King City, Ontario L0G 1K0. Canada.

U.S. Address: *Mother of Consolation Monastery,* 3103 Arlington Ave., Bronx, NY 10463. Tel: 718-548-0888. Revs. Cyril Smetana, O.S.A., Prov.; Leo Cameronosa, O.S.A.; Blaise Pelerine, O.S.A.; Lawrence MacQuarrie, O.S.A.; Othmar Mussmaecher, O.S.A.; S. K. Treu, O.S.A.; Arnold C. Diederich, O.S.A., Treas.

Priests 26; Professed Brothers 18; Seminarians 6.

Represented in the Archdiocese of New York.

Province of St. Thomas Villanova: *St. Augustine Preparatory School,* Richland, NJ 08350. Tel: 609-697-2600; Fax: 609-697-8389. Rev. Stephen LaRosa, O.S.A.; Bro. Frank Cucinotta, O.S.A.; Revs. Cherubin F. Kerr, O.S.A.; Paul Galetto, O.S.A.

St. Augustine Preparatory School.

Represented in the Archdiocese Philadelphia and in the Diocese of Camden.

Region U.S.A. (1993): Province of Castile, Spain, XIII Century; Rev. Telesforo R. Blanco, O.S.A., , 3648 61st St., Port Arthur, TX 77642. Tel: 409-962-6777. Rev. Luis Urriza, O.S.A., , 767 Ave. A, Beaumont, TX 77701. Tel: 409-835-7788. Rev. Severiano Fernandez, O.S.A., , 1600 N. Main, Vidor, TX 77662. Tel: 409-769-2865.

Fathers 5.

Parishes 5.

Represented in the Archdiocese of San Antonio and in the Diocese of Beaumont.

[0150] (O.A.R.)—ORDER OF THE AUGUSTINIAN RECOLLECTS
(Ordo Augustinianorum Recollectorum)

General Motherhouse: Rome, Italy. viale dell' Astronomia 27 (E.U.R.); Most Rev. Javier Pipaon, O.A.R., Prior Gen.

Province of St. Augustine (1944): *Augustinian Recollects,* 29 Ridgeway Ave., West Orange, NJ 07052. Tel: 201-731-0616; Fax: 201-731-1033. Very Rev. Francis E. Peluso, O.A.R., Prior Prov.; Revs. Francis de la Vega, O.A.R., 1st Councillor, Vicar of Prov.; Anthony Palos, O.A.R., 2nd Councillor; John Gruben, O.A.R., 3rd Councillor; Bro. Michael Stechmann, O.A.R., 4th Councillor & Prov. Sec.

Priests 43; Brothers 10; Professed Clerics 12; Novices 1; Prepostulants 17.

Represented in the Archdioceses of Los Angeles, Newark and New York and in the Diocese of Orange.

Province of St. Nicholas of Tolentine, (Delegation in the South of U.S.A.): P.O. Box 310, Mesilla, NM 88044. Tel: 505-523-7030; 523-7038. Rev. Narciso Rivera, Prov. Delegate Supr.

Province of St. Nicholas (NY Delegation): 2800 Schurz Ave., Bronx, NY 10465. Tel: 718-823-0460. Rev. Jose Luis Duenas, O.A.R., Prov. Delegate.

Priests 10.

Represented in the Archdiocese of New York.

[0160] (C.R.S.P.)—CLERICS REGULAR OF ST. PAUL
(Barnabite Fathers)
(Ordo Clericorum Regularium Sancti Pauli)

Founded in Milan, Italy in 1533. First foundation in the United States in 1952 in Buffalo, NY.

Historical Motherhouse: *Church of St. Barnabas,* Milan, since 1545.

General Motherhouse: Via Giacomo Medici, 15, Rome, Italy. Rt. Rev. Luigi M. Villa, C.R.S.P., Supr. Gen.

North American Province: *Provincial Motherhouse,* 1023 Swann Rd., Youngstown, NY 14174. Tel: 716-754-7489. Very Rev. Julio M. Ciavaglia, C.R.S.P., Prov.

Legal Title: *Barnabite Fathers, Inc.*

Priests 16; Theology Students 2.

Fathers staff and serve: Parishes 4; Marian Shrine 1; Colleges 1; Philippine Mission 1; Spiritual Center 1.

Properties Owned: *Our Lady of Fatima Shrine and Barnabite Fathers Seminary,* Youngstown, NY; *Barnabite Spiritual Center,* Bethlehem, PA.

Represented in the Dioceses of Allentown, Buffalo and San Diego. Also in Ontario, Canada and the Philippines.

[0170] (C.S.B.)—BASILIAN FATHERS
(Congregatio Presbyterorum a S. Basilio)

General Curia: *Cardinal Flahiff Basilian Centre,* 95 St. Joseph St., Toronto, Ont, M5S 3C2. Canada. Tel: 416-921-6674; Fax: 416-920-3413. Very Rev. Robert J. Barringer, C.S.B., Supr. General.

Eastern U.S.: 445 King's Hwy., Rochester, NY 14617. Tel: 716-266-1288. Rev. Joseph A. Trovato, C.S.B.

Western U.S.: 4500 Memorial Drive, Houston, TX 77007. Tel: 713-861-2949. Rev. Carl L. Belisch, C.S.B.

Western U.S.: *Basilian Fathers,* 4500 Memorial Dr., Houston, TX 77007. Tel: 713-861-2949. Rev. Carl L. Belisch, C.S.B.

Fathers in U.S. 132; Students in Major Seminary 9; Associates 8.

Parishes 11; Colleges 2; High Schools 6.

Represented in the Archdioceses of Detroit, Hartford, and Santa Fe, and in the Dioceses of Austin, Galveston-Houston, Gary, Las Cruces, Oakland, Phoenix, Rochester and Victoria.

[0180] (O.S.B.M.)—ORDER OF ST. BASIL THE GREAT
(Ordo Sancti Basilii Magni)

General Superior "Protoarchimandrita": Rt. Rev.

Dionysius Lachovicz, O.S.B.M., Rome, Italy, 00153 (Aventino). Via San Giosafat 8.

AMERICAN PROVINCE (1948): 31-12 30th St., Long Island City, NY 11106. Tel: 718-278-6622; Fax: 718-726-0686. Very Rev. Christopher Woytyna, O.S.B.M., Prov.

Fathers 24; Scholastics 8; Brothers 3; Novices 2.

Parishes 7; Community Houses 7; House of Studies; Novitiate; Monasteries 3; Retreat House; Library.

Represented in the Byzantine Rite Archdiocese of Philadelphia, and in the Byzantine Rite Dioceses of Chicago, Parma, Passaic and Stamford.

[0190] (B.S.O.)—BASILIAN SALVATORIAN FATHERS

GENERAL MOTHERHOUSE: *Holy Savior Monastery,* Saida, Lebanon. Rt. Rev. Salim Ghazal, B.S.O., Supr. Gen.

AMERICAN HEADQUARTERS: *Basilian Salvatorian Fathers,* 30 East St., Methuen, MA 01844. Rt. Rev. Gerasimos Murphy, B.S.O., J.C.D., Prov. Supr.; Revs. Simon Hage, B.S.O.; Lawrence Tumminelli, B.S.O.; John Jadaa, B.S.O.; Youssef Aziz, B.S.O.; Adib Badaoui, B.S.O.; George Dagher, B.S.O.; Eugene Mitchell, B.S.O., General Economos; Martin A. Hyatt, B.S.O., Local Supr.

Fathers in American Region 23.

Novitiate and House of Studies: *St. Basils Seminary,* Methuen, MA.

Parishes: Canada 4; U.S.A. 7.

Represented in the Archdioceses of Atlanta, Boston and Miami, and in the Dioceses of Cleveland, Manchester and Norwich.

[0200] (O.S.B.)—BENEDICTINE MONKS

(Ordo Sancti Benedicti)

American Cassinese Congregation (Established by Pope Pius IX, Aug. 24, 1855)

HEADQUARTERS: *Newark Abbey,* 520 Dr. M.L. King Blvd., Newark, NJ 07102. Tel: 201-733-2822; Fax: 201-643-6922. Rt. Rev. Melvin J. Valvano, O.S.B., Abbot Pres.

President's Council: Rt. Rev. Douglas Nowicki, O.S.B., Saint Vincent Archabbey; Rt. Rev. Hugh Anderson, O.S.B., Saint Procopius Abbey; Revs. Claude Peifer, O.S.B., Saint Bede Abbey, Daniel Ward, O.S.B., Saint John Abbey, Roman Galiardi, O.S.B., Saint Procopius Abbey.

The Abbeys and Priories belonging to this Congregation are as follows:

ST. VINCENT ARCHABBEY: 300 Fraser Purchase Rd., Latrobe, PA 15650-2686. Tel: 412-532-6600. Rt. Rev. Douglas R. Nowicki, O.S.B., Archabbot; Rt. Rev. Paul R. Maher, O.S.B., Archabbot (Resigned); Rt. Rev. Egbert H. Donovan, O.S.B., Archabbot (Resigned); Most Rev. Rembert G. Weakland, O.S.B., Archbishop of Milwaukee.

Legal Title: *The Benedictine Society of Westmoreland County; Saint Vincent College Corporation; The Wimmer Corporation; The Saint Vincent Cemetery Corporation.*

Priests 147; Deacons 4; Solemn Professed Choir-Monks 24; Junior Professed Monks 7; Brothers 7; Choir Novices 9.

Represented in the Archdiocese of Baltimore, and in the Dioceses of Altoona-Johnstown, Erie, Greensburg, Pittsburgh, Richmond and Savannah.

ST. JOHN'S ABBEY: P.O. Box 2015, Collegeville, MN 56321-2015. Tel: 612-363-2011; Fax: 612-363-3082. Monastery founded in 1856 and raised to an Abbey in 1866; Rt. Rev. Timothy Kelly, O.S.B., Abbot; Very Rev. Geoffrey Fecht, O.S.B., Prior; Very Ven. Alan Reed, O.S.B., Subprior.

Fathers 153; Professed Brothers 63.

Abbeys 1; Dependent Priories 2; Parishes 21; Chaplaincies 16; Indian Mission Residences 1; Japanese Residences 2; School of Theology 1; College 1; High Schools 1; Novitiates 5.

Legal Holdings: *Saint John's Seminary; Saint John's University; Saint John's Preparatory School; Saint John's Abbey.*

Represented in the Archdiocese of St. Paul-Minneapolis, and the Dioceses of Crookston, Duluth, Metuchen, New Ulm, Norwich, St. Cloud and San Bernardino. Also in Austria, Germany, Japan, The Bahamas and Republic of China.

ST. BENEDICT'S ABBEY: Atchison, KS 66002. Tel: 913-367-5341; Fax: 913-367-6230. Founded in 1857 and raised to an Abbey in 1876; Rt. Rev. Barnabas Senecal, O.S.B., Abbot; Rt. Rev. Owen Purcell, O.S.B., Retired Abbot; Rt. Rev. Ralph Koehler, O.S.B., Retired Abbot; Very Revs. Michael Santa, O.S.B., Prior & Dir. Formation; Rev. Meinrad Miller, Subprior.

Bishops 1; Fathers 50; Brothers Professed 18; Novices 3.

Abbeys 1; Parishes 11; Missions 3; Foreign Missions 1; Chaplaincies 3; Colleges 1; High Schools 1.

Represented in the Archdiocese of Kansas City in Kansas and the Dioceses of Lansing and Springfield-Cape Girardeau. Also in Brazil.

ST. MARY'S ABBEY: Delbarton, Morristown, NJ 07960. Tel: 201-538-3231. Monastery founded in 1857 and raised to an Abbey in 1884; Rt. Rev. Gerard P. Lair, O.S.B., Abbot; Very Rev. Elias R. Lorenzo, O.S.B., Prior; Bro. Paul J. Diveny, O.S.B., Subprior.

Priests 42; Brothers 9.

Parishes 2; Schools Preparatory School 1.

Represented in the Archdiocese of Newark and in the Dioceses of Paterson and Trenton.

NEWARK ABBEY: 528 Dr. Martin Luther King, Jr. Blvd., Newark, NJ 07102. Tel: 201-643-4800; Fax: 201-643-6922. Priory founded 1857, Abbey in 1884; title transferred from Newark to Morristown, N.J. in 1956; became Abbey again in 1968 and known as Newark Abbey under the patronage of the Immaculate Conception; Rt. Rev. Melvin J. Valvano, O.S.B., Abbot; Very Revs. Mark M. Payne, O.S.B., Prior; Boniface J. Treanor, O.S.B., Subprior.

Priests 20; Brothers 7.

Legal Holding: *St. Benedict Preparatory School,* Newark, NJ.

Abbeys 1; Dependent Priories 1; Parishes 1; Preparatory (High) School 1.

Represented in the Archdioceses of Indianapolis and Newark.

BELMONT ABBEY: 100 Belmont-Mount Holly Rd., Belmont, NC 28012-1802. Tel: 704-825-6675; Fax: 704-825-6680. Monastery founded in 1876, raised to an Abbey in 1884 and erected into an Abbey Nullius in 1910; Abbey Nullius suppressed January 1, 1977 and incorporated into Diocese of Charlotte; Rt. Rev. Oscar C. Burnett, O.S.B., Abbot; Rt. Rev. Walter A. Coggin, O.S.B., Retired Abbot; Very Rev. Kenneth A. Geyer, O.S.B., Prior; Ven. Bro. Paul J. Shanley, O.S.B., Subprior & Master of Novices.

Priests 19; Brothers 2.

Legal Title: *Southern Benedictine Society of North Carolina, Incorporated.*

Properties owned or sponsored: *Belmont Abbey College,* Belmont, NC.

Represented in the Archdiocese of Washington.

ST. BERNARD ABBEY (1891): Cullman, AL 35055. Tel: 205-734-8291; Fax: 205-734-2925. Rt. Rev. Cletus D. Meagher O.S.B., Abbot; Very Rev. Edward Markley, O.S.B., Prior; Rev. Thomas O'Connor, O.S.B., Subprior.

Legal Title: *Benedictine Society of Alabama, Inc.*

Priests 24; Brothers 12.

Represented in the Archdiocese of Mobile and the Diocese of Birmingham.

ST. PROCOPIUS ABBEY: 5601 College Rd., Lisle, IL 60532. Tel: 630-969-6410; Fax: 630-969-6426. Monastery founded in 1885 and raised to an Abbey in 1894; Rt. Rev. Hugh Anderson, O.S.B., Abbot; Very Ven. Columban Trojan, O.S.B., Prior; Revs. James Flint, O.S.B., Subprior; Kevin Sheeran, O.S.B., Procurator & Business Mgr.

Legal Holdings or Titles: *Illinois Benedictine College,* Lisle, IL, *Benet Academy,* Lisle, IL, *Benedictine Chinese Missions,* Lisle, IL, *Slav Mission,* Lisle, IL, *King of Martyrs Priory,* Fifield, WI.

Bishops 1; Priests 37; Brothers 14; Oblates 3.

Represented in the Archdiocese of Denver and in the Dioceses of Alexandria, Joliet and Superior. Also in Taiwan.

ST. GREGORY'S ABBEY: Shawnee, OK 74801. Tel: 405-878-5490; Fax: 405-878-5198. Monastery founded in 1875 and raised to an Abbey in 1896.

Legal Title: *Benedictine Fathers of Sacred Heart Mission, Inc.*

Rt. Rev. Charles Massoth, O.S.B., Resigned Abbot; Rt. Rev. Philip Berning, O.S.B., Resigned; Rt. Rev. Adrian Vorderlandwehr, O.S.B., Resigned; Very Revs. Martin Lugo, O.S.B., Admin.; Patrick McCool, O.S.B., Prior; Rev. Joachim Spexarth, O.S.B., Subprior.

Properties owned or sponsored: *National Shrine of the Infant of Prague,* Prague, OK *Mabee-Gerrer Museum of Art,* Shawnee, OK *St. Gregory's College,* Shawnee, OK.

Ministries in 18 Parishes.

Priests 24; Brothers 10; Deacons 1.

Represented in the Archdioceses of Los Angeles and Oklahoma City and in the Diocese of Tulsa.

ST. LEO ABBEY: Saint Leo, FL 33574. Founded in 1889 and raised to an Abbey in 1902; Rev. Simeon J. Thole, O.S.B., Apostolic Admin.

Legal Title: *Order of St. Benedict of Florida, Inc.*

Fathers 14; Brothers 20; Internal Oblates 1.

Represented in the Dioceses of Covington, Phoenix and St. Petersburg.

ASSUMPTION ABBEY: P.O. Box A, Richardton, ND 58652. Tel: 701-974-3315. Founded in 1893 and raised to an Abbey in 1903; Rt. Rev. Patrick Moore, O.S.B., Abbot; Rt. Rev. Lawrence Wagner, O.S.B., Resigned Abbot; Rt. Rev. Robert West, O.S.B., Resigned Abbot; Very Rev. Valerian Odermann, O.S.B., Prior; Rev. Thomas Wordekemper, O.S.B., Subprior; Bro. Alban Petesch, O.S.B., Formation Dir.

Priests 34; Brothers 25.

Properties owned or sponsored: Abbey; Dependent Priory; Parishes 9; Chaplaincies 4; Indian Mission.

Represented in the Dioceses of Bismarck, Fargo, Great Falls and Indianapolis. Also in Colombia. Monastery founded and raised to an Abbey in 1910; Rt. Rev. Marion Balsavich, O.S.B., Resigned Abbot; Rt. Rev. Roger Corpus, O.S.B., Abbot; Very Rev. Philip Davey, O.S.B., Prior; Very Ven. Nathaniel Grossman, O.S.B., Subprior.

Priests 29; Brothers 6.

Legal Title: *The Benedictine Society of Saint Bede.*

Properties owned or sponsored: Parishes 5.

Represented in the Archdiocese of Chicago and in the Diocese of Peoria.

ST. MARTIN'S ABBEY: 5300 Pacific Ave. S.E., Lacey, WA 98503-1297. Monastery founded in 1895 and raised to an Abbey in 1914; Rt. Rev. Neal G. Roth, O.S.B.; Rt. Rev. Conrad R. Rausch, O.S.B., Resigned Abbot; Rt. Rev. Adrian Parcher, O.S.B., Resigned Abbot; Very Revs. Urban C. Feucht, O.S.B., Prior; Nicholas B. Rausch, O.S.B., Subprior; Rev. Sean R. Malvey, O.S.B., Formation Dir.; Rev. Alfred J. Hulscher, O.S.B., Treas. & Financial Dir.

Legal Holdings or Titles: *St. Martin's Abbey, St. Martin's College.*

Priests 29; Brothers 16.

Represented in the Archdioceses of Seattle and Portland in Oregon and in the Dioceses of Spokane and Yakima.

HOLY CROSS ABBEY: P.O. Box 1510, Canon City, CO 81215-1510. Tel: 719-275-8631. Founded in 1886 and raised to an Abbey in 1925; Revs. Kenneth Hein, O.S.B., Admin.; Ignatius Smith, O.S.B., Prior.

Fathers 18; Brothers 6; Oblates 2.

Parishes 5; Chaplaincies 2; Missions 1.

Represented in the Archdiocese of Denver and in Dioceses of Cheyenne, Colorado Springs and Pueblo.

ST. ANSELM ABBEY: 100 St. Anselm Dr., Manchester, NH 03102-1310. Tel: 603-641-7000; Fax: 603-641-7116. Monastery founded in 1889 and raised to an Abbey in 1927; Rt. Rev. Matthew K. Leavy, O.S.B., Abbot; Most Rev. Joseph J. Gerry, O.S.B., 3rd Abbot, Tenth Bishop of Portland, ME; Rt. Rev. Gerald F. McCarthy, O.S.B., 2nd Abbot, Resigned; Very Rev. John R. Fortin, O.S.B., Prior; Very Rev. Peter J. Guerin, O.S.B., Subprior.

Legal Title: *Order of Saint Benedict of New Hampshire.*

Bishops 1; Abbots 2; Fathers 32; Brothers 7.

Represented in the Archdiocese of San Francisco and the Diocese of Manchester.

ST. ANDREW ABBEY: 10510 Buckeye Rd., Cleveland, OH 44104. Tel: 216-721-5300. Founded in 1922 and raised to an Abbey in 1934; Rt. Rev. Roger Gries, O.S.B., Abbot; Very Rev. Joachim Pastirik, O.S.B., Prior; Ven. Bro. Peter Ancell, O.S.B., Subprior.

Legal Holdings or Titles: *Benedictine Order of Cleveland, Benedictine High School.*

Priests 27; Brothers 13; Simple Vows 2; Novices 1.

Abbeys 1; Parishes 2; High School; Chaplaincies 4.

Represented in the Dioceses of Cleveland and Great Falls-Billings.

ST. MAUR PRIORY: 4615 N. Michigan Rd., Indianapolis, IN 46228. Tel: 317-925-9095. Very Rev. Charles W. Henry, O.S.B., Prior.

Priests 3; Professed Brothers 4.

Represented in the Archdiocese of Indianapolis.

HOLY TRINITY PRIORY: P.O. Box 990, Butler, PA 16003. Tel: 412-287-4461. Rt. Rev. Leo R. Schlosser, O.S.B., Hegumen.

Monks 12.

Represented in the Byzantine Archdiocese of Pittsburgh.

BENEDICTINE PRIORY: P.O. Box 13577, 6502 Seawright Dr., Savannah, GA 31406. Tel: 912-356-3520; Fax: 912-356-3527. Founded 1877, dependent priory of St. Vincent Archabbey, Latrobe, PA; Very Rev. Meinrad Lawson, O.S.B., Prior.

Priests 6; Brothers 3.

High Schools 1.

Represented in the Diocese of Savannah.

WOODSIDE PRIORY: 302 Portola Rd., Portola Valley, CA 94028. Tel: 415-851-8220. Founded in 1956, erected as Conventual Priory 1958, became a dependent Priory upon St. Anselm's Abbey, Manchester, NH, 1976; Very Rev. William J. Sullivan, O.S.B., Prior; Very Rev. Martin J. Mager, O.S.B., Subprior.

Priests 6; Brothers 2.

Legal Title: *Benedictine Fathers of the Priory, Inc.*

High Schools 1; Middle Schools 1.

Represented in the Archdiocese of San Francisco.

BENEDICTINE ABADIA DE SAN ANTONIO ABAD: P.O. Box 729, Humacao, PR 00792. Tel: 809-852-1616; 852-1766; Fax: 809-852-1920. Monastery founded in 1947 and became an abbey in 1984; Rt. Rev. Jose M. Rodriguez Santiago, O.S.B., Abbot; Rev.

Eduardo Torrellas, O.S.B., Prior; Bro. Aristides Pacheco, Subprior.
Priests 10; Brothers 7.
Mary Mother of the Church Abbey: 12617 River Rd., Richmond, VA 23233. Tel: 804-784-3508; Fax: 804-784-3508, Ext. 245. Community founded in 1911 and became an Abbey in 1989; Rt. Rev. Benedict R. McDermott, O.S.B., Abbot; Very Rev. Theophile Brown, O.S.B., Prior & Novice Master.
Priests 9; Brothers 5.
Abbeys 1; Parishes 1; Chaplaincies 2; High Schools 1.
Legal Holdings: *Benedictine High School of Richmond, Mary Mother of the Church Abbey.*
Represented in the Diocese of Richmond.

Swiss-American Congregation

Founded by Pope Pius IX, 1870, and Pope Leo XIII, April 5, 1881.
The Abbeys and Priories belonging to this Federation are as follows:.
St. Meinrad Archabbey: St. Meinrad, IN 47577. Tel: 812-357-6611; Fax: 812-357-6551. Founded 1854; raised to an Abbey in 1870; Rt. Rev. Lambert Reilly, O.S.B., Archabbot; Rt. Rev. Bonaventure Knaebel, O.S.B., Retired Archabbot; Very Rev. Keith McClellan, O.S.B., Prior.
Archbishops 1; Priests 95; Brothers 40; Novices 1.
Parishes 16; Schools of Theology 1; Colleges 1; Chaplaincies 8.
Represented in the Archdioceses of Indianapolis, and Washington, and in the Dioceses of Baton Rouge, Evansville, Hartford, Little Rock, Owensboro, Sioux Falls and Venice.
Conception Abbey: Conception, MO 64433. Tel: 816-944-2211; Fax: 816-944-2800. Founded December 8, 1873; Abbey April 5, 1881; Rt. Rev. Gregory Polan, O.S.B., Abbot; Rt. Rev. Anselm Coppersmith, O.S.B., Retired Abbot; Rt. Rev. James Jones, O.S.B., Retired Abbot; Very Rev. Kenneth Reichert, O.S.B., Prior; Bro. Michael Marcotte, O.S.B., Subprior.
Legal Title: *Conception Abbey, Inc.*
Archbishops 1; Fathers 55; Brothers 20; Oblates 1.
Parishes 14; Seminary College 1; Chaplaincies 7.
Represented in the Archdiocese of Omaha and the Dioceses of Cheyenne, Des Moines, Dodge City, Kansas City-St. Joseph, Salina and Springfield-Cape Girardeau.
Mount Michael Abbey: 22520 Mount Michael Rd., Elkhorn, NE 68022-3400. Tel: 402-289-2541; Fax: 402-289-4539. Rt. Rev. Theodore Wolff, O.S.B., Abbot; Very Rev. Robert Halter, O.S.B., Prior; Bro. Jerome Kmiecik, Subprior.
Legal Holdings & Titles: Benedictine Fathers, Inc., Mount Michael Benedictine High School, Elkhorn, NE, *Mt. Michael Foundation, Inc.*
Fathers 17; Brothers 9.
Monks serve & staff: Parishes 4.
Represented in the Archdiocese of Omaha and the Diocese of Pueblo.
Subiaco Abbey: Subiaco, AR 72865. Tel: 501-934-4295; Fax: 501-934-4328. Rt. Rev. Jerome Kodell, O.S.B., Abbot; Bro. Eric Loran, O.S.B., Prior; Rev. Angelo Dobrzynski, O.S.B., Subprior.
Legal Title: *Subiaco Abbey,* Subiaco, AR 72865.
Fathers 41; Perpetually Professed Brothers 28; Temporarily Professed Brothers 5; Students in Major Seminaries 1.
Properties staffed or sponsored: Parishes 13; High School 1; Missions 3.
Represented in the Dioceses of Fort Worth and Little Rock. Also in Belize City.
St. Joseph Abbey: St. Benedict, LA 70457. Tel: 504-892-1800. Rt. Rev. Patrick Regan, O.S.B., Abbot; Very Rev. Gregory Boquet, O.S.B., Prior; Rev. Dominic Braud, O.S.B., Subprior.
Fathers 31; Brothers 17.
Legal Holdings: *St. Joseph Seminary College,* St. Benedict, LA.
Parishes 4; Novitiates 1; Seminary College 1.
Represented in the Archdiocese of New Orleans.
Mt. Angel Abbey: St. Benedict, OR 97373. Tel: 503-845-3030; Fax: 503-845-3594. Founded on Oct. 30, 1882, from Engelberg in Switzerland and raised to an abbey on March 24, 1904; Rt. Rev. Peter Eberle, O.S.B., Abbot; Very Rev. Paul Thomas, O.S.B., Prior; Very Rev. Paschal Cheline, O.S.B., Subprior.
Legal Holdings or Titles: *Mt. Angel & Jerome, Ascension Priory,* Jerome, ID, *Our Lady of the Angels,* Cuernavaca, Morelos, Mexico.
Finally Professed Monks: Priests 61; Brothers 27; Temporarily Professed Monks:; Brothers 8; Novices 2.
Marmion Abbey: Butterfield Rd., Aurora, IL 60504. Tel: 708-897-7215. Founded as Dependent Priory of St. Meinrad's Abbey, June 20, 1943; Abbey since March 21, 1947; Rt. Rev. Vincent de Paul Bataille, O.S.B., Abbot; Rt. Rev. Gerald Benkert, O.S.B., Abbot Emeritus; Rt. Rev. David J. Cyr, O.S.B., Abbot Emeritus; Very Rev. Kenneth Theisen, O.S.B., Prior; Ven. Bro. Anselm Mangano, O.S.B., Subprior.
Priests 33; Brothers 11.
Properties staffed or sponsored: Parishes 2; High Schools 2.
Represented in the Dioceses of Rockford and Sioux Falls. Also in Quetzaltenango, Guatemala.
St. Benedict's Abbey: Benet Lake, WI 53102. Tel: 414-396-4311. Monastery founded in 1945 and raised to an Abbey in 1952; Rt. Rev. Leo Ryska, O.S.B., Abbot; Rt. Rev. Robert Schoofs, O.S.B., Abbot Resigned; Rt. Rev. Andrew Garber, O.S.B., Abbot Resigned; Very Rev. Edmund Boyce, O.S.B., Prior; Bro. Richard Aplington, O.S.B., Subprior.
Legal Title: *Benedictine Monks, Inc., St. Benedict's Home Missionary Society.*
Priests 13; Brothers 16.
Represented in the Archdiocese of Milwaukee. Also in Mexico.
Glastonbury Abbey: 16 Hull St., Hingham, MA 02043. Tel: 617-749-2155; Fax: 617-749-7236. Rt. Rev. Nicholas J. Morcone, O.S.B., Abbot.
Property owned: Lincoln School Apartments for the Elderly & Handicapped, Hingham, MA.
Monks in Solemn Vows 9; Monks in Simple Vows 2.
Represented in the Archdiocese of Boston.
Blue Cloud Abbey: Marvin, SD 57251. Tel: 605-432-5528; Fax: 605-432-4754. Monastery founded June 24, 1950; raised to a Priory August 5, 1952; raised to an Abbey March 21, 1954; Rt. Rev. Thomas Hillenbrand, O.S.B., Abbot. Retired Abbots: Rt. Rev. Alan Berndt, O.S.B.; Rt. Rev. Denis Quinkert, O.S.B.; Rev. George Lyon, O.S.B., Prior.
Legal Title: *Blue Cloud Abbey, Inc.*
Priests 28; Brothers 16.
Represented in the Dioceses of Fargo and Sioux Falls. Also in Guatemala.
Corpus Christi Abbey: HCR 2, Box 6300, Sandia, TX 78383. Rt. Rev. Bonaventure Knaebel, O.S.B., Admin.; Very Rev. Bartholomew Leon, O.S.B., Prior.
Fathers 12; Professed Brothers 12.
Property owned: Benedictine Retreat Center, Sandia, TX.
Represented in the Diocese of Corpus Christi.
Prince Of Peace Abbey: 650 Benet Hill Rd., Oceanside, CA 92054. Tel: 619-430-1305; 430-1306. Rt. Rev. Charles Wright, O.S.B., Abbot; Rt. Rev. Claude Ehringer, O.S.B., Abbot (Retired); Very Rev. Basil Mattingly, Prior.
Fathers 11; Brothers 14; Novices 1; Postulants 1.
St. Benedict Abbey: 252 Still River Rd., P.O. Box 67, Still River-Harvard, MA 01467. Tel: 508-456-3221; Fax: 508-456-8181. Rt. Rev. Gabriel Gibbs, O.S.B., Abbot; Very Rev. Xavier Connelly, O.S.B., Prior.
Priests 7; Brothers 13; Oblates 1.
Represented in the Diocese of Worcester.

Congregation of St. Ottilien For Foreign Missions

St. Paul's Abbey: Newton, NJ 07860. Tel: 201-383-2470; Fax: 201-383-5782. (Benedictine Missionaries). Monastery established March 15, 1924; elevated to an Abbey June 9, 1947; Rt. Rev. Justin E. Dzikowicz, O.S.B., Abbot; Rt. Rev. Augustine J. Hinches, O.S.B., Resigned Abbot; Rt. Rev. Charles V. Coriston, O.S.B., Resigned Abbot; Very Rev. Joel P. Macul, O.S.B., Prior.
Solemnly professed monks 17 (14 priests).
Represented in the Archdiocese of Military Services and the Diocese of Paterson.
Christ The King Priory - Benedictine Mission House: Schuyler, NE 68661. Tel: 402-352-2177; Fax: 402-352-2176. Revs. Germar Neubert, O.S.B., Prior; Volker Futter, O.S.B.; Herman Kornbrust, O.S.B.
Fathers 4; Brothers 7.
Represented in the Archdiocese of Omaha.

Congregation of The Annunciation

St. Andrew's Abbey: Valyermo, CA 93563. Tel: 805-944-2178. Rt. Rev. Francis Benedict, O.S.B., Abbot; Revs. Luke Dysinger, O.S.B., Prior; Simon O'Donnell, O.S.B., Subprior.
Monks solemn vows 16; Simple vows 6; Novices 2.
Represented in the Archdiocese of Los Angeles.

Houses Not In Congregations

Mount Saviour Monastery: (Elmira) Pine City, NY 14871. Tel: 607-734-1688; Fax: 607-734-1689. Monastery founded in 1950, raised to Independent Priory 1957; Very Rev. Martin Boler, O.S.B., Prior; Rev. James Cronin, O.S.B., Subprior.
Professed Monks 16; Oblates 1.
Represented in the Diocese of Rochester.
Conventual Priory of St Gabriel the Archangel (1953): 58 Priory Hill Rd., Weston, VT 05161. Tel: 802-824-5409; Fax: 802-824-3573. (Weston Priory of Benedictine Monks; Very Rev. John Hammond, O.S.B., Prior; Rev. Richard Iaquinto, O.S.B., Asst. Prior.
Monks 14.
Represented in the Diocese of Burlington.

Camaldolese Benedictine Congregation

(Congregatio Camaldulensis Ordinis Sancti Benedicti)
General Motherhouse: The Sacred Hermitage and Monastery of Camaldoli, Arezzo, Italy. Most Rev. Emanuele Bargellini, O.S.B.Cam., Prior Gen.
U.S. Foundation (1958): *New Camaldoli Hermitage,* New Camaldoli, Big Sur, CA 93920. Tel: 408-667-2456. Very Rev. Robert Hale, O.S.B.Cam., Prior.
Fathers 10; Professed Brothers 13.
Represented in the Dioceses of Manchester, Monterey and Oakland.

English Benedictine Congregation

St. Anselm's Abbey: 4501 S. Dakota Ave. N.E., Washington, DC 20017. Tel: 202-269-2300; Fax: 202-269-2312. Rt. Rev. Aidan Shea, O.S.B., Abbot.
Legal Title: *Benedictine Foundation at Washington DC.*
Solemnly Professed Monks 25; Claustral Oblates 1.
Abbey of St. Gregory the Great: Cory's Ln., Portsmouth, RI 02871. Tel: 401-683-2000; Fax: 401-683-5888. Rt. Rev. Mark Serna, O.S.B., Abbot; Rt. Rev. Matthew Stark, O.S.B., Abbot Emeritus; Very Rev. Ambrose Wolverton, O.S.B., Prior.
Choir Religious 20.
Abbey of St. Mary and St. Louis: 500 S. Mason Rd., St. Louis, MO 63141-8500. Tel: 314-434-2557; Fax: 314-434-0795. Founded as a dependent Priory 1955, granted independence 1973, raised to status of Abbey 1989; Rt. Rev. W. Thomas Frerking, O.S.B., Abbot.
Solemnly professed monks 17 (13 priests); Oblates 1.

Benedictines—Sylvestrine Congregation

(Monachorum Silvestrinorum, O.S.B.)
General Motherhouse: Rome, Italy. S. Stefano del Cacco 26; Rt. Rev. Andrew Pantaloni, O.S.B., Abbot Gen.
Foundations in U.S. (1910): *Saint Benedict Priory,* 2711 E. Drahner Rd., Oxford, MI 48370. Tel: 810-628-2249. Very Rev. Daniel Homan, O.S.B., Conventual Prior, *St. Sylvester Monastery,* 17320 Rosemont Rd., Detroit, MI 48219. Tel: 313-532-6064; *Holy Face Monastery,* 1697 State Hwy. S-3, Clifton, NJ 07012. Tel: 201-778-1177.
Brothers 7; Priests 10; Novices 3.
Represented in the Archdiocese of Detroit and in the Diocese of Paterson.

Olivetan Benedictines

(Congregatio Sanctae Mariae Montis Oliveti Ordinis Sancti Benedicti)
General Motherhouse: *The Archabbey of Monte Oliveto Maggiore,* Monte Oliveto, Siena, Italy. Most Rev. Michelangelo M. Tiribilli, O.S.B., Abbot Gen.
U.S. Foundations: *Holy Trinity Monastery,* P.O. Box 298, St. David, AZ 85630. Tel: 602-720-4642; 720-4902. Revs. Louis B. Hasenfuss, O.S.B., Prior; Alcuin Almasy, O.S.B.; Lawrence Fedor, O.S.B.; James Liprie, O.S.B.; Henri Capdeville O.S.B.; Alexander Mills O.S.B.; Bartolome Johnston O.S.B.
Solemnly Professed 12; Temporarily Professed 3; Novices 3.
Represented in the Diocese of Tucson.
Lady of Guadalupe Abbey: Pecos, NM 87552. Tel: 505-757-6415. Order of St. Benedict; Rt. Rev. Andrew J. Miles, O.S.B., Abbot; Rev. Mark J. Norris, O.S.B., Prior.
Priests 9; Brothers 5; Novices 1; Sisters 9.
Represented in the Archdiocese of Santa Fe.
Benedictine Monastery of Hawaii: 67-290 Farrington Hwy., P.O. Box 490, Waialua, HI 96791. Tel: 808-637-7887; Fax: 808-637-8601. Rev. David Barfknecht, O.S.B., Supr.
Priests 3; Brothers 2.

Benedictines Subiaco Congregation

Monastery of Christ in the Desert (1964): Abiquiu, NM 87510. Tel: 505-470-4515. Independent Priory 1983; Rt. Rev. Philip Lawrence, O.S.B., Abbot.
Monks 39.
Represented in the Archdiocese of Santa Fe. Also in Mexico.
Saint Mary's Monastery (1987): P.O. Box 345, Petersham, MA 01366. Tel: 508-724-3350. Dependent Priory 1987; Rev. Dom Anselm Atkinson, O.S.B., Supr.
Monks 6.
Represented in the Diocese of Worcester.

[0220] (S.S.S.)—CONGREGATION OF THE BLESSED SACRAMENT

(Congregatio Sanctissimi Sacramenti)
General Motherhouse: 46 Via Giovanni Battista de Rossi, Rome, 00161. Italy. Very Rev. Norman Pelletier S.S.S., Supr. Gen.
Province of St. Ann (1931): 5384 Wilson Mills Rd., Cleveland, OH 44143. Tel: 216-442-6311. Very Rev. Anthony Schueller S.S.S., Prov.; Rev. Edward Stapleton, S.S.S., Consultor & Prov. Treas. Consultors: Revs. Ernest Falardeau S.S.S., Vicar Provincial; Eugene LaVerdierre, S.S.S., Consultor for Formation; Michael Arkins S.S.S.

Priests 59; Permanent Deacons 1; Clerics 4; Brothers 21.
Properties staffed or owned: Parishes 8; Seminary 1; Community Houses 9; Novitiate 1.
Represented in the Archdioceses of Chicago, New York, San Antonio and Santa Fe and in the Dioceses of Cleveland, Green Bay, Galveston- Houston and Salt Lake City.

[0230] (Er. Cam.)—CAMALDOLESE HERMITS OF THE CONGREGATION OF MONTE CORONA

(Eremitae Camaldulenses Congregationis Montis Coronae)

General Motherhouse: *Sacro Eremo Tuscolano,* 00044, Frascati (Roma), Italy. Rt. Rev. Lanfranco Longhi, Er. Cam., Father Major.
U.S. Foundation (1959): *Holy Family Hermitage,* Rte. 2, Box 36, Bloomingdale, OH 43910. Tel: 614-765-4511. Very Rev. Basil Corriere, Er. Cam., Prior.
Hermit Priests 3; Professed 3; Oblates 1.
Represented in the Diocese of Steubenville.

[0240] (O.S.CAM.)—CAMILLIAN FATHERS AND BROTHERS or ORDER OF ST. CAMILLUS

(Order of the Servants of the Sick)
(Ordo Ministrantium Infirmis)

General Motherhouse: *Casa Generalizia,* Ministri degli Infermi, C.P. 643, 00100, Roma Centro, Italy. Most. Rev. Angelo Brusco, O.S.Cam., Supr. Gen.; Very Rev. Richard O'Donnell, O.S.Cam., Vicar Gen.; Rev. Laurent Zougrana, O.S.Cam., Sec. of Formation; Rev. Anselmo Zambotti, O.S.Cam., Sec. of Missions; Rev. Ademar Rover O.S.Cam., Sec. of Ministry.
North American Province (1923): *Provincialate,* 10101 W. Wisconsin Ave., Wauwatosa, WI 53226. Tel: 414-259-4511; Fax: 414-258-4707. Very Rev. William F. Cronin, O.S.Cam., Prov. Councillors: Revs. Louis Lussier, O.S.Cam.; James Francis Kovarik, O.S.Cam.; Bro. Nelson Edward Deloria, O.S.Cam.; Bro. Thomas Farrell, O.S.Cam.
Legal Title: *St. Camillus Nursing Home,* Whitinsville, MA; *St. Camillus Institute,* Whitinsville, MA; *St. Camillus Health Center Inc.,* Wauwatosa, WI; *St. Camillus Institute,* Wauwatosa, WI; *San Camillo, Inc.,* Wauwatosa, WI; *St. Camillus Ministries Inc.,* Wauwatosa, WI; *St. Camillus Formation House,* St. Francis, WI; *St. Camillus Communities Inc.,* Wauwatosa, WI.
Fathers 16; Professed Brothers 6; Temporary Professed 1; Novices 1.
Represented in the Archdiocese of Milwaukee and the Dioceses of Madison and Worcester.

[0250] (C.R.L.)—CANONS REGULAR OF THE LATERAN

(Ordo Canonicorum Regularium S. Augustini Congregations Ss. Salvatoris Lateranensis)

General House: *Curia Generalizia dei Canonicio Regolari Lateranensi,* Piazza S. Pietro in Vincoli, 4A, 00184, Roma, Italy.
United States: *Canons Regular of the Lateran,* 2317 Washington Ave., Bronx, NY 10458. Tel: 212-295-9600. Rev. Jose L. Biain, C.R.L., Supr. Tel: 212-994-1477.
Priests 6; Brothers 4.
Represented in the Archdiocese of New York and in the Diocese of Arecibo.

[0260] (O.C.D.)—DISCALCED CARMELITE FRIARS

(Ordo Carmelitarum Discalceatorum)

Founded Mt. Carmel, Palestine in the 13th Century.
Generalate: *Carmelitani Scalzi,* Corso d'Italia, 38, 00198, Rome, Italy. Very Rev. Camilo Maccise, O.C.D., Supr. Gen.
California-Arizona Province (1983): *Provincial House,* 926 E. Highland Ave., P.O. Box 2178, Redlands, CA 92373. Tel: 909-793-0424; Fax: 909-335-1304. Very Rev. Gerald Werner, O.C.D., Prov.
Legal Title: *Discalced Carmelite Province of California.*
Fathers 31; Brothers 3; Students 4; Novices 1.
Properties owned, staffed, or sponsored: Parishes 4; Retreat House; Novitiate; House of Studies; House of Prayer; Institute of Spirituality.
Represented in the Archdioceses of Los Angeles and Seattle and the Dioceses of Oakland, San Jose, San Bernardino, Santa Rosa and Tucson.
Province of St. Therese of Oklahoma (1935): *Provincial House-Monastery of Marylake,* 515 Marylake Drive, Little Rock, AR 72206-9424. Tel: 501-888-5827. Very Rev. Aloysius Deeney, O.C.D., Prov.
Fathers 25; Brothers 3; Students of Philosophy 2; Students of Theology 2; Novices 3.
Properties staffed or sponsored: Parishes 3; Community Houses 1; Novitiate 1; Student House 1.
Represented in the Archdioceses of San Antonio, New Orleans and Oklahoma City and in the Dioceses of Dallas and Little Rock.
Province of the Immaculate Heart of Mary (1947): *Discalced Carmelites,* 1233 S. 45th St., Milwaukee, WI 53214. Tel: 414-672-7212; Fax: 414-672-3138. Very Rev. Phillip R. Thomas, O.C.D., Prov.
Fathers 63; Brothers 13; Temporary Professed Clerics 9; Temporary Professed Brothers 2; Community Houses 8; Novices 1.
Represented in the Archdioceses of Boston, Chicago, Milwaukee, Washington and Nairobi (Kenya), and in the Dioceses of Manchester and Wheeling-Charleston.
Polish Province of the Holy Spirit, Poland (1949): *Monastery of Our Lady of Mt. Carmel,* 1628 Ridge Rd., Munster, IN 46321. Tel: 219-838-7111; Fax: 219-838-7214. Rev. Thomas I. Balys, O.C.D., Prior.
Priests 10; Brothers 1; Postulants 2.
Represented in the Diocese of Gary.

[0270] (O.CARM.)—CARMELITE FATHERS & BROTHERS

(Ordo Fratrum Beatissimae Virginis Mariae de Monte Carmelo)

General Curia: 00184, Rome, Italy. Via Giovanni Lanza, 138; Most Rev. Joseph Chalmers, O.Carm., Prior Gen.
Province of the Most Pure Heart of Mary (1864): 1317 Frontage Rd., Darien, IL 60561. Tel: 630-971-0050; Fax: 630-971-0195. Very Rev. Leo McCarthy, O.Carm., Prior Prov.
Commissariat Provincials: Very Rev. Leo McCarthy, O.Carm., Prov., 1317 Frontage Rd., Darien, IL 60561. Tel: 630-971-0050; Fax: 630-971-0195; *Midwest Commissary Provincial;* Rev. Raymond Clennon, O.Carm., 8419 Bailey Rd., Darien, IL 60561. Tel: 630-960-4934; *Western Commissary Provincial;* Rev. Ronald Oakham, O.Carm., 1540 E. Glenn St., Tuscan, AZ 85719; *Eastern Commissary Provincial;* Rev. Robert Wolfe, O.Carm., 158 Prospect St., Englewood, NJ 07631. Tel: 201-568-5612.
Provincial Officers: Revs. Daniel O'Neill, O.Carm., Prov. Treas.; John Welch, O.Carm., Dir. of Education. Councillors: Revs. Farrell Kane, O.Carm.; David Simpson, O.Carm.; Paul Schweizer, O.Carm.; Frederick Tillotson, O.Carm.; Peter Byrth, O.Carm., Lay Carmelite Dir.; Robert Colaresi, O.Carm., Dir. Little Flower Society. *Carmelite Mission Office:* Revs. John Malley, O.Carm., Dir.; Kevin Shanley, O.Carm., Prov. Communications Dir. Vocational Directors: Revs. Robert Colaresi, O.Carm.; John Lord, O.Carm.; Peter McGarry, O.Carm.; Leo Huard, O.Carm.
Priests 234; Clerics 20; Pre-Novitiate College Students 18; Novices 2; Brothers 17.
Properties owned: Spiritual Centers 4; Shopping-center Chapels 2; *Carefree Leisure Village,* residence for senior citizens, Darien, IL; High Schools 5; Community Houses 38; House of Study 2.
Ministries in 36 Parishes.
Represented in the Archdioceses of Boston, Chicago, Kansas City in Kansas, Los Angeles, Louisville, Newark and Washington, and in the Dioceses of Galveston-Houston, Joliet, Pittsburgh, Phoenix, Sacramento, Stockton, Tucson and Venice.
Province of St. Elias (1931): P.O. Box 3079, Middletown, NY 10940-0890. Tel: 914-344-2223. Very Rev. Mario Esposito, O.Carm., Prov.
Legal Holdings or Titles: *The Missionary Society of Our Lady of Mt. Carmel of the State of New York; The Carmelite Fathers, Inc. of New York; Carmelite Fathers, Inc. of the Commonwealth of Massachusetts; Mt. Carmel Hermitage; Order of Carmelites of Palm Beach, Inc.; National Shrine of Our Lady of Mount Carmel, Inc.*
Fathers 65; Clerics 5; Brothers 2; Novices 2; Pre-Novices 2.
Properties staffed, owned, or sponsored: Parishes 11; Priories 14; House of Study 2; Retreat Houses 1; Novitiate 1; High Schools 1; Hermitages 2; Shrines 1.
Represented in the Archdioceses of New York and Washington, and in the Dioceses of Albany, Brooklyn, Greensburg, Memphis, Palm Beach, Rochester, Sioux Falls, Springfield (MA) and Trenton.
Mt. Carmel Hermitage: Pineland, R.D. 3, Box 36, New Florence, PA 15944. Tel: 412-235-2157. Founded in 1970, became dependent upon St. Elias Province in 1995; Revs. Bede Mulligan, O.Carm.; Simeon Marro, O.Carm.
Fathers 2.
Represented in the Diocese of Greensburg.

[0275] (C.M.I.)—CARMELITES OF MARY IMMACULATE

(Congregatio Fratrum Carmelitarum B.V. Mariae Immaculatae)

Founded by Blessed Kuriakose Elias Chavara and Companions at Mannanam, Kerala, India in 1831.
Generalate: *Prior General's House,* P.B. No. 1056 Ernakulam, Cochin 682 011, Kerala, India. Tel: 484-360-137. Very Rev. Alex Ukken, C.M.I., Prior Gen.
North American Headquarters: 21 Nassau Ave., Brooklyn, NY 11222. Tel: 718-388-5145. Rev. Sebastian Kochupurackal, C.M.I., Reg. Coord.
Legal Title: *Carmelites of Mary Immaculate, Inc.*
Priests in the United States and Canada 44.
Ministries in Parishes; Hospitals; Universities; Prisons; Mission to the Syro-Malabar catholics.
Represented in the Archdioceses of New York and Philadelphia, and the Dioceses of Beaumont, Brooklyn, Charlotte, Joliet, Lafayette, Lake Charles, Nashville, Syracuse, Toledo and Tyler. Also in Canada.

[0280] (O.CART.)—ORDER OF CARTHUSIANS

(Ordo Cartusianorum)

Motherhouse: Grande Chartreuse, St. Pierre de Chartreuse (Isere), France. Rev. Father Andre Poisson, Supr. Gen.
U.S. Charterhouse of the Transfiguration (1951): *Carthusian Foundation,* R.R. 2, Box 2411, Arlington, VT 05250. Tel: 802-362-2550. Rev. Lorenzo Maria T. De La Rosa, Jr., O.Cart., Rector.
In Community 23.
Legal Title: *Carthusian Foundation in America, Inc., Carthusian Foundation, Association Fraternelle Romande.*
Represented in the Diocese of Burlington.

[0290] (F.C.)—BROTHERS OF CHARITY

(Congregatio Fratrum Caritate)

General Motherhouse (1807): Via G.B. Pagano 35, C.P. 9082, 00167, Roma, Italia. Bro. Waldebert Devestal, F.C., Supr. Gen.
American District (1963): *District of Our Lady of Charity,* 7720 Doe Ln., Laverock, PA 19038. Bro. Michael Lonsway, District Supr.
Represented in the Archdiocese of Philadelphia.

[0300] (I.C.)—INSTITUTE OF CHARITY

Rosminians
Institutum Charitatis

General Motherhouse: Collegio Rosmini Via Porta Latina 17, Rome, Italy. Most Rev. John Baptist Zantedeschi, I.C., D.D., Supr. Gen.
U.S. Foundation (1877): 2327 W. Heading Ave., Peoria, IL 61604. Tel: 309-676-6341. Very Rev. Christopher Fitzgerald, I.C., Prov.
Fathers in the U.S. 18.
Novitiate 1; Parishes 8.
Represented in the Dioceses of Peoria, St. Petersburg and Venice.

[0310] (C.F.C.)—CONGREGATION OF CHRISTIAN BROTHERS

(Christian Brothers Institute)

Founded in Ireland in 1802. First foundation in the United States in 1906.
General Motherhouse: *Fratelli Cristiani,* Via della Maglianella, 375, 00166, Roma, Italia. Very Rev. Bro. Edmund M. Garvey, Supr. Gen.
Eastern U.S. American Province (1916): 21 Pryer Terrace, New Rochelle, NY 10804. Tel: 914-636-6194. Bros. James B. Moffett, Prov.; Brian M. Walsh, Deputy Prov. Consultors: Bros. L. Alphonsus Killelea; J. Edward Roepke; V. Gregory McNally; Mr. Vincent J. Dougherty, Prov. Treas.
Brothers 220.
Properties owned, staffed, or sponsored: College 1; High Schools 15; Grade Schools 3; Migrant Education Center 1; Care Center 1.
Represented in the Archdioceses of Boston, Miami, Newark and New York, and in the Dioceses of Albany, Providence, Rochester, St. Petersburg and Venice.
Brother Rice Province (Western United States): *Brother Rice Provincialate,* 958 Western Ave., Joliet, IL 60435-6954. Tel: 815-723-5464. Bros. Lawrence J. Mooney, Prov.; Michael D. Lucas, Deputy Prov. Consultors: Bros. Charles D. McKenna; Donald D. Murray; Ross E. Wielatz; Bros. Gregory Smyth, Vocations; Richard L. Stanich, Prov. Bursar.
Development Office: Christian Brothers Association, P.O. Box 42903, Evergreen Park, IL 60805-0903. Tel: 312-233-2949. Bro. William G. O'Donnell, Dir.
Legal Title: *The Christian Brothers of Ireland, Inc.*
Properties administered: *Brother Rice High School (The Christian Bros. Inst. of Mich., Inc.),* Bloomfield, MI; *Brother Rice High School (Brother Rice High School, Inc.),* Chicago, IL; *Damien Memorial*

High School (The Congregation of Christian Bros. of Hawaii, Inc.), Honolulu, HI; *Palma Junior-Senior High School (The Christian Brothers Institute of California, Inc.),* Salinas, CA; *St. Laurence High School, (St. Lawrence High School, Inc.),* Oak Lawn, IL.

Brothers under Vows 101.

Represented in the Archdioceses of Chicago, Detroit and Seattle, and in the Dioceses of Helena, Honolulu, Monterey and Joliet. Also in Peru and West Africa.

[0320] (F.I.C.)—BROTHERS OF CHRISTIAN INSTRUCTION

La Mennais Brothers

(Institutum Fratrum Instructionis Christianae)

General Motherhouse: *Casa Generalizia,* Via della Divina Provvidenz, 44, 00166, Rome, Italy. Tel: 66.41.5618; Fax: 66.41.5652. Rev. Jose Antonio Obeso Vega, F.I.C., Supr. Gen.

American Province (1946): *Notre Dame Province-Notre Dame Institute,* P.O. Box 159, Alfred, ME 04002. Tel: 207-324-0067. Bro. Francis Blouin, F.I.C., Prov.

Brothers 59.

College 1; High Schools 2; Retreat Center 1; Houses of Study (Scholasticate-Novitiate) 1.

Represented in the Archdiocese of Indianapolis, and the Dioceses of Fairbanks, Fall River, Ogdensburg, Portland (ME) and Youngstown.

[0330] (F.S.C.)—BROTHERS OF THE CHRISTIAN SCHOOLS

(Fratres Scholarum Christianarum)

General Motherhouse: *Casa Generalizia,* Via Aurelia 476, CP 9099, 00100, Roma, Italia. Bros. John Johnston, F.S.C., Supr. Gen.; Alvaro Rodriquez Echeverria, Vicar Gen.

Christian Brothers Conference: *USA/Toronto Region,* 4351 Garden City Dr., Ste. 200, Landover, MD 20785-2248. Tel: 800-433-7593; 301-459-9410. Bros. Kevin Gilhooly, F.S.C., Interim Exec. Sec.; Theodore Drahmann, F.S.C., Dir. Education; John Linhardt, F.S.C., Dir. Formation; William Quaintance, F.S.C., Dir. Publications; Mr. John Garry, Dir. Volunteers.

Organizations served by this office: *Regional Conference of USA-Toronto Brothers Provincial; Regional F.S.C. Education Board; Regional F.S.C. Finance Board; Regional F.S.C. Vocation and Formation Board; F.S.C. Publication Board.*

Organizations associated with this office: *Christian Brothers Major Superiors.*

Properties owned and or sponsored: *Bethlehem University of the Holy Land,* P.O. Box 9, Bethlehem, via Israel (Incorporated in the State of New Jersey).

Province of Baltimore (1845): *The Provincialate,* Box 29, Adamstown, MD 21710. Tel: 301-874-5188; Fax: 301-874-5674. Bros. Benedict Oliver, F.S.C., Prov., Visitor; Robert Schieler, F.S.C., Auxiliary-Visitor; Timothy Froehlich, F.S.C., Dir. Finance; Charles Lackes, F.S.C., Dir. St. LaSalle Auxiliary; Patrick Cassidy, Dir. Vocations; Martin Fahey, F.S.C., Sec.

Brothers 212.

Legal Holdings or Titles: *Christian Brothers of Frederick, Inc.; Ammendale Normal Institute of Prince George's County, Inc.; Christian Brothers Community Support Charitable Trust.*

Represented in the Archdioceses of Baltimore, Newark, Philadelphia and Washington, and in the Dioceses of Camden and Pittsburgh.

Brothers Of The Christian Schools (Midwest Province - 1995): 200 S. Frontage Rd., Ste. 300, Burr Ridge, IL 60521-6953. Tel: 630-323-3725; Fax: 630-323-3779. Bros. Thomas Johnson, F.S.C., Prov. Visitor; Francis Carr, F.S.C., Aux. Visitor; Michael Fehrenbach, F.S.C., Aux. Visitor; Ms. Marge Beauvais, Dir. Lasallian Family; Bro. Edwin Dupre, F.S.C., Dir. Development; Bros. Joseph Saurbier, F.S.C., Dir. Finance; Thomas Sullivan, F.S.C., Dir. Vocations/Formation; Nicholas Schumer, F.S.C., Dir. St. La Salle Auxiliary.

Legal Title: *The Christian Brothers of the Midwest, Inc.; The Christian Brothers of Illinois, Brothers of the Christian Schools of the St. Louis, District; The Christian Brothers of Minnesota.*

Brothers 255; Novices 1; Aspirants 6.

Properties owned, staffed, or sponsored: Communities 32; Universities 3; High Schools 17; Retreat Houses 3; Group Homes 2; Publishing House 1; Educational Data Center 1.

Represented in the Archdiocese of Chicago, St. Louis, St. Paul-Minneapolis, and in the Dioceses of Green Bay, Gaylord, Jackson, Jefferson City, Joliet, Kansas City-St. Joseph, LaCrosse, Memphis, Tulsa and Winona.

Province of New York (1848): *La Salle Provincialate Inc.,* 800 Newman Springs Rd., Lincroft, NJ 07738. Tel: 908-842-7420; Fax: 908-530-3504. Bros. Michael Corry, F.S.C., Prov. Chm. Bd.; Stephen McCabe, F.S.C., Auxiliary Prov.; Dir.-Devel. Office & Dir.-Education; Robert Carnaghi, F.S.C., Auxiliary Prov. & Dir.-Formation; John Martin, F.S.C., Treas.; Edward Cleary, F.S.C., Sec.; William Martin, F.S.C., Dir. St. La Salle Auxiliary, P.O. Box 228, Lincroft, NJ 07738. Direct all inquiries to Bro. Michael Corry, F.S.C., Prov. All of these Brothers constitute the Board Members of St. Joseph Normal Institute, De La Salle Institute, Hillside Hall and De La Salle College.

Brothers 208.

College 1; High Schools 10; Elementary Schools 2; Welfare Schools 1; Community Houses 18; House of Study and Formation 1.

Represented in the Archdioceses of Detroit, Newark and New York and in the Dioceses of Albany, Buffalo, Syracuse and Trenton.

Province of Long Island-New England (1957): *Christian Brothers' Center-Provincial Offices, St. La Salle Auxiliary and Office of Public Information and Development,* Narragansett, RI 02882-1314. Tel: 401-789-0244; Fax: 401-783-5303. Bros. William Mann, F.S.C., Prov.-Visitor; Daniel Casey, F.S.C., Auxiliary Prov. Continuing-Initial Formation/Education; Peter Clifford, F.S.C., Dir. Finance; Robert Hazard, F.S.C., Dir. Vocation Ministry.

Legal Title: *Brothers of the Christian Schools, Province of the Long Island-New England, Inc.*

Organizations served by this office: *The Familiares Ocean Tides, Inc.* (1975). Bro. Brendan Gerrity, F.S.C., Pres. Tel: 401-789-1016.

Brothers 105; Aspirants 1.

Properties owned, staffed, or sponsored: High Schools 5; Schools Elementary Schools 2; Community Houses 10.

Represented in the Dioceses of Brooklyn, Providence and Rockville Centre.

Province of San Francisco (1868): *Brothers of the Christian Schools Provincial Office,* P.O. Box 3720, Napa, CA 94558-0372. Tel: 707-252-0222. Bro. David Brennan, F.S.C., Prov.

Brothers 139.

College 1; High Schools 9; Community Houses 15; House of Study 1; Retreat & Conference Center 1.

Represented in the Archdioceses of Los Angeles, Portland (OR) and San Francisco, and in the Dioceses of Fresno, Monterey, Oakland, Sacramento and Santa Rosa. Also in Italy, Mexico, Ethiopia, Guatemala, Israel, Philippines, Kenya, Tijuana, Eritrea and England.

Province of New Orleans-Santa Fe (1921): *De La Salle - Christian Brothers Provincialate,* 1522 Carmel Dr., Lafayette, LA 70501. Tel: 318-234-1973. Bros. Clarence Fioke, F.S.C., Prov.; James Brown, F.S.C., Auxiliary Prov. & Finance Dir.

Legal Holdings or Titles: *Brothers of the Christian Schools of Lafayette, LA., Inc.; St. La Salle Auxiliary; New Orleans-Santa Fe Retirement Plan; The Christian Brothers of J.K. Mullen High School; J.K. Mullen High School Corporation; Christian Brothers Foundation; Christian Brothers Retirement Trust.*

Brothers 126.

Properties owned, staffed, or sponsored: College; High Schools 6; Elementary Schools 2.

Represented in the Archdioceses of Denver, New Orleans and Santa Fe, and in the Dioceses of El Paso and Lafayette (LA).

[0340] (O.CIST.)—CISTERCIAN FATHERS

(Ordo Cisterciensis)

Headquarters: Piazza del Tempio di Diana 14, I-00153, Rome, Italy. Most Rev. Maurus Esteva, O.Cist., S.T.D., Abbot Gen.

Cistercian Abbey: *Our Lady of Spring Bank,* Rte. 3, Box 211, Sparta, WI 54656. Tel: 608-269-8138. Rt. Rev. Blaise J. Fuez, O.Cist., Abbot; Very Rev. Bernard McCoy, O.Cist., Prior; Rev. Gregory Norman, O.Cist.

Professed Priests 3; Solemnly Professed 4; Postulants 1; Novices 1.

Cistercian Monastery: *Our Lady of Dallas,* 1 Cistercian Rd., Irving, TX 75039. Tel: 972-438-2044. Rt. Rev. Denis Farkasfalvy, O.Cist., Abbot; Revs. Peter Verhalen, O.Cist., Prior; Henry Marton, O.Cist., Subprior.

Priests 24.

Staff: Parishes 1; Universities 2; Preparatory School 1; Novitiate 1; Chaplaincies 3.

Properties owned: Abbey & Preparatory School.

Represented in the Dioceses of Dallas and Fort Worth.

Cistercian Monastery: 564 Walton Ave., Mt. Laurel, NJ 08054. Tel: 609-235-1330. Revs. Lino Parente, O.Cist., Prior; Anselmo Florio, O.Cist.; Maurizio Nicoletti, O.Cist. Established in 1961 as a dependent Monastery of the Congregation of Casamari (Italy).

Property owned: *Fatima House and the Monastery.*

Cistercian Conventual Priory: *St. Mary's Priory,* R.D. No. 1, Box 206, New Ringgold, PA 17960. Tel: 717-943-2645. Very Rev. Luke Anderson, O.Cist., Ph.D., Prior.

Legal Title: *The Cistercian Monastery of Pennsylvania.*

Monks 3.

[0350] (O.C.S.O.)—THE CISTERCIAN ORDER OF THE STRICT OBSERVANCE (TRAPPISTS)

(Ordo Cisterciensium Strictioris Observantiae)

General Motherhouse: *Casa Generalizia,* O.C.S.O., 33 Viale Africa, Rome, 00144. Italy. Most Rev. Dom Bernardo Olivera, O.C.S.O., Abbot Gen.

Abbey of Gethsemani (1848): Trappist, KY 40051. Tel: 502-549-3117. Rt. Rev. Timothy Kelly, O.C.S.O., Abbot.

Priests 20; Brothers 50; Novices 5.

Abbey of Our Lady of New Melleray (1849): 6500 Melleray Cir., Peosta, IA 52068. Tel: 319-588-2319. Rt. Rev. Brendan Freeman, O.C.S.O., Abbot; Revs. Thomas MacMaster, O.C.S.O., Prior; Daniel Lenihan, O.C.S.O., Subprior.

Professed Monks 51 (30 are Priests).

St. Joseph's Abbey (1825): Spencer, MA 01562-1233. Tel: 508-885-8700; Fax: 508-885-3999. Rt. Rev. Augustine Roberts, O.C.S.O., Abbot.

Legal Title: *Cistercian Abbey of Spencer, Inc.*

Total in community 85 (38 are Priests); Solemnly Professed 77; Simply Professed 3; Novices 2; Postulants 3.

Monastery of The Holy Spirit, Inc. (1944): 2625 Hwy 212 S.W., Conyers, GA 30208. Tel: 404-483-8705; Fax: 404-760-0989. Rt. Rev. Bernard Johnson, O.C.S.O., Abbot; Rt. Rev. Dom Augustin, O.C.S.O., Retired Abbot.

Professed Monks 53; Priests 33; Novices 5.

Represented in the Archdiocese of Atlanta.

Abbey of Our Lady of Guadalupe (1947): Lafayette, OR 97127. Tel: 503-852-7174; Fax: 503-852-7748. Rt. Rev. Peter McCarthy, O.C.S.O., Abbot; Very Rev. John-Baptist Hasbrouck, O.C.S.O., Prior; Bro. Leonard Luberts, O.C.S.O., Subprior.

Solemnly Professed 37; Priests 18.

Abbey of Our Lady of the Holy Trinity (1947): Huntsville, UT 84317. Tel: 801-745-3784. Rt. Rev. Leander Dosch, O.C.S.O., Abbot.

Priests 14.

Abbey of The Genesee (1951): P.O. Box 900, Piffard, NY 14533. Tel: 716-243-0660. Rt. Rev. John Eudes Bamberger, O.C.S.O., Abbot; Rev. Francis Steger, O.C.S.O., Prior; Bro. Anthony Weber, O.C.S.O., Novice Master.

Retreat House. Tel: 716-243-2220.

Professed Monks 32; Novices 2; Professed Priests 11; Oblates 1.

Mepkin Abbey (1949): 1098 Mepkin Abbey Road, Moncks Corner, SC 29461. Tel: 803-761-8509; Fax: 803-761-6719. Rt. Rev. Francis Kline, O.C.S.O., Abbot; Bro. Stephen Petronek, O.C.S.O., Prior; Bro. Stan Gumula, O.C.S.O., Business Mgr.; Rt. Rev. Christian Aidan Carr, O.C.S.O., (Retired Abbot); Rt. Rev. Anthony Chassagne, O.C.S.O., (Retired Abbot).

Priests 10; Monks in Community 30.

Abbey of Our Lady of the Holy Cross (1950): Rte. 2, Box 3870, Berryville, VA 22611-9526. Tel: 703-955-1425; Fax: 703-955-4006. Bro. Benedict Simmonds, O.C.S.O., Supr.

Legal Title: *Community of Cistercians of the Strict Observance, Inc.*

Solemnly Professed 21; Simply Professed 3; Novices 3; Priests 12.

Assumption Abbey: Rte. 5, Box 1056, Ava, MO 65608. Tel: 417-683-5110. Rt. Rev. James Conner, O.C.S.O., Abbot; Rt. Rev. Cyprian Harrison, O.C.S.O., Abbot (Retired); Rt. Rev. Robert Matter, O.C.S.O., Abbot (Retired).

Priests 8; Professed 15.

Abbey of New Clairvaux (1955): *Trappist-Cistercian Abbey,* Vina, CA 96092. Tel: 916-839-2161. Rt. Rev. Thomas X. Davis, O.C.S.O., Abbot.

Legal Title: *Abbey of New Clairvaux, Inc.*

Solemn Vows 24; Simple Vows 3.

St. Benedict's Monastery (1956): 1012 Monastery Rd., Snowmass, CO 81654. Tel: 970-927-3311. Rt. Rev. Joseph Boyle, O.C.S.O., Abbot; Bros. Raymond Roberts, O.C.S.O., Prior; Charles Albanese, O.C.S.O., Subprior.

Professed Monks 14; Novices 1.

[0360] (C.M.F.)—CLARETIAN MISSIONARIES

Missionary Sons of the Immaculate Heart of Mary

(Congregatio Missionariorum Filiorum Immaculati Cordis Beatae Mariae Virginis.)

General Headquarters: Rome, Via Sacro Cuore di

Maria 5, Italy. Very Rev. Aquilino Bocos, C.M.F., Supr. Gen.

WESTERN PROVINCE: *Provincial Headquarters,* 1119 Westchester Pl., Los Angeles, CA 90019. Tel: 213-734-1824; Fax: 213-737-0301. Rev. Ralph Berg, C.M.F., Prov.

Legal Title: *Claretian Missionaries-Western Province, Inc.,* A not-for-profit corporation under the laws of the State of California having as its purpose the support of any Roman Catholic benevolent, charitable, educational or missionary undertakings of the Claretian Missionaries - Western Province, Inc.

Other Corporations: *Dominguez Seminary, Inc.,* Compton, CA; *Claretian Educational and Renewal Center, Inc.,* Los Angeles, CA; *Claretian Tape Ministry, Inc.,* Los Angeles, CA.

Fathers 81; Brothers 8; Students 5; Novices 5.

Ministries in the following areas: Newman Centers; Parishes; Novitiate; House of Study; Centers for Spanish; Speaking; Renewal Centers; Education; Spiritual Direction.

Represented in the Archdioceses of Los Angeles and San Antonio, and in the Dioceses of Austin, Fort Worth, Fresno, Oakland, Orange and Phoenix.

EASTERN PROVINCE: *Headquarters,* 400 N. Euclid Ave., Oak Park, IL 60302. Tel: 708-848-2076; Fax: 708-848-2069. Very Rev. Theodore Cirone, C.M.F., Prov.; Revs. Mark Brummel, C.M.F., Vicar Prov. & Sec.; Greg Kenny, C.M.F., Consultor; Ronald Stua, C.M.F., Consultor.

Legal Holdings or Titles: *The Congregation of Sons of the Immaculate Heart of Mary of the Eastern Province, Inc., Claret Center,* Chicago, IL; *Claretian Lay Volunteer Program,* Chicago, IL; *Claretian Associates Neighborhood Development Office,* Chicago, IL; *U.S. Catholic Bookstore,* Chicago, IL; *Claretians, Inc.; St. Jude League, Inc.; Claret Hills, Inc.; St. Jude Seminary, Inc.*

Fathers 43; Brothers 4; Professed Students 1.

House of Study 1.

Represented in the Archdioceses of Atlanta and Chicago, and in the Dioceses of Metuchen and Springfield-Cape Girardeau. Also in Guatemala.

[0370] (S.S.C.)—SOCIETY OF ST. COLUMBAN

(Societas Sancti Columbani pro missionibus ad Exteros)

CENTRAL ADMINISTRATION (1918): *St. Columban's,* Grange Rd., Donaghmede, Dublin, 13. Ireland. Very Rev. Nicholas Murray, S.S.C., Supr. Gen.

Members 753.

REGION OF THE UNITED STATES: P.O. Box 10, St. Columbans, NE 68056. Tel: 402-291-1920. Very Rev. Brendan O'Sullivan, S.S.C., Dir.; Rev. James J. Hastings, S.S.C., Vice Dir. Council: Revs. Mark Mengel, S.S.C., Regional Vocation & Lay Missionaries Coord.; Thomas P. Reynolds, S.S.C., Education Coord.; William Morton, S.S.C.; Charles O'Rourke, S.S.C.; Rev. Otto J. Imholte, Reg. Treas.

Legal Title: *St. Columban's Foreign Mission Society; The Columban Fathers.*

Fathers 103; Student Members and Candidates 1.

Represented in the Archdioceses of Boston, Chicago, Los Angeles, Omaha, and Washington, and in the Dioceses of Brooklyn, Dallas, Orange, Providence, San Bernadino and San Diego.

[0380] (M.C.C.J.)—COMBONI MISSIONARIES OF THE HEART OF JESUS

(Verona Fathers)

Missionarii Comboniani Cordis Jesu

(A Pontifical World Missionary Congregation of Priests and Brothers)

Founded by Blessed Bishop D. Comboni in 1867. First foundation in United States in 1939.

GENERAL MOTHERHOUSE: *Missionari Comboniani,* Via Luigi Lilio, 80, 00142, Rome, Italy. Very Rev. David Glenday, M.C.C.J., Supr. Gen.

NORTH AMERICAN PROVINCE (1950): *Comboni Mission Center,* 8108 Beechmont Ave., Cincinnati, OH 45255-3194. Tel: 513-474-4997; Fax: 513-474-0382. Revs. John Converset, M.C.C.J.; Patricia Meder, Editor, *Comboni Mission Newsletter* and *Comboni Press Feature Service.*

Legal Title: *Comboni Missionaries of the Heart of Jesus, Inc.*

Priests 38; Brothers 2; College Students 3; Scholastics 22.

Home Mission Parishes 4; Mission Centers 5.

Represented in the Archdioceses of Chicago, Cincinnati, Los Angeles and Newark.

[0390] (I.M.C.)—CONSOLATA MISSIONARIES

(Institutum Missionum a Consolata)

GENERAL MOTHERHOUSE: Rome, Viale delle Mura Aurelie, 11, Italy. Very Rev. Peter Trabucco, Supr. Gen.

HEADQUARTERS IN THE U.S.: P.O. Box 5550, 2301 Rte. 27, Somerset, NJ 08875. Tel: 908-297-9191; Fax: 908-940-3121. Rev. Anthony Bellagamba, I.M.C., Reg. Supr.

Legal Title: *Consolata Society for Foreign Missions; Mission International, Inc.*

Priests 17; Brothers 1.

Properties owned: Mission Community House 5; House of Studies for Philosophy.

Represented in the Archdiocese of Washington and the Dioceses of Buffalo, Metuchen, Pittsburgh and San Bernardino.

[0400] (O.S.C.)—CANONS REGULAR OF THE ORDER OF THE HOLY CROSS

(Crosier Fathers and Brothers)

Canonici Regulares Ordinis Sanctae Crucis

(Cruciferi)

GENERALATE: Most Rev. Lambert Graus, O.S.C., Master Gen.

GENERAL PROCURE: *Padri Crocigeri,* Lungotevere 10, Rome, Italy. Revs. James H. Remmerswaal, O.S.C., Sec. Gen. & Procurator Gen.; Rein Vaanhold, O.S.C., Gen. Econome.

UNITED STATES PROVINCE: *Province of St. Odilia,* Crosier National Headquarters, 3510 Vivian Ave., Shoreview, MN 55126-3852. Tel: 612-486-7456; Fax: 612-486-7589. Very Rev. John J. Neville, O.S.C., Prov. Provincial Councillors: Revs. Dale Ehrman, O.S.C.; Eugene Plaisted, O.S.C.; Steven Henrich, O.S.C.; Michael Van Sloun, O.S.C.; Rev. Thomas E. O'Brien, O.S.C., Prov. Econome.

Legal Title: *Crosier Fathers and Brothers Province, Inc.; Canons Regular of the Order of the Holy Cross.*

Bishops 1; Fathers 81; Professed Clerics 7; Brothers 26; Novice 1.

Properties owned, sponsored, or staffed: Monasteries 9; Novitiates 2; Parishes 12; Chaplaincies 7; Foreign Mission 1.

Represented in the Archdioceses of Baltimore, Chicago, Detroit, New York, St. Paul-Minneapolis and Washington, and the Dioceses of Duluth, Lincoln, Phoenix and St. Cloud. Also in Tokyo, Japan, Indonesia and Zaire.

[0410] (F.D.P.)—SONS OF DIVINE PROVIDENCE

(Filiorum Divinae Providentiae)

GENERAL MOTHERHOUSE: Via Efruria 6, Roma, Italy. Founded in 1893 by Blessed Don Louis Orione; Very Rev. Roberto Simionato, F.D.P., Supr. Gen.

DELEGATION OF OUR LADY QUEEN OF THE UNIVERSE-U.S. FOUNDATION (1953): III Orient Ave., E. Boston, MA 02128. Tel: 617-569-2100; Fax: 617-561-1138. Very Rev. Lawrence Tosatto, F.D.P., Supr.

Priests 10.

Properties staffed or owned: Parishes 1; Nursing Home 2; Shrine 1.

Represented in the Archdioceses of Boston and New York, and the Diocese of Evansville.

[0420] (S.V.D.)—SOCIETY OF THE DIVINE WORD

(Societas Verbi Divini)

GENERAL MOTHERHOUSE: *Collegio del Verbo Divino,* Via Dei Verbiti 1, Rome, Italy. Very Rev. Henry Barlage, S.V.D., Supr. Gen. Founded 1897, with Headquarters at St. Mary's Mission House (Divine Word Seminary) Techny, Illinois; later separating into four provinces. In 1985 the Eastern and Northern Provinces combined.

CHICAGO PROVINCE (1985): *Province of Blessed Joseph Freinademetz, S.V.D.,* Province Center, 1985 Waukegan Rd., P.O. Box 6038, Techny, IL 60082-6038. Tel: 847-272-2700; Fax: 847-272-2517. Very Rev. Stanley Uroda, S.V.D., Prov.; Bro. Douglas Edmonds, S.V.D., Vice Prov.; Rev. Thomas Griffith, S.V.D., Treas.

Priests 158; Brothers 49; Theologians 49; Minor Seminarians: College 114; Student Brothers 4; Novices 12; Associates 3.

Properties owned: Theologate; College; Prep. Seminary; Retreat House; House of Studies; Conference Center; Chaplaincies 1; Retirement Homes 2.

Legal Title: *Divine Word Funds, Inc.,* 1835 Waukegan Rd., P.O. Box 6099, Techny, IL 60082-6099. Tel: 847-272-7600. Revs. Thomas Krosnicki, S.V.D., Pres.; Francis Kamp, S.V.D., Treas.; Walter Bracken, S.V.D., Delegate Supr.-Missionaries on Leave.

Legal Titles: *Divine Word Missionaries, Inc.; S.V.D. Catholic Universities, Inc.; Divine Word International,* 2001 Waukegan Rd., P.O. Box 176, Techny, IL 60082-0176. *Hlasy z domova A Z missii* (Slovak Department); *Missionarze Slowa Bozego, Werbisci* (Polish Department); *S.V.D. Funds, Inc.; Blessed Arnold Charitable Trust.*

Represented in the Archdioceses of Boston, Chicago, Dubuque, Indianapolis, Milwaukee, Newark, St. Louis, Washington, and the Dioceses of Pittsburgh, Springfield (IL), Toledo, Trenton and Wheeling-Charleston. Also in Canada, Jamaica and the West Indies.

EASTERN PROVINCE: Amalgamated with Northern Province. See Chicago Province.

SOUTHERN PROVINCE (1940): *Southern Province of St. Augustine Provincial Residence,* 201 Ruella Ave., Bay St. Louis, MS 39520. Tel: 601-467-4322. Very Rev. Clifton Labbe, S.V.D., Prov.; Rev. Thomas James, S.V.D., Vice. Prov.; Bro. Richard Chanbers, S.V.D., Treas. Address applications for Retreats and Missions to: Rev. William Kelley, S.V.D.

Fathers 48; Brothers 8.

Parishes 23; Mission Stations 3; Elementary Schools 5.

Represented in the Archdiocese of New Orleans, and in the Dioceses of Baton Rouge, Biloxi, Galveston-Houston, Jackson, Lafayette (LA) and Little Rock.

WESTERN PROVINCE (1964): *Province of St. Therese of the Child Jesus,* 2737 Pleasant St., Riverside, CA 92507. Tel: 909-781-0940. Very Rev. Gerald W. Leonard, S.V.D., Prov.; Rev. Bernard Donaghey, S.V.D., Vice Prov.

Fathers 51; Brothers 6; House of Study 6.

Properties staffed, sponsored, or owned: High Schools 1; Parishes 9; Retreat Centers 1; House of Study 1.

Represented in the Archdioceses of Los Angeles and San Francisco, and in the Dioceses of Las Cruces, Oakland, Orange, San Bernardino and Tucson.

[0430] (O.P.)—ORDER OF PREACHERS

Dominicans

Fratres Sacri Ordinis Praedicatorum

GENERALITIA: *Convento Santa Sabina,* Piazza Pietro d' Illiria, Aventino, 00153, Rome, Italy. Most Revs. Timothy J. Radcliffe, O.P., Master Gen.; D. M. Hynous, O.P., Procurator Gen.

DOMINICAN PROVINCE OF ST. JOSEPH-EASTERN (1805): 869 Lexington Ave., New York, NY 10021. Tel: 212-737-5757; Fax: 212-861-4216.

Corporate Title: *Dominican Fathers Province of St. Joseph.* Very Rev. Urban Voll, O.P., Prov.; Revs. R. A. Morris, O.P., Vicar Prov. & Socius to Prov.; E. T. Myers, O.P., Prov. Econ. Admin.; K. J. Pritzl, O.P., Regent of Studies; G. N. Ingham, O.P., Archivist; J. J. Reid, O.P., Vocation Dir.; P. J. Allen, O.P., Dir. Dominican Laity; J. P. McGuire, O.P., Dir. Angelicum Fund; J. A. McMahon, O.P., Dir.-Health Affairs; T. B. Confer, O.P., Sec. for Nuns; R. F. Halligan, O.P., Dir.-Continuing Formation; W. A. Newman, O.P., Promoter Rosary; J. A. McKeon, O.P., Promoter of Preaching; N. Haddad, O.P., Promoter of Social Justice; G. L. Concordia, O.P., Promoter of the Holy Name & Dir., *St. Jude Shrine; E. L. Martin,* O.P., Dir.,, *Deserving Poor Boys Priesthood Assn. & Dominican Friars Guilds;* bro. T. A. Dolan, O.P., Sec. of Missions & Dir. St. Jude Dominican Mission.

Fathers 261; Cooperator Brothers 15; Professed Clerics 20; Novices 4.

Properties owned, staffed, or sponsored: Parishes 20; Colleges 1; House of Study 1; Retreat Houses 1; Novitiates 1.

Legal Title: *Pension Plan, Dominican Fathers, Province of St. Joseph, Deserving Poor Boys Priesthood Association, Inc., Dominican Friars' Guilds, Inc., St. Jude Dominican Missions, Inc., Dominican Foreign Missions, Handicapped Children's Fund, Peru, St. Martin de Porres Guild, Inc.*

Represented in the Archdioceses of Boston, Cincinnati, Detroit, Hartford, Louisville, Newark, New York, Philadelphia and Washington and in the Dioceses of Columbus, Metuchen, Providence, Richmond, Rockville Centre and Youngstown.

PROVINCE OF THE MOST HOLY NAME OF JESUS-WESTERN DOMINICAN PROVINCE (1912): 5877 Birch Ct., Oakland, CA 94618. Tel: 510-658-8722; Fax: 510-658-1061. Very Rev. Daniel Syverstad, O.P., Prov.; Very Rev. Reginald E. Martin, O.P., Socius, Vicar Prov. & Dir. Devel.; Revs. Luke D. Buckles, O.P., Corporate Sec. & Regent of Studies; Anthony G. Cordeiro, O.P., Prov. Econ. Admin. & Dir. St. Dominic Cemetery; Basil B. Cole, O.P., Western Regional Dir. of the Holy Name Society; Martin Walsh, O.P., Dir. Vocations; Fred Lucci, O.P., Promoter of Social Justice; Donald Bramble, O.P., Dir.-Mission Foundation; Thomas Hayes, O.P., Dir.-Shrine of St. Jude; Reginald Martin, O.P., Co-Dir. Shrine of St. Jude; Sergius Propst, O.P., Dir. Western Dominican Preaching; Friars Michael Dodds, O.P., Master of Students; Vincent Serpa, O.P., Master of Novices.

Legal Title: *Province of the Holy Name, Inc.*

Fathers 119; Professed Clerics 15; Brothers Professed 8.

Parishes 14; Houses 16; Priories 5; House of Studies 1; Novitiates 1.

Represented in the Archdioceses of Anchorage, Los Angeles, Portland in Oregon, San Francisco and Seattle and in the Dioceses of Norwich, Oakland, Phoenix, Providence, Raleigh Sacramento, Salt

Lake City, San Bernardino, San Jose and Tucson. Also in Mexico, Kenya and Guatemala.

PROVINCE OF ST. ALBERT THE GREAT-CENTRAL DOMINICAN PROVINCE (1939): 1909 S. Ashland Ave., Chicago, IL 60608. Tel: 312-666-3244; Fax: 312-829-8471. Very Revs. Edward M. Ruane, O.P., Prov.; David F. Wright, O.P., Socius, Vicar Prov. - Archivist; Gerald L. Stookey, O.P., Vicar Prov.; Revs. Michael A. Winkels, O.P., Economic Admin.; Jesse deP. Cox, O.P., Promoter of Vocations; Charles W. Dahm, O.P., Promoter of Social Justice; Dennis R. Zuzy, O.P., Regent, Dir. Society Vocational Support; Bro. Regis R. Hovald, O.P., Prov. Rep. to Dominican Laity; Revs. Bede R. Jagoe, O.P., Dir. St. Dominic Mission Society; Jerome M. Walsh, O.P., Dir. Shrine of St. Jude; Michael A. Winkels, O.P., Dir. of Dominican Conference Center, 7200 W. Division St., River Forest, IL 60305.

Legal Title: *Dominicans, Province of St. Albert the Great, U.S.A., Shrine of St. Jude Thaddeus, Inc., Society for Vocational Support, Inc., St. Dominic Mission Society, Dominican Social Action Fund, Dominican Laity, Dominican Central Productions, Fra Angelico Art Foundation.*

Fathers 189; Professed Clerics 23; Novices 2; Brothers 26.

Properties owned, staffed, or sponsored: Parishes 8; Convents 8; Houses 11; Houses of Studies 2; Novitiates 2; High Schools 1.

Represented in the Archdioceses of Chicago, Denver, Detroit, the Military Services, St. Louis, St. Paul-Minneapolis and Santa Fe and in the Dioceses of Cheyenne, Dallas, Des Moines, Duluth, Fort Wayne-South Bend, Grand Rapids, Joliet, Las Cruces, Madison, Peoria, St. Cloud, Springfield (IL), Superior and Winona.

SOUTHERN DOMINICAN PROVINCE (1979): 1421 N. Causeway Blvd., Ste. 200, Metairie, LA 70001-4144. Tel: 504-837-2129; Fax: 504-837-6604. Very Revs. Alberto Rodriguez, O.P., Prov.; Carl B. Trutter, O.P., Vicar Prov.; James A. McDonough, O.P., Econ. Admin. & Dir. Southern Dominican Global Missions; Wayne A. Cavalier, O.P., Promoter for Community Life and Permanent Formation; C. Gerard Austin, O.P., Regent of Studies; Henry B. Groover, O.P., Promoter of Vocations.

Legal Holdings or Titles: *Southern Dominican Foundation, Retirement and Community Support Plan, Southern Province, U.S.A., Shrine of St. Martin de Porres.*

Fathers 119; Professed Clerics 12; Brothers 10; Novices 3.

Properties owned, staffed, or sponsored: Parishes 12; Priories 6; Houses 6.

Represented in the Archdioceses of Denver, Los Angeles, Miami, New Orleans, St. Louis, San Antonio, Santa Fe, Washington and the Dioceses of Austin, Baton Rouge, Charleston, Charlotte, Corpus Christi, Dallas, Fort Wayne-South Bend, Galveston-Houston, Houma-Thibodaux, Knoxville, Memphis, Nashville, Pensacola-Tallahassee, Raleigh, San Angelo, Tucson and Tyler.

U.S. FOUNDATION (1926): Province of Spain, P.O. Box 279, San Diego, TX 78384. Tel: 512-279-3596. Very Rev. Candido Aniz, O.P.

Priests 4.

Parishes 3; Missions 3.

Represented in the Diocese of Corpus Christi.

[0440] (S.S.E.)—SOCIETY OF SAINT EDMUND

(Societas Sancti Edmundi)

GENERAL MOTHERHOUSE: Edmundite Generalate, 270 Winooski Park, Colchester, VT 05439. Tel: 802-654-3400; Fax: 802-654-3409. Very Rev. Joseph L. Hart, S.S.E., Supr. Gen. Councillors: Revs. Richard M. Myhalyk, S.S.E.; David G. Cray, S.S.E., Dir. Vocation Ministries; David G. Theroux, S.S.E.; Michael P. Cronogue, S.S.E.; Adalbert Wolski, T.O.R., Procurator Gen.

Legal Titles: Society of St. Edmund, Inc., Bishop Perry Middle School, New Orleans, LA.

Bishops 1; Fathers 51; Brothers 9; Scholastics 1.

Properties owned, staffed, or sponsored: Parishes 13; Missions 5; College 1; Retreat House; Novitiate; Middle School.

Represented in the Archdioceses of Detroit, Mobile and New Orleans and in the Dioceses of Burlington, Norwich and Venice.

[0450] (C.J.M.)—CONGREGATION OF JESUS AND MARY

(Congregatio Jesu et Mariae)
(Eudist Fathers)

GENERAL MOTHERHOUSE: Via dei Querceti, 15, 00184, Rome, Italy. Very Rev. Pierre Drouin, C.J.M., Supr. Gen.

NORTH AMERICAN PROVINCE: 6125 Premiere Ave., Charlesbourg, Quebec G1H 2V9. Canada. Tel: 418-626-6494. Very Rev. Bernard Cantin, C.J.M., Prov.; Revs. Michel Hebert, C.J.M., Asst. Prov. Provincial Council; Ulysses Doiron, C.J.M.; Robert Berger, C.J.M.; Aurele Godbout, C.J.M.; J. Gregory Sampson, C.J.M.; Rene Tousignant, C.J.M., Bursar.

U.S. REGION EUDIST COMMUNITY: 36 Flohr Ave., W. Seneca, NY 14224-1818. Tel: 716-825-4475.

Bishops 1; Fathers 106; Associates 28; Laymen 5.

Represented in the Dioceses of Buffalo and San Diego.

[0460] (C.F.P.)—BROTHERS OF THE POOR OF ST. FRANCIS

(Congregatio Fratrum Pauperum)

Generalate: Aachen, Germany. Very Rev. Bro. James Phelan, C.F.P., Min. Gen.

PROVINCE OF ST. JOSEPH: Provincial Business Office, P.O. Box 187, Burlington, IA 52601-0187. Tel: 319-752-0050; Fax: 319-752-5605. Rev. Bro. Robert Reinke, C.F.P., Prov. Supr. Tel: 201-420-1554; Fax: 201-792-8595.

Professed Brothers 24.

Brothers serve and staff: Development Office 1; High Schools 1; Elementary Schools 5; AIDS Social Service Agency 1; Hospices Social Service Agency 1; Homes for Senior Citizens 2; Group Homes 2.

Brothers' Special Mission:Care & education of neglected youth; elementary & secondary education; human services.

Properties owned: Morris School for Boys, Searcy, AR.

Represented in the Archdioceses of Cincinnati, Denver, Newark and in the Dioceses of Covington, Davenport, El Paso and Little Rock.

[0470] (O.F.M.CAP.)—THE CAPUCHIN FRIARS

(Ordinis Fratrum Minorum Capuccinorum)

GENERALATE: Curia Generalis Ord. Min. Cap. via Piemonte 70, Roma, Italy, 00187. Most Rev. John Corriveau, O.F.M.Cap., General Min.

PROVINCE OF ST. JOSEPH (1857): 1740 Mt. Elliott Ave., Detroit, MI 48207-3496. Tel: 313-579-2100; Fax: 313-579-2275. Revs. Daniel Fox, O.F.M.Cap., Prov. Minister; Perry McDonald, O.F.M.Cap., Prov. Vicar. Councillors: Revs. Daniel Crosby, O.F.M.Cap.; Loran Miller, O.F.M.Cap.; John Scherer, O.F.M.Cap.; T.L. Michael, O.F.M.Cap., Dir.-Capuchin Publications; Mr. Mark McDonough, Prov. Treas.; Revs. James C. Wolf, O.F.M.Cap., Sec. Corporations; David Schwab, O.F.M.Cap., Sec.-Religious Affairs; Edward Foley, O.F.M.Cap., Prov. Dir. of Continuing Education; Richard Hart, O.F.M.Cap., Prov. Dir. of Preaching; Ulric Buening, O.F.M.Cap., Prov. Asst. to Secular Franciscan Order; Michael H. Crosby, O.F.M.Cap., Corp. Responsibility Agent; Bro. Larry LaCross, O.F.M.Cap., Dir. Public Relations & Devel., 1820 Mt. Elliott Ave., Detroit, MI 48207-3496. Bro. Richard Merling, O.F.M.Cap., Dir. The Father Solanus Guild, 1780 Mt. Elliott Ave., Detroit, MI 48207-3496. Tel: 313-579-2100. Bro. Leo Wollenweber, O.F.M.Cap., Vice Postulator for the Cause of Ven. Father Solanus Casey, O.F.M.Cap.

Legal Title: *Province of St. Joseph of the Capuchin Order, Inc.*

Priests 176; Perpetually Professed Lay Friars 53; Professed Friars in Temporary Vows 5.

Properties owned, staffed, or sponsored: Parishes 40; Chaplaincies 19; Retreat Houses 4; House of Prayer 1; Novitiates 1; Preparatory Seminary 1; Mission for the Cheyenne Indians; Mission for the Crow Indians; Foreign Missionaries in The Vicariate of Bluefields, Nicaragua and in Dioceses of Panama City, Panama; Agana, Guam; Naha, Japan; Australia, Costa Rica, Honduras, & Brisbane.

Represented in the Archdioceses of Chicago, Detroit, Los Angeles, Milwaukee, New York, St. Paul-Minneapolis and in the Dioceses of Brooklyn, Fort Wayne-South Bend, Great Falls-Billings, Green Bay, LaCrosse, Las Cruces, Madison, Marquette, Oakland, Pittsburg, Saginaw and San Bernardino.

PROVINCE OF ST. AUGUSTINE (1873): *Provincial Office,* 220 37th St., Pittsburgh, PA 15201. Tel: 412-682-6011; Fax: 412-682-0506. Headquarters of Capuchin Franciscan Volunteer Corps., Inc.; St. Augustine Province of the Capuchin Order; National Headquarters of Archconfraternity of Christian Mothers; Mission Office of Seraphic Mass Association; Secular Franciscan Order of St. Augustine, Province; Capuchin Friars Sick and Elderly Trust Fund; St. Fidelis, Inc.; Capuchin Friars Formation and Education Trust Fund. Very Rev. William J. Wiethorn, O.F.M.Cap., Definitor Gen.; Very Rev. Philip Fink, O.F.M.Cap., Prov. Min.; Very Rev. Gregory Chervenak, O.F.M.Cap., Vicar Prov. Definitors: Revs. Joseph Mindling, O.F.M.Cap.; Frederick Krause, O.F.M.Cap.; John Pavlik, O.F.M.Cap.; William Graham, O.F.M.Cap., Exec. Sec. & Sec. for Finances; Richard Lubomski, Asst. Sec. Finances; Brendon Malloy, O.F.M.Cap., Sec. Communications.

Legal Title: *Province of St. Augustine of the Capuchin Order.*

Bishops 1; Priests 131; Brothers 37; Professed in Formation 7; Novices 3; Postulants 3.

Properties owned, staffed, or sponsored: Parishes 30; Formation Houses 2; Novitiate 1; Friaries 17; Postulancy Houses 3; Hospital Chaplains 12; Military Chaplain 1; Foreign Missions 2.

Represented in the Archdioceses of Baltimore, Philadelphia and Washington and in the Dioceses of Altoona-Johnstown, Cleveland, Columbus, Greensburg, Harrisburg, Pittsburgh and Wheeling-Charleston. Also in Papua New Guinea and Puerto Rico.

PROVINCE OF ST. MARY (1952): St. Conrad Friary, 30 Gedney Park Dr., White Plains, NY 10605. Tel: 914-761-3008; Fax: 914-948-6429. Very Rev. Bernard Smith, O.F.M.Cap., Minister Prov. Definitors: Revs. Regis Armstrong, O.F.M.Cap.; John Gallagher, O.F.M.Cap.; Francis Gasparik, O.F.M.Cap.; Bro. Louis Esposito, O.F.M.Cap.

Legal Title: *The Province of St. Mary of the Capuchin Order, Capuchin Friars International, Inc.*

Development Office: St. John Friary, 210 W. 31st St., New York, NY 10001.

Bishops 2; Priests 151; Professed Clerical Brothers 7; Professed Lay Brothers 46; Novices 2.

Properties staffed or sponsored: Parishes 13; Chaplaincies 27; Major Seminaries 1; Novitiate 1; Foreign Missions 3.

Represented in the Archdioceses of Agana and New York and the Dioceses of Bridgeport, Brooklyn, Honolulu, Manchester, Norwich, Portland (ME), Rochester, Rockville Centre and Springfield (MA). Also in Naha.

PROVINCE OF THE STIGMATA OF ST. FRANCIS (1918): *Our Lady of Guadalupe Friary,* 319 - 36th St., P.O. Box 809, Union City, NJ 07087. Tel: 201-865-0611; Fax: 201-866-7035. Revs. Robert Grix, O.F.M.Cap., Prov. Min.; Cyprian Rosen, O.F.M.Cap., Prov. Vicar. Definitors: Bro. Kellen Mears, O.F.M.Cap.; Revs. Vincent Fortunato, O.F.M.Cap.; Achilles Cassiere, O.F.M.Cap.; Francis Sariego, O.F.M.Cap., Prov. Sec.

Priests 45; Brothers 20; Temporary Professed 4; Novices 1; Postulants 5.

Parishes 11; Friaries 5; Retreat House 1; Hospital Chaplaincies 2.

Represented in the Archdioceses of Newark and New York and in the Dioceses of Arlington, Charlotte, Paterson, St. Petersburg and Wilmington.

OUR LADY OF ANGELS, WESTERN AMERICAN PROVINCE: 1345 Cortez Ave., Burlingame, CA 94010. Revs. Peter Banks, O.F.M.Cap., Prov. Definitors: Revs. Christopher Kearney, O.F.M.Cap.; Dale Trunk, O.F.M.Cap.; Enda Heffernan, O.F.M.Cap.; Revs. Camillus MacRory, O.F.M.Cap., Spiritual Asst. to Secular Franciscans; Flavian Welstead, O.F.M.Cap., Dir. of Devel. Finances; Cyrie Kelleher, O.F.M.Cap., Foreign Mission Office Dir.

Priests 45; Brothers 9; Brothers in Formation 10; Novices 3; Postulants 2.

Ministries in Parishes; High Schools; Novitiates; Chaplaincies; House of Study; Retreats; Foreign Missions.

Represented in the Archdioceses of Los Angeles and San Francisco and in the Dioceses of Baker, Fresno and Oakland. Also in Mexico.

PROVINCE OF SS. STANISLAUS AND ADALBERT (1948): *St. Stanislaus Friary,* 2 Manor Dr., Oak Ridge, NJ 07438. Tel: 201-697-7757. Revs. Henry T. Krajewski, O.F.M.Cap., Supr.; Francis Z. Majewski, O.F.M.Cap., Asst. Supr.

Fathers 9.

Represented in the Dioceses of Metuchen, and Paterson.

VICE PROVINCE OF TEXAS: 2601 Singleton Blvd., Dallas, TX 75212. Tel: 214-631-6267. Rev. Juan Cruz Gaston, O.F.M.Cap., Vice Prov.

Fathers 16; Brothers 2.

Parishes 5; Cursillo Centers 2.

Represented in the Archdiocese of San Antonio and in the Dioceses of Dallas and Fort Worth.

PROVINCE OF MID-AMERICA (1977): *St. Francis of Assisi Friary,* 3553 Wyandot St., Denver, CO 80211-2948. Tel: 303-477-5436; 477-5542; Fax: 303-477-6925.

Legal Title: *Capuchin Province of Mid-America, Inc., St. Francis Seminary Endowment Foundation, Inc.;* Revs. David Gottschalk, O.F.M.Cap., Prov.; Gene Emrisek, O.F.M.Cap., Vicar Prov.; Duane Reinert, O.F.M.Cap., Councillor & Coord. Ongoing Formation; Michael Scully, O.F.M.Cap., Councillor; James Moster, O.F.M.Cap., Councillor; Revs. Harvey P. Dinkel, O.F.M.Cap., Exec. Sec. & Treas.; John Lager, O.F.M.Cap., Sec.-Missions & Dir.-Devel.; Mark Schenk, O.F.M.Cap., Coord.-Initial Formation; William Kraus, O.F.M.Cap., Dir. Vocation Programs; Blaine Burkey, O.F.M.Cap., Communications Dir.; Christian Fey, O.F.M.Cap., Archivist.

Bishops 3; Priests 49; Students 2; Brothers 7.

Represented in the Archdioceses of Denver, Kansas

City in Kansas and St. Louis and in the Diocese of Salina.

Vice Province of St. John The Baptist (1905): *Vice Provincial Offices,* 216 Arzuaga St., P.O. Box 21350, Rio Piedras, PR 00928-1350. Tel: 787-764-3090; Fax: 787-764-4070. Bros. John Bednarik, O.F.M.Cap., Vice Prov. Min.; Jose A. Cruz Callero, O.F.M.Cap., First Councillor; Alberto A. Figueroa Morales, O.F.M.Cap., Second Councillor; Jorge Macias de Cespedes, O.F.M.Cap., Vice Prov. Sec., Treas., Public Rels. Dir. & Newsletter Editor; Joseph McCarthy, O.F.M.Cap., Seraphic Mass Assoc.; Ramon J. Casellas, O.F.M.Cap., Dir. Capuchin Charities; Ramon H. Negron Cruz, O.F.M.Cap., Vocation Dir.

Legal Title: *Asociacion de Frailes Capuchinos, Inc.*

Friars 27; Postulants 2.

Properties owned, staffed and sponsored: Formation Fraternites 3; Parishes 4; Retreat Center 1; Friaries 6; Mission Office 1.

Represented in the Archdiocese of San Juan and the Dioceses of Arecibo and Ponce.

[0480] (O.F.M.CONV.)—CONVENTUAL FRANCISCANS

(Friars Minor Conventual)

(Ordo Fratrum Minorum S. Francisci Conventualium)

General Curia: Piazza SS. Apostoli, 51, Rome, 00187. Italy. Most Rev. Agostino Gardin, O.F.M.Conv.; Most Rev. William Robison, O.F.M.Conv., Asst. Gen.

Province of the Immaculate Conception B.V.M. (1852): *Provincial House-Immaculate Conception Friary,* Rensselaer, NY 12144. Very Rev. Giles Van Wormer, O.F.M.Conv., Minister Prov.; Very Rev. Jude DeAngelo, O.F.M.Conv., Vicar & Sec.; Bros. Stephen Merrigan, O.F.M.Conv.; Michael Snyder, O.F.M.Conv., Dir. Vocations.

Legal Title: *Order of Friars Minor Conventual Immaculate Conception, Province Charitable Trust.*

Fathers 140; Professed Clerics 5; Professed Brothers 22.

Parishes 28; Friaries 20; Chaplaincies 14; Filial Houses 10; Novitiates 1.

Represented in the Archdioceses of Newark, New York and Washington, and in the Dioceses of Albany, Charlotte, Metuchen, Raleigh, Syracuse and Trenton.

Province of St. Anthony of Padua (1906): *Provincial House,* 12300 Folly Quarter Rd., Ellicott City, MD 21042-1419. Tel: 410-531-9200; Fax: 410-531-4881. Very Rev. Mark L. Curesky, O.F.M.Conv., Minister Prov.; Very Rev. Thomas Reist, O.F.M.Conv., Vicar; Revs. Vincent A. Gluc, O.F.M.Conv., Prov. Sec. Definitors: Revs. Robert Twele, O.F.M.Conv.; Ross Syracuse, O.F.M.Conv.; Robert Schlageter, O.F.M.Conv.; Bro. Michael Duffy, O.F.M.Conv.

Legal Title: *St. Francis High School of Athol Springs, NY, Inc., The Father Justin Rosary Hour, Inc., Franciscan Fathers Minor Conventuals of Buffalo, NY, Inc., The Franciscan Center, Inc., St. Anthony of Padua Province, Franciscan Fathers Minor, Conventual, U.S.A., Inc; The Friars Knights of the St. Francis High School, Inc., Order of Friars Minor Conventual, Inc., Conventual Franciscan Friars, St. Anthony of Padua Province,, Franciscan Mission Association, Inc; Franciscan Fathers Minor Conventual, St. Anthony of Padua, Province U.S.A., MA. Inc; Franciscan Friars, St. Anthony of Padua Province, Education, Fund, Inc; Franciscan Friars, St. Anthony of Padua Province, Fund for the, Aged and Infirm, Inc; Franciscan Minor Conventuals of Maryland, of Ellicott, City, MD, Inc; The Franciscan Fathers, Minor Conventuals, of St. Stanislaus, Church of Baltimore City, MD. Inc; St. Francis of Assisi Community, Inc., Order of Friars Minor Conventual, St. Anthony of Padua, Province, U.S.A., Inc; St. Stanislaus Cemetery, Inc.*

Priests 178; Brothers in Solemn Vows 22; Brothers in Temporary Vows 1; Clerics in Temporary Vows 7.

Friaries 39; Filial Houses 3.

Apostolates owned, staffed, or sponsored: Novitiates 1; College 1; House of Study 1; Parishes 36; Campus Ministries 3; High Schools 5; Schools Elementary Schools 1; Youth-Crisis Shelter 1; Sisters' Chaplaincies 2; Hospital-Nursing Home Chaplaincies 4; Apostolates Radio Apostolate; Healing Ministry; Apostolates Preaching Apostolate; Foreign Missions 3; Candidate House 1.

Represented in the Archdioceses of Atlanta, Baltimore, Boston and Hartford and in the Dioceses of Altoona-Johnstown, Birmingham, Bridgeport, Brooklyn, Buffalo, Erie, Fall River, Harrisburg, Norwich, Ogdensburg, Palm Beach, Paterson, Portland (ME), Rochester, Springfield (MA) and Trenton.

St. Bonaventure Province (1939): 6107 Kenmore Ave., Chicago, IL 60660-2797. Tel: 312-274-7681; Fax: 312-274-9751. Very Rev. Anthony Labedis, O.F.M.Conv., Min. Prov.; Very Rev. Justin Kusibab, O.F.M. Conv., Vicar Prov. & Sec.; Rev. William Callahan, O.F.M.Conv., Definitor; Bro. Thomas Surmam, Treas. Definitors: Revs. Patrick Greenough, O.F.M.Conv.; James Ciaramitaro, O.F.M.Conv.; Revs. James Henning, Mission Promoter; Michael Suszynski, O.F.M.Conv., Prov. Spiritual Asst. for Secular Franciscans.

Legal Title: *Conventual Franciscans of St. Bonaventure Province, Franciscan Friars Educational Corp., Conventual Franciscan Friars of Marytown, Shrine of St. Maximillian Kolbe, St. Hedwig Cemetery and Mausoleum, The Conventual Franciscans of Saint Bonaventure Province, Charitable Continuing Care Trust Fund.*

Fathers 34; Professed Clerics 8; Brothers 20; Novices 1.

Parishes 5; Chaplaincies 2; Marian Center 1; Shrine 1.

Represented in the Archdioceses of Chicago, Detroit and Milwaukee and in the Dioceses of Peoria and Rockford. Also in Mexico.

Province of Our Lady of Consolation (1926): 101 Anthony Dr., Mount St. Francis, IN 47146. Tel: 812-923-8444. Very Rev. Kent Biergans, O.F.M.Conv., Min. Prov.; Rev. Richard Kaley, O.F.M.Conv., Vicar Prov.; Bro. Jeff Hines, O.F.M.Conv., Sec.

Fathers 118; Brothers 32; Professed Clerics 2; Candidates 5; Novices 3.

Friaries 19; Parishes 14; Houses of Formation 3; Retreat-Renewal Centers 3; Missions 10; Chaplaincies 4.

Province of St. Joseph of Cupertino (1981): *Cupertino Heights,* P.O. Box 820, Arroyo Grande, CA 93421. Tel: 805-489-1012; Fax: 805-489-8303. Very Rev. Allen Ramirez, O.F.M.Conv., Min. Prov; Rev. Charles Shelton, O.F.M.Conv., Vocation Dir.; Revs. Paul Fazio, O.F.M.Conv., Sec.; Stephen Gross O.F.M.Conv., Definitor, Mission Procurator - National Spiritual Asst. for Secular Franciscan Order; Christopher Lucas, O.F.M.Conv., Regent of Studies; Peter Parchem, O.F.M.Conv., Treas. & Definitor; John Heinz, O.F.M.Conv., Definitor; Bro. James Reiter, O.F.M.Conv., Custos Capitularis; Rev. Christopher Bisett, O.F.M.Conv., Prov. Spiritual Asst. for Secular Franciscan Order.

Legal Title: *Conventual Franciscans of California, Inc.*

Parishes 11; Friaries 10; Chaplaincies 3; High Schools 1; Houses of formation 3; Missions 3.

Priests 36; Brothers 12; Clerics (Professed Seminarians) 7; Novices 4; Candidates 6.

Represented in the Archdiocese of Los Angeles and in the Dioceses of Fresno, Monterey, Oakland, Reno-Las Vegas, San Bernardino and San Diego. Also in Mexico.

[0490] (O.S.F.)—CONGREGATION OF THE RELIGIOUS BROTHERS OF THE THIRD ORDER REGULAR OF ST. FRANCIS

Franciscan Brothers of Brooklyn

Generalate (1858): *St. Francis Monastery,* 135 Remsen St., Brooklyn, NY 11201. Tel: 212-858-8217; Fax: 718-858-8306. Bros. Kevin Smith O.S.F., Supr. Gen.; Joseph Moloney O.S.F., Asst. Supr. Gen.; Edward Bacon, O.S.F., Master of Novices.

Legal Titles and Holdings: St. Francis Monastery, Franciscan Brothers' Generalate, Franciscan Brothers, Inc., Brooklyn, NY, *Mount Alvernia, Inc., St. Francis Center, Inc.,* Rockville Centre, NY.

Brothers 110.

Ministries in the field of Education at all levels; Pastoral Ministries, Social Services; Spirituality Centers.

Represented in the Archdioceses of Hartford, Newark and St. Louis and the Dioceses of Bridgeport, Brooklyn, Paterson, Raleigh and Rockville Centre.

[0500] (O.S.F.)—FRANCISCAN BROTHERS OF CHRIST THE KING

General Motherhouse and Novitiate (1961): 3737 N. Marybelle Ave., Peoria, IL 61615. Tel: 309-688-0094; 0093. Bro. Francis A. Skube, Supr. Gen.

Professed Brothers 4; Novices 1.

Represented in the Diocese of Peoria.

[0510] (F.F.S.C.)—FRANCISCAN BROTHERS OF THE HOLY CROSS

Generalate: St. Josefshaus, Hausen, Linz Rhein, West Germany. Bro. David Sarnecki, Supr. Gen.

American Region (1924): 2500 St. James Rd., Springfield, IL 62707. Tel: 217-544-4876, Ext. 222. Bros. Raphael Kreikemeier, Pres.; Gerald Voycheck, Vice Pres. & Treas.; Luke Morin, Board Member; Anthony McCoy, Sec.; Boniface Shellock, Board Member.

Properties owned, staffed, or sponsored: Home for Mentally Handicapped; Adult Training Center for Mentally Handicapped; Schools Elementary School; Novitiate.

Brothers 17.

Represented in the Dioceses of Little Rock, Madison and Springfield (IL).

[0515] (O.S.F.)—FRANCISCAN BROTHERS OF THE THIRD ORDER REGULAR

Generalate: Franciscan Brothers' Generalate, Mountbellew, Ireland.

United States Region: 2117 Spyglass Trail W., Oxnard, CA 93030. Tel: 805-485-5002; Fax: 213-487-5275. Mailing Address: 4522 Gainsborough Ave., Los Angeles, CA 90027. Bro. Hilarion O'Connor, Reg. Supr.

Brothers 15.

Ministries in the field of secondary education.

Represented in the Archdioceses of Los Angeles and New York.

[0520] (O.F.M.)—FRANCISCAN FRIARS

(Ordinis Fratrum Minorum)

General Headquarters: Via S. Maria Mediatrice, 25, 00165, Rome, Italy. Curia Generalizia dei Frati Minori. Most Rev. Hermann Schalueck, O.F.M., Min. Gen.; Very Rev. Gilles Bourdeau, O.F.M., Vicar Proc. Gen. Tel: 011-39-6-632.241. Very Rev. Robert Karris, O.F.M., English-Speaking General Councillor. Tel: 011-39-6-68491290.

English-Speaking Conference of the Order of Friars Minor: 3140 Meramec St., St. Louis, MO 63118. Tel: 314-353-7729; Fax: 314-353-2790. Rev. Thomas Gardner, O.F.M., Exec. Dir., Includes Order of Friars Minor Provinces 12; Vice Province 2; Custodies 2: of the United States, Canada, England, Ireland and Malta. Associate Member: Commissariat of the Holy Land, Washington DC.

Province of St. John the Baptist (1844): 1615 Vine St., Cincinnati, OH 45210-1222. Tel: 513-721-4700; Fax: 513-421-9672. Revs. John Bok, O.F.M., Prov. Min.; Alan Hirt, O.F.M., Prov. Vicar. Councillors: Revs. Nicholas Lohkamp, O.F.M.; Joseph Rayes, O.F.M.; Frank Jasper, O.F.M.; Rock Travnikar, O.F.M.; Jeffrey Scheeler, O.F.M.; Bro. Ronald Bolfeta, O.F.M.; Bro. Gene Mayer, O.F.M., Prov. Sec.; Revs. Kenan Freson, O.F.M., Prov. Treas.; James Bok, O.F.M., Dir.-Devel.; Maynard Tetreault, O.F.M., Bldg. Coord.; Nicholas Lohkamp, O.F.M., Coord. of Ministry of the Word; Alan Hirt, O.F.M., Dir.-Formation & Studies; Francis Tebbe, O.F.M., Dir. Continuing Education/Formation. Tel: 313-432-5300. Henry Beck, O.F.M., Dir.-Office of Peace, Justice & Integrity of Creation; Bro. Scott Obrecht O.F.M., Dir.-Franciscan Missionary Union; Revs. John Boehman, O.F.M., Dir.-Office of Senior Friars; Daniel Anderson, O.F.M., Prov. Archivist & Libriarian; Marcan Hetteberg, O.F.M., Prov. Archivist & Libriarian; Loren Connell, O.F.M., Prov. Spiritual Asst. for Secular Order; Stanley Bir, O.F.M., Personnel Adv. Vocation Dirs.: Revs. Bruno Kremp, O.F.M.; Rock Travnikar, O.F.M.; Bro. Allan Schmitz, O.F.M. Tel: 513-825-1082.

Priests 163; Temporary Professed 3; Deacons 3; Novices 1; Brothers 58.

Represented in the Archdioceses of Cincinnati, Detroit, Indianapolis, Louisville, New Orleans and the Dioceses of Baton Rouge, Galveston-Houston, Houma-Thibodaux, Lafayette (LA), Lexington, Marquette and Peoria.

Province of The Sacred Heart (1858): 3140 Meramec St., St. Louis, MO 63118. Tel: 314-353-3421. Very Rev. Kurt Hartrich, O.F.M., Prov. Minister; Rev. John Doctor, O.F.M., Prov. Vicar. Councillors: Revs. Louis Davino, O.F.M.; Arthur Anderson, O.F.M.; John Eaton, O.F.M.; Thomas Nairn, O.F.M.; Michael Cusato, O.F.M.; Bro. Herbert Rempe, O.F.M., Prov. Treas. & Councilor; Bro. Christopher Lambert, O.F.M., Prov. Sec.; Bro. William Schulte, O.F.M., Dir. of Public Relations and Fund Raising, Franciscan Charities,, St. Anthony Bread; Revs. Allan DaCorte, O.F.M., Prov. Treas.; Henry Willenborg, O.F.M., Prov. Dir. of Formation & Dir.-Franciscan Vocation Center, 4860 W. 29th St., Cicero, IL 60650. Michael Crosby, O.F.M., Office of Friar Formation & Prov. Spiritual Asst. of Secular Franciscan Order; Thomas Gardner, O.F.M., Prov. Promoter of the Missions, Commissary of the Holy Land.

Legal Title: *An Association of Franciscan Fathers of the State of Illinois, Franciscan Fathers of the State of Missouri, Friars Minor of the Order of St. Francis, Cleveland, Franciscan Fathers of the State of Wisconsin, Inc., Franciscan Press, Franciscan Tertiary Province of the Sacred Heart, Incorporated, Mayslake Village, Franciscan Mayslake Village, Cloister Courts, Chariton Apartments, Employees of the Franciscan Orders.*

Solemnly Professed:; Priests 244; Brothers 82; Simply

Professed: Brothers 16; Novices 3; Permanent Deacons 2.

Properties owned, sponsored or staffed: Friaries 40; Parishes 38; Missions 30; Institutional Chaplaincies 20; Chaplaincies for Religious 9; Formation Houses 2; Novitiates 1; Colleges 1; High Schools 2; Publishing House 1.

Represented in the Archdioceses of Chicago, Indianapolis, New Orleans, St. Louis, St. Paul-Minneapolis and San Antonio and in the Dioceses of Cleveland, Fairbanks, Fort Worth, Gaylord, Jefferson City, Joliet, Knoxville, Little Rock, Memphis, Nashville, Shreveport, Springfield (IL), Superior and Victoria.

PROVINCE OF THE ASSUMPTION OF THE BLESSED VIRGIN MARY (1887): *Provincial Office,* Pulaski, WI 54162. Tel: 414-822-5422; Fax: 414-822-5423. Very Rev. Paul Reczek, O.F.M., Prov.; Rev. Thomas Luczak, O.F.M., Vicar. Definitors: Revs. Leslie Hoppe, O.F.M.; Thomas Wojciechowski, O.F.M.; Placid Strolk, O.F.M.; John Puodziwnas, O.F.M.; Andrew Brophy, O.F.M.; Revs. Richard Tulko, O.F.M., Prov. Sec.; John Puodziunas, O.F.M., Comptroller; Hugh Zurat, O.F.M., Dir. of Evangelization Center; James Buda, Prov. Spiritual Asst. of Secular Franciscan Order.

Legal Holdings or Titles: *St. Francis Friary & Retreat Center,* Burlington, WI, *Holy Name Friary,* Chicago, IL, *Assumption of B.V.M. Friary,* Pulaski, WI.

Priests 142; Professed Clerics 2; Professed Brothers 60.

Properties owned or staffed: Parishes 20; Friaries 16.

Represented in the Archdioceses of Chicago, Detroit, Milwaukee, New York and Philadelphia and in the Dioceses of Brownsville, Burlington, Camden, Cleveland, Fort Wayne-South Bend, Gary, Gaylord, Green Bay, Jackson, Joliet, Pittsburgh, Rochester, Rockford, Saginaw, and St. Petersburg.

PROVINCE OF OUR LADY OF GUADALUPE (1985): *San Antonio Provincial Friary,* 1350 Lakeview Rd., S.W., Albuquerque, NM 87105. Tel: 505-877-5425. Very Rev. Gilbert Schneider, O.F.M., Prov. Min.; Rev. Martan Rademaker, O.F.M., Prov. Vicar & Sec. of Formation & Studies. Councillors: Revs. Salvador Aragon, O.F.M.; Hilaire Valiquette, O.F.M.; Dennis Fountain, O.F.M.; John Friebel, O.F.M.; Crispin Butz, O.F.M., Guardian & Prov. Sec.; Don Billiard, O.F.M., Prov. Treas.; Lawrence Schreiver, O.F.M., Vocation Dir.; Forest McAllister, O.F.M., Sec. Missionary Evangelization; Niles Kraft, O.F.M., Prov. Devel.; Dale Jamison, O.F.M., FMC Dir.; Gerald Grantner, O.F.M., Archivist; Nils Francis Thompson, O.F.M., Prov. Spiritual Asst.-SFO; Forest McAllister, O.F.M., Prov. Communications.

Legal Title: *The Province of Our Lady of Guadalupe of the Order of Friars, Minor, Inc; Southwest Franciscan Missions, Inc., Southwest Franciscan Services, Inc.*

Priests 70; Brothers 18; Temporary Professed 1; Postulants 2; Novices 1.

Represented in the Archdioceses of Denver and Santa Fe and the Dioceses of Gallup and Las Cruces. Also in Mexico and Peru.

ORDER OF FRIARS MINOR OF THE PROVINCE OF THE MOST HOLY NAME (Legal Title) (1901): 126 West 32nd St., New York, NY 10001-3202. Tel: 212-967-6300. Very Rev. John M. Felice, O.F.M., Prov. Minister; Very Rev. Charles J. Miiller, O.F.M., Prov. Vicar. Provincial Councillors: Revs. Hugh Hines, O.F.M.; David Hyman, O.F.M.; Daniel McLellan, O.F.M.; John O'Connor, O.F.M.; Ronald Pecci, O.F.M.; Kevin Mullen, O.F.M.; Bro. F. Edward Coughlin, O.F.M., Prov. Sec.; Revs. Vincent Grogan, O.F.M., Legal & Canonical Counsel; Cassian A. Miles, O.F.M., Dir. Communications; Joseph Hertel, O.F.M., Dir. Office of Devel. & Public Rels.; Dennis Wilson, O.F.M., Treas.; Bro. Gordon (Denis) Clark, O.F.M., Promoter of the Missions & Sec.-Missionary Evangelization; Revs. Peter Brophy, O.F.M., Dir. Vocations; Matthew Gaskin, O.F.M., Prov. Spiritual Asst. for Secular Franciscan Order.

Solemn Profession: Bishops 3; Priests 401; Brothers 77; Permanent Deacons 3; Temporary Profession: Brothers 2; Clerics 15; Novices 8; Perpetual Tertiaries 1; Affiliates 10.

Properties owned or sponsored: Province Parishes 32; Missions 1; Urban Ministry Centers 4; University 1; Colleges 1; Community Houses-Residences 45; Houses of Formation 5; Campus Ministry 8.

Ministries in 11 Chaplaincies; 1 Military Chaplain; 2 Shrine Churches.

Represented in the Archdioceses of Atlanta, Baltimore, Boston, Chicago, Denver, Hartford, Los Angeles, Miami, Newark, New York, Philadelphia, Santa Fe, Washington and the Dioceses of Albany, Bridgeport, Buffalo, Camden, Charleston, Charlotte, Corpus Christi, Fall River, Honolulu, Las Cruces, Ogdensburg, Palm Beach, Paterson, Providence, Raleigh, Rochester, Rockville Centre, St. Petersburg, San Diego, Scranton, Springfield (MA), Steubenville, Trenton, Wilmington and Youngstown.

PROVINCE OF ST. BARBARA (1915), THE FRANCISCAN FRIARS OF CALIFORNIA (1900): 1500 34th Ave., Oakland, CA 94601. Tel: 510-536-3722; Fax: 510-536-3970. Very Rev. Joseph P. Chinnici, O.F.M., Prov.; Rev. Finian McGinn, O.F.M., Vicar Prov. Definitors: Revs. Warren Rouse, O.F.M.; Stephen Barnufsky, O.F.M.; Miguel Obregon, O.F.M.; Michael Doherty, O.F.M.; Bros. John Gutierrez, O.F.M.; William Short, O.F.M.; Rev. Melvin A. Jurisich, O.F.M., Prov. Sec.; Ms. Lupe Aceves, Prov. Treas.

Legal Title: *Franciscan Friars of California, Franciscan Fathers of Arizona, Franciscan Fathers of Oregon, Franciscan Fathers of Washington.*

Priests 165; Solemnly Professed Lay Brothers 75; Simply Professed Brothers 18; Novices 5.

Represented in the Archdioceses of Los Angeles, Portland (OR), and San Francisco and in the Dioceses of Fresno, Gallup, Las Cruces, Monterey, Oakland, Orange, Phoenix, Las Vegas, Sacramento, Salt Lake City, San Diego, San Jose, Spokane and Tucson.

PROVINCE OF THE IMMACULATE CONCEPTION (FRIARS MINOR OF THE ORDER OF ST. FRANCIS) (1871): 147 Thompson St., New York, NY 10012. Tel: 212-674-4388. Very Rev. Robert M. Campagna, O.F.M., Prov.; Rev. Steven M. Sysol, O.F.M., Vicar Prov. Definitors: Revs. Blaise Tranchida, O.F.M.; Armand Padula, O.F.M.; Primo Piscitello, O.F.M.; Antonio Nardoianni, O.F.M.; Michael Bercik, O.F.M.; Simeon Distefano, O.F.M., Prov. Sec.; Claude Scrima, O.F.M., SFO Prov. Spiritual Asst.; Alban Montella, O.F.M., Promoter of the Franciscan Missions; Madeline Bonnici, Exec. Dir., *Franciscan Mission Associates,* 274-280 W. Lincoln Ave., Mount Vernon, NY 10550. Rev. Robert M. Campagna, O.F.M., *Pious League of St. Anthony.*

Fathers 153; Bishops 3; Brothers 29; Permanent Deacons 3.

Properties owned or staffed:: Parishes 33; Residences 20.

Represented in the Archdioceses of Boston, Hartford and New York and in the Dioceses of Albany, Bridgeport, Brooklyn, Fall River, Manchester, Metuchen, Pittsburgh, Portland (ME), Trenton, Wheeling-Charleston and Youngstown. Also in Toronto.

CUSTODY OF THE HOLY CROSS (1912): 14246 Main St., P.O. Box 608, Lemont, IL 60439. Tel: 630-257-2494; Fax: 630-257-8559. Rev. Blase Chemazar, O.F.M., Custos. Councillors: Revs. Vendelin Spendov, O.F.M.; Bernard Karmanocky, O.F.M.; Bro. Robert Hochevar, O.F.M.

Legal Title: *The Slovene Franciscan Fathers, Order of Friars Minor,, Commissariat of the Holy Cross,* Lemont, IL, *St. Mary's Retreat House,* Lemont, IL.

Fathers 14; Brothers 1.

Parishes 4; Monastery 1; Retreat House 1; Mission Center 1.

Represented in the Archdioceses of Chicago and New York and in the Diocese of Altoona-Johnstown.

VICE PROVINCE OF THE HOLY SAVIOR: Provincial House-Holy Family Friary, 232 S. Home Ave., Pittsburgh, PA 15202. Tel: 412-761-2550; 761-8470. Friar. David Kohut, O.F.M., Prov.; Friar John Joseph Gonchar, Vicar Prov. Councillors: Friar Michael Dubec, O.F.M.; Friar Richard Portasik, O.F.M.; Friar Mark Hudak, O.F.M.; Friar David Moczulski, O.F.M.

Fathers 23; Brothers 6.

Friaries 4.

Represented in the Dioceses of Allentown, Greensburg and Pittsburgh.

FRANCISCAN FRIARS: Mt. Alverna Friary, 517 S. Belle Vista Ave., Youngstown, OH 44509. Tel: 216-799-1888. Revs. John Reiss, O.F.M., Vicar; Matthew J. Kiss, O.F.M., Guardian; Nicholas Dengl, O.F.M.; Bros. Reginald Antal, O.F.M.; Emery Kish, O.F.M.

Represented in the Diocese of Youngstown.

CROATIAN FRANCISCAN CUSTODY OF THE HOLY FAMILY OF U.S. & CANADA (1926): 4848 S. Ellis Ave., Chicago, IL 60615. Tel: 312-536-0552; Fax: 312-536-0552. Rev. Slavko Soldo, O.F.M., Custos. Councillors: Revs. Matthew Ruyechan, O.F.M.; Jozo Cuic, O.F.M.; Marko Puljic, O.F.M.; Jerome Kucan, O.F.M.

Fathers 34; Cleric 1.

Friaries 1; Parishes 9; Missions in Canada 8; Printery 1.

Represented in the Archdioceses of Chicago, Detroit, Milwaukee, New York and St. Louis and in the Dioceses of Allentown and Erie. Also in Canada.

LITHUANIAN FRANCISCAN VICE-PROVINCE OF ST. CASIMIR: Franciscan Friary, P.O. Box 980, Kennebunkport, ME 04046. Tel: 207-967-2011; Fax: 207-967-5721. Very Rev. Placid Barius, O.F.M., Prov. Minister; Rev. Augustine Simanavicius, O.F.M., Prov. Vicar. Councillors: Revs. Francis Giedgaudas, O.F.M.; Raphael Sakalys, O.F.M.; John Bacevicius, O.F.M.; Benedict Jurcys, O.F.M.

Bishops 1; Fathers 34; Brothers 4; Seminarians 14.

Properties owned or sponsored: Parishes 4; Summer Camps 1; Guest House; Retreat House 1; Printery 1.

Represented in the Dioceses of Brooklyn, Portland (ME), and St. Petersburg. Also in Toronto, Canada.

U.S. FOUNDATION (1940): *Province of the Holy Gospel,* Roger Bacon College, 2400 Marr St., El Paso, TX 79903. Rev. Alberto Hernandez, O.F.M.

Priests 3; Brothers 1.

Represented in the Diocese of El Paso.

COMMISSARIAT OF THE HOLY LAND, FRANCISCAN MONASTERY OF MT. ST. SEPULCHRE: 1400 Quincy St., N.E., Washington, DC 20017. Tel: 202-526-6800; Fax: 202-529-9889. Bro. Callistus Welch, O.F.M., Guardian & Commissary of the Holy Land; Revs. Mark Hurst, O.F.M., Moderator - Knights; James Brabandt, O.F.M., Dir.-Postulants; Stephen F. Sabbagh, O.F.M., Prov. Spiritual Asst. to the Secular Franciscan Order; Joshua Doyle, O.F.M.; Sabin Plechta, O.F.M.; Kevin Treston, O.F.M., Public Rels., Editor of Cursador's Almanac; Francis Sihuay, O.F.M. (Peru); Manuel Ybarra, O.F.M., Vicar, Vice Commissary, Treas.; Patrick Flanigan, O.F.M.

Priests 11; Brothers 14; Solemnly Professed 14; Novices 4.

Represented in the Archdiocese of Washington.

FRANCISCAN CUSTODY OF ST. MARY OF THE ANGELS (BYZANTINE-SLAVONIC RITE): *Holy Dormition Monastery,* P.O. Box 270, Sybertsville, PA 18251. Tel: 717-788-1212; Fax: 717-788-2431. Very Rev. Anthony Skurla, O.F.M., Protohegumen.

Represented in the Byzantine Rite Dioceses of St. Nicholas in Chicago, Parma, Passaic, Philadelphia, Pittsburgh and Stamford.

ACADEMY OF AMERICAN FRANCISCAN HISTORY: 1712 Euclid Ave., Berkeley, CA 94709.

Legal Title: *Academy of American Franciscan History;* Dr. John F. Schwaller, Dir.

FRANCISCAN VOCATION CONFERENCE (F.V.C.) (1944): *Sacred Heart Province,* 4860 W. 29th St., Cicero, IL 60804. Tel: 708-656-2570. Rev. Henry V. Willenborg, O.F.M., Pres., Franciscan Society organized nationally to promote cooperative and unified vocational effort in the Franciscan Provinces, Vice-Provinces and Custodies of the U.S.A.

NATIONAL FRATERNITY OF THE SECULAR FRANCISCAN ORDER, U.S.A. (formerly NORTH AMERICAN FEDERATION, THIRD ORDER OF ST. FRANCIS): 3191 71st St. E., Inver Grove Heights, MN 55076. Richard Morton, S.F.O., Natl. Minister. Founded by St. Francis of Assisi in 1209, to give secular, clergy and laity, an opportunity to live according to the Gospel through the observance of an approved rule of life. In 1921 the Fraternities in the United States united in Secular Franciscan Provinces, and are officially known as the National Fraternity of the Secular Franciscan Order, U.S.A. Present membership in the United States is 20,000 in 800 local fraternities and 33 regional fraternities.

[0530] (S.A.)—FRANCISCAN FRIARS OF THE ATONEMENT

(Societas Adunationis T.O.R.)

GENERALATE: St. James Friary, P.O. Box 5, Garrison, NY 10524-0005. Tel: 914-424-3038. Very Rev. Emil F. Tomaskovic, S.A., Minister Gen.; Rev. Thomas Gumprecht, S.A., Vicar General; Bro. Raymond Saville, S.A., Sec. Gen. General Councillors: Revs. Elias Mallon, S.A.; Henry Marchese, S.A.; Dennis Polanco, S.A.; Rev. Bernard Palka, S.A., Treas. Gen.; Bro. William Martyn, S.A., Procurator General to the Holy See, Frati Dell'Atonement, Piazza S. Onofrio, 2, 00165 Rome, Italy.

Motherhouse: St. Paul's Friary, Graymoor, Garrison, NY 10524. Tel: 914-424-3671.

Legal Title: *St. Chistopher's Inn, St. James Friary, St. Paul's Friary, St. Francis of Assisi Novitiate.*

Priests 100; Professed Seminarians 4; Professed Brothers 49.

Friaries 13; Novitiates 1; Parishes (U.S. and Canada) 9; Overseas Ministries: England, Italy, and Japan; Ecumenical Institute 1; Pastoral Center 1; Campus Ministries; Retreat and Conference Center 1; Rehabilitation Center for Alcoholics 1; Shelter for Homeless men; Military Chaplaincies 2.

Represented in the Archdioceses of Boston, Los Angeles, New York and Washington and in the Dioceses of Arlington, Monterey, Ogdensburg and Raleigh.

[0533] (F.F.I.)—FRANCISCAN FRIARS OF THE IMMACULATE

GENERAL MOTHERHOUSE: Benevento, Italy. Founded 1990.

OUR LADY'S CHAPEL: *Marian Friary of Our Lady Queen of the Seraphic Order,* 600 Pleasant St., New Bedford, MA 02740-6299. Tel: 508-996-8274. P.O. Box

3003, New Bedford, MA 02741-3003. Rev. Francis Mary of the Angels Pimental, F.F.I., American Supr.
Legal Title: *Marian Friary of Our Lady of Guadalupe*, Baltic, CT.
Represented in the Dioceses of Fall River and Norwich.

[0535] (C.F.R.)—FRANCISCAN FRIARS OF THE RENEWAL

CENTRAL HOUSE: Saint Crispin Friary, 420 E. 156th St., Bronx, NY 10455. Tel: 718-665-2441. Rev. Andrew Apostoli, C.F.R., Community Servant. Counselors: Revs. Robert Stanion, C.F.R.; Benedict J. Groeschel, C.F.R.; Glenn Sudano, C.F.R.
Represented in the Archdiocese of New York.

[0540] (O.S.F.)—FRANCISCAN MISSIONARY BROTHERS OF THE SACRED HEART OF JESUS

(Fratres Missionarii sti Francisci de Sso. Corde Jesu)
MOTHERHOUSE (1927): *Our Lady of Angels Monastery, St. Joseph Rd., Eureka, MO 63025. Tel: 314-587-3661. Bros. Matthew Gallagher,* O.S.F., Dir. Gen.; Damien De Braekeleer, O.S.F., Asst. Dir. Gen.
Legal Holdings or Titles: *The Black Madonna Shrine and Grottos (Our Lady of Czestoehowa), St. Joseph's Hill Infirmary, Inc., Price Memorial,* Eureka, MO, *Merkle-Knipprath Nursing Home & Apartment Community,* Clifton, MO.
Brothers 13.
Represented in the Archdiocese of St. Louis and the Diocese of Joliet.

[0560] (T.O.R.)—THIRD ORDER REGULAR OF SAINT FRANCIS

(Tertius Ordo Regularis de Poenitentia)
GENERAL MOTHERHOUSE: SS. Cosmas and Damian, Via dei Fori Imperiali, 1, Rome, Italy. Most Rev. Bonaventure Midili, T.O.R., Minister Gen.; Revs. Edmund F. Carroll, T.O.R., Sec.-Treas., *American Parish Youth Center, Inc; Robert Sisk,* T.O.R., Gen. Councilor; Kevin Queally, T.O.R., Sec. Gen.
PROVINCE OF THE MOST SACRED HEART OF JESUS (1910): *Provincial Residence,* 215 57th St., Pittsburgh, PA 15201. Tel: 412-781-1232; Fax: 412-781-1219. Very Rev. Edmund F. Carroll, T.O.R., Minister Prov.; Rev. Christian R. Oravec, T.O.R., Vicar Prov. Councillors: Revs. Michael Scanlan, T.O.R.; Thomas Bourque, T.O.R.; Daniel Sinisi, T.O.R.; Bro. Mark McBride, T.O.R., Treas. & Dir.-Missions; Revs. Fidelis Weber, T.O.R., Prov. Sec. Formation; Terence Henry, T.O.R., Dir.-Postulants; Peter A. Lyons, T.O.R., Dir. Post-Novitiate Formation; Michael Higgins, T.O.R., Dir.-Novices; Richard Davis, T.O.R., Dir.-Vocations; Bernard Tickerhoof, T.O.R., Secular Franciscans Prov. Spiritual Asst.
Fathers 129; Professed Clerics 8; Brothers 26; Novices 4; Postulants 2.
Legal Title: *Province of the Most Sacred Heart of Jesus, Third Order Regular of Saint Francis (USA), Loretto, PA.*
Ministry in Ministries in Parishes; Universities and Colleges; High School; Chaplaincies; Foreign Mission in Brazil & Republic of South Africa; House of Study 1; Novitiates 1; Laymen's Retreat League.
Represented in the Archdioceses of Philadelphia and Washington and in the Dioceses of Altoona-Johnstown, Arlington, Fort Worth, Harrisburg, Pittsburgh, St. Augustine, St. Petersburg, Sioux Falls, Steubenville, Trenton, Venice and Wheeling-Charleston.
PROVINCE OF THE IMMACULATE CONCEPTION: San Pedro Center, 2400 Dike Rd., Winter Park, FL 32792. Tel: 407-677-6406; Fax: 407-677-6489. Very Rev. Robert J. D'Aversa, T.O.R., Minister Prov.; Very Rev. Theodore Midile, T.O.R., Vicar Prov.; Revs. Carl Vacek, T.O.R.; Alexis Nagle, T.O.R.; William Ellert, T.O.R.; Guy Noonan, T.O.R. Prov. Councillors: Rev. Patrick Quinn, T.O.R., Prov. Sec.; Most Rev. Bonaventure Midili, Minister Gen. of the Order, Rome, Italy; Rev. Cyprian Mercieca, South Africa.
Legal Title: *Third Order Regular of St. Francis, Province of the Immaculate, Conception (USA).*
Priests 52; Brothers 9; Permanent Deacons 1; Student Friars 2.
Represented in the Archdioceses of Miami, St. Paul-Minneapolis, Washington, and the Dioceses of Altoona-Johnstown, Davenport, Orlando, Owensboro, Scranton, Wheeling-Charleston and Wilmington.
U.S.A. FRANCISCAN COMMISSARIATE T.O.R., OF THE SPANISH PROVINCE (1924): 301 Jefferson Ave., Waco, TX 76701. Tel: 817-752-8434; Fax: 817-752-2415. Very Rev. Joseph A. Martorell, T.O.R., Commissary. Councillors: Revs. Lawrence Soler, T.O.R.; Antonio Terrassa, T.O.R.
Fathers 12.
Parishes 6.
Represented in the Archdiocese of Newark and in the Dioceses of Austin and Fort Worth.

[0570] (Glmy.)—THE GLENMARY HOME MISSIONERS

(Societas Missionariorum Domesticorum Americas)
(The Home Missioners of America)
GENERAL HEADQUARTERS: P.O. Box 465618, Cincinnati, OH 45246-5618. Tel: 513-874-8900. Revs. Jerry Dorn, Pres.; Will Steinbacher, 1st Vice Pres.; Bros. Jack Henn, 2nd Vice Pres. & Office Operation Mgr.; Mike Springer, Senior Member Coord.; Mr. Bob Knueven, Treas.; Mr. Geoffrey Goodnow, Dir. Devel. Senior Members: Revs. Joseph Gartner; Robert Healy; Joseph Dean; Del Holmes; James P. Kelly; George Mathis; Raymond Orlett; Frank Schenk; William Smith; Ed Haggerty; Pat O'Donnell; Charles Hughes; John McNearney; John Otterbacher; Bob Berson; Bros. George Sauer; Paul Wilhelm; Arthur Miller; Vincent Wilmes.
Vocation Center: P.O. Box 465618, Cincinnati, OH 45246. Rev. Mike Caroline, Dir. Vocations.
Houses of Formation: Glenmary House of Studies and Glenmary Novitiate, 1323 Quincy St., N.E., Washington, DC 20017. Tel: 202-526-1337. Rev. Chet Artysiewicz, Dir. House of Studies; Rev. Mike Kerin, Dir. Novitiate.
Glenmary Research Center, 235 E. Ponce de Leon Ave., Ste. 226, Decatur, GA 30030. Tel: 404-377-7010. Sr. Mary Priniski, O.P., Interim Dir., Works exclusively in the rural missionary apostolate, to serve the needs of the Catholic Church as a whole in small town and rural America.
Glenmary Department of Pastoral Services, 1312 Fifth Ave. N., Nashville, TN 37208. Tel: 615-256-1900. Rev. Dennis Holly, Dir., Assists in educational programs, teacher training, parish evaluations and long range planning. Maintains extensive library of publications and audio visuals.
Fathers 64; Students in Theology 2; Professed Brothers 20.
Properties owned, sponsored or staffed: Mission Bases 38; Houses of Study 2; Vocational Centers.
Represented in the Archdioceses of Atlanta, Cincinnati and Washington and in the Dioceses of Birmingham, Charlotte, Covington, Jackson, Knoxville, Lexington, Little Rock, Nashville, Owensboro, Richmond, Savannah, Tulsa, Tyler and Wheeling-Charleston.

[0580] (B.G.S.)—LITTLE BROTHERS OF THE GOOD SHEPHERD

VILLA MATHIAS: Foundation House: Little Brothers of The Good Shepherd, 901 Bro. Mathias Pl. N.W., P.O. Box 389, Albuquerque, NM 87102. Tel: 505-243-4238; Fax: 505-764-9721.
GENERAL HEADQUARTERS (1987): *Good Shepherd Centre,* 135 Mary St. -P.O. Box 1003, Hamilton, Ontario , Canada, L8N 3R1. Tel: 416-528-9109. Rev. Bros. Justin Howson, B.G.S., Supr. Gen; Fax: 905-526-1184, Mailbox 00. David Lynch, B.G.S., Vicar Gen.; Bros. Majella Marchand, B.G.S., Sec. Gen.; Paul Johnson, B.G.S., Gen. Treas., Gen Counselor & Dir. of Novices; Gerard Sullivan, B.G.S.; Mark Kijnsella, B.G.S., Vocation Counselor, U.S.A.; William Osmanski, B.G.S., Vocation Counselor, U.S.A.; Thomas Liss, B.G.S., Vocation Counselor, U.S.A.; Simon Iddon, B.G.S., Vocation Counselor, England; Richard MacPhee, B.G.S., Vocation Counselor, Canada.
Legal Holdings and Titles: *Caritas Deus, Inc. of New Mexico; Camillus House Inc. of Florida; Camillus Health Concern Inc. of Florida; Charity Unlimited, Inc. of New Mexico; BGS Charitable of Illinois; Brother Mathias Barrett Inc. of Illinois; Brother Mathias Barrett Inc. of New Mexico; Brothers of Good Sheperd Inc. of Pennsylvania; Little Brothers of the Good Shepherd (Philadelphia); Brothers of Good Sheperd Inc. of Florida; Brothers of The Good Shepherd Inc. of New Mexico; Brother Maathias Barrett Inc. of New Mexico (Good Shepherd Manor); Good Shepherd Center Inc. of New Mexico,* Albuquerque, NM; *Good Shepherd Center Auxiliary Inc. of New Mexico; Good Shepherd Manor, Inc.,* Momence, IL; *Little Brothers of Good Sheperd Inc. of Illinois; Villa Mathia, Inc. of New Mexico.*
Professed Brothers 37; Novice Brothers 7.
Represented in the Archdioceses of Miami, Philadelphia and Santa Fe and the Diocese of Joliet.

[0590] (M.Ss.A.)—MISSIONARIES OF THE HOLY APOSTLES

GENERAL ADMINISTRATION: Missionaries of the Holy Apostles, 8594 rue Berri, Montreal, Quebec, Canada, H2P 2G4. Tel: 514-387-2222. Very Rev. Yvon Archambault, M.Ss.A., Supr. Gen. Adminator.
MISSIONARIES OF THE HOLY APOSTLES HEADQUARTERS: Provincial Administration, 33 Prospect Hill Rd., Cromwell, CT 06416. Tel: 203-632-3039; Fax: 203-632-3035. Very Rev. Benedict Klucinec, M.Ss.A., Prov. Animator; Rev. Martin D. Rooney, M.Ss.A., Sec.
Priests 48; Brothers 7.
Properties owned, staffed, or sponsored: Holy Apostles College and Seminary, 6 Parishes Hermitage 3 Hospital Chaplaincies.
Represented in the Archdioceses of Denver, Washington and the Dioceses of Norwich, Pennsacola-Tallahassee and Wheeling-Charleston.

[0600] (C.S.C.)—BROTHERS OF THE CONGREGATION OF HOLY CROSS

(Congregatio A Sancta Cruce)
GENERALATE: Congregazione di Santa Croce, Via Framura, 85, 00168, Rome, Italy. Rev. Claude Grou, Supr. Gen.; Bro. Patrick Sopher; Rev. Robert Morin; Bro. Joel Giallanza; Rev. Leo D'Souza.
MIDWEST PROVINCE OF THE BROTHERS OF HOLY CROSS (1841): *Provincial House,* Box 460, Notre Dame, IN 45656. Tel: 219-239-8311; Fax: 219-289-0487. Bros. William Geenen, C.S.C., Prov. Supr.; Donald Gibbs, C.S.C., Asst. Prov.; Robert Fillmore, C.S.C., Sec.; Donald Bailer, C.S.C., Steward & Treas.; Bro. Richard Gilman, C.S.C., Councillor.
Legal Title: *Notre Dame, Ind. Brothers of Holy Cross, Inc.*
Professed Brothers 236; Temporarily Professed 1; Aspirants 7.
Properties owned, staffed, or sponsored: Community Houses 2; Junior College; High Schools 9; Boarding Military Grade School; Scholasticates 2; Foreign Mission Schools 3.
Represented in the Archdioceses of Anchorage, Chicago, Detroit, Indianapolis, Los Angeles, Miami, Milwaukee, New Orleans, Portland (OR), San Antonio and Washington and in the Dioceses of Austin, Cleveland, Colorado Springs, Erie, Evansville, Fort Wayne-South Bend, Gary, Grand Rapids, Lansing, Nashville, Oakland, Phoenix, Providence, St. Petersburg, Savannah, Scranton and Venice.
SOUTH-WEST PROVINCE OF THE BROTHERS OF HOLY CROSS (1956): *Brother John Baptist Province Center,* St. Edward University, No. 1046, Austin, TX 78704. Tel: 512-442-7856. Bros. Donald Blauvelt, C.S.C., Prov.; Matthew Lyons, C.S.C., Asst. Prov.; Richard Critz, Sec.; Harold Ehlinger, C.S.C., Steward. Councillors: Bros. Stanley Culotta; Richard Daly; Stephen Walsh.
Professed Brothers 128; Temporarily Professed 7.
Properties owned, staffed, or sponsored: Colleges 1; High Schools 7; Home for Boys 1; Schools Foreign Mission Schools 2.
Represented in the Archdioceses of Los Angeles, Louisville, New Orleans, Portland (OR), San Antonio and Santa Fe and in the Dioceses of Austin, Beaumont, Cheyenne, Cleveland, Fort Wayne-South Bend, Knoxville, Lake Charles, Oakland, San Jose and Savannah.
EASTERN PROVINCE OF THE BROTHERS OF HOLY CROSS (1956): 85 Overlook Cir., New Rochelle, NY 10804. Tel: 914-632-4468; 4469; Fax: 914-632-2490. Bros. John Gleason, C.S.C., Prov.; John McGovern, C.S.C., Asst. Prov. & Councillor for Schools; Mark Knightly, C.S.C., Sec.; Peter Martin, C.S.C., Councillor for Financial Services; Stephen LaMendola, C.S.C., Councillor; John Thornton, C.S.C., Councillor; Paul Bednarcyzk, C.S.C., Councillor.
Legal Title: *Brothers of the Holy Cross of the Eastern Province of the United States of America, Inc.*
Professed Brothers 127; Temporarily Professed 5; Novices 1.
High Schools 4; Foreign Mission Houses 6; Schools Middle School; Spiritual Life Center; Boys Home.
Represented in the Archdioceses of Hartford, Indianapolis, New York, San Antonio, Washington and in the Dioceses of Albany, Allentown, Austin, Brooklyn, Colorado Springs, Fall River, Rockville Centre, Salt Lake City, Savannah, Scranton, and Wilmington.

[0610] (C.S.C.)—PRIESTS OF THE CONGREGATION OF HOLY CROSS

Congregatio a Sancta Cruce
GENERALATE: Curia Generalizia di Santa Croce, Via Framura 85, 00168, Rome, Italy. Rev. Claude Grou, C.S.C., Supr. Gen. General Assts.: Bro. Patrick Sopher, C.S.C.; Rev. Robert Morin, C.S.C.; Bro. Joel Giallanza, C.S.C.; Rev. Leo D'Souza, C.S.C.
CONGREGATION OF HOLY CROSS, INDIANA PROVINCE (1841): *Provincial House,* 1304 E. Jeffersen Blvd., South Bend, IN 46617. Tel: 219-289-6850. Revs. Carl F. Ebey, C.S.C., Prov. Supr.; Robert L. Epping, C.S.C., Asst. Prov.; William D. Dorwart, C.S.C., Prov. Sec.; James E. McDonald, C.S.C., Prov. Steward. Prov. Councillors: Revs. David L. Guffey, C.S.C.; Thomas F. Lemos, C.S.C.; Kennth M. Molinaro, C.S.C.; Anthony V. Szakaly, C.S.C.; M. Terrance Lally, C.S.C.; Mark L. Poorman, C.S.C.;

Richard V. Warner, C.S.C.; Bro. John J. Platte, C.S.C.

Legal Title: *Priests of Holy Cross, Indiana Province, Inc.*

Fathers 317; Professed Clerics 8; Temporarily Professed Clerics 19; Novices 13; Candidates 50; Professed Brothers 22.

Properties owned, sponsored, or staffed: College Seminary; Theological Seminary; Novitiate; Mission Center; Provincial House; Postulate; Universities 2; Colleges 2; High Schools 2; Parishes 15; Chaplaincies 19; Home Mission Band; Publishing House; Retreat House.

Holy Cross Associates Lay Missionary Program, P.O. Box 668, Notre Dame, IN 46556. Mr. John Pinter, Dir.

Holy Cross Association, Box K, Notre Dame, IN 46556. Rev. Herbert C. Yost, C.S.C., Dir.

Represented in the Archdioceses of Anchorage, Chicago, Los Angeles, New Orleans, New York, Portland (OR), San Antonio, San Francisco, Washington and in the Dioceses of Austin, Colorado Springs, Fall River, Fort Wayne-South Bend, Gary, Grand Rapids, Kalamazoo, Monterey, Oakland, Phoenix, San Bernardino, San Diego and San Jose.

Congregation of Holy Cross–Eastern Province, Inc. (1952): *Provincial Headquarters,* 835 Clinton Ave., Bridgeport, CT 06604. Tel: 203-367-7252; 367-1152; Fax: 203-366-7886. Revs. Hugh W. Cleary, C.S.C., Prov. Supr.; Wilfred J. Raymond, C.S.C., Asst. Prov. Supr.; R. Bradley Beaupre, C.S.C., Treas. Prov. Councillors: Revs. Mark T. Cregan, C.S.C.; Robert J. Kruse, C.S.C.; James R. Lackenmier, C.S.C.; Joseph J. Long, C.S.C.; Charles L. Wallen, C.S.C.; Bro. Herman Zaccarelli, C.S.C.

Fathers 131; Temporarily Professed Clerics 5; Candidates 14; Novices 4; Brothers Professed 15; Deacons 2.

Properties owned, sponsored, or staffed: Colleges 2; Mission Houses; Parishes 11; Retreat House; Chaplaincies 22; Campus Ministry 8; Family Rosary Crusade; Family Theater.

Represented in the Archdioceses of Boston, Hartford, Los Angeles, New York and Washington and in the Dioceses of Albany, Bridgeport, Brooklyn, Burlington, Fall River, Norwich, Orlando, Portland (ME), Rochester and Scranton.

Southern Province (1968): *Holy Cross, Southern Province, Provincial House,* 2111 Brackenridge St., Austin, TX 78704. Tel: 512-443-3886; Fax: 512-416-1216. Revs. Leonard J. Collins, C.S.C., Prov. Supr.; John S. Korcsmar, C.S.C., Asst. Prov.; Revs. Barry E. Cabell, Prov. Councillor; L. Peter Logsdon, C.S.C., Prov. Councillor; C. Richard Nowery, C.S.C., Prov. Councillor; Bro. Thomas G. Krieter, C.S.C., Prov. Steward & Sec.

Legal Title: *Congregation of Holy Cross, Southern Province, Inc.*

Fathers 32; Professed Brothers 1; Temporarily Professed 5; Novices 1.

Ministries in Parishes; Foreign Missions; Chaplaincies; Social Service.

Represented in the Archdioceses of New Orleans, St. Louis and San Antonio and in Dioceses of Austin, Baton Rouge, Fort Wayne-South Bend, Lafayette (LA) and Las Cruces.

[0620] (F.S.E.)—BROTHERS OF THE HOLY EUCHARIST

Founded in the United States 1957.

General Motherhouse and Novitiate: P.O. Box 25, Plaucheville, LA 71362. Tel: 318-922-3630; 922-3401. Rev. Bro. Andre M. Lucia, F.S.E., Supr. Gen.

Represented in the Diocese of Alexandria.

[0630] (M.S.F.)—CONGREGATION OF THE MISSIONARIES OF THE HOLY FAMILY

(Congregatio Missionariorum a Sacra Familia)

General Motherhouse: Via di Villa Troili, 56, 00163, Rome, Italy. Very Rev. Egon Farber, M.S.F., Supr. Gen.

General Mission Office - M.S.F., Inc.: P.O. Box 918, West Point, VA 23181. Tel: 804-843-2622. Rev. John Brieffies, M.S.F., Exec. Dir.

Provincial House: North American Province of Missionaries of the Holy Family, 10415 Midland Blvd., St. Louis, MO 63114. Tel: 314-423-6815. Rev. James Wasser, M.S.F., Prov.

Fathers 52; Theology Students 4; Brothers 8.

Ministries in House of Study 2; Parishe 16.

Represented in the Archdioceses of St. Louis and San Antonio, and in the Dioceses of Brownsville, Corpus Christi, Duluth and Richmond. Also in Canada and Mexico.

[0640] (S.F.)—SONS OF THE HOLY FAMILY

(Congregatio Filiorum Sacrae Familiae)

General Motherhouse: Entenza 301, Barcelona, 08029. Spain. Very Rev. Jose Roca, Gen. Superior.

U.S. Foundation (1920): 401 Randolph Rd., P.O. Box 4138, Silver Spring, MD 20914. Tel: 301-622-1184. Rev. Luis Picazo, S.F., Vice Prov.

Fathers 16.

Represented in the Archdioceses of Santa Fe, Washington, and the Archdiocese for the Military Services, U.S.A.

[0650] (C.S.SP.)—HOLY GHOST FATHERS

(Congregation of the Holy Ghost and of the Immaculate Heart of Mary)

Congregatio Sancti Spiritus sub tutela Immaculati Cordis Beatissimae Virginis Mariae)

Generalate: Clivo di Cinna 195, Rome, 00136. Italy. Very Rev. Pierre Schouver, C.S.Sp., Supr. Gen.

Eastern Province of the United States (1872): 6230 Brush Run Rd., Bethel Park, PA 15102. Tel: 412-831-0302; Fax: 412-831-0970. Revs. Christopher P. Promis, C.S.Sp., Prov. Councillors: Revs. William R. Headley, C.S.Sp.; Francis X. Hanley, C.S.Sp.; James P. McCloskey, C.S.Sp.; Leonard J. Tuozzolo, C.S.Sp.; Charles J. Fenner, C.S.Sp.; Robert E. Spangenberg, C.S.Sp.

Legal Holdings: *Provincial Residence, Duquesne University, Holy Ghost Preparatory School, Bethel Holy Ghost Animation Center.*

Fathers in U.S. 85; Professed Theologians 3; Professed Brothers 3.

Properties owned, sponsored, or staffed: 13 Parishes; Theologate; Home for Homeless Boys; Retirement Residences.

Represented in the Archdioceses of Chicago, Cincinnati, Detroit, New York, Philadelphia and Washington and in the Dioceses of Arlington, Pittsburgh, Providence, Saginaw and Venice. Also in Puerto Rico & Africa.

Western Province of the United States (1964): *Congregation of the Holy Ghost,* 1700 W. Alabama St., Houston, TX 77098-2808. Tel: 713-522-2882; Fax: 713-522-8063. Very Rev. Donald S. Nesti, C.S.Sp., Prov. Supr. Prov. Councillors: Rev. Silvio A. D'Ostilio, C.S.Sp., 1st Asst.; Bro. Michael E. Suazo, C.S.Sp., 2nd Asst. & Prov. Sec.; Rev. Frankie L.G. Santos, C.S.Sp.; Rev. Daniel L. Walsh, C.S.Sp.; Rev. Joseph Gaglione, C.S.Sp., Prov. Bursar.

Priests 54; Professed Brothers 2; Lay Associates 8; Scholastics 12; Priest-Novice 3.

Properties owned, sponsored, or staffed: Holy Spirit Provincialate & Holy Ghost Hall, Houston, TX Libermann House at Spiritan Renewal Center, New Braunfels, TX Casa Laval and Holy Ghost Novitiate, Hemet, CA Iglesia de Santa Ana Maison Brottier, Natchitoches, LA Mision San Juan Bautista Staff: 15 Parishes & 2 Training Centers.

Represented in the Archdioceses of New Orleans and San Antonio and in the Dioceses of Alexandria, Fresno, Galveston-Houston, Lafayette (LA), Little Rock, Phoenix and San Bernardino. Also in Valles, Mexico.

Holy Ghost Fathers of Ireland (1971): Very Rev. Vincent O'Connell, C.S.Sp., Prov. Delegate U.S.A. East, 4849 37th St., Long Island City, NY 11101. Tel: 718-729-5273; Fax: 718-729-6949. Very Rev. Francis Mulloy, C.S.Sp., Prov. Delegate U.S.A. West, St. Dunstan's Church, 1133 Broadway, Mill Brae, CA 94030. Very Rev. Matthias Moore, C.S.Sp., Prov. Delegate Louisiana, St. John the Baptist Church, 1139 Dryades St., New Orleans, LA 70113. Councillors: Revs. Cornelius C. Woulfe, C.S.Sp.; Michael McCarthy, C.S.Sp.; Peter Nolan, C.S.Sp.; Andrew F. Duffy, C.S.Sp.; James Delaney, C.S.Sp.

Fathers 69.

Represented in the Archdioceses of Boston, Miami, New Orleans, New York and San Francisco and in the Dioceses of Brooklyn, Fargo, Metuchen, Palm Beach and St. Augustine.

[0660] (M.Sp.S.)—MISSIONARIES OF THE HOLY SPIRIT

General Motherhouse: Av. Universidad 1702, 04010, Mexico, D.F., Mexico. Tel: 5-658-74-33; 5-658-7851. Very Rev. Melecio Picazo, M.Sp.S., Supr. Gen.

American Headquarters: Our Lady of Guadalupe, 500 N. Juanita Ave., P.O. Box 1091, Oxnard, CA 93030. Tel: 805-483-0987.

Priests 17; Professed 17; Novices 16.

Parishes 5; House of Study 1; Novitiates 1; Theologate 1.

Represented in the Archdiocese of Los Angeles and the Diocese of Fresno.

[0670] (O.H.)—HOSPITALLER BROTHERS OF ST. JOHN OF GOD

General Motherhouse: Hospitaller Brothers of St. John of God, via della Nocetta 263, Rome, Italy, 00164. Most Rev. Bro. Pascual Piles, O.H., Prior Gen. Order founded by St. John of God at Granada, Spain, in 1537.

American Province of Our Lady Queen of Angels (1970): *Villa Maria-Provincial Curia,* 2425 S. Western Ave., Los Angeles, CA 90018. Tel: 213-734-0233; 731-0641; Fax: 213-731-5987. Bro. Edward Francis McEnroe, O.H., Prov.

Brothers 36; Solemn Professed 28; Simple Professed 2; Priests 2; Novices 1.

Legal Holdings: *St. John of God Retirement and Care Center, Los Angeles, CA St. Joseph Health & Care Center, Ojai, CA St. John of God Health Care Services, Victorville, CA.*

Represented in the Archdiocese of Los Angeles and the Dioceses of Camden and San Bernardino.

[0680] (I.H.M.)—BROTHERS OF THE IMMACULATE HEART OF MARY

General Motherhouse (1948): 609 N. 7th St., Steubenville, OH 43952. Tel: 614-283-2462. Bro. Dominic Carroll, I.H.M., Supr. Gen.; Bro. Anthony Motto, I.H.M., Novice Master.

Professed Brothers 5.

Novitiate 1; Bishop's Residence; CCD Center 1; Pastoral Associates 3; Diocesan Office 1.

Represented in the Diocese of Steubenville.

[0690] (S.J.)—JESUIT FATHERS AND BROTHERS

(Societas Jesu)

Generalate: Casella Postale 6139, 00195, Rome, Italy. Very Rev. Peter-Hans Kolvenbach, S.J., Gen.; Revs. Hans Zwiefelhofer, Sec.; Francis E. Case, S.J., U.S. Assistant.

Jesuit Conference: The Society of Jesus in the United States National Offices, 1616 P Street, Suite 400, Washington, DC 20036-1405. Tel: 202-462-0400; Fax: 202-328-9212. Revs. Gregory F. Lucey, S.J., Pres.; Daniel C. McDonald, S.J., Exec. Sec. & Treas.; Charles J. Jackson, S.J., Sec. Formation; British Robinson, S.J., Sec. Social Ministries; Robert W. Chesney, S.J., Sec. Intl. Ministries and Refugee Apostolates; Thomas M. Rochford, S.J., Sec. for Communications.

Maryland Province (1833): 5704 Roland Ave., Baltimore, MD 21210. Tel: 410-532-1400; Fax: 410-532-1419.

Legal Title: *Corporation of the Roman Catholic Clergymen, Maryland;* Very Rev. Edward Glynn, S.J., Prov.; Revs. James R. Stormes, S.J., Socius to the Prov. & Asst. Prov. Pastoral Ministries &, Intl. Apostolates; James A. Casciotti, S.J., Supr.; Sec. to Prov.; Dir. Communication; James F. Salmon, S.J., Treas.; Thomas P. Gaunt, S.J., Asst. Prov. for Jesuit Students; Hugh A. Kennedy, S.J., Assist. Sec. to Prov.; Ms. Suzanne M. Geaney, Dir. Social Ministries; Revs. William F. Lamm, S.J., Asst. Treas. & Sec.; Thomas P. Martin, S.J., Asst. Treas.; Francis H. McGauley, S.J., Health Care Coord.; William K. McGroarty, S.J., Asst. Treas. for Properties; Mr. James S. Schaefer, Bus. Mgr.; Revs. Bradley Murray, S.J., Computer Consultant; T. Donald Rinfret, S.J., Dir. Mission Bureau & Jesuit Seminary Guild, Maryland Province; Francis R. Carmody, S.J., Asst. Dir.; Richard J. Colgan, S.J., Asst. Dir.; Herbert F. Smith, S.J., Sec. Gen. of the League of the Sacred Heart; Joseph S. Costantino, S.J., Dir. Vocations; Gerald P. Fogarty, S.J., Archivist; James A. O'Brien, S.J., Promoter, Christian Life Communities; Henry B. Haske, S.J., Tertian Instructor.

Jesuit Volunteer Corps, East, 17th & Thompson Sts., Philadelphia, PA 19121.

Fathers 427; Scholastics 43; Brothers 28.

Properties owned, sponsored, or staffed: Parishes 13; Universities 3; Colleges 2; High Schools 5; Houses of Retreats 2; Residences 9.

Represented in the Archdioceses of Baltimore, Philadelphia and Washington and in the Dioceses of Allentown, Arlington, Camden, Charlotte, Erie, Pittsburgh, Raleigh, Richmond, Scranton, Wheeling-Charleston and Wilmington.

Province of New York (1943): 39 E. 83rd St., New York, NY 10028. Tel: 212-774-5500; Fax: 212-774-5510.

Legal Title: *The New York Province of the Society of Jesus, New York, N.Y.;* Very Rev. Joseph P. Parkes, S.J., Prov.; Revs. Thomas E. Smith, S.J., Exec. Asst. to Prov.; Bro. Gilbert J. Scott, S.J., Asst. to the Prov.; Revs. J. Raymond Johnson, S.J., Prov. Treas.; J. Raymond Johnson, S.J., Auditor & American Rep. for the Missions of the Society of Jesus, Vatican City; Thomas P. Gaunt, S.J., Asst. for Formation; Frederick J. O'Brien, S.J., Asst. for Sec. Education; James F. Joyce, S.J., Asst. for Social & Pastoral Ministries; William T. Wood, S.J., Asst. for Intl. Apostolate; Joseph S. Costantino, S.J., Dir.

of Vocations; John G. Marzolf, S.J., Dir. of the Jesuit Seminary & Mission Bureau.

Fathers 546; Scholastics 87; Brothers 39.

Properties owned, sponsored, or staffed: Parishes 9; Universities 1; Colleges 3; High Schools 8; Houses for Laymen's Retreats 4; House of Study 1; Novitiates 2; Community Houses 3.

Represented in the Archdioceses of Newark and New York and in the Dioceses of Albany, Brooklyn, Buffalo, Paterson, Rochester, Rockville Centre and Syracuse. Also in Guam, the Caroline Islands, Chalan Kanoa, and the Prefecture Apostolic of Marshall Islands.

The Jesuits of the Missouri Province (Missouri Province of the Society of Jesus): *Province Offices,* 4511 W. Pine Blvd., St. Louis, MO 63108-2191. Tel: 314-361-7765 Mon.-Fri. 9-5; Fax: 314-758-7164. Very Rev. E. Edward Kinerk, S.J., Prov.; Revs. Louis J. McCabe, S.J., Exec. Asst.; Robert F. Weiss, S.J., Treas.; Frank Reale, S.J., Asst. for Jesuits in Training and Asst. for Secondary Education; Robert L. Sullivan, S.J., Asst. for Jesuits in Pastoral and Intl. Apostolates; William T. Oulvey, S.J., Asst. for Prov. Planning and Vocation Dir.; L. Gene Martens, S.J., Assoc. Dir. Jesuit Devel. Office; Ms. Mary Flick, S.J., Dir. of Publications & Editor, *The Jesuit Bulletin & Panarama.* Tel: 314-361-7765. William B. Faherty, S.J., Prov. Archivist.

Fathers 294; Students in Major Seminary 28; Novices 7; Brothers 33.

Legal Title: *Regis Jesuit High School Corporation,* Aurora, CO, *Jesuit Novitiate - The Jesuits of the Missouri Province, Regis University,* Denver, CO, *Rockhurst University, Rockhurst High School,* Kansas City, KS, *The Province - The Jesuits of the Missouri Province, Bellarmine House of Studies - The Jesuits of the Missouri Province, Fusz Pavilion - The Jesuits of the Missouri Province, Institute of Jesuit Sources - The Jesuits of the Missouri Province, Jesuit Mission Bureau - The Jesuits of the Missouri Province, Review for Religious - The Jesuits of the Missouri Province, DeSmet Jesuit High School, Jesuit Community Corporation at St. Louis University, St. Louis University, St. Louis University High School, The Sacred Heart Program, Inc., White House Retreat, Inc.,* St. Louis, MO, *Society of Jesus in Belize, Inc., St. John's College, Inc.,* Belize, *Jesuit Retreat House,* Sedalia.

Ministries in Parishes; Universities; High Schools; Colleges; Novitiates; Curia; Retreat Houses.

Represented in the Archdioceses of Denver, Kansas City in Kansas and St. Louis and the Dioceses of Belleville, Cheyenne, Colorado Springs, Dodge City, Jefferson City, Kansas City-St. Joseph, Pueblo, Springfield-Cape Girardeau, Springfield in Illinois, Tulsa and Wichita.

Province of New Orleans (1907): 500 S. Jefferson Davis Pky., New Orleans, LA 70119-7192. Tel: 504-821-0334; Fax: 504-822-5322.

Legal Title: *Catholic Society of Religious and Literary Education, A Louisiana Corporation;* Very Rev. Edward B. Arroyo, S.J., Prov.; Revs. Donald J. Martin, S.J., Asst. for Parishes; Michael S. Gallagher, S.J., Asst. for Social Apostolate; Joseph H. Reising, S.J., Asst. for Formation & Retreat Apostolate; John F. Armstrong, S.J., Socius & Asst. for Secondary Education; Robert J. Ratchford, S.J., Staff Assist.; Bro. Lawrence J. Lundin, S.J., Treas.

Fathers 234; Students in Major Seminary 25; Novices 12; Brothers 33.

Properties owned, sponsored, or staffed: Parishes 14; Universities 1; Colleges 1; High Schools 4; Novitiate 1; Houses of Retreat 5.

Represented in the Archdioceses of Atlanta, Miami, New Orleans, San Antonio and Santa Fe and in the Dioceses of Alexandria, Amarillo, Austin, Baton Rouge, Charleston, Corpus Christi, Dallas, El Paso, Fort Worth, Galveston-Houston, Gallup, Lafayette (LA), Las Cruces, Little Rock, Mobile, Nashville, Orlando, Palm Beach, Pensacola-Tallahassee, St. Augustine, St. Petersburg and Venice.

California Province (1909): Executive Assistant, 300 College Ave., P.O. Box 519, Los Gatos, CA 95031-0519. Tel: 408-354-6143.

Legal Title: *The California Province of the Society of Jesus;* Very Rev. John A. Privett, S.J., Prov.; Revs. John T. Mitchell, S.J., Exec. Asst. & Dir. Vocations; Gerdenio M. Manuel, S.J., Asst. for Formation; Alfred E. Naucke, S.J., Asst. for Secondary Education; Michael J. Mandala, S.J., Asst. for Social-Pastoral Ministries; Michael E. Engh, S.J., Dir. Studies; Robert L. St. Clair, S.J., Prov. Treas.; William J. Maring, S.J., Prov. Dir.-Devel.; Bros. Thomas A. Marshall, S.J., Prov. Archivist; Jack A. Hughes, S.J., Asst. Sec.; Revs. Paul J. Bernadicou, S.J., Tertian Instructor; David Fitch, S.J., Promoter, *Christian Life Communities; Theodore T. Taheny,* S.J., Dir., *California Jesuit Missionaries* 284 Stanyan St., San Francisco, CA 94118-4299. Tel: 415-221-1588. George M. Twigg-Porter, S.J., Apostleship of Prayer; Andrew F. Maginnis, S.J., Dir. Jesuit Seminary Association & Editor—"The Western Jesuit"; Bro. John E. Maloney, S.J., Asst. Dir., *Jesuit Sem. Assn.* Mr. Kevin O'Neill, Dir. Jesuit Volunteer Corps Southwest.

Legal Title: *JVC Center,* P.O. Box 23404, Oakland, CA 94623-9991. Tel: 510-465-5016.

Fathers 419; Brothers 38; Scholastics 62; Scholastic Novices 13; Brother Novices 1.

Properties owned, sponsored, or staffed: Parishes 14; Universities 3; High Schools 5; Novitiates 1; Theologate 1; Retreat Houses 1.

Represented in the Archdioceses of Los Angeles and San Francisco and in the Dioceses of Fresno, Honolulu, Monterey, Orange, Phoenix, Reno, Sacramento, Salt Lake City, San Bernardino, San Diego, San Jose, Santa Rosa, Stockton and Tucson.

New England Province (1926): 771 Harrison Ave., Boston, MA 02118-2311. Tel: 617-266-7233; Fax: 617-536-8074.

Legal Title: *The Society of Jesus of New England;* Revs. William A. Barry, S.J., Prov.; James F. Lafontaine, S.J., Asst. for Formation & Secondary Education; Robert J. Levens, S.J., Socius, Asst. for Social Justice Issues; Martin P. MacDonnell, S.J., Asst. for Intl. & Pastoral Ministries; William C. Russell, S.J., Asst. for Devel. & Assoc. Dir. Jesuit Seminary Guild & Mission, Bureau, Vocation Dir. Rev. Thomas J. Gibbons, S.J., Asst. for Prov. Finances.

Fathers 467; Scholastics 32; Brothers 24.

Parishes 3; Universities 2; Colleges 1; High Schools 3; Houses of Retreats 2; Seminaries 1; Novitiates 1; Residences 1.

Represented in the Archdioceses of Baltimore, Boston, Detroit, Hartford, Los Angeles, Louisville, Miami, New York, Philadelphia, St. Louis, San Francisco, and Washington, and in the Dioceses of Bridgeport, Burlington, Camden, Charleston, Fall River, Gallup, Kansas City-St. Joseph, Manchester, Norwich, Oakland, Portland (ME), Rapid City, St. Petersburg, San Diego, San Jose, Scranton, Spokane, Springfield (MA), Wheeling-Charlestown and Worcester.

Chicago Province - Society of Jesus (S.J.) (1928): 2050 N. Clark St., Chicago, IL 60614. Tel: 773-975-6363; Fax: 773-975-0230.

Legal Title: *Chicago Province of the Society of Jesus;* Very Rev. Bradley M. Schaeffer, S.J., Prov.; Revs. Francis J. Daly, S.J., Exec. Asst. & Asst. for Formation; Daniel L. Flaherty, S.J., Prov. Treas. and Asst. for Bus. and Finance; James A. Stoeger, S.J., Asst. Secondary Education; Brian G. Paulson, S.J., Asst. for Vocation Promotion; Paul V. Robb, S.J., Asst. Treas.; Gerald P. Grace, S.J., Asst. for Intl. Apostolates & Dir. of Jesuit Intl. Missions; Joseph F. Small, S.J., Asst. for Records & Research; James P. Gschwend, S.J., Asst. for Continuing Education & Asst. for Jesuits in Diaspora; Richard H. McGurn, S.J., Asst. for Pastoral & Social Ministries.

Jesuit Development Office, 2059 N. Sedgwick St., Chicago, IL 60614. Tel: 773-975-8181; Fax: 773-975-2042. Revs. John F. Costello, S.J., Coord.-Planned Giving; John J. Foley, S.J., Asst. to Devel. Dir. for Jesuit Seminary Assoc.; John A. McGrail, S.J., Dir. Apostleship of Prayer.

Quarterly Publication: *Company Magazine,* Offices, 3441 N. Ashland Ave., Chicago, IL 60657. Tel: 773-281-1534; Fax: 773-281-2667.

Fathers 229; Scholastics 21; Brothers 17; Scholastic Novices 4.

Properties Sponsored: Parishes 4; Universities 2; High Schools 4; Retreat Houses 2; Diocesan Major Seminary 1; Residences 9; House of Writers 1.

Represented in the Archdioceses of Chicago, Cincinnati, Indianapolis and Louisville and in the Dioceses of Covington, Evansville, Fort Wayne-South Bend, Gary, Joliet, Lafayette (IN), Peoria and Rockford.

Oregon Province - Society of Jesus (1932): 2222 N.W. Hoyt, Portland, OR 97210. Tel: 503-226-6977. Very Rev. Robert B. Grimm, S.J., Prov.; Rev. Michael A. Tyrrell, S.J., Treas.; Rev. Charles E. Schmitz, S.J., Exec. Assist. to Prov., Socius and Legal Sec.; Mr. William L. Lockyear, CFO; Mr. Matthew Senecal, Dir. Devel. & Public Rels.; Joyceann Hagen, Asst. Ministries; Revs. Brad R. Reynolds, S.J., Prov. Asst. for Formation; Charles E. Schmitz, S.J., Province Coord.-Intl. Apostolate; Gary N. Smith, S.J., Province Coord. Social Ministries.

Legal Title: *Society of the Jesus, Oregon Province,* Portland, OR, *The Pioneer Educational Society,* Spokane, WA, *Montana Catholic Mission.*

Fathers 252; Scholastics 27; Brothers 22; Students in Major Seminaries 8; Novices 6; Special Students 4.

Properties owned, sponsored, or staffed: Parishes 33; Universities 2; High Schools 4; House of Study 1; Novitiates 1.

Represented in the Archdioceses of Anchorage, Portland in Oregon and Seattle and in the Dioceses of Baker, Boise, Fairbanks, Great Falls-Billings, Helena, Spokane and Yakima.

Detroit Province- Society of Jesus (S.J.) (1955): 7303 W. Seven Mile Rd., Detroit, MI 48221. Tel: 313-861-7500; Fax: 313-861-4230. Very Rev. John F. Libens, S.J., Prov. Supr.; Revs. Keith J. Esenther, S.J., Exec. Asst.; Walter L. Farrell, S.J., Treas.; Norman J. Dickson, S.J., Asst.-Intl. Apostolates & Vocation Training; John E. Dister, S.J., Asst for Pastoral & Social Ministries; Timothy J. Shepard, S.J., Asst. Formation.

Fathers 177; Scholastics 17; Brothers 25.

Properties owned, sponsored, or staffed: Parishes 8; Universities 2; High Schools 5; Retreat Houses 3.

Legal Title: *Detroit Province of the Society of Jesus, Colombiere Center,* Clarkston, MI, *Jesuit Retreat House of Cleveland, Ohio, Jesuit Seminary Association, Jesuit International Missions, John Carroll University of Cleveland, Ohio, John Carroll Jesuit Community Corporation, Loyola Academy,* Detroit, MI, *Loyola of the Lakes Jesuit Retreat House, Inc., Manresa Jesuit Retreat House, Patna Jesuit Mission Society, Inc., St. Ignatius High School of Cleveland, Ohio, St. John's Jesuit High School of Toledo, Ohio, University of Detroit Mercy, The Jesuit Community Corporation at the University of Detroit, University of Detroit Jesuit High School and Academy, Walsh Jesuit High School.*

Represented in the Archdioceses of Boston, Chicago, Cincinnati, Detroit, New York, Washington and the Dioceses of Buffalo, Cleveland, Columbus, Davenport, Fort Wayne-South Bend, Lexington, Oakland, Richmond, Saginaw, Toledo, Wheeling-Charleston and Worcester.

Wisconsin Province- Society of Jesus (S.J.) (1955): 3400 W. Wisconsin Ave., P.O. Box 08277, Milwaukee, WI 53208-0277. Tel: 414-937-6949; Fax: 414-937-6950.

Legal Title: *Wisconsin Province of the Society of Jesus;* Very Rev. D. Edward Mathie, S.J., Prov. & Coord. for Higher Education; Revs. James E. Grummer, S.J., Asst. Prov. & Asst. for Intl. Ministries; Asst. for Secondary Education; James M. Kubicki, S.J., Asst. for Formation; J. Robert Hilbert, S.J., Asst. for Pastoral & Retreat Ministries; Eugene M. Dutkiewicz, S.J., Treas.; Warren J. Sazama, S.J., Pres.- Jesuit Partnership; Robert M. Frommelt, S.J., Asst. Pres.-Jesuit Partnership.

Fathers 336; Students in Major Seminary 48; Novices 7; Brothers 28.

Properties owned, sponsored, or staffed: Parishes 5; Universities 2; High Schools 3; Middle Schools 2; Community Houses 19; Novitiate; Native American Missions 3; Negro Mission; Ethnic Parishes 2; Retreat Houses 3.

Represented in the Archdioceses of Milwaukee, Omaha and St. Paul-Minneapolis and in the Dioceses of Green Bay, La Crosse, Rapid City, Winona, and Cheyenne.

Province of the Antilles (1947): Correa y Cindron, 28; P.O. Box 76, Santo Domingo, Dominican Republic. Tel: 809-532-5628.

U.S. Address: 13339 S.W. 9 Terrace, Miami, FL 33184. Very Rev. Benjamin Gonzalez-Buetta, S.J., Prov.; Revs. Pedro Suarez, S.J., Miami Reg. Supr.; Eduardo Alvarez, S.J., Supr.

Fathers 101; Scholastics 46; Brothers 18.

High Schools: Loyola in Dominican Republic Belen Jesuit Prep in Miami; Novitiate 1; House of Retreat 3 in Santo Domingo; Juan Pablo II in Miami; Residences 2.

Represented in the Archdiocese of Miami. Also in Santo Domingo.

[0700] (S.S.J.)—ST. JOSEPH'S SOCIETY OF THE SACRED HEART

(The Josephites)

(Societas Sancti Joseph SSmi Cordis)

Central House of Administration: 1130 N. Calvert St., Baltimore, MD 21202. Tel: 410-727-3386; Fax: 410-385-2331. Very Rev. Robert M. Kearns, S.S.J., Supr. Gen.

Fathers 125; Brothers 10; Students in House of Studies 3; Seminarians 3.

Legal Title: *St. Joseph's Society of the Sacred Heart, Inc.*

Properties owned, staffed, or sponsored: Parishes 62; Missions attached 7; Schools Grade Schools 21; High School; House of Study; Major Seminary; Novitiate.

Represented in the Archdioceses of Baltimore, Los Angeles, Mobile, New Orleans and Washington and in the Dioceses of Arlington, Baton Rouge, Beaumont, Biloxi, Birmingham, Fort Worth, Galveston-Houston, Houma-Thibodaux, Lafayette (LA), Lake Charles, Jackson, and Wilmington.

[0710] (C.J.)—JOSEPHITE FATHERS
(Congregatio Iosephitarum Gerardimontensium)
GENERAL MOTHERHOUSE: Melle (Ghent), Belgium. Very Rev. Richard Lear, C.J., Supr. Gen.
U.S. FOUNDATION (1963): *St. Joseph Seminary, Provincialate and Novitiate,* 180 Patterson Road, Santa Maria, CA 93455. Tel: 805-937-5378. Very Rev. Edward Jalbert, Prov. Supr.
Fathers 14; Brothers 1.
Parishes 3; High Schools 2; Hospitals 1; Air Force Chaplains 1.
Represented in the Archdiocese of Los Angeles.

[0720] (M.S.)—THE MISSIONARIES OF OUR LADY OF LA SALETTE
(Congregatio Missionariorum Vulgo "De la Salette")
GENERAL HOUSE: Piazza Madonna Della Salette 3, Rome, 00152. Italy. Very Rev. Isidro Perin, M.S., Supr. Gen.
American Region was established 1892; Canonically erected 1934; Divided into other Provinces in 1945, 1958 and 1967.
PROVINCE OF OUR LADY OF SEVEN DOLORS (1934): 915 Maple Ave., Hartford, CT 06114-2330. Tel: 860-956-8870.
Legal Title: *Missionaries of LaSalette Corp., Religious Trust of the Missionaries of Our Lady of La Salette, Province of Our Lady of Seven Dolors;* Very Rev. Thomas A. Reilly, M.S., Prov.; Revs. James H. Kuczynski, M.S., Asst. & Vicar; Joseph G. Bachand, M.S., Asst. & Sec.; Bro. G. Peter Collins, M.S., Treas.
Priests 89; Brothers 19; Novices 1; Oblate Brothers 1.
Represented in the Archdioceses of Atlanta, Boston, Hartford, New York, St. Paul-Minneapolis and Washington and in the Dioceses of Albany, Manchester, Norwich, Orlando, Raleigh, Springfield (MA) and Worcester.
PROVINCE OF THE IMMACULATE HEART OF MARY (1945): *Missionaries of Our Lady of La Salette,* 947 Park St., P.O. Box 2965, Attleboro, MA 02703-0965. Tel: 617-222-7171; Fax: 508-222-6178. Very Rev. Gilles Genest, M.S., Prov. Supr.; Rev. Rene J. Gelinas, M.S., Vicar & Sec.; Bro. Claude Rheaume, M.S., Treas. & Councillor.
Priests 52; Brothers 23; Oblates 1.
Missionaries (priests and brothers) serve: Parishes 7; Shrines 2; Retreat House 1; Hospital Chaplaincies 3; College Chaplaincies 2.
Properties owned: La Salette Shrine, Provincial House and Center for Christian Living, Attleboro, MA La Salette Shrine, Enfield, NH.
Represented in the Dioceses of Burlington, Fall River, Manchester and Tucson. Also in Canada.
PROVINCE OF MARY QUEEN (1958): *La Salette Missionaries,* 4650 S. Broadway, St. Louis, MO 63111-1303. Tel: 314-353-5000; Fax: 314-353-4582.
Legal Title: *Missionaries of La Salette Corporation of Missouri;* Very Rev. Dennis J. Meyer, M.S., Prov. Supr.; Revs. Edward J. Brunnert, M.S., Vicar; Peter D. Kohler, M.S., Prov. Asst. & Sec.; John Nuelle, M.S., Procurator Missions of Morondava; Joseph Shea, M.S., Procurator Missions of Morondava; Bro. Timothy A. Schultz, M.S., Prov. Treas.
Fathers 37; Professed Brothers 6; Oblate Brothers 2.
Parishes 13; Religious Houses 5; Chaplaincies 6.
Represented in the Archdiocese and St. Louis and in the Dioceses of Beaumont, Galveston-Houston, Jefferson City, Lake Charles, and Tyler.
PROVINCE OF MARY, QUEEN OF PEACE (1967): P.O. Box 250, Twin Lakes, WI 53181. Tel: 414-877-3123. Revs. James Stajkowski, M.S., Prov.; Terrence Niziolek, M.S., Vicar; James Winiarski, M.S., Councillor; Thaddeus Galuszka, M.S., Treas.
Priests 16; Missionary Brothers 4; Oblate Brothers 1.
Represented in the Archdiocese of Milwaukee and the Diocese of Peoria.

[0730] (L.C.)—LEGIONARIES OF CHRIST
Founded in Mexico 1941, first foundation in United States 1965.
General Headquarters: Via Aurelia 677, Rome, Italy. Very Rev. Marcial Maciel, L.C., Founder and Supr. Gen.
U.S. HEADQUARTERS: 393 Derby Ave., Orange, CT 06477. Tel: 203-795-2800; Fax: 203-795-2808. Rev. Anthony Bannon, L.C., Natl. Dir.
Novitiate and Juniorate, 475 Oak Ave., Cheshire, CT 06410. Tel: 203-271-0805. Rev. William Meade, L.C., Rector.
Residences include addresses at the following locations, 815 Boston Post Rd., Rye NY; 11917 Falls Rd., Potomac MD; 2460 Opdyke Rd., Bloomfield Hills MI; 4522 Crown Ave., La Canada CA; Immaculate Conception Apostolic School, P.O. Box 936, Center Harbor, NH; 432 Liguori Rd., Edgerton, WI; 2424 Briarcliff Ct., Irving TX.
Priests 48; Religious 62; Novices 85; Juniors 48.
Represented in the Archdioceses of Atlanta, Detroit, Hartford, Los Angeles, New York Washington and the Dioceses of Dallas, Lincoln, Manchester, Madison and Providence.

[0740] (M.I.C.)—CONGREGATION OF MARIANS OF THE IMMACULATE CONCEPTION
(Congregatio Clericorum Marianorum sub titulo Immaculatae Conceptionis Beatae Mariae Virginis)
GENERAL MOTHERHOUSE: via Corsica no. 1, Rome, Italy. Very Rev. Adam Boniecki, M.I.C.; Very Rev. Vaclovas Aliulis, M.I.C., Vicar Gen.
AMERICAN PROVINCE OF ST. CASIMIR (1913): 6336 S. Kilbourn Ave., Chicago, IL 60629. Tel: 312-582-1666. Very Rev. Donald Petraitis, M.I.C., Prov.; Revs. Victor Rimselis, M.I.C.; Timothy Roth, M.I.C.; Boniface Vaisnoras, M.I.C.; Bro. Donald Schaefer, M.I.C., Prov. Treas.
Fathers 32; Seminarians 7; Brothers 2.
Parishes 6; High School 1; Community Houses 8.
Represented in the Archdioceses of Chicago and Milwaukee and in the Dioceses of Joliet, Norwich and Worcester. Also in Argentina.
ST. STANISLAUS KOSTKA PROVINCE: Eden Hill, Stockbridge, MA 01262-0951. Tel: 413-298-3931. Very Rev. Walter Dziordz, M.I.C., Prov. Supr. Councilors: Revs. Kazimierz Chwalek, M.I.C.; Seraphim Michalenko, M.I.C.; Mark Lamprich, M.I.C.; Bro. Andrew Maczynski, M.I.C., Dir. Marian Helpers Center.
Legal Holdings: *Marian Helpers Center Marian Scholasticate Divine Mercy International John Paul II Institute of Divine Mercy Shrine of Divine Mercy.*
Fathers 23; Brothers 7; Seminarians 7; Novices 3.
Properties owned, staffed or sponsored: 4 Community Houses; Novitiate; Filial House; 1 Residence.
Represented in the Archdioceses of Detroit and Washington and the Dioceses of Charlotte and Springfield. Also in Portugal.

[0750] (C.M.M.)—CONGREGATION OF MARIANNHILL MISSIONARIES, MARIANNHILL FATHERS AND BROTHERS
(Congregatio Missionariorum de Mariannhill)
GENERALATE: Via S. Giovanni Eudes 91, 00163, Rome, Italy. Very Rev. Yves LaFontaine, C.M.M., Supr. Gen.
AMERICAN-CANADIAN PROVINCE (1938): *Our Lady of Grace Monastery,* 23715 Ann Arbor Trail, Dearborn Hts., MI 48127. Tel: 313-274-2893. Revs. Aloysius Blonigen, C.M.M., American Reg.; Timothy Mock, C.M.M., Procurator.
Fathers 12; Brothers 4.
Legal Holdings: *Mariannhill Retreat Center,* Dearborn MI.
Represented in the Archdiocese of Detroit.

[0760] (S.M.)—SOCIETY OF MARY
(Marianists—Brothers of Mary)
(Societas Mariae—Marianistae)
GENERAL MOTHERHOUSE: Via Latina 22, 00179 Rome. Italy. Very Rev. David Fleming, S.M., Supr. Gen.
PROVINCE OF CINCINNATI (1849): *Marianist Provincialate,* 4435 E. Patterson Rd., Dayton, OH 45430-1095. Tel: 937-429-0794; Fax: 937-429-3195. Very Rev. James F. Fitz, S.M., Prov. Supr. Councillors: Rev. Bertrand A. Buby, S.M.; Bros. Joseph H. Kamis, S.M.; Ronald L. Overman; Thomas J. Pieper, S.M.
Legal Holdings or Titles: *Mount St. John, Bergamo Center, University of Dayton, Chaminade-Julienne High School, Marianist Mission,* Dayton OH, *Governor's Island,* Huntsville, OH, *Marianist Communities,* Cleveland, OH, Cincinnati, OH, Dayton, OH, Kalamazoo, MI, Pittsburgh, PA.
Fathers 60; Brothers 166; Brothers Perpetual Professed 146; Temporary Professed 20; Novices 11; Aspirants 13.
Properties owned, sponsored, or staffed: Universities 1; High Schools 5; Parishes 5; Apostolic Centers 1; Novitiates 2.
Represented in the Archdiocese of Cincinnati and in the Dioceses of Cleveland, Kalamazoo and Pittsburgh.
PROVINCE OF ST. LOUIS (1908): *Marianist Provincialate,* P.O. Box 23130, St. Louis, MO 63156. Tel: 314-367-0390; Fax: 314-361-3131. Rev. Timothy Dwyer, S.M., Prov. Supr.; Bros. Jerome Bommer, S.M., Asst. Prov.; Richard Dix, S.M., Temporalities; Rev. John Moder, S.M., Councillor.
Fathers 65; Brothers 185; Novices 20.
Members serve and staff: Parishes 6; University 1; High Schools 5; Retreat House 1; Missions in India & Mexico.
Properties owned: St. Mary's University, San Antonio, TX Central Catholic Marianist High School, San Antonio, TX Chaminade Preparatory, St. Louis, MO Vianney High School, St. Louis, MO Marianist Retreat & Conference Center, Eureka, MO.
Represented in the Archdioceses of New Orleans, St. Louis and San Antonio and in the Dioceses of Belleville, Fort Worth and Galveston-Houston.
PROVINCE OF THE PACIFIC (1948): *Marianist Provincial Residence,* 22825 San Juan Rd., Cupertino, CA 95014-3934. P.O. Box 1775, Cupertino, CA 95015-1775. Tel: 408-253-4841; Fax: 408-253-5280.
Legal Title: *Marianist Province of the Pacific, a Hawaii Corp;* Very Rev. Timothy Eden, S.M., Prov.; Bro. Gary Morris, S.M., Asst. Prov.; Rev. John McEnhill, S.M., Religious Life; Bro. John Haster, S.M., Temporalities.
Fathers 30; Brothers 91; Parishes 2; University 1; High Schools 4; Middle Schools 1.
Legal Holdings: *Marianist Community,* Santa Clara, CA, *Marianist Community,* San Jose, CA, *Marianist Center, Villa St. Joseph, Marianist Provincialate,* Cupertino, CA.
Represented in the Archdioceses of Los Angeles and San Francisco and in the Dioceses of Honolulu, Monterey and San Jose. Also in Korea.
PROVINCE OF NEW YORK (1961): *Marianist Provincial House,* 4301 Roland Ave., Baltimore, MD 21210. Tel: 410-366-1300. Bro. Stephen M. Glodek, S.M., Prov.; Rev. George J. Cerniglia, S.M., Asst. Prov. Councillors: Bros. Frank J. O'Donnell, S.M.; Francis M. Ouellette, S.M.; Rev. Theodore K. Cassidy, S.M.
Legal Titles & Holdings: Marianist Society, Inc. - A Maryland Corporation, Marianist Society of Floria, Inc. - A Florida Corporation, Marianist Provincial House, Baltimore, MD, *Marianist Community Residence,* Baltimore, MD, *Marianist Family Center,* Cape May Point, NJ, *Marianist Community Residence,* Vernon, CT, *Marianist Community Residence,* Hollywood, FL, *Chaminade/Madonna High School,* Hollywood, FL, *Mission Noell,* Villalba, PR, *Colegio San Jose,* Rio Piedras, PR.
Fathers 30; Brothers 60.
Properties owned, sponsored, or staffed: High Schools 2; Orphanage 1; Parishes 2; Apostolic Centers 3.
Represented in the Archdioceses of Baltimore, Boston, Miami, Philadelphia and the Dioceses of Brooklyn, Camden, Fort Wayne-South Bend, Hartford, Raleigh, Rockville Centre and Trenton. Also in the Archdiocese of San Juan and the Diocese of Ponce.
PROVINCE OF MERIBAH (1976): *Marianist Provincial Residence,* 240 Emory Rd., Mineola, NY 11501. Tel: 516-742-5555. Bro. George E. Endres, S.M., Prov.; Rev. Thomas A. Cardone, S.M., Asst. Prov. & Asst. for Rel. Life; Bro. Kenneth M. Hoagland, S.M., Asst. for Education; Rev. Philip K. Eichner, S.M., Asst. for Temporalities; Bro. Michael J. Gillen, S.M., Councillor; Rev. Francis T. Keenan, S.M., Councillor; Bro. Michael J. McAward, S.M., Councillor.
Legal Holdings: *Chaminade High School,* Mineola, NY, *Kellenberg Memorial High School,* Uniondale, NY.
Fathers 6; Brothers 37.
Properties owned, sponsored, or staffed: High Schools 2; Retreat Houses 2.

[0770] (F.M.S.)—THE MARIST BROTHERS
(Fratres Maristae a Scholis)
GENERALATE: Rome, Italy. Rev. Bro. Benito Arbues, F.M.S., Supr. Gen.; Rev. Bro. Sean D. Sammon, F.M.S., Vicar Gen.
PROVINCE OF ESOPUS (1959): *Provincial Office,* 1241 Kennedy Blvd., Bayonne, NJ 07002. Tel: 201-823-1115. Bros. John Klein, F.M.S., Prov.; Leo Shea, F.M.S., Asst. Prov. Councillors: Bros. Vincent Damian; John McDonnell; Robert Clark; Stephen Schlitte; John Venturella; Henry Sammon, F.M.S., Prov. Treas.; Michael Sheerin, F.M.S., Vocation Dir.
Brothers 147; Candidates in Formation 1.
Represented in the Archdioceses of Miami, Newark and New York and in the Dioceses of Brooklyn, Brownsville, Corpus Christi, Houma-Thibodaux, Rockville Centre, Savannah and Wheeling-Charleston.
POUGHKEEPSIE PROVINCE (1959): *Provincial Administration,* 26 First Ave., Pelham, NY 10803. Tel: 914-738-0740. Bros. Patrick Mcnamara, F.M.S., Prov.; Dermot Healy, F.M.S., Vice Prov.; Henry Sammon, F.M.S., Treas.; Hugh Turley, F.M.S., Devel.; Patrick Tyrrell, F.M.S., Dir. Marist Foreign Missions. Councillors: Bros. Vito Aresto, F.M.S.; Richard Carey, F.M.S.; Dennis Dunne, F.M.S.
Brothers 119.
High Schools 8; Community Houses 19; Junior High School 1; Two community schools located in Japan.
Represented in the Archdioceses of Boston, Chicago, Miami and New York and in the Diocese of Houma-Thibodaux and Wheeling-Charleston.

[0780] (S.M.)—MARIST FATHERS
(Societas Mariae)

General Motherhouse: via Alessandro Poerio 63, Rome, 00152. Italy. Very Rev. Joaquin Fernandez, S.M., Supr. Gen.; Rev. John Crispin, S.M., Treas. Gen., The first Marist foundation in the United States was in 1863, St. Michael's in Convent, Louisiana. The first Marist Province in the United States was established in 1889 under the name of American Province. This Province was subdivided in 1924 into the Washington Province and the Boston Province; On January 1, 1962, the San Francisco Province was established.

Washington Province (1924): 815 Varnum St., N.E., Washington, DC 20017-2199. Tel: 202-529-4800. Very Rev. William F. Rowland, S.M., Prov.; Revs. James F. McGoldrick, S.M., Vicar Prov.; H. Joseph Wilhelm, S.M., Prov. Treas.; Timothy F. Sugrue, S.M., Business Mgr. Prov. Council: Revs. Thomas E. Ellerman, S.M.; Edwin L. Keel, S.M.; John M. Ulrich, S.M., Dir. Vocations; Peter R. Blanchard, S.M., Dir. Third Order of Mary; Timothy F. Sugrue, S.M., Mission Promoter.

Legal Holdings & Titles: Marist Society, Inc., Marist College, Marist Provincial House, Washington, DC, *Marist Society of OH,* Cleveland, OH, *Marist Society of LA, Marist Community,* New Orleans, LA, *Marist Society of PA,* Philadelphia, PA.

Fathers 86; Brothers 9; Scholastics 1.

Properties owned, sponsored, or staffed: Community Houses 4; Parishes 14; Diocesan Seminaries/Houses of Study and High School.

Represented in the Archdioceses of Atlanta, Chicago, US Military Services, New Orleans, New York, Philadelphia, St. Paul-Minneapolis, Washington and the Dioceses of Austin, Baton Rouge, Brooklyn, Brownsville, Cleveland, Lubbock, Orlando St. Petersburg, Savannah and Wheeling-Charleston.

Boston Province (Marist Fathers) (1924): *Marist Provincial House,* 27 Isabella St., Boston, MA 02116-5216. Tel: 617-426-5297; Fax: 617-482-1570. Very Rev. Joseph Hindelang, S.M., Prov.; Rev. Michael McElhinny, S.M., Vicar Prov. Prov. Council: Revs. Ronald Saunders, S.M.; Leon Olszamowski, S.M.; Gerard Demers, S.M.; Albert DiIanni, S.M.; Revs. Raymond Arsenault, S.M., Prov. Treas.; Robert Graham, S.M., Prov. Archivist; J. Armand Robichaud, S.M., Marist Missions; Albert Dilanni, S.M., Prov. Dir. of Third Order of Mary & Vocation Dir.; Gerard Caron, S.M., Dir. Paratours Inc. & Lourdes Center. Tel: 617-247-2533.

Legal Title: *Marist Fathers of Boston, Marist Fathers of Detroit, Inc., Marist Fathers of New York.*

Fathers 75; Brothers 6; Seminarians 3.

Properties owned, sponsored, or staffed: Community Houses 7; Parishes 10; High Schools 2; Retreat House 1.

Represented in the Archdioceses of Anchorage, Boston, Hartford, Detroit and the Dioceses of Brooklyn, Burlington, Honolulu, Portland (ME), Rapid City, and St. Petersburg.

Third Order of Mary: Envisioned as the Third or Lay Branch of the Society of Mary by its Founder, Father Jean-Claude Colin. The Third Order of Mary was approved in 1850 for lay men and women, as well as for members of the Diocesan Clergy. The rule was written by Rev. Jean Claude Colin, founder of the Society of Mary, the Marist Fathers and Brothers. It was approved by the Holy See in 1836. There are confraternities throughout the world. New styles of confraternities are being formed to help evangelize the world after the spirit of Jesus and Mary. Information concerning this Third Order of Mary or the Marist Laity Movement may be obtained from: Third Order of Mary-Marist Laity, 518 Pleasant St., Framingham, MA 01701-2898. Tel: 508-875-6075; 879-1620; Fax: 508-879-0719. Rev. Albert Dilanni, S.M., Dir.

San Francisco Western Province (1962): *Marist Center Provincial House,* 625 Pine St., San Francisco, CA 94108-3210. Tel: 415-398-3543. Very Rev. John F. McGregor, S.M., Prov.; Very Rev. Dennis J. Steik, S.M., Vicar Prov.; Revs. Etienne Siffert, S.M., Archivist; Francis Springer, S.M., Mission Promoter; Thomas Hamilton, S.M., Prov. Councillor, Vocation Dir. & Formation Dir. Prov. Councillors: Revs. Dennis Steik, S.M.; Bruce Lery, S.M.; James Pratt, S.M.; Rene Iturbe, S.M.; Rev. Bro. Ernest Morasci, S.M.; Rev. Michael Galinada, S.M., Vocation Dir.

Fathers 26; Brothers 6; Deacon 1; Students in Theology 4.

Properties owned, sponsored, or staffed: Parishes 5; Preparatory Seminaries 1.

Represented in the Archdioceses of Portland (OR) and the Dioceses of Boise, Honolulu, Oakland, and Monterey.

[0785] (C.M.L.M.)—THE CONGREGATION OF MARONITE LEBANESE MISSIONARIES

Founded at the Monastery of Kreim-Ghosta (Mountain of Lebanon), in the year 1865. Established in the United States March of 1991: Agreement between Archbishop Zayek of the Diocese of St. Maron and the Congregation to serve the parishes of San Antonio, Dallas and Houston.

U.S. Foundation: Saint George Maronite Church, 6070 Babcock Rd., San Antonio, TX 78240. Tel: 210-690-9569; Fax: 210-690-5093. Rev. Abdallah Zaidan, C.M.L.M.; Supr.

Bishops 2; Priests 62; Brothers 1; Seminarians 26; Novices 5; Postulants 12.

Represented in the Dioceses of Our Lady of Lebanon.

[0790] (O.Mar.)—CONGREGATION OF MARONITE MONKS

Monastery of the Most Holy Trinity: 67 Dugway Rd., Petersham, MA 01366-0605. Tel: 508-724-3347. Rt. Rev. William J. Driscoll, O. Mar., Supr.; Revs. Giles R. Goyette, O. Mar., 1st Councillor; Michael Cermak, O. Mar., Asst. Supr.

Priests 12; Brothers 4.

Monastery of the Holy Nativity: (a dependency of Holy Trinity Monastery, Petersham, MA) Bethlehem, SD 57708. Tel: 606-787-4606. Rev. Louis Marie Dauphinais, O.Mar., Supr.

Priests 4; Brothers 1.

Represented in the Diocese of St. Maron, Brooklyn.

[0800] (M.M.)—MARYKNOLL

Catholic Foreign Mission Society of America, Inc.

U.S. Foundation (1911): *Maryknoll Society Center & Admin. Offices,* Maryknoll, NY 10545-0305. Tel: 914-941-7590; Fax: 914-762-0316. Revs. Raymond J. Finch, M.M., Supr. Gen.; Jeremiah R. Burr, M.M., Vicar Gen. Assts. General: Revs. Thomas P. Henehan, M.M.; Michael J. Snyder, M.M.; Bro. Wayne J. Fitzpatrick, M.M.

Legal Title: *Catholic Foreign Mission Society of America Incorporated.*

Training Center: Maryknoll Society Center, Maryknoll, NY 10545.

Houses in Archdioceses and Dioceses

Boston: Maryknoll Fathers and Brothers, 80 Emerson Rd., East Walpole, MA 02032. Tel: 508-668-6831; Fax: 508-660-0252.

Buffalo: Maryknoll Fathers and Brothers, 71 Jewett Pkwy., Buffalo, NY 14214-2396. Tel: 716-834-6065.

Chicago: Maryknoll Fathers and Brothers, 3600 Seeley Ave., Chicago, IL 60609-1148. Tel: 312-927-9257; Fax: 312-927-7305.

Seminary Residence: 5508 S. Cornell Ave., Chicago, IL 60637. Tel: 312-288-3143; Fax: 312-288-3950.

Cincinnati: Maryknoll Fathers and Brothers, 104 Elm Ave. (Wyoming), Cincinnati, OH 45215. Tel: 513-761-5888.

Cleveland: Maryknoll Fathers and Brothers, 10309 Edgewater Dr., Cleveland, OH 44102. Tel: 216-651-2121; Fax: 216-651-8242.

Denver: Maryknoll Fathers and Brothers, 4460 Federal Blvd., Denver, CO 80211. Tel: 303-455-5669; Fax: 303-455-5753.

Detroit: Maryknoll Fathers and Brothers, 12709 Pembroke Ave., Detroit, MI 48235. Tel: 313-342-0330.

Galveston-Houston: Maryknoll Fathers and Brothers, 2360 Rice Blvd., Houston, TX 77005. Tel: 713-529-1912; Fax: 713-529-0372.

Newark: Maryknoll Fathers and Brothers, 64 Fielding Ct., South Orange, NJ 07079. Tel: 201-761-5883.

New York: Maryknoll Fathers and Brothers, 121 E. 39th St., New York, NY 10016. Tel: 212-697-4470.

Los Angeles: Maryknoll Fathers and Brothers, 745 W. Adams Blvd., Los Angeles, CA 90007. Tel: 213-747-9676; Fax: 213-747-8923.

Philadelphia: Maryknoll Fathers and Brothers, 6367 Overbrook Ave., Philadelphia, PA 19151. Tel: 215-477-5892; Fax: 215-477-3088.

Rockville Centre: Maryknoll Fathers and Brothers, 813 Myrna Dr., West Hempstead, NY 11552. Tel: 516-489-7799.

St. Augustine: Maryknoll Fathers and Brothers, 2243 Saragossa Ave., Jacksonville, FL 32217-2685. Tel: 904-739-1112.

St. Louis: Maryknoll Fathers and Brothers, 4542 W. Pine Blvd., St. Louis, MO 63108. Tel: 314-361-7729; Fax: 314-361-0718.

St. Paul: Maryknoll Fathers and Brothers, 10345 Portland Ave. S., Minneapolis, MN 55420. Tel: 612-884-7743; Fax: 612-884-7744.

San Francisco: Maryknoll Fathers and Brothers, 2555 Webster St., San Francisco, CA 94115. Tel: 415-921-1100; Fax: 415-775-8261; *Casa Maryknoll,* 453 Miller Ave., So. San Francisco, CA 94080. Tel: 415-952-5500; Fax: 415-775-8261.

San Jose: Maryknoll Residence, 23000 Cristo Rey Dr., Los Altos, CA 94024. Tel: 415-967-3822.

Seattle: Maryknoll Fathers and Brothers, 958 16th Ave., E., Seattle, WA 98112. Tel: 206-322-8831; Fax: 206-324-6909.

Washington: Maryknoll Fathers and Brothers, 4834 16th St., N.W., Washington, DC 20011. Tel: 202-726-4252; 726-4281; Fax: 207-726-0466.

Priests 559; Students in Theology 15; Brothers 71; Priests Associates 8.

Properties owned or sponsored: Major Society Center; House of Formation; U.S. Community Houses 25.

Represented in the Archdioceses of Boston, Chicago, Cincinnati, Denver, Detroit, Los Angeles, New Orleans, New York, Newark, Philadelphia, St. Louis, St. Paul-Minneapolis, San Francisco, Seattle and Washington and in the Dioceses of Buffalo, Cleveland, Galveston-Houston and San Jose.

[0810] (F.M.M.)—BROTHERS OF MERCY

General Motherhouse: 5430 Montabaur, West Germany. Bro. Ferdinand Frink, Supr. Gen.

American Province: 4520 Ransom Rd., Clarence, NY 14031. Tel: 716-759-8341. Bros. Jude Holzfoerster, F.M.M., Prov. Supr. Councillors: Bros. Edward Lewis; Christopher Sullivan.

Brothers 15; Candidate 2.

Legal Holdings or Titles: *Brothers of Mercy Nursing Home Co., Inc., Brothers of Mercy Housing Co., Inc., Brothers of Mercy Sacred Heart Home, Inc.*

Represented in the Diocese of Buffalo.

[0820] (C.P.M.)—CONGREGATION OF THE FATHERS OF MERCY

(Congregatio Presbyterorum a Misericordia)

Generalate and Novitiate (1808): South Union, KY 42283. Tel: 502-542-4146. Very Rev. John O'Brien, C.P.M., Supr. Gen. Consultors: Revs. John Molloy, C.P.M.; William Casey, C.P.M.; David Wilton, C.P.M.; Albert Heidecke, C.P.M.

Priests 12; Novices 3; Students 12.

Represented in the Archdioceses of Louisville and New York and in the Dioceses of Lafayette (LA), and Owensboro.

[0825] M.S.S.—MISSIONARIES OF THE BLESSED SACRAMENT

Missionaries of the Blessed Sacrament

Regional Headquarters: P.O. Box 4337, Corpus Christi, TX 78469. Tel: 512-881-5025; Fax: 512-883-1581. Revs. Martin V. Lucia, M.S.S., Supr.

Fathers 4.

Ministries in Special Apostolate: Promotion of perpetual Eucaristic adoration.

Represented in the Dioceses of Alexandria, Baton Rouge, Corpus Christi, Lafayette, and Lake Charles.

[0830] (M.H.M.)—MILL HILL MISSIONARIES

St. Joseph's Missionary Society of Mill Hill

International Headquarters: St. Joseph's College, Mill Hill, London NW7 4JX, England. Very Rev. Maurice McGill, M.H.M., Supr. Gen.

American Headquarters: Mill Hill Missionaries, 222 W. Hartsdale Ave., Hartsdale, NY 10530-1667. Tel: 914-682-0645; Fax: 914-682-0862. Very Rev. Terence J. Lee, M.H.M., Reg. Rep.

Fathers 17; Brothers 2; Associates 1.

Represented in the Archdioceses of Los Angeles & New York.

[0835] (O.M.)—MINIM FATHERS

General Motherhouse: Via S. Andrea delle Fratte, 1, 00184, Rome, Italy. Tel: 011-39-6-678-0407; Fax: 011-39-6-678-0752. Very Rev. Giuseppe Morosini, O.M., Supr. Gen.

North American Delegation (1970): 3431 Portola Ave., Los Angeles, CA 90032. Tel: 213-223-1101. Friar Constantino Mandarino, O.M., Delegate Gen.

Legal Title: *Minim Fathers.*

Priests 3.

Vocation Center: 6043 N. Barranca Ave., Azusa, CA 91702.

Represented in the Archdiocese of Los Angeles.

[0840] (S.T.)—MISSIONARY SERVANTS OF THE MOST HOLY TRINITY

(Missionarii Servi Sanctissimae Trinitatis)
(Trinity Missions)

Generalate-Missionary Servants of the Most Holy Trinity: 1215 N. Scott St., Arlington, VA 22209-3097. Tel: 703-276-8646; Fax: 703-522-2656. Revs. Dominigo Rodriguez, S.T., Gen. Custodian; Leon Buggy, S.T., Vicar Gen.; Revs. John P. McSpiritt, S.T., Gen. Councillor & Vicar for Personnel; Jesus Rivera, S.T., Gen. Councillor & Vicar for Spanish-speaking Personnel &, Apostolates; Bros. Hilary Mettes, S.T., Sec. Gen.; Alexis Norton, S.T., Treas. Gen.; Jordan Baxter, S.T., Asst. Treas. Gen.; Paul Michalenko, S.T., Gen. Councillor & Vicar for Apostolates.

Legal Title: *Missionary Servants of The Most Holy Trinity (a.k.a) Trinity Missions, Missionary Servants Charitable Trust, Father Judge Charitable Trust.*
Priests 112; Brothers 34; Student Brothers 10; Novices 12; Candidates 46.
Ministry in the following areas: Missionary Cenacles; Parishes; Missions; Stations and Specialized Apostolates; Lay Apostolate Secretariat; Halfway House; Auxiliary Military Chaplaincies; Counseling Centers; Hospitals and Rest Home Chaplains; AA Programs; Protective Institutions; Prison Chaplains; V.A. Chaplains; Community Centers; Elementary Schools.
Properties owned and or sponsored: Generalate, Arlington, VA; Parish, rectory and school, Holy Trinity, AL; Former Retreat Center, New Orleans, LA, Philadelphia, PA, Rio Piedras, PR; Seminary and Fund Raising Office Buildings, Silver Spring, MD; School Buildings, Camden, MS; St. Joseph Shrine, Stirling, NJ; Trinity Ministries Center, Stirling, NJ; Former minor seminary building, Monroe, VA; Residences, Winona Lake, PA, Harpers Ferry, WV, Sound Beach, NY; Residence Senior Ministry Residence, Adelphi, MD; Residence Post-Novitiate Formation House, Adelphi, MD; Holy Trinity Missionary Cenacle, University Park, MD.
Represented in the Archdioceses of Boston, Chicago, Indianapolis, Los Angeles, Military Services-USA, Mobile, Newark, New Orleans, Philadelphia, St. Paul-Minneapolis and Washington and in the Dioceses of Arlington, Biloxi, Birmingham, Boise, Cleveland, Jackson, Lake Charles, Orange, Paterson, Richmond, St. Augustine, San Diego, Savannah, Tucson and Wheeling-Charleston. Also in Mexico, Puerto Rico and Costa Rica.

[0850] (M.AFR.)—MISSIONARIES OF AFRICA

(Societas Missionariorum Africae)

GENERALATE: 269 via Aurelia, C.P. 9078, I-00165, Rome, Italy. Rev. Gotthard Rosner, M.Afr., Supr. Gen.
U.S. PROVINCIAL HEADQUARTERS: 1624 21st St., N.W., Washington, DC 20009-1055. Tel: 202-232-5154; Fax: 202-332-8640. Revs. William Moroney, M.Afr., Prov.; David J. Goergen, M.Afr., Treas.; Roger L. Bisson, M.Afr., Dir. of Planned Giving Dept.; William Dyer, M.Afr., Justice & Peace.
Priests 29; Brothers 2.
Represented in the Archdioceses of Chicago, Los Angeles and Washington, and in the Diocese of St. Petersburg.

[0853] (M.S.C.)—MISSIONARY SERVANTS OF CHRIST

Founded in the United States in 1979 by Bro. Edwin Baker.
HEADQUARTERS AND NOVITIATE: St. Anthony in the Hills, 6730 Limestone Rd., Avondale, PA 19311. Tel: 610-268-2747; Fax: 610-268-2747. Bro. Edwin Baker, M.S.C., Supr.
Professed Brothers 8; Novices 3; Postulants 3.
Represented in the Diocese of Wilmington.

[0854] (M.S.P.)—MISSIONARY SOCIETY OF ST. PAUL OF NIGERIA

GENERALATE: Gwagwalada P.O. Box 23, Abuja, Nigeria. Very Rev. Felix Elosi, M.S.P., Supr. Gen.
U.S. REGION: Missionary Society of St. Paul, Inc., 12606 Crosby-Lynchburg Rd., P.O. Box 3200, Barrette Station, TX 77532-2200. Tel: 713-328-8931; Fax: 713-328-7306. Rev. Paul N. Ofoha, M.S.P., Local Supr.
Universal number of Priests 104; Priests in U.S. 17.
Legal Title: Missionary Society of St. Paul, Inc., Barrette Station, TX.
Represented in the Diocese of Galveston-Houston.

[0855] (F.M.M.)—MISSIONARY FRATERNITY OF MARY

GENERAL HEADQUARTERS: 6A Calle 48-98, Zona 7-Apartado Postal 623-I, Zona 7, Guatemala, Central America. Rev. Msgr. Eduardo Aguirre-Oestmann, General Moderator.
U.S. FOUNDATION (1991): 340 Pine St., Seaford, DE 19973. Tel: 302-629-5705; Fax: 302-629-7403. Revs. Ruben A. Soto, F.M.M., U.S. Regional Vicar; Juan Vicente Hidalgo, F.M.M.
Represented in the Archdiocese of Miami and in the Dioceses of Beaumont, TX and Wilmington, De.

[0860] (C.I.C.M.)—MISSIONHURST CONGREGATION OF THE IMMACULATE HEART OF MARY

(Congregatio Immaculati Cordis Mariae)
Foreign and home missions

GENERAL MOTHERHOUSE: Casa Generalizia C.I.C.M., Via S. Giovanni Eudes, 95, 00163, Roma, Italy. Very Rev. Jacques Thomas, C.I.C.M., Supr. Gen.
U.S. PROVINCE (1946): *Missionhurst,* 4651 N. 25th St., Arlington, VA 22207. Tel: 703-528-3800; Fax: 703-528-5355. Rev. Joseph Lapauw, C.I.C.M., Prov. Supr.
Legal Title: *American I.H.M. Province, Inc., Immaculate Heart Missions, Inc., Missionhurst, Inc.*
Fathers 56; Brothers 9.
Ministries in Parishes and Hospital Pastoral Work.
Represented in the Archdioceses of Detroit, Hartford, New York, Philadelphia and San Antonio and in the Dioceses of Arlington, Brooklyn and Brownsville.

[0870] (S.M.M.)—MONTFORT MISSIONARIES

(Missionaries of the Company of Mary)
(Societas Mariae Montfortana)

GENERALATE: Viale Dei Monfortani 65, Rome, 12. Italy. Very Rev. William J. Considine, S.M.M.
UNITED STATES PROVINCE (1948): *Montfort Missionaries,* 101-18 104th St., Ozone Park, NY 11416. Tel: 718-849-5885; Fax: 718-849-7518. Very Rev. Gerald J. Fitzsimmons, S.M.M. Counselors: Revs. Richard Schebera, S.M.M.; Donald LaSalle, S.M.M.; Eugene Lynch, S.M.M.; Matthew Considine, S.M.M.
Fathers 32; Brothers 4.
Parishes 3; Community Houses 6.
Represented in the Archdioceses of Hartford, St. Louis and Washington and in the Dioceses of Brooklyn, Fall River and Rockville Centre.

[0895] (O.Ss.S.)—BRIGITTINE MONKS

(The Order of the Most Holy Savior)

MONASTERY OF OUR LADY OF CONSOLATION: 23300 Walker Ln., Amity, OR 97101. Tel: 503-835-8080; Fax: 503-835-9662. Bro. Benedict Kirby, O.Ss.S., Prior.
Professed Monks 13; Novices 2.
Represented in the Archdiocese of Portland in Oregon.

[0897] (M.E.P.)—PARIS FOREIGN MISSION SOCIETY

(Societas Parisiensis Missionum Ad Exteros)
Society of secular priests, without vows, of Pontifical Right

HEADQUARTERS: 128 Rue du Bac, Paris, France. Very Rev. Raymond Rossignol, Supr. Gen.; Rev. Jean-Baptiste Etcharren.
U.S. ESTABLISHMENT: Paris Foreign Mission Society, 930 Ashbury St., San Francisco, CA 94117. Tel: 415-664-6747. Rev. Jacques R. Didier, M.E.P., Dir.
Legal Title: *American Auxiliary of Paris Foreign Missions, Inc.*
Priests 3.
Represented in the Archdiocese of San Francisco.

[0900] (O. PRAEM.)—CANONS REGULAR OF PREMONTRE

(Norbertines, Order of St. Norbert, Premonstratensians)
(Ordo Canonicorum Regularium Praemonstratensium)

Founded in France in the 12th century. First foundation in the United States in 1893.
ABBOT GENERAL: Most Rev. Hermenegild J. Noyens, O.Praem, Norbertine Generalate, 27 Viale Giotto, 00153, Rome, Italy. Tel: 011-39-6-57-46-979; 011-39-6-57-42-397; Fax: 011-39-6-574-0241.
UNITED STATES: St. Norbert Abbey - Eugene E. Gries, O.Praem., 1016 N. Broadway, De Pere, WI 54115-2697. Tel: 414-337-4300; Fax: 414-337-4328; *St. Norbert Abbey, Ministry and Life Center,* 1016 N. Broadway, De Pere, WI 54115-2697. Tel: 414-337-4315. Rt. Rev. E. Thomas De Wane, O.Praem., Abbot; Rt. Rev. Sylvester M. Killeen, O.Praem., Abbot Emeritus; Rt. Rev. Jerome G. Tremel, O.Praem.; Rt. Rev. Benjamin T. Mackin, O.Praem., Abbot Emeritus; Very Rev. Eugene E. Gries, O.Praem., Prior; Revs. James T. Baraniak, O.Praem., Vocation Coord.; Robert K. Finnegan, O.Praem., Provisor/Sec.-Treas.; Anthony J. Wieczorek, O.Praem.
Legal Title: *The Premonstratensian Fathers, NORBERT & CO., a nominee of The Premonstratensian Fathers, Norbertine Fathers, St. Norbert Abbey, Inc., The Walnut Markets, Inc., Los Amigos del Peru, Inc., Norbertine Generalate, Inc.*
Fathers 85; Seminarians 9; Brothers 6.
Properties owned, staffed, or sponsored: Dependent Priories 4; House of Studies 1; Colleges 1; Chaplaincies 5; Parishes 12.
Represented in the Archdioceses of Boston, Chicago, Military Services for the U.S.A., and Santa Fe and in the Dioceses of Green Bay, Jackson, Madison and Providence. Also in Peru.
DAYLESFORD ABBEY: Norbertine Fathers and Brothers Canonry, 220 S. Valley Rd., Paoli, PA 19301-1900. Tel: 610-647-2530. Rt. Rev. Jerome G. Tremel, O.Praem., Abbot/Admin.; Very Rev. Robert F. Kelly, O.Praem., Prior; Revs. Theodore J. Antry, O.Praem, Vocation Dir.; Robert F. Kelly, O.Praem., Master of Novices; Edward J. Smith, O.Praem., Sec.- Treas.
Legal Title: *Norbertine Fathers of Pa., Inc.*
Fathers 47; Brothers 3; Seminarians 1; Novice 1.
Properties owned, staffed, or sponsored: Chaplaincies 1; Dependent Priories 2; Seminary; Parishes 6.
Represented in the Archdioceses of Baltimore, Philadelphia, Santa Fe and Washington and the Dioceses of Harrisburg, Fort Wayne-South Bend and Wilmington. Also in Peru.
ST. MICHAEL'S ABBEY: 19292 El Toro Rd., Silverado, CA 92676. Tel: 714-858-0222; Fax: 714-858-4583.
Legal Title: *The Norbertine Fathers of Orange, Inc.;* Rt. Rev. Eugene J. Hayes, O.Praem., Abbot; Very Rev. Hugh Barbour, O.Praem., Prior; Revs. John Caronan, O.Praem., Treas.; Werenfried van Straaten, O.Praem., Germany.
Pious Association (Aid to the Church in Need, Inc.), P.O. Box 819, El Toro, CA 92630. Tel: 714-858-0222.
Priests 41; Deacons 1; Clerics 10; Postulants 4; Novices 3.
Properties owned: St. Michael's College Preparatory High School, Orange, CA Summer Camp, Orange, CA.
Represented in the Archdiocese of Los Angeles and in the Diocese of Orange.

[0910] (O.M.I.)—OBLATES OF MARY IMMACULATE

GENERAL HOUSE: Oblati di Maria Immacolata, C.P. 9061, 00100, Roma-Aurelio-Italy; Most Rev. Marcello Zago, O.M.I., Supr Gen.; Very Rev. Daniel Corijn, O.M.I., Vicar Gen.
U.S. CONSULATE: 290 Lenox Ave., Oakland, CA 94610; Fax: 510-452-3421. Rev. Ronald Carignan, O.M.I., General Councillor.
Legal Title: *Western Oblates Support Trust Fund, Oblate Fathers Western Province, Inc.*
SOUTHERN U.S. PROVINCE (1904): *Provincial Admin. Office,* 7711 Madonna Dr., San Antonio, TX 78216-6696. Tel: 512-349-1475. Very Rev. Eugene Canas, O.M.I., Prov. Admin.; Rev. Charles Banks, O.M.I., Vicar Prov.; Revs. Richard Houlahan, O.M.I.; F. Kelly Nemeck, O.M.I.; Robert Wright, O.M.I., Prov. Archivist; Jerome Burnet, O.M.I., Bursar.
Fathers 138; Brothers 5; Scholastics 18.
Properties owned, staffed, or sponsored: Seminaries; Retreat Centers; Religious Residences & Houses.
Represented in the Archdioceses of New Orleans, San Antonio and Washington and in the Dioceses of Austin, Brownsville, Corpus Christi, Galveston-Houston, Juneau, San Angelo, Springfield (IL) and Tucson. Also in Zambia.
EASTERN AMERICAN PROVINCE (1883): *Our Lady of Hope,* 391 Michigan Ave., N.E., Box 29152, Washington, DC 20017. Revs. William Sheehan, O.M.I., Prov.; William O'Donnell, O.M.I., Vicar Prov. Councillors: Revs. Henry Lemoncelli, O.M.I.; Stephen Conserva, O.M.I.; Thomas Coughlin, O.M.I.; James Fee, O.M.I.; John Madigan, O.M.I.
Fathers 118; Brothers 9; Professed Clerics 10.
Staff and-or serve: Parishes 23; Prisons 1; Hospitals 2; Community Houses 5; Scholasticate 1; Novitiate 1; Pre-Novitiate 1.
Represented in the Archdioceses of Boston, Miami, New York and Washington and in the Dioceses of Buffalo, Columbus, Grand Rapids, Harrisburg, Juneau, Lexington, Palm Beach and Pensacola-Tallahassee. Also in Puerto Rico.
THE NORTHERN U.S. PROVINCE (ST. JOHN THE BAPTIST) (1921): 61 Burns Hill Rd., Hudson, NH 03051-4423. Tel: 603-883-3233; Fax: 603-883-6089. Very Rev. George G. Capen, O.M.I., Prov.; Rev. Charles Breault, O.M.I., Treas. Councillors: Revs. Roger E. Lamoureux, O.M.I.; Roger Couture, O.M.I.; Arthur Obin, O.M.I.; James Robichaud, O.M.I.
Legal Title: *Missionary Oblates of Mary Immaculate.*
Fathers 79; Scholastics (Theology) 1; Brothers 12.
Ministries in Parishes; Retreat Houses; Hospital Chaplaincies; Men's Correctional Institutions; Nursing Home Res. Chaplains; Religious Community Resident Chaplains; Special; Ministries; U.S. Military.
Legal Holdings: Oblate Provincial House, Hudson, NH, *Andre Garin Residence,* Lowell, MA, *St. Paul Center,* Augusta, ME, *Oblate Seminary Residence,* Brighton, MA, *Shrine of Our Lady of Grace,* Colebrook, NH, *Oblate Retreat House,* Hudson, NH, *Oblate Foreign Missions Office,* Lowell, MA, *Oblate Ministry Development Office,* Lowell, MA, *St. Joseph the Worker Shrine & Center,* Lowell, MA, *Ephpheta House,* Manville, RI, *Immaculata Retreat House,* Willimantic, CT, *St. Joseph Cemetery,* East Chelmsford, MA.
Represented in the Archdioceses of Boston, Miami, New Orleans, Washington and the Dioceses of

Manchester, Norwich, Oakland, Ogdensburg, Portland (ME), Providence, Richmond and Worcester. Also in Canada and French Polynesia.

CENTRAL U.S. PROVINCE (1924): 267 E. 8th St., St. Paul, MN 55101; Fax: 612-292-8769. Revs. David A. Kalert, O.M.I., Prov.; Thomas J. Singer, O.M.I., Vicar Prov. & Personnel Dir.; William P. Clark, O.M.I.; James F. Allen, O.M.I.; Louis B. Studer, O.M.I.; Joseph H. Hitpas, O.M.I.; William L. Johnson, O.M.I.; Robert F. Moobrugger, O.M.I., Treas.

Priests 122; Brothers 16; Scholastics 8; Novices 2; Post College Seminarians 2.

Ministries in Parishes; House of Study and Retreat Houses.

Represented in the Archdioceses of Chicago, St. Paul-Minneapolis and St. Louis and in the Dioceses of Belleville, Crookston, Duluth, Green Bay, Superior, Sioux Falls, Springfield-Cape Girardeau and Springfield (IL).

WESTERN PROVINCE (1953): 290 Lenox Ave., Oakland, CA 94610. Tel: 510-452-1550; Fax: 510-452-3421. Very Rev. David Ullrich, O.M.I., Prov.; Revs. Leo Dummer, O.M.I., Bursar; Richard Haslam, O.M.I.; William Antone, O.M.I.; Paul Waldie, O.M.I.; Thomas Rush, O.M.I.

Fathers 50; Scholastic Brothers 2; Brothers 2.

Legal Title: *Western Oblates Support Trust Fund, Oblate Fathers Western Province Inc.*

Ministries in Parishes; Missions; Retreat Houses; Chaplaincies.

Represented in the Archdioceses of Los Angeles, Portland (OR), Seattle and the Dioceses of Boise, Fresno, Monterey, Oakland and San Diego. Also in Mexico.

[0920] (O.S.F.S.)—OBLATES OF ST. FRANCIS DE SALES

(Congregatio Oblatorum Sancti Francisci Salesii)

GENERAL MOTHERHOUSE: Via Dandolo 49, Rome, Italy. In July 1966, the American Province divided into two provinces.

WILMINGTON-PHILADELPHIA PROVINCE (1906): 2200 Kentmere Pky., Box 1452, Wilmington, DE 19899. (Direct all communications to Box 1452, Wilmington, DE 19899; Very Rev. Joseph G. Morrissey, O.S.F.S., Prov. Councillors: Revs. Edward T. Fitzpatrick, O.S.F.S.; Francis W. Danella, O.S.F.S.; James J. Behan, O.S.F.S., Prov.; Thomas B. Curran, O.S.F.S. Provincial Staff: Revs. Edward T. Fitzpatrick, O.S.F.S., Dir. Personnel; Francis W. Danella, O.S.F.S., Asst. Prov.; Robert A. Mancini, O.S.F.S., Treas.; Richard R. De Lillio, O.S.F.S., Dir. Development; Joseph P. Jocco, O.S.F.S., Dir. Vocations; John J. Hurley, O.S.F.S., Dir. Missions; Nicholas R. Waseline, O.S.F.S., Formation Advisor.

Fathers 212; Scholastics 14; Brothers 26.

Properties owned, staffed, or sponsored: Parishes 23; Colleges 1; Scholasticates 1; Novitiates 1; High Schools 6; Retreat Houses 1; Armed Forces 3; Chaplaincies 20; Foreign Missions 10.

Properties owned: Provincial Residence, Wilmington, DE; Salesianum School, Wilmington, DE; DeSales House, Wilmington, DE; Center for New Life, Childs, MD; Oblate Novitiate, Wyndmoor, PA; Villa St. Joseph, Newfield, NJ; Oblate Residence, Cape May, NJ; Brisson Seminary, Center Valley, PA; DeSales Theological Center, Washington, DC; Deshairs House, Washington, DC.

Represented in the Archdioceses of Philadelphia and Washington and in Dioceses of Allentown, Arlington, Camden, Charlotte, Harrisburg, Providence, Raleigh, Richmond, Trenton, Venice and Wilmington.

TOLEDO-DETROIT PROVINCE (1966): 2056 Parkwood Ave., Toledo, OH 43620-1616. Tel: 419-243-5105; Fax: 419-243-8827. Very Rev. James F. Cryan, O.S.F.S., Prov.; Revs. John J. Loughran, O.S.F.S., Asst. Prov.; Richard E. Morse, O.S.F.S., Treas. Prov. Councillors: Revs. Richard E. Morse, O.S.F.S.; Ronald W. Olszewski, O.S.F.S.; Rev. Francis J. Gross, O.S.F.S., Oblate Mission Procurator, 259 4th St., Niagra Falls, NY 14303.

Legal Title: *Oblates of St. Francis de Sales, Inc.*

Priests 75; Brothers 14; Professed Scholastics 1.

Properties owned, staffed, or sponsored: Provincial Residence, Toledo, OH St. Francis de Sales High School, Toledo, OH Oblate Residence, Jackson, MI Oblate Residence, Toronto, Canada Oblate Residence, Lewiston, NY Oblate Residence, Livonia, MI Oblate Residence, Buffalo, NY.

Ministries in Parishes; Highschools; Chaplaincies; Armed forces; Senior Citizens Residence.

Represented in the Archdioceses of Detroit, Miami, Military Services, Oklahoma City and Philadelphia, and in the Dioceses of Buffalo, Erie, Lansing, Oakland, Saginaw, Salt Lake City, Stockton and Toledo. Also in Canada and the Virgin Islands.

[0930] (O.S.J.)—OBLATES OF ST. JOSEPH

(Congregatio Oblatorum S. Joseph)

Founded in Italy in 1878. Founder: Blessed Bishop Joseph Marello (1844-1895). Cause of Beatification introduced May 28, 1948. Beatified 1993. First foundation in U.S. in 1929.

Motherhouse: Corso Alfieri 384, Asti, Italy.

GENERAL HOUSE: Via Boccea, 364, Rome, Italy. Very Rev. VITO CALABRESE, O.S.J., Supr. Gen.; Very Rev. VITO ACCETTURA, O.S.J., Vicar Gen.; Very Rev. TARCISIO STRAMARE, O.S.J., Procurator Gen.

EASTERN PROVINCE: Rte. 315, R.R. 4, Box 14, Pittston, PA 18640; Fax: 717-654-8621. Rev. Mario S. Buttini, O.S.J., Prov. Councillors: Revs. Silvio Chini, O.S.J.; Paul J. Pavese, O.S.J.

Priests 12; Students 1.

Parishes 4; Community Houses 5; Houses of Studies 1.

Properties owned: St. Joseph's Oblate Seminary, Pittston, PA.

Represented in the Dioceses of Norwich and Scranton.

CALIFORNIA PROVINCE: 544 W. Cliff Dr., Santa Cruz, CA 95060. Tel: 408-457-1868; Fax: 408-457-1317. Rev. Larry Toschi, O.S.J., Prov. Councillors: Revs. Philip Massetti, O.S.J.; Arnold Ortiz, O.S.J.; Carlos Esquivel, O.S.J.; Brian Crawford, O.S.J.

Legal Title: *Oblates of St. Joseph.*

Priests 17; Brothers 4; Temporary Professed Clerical Student 2; Aspirants 6.

Parishes 4; Community Houses 6; Houses of Study 2; Shrines 1.

Properties owned: St. Joseph House of Studies, Berkeley, CA Mount St. Joseph Seminary, Loomis, CA Shrine of St. Joseph, Guardian of the Redeemer, Santa Cruz, CA Blessed Marello House of Studies, Oxnard CA St. Joseph's Villa, Soda Springs, CA.

Represented in the Archdiocese of Los Angeles and in the Dioceses of Fresno, Monterey and Sacramento.

[0940] (O.M.V.)—OBLATES OF THE VIRGIN MARY

Congregation of the Oblates of the Virgin Mary)
(Congregatio Oblatorum Beatae Mariae Virginis)

GENERALATE: Viale XXX Aprile, 17, 00153, Rome, Italy. Very Rev. Peter Gojuk, O.M.V., Rector Major.

ST. IGNATIUS PROVINCE: 2 Ipswich St., Boston, MA 02215-3607. Tel: 617-536-7471. Rev. Timothy Gallagher, O.M.V., Prov.

Priests in U.S. 36; Brothers 3.

Legal Holdings: *St. Clement's Eucharistic Shrine,* Boston, MA, *St. Joseph House of Studies,* Milton, MA, *St. Ignatius Province of the Oblates of the Virgin Mary, Inc.,* Boston, MA.

Ministries in Parishes; Hospital and Prison Chaplaincies; Retreats & Parish Missions; Retreat House; Novitiate; Community Houses; College Seminary Shrine Chaplaincies.

Represented in the Archdioceses of Boston and Los Angeles and in the Dioceses of Metuchen and Springfield. Also in Chile.

[0950] (C.O.)—ORATORIANS

(Confederatio Oratorii S. Philippi Nerii)

A Confederation of Autonomous Houses first founded in Rome, 1575

GENERAL CONFEDERATION: Confederazione dell'Oratorio S. Philippi Neri, Via S. Girolamo della Carita 63, 00186, Roma, Italia. Revs. Edoardo Cerrato, C.O., Procurator Gen.; Antonio Chavez Rios, C.O., Delegate of the Holy See, The Oratory, La Professa, Isabel La Catolica, 21 Apartado Postal 7113, Mexico, DF 06000.

THE ORATORY OF ROCK HILL: P.O. Box 11586, Rock Hill, SC 29731. Tel: 803-327-2097. Very Rev. Joseph Wahl, C.O., Father Provost.

Fathers 10; Brothers 4; Novices 2.

Represented in the Diocese of Charleston.

THE ORATORIAN COMMUNITY OF MONTEREY: P.O. Box 1688, Monterey, CA 93942. Tel: 408-373-0476. Very Rev. Peter C. Sanders, Provost & Major Supr.; Revs. Michael P. Drury, Vicar; Lidio Limon, Sec. & Assoc. Vocational Apostolate; Thomas A. Kieffer, Treas.

Total in community 4.

Oratorian Foundation Inc., Arizona, P.O. Box 241, Yarnell, AZ 85362. An outreach of the Oratorian Community in Monterey.

Represented in the Diocese of Monterey.

THE PITTSBURGH ORATORY: Congregation of the Oratory of St. Philip Neri, 4450 Bayard Street, Pittsburgh, PA 15213-1506. Tel: 412-681-3181. Very Rev. Bryan F. Summers, C.O., Provost; Revs. Drew P. Morgan, C.O., Vicar; David S. Abernethy, C.O., Treas.

Fathers 4; Deacons 1; Novices 1.

Represented in the Diocese of Pittsburgh.

THE ORATORY OF PHARR: P.O. Box II, Pharr, TX 78577-1235. Tel: 210-843-8217; Fax: 210-843-2946. Residence, end of S. Jackson Rd., FM 2061, near Hidalgo. Very Rev. Leo Francis Daniels, C.O., Provost; Rev. Jose Encarnacion Losoya, C.O., Sec. Treas.; Bro. Mario Aviles Campos, C.O., Assist. Sec.; Rev. David Garcia, C.O., In Residence; Very Rev. Antonio Rios, C.O., Delegate of the Holy See.

Properties owned: Casa Maria of the Oratory, Pharr, TX Oratory Academy-Academia Oratoriana, Pharr, TX Pharr Oratory of St. Philip Neri of Pontifical Right.

Ministries in Parish work; Services to the poor; promotion of Mexican-American cultural services.

Secular Oratory, Lay Institute founded by St. Philip Neri. Principal Work:.

Federacion Mexicana del Oratorio de San Felipi Neri, American Office, The Oratory, Rte. 1, Box 118, Pharr, TX 78577. Rev. Antonio Ortega, C.O., Natl. Procurator, Mexican Office, Oratorio de San Felipe Neri,, Apdo. Postal M-7852, C.P. 06000, Mexico, D.F.. Rev. Agustin Martinez, C.O., Natl. Sec., The Pharr Oratory is a member of the Mexican Federation of Oratories, and at present serves as the American office of all eleven houses.

Represented in the Diocese of Brownsville. Also in Mexico and Costa Rica.

THE ORATORY OF ST. PHILIP NERI: 109 Willoughby St., Brooklyn, NY 11201. Tel: 718-875-2096; Fax: 718-875-4678. Very Rev. Dennis M. Corrado, C.O., Provost.

Fathers 4; Brothers 2.

[0960] (F.S.R.)—BROTHERS OF THE CONGREGATION OF OUR LADY OF THE HOLY ROSARY

Founded in the United States in 1957.

General Motherhouse and Novitiate: 1725 S. McCarran Blvd., Reno, NV 89502. Tel: 702-358-6806. Bros. Matthew Cunningham, F.S.R., Supr.; Philip Napolitano, F.S.R., Asst. Supr.

Brothers 3.

Ministries in the field of Education and Pastoral Ministry.

Represented in the Diocese of Reno.

[0970] (O.de.M.)—ORDER OF OUR LADY OF MERCY

(Mercedarians Friars)
(Ordo de Beatae Mariae Virginis de Mercede)
(Founded in Barcelona, Spain on August 10, 1218)

GENERALATE: Curia Generalizia dei PP. Mercedari,, Via Monte Carmelo 3, 00166, Rome, Italy. Most Rev. Emilio Aguirre Herrera, O.de.M., Master Gen.

U.S. VICARIATE: St. Rocco Rectory, 3205 Fulton Rd., Cleveland, OH 44109. Tel: 216-961-8331. Rev. Marino Frascati, O.de.M., Vicar Prov.

Priests 16; Brothers 4; Clerics 4; Novices 2.

Properties owned: St. Raymond Nonnatus Novitiate, Le Roy, NY Monastery of Our Lady of Mercy, Philadelphia, PA Saint Peter Nolasco Residence, St. Petersburg, FL.

Represented in the Archdiocese of Philadelphia and in the Dioceses of Buffalo, Cleveland and St. Petersburg.

[0975] (S.O.L.T.)—SOCIETY OF OUR LADY OF THE MOST HOLY TRINITY

HEADQUARTERS: Casa San Jose, 109 W. Avenue F, P.O. Box 152, Robstown, TX 78380. Tel: 512-387-2754. Rev. James H. Flanagan, S.O.L.T., Gen. Priest Servant.

Priests 72; Deacons 3; Novices 21; Seminarians 81.

Pastoral Ministries: Community House; House of Study-Novitiate; Migrant Ministry.

Represented in the Archdioceses of Hartford and Santa Fe and in the Dioceses of Albany, Cheyenne, Corpus Christi, Gallup, Kansas City-St. Joseph, Lafayette, Norwich and Wheeling-Charleston.

[0980] (C.F.M.M.)—BROTHERS OF OUR LADY, MOTHER OF MERCY

(Congregatio Fratrum Beatae Mariae Virginis, Matris Misericordiae)

GENERALATE: Gasthuisring 54, 5041 DT, Tilburg, The Netherlands.

U.S. REGION: 2336 S. C St., Oxnard, CA 93033. Tel: 805-486-3692. Bro. C. W. Gresnigt, C.F.M.M., Reg. Supr.

Brothers 8.

Represented in the Archdiocese of Los Angeles.

[0990] (S.A.C.)—SOCIETY OF THE CATHOLIC APOSTOLATE

(Pallottines)

GENERALATE: Pallottines, Piazza S.V. Pallotti 204, 00186, Rome, Italy.

PROVINCE OF THE IMMACULATE CONCEPTION (EASTERN) (1953): P.O. Box 979, South Orange, NJ 07079. Tel: 201-762-2926. 204 Raymond Ave., South Orange,

NJ 07079. Very Rev. Peter T. Sticco, S.A.C., Prov.; Revs. Frank Amato, S.A.C., 1st Consultor; Frank Gaetano, S.A.C., Bursar. Consultors: Revs. Louis Micca, S.A.C.; Oreste Pandola, S.A.C.; Frank Gaetano, S.A.C.

Fathers 30; Professed Clerics 1; Professed Brothers 5.

Properties owned, sponsored, or staffed: Parishes 4; Seminary; High School; Novitiate; Shrine of St. Jude, Pallottine Center for Apostolic Causes.

Represented in the Archdioceses of Baltimore, Newark and Washington and in the Dioceses of Brooklyn and Camden.

Mother of God Province (1946): *Pallottine Father and Brothers, Inc.,* 5424 W. Blue Mound Rd., Milwaukee, WI 53208. Tel: 414-259-0688; Fax: 414-258-9314. Very Rev. Robert V. Carney, S.A.C., Prov.; Revs. Leon Martin, S.A.C., 1st Consultor; Harold J. Liebl, S.A.C., Consultor & Prov. Treas.; Francis Hueller, S.A.C., Consultor; Richard J. Gunderman, S.A.C., Consultor.

Fathers 20; Brothers 1.

Ministries in Parishes; Retreat House; Hospital Chaplaincies; High School.

Represented in the Archdiocese of Milwaukee and the Diocese of Fargo.

Irish Province (1909): Homestead, Sandyford Rd., Dundrum, Dublin 16, Republic of Ireland. Very Rev. William Hanly, S.A.C., Prov.

U.S. Foundation: 3352 4th St., P.O. Box 249, Wyandotte, MI 48192. Very Rev. Philip McNamara, S.A.C., Prov. Delegate.

Fathers 20.

Parishes 19; Missions 10.

Represented in the Archdiocese of Detroit and in the Diocese of Fort Worth, Lubbock and Reno-Las Vegas.

Queen of the Apostles Province (1909): Via Giuseppe Ferrari, 1-Rome, Italy. Very Rev. Gaetano Iann, S.A.C., Prov.

U.S. Foundation: Our Lady of Mt. Carmel Shrine and Church, 448 E. 116th St., New York, NY 10029. Tel: 212-534-0681. Very Rev. Terzo Vinci, S.A.C., Prov. Delegate.

Our Lady of Mt. Carmel, 70 Park Hill Ave., Yonkers, NY 10701.

Fathers 8.

Parishes 4.

Represented in the Archdiocese of New York and the Diocese of Albany and Pensacola-Tallahassee.

Infant Jesus Delegature of Christ The King Province: Mission House and Infant Jesus Shrine, 3452 Niagara Falls Blvd., North Tonawanda, NY 14120. Rev. Anthony Zemula, S.A.C., Supr. & Prov. Delegate, Motherhouse, Poznan, Poland; *Society of the Catholic Apostolate.*

Priests 11.

Represented in the Dioceses of Brooklyn and Buffalo.

[1000] (C.P.)—CONGREGATION OF THE PASSION

(Congregatio Passionis Jesu Christi)

Founded in Italy in 1720 by St. Paul of the Cross. First foundation in United States in 1853.

General Motherhouse: SS. Giovanni e Paolo Monastery, Rome, 00184. Italy. Most Rev. Jose A. Orbegozo, C.P., Supr. Gen.

Eastern Province, Province of St. Paul of the Cross (1852): *Province Pastoral Center,* 80 David St., South River, NJ 08882. Tel: 908-257-7177. Very Revs. Robert Joerger, C.P., Prov.; Lucian Clark, C.P., 1st Consultor; Paul Ruttle, C.P., 2nd Consultor; Richard Burke, C.P., 3rd Consultor; Terence Kristofak, C.P., 4th Consultor; Victor Hoagland, C.P., 5th Consultor; Paul Fagan, C.P., 6th Consultor; Rev. Dominic Papa, C.P., Dir., Office of Preaching Ministry.

Legal Title: *St. Paul's Benevolent, Educational and Missionary Institute of West Hoboken, New Jersey, Passionist Missions, Inc., Passionist Missionaries, Inc.*

Fathers 201; Professed Clerics 1; Brothers 31; Postulants 2.

Properties owned, sponsored, or staffed: Parishes 13; Community Houses 24; House of Study; Novitiate.

Represented in the Archdioceses of Atlanta, Baltimore, Boston, Hartford, Newark, New York and Philadelphia and in the Dioceses of Altoona-Johnstown, Brooklyn, Metuchen, Palm Beach, Pittsburgh, Raleigh, Rockville Centre, Scranton, Springfield (MA), Wheeling-Charleston and Worcester. Also in Canada.

Western Province, Province of the Holy Cross: Passionist Provincial Office, 5700 N. Harlem Ave., Chicago, IL 60631. Tel: 773-631-6336.

Legal Title: *Congregation of the Passion, Holy Cross Province;* Very Rev. Michael J. Stengel, C.P., Prov. Consultors: Revs. Michael Higgins, C.P., Assist. Prov.; Blaise Czaja, C.P., Prov. Consultor; Clemente Barron, C.P.; James Thoman, C.P., Consultor.

Fathers 124; Brothers 20.

Properties owned or sponsored: Passionist Provincial Office Stauros International Immaculate Conception Monastery Daneo Hall Passionist Community CTU Immaculate Conception Parish, Chicago, IL.

Represented in the Archdioceses of Chicago, Detroit, Los Angeles, Louisville, San Antonio and in the Dioceses of Birmingham, Galveston-Houston, Orlando and Sacramento.

[1010] (O.S.P.P.E.)—PAULINE FATHERS

(Ordo Sancti Pauli Primi Eremitae)

Founded in Hungary in the 13th Century. First foundation in the United States in 1953.

General Motherhouse: Ojcowie Paulini - Jasna Gora ul. Kordeckiego 2, 42-200, Czestochowa, Poland. Very Rev. Jan Nalaskowski, O.S.P.P.E., Supr. Gen.

American Province (1984): Beacon Hill, P.O. Box 2049, Ferry Rd., Doylestown, PA 18901. Tel: 215-345-0607; *Provincial Motherhouse - Monastery - Shrine of Our Lady of Czestochowa;* Very Rev. Zdzislaw Kikowski, O.S.P.P.E., Prov. Supr.; Revs. Stephen Wozniczka, Shrine Dir.; Jan Michalak, O.S.P.P.E., Sub-Prior.

Priests in U.S. 16; Brothers 4.

Represented in the Archdioceses of New York and Philadelphia and in the Diocese of Greensburg.

[1020] (S.S.P.)—PAULINE FATHERS AND BROTHERS

Society of St. Paul for the Apostolate of Communications

General Motherhouse: Via della Fanella 39, 00148, Rome, Italy. Very Rev. Silvio Pignotti, S.S.P., Supr. Gen.; Very Rev. Teofilo Perez, S.S.P., Vicar Gen.

New York Province (1932): 6746 Lake Shore Rd., Box 757, Derby, NY 14047. Tel: 716-947-5407. Very Rev. Jeffrey J. Mickler, S.S.P., Prov. Supr.; Very Rev. Anthony C. Warren, S.S.P., Vicar Prov.; Rev. Ignatius W. Staniszewski, S.S.P., Publishing Editor, *Alba House.* Tel: 718-761-0047. Rev. Timothy Chenevey, S.S.P., Editor, *Pastoral Life Magazine, Alba House.* Tel: 216-533-5503. Bro. Dismas Beique, S.S.P., Editor, *Alba House AV Communications.* Tel: 216-533-5503. Bro. Peter C. Lyne, S.S.P., Vocation Dir. Tel: 718-698-3698.

Priests 14; Brothers 26; Postulants 2.

Represented in the Archdioceses of Detroit and New York and in the Dioceses of Buffalo and Youngstown.

Los Angeles Province: 112 S. Herbert Ave., Los Angeles, CA 90063. Tel: 213-269-9814; 268-5010 (Bookstore); Fax: 213-268-4583. Revs. Gonzalo Ponce, S.S.P., Supr.; Gilberto Martinez, S.S.P., Vice Supr.; Valeriano Giachino, S.S.P.; Thomas Martinez, S.S.P.; Everardo Monroy, S.S.P.

Priests 5.

[1030] (C.S.P.)—PAULIST FATHERS

(Societas Missionaria a S. Paulo Apostolo)

Paulist Fathers Motherhouse (1858): 86-11 Midland Pkwy., Jamaica Estates, NY 11432. Tel: . Very Rev. Frank P. DeSiano, C.S.P., Pres.

Legal Title: *Missionary Society of St. Paul the Apostle in the State of New York.*

Fathers 205; Students in Major Seminary 13; Novices 4.

Properties owned or sponsored: Newman Campus Chaplaincies; Information Centers; Paulist Press; Paulist Radio-TV-Film Communications Svcs. Paulist National Catholic Evangelization Association; House of Study; Novitiate.

Represented in the Archdioceses of Boston, Chicago, Denver, Los Angeles, New York, Portland (OR), St. Paul-Minneapolis, San Francisco and Washington and in the Dioceses of Austin, Charleston, Columbus, Grand Rapids, Knoxville, Memphis, Oakland, Paterson, San Diego, Tucson and Wheeling-Charleston.

[1040] (SCH.P.)—PIARIST FATHERS

(Ordo Clericorum Regularum Pauperum Matris Dei Scholarum Piarum)

General Motherhouse: San Pantaleo, Piazza De Massimi, 4, Rome, Italy, 00186. Most Rev. Joseph M. Balcells, Sch.P., Supr. Gen.

U.S. Province (1975): *Devon Preparatory School,* 363 Valley Forge Rd., Devon, PA 19333. Tel: 215-688-7337; 688-6807. Very Rev. Richard S. Wyzykiewicz, Sch.P., Prov. Supr.; Rev. James J. Shea, Sch.P., Prov. Sec.

Legal Titles and Holdings: Piarist Fathers, Inc., Order of the Pious Schools, Inc., Piarist Fathers House of Studies, Washington, DC, *Piarist Fathers Residence,* Derby, NY, *Piarist Fathers Residence,* Martin, KY, *Devon Preparatory School,* Devon, PA.

Priests 22.

Represented in the Archdioceses of Miami, Philadelphia and Washington and the Dioceses of Buffalo, Lexington and Paterson.

New York-Puerto Rico Vice Province: Seminario Escolapio, P.O. Box 118, Playa Sta., Ponce, PR, 00734. Tel: 809-840-0610; Fax: 809-841-6861. Rev. Joseph Mateo, Sch.P., Vice Prov.

Priests 23; Cleric Students 2.

Houses 5; Parishes 3; High Schools 2; Schools 4.

Represented in the Archdioceses of New York and San Juan and the Diocese of Ponce Also, Calasanzian Fathers and Padres Escolapios de P.R.

California Provincial Vice Province: Piarist Fathers, 3951 Rogers St., Los Angeles, CA 90063. Tel: 213-261-4432; Fax: 213-266-0646. Rev. Antonio Tort, Sch.P., Vice Prov.

Properties owned, staffed, or sponsored: Parishes 5; Grammar Schools 2; House of Formation 3.

Priests 17; Novices 6; Prenovices 7; Seminarians 15.

Represented in the Archdiocese of Los Angeles.

[1050] (P.I.M.E.)—PONTIFICAL INSTITUTE FOR FOREIGN MISSIONS (P.I.M.E.), Inc.

General Motherhouse: Via F. D. Guerrazzi 11, Rome, Italy, 00152. Very Rev. Franco Cagnasso, P.I.M.E., Supr. Gen.

U.S. Region: 17330 Quincy Ave., Detroit, MI 48221. Tel: 313-342-4066; Fax: 313-342-6816. Very Rev. Bruno Piccolo, P.I.M.E., Prov. Supr.

Fathers 21; Brothers 1; Seminarians 5.

Legal Titles and Holdings: P.I.M.E. Mission Center, Newark, OH, *PIME Missionaries - PIME Mission Center, PIME College Community,* Detroit, MI, *PIME Missionaries,* Wayne, NJ, Tequesta, FL.

Formation Communities 1; Parishes 1; Mission Houses 3.

Represented in the Archdiocese of Detroit and the Dioceses of Paterson, Columbus and Palm Beach.

[1060] (C.PP.S.)—SOCIETY OF THE PRECIOUS BLOOD

(Congregatio Missionariorum Pretiosissimi Sanguinis Domini Nostri Jesu Christi)

General Motherhouse: Viale di Porta Ardeatina 66, Rome, Italy, 00154. Very Rev. Barry Fischer, C.PP.S., Moderator.

Cincinnati Province: 431 E. Second St., Dayton, OH 45402. Tel: 513-228-9263. Very Rev. Kenneth F. Pleiman, C.PP.S., Prov. Dir. Prov. Council: Revs. James F. McCabe, C.PP.S., Vice Prov.; Clarence Williams, C.PP.S.; William O'Donnell, C.PP.S.; James Seibert, C.PP.S.; Bros. Joseph Fisher, C.PP.S., Treas. & Mission Procurator; Benjamin Basile, C.PP.S.; Rev. Angelo Anthony, C.PP.S.

Fathers 203; Brothers 38; Students in Major Seminaries 8; Students in Preparatory Seminary 22.

Ministries in Parishes; Missions; Chaplaincies; Shrine; Community Houses; Houses of Study; Military Chaplains.

Represented in the Archdioceses of Chicago, Cincinnati, Detroit, Miami, Military Services and in the Dioceses of Cleveland, Columbus, Fort Wayne-South Bend, Gary, Harrisburg, Lafayette in Indiana, Lansing, Orlando, Pensacola-Tallahassee, Steubenville, Toledo and Youngstown.

Kansas City Province: Precious Blood Society Provincial Office, P.O. Box 339, Liberty, MO 64068. Tel: 816-781-4344; Fax: 816-781-3639. Very Rev. Mark Miller, C.PP.S., Prov. Dir.; Revs. William Walter, C.PP.S., 1st Consultor; Joseph Nassal, C.PP.S., 2nd Consultor; Ronald Will, C.PP.S., 3rd Consultor; William Miller, C.PP.S., 4th Consultor; Ronald Will, C.PP.S., Prov. Sec.; William Dineen, C.PP.S., Prov. Treas.

Bishops 1; Fathers 69; Brothers 5; Deacons 2; Seminarians 2.

Ministries in Parishes; Missions; Houses of Study; Community House; Chaplaincies.

Represented in the Archdioceses of Cincinnati, Kansas City in Kansas and in the Dioceses of Davenport, Dodge City, Jefferson City, Kansas City-St. Joseph, Salina, San Angelo, Superior, and Wichita.

Province of the Pacific of the Precious Blood: Society of the Precious Blood, 2337 134th Ave. West, San Leandro, CA 94577-4132. Tel: 510-357-4982; Fax: 510-357-4036. Very Rev. James Franck, C.PP.S., Prov. Dir. Councillors: Revs. Ronald Wiecek, C.PP.S., Vice Prov.; Gregory Comella, C.PP.S.; James Sloan, C.PP.S.; Jeffrey Finley, C.PP.S.; Deacon Joseph Brown, C.PP.S., Treas.; Revs. John Klopke, C.PP.S., Sec.; Jeffrey Finley, C.PP.S., Vocation Dir.

Fathers 22; Deacons21.

Ministries in Parishes; Chaplaincies; Community Houses; Center of Spirituality.

Represented in the Archdioceses of Los Angeles, St. Louis, and the Dioceses of Oakland, and Salt Lake City.

Atlantic Province: Society of the Precious Blood, St. Alphonsus Church, 540 St. Clair Ave. W., Toronto, Ontario M6C 1A4. Canada. Tel: 416-658-3735.

Very Rev. Peter Nobili, C.PP.S., Prov.; Rev. John Colacino, C.PP.S., Sec.
Priests in the U.S. 9.
Represented in the Archdioceses of Miami, Washington and the Dioceses of Rochester and Youngstown. Also in Canada.

[1065] (F.S.S.P.)—PRIESTLY FRATERNITY OF ST. PETER

Founded in Switzerland in 1988. First foundation in United States in 1991.
General Motherhouse: Priesterseminar Sankt Petrus, Kirchstrasse 20, 88145, Opfenbach-Wigratzbad, Germany. Tel: 49-8385/645; Fax: 49-8385/1840. Very Rev. Josef Bisig, F.S.S.P., Supr. Gen.
U.S. Headquarters and House of Formation: Our Lady of Guadalupe Seminary, Griffin Rd., P.O. Box 196, Elmhurst, PA 18416. Tel: 717-842-4000; Fax: 717-842-4001. Revs. Arnaud J. Devillers, F.S.S.P., District Supr.; Nathan R. Vail, F.S.S.P., Rector; James B. Buckley, F.S.S.P., Novice Master; Dennis M. Duvelius, F.S.S.P., Admin. Asst. & Dir.-Admissions.
Priests 22; Seminarians 46; Novices 13.
Properties owned or sponsored: Houses 12; Elementary & High Schools.
Represented in the Archdioceses of Atlanta, Denver, Kansas City, New York, Oklahoma City, Omaha, and the Dioceses of Corpus Christi, Dallas, Lincoln, Little Rock, Paterson, Rapid City, Scranton, Tulsa, and Youngstown.

[1070] (C.SS.R.)—REDEMPTORIST FATHERS

(Congregatio Sanctissimi Redemptoris)
(Redemptorist Fathers and Brothers)
Generalate: Sant' Alphonso, Via Merulana 31. C.P. 2458, 1-00100, Roma, Italia. Most Rev. Juan Lasso de la Vega, C.Ss.R., Supr. Gen.; Very Rev. Michael Kratz, C.Ss.R., Vicar Gen.; Rev. Jose Sousa, C.Ss.R., Proc. Gen.
Province of Baltimore (1850): *Provincial Residence,* 7509 Shore Rd., Brooklyn, NY 11209. Tel: 718-833-1900. Very Rev. George J. Keaveney, C.Ss.R., Prov. Supr.; Revs. Patrick F. Woods, C.Ss.R., Prov. Vicar; Francis J. O'Rourke, C.Ss.R., Prov. Consultor; Very Rev. Francis Nelson, C.Ss.R., Prov. Procurator; Rev. Ruskin Piedra, C.Ss.R.; Bros. Albert R. Schreiber, C.Ss.R., Prov. Sec.; Thomas Rochacewicz, C.Ss.R.; Revs. Carl Hoegerl, C.Ss.R., Prov. Archivist; Gerard Knapp, C.Ss.R., Asst. Procurator.
Bishops 3; Priests 243; Brothers 25; Novices 4; Minor Seminarians 14.
Properties owned, staffed, or sponsored: Parishes 38; Novitiate 1; Residences 5; Retreat Houses 3; Community Houses 45.
Represented in the Archdioceses of Baltimore, Boston, Hartford, New York, Philadelphia and Washington and in the Dioceses of Albany, Brooklyn, Harrisburg, Rockville Centre, Toledo, Trenton and Wilmington. Also in St. Thomas, V.I. and West Indies.
Richmond Vice Province (1942): *Vice Provincial Headquarters,* 313 Hillman St., P.O. Box 1529, New Smyrna Beach, FL 32170. Tel: 904-427-3094. Very Rev. Edward J. Gray, C.Ss.R., Vice Prov.; Revs. Eugene S. Daigle, C.Ss.R., Vicar. Consultors; Joseph Majewski, C.Ss.R.; Mark Knoll, C.Ss.R., Vice Prov. Procurator; Michael Koncik, C.Ss.R., Vocation Dir.; Bro. Thomas Kuhn, C.Ss.R., Asst. Procurator.
Legal Title: *Congregation of the Most Holy Redeemer.*
Priests 60; Professed Students 3.
Properties owned, staffed, or sponsored: Parishes 10; Retreat Houses 1; Retirement Home 1; Residences 1; Missions 6.
Represented in the Archdiocese of Atlanta and the Dioceses of Charleston, Charlotte, Orlando, Richmond, St. Augustine, St. Petersburg and Venice.
The Redemptorist-Denver Province (1875): *The Redemptorists Provincial Residence,* 2130 E. Fourteenth Ave. - Box 300399, Denver, CO 80203-0399. Tel: 303-370-0035; Fax: 303-370-0036. Very Rev. Richard Thibodeau, C.Ss.R., Prov. Supr.; Revs. J. Robert Fenili, C.Ss.R., Prov. Vicar; Stephen Meyer, C.Ss.R., Prov. Consultor; John Steingraeber, C.Ss.R., Co-Dir. - Office of Fin. Servicesmptroller; Bro. Tom Wright, C.Ss.R., CO-Dir. - Office of Fin. Services.
Total in community Priests 21; Brothers 2.
Properties owned, sponsored or staffed: Parishes 15; Retreat Houses 3; Residences 5; Community Houses 19.
Represented in the Archdioceses of Chicago, Denver, Detroit, Milwaukee, Omaha, St. Louis and St. Paul-Minneapolis and in Dioceses of Davenport, Grand Rapids, Kansas City-St. Joseph and Wichita. Also in Foreign Missions.
Bangkok Vice-Province: Redemptorist Fathers, 123-19 Ruam Rudi Lane, Bangkok, 10500. Thailand. Very Rev. Philip Banchong Chaiyara, C.SS.R., Vice Prov.
Manaus Vice-Province: Padres Redentoristas, Caixa Postal 217, 69.011 Manaus, Amazonas, Brazil, South America. Very Rev. Jacson Rodrigues, C.SS.R., Vice Prov.
New Orleans Vice-Province: Redemptorist Fathers and Brothers, 5354 Plank Rd.-P.O. Box 53900, Baton Rouge, LA 70892-3900. Tel: 504-355-2600; Fax: 504-355-6200. Very Rev. Monroe G. Perrier, C.Ss.R., Vice Prov.; Revs. Samuel Maranto, C.Ss.R., Vice Prov. Consultor, Local Supr. & Archivist; Joseph L. Buhler, C.Ss.R., Vice Prov. Archivist Emeritus; Bro. Charles E. Fucik, C.Ss.R., Vice Prov. Treas.; Revs. Eugene E. Staub, C.Ss.R.; John C. Vargas, C.Ss.R., (Redemptorist Generalate - Rome); Bro. Steven E. Fruge, C.Ss.R.
Priests 56; Brothers 6; Professed Students 4.
Properties owned, staffed, or sponsored: Parishes 6; Retreat House; Residences.
Represented in the Archdioceses of New Orleans, San Antonio and the Dioceses of Amarillo, Baton Rouge, Biloxi, Corpus Christi, Galveston-Houston, Lafayette (LA) and San Angelo.

[1080] (C.R.)—CONGREGATION OF THE RESURRECTION

(Congregatio a Resurrectione Domini Nostri Jesu Christi)
Generalate: Via San Sebastianello 11, 00187, Rome, Italy. Very Rev. Sutherland MacDonald, C.R., Supr. Gen.
U.S. of America Province: 2250 North Latrobe Ave., Chicago, IL 60639. Tel: 773-637-0999. Very Rev. Richard P. Balazs, C.R., Prov. Supr. Councillors: Revs. Joseph Glab, C.R.; John Nowak, C.R., Dir. of Vocations; Eugene Szarek, C.R.; Bro. William Hallas, C.R.; Rev. Marion Wroblewski, C.R., Treas.
Fathers 72; Brothers 5.
Ministries in Parishes; Missions; High Schools; Retreat House; Chaplaincies.
Represented in the Archdioceses of Chicago, Mobile, St. Louis and the Dioceses of Pensacola-Tallahassee, Rockford and San Bernardino. Also in Oaxaca, Mexico, St. George's & Bermuda.
Ontario Kentucky Province:.
U.S. Address: St. Cecilia House, 338 N. 25th St., Louisville, KY 40212. Tel: 502-772-3694; Fax: 502-772-3695. Revs. Ray Hofmann, C.R.; Ernest Schumacher, C.R.; John Lesousky, C.R.; Charles Schoenbaechler, C.R.; Fabian Avers, C.R.
Provincialate: Resurrection College, Waterloo, Ontario , Canada, N2L 3G7; Fax: 519-885-4951. Revs. Lory A. Keasey, C.R.; Charles Fedy, C.R. Councillors: Revs. Robert Liddy, C.R.; Larry Bordanero, C.R.; James Link, C.R.; Chris Buda, C.R.; Bro. D. Taylor, C.R., Bursar.
Properties owned, sponsored, or staffed: Resurrection College Parishes 2; University; High Schools 3; Community Houses 15 ; House of Study.
Represented in the Archdiocese of Louisville.

[1090] (R.C.J.)—ROGATIONIST FATHERS

Congregatio Rogationis-a-Corde-Jesu
Generalate:: via Tuscolana 167, 00182, Roma, Italy. Very Rev. Pietro Cifuni, R.C.J., Supr. Gen.
U.S.A. Delegation: 2688 S. Newmark Ave., Box 37, Sanger, CA 93657. Tel: 209-875-5808; 875-2025; Fax: 209-875-1281. Rev. John Bruno, R.C.J., Delegation Supr.
U.S. Foundations: St. Mary's Church, 828 O St., P.O. Box 335, Sanger, CA 93657. Tel: 209-875-2025. Revs. Salvatore Ciranni, R.C.J.; John Bruno, R.C.J.; Loji Pilones, R.C.J.
Vocation Center, 9815 Columbus Ave., North Hill, CA 91343. Tel: 818-894-2546. Revs. Rodolfo D'Agostino, R.C.J.; Vincent Buccheri, R.C.J.
Legal Title: *Congregation of Rogationists, Inc.*
Priests 7.
Ministries in Parishes; Vocation Center; Formation House; Social Service Center.
Represented in the Archdiocese of Los Angeles and the Diocese of Fresno.

[1100] (S.C.)—BROTHERS OF THE SACRED HEART

(Societas Fratrum Sacris Cordis)
Founded in Lyons, France in 1821. First foundation in the United States in Mobile in 1847.
Generalate: Piazza Sacro Cuore, No. 3, Rome, Italy, 00152. Bro. Bernard Couvillion, S.C., Supr. Gen. Provinces.
New Orleans Province (1847): *Provincial Office,* 4540 Elysian Fields Ave., New Orleans, LA 70122. Tel: 504-282-5693; Fax: 504-288-9920. Bro. Paul Montero, S.C., Prov. Prov. Councillors: Bros. Matthias Amos, S.C.; Ivy LeBlanc, S.C.; Francis David, S.C.; Donnan Berry, S.C.; Bro. Mark Thornton, S.C., Treas.
Perpetual Professed 79; Temporary Professed 3; Ordained Brothers 6.
Incorporated Schools: Brother Martin High School, New Orleans, LA Catholic High School, Baton Rouge, LA Saint Stanislaus College, Bay St. Louis, MS.
Legal Title: *Brothers of the Sacred Heart, (a Louisiana Corporation), Vocational Development Fund of the Brothers of the Sacred, Heart, Inc.*
Represented in the Archdioceses of Mobile and New Orleans and the Dioceses of Baton Rouge, Biloxi and Houma-Thibodaux. Also in the Diocese of Gulu, Uganda.
New England Province (1945): *Provincial House - Brothers of the Sacred Heart,* 685 Steere Farm Rd., Pascoag, RI 02859-4601. Tel: 401-568-3361; Fax: 401-568-9810. Bro. Roland Ouellette, S.C., Prov. Supr. Councillors: Bros. Robert Croteau, S.C.; Donald Tardif, S.C.; Clifford King, S.C.; Frederick U. Bouchard, S.C.; Edward Breault, S.C., Prov. Sec.; Louis Laperle, S.C., Exec. Asst. Finances; Paul Hebert, S.C., Missions Procurator; Leon Cyr, S.C., Recruiter & Vocation Dir.; Charles L. Amand, S.C., Devel. Dir.
Brothers 99.
Properties owned: Brothers of the Sacred Heart Provincial House, Pascoag, RI; Mt. St. Charles Academy, Woonsocket, RI; Bishop Guertin High School, Nashua, NH; St. John Residence, Woonsocket, RI; Brothers of the Sacred Heart Residence, Nashua, NH.
Represented in the Archdiocese of Hartford and in the Dioceses of Burlington, Manchester and Providence. Also in England, Lesotho, Zambia, Zimbabwe, and Uganda.
Province of New York (1960): *Brothers of the Sacred Heart Provincial House,* P.O. Box 68, Belvidere, NJ 07823. Tel: 908-475-4694; Fax: 908-475-2623. Bro. Donald Sukanek, S.C., Prov.
Final Professed Brothers 42; Temporary 1; Novices 1; Candidates 1.
Ministries in the field of Education; Spiritual Centers; Kenya Missions.
Properties owned: Sacred Heart Center, Belvidere, NJ Msgr. McClancy High School, East Elmhurst, NY St. Joseph High School, Metuchen, NJ.
Represented in the Dioceses of Brooklyn, Metuchen and Rockville Center. Also in Kenya.

[1110] (M.S.C.)—MISSIONARIES OF THE SACRED HEART

(Societas Missionariorum Sacratissimi Cordis Jesu)
General Motherhouse: Via Asmara 11, 00199, Rome, Italy. Very Rev. Michael Curran, M.S.C., Supr. Gen.
United States Province (1939): P.O. Box 270, 305 S. Lake St., Aurora, IL 60507. Tel: 630-892-8400; 892-2371; Fax: 630-892-3071. Very Rev. Mark McDonald, M.S.C., Prov. Supr. Consultors: Revs. David Foxen, M.S.C., Vice Prov.; Eugene Jung, M.S.C.; Peter Campbell, M.S.C.; Tony Ripp, M.S.C.; John Kavcak, M.S.C.
Legal Title: *Society of the Missionaries of the Sacred Heart.*
Fathers 71; Brothers 22; Foreign Missionaries 18; Professed Students 3.
Properties owned, staffed, or sponsored: Renewal Centers 1; Residential Houses 6; Parishes 9; Chaplaincies 5; Foreign Missions 2.
Represented in the Archdioceses of Baltimore, Chicago, Philadelphia and Washington and in the Dioceses of Allentown, Gary, Ogdensburg, Providence, Rockford, San Bernardino, Toledo and Youngstown. Also in Colombia, Papua New Guinea, Namibia and Slovakia.
U.S. Section of the Irish Province for California and Southern States: Sectional Headquarters, 207 Rio Seco, San Antonio, TX 78232. Tel: 210-402-0354; Fax: 210-402-0346. Very Rev. Bill Clarkson, M.S.C., Sectional Supr. Sectional Consultors: Revs. Patrick O'Shea, M.S.C.; James Dudley, M.S.C.; Jeremiah McCarthy, M.S.C.; Aidan O'Donovan, M.S.C.
Priests 18.
Represented in the Archdioceses of Los Angeles, San Antonio and Washington and the Dioceses of Beaumont, Corpus Christi, Dallas and San Angelo.

[1120] (M.SS.CC.)—MISSIONARIES OF THE SACRED HEARTS OF JESUS AND MARY

(Missionarii a Sacris Cordibus Jesus et Mariae)
Founded in Italy in 1833.
General Motherhouse: Via dei Falegnami 23, Rome, Italy. Very Rev. Anthony Palmiero, M.SS.CC., Supr. Gen.
American Headquarters: 2249 Shore Rd., Linwood, NJ 08221. Tel: 609-927-5600; Fax: 609-927-5262. Revs. Anthony Patrizio, M.SS.CC., Reg. Supr.; John Perdue, M.SS.CC., Mission Procurator.

Legal Title: *Villa Pieta,* Linwood, NJ.
Priests 10; Brothers 3; Postulants 1.
Represented in the Dioceses of Camden and Harrisburg.

[1130] (S.C.J.)—CONGREGATION OF THE PRIESTS OF THE SACRED HEART
(Priests of the Sacred Heart)
(Congregatio Sacerdotum a Corde Jesu)

General Motherhouse: Curia Generalizia, S.C.J., Via Casale S. Pio v, no. 20, 00165, Rome, Italy. Very Rev. Virginio Domingo Bressanelli, S.C.J., Supr. Gen.
United States Province (1933): *Provincialate Offices,* P.O. Box 289, Hales Corners, WI 53130-0289. Tel: 414-425-6910. Very Rev. John Czyzynski, S.C.J., Prov. Supr.
Bishops 2; Priests 103; Clerics 6; Brothers 23; Deacons 1.
Represented in the Archdioceses of Chicago, Milwaukee and San Antonio and in the Dioceses of Brownsville, Galveston-Houston, Green Bay, Jackson, Memphis, Rapid City, St. Petersburg and Sioux Falls.

[1140] (SS.CC.)—CONGREGATION OF THE SACRED HEARTS OF JESUS AND MARY
(Congregatio Sacrorum Cordium)

General Motherhouse: Casa Generalizia-Padri Dei Sacri Cuori-via Rivarone 85, 00166, Rome, Italy. Very Rev. Enrique Losada, SS.CC., Supr. Gen.
Legal Title: *Congregation of the Sacred Hearts of Jesus and Mary.*
Eastern Province (1946): *Provincial House,* Box 111 - 77 Adams St., Fairhaven, MA 02719-0111. Tel: 508-993-2442; Fax: 508-996-5499. Very Rev. Columban Crotty, SS.CC., Prov.; Rev. Fintan D. Sheeran, SS.CC., Vicar Prov. Councillors: Revs. Martin Gomes, SS.CC.; Stanley Kolasa, SS.CC.; Robert Charlton, SS.CC.
Priests 63; Novices 3; Brothers 8.
Properties owned or staffed: Parishes 7; Community Houses 3; House of Studies 1.
Represented in the Archdiocese of Washington and the Dioceses of Brownsville, and Fall River.
Western United States Province (1970): *Congregation of the Sacred Hearts of Jesus and Mary,* 724 East Bonita Ave., San Dimas,, CA 91773. Tel: 909-599-1243; 5441; Fax: 909-593-3971. Very Rev. Martin P. O'Loghlen, SS.CC., Prov.
Priests 28; Seminarians 2.
Ministries in the field of Religious and Academic Education; Parishes; Chaplaincies.
Represented in the Archdiocese of Los Angeles and the Dioceses of Oakland, Orange and San Bernardino. Also in the Philippines.
Hawaii Province: Sacred Hearts Center, Box 797, Kaneohe, Oahu, HI 96744; Fax: 808-235-8849. Very Rev. Joseph Bukoski, III, SS.CC., Prov.
Fathers 35; Scholastics 1; Brothers 7.
Properties owned, staffed, or sponsored: Churches 11; Mission 1; Chaplaincies 2.

[1144] (L.B.S.F.)—LITTLE BROTHERS OF SAINT FRANCIS

Founded in the United States in 1970 by Bro. James Curran, L.B.S.F.
Regional Fraternity and Novitiate (1970): 785-789 Parker St., Roxbury, MA 02120. Tel: 617-442-2556.
Legal Title: *Little Brothers of Saint Francis - Franciscan Fraternity of, Peace and Love, Inc.*
Professed Brothers 3; Novices 2; Postulants 3.
Represented in the Archdiocese of Boston.

[1150] (C.S.J.)—CONGREGATION OF ST. JOSEPH
(Congregatio Sancti Joseph)

Founded in Turin, Italy in 1873. First foundation in United States in 1951.
General Motherhouse: Via Belvedere Montello 77, 00166, Rome, Italy. Very Rev. Luigi Pierini, C.S.J., Supr. Gen.
U.S. and Mexico Vice Province: 338 N. Grand Ave., San Pedro, CA 90731. Tel: 310-547-2969. Rev. John Trimaglio, C.S.J., Prov. Supr.
Priests 24; Novices 3.
Properties owned, staffed, or sponsored: Parishes 5; High Schools 2; Center for troubled youths.
Properties owned: St. Leonard House, Avon, OH.
Represented in the Archdiocese of Los Angeles and the Diocese of Cleveland. Also in Mexico.

[1160] (F.S.P.)—BROTHERS OF ST. PATRICK
(Patrician Brothers)

Founded in Ireland 1808 by Bishop Daniel Delaney.
U.S. Foundation (1948): *St. Patrick's Novitiate,* 7820 Bolsa Ave., Midway City, CA 92655. Tel: 714-897-8181; Fax: 714-898-9020. Bro. Aquinas Cassin, F.S.P., Prov.
Brothers 8.
Represented in the Archdiocese of Los Angeles and Diocese of Orange.

[1170] (S.P.S.)—ST. PATRICK'S MISSIONARY SOCIETY
(St. Patrick Fathers)

Founded March 17, 1932 with the approval of Pope Piux XI. A Pontifical Society of secular priests devoted entirely to the missionary needs of the Church.
International Headquarters: St. Patrick's, Kiltegan, Wicklow , Ireland. Very Rev. Sean Barry, S.P.S., Supr. Gen.; Very Rev. Timothy J. Barry, S.P.S., Supr. for North America; Very Rev. James Bermingham, S.P.S., Proc. Gen.-Rome.
Total number of Priests 370; Priests in the U.S. 16.
U.S. Foundations (1965): *St. Patrick's,* 70 Edgewater Rd., Cliffside Park, NJ 07010. Tel: 201-943-6575; Fax: 201-943-9426. Very Rev. Timothy J. Barry, S.P.S., Supr., *St. Patrick's,* (1967), 19536 Eric Dr., Saratoga, CA 95070. Tel: 408-253-3135. Rev. Eamonn Hayden, S.P.S., Supr., *St. Patrick's,* (1968), 1347 W. Granville Ave., Chicago, IL 60660. Tel: 312-973-3737. Rev. Karl Langsdord, S.P.S., Supr.
Legal Title: *St. Patrick Missionary Society, Camden, N.J.*
Represented in the Archdioceses of Chicago, New Orleans, Newark and San Francisco and in the Dioceses of Palm Beach, Paterson and San Jose.

[1180] (C.S.P.X.)—BROTHERS OF SAINT PIUS X

Founded in the United States in 1952.
Motherhouse: P.O. Box 217, DeSoto, WI 54624. Tel: 608-648-2087. Bro. Charles Bisenius, Dir.
Ministries in the field of Religious and Academic Education; Health Care; Community services and Administration.
Represented in the Diocese of La Crosse.

[1190] (S.D.B.)—SALESIANS OF DON BOSCO
Societas Sancti Francisci Salesii

Generalate: Salesian D. Bosco, via Della Pisana, 1111, C.P., 9092-00163, Roma-Aurelio, Italy. Very Rev. Juan Vecchi, S.D.B., Vicar. Gen.
Province of St. Philip the Apostle (1902): 148 Main St., New Rochelle, NY 10802. Tel: 914-636-4225. Very Rev. Timothy C. Ploch, S.D.B., Prov.; Revs. David Moreno, S.D.B., Sec.; David Gonder, S.D.B., Prov. Economer & Councillor; Bro. Gerald Meegan, S.D.B., Dir. Social Communication & Councillor; Revs. Clement Cardillo, S.D.B., Vice Prov.; Joseph Tyminski, S.D.B., Dir. of Formation & Councillor; Stephen Schenck, S.D.B., Dir. of Religious Education & Councillor; James Marra, S.D.B., Mission Procurator.
Legal Title: *Salesian Society, Inc.,* New Rochelle, NY.
Fathers 148; Professed Clerics 15; Students in Major Seminaries 7; Coadjutor-Brothers 48.
Ministries in Parishes; High Schools; Trade Schools; Technical Schools; Boys Clubs; Camps.
Represented in the Archdioceses of Boston, Miami, Newark, New Orleans and New York and in the Dioceses of Birmingham, Columbus, Palm Beach, Passaic, Paterson, St. Petersburg and Scranton. Also in Canada.
San Francisco Province (1926): *Salesian Society - San Francisco,* 1100 Franklin St., San Francisco, CA 94109. Tel: 415-441-7144; Fax: 415-563-5394. Very Rev. William Schafer, S.D.B., Prov.; Rev. Carmine Vairo, S.D.B., Vice Prov. Councillor: Revs. Nicholas Reina, S.D.B.; Joseph Boenzi, S.D.B.; David Purdy, S.D.B.; Bro. Joseph Lockwood, S.D.B., Treas.
Fathers 86; Professed Clerics 12; Professed Brothers 29; Novices 6; Students in Seminaries 2.
Ministries in Parishes; High Schools; Retreat House; Youth Centers.
Represented in the Archdioceses of Los Angeles, Santa Fe, San Francisco and the Dioceses of Corpus Christi, Monterey, Oakland, San Bernardino, San Diego, Santa Rosa, Stockton, and Van Nuys. Also in Canada and Sierra Leone.

[1200] (S.D.S.)—SOCIETY OF THE DIVINE SAVIOR
Salvatorian Fathers and Brothers
(Salvatorians - Societas Divini Salvatoris)

General Headquarters: Curia Generalizia dei Salvatoriani, Via della Conciliazione 51, 00193, Rome, Italy. Very Rev. Karl Hoffman, S.D.S., Supr. Gen.
U.S.A. Province (1896): *Salvatorian Provincial Residence,* 1735 Hi-Mount Blvd., Milwaukee, WI 53208-1720. Tel: 414-258-1735; Fax: 414-258-1934. Very Rev. Dennis D. Thiessen, S.D.S., Prov.; Revs. Michael A. Shay, S.D.S., Vicar & Dir. Finance; Jean F. Blais, S.D.S., Dir. Personnel; Joseph Rodrigues, S.D.S., Dir. Planning & Communications.
Legal Title: *Society of the Divine Savior, Society of the Divine Savior Ongoing Community Support Plan and Trust.*
Fund Raising and Public Relations Center: Salvatorian Center, New Holstein, WI 53061.
Fathers 106; Professed Clerics 6; Brothers 53.
Properties owned, staffed, or sponsored: Parishes 5; Houses of Study and Formation 22.
Represented in the Archdioceses of Baltimore, Chicago, Louisville, Milwaukee, New York, Portland, San Francisco, Washington and the Dioceses of Camden, Birmingham, Bismarck, Erie, Fresno, Gallup, Green Bay, LaCrosse, Mobile, Nashville, Oakland, Orlando, Phoenix, Sacramento, Savannah, Tucson, Wilmington and Richmond.

[1210] (C.S.)—MISSIONARIES OF ST. CHARLES-SCALABRINIANS
(Congregatio Missionariorum A Sancto Carolo)

General Motherhouse: Via Calandrelli, 42, 00153, Rome, Italy. Very Rev. Luigi Favero, C.S., Supr. Gen.
Province of St. Charles Borromeo (1888): *Provincial Curia,* 27 Carmine St., New York, NY 10014. Tel: 212-675-3993; Fax: 212-727-2866. Very Rev. Joseph Fugolo, C.S., Prov. Supr.; Revs. Joseph Cogo, C.S., Vicar & 1st Councillor; Charles Zanoni, C.S., Sec. & 2nd Councillor; Ezio Marchetto, C.S., 3rd Councillor; Dominic Rodighiero, C.S., Treas. & 4th Councillor.
Legal Title: *The Pious Society of the Missionaries of St. Charles Borromeo, Inc.*
Fathers 96; Brothers 3.
Properties staffed or owned: Parishes 30; Missions 7; Homes for Aged 2; Seminaries 3; Center for Migration Studies; Assistance Agency for Migrants.
Represented in the Archdioceses of Boston, Hartford, Newark, New York and Washington and the Dioceses of Brooklyn, Buffalo, Palm Beach, Providence, Syracuse and Venice. Also in Eastern Canada, Venezuela, Colombia, the Dominican Republic and Haiti.
Province of St. John Baptist (1903): *Missionaries of St. Charles - Fathers of St. Charles,* 546 N. East Ave., Oak Park, IL 60302. Tel: 708-386-4430; Fax: 708-386-4457. Very Rev. Livio Stella, C.S., Prov.
Legal Title: *The Fathers of Saint Charles, Scalabrinian Community Support Corp., Scalabrinian Community Formation Corp.*
Fathers 75; Brothers 4.
Ministries in 25 Parishes; 2 Homes for the Aged; 3 Missions; 4 Seminaries; 4 Centers for Migrants and Refugees.
Represented in the Archdioceses of Chicago, Cincinnati and Los Angeles and the Dioceses of Galveston-Houston, Kansas City-St. Joseph, San Diego and San Jose. Also in Canada, Mexico and Italy.

[1220] (S.C.)—SERVANTS OF CHARITY
(Guanellians)
(Congregatio Servorum a Charitate)

General Motherhouse: Vicolo Clementi 41, Rome, Italy. Very Rev. Nino Minetti, Supr. Gen.
U.S. Headquarters: Servants of Charity, 16195 Old U.S. 12, Chelsea, MI 48118-9646. Tel: 313-475-8430; Fax: 313-475-0310. Rev. Joseph Rinaldo, Supr. USA Province.
Priests 12; Brothers 1; Theologian 1; Novices 1.
Schools Schools for mentally handicapped boys 2; Residences for mentally handicapped adults 2; Parishes 1; House of Formation 1; Group Home 1; Chaplaincies 1.
Represented in the Archdioceses of Chicago and Philadelphia and in the Dioceses of Lansing and Providence.

[1230] (s.P.)—SERVANTS OF THE PARACLETE

Generalate & U.S. Motherhouse (1952): *Foundation House,* Jemez Springs, NM 87025. Tel: 505-829-3586; Fax: 505-829-3706. Very Rev. Liam Hoare, s.P., Servant Gen.; Revs. Michael Foley, s.P., Vicar Gen.; Benedict Livingston, s.P., Dir. Formation; James Sampson, s.P.; Patrick Coffey, s.P.; Raymond Gunzel, s.P.; Paul Valley, s.P.; Bros. J. Paul Pelletier s.P.; Conrad Rydel, s.P.
Professed Priests 26; Professed Brothers 5.
Represented in the Archdioceses of St. Louis and Santa Fe and the Diocese of San Bernardino.

[1240] (O.S.M.)—SERVITES
Order of Friar Servants of Mary
(Ordo Fratrum Servorum Beatae Virginis Mariae)

Generalate: Curia Generalizia dei Servi di Maria, Piazza San Marcello al Corso, 5, 00187, Rome, Italy.
Eastern Province (1967): *Servite Friars-Eastern Prov-*

ince, 3121 W. Jackson Blvd., Chicago, IL 60612. Tel: 773-533-0360; Fax: 773-533-8307. Very Rev. Michael M. Guimon, O.S.M., Prior Prov.; Rev. Joseph M. Chamblain, O.S.M., Asst. Prov. Councillors; James M. Dore, O.S.M.; Paul M. Cullen, O.S.M.; Paul M. Novak, O.S.M.; Bro. Edmund M. Baran, O.S.M., Prov. Treas.; Bro. Michael M. Callary, O.S.M., Prov./Corporate Sec.; Bro. Donald M. Siple, O.S.M., Natl. Vocation Dir.; Conrad M. Borntrager, O.S.M., Archivist & Historian.

Legal Title: *Servite Friars-Eastern Province, Inc., Chicago, IL Servite Friars-Eastern Province Retirement Trust, Chicago, IL St. Anthony Pucci Charitable Trust, Chicago, IL Servants of Mary, Inc., Chicago, IL.*

Parishes 8; Residences 12; Hospital Chaplaincies; Military Chaplaincies; V.A. Chaplaincies.

Priests 56; Professed Brothers 9.

Represented in the Archdioceses of Chicago, Detroit, Military Services, Portland (OR), St. Louis, Santa Fe and the Dioceses of Orange, Orlando, St. Petersburg, Springfield-Cape Girardeau and Tucson. Also in Germany, Ireland, and South Africa.

Western Province (1967): *Servite Provincial Center,* 5210 Somerset St., Buena Park, CA 90621-1498. Tel: 714-523-5810; Fax: 714-523-8129. Revs. Ignatius M. Kissel, O.S.M., Prov.; Peregrine M. Graffius, O.S.M., Asst. Prov. Councillors: Revs. Gerald M. Horan, O.S.M., Archivist; Eugene M. Smith, O.S.M.; Justin M. Pisciotta, O.S.M.; Michael M. Pontarelli, O.S.M., Prov. Treas.; Donald M. Siple, O.S.M., Vocation Dir.

Legal Title: *The Western Province of the Servites, Inc., The Western Province of the Servites Inc. Charitable Trust.*

Fathers 38; Professed Brothers 5; Temporarily Professed Brothers 1.

Properties owned, staffed, or sponsored: Parishes 9; High Schools 1; Community Houses 9; Hospital Chaplaincies 3.

Represented in the Archdioceses of Denver, Los Angeles and Portland in Oregon and in the Dioceses of Oakland, Orange and Tucson.

[1250] (C.R.S.)—SOMASCAN FATHERS

(Clericorum Regularium Somaschensium)
Order of St. Jerome Aemilian

General Motherhouse: Largo Alessandria del Carretto, 00040, Morena - Rome, Italy. Most Rev. Bruno Luppi, C.R.S., Ph.D., Father Gen.

U.S. Foundation: Pine Haven Boys Center, River Rd., P.O. 162, Suncook, NH 03275. Tel: 603-485-7141. Rev. Julian Gerosa, C.R.S., Supr.

Priests 3; Total in U.S. 8.

Represented in the Archdiocese of Hartford and in the Dioceses of Galveston-Houston and Manchester.

[1260] (S.Ch.)—SOCIETY OF CHRIST

(Societas Christi Pro Emigrantibus Polonis)

General Motherhouse: 60-962 Poznan Ulica Panny Marii 4, Poland. Very Rev. Tadeusz Winnicki, S.Ch., Supr. Gen.; Rev. Marian Burniak, Procurator Gen., Via Botteghe Oscure 15, 00186, Rome, Italy.

American-Canadian Province: Provincial Residence, 3000 Eighteen Mile Rd., Sterling Heights, MI 48314. Tel: 810-939-5022. Very Rev. Andrzej Maslejak, S.Ch., Prov.; Revs. Stanislaw Kuczaik, S.Ch., Vice-Prov.; Gerald Grupczynski, S.Ch., Treas.

Priests 50.

Represented in the Archdioceses of Baltimore, Chicago, Detroit, Hartford, Los Angeles, Miami, Portland (OR), St. Paul-Minneapolis, San Francisco, Seattle and Washington and the Dioceses of Dallas, Galveston-Houston, Passaic, San Diego, San Jose and Toledo. Also in Canada.

[1270] (F.M.S.I.)—SONS OF MARY MISSIONARY SOCIETY

Sons of Mary, Health of the Sick
(Filii Mariae Salutis Infirmorum)

General Headquarters: 567 Salem End Rd., Framingham, MA 01701. Tel: 508-879-6711. Bro. Kevin Courtney, Major Coord.; Revs. John Coss, Financial Coord.; Henry Cicale, F.M.S.I., Councilor.

Professed 12.

Represented in the Archdiocese of Boston. Also in the Philippines.

[1280] (C.S.S.)—STIGMATINE FATHERS AND BROTHERS

(Congregation of the Sacred Stigmata)

General Motherhouse: Via Mazzarino No. 16, Rome, Italy. Very Rev. Jose Luiz Nemes, C.S.S., Supr. Gen.; Rev. Giampietro DePaoli, C.S.S., Vicar Gen.

North American Province (1940): 554 Lexington St., Waltham, MA 02154. Tel: 617-894-7713; Fax: 617-894-9785. Very Rev. Robert S. White, C.S.S., Prov. Supr.

Priests 45; Brothers 4.

Legal Title: *Stigmatine Fathers & Brother, Inc.*

Properties owned, staffed, or sponsored: Parishes 7; Retreat & Conference Center.

Represented in the Archdioceses of Boston, New York, and the Dioceses of Springfield (MA) and Worcester.

[1290] (S.S.)—SOCIETY OF THE PRIESTS OF SAINT SULPICE

(Societas Presbyterorum a S. Sulpitio)

General Motherhouse: 6 rue du Regard, Paris, 75006. France. Very Rev. Lawrence B. Terrien, S.S., Supr. Gen.

U.S. Provincial House: 5408 Roland Ave., Baltimore, MD 21210. Tel: 301-323-5070; Fax: 410-433-6524. Very Rev. Gerald L. Brown, S.S., Prov.; Mr. Joseph M. Reynolds, Exec. Asst. to Prov. & Operations Mgr.; Revs. Louis M. Reitz, S.S., Prov. Treas.; Melvin C. Blanchette, S.S., Dir. Formation & Personnel Services, Dir. Discernment & Admissions; Thomas R. Ulshafer, S.S., Prov. Sec.

Legal Title: *The Associated Sulpicians of the United States.*

Fathers 89.

Represented in the Archdioceses of Baltimore, San Francisco, Seattle and Washington and the Dioceses of Honolulu and San Jose.

[1300] (C.R.)—THEATINE FATHERS

(Congregatio Clericorum Regularium)

General Motherhouse: Sant' Andrea della Valle, Piazza Vidoni, 6, 00186, Rome, Italy. Most Rev. Gabriele Darida, C.R., Supr. Gen.

U.S. Headquarters: 1050 S. Birch St., Denver, CO 80222. Tel: 303-756-5522. Very Rev. Patrick Valdez, C.R.

Fathers 17; Clerics 5.

Parishes 9; House of Formation 1; Provincial House 1.

Represented in the Archdioceses of Denver and New York and in the Diocese of Pueblo.

[1310] (O.SS.T.)—ORDER OF THE MOST HOLY TRINITY

Holy Trinity Fathers, Inc.
(Ordo Sanctissimae Trinitatis; *The Trinitarians*)

Founded in France in 1198 by St. John De Matha for the ransom of Christian slaves. First settlement in the United States in 1911.

General Curia: Via Massimi, 114C, 00136, Rome, Italy. Most Rev. Jose Hernandez Sanchez, Minister Gen.

U.S.A. Province (1950): *Province of the Immaculate Heart of Mary,* P.O. Box 5719, 8400 Park Heights Ave., Baltimore, MD 21282. Tel: 410-486-5171. Very Rev. John L. Dorn, O.SS.T., Minister Prov.; Rev. Thomas Cerulo, O.SS.T., Vicar Prov. Prov. Councillors: Revs. William Axe, O.SS.T.; Joseph Gidaro, O.SS.T.; Albert Anuszewski, O.SS.T., Dir.-Vocation; Charles J. Flood, O.SS.T., Sec. & Treas.

Trinitarian Communities in the U.S. 14; Fathers 55; Brothers 24; Novices 2.

Ministries in 12 parishes; Seminary Facility Positions; High Schools; Prison Chaplaincies; Hospital Chaplaincies; Social Apostolate to the Homeless; Seminary; Faculty Member; India Foundation; Mission for Persecuted Christians.

Properties owned: DeMatha Catholic High School, Hyattsville, MD; Holy Trinity Monastery, Pikesville, MD; Redeemer House, Baltimore, MD; Trinity House, Victoria, TX.

Represented in the Archdioceses of Baltimore, Cincinnati, Los Angeles, New Orleans, Philadelphia, New York, Washington and in the Dioceses of Corpus Christi, Trenton, Rockville Centre, Memphis, Palm Beach, Trenton and Victoria. Also in India.

[1320] (C.S.V.)—CLERICS OF ST. VIATOR

(Congregatio Clericorum Sancti Viatoris)

General Motherhouse: Via Padre A. Paoli, 41, Rome, Italy. Casella Postale 10793, 00144, Roma, Italia. Very Rev. Leonard Audet, C.S.V., Supr. Gen.

Province of Chicago (1882): 1212 East Euclid St., Arlington Heights, IL 60004. Tel: 708-398-1354. Very Rev. Robert M. Egan, C.S.V., Prov.; Revs. Richard A. Rinn, C.S.V., Councillor and Asst. Prov.; Robert E. Erickson, C.S.V., Prov. Treas.

Fathers 93; Brothers 21.

Properties owned, staffed, or sponsored: Parishes 15; High Schools 4; Formation Houses 2.

Represented in the Archdioceses of Chicago, Kansas City in Kansas, Military Services and the Dioceses of Arlington, Joliet, Manchester, Monterey, Oakland, Peoria, Las Vegas, Rockford, San Diego, San Jose, Springfield (IL) and Tucson. Also in Colombia and Italy.

[1330] (C.M.)—CONGREGATION OF THE MISSION

Vincentians
(Congregatio Missionis Sti. Vincentii a Paulo)

Founded in France in 1625. First foundation in the United States in 1818.

General Motherhouse: Curia Generalizia, Via dei Capasso, 30, 00164, Roma, Italia. Very Rev. Robert P. Maloney, C.M., Supr. Gen.

Eastern Province of the U.S.A. (1867): *St. Vincent's Seminary,* 500 E. Chelten Ave., Philadelphia, PA 19144. Tel: 215-848-1985; Fax: 215-844-2085. Very Rev. Joseph L. Levesque, C.M., Prov.; Revs. Thomas F. McKenna, C.M., Asst. Prov.; John W. Gouldrick, C.M., Prov. Treas. Consultors: Revs. William W. Sheldon, C.M.; John Kettelberger, C.M.; Michael J. Carroll, C.M., Prov. Planner; Bro. Peter A. Campbell, C.M.

Legal Title: *Congregation of the Mission of St. Vincent de Paul in Germantown, Inc.*

Fathers 194; Brothers 12; Students in Major Seminaries 6; College Seminarians 10; Students in Preparatory Seminaries 9; Novice 3.

Properties owned, sponsored, or staffed: Parishes 15; Missions in Republic of Panama 8; Universities 2; Major Seminary Residences 2; College Seminary Residences 1; Novitiates 2; Retreat Houses 2.

Represented in the Archdioceses of Baltimore, New York, Miami, Mobile, Philadelphia, Washington and the Dioceses of Albany, Allentown, Birmingham, Brooklyn, Buffalo, Charleston, Charlotte, Grand Rapids, Lansing, Metuchen, Palm Beach, Rockville Centre and St. Augustine.

Midwest Province - Vincentians (1888): 13663 Rider Trail N., Earth City, MO 63045-1512. Tel: 314-344-1184; Fax: 314-344-2989. (Motherhouse St. Mary's Seminary, Perryville, MO.; Very Rev. William E. Hartenbach, C.M., Prov.; Revs. Ignatius M. Melito, C.M., Communication Coord.; Michael P. Joyce, C.M.; Bro. F. Joseph Hess, C.M., Prov. Treas.

Priests 137; Brothers 19; Students in Major Seminaries 3.

Dioceses served 19; University 1; Foreign Mission Stations 1; Houses of Apostolic Activity 7; Total houses of the Province 18.

Represented in the Archdioceses of Chicago, Denver, Kansas City in Kansas, Milwaukee, San Francisco, St. Louis, and the Dioceses of Belleville, Buffalo, Cheyenne, Colorado Springs, Evansville, Galveston-Houston, Jefferson City, Kansas City-St. Joseph, Phoenix, Pueblo, Salt Lake City and Springfield-Cape Girardeau. Also in Kenya.

The New England Province of the Vincentian Fathers (1975): *Vincentian Provincial House,* 234 Keeney Street, Manchester, CT 06040-7023. Tel: 860-643-2828; Fax: 860-533-9462. Very Rev. John S. Sledziona, C.M., Prov.

Fathers 32; Brothers 5.

Legal Title: *New England Province of the Congregation of the Mission, Inc., Charitable Trust of the New England Province of the, Congregation of the Mission.*

Parishes 8; Mission Houses 1.

Represented in the Archdiocese of Hartford and the Dioceses of Brooklyn, Manchester, Portland (ME) and Syracuse.

American Italian Branch (Naples, Italy) (1922): *Our Lady of Pompei Church,* 3600 Claremont St., Baltimore, MD 21224. Tel: 301-675-7790. Rev. Luigi Esposito, C.M., Supr.

Legal Title: *Vincentian Fathers of the Neapolitan Province of Maryland Charities, Inc.*

Fathers 3.

Represented in the Archdiocese of Baltimore.

American Spanish Branch (Barcelona, Spain): 234 Congress St., Brooklyn, NY 11201. Tel: 718-624-3425. Rev. Gabriel Del-Real, C.M., Supr.

Fathers 7.

Represented in the Diocese of Brooklyn.

American Spanish Branch (Zaragoza, Spain) (1926): *Holy Agony Church,* 1834 3rd Ave., New York, NY 10029. Tel: 212-289-5589; Fax: 212-289-8321. Revs. Jesus M. Oses, C.M.; Candido Arrtzurieta, C.M.; Santiago Lluch, C.M.

Legal Title: *Padres Paules Community - Vincentians Inc.*

Fathers 13.

Represented in the Archdioceses of Los Angeles, and New York.

(Vincentian) Province of the West (1975): 650 W. 23rd St., Los Angeles, CA 90007-2036. Tel: 213-749-1865; Fax: 213-749-1554. Very Rev. Bernard J. Quinn, C.M., Prov.

Fathers 51; Brothers 3; Permanent Deacons 3; Major Theologians 3.

Members serve and staff: Parishes 4; Seminaries 2; Evanglization Centers 2; Community Houses 10.

Legal Title: *Congregation of the Mission in California, A Corporation, Vincentian Community Charitable Trust, Vincentian Foreign Mission Society, DePaul Center Corp. (Formerly St. Vincent's Semi-*

nary Corp.), Vincentians Province of the West Support Trust Fund.
Properties owned: DePaul Center, Montebello, CA St. Mary's Seminary, Santa Barbara, CA Amat House, Los Angeles, CA.
Represented in the Archdioceses of Chicago and Los Angeles, and the Dioceses of Fresno, Phoenix, San Jose and Stockton. Also in Belgium.
The Congregation of the Mission Southern Province (1975): 3826 Gilbert Ave., Dallas, TX 75219-4346. Tel: 214-526-2421; Fax: 214-526-3477. Very Rev. George Weber, C.M., Prov.; Rev. Miles Heinen, C.M., Treas.
Priests 34; Brothers 1.
Properties owned, sponsored, or staffed: Parishes 9; Community Houses 5; Mission Churches 3.
Represented in the Archdioceses of New Orleans, St. Louis, San Antonio and the Dioceses of Alexandria, Gallup, Galveston-Houston, Dallas, and Little Rock.

[1340] (S.D.V.)—VOCATIONIST FATHERS

(Society of The Divine Vocations)

Generali: Via Cortina D'Ampezzo, 138, 00135, Rome, Italy. Very Rev. James Capraro, S.D.V., Supr. Gen.
American Headquarters: 90 Brooklake Rd., Florham Park, NJ 07932. Tel: 201-966-6262. Rev. Mario Muccitelli, S.D.V., Delegate of Supr. Gen. for U.S.A.
U.S. Foundations: Our Lady of Perpetual Help Center, 170 Broad St., Newark, NJ 07104. Revs. Louis Caputo, S.D.V., Pastor-Religious Supr. & Vocation Dir.; Giosue DiCesare, S.D.V.; Felix Antonitti, S.D.V.; Bro. Harold Hernandez, S.D.V.; Revs. Antonio da Silva, S.D.V.; Anthony Basso, S.D.V.
Represented in the Archdiocese of Newark and the Diocese of Paterson.

[1350] (C.F.X.)—BROTHERS OF ST. FRANCIS XAVIER

(Congregatio Fratrum Sti Francisci Xaverii)

Generalate: Bros. Matthew Burke, C.F.X., Supr. Gen.; Cornelius E. Hubbuch, C.F.X., Vicar.
Sacred Heart Province: 10318-B Baltimore National Pike, Ellicott City, MD 21042. Tel: 410-750-2850; Fax: 410-465-4220. Bros. Richard Murphy, C.F.X., Prov.; Cornelius Hubbuch, C.F.X., Dir. Staff Formation; John Olsen, C.F.X., Dir. Xaverian Sponsored Schools; Henry Marino, C.F.X., Dir. Devel.
Legal Title: *American Central Province of Xaverian Brothers Inc.*
Brothers 123.
Represented in the Archdioceses of Baltimore, Boston, Chicago, Los Angeles, Louisville, Milwaukee, Newark, New Orleans, New York, St. Louis, Santa Fe, Washington and the Dioceses of Birmingham, Brooklyn, Charleston, Fairbanks, Fort Wayne-South Bend, Houma-Thibodaux, Jackson, Memphis, Richmond, Rapid City, Rockville Centre, Scranton, St. Augustine, St. Petersburg, Venice and Worcester.
St. Joseph Province (Xaverian Brothers): 704 Brush Hill Rd., Milton, MA 02186. Tel: 617-333-0970; Fax: 617-333-0742. Bros. Edward Keefe, C.F.X., Prov.; Robert Green, C.F.X., Vicar Prov. Prov. Councillors: Bros. Brian Davos, C.F.X.; Paul Feeney, C.F.X.; Lawrence Harvey, C.F.X., Dir.-Education; Charles Moran, C.F.X., Treas.; David Wiggin, C.F.X., Archivist; Arcadius Alkonis, C.F.X.
Legal Title: *American Northeastern Province of Xaverian Brothers Inc., Xaverian Brothers Northeastern Community Support Charitable Trust Fund.*
Brothers Professed 112.
Ministries in the field of Religious and Academic Education at all levels; Diocesan Offices; Pastoral Ministry; Mission Schools; Community; Houses; House of Formation.
Properties owned: St. John's Preparatory School, Danvers, MA St. John's High School, Shrewsbury, MA Malden Catholic High School, Malden, MA Xaverian Brothers High School, Westwood, MA Provincialate, Milton, MA Community houses in Malden, Danvers & Melrose, MA & Venice, FL.
Represented in the Archdioceses of Boston, Chicago, Hartford, Louisville, New York, Newark, Los Angeles, and the Dioceses of Brooklyn, Charleston, Memphis. Monterey, Norwich, Rapid City, Richmond, Venice and Worcester. Also in Kenya, Uganda, Haiti, Zaire and England.

[1360] (S.X.)—XAVERIAN MISSIONARY FATHERS

Saint Francis Xavier Foreign Mission Society
(Pia Societas Sancti Francisci Xaverii pro Exteris Missionibus)

General Motherhouse: *Istituto Saveriano Missioni Estere,* Viale Vaticano 40, 00165, Rome, Italy. Very Rev. Francesco Marini, S.X., Supr. Gen.
U.S. Province: *Xaverian Missionary Fathers,* 12 Helene Ct., Wayne, NJ 07470. Tel: 201-942-2975; Fax: 201-942-5012. Very Rev. Francis Signorelli, S.X., Prov.
Fathers 20; Seminarians 9.
Mission Houses 2; Houses of Formation 2.
Represented in the Archdioceses of Boston, Chicago and Milwaukee and in the Diocese of Paterson.

Index for Religious Institutes of Women

Religious Institutes of Women

Leadership Conference of Women Religious of the United States of America—National Office: 8808 Cameron St., Silver Spring, MD 20910. Tel: 301-588-4955. Sr. Margaret Cafferty, P.B.V.M., Exec. Dir.; Sr. Nancy Schreck, O.S.F., Pres.; Sr. Andree Fries, C.PP.S., Past Pres.; Sr. Anne Munley, I.H.M., Vice Pres.; Sr. Mary Ann Gschwind, F.S.P.A., Sec.; Sr. Anne Guinan, O.P., Treas. *Council Major Superiors of Women Religious in the United States of America*—4200 Harwood Rd., N.E., P.O. Box 4467, Washington, DC 20017-0467. Tel: 202-832-2575; Fax: 202-832-6325. Mother Vincent Marie Finnegan, O.C.D., Pres.

(The initial* D *or* P *indicates Diocesan or Pontifical Jurisdiction)

[0100] (A.S.C.)—ADORERS OF THE BLOOD OF CHRIST P

Founded in Acuto, Italy, in 1834. First foundation in the United States in 1870.

General Motherhouse: Via Beata Maria De Mattias 10, Rome, 00183. Italy. Sr. Giuseppina Fragasso, A.S.C., Supr. Gen.

Province of Ruma (1876): *Provincial House,* 2 Pioneer Ln., Red Bud, IL 62278. Tel: 618-282-3848; 282-6229. Sr. Margaret Mary Kopish, A.S.C., Prov. Supr.

Professed Sisters 208.

Sisters serve and staff: Colleges, Secondary & Elementary Schools, Special and Religious Education; Hospitals; Pastoral Care; Nursing Homes; Domestic Service in Communities and Institutions; Administration in Religious Orders and Parishes; Prayer Ministry; Retreat Ministry; Social Service; Pastoral and Chaplaincy Ministry; Prison and Minority Ministries.

Properties owned: *St. Clement Hospital,* Red Bud, IL; *St. Joseph Memorial Hospital,* Murphysboro, IL; *St. Vincent Memorial Hospital,* Taylorville, IL; *MariaCare,* Red Bud, IL.

Represented in the Archdioceses of St. Louis, and San Antonio, and the Dioceses of Belleville, Dodge City, Fort Wayne-South Bend, Gallup, Harrisburg, Jefferson City, Joliet, Springfield-Cape Girardeau, Oakland, Springfield (IL) and Tucson.

Province of Wichita (1929): *Provincial House,* 1400 S. Sheridan, Wichita, KS 67213-1394. Tel: 316-943-1203. Sr. Charlotte Rohrbach, A.S.C., Prov. Supr.; Sr. Helen Streck, Community Archivist.

Finally Professed Sisters 228; Scholasticates 7; Postulants 1; Novices 1.

Sisters Serve and Staff: College and Universities; High Schools; Elementary Schools; CCD-Parish Ministry; Social Work; Diocesan Offices; Hospitals-Clinics; Prayer Center; Homes for the Aged; Foreign Missions.

Properties owned: *Villa Maria,* Mulvane, KS; *Kansas Newman College,* Wichita, KS; *St. Joseph's Villa,* David City, NE.

Represented in the Archdioceses of Kansas City in Kansas, Oklahoma City, St. Louis, San Antonio and Washington, and the Dioceses of Beaumont, Brownsville, Dodge City, El Paso, Fort Worth, Gallup, Jefferson City, Kansas City - St. Joseph, Las Cruces, Lincoln, Oakland, Owensboro, Salina, San Angelo, Springfield (IL), Tulsa and Wichita.

Province of Columbia (1925): *Adorers of the Blood of Christ Provincial House,* 3950 Columbia Ave., Columbia, PA 17512-9714. Tel: 717-285-4536. Sr. Agatha Marie Groft, A.S.C., Prov. Coord.

Legal Title: *Adorers of the Blood of Christ, Province of Columbia, PA, Inc.*

Total number in community 85.

Ministry in the field of Academic and Religious Education through College; Home for the; Aged; Home Nursing; Independent Living Retirement Village; Domestic Service at; Bishops' Residence; Religious Education Resource Center; Retreat House; Pastoral Assistants; Hospital Chaplaincy; Ministry to Abused Children and; Children with AIDS.

Properties owned: *St. Joseph Convent-Provincial House; Precious Blood Spiritual Center; St. Anne's Home for the Aged, Inc.; De Mattias Residence; St. Anne's Independent Living Retirement Village,* Columbia, PA.

Represented in the Archdioceses of Baltimore, Chicago, New York, Newark and St. Louis, and the Dioceses of Altoona-Johnstown, Harrisburg, Savannah, Wilmington and Youngstown. Also in Guatemala and Slovak Republic.

[0110] (A.P.B.)—THE SISTERS ADORERS OF THE PRECIOUS BLOOD P

(Cloistered Contemplative Order)

American Federation: Consisting of six autonomous monasteries: 166 State St., Portland, ME 04101-3794. Sr. Mary Jo Divney, A.P.B., Pres. American Federation.

New York: 54th & Ft. Hamilton Pkwy., Brooklyn, NY 11219. Tel: 718-438-6371.

New Hampshire: 700 Bridge St., Manchester, NH 03104. Tel: 603-623-4264.

Indiana: 1106 State St., Lafayette, IN 47905. Tel: 317-742-8227.

New York: 400 Pratt St., Watertown, NY 13601. Tel: 315-788-1669.

Maine: 166 State St., Portland, ME 04101. Tel: 207-774-0861.

Canada: 9415 - 165th St., Edmonton, Alberta , Canada, T5R 2S5. Tel: 403-484-6691.

Professed Sisters 80; Novices 6; Postulants 2.

Represented in the Dioceses of Brooklyn, Lafayette (IN), Manchester, Ogdensburg and Portland (ME).

[0130] (A.S.C.J.)—APOSTLES OF THE SACRED HEART OF JESUS P

Founded in Italy in 1894. First foundation in United States 1902.

General Motherhouse: Via Germano Sommeiller, No. 38 Rome, Italy. Mother Auxiliadora deGodoy, Supr. Gen.; Sr. Leopoldina Euclidi, Archivist.

U.S. Provincial Motherhouse: *Mt. Sacred Heart,* 265 Benham St., Hamden, CT 06514. Tel: 203-248-4225; Fax: 203-230-8341.

Professed Sisters 196.

Ministry in the field of Education, Health Care, Parishes and Adult Day Care.

Properties owned: *Mary, Mother of the Church Convent,* Hamden, CT; *Mount Sacred Heart College for Sisters; Sacred Heart Academy; Sacred Heart Manor; Sacred Heart Manor Kindergarten and Nursery, Clelian Adult Day Care,* Hamden, CT; *Sacred Heart on the Lake,* Higganum, CT; *Cor Jesu Academy, Sacred Heart Villa Nursery,* St. Louis, MO; *Our Lady Queen of Apostles* (Convent & Nursery), Imperial, MO; *Clelian Heights School for Exceptional Children,* Greensburg, PA; *Sacred Heart Private Elementary School,* Bronx, NY.

Represented in the Archdioceses of Hartford, Newark, New York and St. Louis and in the Dioceses of Bridgeport, Greensburg, Metuchen, Norwich, Palm Beach, Pensacola-Tallahassee, Pittsburgh, Providence, Sacramento and St. Petersburg.

[0140] (S.A.A.)—SISTERS AUXILIARIES OF THE APOSTOLATE D

Founded in Canada in 1903. First United States foundation in 1911.

General Motherhouse: *Ss. Peter and Paul,* P.O. Box 9086, 689 Maple Terr., Monongah, WV 26555-9086. Tel: 304-534-3081. Sr. Angela Marie Pastore, Supr.

Total in Congregation 6; Professed Sisters 6.

Legal Holdings: *Ss. Peter and Paul Catholic School.*

Represented in the Diocese of Wheeling-Charleston.

[0150] (S.A.S.V.)—SISTERS OF THE ASSUMPTION P

Founded in Saint-Gregoire, P.Q., Canada in 1853. First foundation in the United States in 1891.

General Motherhouse: Nicolet, P.Q. Canada. Sr. Aline Vadnais, S.A.S.V., Supr. Gen.

Province Of The United States: *Provincial House,* 316 Lincoln St., Worcester, MA 01605. Sr. Muriel Lemoine, S.A.S.V., Prov. Supr. Tel: 508-856-9383. Sr. Lorraine Normand, S.A.S.V., Prov. Treas. Tel: 508-856-9450.

Total in Province 122; Total Professed 120; Junior Professed 2.

Ministry in all levels of education.

Legal Holdings: *Assumption Residence of the Sisters of the Assumption of the Blessed Virgin,* Petersham, MA; *Provincial House,* Worcester, MA; *Harper Residence,* Worcester, MA.

Represented in the Archdioceses of Boston and Hartford, and the Dioceses of Manchester, Portland in Maine, Providence, Springfield (MA) and Worcester. Missions in Japan, Brazil and Ecuador.

[0160] (O.S.A.)—AUGUSTINIAN NUNS OF CONTEMPLATIVE LIFE P

Augustinian Contemplative Nuns: *Mother of Good Counsel Convent,* 4328 Westminster Pl., St. Louis, MO 63108. Sr. Mary Grace, O.S.A., Prioress.

Total number in community 6.

Legal Title: *Augustinian Cloistered Nuns, Inc.*

Represented in the Archdiocese of St. Louis.

[0170] (O.S.B.)—BENEDICTINE NUNS OF THE CONGREGATION OF SOLESMES P

Order originated in Italy, c.529. Congregation of Solesmes formed in France in 1837.

U.S. Establishment (1981): *Monastery of the Immaculate Heart of Mary,* H.C.R. # 13, Box 11, Westfield, VT 05874. Tel: 802-744-6525. Rev. Mother Marguerite Derome, O.S.B., Prioress.

Total in Congregation 290; Total in community 14.

Represented in the Diocese of Burlington.

[0180] (O.S.B.)—BENEDICTINE NUNS OF THE PRIMITIVE OBSERVANCE P

First founded in Italy in about c. 529. First United States establishment in 1948.

Abbey of Regina Laudis: Bethlehem, CT 06751. Tel: 203-266-7727; Fax: 203-266-5915. Rt. Rev. Mother Benedict Duss, O.S.B., Abbess.

Professed Nuns 27; Sisters in First Vows 6; Novices 5; Postulants 1.

[0190] (O.S.B.)—BENEDICTINE SISTERS P

First founded in Italy c.529. Founded in the United States in 1931 from St. Walburg Abbey, Eichstatt, Bavaria, Germany.

The Sisters of St. Benedict of Westmoreland County: *St. Emma Monastery,* 1001 Harvey Ave., Greensburg, PA 15601-1494. Tel: 412-834-3060; Fax: 412-834-5772. Mother Mary Anne Noll, O.S.B., Prioress.

Professed Sisters 20; Postulants 1.

Ministry in Monastic Life; Benedictine hospitality extended through St. Emma Retreat House.

Represented in the Diocese of Greensburg.

Benedictine Nuns: *Abbey of St. Walburga,* 6717 S. Boulder Rd., Boulder, CO 80303. Tel: 303-494-5733; Fax: 303-494-4357. Mother Maria-Thomas Beil, O.S.B., Abbess.

Sisters 22; Postulants 1.

Represented in the Archdiocese of Denver.

[0200] (O.S.B.)—BENEDICTINE SISTERS D

(Regina Pacis)

The first Monastery was founded 1680 in Kaunas, Lithuania by a Polish Abbess Eufemia Skorulska.

Founded in United States in 1957 by Mother M. Raphaela Simonis, O.S.B.

U.S. Foundation: Regina Pacis Benedictine Sisters, 333 Wallace Rd., Bedford, NH 03110. Tel: 603-472-3239. Mother M. Raphaela Simonis, O.S.B., Supr.

Novitiate; Kindergarten and Nursery School.

Represented in the Diocese of Manchester.

[0210] (O.S.B.)—MISSIONARY BENEDICTINE SISTERS P

The Congregation of Missionary Benedictine Sisters is of Pontifical Jurisdiction. Its Constitutions were approved by Rome on June 25, 1934; Revised approval June 29, 1983.

Generalate: Rome, Italy.

Provincial Motherhouse and Novitiate: *Immaculata Convent,* (1923), 300 N. 18th St., Norfolk, NE 68701-3687. Tel: 402-371-3438; Fax: 402-379-2877. Sr. M. Agnes Salber, O.S.B., Prioress.

Professed Sisters 52; Juniorates 6; Postulants 3; Novices 3.

Ministry in the fields of Education; Health & Hospitals; Nursing Homes.
Legal Holdings or Titles: *Immaculata Convent,* Norfolk, NE; *Our Lady of Lourdes Hospital,* Norfolk, NE; *St. Joseph Nursing Home,* Norfolk, NE; *Providence Medical Center,* Wayne, NE; *Graceville Missionary Benedictine Sisters, Inc., dba Holy Trinity Hospital - Grace Home,* Graceville, MN.
Represented in the Archdiocese of Omaha and the Diocese of New Ulm.

[0220] (O.S.B.)—CONGREGATION OF THE BENEDICTINE SISTERS OF PERPETUAL ADORATION OF PONTIFICAL JURISDICTION

P

Founded from Maria Rickenbach, Switzerland, in 1874 with first monastery at Clyde, MO. Congregation erected by decree of the Holy See on June 16, 1936. Generalate, Novitiate and Healthcare community transferred to St. Louis in 1966.
General Motherhouse and Novitiate: *Benedictine Monastery of Perpetual Adoration,* 8300 Morganford Rd., St. Louis, MO 63123. Tel: 314-638-6427. Sr. Mary Jane Romero, Prioress Gen., General Council; Sr. M. Bede Luetkemeyer; Sr. Sarah Schwartzberg; Sr. Joan Therese Anderson; Sr. Cathleen Marie Timberlake.
Total number in community: Professed 134; Novices 5.
Interdependent Monasteries: R.R. 1, Box 101, Clyde, MO 64432. 800 N. Country Club Rd., Tucson, AZ 85716. Osage Monastery, 18701 W. Monastery Rd., Sand Springs, OK 74063. San Benito Monastery, Box 520, Dayton, WY 82836.
Ministry in Monastic/Contemplative/Eucharistic Apostolate of Prayer; Liturgy of the Hours four times daily in Choir; Contemplative Prayer and Monastic Atmosphere Shared with Others; Prayer Days and Retreats for Sisters; Editing and Publishing Bimonthly Magazine: "Spirit & Life"; Production and Distribution of Altar Breads; Liturgical Vestments; Correspondence.
Represented in the Archdiocese of St. Louis, and the Dioceses of Cheyenne, Kansas City-St. Joseph, Tucson and Tulsa.

[0230] (O.S.B.)—BENEDICTINE SISTERS OF PONTIFICAL JURISDICTION

P

(1) The Federation Of St. Scholastica.
Erected by Decree of the Holy See, Feb. 25, 1922, with final approbation by Decree of June 10, 1930.
Twenty-two Motherhouses in the United States and two in Mexico. Total number in the Federation 1,288; Sr. Regina Crowley, O.S.B., Pres., residing at 5807 N. Kolmar Ave., Chicago, IL 60646. Tel: 773-973-6845.
Benedictine Sisters of Baltimore, Inc.: *Emmanuel Monastery,* 2229 W. Joppa Rd., Lutherville, MD 21093. Tel: 410-821-5792. Sr. Patricia Kirk, O.S.B., Prioress.
Total number in community 15.
Ministry in the field of Education; Parish Ministry; Retreats and Spiritual Direction; Justice Ministry; Social Services; Hospice Chaplaincy.
Represented in the Archdioceses of Baltimore and Newark.
Benedictine Sisters of the Byzantine Rite (1969): *Queen of Heaven Monastery,* 8640 Squires Ln., N.E., Warren, OH 44484. Tel: 330-856-1813. Sr. Barbara Pavlik, O.S.B., Prioress.
Professed Sisters 12.
Legal Holding: *BEL-Center (Benedictine Early Learning Center).*
Ministry in Religious and Academic Education; Pastoral Ministry; Child Care; Administration.
Represented in the Archdiocese of Pittsburgh Byzantine Rite.
Mount St. Scholastica, Inc. (1863): *Motherhouse of the Sisters of St. Benedict,* 801 S. Eighth St., Atchison, KS 66002-2778. Tel: 913-367-6110; Fax: 913-367-3866. Sr. Mary Agnes Patterson, O.S.B., Prioress.
Total number in community 244.
Legal Holdings: *Dooley Center, Inc.; The Mount Community Center, Inc.; Mount St. Scholastica, Inc.,* Atchison, KS.
Ministry in the field of Academic Education at all levels; Special Education; Music Conservatory; Pastoral Ministry; Counseling; Retreats; Spirituality Center; Spiritual Direction; Social Services; Diocesan Offices; Ministry to the Aged; Child Day Care; Hospitality; Community & Conference Center Work; Special Services to the needy; Ministry to the sick; Missionary Work in Brazil.
Represented in the Archdioceses of Chicago, Kansas City in Kansas, New Orleans, St. Louis and Washington, and the Dioceses of Des Moines, Dodge City, Kansas City-St. Joseph, Arlington, and Tulsa. Also in Brazil.
Benedictine Sisters of Elk Co. (1852): *St. Joseph Monastery,* St. Marys, PA 15857. Tel: 814-834-2267. Sr. Raphael Baker, O.S.B., Prioress.
Professed Sisters 50.
Ministry in the fields of Academic and Religious Education; Pastoral Ministry; Child Welfare; Retreats; Diocesan Marriage Tribunal.
Benedictine Sisters of Erie (1856): *Mt. St. Benedict Monastery,* 6101 East Lake Rd., Erie, PA 16511. Tel: 814-899-0614; Fax: 814-898-4004. Sr. Phyllis Schleicher, O.S.B., Prioress.
Total in Congregation 147; Professed Sisters 138; In Formation 9.
Sisters serve and staff: High Schools; Elementary Schools; Colleges; Day Care Centers; Residence for Elderly and Handicapped; Hospitals; Social Services; Diocesan Offices; Pastoral Ministry; Religious Education.
Properties owned: *Mount Saint Benedict Monastery; Glinodo Conference Center; St. Benedict Education Center; Benet Center Om Shanti; St. Scholastica Priory Kraus House,* Erie, PA; *Benetwood Apartments,* Harborcreek, PA; *Holy Family Priory,* Benet Lake, WI; *St. Walburga Priory; Sophia House Benedita Reipp Priory,* Erie, PA.
Represented in the Archdiocese of Chicago and Milwaukee, and the Dioceses of Arlington, Cleveland, Erie, Orlando and Syracuse.
Benedictine Sisters of Chicago O.S.B. (1861): *St. Scholastica Priory,* 7430 Ridge Blvd., Chicago, IL 60645. Tel: 312-764-2413. Sr. Karen Bland, Prioress; Sr. Vivian Ivantic, Community Archivist.
Professed Sisters 92; Scholastics 1; Novices 1.
Ministry in High Schools; Elementary Schools; Pastoral Ministry; Religious Education; University staff; Management Consultant; Campus Ministry; Spiritual Direction; Peace and Shelter Ministry; Community Center Work; Jail and Hospital Chaplains.
Properties owned: *St. Scholastica Priory,* Chicago, IL; *St. Scholastica High School,* Chicago, IL; *St. Scholastica Academy,* Canon City, CO.
Represented in the Archdioceses of Chicago and the Diocese of Pueblo.
Benedictine Sisters of the Sacred Heart O.S.B. (1895): *Sacred Heart Monastery,* 1910 Maple Ave., Lisle, IL 60532-2184. Tel: 630-969-7040. Sr. Judith Ann Heble, O.S.B., Prioress.
Legal Title: *Benedictine Sisters of the Sacred Heart Charitable Trust.*
Professed Sisters 52.
Sisters serve and staff: High Schools; Elementary Schools; Colleges; Queen of Peace Center; Religious Education; Pastoral Ministry; Nurses Administration; P.A.D.S.; Independent Positions involving Secretarial, Counseling, Liturgical Works, Occupational Therapy, Internal Ministry and Altar Bread Baking.
Represented in the Archdiocese of Chicago and the Diocese of Joliet.
Benedictine Sisters of Elizabeth, NJ O.S.B. (1868): *St. Walburga Monastery and Novitiate,* 851 N. Broad St., Elizabeth, NJ 07208. Tel: 201-352-4278. Sr. Germaine Fritz, O.S.B., Prioress.
Professed Sisters 72.
Legal Holdings and Titles: *Benedictine Hospital,* Kingston, NY; *Benedictine Academy,* Elizabeth, NJ; *Bender Memorial Academy,* Elizabeth, NJ.
Represented in the Archdioceses of New York, Newark and Washington, and the Dioceses of Paterson and Trenton.
Benedictine Sisters of Pittsburgh, PA. O.S.B. (1870): *St. Benedict Monastery,* 4530 Perrysville Ave., Pittsburgh, PA 15229-2296. Tel: 412-931-2844. Sr. Roberta Campbell, O.S.B., Prioress.
Total in Congregation 90; Professed Sisters 89.
Ministry in the field of Education in all levels; Religious and Special Education; Pastoral Ministry; Childcare; House of Prayer; Social Service; Campus Ministry; Hospital Chaplaincy; Art Education; Ministry Resource; Peace & Justice Commission; Outreach with Poor; Benedictine Center for Senior Citizens; Adult Day Care.
Properties owned: *Saint Benedict Academy,* Pittsburgh, PA; *Pittsburgh Benedictine Ministries, Inc.*
Represented in the Dioceses of Greensburg, Lexington and Pittsburgh.
Sisters of Benedict O.S.B. (1968): *Red Plains Monastery,* 728 Richland Rd., S.W., Piedmont, OK 73078-9324. Tel: 405-373-4565 & 4569. Sr. Marie Ballmann, O.S.B., Prioress.
Professed Sisters 12.
Ministry in the fields of Education, CCD and Adult Religious Education; Spiritual Formation; Spiritual Direction; Retreats.
Represented in the Archdiocese of Oklahoma City.
Benedictine Sisters O.S.B. (1879): *St. Joseph Monastery, Priory and Novitiate,* 2200 S. Lewis, Tulsa, OK 74114-3100. Tel: 918-742-4989. Sr. Barbara Austin, O.S.B., Prioress; Sr. Anita Marie Gilpin, O.S.B., Archivist.
Professed Sisters 36; In Formation 2.
Ministry in the field of Academic Education; Catechetics; Evangelization; Nursing; Pastoral Ministry; Social Civic & Ecumenical Group Work; Counselling & Spiritual Direction; Prison Ministry; Religious Education & Religious Formation.
Legal Titles & Holdings: *Congregation of the Benedictine Sisters of the Sacred Hearts Monte Cassino School.*
Represented in the Archdiocese of Oklahoma City and the Diocese of Tulsa.
Benedictine Sisters of Pontifical Jurisdiction O.S.B. (1857): *St. Gertrude Monastery,* 14259 Benedictine Ln., Ridgely, MD 21660. Tel: 301-634-2497.
Professed Sisters 42; Temporary Professed 2.
Ministry in Special Schools and Elementary & Secondary Education; Job Training Center for the Mentally Handicapped; Open Community Houses for Mentally Handicapped; Do-It-Yourself Retreat Facility: Berg Center; Outreach facility for the poor: St. Martin's Barn; Transitional home for homeless women and children.
Legal holdings & titles: *The Benedictine School for Exceptional Children; Berg Retreat Facility; St. Martin's Barn; St. Martin House,* Ridgely, MD; *St. Benedict-at-Innisfail,* Hockessin, DE.
Represented in the Archdiocese of Washington, and the Dioceses of Camden and Wilmington.
St. Walburg Monastery of Benedictine Sisters of Covington, KY. O.S.B. (1859): *St. Walburg Monastery,* 2500 Amsterdam Rd., Villa Hills, KY 41017-5316. Tel: 606-331-6324; Fax: 606-331-2136. Motherhouse and Novitiate. Sr. M. Catherine Wenstrup, O.S.B., Prioress; Sr. Teresa Wolking, O.S.B., Community Archivist.
Professed Sisters 110.
Sisters serve and staff: Diocesan and Archdiocesan Offices; Hospitals; Pastoral and Social Ministry; Home or Public Health Care; Seminary; all levels of academic education.
Legal titles & holdings: *Madonna Manor Nursing-Senior Citizens Home Villa Madonna Early Learning Center Villa Madonna Academy Villa Madonna Center - Spirituality Center.*
Represented in the Archdiocese of Cincinnati, and the Dioceses of Covington, Lexington and Pueblo.
Benedictine Sisters (1902): *Sacred Heart Monastery,* Cullman, AL 35056. Tel: 205-734-2199; 734-4622; Fax: 205-734-3835. Sr. Treva Heinberg, O.S.B., Prioress; Sr. Benedicta Karter, O.S.B., Community Archivist.
Professed Sisters 63.
Sisters staff and serve: in all levels of Academic Education; Pastoral Ministry; Diocesan Offices; Retirement Homes; Conference Centers.
Properties owned: *Benedictine Spirituality and Conference Center; Benedictine Manor Retirement Home.*
Represented in the Archdioceses of Atlanta, and New Orleans and in the Dioceses of Birmingham and Orlando.
Benedictine Sisters O.S.B. (1870): *St. Scholastica Priory,* 75512 Louisiana Hwy. 1081, Covington, LA 70433. Sr. Regina Crowley, O.S.B., Admin., 5807 N. Kolmar, Chicago, IL 60646. Tel: 312-736-0876.
Professed Sisters 2.
Sisters serve and staff: Parish & Social Ministries.
Represented in the Archdiocese of New Orleans.
Benedictine Sisters of Virginia O.S.B. (1868): *St. Benedict Monastery,* Bristow, VA 20136-1217. Tel: 703-361-0106. Sr. Cecilia Dwyer, O.S.B., Prioress.
Total in Congregation 43; Professed Sisters 41.
Legal Holdings and Titles: *Benedictine Sisters of Virginia, Inc., St. Gertrude High School,* Richmond, VA; *Linton Hall School, Benedictine Pastoral Center; Benedictine Counseling Services,* Bristow, VA.
Represented in the Dioceses of Arlington and Richmond.
Benedictine Sisters (1911): *St. Scholastica's Monastery and Novitiate,* 416 W. Highland Dr., Boerne, TX 78006. Tel: 210-249-2645. Sr. Mary Agnes Zinni, O.S.B., Prioress.
Total number in community 24.
Properties owned: *St. Scholastica Monastery; St. Albert Early Learning Center,* Boerne, TX; *Benedictine Resource Center,* San Antonio, TX, Convents 4.
Represented in the Archdiocese of San Antonio,, and the Dioceses of Austin and Gallup.
Benedictine Sisters of St. Lucy's Priory Inc. O.S.B. (1956): *St. Lucy's Priory,* 19045 E. Sierra Madre Ave., Glendora, CA 91741. Tel: 818-335-1682. Sr. Elizabeth Brown, O.S.B., Prioress.
Professed Sisters 27.
Sisters serve & staff: all levels of Academic Education; Continuing Education; Home for Developmentally Disabled Adults; Pastoral Ministry; Hospital Chaplaincy.
Legal holdings: *St. Lucy's Priory High School; St. Lucy's Benedictine Child Development Center.*

Represented in the Archdiocese of Los Angeles and the Diocese of San Diego.

BENEDICTINE SISTERS OF FLORIDA (1889): *Holy Name Priory,* P.O. Box H, St. Leo, FL 33574-4002. Tel: 904-588-8320; Fax: 904-588-8319. Sr. Germaine Bevans, O.S.B., Prioress; Sr. Jerome Leary, O.S.B., Community Archivist.
Professed Sisters 25; Temporary Professed 3.
Represented in the Diocese of St. Petersburg.

SISTERS OF ST. BENEDICT (1963): *Benet Hill Monastery-Motherhouse,* 2555 N. Chelton Rd., Colorado Springs, CO 80909-1399. Tel: 719-633-0655; Fax: 917-471-0403. Sr. Anne Stedman, O.S.B., Prioress; Sr. Diane Liston, Community Archivist.
Total number in community 47.
Properties owned: Benet Hill Center; Benet Pines Retreat Center.
Represented in the Archdiocese of Denver, and the Dioceses of Colorado Springs, Salina, and Pueblo. Also in Jamaica.

BENEDICTINE SISTERS O.S.B. (1989): *Queen of Angels Monastery,* 717 Kings Hwy., Liberty, MO 64068. Tel: 816-781-6246; 781-4613. Sr. Imelda Koch, O.S.B., Prioress.
Professed Sisters 5; Temporary Professed 2; Novices 1; Pre-Novitiate 3.
Ministry in Residential Care Facility for Developmentally Disabled Women.
Represented in the Diocese of Kansas City-St. Joseph.

(II) THE FEDERATION OF ST. GERTRUDE.
Erected by Decree of the Apostolic See on April 14, 1937, with final approbation by Decree of April 4, 1950. *Federation Office,* Sacred Heart Monastery, P.O. Box 364, Richardton, ND 58652. Tel: 701-974-2121; Fax: 701-974-2124. Sr. Ruth Fox, O.S.B., Federation Pres.
Total in the Federation 1,197. Eighteen member monasteries form this Federation as follows:.

SISTERS OF ST. BENEDICT OF BEECH GROVE, IND., INC.: *Our Lady of Grace Monastery, (1956),* 1402 Southern Ave., Beech Grove, IN 46107. Tel: 317-787-3287; Fax: 317-780-2368. Sr. Rachel Best, O.S.B., Prioress.
Total Professed Sisters 85.
Ministry in Education; Parish Ministries; Retirement Home; Educational Center; Religious Education; Hospitals.
Properties owned and sponsored: Our Lady of Grace Monastery; Beech Grove Benedictine Center; St. Paul Hermitage Regina Retreat.
Legal Title: *Sisters of St. Benedict of Beech Grove, Ind., Inc.; Charitable Trust of the Monastery of Our Lady of Grace; Sisters of the Order of St. Benedict.*
Represented in the Archdioceses of Cincinnati and Indianapolis and the Diocese of Evansville.

BENEDICTINE SISTERS OF BELCOURT O.S.B.: *Queen of Peace Monastery, (1963),* P.O. Box 370, Belcourt, ND 58316. Tel: 701-477-6167; Fax: 701-477-5575. Sr. Maura Schnur, O.S.B., Prioress.
Professed Sisters 7.
Ministry in Counselling; Religious Education; Parish Ministry and Administration; Home Ministry.

BENEDICTINE SISTERS O.S.B.: *Our Lady of Peace Monastery,* 3710 West Broadway, Columbia, MO 65203. Tel: 314-446-2300. Sr. JoAnn Schmidt, O.S.B., Prioress.
Professed Sisters 13.
Ministry in Education; Home Health Care; Parish & Social Ministries; Counseling.
Represented in the Dioceses of Jefferson City, Kansas City-St. Joseph, Little Rock, Springfield in Illinois and Springfield-Cape Girardeau.

MONASTERY OF ST. GERTRUDE: (1882), HC 3 Box 121, Cottonwood, ID 83522-9408. Tel: 208-962-3224.
Legal Title: *Idaho Corporation of Benedictine Sisters;* Sr. Mary Kay Henry, O.S.B., Prioress.
Professed Sisters 89.
Sisters serve in: Education; Parish Ministry; Foreign Mission; Health Care; Retreat Ministry; Social Work; St. Gertrude's Museum.
Sisters sponsor: *St. Benedict's Family Medical Center,* Jerome, ID.
Represented in the Archdioceses of Los Angeles, Portland (OR) and Seattle, and the Dioceses of Boise and Spokane.

SISTERS OF ST. BENEDICT OF CROOKSTON O.S.B.: *Mount St. Benedict Monastery,* (1919), 620 E. Summit Ave., Crookston, MN 56716-2799. Tel: 218-281-3441. Sr. Michelle McGurran, O.S.B., Prioress.
Professed Sisters 156.
Sisters serve and staff: Elementary, High Schools & Colleges; Nursing Homes; Board, Care and Assisted Living Home; Religious Education Center; Adult Education; Parish Ministry; Pastoral Care; Retreat Centers & Social Services; Child Care; Nursery School.
Legal Holding: *St. Vincent,* Crookston, MN.
Represented in the Dioceses of Brownsville, Crookston, Fargo, New Ulm and St. Cloud.

BENEDICTINE SISTERS O.S.B.: *Monastery Immaculate Conception,* (1867), 802 E. 10th St., Ferdinand, IN 47532-9239. Tel: 812-367-1411. Sr. Kathryn Huber, O.S.B., Prioress.
Professed Sisters 228.
Legal Title: *Sisters of St. Benedict of Ferdinand, Indiana, Inc.*
Sisters serve and staff: on all levels of Academic Education; Religious Education Centers; Parish Ministry; Special Education Centers; Hospitals; Public Health-Social Service Agencies; Diocesan Offices; Foreign Missions; Retreat House.
DEPENDENT MONASTERIES: *Monasterio Paz de la Cruz,* Morropon, Peru, *Monasterio Reina de la Paz,* Coban, Guatemala.
Sisters Sponsor: *Marian Heights Academy; Kordes Enrichment Center,* Ferdinand, IN.
Represented in the Archdioceses of Chicago, Indianapolis, Louisville,, and the Dioceses of Evansville, Fort Wayne-South Bend, Joliet, Lafayette (IN), Memphis, Owensboro, and Richmond.

BENEDICTINE SISTERS, O.S.B. OF ST. SCHOLASTICA MONASTERY: *St. Scholastica Monastery,* (1879), P.O. Box 3489, Fort Smith, AR 72913. Tel: 501-783-4147. Sr. Elise Forst, O.S.B., Prioress.
Professed Sisters 126.
Ministry in the fields of Elementary and Religious Education; Retreat Center; Day Care Center; Parish Ministry; Hospital Chaplaincy; House of Prayer; Spiritual Direction.
Dependent Monastery: *St. Benedict Monastery,* Canyon, TX.
Represented in the Dioceses of Amarillo, Little Rock, and Tulsa.

SISTERS OF ST. BENEDICT OF RIVERSIDE, INC.: *Holy Spirit Monastery, (1972),* 22791 Pico St., Grand Terrace, CA 92313-5750. Tel: 909-783-4446. Sr. Carolyn Gries, O.S.B., Prioress.
Professed Sisters 11.
Ministry in Elementary Education; Parish & Diocesan Ministry; Counseling and Spiritual Direction; Hospital Chaplaincy; Work with the Elderly; Retreat Centers; Educating the Handicapped.
Represented in the Dioceses of Orange and San Bernardino.

BENEDICTINE SISTERS: *Spirit of Life Monastery,* 10760 W. Glennon Dr., Lakewood, CO 80226. Tel: 303-986-9234. Sr. Charlotte Redpath, O.S.B., Prioress.
Corporate Minsitry: *Spirit of Life Center.*
Sisters serve in: Retreat and Prayer Ministry; Counseling and Spiritual Direction.
Professed Sisters 2.

SISTERS OF ST. BENEDICT OF MADISON, WISCONSIN, INC.: *Monastery of St. Benedict Center, (1897),* P.O. Box 5070, Madison, WI 53705-0070. Tel: 608-836-1631. Sr. Mary David Walgenbach, O.S.B., Prioress.
Professed Sisters 6.
Sisters serve: Community Building, Prayer, Education, Retreat and Conference Ministries.
Corporate Ministries: *St. Benedict Center.*
Legal Title: *Sisters of St. Benedict, Sioux City, Iowa, Inc.; Sisters of St. Benedict of Madison, Wisconsin, Inc.*
Represented in the Dioceses of Madison and Sioux City.

BENEDICTINE SISTERS OF MT. ANGEL, OREGON: *Queen of Angels Monastery,* (1882), 840 S. Main St., Mt. Angel, OR 97362. Tel: 503-845-6141. Sr. Jeanette von Herrmann, O.S.B., Prioress.
Professed Sisters 63.
Sisters serve: Elementary and High Schools; Colleges; Parish Ministry; Retreat and Prayer Ministry; Nursing; Counseling and Spiritual Direction; Work with Handicapped and Aging; Home Health Care; Hospital Chaplaincy; Ministry to Poor and Hispanics.
Corporate Ministries: *Shilom Prayer Center; St. Joseph's Shelter,* Mt. Angel, OR.
Institution Sponsors: *Benedictine Nursing Center,* Mt. Angel, OR.
Represented in the Archdiocese of Portland (OR) and the Diocese of Boise, and Honolulu. Also in Victoria, B.C.

BENEDICTINE CONVENT OF ST. MARTIN: (1889), 2110-C St. Martin's Dr., Rapid City, SD 57702. Tel: 605-343-8011; Fax: 605-399-2723. Sr. Florence McManamen, O.S.B., Prioress.
Professed Sisters 43.
Properties owned: *St. Martin's Academy Learning Center and Retreat Center.*
Sisters serve and staff: Elementary Schools; Retreat Center; Home care; Adult Religious Education; Parish Ministries; Chancery Staff; Hospital Chaplaincies, Nursing and Counseling.
Dependent Monastery: *Epiphany Monastery,* Columbia Falls, MT.
Represented in the Archdioceses of Seattle, Portland (OR), and the Dioceses of Great Falls-Billings, Helena, Madison, Orange, Rapid City, and Tyler.

BENEDICTINE SISTERS OF RICHARDTON, O.S.B.: *Sacred Heart Monastery,* (1916), P.O. Box 364, Richardton, ND 58652. Tel: 701-974-2121; Fax: 701-974-2124. Sr. Paula Larson, O.S.B., Prioress.
Professed Sisters 40.
Ministry in the fields of Academic Education; Summer Vacation Schools; Hospital Chaplaincy; Indian ministry; Parish ministry; Health Care.
Legal Titles or Holdings: *St. Vincent's Nursing Home, Inc. Marillac Manor, Inc. Subiaco Manor Inc. Sacred Heart Benedictine Foundation.*
Represented in the Diocese of Bismarck.

THE BENEDICTINE SISTERS OF MOTHER OF GOD MONASTERY O.S.B.: *Mother of God Monastery,* (1961), 120 S.E. 28th Ave., Watertown, SD 57201. Tel: 605-886-6777. Sr. Sandra Meek, O.S.B., Prioress.
Professed Sisters 89.
Sisters serve and staff: in Elementary and College Education; CCD Centers; Ecumenical Monastery; Social Justice Center; Parish Ministry; Social Services; Hospitals and Hospices; Retreat Center; Homes for Aged; Juvenile Services; Continuing Education Center; Native American Ministeries; Hispanic Ministries; Foreign Mission in Guatemala; and Congregate Housing for Elderly.
Legal Title: *The Benedictine Sisters of Mother of God Monastery, St. Ann's Corporation (includes Benet Place),* Watertown, SD; Harmony Hill Corporation, Watertown, SD.
Represented in the Archdioceses of Chicago, Omaha, St. Paul-Minneapolis and San Antonio, and the Dioceses of Arlington, Bismarck, Boise, Crookston, Dubuque, Duluth, Fargo, La Crosse, Lincoln, Madison, Sioux Falls, Tyler and Yakima. Also in Guatemala and Germany.

ST. BENEDICT'S MONASTERY (1912): 225 Masters Ave., Winnipeg, Manitoba , Canada, R4A 2A1. Tel: 204-338-4601. Sr. Virginia Euard, Prioress.
Professed Sisters 53.
Ministry in Retreat Center; Education and Health Care.
Represented in the Dioceses of Calgary, St. Boniface and Winnipeg in Canada.

BENEDICTINE CONVENT OF THE SACRED HEART: *Sacred Heart Monastery, (1880),* 1005 W. 8th St., Yankton, SD 57078. Tel: 605-668-1011. Sr. Kathryn Easley, O.S.B., Prioress.
Professed Sisters 173.
Sisters serve and staff: in Health Care Institutions; all levels of Academic Education; Social Services; Parish Ministry; Pastoral Care; Diocesan Offices; Counseling & Religious Education.
Represented in the Archdioceses of Chicago, Detroit, Dubuque, Omaha, St. Louis, Washington, and the Dioceses of Arecibo, Bismarck, Lincoln, Pueblo, St. Cloud, Sioux Falls and Tucson.

BENEDICTINE SISTERS, O.S.B.: *The Dwelling Place Monastery, (1993),* 150 Mt. Tabor Rd., Martin, KY 41649. Tel: 606-886-9624. Sr. Judy Yunkers, O.S.B., Prioress.
Professed Sisters 4.
Sisters serve and staff: Elementary and Adult Education; Mentally Handicapped; Retreat Center; Volunteer Program.
Represented in the Diocese of Lexington.

BENEDICTINE SISTERS OF NANAIMO: *House of Bread Monastery, (1993),* 2329 Arbot Rd., Nanaimo, British Columbia, Canada, V9R 6S8. Tel: 604-753-1763; Fax: 604-753-6742. Sr. Jean Ann Berning, O.S.B., Prioress.
Sisters serve: Counselling; Retreat and Prayer Ministry; Nursing; Artist; Corporate Ministries; Bethlehem Retreat Centre; Bethlehem Counselling Centre.
Represented in the Diocese of Victoria, Canada.
Professed Sisters 9.

(III) THE FEDERATION OF ST. BENEDICT.
Erected by decree of the Holy See March 24, 1947; *St. Benedict's Monastery,* 104 Chapel Lane, St. Joseph, MN 56374. Tel: 320-363-7070; Fax: 320-363-7130. Sr. Colleen Haggerty, O.S.B., Federation Pres.
Legal Title: *Federation of St. Benedict.*
Total number of Sisters in Federation 1,012. Eleven monasteries form this Federation; in addition to the eight American Monasteries listed, three autonomous monasteries exist in Japan. St. Benedict's Monastery (1985) Sapparo, Hokkaido; Taiwan- St. Benedict's Monastery (1988) Tanshui, Taipei; Bahamas - Saint Martin Convent (1994) Nassau.

Sisters of St. Benedict, 1994, Mt. Benedict Priory, 309 E. 5450 South, Ogden, UT 84405. Tel: 801-479-6030. Sr. Mary Zenzen, O.S.B., Prioress.
Professed sisters 11.
Sisters serve and staff: Health Care; Campus Ministry; Diocesan Offices—Retreat Center, Vocation Director.
Represented in the Diocese of Salt Lake City.

SISTERS OF THE ORDER OF ST. BENEDICT-O.S.B. (1857): *St. Benedict's Convent-Motherhouse and Novitiate,* St. Joseph, MN 56374-0277. Tel: 320-363-7100. Sr. Ephrem Hollermann, O.S.B., Prioress; Sr. Ruth Boedigheimer, O.S.B., Archivist.
Total Sisters in Community 451.
Legal Title: *Sisters of the Order of Saint Benedict, St. Joseph, MN.*

Ministry in the field of Education at all levels; Indian Missions; Hospitals; Nursing Homes; Dependent Priory; Individual Apostolates; Diocesan Marriage Tribunal; Diocesan Newspaper; Parish Ministry; Social Work; Counseling.
Represented in the Archdioceses of Mobile, St. Paul-Minneapolis Seattle and Washington, and the Dioceses of Caguas (PR), Crookston, Duluth, Madison, Manchester, New Ulm, St. Cloud, San Diego and San Jose. Also in Brazil and Canada.
SISTERS OF ST. BENEDICT - ST. SCHOLASTICA MONASTERY O.S.B. (1892): 1200 Kenwood Ave., Duluth, MN 55811. Tel: 218-723-6555. Sr. Danile Lynch, O.S.B., Prioress; Sr. Aelred Roehl, Archivist.
Total number in community 177.
Ministry in the field of Academic Education at all levels; Religious Education; Indian Ministry; Residence for Elderly; Nursing Homes; Hospitals; Pastoral Care and Parish Ministries; Prison Ministry; Peace and Justice; Retreat Center.
Properties owned and/or sponsored: *McCabe Renewal Center,* Duluth, MN; *College of St. Scholastica; St. Mary's Medical Center,* Duluth, MN; *Benedictine Foundation, Inc.; BHS Long Term Care, Inc.,* Duluth, MN; *Benedictine Health Center; Polinsky Rehabilitation Center,* Duluth MN; *St. Joseph's Medical Center,* Brainerd, MN; *St. Mary's Regional Health Center,* Detroit Lakes, MN; *St. Francis Regional Medical Center,* Shakopee, MN; *St. Mary's Hospital,* Cottonwood, ID; *Tekakwitha Nursing Center, Inc.,* Sisseton, SD; *Madonna Towers of Rochester, Inc.,* Rochester, MN; *Dickinson Nursing Center; Ellendale Nursing Center; Garrison Nursing Home; LaMoure Healthcare Manor; Wahpeton Healthcare Center,* ND; *Aberdeen Living Center,* SD; *Benedictine Sisters Benevolent Association; Benedictine Health System,* Duluth, MN.
Represented in the Archdioceses of Chicago, Milwaukee, St. Paul-Minneapolis, and Seattle, and the Dioceses of Arlington, Bismarck, Boise, Crookston, Duluth, Fargo, La Crosse, New Ulm, Phoenix, Rochester, St. Cloud, Sioux Falls, and Winona.
ST. BEDE PRIORY (1948): 1190 Priory Rd., P.O. Box 66, Eau Claire, WI 54702. Tel: 715-834-3176. Sr. Margaret Michaud, O.S.B., Prioress; Sr. Lorayne Andre, O.S.B., Archivist.
Total number in community 53.
Properties owned and sponsored: *St. Bede Priory - Motherhouse St. Bede Retreat and Conference Center.*
Represented in the Archdioceses of San Antonio and St. Paul-Minneapolis, and the Dioceses of La Crosse and Springfield-Cape Girardeau. Also in Jamaica.
SISTERS OF THE ORDER OF ST. BENEDICT O.S.B. (1874): *St. Mary Monastery,* Nauvoo, IL 62354. Tel: 217-453-2227. Sr. Ruth Ksycki, O.S.B., Prioress; Sr. Antoinette Fineran, Archivist.
Total number in community 76.
Ministry in the field of Religious and Academic Education; Pastoral Care; Parish Ministry.
Represented in the Dioceses of Davenport, Gary, and Peoria.
BENEDICTINE SISTERS OF THE ANNUNCIATION, BVM (1947): *Annunciation Priory,* 7520 University Dr., Bismarck, ND 58504-9653. Tel: 701-255-1520. Sr. Susan Berger, O.S.B., Prioress.
Professed Sisters 102.
Ministry in Hospitals; Parish Ministry and Catechetical Work; Education and Health Care.
Represented in the Archdiocese Seattle and the Diocese of Bismarck.
SISTERS OF ST. BENEDICT (1948): *St. Paul's Priory,* 2675 Larpenteur Ave. E., St. Paul, MN 55109. Tel: 612-777-8181; Fax: 612-777-4442. Sr. Marie Fugan, O.S.B., Prioress.
Professed Sisters 94.
Sisters serve and staff: School on all levels; Homes for the Aged; Business, Child Care; Retreat Center; Parish Ministry; Social Service and various other apostolic work.
Represented in the Archdiocese of St. Paul-Minneapolis and the Diocese of Great Falls, Jackson, and St. Cloud.
SISTERS OF ST. BENEDICT O.S.B. (1952): *St. Placid Priory,* 500 College St., N.E., Lacey, WA 98516-5338. Tel: 360-438-1771. Sr. Sharon McDonald, O.S.B., Prioress.
Professed Sisters 25.
Sisters serve in the field of Education; Spirituality Centers.
Represented in the Archdiocese of Seattle.

[0233] (O.S.B.)—BENEDICTINE NUNS
Subiaco Congregation

ST. SCHOLASTICA PRIORY: *Benedictine Nuns (Cloistered),* Box 606, 271 N. Main St., Petersham, MA 01366-0606. Tel: 508-724-3213; Fax: 508-724-3574. Very Rev. Mother Mary Clare Vincent, O.S.B., Prioress; Sr. Mary Frances Wynn, O.S.B., Sub-Prioress.
Nuns in Solemn vows 11; Simple vows 1; Novices 1; Claustral Oblates 1.

[0240] (O.S.B.)—OLIVETAN BENEDICTINE SISTERS D

Established in the Diocese of Little Rock in 1887.
MOTHERHOUSE AND NOVITIATE (1887): *Holy Angels Convent,* P.O. Drawer 130, Jonesboro, AR 72403. Tel: 501-935-5810; Fax: 501-935-4210. Sr. M. Henrietta Hockle, O.S.B., Prioress.
Professed Sisters 59.
Sisters serve and staff: High Schools; Grammar Schools; Diocesan Office; CCD Centers & Parish Services.
Properties owned: *Little Angels Day Care Center,* Little Rock, AR; *Immaculate Heart Convent,* Pocahontas, AR; *St. Bernards Regional Medical Center,* Jonesboro, AR.
Represented in the Dioceses of Fort Worth and Little Rock.

[0250] (C.V.D.)—SISTERS OF BETHANY P

Founded in El Salvador in 1928.
GENERAL MOTHERHOUSE: *Instituto Bethania,* Santa Tecla, El Salvador, C.A. Mother Dolores de Maria Zea, Mother Foundrees; Madre Luz Elena Ordonez, Supr. Gen.
U.S. ADDRESS (1949): *Bethany House,* 850 N. Hobart Blvd., Los Angeles, CA 90029. Tel: 213-669-9411; 665-6937. Sr. Maria de Jesus Diaz, Superiora.
Professed Sisters 19.
Ministry in Social Service Centers; Parish Work.
Represented in the Archdiocese of Los Angeles.

[0260] (S.B.S.)—THE SISTERS OF THE BLESSED SACRAMENT FOR INDIANS AND COLORED PEOPLE P

Founded in the United States in 1891.
GENERAL MOTHERHOUSE: *St. Elizabeth's Convent,* Bensalem, PA 19020-8502. Tel: 215-244-9900. Sr. Monica Loughlin, Pres.
Professed Sisters 295.
Sisters serve and staff in: the field of Education on all levels; Catechetical Schools; Houses for Catechetical; Adult Education and Social Service; House of Prayer; Spiritual Center; Evangelization Center.
Properties owned: *St. Catherine Indian School,* Santa Fe, NM; *St. Michael Indian School,* St. Michael's, AZ; *Xavier Prep,* New Orleans, LA.
Represented in the Archdioceses of Atlanta, Boston, Chicago, Los Angeles, New Orleans, New York, Philadelphia, Santa Fe, and the Dioceses of Camden, Evansville, Gallup, Lafayette (LA), Palm Beach, Rockville Centre, Savannah and Tucson. Also in Haiti.

[0270] (C.B.S.)—CONGREGATION OF BON SECOURS P

Founded in France in 1824. First foundation in the United States in 1881.
GENERALATE: 20, rue N.D. des Champs. 75006, Paris, France. Sr. Justine Cyr, Supr. Gen.
UNITED STATES PROVINCE: *Provincial House and Novitiate,* 1525 Marriottsville Rd., Marriottsville, MD 21104. Tel: 410-442-1333; Fax: 410-442-1394. Sr. Anne Marie Mack, Pres.
Total Sisters in U.S. Province 49.
Sisters own and operate: *Bon Secours Spiritual Center; Bon Secours Health System, Inc.*
Represented in the Archdioceses of Baltimore, Detroit, Miami, Philadelphia, and the Dioceses of Altoona-Johnstown, Charleston, Richmond, St. Petersburg and Venice.

[0280] (O.SS.S.)—THE BRIGITTINE SISTERS P

Founded in Sweden in 14th century.
MOTHERHOUSE: Rome, Italy.
CONVENT AND NOVITIATE (1957): *Convent of St. Birgitta,* Vikingsborg, 4 Runkenhage Rd., Darien, CT 06820. Tel: 203-655-1068. Sr. M. Sabina Kavanadi, O.SS.S., Supr. Monastic tradition, more contemplative than active.
Legal Title: *Order of the Most Holy Savior of St. Bridget.*
Professed Sisters 9.
Represented in the Diocese of Bridgeport.

[0300] (O.CARM.)—CALCED CARMELITES P

Carmelite Nuns of the Ancient Observance, Strictly Cloistered, belonging to the Second Order of Carmel.
Founded in Naples, Italy in 1536. First foundation in the United States in 1931. *Carmelite Monastery of St. Therese; Little Flower of Jesus and St. M. Magdalen Di Pazzi,* St. Therese's Valley, 3551 Lanark Rd., Coopersburg, PA 18036-9324. Mother Joseph Marie, O.Carm., Prioress.
Professed Sisters 13.
Legal Title: *The Carmelite Sisters of St. Therese's Valley, Inc.*
Represented in the Dioceses of Allentown, Fargo, San Angelo and Superior.

[0315] (C.C.W.)—CARMELITE COMMUNITY OF THE WORD D

MOTHERHOUSE & NOVITIATE (1971): 1304 13th Ave., Altoona, PA 16601. Tel: 814-943-0088. Sr. Martha Burbulla, C.C.W., Gen. Admin.
Total number in the community 22.
Ministries in Diocesan Administration; the field of Religious and Academic Education at all levels; Pastoral Care to the Imprisoned, Institutionalized, Elderly, Mentally Handicapped, Family Life Support Groups and the Poor; Parish Ministry.
Represented in the Diocese of Altoona-Johnstown.

[0320](O.CARM.)—CARMELITE NUNS OF THE ANCIENT OBSERVANCE P

CARMELITE NUNS OF THE ANCIENT OBSERVANCE.
Strictly Cloistered, belonging to the Second Order of Carmel.
Founded in Guelder, Holland, in 1453. First Foundation in the United States in 1930.
CARMEL OF MARY (1954): 17765 78th St., S.E., Wahpeton, ND 58075. Tel: 701-642-2360. Mother M. Rose of the Sacred Heart, O.Carm., Prioress.
Total number in community 16.
Represented in the Diocese of Fargo.
MONASTERY OF OUR LADY OF GRACE (1989): 1 Saint Joseph Place, San Angelo, TX 76905. Tel: 915-651-4959.
Professed Sisters 5.
Represented in the Diocese of San Angelo.
CARMEL OF THE SACRED HEART (1963): 430 Laurel Ave., Hudson, WI 54016. Tel: 715-386-2156. Sr. Gemma Angelo, O.Carm., Prioress; Sr. Lucia LaMontagne, O.Carm., Archivist.
Professed Sisters 6.
Legal Title: *Carmelite Nuns of the Diocese of Superior, Inc.*
Represented in the Diocese of Superior.

[0330] (O.CARM.)—CARMELITE SISTERS FOR THE AGED AND INFIRM P

Founded in 1929 in New York. Foundress: Mother M. Angeline Teresa, O.Carm.
MOTHERHOUSE AND NOVITIATE: *St. Teresa's Motherhouse and Novitiate,* 600 Woods Rd., Avila on the Hudson, Germantown, NY 12526. Mother Mary Suzanne, O.Carm., Supr. Gen.
Professed Sisters 282; Novices 1.
Legal Holdings: *St. Patrick Home,* Bronx, NY; *Sacred Heart Manor,* Philadelphia, PA; *Villa Teresa,* Harrisburg, PA; *St. Raphael Home,* Columbus, OH; *St. Rita's Home,* Columbus, OH; *St. Margaret's Hall,* Cincinnati, OH; *Carmel Manor,* Fort Thomas, KY; *Kahl Home for the Aged,* Davenport, IA; *St. Patrick's Manor,* Framingham, MA; *Marian Manor,* Boston, MA; *St. Patrick's Residence,* Naperville, IL; *Lourdes - Noreen McKeen Residence,* West Palm Beach, FL; *Our Lady's Manor,* Dublin, Ireland.
Represented in the Archdioceses of Boston, Cincinnati, New York and Philadelphia, and the Dioceses of Albany, Altoona-Johnstown, Bridgeport, Brooklyn, Fall River, Harrisburg, Manchester, Scranton and Syracuse.

[0340] (C.aCh.)—CARMELITE SISTERS OF CHARITY P

Founded in 1826.
MOTHERHOUSE: Vic, Spain.
GENERALATE: Carlo Zucchi, 12, 00165 Rome, Italy. Tel: 06-662-03-52.
PROVINCIAL/FORMATION HOUSE: *Carmelite Sisters of Charity,* 701 Beacon Rd., Silver Spring, MD 20903. Tel: 301-434-6344. Sr. Maria Pilar Chamorro, Prov.
Ministry in Health Clinics; Parishes; Higher Education; Immigrants, Hispanics and Homeless, Educational Centers.
Properties owned or sponsored: *Mount Carmel House Formation House.*
Represented in the Archdiocese of Washington and the Diocese of Brooklyn.

[0350] (O.CARM.)—CARMELITE SISTERS (CORPUS CHRISTI) P

First foundation in the United States in 1920.
GENERAL MOTHERHOUSE: Tunapuna, Trinidad, West Indies. Sr. Ann Parker, O.Carm., Supr. Gen.
U.S. ADDRESS: *Mount Carmel Home-Keens' Memorial,* 412 W. 18th, Kearney, NE 68847. Tel: 308-237-2287. Sr. Emerentiana, O.Carm., Regl. Supr.
Professed Sisters 105.

Ministry in Home and foreign missions; Academic and Religious Education; Social Work.
Represented in the Archdiocese of Portland (OR) and the Dioceses of Grand Island and Providence.

[0360] (Carmel D.C.J.)—CARMELITE SISTERS OF THE DIVINE HEART OF JESUS P

Founded in Germany in 1891. First Convent in the United States in 1912.
General Motherhouse: Sittard, Netherlands. Mother M. Katharina, Supr. Gen.
Northern Province: 1230 Kavanaugh Pl., Milwaukee, WI 53213. Tel: 414-453-4040; Fax: 414-453-6503. Sr. M. Immaculata, Prov. Supr.
Central Province: 10341 Manchester Rd., St. Louis, MO 63122. Tel: 314-965-7616. Sr. M. Angelina, Prov. Supr.
South Western Province: 8585 La Mesa Blvd., La Mesa, CA 92041. Tel: 619-466-3116. Sr. M. Angela Therese, Prov. Supr.
Professed Sisters Worldwide 480; Total in U.S. 90; Novices 18; Postulants 10.
Sisters minister to: Homes for Children 3; Homes for the Aged 9; Day Nurseries 3; Mission work in Africa, Nicaragua, Venezuela & Brazil.
Represented in the Archdioceses of Detroit, Milwaukee, St. Louis and San Antonio, and the Dioceses of Gary, Grand Rapids, Jefferson City, Owensboro and San Diego.

[0370] (O.C.D.)—CARMELITE SISTERS OF THE MOST SACRED HEART OF LOS ANGELES P

General Motherhouse & Novitiate: *Carmelite Sisters of the Most Sacred Heart of Los Angeles,* 920 E. Alhambra Rd., Alhambra, CA 91801. Tel: 818-289-1353; Fax: 818-308-1913. Mother Vincent Marie, O.C.D., Supr. Gen.; Sr. Mary Michael, O.C.D., Archivist.
Total number in community 129.
Legal Title: *Sacred Heart Retreat House Santa Teresita Hospital.*
Sisters serve and staff: Grammar Schools; General Hospital; Skilled Nursing Facility for the care of the Aged; Nursery Schools With Day Care Centers and Kindergarten; Retreat House; Directors of Religious Education; Ministry to elderly, sick and convalescents.
Represented in the Archdioceses of Los Angeles and Miami, and the Dioceses of Cleveland and Tucson.

[0380] (C.S.T.)—CARMELITE SISTERS OF ST. THERESE OF THE INFANT JESUS D

Founded in the United States in 1917 at Bentley, OK.
General Motherhouse: *Villa Teresa,* 1300 Classen Dr., Oklahoma City, OK 73103-2447. Tel: 405-232-7926. Sr. Immaculata Commet, C.S.T., Gen. Supr.
Legal Title: *Carmelite Sisters of St. Therese of the Infant Jesus Motherhouse.*
Properties owned and sponsored: *Villa Teresa School,* Oklahoma City, OK; *Villa Teresa Moore,* Oklahoma City, OK.
Total number in community 28.
Ministry in the field of Academic Education; Religious Education and Parish Ministry.
Represented in the Archdiocese of Oklahoma City.

[0390] (C.M.S.T.)—MISSIONARY CARMELITES OF ST. TERESA P

Founded in Mexico City in 1903.
General Motherhouse: Fresno 150, 06400. Mexico, D.F. Mother Carmen Margarita Pratt, Supr. Gen.
U.S. Holy Family Province (1983): 9548 Deer Trail Dr., Houston, TX 77038. Tel: 713-445-5520; Fax: 713-445-5748. Sr. Victoria Alvarez, Prov. Supr.
Professed Sisters 66.
Ministry in Pastoral; Domestic and Retreats.
Represented in the Archdioceses of Los Angeles, St. Louis and Oklahoma City, and the Dioceses of Corpus Christi, Galveston-Houston and Tulsa.

[0400] (O.CARM.)—CONGREGATION OF OUR LADY OF MOUNT CARMEL P

Founded in France in 1824. First foundation in the United States in 1833.
Generalate: P.O. Box 476, Lacombe, LA 70445. Sr. Rose Marie Penouilh, O.Carm., Pres.; Sr. M. Hyacinth Breaux, O.Carm., Archivist; Sr. Andree Marie Bindewald, O.Carm., Devel. Dir.
Professed Sisters 108.
Ministry in the field of Education on all levels; Hospitals; Social Service; Religious Education; Pastoral Ministry and Retreat Work.
Represented in the Archdiocese of New Orleans, and Washington, DC, and the Dioceses of Alexandria, Baton Rouge, Houma-Thibodaux, Joliet, and Lafayette (LA). Also in the Philippines.

[0410] (O.CARM.)—INSTITUTE OF THE SISTERS OF OUR LADY OF MOUNT CARMEL P

(Istituto delle Suore di Nostra Signora del Carmelo)
Founded in Italy in 1854, First foundation in the United States, 1947.
General Motherhouse: Istituto di Nostra Signora del Carmelo, Via dei Baglioni 10, Roma, Italy.
U.S. Headquarters: *Carmelite Sisters,* 5 Wheatland St., Peabody, MA 01960. Tel: 508-531-4733. Sr. Benedetta Zaccardi, Supr.
Professed Sisters 7.
Ministry in Holy Childhood Nursery and Kindergarten.
Represented in the Archdioceses of Boston and Washington.

[0420] (O.C.D.)—DISCALCED CARMELITE NUNS P

Founded in Spain in 1562. First foundation in the United States in 1790 in Charles County, Maryland; later this monastery was moved to Baltimore.
The Monasteries listed here are strictly contemplative and belong to the Order of Discalced Carmelites.
Carmelite Monastery (1790): 1318 Dulaney Valley Rd., Towson, Baltimore, MD 21286-1399. Tel: 410-823-7415. Sr. Veronica Emmick, O.C.D., Prioress; Sr. Constance FitzGerald, O.C.D., Community Archivist.
Total number in community 16.
Legal Title: *Carmelite Sisters of Baltimore.*
Carmel of St. Joseph (1863): 9150 Clayton Rd., Ladue, St. Louis County, MO 63124-1898. Tel: 314-993-6899; Fax: 314-993-5039. Mother Mary Joseph of Divine Providence, O.C.D., Prioress.
Professed Cloistered Nuns 8; Professed Extern sisters 1.
Monastery of St. Joseph and St. Teresa (1877): *Discalced Carmelite Nuns,* 73530 River Rd., Covington, LA 70435-2206. Carmelite Nuns, Discalced (O.C.D.), Mother Mary Alice Grace, O.C.D., Prioress.
Total number in community 9.
Discalced Carmelite Monastery (1890): 61 Mt. Pleasant Ave., Boston, MA 02119. Tel: 617-442-1411; Fax: 617-442-0203. Sr. Mary Teresa Wisniewski, O.C.D., Prioress.
Total number in community 12.
Carmelite Monastery (1902): 66th Ave. and Old York Rd. (Oak Lane), Philadelphia, PA 19126. Tel: 215-424-6143; Fax: 215-424-6143. Mother Pia of Jesus Crucified, O.C.D., Prioress.
Professed Nuns 8.
Monastery of Our Lady of Mt. Carmel (1907): 745 St. John's Pl., Brooklyn, NY 11216. Mother Josefa Marie, Prioress.
Carmelite Monastery of the Infant Jesus (1908): 1000 Lincoln St., Santa Clara, CA 95050. Tel: 408-296-8412. Sr. Roseanne of Jesus, O.C.D., Prioress.
Sisters Solemn Vows 17.
St. Joseph's Carmelite Monastery (1908): 2215 N.E. 147th, Shoreline, WA 98155. Sr. Marie Suzanne, Prioress.
Professed Sisters 8.
Legal Title: *Carmelite Monastery of Seattle.*
Carmel of the Queen of Heaven (Formerly known as Regina Coeli Monastery) (1911): 17937 250th St., Eldridge, IA 52748. Tel: 319-285-8387. Sr. Mary Joan Loebig, O.C.D., Prioress.
Professed Sisters 12; Novices 2.
Discalced Carmelite Nuns (1930): *Monastery of Mary Immaculate and St. Joseph,* 1740 Newburg Rd., Louisville, KY 40205. Tel: 502-451-6796. Mother Francis, Prioress; Sr. Clare, Archivist.
Professed Sisters 11.
Legal Title: *Carmelite Monastery of Louisville, Inc.*
Order of Discalced Carmelites O.C.D. (1913): *Carmel of St. Teresa of Los Angeles, Inc.,* 215 E. Alhambra Rd., Alhambra, CA 91801. Tel: 818-282-2387; Fax: 818-282-2053. Mother Maria, O.C.D., Prioress.
Total number in community 15.
Carmelite Monastery (1916): 4300 Mount Carmel Dr. N.E., Ada (Parnell), MI 49301. Mother Agnes Therese of the Infant Jesus, O.C.D., Prioress.
Cloistered Nuns 20; Novices 4, Externs 2.
Discalced Carmelite Nuns (1920): *Carmelite Monastery,* 139 DePuyster Ave., Beacon, NY 12508-3540. Tel: 914-831-5572. Sr. Marjorie Robinson, Prioress.
Total number in community 10.
Discalced Carmelite Monastery of St. Therese of the Child Jesus (1920): 75 Carmel Rd., Buffalo, NY 14214. Tel: 716-837-6499. Mother Marie Therese of the Child Jesus, O.C.D., Prioress.
Cloistered Professed Sisters 16; Extern Professed Sisters 3; Novices 2.
Monastery of Discalced Carmelites (1922): 2500 Cold Spring Rd., Indianapolis, IN 46222. Tel: 317-926-5654. Sr. Jean Alice McGoff, O.C.D., Prioress.
Legal Title: *Monastery of the Resurrection, Discalced Carmelites Sisters of Our Lady of Mount Carmel Carmelite Monastery.*
Contemplative Professed Nuns 14; Novices 4.
Carmel of the Holy Family (1923): 3176 Fairmount Blvd., Cleveland Heights, OH 44118. Tel: 216-321-6568. Sr. Patricia O'Brien, O.C.D., Prioress.
Contemplative Professed Nuns 16; Vowed Religious Transfer Sisters in Formation 2.
Discalced Carmelite Nuns of Schenectady, NY, Inc. (1923): *Monastery of St. Teresa of Jesus,* 428 Duane Ave., Schenectady, NY 12304. Mother Elia of the Trinity, O.C.D., Prioress.
Professed Nuns 12; Novices 1; Postulants 2.
Discalced Carmelites of the Order of Our Lady of Mount Carmel O.C.D. (1925): *Monastery of Our Lady and St. Therese,* 27601 Hwy. 1, Carmel, CA 93923. Tel: 408-624-3043; Fax: 408-624-5495. Mother Therese of the Heart of Jesus, O.C.D., Prioress.
Professed Sisters 14.
Legal Title: *Carmelite Monastery of Carmel, California, Inc.*
Discalced Carmelites O.C.D. (1926): *Monastery of the Most Blessed Virgin Mary of Mount Carmel,* 189 Madison Ave., Morristown, NJ 07960. Mother Mary Michael, O.C.D., Prioress.
Professed Sisters 7; Postulants 2.
Order of Discalced Carmelites O.C.D. (1926): *Carmelite Monastery of the Trinity,* 5158 Hawley Blvd., San Diego, CA 92116. Tel: 619-280-5424. Sr. Yvonne Hanke, Prioress.
Professed Nuns 14.
Monastery of St. Therese of the Child Jesus (1926): 35750 Moravian Dr., Clinton Township, MI 48035-2138. Tel: 810-790-7255. Rev. Mother Prioress, O.C.D.
Professed Nuns 8; Professed Extern Sisters 2; Extern Novice 1.
Carmel of St. Therese of Lisieux, Inc. (1927): *Discalced Carmelite Nuns,* P.O. Box 57, Loretto, PA 15940-0057. Tel: 814-472-8620. Mother Teresa of Jesus, Prioress.
Professed Nuns 10; Extern Sisters 1.
Discalced Carmelite Nuns O.C.D. (1928): *Carmelite Monastery of Cristo Rey,* 721 Parker Ave., San Francisco, CA 94118-4297. Sr Mary Joseph, O.C.D., Prioress; Sr. Maria de la Immaculada, O.C.D., Archivist.
Total number in community 16.
Monastery of Discalced Carmelites (1928): 600 Flowers Ave., Dallas, TX 75211. Reverend Mother Prioress, O.C.D.
Professed Nuns 9.
Discalced Carmelite Nuns (1930): *Monastery of Our Lady and St. Joseph,* 1931 W. Jefferson Rd., Pittsford, NY 14534. Tel: 716-427-7094. Mother Miriam of the Angels, Prioress.
Professed Nuns with Solemn Vows 9; Professed Extern Sisters 1.
Legal Title: *Carmelite Monastery of Rochester.*
Monastery of Discalced Carmelites O.C.D. (1930): *Monastery of Our Lady of Mount Carmel and St. Therese of the Child Jesus,* Watson Ave. at Nayatt Rd., Barrington, RI 02806. Tel: 401-245-3421. Sr. Genevieve Lawler, O.C.D., Prioress.
Total number in community 14.
Discalced Carmelite Nuns O.C.D. (1934): *Monastery of the Infant Jesus of Prague and Our Lady of Guadalupe,* 6301 Culebra & St. Joseph Way, San Antonio, TX 78238-4909. Tel: 210-680-1834. Mother Therese Leonard, Prioress.
Total number in community 10.
Carmel of the Holy Family and St. Therese (1935): 6981 Teresian Way, P.O. Box 1720, Georgetown, CA 95634. Tel: 916-333-1617. Mother Christine, Prioress.
Total number in community 16.
Discalced Carmelite Nuns O.C.D. (1936): *Monastery of Mary, Mother of Grace,* 1250 Carmel Ave., Lafayette, LA 70501. Tel: 318-232-4651; Fax: 318-232-3540. Mother Catherine, Prioress.
Total number in community 22.
Discalced Carmelite Nuns O.C.D. (1939): *Carmel of St. Joseph,* 20,000 N. County Line Rd., Piedmont, OK 73078. Sr. Therese Ranallo, O.C.D., Prioress.
Total number in community 11.
Discalced Carmelite Nuns of Milwaukee O.C.D. (1940): *Carmel of the Mother of God,* W267 N2517, Meadowbrook Rd., Pewaukee, WI 53072. Tel: 414-691-0336. Sr. Mary Agnes Kramer, Prioress.
Total number in community 8.
Carmelite Monastery (1943): 716 Dauphin Island Pkwy., Mobile, AL 36606; Fax: 205-471-3991. Mother Agnes of the Infant Jesus, Prioress.
Solemnly Professed Nuns 6.
Discalced Carmelite Monastery (1945): Mount Carmel Rd., Santa Fe, NM 87501-4597. Tel: 505-983-7232. Mother Rose Teresa, O.C.D., Prioress.
Total number in community 13.

Discalced Carmelite Monastery (1946): 275 Pleasant St., Concord, NH 03301-2590. Tel: 603-225-5791. Sr. Thomas Aquinas, O.C.D., Prioress.
Solemnly Professed Nuns 11.

Monastery of Discalced Carmelites O.C.D. (1947): *Monastery of St. Joseph,* Terre Haute, IN, 59 Allendale, Terre Haute, IN 47802-4751. Tel: 812-299-1410; Fax: 812-299-5820. Mother Joseph McKenzie, O.C.D., Prioress.
Professed Nuns 11; Novices 1; Postulants 1.

Discalced Carmelite Nuns of Colorado, Inc. (1948): *Carmel of Holy Spirit,* 6138 S. Gallup St., Littleton, CO 80120-2702. Tel: 303-798-4176. Mother Judith of the Immaculate Heart, D.C., Prioress.
Professed Nuns 9.

Carmel of St. Joseph of Santa Ynez Valley, Inc. O.C.D. (1949): 1883 Ringsted Dr., P.O. Box 379, Solvang, CA 93463. Tel: 805-686-4292. Mother Mary Veronica Arakaki, O.C.D., Prioress.
Professed Sisters 11.

Order of Discalced Carmelites O.C.D. (1949): *Carmel of Mary Immaculate and St. Mary Magdalen,* P.O. Box 785, Flemington, NJ 08822. Mother Teresa of Mary Immaculate, O.C.D., Prioress.
Total in community 14.

Discalced Carmelite Nuns O.C.D. (1950): *Monastery of the Infant Jesus of Prague,* 3501 Silver Lake Rd., Traverse City, MI 49684-8949. Tel: 616-946-4960. Mother Teresa Margaret, O.C.D., Prioress and Archivist.
Total number in community 12.

Carmelite Monastery of Christ, the Exiled King (1950): 68 Rincon Rd., Kensington, CA 94707. Sr. Mary Magdalen, Prioress.
Professed Nuns of Solemn Vows 6.

Discalced Carmelite Nuns O.C.D. (1951): *Monastery of the Holy Cross,* Hwy. U.S. 2, P.O. Box 397, Iron Mountain, MI 49801. Tel: 906-774-0561. Mother Pauline Marie of Jesus Crucified, O.C.D., Prioress.
Total number in community 17.

Discalced Carmelite Nuns O.C.D. (1950): *Monastery of the Immaculate Heart of Mary,* R.R. 2, Box 4784, Barre, VT 05641. Tel: 802-476-8362. Sr. Jeanne Gonyon, O.C.D., Prioress.
Total number in community 10.

Discalced Carmelite Nuns O.C.D. (1950): *Monastery of St. Teresa of Jesus,* 7201 W. 32nd St., Little Rock, AR 72204-4716. Tel: 501-565-5121. Sr. Therese Stewart, O.C.D., Prioress.
Professed Sisters 11; Temporary Professed 2.
Legal Title: *Discalced Carmelite Nuns of Little Rock.*

Discalced Carmelite Nuns O.C.D. (1951): *Monastery of Our Lady of Mount Carmel and The Little Flower,* 2155 Terry Rd., Jackson, MS 39204. Tel: 601-373-1460. Sr. Margaret Mary, O.C.D., Prioress.
Professed Nuns 3; Temporary Professed 1; Postulants 1.

Carmel of the Immaculate Heart of Mary (1952): 5714 Holladay Blvd., Salt Lake City, UT 84121-1599. Tel: 801-277-6075. Mother Margaret Mary Miller, O.C.D., Prioress; Sr. Maureen, O.C.D., Sub-Prioress & 1st Counsellor; Sr. Mary Ann Krajicek, O.C.D., Archivist.
Solemn Vows 7; Finally Professed Externs 1.

Discalced Carmelite Nuns (1952): *St. Joseph's Monastery,* 68 Franklin Ave., Saranac Lake, NY 12983. Tel: 518-891-0655. Sr. Marie Gertrude Haughney, O.C.D., Prioress.
Total number in community 11.

Discalced Carmelite Nuns of St. Paul (1952): *Carmel of Our Lady of Divine Providence,* 8251 De Montreville Trail N., Lake Elmo, MN 55042-9547. Tel: 612-777-3882. Sr. Paula of the Eucharist, O.C.D., Prioress.
Professed Sisters 9; Novices 3; Postulants 1.

Discalced Carmelite Nuns O.C.D. (1953): 70 Monastery Rd., Elysburg, PA 17824-9697. Tel: 717-672-2935. Sr. Christine O'Brien, O.C.D., Prioress; Sr. Joan Lundy, O.C.D., Archivist.
Professed Sisters 18; Postulants 1.

Discalced Carmelite Nuns O.C.D. (1954): *Monastery of Our Lady of the Mountains,* 1950 La Fond Dr., Reno, NV 89509-3099. Tel: 702-323-3236; Fax: 702-322-1532. Sr. Maria, O.C.D., Prioress.
Professed Nuns 15.

Carmel of Maria Regina O.C.D. (1957): 87609 Green Hill Rd., Eugene, OR 97402. Tel: 541-345-8649. Mother Elizabeth Mary, O.C.D., Prioress; Sr. Maria Teresa, O.C.D., Community Archivist.
Total number in community 11.

Monastery of the Holy Family (1957): 510 E. Gore Rd., Erie, PA 16509. Mother Emmanuel of the Mother of God, Prioress.
Professed Sisters 6; Novices 1; Postulants 2.

Discalced Carmelite Nuns (1958): *Coffee Bluff,* 11 W. Back St., Savannah, GA 31419-3219. Tel: 912-925-8505. Sr. Angela Collins, O.C.D., Prioress.
Total number in community 6.

Monastery of the Most Holy Trinity (1958): 5801 Mt. Carmel Dr., Arlington, TX 76017. Tel: 817-468-1781. Mother Anne Teresa of Jesus Kulinski, O.C.D., Prioress.
Total number in community 10.

Discalced Carmelite Nuns O.C.D. (1958): *Carmel of the Most Holy Trinity,* 1100 Parthenon Pl., Roman Forest, New Caney, TX 77357. Mother Mary Angel Mendoza, O.C.D., Prioress; Sr. Angel Teresa Sweeney, O.C.D., 1st Council Sister.
Total number in community 12.

Monastery of Discalced Carmelites (1959): River Rd. and Central, Des Plaines, IL 60016. Tel: 708-298-4241. Mother Catherine of the Mother of God, Prioress.
Total number in community 18.

Order of Discalced Carmelites O.C.D. (1958): *Carmel of St. Therese,* 15 Mt. Carmel Rd., Danvers, MA 01923-3796. Tel: 508-774-3008. Mother Michael of Christ the King, O.C.D., Prioress.
Total number in community 17.
Legal Title: *Discalced Carmelite Nuns of Danvers.*

Discalced Carmelite Nuns O.C.D. (1960): *Monastery of The Sacred Heart and St. Joseph,* 2201 W. Main St., Jefferson City, MO 65109. Tel: 573-636-3364. Mother Mary Teresa, O.C.D., Prioress.
Solemnly Professed Nuns 8; Temporary Professed Nuns 1; Postulants 2.

Carmel of the Assumption (1961): R.D. 6, Box 28, Center Dr., Latrobe, PA 15650. Tel: 412-539-1056. Sr. Barbara Sitter, O.C.D., Prioress.
Professed Sisters 14.

Discalced Carmelite Nuns, Inc. (1962): *Monastery of the Discalced Carmelite Nuns,* 2901 S. Cecelia St., Sioux City, IA 51106-3299. Tel: 712-276-1680. Mother Therese of the Spirit of Love, O.C.D., Prioress.
Total number in community 13.

Carmelite Monastery of the Mother of God (1965): 530 Blackstone Dr., San Rafael, CA 94903. Tel: 479-6872; Fax: 415-491-4964. Mother Anna Marie, O.C.D., Prioress.
Total number in community 7.

Discalced Carmelite Nuns O.C.D. (1965): *Carmel of St. Anne,* 424 E. Monastery Rd., Springfield, MO 65807. Tel: 417-881-2115. Mother Mary Charles, O.C.D., Prioress.
Total number in community 6.

Carmel of the Holy Trinity: 6301 Pali Hwy., Kaneohi, HI 96744. Tel: 808-261-6542. Mother Mary Agnes Tse, O.C.D., Supr.
Total number in community 7.

Discalced Carmelite Nuns of the Byzantine Rite (1980): *Holy Annunication Monastery,* R.R. No. 1, Box 1336, Sugarloaf, PA 18249. Tel: 717-788-1205; Fax: 717-788-3329. Mother Marija of the Holy Spirit, O.C.D., Prioress.
Professed Nuns 11.
Represented in the Diocese of Passaic.

Carmel of Port Tobacco: 4035-A Mt. Carmel Rd., Port Tobacco, MD 20646-9611.
Professed 9; Simple Professed 1.

[0430] (B.V.M.)—SISTERS OF CHARITY OF THE BLESSED VIRGIN MARY P

Founded in America in 1833.

BVM Center: *Mount Carmel,* 1100 Camel Dr., Dubuque, IA 52003. Tel: 319-588-2351; Fax: 319-588-4832. Sr. Dolores Marie McHugh, B.V.M., Pres.
Total number in Congregation 964.
Sisters staff and serve in: the field of Academic Education on all levels; Health Care-Aging; Religious Education; Chaplaincies; Pastoral Ministry; Diocesan School Offices; Diocesan Services-Administration; Social Work; Homeless Shelters; Aids Ministry; Secretarial; Social Justice; Adult Day Care; Extended Day Care.
Represented in the Archdioceses of Atlanta, Chicago, Denver, Dubuque, Indianapolis, Los Angeles, Omaha, Miami, Milwaukee, Mobile, New York, Portland (OR), St. Louis, St. Paul-Minneapolis, San Francisco, Santa Fe, Seattle, and the Dioceses of Baton Rouge, Belleville, Brooklyn, Cheyenne, Davenport, Des Moines, Dodge City, Fort Wayne-South Bend, Fresno, Green Bay, Helena, Honolulu, Jackson, Joliet, Kansas City-St. Joseph, Knoxville, Lafayette, Lexington, Lincoln, Memphis, Oakland, Orange, Orlando, Palm Beach, Peoria, Pensacola-Tallahassee, Phoenix, Reno-Las Vegas, Rockford, Rockville Centre, San Diego, San Bernardino, San Jose, Santa Rosa, Sioux City, Springfield-Cape Girardeau, Springfield (IL), Stockton, Tucson, Venice, Wichita and Winona. Also in Africa,Ecuador, and Guatemala.

[0440] (S.C.)—SISTERS OF CHARITY OF CINCINNATI, OHIO P

Founded by Saint Elizabeth Ann Seton, Emmitsburg, MD 1809. The Cincinnati Community became independent in 1852, Papal approval in 1939.

General Motherhouse (1852): *Mount St. Joseph,* Mt. Joseph, OH 45051. Tel: 513-347-5201; Fax: 513-347-5228. Sr. Mary Ellen Murphy, Pres.
Legal Title: *Sisters of Charity of Cincinnati Ohio,* Cincinnati, OH.
Professed Sisters 686.
Sisters serve and staff: Colleges; Secondary and Elementary Schools; Parishes; Healthcare Facilities and School of Nursing; Foreign Missions; Home for Profoundly Retarded Children; Senior Care Services; Social Services; Congregational Services.
Represented in the Archdioceses of Boston, Chicago, Cincinnati, Denver, Detroit, Indianapolis, Louisville, Newark New York, St. Louis, San Francisco, Santa Fe, Washington, and the Dioceses of Brownsville, Buffalo, Cleveland, Colorado Springs, Columbus, Covington, El Paso, Fort Wayne-South Bend, Gaylord, Galveston-Houston Grand Rapids, Helena, Kalamazoo, Knoxville, Las Cruces, Lansing, Lexington, Memphis, Oakland, Orlando, Palm Beach, Phoenix, Pueblo, Raleigh, Rapid City, Savannah, Saginaw, St. Petersburg, Spokane, Toledo, and Wichita. Also in Peru, Ecuador, Poland and Gautemala.

[0450] (S.C.I.C.)—SISTERS OF CHARITY OF THE IMMACULATE CONCEPTION OF IVREA P

Founded in Italy in the 18th Century. First Foundation in the United States in 1961.

General Motherhouse: della Renella 85, Rome, Italy. Tel: 396-5818145. Sr. Grazia Raffaella Rossi, Supr. Gen.
Total number in Congregation 1,387.

U.S. Foundation (1961): *Immaculate Virgin of Miracles Convent,* R.D. 2, Box 348, Mount Pleasant, PA 15666. Tel: 412-887-6753. Sr. Gemma Mancini, Regl. Supr. Tel: 412-887-0220.
Professed Sisters in the U.S.A. 13.
Sisters serve and staff: Kindergarten and Elementary Schools; Parish Services; Religious Education; Pastoral Ministry.
Properties owned: *Verna Montessori Children's House & Elememtary School; Immaculate Virgin of Miracles Convent,* Mt. Pleasant, PA.
Represented in the Diocese of Greensburg and Norwich.

[0460] (C.C.V.I.)—CONGREGATION OF THE SISTERS OF CHARITY OF THE INCARNATE WORD P

Founded in 1869 at San Antonio, Texas.

Generalate: 4503 Broadway, San Antonio, TX 78209-6209. Tel: 210-828-2224. Sr. Teresa Stanley, Gen. Supr.

U.S. Motherhouse, Provincial and Retirement Center: 4707 Broadway, San Antonio, TX 78209-6200. Tel: 210-829-0987; Fax: 210-830-3743. Sr. Kathleen Coughlin, Prov. Supr.
Universal Total in Congregation 631; U.S. Province 325.
Properties owned and sponsored: Colleges 1; Highschools 2; Hospitals 6; Temporary shelter for homeless women & children 1; Retirement Center 1.
Ministry in the field of Academic Education at all levels; Pastoral Ministry; Nursing Homes; Diocesan Offices; Social Service Agencies; Health Service Agencies.
Represented in the Archdioceses of Chicago, New Orleans, St. Louis, San Antonio, San Francisco and Santa Fe, and the Dioceses of Amarillo, Austin, Brownsville, Corpus Christi, Fort Worth, Galveston-Houston, Jefferson City, Lubbock, Springfield-Cape Girardeau, San Angelo, Spokane, Tucson, Tyler and Victoria. Also in Mexico, & Peru.

[0470] (C.C.V.I.)—THE CONGREGATION OF THE SISTERS OF CHARITY OF THE INCARNATE WORD, HOUSTON, TEXAS P

Founded in the United States in 1866, St. Mary's Infirmary, Galveston, Texas.

Motherhouse: *Villa de Matel,* 6510 Lawndale Ave., P.O. Box 230969, Houston, TX 77223-0969. Tel: 713-928-6053; Fax: 713-928-8148. Sr. Elizabeth Ann Hayes, Gen. Supr.
Total number in congregation 261.
Legal Title: *Incarnate Word Charitable Trust, Evelyn Malloy Education Fund for the Sisters of Charity of the Incarnate Word,* Houston, TX.
Sisters serve and staff: Hospitals; Homes for Aged; Elementary Schools; Social Services.
Represented in the Archdiocese of Los Angeles, and the Dioceses of Alexandria, Austin, Beaumont, Brownsville, Galveston-Houston, Lake Charles, Little Rock, Salt Lake City, San Bernardino, Shreveport, and Tulsa. Also in Ireland, Guatemala, El Salvador and Kenya.

[0480] (S.C.L.)—SISTERS OF CHARITY OF LEAVENWORTH, KANSAS P

Founded in the United States in 1858.

COMMUNITY OFFICES AND MOTHERHOUSE: 4200 S. Fourth St., Leavenworth, KS 66048-5054. Tel: 913-758-6501; Fax: 912-682-2128. Sr. Mary Kathleen Stefani, Community Dir.; Sr. Helen Forge, Archivist.

Total number in community 458.

Properties owned and sponsored: *Saint Mary College,* Leavenworth, KS; *Residential and Day Treatment Centers for Children: Mount St. Vincent Home,* Denver, CO; *Saint John's Child Study Center,* Santa Monica, CA. Health Facilities: *Sisters of Charity of Leavenworth Health Services Corporation,* Cantwell Hall, Leavenworth, KS; *Saint John's Hospital & Health Center,* Santa Monica, CA; *Saint Joseph Hospital,* Denver, CO; *St. Mary's Hospital & Medical Center,* Grand Junction, CO; *Saint John Hospital,* Leavenworth, KS; *St. Francis Hospital and Medical Center,* Topeka, KS; *Saint Vincent Hospital & Health Center,* Billings, MT; *St. James Community Hospital,* Butte, MT; *Marian Clinic,* Topeka, KS; *Marillac Clinic,* Grand Junction, CO; *Providence Medical Center,* Kansas City, KS; *Caritas Clinic, Inc.,* Kansas City, KS.

Sisters serving in Elementary, Secondary, and Higher Education; Nursing Education; Special Education; Religious Education; Ministry Training; Hospitals; Latin American Missions; Diocesan Offices; Parish Administration and Pastoral Ministry; Liturgy-Music Ministry; Campus Ministry; Spiritual Direction; Communications; Social Justice; Housing.

Ministries to AIDS Victims; Cross-culture; Elderly; Prisoners; Handicapped Adults and Youth; Health Service Agencies; Mental Health; Native Americans and Social Service Agencies.

Represented in the Archdioceses of Denver, Kansas City in Kansas, Los Angeles, Louisville, Oklahoma City, Omaha, Santa Fe, and Washington, and the Dioceses of Brownsville, Cheyenne, Gallup, Galveston-Houston, Grand Island, Great Falls-Billings, Helena, Jefferson City, Kansas City-St. Joseph, Oakland, Orange, Pueblo, St. Cloud, Spokane, Tucson and Wichita. Also in Peru and Ecuador.

[0490] (S.G.M.)—SISTERS OF CHARITY OF MONTREAL
(Grey Nuns) P

Founded in 1737 by Saint Marguerite d'Youville at Montreal, Canada. First foundation in the United States 1855.

GENERALATE: *General Administration,* 138 Rue Saint-Pierre, Montreal, Quebec H2Y 2L7. Canada. Tel: 514-842-9411. Aurore Larkin, S.G.M., Supr. Gen.

ST. JOSEPH PROVINCE - U.S.A.: *Provincial Administration,* 10 Pelham Rd., Lexington, MA 02173. Tel: 617-862-4700. Sr. June Ketterer, S.G.M., Prov. Supr.; Sr. Helene Georges, S.G.M., Contact Person - Formation Team.

Legal Title: *The Grey Nuns Charities, Inc.*

Total number in province 68.

Ministry in Hospitals; Schools of Nursing; Nursing Homes; Parish Ministry; Adult Day Health Care; Social Day Care; Social Justice; Pastoral Care; Foreign Missions; Housing for the Elderly & Handicapped; Nutrition Programs for Poor; Elder Health Center; Shelter for Homeless; Emergency Satellite Facilities.

Represented in the Archdiocese of Boston, and the Dioceses of Manchester, Portland (ME) and Toledo. Also in Comodoro Rivadavia, Argentina.

[0500] (S.C.N.)—SISTERS OF CHARITY OF NAZARETH P

Founded in the United States in 1812.

SCN CENTER: P.O. Box 172, Nazareth, KY 40048. Tel: 502-348-1555; Fax: 502-348-1502. Sr. Elizabeth Wendeln, S.C.N., Pres.; Sr. Mary Collette Crone, Archivist.

Legal Title: *Nazareth Literary & Benevolent Institution.*

Total number in Congregation 814.

Properties owned or sponsored: *Health Facilities SCN Health System,* Louisville, KY; *Caritas Home Health,* Nazareth, KY; *Flaget Memorial Hospital,* Bardstown, KY; *Memorial Hospital,* Chattanooga, TN; *Caritas Medical Center,* Louisville, KY; *St. Joseph Hospital,* Lexington, KY; *Caritas Peace Center,* Louisville, KY; *St. Vincent Infirmary-Medical Center,* Little Rock, AR; *Marymount Hospital,* London, KY; *Nazareth Hospital,* Mokama, India; *Educational Facilities Spalding University,* Louisville, KY; *Presentation Academy,* Louisville, KY; *Nazareth Arts for Life,* Nazareth, KY; *Our Lady of Nazareth Academy,* Wakefield, MA; *Nazareth Montessori Children's Center.* Retreat Facilities: *Catherine Spalding Center,* Nazareth, KY; *Bethany Spring,* New Haven, KY; *Camp Maria,* Leonardtown, MD. Facilities for the Elderly and Handicapped: *Nazareth Village I Nazareth Village II,* Nazareth, KY; *Nazareth Home,* Louisville, KY. Missions: *SCN Missions.*

LOUISVILLE REGION: *Regional Office,* 676 Atwood, P.O. Box 17545, Louisville, KY 40217. Tel: 502-636-0411; Fax: 502-636-0412. Sr. Elizabeth Blandford, S.C.N., Regl. Rep.

Final professed sisters 237.

Sisters serve and staff the field of Academic Education on all levels: Special Educational Services; Social Services; Public Library; Counseling; Campus Ministry; Archdiocesan Offices; Health Care Institutions; Pastoral Ministry; Literacy Council and Retirement Center.

Represented in the Archdiocese of Louisville and the Diocese of Evansville.

SOUTHERN REGION: 126 Suburban Ct., Lexington, KY 40503. Tel: 606-277-4744; Fax: 606-277-8652. Sr. Anne Rita Mauck, S.C.N., Regl. Rep.

Final professed sisters 310.

Sisters serve and staff in the field of Academic Education on all levels: Literacy Program; Parish Ministry; Diocesan Centers; Social Services; Retirement Centers; Retreat Centers; Peace & Justice Center; Department of Human Resources; Counseling; Health Care Agencies.

Represented in the Archdioceses of Chicago, Cincinnati, Indianapolis, Louisville and St. Louis, and the Dioceses of Baton Rouge, Birmingham, Brownsville, Covington, Charleston, Jackson, Little Rock, Lexington, Memphis, Nashville, Owensboro, Palm Beach, St. Petersburg and San Jose. Also in Belize City and Independence, Belize.

NORTHERN REGION: *Regional House,* 169 Fenno St., Quincy, MA 02170. Tel: 617-479-4909; Fax: 617-786-0767. Sr. Gwen McMahon, S.C.N., Regl. Rep.

Final professed sisters 86.

Sisters serve and staff in the field of Academic Education on all levels: Social Services; Parish Ministry; Diocesan Center; Health Care Institutions; Retreat Centers; Retirement Centers and Seminary.

Represented in the Archdioceses of Boston, Philadelphia and Washington, and the Dioceses of Arlington, Columbus, Richmond, Steubenville, Wheeling-Charleston and Youngstown.

INDIA REGION: *Regional House,* E. Boring Canal Rd., Post Box 219, Patna, Bihar 800-001. India. Tel: 011-91-612-2341-21. Sr. Bridget Kappalumackal, S.C.N., Prov.

Final professed sisters 178.

Central Leadership Team: Final Professed Sisters 3.

[0510] (O.L.M.)—SISTERS OF CHARITY OF OUR LADY OF MERCY D

Founded in Charleston, South Carolina in 1829.

GENERALATE AND MOTHERHOUSE: 424 Fort Johnson Rd., P.O. Box 12410, Charleston, SC 29422. Tel: 803-795-6083; 795-2866. Sr. Anne Francis Campbell, O.L.M., Gen. Supr.

Total number in community 33.

Sisters serve and staff: Parishes; High School; Elementary Schools; Hospital; Social Services.

Legal Title: *The Sisters of Charity of Our Lady of Mercy Charitable Trust.*

Properties owned: *Motherhouse,* May Forest, Charleston, SC; *Our Lady of Mercy Convent,* Charleston, SC; *Our Lady of Mercy Community Outreach Services, Inc.,* Johns Island, SC.

Represented in the Diocese of Charleston.

[0520] (S.C.M.M.)—SISTERS OF CHARITY OF OUR LADY, MOTHER OF MERCY P

Founded in Holland 1832. First foundation in the United States in 1874.

GENERAL MOTHERHOUSE: Den Bosch, Netherlands.

Universal number in Congregation 1,407.

U.S. PROVINCIAL HOUSE: 520 Thompson Ave., East Haven, CT 06512. Tel: 203-469-7872. Sr. Mary Ellen Ryley, S.C.M.M., Prov.

Total number in community 21.

Represented in the Archdioceses of Chicago, Detroit, Hartford and St. Paul-Minneapolis, and the Dioceses of Bridgeport and San Diego.

[0530] (S.C.M.C.)—SISTERS OF CHARITY OF OUR LADY, MOTHER OF THE CHURCH D

First foundation in the United States in 1970.

GENERAL MOTHERHOUSE: Baltic, CT 06330. Tel: 860-822-8241; Fax: 860-822-9842. Mother M. Theresita, Supr. Gen.

Professed Sisters 81; Junior Professed 9; Novices 5; Postulants 2.

Properties owned, staffed or sponsored: 2 High Schools; 9 Elementary Schools; 4 Home for Aged; Home for Dependent Children; 18 Catechetical Schools; Shelter for the Homeless; Hispanic Ministry.

Represented in the Archdiocese of Hartford, and the Dioceses of Manchester, Madison and Norwich.

[0540] (S.C.O.)—SISTERS OF CHARITY, OF OTTAWA
(Grey Nuns of the Cross) P

Founded in Ottawa, Canada, in 1845. First foundation in the United States in 1857.

GENERAL MOTHERHOUSE: 9 Bruyere St., Ottawa, Ontario K1N 5C9. Canada. Mother Claire Malette, S.C.O., Gen. Supr.

Total number of Sisters in Congregation based in Ottawa 871.

AMERICAN PROVINCE (1950): *St. Joseph,* 975 Varnum Ave., Lowell, MA 01854. Tel: 508-453-4993. Sr. Gabrielle L. Jean, Prov. Supr.; Sr. Claire Cayer, Archivist.

Professed U.S. Sisters 55.

Sisters staff: High Schools; Grammar Schools; CCD Parish Services; Home for Young Ladies; Health Care and Pastoral Ministries; Apostolate of Aging.

Properties owned: *D'Youville Manor; Bachand Hall; St. Joseph Residence,* Lowell, MA.

Legal Title: *Sisters of Charity of Ottawa.*

Represented in the Archdioceses of Boston and Newark.

[0560] (S.C.Q.)—SISTERS OF CHARITY OF QUEBEC
(Grey Nuns) P

Founded in Quebec in 1849. First United States foundation in 1890.

GENERAL MOTHERHOUSE: 2655 Le Pelletier St., Beauport, Quebec GIC 3X7. Canada. Tel: 418-628-8860. Sr. Denise Marcoux, S.C.Q., Supr. Gen.

U.S. HOUSE (1908):

Franco - American School 357 Pawtuckert St., Lowell, MA 01854. Tel: 508-937-8672. Sr. Madeleine Gagnon, S.C.Q., Supr.

U.S. HOUSE (1917): *Sacred Heart Nursing Home,* 359 Summer St., New Bedford, MA 02740. Tel: 508-996-6751. Sr. Blandine d'Amours, S.C.Q., Supr.

Professed U.S. Sisters 17.

Sisters serve and staff: The field of education and care of the elderly; Franco American School, Lowell, MA; Sacred Heart Nursing Home, New Bedford, MA.

Represented in the Archdiocese of Boston and the Diocese of Fall River.

[0570] (S.C.)—SISTERS OF CHARITY OF SETON HILL, GREENSBURG, PENNSYLVANIA P

Foundation from Cincinnati, Ohio to Altoona, Pennsylvania in 1870.

GENERALATE: Mt. Thor Rd., Greensburg, PA 15601. Tel: 412-836-0406; Fax: 412-836-8280. Sr. Gertrude Foley, S.C., Major Supr.; Sr. Mary Catherine Seli, S.C., Archivist.

Total number in the community 556.

Ministry in the field of Academic Education at all levels; Day Care Centers; Community Service Center; Adult Day Care Center; Special Education for the Handicapped.

Properties owned: *Elizabeth Seton Center,* Pittsburgh, PA; *Doran Hall,* Greensburg, PA.

Represented in the Archdioceses of Baltimore, Chicago, Cincinnati, Los Angeles, Santa Fe, Seattle and Washington, and the Dioceses of Altoona-Johnstown, Brooklyn, Erie, Greensburg, Oakland, Orlando, Paterson, Phoenix, Pittsburgh, Raleigh, St. Petersburg, Steubenville, Tucson, and Wheeling-Charleston. Also in South Korea and Israel.

[0580] (C.S.A.)—SISTERS OF CHARITY OF ST. AUGUSTINE D

Founded in Cleveland, Ohio in 1851.

MOTHERHOUSE: *Mount Augustine,* 5232 Broadview Rd., Richfield, OH 44286. Sr. Judith Ann Karam, C.S.A., Major Supr.; Sr. Mary Denis Maher, C.S.A., Archivist.

Total number in Congregation 104.

Properties owned and sponsored: *CSA Health Network,* Cleveland, OH; *Providence Hospital,* Columbia, SC; *Regina Health Center,* Richfield, OH; *Saint Ann Foundation,* Cleveland, OH; *Saint Augustine Academy,* Lakewood, OH; *St. Vincent Charity Hospital & Health Center,* Cleveland, OH; *Sisters of Charity of St. Augustine Health System, Inc.,* Cleveland, OH; *Timken Mercy Medical Center,* Canton, OH; *Westlake Health Campus Association, dba St. John West Shore Hospital,* Westlake, OH.

Represented in the Dioceses of Charleston, Cleveland and Youngstown.

[0590] (S.C.)—SISTERS OF CHARITY OF SAINT ELIZABETH, CONVENT STATION P

Founded in Newark, New Jersey in 1859.

GENERAL MOTHERHOUSE: *Convent of St. Elizabeth - Administration Building,* P.O. Box 476, Convent Station, NJ 07961-0476. Tel: 201-605-3300; Fax: 201-605-3322. Sr. Barbara Conroy, Gen. Supr.; Sr. Elizabeth McLoughlin, Archivist; Sr. Miriam Teresa League of Prayer.

Legal Titles and Properties: *Sisters of Charity of Saint Elizabeth Academy of Saint Elizabeth,* Convent Station, NJ *Saint Vincent Academy,* Newark, NJ *Academy of the Sacred Heart,* Hoboken, NJ *Saint Frances Residence,* Paterson, NJ.

Total number in Congregation 718.

NORTHERN PROVINCE (1967): *Provincial House,* 41 Emory St., Jersey City, NJ 07304. Tel: 201-435-0868. Sr. Mary Morley, Prov., Councilors: Sr. Roseann Mazzeo; Sr. Elizabeth Noonan.

Professed Sisters 225.

Sisters serve and staff: Academy 1; High Schools 2; Elementary Schools 17; Hospitals 2; C.C.D. 7; Parish Work 21; Social Work 5; Health Services 22; College Teaching 13.

Represented in the Archdioceses of Boston, Hartford, Newark, New York St. Louis and Santa Fe, and the Dioceses of Bridgeport, Charlotte, El Paso, Fairbanks, Metuchen, Paterson, St. Petersburg, Syracuse, Trenton, Venice and Wheeling-Charleston. Also in St. Thomas, Virgin Islands.

SOUTHERN PROVINCE (1967): *Provincial House,* 139 Gregory Ave., West Orange, NJ 07052. Tel: 201-731-5425. Sr. Edna Francis Hersinger, S.C., Prov.

Professed Sisters 263.

Ministry in the field of Elementary & High School Education; Hospitals & Homes for Aged; Health and Welfare Services.

Represented in the Archdioceses of Boston, Newark, Omaha, Washington and in the Dioceses of Jackson, Orlando, Palm Beach, Paterson, Pensacola-Tallahassee, Providence, St. Petersburg, Trenton, Wilmington and Wheeling-Charleston. Also in the Virgin Islands.

SISTERS OF CHARITY OF SAINT ELIZABETH - WESTERN PROVINCE (1967): *Western Provincial House,* 31 Jackson St., Paterson, NJ 07501. Tel: 201-278-1424; Fax: 201-523-5848. Sr. Francis Raftery, Prov. Supr.

Total number in Province 249.

Ministry in the field of Education; Diocesan/Parish Ministry; Hospitals; Homes for Aged/Residences for the Aged; Health Care; Social Services.

Represented in the Archdioceses of Boston, Newark, New York, and the Dioceses of Arlington, Lexington, Metuchen, Paterson, Rockville Centre, St. Petersburg, Scranton, Trenton and Wilmington. Also in the Virgin Islands.

[0600] (S.C.S.J.A.)—SISTERS OF CHARITY OF ST. JOAN ANTIDA P

Founded in France in 1799 by Saint Joan Antida Thouret. First foundation in the U.S. 1932.

GENERAL MOTHERHOUSE: *Suore della Carita di Santa Giovanna Antida,* Via S. Maria in Cosmedin 5, 00153, Roma, Italia. Sr. M. Antoine Henriot, Supr. Gen.

NORTH AMERICAN PROVINCE (1976): *Regina Mundi Provincial House,* 8560 N. 76th Pl., Milwaukee, WI 53223. Tel: 414-354-9233; Fax: 414-355-6463. Sr. Mary Joachim Waskovich, S.C.S.J.A., Prov.

Total number in Congregation 49.

Properties owned and sponsored: *St. Joan Antida High School, Inc.; St. Joan Antida Home, Inc.; St. Joan Antida High School Foundation, Ltd.; Hope Nursing Home, Inc.; Guardian Angel Nursery and Kindergarten, Inc.; St. Joan Antida Day Care Center, Inc.*

Ministry also in prisons; neighborhood services and parishes.

Represented in the Archdiocese of Milwaukee and the Diocese of Amarillo.

[0610] (S.C.S.H.)—SISTERS OF CHARITY OF ST. HYACINTHE (Grey Nuns) P

Founded in 1840 in St. Hyacinthe, P.Q., Canada. First United States foundation in 1878.

Legal Title: *The Society of the Sisters of Charity, Lewiston, ME.*

GENERAL HOUSE: 16470 Avenue Bourdages, SUD, St. Hyacinthe, P.Q. Canada, J2T 4J8. Sr. Jeannine Daoust, S.C.S.H., Supr. Gen.; Sr. Jeannine Galipeau, S.C.S.H., Gen. Sec.

Universal number in Congregation 284.

U.S. REGIONAL ADMINISTRATION: 98 Campus Ave., Lewiston, ME 04240-6076. Tel: 207-784-2340. Sr. Jacqueline Corriveau, Supr.

Total number in U.S. 16.

Sisters staff: St. Joseph's Manor, Portland, ME; Catholic Medical Center, Manchester, NH.

Properties owned: *St. Peter's Home,* Manchester, NH.

Represented in the Dioceses of Manchester and Portland (ME). Also in Canada and Haiti.

[0620] (S.C.S.L.)—SISTERS OF CHARITY OF ST. LOUIS P

Founded in France in 1803. First foundation in the United States in 1910.

GENERALATE: Casa Generalizia Via Pecori Giraldi 67, Roma, Italia. Sr. Geraldine Hagel, Supr. Gen.

Total universal number in Congregation 821.

AMERICAN REGION: 4907 S. Catherine St., Plattsburgh, NY 12901. Tel: 518-563-7410; Fax: 518-563-0383. Sr. Bernadette Ducharme, Regl. Supr.

Total number in community 19.

Properties owned and sponsored: *Our Lady of Victory Convent,* Ogdensburg, NY; *House of Formation,* Albany, NY.

Represented in the Dioceses of Albany and Ogdensburg.

[0630] (V.Z.)—SISTERS OF CHARITY OF ST. VINCENT DE PAUL OF ZAGREB P

Founded in Croatia (Austria-Hungary) in 1845. First U.S. Foundation in 1955.

GENERAL MOTHERHOUSE: Zagreb, Croatia. Mother Maria Agneta Tadic-Sutra, Supr. Gen.

U.S. FOUNDATION: *Sisters of Charity Convent,* 171 Knox Ave., West Seneca, NY 14224. Tel: 716-825-5859. Sr. Maria Mirna Matic, V.Z., Supr., U.S. Delegate.

Professed Sisters 25.

Sisters staff: Nursery Schools; CCD Centers and Parish Services; Hospital & Health Services.

Properties owned: Nursery Schools 2.

Represented in the Archdioceses of Chicago and the Diocese of Buffalo.

[0640] (S.C.)—SISTERS OF CHARITY OF ST. VINCENT DE PAUL, HALIFAX P

Founded by Saint Elizabeth Ann Seton, Emmitsburg, Maryland in 1809. Congregation at Halifax became independent in 1856, Papal approval in 1908.

MOTHERHOUSE: *Mount Saint Vincent,* 150 Bedford Hwy., Halifax, N.S, B3M 3J5. Canada. Tel: 902-457-3500; Fax: 902-457-3506. Sr. Mary Louise Brink, Congregational Leader; Sr. Frances Teresa Martin, Archivist.

Legal Title: *Sisters of Charity (Halifax).*

Total universal number in Congregation 840.

BOSTON PROVINCE: *Sisters of Charity of Saint Vincent De Paul, Inc.,* 125 Oakland St., Wellesley Hills, MA 02181. Tel: 617-237-2161. Sr. Mary Louise Brink, S.C., Gen. Supr.

Boston Province: Provincial Office 26 Phipps St., Quincy, MA 02169. Tel: 617-773-6085; Fax: 617-773-4794. Sr. Esther Plefka, Councillor.

Legal Title: *Boston Province, Sisters of Charity of Saint Vincent De Paul, Inc. Elizabeth Seton Residence, Inc.,* Quincy, MA.

New York Province: 84-32 63rd Ave., Middle Village, NY 11379. Tel: 718-779-6284; Fax: 718-651-5645. Sr. Joan Holmberg, Councillor.

Legal Title: *New York Province, Sisters of Charity, Halifax, Inc.*

Ministry in Education at Elementary, Secondary and University Levels; Hospitals; Homes for the Aging; Parish Ministry; Spiritual Directors/Retreats; House of Prayer; Social Services; Pastoral Ministry; Administration.

Represented in the Archdioceses of Boston, New York, and Washington, and the Dioceses of Brooklyn, Manchester and Rockville Centre. Also in Canada and Bermuda. Missionary Region in Dominican Republic and Peru.

[0650] (S.C.)—SISTERS OF CHARITY OF ST. VINCENT DE PAUL, OF NEW YORK D

Founded in Emmitsburg, MD in 1809 by Saint Elizabeth Ann Seton.

GENERAL MOTHERHOUSE: *Sisters of Charity Center, Mount Saint Vincent-on-Hudson,* 6301 Riverdale Ave., Bronx, NY 10471. Tel: 718-549-9200; Fax: 718-884-3013. Sr. Elizabeth A. Vermaelen, Pres.

Total number in Congregation 587.

Sisters serve and staff: Colleges; High Schools; Elementary Schools; Secretarial Science School; Child Caring Homes; General Hospitals; Foundling Hospital; Schools of Nursing; Residence for Senior and Invalid Sisters; Mental Health Divisions, Rest House for Community use; Housing for Homeless.

Represented in the Archdioceses of Atlanta, Baltimore, Newark, New York and Washington, and the Dioceses of Albany, Bridgeport, Brooklyn, Camden, Charlotte, Gary, Oakland, Rockville Centre, and Shreveport. Also in the Bahamas, Guatemala and Puerto Rico.

[0660] (S.C.C.)—SISTERS OF CHRISTIAN CHARITY P

Daughters of the Blessed Virgin Mary of the Immaculate Conception

Founded in Germany in 1849. First foundation in the United States in 1873.

GENERALATE: *Suore della Carita Cristiana Casa Generalizia,* Via di Boccea, 671, 00166, Roma (Casalotti), Italia. Tel: 011-396-6156-0829. Mother Gregoris Michels, Supr. Gen.

Total universal number in congregation 961.

NORTH AMERICAN EASTERN PROVINCE (1927): *Mallinckrodt Convent,* Mendham, NJ 07945. Tel: 201-543-6528. (*Div. of North American Province 1927; Sr. Maria Assumpta Shurer, Prov.; Sr. Pierre Koesters, Archivist,*

Professed Sisters 325.

Ministry in Academic Education; Retreat House; Catechetical Centers; Religion Coordinators; and Hospital work.

Properties owned and/or sponsored: *Villa Pauline, Retreat House,* Mendham, NJ; *Divine Providence Hospital,* Williamsport, PA; *Holy Spirit Hospital,* Camp Hill, PA; *Mallinckrodt Convent Motherhouse,* Mendham, NJ; *Holy Family Convent, Home for Aged and Retired Sisters,* Danville, PA; *Muncy Valley Hospital,* Muncy, PA.

Represented in the Archdioceses of Newark, New York and Philadelphia; and in the Dioceses of Allentown, Camden, Harrisburg, Metuchen, Paterson and Scranton.

NORTH AMERICAN WESTERN PROVINCE: *Sisters of Christian Charity - Daughters of the Blessed Virgin Mary of the Immaculate Conception,* 1041 Ridge Rd., Wilmette, IL 60091-1560. Tel: 847-853-3400; Fax: 847-251-0482. Sr. M. Judith Moran, Prov.; Sr. Mary Thecla Malawey, Archivist.

Professed Sisters 151.

Ministry in the field of Academic Education at all levels; Abused and Neglected Children; Religious Education; Parish Ministry; Ministry to Aged; Vocation Ministry; Prayer Ministry; Ministry to the Poor; Multi-Cultural Ministry.

Properties owned and sponsored: *Maria Immaculata Convent; Sacred Heart Convent,* Wilmette, IL; *Josephinum High School and Convent,* Chicago, IL; *Mallinckrodt College of the North Shore,* Wilmette, IL.

Represented in the Archdioceses of Chicago, New Orleans, St. Louis, Santa Fe, and the Dioceses of Brownsville, Jefferson City, Lansing and Rapid City.

[0670] (O.C.S.O.)—CISTERCIAN NUNS OF THE STRICT OBSERVANCE P

Founded at Citeaux, France, in 1125. First foundation in the United States in 1949.

GENERALATE: Viale Africa 33, 00144, Rome, Italy.

Total universal number of nuns in Order 1,908. Contemplative.

U.S. ESTABLISHMENTS:.

MOUNT ST. MARY'S ABBEY: 300 Arnold St., Wrentham, MA 02093. Tel: 508-528-1282. Rev. Mother M. Agnes Day, O.C.S.O., Abbess.

Total number in community 49.

Represented in the Archdiocese of Boston.

OUR LADY OF THE MISSISSIPPI ABBEY: 8400 Abbey Hill Road, Dubuque, IA 52003. Tel: 319-582-2595; Fax: 319-582-5511. Rev. Mother Gail Fitzpatrick, O.C.S.O., Abbess.

Total number in community 26.

Legal Title: *Trappistine Nuns, Inc.; Iowa Cistercians of the Strict Observance.*

Represented in the Archdiocese of Dubuque.

SANTA RITA ABBEY: HC 1, Box 929, Sonoita, AZ 85637-9705. Tel: 520-455-5595. Mother M. Beverly Aitken, O.C.S.O., Prioress.

Legal Title: *Cistercian Nuns of the Strict Observance.*

Total number in community 13.

Represented in the Diocese of Tucson.

OUR LADY OF THE REDWOODS ABBEY: Whitethorn, CA 95589. Tel: 707-986-7419. Sr. Diane Foster, O.C.S.O., Abbess.

Total number in community 11.

Represented in the Diocese of Santa Rosa.

OUR LADY OF THE ANGELS MONASTERY: 3365 Monastery Dr., Crozet, VA 22932. Tel: 804-823-1452; Fax: 804-823-6379. Mother Marion Rissetto, O.C.S.O., Supr.

Legal Title: *Cistercian Nuns of the Strict Observance in Virginia, Inc.*

Total number in community 9.

Represented in the Diocese of Richmond.

[0680] (O.CIST.)—CISTERCIAN NUNS P

HEADQUARTERS: Piazza del Tempio di Diana, 14, Roma, Italia, 00153. Most Rev. Maurus Esteva, O.Cist., Abbot General.

U.S. HEADQUARTERS: *Valley of Our Lady Monastery,* E. 11096 Yanke Dr., Prairie du Sac, WI 53578. Tel:

608-643-3520; Fax: 608-643-3520. Rev. Mother Paula Hannah, O.Cist., Prioress.
Total number in community 14.

[0685] (R.M.I.)—CLARETIAN MISSIONARY SISTERS P

Religious of Mary Immaculate
Claretian Missionary Sisters

Founded in Santiago de Cuba, August 25, 1855. Established in the United States in 1956.
GENERALATE: Via Callandrelli 16, 00153, Roma, Italy. Eusebia Pizarro, Supr. Gen.
U.S. DELEGATION: 9600 W. Atlantic Ave., Delray Beach, FL 33446. Sr. Regina Tutzo, Local Supr.
Sisters in the World 600 Sisters in Florida 10.
Legal Title: *Claretian Missionary Sisters of Florida, Inc.*
Ministry in Religious Education; Theological formation in Pastoral Institutes and Seminaries; Social Ministries; Youth Ministry; Parish and Diocesan Ministries.
Represented in the Archdiocese of Miami and the Diocese of Palm Beach.

[0690] (C.M.S.)—COMBONI MISSIONARY SISTERS P

Founded in Italy in 1872. An international congregation of 1,869 sisters serving in the mission fields of Africa, Latin America and the Middle East. First United States Foundation in 1950.
GENERALATE: Rome, Italy. Mother Mariangela Sardi, Supr. Gen.
AMERICAN HEADQUARTERS: 1307 Lakeside Ave., Richmond, VA 23228. Tel: 804-262-8827; Fax: 804-264-2906. Sr. Ruth Ann Bryden, Prov. Supr.
Legal Titles & Holdings: *Provincial House Holy Angels Day Care Center Comboni Missionary Sisters, Inc.*, Richmond, VA.
Represented in the Archdioceses of Chicago and Philadelphia and the Diocese of Richmond.

[0700] (O.D.N.)—COMPANY OF MARY P

Founded in Bordeaux, France, April 7, 1607, by St. Jeanne de Lestonnac. First foundation in the United States in 1926, in Douglas, Arizona.
GENERAL MOTHERHOUSE: Rome, Italy. Sr. Margarita Maria Pedraz, O.D.N., Supr. Gen.
Universal number in Congregation 2,290.
U.S. MOTHERHOUSE (1926): *Company of Mary Provincial House,* 16791 E. Main St., Tustin, CA 92680. Tel: 714-541-3125. Sr. Ernestine Velarde, O.D.N., Prov. Supr.; Sr. Kathy Schneider, O.D.N., Community Archivist.
Total number in U.S. 60.
Sisters serve and staff: Kindergartens; Grammar Schools; Religious Instruction Centers; Residences; Parishes & Retreat Centers; Medical Clinic.
Properties owned: *St. Jeanne de Lestonnac Kindergarten & Day Nursery,* Los Angles, CA; *Divine Providence Kindergarten & Day Nursery,* Los Angeles, CA; *St. Joseph Residence for Women,* Los Angeles, CA; *St. Jeanne De Lestonnac School,* Tustin, CA; *Lestonnac Kindergarten & Day Nursery,* Douglas, AZ.
Represented in the Archdiocese of Los Angeles, and the Dioceses of Orange, San Bernardino, and Tucson.

[0710] (C.S.)—THE COMPANY OF THE SAVIOR D

Founded in Spain in 1952. First United States foundation in 1962.
GENERAL MOTHERHOUSE: Aravaca Madrid-23, Spain. Mother Carmen Aige, Supr. Gen.
U.S. FOUNDATION: 820 Clinton Ave., Bridgeport, CT 06604. Tel: 203-368-1875.
Professed Sisters 51; Novices 1.
Represented in the Diocese of Bridgeport.

[0720] (M.C.)—CONSOLATA MISSIONARY SISTERS P

Founded in Italy in 1910. First foundation in United States in 1954.
MOTHERHOUSE: Istituto Suore Missionarie della Consolata, Corso Allamano, Torino, Italy. Mother Rina Carla Salsa, Supr. Gen.
Total universal number in congregation is approximately 975.
U.S. HEADQUARTERS: *Consolata Missionary Sisters,* 6801 Belmont Rd. - P.O. Box 371, Belmont, MI 49306. Tel: 616-361-2072; Fax: 616-361-2049. Sr. Felicia Bertaina, M.C., Supr.
Total number in community 22.
Sisters serve and staff: Grammar Schools; Apostolate among Minorities; Catechetical and Pastoral Work.
Represented in the Dioceses of Birmingham and Grand Rapids.

[0725](M.C-M.)—CORDI-MARIAN MISSIONARY SISTERS CONGREGATION P

Founded in Mexico City in 1921. First United States foundation in 1926.
GENERAL MOTHERHOUSE: Apdo. Postal #1109, Toluca, Mexico C.P., 50091. Sr. Maria Cibrian, M.C-M., Supr. Gen.
U.S. PROVINCIAL HOUSE: 11624 FM 471, Apt. 402, San Antonio, TX 78253. Tel: 210-688-3889. Sr. Mary Catalina Marquez, M.C-M., Prov. Supr.
Total number in Congregation 122; Total number in U.S. community 38.
Properties Owned: *Cordi-Marian Villa—Retreat Center and Provincial House,* San Antonio, TX; *East St. Louis Catholic Day Care Center and Convent,* East St. Louis, IL.
Ministry in Catechetical Centers; Pastoral Ministry Programs; Elementary Education; Kindergarten and Day Care Centers; Retreat Center; Social Service; Migrant Ministry; Prison Ministry; Vestment and Banner Making.
Represented in the Archdioceses of Chicago, Kansas City and San Antonio, and the Dioceses of Austin, Belleville and Galveston-Houston.

[0730] (Fd.CC.)—CANOSSIAN DAUGHTERS OF CHARITY
Canossian Sisters P

Founded in Verona, Italy in 1808.
GENERAL MOTHERHOUSE: via della Stazione di Ottavia 70, Rome, Italy, 00135.
U.S. PROVINCIAL HOUSE: *Cristo Rey Convent,* 5625 Isleta Blvd., S.W., Albuquerque, NM 87105.
Sisters in U.S. 33.
Ministry in Evangelization; Integral Promotion of the Person; Visiting the Sick; Intermediate Care Facility for children with pervasive needs; Residential lay volunteer program.
Represented in the Archdioceses of San Francisco and Santa Fe and the Diocese of Sacramento. Also in Canada and Mexico.

[0740] (D.C.P.B.)—DAUGHTERS OF CHARITY OF THE MOST PRECIOUS BLOOD P

Founded in Pagani, Italy in 1872. First foundation in United States in 1908.
GENERALATE: Via Vigna Fabbri 45, Rome, Italy. Sr. Ofelia Marzocca, Mother Gen.
U.S. ADDRESS: *Daughters of Charity of the Most Precious Blood,* 1482 North Ave., Bridgeport, CT 06604. Tel: 203-334-7000.
Total number in community 20.
Represented in the Dioceses of Albany, Bridgeport and Paterson.

[0750] (F.C.S.C.J.)—DAUGHTERS OF THE CHARITY OF THE SACRED HEART OF JESUS P

First founded in France at La Salle de Vihiers in 1823. First founded in the United States at Newport, Vermont in October 1905.
GENERALATE: Montgeron, France.
GENERAL MOTHERHOUSE: La Salle de Vihiers, France. Sr. Collette Lussier, Supr. Gen.
MOUNT SACRED HEART PROVINCIAL HOUSE: *Daughters of the Charity of the Sacred Heart,* (1949), Grove St. - P.O. Box 642, Littleton, NH 03561-0642. Tel: 603-444-5346; Fax: 603-444-5348. Sr. Rosina Bechard, F.C.S.C.J., Prov. Supr.; Sr. Lucille Grandpre, F.C.S.C.J., Local Supr.; Sr. Yvette Beloin, F.C.S.C.J., Local Supr.
Total number in province 82.
Sisters serve and staff: Grammar Schools and Kindergarten; Catechetical Centers; Spiritual Directors; Pastoral Ministry; Homes for the Aged; Domestic Departments; Pre-schools; Foreign Missions.
Represented in the Archdiocese of Boston, and the Dioceses of Burlington, Fall River, Lafayette (LA), Manchester, Ogdensburg and Portland (ME).

[0760] (D.C.)—DAUGHTERS OF CHARITY OF ST. VINCENT DE PAUL P

Founded in France in 1633. First foundation in the United States in 1809 by Saint Elizabeth Ann Seton, Emmitsburg, MD.
GENERAL MOTHERHOUSE: Paris, France. Sr. Juana Elizondo, Supr. Gen.
EMMITSBURG PROVINCE (SOUTHEAST) (1809): *St. Joseph's Provincial House,* Emmitsburg, MD 21727. Tel: 301-447-3121; Fax: 301-447-6038. Sr. Virginia Ann Brooks, Prov.; Bonnie Weatherly, Archivist.
Legal Title: *Sisters of Charity of St. Joseph's.*
Total number in province 299.
Sisters serve and staff: High Schools; Elementary Schools; Medical Clinics; Hospitals; Nursing Homes; Homes for Unmarried Mothers; Child Caring Homes; Social Service Centers; Catholic Charities; Parish Ministries; Hispanic Ministry.
Represented in the Archdioceses of Baltimore and Washington and in the Dioceses of Arlington, Charleston, Charlotte, Pensacola-Tallahassee, Raleigh, Richmond, Savannah, St. Augustine and Wheeling-Charleston.
WEST CENTRAL PROVINCE (1910): *Marillac Provincial House,* 7800 Natural Bridge Rd., St. Louis, MO 63121-4694. Tel: 314-382-2800; Fax: 314-382-8392. Sr. Nannette Gentile, Prov.; Sr. Genevieve Keusenkothen, Archivist.
Total number in the community 254.
Ministry in the field of Religious and Academic Education at all levels; Seminary Education; Hospitals; Leprosarium; Psychiatric Hospitals; Parish Ministry; Social Service Centers; Schools of Nursing; Day Care Centers; Clinics; Homes for Unwed Mothers; Homes for Children; Housing for the Homeless; Catholic Charities Offices; Refugee Resettlement; Housing; Peace and Justice; Diocesan Offices; Hospice; State Health Care; Home Health Care; Emergency Relief Centers; Spiritual Direction and Retreats.
Sponsors: Clinics— *Centro San Vicente,* El Paso, TX; *Daughters of Charity Services of San Antonio, Inc. Daughters of Charity Services of San Antonio-El Carmen Div.,* San Antonio, TX; *Daughters of Charity Services of San Antonio-De Paul Div.,* San Antonio, TX; *Daughters of Charity Services of San Antonio-St. Philip of Jesus Div.,* San Antonio, TX; *Daughters of Charity Community Services of El Paso (DCCS-EP) Daughters of Charity Healthservices of Austin - East Side Center,* Austin, TX; *Daughters of Charity Health Services of Austin,* Austin, TX. Hospitals— *Seton Medical Center,* Austin, TX; *Seton Northwest,* Austin, TX St. Paul Medical Center, Dallas, TX ; *Providence - De Paul Center Providence Health Center,* Waco, TX; *Support Services— Daughters of Charity National Health System, West Central, Inc.,* St. Louis, MO; *Daughters of Charity Healthcare Foundation of St. Louis,* St. Louis, MO; *Daughters of Charity National Health System,* St. Louis, MO; *Daughters of Charity National Health System, West Central, Data Center,* Dallas, TX.
Represented in the Archdioceses of Kansas City in Kansas, New Orleans, St. Louis and San Antonio, and the Dioceses of Austin, Amarillo, Baton Rouge, Brownsville, Dallas, El Paso, Kansas City-St. Joseph, Little Rock, San Angelo and Springfield-Cape Girardeau.
Charity of St. Vincent de Paul of Indiana, Inc., 9400 New Harmony Rd., Evansville, IN 47720. Tel: 812-963-3341; Fax: 812-963-7589. Sr. Catherine Madigan, D.C., Prov. Supr.; Sr. Margaret Flynn, D.C., Archivist.
Total number in the community 202.
Sponsored Works: Home for Retired Sisters; General Hospitals; Skilled Nursing Facilities; Clinics; Home Health Care; Day Care Centers and Neighborhood Services; Home for Unwed Mothers; Childrens' Residence; Services to Elderly.
Sponsored Organizations: *Daughters of Charity National Health System, East Central, Inc. Daughters of Charity Regional Information Services, Inc.* Local Development Corporations. Shared ownership in Health Maintenance Organizations and Preferred Provider Organizations.
Legal Title: *Mater Dei Provincialate, Inc.*
Ministries of Insertion Religious and Academic Education at all levels; Diocesan Program for Deaf; Campus Ministry; Parish Ministry; Social Services in parishes; Catholic Charities Office; Shelters for homeless; Residences for Elderly.
Represented in the Archdioceses of Chicago, Detroit, Indianapolis, Milwaukee and Mobile, and the Dioceses of Belleville, Biloxi, Birmingham, Evansville, Fort Wayne-South Bend, Lafayette (IN), Nashville, Jackson, Peoria, Saginaw and Springfield (IL).
NORTHEAST PROVINCE (1969): *De Paul Provincial House,* 96 Menands Rd., Albany, NY 12204-1499. Sr. Louise Gallahue, Prov. Supr.; Sr. Elaine Wheeler, Archivist.
Total number in the community 239.
Ministry in the field of Academic Education at all levels; Hospital; Specialized Hospitals; Homes for Unmarried Mothers; Child Caring Homes; Day Care Centers; Social Service Centers; Parish Centers.
Represented in the Archdioceses of Boston, New York, Philadelphia and in the Dioceses of Albany, Allentown, Bridgeport, Brooklyn, Buffalo, Metuchen, Ogdensburg, Rochester, Syracuse and Wilmington.
PROVINCE OF THE WEST (LOS ALTOS HILLS) (1969): *Seton Provincialate,* 26000 Altamont Rd., Los Altos Hills, CA 94022-4398. Tel: 415-941-4490; Fax: 415-949-3874. Sr. Joyce Weller, D.C., Prov.; Sr. Mary William Vinet, D.C., Archivist.
Total number in the community 160.

Properties owned and sponsored: *Seton Medical Center,* Daly City, CA; *Seton Provincialate,* Los Altos Hills, CA; *St. Vincent Medical Center,* Los Angeles, CA; *St. Vincent's Senior Citizen Nutrition Program,* Los Angeles, CA; *St. Francis Medical Center,* Lynwood, CA; *Maryvale,* Rosemead, CA; *Mount St. Joseph-St. Elizabeth,* San Francisco, CA; *O'Connor Hospital,* San Jose, CA; *St. Louise Hospital,* Morgan Hill, CA; *St. Vincent's,* Santa Barbara, CA; *Robert F. Kennedy Medical Center,* Hawthorne, CA.
Represented in the Archdioceses of Los Angeles, San Francisco and in the Dioceses of Fresno, Gallup, Monterey, Oakland, Phoenix, Salt Lake City, and San Jose.

[0770] (D.C.)—DAUGHTERS OF THE CROSS D

Founded in France in 1640. First foundation in the United States in 1855.
MOTHERHOUSE: *Daughters of the Cross Motherhouse,* 1000 Fairview St., Shreveport, LA 71104. Tel: 318-869-3482. Sr. Marietta Welsh, Supr. Gen.
Total number in community 16.
Represented in the Diocese of Dallas and Shreveport.

[0780] (F.C.)—DAUGHTERS OF THE CROSS OF LIEGE P

Founded in Liege, Belgium in 1833. First foundation in the United States in 1958.
PRINCIPAL HOUSE: *St. Bernard Convent,* 165 W. Eaton Ave., Tracy, CA 95376. Sr. M. Eugene Hagan, F.C., Supr.
Total number in community 8.
Represented in the Diocese of Stockton.

[0790] (F.D.C.)—DAUGHTERS OF DIVINE CHARITY P

Founded in Austria on Nov. 21, 1868. First founded in the United States on Oct. 8, 1913, in New York City.
GENERAL MOTHERHOUSE: Grottaferrata, Rome, Italy. Sr. Nicolina Hendges, Supr. Gen.
ST. JOSEPH PROVINCE (1921): *St. Joseph Provincialate,* 205 Major Ave., Staten Island, NY 10305. Tel: 718-720-4377. Sr. Josita DeVita, F.D.C., Prov.; Sr. Marie Claire Weaver, F.D.C., 1st Prov. Councilor.
Total number universally 1,480.
Ministry in Education; Nursing; Residences for Women; Working with the Homeless and the Elderly.
Properties owned: *St. Mary's Residence,* New York, NY; *St. Joseph Hill Academy,* Staten Island, NY; *Villa Madonna,* Hackettstown, NJ.
Represented in the Archdioceses of Newark and New York, and the Dioceses of Bridgeport, Metuchen, San Bernardino and San Diego.

[0793] (D.D.L.)—DAUGHTERS OF DIVINE LOVE CONGREGATION

Founded in Ukpor, Nigeria in 1969. First United States Foundation in 1990.
GENERAL HOUSE: Fifth Avenue, P.O. Box 546, Enugu, Enugu State, Nigeria. Tel: 042-559071; 042-554450. Rev. Mother M. Chilota Elochukwu, D.D.L., Mother Gen.
Total Professed Sisters 521.
U.S. REGIONAL HOUSE: 140 North Ave., Highwood, IL 60040. Tel: 708-432-9003. Sr. Mary Paul Asoegwu, D.D.L., Regl. Supr.
Professed Sisters in U.S. 19.
Ministry in the field of Administration; Religious and Academic Education at all levels; Special Education; Health Services; Parish and Diocesan Services; Retreat Work; Social Work.
Represented in the Archdiocese of Chicago and the diocese of Brooklyn.

[0795] (F.D.Z.)—DAUGHTERS OF DIVINE ZEAL

Founded in Messina, Italy, in 1887 by Blessed Hannibal Maria DiFrancia. First foundation in the United States in 1951.
GENERALATE: *Figlie Del Divino Zelo,* Circonvallazione Appia 144, 00179, Rome, Italy. Mother Ferdinanda Reale, Supr. Gen.
Total universal number in the Congregation 1,000.
U.S. HEADQUARTERS: *Hannibal House Spiritual Center,* 1526 Hill Rd., Reading, PA 19602. Tel: 610-375-1738; 375-9072; Fax: 610-375-2188. Sr. Gesulmina Micali, F.D.Z., Supr.
Total number in community 6.
Ministry in the field of Religious and Academic Education; Parish and Youth Ministry; Retreat, Vocation, Prayer and Apostolate.
Represented in the Diocese of Allentown.
ST. MARY PROVINCE (1950): *Provincial Motherhouse and Novitiate,* 39 N. Portage Path, Akron, OH 44303-1183. Tel: 216-867-4960. Sr. Maria Bakich, Prov. Supr.
Total number in community 23.
Ministry in the field of Education; Home for Working Girls; Home for elderly senior Women and Men.
Properties owned: *Daughters of Divine Charity, Inc.; Leonora Hall Convent; Leonora Hall Residence; Francesca Residence.*
Represented in the Archdioceses of Miami, Milwaukee, and the Dioceses of Cleveland.
HOLY TRINITY PROVINCE (1972): *Provincial House,* 1315 N. Woodward Ave., Bloomfield Hills, MI 48304. Tel: 313-645-5318. Sr. M. Paschal Grand, Prov. Supr.
Professed Sisters 34.
Ministry in Education; Foster Care Residence; Homes for the Aged.
Represented in the Archdiocese of Detroit and the Diocese of Fort Wayne-South Bend.

[0810] (D.H.M.)—DAUGHTERS OF THE HEART OF MARY P

Founded in France in 1790. First United States foundation in 1851.
GENERALATE: 39 rue Notre Dame des Champs, 75006, Paris, France.
PROVINCIALATE: 1339 Northampton St., Holyoke, MA 01040-1913. Tel: 413-532-7406; Fax: 413-533-4217. Sr. Miriam Najimy, D.H.M., Prov.
Properties owned: *Marian Center & Residence,* Holyoke, MA; *Maryhill Retreat Center,* St. Paul, MN; *Nardin Academy,* Buffalo, NY; *Heart of Mary Center,* St. Louis, MO; *St. Isaac Jogues Center,* Philadelphia, PA; *Regina Maria Retreat House,* Plattsburgh, NY; *St. Joseph's School for the Deaf,* Bronx, NY; *Ephpheta Center,* Oak Park, IL.
Professed Sisters 124; Novices 2; Aspirants 1.
Represented in the Archdioceses of Chicago, New York, Philadelphia, St. Louis and St. Paul-Minneapolis, and the Dioceses of Buffalo, Ogdensburg, Springfield (MA) and Trenton.

[0820] (D.H.S.)—DAUGHTERS OF THE HOLY SPIRIT P

Founded in France in 1706. First foundation in the U.S. in 1902.
GENERAL MOTHERHOUSE: St. Brieuc, Cotes du Nord, Bretagne, France. Sr. Yvette LeGrand, F.S.E., Supr. Gen.
PROVINCIAL HOUSE: *Daughters of the Holy Spirit, Inc.,* 72 Church St., Putnam, CT 06260. Tel: 203-928-0891. Sr. Bonnie Morrow, D.H.S., Prov.
Total number in the community 198.
Legal Title: *Daughters of the Holy Spirit Charitable Trust Holy Spirit Health Care Center, Inc.*
Ministry in the field of Academic Education at all levels; Home for Aged; Home/District Nursing; Nursing Home for Daughters of the Holy Spirit; and various social and pastoral ministries of service.
Represented in the Archdioceses of Boston, Hartford, Mobile, New York, Philadelphia, and the Dioceses of Birmingham, Bridgeport, Burlington, Fall River, Fresno Norwich, Ogdensburg, Portland in Maine, Providence, Richmond, Sacramento, Springfield (MA), Stockton and Worcester.

[0830] (F.J.)—CONGREGATION OF THE DAUGHTERS OF JESUS (LES FILLES DE JESUS) P

Founded in France in 1834. First foundation in the U.S. in 1903.
MOTHERHOUSE: Kermaria, 56500, Locmine, France.
GENERALATE: 11, rue d'Arras, 75005, Paris, France. Sr. Ellen Martin, Supr. Gen.
Total universal number in Congregation 2,138.
WESTERN PROVINCE (1902): 9040 84th Ave., Edmonton, Alberta T6C 1E4, Canada. Tel: 403-466-6527. Sr. Irene Magnan, Prov. Supr.
U.S. ADDRESS: 4209 3rd Ave. S., Great Falls, MT 59405. Tel: 406-452-7231.
Total number in community 3.
Represented in the Diocese of Great Falls.

[0840] (F.I.)—DAUGHTERS OF JESUS P

Founded in Spain in 1871. First foundation in the U.S. in 1950.
GENERAL MOTHERHOUSE: Rome, Italy.
U.S. FOUNDATION: 2021 Stuart Ave., Baton Rouge, LA 70808. Tel: 504-344-7131. Sr. Ana Maria Lopez, F.I., Prov.
Professed Sisters 5.
Represented in the Diocese of Baton Rouge.

[0850] (F.M.A.)—DAUGHTERS OF MARY HELP OF CHRISTIANS P

Salesian Sisters of St. John Bosco

Founded in Mornese, Italy, in 1872. First foundation in the U.S. in 1908 at Paterson, New Jersey.
GENERAL MOTHERHOUSE: Via Ateneo Salesiano, 81, 00139, Rome, Italy. Very Rev. Mother Marinella Castagno, F.M.A., Mother Gen.
Total universal number in Congregation 16,701.
PROVINCE OF ST. PHILIP, APOSTLE: *Provincial House,* 655 Belmont Ave., Haledon, NJ 07508-2398. Tel: 201-790-7964; 7965. Mother Theresa Kelly, F.M.A., Prov.
Legal Title: *Missionary Society of the Salesian Sisters, Inc. Salesian Sisters of Tampa, Inc.*
Properties owned: *Provincial House,* Haledon, NJ; *Mary Help of Christians Academy,* North Haledon, NJ; *Sacred Heart Center,* Newton, NJ; *Villa Madonna School-Salesian Sisters of Tampa, Inc.,* Tampa, FL; *Camp Auxilium Learning Center,* Newton, NJ.
Total number in the community 150.
Ministry in the field of Education; Day Nurseries; CCD Centers; Youth Ministry.
Represented in the Archdioceses of Miami, Newark, New York, and the Dioceses of Birmingham, Paterson and St. Petersburg.
PROVINCE OF MARY IMMACULATE: *FMA Provincial House,* 6019 Buena Vista, San Antonio, TX 78237. Tel: 210-432-0089; 0090; Fax: 210-432-4016. Mother Martina Ponce, F.M.A., Prov.
Legal Title: *Institute of the Daughters of Mary Help of Christians - Salesian Sisters of St. John Bosco,* San Antonio, TX; *Salesian Sisters - Mary Help of Christians Youth Center, Inc.,* Corralitos, CA.
Properties owned: *FMA Provincial House & St. John Bosco School,* San Antonio, TX; *Mary Help of Christians School,* Laredo, TX' *Salesian Sisters School - Salesian Sisters: MHC Youth Center, Inc.,* Corralitos, CA.
Total number in community 115.
Ministry in Education; Youth Ministry and Religious Education.
Represented in the Archdioceses of Los Angeles, New Orleans, San Antonio and San Francisco, and the Dioceses of Austin, Corpus Christi, Monterey and Phoenix.

[0860] (D.M.)—DAUGHTERS OF MARY OF THE IMMACULATE CONCEPTION P

Founded in New Britain in 1904.
GENERAL MOTHERHOUSE AND NOVITIATE: 314 Osgood Ave., New Britain, CT 06053. Tel: 203-225-9406. Mother Mary Mark, Supr. Gen.
Total number in community 73.
Legal Title: *Congregation of the Daughters of Mary of the Immaculate Conception, Inc.*
Ministry in the field of Education; Child Day Care Center; Home for the Aged; Homes for Working Girls and Students; Skilled Care Facilities; Catechetical Centers.
Properties owned: *St. Lucian's Home; Our Lady of Rose Hill Day Care Center; Marian Educational Clinic; Monsignor Bojnowski Manor; Mary Immaculate Academy Motherhouse and Novitiate Complex,* New Britain, CT; *St. Joseph's Home,* NY; *St. Agnes Residence,* NY; *Our Lady's Guild House,* Boston, MA; *Sancta Maria Nursing Facility,* Cambridge, MA.
Represented in the Archdioceses of Boston, Hartford and New York and in the Diocese of Springfield (MA).

[0870] (F.M.I.)—CONGREGATION OF THE DAUGHTERS OF MARY IMMACULATE P

Marianist Sisters

Founded in France in 1816.
MOTHERHOUSE: Rome, Italy. Mother M. Blanca Jamar, Supr. Gen.
U.S. FOUNDATION (1949): *Our Lady of the Pillar Convent,* 251 W. Ligustrum Dr., San Antonio, TX 78228. Tel: 210-433-5501; Fax: 210-431-9611. Sr. Evangeline Escobar, Prov. Supr.
Total number in community 19.
Properties owned: *Our Lady of the Pillar Convent,* San Antonio, TX; *Novitiate House,* Dayton, OH.
Represented in the Archdioceses of Cincinnati and San Antonio and the Diocese of Toledo.

[0880] (D.M.J.)—DAUGHTERS OF MARY AND JOSEPH P

Founded in Belgium in 1817. First U.S. Foundation in 1926.
GENERALATE: Via Rivarone, 100, 00166, Rome, Italy. Sr. Joan Roddy, Supr. Gen.
NOVITIATE: 5300 Crest Rd., Rancho Palos Verdes, CA 90275. Tel: 310-541-8194; Fax: 310-544-0387. Sr. Julia Costello, Formation Dir.
PROVINCIALATE: 5300 Crest Rd., Rancho Palos Verdes, CA 90274. Tel: 310-377-9968. Sr. Catherine McShane, Prov.
Professed Sisters 76.

Legal Title: *Daughters of Mary and Joseph, California.*
Sisters staff: Grammar & High Schools; Parish Ministry; Health Ministry; Missionary Work; Detention Ministry; Retreat Work; House of Prayer.
Represented in the Archdioceses of Los Angeles and San Francisco, and in the Dioceses of San Bernardino and San Diego.

[0890] (D.M.)—DAUGHTERS OF OUR LADY OF MERCY P

Founded in Italy in 1837 by Saint Mary Joseph Rossello. First foundation in the United States in 1919.
GENERALATE: Via Monte Grappa, No. 7., Savona, Italy. Rev. Mother M. Celsa Benneti, Supr. Gen.
PROVINCIALATE AND NOVITIATE: *Villa Rossello,* 1009 Main Rd., Newfield, NJ 08344. Tel: 609-697-2983. Sr. Grace Marie Scandale, D.M., Mother Prov.; Sr. Loretta Marie Stevens, D.M., Community Archivist.
Total number in community 68.
Ministry in the field of Education; Health Services; Day Nursery; Convalescent Hospital; C.C.D. and Parish Work.
Legal Holdings: *Misericordia Convalescent Home,* York, PA *Holy Child Nursery,* York, PA *Our Lady of Mercy Academy,* Newfield, NJ.
Represented in the Dioceses of Camden, Harrisburg, Scranton and Springfield (MA).

[0900] (F.D.N.S.C.)—DAUGHTERS OF OUR LADY OF THE SACRED HEART P

Founded in France in 1882.
MOTHERHOUSE: Via Casale S. Pio. V, 37, Rome, Italy. Sr. Mary Ringnalda, Supr. Gen.
U.S. FOUNDATION (1955): *St. Francis de Sales Convent,* 424 E. Browning Rd., Bellmawr, NJ 08031. Tel: 609-931-8973.
Professed Sisters in U.S. 15.
Represented in the Archdiocese of Philadelphia, and the Dioceses of Camden.

[0910] (Bethl.)—BETHLEMITA, DAUGHTER OF THE SACRED HEART OF JESUS P

Founded in Guatemala in 1861. First foundation in United States in Dallas, Texas.
MOTHERHOUSE: Bogota, Colombia, S.A.
U.S. FOUNDATION: *St. Joseph Residence,* 330 W. Pembroke St., Dallas, TX 75208. Tel: 214-948-3597. Sr. Adelaide Bocanegra, Admin.
Professed Sisters 6.
Represented in the Diocese of Dallas.

[0920] (D.S.F.)—DAUGHTERS OF ST. FRANCIS OF ASSISI P

Founded in Austro, Hungary, 1894. First foundation in United States in 1946.
MOTHERHOUSE: *St. Joseph's Convent,* 507 N. Prairie St., Lacon, IL 61540. Tel: 309-246-2175. Sr. M. Vaclava Ballon, D.S.F., Prov. Supr.
Professed Sisters 31.
Represented in the Dioceses of Peoria and Springfield-Cape Girardeau.

[0930] (F.S.J.)—RELIGIOUS DAUGHTERS OF ST. JOSEPH P

Founded in Gerona, Spain in 1875.
GENERAL MOTHERHOUSE: General Asensio Cabanillas, 18, Madrid, 28003, Spain. Mother Carmen Vela, Supr. Gen.
Total universal number in Congregation 880.
Provincial House, Calzada Ermita Istapalapa, Mexico. Sr. Pilar Soto, Prov.
U.S. FOUNDATION: *Santa Marta Hospital,* 319 N. Humphreys Ave., Los Angeles, CA 90022. Sr. Eulalia Yepez, F.S.J., Supr.
Legal Title: *Daughters of St. Joseph of California, Inc.*
Total number in community 9.
Represented in the Archdiocese of Los Angeles.

[0940] (D.S.M.P.)—DAUGHTERS OF ST. MARY OF PROVIDENCE P

Founded in Italy in 1881. First foundation in the U.S. in 1913.
GENERALATE: Rome, Italy. Mother Elena Salarici, Supr. Gen.
NOVITIATE: *Daughters of St. Mary,* 24955 North Highway 12, Lake Zurich, IL 60047. Tel: 847-438-5050. Sr. Caryn Haas, Formation Dir.
PROVINCIALATE: *St. Mary of Providence Institute,* 4200 N. Austin Ave., Chicago, IL 60634. Tel: 312-545-8300. Sr. Bernardine Kauffmann, Prov.
Professed Sisters 100.
Represented in the Archdioceses of Boston, Chicago, Detroit and Philadelphia, and the Dioceses of Camden, Gary, Lansing, New Ulm, Providence and Sioux Falls.

[0950] (F.S.P.)—PIOUS SOCIETY DAUGHTERS OF ST. PAUL P

(Missionary Sisters of the Media of Communications)

Founded in Alba, Piedmont, Italy, on June 15, 1915. First founded in the United States on June 28, 1932, at 78 Fort Place, Staten Island, New York.
GENERAL MOTHERHOUSE: Rome, Italy. Sr. Giovanna Maria Carrara, Supr. Gen.
Total universal number in Congregation 2,592.
PROVINCIAL HOUSE, NOVITIATE, JUNIORATE, PUBLISHING HOUSE: 50 St. Paul's Ave., Boston, MA 02130. Tel: 617-522-8911. Sr. Linda James Smith, Prov. Supr.; Sr. Cecilia Paula Livingston, Local Supr.
Legal Title: *Daughters of St. Paul, Inc.*
Properties owned: *St. Paul Book and Media Centers,* situated in 19 locations throughout the States (see list of (Arch)Dioceses where represented); *Provincialate,* Boston, MA; *St. Thecla Retreat House,* Billerica, MA.
Total number in community 164.
Represented in the Archdioceses of Anchorage, Boston, Chicago, Los Angeles, Miami, New Orleans, New York, Philadelphia, St. Louis, San Antonio and San Francisco, and the Dioceses of Arlington, Charleston, Cleveland, Honolulu, Memphis, Metuchen and San Diego. Also in Canada.

[0960] (D.W.)—DAUGHTERS OF WISDOM P

Founded in France in 1703. First foundation in the United States in 1904.
GENERAL MOTHERHOUSE: St. Laurent-sur-Sevre, Vendee, France.
Superior General Headquarters located in Rome, Italy.
U.S. PROVINCE (1949): *Provincial House,* 385 Ocean Ave., Islip, NY 11751-4600. Tel: 516-277-2660; Fax: 516-277-3274. Sr. Evelyn Eckhardt, D.W., Prov.
Professed Sisters 147.
Ministry in all levels of Education; Retreat House; Hospital & Health Services; Orphanage; Social Work; Pediatrics Clinic.
Properties owned: *Wisdom House Center for Spirituality,* Litchfield, CT; *Our Lady of Perpetual Help Convent* (Rest Home for Sisters), Sound Beach, NY; *Provincial House,* Islip, NY; *Montfort Academy,* Fredericksburg, VA; *Our Lady of Wisdom Convent,* St. Agatha, ME. Property in: Farmingville, NY; Ozone Park, NY; Elmhurst, NY; Coram, NY.
Represented in the Archdioceses of Denver, Hartford, Mobile and Washington, and the Dioceses of Brooklyn, Burlington, Charleston, Charlotte, Metuchen, Portland (ME), Raleigh, Richmond, Rockville Centre, St. Augustine, St. Petersburg and Wheeling-Charleston.

[0965] (D.L.J.C.)—DISCIPLES OF THE LORD JESUS CHRIST

MOTHERHOUSE: P.O. Box 17, Channing, TX 79018. Tel: 806-534-2312; Fax: 806-534-2223. Mother Bernadette Beamsley, Supr. Gen.

[0970] (R.D.C.)—SISTERS OF THE DIVINE COMPASSION D

Founded in the United States in 1886.
GENERAL MOTHERHOUSE: *Good Counsel Convent,* 52 N. Broadway, White Plains, NY 10603. Tel: 914-949-2950; Fax: 914-949-5169. Sr. Helen Coldrick, R.D.C., Pres.
Total number in community 126.
Legal Holdings and Titles: *Academy of Our Lady of Good Counsel High School and Elementary School,* White Plains, NY; *Preston High School,* New York, NY; *Divine Compassion Center for Spiritual Renewal, NY; Migrant Ministry,* Goshen, NY; *Residence,* Hampton Bays, NY; *RDC Center for Counselling and Human Development.*
Ministry in Pre-school, Elementary, Secondary, College and University Education; Religious Education; Educational Consultation; Adult Education; Special Education; Pastoral Ministry; Retreat Work and Spiritual Direction; Counseling; Social Services; Migrant Ministry; Health Services; Administration and Business Services.
Represented in the Archdiocese of New York.

[0980] (P.D.D.M.)—PIOUS DISCIPLES OF THE DIVINE MASTER P

Founded in 1924. First foundation in the United States in 1948.
GENERAL MOTHERHOUSE: Rome, Italy. Mother Mary Paola Mancini, Supr. Gen.
Universal number in Congregation 1,400.
U.S. HEADQUARTERS: 60 Sunset Ave., Staten Island, NY 10314. Tel: 718-494-8597; Fax: 718-494-8521. Sr. M. Lucille Van Hoogmoed, Regl. Supr.
Total number in region 47.
Ministry is a Three Dimensional Mission: Eucharistic, Priestly, Liturgical.
Represented in the Archdioceses of Boston, Los Angeles, and New York, and the Dioceses of Fresno and San Jose.

[0990] (C.D.P.)—SISTERS OF DIVINE PROVIDENCE P

Founded in Germany in 1851. First foundation in United States in 1876.
GENERAL MOTHERHOUSE: Rome, Italy.
ST. PETER'S PROVINCE (1876): *Provincial House,* 9000 Babcock Blvd., Allison Park, PA 15101-2793. Tel: 412-931-5241; Fax: 412-635-5416. Sr. Mary Ellen Rufft, Prov.
Total number in community 281.
Properties owned and sponsored: *La Roche College Providence Heights Alpha,* Allison Park, PA; *Transfiguration House of Prayer,* Butler, PA; *Kearns Spirituality Center,* Allison Park, PA; *Providence Connections, Inc., Providence Child Care Center - South,* Castle Shannan, PA; *Providence Child Care Center, North,* Pittsburgh, PA; *Providence Family Suupport Center,* Pittsburgh, PA; *Amelia House - Safe House,* Clarion, PA.
Ministry in the fields of Education; Social Services; Pastoral Ministry; and Health Care Services.
Represented in the Archdioceses of Atlanta, Baltimore, Boston, Chicago, Denver, Detroit, Kansas City in Kansas, New York, Philadelphia, Santa Fe, and the Dioceses of Bismarck, Brownsville, Charleston, Cleveland, Colorado Springs, Columbus, Davenport, Erie, Greensburg, Orlando, Phoenix, Pittsburgh, Raleigh, San Bernardino, Wheeling-Charleston, Wilmington, Yakima and Youngstown. Also in Puerto Rico, Italy and the Dominican Republic.
ST. LOUIS PROVINCE (1930): *Mount Providence - Sisters of Divine Providence,* 8351 Florissant Rd., St. Louis, MO 63121. Tel: 314-524-3803. Sr. Janet Folkl, C.D.P., Prov. Supr.
Total number in community 59.
Legal Title: *Providence Charitable Trust,* Normandy, MO.
Properties owned and sponsored: *Mount Providence Motherhouse,* Normandy, MO; *St. Elizabeth Medical Center,* Granite City, IL.
Ministry in the fields of Education; Health Services; Parish Ministry; Social Work; Services to Refugees and Homeless People.
Represented in the Archdioceses of Chicago and St. Louis, and the Dioceses of Brownsville, Jefferson City, Nashville, Springfield-Cape Girardeau, and Springfield (IL).
OUR LADY OF DIVINE PROVIDENCE PROVINCE (1957): 363 Bishops Hwy., Kingston, MA 02364. Tel: 617-585-1745. Sr. Claudia Ward, C.D.P., Prov. Supr.
Total number in the community 47.
Sisters minister in the field of Education at all levels; Hospital and other Health Services; Parish Ministries; Diocesan Administration; Elderly Care; Education for Mentally Handicapped; Alcohol Rehabilitation Ministry.
Properties owned: *Provincial Residence; Sacred Heart Junior-Senior High School; Sacred Heart Elementary and PrePrimary School; Visitation Camp Mishannock,* Kingston, MA.
Represented in the Archdiocese of Boston, and the Dioceses of Fall River and Richmond.

[1000] (C.D.P.)—CONGREGATION OF DIVINE PROVIDENCE, MELBOURNE, KENTUCKY P

Founded in France in 1762. First foundation in the United States in 1889.
GENERAL MOTHERHOUSE: *St. Jean de Bassel,* 57930 Fenetrange, France. Sr. Marie Therese Seyler, Supr. Gen.
AMERICAN PROVINCIAL HOUSE (1889): *St. Anne Convent,* Melbourne, KY 41059. Tel: 606-441-0679. Sr. Lynn Stenken, C.D.P., Prov. Supr.; Sr. Mary Joan Dohmen, C.D.P., Archivist.
Total number in community 201.
Ministry in the field of Academic Education at all levels; Montessori Schools; Home for Working Women; Retreat Center; Religious Education & Pastory Ministry; Health & Social Services.
Represented in the Archdioceses of Baltimore, Cincinnati, New York, Washington, and the Dioceses of Charleston, Covington, Duluth, Gallup, Grand Raprids, Lafayette in Indiana, Lexington, Providence, Savannah and Toledo. Also in West Africa.

[1010] (C.D.P.)—CONGREGATION OF DIVINE PROVIDENCE, SAN ANTONIO, TEXAS P

Founded in France in 1762. First Foundation in the United States in 1866.

THE GENERALATE: P.O. Box 197, 18811 Scenic Loop Rd., Helotes, TX 78023. Tel: 210-695-8721; Fax: 210-695-6033. Sr. Lora Ann Quinonez, Supr. Gen., Councilors; Sr. Ann Umscheid; Sr. Regina Decker; Sr. Rose Kruppa; Sr. Lourdes Leal; Sr. L. Suzanne Dancer, Treas.; Sr. Mary Paul Valdez, Community Archivist.

Legal Titles & Holdings: *Congregation of Divine Providence, Inc. Providence Trust,* Helotes, TX.

NOVITIATE AND FORMATION: *Formation/Vocation Office,* 515 S.W. 24th St., San Antonio, TX 78207-4600. Tel: 210-431-3587.

Total number in community 350.

Properties owned: *The Generalate,* Helotes, TX; *Moye Center,* Castroville, TX; *Our Lady of the Lake Retirement Center,* San Antonio, TX.

Ministry in all levels of Education; Catechetical Centers; Hospitals, Clinics; Diocesan Offices; Retreat Houses; Spiritual Direction-Counseling; Pastoral; Social Work; Chaplaincies in Public Institutions; Home-Health Care; Administration.

Represented in the Archdioceses of Chicago, Denver, Kansas City in Kansas, Milwaukee, New Orleans, Oklahoma City, St. Louis, San Antonio, San Francisco, Seattle and in the Dioceses of Alexandria, Austin, Baton Rouge, Beaumont, Brownsville, Corpus Christi, Dallas, El Paso, Fort Worth, Fresno, Gallup, Galveston-Houston, Lafayette (LA), Lake Charles, Lexinton, St. Petersburg, San Angelo, Savannah, Shreveport, Springfield-Cape Giradeau, Tucson, Tulsa, Tyler and Victoria. Also in Ghana, South Africa and Mexico.

[1020] (S.D.R.)—SISTERS OF THE DIVINE REDEEMER P

Founded in 1849 at Niederbronn, France. First founded in the United States on Oct. 6, 1912 at McKeesport, Pennsylvania.

GENERALATE: Rome, Italy. Sr. M. Emelia Grabner, Gen. Supr.

AMERICAN PROVINCE (1922): *Divine Redeemer Motherhouse,* 999 Rock Run Rd., Elizabeth, PA 15037. Tel: 412-751-8600; Fax: 412-751-0355. Sr. M. Monica Kosztolnyik, Prov. Supr.; Sr. Bernard Szeman, Archivist.

Total number in province 60.

Legal Titles and Holdings: *Sisters of the Divine Redeemer Charitable Trust Divine Redeemer Health Care Ministries Corp.,* Elizabeth, PA.

Sisters serve and staff: Elementary Schools; Personal Care Home; Parish Ministry; Nursing Home.

Represented in the Archdiocese of Philadelphia, and the Dioceses of Buffalo, Cleveland and Pittsburgh.

[1030] (S.D.S.)—SISTERS OF THE DIVINE SAVIOR P

Founded in Tivoli, Italy, in 1888. First foundation in the United States in 1895.

GENERAL MOTHERHOUSE: Rome, Italy. Viale Mura Gianicolensi 67; Sr. Jean Schafer, Supr. General.

NORTH AMERICAN PROVINCE: *Sisters of the Divine Savior,* 4311 N. 100 St., Milwaukee, WI 53222-1393. Tel: 414-466-0810; Fax: 414-466-4335. Sr. Sheila Novak, S.D.S., Prov. Leader; Sr. Aquin Gilles, Archivist.

Total number in U.S. Community 139.

Ministry in Novitiate; all levels of Education; Pastoral and Social Services; Health Care; and Homes for the Aged.

Properties owned or sponsored: *St. Anne's Home for the Elderly; St. Mary's Nursing Home; Divine Savior Holy Angels High School,* Milwaukee, WI; *Divine Savior Hospital and Nursing Home,* Portage, WI; *Divine Savior Holy Angels High School Endowment Foundation, Inc.,* Milwaukee, WI; *St. Mary's Convent,* St. Nazianz, WI.

Represented in the Archdioceses of Baltimore, Chicago, Milwaukee, and the Dioceses of Birmingham, Green Bay, Jackson, La Crosse, Madison, Phoenix, Rapid City, Sioux Falls and Tucson.

[1040] (C.D.S.)—CONGREGATION OF THE DIVINE SPIRIT D

First foundation in Erie, Pennsylvania in 1956.

MOTHERHOUSE: 409 W. Sixth St., Erie, PA 16507. Tel: 814-455-3590. Mother Patricia O'Connor, Supr. Gen.

Membership 47.

Sisters serve and staff: Parochial Schools 1; CCD Activities 1; Home for Aged 1; Social Work.

Represented in the Dioceses of Erie and Youngstown.

[1050] (O.P.)—DOMINICAN CONTEMPLATIVE NUNS P

(The Nuns of the Order of Preachers)

Founded in France in 1206. First foundation in the United States in 1880. Monastic contemplative branch of the Order of Preachers. Papal cloister.

MONASTERY OF ST. DOMINIC: 375 13th Ave., Newark, NJ 07103. Tel: 201-622-6622. Sr. Catherine Mary, O.P., Prioress.

Total number in community 20.

NUNS OF THE ORDER OF PREACHERS O.P.: *Corpus Christi Monastery,* 1230 Lafayette Ave., Bronx, NY 10474. Tel: 718-328-6996. Sr. Lee, O.P., Prioress.

Total number in community 22.

MONASTERY OF THE BLESSED SACRAMENT, (CONTEMPLATIVE, CLOISTERED): *Dominican Nuns of Perpetual Adoration,* 29575 Middlebelt, Farmington Hills, MI 48334-2311. Tel: 810-626-8321; 8253; Fax: 810-626-8724. Sr. Mary Thomas, O.P., Prioress.

Cloistered Professed Nuns 37; Extern Professed Sisters 3.

MONASTERY OF THE ANGELS: *Cloistered Dominican Nuns of Perpetual Adoration,* 1977 Carmen Ave., Los Angeles, CA 90068. Tel: 213-466-2186. Sr. Mary Raymond, O.P., Prioress.

Sisters 25.

Legal Title: *The Monastery of the Angels, Inc.*

DAUGHTER HOUSES:.

Monastery of the Angels Karachi, Pakistan. Mother Mary Rose, O.P., Prioress.

Sisters 18.

Queen of Angels Monastery Bocaue, Bulacan, Philippines. Sr. Mary of Jesus, O.P., Prioress.

Sisters 22.

CORPUS CHRISTI MONASTERY: 215 Oak Grove Ave., Menlo Park, CA 94025. Tel: 415-322-1801; Fax: 415-322-6816. Sr. Mary of the Angels, O.P., Prioress.

Cloistered total number in community 24.

DOMINICAN NUNS O.P.: *Monastery of the Mother of God,* 1430 Riverdale St., West Springfield, MA 01089. Tel: 413-736-3639; Fax: 413-736-0850 Ext: 18. Sr. Mary St. John, O.P., Prioress.

Total number in community 28.

DOMINICAN NUNS OF THE PERPETUAL ROSARY: *Monastery of Our Lady of the Rosary,* 335 Doat St., Buffalo, NY 14211-2199. Tel: 716-892-0066. Mother Rose of St. Mary, O.P., Prioress.

Total number in community 30.

MONASTERY OF OUR LADY OF GRACE: North Guilford, CT 06437. Tel: 203-457-0599. Sr. Mary Ann, O.P., Prioress.

Legal Title: *Dominican Nuns of North Guilford, CT Inc.*

Total number in community 45.

MONASTERY OF THE INFANT JESUS: *Dominican Contemplative Nuns O.P.,* 1501 Lotus Ln., Lufkin, TX 75904. Tel: 409-634-4233; Fax: 409-634-2156. Sr. Mary John, O.P., Prioress.

Total number in community 25.

MONASTERY OF OUR LADY OF THE ROSARY (Rosary Shrine): Morris Ave. & Springfield Ave., Summit, NJ 07901. Tel: 908-273-1228. Sr. Mary Martin de Porres of Jesus, O.P., Prioress.

Professed Choir Sisters 21; Novices 1; Postulants 1.

NUNS OF THE ORDER OF PREACHERS O.P.: *Monastery of Mary the Queen,* 1310 W. Church St., Elmira, NY 14905. Tel: 607-734-9506. Sr. Mary of the Sacred Heart, O.P., Prioress.

Total number in community 13.

MONASTERY OF THE DOMINICAN NUNS OF THE PERPETUAL ROSARY (Cloistered): 14th St. & West St., Union City, NJ 07087. Tel: 201-866-7004. Mother Mary Clare, O.P., Prioress.

Professed Sisters 8; Novices 1.

MONASTERY OF THE PERPETUAL ROSARY: 1500 Haddon Ave., Camden, NJ 08103. Mother M. Immaculate Heart, O.P., Prioress.

Professed Nuns 8.

ST. DOMINIC'S MONASTERY (Contemplative): 4901 16th St. N.W., Washington, DC 20011. Sr. Mary Paul, O.P., Prioress.

Nuns 10.

THE DOMINICAN NUNS OF THE PERPETUAL ROSARY (Cloistered-Contemplative): *Monastery of the Immaculate Heart of Mary,* 1834 Lititz Pike, Lancaster, PA 17601-6585. Tel: 717-569-2104. Mother Mary Veronica, O.P., Prioress.

Solemnly Professed 13; Temporarily Professed 2; Postulants 2.

DOMINICAN MONASTERY OF THE PERPETUAL ROSARY: 802 Court St., Syracuse, NY 13208. Tel: 315-471-6762. Sr. Mary Augustine, O.P., Prioress, Solemn Vows, Papal enclosure.

Total number in community 11.

DOMINICAN MONASTERY OF ST. JUDE: P.O. Box 170, Marbury, AL 36051. Tel: 205-755-1322. Dominican Nuns of Perpetual Rosary and Adoration; Mother Mary Aimee of the Holy Spirit, O.P., Prioress.

Professed Nuns 9.

[1060] (O.P.)—DOMINICAN CONTEMPLATIVE SISTERS D

(Cloistered Contemplative)

Founded in Calais, France in 1880.

MONASTERY OF THE DOMINICAN SISTERS OF THE PERPETUAL ROSARY (Cloistered): 217 N. 68th St., Milwaukee, WI 53213. Tel: 414-258-0579. Mother Miriam Leonard, O.P., Prioress.

Professed Sisters 12.

[1070] (O.P.)—DOMINICAN SISTERS

There are thirty Congregations of the Dominican Sisters of the Third Order of St. Dominic in the United States. The list of General Motherhouses follows in the order of seniority. If the Congregation is known under a more familiar name, that name is given under the name of the Congregation.

[1070-01] CONGREGATION OF ST. CATHARINE OF SIENA (1822) P

The first American Foundation of the Dominican Sisters in the United States founded in Kentucky in 1822.

GENERAL MOTHERHOUSE: *Congregational Offices of St. Catharine of Siena,* 2645 Bardstown Rd., St. Catharine, KY 40061. Tel: 606-336-9303; Fax: 606-336-9306. Sr. Joan Scanlon, O.P., Pres.; Sr. Ann Miriam Hickey, O.P., Archivist.

Legal Title: *The Literary Society of Saint Catharine of Siena.*

Total number in community 311.

Sisters serve and staff: Colleges and Universities; High Schools; Elementary Schools; Foreign Missions; Health Care-Facilities; Diocesan Offices; Pastoral Associates-Assistants; Parish Ministry; Chaplain-Pastoral Care; Directors Religious Education, and Human Services.

Properties owned: *Rosary Manor,* Watertown, MA; *Dominican Sisters,* Plainville, MA; *St. Mel Independent School,* Gloucester, MA; *Holy Rosary Academy,* Louisville, KY; *Sansbury Memorial Infirmary, St. Catharine Motherhouse, St. Catharine College,* St. Catharine, KY; *St. Agnes Academy-St. Dominic School,* Memphis, TN.

Represented in the Archdioceses of Boston, Chicago, Louisville, New York, Omaha, St. Louis, Washington, and the Dioceses of Bismarck, Brooklyn, Brownsville, Covington, Fort Wayne-South Bend, Grand Island, Jackson, Joliet, Lincoln, Lubbock, Memphis, Norwich, Providence, Rockford, St. Petersburg, Shreveport and Springfield (MA). Also in San Juan.

[1070-02] DOMINICAN SISTERS OF ST. MARY OF THE SPRINGS (1830) P

CONGREGATIONAL OFFICE: *Dominican Sisters - St. Mary of the Springs,* 2320 Airport Dr., Columbus, OH 43219-2098. Tel: 614-252-2137; Fax: 614-252-7435. Sr. Mary Faith, O.P., Prioress.

Total number in community 340.

Properties sponsored: Dominican Academy, New York, NY; Ohio Dominican College, Columbus, OH; St. Mary's Montessori Pre-school & Kindergarten, Columbus, OH; Albertus Magnus College, New Haven, CT.

Ministry in Diocesan Offices; the field of Academic Education at all levels; Religious Education; Adult Education Programs; Congregational Infirmary; Care of the Elderly; Parish Ministry; Pastoral Care; Justice and Peace Ministry; Family Care; Liturgy Preaching and Spirituality Programs; Research Programs; Missionaries; Counseling and Canon Law Ministry; Campus Ministry; Social Work.

Represented in the Archdioceses of Baltimore, Cincinnati, Denver, Detroit, Hartford, New Orleans, New York, Santa Fe and Washington, and the Dioceses of Brooklyn, Bridgeport, Columbus, Fort Wayne-South Bend, Gary, Green Bay, Greensburg, Lexington, Norwich, Pittsburgh, Providence, Raleigh, Rockford, Steubenville, St. Petersburg and Wheeling-Charleston. Also in Puerto Rico, Korea, Peru and Bolivia.

[1070-03] SINSINAWA DOMINICAN CONGREGATION OF THE MOST HOLY ROSARY (1847) P

GENERALATE: Sinsinawa, WI 53824. Tel: 608-748-4411. Sr. Jean McSweeney, O.P., Prioress of the Congregation.

INTERDEPENDENT PROVINCES (1987):

Eastern Province 533 Ashland Ave., River Forest, IL 60305. Tel: 708-366-0282. Sr. Marise Barry, O.P., Prov.

Southern Province 719 Penn Ave. N.E., Atlanta, GA 30308-1501. Tel: 404-892-6814. Sr. Patricia Caraher, O.P., Prov.

Western Province 3330 Kendall St., Wheat Ridge, CO 80033-4944. Tel: 303-462-0200. Sr. Carol Coenen, O.P., Prov.; Sr. Marjorie Buttner, O.P., Archivist.

Total number in community 941.

Novitiate: Manchester, MO. Tel: 3142-391-4934.

Properties owned or Institutions sponsored: *Sinsinawa Dominicans, Inc., Rosary College,* River Forest, IL; *Bethlehem Academy,* Faribault, MN; *Dominican High School,* Whitefish Bay, WI; *Queen of Peace High School,* Burbank, IL; *Trinity High School,* River Forest, IL; *Dominican Motherhouse,* Sinsinawa, WI; *St. Dominic Villa,* Dubuque, IA; *Camp We-Ha-Kee,* Winter, WI; *The Bridge,* Denmark, WI; *Edgewood Campus School, Edgewood High School, Edgewood College,* Madison, WI; *Dominican Outreach Services,* Spokane, WA; *Dominican Outreach Foundation,* Spokane, WA.

Ministry in a variety of cultures in Preaching & Evangelization; Elementary, Secondary and Higher Education; Medical, Legal and Social Services; Adult and Religious Education; Diocesan and Parish Administration, Spiritual Direction and Counseling; Rural, Migrant and Native American Services; Writing Research.

Represented in the Archdioceses of Anchorage, Atlanta, Chicago, Denver, Dubuque, Indianapolis, Los Angeles, Miami, Milwaukee, Mobile, New Orleans, New York, Oklahoma City, Omaha, St. Louis, St. Paul-Minneapolis, San Antonio, San Francisco, Santa Fe, Seattle and Washington, and the Dioceses of Altoona-Johnstown, Austin, Baker, Beaumont, Birmingham, Brownsville, Camden, Charleston, Charlotte, Cheyenne, Columbus, Crookston, Dallas, Des Moines, Fairbanks, Fort Wayne-South Bend, Gallup, Gary, Gaylord, Grand Island, Great Falls-Billings, Green Bay, Helena, Honolulu, Jackson, Joliet, Juneau, Kansas City-St. Joseph, Knoxville, La Crosse, Lexington, Madison, Memphis, Nashville, New Ulm, Oakland, Ogdensburg, Orange, Orlando, Owensboro, Palm Beach, Pensacola-Tallahassee, Peoria, Phoenix, Richmond, Rockford, Sacramento, Saginaw, San Angelo, San Diego, San Jose, St. Augustine, St. Petersburg, Santa Rosa, Spokane, Superior, Tucson, Tulsa, and Venice. Also in Bolivia, Guatemala, Switzerland and Trinidad.

[1070-04] **CONGREGATION OF THE MOST HOLY NAME (1850)** **P**

GENERALATE: *Dominican Sisters of San Rafael,* 1520 Grand Ave., San Rafael, CA 94901. Tel: 415-453-8303; Fax: 415-453-8367. Sr. Kristin Wombacher, O.P., Prioress Gen.

Total number in community 167.

Legal Holdings and Titles: *Justin Siena High School,* Napa, CA; *San Domenico School,* San Anselmo, CA; *Santa Sabina Retreat Center,* San Rafael, CA *St. Rose Academy,* San Francisco, CA; *St. Joseph's HealthCare Corporation St. Joseph's Medical Center,* Stockton, CA; *St. Mary's Health Care Corporation St. Mary's Regional Medical Center,* Reno, NV; *Sisters of St. Dominic, Congregation of the Most Holy Name,* San Rafael, CA; *Mission Holding Corporation,* San Rafael, CA.

Represented in the Archdioceses of Los Angeles, San Francisco and Seattle and in the Dioceses of Oakland, Reno, Sacramento, San Jose, Santa Rosa and Stockton. And also in Canada and Mexico.

[1070-05] **CONGREGATION OF THE HOLY CROSS (1853)** **D**

GENERAL MOTHERHOUSE: *Queen of the Rosary Motherhouse,* Albany Ave., Amityville, NY 11701. Tel: 516-842-6000; Fax: 516-842-0240. Sr. Mary Hughes, O.P., Prioress; Sr. Margaret Clines, O.P., Archivist.

Total number in community 773.

Sisters are engaged in the ministry of Education at all levels; Catechetical Schools; Handicapped, Adult and Continuing Education; Hospitals; Homes for the Aged; Residence for Senior Citizens; Spiritual Life Centers; Chaplaincy; Advocacy; Communications; Social Service Institutions; Shelters; Pastoral Services; Health Services.

Represented in the Archdioceses of Boston, Hartford, Newark, New York, San Francisco, Seattle, Washington and in Dioceses of Albany, Brooklyn, Kalamazoo, Oakland, Orlando, Paterson, Providence, Rochester, Rockville Centre, St. Augustine, St.Petersburg, and Trenton. Also in Puerto Rico, and Colombia.

[1070-07] **CONGREGATION OF ST. CECILIA (1860)** **P**

GENERAL MOTHERHOUSE: *St. Cecilia Convent,* 801 Dominican Dr., Nashville, TN 37228-1909. Tel: 615-256-5486; Fax: 615-726-1333. Mother Christine Born, O.P., Prioress Gen.; Sr. Rose Marie Masserano, Archivist.

Professed sisters in community 137; Novices 4; Postulants 9.

Ministry in the field of Academic Education at all levels.

Legal Holdings and Titles: *Aquinas Junior College,* Nashville, TN.

Represented in the Archdioceses of Baltimore, Cincinnati, Denver, and the Dioceses of Arlington, Birmingham, Knoxville, Memphis, Nashville and Richmond.

[1070-08] **CONGREGATION OF ST. MARY (1860)** **P**

GENERAL MOTHERHOUSE: *Dominican Sisters,* 580 Broadway, New Orleans, LA 70118. Tel: 504-861-8183; Fax: 504-861-8184. Sr. Therese Leckert, O.P., Prioress.

Total number in community 75.

Ministry in Education and Social Apostolates.

Legal Holdings: *St. Mary's Dominican High School,* New Orleans, LA; *Dominican Conference Center,* New Orleans, LA; *Rosaryville Retreat Center,* Ponchatoula, LA.

Represented in the Archdiocese of New Orleans, and the Diocese of Baton Rouge.

[1070-09] **CONGREGATION OF ST. CATHERINE OF SIENA (1862)** **P**

GENERAL MOTHERHOUSE: *Convent of St. Catherine,* Siena Center, 5635 Erie St., Racine, WI 53402. Tel: 414-639-4100. Sr. Evelyn Lins, O.P., Pres.; Sr. Diane Kenel, Archivist.

Total number in community 275.

Sisters minister in the areas of Elementary, Secondary, Higher and Music-Cultural Education; Adult Education; Religious Education; Administration; Parish and Pastoral Ministry; Prison Ministry; Communications; Social Justice; Campus Ministry; Social Services, Hospital and Health Services; Writing-Research; Hospital Chaplains; Diocesan Services; Retreats-Prayer Programs; Community Services.

Legal Holdings and Titles: *Sisters of St. Dominic,* Racine, WI; *Dominican College of Racine, Inc.,* Racine, WI; *St. Catherine's High School of Racine, Inc.,* Racine, WI; *Racine Dominican Ministries, Inc.,* Racine, WI; *Our Lady of the Oaks Convent,* Pewaukee, WI; *St. Catherine's Infirmary, Inc.,* Racine, WI.

Properties sponsored by the Franciscan Sisters, Daughters of the Sacred Hearts of Jesus and Mary, Wheaton, IL and the Sisters of St. Dominic, Racine, WI: *Catherine Marian Housing Inc.; Villa St. Anna, Inc.,* Racine, WI.

Represented in the Archdioceses of Chicago, Detroit, Louisville, Milwaukee, Newark, St. Louis, Santa Fe and Washington and in the Dioceses of Brownsville, Charleston, Jackson, Gallup, Green Bay, La Crosse, Lexington, Lansing, Madison, Marquette, Nashville, Phoenix, Salt Lake City, Toledo and Wilmington. Also in Kenya.

[1070-10] **DOMINICAN SISTERS OF SPRINGFIELD IN ILLINOIS (1873)** **P**

GENERAL MOTHERHOUSE: *Sacred Heart Convent,* 1237 W. Monroe St., Springfield, IL 62704. Tel: 217-787-0481; Fax: 217-787-8169. Sr. Rose Miriam Schulte, O.P., Prioress Gen.

Total number in community 349.

Apostolic Work: Preaching through a variety of educational, health care, and pastoral ministries in elementary, secondary schools, daycare and learning centers, hearing impaired and literacy; elderly and shut-ins; in spiritual direction, counseling, and social service.

Legal Holdings or Titles: *Dominican Sisters of Springfield, Illinois; Alfred Fortin Villa and Day Care Learning Center,* Bourbonnais, IL; *Benincasa-Dominican Renewal Center,* Riverton, IL; *Marian Catholic High School,* Chicago Heights, IL; Rosary High School, Aurora, IL; *Sacred Heart-Griffin High School,* Springfield, IL; *St. Dominic-Jackson Memorial Hospital,* Jackson, MS.

Represented in the Archdioceses of Chicago and St. Paul-Minneapolis, and the Dioceses of Baton Rouge, Belleville, Duluth, La Crosse, Little Rock, Jackson, Joliet, Peoria, Rockford, and Springfield (IL). Also in Peru.

[1070-11] **CONGREGATION OF OUR LADY OF THE ROSARY (1876)** **D**

GENERAL MOTHERHOUSE AND NOVITIATE: *Dominican Convent of Our Lady of the Rosary,* Sparkill, NY 10976. Tel: 914-359-6400. Sr. Patricia Keating, O.P., Pres.

Legal Title: *Dominican Congregation of Our Lady of the Rosary.*

Total number in community 484.

Ministry in High Schools and Elementary Schools; Parish Associates; Religious Education; Hospital Ministry; Colleges; House of Prayer; Housing and Community Centers; Foreign Missions.

Represented in the Archdioceses of Denver, New York, Newark and St. Louis, and the Dioceses of Belleville, Bridgeport, Brooklyn, Great Falls-Billings, Helena, Jefferson City, Oakland, Paterson, Phoenix, Rockville Centre, San Diego, St. Petersburg, Trenton and Wilmington. Also in Pakistan and Peru.

[1070-12] **CONGREGATION OF THE QUEEN OF THE HOLY ROSARY (1876)** **P**

GENERAL MOTHERHOUSE: *Dominican Convent,* P.O. Box 3908, Mission San Jose, CA 94539. Tel: 510-657-2468; Fax: 510-657-1734. Sr. Rose Marie Hennessy, Prioress Gen.; Sr. M. Evangela Balde, Community Archivist.

Legal Title: *Dominican Sisters of Mission San Jose, a Corporation Queen of the Holy Rosary College, a Corporation, Mission* San Jose, CA; *St. Catherine's Military School, a corp.,* Anaheim, CA; *Immaculate Conception Academy, a corp.,* San Francisco, CA; *Flintridge Sacred Heart Academy, a corp.,* La Canada-Flintridge, CA.

Total number in community 247.

Ministry in Parishes; Colleges; High Schools and Elementary Schools; Kindergarten and Music School.

Represented in the Archdioceses of Los Angeles, Portland (OR) and San Francisco, and the Dioceses of Oakland, Orange, San Jose and Tucson.

[1070-13] **CONGREGATION OF THE MOST HOLY ROSARY (1892)** **P**

GENERAL MOTHERHOUSE: 1257 Siena Heights Dr., Adrian, MI 49221-1793. Tel: 517-265-5135; Fax: 517-265-4733. Sr. Patricia Walter, O.P., Prioress.

MISSION CHAPTERS (1982):

Florida Mission Chapter 810 N. Olive Ave., West Palm Beach, FL 33401-3710. Tel: 561-832-6521. Sr. Marie Carleen Maly, O.P., Chapter Prioress.

Great Lakes Mission Chapter 9400 Courville, Detroit, MI 48224-2517. Tel: 313-882-8484. Sr. Rosemary Asaro, O.P., Chapter Prioress.

Mid-Atlantic Mission Chapter 5735 Dawsonville Hwy., Gainesville, GA 30506-3889. Tel: 770-844-1370. Sr. Mary Kathryn Cliatt, O.P., Chapter Prioress.

Midwest Dominican Mission Chapter 8925 S. Kostner Ave., Hometown, IL 60456-1006. Tel: 708-636-7566. Sr. Joella Miller, O.P., Chapter Prioress.

Motherhouse Mission Chapter 1257 Siena Heights Dr., Adrian, MI 49221-1723. Tel: 517-265-5135. Sr. Celestine Dunne, O.P., Chapter Prioress.

Nokomis Mission Chapter 7506 Inkster Rd., Dearborn Heights, MI 48127-1668. Tel: 313-274-3543. Sr. Nancyann Turner, O.P., Chapter Prioress.

Overseas Mission Chapter c/o 1257 Siena Heights Dr., Adrian, MI 49221. Tel: 809-534-8017. Sr. Rose Ann Schlitt, O.P., Chapter Prioress.

Pacific West Mission Chapter P.O. Box 2235, Santa Cruz, CA 95063-2235. Tel: 408-457-7117. Sr. Molly Giller, O.P., Chapter Prioress.

South East Adrian Mission Chapter 28650 Eleven Mile Rd., Farmington, MI 48336-1502. Tel: 810-426-9185. Sr. Lorraine Mordenski, O.P., Chapter Prioress.

Southwest Mission Chapter 1983 S. Broadway, Grand Junction, CO 81503-9592. Tel: 970-241-6152. Sr. Barbara Stanek, O.P., Chapter Prioress.

Upper Midwest Mission Chapter 8925 S. Kostner Ave., Hometown, IL 60456-1006. Tel: 708-636-8178. Sr. Patricia Brady, O.P., Chapter Prioress.

Total number in community 1,180.

Legal Holdings or Titles: *Benefit Trust of the Adrian Dominican Congregation,* Adrian, MI; *Adrian Dominican Sisters Office of Development,* Adrian, MI *Dominican High School,* Detroit, MI; *Dominican Santa Cruz Hospital,* Santa Cruz, CA; *Maria Health Care Center,* Adrian, MI; *Regina Dominican High School,* Wilmette, IL; *Rosarian Academy,* West Palm Beach, FL; *Siena Heights College,* Adrian, MI; *St. Joseph Academy,* Adrian, MI; *St. Rose Dominican Hospital,* Henderson, NV; *Weber Retreat Center,* Adrian, MI.

Sisters minister in the areas of Formal Education - as administrators, teachers and consultants at elementary, secondary, college, state and diocesan levels; Pastoral Ministry - parishes, hospitals and campuses; Religious Education - coordinators and teachers; Social Services - case workers, administrators, counselors, therapists, consultants, caregivers for elderly and staff for retirement centers; Health Services - administrators, nurses, therapists, doctors, physician assistants, psychologists, technologists, pharmacists and dietitians; Business Services - directors, accountants, secretaries, administrative assistants, typists, bookkeepers, office managers, office staff, drivers and housekeeping staff; Spiritual Direction - retreat work, formation, Congregation leadership and as diocesan Vicars for Religious; Social Justice - coordinators, staff and community organizers; other ministries including research, law, science, public relations, art, communications and full-time study.

Represented in the Archdioceses of Atlanta, Boston, Chicago, Cincinnati, Detroit, Indianapolis, Los Angeles, Louisville, Miami, Milwaukee, Newark, New Orleans, New York, Oklahoma City, Philadelphia, St. Louis, San Antonio, San Francisco, Santa Fe, Seattle, Washington, and the Dioceses of Austin, Birmingham, Charleston, Cleveland, Columbus, Des Moines, Duluth, El Paso, Erie, Fresno, Fort Wayne-South Bend, Gallup, Galveston-Houston, Gary, Gaylord, Grand Rapids, Green Bay, Helena, Jackson, Joliet, Las Vegas, Little Rock, Kalamazoo, Knoxville, La Crosse, Lafayette, Lansing, Lexington, Madison, Manchester, Marquette, Monterey, Oakland, Orange, Orlando, Palm Beach, Pensacola-Tallahassee, Peoria, Phoenix, Pittsburgh, Providence, Pueblo, Raleigh, Rapid City, Richmond, Rockville Centre, Rockford, Saginaw, St. Augustine, St. Cloud, St. Petersburg, San Bernardino, San Diego, San Jose, Santa Rosa, Savannah, Springfield (IL), Toledo, Tucson, and Venice. Also in Belgium, Brazil, Canada, Dominican Republic, Guatemala, Puerto Rico and South Africa.

[1070-14] **CONGREGATION OF OUR LADY OF THE SACRED HEART (1877)** **P**

GENERAL MOTHERHOUSE: *Marywood,* 2025 E. Fulton St., Grand Rapids, MI 49503. Tel: 616-459-2910; Fax: 616-454-6105. Sr. Barbara Hansen, O.P., Prioress; Sr. Mona Schwind, O.P., Archivist.

Legal Holdings or Titles: *Sisters of the Order of St. Dominic of Grand Rapids; Marywood Academy; Sisters of St. Dominic of the Congregation of Our Lady of the Sacred Heart Charitable Trust; Dominican Land Company.*

Total number in community 358.

Sisters are involved in: Elementary and Secondary Education; Liturgy; Religious Education; Pastoral Ministry; Diocesan Offices; Health Care; Congregational Services; Social Work; Foreign Missions; Justice Advocacy.

Represented in the Archdioceses of Baltimore, Chicago, Denver, Detroit, Mobile, New Orleans, Omaha, St. Louis, St. Paul-Minneapolis, Santa Fe, Seattle, Washington, and in the Dioceses of Albany, Brownsville, Charleston, Cleveland, Des Moines, El Paso, Gaylord, Grand Rapids, Lafayette, Kalamazoo, Lansing, Lexington, Providence, Saginaw, San Diego, Shreveport, Sioux Falls and Toledo. Also in Peru, Hungary and Russia.

[1070-15] **CONGREGATION OF SAINT DOMINIC (1878)** **D**

GENERAL MOTHERHOUSE: *Sisters of Saint Dominic of Blauvelt, New York,* Blauvelt, NY 10913. Tel: 914-359-5600; Fax: 914-359-5773. Sr. Barbara Werner, O.P., Pres.; Sr. Judith Campbell, O.P., Archivist.

Total number in community 241.

Sisters serve and staff: Elementary; Secondary; Higher Education; Special Education; Hospital Care; Pastoral Care; Parish Ministry; Retreat Work; Child Care; Neighborhood Services; Services to Migrants; Services to Chemically Dependent.

Represented in the Archdioceses of Boston, Newark and New York and in the Dioceses of Orlando, Paterson, Providence, Rockville Centre and San Bernardino. Also in Jamaica.

[1070-17] **DOMINICAN SISTERS CONGREGATION OF ST. CATHERINE DE RICCI (1880)** **P**

GENERAL MOTHERHOUSE: *Fanjeaux,* 750 Ashbourne Rd., Elkins Park, PA 19027-2596. Tel: 215-635-6027. Sr. Rita McManus, O.P., Pres.

Professed Sisters 101; Novices 1.

Sisters serve and staff: Retreat Houses; CCD Centers and Parish Services; Hospital; Pastoral Ministry; College; Diocesan Offices; Residence for Women; Campus Ministry; Special Services; Residence for Aging; Spiritual Direction; Counselling Center; House of Prayer; Liturgical Art Studio.

Properties owned: *Dominican Retreat House / Convent of Our Lady of Prouille,* Elkins Park, PA; *St. Dominic Hall,* Elkins Park, PA; *Dominican Retreat, Immaculate Heart of Mary Convent,* McLean, VA; *Dominican Retreat House / Our Lady of Grace Convent,* Schenectady, NY; *Dominican Retreat House / Queen of Apostles Convent,* Miami, FL; *The Lucy Eaton Smith Residence,* Philadelphia, PA; *St. Catherine Hall,* Elkins, PA; *Efharisto Studio, Inc.,* Baltimore, MD.

Represented in the Archdioceses of Baltimore, Cincinnati, Detroit, Miami, Newark, Philadelphia, San Juan, Santa Fe, and the Dioceses of Albany, Arlington, Camden, Harrisburg, Metuchen, Orlando, Palm Beach, Providence, Raleigh, St. Petersburg, and Scranton.

[1070-18] **SISTERS OF ST. DOMINIC OF THE AMERICAN CONGREGATIONOF THE SACRED HEART OF JESUS (1881)** **D**

DOMINICAN MOTHERHOUSE: 1 Ryerson Ave., Caldwell, NJ 07006. Tel: 201-403-3331; Fax: 201-228-9611. Sr. Joan Doyle, O.P., Prioress; Sr. Helen Marguerite, Archivist.

Total number in community 234.

Legal Title: *Sisters of St. Dominic of Caldwell, N.J.*

Properties owned: *Caldwell College,* Caldwell, NJ; *Mount Saint Dominic Academy,* Caldwell, NJ; *St. Dominic Academy,* Jersey City, NJ; *Lacordaire Academy,* Upper Montclair, NJ.

Ministry in Education at all levels; Pastoral Ministry; Health and Human Services.

Represented in the Archdioceses of Boston, Newark, Portland,, and the Dioceses of Alexandria, Metuchen, Orange, Paterson, Savannah, Springfield (IL) and Trenton.

[1070-19] **DOMINICAN SISTERS OF HOUSTON, TEXAS (CONGREGATION OF THE SACRED HEART) (1882)** **P**

GENERAL MOTHERHOUSE & NOVITIATE: *Dominican Sisters,* 6501 Almeda Rd., Houston, TX 77021. Tel: 713-747-3310; Fax: 713-747-4707. Sr. Paula Enderle, O.P., Prioress.

Legal Title: *Dominican Sisters of Houston, Texas, Inc. (aka Sacred Heart Convent of Houston).*

Total number in community 150.

Properties owned and sponsored: *St. Agnes Academy; St. Agnes Academy Foundation; St. Pius X High School; St. Pius X High School Foundation, Inc.; The Sacred Heart Convent Retirement Trust.*

Ministry in the field of Academic Education at all levels and Parish Ministry.

Represented in the Archdioceses of Los Angeles, San Antonio and Seattle, and the Dioceses of Austin, Beaumont, Galveston-Houston, San Angelo, San Bernardino, San Jose and Tyler. Also in Guatemala.

[1070-20] **CONGREGATION OF ST. THOMAS AQUINAS (1888)** **P**

MOTHERHOUSE: *Tacoma Dominican Center,* 935 Fawcett Ave. S., Tacoma, WA 98402. Tel: 206-272-9688; Fax: 206-272-8790. Sr. Agnes Huck, O.P., Pres.

Total number in community 87.

Ministry in a variety of apostolacies.

Legal Holdings and Titles: *Sisters of St. Dominic, Tacoma Dominican Center Sisters of St. Dominic - Tacoma Charitable Trust.*

Represented in the Archdioceses of Los Angeles, New York, San Francisco and Seattle, and the Dioceses of Baker, Fresno, St. Augustine, San Diego, San Bernardino, and Yakima. Also in Canada.

[1070-21] **DOMINICAN SISTERS CONGREGATION OF HOLY CROSS (1890)** **P**

GENERAL MOTHERHOUSE & NOVITIATE: *Rosary Heights,* P.O. Box 280, Edmonds, WA 98020. Tel: 206-542-7511; 542-3212. Sr. Judy Byron, O.P., Prioress.

Total number in community 74.

Sisters minister in Elementary, Secondary and University Education; Diocesan, Parish and Hospital Pastoral Ministry; Health Care; Mental Health; Detention; Political; Direct Service and Advocacy with Women and Children; Housing; Peace and Justice; Community Service.

Represented in the Archdioceses of Los Angeles, St. Paul-Minneapolis, San Francisco, Santa Fe and Seattle, and the Dioceses of Boise, Fairbanks and San Diego. Also in Haiti, & Mexico.

[1070-23] **CONGREGATION OF ST. ROSE OF LIMA (1896)** **D**

THE SERVANTS OF RELIEF FOR INCURABLE CANCER IN THE U.S.

GENERAL MOTHERHOUSE: *Rosary Hill Home,* Hawthorne, NY 10532. Tel: 914-769-0114. Mother Anne Marie, O.P., Mother Gen.

Total number in community 80.

The work of these sisters is confined entirely to the incurable cancerous poor.

Represented in the Archdioceses of Atlanta, New York, Philadelphia and St. Paul-Minneapolis and in the Dioceses of Cleveland and Fall River.

[1070-24] **DOMINICAN SISTERS OF GREAT BEND (1902)** **P**

MOTHERHOUSE & NOVITIATE: *Immaculate Conception Convent,* 3600 Broadway, Great Bend, KS 67530. Tel: 316-792-1232. Sr. Betty Werner, O.P., Prioress.

Total number in community 135.

Legal Title: *The Nuns of the Third Order of St. Dominic.*

Sisters serve in Grade Schools, Secondary Schools; Colleges; Special Education; CCD Centers and Centers for Retreats and Spirituality; Hospitals; Nursing Homes; Infirmary; Home Health Services; Health Care Ministries; Foreign Missions; Ministry to Minorities; Ministry to Aging; Housing; Parish Ministry; Office of Mission and Ministry.

Properties owned: *Central Kansas Medical Center,* Great Bend, KS with campus at *St. Joseph Memorial Hospital,* Larned, KS and *St. Rose Campus,* Great Bend, KS; *St. Catherine Hospital,* Garden City, KS; *Hospitality House,* Wichita, KS; several residential convents Pilgrim House of Praise, Great Bend, KS; *Heartland Farm,* Pawnee Rock, KS; *Novitiate House,* Great Bend, KS.

Properties owned and sponsored: *Heartland Center for Spirituality,* Great Bend, KS; *St. Martin de Porres Association Dominican Retreat Center,* Great Bend, KS; *Cedar Park Place, Inc.* (low and middle income housing for elderly and handicapped), Great Bend, KS; *Heartland Center for Wholistic Health Association,* Great Bend, KS; *Office of Mission and Ministry,* Great Bend, KS; *Art of Learning Center,* Wichita, KS.

Represented in the Archdioceses of Denver, Kansas City in Kansas, Mobile, Oklahoma City, St. Louis and in the Dioceses of Dodge City, Phoenix, Pueblo, Salina, San Angelo, Springfield-Cape Girardeau, and Wichita. Also in Africa.

[1070-25] **CONGREGATION OF THE DOMINICAN SISTERS OF ST. CATHERINE OF SIENA OF KENOSHA (1911)** **P**

GENERAL MOTHERHOUSE & NOVITIATE: P.O. Box 1288, Kenosha, WI 53141. Tel: 414-694-2067; Fax: 414-694-6542. sr. Susan Anne Snyder, O.P., Prioress.

Legal Title: *Congregation of the Dominican Sisters of St. Catherine of Siena of Kenosha, Inc.*

Total number in community 37.

Properties owned: *Holy Rosary Medical Center,* Ontario, OR; *St. Catherine's Hospital,* Kenosha, WI; *Our Lady of Fatima Villa,* Saratoga, CA; *Mercy Hospital,* Merced, CA.

Represented in the Archdioceses of Milwaukee and San Francisco, and the Dioceses of Baker, Columbus, and Fresno. Also in Ecuador.

[1070-26] **CONGREGATION OF ST. ROSE OF LIMA (1923)** **D**

GENERAL MOTHERHOUSE: *St. Joseph's Convent,* 775 Drahner Rd., Box 167, Oxford, MI 48371. Tel: 810-628-2872. Sr. Frances Mary Kernasovich, O.P., Pres.; Sr. Mary Ann Fedor, O.P., Vice Pres.; Sr. Virginia Berak, O.P., Vice Pres.

Total number in community 47.

Properties owned and sponsored: *St. Mary's Retreat House,* Oxford, MI; *St. Jude Home,* Waterford, MI; *Dominican Center* (retreat house for teenagers), Oxford, MI; *Lourdes Nursing Home Fox Manor,* Waterford, MI.

Sisters minister in Elementary Schools; Nursing Homes; Retreat House; Parish Ministry; Religious Education; Senior Citizens Residence; Hospital Ministry; Pastoral Assistant.

Represented in the Archdiocese of Detroit, and the Dioceses of Gaylord, Lansing and Saginaw.

[1070-27] **CONGREGATION OF THE IMMACULATE CONCEPTION (1929)** **D**

PROVINCIAL HOUSE: *Immaculate Conception Provincial House,* 9000 W. 81st. St., Justice, IL 60458. Tel: 708-458-3040. Mother M. Natalie, O.P., Prov. Supr.

Total number in community 25.

Represented in the Archdioceses of Chicago and Milwaukee. Also in Canada.

[1070-28] **CONGREGATION OF THE SISTERS OF ST. DOMINIC OF THE IMMACULATE HEART OF MARY (1929)** **D**

GENERAL MOTHERHOUSE: *Our Lady of the Elms Convent,* 1230 W. Market St., Akron, OH 44313-7185. Tel: 330-836-4908; Fax: 330-836-5913. Sr. Bernadine Baltrinic, O.P., Pres.; Sr. Rebecca Betz, O.P., Archivist.

Total number in community 112.

Properties owned: *Our Lady of the Elms High School; Our Lady of the Elms Elementary School; Our Lady of the Elms Preschool.*

Represented in the Archdioceses of Chicago, Seattle, St. Louis, Washington, and the Dioceses of Cleveland, Fort Wayne-South Bend, Lansing, Little Rock, Phoenix, Portland (ME), St. Augustine, St. Petersburg, Toledo and Youngstown. Also in Central America.

[1070-30] **DOMINICAN SISTERS OF OAKFORD** **P**

MOTHERHOUSE: *Oakford Priory,* P.O. Verulam, Natal, Republic of South Africa. Sr. Gisela Wittershagen, O.P., Supr. Gen.

U.S. Regional Center: 1855 Miramonte Ave., Mountain View, CA 94040. Tel: 415-965-1903; Fax: 415-965-1456. Sr. Ursula Bomholt, O.P., Regl. Supr.
Total number in community 19.
Ministries in Care for the Aged; Pastoral Care; Community Services; Parish Work; Adult Education.
Properties owned: *Villa Siena* (Home for the Aged), Mountain View, CA; *Regional Center,* Mountain View, CA; *Formation House,* San Leandro, CA.
Represented in the Dioceses of Oakland, Phoenix and San Jose.

[1100] (O.P.)—DOMINICAN SISTERS OF CHARITY OF THE PRESENTATION OF THE BLESSED VIRGIN P

Founded in France in 1696. First foundation in the United States in 1906.
Motherhouse: 15 Quai Portillon, 37081, Tours Cedex 2, France.
Universal total in Congregation 3,377.
Provincial House: 3012 Elm St., Dighton, MA 02715. Tel: 508-669-5425. Tel: 508-669-5023. Sr. Joanna Fernandes, O.P., Prov. Supr.
Total number in province 45.
Ministry in Hospitals; Homes For the Aged; Residence for Working Women & Students; Dispensaries; Migrant Clinic; Education; Pastoral Ministry.
Represented in the Archdiocese of Washington, and the Dioceses of Brownsville, Fall River and Providence. Present in 34 countries.

[1105] (O.P.)—DOMINICAN SISTERS OF HOPE P

Founded July 20, 1995, as a merging of three former Congregations: Dominican Sisters of the Congregation of the Most Holy Rosary of Newburgh, NY; Dominican Sisters of the Sick Poor of Ossining, NY.
General Administrative Offices: *Dominican Sisters of Hope,* 299 N. Highland Ave., Ossining, NY 10562. Tel: 914-941-4420; Fax: 914-941-1125. Sr. Catherine Walsh, O.P., Prioress.
Total number in community 338.
Legal Titles and Holdings: *Dominican Sisters of Hope Ministry Trust.*
Ministry in Religious & Academic Education at all levels; health, social, community and pastoral services in low income area; parish service, counseling, retreats and spiritual direction.
Represented in the Archdioceses of Cincinnati, Denver, Detroit, Hartford, Newark, New York, Oklahoma City, Philadelphia, Washington, and the Dioceses of Albany, Allentown, Arlington, Bridgeport, Brooklyn, Burlington, Camden, Fall River, Gallup, Jackson, Lexington, Metuchen, Ogdensburg, Palm Beach, Paterson, Providence, Richmond, Rockville Centre.

[1110] (O.P.)—DOMINICAN SISTERS OF OUR LADY OF THE ROSARY AND OF SAINT CATHERINE OF SIENA, CABRA P

Founded in Ireland in 1644.
General Motherhouse: Cabra, Dublin 7, Ireland.
Region of Louisiana established in 1978.
Regional House: *Dominican Sisters, Cabra,* 1930 Robert E. Lee, New Orleans, LA 70122. Tel: 504-288-1593. Sr. Elizabeth Ferguson, O.P., Regl. Vicar.
Total number in local community 13.
Ministry in Elementary Schools; Parish Ministry; Neighborhood Social Service Agency; Prison Ministry; Adult Education; Social Apostolate; Retreats; Spiritual Direction.
Represented in the Archdiocese of New Orleans.

[1120] (O.P.)—DOMINICAN SISTERS OF THE ROMAN CONGREGATION P

Founded in France in 1621. First United States foundation in 1904.
General Motherhouse: Rome, Italy. Sr. Rosario de Meer, Supr. Gen.
Universal total in Congregation 734.
U.S. Provincial Office: 304 Oberlin St., Iowa City, IA 52245. Sr. Jacqueline Provencher, O.P., Prov. Prioress.
Total number in community 36.
Properties owned: Residences 5.
Ministry in the field of Religious & Academic Education; Adult Education; Indian Reservation; Pastoral Ministry; Health Care; Social Work; Para-Legal.
Represented in the Archdioceses of Chicago, New York and Portland (OR), and in the Dioceses of Davenport, Des Moines, Gallup, Phoenix and Portland (ME).

[1140] (O.P.)—EUCHARISTIC MISSIONARIES OF ST. DOMINIC D

Founded in Louisiana in 1927.
General Motherhouse: 3801 Canal St. - Suite 400, New Orleans, LA 70119. Tel: 504-486-1133; Fax: 504-486-6547. Sr. Catherine Drawe, O.P., Pres.
Perpetually Professed Sisters 46; Missions 20.
Properties owned: *Regina Coeli Retreat Center,* Covington, LA.
Sisters Staff and Serve: Parish and Diocesan Religious Education; Parish and Diocesan Social Services; Parish Administrators; Parish Census; Home Health Nursing; Literacy ministry to immigrants; Hospital Chaplaincy and Parish ministry.
Represented in the Archdiocese New Orleans, and the Dioceses of Baton Rouge, Beaumont, Biloxi, Houma-Thibodeaux, Lafayette (LA), Palm Beach, Phoenix, St. Petersburg and Tucson.

[1145] (O.P.)—RELIGIOUS MISSIONARIES OF ST. DOMINIC

General Motherhouse: Via di Val Cannuta 138, 00166, Rome, Italy. Mother Catalina Civit, O.P., Supr. Gen., *U.S. Headquarters,* 2237 Waldron Rd., Corpus Christi, TX 78418. Tel: 512-939-8102; Fax: 512-939-8203. Sr. Maria Purificacion Palis, O.P., Delegate of the Supr. Gen.
Total number in congregation 570; Sisters in the United States 34.
Legal Title: *Religious Missionaries of St. Dominic, Inc.,* Corpus Christi, TX.
Represented in the Archdiocese of Los Angeles, and the Diocese of Corpus Christi.

[1150] (E.F.M.S.)—EUCHARISTIC FRANCISCAN MISSIONARY SISTERS D

Founded in Mexico in 1943. Mother Maria Gemma de Jesus Aranda, Founderess & Supr. Gen.
Motherhouse: *Our Lady's Convent,* 943 S. Soto St., Los Angeles, CA 90023. Tel: 213-264-6556. 1421 Cota Ave., Torrance, CA 90501. Tel: 213-328-6725. Sr. Gloria de Jesus, E.F.M.S., Gen. Sec.
Total number in community 22.
Legal Title: *Eucharistic Franciscan Missionary Sisters of Los Angeles.*
Sisters serve and staff: The field of Education; Missionary Activities; Catechetics; Social Work; Diocesan and Administration offices.
Represented in the Archdiocese of Los Angeles and the Diocese of Stockton.

[1170] (C.S.S.F.)—FELICIAN SISTERS P

(Congregation of Sisters of St. Felix of Cantalice, of the III Order of St. Francis)
Founded in Poland in 1855. First foundation in the United States in 1874.
General Motherhouse: Via del Casaletto 540, 00151, Rome, Italy. Sr. Mary Cynthia Strzalkowski, C.S.S.F., Min. Gen.
Presentation of the B.V.M. Province (1874): *Motherhouse and Novitiate-Provincialate,* 36800 Schoolcraft Rd., Livonia, MI 48150. Tel: 313-591-1730; Fax: 313-591-1710. Sr. Mary Dennis Glonek, C.S.S.F., Prov. Min.
Professed 271; Novices 3.
Ministry in the Field of Academic Education at all levels; Catechetical Center; CCD Programs; Archival and Secretarial Services in Seminary; Diocesan Nursing Home; Youth Ministry Center; Pastoral Ministry Programs; DRE Offices; Hospital; Nursing Homes; Assisted Living; Archdiocesan Tribunal and Office of Delegate for Religious; Parish Soup Kitchen; Hospice Inpatient and Home Care Program; Day Care Centers; Retreat Centers; House of Prayer; Senior Clergy Residence.
Properties owned: *Madonna University; Ladywood High School; Montessori Center of Our Lady; St. Mary Hospital,* Livonia, MI; *St. Joseph Day Care; Presentation Prayer Center,* Jackson, MI; Maryville Center, Holly, MI; *Angela Hospice Home Care and Inpatient Facility; Marian Professional Building,* Livonia, MI.
Represented in the Archdiocese of Detroit, and the Dioceses of Fort Wayne-South Bend, Gaylord, Kalamazoo, Lansing, Saginaw and Toledo.
Immaculate Heart of Mary Province (1900): *Provincial House and Novitiate-Villa Maria,* 600 Doat St., Buffalo, NY 14211. Tel: 716-892-4141. Sr. Mary Raymond Kasprzak, C.S.S.F., Prov. Minister; Sr. Mary Simplicia Wytrwal, C.S.S.F., Prov. Archivist.
Total number in community 338.
Ministry in the field of Academic Education on all levels; Day Care Center; School for Mentally and Multiply Handicapped; Institute of Music; Religious Education Centers; Outreach Centers; Diocesan Offices.
Properties owned: *Villa Maria College of Buffalo, Villa Maria Academy, Villa Maria Institute of Music,* Buffalo, NY.
Represented in the Dioceses of Buffalo, Charleston, Erie, Syracuse and Wilmington. Also in Canada, and Italy.
Mother of Good Counsel Province (1910): *Mother of Good Counsel Provincialate, Novitiate, & Convent,* 3800 W. Peterson Ave., Chicago, IL 60659. Tel: 773-463-3020. Sr. Mary Barbara Ann Bosch, C.S.S.F., Prov. Minister; Sr. M. Adolphine Ksioszk, C.S.S.F., Community Archivist.
Total number in the community 289.
Ministry in the field of Academic and Religious Education at all levels; Homes for Aged; Independent Living for the Elderly; Assisted Living for the Elderly; Pastoral Ministry; Social Workers; Family Therapists; Day Care Centers; Hospitals; Infirmary for Sisters; Foreign Missions; Recreation House for Children.
Represented in the Archdioceses of Chicago and Milwaukee, and the Dioceses of Belleville, Green Bay, Joliet, La Crosse and Rockford.
Immaculate Conception Provincial House (1913): *Provincial House & Novitiate-Immaculate Conception Convent,* 260 S. Main St., Lodi, NJ 07644-2196. Tel: 201-473-7447; Fax: 201-473-7126. Sr. Mary Antonelle Chunka, C.S.S.F., Prov. Minister; Sr. Mary Alicia Adametz, Prov. Sec.; Sr. Mary Raphael Monczewska, Archivist.
Total number in community 248.
Properties sponsored: *Immaculate Conception High School; Felician College; Felician College Child Care Center; Felician School for Exceptional Children, Lodi, NJ; Felician Retreat Center; Our Lady of Grace Home; St. Ignatius Nursing Home.*
Sisters Serve and Staff: Colleges; High Schools; Elementary Schools; Hospitals; Home for Neglected Children; Home for Aged; Infirmary for Sisters; Day Care Center; School for Exceptional Children; Religious Education; Parish Ministries.
Represented in the Archdioceses of Baltimore, Newark, Philadelphia, and the Dioceses of Arlington, Camden, Metuchen, Paterson, Trenton and Wilmington.
Our Lady of the Sacred Heart Province (1921): *Provincial House and Novitiate, Felician Sisters of Pennsylvania,* 1500 Woodcrest Ave., Coraopolis, PA 15108. Tel: 412-264-2890; Fax: 412-264-7047. Sr. Mary Cabrini Procopio, C.S.S.F., Prov. Min.
Total number in community 149 Postulants 1.
Ministry in the field of Academic Education at all levels; Hospital Work; Religious Education; CCD Centers; Youth and Pastoral Ministry; Home for Mentally Retarded Children; Infirmary; Nursing Homes; Missionary Work.
Legal Holdings and Titles: *Felician Sisters of Pennsylvania Our Lady of the Sacred Heart High School.*
Represented in the Dioceses of Altoona-Johnstown, Charleston, Cleveland, Greensburg, Harrisburg, Pittsburgh, and Venice. Also in Kenya.
Our Lady of the Angels Province (1932): *Felician Sisters,* 1315 Enfield St., Enfield, CT 06082-4920. Tel: 860-745-7791; Fax: 860-741-0819. Sr. Mary Laureann Alezandrowicz, C.S.S.F., Prov. Minister.
Universal total 154; Postulants 2.
Properties owned and sponsored: *Montessori School, The Felician Adult Day Care,* Enfield, CT; *St. Joseph Hospital,* Bangor, ME.
Ministry in the field of Religious and Academic Education on all levels; Pastoral Ministry; Social Services; Healthcare.
Represented in the Archdioceses of Boston, Hartford, New York, and the Dioceses of Albany, Manchester, Norwich, Portland (ME), Providence, Springfield (MA) and Worcester.
Assumption of the B.V.M. Province (1953): *Provincial House - Novitiate,* P.O. Box 15096, 4210 Meadowlark Ln., S.E., Rio Rancho, NM 87124-1021. Sr. Rosemarie Goins, C.S.S.F., Prov. Min.
Total number in community 77.
Legal Titles and Holdings: *Felician Sisters of the Southwest, Inc. St. Felix Pantry Inc.*
Sisters serve and staff: High Schools; Elementary Schools; Foreign and Rural Missions; Religious Education Centers & Classes; Health Care; Pastoral Care; Food & Clothing Pantry; Youth Ministry; Adult Education.
Represented in the Archdioceses of Los Angeles, San Antonio and Santa Fe, and the Dioceses of Austin and Fort Worth. Also in Mexico and Italy.

[1180] (O.S.F.)—FRANCISCAN SISTERS OF ALLEGANY, NEW YORK P

Founded in the United States in 1859.
General Motherhouse (1859): *St. Elizabeth Motherhouse,* Allegany, NY 14706. Tel: 716-373-0200; Fax: 716-372-5774. Sr. Margaret Mary Kimmins, O.S.F., Gen. Minister; Sr. Marigene Kennedy, O.S.F., Local Minister.
Total number in community 458.
Legal Titles and Holdings: *Franciscan Sisters of Allegany, NY, Inc.; Franciscan Center, Inc.,* Tampa, FL; *Dwelling Place, Inc.,* New York, NY; *St. Joseph*

Villa, Catskill, NY; *Franciscan Sisters of Allegany Residence of Miami Beach*, Inc., Miami, FL.

Ministry to Evangelization in all levels of Education; Health Care; Social Services; Pastoral and Campus Ministries; Spiritual Ministries and Social Advocacy.

Represented in the Archdioceses of Boston, Hartford, Miami, Newark, New York and Philadelphia, and the Dioceses of Albany, Buffalo, Camden, Charlotte, Metuchen, Orlando, Palm Beach, Paterson, Rochester, Rockville Centre, St. Petersburg, Scranton, Springfield (MA), Syracuse, Trenton, Venice and Wilmington. Also in Bolivia, Brazil and Jamaica.

REGION I OFFICE: *Franciscan Sisters of Allegany*, (1984), 115 E. Main St., Allegany, NY 14706. Tel: 716-373-1888. Sr. Rosemary Higgins, O.S.F., Region I Minister.

Represented in the Dioceses of Albany, Buffalo, Rochester and Syracuse. Also in Bolivia.

REGION II: *Franciscan Sisters of Allegany*, (1972), 168 Hopkins Ave., Haddonfield, NJ 08033. Tel: 609-429-1739. Sr. Victoria Masterpaul, O.S.F., Region II Minister.

Represented in the Archdioceses of Boston, Hartford, Newark, New York and Philadelphia, and the Dioceses of Camden, Charlotte, Metuchen, Paterson, Rockville Centre, Springfield (MA), Trenton and Wilmington.

REGION III: *Franciscan Sisters of Allegany*, (1972), 601 12th St., North, St. Petersburg, FL 33705. Tel: 813-824-0857. Sr. Gladys T. Sharkey, O.S.F., Region III Minister.

Represented in the Archdiocese of Miami and in Dioceses of Orlando, Palm Beach, St. Petersburg and Venice. Also in Bolivia.

REGION IV: *Franciscan Sisters of Allegany*, 152 Constant Spring Rd., Box 1654, Kingston, Jamaica, West Indies. Tel: 809-924-1719. Sr. Teresita Marie De Souza, O.S.F., Region IV Minister.

REGION V: *Franciscan Sisters of Allegany*, C.P. 322, 75001-970 Anapolis, Goias, Brazil, South America. Tel: 011-55-62-321-0805. Sr. Maria do Socorro de Rosal, O.S.F., Region V Minister.

[1190] (S.A.)—FRANCISCAN SISTERS OF THE ATONEMENT P

Founded in the United States in 1898.

MOTHERHOUSE: *St. Francis Convent*, Graymoor, Garrison, NY 10524. Tel: 914-424-3623; Fax: 914-424-3298. Sr. Diane Bernier, S.A., Congregational Minister; Sr. Mary Annunciata Griffitts, S.A., Archivist.

Total number in community 238.

Properties owned: *St. Francis Convent - Complex*, Garrison, NY; *Mother Lurana House*, Garrison, NY; *Washington Retreat House*, Washington, DC.

Represented in the Archdioceses of Boston, Detroit, Newark, New York, Washington, and the Dioceses of Albany, Brooklyn, Bridgeport, Burlington, Fresno, Manchester, Metuchen, Monterey, Nashville, Norwich, Ogdensburg, Paterson, Pittsburgh, Portland (ME), Raleigh, Reno-Las Vegas, Sacramento, Salt Lake City, Savannah and Syracuse. Also in Canada, Brazil, Ireland, Italy and Japan.

[1200] (O.S.F.)—THE FRANCISCAN SISTERS OF BALTIMORE P

Founded in England in 1868. First foundation in the United States in 1881.

GENERAL MOTHERHOUSE: 3725 Ellerslie Ave., Baltimore, MD 21218. Tel: 410-235-0139; Fax: 410-243-2569. Sr. Ritamary Tan, O.S.F., Dir. Gen.

Total number in community 50.

Legal Title: *Franciscan Sisters of Baltimore, Inc.*

Sisters serve and staff: Parochial Schools; Schools of Special Education; AIDS Ministry; Emergency Welfare Center; Youth Center; Religious Education Centers; Pastoral Ministry; Lay Volunteer Program; Chaplaincy Programs; Hispanic & African-American Evangelization.

Properties owned: Residences for the mentally handicapped; St. Elizabeth School, Inc.; Francis House, Inc.; Franciscan Center, Inc.; General Motherhouse, Baltimore, MD.

Represented in the Archdioceses of Baltimore and Washington, and the Dioceses of Brownsville and Trenton.

[1210] (O.S.F.)—FRANCISCAN SISTERS OF CHICAGO P

Founded in Chicago, Illinois in 1894 by Mother Mary Theresa (Josephine Dudzik) Venerable Servant of God.

GENERAL MOTHERHOUSE: *Our Lady of Victory Convent*, 14700 Main St., Lemont, IL 60439-0956. Tel: 630-257-7776; Fax: 630-257-7887. Sr. M. Francis Clare Radke, Gen. Supr.; Sr. Emilie Marie Lesniak, Archivist.

Total number in community 138.

Sisters serve and staff: Elementary Schools 3; CCD Programs 5.

Properties owned: *Madonna High School*, Chicago, IL; *St. Anthony Medical Center, Inc.*, Crown Point, IN; *St. Anthony Home, Inc.*, Crown Point, IN; *St. Joseph Home of Chicago, Inc.*, Chicago IL; *Mount Alverna Home, Inc., Mount Alverna Home Annex, Inc.*, Parma, OH; *Mother Theresa Home, Inc., Franciscan Village*, Lemont, IL; *St. Francis House of Prayer, Franciscan Sisters of Chicago Service Corp., Our Lady of Victory Convent*, Lemont IL.

Represented in the Archdiocese of Chicago, and the Dioceses of Cleveland and Gary.

[1230] (O.S.F.)—FRANCISCAN SISTERS OF CHRISTIAN CHARITY P

Founded in the United States in 1869.

MOTHERHOUSE: *Holy Family Convent*, 2409 S. Alverno Rd., Manitowoc, WI 54220. Tel: 414-682-7728; Fax: 414-682-4195. Sr. Paula Vanden Hogen, Community Dir.; Sr. Donna Marie Kessler, Community Archivist.

Total number in community 563.

Properties owned or sponsored: *Holy Family Convent*, Manitowoc, WI; *Holy Family Medical Center*, Manitowoc, WI; *St. Francis Memorial Hopital*, West Point, NE; *Good Samaritan Medical Center*, Zanesville, OH; *St. Joseph Retirement Community*, West Point, NE; *St. Paul Home*, Kaukauna, WI; *Silver Lake College*, Manitowoc, WI; *Franciscan Sisters of Christian Charity HealthCare Ministry, Inc.*, Manitowoc, WI; *Holy Family Conservatory of Music*, Manitowoc, WI; *St. Clare Convent*, Manitowoc, WI; *St. Francis Convent*, Manitowoc, WI; *San Damiano Convent*, Slinger, WI.

Represented in the Archdioceses of Chicago, Los Angeles, Milwaukee and Omaha and in the Dioceses of Columbus, Gaylord, Green Bay, Honolulu, Lexington, Marquette, Phoenix, Steubenville, Superior and Tucson. Also in Peru.

[1235] (F.H.M.)—FRANCISCAN SISTERS DAUGHTERS OF MERCY

Franciscanas Hijas de la Misericordia

Founded in Pina, Mallorca, Spain in 1856. First U.S. establishment in 1962.

GENERAL MOTHERHOUSE: Calle Moral 4, 07001 Palma de Mallorca, Spain. Sr. Antonia Barrilero Canadas, Supr. Gen.

Universal number in Congregation 447.

U.S. REGIONAL DELEGATION: 612 N. 3rd St., Waco, TX 76701. Tel: 817-753-5565. Sr. Rose Moreno, Regl. Delegate.

Professed Sisters 15.

Ministry in Kingergarten; Catechetical Work; Pastoral Work; Social Work.

Represented in the Diocese of Austin.

[1240] (O.S.F.)—FRANCISCAN SISTERS, DAUGHTERS OF THE SACRED HEARTS OF JESUS AND MARY P

Founded in Germany in 1860. First foundation in the United States in 1872.

GENERALATE: Via di Sant' Alessio, 22-24, 00153, Rome, Italy. Sr. Clare Nyderek, Gen. Dir.

Universal number in Congregation 968.

ST. CLARA'S PROVINCE (1877): *Convent of Our Lady of the Angels, Motherhouse and Novitiate*, P.O. Box 667, Wheaton, IL 60189. Tel: 630-462-7422. Sr. Mary Ellen McAleese, Prov. Dir.

Total number in province 129.

Sisters serve and staff: Hospitals; Housing Development; Grammar Schools; Universities; Parish Ministry; Spirituality Center; Home Health Care; Corporate Offices; System Ministries; Long-term Care; Social Services; Wellness; Spiritual Direction; Campus Ministry; Foreign Mission.

Legal Holdings and Titles: *All Saints Healthcare System, Inc.*, Racine, WI *All Saints Healthcare Foundation, Inc.- (formerly known as St. Mary's and St. Luke's Health Care Foundation, Inc.) All Saints Visiting Nurse Association & Hospice of Racine, Inc. Assisi Community Organization, Inc.- (formerly known as Project Hope, Inc.) Assisi Homes - Batavia Apartments, Inc.*, Joliet, IL *Assisi Homes - Colony Park, Inc.; Assisi Homes - Constitution House, Inc. Assisi Homes - DeKalb, Inc. Assisi Homes of Gurnee, Inc. Assisi Homes - Eldr Manor, Inc. Assisi Homes - Gateway, Inc.* Assisi Homes - *Howard Woods, Inc. Assisi Homes - Jefferson Court, Inc. Assisi Homes - Kenosha, Inc. Assisi Homes - Rock View, Inc. Assisi Homes - Saxony, Inc. Assisi Homes of Milwaukee, Inc. Assisi Homes - Aurora, Inc. Assisi Homes of Illinois, Inc.*, Wheaton, IL *Assisi Homes of Neenah, Inc.*, Neenah, WI *Assisi Homes of Wisconsin, Inc. Canticle Place, Inc. Canticle Place Ministries, Inc. Clare of Assisi Homes - Westminster, Inc.*, Denver, CO *Clare Gardens, Inc. Clara Pfaender Fund, Inc.*, Wheaton, IL - *(Joliet Diocese) Covenant Community Foundation, Inc.- (formerly known as WFSI-Milwaukee Foundation, Inc. Covenant Foundation, Inc. Covenant Health System, Inc.- (formerly known as WFSI-Iowa, Inc.) Covenant Healthcare System, Inc. Covenant Medical Center, Inc. Dayspring Villa, Inc.*, Denver, CO *Elmbrook Memorial Hospital*, Brookfield, WI *First Care North, Inc.*, Appleton, WI *Franciscan Care Center, Inc.*, Appleton, WI *Franciscan Health and Education Corporation, Inc. Franciscan Seniors, Kenosha, Inc. Francis of Assisi Foundation of Colorado, Inc.*, Denver, CO - *(Denver Archdiocese) Francis Heights, Inc. Franciscan Home Health, Inc. Franciscan Ministries, Inc. Franciscan Shared Laboratory, Inc. Kaukauna Community Hospital*, Kaukauna, WI - *(Green Bay Diocese) Marian Catholic Home, Inc. Marian Center of Racine, Inc.*, Racine, WI *Marian Franciscan Center, Inc. M.F.S.I., Inc. - (formerly known as Marian Franciscan Services, Inc.) Marian Housing Center, Inc.*, Racine, WI *Marianjoy, Inc. Marian Park, Inc. Mercy Hospital of Franciscan Sisters, Inc. Oak Park Hospital*, Oak Park, IL - *(Chicago Archdiocese) O.S.F. Services, Inc. Rosalie Manor, Inc. Ridgeway Place, Inc.*, Waterloo, IA *S.E.T. Ministry, Inc. S.F.H., Inc. S.F.A. of Racine, Inc. St. Elizabeth Hospital Inc. St. Elizabeth Hospital Community Foundation, Inc. St. Francis Health Care Corporation of Racine*, Racine, WI - *(Milwaukee Archdiocese) St. Joseph's Hospital of Franciscan Sisters of Milwaukee, Inc.*, Milwaukee, WI *St. Mary's Medical Center, Inc.*, Racine, WI *St. Michael Hospital Community Foundation, Inc.*, Milwaukee, WI *St. Michael Hospital of Franciscan Sisters of Milwaukee, Inc.*, Milwaukee, WI *Villa Maria, Inc. Villa St. Anna, Inc. Villa St. Clare, Inc.*, Neenah, WI *Villa St. Joseph, Inc. Villa St. Theresa, Inc. WFSI-Fox Valley*, Appleton, WI *WFSI-Illinois Wheaton Franciscan Sisters Corporation Wheaton Franciscan Sisters Religious Charitable Trust Wheaton Franciscan Services, Inc.*

Represented in the Archdioceses of Chicago, Denver, Dubuque, Milwaukee and St. Louis, and the Dioceses of Green Bay, Joliet and Springfield-Cape Girardeau. Also in Brazil, Italy and Nigeria.

[1250] (F.S.E.)—THE INSTITUTE OF THE FRANCISCAN SISTERS OF THE EUCHARIST P

Founded December 2, 1973.

MOTHERHOUSE: *John Lateran Center*, 405 Allen Ave., Meriden, CT 06451. Tel: 203-237-0841. Team Members: Mother Rosemae Pender, Mother Gen.; Mother Shaun Vergauwen, Mother Asst.; Mother Rita Brunner; Mother Mary Ann Schmitz; Mother Mary Michael Costello; Mother Mona Brunner.

Total number in community 76.

Legal Title: *Franciscan Sisters of the Eucharist, Incorporated.*

Schools and programs operated under Franciscan Life Center Network, Inc.

Represented in the Archdioceses of Hartford, Portland (OR), Seattle, Washington, and the Dioceses of Boise, Duluth and Grand Rapids. Also in Israel and Italy.

[1260] (F.H.M.)—FRANCISCAN HANDMAIDS OF THE MOST PURE HEART OF MARY D

Founded in the United States in 1916.

GENERAL MOTHERHOUSE: 15 W. 124th St., New York, NY 10027. Tel: 212-289-5655.

Novitiate; 444 Woodvale Ave., Pleasant Plains, Staten Island, NY 10309. Sr. Loretta Theresa, Supr. Gen.; Sr. Maria Goretti, Dir. Formation; Sr. Jacqueline, Community Archivist.

Total number in community 24.

Properties owned: *St. Benedict Day Nursery; Camp Saint Edward; Franciscan Handmaids of Mary Novitiate; Franciscan Handmaids of Mary Motherhouse.*

Ministry in the field of Education, Social Work and Pastoral Care.

Represented in the Archdiocese of New York.

[1270] (F.H.I.C.)—FRANCISCAN HOSPITALLER SISTERS OF THE IMMACULATE CONCEPTION P

Founded in Portugal in 1876.

GENERAL MOTHERHOUSE: Linda-a-Pastora, Portugal. Sr. Maria Isilda Freitas, F.H.I.C., Supr. Gen.

U.S. FOUNDATION (1960): *St. Joseph Novitiate*, 300 S. 17th St., San Jose, CA 95112-2245. Tel: 408-998-2896; Fax: 408-998-3407. Sr. Lucinda D. Fonseca, Supr.

Total number in community 17.

Sisters serve and staff: Parishes; Schools; Hospitals; Social Work.
Represented in the Dioceses of Fresno, Monterey and San Jose.

[1280] (O.S.F.)—FRANCISCAN SISTERS OF THE IMMACULATE CONCEPTION P

First foundation in United States in 1928.
GENERAL MOTHERHOUSE: Kloster Bonlanden, Germany. Sr. M. Fredigundis Fratz, O.S.F., Supr. Gen.
PROVINCE OF THE BLESSED VIRGIN MARY: 291 W. North St., Buffalo, NY 14201; Fax: 716-881-1578. Sr. M. Bernard, O.S.F., Prov.
Professed Sisters 8.
Represented in the Archdiocese of New York and the Diocese of Buffalo.

[1300] (O.S.F.)—FRANCISCAN SISTERS OF THE IMMACULATE CONCEPTION AND ST. JOSEPH FOR THE DYING D

Founded in the United States in December, 1919 at San Carlos Parish, Monterey, California.
GENERAL MOTHERHOUSE: *c/o Ave Maria Convent,* 1249 Josselyn Canyon Rd., Monterey, CA 93940. Tel: 408-373-1216. Sr. M. Constance, O.S.F., Supr. Gen.; Sr. M. Bernadette, O.S.F., Archivist.
Total number in community 7.
Legal Holding: *Ave Maria Convalescent Hospital,* Monterey, CA.
Represented in the Diocese of Monterey.

[1302] (F.I.H.M.)—FRANCISCAN OF THE IMMACULATE HEART OF MARY D

GENERAL MOTHERHOUSE: *Immaculate Heart of Mary Generalate,* St. Therese St., Pondicherry, India, 6050-01. Sr. Regina Savarinathan, F.I.H.M., Supr. Gen.
PROVINCE IN THE U.S.: *St. Catherine's Convent,* 49 King St., Hillside, NJ 07205. Tel: 908-354-9131. Sr. Urmila Selvi, F.I.H.M., Supr.
Total number in community.
Represented in the Archdiocese of Newark.

[1310] (O.S.F.)—FRANCISCAN SISTERS OF LITTLE FALLS, MINNESOTA P

Founded in the United States in 1891.
GENERAL MOTHERHOUSE: *St. Francis' Convent,* Little Falls, MN 56345. Tel: 612-632-2981. Sr. Rose Margaret Schneider, O.S.F., Pres.; Sr. Sabina Collins, Archivist.
Total number in community 259.
Ministry in the field of Academic Education at all levels; Health Care in Nursing Homes, Hospitals, Apartment for the Elderly, Children's Home, Clinics; Religious Education; Parish Ministry; Retreat Houses; Liturgical Music; Music Center; Wholistic Growth Center; Ministry to Refugees; Health and Recreation Center; Diocesan Offices; Social Services; Counseling-spiritual Direction; Consulting; Ministry to AIDS and Chemical Dependency Victims; Ministry to the Poor; Ministry to Migrants; Ministry to the Hearing Impaired; Altar Breadmaking, and Craft Activities; Horticulture; Social Justice and Nonviolent Activities; Spirituality Farm; Native Americans.
Properties owned or sponsored: *Wholistic Growth Resources Program; St. Francis Music Center; St. Francis Health & Recreation Center; Clare's Well.*
Represented in the Archdioceses of Chicago, Los Angeles, Milwaukee, New York, St. Louis, St. Paul-Minneapolis, San Antonio, Washington, and the Dioceses of Arlington, Belleville, Buffalo, Brownsville, Charleston, Crookston, Fargo, Jackson, La Crosse, Madison, Memphis, New Ulm, Oakland, Palm Beach, St. Cloud, St. Petersburg, Scranton, Sioux Falls, Spokane, Tucson, Tyler and Winona. Also in Cameroon, Ecuador, Guatemala, Nicaragua and Tanzania.

[1320] (O.S.F.)—FRANCISCAN MISSIONARY SISTERS FOR AFRICA P

GENERALATE: *Franciscan Convent,* Mount Oliver, Dundalk Co. Louth, Ireland.
AMERICAN HEADQUARTERS: 172 Foster St., P.O. Box 35095, Brighton, MA 02135. Tel: 617-254-4343. Sr. Nora Doyle, O.S.F.
Total number in community 7.
Represented in the Archdiocese of Boston.

[1330] (S.F.M.A.)—FRANCISCAN MISSIONARY SISTERS OF ASSISI P

GENERAL MOTHERHOUSE: Via San Francesco 13, Assisi, Italy. Sr. Serena Picchio, Mother Gen.
U.S. FOUNDATION (1961): *St. Francis Convent,* 1039 Northampton St., Holyoke, MA 01040. Tel: 413-532-8156.
Total number in community 12.
Represented in the Diocese of Springfield (MA).

[1340] (F.M.D.C.)—FRANCISCAN MISSIONARY SISTERS OF THE DIVINE CHILD D

First founded in the United States on August 15, 1927, in Buffalo, New York.
MOTHERHOUSE: *Franciscan Missionary Sisters of the Divine Child Motherhouse,* 6380 Main St., Williamsville, NY 14221. Tel: 716-632-3144; Fax: 716-626-1332. Sr. Margaret Krantz, F.M.D.C., Minister Gen.
Total number in community 33.
Sisters serve and staff: Catechetical Centers; CCD Coordinators; Education in Elementary, High School and College; Parish Ministry; Social Work; Census work; Adult education and Bereavement Ministry.
Represented in the Diocese of Buffalo.

[1350] (O.S.F.)—FRANCISCAN SISTERS OF THE IMMACULATE CONCEPTION P

Founded in Mexico in 1874. First foundation in the United States in 1926.
PROVINCIAL HOUSE: 11320 Laurel Canyon Blvd., San Fernando, CA 91340. Tel: 818-365-2582. Sr. Maria de la Paz Ulloa, O.S.F., Prov. Supr.; Sr. Mary Gabriel De Leon, O.S.F., Community Archivist.
Total number in community 111.
Legal Holdings and Titles: *Franciscan Missionary Sisters of the Immaculate Conception, Inc.; Poverello of Assisi Retreat House,* San Fernando, CA; *St. Francis Home,* Santa Ana, CA; *Mother Gertrude Balcazar Home,* San Fernando, CA; *Immaculate Conception Home,* Los Angeles, CA.
Ministry in the field of Education and Religious Education to Children and Adults; Health Care in Hospitals and Home Visitation to the Sick.
Represented in the Archiocese of Los Angeles, and the Dioceses of Gallup and Orange.

[1360] (M.F.I.C.)—MISSIONARY FRANCISCAN SISTERS OF THE IMMACULATE CONCEPTION P

Founded in the United States in 1873 in Belle Prairie, Minnesota.
GENERAL MOTHERHOUSE: Rome, Italy. Sr. Marian Bandille, M.F.I.C., Gen. Minister.
PROVINCIALATE: *Immaculate Conception Convent,* 790 Centre St., Newton, MA 02158. Tel: 617-527-1004; Fax: 617-527-2528. Sr. Mary Michele Craig, M.F.I.C., Prov.
Total number in province 265.
Represented in the Archdioceses of Boston, Hartford, Newark, New York, Philadelphia, and the Dioceses of Bridgeport, Brooklyn, Savannah, Syracuse and Venice.

[1365] (F.M.I.J.)—FRANCISCAN MISSIONARY SISTERS OF THE INFANT JESUS P

Founded in Aquila, Italy in 1879 by Sr. Maria Giuseppa Micarelli. First Foundation in the U.S. in 1961.
GENERALATE: Piazza Nicoloso da Recco 13, Rome, Italy, 00154. Tel: 6-575-8358. Mother Maria Felicita Decio, F.M.I.J., Supr. Gen.
U.S. PROVINCE AND NOVITIATE: 1215 Kresson Rd., Cherry Hill, NJ 08003. Tel: 609-428-7930; Fax: 609-428-7930. Sr. Chiara Lilia Ferrario, F.M.I.J., Delegate Supr.
Ministries of Evangelization; Education; Health Care; Social-Pastoral Services.
Professed Sisters 17; Junior Professed 1.
Represented in the Dioceses of Camden and Trenton.

[1370] (F.M.M.)—THE FRANCISCAN MISSIONARIES OF MARY P

Founded in India in 1877. First foundation in the United States in 1904.
GENERAL MOTHERHOUSE: 12 via Giusti, Rome, Italy. Sr. Christiane Megarbane, F.M.M., Supr. Gen.
FRANCISCAN MISSIONARIES OF MARY -U.S. PROVINCE (1920): 3305 Wallace Ave., Bronx, NY 10467. Tel: 718-547-4604. Sr. Mary Petrosky, F.M.M., Prov.
Total number in community 210.
Educational Projects among Minority Group of Immigrants; Child Care Agencies; Cardiac and General Hospital; General Pediatric Hospital with Rehabilitation Specialty; Chaplaincy; Retreat Work; Day Care for Elderly; Catechetics; Home Visiting & Community Development.
Represented in the Archdioceses of Boston, Chicago, New York, St. Louis, San Francisco and in the Dioceses of Fall River, Las Cruces, Providence, Rockville Centre, Savannah, and St. Petersburg.

[1380] (O.S.F.)—FRANCISCAN MISSIONARIESOF OUR LADY P

Founded in Calais, France in 1854. First U.S. foundation in 1913.
GENERAL MOTHERHOUSE: Desvres, France.
GENERALATE: Paris, France.
PROVINCIAL AND NOVITIATE HOUSE: *Maryville Novitiate,* 4200 Essen Ln., Baton Rouge, LA 70809. Tel: 504-926-1627; Fax: 504-926-4846. Sr. Brendan M. Ronayne, Supr.
Total number in community 30.
Properties owned and sponsored: *Our Lady of the Lake Regional Medical Center, Inc.,* Baton Rouge, LA; *Ollie Steele Burden Manor, Inc.,* Baton Rouge, LA; *Our Lady of Lourdes Regional Medical Center, Inc.,* Lafayette, LA; *St. Francis Medical Center, Inc.,* Monroe, LA; *FMOL Health System, Inc.,* Baton Rouge, LA.
Represented in the Dioceses of Baton Rouge, Lafayette (LA) and Shreveport.

[1390] (O.S.F.)—FRANCISCAN MISSIONARY SISTERS OF OUR LADY OF SORROWS D

Founded in Hunan China in 1939. First United States foundation in 1950.
COMMUNITY HEADQUARTERS: *Our Lady of Peace Retreat House,* 3600 S.W. 170th Ave., Beaverton, OR 97006. Tel: 503-649-7127; Fax: 503-649-8382. Sr. Anne Marie Warren, O.S.F., Supr. Gen.
Total number in community 50.
Legal Titles and Holdings: *Our Lady of Peace Retreat,* Beaverton, OR; *St. Clare Retreat House,* Soquel, CA; *Our Lady of Mt. Carmel Group Home,* Gallup, NM.
Ministry in religious and academic education and foreign missions.
Represented in the Archdioceses of Portland (OR), San Francisco, and the Dioceses of Gallup and Monterey.

[1400] (F.M.S.C.)—FRANCISCAN MISSIONARY SISTERS OF THE SACRED HEART P

Founded in Italy in 1861. First foundation in the U.S. in New York City (1865).
GENERAL MOTHERHOUSE: Rome, Italy. Sr. Ines Pavan, Supr. Gen.
ST. FRANCIS PROVINCE (1869): *Mt. St. Francis,* 250 South St., Peekskill, NY 10566. Tel: 914-737-5409; Fax: 914-736-9614. Sr. M. Raphael Conlon, Prov.
Universal number in Congregation 782; Number in United States Province 60.
Legal Title: *Missionary Sisters of the Third Order of St. Francis.*
Ministry in Religious and Academic Education; Health Care for Retired Sisters; Pastoral Ministry; Prison Apostolate; Hospital Ministry.
Represented in the Archdioceses of Newark, New York and in Dioceses of Brooklyn and Paterson.

[1410] (F.M.S.J.)—MILL HILL SISTERS P
Franciscan Missionaries of St. Joseph

Founded in 1883. First United States foundation in 1952.
GENERALATE: *St. Joseph's Convent,* Worsley Manchester, England. Sr. Theodora Slot, F.M.S.J., Supr. Gen.
AMERICAN HEADQUARTERS: *Franciscan House,* 1006 Madison Ave., Albany, NY 12208. Tel: 518-482-1991. Sr. Judith Dever, F.M.S.J., Reg Supr.
Total number in community 12.
Represented in the Dioceses of Albany and Norwich.

[1415] (F.S.M.)—FRANCISCAN SISTERS OF MARY P

Founded in the United States in 1872.
ADMINISTRATIVE OFFICES & NOVITIATE: *Franciscan Sisters of Mary,* 1100 Bellevue Ave., St. Louis, MO 63117. Tel: 314-768-1824; Fax: 314-768-1880. Sr. Jacqueline Motzel, F.S.M., Pres.
Total number in community 223.
Properties owned or sponsored: *St. Mary of the Angels,* St. Louis, MO; *St. Mary's Ringling,* Baraboo, WI.
Ministry in Hospitals; Skilled Nursing Facilities; Rehabilitation Unit; Hospice; Counseling Center; Foreign Missions; Adult Living Center; Birthing Centers; Pastoral Services; Consultation Services; Education.
Represented in the Archdioceses of Chicago, Oklahoma City, St. Louis, and the Dioceses of Albany, Brownsville, Charleston, Jefferson City, Kansas City-St. Joseph, Madison, St. Petersburg and Springfield-Cape Girardeau. Also in Brazil & South Africa.

[1420] (F.S.R.)—FRANCISCAN SISTERS OF RINGWOOD D

Founded in the United States in Passaic, New Jersey on Nov. 21, 1929.
GENERAL MOTHERHOUSE AND NOVITIATE: *Mt. St. Francis,* Ringwood, NJ 07456. Tel: 201-962-7411; Fax: 201-962-0445. Sr. Francis Clare Verderosa, Gen. Coord.
Total number in community 34.

Ministry in the field of academic and religious education and as pastoral associates.
Represented in the Archdioceses of Newark and the Diocese of Paterson.

[1425] (F.S.P.)—FRANCISCAN SISTERS OF PEACE D

SISTERS OF ST. FRANCIS OF PEACE: Congregation Center, 20 Ridge St., Haverstraw, NY 10927. Tel: 914-942-2527. Sr. Margaret Gaffikin, Congregation Minister.
Total number in the community 93.
Legal Titles and Holdings: *Our Lady of Hope Convent,* Cortlandt Manor, NY; *St. Joseph's Villa by the Sea,* Ventnor, NJ; *Congregation Center,* Haverstraw, NY.
Ministry in Youth & Campus Ministries; Care for the Aged; Pastoral; Education; Nursing; Catechetical; Social Work; Prison Ministry; Ministry to Unwed mothers and the Native American Indians in Arizona; New Mexico.
Represented in the Archdioceses of Newark, New York, Philadelphia, San Francisco and the Diocese of Albany, Brooklyn, Camden, Gallup, Paterson, and Rockville Centre.

[1430] (O.S.F.)—FRANCISCAN SISTERS OF OUR LADY OF PERPETUAL HELP P

Founded in the United States in 1901.
MOTHERHOUSE AND NOVITIATE: *Villa St. Joseph,* 201 Brotherton Ln., St. Louis (Ferguson), MO 63135. Tel: 314-522-6800. Sr. Monica Marie Laws, O.S.F., Supr. Gen.; Rev. Larry Nickels, O.F.M., Chap.
Total number in community 152.
Legal Holdings and Titles: *Villa St. Joseph Motherhouse and Novitiate,* St. Louis, MO; *Villa St. Joseph Child Care and Education Center,* St. Louis, MO; *St. Francis Rehabilitation and Nursing Home,* Green Springs, OH; *Perpetual Help Charitable Trust,* St. Louis, MO.
Ministry in Education; Nursing Homes; Rehabilitation Hospital; Child Day Care Center; Indian Missions.
Represented in the Archdioceses of Chicago, Kansas City in Kansas, Milwaukee, Omaha, St. Louis and Santa Fe, and the Dioceses of Belleville, El Paso, Las Cruces, Phoenix, Shreveport, Toledo and Wichita.

[1440] (S.F.P.)—FRANCISCAN SISTERS OF THE POOR P

Founded in Aachen, Germany in 1845. First foundation in the United States in 1858.
CONGREGATIONAL OFFICE: 133 Remsen St., Brooklyn, NY 11201. Tel: 718-643-1919; Fax: 718-643-9710. Sr. Jeanne M. Glisky, S.F.P., Congregational Min.
Total number in community 207.
U.S. REGION: 1 McWilliams Pl., Rm. 305, Jersey City, NJ 07302. Tel: 201-795-7431. Sr. Rose Margaret Delaney, Regl. Min.
Congregation Sponsors: *Franciscan Sisters of the Poor; St. Joseph Franciscan House, Inc.,* Brooklyn, NY; *Franciscan Sisters of the Poor Foundation, Inc.; Franciscan Sisters of the Poor Health System, Inc.,* Brooklyn Heights, NY; *Franciscan Health Services, Inc.,* Cincinnati, OH. Parent: *Franciscan Health System of Central Ohio, Inc.—Subsidiaries: St. Anthony Medical Center, Inc.,* Columbus, OH; *St. Anthony Mercy Hospital,* Columbus, OH; *Providential Corp., Inc. MedOne Health Plan, Inc.* Parent: *Franciscan Health System of Cincinnati, Inc.—Subsidiaries: Emerson A. North Hospital, Inc., Providence Hospital, Inc. St. Francis-St. George Hospital, Inc.; St. John Social Service Center, Inc.; West Park Retirement Community, Inc.,* Cincinnati, OH; *St. Raphael Social Service Center, Inc.,* Hamilton, OH; *West Park II, Inc.; Franciscan Health Network, Inc. Franciscan Home Development, Inc.; St. Clare Retirement Community, Inc.* Parent: *Franciscan Health System of Dayton, Inc.—Subsidiaries: St. Elizabeth Medical Center, Inc.,* Dayton, OH; *St. Leonard Center,* Centerville, OH; *Mary Black Schroder Home for the Aging, Inc.,* Hamilton, OH. Parent: *Franciscan Health System of Illinois, Inc.—Subsidiaries: St. Mary Hospital Health Development Association of Quincy,* Quincy, IL. Parent: *Franciscan Health System of New Jersey, Inc.— Subsidiaries: St. Francis Hospital, Inc.,* Jersey City, NJ; *St. Mary Hospital, Inc. F+A+I+T+H Services, Inc.,* Hoboken, NJ. Parent: *Franciscan Health System of New York, Inc.—Subsidiaries: Frances Schervier Home & Hospital,* Bronx, NY; *Franciscan Community Services of NY, Inc.; Frances Schervier Housing Development Fund Corporation Frances Schervier Nutrition Services, Inc.; Frances Schervier Child Care and Learning Center, Inc.* Parent: *Franciscan Health System of South Carolina, Inc.—Subsidiaries: St. Francis Hospital, Inc.,* Greenville, SC. Parent: *Franciscan Health System of Kentucky, Inc.—Subsidiaries: Our Lady of Bellefonte Hospital, Inc.,* Ashland, KY *—Subsidiaries: St. Anthony Community Hospital, Inc. Mt. Alverno Center & Convent,* Warwick, NY; *Mt. Alverno Residency Corp. Inc. Mercy Community Hospital,* Port Jarvis, NY; *Mt. Alverno Catering Service St. Francis Center at the Knolls, Inc. Villa Frances at the Knolls.* Co-sponsors: *St. Clare Holding Company,* Schenectady, NY; *St. Clare Hospital; St. Clare Foundation St. Clare Center Regional House,* Brazil; *Regional House and Frascati Complex,* Italy.
Represented in the Archdioceses of Cincinnati, Detroit, Newark, New York, Philadelphia and Santa Fe, and the Dioceses of Albany, Brooklyn, Charleston, Columbus, Gallup, Lansing, Lexington, Phoenix and Springfield (IL). Also in Italy, Senegal and Brazil.

[1450] (O.S.F.)—FRANCISCAN SISTERS OF THE SACRED HEART P

Congregation of the Franciscan Sisters of the Sacred Heart. Founded in Germany 1866. Established in the United States in 1876.
MOTHERHOUSE, NOVITIATE, POSTULANCY, SACRED HEART RESIDENCE AND PORTIUNCULA CENTER FOR PRAYER: *St. Francis Woods,* 9201 W. St. Francis Rd., Frankfort, IL 60423-8835. Tel: 815-469-4895; Fax: 815-469-4864. Sr. Karen Marie Lanigan, Gen. Supr.
Legal Title: *An Association of Franciscan Sisters of the Sacred Heart; The Franciscan Sisters of the Sacred Heart in California.*
Legal Titles for Health Care entities: *Franciscan Sisters Health Care Corporation; Queen of Angels Hospital; St. Anne's Maternity Home; St. Francis Medical Center of Santa Barbara; Franciscan Foundation.*
Sisters sponsor: *St. Joseph Medical Center, Joliet, IL; St. Joseph Hospital,* Elgin, IL; *St. Francis Medical Center,* Santa Barbara, CA; *St. Joseph College of Nursing,* Joliet, IL; Villa Franciscan, Joliet, IL; *Sacred Heart Home,* Avilla, IN; *LaVerna Terrace,* Avilla, IN; *St. Anne's Maternity Home,* Los Angeles, CA; *United Samaritans Medical Center,* Logan Campus-Danville, IL; *United Samaritans Medical Center,* Sager Campus-Danville, IL; *St. Therese Medical Center,* Waukegan, IL; *Franciscan Sisters Health Care Foundation,* Frankfort, IL.
Total number in community 167.
Sisters serve and staff: Elementary Schools; Religious Education Centers; Neighborhood Health Care Centers; Foreign Mission Centers; Direct Domestic Work at Retreat Houses; Canon Lawyer; Diocesan Offices; Retreat Centers; Clinics, Home Health Agencies, Health Care Systems, Hospitals, Schools of Nursing, Nursing and Retirement Homes; Home for Unwed Mothers; Apartments-Well Elderly; Parish & Youth Ministry; Hispanic Ministry; Liturgical Ministry; Social Work; Congregate Care Facility.
Represented in the Archdioceses of Chicago and Los Angeles, and the Dioceses of Fort Wayne-South Bend, Gary, Joliet, Peoria and Rockford. Also in Brazil.

[1460] (F.S.S.E.)—FRANCISCAN SISTERS OF ST. ELIZABETH P

(Suore Franciscane Elisabettine)
First founded in Naples, Italy, 1865. Founded in United States in Newark, New Jersey in 1919.
GENERAL MOTHERHOUSE: Via Marsico Nuovo 35, Rome, Italy. Mother Enrichetta Casa, Supr. Gen.
DELEGATE HOUSE: 499 Park Rd., Parsippany, NJ 07054. Tel: 201-539-3797. Mother Gina Maria Amico, Delegate Gen.
Total number in U.S. 66; Total in Community 300.
Ministry in Day Nurseries; Mission Houses; Elementary Schools and Montessori Schools.
Sister serve Christ in the person of the poor in Orphanages; Schools; Day Nursery Schools; Catechetical Instruction; Hospitals; Homes for the Poor, Aged, and Physically Handicapped.
Represented in the Archdiocese of Newark and the Diocese of Paterson. Also in India, Italy, Panama, and Philippines.

[1470] (F.S.S.J.)—FRANCISCAN SISTERS OF ST. JOSEPH P

Founded in the United States in 1897.
GENERAL MOTHERHOUSE: *Immaculate Conception Convent,* 5286 S. Park Ave., Hamburg, NY 14075. Tel: 716-649-1205; Fax: 716-649-5958. Sr. Mary Andrea Ciszewski, F.S.S.J., Gen. Min.
Total number in community 210.
Properties owned: *St. Clare Convent,* Hamburg, NY; *Immaculata Academy,* Hamburg, NY; *Hilbert College,* Hamburg, NY; *Marycrest Manor,* Livonia, MI; *St. Joseph Hospital,* Cheektowaga, NY.
Ministry in Education; Health Care; Home and Foreign Mission Work and other diverse ministries.
Represented in the Archdioceses of Baltimore, Detroit, Milwaukee and in the Dioceses of Bridgeport, Brooklyn, Buffalo, Harrisburg, Norwich, Saginaw, Savannah, Springfield (MA) and Trenton. Also in Brazil.

[1480] (F.S.S.J.)—FRANCISCAN SISTERS OF ST. JOSEPH D

Founded in Mexico.
MOTHERHOUSE: Ave. Revolucion No. 431, Delegacion Benito Juarez, Mexico, D.F, 03801. Tel: 515-17-74. Rev. Madre Maria del Rocio Garcia, H.F.J.
U.S. ADDRESS: *St. Paul's College,* 3015 4th St., N.E., Washington, DC 20017-1199. Tel: 202-832-6262; 269-2515.
Total number in community 5.
Ministry in domestic areas.
Represented in the Archdiocese of Washington.

[1485] (O.S.F.)—FRANCISCAN SISTERS OF ST. PAUL, MN. P

Franciscan Sisters of the Blessed Virgin Mary of the Holy Angels
(Beatae Mariae Virginis Angelorum)
Founded in Germany in 1863. First foundation in the United States in St. Paul in 1923.
GENERAL MOTHERHOUSE (1863): *St. Marienhaus,* Waldbreitbach, bei Neuwied, Rhine, Germany. Sr. Irmgard Schmitt, O.S.F., Supr. Gen.
Universal total in Congregation 651.
U.S. FOUNDATION: *Franciscan Regional Center,* 1388 Prior Ave. S., St. Paul, MN 55116. Tel: 612-690-1501; Fax: 612-690-2509. Sr. Mary Lucy Scheffler, Prov.
Total number in community 15.
Represented in the Archdiocese of St. Paul-Minneapolis.

[1490] (O.S.F.)—SISTERS OF THE THIRD FRANCISCAN ORDER P

Founded in the United States in 1860.
GENERALATE OFFICES: *Sisters of the Third Franciscan Order,* 2500 Grant Blvd., Syracuse, NY 13208-1794; Fax: 315-425-0610. Sr. Grace Anne Dillenschneider, Gen. Supr.
MOTHERHOUSE: *St. Anthony Convent,* 1024 Court St., Syracuse, NY 13208-1794.
Total number in community 360.
Ministry in Academic Education at all levels; Hospitals; Schools of Nursing; Religious Education & Pastoral Ministry; Retreat Houses; Rehabilitation Centers; Intentional Communities; Home for Dying; Adult & Child Day Care.
Legal Holding: *Sisters of the Third Franciscan Order-Retirement Trust Fund.*
Properties Owned and/or Sponsored: *Sister Patricia Anns Preschool, dba Gingerbread House,* Syracuse, NY; *St. Anthony Convent and Motherhouse,* Syracuse, NY; *St. Joseph Hospital,* Syracuse, NY; *St. Elizabeth Hospital,* Utica, NY; *Stella Maris Retreat Center,* Skaneateles, NY; *St. Francis Social Adult Day Service,* Syracuse, NY; *St. Francis Medical Center,* Honolulu, HI; *St. Francis Medical Center, West,* Ewa Beach, HI; *The Sister Maureen Keleher Hospice,* Honolulu, HI; *St. Francis School,* Honolulu, HI; *Mercy Rehabilitation Center,* Auburn, NY.
Represented in the Archdioceses of Boston, Los Angeles, Newark, New York, Philadelphia, San Antonio, Washington, and the Dioceses of Albany, Camden, Charlotte, Gallup, Harrisburg, Honolulu, Kansas City-St. Joseph, Las Cruces, Metuchen, Orange, Orlando, Richmond, Rochester, San Diego, St. Petersburg, Scranton, Syracuse, Trenton, Venice and Wilmington. Also in Italy and Peru.

[1500] (F.M.I.)—FRANCISCAN SISTERS OF MARY IMMACULATE OF THE THIRD ORDER OF ST. FRANCIS OF ASSISI P

Founded in Switzerland in the 16th Century. First founded in the United States on Aug. 15, 1932 at Amarillo, Texas.
GENERAL MOTHERHOUSE: Carrera 79 No. 40A-20, Bogota, Colombia, South America. Sr. Remberta Bischof, Supr. Gen.
Universal total in congregation 648.
U.S. PROVINCIAL HOUSE AND NOVITIATE (1964): *St. Francis Convent (1932),* 4301 N.E. 18th Ave., Amarillo, TX 79107. Tel: 806-383-5769. Sr. Mary Magdalene Baca, Prov. Supr.
Total number in community 47.
Represented in the Archdioceses of Los Angeles and Santa Fe and the Diocese of Amarillo.

[1505] (O.S.F.)—ST. FRANCIS MISSION COMMUNITY

Established 1981 in the United States of America in Amarillo, Texas, as an autonomous province of the Franciscan Sisters of Mary Immaculate.

General Motherhouse: *St. Francis Convent,* 4305 54th St., Lubbock, TX 79413-4617. Tel: 806-793-9859. Sr. Celine Thames, O.S.F., Mission Community Coord.

Professed Sisters 22; Novices 1; Postulants 1.

Ministry in the field of Religious and Academic Education in Elementary and Middle Schools; Parish Work; Pastoral Care in Hospitals.

Properties owned: *La Verna Convent,* Amarillo, TX; *St. Francis Convent,* Lubbock, TX; 55 acres of real estate.

Represented in the Archdiocese of Los Angeles, and the Dioceses of Amarillo and Lubbock. Also in Mexico.

[1510] (O.S.F.)—SISTERS OF ST. FRANCIS D

Sisters of St. Francis of the Mission of the Immaculate Virgin. Founded in New York in 1893.

General Motherhouse: *Sisters of St. Francis-Immaculate Conception Motherhouse,* 49 Jackson Ave., Hastings-on-Hudson, NY 10706-3217. Tel: 914-478-3930; Fax: 914-478-5470. Sr. Marie Bernadette Wyman, Gen. Minister.

Total number in community 89.

Properties owned and sponsored: *St. Francis Hospital,* Poughkeepsie, NY; *Nazareth Day Nursery,* New York, NY.

Ministry in Education; Day Nurseries; Hospitals and Parishes.

Represented in the Archdiocese of New York.

[1520] (O.S.F.)—SISTERS OF ST. FRANCIS OF CHRIST THE KING P

Founded in Austria in 1869. First founded in the United States at Kansas City, Kansas, in 1909.

General Motherhouse: Rome, Italy. Mother Natalia Alvarenga, Supr. Gen.

Universal number in Congregation 1,400.

St. Francis of Assisi of Christ the King Province (1926): *Mt. Assisi Convent,* 13900 Main St., Lemont, IL 60439. Tel: 630-257-7495. Sr. M. Ann Barbara Plavac, Prov. Supr.

Total number in community 80.

Properties owned and sponsored: *Mount Assisi Convent and Academy,* Lemont, IL; *Alvernia Manor,* Lemont, IL.

Ministry in Education and Care in Homes for the Aged.

Represented in the Archdioceses of Chicago and Milwaukee, and the Diocese of Joliet.

[1530] (O.S.F.)—SISTERS OF ST. FRANCIS OF THE CONGREGATION OF OUR LADY OF LOURDES, SYLVANIA, OHIO P

Founded in the United States in 1916 at Sylvania, Ohio. Foundation from Rochester, Minnesota.

General Motherhouse: *Convent and Novitiate,* 6832 Convent Blvd., Sylvania, OH 43560-2897. Tel: 419-882-2016; Fax: 419-885-8643. Sr. Ruth Marie Kachelek, Minister Gen.

Total number in the Congregation 315.

Properties owned and sponsored: *Lourdes College,* Sylvania, OH; *Franciscan Services Corporation, Hospital System,* Sylvania, OH. Sponsored Facilities: *Holy Cross Hospital, Inc.,* Detroit, MI; *Providence Hospital, Inc.,* Sandusky, OH; *St. John Medical Center,* Steubenville, OH; *Trinity Community Medical Center,* Brenham, TX; *St. Joseph Regional Health Center,* Bryan, TX; *Franciscan Shelters (Bethany House),* Toledo, OH; *Franciscan Center, Sylvania,* OH; Convent Park, Sylvania, OH *Providence Care Center,* Sandusky, OH.

Ministry in the field of Religious and Academic Education at all levels; Hospitals; Parish Ministries; Retreat Center; Social Services.

Represented in the Archdioceses of Baltimore, Cincinnati, Detroit, Indianapolis, Los Angeles, Milwaukee, New Orleans, Portland (OR), St. Paul-Minneapolis, Santa Fe and Washington, and the Dioceses of Arlington, Austin, Biloxi, Buffalo, Cleveland, Columbus, Dallas, Grand Rapids, Harrisburg, Joliet, Lansing, Lafayette, Phoenix, Raleigh, Richmond, St. Cloud, San Angelo, Shreveport, Steubenville, Toledo, Wheeling-Charleston, Winona and Youngstown. Also in Africa.

[1540] (O.S.F.)—SISTERS OF SAINT FRANCIS, CLINTON, IOWA P

Founded in the United States in 1866.

General Motherhouse: *Sisters of St. Francis Administrative Office,* 400 N. Bluff Blvd., Clinton, IA 52732. Tel: 319-242-7611. Sr. Maria Zeimen, Pres.

Total number in community 119.

Legal Holdings and Properties: *Mount St. Clare College; Mount St. Clare Convent; The Alverno Health Care Facility; Mount St. Clare Speech and Hearing Center; Sisters of St. Francis,* Clinton, IA; *Charitable Trust,* Clinton, IA.

Ministry in the field of Academic Education at all levels; Health Care in Centers and Homes for the aged; Hospitals; Pastoral Ministry; Hospital Chaplaincy; Religious Education and Spiritual Direction; Ministry to the Poor in Legal Aid and Housing as well as to Persons with AIDS.

Represented in the Archdioceses of Chicago, Detroit, Dubuque, Indianapolis, Louisville, Mobile, St. Louis, and the Dioceses of Belleville, Charleston, Davenport, Des Moines, Fresno, Joliet, Lansing, Lexington, Kansas City-St. Joseph, Oakland, Peoria, Phoenix, Portland, San Bernardino, San Diego, Sioux City, Toledo and Wichita. Also in the Bahamas & Peru.

[1550] (O.S.F.)—SISTERS OF ST. FRANCIS OF THE HOLY CROSS D

Founded in Wisconsin in 1881.

Motherhouse and Novitiate: *St. Francis Convent,* 3025 Bay Settlement Rd., Green Bay, WI 54311-7301. Tel: 414-468-1828; Fax: 414-468-1207. Sr. Paulette Hupfauf, Pres.

Total number in community 98.

Legal Title: *Sisters of St. Francis of the Holy Cross, Inc.; Francis & Co., a nominee of Sisters of St. Francis of the Holy Cross, Inc.; community related institution.*

Ministries in the following areas: Education; Pastoral Ministry and Religious Education; Ministry to the Elderly; Health Care; Retreat Work; Foreign Missions.

Represented in the Archdiocese of Milwaukee, and the Dioceses of Baton Rouge, Gary, Green Bay, Jackson, and La Crosse. Also in Nicaragua.

[1560] (O.S.F.)—SISTERS OF ST. FRANCIS OF THE HOLY EUCHARIST D

Founded in Grimmenstein, Switzerland in 1378. First foundation in United States in 1892.

Motherhouse, Novitiate and Prayer Center: *St. Francis Convent,* 2100 N. Noland Rd., Independence, MO 64050. Tel: 816-252-1673; Fax: 816-252-5574. Sr. Connie Boulch, Supr.; Sr. M. Lucy Lang, Vicar; Sr. Doris Engeman, Vocation Dir.

Total number in community 24.

Ministry in the following areas: Education at all levels; Retreat; Evangelization; Pastoral; Health Care.

Legal Title: *Franciscan Prayer Center,* Independence, MO; *Sisters of St. Francis of the Holy Eucharist Foundation,* Independence, MO.

Represented in the Archdiocese of Kansas City in Kansas and the Diocese of Kansas City-St. Joseph.

[1570] (O.S.F.)—SISTERS OF ST. FRANCIS OF THE HOLY FAMILY P

Founded in Germany in 1864. First foundation in the United States in 1875.

Motherhouse and Novitiate: *Mount St. Francis,* 3390 Windsor Ave., Dubuque, IA 52001-1311. Tel: 319-583-9786; Fax: 319-583-3250. Sr. Margaret Jungers, Pres.; Sr. Elvira Kelley, Community Archivist.

Total number in community 490.

Ministry in the following areas: Elementary and High Schools; Intercommunity High Schools; Religious Education-Parish Ministry; Health-Pastoral Care; Diocesan Offices; Social Service-Social Justice Centers; Food Service-Dietary; Communication Centers; Clerical Work-Business; Administration; Campus Ministry; Deaf Ministry; Art Studios; Foreign Missions.

Properties owned and sponsored: *Briar Cliff College,* Sioux City, IA; *Stonehill Care Center; Home for Aging; Alverno Apartments; Residence for the Elderly; Shalom Retreat Center and Mercy Health Center* (co-sponsors), Dubuque, IA.

Represented in the Archdioceses of Anchorage, Atlanta, Baltimore, Chicago, Cincinnati, Detroit, Dubuque, Indianapolis, Omaha, Philadelphia, Portland (OR), St. Paul-Minneapolis, San Antonio, San Francisco, Santa Fe, Washington, and the Dioceses of Allentown, Austin, Bismarck, Charleston, Charlotte, Colorado Springs, Columbus, Davenport, Des Moines, Duluth, Erie, Fort Wayne-South Bend, Jackson, Joliet, Las Cruces, Lexington, Madison, Manchester, New Ulm, Orlando, Owensboro, Phoenix, Providence, Pueblo, Rapid City, Richmond, Rockford, Saginaw, St. Cloud, St. Petersburg, San Angelo, San Jose, Santa Rosa, Sioux City, Springfield-Cape Girardeau, Springfield (IL), Stockton, Tucson, Tulsa, Tyler and Winona. Also in Canada, El Salvador, and Poland.

[1580] (O.S.F.)—SISTERS OF ST. FRANCIS OF THE IMMACULATE CONCEPTION D

Founded in the United States in 1890.

Motherhouse: *Immaculate Conception Convent Inc.,* 2408 W. Heading Ave., West Peoria, IL 61604-5096. Tel: 309-674-6168. Sr. Mary Barbara Buckley, Pres.; Sr. Mary Virginia Butkovich, Archivist.

Total number in community 62.

Properties owned and sponsored: *Immaculate Conception Convent,* Peoria, IL; *St. Joseph's Home of Peoria, St. Joseph's Home of Springfield,* in Illinois.

Represented in the Dioceses of Joliet, Peoria, Rapid City, and Springfield (IL).

[1590] (O.S.F.)—SISTERS OF ST. FRANCIS OF THE IMMACULATE HEART OF MARY (HANKINSON, NORTH DAKOTA) P

Founded in 1241 in Bavaria. First founded in the United States in 1913 at Collegeville, Minnesota.

General Motherhouse: Rome, Italy. Mother M. Irmtraud Eichelbronner, Supr. Gen.

Province of Hankinson (1928): *Sisters of St. Francis Motherhouse,* Hankinson, ND 58041. Tel: 701-242-7197. Sr. Ann Marie Friederichs, Prov.

Professed Sisters 76.

Legal Holdings or Titles: *St. Gerard's Community Nursing Home,* Hankinson, ND; *Oakes Community Hospital,* Oakes, ND; *St. Anne's Guest Home, Grand Forks,* ND.

Ministry in the field of Religious and Academic Education; Health Care in Hospitals; Homes for the Aged.

Represented in the Dioceses of Crookston and Fargo.

[1600] (O.S.F.)—SISTERS OF ST. FRANCIS OF THE MARTYR ST. GEORGE P

Founded in Thuine, Germany. First United States foundation in 1923.

General Motherhouse: Thuine, Germany. Mother Margaretha Maria Brand, Supr. Gen.

American Province St. Elizabeth: *Provincial Motherhouse, St. Francis Convent and Novitiate,* 2120 Central Ave., P.O. Box 9020, Alton, IL 62002-9020. Tel: 618-463-2750; 463-2755. Mother M. Ingeborg Rohner, O.S.F., Prov.

Worldwide Total 1,900.

Total in American Province 159.

Properties owned and sponsored: *Saint Anthony's Hospital,* Alton, IL; *St. Francis Day Care Center,* Alton, IL; *Mother of Good Counsel Home,* St. Louis, MO; *Saint Clare Hospital in Alton, Illinois.*

Sisters serve and staff: Hospitals; Home for Chronically ill; Social Service Center; Foreign Missions; Day Care Centers; Retirement Homes for the Aged; Grade & High Schools; Retirement Homes for Priests.

Represented in the Archdioceses of St. Louis and Washington, and the Dioceses of Lincoln, Metuchen, Peoria, Springfield (IL) and Tulsa.

[1620] (O.S.F.)—SISTERS OF SAINT FRANCIS OF MILLVALE, PENNSYLVANIA P

Motherhouse and Novitiate (1871): *St. Francis Convent,* Mt. Alvernia, 146 Hawthorne Rd., Millvale P.O., Pittsburgh, PA 15209. Tel: 412-821-2200; Fax: 412-821-3318. Sr. Joanne Bich, O.S.F., Supr. Gen.; Sr. M. Thomasita Heller, O.S.F., Community Archivist.

Total number in community 233.

Properties owned: *Mt. Alvernia High School,* Millvale, PA; *Mt. Alvernia Day Care & Learning Center,* Pittsburgh, PA.

Sponsored or managed facilities: *St. Francis Health System; St. Francis Hospital,* New Castle, PA.

Ministry in the following areas: Parochial Schools; Academic High Schools; Catechetical Centers; Hospitals; Consolidated Elementary Schools; Schools of Nursing; Day Care and Learning Center; Montessori School.

Represented in the Archdioceses of Baltimore, Buffalo, Chicago, Cleveland, Los Angeles, Miami, Newark, New York, Santa Fe, and the Dioceses of Altoona-Johnstown, Erie, Gaylord, Greensburg, Lansing, Lubbock, and Pittsburgh. Also in Canada, Nigeria, San Juan.

[1630] (O.S.F.)—SISTERS OF ST. FRANCIS OF PENANCE AND CHRISTIAN CHARITY P

Founded in Holland in 1835. First Foundation in the U.S. in 1874.

General Motherhouse: Rome, Italy. Sr. Christina Pecoraro, Gen. Min.

Universal number in Congregation 2,374.

Holy Name Province (1928): *Sisters of St. Francis,* 4421 Lower River Rd., Stella Niagara, NY 14144. Tel: 716-754-4312. Sr. Mary McCarrick, O.S.F., Prov. Minister.

Total number in community 220.

Legal Holdings: *Stella Niagara Education Park,* Stella Niagara, NY; *Buffalo Academy of the Sacred Heart,* Eggertsville, NY.

• 1947 CCS Founded • 1948 LaSalle Military Academy, NY • 1949 St. Joseph Church, Brooklyn • 1950 St. Anastasia Church, Douglaston, NY • 1951 St. Ann Church, Flushing, NY • 1952 Holy Cross Church, NY, NY • 1953 St. John the Bapti

50 Successful Fund Raising Years as Counsel to Catholic Institutions Worldwide.

In 1947, Community Counselling Service Co., Inc. was founded in Brooklyn, New York as a Catholic parish fund-raising company, conducting campaigns for the important needs of local churches. Over the past five decades, CCS has become a global company serving as counsel to more Catholic parishes, dioceses, institutions and organizations than any other firm in the world. We have raised close to $3,000,00,000 for Catholic causes during our history – and nearly $2,000,000,000 in the past 10 years alone.

We are extremely proud of our deep rooted association with the Catholic Church and we pledge to provide the same high quality services for the next 50 years.

CCS

CELEBRATES 50 YEARS

Community Counselling Service Co., Inc.

Fund Raising/Public Relations

800.233.6733

New York • Chicago • San Francisco • London • Toronto • Dublin

ARCHDIOCESE OF BALTIMC

ARCHDIOCESE OF DETRO

ARCHDIOCESE OF NEW YC

DIOCESE OF BRIDGEPOR

DIOCESE OF NEW ULM

1987 Diocese of Raleigh • 1988 Diocese of Columbus • 1989 Diocese of St. Cloud • 1990 Archdiocese of New York • 1991 Archdiocese of Philadelphia • 1992 Diocese of Trenton • 1993 Archdiocese of New Orleans • 1994 Archdiocese of Detroit • 1995 Diocese of Bridgeport • 1996 Diocese of Providence • 1997 Diocese of Brooklyn

• 1980 St. Patrick's College, Maynooth, Ireland • 1981 Archdiocese of Portland • 1982 Archdiocese of San Francisco • 1983 Diocese of Metuchen • 1984 Diocese of Nassau in the Bahamas • 1985 Providence College • 1986 Paulist Fathers, NY •

Ministry in the field of Academic Education at all levels; Foreign Mission Work; Health and Hospital Care; Social Work; Pastoral Ministry.

Represented in the Archdioceses of Chicago, Cincinnati, Louisville, Miami, Sante Fe, Seattle, and the Dioceses of Buffalo, Columbus, Orlando, Paterson, Raleigh, St. Petersburg, Trenton, Venice, Wheeling-Charleston and Youngstown.

Sacred Heart Province (1939): *Provincial Motherhouse-Marycrest,* 2851 W. 52nd Ave., Denver, CO 80221. Tel: 303-458-6270. Sr. Gloria Shuffer, Prov. Minister.

Total number in community 85.

Sisters Serve and Staff: High Schools, Grammar Schools; Parish Ministries; Apostolate of Aging; Diocesan Biblical School; Hospital Pastoral Ministry; Emergency Housing; Home for Neglected Children; Retreat Ministry; Hospital and Parish Nursing; Formation Programs; Administrative.

Legal Holdings or Titles: *Kenmare Community Hospital,* Kenmare, ND; *St. Joseph's Hospital; St. Joseph's Hospital Foundation; St. Elizabeth Convent,* Minot, ND; *Marycrest Motherhouse Queen of Peace Convent, House of Prayer Damen House - Home for Single Women & Children; Sacred Heart Corporation Sisters of St. Francis Foundation-Sacred Heart Province,* Denver, CO; *St. Anthony's Hospital St. Anthony's Convent,* O'Neill, NE; *St. Francis Home, (Home for Abused Native American Children),* Manderson, SD; *St. Mary's Home, (Home for the Aged),* St. Paul, MN; *Marian Residence, Convent for Retired Sisters,* Alliance, NE; *St. Francis Convent St. Clare Convent,* Alliance, NE.

Represented in the Archdioceses of Denver, Omaha, St. Paul-Minneapolis and Sante Fe, and the Dioceses of Bismarck, Grand Island, Oakland, Rapid City, Las Vegas and Tulsa.

St. Francis Province (1939): *Mt. Alverno,* 3910 Bret Harte Dr., P.O. Box 1028, Redwood City, CA 94064. Tel: 415-369-1725. Sr. Michele Mangan, Prov. Minister.

Total number in community 109.

Legal Title: *Sisters of St. Francis Charitable Trust; Sisters of St. Francis - Mount Alverno.*

Ministry in the following areas: Grammar Schools; Formation House; Colleges; Diocesan Offices; Parish Ministry; Pastoral Ministry; Catholic Social Services Agencies; Education Programs; Secondary Education; Hospitals; Residence for Retired Men and Women; Day Home; CCD Centers; Retreat-Conference Centers; Apostolic Projects; ESL.

Represented in the Archdioceses of Los Angeles, Portland (OR), San Francisco and Seattle, and the Dioceses of Monterey, Oakland, Reno-Las Vegas, Sacramento, San Diego, San Jose and Stockton.

[1640] (O.S.F.)—SISTERS OF ST. FRANCIS OF PERPETUAL ADORATION P

Founded in Germany in 1863. First foundation in the United States in 1875.

Generalate: Olpe, Westfalen, West Germany. Sr. Xaveria Kronen, Supr Gen.

Universal total in congregation 821.

Province of the Immaculate Heart of Mary (1875): *Provincial House and Novitiate, St. Francis Convent,* Box 766, Mishawaka, IN 46546-0766. Tel: 219-259-5427. Sr. M. Rose Agnes Pfautsch, O.S.F., Prov.

Total number in community 181.

Ministry in the field of Academic Education at all levels; Health Care in Hospitals and Nursing Homes.

Properties owned: *Sisters of St. Francis of Perpetual Adoration, Inc.; St. Francis Convent,* Mishawaka, IN; *St. Francis College of Fort Wayne, Inc.,* Fort Wayne, IN; *Sisters of St. Francis Health Services, Inc.; Alverno Administrative Services, Alverno Health Corporation,* Mishawaka, IN. *Sisters of St. Francis Health Services, Inc.,* Corporate Office, Mishawaka, IN, owns the following: *St. Elizabeth Healthcare Center,* Delphi, IN; *St. Francis Hospital & Health Centers,* Beech Grove, IN; *St. James Hospital and Health Centers,* Chicago Heights, IL; *St. Francis Hospital,* Evanston, IL; *St. Margaret Mercy Health Care Centers, North Campus,* Hammond, IN; *St. Margaret Mercy Health Care Centers, South Campus,* Dyer, IN; *St. Elizabeth Hospital Medical Center,* Lafayette, IN; *St. Joseph Hospital and Health Centers,* Memphis, TN; *St. Anthony Hospital and Health Centers,* Michigan City, IN; *St. James-Hospital Medical Clinic,* Beecher, IL; *St. James Manor,* Crete, IL; *St. Francis Extended Care,* Evanston, IL; *Franciscan Health Care Center,* Louisville, KY; *St. Joseph Family Health Center,* Memphis, TN; *St. Joseph Family Health Center,* Fraser Blvd., Memphis, TN; *Alverno Administrative Services,* Beech Grove, IN; *St. Francis Health Center,* Lincolnwood, IL; *Suburban Heights-St. James Hospital Medical Clinic,* Frankfort, IL; *St. James Hospital Medical Clinic,* Lansing, IL. *Alverno Health Corporation* owns the following: *Northern Indiana Medical Laboratory Services,* Michigan City, IN.

Represented in the Archdioceses of Chicago, Indianapolis, Louisville and New Orleans, and the Dioceses of Fort Wayne-South Bend, Gary, Joliet, Lafayette (IN) and Memphis.

Province of St. Joseph (March 19, 1932): *Provincial House and Formation House-Mt. St. Francis,* 7665 Assisi Heights, Colorado Springs, CO 80919. Tel: 719-598-5486. Sr. Clarice Gentrup, Prov.

Professed Sisters 132.

Ministry in Education; Hospitals; Homes for the Aged; Parish/Pastoral Ministry; Religious Education Centers.

Represented in the Archdioceses of Denver, Omaha and Santa Fe, and the Dioceses of Amarillo, Colorado Springs, Gallup, Grand Island, Lincoln and Rapid City.

[1650] (O.S.F.)—THE SISTERS OF ST. FRANCIS OF PHILADELPHIA P

Founded in the United States in 1855.

Congregational Motherhouse: *Convent of Our Lady of Angels,* Aston, PA 19014. Tel: 215-459-4125. Sr. Marie Lucey, O.S.F., Congregational Min.; Sr. Esther Anderson, O.S.F., Asst. Congregational Min.; Sr. M. Andrew, Community Archivist.

Total number in community 918.

Properties owned: *Formation House,* Puerto Rico; *Sisters of St. Francis,* Sea Isle City, NJ; *Franciscan Residence,* Hamilton Square, NJ; *Bay House,* Tacoma, WA; *Marion House,* Tacoma, WA; *St. Ann Convent,* Tacoma, WA; *Neumann College,* Aston, PA; *Assisi House,* Aston, PA; *Franciscan Health System,* Aston, PA; *Portiuncula Convent,* Aston, PA; *St. Mary Convent,* Langhorne, PA; *St. Francis Convent,* Lancaster, PA; *Franciscan Residence,* Langhorne, PA; *St. Agnes Convent,* Philadelphia, PA; *Neumann Convent,* Reading, PA; *The Catholic High School of Baltimore,* Baltimore, MD; *St. Joseph Counseling Center,* Spokane, WA; *Convent of Our Lady of Angels,* Portland, OR; *Portiuncula Convent,* Philadelphia, PA; *Franciscan Renewal Center,* Portland, OR; *Sisters of St. Francis of Philadelphia, Canticle House,* Philadelphia, PA; *Sisters of St. Francis of Philadelphia, TAU Convent,* Philadelphia, PA; *St. Clare Renewal Center,* Aston, PA; *Sisters of St. Francis of Philadelphia, Our Lady of the Valley,* Aston, PA; *Mt. Alvernia Convent,* Aston, PA; *St. Clare Convent,* Trenton, NJ.

Ministry in Health Care; Eldercare; Academic and Religious Education at all Levels; Specialized Education; Parish Ministry; Social Services; Family Centers; Renewal Centers; Seminaries; Diocesan Offices; Retreat Ministry; National Organizations.

Represented in the Archdioceses of Anchorage, Baltimore, Boston, Hartford, Los Angeles, Miami, Mobile, New Orleans, New York, Newark, Philadelphia, Portland (OR), San Juan, Seattle, Santa Fe, St. Louis, Washington, and the Dioceses of Albany, Allentown, Arlington, Baker, Birmingham, Caguas (PR), Camden, Charleston, Cheyenne, Fort Wayne-South Bend, Gallup, Harrisburg, Honolulu, La Crosse, Las Cruces, Lexington, Metuchen, Oakland, Orlando, Raleigh, San Bernardino, San Diego, Spokane, Trenton, Tucson, Venice, Wilmington and Wheeling-Charleston. Also in Ireland, Canada, Central America, England, Zambia, Kenya, Ethiopia, West Indies and Dominican Republic.

[1660] (O.S.F.)—SISTERS OF SAINT FRANCIS OF THE PROVIDENCE OF GOD P

Founded in Pittsburgh in 1922.

Motherhouse: *St. Francis Convent,* 3603 McRoberts Rd., Pittsburgh, PA 15234-2398. Tel: 412-882-9911; Fax: 412-885-7210. Sr. Joanne Brazinski, O.S.F., Gen. Supr.

Total professed 118.

Properties owned and sponsored: *Sisters of St. Francis of the Providence of God; Sisters of St. Francis,* Mt. Vernon Ill., Inc.; *Sisters of St. Francis of the Providence of God Ministries Corporation; St. Francis Academy Franciscan Child Day Care Center; Franciscan Spirit and Life Center.*

Ministry in the field of Education; Health Care; Social Service; Pastoral, Parish & Retreat Ministries; Retreat Directors; Prison Chaplains; Foreign Mission work in Brazil & Lithuania.

Represented in the Dioceses of Albany, Belleville, Galveston-Houston, Grand Rapids, Greensburg, and Pittsburgh.

[1670] (O.S.F.)—SISTER OF ST. FRANCIS OF SAVANNAH, MO. P

Founded in Austria, 1850. Founded in the United States, August 22, 1922.

Provincial House and Novitiate: La Verna Heights, Box 488, 104 E. Park, Savannah, MO 64485-0488. Tel: 816-324-3179; Fax: 816-324-6512. Sr. Kathleen Reichert, Prov. Supr.

Total number in community 31.

Ministry in the field of Education; CCD Centers; Health Care and Hospital Work; Housing for Elderly, Persons with Aids, Abuse Victims and Unwed Mothers; Pastoral Care; Food Pantry.

Legal Holdings and Titles: *Sisters of St. Francis of Savannah, Inc. Maintenance and Custodial Care Trust of the Franciscan Sisters of Savannah La Verna Village Apartment Units for Senior Citizens and Handicapped La Verna Village Nursing Home, Inc. La Verna Heights Provincial House and Retirement Center.*

Represented in the Archdioceses of Kansas City in Kansas, New Orleans and in the Dioceses of Jefferson City and Kansas City-St. Joseph.

[1680] (O.S.F.)—SCHOOL SISTERS OF ST. FRANCIS P

Founded in the United States in 1874.

General Motherhouse: 1501 S. Layton Blvd., Milwaukee, WI 53215. Tel: 414-384-4105; Fax: 414-645-7198. Sr. Frances Brenner, O.S.F., Pres.; Sr. Phyllis Vater, First Vice Pres.; Sr. Raphaela Munch, Vice Pres.; Sr. Alida Lopez, Vice Pres.; Sr. Charlita Foxhoven, Treas.; Sr. Constance Halbur, Archivist.

Total in Congregation 1,638; Total in U.S. 1,084.

Properties owned: *St. Joseph Convent,* Milwaukee, WI; *Generalate-School Sisters of St. Francis, Inc., School Sisters of St. Francis of St. Joseph's Convent, New Castle, Inc.*

U.S. Province: 1515 S. Layton Blvd., Milwaukee, WI 53215. Tel: 414-384-1515. Provincial Team: Sr. Celestine Schall; Sr. Therese Thoenen; Sr. Jane Elyse Russell.

Sisters serve and staff: Universities, Colleges, Seminaries, High Schools, Grade Schools, Pre Schools, Adult and Special Education; National and Diocesan Offices; Hospitals and Nursing Homes; School & Parish Musicians; Retreat and Spiritual Direction; Social Ministries; Campus Ministry; Psychotherapy; Home Health Care Service; Religious Education and CCD; Pastoral Ministry; Pastoral Associate; Health Pastoral Care; Retirement Homes; Overseas Missions; Mission Projects; Special Service to Women; Fine Arts; Home Missions.

Properties owned and sponsored: *Alverno College,* Milwaukee, WI; *Clement Manor,* Greenfield, WI; *Villa Clement,* West Allis, WI; *Maryhill Manor,* Niagra, WI; *New Cassel,* Omaha, NE; *Clare Towers I,* Milwaukee, WI; *Clare Towers II,* Milwaukee, WI; *Telos, Inc.,* Milwaukee, WI; *St. Clare Management, Inc.,* Milwaukee, WI; *Marian Hall,* Milwaukee, WI; *Sacred Heart Convent,* Milwaukee, WI; *St. Joseph Convent,* Campbellsport, WI; *School Sisters of St. Francis Foundation, Inc.,* Omaha, NE; *School Sisters of St. Francis of St. Joseph's Convent, Milwaukee, Wisconsin, Inc.; Convergence, Inc.,* Milwaukee, WI; *Vision Ministries,* Milwaukee, WI; *The School Sisters of Saint Francis of St. Joseph's Convent, Milwaukee, Wisconsin, Inc. - Congregational Support Charitable Trust,* Milwaukee, WI.

Represented in the Archdioceses of Anchorage, Chicago, Denver, Dubuque, Indianapolis, Los Angeles, Milwaukee, New York, Oklahoma City, Omaha, Portland (OR), St. Louis, St. Paul-Minneapolis, San Antonio, Santa Fe, Washington, and the Dioceses of Buffalo, Charleston, Davenport, Des Moines, Dodge, El Paso, Great Falls, Green Bay, Jackson, Jefferson City, Joliet, Kansas City-St. Joseph, Knoxville, La Crosse, Lexington, Lincoln, Madison, Memphis, Nashville, New Ulm, Orange, Palm Beach, Phoenix, Rapid City, Rockford, St. Cloud, San Bernardino, San Diego, Santa Rosa, Springfield (IL), St. Petersburg, Superior, Trenton, Tucson, Venice, Wheeling-Charleston and Winona.

[1690] (O.S.F.)—SCHOOL SISTERS OF THE THIRD ORDER OF ST. FRANCIS (PITTSBURGH, PA.) P

First foundation in the U.S. in 1913.

General Motherhouse: Rome, Italy.

Motherhouse and Novitiate: *Mount Assisi Convent,* 934 Forest Ave., Bellevue, Pittsburgh, PA 15202. Tel: 412-761-6004. Sr. Elaine Hromulak, O.S.F., Prov. Supr. Tel: 412-761-2855.

Total number in community 91.

Legal Title: *School Sisters of the Third Order of St. Francis; School Sisters of the Third Order of St. Francis, of Texas.*

Ministry in the following areas: the field of academic education at all levels; CCD Centers; Pastoral Ministry; Pastoral Associate; Residence Home for Aged Women; Mission Work in Chile & South Africa; Hospital Ministry; Campus Ministry; House of Prayer.

Represented in the Archdiocese of San Antonio, and the Dioceses of Erie, Greensburg, Phoenix, Pitts-

burgh and San Angelo. Also in South Africa and Chile.

[1695] (O.S.F.)—SCHOOL SISTERS OF THE THIRD ORDER OF ST. FRANCIS (PANHANDLE, TEXAS) P

Founded in Austria, 1723; The Vienna Foundation in 1845. First founded in the United States, 1931.

GENERAL MOTHERHOUSE: Vienna, Austria.

AMERICAN CENTER AND NOVITIATE: P.O. Box 906, Panhandle, TX 79068. Tel: 806-537-3182. Mother M. Bernadette, Supr.

Total number in U.S. 26.

Ministry in the following areas: Grammar Schools; Confraternity Classes; Home for the Aged.

Represented in the Dioceses of Amarillo and Victoria.

[1700] (O.S.F.)—SCHOOL SISTERS OF THE THIRD ORDER OF ST. FRANCIS (BETHLEHEM, PA.) P

Founded in Austria, 1843. First founded in the United States, 1913.

GENERAL MOTHERHOUSE: Rome, Italy.

BETHLEHEM PROVINCE AND NOVITIATE: 395 Bridle Path Rd., Bethlehem, PA 18017. Tel: 610-866-2597; Fax: 610-861-7478. Sr. M. Xavier Bomberger, Prov. Supr.

Sisters 63.

Properties owned: *St. Francis Academy Kindergarten; St. Francis Day Care; St. Francis Center for Renewal,* Bethlehem, PA.

Represented in the Archdiocese of Newark, and the Dioceses of Allentown, Metuchen, Paterson, Scranton and Springfield (MA). Also in Chile, India and Rome, Italy.

[1705] (O.S.F.)—THE SISTERS OF ST. FRANCIS OF ASSISI P

(Sisters of Penance and Charity)

Founded in the United States in 1849.

GENERAL MOTHERHOUSE: *St. Francis Convent,* 3221 S. Lake Dr., St. Francis, WI 53235-3799. Tel: 414-744-1160; Fax: 414-744-7193. Sr. Marita Maschmann, O.S.F., Dir.

Total number in community 378.

Legal Titles: *The Sisters of St. Francis of Assisi; The Ongoing Community Support Fund of the Sisters of St. Francis.*

Goals of the Congregation are: to bring the healing, teaching, reconciling and liberating power of Jesus into the human situations in which we live and minister; to be in solidarity with the poor through the work of justice and peace; to appreciate and affirm and to encourage the development of each community member and each community apostolate for the sake of full effectiveness in the ministry of the Church; and to work effectively toward implementing co-responsibility, subsidiarity and accountability at all levels within the Congregation.

Sponsored Corporations: *St. Ann Adult Day Care,* St. Francis, WI; *St. Mary's Academy,* Milwaukee, WI; *Cardinal Stritch College,* Milwaukee, WI; *St. Coletta's,* Jefferson, WI; *St. Coletta School Foundation of Jefferson Charitable Trust,* Jefferson, WI; *St. Coletta's of Illinois,* Palos Park, IL; *The Lt. Joseph P. Kennedy Jr. School for Exceptional Children,* Palos Park, IL; *St. Coletta's of Illinois Foundation,* Palos Park, IL; *St. Coletta's of Massachusetts: Cardinal Cushing School and Training Center,* Hanover, MA; *Cushing Residence, Inc.,* Hanover, MA; *The Cardinal Cushing School Foundation of Hanover Charitable Trust,* Hanover, MA; *St. Coletta Day School,* Braintree, MA. Services to the Elderly: *Alverno Housing Corporation,* Jefferson, WI; *Canticle Court, Inc.; Juniper Court, Inc.,* Milwaukee, WI.

Represented in the Archdioceses of Boston, Chicago, Denver, Los Angeles, Milwaukee, Philadelphia, San Antonio, San Francisco, Santa Fe and Seattle, and the Dioceses of Birmingham, Cheyenne, Davenport, Des Moines, Fall River, Joliet, Gary, Green Bay, La Crosse, Little Rock, Madison, New Ulm, Palm Beach, Peoria, Phoenix, Reno-Las Vegas, Rockford, San Diego, San Jose, Santa Rosa, Steubenville, Superior, Toledo, Tucson and Winona. Also in Taiwan.

[1710] (O.S.F.)—CONGREGATION OF THE THIRD ORDER OF ST. FRANCIS OF MARY IMMACULATE, JOLIET, IL P

Founded in the United States, Joliet, Illinois, in 1865.

GENERAL MOTHERHOUSE: *St. Francis Convent,* 520 Plainfield Ave., Joliet, IL 60435. Tel: 815-727-3686. Sr. Mary Jean Morris, O.S.F., Pres.; Sr. Marian Voelker, O.S.F., Community Archivist.

Total number in community 351.

Legal Title: *Congregation of the Third Order of St. Francis of Mary Immaculate,* Joliet, IL; *Retirement Plan Trust of the Congregation of the Third Order of St. Francis of Mary Immaculate,* Joliet, IL.

Ministry in the following areas: School and Adult Education; Home for Emotionally Disturbed Children; Retirement Home; House of Prayer. Also engaged in Religious Education; Social Services; Spiritual Direction; Nursing and Health Services; Hospital and Parish Ministry; Food Service; and Prison ministry.

Represented in the Archdioceses of Boston, Chicago, Cincinnati, Denver, Detroit, Dubuque, Indianapolis, Los Angeles, Miami, New York, Omaha, St. Louis, Washington, and the Dioceses of Cleveland, Colorado Springs, Columbus, Dodge City, Fort Wayne-South Bend, Gary, Joliet, Lansing, Lexington, Palm Beach, Phoenix, Peoria, Rockford, St. Cloud, St. Petersburg, San Diego, Springfield, Springfield-Cape Girardeau, Springfield (IL), Stockton, Superior, Toledo, Tucson, Venice and Youngstown. Also in Agana, Guam and Brazil.

[1720] (O.S.F.)—SISTERS OF THE THIRD ORDER REGULAR OF ST. FRANCIS OF THE CONGREGATION OF OUR LADY OF LOURDES P

Founded in the United States in 1877.

ADMINISTRATION CENTER: *Assisi Heights,* Rochester, MN 55903. Tel: 507-280-2198; Fax: 507-282-7762. Sr. Valerie Usher, O.S.F., Pres./Community Min. Tel 507-280-2198. Sr. Mary Lonan Reilly, Community Archivists.

Total number in community 420.

Properties owned and sponsored: *Tau Center,* Winona, MN; *Assisi Heights,* Rochester, MN; *Saint Anne Hospice,* Winona, MN.

Ministry in the following areas: Education Services; Pastoral Concerns Development; Religious Life Development; Spiritual Life Development; Community Life Development; Social Concerns Development; Business Services; Health Care Services; Support Services.

Represented in the Archdioceses of Baltimore, Boston, Chicago, Denver, Dubuque, Indianapolis, Milwaukee, Newark, Oklahoma City, St. Paul-Minneapolis, St. Louis, Santa Fe, Seattle and Washington, and the Dioceses of Brownsville, Charleston, Charlotte, Columbus, Colorado Springs, Covington, Duluth, Fargo, Fort Wayne-South Bend, Great Falls-Billings, Helena, Joliet, La Crosse, Lexington, Madison, Memphis, New Ulm, Orange, Owensboro, Pueblo, St. Cloud, San Bernardino, San Diego, Savannah, Sioux City, Sioux Falls, Springfield-Cape Girardeau, Springfield (IL), Superior, Tucson and Winona. Also in Thailand, Colombia, Peru and Kenya.

[1730] (O.S.F.)—CONGREGATION OF THE SISTERS OF THE THIRD ORDER OF ST. FRANCIS, OLDENBURG, IN. P

Founded in U.S., Oldenburg, Indiana in 1851.

GENERAL MOTHERHOUSE AND NOVITIATE: *Convent of the Immaculate Conception,* Oldenburg, IN 47036. Tel: 812-934-2475. Sr. Amy Kistner, Congregational Minister.

Total number in community 385.

Sisters serve & staff: Liberal Arts College, Academy, High Schools, Elementary Schools; Navajo, Crow Indian and Cheyenne Missions; Religious Education Centers; Hospital & Parish Ministry; Apostolate of Aging; Diocesan Offices; Retreat & Counseling Ministry; Hispanic Ministry; Justice & Peace Offices; Clerical Staff; Social Services.

Properties owned: *Marian College,* Indianapolis, IN; *ICA Academy,* Oldenburg, IN.

Represented in the Archdioceses of Chicago, Cincinnati, Detroit, Indianapolis, Los Angeles, New York, St. Louis, and the Dioceses of Cleveland, Columbus, Covington, Evansville, Fort Wayne, Gallup, Great Falls-Billings, Helena, Jefferson City, Lexington, Peoria, St. Augustine and Wheeling-Charleston. Also in Korea and Mexico.

[1760] (O.S.F.)—SISTERS OF THE THIRD ORDER OF ST. FRANCIS OF PENANCE AND OF CHARITY P

Founded in Tiffin, Ohio in 1869.

GENERAL MOTHERHOUSE: *St. Francis Convent,* St. Francis Ave., Tiffin, OH 44883. Tel: 419-447-0435; Fax: 419-447-1612. Sr. Jacquelyn Doepker, Community Minister.

Total number in community 153.

Legal Title: *Sisters of St. Francis of Tiffin, OH.*

Properties Owned or Sponsored: *St. Francis Villas, Inc., St. Francis Home, Inc.,* Tiffin, OH.

Ministry in the following areas: Parochial Schools; Ministry to the Aged; Parish Ministry; Retreat and Renewal Centers; Diocese Offices; Health Care; Health-Pastoral Care; Administration.

Represented in the Archdioceses of Cincinnati, Indianapolis, Santa Fe, and the Dioceses of Brownsville, Columbus, Charlotte, Davenport, Evansville, Jackson, Lansing, Lexington, Owensboro, Rockford, Toledo, Venice and Wheeling-Charleston. Also in Mexico.

[1770] (O.S.F.)—THE SISTERS OF THE THIRD ORDEROF ST. FRANCIS (EAST PEORIA, ILLINOIS.) P

Founded in the United States in 1877.

MOTHERHOUSE: St. Francis Lane, East Peoria, IL 61611. Tel: 309-699-7215. Sr. Mary Ellen Flannery, Major Supr.

Total number in community 75.

Properties owned and sponsored: *Saint Francis Medical Center,* Peoria, IL; *St. Joseph Medical Center,* Bloomington, IL; *St. Mary Medical Center,* Galesburg, IL; *Saint James Hospital,* Pontiac, IL; *Saint Anthony Medical Center,* Rockford, IL; *Saint Francis Hospital,* Escanaba, MI; *St. Francis Continuation Care and Nursing Home Center,* Burlington, IA; *Saint Joseph Hospital,* Belvidere, IL; *St. Anthony's Continuing Care Center,* Rock Island, IL; *St. Mary of the Angels Convent,* Rock Island, IL; *OSF Healthcare System,* Peoria, IL; *OSF Healthcare Foundation,* Peoria, IL; *Motherhouse,* East Peoria, IL.

Represented in the Dioceses of Davenport, Marquette, Peoria and Rockford.

[1780] (F.S.P.A.)—CONGREGATION OF THE SISTERS OF THE THIRD ORDER OF ST. FRANCIS OF PERPETUAL ADORATION P

(Francisan Sisters of Perpetual Adoration)

Founded in the United States in 1849.

GENERALATE: 912 Market St., La Crosse, WI 54601. Tel: 608-782-5610; Fax: 608-782-6301. Sr. Marla Lang, Pres.; Sr. Jolyce Greteman, Archivist.

Total number in Congregation 525.

Properties owned and sponsored: *St. Joseph Memorial Hospital, Inc.,* Hillsboro, WI; *St. Anthony Regional Hospital, Inc.,* Carroll, IA; *Viterbo College, Inc.,* La Crosse, WI.

EASTERN REGION: 3560 Hwy. 51 N, Arbor Vitae, WI 54568-9540. Tel: 715-385-2732; 385-3243. Sr. Michon Desmond, Regl. Leader.

Total number in region 286.

Represented in the Archdioceses of Chicago, Milwaukee, Mobile, St. Paul-Minneapolis, Spokane, Seattle, Washington, and the Dioceses of Albany, Amarillo, Davenport, Erie, Green Bay, Helena, Joliet, La Crosse, Lexington, Lafayette, Lexington, Madison, Rockford, Savannah, Springfield-Cape Girardeau and Superior. Also in Canada and Mexico.

CENTRAL REGION OF FRANCISCAN SISTERS OF PERPETUAL ADORATION (1966): P.O. Box 190, Hiawatha, IA 52233-0190. Tel: 319-393-5982; Office Sec. 393-6092. Sr. Karen Flottmeier, Regl. Admin.

Total number in region 178.

Ministry in the field of Academic Education at all Levels; Religious Education and Parish Centers; Health Care; Hospital and Parish Ministry; Diocesan Offices; Mission Centers.

Represented in the Archdioceses of Chicago, Dubuque, Milwaukee, Mobile, Santa Fe, St. Louis and St. Paul-Minneapolis, and the Dioceses of Belleville, Davenport, Des Moines, El Paso, Jackson, La Crosse, Madison, Oakland, Peoria, Reno-Las Vegas, St. Cloud, Sioux City, Springfield-Cape Girardeau and Winona. Also in Caroline-Marshall Islands, Guatemala, Mexico and Zimbabwe.

WESTERN REGION (1985): *Mary of the Angels,* 4624 E. Jamieson, Spokane, WA 99223-2028. Tel: 509-448-0674. Sr. Patricia Gordon, Regl. Admin.

Professed Sisters 67.

Sisters serve and staff: Religious Education; Education-University, College, High School, Elementary, Special Education; Home Health Care; Pastoral Ministry; Religious Education-Administrative, Adult, Consultative, Secondary, Elementary; Secretarial; Social Services; Health Services; Spiritual Direction.

Represented in the Archdioceses of Denver, Los Angeles, Portland (OR), Santa Fe and Seattle, and the Dioceses of Boise, Helena, Honolulu, La Crosse, Oakland, Orange, Phoenix, Reno-Las Vegas, San Jose, Spokane and Tuscon. Also in Guam and El Salvador.

[1800] (O.S.F.)—SISTERS OF ST. FRANCIS OF THE THIRD ORDER REGULAR (WILLIAMSVILLE, NEW YORK) P

MOTHERHOUSE: *St. Mary of the Angels Convent of Perpetual Adoration,* 400 Mill St., P.O. Box 275, Wil-

liamsville, NY 14231. Tel: 716-632-2155. Sr. Patricia Burkard, Gen. Minister.
Total number in community 143.
Sisters serve and staff: Universities; High Schools Grammar Schools; Hospitals; Nursing Homes & Homes for the Aged; Pastoral Ministry in Parishes, Hospitals & Nursing Homes; Diocesan Offices.
Properties owned and/or sponsored: *Mount St. Mary's Hospital,* Lewiston, NY; *Mount St. Mary's LTC Facility, Inc.,* Niagara Falls, NY; *St. Francis Geriatric & Health Care Services,* Buffalo, NY; *Holy Family Home,* Williamsville, NY.
Represented in the Archdioceses of Chicago and San Juan, and the Dioceses of Buffalo, Charleston, Gallup, Harrisburg, Ogdensburgh, Rochester, and Syracuse. Also in Africa.

[1810] (O.S.F.)—BERNARDINE FRANCISCAN SISTERS P

Founded in the United States in 1894.
Bernardine Franciscan Sisters Generalate: 403 Allendale Rd., King of Prussia, PA 19406. Tel: 610-337-3864; Fax: 610-337-4359. Sr. Mary Margaret Jackson, O.S.F., Gen. Min.
Universal number in Congregation 573; total number in U.S. Provinces 460.
Bernardine Franciscan Sisters: United States Province Offices, 460 St. Bernardine St., Reading, PA 19607-1737. Tel: 610-777-4174; Fax: 610-777-3973. Sr. Deborah Ann Surgot, O.S.F., Co-Dir., Office of Communications; Sr. Patrice Marie Klausing, O.S.F., Co-Dir., Office of Communications; Sr. Kateri Peake, O.S.F., Dir. Personnel; Sr. Dolorice Domin, O.S.F., Dir. Life Development; Sr. Rosemary Stets, O.S.F., Dir. Vocations and Assocs.; Sr. Miriam Keiser, O.S.F., Dir. Finance and Health Benefits Office.
Ministry in the field of academic education at all levels - preschool to college; religious education of children & adults; hospitals, health & home care; retreat work; social work.
Represented in the 24 Archdioceses and Dioceses and 5 Overseas Dioceses.
Our Lady of the Rosary Convent (Area 1): 27405 West Ten Mile Rd., Farmington Hills, MI 48336. Tel: 810-476-3576; Fax: 810-476-6950. Sr. Maria Christine Keller, O.S.F., Prov. Minister.
Represented in the Archdioceses of Detroit, Los Angeles, St. Paul-Minneapolis and in the Dioceses of Allentown, Harrisburg, Lansing, and Tucson.
Our Lady of Grace Convent (Area 2): 106 S. Seventh Ave., West Reading, PA 19611. Tel: 610-372-3390; Fax: 610-372-2786. Sr. Mary Sninsky, O.S.F., Provincial Min.
Represented in the Archdioceses of Miami, Philadelphia, San Antonio, San Juan, Washington, and the Dioceses Arlington, Lexington, Richmond, and Trenton.
Our Lady of Grace Convent (Area 3): 106 S. Seventh Ave., West Reading, PA 19611. Tel: 610-372-3544; Fax: 610-372-2786. Sr. Lynn Rachelle Pascoe, O.S.F., Provincial Min.
Represented in the Archdioceses of Boston, Hartford, Newark,, and the Dioceses of Bridgeport, Metuchen, Providence, Saginaw, and Scranton.
Properties owned and sponsored in the U.S.: *Alvernia Montessori School,* Reading, PA; *Bernardine Franciscans, Delaware County,* Villanova, PA; *Heart of Mary Convent,* Stamford, CT; *Lt. Joseph P. Kennedy Memorial School,* Hyde Park, MA; *Mary's Home,* Farmington, MI; *Our Lady of Grace Convent,* West Reading, PA; *Our Lady of the Rosary Convent,* Farmington, MI; *Sacred Heart Convent - Retirement Facility for Bernardine Sisters,* Reading, PA; *St. Joseph Villa,* Reading, PA; *St. Clare Convent,* Reading, PA; *Villa Maria Retreat Center,* Stamford, CT; *Villa Maria Education Center,* Stamford, CT; *Villa of Our Lady of the Poconos Retreat House,* Mt. Pocono, PA. Sponsored: *Alvernia College,* Reading, PA; *Hazleton-St. Joseph Medical Center,* Hazleton, PA; *Mary Immaculate Hospital,* Newport News, VA.
Sisters engaged in the field of Religious and Academic education at all levels; Parish and Pastoral ministry; Spiritual Direction and Retreat House; Ministry to women, the poor, homeless, mentally and physically challenged; Gerontology, Hospital and Health Care; Day care; Overseas Missions; Business & Clerical.

[1820] (O.S.F.)—HOSPITAL SISTERS OF THE THIRD ORDER OF ST. FRANCIS P

Founded in Germany in 1844. First foundation in the United States in 1875.
General Motherhouse: Muenster in Westphalia, Germany. Sr. Mary Ann Minor, O.S.F., Gen. Supr.
American Province (1875): *St. Francis Convent, Motherhouse and Novitiate,* Box 19431, Springfield, IL 62794. Tel: 217-522-3386. Sr. Bernadine Gutowski, O.S.F., Prov. Supr.; Sr. Maureen O'Connor, O.S.F., Prov. Sec.
Total number in the community 233.
Sisters serve and Staff: Hospitals; Home Health Services; Catechetical; Care of Chemically Dependent; Social Ministries; Pastoral Ministries; Overseas Missions.
Properties Owned or Sponsored: Residence 18; *St. Francis Convent, Motherhouse, Novitiate,* Springfield, IL; *Fields Wright Medical Facility, Inc.,* Sullivan, IL; *Hospital Sisters Services, Inc., Hospital Sisters of St. Francis Foundation, Hospital Sisters Health System, St. John's Hospital, St. John's College of Nursing,* Springfield, IL; St. Mary's Hospital, Decatur, IL; *St. Anthony Memorial Hospital,* Effingham, IL; *St. Joseph's Hospital,* Highland, IL; *St. Francis Hospital,* Litchfield, IL; *St. Elizabeth's Hospital,* Belleville, IL; *St. Joseph's Hospital,* Breese, IL; *St. Mary's Hospital Medical Center, St. Vincent Hospital,* Green Bay, WI; *St. Joseph's Hospital, L.E. Phillips Treatment Center for the Chemically Dependent, Hospital Sisters Health Care West, Inc., Transitus House,* Chippewa Falls, WI; *Sacred Heart Hospital, St. Francis Apartments,* Eau Claire, WI; *St. Nicholas Hospital,* Sheboygan, WI; *St. Mary's Hospital,* Streator, IL.
Represented in the Archdioceses of Chicago, Milwaukee, Santa Fe, and the Dioceses of Belleville, Green Bay, La Crosse, Peoria and Springfield (IL). Also in Haiti, Taiwan and Japan.

[1830] (R.G.S. - C.G.S.)—THE SISTERS OF THE GOOD SHEPHERD P

Congregation of Our Lady of Charity of the Good Shepherd

Founded in France in 1835. First foundation in the United States in Louisville, KY 1842.
Generalate for the Provinces: *Suore del Buon Pastore,* via Raffaello Sardiello 20, 00165, Rome, Italy. Sr. Liliane Tauvette, Supr. Gen.
Province of Cincinnati (Carthage) (1857): 2849 Fischer Pl., Cincinnati, OH 45211. Tel: 513-661-1833. Sr. Dolores Kalina, Prov.
Legal Titles: *The Sisters of the Good Shepherd; Cincinnati Province; The Congregation of Our Lady of Charity of the Good Shepherd Community Support Trust,* Cincinnati, OH.
Professed Sisters 54.
Ministry in Adolescent Treatment Centers; Parish Ministry; Social Service and Education Agencies.
Properties Owned and Sponsored: *Good Shepherd Provincialate and Gilead House,* Cincinnati, OH; *The Sisters of the Good Shepherd, Cincinnati Province Inc. aka Good Shepherd Pelletier, Inc.; Sisters of the Good Shepherd, Grand Rapids,* Grand Rapids, MI; *Sisters of the Good Shepherd of Detroit aka Vista Maria,* Dearborn Heights, MI; Sisters of the Good Shepherd of the City of Cleveland aka Marycrest, Independence, OH; *House of the Good Shepherd of Columbus aka Rosemont,* Columbus, OH; *Sisters of the Good Shepherd, Maryhurst, Inc. aka Maryhurst,* Louisville, KY.
Contemplatives of the Good Shepherd, 1400 Morgan Pl., Grand Rapids, MI 49504; 7800 Brookside Rd., Independence, OH 44131; 20651 W. Warren Ave., Dearborn Heights, MI 48127.
Professed sisters 45.
Represented in the Archdioceses of Cincinnati, Detroit, Louisville and in the Dioceses of Cleveland, Columbus, Covington and Grand Rapids.
Province of New York (1857): Sisters of the Good Shepherd, 82-31 Doncaster Pl., Jamaica, NY 11432. Tel: 718-380-3270; Fax: 718-591-9376. Sr. Helene Hayes, Prov.
Legal Title: *Sisters of the Good Shepherd, Province of New York.*
Professed Active Sisters 117; Contemplative Sisters 77.
Ministry in Counseling Centers; Social Service Agencies; Special Education Schools; Neighborhood Family Services; Adolescent Residential Programs; Human Services Workshops; Pastoral Ministry; Prison Ministry; Hospital Chaplaincy.
Legal Holdings or Titles: *Sisters of the Good Shepherd,* New York, NY; *House of the Good Shepherd, Villa Loretto,* Peekskill, NY; *Sisters of the Good Shepherd,* Albany, NY; *Sisters of the Good Shepherd,* Huntington, NY; *House of the Good Shepherd in the City of Hartford,* Hartford, CT; *Good Shepherd Association,* Springfield, MA; *Sisters of the Good Shepherd,* Marlboro, MA; *Madonna Hall,* Marlboro, MA; *Maria Droste Services (Madonna Hall) Sisters of the Good Shepherd,* Morristown, NJ.
Programs Sponsored: *Good Shepherd Services,* New York, NY; *Maria Droste Services (St. Germaine's Services),* New York, NY; *Collier Services,* Wickatunk, NJ; *Good Shepherd Volunteers (St. Germaine's Services).*
Represented in the Archdioceses of Boston and New York, and the Dioceses of Albany, Brooklyn, Fall River, Metuchen, Paterson, Rockville Centre, Springfield (MA) and Trenton.
Province of Washington, DC (1850): Sisters of the Good Shepherd, 504 Hexton Hill Rd., Silver Spring, MD 20904-3300. Tel: 301-384-1169; Fax: 301-384-8889. Sr. Mary Brigid Lawlor, Prov.
Legal Title: *Sisters of the Good Shepherd of the City of Washington, D.C.*
Professed Sisters 74.
Ministry in the field of Adolescent Residential and Day Treatment Centers; Neighborhood Justice Center; Counseling and Referral Center for Families and Children; Family & Youth Services; Parish Ministry; Spousal Abuse Center; Refugee Services; Children's Shelter; Women-in-Transition; Women-with-AIDS.
Properties owned or sponsored: *Good Shepherd Corporation,* Philadelphia, PA; *Good Shepherd Corporation of Orlando, Inc.,* Orlando, FL; *Cora Services Inc., Philadelphia, PA; Good Shepherd Mediation Program,* Philadelphia, PA; *Good Shepherd Corporation, Lourdesmont Good Shepherd Youth & Family Services,* Clarks Summit, PA; *Alee Shelter and Children's Shelter,* Agana, GU; *Sisters of the Good Shepherd of the City of Washington, DC; House of the Good Shepherd,* Baltimore, MD; *Sisters of the Good Shepherd, A Corporation,* Baltimore, MD; *Good Shepherd Corporation of Clarks Summit, PA; Good Shepherd Center,* Baltimore, MD; *CORA Services,* Philadelphia, PA; *Euphrasia House, Inc.,* Philadelphia, PA; *Good Shepherd Corporation (dba Shepherd's Dwelling),* Washington, DC; *Good Shepherd Services,* Atlanta, GA.
Contemplative Sisters of the Good Shepherd, 3601 Reservoir Rd., N.W., Washington, DC 20007-2339. Tel: 202-338-1571. Sr. Louise Cecilia Greenfield, Supr.
Sisters 9.
Contemplative Sisters of the Good Shepherd, 715 Susquehanna Rd., Philadelphia, PA 19111-1396. Tel: 215-722-3970. Sr. Jude Ellen Golumbieski, Supr.
Sisters 13.
Represented in the Archdioceses of Agana, Atlanta, Baltimore, Philadelphia, Washington and in the Dioceses of Orlando, Raleigh and Scranton.
Province of St. Louis (1849): *Provincialate,* 7654 Natural Bridge Blvd., St. Louis, MO 63121. Tel: 314-381-3400; Fax: 314-381-6449. Sr. Nora Patricia O'Flannigan, Prov.
Legal Title: *Sisters of the Good Shepherd St. Louis Province.*
Professed Sisters 81; Contemplatives 24.
Properties owned and staffed: *Good Shepherd Shelter* (for battered women with children), Los Angeles, CA; *Gracenter* (women in need), San Francisco, CA; *Marian Manor,* New Orleans, LA; *De Neuville Heights* (adolescent residential program), Memphis, TN; *Droste Residence* (women in need), St. Louis, MO; *House of the Good Shepherd* (battered women with children), Chicago, IL; *Immaculate Heart Convent* (retired Good Shepherd Sisters), St. Louis, MO; *Good Shepherd Provincialate,* St. Louis, MO.
Ministry in parishes and prisons.
Represented in the Archdioceses of Chicago, Los Angeles, New Orleans, St. Louis and San Francisco, and the Dioceses of Gallup, and Memphis. Also in Guam.
Contemplative Sisters of the Good Shepherd 2711 Mullanphy Lane, Florissant, MO 63031. Tel: 314-837-1719. Sr. Magdalen Clark, C.G.S., Supr.
Total number in the community 24.
Province of St. Paul (1868): *Provincialate,* 5100 Hodgson Rd., St. Paul, MN 55126. Tel: 612-482-5251. Sr. Joan Spiering, Prov.
Professed Sisters 56.
Represented in the Archdioceses of Denver, Omaha, Portland (OR), St. Paul-Minneapolis and Seattle and the Diocese of Honolulu.
Contemplative Sisters of the Good Shepherd, 5104 Hodgson Rd., St. Paul, MN 55126. Tel: 612-482-5240. Sr. Teresita Mater, Supr.
Total number of Professed Sisters 34.
Represented in the Archdioceses of St. Paul-Minneapolis and Omaha.

[1840] (G.N.S.H.)—GREY NUNS OF THE SACRED HEART P

General Motherhouse (1921): 1750 Quarry Rd., Yardley, PA 19067-3998. Tel: 215-968-4236; Fax: 215-968-6656. Sr. Jean Liston, Supr. Gen.; Sr. R. Patricia Smith, Archivist; Sr. Mary O'Connell, Dir. Congregational Advancement Committee.
Total number in community 191.
Sisters staff: College, Secondary and Elementary Education; Hospitals; Nursing Homes; Rehabilitation Care of Aging; Pastoral Care; Personal Care

Home; CCD-Parish Services; Diocesan Offices; Campus Ministry; Prison Ministry; Homeless Housing.
Properties owned: *Holy Angels Academy,* Buffalo, NY; *Motherhouse Complex,* Yardley, PA.
Represented in the Archdioceses of Anchorage, Atlanta, Baltimore, Newark, New York and Philadelphia, and the Dioceses of Brooklyn, Buffalo, Cleveland Erie, Manchester, Ogdensburg, Paterson, Richmond, Rochester, Rockville Centre and Trenton. Also in Canada.

[1845] (M.G.Sp.S.)—GUADALUPAN MISSIONARIES OF THE HOLY SPIRIT P
(Misioneras Guadalupanas del Espiritu Santo)

Founded in Morelia, Michoacan, Mexico in 1930 by Rev. Felix de Jesus Rougier, M.Sp.S.
General Motherhouse: Soja #44 Col. Esmeralda, Del. Iztapalapa 09810, Mexico, D.F. Mother Felicitas Almanza, Supr. Gen.
U.S. Delegation Headquarters: 2483 S.W. 4th St., Miami, FL 33135-2907. Tel: 305-642-9544.
U.S. Novitiate 758 S. Dunsmuir Ave., Los Angeles, CA 90036. Tel: 213-936-0135.
Legal Title: *Missionary Guadalupanas of the Holy Spirit, Inc.*
Total Sisters in U.S. 43; Novices 2; Postulants 2.
Ministry in Religious Education; Pastoral and Parish Ministries.
Represented in the Archdiocese of Los Angeles and Miami, and the Dioceses of Fall River, Palm Beach, Pueblo, and Venice. Also in San Juan, Puerto Rico.

[1850] (S.A.C.)—SISTERS OF THE GUARDIAN ANGEL

Founded in Quillan, France in 1839.
General Motherhouse: Avda, del Valle, 42, Madrid 3, Spain. Sr. Sagrario Escudero, S.A.C., Supr. Gen.
U.S. Foundation: c/o 4529 New York St., Los Angeles, CA 90022.
Represented in the Archdiocese of Los Angeles.

[1855] (H.H.C.J.)—CONGREGATION OF THE HANDMAIDS OF THE HOLY CHILD JESUS P

Founded in Nigeria in 1931 by Sister Mary Magdalen Charles Walker. Canonically erected in 1937 by Bishop Joseph Moynagh.
General Motherhouse: Ifuho, Ikot Ekpene, Akwa Ibom State, Nigeria. Sr. Mary Langley, H.H.C.J., Supr. Gen.
Congregation of the Handmaids of the Holy Child Jesus: *U.S. Headquarters,* 1707 Bryant Ave.-N., Minneapolis, MN 55411. Tel: 612-521-3127. Sr. Caroline Mbonu, H.H.C.J., Asst. Gen. & Contact Person.
Total Sisters in U.S. 26.
Ministry in elementary and higher education Parish ministry; Health care and social ministry.
Represented in the Archdioceses of St. Paul-Minneapolis, and the Dioceses of Alexandria, Beaumont and St. Petersburg.

[1860] (H.P.B.)—HANDMAIDS OF THE PRECIOUS BLOOD P

Founded in Jemez Springs, New Mexico in 1947.
Motherhouse and Novitiate: *Cor Jesu Monastery,* P.O. Box 90, Jemez Springs, NM 87025. Tel: 505-829-3906. Mother John Paul, Prioress.
Perpetually Professed Sisters 34; First Professed 1; Novices 1.
Ministry as Contemplative, Life of Eucharistic Adoration (Perpetual); for the sanctification of priests and for the entire world.
Represented in the Archdioceses of Chicago and Santa Fe. Also in Italy.

[1870] (A.C.J.)—THE HANDMAIDS OF THE SACRED HEART OF JESUS P

Founded in Spain in 1877. First Foundation in the United States in 1926.
General Motherhouse: Largo dei Monti Parioli, 3, 00197, Rome, Italy. Sr. Rosario Lleo, Supr. Gen.
Universal total in Congregation 1,800.
Provincial Motherhouse: 616 Coopertown Rd., Haverford, PA 19041. Tel: 610-642-5715; Fax: 610-642-3879. Sr. Gloria Petrone, A.C.J., Prov. Supr.
Total number in community 47.
Sisters serve and staff: Elementary Schools; Retreat Center; Mission Center; Parish Ministry; CCD; Diocesan Offices; Hispanic Pastoral Ministry; Vietnamese Pastoral Ministry; Hospital Chaplaincy.
Properties owned: *St. Raphaela Center,* Haverford, PA; *Ancillae Assumpta Academy,* Wyncote, PA.
Represented in the Archdioceses of Atlanta, Miami and Philadelphia.

[1880] (A.R.)—HANDMAIDS OF REPARATION OF THE SACRED HEART OF JESUS P

Founded in Messina, Italy in 1918.
U.S. Foundation (1958): *Sacred Heart Villa,* R.D.3, Sunshine Park, Steubenville, OH 43952. Tel: 614-282-3801. Sr. Rosalba Putrino, A.R., Supr.
Total number in U.S. 6.
Apostolic Work in Religious & Academic Education; Education All Levels; Religious Education; Parish and Diocesan Ministry; CCD Work; Orphanages; Missionary Work in Brazil and Africa.
Represented in the Dioceses of Arlington and Steubenville. Also in Africa, Brazil and Italy.

[1890] (H.H.S.)—SOCIETY OF HELPERS P

Founded in France in 1856. First foundation in the U.S. in 1892.
Generalate: 16 rue St. J. Baptiste de la Salle, Paris, France, 75006. Sr. Silvia Conde, Supr. Gen.
American Province (1921): 303 W. Barry Ave., Chicago, IL 60657.
Provincial Office 2956 S. Lowe Ave., Chicago, IL 60616. Tel: 312-842-1039. Sr. Mary Therese Harrington, Prov. Supr.
Total number in U.S. province 55.
Legal Title: *Society of the Helpers of the Holy Souls Helpers of the Holy Souls; Province of the Helpers of the Holy Souls in the United States.*
Represented in the Archdioceses of Chicago, New York, St. Louis, San Francisco, and the Diocese of San Jose.

[1900] (H.C.G.)—HERMANAS CATEQUISTAS GUADALUPANAS P

Founded in Saltillo, Coahuila, Mexico in 1923. First United States foundation in 1950.
Motherhouse and Novitiate: Saltillo, Coahuila, Mexico.
U.S. Addresses: *Hermanas Catequistas Guadalupanas Convents,* 4110 S. Flores., San Antonio, TX 78214. Tel 512-532-9344. 115 Arlington Ct., San Antonio, TX 78210. Tel: 512-533-2968. Sr. Margarita Vasquez, Regl. Delegate.
Total number in the U.S. 19.
Represented in the Archdioceses of Oklahoma City and San Antonio and the Diocese of Fort Worth.

[1910] (H.J.)—HERMANAS JOSEFINAS P

General Motherhouse: Condor 336, Col. las Aguilas, Delg. Alvaro Obregon 01710, Mexico D.F. Mother Cointa Quijas, H.J., Supr. & Mother Gen.
U.S. Address: *Assumption Seminary,* 2600 W. Woodlawn Ave., P.O. Box 28240, San Antonio, TX 78284. Tel: 210-734-0039.
Sisters 8.
Represented in the Archdioceses of Chicago, Denver, Los Angeles and San Antonio, and the Diocese of El Paso.

[1920] (C.S.C.)—CONGREGATION OF THE SISTERS OF THE HOLY CROSS P

Founded at Le Mans, France in 1841. First foundation in the U.S. in 1843.
General Administration: *Sisters of the Holy Cross Generalate,* Bertrand Hall-Saint Mary's, Notre Dame, IN 46556. Tel: 219-284-5550; Fax: 219-284-5779. Sr. Catherine O'Brien, C.S.C., Pres.; Sr. M. Genevra (Rolf), C.S.C., Gen. Sec.
Professed Members 666; Temporarily Professed 30; Novices 12; Candidates 6.
Legal Title: *Sisters of the Holy Cross, Inc.; Sisters of the Holy Cross, Inc. dba CSC Consultation Services* VA; *Holy Cross Shared Services, Inc.; Holy Cross Health System Corporation; Holy Cross Services Corp.; Sisters of the Holy Cross of California,* Ventura, CA; *Havican Insurance Company Havican-Vermont Insurance Company; The Academy of the Holy Cross, Inc.,* MD; *The Corporation of Saint Mary's College,* Notre Dame, IN; *Sociedade Civil Irmas da Santa Cruz, Brasil, SA; Society of the Congregation of the Sisters of the Holy Cross,* Bangladesh.
Areas and Coordinators—
Area I - USA West, Sunland, CA. Tel: 818-353-3589; Fax: 818-352-3077. Sr. Mary Eliza Martin, C.S.C., Coord.
Area II - USA Midwest, Notre Dame, IN. Tel: 219-232-2683; Fax: 219-232-7669. Sr. Joy O'Grady, C.S.C., Coord.
Area III - USA South & Mexico, Austin, TX. Tel: 512-441-6693; Fax: 512-441-6693. Sr. Judith Hallock, C.S.C., Coord.
Area IV - USA East Wheaton, MD. Tel: 301-942-8549; Fax: 301-942-8549. Sr. Camilla Fitzgerald, C.S.C., Coord.
Area V - USA Retired, Notre Dame, IN. Tel: 219-284-5596; Fax: 219-284-5779. Sr. Joseph Cecile, C.S.C., Coord.
Area VI - South America, Sao Paulo, Brazil. Tel: 011-55-11-604-0229; Fax: 011-55-11-871-3430. Sr. Michael Mary Nolan, C.S.C., Coord.
Area VII - Africa-Middle East, Jinja Uganda, East Africa. Tel: 011-256-432-0977; Fax: 011-256-432-2050. Sr. Mary Alice Bowler, C.S.C., Coord.
Area VIII - Asia, Dhaka, Bangladesh. Tel: 011-880-2-310-493; Fax: 011-880-2-813-123. Sr. Joseph Mary, C.S.C., Coord.
Sisters staff and serve: Colleges; High Schools; Grade Schools; Adult Education Centers; Social Service Centers; Prayer Centers; Counseling Centers; Human Rights Centers; Women's Development Center; Hospitals and other Health Ministries including Administration of Health Systems, Primary Health Care and Long Term Health Care; Parish Ministry; Diocesan Catechetical Services; Other Parish and Diocesan Ministries; Retirement Homes; Senior Citizen Residences; Pastoral Ministry with the Deaf.
Represented in the Archdioceses of Baltimore, Boston, Chicago, Cincinnati, Denver, Indianapolis, Los Angeles, Louisville, Miami, New Orleans, Newark, Portland (OR), St. Louis, San Antonio, San Francisco, Seattle, Washington, and the Dioceses of Arlington, Austin, Biloxi, Boise, Brownsville, Charlotte, Columbus, Corpus Christi, Covington, Des Moines, Fall River, Fort Wayne-South Bend, Fresno, Gary, Harrisburg, Joliet, Kalamazoo, Knoxville, Lafayette (IN), Lansing, Lexington, Monterey, Oakland, Orange, Palm Beach, Peoria, Raleigh, Richmond, Rockford, Rockville Centre, St. Cloud, St. Petersburg, Salt Lake City, San Diego, Sann Jose, Stockton, Tucson, Venice and Wheeling-Charleston. Also in Brasil, Peru, Ghana, Uganda, Lebanon, Mexico, Bangladesh, India, Israel and Italy.

[1930] (C.S.C.)—SISTERS OF HOLY CROSS P

Founded in Le Mans, France in 1841. First foundation in Canada in 1847.
General Administration: 905 rue Basile-Moreau, St-Laurent, Montreal, Quebec H4L 4A1. Canada. Sr. Liette Finnerty, C.S.C., Supr. Gen.
Universal total in Congregation 1,203.
American Regional Office: 377 Island Pond Rd., Manchester, NH 03109. Tel: 603-622-9504. Sr. Lucille Cantin, C.S.C., Regl. Rep.
Total number in region 245.
Ministry in the field of Academic Education at all levels; Religious Education Centers; Social and Family Services; Counselor-Therapist; Parish Ministry; Youth and Hospital Chaplaincies; Administrative Positions; Diocesan Services; Hispanic Ministry; Ministry to Abused Women and Children; Social Work and Elderly Assistance.
Properties owned: *Notre Dame College; Holy Cross Kindergarten,* Manchester, NH; *St. George Manor,* Manchester, NH; *Our Lady of the Sacred Heart Convent,* West Franklin, NH; *Londonderry House,* Londonderry, NH; *Sisters of the Holy Cross,* 454 Island Pond Rd., Manchester, NH 03109; 136 Lynwood Ln., Manchester, NH 03109; 113 Wedgewood Ln., Manchester, NH 03109; 969 & 971 Chestnut St., Manchester, NH 03104; 377 Island Pond Rd., Manchester, NH; Fairview Rd., R.R. 1, Box 191, Pittsfield, NH 03263.
Represented in the Archdioceses of Boston and the Dioceses of Burlington, Fall River, Manchester, Norwich, Rochester and St. Petersburg. Also in Bangladesh, Haiti, Jamaica, Mali and Peru.

[1940] (C.H.F.)—CONGREGATION OF THE SISTERS OF THE HOLY FAITH P

Founded in Ireland in 1856. First foundation in U.S. in 1953. St. John of God School, 13817 Pioneer Blvd., Norwalk, California, 90650.
Motherhouse: Glasnevin, Dublin, Ireland.
U.S. Province: 12322 S. Paramount Blvd., P.O. Box 2085, Downey, CA 90242. Tel: 310-923-4013; Fax: 310-869-4609. Sr. M. Victoire Haran, Regl. Supr.
Total number in community 277.
Represented in the Archdioceses of Los Angeles, New Orleans and San Francisco and the Diocese of Sacramento.

[1950] (S.S.F.)—CONGREGATION OF THE SISTERS OF THE HOLY FAMILY P

Founded in the New Orleans, Louisiana, in 1842.
Motherhouse: 6901 Chef Menteur Hwy., New Orleans, LA 70126. Tel: 504-242-8315. Mother M. de Chantal St. Julien, S.S.F., Supr. Gen.
Total number in community 183.
Ministry in Secondary and Elementary Schools; Day Care Centers; Pastoral and Social Services; Nursing Home and Apartments for the Elderly, Disabled and Handicapped.

Represented in the Archdioceses of Los Angeles, New Orleans and Washington and in the Dioceses of Alexandria, Baton Rouge, Galveston-Houston, and Lafayette (LA). Also in Belize, Central America, and Nigeria, West Africa.

[1960] (S.H.F.)—SISTERS OF THE HOLY FAMILY P

Founded in San Francisco, California, in 1872.

GENERAL MOTHERHOUSE: P.O. Box 3248, Mission San Jose, CA 94539. Tel: 510-624-4500; Fax: 510-624-4537. Sr. Elaine Marie Sanchez, Congregational Pres.

Total number in community 147.

Ministry in the following areas: Day Care Centers; Religious Education Program; Teacher Training for Laity; Parish Homevisiting; Parent Education; Family Programs; Pastoral Ministry; Religious Education Classes for Developmentally Disabled; Associate Pastors; Directors of Retreats; Counselling; Convalescent-Rest Home Visiting.

Properties owned: *St. Elizabeth's Day Home,* San Jose, CA; *St. Vincent's Day Home,* Oakland, CA; *Holy Family Renewal Center,* Pleasant Hill, CA.

Represented in the Archdioceses of Anchorage, Los Angeles, Louisville, San Antonio, San Francisco, Seattle, and the Dioceses of Fresno, Honolulu, Juneau, Monterey, Oakland, Reno, Las Vegas, Sacramento, Salt Lake City, San Diego, San Jose and Stockton.

[1970] (C.S.F.N.)—SISTERS OF THE HOLY FAMILY OF NAZARETH P

Founded in Italy in 1875. First foundation in the United States in 1885.

GENERAL MOTHERHOUSE: Rome, Italy. Mother Maria Teresa Jasionowicz, Supr. Gen.

SACRED HEART PROVINCE (1885): 310 N. River Rd., Des Plaines, IL 60016-1211. Tel: 847-298-6760; Fax: 847-803-1941. Sr. M. Lucille, Prov. Supr.; Sr. M. Alexandra, Supr.; Sr. M. Gemma, Archivist.

Total number in community 187.

Properties owned: *St. Mary of Nazareth Hospital Center; Holy Family Medical Center; Holy Family Health Center,* Nazarethville.

Ministry in Academic Education; Hospitals and Health Care.

Represented in the Archdiocese of Chicago and the Diocese of Rockford.

BLESSED FRANCES SIEDLISKA PROVINCE (1962): *Sisters of The Holy Family of Nazareth,* 1814 Egyptian Way, Box 530959, Grand Prairie, TX 75053. Tel: 972-641-4496. Sr. M. Ancilla Sojka, Prov. Supr.

Total number in community 46.

Legal Holdings or Titles: *Bethania Regional Health Care Center,* Wichita Falls, TX; *Mother Frances Hospital Regional Health Care Center,* Tyler, TX.

Ministry in Education; Health Care; Parish Ministry; Religious Education.

Represented in the Dioceses of Dallas, Fort Worth and Tyler.

IMMACULATE CONCEPTION BVM PROVINCE (1918): *Sisters of the Holy Family of Nazareth Provincial House and Academy,* 4001 Grant Ave., Philadelphia, PA 19114-2999. Tel: 215-637-6464; Fax: 215-637-8475. Sr. M. Michaelann Delaney, Prov. Supr.; Sr. Mary Frances, Community Archivist.

Total number in community 184.

Properties owned: *Holy Family College; Nazareth Academy; Mount Nazareth,* Philadelphia, PA; *St. Mary Villa,* Ambler, PA; *Villa Nazareth,* Meadowbrook, PA.

Ministry in the field of Academic Education at all levels; Child-caring Institution; Hospitals; Nursing Homes; Sisters Retirement Home.

Represented in the Archdioceses of Baltimore, Miami, Philadelphia, San Juan, and the Dioceses of Allentown and Scranton.

SAINT JOSEPH PROVINCE (1918): *Sisters of the Holy Family of Nazareth,* 285 Bellevue Rd., Pittsburgh, PA 15229-2195. Tel: 412-931-4775; Fax: 412-931-9746. Sr. Maria Kruszewski, C.S.F.N., Prov. Supr.

Professed sisters in provincialate 43; Professed sisters 161.

Sisters serve and staff: High Schools; Elementary Schools; Religious Education Centers; Conference center; Hospitals; Parish Pastoral Ministry; Housing Counseling; Low-Income Home Ownership; Family Counseling; Family Life Education; Senior Citizen Apartments; Home for the Elderly; Home for Children; Learning Centers.

Legal Holdings and Titles: *Mt. Nazareth Center, Inc.,* Pittsburgh, PA; *Holy Family Institute,* Emsworth, PA; *St. Leonard's Home, Inc.,* Hollidaysburg, PA.

Represented in the Archdiocese of Detroit and the Dioceses of Altoona-Johnstown, Cleveland, Erie, Pittsburgh and Steubenville. Also in the Philippines.

IMMACULATE HEART OF MARY PROVINCE (1959): *Sisters of Holy Family of Nazareth Provincial Residence - Marian Heights,* 1428 Monroe Turnpike, Monroe, CT 06468. Tel: 203-268-7646. Sr. M. Janice Kobierowski, Prov. Supr.

Legal Title: *C.S.F.N. Congregation of the Sisters of the Holy Family of Nazareth.*

Total number in Province 122.

Ministry in Education; Child Care; Health Care; Religious Education; Retreat Work; House of Prayer; Pastoral Ministry and Hospital Chaplaincy; Prison Ministry.

Represented in the Archdioceses of Hartford and New York, and the Dioceses of Bridgeport, Brooklyn, Rockville Centre, Syracuse, Trenton and Worcester.

[1980] (O.S.F.)—CONGREGATION OF THE SERVANTS OF THE HOLY CHILD JESUS OF THE THIRD ORDER REGULAR OF SAINT FRANCIS P

Founded in Germany in 1855. First founded in the United States on April 9, 1929, at Staten Island, New York.

GENERAL MOTHERHOUSE (1855): Kloster Oberzell, Wuerzburg, Germany. Mother M. Reginarda Holzer, Supr. Gen.

REGIONAL HOUSE: *Villa Maria,* 641 Somerset St., North Plainfield, NJ 07060-4909. Tel: 908-757-3050. Rev. Sr. M. Dominic Ritter, Regl. Supr.

Total number in community 39.

Properties owned: *Villa Maria Sanitarium, Inc.* (Nursing Home and Regional House), North Plainfield, NJ; *St. Elizabeth's Home,* Yardville, NJ.

Ministry in Social Work; Health Care; Teaching.

Represented in the Archdiocese of Newark and Dioceses of Metuchen and Trenton.

[1990] (S.N.J.M.)—SISTERS OF THE HOLY NAMES OF JESUS AND MARY P

Founded by Marie Rose Durocher, in Longueuil, Quebec, Canada in 1843. First foundation in the U.S. in 1859.

GENERALATE: 80, rue Saint-Charles Est, Longueuil, Quebec , Canada, J4H 1A9. Tel: 514-651-8104. Sr. Mary Pat LeRoy, Supr. Gen.

An international congregation of 2,150 religious women with missions in Lesotho, Mexico, Nicaragua, Haiti and Brazil. Congregational sponsored works include colleges; adult centers; secondary, elementary and pre-schools; and health clinics.

Sisters ministering in works sponsored by other institutions/agencies include: Formal Education in Universities, Secondary, Elementary and Preschools; Adult Basic Education/Literacy; Administration in Diocesan Offices; Campus Ministry; Pastoral Ministry; Religious Education, Health Care and Social Services.

Represented in the Archdioceses of Detroit, Los Angeles, Portland (OR), San Francisco, Seattle and Washington, and the Dioceses of Albany, Baker, Fairbanks, Jackson, Monterey, Oakland, Orlando, Palm Beach, Richmond, San Jose, Spokane, St. Petersburg, Venice and Yakima.

OREGON PROVINCE (1859): *Provincial Administration,* Box 25, Marylhurst, OR 97036. Tel: 503-635-3621. Sr. Eileen Brown, Prov. Dir.

Total number in community 245.

Properties owned: *Provincial House,* Marylhurst, OR; *St. Mary's Academy,* Portland, OR.

CALIFORNIA PROVINCE (1868): *Provincial Administration,* P.O. Box 907, Los Gatos, CA 95031. Tel: 408-395-5150. Sr. Sally Slyngstad, Prov.

Total number in community 280.

Properties owned or sponsored: *Provincial House; Casa Maria Montessori School,* Los Gatos, CA; *Holy Names College; Holy Names High School,* Oakland, CA; *Next Step Learning Center,* Oakland, CA; *Ramona Convent Secondary School,* Alhambra, CA; *Villa Maria Del Mar,* Santa Cruz, CA.

NEW YORK PROVINCE (1865): *Provincial Administration,* 1061 New Scotland Ave., Albany, NY 12208. Tel: 518-489-5469; Fax: 518-489-5804. Sr. Virginia Bonan, Prov. Dir.

Total number in community 125.

Properties owned: *Provincial Center; Academy of the Holy Names,* Albany, NY; *Sisters of the Holy Names,* Silver Spring, MD; *Academy of the Holy Names,* Tampa, FL.

WASHINGTON PROVINCE (1962): *Provincial Administration,* 2911 W. Fort Wright Dr., Spokane, WA 99224. Tel: 509-328-7470; Fax: 509-328-9824. Sr. Shirley Roberg, Prov. Dir.

Total number in community 213.

Properties owned: *Provincial House,* Spokane, WA; *Holy Names Academy,* Seattle, WA.

[2000] (C.S.R.)—SISTERS OF THE HOLY REDEEMER P

First foundation in the United States on March 19, 1924 in Baltimore, Maryland.

GENERAL MOTHERHOUSE (1866): Wuerzburg, Germany. Sr. M. Veronika Stauch, Supr. Gen.

AMERICAN PROVINCE OF THE IMMACULATE CONCEPTION: 521 Moredon Rd., Huntingdon Valley, PA 19006. Tel: 215-938-0540; Fax: 215-938-7759. Sr. M. Regina Heilman, C.S.R., Prov.

Legal Holdings and Titles: *Holy Redeemer Health System, Inc.—Subsidiaries: Drueding Center (program for homeless women with children); Holy Redeemer Hospital and Medical Center; Holy Redeemer Foundation; HRH Management Corporation; Holy Redeemer, Nazareth and St. Mary-Home Health Services,* PA; *HR Physician Services; Holy Redeemer Visiting Nurse Agency,* PA; *Holy Redeemer Visiting Nurse Agency, Inc.* NJ; *Redeemer-Nazareth Medical Supply Co., Inc.; Redeemer Village & Redeemer Village II; Redeemer Long Term Care & Elder Services, Inc.; St. Joseph's Manor; The Lafeyette-Redeemer. Convents—Provincialate Emmaus Convent; Angelus-Formation Community; St. Joseph's Convent; Emmanuel Convent; Our Lady of Peace Convent; St. Elizabeth Community.*

Represented in the Archdiocese of Philadelphia, and the Dioceses of Camden and Trenton.

[2010] (O.SS.R.)—ORDER OF THE MOST HOLY REDEEMER P

(Redemptoristine Nuns)

Founded 1731 by St. Alphonsus de Liguori and Ven. Maria Celeste Grostarosa. (Contemplative). Rule approved 1750 by Pope Benedict XIV.

First United States Monastery (1957) Esopus, New York.

MOTHER OF PERPETUAL HELP MONASTERY: *Redemptoristine Nuns,* P.O.Box 220, Esopus, NY 12429-0220. Tel: 914-384-6533; Fax: 914-384-6533. Sr. Paula Schmidt, O.SS.R., Prioress. Solemn Vows, Papal Enclosure.

Total number in community 10.

MONASTERY OF ST. ALPHONSUS (1960): *Order of the Most Holy Redeemer,* Liguori, MO 63057. Tel: 314-464-1093. Sr. Joan Calver, O.SS.R., Prioress.

Total number in community 19; Novices 1; Candidates 1.

Represented in the Archdioceses of New York and St. Louis.

[2020] (C.H.S.)—COMMUNITY OF THE HOLY SPIRIT D

U.S. FOUNDATION (1970): 6151 Rancho Mission Rd. #205, San Diego, CA 92108. Tel: 619-584-0809. Sr. Susann Kernaghan, C.H.S., General Coord.

Total number in community 17.

Ministry in the field of Education; Health Care and Social Services.

Represented in the Dioceses of Oakland, Orange, Portland (OR), Las Vegas, San Diego and San Jose.

[2030] (C.S.Sp.)—SISTERS OF THE HOLY SPIRIT D

Founded in the United States 1929; Decree of Establishment 1932.

MOTHERHOUSE AND NOVITIATE: 10102 Granger Rd., Garfield Heights, OH 44125. Sr. Mary Assumpta, Supr. Gen.

Total number in community 9.

Represented in the Diocese of Cleveland.

[2040] (S.H.S.)—SISTERS OF THE HOLY SPIRIT D

Founded in the United States in 1913 at Donora, Pennsylvania.

MOTHERHOUSE: 5246 Clarwin Ave., Ross Township, Pittsburgh, PA 15229. Tel: 412-931-1917. Sr. Marita Juras, S.H.S., Gen. Supr.

Total number in community 68.

Sisters serve and staff: Elementary Schools; Religious Education; Retreat Services; Health and Social Services; Adult Day Care and Child Day Care; Care Facilities for the Aged.

Facilities owned: *Corporation of Sisters of the Holy Spirit of Pittsburgh.*

Represented in the Dioceses of Greensburg, Pittsburgh and Youngstown.

[2050] (S.H.Sp.)—SISTERS OF THE HOLY SPIRIT AND MARY IMMACULATE P

Founded in America in 1893. Papal Approbation 1930; final Approbation, 1938.

GENERAL MOTHERHOUSE: *Convent of the Holy Spirit and Mary Immaculate,* 301 Yucca St., San Antonio,

TX; 78203. Tel: 210-533-5149. Sr. Anne Finnerty, S.H.Sp., Gen. Supr.
Professed Sisters 133.
Legal Holdings: *Holy Spirit Motherhouse; Healy Murphy Center, Inc.* San Antonio, TX *Mother of Perpetual Help Nursing Home, Inc.* Brownsville, TX.
Ministry in the following areas: Education; Health Care; Pastoral Ministry; Catechetical Centers; Social Apostolate Centers; Retreats.
Represented in the Archdioceses of New Orleans and San Antonio, and the Dioceses of Beaumont, Biloxi, Brownsville, Corpus Christi, Dallas, Fort Worth, Galveston-Houston, Houma-Thibadoux, Jackson, Lafayette (LA) and Shreveport. Also in Mexico and Zambia.

[2060] (O.SS.T.)—SISTERS OF THE MOST HOLY TRINITY P

Founded in Rome in 1198. First foundation in the United States in 1920.
GENERAL MOTHERHOUSE: Rome, Italy.
PROVINCIAL HOUSE: *Immaculate Conception Province,* 21281 Chardon Rd., Euclid, OH 44117. Tel: 216-481-8232; Fax: 216-481-6577. Sr. M. Valentine, Regl. Delegate.
Total number in community 27.
Properties owned: *Our Lady of Lourdes Shrine,* Euclid, OH.
Represented in the Archdiocese of Philadelphia and the Diocese of Cleveland.

[2070] (S.U.S.C.)—SISTERS OF THE HOLY UNION P

Founded in France in 1826. First foundation in the United States in 1886.
GENERALATE: Rome, Italy. Sr. Pauline Cowie, Supr. Gen.
HOLY UNION FALL RIVER PROVINCE: *Provincial House,* 550 Rock St., Fall River, MA 02720-3436. Tel: 508-678-3616; Fax: 508-324-0686. Sr. Theresa M. Horvath, S.U.S.C., Prov.; Sr. Grace Donovan, S.U.S.C., Archivist.
Total number in community 115.
Ministry in the field of Religious and Academic Education; Social Services; Pastoral Care; Pastoral Ministry; Spiritual Renewal; Day Care; Business; Ministry Education; Family Ministry; Nursing; Campus Ministry; Spanish Apostolate; Legal Services; Foreign Mission work in Tanzania.
Represented in the Archdioceses of Baltimore, Boston, Miami, New York, Washington, and the Dioceses of Albany, Brooklyn, Fall River, Jackson, Lexington, Orlando, Pensacola-Tallahassee, Providence, and Rockville Centre.
SACRED HEART PROVINCE: Box 993, Main St., Groton, MA 01450. Tel: 508-448-6049. Sr. Alice Arsenault, S.U.S.C., Prov. Supr.; Sr. Rita Beaudoin, S.U.S.C., Archivist.
Professed Sisters 85.
Legal Title: *Holy Union of the Sacred Hearts Province of the Sacred Heart, Inc.*
Ministry in the fields of Education; Religious Education; Parish Ministry; Handicapped & Refugee Ministry; Foreign Missions; Clerical & Secretarial.
Properties owned: *Country Day School,* Groton, MA; *Convent of the Holy Union,* Lowell, MA.
Represented in the Archdiocese of Boston, and the Dioceses of Fall River and Providence. Also in Cameroon, Africa.

[2080] (G.H.M.S.)—HOME MISSION SISTERS OF AMERICA D

Glenmary Sisters
Founded July 16, 1952.
MOTHERHOUSE: *Glenmary Sisters - Glenmary Center,* P.O. Box 22264, Owensboro, KY 42304-2264. Tel: 502-686-8401. Sr. Christine Beckett, Pres.
Total number in community 14.
Ministry in Social Outreach; Evangelization and Catechesis; Promotional Center.
Represented in the Dioceses of Lexington, Owensboro and Savannah.

[2090] (H.V.M.)—SISTERS HOME VISITORS OF MARY D

Founded in Detroit, Michigan in 1949.
MOTHERHOUSE: 356 Arden Park, Detroit, MI 48202. Tel: 313-875-1123. Sr. Elizabeth Harris, H.V.M., Admin.
Total number in community 16.
Ministry in Urban Parishes; Senior Citizen; Prisons; Sojourner Spiritual Affirmation Center; Seminary Staff; Intercultural Center; Pre-Schools; Religious Education, RCIA.
Represented in the Archdiocese of Detroit, and the Dioceses of Tucson.

[2100] (C.H.M.)—CONGREGATION OF THE HUMILITY OF MARY P

Founded in France in 1854. First United States foundation in 1864.
MOTHERHOUSE: *Humility of Mary Center,* Davenport, IA 52804. Tel: 319-323-9466; Fax: 319-323-5209. Sr. Jude Fitzpatrick, Pres.
Legal Title: *Congregation of the Humility of Mary; Humility of Mary Shelter, Inc.; Congregation of the Humility of Mary Charitable Trust.*
Total number in community 183.
Ministry in Schools and Colleges; Religious Education Centers; Migrant Programs; Pastoral Ministry; Social Services; Inner City Programs; Health Services; and Ministry to the Elderly.
Represented in the Archdioceses of Chicago, Denver, Dubuque, Los Angeles, Seattle and Washington, and the Dioceses of Biloxi, Colorado Springs, Davenport, Des Moines, Dodge City, Fresno, Great Falls-Billings, Helena, Jackson, Joliet, Kansas City, Lexington, Peoria, New Ulm, Richmond, Rockford, St. Cloud, San Angelo, San Jose, Sioux City, Springfield (IL), Tyler, Wheeling-Charleston and Yakima. Also in Panama, Mexico.

[2110] (H.M.)—SISTERS OF THE HUMILITY OF MARY P

Founded in France in 1854. First foundation in the United States in 1864 at Villa Maria, Lawrence County, Pennsylvania, 16155.
MOTHERHOUSE: *Villa Maria Community Center,* Villa Maria, PA 16155. Tel: 412-964-8861; Fax: 412-964-8082. Sr. Celine Metzger, H.M., Major Supr.; Sr. Mary-Joanna Huegle, H.M., Community Archivist.
Total number in community 265.
Ministry in the field of Academic and Religious Education at all levels; Hospitals and Nursing Home, Assisted Living; Parish and Pastoral Ministries; Publishing of Education Materials; Diocesan Offices; Legal Services; Social Services; Ministry to Native Americans, Migrants, Hispanics, Haitians; Housing Ministry to Single Parents, Independent Elderly; Ministry to Deaf; Foreign Missions.
Legal Holdings and Titles: *Sisters of the Humility of Mary (Motherhouse),* Villa Maria, PA; *Sisters of the Humility of Mary Charitable Trust,* Villa Maria, PA; *Humility of Mary Health Care Corporation,* Cleveland, OH; *HM Health Services,* Youngstown, OH; *Lorain Community/St. Joseph Regional Health Center,* Lorain, OH; *Assumption Village,* Youngstown, OH; *Humility of Mary Information Systems,* Youngstown, OH *Magnificat High School, Rocky River,* OH; *Villa Montessori Center, Inc.,* Cleveland, OH; *The Center for Learning, Villa Maria,* PA; *Villa Maria Education Center, Inc.,* Villa Maria, PA; *Humility of Mary Housing Program, Inc.,* Akron, OH; *Life Opportunity Services,* Akron, OH; *HM Center for Women & Children,* Lorain, OH; Villa *Residential Services (Villa Maria Apartments),* Villa Maria, PA; *Christa Center, Inc.,,* Cleveland, OH.
Represented in the Archdioceses of Chicago, Cincinnati, Washington, and the Dioceses of Charleston, Cleveland, Grand Island, Lansing, Palm Beach, Pittsburgh, Richmond, Spokane, Trenton, Tucson, Venice, Wheeling-Charleston and Youngstown. Also in El Salvador and Mexico.

[2120] (C.I.C.)—SISTERS OF THE IMMACULATE CONCEPTION D

Founded in the United States in 1874.
GENERAL MOTHERHOUSE AND CONVENT OF THE IMMACULATE CONCEPTION: P.O. Box 50426, New Orleans, LA 70185-0426. Tel: 504-486-7426. Sr. Ada Missler, C.I.C., Contact Person.
Total number in community 17.
Ministry in Pastoral Ministry.
Represented in the Archdiocese of New Orleans and the Diocese of Houma-Thibodaux.

[2130] (R.C.M.)—SISTERS OF THE IMMACULATE CONCEPTION P

Founded in Spain in 1892.
GENERAL MOTHERHOUSE: Princesa 19 y 21 28008, Madrid, Spain. Mother Maria Mateu, Mother Gen.
U.S. DELEGATION HOUSE (1962): 2230 Franklin, San Francisco, CA 94109. Tel: 415-474-0159.
Represented in the Archdiocese of San Francisco and the Diocese of Fresno.

[2140] SISTERS OF THE IMMACULATE CONCEPTION OF THE BLESSED VIRGIN MARY (LITHUANIAN) D

Founded in Marijampole, Lithuania in 1918. First foundation in the United States in 1936.
AMERICAN HEADQUARTERS: *Immaculate Conception Convent and Novitiate,* 600 Liberty Hwy., Putnam, CT 06260-2503. Tel: 860-928-7955; Fax: 860-928-1930. Sr. M. Paul Savickas, Prov. Supr.
Total number in community 30.
Ministry in Nursing Homes; Retreat House; Catechetical Work in Parishes; Summer Camp for Children and Young Adults; Day Nursery and Kindergarten.
Legal Titles & Holdings: *Immaculate Conception Convent; Matulaitis Nursing Home,* Putnam, CT; *Camp Neringa,* Marlboro, VT.
Represented in the Archdiocese of Chicago, and the Dioceses of Burlington and Norwich. Also in Canada.

[2145] (O.S.A.)—CONGREGATION OF AUGUSTINIAN SISTERS SERVANTS OF JESUS AND MARY P

GENERALATE: via Nomentana 514, Rome, Italy. Mother Atanasia Buhogiar, Gen.
MALTA PROVINCE: 208 Fleur-de-Lys, B'Kara, Malta. Mother Miriam Grech, Mother Prov.
U.S. FOUNDATION: *St. John School,* 513 E. Broadway, Brandenburg, KY 40108. Sr. Lydia Falzon, Supr.
Total number in community 4.
Represented in the Archdiocese of Louisville.

[2150] (I.H.M.)—SISTERS, SERVANTS OF THE IMMACULATE HEART OF MARY P

Founded in the United States in 1845.
SSIHM LEADERSHIP COUNCIL: 610 W. Elm, Monroe, MI 48162-7909. Tel: 313-241-0092; Fax: 313-241-9114. Sr. Mary M. McCann, Pres.; Sr. Rose Matthew Mangini, Archivist.
Total number in Congregation 759.
Ministry in Academic and Religious Education at all levels; Pastoral Ministry (parish, healthcare, campus and prison settings); Diocesan and Parish Administration; Peace and Justice; Social Service and Counseling; Spiritual Growth and Development; Overseas Ministries.
Legal Titles and Sponsored Entities: *SSIHM, Inc., Marygrove College,* Detroit, MI; *Immaculate Heart of Mary High School,* Westchester, *I; Marian High School,* Bloomfield Hills, MI; *St. Mary Center,* Monroe, MI; *Visitation House of Prayer,* Monroe, MI; *SSIHM Charitable Trust (Retired and Infirm Sisters),* Monroe, MI; *Norman Towers (Congregate Living Facility for Senior Citizens),* Monroe, IL.
Co-Sponsor: *Groundwork for a Just World,* Detroit, MI.
Represented in the Archdioceses of Atlanta, Baltimore, Boston, Chicago, Cincinnati, Detroit, Louisville, Miami, Mobile, New York, Oklahoma City, St. Louis, St. Paul-Minneapolis, San Antonio, Santa Fe, Washington, and the Dioceses of Allentown, Austin, Cleveland, Columbus, Duluth, Fort Wayne-South Bend, Gaylord, Grand Rapids, Joliet, Juneau, Kalamazoo, Kansas City, Knoxville, Lafayette, IN, Lansing, Las Cruces, Lexington, Louisville, Marquette, Milwaukee, Oakland, Orlando, Palm Beach, Pensacola-Tallahassee, Phoenix, Pittsburgh, Raleigh, Rockville Centre, Saginaw, St. Augustine, St. Cloud, St. Petersburg, San Diego, Toledo, Tulsa, Venice, Washington, Wichita and Worcester. Also in Brazil, Canada, Italy, Ghana, Haiti, Honduras, Mexico, Puerto Rico, South Africa and Zimbabwe.

[2160] (I.H.M.)—SISTERS, SERVANTS OF THE IMMACULATE HEART OF MARY P

Founded in 1845. Established in Scranton, Pennsylvania in 1871.
GENERAL MOTHERHOUSE: *Immaculate Heart of Mary Center,* 2300 Adams Ave., Scranton, PA 18509. Tel: 717-342-6850; Fax: 717-346-5439. Sr. Anne Munley, I.H.M., Congregation Admin.
Total number in community 698.
Properties owned: *IHM Center Marian Convent Marywood College,* Scranton, PA; *Marian Community Hospital,* Carbondale, PA; *St. Joseph's Center,* Scranton, PA; *Our Lady of Grace Center,* Manhasset, NY.
Ministry in the field of Academic Education; Hospitals; Early Childhood Education Centers; Congregation Retirement and Health Care Centers; Spiritual Renewal Center; Directors of Religious Education; Pastoral Ministries; Social Services; Hospice; Campus Ministry; Peace and Justice Center; Volunteer Services; Family Ministry; Drug and Alcohol Counseling; Ministry to Hispanics; Diocesan Offices; Vicars for Religious; Ministry to Persons with AIDS.
Represented in the Archdioceses of Baltimore, Miami, New York, Philadelphia, Santa Fe and Washington, and the Dioceses of Allentown, Altoona-Johnstown, Bridgeport, Brooklyn, Camden, Harrisburg, Jackson, Norwich, Orlando, Paterson,

Providence, Pittsburgh, Raleigh, Rockville Centre, St. Petersburg, Scranton, Syracuse, Trenton, Venice, Wheeling-Charleston, Wilmington and Yakima. Also in Canada, Guatemala, and Peru.

[2170] (I.H.M.)—SISTERS, SERVANTS OF THE IMMACULATE HEART OF MARY P

Founded in 1845. Established in West Chester, Pennsylvania in 1872.

General Motherhouse: *Villa Maria,* Immaculata, PA 19345. Tel: 610-647-2160; Fax: 610-889-4874. Sr. Marie Angela Natoli, I.H.M., Supr. Gen.

Total number in Congregation 1,350.

Ministry in the field of Academic Education at all levels in the U.S. as well as Peru and Chile and Infirmary work.

Represented in the Archdioceses of Atlanta, Boston, Hartford, Miami, Philadelphia and San Francisco, and the Dioceses of Allentown, Camden, Harrisburg, Metuchen, Richmond, San Jose, Savannah and Trenton.

[2180] (I.H.M.)—SISTERS OF THE IMMACULATE HEART OF MARY P

Founded in Spain in 1848. First foundation in United States in 1871.

General Motherhouse: Rome, Italy.

U.S. Province: 4100 Sabino Canyon Rd., Tucson, AZ 85715. Tel: 602-886-4273. Sr. Alice Martinez, Prov. Supr.; Sr. Mary Evelyn Soto, Sec. & Community Archivist.

Total number in community 35.

Ministry in the field of Academic and Religious Education.

Represented in the Archdiocese of Miami, and the Dioceses of Oakland and Tucson.

[2185] (I.H.M.)—SISTERS OF THE IMMACULATE HEART OF MARY OF WICHITA

Founded in Olot, Spain, in 1848. First foundation in United States in 1871. Wichita foundation in 1979.

Motherhouse: 605 N. Woodchuck, Wichita, KS 67212. Tel: 316-722-9316. Mother M. Giovanni Oliveri, I.H.M., Gen. Supr.

Total number in community 13.

Apostolate: Contemplation of the Word and the spread of His Message of salvation through the various works and levels of education and retreat work:.

Represented in the Diocese of Wichita.

[2190] (C.V.I.)—CONGREGATION OF THE INCARNATE WORD AND BLESSED SACRAMENT P

Founded in France in 1625. First foundation in the United States in 1853.

Motherhouse and Novitiate: *Incarnate Word Convent,* 3400 Bradford Pl., Houston, TX 77025-1398. Tel: 713-668-0423. Sr. Brigid Cummins, Supr.; Sr. Dympna Lyons, Archivist.

Total number in community 65.

Ministry in the field of Academic and Religious Education; Social Service; Administration; Hispanic Ministry; Diocesan Ministry (Secretariat for Christian Formation, Department of Aging, Pastoral Care); Parish Ministry; Renewal Work.

Represented in the Dioceses of Austin, Beaumont and Galveston-Houston.

[2200] (I.W.B.S.)—CONGREGATION OF THE INCARNATE WORD AND BLESSED SACRAMENT P

Founded in France in 1625. First founded in the United States in 1853.

Motherhouse and Novitiate: *Incarnate Word Convent,* 1101 N.E. Water St., Victoria, TX 77901. Tel: 512-575-2266; Fax: 512-575-2165. Sr. M. Stephana Marbach, Supr. Gen.; Sr. M. Andrea Hubnik, Community Archivist.

Total number in community 119.

Legal Title: *Sisters of the Incarnate Word and Blessed Sacrament of Victori; Texas Medical and Retirement Trust,* Victoria, TX.

Properties owned or sponsored: *Nazareth Academy,* Victoria, TX; *Blessed Sacrament Academy,* San Antonio, TX.

Ministry in the field of Education; CCD Centers; Hospitals.

Represented in the Archdiocese of San Antonio, and the Dioceses of Beaumont, Corpus Christi, Dallas, Galveston-Houston and Victoria. Also in Africa and Italy.

[2205] (I.W.B.S.)—SISTERS OF THE INCARNATE WORD AND BLESSED SACRAMENT P

Founded in France in 1625. First Founded in the United States in 1853.

Motherhouse and Novitiate: *Incarnate Word Convent,* 2930 S. Alameda St., Corpus Christi, TX 78404. Tel: 512-882-5413; Fax: 512-880-4152. Sr. Michelle Marie Kuntscher, Supr. Gen.

Legal Title: *Convent Academy of the Incarnate Word; Incarnate Word Academy Foundation.*

Sisters 70.

Sisters serve and staff: Private High Schools; Private Kindergartens; Montessori; Diocesan and Private Middle Schools; Parochial and Private Elementary Schools; Other ministries include Religious Education; Hospital Ministry; Vocation Ministry; Diocesan Offices; Adult Education; General Administration; Retreat Ministry; Parish Ministry.

Represented in the Dioceses of Beaumont, Brownsville, Corpus Christi, and Galveston-Houston. Also in Nakuru, Africa.

[2210] (S.I.W.)—SISTERS OF THE INCARNATE WORD AND BLESSED SACRAMENT D

Founded in France in 1625. First foundation in the United States in 1853.

Motherhouse and Novitiate: 6618 Pearl Rd., (Parma Heights-U.S. Rd. 42), Cleveland, OH 44130. Tel: 216-886-6440. Sr. Margaret Taylor, Congregational Leader.

Total number in community 43.

Ministry includes Evangelization; Elementary and Religious Education; Spiritual Ministry (Retreat and Spiritual Direction); Pastoral Ministry in Parishes, Hospitals and Nursing Homes; Ministry with the Mentally Disabled.

Represented in the Diocese of Cleveland.

[2230] (C.I.J.)—CONGREGATION OF THE INFANT JESUS D

Founded in France in 1835. First foundation in the United States in 1905.

General Motherhouse: 310 Prospect Park W., Brooklyn, NY 11215. Tel: 718-965-7317. Sr. Mary Louise Kelly, Supr. Gen.

Total number in community 76.

Corporate Title: *Nursing Sisters of the Sick Poor Inc.* Congregation sponsors one Hospital and one Home Health Agency.

Ministry in the fields of Nursing; Social Work; Physical Therapy; Services to Disabled Persons; Pastoral Care; Chaplains; Retreat Work; Teaching; Parish Ministry; and other works related to Health Services.

Represented in the Dioceses of Brooklyn and Rockville Centre.

[2240] (I.J.)—SISTERS OF THE INFANT JESUS P

Founded in Rouen, France in 1662. First United States foundation in 1950.

Motherhouse: 8 Rue Abbe Gregoire, Paris, France 75006.

Generalate: *Via Trionfale,* 8062-Palazzina D, Roma, Italy 00135. Sr. Daniel Ee, Supr. Gen.

U.S. Foundation: *Holy Angels School,* 20 Reiner St., Colma, CA 94014.

Represented in the Archdiocese of San Francisco.

[2250] (O.S.B.)—CONGREGATION OF THE BENEDICTINES OF JESUS CRUCIFIED P

Founded in France in 1930. First foundation in the United States in 1955.

General Motherhouse: Brou-sur-Chantereine, France. Mother Godefrieda Bowman, Prioress Gen.

U.S. Foundations: *Regina Mundi Priory,* 550 S. Waterloo Rd., Devon, PA 19333-1798. Tel: 610-688-5130; Fax: 610-995-0477. Sr. Marie Zita Wenker, O.S.B., Prioress.

St. Paul's Priory, Newport, RI 02840. Sr. Marie-Agathe Karunaratne, O.S.B., Prioress.

Total number in the U.S. 29.

Represented in the Archdiocese of Philadelphia and the Diocese of Providence.

[2260] (A.D.)—SISTERS OF THE LAMB OF GOD D

Founded in France in 1945.

General Motherhouse: *Institute of the Lamb of God,* 85 Rt du Vieux Saint Marc, Brest, France 29283. Sr. Claire Marie Ducraux, A.D., Supr. Gen.

U.S. Foundation (1958): *House of Formation,* 2063 Wyandotte Ave., Owensboro, KY 42301. Tel: 502-926-7630. Sr. Marie John, Formation Dir.

Sisters 5; Novices 2.

Other Address 9534 Kentucky Rte. 144, Philpot, KY 42366. Tel: 502-281-5450. Sr. Mary Raymonde, Supr.

Sisters 4.

Represented in the Diocese of Owensboro.

[2270] (L.C.M.)—SISTERS OF THE LITTLE COMPANY OF MARY P

Founded in England in 1877. First foundation in the United States in 1893.

Generalate: *Little Company of Mary Generalate,* 28 Trinity Crescent, Tooting Bec London, England, SW17 7AE.

Universal total for the Congregation 464.

Provincial Office: *Province of the Immaculate Conception, The Little Company of Mary,* 9350 S. California Ave., Evergreen Park, IL 60805. Tel: 708-422-0130. Sr. Carol Pacini, L.C.M., Prov.

Total number in community 32.

Properties owned: *Little Company of Mary Hospital and Health Care Centers,* Evergreen Park, IL; *Memorial Hospital and Health Care Center,* Jasper, IN; *Little Company of Mary Health Services (Little Company of Mary Hospital* - Torrance, CA and *San Pedro Peninsula Hospital* - San Pedro, CA).

Ministry in Hospitals and Health Care; Pastoral/Parish areas.

Represented in the Archdioceses of Chicago and Los Angeles, and the Dioceses of Evansville, Orange and Toledo.

[2280] (P.F.M.)—LITTLE FRANCISCANS OF MARY (U.S.) P

Founded in the United States in 1889.

General Motherhouse: Baie St. Paul, (Charlevoix), Diocese of Quebec, P.Q. Canada. Sr. Madeleine Tremblay, Supr. Gen.

American Region: *St. Francis,* 2 Dupont St., Worcester, MA 01604. Tel: 508-755-0878. Sr. Rena Mae Gagnon, Regl. Supr.

Total number in Congregation including Canada and the United States 313.

Represented in the Dioceses of Portland (ME) and Worcester.

[2290] (L.M.S.C.)—LITTLE MISSIONARY SISTERS OF CHARITY P

Founded in Italy in 1915.

Generalate: Via Monte Acero, 500141, Rome, Italy.

U.S. Address: *Immaculate Conception Convent,* 120 Orient Ave., East Boston, MA 02128; Fax: 508-521-6711. Sr. Mary Gladys, L.M.S.C., Supr.

Professed Sisters 4.

Represented in the Archdiocese of Boston.

[2300] (L.S.I.C.)—LITTLE SERVANT SISTERS OF THE IMMACULATE CONCEPTION P

Founded in Poland on May 3, 1850. First founded in the United States in Reading, Pennsylvania on December 8, 1926.

General Motherhouse: Stara Wies, Brzozow, Poland. Mother Marietta Kopinska, Mother Gen.

Universal total in Congregation 1,500.

Holy Trinity Province: *Little Servants Sisters of the Immaculate Conception Provincialate-Novitiate,* 1000 Cropwell Rd., Cherry Hill, NJ 08003. Tel: 609-424-1962. Mother Mary Leoharda, Prov.; Sr. M. Philomena, Archivist.

Legal Title: *Congregation of the Little Servant Sisters of the Blessed Virgin Mary of the Immaculate Conception.*

Professed Sisters 72.

Ministry in Religious and Academic Education; Nursery Schools; Senior Day Care Center; House of Study; Guest House and Retreat House; Homes for Aged; Nursing Homes; Home Nursing Service; Parish Work; Parish Ministry.

Represented in the Archdioceses of Newark and Philadelphia and Dioceses of Camden and Metuchen.

[2310] (L.S.A.)—LITTLE SISTERS OF THE ASSUMPTION P

Founded in France in 1865. First foundation in the United States in 1891.

General Motherhouse: Paris, France. Sr. Celine Heon, Supr. Gen., 57 rue Violet, Paris, France, 75015.

United States Province: *Little Sisters of the Assumption Provincialate,* 214 E. 30th St., New York, NY 10016. Tel: 212-889-4310. Sr. Jean McCormack, Prov. Coord.

Total number in community 47.

Ministry in Home Health; Community Development Supportive Family Services Located in Poverty Areas; Services are predominantly provided in the Home Setting.

Represented in the Archdioceses of Boston, New York and Philadelphia and in the Diocese of Worcester.

[2315] (L.S.G.)—LITTLE SISTERS OF THE GOSPEL D

Founded in 1963 in France by Rev. Rene Voillaume. First foundation in the United States in 1972 in New York.
GENERALATE: La Courneuve, France, 93120. Tel: 1-48361814.
U.S. HOUSE: Box 305, Mott Haven Sta., Bronx, NY 10454. Tel: 718-292-2867.
Residence: 308 Willis Ave., Bronx NY, 10454.
Professed Sisters 78; Novices 3.
Ministry in Prison Ministry; Service to the Poor and Underserved.
Represented in the Archdiocese of New York.

[2330] (L.S.J.)—LITTLE SISTERS OF JESUS P

Founded in the Sahara in 1939. First foundation in the United States in 1952.
GENERAL MOTHERHOUSE: Rome, Italy. Sr. Iris Mary of Jesus, Prioress Gen.
Universal total in Congregation 1,400.
U.S. REGIONAL HOUSE: 400 N. Streeper St., Baltimore, MD 21224-1230. Tel: 410-327-7863. Sr. Cathy of Jesus, Regl. Dir.
Total number in U.S. 25.
Represented in the Archdioceses of Anchorage, Baltimore, Chicago and Washington, and the Dioceses of Altoona-Johnstown, Fairbanks and Raleigh.

[2331] (L.S.J.M.)—LITTLE SISTERS OF JESUS AND MARY D

Founded in the United States in 1974. Sr. Mary Elizabeth, Foundress.
JOSEPH HOUSE: P.O. Box 1755, Salisbury, MD 21802. Tel: 410-543-1645. Sr. Mary Elizabeth Gintling, Dir.
Total in the community 8.
Represented in the Archdiocese of Baltimore and the Diocese of Wilmington.

[2340] (L.S.P.)—LITTLE SISTERS OF THE POOR P

Founded in France in 1839. First foundation in the United States in 1868.
GENERAL MOTHERHOUSE: La Tour St. Joseph, Tinteniac, France 35190. Mother Celine de la Visitation, Supr. Gen.
Universal total in Congregation 3,709.
PROVINCE OF BROOKLYN (1868): *Queen of Peace Residence,* 110-30 221st St., Queens Village, NY 11429. Sr. Genevieve Regina, Prov.
Total number in Province 181.
Ministry in Homes for the Aging.
Represented in the Archdioceses of Boston, Hartford, Philadelphia and New York, and the Dioceses of Albany, Brooklyn, Metuchen, Paterson, Providence and Scranton. Also in Montreal.
PROVINCE OF BALTIMORE: *Little Sisters of the Poor,* 601 Maiden Choice Ln., Baltimore, MD 21228-3698. Tel: 410-744-9367; Fax: 410-747-0601. Sr. Mary Bernard du St. Esprit, Prov.
Total number in community 160.
Ministry in Homes for the Aged.
Represented in the Archdioceses of Baltimore, Cincinnati, Indianapolis, Mobile, New Orleans and Washington, and the Dioceses of Cleveland, Pittsburgh, Richmond, Toledo and Wilmington.
PROVINCE OF CHICAGO: *Little Sisters of the Poor, Chicago Province, Inc.,* 80 W. Northwest Hwy., Palatine, IL 60067-3580. Tel: 847-358-5700; Fax: 847-934-6852. Sr. Margaret Regina, Prov.
Total number in Province 150.
Ministry in Homes for the Aged.
Represented in the Archdioceses of Chicago, Denver, Los Angeles, Louisville, St. Louis, St. Paul-Minneapolis and San Francisco, and the Dioceses of Evansville, Gallup, and Kansas City-St. Joseph.

[2345] (P.O.S.C.)—LITTLE WORKERS OF THE SACRED HEARTS P

Founded in Italy in 1892. First Foundation in the U.S. in 1948.
GENERAL HOUSE: Via dei Pamphili 300152, Rome, Italy.
MOTHERHOUSE AND NOVITIATE: *Our Lady of Grace Convent,* 635 Glenbrook Rd., Stamford, CT 06906. Tel: 203-348-5531. Mother Lillian Cairo, P.O.S.C., Supr.
Ministry in Day Care Centers; Catechetics.
Represented in the Archdioceses of Philadelphia and Washington and the Diocese of Bridgeport.

[2350] (S.L.W.)—SISTERS OF THE LIVING WORD D

Founded in the United States in 1975.
GENERAL MOTHERHOUSE: *The Living Word Center,* 800 N. Fernandez Ave. B, Arlington Heights, IL 60004-5316. Tel: 847-577-5972; Fax: 847-577-5980. Sr. Mary Ann Zrust, Coord. of Spiritual Life.
Total number in community 80.
Ministry in the field of Academic and Religious Education; Hospitals; Parish Ministry and Social Services.
Represented in the Archdioceses of Chicago, Detroit, New Orleans, St. Louis and St. Paul-Minneapolis, and the Dioceses of Biloxi, Brownsville, Jackson, Jefferson City, Joliet, Lansing, Rockford, San Angelo and Sioux City.

[2360] (S.L.)—SISTERS OF LORETTO AT THE FOOT OF THE CROSS P

Founded in America in 1812.
GENERAL MOTHERHOUSE & NOVITIATE: *Loretto Motherhouse and Novitiate,* Nerinx, KY 40049. Tel: 502-865-5811.
ADMINISTRATIVE OFFICE: 3001 S. Federal Blvd., Denver, CO 80236-2711. Tel: 303-922-8215; Fax: 303-922-4906. Sr. Mary Ann Coyle, S.L., Pres.
Legal Title: *Loretto Literary and Benevolent Institution.*
Total number in Congregation 439.
Ministry in the field of Academic and Religious Education at all levels; Seminaries; Specialized Education; Health Care-Aging; Community Administration; Pastoral Ministry; Social Justice-Social Service; Administration; Diocesan Offices; Medicine and Nursing; Prayer Retreats; Clerical Offices; Consultants; Spirituality Center.
Represented in the Archdioceses of Atlanta, Chicago, Cincinnati, Denver, Indianapolis, Los Angeles, Louisville, Mobile, New Orleans, New York, St. Louis, San Antonio, San Francisco, Santa Fe, and the Dioceses of Cheyenne, Colorado Springs, El Paso, Galveston-Houston, Kansas City-St. Joseph, Nashville, Oakland, Pueblo, Rockford, San Diego, San Jose and Wheeling-Charleston.

[2370] (I.B.V.M.)—INSTITUTE OF THE BLESSED VIRGIN MARY (LORETTO SISTERS) P

Founded in St. Omer, Belgium, 1609. First foundation in Canada in 1847; in the United States in 1880.
GENERAL MOTHERHOUSE NORTH AMERICA: *Loretto Abbey,* 101 Mason Blvd., Toronto, Ontario, Canada M5M 3E2. Sr. Jane McDonell, Supr. Gen.
Universal total in Congregation 254.
REGIONAL OFFICE CANADA: *Canadian Regional Government, Loretto College,* 70 St. Mary St., Toronto, Ontario, Canada M5S 1J3. Sr. Anne Murray, Regl. Supr.-Canada.
REGIONAL OFFICE UNITED STATES: *American Regional Administration, Loretto Convent,* P.O. Box 508, Wheaton, IL 60189. Tel: 630-665-3814; Fax: 630-653-4886. Sr. Barbara Nelson, Regl. Supr.
Total number in community 106.
Properties owned: *Loretto High School,* Sacramento, CA; *Loretto Development Office Loretto Convent,* Wheaton, IL; *Loretto Early Childhood Center,* Wheaton, IL; *Loretto Conference Center,* Wheaton, IL.
Sisters serve and staff: High Schools; Grammar Schools; Missionary Work; Correspondence School; University; Pastoral Ministry; Adult Education; Social Work; Diocesan Office; Director of Religious Education.
Represented in the Archdiocese of Chicago, and the Dioceses of Fairbanks, Joliet, Marquette, Nashville, Phoenix, Sacramento, St. Petersburg and San Bernardino. Also in the West Indies.

[2380] (I.B.V.M.)—INSTITUTE OF THE BLESSED VIRGIN MARY (LORETO SISTERS) P

Founded in St. Omer, Belgium, in 1609. Foundation in Arizona, 1954 from the diocese of Meath, Ireland.
MOTHERHOUSE: Rathfarnham, Dublin, Ireland.
GENERALATE: Viale Appio Claudio, 10, Rome, Italy. Sr. Noni Mitchell, Supr. Gen.
Total number in Congregation 1,147.
U.S. REGIONAL: *Mary Ward House,* 2521 W. Maryland Ave., Phoenix, AZ 85017. Tel: 602-433-0658. Sr. Christine Gilsenan, Regl. Supr.
Total number in community 17.
Represented in the Diocese of Phoenix.

[2390] (L.H.C.)—LOVERS OF THE HOLY CROSS SISTERS
Phat Diem P

Founded in 1670 in Viet Nam by Bishop Pierre Lambert de la Motte. First foundation in the United States in 1976. Established as an autonomous institute of Consecrated Life of Diocesan Right in 1992.
GENERAL MOTHERHOUSE (1976): *Holy Cross Convent,* 14700 South Van Ness Ave., Gardena, CA 90249. Tel: 310-768-1906 or 516-0271; Fax: 310-352-6435. Sr. Monica Phi Tran, L.H.C., Supr. Gen.
Legal Title: *Lovers of the Holy Cross Sisters, Inc.*
Sisters 39; Novices 4; Postulants 7; Aspirants 23; Oblates 2.
Represented in the Archdioceses of Los Angeles and New Orleans and the Diocese of Orange.

[2400] (M.S.)—MARIAN SISTERS OF THE DIOCESE OF LINCOLN D

MARYCREST MOTHERHOUSE: *Marian Center,* R.R. No. 1, Box 108, Waverly, NE 68462. Tel: 402-786-2750. Sr. Ann Divis, M.S., Major Supr.
Total number in community 34.
Ministry in the field of Education; Specialized Education; Health Care; Catechetics.
Represented in the Diocese of Lincoln.

[2410] (M.S.C.)—CONGREGATION OF THE MARIANITES OF HOLY CROSS P

Founded in France in 1841. First foundation in the United States in 1843.
GENERAL ADMINISTRATION HEADQUARTERS: 220 Taylor St., N.E., Washington, DC 20017-1096. Sr. Mary Kay Kinberger, M.S.C., Supr.
NORTH AMERICA HEADQUARTERS: 1011 Gallier St., New Orleans, LA 70117. Tel: 504-945-1620. Congregational Assistants: Sr. Carmelita Centanni, M.S.C.; Sr. Joyce Hanks, M.S.C.; Sr. Gretchen Dysart, M.S.C.
Total number in North America 197.
Legal Holdings or Titles: *Our Lady of Holy Cross Convent,* New Orleans, LA; *Our Lady of Holy Cross College,* New Orleans, LA; *Prompt Succor Nursing Home,* Opelousas, LA; *C'est la Vie (Senior Citizen Independent Living Units),* Opelousas, LA; *Our Lady of Princeton Convent,* Princeton, NJ.
Ministry in Parishes; Social & Health Services; and the field of Education.
Represented in the Archdioceses of New Orleans, New York and Washington, and the Dioceses of Alexandria, Baton Rouge, Biloxi, Camden, Houma-Thibodeaux, Juneau, Lafayette (LA), Manchester, Paterson, Scranton, Syracuse and Trenton. Also in Bangladesh, Canada, Central America, Haiti, and Mexico.

[2420] (S.M.S.M.)—MARIST MISSIONARY SISTERS (MISSIONARY SISTERS OF THE SOCIETY OF MARY) INC. P

Founded in France in 1845-1857. First foundation in the United States in Boston, Massachusetts 1922.
MOTHERHOUSE: Via Cassia, 1243, Roma, Italia, 00189.
Universal total in Congregation 630.
NORTH AMERICAN PROVINCE: *Provincial Office,* 349 Grove St., Waltham, MA 02154. Tel: 617-893-0149; Fax: 617-894-7610. Sr. Rosalie Warpeha, S.M.S.M., Prov., *Vocation Promotion House,* 5142 S. Blackstone, Chicago, IL 60615. Sr. Claire Rheaume, S.M.S.M.
Represented in the Archdioceses of Boston, Chicago, and the Dioceses of Fairbanks, Little Rock, Shreveport, Davenport, Venice, Brownsville, Memphis, St. Petersburg, Peoria, Providence, Rochester, and St. Thomas, Virgin Islands. Also in Jamaica and Fairbanks.

[2430] (S.M.)—MARIST SISTERS/CONGREGATION OF MARY P

Founded in France in 1824 by Venerable John Claude Colin and Jeanne Marie Chavoin.
GENERAL MOTHERHOUSE: Via Aurelia 292, Rome, Italy 00165. Sr. Bridget Burns, S.M., Supr. Gen.; Sr. Linda Sevcik, S.M., Prov. Supr.
Universal total in Congregation 620.
U.S. FOUNDATIONS: *Our Lady of the Snows (1984),* 4810 S. Leamington, Chicago, IL 60638. Tel: 312-767-5392; *St. Barnabas,* (1958), 24262 Johnston, East Detroit, MI 48021. Tel: 313-772-2577; *Marie, Madre de la Iglesia,* (1985), 4419 St. James, Detroit, MI 48210. Tel: 313-846-9220; *St. Albert the Great,* (1956), 4855 Parker, Dearborn Heights, MI 48125. Tel: 313-292-0493.
Total number in the community 16.
Ministry in Elementary & Adult Education; Pastoral Ministry; Counseling; Pastoral Care in Hospitals; Music Ministry.
Represented in the Archdioceses of Chicago and Detroit.

[2440] (S.M.I.)—SISTERS OF MARY IMMACULATE

Catechist Sisters of Mary Immaculate, Help of Christians P

Founded in India in 1948 by the late Bishop Louis LaRavoire Morrow, Bishop of Krishnagar, India.

GENERAL MOTHERHOUSE: Krishnagar, Nadia Dist., West Bengal, India 741 101. Sr. Marie Pothanamala, Supr. Gen.
Universal total in Congregation 475.
U.S. FOUNDATION (1981): *Sisters of Mary Immaculate,* R.D. No.5, Box 1231, Leechburg, PA 15656. Tel: 412-845-2828; 836-0449. Sr. Gratia Kuttianickal, S.M.I., Delegation Supr.; Sr. Tracy Vattakuzihiyil, S.M.I., Supr.
Total number in the community 6.
Legal Holdings & Titles: *St. Joseph Center Convent,* Greensburg, PA; *Bishop Morrow Personal Care Home,* Leechburg, PA.

[2450] (S.M.P.)—SISTERS OF MARY OF THE PRESENTATION P

Founded in France. First foundation in the United States in 1903.
GENERAL MOTHERHOUSE: Broons, Cotes-du-Nord, France. Sr. Anne Grall, Supr. Gen.
U.S. PROVINCIAL HOUSE & NOVITIATE AT MARYVALE: 11550 River Rd., Valley City, ND 58072. Tel: 701-845-2864. Sr. Marlyss Dionne, Prov. Supr.
Total number in the community 62.
Ministry in the field of Religious and Academic Education at all levels; Parish Ministry; Hospitals and Home Health Agencies.
Represented in the Archdiocese of St. Paul-Minneapolis, and the Dioceses of Fargo, Peoria and Rockford.

[2460] (S.M.R.)—SOCIETY OF MARY REPARATRIX P

Founded in France in 1857. First foundation in the United States in 1908.
Total International Membership: 1,000 Sisters.
GENERALATE: *Society Di Maria Riparatrice,* Via dei Lucchesi 3, Roma, Italia 00187. Sr. Mary Henihan, Supr. Gen.
U.S. PROVINCE: 225 E. 234th St., Bronx, NY 10470. Tel: 718-324-2252. Sr. Margaret Hoey, Prov. Supr.
Total number in the community 37.
Represented in the Archdioceses of Detroit, Miami, New York and San Juan, and the Dioceses of Albany and Brooklyn.

[2470] (M.M.)—MARYKNOLL SISTERS OF ST. DOMINIC P

Founded in New York 1912.
CENTER: *Maryknoll Sisters Center,* Maryknoll, NY 10545-0311. Tel: 914-941-7575. Sr. Claudette La Verdiere, M.M., Community Pres.; Sr. Rosemary Healy, Center Coord.; Sr. M. Grace Krieger, M.M., Archivist.
ORIENTATION PROGRAM: *Maryknoll Sisters.* Co-Dirs.: Sr. Rita Burdzy, M.M.; Sr. Aida Manlucu, M.M.
Legal Titles and Holdings: *Maryknoll Sisters of St. Dominic, Inc.; Maryknoll Mission Institute.*
Total number in the Congregation 747.
Represented in the Archdioceses of Baltimore, Boston, Chicago, Cincinnati, Detroit, Hartford, Los Angeles, Louisville, Newark, New York, Philadelphia, Portland (OR), St. Louis, San Francisco and Washington and, and the Dioceses of Albany, Brooklyn, Gallup, Honolulu, Galveston-Houston, Jackson, Las Cruces, Madison, Manchester, Oakland, Palm Beach, Providence, Rochester, Rockville Centre, Sacramento, St. Augustine, St. Petersburg, San Bernardino, San Diego, San Jose, Santa Rosa, Scranton, Stockton and Winona. Also in Samoa.

[2480] (M.M.M.)—MEDICAL MISSIONARIES OF MARY P

Founded in Ireland in 1937. First United States Foundation in 1950.
GENERAL MOTHERHOUSE: *Rosemount,* Booterstown Ave., Blackrock, Co. Dublin, Ireland. Mother Mary Martin, M.M.M., Foundress; Sr. Philomena Sheerin, Supr. Gen.
REGIONAL HEADQUARTERS: 563 Minneford Ave., City Island, NY 10464-1118. Tel: 718-885-0945; Fax: 718-885-0010. Sr. Anne Marie Hubbard, M.M., Regional Supr.
Total number in the Congregation 436.
Represented in the Archdioceses of Boston, Chicago and New York, and the Dioceses of Richmond and San Diego.

[2490] (M.M.S.)—MEDICAL MISSION SISTERS P

GENERALATE: London, England. Sr. Rita Syron, M.M.S., Society Coord.
Universal total in the Congregation 680.
NORTH AMERICAN HEADQUARTERS (1925): 8400 Pine Rd., Philadelphia, PA 19111. Tel: 215-742-6100; Fax: 215-342-3948. Sr. Estelle Demers, M.M.S., North American Coord.
Legal Titles: *Society of Catholic Medical Missionaries, Inc.; Society of Catholic Medical Missionaries Generalate, Inc.*
Total number in North America 149.
Represented in the Archdioceses of Anchorage, Baltimore, Boston, Cincinnati, Hartford, Louisville, New Orleans, New York, Philadelphia, St. Louis and Washington, and the Dioceses of Arlington, Cleveland, El Paso, Harrisburg, Las Cruces, Memphis, Palm Beach, Richmond, St. Augustine, St. Petersburg, San Jose, San Diego, Savannah, Trenton, and Tucson. Also in Mexico.

[2500] (M.S.J.)—MEDICAL SISTERS OF ST. JOSEPH P

Founded in Kerala, South India, 1946.
GENERAL MOTHERHOUSE: Dharmagiri, P.O. Kothamangalam, Kerala, South India, 686691. Mother Cassia, M.S.J., Supr. Gen.
U.S. FOUNDATION (1985): *Medical Sisters of St. Joseph,* 3435 E. Funston, Wichita, KS 67218. Tel: 316-686-4746. Sr. Audrey, M.S.J., Supr.
Total number in Congregation 700.
Ministry as Health Care Apostolates.
Represented in the Diocese of Wichita.

[2515] (C.M.S.)—CASHEL MERCY SISTERS D

U.S. FOUNDATION (ST. MEL'S CONVENT): *Congregation of the Sisters of Mercy of Ireland,* P.O. Box 1180, Fair Oaks, CA 95628. Tel: 916-967-9504. Sr. Kathleen O'Dwyer, Contact Person.
Represented in the Diocese of Sacramento.

[2516] (S.M.)—SISTERS OF MERCY P

Founded in Ireland in 1831.
U.S. FOUNDATION (1956): *St. John's Convent of Mercy,* 11154 San Pablo Ave., El Cerrito, CA 94530. Tel: 415-233-6769.
Other U.S. Convents (1960): St. Nicholas Convent, 12816 S. El Monte Ave., Los Altos Hills CA, 94022. Tel: 415-948-0775.
Professed Sisters 10.
Represented in the Dioceses of Oakland, San Bernardino, San Jose, Santa Rosa and Sioux Falls.

[2517] SISTERS OF MERCY P

Founded in Dublin, Ireland 1831.
HOLY INFANT CONVENT: 239 Nancy P.., Ballwin, MO 63021. Tel: 314-391-1528. Sr. Agnes Nolan, Facilitator.
Total number in the community 4.
Legal Title: *Sisters of Mercy, Ireland.*
Ministry in Education & Pastoral Ministries.
Represented in the Archdiocese of St. Louis.

[2518] (S.M.)—SISTERS OF MERCY P

Founded in Kerry, Ireland, in 1844.
GENERAL MOTHERHOUSE: Mercy Generalate, Tralee County Kerry, Ireland.
U.S. FOUNDATION: *St. John the Evangelist Convent,* 5701 Locust Ave., Carmichael, CA 95608. Tel: 916-482-0163; Fax: 916-481-8326.
Total number in the community 3.
Represented in the Dioceses of Sacramento, and Santa Rosa.

[2519] (R.S.M.)—RELIGIOUS SISTERS OF MERCY OF ALMA, MICHIGAN P

The Religious Sisters of Mercy of Alma was officially founded on September 1, 1973; Diocesan approval on Jan. 25, 1974; Constitutions of Community approved March 17, 1978; Pontifical Status fully approved June 18, 1982.
MOTHERHOUSE AND NOVITIATE: *Religious Sisters of Mercy,* 1835 Michigan Ave., Alma, MI 48801. Tel: 517-463-6035. Mother Mary Quentin Sheridan, R.S.M.
Total number in the community 51.
Represented in the Archdioceses of Hartford, Philadelphia, Washington, and the Dioceses of Lansing, Portland, Saginaw and Winona. Also in Canada, Germany and Italy.

[2520] (R.S.M.)—SISTERS OF MERCY P

Founded in the United States in 1960.
GENERAL MOTHERHOUSE: *Congregation of the Sisters of Mercy,* Elblano Ave., Dun Laoghlaire, Dublin 01-2800448. Ireland. Sr. Dervilla Byrne, Supr. Gen.
U.S. FOUNDATION: *St. Joan of Arc,* 500 S.W. Fourth St., Boca Raton, FL 33432. Tel: 407-368-6655. Sr. Kathleen Sweeney, Supr.
Professed Sisters 5.
Represented in the Diocese of Palm Beach.

[2523] (R.S.M.)—SISTERS OF MERCY OF ARDAGH & CLONMACNOIS

Founded in Dublin, Ireland in 1831.
U.S. FOUNDATION (1962): *Little Flower Convent,* 1280 Casazza Dr., Reno, NV 89502.
Professed Sisters 3.
Represented in the Dioceses of Las Vegas, Orlando, Palm Beach and Reno.

[2530] SISTERS OF MERCY D

Founded in Dublin, Ireland in 1831.
MERCY GENERALATE: Dundalk Co. Louth, Ireland. Sr. M. Rosarii Carville.
U.S. FOUNDATION: *Mailing Address:,* P.O. Box 360937, Melbourne, FL 32936-0937; *Ascension School,* P.O. Box E.G. 937, Melbourne, FL 32935. Sr. M. Joseph Barden, Local Supr.
Represented in the Diocese of Orlando.

[2535] (R.S.M.)—SISTERS OF MERCY (IRELAND)

Founded in Ireland in 1831. First Foundation in United States in 1969.
GENERALATE: Dublin, Ireland. Sr. Dervila Byrne, Supr. Gen.
U.S. ADDRESS: 2766 Navajo Rd., El Cajon, CA 92020. Tel: 619-465-2233.
Ministry in Hospital, Schools and Parishes.
Professed Sisters 7.
Represented in the Diocese of San Diego.

[2540] (R.S.M.)—SISTERS OF MERCY P

GENERAL MOTHERHOUSE: *Congregation of the Sisters of Mercy,* Elblano Ave., Dun Laoghlaire, Dublin 01-2800448, Ireland. Sr. Dervilla Byrne, Supr. Gen.
NOVITIATE AND RELIGIOUS EDUCATION CENTER (1971): 1172 S.W. 26th Ave., Deerfield Beach, FL 33442. Tel: 305-480-8511. Sr. Teresa O'Connell, Regl. Supr.
Total number in the community 13.
Ministry in the field of Education; Parish Work.
Represented in the Archdiocese of Miami and the Diocese of Palm Beach.

[2549] (R.S.M.)—SISTERS OF MERCY (SLIGO) P

Founded in Ireland in 1846. First foundation in United States in 1956.
GENERALATE: St. Peter's Convent, Athlone Roscommon, Ireland. Sr. Patricia Kelly, Supr. Gen.
AMERICAN REGION: 4825 H St., San Bernardino, CA 92447. Tel: 909-886-6172; Fax: 909-883-5954. Sr. Maura Feeley, Regl. Supr.
Total number in the community 25.
Ministry in the field of Religious and Academic Education; Parishes; Social Services; Diocesan Offices.
Represented in the Dioceses of Orange, San Bernardino and San Diego.

[2550] (R.S.M.)—SISTERS OF MERCY D

GENERAL MOTHERHOUSE: *Convent of Mercy,* St. Mary Limerick, Ireland. Sr. Clare Stapleton, Supr. Gen.
U.S. ADDRESSES: *St. Pius X Convent,* 3012 Cottage Hill Rd., #395, Mobile, AL 36606. Tel: 205-470-8453.
Total number in community 1.
St. Mary Convent Rockledge, FL 32955. Tel: 407-636-1341.
Total number in community 6.
Represented in the Archdiocese of Mobile and the Diocese of Orlando.

[2560] SISTERS OF MERCY D

Founded in Ireland.
U.S. ADDRESS (1963): *St. James Convent,* 366 Cowan Rd., Gulfport, MS 39507. Tel: 601-896-3277. Sr. Teresa O'Connell.
Total number in the community 9.
Represented in the Diocese of Biloxi.

[2575] (R.S.M.)—SISTERS OF MERCY OF THE AMERICAS

Catherine McAuley founded the Sisters of Mercy in Dublin, Ireland, in 1831. Ten years later, she received confirmation of the Rule by Pope Gregory XVI. In 1843 the Sisters of Mercy established their first U.S.A. foundation in Pittsburgh. In 1929 several of the independent congregations amalgamated to form the Sisters of Mercy of the Union. In 1991 the members of the nine provinces of the Union and of 16 other Mercy congregations founded the Sisters of Mercy of the Americas, with its 25 regional communities.
Universal total in the Congregation 6,367.
INSTITUTE ADMINISTRATIVE OFFICES: 8300 Colesville Rd., #300, Silver Spring, MD 20910-3243. Tel: 301-

587-0423; Fax: 301-587-0533. Sr. Doris Gottemoeller, R.S.M., Pres.

Mercy Action, Inc. is separately incorporated to foster innovative works of mercy.

McAuley Institute, Inc. is separately incorporated to foster the development of low-income housing ministry as a work of mercy.

Mercy Corps, Inc. is separately incorporated to conduct a volunteer lay ministry program to further the works of mercy.

Albany P

Regional Community of Albany (1863): *Convent of Mercy,* 310 S. Manning Blvd., Albany, NY 12208. Tel: 518-437-3000; Fax: 518-437-3030. Sr. Rosemary J. Sgroi, R.S.M., Pres.

Total number in the community 181.

Properties owned or sponsored: *Maria College; St. Peter's Hospital.*

Ministry in the field of Education; Health Services; Pastoral Ministry; Social Services.

Represented in the Archdioceses of Anchorage, Hartford and Newark, and the Dioceses of Albany and Syracuse.

Auburn P

Regional Community of Auburn: *Convent Of Our Lady Of Mercy Motherhouse,* 535 Sacramento St., Auburn, CA 95603. Tel: 916-887-2000. Sr. Susan McCarthy, R.S.M., Pres.

Total number in the community 93.

Properties owned, staffed or sponsored: *Our Lady of Mercy Convent,* Auburn, CA; *McAuley Convent; Russell House; Mercy Convent,* Sacramento, CA; *Mercy Convent,* Redding, CA; *Mercy San Juan Convent,* Fair Oaks, CA; *Mercy Convent,* Folsom, CA.

Ministry in the field of Education; Parishes; Diocesan Offices; Hospitals; Convalescent Units; Clinics; Pastoral Ministries; Senior Housing; Social Ministries.

Represented in the Diocese of Sacramento.

Baltimore P

Sisters of Mercy, Regional Community of Baltimore: P.O. Box 11448, Baltimore, MD 21239. Tel: 410-435-4400. Sr. Margaret Beatty, R.S.M., Pres.

Total number in community 251.

Legal Holdings and Titles: *Sisters of Mercy, Baltimore, Inc.; The Villa, Inc.,* Baltimore, MD; *House of Mercy,* Baltimore, MD.

Sisters serve and staff: Elementary Schools; High Schools; Institutions of Higher Education; Multi-Level Long-Term Care Facility; Diocesan Child Care Homes; Pastoral Ministry Programs in Parishes; Diocesan Offices; National Conference of Catholic Bishops; United States Catholic Conference; Inner-City Literacy Programs.

Properties Owned or Sponsored: High Schools 3; Hospitals 4; Retirement Facilities for Sisters 4; Leisure-Retreat Houses for Sisters 3; Residential Program for Homeless Women; Neighborhood Center.

Represented in the Archdioceses of Atlanta, Baltimore, Mobile and Washington, and the Dioceses of Birmingham, Pensacola-Tallahassee, Savannah and Wilmington. Also in Belize.

Brooklyn P

Brooklyn Regional Community (1855): 273 Willoughby Ave., Brooklyn, NY 11205. Tel: 718-622-5750. Sr. Camille D'Arienzo, Pres.

Total number in the community 270.

Ministry in the field of Education and Child Care Institutions.

Represented in the Dioceses of Brooklyn and Rockville Centre. Also in Panama.

Buffalo P

Regional Community of Buffalo: 5245 Murphy Rd., Orchard Park, NY 14127. Tel: 716-662-9836; 662-5120; Fax: 716-662-9766. Sr. Peggy Gorman, R.S.M., Pres.

Total number in the community 215.

Legal Holdings and Titles, Sponsored Works: *Trocaire College Mount Mercy Academy,* Buffalo, NY; *Mercy Health System of Western New York,* Buffalo, NY; *Kenmore Mercy Hospital,* Kenmore, NY; *Mercy Hospital,* Buffalo, NY; *St. Jerome Hospital,* Batavia, NY; *Mercy Home Care of Western New York,* Lockport, NY; *Ignatia House,* Buffalo, NY. *Co-sponsor: The McAuley Seton Home Care Agency,* Cheektowaga, NY; *Eastern Mercy Health System,* Radnor, PA.

Ministry in the field of Education at all levels; Catholic Charities; Parish Ministry; Community Table.

Represented in the Archdiocese of Washington, and the Dioceses of Brooklyn, Buffalo, Providence and Rochester. Also in the Philippines.

Burlingame P

Regional Community of Burlingame (1854): 2300 Adeline Dr., Burlingame, CA 94010-5599. Tel: 415-340-7410; Fax: 415-347-2550. Sr. Phyllis Hughes, Pres.; Sr. Marilyn Gouailhardou, Archivist.

Total number in the community 222.

Legal Title: *Sisters of Mercy,* Burlingame, California.

Ministry in Health Care; Religious and Academic Education; Spirituality and Conference Center; Foreign Missions; Social Services including housing; Retreats; Diocesan Offices.

Represented in the Archdioceses of Los Angeles and San Francisco, and the Dioceses of Fresno, Oakland, Orange, Phoenix, San Diego, San Jose and Santa Rosa. Also in Peru.

Cedar Rapids P

Regional Community of Cedar Rapids: *Sacred Heart Convent Motherhouse,* 1125 Prairie Dr., N.E., Cedar Rapids, IA 52402-4737. Tel: 319-364-5196; Fax: 319-364-7383. Sr. Susan O'Connor, R.S.M., Pres.; Sr. Delores Marie Hannon, R.S.M., Vice Pres.

Total number in the community 115.

Ministry in the field of Academic and Religious Education at all levels; Parish Ministry; Pastoral Care; Foreign Mission work; Social Services; Hospitals; Literacy Programs; Transitional Housing; Advocacy; Respite care for AIDS families.

Properties owned or sponsored: *Mount Mercy College; Mercy Medical Center; Sisters of Mercy Charitable Trust; Catherine McAuley Center for Women,* Cedar Rapids, IA.

Represented in the Archdioceses of Chicago, Cincinnati, Detroit, Dubuque, Indianapolis, Kansas City in Kansas, Miami, Milwaukee, St. Louis, St. Paul-Minneapolis, Washington, and the Dioceses of Davenport, Des Moines, Fall River, Helena, Kansas City-St. Joseph, Lincoln, Madison, St. Cloud, Springfield, Wheeling-Charleston and Wichita. Also in Peru.

Chicago P

Regional Community of Chicago: *Administrative Center,* 10024 S. Central Park Ave., Chicago, IL 60655-3132. Tel: 773-779-6011; Fax: 773-779-6094. Sr. Lucille McKillop, R.S.M., Pres.

Total number in community 368.

Sisters serve and staff: Education at all Levels; Social Services; Pastoral Services; Health Care; Spirituality; Foreign Missions.

Legal Holdings and Titles: *Sisters of Mercy of the Americas; Regional Community of Chicago Mercy Housing Corp.; The Warde Corp.; Sisters of Mercy of the Americas; Regional Community of Chicago Charitable Trust.*

Properties Owned and Sponsored: University 1; High Schools 1; Hospitals 3; Residence 2; Retreat Houses 1; Health Care and Rehabilitation Centers 2.

Represented in the Archdioceses of Boston, Chicago, Milwaukee, San Antonio, San Francisco, St. Louis, and the Dioceses of Colorado Springs, Davenport, Des Moines, Joliet, Knoxville, Little Rock, Peoria, Phoenix, Rockford, St. Petersburg, Springfield (IL) and Superior. Also in Honduras.

Cincinnati P

Regional Community of Cincinnati: *Sisters of Mercy Regional Center,* 2335 Grandview Ave., Cincinnati, OH 45206. Tel: 513-221-1800; Fax: 513-221-0207. Sr. Marie Hartmann, R.S.M., Pres.

Total number in community 402.

Sisters staff and serve: Academic Education at all levels; Parish & Diocesan Ministry; Health and Child-Care; Hospitals and Schools of Nursing; Homes for the Aged; Retreat and Renewal Center; Special Education.

Represented in the Archdioceses of Cincinnati and Louisville, and the Dioceses of Cleveland, Knoxville, Lexington, Memphis, Nashville, Owensboro and Toledo. Also in Jamaica and West Indies.

Connecticut P

Regional Community of Connecticut: 249 Steele Rd., West Hartford, CT 06117. Tel: 860-232-8602; Fax: 860-233-0065. Sr. Judith A. Carey, R.S.M., Regl. Pres.; Sr. Dolores Liptak, Archivist.

Total number in the community 276.

Legal Title: *Sisters of Mercy of Connecticut, Inc.*

Properties owned and sponsored: *Mercyknoll, Inc.; Saint Mary Home, Inc.; McAuley Center, Inc.; The Academy of Our Lady of Mercy - Lauralton Hall, Inc.; Saint Joseph College, Inc.; Our Lady of Mercy School, Inc.; Mercy Housing and Shelter, Inc.; Mercy Center, Inc.*

Ministry in the field of Religious and Academic Education at all levels including children with special needs; Spirituality and Retreat Work; Social Services and Health Care.

Represented in the Archdioceses of Boston, Hartford, New York and Washington, and the Dioceses of Bridgeport, Burlington, Kansas City-St. Joseph, Lexington, Manchester, Norwich, Pittsburgh, Portland (ME), Providence, Richmond, Springfield, Wheeling-Charleston and Worcester. Also in Belize, Guatemala and Haiti.

Dallas P

Regional Community of Dallas: *Administrative Office,* P.O. Box 369, Dallas, PA 18612-0369. Tel: 717-675-1966; Fax: 717-675-9051. Sr. Maureen McCann, R.S.M., Pres.; Sr. Mary Sylvia Connell, R.S.M., Community Archivist.

Total number in community 389.

Properties owned or sponsored: *Mercy Center College; Misericordia Mount Aloysius College; Mercy Center Preschool; Catherine McAuley Center; Neuman Housing Services, Inc.; Project REMAIN.*

Ministry in the field of Education; Hospital & Health Care; Art; Communications; Retirement Homes; Housing; Pastoral Services; Social Services; South American Ministries; European Ministries (overseas ministry).

Represented in the Archdioceses of Baltimore, Chicago, Detroit, Hartford, Miami, New Orleans, New York, Omaha, Philadelphia, Seattle, St. Louis, St. Paul-Minneapolis and Washington, and the Dioceses of Albany, Altoona-Johnstown, Biloxi, Brooklyn, Charlotte, Greensburg, Harrisburg, Jackson, Little Rock, Madison, Pittsburgh, Palm Beach, Rockville Centre, St. Cloud, Scranton, Springfield-Cape Giradeau, Trenton and Wheeling-Charleston. Also in Czech Republic, Guyana, Honduras and Ireland.

Detroit P

Regional Community of Detroit: *Sisters of Mercy,* 29000 Eleven Mile Rd., Farmington Hills, MI 48336. Tel: 810-476-8000; Fax: 810-467-4222. Sr. Gretchen Elliott, R.S.M., Pres.; Sr. Michaeline Lewandowski, R.S.M., Archivist.

Total number in community 306.

Legal Title: *Sisters of Mercy - Regional Community of Detroit; Sisters of Mercy of the Americas; Regional Community of Detroit, Charitable Trusts I and II.*

Properties Sponsored: Universities 1; High Schools 2; Mercy Health Services and 7 Subsidiaries & 15 Health Care Facilities; Mercy Center.

Represented in the Archdioceses of Baltimore, Denver, Detroit, Dubuque, Hartford, Indianapolis, Milwaukee, St. Louis, St. Paul-Minneapolis, Washington, and the Dioceses of Albany, Burlington, Charlotte, Cleveland, Columbus, Dodge City, Gaylord, Grand Rapids, Greensburg, Kalamazoo, La Crosse, Lansing, Lexington, Orlando, Owensboro, Saginaw, Sioux City and Toledo. Also in Argentina, & Chile.

Erie P

Regional Community of Erie: 444 E. Grandview Blvd., Erie, PA 16504. Tel: 814-824-2516; Fax: 814-824-2127. Sr. JoAnne Courneen, Regl. Pres.; Sr. Edith Langiotti, Archivist.

Total number in the community 89.

Legal Title: *Sisters of Mercy of Erie County, PA.*

Properties owned and or sponsored: *Mercyhurst College; Mercyhurst Preparatory School; Mercy Center for the Arts* (preschool); *Mercy Center on Aging, Mercy Terrace Apartments,* (housing for elderly); *Mercy Center for Women.*

Ministry in the field of Religious and Academic Education at all levels; Prison Ministry; Health Care Ministry; Diocesan Marriage Tribunal; Social Services.

Represented in the Archdioceses of Detroit and Washington, and the Dioceses of Buffalo, Erie, Little Rock, Pittsburgh and Savannah.

Merion P

Regional Community of Merion: *Motherhouse of The Sisters of Mercy,* Merion, PA 19066. Tel: 610-664-6650; Fax: 610-664-3429. Sr. Christine McCann, R.S.M., Regl. Pres.; Sr. Juliet Ferrari, R.S.M., Local Coord.

Total number in the community 449.

Legal Title: *Sisters of Mercy of Merion, Pennsylvania.*

Properties owned, staffed, or sponsored: *Gwynedd Mercy College; McAuley Convent; Merion Mercy Academy; Waldron Mercy Academy; Gwynedd Mercy Academy; Mercy Vocational High School; St. Mary Residence; Mercy Catholic Medical Center; Walsingham Academy; Mercy Health Corporation.*

Sisters serve and staff: Religious and academic education at all levels; Schools for the Mentally impaired; Hospices; House of Prayer; Social service organizations.

Represented in the Archdioceses of Anchorage, Atlanta, Baltimore, Chicago, Detroit, Miami, New York, Philadelphia, St. Louis and Washington, and the Dioceses of Allentown, Biloxi, Camden, Gallup, Orlando, Raleigh, Richmond, Scranton, St. Petersburg, Trenton, Wheeling-Charleston and Wilmington. Also in Italy, Peru, Bolivia and Canada.

New Hampshire P

Motherhouse of the Sisters of Mercy Inc.: *Sisters of Mercy of the Americas-Regional Community of New Hampshire,* (1858), 21 Searles Rd., Windham, NH 03087-1297. Tel: 603-893-6550; Fax: 603-893-2413. Sr. Patricia Sullivan, Pres.

Total number in the community 191.

Properties owned or sponsored: *Castle College,* Windham, NH; *Marian Court College,* Swampscott, MA; *Mount St. Mary Early Childhood Center,* Manches-

ter, NH; *Manchester Convent of the Sisters of Mercy; Mount Saint Mary Corporation of the Sisters of Mercy; Frances Warde House, Inc.,* Manchester, NH; *Warde Health Center, Inc.,* Windham, NH.

Ministry in the field of Academic Education at all levels; Nursing Homes; Hospitals.

Represented in the Archdioceses of Baltimore, Boston,, and the Dioceses of Brooklyn, Fall River, Orlando, Manchester, Portland (ME), Providence, Pueblo, St. Augustine and St. Cloud.

New Jersey **P**

Regional Community of New Jersey: 1645 U.S. Hwy 22, W., Watchung, NJ 07060-6587. Tel: 908-756-5348; Fax: 908-754-0164. Sr. Diane Szubrowski, R.S.M., Regl. Pres.; Sr. Innocent Dolan, R.S.M., Archivist.

Total number in the community 336.

Legal Title: *Sisters of Mercy of New Jersey.*

Properties owned or sponsored: *McAuley Hall; McAuley School for the Exceptional Child,* Watchung, NJ; *Georgian Court College of the Sisters of Mercy,* Lakewood, NJ; *Mount Saint Mary Academy,* Watchung, NJ; *Mount Saint Mary House of Prayer Mercy Center,* Asbury Park, NJ.

Ministry in the field of Education at all levels; Catholic Charities; Parish Ministry; School for Special Education; Day Care Center for Senior Citizens; Child Day Care Center; Social Services; Medicine; House of Prayer; Center for Peace and Justice.

Represented in the Archdioceses of Hartford, New York, Newark, Philadelphia, Washington, and the Dioceses of Camden, Charlotte, Metuchen, Las Cruces, Paterson, Rochester, Santa Rosa and Trenton.

New York **P**

Regional Community of New York: *Sisters of Mercy,* 150 Ridge Rd., Hartsdale, NY 10530. Tel: 914-328-3200; Fax: 914-328-3761. Sr. Patricia Wolf, R.S.M., Regl. Pres.

Total number in community 219.

Properties owned and sponsored: *Our Lady of Victory Academy,* NY; *St. Catharine Academy,* NY. Co-Sponsor: *Mercy Community Hospital,* Port Jervis, NY; *Nazareth Home for Boys,* Leicester, MA; *Uihlein Mercy Center (skilled nursing facility),* Lake Placid, NY; *Mercy Healthcare Center, Inc.,* Tupper Lake, NY; *St. Joseph's Home,* Worcester, MA.

Ministry in the field of Academic Education at all levels; Health and Child care; Special Education; Social Services; Spirituality and Counseling centers; Catechetical services; Pastoral Ministry.

Represented in the Archdioceses of Hartford, Los Angeles and New York, and the Dioceses of Ogdensburg, St. Petersburg and Worcester.

North Carolina **P**

Sisters of Mercy of the Americas - Regional Community of North Carolina: *Sacred Heart Convent Motherhouse,* 100 Mercy Dr., Belmont, NC 28012. Tel: 704-829-5103; Fax: 704-829-5137. Sr. Rosalind Picot, R.S.M., Regl. Pres.; Sr. Mary Andrew Ray, R.S.M., Community Archivist.

Total number in the community 137.

Legal Title: *Sisters of Mercy of North Carolina; Sisters of Mercy of North Carolina, in Guam, Inc.*

Ministry in the field of Religious and Academic Education at all levels; Aids Ministry; Pastoral Ministry; Hospitals; Developmental Center for Handicapped Children; Social Work; Religious and Academic Education in the Region of Guam, Saipan and Rota; Daycare and Preshool Centers; Shelter for Homeless Women and Children; Psycho-Spiritual Programs.

Represented in the Archdiocese of Miami, and the Dioceses of Charlotte, Charleston, Orlando, Pensacola-Tallahassee, and Wheeling-Charleston. Also in Agana and Chalan Kanoa.

Omaha **P**

Regional Community of Omaha: *Sisters of Mercy Regional Office,* 7262 Mercy Rd., Omaha, NE 68124. Tel: 402-393-8225; Fax: 402-393-8145. Sr. Patricia McDermott, R.S.M., Pres.; Sr. Rita Connell, R.S.M., Community Archivist.

Total number in community 278; Associates 87.

Ministry in the field of Education at all levels; Hospitals; Nursing Centers and Long Term Care Facilities for the Aged; Diocesan and Parish programs & services; Social Service; Housing for Families and Elderly.

Properties owned or sponsored: *Knowles Mercy Center,* Waterloo, NE; *Mercy High School,* Omaha, NE; *Health and Retirement Plan of the Sisters of Mercy of the Americas Regional Community of Omaha.* Co-sponsor: *Catholic Health Corporation,* Omaha, NE; *Mercy Housing Inc.,* Denver, CO.

Represented in the Archdioceses of Chicago, Dubuque, Denver, Detroit, Kansas City in Kansas, Omaha, Philadelphia, Portland (OR), Santa Fe, Seattle, St. Paul-Minneapolis, San Francisco, and the Dioceses of Bismarck, Boise, Cheyenne, El Paso, Des Moines, Fargo, Fresno, Great Falls-Billings, Kansas City-St. Joseph, Lincoln, Las Cruces, Phoenix, Pueblo, Sacramento, Salt Lake City, San Diego, and Springfield-Cape Girardeau. Also in Mexico, Hungary, Jamaica, and South America.

Pittsburgh **P**

Regional Community of Pittsburgh (1843): 3333 Fifth Ave., Pittsburgh, PA 15213. Tel: 412-578-6225; Fax: 412-578-6180. Sr. Sheila Carney, R.S.M., Pres.; Sr. Patricia Hodge, R.S.M., Community Archivist.

Total number in the community 229.

Ministry in the field of Education and Health Services.

Legal Titles & Holdings: *Carlow College Pittsburgh Mercy Health System, Inc.; The Mercy Hospital of Pittsburgh Pittsburgh Mercy Foundation; Mercy Center for Chemical Dependency; Mercy Psychiatric Institute; St. Joseph Nursing and Health Care Center, Inc.; St. Pius X Residence,* Pittsburgh, PA; *Holy Cross Health Corporation, Inc.; Holy Cross Hospital,* Fort Lauderdale, FL.

Represented in the Archdioceses of Boston, Baltimore, Hartford, Miami and Washington, and the Dioceses of Charleston, Erie, Greensburg, Orlando, Pittsburgh, Raleigh and Richmond. Also in Guatemala, Peru and Puerto Rico.

Portland **P**

Regional Community of Portland: *St. Joseph's Convent Motherhouse,* 605 Stevens Ave., Portland, ME 04103. Tel: 207-797-7861; Fax: 207-797-0146. Sr. Mary Laboure Morin, R.S.M., Pres.; Sr. Mary Shaun Sevigny, R.S.M., Community Archivist.

Total number in the community 144.

Ministry in the field of Education; Health Services; Catechetical Centers; Social Services.

Represented in the Archdiocese of New York, and the Dioceses of Manchester, Savannah and Portland (ME). Also in the Bahamas.

Providence **P**

Regional Community of Providence: *Sisters of Mercy of the Americas,* Highland View Rd., Cumberland, RI 02864. Tel: 401-333-6333; Fax: 401-333-6450. Sr. Barbara Riley, R.S.M., Pres.; Sr. Catherine Felton, R.S.M., Community Archivist.

Total number in community 419.

Sisters serve and staff: Houses of Prayer; Hospitality Houses; Transitional House; Literacy Centers; Nursing Home; University; High Schools; Elementary Schools; Office of Peace and Justice; Diocesan Offices; Pre-School and Day Care; Education for Special Groups; Health Services; Pastoral Care; Religious Education; Parish Ministry Centers; Social Service; Spirituality and Counseling Services; Foreign Missionary work.

Legal Holdings or Titles: *Sisters of Mercy of Providence, Inc.; Mount St. Rita Health Centre, Inc.; Mercymount Country Day School; Mercy Lodge House of Hospitality;* Cumberland, RI; *St. Mary Academy,* East Providence, RI; *Salve Regina University,* Newport, RI; *McAuley House; McAuley Village,* Providence, RI.

Represented in the Archdioceses of Baltimore, Boston, Chicago, Hartford, Philadelphia, St. Louis and Washington, and the Dioceses of Fall River, Ogdensburg, Phoenix, Pittsburgh, Portland (ME), Providence, Richmond and St. Petersburg. Also in Australia, Belize, Ireland and Honduras.

Rochester **P**

Regional Community of Rochester (1857): 1437 Blossom Rd., Rochester, NY 14610. Tel: 716-288-2710; Fax: 716-288-2756. Sr. Ann Miller, Pres. Tel: 716-482-0552.

Total number in the community 215.

Properties owned: *Our Lady of Mercy High School,* Rochester, NY; *Mercy Prayer Center,* Rochester, NY; *Mercy Motherhouse,* Rochester, NY.

Ministry in the field of Education at all levels; Inner City and Urban

Renewal Programs; Religious Education Coords.; Parish Associates; Campus Ministry; Social Work; Rural Ministry; Prayer Ministry; Ministry with the Aging; Hospital Ministry; Parish Visitation; Health Apostolates; AIDS Ministry; Foreign Missions (Chile); Care of Foster Children; Ministry to Pregnant Women; Counselling.

Represented in the Archdioceses of Atlanta, and the Dioceses of Jackson, Phoenix, Rochester, San Jose and Yakima. Also in Santiago and Guam.

St. Louis **P**

Regional Community of St. Louis: *Sisters of Mercy,* 2039 N. Geyer Rd., St. Louis, MO 63131-3399. Tel: 314-966-4313. Sr. Richard Mary Burke, R.S.M., Regl. Pres.

Total number in community 359.

Ministry in the following areas: Hospitals; Ambulatory Health Care Center; Long Term Care; Social Work Centers; Education Centers; Care and Counseling; Ministry to Elderly; Parish Ministry-Pastoral Care-Lay Ministry; Universities and Colleges; High Schools; Elementary Schools; Education Research Programs; Schools for Exceptional Children; Adult Education; Parish Directors of Religious Education-Coordinator of Religious Education; staffing of Diocesan Offices; Retreat-Renewal; Basic Formation; On-Going Development; Vocation Offices; Novitiate; Creative Spirituality Department/Office of Mercy/Associates-Volunteers.

Properties owned or sponsored: *Mercy Center,* St. Louis, MO. Hospitals: *Sisters of Mercy Health System, St. Louis, Inc.; St. Edward Health Facilities of Logan County-dba North Logan Mercy Hospital,* Paris, AR; *St. Edward Mercy Medical Center,* Fort Smith, AR; *St. Edward Health Facilities of Franklin County, dba Mercy Hospital/Turner Memorial,* Ozark, AR; *Harbor View Mercy Hospital,* Fort Smith, AR; *Saint Joseph's Regional Health Center, Inc.,* Hot Springs, AR; *St. Edward Health Facilities of Scott County, dba Mercy Hospital of Scott County; Pinewood Nursing Home; Mercy Village,* Waldron, AR; *Mercy Hospitals of Kansas, Inc., dba Mercy Hospital of Fort Scott,* Fort Scott, KS; *St. Mary's Hospital,* Enid, OK; *Mercy Hospital of Independence,* Independence, KS; *St. John's Mercy Medical Center,* St. Louis, MO; *St. John's Regional Health Center,* Springfield, MO; *St. John's Mercy Hospital,* Washington, MO; *Mercy Health Center, Inc.,* Oklahoma City, OK; *Mercy Hospital of Laredo, dba Mercy Regional Medical Center,* Laredo, TX. High Schools: *Mount St. Mary Academy,* Little Rock, AR; *Mount St. Mary High School,* Oklahoma City, OK.

Convent Corporations: *Sisters of Mercy of the Union in the United States of America-Province of St. Louis; St. Joseph's Convent of Mercy in St. Louis, Inc.; Religious Sisters of Mercy of the Province of St. Louis of Springfield, Inc.; Religious Sisters of Mercy of Louisiana, Inc.; Sisters of Mercy of Mississippi, Inc.; Religious Sisters of Mercy of the Province of St. Louis of South Texas, Inc.; Sisters of Mercy of Oklahoma, Inc.; The Sisters of Mercy of St. Joseph's Convent of Hot Springs, Arkansas, Inc.; The Sisters of Mercy of Mt. St. Mary Convent of Little Rock, Arkansas, Inc.; The Sisters of Mercy of Fort Scott, Kansas, Inc.; The Religious Sisters of Mercy of Fredonia, Kansas, Inc.; The Health and Retirement Corporation of the Religious Sisters of Mercy of Arkansas; The Sisters of Mercy of St. Edward Mercy Convent of Fort Smith, Arkansas, Inc.; The Religious Sisters of Mercy of Independence, Kansas, Inc.; Sisters of Mercy Education System, St. Louis, Inc.; Sisters of Mercy of Arkansas Housing, Inc.*

Represented in the Archdioceses of Baltimore, Boston, Cincinnati, Denver, Detroit, Hartford, Mobile, New Orleans, Oklahoma City, Omaha, Portland, St. Louis and San Antonio and in the Dioceses of Amarillo, Baton Rouge, Biloxi, Brownsville, Columbus, Corpus Christi, Covington, Houma-Thibodaux, Jackson, Jefferson City, Lafayette (LA), Little Rock, Lubbock, Oakland, Pittsburgh, St. Cloud, Springfield-Cape Girardeau and Wichita. Also in Dublin, Ireland and Ghana, South Africa.

Vermont **P**

Regional Community of Vermont: *Mt. St. Mary Motherhouse and Novitiate,* 100 Mansfield Ave., Burlington, VT 05401. Tel: 802-863-6835. Sr. Jeannine Mercure, R.S.M., Pres.

Total number in the community 92.

Properties owned or sponsored: *Trinity College of Vermont, Inc.; Institute for Spiritual Development; Mater Christi School Inc.,* Burlington, VT.

Ministry in the field of Education & Spirituality; Parish Ministry.

Represented in the Archdioceses of Hartford and Washington, and the Dioceses of Burlington, Ogdensburg and San Bernardino. Also in Saipan.

[2590] (H.M.S.S.)—SISTERS OF MERCY OF THE BLESSED SACRAMENT **P**

(Sisters of Mercy of the Blessed Sacrament)

Founded in Mexico in 1910. First foundation in the United States in 1926.

General Motherhouse: Fernandez Leal #130, Coyoacan 04330, Mexico. Mother Guadalupe Aguilar Cancino, H.M.S.S., Supr. Gen.

Regional House: *Blessed Sacrament Convent,* 222 W. Cevallos St., San Antonio, TX 78204. Tel: 210-223-5013; 222-1354. Sr. Dolores Munoz, H.M.S.S., Regl. Supr.

Professed Sisters in U.S. 32; Aspirants 1; Novices 1.

Represented in the Archdioceses of Omaha, San Antonio, and the Dioceses of Corpus Christi, San Bernardino and San Diego.

[2600] (S.M.)—SISTERS OF MERCY (CORK AND ROSS) **D**

General Motherhouse: *St. Columba Convent,* Bishopstown Ave., West Cork, Ireland. Sr. M. Imelda O'Shaughnessy, Supr. Gen.

U.S. Address: *Sacred Heart Convent,* 6240 105th St., Jacksonville, FL 32244. Tel: 904-771-3858. Sr. Regina Fahy, Contact Person.
Represented in the Diocese of St. Augustine.

[2610] (S.M.D.C.)—SISTERS OF MERCY OF ST. VINCENT DE PAUL OF (SZATMAR) P

Founded in Hungary in 1842. Mother M. Benedicta Raskovska, Supr. Gen. Slovak Republic. Europe.
U.S. Foundation: *St. Joseph Home, Convent and Novitiate,* 240 Longhouse Dr., Hewitt, NJ 07421. Tel: 201-853-7212. Sr. Mary Innocenta Butko, Supr.
Represented in the Diocese of Paterson.

[2630] (S.C.S.C.)—SISTERS OF MERCY OF THE HOLY CROSS P

Founded in Switzerland in 1856. First foundation in the U.S. in 1912.
General Motherhouse: Ingenbohl, Switzerland. Sr. Louise-Henri Kolly, Supr. Gen.
U.S. Provincial Residence: *Holy Cross Sisters,* 700 E. Riverside Ave., Merrill, WI 54452; Fax: 715-536-5445. Sr. Mary Anthony Menting, Prov.
Total number in community 50.
Legal Title: *Bell Tower Residence, Inc.; Sisters of Mercy of the Holy Cross of Merrill WI Inc.*
Ministry in the following areas: Schools; Hospitals; Home Nursing; Social Ministries; Parishes and Diocesan Offices; Retirement Homes; Adult Education; Campus Ministries.
Represented in the Archdioceses of Cincinnati, Milwaukee, New Orleans, St. Louis, and the Dioceses of Belleville, Baton Rouge, Bismarck, Des Moines, Gaylord, Great Falls-Billings, Green Bay, Superior and Steubenville.

[2655] SISTERS OF MERCY OF PORTLAND D

Motherhouse: *Diocesan Sisters of Mercy of Portland,* 265 Cottage Rd., South Portland, ME 04106. Tel: 207-767-5804. Sr. Eunice Boyd, R.S.M.

[2670] (S.O.L.M.)—SISTERS OF OUR LADY OF MERCY

(Mercedarians)

General Motherhouse: via Ostriana 24, Rome, Italy. Mother Luisa Sanchez, Supr. Gen.
Brooklyn: *Most Precious Blood,* 133 27th Ave., Brooklyn, NY 11214. Sr. Doloretta, Supr.
Sisters 4.
St. Edward, Pine Hill NJ, 08021. Sr. Leonilla, Supr.
Sisters 6.
Represented in the Dioceses of Brooklyn and Camden.

[2675] (C.F.M.M.)—MINIM DAUGHTERS OF MARY IMMACULATE P

Founded in Leon, Guanajuato, Mexico on March 25, 1886. Came to the United States in 1926, fleeing from a Catholic persecution.
General Motherhouse: Leon, Guanajuato, Mexico. Mother Margarita Maria Gutierrez, Mother General.
Total number in community 395.
U.S. Address: *Our Lady of Lourdes High School,* P.O. Box 1865, Nogales, AZ 85628. Tel: 602-287-5659.
Ministry in Academic and Religious Education and Health Care.
Properties owned: *Convent of the Holy Cross Hospital,* Nogales, AZ; *Our Lady of Lourdes Convent,* Nogales, AZ; *Our Lady of Lourdes High School,* Nogales, AZ.
Total Sisters in the U.S. 26.
Represented in the Diocese of Tucson.

[2677] (S.M.M.I.)—SISTERS MINOR OF MARY IMMACULATE D

First foundation in the United States June 13, 1989. Active-contemplative Franciscan Religious Congregation following the spirituality of St. Maximilian Mary Kolbe, O.F.M.Conv.
Central Motherhouse & Novitiate: Via Germanico 198, 00192 Rome, Italy. Tel: 011-39-6-324-2036. Mother Maria Elisabetta Patrizi, S.M.M.I., Foundress.
American Headquarters - St. Francis Villa: *Vice Province of the Immaculate Conception,* 138 Brushy Hill Rd., Danbury, CT 06810-8431. Tel: 203-744-8041. Sr. Theresa Marie Kovacs, S.M.M.I., Vice Prov. Supr.
Legal Title: *Sisters Minor of Mary Immaculate.*
Ministry in the field of Academic and Religious Education; Health Care; Parish & Shrine work; Work with the elderly, youth groups; Newman Centers.
Represented in the Dioceses of Bridgeport, Fargo and Springfield (MA).

[2680] (S.M.)—MISERICORDIA SISTERS P

Founded in Canada in 1848. First foundation in the United States in 1887.
General Motherhouse: 12435 Misericorde Ave., Montreal, Que, Canada H4J 2G3. Tel: 514-332-0550. Sr. Jeannine Vallieres, Supr. Gen.
U.S. Address: 820 Jungles Ave., Aurora, IL 60505.
Represented in the Archdioceses of Chicago, Milwaukee and New York.

[2690] (M.C.D.P.)—MISSIONARY CATECHISTS OF DIVINE PROVIDENCE, SAN ANTONIO, TEXAS P

Autonomy with Pontifical status granted December 12, 1989.
Administrative House: *St. Andrew's Convent,* 2318 Castroville Rd., San Antonio, TX 78237. Tel: 210-432-0113; Fax: 210-432-1709. Sr. Carmen Therese Lazo, Supr.
Properties owned or sponsored: *Benitia Family Center,* San Antonio, TX.
Total number in community 52.
Represented in the Archdioceses of Anchorage, San Antonio, and the Dioceses of Austin, Brownsville, Dallas, El Paso, Fort Worth, Fresno, Galveston-Houston, Monterey, San Angelo and Tyler.

[2700] (M.C.SS.CC.J.M.)—MISSIONARY CATECHISTS OF THE SACRED HEARTS OF JESUS AND MARY D

Founded in Mexico City, D.F. in 1918. U.S. foundation in 1943 in Victoria, Texas.
Central House: Mexico City, Mexico. Sr. Hermila Pena, Supr. Gen.
U.S. Regional Office: 805 S. Liberty St., Victoria, TX 77901-8907. Tel: 512-578-9302. Sr. Eva Sanchez, Prov. Supr.
Total number in U.S. Region 57.
Catechetical familiy ministry in parishes and missions.
Represented in the Dioceses of Fort Worth, Galveston-Houston, Lubbock, Metuchen, Trenton and Victoria.

[2710] (M.C.)—MISSIONARIES OF CHARITY P

Founded in India, 1950.
General Motherhouse: 54A AJC Bose Rd., Calcutta 700016, India. Mother M. Teresa Bojaxhiu, M.C., Mother Gen.
U.S. Foundation & Office (1971): *Missionaries of Charity,* 335 E. 145th St., Bronx, NY 10451. Tel: 718-292-0019. Sr. M. Sabita, M.C., Regl. Supr.
Professed sisters in Congregation 4,500.
Legal Title: *Missionaries of Charity, Inc.*
Sisters serve and staff: Soup Kitchens; Emergency Shelters for Women; Homes for Unwed Mothers; Shelters for Unwed Mothers; Shelters for Men; Religious Education Programs; After-School and Summer Camp Programs for Children; Homes for AIDS Patients; Prison Ministry; Nursing Homes; Hospital and Shut-in Ministry; Family Counseling and Ministry; Home for Infants for Adoption; Foreign Missionary Work.
Represented in the Archdioceses of Atlanta, Boston, Chicago, Denver, Detroit, Los Angeles, Miami, New York, Newark, Philadelphia, San Francisco, St. Louis, Washington, and the Dioceses of Baton Rouge, Brooklyn, Charlotte, Dallas, Fall River, Gallup, Lafayette, Lexington, Little Rock, Peoria, Phoenix and Memphis. Also in Canada and Mexico.

[2715] (M.S.C.K.)—MISSIONARY SISTERS OF CHRIST THE KING D

Founded in Poland in 1959 by Father Ignacy Posadzy. First foundation in the U.S. 1978.
General Motherhouse: *Siostry Misjonarki Chrystusa Krola,* ulica Siostr Misjonarek 10, 61-680 Poznan, Poland. Sr. Teresa Ambroza, M.Chr., Supr. Gen.
Delegation Superior in the U.S.: 3030 18 Mile Rd., Sterling Heights, MI 48314. Tel: 810-979-0255. Sr. Elzbieta Veronica Ilnicka, M.Chr., Prov.; Sr. Irena Gertrude Szymanska, M.Chr., Vice Prov.; Sr. Boguslawa Trus, M.Chr., Treas.
Legal Title: *Missionary Sisters of Christ the King for Polonia.*
Total in Congregation 198; Professed in U.S. and Canada 19.
Ministry among Polish immigrants and people of Polish heritage.
Represented in the Archdioceses of Chicago, Detroit, Los Angeles and in the Diocese of San Jose. Also in Toronto, Canada.

[2717] (M.D.P.V.M.)—MISSIONARY DAUGHTERS OF THE MOST PURE VIRGIN MARY P

Founded in Mexico. First foundatioin in the United States in the Diocese of Corpus Christi 1916.
General Motherhouse: Heroe de Nacocariz, 72 Sur, Aguascalientes, Mexico. Mother Maria Cristina Duran Herrera, M.D.P.V.M., Supr. Gen.
Missionary Daughters of the Most Pure Virgin Mary: 919 N. 9th St., Kingsville, TX 78363. Tel: 512-595-1087. Sr. Rafaela Valadez, M.D.P.V.M., Supr.; Sr. Carmen Villalpando, M.D.P.V.M., Sec.; Sr. Vicenta Aquilar, M.D.P.V.M., Treas.; Sr. Maria Amada Villarreal, M.D.P.V.M., Mission Dir.
Legal Title: *Missionary Daughters of the Most Pure Virgin Mary.*
Total in Congregation 500; Present in U.S. 31.
Ministry in the field of Religious and Academic Education at the elementary level; Pastoral Ministry.
Represented in the Diocese of Camden, Corpus Christi, and Yakima.

[2720] (M.H.S.H.)—MISSION HELPERS OF THE SACRED HEART P

Founded in the United States in 1890.
Mission Helper Center: 1001 W. Joppa Rd., Baltimore, MD 21204-3787. Tel: 410-823-8585; Fax: 410-825-6355. Sr. Catherine Dages, Pres.
Total number in community 113.
Legal Title: *Institute of Mission Helpers of Baltimore City.*
Represented in the Archdioceses of Atlanta, Baltimore, Boston, Cincinnati, Detroit, Indianapolis, New York, San Juan (PR), San Antonio, San Francisco, Washington, and the Dioceses of Erie, Norwich, Orlando, Raleigh, Pensacola-Tallahassee, Pittsburgh, Rochester, St. Petersburg, Tucson, Wilmington, and Youngstown. Also in Venezuela.

[2730] (M.S.H.R.)—MISSIONARY SISTERS OF THE HOLY ROSARY P

Generalate (1924): 23 Cross Ave., Blackrock County Dublin, Ireland. Sr. Monica Devine, Supr. Gen.
U.S. Regional Headquarters (1954): *Missionary Sisters of the Holy Rosary,* 741 Polo Rd., Bryn Mawr, PA 19010. Tel: 610-520-1974. Sr. Paula Molloy, M.S.H.R., Regl. Rep. (U.S. Region).
Total number in community 460.
Represented in the Archdiocese of Philadelphia.

[2740] (M.S.Sp.)—MISSION SISTERS OF THE HOLY SPIRIT D

Motherhouse and Novitiate: 1030 N. River Rd., Saginaw, MI 48609. Tel: 517-781-0934. Sr. Margo Tafoya, Community Coord.
Total number in community 12.
Legal Title: *Society of the Mission Sisters of the Holy Spirit of the Diocese of Saginaw; Holy Spirit Sisters Charitable Trust,* Saginaw, MI.
Ministry in Social Services; Religious Education at all levels including Mentally Retarded and Deaf; Pastoral Ministry; Pastoral Administrator.
Represented in the Diocese of Saginaw.

[2750] (I.C.M.)—MISSIONARY SISTERS OF THE IMMACULATE HEART OF MARY P

Founded in India in 1897. First foundation in the United States in 1910.
Generalate: Via di Villa Troili, 30, Rome, Italy, 00163. Sr. M. Therese De Coninck, I.C.M., Supr. Gen.
Universal total of Congregation 1,055.
American Province: 238 E. 15th St., New York, NY 10003. Tel: 212-677-2959. Sr. Alene Grothues, I.C.M., Prov.
Total number in community 31.
Missionaries Minister in Education; Catechetical; Pastoral and Social Ministry; Health Care; Leprosaria; International Justice and the Promotion of Human Dignity.
Represented in the Archdioceses of Los Angeles, New York and Philadelphia, and the Dioceses of Albany and Brownsville. Also in Belgium, Brazil, Burundi, Cameroon, Guatemala, Hong Kong, India, Italy, Philippines, Taiwan, Outer Mongolia, Tchad, Virgin Islands, West Indies and Zaire.

[2760] (S.M.I.C.)—MISSIONARY SISTERS OF THE IMMACULATE CONCEPTION OF THE MOTHER OF GOD P

Founded in Brazil in 1910. First foundation in the United States in 1922.
Generalate: 48 Garden Ave., West Paterson, NJ 07424-3325. Tel: 201-279-1484. Sr. Luci Fontenele, S.M.I.C., Coord. Gen.
U.S. Province (1960): *Provincialate of the Immaculate Conception,* P.O. Box 3026, Paterson, NJ 07509-3026. Tel: 201-279-3790; Fax: 201-742-8231. Sr. Saundra McKeta, S.M.I.C., Prov. Coord.
Professed Sisters 60.
Properties owned: *Holy Family Residence,* Paterson, NJ.

Sisters serve and staff: Elementary Schools; Universities, Religious Education; Health and Social Services; Sheltered Care Facility for Aged Men and Women.
Represented in the Archdioceses of Newark, San Antonio and Washington, and the Dioceses of Austin, Brownsville, Gallup, Galveston-Houston, Paterson, Portland (ME), San Bernardino, Trenton and Victoria.

[2770] (M.J.M.J.)—MISSIONARIES OF JESUS, MARY AND JOSEPH P

Founded in Spain in 1942. First foundation in United States in 1956. Mother Maria Dolores de la Cruz Domingo, Foundress.
MOTHERHOUSE: Plaza de la In. Concepcion No. 1, Madrid, Spain 28019. Sr. Clementina Martinez, Supr. Gen.
DELEGATION HEADQUARTERS AND FORMATION HOUSE: 12940 Up River Rd., Corpus Christi, TX 78410. Tel: 512-241-1955. Sr. Avelina Sosa, M.J.M.J., Delegation Supr.; Sr. Milagros Tormo, M.J.M.J., Community Supr.
Sisters 22.
Properties owned: *Joseph of the Valley Pre-School,* El Paso, TX.
Represented in the Dioceses of Corpus Christi, El Paso and San Antonio. Also in Mexico.

[2780] (M.SS.S.)—MISSIONARY SISTERS OF THE MOST BLESSED SACRAMENT P

GENERAL MOTHERHOUSE: San Lucas 7, Madrid, Spain. Mother Socorro Musveta, Mother Gen.
U.S. FOUNDATION: *Convent of Mary Immaculate,* 1111 Wordin Ave., Bridgeport, CT 06605. Sr. Presentacion Zabala, Prov.
FORMATION CENTER: 1109-1111 Wordin Ave., Bridgeport, CT 06605.
Represented in the Archdioceses of Boston and Newark and the Diocese of Bridgeport.

[2790] (M.S.B.T.)—MISSIONARY SERVANTS OF THE MOST BLESSED TRINITY P

Founded in United States in 1912.
MOTHERHOUSE-GENERALATE-NOVITIATE AND CANDIDACY: 3501 Solly Ave., Philadelphia, PA 19136. Tel: 215-335-7550. Sr. Siena Marie Wahl, M.S.B.T., Gen. Custodian.
Total number in community 257.
Properties owned and sponsored: *Blessed Trinity Mother Missionary Cenacle,* Philadelphia, PA; *St. Patrick's School,* Phenix City, AL; *Blessed Trinity Shrine Retreat Cenacle,* Holy Trinity, AL; *Trinita Ecumenical Retreat Center,* New Hartford, CT; *Blessed Trinity Missionary Cenacle,* Stirling, NJ; *Blessed Trinity Mother Missionary Cenacle,* Philadelphia, PA.
Represented in the Archdioceses of Boston, Chicago, Hartford, Los Angeles, Newark, Mobile, New York, Philadelphia, Washington, and the Dioceses of Arlington, Biloxi, Birmingham, Brooklyn, Charleston, Camden, Charlotte, Cleveland, Fall River, Gallup, Jackson, Paterson, Pensacola-Tallahassee, Raleigh, Richmond, Rockford, Savannah, Wilmington and Yakima Also in Puerto Rico and Mexico.

[2800] (M.S.C.)—MISSIONARY SISTERS OF THE MOST SACRED HEART OF JESUS (OF HILTRUP) P

Founded in Germany in 1899. First foundation in the United States in 1908.
GENERALATE: Via Martiri di Via Fani, Sutri (Viterbo), Italy. Sr. M. Klara, M.S.C.
AMERICAN PROVINCE-MOTHERHOUSE (1908): *St. Michael's Convent,* 51 Seminary Ave., Reading, PA 19605. Tel: 215-929-5751. Sr. Joanne Leblanc, M.S.C., Coord.; Sr. Theresa Lepera, M.S.C., Coord.
MSC Province Center, 2811 Moyers Ln., Reading PA, 19605. Tel: 215-929-5944. Sr. Teresita Nolden, M.S.C., Prov.
Total number in U.S. Province 147.
Legal Title: *Missionary Sisters of the Most Sacred Heart of Jesus, Inc.*
Ministry in Education; Health Care; Home Health Care; Parish Ministry; Prison Ministry; Counseling; Social Ministry; Spiritual Ministry.
Properties owned or sponsored: *St. Mary's Hospital,* Athens, GA; *MSC Province Center; St. Michael Convent,* Reading, PA.
Represented in the Archdioceses of Atlanta, Philadelphia, Washington,, and the Dioceses of Allentown, Galveston-Houston, Harrisburg, Jackson, Venice and Wheeling-Charleston.

[2810] (M.S.M.G.)—MISSIONARY SISTERS OF MOTHER OF GOD D

(Byzantine Ukrainian Rite-Stamford)
MOTHERHOUSE: 711 N. Franklin St., Philadelphia, PA 19123. Tel: 215-627-7808.
Novitiate, 111 W. North St., Stamford, CT 06902. Tel: 203-323-1237. Sr. Josepha Kruchinsky, M.S.M.G., Supr.
Total number in community 11.
Ministry in the field of Education.
Represented in the Ukrainian Archdiocese of Philadelphia and in the Ukrainian Diocese of Stamford.

[2820] (M.S.O.L.A.)—MISSIONARY SISTERS OF OUR LADY OF AFRICA P

(Sisters of Africa)
Founded in Algiers, N. Africa, in 1869. First foundation in the United States in 1929.
GENERAL MOTHERHOUSE: Rome, Italy. Sr. Marie McDonald, Supr. Gen.
Universal total in Congregation 1,330.
AMERICAN HEADQUARTERS: 47 West Spring St., Winooski, VT 05404. Tel: 802-655-4003. Sr. Lucille Pilotte, District Supr.
Total number in U.S. 15.
Represented in the Archdiocese of Washington and the Diocese of Burlington.

[2830] (M.O.M.)—MISSIONARY SISTERS OF OUR LADY OF MERCY D

Founded in Piaui, Brazil in 1938. First foundation in United States at Lackawanna, New York 1955.
GENERAL MOTHERHOUSE: Salvador, Bahia, Brazil. Mother Raquel Novaes, Supr. Gen.
U.S. HEADQUARTERS: *Rainbow K,* 388 Franklin St., Buffalo, NY 14202. Tel: 716-854-5198. Sr. M. Neves, Supr.
Total number in community 3.
Represented in the Diocese of Buffalo.

[2840] (M.C.)—POOR CLARE MISSIONARY SISTERS P

Founded in Mexico by Mother Maria Ines Teresa Arias.
GENERAL MOTHERHOUSE: Via Cardinale Garampi 17, Pineta Sachetti, Rome, Italy. Mother Maria Teresa Botello, Gen. Supr.
U.S. FOUNDATION: *Regional House and Novitiate,* 1019 N. Newhope, Santa Ana, CA 92703.
Total number in community 42.
Ministry in Day Nurseries; Schools and Retreat House.
Represented in the Archdiocese of Los Angeles and the Diocese of Orange.

[2850] (C.P.S.)—MISSIONARY SISTERS OF THE PRECIOUS BLOOD P

Founded in South Africa on Sept. 8, 1885. First founded in the United States at Princeton, New Jersey on August 15, 1925.
GENERAL MOTHERHOUSE: Casa Generalizia, Suore Missionarie del Preziosissimo Sangue Mariannhill, Via San Giovanni Eudes 93, Roma, Italia, 00163.
Universal number in Congregation 1,018.
AMERICAN PROVINCE: *Novitiate-Precious Blood Convent,* P.O. Box 97, Reading, PA 19607-0097. Tel: 215-777-1624. *Precious Blood Convent,* 1094 Welsh Rd., Reading, PA 19607. Sr. M. Francis Bisland, C.P.S., Prov. Supr.
Total number in community 33.
Represented in the Diocese of Allentown and Gallup.

[2860] (M.S.C.)—MISSIONARY SISTERS OF THE SACRED HEART OF JESUS P
(Cabrini Sisters)

Founded in Italy in 1880, by Saint Frances Xavier Cabrini. First foundation in the United States 1889.
MOTHERHOUSE: Viale Cortina D'Ampezzo, 269, Rome, Italy, 00135. Sr. Lina Colombini, Supr. Gen.
PROVINCIAL OFFICE: 222 E. 19th St., 5B, New York, NY 10003. Sr. Pietrina Raccuglia, M.S.C., Prov. Supr.
Professed Sisters 148.
Total in Congregation 547.
Ministry in the field of Education; Hospitals; Nursing Home; Child Care; Parish Ministry; Pastoral Work; Retreat & Shrine Ministry.
Represented in the Archdioceses of Chicago, Denver, New Orleans, New York, Philadelphia and Seattle and in the Diocese of Brooklyn. Also in Argentina, Australia, Brazil, Central America, England, France, Italy, Philippines, Portugal, Russia, Spain, Swaziland and Taiwan.

[2865] (M.S.C.Gpe.)—MISSIONARIES OF THE SACRED HEART OF JESUS AND OUR LADY OF GUADALUPE

NATIONAL ADDRESS: 1212 E. Euclid Ave., Arlington Heights, IL 60004. Tel: 708-398-1350. Sr. Piedad Fernandez, Pres.; Sr. Esperansa Hernandez, Sec.; Sr. Zoila Alcala, Treas.
Ministry in Schools; Nursing Homes; Seminaries and Foreign Missions.
Represented in the Archdiocese of Boston, Chicago, San Francisco and Washington and the Diocese of Rockford.

[2880] (S.S.C.)—MISSIONARY SISTERS OF ST. COLUMBAN (Columban Sisters) P

Founded in Ireland in 1922. First Foundation in the United States in 1930.
GENERAL MOTHERHOUSE: Wicklow, Ireland. Sr. Mary Nolan, Congregational Leader.
U.S. REGION: *Missionary Sisters of St. Columban,* 73 Mapleton St., Brighton, MA 02135. Tel: 617-782-5683; Fax: 617-789-3569. Sr. Corona Colleary, S.S.C., Regl. Coord.
Professed Sisters 27.
Represented in the Archdioceses of Boston, Chicago and Los Angeles and the Diocese of Buffalo.

[2890] (M.S.S.A.)—MISSIONARY SERVANTS OF ST. ANTHONY D

Founded in the United States in 1929.
GENERAL MOTHERHOUSE: 100 Peter Baque Rd., San Antonio, TX 78209. Tel: 210-824-4553. Sr. Mary Ann Domagalski, M.S.S.A., Supr. Gen.
Total number in community 5.
Represented in the Archdiocese of San Antonio.

[2900] (M.S.C.S.)—MISSIONARY SISTERS OF ST. CHARLES BORROMEO (Scalabrini Sisters)

Founded in Italy in 1895. First United States in 1941.
MOTHERHOUSE: Via Monte del Gallo 68, Rome, Italy, 00165. Sr. Lice M. Signor, Gen.
Universal total in Congregation 825.
NORTH AMERICAN PROVINCIAL HOUSE: *Bishop Scalabrini Community and Provincial House,* 1414 N. 37th Ave., Melrose Park, IL 60160. Tel: 708-343-2162; Fax: 708-343-6452. Sr. Marciana Zambiasi, M.S.C.S., Prov.
Total number in community 63.
Ministry in the fields of Education; Pastoral Care of the Sick; Catechesis; Social Service.
Represented in the Archdioceses of Chicago, New York and Washington and the Diocese of San Jose. Also in Canada, Mexico and the Philippines.

[2920] (M.D.)—MOTHERS OF THE HELPLESS D

Founded in Malaga, Spain in 1881. Founded in the United States in 1916.
GENERAL MOTHERHOUSE: Avda. San Jose de la Montana No.15, Valencia, Spain, 46008. Mother Esperanza Ordonez, Supr. Gen.
U.S. ADDRESS: *Sacred Heart Residence,* 432 W. 20th St., New York, NY 10011. Mother Guadalupe Sordo, Supr.
Professed Sisters in U.S. 8.
Properties owned and sponsored: *San Jose De La Montana Day Nursery; Sacred Heart Residence.*
Represented in the Archdiocese of New York.

[2930] (I.H.M.)—THE CALIFORNIA INSTITUTE OF THE SISTERS OF THE MOST HOLY AND IMMACULATE HEART OF THE BLESSED VIRGIN MARY P

Founded in Spain in 1848. First foundation in the United States in 1871.
GENERALATE, NOVITIATE AND RETREAT HOUSE: 3431 Waverly Dr., Los Angeles, CA 90027. Tel: 213-664-1124.
Professed Sisters 28.
Properties staffed: High Schools; Grammar Schools 2.
Represented in the Archdiocese of Los Angeles.

[2940] (M.H.S.)—SISTERS OF THE MOST HOLY SACRAMENT P

Founded in France in 1851. First foundation in the United States in 1872. Pontifical Approbation 1935.
GENERALATE: *Sisters of the Most Holy Sacrament,* 313 Corona Dr., P.O. Box 30727, Lafayette, LA 70593-0727. Tel: 318-981-8475. Sr. Anthony Richards, M.H.S., Major Supr.
Total number in community 45.

Legal Title: *St. Augustine Trust Fund,* Lafayette, LA; *Bethany Health Care Center,* Lafayette, LA.
Ministry in the field of Education; Homes for the Aged; Pastoral Care.
Represented in the Archdiocese of New Orleans, and the Dioceses of Baton Rouge, Biloxi, Gallup, and Lafayette (LA).

[2950] (N.D.S.)—CONGREGATION OF NOTRE DAME DE SION P

Founded in France in 1850. First foundation in the United States in 1892.
GENERALATE: Rome, Italy. Sr. Patricia Watson, N.D.S., Supr. Gen.
PROVINCIALATE: 349 Westminster Rd., Brooklyn, NY 11218. Tel: 718-282-9043. Sr. Audrey Doetzel, N.D.S., Prov. Supr.
Universal Total in Congregation 1,000.
Total in Community 3.
NOTRE DAME DE SION: 3823 Locust St., Kansas City, MO 64109. Tel: 816-931-1928.
Total number in community 2.
Represented in the Archdiocese of Chicago, and the Dioceses of Brooklyn and Kansas City-St. Joseph.

[2960] (N.D.)—NOTRE DAME SISTERS P

Founded in Czechoslovakia, Europe, in 1853. First foundation in the United States in 1910.
GENERAL MOTHERHOUSE: Hradec Kralove, Republic of Czechoslovakia. Mother M. Purissima Kazdova, Supr. Gen.
U.S. PROVINCIAL MOTHERHOUSE: *Notre Dame Convent,* 3501 State St., Omaha, NE 68112. Tel: 402-455-2994. Sr. Mary Ann Zimmer, N.D., Prov. Supr.
Total number in community 73.
Sisters staff and serve: Elementary and Secondary Education; Hispanic Ministry; Pastoral Care; Social Work; Religious Education; Youth Ministry; Chemical Dependency Counseling; Health Care; TEC; Adult Education; Family Life-Diocesan Offices; Community Administration and Services.
Represented in the Archdioceses of Dubuque, Omaha, and the Dioceses of Davenport, Lincoln, Pueblo, Rapid City, Kansas City-St. Joseph, Springfield-Cape Girardeau, and St. Cloud.

[2970] (S.S.N.D.)—SCHOOL SISTERS OF NOTRE DAME P

Founded in Germany in 1833. First foundation in the United States in 1847.
GENERAL MOTHERHOUSE: Rome, Italy. Sr. Patricia Flynn, Supr. Gen.
MILWAUKEE PROVINCE (1850) MILWAUKEE; (1959) MEQUON; (1983) MILWAUKEE: *Notre Dame Sisters Provincial Offices,* 13105 Watertown Plank Rd., Elm Grove, WI 53122-2291. Tel: 414-782-1450; Fax: 414-782-2349. Sr. Laura Jean Spaeth, S.S.N.D., Leader.
Total number in community 646.
Legal Title: *School Sisters of Notre Dame at Milwaukee; Wisconsin, Inc.; School Sisters of Notre Dame at Milwaukee, Wisconsin, Inc. Charitable Trust.*
Properties owned: *Mount Mary College,* Milwaukee, WI; *Notre Dame of Elm Grove,* Elm Grove, WI; *Our Lady of Mt. Carmel Convent,* Mt. Calvary, WI.
Various ministries to Women, Youth, the Poor, Sick and Elderly; all levels of Academic Education; D.R.E.s; Pastoral Associates.
Represented in the Archdioceses of Chicago, Cincinnati, Detroit, Milwaukee, St. Paul-Minneapolis, Seattle, and the Dioceses of Baker, Fort Wayne-South Bend, Gallup, Gary, Grand Rapids, Green Bay, La Crosse, Lafayette (IN), Lexington, Madison, Manchester, Marquette, Phoenix, Portland, Rockford, Saginaw, Spokane, St. Cloud, Superior, Tulsa, Venice, and Wheeling-Charleston. Also in Africa, Caroline-Marshall Islands, Central America and Guam.
BALTIMORE PROVINCE (1876): *School Sisters of Notre Dame in the City of Baltimore, Villa Assumpta-Motherhouse and Maria Health Care Center,* 6401 N. Charles St., Baltimore, MD 21212-1099. Tel: 410-377-7774; Fax: 410-377-5363. Sr. Jane Burke, Prov. Leader.
Total number in community 430.
Properties Owned: *Villa Assumpta-Motherhouse of Baltimore Province; College of Notre Dame of Maryland; Notre Dame Preparatory School; Institute of Notre Dame,* Baltimore, MD.
Ministries to the Needy and Elderly; Teaching and Administering in the field of Academic Education at all levels; D.R.E.'s and Pastoral Associates.
Represented in the Archdioceses of Baltimore, Boston, Hartford, Los Angeles, Miami, Milwaukee, Newark, Philadelphia, St. Louis, San Antonio, Seattle, Washington, and the Dioceses of Arlington, Birmingham, Brooklyn, Camden, Charleston, Gary, Greensburg, Jackson, Lexington, Paterson, Palm Beach, Pittsburgh, Richmond, St. Petersburg, Tucson, Venice and Wilmington. Also in Boliva, Ghana, Italy, Vienna, El Salvador and Nigeria.
ST. LOUIS PROVINCE (1895): *School Sisters of Notre Dame,* 320 E. Ripa Ave., St. Louis, MO 63125. Tel: 314-544-0455; Fax: 314-544-6754. Sr. Kathleen Wegman, Prov. Supr.
Legal Title: *The School Sisters of Notre Dame of St. Louis.*
Total number in community 727.
Represented in the Archdioceses Atlanta, Baltimore, Boston, Chicago, Los Angeles, Louisville, Milwaukee, New Orleans, Oklahoma City, St. Louis, St. Paul-Minneapolis, San Antonio, Washington, and the Dioceses of Austin, Belleville, Bismarck, Bridgeport, Dallas, Davenport, Evansville, Fresno, Gallup, Jefferson City, Knoxville, Little Rock, La Crosse Monterey, Orange, Peoria, Rapid City, San Angelo, San Bernardino, San Diego, Shreveport, Sioux City, Springfield-Cape Girardeau, Springfield in Illinois, Tucson, and Venice. Also in Ghana, Gautemala, Nepal, Canada, Honduras, Japan, Kenya, South America, Rome and Sierra Leone.
MANKATO PROVINCE (1912): *School Sisters of Notre Dame,* 170 Good Counsel Dr., Mankato, MN 56001-3138. Tel: 507-389-4200; Fax: 507-345-6679. Sr. Katherine Du Val, Prov.; Sr. Irene Feltz, Community Archivist.
Total number in community 492.
Legal Title: *School Sisters of Notre Dame at Mankato, Minnesota, Inc.; School Sisters of Notre Dame at Mankato, Minnesota, Inc. - Charitable Trust School Sisters of Notre Dame Cooperative Investment Fund.*
Represented in the Archdioceses of Chicago, Dubuque, Miami, Milwaukee, New Orleans, New York, St. Louis, St. Paul-Minneapolis, Seattle and Washington, and the Dioceses of Albany, Alexandria, Bismarck, Brownsville, Bridgeport, Charlotte, Dallas, Duluth, Fargo, Forth Worth, New Ulm, Richmond, Rockford, Sioux City, Sioux Falls, Superior, St. Cloud, Tyler and Winona. Also in Guatemala and Kenya.
NORTHEASTERN PROVINCE (1957): *School Sisters of Notre Dame,* Wilton, CT 06897. Tel: 203-762-3318; Fax: 203-762-9434. Sr. Marie Jeannette Blatz, Prov. Leader.
Total number in community 436.
Legal Holdings and Titles: *The Northeastern Province of the School Sisters of Notre Dame in the State of Connecticut; Motherhouse and Lourdes Health Care Center,* Wilton, CT *Academy of the Holy Angels,* Demarest, NJ.
Represented in the Archdioceses of Baltimore, Boston, Hartford, Miami, Newark, New York, Philadelphia and Washington, and the Dioceses of Albany, Allentown, Bridgeport, Brooklyn, Camden, Manchester, Norwich, Paterson, Providence, Richmond, Rochester, Rockville Centre and Venice. Also in Cape Coast, Chile, Dominican Republic, Ghana, and Puerto Rico.
DALLAS PROVINCE (1961): *Notre Dame of Dallas - School Sisters of Notre Dame,* P.O. Box 227275, Dallas, TX 75222. Tel: 214-330-9152; Fax: 214-330-9197. Sr. Elizabeth Newman, Prov. Leader.
Total number in community 203.
Legal Title: *School Sisters of Notre Dame of Dallas Charitable Trust.*
Represented in the Archdioceses of New Orleans and San Antonio and in the Dioceses of Alexandria, Biloxi, Baton Rouge, Brownsville, Dallas, Fort Worth, Galveston-Houston, Jackson, Lafayette (LA), Little Rock, Phoenix, San Angelo, and Tucson Also in Guatemala, Hungary, and West Africa.
CHICAGO PROVINCE: *School Sisters of Notre Dame,* 1431 Euclid Ave., Berwyn, IL 60402. Tel: 708-749-1380. Sr. Catherine Sarther, S.S.N.D., Prov. Leader.
Total number in the community 162.
Properties Owned: *Academy of Our Lady,* Chicago, IL.
Ministry in the field of Academic, Special and Religious Education; Day Care Centers; Foreign Mission work; Nurses; Pastoral Work; Apostolate of the Aging; Vicar for Women Religious.
Represented in the Archdioceses of Baltimore, Chicago, Miami, Milwaukee, St. Louis, Washington, and the Dioceses of Belleville, Bridgeport, Fargo, Joliet, Lafayette, Peoria, Pueblo and Rockford. Also in Rome, Brazil, Japan and Paraguay.

[2980] (C.N.D.)—SISTERS OF THE CONGREGATION DE NOTRE DAME P

Founded in Canada in 1653. First Foundation in United States in 1860. American Novitiate established at Ridgefield, Connecticut; House of Formation in Staten Island, New York.
GENERAL MOTHERHOUSE: 4873 Westmount Ave., Montreal, Quebec , Canada.
GENERALATE: 2330 Sherbrooke St., W., Montreal, Quebec , Canada. Sr. Lorraine Caza, C.N.D., Congregation Leader.
U.S. PROVINCE (1946): *Blessed Sacrament Province,* 223 W. Mountain Rd., Ridgefield, CT 06877. Tel: 203-438-5282; Fax: 203-438-3150. Sr. Anne Leonard, C.N.D., Prov. Leader.
Total number in the U.S. Province 202.
Represented in the Archdioceses of Boston, Chicago, Hartford and New York, and the Dioceses of Albany, Bridgeport, Brooklyn, Brownsville, Charlotte, Fall River, Jackson, Joliet, Gallup, Pensacola-Tallahassee, Providence, Rapid City, Richmond and Scranton.

[2990] (S.N.D.)—SISTERS OF NOTRE DAME P

Founded in Germany in 1850. First foundation in the United States in 1874.
GENERALATE: Rome, Italy. Sr. Mary Joell, Supr. Gen.
Universal total in Congregation 2,727.
CLEVELAND PROVINCE (1874): *Notre Dame Educational Center - Provincial House, Juniorate, & Novitiate,* 13000 Auburn Rd., Chardon, OH 44024. Tel: 216-286-7101; Fax: 216-286-3377. Sr. Mary Frances Murray, Prov. Supr.; Sr. M. Helen Louise Kist, Prov. Sec.
Legal Titles: *The Corporation of the Sisters of Notre Dame of Cleveland; Ohio The Sisters of Notre Dame Charitable Trust.*
Total number in community 472.
Properties owned and sponsored: *Notre Dame Cathedral Latin School,* Chardon, OH; *Notre Dame College of Ohio,* South Euclid, OH; *Notre Dame Elementary School,* Chardon, OH; *Notre Dame Montessori School,* Chardon, OH; *Regina High School,* Cleveland, OH; *Julie Billiart School,* Lyndhurst, OH.
Ministry in the field of Academic Education at all levels; Special Education for Exceptional Children; Foreign Mission Work; Religious Education; Pastoral Ministry; Diocesan and National Offices; Pastoral Associate and D.R.E.; Adult Literacy; Hispanic & Refugee Outreach; Sick and Elderly in Hospitals and Nursing Homes; Youth Ministry; Campus Ministry; Writing Textbooks for Religion Series.
Represented in the Archdioceses of Chicago, Detroit and Washington, and the Dioceses of Arlington, Cleveland, Cincinnati, Lexington, Orlando, Raleigh, St. Petersburg, Scranton, Springfield-Cape Girardeau, Venice and Youngstown.
COVINGTON PROVINCE (1924): *Provincial House and Novitiate of the Sisters of Notre Dame,* 1601 Dixie Hwy., (St. Joseph Heights), Covington, KY 41011. Tel: 606-291-2040; Fax: 606-291-1774. Sr. Shauna Bankemper, S.N.D., Prov.
Total number in the community 186.
Legal Title: *Sisters of Notre Dame of Covington, KY Inc.*
Ministry in the field of Education; Hospital and Health Care Services; Child Care.
Properties sponsored and owned: St. Claire Medical Center, Morehead, KY St. Charles Care Center and Village, Covington, KY Notre Academy, Covington, KY.
Represented in the Archdiocese of Cincinnati, and the Dioceses of Birmingham, Covington and Lexington. Also in Hoima, Uganda, and East Africa.
PROVINCE OF TOLEDO (1924): *Notre Dame Provincialate, Juniorate & Novitiate,* 3837 Secor Rd., Toledo, OH 43623. Tel: 419-474-5485. Sr. Joan Marie Recker, Prov. Supr.
Total number in community 308.
Properties owned and sponsored: *Notre Dame Academy; Ladyfield School; Maria Child Care; Mary Immaculate School; Notre Dame School of Music,* Toledo, OH; *Lial Elementary School; Convent & Renewal Center,* Whitehouse, OH; *Holy Trinity Mission,* Papua, New Guinea.
Ministry in the field of Education; Specialized Education; Foreign Mission Work; Vocational School.
Represented in the Archdiocese of Detroit, and the Dioceses of Fort Wayne-South Bend, Joliet, Lafayette (IN), St. Augustine and Toledo.
PROVINCE OF LOS ANGELES (1924): *Notre Dame Provincialate,* 1776 Hendrix Ave., Thousand Oaks, CA 91360. Tel: 805-496-3243; Fax: 805-379-3616. Sr. Mary Amy, Prov. Supr.
Total number in Province 93.
Legal Title: *Corporation of the Sisters of Notre Dame of Los Angeles; Notre Dame Academy High School; Notre Dame Academy Elementary School,* Los Angeles, CA; *Notre Dame Center La Reina High School,* Thousand Oaks, CA.
Ministry in the field of Education and Parish Ministry; Catechetics; Foreign Mission Work.
Represented in the Archdiocese of Los Angeles.

[3000] (S.N.D.deN.)—SISTERS OF NOTRE DAME DE NAMUR P

Founded in France in 1804. First foundation in the United States in 1840.
GENERALATE: *Suore di Nostra Signora di Namur,* Via Raffaello Sardiello, 20, 00165, Rome, Italy. Sr. Ellen Gielty, S.N.D.deN., Gen. Moderator.

OFFICE OF THE GENERAL TREASURER: Generalate Offices in the U.S., 400 The Fenway, Boston, MA 02115. Tel: 617-738-4547; Fax: 617-566-6068. Sr. Anne Mary Donovan, S.N.D.

BOSTON PROVINCE CENTER (1973): *Sisters of Notre Dame de Namur - Emmanuel College,* 351 Broadway, Everett, MA 02149. Tel: 617-387-2500; Fax: 617-387-1303. Prov. Team: Sr. Margaret Lanen, S.N.D.; Sr. Elizabeth Michaels, S.N.D.; Sr. Janice Waters, S.N.D.

Total number in community 252.

Legal Title: *The Boston Province of the Sisters of Notre Dame de Namur, Inc.*

Properties owned and sponsored: *Notre Dame Academy,* Worcester, MA; *Notre Dame Children's Class,* Wenham, MA.

Ministry in the field of Academic Educational at all levels; Adult Education Programs; Parish Ministries; Religious Education Programs; and Social Services.

Represented in the Archdioceses of Boston, Hartford, Louisville, New York and Washington, and the Dioceses of Albany, Fall River, Gallup, Galveston-Houston, Honolulu, Manchester, Orlando, Portland (ME), Saginaw, Springfield (MA) and Worcester.

IPSWICH PROVINCE (1973): *Sisters of Notre Dame de Namur Provincialate,* 30 Jeffrey's Neck Rd., Ipswich, MA 01938. Tel: 508-356-4381; 927-7589; Fax: 508-356-9759. Prov. Team Admin.: Sr. Mary M. Farren, S.N.D., Prov.; Sr. Marie A. McDonald, S.N.D., Prov.; Sr. Therese J. Fitzmaurice, S.N.D., Prov.

Total number in community 294.

Legal Title: *Notre Dame Training School, Inc.*

Ministry in all fields of Education; Pastoral Ministry; Health, Social and Community Services; Retreat Work.

Properties owned and sponsored: *Academy of Notre Dame,* Tyngsboro, MA; *Julie Country Day School,* Leominster, MA; *Notre Dame Academy,* Hingham, MA; *Notre Dame Long Term Health Care Facility,* Worcester, MA; *St. Jospeh by-the-Sea,* Peaks Island, ME; *Cuvilly Arts and Earth Center,* Ipswich, MA.

Represented in the Archdiocese of Boston, Washington, and the Dioceses of Birmingham, Fall River, Manchester, Nashville, Providence, Springfield (MA) and Worcester.

CONNECTICUT PROVINCE (1959): *The Connecticut Province of the Sisters of Notre Dame de Namur, Inc.;* Sisters of Notre Dame de Namur Province Center, 468 Poquonock Ave., Windsor, CT 06095-2473. Tel: 860-688-1832. Prov. Admin. Team: Sr. Joan Farley, S.N.D.; Sr. Elizabeth McLaughlin, S.N.D.; Sr. Marilyn Pechillo, S.N.D.

Total number in community 165.

Sisters Serve and Staff: Colleges, High Schools, Grammar Schools.

Sisters Engaged in Specialized Educational Programs: Pastoral Ministry and Religious Education, Social Health and Community Services, Diocesan Offices.

Represented in the Archdioceses of Boston, Hartford and Newark, and the Dioceses of Bridgeport, Burlington, Norwich, Providence, St. Augustine, Springfield (MA) and Worcester.

BALTIMORE PROVINCE (1934): *Sisters of Notre Dame de Namur, Maryland Province Center,* 1531 Greenspring Valley Rd., Stevenson, MD 21153. Tel: 410-486-5599. Sr. Marie Kelly, Prov. Moderator. Prov. Leadership: Sr. Bernadette Glodek; Sr. Jeanne McGloue.

The Development Center is a joint activity of the Maryland, Chesapeake & Notre Dame Base Communities Provinces; Sr. Alice Gillen S.N.D., Co-Dir.; Sr. Catharine Lafferty, S.N.D., Co-Dir.

Total in community 170.

Properties owned and sponsored: *Trinity School; Maryland Province Center,* Ellicott City, MD; *Villa Julie Infirmary,* Stevenson, MD; *Maryvale Preparatory School,* Brooklandville, MD; *Notre Dame Academy,* Villanova, PA; *Julie Billiart Residence,* Washington, DC.

Represented in the Archdioceses of Atlanta, Baltimore, Philadelphia, Washington, and the Dioceses of Boston, Brooklyn, Camden, Oakland, Portland (ME), Rochester, Rockville Centre and Wilmington. Also in Japan and Nigeria.

CHESAPEAKE PROVINCE (1990): *Sisters of Notre Dame de Namur Provincial Offices,* 305 Cable St., Baltimore, MD 21210-2511. Tel: 410-243-1993; Fax: 410-243-2279. Administrative Team: Sr. Agnes Rose McNally; Sr. Mary Margaret Pignone.

Total number in community 83.

Represented in the Archdioceses of Baltimore, Cincinnati, Miami, New York, Philadelphia and Washington, and the Dioceses of Brooklyn, Charlotte, Fort Wayne-South Bend, Metuchen, Raleigh, Richmond, Wheeling-Charleston and Wilmington. Also in Brazil, Kenya, Mexico, Rome and Zaire.

OHIO PROVINCE (1840): *Sisters of Notre Dame de Namur Provincial House,* 701 E. Columbia Ave., Cincinnati, OH 45215. Tel: 513-821-7448. Sr. Claire Foley, Prov.

Total number in community 275.

Legal Title: *St. Mary's Educational Institute at Cincinnati; Sisters of Notre Dame de Namur - Ohio Province; Sisters of Notre Dame de Namur, Ohio Province, Charitable Trust.*

Ministry in the field of Education at all levels; Montessori; Reading Centers; Pastoral Ministry; Administration and Services; Social Services; Communication; Health Care; Community Services.

Represented in the Archdioceses of Boston, Chicago, Cincinnati, Detroit, Indianapolis, Louisville and St. Louis, and the Dioceses of Austin, Buffalo, Columbus, Covington, Gallup, Joliet, Lafayette, Lincoln, Memphis, Palm Beach, Phoenix, Saginaw, Salt Lake City, Sioux Falls, Tucson and Trenton. Also in Brazil, Nicaragua, Nigeria, Peru, Rome and Zimbabwe.

CALIFORNIA PROVINCE (1851): *Provincial House Sisters of Notre Dame de Namur,* 14800 Bohlman Rd., Saratoga, CA 95070. Tel: 408-741-0324; Fax: 408-741-5809. Provincial Team: Sr. Claudia McTaggart, S.N.D.deN.; Sr. Jean Stoner, S.N.D.deN.; Sr. Barbara Thiella, S.N.D.deN.

Total number in community 179.

Legal Title: *Sisters of Notre Dame de Namur California Province; Raggio Memorial Trust.*

Ministries Include: Counselors; Convalescent Hospital Ministry; Campus Ministry; Diocesan Administrative Positions; Directors of Religious Education; Health Ministry; Hospice Services; Missionary Work; Parish Ministry; Education at all levels; Religious Education for Adults; Retreat Work; Social Services.

Represented in the Archdioceses of Los Angeles, San Francisco, Seattle, and the Dioceses of Baker, Burlington, Des Moines, Honolulu, Monterey, Oakland, Sacramento, San Jose, Stockton and Wheeling-Charleston.

BASE COMMUNITIES PROVINCE (1989): *Sisters of Notre Dame de Namur Base Communities Province Office,* 3037 Fourth St., N.E., Washington, DC 20017. Tel: 202-832-8770. Communications Network: Sr. Marlene Cunningham; Sr. Barbara Karl; Sr. Theresa Kreibick.

Total in Province 52.

Legal Titles: *Sisters of Notre Dame de Namur Base Communities, Inc.; S.N.D.B.C. Charitable Trust.*

Ministry in Formal Education; Health Care; Social Services/Community Development; Pastoral Ministry.

Represented in the Archdioceses of Baltimore, Hartford, Philadelphia and Washington, and the Dioceses of Brooklyn, Charleston, Harrisburg, Orlando, Richmond and Wilmington.

[3010] (O.S.B.S.)—OBLATE SISTERS OF THE BLESSED SACRAMENT — D

Founded in 1935 by Rev. Sylvester Eisenman, O.S.B.

MOTHERHOUSE: *St. Sylvester's Convent,* P.O. Box 217, Marty, SD 57361. Tel: 605-384-3305. Sr. Patricia Mylott, Supr.

ASSOCIATE & FORMATION HOUSE: *Kateri Convent,* 624 Adams St., Rapid City, SD 57701. Tel: 605-343-6261.

Total number in community 7.

Represented in the Dioceses of Rapid City and Sioux Falls.

[3020] (O.B.T.)—SISTERS OBLATES TO THE BLESSED TRINITY — D

Founded in Italy in 1923. First foundation in the United States in 1987, however, was established in New York 1949.

U.S. NOVITIATE: *St. Aloysius Gonzaga Novitiate,* Beekman Rd. - P.O. Box 98, Hopewell Junction, NY 12533. Tel: 914-226-5671. Mother Gloria Castro, Supr. Gen.

Total number in community 41.

Represented in the Archdioceses of New York, San Juan, and the Dioceses of Ponce and Madison.

[3030] (O.SS.R.)—OBLATES OF THE MOST HOLY REDEEMER — P

Founded in Madrid in 1864.

MOTHERHOUSE: Ciempozuelos, Madrid, Spain. Analita Albani, Mother Gen.

U.S. FOUNDATION: *Our Lady of the Way Residence,* 60-80 Pond St., Jamaica Plain, MA 02130. Tel: 617-524-1640. Sr. Matilde Murillo, Supr.

Total number in community 3.

Represented in the Archdioceses of Boston and New York. Also in Puerto Rico.

[3035] (O.M.O.)—OBLATES OF THE MOTHER OF ORPHANS — P

Founded in Italy on September 8, 1945.

GENERAL MOTHERHOUSE: via Amundsen 10, Milano, Italy. Sr. Lucilla Passoni, General Supr.

Universal Total in Congregation 200.

U.S. ADDRESS: 20 E. 72nd St., New York, NY 10021. Sr. Maria Emanuele, Supr.

Total in community 3.

Represented in the Archdiocese of New York. Also in Cameroon, Colombia, El Salvador, Guatemala and Italy.

[3040] (O.S.P.)—OBLATE SISTERS OF PROVIDENCE — P

Founded in the United States in 1829.

GENERAL MOTHERHOUSE: *Our Lady of Mount Providence Convent,* 701 Gun Rd., Baltimore, MD 21227. Tel: 410-242-8500. Sr. Mary Claudina Sanz, O.S.P., Supr. Gen.; Sr. Mary Alexis Fisher, O.S.P., Asst. Supr. Gen.; Sr. Naomi Smith, O.S.P., Sec. Gen.; Sr. Mary Sharon Young, O.S.P., Treas. Gen.

Professed Sisters 125.

Legal Title: *The Oblate Sisters of Providence of the City of Baltimore.*

Sisters serve as: Pastoral Ministry-Associates; in the field of Education; Reading Centers; Day Care Centers; Teaching; Counseling; Hispanic & Migrant ministry.

Represented in the Archdioceses of Baltimore, Chicago, Detroit, Mobile, Miami, Washington, and the Dioceses of Buffalo, Charleston, and Trenton. Also in Costa Rica and the Dominican Republic.

[3050] (O.S.H.J.)—OBLATE SISTERS OF THE SACRED HEART OF JESUS — P

Founded in 1894. First foundation in the United States in 1949.

GENERAL MOTHERHOUSE: Rome, Italy.

AMERICAN HEADQUARTERS: *Villa Maria Teresa,* 50 Warner Rd., Hubbard, OH 44425. Tel: 330-759-8468; Fax: 330-759-7290. Sr. Joyce Candidi, O.S.H.J., Supr.

Total number in the community 21.

Represented in the Dioceses of Pittsburgh and Youngstown.

[3060] (O.S.F.S.)—OBLATE SISTERS OF ST. FRANCIS DE SALES — P

Founded in France in 1866. First foundation in the United States in 1951.

GENERAL MOTHERHOUSE: 10 rue des Terrasses, Troyes, France.

AMERICAN HEADQUARTERS: *Villa Aviat Convent,* Childs, MD 21916. Tel: 410-398-3699. Sr. John Marie, Supr.

Total number in the community 14.

Ministry in the field of Academic and Religious Education; Retreat work; Summer Camp.

Represented in the Archdiocese of Philadelphia and the Diocese of Wilmington.

[3070] (N.A.U.-O.L.C.)—NORTH AMERICAN UNION SISTERS OF OUR LADY OF CHARITY — P

Founded in Caen, France in 1641, by St. John Eudes. First foundation in the United States in 1855.

The primary work of the Sisters of Our Lady of Charity, is to devote themselves to the needs of women and girls in residential and non-residential settings, also nursing homes, day care centers, teaching, pastoral ministries, CCD program, parish ministry, English and Spanish speaking.

The Autonomous Houses were Federated in 1944 and March 21, 1979 the North American Union of the Sisters of Our Lady of Charity was established and approved by Rome.

North American Union of the Sisters of Our Lady of Charity.

ADMINISTRATION OFFICE: 154 Edgington Ln., Wheeling, WV 26003-1535. Tel: 304-242-0042; Fax: 304-242-8981. Sr. Deana Kohlman, Supr. Gen.

Madison

General Motherhouse and Administrative Centre, Box 327, Wisconsin Dells, WI 53965. Tel: 304-242-0042; Fax: 304-242-8981. Sr. Deana Kohlman, Supr. Gen.

Total Sisters Membership 141.

Legal Title: *North American Union of the Sisters of Our Lady of Charity, Inc.*

Canonical Formation, Wisconsin Dells, WI.

Represented in the Archdioceses of New York and San Antonio and the Diocese of Buffalo, El Paso, Erie, Green Bay, Madison, Pittsburgh, Rochester, San Diego, Venice and Wheeling-Charleston. Also in Canada and Mexico.

Buffalo

NORTH AMERICAN UNION OF THE SISTERS OF OUR LADY OF CHARITY: 3800 Howard Rd., Hamburg, NY 14075. Tel: 716-648-4988. Sr. Rosemary Toth, Local Supr.

Legal Title: *Sisters of Our Lady of Charity of Refuge, Inc.*

El Paso

NORTH AMERICAN UNION OF OUR LADY OF CHARITY: 415 N. Glenwood Dr., El Paso, TX 79905. Tel: 915-722-0737. Sr. Yolana Martinez, Local Supr.

San Juan Day Care Centre, Inc. 5636 Frutas Ave., El Paso, TX 79905. Tel: 915-772-1681. Sr. Cruz Celia Gomez, Dir.; Sr. Ellen Patrick Stapleton, Business Mgr.

Legal Title: *North American Sisters of Our Lady of Charity, Inc.*

Erie

NORTH AMERICAN UNION OF THE SISTERS OF OUR LADY OF CHARITY: 4635 East Lake Rd., Erie, PA 16511. Tel: 814-899-1052. Sr. Carol Pregno, Local Supr.

Legal Title: *Gannondale Residential Center for Girls,* Erie, PA; *North American Union Sisters of Our Lady of Charity, Inc.*

Green Bay

NORTH AMERICAN UNION OF THE SISTERS OF OUR LADY OF CHARITY: 2640 West Point Rd., P.O. Box 10357, Green Bay, WI 54307. Tel: 414-494-8747. Sr. Barbara Jean Arnsmeyer, Local Supr.

Legal Title: *Sisters of Our Lady of Charity of the North American Union, Inc.; McClosky Program, Inc.*, Green Bay, WI.

Pittsburgh

NORTH AMERICAN UNION OF THE SISTERS OF OUR LADY OF CHARITY: Nativity Convent, 4100 Vinceton St., Pittsburgh, PA 15214. Tel: 412-931-2299. Sr. Thomas Aul, Local Supr.

Legal Title: *North American Union Sisters of Our Lady of Charity, Inc.; Eudes Institute.*

Rochester

NORTH AMERICAN UNION SISTERS OF OUR LADY OF CHARITY: 1280 Winton Rd. N., Rochester, NY 14609. Tel: 716-654-8600. Sr. Frances Aguillon, Local Supr.

Legal Title: *Sisters of Our Lady of Charity of Refuge, Inc.*

San Antonio

NORTH AMERICAN UNION SISTERS OF OUR LADY OF CHARITY (1897): 1900 Montana St. - P.O. Box 10443, San Antonio, TX 78210. Tel: 210-534-1231. Sr. Agnes O'Mahony, Local Supr.

Legal Title: *North American Union Sisters of Our Lady of Charity, Inc.; Our Lady of Victory School.*

Walden

NORTH AMERICAN UNION OF THE SISTERS OF OUR LADY OF CHARITY: 257 St. Andrew's Rd., Walden, NY. Tel: 914-778-5941. Sr. Rose Marie Levesque, Local Supr.

Legal Title: *St. Andrew's Retreat House.*

Wheeling

NORTH AMERICAN UNION SISTERS OF OUR LADY OF CHARITY: 141 Edgington Ln., Wheeling, WV 26003. Tel: 304-242-7070. Sr. Martha Teresa Gomez, Local Supr.

Legal Title: *North American Union Sisters of Our Lady of Charity, Inc.; West Virginia Haven Corporation.*

[3071] (O.L.C.)—SISTERS OF OUR LADY OF CHARITY — P

MT. ST. MICHAEL CONVENT OF OUR LADY OF CHARITY: 4500 W. Davis St., Dallas, TX 75211. Tel: 214-331-1754. Sr. Margaret McCaffrey, Supr.

Total number in the community 17.

Legal Holding: *Mt. St. Michael Spiritual Life Center.*

[3072] (R.O.L.C.)—OUR LADY OF CHARITY OF REFUGE — P

MONASTERY OF OUR LADY OF CHARITY OF REFUGE: 1125 Malvern Ave., Hot Springs, AR 71901. Tel: 501-623-9651. Sr. Theresa Marie Lalancette, Supr.

Total number in the community 14; Novices 1.

[3073] (O.L.C.)—SISTERS OF OUR LADY OF CHARITY — P

SISTERS OF OUR LADY OF CHARITY: 620 Roswell Rd., N.W., Carrollton, OH 44615-9399. Tel: 216-627-7647; Fax: 216-627-4411. Sr. Mary Kevin Crain, Supr.

Total number in community 19.

[3080] (R.C.D.)—SISTERS OF OUR LADY OF CHRISTIAN DOCTRINE — D

Founded in New York in 1910 for the work of religious education and social service.

CENTRAL OFFICE: *Marydell Center,* 23 Haskell Ave., Suffern, NY 10901. Tel: 914-357-0046. Sr. Virginia Johnson, R.C.D., Pres.

Total number in the community 39.

Ministry in the field of Religious Education in Parish Centers and Parishes; Social Work and Counseling.

Represented in the Archdioceses of Chicago and New York, and the Dioceses of Manchester, Orlando and Paterson. Also in the Dominican Republic.

[3090] (C.L.H.C.)—CONGREGATION OF OUR LADY, HELP OF THE CLERGY — D

Maryvale Sisters

Founded in the United States in 1961.

MOTHERHOUSE: *Maryvale Motherhouse,* 2522 June Bug Rd., Vale, NC 28168. Tel: 704-276-2626. Mother Mary Louis, Supr.

Total number in the community 5.

Represented in the Diocese of Charlotte.

[3100] (R.S.R.)—CONGREGATION OF OUR LADY OF THE HOLY ROSARY — P

Founded in Rimouski, P.Q., Canada, in 1874. First Foundation in the United States in 1899.

GENERAL MOTHERHOUSE: 300 Alle du Rosaire, Rimouski, P. Q. Canada, G5L 3E3. Tel: 418-724-5940. Sr. Berangere Provost, Supr. Gen.

U.S. ADDRESS: *Our Lady of the Holy Rosary,* 20 Thomas St., Portland, ME 04102. Tel: 207-774-3756; 772-3130 (Office). Sr. Maureen Bellerose, R.S.R., Regl. Supr.

Total number in the region 10.

Our Lady of the Holy Rosary Regional House, 25 Portland Ave., Old Orchard Beach, ME 04064. Tel: 207-934-0592.

Ministry in the fields of Education; Diocesan Ministry; Retreat Ministry.

Represented in the Diocese of Portland (ME).

[3105] (S.O.L.T.)—OUR LADY OF THE MOST HOLY TRINITY CONVENT — D

GENERAL MOTHER HOUSE: P.O. Box 189, Skidmore, TX 78389. Tel: 512-287-3146. Sr. Mary of the Redemption Mansfield, Gen. Sister Servant.

Professed Sisters 47; Novices 8; Candidates 11.

Represented in the Archdiocese of Santa Fe and in the Dioceses of Corpus Christi and Kansas City-St. Joseph.

[3110] (R.C.)—CONGREGATION OF OUR LADY OF THE RETREAT IN THE CENACLE — P

Founded in France in 1826. First foundation in the United States in 1892.

GENERALATE: Piazza Madonna del Cenacolo, 15, Rome, Italy 00136.

EASTERN PROVINCE N.A. (1892): *The Cenacle of St. Regis, Inc.,* Cenacle Rd., Lake Ronkonkoma, NY 11779-0408. Tel: 516-471-6270. Sr. Marian Hahn, Prov

Total number in community 111.

Properties owned and sponsored: *Cenacle of St. Regis, Inc.,* Rockville Centre, NY; *The Religious of Our Lady of the Cenacle of New Brunswick, NJ,* Metuchen, NJ; *Cenacle Center for Spiritual Renewal,* Brooklyn, NY; *Ronkonkoma Cenacle, Inc.,* Rockville Centre, NY; *The Cenacle Convent of Palm Beach Co., Inc.,* Palm Beach, FL.

Represented in the Archdioceses of Atlanta, Baltimore, Boston, New York, and the Dioceses of Albany, Arlington, Brooklyn, Metuchen, Rochester, Rockville Centre, Palm Beach, St. Petersburg, and Wheeling-Charleston. Also in Ghana & Bosnia.

MIDWESTERN PROVINCE (1946): *Congregation Of Our Lady of the Cenacle,* 513 Fullerton Pkwy., Chicago, IL 60614. Tel: 312-528-6300. Sr. Marguerite Gautreau, Prov.

Total number in community 97.

Properties owned and sponsored: *Cenacle Convent, Inc.,* Chicago, IL; *Cenacle Convent, Inc.,* Houston, TX; *Convent of Our Lady of the Cenacle,* Metairie, LA; *Warrenville Cenacle Retreat House,* Warrenville, IL; *Cenacle Retreat House,* Wayzata, MN.

Represented in the Archdioceses of Chicago, New Orleans, Milwaukee, St. Louis, St. Paul-Minneapolis, and the Dioceses of Denver, Galveston-Houston, Joliet, Madison, Oakland and Sacramento. Also in Canada, Ghana and Rome, Italy.

[3120] (O.L.S.)—SISTERS OF OUR LADY OF SORROWS — P

Founded in Italy in 1839. First foundation in the United States in 1947.

GENERAL MOTHERHOUSE: Viale Vaticano 90, Rome, Italy, 00165. Mother Vilge Terzanelli, O.L.S., Supr. Gen.

AMERICAN HEADQUARTERS: *Sisters of Our Lady of Sorrows Convent,* 9894 Norris Ferry Rd., Shreveport, LA 71106. Fax: 318-797-7003. Sr. Seraphine Ricci, Supr.

Total number in community 25.

Ministry in the field of Education; Pastoral Ministry; CCD & Adult Education.

Represented in the Dioceses of Alexandria and Shreveport.

[3130] (O.L.V.M.)—OUR LADY OF VICTORY MISSIONARY SISTERS — P

Founded in the United States in 1922.

MOTHERHOUSE: Victory Noll, Box 109, Huntington, IN 46750. Tel: 219-356-0628; Fax: 219-356-0628. Sr. Lucy Regalado, Pres.

Total number in the community 204.

Legal Holding: *Victory Noll Sisters Community Support Trust.*

Represented in the Archdioceses of Chicago, Cincinnati, Denver, Detroit, Dubuque, Los Angeles, Louisville, Miami, Milwaukee, Oklahoma City, Omaha, San Antonio, Santa Fe, and the Dioceses of Austin, Belleville, Charlotte, Cheyenne, Cleveland, Fort Wayne-South Bend, Gary, Helena, Jefferson City, Kansas City-St. Joseph, Las Cruces, Lubbock, Oakland, Orlando, Phoenix, Pueblo, St. Cloud, Salt Lake City, San Bernardino, San Diego, Toledo and Tucson.

[3140] (C.S.A.C.)—SISTERS OF THE CATHOLIC APOSTOLATE (PALLOTTINE) — P

Founded in Italy in 1835. First foundation in the United States in 1889.

GENERAL MOTHERHOUSE: Viale Kennedy No. 62, Grotta Ferrata, Rome, Italy. Mother M. Ivete Garlet, Supr. Gen.

Universal total in Congregation 650.

PROVINCIAL MOTHERHOUSE IN AMERICA: *St. Patrick's Villa,* Harriman Heights, P.O. Box 118, Harriman, NY 10926. Tel: 914-783-9007. Sr. Michele Ruggiero, Prov. Moderator.

Novitiate, Pallottine House of Formation, Box 350, Harriman, NY 10926. Tel: 914-774-7585.

Total number in the community 72.

Ministry in the field of Academic and Religious Education at Elementary and Secondary Levels; Pastoral Services.

Represented in the Archdioceses of Newark and New York and the Diocese of Brooklyn.

[3150] (S.A.C.)—PALLOTTINE MISSIONARY SISTERS - QUEEN OF APOSTLES PROVINCE — P

(Missionary Sisters of the Catholic Apostolate)

Founded in Rome, Italy, in 1838. First founded in the United States in 1912.

GENERAL MOTHERHOUSE: Rome, Italy. Sr. Maria Knaus, S.A.C., Supr. Gen.

AMERICAN PROVINCIALATE: *Pallottine Renewal Center,* 15270 Old Halls Ferry Rd., Florissant, MO 63034. Tel: 314-837-7100; Fax: 314-837-2385. Sr. M. Elisabeth Heptner, S.A.C., Prov.; Sr. Phyllis Carpenter, S.A.C., Community Archivist.

Total number in the community 720.

Properties Owned: *Pallottine Renewal Center,* Florissant, MO; *Frascati Convent,* Londell, MO; *St. Mary's Hospital & Convent,* Huntington, WV; *Vincent Pallotti House,* Huntington, WV; *St. Joseph's Hospital & Convent,* Buckhannon, WV; *St. Vincent Pallotti Convent, High School & Child Care Center,* Laurel, MD.

Sisters minister in the fields of Health Care; Child Day Care; Education; Retreat and Renewal Ministry; Social Services; Counseling; Parish and Pastoral Work.

Represented in the Archdioceses of St. Louis and Washington and the Diocese of Wheeling-Charleston.

[3160] (P.V.M.I.)—PARISH VISITORS OF MARY IMMACULATE — P

Founded in New York City in 1920 for evangelization through family visitation, religious education and social service assistance.

MOTHERHOUSE, JUNIORATE AND NOVITIATE: *Marycrest,* P.O. Box 658, Monroe, NY 10950-0658. Tel: 914-783-2251. Sr. Carole Marie Troskowski, Gen. Supr.; Sr. Rita Mairelenes, Juniorate Dir.; Sr. Frances Walter, Gen Sec.

Total number in community 73.

Serving the Church in the Pastoral Ministry as a bridge between the people and their pastor and associates; acting as liaison where social needs are present; Visitation and Religious Education in Parishes and Catechetical Centers.

Represented in the Archdioceses of Baltimore, New York, and the Dioceses of Brooklyn, Scranton and Syracuse. Also in the Diocese of Okigwe, Nigeria.

[3170] (C.P.)—RELIGIOUS OF THE PASSION OF JESUS CHRIST P
(Passionist Nuns)

Founded in Italy in 1771, by St. Paul of the Cross. First foundation in the United States in 1910.

Our Lady of Sorrows Convent of the Passionist Nuns (Contemplative): 2715 Churchview Ave., Pittsburgh, PA 15227. Tel: 412-881-1155. Mother Mary Ann, C.P., Supr.

Total number in community 10.

The Religious of the Passion of Jesus Christ (Contemplative) (1926): *St. Gabriel's Monastery,* 631 Griffin Pond Rd., Clarks Summit, PA 18411. Tel: 717-586-2791. Sr. Helen Gallagher, C.P., Pres.

Professed Sisters 16.

Legal Holding: *St. Gabriel's Monastery and Retreat Center.*

Sisters serve and staff: Retreats and other Programs for Women and Men of all Faiths; Clergy and Religious; Ecumenical Groups; Business and Civic Groups.

Passionist Nuns (Cloistered Contemplative) (1946): *St. Joseph's Monastery,* 8564 Crisp Rd., Whitesville, KY 42378. Tel: 502-233-4571. Sr. Mary Agnes, C.P., Supr.

Professed Nuns 18.

Passionist Nuns (Contemplative) (1947): *Monastery of the Sacred Passion,* 1151 Donaldson Hwy., Erlanger, KY 41018. Tel: 606-371-8568. Sr. Margaret Mary, C.P., Supr.

Legal Title: *Passionist Nuns of Covington, KY.*

Total number in community 9.

Passionist Nuns (Cloistered) (1947): *Immaculate Conception Monastery,* 15700 Clayton Rd., Ellisville, MO 63011-2300. Tel: 314-227-5275. Mother Mary Salvador, C.P., Supr.

Total number in community 12; Professed Novices 2.

[3180] (C.P.)—SISTERS OF THE CROSS AND PASSION P
(Passionist Sisters)

Founded in 1852. First foundation in the United States 1924.

Generalate located 14 Oxford Rd., Dewsbury West Yorkshire WF13 4JT England. Sr. Patricia Denny, C.P., Supr. Gen.

Motherhouse-American Provincial Office: *Holy Family Convent,* One Wright Ln., North Kingstown, RI 02852. Tel: 401-294-3554. Sr. Ellen Downes, C.P., Prov.

Professed Sisters 47.

Sisters minister in Retreat Houses; Elementary and Secondary Education; Hospital Chaplaincy; Parish Ministry; Religious Education; Chancery and Tribunal Offices.

Properties owned and operated: *Our Lady of Calvary Retreat,* Farmington, CT.

Represented in the Archdioceses of Hartford, Los Angleles and New York, and the Dioceses of Providence and Rockville Centre. Also in Jamaica, West Indies.

[3190] (A.P.)—NUNS OF THE PERPETUAL ADORATION OF THE BLESSED SACRAMENT P

Founded in Rome in 1807. First foundation in United States in 1925.

El Paso: *Expiatory Shrine of Christ the King and Monastery of Perpetual Adoration,* 145 N. Cotton Ave., El Paso, TX 79901. Tel: 915-533-5323. Mother Maria de Jesus, A.P., Supr.

Sisters 22.

Represented in the Archdioceses of Anchorage and San Francisco and the Diocese of El Paso.

San Francisco: *Monastery of Perpetual Adoration,* 771 Ashbury St., San Francisco, CA 94117. Tel: 415-566-2743. Mother Rosalba Vargas, A.P., Supr.

Sisters 24.

Represented in the Archdiocese of San Francisco. Also in Africa, Chile, Mexico and Spain.

[3195] (A.P.G.)—SISTER OF PERPETUAL ADORATION OF GUADALUPE, INC. P

U.S. Foundation: 2403 W. Travis, San Antonio, TX 78207. Tel: 512-227-5546. Mother Esperanza Teresa Avila, General Counsel; Sr. Ma. del Carmen Sanchez O., Supr.

Total number in community 7.

[3200] (Sch.P.)—SISTERS OF THE PIOUS SCHOOLS (Escolapias) P

Founded in Figueras, Spain in 1829.

Universal total in Congregation 844.

General Motherhouse: Via Crescenzio 77, Rome, Italy, 00193. Mother Isolina Vasquez, Sch.P., Supr. Gen.

U.S. Headquarters (1954): 17601 Nordhoff St., Northridge, CA 91325. Tel: 818-882-5265; Fax: 818-718-6752. Sr. Maria Jesus Jurado, Sch.P., Vice Prov.

Total number in community 26.

Ministry in Religious Education; Parish Schools.

Represented in the Archdiocese of Los Angeles.

[3210] (P.C.P.A.)—POOR CLARES OF PERPETUAL ADORATION P

Founded in France, 1854. First foundation in the United States at Cleveland, Ohio, 1921.

Poor Clares of Perpetual Adoration, cloistered, contemplative, solemn vows. Object: Perpetual Adoration in spirit of Praise and Thanksgiving, and Gospel living. Solemn Exposition day and night. Each monastery is autonomous

Sancta Clara Monastery (1946): 4200 N. Market Ave., Canton, OH 44714. Sr. Kay Marie, Abbess.

Total number in community 12.

Saint Joseph Adoration Monastery (1956): 2311 Stockham Ln., Portsmouth, OH 45662-3049. Tel: 614-353-4713. Mother M. Agnes, Abbess.

Total number in community 8.

Legal Holdings and Titles: *Poor Clares of Perpetual Adoration; St. Joseph Adoration Monastery.*

Adoration Monastery (1921): 4108 Euclid Ave., Cleveland, OH 44103. Tel: 216-361-0783; Fax: 216-361-0979. Mother Mary Angela, Abbess.

Total number in community 23; Novices 1.

Poor Clares of Perpetual Adoration (1954): Our Lady of the Most Blessed Sacrament Monastery, 3900 13th St., N.E., Washington, DC 20017. Tel: 202-526-6808. Mother Margaret Mary, Abbess.

Total number in community 10.

Our Lady of the Angels Monastery: 5817 Old Leeds Rd., Birmingham, AL 35210. Tel: 205-956-5987; Fax: 205-956-5696. Mother M. Angelica, P.C.P.A., Abbess.

Total number in community 31; Novices 5; Postulants 3; Members of the Lay Missionaries of the Eternal Word 50.

Properties owned or sponsored: *Eternal Word Television Network, Inc. (EWTN); WEWN Shortwave Network.*

Legal Title: *Eternal Word Television Network, Inc. (EWTN); WEWN Shortwave Network AM/FM Radio Journey Into Scripture Publishing*, global television, radio, and book apostolates.

Represented in the Diocese of Birmingham.

[3220] (P.C.J.)—SISTERS OF THE POOR CHILD JESUS P

Founded on February 2, 1844 in Germany. First founded in the United States on July 2, 1924 at Parkersburg, West Virginia.

General Motherhouse: Haus Loreto, Simpelveld, Netherlands. Rev. Sr. Maria Kamsiyati, P.C.J., Supr. Gen.

Universal number in Congregation 850.

American Region and Novitiate: *Our Lady of Bethlehem Convent,* 4567 Olentangy River Rd., Columbus, OH 43214. Tel: 614-451-3900; Fax: 614-451-4745. Sr. Frances Teresa Holzberger, P.C.J., Regl. Supr.

Total number in community 7.

Ministry in the field of Education.

Properties owned: *Kindergarten and a Day Care Center.*

Represented in the Dioceses of Columbus and Wheeling-Charleston.

[3230] (P.H.J.C.)—POOR HANDMAIDS OF JESUS CHRIST P
(The Ancilla Domini Sisters)

Founded in Germany in 1851. First foundation in the United States in 1868.

General Motherhouse: Dernbach, Westerwald, Germany. Sr. M. Germaine Hustedde, P.H.J.C., Supr. Gen.

American Province-Provincialate: *Convent Ancilla Domini,* Donaldson, IN 46513. Tel: 219-936-9936; Fax: 219-935-1785. Sr. Annemarie Kampwerth, P.H.J.C., Prov. Councilors: Sr. Nora Hahn, P.H.J.C.; Sr. Jean Christianson, P.H.J.C.; Sr. Linda Volk, P.H.J.C.; Sr. Carleen Wrasman, P.H.J.C.; Sr. M. Jolise May, P.H.J.C., Treas.; Sr. Elizabeth Roberts, P.H.J.C., Communications Dir.; Ms. Mary Chudzynski, Dir. Devel.; Sr. M. Cecelia Bianchino, P.H.J.C., Archivist.

Professed Sisters 210.

Properties owned or sponsored: *Ancilla Domini College; Convent Ancilla; Domini Maria Center; Catherine Kasper Home; Lindenwood Retreat & Ministry Center; Earthworks, Inc.; Ancilla Domini Hospitals; Self Insurance Trust; Poor Handmaids of Jesus Christ Community Support Trust,* Donaldson, IN; *Ancilla Domini Convent,* Milwaukee, WI; *St. Catherine Convent,* East Chicago, IN; *Annunciation Convent,* Hoffman Estates, IL; *Poor Handmaids of Jesus Christ,* 1916 S. Clarence Ave., Berwyn, IL 60402; *Mary Katherine Convent,* Cairo, IL; *Marian Convent, St. Joseph Medical Center,* Fort Wayne, IN; *Beacon House,* Burlington, IA; *Catherine Kasper Center, St. Mary Hospital, St. Mary Convent,* East St. Louis, IL; *Ancilla Systems, Inc., St. Mary Medical Center,* Hobart, IN; *St. Elizabeth Hospital,* Chicago, IL; *St. Catherine Hospital,* East Chicago, IL; *St. Joseph Mishawaka Health Services, Inc.,* Mishawaka, IN.

Ministry in the field of Academic Education at all levels; Hospitals; Parish Ministries; Retreat Ministries; Child Care Institutions; and Retirement Homes.

Represented in the Archdioceses of Chicago, Cincinnati, Milwaukee, St. Paul-Minneapolis, and the Dioceses of Belleville, Davenport, Evansville, Fort Wayne-South Bend, Gary, Joliet, Lansing, Peoria, Savannah, Springfield (IL), Springfield-Cape Girardeau, and Wilmington. Also in Brazil, Germany and Mexico.

[3240] (C.J.C.)—POOR SISTERS OF JESUS CRUCIFIED AND THE SORROWFUL MOTHER D

Founded in the United States in 1924.

General Motherhouse: *Our Lady of Sorrows Convent,* 261 Thatcher St., Brockton, MA 02402-3997. Sr. Celestine Stakutis, C.J.C., Supr. Gen.

Total number in community 56.

Properties owned: *St. Joseph Manor Health Care, Inc.; Mater Dei Adult Day Health Program; Our Lady of Sorrows Convent,* Brockton, MA; *St. Mary's Villa Nursing Home,* Elmhurst, PA; *St. Peter's Convent,* South Boston, MA.

Ministry in Nursing Homes; Education Center; Elementary Schools; Inter-Community High Schools; and Pastoral Ministry.

Represented in the Archdiocese of Boston and in the Dioceses of Allentown and Scranton.

[3242] (P.S.N.)—POOR SISTERS OF NAZARETH P

Founded in England by Mother St. Basil.

Motherhouse: Nazareth House, Hammersmith, London, W6 8DB. England. Mother Mary Bernard, Supr. Gen.

U.S. Region and Novitiate (1924): 3333 Manning Ave., Los Angeles, CA 90064. Tel: 310-839-2361. Mother Margaret Clare, Regl. Supr.

Professed Sisters 35.

Represented in the Archdioceses of Los Angeles and San Francisco, and the Dioceses of Fresno, Madison and San Diego. Also in American Samoa.

[3250] (P.S.S.J.)—POOR SISTERS OF ST. JOSEPH P

Founded in Buenos Aires, Argentina, 1880.

General Motherhouse: Leon Gallardo 734, Muniz, Buenos Aires, Argentina. Mother Agueda Magdalena Padros, Mother Gen.

U.S. Foundation: *Casa Belen,* 305 E. Fourth St., Bethlehem, PA 18015. Tel: 610-867-4030.

U.S. Motherhouse: *St. Gabriel Convent,* 4319 Sano St., Alexandria, VA 22312. Tel: 703-354-0395.

Casa Nazaret 5321 Spruce St., Reading, PA 19602. Tel: 610-378-1947.

Total number in community 15.

Represented in the Dioceses of Allentown and Arlington.

[3260] (C.PP.S.)—SISTERS OF THE PRECIOUS BLOOD (DAYTON, OHIO) P

Founded in Switzerland in 1834. First foundation in the United States in 1844.

Generalate: 4000 Denlinger Rd., Dayton, OH 45426. Tel: 513-837-3302. Sr. Joyce Langhals, C.PP.S., Pres.; Sr. Nancy Raley, C.PP.S., Vice Pres. & Councilor; Sr. Judy Kroeger, C.PP.S., Sec. & Councilor; Sr. Joyce Lehman, C.PP.S., Councilor; Sr. Benita Volk, C.PP.S., Councilor; Sr. Barbara Brown, C.PP.S., Treas.

Total Membership 334.

Properties owned and sponsored: *Generalate,* Dayton, OH; *Salem Heights Convent,* Dayton, OH; *Maria Stein Center,* Maria Stein, OH; *San Luis Rey Academy, Inc.,* San Luis Rey, CA.

Universities, High Schools, Elementary Schools & Seminaries; Diocesan Offices; Pastoral Ministry in Hospitals and Long-term Care Centers; Religious and Adult Education; Nursing Care; Homemaking Services in Homes for the Aged; Ethnic Minorities and Marginalized Peoples; Retreat and Music Ministry; Missionary and Volunteer Services.

Represented in the Archdioceses of Cincinnati, Denver, Detroit, Indianapolis Los Angeles, Philadelphia, Washington, and the Dioceses of Altoona-Johnstown, Cleveland, Columbus, Covington, Dallas, Gallup, Grand Rapids, Kalamazoo, Lafayette (IN), Lansing, Lexington, Marquette, Oakland, Phoenix, Raleigh, Saginaw, San Bernardino San Diego, Toledo and Tucson. Also in Chile, and Guatemala.

[3270] (C.PP.S.)—SISTERS OF THE MOST PRECIOUS BLOOD (O'FALLON, MO.) P

Founded in Switzerland in 1845. First foundation in the United States in 1870.

General Motherhouse: *St. Mary's Institute,* 204 N. Main St., O'Fallon, MO 63366-2299. Tel: 314-240-3420; Fax: 314-272-5031. Sr. Andree Fries, C.PP.S., Supr. Gen. Gen. Councilors: Sr. Susan Borgel; Sr. Cecile Gunelson; Sr. Eileen Schieber; Sr. Marjorie Cordes; Sr. Janice Bader, Treas.; Sr. Charlene Grieshaber, Sec.; Sr. Virginia Volkerding, Community Archivist.

Total number in community 323.

Properties Owned: *St. Mary's Institute, Inc.; Charitable Trust, Sisters of the Most Precious Blood of O'Fallon, O'Fallon, MO; Linda Vista Catholic School,* Chesterfield, MO; *St. Elizabeth Academy,* St. Louis, MO; *St. Elizabeth Adult Day Care Center,* St. Louis, MO; *Centers for Professional and Pastoral Services - Sisters of the Most Precious Blood,* O'Fallon, MO.

Ministry in the field of Education; Care of the Elderly; Pastoral and Parish Ministry; Ecclesiastical Art; Foreign Missions; Social Services; Prayer/Presence.

Represented in the Archdioceses of Anchorage, the Military Services and St. Louis, and the Dioceses of El Paso, Harrisburg, Jefferson City, Kansas City-St. Joseph, Kansas City (KS), Las Cruces, Lexington, Lincoln, Nashville, Sioux City, Springfield-Cape Girardeau, Springfield (IL) and Wheeling-Charleston.

[3310] (P.M.)—SISTERS OF THE PRESENTATION OF MARY P

Founded in France in 1796. First foundation in the United States in 1873.

General Motherhouse: *Presentazione di Maria,* Viale PIO XI, 29 C.P. 104, Castelgandolfo, Italy, 00040. Mother Carmen Barbe, Supr. Gen.

Inter-Provincial Novitiate: 180 Lowell Rd., Hudson, NH 03051. Sr. Colette Barbeau, Dir. Tel: 603-880-8186.

Manchester Province: *Provincial Administration,* 495 Mammoth Rd., Manchester, NH 03104. Tel: 603-669-1080. Sr. Mariette Plante, Prov. Supr.

Sisters 243; Novices 1.

Ministry in the field of Education at all levels; Pastoral Ministry; Youth Ministry; Ministry for Persons with Disabilities.

Properties owned: *Bethany House,* Manchester, NH; *Emmanuel House,* Woonsocket, RI; *Our Lady of Hope House of Prayer,* New Ipswich, NH; *Presentation of Mary Novitiate; Trinity House,* Hudson, NH; *Provincial House Rivier College,* Nashua, NH; *St. Joseph Residence, St. Marie Residence,* Manchester, NH.

Represented in the Dioceses of Galveston-Houston, Manchester and Providence.

Methuen Province: *Provincial Administration,* 209 Lawrence St., Methuen, MA 01844. Tel: 508-687-1369; 685-0980. Sr. Aline Plante, Prov.

Total number in Province 172.

Ministry in High Schools; Elementary Schools; Montessori Kindergartens; Montessorri Day Nurseries; Religious Instruction Centers; Chaplaincy and Pastoral work; Spiritual Retreat Center.

Properties owned: *Montessori Kindergartens; Montessori Day Nurseries; Marie Joseph Spiritual Center,* Biddeford, ME; *Presentation of Mary Academy,* Methuen, MA.

Represented in the Archdiocese of Boston, and the Dioceses of Portland (ME), Springfield (MA) and Worcester.

[3320] (P.B.V.M.)—SISTERS OF THE PRESENTATION OF THE B.V.M. P

Founded in Ireland in 1775. First foundation in San Francisco CA in 1854.

Represented in the United States in the following Archdioceses and Dioceses.

Dubuque P

Mt. Loretto Convent, Motherhouse and Novitiate: 2360 Carter Rd., Dubuque, IA 52001-2997. Tel: 319-588-2008; Fax: 319-588-4463. Sr. Mary Jacqueline Quillin, Congregational Leader.

Legal Title: *Sisters of the Presentation of the B.V.M.,* Dubuque, IA.

Total number in community 174.

Ministry in the field of Religious and Academic Education; Hospital & Prison Chaplaincy; Elder Care; Parish & Campus Ministries; South American Mission; Mission in Guatemala; Diocesan/Metropolitan Offices; Retreat & Spiritual Direction; Property Manager for Housing Project; Food Service; Lobbyist; Photo Editor.

Represented in the Archdioceses of Chicago, Denver Kansas City (KS), Dubuque, Indianapolis, St. Paul-Minneapolis, Washington, and the Dioceses of Austin, Brownsville, Covington, Davenport, Jackson, Orlando Rapid City, Winona and Sioux City. Also in Bolivia and Guatemala.

New York P

Mt. St. Joseph, Generalate, Infirmary and Motherhouse: *Sisters of the Presentation of the Blessed Virgin Mary,* 880 Jackson Ave., New Windsor, NY 12553. Tel: 914-564-0513; Fax: 914-567-0219. Sr. Carla Lorenz, Pres.; Sr. Laura Follmer, Community Archivist.

Total number in community 123.

Ministry in the field of Academic Education in Parochial and High Schools; Pastoral Services; Health Care, and Social Services.

Represented in the Archdioceses of Newark, New York, Washington, and the Dioceses of Brooklyn, Dallas, Metuchen and Paterson. Also in Bolivia and Ghana.

Our Lady of the Presentation, Motherhouse and Novitiate: 419 Woodrow Rd., Staten Island, NY 10312. Tel: 718-356-2121. Sr. Mary O'Keefe, Congregation Leader.

Professed Sisters 34.

Ministry in Elementary and High Schools; University; Campus Ministry; Pastoral Counseling; Adult Education; Healing & Parish Ministry.

Represented in the Archdioceses of New York and Philadelphia.

San Francisco P

Presentation Convent-Motherhouse: 2340 Turk Blvd., San Francisco, CA 94118. Tel: 415-751-0406. Sr. Rosina Conrotto, P.B.V.M., Pres.; Sr. Kathleen Griffin, Archivist.

Legal Title: *Sisters of the Presentation of the Blessed Virgin Mary.*

Total number in community 152.

Ministry in the field of Religious and Academic Education at all levels; Parish Ministry; Social and Health Ministry; College and University Teaching; Retreat Work; Church Related Administrative Positions; Missionary Work; Internal Ministry.

Represented in the Archdioceses of Los Angeles, San Francisco and Washington, and the Dioceses of Monterey, Oakland, San Jose, San Diego and Santa Rosa.

Albany P

St. Colman's Presentation Convent, Motherhouse and Novitiate: *Sisters of the Presentation of the Blessed Virgin Mary PVBM,* Watervliet, NY 12189. Tel: 518-273-4911; Fax: 518-273-3312. Mother Mary Carmel, Supr.

Total number in community 63.

Ministry in the field of Academic Education; Day Care Center; Child Caring Institution; Resident School for Autistic & Emotionally Disturbed Children; Parish Ministry; Residential School for Mentally Retarded; Pre-School Handicapped Program.

Represented in the Diocese of Albany.

Fargo P

Sacred Heart Convent, Motherhouse and Novitiate: *Sisters of Presentation of the Blessed Virgin Mary PBVM,* 1101 32nd Ave., S., Fargo, ND 58103. Tel: 701-237-4857. Sr. Paula Ringuette, Pres.; Sr. Mary Jo Hasey, Archivist.

Total number in community 64.

Sponsored Ministries; *Presentation Prayer Center,* Fargo, ND; *Riverview Place,* Fargo, ND; *Presentation Center,* Fargo, ND; *Friendship,* Fargo, ND; *St. Ansgar's Hospital,* Park River, ND; *Carrington Health Center,* Carrington, ND.

Represented in the Archdioceses of Portland (OR), St. Louis, and the Dioceses of Bismarck, Columbus, Crookston, Fargo, Knoxville, La Crosse, Lexington, Rapid City, Springfield-Cape Girardeau and Winona. Also in Peru & Africa.

Sioux Falls P

Presentation Convent, Motherhouse and Novitiate: *Sisters of the Presentation of the Blessed Virgin Mary,* Aberdeen, SD 57401. Tel: 605-225-0420. Sr. Joyce Meyer, Pres.; Sr. Lois Ann Sargent, Congregation Archivist.

Total number in community 173.

Ministry in the field of Academic Education at all levels; Hospitals; Homes for the Aged; Parish Pastoral Ministry; Missionary Ministry in Mexico.

Represented in the Diocese of Sioux Falls.

Worcester P

Presentation Convent of the Presentation of the B.V.M.: 99 Church St., Leominster, MA 01453. Sr. Catherine Hannigan, Pres.

Total number in community 81.

Sisters Staff or Sponsor: Elementary and High School Education; Spanish Apostolate; Pastoral Ministry; Social Services; Nursing.

Represented in the Archdiocese of Boston, and the Dioceses of Manchester, Norwich, Providence, Sioux Falls and Worcester.

[3330] (P.B.V.M.)—UNION OF THE SISTERS OF THE PRESENTATION OF THE BLESSED VIRGIN MARY P

The Congregation of the Presentation was founded in Cork, Ireland, 1776. By decree of the Sacred Congregation for Religious, the Union of the Sisters of the Presentation was established in Ireland in 1976. First U.S.A. Province in 1989.

Generalate: Monasterevan Co. Kildare, Ireland. Tel: 353-045-2535. Sr. Wiona Engel, Supr. Gen.

Provincialate: 729 W. Wilshire Dr., Phoenix, AZ 85007. Tel: 602-271-9687. Sr. Catherine Burke, Prov.; Sr. Betty O'Dowd, Treas.

Novitiate, 5151 Evergreen Ave., Cypress, CA 90630. Tel: 714-527-4844.

Perpetual Profession 101.

Sisters serve and staff: Elementary and Religious Education; Parish Ministry; Health & Hospital Services; Ministry to Handicapped; Diocesan School Service.

Represented in the Archdioceses of Los Angeles, Mobile, New Orleans, San Antonio and San Francisco, and the Dioceses of Birmingham, Biloxi, Oakland, Orange, Phoenix, Sacramento, San Bernadino, Savannah and Tucson.

[3340] (S.P.)—SISTERS OF PROVIDENCE D

Founded in Kingston, Canada in 1861. First foundation in the United States in 1873. Became independent, diocesan foundation in 1892.

Providence Motherhouse: Gamelin St., Holyoke, MA 01040-4083. Tel: 413-536-7511; Fax: 413-536-7917. Sr. Ruth McGoldrick, S.P., Congregation Pres.

Professed Sisters 132.

Legal Holdings and Titles: *Sisters of Providence, Inc.,* Holyoke, MA; *Sisters of Providence Health System, Inc.,* Springfield, MA; Hospitals: Mercy Hospital, Springfield, MA; *Providence Hospital,* Holyoke, MA; *Sisters of Providence Care Centers, Inc. including: Queen of Peace Centennial House Beaven Kelly Home; St. Luke's Home, Inc.; Mt. St. Vincent Nursing Home,* Holyoke, MA; *Farren Care Center, Inc.,* Turners Falls, MA; *St. Joseph of the Pines Hospital, Inc.,* Southern Pines, NC; *Brightside for Children & Families, Inc.,* West Springfield, MA. *Family Services: Providence Ministries for the Needy, Inc.,* Holyoke, MA;. *Retreat House: Genesis Spiritual Life Center,* Westfield, MA.

Represented in the Archdiocese of Boston, and the Dioceses of Raleigh, Springfield (MA) and Worcester. Also in Santiago, Chile.

[3350] (S.P.)—SISTERS OF PROVIDENCE P

Founded in Montreal in 1843. First foundation in the United States in 1856.

General Motherhouse and Novitiate: 12055 Grenet St., Montreal, Quebec , Canada, H4J 2J5. Sr. Gloria Keylor, Supr. Gen.

Province of the Sacred Heart (1856): *Province and Sisters of Providence-Pariseau Association,* P.O. Box 11038, Seattle, WA 98111-9038. Tel: 206-464-3355. Sr. Roberta Rorke, S.P., Prov. Supr.; Loretta Zwolak Greene, Archivist. Tel: 206-937-4600.

Novitiate-Vocation House, 4727 Stanley Rd. SW, Calgary, Alberta T25 293. Canada. Tel: 403-287-2863.

Total number in community 1,456; Sisters in Sacred Heart Province 165.

Ministry in the field of Academic Education; Health Care Services; Hospitals & Skilled Nursing Facilities; Outpatient Health Care Services; Home, Health and Hospice; Retirement Homes; Children's Nursing Centers; Senior and Handicapped Housing Facilities; Shelters for Homeless Women with Children; Transitional Housing for Women.

Sisters of Providence System Office P.O. Box 11038, Seattle, WA 98111-9038. Tel: 206-464-3355. Sr. Karin Dufault, S.P., Chm. Bd., Acting Pres. & CEO.

Properties, entities and divisions owned or operated: Sisters of Providence in Washington— *Providence Alaska Medical Center,* Anchorage, AK; *Our Lady of Compassion Care Center,* Anchorage, AK; *Providence General Medical Center,* Everett, WA; *System Office Providence Medical Center Heritage House at the Market (leased) Hospice of Seattle Providence Mount St. Vincent Nursing Center and Retirement Apartments Vincent House,* Seattle,

WA; *Providence St. Peter Hospital Providence Mother Joseph Care Center,* Olympia, WA; *Providence Centralia Hospital,* Centralia, WA Providence SoundHomeCare, Olympia, WA; *St. Elizabeth Medical Center,* Yakima, WA; *Providence Hospital,* Toppenish, WA. Sisters of Providence in Oregon— *Oregon Regional Office St. Vincent Hospital and Medical Center Providence Seattle Medical Center Providence Child Center,* Portland, OR; *Providence Milwaukie Hospital,* Milwaukie, OR; *Providence Seaside Hospital (leased),* Seaside, OR; *Providence Hospital and Medical Center,* Medford, OR. Sisters of Providence in California— *Providence High School Saint Joseph Medical Center,* Burbank, CA. Sisters of Providence-Pariseau Association— *Saint Joseph Residence Providence Hospitality House Sojourner Place The Gamelin Association—Providence House,* Yakima, WA; *The Gamelin-Oregon Association—Emilie House,* Portland, OR; *The Gamelin-California Association—Providence House,* Oakland, CA.

Represented in the Archdioceses of Anchorage, Los Angeles, Portland (OR) and Seattle, and the Dioceses of Oakland and Yakima.

Province of St. Ignatius (1891): *Sisters of Providence,* 9 E. Ninth Ave., Spokane, WA 99202-1295. Tel: 509-455-4884; Fax: 509-455-4882. Sr. Eileen Croghan, S.P., Prov. Supr.

Total number in Province 102.

Properties owned or sponsored: *University of Great Falls, Inc.; Benefis Health Care Corporation; St. Thomas Child and Family Center,* Great Falls, MT; *St. Patrick Hospital Corporation,* Missoula, MT; *St. Joseph Hospital Corporation,* Polson, MT; *St. Mary Medical Center,* Walla Walla, WA; *Holy Family Hospital, Holy Family Adult Day Health; Sacred Heart Medical Center; St. Brendan Continuing Care Center; St. Joseph Care Center; Sisters of Providence; St. Ignatius Province,* Spokane, WA; *Mount Carmel Hospital,* Colville, WA; *St. Joseph's Hospital,* Chewelah, WA; *Domini Care,* Chewelah, WI; *Deer Park Health Center and Hospital,* Deer Park, WA.

Represented in the Dioceses of Boise, Great Falls-Billings, Helena and Spokane.

Province of Elizabeth (1911): *Sisters of Charity of Providence, Maryville Convent,* 353 N. River Rd., Des Plaines, IL 60016. Tel: 708-299-7808. Sr. Imelda Caissie, Supr. Tel: 708-299-7808; *Maryville Academy,* 1150 N. River Rd., Des Plaines, IL 60016. Tel: 708-824-6126.

Represented in the Archdioceses of Chicago and Newark, and the Dioceses of Burlington and Manchester.

[3360] (S.P.)—SISTERS OF PROVIDENCE OF SAINT MARY-OF-THE-WOODS, INDIANA P

Founded in France in 1806. First foundation in the United States in 1840.

General Administration: *Sisters of Providence,* St. Mary-of-the-Woods, IN 47876-1089. Tel: 812-535-4193. Sr. Diane Ris, S.P., Gen. Supr.; Sr. Eileen Ann Kelley, S.P., Congregation Archivist.

Legal Titles and Sponsored Institutions: *Mother Theodore Guerin High School,* River Grove, IL; *Saint Mary-of-the-Woods College,* Saint Mary-of-the-Woods, IN; *Woods Day Care/Pre-School, Inc.,* St. Mary-of-the-Woods, IN; *Providence Self-Sufficenty,* New Albany, IN.

Sisters of Providence Community Support Trust (1969); Foundation to provide support for the aged and infirm members of the Congregation.

Total Number in Congregation 693.

Ministry in the fields of Education at all levels; Diocesan Offices; Parish and Pastoral Ministry; Health Care and Retirement Facilities; Congregation Administration; Social Services; Therapeutic/Rehabilitative/Mental Health Services.

Represented in the Archdioceses of Atlanta, Boston, Chicago, Cincinnati, Indianapolis, Louisville, Los Angeles, Milwaukee, New York, Mobile, Omaha, St. Louis, St. Paul-Minneapolis, San Antonio, San Francisco, Washington, and the Dioceses of Albany, Arlington, Belleville, Birmingham, Cheyenne, Corpus Christi, Covington, Evansville, Fort Wayne-South Bend, Galveston-Houston, Gary, Helena, Jackson, Joliet, Kalamazoo, La Crosse, Lafayette (LA), Lafayette (IN), Lexington, Manchester, Norwich, Oakland, Ogdensburg, Oklahoma, Orange, Owensboro, Peoria, Rockford, Raleigh, Sacramento, St.Petersurg, San Bernadino, San Jose, Springfield, Trenton and Venice. Also in China.

Area of Taiwan: *Providence University,* 200 Chung Chi Rd., Shalu 43309, Taichung County, Taiwan, Republic of China. Tel: 011-886-4-631-1182. Sr. Marilyn Baker, S.P., Area Rep.

Total number in community 9.

Ministry in the field of Education; Opportunity Center for Mentally Handicapped.

Property Owned: Mother Marie Gratia Spirituality Center.

Represented in the Archdiocese of Taipei, and the Dioceses of Taichung and Tainan.

[3380] (R.A.)—RELIGIOUS OF THE APOSTOLATE OF THE SACRED HEART OF JESUS P

Religiosas del Apostolado del Sagrado Corazon

General Motherhouse: San Esteban de Gormaz 32, Madrid, Spain, 28033. Leonor Micheo, Mother Gen.

St. Lazaro Convent: 1310 W. 42nd Pl., Hialeah, FL 33012. Tel: 305-823-3232. Sr. Ofelia M. Rasco, R.A., Supr.

Represented in the Archdiocese of Miami. Also in Puerto Rico.

[3390] (R.A.)—RELIGIOUS OF THE ASSUMPTION P

Founded in France in 1839. Established in the United Stats of America in 1919.

Generalate: 17 rue de l'Assomption, 75016, Paris, France.

Universal total in Congregation 1,423.

Represented in the 31 countries through Europe, Africa, Asia, North America, Central America, and South America.

North American Province: *Provincial House,* 227 N. Bowman Ave., Merion Station, PA 19066. Tel: 610-664-3074. Sr. Anne-Francoise Salaun, R.A., Prov. Supr.

Total number in Province 23.

Represented in the Archdiocese of Philadelphia and the Diocese of Worcester.

Ministry in Spiritual Formation; Counseling; Campus Ministry; Pastoral and Social Ministry; Education.

[3400] (R.S.C.)—RELIGIOUS SISTERS OF CHARITY P

Founded in Dublin, Ireland in 1815. Sisters in entire Congregation 650.

Motherhouse: *Caritas,* 15 Gilford Rd., Sandymount, Dublin 4, Ireland. Sr. Una O'Neill, Supr. Gen.

U.S. Headquarters (1953): *Regional Residence,* 1206 N. Edgemont St., Los Angeles, CA 90029. Tel: 213-644-1695; Fax: 213-662-1237. Sr. Carmel Noone, Regl. Supr.

Total in U.S. community 34.

Represented in the Archdiocese of Los Angeles and the Diocese of Orange.

[3410] (R.C.E.)—RELIGIOUS OF CHRISTIAN EDUCATION P

Founded in France in 1817. First foundation in the United States in 1905.

General Motherhouse: France.

Provincial Residence: 14 Bailey Rd., Arlington, MA 02174. Tel: 617-643-3032. Sr. Martha Brigham, R.C.E., Prov. Supr.

Total number in community 40.

Legal Title: *Religious of Christian Education, Inc.*

Ministry in Religious Education Centers; Pastoral Associates; Teaching; Home Care.

Represented in the Archdiocese of Boston and the Diocese of Charlotte.

[3420] (R.E.)—RELIGIOUS OF THE EUCHARIST P

(formerly Society of Perpetual Adoration)

Founded in Belgium in 1857. First Foundation in U.S. in 1900.

General Motherhouse: Watermael, near Brussels, Belgium. Very Rev. Mother Marie Virginie, Supr. Gen.

American Foundation: *Convent of the Religious of the Eucharist,* 2907 Ellicott Terrace, N. W., Washington, DC 20008. Tel: 202-966-3111. Sr. Patricia, Supr.

Ministry in the fields of Education; General.

Professed Sisters 5.

Represented in the Archdiocese of Washington.

[3430] (M.P.F.)—RELIGIOUS TEACHERS FILIPPINI P

(Maestre Pie Filippini)

Founded in Italy in 1692. First foundation in the United States in 1910.

General Motherhouse: *Villa Maria Regina,* Via Stazione Ottavia, 72, Rome, Italy. Sr. Mary DeBacco, M.P.F., Supr. Gen.

St. Lucy Filippini Province: *Villa Walsh,* Morristown, NJ 07960-4928. Tel: 201-538-2886. Sr. Frances Lauretti, Prov. Supr.; Sr. Clare Testa, Community Archivist.

Total number in community 282.

Properties owned and sponsored: *Villa Walsh,* Morristown, NJ; *Villa Victoria,* Trenton, NJ; *St. Joseph by the Sea,* South Mantoloking, NJ.

Ministry in the field of Religious and Academic Education in elementary; and secondary schools; Child Care Centers; Parish Ministry; Pastoral Care; Foreign Mission Work; Special Education; House of Prayer; Retreat House.

Represented in the Archdioceses of Newark and Philadelphia, and the Dioceses of Albany, Brooklyn, Cleveland, Camden, Metuchen, Paterson, Pittsburgh, Scranton and Trenton.

Queen of Apostles Province: *Religious Teachers Filippini M.P.F.,* 474 East Rd., Bristol, CT 06010. Tel: 203-584-2138. Sr. Christine Spirito, M.P.F., Prov.; Sr. Josephine Riccio, M.P.F., Community Archivist.

Total number in community 42.

Ministry in the field of Education; Pastoral Ministry; Catechetical Centers; Youth Retreats; Foreign Mission Work.

Represented in the Archdioceses of Hartford and Washington, and the Dioceses of Bridgeport, Norwich, Orlando and Providence.

[3449] (C.V.I.)—RELIGIOUS OF THE INCARNATE WORD P

Founded in Lyon, France, in 1625. First foundation in United States in 1853, in Mexico 1894.

General Motherhouse: Mexico City, Industria #1-Col.Toriello Guerra, Deleg. Tlalpan, Mexico, D.F., 14050. Sr. Gloria Leticia Ramirez Godoy, Gen. Supr.

U.S. Vice Provincial House: 153 Rainier Ct., Chula Vista, CA 91911. Tel: 619-420-0231. Sr. Mary Paz Mejia, C.V.I., Vice Prov.

Total number in Congregation 490.

Ministry in Parishes; Schools; Diocesan Offices and Missions.

Represented in the Diocese of San Diego. Also in Africa, Argentina, France, Guatemala, Mexico & Spain.

[3450] (R.J.M.)—RELIGIOUS OF JESUS AND MARY P

Founded at Lyons, France, 1818. First foundation in the U.S. in 1877.

Motherhouse: Via Nomentana 325, Rome, Italy. Rev. Mother Aurora Trallero, Supr. Gen.

Universal number in Congregation 1,701.

United States Province Provincialate: 3706 Rhode Island Ave., Mount Rainier, MD 20712. Tel: 301-277-3794; Fax: 301-277-8656. Sr. Rosemary Mangan, Prov.; Sr. Yvette Beaulieu, Archivist.

Legal Title: *Religious of Jesus and Mary, Inc.*

Total in community 159.

Ministry in the field of Academic and Religious Education; Pastoral Ministry; Social Services; QUEST Volunteer Program.

Represented in the Archdioceses of Boston, Los Angeles, New York, Washington, and the Dioceses of El Paso, Fall River, Manchester, Providence and San Diego.

[3460] (R.M.I.)—RELIGIOUS OF MARY IMMACULATE P

Founded in Madrid, Spain in 1876.

Mother House: Madrid, Spain.

Generalate: Rome, Italy.

U.S. Foundation (1954): *Villa Maria,* 719 Augusta St., San Antonio, TX 78215. Tel: 210-226-0025; Fax: 210-226-3305. Sr. Clara Echeverria, Local Supr.

Total number in community 12.

Headquarters: *Centro Maria,* 539 West 54th St., New York, NY 10019. Tel: 212-581-5273. Sr. Maria Christina Lopez, Local Supr.

Total number in community 9.

Represented in the Archdioceses of New York and San Antonio.

[3465] (R.S.H.M.)—RELIGIOUS OF THE SACRED HEART OF MARY P

Founded in France in 1848. First foundation in the United States in 1877.

Generalate: Via Adelaide Ristori 26, Curia Generalizia, Rome, Italy, 00197. Sr. Catherine Dolan, R.S.H.M., Gen. Supr.

Universal number in Congregation 1,120.

Eastern American Province (1907): 50 Wilson Park Dr., Tarrytown, NY 10591. Tel: 914-631-8872; 631-2630. Sr. Martina Crowley, R.S.H.M., Prov.

Total number in community 257.

Ministries including Education; Pastoral Ministry; Retreat and Spiritual Direction; Health Care and Social Work.

Represented in the Archdioceses of Baltimore, New York and St. Louis, and the Dioceses of Arlington, Brooklyn, Norwich, Oakland, Palm Beach, Rich-

mond, Rockville Centre, Trenton, Venice and Winona. Also in Africa and Europe.

WESTERN AMERICAN PROVINCE (1959): *Religious of the Sacred Heart of Mary R.S.H.M.,* R.S.H.M. Provincial Center, 441 N. Garfield Ave., Montebello, CA 90640-2901. Tel: 213-887-8821; Fax: 213-887-8952. Sr. Mary Genino, R.S.H.M., Prov.

Total number in community 95.

Legal Titles or Holdings: *Religious of the Sacred Heart of Mary, California Province, a California corporation; Marymount School, a California corporation.*

Ministry in the field of Academic Education at all levels; Diverse Pastoral Ministries.

Represented in the Archdioceses of Los Angeles and San Francisco, and the Dioceses of San Diego and San Jose. Also in Mexico.

[3470] (S.R.C.M.)—SISTERS OF REPARATION OF THE CONGREGATION OF MARY, INC. D

MOTHERHOUSE AND NOVITIATE: *St. Zita's Villa,* Monsey, NY 10952. Tel: 914-356-2011. Sr. Maureen Francis.

Total number in the community 15.

Represented in the Archdiocese of New York.

[3475] (S.R.)—SISTERS OF REPARATION OF THE SACRED WOUNDS OF JESUS D

Founded in 1959 in New York by Mother Mary Rose Therese, S.R. Established in the Diocese of San Diego in 1959. Motherhouse and Novitiate transferred to the Archdiocese of Portland in Oregon.

GENERAL MOTHERHOUSE AND NOVITIATE: *Sacred Wounds of Jesus Convent,* 2120 S.E. 24th Ave., Portland, OR 97214. Tel: 503-236-4207. Mother Regina Rose, S.R., Supr.

Sisters 4: Donne members 80.

Legal Title: *Sisters of Reparation of the Sacred Wounds of Jesus,* Portland, OR.

Health Care; Education; Pastoral Animation.

Represented in the Archdiocese of Portland.

[3480] (C.R.)—SISTERS OF THE RESURRECTION P

Founded in Rome, Italy, in 1891. First foundation in the United States in 1900.

GENERAL MOTHERHOUSE: Via Marcantonio Colonna 52A, Rome, Italy. Rev. Mother Dolores Stepien, C.R., Supr. Gen.

Universal total in Congregation 612.

WESTERN PROVINCE PROVINCIALHOUSE AND NOVITIATE: 7432 Talcott Ave., Chicago, IL 60631. Tel: 773-792-6363. Sr. Virginia Ann Wanzek, C.R., Prov. Supr.

Total number in community 83.

Properties owned or sponsored: *Resurrection Medical Center; Our Lady of Resurrection Medical Center; Resurrection Nursing and Rehabilitation Center; Resurrection Retirement Community; Resurrection Day Care Center; Resurrection High School; Resurrection Health Care Corp.; Queen of Resurrection House of Prayer.*

Represented in the Archdioceses of Chicago, Mobile and Milwaukee.

EASTERN PROVINCE PROVINCIALHOUSE AND NOVITIATE: *Sisters of the Resurrection - Mount St. Joseph,* 35 Boltwood Ave., Castleton-on-Hudson, NY 12033. Tel: 518-732-2226; Fax: 518-732-2898. Sr. Jeanne Marie Harla, C.R., Prov. Supr.

Total number in community 82.

Legal Title: *Sisters of the Resurrection, New York, Inc.*

Ministry in Nursing Homes; Elementary Schools; Christian Doctrine Centers; High School for Girls; Day Care Centers; Pre-schools.

Represented in the Archdiocese of New York, and the Dioceses of Albany, Bridgeport, Fall River and Trenton.

[3490] (O.S.S.)—RELIGIOUS OF THE ORDER OF THE BLESSED SACRAMENT AND OF OUR LADY P

Sacramentine Nuns

Cloistered Contemplative.

Founded in France in 1639. First foundation in the United States in 1912. The Sisters devote their lives to the perpetual adoration of Christ in the Eucharist.

BLESSED SACRAMENT MONASTERY: 235 Bellvale Lakes Rd., Warwick, NY 10990-3403. Tel: 914-988-5424. Sr. Mary Veronica, O.S.S., Prioress.

Professed Sisters 17.

MONASTERY OF PERPETUAL ADORATION (1951): U.S. 31, P.O. Box 86, Conway, MI 49722-0086. Tel: 616-347-0447. Sr. Rosalie, O.S.S., Prioress.

Professed Sisters 4.

Represented in the Archdiocese of New York and the Diocese of Gaylord.

[3499] (S.J.S.)—SISTERS SERVANTS OF THE BLESSED SACRAMENT P

Founded in Mexico in 1904. First foundation in the United States in 1926.

GENERAL MOTHERHOUSE: Juan Bernardino 650, Guadalajara, Jalisco , Mexico, 45000. Sr. Bertha Munoz, Supr. Gen.

U.S. VICE PROVINCE: 215 Lomita St., El Segundo, CA 90245. Tel: 310-615-0766; Fax: 310-615-0571. Sr. Ana Rosa Aceves, S.J.S., Vice Prov.

Total number in the community 62.

Legal Title: *Sisters Servants of the Blessed Sacrament, Inc.*

Ministry in the field of Education.

Represented in the Archdiocese of Los Angeles and the Diocese of Fresno, Sacramento and San Diego.

[3500] (S.S.S.)—SERVANTS OF THE BLESSED SACRAMENT P

Founded in France in 1858; First foundation in the United States in 1947.

GENERAL MOTHERHOUSE: Via Aurelia, 145-Int. C-2, Rome, Italy 00165.

AMERICAN PROVINCIAL HOUSE: *St. Charles Borromeo Parish,* 1818 Coal Pl. S.E., Albuquerque, NM 87106. Tel: 505-242-3692. Sr. Catherine Marie Caron, S.S.S., Prov.

Total number in the community 22.

Represented in the Archdiocese of Santa Fe, and the Dioceses of Portland (ME) and Pueblo.

[3510] (S.S.C.K.)—SISTER SERVANTS OF CHRIST THE KING D

Founded in the United States in 1936.

GENERAL MOTHERHOUSE: *Loretto Convent,* Mt. Calvary, WI 53057. Tel: 414-753-3211. Mother Mary Rose, Supr.

Professed Sisters 11.

Represented in the Archdiocese of Milwaukee and the Diocese of Fargo.

[3520] (S.S.C.M.)—SERVANTS OF THE HOLY HEART OF MARY P

Founded in Paris, France in 1860. First foundation in the United States in 1889.

GENERALATE: 2029 rue Holy Cross, Montreal, Quebec , Canada, H4E 2A4. Sr. Fernande Dionne, S.S.C.M., Gen. Supr.

UNITED STATES REGION-HOLY FAMILY PROVINCE: *Provincialate,* 145 S. Fourth Ave., Kankakee, IL 60901-3603. Tel: 815-937-2380; Fax: 815-937-5520. Sr. Kathleen Mulchay, S.S.C.M., Prov. Supr.

Total number in region 62.

Legal Title: *ServantCor; HealthCor; Service Cor, Inc.; Servants United Foundation.*

Ministry in Grammar Schools; Nursing Homes; Health Care; Education; Pastoral Ministry; Parishes; Ministry to the Aged; and Home Missions.

Represented in the Archdioceses of Chicago and Washington, and the Dioceses of Joliet, Peoria and Rockford.

[3530] (S.Sp.S.)—MISSIONARY SISTERS SERVANTS OF THE HOLY SPIRIT P

Founded in Holland in 1889. First foundation in the United States in 1901.

GENERAL MOTHERHOUSE: *Convento dello Spirito Santo,* Via Cassia 645, Roma, Italy 00189. Sr. Agada Brand, Supr. Gen.

Universal total in Congregation 3,750.

AMERICAN MOTHERHOUSE (1901): *Convent of the Holy Spirit,* Techny, IL 60082-6026. Tel: 847-272-5930; Fax: 847-272-0113. Sr. Priscilla Burke, Prov.

Total number in the community 125.

Affiliates: *Missionary Sisters Sponsorship, Inc.,* Techny, IL; *Missionary Sisters Health Care System,* McHenry, IL; *Sacred Heart Home, Inc.,* Hyattsville, MD; *Arnold Janssen Foundation,* Techny, IL.

Ministry in Schools; Health Care; Home for the Aged; Central Houses for Catechetical Work; Parish Ministry & Administration.

Represented in the Archdioceses of Chicago, Los Angeles, Washington and the Diocese of Jackson.

[3540] (S.Sp.S.deA.P.)—SISTER-SERVANTS OF THE HOLY SPIRIT OF PERPETUAL ADORATION P

Cloistered Contemplative.

Founded in Holland in 1896. First foundation in the United States in 1915.

GENERALATE: Convent of the Most Holy Trinity, Bad Driburg, Germany. Mother Mary Aurora, Supr. Gen.

U.S. NOVITIATE HOUSE: *Convent of Divine Love,* 2212 Green St., Philadelphia, PA 19130. Tel: 215-567-0123. Sr. Mary Victoria, Supr.

Professed Sisters 26; *Mount Grace Convent,* 1438 E. Warne Ave., St. Louis, MO 63107. Tel: 314-381-5686. Sr. Mary Margaret, Supr.

Professed Sisters 26; *Convent of the Blessed Sacrament,* 4105 Ocean Dr., Corpus Christi, TX 78411. Tel: 512-852-6212. Sr. Mary Lourdes, Supr.

Professed Sisters 19; *Adoration Convent of Christ the King Church,* 1040 S. Cotner Blvd., Lincoln, NE 68510. Tel: 402-489-0765. Sr. Mary Catherine, Supr.

Professed Sisters 8.

[3550] (S.C.I.M.)—SERVANTS OF THE IMMACULATE HEART OF MARY P

Good Shepherd Sisters of Quebec

Founded in Canada in 1850. First foundation in the United States in 1882.

GENERALATE: 2550, rue Marie-Fitzbach, Ste-Foy, Quebec , Canada. Sr. Denise Rodrigue, Supr. Gen.

Universal total in Congregation 889.

PROVINCIAL HOUSE: *St. Joseph Province at Bay View,* 313 Seaside Ave., Saco, ME 04072. Tel: 207-283-3433; Fax: 207-282-7376. Sr. Theresa Rounds, Prov. Supr.

Total number in community 117.

Ministry in High Schools; Grammar Schools; Adoption Agency; Group Homes for Unmarried Mothers; Group Home for Troubled Adolescents; C.C.D. Centers; Youth (Retreat Work); Apostolate to the Elderly and Homeless; Foreign Mission Work in Brazil.

Represented in the Archdiocese of Boston and the Diocese of Portland (ME). Also in the Dioceses of Natal and Caico, Brazil.

[3560] (S.J.)—SERVANTS OF JESUS D

SERVANTS OF JESUS (1974): *Central Office,* 9075 Big Lake Rd., P.O. Box 128, Clarkston, MI 48347. Tel: 313-625-8483. Leadership Team: Sr. Jane Przygocki, Pres.; Sr. Barbara Celeskey; Sr. Patricia Radomski.

Total number in community 24.

Legal Title: *Servants of Jesus Community Support Trust.*

Represented in the Archdiocese of Detroit, and the Dioceses of Gaylord, Grand Rapids and Saginaw.

[3570] (O.S.M.)—MANTELLATE SISTERS, SERVANTS OF MARY OF BLUE ISLAND P

Founded in Italy in 1861. First foundation in the United States in 1916.

GENERALATE AND NOVITIATE: Rome, Italy.

U.S. MOTHERHOUSE & NOVITIATE: *Convent of Our Mother of Sorrows,* 13811 S. Western Ave., Blue Island, IL 60406. Tel: 708-385-2103. Sr. M. Assuntina DeMato, O.S.M., Prov.

Professed Sisters 22.

Ministry in Grammar Schools; Nursery and Kindergartens; Catechetical Work.

Represented in the Archdiocese of Chicago.

[3572] (O.S.M.)—MANTELLATE SISTERS SERVANTS OF MARY OF PLAINFIELD

Founded October 6, 1861 in Treppi, Italy. First founded in the United States 1916.

Universal number of Mantellate Sisters 800.

MANTELLATE SISTERS SERVANTS OF MARY OF PLAINFIELD (1977): 16949 S. Drauden Rd., Plainfield, IL 60544-9219. Tel: 815-436-5796. Sr. Francis Gresser, O.S.M., Regl. Supr.

Sisters 12.

Ministry in the field of Academic Education; Parish Ministry; Social Work; Nursing; Homes for the Aged; Foreign Missions.

Represented in the Archdiocese of Chicago and the Diocese of Joliet.

[3580] (O.S.M.)—SERVANTS OF MARY P

Founded in Italy in the 13th Century. First foundation in the United States in 1893.

GENERAL MOTHERHOUSE: 89, St. Bernard's Rd., Solihull, B92 7DG. England. Sr. M. Felicity McKeon, O.S.M., Prioress Gen.

AMERICAN PROVINCE (1893): *Provincial Motherhouse, Convent of Our Lady of Sorrows,* 7400 Military Ave., Omaha, NE 68134-3398. Tel: 402-571-2547; Fax: 402-573-6055. Sr. Terese Lux, O.S.M., Prov.

Total number in community 126.

Ministry in the field of Religious and Academic Education at all levels; Parishes; Social Service Agencies; Diocesan Offices; Hospital Pastoral Care; Counseling Agencies; Peace and Justice Offices; Campus Ministry; Hospice; Jail Ministry; Develop-

ment; Health Care Services; Medical Research; Consulting; Spiritual Direction; Retreat Work; Missionary Work in Foreign Countries and in the United States.
Properties owned: *Marian High School,* Omaha, NE; *Our Lady of Sorrows Convent,* Omaha, NE.
Represented in the Archdioceses of Denver, Detroit, Kansas City in Kansas, Omaha, Portland (OR), St. Paul-Minneapolis, and the Dioceses of Belleville, Colorado Springs, Des Moines, Gaylord, Grand Island, Lexington, Metuchen, Ogdensburg, Rapid City, Salina, St. Cloud, Sioux City, and Tucson. Also in Jamaica.

[3590] (O.S.M.)—SERVANTS OF MARY (SERVITE SISTERS) D

Founded in Italy in the 13th Century. First United States foundation in 1912.
GENERAL MOTHERHOUSE: *Servants of Mary,* 1000 College Ave. W., Ladysmith, WI 54848. Tel: 715-532-3364; Fax: 715-532-6153. Sr. Anita C. Swansen, O.S.M., Pres.
Total number in community 95.
Ministry in the field of Academic Education; Parish and Pastoral Ministry; Health Care; Social Services, Law; and Administration.
Represented in the Archdioceses of Boston, Chicago, Louisville, Milwaukee and St. Paul-Minneapolis, and the Dioceses of Duluth, Fresno, Gary, Green Bay, Joliet, La Crosse, Orange, Orlando, Superior, St. Petersburg, Tucson and Wheeling-Charleston.

[3595] (S.S.J.)—SERVANTS OF ST. JOSEPH P

Founded in Spain in 1874.
MOTHERHOUSE: Salamanca, Spain.
GENERAL HOUSE: Rome, Italy. Mother Josefa Somoza, Supr. Gen.
U.S. ADDRESS (1957): *Servants of St. Joseph,* 203 N. Spring St., Falls Church, VA 22046. Tel: 703-533-8441. Sr. Fabiola Ospina, Supr. Tel: 703-534-9549.
Total number in community 16.
Represented in the Archdiocese of Newark and Diocese of Arlington.

[3600] (S.M.)—SISTERS SERVANTS OF MARY P
(Ministers to the Sick)

Founded in Madrid, Spain by St. Maria Soledad Torres, August 15, 1851. First foundation in the United States in 1914. Total Membership 1,974 Sisters.
GENERAL MOTHERHOUSE: via Antonio Musa 16, Rome, Italy. Mother Josefa Oyarzabal, Supr. Gen.
PROVINCIAL MOTHERHOUSE: 800 N. 18th St., Kansas City, KS 66102. Sr. Alfonsa Bellido, Prov. Supr.; Sr. Esther Betancourt, Locale Supr.; Sr. Carmela Sanz, Community Archivist.
Total number in the province 255.
Represented in the Archdioceses of Kansas City in Kansas, Los Angeles, New Orleans and New York.

[3610] (S.S.M.I.)—SISTERS SERVANTS OF MARY IMMACULATE P

Founded in Zuzel, Ukraine on August 28, 1892. Approved by the Holy See, 1932. Arrived in the United States on August 15, 1935 at Stamford, Connecticut.
GENERALATE: Via Cassia Antica 104, Rome, Italy 00191. Sr. Teresa Kito, Supr. Gen.
SISTERS SERVANTS OF MARY IMMACULATE: Sisters Servants Ln., 9 Emmanuel Dr., P.O. Box 6, Sloatsburg, NY 10974-0006. Tel: 914-753-2840. Sr. Michele Yakymovitch, Prov. Supr.; Sr. Thadea Nykolayow, S.S.M.I., Prov. Archivist.
Total number in community 54.
Properties owned: *Home of Divine Providence,* Philadelphia, PA; *Immaculate Conception Provincialate & Novitiate, St. Joseph's Home (for the aged), Saint Mary's Villa Spiritual, Cultural and Educational Center,* Sloatsburg, NY.
Ministry in the field of Education; Parish and Pastoral ministry; Health Care; Administration; Hospitality; Holy Dormition Pilgrimage.
Represented in the Ukrainian and Byzantine Rite Catholic Dioceses of the United States.

[3620] (S.S.M.I.)—SISTERS SERVANTS OF MARY IMMACULATE P

First founded in Poland 1878.
GENERAL MOTHERHOUSE: Mariowka-Opoczynska, Poland. Mother Maria Floryn, Mother Gen.
Universal total in Congregation 1,100.
AMERICAN PROVINCE (1935): 1220 Tugwell Dr., Catonsville, MD 21228. Tel: 410-747-1353. Sr. Bernadette Kozyra, Prov. Supr.; Sr. Marianna Danko, Community Archivist.
Total in the community 36.
Represented in the Archdioceses of Baltimore and Washington and the Diocese of Cleveland.

[3630] (S.S.C.J.)—SERVANTS OF THE MOST SACRED HEART OF JESUS P

Founded in Poland in 1894.
GENERAL MOTHERHOUSE: Garncarska St., Cracow, Poland. Mother Szczesna Niemiec, Supr. Gen.
SISTER SERVANTS OF THE MOST SACRED HEART OF JESUS (1959): *Sacred Heart Province,* 866 Cambria St., Cresson, PA 16630-1713. Sr. Theresa Marie, S.S.C.J., Prov. Supr.
Total number in U.S. Province 32.
Represented in the Archdiocese of Philadelphia, and the Dioceses of Altoona-Johnstown and Metuchen.

[3640] (S.M.G.)—POOR SERVANTS OF THE MOTHER OF GOD P

Founded in London, England in 1869. First foundation in the United States in 1947.
GENERAL MOTHERHOUSE: Maryfield, Roehampton, London S.W. 15, England. Sr. Rosarii O'Connor, S.M.G., Supr. Gen.
AMERICAN FOUNDATIONS: *Maryfield Nursing Home,* High Point, NC 27260. Tel: 919-886-2444. Sr. Clare Francis, Regl. Supr.
Total number in the community 26.
Ministry in Hospitals; Parish; Nursing Homes; Schools; Retreat House.
Represented in the Archdiocese of Philadelphia, and the Dioceses of Charlotte, Metuchen, Richmond and Tulsa.

[3650] (S.R.C.)—SERVANTS OF OUR LADY, QUEEN OF THE CLERGY D

Founded in Canada December 8th, 1929. First foundation in the United States in 1934.
GENERAL MOTHERHOUSE: 57 Jules-A. Brillant, Rimouski, Quebec G5L 1X1. Canada. Tel: 418-722-4402. Mother Pierrette Pelletier, S.R.C., Supr. Gen.
Sisters working in the United States 4.
Sister serve in the area of Domestic work.
Represented in the Dioceses of Fall River, Manchester and Providence.

[3658] (S.S.H.J.)—SISTERS OF THE SACRED HEART OF JESUS P

Founded in Ragusa, Italy in 1889. First foundation in the United States in 1950. Generalate House: Instituto Sacro Cuore di Ragusa, Via Cassia 1714, 00123 Rome, Italy.
Universal total in Congregation 602.
MOTHERHOUSE: *Instituto Sacro Cuore,* Via Suor Maria Schinina 2, 97100 Ragusa, Italy.
AMERICAN HEADQUARTERS: *Sacred Heart Villa School & Convent,* 5269 Lewiston Rd., Lewiston, NY 14092. Tel: 716-284-8273. Sr. M. Terenzia Giudice, S.S.H.J., Supr.
Legal Title: *Sacred Heart Villa School & Convent,* Lewiston, NY; *Saint Frances Cabrini Nursery and Convent,* North Haven, CT.
Ministry in the field of Religious and Academic Education at all levels; Hospitals; Homes for the Aged; Orphanages; Parish Ministry; Youth Ministry; Foreign Missions; Social Services.
Represented in the Archdiocese of Hartford and the Diocese of Buffalo.

[3660] (S.S.H.J.P.)—SERVANTS OF THE SACRED HEART OF JESUS AND OF THE POOR P

Founded in Leon, Gto., Mexico in 1885. First foundation in U.S. in 1907.
MOTHERHOUSE: Apartado 92, Puebla, Pue, Mexico. Tel: 01152-22-42-1869. Mother Guadalupe Lucia Bertoglio, Mother Gen.
U.S. ADDRESS: *Sacred Heart Children's Home Convent,* 3310 S. Zapata Hwy., Laredo, TX 78046. Sr. Maria Teresa Grajeda, Admin.
U.S.A. REGIONAL HOUSE: 3119 Pera St., El Paso, TX 79905.
Professed Sisters in U.S. 44.
Ministry in High School; Grammar School; Children's Home; Kindergarten; Language School.
Represented in the Dioceses of Corpus Christi and El Paso.

[3670] (S.S.C.J.)—SISTERS OF THE SACRED HEART OF JESUS OF SAINT JACUT P

Founded in France in 1816. First foundation in the United States in 1903.
GENERALATE: Paris, France.
MOTHERHOUSE: St. Jacut, Brittany, France.
USA/MEXICO PROVINCE (1916): *Mt. Sacred Heart Convent and Novitiate,* 5922 Blanco Road, San Antonio, TX 78216. Tel: 512-344-4805. Tel: 512-344-7203. Sr. Laura Gonzalez, Prov. Tel: 512-344-3610.
Total number in community 63.
Properties owned or sponsored: *Mount Sacred Heart Convent; Mount Sacred Heart School; Mount Sacred Heart School for Girls,* San Antonio, TX; *Casa Angelique; Mexico Casa San Antonio,* San Antonio, TX.
Ministry in Education; Domestic Work Houses; Schools of Religion; Health Care; Mexico Missions.
Represented in the Archdioceses of San Antonio and Santa Fe, and the Dioceses of Amarillo, Brownsville and Galveston-Houston. Also in Mexico City.

[3680] (S.H.J.M.)—SISTERS OF THE SACRED HEARTS OF JESUS AND MARY P

Founded in France in 1866. First foundation in United States in 1953.
MOTHERHOUSE: Essex, England.
REGIONAL HOUSE: 8644 Don Carlo Dr., El Cerrito, CA 94530. Tel: 415-527-3328.
Total number in community 250.
Represented in the Dioceses of Oakland, Sacramento and Stockton.

[3690] (SS.CC.)—CONGREGATION OF THE SACRED HEARTS AND OF PERPETUAL ADORATION P

Founded in France in 1800 as a Congregation of men and women. Members are consecrated to the Hearts of Jesus and Mary. Special Ministries are Perpetual Adoration, the education of youth, especially the poor, parish work and foreign missions. First Catholic missionaries to Hawaii in 1827: Sisters started Catholic Schools for girls in Hawaii 1859. First foundation in the continental United States in 1908.
GENERALATE: Via Aurelia 145, Scala C-Int 10-14-00165, Rome, Italy. Mother Jeanne Cadiou, SS.CC., Supr. Gen.
PACIFIC PROVINCE: *Sisters of the Sacred Hearts,* 1120 Fifth Ave, Honolulu, HI 96816. Tel: 808-737-5822. Sr. Regina Mary Jenkins, SS.CC., Prov.
Total number in community 57.
Legal Holdings and Titles: *Sisters of the Sacred Hearts Corporation; Regina Pacis Convent; Sacred Hearts Academy Corporation; Saint Anthony Home Corporation.*
EAST COAST REGION: *Sisters of the Sacred Hearts,* 419 Hood St., Fall River, MA 02720. Sr. Dolores Pavao, SS.CC., Regl. Supr.
Total number in community 14.
Properties owned or sponsored: *Sisters of the Sacred Hearts Residences,* at 35 Huttleston Ave. and 44 Adams St., Fairhaven, MA.
Represented in the Archdioceses of Los Angeles, and the Dioceses of Fall River and Honolulu.

[3710] (C.S.A.)—CONGREGATION OF THE SISTERS OF SAINT AGNES P

Founded in the United States in 1858.
GENERAL MOTHERHOUSE: *St. Agnes Convent,* 475 Gillett St., Fond du Lac, WI 54935. Tel: 414-923-2121. Sr. Mary Mollison, Gen. Supr.; Sr. Mary Christine Felerhoff, Gen. Vicar. Councillors: Sr. Donna Innes; Sr. Deborah Walter.
Total number in Congregation 428.
Properties owned or sponsored: *Hazotte Ministries, Inc.; Nazareth Heights, Inc.; Marian College of Fond du Lac; Genesys HealthCare of Fond du Lac, Inc.,* Fond du Lac, WI; *St. Francis Home,* Fond du Lac, WI; *Waupun Memorial Hospital,* Waupun, WI; *The Monroe Clinic (corporate title: St. Clare Hospital),* Monroe, WI.
Ministry in the field of Academic and Religious Education; Hospitals; Homes for Aged; Parish Ministry; Foreign Missions; Social Services; Healthcare.
Represented in the Archdioceses of Chicago, Cincinnati, Miami, Milwaukee, Mobile, New York, Philadelphia, St. Paul-Minneapolis,, and the Dioceses of Allentown, Altoona-Johnstown, Fort Wayne-South Bend, Gallup, Gary, Grand Island, Green Bay, Jackson, Joliet, Lafayette, Lexington, Madison, Marquette, Memphis, Oakland, Orlando, Phoenix, Raleigh, Rockford, Salina, St. Petersburg, Superior, Toledo, Tucson and Wichita. Also in Nicaragua, Honduras and Siberia.

[3718] (S.S.A.)—SISTERS OF ST. ANN P

Founded in Italy in 1834.
GENERAL MOTHERHOUSE: V.d. Aldobrandeschi, 100-00163, Rome, Italy. Franceschina Milanesio, S.S.A., Supr. Gen.
Universal total in Congregation 1,500.

U.S. Delegation (1952): *Mount St. Ann,* Ebensburg, PA 15931. Tel: 814-472-9354. Sr. Anna Maria Lorenzon, S.S.A., Delegate; Sr. Melany Pereira, S.S.A., Community Archivist.
Total number in community 9.
Ministry in the field of Education; Retreat Ministry; Foreign Mission; Pastoral Ministry.
Represented in the Dioceses of Altoona-Johnstown and Corpus Christi.

[3720] (S.S.A.)—SISTERS OF SAINT ANNE P

Founded in Vaudreuil, Province of Quebec, Canada, 1850. First foundation in the United States in 1866.
Legal Title: *The Community of the Sisters of St. Anne.*
General Motherhouse: 1950 Provost St., Lachine, Quebec , Canada. Sr. Yvette Bellerose, S.S.A., Supr. Gen.
Saint Marie Province (1887): 720 Boston Post Rd., Marlboro, MA 01752. Tel: 508-485-3791. Prov. Leaders: Sr. Therese Noury, S.S.A.; Sr. Michele Jacques, S.S.A. Tel: 508-481-4934.
Total number in Province 166; In community 1,002.
Properties owned: *Saint Anne Convent; Mary Martha House,* Marlboro, MA; *Emmanuel House,* Wayland, MA; *Esther House,* Worcester, MA; *Marie Esther Health Center, Inc.,* Marlboro, MA.
Ministry in the field of Academic and Religious Education at all levels; Center for Spiritual Renewal; Campus Ministry; Various Apostolates; Retreat Work; Pastoral Ministry; Ministry to the Aged, Shut-ins and the Poor; Hospital and Infirmary Nursing; Prison and Hospital Chaplaincies; Foreign Missions.
Represented in the Archdioceses of Boston, Hartford, Washington, and the Dioceses of Fall River, Manchester, Norwich, Providence, St. Petersburg, Springfield (MA), Venice, Wheeling-Charleston and Worcester.

[3730] (O.S.B.M.)—SISTERS OF THE ORDER OF ST. BASIL THE GREAT P
(International Byzantine Rite)

Founded in Cappadocia in the 4th Century by St. Basil the Great and his sister St. Macrina. First foundation in the United States in 1911.
Basilian Generalate: Via San Alessio 26, Roma, Italy 00153. Sr. M. Dia Stasiuk, Gen. Supr.

Philadelphia-Ukrainian Byzantine Rite

Provincial and Motherhouse: 710 Fox Chase Rd., Fox Chase Manor, PA 19046. Tel: 215-379-2817; 663-9153; Fax: 215-728-6129. Sr. Dorothy Ann Busowski, O.S.B.M., Prov.
Solemnly Professed Sisters 73.
Ministry in Education at all levels; Pastoral Ministry.
Represented in the Ukrainian Archdiocese of Philadelphia and the Ukrainian Dioceses of Chicago, Parma and Stamford.

Pittsburgh Ruthenian Byzantine Rite

Motherhouse and Novitiate: *Mount St. Macrina,* 500 W. Main St., P.O. Box 878, Uniontown, PA 15401. Tel: 412-438-8644. Sr. Ruth Plante, O.S.B.M., Prov.
Professed Sisters 96.
Sisters serve in: Diocesan, Parish and Religious Education Ministry; Health Care & Pastoral Ministry.
Legal Title: *Declaration of Trust of the Sisters of the Order of St. Basil the Great Community Support Program,* Uniontown, PA; *Declaration of the Sisters of the Order of St. Basil the Great Endowment Trust,* Uniontown, PA.
Represented in the Byzantine Archdiocese of Pittsburgh, and the Dioceses of Parma, Passaic and Van Nuys.

[3735] (C.S.B.)—CONGREGATION OF ST. BRIGID P

Founded in Ireland in 1807.
U.S. Foundation (1953): *St. Brigid's Convent,* 5118 Loma Linda Dr., San Antonio, TX 78201. Tel: 210-733-0701 & 736-1671. Sr. Teresa Carter, C.S.B., Regl. Coord.
Total number in community 20.
Properties owned: *Regional House; St. Brigid's Kindergarten,* San Antonio, TX.
Ministry in Seminaries; Pastoral ministry in parishes, hospitals, hospices, & detention facilities; Education in Elementary Schools; Counseling; Music Ministry.
Represented in the Archdioceses of Boston and San Antonio. Also in Ireland, England, Wales, Australia, Mexico, New Zealand, and Kenya.

[3740] (S.S.C.)—SISTERS OF ST. CASIMIR P

Founded by Mother Maria Kaupas in the United States in 1907.
General Motherhouse: 2601 W. Marquette Rd., Chicago, IL 60629. Tel: 773-776-1324; Fax: 773-776-8755. Sr. Marilyn Kuzmickus, S.S.C., Gen. Supr.; Sr. M. Christella, S.S.C., Archivist.
Total number in community 208.
Properties owned: *Maria High School; Holy Cross Hospital,* Chicago, IL; *Villa Joseph Marie High School,* Holland, PA; *St. Joseph Home for the Aged,* Holland, PA.
Ministry in the field of Academic Education; Foreign Missions; Hospitals; Homes for the Aged; Pastoral Ministry.
Represented in the Archdioceses of Baltimore, Chicago, Miami, Philadelphia and Washington, and the Dioceses of Allentown, Joliet and Las Cruces. Also in Argentina.

[3750] (S.S.Ch.)—SISTERS OF ST. CHRETIENNE P

Founded in France in 1807. First foundation in the United States in 1903.
General Motherhouse: Metz (Moselle), 57000, France.
Provincial House: 297 Arnold St., Wrentham, MA 02093-1798. Tel: 508-384-8066; Fax: 508-384-3170. Sr. Suzanne Beaudoin, S.S.Ch., Prov. Supr. Tel: 508-384-7841.
Novitiate, 30 Basset St., Lynn, MA 01902.
Total number in community 74.
Legal Titles: *St. Chretienne Educational Institute, Inc.,* Marlboro, MA; *St. Chretienne Educational Institute Trust,* Wrentham, MA.
Properties Owned: *Nazareth Spiritual Enrichment Center,* Newport, RI; *Retirement Home and Infirmary,* Marlboro, MA; *Our Lady Preschool Learning Center,* Marlboro, MA; *Novitiate,* Lynn, MA.
Represented in the Archdiocese of Boston, and the Dioceses of Lexington, Manchester, Portland (ME), Providence, and St. Petersburg.

[3760] (P.C.C. or O.S.C.)—ORDER OF ST. CLARE P

Poor Clares—Poor Clares of the Primitive Observance—Poor Clares of the Reform of St. Colette—Poor Clares of the Capuchin Branch of Poor Clares.
Founded in Assisi, Italy in 1212. First foundation in the United States in 1875.
Motherhouse: Monastery of St. Clare, Assisi, Italy, is called the Motherhouse of the Order, but the Abbess of said Monastery has no jurisdiction over other Communities of Poor Clares. Some Monasteries, such as those at Omaha, Evansville, New Orleans, Memphis, Jamaica Plain, Greenville, Lowell and Spokane, are subject to a Father General and to the Provincial of the Franciscan Province in which the Monastery is located. Monasteries at Aptos, Cleveland, Kokomo. Los Altos Hills, Newport News, Rockford, Roswell and Santa Barbara are Colettines.
Franciscan Monastery of St. Clare: 3626 N. 65th Ave , Omaha, NE 68104-3299. Tel: 402-558-4916. Sr. Veronica Leubbert, O.S.C., Abbess.
Solemnly Professed Sisters 9; Simply Professed Sisters 1.
St. Clare's Monastery of the Blessed Sacrament O.S.C.: 720 Henry Clay Ave., New Orleans, LA 70118. Tel: 504-895-2019. Sr. Elizabeth Mortell, O.S C., Abbess.
Total number in cloistered community 11.
Franciscan Monastery of St. Clare O.S.C.: 6825 Nurrenbern Rd., Evansville, IN 47712. Tel: 812-425-4396. Sr. Anna Scheessele, O.S.C., Supr.; Sr. Mary Martha, O.S.C., Community Archivist.
Total number in community 17.
Monastery of St. Clare (1932): 1310 Dellwood Ave., Memphis, TN 38127. Tel: 901-357-6662. Sr. Mary Helen Kelley, O.S.C., Abbess.
Solemnly Professed Cloistered Total number in community 10.
The Franciscan Monastery of St. Clare: 920 Centre St., Jamaica Plain, MA 02130. Tel: 617-524-1760. Sr. Clare Frances McAvoy, O.S.C., Abbess.
Total number in community 25.
Monastery of St. Clare O.S.C.: 201 Crosswicks St., Bordentown, NJ 08505. Tel: 609-298-0016. Sr. Mary McCourt, O.S.C., Abbess.
Total number in community 13.
Franciscan Monastery of Saint Clare: 1271 Langhorne-Newtown Rd., Langhorne, PA 19047-1297. Tel 215-968-5775. Sr. Mary Alfred Beattie, O.S.C., Abbess.
Total number in community 15.
Franciscan Monastery of St. Clare, Spokane, Washington: *Poor Clare Nuns,* 4419 N. Hawthorne St., Spokane, WA 99205. Tel: 509-327-4479; Fax: 509-327-5171. Sr. Mary Rita Dolan, O.S.C., Abbess; Sr. Patricia Proctor, O.S.C., Community Archivist, Solemn Vows, Papal Enclosure *Franciscan Province of Santa Barbara. Mother Bentivoglio Federation of Poor Clares.*
Professed Nuns 9.
Monastery of St. Clare: 142 Hollywood Ave., Bronx, NY 10465. Sr. Mary Bernadette Quinn, O.S.C., Abbess., Solemn Vows, Papal Enclosure.
Total number in community 14.
St. Clare's Monastery: 421 S. Fourth St., Sauk Rapids, MN 56379. Tel: 320-251-3556. Mother Mary Peter, O.S.C., Abbess.
Solemn Professed Cloistered. Total number in community 16; Simple Professed 1.
St. Clare's Monastery of the Infant Jesus (1953): *Franciscan Poor Clare Nuns,* 8650 Russell Ave. S., Minneapolis, MN 55431. Tel: 612-881-4766. Sr. Mary Catherine Martin, O.S.C., Abbess.
Legal Title: *Franciscan Poor Clare Nuns.*
Total number in community 16.
Monastery of Poor Clares: *Order of St. Clare-Poor Clare Colettine Nuns P.C.C.,* 3501 Rocky River Dr., Cleveland, OH 44111-2998. Tel: 216-941-2820. Mother Mary St. Paul, P.C.C., Abbess, Poor Clare Nuns (Colettines), observing the Primitive Rule of St. Clare. Strictly cloistered, Solemn Vows, Perpetual Exposition of the Most Blessed Sacrament.
Total number in community 26.
St. Joseph Monastery of the Poor Clares Colettines P.C.C.: 1671 Pleasant Valley Rd., P.O. Box 160, Aptos, CA 95001-0160. Tel: 408-761-9659. Mother Mary Clare, Abbess, (Reform of St. Colette) Daily Exposition of the Most Blessed Sacrament.
Total number in community 15; Postulants 1; Novices 2.
Corpus Christi Monastery (Solemn Vows, Papal Enclosure): *Poor Clare Colettines P.C.C.,* 2111 S. Main St., Rockford, IL 61102. Tel: 815-963-7343. Mother Mary Dorothy, P.C.C., Abbess.
Cloistered. Total number in community 32.
Monastery of Poor Clares-P.C.C. (1928): 215 E. Los Olivos St., Santa Barbara, CA 93105. Tel: 805-682-7670. Mother M. Clare of Jesus, Abbess.
Total number in community 15.
Monastery of St. Clare: 460 River Rd., Andover, MA 01810-4260. Tel: 508-851-6743. Sr. Therese Lacroix, O.S.C., Abbess.
Cloistered. Total number in community 16.
Poor Clare Monastery of Our Lady of Guadalupe: 809 E. 19th St., Roswell, NM 88201. Tel: 505-622-0868. Mother M. Francis, Abbess.
Legal Title: *Community of the Poor Clares of New Mexico, Inc.*
Cloistered. Total number in community 32.
Immaculate Heart Monastery of Poor Clares: 28210 Natoma Rd., Los Altos Hills, CA 94022. Tel: 415-948-2947. Mother Maura, P.C.C., Abbess.
Total number in community 19.
Monastery of St. Clare: 1916 N. Pleasantburg Dr., Greenville, SC 29609-4080. Tel: 864-244-4514. Sr. Maryalice Pierce, O.S.C., Abbess.
Cloistered. Total number in community 17.
Monastery of Poor Clares Colettine P.C.C.: 28 Harpersville Rd., Newport News, VA 23601. Tel: 757-596-5942. Solemn Vows. Mother Mary Colette, P.C.C., Abbess; Sr. Mary Charitas, P.C.C., Archivist.
Cloistered. Total number in community 13.
Maria Regina Mater Monastery P.C.C.: *Poor Clare Nuns,* 1175 N., 300 W., Kokomo, IN 46901. Tel: 317-457-5743. Mother Miriam, Abbess.
Cloistered. Total number in community 9.
Christ the King Monastery of St. Clare O.S.C.: 3900 Sherwood Blvd., Delray Beach, FL 33445. Tel: 561-498-3294. Sr. Mary Veroncia Butler, O.S.C., Abbess.
Total number in community 11.
Monastery of St. Clare of the Immaculate Conception O.S.C.: *Poor Clares,* 200 Marycrest Dr., St. Louis, MO 63129. Tel: 314-846-2618. Mother Mary Leo Hoffmann, O.S.C., Abbess.
Legal Title: *Nuns of the Order of St. Clare of St. Louis.*
Total number in community 9.
San Damiano Monastery of St. Clare: 6029 Estero Blvd., Fort Myers Beach, FL 33931-4325. Tel: 941-463-5599. Sr. Mary Emmanuel Kilkenny, O.S.C., Abbess.
(Solemn Vows, Papal Enclosure); Cloistered Sisters 4.
Monastery of St. Clare: 9300 Hwy 105, Brenham, TX 77833. Tel: 409-836-2444; Fax: 409-836-9652. Sr. Mary Angela Chandler, O.S.C., Abbess.
Sisters in Community 8.

[3765] (O.S.C.CAP.)—CAPUCHIN POOR CLARES P

Federation of Our Lady of the Angels in North America (1991): *Monastery of the Blessed Sacrament,* 4201 N.E. 18th St., Amarillo, TX 79107. Tel: 806-383-6771; Fax: 806-383-9877. Mother Catalina de Maria Banuelos, Pres.

[3770] (O.S.C.)—SISTERS OF ST. CLARE P

Generalate: 63 Harold's Cross Rd., Dublin 6W, Ireland. Sr. Helen Conway, Abbess Gen.

Regional Superior California: *St. Francis Convent,* 326 Santa Clara Dr., Vista, CA 92083. Sr. Madeline Fitzgerald, O.S.C., Regl. Supr.
Regional Superior Florida: *St. Vincent De Paul Convent,* 2109 Tilogia Ct., Holiday, FL 34690. Sr. Josephine Rooney, O.S.C., Regl. Supr.
Ministry in the Fields of Academic and Religious Education at All Levels; Pastoral Ministry; Youth Ministry; Retreat Ministry.
Represented in the Dioceses of Orange, St. Petersburg, San Bernardino and San Diego. Also in Albania, Australia, El Salvador, England, Guatemala, Ireland and Wales.

[3780] (SS.C.M.)—SISTERS OF SAINTS CYRIL AND METHODIUS P

Founded in the United States in 1909.
General Motherhouse: *Villa Sacred Heart,* Danville, PA 17821-1698. Tel: 717-275-3581; Fax: 717-275-5997. Sr. M. Paracleta, Gen. Supr.
Total number in community 205.
Properties owned or sponsored: *St. Cyril Academy; Villa Sacred Heart; Sacred Heart Institute; Maria Hall; Maria Joseph Manor; The Meadows at Maria Joseph Manor,* Danville, PA; *Villa St. Cyril,* Highland Park, IL.
Ministry in the field of Education; Pastoral; Homes for the Aged; Music Conservatory; Education Resource Centers; Continuing Care Retirement Community.
Represented in the Archdioceses of Chicago, Detroit, Hartford, and the Dioceses of Allentown, Altoona-Johnstown, Bridgeport, Charleston, Gary, Harrisburg, Scranton and Syracuse.

[3790] (S.S.D.)—INSTITUTE OF THE SISTERS OF ST. DOROTHY P

Founded in Italy in 1834. First foundation in the United States in 1911.
General Motherhouse: Via del Gianicolo 4-a, Rome, Italy 00165. Sr. Teresa Lopez, Gen. Coord.
Province of United States of America (1920): *Mt. St. Joseph,* 13 Monkeywrench Lane, Bristol, RI 02809. Tel: 401-253-7835. Sr. Eileen Egan, S.S.D., Prov. Coord.
Total number in community 59.
Properties owned or sponsored: *Villa Fatima,* Taunton, MA; *Mt. St. Joseph,* Bristol, RI; *Our Lady of Fatima High School,* Warren, RI; *St. Dorothy Academy,* Staten Island, NY.
Ministry in the fields of Education; Spiritual Life Centers; Social work with immigrants.
Represented in the Archdiocese of New York, and the Dioceses of Brownsville, Fall River and Providence.

[3810] (X.S.)—SOCIETY OF CATHOLIC MISSION SISTERS OF ST. FRANCIS XAVIER, INC. D
(Xavier Sisters)

Founded in the United States in 1946.
Convent: 37179 Moravian Dr., Clinton Township, MI 48036. Tel: 810-465-5082. Sr. Miriam Kennedy, Coord.
Total number in community 3.
Represented in the Archdiocese of Detroit.

[3820] (C.S.J.B.)—SISTERS OF ST. JOHN THE BAPTIST P

Founded in Italy in 1878. First foundation in the United States in 1906.
Legal Title: *Sisters of St. John the Baptist, Inc.*
General Motherhouse: Rome, Italy. Mother John Marie White, Supr. Gen.
U.S. Provincial House: 3308 Campbell Dr., Bronx, NY 10465. Tel: 718-518-7820. Sr. Mary Cecile Swanton, C.S.J.B., Prov. Supr.
Total number in community 124.
Legal Titles and Holdings: *Mt. St. John Convent,* Purchase, NY; *St. John Villa Academy,* Staten Island, NY; *Providence Rest Nursing Home,* Bronx, NY; *St. Lucy School,* Newark, NJ; *Mt. St. John Convent,* Gladstone, NJ; *St. Joseph Villa,* Peapack, NJ.
Ministry in the field of Education; Health Care for Aged; Private Guest House.
Represented in the Archdioceses of Newark and New York, and the Dioceses of Metuchen and Paterson.

[3830] (C.S.J. or S.S.J.)—SISTERS OF ST. JOSEPH

The Independent Motherhouses of the Sisters of St. Joseph are represented in the United States in the following Archdioceses and Dioceses:.

[3830-01] BOSTON D

Motherhouse of the Congregation of the Sisters of St. Joseph of Boston-CSJ (1873): 637 Cambridge St., Brighton, MA 02135. Tel: 617-783-9090; Fax: 617-783-8246. Sr. Kathleen McCluskey, C.S.J., Pres.; Sr. Therezon Sheerin, C.S.J., Community Archivist.
Total number in community 801.
Legal Holdings or Titles: *Motherhouse of the Sisters of Saint Joseph of Boston,* Brighton, MA; *Bethany Health Care Center, Inc. Bethany Hill School, Inc.,* Framingham, MA; *Fontbonne Hall,* Framingham, MA; *Retreat Center,* Cohasset, MA; *The Merrimack Montessori School,* Haverhill, MA; *Walnut Park Montessori School,* Newton, MA; *Jackson School Continuous Progress Elementary,* Newton, MA; *Fontbonne Academy,* Milton, MA; *Mount Saint Joseph Academy, Brighton,* MA; *Aquinas College, Milton,* MA; *Aquinas College,* Newton, MA; *Regis College,* Weston, MA.
Ministry in the field of Education at all levels; Health and Hospital services; Human Services and Pastoral Ministries.
Represented in the Archdioceses of Boston and Santa Fe.

[3830-02] CHICAGO D

Sisters of St. Joseph of La Grange CSJ (1899): 1515 W. Ogden Ave., La Grange Park, IL 60526. Tel: 708-354-9200. Leadership Team: Sr. Carol Crepeau, Pres.; Sr. Peter Mary Hettling; Sr. Terry Middendorf; Sr. Marlene Schemmel; Sr. Ethel Vaca.
Total number in community 114.
Ministry in the field of Education; School Administration; Nursing; Pastoral Care in Hospitals; Nursing Homes; Work with the Elderly; Parish Ministry; Archdiocesan Administration; Spiritual Direction and Retreats.
Legal Titles and Holdings: *Bethlehem Woods Retirement Living Center; Nazareth Academy High School; Sisters of St. Joseph of LaGrange Charitable Trust,* LaGrange Park, IL.
Represented in the Archdioceses of Chicago and Milwaukee, and the Dioceses of Cheyenne, Fort Wayne-South Bend, Jackson, Joliet, New Ulm, Rockford and Springfield-Cape Girardeau.

[3830-03] ORANGE P

Motherhouse of the Sisters of St. Joseph of Orange CSJ: 480 S. Batavia St., Orange, CA 92868. Tel: 714-633-8121; Fax: 714-744-3165. Sr. Nancy O'Connor, Gen. Supr.; Sr. Annette Bachand, C.S.J., Community Archivist.
Total number in community 232.
Ministry in the field of Education; Health & Hospital Services; Pastoral and Social Services.
Legal Holdings and Titles: *St. Joseph Hospital of Orange,* Orange, CA; *St. Joseph Health System, A Sisters of St. Joseph of Orange Corporation,* Orange, CA; *St. Jude Medical Center,* Fullerton, CA; *Center for Spiritual Development,* Orange, CA; *St. Joseph College,* Orange, CA; *Santa Rosa Memorial Hospital,* Santa Rosa, CA; *St. Joseph Hospital of Eureka,* Eureka, CA; *Redwood Memorial Hospital,* Fortuna, CA; *Queen of the Valley Hospital of Napa,* Napa, CA; *St. Mary of the Plains Hospital,* Lubbock, TX; *St. Joseph Health System Foundation,* Orange, CA; *St. Jude Memorial Foundation,* Fullerton, CA; *Redwood Memorial Foundation,* Fortuna, CA; *St. Jude Hospital Yorba Linda,* Yorba Linda, CA; *Sisters of St. Joseph Healthcare Foundation,* Orange, CA; *Mission Hospital Regional Medical Center St. Mary Desert Valley Hospital,* Apple Valley, CA.
Represented in the Archdioceses of Los Angeles and San Francisco, and the Dioceses of El Paso, Lubbock, Oakland, Orange, San Bernardino, San Diego and Santa Rosa. Also in El Salvador, Mexico, Hungary, Israel and Australia.

[3830-05] ROCKVILLE CENTRE D

St. Joseph's Convent - Congregation of the Sisters of Saint Joseph of Brentwood, NY CSJ: Brentwood, NY 11717. Tel: 516-273-4531. Sr. Angela Gannon, Gen. Supr.; Sr. Edna McKeever, Community Archivist.
Total number in community 997.
Ministry in the field of Education; Health & Hospital Services.
Represented in the Dioceses of Brooklyn and Rockville Centre. Also in Puerto Rico.

[3830-06] BUFFALO P

Generalate - Congregation of the Sisters of St. Joseph SSJ: 23 Agassiz Cir., Buffalo, NY 14214. Tel: 716-838-4400. Sr. Bea Manzella, Pres.; Sr. Mary Anne Butler, S.S.J., Community Archivist.
Total number in community 158.
Properties owned or sponsored: *Mt. St. Joseph Academy Administrative Office; Sisters of St. Joseph Residence; Center for Justice.*
Ministry in the field of Education at all levels; Hospital; Infant Home; School for Deaf; Youth Ministry; Justice Ministry; Pastoral Ministry; Hospital Chaplaincy; Prison Ministry; Spirituality Center.
Represented in the Archdioceses of Cincinnati, Detroit, and the Dioceses of Buffalo, Pensacola-Tallahassee, and Tucson. Also in Peru.

[3830-07] BURLINGTON D

Sisters of St. Joseph SSJ: 129 Convent Ave., Rutland, VT 05701. Tel: 802-775-0665. Sr. Miriam Francis Preedom, Pres.
Total number in community 56.
Properties owned or sponsored: *Mt. St. Joseph Convent; Fontbonne Hall; St. Francis Residence; Reading Nook; Mt. St. Joseph Academy,* Rutland, VT; *St. Joseph Convent,* Bennington, VT.
Ministry in the field of Education; Pastoral Ministry; Health Care; Social Services.
Represented in the Diocese of Burlington.

[3830-08] CLEVELAND D

St. Joseph Convent - Sisters of St. Joseph CSJ: 3430 Rocky River Dr., Cleveland, OH 44111. Tel: 216-252-0440. Executive Team: Sr. Barbara Green; Sr. Donna Hawk; Sr. Marietta Starrie; Sr. Ruth Rogers, Community Archivist.
Total number in community 183.
Legal Holdings & Titles: *Saint Joseph Academy; Sisters of Saint Joseph Community Support Charitable Trust Fund.*
Ministry in the field of Academic and Religious Education at all levels; Parish and Pastoral Ministry; Deaf Apostolate; Parish Team Member; Justice Work; Health Care; Social Services; Chancery Offices; Social Concerns; Retreat Work; House of Prayer.
Represented in the Archdiocese of Miami and Washington, and the Dioceses of Cleveland, Columbus, Galveston-Houston, Knoxville, Oakland, Steubenville, Venice and Youngstown.

[3830-09] ERIE D

Sisters of St. Joseph SSJ: *Villa Maria,* 5031 W. Ridge Rd., Erie, PA 16506-1249. Tel: 814-838-4100; Fax: 814-838-5167. Sr. Mary Fromknecht, Congregational Admin.
Total number in the community 190.
Legal Title: *Sisters of St. Joseph of Northwestern Pa.*
Institutions sponsored: Saint Vincent Health Center; Saint Mary's Home of Erie; Villa Maria Elementary; Villa Maria Academy; Villa Maria Center.
Ministry in the field of Education at all levels; Social Ministries; Nursing Home; Health Care; Pastoral Work and other Diocesan Ministries.
Represented in the Archdioceses of Chicago, Louisville, Miami, Milwaukee and Washington, and the Dioceses of Arlington, Cleveland, Memphis, Pittsburgh, Rochester and Steubenville.

[3830-10] LAFAYETTE-IN-INDIANA D

St. Joseph Center - Sisters of St. Joseph of Tipton CSJ: 1440 W. Division Rd., Tipton, IN 46072. Tel: 317-675-6203; Fax: 317-675-7471. Sr. Dorothy Gall, Pres.
Total number in community 54.
Ministry in Education; Health Care; Pastoral Ministry; Social Service; Evangelization.
Represented in the Archdiocese of Indianapolis, and the Dioceses of Baker and Lafayette (IN). Also in Haiti.

[3830-11] KALAMAZOO P

Motherhouse and Novitiate - Sisters of St. Joseph of Nazareth SSJ: Nazareth, MI 49074. Tel: 616-381-6290; Fax: 616-381-4909. Leadership Team: Sr. Janet Fleischhacker, Pres.; Sr. Christine Parks; Sr. Rita Ann Teichman; Sr. Judy Schroeder.
Total number in community 359.
Properties owned or sponsored: Hospitals; Holding Companies for Health Service Corporation; Nursing Homes; Day Care Center for handicapped and senior citizens; Residence for Senior Citizens; Home Health Care Organizations; Ambulatory Care Services; Residential Treatment Center; Family Clinic; Gerontology Research Center; Outpatient Mental Health Clinic.
Ministry in the field of Educational Services; Social Services; Parish and Church-related Ministries; Foreign Missions.
Represented in the Archdioceses of Chicago, Detroit, Los Angeles, New Orleans, Omaha, Sante Fe and Washington, and the Dioceses of Gary, Gaylord, Grand Rapids, Jackson, Jefferson City, Kalamazoo, Lafayette in Indiana, Lansing, Memphis, Phoenix, Saginaw, and St. Petersburg. Also in Peru and France.

[3830-12] **OGDENSBURG** D

MOTHERHOUSE OF THE SOCIETY OF THE SISTERS OF ST. JOSEPH SSJ: 1425 Washington St., Watertown, NY 13601. Tel: 315-782-3460. Sr. Jennifer Votraw, Supr. Gen.; Sr. Mary Joseph Meichelbeck, Community Archivist.

Total number in community 77.

Ministry in the field of Education at all levels.

Represented in the Diocese of Ogdensburg.

[3830-13] **PITTSBURGH** P

SISTERS OF ST. JOSEPH CSJ - MOTHERHOUSE & MT. GALLITZIN ACADEMY: Baden, PA 15005. Tel: 412-869-2151 & 761-3700; Fax: 412-869-3336. Leadership Team: Sr. Jeanette Bussen; Sr. Cynthia Comiskey; Sr. Anna Marie Gaglia; Sr. Dolores Montini; Sr. Patricia Phillips; Sr. Helen Marie Shrift, Community Archivist.

Total number in community 335.

Properties owned: Motherhouse and 7 residences for sisters.

Ministry in the field of Religious and Academic Education; Campus Ministry; Hospital Ministry; Health Care; Social Work; Parish Social and Pastoral Ministry; Family Life Ministry; Missionary Work; Housing Managers; Prison Ministry; Diocesan Administrative Services.

Represented in the Archdioceses of Baltimore, Boston, Detroit, Hartford, Miami, New York, Washington, and the Dioceses of Altoona-Johnstown, Arlington, Charlotte, Cheyenne, Columbus, Covington, Fresno, Greensburg, Harrisburg, Jackson, Memphis, Pittsburgh, Richmond, Sioux Falls, Tuscon and Wheeling-Charleston. Also in Jamaica and London.

[3830-14] **ROCHESTER** P

SISTERS OF ST. JOSEPH SSJ - MOTHERHOUSE: 4095 East Ave., Rochester, NY 14618-3798. Tel: 716-586-1000; Fax: 716-586-1193. Sr. Rosemary St. Peter, Congregational Pres.; Sr. Jeanne Agnes Michaud, Archivist.

Total number in community 446.

Properties owned and sponsored: *Nazareth Academy; Nazareth Hall; Nazareth Academy Convent; Motherhouse; St. Joseph Convent Infirmary.*

Ministry in the field of Education at all levels; Homes for Aging; Health Care; Pastoral Ministry; School for Special Children and Adults; Homes for Emotionally Disturbed Children; Parish and Diocesan Evangelization; College Campus Ministry; Social Service; Justice and Peace Offices; Drug Dependency Programs; Prison Ministry.

Sisters sponsor: 2 Foster Care Homes, 1 Food Kitchen and 1 Community Neighborhood Center.

Represented in the Archdioceses of Atlanta, Boston, Mobile, New York, and the Dioceses of Albany, Rochester and Syracuse. Also in Brazil.

[3830-15] **SALINA** P

GENERAL ADMINISTRATION OFFICE (1884): *Sisters of St. Joseph of Concordia CSJ,* 215 Court St., P.O. Box 279, Concordia, KS 66901. Tel: 913-243-2149. Sr. Christine Doman, Pres.

MOTHERHOUSE: *Sisters of St. Joseph,* 1300 Washington St., Concordia, KS 66901. Tel: 913-243-2113.

Total sisters in community 247.

Properties owned: Residences for Retired Sisters; *St. Mary's Convent,* Concordia, KS; *Medaille Center,* Salina, KS; *Manna House of Prayer,* Concordia, KS; *Saint Joseph Foundation for Apostolic and Charitable Purposes, Inc.*

Ministries: Care for Elderly; Homeless; Education; Parish and Diocesan Evangelization; Social Services; Justice and Peace Offices; Marriage and Family Counseling; Youth Formation; Handicapped Adults; Healthcare; College Campus Ministry; Drug Dependency Programs; Prisons; Consultants; Refugees; Continuous Prayer.

Represented in the Archdioceses of Atlanta, Boston, Denver, Kansas City in Kansas, St. Louis, St. Paul-Minneapolis, Seattle and Washington, and the Dioceses of Davenport, Dodge City, El Paso, Fargo, Grand Island, Jackson, Jefferson City, Kansas City-St. Joseph, Las Cruces, Marquette, Oakland, Phoenix, Pueblo, Rockford, St. Cloud and Salina.

[3830-16] **SPRINGFIELD (MA)** D

MOTHERHOUSE: *Mont Marie - Sisters of St. Joseph of Springfield SSJ,* Holyoke, MA 01040. Tel: 413-536-0853; Fax: 413-533-3275. Sr. Constance Quinlan, Pres.; Sr. Rita Morey, Archivist.

Total number in community 408.

Legal Holdings and Titles: *Mont Marie Child Care Center, Inc.; Mont Marie Health Care Center, Inc.; Mont Marie Conference Center,* Holyoke, MA.

Ministry in the field of Education at all levels; Spiritual Direction; Retreat Work; Diocesan Administration; Pastoral Ministry; Campus Ministry; Hospital Chaplaincy; Ministry to the Elderly; Youth Ministry; Counseling; Social Services; Health Care; Peace and Justice; Spanish Apostolate and Communications.

Represented in the Archdioceses of Hartford and Washington, and the Dioceses of Baton Rouge, Fall River, Lake Charles, Providence, Springfield (MA) and Worcester. Also in Kenya and Tanzania.

[3830-17] **WHEELING** D

MOTHERHOUSE: *Mt. St. Joseph-Sisters of St. Joseph of Wheeling SSJ,* Pogue Run Rd., Wheeling, WV 26003. Tel: 304-232-8160. Sr. Christine Riley, Pres.; Sr. Mary Thomas Camilletti, Community Archivist.

Total number in community 113.

Legal Holdings and Titles: *Sisters of St. Joseph of Wheeling Foundation; St. Joseph Hospital,* Parkersburg, WV.

Ministry the following areas: Parish Ministry; Pastoral Services; Elementary, Secondary, College Education; Health Care; Social Services; Spiritual Formation, Direction and Retreat Ministries; Diocesan; Administration and Service.

Represented in the Diocese of Wheeling-Charleston.

[3830-18] **WICHITA** P

MOTHERHOUSE: *Mt. St. Mary Convent - Sisters of St. Joseph of Wichita, CSJ,* 3700 E. Lincoln St., Wichita, KS 67218. Tel: 316-686-7171; Fax: 316-689-4056. Sr. Veronice Born, Pres.; Sr. Denise Seuart, Archivist.

Total number in community 232.

Legal Holdings and Titles: *Mt. St. Mary Convent* (Motherhouse), Parent organization for: 5 residences, Wichita, KS; 1 residence, Pittsburg, KS; 1 residence, Ponca City, OK; 1 residence, Hayward, CA; *Via Christi Health System, Inc.,* Parent organization for: *Via Christi Regional Medical Center, Inc.; St. Francis Campus; St. Joseph Campus Via Christi Rehabilitation Hospital, Inc. - Lourdes Campus GeorgeTown Village, Inc.,* Wichita, KS; *Mount Carmel Medical Center, Inc. Parent organization for: Mount Carmel Foundation,* Pittsburg, KS; *Mount Joseph Senior Community, Inc.; The St. Mary Hospital of Manhattan; St. Joseph Senior Community, Inc.,* Manhattan, KS; *St. John's Regional Health Center, Inc.; St. John's Hospital Foundation, Inc.,* Salina, KS; *St. Joseph Regional Medical Center of Northern Oklahoma, Inc.; Sisters of St. Joseph Convent Westminster Village, Inc.,* Ponca City, OK; *Hayward Sisters Hospital, dba St. Rose Hospital, Parent organization for: St. Rose Medical Building, Inc.; St. Rose Hospital Foundation,* Hayward, CA.

Ministry in the field of Religious and Academic Education; Adult Religious Correspondence Courses; Diocesan Program for the Handicapped; School of Special Education; Day Nursery; Home for Aged; Pro-Life Ministry to Women; Catholic IndoChinese Resettlement Center; ESL Language School; G.E.D. Program; Home Hospice; Hospital and Clinical Care; Pastoral Ministry; Campus Ministry.

Represented in the Archdioceses of Kansas City in Kansas, Oklahoma City, and the Dioceses of Oakland, Salina and Wichita. Also in Japan.

[3840] **(C.S.J.)—SISTERS OF ST. JOSEPH OF CARONDELET** P

Founded in France in 1650. First foundation in the United States in 1836.

CONGREGATIONAL OFFICES: 2307 S. Lindbergh Blvd., St. Louis, MO 63131. Sr. Lynn Levo, C.S.J., Congregational Dir. for the Provinces and Vice Province listed below.

PROVINCE OF ST. LOUIS (1836): *St. Joseph's Provincial House,* 6400 Minnesota Ave., St. Louis, MO 63111. Tel: 314-481-8800; Fax: 314-481-2366. Sr. Barbara Dreher, C.S.J., Prov. Dir. Team Members: Sr. Paulette Gladis, C.S.J.; Sr. Suzanne Giblin, C.S.J.

Total number in community 647.

Sponsored Institutions: Colleges 2; Academies 2; Hospitals 3; Institute for the Deaf 1; Long Term Care Facility 1.

Legal Title: *Sisters of St. Joseph of Carondelet,* St. Louis, MO.

Ministries in the field of Academic Education; Pastoral Ministries; Diocesan Offices; Health Care; Child Care; Geriatric Care; Foreign Missions; Social Servies; Community Services; Special Services; Fine Arts.

Represented in the Archdioceses of Atlanta, Chicago, Cincinnati, Denver, Indianapolis, Kansas City in Kansas, Los Angeles, Miami, Mobile, New Orleans, Oklahoma City, St. Louis, St. Paul-Minneapolis, San Francisco, Seattle, and the Dioceses of Belleville, Brownsville, Charleston, Colorado Springs, Davenport, Evansville, Green Bay, Helena, Jackson, Jefferson City, Kansas City-St. Joseph, Lafayette, Marquette, Memphis, Oakland, Orange, Palm Beach, Peoria, Reno-Las Vegas, St. Petersburg, San Diego, San Jose, Savannah, Shreveport, Springfield-Cape Girardeau, Steubenville, Syracuse, Tucson, Venice and Wilmington.

PROVINCE OF ST. PAUL (1851): *St. Joseph's Administration Center,* 1884 Randolph Ave., St. Paul, MN 55105. Tel: 612-690-7000; Fax: 612-690-7039. Province Admin. Team: Sr. Ann Vivia Walton, C.S.J.; Sr. Margaret Belanger, C.S.J.; Sr. Margaret L. Kvasnicka, C.S.J.; Sr. Mary Kraft, C.S.J., Archivist.

Total number in community 469.

Legal Holdings or Titles: *St. Joseph of Carondelet - St. Paul Province Provincial House; The College of St. Catherine Bethany Convent for Retired Sisters,* St. Paul, MN.

Ministry in the fields of Education; Health; Social Services; Spirituality.

Represented in the Archdioceses of Los Angeles, New York, Portland (OR), St. Paul-Minneapolis, Seattle, and the Dioceses of Brownsville, Charlotte, Duluth, El Paso, Fargo, Fort Worth, Helena, Jackson, Jefferson City, Kalamazoo, New Ulm, Pittsburgh and Superior.

PROVINCE OF ALBANY (1858): *St. Joseph's Provincial House,* 385 Watervliet-Shaker Rd., Latham, NY 12110. Tel: 518-783-3500. Sr. Sean C. Peters, C.S.J., Prov. Dir.; Sr. Frances Eustace, C.S.J., Prov. Archivist.

Total number in community 614.

Novitiate, 369 Watervliet-Shaker Rd., Latham, NY 12110. Tel: 518-783-3536.

Ministry in the fields of Academic and Special Education at all levels; Hospital and Infirmary Services; Hospital Pastoral Ministries; Parish Ministry and Religious Education; Diocesan Offices; Youth Ministry; Counseling; Retreat and Spiritual Direction; Social and Community Services; Fine Arts; Mortuary Science.

Represented in the Archdioceses of Boston, Cincinnati, Los Angeles, New York, St. Louis, Seattle, San Francisco, Washington, and the Dioceses of Albany, Arlington, Birmingham, Brooklyn, Buffalo, Erie, Fairbanks, Fall River, Harrisburg, Honolulu, Kansas City-St. Joseph, Manchester, Ogdensburg, Orange, Orlando, Palm Beach, Pensacola-Tallahassee, Pittsburgh, Providence, Rochester, Scranton, Spokane, Springfield in Illinois, Syracuse, Trenton, Tucson and Worcester. Also in Chile, Japan and Peru.

PROVINCE OF LOS ANGELES (1878): *St. Mary's Provincialate and Carondelet Center,* 11999 Chalon Rd., Los Angeles, CA 90049-1524. Tel: 310-272-8016; Fax: 310-476-8735. Sr. Joyce Marie Gaspardo, C.S.J., Prov. Supr.; Sr. Mary Ellen Sprouffske, C.S.J., Archivist.

Professed Sisters 505.

Legal Titles or Holdings: *Sisters of St. Joseph in California; Sisters of St. Joseph in Arizona; Sisters of St. Joseph Ministerial Services.*

Sisters serve in the fields of Education, Health and Hospital services; Social Services; and other related services.

Represented in the Archdioceses of Boston, Los Angeles, San Francisco, Seattle and Washington, and the Dioceses of Boise, Fresno, Honolulu, Monterey, Oakland, Orange, Phoenix, Sacramento, San Bernardino, San Diego, San Jose, Santa Rosa, Spokane, Stockton, Tucson and Yakima.

HAWAII VICE-PROVINCE (1956): *Sisters of St. Joseph of Carondelet,* Carondelet Convent, 5311 Apo Dr., Honolulu, HI 96821-1829. Tel: 808-373-3850. Sr. Ruth Margaret Raupp, Vice-Prov. Supr.

Legal Title: *Sisters of St. Joseph of Carondelet-Hawaii Vice-Province.*

Professed Sisters 47.

Ministries Include: Elementary and Secondary Schools; Pastoral Associates; Prayer & Spirituality; Administering Diocesan Offices; Religious Education Directors; Campus Ministry; Social Ministry.

Represented in the Diocese of Honolulu. Also in Chile.

[3850] **(C.S.J.)—SISTERS OF ST. JOSEPH OF CHAMBERY** P

Founded in France in 1650. First foundation in United States in 1885.

GENERALATE: Via Calandrelli 7, 00153, Rome, Italy. Sr. Marie Pierre Ruche, Supr. Gen.

PROVINCIAL HOUSE: *Convent of Mary Immaculate,* 27 Park Rd., West Hartford, CT 06119. Tel: 860-233-5126. Sr. Suzanne Brazauskas, C.S.J., Prov. Supr. Tel: 860-232-8252.

Total number in community 201.

Legal Title: *Sisters of St. Joseph Corporation.*

Ministry in the field of Academic and Religious Education at all levels; Social Services; Pastoral and Parish Ministries; Prisons; Law and Business;

Child Day Care Center; Foreign Missions; Hospitals and Health Care.
Represented in the Archdioceses of Baltimore, Hartford, Miami, Mobile, New York, Washington, and the Dioceses of Bridgeport, Burlington, El Paso, Fairbanks, Lexington, Norwich, Springfield (MA) and Trenton.

[3860] (S.J.C.)—SISTERS OF ST. JOSEPH OF CLUNY P

Founded in France in 1807.
GENERALATE: Paris, France. Sr. Marie Noel LeFrancios, Supr. Gen.
AMERICAN NOVITIATE: *Mary Immaculate Queen Novitiate,* 20955 Halldale Ave., Torrance, CA 90501. Tel: 310-328-1807.
Provincialate, Brenton Rd., Newport, RI 02840. Tel: 401-846-4757. Sr. Marie Cooper, Prov. of U.S. & Canada.
Professed Sisters in U.S. & Canada 45.
Legal Title: *Sisters of St. Joseph of Cluny, Inc.*
Represented in the Archdiocese of Los Angeles, and the Dioceses of Orange, Providence and Wheeling-Charleston. Also in Canada.

[3870] (C.S.J.)—SISTERS OF ST. JOSEPH OF LYONS, FRANCE P

Founded in France October 15, 1650. First foundation in United States in 1906 in Jackman, Maine.
GENERAL MOTHERHOUSE: Lyons, France. Sr. Joelle Peillon, Supr. Gen.
MAINE PROVINCE: *Sisters of St. Joseph,* 93 Halifax St., Winslow, ME 04901. Tel: 207-873-4512; Fax: 207-873-1976. Sr. Janet Gagnon, Prov.
Total number in community 60.
Properties owned and sponsored: *Mount St. Joseph Nursing Home,* Waterville, ME; *St. Joseph Child Care Center,* Auburn, ME.
Ministry in Catechetical Centers; Nursing Homes; Day Care Centers; Renewal Center; Pastoral Ministry; Education; Drug and Substance Abuse; Rehabilitation.
Represented in the Dioceses of El Paso, Fairbanks, and Portland (ME). Also in Brazil.

[3880] (C.S.J.)—SISTERS OF ST. JOSEPH OF MEDAILLE P

Founded in France in 1650. First foundation in the United States in 1855. Classified as an American Congregation November 30, 1977.
CENTRAL OFFICE: *Congregation of the Sisters of Saint Joseph of Medaille,* 1821 Summit Rd., Suite 210, Cincinnati, OH 45237. Tel: 513-761-2888; Fax: 513-761-9957. Sr. Lucy Silvio, Pres.; Sr. Maria Hill, Vice Pres. General Councilors: Sr. Joan Hartlaub; Sr. Janice Miller.
Total number in community 198.
Legal Title: *Sisters of St. Joseph of Medaille, Ohio Corporation.*
Ministry in the field of Academic Education at all levels; Montessori; Hospital and Clinic Care; Pastoral Ministry; Religious Education; Foreign Missions; Social Service; Centers for Christian Renewal; Services to Poor and Minorities; Community Service; Diocesan Offices; Activities Programs for Retired-Elderly; Chemical Dependency; Adult Mentally Retarded; Care for Retired Sisters.
Represented in the Archdioceses of Cincinnati, New Orleans, St. Paul-Minneapolis and Washington, and the Dioceses of Baton Rouge, Crookston, El Paso, Fargo, Fort Wayne-South Bend, Green Bay, Houma-Thibodaux, St. Petersburg and Superior. Also in Managua, Nicaragua.

[3890] (C.S.J.P.)—SISTERS OF ST. JOSEPH OF PEACE P

Founded in England 1884. First United States foundation 1885.
GENERALATE: *Sisters of St. Joseph of Peace Generalate, Inc.,* 1225 Newton St. N.E., Washington, DC 20017. Tel: 202-529-7015; Fax: 202-529-7015. Sr. Suzanne Golas, C.S.J.P., Congregation Leader.
St. Joseph Province-Eastern Province (1885): Sr. Ann Rutan, C.S.J.P., Congregation Leader; Sr. Mary McLeod, C.S.J.P., Asst. Congregation Leader; Sr. Mary Rattigan, C.S.J.P., Prov.
Total number in the community 362, Total number in the Province 169.
Ministry in the field of Education; Health and Social Services.
Properties owned or sponsored: *St. Joseph's Home for the Blind; The Kenmare School; St. Ann's Home for The Aged; St. Mary's Residence; Stella Maris Retreat House; School of Nursing; Senior Sisters Residence; St. Joseph's Home Messenger; The Guild for the Sisters of St. Joseph of Peace; Retirement Trust Fund for St. Joseph Province (Eastern); St. Joseph Province Offices, Shalom Center,* Englewood Cliffs, NJ. Affiliated Corporations: *St. Joseph's Village; Englewood Cliffs College; Holy Name Hospital; St. Joseph's School for the Blind; St. Michael's Villa; Villa Marie Claire; Holy Name Health Care Foundation; St. Joseph's Home for the Blind-Sisters of St. Joseph of Peace; St. Joseph's Home,* Jersey City, NJ; *The Nurturing Place (York Street Child Development Center).*
Represented in the Archdioceses of Baltimore, Los Angeles, Newark, New York and Washington, and the Dioceses of Camden, Metuchen, Paterson, St. Petersburg and Trenton.
OUR LADY PROVINCE (WESTERN) (1909): *St. Mary's Provincialate,* 1663 Killarney Way, Box 248, Bellevue, WA 98009-0248. Tel: 206-451-1770; Fax: 206-462-9760. Sr. Sheila Lemieux, C.S.J.P., Prov. Leader.
Properties owned: *St. Mary's Residence and Novitiate,* Bellevue, WA; *Prospect House,* Seattle, WA; *St. Therese Residence,* Seattle, WA; *Grace House,* Seattle, WA; *Alicia Park House,* Seattle, WA; *Bellingham Residence,* Bellingham, WA; *Eugene Residence,* Eugene, OR.
Corporate Titles: *Sisters of St. Joseph of Peace; Our Lady Province (Western); Sisters of St. Joseph of Peace Charitable Trust; Health and Hospital Services Sisters of St. Joseph of Peace,* Bellevue, WA; *Jubilee Women's Center,* Seattle, WA.
Total number in community 107.
Ministry in the field of Education; Health and Hospital; Services; Social Services; Religious Education; Parish Ministry, Retreat Ministry, Social and Minority Ministry.
Represented in the Archdioceses of Anchorage, Los Angeles, Portland (OR), San Francisco and Seattle, and the Dioceses of Juneau, San Diego, Spokane and Yakima. Also in Canada.

[3893] (S.S.J.)—SISTERS OF SAINT JOSEPH OF CHESTNUT HILL, PHILADELPHIA P

Founded in France in 1650. First foundation in Philadelphia in 1847.
MOTHERHOUSE (1847): *Mount St. Joseph Convent,* Chestnut Hill, Philadelphia, PA 19118-2694. Tel: 215-248-7200. Sr. Margaret Fleming, Supr. Gen.; Sr. Lawrence Joseph Murphy, Community Archivist.
Total number in Congregation 1,399.
Legal Holdings or Titles: *Saint Joseph Villa Saint Joseph Guild; Bethelehem Retirement Village,* Flourtown, PA; *Academy Village,* McSherrystown, PA; *Saint Joseph Housing Corporation; Saint Mary by-the-Sea Convent,* Cape May Point, NJ; Cecilian Academy, Philadelphia, PA; *Mount Saint Joseph Academy,* Flourtown, PA; *Norwood-Fontbonne Academy for Boys and Girls,* Philadelphia, PA; *Holy Family Academy,* Bayonne, NJ; *Chestnut Hill College,* Philadelphia, PA; *Saint Joseph Academy,* McSherrystown, PA; *The Convent of the Sisters of St. Joseph,* Chestnut Hill, PA.
Ministry in the field of Academic and Religious Education at all levels; Institutes for Dependent Children; Pastoral Ministry; Campus Ministry; Care of the Aged; Social Services; Prison Ministry; Health Care; Psychologists; Hospice Ministry; Hospital Chaplaincy; Spiritual Directors; Drug and Alcohol Counsellors; Legal Services Ministry; Delegates for Religious.
Represented in the Archdioceses of Baltimore, Chicago, Mobile, Newark, Philadelphia, San Antonio, Washington, and the Dioceses of Allentown, Arlington, Belleville, Brooklyn, Camden, Charlotte, Fort Wayne-South Bend, Harrisburg, Jackson, Juneau, Lexington, Metuchen, Paterson, Raleigh, St. Petersburg, Trenton and Wilmington. Also in Canada, Peru, and the Dominican Republic.

[3900] (S.S.J.)—SISTERS OF ST. JOSEPH OF ST. AUGUSTINE, FLORIDA D

Founded in France in 1650. First foundation in the United States in 1866. Classified as an American Congregation in 1899.
MOTHERHOUSE: *St. Joseph Convent,* 241 St. George St. P.O. Box 3506, St. Augustine, FL 32085. Tel: 904-824-1752. Sr. Florence Bryan, S.S.J., General Supr.; Sr. Mary Albert Lussier, S.S J., Community Archivist.
Legal Title: *The Sisters of St. Joseph Continuing Community Support Trust Fund.*
Total number in community 116.
Ministry in Hospital-Health Care Services; Social Services; Hospital Pastoral Care; Care of Aged; Academic and Religious Education at all levels; Parish Ministry; Diocesan Office Administration; House of Prayer; Ministry to the Handicapped.
Represented in the Archdiocese Miami, and the Dioceses of Orlando, Palm Beach, Pensacola-Tallahassee, St. Augustine and St. Petersburg.

[3910] (S.J.S.M.)—SISTERS OF ST. JOSEPH OF ST. MARK D

Founded in France in 1845. First foundation in the United States in October, 1937.
GENERALATE: Colmar, France. Sr. Sophie Moog, Gen. Supr.
Universal total number in Congregation 256.
YOUNGSTOWN DIOCESE: *Community Center,* 2337 Reno Dr., Louisville, OH 44641. Tel: 330-875-5946. Sr. M. Leo Hauck, Supr.
Total number in U.S. 9.
GENERAL MOTHERHOUSE (CLEVELAND) (1939): 21800 Charden Rd., Euclid, OH 44117. Mother Mary Therese Trunk, Supr. Gen.
Represented in the Diocese of Cleveland.

[3920] (S.J.W.)—SISTERS OF ST. JOSEPH THE WORKER D

GENERAL MOTHERHOUSE: *St. William Convent,* 1 St. Joseph Ln., Walton, KY 41094. Mother Ellen Curran, S.J.W., Supr.
Total number in the community 21.
Properties owned and operated: *Taylor Manor Nursing Home,* Versailles, KY; 16-acre property in Walton, KY; *Motherhouse Formation House.*
Represented in the Dioceses of Covington and Lexington.

[3930] (SSJ-TOSF)—SISTERS OF ST. JOSEPH OF THE THIRD ORDER OF ST. FRANCIS P

Founded in the United States in 1901.
SISTERS OF ST. JOSEPH TOSF: *Corporate Offices,* 1300 Maria Dr., Stevens Point, WI 54481. Tel: 715-341-8457; Fax: 715-341-8830. Sr. Jeanne Conzemius, Pres.; Sr. Beth Konkol, Vice Pres.; Sr. Mary Alice Jarosz, Vice Pres.; Sr. Katherine Wyszynski, Vice Pres.
Total number in the Congregation 528.
Ministries in the following areas: Academic Education at all levels; Pastoral Ministry; Health Care Services; Ministry abroad in South America and Puerto Rico; 8th Day Center for Social Justice; Social Services.
Sponsors: 1 Learning Center; 3 High Schools; 1 Health Care Facility.
Represented in the Archdioceses of Chicago, Denver, Detroit, Hartford, Los Angeles, Milwaukee, Newark, St. Paul-Minneapolis and San Francisco, and the Dioceses of Cleveland, Dallas, Fort Wayne-South Bend, Gary, Grand Island, Great Falls-Billings, Green Bay, Harrisburg, Jackson, Joliet, Kalamazoo, Knoxville, La Crosse, Lafayette (IN), Lansing, Madison, Norwich, Oakland, Phoenix, Rockford, Superior, Youngstown. Also in Brazil Peru, Puerto Rico and South Africa.

[3935] (S.S.L.)—THE CONGREGATION OF THE SISTERS OF ST. LOUIS, JUILLY - MONAGHAN P

Founded in France in 1842. First foundation in the United States in 1949.
GENERAL MOTHERHOUSE: Louisville Monaghan, Ireland. Sr. Anne Kavanagh, S.S.L., Supr. Gen.
REGIONAL HOUSE: *Louisville Convent,* 22300 Mulholland Dr., Woodland Hills, CA 91364. Tel: 818-883-1678. Sr. Bernadette Murphy, S.S.L., Regl. Supr.
Legal Title: *Sisters of St. Louis (Monaghan), Inc.*
Finally Professed Sisters 80.
Ministry in the field of Education; Pastoral and Social Ministries.
Represented in the Archdioceses of Indianapolis, Los Angeles and Washington, and the Dioceses of Orange, Raleigh and San Diego.

[3950] (S.S.M.N.)—SISTERS OF SAINT MARY OF NAMUR P

Founded in Namur, Belgium, in 1819. First foundation in the United States in 1863.
GENERAL MOTHERHOUSE: Namur, Belgium; Sr. Marie Julianne Farrington, Gen. Supr.
Universal Total in Congregation 550.
EASTERN PROVINCE: *Provincial House,* 250 Bryant, Buffalo, NY 14222. Tel: 716-884-8221; Fax: 716-884-2950. Sr. Nancy Charlesworth, Prov. Supr.
Total number in community 110.
Legal Holdings or Titles: *St. Joseph Convent,* Lockport, NY.
Ministry in the field of Religious and Academic Education; Pastoral Ministry; Social Services; Refugee Assistance.
Represented in the Archdiocese of Boston, and the Dioceses of Buffalo, Charleston, Jackson, Rochester, Savannah and Syracuse.
WESTERN PROVINCE: *Provincial House - Our Lady of Victory Center,* 909 W. Shaw St., Fort Worth, TX 76110. Tel: 817-923-8393. Sr. Joan Markey, Prov. Supr.
Total number in community 75.

Properties owned or sponsored: *Our Lady of Victory Center,* Fort Worth, TX; *Our Lady of Victory Elementary School,* Fort Worth, TX; *Casa de Esperanza,* Houston, TX; *Sisters of St. Mary of Namur,* Fort Worth, TX; *Notre Dame Convent Mercy Convent,* Wichita Falls, TX.
Ministry in the field of Religious and Academic Education; Diocesan Offices; Pastoral Ministry; Social Services; Health Care.
Represented in the Archdiocese of Seattle, and the Dioceses of Dallas, Fort Worth, Galveston-Houston and Richmond.

[3960] (S.S.M.O.)—SISTERS OF ST. MARY OF OREGON P

Founded in Oregon in 1886.
GENERAL MOTHERHOUSE: *St. Mary of the Valley,* 4440 S.W. 148th Ave., Beaverton, OR 97007. Tel: 503-644-9181. Sr. Delores Adelman, Supr. Gen.
Total number in Congregation 99.
Properties owned or sponsored: *St. Mary of the Valley School & Convent; Valley Catholic School, Maryville Nursing Home; Little Flower Development Center,* Beaverton, OR.
Ministry in the field of Education; Nursing Homes; and Parish Services.
Represented in the Archdioceses of Los Angeles, Portland (OR), Seattle, and the Dioceses of Baker, and Helena.

[3980] (S.P.C)—SISTERS OF SAINT PAUL DE CHARTRES P

Founded in France in 1696.
GENERAL HOUSE: 193 Via della Vignaccia, Rome, I-00163. Italy. Sr. Ann-Marie Audet, Supr. Gen.
Universal total in Congregation 4,000.
U.S. PROVINCE: 1300 County Rd. 492, Marquette, MI 49855. Tel: 906-226-3932; 226-6133. Sr. Mary Carol Goodman, Prov. Supr.
Total number in community 21.
Legal Holding: *Bishop Noa Home for Senior Citizens,* Escanaba, MI.
Ministry in the field of Academic and Religious Education; Pastoral Associates; Ministry to the Aged.
Represented in the Archdiocese of Washington and the Diocese of Marquette.

[3990] (S.S.P.C.)—MISSIONARY SISTERS OF ST. PETER CLAVER P

Founded in 1894. First Foundation in the United States, 1914.
Legal Title: *The Sodality of St. Peter Claver for the African Missions.*
GENERAL HOUSE: 16 via dell' Olmata, Rome, Italy. Mother Elizabeth Adamiak, S.S.P.C., Supr. Gen.
AMERICAN HEADQUARTERS: 667 Woods Mill Rd., S. P.O. Box 401, Chesterfield, MO 63006-0401. Tel: 314-434-8084. Sr. M. Aidan, S.S.P.C., Supr.
Total number in community 23.
Represented in the Archdioceses of Chicago, St. Louis and St. Paul-Minneapolis.

[4010] (O.S.A.)—SISTERS OF ST. RITA D

GENERAL MOTHERHOUSE: F. Spee Str., Wurzburg, 87 Germany. Sr. M. Dolores Schneider, Gen.
Universal total in Congregation 190.
U.S. ADDRESS: *St. Monica's Convent,* 3920 Green Bay Rd., Racine, WI 53404. Tel: 414-639-1766. Sr. Hanika, Supr.
Represented in the Archdiocese of Milwaukee.

[4020] (S.T.J.)—SOCIETY OF ST. TERESA OF JESUS P
(Teresian Sisters)

Founded in Spain in 1876. First foundation in the United States in 1910. Total Membership 1,830.
GENERALATE: Rome, 00166, Italy, Via Valcannuta, 134.
PROVINCIAL HOUSE: *St. Francis de Sales Province,* 18080 St. Joseph's Way, Covington, LA 70435-5623. Tel: 504-893-1470; Fax: 504-893-2476.
FORMATION HOUSE: 18158 St. Joseph's Way, Covington, LA 70435-5623. Tel: 504-893-1557. Sr. Martha L. Gonzalez, Community Archivist.
Total number in community 52.
Ministry in the field of Academic Education at all levels; Education in underdeveloped areas; Youth Centers.
Properties owned: *St. Teresa's Academy,* San Antonio, TX; *Blessed Mercedes Prat Convent,* New Orleans, LA; *Henry de Osso Convent,* San Antonio, TX; *Provincialate,* Covington, LA.
Represented in the Archdioceses of Miami, New Orleans and San Antonio.

[4030] (S.S.T.V.)—CONGREGATION OF SISTERS OF ST. THOMAS OF VILLANOVA P

Founded in France in 1661. First foundation in the United States in 1948.
GENERAL MOTHERHOUSE: 52 Blvd. d'Argenson, Neuilly-sur-Seine, France.
Universal total in Congregation 300.
SISTERS OF ST. THOMAS OF VILLANOVA CONVENT: Rocks Rd., Norwalk, CT 06851. Tel: 203-847-2885. Mother Edmond, Supr.
Total number in the community 5.
Properties owned: *Notre Dame Convalescent Home.*
Represented in the Dioceses of Bridgeport.

[4040] (S.U.)—SOCIETY OF ST. URSULA P

Founded in Dole, France, in 1606. First foundation in the United States in 1902.
GENERAL MOTHERHOUSE: St. Cyr-Loire, France. Sr. Marie Bernard, Supr. Gen.
PROVINCIALATE: *Linwood Spiritual Center,* 139 S. Mill Rd., Rhinebeck, NY 12572. Tel: 914-876-4178, 876-4512; Fax: 914-876-6544. Sr. Mary Isaac Jogues Koenig, Prov.
Total number in the community 36.
Ministry in the field of Education; Parish Ministry; Social Work.
Represented in the Archdioceses of Boston, New York and Washington, and the Dioceses of Providence and Raleigh.

[4048] (F.C.J.)—SOCIETY OF THE SISTERS, FAITHFUL COMPANIONS OF JESUS P

Founded in France in 1820. First founded in United States 1895.
GENERAL MOTHERHOUSE: *Stella Maris Convent,* North Foreland, Broadstairs Kent, England.
AMERICAN PROVINCE: *St. Philomena Convent,* Cory's Ln., Portsmouth, RI 02871. Tel: 401-683-5422. Sr. Paula Terroni, F.C.J., Supr. Gen.; Sr. Carmel Hamilton, F.C.J., Local Supr.; Sr. Susan Donohue, F.C.J., Prov. Supr.; Sr. Marie Therese Dyer, Novice Dir.
Sisters 11.
Represented in the Dioceses of Fall River, Providence and Raleigh.

[4050] (S.D.S.H.)—SISTERS OF THE SOCIETY DEVOTED TO THE SACRED HEART D

Founded in Hungary in 1940.
MOTHERHOUSE (1956): 9814 Sylvia Ave., Northridge, CA 91324. Tel: 818-772-9961; Fax: 818-772-2742. Sr. Jane Stafford, Supr. Gen.; Sr. Ida Peterfy, Foundress.
Novitiate House 10480 Winnetka, Chatsworth, CA 91313. Tel: 818-831-9710; Fax: 818-831-0790.
Total number in community 54.
Ministry in Parish Religious Education Centers; Catechist Formation Centers; Camp for year-round Retreats and for summer Family Retreats; Catechesis; Youth Leadership Programs; Day Retreat Center for Children and Adults; Catechesis in Parochial Schools and Catholic High Schools; "Sacred Heart Kids' Club" Video Catechesis; Hispanic, Chinese and Korean Catechetical Centers; Catechetical Programs on Military Bases; Catechetical Missions to Dioceses; Far East Mission in Taiwan; Mission in Hungary.
Properties owned: *Heart of Jesus Retreat Center,* Santa Ana, CA; *Sacred Heart Retreat Camp,* Big Bear Lake, CA; *Sacred Heart Novitiate,* Chatsworth, CA.
Represented in the Archdiocese of Los Angeles, and the Dioceses of Orange, Reno, and San Bernardino. Also in Hungary and Taiwan.

[4060] (S.H.C.J.)—SOCIETY OF THE HOLY CHILD JESUS P

Founded in England in 1846. First foundation in the United States in 1862.
MOTHERHOUSE: Via della Maglianella 379, Rome, Italy 00166. Sr. Mary Ann Buckley, Supr. Gen.
AMERICAN PROVINCE: *Provincial Offices,* 460 Shadeland Ave., Drexel Hill, PA 19026. Tel: 610-626-1400. Sr. Susan Slater, Prov.; Sr. Dorothy Cropper, Archivist.
Total number in Province 272.
Properties owned or sponsored: *Connelly School of the Holy Child,* Potomac, MD; *Cornelia Connelly School,* Anaheim, CA; *Mayfield Junior School of the Holy Child Jesus; Mayfield Senior School of the Holy Child Jesus,* Pasadena, CA; *Oak Knoll School of the Holy Child,* Summit, NJ; *Old Westbury School of the Holy Child,* Old Westbury, NY; *Rosemont School of the Holy Child,* Rosemont, PA; *School of the Holy Child,* Drexel Hill, PA; *School of the Holy Child,* Rye, NY; *Providence Center,* Philadelphia, PA.
Sisters minister in a variety of Educational and Pastoral Work.
Represented in the Archdioceses of Boston, Chicago, Cincinnati, Denver, Hartford, Los Angeles, Louisville, Milwaukee, Newark, New Orleans, New York, Philadelphia, Portland (OR) and Washington, and the Dioceses of Baker, Brooklyn, Camden, Charlotte, Erie, Jackson, Las Cruces, Metuchen, Orange, Paterson, Pueblo, Rockville Centre, Sacramento, San Diego, Trenton, Toledo, Venice, Wheeling-Charleston, and Wilmington.

[4070] (R.S.C.J.)—SOCIETY OF THE SACRED HEART P

Founded in France in 1800. First foundation in the United States in 1818.
GENERALATE: Via Tarquinio Vipera, 16, 00152, Rome, Italy. Sr. Patricia Garcia de Quevedo, Supr. Gen.
UNITED STATES PROVINCIAL HOUSE: 4389 W. Pine Blvd., St. Louis, MO 63108. Tel: 314-652-1500; Fax: 314-534-6800. Sr. Barbara Dawson, Prov.; Sr. Elizabeth Farley, Prov. Archivist.
Total number in the Province 539.
Province Corporations: *California Province of the Society of the Sacred Heart, Inc.; Society of the Sacred Heart, Chicago Province, Inc.; Religious of the Sacred Heart, Washington Province, Inc.; Religious of the Sacred Heart, New York Province, Inc.; Ladies of the Sacred Heart, MO; Religious of the Sacred Heart in Massachusetts, Inc.*
Network of Sacred Heart Schools, Inc. 860 Beacon St., Newton, MA 02159-1879. Tel: 617-244-9260.
Ministry in the field of Religious and Academic Education at all levels; Adult Education; Parish, Pastoral, Social and Health Care Ministries.
Represented in the Archdioceses of Boston, Chicago, Detroit, Miami, New Orleans, New York, Omaha, St. Louis, San Francisco, Seattle and Washington, and the Dioceses of Albany, Bridgeport, Galveston-Houston, Lafayette (LA), Richmond, San Diego, San Jose, Trenton and Venice.

[4080] (S.S.S.)—SISTERS OF SOCIAL SERVICE OF LOS ANGELES, INC. P

Founded in Hungary. Established in the United States at Los Angeles, California in 1926.
GENERAL MOTHERHOUSE: 2303 S. Figueroa Way, Los Angeles, CA 90007. Tel: 213-746-2117; Fax: 213-747-4499. Sr. Simone Campbell, Gen. Dir.
Total number in the community 104.
Legal Title: *Sisters of Social Service of Los Angeles; Sisters of Social Service Support Trust Fund.*
Social Service Work in Parish, Diocesan Agency & Secular settings; Leadership Training of Youth and Adults; Summer Camps for Children and Families; Programs for the Elderly; Peace and Justice Work; Religious Education; Settlement Houses; Health Programs; Low Cost Legal Services; Family Counseling Services; International houses in Mexico, Philippines and Taiwan.
Represented in the Archdioceses of Baltimore, Boston, Los Angeles, New York, Portland (OR), San Francisco, Seattle, and the Dioceses of Dallas, Great Falls-Billings, Oakland, Sacramento and San Diego.

[4090] (S.S.S.)—SISTERS OF SOCIAL SERVICE D

Founded in Budapest, Hungary in 1923. Sr. Margaret Slachta, Foundress.
GENERALATE RESIDENCE: 296 Summit Ave., Buffalo, NY 14214. Tel: 716-834-0197. Sr. Anne Lehner, S.S.S., General Moderator.
U.S. RESIDENCE: 440 Linwood Ave., Buffalo, NY 14209. Tel: 716-883-0112. Sr. Angela Homoki-Szabo, S.S.S., District Moderator.
Total number in the United States 21.
Social Work in private and public agencies; Religious Education; Parish Ministry; Ministry for Justice and Human Rights; Spanish Apostolate.
Represented in the Archdiocese of Miami, and the Dioceses of Buffalo and Ponce, PR.

[4100] (S.S.M.)—SISTERS OF THE SORROWFUL MOTHER (THIRD ORDER OF ST. FRANCIS) P

Founded in Italy in 1883. First foundation in the United States in 1889.
GENERAL MOTHERHOUSE: *Casa Generalizia della Suore dell'Addolorata,* Via Paolo III, 7-9, I-00165, Roma, Italy.
U.S./CARIBBEAN PROVINCE: *Our Lady of Sorrows Convent,* 17600 E. 51st St., S., Broken Arrow, OK 74012. Tel: 918-355-1148; Fax: 918-355-3534. Sr. Catherine Marie Hanegan, S.S.M., Prov. Supr.
Total number in the U.S. community 233.

Legal Holding: *Sisters of the Sorrowful Mother - US Health System, Inc.; Sisters of the Sorrowful Mother - US / Caribbean Province, Inc.*
Ministry in the fields of Religious and Academic Education; Nursing Homes; Social Work; Hospitals and Hospital Administration.
Represented in the Archdioceses of Milwaukee and Santa Fe, and the Dioceses of El Paso, Green Bay, La Crosse, Paterson, Superior, Tulsa, Wichita and Winona. Also in Dominican Republic, Jamaica, Grenada and Castries.

[4110] (O.S.U.)—URSULINE NUNS P
(Roman Union)
Founded in Italy in 1535. First foundation in the United States New Orleans, Louisiana in 1727.
GENERALATE: Via Nomentana, 236, Rome, 00162. Italy. Mother Colette Lignon, O.S.U., Prioress Gen.
EASTERN PROVINCE OF THE U.S. (1900): *Ursuline Provincialate-St. Mary's Hall,* 323 E. 198th St., Bronx, NY 10458. Tel: 718-365-7410; Fax: 718-733-4498. Sr. Madeline Welch, O.S.U., Prov.
Total number in the Province 216.
Legal Title: *Ursuline Provincialate, Eastern Province of the United States, Inc.*
Ministry in the field of Academic Education at all levels; Varied Pastoral and Social Services.
Represented in the Archdioceses of Baltimore, New York and Washington, and the Dioceses of Ogdensburg, Orlando, Raleigh, and Wilmington.
CENTRAL PROVINCE OF THE U.S.: *Ursuline Provincialate,* 210 Glennon Heights Rd., Crystal City, MO 63019. Tel: 314-937-6206; Fax: 314-937-7627. Sr. Pauline Lorch, O.S.U., Prov. Prioress.
Total number in the community 224.
Ministry in the field of Religious and Academic Education.
Represented in the Archdioceses of Cincinnati, New Orleans, St. Louis, St. Paul-Minneapolis, San Antonio, and the Dioceses of Corpus Christi, Dallas, Jackson, Galveston-Houston, Springfield-Cape Girardeau and Springfield (IL).
WESTERN PROVINCE U.S. (1932): *Ursuline Provincialate,* 639 Angela Dr., Santa Rosa, CA 95403-1793. Tel: 707-545-6811; Fax: 707-579-8571. Sr. Francis Xavier Porter, O.S.U., Prov. Prioress.
Total number in the Province 47.
Ministry in the field of Elementary and Secondary Education; Work with the Eskimos, American Indians, Hispanics & Blacks; Parish Ministry; Catechetical Coordinators; Blind Apostolate; Spiritual Growth Centers; Counseling Services.
Represented in the Archdioceses of Anchorage, Los Angeles and San Francisco, and the Dioceses of Boise, Fairbanks, Great Falls-Billings, Oakland, San Jose and Santa Rosa.
NORTHEASTERN PROVINCE: *Ursuline Provincialate,* 45 Lowder St., Dedham, MA 02026-4200. Tel: 617-326-6219; Fax: 617-326-7296. Sr. Dorothy Doyle, O.S.U., Prov.
Total number in the community 65.
Ministry in the field of Education.
Represented in the Archdiocese of Boston and the Diocese of Portland (ME).

[4120] (O.S.U.)—URSULINE NUNS, OF THE CONGREGATION OF PARIS P
Founded in Italy in 1535. First foundation in the United States in New Orleans, Louisiana in 1727.
MOTHERHOUSE (1845): *Immaculate Heart of Mary Convent,* 20860 St. Rte. 251, St. Martin, OH 45118-9705. Tel: 513-875-2020. Sr. Anne Maureen Maher, Supr.
Total number in the community 43.
Ministry in the field of Academic Education at all levels; Special Education; Adult Education; Catechetical Instruction; Administration; Retreats; Counseling; Organization Consultation; Social-Inner City & Rural; Hospital; Senior Services; Campus and Parish Ministry.
Legal Title: *St. Ursula Literary Institute; Ursulines of Brown County; Ursuline Academy of Cincinnati Chatfield College.*
Represented in the Archdiocese of Cincinnati, and the Dioceses of Covington, Trenton and Toledo.

[4120-01] Cincinnati P
MOTHERHOUSE: *Ursulines of Cincinnati, St. Ursula Convent,* 1339 E. McMillan St. (Walnut Hills), Cincinnati, OH 45206. Tel: 513-961-3410. Sr. Mary Cabrini Durkin, Supr.
Total number in the community 31.
Legal Title: *Ursulines of Cincinnati.*
Ministry in the field of Academic Education at all levels; Administration; Adult Education; Pastoral Ministry; Social Services; Hospices.
Properties Owned and Operated: *St. Ursula Convent & Academy,* Cincinnati, OH.
Represented in the Archdiocese of Cincinnati and the Diocese of Covington.

[4120-02] Kansas City in Kansas D
URSULINE CONVENT OF OUR LADY OF LOURDES: 901 E. Miami St., Paola, KS 66071. Tel: 913-294-2349. Sr. Pat Lynch, O.S.U., Supr.
Total number in the community 43.
Legal Title: *Ursuline Sisters, Inc.; Ursuline Sisters, Inc. Charitable Trust.*
Ministry in the field of Academic Education at all levels; Parish and Diocesan Services; Health Services.
Represented in the Archdioceses of Kansas City in Kansas and New Orleans, and the Dioceses of Kansas City-St. Joseph, Sacramento and Tulsa.

[4120-03] Louisville P
URSULINE MOTHERHOUSE OF THE IMMACULATE CONCEPTION: 3115 Lexington Rd., Louisville, KY 40206. Tel: 502-893-0125; Fax: 502-896-3913. Sr. Sarah Stauble, O.S.U., Pres.; Sr. Amelia Dues, O.S.U., Community Archivist.
Total number in the community 236.
Legal Title: *Ursuline Society and Academy of Education aka Ursuline Sisters.*
Properties owned and sponsored: *Sacred Heart Academy; Sacred Heart Model School; Ursuline Montessori; Ursuline Child Development Center; Ursuline School of Music & Drama; Marian Home,* Louisville, KY.
Ministry in the field of Academic Education; Child Care; Pastoral Ministry; Retreat Work; Social Services; Health Care.
Represented in the Archdioceses of Baltimore, Chicago, Indianapolis, Louisville, Omaha, Philadelphia, San Francisco, and the Dioceses of Brooklyn, Charleston, Cheyenne, Davenport, Grand Island, Jackson, Lexington, Pittsburgh, Richmond, St. Petersburg and Wheeling-Charleston.

[4120-04] Cleveland P
URSULINE MOTHERHOUSE AND EDUCATIONAL CENTER: 2600 Lander Rd., Cleveland, OH 44124; Fax: 216-449-3588. Sr. Virginia DeVinne, Supr. Gen.; Sr. Joann Kessler, Community Archivist.
Total number in the community 287.
Legal Title: *The Ursuline Academy of Cleveland; The Ursuline Sisters of Cleveland.*
Properties sponsored: *Ursuline College; Ursuline Sophia Center; Beaumont High School.*
Ministry in the field of Academic Education at all levels; Parish Ministry; Diocesan Offices; Seminary; Social Service Agency; Hospital Ministry; Foreign Mission.
Represented in the Dioceses of Buffalo, Cleveland, Columbus, Evansville, Great Falls, Fort Wayne-South Bend, Kansas City-St. Joseph, Pittsburgh, Orlando and Youngstown.

[4120-05] Owensboro P
MT. ST. JOSEPH URSULINE MOTHERHOUSE: Maple Mount, KY 42356. Tel: 502-229-4103. Sr. Rose Marita O'Bryan, Major Supr.
Total number in community 226.
Legal Holdings & Titles: *St. Joseph Female Ursuline Academic, Inc.; Brescia College; Mount St. Joseph Center,* Maple Mount, KY.
Ministry in Colleges; High Schools; Elementary Schools; Pastoral Ministries; Retreat Care; Pastoral Care; Social Services; Chancellor, Diocesan Offices.
Represented in the Archdioceses of Chicago, Cincinnati, Indianapolis, Louisville, St. Louis, Washington, Santa Fe, and the Dioceses of Beaumont, Evansville, Gallup, Kansas City-St. Joseph, Lincoln, Memphis, Owensboro, Richmond, and Springfield-Cape Girardeau.

[4120-06] Toledo P
URSULINE CONVENT OF THE SACRED HEART OFFICES: 4045 Indian Rd., Toledo, OH 43606. Tel: 419-536-9587; Fax: 419-536-0019. Sr. Nancy Mathias, Gen. Supr.
Total number in the community 108; Associates 116.
Legal Title: *Ursuline Convent of the Sacred Heart.*
Properties owned or sponsored: *St. Ursula Academy,* Toledo, OH.
Ministry in the field of Administration; Religious and Academic Education; Health Care; Counseling Services; Diocesan Education Office; Pastoral Ministry; Pastoral Care; Retreat Work; Spiritual Direction; Education in Music; Home Health Care.
Represented in the Archdiocese of Washington, and the Dioceses of Fresno and Toledo. Also in Lima, Peru.

[4120-07] Youngstown P
MOTHERHOUSE: *Ursuline Motherhouse and Educational Center,* 4250 Shields Rd., Canfield, OH 44406. Tel: 330-792-7636. Sr. Nancy Dawson, Gen. Supr.
Total number in the community 82.
Legal Title: *Ursuline Sisters of Youngstown.*
Properties Owned: *Ursuline Motherhouse; Ursuline Center; Ursuline Preschool & Kindergarten; Beatitude House.*
Ministry in the field of Religious and Academic Education at all levels; Parish Ministry; Diocesan Offices; Social Services; Hospital Services; AIDS ministry; Single Parenting; Preschool; Kindergarten; Nursing Home Administration; Nursing Home Service; Audiology; Speech Pathology; Music.
Represented in the Archdioceses of Washington, and the Dioceses of Cleveland, and Youngstown.

[4130] (O.S.U.)—URSULINE SISTERS OF THE CONGREGATION OF TILDONK, BELGIUM P
International Congregation.
Founded in Italy in 1535 by St. Angela Merici (Ursulines). Congregation of Tildonk founded in Belgium in 1832. First foundation in the United States in Ozone Park, New York, in 1924.
GENERALATE: Brussels, Belgium. Sr. Judith O'Connor, O.S.U., Gen. Supr.
URSULINE PROVINCIALATE: 81-15 Utopia Pkwy., Jamaica, NY 11432. Tel: 718-591-0681; 380-3459 (Residence). Sr. Catherine Talia, O.S.U., Prov. Supr.
Properties owned: *St. Ursula Center,* (Convent & Retreat center), Blue Point, NY; *Ursuline Provincialate,* Jamaica, NY.
Total number in the community 71.
Ministry in the field of Education in all its aspects.
Represented in the Archdioceses of Hartford and New York, and the Dioceses of Bridgeport, Brooklyn, Burlington, Richmond and Rockville Centre.

[4140] (O.S.U.)—URSULINE SISTERS OF BELLEVILLE D
Founded in Italy in 1535. First foundation in the United States in 1910. Newly established as Diocesan Community August 13, 1983.
CENTRAL HOUSE: 1026 N. Douglas Ave., Belleville, IL 62220-4198. Tel: 618-235-3444. Sr. Dorothy Hebling, Community Leader.
Total number in the community 18.
Ministry in the field of Religious and Academic Education; Retreat Work; Pastoral Ministry.
Represented in the Diocese of Belleville.

[4150] (O.S.U.)—IRISH URSULINE UNION P
THE GENERALATE: 17 Trimleston Park, Booterstown, Dublin, Ireland. Sr. Mary Gilbride, O.S.U., Supr. Gen.
U.S. FOUNDATION: *Our Lady of Lourdes Convent,* 1973 Torch Hill Rd., Columbus, GA 31903. Tel: 706-689-5184. Sr. Kathleen Twomey, O.S.U., Supr.
Total number in community 4.
Ministry in Domestics; Teaching and Parishes.
Represented in the Diocese of Savannah.

[4155] (M.T.G.)—VIETNAMESE ADORERS OF THE HOLY CROSS P
Founded in 1670 in Viet Nam by Bishop Pierre Lambert de la Motte. First foundation in the United States 1976.
GENERAL MOTHERHOUSE: *Vietnamese Adorers of the Holy Cross,* Holy Cross Convent, 7408 S.E. Adler, Portland, OR 97215. Tel: 503-254-3284. Sr. Mary Kim Phuong T. Nguyen, M.T.G., Supr.
Sisters 14: Novices 5; Candidates 10.
Legal Title: *Vietnamese Adoreres of the Holy Cross,* Portland, OR.
Represented in the Archdiocese of Portland, OR and the Diocese of Arlington.

[4160] (V.S.C.)—VINCENTIAN SISTERS OF CHARITY P
First foundation in the United States in 1902.
GENERAL MOTHERHOUSE AND NOVITIATE: *St. Vincent Hill,* 8200 McKnight Rd., Pittsburgh, PA 15237. Tel: 412-364-3000; Fax: 412-364-9055. Sr. Rita Gesue, Supr. Gen.
Professed sisters 194.
Properties owned or sponsored: *Vincentian Child Care Center; Vincentian High School; Vincentian Home, Inc.; Villa de Marillac Nursing Home; Regency Hall Nursing Home and Adult Day Care; St. Louise De Marillac Mission Convent,* Talara, Peru.
Ministry in the Field of Education at All Levels; Health Care in Nursing Homes; Child Care Center; Adult Day Care; Catechetical Centers; Social Apostolates; Montessori; Pastoral Ministries.
Represented in the Archdiocese of Mobile and in Dioceses of Altoona-Johnstown, Greensburg, Madison, Pittsburgh, Springfield-Cape Girardeau, Steubenville, Venice, Wheeling-Charleston and Youngstown. Also in Canada, Peru.

[4170] (V.S.C.)—VINCENTIAN SISTERS OF CHARITY D

Founded in Bedford in 1928.

MOTHERHOUSE & NOVITIATE: *Villa San Bernardo,* 1160 Broadway, Bedford, OH 44146-4523. Tel: 216-232-4755; Fax: 216-232-7832. Sr. Margaret Mach, Gen. Supr.; Sr. Dorothy Ann Blatnica, Dir. Formation.

Professed 77; Novices 1.

Ministry in the field of Education at all levels; Pastoral Ministry and Counseling; Social Services; Nursing care of the Elderly; Marian Shrine and Poustinia; Hospice; Poor in Appalachia; Facility for Elderly - Independent and Assisted Living; Light of Hearts Villa (Assisted Living Facility).

Represented in the Dioceses of Cleveland, and Lexington.

[4180] (M.P.V.)—RELIGIOUS VENERINI SISTERS P

Founded in Italy in 1685. First foundation in the United States in 1909.

GENERAL MOTHERHOUSE: via Gioachino Belli 31, Rome, Italy. Rev. Mother Marcella Lorenzetti, Supr. Gen.

Universal total in Congregation 490.

PROVINCIALHOUSE FOR THE U.S.: 23 Edward St., Worcester, MA 01605. Sr. Hilda Ponte, Prov.

Total number in the community 36.

Legal Holdings: *Venerini Academy,* Worcester, MA.

Ministry in the field of Education; Health Care; Social Services; Parish and Diocesan Ministry; Foreign Missions.

Represented in the Dioceses of Albany, Fall River, St. Petersburg and Worcester.

[4190] (V.H.M.)—VISITATION NUNS P

Founded in France in 1610. First foundation in the United States in Georgetown, Washington, DC in 1799.

First Federation of North America

Major pontifical enclosure. Mother Mary Jozefa, Federation Pres., residing at the Monastery of Visitation, Snellville GA.

Listed in the Order of Foundation established:

MONASTERY OF THE VISITATION (1833): 2300 Springhill Ave., Mobile, AL 36607-3202. Tel: 334-473-2321. Sr. Rose Marie Kinsella, Supr.

Total number in the community 13.

MONASTERY OF THE VISITATION: Beach Rd., Tyringham, MA 01264. Tel: 413-443-0468. Mother Mary Francis Metz, Supr.

Legal Title: *Visitation of Holy Mary.*

Total number in the community 19.

MONASTERY OF THE VISITATION: 12221 Bievenue Rd., Rockville, VA 23146. Tel: 804-749-4885. Mother Margaret Mary McGuire, Supr.

Legal Title: *Visitation of Holy Mary.*

Professed Sisters 17; Novices 3.

MONASTERY OF THE VISITATION: 5820 City Ave., Philadelphia, PA 19131-1295. Tel: 215-473-5888. Mother Frances de Sales Paganelli, Supr.

Legal Title: *Sisters of the Visitation of Philadelphia.*

Professed Sisters Cloistered 11; Externs: Professed 1.

MONASTERY OF THE VISITATION (CONTEMPLATIVE): 1745 Parkside Blvd., Toledo, OH 43607. Tel: 419-536-1343. Mother Sharon Elizabeth Gworek, Supr.

Professed Sisters 15; in Formation 4.

MONASTERY OF THE VISITATION (STRICTLY CLOISTERED): 2055 Ridgedale Dr., Snellville, GA 30278. Tel: 770-972-1060. Mother Mary Jozefa Kowalewski, Federation Pres. & Supr.

Legal Title: *Order of the Visitation.*

Professed Sisters 14; Novices 2.

Second Federation of North America

Sister Anne Madeleine Godefroy residing at Monastery of the Visitation, St. Louis, Missouri.

Total number of nuns in this federation 160.

MONASTERY OF THE VISITATION OF GEORGETOWN: 1500 35th St., Washington, DC 20007. Tel: 202-337-0350. Mother Mary de Sales McNabb, Supr.; Sr. Mada-anne Gell, Community Archivist.

Legal Titles & Holdings: *Sisters of the Visitation of Georgetown; Georgetown Visitation Preparatory School.*

Total number in the school community 417; Total number in religious community 29.

MONASTERY OF THE VISITATION (1833): 3020 N. Ballas Rd., St. Louis, MO 63131. Tel: 314-432-5353. Sr. Anne Madeleine Godefroy, Supr.

Total number in the community 26.

Ministry in Education.

Legal Holdings: *Visitation Academy of St. Louis County; Monastery of the Visitation,* St. Louis, MO.

MONASTERY OF THE VISITATION (1846): 200 E. Second St., Frederick, MD 21701. Tel: 301-622-3322. Mother Marguerite Therese Leary, V.H.M., Supr.

Total number in the community 6.

Legal Holdings or Titles: *Monastery of the Visitation - Frederick, Maryland; Frederick Academy of the Visitation Cloistered Contemplative Order with Elementary School as Apostolate.*

SISTERS OF THE VISITATION OF HOLY MARY OF MOUNT DE CHANTAL, INC. (1848): Wheeling, WV 26003. Tel: 304-232-1283. Sr. Mary Grace Flynn, V.H.M., Supr.

Total number in the community 29.

Legal Holdings or Titles: *Sisters of the Visitation of Holy Mary of Mount de Chantal, Inc.; Mount de Chantal Visitation Academy, Inc.*

Ministry in the field of Education.

MONASTERY OF THE VISITATION (1855): 8902 Ridge Blvd., Brooklyn, NY 11209-5716. Tel: 718-745-5151. Sr. Marie Anatrella, Supr.

Professed Sisters 22.

Ministry: Comtemplative Prayer and limited participation in Elementary School.

VILLA DE CHANTAL: 2936 36th St., Rock Island, IL 61201. Sr. Mary Veronica Haronik, V.H.M., Pres.

Legal Title: *Sisters of the Visitation.*

Ministry in Spiritual and Educational Center.

MONASTERY OF THE VISITATION: 2455 Visitation Dr., Mendota Heights, MN 55120. Tel: 612-683-1700. Sr. Mary Denise Villaume, V.H.M., Supr.

Total number in the community 23.

Ministry in the field of Education.

[4200] (S.V.M.)—SISTERS OF THE VISITATION OF THE CONGREGATION OF THE IMMACULATE HEART OF MARY D

Founded in France in 1610. First foundation in the United States in 1799.

VISITATION CONVENT: 2950 Kaufmann Ave., Dubuque, IA 52001-1655. Tel: 319-556-2440. Sr. Ruth Jackson, Pres.

Total number in community 9.

Ministry in Elementary & Higher Education; Adult Education; Parish Ministry.

Represented in the Archdiocese of Dubuque and the Diocese of Fort Wayne-South Bend.

[4210] (S.D.V.)—VOCATIONIST SISTERS P

(Sisters of the Divine Vocations)

Founded in Italy in 1921. First established in the United States in 1967.

GENERAL MOTHERHOUSE: Corso Duca D'Aosta, 22 Pianura, 80126, Naples, Italy. Sr. Giannina Di Francia, Mother Supr. Gen.

U.S. FOUNDATION: *Perpetual Help Day Nursery,* 172 Broad St., Newark, NJ 07104. Tel: 201-484-3535. Sr. Louisa Gargione, Supr.

Total number in community 5.

Ministry in Nursery Schools & Kindergartens; CCD Program and Parish Services.

Represented in the Archdiocese of Newark.

SISTER JOANNA FORMATION HOUSE: 88 Brooklake Rd., Florham Park, NJ 07932. Tel: 201-966-9762. Sr. Anna Maria Mancino, Delegate; Sr. Gelsomina Mosca, Supr.

Total number in community 7.

Ministry in Nursery School; Formation House.

Represented in the Diocese of Paterson.

[4230] (X.M.M.)—XAVERIAN MISSIONARY SOCIETY OF MARY, INC. P

Founded in Italy in 1945. First established in the United States in 1954.

GENERAL MOTHERHOUSE: Missionarie Saveriane Di Maria, Via Omero 4, Parma, Italy. Sr. Giuseppina Caccia, X.M.M., Supr. Gen.

Total Membership 250.

U.S. HEADQUARTERS: *Xaverian Missionary Society of Mary,* 242 Salisbury St., Worcester, MA 01609. Tel: 508-757-0514. Sr. Rita Davoli, X.M.M., Gen. Delegate.

Ministry to Hispanics; Elderly; Families; CCD Programs and Mission Education.

Represented in the Archdiocese of New York and the Diocese of Worcester.

COLLEGES AND UNIVERSITIES

ALABAMA

Mobile
Archdiocese of Mobile

Spring Hill College (1830)
4000 Dauphin St.
Mobile, AL 36608
Tel: 334-380-3866; Fax: 334-460-2111
Revs.:
WILLIAM J. REWAK, S.J., Pres.
JOHN R. PAYNE, S.J., Rector of Jesuit Community
FREDERICK W. GUNTI (LR)
J. WILLIAM HARMLESS, S.J.
LAURIE FURMAN, S.J.
DAVID BORBRIDGE, S.J.
EVERETT H. LARGUIER, S.J.
GERALD T. REGAN, S.J. (Wisconsin)
ROBERT B. RIMES, S.J.
SIDNEY A. TOMSMEIRE, S.J.
MICHAEL A. WILLIAMS, S.J. (Maryland)
STEPHEN CAMPBELL, S.J.
CHRISTOPHER J. VISCARDI, S.J.
Bros.:
FERRELL BLANK
CLAUDE L. ORY, S.J.
Priests of Faculty 8
Brothers 2
Lay Teachers 54
Students 946

CALIFORNIA

Belmont
Archdiocese of San Francisco

College of Notre Dame
1500 Ralston Ave.
Belmont, CA 94002
Tel: 415-593-1601; Fax: 415-637-0493
Sisters of Notre Dame de Namur
Dr. MARGARET A. HUBER, Pres.
Dr. JANIFER STACKHOUSE, Academic Dean
Rev. BASIL POSTLETHWAITE, Chap.
JOHN BOLLARD, Dir. Campus Ministry
Priests 1
Sisters 7
Lay Faculty 53
Students 1,627

Fremont
Diocese of Oakland

Queen of the Holy Rosary College
Mailing Address:
P.O. Box 3908
Mission San Jose, CA 94539
Tel: 510-657-2468; Fax: 510-657-1734
Legal Title: *Queen of the Holy Rosary College*
Dominican Sisters of Mission San Jose
Sr. ROSE MARIE HENNESSY, O.P., Pres.
Sr. MARY PAUL MEHEGAN, O.P., Dean
Total Enrollment 225

Los Angeles
Archdiocese of Los Angeles

Loyola Marymount University
7101 W. 80th St.
Los Angeles, CA 90045-2699
Tel: 310-338-2700
Sponsored by the Society of Jesus (Jesuit Fathers), Religious of Sacred Heart of Mary, Sisters of St. Joseph of Orange
Revs.:
THOMAS P. O'MALLEY, S.J., Pres.
DONALD P. MERRIFIELD, S.J., Chancellor
Dr. JOSEPH G. JABBRA, Academic Vice Pres.
Mr. JOHN R. OESTER, Vice Pres. Business and Finance
Dr. LANE BOVE, Vice Pres. Student Affairs
Rev. RICHARD A. ROBIN, S.J., Asst. to the Pres.
Mr. DAVID G. TRUMP, Vice Pres. Facilities Mgmt.
Ms. ROSE ST. ONGE, Registrar
Mr. MATTHEW FISSINGER, Dir. Admissions
Ms. DONNA PALMER, Dir. Financial Aid
Ms. JOANNE THOMPSON, Dir. Personnel Svcs.
Mr. FERNANDO D. MORENO, Dir. Campus Ministry
Dr. JOHN T. WHOLIHAN, Dean of Business Admin.
Dr. GERALD S. JAKUBOWSKI, Dean of Science and Engrg.
THOMAS KELLY, Dean of Communication & Fine Arts
Sr. MARY MILLIGAN, R.S.H.M., Dean, Liberal Arts
Jesuit Community
P.O. Box 45041
Los Angeles, CA 90045
Tel: 310-338-7445
Very Rev. MICHAEL ENGH, S.J., Rector
Rev. TERRANCE L. MAHAN, S.J.
In res.,
Revs.:
CLINTON E. ALBERTSON, S.J.
JAMES ARENZ, S.J.
JOHN L. BOYLE, S.J.
ANTHONY B. BRZOSKA, S.J.
THOMAS E. BUCKLEY, S.J.
PETER BURNS, S.J.
ROBERT I. BURNS, S.J.
WILLIAM F. CAIN, S.J.
ROBERT V. CARO, S.J.
GEORGE L. CRAIN, S.J.
JOHN P. DALY, S.J.
WILLIAM K. DELANEY, S.J.
GEORGE H. DUNNE, S.J.
MICHAEL E. ENGH, S.J.
Bro. WILLIAM C. FARRINGTON, S.J.
Revs.:
D. THEODORE FISHER, S.J.
JOHN J. FLYNN, S.J.
WILLIAM J. FULCO, S.J.
THOMAS P. HIGGINS, S.J.
FLOYD A. JENKINS, S.J.
CHARLES L. JURGENSMEIER, S.J.
CHARLES J. KAVANAGH, S.J.
JAMES H. KEENE, S.J.
JOHN F. KILLEEN, S.J.
LOUIS E. LIBBEY, S.J.
TERRANCE L. MAHAN, S.J.
THOMAS J. MALONEY, S.J.
SHANE P. MARTIN, S.J.
DONALD P. MERRIFIELD, S.J.
MICHAEL R. MOODIE, S.J.
THOMAS P. O'MALLEY, S.J.
THOMAS P. RAUSCH, S.J.
RICHARD A. ROBIN, S.J.
RICHARD W. ROLFS, S.J.
HERBERT J. RYAN, S.J.
ERNEST S. SWEENEY, S.J.
MICHAEL R. TANG, S.J.
ROBERT H. TAYLOR, S.J.
RICHARD H. TRAME, S.J.
Bro. RAYMOND W. UPTON, S.J.
Revs.:
RICHARD P. VAUGHAN, S.J.
KARL E. VON DER AHE, S.J.
CLARENCE J. WALLEN, S.J.
HANFORD E. WECKBACH, S.J.
MICHAEL F. WEILER, S.J.
ROBERT J. WELCH, S.J.
JOHN B. WELING, S.J.
Priests 15
Brothers 2
Sisters 7
Lay Teachers 245
The Sacred Heart of Mary and Sisters of St. Joseph of Orange
7101 W. 80th St.
Los Angeles, CA 90045
Tel: 310-338-2700; 641-4682
Legal Title: *Communities of the Religious of the Sacred Heart of Mary and Sisters of St. Joseph of Orange*
Loyola School of Law
919 S. Albany St., P.O. Box 15019
Los Angeles, CA 90015
Tel: 213-736-1000
Mr. GERALD T. MCLAUGHLIN, Dean

Mount St. Mary's College
Chalon Campus
12001 Chalon Rd.
Los Angeles, CA 90049
Tel: 310-476-2237; Fax: 310-471-9028
Doheny Campus
10 Chester Pl.
Los Angeles, CA 90007
Tel: 213-746-0450; Fax: 213-744-0833
Conducted by the Sisters of St. Joseph of Carondelet
Resident and non-resident students.
Sr. KAREN M. KENNELLY, Pres.
Dr. JANE LINGUA, Vice Pres. for Student Affairs
Mr. LARRY SMITH, Asst. Vice Pres. for Info. Support Services
Dr. JACQUELINE DOWD, Academic Vice Pres.
Mr. WILLIAM EVERHART, Vice Pres. for Business & Finance
Sr. KATHLEEN KELLY, Vice Pres. Doheny Campus and Dean Graduate and Assoc. Divisions
PAMELA HILLMAN, Vice Pres. for Institutional Advancement
Ms. KATY MURPHY, Executive Dir. of Enrollment Mgt.
Sisters 32
Priests 3
Lay Teachers 212
Students 1,974

Moraga
Diocese of Oakland

Saint Mary's College
Moraga, CA 94575
Tel: 510-631-4000
Legal Title: *Saint Mary's College of California*
Brothers of the Christian Schools
Coed. Resident and Non-Resident Students.
Bros.:
T. MEL ANDERSON, F.S.C., Pres.
JEROME WEST, F.S.C., Vice Pres., College Rels.
Saint Mary's College Community:
Bros.:
ARNOLD STEWART, F.S.C., Dir.
RICHARD LEMBERG, F.S.C., Sub-Dir.
Alemany Community:
Bro. ROBERT LEE F.S.C., Dir.
Rev. JOHN MCDONOUGH, Chap. & Dir. Campus Ministry
Campus Ministers:
Rev. MICHAEL CAREY, O.P.
Sr. INGRID CLEMMENSEN, O.P.
Revs.:
DAVID DEIBEL
SALVATORE RAGUSA, S.D.S.
Faculty:
Rev. OWEN CARROLL (Canada)
Rev. Msgr. EDGAR P. MCCARREN (RVC)
Revs.:
JOHN MORRIS, O.P.
MICHAEL MORRIS, O.P.
MICHAEL A. RUSSO (NEW)
Sr. CLARE WAGSTAFFE
Priests 9
Sisters 2
Brothers 35
Professors 221
Total Enrollment 4,318

Oakland
Diocese of Oakland

Holy Names College (1868)
3500 Mountain Blvd.
Oakland, CA 94619
Tel: 510-436-1000
Chartered 1880. Resident and Non-Resident Students.
Sisters of the Holy Names of Jesus and Mary
Legal Title: *Sisters of the Holy Names of Jesus and Mary, A Corporation*
Legal Title: *Holy Names College, A Corporation*
Administration:
MARY ALICE MUELLERLEILE, Pres.
JUDIE GRAFFIN WEXLER, Vice Pres. for Academic Affairs
Sr. CAROL SELLMAN, S.N.J.M., Assoc. Dean
LISA LEMON, Assoc. Dean, Academic Affairs
ROBERT D. HITE, Vice Pres. for Finance
MICHAEL A. PETRINI, Vice Pres. for College Advancement
XAVIER E. ROMANO, Vice Pres. for Student Services
Administrative Staff:
LUCY HOLMAN, Dir., Residence Life
BETH HOENNINGER, Dir. of Development
MARIANNE STICKEL, Registrar
FRANCES HUI, Dir., Library Services
TO AHN NGUYEN, Dir., Financial Aid
SHARON CASEY, Dir., Campus Ministry
Religious Faculty:
Sr. ELIZABETH ADAMS, S.N.J.M.
Sr. MARY ANDERSON, S.N.J.M.
Sr. MARGARET CAMPBELL, S.N.J.M.
Sr. DEBORAH CHURCH, S.N.J.M.
Rev. JAMES CONLON
Sr. ROSE ELEANOR EHRET, S.N.J.M.
MARCIA FRIDEGER
Sr. JEAN ELIZABETH GRIFFIN, S.N.J.M.
Sr. MAUREEN HESTER, S.N.J.M.
Sr. DONNA MAYNARD, S.N.J.M.
Sr. JUNE KEARNEY, S.N.J.M.
Rev. HENRY ORMOND, O.Carm.
Sr. JOANNE QUINLIVAN, S.N.J.M.
Sr. DELORES RASHFORD, S.N.J.M.
Sr. NANCY TESKEY, S.N.J.M.
Sr. CHRISTINE PATRINOS, S.N.J.M.
Sr. ETHEL MARY TINNEMANN, S.N.J.M.
Sr. FRANCESCA CABRINI WEBER, S.N.J.M.
Sr. IRENE WOODWARD, C.F.C.
Religious Staff:
Sr. SYLVIA BARTHELD, S.N.J.M.
Sr. MARGUERITE KIRK, S.N.J.M.
Sr. MARY CHRISTINE FLEITZ, S.N.J.M.
Sr. ANN MARTINOVICH, S.N.J.M.
Priests 2

Sisters 17
Lay Professors 55
Students 923

Orange
Diocese of Orange in California

St. Joseph College, Orange
480 S. Batavia St.
Orange, CA 92868
Tel: 714-633-8121; Fax: 714-744-3165
Branch Campus of University of San Francisco; St. Joseph College Library.

Rancho Palos Verdes
Archdiocese of Los Angeles

Marymount College, Palos Verdes, California
30800 Palos Verdes Dr., E.
Rancho Palos Verdes, CA 90275-6299
Tel: 310-377-5501
An Independent and Catholic Co-Educational Two-Year Liberal Arts College; Resident and Non-Resident.
Dr. THOMAS M. MCFADDEN, Pres.
Dr. ROBERT MATTHES, Dean of Academic Affairs
Mr. JAMES REEVES, Vice Pres. of College Atomerations & Student Svcs.
Mr. ED OGLE, Registar
Rev. SEAN CRONIN, Chap.
Sisters 4
Lay Teachers 72
Students 853

Rosemead
Archdiocese of Los Angeles

Don Bosco Technical Institute
(Junior College)
1151 San Gabriel Blvd.
Rosemead, CA 91770-4299
Tel: 818-307-6500; Fax: 818-280-9316
Two-year college program leading to Associate in Science degree in seven technical areas. (Staffed by Salesians of St. John Bosco).
Revs.:
NICHOLAS J. REINA, S.D.B., Pres.
MICHAEL GERGEN, S.D.B., Admin. Vice Pres.
PETER BUI, S.D.B.
MARC ROUGEAU, S.D.B.
Bros.:
PATRICK BARBARIOL, S.D.B.
JOHN KORNAK, S.D.B.
GENE MYLAN, S.D.B.
Priests 4
Brothers 3
Lay Teachers 26
Students 123
Don Bosco High School
Rev. MICHAEL ALVAREZ, S.D.B., Prin.
Priests 4
Brothers 10
Sisters 1
Lay Teachers 70
Students 758

San Diego
Diocese of San Diego

Austin House - House of Formation
1605 28th St.
San Diego, CA 92102
Tel: 619-233-9141 (Prov. Office)
Very Rev. JAMES A. MOTT, O.S.A., Prior Prov. & Vocation Dir., Tel: 619-235-0247; Fax: 619-231-2814
Revs.:
WALTER P. VOGEL, O.S.A., Prior
JEROME BEVILACQUA, O.S.A.
Deacon RICHARD HARDICK, O.S.A.

University of San Diego
5998 Alcala Park
San Diego, CA 92110-2492
Tel: 619-260-4600
Dr. ALICE BOURKE HAYES, Pres.
Dr. FRANCIS M. LAZORUS, Vice Pres. and Provost
Rev. Msgr. I. BRENT EAGEN, Vice Pres. Mission and Ministry
Sr. MAUREEN CRONIN, R.S.C.J., Assoc. Provost and Dir. Institutional Research
Dr. PATRICK DRINAN, Dean, College of Arts and Sciences
Dr. JAMES M. BURNS, Dean, School of Business Administration
Dr. EDWARD F. DE ROCHE, Dean, School of Education
Dr. KRISTINE STRACHAN, Dean, School of Law
Dr. JANET RODGERS, Dean, Hahn School of Nursing
Dr. CYNTHIA VILLIS, Dean, Academic Services
University Ministers:
Revs.:
JOHN D. KELLER, O.S.A., Dir. of Univ. Ministry
BARRY E. VINYARD
PAUL A. DONOVAN, S.J.
Sr. IRENE CULLEN, R.S.C.J.
Bro. TOM THING, O.F.M.
MIKE MCINTYRE
KATHY VALDIVIA
ANNETTE WELSH
Mr. EDWARD P. STARKEY, Librarian
Dr. JANE GORMAN, Dir., Institute for Christian Min.
Rev. Msgr. WILLIAM L. SHIPLEY
Revs.:
STEPHEN DUNN
DENNIS W. KROUSE
JAMES W. MCGRAY
ORLANDO O. ESPIN (VEN)
RONALD A. PACHENCE (SAV)
NORBERT J. RIGALI, S.J.
MATTHEW D. SPAHR
Faculty:
Priests 8
Sisters 6
Lay Faculty 499
Students 6,603
Graduate Division:
Dr. EREN BRANCH, Dean, Graduate & Continuing Educ.
Students 1,224
School of Law:
Dr. KRISTINE STRACHAN, Dean
Lay Teachers 85
Students 1,080

San Francisco
Archdiocese of San Francisco

**University of San Francisco*
2130 Fulton St.
San Francisco, CA 94117-1080
Tel: 415-422-5555; Fax: 415-422-2303
Jesuit Fathers
Established 1855; Chartered by State, 1859.
Revs.:
JOHN P. SCHLEGEL, S.J., Pres.
JOHN J. LOSCHIAVO, S.J., Chancellor
CHARLES W. DULLEA, S.J., Chancellor Emeritus
JOHN W. CLARK, S.J., Provost & Vice Pres. Academic Affairs
ROBERT F. CURRAN, S.J., Vice Pres. for Legal Affairs
PHILIP P. CALLAGHAN, S.J., Sec. of the Univ.
Dr. CARMEN A. JORDAN-COX, Vice Pres. Student Affairs
Mr. WILLARD H. NUTTING, Vice Pres. Business & Finance
Mr. ALFRED P. ALESSANDRI, Vice Pres. Univ. Rels.
Mr. DAVID F. MACMILLAN, Vice Pres. Devel.
MAUREEN L. PRYOR, Dir. of Campus Ministry
The following are the Schools and Colleges that compose the University:
College of Arts and Sciences—
Dr. STANLEY D. NEL, Dean
McLaren School of Business—
Dr. GARY G. WILLIAMS, Dean
School of Nursing—
Dr. NORMA L. CHASKA, Dean
School of Education—
Dr. PAUL B. WARREN, Dean
School of Law—
Dr. H. JAY FOLBERG, Dean
College of Professional Studies—
Dr. BETTY E. TAYLOR, Dean
Priests 19
Sisters 5
Lay Faculty 263
Students 7,888

San Rafael
Archdiocese of San Francisco

Dominican College
50 Acacia Ave.
San Rafael, CA 94901-2298
Tel: 415-457-4440; Fax: 415-485-3205
An Independent and Catholic Coeducational Liberal Arts College.
Dr. JOSEPH R. FINK, Pres.
Dr. KATHERINE HENDERSON, Vice Pres. for Academic Affairs
Resident and non-resident students.
Sisters 6
Lay Teachers 146
Students 1,415

Santa Clara
Diocese of San Jose in California

Santa Clara University
500 El Camino Real
Santa Clara, CA 95053-0460
Tel: 408-554-4764; Fax: 408-554-2700
Mission Santa Clara. Founded in 1777. University established in 1851 and chartered by the State in 1855.
Society of Jesus
Administrators:
Rev. PAUL L. LOCATELLI, S.J., Pres.
Mr. ROBERT WARREN, Vice Pres. Business & Finance
Rev. STEPHEN A. PRIVETT, S.J., Academic Vice Pres.
Mr. JAMES I. BRIGGS, Vice Pres. Student Devel.
Dr. PETER A. FACIONE, Dean, College of Arts and Sciences
Dr. ALEX FIELD, Acting Dean, School of Business
Dr. TERRY E. SHOUP, Dean, School of Engrg.
Dr. MARK A. PLAYER, Dean, School of Law
Rev. MARIO J. PRIETTO, S.J., Dir. Campus Ministry
Jesuit Community
500 El Camino Real
Santa Clara, CA 95053-0001
Legal Title: *Jesuit Community at Santa Clara University, Inc.*
Tel: 408-554-4124; Fax: 408-554-4795
Revs.:
GERALD L. MCKEVITT, S.J., Rector
PETER F. FILICE, S.J., Min.
LOUIS I. BANNAN, S.J.
LUIS F. CALERO, S.J.
PAUL G. CROWLEY, S.J.
WILLIAM F. DONNELLY, S.J.
CARLO A. FARINA, S.J.
JAMES W. FELT, S.J.
DANIEL V. GERMANN, S.J.
PAUL J. GODA, S.J.
CARL H. HAYN, S.J.
JOHN R. LEVECKE, S.J.
ARTHUR F. LIEBSCHER, S.J.
PAUL L. LOCATELLI, S.J.
NORMAN F. MARTIN, S.J.
DENNIS R. PARNELL, S.J.
CHARLES T. PHIPPS, S.J.
STEPHEN A. PRIVETT, S.J.
JAMES W. REITES, S.J.
MARIO J. PRIETTO, S.J.
LEO P. ROCK, S.J.
THEODORE J. RYNES, S.J.
STEPHEN R. SCHLOESSER, S.J.
ROBERT M. SENKEWICZ, S.J.
THOMAS E. SHANKS, S.J.
ANTHONY E. SHOLANDER, S.J.
FRANCIS R. SMITH, S.J.
DENNIS C. SMOLARSKI, S.J.
PAUL A. SOUKUP, S.J.
GERALD P. SULLIVAN, S.J.
SALVATORE A. TASSONE, S.J.
FREDERICK P. TOLLINI, S.J.
EDWARD V. WARREN, S.J.
WILLIAM J. WOOD, S.J.
TENNANT C. WRIGHT, S.J.
Bro. THOMAS C. BRACCO, S.J.
Mr. THOMAS J.E. SCHWARZ, S.J., (Scholastic)
Priest Teachers 36
Brothers 2
Scholastics 1
Lay Teachers 329
Students 7,863

Santa Paula
Archdiocese of Los Angeles

Thomas Aquinas College
10000 N. Ojai Rd.
Santa Paula, CA 93060
Tel: 805-525-4417
Four-year undergraduate program in the Liberal Arts leading to the B.A. Degree; Coeducational.
Dr. THOMAS E. DILLON, Pres.
Dr. R. GLEN COUGHLIN, Dean
Mr. PETER L. DELUCA, III, Vice Pres. Finance and Admin.
Mr. DANIEL J. GRIMM, Vice Pres. Devel.
Chaplains:
Revs.:
BARTHOLOMEW DE LA TORRE, O.P.
THOMAS V. CONN, S.J.
WILFRED F. BORDEN, O.M.I.
Lay Teachers 24
Students 222

COLORADO

Denver
Archdiocese of Denver

Regis University
3333 Regis Blvd.
Denver, CO 80221-1099
Tel: 303-458-4100

A University conducted under the auspices of the Society of Jesus.
Revs.:
WILLIAM J. FORTUNE, Chm. Board of Trustees
MICHAEL J. SHEERAN, S.J., Pres.
DAVID M. CLARKE, S.J., Chancellor
Dr. ALLAN L. SERVICE, Vice Pres. Academic Affairs
Dr. JAMES R. SCHOEMER, Vice Pres. Admin.
Dr. THOMAS E. REYNOLDS, Vice Pres. Student Life
Mr. JOHN A. ALEXANDER, Vice Pres. Devel. & Public Affairs
Dr. STEPHEN DOTY, Dean, Regis College
Dr. WILLIAM J. HUSSON, Dean, School for Professional Studies
Dr. PATRICIA A. LADEWIG, Dean, School for Health Care Professions
Mr. ANDREW D. SCRIMGEOUR, Dean Libraries
Ms. KATHLEEN M. SCHAEFER, Dir. Campus Ministry
Priests 16
Sisters 3
Lay Teachers 500
Students 9,648

CONNECTICUT

Bridgeport
Diocese of Bridgeport

St. Vincent's College
2800 Main St.
Bridgeport, CT 06606
Tel: 203-576-5235
ANNE T. AVALLONE, M.A., Pres.
BARBARA B. DAVIS, M.S., Dean/Provost
ROBERT S. TROJANOWSKI, M.B.A., J.D., CFO
JANICE NOLAN FAYE, Exec. Asst.
DEBRA POPILOWSKI-DIZENZO, M.A., Asst. Dean of Admin. Svcs., Registrar
SHIRLEY FLANAGAN, Dir. Housing & Facilities
ANITA K. MCCAIN, Ed.D., Assoc. Dean of Academic Svcs.
COLETTE T. DZIADUL, M.S., Asst. Dean of Student & Alumni Svcs, Dir. of Admissions
Students 212

Fairfield
Diocese of Bridgeport

**Fairfield University*
(Coed)
1073 N. Benson Rd.
Fairfield, CT 06430-5195
Tel: 203-254-4000
The Society of Jesus. College of Arts and Sciences; School of Business; School of Continuing Education; School of Nursing; BEI School of Engineering; Graduate School of Education & Allied Professions; Graduate Program in Financial Management; Graduate Program in Nursing; and Masters in Business Administration.
Revs.:
ALOYSIUS P. KELLEY, S.J., Pres.
TIMOTHY E. TOOHIG, S.J.
CHARLES H. ALLEN, Exec. Asst. to Pres.
Mr. L. WILLIAM MILES, Vice Pres. Admin.
Dr. ROBERT E. WALL, Academic Vice Pres.
Mr. ROBERT C. RUSSO, University Registrar
Mr. STEPHEN P. JAKAB, Assoc. Vice Pres. Admin.
Rev. W. LAURENCE O'NEIL, S.J., Dir. Student Support Svcs.
Dr. RUSSELL P. BOISJOLY, Dean, School of Business
Dr. THERESA M. VALIGA, Dean, School of Nursing
Dr. ORIN L. GROSSMAN, Dean of Arts & Sciences
Dr. EVANGELOS HADJIMICHAEL, Dean, BEI, School of Engrg.
Dr. J. MICHAEL SWEENEY, Dean of Continuing Education
Dr. ANTONIO SIMOES, Dean of Graduate School of Education & Allied Professions
Rev. HENRY J. MURPHY, S.J., Dean of Freshmen
Ms. MARY SPIEGEL, Acting Dean of Admissions
Mrs. SUSAN KADIR, Dir. of Financial Aid
Mr. JAMES ESTRADA, University Librarian
Mr. WILLIAM P. SCHIMPF, Vice Pres. Student Svcs.
Dr. GWENDOLYN M. VENDLEY, Dean of Students
Dr. SUSAN BIRGE, Dir. Counseling Svcs.
Mr. JAMES D. FITZPATRICK, Assoc. Dean of Students & Dir. University Activities
Rev. PAUL E. CARRIER, S.J., University Chap.
Mr. ROBERT W. CARTER, S.J., Asst. University Chap.
Revs.:
JOSEPH J. SCHAD, S.J., Asst. Chap.
RICHARD J. STANLEY, S.J., Asst. Chap.
Mr. GEORGE E. DIFFLEY, Vice Pres. Advancement
Mr. MURRAY FARBER, Dir. Public Rels.
Ms. JANET CANEPA, Dir. Alumni Rels.
Mr. FREDRIC WHEELER, Assoc. Vice Pres. Devel.
Mr. WILLIAM J. LUCAS, Vice Pres. Finance
Mr. MICHAEL S. MACCARONE, Controller
Revs.:
JAMES R. BLAETTLER, S.J.
VINCENT M. BURNS, S.J.
ALBERT A. CARDONI, S.J.
WILLIAM F. CARR, S.J.
JOHN W. ELDER, S.J.
G. SIMON HARAK, S.J.
VICTOR F. LEEBER, S.J.
FRANCIS W. LEWIS, S.J.
DONALD D. LYNCH, S.J.
JOSEPH F. MACDONNELL, S.J.
Mr. MICHAEL CROWLEY, S.J.
Mr. LUIS A. TAMPE, S.J.
Mr. MICHAEL F. ANDREWS, S.J.
Revs.:
JAMES J. MAYZIK, S.J.
G. PAUL PETERSON, S.J.
ALBERT F. REDDY, S.J.
THOMAS J. REGAN, S.J.
MAURICE WONG, S.J.
Sisters 1
Lay Teachers 187
Students 5,111
(See separate listing for Fairfield College Prep).

* *Sacred Heart University*
5151 Park Ave.
Fairfield, CT 06432-1000
Tel: 203-371-7999
Coeducational and Comprehensive University. Courses offered year round, day & evening.
Dr. ANTHONY J. CERNERA
Dr. DAVID HARNETT, Provost & Vice Pres. for Academic Affairs
Dr. DONNA DODGE, S.C., Vice Pres. Mission & Planning
Mr. JAMES M. BARQUINERO, Vice Pres. Enrollment, Planning & Student Affairs
Dr. PAUL K. MADONNA, Vice Pres. Admin. & Finance
Institute for Religious Education and Pastoral Studies
Rev. Msgr. GREGORY M. SMITH, Ed.D., Dir.
Rev. THOMAS M. MCLERNON
Sr. MARGARET PALLISER, O.P, S.T.D., Dir. Campus Ministry
Priests 3
Sisters 4
Lay Teachers 132
Students 5,545

Hamden
Archdiocese of Hartford

Mt. Sacred Heart College
265 Benham St.
Hamden, CT 06514
Tel: 203-248-4225; Fax: 203-230-8341
Chartered by the State of Connecticut for Sisters of Community of Apostles of the Sacred Heart of Jesus.
Sr. DEBORAH LOPEZ, A.S.C.J., Pres./Dean
Sisters 3
Students 1

New Haven
Archdiocese of Hartford

Albertus Magnus College
700 Prospect St.
New Haven, CT 06511-1189
Tel: 203-773-8500; Fax: 203-773-3117
Dominican Sisters (St. Mary of the Springs, Columbus, OH)
Dr. JULIA M. MCNAMARA, Pres.
Sr. CHARLES MARIE BRANTL, O.P., Vice. Pres.
KEVIN CANAVAN, Dir. of Devel.
JEANNE MANN, Treas.
EILEEN PERILLO, Registrar
JANICE CRISCI, Vice Pres. Student Svcs.
BETSEY P. TODT, Dir. of Public Rels. & Contact
Sisters 5
Priests 2
Lay Teachers 45
Total Enrollment 1,167

West Hartford
Archdiocese of Hartford

Saint Joseph College
1678 Asylum Ave.
West Hartford, CT 06117
Tel: 860-232-4571; Fax: 860-233-5695
Women.
Sisters of Mercy
Chartered by the State of Connecticut.
WINIFRED E. COLEMAN, M.A., Pres.
Dr. MARTIN D. SNYDER, Provost
Dr. DOROTHY ZEISER, Academic Dean
Dr. MARK EBERSOLE, Vice Pres. for Academic
Dr. MAUREEN REARDON, Dean of Enrollment Mgmt. & Contact, Exec. Vice Pres.
NANCY M. CONNELLY, Dean of Students, Vice Pres. for Student Affairs
IRENE RIOS, Registrar
Revs.:
DAVID CINQUEGRANI, C.P.
JOHN J. STACK, S.T.D.
JOHN W. MCHUGH
CHARLES J. TOPPER, Ed.D.
TERENCE KRISTOFAK, C.P.
JAMES F. LEARY, M.A.
Priests 6
Sisters 12
Lay Teachers 70
Students 1,919
Undergraduates:
Women 1,169
Men 37
Graduates Coed 713
School for Young Children 96
Gengras Center for Exceptional Children 120

DISTRICT OF COLUMBIA

Washington
Archdiocese of Washington

Catholic University of America, The (1887)
Nugent Hall/Executive Offices
Washington, DC 20064
Tel: 202-319-5000
His Eminence JAMES CARDINAL HICKEY, Chancellor (Ex Officio)
His Eminence BERNARD CARDINAL LAW, Chm., Bd. of Trustees
Bro. F. PATRICK ELLIS, F.S.C., Ph.D., Pres.
Sr. ROSEMARY DONLEY, S.C., Ph.D., Exec. Vice Pres.
Mr. VINCENT P. WALTER, JR., M.M., Sec. of the University, Bd. of Trustees & Chief of Staff
Rev. MICHAEL MANNION (CAM) Univ. Chap. & Dir. Campus Ministry
Rev. Msgr. DENNIS MAHON, Ph.D., Vice Pres. Devel.
Rev. Msgr. JOHN F. WIPPEL, Ph.D., Academic Vice Pres.
Rev. JOHN E. LYNCH, C.S.P., Ph.D., Assoc. Academic Vice Pres., Graduate Studies
INGRID MERKEL, Ph.D., Assoc. Academic Vice Pres., Undergraduate Prog.
JAMES W. MAYO, Asst. Academic Vice Pres., Sponsored Prog. & Research Svcs.
Rev. RAYMOND F. COLLINS, S.T.D., Dean, School of Religious Studies
JUDE P. DOUGHERTY, Ph.D., Dean, School of Philosophy
ANTANAS SUZIEDELIS, Ph.D., Dean, School of Arts and Sciences
WILLIAM E. KELLY, D. Civil Eng., Dean, School of Engrg.
BERNARD DOBRANSKI, J.D., Dean, Columbus School of Law
Sr. MARY JEAN FLAHERTY, S.C., Ph.D., Dean, School of Nursing
ELAINE R. WALTER, Ph.D., Dean, Benjamin T. Rome School of Music
ELIZABETH SMITH EVERSA, Ph.D., Dean, School of Library and Information Science
Sr. ANN PATRICK CONRAD, D.S.W., Acting Dean, National Catholic School of Social Svc.
STANLEY I. HALLET, F.A.I.A., Dean, School of Architecture and Planning
JAMES S. PULA, Ph.D., Dean, Metropolitan College
Rev. EUGENE HEMRICK, Dir., Diocesan Rels.
ADELE CHWALEK, M.S.L.S., Dir. Libraries
ARTHUR M. CAVANAGH, M.A., Registrar
RALPH H. BEAUDOIN, Vice Pres. Finance and Treas.
SUSAN D. PERVI, M.A., Vice Pres. Admin.
GREGORY K. HUNT, A.I.A., Dean, School of Architecture and Planning
Rev. ROBERT M. FRIDAY, S.T.D. (PIT) Vice Pres. Student Affairs
Priests Associated with the University Full-Time:
Revs.:
C. GERARD AUSTIN, O.P., S.T.D.
JOHN P. BEAL, J.C.D.
CHRISTOPHER T. BEGG, S.T.D., Ph.D.
HOWARD P. BLEICHNER, S.S., D.Th.
ANDREW C. BUECHELE, Sch.P., Ph.D.
WILLIAM CENKNER, O.P., Ph.D.
RAYMOND F. COLLINS, S.T.D.
ALEXANDER A. DI LELLA, O.F.M., Ph.D.
ROBERT B. ENO, S.S., S.T.D.
JOHN T. FORD, C.S.C., S.T.D.
ROBERT M. FRIDAY, S.T.D. (PIT)
JOHN P. GALVIN, D.Th.(BO)
ALBERT C. GIAQUINTO, S.S., M.A., S.T.L.
FRANCIS T. GIGNAC, S.J., D.Phil.
PATRICK GRANFIELD, O.S.B., J.D., Ph.D., S.T.D.
THOMAS J. GREEN, J.C.D. (BGP)
JACQUES GRES-GAYER, D.Th. (France)
SIDNEY H. GRIFFITH, S.T., Ph.D.
THOMAS P. HALTON, Ph.D. (Ireland)
STEPHEN W. HAPPEL, S.T.D., Ph.D.
THOMAS R. HURST, S.S., Ph.D.
KEVIN W. IRWIN, S.T.D. (NY)

JOSEPH JENSEN, O.S.B., S.T.D.
DAVID W. JOHNSON, S.J., Ph.D.
THOMAS C. KANE, O.P., S.T.D.
ROBERT T. KENNEDY, J.U.D. (NY)
JOSEPH A. KOMONCHAK, Ph.D. (NY)
LOUIS M. LAFAVIA, C.PP.S., Ph.D.
JOHN E. LYNCH, C.S.P., Ph.D.
Rev. Msgr. DENNIS MAHON, Ph.D.
Revs.:
MICHAEL MANNION, C.A.M.
BERARD L. MARTHALER, O.F.M.Conv., Ph.D., S.T.D.
FRANK J. MATERA, Ph.D. (HRT)
JOHN P. MEIER, S.S.D. (NY)
RAYMOND C. O'BRIEN, J.D.
EDWARD G. PFNAUSCH, J.C.L.
CARL L. PIEBER, C.M., Ph.D.
PETER C. PHAN, Ph.D., S.T.D. (DAL)
DAVID N. POWER, O.M.I., S.T.D.
KURT PRITZL, O.P., Ph.D.
JAMES H. PROVOST, J.C.D. (HEL)
PAUL G. ROBICHAUD, C.S.P., Ph.D.
BRIAN J. SHANLEY, O.P., Ph.D.
ROBERT S. SOKOLOWSKI, Ph.D. (HRT)
RAYMOND STUDZINSKI, O.S.B., Ph.D.
ROBERT F. TRISCO, H.E.D. (CHI)
JOHN J. TUOHEY, Ph.D (SPR)
WILLIAM L. VIOLA, S.T.M., S.T.L.
Rev. Msgr. JOHN F. WIPPEL, Ph.D. (STU)
Rev. JAMES A. WISEMAN, O.S.B., S.T.D.
Priests Associated with the University Part-Time:
Very Rev. SEELY BEGGIANI, S.T.D. (SAM)
Revs.:
WILLIAM J. CONLAN, O.P.
PETER J. DALY, J.D.
GEORGE T. DENNIS, S.J., S.E.D.
COLUMBA ENRIGHT, T.O.R.
JOSEPH A. FITZMYER, S.J., Ph.D.
LEO FOLEY, S.M.
BERNARD K. HARKINS, O.P.
Rev. Msgr. GEORGE G. HIGGINS, Ph.D. (CHI)
Revs.:
WILLIAM J. HILL, O.P., S.T.D.
JOHN FREDERICK HINNEBUSCH, O.P.
Rev. Msgr. FREDERICK R. MCMANUS, J.C.D., L.L.D. (BO)
Rev. Msgr. ROBERT PAUL MOHAN
Revs.:
THOMAS PATER (CIN)
EDWARD G. PFNAUSCH, J.C.L.
RAYMOND H. POTVIN, Ph.D. (SPR)
WILLIAM J. ROONEY (CHI)
JOHN F. SMOLKO (BGP)
Clerical Members, Board of Trustees:
Most Rev. Robert J. Banks; His Eminence, Anthony Cardinal Bevilacqua; His Excellence, Joseph Cardinal Bernardin; Rev. Msgr. Michael Bransfield; Most Rev. Daniel M. Buechlein; Most Rev. Charles J. Chaput; Most Rev. Thomas V. Daily; Most Rev. Francis E. George; His Eminence, James Cardinal Hickey, Chancellor (Ex-Officio); His Eminence, William Cardinal Keeler; His Eminence, Bernard Cardinal Law, Chm.; Most Rev. John J. Leibrecht; Rev. Msgr. Paul A. Lenz; Most Rev. William J. Levada; Most Rev. Oscar H. Lipscomb; His Eminence, Adam Cardinal Maida; Most Rev. James W. Malone; Most Rev. Theodore E. McCarrick; Most Rev. Robert E. Mulvee; Most. Rev. Thomas Murphy; Most Rev. Thomas O'Brien; His Eminence, John Cardinal O'Connor; Most Rev. Frances B. Shulte; Most Rev. J. Frances Stafford; Most Rev. Donald W. Wuerl; Most Rev. Philip M. Hannan, Emeritus.
Religious 56
Lay Teachers 315
Students 6,108

**Georgetown University* (1789)
37th and O Sts., N.W.
Washington, DC 20057
Tel: 202-687-0100
Rev. LEO J. O'DONOVAN, S.J., Pres.
VIRGINIA M. KEELER, Sec.
JOHN F. GRIFFITH, M.D., Exec. Vice Pres., Health Science & Dir., Medical Center
JUDITH AREEN, Exec. Vice Pres. for Law Center Affairs and Dean of the School of Law
JAMES M. WAGNER, Acting Vice Pres. for Admin. and Facilities
NICOLE MANDEVILLE, Vice Pres. & Treas.
JOSEPH PETTIT, Ph.D., Vice Pres. Planning and Inst. Research
KATHLEEN T. JONES, Acting Vice Pres. Alumni & Univ. Rels.
Rev. JOHN B. BRESLIN, S.J., University Chap.
JAMES A. DONAHUE, Dean Student Affairs
The following are the Schools and Colleges which compose the University:
Rev. ROBERT B. LAWTON, S.J., Dean
College of Arts and Sciences (1789)—
Graduate School:
RICHARD B. SCHWARTZ, Ph.D., Dean
School of Medicine (1851)
3900 Reservoir Rd., N.W.
Washington, DC 20007
WILLIAM MAXTED, M.D., Dean
Law Center (1870)
600 New Jersey Ave., N.W.
Washington, DC 20001
JUDITH AREEN, Esq., Dean
School of Nursing (1903)
3700 Reservoir Rd., N.W.
Washington, DC 20007
ELAINE L. LARSON, Ph.D., Dean
Edmund A. Walsh School of Foreign Service (1919).
School of Business (1958)—
ROBERT S. PARKER, Ph.D., Dean
School for Summer and Continuing Education (1954)—
MICHAEL J. COLLINS, Ph.D., Dean
Georgetown University Hospital
3800 Reservoir Rd., N.W.
Washington, DC 20007
ANATOLY DRITSCHILO, M.D., Medical Dir.
Undergraduate Admissions and Records—
CHARLES A. DEACON, M.A., Dean
Language Memorial Library—
SUSAN K. MARTIN, M.S.L.S., Librarian
Alumni Associates:
Alumni House
3604 O St., N.W.
Washington, DC 20057
CONAN N. LOUIS, Exec. Sec. Alumni Assoc. & Assoc. Vice Pres. Alumni Rels.
Affirmative Action Programs
3800 Reservoir Rd., N.W.
Washington, DC 20007
ROSEMARY KILKENNY, M.A., Special Asst. to Pres. for AAP
Jesuits 26
Sisters 1
Lay Teachers 131
Total Enrollment 12,618

Trinity College
Michigan Ave. and Franklin St., N.E.
Washington, DC 20017
Tel: 202-939-5000
Sisters of Notre Dame de Namur
PATRICIA A. MCGUIRE, Pres.
Sr. CATHERINE MARIE LEE, S.N.D., Community Rep.
Dr. PATTY WEITZEL-O'NEILL, Vice Pres. Academic Affairs
Priests 2
Sisters 6
Lay Professors 44
Students 1,450

FLORIDA

Miami
Archdiocese of Miami

Barry University
11300 N.E. 2nd Ave.
Miami, FL 33161
Tel: 305-899-3000
Sisters of St. Dominic (Adrian, MI)
Sr. JEANNE O'LAUGHLIN, O.P., Ph.D., Pres.
Sr. PEGGY ALBERT, O.P., Ph.D., Exec. Asst. Pres.
Dr. J. PATRICK LEE, Ph.D., Provost & Vice Pres. Academic Affairs
Sr. CORINNE SANDERS, O.P., Ed.D., Dir. of Mission & Ministry
Mrs. GRACE MERINO SCHOLLMEYER, Dean Records & Registrar
Mr. TIMOTHY H. CZERNIEC, Vice Pres. Business & Finance
Dr. GEORGE J. WANKO, Ph.D., Vice Pres. Student Svcs.
Sr. MARGARET JOHNSON, O.P., Vice Pres. Planning, Research & Evaluation
Sr. LORETTA MULRY I.H.M., Ed.D., Dean School of Adult & Continuing Education
Ms. JANE BOWER, Assoc. Vice Pres. Student Svcs.
Revs.:
MARK WEDIG, O.P.
GEORGE BOUDREAU, O.P.
DANIEL P. MADDEN, O.P.
PEDRO A. SUAREZ, S.J.
JOHN F. O'GRADY, S.S.D., S.T.D. (ALB)
EMILIANO ZAPATA, O.P.
Bro. EDWARD VAN MERRIENBOER, O.P.
Sr. EVELYN PICHE, O.P., Ph.D., Dean of School of Education
Mr. GREGORY MILLER, Dean of Admissions & Enrollment Planning
Sr. JOHN KAREN FREI, O.P., Ph.D., Assoc. Vice Pres. Academic Affairs & Dean of School of Natural and Health Science
CHESTER A. EVANS, D.P.M., Assoc. Vice Pres. & Dean, School of Podiatric Medicine
MARY EILEEN MCDONOUGH, Ed.D., Dean, Academic & Instructional Svcs.
LEWIS W. LASH, Ph.D., Dean, School of Business
LAURA S. ARMESTO, Ph.D., Dean, School of Arts & Sciences
HUGH W. RIPLEY, M.S.L.S., Dean, Library Svcs.
JUDITH A. BALCERSKI, Ph.D., Dean, School of Nursing
STEPHEN M. HOLLOWAY, Ph.D., Dean, School of Social Work
GENE AUTREY, B.E.E., Vice Pres., Institutional Advancement & Chm. Capital Campaign
Sr. SARAH CAVANAUGH, O.P., M.S., Assoc. Vice Pres. Institutional Advancement
G. JEAN CERRA, Ph.D., School of Human Performance & Leisure Sciences
Sisters 32
Priests 5
Lay Teachers 228
Students 7,135

Opa Locka
Archdiocese of Miami

St. Thomas University
(Coed)
16400 N.W. 32nd Ave.
Opa Locka, FL 33054
Tel: 305-625-6000; Fax: 305-628-6511
Board of Trustees:
THOMAS A. BASTIAN, C.P.A.
C. CLYDE ATKINS
JULIO CAPO
JOSEPH M. CATANIA
EILEEN CORNACCHIA
RONALD E. FRAZIER
WILLIAM O. CULLOM
FRANK R. ESPOSITO, Trustee Emeritus
GEORGE GOLDBLOOM
STEVEN D. HAYWORTH
Rev. Msgr. WILLIAM HENNESSEY, V.G.
Most Rev. ROBERT N. LYNCH
Very Rev. TOMAS M. MARIN
SAMUEL L. HIGGINBOTTOM
Rev. Msgr. GERARD T. LACERRA
MARIA C. LEIVA
ANN P. MACHADO
Revs.:
GUSTAVO J. MIYARES
JOSE P. NICKSE
HERMAN J. RUSSOMANO, Esq.
RAFAEL A. SANCHEZ
STEPHEN HAROLD SCHOTT
Dr. P. ALAN SMURFIT
Sr. ELIZABETH ANNE WORLEY, S.S.J.
The Member:
Most Rev. JOHN CLEMENT FAVALORA
Of Counsel:
J. PATRICK FITZGERALD
Administration:
Rev. GARY N. MCCLOSKEY, O.S.A., Ph.D., Vice Pres. for Academic Affairs
Mr. NORMAN BLAIR, Vice Pres. for Admin. & Treas.
ANA GLORIA RIVAS-VASQUEZ, Esq., Vice Pres. for Devel. & External Affairs
Mr. STEPHEN CONDON, Acting Dean of Student Affairs
Dr. JOSEPH IANNONE, Dean of the School of Graduate Studies
DANIEL MORRISSEY, Esq., Dean of the School of Law
Rev. EDWARD A. BLACKWELL, Dir. of Campus Ministry
Clergy and Religious Full-Time Faculty:
Revs.:
RAYMOND E. GEISSER, O.S.A.
JAMES GAUGHAN
DANIEL KENT
JAMES L. MACDOUGALL, O.S.A.
Sr. HELEN ROSENTHAL, R.S.C.J.
Priests 8
Sisters 2
Lay Teachers 100
Students 3,055

St. Leo
Diocese of St. Petersburg

Saint Leo College
Mailing Address:
P.O. Box 2187
St. Leo, FL 33574
Tel: 352-588-8200
An Independent and Catholic Coeducation Liberal Arts College.
Dr. ARTHUR F. KIRK, JR., Pres.
Dr. MAUREEN POWERS, Vice Pres. Student Affairs
Mr. JOHN WEICHERDING, Vice Pres. Business Affairs
Mr. BERNARD SCHNEIDER, Vice Pres. Institutional Advancement
Ms. BONNIE BLACK, Dir. Admissions
Dr. STEVE LOGAN, Dir. Residential Life
Mr. RICHARD RITZMAN, Dir. Financial Aid & Veterans Affairs

Sr. CANDICE TUCCI, O.S.F., Asst. to Pres. for Campus Ministry
Rev. ANTHONY KISSEL, Asst. Dir. Campus Ministry
Legal Title: *Saint Leo College, Inc.*
Legal Title: *Saint Leo College Educational Fund, Inc.*
Priests 2
Sisters 6
Lay Teachers 460
Students 7,124

HAWAII

Honolulu
Diocese of Honolulu

**Chaminade University of Honolulu*
3140 Waialae Ave.
Honolulu, HI 96816
Tel: 808-735-4711
MARY C. WESSELKAMPER, Pres.
Campus Ministry:
Rev. MARIO PARIANTE, S.M., Dir.
Sr. ST. JOSEPH BRENNION, O.S.F.
Bro. THOMAS SPRING, S.M.
Priests 3
Brothers 3
Sisters 3
Lay Teachers 157
Students 2,430

ILLINOIS

Cahokia
Diocese of Belleville

Parks College of Saint Louis University
62206
Dr. CHARLES KIRKPATRICK, Dean, Tel: 618-337-7575 Ext. 203
DONALD W. RECK, S.J., Dir. Campus Ministry, Tel: 618-337-7575 Ext. 284
5047 Washington Pl.
St. Louis, MO 63108
Tel: 314-367-8013
Rev. JAMES H. BAKER, S.J. Tel: 618-337-7575 Ext. 287
3601 Lindell Blvd.
St. Louis, MO 63108
Tel: 314-658-2588
Sr. BETTY LEIWE, C.S.J. Tel: 618-337-7575 Ext. 451
Lay Teachers 78
Students 632

Chicago
Archdiocese of Chicago

De Paul University
One E. Jackson Blvd.
Chicago, IL 60604
2320 N. Kenmore Ave.
Chicago, IL 60614
Tel: 312-362-8000; Fax: 312-362-6606
Conducted by the Priests of the Congregation of the Mission (Vincentian Fathers and Brothers)
Revs.:
JOHN P. MINOGUE, C.M., Pres.
JOHN T. RICHARDSON, C.M., Chancellor
Rev. Msgr. JOHN J. EGAN, Asst. to the Pres. Office Community Affairs
Dr. RICHARD J. MEISTER, Exec. Vice Pres. Academic Affairs
Rev. PAUL GOLDEN, C.M., Sr. Exec. University Mission
Ms. ANNE M. KENNEDY, Vice Pres. Enrollment Mgmt.
Mr. KENNETH A. MCHUGH, Exec. Vice Pres. Oper.
Mr. JAMES R. DOYLE, Vice Pres. Student Affairs
Mr. HERBERT E. NEWMAN, Vice Pres. Devel. & Alumni
Dr. SUSY S. CHAN, Vice Pres. Univ. Planning & Information Technology
Mr. ROBERT KOZOMAN, Treas.
Mrs. SUSAN WALLACE, Controller
NANCY E. GALL, Registrar
LYNN SCHUMACHER, Dir. Ctr. for Professional Career Devel.
Rev. PAUL L. GOLDEN, C.M., Sec.
Mr. JOHN SCHOULTZ, Dir. Financial Aid
Ms. LUCY LEUSCH, Enrollment Management/Dean of Admissions
ROBERT A. LUDWIG, Ph.D., Dir. Univ. Ministry
Rev. THOMAS P. MUNSTER, C.M., Assoc. Chancellor
Priests 20
Brothers 3
Sisters 12
Faculty 495
Students 16,747
College of Liberal Arts and Sciences
2320 N. Kenmore Ave.
Chicago, IL 60614
MICHAEL L MEZEY, Ph.D., Acting Dean
College of Law
One E. Jackson Blvd.
Chicago, IL 60604
Mr. JOHN C. ROBERTS, Dean
College of Commerce
One E. Jackson Blvd.
Chicago, IL 60604
RONALD J. PATTEN, Dean
School of Music
804 W. Belden
Chicago, IL 60614
FREDERICK MILLER, D.M.A., Dean
School for New Learning
One E. Jackson Blvd.
Chicago, IL 60604
DAVID O. JUSTICE, Dean
The Theatre School
2135 N. Kenmore Ave.
Chicago, IL 60614
JOHN R. WATTS, Ph.D., Dean
School of Education
2320 N. Kenmore Ave.
Chicago, IL 60614
BARBARA SIZEMORE, Ph.D., Dean

Jesuit Community at Loyola University of Chicago
Jesuit Residence, 6525 N. Sheridan Rd.
Chicago, IL 60626
Tel: 773-508-8800; Fax: 773-508-2098
Legal Title: *The Jesuit Community Corporation at Loyola University*
Revs.:
LAWRENCE REUTER, S.J., Rector
KEITH ABRANCHES, S.J.
ALBERT A. AGRESTI, S.J.
DENNIS P. AHERN, S.J.
RICHARD W. ANDERSON, S.J.
MARIA S. AUGUSTINE, S.J.
JOHN D. BAGGARLY, S.J.
RAYMOND C. BAUMHART, S.J.
FRANS J. VAN BEECK, S.J.
FRED F. BERGEWISCH, S.J.
ROBERT L. BIRELEY, S.J.
CHARLES J. BRANNEN, S.J.
DONALD E. BRUGGER, S.J.
TIMOTHY R. CLANCY, S.J.
Bro. BRUTUS J. CLAY, S.J.
Revs.:
MICHAEL W. COOPER, S.J.
RICHARD F. COSTIGAN, S.J.
MATTHEW E. CREIGHTON, S.J.
WILLIAM A. DEHLER, S.J.
CARL L. DEHNE, S.J.
JOHN T. DILLON, S.J.
ROBERT L. DOLAN, S.J.
CARIDADE DRAGO, S.J.
EUGENE F. DWYER, S.J.
RONALD J. FERGUSON, S.J.
KEVIN T. FITZGERALD, S.J.
PETER D. FOX, S.J.
EUGENE M. GEINZER, S.J. (MAR)
Bro. MICHAEL J. GRACE, S.J.
Revs.:
JOSEPH R. HACALA, S.J.
PAUL F. HARMAN, S.J.
JOHN C. HAUGHEY, S.J. (MAR)
F. TORRENS HECHT, S.J.
WILLIAM H. HOGAN, S.J.
JOHN J. KILGALLEN, S.J.
STEVEN KIMMONS, S.J. (NOR)
JOHN J. KINSELLA, S.J.
ALLAN F. KIRK, S.J.
EDWARD H. KONERMAN, S.J.
WALTER P. KROLIKOWSKI, S.J.
JOHN P. LANGAN, S.J. (DET)
MARK J. LINK, S.J.
JAMES F. MAGUIRE, S.J.
PATRICK J. MCATEER, S.J.
JAMES M. MCCANN, S.J.
JOHN M. MCMANAMON, S.J. (DET)
LUTZ MULLER, S.J.
ROBERT W. MULLIGAN, S.J.
JOHN J. O'CALLAGHAN, S.J.
ROBERT C. O'CONNOR, S.J.
JEROME T. OVERBECK, S.J.
BRIAN G. PAULSON, S.J.
F. MICHAEL PERKO, S.J.
GENE D. PHILLIPS, S.J.
JOHN J. PIDERIT, S.J. (NY)
JOHN J. POWELL, S.J.
EDWARD J. QUINNAN, S.J. (NY)
JOHN E. REILLY, S.J.
JOHN H. REINKE, S.J.
LIBORIUS REPSCHINSKI, S.J.
HUGH B. RODMAN, S.J.
CHARLES E. RONAN, S.J.
THEODORE C. ROSS, S.J. (DET)
DONALD F. ROWE, S.J.
THOMAS SARJUMANARSA, S.J.
ROBERT T. SEARS, S.J.
MYLES N. SHEEHAN, S.J.
AMADEUS SHIRIMA, S.J.
JOSEPH F. SMALL, S.J.
EARL L. SMITH, S.J.
WILLIAM J. SPINE, S.J.
JAMES A. STOEGER, S.J.
LEO C. SWEENEY, S.J.
RALPH H. TALKIN, S.J.
THOMAS H. TOBIN, S.J.
THEODORE J. TRACY, S.J.
J. RICHARD VANDEVELDE, S.J.
MUREL R. VOGEL, S.J.
GERALD C. WALLING
EARL A. WEIS, S.J. (DET)
ROBERT J. WILLMES, S.J.
JOHN C. WRONSKI, S.J

Loyola University-Chicago
6525 N. Sheridan Rd.
Chicago, IL 60626
Tel: 312-274-3000
Mailing Address:—President's Office
820 N. Michigan Ave.
Chicago, IL 60611
Tel: 312-915-6400
Legal Title: *Loyola University of Chicago, Illinois*
FRANK W. CONSIDINE, Chm. Bd.
Rev. JOHN J. PIDERIT, S.J., Pres.
Dr. RONALD E. WALKER, Exec. Vice Pres.
Dr. ANTHONY L. BARBATO, Pres. & C.E.O, Loyola Univ. Medical Center
PAUL G. MCFARLAND, Vice Pres. Finance
Dr. JOSEPH SANDMAN, Vice Pres. Advancement
Dr. DANIEL BARNES, Acting Vice Pres. Student Affairs
Mr. ALLAN O. BALDWIN, Vice Pres. Information Technologies
Rev. LAWRENCE REUTER, S.J., Vice Pres. University Ministry
Dr. JAMES L. WISER, Senior Vice Pres. & Dean Faculties
Mr. JOHN KAMBANIS, Vice Pres. Human Resource Mgmt.
Ms. ELLEN WAITE, Vice Pres. Academic Svcs.
Mr. DAVID MEAGHER, Vice Pres. Finance & Treasury
Mrs. ELLEN KANE MUNRO, Vice Pres. and General Council
The following are the Schools and Colleges which compose the University:
The College of Arts and Sciences (1870)
Lake Shore Campus
6525 N. Sheridan Rd.
Chicago, IL 60626
Water Tower Campus
820 N. Michigan Ave.
Chicago, IL 60611
Dr. KATHLEEN MCCOURT, Dean
The School of Law (1908)
1 E. Pearson St.
Chicago, IL 60611
NINA APPEL, Dean
The Stritch School of Medicine (1909)
2160 S. First Ave.
Maywood, IL 60153
Dr. DANIEL H. WINSHIP, Dean
School of Social Work (1914)
820 N. Michigan Ave.
Chicago, IL 60611
Dr. JOSEPH WALSH, Dean
Mundelein College of Loyola
6525 N. Sheridan Rd.
Chicago, IL 60626
Dr. STEPHEN FREEDMAN, Dean
The School of Business Administration (1922)
820 N. Michigan Ave.
Chicago, IL 60611
Dr. WILLIAM BRYAN, Dean
The Graduate School (1926)
820 N. Michigan Ave.
Chicago, IL 60611
Dr. JAMES BRENNAN, Dean
The School of Nursing (1935)
6525 N. Sheridan Rd.
Chicago, IL 60626
Dr. SHIRLEY DOOLING, Dean
The School of Education (1969)
Mallinkrodt Campus, 1041 Ridge Rd.
Wilmette, IL 60091
Dr. TERRY E. WILLIAMS, Acting Dean
Total University enrollment 14,001
Total full-time faculty 900
St. Joseph's Seminary
6551 N. Sheridan Rd.
Chicago, IL 60631
Rev. DENNIS LYLE, Academic Dean
Mallinckrodt Campus
1041 Ridge Rd.
Wilmette, IL 60626
Dr. MARJORIE BEANE, Assoc. Vice Pres.

Saint Xavier University
3700 West 103rd St.

Chicago, IL 60655
Tel: 773-298-3000
Dr. RICHARD A. YANIKOSKI, Pres.
Sisters of Mercy of the Union in the U.S. 10
Order of St. Francis 1
Sisters of Charity of Blessed Virgin Mary 1
Lay Teachers 262
Students 4,100

Vincentian Community at DePaul University
2233 N. Kenmore Ave.
Chicago, IL 60614
Tel: 312-880-2968
Legal Title: *Society of Priests of the Congregation of the Mission of Chicago*
Revs.:
RALPH C. PANSZA, C.M., Supr.
JOSEPH C. GEDERS, C.M., Treas.
Members of the Vincentian Community (Congregation of the Mission):
Revs.:
WILLIAM V. BRENNAN, C.M.
KEVIN COLLINS, C.M.
JOHN R. CORTELYOU, C.M.
WILLIAM R. PILETIC, C.M.
Bros.:
PAUL P. JOSEPH, C.M.
LEO KEIGHER, C.M.
Revs.:
JOHN HICKEY, C.M.
JAY JUNG, C.M.
THOMAS J. MEIK, C.M.
AUSTIN F. MINOGUE, C.M.
JOHN P. MINOGUE, C.M.
PATRICK MULLINS, C.M.
THOMAS P. MUNSTER, C.M.
MANUEL J. PELLETERI, C.M.
RONALD W. RAMSON, C.M.
JOHN T. RICHARDSON, C.M.
WILLIAM A. RYAN, C.M.
EDWARD J. TOMASIEWICZ, C.M.
CHARLES J. WELTER, C.M.
RAYMOND F. WHITE, C.M.
MARTIN J. CULLIGAN, C.M.
DONALD OURS, C.M.

Joliet
Diocese of Joliet in Illinois

College of St. Francis
500 N. Wilcox
Joliet, IL 60435
Tel: 815-740-3360
A coed resident and commuter school.
JOHN C. ORR, Chancellor
Dr. JAMES A. DOPPKE, Pres.
Sr. DOLORES ZEMONT, O.S.F., Dir. Campus Ministry
Priests 1
Sisters of St. Francis of Mary Immaculate 5
Lay Teachers 51
Students 1,105
Total Staff 205

Saint Joseph College of Nursing (1988)
(Coed Commuter College)
290 N. Springfield Ave.
Joliet, IL 60435
Fax: 815-741-7131
VIRGINIA E. KECK, Pres.
Lay Teachers 19
Students 231

Lake Forest
Archdiocese of Chicago

Barat College
700 Westleigh Rd.
Lake Forest, IL 60045
Tel: 708-234-3000
Dr. LUCY S. MORROS, Pres.
Dr. DAVID THROGMORTON, Dean of College & Vice Pres. Academic Affairs
Religious of the Sacred Heart 2
Lay Teachers 88
Students 731

Lisle
Diocese of Joliet in Illinois

Benedictine University
5700 College Rd.
Lisle, IL 60532-0900
Tel: 630-829-6000; Fax: 630-960-1126
Rt. Rev. HUGH R. ANDERSON, O.S.B., Chancellor
Dr. WILLIAM J. CARROLL, Pres.
Mr. SAM ROSS, Vice-Pres. Univ. Advancement
Dr. JOHN E. EBER, Dean of Graduate & Adult Education
Dr. PHYLLIS M. KITTEL, Vice Pres. for Academic Affairs
Ms. BARBARA BERNHARD, Vice Pres. for Student Affairs
Mr. ROBERT HEAD, Vice-Pres. Finance & Admin.
DAVID TURNER, Univ. Chap.
Revs.:
KEVIN J. SHEERAN, O.S.B., Sec. & Treas.
STANLEY G. VESELY, O.S.B.
PHILIP S. TIMKO, O.S.B.
CHRISTIAN W. CEPLECHA, O.S.B.
MICHAEL E. KOMECHAK, O.S.B.
ODILO CRKVA, O.S.B.
THEODORE D. SUCHY, O.S.B.
JOHN PALMER, C.S.V.
JAMES FLINT, O.S.B.
PASCHAL D. HONNER, O.S.B.
Bros.:
SEBASTIAN KUHN, O.S.B.
AUGUSTINE MALLAK, O.S.B.
FINIAN D. TAYLOR, O.S.B.
ROBERT L. LORITZ, O.S.B.
Fathers 12
Brothers 4
Sisters 1
Lay Teachers 250
Administrators 94
Students 2,571

Quincy
Diocese of Springfield in Illinois

Quincy University (1860)
1800 College Ave.
Quincy, IL 62301
Tel: 217-222-8020; 228-5318
Franciscan Friars, Sacred Heart Province
Revs.:
JAMES F. TOAL, O.F.M. (New York) Pres.
VICTOR KINGERY, O.F.M., Librarian
JAMES KELLY, O.F.M.
KENNETH CAPALBO, O.F.M.
Bros.:
GREGORY BUMM, O.F.M.
JAMES EDMISTON, O.F.M.
JAMES FINNEGAN, O.F.M.
JACK HARDESTY, O.F.M.
Rev. PHILIBERT HOEBING, O.F.M.
Bro. HERMAN JOE JAMES, O.F.M.
Revs.:
RICHARD M. JESKE, O.F.M., Chap., Illinois Veteran's Home
WILLIAM BURTON, O.F.M.
JOHN J. LAKERS, O.F.M.
Bros.:
JAMES LAMMERS, O.F.M.
THOM SMITH O.F.M., Campus Minister
Revs.:
JOSEPH TAN DOAN NGUYEN, O.F.M.
DENNIS SCHAFER, O.F.M.
HARRY SPECKMAN, O.F.M., Exec. Vice Pres. & Dir., Radio Station
RICHARD BENDEROF, O.F.M.
DUNSTAN VELESZ, O.F.M.
GEORGE WINDOLPH, O.F.M.
JOSEPH ZIMMERMAN, O.F.M.
Sr. KATHLEEN EAGAN, C.S.V., Registrar
Priests 15
Brothers 7
Sisters 2
Lay Faculty - Administrators 99
Students 1,141

River Forest
Archdiocese of Chicago

Dominican University (Formerly Rosary College)
7900 W. Division St.
River Forest, IL 60305
Tel: 708-366-2490
Legal Title: *Dominican University*
Dominican Sisters of Sinsinawa, WI
Dr. DONNA M. CARROLL, Pres.
Sr. DIONA MCNICHOLS, O.P., Prioress
Dr. NORMAN CARROLL, Vice Pres. of Academic Affairs & Dean of Faculty
Rosary College of Arts and Sciences at Dominican University
Dr. HUGH MCELWAIN, Dean
School of Business
Dr. MOLLY BURKE, Dean
School of Education
Sr. COLLEEN MCNICHOLAS, Dean
Graduate School of Library and Information Science
Dr. PEGGY SULLIVAN, Dean
Sisters 11
Lay Teachers 59
Students 1,789

Romeoville
Diocese of Joliet in Illinois

Lewis University
(Coed University)
Rt. 53
Romeoville, IL 60446
Tel: 815-838-0500
Bros.:
JAMES GAFFNEY, F.S.C., Pres.
ROBERT MURPHY, O.Carm., Dir. Campus Ministry
Priests 3
Sisters 4
Brothers of the Christian Schools 11
Lay Teachers 103
Students 4,264

Springfield
Diocese of Springfield in Illinois

Springfield College in Illinois
1500 N. Fifth St.
Springfield, IL 62702
Tel: 217-525-1420
Dr. H. BRENT DELAND, Pres.
Rev. DAVID S. LANTZ, Dir.
Ursuline Sisters 1
Priests 1
Lay Teachers 39
Students 536

INDIANA

Donaldson
Diocese of Fort Wayne - South Bend

Ancilla Domini College
Mailing Address:
P.O. Box 1
Donaldson, IN 46513
Poor Handmaids of Jesus Christ (Ancilla Domini Sisters)
Dr. WILLIAM J. SHUSTOWSKI, JR., Pres.
RAYMOND GIRRES, Business Officer
Dr. MARCIA MITTELSTADT, Academic Dean
SHARON BLUBAUGH, Registrar
SARAH ROBINSON, Dir. of Student Svcs.
GLENDA BOCKMAN, Head Librarian
JACKIE WALORSKI, Dir. Inst. Advancement
Sisters 5
Lay Teachers 8
Students 660

Fort Wayne
Diocese of Fort Wayne - South Bend

Saint Francis College of Fort Wayne, Inc.
2701 Spring St.
Fort Wayne, IN 46808-3994
Tel: 219-434-3100; Fax: 219-434-3183; 434-3194
Conducted by Sisters of St. Francis of Perpetual Adoration.
Sr. M. ELISE KRISS, O.S.F., Pres.
Rev. JEREMIAH J. CULLINANE (WH) Residence Chap.
Priests 1
Sisters 11
Lay Teachers 41
Students 948

Indianapolis
Archdiocese of Indianapolis

Marian College
(Coed)
3200 Cold Spring Rd.
Indianapolis, IN 46222
Tel: 317-929-0123; Fax: 317-929-0263
Sisters of the Third Order Regular of St. Francis
Sr. NORMA ROCKLAGE, O.S.F., Ph.D., Vice Pres. Mission Effectiveness & Planning
EDWARD C. BALOG, Ph.D., Dean of Academic Affairs
DANIEL A. FELICETTI, Ph.D., Pres.
Revs.:
FRANCIS E. BRYAN
LEOPOLD KEFFLER, O.F.M.Conv.
Priests 2
Sisters 6
Lay Teachers 68
Students 1,304

Notre Dame
Diocese of Fort Wayne - South Bend

Holy Cross College, Holy Cross College, Inc.
1801 N. Michigan, P.O. Box 308
Notre Dame, IN 46556-0308
Tel: 219-239-8400; Fax: 219-233-7427
Legal Title: *Holy Cross College, Inc.*
Bros.:
RICHARD GILMAN, C.S.C., Pres.
JAMES BLUMA, C.S.C., Dean of Student Life
R. DOUGLAS IRVINE, Dir. Financial Aid
MARK P. MULLANEY, Vice Pres. Finance
Bro. CHARLES GREGG, C.S.C., Librarian
JOSEPH GOEPFRICH, Vice Pres. Advancement
CHRISTOPHER J. RUHE, Dir. Residence Life

Richard Sullivan, Registrar
Vincent M. Duke, Dir. Admissions
Sr. Anna Mae Golden, C.S.C., Academic Dean
Priests 6
Sisters 3
Brothers 12
Lay Professors 19
Students 445

Saint Mary's College
Notre Dame, IN 46556
Tel: 219-284-4000; Fax: 219-284-4716
An institution of higher education for women.
Sisters of the Holy Cross
William A. Hickey, Pres.
Sisters 4
Lay Professors 159
Students 1,474

**University of Notre Dame Du Lac* (1842)
Corby Hall
Notre Dame, IN 46556
Tel: 219-631-5000
The Graduate School (29 departments). The Law School. The Undergraduate School (four colleges, 36 departments). Institutes and Radiation Laboratory, Center for Study of Man, Institute for Urban Studies and Institute for International Studies.
Officers Group:
Rev. Edward A. Malloy, C.S.C., Pres. & C.S.C. Faculty and Personnel
Nathan O. Hatch, Ph.D., Provost
Revs.:
E. William Beauchamp, C.S.C., Exec. Vice Pres.
Timothy R. Scully, C.S.C., Vice Pres. & Assoc. Provost
Dr. Patricia O'Hara, Vice Pres. Student Affairs
Jeffrey C. Kantor, Ph.D., Vice Pres. & Assoc. Provost
Carol A. Mooney, J.D., Vice Pres. & Assoc. Provost
Thomas J. Mason, Vice Pres. Business Affairs
Dr. William P. Sexton, Vice Pres. Univ. Rels.
James L. Merz, Ph.D., Vice Pres. Graduate Studies & Research
James J. Lyphout, Assoc. Vice Pres. for Business Operations
Scott C. Malpass, Assoc. Vice Pres. for Finance
Rev. Richard V. Warner, C.S.C.
Carol C. Kaesebier, J.D., Vice Pres. & General Counsel
Mr. Matthew S. Cullinan, Asst. to Pres.
Rev. Richard V. Warner, C.S.C., Counselor to the Pres., Dir. of Campus Ministry
Administrative Group:
Dr. Steven Buechler, Assoc. Provost
Sr. Kathleen Cannon, O.P., Assoc. Provost
Dr. Anthony Hyder, Assoc. Vice Pres. Graduate School
Dr. Thomas L. Sweeney, Asst. Vice Pres. Research
Dr. James H. Powell, Asst. Vice Pres. & Dir. Summer Session
Kevin M. Rooney, Dir. Admissions
Robert C. Miller, Dir. Univ. Libraries
James J. Lyphout, Assoc. Vice Pres. Business Affairs
Roger V. Mullins, Dir. Human Resources
Joseph A. Russo, Dir. Financial Aid
Michael A. Wadsworth, Dir. Athletics
Richard W. Conklin, Assoc. Vice Pres. Univ. Rels.
William W. Kirk, Asst. Vice Pres. Student Affairs
Sr. Jean Lenz, O.S.F., Asst. Vice Pres. Student Affairs
Rev. Peter D. Rocca, C.S.C., Asst. Vice Pres. Student Affairs
Iris Outlaw, Dir. Minority Students
Scott C. Malpass, Vice Pres. of Finance
C.S.C. Faculty & Personnel:
Most Rev. Mark McGrath, C.S.C.
Revs.:
Robert Austgen, C.S.C.
Nicholas Ayo, C.S.C.
Leonard N. Banas, C.S.C.
Ernest J. Bartell, C.S.C.
Michael Baxter, C.S.C.
E. William Beauchamp, C.S.C.
Thomas E. Blantz, C.S.C.
William Botzum, C.S.C.
Richard S. Bullene, C.S.C.
David B. Burrell, C.S.C.
Bro. John Campbell
Revs.:
Charles M. Carey, C.S.C.
Joseph H. Carey, C.S.C.
Austin I. Collins, C.S.C.
John E. Conley, C.S.C.
Michael E. Connors, C.S.C.
Raymond F. Cour, C.S.C.
Alfred F. D'Alonzo, C.S.C.
William J. Dohar, C.S.C.
Paul F. Doyle, C.S.C., Religious Supr.
John S. Dunne, C.S.C.
Clarence R. Durbin, C.S.C.
Mark J. Fitzgerald, C.S.C.
James F. Flanigan, C.S.C.
Patrick Gaffney, C.S.C.
David A. Garrick, C.S.C.
Thomas E. Gaughan, C.S.C.
Mark Ghyselinck, C.S.C.
Edmund N. Goedert
Bro. Francis Gorch, C.S.C.
Revs.:
Gregory A. Green, C.S.C.
Carl G. Hager, C.S.C.
Michael J. Heppen, C.S.C.
Theodore M. Hesburgh, C.S.C.
Bro. Louis Hurcik, C.S.C.
Revs.:
John J. Jenkins, C.S.C.
Daniel R. Jenky, C.S.C.
Edmund P. Joyce, C.S.C.
Thomas P. King, C.S.C.
Jerome Knoll, C.S.C.
Robert A. Krieg, C.S.C.
Bro. Richard Kyle, C.S.C.
Revs.:
John F. Lahey, C.S.C.
William Lewers, C.S.C.
Jim Lies, C.S.C.
Bro. Edward Luther, C.S.C.
Revs.:
Patrick H. Maloney, C.S.C.
James J. McGrath, C.S.C.
Most Rev. Mark G. McGrath, C.S.C.
Revs.:
Donald P. McNeill, C.S.C.
Jose M. Martelli, C.S.C.
Leon J. Mertensotto, C.S.C.
Bro. Dennis Meyers, C.S.C.
Revs.:
Matthew M. Miceli, C.S.C.
Wilson D. Miscamble, C.S.C.
Robert Moss, C.S.C.
Michael J. Murphy, C.S.C.
Patrick Neary, C.S.C.
Stephen P. Newton, C.S.C.
Martin Lam Nguyen, C.S.C.
Edward D. O'Connor, C.S.C.
John H. Pearson, C.S.C.
Robert S. Pelton, C.S.C.
Mark Poorman, C.S.C.
Louis Putz, C.S.C.
Herman R. Reith, C.S.C.
James L. Riehle, C.S.C.
James A. Rigert, C.S.C.
Peter D. Rocca, C.S.C.
Joseph D. Ross, C.S.C.
George A. Rozum, C.S.C.
Bro. Beatus Schlenker, C.S.C.
Revs.:
David J. Scheidler, C.S.C.
Timothy R. Scully, C.S.C.
William D. Seetch, C.S.C.
Thomas G. Streit, C.S.C.
Michael Bruce Sullivan, C.S.C.
Thomas Tallarida, C.S.C.
Merwyn J. Thomas, C.S.C.
Joseph L. Walter, C.S.C.
Charles F. Weiher, C.S.C.
Oliver F. Williams, C.S.C.
George C. Wiskirchen, C.S.C.
Non-C.S.C. Religious Faculty:
Revs.:
Joseph P. Amar (SAM)
Paul F. Bradshaw
Sr. Susan Bruno, O.S.F.
Revs.:
Brian Daley, S.J.
Michael Driscoll
Sr. Sally Duffy, S.C.
Sr. Carrine Etheridge, I.H.M.
Rev. Patrick Timothy Fitzgerald
Rt. Rev. Astrik L. Gabriel
Sr. Joann Haney, O.S.F.
Sr. Mary Catherine Hikert, O.P.
Revs.:
Robert Lee Kerby
Eugene F. Lauer
Richard P. McBrien
Ernan McMullin
Richard A. McCormick, S.J.
John A. Melloh, S.M.
George Minamicki, S.J.
Sr. Mary Ann Mueninghoff, O.P.
Rev. Jerome H. Neyrey, S.J.
Sr. Mary Catherine Nolan, O.P.
Revs.:
Marvin O'Connell
Thomas O'Meara, O.P.
Hugh H. Page
Frederick W. Pfotenhauer
Bro. Bonaventure Scully, C.F.X.
Rev. Lourdes Sheehan, R.S.M.
Brian Spinks
Revs.:
Paul Philibert, O.P.
James F. White
D. Reginald Whitt, O.P.
Total Staff 1,251

Rensselaer
Diocese of Lafayette in Indiana

Saint Joseph's College
Rensselaer, IN 47978
Tel: 219-866-6000
The Society of the Precious Blood
Dr. Albert Shannon, Ph.D., Pres.
Revs.:
Charles H. Banet, C.PP.S., (Retired)
Raymond M. Cera, C.PP.S., (Retired)
James E. Froelich, C.PP.S.
Dominic B. Gerlach, C.PP.S.
Philip F. Gilbert, C.PP.S.
Lawrence F. Heiman, C.PP.S.
Dennis J. Kinderman, C.PP.S.
Leonard J. Kostka, C.PP.S., (Retired)
William J. Kramer, C.PP.S., (Retired)
Edward P. McCarthy, C.PP.S., (Retired)
Timothy D. McFarland, C.PP.S.
Charles J. Robbins, C.PP.S., (Retired)
Joseph V. Rodak, C.PP.S.
Charles R. Rueve, C.PP.S.
William J. Stang, C.PP.S.
Ralph C. Verdi, C.PP.S.
Paul R. White, C.PP.S., (Retired)
Diocesan Priests:
Rev. James Challancin (MAR) Chap.
Bros.:
Timothy P. Hemm, C.PP.S., Religious Supr.
Hugh Henderson, C.PP.S.
Sr. Catherine Fay, B.V.M.
Sr. Patricia Robinson, B.V.M.
Sr. Linda Kors, C.S.C.
Priests 19
Sisters 3
Lay Teachers 70
Brothers 2
Students 876

Saint Mary-of-the-Woods
Archdiocese of Indianapolis

Saint Mary-of-the-Woods College
Saint Mary-of-the-Woods, IN 47876
Tel: 812-535-5151; Fax: 812-535-4613
Dr. Barbara Doherty, S.P., Pres.
Priests 2
Sisters of Providence 7
Sisters of St. Francis 1
Lay Teachers 50
Students 1,245

St. Meinrad
Archdiocese of Indianapolis

St. Meinrad Seminary-College of Liberal Arts
St. Meinrad, IN 47577
Tel: 812-357-6611; Fax: 812-357-6964
Very Rev. Mark O'Keefe, O.S.B., Pres. & Rector
Revs.:
Damian Schmelz, O.S.B., Vice Rector & Provost
Gavin Barnes, O.S.B.
Freddie Byrd, O.S.B. (OWN)
Bede Cisco, O.S.B.
Thomas Crouse, O.S.B. (ANC)
Simeon Daly, O.S.B.
Guerric DeBona, O.S.B.
Jonathan Fassero, O.S.B.
Theodore Heck, O.S.B.
Eugene Hensell, O.S.B.
Columba Kelly, O.S.B.
Jeremy King, O.S.B.
Michaes Langston, O.S.B.
Guy Mansini, O.S.B.
Noel Mueller, O.S.B.
Matthias Neuman, O.S.B.
Austin Newberry, O.S.B.
Julian Peters, O.S.B.
David Rabenecker, O.S.B.
Christopher Shappard, O.S.B.
Donald Walpole, O.S.B.
Samuel Weber, O.S.B.
Cajetan White, O.S.B.
Deacon Thomas Holsworth (EVN)
Other Faculty and Staff 29
Sisters 4
Lay Women 9
Lay Men 22
Students 101

Whiting
Diocese of Gary

Calumet College of St. Joseph
2400 New York Ave.

Whiting, IN 46394
Tel: 219-473-7770
Dr. DENNIS RITTENMEYER, Pres.
Rev. ERNEST KRANTZ, C.PP.S., Chap.
Bros.:
BENJAMIN BASILE, C.PP.S., Religious Supr., Registrar
JAMES BALLMANN, C.PP.S., Dir. Computer Svcs.
GABRIEL BRIDGES, C.PP.S., Dir. Information Svcs., Campus Ministry
GERARD VON-HAGEL, C.PP.S., Alumni Assoc.
In res.,
Bro. JEROME SCHULTE, C.PP.S
Priests 1
Brothers 3
Sisters 1
Lay Teachers 62
Total Staff 105
Enrollment 1,022

IOWA

Cedar Rapids
Archdiocese of Dubuque

Mount Mercy College
1330 Elmhurst Dr., N.E.
Cedar Rapids, IA 52402
Tel: 319-363-8213; Fax: 319-363-5270
Dr. THOMAS R. FELD, Pres.
VICKY VAN WINKLE, Registrar
Dr. JEAN F. SWEAT, Vice Pres. Academic Affairs
Sisters 1
Lay Teachers 63
Students 1,131

Clinton
Diocese of Davenport

Mt. St. Clare College
(Coed)
Bluff Blvd. & Springdale Dr.
Clinton, IA 52732
Tel: 319-242-4023
Sisters of St. Francis, Clinton, IA
Dr. JAMES ROSS, Pres.
Sisters 3
Lay Teachers 37
Students 515

Davenport
Diocese of Davenport

St. Ambrose University
Davenport, IA 52803-2898
Tel: 319-333-6300; Fax: 319-333-6243
EDWARD ROGALSKI, Ph.D., Pres.
DONALD J. MOELLER, Provost
ANN FREEBERG, Ph.D., Vice Pres. Inst. Research
EDWARD J. HENKHAUS, Vice Pres. Finance
Rev. DRAKE R. SHAFER, Vice Pres. Univ. Ministry
Rev. Msgr. CLETUS P. MADSEN, Asst. to Pres.
WILLIAM T. TRACY, Ed.D., Vice Pres. Academic Support Svcs.
STEVEN R. GOEBEL, Vice Pres. Univ. Rels.
SHEILA FUNDERBURK, Campus Min.
Priest Faculty:
Revs.:
CHARLES ADAM
EDWARD A. BOTKIN
WILLIAM F. DAWSON, Ph.D.
JOSEPH DE FRANCISCO, Ph.D. (BEA)
EDMOND J. DUNN, Ph.D.
ROBERT L. GRANT
JOSEPH KOKJOHN, Ph.D.
GEORGE MCDANIEL, Ph.D.
CARROLL A. MCGIVERN
FREDERICK J. MCMAHAN, Ph.D.
RICHARD POSTER
DRAKE R. SHAFER
CHARLES C. SHEPLER
BRIAN MICLOT, Ph.D.
Priests 7
Lay Teachers 111
Total Staff 207
Students 2,640

Dubuque
Archdiocese of Dubuque

Clarke College
1550 Clarke Dr.
Dubuque, IA 52001
Tel: 319-588-6300; Fax: 319-588-6789
Liberal Arts College. (Coed)
Conducted by Sisters of Charity, B.V.M.
Sr. CATHERINE DUNN, B.V.M., Ph.D., Pres.
Sr. THERESE MACKIN, B.V.M., Asst. to Pres.
Bro. JOHN WAZNIAK, F.S.C., Vice Pres. Academic Affairs
KATE ZANGER, Vice Pres. Student Affairs
GAIL NAUGHTON, Vice Pres. of Institutional Advancement
BOBBE AMES, Vice Pres. Inst. Mktg. Recruitment
JAMES PRINCE, Vice Pres. Business & Finance
Rev. MARK RESSLER, Chap.
Brothers 1
Sisters 23
Lay Teachers 53
Students 1082

Loras College
1450 Alta Vista St.
Dubuque, IA 52004-0178
Tel: 319-588-7100; Fax: 319-588-7964
(Accredited by the North Central Assoc. of Colleges and Secondary Schools)
Dr. JOACHIM FROEHLICH, Pres.
Dr. RONALD BECHT, Vice Pres. of Academic Affairs
Dr. SUZANNE DEXTRAS, Vice Pres. for Student Devel.
JAMES COLLINS, Vice Pres. for Institutional Advancement
KENNETH J. TEKIPPE, Vice Pres. Finance & Admin. Svcs.
TEDDI JOYCE, Dean of Admissions & Financial Planning
KATHY BLAU, Dir. Placement
Mr. JON CHRISTY, Registrar
Rev. DAVID H. O'CONNOR, Chap.
MARY MOODY, Dir. of Campus Ministry
College Faculty:
Revs.:
ROBERT R. BECK, D.Min.
DENNIS J. COLTER
JOHN C. FRIEDELL, Ph.D.
JOHN J. MCDERMOTT, S.S.L.
MARK A. RESSLER, Ph.D.
RICHARD L. SCHAEFER, M.A.
KARL G. SCHROEDER, M.A., (Oxon)
Rev. Msgr. ROBERT R. VOGL, M.A.
Revs.:
DOUGLAS O. WATHIER, S.T.D.
WILLIAM E. WILKIE, Ph.D.
Priests 8
Sisters 1
Lay Teachers 112
Students 1,815

Sioux City
Diocese of Sioux City

Briar Cliff College
3303 Rebecca St., P.O. Box 2100
Sioux City, IA 51104-2100
Tel: 712-279-5321; Fax: 712-279-5410
Sisters of St. Francis of the Holy Family of Dubuque, Iowa
Liberal Arts College. Coed. Day and Resident Students.
Sr. MARGARET WICK, Pres.
ROSE REINHART, Registrar
LAURIE GROTHAUS, Admissions Dir.
Revs.:
ROBERT M. CONDON
TIMOTHY A. FRIEDRICHSEN
BRIAN C. HUGHES
Sisters 17
Lay Teachers 56
Lay Admins. and Staff 99
Students 1,116

KANSAS

Atchison
Archdiocese of Kansas City in Kansas

Benedictine College
Atchison, KS 66002
Tel: 913-367-5340; Fax: 913-367-3673
E-mail:beregis@raven.benedictine.edu
DANIEL J. CAREY, Ph.D., Pres.
FRANK CARPINELLI, Ph.D., Business Mgr.
Sr. MARY BLAISE CILESSEN, O.S.B., Registrar
Revs.:
BERTRAND LANOUE, O.S.B.
DENIS MEADE, O.S.B.
BLAINE SCHULTZ, O.S.B.
EUGENE DEHNER, O.S.B.
MARK BROSKI, O.S.B.
MEINRAD MILLER, O.S.B.
Bros.:
VINCENT FITZGERALD, O.S.B.
LAWRENCE BRADFORD, O.S.B.
Coed College of St. Benedict's & Mount St. Scholastica.
Priests 1
Brothers 1
Benedictine Sisters 7
Laypeople 37
Students 964

Kansas City
Archdiocese of Kansas City in Kansas

Donnelly College
608 N. 18th St.
Kansas City, KS 66102
Tel: 913-621-6070; Fax: 913-621-0354
Dr. JOHN MURRY, Pres.
Sr. PAULA HOWARD, O.S.B., Dean
Mrs. PEGGY HOYTAL, Registrar
Benedictine Sisters 7
Other Order Sisters 6
Lay Teachers 28
Students 807

Leavenworth
Archdiocese of Kansas City in Kansas

Saint Mary College
Leavenworth, KS 66048
Tel: 913-682-5151; Fax: 913-758-6140
JAMES F. REID, Ph.D., Pres.
Lay Teachers 24
Sisters of Charity of Leavenworth 11
Notre Dame Sisters 1
Students 659

Wichita
Diocese of Wichita

Kansas Newman College
3100 McCormick Ave.
Wichita, KS 67213
Tel: 316-942-4291; Fax: 316-942-4483
Sr. TARCISIA ROTHS, A.S.C., Ph.D., Pres.
ANDREW BOGNER, Ph.D., Vice Pres. Academic Affairs
EDWARD G. LITTIG, Ph.D., Vice Pres. Advancement
MARK DRESSELHAUS, Vice Pres. Finance & Admin.
KIM MILLER JACOBS, Vice Pres. Student Affairs
SHIRLEY RUEB, Registrar
Coeducational liberal arts college, founded in 1933 by the Sisters Adorers of the Blood of Christ. (Accredited by the North Central Association of Colleges and Secondary Schools).
Sisters 20
Lay Teachers 74
Students 1,984

KENTUCKY

Covington
Diocese of Covington

Thomas More College
(Coed)
Crestview Hills
Covington, KY 41017-3428
Tel: 606-341-5800
Rev. WILLIAM F. CLEVES, Ph.D., Pres.
Mr. JOHN M. MURPHY, Vice Pres. Admin. & Finance
MARY B. FISHER, Vice Pres. for Institutional Advancement
LAURA A. KOEHL, Vice Pres. Student Devel.
Dr. RAYMOND G. HEBERT, Vice Pres. Academic Affairs & Dean of College
Dr. DALE MYERS, Assoc. Vice Pres. Academic Affairs
Mr. JAMES MCKELLOGG, Dir. Library
Ms. PATSY KENNER, Registrar
Ms. VICTORIA H. WALKER, Dir. Financial Aid
Ms. BARBARA DAVIS, Dir. Student Support Svcs.
Sr. RITA MARIE MUELLER, S.N.D., Dir. Inst. Research
Priests 3
Lay Teachers 59
Sisters 4
Administration:
Priests 1
Sisters 5
Lay People 19
Students 1,426

Thomas More College
Student Dormitory, 333 Thomas More Pkwy.
Covington, KY 41017
In res.,
Rev. GERALD TWADDELL, Chap.

Louisville
Archdiocese of Louisville

Bellarmine College
2001 Newburg Rd.
Louisville, KY 40205-0671
Tel: 502-452-8211
Administration Officers:
Most Rev. THOMAS C. KELLY, O.P., J.C.D., Archbishop of Louisville, Chancellor
Dr. JOSEPH J. MCGOWAN, JR., Pres.
Dr. NEIL THORBURN, Vice Pres. Academic Affairs
JOHN O. KAMPSCHAEFER, JR., Vice Pres. Admin. & Finance

Dr. Fred W. Rhodes, Vice Pres. Student Affairs & Dean of Students
Dr. Leonard J. Moisan, Ph.D., Vice Pres. Inst. Advancement
Dr. Susan Hockenberger, Dean of the Lansing Nursing
Mr. Edwin Wilkes, Vice Pres. for Enrollment Management
Dr. Theresa Sandok, O.S.M., Dean of the College of Arts and Sciences
Dr. Edward Popper, Dean of the Rubel School of Business
Revs.:
Nelson Belizario
Clyde F. Crews
W. Frederick Hendrickson
George A. Kilcourse
Eugene L. Zoeller
Priests 5
Sisters 4
Students 2,173

Spalding University
851 S. 4th St.
Louisville, KY 40203
Tel: 502-585-9911; Fax: 502-585-7158
Thomas R. Oates, Pres.
Mr. Ishmon Burks, Vice Pres. Administrative Svcs.
Mr. Edward Galanif, Vice Pres. for Finance
M. Janice Murphy, Provost & Dean of Graduate Studies
Byron Wunderlich, Registrar
Phyllis Passafiume, Dean, College of Arts & Sciences
Mary Burns, S.C.N., Dean, School of Education
Marjorie Perrin, Dean, School of Nursing & Health Sciences
Thomas G. Titus, Chm. Dept. of Psychology
Jill G. McKelvy, Chm. Dept. of Social Work
Vandelia VanMeter, Dir. Library
Deborah A. Ford, Dir. Student Svcs.
Emily Whalin, Dir. Public Rels.
Brian Kesse, Dir. of Enrollment Mgmt.
Dorothy Allen, Dir. Admissions
Betty Harlan, Dir. Student Financial Aid
Priests 1
Sisters 8
Brothers 2
Lay Teachers 6
Students 1,421

Owensboro
Diocese of Owensboro

Brescia College
717 Frederica St.
Owensboro, KY 42301
Tel: 502-685-3131
Sr. Vivian Marie Bowles, O.S.U., Pres.
Sr. JoAnn Mark, A.S.C., Dean
Sr. Helena Fischer, O.S.U., Registrar
Sr. Rose Jean Powers, O.S.U., Campus Min.
Revs.:
Leonard J. Alvey
Anthony Shonis
Priests 1
Sisters 5
Lay Teachers 30
Students 760

St. Catharine
Archdiocese of Louisville

St. Catharine College
2735 Bardstown Rd.
St. Catharine, KY 40061
Tel: 606-336-5082
Dominican Sisters
Sr. Marina Gibbons, O.P., Vice Pres. & Academic Dean
Priests 1
Sisters 4
Lay Teachers 20
Students 400

LOUISIANA

Baton Rouge
Diocese of Baton Rouge

Our Lady of the Lake College
5345 Brittany Dr.
Baton Rouge, LA 70808-4398
Tel: 504-768-1710; Fax: 504-768-1726
Dr. James W. Firnberg, Pres.
Lay Teachers 35
Students 869

New Orleans
Archdiocese of New Orleans

Loyola University (1912)
6363 St. Charles Ave.
New Orleans, LA 70118-6195
Tel: 504-865-2011; Fax: 504-865-3851
Revs.:
Bernard P. Knoth, S.J., Pres.
James C. Carter, S.J., Chancellor
Dr. David C. Danahar, Provost/Vice Pres. for Academic Affairs
Revs.:
Robert S. Gerlich, S.J., Rector
Robert L. Anderson, S.J.
John F. Armstrong, S.J.
Edward B. Arroyo, S.J.
Emmett M. Bienvenu, S.J.
Thomas F. Clancy, S.J.
Harold F. Cohen, S.J.
Joseph A. Currie, S.J.
Gregory F. Curtin, S.J.
Stephen Duffy, S.T.D.
Gerald M. Fagin, S.J.
Ernest Ferlita, S.J.
Alvin J. Holloway, S.J.
Theodore M. Kalamaja, S.J.
John F. Keller, S.J.
Marvin C. Kitten, S.J.
John J. Konicek, S.J.
C. Franklyn Lynette, S.J.
Ransom Marlow, S.J.
Lawrence Moore, S.J.
Thomas Mulcrone, S.J.
Leo A. Nicoll, S.J.
Charles E. O'Neill, S.J.
Robert J. Ratchford, S.J.
W. Wayne Roca, S.J.
Peter S. Rogers, S.J.
Raymond A. Schroth, S.J.
John L. Vessels, S.J.
George F. Wiltz, S.J.
Benjamin L. Wren, S.J.
Dr. David A. Boileau
Dr. Kenneth P. Keulman
Dr. Bernard J. Lee, S.M.
Dr. Robert J. Rowland, Jr., Dean, College of Arts and Sciences
Dr. David Swanzy, Dean, College of Music
Marcel Garsaud, Interim Dean, School of Law
Dr. J. Patrick O'Brien, Dean, College of Business Admin.
Dr. Marcel Dumestre, Interim Dean, City College
Priests 30
Brothers 1
Lay Teachers 407
Students 5,530

Our Lady of Holy Cross College
4123 Woodland Dr.
New Orleans, LA 70131-7399
Tel: 504-394-7744; Fax: 504-391-2421
Rev. Thomas E. Chambers, C.S.C., Ph.D., Pres.
Dr. Gerald F. DeLuca, Vice Pres. Academic Affairs
Mr. Thomas O. Porteous, Jr., Vice Pres. Business Affairs
Ms. June H. Amundson, Registrar
Rev. Thomas Ellerman, S.M., Chap.
Priests 3
Brothers 1
Congregation of the Sisters Marianites of Holy Cross 11
Lay Teachers 94
Students 1,316

Xavier University of Louisiana
Palmetto and Pine Sts.
New Orleans, LA 70125-1098
Tel: 504-486-7411; Fax: 504-482-2801
(Coed)
Dr. Norman C. Francis, Pres.
Dr. Antoine Garibaldi, Vice Pres. Academic Affairs
Dr. Deidre Labat, Dean, College of Arts and Sciences
Mr. Joseph Byrd, Vice Pres., Student Svcs.
Anthony M. Rachal, Jr., Exec. Vice Pres.
Calvin S. Tregre, Vice Pres., Fiscal Services
Clarence J. Jupiter, Vice Pres., Devel.
Dr. Marcellus Grace, Dean, College of Pharmacy
Mrs. Lisa Lewis McClain, Dir., Office of Campus Ministry
Rev. Bryan Fontenot, O.P., Assoc. Dir. & Chap.
Priests 6
Sisters of the Blessed Sacrament 12
Lay Teachers 189
Students 3,450

MAINE

Standish
Diocese of Portland (In Maine)

Saint Joseph's College
278 Whites Bridge Rd.
Standish, ME 04084-5263
Tel: 207-893-7711; Fax: 207-893-7867
Dr. David B. House, Pres.
Sr. Mary Ellen Murphy, R.S.M., Vice Pres. for Academic Affairs and Dean
Dr. Timothy O'Leary, Vice Pres. for Student Affairs
Sr. Mary Kneeland, R.S.M., Treas.
Rev. Thomas M. Murphy, Campus Min.
Sr. Sylvia Comer, R.S.M.
Rev. Emmanuel Sullivan, O.C.D. (BO) Assoc. Prof. Religious Studies
Priests 1
Sisters 19
Lay Professors 90
Students 1,105
Undergraduate Students in Distance Education 2,350
Graduate Students 1,330

MARYLAND

Baltimore
Archdiocese of Baltimore

College of Notre Dame of Maryland
4701 N. Charles St.
Baltimore, MD 21210
Tel: 410-435-0100
School Sisters of Notre Dame
Sr. Jane Burke, S.S.N.D., Chm. of the Bd. of Trustees
Dr. Dorothy M. Brown, S.S.N.D., Interim Pres.
Dr. Joseph DiRienzi, Interim Academic Dean
Patricia A. Grega, Registrar
Dr. Jeanne Ortiz, Dean of Students
Ms. Martha Scholz, Dir. Inst. Advancement
Sr. Kathleen Jager, S.S.N.D., Campus Min.
Sisters 16
Lay Professors 58
Students 3,220
Residents 420

**Loyola College*
4501 N. Charles St.
Baltimore, MD 21210
Tel: 410-617-2000
Other locations at which courses are offered: For information call Graduate Admissions.
Tel: 410-617-5012, Ext. 5012
I-97 Business Park
1110 Benfield Blvd., Ste F
Millersville, MD 21108
Harford County, H.E.A.T. Center
5336 Churchville Rd.
Aberdeen, MD 21001
Hunt Valley
Longview Executive Park, 311 International Cir.
Hunt Valley, MD 21031
Cecil County - Booth Street Center
Elkton, MD 21921
Loyola College Business Center
7135 Minstrel Way
Columbia, MD 21045
College Established 1852. Combined with Mt. St. Agnes College 1971.
Legal Title: *Loyola College in Maryland, Inc.*
Rev. Harold Ridley, S.J., Pres.
Dr. Thomas Scheye, Academic Vice Pres. & Provost
Dr. Francis J. McGuire, Dean, Graduate Studies
Dr. David Roswell, Dean, College of Arts and Sciences
Dr. Peter Lorenzi, Dean, Sellinger School of Business & Mgmt.
Revs.:
Ronald J. Anton, S.J.
John L. Brunett, S.J.
Timothy B. Brown, S.J.
Edwin H. Convey, S.J.
William M. Davish, S.J.
William M. Driscoll, S.J.
Patrick F. Earl, S.J.
Michael D. French, S.J.
C. Kevin Gillespie, S.J.
Edgar B. Graham, S.J.
John H. Gray, S.J.
Frank R. Haig, S.J.
Francis G. Hilton, S.J.
Joseph M. Kennedy, S.J.
William K. McGroarty, S.J.
Daniel J. McGuire, S.J.
Francis G. McManamin, S.J.
Francis J. Nash, S.J.
Harold E. Ridley, S.J.
Joseph S. Rossi, S.J.
Peter F. Ryan, S.J.
William P. Ryan, S.J.
William J. Sneck, S.J.
Joseph A. Sobierajski, S.J.
Robert K. Judge, S.J.
James F. Salmon, S.J.
Paul Sun, S.J.
Students 6,245
Priests 8

Sisters 1
Lay Teachers 209
Jesuit Community of Loyola College, Inc.
Revs.:
PATRICK F. EARL, S.J., Rector
JOHN H. GRAY, S.J., Asst. to the Rector
EDGAR B. GRAHAM, S.J., Treas.
Mount St. Agnes College (Merged to Loyola College. Corporation remains in existence.)
Sisters of Mercy of the Americas
Sr. ANGELA MARIE EBBERWEIN, R.S.M., Chm. of the Board of Trustees

Emmitsburg
Archdiocese of Baltimore

Mount Saint Mary's College (1808)
Emmitsburg, MD 21727
Tel: 301-447-6122
GEORGE R. HOUSTON, JR., Pres.
Dr. STEPHEN ROCKWOOD, Librarian
Mr. LEO B. TOPPER, Vice Pres. Finance and Admin.
Mr. JOSEPH P. ZANELLA, Dir. Financial Aid
Dr. CAROL L. HINDS, Vice Pres. & Dean of College
Mr. FRANK DELUCA, Vice Pres. for Inst. Advancement
Dr. WILLIAM J. CRAFT, Dean of Undergraduate Studies
Dr. BYRON STAY, Assoc. Dean
Mr. GUY A. BAKER, JR., Registrar
Mr. JOHN C. GILL, Dir. Admissions
Dr. CHRISTOPHER B. SMITH, Dean of Student Devel.
Rev. Msgr. KENNETH W. ROELTGEN, Rector of the Seminary
Rev. Msgr. ROBERT R. KLINE, Ph.D. (SCR) Pres. Emeritus
Rev. Msgr. HUGH PHILLIPS, Chap. of the Grotto Shrine and Pres. Emeritus
Revs.:
GERARD FRANCIK, Chap.
DANIEL C. NUSBAUM (ALB)
JAMES T. DELANEY (WIL)
PAUL V. REDMOND (ALB)
DAVID W. SHAUM, Ph.D.
JOHN ZEC (TR)
CARL J. FIVES (SCR)
THOMAS J. BYRD
ROBERT TERENTIEFF (BGR)
JAMES DONOHUE, C.R.
Priests 16
Sisters 5
Lay Teachers 112
Total Enrollment 1,900

MASSACHUSETTS

Boston
Archdiocese of Boston

Emmanuel College
400 The Fenway
Boston, MA 02115
Tel: 617-277-9340; 735-9825
Sr. JANET EISNER, S.N.D., Ph.D., Pres. Sisters of Notre Dame de Namur
Rev. RICHARD CLANEY, Campus Minister
Priests 1
Sisters 13
Lay Teachers 42
Students 1,560

Chestnut Hill
Archdiocese of Boston

**Boston College*
(Coed)
Chestnut Hill, MA 02167
Tel: 617-552-8000
Revs.:
WILLIAM P. LEAHY, S.J., Pres.
WILLIAM B. NEENAN, S.J., Academic Vice Pres.
Students 14,830
College of Arts and Sciences.
Students 5,541
Rev. J. ROBERT BARTH, S.J., Dean
Summer Session.
Rev. JAMES A. WOODS, S.J., Dean
Graduate School of Arts and Sciences.
Students 1,095
Dr. MICHAEL A. SMYER, Dean
School of Law.
Students 804
AVIAM SOIFER, J.D., Dean
College of Advancing Studies.
Students 1,354
Rev. JAMES A. WOODS, S.J., Dean
Graduate School of Social Work.
Students 595
Dr. JUNE G. HOPPS, Dean
School of Management.
Students 2,339
Dr. JOHN J. NEUHAUSER
Graduate School of Management.
Students 910
School of Nursing.
Students 306
Dr. BARBARA HAZARD MUNRO, Dean
School of Education.
Students 772
Priests 34
Sisters 3
Lay Teachers 578
Graduate School of Nursing
Students 143
Dr. BARBARA HAZARD MUNRO, Dean
Graduate School of Education
Students 971
Dr. MARY M. BRABECK, Dean

Chicopee
Diocese of Springfield in Massachusetts

College of Our Lady of the Elms
Chicopee, MA 01013
Tel: 413-594-2761; Fax: 413-592-4871
Sisters of St. Joseph
Most Rev. THOMAS L. DUPRE, Bishop of Springfield
Sr. KATHLEEN C. KEATING, S.S.J., Pres.
Sr. NORA T. HARRINGTON, S.S.J., Exec. Vice Pres.
PATRICK F. DELANEY, Vice Pres. Academic Affairs & Dean
Sisters 28
Professors 54
Lay Teachers 46
Students 1,187

North Andover
Archdiocese of Boston

Merrimack College
North Andover, MA 01845
Tel: 508-683-7111; 837-5000
Revs.:
THOMAS D. BOGARDUS, O.S.A.
ROBERT M. BURKE, O.S.A.
THOMAS M. CASEY, O.S.A.
KEVIN F. DWYER, O.S.A.
TERRANCE W. HYLAND, O.S.A.
In res.,
Revs.:
STANLEY C. SMITH, O.S.A.
SALVATORE S. BONACCORSI, O.S.A.
Bros.:
THOMAS C. KENNY, O.S.A., Prior
JOHN V. CASEY, O.S.A.
CARMEN J. COLETTA, O.S.A.
KEVIN F. DWYER, O.S.A.
ALBERT P. MACPHERSON, O.S.A.
WILLIAM J. WYNNE, O.S.A.
ALFRED E. MURPHY, O.S.A.
Priests 11
Lay Teachers 135
Students 2,105
Continuing Education 1,000

North Easton
Diocese of Fall River

Holy Cross Fathers Religious
480 Washington St.
North Easton, MA 02356
Tel: 508-238-6089
Revs.:
FRANCIS M. WALSH, C.S.C., Supr., Tel: 508-238-7838; Fax: 508-230-7455
PAUL J. DUFF, C.S.C., Asst. Supr.
GENARO P. AGUILAR, C.S.C.
WILLIAM J. BESTON, C.S.C.
Bros.:
RONALD L. CHRISTESON, C.S.C.
STEPHAN CLARKE, C.S.C.
Revs.:
ALBERT J. CROCE, C.S.C.
JOHN F. DENNING, C.S.C.
Bro. JAMES W. MADIGAN, C.S.C.
Revs.:
JOHN J. MURPHY, C.S.C.
AUGUSTINE J. PEVERADA, C.S.C.
JOHN J. PHALEN, C.S.C.
JAMES T. PRESKENIS, C.S.C.
G. MICHAEL SCULLY, C.S.C.
RICHARD J. SEGREVE., C.S.C.
KEVIN P. SPICER, C.S.C.
DENIS B. SUGHRUE, C.S.C.
PETER J. WALSH, C.S.C.
FRANCIS T. ZLOTKOWSKI, C.S.C.

Stonehill College
North Easton, MA 02357
Tel: 508-238-1081; Fax: 508-230-3732
Revs.:
FRANCIS M. WALSH, C.S.C., Supr., Tel: 508-238-7838; Fax: 508-230-7455
BARTLEY J. MACPHAIDIN, C.S.C., Pres.
DANIEL J. ISSING, C.S.C., College Chap.
DAVID J. ARTHUR, C.S.C.
F. JAMES BURBANK, C.S.C.
RUDOLPH V. CARCHIDI, C.S.C.
JAMES W. CHICHETTO, C.S.C.
ANTHONY J. DECONCILIIS, C.S.C.
HARRY B. EICHORN, C.S.C.
THOMAS M. FEELEY, C.S.C.
THOMAS P. GARIEPY, C.S.C.
RICHARD E. GRIBBLE, C.S.C.
THOMAS M. HALKOVIC, C.S.C.
FRANCIS J. HURLEY, C.S.C.
ROBERT J. KRUSE, C.S.C.
JOHN E. MCCARTHY, C.S.C.
LOUIS A. MANZO, C.S.C.
Priests 9
Sisters 2
Lay Teachers 109
Students 2,882

Paxton
Diocese of Worcester

Anna Maria College
Paxton, MA 01612
Tel: 508-849-3300
E-mail: psadin@anna-maria.edu
A Coeducational Catholic College.
Sisters of St. Anne
Dr. BERNARD PARKER, Pres.
Sr. ROLLANDE QUINTAL, S.S.A., Registrar
Priests 1
Sisters 1
Lay Undergrad. Teachers 32
Grad. Teachers 90
Students 1,927

Weston
Archdiocese of Boston

Regis College
Wellesley St.
Weston, MA 02193
Tel: 617-893-1820
Sr. SHEILA E. MEGLEY, Ph.D., Pres.
Sr. MILDRED CROWLEY, S.C., Campus Min.
Sisters of St. Joseph 15
Lay Teachers 106
Students 1,121

Worcester
Diocese of Worcester

Assumption College
500 Salisbury St.
Worcester, MA 01615-0005
Tel: 508-767-7000; Fax: 508-799-5411
A Catholic Liberal Arts College under the Auspices of the Augustinians of the Assumption (Assumptionists).
Dr. JOSEPH H. HAGAN, Pres.
Revs.:
WILFRID J. DUFAULT, A.A., Chancellor
LOUIS F. DION, A.A., Vice Chancellor
FRANCIS P. GURLEY, Exec. Vice Pres.
CHARLES L. FLYNN, Provost
RICHARD P. BURKE, Vice Pres.
ROBERT D. BRILL, Vice Pres.
J. RICHARD CHRISTIANSEN, Vice Pres.
THOMAS E. DUNN, Vice Pres.
DAVID AALTO, Registrar
Rev. CLAUDE L. GRENACHE, A.A., Vice Pres. Religious Affairs & Dir. Campus Ministry
Priests 6
Sisters 1
Lay Teachers 106
Students 2,596

College of the Holy Cross, Inc
Worcester, MA 01610
Tel: 508-793-2011
A College for Boarders and Day Scholars.
Revs.:
GERARD REEDY, S.J., Pres.
WILLIAM J. O'HALLORAN, S.J., Vice Pres.
Priests 28
Deacons 1
Sisters 3
Lay Teachers 202
Students 2,720
Jesuit Teachers 12

MICHIGAN

Adrian
Diocese of Lansing

Siena Heights College - President
1247 E. Siena Heights Dr.

Adrian, MI 49221-1796
Tel: 517-263-0731; Fax: 517-264-7702
RICHARD B. ARTMAN, Ph.D., Pres.
Sr. SHARON R. WEBER, O.P., Ph.D., Academic Dean
Sisters 14
Brothers 1
Priests 1
Faculty 72
Staff 118
Students 2,026
Sponsored by the Adrian Dominican Sisters.

Detroit
Archdiocese of Detroit

Marygrove College
8425 W. McNichols Rd.
Detroit, MI 48221
Tel: 313-862-8000
(Coed)
Dr. JOHN E. SHAY, JR., Pres.
Sr. ANDREA LEE, I.H.M., Exec Vice Pres.
Dr. JOHN R. NOVAK, Academic Dean
Faculty:
I.H.M. Sisters 9
Sisters 2
Priests 1
Lay 66
Students 2,381
Incorporated.
Sisters, Servants of the Immaculate Heart of Mary

University of Detroit Mercy
McNichols Campus, 4001 W. McNichols Rd. at Livernois
Detroit, MI 48219-0900
Tel: 313-993-1000
Outer Drive Campus
8200 W. Outer Dr.
Detroit, MI 48219-0900
Law School
851 E. Jefferson
Detroit, MI 48226
Dental School
2985 E. Jefferson
Detroit, MI 48207
Sr. MAUREEN FAY, O.P., Pres.
Rev. GERALD F. CAVANAGH, S.J., Vice Pres. Academic Affairs & Provost
Mr. JOE CLARK, Vice Pres. Finance
BARBARA MILBAUER, Vice Pres. Contract Learning & Continuing Education
PETER REMINGTON, Vice Pres. Univ. Rels.
Priests 22
Brothers 2
Sisters 18
Lay 400
Students 7,888

Grand Rapids
Diocese of Grand Rapids

Aquinas College
1607 Robinson Rd., S.E.
Grand Rapids, MI 49506
Tel: 616-459-8281
R. PAUL NELSON, M.Ed., Pres.
GARY G. KONOW, Ph.D., Academic Vice Pres.
Sr. MAUREEN GEARY, O.P., J.D., C.P.A., Vice Pres. Finance
MARIBETH WARDROP, B.A., Vice Pres. Devel.
Sr. M. AQUINAS WEBER, O.P., M.A., Chancellor
BARRY R. KANTZ, J.D., Vice Pres. Operations
MICHAEL C. KELLER, M.S.A., Vice Pres. Enrollment Mgmt.
JOYCE MCNALLY, D.B.A., Dean Graduate Studies
LOIS B. KALMAN, B.A., Registrar
Sisters 8
Lay Teachers 70
Students 2,385

Livonia
Archdiocese of Detroit

Madonna University
36600 Schoolcraft Rd.
Livonia, MI 48150
Tel: 313-432-5300; Fax: 313-432-5393
Coeducational, resident and non-resident.
Conducted by the Felician Sisters.
Sr. M. FRANCILENE VAN DE VYVER, C.S.S.F., Pres.
Sr. M. LAURIANA GRUSZCYNSKI, C.S.S.F., Vice Pres. Univ. Advancement
Dr. ERNEST NOLAN, Vice Pres. Academic Affairs
Sr. NANCY MARIE JAMROZ, C.S.S.F., Vice Pres. Student Life
Sr. ALICIA BOMYA, C.S.S.F., Registrar
Mr. L. EONARD WILHELM, Vice Pres. Finance
Mr. LOU BROHL, Dir. Admissions
Ms. DONNA BERRY, Dir. Admin. Computer Center & Inst. Research
Mr. CHRIS ZIEGLER, Dir. Financial Aid
Deacon EUGENE DESJARLAIS, Dir. Campus Ministry
Rev. FRANCIS TEBBE, O.F.M., Vice Pres. Planning and Mission Effectiveness
Priests 8
Sisters 20
Lay Staff 489
Students 3,972

Orchard Lake
Archdiocese of Detroit

Saint Mary's College
3535 Indian Trail
Orchard Lake, MI 48324
Tel: 810-682-1885
(Coed, resident and non-resident)
Rev. Msgr. STANLEY E. MILEWSKI, Chancellor of the Orchard Lake Schools and Centers
THADDEUS C. RADZILOWSKI, Pres.
RONALD P. MULLER, Ph.D., Academic Dean
MICHAEL LOEFFLERCHACZYK, Business Office
Rev. FRANCIS B. KOPER (WIL) Dir. Prog. of Priestly Formation
DEBORAH GRACZYK, Dir. Financial Aid & Dir. Admissions
JOANNE BELLAIRE, Dean of Students
Rev. JAMES K. MAZUREK (PIT) Exec. Sec. Natl. Alumni Association
NANCY WARD, Dir. Library
DEBORAH GRACZYK, Ph.D., Registrar Faculty
Faculty 34
Students 276

MINNESOTA

Collegeville
Diocese of St. Cloud

St. John's University (1857)
(Men)
Collegeville, MN 56321-2000
Tel: 320-363-2011; Fax: 320-363-2504
Sponsored by the Collegeville Benedictine Monks as a division of the corporate Order of St. Benedict, Collegeville, MN.
The Graduate School of Theology (Coed)/Saint John's Seminary (Men): M.A. in Theology, Liturgical Studies, Liturgical Music, Pastoral Ministry and a Master of Divinity. The Undergraduate College of Liberal Arts and Sciences (Men), in full coordinate academic relation with the College of St. Benedict, St. Joseph (Women), offers forty departments, ten pre-professional and ten special academic programs.
Rt. Rev. TIMOTHY KELLY, O.S.B., M.A., Abbot, Chancellor
Sponsored Programs: The Hill Monastic Manuscript Library, the College of St. Benedict/Saint John's University Bahamas Campus, the Interfaith Sexual Trauma Institute, the Saint John's Pottery.
Officers Group:
Bro. DIETRICH REINHART, O.S.B., Pres.
Dr. CLARK HENDLEY, Provost, Academic Affairs
Dr. GAR KELLOM, Vice Pres., Student Devel.
Mr. WARREN JANZEN, Vice Pres., Admin. Svcs.
Mr. JOHN CROSBY, Institutional Advancement
Mr. RICK SMITH, Vice Pres., Enrollment Mgmt./Dean of Admissions
Bro. BENEDICT LEUTHNER, O.S.B., Corp. Treas.
Rev. DALE LAUNDERVILLE, O.S.B., Dean, School of Theology
Dr. JOSEPH FARRY, Dean of the College
Administrative Group:
Rev. ALBERIC CULHANE, O.S.B., Exec. Asst. to the Pres. for Univ. Rels.
Dr. CHARLES VILLETTE, Vice Pres. Special Academic Prog.
Mr. HERB TRENZ, Dir. Human Resources
Mr. JAMES HARDWICK, Dean of Students
Bro. ISAAC CONNELLY, O.S.B., Dir. Residential Prog.
Rev. TIMOTHY BACKOUS, O.S.B., Chap., Dir. Campus Ministry
Dr. BERNARD EVANS, The Butler Family's Virgil Michel Ecumenical Chair in Rural Social Ministries
Dr. DANIEL RUSH FINN, The William & Virginia Clemens Chair in Economics and the Liberal Arts
Dr. EUGENE GARVER, The McNeely Chair in Thinking
Dr. CHARLES THORNBURY, The Michael Blecker Professorship
Mr. MICHAEL WHITE, Dir. Financial Aid
Dr. DAVID BENNETTS, Dir. Summer Academic Prog.
Mr. MICHAEL KATHMAN, Dir. Libraries and Media
Mr. JAMES KOENIG, Dir. Computing Svcs.
Mr. DAVID LYNDGAARD, Registrar
Revs.:
JONATHAN LICARI, O.S.B., Vice Rector, Saint John's Seminary
ERIC HOLLAS, O.S.B., Dir. Hill Monastic Manuscript Library
ROMAN PAUR, O.S.B., Dir. Interfaith Sexual Trauma Institute
Mr. RICHARD BRESNAHAN Potter, The St. John's Pottery
Mr. JOSE BOURGET-TACTUK, Dir. Cultural Enrichment
Mr. JAMES SMITH, Dir. Athletics
Dr. GENE SANDS, Exec. Dir. Public Affairs
Mr. JON GALLOWAY, Exec. Dir. Devel. and Univ. Rels.
Bros.:
LINUS ASCHEMAN, O.S.B., Dir. Buildings and Grounds
DAVID KLINGEMAN, O.S.B., Archivist
W. CLARK HENDLEY, Provost
Priests 24
Brothers 4
Sisters 5
Faculty 107
Administrators 96
Students 1,796
Bahamas Campus Students 212

Duluth
Diocese of Duluth

College of St. Scholastica
1200 Kenwood Ave.
Duluth, MN 55811
Tel: 218-723-6000; Fax: 218-723-6290
A coed Benedictine college for resident and day students.
Dr. DANIEL H. PILON, Ed.D., Pres.
Sr. MARY ODILE CAHOON, O.S.B., Senior Vice Pres.
JOHN SIEBENAND, Dean of Student Affairs
Sisters 10
Lay Faculty 114
Students 1,895

Minneapolis
Archdiocese of St. Paul and Minneapolis

The College of St. Catherine-Minneapolis
601 25th Ave. S.
Minneapolis, MN 55454
Tel: 612-690-7702
ANITA M. PAMPUSCH, Pres.
MARY E. BRODERICK, Vice Pres. & Academic Dean
DAN JOHNSON, Assoc. Dean
Coed Health Occupation Human Service and Continuing Education Programs.
Sisters of St. Joseph of Carondelet 1
Students 1,237

St. Joseph
Diocese of St. Cloud

College of St. Benedict (1913)
(Women)
37 S. College Ave.
St. Joseph, MN 56374-2099
Tel: 320-363-5407 (Public Affairs); Fax: 320-363-5136 (Public Affairs)
Legal Title: *College of Saint Benedict*
Affiliation: Roman Catholic, established for the undergraduate education of women by the Sisters of the Order of Saint Benedict.
Sisters of the Order of St. Benedict
Partnership: In 1964 CSB began its first faculty exchange with Saint John's University (SJU) for men. Its present partnership with SJU offers complete coeducational academics, and a variety of coed social, cultural and spiritual programs. Sponsored Programs: CSB/SJU Bahamas Campus; corporate sponsors of Minnesota Public Radio (KNSR).
Officers Group:
Sr. MARY E. LYONS, Pres.
W. CLARK HENDLEY, Provost, Academic Affairs
KATHLEEN ALLEN, Vice Pres. Student Devel.
MIRIAM ARDOLF, Vice Pres. of Fin.
BARB CARLSON, Vice Pres. of Institutional Advancement
MARY MILBERT, Acting Dean/Dir. of Admission
RITA KNUESEL, Dean of the College
MIKE RYAN, Vice Pres. of Admin. Svcs.
CHARLES VILLETTE, Vice Pres. for Special Academic Prog.
Administrative Group:
HERB TRENZ, Dir. Human Resources
MARY GELLER, Dean of Students
JODY TERHAAR, Dir. of Residence Life/Housing
MARY HOLICKY, Dir. Campus Ministry
JANE HAUGEN, Dir. of Fin. Aid
MICHAEL KATHMAN, Dir. of Libraries and Media
JAMES KOENIG, Dir. of Computing Svcs.
DAVID LYNDGAARD, Registrar
MICHELLE SAUER, Dir. of Academic Advising
JOSE BOURGET-TACTUK, Dir. of Cultural Enrichment
STEPHEN BURMEISTER-MAY, Dir. of Intl. Education
CAROL HOWE-VEENSTRA, Dir. of Athletics
MARY HARLANDER-LOCKE, Dir. of Career Svcs.

GENE SANDS, Exec. Dir. of Public Affairs
CONNIE CROSS, Dir. of Public Affairs
GREG HOYE, Dir. of Publications
MIKE DURBIN, Dir. of Sports Information
ANN RUFF, Exec. Dir. Devel.
MERLE JERZAK, Dir. of Physical Plant
SUSAN HARRISON, Archivist
Sisters 34
Priests 1
Faculty 129
Administrators 112
Students 1,893
Bahamas Campus Students 135

St. Paul
Archdiocese of St. Paul and Minneapolis

College of St. Catherine
2004 Randolph Ave.
St. Paul, MN 55105
Tel: 612-690-6000
ANITA M. PAMPUSCH, Ph.D., Pres.
MARILOU ELDRED, Ph.D., Vice Pres. and Academic Dean
WILLIAM HALLORAN, Vice Pres. Business and Financial Affairs
JANET MINER, Vice Pres. Institutional Advancement
COLLEEN HEGRANES, Dean of Students & Vice Pres. Enrollment Management
MARY BRODERICK, Ph.D., Academic Dean, St. Mary's Campus
COLLEEN HEGRANES, Vice Pres. Enrollment Management & Dean of Students
DOROTHY CORRIGAN, M.Div., Dir. Campus Ministry
Rev. RODNEY ADAMS, M.Div. (OM) Assoc. Dir. Campus Ministry
MICHELLE PLOMBON, Assoc. Dir. Campus Ministry
Sisters of St. Joseph of Carondelet 17
Lay Teachers 214
Students 2,763

University of St. Thomas
2115 Summit Ave.
St. Paul, MN 55105
Tel: 612-962-5000; Fax: 612-962-6504
Rev. DENNIS J. DEASE, Pres.
Rev. Msgr. TERRENCE J. MURPHY, Chancellor
Dr. CHARLES J. KEFFER, Provost
Dr. MIRIAM Q. WILLIAMS, Assoc. Vice Pres. Academic Affairs
Dr. PAULINE LAMBERT, Exec. Asst. to the Pres.
Dr. NOREEN CARROCCI, Dean of the College
Dr. RALPH PEARSON, Vice Pres. Academic Affairs
Dr. MICHAEL SULLIVAN, Vice Pres. Business Affairs
Mr. GREGORY ROBERTS, Vice Pres. Students Affairs
Dr. JEROME HALVERSON, Dean, New College
Dr. TED FREDRICKSON, Dean, Graduate School of Business
Mr. QUENTIN J. HIETPAS, Senior Vice Pres. External Affairs
Dr. NONA MASON, Dir., Masters in Business Communications
Dr. BERNICE FOLZ, Dir., Graduate Program in the Software Design and Devel. Dept.
Mr. ALAN SICKBERT, Dean of Student Life
Dr. RONALD BENNETT, Chair, Manufacturing Systems Engineering Dept.
JEAN WALSTROM HALEY, Associate Provost for Information Technology
Rev. PHILLIP J. RASK, Vice Pres. & Rector of St. Paul Seminary School of Divinity
Dr. VICTOR KLIMOSKI, Dean, St. Paul Seminary School of Divinity
Rev. Msgr. JAMES M. LAVIN, Alumni Affairs
Rev. Msgr. ROBERT L. PROBST, Computing & Communication Svcs.
Rev. Msgr. JOHN P. SANKOVITZ, Theology Dept.
Revs.:
RONALD BOWERS, J.C.D., Assoc. Prof. of Canon Law, Vice Rector
J. MICHAEL BYRON, M.Div., Instructor, Dogmatic Theology
PETER CHRISTENSEN, Rector, St. John Vianney Seminary
KEVIN CONNOR, S.T.L., Instructor in Theology
THOMAS J. CONROY, Asst. Prof. Theology
DOUGLAS DANDURAND, M.Div., Spiritual Formation Advisor
JEROME M. DITTBERNER, S.T.D., Prof. Dogmatic Theology
JOHN ECHERT, S.S.L., Instructor, Sacred Scripture
PAUL F. FEELA, M.A., Instructor, Sacramental Theology & Liturgy
PETER FELDMEIER, Ph.D., Instuctor, Dogmatic Theology
JAY M. HARRINGTON, O.P., Prior, St. Albert the Great
JAN MICHAEL JONCAS, Dept. Theology, School of Divinity
ARTHUR L. KENNEDY (BO) Dept. Theology
THOMAS KRENIK, Spiritual Dir.
JOHN M. MALONE, Assoc. Prof. Business
WILLIAM C. MCDONOUGH, Asst. Prof. Moral Theology
JAMES R. MOTL, O.P., Ph.D., Assoc. Prof. Homiletics
LEE PICHE, Assistant Prof. Theology
THADEUS J. POSEY, O.F.M.Cap., Assoc. Prof. of Theology
JAMES REIDY, Dept. English
DOMINIC SERRA, Asst. Prof. Sacramental Theology & Liturgy
PAUL SIRBA, Spiritual Dir.
DAVID W. SMITH, Prof. Philosophy
JAMES S. STROMBERG, Dept. Philosophy
XAVIER THELAKKART, Spiritual Dir.
GREGORY TOLAAS, Campus Ministry
JOHN UBEL, Co-Dir of Vocations
ROBERT B. WELLISCH, Dept. English
Students 10,324

Winona
Diocese of Winona

Saint Mary's University of Minnesota
(Coed)
700 Terrace Hts.
Winona, MN 55987-1399
Tel: 507-452-4430; Fax: 507-457-1566
Brothers of the Christian Schools
Bro. LOUIS DE THOMASIS, F.S.C., Pres.
Dr. JEFFREY HIGHLAND, Vice Pres., Academic Affairs
Mr. ANTHONY PISCITIELLO, Exec. Vice Pres., Admissions
SHARON GOO, Vice Pres., Student Devel.
MARY C. FOX, Vice Pres., Institutional Advancement
Dr. SUZANNE G. JAMES, Vice Pres., Graduate and Special Prog.
CYNTHIA MAREK, Vice Pres., Financial Affairs
LORAS SIEVE, Vice Pres., Corporate and Community Rels.
TIM BURCHILL, Pres., Metanoia
ANN MERCHLEWITZ, Vice Pres., General Counsel
Dr. JAMES TOWERS, Dean, School of Education
Dr. ROBERT PEVITTS, Dean, School of Arts and Humanities
JAMES BEDTKE, Dean, School of Business and Social Sciences
Bro. CRAIG FRANZ, Dean, School of Sciences and Mathematics
Priests 3
Brothers 10
Sisters 11
Lay Faculty 471
Students 1,387

MISSOURI

Kansas City
Diocese of Kansas City-St. Joseph

Avila College
11901 Wornall Rd.
Kansas City, MO 64145-1698
Tel: 816-942-8400; Fax: 816-942-3362
Dr. LARRY KRAMER, Ed.D., Pres.
Mr. THOMAS LEASE, Vice Pres. & Dean for Student Affairs
Sr. MARIE JOAN HARRIS, C.S.J., Ph.D., Vice Pres. & Dean for Academic Affairs
Mr. NORMAN GERHART, Vice Pres. for Fiscal Affairs
Dr. JAMES T. "TIM" BARRY, Ed.D., Vice Pres. Advancement
Rev. DANIEL TORSON, C.PP.S., Dir. Campus Ministry & Chap.
Sisters of St. Joseph of Carondelet 16
Lay Teachers 58
Students 1,275

Rockhurst College
1100 Rockhurst Rd.
Kansas City, MO 64110-2561
Tel: 816-501-4000; Fax: 816-501-4588
Revs.:
PETER B. ELY, S.J., Pres.
MAURICE E. VAN ACKEREN, S.J., Chancellor
THOMAS A. MARTZ, Vice Pres. Inst. Advancement
JOHN HAYES, Chm., Board of Trustees
ROBERT A. LAYTON, Chief Financial Officer
NANCY TONJES, Dir. Enrollment Svcs.
JEAN LANGDON, Dir. of the Library
JOHN DAVIS, Controller
Revs.:
THOMAS N. LAY, S.J., Rector
FRANCIS L. PEDROTTI, S.J.
College of Arts & Sciences:
JANET SHEERAN, Dean
ELIZABETH KRAMER, Dean of Students
School of Management:
ROBERT CLARK, Dean
Research College of Nursing:
NANCY DEBASIO, Pres./Dean
2316 E. Meyer Blvd.
Kansas City, MO 64123
Tel: 816-276-4700
Rockhurst College Continuing Education Center/ National Seminars Group:
MARK TRUITT, Exec. Dir.
GARY TRUITT, Mng. Dir.
6901 West 63rd St.
Kansas City, KS 66205
Tel: 913-432-7755
Revs.:
E. EUGENE ARTHUR, S.J.
JULES M. BRADY, S.J.
MARTIN J. BREDECK, S.J.
EDWARD K. BURGER, S.J.
ROBERT R. BURKE, S.J.
THOMAS J. CASEY, S.J.
THOMAS F. DENZER, S.J.
JOSEPH M. FREEMAN, S.J.
JOSEPH E. GOUGH, S.J.
WILFRED L. LACROIX, S.J.
ROBERT J. MAHONEY
FRANCIS J. MURPHY, S.J.
WALTER G. NESBIT, S.J.
JAMES D. WHEELER, S.J.
MICHAEL P. CARUSO, S.J.
Bros.:
JOHN R. OLSON, S.J.
GERARD A. SCHROEDER, S.J.
Sisters 1
Priests 21
Lay Professors 162
Students 2,623

St. Louis
Archdiocese of St. Louis

Fontbonne College
6800 Wydown Blvd.
St. Louis, MO 63105
Tel: 314-862-3456
DENNIS C. GOLDEN, Ed.D., Pres.
Sisters 5
Lay Teachers 43
Students 1,786

Saint Louis University
Corporate Title: St. Louis University
221 N. Grand Blvd., DB 261
St. Louis, MO 63103-2097
Tel: 314-977-2222
Revs.:
LAWRENCE BIONDI, S.J., Pres.
PAUL C. REINERT, S.J., Chancellor Emeritus
J. BARRY MCGANNON, S.J., Chancellor
ROBERT ALTHOLZ, Acting Vice Pres. for Business and Finance
Mr. JOE ADORJAN, Chm., Bd. of Trustees
Dr. JAMES KIMMEY, Vice Pres. Sciences Ctr.
Rev. MICHAEL J. GARANZINI, S.J., Academic Vice Pres.
Dr. FRANCES BENHAM, Dir. Univ. Libraries
Mr. MARK SCHMOTZER, Controller
I. College of Arts and Sciences
200 N. Grand Blvd.
St. Louis, MO 63103
Dr. SHIRLEY DOWDY, Dean
II. College of Philosophy and Letters
221 N. Grand Blvd.
St. Louis, MO 63103
Rev. GARTH L. HALLETT, S.J., Dean
III. Graduate School
3663 Lindell
St. Louis, MO 63108
Dr. DONALD G. BRENNAN, Dean
IV. School for Professional Studies
221 N Grand Blvd.
St. Louis, MO 63103
Dr. ROBERT HASENSTAB, Dean
V. Parks College/Science, Technology and Aviation
St. Louis, MO 63103
Dr. CHARLES KIRKPATRICK, Dean
VI. School of Business and Administration
3674 Lindell Blvd.
St. Louis, MO 63103
Dr. NEIL SEITZ, Dean
VII. School of Law
3642 Lindell Blvd.
St. Louis, MO 63103
Dr. JOHN B. ATTANSIO, Dean
VIII. School of Medicine
1402 S. Grand Blvd.
St. Louis, MO 63104
Dr. PATRICIA MONTELEONE, Dean
IX. School of Nursing
1402 S. Grand Blvd.
St. Louis, MO 63104
Dr. JOAN HRUBETZ, Dean
X. School of Allied Health Professions
1402 S. Grand Blvd.
St. Louis, MO 63104
Dr. FRANCES HORVATH, Dean

XI. School of Social Service
3550 Lindell Blvd.
St. Louis, MO 63103
Dr. SUSAN TEBB, Dean
XII. School of Public Health
3663 Lindell
St. Louis, MO 63108
Dr. RICHARD KURZ, Dean
Revs.:
A. JAMES BLUMEYER, S.J.
JAMES H. BAKER, S.J.
MICHAEL D. BARBER, S.J.
Bro. WILLIAM BIERNATZKI
Revs.:
JOSEPH E. BROWN, S.J.
ROBERT A. BRUNGS, S.J.
FRANCIS X. CLEARY, S.J.
ANTHONY C. DALY, S.J.
DENIS E. DALY, S.J.
TERRENCE E. DEMPSEY, S.J.
MICHAEL J. DOODY, S.J.
PAUL J. DUFFY, S.J.
RICHARD W. DUNPHY, S.J.
JOHN B. FOLEY, S.J.
IGNATIUS FUTO, S.J.
MICHAEL J. GARANZINI, S.J.
EUGENE E. GROLLMES, S.J.
GARTH L. HALLETT, S.J.
CHARLES HEISER, S.J.
THOMAS E.J. KELLY, S.J.
JOHN J. MUELLER, S.J.
JOHN F. KAVANAUGH, S.J.
EDWIN L. LISSON, S.J.
FREDERICK G. MCLEOD, S.J.
MICHAEL K. MAY, S.J.
MARTIN D. O'KEEFE, S.J.
CLAUDE N. PAVUR, S.J.
DONALD W. RECK, S.J.
Bro. WILLIAM R. REHG, S.J.
Revs.:
RALPH C. RENNER, S.J.
LARS REUTER, S.J.
ALBERT C. ROTOLA, S.J.
JAMES A. SEBESTA, S.J.
JOHN F.X. SHEEHAN, S.J.
WILLIAM V. STAUDER, S.J.
PAUL V. STARK, S.J.
JAMES V. VELTRIE, S.J.
For further staff see the listing for the Jesuit Community at Saint Louis University under the Monasteries and Residences of Priests and Brothers.
Priests 39
Brothers 2
Sisters 4
Lay Teachers 810
Total Enrollment 10,572

MONTANA

Great Falls
Diocese of Great Falls - Billings

University of Great Falls (1932)
1301 20th St. S.
Great Falls, MT 59405
Tel: 406-761-8210
Conducted by the Sisters of Providence
Dr. FREDERICK GILLARD, Pres.
Dr. B. LEE COOPER, Academic Vice Pres.
AUDREY THOMPSON, Vice Pres. Student Svcs.
JAMES B. WASHBURN, JR., Vice Pres. Finance
BILL COYLE, Vice Pres. Devel.
JO MARIE EINAN, Dir. of Campus Ministry
Assoc. Profs. of Religious Studies:
Revs.:
JAMES R. SIKORA
JON TAYLOR, A.B.D.
Priests 3
Lay Teachers 98
Students 1,426

Helena
Diocese of Helena

Carroll College (1909)
Tel: 406-447-4300; Fax: 406-447-4533
Four year Diocesan College of Liberal Arts and Sciences.
Most Rev. ALEX J. BRUNETT, Chancellor
Dr. MATTHEW J. QUINN, Pres.
Dr. JAMES TRUDNOWSKI, Vice Pres. Academic Affairs
Ms. LYNN ETCHART, Vice Pres. Business Affairs
Mr. THOMAS J. MCCARVEL, Vice Pres. Inst. Advancement
Mr. ROBERT PASTOOR, Vice Pres. Student Affairs
Revs.:
JOSEPH D. HARRINGTON, Episcopal Vicar
WILLIAM GREYTAK
DANIEL P. HILLEN
JEREMIAH LOWNEY
J. EUGENE PEOPLES
LEO G. PROXELL
DANIEL B. SHEA
JEREMIAH T. SULLIVAN
In res.,
Revs.:
HUMPHREY J. COURTNEY, (Retired)
CHARLES FABING, (Retired)
GERALD LYNAM, (Retired)
Priests 9
Lay Professors 68
Students 1,418
Total Staff 114

NEBRASKA

Omaha
Archdiocese of Omaha

College of St. Mary
1901 S. 72 St.
Omaha, NE 68124
Tel: 402-399-2400
Sr. MARYANNE STEVENS, R.S.M., Pres.
ELIZABETH Y. MULLIKEN, Vice-Pres. for Academic Affairs & Dean of the College
NANCY HEMESATJ, Dir. of Campus Ministry

**Creighton University*
2500 California Plaza
Omaha, NE 68178
Tel: 402-280-2700
Rev. MICHAEL G. MORRISON, S.J., Pres. & Contact
The University is comprised of the following schools:
College of Arts and Sciences—
Rev. MICHAEL PROTERRA, S.J., Dean
College of Business Administration—
Mr. BERNARD W. REZNICEK, Dean
Graduate School—
Dr. BARBARA J. BRADEN, Dean
School of Law—
LAWRENCE RAFUL, J.D., Dean
University College/Summer Sessions—
Dr. WESLEY G. WOLFE, Dean
School of Dentistry—
Dr. WAYNE W. BARKMEIER, Dean
School of Medicine—
Dr. THOMAS J. CINQUE, Dean
School of Nursing—
Dr. EDITH K. KITCHENS, Dean
School of Pharmacy and Allied Health Professions—
Dr. SIDNEY J. STOHS, Dean

NEW HAMPSHIRE

Manchester
Diocese of Manchester

Notre Dame College
2321 Elm St.
Manchester, NH 03104
Tel: 603-669-4298; Fax: 603-644-8316
Founded by Sisters of Holy Cross.
Sr. CAROL J. DESCOTEAUX, C.S.C., Ph.D., Pres.
Sr. EDIE DALY, S.N.D.deN., Dir. Campus Ministry
Sisters 16
Lay Teachers 107
Students 1,290

Saint Anselm College
Manchester, NH 03102
Tel: 603-641-7000
Order of St. Benedict
Rt. Rev. MATTHEW K. LEAVY, O.S.B., Ph.D., Chancellor
Rev. JONATHAN P. DEFELICE, O.S.B., J.C.L., Pres. Admin. & Faculty
Priests 3
Lay Teachers 106
Sisters 2
Students 1,928

Merrimack
Diocese of Manchester

The Thomas More College of Liberal Arts
6 Manchester St.
Merrimack, NH 03054
Tel: 603-880-8308; Fax: 603-880-9280
PETER V. SAMPO, Pres.
Total Staff 8
Students 78

Nashua
Diocese of Manchester

Rivier College
Nashua, NH 03060
Tel: 603-888-1311
Sisters of the Presentation of Mary
Sr. JEANNE PERREAULT, Pres.
Rev. PAUL R. DEMERS, S.C., Chap.
Presentation Sisters 44
Teaching Sisters 10
Teaching Priests 2
Lay Teachers 196
Students 2,950

Warner
Diocese of Manchester

Magdalen College
511 Kearsarge Mountain Rd.
Warner, NH 03278-9206
Tel: 603-456-2656
JOHN D. MEEHAN, Pres.
MARY L. PRIETO, Dean of Students
Dr. GEORGE N. STANCIU, Academic Dean
Rev. THOMAS J. SPARKS, Chap.
Lay Teachers 9
Total Staff 19
Students 70

Windham
Diocese of Manchester

Castle College
21 Searles Rd.
Windham, NH 03087-1297
Tel: 603-893-6111
Degree-Granting Program: Associate in Business Science (A.B.S.), Associate in Early Childhood Education (A.E.C.E.), Associate of Science in Human Services (A.H.S.S.), Associate Degree in Recreation Therapy (A.R.T.), collaborative program with St. Joseph Healthcare.
Sisters of Mercy
Sr. OLIVIA KIDNEY, R.S.M., Pres.
Sisters 3
Lay Teachers 5
Students 445

NEW JERSEY

Caldwell
Archdiocese of Newark

Caldwell College
9 Ryerson Ave.
Caldwell, NJ 07006
Tel: 201-228-4424
Incorporated under the laws of the State of New Jersey with full power to confer degrees.
College Faculty:
Sr. PATRICE WERNER, O.P., Ph.D., Pres.
Dr. WILLIAM ALEXANDER, Ph.D., Vice Pres., Dean for Academic Affairs
Rev. CHRISTOPHER L. SENK, Dir. Campus Ministry
Priests 4
Sisters 2
Sisters of St. Dominic 8
Lay Teachers 99
Students 1,750

Haledon
Diocese of Paterson

Salesian College
655 Belmont Ave.
Haledon, NJ 07508
Sr. THERESA KELLY, F.M.A., Pres., Dean
Sr. IDA OSSI, F.M.A., Registrar
Students 15

Jersey City
Archdiocese of Newark

Saint Peter's College
2641 Kennedy Blvd.
Jersey City, NJ 07306-5997
Tel: 201-915-9000; Fax: 201-451-0036
Rev. JAMES N. LOUGHRAN, S.J., Pres.
EILEEN L. POIANI, Ph.D., Asst. to the Pres. for Planning
Dr. GEORGE E. MARTIN, Academic Vice Pres.
Mr. FRANK J. BARLETTA, Vice Pres. Finance and Admin. Svcs.
Mr. EDWARD W. REUTER, Vice Pres. Student Affairs
Mr. JAMES J. MORGAN, Vice Pres. Advancement
BARBARA A. CHRYST, Dean of Students
Dr. PETER ALEXANDER, JR., Academic Dean-Day Session
Mr. MARK JOHN HOESLY, Asst. Dean-Day Session
Ms. SUSAN E. NELSON, Asst. Dean-Day Session
Dr. KATHERINE M. RESTAINO, Dean-Englewood Cliffs Campus
Ms. BARBARA PENNIPEDE, Assoc. Dean, Englewood Cliffs Campus
Mr. HENRY A. SHIELDS, JR., Academic Dean, Evening

and Summer Sessions
Mr. COREY VIGDOR, Asst. Dean-Evening Session
Mr. MICHAEL WORLDS, Dir. Admissions
Ms. JOAN Z. SHIELDS, Registrar
Priests 30
St. Peter's College Jesuit Community
Gothic Towers, 50 Glenwood Ave.
Jersey City, NJ 07306-4606
Tel: 201-433-2527; Fax: 201-432-7397
Jesuit Center
St. Peter Hall, 2652 Kennedy Blvd.
Jersey City, NJ 07306
Tel: 201-433-2527; 2528 (Rector's Office); Fax: 201-433-7139
Revs.:
WILLIAM ABBOTT
THOMAS BLESSIN
EDWARD BRANDE
JOHN BUCKLEY
LAURENCE CASSIDY
EUGENE CULHANE
JAMES DAHLINGER
MARK DESTEPHANO
EUGENE DEVLIN
JUAN DIAZ VILAR
JAMES DOLAN
Bro. PATRICK FLANAGAN
Revs.:
CHARLES GALLAGHER
EDWARD GILLEN
JEROME GRUSZCZYK
EDWARD HEAVEY
JOSEPH KELLY
ROBERT KENNEDY
JAMES LOUGHRAN
JOSEPH LUX
T. PATRICK LYNCH
DONAL MACVEIGH
OSCAR MAGNAN
WILLIAM MAHER
EDMUND MAJEWSKI
CARSTEN MARTENSEN
ROBERT MCCARTY
WILLIAM MCKENNA
AIDAN MCMULLEN
JOHN J. O'BRIEN
JOHN RUANE
JOHN ST. GEORGE
DAVID STUMP
THOMAS SHERIDAN
JOHN WRYNN
Full-time Faculty:
Priests 15
Lay Teachers 103
Students 3,863

Lakewood
Diocese of Trenton

Georgian Court College
900 Lakewood Ave.
Lakewood, NJ 08701-2697
Tel: 908-364-2200; Fax: 908-367-3920
Sisters of Mercy
Sr. BARBARA WILLIAMS, R.S.M., Pres.
Sr. MARIE COOK, R.S.M., Academic Dean
Revs.:
DENNIS BAJKOWSKI
NORMAN DEMECK, C.P.
Priests 3
Sisters 18
Lay Teachers 170
Students 2,422

Lodi
Archdiocese of Newark

Felician College
262 S. Main St.
Lodi, NJ 07644
Tel: 201-778-1190; Fax: 201-778-4111
Sr. THERESA MARY MARTIN, C.S.S.F., Pres.
Rev. DAMIAN COLICCHO, Dir. of Campus Ministry
Priests 1
Sisters 25
Lay Teachers 102
Students 1,231

Mendham
Diocese of Paterson

Assumption College for Sisters
Mendham, NJ 07945
Fax: 201-543-9459
Conducted by Sisters of Christian Charity.
Sr. MARY GERARD GEBLER, S.C.C., Pres.
Sr. JULITTA HEINEN, S.C.C., Academic Dean
Sr. MARY RENEE NELSON, S.C.C., Registrar
Sr. DE SALES TONERO, S.C.C., Treas.
Religious 20
Students 20

Morristown
Diocese of Paterson

College of Saint Elizabeth
2 Convent Rd.
Morristown, NJ 07961
Tel: 201-292-6300
Sisters of Charity
Sr. JACQUELINE BURNS, Pres.
Dr. JOHANNA GLAZEWSKI, Vice Pres. for Academic Affairs and Dean of Studies
MARIA CAMMARATA, Vice Pres. for Finance & Admin. and Treas.
Mrs. ROSEMARIE GENCO, Comptroller
Mrs. SONIA SALADUCHIN, Registrar
Mrs. DONNA YAMANIS, Dean of Admissions and Financial Aid
Rev. ANTHONY J. CIORRA, O.F.M.Cap., Chap.
Tel: 201-292-6510
Full-time Admin. and Faculty:
Priests 1
Religious 34
Lay Teachers 58
Students 1,587

South Orange
Archdiocese of Newark

Seton Hall University (1856)
400 South Orange Ave.
South Orange, NJ 07079
Tel: 201-761-9000; Fax: 201-275-2361
Rev. THOMAS R. PETERSON, O.P., S.T.D., Ph.D., Chancellor
Rev. Msgr. ROBERT T. SHEERAN S.T.D., Pres.
Officers of University:
MARY MEEHAN, Vice Pres.
BERNARD W. SCHOLZ, Ph.D., Provost
JAMES O. ALLISON, M.B.A., Exec. Vice Chancellor
CRAIG J. LEACH, Vice Pres. University Affairs
LAURA A. WANKEL, Ed.D., Vice Pres. Student Affairs
Rev. Msgr. WILLIAM C. HARMS, D.Min., Vice Pres. Planning
Administrators:
CATHERINE KIERNAN, University Counsel
LISA GRIDER, Dir. Publications and Public Rels.
KATHERINE REDDICK, Dir. Bd. Affairs
JANE V. NORTON, Ed.D., Asst. Provost for Academic Services
PATRICIA L. BURGH, M.A., Asst. Provost for Enrollment Mgmt.
FRANCISCO MORALES, Dir. Special Academic Programs
PETER G. AHR, Ph.D., Dean Freshman Studies
Sr. ANITA TALAR, M.L.S., Dean University Libraries
MARY ELLEN FARRELL, Registrar
MICHAEL MENENDEZ, Dir. Financial Aid
EDWIN MILLAR, Chief Financial Mgr.
DEBORAH KROEGER, Dir. Human Resources
DANIEL MURRAY, Dir. Alumni Rels.
Dr. ROBERT HALLISSEY, Dir. Grants & Contracts
LAURENCE KEATING, Dir. University Athletics
Rev. Msgr. HAROLD P. DARCY, J.C.D., Min. to Priest Community
Revs.:
JAMES F. SPERA, M.Div., Dir. Campus Ministry
ROBERT S. MEYER, S.T.L., Asst. to Vice Pres. Student Affairs
Rev. Msgr. ANDREW T. CUSACK, Ph.D., Dir. National Inst. for Clergy Formation
College of Arts and Sciences
JO RENEE FORMICOIA, Ph.D., Acting Dean, Tel: 201-761-9022
School of Business
JOHN H. SHANNON, J.D., Dean, Tel: 201-761-9013
College of Education and Human Services
SYLVESTER KOHUT, JR., Ph.D., Dean, Tel: 201-761-9025
College of Nursing
BARBARA A. BEEKER, R.N. Ed.D., Dean, Tel: 201-761-9014
School of Law
RONALD J. RICCIO, J.D., Dean
One Newark Center
Newark, NJ 07102
Tel: 201-642-8750
School of Theology
Rev. JOHN W. FLESEY, S.T.D., Rector/Dean, Tel: 201-761-9016
School of Graduate Medical Education
JOHN PATERSON, D.D.S., Dean, Tel: 201-761-9710
College Seminary
Rev. Msgr. ROBERT FUHRMAN, M.A., Rector, Tel: 201-761-9420
University College
JANE V. NORTON, Ed.D. Tel: 201-761-9430
Priest Community:
Rev. Msgr. HAROLD P. DARCY, J.C.D., Min. to Priest Community
Rev. Msgr. ANDREW T. CUSACK, Ph.D.
Rev. Msgr. WILLIAM N. FIELD, M.L.S., M.A.
Rev. Msgr. EDWARD J. FLEMING, Ph.D., (Retired)
Rev. Msgr. ROBERT J. FUHRMAN, M.A.
Rev. Msgr. WILLIAM C. HARMS, D.Min.
Rev. Msgr. WALTER G. JARVAIS
Rev. Msgr. RICHARD M. LIDDY, Ph.D.
Rev. Msgr. ROBERT T. SHEERAN, S.T.D.
Rev. Msgr. EDWIN V. SULLIVAN, Ph.D., (Retired)
Rev. Msgr. JAMES C. TURRO, Ph.D., (Retired)
Rev. Msgr. ROBERT J. WISTER, S.T.M.
Revs.:
JOHN M. BALLWEG, M.A., Holy Spirit, Union, NJ
W. JEROME BRACKEN, Ph.D.
JAMES M. CAFONE, S.T.D.
ALFRED V. CELIANO, Ph.D., (Retired)
ROBERT F. COLEMAN, J.C.D.
GABRIEL B. COSTA, Ph.D.
EUGENE J. COTTER, D.Lett
DECLAN J. CUNNIFF, Th.M., M.L.S., D.Min.
WALTER A. DEBOLD, M.A., (Retired)
ARNOLD P. DE ROSA, Ph.D.
JOHN W. FLESEY, S.T.D.
LAWRENCE E. FRIZZELL, D.Phil.
FRANCIS T. GAVIN, M.A., (Retired)
NICHOLAS S. GENGARO, S.T.D.
THOMAS G. GUARINO, S.T.D.
KEVIN M. HANBURY, Ed.D.
PAUL A. HOLMES, S.T.D.
CHRISTOPHER J. HINES, Ed.S.
PETER F. LENNON, Ph.D.
GERALD H. MCCARREN, S.T.D.
ROBERT S. MEYER, S.T.L.
DOUGLAS J. MILEWSKI, S.T.L.
JOHN F. MORLEY, Ph.D.
DANIEL A. MURPHY, Ph.D., (Retired)
RICHARD M. NARDONE, Ph.D.
ROBERT P. NESTOR, Ed.D.
MARTIN F. O'BRIEN, M.S.
THOMAS R. PETERSON, O.P., S.T.D., Ph.D.
LAWRENCE B. PORTER, O.P., Ph.D.
JOHN J. RANIERI, Ph.D.
JOHN F. RUSSELL, O.Carm., S.T.D.
HENRY J. SCHREITMUELLER, Ed.D.
ARTHUR J. SERRATELLI, S.T.D.
WILLIAM P. SHERIDAN, M.Div.
DONALD C. SMITH, M.A.
JAMES F. SPERA, M.Div.
C. ANTHONY ZICCARDI, S.T.L., S.S.L.
In res.,
Revs.:
JOSEPH R. CHAPEL, S.T.D.
JAMES S. CHOMA, M.Div.
MARTIN J. FORAN, M.A.
JOSEPH F. WORTMANN, M.A.
Priests 55
Lay Teachers 350
Students 9,408

NEW MEXICO

Santa Fe
Archdiocese of Santa Fe

College of Santa Fe (1947)
(Coed Four Year Liberal Arts College)
Santa Fe, NM 87501
Tel: 505-473-6011
Brothers of the Christian Schools
Dr. JAMES FRIES, Pres.
Dr. JIM LAWRENCE, Sr. Vice Pres. & Dean of the College
DALE REINHART, Dir. Admissions and Enrollment Mgmt.
Ms. YVONNE RUSSELL, Dean of Students
Revs.:
LEONA STUCKY-ABBOTT, Dir. Campus Ministry
JAMES CRONIN
Brothers 7
Lay Teachers 110
Students 1,600

NEW YORK

Albany
Diocese of Albany

The College of Saint Rose
(Corporate Name)
432 Western Ave.
Albany, NY 12203
Tel: 518-454-5111; 800-657-8556; Fax: 518-458-5447
Founded by the Sisters of St. Joseph of Carondelet in 1920.
Dr. MARK SULLIVAN, Pres.
Sr. ANNE CLARK, Acting Vice Pres. for Academic Affairs and Provost
KATHLEEN M. SINEL, Vice Pres. for Finance & Admin.
Ms. JEANNE KOBUSZEWSKI, Vice Pres. Devel. & Alumni Rels.
CHARLES E. GREENE, JR., Comptroller

JUDITH A. KELLY, Registrar
MARGARET KIRWIN, Dean of Studies
DENNIS MCDONALD, Dean of Student Svcs.
MICHAEL FISHBEIN, Dean of Instructional Resources
MARY GRONDAHL, Dean of Enrollment Svcs.
Revs.:
CHRISTOPHER DEGIOVINE, Chap. & Dir. of Campus Ministry
ANTHONY D. GULLEY, Non-Resident Priest
Priests 2
Sisters 14
Lay Teachers 125
Students 3,800

Maria College
700 New Scotland Ave.
Albany, NY 12208
Two Year College
Sr. LAUREEN FITZGERALD, Pres.
Sr. JOSEPHINE REYNOLDS, Dean for Academic Affairs
Ms. LAURIE GILMORE, Dir. Admissions
Ms. DEBORAH CORRIGAN, Dean Students
Mrs. FRANCES BERNARD, Dir. Business Affairs
Revs.:
MICHAEL HOGAN
PAUL R. SMITH
THOMAS BERARDI
Sisters of Mercy 16
Lay Teachers 34
Students 860

St. Bernard's Institute at Albany
Extension Program of St. Bernard's Institute, Rochester, NY.
40 N. Main St.
Albany, NY 12203
Tel: 518-453-6760
Graduate School of Theology & Ministry Studies.
Sr. MARGERY HALPIN, R.S.M., Dir.

Bronx
Archdiocese of New York

*_Fordham University_ (1841)
Fordham Rd.
Bronx, NY 10458
Fax: 718-817-4925
Second campus and Branch campus at Lincoln Center, New York, NY 10023 and Marymount College, Tarrytown, NY 10591. Chartered by the Legislature of the State of New York.
Revs.:
JOSEPH A. O'HARE, S.J., Pres.
GERARD C. REEDY, S.J., Vice Pres. Academic Affairs
Dr. BARBARA ELLEN BLACK, Financial Vice Pres. and Treas.
Mr. BRUNO M. SANTONOCITO, Vice Pres. Devel. & Univ. Rels.
Revs.:
GEORGE J. MCMAHON, S.J., Vice Pres. Lincoln Center
JOHN J. SHEA, S.J., Vice Pres. Students Affairs
Dr. BRIAN BYRNE, Vice Pres. Admin.
Dr. JOHN W. HEALEY, Vice Pres. Planning & Budget
Mr. RICHARD T. WALDRON, Vice Pres., Institutional Research
Dr. ROBERT F. HIMMELBERG, Dean of Graduate School of Arts and Sciences
Rev. JOSEPH M. MCSHANE, S.J., Dean of Fordham College
Dr. SHARON SMITH, Dean of College of Business Admin.
Mr. WILLIAM SMALL, Dean of Graduate School of Business Admin.
Dr. MAX WEINER, Dean of Graduate School of Education
JOHN D. FEERICK, LL.B., Dean of School of Law
Dr. MARY ANN QUARANTA, Dean of Graduate School of Social Service
Dr. EDWARD BRISTOW, Dean of College at Lincoln Center
Dr. MICHAEL GILLAN, Dean of Ignatius College
Rev. VINCENT M. NOVAK, S.J., Dean of Graduate School of Religion and Religious Education
Sr. MONICA KEVIN, O.S.U., Dean of Summer Session

Manhattan College
Manhattan College Pkwy.
Bronx, NY 10471
Tel: 718-862-7200; 800-MC2-XCEL
Bro. THOMAS SCANLAN, F.S.C., Pres.
Priests 3
Brothers 19
Sisters 2
Lay Staff 165
Total Enrollment 3,400

Brooklyn
Diocese of Brooklyn

*_St. Francis College_
180 Remsen St.
Brooklyn, NY 11201
Tel: 718-522-2300

*_St. Joseph's College_
245 Clinton Ave.
Brooklyn, NY 11205
Tel: 718-636-6800
Branch Campus
155 Roe Blvd.
Brooklyn, NY 11772
Tel: 516-447-3200
Under supervision of Board of Trustees.
Sr. GEORGE AQUIN O'CONNOR, C.S.J., Ph.D., Pres.
Sr. MARY FLORENCE BURNS, C.S.J., Ph.D., Academic Vice Pres.
Sr. MARGARET BUCKLEY, C.S.J., Ed.D., Academic Dean
THOMAS G. TRAVIS, Ph.D., Dean, Div. General Studies
Sisters 18
Lay Teachers 31
Students 1,381

Buffalo
Diocese of Buffalo

Canisius College
2001 Main St.
Buffalo, NY 14208-1098
Tel: 716-883-7000; Fax: 716-888-2525
Revs.:
VINCENT M. COOKE, S.J., Pres.
JAMES P. HIGGINS, S.J., Asst. to the Pres.
Sr. MARLENE G. BUTLER, G.N.S.H., Dir., Campus Min.
Dr. THOMAS E. MILLER, Vice Pres. for Student Affairs
Mr. EDWARD A. ENGEL, Vice Pres. for College Relations
Dr. LAURENCE W. FRANZ, Vice Pres. of Business & Finance & Treas.
Dr. HERBERT J. NELSON, Interim Vice Pres. for Academic Affairs
Dr. ELLEN O. CONLEY, Dean, College of Arts & Sciences
Dr. RICHARD A. SHICK, Dean, Wehle School of Business
Dr. JAMES M. MCDONNELL, Acting Dean, School of Educ. & Human Svcs.
Mr. GEORGE M. TELATNIK, Dir. Library
Dr. JOEL A. COHEN, Dir., Information Technology Svcs.
Total Enrollment 4,836

*_D'Youville College_
320 Porter Ave.
Buffalo, NY 14201
Tel: 716-881-3200; Fax: 716-881-7780
Sr. DENISE A. ROCHE, G.N.S.H., Ph.D., Pres.
Dr. ROBERT A. DISIBIO, Dean Arts & Sciences
Dr. SUSAN E. BENNETT, Dean School of Health & Human Services, Prof. Studies
Bro. JAMES SARACH, Dir. Campus Ministry
Students 1,901

Trocaire College
110 Red Jacket Pkwy.
Buffalo, NY 14220
Tel: 716-826-1200
Sr. BARBARA CIARICO, R.S.M., Pres.
Mrs. MARY JO O'SULLIVAN, Exec. Vice Pres.
Sisters 1
Lay Teachers 42
Students 1,196
Total Staff 43

Villa Maria College of Buffalo
240 Pine Ridge Rd.
Buffalo, NY 14225-3999
Tel: 716-896-0700; Fax: 716-896-0705
Sr. MARCELLA MARIE GARUS, Pres.
NATALIE J. MOUDGIL, Ph.D., Vice Pres. Academic Affairs
Sr. MARY DE ANGELIS NOWAK, Vice Pres. Business Affairs
Sr. MARY MARCINE BOROWIAK, Vice Pres. Inst. Advancement
Sr. MARY LOUIS RUSTOWICZ, Vice Pres. Student Affairs
Sisters 3
Lay Teachers 17
Students 392
Total Staff 116

Dobbs Ferry
Archdiocese of New York

Mercy College in Dobbs Ferry
541 Broadway
Dobbs Ferry, NY 10522
Tel: 914-693-4500

Hamburg
Diocese of Buffalo

Hilbert College
5200 S. Park Ave.
Hamburg, NY 14075
Tel: 716-649-7900
Franciscan Sisters of Saint Joseph
Sr. EDMUNETTE PACZESNY, F.S.S.J., Pres.
Rev. BERNARD OLSZEWSKI, O.F.M.Conv., Chap.
Priests 1
Sisters 3
Lay Teachers 65
Students 888
Total Staff 69

Jamaica
Diocese of Brooklyn

St. John's University
8000 Utopia Pkwy.
Jamaica, NY 11439
Tel: 718-990-1924; Fax: 718-990-5886
Composed of the following schools and colleges:
St. John's College, Queens Campus
Rev. DAVID M. O'CONNELL, C.M.
Faculty 200
Students 2,153
The School of Education and Human Services
8000 Utopia Pkwy.
Jamaica, NY 11439
300 Howard Ave.
Staten Island, NY 10301
Dr. JERROLD ROSS, Dean
Sr. COLLEEN FOGARTY, Asst. Dean.
Faculty 102
Students 3,460 (Total, Undergraduate and Graduate - Queens and Staten Island campuses)
Colleges of Business Administration
Dr. CHARLES O. KRONCKE, Dean
Faculty 102
Students 3,460 (Total, Undergraduate and Graduate - Queens, Staten Island and Rome campuses)
College of Pharmacy and Allied Health Professions
Dr. THOMAS H. WISER, Dean
Faculty 44
Students 1,912 (Total, Undergraduate and Graduate - Queens Campus)
Graduate School of Arts and Sciences
Dr. WILLARD GINGERICH, Assistant Provost for Research & Dean
Students 1,022
School of Law
RUDOLPH C. HASL, Dean
Faculty 45
Students 1,134
St. Vincent's College
Dr. KATHLEEN VOUTE MACDONALD, Dean
Faculty 97
Students 4,436 (Total, Queens and Staten Island)
Notre Dame College
300 Howard Ave.
Staten Island, NY 10301
Dr. JUDITH DWYER, Dean
Faculty 40
Students 1,014

Loudonville
Diocese of Albany

Siena College
Loudonville, NY 12211
Tel: 518-783-2300
Founded in 1937 by the Franciscan Friars, Order of Friars Minor, Province of the Most Holy Name of Jesus.
Rev. KEVIN E. MACKIN, Pres.
Bro. JOHN MAHON, O.F.M., Asst. to Pres.
Dr. DOUGLAS M. ASTOLFI, Vice Pres. Academic Affairs
ANTHONY PONDILLO, Vice Pres. Finance & Admin.
Dr. GREGORY STAHL, Vice Pres. for Inst. Advancement
NOEL HOGAN, Dean of Enrollment Mgmt.
NED JONES, Dir. of Admissions
Rev. JOHN FRAMBES, O.F.M., Vice Pres. for Student Affairs
Dr. FREDERICK J. DECASPERIS, Dean of Continuing Education
Rev. FRANCIS X. GUNN, O.F.M., Dir. of Campus Ministry
ANN WHITE, Dir. Financial Aid
Dr. KENNETH WITTIG, Asst. Vice Pres. Inf. & Tech. Svcs.
WILLIAM KELLEY, Dir. of Physical Plant
JAMES A. SERBALIK, Registrar
KATHERINE HARRINGTON, Dir. Career Resources
Legal Title: *Siena College*
Students 3,138
The Friary:
Bro. JOHN P. MAHON, O.F.M., Guardian

Revs.:
Capistran J. Hanlon, O.F.M., Vicar
Callistus M. Bamberg, O.F.M., Dir. Northway Mall Chapel
Bros.:
Romuald Chinetsky, O.F.M.
Gary Maciag, O.F.M.
Michael Harlan, O.F.M.
Revs.:
Matthew T. Conlon, O.F.M.
Julian A. Davies, O.F.M.
William DeBiase, O.F.M.
Daniel P. Dwyer, O.F.M.
Kevin Daly, O.F.M.
Peter A. Fiore, O.F.M.
John C. Frambes, O.F.M.
Berard A. Giblin, O.F.M.
Francis Gunn, O.F.M.
Kevin E. Mackin, O.F.M.
Henry L. Madden, O.F.M.
William E. McConville, O.F.M.
Daniel C. Nelson, O.F.M.
Luke A. O'Connell, O.F.M.
Laurence P. Rainville, O.F.M.
Reginald J. Reddy, O.F.M.
Blaise R. Reinhart, O.F.M.
Sennen C. San Fratello, O.F.M.
Dennis Tamburello, O.F.M.
John E. Van Hook, O.F.M.

New Rochelle
Archdiocese of New York

**College of New Rochelle*
29 Castle Pl.
New Rochelle, NY 10805
Tel: 914-654-5000; Fax: 914-654-5290
Founded in 1904 by the Religious of the Order of St. Ursula. Chartered by the Regents of the University of the State of New York. The College is composed of four schools: School of Arts and Sciences (Women); Graduate School; School of New Resources; School of Nursing (Coed).
Sr. Dorothy Ann Kelly, O.S.U., Pres.
Dr. Stephen Sweeny, Vice Pres. Academic Affairs
Dr. Joan Bailey, Dean, School of Arts and Sciences
Dr. Laura Ellis, Dean, Graduate School
Dr. Connie Vance, Dean, School of Nursing
Dr. Bessie Blake, Dean of School of New Resources
Walter McCarthy, Vice Pres. Financial Affairs
Rev. John Rathschmidt, O.F.M.Cap., Chap.
Sr. Joan Garvey, O.P., Dir., Campus Ministry
Rev. Bernard McMahon, Asst. Chap.
Sr. Patricia McLoughlin, S.C., Dir. Grants
Priests 2
Sisters 14
Lay Teachers 630
Students 7,054

Iona College
715 North Ave.
New Rochelle, NY 10801
Tel: 914-633-2000
(Coed)
Branch Orangeburg Campus
One Dutch Hill Rd.
Orangeburg, NY 10962
Tel: 1-800-231-IONA
Branch Manhattan Campus.
St. Michael High School
425 W. 33rd St.
New York, NY 10001
Education in the tradition of the Christian Brothers. Independent College.
Bro. James A. Liguori, Ed.D., Pres.
Dr. Judson R. Shaver, Vice Pres. for Academic Affairs/Provost
Mr. John Braunstein, Vice Provost for Enrollment Management
Dr. Michael McGrath, Vice Provost for Student Development
Mr. Gregory Puchalski, Vice Pres. for Finance/Admin.
Mr. James Link, Vice Pres. for Advancement
Dr. Gloria Moldow, Dean of the Columbia School
Ms. Joy Collins, Dir. of Libraries
Priests 3
Brothers 21
Sisters 11
Lay Teachers 375
Students 5,182

New York
Archdiocese of New York

College of Mount Saint Vincent
(Coed)
6301 Riverdale Ave.
New York, NY 10471-1093
Tel: 718-405-3200; Fax: 718-549-2603
Founded by the Sisters of Charity of Saint Vincent de Paul. Chartered by the University of the State of New York.
Mary C. Stuart, Ph.D., Pres.
Michael J. McGovern, Ed.D., Vice Pres., Academic Affairs
Theresa D. Whitesall
Brothers 1
Sisters 8
Lay Faculty 57
Total Enrollment 1,521

Marymount Manhattan College
Chartered by the Univ. of the State of NY.
221 E. 71st St.
New York, NY 10021
Tel: 212-517-0400
Dr. Regina S. Peruggi, Pres.
Paula Mayhew, Vice Pres. Academic Affairs
Rosemarie Dackerman, Vice Pres. Student Affairs
Arnold Dimond, Vice Pres. Business & Financial Affairs
Mary Kay Demetry-Jeynes, Dean Courses for Adults
Diana Zwirn, Dir. College Rels. & Inst. Advancement
Sisters 4
Students 1,330

Newburgh
Archdiocese of New York

Mt. St. Mary College Grades(1954)
Newburgh, NY 12550
Tel: 914-561-0800
(Coed)
Sr. Ann Sakac, O.P., Pres.
Sr. Agnes Boyle, O.P., Academic Dean
Gerald Jilbert, Registrar
Rev. James Gilhooley, Chap.
Divisions: Arts & Letters; Education; Business; Nursing; Natural Sciences; Mathematics & Computer Science; Philosophy & Religious Studies; Social Sciences.
Sisters 7
Lay Teachers 46
Students 1,845

Niagara University
Diocese of Buffalo

Niagara University
Lewiston Rd.
Niagara University, NY 14109-2016
Tel: 716-285-1212; Fax: 716-286-8355
Rev. Paul L. Golden, C.M., Pres.
Richard M. Bernard, Ph.D., Executive Vice Pres. for Academic Affairs
David M. Alexander, Interim Vice Pres. for Bus. Affairs
Rev. Francis X. Prior, C.M., Vice Pres. Devel. & Univ. Rels.
Sheila L. Hausrath, M.S.Ed., Vice Pres. for Student Life
Rev. Vincent J. O'Malley, C.M., Special Advisor to the Pres.
Dr. Judith S. Willard, Asst. Pres. for Planning
Dolores A. Bower, R.N., Ph.D., Dean, College of Nursing
Susan E. Mason, Ph.D., Dean, College of Arts & Science
Keith T. Miller, Ph.D., Dean, College of Business Administration
Rev. Daniel F. O'Leary, O.M.I., Dean, College of Education
George C. Pachter, Jr., M.S.Ed., Dean, Enrollment Management
JoAnne E. Wray, M.S., Dean, Division of Lifelong Learning
Mark D. LaRoach, M.S., Asst. to Exec. Vice Pres.
Patricia G. Kinner, M.A., Dir., Academic Support
Leslie Morris, M.L.S., Dir. Library
Sandra H. Olsen, Ph.D., Dir. Castellani Art Museum
Maureen Salfi, M.S.Ed., Dir. Fin. Aid
John B. Stranges, Ph.D., Prof.
James Williams, Ed.D., Chair, Center for Study and Stabilization of Black Families
David J. Boyda, M.S.Ed., Dir., Campus Activities
Mary Beth Coates, M.S., Dir. Campus Min.
Joseph H. Cuda, M.A., Dean Student Affairs
Elizabeth Deletka, R.N., Dir. Health Serv.
Blake H. Dye, M.P.A., Dir. Multicultural Student Affairs
Thomas McDermott, M.S., Dir. Counseling Serv.
Martha E. Troia, M.S., Dir. Career Dev.
Kimberly J. Zukowski, M.S.Ed., Dir. University Housing
Richard S. Hopkins, B.S., Dir. of Development
Sandra Mann Ormsby, B.A., Alumni Dir.
Linus L. Ormsby, M.S.Ed., Dir. Public Relations
Jeannine Brown Miller, M.A., Dir. Human Resources
Revs.:
John C. Bowes, C.M., Assistant Prof. of Rel. Studies
Edward J. Burke, C.M., Emeritus Prof. English
Kevin G. Creagh, C.M., Campus Min.
Patrick S. Flanagan, C.M., Campus Min.
William L. Green, C.M., Dir. SELF
Joseph G. Hubbert, C.M., Asst.Prof. Rel. Studies
John Kettelberger, C.M., Supr. of Vincentian Community
Gregory L. Klein, O.Carm., Asst. Prof. of Rel. Studies
Thomas P. McGourty, C.M., Adjunct Prof. of Rel. Studies
Louis P. Trotta, C.M., Asst. Pres. Alumni Relations
Michael J. Tumulty, C.M., Adjunct Prof. English
Bros.:
Stephen J. Kennedy, C.M., Dir. St. Vincent de Paul
Martin Schneider, C.M., Coordinator Conv.
Augustine D. Towey, C.M., Prof. of English
Priests 15
Lay Brother 3
Lay Faculty 117
Sisters 2
Students 2,935
Total Staff 247
Founded in 1856 by the Congregation of the Mission (Vincentian Community of Priests & Brothers). Niagara University is composed of the College of Arts & Sciences; Business Education; Nursing; The Division of Lifelong Learning; and The Institute of Travel & Hotel- Restaurant Administration
E-mail: jbm@niagara.edu

Ogdensburg
Diocese of Ogdensburg

Mater Dei College
5428 State Hwy. 37
Ogdensburg, NY 13669
Tel: 315-393-5930
Sisters of St. Joseph 3
Lay Teachers 30
Students 508

Orangeburg
Archdiocese of New York

Dominican College of Blauvelt
Orangeburg, NY 10962
Tel: 914-359-7800
Chartered by Univ. of the State of NY.
Sr. Kathleen Sullivan, O.P., Pres.
Dr. Leigh Holt, Dean
Sr. M. Noel Dwyer, O.P., Registrar
Sisters 14
Lay Teachers 51
Students 1,811

Patchogue
Diocese of Rockville Centre

St. Joseph's College
155 W. Roe Blvd.
Patchogue, NY 11772-2399
Tel: 516-447-3200; Fax: 516-654-1782
Sr. Loretta McGrann, C.S.J.
Priests on Faculty:
Revs.:
Angelo Ditta
Thomas Petriano
Frank Pizzarelli, S.M.M.
Sisters 16
Lay Teachers 52
Students 2,398

Poughkeepsie
Archdiocese of New York

Marist College
(Coed)
Poughkeepsie, NY 12601-1328
Tel: 914-575-3000
Dennis J. Murray, Ph.D., Pres.
Rev. Luke W. Cann, Ph.D., Chap.
Brothers 4
Lay Teachers 150
Students 4,300
Marist Foreign Missions
Bro. Paul Ambrose, F.M.S.

Queens and Staten Island
Diocese of Brooklyn

St. John's University (1870)
Main Campus
8000 Utopia Pkwy.
Jamaica, NY 11439

Tel: 718-990-6161; Fax: 718-990-6555
Branch Campus
300 Howard Ave.
Staten Island, NY 10301
Tel: 718-390-4545
Under supervision of the Congregation of the Mission Vincentian Fathers.
Rev. DONALD J. HARRINGTON, C.M., Pres of the Univ.
Dr. ANDREW J. BARTILUCCI, Exec. Vice Pres.
Dr. TONY BONAPARTE, Provost
Revs.:
DAVID M. O'CONNELL, C.M., Assoc. V.P. & Dean of St. John's College of Liberal Arts & Sciences
JOSEPH V. DALY, C.M., Asst. to the Pres.
Hon PHILIP ROACHE, Asst. to Pres.
Mr. HERBERT D. SCHWARTZMAN, Asst. to Pres. and Gen. Counsel
Rev. THOMAS V. CONCAGH, C.M., Vice Pres. for Auxiliary Svcs. and Alumni Rels.
JOHN P. CONNOLLY, Treas.
SUZANNE HALPIN, Exec. Dir. for Public Rels.
EDWARD J. MANETTA, Dir. Athletics
Rev. JAMES O. KIERNAN, C.M., Senior Vice Pres. for Staten Island Campus
Mr. JAMES MASUGA, Vice Pres. Enrollment Mgmt. & Univ. Registrar for In State Advancement
Dr. EDWARD G. SKIRDE, Vice Pres. Devel.
Revs.:
MICHAEL J. CARROLL, C.M., Assoc. Vice Pres. Campus Ministry
PETER J. ALBANO, C.M.
STEPHEN C. BICSKO, C.M.
MICHAEL J. CALLAGHAN, C.M.
MICHAEL J. CUMMINS, C.M.
STEPHEN J. DENIG, C.M.
RICHARD J. DEVINE, C.M.
JAMES F. DORR, C.M.
JOSEPH P. FOLEY, C.M.
JOHN B. FREUND, C.M.
PETER D. GOLDBACH, C.M.
RICHARD J. KEHOE, C.M.
JAMES M. KELLY, C.M.
JAMES J. MAHER, C.M.
JOHN J. MCDONNELL, C.M.
JOHN H. MCKENNA, C.M.
THOMAS F. MCKENNA, C.M.
JOSEPH A. MORRIS, C.M.
JOHN B. MURRAY, C.M.
DAVID M. O'CONNELL, C.M.
JOSEPH M. O'DONNELL, C.M.
ROBERT J. RIVARD, C.M.
FRANCIS W. SACKS, C.M.
KENNETH F. SLATTERY, C.M.
DANIEL J. SULLIVAN, C.M.
BERNARD M. TRACEY, C.M.
ROBERT R. VIGNOLA, C.M.
Priests 20
Brothers 1
Sisters 2
Lay Faculty 593
Students 17,422

Rochester
Diocese of Rochester

St. Bernard's Institute
1100 S. Goodman St.
Rochester, NY 14620
Tel: 716-271-3657
Dr. PATRICIA A. SCHOELLES, S.S.J., Pres.
MARGERY HALPIN, Dir. at Albany
Dr. STEPHEN GRAFF, Coord. Certificate for Designated Ministry & Perm. Diaconate Formation
Dr. CY YOUNG, Dir. of Development
JUDITH ANN KOLLAR, Dir. Continuing Education
Dr. MARVIN MICH, Dean
Ms. MARY ANN LACOUR, Dir. Business Affairs
Dr. DEVADASAN PREMNATH, Registrar
Rev. ROBERT KENNEDY, Coord. of Student Formation
Total Staff 9
Total enrollment 150

Rockville Centre
Diocese of Rockville Centre

Molloy College
1000 Hempstead Ave.
Rockville Centre, NY 11571-5002
Tel: 516-678-5000; 800-229-1020
MARTIN D. SNYDER, Ph.D., Pres.
Sr. PATRICIA MORRIS, O.P., Ph.D., Vice Pres. Academic Affairs (Academic Dean)
Sr. DOROTHY ANNE FITZGIBBONS, O.P., Ed.D., Asst. to Pres. for Planning
Rev. MICHAEL MCCORMACK, Chap.
CATHERINE C. KREIN, M.A., Vice Pres. College Rels.
ANTHONY J. RISO, M.B.A., Vice Pres. Business & Finance
WAYNE F. JAMES, M.S., Dir. Admissions and Freshmen-Transfer Aid
JAMES A. O'REILLY, JR., M.A., Registrar
KATHLEEN F. BONNICI, Dir. Financial Aid
Sr. DORIS NEVITT, O.P., M.A., Dir. Student Financial Svcs.
Rev. JOHN A. MADIGAN, O.P., M.B.A., Chap. for Sisters
Priests 3
Ministers 4
Sisters of St. Dominic (Amityville Community) 45
Lay Teachers 232
Students 2,340

Sparkill
Archdiocese of New York

St. Thomas Aquinas College
Sparkill, NY 10976
Tel: 914-398-4000; Fax: 914-359-8136
Founded by Dominican Sisters of Sparkill in 1952. Senior coed college, chartered by Univ. of the State of New York.
Sr. MARGARET M. FITZPATRICK, S.C., Ed.D., Pres.
Dr. PETER O'CONNOR, Vice Pres. Academic Affairs
Priests 1
Sisters 9
Lay Professors 65
Students 2,100

St. Bonaventure
Diocese of Buffalo

St. Bonaventure University
St. Bonaventure, NY 14778
Tel: 716-375-2000; Fax: 716-375-2055
Franciscan Friars, Province of the Holy Name, Order of Friars Minor.
School of Arts and Sciences, School of Education, Business Admin.; School of Journalism/Mass Communication; Franciscan Studies and the Franciscan Institute; Graduate Studies.
Administration:
ROBERT J. WICKENHEISER, Ph.D., Pres.
EDWARD K. ECKERT, Ph.D., Vice Pres. Academic Affairs
DONALD ZEKAN, Ed.D., Vice Pres. Business & Finance
Rev. ANTHONY M. CARROZZO, O.F.M., D.Min., Vice Pres. for the Franciscan Charism
GEORGE F. SOLAN, M.S., Vice Pres. Student Life
ANTONIO E. PIOTTI, B.A., Vice Pres. Univ. Advancement
MARY E. FREEMAN, B.A., Dir. Public Relations
DAVID L. DILES, Ed.D., Dir. Athletics
Rev. FRANCIS STORMS, O.F.M., M.A., Asst. to Pres.
JAMES P. WHITE, Ph.D., Dean, School of Arts & Sciences
Rev. ANTHONY M. CARROZZO, O.F.M., D.Min., Ph.D., Dean, School of Franciscan Studies; Dir. The Franciscan Institute
JOHN H. BURNS, Ph.D., School of Graduate Studies
JON BOECKENSTEDT, B.A., Dean, Enrollment Mgmt.
ALEX P. NAZEMETZ, M.S., Dir. Admissions
MARY K. PICCIOLI, M.B.A., Dir. Financial Aid
BARBARA RUSSELL, M.S., Registrar
DONALD KORBEN, Ed.D., Dir. Counseling & Career Development
STEPHEN PLESAC, M.S., Dir. Student Activities
JOHN FRAZIER, M.A.E.D., Dir. Residence Life
JOSEPH FLANAGAN, M.S., Dir. Alumni Services
JUNE T. SOLAN, M.S., Dir. Human Resources
MARGARET T. BRYNER, M.S., Dir. Higher Educ. Opportunities Program (HEOP)
JEAN T. EHMAN, M.A., Dir. The Teaching & Learning Center
RAJEEV N. PARIKH, Ph.D., Lifelong Learning
ALICE F. SAYEGH, M.S., Advisor, International Student Advisement
CHARLES SHAFFER, B.S., Exec. Dir. Technology Svcs.
PAUL J. SPAETH, M.L.S., M.A., Dir. Library
CONSTANCE F. WHITCOMB, M.S.Ed., Dir. Career Devel.
Bro. THOMAS J. COLE, O.F.M.,, B.S., Coord. of University Ministries
Rev. JACK ZILBERT, O.F.M., Ph.D., Guardian of the Friary
Priests 22
Brothers 6
Sisters 4
Lay Professors 163
Students 2,723

Staten Island
Archdiocese of New York

St. John's University Staten Island Campus
300 Howard Ave.
Staten Island, NY 10301
Tel: 718-390-4545; Fax: 718-816-4520
Vincentian Community
Very Rev. DONALD J. HARRINGTON, C.M., Pres.
Rev. JAMES F. KIERNAN, C.M., Senior Vice Pres.-Staten Island
Dr. JUDITH DWYER, Assoc. Vice Pres. & Dean Notre Dame College
DONNA NARDUCCI, Asst. Dean & Dir. Programs Colleges of Business
KATHLEEN MACDONALD, Dean St. Vincent's College
Dr. STEPHEN KUNTZ, Asst. Dean, School of Education, Graduate Div.
Mr. JAMES R. GUILBERT, Dean, Office of Student Life

Syracuse
Diocese of Syracuse

Le Moyne College
Syracuse, NY 13214
Rev. ROBERT A. MITCHELL, S.J., Pres.
Dr. WILLIAM BARNETT, Academic Vice Pres.
Dr. MICHAEL W. YOST, Vice Pres. Student Life
Dr. JAMES J. BOYLE, Vice Pres. for Institutional Advancement
Ms. GENEVIEVE R. SAYA, Vice Pres. Campus Svcs. & Asst. to Pres.
Mr. THOMAS E. O'NEIL, Vice Pres. for Finance & Treasurer
Mrs. BARBARA M. MAYLONE, Assoc. Dean Student Life/Dir. Campus Activities
Mr. C. JOSEPH BEHAN, Asst. Dean of Student Life
Rev. EDMUND G. RYAN, S.J., Special Asst. to the Pres. for Mission & Planning & Interim Dir. Campus Ministry
Dr. MARCIA ROWE, Academic Dean
Miss DOROTHY A. NAMISHIA, Registrar
Mr. DENNIS R. DEPERRO, Dean of Enrollment Management

Tarrytown
Archdiocese of New York

Marymount College
Tarrytown, NY 10591
Tel: 914-631-3200
Founded by the Religious of the Sacred Heart of Mary. Women Resident and non-resident.
Sr. BRIGID DRISCOLL, R.S.H.M., Ph.D., Pres.
Sr. MARGARET ELLEN FLANNELLY, R.S.H.M., Ph.D., Vice Pres. Academic Affairs & Dean of Faculty
Sisters 4
Lay Teachers 54
Students 1,101

NORTH CAROLINA

Belmont
Diocese of Charlotte

**Belmont Abbey College*
100 Belmont-Mount Holly Rd.
Belmont, NC 28012-2795
Tel: 704-825-6700; Fax: 704-825-6670
(Coed) Liberal Arts Senior College.
Dr. ROBERT PRESTON, Pres.
Rt. Rev. OSCAR BURNETT, O.S.B., Chancellor
Rev. PLACID SOLARI, O.S.B., Academic Dean
MARGARET SKIDMORE, Registrar
Rev. FREDERICK GEORGE, O.S.B., Dir. Campus Ministry
Dr. MIKE MCLEOD, Vice Pres. Student Affairs
Mr. JAMES SCHUPPENHAUER, Vice Pres. Admin. & Finance
Mr. DENIS M. STOKES, Vice Pres. Enrollment Mgmt.
Bro. LEO FOWLER, O.S.B., Librarian
Priests 2
Lay Teachers 34
Students 902
The Ecumenical Institute of Wake Forest University and Belmont Abbey College
Rev. W. ROBERT SPINKS, Dir.

Sacred Heart College
Belmont, NC 28012
Tel: 704-829-5100; Fax: 704-829-5137
Sisters of Mercy
Sr. M. ROSALIND PICOT, R.S.M., Pres.
College ceased academic operation, effective August 1987. Corporation intact.

NORTH DAKOTA

Bismarck
Diocese of Bismarck

University of Mary
7500 University Dr.
Bismarck, ND 58504-9652
Tel: 701-255-7500
Sr. THOMAS WELDER, O.S.B., Pres.
THOMAS P. JOHNSON, Vice Pres. Academic Affairs
Revs.:

DANIEL MALONEY, O.S.B.
RICHARD WILHELMI, O.S.B.
DENIS FOURNIER, O.S.B.
VICTOR FESER, O.S.B.
VALERIAN ODERMANN, O.S.B., Chap.
Priests 5
Brothers 1
Sisters 15
Lay Teachers 112
Students 2,016

OHIO

Cincinnati
Archdiocese of Cincinnati

College of Mount St. Joseph
5701 Delhi Rd.
Cincinnati, OH 45233-1670
Tel: 513-244-4200
Coed. Chartered by the State of Ohio.
Sr. FRANCIS MARIE THRAILKILL, O.S.U., Pres.
GEORGE BANZIGER, JR., Ph.D., Academic Dean
Rev. ANGELO A. DELLA PICCA (Italy)
Faculty:
Priests 1
Sisters 20
Brothers 1
Lay Teachers 98
Students 2,205

Xavier University
3800 Victory Pkwy. at Dana Ave.
Cincinnati, OH 45207
Tel: 513-745-3000
Revs.:
JAMES E. HOFF, S.J., Pres.
J. LEO KLEIN, S.J., Vice Pres.
MICHAEL GRAHAM, S.J., Vice Pres.
Vice Presidents:
Dr. JAMES E. BUNDSCHUH
Dr. RONALD SLEPITZA
Dr. J. RICHARD HIRTE
Mr. JOHN F. KUCIA
Revs.:
JOSEPH A. BRACKEN, S.J., Rector, Jesuit Community
RICHARD BOLLMAN, S.J., Pastor, Bellarmine Chapel
Mr. DAVID SAUTER, Registrar
VALERIE WITHIAM, Assoc. V.P. for Marketing
Dr. MAX KECK, Dean, College of Arts & Sciences
Rev. THOMAS P. KENNEALY, S.J., Assoc. Dean, College of Arts & Sciences and College of Social Sciences
Dr. DANIEL W. GEEDING, Dean, College of Business Admin.
Dr. PHILLIP JONES, Assoc. Dean, College of Business Administration
Dr. NEIL R. HEIGHBERGER, Dean, College of Social Sciences
Ms. SUSAN G. WIDEMAN, Dean, Center for Adult and Part-Time Students
Dr. DAVID KALSBEEK, Assoc. Vice Pres. Enrollment Svcs.
Enrollment: College of Arts & Sciences:
Students 1,853
College of Business Administration:
Students 625
College of Social Sciences:
Students 1,051
Center for Adult and Part-Time Students:
Students 335
Graduate Programs:
Students 2,559
Permanent Staff:
Priests 21
Brothers 1
Sisters 6
Faculty (full-time):
Priests 9
Lay Teachers 235

Cleveland
Diocese of Cleveland

John Carroll Jesuit Community
John Carroll University
University Heights
Cleveland, OH 44118
Tel: 216-397-1886; Fax: 216-397-4228
Revs.:
PETER J. FENNESSY, S.J., Rector
JOHN A. KNAPEK, S.J., Min.
FREDERICK J. BENDA, S.J.
WILLIAM M. BICHL, S.J.
CASIMIR R. BUKALA, S.J.
EMMANUEL M. CARREIRA, S.J. (Spain)
FRANCIS P. LIHVAR, S.J.
WILLIAM H. NICHOLS, S.J.
JOSEPH P. OWENS, S.J.
DANIEL T. REIM, S.J.
GERALD J. SABO, S.J.
RICHARD P. SALMI, S.J.
JOSEPH O. SCHELL, S.J.
THOMAS L. SCHUBECK, S.J.
JOHN J. SHEA, S.J.
FRANCIS J. SMITH, S.J.
ERNEST G. SPITTLER, S.J.
MICHAEL J. VJECHA, S.J.
MICHAEL L. NUSBAUM
Bro. RAYMOND P. FREISEN, S.J.
Scholastics:
Bros.:
MARK R. BANDSUCH, S.J.
DONALD J. DUNBAR, S.J.
Priests 18
Brothers 2
Scholastics 2

John Carroll University
North Park & Miramar Blvd.
Cleveland, OH 44118
Tel: 216-397-1886
Rev. JOHN J. SHEA, S.J., Pres.
Mr. W. D. BOOKWALTER, Vice Pres. & Asst. to the Pres.
Revs.:
PETER FENNESSY, S.J., Vice Pres. & Dir. Campus Ministry, Religious Affairs
RICHARD P. SALMI, S.J., Vice Pres. Student Affairs
Mr. PAUL KANTZ, Vice Pres. Devel.
Mr. JONATHAN IVEC, Vice Pres. Business
Mr. JOHN T. REALI, Vice Pres. Services
Dr. DAVID M. LAGUARDIA, Asst. Academic Vice Pres.
Dr. FREDERICK F. TRAVIS, Provost and Academic Vice Pres.
Dr. FRANK J. NAVRATIL, Dean, School of Business
Dr. NICK BAUMGARTNER, Dean, College of Arts & Sciences
Dr. SALLY WERTHEIM, Dean of Graduate School
Dr. JOSEPH B. MILLER, Assoc. Dean, College of Arts & Sciences
Rev. WILLIAM M. BICHL, S.J., Asst. Dean, College of Arts & Sciences
Mrs. MARTHA A. MACKIE, Asst. Dean, College of Arts & Sciences
Dr. JAMES DALEY, Assoc. Dean, School of Business
Priests 13
Sisters 2
Lay Faculty 214
Students 4,326

Notre Dame College of Ohio
(Women)
4545 College Rd.
South Euclid, OH 44121
Tel: 216-381-1680; Fax: 216-381-3802
ANNE L. DEMING, Ph.D., Pres.
Sr. MARGARET GORMAN, S.N.D., Interim Vice Pres. for Academic Affairs, Dean of Faculty
CAROL PROBSTFELD, Vice Pres. Finance
Priests 1
Sisters of Notre Dame 10
Lay Teachers 27
Total Staff 102
Students 644

Ursuline College
2550 Lander Rd.
Pepper Pike, OH 44124
Tel: 216-449-4200; Fax: 216-646-8102
LAURENCE W. MAZZENO, Ph.D., Interim Pres. and Vice Pres. Acad. Affairs
VALERIE A. HUGHES, Vice Pres. Fin. & Admin.
SANDRA M. ESTANEK, Vice Pres. Student Services
Sr. ANNA MARGARET GILBRIDE, O.S.U., Ph.D., Asst. to the Pres.
Sr. DIANA STANO, O.S.U., Ph.D., Dean of Graduate Studies
Ursuline Nuns of Cleveland 21
Lay Professors 50
Students 1,220

Columbus
Diocese of Columbus

Ohio Dominican College
1216 Sunbury Rd.
Columbus, OH 43219
Tel: 614-253-2741; Fax: 614-252-0776
Dominican Sisters of the Third Order of St. Dominic
Sr. MARY ANDREW MATESICH, O.P., Pres.
ANDREW KEOGH, Vice Pres. Academic Affairs
JAMES SAGONA, Vice Pres. Admissions & Student Svcs.
MICHAEL D. BROMBERG, Vice Pres. Business Affairs
LYNDA HUEY, Vice Pres. College Advancement
JAMES GROVE, Dir. Campus Ministry & Lecturer in Theology Studies
E-mail: admission @ odc. edu
Sisters 16
Lay Teachers 99
Students 1,883

Dayton
Archdiocese of Cincinnati

The University of Dayton (1850)
(Coed)
300 College Park Ave.
Dayton, OH 45469-1624
Tel: 937-229-1000
Bro. RAYMOND L. FITZ, S.M., Pres.
Rev. JAMES L. HEFT, S.M., Chancellor & Prof. of Faith
Dr. JOHN O. GEIGER, Acting Provost
Dr. PATRICK F. PALERMO, Assoc. Provost Undergraduate Education
Mr. CHRISTOPHER MUNOZ, Assoc. Provost, Enrollment Mgmt.
Bro. BERNARD J. PLOEGER, S.M., Senior Vice Pres.-Admin.
Mr. THOMAS E. BURKHARDT, Vice Pres. for Financial Affairs & Treas.
Mr. THEODORE L. KISSELL, Dir. of Athletics
Dr. WILLIAM C. SCHUERMAN, Vice Pres. Student Devel. & Dean of Students
Rev. EUGENE CONTADINO, S.M., Rector
Mrs. MARY A. NEACY, Exec. Asst. to the Pres.
Mr. RICHARD T. FERGUSON, Asst. to the Pres. for Regional & Government Relations
Mr. HERMAN A. COLE, Dir. Facilities Mgmt.
Mr. DANIEL F. PALMERT, Registrar
Mr. MYRON H. ACHBACH, Dir. Admissions
Mrs. JOYCE J. WILKINS, Dir. Financial Aid
Revs.:
NORBERT C. BURNS, S.M.
GERALD T. CHINCHAR, S.M.
MATTHEW F. KOHMESCHER, S.M.
WILLIAM P. FROST
JOSEPH F. KOZAR, S.M.
ROBERT J. HATER
JAMES L. HEFT, S.M.
PAUL F. VIESON, S.M.
THEODORE A. KOEHLER, S.M.
JOSEPH H. LACKNER, S.M.
THOMAS A. SCHROER, S.M.
JOHN S. PUTKA, S.M.
BERTRAND A. BUBY, S.M.
CHRISTOPHER W. CONLON, S.M., Dir., Campus Ministry
JOHN A. MCGRATH, S.M.
JOHANN G. ROTEN, S.M.
THOMAS A. SCHOEN, S.M.
THOMAS A. THOMPSON, S.M., Dir. and Curator, Marian Library
JOSEPH D. MASSUCCI
Sr. NANCY H. BRAMLAGE, S.C.
Sr. LAURA M. LEMING, F.M.I., (On Leave)
Sr. KATHLEEN A. ROSSMAN, O.S.F.
Sr. JUDITH G. MARTIN, S.S.J.
Sr. JODY O'NEIL, S.P.
Sr. PAMELA L. THIMMES, O.S.F.
Sr. FRANCES M. TRAMPIETS, S.C.
Sr. ANGELA ANN ZUKOWSKI, M.H.S.H.
Sr. M. JEAN FRISK
Sr. MONICA M. GUNDLER, S.C.
Sr. MARY LOUISE FOLEY, F.M.I.
Sr. EILEEN J. CEHYRA, F.M.I.
Sr. JUDITH KEEHNEN, C.S.J.
Sr. LEANNE M. JABLONSKI, F.M.I.
Sr. ELLEN M. MURPHY, O.P.
Society of Mary (Marianists)
College of Arts and Sciences
Dr. PAUL J. MORMAN, Dean
Dr. R. GERALD KEIL, Assoc. Dean Graduate & Admin. Affairs
Dr. MARY JO VESPER, Assoc. Dean Undergraduate & Student Affairs
Mr. SAM F. JOHNSON, Asst. Dean
Mrs. RAE ELLEN HUFF, Asst. Dean.
Professors 227
Students 3,188
Graduate Studies and Research
Dr. GORDON A. SARGENT, Vice Pres. Graduate Studies & Research and Dean Graduate School
Dr. JOSEPH E. ROWE, Assoc. Vice Pres. for Research & Dir. Research Institute (UDRI)
Dr. KITAYUN E. MARRE, Assoc. Dean of the Grad. School
Ms. CAROL M. SHAW, Dir. Center for Competitive Change
Students 2,989
School of Business Administration
Dr. SAM GOULD, Dean
Dr. JOHN E. RAPP, Assoc. Dean
Dr. E. JAMES DUNNE, Assoc. Dean & Dir., MBA Prog.
Professors 51
Students 1,045
School of Education
Dr. PATRICIA F. FIRST, Dean
Dr. JOSEPH F. ROGUS, Assoc. Dean for Graduate Studies

Dr. DONALD J. FRERICKS, Asst. Dean for Catholic Education
Dr. JAMES R. BIDDLE, Assoc. Dean for Undergraduate Studies
Professors 40
Students 767
School of Engineering
Dr. JOSEPH LESTINGI, Dean
Mr. NORMAN S. PHILLIPS, Assoc. Dean for Undergraduate Engineering Programs
Dr. DONALD L. MOON, Assoc. Dean for Graduate Engineering Programs & Research
Professors 69
Students 1,262
School of Law
FRANCIS J. CONTE, Dean
Mr. RICHARD P. PERNA, Assoc. Dean for Academic Affairs
Mr. CHARLES ROBOSKI, Asst. Dean and Dir. of Admissions and Financial Aid
Mr. TIMOTHY P. STONECASH, Asst. Dean of Law School Development
Professors 21
Students 475
Libraries and Information Technologies
Dr. EDWARD D. GARTEN, Dean of Libraries and Information Technology
Total Enrollment 9,908
Faculty 408
The Marian Library / International Marian Research Institute (IMRI)
Revs.:
JOHANN G. ROTEN, S.M., S.T.D., Dir.
THOMAS A. THOMPSON, S.M., Dir. & Curator
THEODORE A. KOEHLER, S.M., S.T.D., Dir. Emeritus
University of Dayton
Dayton, OH 45469-1390
Tel: 937-229-4214

North Canton
Diocese of Youngstown

Walsh University
(Coed)
2020 Easton St., N.W.
North Canton, OH 44720-3396
Tel: 330-499-7090
Brothers of Christian Instruction
Revs.:
RICHARD J. MUCOWSKI, O.F.M., Ed.D., Ph.D., (Holy Name Province)
DONALD A. MILLER, O.F.M., Ph.D., (St. John the Baptist Province)
MICHAEL J. PUTICH, O.F.M., (Holy Name Province)
Sr. CAROL HEBERT, S.S.J., Campus Min.
Mr. DALE HOWARD, Vice Pres. for Student Affairs
Dr. RICK NIECE, Ph.D., Exec. Vice Pres.
Dr. JAMES C. FOSTER, Ph.D., Interim Pres. for Academic Affairs & Dean
Mr. JAMES ABBUHL, Vice Pres. of Enrollment Mgmt.
Mr. NORMAN KUTZ, Asst. to the Pres.
Mr. JOHN JONES, Vice Pres. for Finance & Business Affairs
Brothers 9
Sisters 1
Lay Teachers 151
Total Staff 190
Students 1,447

Saint Martin
Archdiocese of Cincinnati

Chatfield College
Brown County Ursulines, 20918 State Rte. 251
Saint Martin, OH 45118
Tel: 937-875-3344; Fax: 937-875-3912
Sr. ELLEN DOYLE, O.S.U., Pres.
Students 300

Steubenville
Diocese of Steubenville

Franciscan University of Steubenville
University Blvd.
Steubenville, OH 43952
Tel: 614-283-3771
Rev. MICHAEL SCANLAN, T.O.R., Pres.
Mr. DAVID SKIVIAT, Vice Pres. Finance & Admin.
Dr. MICHAEL J. HEALY, Dean of Faculty
Mr. NICHOLAS HEALY, JR., Vice Pres. Univ. Rels.
Mr. JOHN MADIGAN, Vice Pres. Alumni & Community Rels.
Mr. RANDALL CIRNER, Dean of Students
Ms. SHARON KILZER, Sec. of the Univ.
Revs.:
JAMES ANGERT, T.O.R., (Austria) Asst. Prof. & Campus Min.
BRIAN CAVANAUGH, T.O.R., Student Svcs.
ROBERT CONLIN, T.O.R., Chap.
RICHARD DAVIS, T.O.R., Alumni Rels.
JOSE DEL TORO, T.O.R., Admissions Counselor
GILES DIMOCK, O.P., Assoc. Prof.
AUGUSTINE DONEGAN, T.O.R., (Austria) Campus Ministry
CONRAD HARKINS, O.F.M., Assoc. Prof.
ROBERT HILZ, T.O.R.
STAN HOLLAND, T.O.R., Dir. of Works of Mercy
ANTHONY MASTROENI (Austria) (PAT) Assoc. Prof.
RONALD MOHNICKEY, T.O.R., Religious Admin.
AIDAN MULLANEY, T.O.R., Dir. Franciscan Heritage Office
DANIEL PATTEE, T.O.R, Lecturer
DAVID PIVONKA, T.O.R., Campus Ministry & Lecturer
DANIEL SINISI, T.O.R., Assoc. Prof.
EDMUND J. SYLVIA (BGP) Counseling
DAVE TESTA (ALB) Campus Min.
LAURENCE UHLMAN, T.O.R., Chap.
Bro. JOHN MARK KLAUS, T.O.R., Campus Min.
Priests 5
Lay Teachers 84
Students 1,936

Sylvania
Diocese of Toledo

Lourdes College
6832 Convent Blvd.
Sylvania, OH 43560
Tel: 419-885-3211
Sisters of St. Francis of the Congregation of Our Lady of Lourdes, (O.S.F.).
Sr. M. ANN FRANCIS KLIMKOWSKI, O.S.F., Pres.
Sr. M. CABRINI WARPEHA, O.S.F., Vice Pres. Academic Affairs
Sr. NANCY ANN SURMA, O.S.F., Vice Pres. Admin. Svcs.
ROBERT TUREK, Vice Pres. Student Svcs.
G. PATRICK WILLIAMS, Vice Pres. Inst. Advancement
SUE BUCHER, Registrar
Full-time faculty 67
Lay instructors 58
Enrollment 1,670

OKLAHOMA

Shawnee
Archdiocese of Oklahoma City

St. Gregory's College
(Coed)
Shawnee, OK 74801
Tel: 405-878-5100; Fax: 405-878-5198
Liberal Arts and Sciences.
Benedictine Monks
Mr. FRANK PFAFF, Ph.D., Pres.
Priests 6
Brothers 3
Sisters 2
Lay Teachers 18
Students 335

OREGON

Marylhurst
Archdiocese of Portland in Oregon

Marylhurst College
Marylhurst, OR 97036
Tel: 503-636-8141
Dr. NANCY WILGENBUSCH, Pres.
DENIS LAWRENCE, Vice Pres. Academic Affairs & Contact Person
Sisters 8
Lay Teachers 219
Students 2,800

Portland
Archdiocese of Portland in Oregon

**University of Portland*
5000 N. Willamette Blvd.
Portland, OR 97203
Tel: 503-283-7911
Endowed by the Congregation of Holy Cross; established 1901.
Exec. Officers of the Univ.:
Rev. DAVID T. TYSON, C.S.C., Pres.
Dr. ARTHUR A. SCHULTE, JR., Special Asst. to the Pres.
Bro. DONALD J. STABROWSKI, C.S.C., Academic Vice Pres.
Mr. ANTHONY J. DISPIGNO, Vice Pres. Univ. Rels.
Dr. GUY D. SIEVERT, Vice Pres. Student Svcs.
Dr. ROY HEYNDERICKX, Financial V.P.
Faculty Staff:
Revs.:
RICHARD F. BERG, C.S.C.
GEORGE C. BERNARD, C.S.C.
JAMES CONNELLY, C.S.C.
JOHN CHAPLIN, C.S.C.
MICHAEL M. DELANEY, C.S.C.
BARRY J. HAGAN, C.S.C.
THOMAS HOSINSKI, C.S.C.
WILLIAM HUND, C.S.C.
JOHN KURTZKE, C.S.C.
DENNIS O'HARE, C.S.C.
CLAUDE POMERLEAU, C.S.C.
RICHARD RUTHERFORD, C.S.C.
JEFFREY SCHNEIBEL, C.S.C.
CHARLES D. SHERRER, C.S.C.
JEFFREY SOBOSAN, C.S.C.
PHILIP SOPKE, C.S.C.
ARTHUR F. WHEELER, C.S.C.
In res.,
Revs.:
FREDERICK BARR, C.S.C.
THOMAS BILL, C.S.C.
HARRY BRIDE, C.S.C.
CHARLES CORSO, C.S.C.
Bros.:
KEN ALLEN, C.S.C.
FLUGENCE DOUGHERTY, C.S.C.
FREDERICK WILLIAMS, C.S.C.
Revs.:
PAUL FRYBERGER, C.S.C.
W. PATRICK HANNON, C.S.C.
JAMES KING, C.S.C.
JAMES CONNELLY, C.S.C., Religious Supr.
EDWIN OBERMILLER, C.S.C.
ADRIEN STE. MARIE, C.S.C.
CHESTER PRUSYNSKI, C.S.C.
ARTHUR SCHOENFELDT, C.S.C.
STEPHEN SEDLOCK, C.S.C.
Priests 35
Brothers 4
Sisters 5
Lay Teachers 126
Adjunct Faculty 104
Students 2,375
Following is the Academic Structure of the University:
College of Arts and Sciences—
Dr. MARLENE MOORE, Dean
School of Nursing—
Dr. SUSAN MOSCATO, Interim Dean
School of Business Administration—
Dr. RONALD HILL, Dean
School of Engineering—
Dr. ZIA J. YAMAYEE, Dean
School of Education—
Sr. MARIA CIRIELLO, O.P., Dean
Graduate School—
Dr. KARL J. WETZEL, Dean

PENNSYLVANIA

Aston
Archdiocese of Philadelphia

Neumann College
One Neumann Dr.
Aston, PA 19014-1298
Tel: 610-459-0905
Opened September 1965.
Conducted by the Sisters of St. Francis of Philadelphia
Dr. ROSALIE M. MIRENDA, Ph.D., Pres.
Rev. JUDE MICHAEL KRILL, O.S.F.Conv., Chap.
Priests 1
Sisters 21
Administrators 33
Faculty and Staff 51
Adjuncts 89
Lay Teachers 44
Students 1,150

Center Valley
Diocese of Allentown

Allentown College of St. Francis de Sales
2755 Station Ave.
Center Valley, PA 18034-9568
Tel: 610-282-1100
Coeducational liberal arts college conducted by the Oblates of St. Francis de Sales (1965); Accredited.
Very Rev. DANIEL G. GAMBET, O.S.F.S., Ph.D., Pres.
Revs.:
ALEXANDER T. POCETTO, O.S.F.S., Ph.D., Senior Vice Pres.
BERNARD F. O'CONNOR, O.S.F.S., Ph.D., Academic Dean
JOHN HANLEY, O.S.F.S., Dir. Campus Ministry
JOHN F. MCGINLEY, O.S.F.S., M.A., Vice Pres. for Continuing Education
Mrs. MARGARET KENDER, M.A., Vice Pres. Student Svcs.
Mr. GEORGE KELLY, Vice Pres. Enrollment Mgmt.
Mrs. JAN HOLLY, Registrar
Mr. WILLARD CRESSMAN, Treasurer

Mr. DENNIS CAMPBELL, Vice Pres. Development
Mr. MICHAEL THOMPSON, Vice Pres. Admin.
Dr. KAREN DOYLE WALTON, Vice Pres. Academic Affairs
Revs.:
JOHN F. HARVEY, O.S.F.S., S.T.D.
JAMES P. FINNEGAN, O.S.F.S., Ph.D.
GERARD H. SCHUBERT, O.S.F.S., Ph.D.
BERNARD F. DONAHUE, O.S.F.S., Ph.D.
PETER LEONARD, O.S.F.S., M.A.
A. ROBERT MCGILVARY, O.S.F.S., Ph.D.
THOMAS DAILEY, O.S.F.S., S.T.L.
JACOB WELLE, M.S.C., M.A.
ROBERT RUTLEDGE, O.S.F.S.
Priests on Faculty 14
Lay Teachers 99
Students 1,670

Cresson
Diocese of Altoona-Johnstown

Mount Aloysius College
7373 Admiral Peary Hwy.
Cresson, PA 16630
Tel: 814-886-4131
Sisters of Mercy
Dr. EDWARD F. PIERCE, Pres.
Ms. SYLVIA HIRSCH, Dean Enrollment Mgmt.
Dr. PAUL KESSLER, Vice Pres. Academic Affairs
Ms. BEIRNE B. COFIELD, Dean Inst. Advancement
Rev. GEORGE J. VALKO, M.A., M.Div., Chap.
Priests 1
Sisters 4
Lay Faculty 57
Students 4,950

Dallas
Diocese of Scranton

College Misericordia
Dallas, PA 18612
Tel: 717-674-6400
Religious Sisters of Mercy of the Union in the U.S.A.
Administration:
ALBERT B. ANDERSON, Ph.D., Pres.
Mr. JOHN RISBOSKIN, Dean of Financial & Admin. Affairs
Rev. MICHAEL M. BRYANT, M.Th., Chap.
Sr. MARY GLENNON, R.S.M., Ed.D., Academic Dean
Mr. FRANK OLIVER, Dean, Institutional Advancement
Sr. JEAN MESSAROS, R.S.M., Dean of Students
Mrs. JANE DESSOYE, M.S., Exec. Dir., Admissions & Financial Aid
Mr. EDWARD LAHART, Registrar
Mr. MICHAEL JOSEPH, B.A., Dean, Enrollment Mgmt.
JENNIFER A. MCCARTHY, Dir., Career Svcs.
Ms. GERALDINE WALL, M.S., Dir., Counseling
Mr. JOSEPH MACK, M.B.A., Dir., Mgmt. Information Svcs.
Sr. MARY SHARON GALLAGHER, R.S.M., M.S.L.S., Dir., Library Svcs.
Ms. KATHLEEN A. FOLEY, B.S., M.S., Asst. Dean of Students
Mr. RONALD HROMISIN, C.P.A., Comptroller
Mr. JOSEPH J. HAYER, M.B.A., Business Mgr.
Mr. MARK LIPPI, Project Mgr.
Mrs. GAIL SMALLWOOD, Dir. of Public Communications
Priests 1
Sisters Teaching 18
Students 1,779

Erie
Diocese of Erie

Gannon University
University Square
Erie, PA 16541
Tel: 814-871-7000
Rev. Msgr. DAVID A. RUBINO, Ph.D., Pres.
Rev. Msgr. ADDISON YEHL, M.S.
Very Rev. CHARLES H. DREXLER, S.T.D.,V.F.
Revs.:
JOHN P. SCHANZ, Censor Librorum
PAUL J. DESANTE, Ph.D.
SCOTT P. DETISCH
GILIO L. DIPRE, Ph.D.
ROBERT G. FIN, Ph.D., (Retired)
JOSEPH C. GREGOREK
EDWARD C. KRAUSE, C.S.C., Ph.D.
ROBERT J. LEVIS, Ph.D.
JAMES MCCULLOUGH, M.S.
GERALD L. ORBANEK, M.A.
DAVID L. POULSON, Ph.D.
NICHOLAS J. ROUCH
JOHN P. SCHANZ, Ph.D.
ROBERT P. SUSA, M.A.
CASIMIR J. WOZNIAK
MICHAEL KISICKI
CHRISTOPHER HAMLETT
RONALD GMEREK
Priests 21
Sisters 8
Lay Teachers 161
Students 3,327

Mercyhurst College
501 E. 38th St. Blvd.
Erie, PA 16546
Tel: 814-824-2000
Dr. WILLIAM P. GARVEY, Pres.
Dr. JOSEPH GOWER, Dean
Rev. STEPHEN A. ANDERSON, Chap.
Priests 1
Sisters 2
Lay Teachers 103
Students 2,700

Greensburg
Diocese of Greensburg

Seton Hill College
Greensburg, PA 15601
Tel: 412-834-2200; Fax: 412-830-4611
Sisters of Charity of Seton Hill
Dr. JOANNE W. BOYLE, Pres.
MARY ANN GAWELEK, Ed.D., Vice Pres. Academic Affairs & Dean of College
Rev. JOSEPH P. MADDALENA, Chap.
Sisters 4
Lay Teachers 41
Students 902

Gwynedd Valley
Archdiocese of Philadelphia

Gwynedd-Mercy College
Gwynedd Valley, PA 19437
Tel: 215-646-7300; Fax: 215-641-5509
Rev. JOSEPH B. SMITS, C.I.C.M., Chap.
Sisters of Mercy 29
Lay Teachers 161
Students 1,979

Immaculata
Archdiocese of Philadelphia

Immaculata College
Immaculata, PA 19345
Tel: 610-647-4400
Sisters, Servants of the Immaculate Heart of Mary
Sr. MARIE ROSEANNE BONFINI, I.H.M., Pres.
Sr. GEORGINE MARIE, I.H.M., Registrar
Sr. KATHLEEN MCKEE, Vice Pres. for Academic Affairs
Rev. HANS A.L. BROUWERS, Chap.
Priests 2
Sisters 61
Lay Teachers 119
Day Students 2,391

Jenkintown
Metropolitan Archdiocese of Philadelphia Ukrainian

Manor Junior College
700 Fox Chase Rd.
Jenkintown, PA 19046
Tel: 215-885-2360; Fax: 215-576-6564
Approved by the Commonwealth of Pennsylvania and accredited by the Middle States Association of Colleges and Secondary Schools.
Sisters of St. Basil the Great
Sr. M. CECILIA JURASINSKI, O.S.B.M., Pres.
SALLY MYDLOWEC, Academic Dean
OLGA UDVARI, Contact Person

Latrobe
Diocese of Greensburg

St. Vincent College
300 Fraser Purchase Rd.
Latrobe, PA 15650-2690
Tel: 412-539-9761
Legal Title: *Saint Vincent College Corporation*
Rt. Rev. DOUGLAS R. NOWICKI, O.S.B., Chancellor
Rev. MARTIN R. BARTEL, O.S.B., Pres.
Bro. NORMAN W. HIPPS, O.S.B., Provost
Priests 18
Brothers 6
Lay Teachers 55
Students 1,215

Loretto
Diocese of Altoona-Johnstown

St. Francis College
P.O. Box 600
Loretto, PA 15940-0600
Tel: 814-472-3000
Rev. CHRISTIAN R. ORAVEC, T.O.R., Pres.
Dr. RICHARD CRAWFORD, Asst. to the Pres.
Dr. KATHLEEN OWENS, Vice Pres. Academic Affairs
Rev. CARL SZURA, T.O.R., Dir. Campus Ministry
Mr. F. DENNIS RIEGELNEGG, Vice Pres. Student Devel.
Mr. RICHARD GAJEWSKI, Vice Pres. Finance
Rev. THOMAS BOURQUE, T.O.R., Dir. Continuing Education
Mr. RAYMOND PONCHIONE, Dir. Devel.
Dr. MICHAEL MCKALE, Dir. Pastoral Ministry Center
Mr. RANDY FRYE, Dir. M.B.A. Prog.
Dr. WILLIAM DURYEA, Dir. M.M.S. Prog.
Ms. GLENDA GRIFFITH, Dir. Residence Life
Ms. PATRICIA SEROTKIN, Dir. Library
Mr. MICHAEL SARAKA, Dir. Career Devel.
Rev. JOSEPH A. CHANCLER, T.O.R., Dir. Computer Svcs.
Dr. PHILIP BENHAM, Dir. Graduate School Human Resource Mgmt./Industrial Rels.
Mr. DOMINICK PERUSO, Dir. Student Activities
Ms. DENISE KOVACH, Dir. Learning Resource Center
Mr. FRANK PERGOLIZZI, Dir. Athletics
Mr. MICHAEL PRICE, Dir. Student Financial Aid
Ms. KATHLEEN GILMOUR, Dir. Public Rels.
Mr. DAVID WILSON, Dir. Counseling
Revs.:
BEDE F. HINES, T.O.R.
THOMAS CARAPELLA, T.O.R.
JAMES MORMAN, T.O.R.
EMIL C. RESCONICH, T.O.R., (Retired)
OLIVER J. HEBERT, T.O.R.
THOMAS BOURQUE, T.O.R.
CARL SZURA, T.O.R.
MICHAEL HIGGINS, T.O.R.
JOSEPH CHANCLER, T.O.R.
Priests 1
Sisters 1
Lay Professors 76
Students 1,853

Philadelphia
Archdiocese of Philadelphia

Chestnut Hill College
Philadelphia, PA 19118
Tel: 215-248-7000; Fax: 215-248-7155
Sr. CAROL JEAN VALE, Ph.D., Pres.
Rev. EUGENE R. KOLE, O.F.M.Conv., D. Min., Dean of Graduate Division
Sisters 23
Lay Teachers 36
Students 1,340

Holy Family College (1954)
Grant and Frankford Aves.
Philadelphia, PA 19114
Tel: 215-637-7700; Fax: 215-637-3787
E-mail:fonley@hslc.org
Congregation of the Sisters of the Holy Family of Nazareth
Sr. FRANCESCA ONLEY, C.S.F.N., Pres.
Rev. ALBERT J. SMITH, O.S.F.S., Chap. & Campus Minister
In res.,
Rev. JAMES J. COLLINS, S.O.E.D., Dept. of Religious Studies
Priests 7
Sisters 28
Lay Faculty 241
Undergraduate Students 2,161
Graduate 466

LaSalle University
1900 W. Olney Ave.
Philadelphia, PA 19141
Tel: 215-951-1000; Fax: 215-951-1783
(Incorporated under the auspices of the Brothers of the Christian Schools)
Bros.:
JOSEPH F. BURKE, F.S.C., Ph.D., Pres.
DANIEL C. PANTALEO, Ph.D., Provost
RAYMOND P. HEATH, Ph.D., Vice Pres. Student Affairs
DAVID C. FLEMING, M.B.A., Vice Pres. Business Affairs
FRED J. FOLEY, JR., Ph.D., Vice Pres. Devel.
RAYMOND A. RICCI, Ed.M., Vice Pres. Enrollment Svcs.
BARBARA C. MILLARD, Ph.D., Dean of the School of Arts and Sciences
JOSEPH A. KANE, Ph.D., Dean of the School of Business Admin.
MARYANNE R. BEDNAR, Ph.D., Interim Dean, School of Continuing Studies
Bros.:
CHRISTOPHER LYDON, Dir., Admissions
CHARLES ECHELMEIER, F.S.C., Dir. Campus Ministry
GLORIA A. DONNELLY, Ph.D., Dean, School of Nursing
Brothers 24

Priests 5
Sisters 1
Lay Teachers 194
Students 5,376

St. Joseph's University
5600 City Ave.
Philadelphia, PA 19131
Tel: 610-660-1000; Fax: 610-660-1201
Jesuit Fathers
Tel: 610-660-1400
Under the direction of the Jesuit Fathers. Incorporated January 29, 1852.
Revs.:
NICHOLAS J. RASHFORD, S.J., Pres.
JAMES W. MOORE, S.J., Assoc. Dean College of Arts and Sciences
JOSEPH A. ARROYO, S.J., (Spain) Assoc. Dean, College of Business and Admin.
JOHN E. BENNETT, S.J., Campus Min.
ANTHONY J. BERRET, S.J.
H. CORNELL BRADLEY, S.J.
FRANCIS F. BURCH, S.J.
JOSEPH F. CHORPENNING, O.S.F.S.
DONALD G. CLIFFORD, S.J.
JEROME B. COLL, S.J.
MARK J. CONNELLY, S.J.
CHARLES L. CURRIE, S.J.
JOSEPH J. FEENEY, S.J.
GERALD F. FINNEGAN, S.J.
VINCENT J. GENOVESI, S.J.
JOSEPH J. GODFREY, S.J.
HOWARD J. HEIM, S.J.
FREDERICK A. HOMANN, S.J.
MICHAEL A. HRICKO, S.J.
ALBERT H. JENEMANN, S.J.
JOSEPH M. KAKALEC, S.J.
JOSEPH L. LOMBARDI, S.J.
MICHAEL A. MCELNEE, S.J.
DENNIS E. MCNALLY, S.J.
SCOTT R. PILARZ, S.J.
MARTIN R. TRIPOLE, S.J.
Bro. JOHN J. MCLANE S.J.
Sr. ANN BERNADETTE, G.N.S.H.
Sr. NORMANDIE GAITLEY, S.S.J.
Sr. FRANCES HART, S.S.J.
Sr. FRANCIS JOSEPH, R.A.
Sr. ELIZABETH ANN LINEHAN, R.S.M.
Sr. ANNE MCCOY, S.S.J.
Priests 26
Sisters 4
Lay Teachers 360
Students 6,502

Pittsburgh
Diocese of Pittsburgh

Carlow College
3333 5th Ave.
Pittsburgh, PA 15213
Tel: 412-578-6000
Sisters of Mercy
Sr. GRACE ANN GEIBEL, R.S.M., Ph.D., Pres.
MARIE IMMACULEE DANA, R.S.M., Ph.D., Vice Pres. for Academic Affairs
Sisters 8
Lay Teachers 221
Students 2,339

Duquesne University of the Holy Ghost
600 Forbes Ave.
Pittsburgh, PA 15282
Tel: 412-396-6000; Fax: 412-396-5785
Dr. JOHN E. MURRAY, JR., Pres.
Holy Ghost Fathers
Revs.:
CHARLES J. FENNER, C.S.Sp., Univ. Sec.
DAVID T. COTTINGHAM, C.S.Sp.
WILLIAM CROWLEY, C.S.Sp.
REGINALD DEFOUR, C.S.Sp.
EDWARD A. BUSHINSKI, C.S.Sp.
JOSEPH A. DUCHENE, C.S.Sp.
WILLIAM R. HEADLEY, C.S.Sp.
J. CLIFTON HILL, C.S.Sp.
SEAN M. HOGAN, C.S.Sp., Exec. Vice Pres. Student Life
SEAN KEALY, C.S.Sp.
DONALD MCEACHIN, C.S.Sp.
RAYMOND FRENCH, C.S.Sp.
EDWARD L. MURRAY, C.S.Sp.
JOSEPH PUDICHERY
DAVID L. SMITH, C.S.Sp.
WILLIAM SMITH, C.S.Sp.
EDMUND R. SUPPLE, C.S.Sp.
RICHARD F. WERSING, C.S.Sp.
ADRIAN VAN KAAM, C.S.Sp.
DAVID F. KELLY
MICHAEL SLUSSER
THOMAS SCHAEFER, C.S.Sp.
JOCELYN GREGORIE, C.S.Sp.
MICHAEL GREY, C.S.Sp.
FRANCIS MALINOWSKI, C.S.Sp.
GERALD WALSH, C.S.Sp.
Priests 26
Sisters 6
Lay Teachers 350
Students 9,285
The University is coeducational and comprises the following Colleges and Schools and Institutes:
College of Library Arts—
Dr. CONSTANCE RAMIREZ, Dean, College & Graduate School of Liberal Arts
School of Business Administration—
Mr. THOMAS J. MURRIN, Dean
School of Music—
D. MICHAEL KUMER, Dean
School of Law—
NICHOLAS CAFARDI, Dean
Division of Continuing Education—
Dr. BENJAMIN HODES, Dean
School of Education—
Dr. JAMES E. HENDERSON, Interim Dean
School of Nursing—
Dr. MARY DE CHESNAY, Dean
School of Pharmacy—
Dr. DOUGLAS H. KAY, Dean
School of Health Sciences—
Dr. JEROME L. MARTIN, Dean
Dr. HEINZ MACHATZKE, Dean, School of Natural & Environmental Sciences
Dr. MICHAEL P. WEBER, Provost and Academic Vice Pres.
Mr. ISADORE R. LENGLET, Executive Vice Pres. Mgmt. and Business
Dr. PAUL J. PUGLIESE, Librarian
Dr. FRANK YINING LIU, Law Librarian

La Roche College
9000 Babcock Blvd.
Pittsburgh, PA 15237
Tel: 412-367-9300
Sisters of Divine Providence
Rev. Msgr. WILLIAM A. KERR, Ph.D., Pres.
Sr. CAROLYN WINSCHEL, C.D.P., Ph.D., Exec. Vice Pres.
Rev. W. PETER HORTON, M.A., M.Div., Campus Minister
PATRICIA D. O'DONOGHUE, Ph.D., Vice Pres. Academic Affairs & Academic Dean
ROGER CAROTHERS, Vice Pres. Business Affairs
ARTHUR SHUKER, Vice Pres. Finance
Rev. PATRICK O'BRIEN, S.T.D., M.S.Ed., Div. Chair Humanities
Priests 3
Sisters 10
Lay Teachers 145
Students 1,641

Radnor
Archdiocese of Philadelphia

Cabrini College (1957)
610 King of Prussia Rd.
Radnor, PA 19087
Tel: 610-902-8100
Missionary Sisters of the Sacred Heart
Dr. ANTOINETTE IADAROLA, Pres.
Campus Ministers:
JOHN DIMUCCI
ARLENE SMITH
Lay Teachers 150
Students 2,119

Reading
Diocese of Allentown

Alvernia College
Reading, PA 19607
Tel: 610-796-8200; Fax: 610-796-8324
Bernardine Sisters of the Third Order of St. Francis
Deacon DANIEL N. DELUCCA, Pres.
Priests 1
Sisters 4
Lay Teachers 57
Students 1,313

Rosemont
Archdiocese of Philadelphia

Rosemont College of the Holy Child Jesus
Rosemont, PA 19010-1699
Tel: 610-526-2984; Fax: 610-527-0341
E-mail:jtrogers@rosemont.edu
MARGARET M. HEALY, Pres.
Sr. KATHY RONEY, S.H.C.J., Campus Minister
Sisters of the Holy Child Jesus 5
Full Time Lay Teachers 39
Part Time Lay Teachers 59
Students 1,180

Scranton
Diocese of Scranton

Marywood College
Scranton, PA 18509
Tel: 717-348-6211
Sisters, Servants of the Immaculate Heart of Mary
Sr. MARY REAP, I.H.M., Ph.D., Pres.
Sr. PATRICIA ANN MATTHEWS, I.H.M., Ph.D., Vice Pres., Academic Affairs
Sr. M. MARTIN DE PORRES MCHALE, I.H.M., M.B.A., Vice. Pres., Business Affairs
Dr. CLAYTON N. PHEASANT, Vice Pres., College Advancement
Dr. RAYMOND P. HEATH, Vice Pres., Student Affairs
Dr. JANET R. REOHR, Dean, Undergraduate School
Dr. JAMES L. GEARITY, Dean, Graduate School of Arts & Sciences
Dr. TERRY L. SINGER, Dean, School of Social Work
Dr. EDNA FARACE WILSON, Dean, School of Continuing Education
Sr. DOLORES FILICKO, I.H.M., M.B.A., Registrar
MARY ANNE FEDRICK, M.S.L.S., M.A., Asst. Vice Pres., Academic Affairs
Dr. BARBARA R. SADOWSKI, Dir., Planning & Institutional Research
Faculty:
Sisters 21
Lay Teachers 117
Students 2,926

University of Scranton
(Society of Jesus)
18510
Tel: 717-941-7533
Rev. JOSEPH A. PANUSKA, S.J., Pres.
Dr. RICHARD H. PASSON, Provost & Academic Vice Pres.
Rev. ROYDEN B. DAVIS, S.J., Rector of the Jesuit Community
Mr. DAVID E. CHRISTIANSEN, Vice Pres., Finance & Treas.
Mr. ROBERT J. SYLVESTER, Vice Pres., Devel. & Pub. Rels.
Revs.:
BERNARD R. MCILHENNY, S.J., Dean of Admissions
THOMAS D. MASTERSON, S.J., Vice Pres., Univ. Ministries
Dr. PAUL F. FAHEY, Dean of the College of Arts and Sciences
Dr. JOSEPH J. HORTON, Dean of the School of Mgmt.
Dr. SHIRLEY M. ADAMS, Dean of the Dexter Hanley College
Dr. THOMAS P. HOGAN, Dean of the Graduate School
Mr. LAIPENG REHFIELD, Registrar
Dr. JAMES J. PALLANTE, Dean, College of Health, Education & Human Resources
Dr. SUSAN WILLIAMS-QUINLAN, Dir., Counseling Center
Dr. JAMES T. BRYAN, Vice Pres., Student Affairs
Dr. LAWRENCE J. MORTON, Asst. to Vice Pres., Student Affairs
Mr. MARTIN L. LANGAN, Assoc. Vice Pres., Admin. Svcs.
Mr. CHARLES E. KRATZ, Dir., Library
Mr. GLENN PELLINO, Vice Pres., Planning
Miss MARILYN COAR, Exec. Asst. to the Pres.
Revs.:
JOSEPH D. AYD, S.J.
JOHN J. BEGLEY, S.J.
PAUL R. BEINING, S.J.
BRUCE M. BIDINGER, S.J.
THOMAS F. CLIFFORD, S.J.
JAMES J. CONLIN, S.J.
HENRY G. COSTER, S.J.
JOHN H. DUGGAN, S.J.
JOSEPH M. HAMERNICK, S.J.
WILLIAM B. HILL, S.J.
FRANCIS J. KOWNACKI, S.J.
BRENDAN G. LALLY, S.J.
JOHN W. LANGE, S.J.
JOHN J. LEVKO, S.J.
KENNETH G. LOFTUS, S.J.
FRANCIS J. MACENTEE, S.J.
LEONARD A. MARTIN, S.J.
RICHARD S. MCCOUCH, S.J.
WILLIAM J. MCGRATH, S.J.
RONALD H. MCKINNEY, S.J.
NEIL P. MCLAUGHLIN, S.J.
J. PATRICK MOHR, S.J.
OLIVER J. MORGAN, S.J.
EUGENE A. NOLAN, S.J.
FRANK MCG. NUGENT, S.J.
G. DONALD PANTLE, S.J.
EDWARD R. POWERS, S.J.
JOHN J. QUINN, S.J.
JOSEPH L. QUINN, S.J.
RICHARD W. ROUSSEAU, S.J.
THOMAS F. SABLE, S.J.
GEORGE J. SCHEMEL, S.J.
THOMAS R. SLON, S.J.

ROBERT F. YOUNG, S.J.
FREDERICK P. ZAGONE, S.J.
Bro. JAMES C. LEMON, S.J.
Priests 36
Students 4,931
Center for Eastern Christian Studies
University of Scranton
Scranton, PA 18510
Tel: 717-941-6116
Revs.:
JOHN J. LEVKO, S.J., Dir.
THOMAS F. SABLE, S.J., Editor Diakonia
Sr. JOAN L. ROCCASALVO, C.S.J., Coord. & Mng. Editor

Villanova
Archdiocese of Philadelphia

Villanova University
Villanova, PA 19085
Tel: 610-519-4500; Fax: 610-519-4514
Founded 1842 by the Augustinians, Province of St. Thomas of Villanova. Colleges of Liberal Arts and Sciences, Engineering, Commerce and Finance, Nursing, University College (part time), Graduate Studies and the School of Law.
E-mail:fmcguire@email.vill.edu
Board of Trustees:
Revs.:
EDMUND J. DOBBIN, O.S.A., Pres.
GEORGE F. BURNELL, O.S.A.
THOMAS M. CASEY, O.S.A.
JOHN E. DEEGAN, O.S.A.
JOHN M. DRISCOLL, O.S.A.
KEVIN F. DWYER, O.S.A.
DONALD F. REILLY, O.S.A.
JOSEPH F. WIMMER, O.S.A.
EDSON J. WOOD, O.S.A.
Mr. LAWRENCE E. BATHGATE, II
JAMES R. BIRLE
ROBERT M. BIRMINGHAM
DAVID R. COOK
NANCE K. DICCIANI, Ph.D.
JAMES A. DROBILE
ROSA M. GATTI
JOHN G. GILFILLAN, III, ESQ.
ARTHUR J. HALLERAN, JR.
HARRY R. HALLORAN, JR.
HAZEL W. JOHNSON-BROWN, Ph.D.
JOHN H. KOLMER, JR.
ANDREW J. MARKEY, JR.
MAUREEN H. MCCULLOUGH, Esq.
JOSEPH M. MCNAMARA
MICHAEL P. MONACO
ANTHONY T. RANDAZZO
EMILY C. RILEY
Dr. MARIELLEN WHELAN
Administration:
Dr. JOHN R. JOHANNES, Vice Pres. Academic Affairs
Dr. HELEN K. LAFFERTY, Univ. Vice Pres.
Mr. GARY B. FENNER, Vice Pres., Financial Affairs
Rev. PATRICK J. RICE, O.S.A., Vice Pres. Admin.
Mr. JOHN M. ELIZANDRO, Vice Pres. Institutional Advancement
Dr. RICHARD A. NEVILLE, Vice Pres. Student Life
Rev. GEORGE F. RILEY, O.S.A., Special Asst. to Pres./Alumni & External Affairs
STEVEN P. FRANKINO, J.D., Dean of the School of Law
Rev. KAIL C. ELLIS, O.S.A., Dean of Liberal Arts and Sciences
Dr. M. LOUISE FITZPATRICK, Dean of Nursing
Dr. ROBERT LYNCH, Dean of Engineering
Rev. WILLIAM A. MCGUIRE, O.S.A., Dean of Enrollment Management
Dr. THOMAS F. MONAHAN, Dean of Commerce of Finance
Rev. JOHN P. STACK, O.S.A., Dean of Students
Dr. DANIEL J. ZIEGLER, Dean, Graduate School of Liberal Arts & Sciences
Dr. EDWARD L. COLLYMORE, Dir.. Multicultural Affairs
Revs.:
EDWARD T. HASTINGS, O.S.A., Exec. Dir., Campus Ministry
T. SHAWN TRACY, O.S.A., Campus Ministry
KEVIN J. KEELEN, O.S.A., Campus Ministry
JOHN P. BETONI, O.S.A., Asst. Registrar
JOHN F. MCATEE, O.S.A.
Revs.:
FRANCIS A. FARSACI, O.S.A., Residence Life
DENNIS J. GALLAGHER, O.S.A., Archivist
THOMAS J. MAHONY, O.S.A., Facilities Mgmt.
FRANCIS CHAMBERS, O.S.A., Office of Undergraduate Admission
Clerical Faculty:
Revs.:
DONALD X. BURT, O.S.A.
JAN BUSCH, O.S.A.
ARTHUR B. CHAPPELL, O.S.A.
PETER M. DONOHUE, O.S.A.
DANIEL E. DOYLE, O.S.A.
FRANCIS A. EIGO, O.S.A.
EDWARD J. ENRIGHT, O.S.A.
JOHN J. FARRELL, O.S.A.
ALLAN D. FITZGERALD, O.S.A.
JOHN J. HAGEN, O.S.A.
OWEN R. JACKSON, O.S.A.
CHARLES P. LAFERTY, O.S.A.
BERNARD A. LAZOR, O.S.A.
JOSEPH LOYA, O.S.A.
LEE J. MAKOWSKI, O.S.A.
THOMAS MARTIN, O.S.A.
JAMES J. MCCARTNEY, O.S.A.
NEIL MCGETTIGAN, O.S.A.
JOHN J. MCKENZIE, O.S.A.
ROBERT J. MURRAY, O.S.A.
MICHAEL J. SCANLON, O.S.A.
RALPH C. SHURER, O.S.A.
DENNIS G. WILDE, O.S.A.
Bros.:
RICHARD CANNULI, O.S.A.
JOHN STAGLIANO, O.S.A.
Full-Time Enrollment 6,271
Part-Time Enrollment 449
Total Enrollment 10,156
Priests 42
Brothers 2
Sisters 2
Lay Teachers 486
Students 10,156

Wilkes-Barre
Diocese of Scranton

**Kings College*
Wilkes-Barre, PA 18711
Tel: 717-826-5900
Officers of the College:
Rev. JAMES R. LACKENMIER, C.S.C., Pres.
Dr. DONALD W. FARMER, Vice Pres., Academic Affairs
Mr. STEVEN H. SEITCHIK, Vice Pres., Business Affairs & Treas.
Rev. EUGENE F. GORSKI, C.S.C., Vice Pres., Student Affairs
Mr. TERRENCE F. MECH, Vice Pres., Information & Instructional Technologies & Dir., Corgan Library
Mr. FRANK J. PASQUINI, Vice Pres., Development
Rev. JAMES J. DOHERTY, C.S.C., College Chap. & Dir., Campus Ministry
Dr. EDWARD J. SCHOEN, Dean of the William J. McGowan School of Business
Dr. WILLIAM A. SHERGALIS, Dean of the College of Arts and Sciences
Revs.:
THOMAS F. CARTEN, C.S.C., Assoc. Campus Min.
JOHN R. GERACCI, C.S.C., Assoc. Campus Min.
Mr. DANIEL P. CONRY, Dean of Admissions
Dr. JEAN P. ANDERSON, Registrar
Rev. JOSEPH A. SIDERA, C.S.C., Religious Supr.
Religious Faculty:
Revs.:
ANTHONY R. GRASSO, C.S.C.
DONALD J. GRIMES, C.S.C.
JAMES E. KELLY, C.S.C.
CHARLES J. KOCIOLEK, C.S.C.
THOMAS J. O'HARA, C.S.C.
THOMAS P. LOONEY, C.S.C.
WILLIAM R. RIBANDO, C.S.C.
JOHN J. RYAN, C.S.C.
RONALD J. WASOWSKI, C.S.C.
In res.,
Revs.:
JAMES J. DOYLE, C.S.C.
JOSEPH J. LONG, C.S.C.
CLEMENT J. PODSKOCH, C.S.C.
Bros.:
JAMES H. MILLER, C.S.C.
HAROLD J. ROGAN, C.S.C.
THOMAS SAWYER, C.S.C.
HERMAN F. ZACCARELLI, C.S.C.
Sr. CATHERINE M. HENNESSY, M.S.C.
Priests 17
Brothers 4
Sisters 2
Lay Teachers 97
Students 2,263

PUERTO RICO

Ponce
Diocese of Ponce, Puerto Rico

The Pontifical Catholic University of Puerto Rico
2250 Avenida de las Americas
Ponce, PR 00731-6382
Tel: 787-841-2000
The University is composed of the following: College of Arts and Humanities and Graduate Studies in Hispanic Studies; College of Business Administration and Graduate Studies; College of Education and Graduate Studies; College of Science and Graduate Studies; School of Law; Institute of Social Doctrine of the Church; Program for Special Services; Post-Baccalaureate Achievement Program; Upward Bound Program.
Administration:
Most Revs.:
FREMIOT TORRES OLIVER, D.D., Chancellor
RICARDO A. SURINACH, Vice Chancellor
Rev. Msgr. LORENZO M. ALBACETE-CINTRON, C.S.Sp., Pres.
Mrs. MARCELINA V. DE SANTIAGO, Vice Pres. Academic Affairs
IRMA RODRIGUEZ, Prof. & Assoc. Vice Pres. Academic Affairs
JULIO COLON, Vice Pres. Financial Affairs
CARL B. SAUDER, Prof. & Vice Pres. Student Affairs
Mrs. LISANIA MORALES DE AULET, Special Asst. to the Vice Pres. Student Affairs
Dr. ENID MIRANDA, Dean, College of Arts and Humanities
JAIME SANTIAGO CANET, College of Business Admin.
Dr. LILLIAN NEGRON, Dean, College of Education
Mr. JULIO RIVERA, Dean, College of Science
JOSE I. IRIZARRY YORDAN, ESQ., Dean, School of Law
INES CARRAU, Assoc. Dean, School of Law
Mr. IVAN E. DAVILA, Registrar
Mrs. CARIDAD C. DE FRAU, Dir., Admissions
Mrs. ANA O. BONILLA DE SANCHEZ, Dir., Freshmen Prog.
Mrs. GLADYS M. VIDAL, Dir., Guidance Ctr.
Mrs. ESTHER IRIZARRY, Dir. Libraries
NOELIA PADUA, ESQ., Dir. Law Library
Faculty:
Rev. Msgr. JOAQUIN A. ALICEA
Rev. Msgr. HERMINIO DE JESUS
Rev. Msgr. ROBERTO GARCIA
Rev. Msgr. JESUS R. DIAZ, 57
Revs.:
TOSELLO GIANGIACOMO, C.S.Sp.
FELIX LAZARO, Sch.P.
JOSE LUIS LARREATEGUI, Sch.P.
PERFECTO ALVAREZ, O.S.A.
JOSE M. HERRERO
ABEL A. DI MARCO
BRIAN W. HARRISON, O.S.
MOISES NAVASCUES, Sch.P.
ADALIN RIVERA
ALVARO HUERGA, O.P.
ESTEBAN SANTAELLA
ALFREDO ALVAREZ LACRUZ
ROMEO SALCIDO, M.J.
Ponce:
Revs.:
ALEXIO JOSE DE ARMAS, O.C.D.
SEGISMUNDO CINTRON
CARMELO DE JESUS, O.C.D.
JUAN J. INIGO, C.M.
JUAN RODRIGUEZ
VICENTE SALAS, O.M.
JOSE L. ALONSO, O.P.
MIGUEL ALVAREZ, Sch.P.
CARLOS R. ROMAN TORO
FRANCISCO SIRVENT
Arecibo:
Rev. SERAPIO FERNANDEZ, O.F.M.
CARLOS E. GRANADOS
CESAR E. SANTOS
ANTONIO J. VAZQUEZ
Guayama:
EMILIANO ALAMO
FELIX E. ALVARADO
Mayaguez:
JOSE FRANCISCO BAEZ
Revs.:
ANTONIO A. HERNANDEZ, C.SS.R.
JUAN LAMELA, C.M.
JOSE R. LINARES
EDGARDO LOPEZ
LUIS ALBERTO RODRIGUEZ
DELROY E. THOMAS
LUIS F. FAJARDO
Priests 18
Sisters 4
School of Law 34
Lay Teachers 398
Students 11,462

RHODE ISLAND

Newport
Diocese of Providence

Salve Regina University
Newport, RI 02840-4192
Tel: 401-847-6650; Fax: 401-847-0372
Legal Title: *Salve Regina University*
Sisters of Mercy of the Americas
Dr. M. THERESE ANTONE, R.S.M., Pres.
Dr. JUDITH MILLS, Vice Pres. for Academic Affairs
DOMINIC C. VARISCO, Exec. Vice Pres.
WILLIAM B. HALL, Vice Pres. for Business and Financial Affairs
THOMAS P. FLANAGAN, Vice Pres. for Admin./Services and Community Relations

John J. Rok, Vice Pres. for Student Life
Laura E. McPhie, Dean of Enrollment Svcs.
Frederick C. Promades, Dir. Institutional Research
Lucile Flanagan, Dir. Financial Aid
Michael Semenza, Vice Pres. Institutional Advancement
Kathleen Willis, Registrar/Asst. Academic Dean
David Kim, Dean of Library Sciences
John Quinn, Dean of Students
Thomas H. Brennan, Dir. of Information Systems
Revs.:
Donald L. Paradis, M.S.
Eugene L. Hillman, C.S.Sp.
Michael T. Malone, C.S.Sp.
Priests 3
Brothers 6
Sisters 19
Lay Teachers 91
Students-Men 786
Women 1,277

Providence
Diocese of Providence

Providence College
River Ave. & Eaton St.
Providence, RI 02918
Tel: 401-865-1000; Fax: 401-865-2057
Legal Title: *Providence College*
Conducted by the Dominican Friars.
Revs.:
Philip A. Smith, O.P.
Terence J. Keegan, O.P., Exec. Vice Pres.
Thomas L. Canavan, O.P., Vice Pres. Academic Admin.
Mr. Michael V. Frazier, Vice Pres. Finance & Business
Rev. J. Stuart McPhail, O.P., Vice Pres. Student Svcs.
Mr. Joseph P. Brum, Vice Pres. Alumni/Devel.
Mr. Edward J. Caron, Vice Pres. College Relations
Rev. Robert E. Bond, O.P., Dean Undergraduate Studies
Judith K. Jamieson, Dean School of Continuing Education
Revs.:
Robert J. Hennessey, O.P., Dir. Academics for Graduate Religious Studies Prog.
James A. Driscoll, O.P., Dir. Promotions and Publicity of the Grad. School of Relg. & Biblical Studies
Richard J. Barranger, O.P., Chap.
Mr. Edgar C. Bailey, Jr., Dir. Library
Dominican Priests Teaching 39
Diocesan Priests Teaching 4
Sisters Teaching 6
Lay Professors 260
Enrollment-Day School:
Men 1,520
Women 2,069
Graduate School:
Men 361
Women 666
Evening Division:
Men 406
Women 599

SOUTH DAKOTA

Aberdeen
Diocese of Sioux Falls

Presentation College
Aberdeen, SD 57401
Tel: 605-225-1634; Fax: 605-229-8430
Sisters of the Presentation of the B.V.M.
Dr. Lorraine M. Hale, Pres.
Rev. Joseph Sheehan, O.Carm., Chap.
Priests 1
Sisters 6
Lay Teachers 26
Students 384

Yankton
Diocese of Sioux Falls

Mount Marty College
1105 W. 8th St.
Yankton, SD 57078
Fax: 605-668-1357
Benedictine Sisters
Dr. Mark Hurtubise, Pres.
Rev. Denis Quinkert, O.S.B., Chap.
Priests 1
Sisters 15
Lay Teachers 42
Students 1,142

TENNESSEE

Memphis
Diocese of Memphis

**Christian Brothers University* (1871)
(Coed)
650 E. Parkway S.
Memphis, TN 38104
Tel: 901-321-3000
Legal Title: *Christian Brothers Univ. of Memphis, Tenn.*
Bro. Michael J. McGinniss, Pres.
Four-Year university with Schools of Business, Engineering, Liberal Arts, and Science-Mathematics. Graduate programs in Business and Engineering.
Dr. Mark Smith, Vice Pres. Academic Affairs
Mr. J. Christopher Mathis, Vice Pres. Admin. Affairs
Mr. Nick Scully, Vice Pres. Institutional Advance
Bro. Frank Osage, F.S.C., Vice Pres. Student Affairs
Mrs. Debra Czestochowski, Dir. University Rels.
Ms. Betty McWillie, Dir. Career Devel. & Placement
Bro. John Edward Doody, F.S.C., Dir. Grants & Proposals
Rev. Francis Dixon, Dir. Campus Ministry
Mr. Thomas Faulkner, Business Office Mgr.
Sr. Sue Russell, R.S.M., Campus Minister
Brothers 21
Sisters 2
Lay Teachers 130
Students 1,784

Nashville
Diocese of Nashville

Aquinas College
4210 Harding Rd.
Nashville, TN 37205
Tel: 615-297-7545
Dominican Sisters of St. Cecilia Congregation
Mother Christine Born, O.P., Chm.
Sr. Evelyn Potts, O.P., Pres.
Sr. Mary Dominic Pitts, Academic Dean
Sisters 10
Lay Teachers 37
Students 415

TEXAS

Austin
Diocese of Austin

Brothers of the Congregation of the Holy Cross (1881)
St. Edward's University, 3001 S. Congress Ave.
Austin, TX 78704
Tel: 512-448-8400
Faculty and Officers:
Dr. Patricia A. Hayes, Pres.
Sr. Donna Jurick, S.N.D., Vice Pres. Academic Affairs
Dr. Sandra Pacheco, Dean Student Devel.
John Lucas, Vice Pres. Enrollment & Student Svcs.
David A. Dickson, Jr., Vice Pres. Financial Affairs
Faculty:
Dominican Priests 1
Holy Cross Brothers 15
Sisters 2
Lay Professors 205
Students 3,110

Houston
Diocese of Galveston—Houston

University of St. Thomas
3800 Montrose Blvd.
Houston, TX 77006-4696
Tel: 713-522-7911
E-mail:basil.stthom.edu
Founded in 1947, Graduate Division (Four Schools). Undergraduate Division (21 Departments). Center for Thomistic Studies. Center for International Studies.
Dr. Joseph M. McFadden, Pres.
Dr. Lee Williames, Vice Pres., Academic Affairs
Rev. William J. Young, C.S.B., Pres. Emeritus, Dir., Community Svcs. of the Univ.
Rodney Crowl, Institutional Advancement
Deacon Richard Glor, Registrar
Mrs. Elsie Biron, Dir., Admission
Mr. James Piccininni, Dir., Doherty Library
Rev. Louis Brusatti, C.M., Dean, School of Theology
Dr. Yhi Min Ho, Dean, Cameron School of Business
Dr. Anna Dewald, Dean, School of Education
Dr. Jerome Kramer, Assoc. Vice Pres., Academic Affairs
Dr. John Freed, Dean, Special Programs
Rev. Thomas A. Russman, O.F.M.Cap., Dir., Center for Thomistic Studies (Graduate Philosophy)
Dr. Ronald Hatchett, Dir., Center for International Studies
Dr. Eugene Connors, Dir., Human Resources
Ms. Linda Ballard, Dir., Financial Aid
Mr. Jack Hank, Dean, Student Svcs.
Dr. Deborah Baker, Dir., Counseling Center
Rev. Mark Gazin, C.S.B., Coord., Campus Ministry
Mr. James Rodriguez, Dir., Alumni Rels.
Ms. Marionette Mitchell, Dir. of Publications
Rev. Edward A. Bader, C.S.B., Curator, University Art Collection
Teachers:
Dr. Khalil Yazdi, Asst. Vice Pres. Academic Affairs & Dir. of Institutional Research
Priests 22
Sisters 6
Lay Professors 176
Total Staff 120
Students 2,504

Irving
Diocese of Dallas

University of Dallas
President's Office, 1845 E. Northgate
Irving, TX 75062
Tel: 214-721-5000; Fax: 214-721-5017
Administrative Officers:
Most Rev. Charles V. Grahmann, D.D., Grand Chancellor
Rev. Msgr. Milam Joseph, Pres.
Mr. George Herbst, Vice Pres. Admin.
Dr. Glen E. Thurow, Provost & Dean
Dr. Paula Hughes, Acting Dean
Mrs. Sybil Novinski, Assoc. Provost
Mr. Donald Miller, Dean of Students
Rev. Thomas Cloherty, Chap.
Diocesan Priests:
Rev. Enrique Nardoni, S.S.D.
Cistercian Priests:
Revs.:
David Balas, O.Cist.
Placid Csizmazia, O.Cist.
James Lehrberger, O.Cist.
Robert Maguire, O.Cist.
Moses Nagy, O.Cist.
Lay Teachers 189
Students 2,747

San Antonio
Archdiocese of San Antonio

Oblate School of Theology (1903)
(Coed) (Graduate Theology)
285 Oblate Dr.
San Antonio, TX 78216-6693
Tel: 210-341-1366; Fax: 210-341-4519
Conducted by the Missionary Oblates of Mary Immaculate
Revs.:
J. William Morell, O.M.I., M.Div., Pres.
Rufus J. Whitley, O.M.I., J.D., Interim Vice Pres.
Mrs. Christiane B. Scheel, Dir. Admissions, Registrar
Mr. Hector Rodriguez, Dir. Finance
Mrs. Peggy Piper, Admin. Asst. Pres.
Faculty:
Revs.:
Warren Brown, O.M.I., L.C.L., M.C.L.
Kevin Collins, O.M.I., M.Div., Dir. Oblate Renewal Center
Kenneth G. Davis, O.F.M.Conv., D.Min., Dir. D.Min. Prog.
Vaughn J. Fayle, O.M.I., Ph.D. (Canada) Dir. Phil. Program
Mark A. Garrett, O.S.A., Ph.D. (Canada)
Ken Hannon, O.M.I., Ph.D.
Jan Heemrood, O.M.I., S.S.L.
Robert E. Lambert, Ph.D. (STL)
Jose A. Lopez, Ph.D. (Canada)
John M. Makothakat, Ph.D., J.C.D., S.T.D.
Francis Kelly Nemeck, O.M.I., S.S.D.
Thomas Ovalle, O.M.I., M.Div., Dir. Oblate Renewal Center
Leopoldo Perez, O.M.I., S.T.D., Co-Dir. M.Div.
Frederick Sackett, O.M.I., J.C.D.
Stephen K. Sherwood, C.M.F., S.T.D.
James K. Sullivan, M.A. (SPC) Dir. Ministry to Ministers Prog.
Robert E. Wright, O.M.I., Ph.D.
Ronald W. Young, O.M.I., S.T.L.
Margaret Escobedo, M.T.S., Dir. Lay Ministry
Priests 16
Sisters 2
Lay Professors 11
Students 239

Our Lady of the Lake University
411 S.W. 24th
San Antonio, TX 78207-4689
Tel: 210-434-6711; Fax: 210-436-0824
Sponsored by Sisters of Divine Providence
Sr. ELIZABETH ANNE SUELTENFUSS, C.D.P., Ph.D., Pres.
Dr. ROBERT E. GIBBONS, Ph.D., Exec. Vice Pres.
Dr. HOWARD BENOIST, Ph.D., Vice Pres. & Dean Academic Affairs
ALLEN R. KLAUS, B.B.A., C.P.A., Vice Pres. Finance and Facilities
Dr. ANTONIO R. RIGUAL, Ph.D., Vice Pres. Inst. Advancement
MARY ELLEN SMITH, M.S., Vice Pres. & Dean of Student Life
FRED C. SCOTT, B.A.A.S., Inst. Research Officer
Dr. SANTOS H. HERNANDEZ, Ph.D., Dean, Worden School of Social Svcs.
Sr. ISABEL BALL, C.D.P., Ph.D., Dean, College of Arts & Sciences
Dr. W. EARL WALKER, J.D., Interim Dean, School of Business & Public Admin.
Dr. JACQUELYN ALEXANDER, Ph.D., Dean, School of Education & Clinical Studies
Ms. LORETTA SCHLEGEL, M.Ed., Dean, Enrollment Mgmt.
Campus Ministry Team:
Rev. JOHN W. LUBBERS, C.S.C., M.A.
WAYNE ROMO, M.T.S.
Sisters 20
Full-time Faculty 164
Lay Teachers 144
Students 3,468

St. Mary's University of San Antonio, Texas (1852) (Coed)
One Camino Santa Maria
San Antonio, TX 78228-8572
Tel: 210-436-3011
Conducted by the Society of Mary
Rev. JOHN J. MODER, S.M., Pres.
Dr. CHARLES COTRELL, Academic Vice Pres.
Ms. RUTH RODGERS, Vice Pres. Student Devel.
Mr. DANIEL J. WHITE, Vice Pres. Admin. & Finance
Rev. CHARLES MILLER, S.M., Dean, School of Humanities and Social Sciences
Dr. DAVID MANUEL, Dean, School of Business
Dr. ANTHONY J. KAUFMANN, Dean, School of Science, Engrg. and Technology
Dr. RONALD MERRELL, Dean, Graduate School
BARBARA BADER ALDAVE, Dean, School of Law
LOUISA AVITUA-TREVINO, Registrar
Mr. RICHARD CASTILLO, Dir. Admissions
Dr. H. PALMER HALL, Dir. Academic Library
Mr. ROBERT L. SUMMERS, JR., Dir. Law Library
Revs.:
MIGUEL BRISENO, O.F.M.Conv., Dir. Campus Ministry
CHARLES NEUMANN, S.M.
JOHN RECHTEIN, S.M.
W. FRANZ SCHORP, S.M.
CONRAD KACZKOWSKI, S.M.
JOHN MODER, S.M.
CHARLES MILLER, S.M.
JOHN A. LEIES, S.M.
J. WILLIS LANGLINAIS, S.M.
NORBERT C. BROCKMAN, S.M.
GEORGE MONTAGUE, S.M.
WILLIAM ELLOS, S.J.
ROBERT HOGAN, S.M.
Priests 12
Brothers 20
Sisters 6
Lay Teachers 149
Students 4,212

The United Colleges of San Antonio
(A Consortium of Catholic Colleges in San Antonio)
285 Oblate Dr.
San Antonio, TX 78216
Revs.:
WILLIAM MORELL, O.M.I.
JOHN MODER, S.M.
Dr. LOUIS AGNESE, JR., Ph.D.
Sr. ELIZABETH ANNE SUELTEN FUSS, C.D.P.
San Antonio, TX 78212
Tel: 210-341-1366

University of the Incarnate Word
4301 Broadway
San Antonio, TX 78209
Tel: 210-829-6000
Dr. LOUIS J. AGNESE, JR., Ph.D., Pres.
Sr. MARGARET PATRICE SLATTERY, C.C.V.I., Ph.D., Chancellor
Dr. EDUARDO PADERON, Ph.D., Vice Pres. Academic Affairs
DOUGLAS B. ENDSLEY, M.B.A, Vice Pres. Business & Finance
THOMAS PLOFCHAN, M.A., Vice Pres. Inst. Advancement
FRANK AYALA, Ph.D., Vice Pres. Student Affairs
DAVID JURENOVICH, Ph.D., Vice Pres. Mktg. and Planning
GILBERT HINOJOSA, Ph.D., Dean of Arts and Sciences
REGINALD TRAYLOR, Ph.D., Dean of Graduate Studies
WILLARD PLATZER, Ph.D., Dean of Professional Studies
RENEE MOORE, Acting Dean of Student Life
BRIAN DALTON, Dean of Student Enrollment
Sr. MARGARET SNYDER, C.C.V.I., Dir. Campus Ministry
Rev. GREGORY NEVLUD, Chap.
Sr. EILISH RYAN, Ph.D., Dir. Pastoral Institute
NOEL MCCOY, Registrar
Priests 1
Sisters of the Incarnate Word 19
Lay Faculty 278
Students 3,287

VERMONT

Burlington
Diocese of Burlington

Trinity College of Vermont
President's Office, 208 Colchester Ave.
Burlington, VT 05401
Tel: 802-658-0337
Dr. LORNA DUPHINEY EDMUNDSON, Ed.D., Pres.
Sisters 2
Lay Teachers 42
Students 913

Colchester
Diocese of Burlington

St. Michael's College
Winooski Park
Colchester, VT 05439
Tel: 802-654-2211; Fax: 802-655-4079
Dr. MARC A. VANDERHEYDEN, Pres.
Mr. WILLIAM H. CHADWICK, Chm. of the Board
Ms. MARILYN CORMIER, Asst. to Pres.
Dr. JOHN J. MCDONALD, Vice Pres., Academic Affairs
Mr. STEVEN KARCHER, Assoc. Vice Pres. Budget
Mr. MICHAEL D. SAMARA, Vice Pres. for Student Affairs
Mr. JOHN T. GUTMAN, Vice Pres. for Admin.
Ms. ANNE M. BERRY, Vice Pres. Inst. Advancement
Mr. RICHARD V. DIVENERE, Assoc. Vice Pres. Alumni Relations & Devel.
Dr. JOHN P. KENNEY, Dean of the College
Mr. JERRY E. FLANAGAN, Assoc. Vice Pres. for Admissions & Enrollment Mgmt.
Mr. JOHN D. SHEEHEY, Registrar
Dr. BONNIE TANGALOS, Dean of the School for Intl. Studies
Dr. SUSAN W. KUNTZ, Dean of the Prevel School
Dr. EDWARD MAHONEY, Chm. Graduate Theology & Pastoral Ministry Prog.
Rev. MICHAEL P. CRONOGUE, S.S.E., Dir. Edmundite Campus Ministry
Ms. DIANE FOSTER, Edmundite Campus Min. (Religious Education)
Ms. ANN GIOMBETTI, Dir. of Volunteer Programs
Priests 4
Lay Teachers 117
Students 2,642

Rutland
Diocese of Burlington

College of St. Joseph in Vermont
71 Clement Rd.
Rutland, VT 05701-3899
Tel: 802-773-5900
Dr. FRANK G. MIGLORIE, JR., Pres.
Lay Teachers 13
Students 474

VIRGINIA

Arlington
Diocese of Arlington

Marymount University
2807 N. Glebe Rd.
Arlington, VA 22207
Tel: 703-522-5600
Religious of the Sacred Heart of Mary
Resident and Non-resident coed students.
Sr. EYMARD GALLAGHER, R.S.H.M., Pres.
Sisters 10
Lay Teachers 357
Students 3,778

Front Royal
Diocese of Arlington

Christendom College
Tel: 540-636-2900
Resident and Non-resident students.
TIMOTHY T. O'DONNELL, S.T.D., Pres.
In res.,
Rev. ROBERT A. SKERIS, Adjunct Prof., Theology
Priests 3
Lay Teachers 27
Students 214

WASHINGTON

Lacey
Archdiocese of Seattle

St. Martin's College
5300 Pacific Ave., S.E.
Lacey, WA 98503
Tel: 360-491-4700
Dr. DAVID R. SPANGLER, Pres.
Dr. RICHARD LANGILL, Vice Pres. Academic Affairs
Order of St. Benedict College of Liberal Arts and Sciences. Resident and non-resident students.
Main Campus 958
Extension Campuses 547
Priests 5
Brothers 1
Lay Teachers 64

Seattle
Archdiocese of Seattle

Seattle University
900 Broadway
Seattle, WA 98122
Tel: 206-296-6000
Dr. JOHN D. ESHELMAN, Acting Pres.
Revs.:
ALEXIUS W. BYRNE, S.J.
GREGG D. WOOD, S.J.
PATRICK J. CONROY
PHILIP BOROUGHS, S.J., Rector
EMMETT H. CARROLL, S.J.
GERALD T. COBB, S.J.
JOHN F. FOSTER, S.J.
RONALD R. FUNKE, S.J.
THOMAS R. GARVIN, S.J.
ROGER S. GILLIS, S.J.
JAMES M. HARBAUGH, S.J.
PATRICK J. HOWELL, S.J.
PAUL A. JANOWIAK, S.J.
MICHAEL M. KELLIHER, S.J.
WILLIAM F. LEROUX, S.J.
DAVID J. LEIGH, S.J.
FRANCIS A. LOGAN, S.J.
PHILIP J. LUCID, S.J.
JOSEPH O. MCGOWAN, S.J.
PATRICK B. O'LEARY, S.J.
LAMMERT B. OTTEN, S.J.
JAMES B. REICHMANN, S.J.
JOHN D. WHITNEY, S.J.
JOSEF V. VENKER, S.J. (MIS)
Bros.:
JAMES P. SELINSKY, S.J.
FREDERICK O. MOREY, S.J.
Revs.:
ROBERT J. SPITZER, S.J.
JOSEPH R. STOCKING, S.J.
WILLIAM J. SULLIVAN, S.J.
MICHAEL J. TAYLOR, S.J.
L. JOHN TOPEL, S.J.
THEODORE E. ZEMBAL, S.J. (BGP)
Priests 30
Sisters 3
Brothers 2
Lay Teachers 220
Students 5,998

Spokane
Diocese of Spokane

Gonzaga University
Spokane, WA 99258
Tel: 509-328-4220
College of Arts and Sciences, and Schools of Law, Engineering, Education, Business Administration, Graduate School. Professional Studies Education conducted by the Fathers of the Society of Jesus.
Very Rev. EDWARD GLYNN, S.J. (Maryland) Pres.
Revs.:
PATRICK J. FORD, S.J., Academic Vice Pres.
ROBERT J. ARAVJO, S.J.
ROBERT M. BICKFORD, S.J.
J. ALFRED CARROLL, S.J.
SCOTT W. COBLE, S.J.
MICHAEL J. CONNOLLY, S.J. (New England)
MICHAEL L. COOK, S.J.
FRANK B. COSTELLO, S.J.
BERNARD J. COUGHLIN, S.J. (Missouri)
TIMOTHY F. CRONIN, S.J.
ROBERT R. DORIN, S.J. (New England)
ROBERT J. EGAN, S.J.
JOHN J. EVOY, S.J.

FRANCIS J. FALSETTO, S.J.
GERALD R. GORDON, S.J.
DONALD E. HIGHBERGER, S.J. (Missouri)
CLIFFORD KOSSEL, S.J.
KENNETH R. KRALL, S.J.
STEPHEN R. KUDER, S.J.
WALTER F. LEEDALE, S.J.
ANTHONY LEHMANN, S.J.
ROBERT LYONS, S.J.
MICHAEL MCFARLAND, S.J.
KEVIN P. MCGINLEY, S.J.
ALFRED MORISETTE, S.J.
GEORGE O. MORRIS, S.J.
JOHN P. MOSSI, S.J. (California)
MICHAEL E. MOYNAHAN, S.J.
JAMES G. POWERS, S.J.
KENNETH J. RUDNICK, S.J.
WILLIAM F. RYAN, S.J.
FREDRIC SCHLATTER, S.J.
MICHAEL SICONOLFI, S.J. (New York)
LEONARD F. SITTER, S.J.
M. DELMAR SKILLINGST, S.J.
J. PATRICK STEWART, S.J.
MICHAEL TRELEAVEN, S.J.
RICHARD E. TWOHY, S.J.
BERNARD J. TYRRELL, S.J.
GARY D. UHLENKOTT, S.J.
ANTHONY P. VIA, S.J.
J. KEVIN WATERS, S.J.
Bros.:
MICHAEL J. BENNETH, S.J.
DONALD A. JELLISON, S.J.
EDWARD S. JENNINGS, S.J.
THOMAS J. O'SHEA, S.J.
MAURICE C. PAQUET, S.J.
STEPHEN J. SOUZA, S.J.
BENJAMIN A. TRAUTMAN, S.J.
ADAM C. WEISGERBER, S.J.
Priests 33
Brothers 4
Sisters 7
Lay Teachers 238
Students 4,253

Toppenish
Diocese of Yakima

******Heritage College*
(Interdenominational University with an Independent Board)
3240 Fort Rd.
Toppenish, WA 98948
Tel: 509-865-2244
Sisters 6
Lay Teachers 38
Students 1,067

WEST VIRGINIA

Wheeling
Diocese of Wheeling-Charleston

Wheeling Jesuit University
316 Washington Ave.
Wheeling, WV 26003-6295
Tel: 304-243-2000
Jesuit Fathers
Tel: 304-243-2375
Very Rev. JOSEPH J. HAYDEN, S.J., Rector
Revs.:
THOMAS S. ACKER, S.J., Pres.
FRANK C. BOURBON, S.J.
WALTER A. BUCKIUS, S.J.
JAMES J. GORMLEY, S.J.
JOSEPH A. BURKE, S.J.
GEORGE R. HOHMAN, S.J.
JOHN J. KARWIN, S.J.
JOSEPH E. KOLB, S.J.
VINCENT J. LAGOMARSINO, S.J.
JAMES A. O'BRIEN, S.J.
JOSEPH P. SANDERS, S.J.
PATRICK T. QUINN, S.J.
JOHN J. ROCK, S.J.
DONALD M. SERVA, S.J.
MICHAEL F. STELTENKAMP, S.J.
CARL PIEBER, C.M.
Bro. NOAH A. KACUR, S.J.
Priests 17
Brothers 1
Sisters 1
Lay Teachers 87
Students 1,527

WISCONSIN

De Pere
Diocese of Green Bay

St. Norbert College
De Pere, WI 54115-2099
Tel: 414-337-3181
Legal Title: *St. Norbert College, Inc.*
Dr. THOMAS A. MANION, Pres.
Dr. THOMAS J. TREBON, Vice Pres. Academic Affairs & Dean of College
Mr. WILLIAM C. KOMSI, Vice Pres., Business & Finance
Dr. RICHARD RANKIN, Vice Pres. Student Life
Mr. DONALD L. SALMON, Vice Pres., Institutional Advancement
Revs.:
GERY MEEHAN, O.Praem, Dir. Campus Min. & Pastor St. Norbert College Parish
DENNIS M. BURKE, O.Praem., S.T.D., J.C.D., LL.D., Chancellor Emeritus
Faculty:
Revs.:
RICHARD M. VER BUST, Ph.D.
ROBERT J. CORNELL, O.Praem
JOHN P. KASTENHOLZ, O.Praem.
DAVID M. KOMATZ, O.Praem.
Priests 5
Sisters 2
ROTC 1
Lay Teachers 142
Students 2,100
St. Norbert College Summer School
Tel: 414-337-3051
Dr. JOHN SUTTON, Assoc. Dean Instructional Svcs.

Fond du Lac
Archdiocese of Milwaukee

Marian College of Fond du Lac
45 S. National Ave.
Fond du Lac, WI 54935
Tel: 414-923-7600
MATTHEW G. FLANIGAN, Pres.
Dr. GARY J. BOELHOWER, Academic Dean
Rev. ROY A. MATELJAN, Chap.
Sr. MARIE SCOTT, C.S.A., Campus Min.
Sisters of the Congregation of St. Agnes 2
Lay Teachers 75
Students 2,432
Total Staff 114

La Crosse
Diocese of La Crosse

Viterbo College
815 S. 9th
La Crosse, WI 54601-4797
Tel: 608-796-3000; Fax: 608-796-3050
A Catholic four-year coed liberal arts college founded by the Franciscan Sisters of Perpetual Adoration. Fully accredited Resident, Day and Evening Students.
Dr. WILLIAM J. MEDLAND, Ph.D., Pres.
LORILEE REBHAN, Vice Pres. Inst. Advancement
JANET LINDERBAUM, Registrar
Dr. ROLAND NELSON, Ph.D., Dir. Admissions
Rev. THOMAS M. O'NEILL, Chap. & Dir. Campus Ministry, Tel: 608-796-3804
Sisters 9
Lay Teachers 144
Students 1,635
Nursing Department
Students 409

Madison
Diocese of Madison

Edgewood College
855 Woodrow St.
Madison, WI 53711
Tel: 608-257-4861
Dominican Sisters, Sinsinawa, WI
Dr. JAMES A. EBBEN, Pres.
Sr. MAUREEN MCDONNELL, O.P., Campus Minister
Sr. MARGARET HOPKINS, O.P., Dir., Church Relations
STEPHEN BULLOCK, Campus Min.
Sisters 22
Lay Teachers 153
Students 2,056

Manitowoc
Diocese of Green Bay

Silver Lake College of the Holy Family
2406 S. Alverno Rd.
Manitowoc, WI 54220-9340
Tel: 414-684-6691; Fax: 414-684-7082
Connected with Holy Family Motherhouse of Franciscan Sisters of Christian Charity.
Sr. BARBARA BELINSKE, O.S.F., Pres.
Rev. JUSTIN A. PIERCE, S.D.S., Chap.
Priests 16
Sisters 58
Lay Teachers 86
Students 3,000

Milwaukee
Archdiocese of Milwaukee

Alverno College
3401 S. 39th St., P.O. Box 343922
Milwaukee, WI 53234-3922
Tel: 414-382-6000; Fax: 414-362-6354
Mr. GUY A. OSBORN, Chm., Bd. of Trustees
Sr. JOEL READ, O.S.F., Pres.
Sr. AUSTIN DOHERTY, O.S.F., Vice Pres. Academic Affairs
ELLEN S. BARTEL, Vice Pres., Institutional Advancement
Sisters 15
Lay Teachers 100
Students 2,191
Total Staff 217

Cardinal Stritch College
6801 N. Yates Rd.
Milwaukee, WI 53217
Tel: 414-352-5400
Conducted by Sisters of St. Francis of Assisi
Sr. MARY LEA SCHNEIDER, O.S.F., Pres.
Dr. MARNA BOYLE, Vice Pres. Academic Affairs
Revs.:
JAMES E. LOBACZ, Office of Campus Ministry
RICHARD C. BREITBACH
Sisters 8
Priests 1
Lay Teachers 68
Students 5,176
Total Staff 406

******Marquette University*
P.O. Box 1881
Milwaukee, WI 53201-1881
Tel: 414-288-7250
Legal Title: *Marquette University*
Opened in 1881. Conducted under the auspices of the Society of Jesus.
EDWARD A. BRENNAN, Chm. Bd. of Trustees
Rev. ROBERT A. WILD, S.J., Pres.
Internet Address: WildR@VMS.CSD.MU.EDU
Revs.:
PATRICK J. BURNS, S.J., Corp. Vice Pres., & Asst. to the Pres.
JOHN P. RAYNOR, S.J., Chancellor
Dr. DAVID R. BUCKHOLDT, Acting Vice Pres. Academic Affairs
Mr. KENNETH H. SMITS, Vice Pres. Administrative Affairs & Acting Vice Pres. for Academic Affairs
DOROTHY H. BIWER, Vice. Pres. Univ. Advancement
Dr. SHERRI COE-PERKINS, Vice Pres. Student Affairs
Mr. NORBERT J. TLACHAC, Asst. to Pres.
Dr. MARY FEELEY, Dir. Univ. Min.
The University is comprised of the following divisions:
College of Arts and Sciences—
Dr. THOMAS E. HACHEY, Dean
College of Business Administration—
Dr. LEWIS MANDELL, Dean
School of Dentistry—
Dr. THOMAS S. RYPEL, Interim Dean
School of Education—
Dr. MARY P. HOY, Dean
College of Engineering—
Dr. ROBERT L. REID, Dean
Graduate School—
Rev. THADDEUS J. BURCH, S.J., Dean
College of Communication—
Dr. WILLIAM R. ELLIOT, Dean
Law School—
Mr. HOWARD B. EISENBERG, Dean
College of Nursing—
Dr. MADELINE WAKE, Dean
College of Health Sciences—
Dr. JACK C. BROOKS, Dean
MU College of Professional Studies—
Dr. ROBERT J. DEAHL, Dean
Division of Continuing Education—
Ms. LORRAINE LOMBARDI, Dir.
Priests 23
Sisters 4
Lay Staff 511
Students 10,309
Total Staff 1,672

Mount Mary College
2900 N. Menomonee River Pkwy.
Milwaukee, WI 53222-4545
Tel: 414-258-4810
Sponsored by the School Sisters of Notre Dame.
Most Rev. REMBERT G. WEAKLAND, O.S.B., D.D., Chancellor
SALLY MAHONEY, Interim Pres.
Rev. ROBERT J. LOTZ, Th.M., Campus Minister
Sisters 47
Lay Teachers 58
Students 1,287
Total Staff 308

HOSPITALS

ALABAMA

Birmingham
Diocese of Birmingham

St. Vincent's Hospital
P.O. Box 12407
Birmingham, AL 35202-2407
Tel: 205-939-7000
810 St. Vincent's Dr.
Birmingham, AL 35205
Sponsored by Daughters of Charity
Mr. VINCENT CAPONI, Pres.
Sisters 5
Full-Time Nurses 349
Patients assisted annually 119,158
Beds 338

Seton Health Corporation of North Alabama
P.O. Box 12407
Birmingham, AL 35202-2407
Tel: 205-458-4040
Daughters of Charity
Mr. VINCENT CAPONI, Pres.
Sisters 1
Full-Time Nurses 275
Patients assisted annually 893,212

Mobile
Archdiocese of Mobile

Providence Foundation
6701 Airport Blvd., Ste. C-130, P.O. Box 850429
Mobile, AL 36608
Tel: 334-639-2050
THOMAS T. ZIEMAN, JR., Chm. of the Board
BETH MCFADDEN ROUSE, Vice Chm. of the Board
GAVIN J. BENDER, Sec.
FRANK J. LOTT, JR., Treas.

Providence Healthcare Services
6801 Airport Blvd., P.O. Box 850429
Mobile, AL 36685
Tel: 334-633-1000; Fax: 334-633-1679
Sr. ELISE BOUDREAUX, D.C., Chm.
JOHN R. ROEDER, Pres.
W. CARL MARTIN, Sec. & Treas.
Patients assisted annually 177,920

Providence Hospital
6801 Airport Blvd., P.O. Box 850429
Mobile, AL 36608(36685)
Tel: 334-633-1000; Fax: 334-633-1679
JOHN R. ROEDER, Pres. & CEO
Sr. ELISE BOUDREAUX, D.C., Chm.
Rev. LEO WEISHAAR, Chap.
Daughters of Charity of St. Vincent de Paul 8
Beds 349
Patients assisted annually 177,920
Nurses 499

Seton Health Corp. of South Alabama
6801 Airport Blvd., P.O. Box 850429
Mobile, AL 36608(36685)
Tel: 334-633-1660; Fax: 334-633-1679
Sr. ELISE BOUDREAUX, D.C., Chair
JOHN R. ROEDER, Pres.
Sr. ANTOINE SPEYRER, Sec. & Treas.

Seton Medical Management, Inc.
6801 Airport Blvd., P.O. Box 850429
Mobile, AL 36685
Tel: 334-633-1600
Sr. ELISE BOUDREAUX, D.C., Chm.
JOHN R. ROEDER, Pres.
Mr. ROBERT B. ANDREWS, Sec. & Treas.

ALASKA

Anchorage
Archdiocese of Anchorage

Providence Alaska Foundation
3200 Providence Dr., P.O. Box 196604
Anchorage, AK 99519
Tel: 907-261-3600; Fax: 907-261-3048
VINCENT J. WALKER, Pres.

Providence Alaska Medical Center
3200 Providence Dr., P.O. Box 196604
Anchorage, AK 99519
Tel: 907-562-2211; Fax: 907-261-3041
Mr. DOUGLAS BRUCE, Admin.
MONICA ANDERSON, Dir. Pastoral Care
Sr. KAYE BELCHER, S.P., Admin. Mission Integration Svcs.
Bed Capacity 341
Patients assisted annually 287,000
Staff 1,700

Ketchikan
Diocese of Juneau

Ketchikan General Hospital
3100 Tongass
Ketchikan, AK 99901
Tel: 907-225-5171; Fax: 907-225-2173
EDWARD F. MAHN, Admin.
Licensed Bed Capacity 92
Patients assisted annually 2,057
Island View Nursing Home

ARIZONA

Nogales
Diocese of Tucson

Holy Cross Hospital, Inc.
Div. of Carondelet Health Care Corporation,
1171 W. Target Range Rd.
Nogales, AZ 85621
Tel: 520-287-2771; Fax: 520-287-7314
Sr. ST. JOAN WILLERT, C.S.J., CEO
C. RAY HONAKER, Admin., Sr. Vice Pres.
Sr. AUGUSTINA HERNANDEZ, Chaplain
Beds 31
Patients assisted annually 38,370
Holy Cross Geriatric Center
Patients assisted annually 49
Holy Cross Hospital, Inc.

Phoenix
Diocese of Phoenix

Mercy Services Corporation
350 W. Thomas Rd.
Phoenix, AZ 85013
Skilled Nursing, Rehabilitation, Restorative & Custodial Care, Home Care, Senior Services, Functional Assessment, Psychological Services.
MICHAEL NANKO, Ph.D., Vice Pres.

St. Joseph's Hospital and Medical Center
350 W. Thomas Rd., P.O. Box 2071
Phoenix, AZ 85001
Tel: 602-285-3000
MARY YARBROUGH, Pres. & CEO
Chaplaincy Services:
THERESA M. EHRSAM, Dir.
Revs.:
CHARLES PARKER, Chap.
MILTON N. ADAMSON, C.S.C.
MICHAEL CENERINI
Sr. M. LAURANA, R.S.M.
Sr. DIANA DURLING, S.C.
ED BURKE
MICHAEL HUNDEMER
Sisters of Mercy 7
Beds 570
Patients assisted annually 311,481
Total Staff 3,665

Tucson
Diocese of Tucson

Carondelet Health Care Corporation of Arizona, Inc.
1601 W. St. Mary's Rd.
Tucson, AZ 85745-2682
Sr. ST. JOAN WILLERT, C.S.J., Pres. & CEO
St. Joseph and St. Mary Hospitals and Health Centers
1601 W. St. Mary's Rd.
Tucson, AZ 85745-2682
St. Joseph Hospital Div. of Carondelet Health Care Corporation of Arizona, Inc.
350 N. Wilmot Rd., P.O. Box 12069
Tucson, AZ 85711-2678
Tel: 520-296-3211
Sr. ST. JOAN WILLERT, C.S.J., Pres. & CEO
Revs.:
ROBERT FOSTER, C.S.V.
JAMES A. FREEMAN
Sr. PATRICK BERNARD LYON, C.S.J., Dir. Chaplain Svcs.
Sisters of St. Joseph of Carondelet 7
Beds 303
Bassinets 30
Patients assisted annually 101,333
St. Mary's Hospital Div. of Carondelet Health Care Corporation.
1601 W. St. Mary's Rd.
Tucson, AZ 85745-2682
Tel: 520-622-5833
Sr. ST. JOAN WILLERT, C.S.J., CEO
Revs.:
JOSEPH SABA
JAMES MODEEN
Sisters of St. Joseph 14
Beds 374
Patients assisted annually 121,350
Carondelet Foundation
P.O. Box 13190
Tucson, AZ 85732-3170
BEVERLY OWNING, Pres.
Holy Family Center, Inc.
1802 W. St. Mary's Rd.
Tucson, AZ 85745
Tel: 520-628-1991
WAYNE WISNIEWSKI, Admin. Dir.
Sisters of St. Joseph of Carondelet 1
Sisters of St. Joseph in Arizona
1601 W. St. Mary's Rd.
Tucson, AZ 85745
Sr. JOYCE MARIE GASPARDO, C.S.J., Pres.

St. Elizabeth of Hungary Out-Patient Clinic
140 W. Speedway Blvd.
Tucson, AZ 85705
Tel: 520-628-7871
Sr. BARBARA ANNE STOWASSER, C.S.J., Exec. Dir., Admin.
Patients assisted annually 23,000

ARKANSAS

Fort Smith
Diocese of Little Rock

Northside Community Health Center
3202 North 6th
Fort Smith, AR 72904
Tel: 501-782-1456

St. Edward Mercy Medical Center
7301 Rogers Ave.
Fort Smith, AR 72917
Tel: 501-484-6000; Fax: 501-452-1770
Sr. JUDITH MARIE KEITH, R.S.M., CEO
Rev. VINCENT E. MAGUIRE, Chap., Tel: 501-484-6082
Beds 343
Patients assisted annually 102,700
St. Edward Mercy Foundation
2713 S. 74th St., Ste. 103
Fort Smith, AR 72903
Tel: 501-484-6040

St. Edward Mercy Medical Center, dba Harbor View Mercy Hospital and Counseling Center
10301 Mayo Rd., P.O. Box 17000
Fort Smith, AR 72917-7000
Tel: 501-484-5550
Mr. RON SUMMERHILL, Admin.
Sr. JUDITH MARIE KEITH, R.S.M., President/CEO
Beds 80
Patients assisted annually 1,085

Hot Springs National Park
Diocese of Little Rock

St. Joseph's Regional Health Center
300 Werner St.
Hot Springs National Park, AR 71913
Tel: 501-622-1000
RANDALL J. FALE, Pres. & CEO
Rev. ALAN ROSENAU, Priest Chap.
Sisters of Mercy of St. Joseph Convent of Hot Springs, Arkansas, Inc.
Patients assisted annually 216,777
Bed Capacity 317

Jonesboro
Diocese of Little Rock

St. Bernard's Regional Medical Center
224 E. Matthews St.
Jonesboro, AR 72401
Tel: 501-972-4100
BEN E. OWENS, Pres.
Rev. NICHOLAS FUHRMAN, O.S.B., Chap.
Olivetan Benedictine Sisters 10
Patients assisted annually 108,767
Beds 375

Little Rock
Diocese of Little Rock

St. Vincent Infirmary Medical Center
No. 2 St. Vincent Circle
Little Rock, AR 72205

Tel: 501-660-3000; Fax: 501-671-4241
DIANA HUETER, Pres. & CEO
Sisters 17
Beds 717
Patients assisted annually 149,000

Morrilton
Diocese of Little Rock

Conway County Hospital
#4 Hospital Dr.
Morrilton, AR 72110-4510
JOHNSON L. SMITH, Admin.
Sponsored by St. Vincent Infirmary Medical Center, a division of the Sisters of Charity of Nazareth, KY.
Patients assisted annually 20,464
Beds 84

Ozark
Diocese of Little Rock

St. Edward Health Facilities of Franklin County, dba Mercy Hospital / Turner Memorial
801 W. River St., P.O. Box 527
Ozark, AR 72949
Fax: 501-667-4751
Sr. JUDITH MARIE KEITH, R.S.M., C.E.O.
Sr. MARY WERNER KEITH, R.S.M., Admin.
Patients assisted annually 7,683
Beds 39

Paris
Diocese of Little Rock

St. Edward Health Facilities of Logan Co., dba North Logan Mercy Hospital
500 E. Academy
Paris, AR 72855
Sr. JUDITH MARIE KEITH, R.S.M., C.E.O.
JIM L. MADDOX, Admin., Tel: 501-963-6101, FAX: 501-963-6155
Patients assisted annually 9,150
Beds 16

Rogers
Diocese of Little Rock

St. Mary-Rogers Memorial Hospital
72756
Tel: 501-636-0200, Ext. 705; Fax: 501-936-2906
Sr. SHARON THERESE ZAYAC, O.P., Pres.
Rev. STANISLAUS OLEKSY, Chap.
Sr. MICHAEL J. PACKNETT, Pres./C.E.O.
1119 W. Poplar St.
Rogers, AR,
Tel: 501-636-2548
Sisters of St. Dominic 9
Beds 165
Patients assisted annually 64,420
St. Mary Hospital Foundation
Tel: 501-636-0200

Waldron
Diocese of Little Rock

St. Edward Health Facilities of Scott County dba Mercy Hospital
Hwy. 71 & 80, Box 2230
Waldron, AR 72958
Tel: 501-637-4135; Fax: 501-637-3523
Sr. MARY ALVERA SIMON R.S.M., Admin.
Sr. MARITA POZEK, V.S.C., Asst. Admin.
Sr. JUDITH MARIE KEITH, R.S.M., C.E.O.
Vincentian Sisters of Charity 1
Patients assisted annually 14,240
Beds 27
Pinewood Nursing Home, Waldron (Skilled nursing facility)
Beds 105
Mercy Village (Assisted Living) (Residential care facility)
Apartments 22
Patients assisted annually (Mercy Village) 214

CALIFORNIA

Apple Valley
Diocese of San Bernardino

St. Mary Regional Medical Center
18300 Hwy. 18, P.O. Box 7025
Apple Valley, CA 92307.
Tel: 619-242-2311; Fax: 619-242-9750
St. Joseph Health System
Sr. DIANE HEJNA, Pres. & CEO
Sisters 3
Brothers 2
Beds 195
St. Mary Regional Medical Center Auxiliary
St. Mary Desert Valley Hospital Foundation

Bakersfield
Diocese of Fresno

Mercy Healthcare Bakersfield
2215 Truxtun Ave.
Bakersfield, CA 93301
Tel: 805-632-5000; Fax: 805-327-2592
Mailing Address:
P.O. Box 119
Bakersfield, CA 93302
BERNARD J. HERMAN, Pres.
Rev. ROY BURKHART, C.S.Sp., Chap.
Mercy Southwest Hospital
400 Old River Rd.
Bakersfield, CA 93311
Tel: 805-663-6000
Mailing Address:
P.O. Box 119
Bakersfield, CA 93302
Mercy Foundation - Bakersfield
2215 Truxtun Ave.
Bakersfield, CA 93301
Tel: 805-632-5683
Mailing Address:
P.O. Box 119
Bakersfield, CA 93302
SID SHEFFIELD, Exec. Dir.
Patients assisted annually 136,000
Beds 261
Sisters 5
Staff 1,506

Burbank
Archdiocese of Los Angeles

Providence Health System
(Los Angeles Service Area)
501 S. Buena Vista St.
Burbank, CA 91505
Tel: 818-365-8051; Fax: 818-898-4569
Sisters of Providence
MICHAEL J. MADDEN, CEO
Rev. KENNETH O. MCCABE, SS.CC., Chap.
Sr. COLLEEN SETTLES, O.P., D.Min., Dir. Chaplaincy Svcs.
Bed Capacity 309
Sisters 6
Patients assisted annually 98,000
Providence Care Center
10425 Magnolia Blvd.
N. Hollywood, CA 91601
Tel: 818-980-3872
Providence St. Joseph Medical Center
501 Buena Vista St.
Burbank, CA 91505
Tel: 818-843-5111; Fax: 818-843-0641
Sisters of Providence
MICHAEL J. MADDEN, CEO
GERALD FITZGERALD, Spiritual Care
Sisters 13
Bed Capacity 454
Patients Assisted Annually 182,000

Providence Saint Joseph Medical Center
501 S. Buena Vista
Burbank, CA 91505
Tel: 818-843-5111; Fax: 818-843-0641
Conducted by the Sisters of Providence Health System
Revs.:
JAMES TOAL
HAROLD J. FREE, S.J.
Deacon GERALD FITZGERALD, Dir. of Spiritual Care
Bed Capacity 604
Patients assisted annually 16,290
Total Staff 2,000

Carmichael
Diocese of Sacramento

Mercy American River Hospital
4747 Engle Rd.
Carmichael, CA 95608
Tel: 916-484-2222
MICHAEL UBOLDI, Vice Pres., COO
NORM HARRIS, Dir. Support Services
KATHY RICHERSON, Dir. Inpatient Svcs.
Sr. CLARE DALTON, R.S.M., Sister Liaison
Sisters of Mercy 1
Nurses 463
Beds 165
Patients assisted annually 30,176
Affiliated with Mercy Healthcare Sacramento.
Mercy San Juan Hospital / Mercy American River Hospital
6501 Coyle Ave.
Carmichael, CA 95608
Tel: 916-537-5000
Sisters of Mercy 5
Beds 238
Nurses 648
Patients assisted annually 159,857
MICHAEL UBOLDI, Vice Pres., COO

Daly City
Archdiocese of San Francisco

Seton Medical Center
1900 Sullivan Ave.
Daly City, CA 94015
Tel: 415-992-4000
Daughters of Charity of St. Vincent de Paul
BARBARA O'BRIEN, Interim Vice-Pres. & CEO
RICHARD OLSEN, Chap. Svcs.
Daughters of Charity 12
Patients assisted annually 261,546
Catholic Healthcare West
Seton Health Services Foundation
San Francisco Heart Institute
Seton Institute for International Development
Seton Medical Center
Daughters of Charity of St. Vincent de Paul
2000 Sullivan Ave.
Daly City, CA 94015
Sisters 12
Sr. NOREEN MCPARTLAND, D.C., Supr.

Duarte
Archdiocese of Los Angeles

Santa Teresita Hospital
819 Buena Vista St., P.O. Box I
Duarte, CA 91010
Tel: 818-359-3243; Fax: 818-357-7166
MICHAEL J. COSTELLO, JR., CEO
Mother VINCENT MARIE, O.C.D., Pres. Bd. Dir.
Chaplains:
Revs.:
FELIX MAIZA, S.J.
ROBERT GRIFFIN, S.J.
Bed Capacity 253
(With 156 for skilled nursing facility-women)
Sisters 44
Total Staff 410

Eureka
Diocese of Santa Rosa in California

St. Joseph Hospital of Eureka
2700 Dolbeer St.
Eureka, CA 95501
Tel: 707-445-8121
Sisters of St. Joseph of Orange
Mr. PAUL CHODKOWSKI, Area Pres. & CEO
KEN MEECE, Area Dir. of Pastoral Care
ADRIENNE BENSEN, Area Chap.
Rev. JAMES THOTTAPALLY (India)
Bed capacity 92
Priests 1
Sisters 4
Employees 410
Patients assisted annually 132,978

Folsom
Diocese of Sacramento

Mercy Hospital of Folsom
1650 Creekside Dr.
Folsom, CA 95630
Tel: 916-983-7400
DON HUDSON, Vice Pres., Chief Oper. Officer
Sisters of Mercy 2
Beds 95
Nurses 154
Patients assisted annually 14,406
Attended by St. John the Baptist, Folsom.
Corporate Name: Mercy Hospital of Folsom

Fortuna
Diocese of Santa Rosa in California

Redwood Memorial Hospital
3300 Renner Dr.
Fortuna, CA 95540
Tel: 707-725-3361; Fax: 707-725-7212
Sisters of St. Joseph of Orange
Mr. PAUL CHODKOWSKI, Area Pres. & CEO
Sisters 3
Staff 168
Bed capacity 47
Patients assisted annually 33,563
Redwood Memorial Foundation
JOANN CENTER, Pres.

Fresno
Diocese of Fresno

Saint Agnes' Medical Center
1303 E. Herndon

Fresno, CA 93720
Tel: 209-449-3000
Sisters of the Holy Cross
Sr. Ruth Marie Nickerson, C.S.C., Pres. & CEO
Mr. Samuel Reeves, Chm., Bd. of Trustees
Chaplains:
Revs.:
Michael Kendall, S.D.S.
James E. Cairns, C.M.
Sergio Negro, Ethicist Consultant
Sisters 11
Nurses 673
Priests 3
Bed Capacity 326
Patients assisted annually 317,646
Professional Office Corporation
Saint Agnes Medical Center, 1303 E. Herndon Ave.
Fresno, CA 93720
Tel: 209-449-3000
Sr. Ruth Marie Nickerson, C.S.C., CEO
Thomas Mac Michael, Chm. Bd. of Trustees

Fullerton
Diocese of Orange in California

St. Jude Medical Center
101 E. Valencia Mesa Dr.
Fullerton, CA 92834
Tel: 714-871-3280
Sharon Richardson, L.I.C.S.W., Admin. Dir. Patient/Family Support Svcs.
Chaplains:
Revs.:
William Patrick
Gil Mangampo
Sr. Dorothy Morris, C.S.J.
Sr. Dolores Mikula, C.S.J.O.F.
Rev. Jean Watkins
Mr. Jim Erixson
Beds 347
Nurses 607
Patients assisted annually 12,763

St. Jude Memorial Foundation
P.O. Box 4138
Fullerton, CA 92834
Fax: 714-992-3033

Hawthorne
Archdiocese of Los Angeles

**Hawthorne Community Hospital, Inc.*
711 Grevilles Ave.
Hawthorne, CA 90250

Hayward
Diocese of Oakland

St. Rose Hospital
27200 Calaroga Ave.
Hayward, CA 94545
Tel: 510-782-6200
Affiliated with Via Christi Health System, Inc.
Sisters of St. Joseph of Wichita, Kansas
Mr. Michael Mahoney, Pres.
Sr. Mary Alice Girrens, C.S.J., Dir. of Mission Services
Chaplains:
Revs.:
Roy V. Eco
Bruce Klikunas, O.S.M.
David F. Pace, Dir. Pastoral Care
Sr. Donalda Winfrey, C.S.J.
Sally Hussey
Joan M. Silva
Religious 5
Beds 175
Total Staff 730
Patients assisted annually 78,153
St. Rose Medical Office Bldg.
27200 Calaroga
Hayward, CA 94545
Tel: 510-782-6200
St. Rose Hospital Foundation
Sr. Antoinette Yelek, C.S.J., Exec. Dir.
27200 Calaroga Ave.
Hayward, CA 94545-4383
Tel: 510-264-4008
Silva Pediatric Clinic
680 W. Tennyson Rd.
Hayward, CA 94544
Tel: 510-782-4470

Inglewood
Archdiocese of Los Angeles

Daniel Freeman Memorial Hospital
Division of Daniel Freeman Hospitals, Inc.
333 N. Prairie Ave.
Inglewood, CA 90301
Tel: 310-674-7050; 678-0361; Fax: 310-419-8273
Peter F. Bastone, CEO
Britt Berrett, COO and Admin.
Sr. Regina Clare Salazar, C.S.J., Corp. Vice Pres. Sponsorship and Mission
G. Arnold Mulder, M.D., Chief of Staff
Rev. Francis X. Chrysostom (Sri Lanka) Chap.
Sr. Jean O'Leary, C.S.J., Dir. of Pastoral Care
Sisters of St. Joseph of Carondelet 25
Bed Capacity 360
Patients assisted annually 84,000
Total Staff 2,000
Sisters of St. Joseph of Carondelet in California
Sr. Kathleen Mary McCarthy, C.S.J., Chm.
Freeman Hospitals Foundation
Sr. Mary Esther McCann, C.S.J., Pres. Emeritus
Brian Gauthier, Vice Pres.
Bernie Sklar, Chm.

Long Beach
Archdiocese of Los Angeles

St. Mary Medical Center
1050 Linden Ave.
Long Beach, CA 90813

St. Mary Medical Center Foundation
P.O. Box 887
Long Beach, CA 90801
Bed Capacity 551
Total Assisted Annually 35,000
Total Staff 1,800

St. Mary Professional Building, Inc.
1045 Atlantic Ave.
Long Beach, CA 90813
James Riedel, Sec., Tel: 310-491-9010
David B. Tillman, M.D., Pres.

Los Angeles
Archdiocese of Los Angeles

Queen of Angels-Hollywood Presbyterian Medical Center
A California Corporation is the lessee-operator of the Hospital at:
1300 N. Vermont Ave.
Los Angeles, CA 90027
Tel: 213-413-3000
Rev. Steve Ryan, O.S.M., Dir. of Chap.
Mr. S. M. Graff, Admin.
Chaplains:
Revs.:
George Whedbee, C.M.F.
Carlos Castillo, C.M.F.
John Hubbard, Presbyterian Chap.
Mrs. Inge Famularo, Presbyterian Chap.
Sr. Diane Martin, O.S.F.
Sr. Magdalene Mylang
Sisters 2
Bed Capacity 427
Patients assisted annually 150,000

St. Vincent Medical Center
2131 W. 3rd St.
Los Angeles, CA 90057
Tel: 213-484-7111
Daughters of Charity of St. Vincent de Paul
Mr. Vincent F. Guinan, Jr., Pres.
Rev. John P. Fahey, Chap.
Sisters 13
Bed Capacity 380
Nurses 327
Patients assisted annually 49,598

Santa Marta Hospital
319 N. Humphreys Ave.
Los Angeles, CA 90022
Tel: 213-266-6500; Fax: 213-260-8641 (Admin.)
Mr. Wilfred G. Mallari, Pres. & CEO
Sr. Catherine Marie Kreta, C.S.J., Vice Pres. Mission
Sponsored by Carondelet Health System, which is Sponsored by Sisters of St. Joseph of Carondelet.
Bed Capacity 110
Patients assisted annually 31,000
Total Staff 430

Lynwood
Archdiocese of Los Angeles

Catholic Health Care West-Southern California
3630 E. Imperial Hwy.
Lynwood, CA 90262
Tel: 310-603-6000
Diane Carter, Esquire, Tel: 415-438-5610
Operating Divisions:
Robert F. Kennedy Medical Center
St. Bernadine Medical Center (San Bernadino Diocese)
St. Francis Medical Center
St. Mary Medical Center
St. Vincent Medical Center

St. Francis Medical Center
3630 E. Imperial Hwy.
Lynwood, CA 90262
Tel: 310-603-6000
Gerald T. Konzai, Pharm.D., Admin./Chief Operating Officer
Bro. Richard Hirbe, B.F.C.C., Dir. Pastoral Care
Revs.:
J. Paul Fernando, Assoc. Chap.
Boctor Bishara, Assoc. Chap.
Sponsered by the Daughters of Charity of St. Vincent de Paul. (Member of CHW Southern California Region)
Patients assisted annually 100,000
Bed Capacity 520
Total Staff 1,650

Manteca
Diocese of Stockton

St. Dominic's Hospital
(Sub. of St. Joseph's Regional Health System)
1777 W. Yosemite Ave., P.O. Box 1307
Manteca, CA 95337
Tel: 209-825-3500
Acute care community hospital.
Lawrence A. Philipp, CEO
Beds 63
Staff 226
Patients assisted 36,014

Marina Del Rey
Archdiocese of Los Angeles

Daniel Freeman Marina Hospital
Division of Daniel Freeman Hospitals, Inc.
4650 Lincoln Blvd.
Marina Del Rey, CA 90292
Tel: 310-823-8911
Mailing Address:—c/o Daniel Freeman Hospitals, Inc.
333 N. Prairie
Inglewood, CA 90301
Joseph W. Dunn, Ph.D., CEO, D.F. Marina Hospital
Christopher Gray, M.D., Chief of Staff
Sr. Anna Mary Meyer, C.S.J., Dir. Pastoral Care
Priests 1
Sisters 4
Bed Capacity 180
Patients assisted annually 23,800

Merced
Diocese of Fresno

Mercy Hospital & Health Services
2740 M St.
Merced, CA 95340
Tel: 209-384-6444; Fax: 209-722-2902
Mr. Kelly C. Morgan, Pres. & CEO
Sr. Jeannine Percy, O.S.M., Vice Pres., Mission Devel.
Catholic Healthcare West
Sacramental Ministry by Priests of Merced.
Sponsored by Sisters of the Third Order of St. Dominic (O.P.).
Sr. Imelda Michaud, D.H.S., Dir. Spiritual Services
Chaplaincy Services by Daughters of the Holy Spirit (DHS) and Dominican Sisters.
Mercy Surgical & Diagnostic Center
Patients assisted annually 30,000
Mercy Home Care
Annually assisted 23,000
Sisters 5
Beds 101
Patients assisted annually 60,000

Mission Viejo
Diocese of Orange in California

Mission Hospital Regional Medical Center
27700 Medical Center Rd.
Mission Viejo, CA 92691
Tel: 714-364-1400
Sponsored by Sisters of St. Joseph of Orange
Peter Bastone, Pres. & CEO
Patients assisted: Inpatient days 46,481
Outpatients 100,341
Bed Capacity 271

Morgan Hill
Diocese of San Jose in California

O'Connor Hospital dba Saint Louise Hospital & Health Center
Admin. Office, 18500 Saint Louise Dr.
Morgan Hill, CA 95037

Tel: 408-779-1500
Member of Catholic Healthcare West
Rev. Walter Johnson, M.M., Pastoral Care Svcs.
Mr. William C. Finlayson, Pres. & CEO
Sisters 3
Staff 179
Patients assisted annually 23,124

Moss Beach
Archdiocese of San Francisco

Seton Medical Center Coastside
600 Marine Blvd.
Moss Beach, CA 94038
Tel: 415-728-5521
Daughters of St. Vincent de Paul
Deborah E. Stebbins, Pres. & CEO
Katy Innerst, R.N., Mgr.
Sr. Ann D.C., Patient Advocate
Religious 1
Patients assisted annually 8,451

Mt. Shasta
Diocese of Sacramento

Mercy Medical Center
914 Pine St., P.O. Box 239
Mt. Shasta, CA 96067
Tel: 916-926-6111
Mr. James Hoss, Pres.
Beds 80
Patients assisted annually 32,201

Napa
Diocese of Santa Rosa in California

Queen of the Valley Hospital of Napa
1000 Trancas St.
Napa, CA 94558
Tel: 707-252-4411; Fax: 707-257-4073
Sisters of St. Joseph of Orange, California
Howard LeVant, Pres.
Chaplains:
Rev. Gerard Heintzelman (HBG)
Priests 1
Sisters 6
Lay Staff 1,200
Bed Capacity 159
Patients assisted annually 30,6264

Orange
Diocese of Orange in California

St. Joseph Health System
440 S. Batavia St.
Orange, CA 92868

St. Joseph Health System, A Sisters of St. Joseph of Orange Corporation
440 S. Batavia St.
Orange, CA 92868
Tel: 714-997-7690
Sr. Marianna Gemmet, C.S.J., Chm. of the Board
Mr. Richard Statuto, Pres. & CEO

St. Joseph Hospital of Orange
1100 W. Stewart Dr., P.O. Box 5600
Orange, CA 92867
Tel: 714-633-9111
Sisters of St. Joseph of Orange
Larry Ainsworth, Pres. & CEO
Rev. Elly S. Tavarro (Philippines) Contact Person
Patients assisted annually 30,848
Beds 457
Other Employees 1,818
Nurses 797

SRM Alliance Hospital Services
St. Joseph Health System, 440 S. Batavia St.
Orange, CA 92668-3995
Eli H. Glovinsky, Contact Person

Oxnard
Archdiocese of Los Angeles

St. John's Regional Medical Center
1600 N. Rose Ave.
Oxnard, CA 93030
Tel: 805-988-2500
Daniel Herlinger, Pres. & CEO
Christine Picchi, Dir. Chap. Svcs.
Elizabeth Cook, Dir. of Clinical Pastoral Education
Sisters of Mercy 6
Bed Capacity 264
Patients assisted annually 104,006
Total Staff 1,336
St. John's Pleasant Valley Hospital
2309 Antonio Ave.
Camarillo, CA 93010
Daniel Herlinger, Pres. & CEO
Elizabeth Cook, Dir. of Clinical Pastoral Education
Sisters 6
Acute Beds 81
Skilled Nursing 99
Patients assisted annually 43,022
Total Staff 645

Rancho Cordova
Diocese of Sacramento

Mercy Healthcare Sacramento
10540 White Rock Rd.
Rancho Cordova, CA 95670
Tel: 916-851-2000
Sr. Bridget McCarthy, Pres.
(Parent Company - Catholic Healthcare West)
Corporate Office
1700 Montgomery St., Ste. 300
San Francisco, CA 94111
Tel: 415-397-9000
Mr. Richard Kramer, Pres.
Sponsored by Sisters of Mercy of Auburn and Burlingame, Adrian Dominican Sisters, and Daughters of Charity National Health System West
This organization provides regional management and support functions for the following affiliated non-profit organizations: Mercy General Hospital of Sacramento; Mercy American River/Mercy San Juan Hospital, Carmichael (these hospitals are now operating under a single license); Mercy Hospital of Folsom; and the subsidiary corporations of Mercy McMahon Terrace and Mercy Medical Foundation.

Red Bluff
Diocese of Sacramento

Mercy Healthcare North dba St. Elizabeth Community Hospital
2550 Sr. Mary Columba Dr.
Red Bluff, CA 96080-4397
Tel: 916-529-8000; Fax: 916-529-8009
Mr. George A. Govier, Pres. & CEO
Mr. Thomas F. Grimes, Exec. Vice Pres. & COO
Sisters of Mercy 3
Nurses 137
Beds 76
Patients assisted annually 50,000
Total Staff 439
Attended by Sacred Heart, Red Bluff.

Redding
Diocese of Sacramento

Mercy Medical Center
Clairmont Heights, P.O. Box 496009
Redding, CA 96049
Tel: 916-225-6000
Mr. George A. Govier, Pres. & CEO
Rev. Michael Brennan, C.P., Chap.
Sisters of Mercy 6
Beds 256
Patients assisted annually 49,000
Corporate Name: Mercy Healthcare North dba Mercy Medical Center of Redding

Sacramento
Diocese of Sacramento

Mercy General Hospital
4001 J St.
Sacramento, CA 95819
Tel: 916-453-4545
Mr. Tom Peterson, Vice Pres., COO
Margaret Mette, Vice Pres. Cardiovascular Serv.
Rev. John J. Healy, Chap.
Sisters of Mercy 14
Sisters of St. Francis 1
Nurses 680
Patients assisted annually 85,000
Beds 489
Mercy Care
862 39th St.
Sacramento, CA 95819

San Bernardino
Diocese of San Bernardino

St. Bernardine Medical Center
2101 N. Waterman Ave.
San Bernardino, CA 92404
Tel: 909-883-8711; Fax: 909-881-4546
Gregory A. Adams, Admin. & CEO
Revs.:
Bernard Donaghey, S.V.D., Chap.
Barnabas Laubach, O.S.B., Chap. & Dir. Pastoral Care
Sisters 8
Beds 443
Patients assisted annually 403,000

San Diego
Diocese of San Diego

Mercy Hospital and Medical Center dba Mercy Healthcare San Diego
4077 Fifth Ave.
San Diego, CA 92103
Tel: 619-294-8111; Fax: 619-686-3530
Robert Cooley, M.D., Sr. Vice Pres., Admin.
Sr. Mary Jo Anderson, Vice Pres. Community Rels.
Revs.:
Francis W. McDonnell
Benjamin Bachmeier
N.A.C.C. Certified Chaplains:
Benjamin Bachmeier
Joan Krogmeier
Elaine Martin
Sr. Barbara Checkhart, R.S.M.
Josie Rodriquez
John Gillman
Sr. Mary Sutherland, R.S.C.J.
Bed Capacity 520
Patients assisted annually 487,930
Mercy Clinic (Mercy Hospital)
Sisters of Mercy
Mercy Clinic Out Patients 32,727
Mercy Hospital Foundation
San Diego Mercy Hospital Auxiliary

San Francisco
Archdiocese of San Francisco

St. Mary's Medical Center
450 Stanyan St.
San Francisco, CA 94117
Tel: 415-668-1000
Mr. John G. Williams, Pres. & CEO
Chaplains:
Revs.:
Anthony Baumann, O.F.M.
Edward Murray
Sr. Joseph Mary Galli, R.S.M.
Sr. Sharon Krenn, R.S.M.
Sr. Kathleen Sickley, P.B.V.M.
Priests 2
Religious 18
Patients assisted annually 182,405

San Jose
Diocese of San Jose in California

Alexian Brothers Hospital
225 N. Jackson Ave.
San Jose, CA 95116
Tel: 408-259-5000
Legal Title: *Alexian Brothers of San Jose, Inc.*
Parent Corporation: Alexian Brothers of California, Inc.
Congregation of Alexian Brothers, Immaculate Conception Province
Bro. Edward Walsh, C.F.A., Prov.
Mr. Steve Barron, CEO
Bros.:
Jim Classon, C.F.A., Dir., Alexian Bros. Community
James Johnston, C.F.A., Info. Desk
Larry Looby, C.F.A., Nursing Dept.
John O'Connor, C.F.A., Pastoral Care Dept.
Sr. Rosaline Lieu Nguyen, L.H.C., Pastoral Care Dept.
Revs.:
Art Mateo, M.S.C., Pastoral Care Dept.
Thai Q. Trinh, Dir., Pastoral Care Dept. & Supvr., Clinical Pastoral Educ.
Brothers 4
Priests 2
Sisters 1
Pastoral Care Volunteers 40
Staff 950
Bed Capacity 204
Patients assisted annually 94,780
Employees 1,150

O'Connor Hospital
2105 Forest Ave.
San Jose, CA 95128
Tel: 408-947-2500
Legal Title: *O'Connor Hospital*
Member of Catholic Healthcare West
Mr. William Finlayson, Pres. & CEO
Revs.:
Robert Cary, Pastoral Care Svcs.
Toribio Ives Aniban
Sisters 5
Patients assisted annually 127,439
O'Connor Foundation
2105 Forest Ave.
San Jose, CA 95128
Tel: 408-947-2717
Marie Bernardy, Vice Pres.

San Pedro
Archdiocese of Los Angeles

San Pedro Peninsula Hospital
(Affiliate of Little Company of Mary Health Services)
1300 W. Seventh St.
San Pedro, CA 90732
Tel: 310-832-3311
Patients assisted annually 36,962
Total Staff 1,200

Santa Barbara
Archdiocese of Los Angeles

St. Francis Medical Center of Santa Barbara
601 E. Micheltorena St.
Santa Barbara, CA 93103
Tel: 805-962-7661; Fax: 805-966-5704
Franciscan Sisters of the Sacred Heart
Mr. RON BISCARO, Pres. & CEO
Sisters 5
Bed Capacity 110
Patients assisted annually 17,533

Santa Cruz
Diocese of Monterey in California

Dominican Santa Cruz Hospital
(Acute and Rehabilitation Services)
1555 Soquel Dr.
Santa Cruz, CA 95065
Tel: 408-462-7700; Fax: 408-462-7555
Sisters of St. Dominic (Adrian, MI)
Sr. JULIE HYER, O.P., Pres.
Bed Capacity 375
610 Frederick St.
Santa Cruz, CA 95062
Tel: 408-462-7700
Sr. JULIE HYER, O.P., Pres. & CEO
Total Assisted in Hospital 166,586
Total Staff 1,318

Santa Maria
Archdiocese of Los Angeles

Marian Medical Center
1400 E. Church St.
Santa Maria, CA 93454
Tel: 805-739-3000
Sponsored by Sisters of St. Francis of Penance and Christian Charity
MICHAEL A. SCAVOTTO, CEO
CHARLES J. COVA, Exec. Vice Pres.
Deacon ZENON L. NAWROCIK, Dir. Pastoral Care
Sisters 9
Bed Capacity 130
Patients assisted annually 54,194
Marian Medical Center Extended Care Facility
Skilled Nursing Facility.
Beds 95
Marian Medical Center Day Care Facility for Children
Capacity 52
Marian Residence Retirement Home
124 S. College Dr.
Santa Maria, CA 93454
Tel: 805-922-7731
Marian Medical Center Foundation
1406 E. Main St., Ste. E.
Santa Maria, CA 93454
Tel: 805-349-9486

Santa Monica
Archdiocese of Los Angeles

Saint John's Hospital and Health Center
1328 22nd St.
Santa Monica, CA 90404
Tel: 310-829-5511; Fax: 310-315-6134
Sisters of Charity of Leavenworth
Sr. MARIE MADELEINE SHONKA, Pres.
Rev. PATRICK COMERFORD, Chap.
Sisters 9
Bed Capacity 317
Patients assisted annually 150,000
Saint John's Hospital and Health Center Foundation
The Michael Burke Foundation
The Hope Guild
The Irene Dunne Guild
John Wayne Cancer Institute Benefactors
John Wayne Cancer Institute Auxiliary
The ABC's, Associates for Breast Cancer Studies

Santa Rosa
Diocese of Santa Rosa in California

Santa Rosa Memorial Hospital
1165 Montgomery Dr.
Santa Rosa, CA 95405
Tel: 707-546-3210
Sisters of St. Joseph of Orange Corporation
Mr. ROBERT FISH, Acting CEO & Pres.
Rev. MARK G. O'LEARY, O.P., Chap.
Rev. Msgr. PATRICK MCCOY (England) Chap.
Priests 2
Sisters 5
Employees 1,042
Bed capacity 225
Patients assisted annually 68,368

Stockton
Diocese of Stockton

St. Joseph's Behavioral Health Center
(Sub. of St. Joseph's Regional Health System)
2510 N. California St.
Stockton, CA 95204
Tel: 209-948-2100
Psychiatric and chemical dependency care hospital.
NORMA BROWN, Admin.
Beds 35
Staff 157
Patients assisted 2,650

St. Joseph's Medical Center of Stockton
(Sub. of St.Joseph's Regional Health System)
1800 N. California St., P.O. Box 213008
Stockton, CA 95213-9008
Tel: 209-943-2000
Acute care community hospital.
EDWARD G. SCHROEDER, Pres. & CEO
Beds 319
Staff 2,005
Patients assisted 286,500

St. Joseph's Regional Health System of Northern San Joaquin Valley
1800 N. California St., P.O. Box 213008
Stockton, CA 95213-9008
Tel: 209-943-2000
Sponsored by the Sisters of Mercy, Auburn and Burlingame Regional Communities; Adrian Dominican Sisters; Daughters of Charity, Province of the West; Sisters of Charity of the Incarnate Word of Houston, Texas; Dominican Sisters of San Rafael and Dominican Sisters of St. Catherine of Siena of Kenosha, Wisconsin.
Mr. EDWARD G. SCHROEDER, Pres. & CEO
Northern San Joaquin Region
1700 Montgomery St., Ste. 300
San Francisco, CA 94111
Tel: 415-438-5500
This organization provides regional management and support functions for the following affiliated non-profit organizations: St. Joseph's Medical Center of Stockton; St. Dominic's Hospital of Manteca; Mark Twain St. Joseph's Hospital of San Andreas; St. Joseph's Behavioral Health Center of Stockton and Mercy Hospital and Health Services of Merced.
Medical Staff 861
Licensed Acute Beds 560
Full-Time Employees 2,631

Susanville
Diocese of Sacramento

Lassen Community Hospital
560 Hospital Ln.
Susanville, CA 96130
Tel: 916-257-5325
St. Mary's Health Care Corp. Affiliate.
235 W. Sixth St.
Reno, NV 89520
Mr. DAVID S. ANDERSON, Admin.
Beds 59
Bassinets 5
Patients assisted annually 20,114
Corporate Name: Lassen Community Hospital, Inc.

Torrance
Archdiocese of Los Angeles

Little Company of Mary Health Services
4101 Torrance Blvd.
Torrance, CA 90503
Tel: 310-540-7676; Fax: 310-540-8408
JAMES C. LESTER, Pres.
Little Company of Mary Hospital
4101 Torrance Blvd.
Torrance, CA 90503
Tel: 310-540-7676; Fax: 310-540-8408
MARK COSTA, Pres.
Chaplains:
BARBARA FLOWERS
Rev. GARY KLAUER, O.F.M.Conv.
Deacon RICHARD PRUITT
JUANITA MELLER
EILEEN CRONIN, D.M.J.
Little Company of Mary Sisters 6
Bed Capacity 374
Patients assisted annually 85,598
American Province of Little Company of Mary Sisters.
Total Staff 1,533
Little Company of Mary Hospital Foundation
Little Company of Mary Pavilion (SNF)
Torrance Care Station
Patients assisted annually 20,142
Manhattan Beach Care Station
Patients assisted annually 19,976
Care Stations' Combined Staff: 36
South Bay Family Medical Group Clinic
Del Amo Diagnostic Center
San Pedro Peninsula Hospital
1300 W. 7th St.
San Pedro, CA 90732
JOHN M. WILSON, Pres.
Chaplains:
LES RONSBERG
Rev. FRANCIS SHIGO
Little Company of Mary Sisters 1
Bed Capacity 393
Patients assisted annually 57,640
Staff 889
American Province of Little Company of Mary Sisters
San Pedro Peninsula Hospital Foundation
San Pedro Peninsula Home Health & Hospice
San Pedro Peninsula Pavilion (SNF)
San Pedro Care Station
Patients assisted annually 9,657
Staff 12
Peninsula Diagnostic Center
Peninsula Recovery Center

West Covina
Archdiocese of Los Angeles

Queen of the Valley Hospital
1115 S. Sunset Ave., P.O. Box 1980
West Covina, CA 91793
Tel: 818-962-4011; Fax: 818-814-2482
Mr. PETER MAKOWSKI, CEO
Bed Capacity 263
Patients assisted annually 116,640

COLORADO

Canon City
Diocese of Pueblo

St. Thomas More Hospital and Progressive Care Center
1338 Phay Ave.
Canon City, CO 81212
Tel: 719-269-2000
Mr. WILLIAM A. BURNS, CEO
Revs.:
MARTIN MUHEIM, O.S.B., Chap.
IGNATIUS SMITH, O.S.B.
BERNARD GERVAIS, O.S.B.
Sr. KATHLEEN COGAN, O.S.B., Dir. of Pastoral Care
Benedictine Sisters of Yankton 2
Benedictine Sisters of Colorado Springs 1
Priests 3
Beds 245
Patients assisted annually 72,252

Colorado Springs
Diocese of Colorado Springs

The Penrose Foundation
(Formerly the Penrose-St. Francis Healthcare Foundation)
7606 N. Union Blvd., Ste. D
Colorado Springs, CO 80920
Tel: 719-528-5883
A division of Sisters of Charity Health Services Colorado.

Penrose-St. Francis Health Services
Penrose Hospital
2215 N. Cascade Ave.
Colorado Springs, CO 80907
Tel: 719-776-5000; Fax: 719-776-2494
An operating unit of Sisters of Charity Health Services Colorado.
Sisters of Charity of Cincinnati, OH
Chaplains:
Revs.:
GERALD H. BRUGGEMAN, Sacramental Min.
ALAN FILIPPI, Protestant Chap.
Sr. LUCILLE KRIPPEL, O.S.F., Dir. Spiritual Care
Sr. JANE GROSHEIDER, S.C.
Sr. IMMACULATA PARK, O.S.F.
Rev. TOM STELLA
JOHN ZAY
MICHAEL CRINO
Sisters 3

Penrose Community Hospital
3205 N. Academy Blvd.
Colorado Springs, CO 80917
Tel: 719-776-3000; Fax: 719-591-3477
An operating unit of Sisters of Charity Health Services Colorado.
Sisters of Charity of Cincinnati, OH
Sr. JOAN CROCKER, S.C.
Sisters 1
St. Francis Health Center
825 E. Pikes Peak Ave.
Colorado Springs, CO 80903
Tel: 719-776-8800; Fax: 719-636-8871
An operating unit of Sisters of Charity Health Services Colorado.
Sisters of Charity of Cincinnati, OH

Denver
Archdiocese of Denver

**Centura Health*
1601 Lowell Blvd.
Denver, CO 80204
St. Anthony Hospital Central
4231 W. 16th Ave.
Denver, CO 80204
Tel: 303-629-3511; Fax: 303-595-6060
An operating unit of Sisters of Charity Health Services Colorado.
St. Anthony Hospital North
2551 W. 84th Ave.
Denver, CO 80030
Tel: 303-426-2151; Fax: 303-426-2533
An operating unit of Sisters of Charity Health Services Colorado.
Gardens at St. Elizabeth
2835 W. 32nd Ave.
Denver, CO 80211
Tel: 303-477-4442; Fax: 303-964-2340
An operating unit of Sisters of Charity Health Services Colorado.
Centura Senior Life Center
1601 Lowell Blvd.
Denver, CO 80204
Tel: 303-825-2190; Fax: 303-899-5059
An operating unit of Sisters of Charity Health Services Colorado.
Centura Adult Day Care
4165 Eaton St.
Denver, CO 80033
Tel: 303-422-9000
An operating unit of Sisters of Charity Health Services Colorado.

St. Joseph Hospital
1835 Franklin St.
Denver, CO 80218
Tel: 303-837-7111
Sr. MARIANNA BAUDER, Pres. & CEO
Rev. R. PHILIP NEGELE, O.C.S.O.
Sisters of Charity of Leavenworth 14
Bed Capacity 601
Patients assisted annually 104,567
Outpatients assisted annually 252,265

Durango
Diocese of Pueblo

Mercy Medical Center
375 E. Park Ave.
Durango, CO 81301
Tel: 970-247-4311; Fax: 970-382-1082
Mr. RENATO V. BACIARELLI, Admin.
Rev. MICHAEL MCCLEARY
Sr. SHARON EKLER, Vice Pres., Mission & Ministry
MYRON DARMOUR, Chap.
Sisters of Mercy of the Americas 2
Beds 111
Patients assisted annually 203,170

Florence
Diocese of Pueblo

St. Joseph Manor
600 W. Third St.
Florence, CO 81226-1117
Tel: 719-269-2000
Mr. WILLIAM A. BURNS, CEO
Clearview of Colorado, Tertiary Substance Abuse Facility

Grand Junction
Diocese of Pueblo

Marillac Clinic, Inc.
600 Center Ave., Bldg. 3A
Grand Junction, CO 81501
Ms. JANET K. CAMERON, Exec. Dir.
Legal Title: *Sisters of Charity of Leavenworth, Health Services Corp.*

St. Mary Hospital and Medical Center
P.O. Box 1628
Grand Junction, CO 81502
Tel: 970-244-2273; Fax: 970-244-7510
Sr. LYNN CASEY, S.C.L., Pres.
Rev. ALOYSIUS J. BERTRAND, Chap.
Sisters of Charity of Leavenworth, Kansas 10
Beds 294
Patients assisted annually 280,067

Pueblo
Diocese of Pueblo

St. Mary-Corwin Hospital
1008 Minnequa Ave.
Pueblo, CO 81004
Tel: 719-560-4000
Chaplains:
Rev. MICHAEL C. DESCIOSE
Sr. MARGARET DONNELLY, S.C.
Sr. DARLENE MAHONEY, O.S.F.
Rev. PHIL SORENSON, Prot. Chap.
Sisters of Charity of Cincinnati 3
Beds 200
Patients assisted annually 303,204

CONNECTICUT

Bridgeport
Diocese of Bridgeport

St. Vincent's Development Corporation
2800 Main St.
Bridgeport, CT 06606
Tel: 203-576-5459
Mr. JOSEPH CLANCY, Chm.
Mr. RICHARD D'AQUILA, CEO

St. Vincent's Health Services Corporation
2800 Main St.
Bridgeport, CT 06606
Tel: 203-576-5455
Sr. MARY PATRICIA FINNERAN, D.C., Chm.
Mr. WILLIAM J. RIORDAN, Pres. & CEO

St. Vincent's Medical Center
2800 Main St.
Bridgeport, CT 06606
Tel: 203-576-6000
Daughters of Charity of St. Vincent de Paul (Albany, NY)
Sr. MARY PATRICIA FINNERAN, D.C., Chm.
Mr. WILLIAM J. RIORDAN, Pres. & CEO
Revs.:
BARTHOLOMEW SALTER, C.S.C.
JOHN V. BORGO, S.J.
DANIEL KENNELLY
THOMAS ELLIOTT, C.S.C.
St. Vincent's College
Students 201

St. Vincent's Medical Center Foundation
2800 Main St.
Bridgeport, CT 06606
Tel: 203-576-5451
Mr. JOSEPH H. MALONEY, Chm.
Mr. RONALD J. BIANCHI, Pres.

Hartford
Archdiocese of Hartford

Saint Francis Hospital and Medical Center
114 Woodland St.
Hartford, CT 06105-1299
Tel: 714-548-4000; Fax: 714-493-7809
Dr. DAVID D'ERAMO, Pres. & CEO
Chaplains:
Revs.:
LIAM C. CASEY, Dir. Pastoral Care
MARK BONSIGNORE
THOMAS PUTHIYADOM
PETER G. MITCHELL
Licensed Beds 617
Bassinets 65
Out-Patient Visits 273,911
In-Patient Visits 128,319
Staff 3,804
The Women's Auxiliary of Saint Francis Hospital and Medical Center
Mrs. RANJANA CHAWLA, Pres.
Asylum Hill Family Medicine Center, Inc.
Woodland Physician Associates, Inc.
Camillus Corporation
The One Thousand Corporation
One Thousand One Corporation
Saint Francis Hospital and Medical Center Foundation, Inc.
114 Woodland St.
Hartford, CT 06105
The Rehabilitation Hospital of Connecticut, Inc.
480 Blue Hills Ave.
Hartford, CT 06112
Tel: 714-548-4000
Nurses School
260 Ashley St.
Hartford, CT 06105
Student Nurses 54

New Haven
Archdiocese of Hartford

Hospital of St. Raphael
1450 Chapel St.
New Haven, CT 06511
Tel: 203-789-3000; Fax: 203-789-3653
Sisters of Charity (Convent Station)
JAMES J. CULLEN, Pres.
CINDY VON BEREN, Admin. & Contact
Chaplains:
Revs.:
CHACKO KUMPLAMTHANAM
GERARD PELLETIER, S.M.
ROBERT STRUMINSKI, S.M.
THOMAS J. KELLY
Chaplains 5
Sisters 12
Bed Capacity 511
Bassinets 22
Patients assisted annually 110,000
Staff 3,200
Legal Holdings: Saint Raphael Healthcare System; Saint Raphael Foundation, Inc.; DePaul Health Services Corporation; Seton Real Estate, Inc.; Saint Regis Health Center, Inc. (Non-profit charitable corporations affiliated with the Hospital of Saint Raphael).

Saint Regis Health Center, Inc.
1354 Chapel St.
New Haven, CT 06511
Tel: 203-867-8300
KIM CZEPIGA, Exec. Dir. & Contact
125-bed skilled nursing facility.

Stamford
Diocese of Bridgeport

St. Joseph Medical Center
128 Strawberry Hill Ave.
Stamford, CT 06904-1222
Tel: 203-353-2001
Most Rev. EDWARD M. EGAN, Chm.
Mr. WILLIAM J. RIORDAN, Pres. & CEO

St. Joseph Medical Center Corporation
128 Strawberry Hill
Stamford, CT 06904-1222
Most Rev. EDWARD M. EGAN, Chm.

St. Joseph Medical Center Foundation, Inc.
128 Strawberry Hill Ave.
Stamford, CT 06904
Mr. JACKSON E. SPEARS, K.S.G., Pres.

Waterbury
Archdiocese of Hartford

St. Mary Hospital
56 Franklin St.
Waterbury, CT 06706
Tel: 203-574-6000; Fax: 203-597-3238
Sisters of St. Joseph of Chambery
Sr. MARGUERITE WAITE, C.S.J., Pres.
Revs.:
GREGORY ALTERMATT
STANLEY R. STARON
Sisters 13
Bed Capacity 347
Bassinets 32
Patients assisted annually 203,056
The Slocum Corporation-St. Mary's Hospital Foundation, Inc., Non-profit corporations for the exclusive benefit of St. Mary Hospital.

West Hartford
Archdiocese of Hartford

McAuley Center, Inc.
275 Steele Rd.
West Hartford, CT 06117
Tel: 860-236-6300
MICHAEL ESCAMILLA, Exec. Dir. & Contact
Continuing care retirement community; Sisters of Mercy. 255 residential apartment units for individuals age 62 and over. Nursing care at St. Mary's Home included.

DELAWARE

Wilmington
Diocese of Wilmington

St. Francis Hospital, Inc.
7th and Clayton Sts., P.O. Box 2500

Wilmington, DE 19805-0500
Tel: 302-575-8300
STEVEN C. BJELICH, Pres./Chief Exec. Officer
Sr. MARGARET ALOYSIUS MCGRAIL, O.S.F., V.P. Mission & Ministry
Rev. JOSEPH NARIMATTAM, Chap.
Beds 395
Staff 1,500
Patients assisted annually 298,000

DISTRICT OF COLUMBIA

Washington
Archdiocese of Washington

Center for Life of Providence Hospital
1150 Varnum St., N.E.
Washington, DC 20017
Non-Profit Corporation to Render Service, Support and Assistance in the Provision of Community Services Which Foster Human Dignity, Family Unity and Respect for Life. Services Include: Reduced Fee Maternity Programs.
Total Assisted 109,400
Total Staff 1,571

De Paul Foundation, Inc.
1150 Varnum St., N.E.
Washington, DC 20017
De Paul Foundation, Inc. was Organized to Provide Fund Development, Financial and Other Assistance to Provide Hospital and Other Subsidiaries of De Paul Foundation for the Health Care, Medical, Educational and Human Needs of the District of Columbia and Vicinity, by Functioning as a Charitable Nonprofit, Nonstock Corporation.
Providence Health Foundation
1150 Varnum St., N.E.
Washington, DC 20017
Providence Health Foundation, Inc. (PHF), a District of Columbia Charitable Nonprofit Corporation, was Organized to Support the Mission of Providence Hospital by Conducting Fundraising and Development Activities, by Receiving and Managing Donations, by Making Grants, and by Promoting Educational Activities and Scientific Research.

Georgetown University Hospital
3800 Reservoir Rd., N.W.
Washington, DC 20007
Tel: 202-784-3000
DAN J. OLDANI, Admin.
Rev. JAMES M. SHEA, S.J., Dir. Pastoral Care
Chaplains:
Revs.:
TERRENCE W. CURRY, S.J.
JAMES J. DENN, C.S.C.
GUSTAAF KEPPENS, S.J.
Sr. JEANNE BRIDGEMAN, C.S.J.
CHRISTINE SWIFT
DIANA DIXON-PROCTOR
Bed Capacity 530
Patients assisted annually 153,000

Providence Hospital
(See Separate Listing for Details.)
Carroll Manor Inc.
4922 LaSalle Rd.
Hyattsville, MD 20782
Tel: 301-864-2333; Fax: 301-864-2333, Ext. 152
Nursing Home for the Aged.
Priests 1
Licensed Skilled and Intermediate Beds 382
Licensed Domicillay Beds 17
Providence Health Services Inc.
1150 Varnum St., N.E.
Washington, DC 20017
Ambulatory-Outpatient Care, Promote Wellness and Carry Out of Educational Activities & Scientific Research.

Providence Hospital
1150 Varnum St., N.E.
Washington, DC 20017
Tel: 202-269-7000; Fax: 202-269-7160
Daughters of Charity of St. Vincent de Paul
Sr. CAROL KEEHAN, D.C., Pres.
Sr. REGINA LOUGHLIN, D.C., Dir. Pastoral Care
Chaplains:
Revs.:
JAMES POWER, C.M.
BRIAN J. O'CONNELL, C.M.
Sisters 17
Bed Capacity 382
Patients assisted annually 70,459
Carroll Manor Nursing and Rehabilitation
1150 Varnum St., N.E.
Washington, DC 20017-2180
Tel: 202-269-7100; Fax: 202-269-7816
Rev. Msgr. LEONARD F. HURLEY, Chap.
Bed Capacity 240

FLORIDA

Clearwater
Diocese of St. Petersburg

St. Michael's Housing Corporation dba Casa Miguel
Independent Living.
2285 State Rd. #580
Clearwater, FL 34623
Tel: 813-797-8551
Mrs. JOANN LUNGARO, Admin.
Total Staff 5
Residents 82

The Tepeyac Corporation dba Clinica Guadalupana
1215 Drew St., Ste. 7B
Clearwater, FL 34615
Tel: 813-461-7730
Rev. PETER SCHWEITZER, Pres.

Fort Lauderdale
Archdiocese of Miami

Holy Cross Hospital
4725 N. Federal Hwy.
Fort Lauderdale, FL 33308
Tel: 954-771-8000; Fax: 954-492-5741
RAY BUDRYS, Pres.
Rev. ROBERT M. HANLON, S.J., Assoc. Chap.
Sisters of Mercy 14
Staff 1,550
Bed Capacity 587
Patients assisted annually 294,519 (includes Home Health & Holy Cross Medical Group Visits)

Jacksonville
Diocese of St. Augustine

St. Vincent's Medical Center, Inc.
1800 Barrs St., P.O. Box 2982
Jacksonville, FL 32203
Tel: 904-387-7300
Daughters of Charity of St. Vincent de Paul
Revs.:
ROBERT GALCHUS, O.M.
EDWARD MCQUILLAN, C.M.
LESTER DEMOTT, C.M., Chap.
Nurses 724
Beds 518
Bassinets 25
Outpatients 254,166
Inpatient 124,878
St. Vincent's Foundation, Inc.
St. Vincent's Ambulatory Care, Inc.
The Heart And Lung Institute, Inc.
Riverside Hospital, Inc.
St. Catherine Laboure Manor, Inc.

Miami
Archdiocese of Miami

Mercy Hospital
3663 S. Miami Ave.
Miami, FL 33133
Tel: 305-854-4400
Sponsored by the Sisters of St. Joseph of St. Augustine, FL
Sr. ELIZABETH ANNE WORLEY, S.S.J., Chm. Board of Trustees, Contact
Sr. LORRAINE KRAVERATH, S.S.J., Dir. Mission and Ministry
Mercy North, Inc.
3665 S. Miami Ave.
Miami, FL 33133
Tel: 305-285-2121; 854-4000
Sponsored by the Sisters of St. Joseph of St. Augustine, FL
Mercy Mission Services (Subsidiary of Mercy Hospital)
Chaplains:
Revs.:
CARL MORRISON
LUIS MARQUINA
WILLIAM KIDWELL, S.J.
ANTHONY ACEVEDO
Sisters 16
Staff 1,905
Bed Capacity 530
Patients assisted annually 232,628

Pensacola
Diocese of Pensacola-Tallahassee

The Mother Seton Guild of Sacred Heart Hospital, Inc.
Pensacola, FL 32504
Mr. DONALD HOLLAND, Pres.

Sacred Heart Foundation, Inc.
5225 Carmel Heights Dr.
Pensacola, FL 32504
P.O. Box 2700
Pensacola, FL 32513-2700
ROBERT K. WILSON, JR., M.D., Pres.

Sacred Heart Hospital of Pensacola
5151 N. Ninth Ave.
Pensacola, FL 32513
Tel: 904-416-7000
PATRICK J. MADDEN, Pres. & CEO
Annual Admissions 19,990
Staff 2,756

Port Charlotte
Diocese of Venice

Bon Secours-St. Joseph Hospital
2500 Harbor Blvd.
Port Charlotte, FL 33952
Tel: 941-625-4122
Mr. MICHAEL HARRINGTON, EVP/Admin.
Sisters 9
Beds 212
Patients assisted annually 55,742
Total Staff 850
Bon Secours-St. Joseph Healthcare Group, Inc.
2500 Harbor Blvd.
Port Charlotte, FL 33952
Sr. ROSE MARIE JASINSKI, C.B.S., Pres.
Mr. MICHAEL HARRINGTON, EVP/Admin.
BETTY ANNE DARCH, O.S.F., Vice Pres., Mission
Chaplains:
Revs.:
PAUL ORTNER, S.S.J.
OTMAR GALLAGHER, O.F.M.Cap.
Sr. KATHLEEN MORONEY, C.B.S., NACC Cert.
JAMES E. HOFF, Coord., NACC Cert.
KAREN RILEY, Coord. Parish Nurse, NACC Cert.

**Bon Secours-St. Joseph Healthcare Group Foundation, Inc.*
Bon Secours-St. Joseph Home Health Agency, Inc.
Bon Secours-St. Joseph Nursing Care Center
Bon Secours Hospice
Sr. DOROTHY BROGAN, C.B.S., NACC Cert.

St. Petersburg
Diocese of St. Petersburg

**Bon Secours-Maria Manor Nursing Care Center, Inc.*
10300 Fourth St., N.
St. Petersburg, FL 33716
Tel: 813-576-1025
Sisters of Bon Secours
Mr. MICHAEL WARD, Admin.
Sr. KARLA BOGNAR, Dir. Pastoral Care
Rev. PETER ZEMANICK, O.C.S.O., Chap., 813-576-6370
JEWEL CURLEY, Asst. Admin.
Bed Capacity 274

Holy Cross Housing dba Casa Santa Cruz
7851 54th Ave. N.
St. Petersburg, FL 33709
Mr. JOSEPH A. DIVITO, Registered Agent
Total Staff 5
Total in Residence 82

St. Anthony's Hospital, Inc.
1200 Seventh Ave., N.
St. Petersburg, FL 33705
Tel: 813-825-1100
Legal Title: *St. Anthony's Hospital, Inc.*
Legal Title: *St. Anthony's Ancillary Services, Inc.*
Legal Title: *St. Anthony's Professional Buildings, Inc.*
Legal Title: *St. Anthony's Professional Buildings and Services, Inc.*
Legal Title: *St. Anthony's Health Care Foundation, Inc.*
Legal Title: *St. Anthony's Hospital, Inc.*
Legal Title: *Restated and Consolidated Insurance Fund.*
Franciscan Sisters of Allegany 14

Tampa
Diocese of St. Petersburg

Christ the King Housing II, Inc. dba Kings Manor
2946 W. Columbus Dr.
Tampa, FL 33607
Tel: 813-875-0139; Fax: 813-875-6061
Mr. PATRICK O'SULLIVAN, Admin.
Residents 121

Christ the King Housing, Inc. dba Kings Arms
4125 N. Lincoln Ave.
Tampa, FL 33607
Tel: 813-873-0234
Mr. PATRICK O'SULLIVAN, Admin.

Total Staff 4
Total in Residence 89

St. Joseph's Hospital, Inc.
3001 W. Martin Luther King Blvd.
Tampa, FL 33607
Mailing Address:
P.O. Box 4227
Tampa, FL 33677
Tel: 813-870-4000
Franciscan Sisters of Allegany
Licensed Beds 883
Patients assisted annually 204,341
Legal Title: *St. Joseph's Hospital, Inc.*
Legal Title: *St. Joseph's Ancillary Services, Inc.*
Legal Title: *St. Joseph's Health Care Center, Inc.*
Legal Title: *St. Joseph's Hospital of Tampa Foundation, Inc.*
St. Francis Residence, Inc.

St. Patrick's Housing Corporation dba Patrician Arms
4516 S. Manhattan Ave.
Tampa, FL 33611
Tel: 813-835-8227
Total Staff 4
Total in Residence 86

Venice
Diocese of Venice

Bon Secours-Venice Healthcare Corp.
540 The Rialto
Venice, FL 34285
Tel: 941-483-7664
Sr. Mary Catherine Rogers, C.B.S., Pres.
Mr. Roy Hess, Exec. Vice Pres.
Sisters 1
Total Beds 462
Total Patients 177,102

West Palm Beach
Diocese of Palm Beach

St. Mary's Hospital, Inc.
901 45th St.
West Palm Beach, FL 33407-2495
Tel: 561-881-2865; Fax: 561-881-2864
Mailing Address:
P.O. Box 24620
West Palm Beach, FL 33416-4620
Rev. Msgr. Ronald Bershara, Dir. Pastoral Care
Chaplains:
Rev. Msgr. Ronald N. Beshara, Dir. Mission Integration
Revs.:
Emmett Mulligan, O.F.M.
Dominic Novoa (HRT)
Franciscan Sisters of Allegany 9
Beds 450
Patients assisted annually 640,000
Total Discharges 16,250
Affiliated Support Organizations:
St. Mary's Medical Center, Inc.
St. Mary's Hospital Foundation, Inc.
St. Mary's Ancillary Services, Inc.
St. Mary's Imaging Center, Inc.
St. Mary's Care Services, Inc.
St. Mary's Pain Center, Inc.
St. Mary's A.S.C., Inc.
St. Mary's Women's Health Services
Mid-County Medical Center, Inc.
United Medical Management

GEORGIA

Athens
Archdiocese of Atlanta

St. Mary's Hospital
1230 Baxter St.
Athens, GA 30606-3791
Tel: 706-354-3033; Fax: 706-354-3197
Missionary Sisters of the Most Sacred Heart of Jesus
Mr. Edward J. Fechtel, Jr., Admin.
Sr. M. Georgette, M.S.C., Community Care Coord.
Nursing Sisters 4
Other Sister Personnel 4
Nurses 391
Beds 196
Patients assisted annually 106,691

Atlanta
Archdiocese of Atlanta

Saint Joseph's Hospital of Atlanta, Inc.
5665 Peachtree Dunwoody Rd., N.E.
Atlanta, GA 30342
Tel: 404-851-7001
Sisters of Mercy of Americas, Baltimore Regional Community
Ronald P. Hogan, CEO
Sisters 16
Total Staff 2,344
Bed Capacity 346
Patients assisted annually 120,000

Augusta
Diocese of Savannah

St. Joseph Center For Life, Inc.
2260 Wrightsboro Rd.
Augusta, GA 30910
William Paugh, Pres./CEO

St. Joseph Hospital, Augusta, GA, Inc.
2260 Wrightsboro Rd.
Augusta, GA 30910
Tel: 706-481-7400; Fax: 706-481-7599
J. William Paugh, Pres./CEO
Rev. Daniel M. Munn, Chap. & Dir., Mission Effectiveness
Bed Capacity 144
Patients assisted annually 110,000
Staff Chaplains 5
Sisters 5

Columbus
Diocese of Savannah

St. Francis Hospital
2122 Manchester Expwy., P.O. Box 7000
Columbus, GA 31908-7000
Tel: 706-596-4000
SSM Health Care System of St. Louis, MO.
Michael E. Garrigan, FACHE, Pres.
Rev. Hugh Marshall, S.T., Chap.
Beds 376
Patients assisted annually 82,000

Savannah
Diocese of Savannah

St. Joseph's Hospital
11705 Mercy Blvd., P.O. Box 60129
Savannah, GA 31419-1791
Tel: 912-925-4100
Mr. Paul P. Hinchey, Pres./C.E.O., Tel: 912-927-5404
Sr. Bernadette LaFlamme, R.S.M., Dir. Pastoral Care, Tel: 912-927-5582
Sr. Grace Marie Dillard, R.S.M., Vice Pres., Mission Effectiveness, Tel: 912-925-4100
Rev. Rodolfo P. Roxas, Chap.
Sisters of Mercy of the Americas 7
Bed Capacity 305
Bassinets 20
Patients assisted annually 89,620

HAWAII

Honolulu
Diocese of Honolulu

St. Francis Healthcare System of Hawaii
P.O. Box 30100
Honolulu, HI 96820
Tel: 808-566-4783
Sr. Beatrice Tom, O.S.F., CEO
Total Staff 142
St. Francis Medical Center
2230 Liliha St.
Honolulu, HI 96817
Tel: 808-547-6011
Sr. Gretchen Gilroy, O.S.F., CEO
Chaplains:
Revs.:
Edward Popish, SS.CC.
Paulo Tuugamusu
David Schwartz
Bed Capacity 308
Patients assisted annually 343,985
Total Staff 1,626
Women's Addiction Treatment Center
2230 Liliha St.
Honolulu, HI 96817
Patients assisted annually 150
Bed Capacity 14
St. Francis Medical Center - West
91-2141 Fort Weaver Rd.
Ewa Beach, HI 96706
Tel: 808-678-7000
Sr. Gretchen Gilroy, O.S.F., CEO
Rev. Gordon Combs, O.F.M.Cap., Chap.
Bed Capacity 82
Patients assisted annually 38,030
Total Staff 630
St. Francis Healthcare Foundation of Hawaii
Mr. Eugene Tiwanak, CEO
The Sister Maureen Keleher Center (Hospice)
24 Puiwa Rd.
Honolulu, HI,
Tel: 808-595-7566
Sr. Francine Gries, O.S.F., Dir.
Bed Capacity 12
Patients assisted annually 719
St. Francis Health Centers (Iwilei, Downtown, Pali)
Patients assisted annually 8,772
Health Services for Senior Citizens
1149 Bethel St.
Honolulu, HI 96813
Patients assisted annually 26,085
Northern Koolau Health Education Center
54-316 Kamehameha Hwy.
Honolulu, HI 96717
Patients assisted annually 3,630

IDAHO

Boise
Diocese of Boise

St. Alphonsus Regional Medical Center, Inc.
1055 N. Curtis Rd.
Boise, ID 83706
Tel: 208-378-2121
Karl B. Kurtz, Interim Pres. & CEO
Rev. Morse Later, Priest Chap.
Sisters of the Holy Cross 4
Bed Capacity 269
Patients assisted annually 257,000
Legal Title: *St. Alphonsus Regional Medical Center.*
Legal Title: *St. Alphonsus Building Co., Inc.*
Legal Title: *St. Alphonsus Diversified Care.*

Cottonwood
Diocese of Boise

St. Mary's Hospital
(Sub. of Benedictine Health System)
Cottonwood, ID 83522
Tel: 208-962-3251; Fax: 208-962-3722
Mrs. Casey Uhling, Admin.
Rev. Liam Davitt, Chaplain
Iris Hawley, D.N.S., Dir., Nursing
Sponsored by Sisters of St. Benedict, Duluth, MN
Sisters 1
Bed Capacity 28
Patients assisted annually 12,500

Jerome
Diocese of Boise

St. Benedict Family Medical Center
709 N. Lincoln
Jerome, ID 83338
Tel: 208-324-4301
Mr. David Farnes, Admin.
Sponsored by Sisters of St. Benedict, Cottonwood, ID
Sisters 3
Bed Capacity 40
Patients Assisted Annually 38,378
Skilled Nursing Facility in connection with Medical Center.

Lewiston
Diocese of Boise

St. Joseph Regional Medical Center
415 6th St., P.O. Box 816
Lewiston, ID 83501
Tel: 208-743-2511
Howard A. Hayes, Pres. & CEO
Rev. Harry Holwell, Chap.
Sr. Mary Ann Farley, S.N.J.M., Dir., Pastoral Care
Sisters of St. Joseph of Carondelet 2
Bed Capacity 165
Nursing Education is in affiliation with Lewis-Clark State College and with Walla-Walla Community College, Clarkston Branch.

Nampa
Diocese of Boise

Mercy Medical Center
1512 12th Avenue Rd.
Nampa, ID 83686
Tel: 208-467-1171
Joseph A. Messmer, Pres. & CEO
Rev. John J. Tivenan (BRK) Vice Pres., Mission Effectiveness
Sr. Alice Marie Schmid, O.P.
Cheri Bain, M.A.
Sr. Joan Marie Martin, R.S.M.
Rev. Joseph Newcomer, Min.
Sisters 2
Bed Capacity 152
Patients assisted annually 115,443

ILLINOIS

Alton
Diocese of Springfield in Illinois

Saint Anthony's Health Center
Saint Anthony's Way, P.O. Box 340
Alton, IL 62002-0340
Tel: 618-465-2571
Two Campuses: Saint Anthony's Hospital and Saint Clare's Hospital.
WILLIAM E. KESSLER, Pres.
Rev. CRAIG MACMAHON, O.M.V., Chap.
Sisters of St. Francis of the Martyr St. George 19
Bed Capacity 292
Patients assisted annually 137,051

Aurora
Diocese of Rockford

Mercy Health Corporation
1325 N. Highland Ave.
Aurora, IL 60506
Tel: 630-859-2222
Mr. JOHN K. BARTO, JR., Pres.
Sr. JENNIFER KEHRWALD, O.S.F., Pastoral Assoc.
Chaplains:
Rev. JOSEPH LESSARD (PHX)
Sisters 1
Beds 356
Patients assisted annually 93,000
The following are subsidiaries of Mercy Health Corporation: Mercy Center for Health Care Services; McAuley Medical Properties; Bennett Operating Company.

Belleville
Diocese of Belleville

St. Elizabeth Hospital
211 S. Third St.
Belleville, IL 62222
Tel: 618-234-2120; Fax: 618-234-4391
Hospital Sisters of the Third Order of St. Francis
Clinically Affiliated with Southern Illinois University School of Medicine.
Mr. GERALD M. HARMAN, Exec. Vice Pres.
Rev. DENNIS F. VOSS, Chap.
Sisters 5
Bed Capacity 498
Patients assisted annually 94,025

Belvidere
Diocese of Rockford

Saint Joseph Hospital
1005 Julien St.
Belvidere, IL 61008
Tel: 815-544-3411; Fax: 815-547-5977
Mr. DAVID A. SCHERTZ, Admin.
Rev. ROBERT JACKSON, Chap.
O.S.F. Healthcare System.
Beds 72
Inpatient Days 12,434
Outpatient Visits 12,217

Bloomington
Diocese of Peoria

St. Joseph Medical Center
2200 E. Washington
Bloomington, IL 61701
Tel: 309-662-3311; Fax: 309-662-7143
Mailing Address:
607 NE Madison Ave.
Peoria, IL 61603
Mr. KENNETH J. NATZKE, Admin.
Sr. M. GRACE, O.S.F., Supr.
Rev. Msgr. JOSEPH MCGOWAN, Chap.
Sisters of the Third Order of St. Francis 3
Beds 152
Patients assisted annually 87,434
Total Staff 717

Blue Island
Archdiocese of Chicago

St. Francis Hospital and Health Center
12935 S. Gregory St.
Blue Island, IL 60406
Tel: 708-597-2000
Owned and operated by SSM Health Care, a member of the SSM Health Care System.
Mr. JAY KREUZER, Pres.
Revs.:
EDWARD GLANZMANN, Monastery of the Holy Cross
ROBERT MILLER, O.P., Chap.
Sisters 2
Bed Capacity 410
Patients assisted annually 97,909
St. Francis Family Health Center
13000 S. Maple Ave.
Blue Island, IL 60406

Breese
Diocese of Belleville

St. Joseph Hospitcl
9515 Holy Cross Ln.
Breese, IL 62230
Tel: 618-526-4511
Hospital Sisters of the Third Order of St. Francis
JACOLYN M. SCHLAUTMAN, Exec. Vice Pres.
Rev. ROBERT J. O'SHEA, Chap.
Sisters 2
Bed Capacity 85
Patients assisted annually 40,907

Centralia
Diocese of Belleville

St. Mary's Hospital
400 N. Pleasant Ave.
Centralia, IL 62801
Tel: 618-532-6731
Mr. JAMES W. MCDOWELL, Pres. & CEO
Rev. JOEL BURGET, O.F.M.Conv., Chap.
Sisters 10
Bed Capacity 276
Patients assisted annually 111,606

Chicago
Archdiocese of Chicago

Columbus Hospital
Daughters of Charity of St. Vincent de Paul & Missionary Sisters of the Sacred Heart.
2520 N. Lakeview Ave.
Chicago, IL 60614
Legal Title: *Catholic Health Partners Services.*
Mr. JEFFREY FRERICHS, Board Chmn.
Sr. THERESA PECK, D.C., Pres. & C.E.O.
GORDON BASS, C.O.O.
Rev. THEODORE PLOPLIS, Dir. Pastoral Care Dept.
Chaplains:
Rev. RICHARD B. BARTZ
Sr. JOAN BERNICH
Sisters 9
Bassinets 28
Bed Capacity 535
Patients assisted annually 82,359
Chicago Institute for Neuro Surgery & Neuro Research (Affiliate)
420 W. Deming Pl.
Chicago, IL 60614
Tel: 773-883-8585
LEONARD CERULLO, M.D., Dir.

Holy Cross Hospital
2701 W. 68th St.
Chicago, IL 60629
Tel: 312-471-8000
Legal Title: *Holy Cross Hospital*
Sisters of St. Casimir of Chicago
MARK C. CLEMENT, Pres. & CEO
ALICE KILGALLON, Dir. Pastoral Care
Chaplains:
Revs.:
THOMAS MORRISON, O.P.
WALTER MCNICHOLAS, O.S.A.
ERWIN J. DODGE, O.S.A.
THOMAS GRIFFIN, O.S.A.
Sr. MAUREEN JUOZAPAVICIUS, S.S.C.
Sisters 26
Licensed Beds 400
Patients assisted annually 185,123
Holy Cross Hospital and Sisters of St. Casimir Foundation

Mercy Hospital and Medical Center
Fiscal Management.
2525 S. Michigan Ave.
Chicago, IL,
Stevenson Expwy. at King Dr.
Chicago, IL 60616
Tel: 312-567-2100; Fax: 312-567-6575
WINKLE LEE, Pres.
LILIA ZAMAR, Chief Financial Officer, Tel: 312-567-2012
Rev. MARTIN J. HEBDA, Dir. Pastoral Care, Tel: 312-567-2045
Sisters 11
Bed Capacity 386
Bassinets 30
Patients assisted annually 371,287
Affiliates:
Mercy Diagnostic & Treatment Center
Mercy Health Care Corp.
Mercy Services Corp.
Mercy Foundation, Inc.
Mercy Health Care & Rehabilitation Center
Mercy Medical at Presidential Towers (Outpatient Satellite Facility & Alcohol-Drug Dependency Program)
Tower Three, 614 W. Madison St.
Chicago, IL 60606
Tel: 312-902-4000
Ms. PAT O'NEILL, Admin.
Ms. MARY KAY KACMAREK, Admin.
Mercy Medical in Chinatown (Outpatient Satellite Facility)
2347 S. Wentworth
Chicago, IL 60616
Tel: 312-842-0100
Mercy Medical in Justice (Ambulatory Care & Alcohol-Drug Dependency Program)
81st & Kean Ave.
Chicago, IL 60458
Tel: 708-594-3500
Mercy Medical on Pulaski (Outpatient Satellite Facility & Alcohol-Drug Dependency Program)
5635 S. Pulaski
Chicago, IL 60629
Tel: 312-585-1955
St. Patrick's Family Health Center (Outpatient Satellite Facility)
3344 S. Halsted
Chicago, IL 60608
Tel: 312-523-9550
Mercy Medical in Chicago Ridge (Outpatient Satellite Facility)
9830 S. Ridgeland
Chicago, IL 60415
Tel: 708-636-8200
Mercy Medical in Little Village (Outpatient Satellite Facility)
3649 W. 26th St.
Chicago, IL 60623
Tel: 312-521-2080
Mercy Medical on Michigan (Outpatient Satellite Facility)
2930 S. Michigan Ave.
Chicago, IL 60616
Tel: 312-808-0400
Mercy Medical in Mt. Greenwood, Chicago
11055 S. St. Louis Ave.
Chicago, IL 60655
Tel: 312-445-5800
Mercy Works on Ashland
3316 S. Ashland
Chicago, IL 60608
Tel: 312-890-2489
Arlington Heights (Alchohol, Drug Dependency Program)
115 S. Wilke Rd., Ste. 101
Arlington Heights, IL 60005
Tel: 708-398-0045
Hazel Crest (Alcohol, Drug Dependency Program)
17577 S. Kedzie Ave., Ste. 204
Hazel Crest, IL 60429
Tel: 708-922-1983
Mercy Medical in Lincoln Park, Chicago
990 W. Fullerton, Ste. 495
Chicago, IL 60616
Tel: 312-327-8848
Mercy Medical in Chatham
8529-33 S. State St.
Chicago, IL 60619
Bryn Mawr
8610 W. Bryn Mawr
Chicago, IL 60631
Tel: 312-380-0400

**Our Lady of the Resurrection Medical Center*
5645 W. Addison
Chicago, IL 60634
Tel: 312-282-7000
Sisters of the Resurrection
JOSEPH F. TOOMEY, Pres.
JOHN SULLIVAN, CEO
Sr. DONNA SIEGL, O.S.F., Dir. Pastoral Care
Chaplains:
Revs.:
LEON GRANTZ, C.P.
JEROME ANDRACKI, C.R.
Sr. LYDIA MARY YOKIEL, C.R.
Sr. MARY LEONETTE KLAFETA, C.R.
Sr. BARBARA FARIS, O.S.F.
Sisters 3
Bed Capacity 286
Patients assisted annually 66,987

Resurrection Medical Center
7435 Talcott Ave.
Chicago, IL 60631
Tel: 773-774-8000
Sisters of the Resurrection
JOSEPH F. TOOMEY, Pres.
Sr. DONNA MARIE, C.R., CEO
Sr. MARY FLORENCE, C.R., Supr.
Chaplains:
Revs.:

William Bilinsky
Robert Kownacki (SAT)
Chester Ubowski
Gordon Van Hoof, O.S.C.
Sisters 15
Bed Capacity 428
Patients assisted annually 243,780
Student Nurses affiliated with Nurses-Triton College 40
Students Nurses, Oakton Community College 20
Chicago Board of Education 12
Affiliates:
Resurrection Health Care Corporation
Resurrection Ambulatory Care Services
Resurrection Development Foundation

St. Anthony Hospital
Daughters of Charity of St. Vincent de Paul & Missionary Sisters of the Sacred Heart.
2875 W. 19th St.
Chicago, IL 60623
Tel: 773-521-1710
Legal Title: *Catholic Health Partners Services*
Mr. Jeffrey Frerichs, Board Chmn.
Sr. Theresa Peck, D.C., Pres. & C.E.O.
Rev. Theodore Ploplis, Dir. Pastoral Care Dept.
Chaplains:
Rev. Donald Craig
Sr. Benigna Morais, M.S.C., Dir. of Pastoral Care
Missionary Sisters of the Sacred Heart 3
Bassinets 28
Bed Capacity 184
Patients assisted annually 45,246

St. Basil Health Service - Free People's Clinic
1850 W. Garfield
Chicago, IL 60609
Tel: 773-436-6496
Patients assisted annually 4,500

St. Bernard Hospital
326 W. 64th St.
Chicago, IL 60621
Tel: 773-962-3900
Legal Title: *St. Bernard Hospital*
Religious Hospitallers of St. Joseph
Sr. Janet Wahleithner, R.H.S.J., Supr.
Sr. Elizabeth Van Straten, R.H.S.J., Pres. & CEO
Sr. Janet Wahleithmer, R.H.S.J., Dir. Pastoral Care Dept.
Sisters 2
Bed Capacity 233
Patients assisted annually 52,000

St. Elizabeth's Hospital
1431 N. Claremont Ave.
Chicago, IL 60622
Tel: 773-278-2000
Legal Title: *St. Elizabeth's Hospital of Chicago, Inc.*
Operated by the Ancilla Systems, Inc.
JoAnn Birdzell, CEO
Bed Capacity 302
Patients assisted annually 126,580

St. Joseph Hospital
Daughters of Charity of St. Vincent de Paul & Missionary Sisters of the Sacred Heart.
2900 N. Lake Shore Dr.
Chicago, IL 60657
Tel: 773-665-3000
Legal Title: *Catholic Health Partners Services*
Daughters of Charity of St. Vincent de Paul of Indiana, Inc.
Mr. Jeffrey Frerichs, Board Chm.
Sr. Theresa Peck, D.C., Pres. & CEO
Margaret Sullivan McDermott, C.O.O.
Rev. Theodore Ploplis, Dir. Pastoral Care Dept.
Chaplains:
Revs.:
Anthony J. Adducci
John Gomes
Robert Lucas
Robert A. Walsh
Sr. Alverda Bonifas, O.F.
Rabbi Norman Lewison
Sisters 4
Bassinets 33
Bed Capacity 492
Patients assisted annually 114,428
Seton Health Care of Northern Illinois Affiliate.

St. Mary of Nazareth Hospital Center
2233 W. Division
Chicago, IL 60622
Tel: 312-770-2000
Sisters of the Holy Family of Nazareth
Sr. Kathleen Ann Stadler, C.S.F.N., Supr.
Sr. Stella Louise, C.S.F.N., Pres.
Revs.:
John Kobus
Paul Liwanag
Abraham Miller
Sisters 22
Bed Capacity 428
Bassinets 32
Patients assisted annually 156,641

Chicago Heights
Archdiocese of Chicago

Alverno Lakeside Corporation
1423 Chicago Rd.
Chicago Heights, IL 60411
Lincoln Hwy. at Chicago Rd.
Chicago Heights, IL 60411
Sisters 2

St. James Hospital and Health Centers
1423 Chicago Rd.
Chicago Heights, IL 60411
Tel: 708-756-1000
Legal Title: *Sisters of St. Francis Health Services, Inc., Mishawaka, Indiana*
Sisters of St. Francis of the Perpetual Adoration
Mr. Peter J. Murphy, Pres. & CEO
Sr. Marlene Shapley, O.S.F., Vice Pres.-Resource Management Services
Sr. M. Ruth Luthman, O.S.F., Vice Pres. Mission Services
Rev. Ronald L. Kondziolka, Chap.
Sisters 3
Bed Capacity 361
Patients assisted annually 83,248

Crestwood
Archdiocese of Chicago

St. Francis Family Health Center
13755 Cicero Ave.
Crestwood, IL 60445

Danville
Diocese of Peoria

United Samaritans Medical Center
812 N. Logan
Danville, IL 61832
Tel: 217-443-5000; Fax: 217-443-1965
Mailing Address:
607 NE Madison Ave.
Peoria, IL 61603
Legal Title: *Div. of Franciscan Sisters Health Care Corp.*
Dennis J. Doran, Pres.
Rev. Robert G. Mann, Chap.
Franciscan Sisters of the Sacred Heart 4
Capacity 359
Patients assisted annually 93,814
Franciscan Home Health
812 N. Logan Ave.
Danville, IL 61832
United Samaritans Medical Center Foundation
600 Sager Ave.
Danville, IL 61832
United Samaritans Medical Center Apothecary
800 N. Logan Ave.
Danville, IL 61832
Family Care Center
Danville, IL 61832
Catlin Family Practice
P.O. Box 380
Catlin, IL 61817
John Mason, P.A.-C
Chrisman Clinic
139 N. Monroe
Chrisman, IL 61924
Michael Gibson, P.A.-C
East Main Family Practice
1415 E. Main
Danville, IL 61832
William Hensold, M.D.
Rusty Martin, P.A.-C
Family Practice Center
7 N. Virginia
Danville, IL 61832
James Hensold, M.D.
William Hensold, M.D.
Timothy Horner, M.D.
Rusty Martin, P.A.-C
Westville Family Practice
302 N. State
Westville, IL 61883
Bruce Ferguson, P.A.-C
800 N. Logan, Suite 204
Danville, IL 61832
David Hurley, Jr., M.D.
Robert Klausner, M.D.
800 N. Logan Ave.
Danville, IL 61832
David Lehman, M.D.
Victoria Bignal, M.D.
806 N. Logan Ave.
Danville, IL 61832
Karuna Koneru, M.D.
Marvin Hoovis, M.D.
Franciscan Home Health
812 N. Logan
Danville, IL 61832
United Samaritans Medical Center Apothecary
800 N. Logan Ave.
Danville, IL 61832

Decatur
Diocese of Springfield in Illinois

St. Mary's Hospital
1800 E. Lake Shore Dr.
Decatur, IL 62521
Tel: 217-464-2966; Fax: 217-464-1616
Keith L. Callahan, Exec. Vice Pres.
Hospital Sisters of the Third Order of St. Francis 7
Patients assisted annually 112,500
Bed Capacity 376

Des Plaines
Archdiocese of Chicago

Holy Family Medical Center
100 N. River Rd.
Des Plaines, IL 60016
Tel: 847-297-1800; Fax: 847-297-1863
Legal Title: *Holy Family Medical Center*
Sisters of the Holy Family of Nazareth
Sr. Patricia Ann Koschalke, C.S.F.N., Pres. & CEO
Rev. Ricardo Recera (Philippines) Chap.
Sisters 8
Bed Capacity 252
Patients assisted annually 117,334

Dolton
Archdiocese of Chicago

St. Francis Family Health Center
13826 S. Lincoln Ave.
Dolton, IL 60419

East St. Louis
Diocese of Belleville

St. Mary's Hospital
129 N. 8th St.
East St. Louis, IL 62201
Tel: 618-274-1900
Sponsored by the Poor Handmaids of Jesus Christ. Affiliate of Ancilla Systems, Inc.
Richard Mark, Pres. & CEO
Sisters 2
Bed Capacity 169
Patients assisted annually 32,141

Effingham
Diocese of Springfield in Illinois

St. Anthony's Memorial Hospital
503 N. Maple St.
Effingham, IL 62401
Tel: 217-342-2121
Anthony D. Pfitzer, Admin.
Sr. Helen Marie Plummer, O.S.F., Religious Leader
Rev. Gabriel Brinkman, O.F.M., Chap.
Hospital Sisters of the Third Order of St. Francis 5
Bed Capacity 146
Patients assisted annually 63,572

Elgin
Diocese of Rockford

St. Joseph Hospital
77 N. Airlite St.
Elgin, IL 60123
Tel: 847-695-3200
Legal Title: *Franciscan Sisters Health Care Corp.*
Sponsored by Franciscan Sisters of the Sacred Heart, Frankfort, IL.
Mr. Larry Narum, Pres.
Edward J. Hunter, Dir., Pastoral Care
Chaplains:
Revs.:
Dominic J. Cassidy (DAV)
William P. Knott
Sisters 3
Beds 280
Patients assisted annually 231,592
St. Joseph Hospital Foundation
St. Joseph Hospital Auxiliary
Franciscan Home Health of St. Joseph Hospital

Elk Grove Village
Archdiocese of Chicago

Alexian Brothers Medical Center, Inc.
800 Biesterfield Rd.

Elk Grove Village, IL 60007-3397
Tel: 708-437-5500
Congregation of Alexian Brothers, Immaculate Conception Province
Associated with Stritch School of Medicine of Loyola University.
Bro. PHILIP KENNEDY, C.F.A., Pres.
Chaplains:
Sr. SUSAN HART, O.P., Chap.-Supvr.
Revs.:
JAMES W. KELLY, O.P.
RICHARD LAPATA, O.P.
WILLIAM E. VEITH
Brothers 12
Licensed Beds 473
Lay Staff 2,200
Patients assisted annually 150,000
Parent: Alexian Brothers of Illinois, Inc.

Evanston
Archdiocese of Chicago

Saint Francis Hospital of Evanston
355 Ridge Ave.
Evanston, IL 60202
Tel: 708-316-4000
Legal Title: *Sisters of St. Francis Health Services Inc., Mt. Alverno, Mishawaka, IN*
Legal Title: *Alverno-Evanston Corporation*
Headquarters Address, St. Francis Provincialate
P.O. Box 766
Mishawaka, IN 46544
Sisters of St. Francis of Perpetual Adoration
Chaplains:
Revs.:
DANIEL J. COLLINS
KEVIN FANE, O.P.
Sisters 5
Bed Capacity 367
Patients assisted annually 250,000
St. Francis School of Nursing
Students 41

Evergreen Park
Archdiocese of Chicago

Little Company of Mary Hospital and Health Care Centers
2800 W. 95th St.
Evergreen Park, IL 60642
Tel: 708-422-6200; Fax: 708-425-9369
Legal Title: *The Little Company of Mary Hospital and Health Care Centers*
Sr. KATHLEEN MCINTYRE, L.C.M., Pres.
Ms. ROSEANN KELLER, Dir.
Chaplains:
Revs.:
LAMBERT KEMPKES, C.M.M.
LAURENCE COLLINS
JAMES GALLAGHER
Sr. ELIZABETH DONLAN, S.F.C.C.
MARGARET SCHNEIDER
Sisters of the Little Company of Mary 32
Bed Capacity 403
Bassinets 24
Patients assisted annually 175,221
Subsidiaries:
Little Company of Mary Adult Day Care
2800 W. 95th St.
Evergreen Park, IL 60805
Tel: 708-425-3100
Little Company of Mary Auxiliary
2800 W. 95th St.
Evergreen Park, IL 60805
Tel: 708-422-6200, Ext. 5066
Little Company of Mary Affiliated Services, Inc.
2800 W. 95th St.
Evergreen Park, IL 60805
Tel: 708-422-6200, Ext. 5100
Oak Lawn Care Station
5660 W. 95th St.
Oak Lawn, IL 60453
Tel: 708-499-2273
Burbank Care Station
4901 W. 79th St.
Burbank, IL 60459
Tel: 708-424-2273
Mary Potter Pavilion
2850 W. 95th St.
Evergreen Park, IL 60805
Little Company of Mary at Home (Home Health Care)
2800 W. 95th St.
Evergreen Park, IL 60805
Tel: 708-425-4211
Little Company of Mary Hospital Foundation
2800 W. 95th St.
Evergreen Park, IL 60805
Tel: 708-229-5022
MARY JO MAY, Exec. Dir.

Galesburg
Diocese of Peoria

St. Mary Medical Center
3333 N. Seminary St.
Galesburg, IL 61401-1299
Tel: 309-344-3161; Fax: 309-344-9494
Mailing Address:
607 NE Madison Ave.
Peoria, IL 61603
Sr. M. BERNARDA, O.S.F., Supr.
Rev. MICHAEL R. VAN ACKER, Chap.
Sisters of the Third Order of St. Francis 2
Capacity 156
Patients assisted annually 30,000
The Galesburg St. Mary Medical Center Foundation
3333 N. Seminary St.
Galesburg, IL 61401

Granite City
Diocese of Springfield in Illinois

St. Elizabeth Medical Center
2100 Madison Ave.
Granite City, IL 62040
Tel: 618-798-3000; Fax: 618-798-3508
Sr. M. THOMAS, C.D.P., Chm. Bd.
TED EILERMAN, Pres.
Rev. FINIAN MCMULLIN, O.F.M., Chap.
Sisters of Divine Providence, IL 8
Patients assisted annually 222,873
Bed Capacity 403

Highland
Diocese of Springfield in Illinois

St. Joseph's Hospital
1515 Main St.
Highland, IL 62249
Tel: 618-654-7421; Fax: 618-654-2012
Hospital Sisters of the Third Order of St. Francis 4
Patients assisted annually 30,000
Bed Capacity 106

Joliet
Diocese of Joliet in Illinois

St. Joseph Medical Center
Franciscan Sisters Health Care Corporation.
333 N. Madison St.
Joliet, IL 60435
Tel: 815-725-7133
DAVID W. BENFER, Pres.
Deacon ED PETAK, Dir. Pastoral Care
Sisters 13
Chaplains 9
Bed Capacity 542
Patients assisted annually 337,696
Total Staff 2,442
Industrial Rehab Center
Rte. 59
Joliet, IL 60435
Franciscan Home Health
333 N. Madison St.
Joliet, IL 60435
St. Joseph College of Nursing
333 N. Madison St.
Joliet, IL 60435
VIRGINIA E. KECK, Ph.D., R.N., Pres.
Coal City Family Health Center
410 N. Broadway St.
Coal City, IL 60416
New Lenox Family Health Center
305 Vine St.
New Lenox, IL 60451
Mokena Family Health Center
19401 Wolf Rd.
Mokena, IL 60448
St Joseph Medical Center Foundation
333 N. Madison St.
Joliet, IL 60435
St. Joseph Medical Center Women Auxiliary
333 N. Madison St.
Joliet, IL 60435
St. Joseph Medical Center Physical Rehabilitation and Sports Injury Center
2400 Glenwood Ave.
Joliet, IL 60435
Plainfield Family Health Center
138 S. Division St.
Plainfield, IL 60544
Wheatland Family Health Center
24024 W. Brancaster Dr.
Naperville, IL 60564
Weber Road Family Health Center
1280 Windham Pkwy.
Romeoville, IL 60441

Kankakee
Diocese of Joliet in Illinois

St. Mary's Hospital
500 West Court St.
Kankakee, IL 60901
Tel: 815-937-2490
Servants of the Holy Heart of Mary.
Sr. VIRGINIA MARIE DERK, Supr., Tel: 815-937-2384
Mr. ALLAN C. SONDUCK, Pres.
Rev. EDWARD POFF, Chap.
Bed Capacity 222
Patients assisted annually 91,605
Staff 992

Litchfield
Diocese of Springfield in Illinois

St. Francis Hospital
1215 E. Union, P.O. Box 1215
Litchfield, IL 62056
Tel: 217-324-2191
MICHAEL SIPKOSKI, Admin.
Rev. THEODOSIUS A. SCHELICH, O.F.M., Chap.
Sr. PAULETTE COLLINGS, O.S.F., Religious Coord.
Hospital Sisters of the Third Order of St. Francis 3
Patients assisted annually 61,402
Bed Capacity 138

Maywood
Archdiocese of Chicago

Foster G. McGaw Hospital of Loyola University of Chicago
2160 S. First Ave.
Maywood, IL 60153
Tel: 708-216-9056
Revs.:
THOMAS M. HESKIN, O.S.M.
JOHN P. COAKLEY, S.J.
Mr. JERRY KAELIN
Revs.:
ALLEN F. KIRK, S.J.
JAMES J. CREIGHTON, S.J., CPE Supvr.
Ms. LINDA BRONERSKY, M.P.S., Supvr.
Mr. DAVID CORCORAN, M.Ed.
Sr. KATHLEEN CONWAY, B.V.M.
Sr. JOANETTA BRUENE, O.P.
Ms. BETH BUTLER
MARIE COGLIANESE, M.P.S., Dir.
JOELLA DOGGETT, M.P.S.
Deacon ALBIN WEGNER
Rev. KEENAN SCHULER, Evangelical Free Church
Bed Capacity 561
Patients assisted annually 275,000

Mount Vernon
Diocese of Belleville

Good Samaritan Regional Health Center
605 N. 12th St.
Mount Vernon, IL 62864
Tel: 618-242-4600
A member of the SSM Health Care System.
LEO F. CHILDERS, JR., Pres.
Sr. DENISE SHARP, S.S.J., Chap.
Sisters 4
Bed Capacity 175
Patients assisted annually 65,306

Murphysboro
Diocese of Belleville

St. Joseph Memorial Hospital
800 N. Second St., P.O. Box 580
Murphysboro, IL 62966
Tel: 618-684-3156
A service of Southern Illinois Healthcare.
Adorers of the Blood of Christ
Ms. BETTY GAFFNEY, Senior Vice Pres. & Admin.
Sr. MILDRED GROSS, A.S.C., Corporate Dir. of Spritual Care
Sr. MARY BEDE, A.S.C., Dir. of Pastoral Care
Sisters 6
Bed Capacity 59
Patients assisted annually 24,746

Oak Park
Archdiocese of Chicago

Oak Park Hospital
520 S. Maple Ave.
Oak Park, IL 60304
Tel: 708-383-9300
Legal Title: *Oak Park Hospital*
Wheaton Franciscan Sisters
Mr. LEONARD J. MULLER, Pres. & CEO
Ms. LEE KOTNOUR, EVP
Chaplains:
Rev. RAYMOND ZSOLCZAI, O.F.M.

Bro. Michael May, O.F.M.
Sylvia Fromme
Bed Capacity 296
Patients assisted annually 45,306
Oak Park Hospital Endowment Fund Affiliate.

Peoria
Diocese of Peoria

OSF Healthcare System
800 N.E. Glen Oak Ave.
Peoria, IL 61603
Mailing Address:
607 NE Madison Ave.
Peoria, IL 61603
Sr. Frances Marie Masching, O.S.F., Pres.
OSF Healthcare Foundation
800 N.E. Glen Oak Ave.
Peoria, IL 61603
Mr. Kevin Schoeplein, Pres.
Total Annually Assisted 26,850,000
Total Staff 6,505

St. Francis' Medical Center
530 N.E. Glen Oak Ave.
Peoria, IL 61637
Tel: 309-655-2000; Fax: 309-655-2347
Mailing Address:
607 NE Madison Ave.
Peoria, IL 61603
Sr. M. Canisia, O.S.F., Admin.
Mr. Kevin Steffen, Assoc. Admin.
Sr. M. Ildefonsa, O.S.F., Supr.
Revs.:
Thomas Mizeur, Dir.
Michael Bliss
Capacity: Beds 590
Patients assisted annually 439,600
Saint Francis Medical Center College of Nursing Students 156

Pontiac
Diocese of Peoria

Saint James Hospital
610 E. Water
Pontiac, IL 61764
Tel: 815-842-2828; Fax: 815-842-4912
Mailing Address:
607 NE Madison Ave.
Peoria, IL 61603
David T. Ochs, Admin.
Sr. M. Gaudentia, O.S.F., Supr.
Rev. David Roche, Chap.
Sisters of the Third Order of St. Francis 5
Capacity 81
Patients assisted annually 73,314
Total Staff 330

Red Bud
Diocese of Belleville

St. Clement Health Services
One St. Clement Blvd.
Red Bud, IL 62278
Tel: 618-282-3831; Fax: 618-282-6101
Adorers of the Blood of Christ
Mary Saolis, Dir. of Pastoral Care
Mr. Michael McManus, Pres.
Rev. William J. Kane, S.J., Chap.
Sisters 2
Bed Capacity 105
Patients assisted annually 1,939

Rockford
Diocese of Rockford

Saint Anthony College of Nursing
5658 E. State St.
Rockford, IL 61108
Tel: 815-395-5090
Terese A. Burch, Ph.D., R.N., Dean of Academic Affairs
Students 100

Saint Anthony Medical Center
5666 E. State St.
Rockford, IL 61108
Tel: 815-226-2000
Mr. David Schertz, Admin.
Rev. William R. Wentink, Chap. & Dir., Pastoral Care
Center for cancer care.
Sisters of the Third Order of St. Francis (Peoria, IL) 5
Beds 303
Patients assisted annually 128,403

Spring Valley
Diocese of Peoria

St. Margaret's Hospital
600 E. First St.
Spring Valley, IL 61362
Tel: 815-664-5311; Fax: 815-664-1335
Mailing Address:
607 NE Madison Ave.
Peoria, IL 61603
Timothy Muntz, Pres.
Sr. Frances Ann Bellmare, Chap.
Sisters of Mary of the Presentation 7
Bed Capacity 127
Patients assisted annually 47,133
Total Staff 498

Springfield
Diocese of Springfield in Illinois

St. John's Hospital
800 E. Carpenter St.
Springfield, IL 62769
Tel: 217-544-6464
Mr. Scott Kastel, Exec. Vice Pres.
Rev. Thomas Hagstrom, Acting Dir. Pastoral Care
Patients assisted annually 204,164
Bed Capacity 609
St. John's College of Nursing
Jane Schachtsiek, R.N., Ph.D., Chancellor
Students 112

Streator
Diocese of Peoria

St. Mary's Hospital
111 E. Spring St.
Streator, IL 61364
Tel: 815-673-2311; Fax: 815-673-4541
Hospital Sisters of St. Francis
James F. Dover, Executive Vice Pres.
Thomas Whelan Asst. Admin.
Sisters 3
Patients assisted annually 49,056
Bed Capacity 251
Bassinets 28
Total Staff 487

Taylorville
Diocese of Springfield in Illinois

St. Vincent Memorial Hospital
201 E. Pleasant St.
Taylorville, IL 62568
Tel: 217-824-3331; Fax: 217-824-2099
Rev. Richard Trutter, Chap.
Adorers of the Blood of Christ 6
Patients assisted annually 35,569
Bed Capacity 129
Bassinets 8
Extended care facility 50

Tinley Park
Archdiocese of Chicago

St. Francis Family Health Center
17148 S. Harlem Ave.
Tinley Park, IL 60477

Urbana
Diocese of Peoria

Covenant Medical Center of Champaign/Urbana
1400 W. Park Ave.
Urbana, IL 61801
Tel: 217-337-2000; Fax: 217-337-4541
Mailing Address:
607 NE Madison Ave.
Peoria, IL 61603
Servants of the Holy Heart of Mary
Sr. Mary K. Himens, S.S.C.M., Supr.
Sr. Evelyn Var Boncouer, S.S.C.M., Chm. Bd.
Mr. Joseph Beard, Pres.
Chaplains:
Sr. Mary Robert Morton, S.S.C.M., Dir.
Vera Duncanson
Ginny Conron
Peter Duck
Bob Mulligan
Harry Litzenberg
Sisters 8
Capacity 280
Patients assisted annually 126,341
Total Staff 1,102

Waukegan
Archdiocese of Chicago

Saint Therese Medical Center
2615 Washington St.
Waukegan, IL 60085
Tel: 708-249-3900
Legal Title: *Franciscan Sisters Health Care Corp.*
Sponsored by Franciscan Sisters of the Sacred Heart (Frankfort, IL).
Timothy Selz, Pres.
Sr. M. Norma Janssen, O.S.F., Chm. Board.
Rev. Donald E. Cusack, Chap.
Sisters 2
Bed Capacity 388
Patients assisted annually 54,200
Franciscan Sisters Health Care Corp. Affiliate

Worth
Archdiocese of Chicago

St. Francis Family Health Center
11415 S. Harlem Ave.
Worth, IL 60482

INDIANA

Anderson
Diocese of Lafayette in Indiana

Saint John's Health System
2015 Jackson St.
Anderson, IN 46016
Tel: 317-649-2511
Mr. James H. Stephens, Pres. & CEO
Mrs. Christine A. Loftus, Dir. Chaplaincy Svcs.
Anderson Center of Saint John's
2210 Jackson St.
Anderson, IN 46016-4363
Tel: 317-646-8444
A 63-bed psychiatric/chemical dependency hospital.
Sisters of the Holy Cross 5
Bed Capacity 371
Patients assisted annually 183,531

Beech Grove
Archdiocese of Indianapolis

St. Francis Hospital and Health Centers
1600 Albany St.
Beech Grove, IN 46107
Tel: 317-787-3311
Sisters of St. Francis Health Services, Inc.
Mr. Robert J. Brody, Pres. & CEO
Chaplains:
Revs.:
Fred Deters
Ruta A. Cabazi (Tanzania)
John H. Mannion (LFT)
Sisters 6
Staff 2,800
Beds 540
Patients assisted annually 130,000

Crown Point
Diocese of Gary

St. Anthony Medical Center, Inc.
1201 S. Main St.
Crown Point, IN 46307-8483
Tel: 219-738-2100
Mr. Stephen O. Leurck, Pres.
Pastoral Care Team:
Revs.:
Anthony Janik, O.F.M.
Carmen Scuderi, O.F.M.
Franciscan Sisters of Chicago 24
Beds 411
Total Staff 981
Patients assisted annually 96,353

Dyer
Diocese of Gary

St. Margaret Mercy Healthcare Centers, South Campus
(Div. of the Sisters of St. Francis Health Services, Inc.)
24 Joliet
Dyer, IN 46311
Tel: 219-932-2300
Rev. Michael Maginot
Sisters of St. Francis of Perpetual Adoration 2
Beds 319
Bassinets 16
Total Staff 1,017
Patients assisted annually 45,659

East Chicago
Diocese of Gary

St. Catherine Hospital
4321 Fir St.
East Chicago, IN 46312
Tel: 219-392-1700; Fax: 219-392-7002
(Operated by Lakeshore Health Systems, Inc.)
Sponsored by the Poor Handmaids of Jesus Christ.
Affiliates of Ancilla Systems.
John Birzdell, CEO

MARK ROGERS, Chief Oper. Officer & Chief Fin. Officer
Sr. MARY ELLEN GOELLER, P.H.J.C., Reg. Vice Pres. Mission Effectiveness
Sisters 11
Beds 290
Bassinets 20
Total Staff 984
Patients assisted annually 45,987
St. Catherine Hospital Foundation, Inc.
Transitional Care Unit (TCU)
Nazareth Home

Elwood
Diocese of Lafayette in Indiana

St. Vincent Mercy Hospital, Inc.
1331 South A St.
Elwood, IN 46036-1942
Tel: 317-552-3336; Fax: 317-552-6945
Mr. JAMES BAER, Admin.
ROSEMARY J. COUGHLIN, C.S.J., Chap.
Daughters of Charity National Health System
Bed Capacity 49
Patients assisted annually 36,461
Staff 151

Evansville
Diocese of Evansville

St. Mary's Medical Center of Evansville, Inc.
3700 Washington Ave.
Evansville, IN 47750
Tel: 812-485-4000
RICHARD BREON, Pres. & CEO
Sr. CATHERINE KELLY, D.C., Vice Pres. Mission Svcs.
Rev. RALPH SCHIPP, Chap.
Daughters of Charity of St. Vincent de Paul 4
Beds 502
Patients assisted annually 230,837

Fort Wayne
Diocese of Fort Wayne - South Bend

St. Joseph Medical Center
700 Broadway
Fort Wayne, IN 46802
Tel: 219-425-3000; Fax: 219-425-3222
Sponsored by the Poor Handmaids of Jesus Christ.
Affiliate of Ancilla Systems Incorporated.
JOHN T. FARRELL, SR., CEO & Pres.
Sr. M. CONRAD KIRCHHOFF, P.H.J.C., Vice Pres. Mission Effectiveness
GEORGIA K. FLOYD, D.Min., Dir. Pastoral Care
Rev. MATTHEW S. KAFKA, Priest Chap.
Staff Chaplains:
Sr. MARY RUTH KRACK, O.S.B.
Rev. JOSEPH W. ANDREWS
Deacon FRANCIS C. WALSH
DORIS A. MATHER
JANE F. TILL
Sisters 8
Bed Capacity 218
Nursery beds 20
Licensed 218
Patients assisted annually 130,571

Hammond
Diocese of Gary

St. Margaret Mercy Healthcare Centers - North Campus
5454 Hohman Ave.
Hammond, IN 46320
Tel: 219-932-2300
Sisters of St. Francis Health Services, Inc.
Rev. GREGORY HOLICKY
Sisters of St. Francis of Perpetual Adoration 5
Beds 487
Bassinets 45
Total Staff 2,003
Patients assisted annually 84,766

Hobart
Diocese of Gary

St. Mary Medical Center
1500 S. Lake Park Ave.
Hobart, IN 46342
Tel: 219-942-0551; Fax: 219-947-6037
Sponsored by the Poor Handmaids of Jesus Christ
Operated by Lakeshore Health System, Inc. Affiliate of Ancilla Systems, Inc.
JOE MARK, CEO
MILTON TRIANA, CEO
Sr. MARY ELLEN GOELLER, P.H.J.C., Reg. Vice Pres. Mission Effectiveness
Revs.:
MIKE MAGINOT, Chap.
ANDREW MALARZ
Sisters 4
Beds 194
Bassinets 12
Total Staff 804
Patients assisted annually 41,204
St. Mary Medical Center Foundation, Inc.

Indianapolis
Archdiocese of Indianapolis

St. Vincent Hospital and Health Care Center, Inc.
2001 W. 86th St.
Indianapolis, IN 46260
Tel: 317-338-7000; Fax: 317-338-7005
Daughters of Charity of St. Vincent de Paul
DOUGLAS D. FRENCH, Pres. & CEO
Sr. SHARON RICHARDT, D.C., Vice Pres. Mission Svcs.
Revs.:
CHARLES HENRY, O.S.B.
GEORGE F. PLASTER (LAF)
JOSEPH F. RAUTENBERG (IND)
DONALD J. EVRARD (IND)
Ms. JOAN M. BUMPUS, Dir. Pastoral Care
Sisters 9
Bed Capacity 741
Total Staff 4,585
Inpatient Admissions 30,662
Outpatient Visits 841,512
Chaplains 21

**St. Vincent New Hope, Inc.*
8405 N. Payne Rd.
Indianapolis, IN 46268
Tel: 317-872-4210
Daughters of Charity of St. Vincent de Paul
Bed Capacity 269
Total Staff 389
Patients assisted annually 185

Seton Health Corporation of Central Indiana
2001 W. 86th St.
Indianapolis, IN 46260
Tel: 317-338-7000; Fax: 317-338-7005
Daughters of Charity of St. Vincent de Paul
Mr. DOUGLAS D. FRENCH, Pres. & CEO

**St. Vincent Cardiac Services, Inc.*
2001 W. 86th St.
Indianapolis, IN 46260
Tel: 317-338-7000; Fax: 317-338-7005
Mr. SCOTT C. MALANEY, Vice Chm.

Jasper
Diocese of Evansville

Memorial Hospital and Health Care Center, Little Company of Mary of Indiana, Inc.
800 W. Ninth St.
Jasper, IN 47546
Tel: 812-482-2345
Sr. MARY ADRIAN DAVIS, L.C.M., Pres. & CEO
Sr. MAURA BECKMAN, O.S.B., Chap.
Sisters of the Little Company of Mary 2
Beds 131
Patients assisted annually 101,638

Memorial Hospital Foundation, Inc.
Jasper, IN 47546
WILLIAM RUBINO, Pres.

Kokomo
Diocese of Lafayette in Indiana

Saint Joseph Hospital & Health Center of Kokomo, Indiana, Inc.
1907 W. Sycamore St.
Kokomo, IN 46901
Tel: 317-452-5611
Sr. M. MARTIN MCENTEE, C.S.J., Pres.
Dr DWIGHT G. LEE, Dir. Pastoral Care
Total Staff 950
Sisters 1
Bed Capacity 220
Patients assisted annually 85,000
Saint Joseph Foundation of Kokomo, Indiana, Inc.

Lafayette
Diocese of Lafayette in Indiana

St. Elizabeth Hospital Medical Center
1501 Hartford St., P.O. Box 7501
Lafayette, IN 47903
Tel: 317-423-6011
Legal Title: *Sisters of St. Francis Health Services, Inc., Mishawaka, IN*
Mr. DOUGLAS W. EBERLE, Pres.
Sr. ANNETTE CRONE, O.S.F., Senior Vice Pres.
Revs.:
VICTOR SCHOTT
PAUL GRAF
School of Nursing
Students 160
Sisters of St. Francis of Perpetual Adoration 5
Operational Beds 205
Patients assisted annually 134,079
Staff 1,134

Michigan City
Diocese of Gary

St. Anthony Hospital and Health Centers
301 W. Homer St.
Michigan City, IN 46360
Tel: 219-879-8511
Sisters of St. Francis Health Services, Inc.
Rev. LARRY HENRY, C.S.C., Chap.
Sisters of St. Francis of Perpetual Adoration 3
Beds 190
Bassinets 20
Total Staff 667
Patients assisted annually 199,639

Mishawaka
Diocese of Fort Wayne - South Bend

**St. Joseph Community Hospital*
215 W. 4th St.
Mishawaka, IN 46544
Tel: 219-259-2431
Poor Handmaids of Jesus Christ.
Affiliate of Ancilla Systems Incorporated.
STEPHEN CRAIN, Pres. & CEO
Sr. PAULINE BRIDEGROOM, P.H.J.C., Vice Pres. Mission Effectiveness
Bed Capacity 125
Lay Staff 500
Patients assisted annually 60,236

Plymouth
Diocese of Fort Wayne - South Bend

Saint Joseph's Hospital of Marshall County, Inc.
1915 Lake Ave., P.O. Box 670
Plymouth, IN 46563
Tel: 219-936-3181
Sponsored by Congregation of Sisters of the Holy Cross.
BRIAN DIETZ, Pres.
MARY COURSEY, Vice Pres. Diagnostic Svcs.
Mr. JEFF NIXA, N.A.C.C. Cert., Chap.
LORI PRICE, Vice Pres. Patient Care Svcs.
Staff 297
Bed Capacity 58
Patients assisted annually 42,277

South Bend
Diocese of Fort Wayne - South Bend

Saint Joseph's Medical Center, Inc.
801 E. LaSalle St.
South Bend, IN 46617
Tel: 219-237-7111
DENNIS HECK, Pres. & CEO
ALAN BOWMAN, Dir. Chaplaincy Services
Sisters 17
Bed Capacity 339
Patients assisted annually 131,323

St. Mary Community Hospital
2515 E. Jefferson Blvd.
South Bend, IN 46615
Tel: 219-288-8311
Poor Handmaids of Jesus Christ (Affiliate of Ancilla Systems Incorporated)
STEPHEN CRAIN, Pres. & CEO
Sr. PAULINE BRIDEGROOM, P.H.J.C., Vice Pres. Mission Effectiveness

IOWA

Carroll
Diocese of Sioux City

St. Anthony Regional Hospital
Carroll, IA 51401
Tel: 712-792-3581
GARY P. RIEDMANN, Pres.
Rev. ROBERT LEITING, Chap.
Franciscan Sisters of Perpetual Adoration 3
Bed Capacity 99
Patients assisted annually 43,364
St. Anthony Regional Nursing Home
Rev. ROBERT L. LEITING, Chap.
Orchard View, Inc.
S. Clark St.
Carroll, IA 51401
Tel: 712-792-3581

Cedar Rapids
Archdiocese of Dubuque

Mercy Care Management, Inc.
P.O. Box 786

Cedar Rapids, IA 52406
Tel: 319-398-6144
Mr. MARC GULLICKSON, Chief Admin. Officer
Mr. LEE LIU, Chm.

Mercy Medical Center, Cedar Rapids, Iowa
(Sub. of Mercy Care Service Corp.)
701 Tenth St., S.E.
Cedar Rapids, IA 52403
Tel: 319-398-6011
Sponsored by the Sisters of Mercy, Cedar Rapids Regional Community.
A. JAMES TINKER, CEO
Rev. JOHN R. GALLAGHER, Res. Chap.
Sr. MARY LOU PODZIMEK, R.S.M., Dir. Pastoral Care Office
Chaplains:
Rev. GARY DEVRIES
Sr. BERNICE KURT, R.S.M.
Sr. MADONNA SCHMITT, O.S.B.
Staff 1,120
Bed Capacity 382
Patients assisted annually 116,913

Mercy Medical Center, Cedar Rapids, Iowa, Endowment Foundation, Inc.
701 Tenth St., S.E.
Cedar Rapids, IA 52403
Tel: 319-398-6519
Sr. MARY LAWRENCE HALLAGAN, R.S.M., Pres.

Mercycare Service Corporation
(Parent Corp.)
701 10th St., S.E.
Cedar Rapids, IA 52403
Tel: 319-398-6011
Sponsored by the Sisters of Mercy, Cedar Rapids Regional Community.
A. JAMES TINKER, CEO

Centerville
Diocese of Davenport

St. Joseph's Mercy Hospital
One St. Joseph's Dr.
Centerville, IA 52544
Tel: 515-437-4111
WILLIAM C. ASSELL, Pres.
Bro. DARYL CHARRON, C.PP.S., Pastoral Assoc.
Owned by Mercy Hospital Medical Center, Des Moines.
Attended from St. Mary's, Centerville.
Legacies, The Foundation of St. Joseph's Mercy Hospital
Tel: 515-437-3434
Beds 60
Patients assisted annually 34,953

Clinton
Diocese of Davenport

Samaritan Health System, Inc.
A subsidiary of Mercy Health Services.
1410 N. Fourth St.
Clinton, IA 52732
Tel: 319-244-5555
THOMAS J. HESSELMANN, Pres.
Revs.:
HORST HEHR, Chap.
JOHN J. STACK
Beds 201
Staff 1,016
Patients assisted annually 66,713
Samaritan Hospital South
638 S. Bluff Blvd.
Clinton, IA 52732
Tel: 319-244-5555
Samaritan Hospital North
1410 N. Fourth St.
Clinton, IA 52732
Tel: 319-244-5555
Samaritan Services for Aging
Bluff Terrace Nursing Home, 638 S. Bluff Blvd.
Clinton, IA 52732
Beds 64
Wyndcrest Nursing Home
600 14th Ave. N.
Clinton, IA 52732

Corning
Diocese of Des Moines

Mercy Midlands: Mercy Hospital
Rosary Dr., P.O. Box 368
Corning, IA 50841
Tel: 515-322-3121; Fax: 515-322-4872
JAMES C. RUPPERT, Admin.
Rev. DAN SIEPKER, Chap.
Patients assisted annually 3,342

Council Bluffs
Diocese of Des Moines

Bergan Mercy Health System: Mercy Hospital
800 Mercy Dr.
Council Bluffs, IA 51502
Tel: 712-328-5000; Fax: 712-328-5202
Sisters of Mercy of the Americas
The Mercy Center
Mercy Medical Office Bldgs., Inc.
Revs.:
DENNIS TRAUSCH
CHARLES SCOTT
Chaplains 5
Beds 300
Patients assisted annually 67,820

Des Moines
Diocese of Des Moines

Mercy Hospital Medical Center
6th & University Ave.
Des Moines, IA 50314
Tel: 515-247-3121
Sisters of Mercy of the Americas (Omaha Province)
Rev. PAUL SOLOMIA (Philippines) Dir. Pastoral Care
Chaplains:
Rev. BRAULIO TOLOSA (Philippines)
Sr. ALICIA GALLAGHER, R.S.M.
Sr. CAROLA BRODERICK, B.V.M.
Sr. MARGARET O'NEIL, O.P.
Sisters 29
Patients assisted annually 143,767
Mercy Health Center of Central Iowa
Mercy Health and Human Services
Mercy Geriatric Service
Mercy Court
Mercy Properties
Mercy School of Health Sciences
Clark Street House of Mercy

Dubuque
Archdiocese of Dubuque

Mercy Health Center-St. Joseph's Unit
(Div. of Mercy Health Services)
Mercy Dr.
Dubuque, IA 52001
Tel: 319-589-8000; Fax: 319-589-8073
Sr. HELEN HUEWE, O.S.F., Pres.
Sr. JEANNE WICKHAM, O.S.F., Dir. Pastoral Care Dept.
Chaplains:
Rev. STEPHEN A. LUNDGREN
Sr. MARILYN SCHLOSSER, O.P.
Sr. ROSALYN ULFERS, P.B.V.M.
JOAN HAUG
Bed Capacity 402
Total Staff 1,006
Patients assisted annually 43,521

Dyersville
Archdiocese of Dubuque

Mercy Health Center-St. Mary's Unit
(Div. of Mercy Health Services)
1111 Third St., S.W.
Dyersville, IA 52040
Tel: 319-875-7101; Fax: 319-875-2957
Sr. HELEN HUEWE, O.S.F., Pres.
Bed Capacity 49
Total Staff 76
Patients assisted annually 4,514

Estherville
Diocese of Sioux City

Holy Family Hospital
826 N. Eighth St.
Estherville, IA 51334
Tel: 712-362-2631
Sisters of the Presentation of the B.U.M. (Aberdeen, S.D.).
Bed Capacity 58
Patients assisted annually 16,933
Total Staff 203
Holy Family Hospital Foundation.

Iowa City
Diocese of Davenport

Mercy Hospital
Iowa City, IA 52240
Tel: 319-339-0300; Fax: 319-339-3788
RONALD R. REED, Admin.
Chaplains:
Revs.:
ANDREW KELLY
FRANCIS BASS
Sisters 3
Beds 222

Mason City
Archdiocese of Dubuque

North Iowa Mercy Health Center
(Div. of Mercy Health Services)
84 Beaumont Dr.
Mason City, IA 50401
Tel: 515-424-7211; Fax: 515-424-7827
DAVID H. VELLINGA, Pres. & CEO
Chaplains:
JULIE WEBER, Dir. Mission Services
Revs.:
KENNETH B. GEHLING
ROGER KATZ
Sr. ELAINE FRANK, O.S.F.
Rev. KIRK JOHNSON
ROSE SCHLEUTER
Bed Capacity 350
Patients assisted annually 547,908

New Hampton
Archdiocese of Dubuque

St. Joseph Community Hospital
(Div. of Mercy Health Services)
308 N. Maple Ave.
New Hampton, IA 50659
Tel: 515-394-4121; Fax: 515-394-5628
THOMAS R. THOMPSON, Pres. & CEO
MARGE TEKIPPE, Chm. Board, Community Health Care System
Rev. JOHN HARPEL, S.V.D., Chap.
Staff 20
Bed Capacity 49
Patients assisted annually 18,300

Oelwein
Archdiocese of Dubuque

Mercy Hospital of Franciscan Sisters
Oelwein, IA 50662
Tel: 319-283-6000; Fax: 319-283-6004
Franciscan Sisters. Daughters of the Sacred Hearts of Jesus and Mary, Wheaton, IL
KATHY HINTZ, Interim Admin.
Sr. ALICE MAIERS, R.S.M., Chap.
Rev. FREDERICK FANGMAN, Chap.
Bed Capacity 64
Patients assisted annually 41,984

Sioux City
Diocese of Sioux City

Marian Health Center
801 Fifth St.
Sioux City, IA 51101
Tel: 712-279-2010; Fax: 712-279-2034
Mercy Health Services, Regional Community of Detroit.
Mr. DOUGLAS V. JOHNSON, Pres. & CEO
Chaplains:
Rev. RICHARD A. SITZMANN
Sr. MARLYS BECKER, O.S.F.
Rev. JOHN LEE, Lutheran Chap.
PATRICK MCCRUDEN
Sisters 3
Bed Capacity 484
Patients assisted annually 258,000

Waterloo
Archdiocese of Dubuque

Covenant Medical Center
3421 W. Ninth St.
Waterloo, IA 50702
Tel: 319-236-4111
Franciscan Sisters. Daughters of the Sacred Hearts of Jesus and Mary, Wheaton, IL
Mr. RAYMOND BURFEIND, Pres.
Revs.:
A. W. KLEVE, Res. Chap.
PAUL C. MCMANUS, Chap.
S.F.H., Inc.
3421 W. Ninth St.
Waterloo, IA 50702
Tel: 319-236-4111
Franciscan Sisters. Daughters of the Sacred Heart of Jesus and Mary, Wheaton, IL
Mr. WILFED F. LOEBIG, JR., Pres.
Covenant Health System, Inc.
3421 W. Ninth St.
Waterloo, IA 50702
Tel: 319-236-4013
RAYMOND F. BURFEIND, Pres.
Covenant Foundation, Inc.
3421 W. Ninth St.
Waterloo, IA 50702
Tel: 319-236-4030

DON L. HOTH, Exec. Dir.
Sisters 1
Staff 1,950
Bed Capacity 346
Patients assisted annually 12,971

KANSAS

Fort Scott
Diocese of Wichita

Mercy Hospital
821 Burke St.
Fort Scott, KS 66701
Tel: 316-223-7057; Fax: 316-223-5327
SUSAN BARRETT, Admin.
Rev. EUGENE GRABNER, O.S.B.
Sisters of Mercy 26
Lay Staff 482
Bed Capacity 110
Bassinets 15
Patients assisted annually 23,716

Garden City
Diocese of Dodge City

St. Catherine Hospital
410 E. Walnut
Garden City, KS 67846-5672
Tel: 316-272-2222; Fax: 316-272-2566
GARY L. ROWE, Pres. & CEO
MARK STEADHAM, Sr. Vice Pres. Operations
LEANNE IRSIK, Vice Pres. of Patient Svcs.
Rev. FRANCIS JORDAN, Chap.
SUSAN STEELE, Chap.
Sr. KATHY SALEWSKI, Exec. Assistant Mission
MARK TOZZIO, Chief Development & Marketing
DAVID MOODY, Human Resources Dir.
TERRY STOFFERSON, CFO
Sisters 1
Bed Capacity 95
Patients assisted annually 40,280

Great Bend
Diocese of Dodge City

Central Kansas Medical Center
3515 Broadway
Great Bend, KS 67530
Tel: 316-792-2511
Sisters of the Third Order of St. Dominic
GARY L. BARNETT, Pres. & CEO
Sr. KATHLEEN ANDREWS, R.N., Vice Pres. Patient Care Svcs.
TOM SOMMERS, Vice Pres. Fiscal Svcs.
Sisters 9
Bed Capacity 302
Total Staff 509
Patients assisted annually 54,938

Independence
Diocese of Wichita

Mercy Hospitals of Kansas-Independence
800 W. Myrtle St.
Independence, KS 67301
Tel: 316-331-2200
SUSAN BARRETT, COO
Sisters of Mercy 3
Bed Capacity 93
Patients assisted annually 33,267
Home Health visits 22,303

Kansas City
Archdiocese of Kansas City in Kansas

Providence Medical Center
8929 Parallel Pkwy.
Kansas City, KS 66112
Fax: 913-596-4098
An affiliate of the Sisters of Charity of Leavenworth Health Services Corporation.
Mr. FRANK CREEDEN, Pres. & CEO
Sisters 4
Bed Capacity 400
Bassinets 13
Employees 970
Physicians 300
Patients assisted annually 57,131

Larned
Diocese of Dodge City

Central Kansas Medical Center, St. Joseph Campus
923 Carroll St.
Larned, KS 67550
Tel: 316-285-3161
GARY BARNETT, Pres. & CEO
Bed Capacity 50
Total Staff 87

Leavenworth
Archdiocese of Kansas City in Kansas

St. John Hospital
3500 S. 4th St.
Leavenworth, KS 66048
Tel: 913-682-3721
Mr. FRANK CREEDEN, Pres.
Sisters of Charity of Leavenworth 3
Bed Capacity 76
Patients assisted annually 42,612

Pittsburg
Diocese of Wichita

Mount Carmel Medical Center; Mount Carmel Foundation
Centennial and Rouse
Pittsburg, KS 66762
Tel: 316-231-6100
DAN LINGOR, Admin.
Revs.:
SAMUEL J. PINKERTON, Chap.
LARRY PARKER, Chap.
Sisters of St. Joseph 3
Bed Capacity 188
Bassinets 12
Patients assisted annually 70,349

Topeka
Archdiocese of Kansas City in Kansas

St. Francis Hospital and Medical Center
1700 W. 7th St.
Topeka, KS 66606
Tel: 913-295-8000
Sr. LORETTO MARIE COLWELL, S.C.L., Pres.
Sisters of Charity of Leavenworth 3
Bed Capacity 378
Total Staff 1,603
Patients assisted annually 227,411

Wichita
Diocese of Wichita

St. Joseph Health Corporation
929 N. St. Francis
Wichita, KS 67214
Tel: 316-268-5000
Legal Title: *St. Joseph Health Corporation*

Via Christi Regional Medical Center, Inc.
929 N. St. Francis
Wichita, KS 67214
Tel: 316-268-5000
St. Joseph Campus
3600 E. Harry
Wichita, KS 67218
Tel: 316-685-1111
Mr. LEROY E. RHEAULT, Pres. & CEO
Sr. HELENE LENTZ, C.S.J., Vice Pres. Mission Svcs.
Bed Capacity 1222
Patients assisted annually 350,419

Via Christi Rehabilitation Hospital, Inc.
Lourdes Campus, 1151 N. Rock Rd.
Wichita, KS 67206
Tel: 316-634-3400
Mr. ANTHONY ISAAC, Chm.
Ms. LAURIE LABARCA, COO
Mr. TIM LYTLE, Pastoral Svcs.
Staff 155
Bed Capacity 60
Patients assisted annually 1,479

KENTUCKY

Ashland
Diocese of Lexington

Our Lady of Bellefonte Hospital, Inc.
St. Christopher Dr.
Ashland, KY 41101
Tel: 606-833-3333; Fax: 606-833-3695
(Member of Franciscan Health System of Kentucky, Inc.).
Rev. JOHN P. NOE, Chap.
Franciscan Sisters of the Poor 3
Beds 189
Patients assisted annually 61,957

Bardstown
Archdiocese of Louisville

Flaget Memorial Hospital
Bardstown, KY 40004
Tel: 502-348-3923, Ext. 242
Sisters of Charity of Nazareth Health System
SUZANNE REASBECK, Pres. & CEO
Sisters 5
Bed Capacity 52
Bassinets 8
Patients assisted annually 28,698
Attended from St. Joseph Church.

Covington
Diocese of Covington

St. Elizabeth Medical Center, North
401 E. 20th St.
Covington, KY 41014-1585
Tel: 606-292-4000; Fax: 606-292-4487
Mr. JOSEPH W. GROSS, Pres. & CEO
Mr. MARC A. HOFFMAN, Senior Vice Pres. & COO
Ms. ROSEMARY HOOK, Vice Pres. Nursing
Mr. MICHAEL ARTHUR, Vice Pres. Finance
Mr. THOMAS HORTON, Vice Pres. Human Resources
Mr. LEN PUTHOFF, Vice Pres. General Svcs.
Mr. THOMAS E. SAALFIELD, Vice Pres. Professional Svcs.
Mr. MICHAEL J. WALTERS, Vice Pres. Systems Devel.
Mr. ALLEN ZOBAY, M.D., Vice Pres. Medical Affairs
Chaplains:
Rev. ROBERT J. ROSS, S.J., Dir. Pastoral Care
Res.,
2028 Mackoy St.
Covington, KY 41014-1543
Rev. ROBERT ROSING
Res.,
Marydale Retreat Center, 945 Donaldson Hwy.
Erlanger, KY 41018-1093
Beds 149
Patients assisted annually 58,526
St. Elizabeth Medical Center Foundation, Inc.

Edgewood
Diocese of Covington

St. Elizabeth Medical Center, South
One Medical Village Dr.
Edgewood, KY 41017-3441
Tel: 606-344-2000
Mr. JOSEPH GROSS, Pres. & CEO
Mr. MARC A. HOFFMAN, Senior Vice Pres. & COO
Chaplains:
Rev. ROBERT J. ROSS, S.J., Dir. Pastoral Care
Deacon DAVID FLYNN, Assoc. Dir. Pastoral Care
Rev. JOHN P. WERNER
Beds 339
Patients assisted annually 162,196

Frenchburg
Diocese of Lexington

Menifee Medical Center
P.O. Box 49
Frenchburg, KY 40322
Tel: 606-768-2191
(Div. of St. Claire Medical Center).
DAVID BOLT, Vice Pres.
Patients assisted annually 13,551

Irvine
Diocese of Lexington

Marcum and Wallace Memorial Hospital
201 Richmond Ave.
Irvine, KY 40336
Tel: 606-723-2115; Fax: 606-723-6549
(Member of Mercy Health System, Cincinnati, OH).
CHRISTOPHER M. GODDARD, Admin.
Sisters 1
Beds 26
Patients assisted annually 27,500

Lexington
Diocese of Lexington

St. Joseph Hospital
1 St. Joseph Dr.
Lexington, KY 40504
Tel: 606-278-3436
(Member of Sisters of Charity of Nazareth Health System).
THOMAS MURRAY, Pres. & CEO
Mr. MARK DUNDON, Pres. & CEO, Sisters of Charity of Nazareth Health System
Revs.:
HERB OSBORNE, Dir. Chap. Svcs.
JOSEPH E. WHALEN (GI) Chap.
Sisters of Charity of Nazareth 12
Bed Capacity 468
Patients assisted annually 61,314

London
Diocese of Lexington

London, Marymount dba Marymount Medical Center
310 E. Ninth St.

London, KY 40741
Tel: 606-878-6520
(Member of Sisters of Charity of Nazareth Health System).
Mr. LOWELL JONES, Pres. & CEO
MARK W. DUNDON, Pres.
Bed Capacity 100
Patients assisted annually 119,296

Louisville
Archdiocese of Louisville

Caritas Medical Center
1850 Bluegrass Ave.
Louisville, KY 40215
Tel: 502-361-6000
Sisters of Charity of Nazareth
Rev. JOSEPH STOLTZ, Chap.
Sisters 9
Bed Capacity 331
Patients assisted annually 101,944

Martin
Diocese of Lexington

Our Lady of the Way Hospital, Inc.
Box 910
Martin, KY 41649
Tel: 606-285-5181
Sisters of Charity, Cincinnati, OH
Mr. LOWELL JONES, Admin.
Beds 39
Patients assisted annually 16,752

Morehead
Diocese of Lexington

Saint Claire Medical Center
Morehead, KY 40351
Tel: 606-784-6661
Sisters of Notre Dame
Mr. MARK NEFF, Pres. & CEO
Sisters 5
Beds 133
Bassinets 10
Patients assisted annually 71,750
Patients with Primary Care Centers 323,327

Olive Hill
Diocese of Lexington

Carter County Medical Clinic
P.O. Box V, U.S. 60 W.
Olive Hill, KY 41164
Tel: 606-286-4152
(Div. of St. Claire Medical Center).
DAVID BOLT, Vice Pres.
Patients assisted annually 14,594

Owingsville
Diocese of Lexington

Bath County Medical Clinic
632 Slate Ave.
Owingsville, KY 40360
Tel: 606-674-6386
(Div. of St. Claire Medical Center).
Mr. DAVID BOLT, Vice Pres.
Patients assisted annually 20,076

Paducah
Diocese of Owensboro

Lourdes Hospital
1530 Lone Oak Rd., P.O. Box 7100
Paducah, KY 42002-7100
Tel: 502-444-2444
W. JEFFERSON COMER, Pres.
Rev. JOSEPH EKWEARIRI
Sr. MARIE MOORE, Vice. Pres. of Mission Svcs.
Legal Title: *Lourdes Hospital, Inc.*
Beds 389
Patients assisted annually 85,000

Sandy Hook
Diocese of Lexington

Elliot County Medical Clinic
P.O. Box 748
Sandy Hook, KY 41171
Tel: 606-738-5155
(Div. of St. Claire Medical Center).
Mr. DAVID BOLT, Vice Pres.
Patients assisted annually 11,781

Williamstown
Diocese of Covington

St. Elizabeth Medical Center, Grant County
238 Barnes Rd.
Williamstown, KY 41097-9482
Tel: 606-291-6738
Mr. JOSEPH GROSS, Pres. & CEO
Mr. MARC A. HOFFMAN, Senior Vice Pres. & COO
Mr. CHRIS CARLE, Admin.
Rev. ROBERT J. ROSS, S.J., Chap. & Dir. Pastoral Care
Beds 30
Patients assisted annually 17,591

LOUISIANA

Alexandria
Diocese of Alexandria

St. Frances Cabrini Hospital
3330 Masonic Dr.
Alexandria, LA 71301
Tel: 318-487-1122
Sr. OLIVE BORDELON, C.C.V.I., Admin. & CEO
Revs.:
CHRISTUDAS NAYAK (India) Dir. Pastoral Care
FERREOLUS D'CRUZ (India) Chap.
Sisters of Charity of the Incarnate Word 12
Bed Capacity 302
Patients assisted annually 73,946
St. Frances Cabrini Hospital Foundation of Alexandria, Inc.
3330 Masonic Dr.
Alexandria, LA 71301

Baton Rouge
Diocese of Baton Rouge

Our Lady of the Lake Regional Medical Center
5000 Hennessy Blvd.
Baton Rouge, LA 70808-4398
Tel: 504-765-6565; Fax: 504-766-5645
Franciscan Missionaries of Our Lady (North American Province)
Sr. BRENDAN MARY RONAYNE, O.S.F., Supr.
Mr. ROBERT C. DAVIDGE, Pres.
Revs.:
GEORGE E. GOODBOUT (STU) Dir. Pastoral Care
ANTHONY WALTER, O.F.M., Chap.
FRANCIS FERRIER, S.J.
Bed Capacity 838
Sisters 9
Patients assisted annually 200,000
Tau Center
8080 Margaret Ann Dr.
Baton Rouge, LA 70809-3444
Tel: 504-767-1320; Fax: 504-767-1327

Lafayette
Diocese of Lafayette

Our Lady of Lourdes Regional Medical Center, Inc.
611 St. Landry St., P.O. Box 4027
Lafayette, LA 70502
Tel: 318-234-7381
Mr. MIKE HAMMER, Chm. of the Governing Board
Mr. DUDLEY ROMERO, CEO
Revs.:
THOMAS KAMENSKI, O.F.M.
LAWRENCE N. ABARA
Franciscan Missionaries of Our Lady 3
Beds 397
Patients assisted annually 80,860
St. Mary's Imaging Center, Inc.
P.O. Box 4424
Lafayette, LA 70502
Patients assisted annually 15,100
A wholly owned, non-profit subsidiary of Our Lady of Lourdes Regional Medical Center, Inc. Operating as an outpatient diagnostic facility.

Lake Charles
Diocese of Lake Charles

St. Patrick Hospital of Lake Charles
524 S. Ryan St.
Lake Charles, LA 70601
Tel: 318-436-2511
Owned and operated by the Sisters of Charity of the Incarnate Word (Houston, TX).
J. WILLIAM HANKINS, Admin.
Revs.:
BRIAN M. KING, Dir. Pastoral Care & Chap.
SAMUEL OSUJI, Chap.
Sisters 8
Beds 257
Patients assisted annually 104,497
Total Staff 1,300

Monroe
Diocese of Shreveport

St. Francis Medical Center
P.O. Box 1901
Monroe, LA 71210-1901
Tel: 318-327-4000; Fax: 318-327-4142
Mr. H. GERALD SMITH, Pres. & CEO
Revs.:
JOSEPH PUTHUPPALLY (India) Chap.
ZACHARIAS PRAKUZHY, C.M.I., (India) Chap.
Franciscan Missionaries of Our Lady 4
Beds 400
Patients assisted annually 60,698
Total Staff 1,559
Hospice & Ancillary Care
30,163

**St. Francis Specialty Hospital* (1995)
309 Jackson St., P.O. Box 1532
Monroe, LA 71210
Tel: 318-327-4600
Mr. MICHAEL G. RYAN, Pres. & CEO
Licensed Beds 50
Physicians 103
Employees 131
Patient admissions 283

New Orleans
Archdiocese of New Orleans

Daughters of Charity Services of New Orleans
3900 S. Carrollton Ave.
New Orleans, LA 70118-4712
Tel: 504-482-2080; Fax: 504-483-6016
Mr. DAVID J. WARD, Pres. & CEO

St. John's Place of New Orleans, Inc. dba Mercy Family Center
3816 Bienville St.
New Orleans, LA 70119-5206
Tel: 504-482-6600
Mr. BERNARD A. DUCO, Pres.

Shreveport
Diocese of Shreveport

Schumpert Medical Center (1907)
One St. Mary Pl., P.O. Box 21976
Shreveport, LA 71120-1976
Tel: 318-681-4500
Sisters of Charity of the Incarnate Word
Dr. ARTHUR GONZALEZ, P.H., CEO & Pres.
Sr. ROSE MARIE MCDERMOTT, Senior Vice Pres., Mission
BETSY WILLIAMS, Chap., Dir. of Pastoral Care
Rev. GONZALO FERRER, T.O.R., (Spain) Chap.
Sisters 9
Beds 505
Patients assisted annually 130,546
Total Staff 2,300

MAINE

Bangor
Diocese of Portland (In Maine)

St. Joseph Hospital
360 Broadway
Bangor, ME 04401
Tel: 207-262-1000
Sr. MARY EDITH, C.S.S.F., Supr.
Sr. MARY NORBERTA, C.S.S.F., Pres.
Felician Sisters 9
Nursing Sisters 1
Lay Nurses 198
Patients assisted annually 69,840
Pastoral Care Dept.
360 Broadway
Bangor, ME 04401
Rev. RICHARD V. ROKOS

Bucksport
Diocese of Portland (In Maine)

Bridgewell, Inc.
Box 836
Bucksport, ME 04416
Sr. MIRIAM DEVLIN, Contact Person
Health Care Facility.

Lewiston
Diocese of Portland (In Maine)

**St. Mary's Regional Medical Center*
Campus Ave., P.O. Box 291
Lewiston, ME 04243-0291
Tel: 207-777-8100
Legal Title: *Sisters of Charity Sponsorship, Inc.*
Legal Title: *Sisters of Charity Health Systems, Inc.*
Legal Title: *Sisters of Charity of Montreal "Grey Nuns"*
Mr. JAMES E. CASSIDY, Pres. & CEO
Chaplains:

Sr. HUGUETTE ALLARD, S.G.M.
Sr. MADELEINE NORMAND, P.M.
Sr. SHARON LEAVITT, S.C.I.M.
GLORIA JENKINS, Dir.
KENN RANCOURT
Rev. BERTRAND R. POUSSARD, Sacramental Min.
Sisters 3
Lay Nurses 214
LPN 15
CNA 133
Beds 233
Patients assisted annually 72,872

Portland
Diocese of Portland (In Maine)

**Mercy Hospital*
144 State St.
Portland, ME 04101
Tel: 207-879-3000
Mr. HOWARD R. BUCKLEY, Pres.
Rev. DONALD MCALLISTER, Chap.
Lay Nurses (RN's and LPN's) 305
Beds 200
Patients assisted annually 78,360
School of Radiology Students 17

MARYLAND

Baltimore
Archdiocese of Baltimore

Bon Secours Baltimore Health System, Inc.
2000 W. Baltimore St.
Baltimore, MD 21223
Tel: 410-362-3000
Sisters of Bon Secours
Sr. NANCY GLYNN, C.B.S., Pres.
Sr. MARY SKOPAL, S.S.J., Dir. of Pastoral Care
Sisters 6
Beds 208
Patients assisted annually 131,465
Bon Secours Hollins Terrace (Apts. for the Elderly)
Bon Secours Benet House (Apts. for the Elderly)
Bon Secours Home Health & Hospice Program
Bon Secours Rental Dialysis Centers (Baltimore, Glen Burnie and Catonsville)
Bon Secours New Hope Treatment Center (Substance Abuse)
Bon Secours of Maryland foundation
Washington Village Community Medical Center
St. Edward's Family Health Center
St. Anne's Continuing Care Center (Sub-acute, 32 beds)

Mercy Medical Center, Inc.
301 St. Paul Pl.
Baltimore, MD 21202
Tel: 410-332-9000; Fax: 410-783-5993
Institute of the Sisters of Mercy of the Americas
Sr. HELEN AMOS, R.S.M., Pres. & CEO
Chaplains:
Revs.:
THEODORE E.A. BRADY, S.J.
BERNARD A. SUPPE, S.J.
FRANCIS L. DUFFY, S.J.
Sr. M. BENEDICT BRADY, R.S.M.
Sr. MARY HARPER, R.S.M.
Sr. JUDITH MONTONE, R.S.M.
Sr. NAOMI ZERHUSEN, R.S.M.
Sisters 9
Employees 2,042
Patients assisted annually 419,894
Mercy Medical Center Subsidiaries: St. Paul Place Specialists, Inc.; Mercy Home Health Services, Inc.; Mercy Primary Care Group, Inc.; Mercy Ventures, Inc.; Northeast Medical Center; Mercy Southern; Mercy Little Italy; Mercy Basilica Place; Healthcare for the Homeless; Mercy Family Care; Fellowship House; New Song Health Center; South Baltimore Health Center (Cherry Hill); Maryland Personal Physicians, Inc.; Mercy Transitional Care; Stella Maris Hospice at Mercy.

St. Agnes HealthCare, Inc.
900 Caton Ave.
Baltimore, MD 21229-5299
Tel: 410-368-6000
Daughters of Charity of St. Vincent de Paul
ROBERT E. PEZZOLI, Pres. & CEO
Rev. DANIEL FREE, C.P., Chap.
Sisters 10
Bed Capacity 407
Patients assisted annually 196,748
St. Agnes Foundation, Inc. (Subsidiary of St. Agnes HealthCare, Inc.)

St. Joseph Medical Center
7620 York Rd.
Baltimore, MD 21204
Tel: 410-337-1000; Fax: 410-337-1017
Sisters of St. Francis of Philadelphia
JOHN S. PROUT, Pres. & CEO
Rev. LEO J. FARRAGHER, S.S.J., Chap.
Sisters 35
Nurses 640
Beds 460
Patients assisted annually 70,550
Total Staff 602

Cumberland
Archdiocese of Baltimore

Sacred Heart Hospital
900 Seton Dr.
Cumberland, MD 21502
Tel: 301-759-4200
Daughters of Charity of St. Vincent de Paul
EDWARD M. DINAN, Pres.
Sr. GENEVIEVE KURETH, Supr.
Rev. ALFRED CUTAJAR, S.J., Chap.
Beds 240
Sisters 12
Nurses 375
Patients assisted annually 96,548

Silver Spring
Archdiocese of Washington

Holy Cross Hospital of Silver Spring, Inc.
1500 Forest Glen Rd.
Silver Spring, MD 20910
Tel: 301-905-0100; Fax: 301-905-1011
Sisters of the Holy Cross
Mr. JAMES P. HAMILL, Pres.
Sr. VIRGINIA MCLAUGHLIN, C.S.C., Dir. Pastoral Care
Revs.:
ELIOT NITZ, S.D.S.
LOUIS TOU
Sisters 15
Bed Capacity 454
Patients assisted annually 202,651
Total Staff 2,300

MASSACHUSETTS

Boston
Archdiocese of Boston

Carney Hospital
2100 Dorchester Ave.
Boston, MA 02124
Tel: 617-296-4000
MATTHIAS D. MAGUIRE, Pres.
Sr. DECHANTAL LAROW, D.C., Chm. Bd.
Rev. LUCIEN A. SAWYER, O.M.I.
Daughters of Charity of St. Vincent de Paul 12
Bed Capacity 285
Patients treated during the year 111,326

Brighton
Archdiocese of Boston

St. Elizabeth's Hospital of Boston
736 Cambridge St.
Brighton, MA 02135
Tel: 617-789-3000
School of Nursing.
3 Year course (4 years of complete day high school).
Mr. THEODORE DRUHOT, Pres.
Revs.:
BRIAN F. MCMAHON, Chap.
JAMES J. FOLEY, Asst. Chaplain
Rev. Msgr. CHARLES W. MCCARTHY
Sr. VIRGINIA MURRAY, C.S.J.
Sr. IVAN CADIGAN, C.S.J.
Sr. REATA KELLEHER, C.S.J.
Sr. MARGARET SHEEHAN, C.S.J.
Sr. LOUISE MURRAY, C.S.J.
Student Nurses 160
Bed Capacity 350
Bassinets 30
Patients treated during the year 176,302

Brockton
Archdiocese of Boston

Good Samaritan Medical Center
235 N. Pearl St.
Brockton, MA 02401
Tel: 508-427-3000; 427-3151
FRANK J. LARKIN, Pres. & CEO
Sisters of Charity of Nazareth 1
Sisters of Jesus Crucified 1
Holy Union Sisters 1
Revs.:
RICHARD W. VISBISKY, Chap. & Dir. of Pastoral Care
SUZANNE HIGGINS, (Congregational)
Mr. RICHARD MESSING, (Rabbi)
Total Assisted 110,000
Total Staff 1,400

Fall River
Diocese of Fall River

Saint Anne's Health Care Management Services, Inc.
795 Middle St.
Fall River, MA 02721-1798
JOSEPH W. WILCZEK, Pres.

Saint Anne's Health Care System, Inc.
795 Middle St.
Fall River, MA 02721-1798
JOSEPH W. WILCZEK, Pres.

Saint Anne's Hospital
795 Middle St.
Fall River, MA 02721-1798
Tel: 508-674-5741
Dominican Sisters of Charity of the Presentation of the Blessed Virgin Mary
Rev. ROBERT ROCHON
Sisters 8
Total Staff 912
Bed Capacity 165
Patients assisted annually 54,062

Holyoke
Diocese of Springfield in Massachusetts

Providence Hospital, Inc.
1233 Main St.
Holyoke, MA 01040
Tel: 413-536-5111; Fax: 413-539-0429
Sisters of Providence
Department of Pastoral Care:
Mr. VINCENT J. MCCORKLE, Pres./CEO
Pastoral Care Dept. 1
Beds 140
Staff 275
Patients assisted annually 5,000

Lowell
Archdiocese of Boston

Saints Memorial Health System, Inc.
P.O. Box 30
Lowell, MA 01852
Tel: 508-458-1411; Fax: 508-458-8369
THOM CLARK, Pres. & CEO
Sisters of Charity of Ottawa
Bed Capacity 225
Total Assisted 11,000
Total Staff 1,250

Methuen
Archdiocese of Boston

Holy Family Hospital and Medical Center
Caritas Christi, Inc.
70 East St.
Methuen, MA 01844-4597
Tel: 508-687-0151
WILLIAM L. LANE, Pres.
Rev. JOHN T. CRABB, S.J., Chap.
Bed Capacity 247
Bassinets 30
Patients assisted annually 150,000
Affiliating Hospital for: St. Anselm's Collegiate School of Nursing; Northern Essex Community College; University of Lowell; Salem State College; Boston University School of Public Health; Essex Agricultural School; New Hampshire Technical School; Massachusetts Bay Community College; Northeastern University; Rivier College; Woodmill Nursing Home; Greater Lowell Vocational School; Whittier Regional Vocational Technical School; Greater Lawrence Vocational School; and Salem High School.
Priests 1
Holy Family Hospital Auxiliary
70 East St.
Methuen, MA 01844-4597

Springfield
Diocese of Springfield in Massachusetts

Mercy Hospital
271 Carew St., Box 9012
Springfield, MA 01102-9012
Tel: 413-748-9000
VINCENT J. MCCORKLE, Pres. & CEO
Sr. MARGARET M. MCCARTHY, S.N.D., Dir. Dept. of Pastoral Care
Chaplains:
Revs.:
HERBERT C. BALOGA, O.F.M.Conv.
WILLIAM J. DOHERTY, M.S.
STANLEY ARNOLD
Sr. THERESA DUBE, S.A.S.V.

Sr. MARIE DANIEL, S.P.
Sr. MADELINE JOY, S.D.
SANDRA MATTUCCI
SUZANNE NOLAN
JAMES LORD
Sisters of Providence 4
Beds 299
Patients assisted annually 87,000
Nurses:
RNs 312
LPNs 32

Turners Falls
Diocese of Springfield in Massachusetts

Farren Care Center, Inc.
340 Montague City Rd.
Turners Falls, MA 01376
Tel: 413-774-3111
WILLIAM E. CASPER, Pres.
DENNIS P. LOPATA, Admin.
Sisters of Providence 7
Beds 122
Total Staff 195
Total Assisted 140

Worcester
Diocese of Worcester

Our Lady of Mercy Health Care Center, Inc.
101 Barry Rd.
Worcester, MA 01609
Tel: 508-798-3727
Sr. SUZANNE ELLIOTT, R.S.M., Chm.

Pernet Family Health Service
237 Millbury St.
Worcester, MA 01610
Tel: 508-755-1228
Mission of the Little Sisters of the Assumption.
Certified Home Health and Social Service Agency. Focus of services toward the parent and young child. Parenting groups, family activities available, Early Childhood Development services also available.
HARRI THIBEAULT, Exec. Dir.
Total Staff 33
Little Sisters of the Assumption 4
Total Volunteers 5

Saint Vincent Hospital, Inc.
25 Winthrop St.
Worcester, MA 01604
Tel: 508-798-1234; Fax: 508-798-1240
Mr. ROBERT MAHER, CEO
Rev. TERENCE T. KILCOYNE, D.Min., Dir. Pastoral Svcs.
Chaplains:
Rev. FRANCIS ROACH
Sr. MARY O'LEARY, S.P.
Deacon MATTEO PAGANO
Sisters 1
Beds 350
Patients assisted annually 80,000
Saint Vincent Healthcare System, Inc.
25 Winthrop St.
Worcester, MA 01604
Saint Vincent Management Corporation
25 Winthrop St.
Worcester, MA 01604

MICHIGAN

Ann Arbor
Diocese of Lansing

Catherine McAuley Health Services Corporation
(Subsidiary of Mercy Health Services)
5305 E. Huron River Dr., P.O. Box 992
Ann Arbor, MI 48106
Tel: 313-712-3789
Health Care Center, Ancillary Care Systems: (Primary Care Physician Practices)
HELEN V. BERG, Pres.
Staff 135
Patients assisted annually 57,860

Catherine McAuley Health System
(Sponsored by Mercy Health Services - A unit of Mission Health Corporation)
5305 E. Huron River Dr., Box 992
Ann Arbor, MI 48106
Tel: 313-712-4025
BRIAN CONNOLLY, CEO
Beds 918
Gen. Hospitals 3
Staff 4,324
Annually Assisted 644,152

McAuley Clinic Corporation
(Subsidiary of Mercy Health Services)
5333 McAuley Dr., Box 994
Ann Arbor, MI 48106
Tel: 313-712-3788
ROBERT L. RAVIN, Pres.
Health Care Center, Ancillary Care Systems:
Staff 8
Patients assisted annually 6,323

St. Joseph Mercy Hospital
(A Unit of Mission Health Corporation)
5301 E. Huron River Dr., P.O. Box 995
Ann Arbor, MI 48106
Tel: 313-712-3456
Mr. GARRY C. FAJA, CEO
Sr. FRANCES GERHARD, R.S.M., Consultant, Mission Services
Chaplains:
Revs.:
TIMOTHY DOMBROWSKI
MICHAEL BRAND, C.S.B.
Beds 905
Gen. Hospitals 1
Total Staff 4,751
Patients assisted annually 822,937

Sisters of St. Joseph Health Services Corp.
455 E. Eisenhower, Ste. 300
Ann Arbor, MI 48108
Tel: 313-741-1700

Sisters of St. Joseph Health System, Inc.
455 E. Eisenhower, Ste. 300
Ann Arbor, MI 48108
Tel: 313-741-1700
Mr. JOHN LORE, Pres. & CEO
Beds 2,845
Total Staff 17,528

Battle Creek
Diocese of Kalamazoo

Battle Creek Health System
300 North Ave.
Battle Creek, MI 49016
Tel: 616-966-8000; Fax: 616-966-8010
Div. of Sisters of Mercy Health Corp.
Mr. STEPHEN L. ABBOTT, Pres. & CEO
Bed Capacity 490
Patients assisted annually 140,932

Cadillac
Diocese of Gaylord

Mercy Hospital
Mercy Health Services North, Division of Sisters of Mercy Health Corp., Sisters of Mercy Detroit Prov.
400 Hobart St.
Cadillac, MI 49601
Tel: 616-779-7200
Mr. DENNIS RENANDER, Pres. & CEO
Bed Capacity 174
Patients assisted annually 40,000

Clinton Township
Archdiocese of Detroit

Mercy Mount Clemens Corporation
(Acting under the assumed name of St. Joseph's Mercy of Macomb or St. Joseph's Mercy Hospitals and Health Services). A subsidiary of Mercy Health Services.
15855 Nineteen Mile Rd.
Clinton Township, MI 48038
Tel: 810-263-2707
Provides acute care hospital services, home health care services, outpatient medical center services, hospice care services, long term service and fund-raising services.
ROBERT L. BEYER, Pres. & C.E.O.
DEBORA MURRAY, Dir., Spiritual Care Svcs.
Bed Capacity 512 acute care
St. Joseph's Mercy - West
15855 Nineteen Mile Rd.
Clinton Township, MI 48038
Tel: 810-263-2300; 263-2330
St. Joseph's Mercy - East
215 North Ave.
Mt. Clemens, MI 48043
Tel: 810-466-9300
St. Joseph's Mercy - North
80650 Van Dyke
Romeo, MI 48065
Tel: 810-752-3551
Additional divisional operations:
St. Joseph's HomeCare
St. Joseph's Medical Centers
St. Joseph's Mercy Foundation
St. Joseph's Mercy Healthier Image

Detroit
Archdiocese of Detroit

Holy Cross Hospital
4777 E. Outer Dr.
Detroit, MI 48234
Tel: 313-369-9100
Sisters of St. Joseph (Nazareth, MI)
JAMES E. KOERPER, Pres.
Sisters 4
Bed Capacity 229
Patients assisted annually 30,850

Mercy Family Care Program Unit
5555 Conner Ave.
Detroit, MI 48213
Tel: 313-579-4300
TOMMYE H. ARNOLD, Vice Pres. Ambulatory Svcs.
Mercy-Family Practice Center, St. Joseph Center, Chandler Center, Mercy-Nurse Managed Center, Gratiot Center.

Mercy Hospital
A division of Sisters of Mercy Health Corporation.
5555 Conner Ave.
Detroit, MI 48213
Tel: 313-579-4000
BRENITA CRAWFORD SEARCY, Pres. & CEO
Sr. ROSE PETRUZZO, O.P., Dir. Pastoral Care
Bed Capacity 238
Patients assisted annually 48,247

St. John Hospital and Medical Center
(Subsidiary of St. John Health System)
22101 Moross Rd.
Detroit, MI 48236
Tel: 313-343-4000
TIMOTHY GRAJEWSKI, Pres. & CEO
Sr. SUZANNE ZIESKE, S.S.J., Vice Pres. Mission Effectiveness
Sisters of Saint Joseph (Nazareth) 15
Bed Capacity 607
Patients assisted annually 154,939
Outpatients 66,007
Affiliates:
St. John Ambulatory Care, Detroit
St. John Dialysis Center, Detroit
Eastwood-Oxford Network of Care, Detroit
Affiliated Health Services, Inc., Detroit
St. John Hospital-Macomb Center, Morrison Township
St. John-Bon Secour Senior Community, Detroit

Dowagiac
Diocese of Kalamazoo

Lee Memorial Hospital
420 W. High St.
Dowagiac, MI 49047
Tel: 616-782-8681; Fax: 616-782-7611
Mr. FRITZ FAHRENBACHER, CEO
Bed Capacity 74
Patients assisted annually 32,000

Escanaba
Diocese of Marquette

O.S.F. St. Francis Hospital
Escanaba, MI 49829
Tel: 906-786-3311
O.S.F. Healthcare System.
Mr. ROGER BURGESS, Admin.
Sisters 4
Patients assisted annually 63,603
Beds 110

Flint
Diocese of Lansing

Center for Gerontology
An affiliate of Genesys Health System.
303 W. Water St.
Flint, MI 48503
Tel: 810-767-7080
Provides adult day care, care management programs, and educational training.
Annually Assisted 775
Total Staff 39

Genesys Ambulatory Health Services, Inc.
An affiliate of Genesys Health System.
302 Kensington Ave.
Flint, MI 48503
Tel: 810-232-9900
Provides private duty home care services and manages shared services. Also provides outpatient psychiatric services.
Annually Assisted 6,521
Total Staff 496

Genesys Health System
302 Kensington Ave.

Flint, MI 48503-2000
Tel: 810-762-8899
Mr. YOUNG S. SUH, Pres. & CEO
Sr. ELIZABETH GRANGER, S.S.J., Vice Pres., Mission Effectiveness

Genesys Home Health & Hospice
An affiliate of Genesys Health System.
100 S. Dort Hwy.
Flint, MI 48503
Tel: 810-762-7500
Provides professional home care and rehabilitation services.

Genesys Regional Medical Center/Flint Osteopathic Campus
An affiliate of Genesys Health System.
3921 Beecher Rd.
Flint, MI 48532-3699
Tel: 810-762-4000
Mr. YOUNG S. SUH, Pres. & CEO
Beds 297
Annually Assisted 125,053

Genesys Regional Medical Center/St. Joseph Campus
An affiliate of Genesys Health System.
302 Kensington Ave.
Flint, MI 48503-2000
Tel: 810-762-8000
Mr. YOUNG S. SUH, Pres. & CEO
KATHLENE O'DONNELL, S.S.J., Dir. Pastoral Care
Bassinets 39
Beds 374
Patients assisted annually 209,227

Goodrich
Diocese of Lansing

Genesys Regional Medical Center/Wheelock Memorial Campus
An affiliate of Genesys Health System.
7280 State Rd.
Goodrich, MI 48438
Tel: 810-636-2221
Mr. YOUNG S. SUH, Pres. & CEO
Beds 27
Patients assisted annually 25,941

Grand Blanc
Diocese of Lansing

Genesys Convalescent Center, Grand Blanc, Inc.
An affiliate of St. Genesys Health Systems.
8481 Holly Rd.
Grand Blanc, MI 48439-1899
Tel: 810-694-1711
Nursing Home
Beds 140
Patients assisted annually 222
Total Staff 180

Genesys Regional Medical Center/Health Park
An affiliate of Genesys Health System.
One Genesys Pkwy.
Grand Blanc, MI 48439
Tel: 810-606-5000
Mr. YOUNG S. SUH, Pres. & CEO
Beds 379
Annually Assisted 12,720

Grand Rapids
Diocese of Grand Rapids

St. Mary's Health Services
200 Jefferson, S.E.
Grand Rapids, MI 49503
Tel: 616-774-6090
Religious Sisters of Mercy (Detroit Regional Community)
DAVID AMEEN, Pres. & CEO
Rev. ROBERT C. STEIGMEYER, C.S.C.
Beds 280
Patients assisted annually 169,730
Mercy Central School of Nursing
Affiliation with Mercy College, Detroit.

Grayling
Diocese of Gaylord

Mercy Hospital
Mercy Health Services North, Division of Sisters of Mercy Health Corp., Sisters of Mercy Detroit Prov.
1100 Michigan Ave.
Grayling, MI 49738
Tel: 517-348-5461; Fax: 517-348-4839
DENNIS RENANDER, Pres. & CEO
Bed Capacity 120
Patients assisted annually 56,020

Grosse Pointe
Archdiocese of Detroit

Bon Secours Hospital
468 Cadieux Rd.
Grosse Pointe, MI 48230
Tel: 313-343-1000
HENRY DEVRIES, CEO
GARY A. JANKOWSKI, Chief Finance Officer
Sr. ANNE MARIE MACK, C.B.S., V.P. Mission Effectiveness
MARY ALICE PURCELL, Dir. of Pastoral Care
Sisters of Bon Secours 4
Sisters 1
Registered Nurses 450
Practical Nurses 102
Bed Capacity 311
Bassinets 28
Patients assisted annually 130,000

**Bon Secours of Michigan Health Care System, Inc.*
Bon Secours of Michigan Foundation
VANU BAGCHI, Vice Pres.
MICHAEL SERILLA, Vice Pres. Operation

Howell
Diocese of Lansing

McPherson Hospital
(A unit of Mission Health Corporation)
620 Bryon Rd.
Howell, MI 48843-1093
Tel: 517-546-1410
ROBERT B. CARBECK, M.D., Pres. & CEO
Beds 136
Gen. Hospitals 1
Patients assisted annually 155,160
Total Staff 503

Kalamazoo
Diocese of Kalamazoo

Borgess Medical Center
1521 Gull Rd.
Kalamazoo, MI 49001
Tel: 616-226-7000; Fax: 616-226-7396
Mr. R. TIMOTHY STACK, Pres.
Rev. MATHEW ALAPATT, Chap.
542 W. Michigan Ave.
Kalamazoo, MI 49007
Sisters of St. Joseph 7
Bed Capacity 469
Patients assisted annually 338,957

Lansing
Diocese of Lansing

St. Lawrence Hospital and Healthcare Services
1210 W. Saginaw St.
Lansing, MI 48915
Tel: 517-372-3610; Fax: 517-377-0382
(A Division of Mercy Health Services)
ARTHUR A. KNUEPPEL, Pres. & CEO
Chaplains:
Revs.:
FRANCIS MARTIN
RICHARD PRESTON
STANLEY CZARNOTA
Sr. MERCITA LOGAN, R.S.M., Coord. of Pastoral Ministry
Sr. KATHLEEN BOTSFORD, R.S.M.
Ms. SUSAN LIED
Rev. REBECCA EBB-SPEESE, Lutheran (ELCA)
Beds 257
Patients assisted annually 286,119
Total Staff 1,314

Livonia
Archdiocese of Detroit

Marian Village Corporation
36475 Five Mile Rd.
Livonia, MI 48154
Tel: 313-464-4800, Ext. 2300
Sr. MARY MODESTA PIWOWAR, C.S.S.F., Pres. & C.E.O.

St. Mary Hospital
36475 W. Five Mile Rd.
Livonia, MI 48154
Tel: 313-655-4800
Sr. MARY MODESTA, C.S.S.F., Pres.
Sr. MARY RENETTA C.S.S.F., Exec. Vice Pres.
Revs.:
JOHN ANTHONY PARENZA
KAZIMIERZ JASINSKI
Sisters 17
Bed Capacity 304
Patients assisted annually 176,920
RN's 360
LPN's 30
Congregation of the Sisters of St. Felix Felician Sisters
36800 Schoolcraft
Livonia, MI 48150

Muskegon
Diocese of Grand Rapids

Mercy Hospital
1500 E. Sherman Blvd., P.O. Box 358
Muskegon, MI 49443
Tel: 616-739-9341; Fax: 616-733-0957
Sisters of Mercy (Detroit Regional Community)
SANDRA BENNETT BRUCE, Pres. & CEO
LYNNE GORDON, Dir. Pastoral Care
Sisters 2
Beds 175
Patients assisted annually 125,533
Amicare Home Health Services-Western Michigan, Inc.
1500 E. Sherman Blvd.
Muskegon, MI 49444
Tel: 616-733-4064

Okemos
Diocese of Lansing

Majorie J. Gardner Wellness Center for Women
5100 Marsh Rd.
Okemos, MI 48864
Patients assisted annually 6,281

Pontiac
Archdiocese of Detroit

St. Joseph Mercy - Oakland
(Div. of Mercy Health Services)
900 Woodward Ave.
Pontiac, MI 48341-2985
Tel: 810-858-3000
Sponsored Work of the Sisters of Mercy Regional Community of Detroit.
A community healthcare system comprised of: Mercy Bellbrook Living Center, Rochester Hills; Alexander Living Center, Royal Oak; Orchard Hills Living Center, Pontiac; Amicare, West Bloomfield; Mercy Cranbrook Hospice, West Bloomfield; Seven Clinics & St. Joseph Mercy Hospital, Pontiac, MI.
THOMAS L. FEURIG, Pres. & CEO
RICHARD L. BROCHU, B.A., Th.M., Dir. Mission/Values & Ethics
Chaplains:
Revs.:
JOSEPH SZEWCZYK
DONALD WORTHY, O.S.C.
JAMES VON DREMLE
FREDERICK B. MOORE
Sr. DIANE RONDEAU, R.S.M.

Port Huron
Archdiocese of Detroit

Mercy Hospital of Port Huron
(Div. of Sisters of Mercy Health Corporation)
2601 Electric
Port Huron, MI 48060-6518
Tel: 810-985-1500
MARY R. TRIMMER, Pres. & CEO
Sr. IMELDA SHERRETT, R.S.M., Dir. Resource Devel.
Chaplains:
Rev. C. PAUL HIGDON
EVELYN DENEAU
Sr. MARGARET WEBER, R.S.M.
Sr. FRANCIS VILLEROT, R.S.M., Patient Rep.
Bed Capacity 119
Patients assisted annually 26,409

Saginaw
Diocese of Saginaw

St. Mary's Medical Center of Saginaw, Inc.
830 S. Jefferson Ave.
Saginaw, MI 48601-2594
Daughters of Charity of St. Vincent de Paul, East Central Province, Evansville, IN
FREDERIC L. FRAIZER, Pres. & CEO
Sr. DINAH WHITE, D.C., Vice Pres. Mission Svcs.
Chaplains:
Rev. RAYMOND MOEGGENBERG
Sr. ADELAIDE CURTIS, D.C., Patient Rep.
DELMAR SMOLINSKI
RICHARD MCCOOL
JOYCE M. SWARTZ
Sisters 3
Beds 268
Patients assisted annually 67,100
Field Neurosciences Institute
830 S. Jefferson Ave.
Saginaw, MI 48601
FREDERIC L. FRAIZER, Chm.

Saline
Diocese of Lansing

Saline Community Hospital
(A unit of Mission Health Corporation)

400 W. Russell
Saline, MI 48176
Tel: 313-429-1600
GARRY FAJA, CEO
Beds 82
Gen. Hospitals 1
Patients assisted annually 85,000
Total Staff 286

Southfield
Archdiocese of Detroit

Providence Hospital
(A unit of Mission Health Corporation)
16001 W. Nine Mile Rd., P.O. Box 2043
Southfield, MI 48037
Tel: 810-424-3000
BRIAN M. CONNOLLY, Pres.
Sr. JANE BURGER, D.C., Vice Pres., Mission/Ethics Services
Rev. GEORGE HAZLER, Vice Pres. Mission Health Mission Svcs.
Chaplains:
Revs.:
KENT HAJDUK, O.F.M.
RONALD HEIDELBERGER
JOHN GAGALA
JOSEPH DROGOWSKI
FELIX ALSOLA
Ms. CAROL CROWLEY
Sr. ANGELE HINKEY, D.C.
Daughters of Charity of St. Vincent de Paul 4
Bed Capacity 440
Bassinets 65
Lay Staff 2,888
Patients assisted annually 809,721
Medical and Surgical Residences.

Tawas City
Diocese of Gaylord

**Saint Joseph Huron Home Health and Hospice*
716 German St., Ste. B, P.O. Box 208
Tawas City, MI 48764
Tel: 517-362-4611
ANN BALFOUR, Pres.
Patients assisted annually 774

Tawas St. Joseph Hospital
200 Hemlock, M-55
Tawas City, MI 48764-0659
Tel: 517-362-3411; Fax: 517-362-7277
Mr. PAUL SCHMIDT, Pres.
Sr. MARGOT EDER, S.S.J., Chap.
Sr. PATRICIA MULLEN, S.S.J., Vice Pres. Sponsorship
Sisters of St. Joseph (Nazareth, MI) 2
Bed Capacity 60
Patients assisted annually 93,759

MINNESOTA

Albany
Diocese of St. Cloud

Albany Area Hospital
300 Third Ave.
Albany, MN 56307
Tel: 320-845-2121
BEN KOPPELMAN, Admin.
Chaplains:
Sr. LORETTO SCHNEIDER, O.F.M.
WINI HERDA
Sisters of St. Francis 2
Beds 17
Patients assisted annually 5,987

Baudette
Diocese of Crookston

LakeWood Health Center
600 South Main Ave., Box 2120
Baudette, MN 56623
Tel: 218-634-2120; Fax: 218-634-1307
DAVID A. NELSON, Pres. & CEO
Bed Capacity 34
Staff 55
Patients assisted annually 11,737
LakeWood Care Center
410 Third Ave. S.E., Rte. 1, Box 1180
Baudette, MN 56623
Tel: 218-634-2120; Fax: 218-634-1589
Sisters 1
Beds 52
Staff 48
Residents assisted annually 108

Brainerd
Diocese of Duluth

St. Joseph's Medical Center
523 N. Third St.
Brainerd, MN 56401
Tel: 218-829-2861; Fax: 218-828-3103
Sr. GEORGIA THEIS, O.S.B., Dir. Pastoral Care
Sr. LYNNETTE BOUTA, V.P. Operations
Sr. VIVIAN ARTS, Dir. of Mission
VERN BROUGHTON, Chap.
Sisters of St. Benedict 6
Nurses 203
Patients assisted annually 43,596
Beds 162

Breckenridge
Diocese of St. Cloud

St. Francis Medical Center
415 Oak St.
Breckenridge, MN 56520
Tel: 218-643-3000
MARK C. MCNELLY, Pres.
KAREN STOKES, Pastoral Care Dir.
Rev. STANLEY WIESER, Chap.
Sisters 3
Beds 95
Patients assisted annually 22,000

Detroit Lakes
Diocese of Crookston

**St. Mary's Regional Health Center*
(Sub. of Benedictine Health System)
1027 Washington Ave.
Detroit Lakes, MN 56501
Tel: 218-847-5611; Fax: 218-847-7674
JOHN SOLHEIM, CEO
Rev. TIM COOK, Pastoral Care
St. Mary's EMS (Sub. of St. Mary's Regional Health Center)
1240 Washington Ave., P.O. Box 1410
Detroit Lakes, MN 56502
Tel: 218-847-1631; Fax: 218-847-0673
JOHN SOLHEIM, CEO
Beds: Acute 87
Long Term Care 100
Patients Treated Annually:
Hospital Inpatients 2,748
Hospital Outpatients 11,768
Nursing Home Residents 227

Duluth
Diocese of Duluth

St. Mary's Medical Center
407 E. Third St.
Duluth, MN 55805
Tel: 218-726-4000; Fax: 218-726-4383
Sr. KATHLEEN HOFER, O.S.B., Pres.
Rev. JOHN GIBBS, Chap., Dir. of Chaplaincy Svcs.
Sisters 7
Nurses 637
Patients assisted annually 128,285
Beds 286
Bassinets 43

Graceville
Diocese of New Ulm

Graceville Health Center dba Holy Trinity Hospital and Grace Home
115 W. 2nd St.
Graceville, MN 56240-0157
Tel: 320-748-7223
Hospital:
Beds 32
Inpatients 322
Outpatients 6,992
Clinic Patients 7,000
Staff 34
Nursing Home:
Beds 60
Patients assisted annually 80
Staff 49
Board & Lodging:
Beds 13

Hastings
Archdiocese of St. Paul and Minneapolis

Regina Medical Center
1175 Nininger Rd.
Hastings, MN 55033
Tel: 612-480-4100
LYNN W. OLSON, Admin.
Rev. JAMES J. DUNNE, S.S.C., Chap.
Bed capacity 57
Patients assisted annually 22,585
Other Sister Personnel 3
Personnel 455

Ivanhoe
Diocese of New Ulm

Divine Providence Health Center
312 E. George St., P.O. Box G
Ivanhoe, MN 56142-0136
Schoenstatt Sisters of Mary (Waukesha, WI)
JAMES ROSSOW, Admin.
Rev. MARION CASEY, Chap.
Sisters 6
Lay Workers 115
Aged Residents 51
Other Nurses 22
Patients assisted annually 180
Bed Capacity 18

Little Falls
Diocese of St. Cloud

St. Gabriel's Hospital
815 S.E. Second St.
Little Falls, MN 56345
Tel: 320-632-5441; Fax: 320-632-1190
LARRY A. SCHULZ, Admin.
BEA BRITZ, Chap.
Sisters 3
Beds 55
Bassinets 20
Patients assisted annually 20,111

New Prague
Archdiocese of St. Paul and Minneapolis

Queen of Peace Hospital
302 Second St., N.E.
New Prague, MN 56071
Tel: 612-758-4431; Fax: 612-758-5009
Sr. JEAN JUENEMANN, O.S.B., Admin.
Mr. LOY J. JEFFREY, Dir. Pastoral Care, Chap.
ANN SCHOENBAUER, Chap.
Sisters 3
Bed Capacity 28
Bassinets 6
RNs 53
LPNs 13
Other Personnel 146
Patients assisted annually 73,970

Park Rapids
Diocese of Crookston

St. Joseph's Area Health Services
600 Pleasant Ave.
Park Rapids, MN 56470
Tel: 218-732-3311
Mr. DAVID R. HOVE, Pres./CEO
Sisters 1
Bed Capacity 50
Patients assisted annually 21,228

Rochester
Diocese of Winona

Poverello Foundation
St. Marys Hospital, 1216 S.W. Second St.
Rochester, MN 55902
Tel: 507-255-5158
Sr. GENEROSE GERVAIS, O.S.F., Pres.

**Saint Marys Hospital*
Rochester, MN 55902-1970
Tel: 507-255-5123; Fax: 507-255-3125
GERALD T. MAHONEY, Admin.
Sisters of the Third Order Regular of St. Francis of the Congregation of Our Lady of Lourdes 32
Bed Capacity 1,157
Patients assisted annually 98,803

Shakopee
Archdiocese of St. Paul and Minneapolis

St. Francis Regional Medical Center
1455 St. Francis Ave.
Shakopee, MN 55379
Tel: 612-403-3000; Fax: 612-403-3820
Subsidiary of Benedictine Health System.
VENETIA KUDRLE, Pres.
Sr. ANTONICE DELURY, O.S.F., Dir., Pastoral Care
MARY BECKFELD, Chap.
Sisters of St. Francis 1
Nurses 132
Bed Capacity 40
Patients assisted annually 36,000

St. Cloud
Diocese of St. Cloud

St. Cloud Hospital
1406 Sixth Ave. N.

St. Cloud, MN 56303
Tel: 320-251-2700
JOHN FROBENIUS, Pres.
Rev. ROGER BOTZ, O.S.B., Chap.
Sisters of St. Benedict 7
Students 23
Beds 320
Bassinets 40
Patients assisted annually 108,229

St. Peter
Diocese of New Ulm

St. Peter Regional Treatment Center
100 Freeman Dr.
St. Peter, MN 56082-1599
Tel: 507-931-7114
Mental Health Division
Forensic Division
Developmental Disabilities Division:
Patients assisted annually 985

Wabasha
Diocese of Winona

St. Elizabeth's Hospital
1200 5th Grant Blvd., W.
Wabasha, MN 55981
Tel: 612-565-4531
Mr. THOMAS CROWLEY, Pres.
Rev. JOSEPH R. MCGINNIS
Sisters of the Third Order of St. Francis of the Sorrowful Mother 5
Beds 31
Patients assisted annually 675

Winsted
Diocese of New Ulm

St. Mary's Care Center
551 4th St. N., P.O. Box 750
Winsted, MN 55395-0750
Tel: 612-485-2151; Fax: 612-485-4241
HELEN J. GUGGEMOS, Admin.

MISSISSIPPI

Jackson
Diocese of Jackson

St. Dominic-Jackson Memorial Hospital
969 Lakeland Dr.
Jackson, MS 39216
Tel: 601-982-0121
Sr. MARY KAREN O'KELLY, Prioress
Mr. CLAUDE W. HARBARGER, Pres.
Rev. ROBERT OLIVIER, Res. Chap.
Sisters of St. Dominic of Springfield, IL 11
Beds 571
Patients assisted annually 65,812

Tutwiler
Diocese of Jackson

Tutwiler Clinic, Inc.
205 Alma St., P.O. Box 462
Tutwiler, MS 38963-0462
Tel: 601-345-8334; Fax: 601-345-8336
Sr. ANNE BROOKS, S.N.J.M., D.O., Dir.
Patients assisted annually 8,465

MISSOURI

Blue Springs
Diocese of Kansas City-St. Joseph

St. Mary's Hospital of Blue Springs
201 W. R.D. Mize Rd.
Blue Springs, MO 64014
Tel: 816-228-5900; Fax: 816-228-7555
Sponsored by the Sisters of St. Joseph of Carondelet. Acute care facility, having medical, surgical, obstetrical and pediatric services.
Mr. N. GARY WAGES, Pres.
Sisters 4
Bed Capacity 111
Patients assisted annually 52,000

Bridgeton
Archdiocese of St. Louis

De Paul Health Center
12303 De Paul Dr.
Bridgeton, MO 63044
Tel: 314-344-6000
Owned & operated by St. Louis Health Care Network, a member of the SSM Health Care System.
ROBERT G. PORTER, Pres.
Chaplains:
Revs.:
JULES G. YALLALY, C.M.
LAWRENCE ASMA, C.M.
FREDERICK LENCZYCKI (JOL)
Sisters 10
Patients assisted annually 114,456
Staff 1,762
DePaul General Hospital Division
(Operating) Excluding Nursery-Including 14 Bed Acute Rehabilitation Unit 219
(Licensed) Excluding Nursery-Including 14 Bed Acute Rehabilitation Unit 344
St. Anne Division
12303 De Paul Dr.
Bridgeton, MO 63044
Tel: 314-344-6000
Skilled Nursing Facility, Certified for Medicare, for Men and Women.
Operating 94
Licensed 96
St. Vincent Division
12303 De Paul Dr.
Bridgeton, MO 63044
Tel: 314-344-6000
Pre-Adolescent, Adolescent, Adult & Gero Psychiatric Care and Chemical Dependency.
Operating 59
Licensed
98

Cape Girardeau
Diocese of Springfield-Cape Girardeau

**St. Francis' Medical Center*
211 St. Francis Dr.
Cape Girardeau, MO 63703
Tel: 573-335-1251
(Owned and operated by a lay board with Diocesan sponsorship)
Mr. JOHN E. FIDLER, Pres.
Chapel St. Francis.
Mr. JOHN CANTORE, C.M., Chap.
Sisters 2
Bed Capacity 264
Inpatients 8,996
Outpatients 52,261
St. Francis Medical Center
211 St. Francis Dr.
Cape Girardeau, MO 63703
St. Francis Foundation
211 St. Francis Dr.
Cape Girardeau, MO 63703
St. Francis Continuing Care Center
211 St. Francis Dr.
Cape Girardeau, MO 63703
St. Francis Hospital of Franciscan Sisters
211 St. Francis Dr.
Cape Girardeau, MO 63703

Creve Coeur
Archdiocese of St. Louis

St. John's Mercy Medical Center
615 S. New Ballas Rd.
Creve Coeur, MO 63141
Tel.: 314-569-6000; Fax: 314-569-6910
Conducted by the Religious Sisters of Mercy of the Americas-St. Louis Region
(See Branch Unit under Washington, MO)
Mr. MARK F. WEBER, Pres. & CEO
Chaplains:
Revs.:
DAVID D. SULLIVAN
LOWRIE DALY, S.J.
PHILIP KRAHMAN
Deacon KEN POTZMAN
Sisters 25
Other Nurses 984
Bed Capacity 892
Patients assisted annually 482,015
Capacity Includes: Chemical Dependency Unit of 35 beds
Skilled Nursing facility of 120 Beds

Jefferson City
Diocese of Jefferson City

St. Marys Health Center
100 St. Marys Medical Plaza
Jefferson City, MO 65101
Tel: 573-761-7000
Owned and operated by St. Louis Health Care Network, a member of the SSM Health Care System.
JOHN S. DUBIS, Pres.
Chaplains:
Revs.:
ERWIN R. KONRAD
JAMES CARTER, American Baptist Min., C.O.C. Certified Chap.
Ms. JAN SCHUPP, NACC Certified Chap. Dept. Mgr.
Sr. EVELYN SCHNIEDERS, O.S.F., NACC Certified Chap.
Sr. EVELYN MARIE PETERMAN, F.S.M.
Bed Capacity 167
Patients assisted annually 99,202
Clinics 14
Clinic visits 129,478
Home health visits 14,645

Joplin
Diocese of Springfield-Cape Girardeau

St. John's Regional Medical Center; Mercy Lifecare Systems, Inc.
2727 McClelland Blvd.
Joplin, MO 64804
Tel: 417-781-2727
Sisters of Mercy (Omaha)
Mr. ROBERT G. BRUECKNER, Pres.
Rev. BENEDICT W. HARTER, Chap.
Sisters 6
Bed Capacity 367
Patients assisted annually 63,000
Mercy Regional Health Foundation, Inc.
2727 McClelland Blvd.
Joplin, MO 64804

Kansas City
Diocese of Kansas City-St. Joseph

Saint Joseph Health Center
1000 Carondelet Dr.
Kansas City, MO 64114
Tel: 816-942-4400
Sponsored by the Sisters of St. Joseph of Carondelet.
Mr. RICHARD M. ABELL, Pres. & CEO
CAROL NASH, Chap.
Sisters 11
Bed Capacity 300
Nurses 362
Patients assisted annually 100,692
Affiliates:
Carondelet Health Corporation
1000 Carondelet Dr.
Kansas City, MO 64114
Tel: 816-942-4400
Parent Co. Sponsored by the Sisters of St. Joseph of Carondelet.
RICHARD M. ABELL, Pres.
Saint Joseph Health Center Foundation
1000 Carondelet Dr.
Kansas City, MO 64114
Tel: 816-942-4400
Sponsored by the Sisters of St. Joseph of Carondelet.
KENNETH MELLARD, Chm.
Mr. RICHARD M. ABELL, Pres.
Carondelet Manor
621 Carondelet Dr.
Kansas City, MO 64114
Tel: 816-941-3370
DIANNE DOCTOR, Admin.
Bed Capacity 180
Legal Title: *Carondelet Long Term Care Facilities, Inc.*
Owned and operated by Carondelet Long Term Care Facilities, Inc. Sponsored by Sisters of St. Joseph of Carondelet.
Carondelet Home Care Services Inc.
11050 Roe Ave., Ste. 120
Kansas City, KS 66211
Tel: 816-943-4700
KAREN STEFFEN, Admin.
Home health agency affiliated with Saint Joseph Health Center.
Villa Saint Joseph
11901 Rosewood
Overland Park, KS 66209
Tel: 913-345-1745
KATHARINE ENSIGN, Admin.
Bed Capacity 120

Kirkwood
Archdiocese of St. Louis

St. Joseph Hospital of Kirkwood
525 Couch Ave.
Kirkwood, MO 63122
Tel: 314-966-1601
A Member of the SSM Health Care System.
CARLA S. BAUM, Pres.
Rev. MARK FULLER, Supr. & Chap.
Bed Capacity 281
Sisters 2
Nurses 204
Patients assisted annually 50,000

Lake St. Louis
Archdiocese of St. Louis

St. Joseph Hospital West
100 Medical Plaza
Lake St. Louis, MO 63367
Tel: 314-625-5200; Fax: 314-625-5314
Owned and Operated by St. Louis Health Care Network, a member of the SSM Health Care System.
Mr. Kurt L. Weinmeister, Pres.
Rev. Jerome G. Stowell, C.P., Chap.
Bed Capacity 100
Patients assisted annually 19,792

Maryville
Diocese of Kansas City-St. Joseph

St. Francis Hospital & Health Services
2016 S. Main
Maryville, MO 64468
Tel: 816-562-2600; Fax: 816-562-2411
A member of the SSM Health Care System. Sponsored by Franciscan Sisters of Mary, St. Louis, MO. Acute care facility.
Nellie Agyagos, Interim Pres.
Rev. Philip Schuster, O.S.B., Chap.
Sisters 3
Bed Capacity 90
Total Staff 360

Mountain View
Diocese of Springfield-Cape Girardeau

St. Francis Hospital
P.O. Box 82
Mountain View, MO 65548
Tel: 417-934-2246
Daughters of St. Francis of Assisi
Sr. M. Cornelia Blasko, D.S.F., Admin., C.E.O.
Sisters 7
Bed Capacity 42
Patients assisted annually 14,256

Pilot Knob
Diocese of Springfield-Cape Girardeau

Arcadia Valley Hospital
P.O. Box 548
Pilot Knob, MO 63663
Tel: 573-546-3924
Owned & Operated by SSM Health Care System. A member of the SSM Health Care System.
Rev. Anthony M. Gaydos, O.S.M., Chap.
Sisters 5
Bed Capacity 60

Springfield
Diocese of Springfield-Cape Girardeau

St. John's Regional Health Center
1235 E. Cherokee St.
Springfield, MO 65804
Tel: 417-885-2000
Sisters of Mercy Health System (St. Louis)
Mr. Allen L. Shockley, Pres.
Rev. Anthony Shidler, O.S.B., Chap.
Sisters 15
Bed Capacity 866
Patients assisted annually 202,101

St. Charles
Archdiocese of St. Louis

St. Joseph Health Center
300 First Capitol Dr.
St. Charles, MO 63301
Tel: 314-947-5000; Fax: 314-947-5090
Franciscan Sister of Mary
Owned and Operated by SSM Health Care II. A Member of the SSM Health Care System.
Mr. Kevin F. Kast, Pres.
Mr. Dave W. Fitzgerald, Dir. of Pastoral Care
Rev. Ray Hampe
Sisters 3
Bed Capacity 362
Patients assisted annually 118,216
Staff 1,021

St. Louis
Archdiocese of St. Louis

Alexian Brothers Hospital
3933 S. Broadway
St. Louis, MO 63118
Tel: 314-865-3333
Congregation of Alexian Brothers, Immaculate Conception Province
Legal Title: *Alexian Brothers of St. Louis, Inc.*
Bro. Edward Yochim, C.F.A., Dir. of Community
Brothers 8
Bed Capacity 203
Patients assisted annually 52,000
Total Staff 802
Parent Corporation: Alexian Brothers of Missouri, Inc.

Incarnate Word Hospital
3545 Lafayette
St. Louis, MO 63104
Tel: 314-865-6500; Fax: 314-865-6526
Conducted by the Congregation of Sisters of Charity of the Incarnate Word.
Joan I. Holden, C.C.V.I., D.Min.
Linda M. Allin, CEO
Sisters 5
Other Nurses 151
Bed Capacity 336
Patients assisted annually 29,524
Total Staff 1,500

Saint Louis University Hospital
3635 Vista Ave., P.O. Box 15250
St. Louis, MO 63110-0250
Tel: 314-577-8000, Ext. 8066; Fax: 314-577-8003 (Exec. Office)
Owned and Operated by St. Louis University, Society of Jesus.
Mary Lou Bennett, Dir.
Chaplains:
Revs.:
Robert J. Chenoweth (JC)
Gregory Kirsch
Paul Mandziuk, M.S.
Sr. Ann Johnston, O.P.
Deacon Louis A. Menard
Mary Salois
Sandra Spencer
Rev. Kathy Spivey
Kathy Herron, Pastoral Care Asst.
Nurses 537
Bed Capacity 356
Patients assisted annually 139,019

St. Mary's Health Center
6420 Clayton Rd.
St. Louis, MO 63117
Tel: 314-768-8000; Fax: 314-768-8011
Owned & operated by St. Louis Health Care Network, a member of the SSM Health Care System.
Michael Zilm, Pres.
Rev. James Krings, Chap.
Rick Erickson, Pastoral Care Dir.
Franciscan Sisters of Mary 5
Bed Capacity 690
Patients assisted annually 85,975
Total Staff 1,600

Washington
Archdiocese of St. Louis

St. John's Mercy Hospital
200 Madison Ave.
Washington, MO 63090
Tel: 314-239-8000
Rev. Timothy J. Toohey, Chap.
Terry M. Rose, Admin.
Beds 185
Staff 700
(See Listing Under Creve Coeur, MO)

MONTANA

Billings
Diocese of Great Falls - Billings

Saint Vincent Hospital and Health Center
1233 N. 30th St., P.O. Box 35200
Billings, MT 59107-5200
Tel: 406-657-7000
Sisters of Charity of Leavenworth, Kansas
Mr. James T. Paquette, Pres.
Pastoral Care:
Luke Larson, Dir.
Revs.:
Martin Fisher
Anthony J. Ozimek, OSB
Robert H. Koerner, .
Sisters 5
Beds 302
Patients assisted annually 12,000

Butte
Diocese of Helena

St. James Community Hospital, Inc.
400 S. Clark St.
Butte, MT 59701
Mailing Address:
P.O. Box 3300
Butte, MT 59702
Tel: 406-723-2500; Fax: 406-782-1967
Mr. Thomas R. Hochwalt, Pres.
Rev. James C. McCarthy, Chap.
Sr. Joy Duff, S.C.L., Pastoral Care
Bed Capacity 156
Sisters of Charity of Leavenworth 7
Lay Staff 441
Patients assisted annually 38,171

Great Falls
Diocese of Great Falls - Billings

Benefis Health Care
500-15th Ave. S., P.O. Box 5013
Great Falls, MT 59403
Tel: 406-727-3333
Sisters of Providence
Rev. James E. Birkmaier, Dir. Pastoral Care & Chap.
Lloyd V. Smith, FACHE-Pres./CEO
Sisters 2
Student Nurses 60
Patients assisted annually 94,271

Miles City
Diocese of Great Falls - Billings

Holy Rosary Health Center
2600 Wilson St.
Miles City, MT 59301
Tel: 406-233-2600; Fax: 406-233-2601
Presentation Sisters
Mr. H. Ray Gibbons, Pres.
Sisters 1
Beds 44
Patients assisted annually 15,897

Missoula
Diocese of Helena

St. Patrick Hospital Corporation
500 W. Broadway
Missoula, MT 59802
Mailing Address:
P.O. Box 4587
Missoula, MT 59806
Tel: 406-543-7271; Fax: 406-329-5693
Mr. Lawrence L. White, Jr., Pres.
Rev. Roger E. Blanchette, S.J., Chap.
Pastoral Care:
Sr. Marie L. Corr, B.V.M.
Sr. Elizabeth Olsen, B.V.M.
Sr. Catherine Palmatier, S.P.
Rev. Henry Littlehales, (Presbyterian)
Sr. Vivian Ripp, S.N.J.M.
Sisters 5
Lay Staff 1,165
Bed Capacity 213
Patients assisted annually 114,984

Polson
Diocese of Helena

St. Joseph Hospital Corporation
Skyline Dr., P.O. Box 1010
Polson, MT 59860
Tel: 406-883-5377; Fax: 406-883-4388
John W. Glueckert, Admin.
Deacon Wes Vert
Sr. Mary K. Cummings, S.P., Pastoral Care
Sisters 1
Bed Capacity 40
Lay Staff 110
Patients assisted annually 19,956

NEBRASKA

Grand Island
Diocese of Grand Island

Saint Francis Medical Center
2620 W. Faidley Ave., P.O. Box 9804
Grand Island, NE 68802
Tel: 308-384-4600; Fax: 308-389-5589
Mr. Michael Gloor, Pres.
Sisters of Charity Health Care Systems
Beds 216
Bassinets 17
Patients assisted annually 68,659

Kearney
Diocese of Grand Island

Good Samaritan Health Systems dba Good Samaritan Hospital
10 E. 31st St.

Kearney, NE 68847-2926
Tel: 308-236-8511
WILLIAM W. HENDRICKSON, Pres.
Sisters 3
Beds 187
Patients assisted annually 69,986
Richard H. Young Hospital
4600 17th Ave.
Kearney, NE 68847
Tel: 308-236-2000
Beds 80
Patients assisted annually 898

Lincoln
Diocese of Lincoln

St. Elizabeth Community Health Center
555 South 70th St.
Lincoln, NE 68510
Tel: 402-489-7181
Mr. ROBERT LANIK, Pres.
Rev. PATRICK MURPHY, B.A., Chap.
Priests 1
Sisters 2
Beds 208
Patients assisted annually 137,934

Nebraska City
Diocese of Lincoln

St. Mary's Hospital
1314 Third Ave.
Nebraska City, NE 68410
Tel: 402-873-3321
RICHARD W. WALLER, Interim Admin.
Beds 38
Patients assisted annually 22,882

Norfolk
Archdiocese of Omaha

Our Lady of Lourdes Hospital
1500 Koenigstein Ave.
Norfolk, NE 68701
Tel: 402-371-3402; Fax: 402-644-7468
The Missionary Benedictine Sisters
Sr. MARY JAMES UHING, O.S.B., Pres.
Sr. M. AGNES SALBER, O.S.B., Contact & Prioress
Rev. DUANE LUKES, Chap.
Sisters 2
Beds 100
Patients assisted annually 39,500
New Born 318

O'Neill
Archdiocese of Omaha

St. Anthony's Hospital
O'Neill, NE 68763
Tel: 402-336-2611; Fax: 402-336-2815
Sisters of St. Francis of Penance and Christian Charity
RONALD J. CORK, Contact
Beds 44
Bassinets 10
Patients assisted annually 14,815
Attended by St. Patrick Church.

Omaha
Archdiocese of Omaha

Alegent Health
1018 N. 96th St., Ste. 200
Omaha, NE 68114
Tel: 402-343-4430; Fax: 402-343-4337
Sr. NORITA COONEY, R.S.M., Board Chair

**Alegent Health - Bergan Mercy Health System dba Algent Health - Bergan Mercy Medical Center*
7500 Mercy Rd.
Omaha, NE 68124
Tel: 402-398-6060
RICHARD A. HACHTEN, II, Pres.
Chaplains:
Revs.:
ROBERT E. BRODZELLER, S.J.
HARRY EGLSAER, S.J.
Sr. ELAINE ABELS, R.S.C.J.
KATHY KASHER
MARY LOU RUH
MARY SUE STURGEON
Deacon TOM MURPHY
MARY EILEEN ANDREASEN, Congregational Nurse Min.
MARIAN STANDEVEN, Dir. Mission Svcs./ Community Affairs
PEGGY O'MALLEY, Coord. Health Ministry Prog.
Priests 2
Sisters 1
Bed Capacity 470
Inpatients assisted annually 15,718
Outpatients assisted annually 103,182
Bergan Mercy Foundation, Inc.
RICHARD A. HACHTEN, II, Pres.
MARIAN STANDEVEN, Contact

Boys Town National Research Hospital
555 N. 30 St.
Omaha, NE 68131
Tel: 402-498-6511; Fax: 402-498-6357
Dr. PATRICK BROOKHOUSER, Dir.

Catholic Health Corp.
920 S. 107 Ave.
Omaha, NE 68114
Tel: 402-393-7661
ELEANOR G. CLAUS, Interim CEO & Contact
Catholic Health Care Federation
Catholic Health Corporation Retirement Plan
Health Services Self Protection Fund
Health Facilities, Inc.

Wayne
Archdiocese of Omaha

Providence Medical Center
1200 Providence Rd.
Wayne, NE 68787
Missionary Benedictine Sisters
MARCILE THOMAS, Admin.
Sr. KEVIN HERMSEN, Asst. Admin.
Sr. MONICA BACKES, Supr.
Rev. DONALD M. CLEARY, Chap.
Sr. GERTRUD MARIE WOLFER, O.S.B., Pastoral Care
Sr. KEVIN HERMSEN, Contact
Beds 34
Patients assisted annually 6,900

West Point
Archdiocese of Omaha

Franciscan Care Services, Inc., (d.b.a. St. Francis Memorial Hospital
430 N. Monitor St.
West Point, NE 68788-1595
Tel: 402-372-2404; Fax: 402-372-2360
Franciscan Sisters of Christian Charity
RONALD O. BRIGGS, CEO & Contact
Revs.:
GARY OSTRANDER
STEVE EMANUEL
Sisters 6
Bed Capacity 49
Patients assisted annually 59,873

NEVADA

Henderson
Diocese of Las Vegas

St. Rose Dominican Hospital
102 Lake Mead Dr.
Henderson, NV 89015
Tel: 702-564-2622
Sisters of the Third Order of St. Dominic, Congregation of the Most Holy Rosary (Adrian, MI)
Mr. ROD A. DAVIS, Pres. & CEO
Affiliated with the University of Nevada-Las Vegas School of Nursing
Sisters 13
Beds 147
Total Staff 850
Patients assisted annually 77,190

Reno
Diocese of Reno

St. Mary's Regional Medical Center
235 W. Sixth St.
Reno, NV 89520-0108
Tel: 702-323-2041; Fax: 702-789-3963
Dominican Sisters of San Rafael
Sr. JEREMY CARMODY, O.P., Congregational Rep.
JEFF K. BILLS, Pres. & CEO, Tel: 702-789-3004
BENEDICT DASHER, Chm.
Sr. JULIANA JERVIS, O.P., Natural Family Planning
Deacon RANDOL G. BATSON, Mgr. Chaplaincy Svcs.
Chaplaincy Services:
Revs.:
JOHN COEN, S.A.C.
WILLIAM FAUST
Sr. MARRIANNA HARRISON, O.P.
LARRY WISE, Senior Vice Pres. Chief Operating Officer
Sisters 4
Beds 367
Patients assisted annually 98,022

NEW HAMPSHIRE

Manchester
Diocese of Manchester

Catholic Medical Center of Manchester, NH, Inc.
100 McGregor St.
Manchester, NH 03102
Tel: 603-668-3545
Sr. ANDREA MCDONALD, R.S.M., Dept. Dir.
Sisters 4
Beds 266
Bassinets 15
Patients assisted annually 104,909

Nashua
Diocese of Manchester

St. Joseph Hospital
172 Kinsley St.
Nashua, NH 03061
Tel: 603-882-3000
PETER B. DAVIS, Pres.
Sr. JOSEPHINE PATTIGASH, Vice Pres., Mission Effectiveness
Dr. JOHN A. GIANINO, Pastoral Care Dir.
Staff Chaplains:
Rev. JOHN C. BLAIR
Deacon JOHN MARTIN
Grey Nuns 1
Beds 218
Total Staff 1,089
Patients assisted annually 2,299
Rivier-St. Joseph School of Nursing
Students 635

NEW JERSEY

Camden
Diocese of Camden

Our Lady of Lourdes Medical Center, Inc.
(Formerly Our Lady of Lourdes Hospital).
1600 Haddon Ave.
Camden, NJ 08103
Tel: 609-757-3500
Revs.:
WARREN RECTOR, O.F.M.
ARTHUR T. ANDERSON
Our Lady of Lourdes Associates Foundation, Inc.
853 Haddon Ave.
Collingswood, NJ 08108
Tel: 609-858-5097
Lourdes HomeHealth Services
1600 Haddon Ave.
Camden, NJ 08103
Tel: 609-869-0900
Haddon HealthCare
900 Haddon Ave., Suite 318
Camden, NJ 08108
Tel: 609-869-0800
Osborn Family Health Center, Inc.
1601 Haddon Ave.
Camden, NJ 08103
Tel: 609-757-3700
Lourdes Ancillary Services, Inc.
1565 Vesper Blvd.
Camden, NJ 08103
Tel: 609-757-3500
Our Lady of Lourdes School of Nursing, Inc.
1565 Vesper Blvd.
Camden, NJ 08103
Tel: 609-757-3730
Our Lady of Lourdes Medical Center, Inc. Auxiliary
1600 Haddon Ave.
Camden, NJ 08103
Tel: 609-757-3500
Our Lady of Lourdes Health Care Services, Inc.
1600 Haddon Ave.
Camden, NJ 08103
Tel: 609-757-3500

Saint Luke's Catholic Medical Services, Inc.
511 State St.
Camden, NJ 08102
Tel: 609-365-4642
Rev. MARK C. AITA, S.J., M.D., Medical Dir.

Denville
Diocese of Paterson

Sisters of the Sorrowful Mother Health Care Ministry Corp.
22 Bloomfield Ave.
Denville, NJ 07834
Tel: 201-586-1961
Sr. M JOHNICE THONE, S.S.M., Chairperson
JOSEPH TRUNFIO, Pres.
Chaplains:
Revs.:

Thomas A. Heffernan
Charles Lovato, S.F.
James Sullivan, S.M.A.
Stuart Baer
Joseph McNamara, O.S.F.S.
Carmine Fazio, O.F.M.Cap.
Deacons:
Ed Lally
Frank Padden
Sisters of the Sorrowful Mother 10
Bed Capacity 927
Patients assisted annually 315,000
Northwest Covenant Medical Center, Inc.
St. Clares-Riverside Campus-Denville
St. Clares-Riverside Campus-Boonton Township
Dover General Campus
St. Clares-Riverside Campus-Sussex
St. Clares-Riverside Foundation, Inc.
Sisters of the Sorrowful Mother Ambulatory Care Corporation
St. Francis Life Care Corporation
St. Francis Assisted Living Corporation
St. Francis Health Resort, Inc.
Wallkill Valley Health Care Foundation, Inc.
Sisters of the Sorrowful Mother Housing Corporation I, Inc.
Sisters of the Sorrowful Mother Housing Corporation II, Inc.

Elizabeth
Archdiocese of Newark

St. Elizabeth Hospital
225 Williamson St.
Elizabeth, NJ 07207
Tel: 908-527-5000; Fax: 908-820-0554
Sisters of Charity of Saint Elizabeth
Sr. Elizabeth Ann Maloney, S.C., Pres.
Sr. Dorothy Apprich, S.S.J., Dir. Pastoral Care
Chaplains:
Revs.:
Joseph Fiorino
Virgilio P. Chagas (Philippines)
Sisters 14
Bed Capacity 329
Bassinets 31
Patients assisted annually 103,020

Hoboken
Archdiocese of Newark

St. Mary Hospital
(Sub. of Franciscan Health System of New Jersey, Inc.)
308 Willow Ave.
Hoboken, NJ 07030
Tel: 201-418-1000; Fax: 201-418-1013
Franciscan Sisters of the Poor
Ulrich J. Rosa, Pres. & CEO
Sr. Mary Meehan, S.S.N.D., Corporate Vice Pres., Mission
Sr. Rita Marie Donnelly, S.F.P., Pastoral Care
Sr. Maria Teresa Romeo, S.F.P., Pastoral Care
Sr. Jo-Ann Jackowski, S.F.P., Project Coord., Mission
Revs.:
Allen Guglielmo, Chap.
Thomas Kunnath
Franciscan Sisters of the Poor 3
Bed Capacity 328
Patients assisted annually 121,722

Jersey City
Archdiocese of Newark

St. Francis Hospital
(Sub. of Franciscan Health System of New Jersey, Inc.)
25 McWilliams Pl.
Jersey City, NJ 07302
Tel: 201-418-1000; Fax: 201-418-2011
Ulrich J. Rosa, Pres. & CEO
Sr. Mary Meehan, S.S.N.D., Corp. Vice Pres., Mission
Sr. Jo-Ann Jackowski, S.F.P., Project Coord., Mission
Sr. Loretta Kirby, S.F.P., Pastoral Care
Revs.:
Gerard Sudol, Chap.
Thomas Kunnath
Franciscan Sisters of the Poor 2
Bed Capacity 243
Patients assisted annually 37,132

New Brunswick
Diocese of Metuchen

St. Peter's Medical Center
254 Easton Ave.
New Brunswick, NJ 08901
Tel: 732-745-8600; Fax: 732-745-7938
John E. Matuska, Pres.
Chaplains:
Revs.:
Cecilio E. Sipaco (Philippines)
Guy I. McPartland, O.Carm.
Peter J. Murray, S.J. (New York)
Beds 416
Bassinets 112
Patients assisted annually 150,274

Newark
Archdiocese of Newark

Catholic Community Services (C.C.S.) Mt. Carmel Guild Hospital
1160 Raymond Blvd.
Newark, NJ 07102
Tel: 201-596-4084
Rev. Msgr. Nicholas Di Marzio, Ph.D., L.S.W., Exec. Dir., C.C.S.
Julie Willis, L.S.W., Admin. Dir.
Ambrose Mgbako, M.D., Medical Dir.
Operated by Catholic Community Services. The hospital has two adult units: Psychiatric Unit; Substance Abuse Detoxification Unit. Also available are Extensive outpatient and day treatment services in the area of substance abuse and mental health for adults.
Bed Capacity 20
Staff 23
Patients assisted annually 366

St. James Hospital
155 Jefferson St.
Newark, NJ 07105
Tel: 201-589-1300
Ceu Cirne-Neves, Admin.
Olimpia Escudero, Vice Pres. Operations
Chaplains:
Sr. Dolores Cervi
Mary Ellen Doran
Traudel Pannullo, M.D., Pres. of Medical Staff
Bed Capacity 189
Bassinets 23
Staff 550
Patients assisted annually 30,000

Saint Michael's Medical Center
268 Dr. Martin Luther King. Jr. Blvd.
Newark, NJ 07102-9880
Tel: 201-877-5411; Fax: 201-877-2714
Dominick R. Calgi, Admin.
Rev. Michael A. Scheip, Mgr. Pastoral Care
James Amato, M.D., Pres. Medical Staff
Division of Cathedral Health Services, Inc.
Bed Capacity 411
Sisters 5
Bassinets 32
Admissions 11,700
Outpatient Visits 88,740

Orange
Archdiocese of Newark

Saint Mary Life Center, Inc. - Pope John Paul II Pavillion
135 S. Center St.
Orange, NJ 07050
Tel: 201-266-3000
Michael Shipley, Admin.
Patients assisted annually 113

Passaic
Diocese of Paterson

St. Mary's Hospital
211 Pennington Ave.
Passaic, NJ 07055
Tel: 201-470-3000
Patricia Peterson, Pres. & CEO
Rev. Vincent Liuzzo, O.F.M.Cap., Dir. Pastoral Care
Sisters of Charity of St. Elizabeth, NJ 10
Bed Capacity 229
Patients assisted annually 67,683
St. Mary Health Corporation
Sr. Barbara Conroy, S.C.
St. Mary's Hospital Corporation
Patricia Peterson, Pres.
Gillen Property Holding Corporation
Patricia Peterson, Pres.

Paterson
Diocese of Paterson

St. Joseph's Hospital and Medical Center
703 Main St.
Paterson, NJ 07503
Tel: 201-754-2000
Sr. Jane Frances Brady, Pres.
Revs.:
Francis Hanudel, O.F.M.
William Cramer
Sisters of Charity of St. Elizabeth, NJ 35
Bed Capacity 787
Patients assisted annually 315,607

Teaneck
Archdiocese of Newark

Holy Name Hospital
718 Teaneck Rd.
Teaneck, NJ 07666
Tel: 201-833-3000; Fax: 201-833-3230
Sisters of St. Joseph of Peace
Sr. Patricia A. Lynch, FACHE., Pres. & CEO
Bed Capacity 361
Bassinets 36
School of Nursing
Sr. Clare Tynan C.S.J.P., Vice Pres.
Pastoral Care:
Sr. Lois Jablonski, S.S.J., M.S., Dir.
Chaplains:
Revs.:
Paterno Gorospe
James F. Reilly
Constance Forcillo, R.N.
Sr. Donna Conroy, R.S.M.
Mary Ellen Doran, M.S.
Jane Selinske, Ed.D., M.S.W.
Sisters 12

Trenton
Diocese of Trenton

St. Francis Medical Center
601 Hamilton Ave.
Trenton, NJ 08629
Tel: 609-599-5000
Sisters of St. Francis of Philadelphia 10
Bed Capacity 436
Patients assisted annually 137,644
Bassinets 27
Schools for Nurses
Judith M. Persichilli, Pres. & C.E.O.
Bonnie Ross, Dir. School of Nursing
Revs.:
Joel F. Szydlowski, O.F.M., Dir. Pastoral Care
Linus E. Kopczewski, O.F.M.
Rudolph Wieszczek, O.F.M.
Student Nurses 150

NEW MEXICO

Albuquerque
Archdiocese of Santa Fe

St. Joseph Healthcare System
7850 Jefferson, N.E., Ste. 100
Albuquerque, NM 87109
Tel: 505-727-2804; Fax: 505-727-2814
Sisters of Charity of Cincinnati, Ohio
Member of St. Joseph Healthcare System.
Ray H. Barton, III, Pres. & CEO
Sr. Marie Raphael Morell, O.P., Dir. Pastoral Care
Priests 2
Chaplains 8
Patients assisted annually 16,591
Beds 697
Total Staff 2,186

St. Joseph Medical Center
601 Dr. Martin Luther King, Jr. Ave., N.E.
Albuquerque, NM 87102
Tel: 505-727-2804; Fax: 505-727-2814
Sisters of Charity of Cincinnati, Ohio
Member of St. Joseph Healthcare System.
Steven J. Smith, Admin.
Sr. Marie Raphael Morell, O.P., Dir. Pastoral Care
Priests 1
Chaplains 4
Beds 275
Patients assisted annually 9,537
Total Staff 959

St. Joseph Northeast Heights Hospital
4701 Montgomery, N.E.
Albuquerque, NM 87109
Tel: 505-727-2804; Fax: 505-727-2814
Sisters of Charity of Cincinnati, Ohio
Member of St. Joseph Healthcare System.
C. Vincent Townsend, Jr., Admin.
Chaplains 1
Priests 1
Beds 112
Patients assisted annually 3,509
Total Staff 226

St. Joseph Rehabilitation Hospital
505 Elm St., N.E.
Albuquerque, NM 87102

Tel: 505-727-2804; Fax: 505-727-2814
Sisters of Charity of Cincinnati, Ohio
Member of St. Joseph Healthcare System.
MARY LOU COORS, Admin.
Priests 1
Beds 63
Patients assisted annually 865
Total Staff 209

St. Joseph West Mesa Hospital
10501 Golf Course Rd., N.W.
Albuquerque, NM 87114
Tel: 505-727-2804; Fax: 505-727-2814
Sisters of Charity of Cincinnati, Ohio
Member of St. Joseph Healthcare System.
C. VINCENT TOWNSEND, JR., Admin.
Chaplains/Priests Available 1
Beds 112
Patients assisted annually 2,680
Total Staff 216

NEW YORK

Albany
Diocese of Albany

Mercycare Corporation
315 S. Manning Blvd.
Albany, NY 12208
Tel: 518-454-1084; Fax: 518-454-1520

Mercycare Corporation, St. Peter's Hospital
315 S. Manning Blvd.
Albany, NY 12208
Tel: 518-454-1540
Mr. STEVEN P. BOYLE, Pres. & CEO
Rev. JOHN YANAS, Chap.
Bed Capacity 437
Patients assisted annually 193,077
Hospice
Tel: 518-454-1563
Sr. JEAN ROCHE, R.S.M., Contact Person
Hospice of Rensselaer Co.
258 Broadway
Albany, NY 12180
Tel: 518-271-1901
Sr. MARLENE HORRIGAN, C.S.J., Contact Person
Our Lady of Mercy Life Center
2240 Western Ave.
Guilderland, NY 12084
Tel: 518-464-8100
WESLEY I. HALE, Exec. Dir.

Amsterdam
Diocese of Albany

St. Mary's Hospital
427 Guy Park Ave.
Amsterdam, NY 12010
Tel: 518-842-1900
Mr. PETER E. CAPOBIANCO, Pres. & CEO
Rev. JOSEPH J. DWORAK, Chap.
Sisters of St. Joseph of Carondelet 14
Bed Capacity 143
Patients assisted annually 150,355

Auburn
Diocese of Rochester

Mercy Health & Rehabilitation Center Nursing Home Co., Inc. (1972)
St. Anthony St.
Auburn, NY 13021
Tel: 315-253-0351; Fax: 315-258-3904
Sr. MARY NORBERT STANG, Dir. Pastoral Care
Sr. LINDA ANN PALMISANO, CEO
Sisters of the Third Franciscan Order
Nursing Facility Beds 297

Batavia
Diocese of Buffalo

St. Jerome Hospital
16 Bank St.
Batavia, NY 14020
Tel: 716-343-3131
Mr. CHARLES W. SMITH, Admin.
LINDA PROUTY, R.N., Dir. Nursing Services
Sisters of Mercy 4
Capacity 96
Patients assisted annually 76,132
Total Staff 369

Beacon
Archdiocese of New York

St. Francis Hospital
Delavan Ave.
Beacon, NY 12508
Tel: 914-831-3500
LAWRENCE M. WITTE, FACHE

Binghamton
Diocese of Syracuse

Our Lady of Lourdes Memorial Hospital
169 Riverside Dr.
Binghamton, NY 13905
Tel: 607-798-5111
Mr. MICHAEL GULEY, Pres.
Daughters of Charity of St. Vincent de Paul 9
Beds 277
Patients assisted annually 316,481

Buffalo
Diocese of Buffalo

McAuley Mercy Corporation
515 Abbott Rd.
Buffalo, NY 14220
Tel: 716-828-2750
ROBERT V. STANEK, Pres.
Sponsored by the Sisters of Mercy of the Buffalo Diocese.

Mercy Health System of Western New York
Marian Professional Center
515 Abbott Rd., Ste. 508
Buffalo, NY 14220
Tel: 716-828-2750
ROBERT V. STANEK, Pres./ C.E.O.
Annually Assisted 581,114
Total Staff 2,932

Mercy Hospital
565 Abbott Rd.
Buffalo, NY 14220
Tel: 716-826-7000
Sisters of Mercy
Sr. KATHI SWEENEY, R.S.M., CEO
Rev. Msgr. FRANCIS A. KRUPA, Chap.
Rev. Msgr. FRANCIS J. STAEBELL, S.J., Assoc. Chap.
Sisters 17
Patients assisted annually 16,165
Beds 349
Skilled Nursing Beds 74
Bassinets 60
Total Staff 2,300

Sisters Hospital Foundation, Inc.
2130 Main St.
Buffalo, NY 14214
Tel: 716-862-2533

Sisters of Charity Hospital of Buffalo, NY
2157 Main St.
Buffalo, NY 14214
Tel: 716-862-1000; Fax: 716-862-1899
Chaplains:
Revs.:
LOUIS S. KLEIN
RICHARD E. ZAJAC
Sr. MARGARET DOUGHERTY, D.C., Dir., Pastoral Care
Sr. M. CAROLINE HRICZKO, D.C.
Sr. DIANE LOUTTIT, D.C.
Deacon KAREN GOUGH
Ms. JUDITH MILLER
Daughters of Charity of St. Vincent de Paul 11
Bed Capacity 493
Bassinets 60
Patients assisted annually 317,000
Total Staff 2,000
School for Nurses
Student Nurses 100

Cheektowaga
Diocese of Buffalo

McAuley-Seton Home Care
14 Apple Tree Business Park
Cheektowaga, NY 14227
Tel: 716-685-4870
ROBERT STANEK, Pres.

St. Joseph Hospital
2605 Harlem Rd.
Cheektowaga, NY 14225-4097
Tel: 716-891-2400; Fax: 716-891-2616
Franciscan Sisters of St. Joseph
Bed Capacity 208
Patients assisted annually 130,965

Elmira
Diocese of Rochester

St. Joseph's Hospital
555 E. Market St.
Elmira, NY 14902
Tel: 607-733-6541
Sisters of St. Joseph
Skilled Nursing Facility.
Sr. MARIE CASTAGNARO, Pres.
Bed Capacity 224
Skilled Nursing Facility 31
Patients assisted annually 114,158

St. Joseph's Hospital Foundation, Inc.
555 E. Market St.
Elmira, NY 14902
Tel: 607-737-7004; Fax: 607-737-7837
DAVID P. SULLIVAN, Pres.

Hornell
Diocese of Rochester

St. James Mercy Hospital
411 Canisteo St.
Hornell, NY 14843
Tel: 607-324-8000
PAUL E. SHEPHARD, CEO
Sisters of Mercy 4
Bed Capacity 232
Patients assisted annually 5,333
School of Nursing
Sr. AUGUSTINE MALLEY, Pastoral Care
Students 28

Jamaica
Diocese of Brooklyn

Catholic Medical Center of Brooklyn & Queens
88-25 153rd St.
Jamaica, NY 11432
Tel: 718-558-6900
Corporate Staff:
Most Rev. JOSEPH M. SULLIVAN, Chm.
WILLIAM D. MCGUIRE, Pres. & CEO
LEWIS LESSER, Exec. Vice Pres. Planning
RAYMOND RUSSO, M.D., Exec. Vice Pres. Medical Affairs
WILLIAM ARMSTRONG, Vice Pres., Admin.
THOMAS CHARDAVOYNE, Vice Pres. Public Affairs
Sr. ANNELLE FITZPATRICK, C.S.J., Vice Pres. Mission Svcs.
STEVE KALLOS, Vice Pres. Info. Svcs.
PATRICK B. MCENEANEY, Vice Pres. Human Resources
DANIEL J. RINALDI, Treas.
KATHLEEN M. SCHER, Vice Pres., Nursing Services
MILDRED A. SHANLEY, Vice Pres., Legal Services
JOSEPH SKARZYNSKI, M.D., Acting Medical Dir. Quality Assurance
MARGARET FERNANDEZ, Admin. Asst. to the Pres.
Executive Staff:
REGINA ALLEVA, Asst. to the Vice Pres. of Legal Affairs
I. JOSEPH APRILE, M.D., Senior Medical Advisor to the Pres.
WILLIAM ARMSTRONG, Dir. of Finance, SNF/HHA
ADRIENNE AURYANSEN, Dir. of Insurance and Claims Mgmt.
HOWARD BALSAM, Dir. of Finance, Corp. Admin.
MAUREEN BARRON, Corp. Dir. of Risk Mgmt.
SANDRA BLOOMBERG, Ph.D., Dir. of Medical and Allied Health Education
JOSEPH CIANCIOTTO, Dir. of Finance and Patient Accounting
CATHERINE CORBELLI, R.N., Corp. Dir. of Nursing Education
SAMUEL FADEN, Dir., Corp. Info. Systems
Sr. CHRISTINE GAYLOR, C.S.J., Dir. of Mission Ethics
DOROTHY HURLEY, Dir. of Training & Organizational Devel.
SAM JOSEPH, Admin. Dir. for Mental Health Svcs.
WILLIAM LISS-LEVINSON, Ph.D., Dir. of Prog. Devel.
JOSEPH MARINO, AIA, Dir. of Facilities Planning and Construction
JOHN MCKEON, Assoc. Dir. of Human Resources
GERARD MORAN, Dir. Corp. Benefit and Compensation
ANTHONY PELLICANO, Dir. of Employee Rels.
STEPHEN E. PHELPS, JR., Dir. of Public Rels.
SEAN PHILLIPS, Dir. of Devel.
VINCENT RAAB, Dir. of Financial Planning
RICHARD ROSENHAGEN, Dir. of Clinical Data Mgmt.
PATRICIA A. ROZZI, R.N., Corp. Dir., Nursing Financial Systems
ARTHUR RUBIN, Dir. of Materials Mgmt.
JOHN SALANDRA, Dir. of Financial Operations
RONALD STEIMEL, Corp. Controller
Mary Immaculate Hospital Division
152-11 89th Ave.
Jamaica, NY 11432
Tel: 718-558-2000
ANN ALLEN-RYAN, Assoc. Exec. Dir.
GREGORY BRADLEY, Assoc. Exec. Dir.
RONALD WEINGARTNER, Assoc. Exec. Dir. & Controller
FRANK RAMPINO, Asst. Exec. Dir.

ROSE ANN SCISCENTE, R.N., Senior Nurse Exec.
Pastoral Care Office:
Sr. ROSEMARY CORR, O.P., Dir.
Rev. JAMES P. SWEENEY
Sr. ROSE DAMIEN KILLEEN, C.S.J.
Sr. THERESA DORAN, P.B.V.M., Chap.
Rev. PATRICK O'CONNOR, Protestant Chap.
Beds 261
St. John's Queens Hospital Division
90-02 Queens Blvd.
Elmhurst, NY 11373
Tel: 718-558-1000
EDWARD M. STEIN, Exec. Dir.
MATTHEW WISSEMANN, Assoc. Exec. Dir.
DEBORAH PARDIO-MALLON, Asst. Exec. Dir.
DAVE WALZ, Asst. Exec. Dir. & Controller
PATRICIA CLARK, Senior Nurse Exec.
Pastoral Care Office:
Bro. JOHN CHERRY, F.M.S., Dir.
Rev. SOFRONIO LOFRANCO (Philippines)
Sr. JAMES CECILIA, M.S.B.T.
Sr. STELLA SLONSKI, C.S.J., Asst. Dir.
Beds 358
St. Joseph's Hospital Division
158-40 79th Ave.
Flushing, NY 11366
Tel: 718-558-6200
ANN ALLEN-RYAN, Acting Exec. Dir.
NANCY COLE, Assoc. Exec. Dir.
ANDREA DELL ENSLEY-WILLIAMS, Asst. Exec. Dir.
THERESE RYAN, Senior Nurse Exec.
ROBERT ELLIOT, Controller
Pastoral Care Office:
Sr. ELIZABETH EHLERS, O.P., Dir.
BERNADETTE SKUSE, Chap.
Beds 200
St. Mary's Hospital of Brooklyn Affiliate
170 Buffalo Ave.
Brooklyn, NY 11213
Tel: 718-221-3000
ENID MCCOY, Exec. Dir.
CLARENCE HOWARD, Assoc. Exec. Dir.
JOAN BURNS-FLANDERS, Asst. Exec. Dir.
HENRY H. RAY, JR., Asst. Exec. Dir.
Sr. HELEN KUC, Asst. Exec. Dir.
HAZEL SIMON, R.N., Senior Nurse Exec.
PETER TURCHI, Dir. of Finance
Pastoral Care Office:
Sr. CARMELITA SHAUGHNESSY, R.S.M., Acting Dir.
Rev. JAMES REDDICK, Chap.
Beds 285
Mary Immaculate Hospital Home Health Agency
95-25 Queens Blvd.
Rego Park, NY 11374
Tel: 718-830-4500
CATHERINE BARBERA, Exec. Dir., Home Care Agency
St. Mary's Hospital of Brooklyn Home Health Agency
170 Buffalo Ave.
Brooklyn, NY 11213
Tel: 718-221-3844
CATHERINE BARBERA, Exec. Dir., Home Care Agency
St. Mary's Hospital of Brooklyn Long Term Home Health Program
170 Buffalo Ave.
Brooklyn, NY 11213
Tel: 718-221-3844
CATHERINE BARBERA, Exec. Dir., Home Care Agency
St. Anthony Health Professions & Nursing Institute
175-05 Horace Harding Expwy.
Fresh Meadows, NY 11365
Tel: 718-805-4381
SANDRA BLOOMBERG, Ph.D., Admin.
Catholic Medical Center Physician Assistant Program
175-05 Horace Harding Expwy.
Fresh Meadows, NY 11365
Tel: 718-805-7599
JOANN DEASY, M.P.H., PA-C, Dir.
Catholic Medical Center School of Nursing
175-05 Horace Harding Expwy.
Fresh Meadows, NY 11365
Tel: 718-805-5602
ELISA DALMAN-HESS, Dir.
Catholic Medical Center Program of Medical Technology
175-05 Horace Harding Expwy.
Fresh Meadows, NY 11365
Tel: 718-805-4758
ANN PAULA ZERO, Dir.
Catholic Medical Center Program of Radiography
175-05 Horace Harding Expwy.
Fresh Meadows, NY 11365
Tel: 718-805-7099
Ms. BARBARA WILSON CHAKMAKJIAN, M.S., R.T., Dir.
Catholic Medical Center Emergency Medical Services Institute
7200 Douglaston Pkwy.
Douglastown, NY 11362
Tel: 718-428-0602
MICHAEL TRETOLA, Dir.
Catholic Medical Center Pathology Assistants Program
152-11 89th Ave.
Jamaica, NY 11432
Tel: 718-558-6732
USHA RUDER, M.D., Dir.
Catholic Medical Center Catholic Hospital Administration Personnel (CHAP) Program
88-25 153rd St.
Woodhaven, NY 11432
Tel: 718-558-7102
Sr. ANNELLE FITZPATRICK, C.S.J., Ph.D., Dir.
Co-sponsored with St. John's University. Educational Forum.

Kenmore
Diocese of Buffalo

Kenmore Mercy Foundation Inc.
2950 Elmwood Ave.
Kenmore, NY 14217
Tel: 716-879-6204

Kenmore Mercy Hospital
2950 Elmwood Ave.
Kenmore, NY 14217
Tel: 716-447-6100; Fax: 716-447-6090
Sisters of Mercy
Sr. MARY JOEL SCHIMSCHEINER, R.S.M., CEO
Chaplains:
Rev. VINCENT J. FERRARO
DONNA KROPIDLOWSKI, Dir.
Bed Capacity 219
Total Staff 841
Outpatient Visits 174,784
Admissions 7,392

Kingston
Archdiocese of New York

Benedictine Hospital
105 Mary's Ave.
Kingston, NY 12401
Tel: 914-338-2500
Sr. LOUISE GARLEY O.S.B., Pres.
Revs.:
MARTIN SVITAN
LIONEL TRUDEL, M.M.
Sisters of St. Benedict (Federation of St. Scholastica) 7
Capacity 222
Patients assisted annually 59,065

Lackawanna
Diocese of Buffalo

Our Lady of Victory Hospital
55 Melroy at Ridge Rd.
Lackawanna, NY 14218
Tel: 716-825-8000; Fax: 716-825-4681
Mr. ALBERT L. CONDINO, Pres. & CEO
Revs.:
FRANCIS N. MILLER, Dir. Emeritus
ROBERT J. MCARTNEY, Dir. Pastoral Care
RAYMOND MAHAR
Rev. Msgr. ROBERT C. WURTZ, Chm.
Sisters of St. Joseph 4
Capacity 242
Patients assisted annually 72,939
Total Staff 951
Affiliated Programs:
BOCES
Food & Nutritional Services, Nursing Asst., LPN.
Daemen College
Medical Technology, Medical Records Admin., Physical Therapy.
D'Youville College
Physical Therapy, Nutritional Services, Registered Nurses.
Edinboro University of PA
Speech-Language Pathology.
Erie Community College
Dietetic Technology, Emergency Medical Technology.
Genesee Community College
Physical Therapy.
Niagara Community College
Physical Therapy Asst.
Trocaire College
Registered Nurses, Medical Records, EKG/Cardiac Monitor Technology, Surgical Technology, Phlebotomy, Radiologic Technology.
S.U.N.Y. at Buffalo
Speech Language Technology, Dietary, Physical Therapy, Pharmacy, Social Work, Clinical Nutrition.
S.U.N.Y. at Alfred
Medical Records.

Our Lady of Victory Hospital Auxiliary
55 Melroy Ave.
Lackawanna, NY 14218
Tel: 716-825-8000
CAROLYN HETEY, Dir.

Lewiston
Diocese of Buffalo

Mount St. Mary's Hospital of Niagara Falls
5300 Military Rd.
Lewiston, NY 14092-1997
Tel: 716-297-4800
Sisters of St. Francis of the Third Order Regular
HENRY G. LOBL, Pres./CEO
Rev. PAUL C. SCHRECK, Chap.
Capacity 179
Bassinets 22
Patients assisted annually 126,080
Total Staff 798

Lockport
Diocese of Buffalo

Niagara Homemaker Services, dba Mercy Home Care of Western New York
111 Main St.
Lockport, NY 14094
Tel: 716-434-2388
Directors:
J. THOMAS BRIODY
Sr. MARY ANNUNCIATA
Sr. SALLY MALONEY

New York
Archdiocese of New York

Bayley Seton Hospital
75 Vanderbilt Ave.
Staten Island, NY 10304
Tel: 718-390-6000
Annually Assisted 59,000
JOHN DEPIERRO, Pres.
Rev. EDWARD J. DATTY, S.A., Chap.

Cabrini Medical Center (Cabrini Development Council, Inc.)
227 E. 19th St.
New York, NY 10003
Tel: 212-995-6000
Mr. JEFFREY FRERICHS, Pres.
Sr. ARLENE PRIMUS, M.S.C., Asst. to the Pres. for Mission & Chaplaincy Svcs.
Bed Capacity Acute Hospital 493
Skilled nursing facility at Dobbs Ferry 304
Home Care 150
New York City, Beds 240 (Cabrini Nursing Home)
Missionary Sisters of the Sacred Heart 11
Patients assisted annually 44,588
Cabrini Hospice Program (home care) 710
Stuyvesant Polyclinic, Inc.
Tel: 212-674-0220
Patients assisted annually 45,382

Our Lady of Mercy Medical Center
233rd St. Division
600 E. 233 St.
Bronx, NY 10466
Tel: 718-920-9000
Florence D'Urso Pavilion
1870 Pelham Pkwy. S.
Bronx, NY 10461
Tel: 718-430-6000
Acute Care General Hospital.
Mr. GARY S. HORAN, Pres. & CEO
Revs.:
FREDERICK J. BECKER, Vice Pres. Pastoral Svcs.
THOMAS D'ANGELO, Catholic Chap.
BERNARD OBEARA IHEOHA, Catholic Chap.
Capacity 612
Patients assisted annually 229,069
Total Staff 2,301
Rosalie Hall Shelter for Unwed Mothers
DIANE PRUSINSKI, S.M., Dir.
Capacity 28

St. Clare's Hospital and Health Center
415 W. 51st St.
New York, NY 10019
Tel: 212-586-1500
RICHARD N. YEZZO, Pres.
Rev. JOHN J. DONAHUE, C.S.C., Chap.
Bed Capacity 250
Patients assisted annually 15,903

St. Vincent's Hospital and Medical Center of New York
153 W. 11th St.
New York, NY 10011
Tel: 212-604-7000
KARL P. ADLER, M.D., Pres. & CEO
Sr. KAREN HELFENSTEIN, Senior Vice Pres. Mission
Chaplains:
Revs.:

Timothy Colon, O.S.C., Supvr.
Jefferson Hammer
Praxid DeSilva
Martin Raju
Sr. Eileen Lambert O.S.F.
Sr. Patricia Lawlor, S.C.
Sr. Bernadette Baer, S.C.
Sr. Alberta Jurewicz, C.S.F.N.
Bros.:
John Conway, O.F.M.
Michael Moran, C.P.
Sisters of Charity, Mt. St. Vincent on Hudson 31
Capacity 813
Patients assisted annually 195,000
School of Nursing: Students 140

Saint Vincent's Medical Center of Richmond
355 Bard Ave.
Staten Island, NY 10310
Tel: 718-876-1234
Sisters of Charity of St. Vincent de Paul of NY 2
Capacity 440 beds
Patients assisted annually 70,000
School of Nursing Students 110
School of Nursing Staff 23
Total Staff 2,500
Sr. Catherine Sherry, S.C., Treas.
Sr. Therese Monaghan, O.P., Ed.D., Dir. Pastoral Care
Chaplains:
Revs.:
Ralphy Dawis
Dorothy Caldwell, M.Div., C.P.E.
Sr. Mary Alice Duggan, O.S.U.
Rabbi Morris Zacharish
Rabbi Gerald Sussman
Revs.:
Joanna White, M.Div., C.P.E.
Joseph Nietlong
Priests from Our Lady of Mt. Carmel.

Old Brookville
Diocese of Rockville Centre

The St. Francis-Mercy Corporation
Northern Blvd.
Old Brookville, NY 11545-1111
Tel: 516-562-6904

Port Jefferson
Diocese of Rockville Centre

The St. Charles Corporation
200 Belle Terre Rd.
Port Jefferson, NY 11777
Tel: 516-474-6000
Barry T. Zeman, Pres. & CEO
Revs.:
Juniper Jones Thomas
Augustine L. Fahnbulleh
Chaplains:
Sr. Mona Guerrette, D.W.
Sr. Martha Winum, D.W.
Sr. Rodriguez O.P.
Beds 269
Bassinets 41
Total Annually Assisted 145,065
Total Staff 1,015

St. Charles Hospital, Port Jefferson, New York
Port Jefferson, NY 11777
Tel: 516-474-6000
Barry Zeman, Pres. & CEO
Revs.:
Juniper Jones Thomas
James Miller
Chaplains:
Sr. Martha Winum, D.W.
Sr. Mona Guerrette, D.W.
Patients assisted annually 93,800
Beds 271
Bassinets 41
Staff 980

Port Jervis
Archdiocese of New York

Mercy Community Hospital
160 E. Main St.
Port Jervis, NY 12771
Tel: 914-856-5351; Fax: 914-856-5659
R. Andrew Brothers, CEO, Acute Care
Capacity 141
Sisters of Mercy 4
SNF Beds 46
Annually assisted 4,014

Poughkeepsie
Archdiocese of New York

St. Francis Hospital
North Rd.
Poughkeepsie, NY 12601
Tel: 914-471-2000
Sisters of St. Francis of Hastings-on-Hudson
Donald F. Murphy, Exec. Vice Pres.
Sr. M. Ann Elizabeth, O.S.F., Pres.
Rev. Thomas A. McDonald, Dir. Pastoral Care
Capacity 295
St. Francis Health Care Foundation
North Rd.
Poughkeepsie, NY 12601
Sr. M. Ann Elizabeth, Pres.
Saint Francis Hospital, Beacon
Delavan Ave.
Beacon, NY 12538
Tel: 914-831-3500
Lawrence M. Witte, Exec. Dir.
Capacity 116 beds
Total Annually Assisted 150,000
Total Staff 1,300

Rochester
Diocese of Rochester

St. Mary's Hospital
89 Genesee St.
Rochester, NY 14611
Tel: 716-464-3000
Stewart C. Putnam, Pres.
Sr. Maura Hobart, D.C., Supr.
Rev. Frederick Helfrich, Chap.
Daughters of Charity of St. Vincent de Paul 7
Total Staff 1,453
Bed Capacity 230
Patients assisted annually 116,000

Rockville Centre
Diocese of Rockville Centre

Mercy Medical Center
1000 N. Village Ave.
Rockville Centre, NY 11570
Tel: 516-255-0111
Under the sponsorship of The Congregation of the Infant Jesus (Nursing Sisters of the Sick Poor).
George P. Dunn, Chm.
Vincent Di Rubbio, Pres. & CEO
Chaplains:
Revs.:
Denis Sheridan
Asir Antony
Legal Title: *Mercy Medical Center*

Mercy Medical Center
1000 N. Village Ave.
Rockville Centre, NY 11570
Tel: 516-255-2331
Legal Title: *Mercy Medical Center-Mental Health Services Inpatient and Outpatient Psychiatric-Alcohol Inpatient and Outpatient Services*
Patrick F. Carone, M.D., Dir. Psychiatry
Christine Lefkowitz, M.P.S., R.N., Vice Pres. & Dir. Mental Health and Substance Abuse Services

Roslyn
Diocese of Rockville Centre

St. Francis Hospital
100 Port Washington Blvd.
Roslyn, NY 11576
Tel: 516-562-6000
Under the supervision of the Franciscan Missionaries of Mary.
Patrick J. Scollard, Pres. & CEO
Sr. Lois Van Delft, F.M.M., Asst. to the CEO Pastoral Care
Annual Admissions 12,695
Bed Capacity 247
Staff 1,952

Schenectady
Diocese of Albany

St. Clare's Holding Company, Inc.
600 McClellan St.
Schenectady, NY 12304

St. Clare's Hospital
600 McClellan St.
Schenectady, NY 12304
Tel: 518-382-2000
Jerome G. Stewart, Pres. & CEO
Rev. Richard J. Leskovar, Chap., Dir. Pastoral Care
Sr. Susan DiDomenicantonio, I.C.M.
Sr. Donna Marie Irvine, S.S.N.D.
Sr. Miriam Natale, O.S.F.
Bed Capacity 200
Patients assisted annually 159,153

Suffern
Archdiocese of New York

Good Samaritan Hospital of Suffern
Suffern, NY 10901
Tel: 914-368-5000
Joan Regan, Pres.
Sr. Sheila M. Mullins, O.P., Dir. Pastoral Care
Chaplains:
Revs.:
George Mattioni, O.A.R.
Francis Cregan, O.A.R.
Bro. Gerardo J. De Fillippo, O.A.R.
Sr. Anne Veronica Tonne, S.C.
Sisters of Charity of St. Elizabeth 3
Capacity 370
Patients assisted annually 150,000
Total Staff 1,400

Syracuse
Diocese of Syracuse

St. Joseph's Hospital Health Center
301 Prospect Ave.
Syracuse, NY 13203
Tel: 315-448-5111; Fax: 315-448-6161
Mr. Theodore M. Pasinski, Pres. & CEO
Chaplains:
Revs.:
Firmin Finn, O.F.M.Conv.
Robert Amrhein, O.F.M.Conv.
Sisters of the Third Franciscan Order 25
Bed Capacity 431
Patients assisted annually 240,000
School for Nurses
Students 203

Troy
Diocese of Albany

Seton Health System, Inc.
1300 Massachusetts Ave.
Troy, NY 12180
Tel: 518-272-5000
Daughters of Charity of St. Vincent de Paul
Dr. Edward Murphy, Pres. & CEO
Sr. Ellen Boyle, Dir. of Pastoral Care
Rev. Timothy Harrison, Chap.
Sr. Mary Agnes O'Neil, Chm. Bd. of Dir.
Sisters 11
Bed Capacity 201
Patients assisted annually 315,000
Legal Title: *Seton Health System, Inc.*

Utica
Diocese of Syracuse

St. Elizabeth Hospital
2209 Genesee St.
Utica, NY 13501
Tel: 315-798-8100
Sr. Rose Vincent Gleason, CEO
Sr. M. Johanna Delelys, COO
Rev. Matthew Thelly
Sisters of the Third Franciscan Order 17
Beds 201
Patients assisted annually 229,171
College of Nursing
Students 115

Warwick
Archdiocese of New York

St. Anthony Community Hospital, Inc.
Franciscan System of Warwick, Inc.
15-19 Maple Ave.
Warwick, NY 10990
Tel: 914-986-2276
F. Dennis Harrington, Pres.
Leena Rinaldi, R.N., Vice Pres. Mission
Rev. Edward Sullivan, O.F.M., Chap.
Capacity 73
Patients assisted annually 34,262

West Islip
Diocese of Rockville Centre

The Samaritan Corporation
1000 Montauk Hwy.
West Islip, NY 11795
Tel: 516-376-4001
Daniel P. Walsh, Pres.
Revs.:
Bernard M. Blood, S.M.M.
Lawrence Bellew, C.P.
Vincent P. Cunningham, S.M.M.
Paul Dahm, Assoc. Dir.
NOTE: The Samaritan Corporation is the parent corporation of Good Samaritan Hospital Medical Center. Refer to Good Samaritan Hospital Medical

Center for statistics.
Good Samaritan Hospital Medical Center
1000 Montauk Hwy.
West Islip, NY 11795
Tel: 516-376-4001
DANIEL P. WALSH, Pres.
Revs.:
LAWRENCE BELLEW, C.P., Dir.
VINCENT P. CUNNINGHAM, S.M.M.
BERNARD M. BLOOD, S.M.M.
PAUL DAHM, Assoc. Dir.
Annually Assisted 110,640
Staff 2,400
Good Samaritan Nursing Home
Patients Cared For 160
Good Samaritan Chronic Dialysis Center
Treatments 34,064
Good Samaritan Certified Home Health Agency
Visits 96,547
Good Samaritan Long Term Home Health Care Program
Visits 21,892
Martin Luther King Jr. Health Center
Visits 36,214

White Plains
Archdiocese of New York

St. Agnes Hospital and Children's Rehabilitation Center
305 North St.
White Plains, NY 10605
Tel: 914-681-4500; Fax: 914-681-4974
GARY HORAN, Pres. & CEO
Sr. MARY VIRGINIA R.D.C., Dir. Pastoral Care
Capacity 184
Childrens Rehabilitation Center for multi-handicapped children 690
Patients assisted annually 64,789

Yonkers
Archdiocese of New York

St. Joseph's Medical Center
127 S. Broadway
Yonkers, NY 10701
Tel: 914-378-7000; Fax: 914-965-4838
Sr. MARY LINEHAN Pres.
Rev. THOMAS MURPHY, O.F.M.Cap.
Sr. CAROLINE PARKER, Dir. of Pastoral Care
Beds 194
Nursing Home Beds 200
Sisters of Charity of St. Vincent de Paul 9
Patients assisted annually 9,000

NORTH CAROLINA

Asheville
Diocese of Charlotte

St. Joseph's Health Services Corporation
345 Biltmore Ave.
Asheville, NC 28801
Sr. M. VERONICA SCHUMACHER, R.S.M., Chm. & CEO
G. JOHN COLI, Ph.D., Pres. & COO
Sr. M. ANITA SHEERIN, Sec. & Treas.

St. Joseph's Hospital
428 Biltmore Ave.
Asheville, NC 28801
Tel: 704-255-3100
Sr. MARY VERONICA SCHUMACHER, R.S.M., Chm.
G. JOHN COLI, Ph.D., Vice Chm.
Mr. J. LEWIS DANIELS, Pres. & CEO
Sr. MARY ANITA SHEERIN, Sec. & Treas.
Sisters 7
Beds 331
Patients assisted annually 82,452

St. Joseph's Urgent Care, Inc.
345 Biltmore Ave.
Asheville, NC 28801
Tel: 704-258-6569
Patients assisted annually 138,235

Charlotte
Diocese of Charlotte

Selwyn Life Center at Mercy
1921 Vail Ave.
Charlotte, NC 28207
Tel: 704-379-5005
RUTH HUEY, R.N., M.S.N., Dir.
Adult Health Facility.

Southern Pines
Diocese of Raleigh

St. Joseph of the Pines Hospital
590 Central Dr.
Southern Pines, NC 28387
Tel: 910-692-2212
Legal Title: *St. Joseph of the Pines, Inc.*
Mr. GEORGE KECATOS, Pres.

NORTH DAKOTA

Bismarck
Diocese of Bismarck

St. Alexius Medical Center
P.O. Box 5510
Bismarck, ND 58502
Tel: 701-224-7000; Fax: 701-224-7284
Sisters of St. Benedict
RICHARD A. TSCHIDER, Admin. & CEO
TOM HELMICK, Dir. Pastoral Care
Priests 1
Sisters 14
Bed Capacity 287
Total Staff 1,416
Patients assisted annually 147,767

Bottineau
Diocese of Fargo

St. Andrew's Health Center
316 Ohmer St.
Bottineau, ND 58318
Tel: 701-228-2255
Sr. CORINNE S.M.P., Supr.
KEITH KORMAN, Pres.
Sisters of Mary of the Presentation 3
Beds 67
Staff 80
Bassinets 4
Patients assisted annually 5,000

Carrington
Diocese of Fargo

Carrington Health Center
800 N. Fourth St.
Carrington, ND 58421
Tel: 701-652-3141
MICHAEL BAUMGARTNER, CEO
Sister of the Presentation of the Blessed Virgin Mary 3
Acute Beds 30
LTC Beds 40
Staff 143
Patients assisted annually 654

Devils Lake
Diocese of Fargo

Mercy Hospital
1031 Seventh St.
Devils Lake, ND 58301
Tel: 701-662-2131; Fax: 701-662-4862
MARLENE KREIN, Pres.
In res.,
Rev. DENNIS SCHUE
Sisters of Mercy of the Americas 2
Staff 223
Beds 50
Bassinets 7
Patients assisted annually 15,649

Dickinson
Diocese of Bismarck

St. Joseph's Hospital and Health Center
30 W. Seventh St.
Dickinson, ND 58601
Tel: 701-225-7271
JOHN S. STUDSRUD, M.H.A., Pres. & CEO
Nurses 190
Total Staff 365
Beds 109
Patients assisted annually 40,236

Garrison
Diocese of Bismarck

Garrison Memorial Hospital
P.O. Box 39
Garrison, ND 58540
Tel: 701-463-2275
RICHARD SPILOVOY, Admin.
Sisters of St. Benedict (Bismarck) 4
Nurses 45
Total Staff 110
Bed Capacity 56
Patients assisted annually 1,353

Harvey
Diocese of Fargo

St. Aloisius Medical Center
325 E. Brewster St.
Harvey, ND 58341
Tel: 701-324-4651
Sisters of Mary of the Presentation.
RONALD J. VOLK, Admin./Pres.
RALPH J. LLEWELLYN, CFO
Staff 265
Beds 49
Nursing Home 116
Patients assisted annually 5,370

Kenmare
Diocese of Bismarck

**Kenmare Community Hospital*
P.O. Box 697
Kenmare, ND 58746
Tel: 701-385-4296
Sisters of St. Francis of Penance and Christian Charity (Denver)
VERLIN BUECHLER, Pres. & CEO
Nurses 38
Total Staff 75
Bed Capacity 42
Patients assisted annually 13,870

Minot
Diocese of Bismarck

St. Joseph's Hospital dba UniMed Medical Center
Attn: Administration, P.O. Box 5001
Minot, ND 58702
Tel: 701-857-2000; Fax: 701-839-8947
Rev. PAUL D. BECKER, Res. Chap.
GARY A. KENNER, Pres. & CEO
Priests 1
Sisters of St. Francis of Penance and Christian Charity 3
Nurses 160
Bed Capacity 186
Patients assisted annually 54,000

UniMed Medical Center Foundation
3rd St. S.E. & Burdick Expwy.
Minot, ND 58701
Tel: 701-857-2070
BRUCE CHRISTENSON, Dir. Devel.
Total Staff 1

Oakes
Diocese of Fargo

Oakes Community Hospital
314 S. Eighth St.
Oakes, ND 58474
Tel: 701-742-3291
Sr. M. DIANNA HELL, O.S.F., Supr.
Sr. MARY JANE REIBER, O.S.F., Admin.
Sr. SUSAN MARIE LOEFFEN, O.S.F., Admin.
Sisters of St. Francis of the Immaculate Heart of Mary (Hankinson, ND) 5
Beds 30
Bassinets 4
Patients assisted annually 6,877

Park River
Diocese of Fargo

St. Ansgar's Health Center
115 Vivian St.
Park River, ND 58270
Tel: 701-284-7500
Mr. MICHAEL MAHRER, CEO
Staff 82
Beds 30
Patients assisted annually 5,995

Rolla
Diocese of Fargo

Presentation Medical Center
213 N.E. Third St.
Rolla, ND 58367
Tel: 701-477-3161
KIMBER L. WRAALSTAD, Pres. & CEO
Sisters of Mary of the Presentation 3
Beds 54
Patients assisted annually 6,000

Valley City
Diocese of Fargo

Mercy Hospital
570 Chautauqua Blvd.
Valley City, ND 58072
Tel: 701-845-0440
Mr. GREG HANSON, Pres.
Sisters of Mercy of the Americas 2
Beds 74
Bassinets 15
Patients Assisted 15,253

Staff 185

Williston
Diocese of Bismarck

Mercy Hospital
1301 15th Ave. W.
Williston, ND 58801
Tel: 701-774-7400; Fax: 701-774-7409
Sisters of Mercy
DUANE JERDE, CEO
Sr. JEANINE SALAK, R.S.M., Dir. Pastoral Care
Sisters 2
Bed Capacity 134
Total Staff 426
Patients assisted annually 25,378

Mercy Medical Center
1301 15th Ave., W.
Williston, ND 58801
Tel: 701-774-7401
DUANE JERDE, Pres.

Mercy Medical Foundation
1301 15th Ave., W.
Williston, ND 58801
Tel: 701-774-7404
KELLY S. BUECHLER, Dir.

Mercy Recovery Center
1301 15th Ave. W.
Williston, ND 58801
Tel: 701-774-7409; Fax: 701-774-7479
Mr. DONALD WAHUS, Dir.
Bed Capacity 14

OHIO

Batavia
Archdiocese of Cincinnati

Clermont Mercy Hospital
3000 Hospital Dr.
Batavia, OH 45103
Tel: 513-732-8200
Sisters of Mercy
KAREN S. EHRAT, Ph.D., Pres.
Sr. KATHY GREEN, R.S.M., Vice Pres., Mission Svcs.
Bed Capacity 157
Patients assisted annually 57,238

Cincinnati
Archdiocese of Cincinnati

Franciscan Hospital, Mt. Airy Campus
A member of the Franciscan Health System of Cincinnati, Inc.
2446 Kipling Ave.
Cincinnati, OH 45239
Tel: 513-853-5000
R. CHRISTOPHER WEST, Pres. & CEO
Sr. ARLENE MCGOWAN, Vice Pres. Mission & Support Svcs.
JOHNNY RILEY, Dir., Pastoral Care
Chaplains:
Revs.:
MICHAEL PARANIUK
DOMINIC WACHTEL, O.F.M.
Sr. MARGARET SCHLSTEDT, M.M.
Sr. DONNA DE MANGE, O.S.F.
Sr. YVONNE FACKLER, S.F.P.
Sisters 3
Beds 299
Patients assisted annually 85,000

Franciscan Hospital, Western Hills Campus
A member of the Franciscan Health System of Cincinnati, Inc.
3131 Queen City Ave.
Cincinnati, OH 45238
Tel: 513-389-5000
R. CHRISTOPHER WEST, Pres. & CEO
Sr. ARLENE MCGOWAN, Vice Pres. of Mission & Support Svcs.
JOHN RILEY, Dir. Pastoral Care
Chaplains:
Sr. JOANNE BURKHART, S.F.P.
Sr. ADRIENNE COLSON, O.P.
Sr. LAURENE HAGMAN, O.P.
Mrs. JOAN OWENS
Ms. ALBERTA UTRUP
Revs.:
PAUL WALSMAN, O.F.M.
MICHAEL PARANIUK
Sisters 8
Beds 281
Patients assisted annually 90,000

Good Samaritan Hospital
375 Dixmyth Ave.
Cincinnati, OH 45220
Tel: 513-872-1400; Fax: 513-872-3435
Sisters of Charity of Cincinnati, OH
Sr. MYRA JAMES BRADLEY, S.C., CEO
Revs.:
GERALD R. NIKLAS
EUGENE J. NEVINS, S.J.
Bed Capacity 673
Bassinets 62
Long-term Care 15
Patients assisted annually 200,000
Registered Training School for Nurses
Students 235

Mercy Hospital Anderson
7500 State Rd.
Cincinnati, OH 45255
Tel: 513-624-4500
Sisters of Mercy
KAREN S. EHRAT, Ph.D., Pres.
Sr. KATHY GREEN, R.S.M., Vice Pres., Mission Svcs.
Rev. DAVID J. KELLEY, Chap.
Bed Capacity 186
Patients assisted annually 10,280

Cleveland
Diocese of Cleveland

Marymount Hospital, Inc.
12300 McCracken Rd.
Cleveland, OH 44125
Tel: 216-581-0500
Mr. THOMAS J. TRUDELL, Pres.
JUDITH SHEMKOVITZ, Dir. Pastoral Care
Revs.:
JOSEPH O'DONNELL, Chap. & Coord. Sacramental Svcs. & Priest Chaplains
THADDEUS C. MICHALSKI, Senior Chap. Emeritus
Pastoral Assocs.:
Sr. ANNE MASLANKA, S.S.J.-T.O.S.F.
Sr. BERNICE THERESE, S.S.J.-T.O.S.F.
Sisters of St. Joseph of Third Order of St. Francis 7
Bed Capacity (med/surg) 259 (skilled nursing) 20
Bassinets 18
Patients assisted annually 134,514
Total Staff 1,331

St. John Hospital
2351 E. 22nd St.
Cleveland, OH 44115
Tel: 216-696-5560
Sr. MARY PATRICIA BARRETT, C.S.A., Chm. Bd. of Trustees

Columbus
Diocese of Columbus

Holy Cross Care Services, Inc. dba Northland Terrace Medical Center
5700 Karl Rd.
Columbus, OH 43229
Tel: 614-846-5420; Fax: 614-438-5873

Mohun Health Care Center
2320 Airport Dr.
Columbus, OH 43219
Tel: 614-253-8517
Sr. JACQUELINE BAUM, O.P., Admin.

Mount Carmel Health System
793 W. State St.
Columbus, OH 43222
Tel: 614-234-5423; Fax: 614-234-5985
DALE ST. ARNOLD, Pres. & CEO
Beds 945
Staff 6,000
Patients assisted annually 750,000
Legal Holdings:
Mount Carmel Health
Mount Carmel Medical Center - Medical Center
Mount Carmel East Hospital - General Hospital
Mount Carmel Health Community Services Corporation
Hospice, Home Care and Transportation.
Mount Carmel College of Nursing
Mount Carmel Auxiliary
St. Ann's Hospital
St. Ann's Hospital - General Hospital
St. Ann's Auxiliary
St. Ann's Home Health
Niagara Health Corporation
Mount Carmel Health System Foundation

Dayton
Archdiocese of Cincinnati

Good Samaritan Hospital
2222 Philadelphia Dr.
Dayton, OH 45406
Tel: 937-278-2612
Mr. DOUGLAS DECK, Pres.
Bed Capacity 560
Patients assisted annually 160,000

St. Elizabeth Medical Center, Inc.
601 Edwin C. Moses Blvd.
Dayton, OH 45408
Tel: 513-229-6000
A facility of the Franciscan Health System of Dayton.
Sponsored by Franciscan Sisters of the Poor
Mr. JAMES M. STRIEBY, Pres. & CEO
Chaplains:
Revs.:
ALLEN WEIMER, D.Min., Dir.
GARY M. SCHERER, C.PP.S.
THOMAS BEISCHEL, C.PP.S.
CRAIG SCHNEIDER, M.Div.
EDNA LEWIS, M.Div.
JO ANN THIELE
MYRA WENTWORTH
Sisters 1
Bed Capacity 622
Bassinets 30
Patients assisted annually 314,285

Fairfield
Archdiocese of Cincinnati

Mercy Health Plaza
2990 Mack Rd.
Fairfield, OH 45014
Tel: 513-874-6440
BROOKS SUTTON, Vice Pres., Clinical/Service Integration
Ambulatory Surgery Center.

Hamilton
Archdiocese of Cincinnati

Mercy Hospital of Hamilton-Fairfield
100 Riverfront Plaza, P.O. Box 418
Hamilton, OH 45011
Tel: 513-867-6400; Fax: 513-867-9043
3000 Mack Rd.
Fairfield, OH 45014
Tel: 513-870-7000; Fax: 513-870-7065
Sisters of Mercy of Hamilton, OH
Mr. THOMAS S. URBAN, Pres. & CEO
Sr. MONICA MARIE KNIPFER, Vice Pres. Missions
Sisters 9
Bed Capacity 326
Patients assisted annually 121,510

Lima
Diocese of Toledo

St. Rita's Medical Center
730 W. Market St.
Lima, OH 45801
Tel: 419-227-3361
Mr. JAMES P. REBER, Pres.
Mr. KENNETH G. PAYNE, Vice Pres. Finance
Mr. MARK SKAJA, Vice Pres. Mission Svcs.
Chaplains:
Revs.:
JOHN STITES
BEN LOWELL
GRETA WAGNER
Sr. NATALIE HAAS, R.S.M.
Sr. NOEL FREY, R.S.M.
Deacon WALT MILLER
Sisters 3
Bed Capacity 424
Patients assisted annually 223,400
Total Staff 2,042

Oregon
Diocese of Toledo

St. Charles Hospital
2600 Navarre Ave.
Oregon, OH 43616
Tel: 419-698-7200; Fax: 419-698-7328
Sisters of Mercy of the Americas
CATHLEEN K. NELSON, Pres. & CEO
Chaplains:
Revs.:
GEORGE M. KOERBER
CHARLES DENNY
DON CORBIN, Pastoral Care Dir.
Sisters 3
Bed Capacity 316
Patients assisted annually 114,549
Total Staff 1,359

Sandusky
Diocese of Toledo

Providence Hospital Inc.
1912 Hayes Ave.

Sandusky, OH 44870
Tel: 419-621-7000
Sisters of St. Francis of Sylvania, Ohio
Sr. NANCY LINENKUGEL, O.S.F., Pres. & CEO
Rev. JOHN R. LAUDICK, Chap.
Providence Hospital School of Nursing
Student Nurses 93
Providence Hospital School of Radiology
Student Radiology Techs. 11
Sisters 9
Bed Capacity 261
Patients assisted annually 35,492
Total Staff 599

Springfield
Archdiocese of Cincinnati

Mercy Medical Center
1343 N. Fountain Blvd.
Springfield, OH 45501-1380
Tel: 937-390-5000; Fax: 937-328-8003
Sisters of Mercy
Mr. JERROLD MAKI, Pres. & CEO
Sr. MACRINA DORRIAN, R.S.M., Mission Services
Rev. MARVIN R. HACKMAN, Chap.
Sisters 6
Bed Capacity 329
Patients assisted annually 128,357

Steubenville
Diocese of Steubenville

Trinity Health System
Trinity Medical Center, West
4000 Johnson Rd.
Steubenville, OH 43952
Tel: 614-264-8000; Fax: 614-264-8620
Chaplains:
Sr. LADONNA PINKELMAN, O.S.F.
Rev. JOHN MCCOY
Trinity Medical Center, East
380 Summit Ave.
Steubenville, OH 43952
Tel: 614-283-7000
Chaplains:
Sr. MARIA CONSUELO
Rev. JOHN MCCOY
Beds 624
Patients assisted annually:
Admissions: 12,458
Outpatients: 170,982
Emergency Room: 52,900
Births: 734
Sisters 6
Nursing Sisters 4
RNs 263
LPNs 26
Nurse Anesthetists 9

Tiffin
Diocese of Toledo

Mercy Hospital
Sr. Janet Hay
Tiffin, OH 44883
Tel: 419-447-3130
Sisters of Mercy of the Americas
Sisters 2
Bed Capacity 70
Patients assisted annually 54,848
Total Staff 431

Toledo
Diocese of Toledo

Mercy Hospital
2200 Jefferson Ave.
Toledo, OH 43624-9988
Tel: 419-259-1500
Sisters of Mercy of the Americas
CATHLEEN K. NELSON, Pres.
Rev. VINCENT HOYING
Sisters 8
Mercy College of Northwest Ohio
Student Nurses 174
Bed Capacity 311
Patients assisted annually 78,000
Total Staff 960

St. Vincent Medical Center
2213 Cherry St.
Toledo, OH 43608
Tel: 419-321-3232; Fax: 419-321-3810
Sisters of Mercy
Affiliated with Mercy Health System.
Mr. STEVEN L. MICKUS, Pres. & CEO
Chaplains:
Revs.:
WILLIAM FOSTER, Dir. Pastoral Care
JOEL BUCHMAN
Sr. SHARON BELISLE
Sr. ELAINE LADD
Sisters 6
Patients assisted annually 272,242
Bed capacity 588

Urbana
Archdiocese of Cincinnati

Mercy Memorial Hospital
904 Scioto St.
Urbana, OH 43078
Tel: 937-653-5231
Sisters of Mercy
Sisters 3
Bed Capacity 73

Warren
Diocese of Youngstown

St. Joseph Health Center
667 Eastland Ave., S.E.
Warren, OH 44484
Tel: 330-841-4000; Fax: 330-841-4048
Mr. KEVIN E. NOLAN, Pres. & CEO
Rev. GEORGE POPOVICH, Chap.
Ms. BETH JACAOB, Dir. Pastoral Care
Sisters of the Humility of Mary 4
Bed capacity 239
Bassinets 20
Patients assisted annually 70,267
Total Staff 853

Willard
Diocese of Toledo

Mercy Hospital, Willard
110 E. Howard St.
Willard, OH 44890
Tel: 419-933-2931
Sisters of Mercy of the Americas
Mr. JAMES O. DETWILER, Pres.
Sisters 1
Bed Capacity 63
Total Staff 200

Youngstown
Diocese of Youngstown

HM Health Services
4964 Belmont Ave.
Youngstown, OH 44505-1046
Tel: 330-759-7484
KEVIN E. NOLAN, Pres. & CEO

HM Health Services, St. Elizabeth Health Center
1044 Belmont Ave., Box 1790
Youngstown, OH 44501
Tel: 330-746-7211
NANCY VOITUS, Dir. of Social Work
MICHAEL S. SENCHAK, Vice Pres. of Shared & Support Svcs.
Sisters of the Humility of Mary 8
Bed Capacity 550
Bassinets 60
Patients assisted annually 20,415
Referred Outpatient Visits 195,945
Total Staff 2,549
HM Home Care Staff 152

St. Elizabeth Health Resources, Inc.
1044 Belmont Ave., Box 1790
Youngstown, OH 44501
Patients assisted annually 3,051
Total Staff 154

Zanesville
Diocese of Columbus

Good Samaritan Medical Center and Rehabilitation Center
800 Forest Ave.
Zanesville, OH 43701
Tel: 614-454-5000
Mr. THOMAS A. BARONE, Pres.
Franciscan Sisters of Christian Charity 7
Bed Capacity 368
Patients assisted annually 156,461

OKLAHOMA

Enid
Archdiocese of Oklahoma City

St. Mary Mercy Hospital
305 S. 5th St., Box 232
Enid, OK 73701
Tel: 405-233-6100
FRANK LOPEZ, Pres.
Rev. HENRY ROBERSON, Chap.
Sisters 8
Beds 277
Patients assisted annually 96,975

Oklahoma City
Archdiocese of Oklahoma City

Hillcrest Health Center, Inc.
2129 S.W. 59th St.
Oklahoma City, OK 73119
Tel: 405-685-6671; Fax: 405-680-2817
Mr. RAY BRAZIER, Pres.
A member of the SSM Health Care System.
Beds 193
Patients assisted annually 53,350

Mercy Health Center
4300 W. Memorial Rd.
Oklahoma City, OK 73120
Tel: 405-755-1515
Owned and operated by Sisters of Mercy Health System, St. Louis.
BRUCE F. BUCHANAN, Pres. & CEO
Revs.:
CLETUS BASH
GARY KAYLER
JOHN TUOHEY
Sisters 4
Beds 396
Patients assisted annually 125,825
Chaplains 8

St. Anthony Hospital
1000 N. Lee St., P.O. Box 205
Oklahoma City, OK 73101
Tel: 405-272-7000; Fax: 405-272-7075
Franciscan Sisters of Mary (St. Louis, MO)
Mr. STEVEN HUNTER, Pres.
Rev. JOSEPH S. VAS, Chap.
A member of the SSM Health Care System.
Sisters 6
Beds 664
Patients assisted annually 195,967
Bone and Joint Hospital
1111 N. Dewey Ave.
Oklahoma City, OK 73103
Patients assisted annually 5,680
A member of the SSM Health Care System.

Ponca City
Archdiocese of Oklahoma City

St. Joseph Regional Medical Center
14th and Hartford
Ponca City, OK 74602
Tel: 405-765-3321; Fax: 405-765-0379
Sisters of St. Joseph of Wichita/Sisters of the Sorrowful Mother of Broken Arrow, OK
GARRY L. ENGLAND, Pres.
Sr. CLARITA WANER, C.S.J., Dir. Pastoral Care
Sr. MARY KAY LISTON, C.S.J., Asst. Admin. Mission Devel.
Sisters 3
Beds 169
Patients assisted annually 50,000

Tulsa
Diocese of Tulsa

Saint Francis Hospital, Inc.
6161 S. Yale Ave.
Tulsa, OK 74136
Tel: 918-494-2200
C. T. THOMPSON, Interim Chief Exec. Officer
Revs.:
DENIS CASEY, Dir. Pastoral Care
URBAN J. KRAMER, S.J.
JOSEPH W. HOWELL
Sisters of Charity of the Incarnate Word (Houston) 5
Beds 897
Bassinets 94
Patients assisted annually 154,308

St. John Medical Center, Inc.
1923 S. Utica Ave.
Tulsa, OK 74104
Tel: 918-744-2345
Sisters of the Sorrowful Mother (Third Order of St. Francis)
Sr. MARY THERESE GOTTSCHALK, Admin.
Chaplains:
Revs.:
KENNETH HEBERLEIN, Dir. of Pastoral Care
JOHN WADE
LAWRENCE P. COURTRIGHT
Sisters 15
Beds 609
Patients assisted annually 121,560

Sisters of the Sorrowful Mother-St. John Ministry Corporation
1923 S. Utica

Tulsa, OK 74104
Fax: 918-744-2716
Sr. M. THERESE GOTTSCHALK, Pres.

Sisters of the Sorrowful Mother-US Health System, Inc.
P.O. Box 4753
Tulsa, OK 74159-0753
Sr. M. THERESE GOTTSCHALK, Pres.

OREGON

Baker City
Diocese of Baker

St. Elizabeth Health Services, Inc.
3325 Pocahontas Rd.
Baker City, OR 97814
Tel: 541-523-6461
JEFFREY DROP, Pres.
Sisters of St. Francis of Philadelphia 2
Bed Capacity 42
Nursing Home Beds 112
Patients assisted annually 26,938

Bend
Diocese of Baker

St. Charles Medical Center
2500 N.E. Neff Rd.
Bend, OR 97701
Tel: 541-382-4321; Fax: 541-388-7723
Sisters of St. Joseph
Sr. CATHERINE HELLMANN, C.S.J., Pres. Emeritus
Mr. JIM LUSSIER, Pres. & CEO
JEROID ROUSSELL, JR., D.Min., Pastoral Care Coord.
Bed Capacity 181
Patients assisted annually 106,523

Eugene
Archdiocese of Portland in Oregon

**Sacred Heart Medical Center*
1255 Hilyard St., P.O. Box 10905
Eugene, OR 97440
Tel: 503-686-7300
Div. of Peace Health.
Sisters of St. Joseph of Peace
ANDREW MCCULLOCH, Admin. & CEO
Chaplains:
ROBERT V. SCHERI, Dir. Pastoral Care
Rev. J. NOEL HICKIE (BAK)
Sr. KATHERINE MCCARRY
Sr. RITACLARE JOHNSON, O.S.F.
Sisters 2
Bed Capacity 432
Patients assisted annually 286,846

Florence
Archdiocese of Portland in Oregon

Peace Harbor Hospital
400 Ninth St.
Florence, OR 97439
Tel: 503-997-8412
Acute care hospital owned and operated by Peace Health, Bellevue, WA.
JAMES BARNHART, Admin.
Sr. NOREEN TERRAULT, C.S.J.P., Pastoral Care
Bed Capacity 21
Patients assisted annually 64,232

Medford
Archdiocese of Portland in Oregon

Providence Medford Medical Center
1111 Crater Lake Ave.
Medford, OR 97504
Tel: 541-732-6611
Legal Title: *Sisters of Providence in Oregon.*
Mr. CHARLES T. WRIGHT, Chief Executive, Southern Oregon Service Area
Rev. JOSEPH SHIREY, S.J., (Part-time)
Sr. THERESE KOHLES, S.P., Sr. Representative to Foundation Board
Sr. PATRICIA MARIE LANDIN, S.S.M.O., Chap.
Sisters 2
Bed Capacity 184
Patients assisted annually 57,000

**Providence Community Health Foundation, Medford*

Milwaukie
Archdiocese of Portland in Oregon

**Providence Milwaukie Hospital*
10150 S.E. 32nd Ave.
Milwaukie, OR 97222
Tel: 503-652-8300
Legal Title: *Sisters of Providence in Oregon.*
CAMELIA HANEMANN, Dir. Pastoral Care
Bed Capacity 56
Patients assisted annually 70,000

**Providence Milwaukie Foundation, Milwaukie*

Newberg
Archdiocese of Portland in Oregon

Providence Newberg Hospital
501 Villa Rd.
Newberg, OR 97132
Tel: 503-537-1701
MARK MEINERT, CEO
Bed Capacity 35
Patients assisted annually 70,101

Ontario
Diocese of Baker

Holy Rosary Medical Center
351 S.W. Ninth St.
Ontario, OR 97914
Tel: 541-889-5331; Fax: 541-889-7642
Mr. BRUCE JENSEN, Admin.
Mr. LEONARD SHERMAN, D.V.M., Chm.
Rev. CLETUS KIRKPATRICK, Chap.
Dominican Sisters of St. Catherine of Siena (Kenosha, WI) 4
Bed Capacity 92
Patients assisted annually 70,655

Pendleton
Diocese of Baker

St. Anthony Hospital
1601 S.E. Court Ave.
Pendleton, OR 97801
Tel: 541-276-5121
JEFFREY DROP, Pres.
Sisters of St. Francis of Philadelphia 6
Bed Capacity 49
Patients assisted annually 26,150

Portland
Archdiocese of Portland in Oregon

Providence Portland Medical Center
4805 N.E. Glisan St.
Portland, OR 97213
Tel: 503-215-1111
Legal Title: *Providence Health Systems, Oregon Region*
Revs.:
NORBERT NOVAK, O.S.B.
HERBERT WHEATLEY, O.F.M.
JON BUFFINGTON (EST)
ELAINE K. FORREST, CPE Supervisor (Protestant)
CINDY MCNUTT-KAESTNER, Methodist Staff Chaplain (Protestant)
Sr. KATHLEEN KIRCHER, S.N.J.M., Dir. Pastoral Care & Contact Person
Sr. ROSALIE ORR, S.N.J.M., Geriatrics
Sr. MAUREEN NIEDERMEYER, O.S.B., Cardiology
Sr. BRIGID CAREY, P.B.V.M., Staff Chaplain
Sr. LORRAINE HOFMEISTER, S.P., Elder Place
Lay Chaplains:
MICHELE SAKURAI, Oncology
JOSEPH JOYCE, Addiction Treatment
BONITA STILLER, Hospice Home Health (Protestant)
Bed Capacity 483
Sisters 8
Patients assisted annually 241,203
Providence Medical Foundation
4805 N.E. Glisan
Portland, OR 97213
BRYCE STRANG, Exec. Dir.

Providence St. Vincent Medical Center
9205 S.W. Barnes Rd.
Portland, OR 97225
Tel: 503-297-4411; Fax: 503-291-2468
Providence Health System.
Legal Title: *Sisters of Providence Health System.*
RUSS DANIELSON, Admin. Health Care Oper., Providence Health System
DONALD S. ELSOM, Admin., Providence St. Vincent Medical Center
Sr. LUCY ST. HILAIRE, S.P., Sister Rep.
Sr. FARROEL RICHARDSON, S.N.J.M., Dir. Pastoral Svcs.
Revs.:
EDWARD P. MCTIGHE, S.J., Chap.
JOSEPH REEVES
Bro. LARRY ESCHWEILER, O.H.
Sr. MARY LOUISE OLBERDING, O.S.B.
Sr. KATHLEEN WALSH, S.N.J.M.
Sr. SCHOLASTICA LEE, S.P.
Ms. SHIELA SCHAEFFER, Catholic Chap.
Mr. TIMOTHY G. SERBAN, Catholic Chap.
Mrs. EILEEN NORRIS
Ms. JOANNE FLANAGAN
Ms. PAT FRANZ, Protestant Chap. (Presbyterian)
Patients assisted annually 480,864
Bed Capacity 451
Sisters 5
Brothers 1

**St. Vincent Medical Foundation, Portland*

Roseburg
Archdiocese of Portland in Oregon

Mercy Medical Center, Inc.
2700 Stewart Pkwy.
Roseburg, OR 97470
Tel: 541-673-0611; Fax: 541-440-4830
VICTOR J. FRESOLONE, Pres. & CEO
Rev. WALLY GWALTNEY, Chap.
SUSAN LAVIN, Vice Pres. Mission Devel.
Sisters 1
Bed Capacity 111
Patients assisted annually 176,614
Mercy Healthcare, Inc.
2700 Stewart Pkwy.
Roseburg, OR 97470
Tel: 541-673-0611
SANDRA R. PEARSON, Exec. Asst.
Mercy Foundation, Inc.
2700 Stewart Pkwy.
Roseburg, OR 97470
Tel: 541-673-0611
Parkway Medical Buildings, Inc.
2700 Stewart Pkwy.
Roseburg, OR 97470
Tel: 541-673-0611
Mercy Health Promotion, Inc.
2700 Stewart Pkwy.
Roseburg, OR 97470
Tel: 541-673-0611

Seaside
Archdiocese of Portland in Oregon

Providence Seaside Hospital
725 S. Wahanna Rd.
Seaside, OR 97138-7735
Tel: 503-717-7000; Fax: 503-717-7505
RON SWANSON, Admin.
Sr. JERI REINER, O.P., Dir. Pastoral Svcs.
Legal Title: *Sisters of Providence in Oregon.*
Bed Capacity 34
Extended Care 22
Patients assisted annually 60,000

**Providence Seaside Hospital Foundation*

PENNSYLVANIA

Allentown
Diocese of Allentown

Sacred Heart Hospital
421 Chew St.
Allentown, PA 18102-3490
Tel: 610-776-4500
JOSEPH M. CIMEROLA, Pres. & CEO
Rev. MICHAEL J. VASTI, M.S.C., Chap. & Dir. Pastoral Care
Sisters 10
Beds 287
Total Staff 1,155
Patients assisted annually 320,680

Altoona
Diocese of Altoona-Johnstown

Mercy Regional Health System
2500 Seventh Ave.
Altoona, PA 16602
Tel: 814-944-1681
Chaplains:
Sr. CONSTANCE A. BAHL, S.C.
Revs.:
LEO A. LYNCH
EDWARD L. ECKENROD
Sisters of the Holy Family of Nazareth 4
Beds 183
Patients assisted annually 95,484
Total Staff 711

Camp Hill
Diocese of Harrisburg

Holy Spirit Hospital and Community Mental Health Center
503 N. 21st St.

Camp Hill, PA 17011-2288
Tel: 717-763-2100; Fax: 717-763-2183
Sisters of Christian Charity
Sr. ROMAINE NIEMEYER, S.C.C., Pres.
Rev. FRANCIS M. LAHOUT, Chap.
Legal Title: *Sisters of Christian Charity Health Care Corporation.*
Legal Title: *Comfort Care of Holy Spirit Hospital, Inc.*
Legal Title: *Holy Spirit Ventures, Inc.*
Legal Title: *Holy Spirit Corporation.*
Legal Title: *West Shore ALS, Inc.*
Legal Title: *Holy Spirit Hospital.*
Legal Title: *Spirit Physician Services, Inc.*
Patients assisted annually 12,002
Bed Capacity 335
Bassinets 14
Sisters 32
Total Staff 1,645

Carbondale
Diocese of Scranton

Marian Community Hospital
100 Lincoln Ave.
Carbondale, PA 18407
Tel: 717-282-1000; Fax: 717-282-7177
Sr. JEAN COUGHLIN, I.H.M., Pres. & CEO
WILLIAM ROE, Vice Pres. & CFO
Rev. LEO P. CUMMINGS, Chap.
Sisters, Servants of the Immaculate Heart of Mary
Bed Capacity 112
Patients assisted annually 53,020

Marian Community Hospital Foundation
100 Lincoln Ave.
Carbondale, PA 18407
Tel: 717-281-1000

Maxis Medical Services
100 Lincoln Ave.
Carbondale, PA 18407
Tel: 717-281-1000

Cranberry Twp.
Diocese of Pittsburgh

St. Francis Nursing Center-North
One St. Francis Way
Cranberry Twp., PA 16066
Tel: 412-772-5350
JOHN L. SPIELER, Ph.D., Admin.
Rev. JOHN GALLAGHER, Chap.
Bed Capacity 150
Total Staff 125
Patients assisted annually 136

Darby
Archdiocese of Philadelphia

Mercy Catholic Medical Center
Fitzgerald Mercy Hospital, Lansdowne Ave. and Baily Rd.
Darby, PA 19023
Tel: 215-237-4000
Opened July 1, 1933. Incorporated May 1, 1969.
Sr. RITA POWELL, R.S.M., Chm. Bd.
PLATO A. MARINAKOS, Pres. of the Center
Chaplains:
Revs.:
LAWRENCE H. HANSEN
WILLIAM R. CRAIG, O.Praem.
JOSEPH LAENEN, O.Praem.
Sisters of Mercy 10
Bed Capacity 469
Patients assisted annually 96,905

Erie
Diocese of Erie

**Saint Vincent Health Center*
232 W. 25th St.
Erie, PA 16544
Tel: 814-452-5000
Sr. CATHERINE MANNING, S.S.J., Corp. Leader
Revs.:
RAYMOND GRAMATA, Chap.
DENIS A. MARTIN, Chap.
Saint Vincent Health System
Sr. CATHERINE MANNING, S.S.J., Pres. & CEO, St. Vincent Health System

Haverford
Archdiocese of Philadelphia

Mercy Haverford Hospital
2000 Old West Chester Pike
Haverford, PA 19083
Tel: 215-645-3600
Opened Haverford Hospital in 1958; Haverford Community Hospital in 1977; Mercy Haverford Hospital June 28, 1991.
FRANK C. VIDEON, SR., Chm. Bd.
JOHN BUCKLEY, SR., Vice Pres. & CEO
Attended by Local Parishes.
Sisters of Mercy
Bed Capacity 107
Patients assisted annually 27,208

Hazleton
Diocese of Scranton

Hazleton-Saint Joseph Medical Center
687 N. Church St.
Hazleton, PA 18201
Tel: 717-459-4444
Mr. BERNARD C. RUDEGEAIR, Pres.
Sr. M. FRANCESCA, O.S.F., Supr.
Rev. AUSTIN E. FLANAGAN, Chap.
Bernardine Sisters of the Third Order of St. Francis 12
Beds 137
Patients assisted annually 153,490

Huntingdon Valley
Archdiocese of Philadelphia

Holy Redeemer Foundation
521 Moredon Rd.
Huntingdon Valley, PA 19006
Tel: 215-938-0505; Fax: 215-938-8717
Subsididary of Holy Redeemer Health System, Inc.; Sponsor: Sisters of the Holy Redeemer, C.S.R.
Communications Department
c/o 1648 Huntingdon Pike
Meadowbrook, PA 19046
Foundation solicits and manages funds for future growth and development.

HRH Management Corporation
727 Welsh Rd.
Huntingdon Valley, PA 19006
Tel: 215-938-0180; Fax: 215-938-1237
Subsidiary of Holy Redeemer Health System, Inc. Sponsor: Sisters of the Holy Redeemer, C.S.R.
Communications Department
c/o 1648 Huntingdon Pike
Meadowbrook, PA 19046

Jeannette
Diocese of Greensburg

Jeannette District Memorial Hospital
Jefferson Ave.
Jeannette, PA 15644
Tel: 412-527-3551
Mr. ROBERT J. BULGER, Pres. & CEO
Revs.:
DOMINIC J. PETROY, O.S.B., Chap.
JUSTIN WITHROW, O.S.B., Assoc. Chap.
Sisters of Charity of Seton Hill 5
Bed Capacity 170

Johnstown
Diocese of Altoona-Johnstown

Good Samaritan Medical Center
1020 Franklin St.
Johnstown, PA 15905
Tel: 814-533-1000; 533-1410; Fax: 814-533-1819
Mr. TIMOTHY J. KARNES, Pres. & CEO
Revs.:
ADREW C. STANKO
BERNARD V. GRATTAN
LEONARD BLOSTIC, T.O.R.
Beds 167
Bassinets 12
Patients assisted annually 83,806
Nursery 374
Skilled Nursing Care Center Beds 73
Patients assisted annually 143

Lancaster
Diocese of Harrisburg

St. Joseph Hospital
250 College Ave., P.O. Box 3509
Lancaster, PA 17604
Tel: 717-291-8211; Fax: 717-291-8516
Sisters of St. Francis of Philadelphia
JOHN K. TOLMIE, Pres.
BARBARA R. MCLAUGHLIN, M.Div., Regional Dir. of Pastoral Care
Rev. EMMANUEL CAMILLERI, Chap.
Bed Capacity 309
Sisters 3
Total Staff 1,231
Patients assisted annually 194,430
Accredited Schools:
School of Respiratory Therapy 28
Paramedic Institute 28

Langhorne
Archdiocese of Philadelphia

St. Mary Medical Center
Langhorne-Newton Rd.
Langhorne, PA 19047
Tel: 215-750-2000
Sisters of St. Francis of Philadelphia 18
Bed Capacity 287
Total Staff 1,141
Patients assisted Annually 97,000
Opened February 21, 1973.
Sr. CLARE CARTY, O.S.F., Pres.
Rev. GEORGE WALLACE, S.M., Chap.

Meadowbrook
Archdiocese of Philadelphia

Holy Redeemer Hospital and Medical Center
1648 Huntingdon Pike
Meadowbrook, PA 19046
Tel: 215-947-3000
Subsidiary of Holy Redeemer Health System, Inc.
Sponsor: Sisters of the Holy Redeemer, C.S.R.
MARK JONES, Pres.
Rev. KULANDIASAMY AROKIASAMY, Chap.
Acute care community hospital, providing broad spectrum of services, including preventive, rehabilitative, emergency and obstetrical care plus pastoral counseling.

Muncy
Diocese of Scranton

Muncy Valley Hospital
215 E. Water St.
Muncy, PA 17756
Tel: 717-546-4242
KIRBY O. SMITH, Pres.
Sr. SHARON HARTMAN, S.C.C., Dir., Pastoral Care
Capacity 104
Patients assisted annually 48,492

Nanticoke
Diocese of Scranton

Mercy Care Corporation, Home Health Agency
128 W. Washington St.
Nanticoke, PA 18634
Tel: 717-735-9375; Fax: 717-735-9318
Staff 70
Total Visits 40,000

Mercy Special Care Hospital
128 W. Washington St.
Nanticoke, PA 18634
Tel: 717-735-5000; Fax: 717-735-9220
ROBERT D. WILLIAMS, Admin.
Bed Capacity 94
Patients assisted annually 30,000

New Castle
Diocese of Pittsburgh

St. Francis Hospital of New Castle
(Affiliate of St. Francis Health System)
1000 S. Mercer St.
New Castle, PA 16101
Tel: 412-658-3511
Sr. DONNA ZWIGART, O.S.F., CEO
Chaplains:
Rev. FRANK G. ERDELJAC
Sr. JANE FISCHER
Schools:
Nursing 65
Radiology 17
St. Francis Hospice of New Castle:
Total Staff 4
Patients assisted annually 469
Sisters of St. Francis of Millvale 11
Total Staff 622
Bed Capacity (includes 45 skilled nursing beds) 193
Patients assisted annually 71,161

Norristown
Archdiocese of Philadelphia

Sacred Heart Hospital and Rehabilitation Center
1430 DeKalb St.
Norristown, PA 19401
Tel: 215-278-8200
Opened 1936.
Missionary Sisters of the Most Sacred Heart of Jesus
Sr. M. EILEEN, M.S.C., Coord.
Mr. J. RUSSELL WALSH, Pres.
Chaplains:
Revs.:

Joseph F. Sabadish
John F. Lipp, O.S.A.
Bed Capacity 256
Student Nurses 40
Patients assisted annually 7,000

Philadelphia
Archdiocese of Philadelphia

Mercy Catholic Medical Center
Misericordia Hospital, 54th St. and Cedar Ave.
Philadelphia, PA 19143
Tel: 215-748-9000
Opened July 2, 1918. Incorporated May 1, 1969.
Sr. Christine McCanne, Chm. Bd.
Plato A. Marinakos, Pres. & CEO
Wesley Mc Gavock, Senior Vice Pres. & CEO
Chaplains:
Revs.:
Lawrence H. Hansen
William Craig
Sisters of Mercy 14
Bed Capacity 266
Patients assisted annually 37,880
Attended from Transfiguration of Our Lord Church & St. Carthage Church.

Nazareth Hospital
2601 Holme Ave.
Philadelphia, PA 19152
Tel: 215-335-6000
Daniel J. Sinnott, Pres.
Revs.:
Edward V. Avery
Michael Kerper
Bed Capacity 347
Total Staff 850
Patients assisted annually 155,000

St. Agnes Medical Center
1900 S. Broad St.
Philadelphia, PA 19145
Tel: 215-339-4100
Opened May 15, 1888.
Daniel J. Sinnott, Pres.
Rev. John P. Gutekunst, Chap.
Bed Capacity 240
Total Staff 653
Annually Assisted 24,417

Pittsburgh
Diocese of Pittsburgh

Mercy Hospital of Pittsburgh
1400 Locust St.
Pittsburgh, PA 15219
Tel: 412-232-8111
Howard A. Zaren, M.D., Exec. Vice Pres., Acute Care & Hospital Svcs.
Total Assisted 21,799
Total Staff 2,654

Mercy Providence Hospital
1004 Arch St.
Pittsburgh, PA 15212
Tel: 412-323-5600; Fax: 412-323-5685
Sr. Susanne Cherney, Dir. Pastoral Care
Rev. Bob Mellott, Chap.
Sisters 12
Bed Capacity 160
Patients assisted annually 22,721

Pittsburgh Mercy Foundation
Forbes-Stevenson Bldg., 1401 Locust St., Ste. 2, 3rd Fl.
Pittsburgh, PA 15219-5125
Mr. Douglas G. Smith, Pres.
Total Assisted 100,000
Total Staff 3,000

Pittsburgh Mercy Health System, Inc.
1400 Locust St.
Pittsburgh, PA 15219
Tel: 412-232-7510
Sr. Joanne Marie Andiorio, R.S.M., Dr.P.H., Pres. & CEO
Parent company of the following subsidiaries:
The Mercy Hospital of Pittsburgh
Pittsburgh Mercy Foundation
Mercy Life Center Corporation
St. Joseph Nursing and Health Care Center, Inc.
St. Pius X Residence, Inc.
Mercy Behavioral Health Services, Inc.
Brighton Woods, Inc.
Mercy Providence Hospital, Inc. (Formerly Divine Providence Hospital of Pittsburgh)
Total Assisted 181,199
Total Staff 3,430

St. Francis Central Hospital
(Affiliate of St. Francis Health System)
1200 Centre Ave.
Pittsburgh, PA 15219
Tel: 412-562-3301
Ms. Robin Z. Mohr, CEO
Chaplains:
Rev. Gary Patriquin
Sr. Germaine Convery
Sisters of St. Francis of Millvale 1
Bed Capacity 202
Total Staff 546
Patients assisted annually 55,835

St. Francis Medical Center
(Affiliate of St. Francis Health System)
400 45th St.
Pittsburgh, PA 15201
Tel: 412-622-4343
Sr. Florence Brandt, O.S.F., CEO
Chaplains:
Rev. Robert Craig, O.F.M.Cap.
Sr. Mary Joseph Trimbur
Revs.:
Bonaventure Stefun, O.F.M.Cap.
Pius Ng'iela
Schools:
Professional Nursing 63
Practical Nursing 18
Anesthesia 16
Respiratory Care 13
Sisters 31
Bed Capacity 720
Total Staff 2,508
Patients assisted annually 309,623

St. Francis Nursing Center-East
745 N. Highland Ave.
Pittsburgh, PA 15206
Tel: 412-362-6622
Kathleen Euwer, Acting Admin.
Chaplains:
Rev. Edward Hoffman
Sr. M. Sara Magaldi
Sisters of St. Francis of Millvale 1
Bed Capacity 150
Sisters 1
Total Staff 116
Patients assisted annually 157

**St. Francis Health System*
4401 Penn Ave.
Pittsburgh, PA 15224-1890
Tel: 412-633-4343
Sr. M. Rosita Wellinger, O.S.F., Pres. & CEO
Sr. M. Sylvia Schuler, Consultant
Parent company for the following affiliates:
St. Francis Medical Center
St. Francis Nursing Center-North
St. Francis Nursing Center-East
St. Francis Hospital of New Castle
St. Francis Central Hospital

**St. Francis Plaza, Inc.*

**St. Francis Health Foundation*

**St. Francis Financial Corporation*

**St. Francis Health Care Services*

Pottsville
Diocese of Allentown

Good Samaritan Regional Medical Center
700 E. Norwegian St.
Pottsville, PA 17901
Tel: 717-621-4000; Fax: 717-622-7950
Mr. Gino J. Pazzaglini, Pres.
Sr. Helen Edward Dodd, Dir. of Pastoral Care
Rev. James Morgan, Chap.
Daughters of Charity 12
Beds 221
Bassinets 20
Patients assisted annually 128,550
Good Samaritan Health Corporation
700 E. Norwegian St.
Pottsville, PA 17901
Tel: 717-621-4003
Good Samaritan Foundation, Inc.
700 E. Norwegian St.
Pottsville, PA 17901
Tel: 717-621-4252
Good Samaritan Regional Medical Center Auxiliary
700 E. Norwegian St.
Pottsville, PA 17901
Tel: 717-621-4000

Reading
Diocese of Allentown

Bornemann Health Corporation
c/o Saint Joseph Hospital, 12th St. & Walnut St., P.O. Box 316
Reading, PA 19603
Tel: 610-378-2300
Mr. David A. Ferrell, Pres.

Saint Joseph Medical Center
215 N. 12th St., P.O. Box 316
Reading, PA 19603
Tel: 610-378-2000
Opened Aug. 26, 1873.
David A. Ferrell, Pres. & CEO
Rev. Thomas Kuller, S.J., Chap.
Sisters of St. Francis of Philadelphia 17
Beds 289
Bassinets 16
Patients assisted annually 183,362

Scranton
Diocese of Scranton

Mercy Hospital
Mercy Health System Northern Region.
746 Jefferson Ave.
Scranton, PA 18501
Tel: 717-348-7100
John L. Nespoli, Pres. & CEO
Sr. JoMarie Kaczanowski, R.S.M., Local Coord.
Rev. John C. Ruth, Chap.
Sisters of Mercy 14
Bed Capacity 362
Bassinets 12
Total Capacity 374
Patients assisted annually 219,537

Wilkes-Barre
Diocese of Scranton

Mercy Hospital
Mercy Health System Northeast Region.
25 Church St., P.O. Box 658
Wilkes-Barre, PA 18765
Tel: 717-826-3100; Fax: 717-831-8989
John L. Nespoli, Pres. & CEO
Sr. Carol Gallagher, R.S.M., Sisters Liasion
Rev. Joseph C. Streit, Chap.
Sisters of Mercy 10
Bed Capacity 223
Bassinets 24
Patients assisted annually 79,440

Mercy Med-Care, Inc.
25 Church St., Box 658
Wilkes-Barre, PA 18765
Tel: 717-826-3100

Williamsport
Diocese of Scranton

Divine Providence Hospital of the Sisters of Christian Charity
1100 Grampian Blvd.
Williamsport, PA 17701
Tel: 717-320-7007
Kirby O. Smith, Pres.
Sr. Grace Kerekes, S.C.C., Supr.
Rev. Edward J. Williams, Chap.
Bed Capacity 213
Bassinets 20
Patients assisted annually 106,334

**Grampian Health Services, Inc.*
1201 Grampian Blvd.
Williamsport, PA 17701
Tel: 717-326-8214

Providence Foundation
1100 Grampian Blvd.
Williamsport, PA 17701
Tel: 717-321-5467
Geoffrey Harrington, Exec. Dir.

Providence Health System, Inc.
1100 Grampian Blvd.
Williamsport, PA 17701
Tel: 717-320-7007
Kirby O. Smith, Pres. DPH/MVH

Sisters of Christian Charity Healthcare Corporation
1100 Grampian Blvd.
Williamsport, PA 17701
Tel: 717-326-8181

**Susquehanna Regional Home Health & Services*
1201 Grampian Blvd.
Williamsport, PA 17701
Tel: 717-323-9891
Patients assisted annually 49,752

PUERTO RICO

Rio Piedras
Archdiocese of San Juan, Puerto Rico

Hospital del Maestro
Calle Flamboyanes #218, Hyde Park

Rio Piedras, PR 00929
Tel: 809-763-8383
Rev. Msgr. ANGEL VALDES, Chap.

San German
Diocese of Mayaguez, Puerto Rico

Hospital of the Immaculate Conception
Box 285
San German, PR 00683
Sisters of Charity
Sr. MARIA TERESA DIAZ BIRD, Supr.
Rev. Msgr. ROMUALDO M. ORTIZ, Chap.
Mr. HERSON E. MORALES, Admin.
Sisters 10
Beds 124
Patients assisted annually 112,300

San Juan
Archdiocese of San Juan, Puerto Rico

Centro Medico de P.R.
Calle 10 #1030, Pto Nuevo, 00920. Apdo. 347
San Juan, PR 00936
Tel: 809-763-7272
Revs.:
PEDRO L. ZABALLA, Chap.
MANUEL GARCIA, Chap. Hospital Municipal
Calle E., I-90; Urb. Costa de Oro
San Juan, PR 00646
Tel: 809-766-2222; 796-3418 (Res.)
Rev. FLORENTINO ZANS, Chap., Tel: 809-754-2525; 790-2014 (Res.)

Our Lady Of Providence
Dispensary and Health Center.
Mailing Address:
Box 614
San Juan, PR 00903
Tel: 809-725-5358
Sisters Oblates of the Divine Redemptor 2

VA Medical Center
One Veterans Plaza
San Juan, PR 00927-5800
Tel: 809-758-7575, Ext. 3324
Revs.:
JOSE E. COLON, Chief Chap. Serv.
HECTOR DIAZ ESTRADA, Chap.

Santurce
Archdiocese of San Juan, Puerto Rico

Hospital de Diego
Ave. de Diego #310, Pda. 22
Santurce, PR 00908
Tel: 809-724-1700
Rev. JESUS VALLEJO, Chap.

RHODE ISLAND

North Providence
Diocese of Providence

St. Joseph Health Services of Rhode Island - Our Lady of Fatima Hospital
200 High Service Ave.
North Providence, RI 02904
Tel: 401-456-3000
Mr. H. JOHN KEIMIG, Pres.
Revs.:
JOHN PETROCELLI, Dir. Pastoral Care
ARMAND V. VENTRE, Chap.
Miss ELIZABETH DECOSTA, R.N., Dir. School of Nursing
Student Nurses 100
Beds 386
Births 485
Patients assisted annually 201,000

Providence
Diocese of Providence

St. Joseph Corporate Care
Occupational Health and Safety Services
Providence, RI,
Tel: 401-456-4020
RANDALL UPDEGROVE, M.D., M.P.H., Med. Dir.

St. Joseph Health Services of Rhode Island - St. Joseph Hospital for Specialty Care
21 Peace St.
Providence, RI 02907
Tel: 401-456-3000
Mr. H. JOHN KEIMIG, Pres.
Revs.:
C. LEON KACHEL, Chap.
JAMES PATRICK KELLY, O.S.F.S., Chap.
Includes:
Southern New England Rehabilitation Center
Tel: 401-456-4500
JON A. MUKAND, M.D., Medical Dir.
A joint venture of St. Joseph Hospital and Rhode Island Hospital.
St. Joseph Center for Health & Human Services
Tel: 401-456-4321
JAMES HARDIMAN, M.D., Medical Dir.
St. Joseph Center for Psychiatric Services
Tel: 401-456-4232
RONALD GOBEIL, M.D., Medical Dir.

SOUTH CAROLINA

Charleston
Diocese of Charleston

Bon Secours-St. Francis Xavier Hospital
2095 Henry Tecklenburg Dr.
Charleston, SC 29414
Tel: 803-402-1000
Sponsored by the Sisters of Bon Secours, Marriottsville, MD.
Sr. ANNE MACK, C.B.S., Pres., Sisters of Bon Secours USA
Mr. ALLEN P. CARROLL, CEO
Sr. MARY GEMMA NEVILLE, C.B.S., Dir. Pastoral Svcs. & Clinical Pastoral Education
Rev. TIMOTHY J. WATTERS, Chap.
Sr. KATHLEEN OWEN, O.P., Assoc. Dir. Pastoral Svcs.
Sr. CHARLOTTE MCAULIFFE, O.L.M., Pastoral Visitor
Sr. HELEN WAUGH, C.P.E., Supr.
Bed Capacity 141
Staff 650
Patients assisted annually 144,881

**St. Francis Xavier Home Health Care, Inc.*

Dillon
Diocese of Charleston

Saint Eugene Community Hospital
301 E. Jackson St.
Dillon, SC 29536
Tel: 803-774-4111; Fax: 803-774-1563
Owned and operated by SSM Health Care. A member of the SSM Health Care System.
Mr. RONALD W. WEBB, FACHE, Pres.
Franciscan Sisters of Mary (St. Louis, MO) 3
Bed Capacity 92
Patients assisted annually 31,211

Greenville
Diocese of Charleston

**Franciscan Health System of South Carolina, Inc.*
One St. Francis Dr.
Greenville, SC 29601
Tel: 803-255-1000

**St. Francis Hospital, Inc.*
Mr. RICHARD NEUGENT, Pres.
Rev. PAUL C. WILDEROTTER (CHL) Dir. of Pastoral Care
Franciscan Sisters of the Poor 2
Bed Capacity 319
Patients assisted annually 126,456

SOUTH DAKOTA

Aberdeen
Diocese of Sioux Falls

St. Luke's Midland Regional Medical Center
Aberdeen, SD 57401
Tel: 605-622-5000
DALE STEIN, Pres. & CEO
Rev. CHARLES EMEZIE (Nigeria)
ELAINE VAN DOVER, Dir. Pastoral Care
Sisters of the Presentation of the B.V.M. (Aberdeen, SD) 16
Bed Capacity 225
Bassinets 20

Gettysburg
Diocese of Sioux Falls

Gettysburg Medical Center
57442
Tel: 605-765-2488
BRIAN J. MCDERMOTT, CEO
Gettysburg Day Care Center
700 E. Garfield
Gettysburg, SD 57442
Tel: 605-765-2541
Staff 4
Children 25
BETTY BROWN, Dir.
Beds 67
Residential Living Units 12

Milbank
Diocese of Sioux Falls

St. Bernard Providence Hospital
Milbank, SD 57252
Tel: 605-432-4538
Sr. GENEVIEVE KARELS, D.S.M.P., Supr.
Daughters of St. Mary of Providence 5
Bed Capacity 35

Mitchell
Diocese of Sioux Falls

Queen of Peace Hospital
525 N. Foster
Mitchell, SD 57301
Tel: 605-995-2000; Fax: 605-995-2441
Sisters of the Presentation of the B.V.M.
Sisters 3
Beds 120

Parkston
Diocese of Sioux Falls

St. Benedict Health Care Center; Borman Manor; Parkston Supervised Living
Parkston, SD 57366
Tel: 605-928-3311
GALE N. WALKER, Admin.
Benedictine Sisters (Yankton, SD) 2
Bed Capacity 102

Pierre
Diocese of Sioux Falls

St. Mary's Foundation
800 E. Dakota
Pierre, SD 57501
Tel: 605-224-3451
ELLEN J. LEE, Exec. Dir.

St. Mary's Healthcare Center of Pierre, South Dakota
800 E. Dakota
Pierre, SD 57501
Tel: 605-224-3100
JAMES D.M. RUSSELL, CEO
Benedictine Sisters 7
Beds 86
Maryhouse Residential Nursing Facility
Guests 105
Parkwood Retirement Apartments
Units 60

Sioux Falls
Diocese of Sioux Falls

McKennan Hospital
Sioux Falls, SD 57117-5045
Tel: 605-339-8000
Mr. FREDRICK W. SLUNECKA, Pres. & CEO
Mr. PAUL CONNELLY, Chm. Bd. of Trustees
Sr. NORMA NORTON, O.S.B., Dir. Pastoral Care
Rev. BASIL MADUIKE (Nigeria) Chap.
Sisters of the Presentation of the B.V.M. (Aberdeen, SD) 16
Bed Capacity 407

Tyndall
Diocese of Sioux Falls

St. Michael's Hospital
Tyndall, SD 57066
Tel: 605-589-3341
CAROL DEURMIER, CEO
Bed Capacity 25
Nursing Home Beds 9

Yankton
Diocese of Sioux Falls

Sacred Heart Health Services
501 Summit
Yankton, SD 57078
Tel: 605-668-8000
Mr. DENNIS SOKOL, Pres.
Sisters 7
Beds 144
St. James Nursing Home Beds 113

TENNESSEE

Chattanooga
Diocese of Knoxville

Memorial Hospital (1952)
(Div. of Sisters of Charity of Nazareth Health Corp., S.C.N.H.C.)

2525 DeSales Ave.
Chattanooga, TN 37404
Tel: 423-495-2525
Mr. CLARK TAYLOR, Pres. & CEO
Rev. LOUIS JUNOD, Chap.
Sisters 12
Bed Capacity 322
Patients assisted annually 101,348
Total Staff 1,640

Knoxville
Diocese of Knoxville

St. Mary's Medical Center, Inc. (1930)
900 E. Oak Hill Ave.
Knoxville, TN 37917
Tel: 423-545-8000
Conducted by Sisters of Mercy of the Americas
RICH WILLIAMS, Pres.
Rev. BERTRAND DEMERS, Chap.
Sisters 7
Bed Capacity 531
Patients assisted annually 203,726
St. Mary's Health System, Inc.
St. Mary's Foundation, Inc.

Memphis
Diocese of Memphis

St. Joseph Hospital (1889)
220 Overton Ave.
Memphis, TN 38105
Tel: 901-577-2700; Fax: 901-577-3620
Title of Incorporation: Sisters of St. Francis Health Services, Incorporated.
JOAN M. CARLSON, CEO
Sr. ELIZABETH ANN SCHILDMEYER, O.S.F., Pastoral Care Dir.
Beds 440
Patients assisted annually 47,062
School for Nurses
Students 173
Teaching Personnel 15
Graduate Nurses 53

Nashville
Diocese of Nashville

St. Thomas Hospital (1898)
4220 Harding Rd.
Nashville, TN 37205
Tel: 615-222-2111
Legal Title: *St. Thomas Hospital.*
Daughters of Charity of St. Vincent de Paul, (East Central Prov., Evansville, IN)
Revs.:
MARK GEARY, O.P.
JOHN I. REARDON, O.P.
JOHN F. TIGHE, Pres. & CEO
Sr. PRISCILLA GRIMES, D.C., Supr.
Sisters 6
Beds 571
Chaplains 6
Patients assisted annually 144,084
Saint Thomas Foundation
St. Thomas Medical Plaza East
Seton Health Corporation of Tennessee, Inc.

TEXAS

Amarillo
Diocese of Amarillo

St. Anthony's Hospice and Life Enrichment Center
600 N. Tyler, P.O. Box 950
Amarillo, TX 79176
Tel: 806-378-6777; Fax: 806-378-5031
LEZLIE ROBERSON Dir.

**St. Anthony's Hospital*
200 N.W. Seventh St., P.O. Box 950
Amarillo, TX 79176
Tel: 806-376-4411
Sisters of Charity of the Incarnate Word (C.C.V.I.)
Mr. BRAD HORST, Dir. Pastoral Care
Sr. HELEN ANN COLLIER, C.C.V.I., Coord. Mission & Ministry
Rev. Msgr. HAROLD L. WALDOW, Chap.

**The Auxiliary of St. Anthony's Hospital, Inc.*

**St. Anthony's Health Corporation*

Austin
Diocese of Austin

Seton East Community Health Center
2811 E. Second St.
Austin, TX 78702
Tel: 512-323-4930
Mr. LARRY MEJIA, Dir.
Total clients assisted annually 30,000

Seton Medical Center
1201 W. 38th St.
Austin, TX 78705
Tel: 512-323-1000
Daughters of Charity Health Services of Austin
Mr. CHARLES J. BENNETT, Pres. & CEO
Rev. JIM DENHAM, Dir. Pastoral Care
Chaplains:
Revs.:
DON OLIVER WEERAKKODY
JOSEPH GENIESSE
Daughters of Charity of St. Vincent de Paul 10
Bed Capacity 585
Patients assisted annually 30,053
Equivalent Patients 7,307

Seton Northwest Hospital
1113 Research Blvd.
Austin, TX 78759
Tel: 512-795-1000
Daughters of Charity Health Services of Austin
CAROL A. HOKE, Senior Vice Pres. Admin.
JIM DENHAM, Dir. Pastoral Care
Bed Capacity 82
Patients assisted annually 46,411
Staff 305

Seton South Community Health Center
3706 S. First St.
Austin, TX 78704
Tel: 512-323-4940
Mr. LARRY MEJIA, Dir.

Beaumont
Diocese of Beaumont

St. Elizabeth Hospital of Beaumont
2830 Calder Ave., P.O. Box 5405
Beaumont, TX 77726-5405
Tel: 409-892-7171
Operated by Sisters of Charity of the Incarnate Word
Sr. M. FATIMA MCCARTHY, C.C.V.I., Admin.
Chaplains:
Revs.:
JAMES DEMPSEY
JOSEPH BERTRAND
Sisters 12
Bed Capacity 474
Patients assisted annually 310,815

Brenham
Diocese of Austin

Trinity Community Medical Center of Brenham
700 Medical Pkwy.
Brenham, TX 77833
Tel: 409-836-6173
JOHN SIMMS, Admin.
Sr. GERALDINE PALUSZAK, O.S.F., Dir. Pastoral Care
Attended from St. Mary's Church.
Sisters of St. Francis of Sylvania, OH 3
Bed Capacity 60
Patients assisted annually 24,000
Staff 287

Bryan
Diocese of Austin

Burleson Lease Corp. Inc./dba Burleson St. Joseph Health Center
2801 Franciscan Dr.
Bryan, TX 77802
Tel: 409-776-2464
WILLIAM F. HYER, JR., Sec.

Burleson-St. Joseph Services Corp.
2801 Franciscan Dr.
Bryan, TX 77802
Tel: 409-776-3777
JOHN HALL, M.D., Chm. Bd.

St. Joseph Hospital and Health Center of Bryan, Inc.
2801 Franciscan Dr.
Bryan, TX 77802
Tel: 409-776-3777
Sr. GRETCHEN KUNZ, O.S.F., Pres.
Rev. Msgr. JOHN C. MALINOWSKI, Chap.
Sisters of St. Francis of Sylvania, OH 7

Corpus Christi
Diocese of Corpus Christi

Spohn Hospital
600 Elizabeth St.
Corpus Christi, TX 78404
Tel: 512-881-3000; Fax: 512-881-3149
JAKE HENRY, JR., Pres. & CEO
GARY DEER, Admin.
Chaplains:
Revs.:
JOSE GUTIERREZ
ROBERT FRIMTONG-MANSO
TERENCE A. HOLACHECK, O.P.
Sr. MARY EUSTACE FARRELL, C.C.V.I.
Staff 1,655
Beds 458
Sisters 7
Patients assisted annually 113,670

Spohn Hospital South
5950 Saratoga Blvd.
Corpus Christi, TX 78414
Tel: 512-985-5000; Fax: 512-985-5109
Sisters of Charity of the Incarnate Word (San Antonio, TX)
JAKE HENRY, Pres. & CEO
Ms. JANE BAKOS, Admin.
Sr. SARA CARTER, C.C.V.I., Chap.
A member of the Spohn Health System.
Sisters 1
Staff 350
Beds 102
Patients assisted annually 30,000

Spohn Memorial Hospital
Mailing Address:
P.O. Box 5280
Corpus Christi, TX 78465-5280
2620 Hospital Blvd.
Corpus Christi, TX 78405-1818
Tel: 512-902-4000; Fax: 512-902-4949
Mr. ANTHONY W. HEEP, Admin.

Dallas
Diocese of Dallas

Parkland Hospital
5201 Harry Hines Blvd.
Dallas, TX 75235
Tel: 214-590-8512
Pastoral Care:
Rev. L. AIDAN O'DONOVAN, M.S.C.
Sr. MARY WILFRED OLTIVEROS, M.C.D.P.

St. Paul Medical Center
5909 Harry Hines Blvd.
Dallas, TX 75235
Tel: 214-879-1000
Sr. MARY ANGELYN PERA, D.C., Supr.
Mr. FRANK TIEDEMANN, Pres., CEO & Community Mgr.
Department of Chaplain Services,
Revs.:
F. PATRICK HANSER, C.M., Dir.
JOHN ALPHONSO (India)
RUDY RENTERIA (FWT)
VIRGINIA GORDON, Lay Chap.
GARY CARRUTH, Lay Chap.
ROYCE TAYLOR, Baptist Chap.
Sr. EDITH THOMPSON, D.C.
Sr. MICHAEL FRIEBE, D.C.
Sr. HELEN SONNIER, D.C., Volunteer Sacristan
Sr. MARY ANGELYN PERA, D.C., Volunteer
Daughters of Charity of St. Vincent de Paul 12
Bed Capacity 600

St. Paul Medical Center
5909 Harry Hines Blvd.
Dallas, TX 75235
(Texas Non-Profit Corp.)

St. Paul Medical Center Foundation Inc.
2777 Stemmons Fwy., #957
Dallas, TX 75207
(Texas Non-Profit Corp.)
JIM CHAMBERS, Pres.

El Paso
Diocese of El Paso

Centro San Vicente
(Affiliated with Daughters of Charity National Health System)
8061 Alameda
El Paso, TX 79915
Tel: 915-859-7545
JIM C. PARKER, Exec. Dir.
Legal Title: *Centro San Vicente*
Community Oriented Primary Health Care Center (Medical Care).
Total Assisted 23,000

La Clinica Guadalupana, Inc.
901 Ascencion
El Paso, TX 79927
Tel: 915-852-3328

Sr. PEGGY DENEWETH, Contact Person
Sr. JANET GILDEA, M.D., Staff Physician & Medical Dir.

Houston
Diocese of Galveston—Houston

St. Joseph Hospital
1919 LaBranch
Houston, TX 77002
Tel: 713-757-1000
Operated by Sisters of Charity of the Incarnate Word, Houston, Texas.
RAYMOND KHOURY, Admin.
Chaplains:
Revs.:
BEN MEYER, O.P.
RICHARD MARTIN PATRICK, O.P.
Bed Capacity 792
Patients assisted annually 163,809

Sisters of Charity of the Incarnate Word, Houston, Texas
2600 N. Loop W.
Houston, TX 77092
Tel: 713-681-8877
Sr. CHRISTINA MURPHY, Pres. & CEO
SCH Corporate Offices
SCH Health Care System
SCH Employee Benefit Plans
Sisters of Charity of the Incarnate Word Retirement Trust
Sisters of Charity/City of Houston Southwest Community Health Clinic
SCH Liability Retention Trust
St. Elizabeth Hospital of Houston, Texas, 2600 N. Loop West
Houston, TX 77092

Kingsville
Diocese of Corpus Christi

Spohn-Kleberg Memorial Hospital
1300 General Cavazos Blvd.
Kingsville, TX 78363
Tel: 512-595-1661; Fax: 512-595-9888
Mr. ANDREW HARRIS, Admin.
Operated by the Sisters of Charity of the Incarnate Word (San Antonio, TX).
Beds 100
Patients assisted annually 41,798

Laredo
Diocese of Corpus Christi

Mercy Regional Medical Center
1515 Logan, P.O. Box 2068
Laredo, TX 78044
Tel: 210-718-6222; Fax: 210-718-6904
MICHAEL L. MORGAN, Pres. & CEO
Chaplains:
Revs.:
HERNANDO RAMIREZ, S.J.
THOMAS P. O'DONOVAN
Deacon GUILLEMO DE LA GARZA
Sr. CARMEN AVILA, M.C.P.
Sisters of Mercy of the St. Louis Region of South Texas 15
Beds 326
Staff 1,581
Patients assisted annually 183,137

Lubbock
Diocese of Lubbock

St. Mary of the Plains Hospital
4000 24th St.
Lubbock, TX 79410-1894
Tel: 806-796-6000; Fax: 806-796-6081
Sisters of St. Joseph of Orange, CA
Mr. CHARLEY TRIMBLE, CEO
DAVID HARTMAN, Dir. Pastoral Care
Sr. MARY C. GERRIOR, O.P., CPE Supvr.
Chaplains:
Revs.:
JAMES FURLONG
GEORGE THEKKEDAM
Sisters 7
Bed Capacity 420
Total Staff 2,034
Patients assisted annually 391,647

Nassau Bay
Diocese of Galveston—Houston

St. John Hospital
2050 Space Park Dr.
Nassau Bay, TX 77058
Tel: 713-333-5503; Fax: 713-333-8891
Operated by Sisters of Charity of the Incarnate Word, Houston, Texas.
Rev. THOMAS F. MCNAMARA, M.S., Chap.
THOMAS PERMETTI, Admin.
Bed Capacity 140
Patients assisted annually 106,476
Total Staff 610

Paris
Diocese of Tyler

St. Joseph Hospital and Health Center
820 Clarksville St., P.O. Box 9070
Paris, TX 75461
Tel: 903-785-4521; Fax: 903-737-3848
Mr. MONTY MCLAURIN, Pres./CEO
Sisters 5
Beds 212
Patients assisted annually 20,686
Staff 753
Health Care Centers, Ancillary Care Systems 4
Patients Assisted Annually at St. Joseph's Family Clinic: 3,356 at Cooper, TX; 1,849 at Honey Grove, TX; 1,225 at DePort, TX; 1,883 at Paris,TX
St. Joseph's Foundation of Paris, Texas

Port Arthur
Diocese of Beaumont

St. Mary Hospital
3600 Gates Blvd., P.O. Box 3696
Port Arthur, TX 77643
Tel: 409-985-7431; Fax: 409-985-9404
Sisters of Charity of the Incarnate Word
Sr. MAURO THERIOT, C.C.V.I., Treas.
Mr. JIM GARDNER, Admin.
Rev. DONALD E. DONAHUGH (RCK) Chap.
Sisters 6
Bed Capacity 270
Patients assisted annually 108,938

San Antonio
Archdiocese of San Antonio

Incarnate Word Health System
9311 San Pedro #1250
San Antonio, TX 78216-4496
Tel: 210-524-4100
JOSEPH BLASKO, Pres. & CEO
IWHS Forth Worth Health Care Corporation
9311 San Pedro #1250
San Antonio, TX 78216
Tel: 210-524-4100
St. John's Hospital and Health Center
9311 San Pedro #1250
San Antonio, TX 78216

Santa Rosa Children's Hospital
519 W. Houston St.
San Antonio, TX 78207-3198
Tel: 210-704-2011
A Division of Santa Rosa Health Care.
RICHARD WAYNE, MD, CEO
Licensed Beds 325

Santa Rosa Health Care System
519 W. Houston St.
San Antonio, TX 78207-3198
Tel: 210-704-2011
Sisters of Charity of the Incarnate Word
ROBERT J. NOLAN, Pres. & CEO
RICH WOODLEY, Dir. Pastoral Ministry
Revs.:
MICHAEL NORTON, C.PP.S.
PALMER MAXWELL, O.C.D.
Health related activities.
Nurses 917 (Full time registered & licensed)
Patients assisted annually 90,983
Sisters 23
Santa Rosa Home Health
5115 Medical Dr., Cottage E.
San Antonio, TX 78229
Tel: 210-705-5200
ESMER SANCHEZ, Interim Dir.
Santa Rosa Hospice
5115 Medical Dr.
San Antonio, TX 78229
Tel: 210-705-5252
KIMBERLY CAMP, Dir.
Rev. MARK SCHEFFLER, C.S.S.R.

Santa Rosa Hospital
519 W. Houston St.
San Antonio, TX 78207-3198
Tel: 210-704-2011
A Division of Santa Rosa Health Care.
Patients assisted annually 35,000
Licensed Beds 370

Santa Rosa Northwest Hospital
2827 Babcock Rd.
San Antonio, TX 78229
Tel: 210-705-6300
A Division of Santa Rosa Health Care.
RICH WOODLEY, Dir. Pastoral Ministry
Licensed Beds 157
Villa Rosa Hospital
5115 Medical Dr.
San Antonio, TX 78229
Tel: 210-705-5600
A Division of Santa Rosa Health Care.
Licensed Beds 258
Santa Rosa Rehabilitation Hospital
2827 Babcock
San Antonio, TX 78229
Tel: 210-705-6100
A Division of Santa Rosa Health Care.
Beds 59

Santa Rosa Skilled Nursing Facility
519 W. Houston St.
San Antonio, TX 78207-3198
Tel: 210-704-2011
WANDA LEO FORD, Dir.
Licensed Beds 20

Texarkana
Diocese of Tyler

St. Michael Health Care Center
2600 St. Michael Dr.
Texarkana, TX 75503
DON A. BEELER, CEO
Operated by Sisters of Charity of the Incarnate Word, Houston, TX.
General Hospital
Annually Assisted 10,028
Staff 1,095
Bed Capacity 239

St. Michael Rehabilitation Hospital
2400 St. Michael Dr.
Texarkana, TX 75503
CHRISTOPHER KARAM, Admin.
Operated by Sisters of Charity of the Incarnate Word, Houston, Texas.
Health Care Centers, Ancillary Care Systems:
Annually Assisted 947
Staff 228
Bed Capacity 80

Tyler
Diocese of Tyler

Trinity Mother Frances Health System
800 E. Dawson St.
Tyler, TX 75701
Tel: 903-593-8441
Mr. J. LINDSEY BRADLEY, JR., Pres.
Rev. Msgr. JOHN BRENNAN, V.G., Chap.
Sisters of the Holy Family of Nazareth 8
Bed Capacity 358
Staff 1,600
Annually Assisted 248,253

Waco
Diocese of Austin

Providence Health Center
6901 Medical Pkwy., P.O. Box 2589
Waco, TX 76702-2589
Tel: 817-751-4763
KENT A. KEAHEY, Pres.
Sr. ROSEMARY BURKE, C.C.V.I., Dir. Chaplain Services
Sr. CECILE MATUSHEK, D.C., V.P. Mission
Medical & Surgical acute care; Depaul Center - Psychiatric care; St. Catherine's Center - Long Term care; Providence Medical Clinic; Providence Home Health/Hospice.
Daughters of Charity of St. Vincent de Paul 6
Bed Capacity 136

Wichita Falls
Diocese of Fort Worth

Bethania Regional Health Care Center
1600 Eleventh St.
Wichita Falls, TX 76301
Tel: 817-723-4111
Sisters of the Holy Family of Nazareth
Mr. DAVID D. WHITAKER, FACHE, Pres. & CEO
Sr. M. IRENA, C.S.F.N., Supr.
Rev. AIDAN DONLON, S.A.C., Chap.
Sisters 5
Bed Capacity 242
Patients assisted annually 60,000

UTAH

Murray
Diocese of Salt Lake City

Holy Cross Ministries
Mailing Address:

P.O. Box 57672
Murray, UT 84157-0672
404 E. 5600 South
Murray, UT 84107-6218
Tel: 801-281-1457; Fax: 801-281-1602
Sr. ALICE MARY QUINTANA, C.S.C., Exec. Dir.
Outreach Programs, Health Center, Wellness & Literacy Programs, Seniors, Children, Women.
Total Staff 16
Total Annually Assisted 8,156

Ogden
Diocese of Salt Lake City

The St. Benedict's Foundation
319 E. Ridgeline Dr.
Ogden, UT 84405-6925
Tel: 801-479-1800; Fax: 801-479-3216
ESTELLE G. DAHLEMPER, Exec. Dir.
STEVE SPURLOCK, Foundation Bd. Chm.

VERMONT

Colchester
Diocese of Burlington

Fanny Allen Hospital
101 College Pkwy.
Colchester, VT 05446
Tel: 802-655-1234; Fax: 802-654-1109
DAVID R. LINCOLN, Pres. & C.E.O., Board of Directors

VIRGINIA

Newport News
Diocese of Richmond

Mary Immaculate Hospital
2 Bernardine Dr.
Newport News, VA 23602-4499
Tel: 757-886-6600
KIRBY H. SMITH, JR., CEO
Sr. BERNARD MARIE MAGILL, O.S.F., M.S., Dir. Pastoral Care Dept.
Rev. CHARLES A. SAGLIO, Chap.
Bernardine Franciscan Sisters Foundation, Inc.
3 Bernardine Dr.
Newport News, VA 23602
The Bernardine Sisters of the Third Order of St. Francis 13
Beds 110
Nurses 252
Patients assisted annually 65,880

Norfolk
Diocese of Richmond

Bon Secours - De Paul Medical Center, Inc.
150 Kingsley Ln.
Norfolk, VA 23505
Tel: 804-889-5000
Daughters of Charity of St. Vincent de Paul
KEVIN P. CONLIN, Pres.
Revs.:
JEROME TURNER
PATRICK DOODY, C.S.Sp.
Clinic is connected with hospital.
Sisters 11
Beds 366
Patients assisted annually 9,356
Nursing Sisters 1
Nursing School
Students 103
Legal Title: *DePaul Medical Center*
Legal Title: *DePaul Health Foundation*
Legal Title: *Bayley Properties*

Norton
Diocese of Richmond

St. Mary's Hospital, Inc.
P.O. Box 620
Norton, VA 24273
Tel: 540-679-9100
Poor Servants of the Mother of God
GARY L. DELFORGE, Admin.
Sisters 6
Beds 133
Patients assisted annually 60,908
Nurses 174

Portsmouth
Diocese of Richmond

Maryview Medical Center
3636 High St.
Portsmouth, VA 23707
Tel: 804-398-2200
Legal Title: *Bon Secours-Maryview Health Corporation*
Sisters of Bon Secours
H. WAYNE JONES, Exec. Vice Pres./Admin.
MARYANN CHICHESTER, Dir. Pastoral Care
Chaplains:
Rev. PANTALEON O. MANALO
Sr. GRACE MALONZO
KATHY KOFRON
Beds 321
Patients assisted annually 126,694

Richmond
Diocese of Richmond

St. Mary's Hospital
5801 Bremo Rd.
Richmond, VA 23226
Tel: 804-285-2011
Sisters of Bon Secours
CHRISTOPHER M. CARNEY, CEO
Sr. PATRICIA A. ECK, V.P., Pres.
Rev. JAMES H. BONOMO, Chap.
Sisters 4
Beds 391
Patients assisted annually 216,757
Bon Secours-Richmond Health Corporation
Bon Secours-Maryview Health Corporation

**Bon Secours-Maryview Foundation, Inc.*
Bon Secours-St. Mary's Health Care Foundation
Bon Secours-Stuart Circle Hospital
Bon Secours-Richmond Community Hospital
Bon Secours-Richmond Health System

WASHINGTON

Bellingham
Archdiocese of Seattle

St. Joseph Hospital
2901 Squalicum Pkwy.
Bellingham, WA 98225
Tel: 360-734-5400; Fax: 360-738-6393
Sisters of St. Joseph of Peace and PeaceHealth
Mr. JOHN HAYWARD, Admin.
Sr. PAULINE DIBB, Dir. Values Integration/Spiritual Care
Sisters 4
Beds 253
Patients assisted annually 74,033

Centralia
Archdiocese of Seattle

Providence Centralia Hospital
1820 Cooks Hill Rd.
Centralia, WA 98531
Tel: 360-736-2803
Legal Title: *Sisters of Providence in Washington*
Sr. MAUREEN COMER, O.P., Admin.
Rev. TIMOTHY BERG, Chap.
Sisters 3
Patients assisted annually 111,583
Beds 191

Chewelah
Diocese of Spokane

St. Joseph's Hospital of Chewelah
E. 500 Webster
Chewelah, WA 99109
Tel: 509-935-8211
GARY V. PECK, CEO
Pastoral Care:
Sr. HUMILITAS LAMBER, O.P.
Sr. ALBERTA NETT, O.P.
Sr. MARY TOECKES, O.P.
Ms. MARGARET RETHERFORD
Sisters 3
Bed Capacity 65
Patients assisted annually 14,487

Colville
Diocese of Spokane

Mount Carmel Hospital
982 E. Columbia, Box 351
Colville, WA 99114
Tel: 509-684-2561
GLORIA P. COOPER, CEO
Sisters 3
Bed Capacity 55
Patients assisted annually 27,694

Deer Park
Diocese of Spokane

Deer Park Health Center and Hospital
P.O. Box 742
Deer Park, WA 99006
CATHY J. SIMCHUK, R.N., COO

Everett
Archdiocese of Seattle

Providence General Medical Center
14th & Colby, P.O. Box 1147
Everett, WA 98206
Tel: 206-261-2000
Operations Administrators:
Ms. BETH O'BRIEN
Mr. MEL PYNE
Sisters 5
Patients assisted annually 115,751
Beds 475

Federal Way
Archdiocese of Seattle

St. Francis Hospital of Federal Way
34515 9th Ave. S.
Federal Way, WA 98003
Tel: 206-927-9700; 838-9700
Sisters of St. Francis of Philadelphia
Mr. CRAIG L. HENDRICKSON, COO
Patients assisted annually 62,271
Beds 110

Longview
Archdiocese of Seattle

St. John Medical Center
1614 E. Kessler Blvd.
Longview, WA 98632
Tel: 360-423-1530; Fax: 360-636-4952
Sisters of St. Joseph of Peace and PeaceHealth
MARK MCGOURTY, Regl. CEO
Sisters of St. Joseph of Peace 4
Patients assisted annually 124,573
Beds 192

Olympia
Archdiocese of Seattle

Providence St. Peter Hospital
413 Lilly Rd., N.E.
Olympia, WA 98506
Tel: 360-491-9480
Legal Title: *Sisters of Providence in Washington*
Mr. SCOTT BOND, Admin.
Chaplains:
Revs.:
URBAN FEUCHT, O.S.B.
KIERAN CUNNINGHAM, O.S.B.
Beds 390
Patients assisted annually 89,897

Pasco
Diocese of Spokane

Our Lady of Lourdes Health Center
520 N. Fourth Ave., P.O. Box 2568
Pasco, WA 99302
Tel: 509-547-7704
THOMAS CORLEY, Admin.
In res.,
Rev. JOHN BIRK
Sisters of St. Joseph of Carondelet 5
Bed capacity 132
Patients assisted annually 38,701

Richland
Diocese of Yakima

Carondelet Behavioral Health Center
1175 Carondelet Dr.
Richland, WA 99352
Tel: 509-943-9104
BARBARA MEAD, Interim Admin. Dir.
Beds 32
Patients assisted annually 18,784

Seattle
Archdiocese of Seattle

Legal Title: *Sisters of Providence in Washington*
Sr. MAUREEN COMER, O.P., Admin.
Rev. TIMOTHY BERG (SFE) Chap.

Providence Seattle Medical Center
500 17th Ave., Box 34008
Seattle, WA 98124
Tel: 206-320-2000
Legal Title: *Sisters of Providence in Washington*
NANCY GUINTO, Admin.
Sr. LAURENTILLA BACK, S.S.N.D., Dir. Pastoral Care
Sr. SUSANNE HARTUNG, S.P., Dir., Mission & Ethics
Rev. AUGUSTINE HARTMAN, O.P., Chap.

Sisters of Providence 3
Patients assisted annually 110,050
Beds 436

Spokane
Diocese of Spokane

Holy Family Hospital
N. 5633 Lidgerwood St.
Spokane, WA 99207
Tel: 509-482-0111
Mr. Ron Schurra, Pres.
Mr. Richard Spinal, Dir. Pastoral Care
Chaplains 5
Sisters 3
Bed capacity 272
School of Radiology
Students 18

Holy Family Hospital Adult Day Health
c/o Dominican Network
N. 5633 Lidgerwood
Spokane, WA 99207
Tel: 509-482-2475
Mrs. Marie Raschko, Exec. Dir.
Purpose: to perform and provide health care services to the elderly and disadvantaged.

Sacred Heart Medical Center
W. 101 Eighth Ave., TAF-C9
Spokane, WA 99220
Tel: 509-455-3131
Mr. Ryland P. Davis, Pres.
Priest Chaplains:
Revs.:
Donald R. Cadden, S.J.
Gerald R. Gordon, S.J.
Michael Venneri
Chaplains 21
Bed Capacity 623
Patients assisted annually 10,553

Tacoma
Archdiocese of Seattle

St. Clare Hospital
11315 Bridgeport Way S.W.
Tacoma, WA 98499
Tel: 206-588-1711; Fax: 206-584-3001
Sisters of St. Francis of Philadelphia
Mr. Craig Hendrickson, COO
Sr. Jude Connelly, O.S.F., Vice Pres., Mission & Ministry
Sisters 1
Beds 86
Patients assisted annually 50,254

St. Joseph Medical Center
1717 S. J St.
Tacoma, WA 98405
Tel: 206-627-4101
Sisters of St. Francis of Philadelphia
Mr. Craig Hendrickson, COO
Sr. Jude Connelly, O.S.F., Dir. Pastoral Care
Revs.:
Michael Feeney, O.S.B., Chap.
James Poole
Emmanuel Quick (Nigeria)
Sisters 9
Beds 340
Patients assisted annually 330,164

Toppenish
Diocese of Yakima

Providence Hospital
504 W. 4th Ave., P.O. Box 672
Toppenish, WA 98948
Tel: 509-865-3105
Mr. Steve Burdick, Operations Admin.
Sr. Betty Kane, C.S.J.P., Dir. Pastoral Care
Patients assisted annually 48,000
Beds 63

Walla Walla
Diocese of Spokane

St. Mary Medical Center
401 W. Poplar St.
Walla Walla, WA 99362
Tel: 509-525-3320
Sisters of Providence
Mr. John A. Isely, Pres.
Bed capacity 142
Patients assisted annually 58,000

Yakima
Diocese of Yakima

Providence Yakima Medical Center
110 S. 9th Ave.
Yakima, WA 98902
Tel: 509-575-5000
Mr. Richard Brown, Operations Admin.
Sr. Patricia Glen, Dir., Pastoral Care
Revs.:
Justin McCreedy, O.S.B.
John Rashford, S.J.
Sr. Patricia Glen, S.P., Dir., Pastoral Care
Sisters of Providence 3
Patients assisted annually 224,997
Beds 226

WEST VIRGINIA

Buckhannon
Diocese of Wheeling-Charleston

St. Joseph's Hospital of Buckhannon, Inc.
1 Amalia Dr.
Buckhannon, WV 26201
Tel: 304-473-2000
Mr. Wayne B. Griffith, Admin.
Sisters of the Pallottine Missionary Society 4
Bed Capacity 95
Patients assisted annually 42,799
Home Health Care & Hospice Patients
Attended by Marist Fathers
St. Joseph's Foundation of Buckhannon, Inc.
1 Amalia Dr.
Buckhannon, WV 26201

Huntington
Diocese of Wheeling-Charleston

Pallottine Health Services, Inc.
2900 First Ave.
Huntington, WV 25702
Tel: 304-526-1028
Pallotine Missionary Sisters
Parent Corp. for:
St. Mary's Hospital of Huntington, Inc.
St. Joseph's of Buckhannon, Inc.
Sr. M. Diane Bushee, S.A.C.

St. Mary's Hospital of Huntington, Inc.
2900 First Ave.
Huntington, WV 25702
Tel: 304-526-1234
J. Thomas Jones, Exec. Dir.
Pallottine Missionary Sisters 9
Bed Capacity 440
Patients assisted annually 101,340
School of Nursing
Student Nurses 138

Pineville
Diocese of Wheeling-Charleston

Children's Health Care, Inc.
Pineville Children's Clinic, Box 1419
Pineville, WV 24874
Tel: 304-732-7069
Sr. Eileen Catterson, D.W.M.D., Dir.

Rhodell
Diocese of Wheeling-Charleston

Rhodell Health Clinic
P.O. Box 158
Rhodell, WV 25915
Tel: 304-683-4318
Legal Title: *Appalachian Health Cooperative, Inc.*

Wheeling
Diocese of Wheeling-Charleston

Bishop Joseph H. Hodges Continuous Care Center
Medical Park
Wheeling, WV 26003
Tel: 304-243-3800
Deborah A. Cox, R.N., B.S.N., Admin.
Bed Capacity 120
Skilled and Intermediate Care.

Children's Health Care, Inc.
1300 Byron St.
Wheeling, WV 26003

Wheeling Hospital
Medical Park
Wheeling, WV 26003
Tel: 304-243-3000
Donald H. Hofreuter, M.D., Admin
Rev. Gregory Monahan, T.O.R., Pastoral Care Dir.
Sisters of St. Joseph 4
Marist Brother 1
Bed Capacity 276
Patients assisted annually 123,731

WISCONSIN

Antigo
Diocese of Green Bay

Langlade Memorial Hospital
112 E. 5th Ave.
Antigo, WI 55409
Tel: 715-623-2331
Religious Hospitallers of St. Joseph
Sr. Dolores Demulling, R.H.S.J., Supvr., Mission and Philosophy Advocate & Trustee, Dir. of LeRoyer Hospice
Mr. David Schneider, Exec. Dir.
Sr. Jean Bricco, Dir. Pastoral Care, Trustee & Contact Person
Sr. Adele Demulling, Coord. LeRoyer Hospice
Rev. Omer Kelley, Part-time Chap.
Sisters Res.
644 Longlade Rd.
Antigo, WI 55409
Tel: 715-623-4615
Sisters 3
Priests 1
Bed Capacity 49
Patients assisted annually 46,100

Appleton
Diocese of Green Bay

Kaukauna Community Hospital
Mailing Address:—c/o St. Elizabeth Hospital
1506 S. Oneida St.
Appleton, WI 54915-1305
308 E. 14th St.
Kaukauna, WI 54130
Tel: 414-766-4211; Fax: 414-766-0712
Gregory Holub, Pres.
Legal Title: *Wheaton Franciscan Services, Inc.*
Bed Capacity 40
Patients assisted annually 7,289

St. Elizabeth Hospital
1506 S. Oneida St.
Appleton, WI 54915-1305
Tel: 414-738-2665; Fax: 414-738-0949
Legal Title: *St. Elizabeth Hospital, Inc.*
Mr. Otto L. Cox, Pres.
Rev. James M. Gilsoul, Chap.
Sr. Johnette Marek, Dir. Spiritual Svcs. & Contact Person
Priests 1
Franciscan Sisters, Daughters of the Sacred Hearts of Jesus and Mary (Wheaton, IL) 5
Bed Capacity 155
Patients assisted annually 165,454

Arcadia
Diocese of La Crosse

Franciscan Skemp Healthcare, Mayo Health System, Arcadia Campus Hospital
464 S. St. Joseph Ave.
Arcadia, WI 54612
Tel: 608-323-3341
Franciscan Sisters of Perpetual Adoration and Mayo Foundation
Robert Tracey, Admin.
Rev. Robert F. Pelcyn, O.F.M., Chap.
Sr. Arlene Melder, F.S.P.A., Pastoral Care Dir.
Bed Capacity 26
Patients assisted annually 15,000

Baraboo
Diocese of Madison

St. Clare Hospital and Health Services
707 14th St.
Baraboo, WI 53913
Tel: 608-356-5561
Owned and operated by SSM Health Care. A member of the SSM Health Care System.
David Jordahl, Pres.
Sr. Claire Marie Borst, F.S.M., Dir. Pastoral Care
Franciscan Sisters of Mary (St. Louis, MO) 3
Bed Capacity 100
Patients assisted annually 37,000
Staff 292

Brookfield
Archdiocese of Milwaukee

Elmbrook Memorial Hospital, Inc.
19333 W. North Ave.
Brookfield, WI 53045
Tel: 414-785-2000
Franciscan Sisters, Daughters of the Sacred Hearts of Jesus and Mary (Wheaton, IL)
Kimry A. Johnsrud, Pres.
Rev. Robert J. Artmann, Chap.

Bed Capacity 166
Patients assisted annually 57,587
Total Staff 508

Chippewa Falls
Diocese of La Crosse

St. Joseph's Hospital
2661 County Rd. I
Chippewa Falls, WI 54729
Tel: 715-723-1811
Hospital Sisters Health System.
Hospital Sisters of the Third Order of St. Francis
DAVID B. FISH, Exec. Vice Pres.
Sr. FRANCES E. SCHMITZ, O.S.F., Spiritual Svcs.
Sisters 6
Bed Capacity 147
Patients assisted annually 122,293

Eau Claire
Diocese of La Crosse

Sacred Heart Hospital
900 W. Clairemont Ave.
Eau Claire, WI 54701-5105
Tel: 715-839-4121
MATTHEW W. HUBLER, Exec. Vice Pres.
Rev. EDMUND J. KLIMEK, Chap.
Sr. AUGUSTA SPERL, O.S.F., Dir. Pastoral Care
Hospital Sisters of the Third Order of St. Francis 6
Bed Capacity 344
Patients assisted annually 96,259

Fond du Lac
Archdiocese of Milwaukee

Genesys HealthCare of Fond du Lac, Inc.
430 E. Division St.
Fond du Lac, WI 54935
Tel: 414-929-2300; Fax: 414-929-1866
Mr. ROBERT A. FALE, Pres. & CEO
Rev. HILARY ZACH, O.F.M.Cap., Chap.
Sisters 5
Bed Capacity 161
Patients assisted annually 61,437
Total Staff 913

Green Bay
Diocese of Green Bay

Libertas Treatment Center for Chemically Dependent
1701 Dousman St.
Green Bay, WI 54303-3282
Tel: 414-498-8600
Hospital Sisters Health System.
Hospital Sisters of the Third Order of St. Francis
DAVID B. FISH, Exec. Vice Pres.
PATRICK W. RYAN, Prog. Dir.
Bed Capacity 24
Patients assisted annually 500

St. Mary's Hospital-Medical Center
1726 Shawano Ave.
Green Bay, WI 54303-3282
Tel: 414-498-4200
Hospital Sisters of Third Order of St. Francis
Mr. JAMES G. COLLER, Admin.
DAVID J. SCHMIDT, Dir. Pastoral Care & Social Svc. Depts.
Revs.:
JOHN H. VAN DEUREN, Dir. Clinical Pastoral Education
FRANK P. SCHRAGE, Chap.
Bed Capacity 158
Patients assisted annually 91,639

St. Vincent Hospital
P.O. Box 13508
Green Bay, WI 54307-3508
Tel: 414-433-0111; 433-8162
Mr. JOSEPH J. NEIDENBACH, Vice Pres. & Exec.
Chaplains:
Revs.:
CONAN MULROONEY, O.Praem.
PETER J. RENARD, O.Praem.
WILLIAM J. STENGEL
CAMPION KLUCZYNSKI, O.F.M.
Sr. IRENE BUSHMAN, O.S.F.
Sr. BERNADINE POHL, O.P.
Sr. MARILYN HERR, O.S.F.
Hospital Sisters of the Third Order of St. Francis 2
Bassinets 25
Beds 547
Patients assisted annually 115,285

Hillsboro
Diocese of La Crosse

St. Joseph's Memorial Hospital, Inc.
400 Water Ave., P.O. Box 527
Hillsboro, WI 54634
Tel: 608-489-2211
Franciscan Sisters of Perpetual Adoration
Sr. RUTH BERRA, F.S.P.A., Dir. Pastoral Care
Rev. JAMES ENNIS, Chap.
Sisters 1
Bed Capacity 34
Patients assisted annually 3,440
Connected with the hospital is a home for the aged. Under care 65 infirm and aged men and women.

Kenosha
Archdiocese of Milwaukee

St. Catherine's Hospital
3556 Seventh Ave.
Kenosha, WI 53140
Tel: 414-656-3011
Mr. RYLAND P. DAVIS, Pres. & CEO
JEROLD FRANKE, Sec., Board of Directors
JILL HOFFMAN, Chap.
Legal Title: *St. Catherine's Hospital, Inc.*
Sisters 9
Bed Capacity 247
Patients assisted annually 75,000

Kewaunee
Diocese of Green Bay

St. Mary Kewaunee Area Memorial Hospital
810 Lincoln St., P.O. Box 217
Kewaunee, WI 54216
Tel: 414-388-2210
DENNIS MACK, Admin.
Patients assisted annually 13,991

La Crosse
Diocese of La Crosse

Franciscan Skemp Healthcare, Mayo Health System, La Crosse Campus Medical Center
700 West Ave. S.
La Crosse, WI 54601-4796
Tel: 608-785-0940; Fax: 608-791-9429
BRIAN CAMPION, M.D., CEO
Rev. PAUL SANKOORIKAL, Chap.
Franciscan Sisters of Perpetual Adoration and Mayo Foundation
Sisters 7
Bed Capacity 345
Patients assisted annually 51,638

Madison
Diocese of Madison

St. Marys Hospital Medical Center
707 S. Mills St.
Madison, WI 53715
Tel: 608-251-6100
Owned and operated by SSM Health Care. A member of the SSM Health Care System.
Franciscan Sisters of Mary (St. Louis, MO)
Mr. GERALD W. LEFERT, Pres.
Sisters 4
Capacity 440
Patients assisted annually 58,228
Pastoral Care Department
Revs.:
GARRETT KEEGSTRA, O.F.M., Cap.
TED LINDQUIST
HUGO WREISNER, O.P.
Sr. MARY ELLEN LEWIS, F.S.M., Dir.
Sr. CLEMENT SABOL, V.S.C.
JOAN CARLSON, Chap.
PAULA MCKENZIE

Manitowoc
Diocese of Green Bay

Holy Family Memorial, Inc.
2300 Western Ave., P.O. Box 1450
Manitowoc, WI 54221-1450
Tel 414-684-2011; Fax: 414-684-2522
Mr. DANIEL MCGINTY, Pres.
Ms. MARY J. BUSH, Dir. Pastoral Care
Chaplains:
Revs.:
RICHARD H. KLINGEISEN
KIERAN HICKEY, O.F.M.Cap.
Sr. STEPHEN MARIE LUEBBERT, O.S.F.
Deacon RAHLF PROULX
Franciscan Sisters of Christian Charity Sisters 9
Licensed Beds 303
Bassinets 26
Patients assisted annually 60,760

Marshfield
Diocese of La Crosse

St. Joseph's Hospital
611 St. Joseph Ave.
Marshfield, WI 54449
Tel: 715-387-1713
MICHAEL SCHMIDT, Pres. & CEO
Sr. ANTONIENNE THOMA, O.S.F., Acting Manager
Chaplains:
Revs.:
DONALD F. WILGER
LAWRENCE M. FEDOR, O.S.B.
MARY ELLA COLLINS, Catholic Lay Chap.
Protestant Chaplains:
Revs.:
STEVEN E. SUTTERER
LINDEN NELSON
DENNIS OLSON
Sisters of the Sorrowful Mother 5
Bed Capacity 524
Patients assisted annually 57,590
Training School for Nurses (Affiliated with U.W.-Eau Claire).

Mequon
Archdiocese of Milwaukee

St. Mary's Hospital Ozaukee, Inc.
13111 N. Port Washington Rd.
Mequon, WI 53097
Tel: 414-243-7300; 800-848-2844; Fax: 414-243-7416
THERESE PANDL, Sr. Vice Pres.
Rev. JOHN R. PACZESNY, Chap.
Bed Capacity 82
Patients assisted annually 148,369

Merrill
Diocese of Superior

Good Samaritan Health Center of Merrill, Wisconsin, Inc.
601 S. Center Ave.
Merrill, WI 54452
Tel: 715-536-5511
MICHAEL HAMMER, Pres. & CEO
Good Samaritan Health Center Foundation of Merrill, Wisconsin, Inc.
A not-for-profit corporation for the purpose of soliciting and receiving contributions for the benefit of Good Samaritan Health Center of Merrill, Wisconsin, Inc.
Bed Capacity 73
Patients assisted annually 33,627

Milwaukee
Archdiocese of Milwaukee

St. Francis Hospital
3237 S. 16th St.
Milwaukee, WI 53215
Tel: 414-647-5000
Sponsored by the Congregation of the Sisters of St. Felix of Cantalice of the United States of America, Chicago Province (Felician Sisters).
GREG BANASZYNSKI, Pres.
Chaplains:
Revs.:
JOSEPH L. BISOFFI, O.S.Cam.
GEORGE BALDERRAMA, S.C.J.
Sisters 6
Bed Capacity 260
Patients assisted annually 107,000

St. Joseph's Hospital of Franciscan Sisters, Milwaukee, Inc.
5000 W. Chambers St.
Milwaukee, WI 53210
Tel: 414-447-2000
JON L. WACHS, Pres.
Chaplains:
Revs.:
DAVID J. HANSER
NEAL DURHAM, S.D.S.
NORMAN R. SCHWARTZ
Corporate title: St. Joseph Hospital of Franciscan Sisters, Milwaukee, Inc.
Franciscan Sisters, Daughters of the Sacred Hearts of Jesus and Mary (Wheaton, IL) 8
Bed Capacity 567
Patients assisted annually 172,989

St. Mary's Hospital of Milwaukee
2323 N. Lake Dr., P.O. Box 503
Milwaukee, WI 53201-0503
Tel: 414-291-1000; Fax: 414-291-1048
CHARLES LOBECK, CEO
Chaplains:
Revs.:
JOHN R. PACZESNY
RUSSELL F. TIKALSKY
ALLEN BRATKOWSKI, O.S.Cam.
Sr. ROSALYNN DZIKONSKI, O.S.F.
Sr. MARGARET WENZEL, F.S.P.A.
Sr. MARGARET ANN ARNOLD, S.S.S.F.
Corporate title: St. Mary's Hospital of Milwaukee.

Daughters of Charity of St. Vincent de Paul 6
Bed Capacity 314
Patients assisted annually 134,026

St. Michael Hospital of Franciscan Sisters of Milwaukee, Inc.
2400 W. Villard Ave.
Milwaukee, WI 53209
Tel: 414-527-8000
Mr. JEFFREY K. JENKINS, Pres.
Sr. JOELISE RESTLE, Dir. of Pastoral Care Dept.
Corporate title: St. Michael Hospital of Franciscan Sisters, Milwaukee, Inc.
Franciscan Sisters, Daughters of the Sacred Hearts of Jesus and Mary (Wheaton, IL) 6
Bed Capacity 405
Patients assisted annually 128,269

Monroe
Diocese of Madison

St. Clare Hospital
515 22nd Ave.
Monroe, WI 53566
Tel: 608-324-1000
Sisters of the Congregation of St. Agnes
KENNETH E. BLOUNT, Pres. & CEO
Chaplains:
Rev. THOMAS F. CAMPION
Sr. AGNES KIRCHER
Bed Capacity 221
Nurses 179
Patients assisted annually 222,550

New Richmond
Diocese of Superior

Holy Family Hospital
535 Hospital Rd.
New Richmond, WI 54017
Tel: 715-246-2101
JEAN NEEDHAM, Pres.
Sr. MARIAN SCHMIT C.S.J., Pastoral Care
Sisters of St. Joseph of Carondelet 1
Bed Capacity 40
Patients assisted annually 15,000

Oshkosh
Diocese of Green Bay

Mercy Medical Center
631 Hazel St., P.O. Box 1100
Oshkosh, WI 54902-1100
Tel: 414-236-2000; Fax: 414-231-5677
Mr. OTTO COX, CEO
Rev. DAVID J. FUNK, O.F.M.Cap., Chap.
Chaplains:
Sr. RITA SCHMIDT, S.S.J.
Sr. JOHNETTE MAREK, S.S.M., Dir. Spiritual Svcs., Tel: 414-236-2125; 231-7652 (Fax)
Sisters of the Sorrowful Mother 4
Bed Capacity 232
Bassinets 14
Patients assisted annually 7,930

Portage
Diocese of Madison

Divine Savior Hospital & Nursing Home, Inc.
1015 W. Pleasant St.
Portage, WI 53901
Tel: 608-742-4131; Fax: 608-742-6098
Sisters of the Divine Savior
Mr. DELMAR MEDILL, Pres.
Chaplains:
Sr. DEBRA REED, S.D.S.
Sr. KATHLEEN DOOLEY, S.D.S.
Sisters 4
Bed Capacity 69
Patients assisted annually 39,093

Racine
Archdiocese of Milwaukee

St. Mary's Medical Center
3801 Spring St.
Racine, WI 53405
Tel: 414-636-4011; Fax: 414-636-4540
Mr. EDWARD P. DEMEULENAERE, Pres.
Rev. WILLIAM J. DIETZLER, Dir. Pastoral Care & Chap.
Corporate Title: St. Mary's Medical Center, Inc.
Franciscan Sisters, Daughters of the Sacred Hearts of Jesus and Mary 4
Bed Capacity 225
Patients assisted annually 180,200
Total Staff 1,036
Ambulatory Clinics
Patients assisted annually 500,000
Total Staff 652
All Saints Medical Group-Northwestern Campus
2405 Northwestern Ave.
Racine, WI 53404
All Saints Medical Group-Spring St. Campus
3807 Spring St.
Racine, WI 53405
Family Practice Associates of Kenosha
3535 30th Ave.
Kenosha, WI 53144

Rhinelander
Diocese of Superior

Sacred Heart-St. Mary's Hospitals, Inc.
1044 Kabel Ave.
Rhinelander, WI 54501
Tel: 715-369-6600
Mr. KEVIN J. O'DONNELL, Pres.
Sisters of the Sorrowful Mother Ministry Corporation
Bed Capacity 99
Annually Assisted 35,112

Sheboygan
Archdiocese of Milwaukee

St. Nicholas Hospital
1601 N. Taylor Dr.
Sheboygan, WI 53081
Tel: 414-459-8300
MICHAEL J. STENGER, Exec. Vice Pres. & Admin.
Sr. RENELLE BRUEGGEMANN, O.S.F., Rel. Coord.
MARY FLEISCHMAN, Dir. Pastoral Care
Hospital Sisters of the Third Order of St. Francis 3
Bed Capacity 185
Patients assisted annually 112,578
Total Staff 588

Sparta
Diocese of La Crosse

Franciscan Skemp Healthcare, Mayo Health System, Sparta Campus Hospital
310 W. Main St.
Sparta, WI 54656-2142
Tel: 608-269-2132
Franciscan Sisters of Perpetual Adoration and Mayo Foundation
WILLIAM P. SEXTON, M.H.A., Admin.
Sisters 1
Bed Capacity 50
Patients assisted annually 20,000

Stanley
Diocese of La Crosse

**Victory Medical Center, Inc.*
230 E. Fourth Ave.
Stanley, WI 54768
Tel: 715-644-5571; Fax: 715-644-5665
Mrs. CYNTHIA EICHMAN, CEO
Rev. ROBERT W. NELSON, Chap.
Sisters of the Sorrowful Mother-Ministry Corporation
Beds 127
Patients assisted annually 26,528

Stevens Point
Diocese of La Crosse

St. Michael's Hospital and School for Med. Technology
900 Illinois Ave.
Stevens Point, WI 54481
Tel: 715-346-5000; Fax: 715-346-5077
Mr. JEFFREY L. MARTIN, Pres. & CEO
Rev. ROBERT W. GREATOREX, Chap.
Mr. DAVID C. BAKER, Dir. Spiritual Services
Mrs. JANET JACOBY, Spiritual Services
Sr. MARY LEE SLOWEY, S.S.M., Patient Concerns Rep.
Sisters of the Sorrowful Mother 2
Bed Capacity 144
Patients assisted annually 60,000

Superior
Diocese of Superior

St. Mary's Hospital of Superior
3500 Tower Ave.
Superior, WI 54880
Tel: 715-392-8281
Mr. TERRY R. JACOBSON, Admin.
Bed Capacity 42
Patients assisted annually 13,890

Tomahawk
Diocese of Superior

Sacred Heart-St. Mary's Hospitals, Inc.
216 N. 7th St.
Tomahawk, WI 54487
Tel: 715-453-7700
Sisters of the Sorrowful Mother Ministry Corporation (Third Order of St. Francis)
Mr. KEVIN J. O'DONNELL, Pres.
Bed Capacity 60
Patients assisted annually 9,617

Waupun
Archdiocese of Milwaukee

Waupun Memorial Hospital
Waupun, WI 53963
Tel: 414-324-5581
RONALD J. FOUGHT, Interim COO
Bed Capacity 49
Patients assisted annually 39,456
Staff 265
Corporate title: Franciscan Sisters Hospital, Inc.

SPECIAL CARE FACILITIES

ALABAMA

Daphne
Archdiocese of Mobile

Mercy Medical
A Corporation.
P.O. Box 1090
Daphne, AL 36526
Tel: 334-626-2694
Sr. MARY EILEEN WILHELM, R.S.M., Admin.
Rev. Msgr. J. EDWIN STUARDI, Chap.
A Regional Specialized Hospital Facility, Hospice, Home Health Service.
The Birches—A residential care facility.
McAuley Place—A residential care facility.
Portier Place—An independent living facility.
Sisters of Mercy 7
Nursing Sisters 1
Professional Nurses 191
Beds 157
Daughters of Wisdom 1
Patients assisted annually 4,402
Residential Care Units 120

Marbury
Archdiocese of Mobile

Resurrection Catholic Nursing Home
165 County Rd. 20 E., P.O. Box 89
Marbury, AL 36051-0089
Skilled Nursing Facility.
Rev. MANUEL WILLIAMS, C.R., Dir.
Registered Nurses 1
Licensed Practical Nurses 4
Beds 20
In-Patients 20

Mobile
Archdiocese of Mobile

Allen Memorial Home Skilled Nursing Facility
735 S. Washington Ave.
Mobile, AL 36603
Tel: 334-433-2642
Sr. MARILYN MOORE, D.C., Admin.
Daughters of Charity of St. Vincent de Paul 4
Beds 119
Patients assisted annually 155

Cathedral Place
351 Conti St.
Mobile, AL 36602
Tel: 334-434-1590
Mrs. JO ANN SCANLAND, Mgr.
Sr. CLARE CHAREST, D.C., Social Dir.
Sr. DELPHINE FLEMING, D.C., Asst. Social Dir.
Residents 185

Little Sisters of the Poor, Home For the Aged, Inc.
Sacred Heart Residence, 1655 McGill Ave.
Mobile, AL 36604
Tel: 334-476-6335; Fax: 334-478-6519
Rev. LOUIS M. SUFFREDINI, Chap.
Sr. JUDITH MARY, L.S.P. (STP) Supr. & Admin.
Rev. Msgr. JOSEPH G. MCARDLE
Rev. Msgr. JAMES J. MADIGAN
Rev. Msgr. GEORGE ROYER
Revs.:
JAMES MELDRUM, O.C.D.
MICHAEL FINBAR DESMOND
Sisters 14
Residents 84

St. Mary's Home
4350 Moffat Rd.
Mobile, AL 36618
Tel: 334-344-7733
Mr. PHILLIP A. WYNNE, Admin.
Dependent Children 48

Montgomery
Archdiocese of Mobile

City of St. Jude, Inc., The
2048 W. Fairview Ave.
Montgomery, AL 36108
Tel: 334-265-6791
Rev. MATTHEW SINDIK
Includes:
St. Jude Administration Building
St. Jude Church and Rectory
St. Jude Elementary and High School
St. Jude Exceptional Children's Center
St. Jude Head Start
St. Jude Social Services Center
Vincentian Sisters' Convent
The Old Convent
Central Alabama Laubach Literacy
St. Jude Apartments

Father Purcell Memorial Exceptional Children Center
2048 W. Fairview Ave.
Montgomery, AL 36108
Tel: 334-834-5590; Fax: 334-834-5592
Deacon FRANK J. MAY, JR., Admin.
Bed Capacity 58
Patients assisted annually 58

Father Walter Memorial Center for Handicapped Children
2815 Forbes Dr.
Montgomery, AL 36199
Tel: 334-262-6421; Fax: 334-262-2265
Rev. MANUEL WILLIAMS, C.R., Dir.
AUDREY C. WRIGHT, R.D., Admin.
BETTY THOMAS, Asst. Admin.
A skilled nursing facility for the mentally and physically handicapped child. Operated by The Resurrection Catholic Missions.
R.N. 5
L.P.N. 8
Beds 44
Patients assisted annually 44

Laboure Complex Foundation
P.O. Box 3074
Montgomery, AL 36109
Tel: 334-277-5213
Board of Directors:
LARRY NEUHOFF, Pres.
BARBARA DUKE, Vice Pres.
EDWARD AZAR, Sec./Treas.

St. Bede's Children's Center
3840 Atlanta Hwy.
Montgomery, AL 36109

St. John Resurrection Early Childhood Center
2815 Forbes Dr.
Montgomery, AL 36110
Sr. INEZ THERESA, O.S.P., Prin.
Licensed by Alabama State Dept. of Human Resources for 45 Students, Ages 2 1/2 to 5 years.

Seton Haven
3721 Wares Ferry Rd.
Montgomery, AL 36109
Tel: 334-272-4000
Sr. MARY CAROL MAUTEMPS, D.C., Admin.
Sr. MARILLAC CLARKE, D.C., Admin. Asst.
Residents 104

Prichard
Archdiocese of Mobile

Queen's Court I Apartments
W. Clark Ave.
Prichard, AL 36610

ALASKA

Anchorage
Archdiocese of Anchorage

**Mary Conrad Center*
9100 Centennial Dr.
Anchorage, AK 99504
Tel: 907-333-8100; Fax: 907-338-6789
JOAN FISHER, Admin.
Sr. FRANCESCA KOLLER, O.P., Pastoral Care Coord.
Patients assisted annually 89
Staff 140
A long term care facility for the elderly, owned by Cook Inlet Housing Development Corporation and managed by Sisters of Providence in Washington.

Providence Extended Care Center
4900 Eagle St.
Anchorage, AK 99503
Tel: 907-562-2281
THOMAS E. BOLING, Admin.
Sr. PATRICIA COLLINS, R.S.M., Mission Integration
Legal Title: *Sisters of Providence in Washington.*
Patients assisted annually 380
Staff 340
Bed Capacity 224

Juneau
Diocese of Juneau

St. Ann's Care Center, Inc.
415 Sixth St.
Juneau, AK 99801
Tel: 907-586-3883
Skilled and intermediate care facility.
VACANT, Admin.
Bed Capacity 45

American Samoa

Pago Pago
Diocese of Samoa-Pago Pago

Nazareth House
P.O. Box 1510
Pago Pago, American Samoa 96799
Tel: 684-699-2101; Fax: 684-699-1459
Conducted by Poor Sisters of Nazareth.
Sr. ENID HEALY, Dir.
Sisters 5
Aged Residents 17
Special Care Children 11
Montessori Early Education 144
Day Care Center 120

ARIZONA

Avondale
Diocese of Phoenix

Vianney Villas Apartments
(Retirement)
750 S. Fourth St.
Avondale, AZ 85323
Tel: 602-932-2036

Kingman
Diocese of Phoenix

Kingman Heights Apartments
(Retirement)
1020 Detroit Ave.
Kingman, AZ 86401
Tel: 602-753-2425

Lake Havasu City
Diocese of Phoenix

Becket House Apartments
(Retirement)
865 Cashmere Dr.
Lake Havasu City, AZ 86403
Tel: 602-855-7178

Mesa
Diocese of Phoenix

Sun Terrace Apartments
(Retirement)
1825 W. Emelita Ave.
Mesa, AZ 85202-4031
Tel: 602-964-9866
Sun Terrace Senior Adult Community
1825 W. Emelita Ave.
Mesa, AZ 85202
Tel: 602-964-0410

Phoenix
Diocese of Phoenix

Desert Crest Apartments
(Retirement)
2101 E. Maryland Ave.
Phoenix, AZ 85016
Tel: 602-264-6427

Senior Village
3541 W. Vogel
Phoenix, AZ 85051
Tel: 602-843-3008

Sweetwater Gardens Apartments
(Handicapped)
2035 E. Sweetwater
Phoenix, AZ 85022
Tel: 602-867-4549

Wickenburg
Diocese of Phoenix

Padua Hills Apartments
(Retirement)
460 S. West Rd.
Wickenburg, AZ 85390
Tel: 602-684-7034

Williams
Diocese of Phoenix

St. Agnes Apartments
(Retirement)

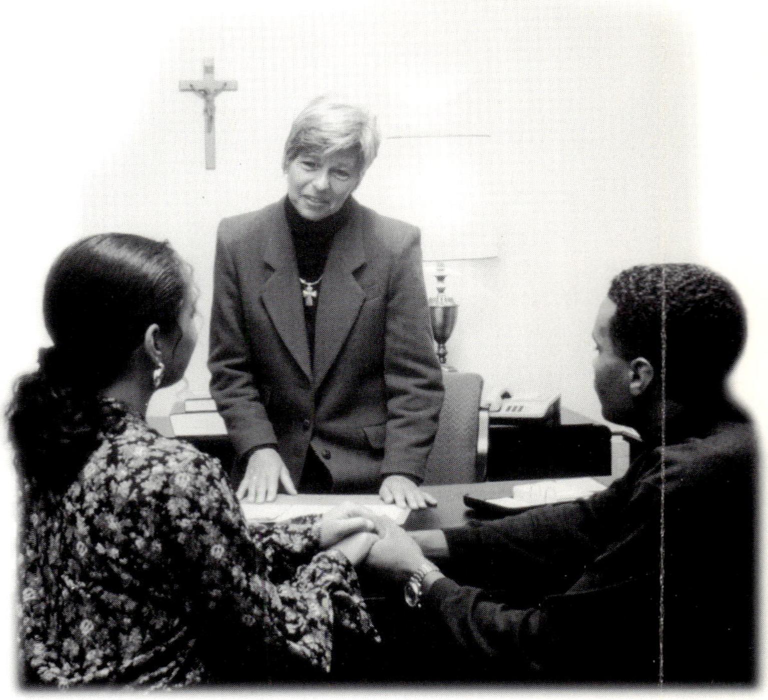

200 S. Ninth
Williams, AZ 86046
Tel: 602-635-2913

ARKANSAS

Barling
Diocese of Little Rock

Mercy Crest of Arkansas, Inc.
1300 Strozier Ln.
Barling, AR 72923
Tel: 501-478-3000
Sponsored by the Religious Sisters of Mercy
Retirement Facility: 30 beds. Residential Care Facility for Elderly: 60 beds.

Hot Springs
Diocese of Little Rock

Benedictine Manor
101 Second St.
Hot Springs, AR 71913
Tel: 501-623-6308
Retirement home and motel for senior citizens, conducted by the Olivetan Benedictine Sisters.
Sr. CECILIA MARIE SHANNON
Sisters 2
Residents 47

Hot Springs National Park
Diocese of Little Rock

Monastery of Our Lady of Charity of Refuge (Good Shepherd)
1125 Malvern Ave.
Hot Springs National Park, AR 71901
Tel: 501-623-9651
Sr. THERESA MARIE LALANCETTE, Supr.
Rev. ANDREW J. DUFAULT, M.Afr., Chap.
Sisters 14
Novices 1

St. Michael's School
1125 Malvern Ave.
Hot Springs National Park, AR 71901
Sr. THERESA MARIE LALANCETTE, Supr.
Sisters of Our Lady of Charity of Refugee (Good Shepherd) 14
Elementary students 50
Kindergarten 18
Day Care Center 96

Little Rock
Diocese of Little Rock

ABBA House
1014 S. Oak St.
Little Rock, AR 72204
Tel: 501-666-9718
Home for expectant mothers.
Missionaries of Charity 4

Catherine's House c/o Sisters of Mercy Health System
1020 W. 14th St.
Little Rock, AR 72202
Tel: 501-370-9100
Home for the first time expectant mothers or parenting teenagers.
Mr. ED APPLER, Dir.
Number Served 27
Lay Personnel 15

CALIFORNIA

Chatsworth
Archdiocese of Los Angeles

Rancho San Antonio
21000 Plummer St.
Chatsworth, CA 91311
Tel: 818-882-6400
Sponsored by Catholic Archdiocese of Los Angeles.
Directed by the Brothers of Holy Cross.
Bro. JOHN CROWE, C.S.C., Exec. Dir.
In res.,
Rev. JAMES BLANTZ, C.S.C.
Brothers 4
Boys (13-17 yrs.) 102

Culver City
Archdiocese of Los Angeles

Marycrest Manor, Convalescent Home
10664 St. James Dr.
Culver City, CA 90230-5498
Tel: 310-838-2778
Religious Sisters of Charity.
Skilled Nursing Facility attended by priests from Loyola University and St. Augustine Parish.
Mrs. ESTHER MOSSE, Admin.
Sr. FRANCIS MARIA
Pastoral Care Sisters 2
Bed Capacity 57
Residents 57
Total Staff 85

Fortuna
Diocese of Santa Rosa in California

St. Joseph Nazareth Residence
2280 Newburg Rd.
Fortuna, CA 95540
Tel: 707-725-3512
JACQUELINE KELLER, Prog. Dir.
Residents 6

Fresno
Diocese of Fresno

Nazareth House
2121 N. First St.
Fresno, CA 93703
Tel: 209-237-2257
Sr. TERESA GRANT, P.S.N., Supr.
Rev. MICHAEL O'SHEA, O.F.M.Cap.
Poor Sisters of Nazareth of Fresno Inc. 7
Residential Care 85
Skilled Nursing 39
Total Staff 79

La Mesa
Diocese of San Diego

Little Flower Haven
8585 La Mesa Blvd.
La Mesa, CA 91941
Tel: 619-466-3163
Sr. BARBARA LEARY, D.C.J., Co-Adm.
Sr. CARMELA LOVATO, Co-Adm.
Rev. PHILIP BRONK, S.T., Chap.
Postulants 1
Novices 1
Aged Residents 82

Los Angeles
Archdiocese of Los Angeles

Convent of the Good Shepherd-Good Shepherd Shelter
2561 Venice Blvd.
Los Angeles, CA 90019
Tel: 213-737-6111
Conducted by Sisters of the Good Shepherd.
Shelter for Battered Women and Their Children.
Sisters 10
Women Assisted Annually 40
Children 166

Franciscan Health Center
2859 Glassell St.
Los Angeles, CA 90026
Tel: 213-413-1050
ROSIE ORTEGA, Clinic Mgr.
Community Clinic Offering Surgical, Medical, OB-GYN, Optometry, Opthamology, Pediatrics, & Dental patients. Payment based on ability to pay.
A United Way Agency. Sponsored by Franciscan Sisters of the Sacred Heart.
Patients assisted annually 5,700

Immaculate Conception Home for Girls
1923 Micheltorena St.
Los Angeles, CA 90039
Tel: 213-664-7070
Sr. BENIGNA, Dir. Franciscan
Missionary Sisters of the Immaculate Conception.
Capacity 10

Knights of Malta Free Clinic, Inc.
2222 W. Ocean View #112
Los Angeles, CA 90057
Tel: 213-384-4323; Fax: 213-384-4097
Conducted by Knights of Malta Physicians.
Primary Health Care for Senior Citizens.
DAVID FRELINGER, M.D., K.M., Medical Dir.
DAVID JOHNSON, Admin.
Visitation 7,500

Little Flower Missionary House
2434 Gates St.
Los Angeles, CA 90031
Tel: 213-221-9248
Sr. MARY JEANNE CODERRE, O.C.D., Supr., Ctr. Admin.
Mrs. CATHERINE CATANO, Dir. & Prin.
Attended by Salesian priests.
Child and Kindergarten Care Center.
Sisters 10
Lay Teachers 10
Capacity 197
Kindergarten Capacity 50

Missionary Brothers of Charity
1345 Alvarado Ter.
Los Angeles, CA 90006
Tel: 213-251-9707
Day Center and Residence for Homeless Youth.

Nazareth House
3333 Manning Ave.
Los Angeles, CA 90064
Tel: 310-839-2361; Fax: 310-839-4204
Conducted by the Poor Sisters of Nazareth.
Mother MALACHY MCSWEENEY, Local Supr.
Rev. PAUL PETERSON, S.S.C., Chap.
In res.,
Sisters 8
Retired Priests 18
Total Staff 185
Residents 150

St. Anne's
155 N. Occidental Blvd.
Los Angeles, CA 90026
Tel: 213-381-2931; Fax: 213-381-7804
Residential care and community counseling programs for pregnant and parenting adolescents.
Sponsored by the Franciscan Sisters of the Sacred Heart
TOM OWENSON, Pres. & CEO
Revs.:
HERBERT PATTERSON, O.F.M., Chap.
WILLIAM BRAND, O.F.M., Youth Minister
Beds Licensed for Children Under 18 years of age 96
Children Served Annually in Residential Care 300
St. Anne's also provides community counseling centers at the following locations to serve pregnant/parenting young women in their homes:
155 N. Occidental Blvd.
Los Angeles, CA 90026
Tel: 213-381-2931
11401 Valley Blvd., #102
El Monte, CA 91731
Tel: 818-443-2577
2301 Daily Dr., #202
Camarillo, CA 93010
Tel: 805-383-7277
Support groups include:
St. Anne's Foundation
St. Anne's Guild
St. Anne's Guild of Ventura
St. Anne's Guild of Orange County
St. Anne's Junior Guild
Roney League
Helen Clark Auxiliary
Mabel Mosler Auxiliary
Loretta Young Auxiliary
Sister Winifred Auxiliary
Assisted Annually 18,000

St. John of God Retirement and Care Center
2035 W. Adams Blvd.
Los Angeles, CA 90018
Tel: 213-731-0641
JOHN WILLIAMS, Admin.
Bros.:
STEPHEN DE LA ROSA, O.H., Local Supr.
EDWARD FRANCIS MCENROE, O.H., Prov.
PAUL HANSON, O.H., Novice Master
Conducted by the Brothers of the Hospitaller Order of St. John of God.
Brothers 14
Bed Capacity 214
SNF 131
Residential Care 33
Independent Living 51
Patients assisted annually 258
Supporting Organizations:
Hospitaller Foundation of California, Inc.
Tel: 213-731-7141
Bro. PATRICK CORR, O.H., Pres.
Women's League of St. John of God, Inc., Helpers Club of St. John of God, Inc.

Monterey
Diocese of Monterey in California

Ave Maria Convalescent Hospital
1249 Josselyn Canyon Rd., P.O. Box 1977
Monterey, CA 93940
Tel: 408-373-1216
Rev. FELIX MIGLIAZZO, Chap.
Franciscan Sisters of the Immaculate Conception 2
Bed Capacity 31
Patients assisted annually 43
Total Staff 42

Mountain View
Diocese of San Jose in California

Villa Siena
1855 Miramonte Ave.

Mountain View, CA 94040
Tel: 415-961-6484
Residential Care and Skilled Nursing Facility.
Mr. Carl Braginsky, Admin.
Sr. Ursula Bomholt, O.P., Pres.
Rev. Salvatore M. DiNardo, O.P., Chap.
In res.,
Rev. Guy B. Hayden, (Retired)
Dominican Sisters of Oakford, dedicated to St. Catherine of Siena. S.A. Motherhouse.
Professed Sisters 9
Residents 46
Nursing Staff 20
Total Staff 20

Newbury Park
Archdiocese of Los Angeles

Mary Health of the Sick Convalescent and Nursing Hospital
2929 Theresa Dr.
Newbury Park, CA 91320
Tel: 805-498-3644; Fax: 805-498-5112
Sisters Servants of Mary
Skilled Nursing Facility.
Sr. Purificacion Ferrero, S.M., Supr./Exec. Dir.
Sisters 15
Bed Capacity 61
Residents Assisted Annually 90
Total Staff 90

Oakland
Diocese of Oakland

Bishop Begin Villa
(Retired Priests)
3418 E. 18th St.
Oakland, CA 94601
Rev. Msgr. Martin E. Walsh
Revs.:
Edmund L. Hayburn
Adrian L. Murray
Edmond Cloutier
Thomas B. Gallagher
Residents 5
Total Assisted 5

Mercy Retirement and Care Center
3431 Foothill Blvd.
Oakland, CA 94601
Tel: 510-534-8540; Fax: 510-261-7551
Else Marie Kiefer, Pres.
Sr. Patrick Curran, Vice Pres.
Sponsored by the Sisters of Mercy.
Sisters of Mercy 4
Sisters of the Holy Names 2
Employees 160
Convalescent Hospital - Skilled Nursing Facility
Residential Care, Assisted Living, Personal Care.
Bed capacity 135
Retirement Facility for Priests in the Oakland Diocese Extensive community services.

Ojai
Archdiocese of Los Angeles

St. Joseph's Health and Retirement Center
2464 E. Ojai Ave., P.O. Box 760
Ojai, CA 93024
Tel: 805-646-1466
Hospitaller Brothers of St. John of God.
Bros.:
Pascal Barry, Prior
Michael Bassemier, O.H., Admin.
Andre Arculetta, O.H., Res. Mgr.
Rev. Sebastian Ward, O.F.M.Cap.
Capacity 28
Independent Living 25 elderly
Total Staff 50

Palm Desert
Diocese of San Bernardino

La Paz Villas
P.O. Box 1962
Palm Desert, CA 92261
Tel: 619-346-6033
Units 24

Rosemead
Archdiocese of Los Angeles

Maryvale
P.O. Box 1039
Rosemead, CA 91770-1003
Tel: 818-280-6510; 213-283-9311; Fax: 818-288-8903
Sr. Linda Ann Cahill, D.C., Exec. Dir.
Daughters of Charity of St. Vincent de Paul 6
Children:
Residential Treatment 85
Day Care 80
The Los Angeles Orphan Asylum
7600 E. Graves Ave.
Rosemead, CA 91770
Los Angeles Orphanage Guild
7600 E. Graves Ave.
Rosemead, CA 91770

Sacramento
Diocese of Sacramento

Mercy-McMahon Terrace
3865 J St.
Sacramento, CA 95816
Tel: 916-733-6510; Fax: 916-733-6515
Sr. Mary St. John, R.S.M., Admin.
Licenced Units 118
Total Assisted 118
Total Staff 45

San Bernardino
Diocese of San Bernardino

St. Bernardine Plaza
550 W. Fifth St.
San Bernardino, CA 92401
Tel: 909-888-0153; Fax: 909-381-1589
Staff 4
Units 150

San Diego
Diocese of San Diego

Cathedral Plaza
1551 Third Ave.
San Diego, CA 92101
Tel: 619-234-0093
Legal Title: *Cathedral Plaza Development Corp. A California Nonprofit Corporation*
Mr. & Mrs. Lance Jobson, Res. Mgrs.
Apartments 222
In Residence 270

Guadalupe Plaza
4142 42nd St.
San Diego, CA 92105
Tel: 619-584-2414
Legal Title: *Guadalupe Plaza Development Corp., A California Nonprofit Corporation*
Mr. & Mrs. George Pettinga, Res. Mgrs.
Apartments 127
In Residence 130

Nazareth House
6333 Rancho Mission Rd.
San Diego, CA 92108
Tel: 619-563-0480
Sr. Margaret Brody, P.S.N., Supr.
Poor Sisters of Nazareth 9
Dependent Children 9
Day Students 358

Nazareth House Retirement Home
6333 Rancho Mission Rd.
San Diego, CA 92108
Tel: 619-563-0480
Retired Priests Residential and Nursing
Rev. Msgr. Patrick J. Kearney, Chap.
Margaret Brody, Mgr.
Capacity 139
Priests 25
Poor Sisters of Nazareth of San Diego 10

St. John's Plaza
8150 Broadway
Lemon Grove, CA 91945
Tel: 619-466-5354
Legal Title: *Calexico Plaza Development Corp., A California Nonprofit Corporation*
Mr. & Mrs. Robert Partiss, Res. Mgrs.
Residences 99
Total In Residence 106

San Fernando
Archdiocese of Los Angeles

Mother Gertrude Home for Senior Citizens
(Franciscan Missionary Sisters of the Immaculate Conception, Inc.)
11320 Laurel Canyon Blvd.
San Fernando, CA 91340
Tel: 818-898-1546; Fax: 818-365-3159
Capacity 98
Total Staff 19
Total in Residence 36

San Francisco
Archdiocese of San Francisco

Alexis Apartments of St. Patrick's Parish
390 Clementina St.
San Francisco, CA 94103
756 Mission St.
San Francisco, CA 94103
Tel: 415-495-3690; Fax: 415-495-3629
Brenda Thomas, Property Admin.
Residents 200

The Good Shepherd Gracenter
1310 Bacon St.
San Francisco, CA 94134
Tel: 415-586-2822
Jean Marie Fernandez, Dir.
A treatment program for chemically dependent women.
Sisters 4
Lay Staff 11
Residence capacity 13

Home for the Aged of the Little Sisters of the Poor
St. Anne's Home, 300 Lake St.
San Francisco, CA 94118
Tel: 415-751-6510; Fax: 415-751-0650
Sr. Margaret Hogarty, L.S.P., Supr.
In res.,
Rev. Msgr. Edwin J. Kennedy
Revs.:
Joseph Sanchez, Chap.
Joseph Jaszovsky
W. Adalbert Gluszek
Ralph Carpenter, C.S.P.
David I. Walsh
Religious 15
Residents 90

Madonna Residence
1055 Pine St.
San Francisco, CA 94109
Tel: 415-928-0743
Cathy Koger, Mgr.
Total in Residence 37
Nonprofit residence for women over 60 with low income. Meal program, social services program.

Mercy Terrace Corporation Apartments
333 Baker St.
San Francisco, CA 94117
Tel: 415-931-2325
Mr. Todd Landreneau, Admin.
The purpose of this corporation is to develop, construct, own, and operate housing for low- and moderate-income persons and families.
Residents 155

Mount St. Joseph-St. Elizabeth (1976)
100 Masonic Ave.
San Francisco, CA 94118
Tel: 415-567-8370; Fax: 415-292-5531
Michael M. Sullivan, Exec. Dir.
Successor Corporation to Mount St. Joseph Home for Girls and St. Elizabeth Infant Hospital.
Sisters 7
Mount St. Joseph Program-Benita House. Residential group homes for abused and neglected girls, ages 11-19, with emotional and behavioral problems.
Number assisted 34
St. Elizabeth Adolescent Parenting Program. Residential care for pregnant teens, teen mothers, and their children.
Girls 34
Babies 24
Shelter Nursery for Drug Exposed Babies
Individuals assisted 42
Simpatico School. On-site junior-senior high school offering basic education and vocational training to school-age residents of our group home and adolescent parenting programs.
Students 40
Epiphany Center for Families in Recovery. Comprehensive support and reunification program for the parents and family members of drug-exposed infants.
Families served 80

San Jose
Diocese of San Jose in California

Jeanne d'Arc Manor
85 S. Fifth St.
San Jose, CA 95112
Tel: 408-288-7421
Housing project for low-income elderly and handicapped. Sponsored by the Roman Catholic Bishop of San Jose, A Corporation Sole.
Carol George, Admin.
Lay Staff 13
Residents 87

San Pedro
Archdiocese of Los Angeles

Little Sisters of the Poor
Jeanne Jugan Residence, 2100 S. Western Ave.

San Pedro, CA 90732
Tel: 310-548-0625
Sr. MARY ANTHONY, Supr.
Legal Title: *Little Sisters of the Poor of Los Angeles. A Corporation*
Sisters 16
Residents 86

San Rafael
Archdiocese of San Francisco

Nazareth House
245 Nova Albion Way
San Rafael, CA 94903
Tel: 415-479-8282
Sr. MARY ANTOINETTE FARRELL, P.S.N., Supr.
Rev. PATRICK F. CONWAY, C.S.Sp., (Ireland) Chap.
Poor Sisters of Nazareth 5
Residents 151
In res.,
Most Rev. JOHN J. SCANLAN
Rev. Msgr. THOMAS I. KENNEDY
Rev. Msgr. ANDRE TOURNEIR
Rev. Msgr. GEORGE MONAGHAN
Rev. Msgr. WALTER TAPPE
Rev. Msgr. CLYDE TILLMAN
Rev. ANTHONY SPIKA

Santa Barbara
Archdiocese of Los Angeles

St. Vincent Residence
4200 Calle Real, P.O. Box 669
Santa Barbara, CA 93102-0669
Tel: 805-683-6381; Fax: 805-967-7508
For female youthful offenders, ages 12-17.
Daughters of Charity of St. Vincent de Paul Sisters 4
Residents 21
Total Assisted 35
Total Staff 55

Santa Cruz
Diocese of Monterey in California

Dominican Health Services
1555 Soquel Dr.
Santa Cruz, CA 95065
Tel: 408-462-7700; Fax: 408-462-7555
Sr. JULIE HYER, O.P., Pres.
Total in Residence 336
Total Staff 124

Santa Maria
Archdiocese of Los Angeles

Marian Residence
124 S. College Dr.
Santa Maria, CA 93454
Conducted by Sisters of St. Francis of Penance and Christian Charity.
Sisters 32
Residents 31
Total Staff 42

Santa Rosa
Diocese of Santa Rosa in California

**Vigil Light Apartments (The Vigil Light, Inc.)*
1945 Long Dr.
Santa Rosa, CA 95405
Tel: 707-544-2810
Sr. ERNESTINA MOLINARI, B.V.M., Mgr.
Sisters 2
Residents 54

Saratoga
Diocese of San Jose in California

Our Lady of Fatima Villa
20400 Saratoga-Los Gatos Rd.
Saratoga, CA 95070
Tel: 408-741-2950; Fax: 408-741-4930
Provides skilled nursing care for aged women and men and Special Alzheimer's Unit.
Dominican Sisters of St. Catherine of Siena, Saratoga: Congregation of St. Catherine of Siena, Kenosha, Wisconsin.
SUSAN SNYDER, O.P., Prioress
JOAN S. LUNDELL, Dir. Pastoral Care
Rev. LEONARD TRAVERSO, Chap.
Religious 3
Residents 85

Spring Valley
Diocese of San Diego

Noah Homes
12526 Campo Rd.
Spring Valley, CA 91978
Tel: 619-660-6200; Fax: 619-660-1481
Sr. KATHRYN JENNINGS, O.S.B., Exec. Dir.

Stockton
Diocese of Stockton

Casa Manana Inn
3700 N. Sutter St.
Stockton, CA 95204
Tel: 209-466-4046
SANDY HUFFSTUTLER, Mgr.
Total in Residence 172
Total Staff 4

Garden Oaks
3334 Wagner Heights Rd.
Stockton, CA 95209
Tel: 209-956-3401
Assisted living facility.
Sisters of the Third Order of St. Dominic, Congregation of the Most Holy Name.
ARLENE LIND, Dept. Mgr.
Total Staff 9
Units 48

St. Joseph's Regional Housing Corp.
1805 N. California St., Ste. 407
Stockton, CA 95204
Tel: 209-467-6312
O'Connor Woods Housing Corp. dba Garden Oaks
3334 Wagner Heights Rd.
Stockton, CA 95209
Tel: 209-956-3400
O'Connor Woods, A Calif. Corp.
3400 Wagner Heights Rd.
Stockton, CA 95209
Tel: 209-3400
St. Joseph's Regional Health System provides regional management and support functions for St. Joseph's Regional Housing Corp. Sponsored by the Sisters of the Third Order of St. Dominic, Congregation of the Most Holy Name, this non-profit Corp. provides a residential community for seniors offering a variety of living arrangements from active to assisted, and coordinates skilled nursing and rehabilitation services with St. Joseph's Medical Center's subsidiary operation, MEADOWOOD.
SCOTT SINCLAIR, Exec. Dir.
Total Assisted 322
Total Staff 113

Sun Valley
Archdiocese of Los Angeles

Villa Scalabrini
10631 Vinedale St.
Sun Valley, CA 91352
Tel: 818-768-6500; Fax: 818-767-1410
Retirement Center and Special Care Unit.
Missionary Fathers of St. Charles
MARLENE RAINEN, Admin. Retirement Center
Sr. SIENA WALD, O.S.E., Admin. Skilled Nursing Facility
Revs.:
AUGUSTO FECCIA, C.S., Exec. Dir.
SALVINO ZANON, C.S., Pastoral Care
Sisters of the Poor of St. Catherine of Siena.
Bed Capacity 188
Retirement Center 130
Skilled Nursing Unit 58

COLORADO

Colorado Springs
Diocese of Colorado Springs

Medalion (East)
1719 E. Bijou St.
Colorado Springs, CO 80909
Tel: 719-471-4800; Fax: 719-471-4807
An operating unit of Sisters of Charity Health Services Colorado.
Skilled Nursing 45
Assisted Living 25
Apartments 79

Medalion West
417 E. Kiowa St.
Colorado Springs, CO 80903
Tel: 719-471-2578; Fax: 719-471-4807
An operating unit of Sisters of Charity Health Services Colorado.
Assisted Living 32
Apartments 89

Namaste Alzheimer Center
2 Penrose Blvd.
Colorado Springs, CO 80906
Tel: 719-560-2000
An operating unit of Sisters of Charity Health Services Colorado.
Beds 64

**St. Francis Nursing Center*
7550 Assisi Heights
Colorado Springs, CO 80920
Tel: 719-598-1336
Sisters of St. Francis.
JUDITH R. FINE, N.H.A., C.H.E., Admin.

Denver
Archdiocese of Denver

Archdiocesan Housing Committee
1544 Pearl St.
Denver, CO 80203
Tel: 303-830-0215; Fax: 303-830-2885
Archdiocesan Family Housing, Inc., Housing for Low-Income Families:
3700 Humboldt
Denver, CO 80205
1900 S. Raritan
Denver, CO 80223
1300 S. Irving
Denver, CO 80204
800 S. Monaco
Denver, CO 80224
Cathedral Plaza Inc.
1575 Pennsylvania St.
Denver, CO 80203
Tel: 303-837-1424
Housing for Low-Income Elderly:
Holy Family Plaza, Inc.
4300 Vrain
Denver, CO 80212
Tel: 303-455-4433
Marian Plaza, Inc.
1818 Marion St.
Denver, CO 80218
Tel: 303-837-1818
Higgins Plaza, Inc.
1380 Detroit St.
Denver, CO 80206
Tel: 303-320-4990
Madonna Plaza, Inc.
6275 Kearney St.
Commerce City, CO 80022
Tel: 303-289-2626
St. Martin Plaza, Inc.
1300 Bruce Randolph Ave.
Denver, CO 80205
Tel: 303-297-1414
Colorado Affordable Catholic Housing Corporation
1544 Pearl St.
Denver, CO 80203
Tel: 303-830-0215

Damen House
2851 W. 52nd Ave., P.O. Box 11580
Denver, CO 80211
Tel: 303-433-4280
Shelter and Safehouse for Homeless Women and Children.
MARY DOMENICO, Contact person

Dayspring Villa, Inc.
3777 W. 26th Ave.
Denver, CO 80211
Tel: 303-455-5066 (local)
CAROLE HULL, Contact Person

Francis Heights
3805 W. 26th Ave.
Denver, CO 80212
Tel: 303-433-6268
Franciscan Sisters, Daughters of the Sacred Hearts of Jesus and Mary (Wheaton, IL).
Rev. DECLAN A. MADDEN, O.F.M.Conv., Chap.
Housing ministry, low-income family units.
Housing Units 128
Residents 600

Francis Heights, Inc.
3805 W. 26th Ave.
Denver, CO 80211
Tel: 303-433-6268
Franciscan Sisters, Daughters of the Sacred Hearts of Jesus and Mary, (Wheaton, IL).
Rev. DECLAN A. MADDEN, O.F.M., Chap.
Housing Ministry, Senior Citizens and Handicapped.
Housing Units 384
Assisted living units 12
Residents 411

Franciscan Ministries, Inc.
3805 W. 26th Ave.
Denver, CO 80212
Tel: 303-433-6268; Fax: 708-462-4977
Housing for low-income elderly and families.

**Gardens at St. Elizabeth*
(Men and Women)
2835 W. 32nd Ave.
Denver, CO 80211
Tel: 303-477-4442
A division of Centura Health.
Sisters of St. Francis of Colorado Springs (O.S.F.).
CATHEY REE, Admin.
Rev. CHARLES SALMON, Res. Chap.
Sisters 5
Aged Residents 320

Hospice of Peace
1601A Lowell Blvd.
Denver, CO 80204-1545
Tel: 303-575-8393; 575-8350
Home Hospice Care.
JOSEPHINE MONTEZ, Dir.

Mullen Home
3629 W. 29th Ave.
Denver, CO 80211
Tel: 303-433-7221
Sr. PATRICIA FRIEL, Supr.
Rev. Msgr. J. HARLEY SCHMITT, Chap.
Little Sisters of the Poor 13
Aged Residents 67

Westminster
Archdiocese of Denver

Villa Maria, Inc.
2451 W. 82nd Pl.
Westminster, CO 80030-4065
Tel: 303-433-6268 (local); 303-427-4406
CINDY DOHMAN, Admin.

CONNECTICUT

Bethel
Diocese of Bridgeport

Augustana Homes/Bishop Curtis Homes
Simeon Rd.
Bethel, CT 06801
Tel: 203-743-2508
BERNARD E. REIDY, K.C.S.G., Exec. Dir.
CLAIRE HIPP, Project Mgr.

Bridgeport
Diocese of Bridgeport

Augustana Homes Bishop Curtis Homes - Danbury
238 Jewett Ave.
Bridgeport, CT 06606
BERNARD E. REIDY, K.C.S.G., Exec. Dir.

Augustana Homes/Bishop Curtis Homes
525 Palisade Ave.
Bridgeport, CT 06610
Tel: 203-366-4333; Fax: 203-576-6790
Mr. JAMES J. CASEY, Manager
Mrs. LILLIAN ARAUJO, Site Mgr.

Augustana Homes/Bishop Curtis Homes
230 Jewett Ave.
Bridgeport, CT 06606
Tel: 203-372-4301
Mr. BERNARD E. REIDY, K.C.S.G., Exec. Dir.

Bridgeport Diocesan Health Care Corporation
238 Jewett Ave.
Bridgeport, CT 06606
Tel: 203-372-4301
Mr. CARLETON H. PEMBER, III, Dir.

Roncalli Apartments
430 Grant St.
Bridgeport, CT 06610
Tel: 203-384-9984
Rev. EDWARD C. DOHERTY, M.SS.A., Pres.
MARIANN CALLAHAN, L.P.N., Admin.
Affiliate of the Roncalli Institute, Supervised Apartments for the Elderly & Handicapped.

Roncalli Charities Inc.
430 Grant St.
Bridgeport, CT 06610
Tel: 203-384-9984
Rev. EDWARD C. DOHERTY, M.SS.A., Pres.

St. Camillus Home Foundation, Inc.
238 Jewett Ave.
Bridgeport, CT 06606
Fax: 203-353-0550
BERNARD E. REIDY, K.C.S.G., Exec. Dir.

Danbury
Diocese of Bridgeport

The Pope John Paul II Center for Health Care, Inc.
33 Lincoln Ave.
Danbury, CT 06810
Tel: 203-797-9300
Mrs. DIANE A. PIMENTEL, Admin.
Rev. Msgr. DANIEL J. FOLEY, Chap.
Sr. FRANCES SMALKOWSKI, C.F.S.N., Co-Dir. Pastoral Care

The Pope John Paul II Foundation, Inc.
238 Jewett Ave.
Danbury, CT 06606
Most Rev. EDWARD M. EGAN, Chm.
Mr. BERNARD REIDY, K.C.S.G., Exec. Dir.

Deep River
Diocese of Norwich

Mount St. John
135 Kirtland St.
Deep River, CT 06417
Tel: 203-526-5391; Fax: 203-526-3846
Bro. K. PAUL MCGLADE, C.F.C., Exec. Dir.
Rev. THADDEUS (TED) SEWERTZ, C.S.C.
In res.,
Rev. NOEL G. AHREN, O.Carm.
Lay Staff 100
Boys 77

Enfield
Archdiocese of Hartford

The Home for the Aged of the Little Sisters of the Poor
Incorporated Operating as St. Joseph's Residence
1365 Enfield St.
Enfield, CT 06082-4900
Tel: 860-741-0791
Rev. ANDREW SCOPP, S.J.
Little Sisters of the Poor 15
Residents 93
Senior Center 18
Total Assisted 27

Fairfield
Diocese of Bridgeport

Augustana Homes/Bishop Curtis Homes
1677 Post Rd.
Fairfield, CT 06430
Mr. JAMES J. CASEY, Manager, Tel: 203-576-0823

Meriden
Archdiocese of Hartford

Franciscan Family Care Center
267 Finch Ave.
Meriden, CT 06450
Tel: 203-237-8084
Legal Title: *Franciscan Family Care Center, Inc.*
Sr. SHAUN VERGAUWEN, F.S.E., Dir.
Sr. SUZANNE GROSS, F.S.E., Dir. Franciscan Home Care, Tel: 203-238-1441
Franciscan Sisters of the Eucharist 8
Total Assisted 330
Total Staff 75

New Britain
Archdiocese of Hartford

Marian Educational Clinic
314 Osgood Ave.
New Britain, CT 06053
Tel: 860-223-0501
Daughters of Mary of the Immaculate Conception.
Sr. MARY EDMUNDA, D.M., Dir. & Contact
Sisters 2

Monsignor Bojnowski Manor, Inc.
50 Pulaski St.
New Britain, CT 06053
Fax: 860-229-3252
Owned and operated by the Daughters of Mary of the Immaculate Conception.
Sr. MARY DEBORAH, D.M., Exec. Dir.
Skilled Nursing Beds 54
Total Staff 96

St. Lucian's Home for the Aged
532 Burritt St.
New Britain, CT 06053
Tel: 860-223-2123
Daughters of Mary of the Immaculate Conception.
Rev. AUGUSTINE PILATOWSKI, O.F.M.Conv., Chap.
Sisters 2
Residents 42

New Haven
Archdiocese of Hartford

St. Francis Home for Children, Inc.
651 Prospect St.
New Haven, CT 06511
Tel: 203-777-5513; Fax: 203-777-0644
Residential, day treatment, group home, special education, preschool, foster placement adoptions.
Sisters of Mercy, Sisters of Notre Dame.
Rev. JEREMIAH N. MURASSO, Exec. Dir.
Sisters 3
Lay Staff 105
Children 52
Intensive Day Treatment 25
Preschool 25

Norwalk
Diocese of Bridgeport

Notre Dame Convalescent Home
76 W. Rocks Rd.
Norwalk, CT 06851
Tel: 203-847-5893
Sisters of St. Thomas of Villanova.
Mother EDMOND, S.S.T.V., Supr.
Mr. JOHN FARLING, Admin.
Rev. ALBERT W. WATTS, Chap.
Sisters 5
Patients assisted annually 60

Riverside
Diocese of Bridgeport

Augustana Homes of Greenwich/Bishop Curtis Homes
1040 E. Putnam Ave.
Riverside, CT 06878
Mr. JAMES J. CASEY, Manager, Tel: 203-576-0823

Stamford
Diocese of Bridgeport

Augustana Homes/Bishop Curtis Homes - Glenbrook
352 Glenbrook Rd.
Stamford, CT 06902
Tel: 203-576-0823
Mr. JAMES J. CASEY, Manager

St. Camillus Health Center
494 Elm St.
Stamford, CT 06902
Tel: 203-353-0550
Mr. DAVID J. IANACONE, Admin.
LIZ MONTELLI, Asst. Admin.
Rev. PAUL B. LALIC, Chap.
St. Camillus Auxiliary Committee
494 Elm St.
Stamford, CT 06902
Tel: 203-325-0200
St. Camillus Adult Day Care
494 Elm St.
Stamford, CT 06902
Tel: 203-325-0200
AMY HOLLANDER, Dir.

Trumbull
Diocese of Bridgeport

Carmel Ridge
6454 Main St.
Trumbull, CT 06611
Tel: 203-261-2229
Mr. PETER CADY, Site Mgr.

St. Joseph's Housing Corporation
Teresian Towers & Carmel Ridge Estates, 6448 Main St.
Trumbull, CT 06611
Tel: 203-261-2229
Mr. PETER CADY, Site Mgr.

St. Joseph's Manor
6448 Main St.
Trumbull, CT 06611
Tel: 203-268-6204; Fax: 203-268-5271
Sr. MICHELLE ANNE REHO, O.Carm., Admin.
Rev. ALFRED E. RUSSO, Chap.
Most Rev. WALTER W. CURTIS, S.T.D.
Rev. Msgr. THOMAS HENAHAN
Revs.:
CHARLES L. HEWITT (HRT)
JOHN R. O'CONNOR
CHARLES T. KENNEDY (HRT)
PATRICK SPEER (HRT)
Carmelite Sisters for the Aged and Infirm 9
Capacity 297

West Hartford
Archdiocese of Hartford

Saint Agnes Home, Inc.
104 Mayflower St.
West Hartford, CT 06110
Tel: 860-521-7516; Fax: 860-521-6160
For unmarried mothers and their infants.

M. KEEGAN, Exec. Dir.
Bed Capacity 16
Patients assisted annually 43
Total Staff 37

Saint Mary Home
2021 Albany Ave.
West Hartford, CT 06117
Tel: 860-236-1924
Mrs. MAUREEN KOLACZENKO, Admin.
Mrs. GERALYN HINES-IVERSON, R.N., Dir. Nursing
Sr. M. LEO JOSEPH DIVINE, Asst. Admin.
Rev. HERBERT CLARKIN, Res. Chap.
Sisters of Mercy 16
Sisters in Res. 6
Residents 107
Patients assisted annually 217
St. Mary Home, II, Inc.
2021 Albany Ave.
West Hartford, CT 06117
Adult Day Care 21
Staff 6

Willimantic
Diocese of Norwich

Holy Family Home and Shelter, Inc.
88 Jackson St., P.O. Box 884
Willimantic, CT 06226
Tel: 860-423-7719
BONNIE REILEIN, Exec. Dir.
Rev. STEPHEN FRONCKEWICZ, O.S.B., Chap.
Residents 23

Windham
Diocese of Norwich

St. Joseph Living Center
14 Club Rd.
Windham, CT 06280
Tel: 860-456-1107
PATRICIA HAMILL, M.S., Admin.
Dr. MICHAEL KEENAN, Medical Dir.
Sr. MARY ANN, C.S.E., Dir. Nursing Svcs.
Sr. AGNES PATRICIA, C.S.E., Dir. Admissions
JANET GRISWOLD, Dir. Day Care
Rev. WILLIAM J. FLYNN, Chap.
Sisters 3
Lay Staff 141
Capacity 120
Total Assisted 120
Total Staff 144

DELAWARE

Claymont
Diocese of Wilmington

Children's Home, Inc.
2901 Green St.
Claymont, DE 19702
Tel: 302-798-0601
BARBARA GRIECO, M.C., Deputy Dir. & Dir. of Children's Services
Capacity:
Children 40

Hockessin
Diocese of Wilmington

Franciscan Health System/Care at Brackenville
100 St. Clare Dr.
Hockessin, DE 19707
Tel: 302-234-5420

Newark
Diocese of Wilmington

Jeanne Jugan Residence
185 Salem Church Rd.
Newark, DE 19713
Conducted by the Little Sisters of the Poor.
Sr. ANDREA MUNARRIZ, L.S.P., Supr.
Rev. ANTHONY SCHELICH, O.S.F.S.
Residents 83
Sisters 12

Marydale Retirement Village
135 Jeandell Dr.
Newark, DE 19713
Tel: 302-368-2784
Bro. ROBERT GILROY, C.S.C., Admin.
Sr. ALICE PENROSE, S.H.C.J., Pastoral Care Coord.
Apartments for Elderly.
Apartments 108
Residents 120

Our Lady of Grace Home for Children, Inc.
487 E. Chestnut Hill Rd.
Newark, DE 19713
Tel: 302-738-4658; 737-6650
Sr. MARY ANTONEA SLOWIK, C.S.S.F., Admin. & Supr.
Sr. MARY CHARLOTTE WSZOLEK, C.S.S.F., Supr.
Felician Sisters 5
Children 10
Total Assisted 31

Wilmington
Diocese of Wilmington

The Antonian
1701 W. 10th St.
Wilmington, DE 19805
Tel: 302-421-3758
Mrs. CHRISTINE T. SPAGNOLO, Mgr.
Rev. MARIO BUGLIOSI, O.S.F.S., Chap
Congregate Housing for the Elderly.
Residents 150
Apartments 136

Franciscan Health System/Care at Wilmington
801 N. Broom St.
Wilmington, DE 19806
Tel: 302-652-3861

Home of Divine Providence, Inc.-Bayard House
300 Bayard Ave.
Wilmington, DE 19805
Tel: 302-654-1184
EILEEN M. POORTEN, Dir.
Pregnant Teens & Women (12-35)
Residents 25
Staff 13
Total Assisted Annually 400

Ministry of Caring, Inc.
506 N. Church St.
Wilmington, DE 19801-4812
Tel: 302-652-5523; Fax: 302-652-1919
Rev. RONALD GIANNONE, O.F.M.Cap., Exec. Dir.
JAMES A. TEOLI, SR., Assoc. Dir. & Chief Financial Officer
Sr. CAROL SUKITZ, I.H.M., Assoc. Dir. of Program Svcs.
Ms. LOUISA TEOLI, Office Mgr. & Asst.
DEBBE DUNPHY, Exec. Asst.
Sr. MAGDALEN O'HARA, O.S.U., Assoc. Dir. of Human Resources
Sr. SUSAN PLEWS, S.S.N.D., Admin. Asst.
Child Care Center
221 N. Jackson St.
Wilmington, DE 19805-3649
Tel: 302-652-8992; Fax: 302-652-8945
Child care for homeless children, from infancy to 5 years old.
VALERIE MARTIN, Dir.
St. Clare Medical Outreach
7th & Clayton Sts.
Wilmington, DE 19805-3156
Mobile Medical Van which provides health services for the poor.
THOMAS SCOTT, M.D.
MARYANN FAGAN, R.N.
Mary Mother of Hope House Transitional Residence
818 Jefferson St.
Wilmington, DE 19801-1432
Tel: 302-427-9170
Transitional Residence for single women.
Sr. MARY ANNE MATARESE, O.S.B., Mgr.
Capacity 8
House of Joseph II
7-9 W. 18th St.
Wilmington, DE 19802-4833
Hospice for men with AIDS.
Capacity 8
Bro. KEVIN O'LOUGHLIN, O.F.M. Cap., Dir.
Pierre Toussaint Dental Office
830 Spruce St.
Wilmington, DE 19801-4205
Dental office for the homeless.
PAIGE KING, D.M.D.
Angela Merici House
1105 W. 8th St.
Wilmington, DE 19806-4605
Tel: 302-655-4817
Residence for Sisters of St. Francis 3
St. Francis Transitional Residence
103-107 N. Jackson St.
Wilmington, DE 19805-3648
Transitional living for women and children.
EMMA TERRELL, Dir.
House of Joseph Transitional Residence
704 West St.
Wilmington, DE 19801-1523
Transitional residence for men.
Bro. KEVIN O'LOUGHLIN, O.F.M.Cap., Dir.
Samaritan Outreach
1410 N. Claymont St.
Wilmington, DE 19802-5227
Tel: 302-652-0969
Rev. ROBERT LONGO, O.F.M.Cap., Dir.
Social outreach for the homeless.
Mary Mother of Hope House I
1103 W. 8th St.
Wilmington, DE 19806-4605
Tel: 302-652-8532
Sr. MARY ANNE MATARESE, O.S.B., Mgr.
Emergency shelter for homeless women.
Capacity 21
Mary Mother of Hope House II
121 N. Jackson St.
Wilmington, DE 19805-3670
Tel: 302-652-1935
Ms. ELLEN ROBB, Mgr.
Emergency shelter for women with children.
Capacity 23
Mary Mother of Hope House III
515 N. Broom St.
Wilmington, DE 19805-3114
Tel: 302-652-0970
Ms. LINDA MYRIE, Mgr.
Emergency shelter for women with children.
Capacity 21
Job Placement Center
1100 Lancaster Ave.
Wilmington, DE 19805-4009
Tel: 302-652-0917
Ms. JUANITA BEAUFORD, Dir.
Employment agency to assist the poor.
House of Joseph I
1328 W. Third St.
Wilmington, DE 19805-3662
Tel: 302-652-0904
Bro. KEVIN O'LOUGHLIN, O.F.M.Cap., Dir.
Shelter for homeless employable men who are seeking employment.
Capacity 13
Capuchin Friars 2
Emmanuel Dining Room, West
121 N. Jackson St.
Wilmington, DE 19805-3670
Tel: 302-652-3228; Fax: 302-652-2576
Bro. JOHN RUSSO, O.F.M.Cap., Dir.
Ms. MARY TAGGART, Mgr.
Sr. CHRISTINA SEMINATORE, C.D.P., Sec.
Emmanuel Dining Room, East
226 N. Walnut St.
Wilmington, DE 19801-3934
Tel: 302-652-2577
Mr. ODELL PARKER, Mgr.
Emmanuel Dining Room, South
500 Rogers Rd.
New Castle, DE 19720
Tel: 302-577-2951
Ms. EMMA MITCHELL, Mgr.
Ministry of Caring Distribution Center.
1410 N. Claymont St.
Wilmington, DE 19802-5227
Tel: 302-652-0969
Mr. EUGENE MCLAUGHLIN, Mgr.
Ministry of Caring Guild.
506 N. Church St.
Wilmington, DE 19801
BARBRA ANDRISANI, Pres.
ROBERTA CAMPBELL, Treas.

St. Patrick's House, Inc.
115 E. 14th St.
Wilmington, DE 19801
Tel: 302-654-6908
Rev. JAMES F. TRAINOR, Chm. of Board
Affiliated with St. Patrick Parish. Congregate Independent Living Facility for the elderly.
Capacity 16

Seton Villa, Inc.
800 Bellevue Rd.
Wilmington, DE 19809
Tel: 302-762-2982
BARBARA GRIECO, M.C., Deputy Dir. & Dir. Children's Services
Capacity:
Children (ages 5-18) 13

Siena Hall, Inc.
2307 Kentmere Pkwy.
Wilmington, DE 19806
Tel: 302-656-2183
BARBARA GRIECO, M.C., Deputy Dir. & Dir. Children's Services
Capacity:
Children (ages 5-18) 20

DISTRICT OF COLUMBIA

Washington
Archdiocese of New York

Centro Maria, Inc.
650 Jackson St., NE
Washington, DC 20017

Tel: 202-635-1697
For young students and working women.
Sr. MARY CHRISTINE LOPEZ, R.M.I., Supr.
Religious of Mary Immaculate 5
Bed Capacity 54

Archdiocese of Washington

Cardinal O'Boyle Residence for Priests
1150 Varnum St., N.E.
Washington, DC 20017
In res.,
Revs.:
JOSEPH A. O'BRIEN, Rector
JOSEPH BUI-TRANG-NGHIEM, Tribunal
Rev. Msgr. ARMANDO JIMENEZ
Rev. Msgr. JOSEPH W. HARTMAN
Rev. Msgr. LEONARD F. HURLEY, Chap., Carroll Manor
Revs.:
MIGUEL P. QUINONES
ROBERT H. WHARTON
J. GERARD COLE
ROGER P. GALLAGHER
JOHN A. LUBEY
J. EDWARD STUDNEY

Jeanne Jugan Residence-St. Joseph's Villa
4200 Harewood Rd., N.E.
Washington, DC 20017
Tel: 202-269-1831
Little Sisters of the Poor.
Sr. MARY JOSEPH, L.S.P., Admin.
Rev. Msgr. E. ROBERT ARTHUR, Chap.
Sisters 15
Residents 89
Apartments 8
Total Staff 87

FLORIDA

Daytona Beach
Diocese of Orlando

Casa San Pablo
401 N. Ridgewood Ave.
Daytona Beach, FL 32114
Tel: 904-253-2828
Sr. MARY MICHAEL HILL, O.S.F., Admin.
Total Staff 3
Total in Residence 65

Fort Myers
Diocese of Venice

Villa Francisco
2140 Cottage St.
Fort Myers, FL 33901
Tel: 941-332-3229
Very Rev. THOMAS ANGLIM, V.G., Pres.
Sr. MARIE VINCENT CHIARAVALLE, O.S.F., Admin.
Total in Residence 73
Total Staff 2

Jacksonville
Diocese of St. Augustine

All Saints Home
5888 Blanding Blvd.
Jacksonville, FL 32246
ALICE WILBUR, Admin.
Rev. B. BUTLER, Chap.
Physical Therapy, Speech Therapy & Occupational Therapy Available.
Total Staff 110
Residents 120

St. Catherine Laboure Manor
1750 Stockton St.
Jacksonville, FL 32204
Tel: 904-308-4700
Long term health care Skilled Nursing Facility.
Beds 240
Sisters 3
Total Staff 239
Patients assisted annually 884

Melbourne
Diocese of Orlando

Ascension Manor
2960 Pineapple Ave.
Melbourne, FL 32935
Tel: 407-757-9828
JACKIE HAYNES, Mgr.
Total Staff 3
Total in Residence 85

Miami
Archdiocese of Miami

Camillus House, Inc.
P.O. Box 1829
Miami, FL 33101-1829
Food, shelter, clothing, mail, and rehabilitation program.
Bro. PAUL JOHNSON, B.G.S., Exec. Dir., Contact
Little Brothers of the Good Shepherd
Camillus Health Concern, Inc. Medical, legal and social services.
Camillus S.R.O. Residence for graduates of rehabilitation programs.
726 N.E. 1 Ave.
Miami, FL 33132
Tel: 305-374-1065; Fax: 305-372-1402
P.O. Box 1829
Miami, FL 33101-1829
Emergency Service to Homeless, including health care, drug and alcohol rehabilitation, subsidized housing, etc.
Charity Unlimited, Inc.
Buildings & grounds for charitable works.
Total Assisted 433,650
total Staff 70

Gift of Hope, Missionaries of Charity
724 N.W. 17 St.
Miami, FL 33136
Tel: 305-326-0032
Mother TERESA OF CALCUTTA Supr. Gen.
Women's and Children's Shelter
Total Women Assisted 353
Total Children Assisted 142
Soup Kitchen for Men
Total Assisted 45,957
Total Staff 6

Ocala
Diocese of Orlando

Trinity Villas I, Inc.
3728 N.E. 8th Pl.
Ocala, FL 34470-1093
Tel: 904-694-5507; Fax: 904-694-7434
JANE LAMB LAIDLAW, Mgr.
Total Staff 5
Total in Residence 97

Trinity Villas II, Inc.
3728 N.E. 8th Pl.
Ocala, FL 34470-1093
Tel: 904-694-5507; Fax: 904-694-7434
JANE LAMB LAIDLAW, Mgr.
Total Staff 3
Total in Residence 64

Orlando
Diocese of Orlando

Monsignor Bishop Manor Apts., Inc.
824 Borders Cir.
Orlando, FL 32808
Tel: 407-293-3339; Fax: 407-295-3214
Total Staff 6
Total in Residence 182

Ormond Beach
Diocese of Orlando

Prince of Peace Villas, Inc.
664 S. Nova Rd.
Ormond Beach, FL 32174
Tel: 904-673-5080; Fax: 904-673-2008
SUE TYSON, Mgr.

Pensacola
Diocese of Pensacola-Tallahassee

Haven of Our Lady of Peace
5203 N. Ninth Ave.
Pensacola, FL 32504
Tel: 904-477-0531; Fax: 904-477-6782
Daughters of Charity of St. Vincent de Paul.
Mr. J. BRENT WATSON, Admin.
Guests 89
Total Staff 92

Port Charlotte
Diocese of Venice

Bon Secours-St. Joseph Nursing Care Center, Inc.
2370 Harbor Blvd.
Port Charlotte, FL 33952
Tel: 941-624-5966; Fax: 941-624-3963
SCOTT MIXER, Admin.
Patients assisted annually 37,960
Total Staff 128

St. Charles Housing I, Inc.
(aka Villa San Carlos)
2550 Easy St.
Port Charlotte, FL 33952
Tel: 941-624-2266
LYNN STEPHENS, Pres.
Total in Residence 53
Total Staff 8

St. Charles Housing II, Inc.
(aka Villa San Carlos II)
22250 Vick St.
Port Charlotte, FL 33980
Tel: 941-624-4404; Fax: 941-624-5556
Sr. FRANCES KOWALSKI, O.S.F., Resident Mgr.
Ms. LYNN STEPHENS, Pres.
Total in Residence 56
Total Staff 7

Port Orange
Diocese of Orlando

Epiphany Manor
4792 S. Ridgewood Ave.
Port Orange, FL 32127
Total Staff 5
Total in Residence 72

Sarasota
Diocese of Venice

St. Martha's Housing II, Inc.
(Casa Santa Marta II)
800 N. Lemon Ave.
Sarasota, FL 34236
Tel: 941-365-7913
Rev. FAUSTO STAMPIGLIA, S.A.C., Pres.
CORA BEALS, Site Mgr.
Total in Residence 54
Total Staff 2

St. Martha's Housing, Inc.
(Casa Santa Marta)
1576 Eighth St.
Sarasota, FL 34236
Tel: 941-366-4448
Rev. FAUSTO STAMPIGLIA, S.A.C., Pres.
Total in Residence 82
Total Staff 5

Tallahassee
Diocese of Pensacola-Tallahassee

Casa Calderon, Inc.
800 W. Virginia St.
Tallahassee, FL 32304
Tel: 904-222-4026
Rev. Msgr. JAMES AMOS, V.G., Pres.
Mr. ROBERT M. PETERSON, Mgr.

West Palm Beach
Diocese of Palm Beach

Noreen McKeen Residence for Geriatric Care
315 Flagler Dr., S.
West Palm Beach, FL 33401
Tel: 561-655-8544
Sr. M. FIDELIS, O.Carm., Admin.
Rev. EUGENE BANNIN, S.J.

Winter Haven
Diocese of Orlando

Episcopal Catholic Apartments
500 Ave. L N.W.
Winter Haven, FL 33881
Tel: 941-299-4481
Mrs. PEGGY E. KORUSCHAK, Admin.
Total Staff 6
Total in Residence 199

GEORGIA

Atlanta
Archdiocese of Atlanta

Our Lady of Perpetual Help Home
760 Washington St. S.W.
Atlanta, GA 30315
Tel: 404-688-9515
Sisters of St. Dominic.
Legal Title: *Servants of Relief for Incurable Cancer.*
Nursing Home for Free Care of Cancer Patients.
Sr. M. REGIS O.P., Supr.
Rev. RICHARD LOPEZ, Res. Chap.
Sisters 10
Bed Capacity 41
Patients assisted annually 202

Saint Joseph's Mercy Care Services
60 Eleventh St.
Atlanta, GA 30309-3970
Tel: 404-249-8600
Division of Saint Joseph's Health System. Operates

Mercy Mobile Health Care (Atlanta, Georgia). Operates Mercy Senior Care (Rome, Georgia).
Total Staff 102
Sisters 5
Total Assisted 20,000

Savannah
Diocese of Savannah

St. Mary's Home
E. Victory Dr., P.O. Box 3627, Sta. B
Savannah, GA 31404
Tel: 912-236-7164; Fax: 912-236-7164
Sisters of Mercy of the Americas
Sr. MARY ALVIN SEUBOTT, R.S.M., Admin
Sisters 3
Lay Staff 25
Residents 42

HAWAII

Kalaupapa, Molokai
Diocese of Honolulu

Kalaupapa Settlement
Kalaupapa, Molokai, HI 96742
Operated by the State Dept. of Health for treatment of Leprosy.
Mrs. FE AUSTRIA-SCHWIND, Nursing Supvr.
Dr. W. PHILIP JONES, Medical Dir. Settlement
Rev. ARSENE DAENEN, SS.CC., Pastor
Franciscan Sisters of the Third Order 3
Bed Capacity 14
Patients assisted annually 8,782

ILLINOIS

Alton
Diocese of Springfield in Illinois

Catholic Children's Home
1400 State St.
Alton, IL 62002
Tel: 618-465-3594; Fax: 618-465-4023
Mr. LAWRENCE DRURY, Dir.
STEVEN ROACH, Admin.
Children under care 130

Marian Heights Apartments
20 Marian Heights Dr.
Alton, IL 62002
Tel: 618-462-0363
Residence for the Elderly.
Sr. M. ANGELA, O.S.F., Supr.
SUSAN E. BARNETT, Operations Mgr.
Rev. Msgr. JAMES SUDDES, Chap.
Sisters of St. Francis of the Martyr St. George 2
Residents 130

Aurora
Diocese of Rockford

Fox Knoll (Retirement Community)
421 N. Lake St.
Aurora, IL 60506
Tel: 630-844-0380
A Mercy Retirement Community.
Sr. MARCIAN DEISENROTH, R.S.M., Exec. Dir.
Total Staff 60
Total in Residence 165

McAuley Manor
400 W. Sullivan Rd.
Aurora, IL 60506
Tel: 630-859-3700; Fax: 630-264-1862
Sisters of Mercy
Mrs. MARY A. BURNELL, Admin.
Total Staff 130
Bed Capacity 87
Total assisted 120

Bartlett
Archdiocese of Chicago

Bartlett Learning Center
801 W. Bartlett Rd.
Bartlett, IL 60103
Tel: 630-289-4221
Legal Title: *Barlett Learning Center, Inc.*
RUSSELL E. CONRAD, Admin.
Sisters 7
Lay Staff 65
Students 120
Day school program for developmentally delayed and multiple handicapped individuals ages 3 to 21. Accept youth identified LD, BD, EMH, & TMH, Speech/Language Impaired, Autistic.
Sponsored by the Sisters of St. Joseph, Third Order of St. Francis.

Belleville
Diocese of Belleville

Charles and Bertha Hincke Residence for Priests and Sense Residence
2620 Lebanon Ave.
Belleville IL 62221
Tel: 618-234-5722
Owned by Diocese of Belleville.
CAROL KIEFER, Admin.
Guests 15

Meredith Memorial Home
16 S. Illinois St.
Belleville, IL 62220
Tel: 618-233-8780
Owned by the Diocese of Belleville.
Mr. ROBERT L. WEBER, Admin.
Sr. KATHLEEN MORRISSEY, P.H.J.C., Asst. Admin.
Rev. Msgr. LEONARD A. BAUER, Chap., Tel: 618-234-2773
Guests 71

Our Lady of the Snows Apartment Community Retirement Home
9500 W. Illinois Hwy. 15
Belleville, IL 62223
Tel: 618-397-6700
Sr. DORETTA MEIER, Admin.
D. ROBERT MCCARDLE, Exec. Vice Pres.
LUCY NILE, Dir. of Pastoral Care
Revs.:
LINUS J. GARITY (MIL)
RENE P. DU FOUR, O.M.I.
ANDREW G. CHALKEY, O.M.I.
DAVID TARLIZZO, O.M.I.
Guests 175

Bourbonnais
Diocese of Joliet in Illinois

Our Lady of Victory Nursing Home
20 Briarcliff Ln.
Bourbonnais, IL 60914
Tel: 815-937-2022; Fax: 815-937-2026
Servants of the Holy Heart of Mary.
CHERYL GUILD, Admin.
Rev. FRANK CZERWIONKA, C.S.V., Chap.
Bed Capacity 107

Chicago
Archdiocese of Chicago

Big Sisters
203 N. Wabash Ave.
Chicago, IL 60601
Tel: 312-346-0075
Mrs. GERARD V. CRIST, Pres.
Mrs. LAWRENCE J. TARDY, Social Serv. Dir.
Miss VICTORIA R. MANNERINO, Exec. Sec.
Patients assisted annually 200

Catholic Home Care
721 N. LaSalle St.
Chicago IL 60610
Tel: 312-655-7415
Home health agency providing health care to individuals in their homes in Cook and Lake Counties.
ANNE DEMKE, Exec. Dir.

Catholic Home Care Home Services
721 N. LaSalle St.
Chicago, IL 60610
Tel: 312-655-7573
ANNE DEMKE, Exec. Dir.

Cortland Manor Retirement Home
1900 N. Karlov
Chicago, IL 60639
Tel: 773-235-3670
Catholic Charities Housing Development Corporation.
MAUREEN SCHOLLE, Admin.
Capacity 51

House of the Good Shepherd
1114 W. Grace St.
Chicago, IL 60613
Tel: 773-935-3434; Fax: 773-935-3523
Legal Title: *House of the Good Shepherd*
Sisters of The Good Shepherd.
Sisters 7
Part time social workers 6
Abused Women with children.
Capacity 14 Families

Jugan Terrace
2300 N Racine
Chicago, IL 60614
Tel: 773-935-9600; Fax: 773-935-4291
Legal Title: *Little Sisters of the Poor, North Side Chicago, Inc., (HUD subsidized)*
Sr. MARIA CHRISTINE, L.S.P., Admin.
Senior Housing Apts. 50

Little Sisters of the Poor Center for the Aging
2325 N. Lakewood Ave.
Chicago, IL 60614
Tel: 773-935-9600; Fax: 773-935-9614
Legal Title: *Little Sisters of the Poor of Chicago, Inc.*
Sr. MARIA CHRISTINE, L.S.P., Admin. & Supr.
Rev. WALTER HUPPENBAUER, Chap.
Sisters 15
Residents 96
Intermediate and skilled care facility.

Misericordia Home South
2916 W. 47th St.
Chicago, IL 60632
Tel: 773-254-9595
Sr. ROSEMARY R.S.M., Dir.
Sisters of Mercy 9
Patients assisted annually 110
Respite Beds 2
Handicapped children under 22 years of age:
Bed Capacity for Children 110

Misericordia/Heart of Mercy Center
6300 N. Ridge
Chicago, IL 60660
Tel: 773-973-6300
Children and young adults with Developmental disabilities.
Sr. ROSEMARY CONNELLY, R.S.M., Dir.
Sisters 25
Residents 548

Resurrection Retirement Community
7262 W. Peterson Ave.
Chicago, IL 60631
Tel: 773-792-7930
Division of Resurrection Health Care Corporation.
Sr. MARY PAUL SCHUTZ, C.R., Exec. Dir.
Apartments 472

St. Joseph Home of Chicago, Inc.
2650 N. Ridgeway Ave.
Chicago, IL 60647
Tel: 773-235-8600; Fax: 773-235-2933
Legal Title: *St. Joseph Home of Chicago, Inc.*
Franciscan Sisters of Chicago
JANE D. WINTER, Admin.
Rev. CHARLES MROWINSKI, C.R., Chap.
Sisters 6
Licensed Beds 173

St. Joseph's Carondelet Child Center
739 E. 35th St.
Chicago, IL 60616
Tel: 773-624-7443; Fax: 773-624-7676
Legal Title: *St. Joseph's Carondelet Child Center*
Treatment, rehabilitation and education of the dependent emotionally disturbed children and youth.
Sisters of St. Joseph of Carondelet
Mr. JAMES B. MCLAUGHLIN, Exec. Dir.
Rev. CHARLES T. RUBEY, Chap.
Sisters 2
Children 87

St. Mary of Providence
4200 N. Austin Ave.
Chicago, IL 60634
Tel: 773-545-8300; Fax: 773-545-8035
Operated by the Daughters of St. Mary of Providence.
Sr. NANCY MCLENNON, Admin.
Sr. PATRICIA MCCAFFERTY, Supr.
Rev. SALVATORE OGNIBENE, Chap.
Sisters 10
Staff 128
Students 63
Adults 96
Legal Title: *Daughters of St. Mary of Providence*
Education and residential care of developmentally disabled boys, girls and young adults.

Clifton
Diocese of Joliet in Illinois

Merkle-Knipprath Countryside Home
Rte. 1
Clifton, IL 60927
Tel: 815-694-2306
Bro. DAMIEN DEBRAEKELEER, O.S.F., Admin.
Religious 4
Total in Nursing Care 100
Apartment Living 30
Apartment Community and Nursing Center.

Crete
Diocese of Joliet in Illinois

St. James Manor
1251 Richton Rd.

Crete, IL 60417
Tel: 708-672-6700
DIANNE STRUTYNSKI, Admin.
Beds 110
Care of the Elderly.

Darien
Diocese of Joliet in Illinois

Carmelite Carefree Retirement Village
8419 Bailey Rd.
Darien, IL 60561-5361
Tel: 630-960-4060
Rev. RAYMOND J. CLENNON, O.Carm., Dir.
Residents 98

Des Plaines
Archdiocese of Chicago

Holy Family Health Center
2380 Dempster
Des Plaines, IL 60016
Tel: 708-296-3335
Sr. M. ELIZABETH, C.S.F.N., Admin.
Licensed Bed Capacity 362
Intermediate and skilled nursing care facility.
Sponsored by the Sisters of the Holy Family of Nazareth.

Nazarethville
300 N. River Rd.
Des Plaines, IL 60016
Tel: 708-297-5900
Sr. M. AMATA SWEENEY, C.S.F.N., Admin.
Total under care 83
Sponsored by the Sisters of the Holy Family of Nazareth.

Freeport
Diocese of Rockford

St. Joseph Adult Day Care Center
659 E. Jefferson St.
Freeport, IL 61032
Tel: 815-232-6181; Fax: 815-232-6143
Under Auspices of St. Vincent Home for Children.
Mrs. KELLY SCHLEICH, Prog. Dir.
Rev. CLARENCE J. THENNES, Chap.
Sisters 1

St. Joseph Home for the Aged
659 E. Jefferson St.
Freeport, IL 61032
Tel: 815-232-6181; Fax: 815-232-6143
Under auspices of St. Vincent Home for Children.
Mr. RICHARD RIMKUS, Admin.
Rev. CLARENCE J. THENNES, Chap.
Sisters 3
Aged Residents 145

Glenview
Archdiocese of Chicago

Maryhaven Inc.
1700 East Lake Ave.
Glenview, IL 60025
Tel: 708-729-1300; Fax: 708-729-9202
Legal Title: *Maryhaven Inc.*
Home for Aged, intermediate and skilled care facilities, Medicare, Therapy.
Mr. PAUL M. ASSELIN, Admin.
Rev. JOHN E. FLAVIN, Pres.
Capacity 138

Homewood
Archdiocese of Chicago

Mercy Health Care and Rehabilitation Center
19000 S. Halsted St.
Homewood, IL 60430
Tel: 708-957-9200; Fax: 708-799-4787
Affiliate of Mercy Hospital and Medical Center.
Sponsored by the Religious Sisters of Mercy.
Sr. ALICE ANN RHINESMITH, S.P., Admin.
Pastoral Care:
Sr. BERNADETTE MADDEN, R.S.M.
Sr. JOANNE VALLERO, C.S.J.
Bed Capacity 259
Total under care 245

Joliet
Diocese of Joliet in Illinois

Guardian Angel Home
1550 Plainfield Ave.
Joliet, IL 60435
Tel: 815-729-0930; Fax: 815-744-6087
Sponsored by the Sisters of St. Francis of Mary Immaculate.
Child and family welfare agency: residential treatment, therapeutic school, foster care, domestic violence shelter, child abuse prevention center, and counselling.

Our Lady of Angels Retirement Home
1201 Wyoming
Joliet, IL 60435
Tel: 815-725-6631
Sisters of St. Francis of Mary Immaculate
Sr. LILLIAN UJKA, Local Coord.
In res.,
Rev. PATRICK GLEESON, Chap.
Sr. PHYLLIS PITZ, Admin.
Sister Staff 16
Lay Employees 171
Retired Sisters 85
Residents 96

St. Elizabeth Home
704 W. Marion St.
Joliet, IL 60436
Tel: 815-727-0125
Sr. ELLEN THOMAS, R.C., Senior Prog. Dir.
In Residence 11

Villa Franciscan, Franciscan Sisters Health Care Corp.
210 N. Springfield
Joliet, IL 60435
Tel: 815-725-3400; Fax: 815-725-2160
DIANE MIKES, Admin.
Bed Capacity 176
Extended, Intermediate, and Skilled Care, Respite Care, Alzheimer Unit.

Justice
Archdiocese of Chicago

Rosary Hill Home
9000 W. 81st St.
Justice, IL 60458
Tel: 708-458-3040
Operated by the Dominican Sisters of Chicago.
Sr. M. NATALIE, O.P., Supr.
Rev. JOSEPH MIKA, O.F.M., Chap.
Sisters 9
Bed Capacity 48
Number under care 48

Lacon
Diocese of Peoria

St. Joseph's Nursing Home
Lacon, IL 61540
Tel: 309-246-2175
Daughters of St. Francis of Assisi.
Sr. CATHERINE Admin.
Rev. MICHAEL MENNER, Chap.
Sisters 17
Bed Capacity 93
Total Staff 100

Lake Zurich
Archdiocese of Chicago

Mt. St. Joseph Home
24955 North Hwy. 12
Lake Zurich, IL 60047
Tel: 847-438-5050; Fax: 847-438-1561
Intermediate care for developmentally developed women.
Operated by the Daughters of St. Mary of Providence.
Sr. ARLENE RICCIO, Admin.
Rev. ALOYSIUS ROMANSKI, O.F.M.Conv.
Sisters 10
Novices 1
Lay Assistants 190
Residents 137

Lemont
Archdiocese of Chicago

Alvernia Manor
13950 Main St.
Lemont, IL 60439
Tel: 708-257-7721
Sr. GEORGINE HROMA, O.S.F., Admin.
Sisters of St. Francis of Christ King 7
Guests 50

Holy Family Villa
12375 McCarthy Rd.
Lemont, IL 60439
Sisters of St. Casimir
ROBERTA MAGURANY, Admin.
Sisters 3
Residents 99

Mother Theresa Home
1270 Franciscan Dr.
Lemont, IL 60439
Tel: 708-257-5801; Fax: 708-257-1328
Conducted by the Franciscan Sisters of Chicago.
Sr. LORA ANN SLAWINSKI, Admin.
Sisters 5
Residents 150

Lisle
Diocese of Joliet in Illinois

Queen of Peace Center
1910 Maple Ave.
Lisle, IL 60532
Tel: 630-852-5360
Retirement home.
Sr. KAREN NYKIEL, O.S.B., Admin.
Lay Staff 7
Residents 32

Momence
Diocese of Joliet in Illinois

Good Shepherd Manor
P.O. Box 260
Momence, IL 60954
Tel: 815-472-6492; Fax: 815-472-2160
Adult Male DD-MR.
Dr. JAMES CZERWIONKA, Pres. & CEO
DORIS WILLIAMSON, Admin.
Bro. ALPHONSUS BROWN, B.G.S., Asst. Admin.
Rev. ARTHUR LEMRISE, C.S.V., Chap.
Brothers of the Good Shepherd 4
Bed Capacity 120
Permanent Residents 120

Naperville
Diocese of Joliet in Illinois

St. John Vianney Villa
1464 Green Trails Dr.
Naperville, IL 60540-8359
Tel: 630-983-0533
Retirement home for priests.
Revs.:
PATRICK MORAN
WILLIAM RYAN
EUGENE DOHERTY
CARL O'ROURKE
Residents 4

St. Patrick's Residence
1400 Brookdale Rd.
Naperville, IL 60563-2125
Tel: 630-416-6565
Sr. M. ANTHONY DELOURDES, O.Carm., Admin.
Rev. PHILIP DEDERA, Chap.
Carmelite Sisters 10
Beds 210
Residents 210
Total Assisted 300
Total Staff 225

Niles
Archdiocese of Chicago

St. Andrew Home for the Aged
7000 N. Newark Ave.
Niles, IL 60714-4497
Tel: 847-647-8332
Felician Sisters.
JOHN E. KEANE, Admin.
Sr. MARY AGNES, C.S.S.F., Supr.
Sisters 15
Number under care 175

St. Benedict Home for the Aged
6930 W. Touhy Ave.
Niles, IL 60714
Tel: 847-647-0003
Legal Title: *St. Benedict Home for the Aged (Catholic Charities of Chicago)*
Sisters of St. Benedict (Lisle, IL).
KAREN LARSON, Admin.
Rev. FRANCIS SPELLMAN, Chap.
Sisters 7
Residents 130

Northlake
Archdiocese of Chicago

Villa Scalabrini Home for the Aged
480 N. Wolf Rd.
Northlake, IL 60164-1667
Tel: 708-562-0040
Missionaries of St. Charles Scalabrinians.
VIRGINIA BARRY, Admin.
Rev. JOHN DIVITO, C.S., Chap.
Sisters 10
Residents 265

Oak Brook
Diocese of Joliet in Illinois

Mayslake Village
1801 35th St.
Oak Brook, IL 60521
Tel: 630-654-3280
Including Mayslake Villas, Mayslake Manor, and Cloisters Courts.
Senior Citizen Retirement Community.
Rev. LARRY DREFFEIN, O.F.M., Pres.
Mr. MICHAEL A. FRIGO, Admin.
Units 630
Residents 750
Total Staff 35

Oak Park
Archdiocese of Chicago

Ephpheta Center and Hearing Conservation Service
119 S. Harvey Ave.
Oak Park, IL 60302
Legal Title: *Ephpheta Center and Hearing Conservation Service*
Under the direction of the Daughters of the Heart of Mary.
Sr. ANITA BAIRD, D.H.M., Supr.
Sisters 9

Olympia Fields
Archdiocese of Chicago

Mercy Residence at Tolentine Center
20300 Governors Hwy.
Olympia Fields, IL 60461
Tel: 708-748-9500; Fax: 708-481-2090
Sr. ARMELLA GUINEY, R.S.M., Admin.
Sr. CONLETH FOLEY, R.S.M., Asst. Admin.
Sisters 3
Residents 52
Senior citizen housing.

Palatine
Archdiocese of Chicago

St. Joseph's Home for the Elderly
80 W. Northwest Hwy.
Palatine, IL 60067
Tel: 847-358-5700; Fax: 847-358-5763
Legal Title: *Little Sisters of the Poor, Palatine, Inc.*
Operated by the Little Sisters of the Poor.
Sr. ROSE MARIE MAYOCK, Supr.
Rev. ROBERT PIEPER, O.P.
Sisters 15
Guests 68

Palos Park
Archdiocese of Chicago

St. Coletta's of Illinois
123rd and Wolf Rd.
Palos Park, IL 60464
Tel: 708-448-6520
Sponsored by the Sisters of St. Francis of Assisi. Residential care, education, job training & job placement for developmentally disabled children and adults.
Mr. WAYNE A. KOTTMEYER, Exec. Dir.
Residents 138
Students 100
Job Training Clients 165
Infants & Toddlers 30
Divisions:
Lt. Joseph P. Kennedy Jr. School, Palos Hills
Kennedy Job Training Center, Bedford Park
St. Coletta's of Illinois Foundation Affiliate

Park Ridge
Archdiocese of Chicago

Resurrection Nursing and Rehabilitation Center
1001 N. Greenwood
Park Ridge, IL 60068
Tel: 708-692-5600; Fax: 708-692-2305
Legal Title: *Resurrection Health Care*
PATRICIA TIERNAN, Admin.
Skilled Care Bed Capacity 295

Peoria
Diocese of Peoria

Cabrini Hall Maternity Home
2900 W. Heading Ave.
Peoria, IL 61604
Tel: 309-671-5743
For Care of Unwed Mothers.
Staff 12
Capacity 10
Served 38

Catholic Social Service Foster Care Placement
2900 W. Heading Ave.
Peoria, IL 61604
Tel: 309-671-5750; Fax: 309-671-1046
Ms. PEGGY A. ARIZZI, Exec. Dir.
Mr. JEFF TURNBULL, Assoc. Dir.
Mr. TOM FERRUZZA, Primary Care Coord.
ROBERT GAFFRON, Treatment Coord.
RICH COLE, Specialized Foster Care Coord.
TRICIA CUTRER, Training Coord.
ROBERT FOGLESONG, Resource/Licensing Coord.
DEBORAH EASLEY, Chicago Project Coord.
Clients placed in Foster Care during year 1,169
Total in Residence 110
Total Staff 119

Guardian Angel Home
PEGGY ARIZZI
Lawrence Hall, Edward Hall
2900 W. Heading Ave.
Peoria, IL 61604
Tel: 309-671-5760
Treatment for Emotionally Disturbed Youth.
Staff 75
Capacity 38
Served 58

St. Anne Residential Treatment Center
2900 W. Heading Ave.
Peoria, IL 61604
Tel: 309-671-5755
PEGGY ARIZZI, Contact Person
For Single Mothers and Infants/Children.
Staff 43
Served:
Mothers 32
Children 29

St. Augustine Manor
1301 N.E. Glendale Ave.
Peoria, IL 61603
Tel: 309-674-7069
Mr. DICK LANGJAHR, Admin.
In res.,
Most Rev. EDWARD W. O'ROURKE, D.D.
Rev. Msgr. BERNARD A. RENDER
Revs.:
E. C. BLOUGH
JEROME V. MORRISSEY
LAWRENCE M. MORRISSEY
G. RAYMOND SPRAGUE
MICHAEL T. VAN RAES
MARIO W. SHAW
Residents 83
Students 185
Total Staff 21

St. Joseph's Home of Peoria
2223 W. Heading Ave.
Peoria, IL 61604
Tel: 309-673-7425
Sisters of St. Francis of the Immaculate Conception.
Co-Administrators:
Sr. MARY PAUL MAZZORANA
Sr. MARY DRIES
Rev. RICHARD SOSEMAN, Chap.
In res.,
Rev. Msgr. GEORGE A. CARTON
Sisters 10
Residents 189
Retired Sisters 11
Total Assisted 54
Total Staff 105

Red Bud
Diocese of Belleville

Maria Care Center
350 W. South First St.
Red Bud, IL 62278
Tel: 618-282-3891
Under the Sponsorship of the Adorers of the Blood of Christ.
BARBARA WAGNER, Admin.
MARY SAOLIS, Dir. of Pastoral Care
Guests 115

Rock Island
Diocese of Peoria

St. Anthony's Continuing Care Center
767 30th St.
Rock Island, IL 61201
Tel: 309-788-7631
Rev. RAPHAEL FABISH
Sisters 3
Beds 155
Total Assisted 112
Total Staff 123

Rockford
Diocese of Rockford

Cor Mariae Center
3330 Linden Dr.
Rockford, IL 61114
Servant Cor owned and operated retirement center for religious and laypersons assisted living.
Rev. MELVYN J. VLASZ, Sacramental Min.
Ms. CHERYL STOUT, Admin.
Number Assisted 60

St. Anne Center
4405 Highcrest Rd.
Rockford, IL 61107
Tel: 815-229-1999
Servants of the Holy Heart of Mary.
Ms. JUDY K. LARSON, Admin.
Total Staff 165
Bed Capacity 179

St. Anne Place
4444 Brendenwood Rd.
Rockford, IL 61107
Tel: 815-399-6167
Senior Retirement Community.
Total Staff 35
Total Residences
Total in Residence 120

Vianney Oaks
7712 E. McGregor Rd.
Rockford, IL 61102
Tel: 815-965-0910
Office:
1245 N. Court St., P.O. Box 7044
Rockford, IL 61126
Tel: 815-962-3709
A retirement home for priests conducted by the Diocese of Rockford.
Total Staff 1
Total in Residence 4

Springfield
Diocese of Springfield in Illinois

Brother James Court
2500 St. James Rd.
Springfield, IL 62707
Tel: 217-544-4876
Residence for Mentally Retarded Male Adults.
Franciscan Brothers of the Holy Cross.
Bro. RAPHAEL KREIKEMEIER, F.F.S.C., Pres.
Franciscan Brothers of the Holy Cross 3
Bed Capacity 93
Residents 93

Pope John Paul Apartments
1 Pope John Paul Plaza
Springfield, IL 62703
Tel: 217-528-1771; Fax: 217-528-5110
Residence for the Elderly.
Sr. M. BARBARA, O.S.F., Supr.
NORMA JEAN CAPRANICA, Proj. Mgr.
Mr. THOMAS E. REISER, Admin.
Sisters of St. Francis of the Martyr St. George 2
Residents 160

St. Joseph's Home
3306 S. Sixth St. Rd.
Springfield, IL 62703
Tel: 217-529-5596
Residence for the Elderly.
Sr. JUDITH MORRIS, O.S.F., Admin.
Sr. M. PATRICIA MASTERSON, O.S.F., Asst. Admin.
Rev. Msgr. JOHN BRETZ, Chap.
Sisters of St. Francis of the Immaculate Conception 8
Residents 110

St. Monica's Center
109 E. Lawrence Ave.
Springfield, IL 62704
Tel: 217-523-7922; Fax: 217-525-8241
Maternity Home For Care of Unwed Mothers & Residential Care for Adolescent Women.
Mr. LAWRENCE P. DRURY, Dir.
JUDITH A. COMERIO, Admin.
Bed Capacity 17
Patients assisted annually 135
Out-patient Counselling 70

Wheaton
Diocese of Joliet in Illinois

Marian Park, Inc.
26 W. 171 Roosevelt Rd., P.O. Box 667
Wheaton, IL 60187
Tel: 630-665-9100
Franciscan Sisters, Daughters of the Sacred Hearts

of Jesus and Mary, (Wheaton, IL).
RAY WOJCIK, Pres. Housing Ministry
Apartments 208
Senior Citizen Residents 117
Low Income Family Units 91
Residents 470

Wheeling
Archdiocese of Chicago

Addolorata Villa, Inc.
555 McHenry Rd.
Wheeling, IL 60090
Tel: 708-537-2900; Fax: 708-215-5805
Home for the aged and independent living apartments.
Mr. GERALD B. KINNEY, CFACHCA, CEO & Pres.
Sr. PATRICIA A. FERGUSON, O.S.M., Asst. Admin.
Ms. NANCY LABIAK, Dir. Mission Services
Mrs. BETTY SKONIECZNY, Pastoral Care Coord.
Rev. MARION J. SNIEG, Chap.
Servants of Mary 20
Skilled 80
Intermediate 10
Sheltered 45
Independent Living Apartments 100

INDIANA

Avilla
Diocese of Fort Wayne - South Bend

LaVerna Terrace Apartments
517 N. Main St.
Avilla, IN 46710
Tel: 219-897-2093
Conducted by Franciscan Sisters Health Care Corp.
SHARON MASEAR, Mgr.
In res.,
Rev. DANIEL LEEUW Tel: 219-897-3922
Apartments 51
Total Assisted

Sacred Heart Home
515 N. Main St.
Avilla, IN 46710-9602
Tel: 219-897-2841
Legal Title: *Franciscan Sisters Health Care Corporation*
NANCY K. DANIEL, Admin.
Sr. MARY WILLIAM HUGHES, O.S.F., Religious Supr.
Rev. DANIEL LEEUW, Chap.
Staff 155
Total assisted 133

Beech Grove
Archdiocese of Indianapolis

St. Paul Hermitage
501 N. 17th Ave.
Beech Grove, IN 46107
Tel: 317-786-2261
Sisters of St. Benedict of Beech Grove, IN, Inc.
Sr. PATRICIA DEDE, O.S.B., Admin.
Rev. KEVIN RYAN, O.S.B.
Sisters 12
Total Staff 92
Residents 96

Crown Point
Diocese of Gary

St. Anthony Home, Inc.
203 Franciscan Dr.
Crown Point, IN 46307-4824
Tel: 219-757-6281
STEPHEN J. BARDOCZI, Admin.
Pastoral Care Team:
Revs.:
ANTHONY JANIK, O.F.M.
CARMEN SCUDERI, O.F.M.
MYRON LOWICZ, O.F.M.
Priests 2
Franciscan Sisters of Chicago 24
Total Staff 650
Residents 229

Delphi
Diocese of Lafayette in Indiana

St. Elizabeth Healthcare Center
701 Armory Rd.
Delphi, IN 46923
Fax: 317-564-6384
Rev. RICHARD W. PUETZ, Chap.
Managed by St. Elizabeth Hospital, Lafayette. Owned by Sisters of St. Francis Health Services, Inc.
Total Assisted 270
Total Staff 92

East Chicago
Diocese of Gary

Carmelite Home for Girls
4840 Grasselli Ave.
East Chicago, IN 46312
Tel: 219-397-1085; Fax: 219-392-3574
Sr. MARIA GIUSEPPE MOXLEY, Supr.
Carmelite Sisters of the Divine Heart of Jesus 4
Total Staff 30
Girls 54

Evansville
Diocese of Evansville

The Regina Continuing Care Center
3900 Washington Ave.
Evansville, IN 47714
Tel: 812-479-4226
Mrs. ANN M. MORROW, Admin.
Beds 128
Nursing Patients 128

St. John's Home for the Aged
1236 Lincoln Ave.
Evansville, IN 47714
Tel: 812-464-3607
Sr. MARY MICHAEL NICKLES, L.S.P., Supr.
Rev. Msgr. CLARENCE LINDAUER, Chap.
Little Sisters of the Poor 14
Residents 70

Seton Residence
9200 New Harmony Rd.
Evansville, IN 47720-8918
Tel: 812-963-7600
Home for the Senior Sisters of the Daughters of Charity of St. Vincent de Paul.
Sr. ANTHONY PRUGGER, Admin.
Sr. GERTRUDE BASTNAGEL, Supr.
Rev. GLENNON E. FIGGE, C.M., Chap.
Senior Sisters 53

Fort Wayne
Diocese of Fort Wayne - South Bend

Saint Anne Home & Retirement Community
1900 Randallia Dr.
Fort Wayne, IN 46805
Tel: 219-484-5555
A Catholic Charities Service of the Fort Wayne-South Bend Diocese.
MARY E. HAVERSTICK, Admin.
Rev. FRANK KRONEWITTER, Chap.
In res.,
Rev. LOUIS ZENZ
Staff 185
Residents 204

Hammond
Diocese of Gary

Albertine Home
1501 Hoffman St.
Hammond, IN 46327
Tel: 219-937-0575
Sr. LORETTA SOJA, Dir.
Albertine Sisters 11
Guests 35

Carmelite Home for Boys
4007 Sheffield Ave.
Hammond, IN 46327
Tel: 219-931-6451
Sr. M. LUCY CarmelD.C.J., Supr.
Sr. M. FRANCIS XAVIER, Carmel.D.C.J., Admin.
Carmelite Sisters of the Divine Heart of Jesus 4
Total Staff 47
Boys (4-18 yrs.) 62

Indianapolis
Archdiocese of Indianapolis

St. Augustine Home, Little Sisters of the Poor
2345 W. 86th St.
Indianapolis, IN 46260
Tel: 317-872-6420
Sr. JOSEPHINE Supr.
Rev. ADRIAN FIGUEROLA, Chap.
Sisters 13
Total Staff 80
Residents 100

Jasper
Diocese of Evansville

Providence Home, Nursing Home for the Needy
520 W. Ninth St.
Jasper, IN 47546
Tel: 812-482-6603
Conducted by the Sons of Divine Providence.
Revs.:
THADDEUS J. SZTUCZKO, F.D.P., Admin.
ANGELO QUADRINI, Supr.
Priests 4
Residents 60

Lafayette
Diocese of Lafayette in Indiana

St. Anthony Health Care
1205 N. 14th St.
Lafayette, IN 47904
Tel: 317-423-4861; Fax: 317-742-8790
Rev. JOHN A. BACH, Chap.
Total Staff 110
Bed Capacity 120
Residents 115

New Albany
Archdiocese of Indianapolis

Mercy Long Term Care Initiatives dba Providence Retirement Home
703 E. Spring St.
New Albany, IN 47150
Tel: 812-945-5221; Fax: 812-945-2614
Sisters of Mercy.
JANE F. COOK, Admin.
Sisters 4
Total Staff 62
Residents 103

Notre Dame
Diocese of Fort Wayne - South Bend

University Health Services
Notre Dame, IN 46556
Tel: 219-239-8013
In res.,
Rev. EDMUND GOEDERT, C.S.C.
Patients assisted annually 21,000

San Pierre
Diocese of Gary

Holy Cross Care Services dba Little Company of Mary Health Facility, Inc.
7520 S. U.S. Hwy. 421
San Pierre, IN 46374-4275
Tel: 219-828-4111; Fax: 219-828-4172
Comprehensive Nursing Care Home.
Mr. STEVEN J. MINNIEAR, Admin.
EDWARD B. NEWMAN, Pres. & CEO
Rev. WILLIAM J. SPRANGER, Chap.
Priests 1
Beds 200
Patients assisted annually 214

Schererville
Diocese of Gary

Hoosier Boys' Town
7403 Cline Ave.
Schererville, IN 46375
Tel: 219-838-7723
A residential care facility for abused, neglected boys from 10-18 years of age.
Boys 68

Terre Haute
Archdiocese of Indianapolis

Gibault School for Boys
6301 S. U.S. Hwy. 41, P.O. Box 2316
Terre Haute, IN 47802-0316
Tel: 812-299-1156
School for delinquent boys, sponsored by the Knights of Columbus of Indiana.
Mr. DANIEL P. MCGINLEY, A.C.S.W., Exec. Dir.
Boys 147

IOWA

Burlington
Diocese of Davenport

St. Francis Continuation Care and Nursing Home
Burlington, IA 52601
Tel: 319-752-4564
Sr. BERNADETTE DUMAN, C.D.P., Admin.
Sr. M. DOLORITA, O.S.F., Supr.
Rev. THOMAS J. REILMAN, Chap.
Sisters of the Third Order of St. Francis 3
Bed Capacity 88
Independent Living Unit 12
Patients assisted annually 169

**Young House Family Services, Inc.*

Central Office, 724 N. 3rd St., P.O. Box 845
Burlington, IA 52601
Tel: 319-752-4000; Fax: 319-752-6933
JACK ESCORCIA, Admin.
LYNNDA STOGDILL, Asst. Admin./Controller
Woodlands Treatment Center
Sullivan Slough Rd.
Burlington, IA 52601
Tel: 319-753-0700
JOHN KORB, Coord.

**Christamore House Incorporated*
701 Broadway St.
Burlington, IA 52601
Tel: 319-385-3330
JON COON, Coord.
Total Assisted 45
Total Staff 30

Carroll
Diocese of Sioux City

St. Anthony Nursing Home
406 E. Anthony St.
Carroll, IA 51401
Tel: 712-792-3581
GARY RIEDMANN, Admin.
Rev. ROBERT L. LEITING, Chap.
Residents 79

Cedar Rapids
Archdiocese of Dubuque

Hallmar-Mercy Medical Center
701 Tenth St., S.E.
Cedar Rapids, IA 52403
Sisters of Mercy
Cedar Rapids Regional, owned and operated by Mercy Medical Center. Home for Aged.
Mr. A. JAMES TUIKER, CEO
Total Assisted 37
Total Staff 30
Residents 59

Clinton
Diocese of Davenport

The Alverno Health Care Facility
Clinton, IA 52732
Tel: 319-242-1521; Fax: 319-243-3016
Sr. RUTH A. COX, O.S.F., Pres. & CEO
Rev. JOHN STACK, Chap.
Sisters of St. Francis, Clinton, IA 3
Bed Capacity 138
Total Staff 185

Arch Office
Box 278
Clinton, IA 52733-0278
Tel: 319-243-9035
Arch I
402 S. Fourth St.
Clinton, IA 52732
Tel: 319-243-3980
Arch II
734 Fifth Ave. S.
Clinton, IA 52732
Tel: 319-242-5082
Arch III
505 7th Ave. S.
Clinton, IA 52732
Tel: 319-242-8740
Total Assisted 18
Total Staff 10

Cresco
Archdiocese of Dubuque

Elder Hospitality of Iowa, Inc.
Heritage Haven, 301 First Ave.
Cresco, IA 52136
Tel: 319-547-3325
Mailing Address:—c/o Archdiocese of Dubuque
P.O. Box 479
Dubuque, IA 52004-0479
JO GLASSER, Vice Pres.
BONNIE FELTEN, Housing Coord.
RICHARD BERENDES, Admin./Extended Care
Franciscan Sisters of Perpetual Adoration, La Crosse, Wisconsin and Mayo Foundation, Rochester, MN
Elderly housing for low income. HUD section 202.
Units 12
Elder Hospitality of Iowa II, Inc.
Heritage Haven, 509 Goose Island Dr.
Decorah, IA 52101
Tel: 319-382-2863
Mailing Address:—c/o Archdiocese of Dubuque
P.O. Box 479
Dubuque, IA 52004-0479
JO GLASSER, Vice Pres.
BONNIE FELTEN, Housing Coord.
RICHARD BERENDES, Admin./Extended Care
Elderly housing for low income. HUD section 202.
Units 24

Davenport
Diocese of Davenport

Kahl Home for the Aged and Infirm
1101 W. Ninth St.
Davenport, IA 52804
Tel: 319-324-1621
Carmelite Sisters for the Aged and Infirm.
Sr. M. LOIS JOSEPH, O.Carm., Supr. & Admin.
In res.,
Revs.:
PASQUALE FERRARA
JOSEPH A. HRATZ
HERMAN A. STRUB
RICHARD J. VON AH
Sisters 7
Beds 134
Total Staff 150

Des Moines
Diocese of Des Moines

House of Mercy
1409 Clark St.
Des Moines, IA 50314-1964
Tel: 515-243-2424; Fax: 515-243-0318
Mr. TODD BEVERIDGE, Dir.

Dubuque
Archdiocese of Dubuque

Holy Family Hall Infirmary
3340 Windsor Ave.
Dubuque, IA 52001-1300
Tel: 319-583-9786; Fax: 319-583-3250
Sisters of St. Francis, Dubuque.
Rev. WILLIAM E. WILKIE, Chap.
Sr. MARGE STAUDT, O.S.F., Dir. Sister Support Svcs.
Bed Capacity 98
Professed Sisters 89
Patients assisted annually 148

Marian Hall Infirmary
1050 Carmel Dr.
Dubuque, IA 52003
Tel: 319-556-5474
Sr. MARY AGNES O'CONNOR, B.V.M., Admin.
Rev. Msgr. ROBERT R. VOGL, Chap.
Professed Sisters 133
Bed Capacity 133

Padre Pio Health Care Center, Inc. dba Stonehill Care Center
3485 Windsor Ave.
Dubuque, IA 52001-1312
Tel: 319-557-7180; Fax: 319-557-8934
JOHN SCHMIDT, Pres.
Sr. DOLORES ULLRICH, O.S.F., Admin.
Sisters of St. Francis of the Holy Family 10
Staff 246
Residents 250
Stonehill Benevolent Foundation
GEORGE FREUND, Pres. Stonehill Benevolent Foundation Board
Sponsored by Sisters of St. Francis of the Holy Family.

St. Dominic Villa
Cardiff St. and Mazzuchelli Heights
Dubuque, IA 52001-7399
Community infirmary and staff residence.
Dominican Sisters (Sinsinawa, WI).
Sr. MARGARET MARY O'NEILL, O.P., Prioress
Sr. MARIAN DE GROOD, O.P., Asst. Prioress
Sr. MARYANN TRANEL, O.P., Admin.
Part-time Chaplains:
Revs.:
BRIAN BRICKER, O.P.
JOSEPH FOGARTY, O.P.
Sisters 15
Lay Staff 126
Patients assisted annually 110

Villa Raphael
1235 Mt. Loretta Ave.
Dubuque, IA 52003
Tel: 319-583-4904
Administered by the Archdiocese of Dubuque.
Sr. MARY PIERRE KOLLASCH, P.B.V.M., Coord.
Accommodations for 16 priests.
Total Staff 7
Total in Residence 16

Dyersville
Archdiocese of Dubuque

Mercy Health Center St. Mary's Unit-Oakcrest Manor
(Div. of Mercy Health Services)
1111 Third St., S.W.
Dyersville, IA 52040
Tel: 319-875-7101; Fax: 319-875-2957
Sr. HELEN HUEWE, O.S.F., Pres.
Bed Capacity 40
Total Staff 26
Patients assisted annually 60

Fort Dodge
Diocese of Sioux City

The Marian Home
2400 Sixth Ave. N.
Fort Dodge, IA 50501
Mr. GERALD BRUENING Admin.
Rev. EUGENE F. WALDING
Guests 97
Total in Residence 29

Johnston
Diocese of Des Moines

Bishop Drumm Retirement Center
5837 Winwood Dr.
Johnston, IA 50131
Tel: 515-270-1100; Fax: 515-276-1714
In res.,
Rev. THOMAS M. DECARLO, Res. Chap.
Sisters of Mercy of the Americas (Omaha Province) 7
Care Center Residents 150
Apartment Residents 94
McAuley Terrace Apts.
5921 Winwood Dr.
Johnston, IA 50131
Tel: 515-270-6640

Sioux City
Diocese of Sioux City

Holy Spirit Retirement Home
1701 W. 25th St.
Sioux City, IA 51103
Tel: 712-252-2726
PATRICK J. TOMSCHA, Admin.
Rev. LEROY SEUNTJENS
Guests 94

St. Anthony's Orphanage
(Iowa Corporation)
Mailing Address: Catholic Charities of the Diocese of Sioux City
1601 Military Rd., P.O. Box 2025
Sioux City, IA 51104
Tel: 712-252-4547

KANSAS

Concordia
Diocese of Salina

Mount Joseph Senior Community
Concordia, KS 66901
Tel: 913-243-1347; Fax: 913-243-1907
Owned & operated by the Sisters of St. Joseph of Wichita, via Christi, Inc., Wichita, KS.
Mrs. GRETCHEN L. BARCLAY, Admin.
JANET G. CHAPMAN, CEO
Rev. HENRY KIEFFER, Chap.
Sisters 3
Residents 108
Retirement Apartments 12

Hays
Diocese of Salina

St. John's New Horizons
2225 Canterbury
Hays, KS 67601
Tel: 913-628-8742
GEORGE GATSCHET, Admin.
Sr. VERA BITTEL
Residents 45
St. Elizabeth of Hungary Home Health Agency
Semi-independent Living Apartments 10
Assisted Living Units 43

Kansas City
Archdiocese of Kansas City in Kansas

Marian Hall
1920 Tauromee
Kansas City, KS 66102
Tel: 913-621-4302
Sr. SUSAN PRYOR, S.C.L., Admin.
Total in Residence 53
Total Staff 13

Providence Place
8909 Parallel

Kansas City, KS 66112
Tel: 913-596-4200
Sisters 1
Total Staff 60
Total Residents 77

St. Joseph Care Center
LTC
759 Vermont Ave.
Kansas City, KS 66101
Tel: 913-621-6800
Mr. Frank T. Trimboli, Admin.
Owned and operated by Catholic Housing Services, Inc.
Intermediate and skilled nursing care and independent boarding.
In res.,
Most Rev. Marion F. Forst
Sisters of Charity of Leavenworth 4
Total Staff 220
Total Residents 240

Manhattan
Diocese of Salina

St. Joseph Senior Community, Inc.
2423 Kimball Ave.
Manhattan, KS 66502
Tel: 913-539-7671
Owned & operated by the Via Christi Health System of Wichita.
Residents 85

Mulvane
Diocese of Wichita

Villa Maria
116 S. Central
Mulvane, KS 67110
Tel: 316-777-1129; Fax: 316-777-4406
Sandy Schmidt Leach, Admin.
Home for Aging Men and Women.
Adorers of the Blood of Christ 7
Guests 63

Overland Park
Archdiocese of Kansas City in Kansas

Villa St. Joseph Nursing Home
11901 Rosewood
Overland Park, KS 66209
Tel: 913-345-1745
Ms. Katharine Ensign, Admin.
Total Staff 375
Total Assisted 203

Victoria
Diocese of Salina

St. John's Rest Home
701 Seventh St.
Victoria, KS 67671
Tel: 913-735-2208
Bernadette Smith, Admin.
Rev. Frank Grinko, O.F.M.Cap., Chap.
Residents 90

Wichita
Diocese of Wichita

Catholic Care Center, Inc.
6700 E. 45th St., N.
Wichita, KS 67226
Tel: 316-744-2020
Fred Hermes, CEO
Gregory J. Lohkamp, Admin.
Rev. Ronald M. Gilmore, Chap.
Sisters 8
Residents 178
Operated by Catholic Diocese of Wichita.

Georgetown Village, Inc.
1655 Georgetown St.
Wichita, KS 67218
Staff 70
Residences 200
Residents 215

KENTUCKY

Cold Spring
Diocese of Covington

Campbell Lodge Boys Home
150 Skyline Dr.
Cold Spring, KY 41076-2099
Tel: 606-781-1214
Ms. Kathy Lee Kirst, Dir.
Boys 50

Covington
Diocese of Covington

Diocesan Catholic Children's Home
Orphanage Rd., P.O. Box 17007
Fort Mitchell, KY 41017-2730
Sisters of Notre Dame 6
Lay Staff 43
Children in Residence 28
Students 21
Sr. Jean Marie Hoffman, S.N.D., Exec. Dir. & Religious Supr.
Sr. Pamela Mae Geiger, S.N.D., Prin.

Madonna Manor, Inc.
2344 Amsterdam Rd.
Villa Hills, KY 41017-3712
Tel: 606-341-3981
Sisters of St. Benedict 11
Patients assisted annually 60
49 Independent living apartments with 54 residents
Sr. Charles Wolking, O.S.B., Admin.
Rev. Joseph Broering, Chap.

St. Charles Care Center, Inc.
500 Farrell Dr.
Covington, KY 41011-3798
Tel: 606-331-3224
Sr. Mary Luann Bender, S.N.D., Admin.
Rev. Charles E. Weber, Chap.
Sisters of Notre Dame 7
Beds 149
Assisted Living Apartments 60
Independent Living Apartments 12
Independent Living Cottages 35
Total Assisted 371
Adult Day Health Program & Licensed Physical Therapy Department.

Fort Thomas
Diocese of Covington

Carmel Manor
100 Carmel Manor Rd.
Fort Thomas, KY 41075-2395
Tel: 606-781-5111
Carmelite Sisters for the Aged and Infirm.
Sr. Mary David, O.Carm., Admin.
Rev. Gary A. Miller, Chap.
Residents 145

Regina Cleri Home for Retired Priests
100 Carmel Manor Rd.
Fort Thomas, KY 41075-2395
Tel: 606-781-5111
Carmelite Sisters for the Aged and Infirm.
Sr. Mary David, O.Carm., Admin.
Rev. Gary A. Miller, Chap.
Residents 6

Knottsville
Diocese of Owensboro

Bishop Soenneker Home
9545 Kentucky 144
Philpot, KY 42366
Tel: 502-281-4881
Sr. Mary Raymonde Carrat, A.D., Admin.
Residents 63

Louisville
Archdiocese of Louisville

Boys' Haven
2301 Goldsmith Ln.
Louisville, KY 40205
Tel: 502-458-1171; Fax: 502-451-2161
For dependent, neglected, or abused boys, 12 to 18 years of age.
Mr. Jerome A. Weber, Exec. Dir.
Rev. James C. Maloney, Chap.
Number of Boys in Home 30

Caritas Health Services, Inc. dba Caritas Peace Center
2020 Newburg Rd.
Louisville, KY 40205
Tel: 502-451-3330
Hospital for Psychiatric Illness.
Sisters of Charity of Nazareth Health System.
Sisters 7
Bed Capacity 416
Patients assisted annually 2,000

Franciscan Health Care Center/Retirement Center
3625 Fern Valley Rd.
Louisville, KY 40219
Rev. Mark Sandford, O.F.M., Chap.
Nursing Facility Beds 150
Legal Title: *Sisters of St. Francis Health Services, Inc. dba Franciscan Health Care Center*

Marian Home
3105 Lexington Rd.
Louisville, KY 40206
Tel: 502-893-0121; Fax: 502-896-3925
Sr. Assumpta Devine, O.S.U., Admin.
Rev. Joseph T. Merkt, Chap.
Staff Sisters 10
Residents 70

Maryhurst
1015 Dorsey Ln.
Louisville, KY 40223
Tel: 502-245-1576; Fax: 502-245-4737
Sisters of the Good Shepherd.
Sr. M. Bernadette Faulhaber, R.G.S., Supr.
Judith Lambeth, Exec. Dir.
Sisters 3
Students 79

Nazareth Home
2000 Newburg Rd.
Louisville, KY 40205
Tel: 502-459-9681; Fax: 502-456-9077
Sisters of Charity of Nazareth.
Joyce Denczek, CEO & Admin.
Rev. Germain Legere, C.P., Chap.
In res.,
Revs.:
Linus T. Giesler
Paul M. Russell
Fabian Ayers, C.R.
Staff Sisters 14
Residents 168

Sacred Heart Home, Inc.
(Rudd-Taylor Memorial)
2120 Payne St.
Louisville, KY 40206
Tel: 502-895-9888; 895-9425; Fax: 502-894-9619
Sisters of Mercy.
Mercy Health System. Cincinnati Regional Community.
Leslie A. Wilson, Admin.
Rev. Louis Miller, Chap.
Sisters 2
Residents 111
Capacity 112
Mercy Assoc. 1

St. Joseph Catholic Orphan Society
2823 Frankfort Ave.
Louisville, KY 40206
Tel: 502-893-0241; Fax: 502-896-2394
Rev. Herman J. Naber, Exec. Dir.
Mr. Norbert C. Nopper, Pres.

St. Joseph Children's Home
2823 Frankfort Ave.
Louisville, KY 40206
Tel: 502-893-0241; Fax: 502-896-2394
Rev. Herman J. Naber, Exec. Dir.
Mr. Dennis Davis, Assoc. Dir. Residential Care
Ursuline Sisters 1
Children 53

St. Joseph Home for the Aged
15 Audubon Plaza Dr.
Louisville, KY 40217
Fax: 502-636-2239
Sr. Marie Mayock, Admin.
In res.,
Rev. John B. Lenahan
Legal Title: *Home for the Aged of the Little Sisters of the Poor*

St. Thomas Orphan Society, Inc.
P.O. Box 1073
Louisville, KY 40201

St. Vincent's Orphan Society, Inc.
P.O. Box 1073
Louisville, KY 40201

Owensboro
Diocese of Owensboro

Carmel Home
2501 Old Hartford Rd.
Owensboro, KY 42303
Tel: 502-683-0227
Carmelite Sisters of the Divine Heart of Jesus
Sr. M. Francis Teresa Scully, Carmel.D.C.J., Supr.
Rev. Joseph Rhodes, Chap.
Sisters 4
Residents 113

Versailles
Diocese of Lexington

Taylor Manor Nursing Home
300 Berry Ave.

Versailles, KY 40383
Tel: 606-873-4201
Sr. MARY CHRISTINA MURRAY, S.J.W., Admin.
Rev. MAURICE J. BRINKER, Chap.
Sisters of St. Joseph the Worker 4
Patients assisted annually 82

LOUISIANA

Alexandria
Diocese of Alexandria

Our Lady's Manor, Inc.
402 Monroe St.
Alexandria, LA 71301
Tel: 318-473-2560
Mrs. JOANN BARONNE, Admin.
Apartments 114

St. Mary's Residential Training School, Inc.
P.O. Box Drawer 7768
Alexandria, LA 71306
Tel: 318-445-6443; Fax: 318-449-8520
Congregation of the Sisters of Our Lady of Sorrows of the U.S.A., Inc.
Sr. SERAPHINE RICCI, O.L.S., Admin.
Sisters 8
Lay Staff 270
Beds 152
Students 152

Baton Rouge
Diocese of Baton Rouge

Assisi Homes, Inc., of Our Lady of the Lake Medical Center
5000 Hennessy Blvd.
Baton Rouge, LA 70808-4398
Tel: 504-765-6565
Mr. ROBERT C. DAVIDGE, Pres. & CEO
Assisi Village, Inc., of Our Lady of the Lake Medical Center
7585 Bishop Ott Dr.
Baton Rouge, LA 70806-8922
Tel: 504-927-5070
Senior citizens' residence.
Calais House, Inc., of Our Lady of the Lake Medical Center
7545 Bishop Ott Dr.
Baton Rouge, LA 70806-8900
Tel: 504-927-1889
Senior citizens' residence.
Villa St. Francis, Inc., of Our Lady of the Lake Medical Center
7575 Bishop Ott Dr.
Baton Rouge, LA 70806-8906
Tel: 504-927-0070
Housing facilities for elderly and handicapped persons.

Ollie Steele Burden Manor
4250 Essen Ln.
Baton Rouge, LA 70809-2196
Tel: 504-926-0091; Fax: 504-926-4937
Our Lady of the Lake Regional Medical Center.
Rev. MARCELLUS MOORMAN, O.F.M., Chap.
Staff 170
Bed Capacity 184

Belle Chasse
Archdiocese of New Orleans

Padua Community Services Pediatric Residential Program
200 Beta St.
Belle Chasse, LA 70037-1499
Tel: 504-392-0502; Fax: 504-392-5411
Residential Facility for Severely-Profoundly Retarded and Multihandicapped Children.
Ms. JENNY VIEITO, Admin.

Forest Hill
Diocese of Alexandria

Our Lady of Guadalupe Mission
10 Butter Cemetery Rd.
Forest Hill, LA 71430
Mailing Address:
4400 Coliseum Blvd.
Alexandria, LA 71303
Rev. PEDRO J. SIERRA-POSADA
Franciscan Religious of Our Lady of Refuge 3

La Place
Archdiocese of New Orleans

Place Dubourg, Inc.
201 Rue Dubourg
La Place, LA 70068-2433
Tel: 504-652-1981; Fax: 504-651-6147
Ms. CHRISTINE PALMISANO, Admin.
Units 115
Total Staff 8
Total in Residence 119

Lafayette
Diocese of Lafayette

Bethany M H.S. Health Care Center
P.O. Box 2308
Lafayette, LA 70502
Tel: 318-234-2459
Sisters of the Most Holy Sacrament 12
Bed Capacity 42

Village du Lac, Inc.
1404 Carmel Ave.
Lafayette, LA 70501
Tel: 318-234-5106
Community housing for the handicapped and elderly with low income. Sponsored by the Diocese.
Mr. J. BERNEL FONTENOT, Dir.
Residents 200

Mandeville
Archdiocese of New Orleans

Rouquette Lodge
St. Tammany Manor, Inc.
4300 Hwy. 22
Mandeville, LA 70448-2824
Tel: 504-626-5217; Fax: 504-626-9226
Residence for Senior Citizens
Bro. HAROLD EHLINGER, C.S.C., Admin.
Residential Units 120
Rouquette II
Residential Units 51

Marrero
Archdiocese of New Orleans

Hope Haven Center (1925)
1101 Barataria Blvd.
Marrero, LA 70072-3085
Tel: 504-347-5581; Fax: 504-340-2075
Residential Treatment Center and School.
Ms. KAREN YOUNG, Asst. Admin.

St. Elizabeth's at Hope Haven
1101 Barataria Blvd.
Marrero, LA 70072-3085
Tel: 504-347-5581; Fax: 504-340-2075
Ms. KAREN YOUNG, Asst. Admin.

Villa D'Ames Apartments
6305 Fourth St.
Marrero, LA 70072-1513
Tel: 504-347-0474; Fax: 504-347-0476
Ms. YVONNE STEWART, Admin.
Units 200

Wynhoven Apartments and Wynhoven II
4600-10th St.
Marrero, LA 70072-3048
Tel: 504-347-8443; Fax: 504-340-6076
Private Non-Profit Residence for Senior Citizens Sponsored by the Archdiocese.
Sr. EMMA DUNNE, S.S.N.D., Admin.
Sr. MARTIN MARIE BULLARD, S.S.N.D., Mgr., Wynhoven II
Sisters 4
Residents 375

Wynhoven Health Care Center
1050 Medical Center Blvd.
Marrero, LA 70072-3170
Tel: 504-347-0777; 347-3443 (Convent); Fax: 504-341-7240
Mr. JOHN TIEPERMAN, Admin.
Residents 180

Meraux
Archdiocese of New Orleans

St. Bernard Manor, St. Bernard II, and St. Bernard III
2400 Archbishop Hannan Blvd.
Meraux, LA 70075-2640
Tel: 504-277-2441; Fax: 504-277-6300
Ms. DIANE JOHNSON, Admin.
Residents 182

Metairie
Archdiocese of New Orleans

Cascades Apartments, Walmsley Housing Corp.
2212 N. Arnoult Rd.
Metairie, LA 70001-1807
Tel: 504-835-2998; Fax: 504-835-3647
Mrs. THELMA AGUILAR, Admin.
Units 120

Metairie Manor, Metairie II, and Metairie III
4929 York St.
Metairie, LA 70001-1013
Tel: 504-456-1467; Fax: 504-887-3718
Sr. MARY ALOYSIUS OTT, O.P., Admin.
Sr. MARY GRIGNON BAUDOUIN, O.P., Asst. Admin.
Rev. JOHN A. POWERS, O.P., Chap.
Residential Units 287

Rock Creek Apartments, Walmsley Housing Corp.
4817 York St.
Metairie, LA 70001-1168
Tel: 504-455-3886; Fax: 504-455-3888
Ms. DIANA LAMBERT, Admin.
Units 160

Monroe
Diocese of Shreveport

St. Joseph Home
2301 Sterlington Rd., P.O. Box 6057
Monroe, LA 71211-6057
Tel: 318-323-3426
Operated by the Sisters of Charity of the Incarnate Word, Houston, TX.
Ms. JOY ANDERSON, Admin.
Licensed Capacity 132
Sisters 3

Moreauville
Diocese of Alexandria

St. John's Village
116 Beridon St.
Moreauville, LA 71355-3004
Tel: 318-985-2948
Rev. Msgr. JOHN TIMMERMANS, Admin.
Apartments 50

New Iberia
Diocese of Lafayette

Consolata Home
2319 E. Main St.
New Iberia, LA 70560
Tel: 318-365-8226
Mr. DAVID LANDRY, Admin.
Rev. RAYMOND ROBITAILLE, Chap., Tel: 318-365-7477
Residents 114
Bed Capacity 114

New Orleans
Archdiocese of New Orleans

The 1540 House
1540 N. Johnson St.
New Orleans, LA 70116-1721
Tel: 504-945-0253
Mr. MATTHEW ROBINSON, III, Admin.
Residents 12

Annunciation Inn
1220 Spain St.
New Orleans, LA 70117-8369
Tel: 504-944-0512; Fax: 504-944-0514
Residence for Elderly
Sr. HELEN I. BREAUX, S.F.C.C., Admin.
Units 106
Total Staff 8
Residents 112

Boys Hope
4128 Baudin St.
New Orleans, LA 70119-6815
Tel: 504-486-6030
4233 Banks St.
New Orleans, LA 70119-6714
Tel: 504-486-5223
2726 Esplanade
New Orleans, LA 70119-3333
Tel: 504-484-7744; Fax: 504-484-6120
Group Homes for Boys. Jesuit Program for Living and Learning.
Rev. ROBERT C. ALLANACH, O.M.I., Ph.D., Dir.
Total Staff 6
Boys 16

Carriage House Apartments, Pontchartrain Housing Corp. I
10151 Curran Blvd.
New Orleans, LA 70127-1390
Mrs. SHERRI TARDIFF, Admin.
Units 216
Total Staff 5
Total in Residence 212

Chateau de Notre Dame
2832 Burdette St.

New Orleans, LA 70125-2596
Tel: 504-866-2741; Fax: 504-866-6769
Residence and Nursing Home.
Ms. PATRICIA ANN GAUTREAUX, Admin.
Rev. EDWARD J. LAWLOR, S.S.J., Chap.
Residential Units 106
Nursing Beds 180
Priests 1
Sisters 4
Lay Staff 215

Christopher Inn Apts.
2110 Royal St.
New Orleans, LA 70116-1693
Tel: 504-949-0312; Fax: 504-945-2634
Private Non-Profit Residence for Senior Citizens Sponsored by the Archdiocese.
Ms. EVANGELINE WASHINGTON, Acting Admin.
Residents 148

**Covenant House*
622 N. Rampart St.
New Orleans, LA 70112-3540
Tel: 504-584-1111; 800-999-9999 (Hotline); Fax: 504-584-1171
Home for Runaway, Abused & Homeless Youth.
Mrs. MAUDELLE CADE, Exec. Dir.

DeLille Inn
6924 Chef Menteur Hwy.
New Orleans, LA 70126-5260
Tel: 504-241-4877; Fax: 504-241-1828
Sr. M. TEKAKWITHA VEGA, S.S.F., Admin.
Total Staff 5
Residents 55

Haydel Heights Apartments
4402 Reynes St.
New Orleans, LA 70126
Tel: 504-242-4438; Fax: 504-242-4061
Ms. LINDA CHAPMAN, Admin.
Units 65

Josephine Apartments
1410 St. Andrew St., Apt. #6
New Orleans, LA 70130-5344
Tel: 504-522-5425; Fax: 504-522-5446
Mrs. ROSALYN W. TRIPPS, Mgr.
Residents 93

Lafon Nursing Home of the Holy Family
6900 Chef Menteur Hwy.
New Orleans, LA 70126-5296
Tel: 504-246-1100; Fax: 504-241-6672
Sisters of the Holy Family
Sr. ANN ELISE SONNIER, S.S.F., Admin.
Sisters 8
Residents 171

Mary-Joseph Residence for the Elderly (1868)
4201 Woodland Dr.
New Orleans, LA 70131-7398
Tel: 504-394-2200; Fax: 504-391-3347
Sr. CHRISTINE KREUPER, L.S.P., Supr.
Rev. FRANCIS WHATLEY, O.SS.T., Chap.
Sisters 12
Total Staff 140
Residents 110

Nazareth II
9640 Hayne Blvd.
New Orleans, LA 70127-4725
Tel: 504-246-9640; Fax: 504-241-9631
Sr. TERESA CARONIA, S.S.N.D., Dir.
Apartments 120
Total Staff 6
Total in Residence 123

Nazareth Inn
9630 Hayne Blvd.
New Orleans, LA 70127-1260
Tel: 504-241-9630; Fax: 504-241-9631
Legal Title: *Nazareth Manor, Inc.*
Sr. ANNA MARY CARONIA, S.S.N.D., Dir.
Sisters 2
Apartments 150
Total Staff 9
Total in Residence 158

St. John Berchmans Manor
3400 St. Anthony St.
New Orleans, LA 70122-3098
Tel: 504-943-9343; Fax: 504-947-6090
Sr. M. ROSE DE LIMA HAZEUR, S.S.F., Admin.
Rev. VINCENT THEOBALD, S.V.D., Chap., Tel: 504-948-4425
Units 150

St. Margaret's Daughters' Home for Aged Women
6220 Chartres St.
New Orleans, LA 70117-1595
Tel: 504-279-6414; Fax: 504-277-1834
Mrs. PATRICIA G. HEINTZ, Admin.
Residents 113
Total Staff 110
Total Assisted 115

St. Martin Manor
1501 N. Johnson St.
New Orleans, LA 70116-1720
Tel: 504-945-7728; Fax: 504-945-1645
Sr. M. CAMILLUS DURALD, S.S.F., Admin.
Residential Units 140
Total Staff 12
Total in Residence 145

Timber Ridge Apartments Pontchartrain Housing Corp. III
6364 Woodland Hwy.
New Orleans, LA 70131-7474
Tel: 504-391-9841; Fax: 504-391-9996
Legal Title: *Christopher Homes Inc.*
Ms. JOANN ROBERT, Admin.
Units 152

Villa St. Maurice
500 St. Maurice Ave.
New Orleans, LA 70117-1568
Tel: 504-277-8477; Fax: 504-277-8493
Residence for Senior Citizens & Handicapped.
Mrs. JUANITA C. JONES, Admin.
Residential Units 110

Villa St. Maurice II (Villa Additions)
6101 Douglas St.
New Orleans, LA 70117-2100
Tel: 504-277-8731; Fax: 504-277-8493
Residence for Senior Citizens & Handicapped.
Mrs. CAROL MOTEN, Asst. Admin.
Residential Units 75

Opelousas
Diocese of Lafayette

C'est La Vie Center of the Sisters Marianites of Holy Cross
749 E. Prudhomme Ln.
Opelousas, LA 70570
Tel: 318-942-8154
Independent living for the elderly and handicapped.
Sr. KAY KINBERGER, M.S.C., Pres.
Sr. MARY ZITA GUIDRY, M.S.C., Coord.
Sr. JOYCELYN F. LEE, Admin.
Sisters 2

Our Lady of Prompt Succor Home
751 E. Prudhomme Ln.
Opelousas, LA 70570
Tel: 318-948-3634
Mrs. JOAN COLEMAN, Admin.
Sisters 2
Patients assisted annually 78

Shreveport
Diocese of Shreveport

Holy Angels Residential Facility
10450 Ellerbe Rd.
Shreveport, LA 71106-7712
Tel: 318-797-8500; 797-9070
Sisters of Our Lady of Sorrows.
Sr. CONCETTA SCIPIONE, O.L.S., Admin.
Sr. GEMMA FORLANI, O.L.S., Supr.
Most Rev. WILLIAM B. FRIEND, D.D., Pres.
Sisters 4
Lay Personnel 261
Residents 184

St. Rose
Archdiocese of New Orleans

River Road Apartments, Pontchartrain Housing Corp. II
100 A East Club Dr.
St. Rose, LA 70087-9411
Tel: 504-464-0326; Fax: 504-466-1987
Ms. JO ANN ANDRY, Admin.
Units 320
Total Staff 7

MAINE

Bangor
Diocese of Portland (In Maine)

St. Xavier's Home
119 Somerset St.
Bangor, ME 04401
Tel: 207-942-4815
Mailing Address:
Box 429
Orono, ME 04473
Rev. JAMES P. BREWER, Contact Person
Units 19

Biddeford
Diocese of Portland (In Maine)

St. Andre Health Care Facility
407 Pool St.
Biddeford, ME 04005-9716
Tel: 207-282-5171
Sr. MADELEINE D'ANJOU, Admin.
Sponsored by Servants of the Immaculate Heart of Mary S.C.I.M. Good Shepherd, Quebec, Canada.
Beds 96

Lewiston
Diocese of Portland (In Maine)

Marcotte Congregate Housing Inc.
100 Campus Ave.
Lewiston, ME 04240
Tel: 207-786-0062
CECILE Y. MATHIEU, Dir.

**Marcotte Nursing Home - D'Youville Pavilion*
102 Campus Ave.
Lewiston, ME 04240
Tel: 207-777-4200
Rev. J. DONOVAN, O.P., Chap.
Beds 280
Patients assisted annually 95,000

Portland
Diocese of Portland (In Maine)

Deering Pavilion Apartment House for Senior Citizens
880 Forest Ave.
Portland, ME 04103
Tel: 207-797-8777
Mr. OREN W. SCHROEDER, Admin.
Residents 235
Apartments 200

St. Joseph's Manor
1133 Washington Ave.
Portland, ME 04103
Tel: 207-797-0600
Most Rev. JOSEPH J. GERRY, O.S.B., Pres.
Rev. MICHAEL J. HENCHAL
Mr. RONALD G. TARDIF, Dir.
KATHY MURPHY, R.N., Dir. Nurses
Bed Capacity 200

Waterville
Diocese of Portland (In Maine)

Mt. St. Joseph Holistic Care Community
Highwood St.
Waterville, ME 04901
Tel: 207-873-0705
PATRICIA BERGER, Admin.
Sisters of St. Joseph of Lyons, C.S.J.
Bed Capacity 88

Seton Village Inc.
1 Carver St.
Waterville, ME 04901
Tel: 207-873-0178
Most Rev. JOSEPH J. GERRY, Bishop of Portland, Pres.
Rev. J. JOSEPH FORD, Treas.
ARMAND CARON, Chm.
Ms. PAMELA HALL, Admin.
Units 140
Guests 150

MARYLAND

Baltimore
Archdiocese of Baltimore

The Cardinal Shehan Center, Inc.
2300 Dulaney Valley Rd.
Towson, MD 21204
Tel: 410-252-4500; Fax: 410-628-8095
Rev. LAWRENCE M. JOHNSON, Chap.
A holding company for Stella Maris (Formerly: Stella Maris Hospice Properties, Inc.); Outreach Ministry Programs; Home Health Agency; Hospice Care; Saint John Hall-Long Crandon, for retired priests; Saint Elizabeth Hall Apartments; Urban Shelter Program at Blessed Sacrament Residence for the Elderly; Nursing Home; Subacute/Rehab Unit; Outpatient Physical Therapy; Center for Grief & Loss.
4101 1/2 Old York Rd.
Baltimore, MD 21218

St. Charles Villa
603 Maiden Choice Ln.
Baltimore, MD 21228
Tel: 410-747-1211
Revs.:
LAWRENCE A. BENDER, S.S.
JOHN W. BOWEN, S.S.
JAMES H. BRENNAN, S.S.
FREDERICK V. CHUDZINSKI, S.S.
CHARLES P. DILLON, S.S.
CLAUDE H. DUKEHART, S.S.
ANDREW A. FORSTER, S.S.
VINCENT M. EATON, S.S.
JAMES J. HEALY, S.S.
RAYMOND F. HESLER, S.S.
WILLIAM J. LEE, S.S.
WILLIAM MORRIS, S.S.
WILLIAM T. O'KEEFFE, S.S., Supr. & Dir.
WILLIAM A. THIELEMANN, S.S.
JOHN A. WARD, S.S.
J. PAUL WELCH, S.S.
JOSEPH L. WHITE, S.S.
Total in Residence 17
Total Staff 10

St. Elizabeth Home for Nursing Care
3320 Benson Ave.
Baltimore, MD 21227-1088
Tel: 410-644-7100; Fax: 410-644-2154
Legal Title: *The Jenkins Memorial Nursing Home, Inc.*
Sponsored by Associated Catholic Charities.
Mr. GARRET A. FALCONE, Admin.
Sisters 3
Beds 162

St. Joseph's Nursing Home
1222 Tugwell Dr.
Baltimore, MD 21228
Tel: 410-747-0026; Fax: 410-747-0386
Legal Title: *Sisters Servants of Mary Immaculate, Inc.*
Sr. CAROLYN CARNE, Admin.
Rev. JOSEPH SIELSKI, M.I.C., Chap.
Sisters 11
Residents 40
Total Assisted 47
Total Staff 47

St. Martin's Home for Aged, Little Sisters of the Poor
601 Maiden Choice Ln.
Baltimore, MD 21228
Tel: 410-744-9367
Rev. ROBERT G. HAWKINS, Chap.
Sisters 21
Aged Residents 106
Total Staff 130

Stella Maris Operating Corporation
2300 Dulaney Valley Rd.
Baltimore, MD 21204
Tel: 410-252-4500
Sr. LOUIS MARY BATTLE, R.S.M., Pres.
Rev. LAWRENCE M. JOHNSON, Dir. of Pastoral Care
The management corporation for all programs of the Center. All applications for the facilities of the Center are processed directly through the Admissions Office at Stella Maris.
Lay Personnel 753
Sisters 13
Residents 416
Saint John Hall-Long Crandon
Rev. Msgr. STANLEY J. SCARFF
Rev. Msgr. SIMON KENNY
Rev. Msgr. MELVILLE TAYLOR
Revs.:
JOHN C. COLLOPY
PAUL F. DOLAN
FRANCIS J. LE FEVRE
Stella Maris
Rev. Msgr. FRANCIS J. LINN
Revs.:
JOHN TIERNEY
WILLIAM M. DRISCOLL, S.J.
JOSEPH A. KENNEY
LEON KACZKOWSKI
JOHN J. TIERNEY
St. Elizabeth Hall
Revs.:
ROBERT BOZEL
MYLES MULLER

Ellicott City
Archdiocese of Baltimore

Bon Secours Nursing Care Center, Inc.
(Subsidiary of Bon Secours Health Systems, Inc.)
3000 N. Ridge Rd.
Ellicott City, MD 21043
Tel: 410-461-6660; Fax: 410-461-6695
Sisters of Bon Secours.
SHERRY L. BRUNNER, Exec. Dir.
Sr. KATHERINE ANN DURNEY, Chap.
Sisters 1
Beds 187
Total Assisted 266
Total Staff 183

Hyattsville
Archdiocese of Washington

Sacred Heart Home Inc.
5805 Queens Chapel Rd.
Hyattsville, MD 20782
Tel: 301-277-6500
Missionary Sisters, Servants of the Holy Spirit.
Sr. MARY AGNES FAHRLAND, S.Sp.S., Admin.
Rev. ROBERT MERTES, S.V.D.
Sisters 4
Residents 102

St. Ann's Infant and Maternity Home
4901 Eastern Ave.
Hyattsville, MD 20782
Tel: 301-559-5500; Fax: 301-853-6985
Daughters of Charity.
Sr. JOSEPHINE Admin.
Sr. PAULA Local Supr.
Sisters 7
Residential Children 57
Maternity Program 18
Day Care 85
After Care Program:
Mothers 14
Infants 14

Mitchellville
Archdiocese of Washington

Villa Rosa Nursing Home, Inc.
3800 Lottsford Vista Rd.
Mitchellville, MD 20721-4026
Tel: 301-459-4700; Fax: 301-459-0754
Rev. CARMELO NEGRO, C.S., Dir.
Mr. EUGENE L. ZIBRAT, Admin.
Sr. IDALINA BARATTER, M.S.S.C., Supr.
Sisters 6
Residents 100
Comprehensive Care Nursing Facility.

Ridgely
Diocese of Wilmington

St. Martin's Ministries
14259 Benedictine Ln.
Ridgely, MD 21660
Tel: 410-634-2497
Sisters of St. Benedict
Sr. PATRICIA GAMGORT, O.S.B., Exec. Dir.
St. Martin's Barn
14376 Benedictine Ln.
Ridgely, MD 21660
Tel: 410-634-1140
Staff 5
Total Assisted 9,555
Sr. FRANCES WALKER, O.S.F., Dir.
St. Martin's House
14374 Benedictine Ln.
Ridgely, MD 21660
Tel: 410-634-2537
Staff 5
Total Assisted 67
Ms. JUDITH BATES, Dir.

MASSACHUSETTS

Boston
Archdiocese of Boston

Don Orione Nursing Home
111 Orient Ave.
East Boston, MA 02128
Tel: 617-569-2100
Revs.:
LAWRENCE TOSATTO, F.D.P., Supr., Dir. and Admin.
ROCCO CRESCENZI, F.D.P., Vicar & Treas.
GINO MARCHESANI, F.D.P., Counselor
JOHN KILMARTIN, F.D.P., Rector of the Shrine & Counselor
Sons of Divine Providence (Don Orione Fathers) 4
Guests 190
Total Assisted 185
Total Staff 195

Franciscan Children's Hospital and Rehabilitation Center
General Pediatrics, Rehabilitation and Special Education.
30 Warren St.
Brighton, MA 02135
Tel: 617-254-3800
KEVIN W. RYAN, Pres.
Bed Capacity 100
Number under care 58,815
Day Program 90

Marian Manor (1954)
130 Dorchester St.
South Boston, MA 02127
Tel: 617-268-3333
Sr. ANDRE MARIE O.Carm., Admin.
Revs.:
JOSEPH M. KANE, Chap.
HERBERT CLEARY, S.J., Assoc. Chap.
Priests 2
Carmelite Sister for the Aged and Infirm 14
Guests 366

St. Joseph Nursing Care Center
321 Centre St.
Dorchester, MA 02122
Tel: 617-825-6320; Fax: 617-825-7410
PAUL F. SHANNON, Admin.
Rev. JOHN J. JENNINGS, Chap.
123 Bed Nursing Care Center.
St. Joseph Nursing Care Center, Inc.
Sisters 3

St. Mary's Women and Infants Center
90 Cushing Ave.
Dorchester, MA 02125
Center for pregnant women.
(See Guidance Centers for more information.)

Brighton
Archdiocese of Boston

St. John of God Hospital
296 Allston St.
Brighton, MA 02146
Tel: 617-277-5750
WILLIAM K. BRINKERT, Pres.
Rev. JOSEPH K. COLEMAN, Chap., Dir. Pastoral Care, Chronic and Rehabilitation Hospital.
A member of Caritas Christi, the Catholic Health Care System of the Archdiocese of Boston.
Bed Capacity 70
Total Staff 119

Brockton
Archdiocese of Boston

St. Joseph Manor Nursing & Extended Care Facility
215 Thatcher St.
Brockton, MA 02402-3999
Tel: 508-583-5834; Fax: 508-583-8551
THOMAS J. BROWN, CEO
ANNE M. TERI, Admin.
Rev. AUSTIN NAGLE, SS.CC., Chap.
Adult Day Health Center
Total Assisted 30
Total Staff 5
Sisters of Jesus Crucified and the Sorrowful Mother 9
Residents 118

Cambridge
Archdiocese of Boston

**Youville Healthcare Center, Inc.*
1575 Cambridge St.
Cambridge, MA 02138-4398
Tel: 617-876-4344
Mr. T. RICHARD QUIGLEY, Pres. & CEO
Sr. JOAN COYNE, Admin.
Sr. THERESE CAPISTRAN, S.G.M., Vice Pres. Mission Effectiveness
Chaplains:
Revs.:
WILLIAM MULLIGAN, S.J., Chap.
NEIL F. DECKER, S.J.
Ms. PATRICIA KENNEDY, Dir., Pastoral Care Services
Ms. ELIZABETH WALSH
Priests 2
Sisters of Charity (Grey Nuns) 3
Member of Youville Lifecare, Inc.
Bed Capacity 140
Patients assisted annually 1,061
Staff 176

**Youville Hospital & Rehabilitation Center, Inc.*
1575 Cambridge St.
Cambridge, MA 02138-4398
Tel: 617-876-4344
Mr. T. RICHARD QUIGLEY, Pres. & CEO
Sr. THERESE CAPISTRAN, S.G.M., Vice Pres. Mission Effectiveness
Chaplains:
Revs.:

WILLIAM MULLIGAN, S.J.
NEIL F. DECKER, S.J.
Ms. PATRICIA KENNEDY, Dir. Pastoral Care Services
Ms. ELIZABETH WALSH
Priests 2
Sisters of Charity (Grey Nuns) 3
School of Practical Nursing.
Ms. HELEN M. BARRETT, R.N., M.S., Dir.
Member of Youville Lifecare, Inc.
Bed Capacity 146
Patients assisted annually 7,740
Staff 357

Fairhaven
Diocese of Fall River

Our Lady's Haven of Fairhaven Inc.
71 Center St.
Fairhaven, MA 02719
Tel: 508-999-4561
JEAN M. GOLITZ, Admin.
Rev. ROY YURCO, SS.CC., Chap.
Sr. MARIA CRAVEDI, M.P.V., Dir. Pastoral Care
Residents 117

Fall River
Diocese of Fall River

Catholic Memorial Home Inc.
2446-2474 Highland Ave.
Fall River, MA 02720
Tel: 508-679-0011; Fax: 508-672-5858
Sr. SEAN CONNOLLY, O.Carm., Supr. & Admin.
Rev. ARTHUR K. WINGATE, Chap.
Sr. ELAINE HEFFERNAN, R.S.M., Dir. Pastoral Care
Carmelite Sisters 5
Total Assisted 300
Total Staff 379

Rose Hawthorne Lathrop Home
(Servants of Relief for Incurable Cancer)
1600 Bay St.
Fall River, MA 02724
Tel: 508-673-2322; Fax: 508-679-5830
Dominican Sisters of the Congregation of St. Rose of Lima.
Rev. DENNIS M. MCNELIS, C.S.C., Chap.
Total Assisted 120
Sisters 7
Total Staff 30
Bed Capacity 35
Patients assisted annually 120

Framingham
Archdiocese of Boston

Carmel Terrace
933 Central St.
Framingham, MA 01701
Tel: 508-788-8000
Sr. M. JOSEPH AUGUSTINE, Dir.
Carmelite Sisters for the Aged and Infirm 3
Apartments for Assisted Living of the Elderly 62
Total Staff 35

St. Patrick's Manor, Inc.
863 Central St.
Framingham, MA 01701
Tel: 508-879-8000; Fax: 508-626-1604
Sr. M. JOSEPH AUGUSTINE, O.Carm., Admin.
Rev. ROBERT T. FERRICK, S.J., Chap.
Carmelite Sisters for the Aged and Infirm 26

Holyoke
Diocese of Springfield in Massachusetts

Mont Marie Health Care Center, Inc.
34 Lower Westfield Rd.
Holyoke, MA 01040
Tel: 413-536-0853; Fax: 413-533-3275
Sr. ELIZABETH SULLIVAN, S.S.J., Admin.
In res.,
Rev. Msgr. EUGENE GUERLIN
Total Staff 88
Total Assisted 72
Total Resident Days 26,153
Total Census 72 residents

Sisters of Providence Care Centers, Inc.
35 Holy Family Rd.
Holyoke, MA 01040-2758
Mr. WILLIAM E. CASPER, Pres.
Beaven Kelly Home
25 Brightside Dr.
Holyoke, MA 01040
Tel: 413-532-4892
Residents 55
Sr. GERALDINE NOONAN, S.P., Pastoral Care Dir. (Staff)
Mrs. CYNTHIA BROWN, Admin.
Mount St. Vincent Nursing Home
35 Holy Family Rd.
Holyoke, MA 01040-2758
Tel: 413-532-3246
Sisters of Providence 1
Persons under care 125
In res.,
Revs.:
ANDREW B. CEKOVSKY (ALB)
PAUL D. RIEDL
CASIMIR SWITALSKI (SPR)
Sr. MARY CONWAY
Sr. MARY HORGAN, S.P., M.Div., Chap. (Staff)
Mr. DENNIS K. MCKENNA, Admin.
St. Luke's Home
85 Spring St.
Springfield, MA 01105
Tel: 413-736-5494
Residents 89
Sr. DOROTHY YOUNG, S.P., Pastoral Care Dir. (Staff)
Mrs. NANCY HARPER, Admin.
In res.,
Rev. JOSEPH MULLIGAN (HRT)
Sr. MABEL WITHAM, S.S.J.
Sr. JOSEPHINE AHEARN, S.S.J.
Center for Rehabilitation and Nursing Care
217 Westfield St.
West Springfield, MA 01089
Tel: 413-746-0390
Residents 120
Mr. JOEL CAMP, Admin.
Sr. JOAN MANNING, S.P., (CNA - Staff)
Sr. AGNES REICHLIN, (3-11 RN Supvr.) - Staff
In res.,
Sr. MARY KWALA
Bro. EDWARD MURPHY
Total Staff 400
Total Assisted 369

Lawrence
Archdiocese of Boston

**M.I. Adult Day Health Center, Inc.*
189 Maple St.
Lawrence, MA 01841
Tel: 508-682-7575
Sisters of Charity of Montreal (Grey Nuns).
THOMAS L. LUCAS, Pres. & CEO
BARBARA E. GRANT, Admin.
Adult day health and social day care for Senior Citizens.
Total in Residence 100
Total Staff 16

M.I. Nursing-Restorative Center, Inc.
172 Lawrence St.
Lawrence, MA 01841
Tel: 508-685-6321
Sisters of Charity Montreal (Grey Nuns).
THOMAS L. LUCAS, Pres. & CEO
JOANNE MUKERJEE, Admin.
Multi-level Skilled Nursing Facility.
Member of Convenant Health System, Lexington, MA. Unit of: Mary Immaculate Health Care Services.
Residents 250
Total Staff 340

M.I. Residential Community II, Inc.
191 Maple St.
Lawrence, MA 01841
Tel: 508-682-7575
Sisters of Charity of Montreal (Grey Nuns).
THOMAS L. LUCAS, Pres. & CEO
BARBARA E. GRANT, Admin.
Independent & assisted living for Elderly and Handicapped.
Units 106
Total in Residence 120
Total Staff 35

M.I. Residential Community III, Inc.
193 Maple St.
Lawrence, MA 01841
Tel: 508-682-7575
Sisters of Charity of Montreal (Grey Nuns).
THOMAS L. LUCAS, Pres. & CEO
BARBARA E. GRANT, Admin.
Independent & assisted living for Elderly and Handicapped.
Units 88
Total in Residence 95
Total Staff 35

M.I. Residential Community, Inc.
189 Maple St.
Lawrence, MA 01841
Tel: 508-682-7575
Sisters of Charity of Montreal (Grey Nuns).
THOMAS L. LUCAS, Pres. & CEO
BARBARA E. GRANT, Admin.
Independent & assisted living for Elderly and Handicapped.
Units 110
Total in Residence 121
Total Staff 35

**M.I. Transportation, Inc.*
189 Maple St.
Lawrence, MA 01841
Tel: 508-682-7575
Sisters of Charity of Montreal (Grey Nuns).
THOMAS L. LUCAS, Pres. & CEO
BARBARA E. GRANT, Admin.
Total Assisted 75
Total Staff 5

Leominster
Diocese of Worcester

Presentation Health Care Center
99 Church St.
Leominster, MA 01453-3147
Tel: 508-537-7108
Sr. JULIE CICCOLINI, P.B.V.M., Pres.
Purpose: To operate and maintain a nursing home for aged and/or infirmed persons at Presentation Convent.

Lowell
Archdiocese of Boston

D'Youville Manor
981 Varnum Ave.
Lowell, MA 01854
Tel: 508-454-5681
Sisters of Charity of Ottawa (Grey Nuns of the Cross).
STEVE JOHNSON, CEO
Rev. FRANK DOLAN, O.M.I., Chap.
Priests 4
Sisters 5
Total Assisted 196
Total Staff 260
Adult Day Health Care Capacity 22
Total Staff 6

Marlboro
Archdiocese of Boston

Madonna Hall
(Legal Title)
Cushing Hill Dr.
Marlboro, MA 01752
Tel: 508-485-8610
Sr. HELENE HAYES, R.G.S., L.I.C.S.W., Exec. Dir.
Madonna Hall Pelletier
Tel: 508-485-1401
LINDA KELLY, Prog. Dir.
Conducted by Sisters of the Good Shepherd.
Residents 20

Marie Esther Health Center, Inc.
720 Boston Post Rd.
Marlboro, MA 01752
Tel: 508-485-3791
Total Assisted 29
Total Staff 39

Methuen
Archdiocese of Boston

Holy Family Hospital Men's Guild
70 East St.
Methuen, MA 01844

Millbury
Diocese of Worcester

Providence House Nursing Home of Millbury
29 Main St.
Millbury, MA 01527
Tel: 508-865-6106
Member of Saint Vincent Healthcare System, Inc.
Beds 138
Total Assisted 138
Total Staff 180

New Bedford
Diocese of Fall River

Sacred Heart Home
359 Summer St.
New Bedford, MA 02740
Tel: 508-996-6751
Sr. BLANDINE D'AMOURS, S.C.Q., Admin. & Supr.
Sisters of Charity of Quebec 6
Total Staff 310
Residents 217

North Attleboro
Diocese of Fall River

Madonna Manor Inc.
85 N. Washington St.
North Attleboro, MA 02760
Tel: 508-699-2740; Fax: 508-699-0481
Mrs. SUSAN L. CALDWELL, Admin.
Rev. RAYMOND MOQUIM
Sr. CONSTANCE PERRON, D.H.S., Dir. of Pastoral Care
Total Staff 180
Residents 160

Somerville
Archdiocese of Boston

Jeanne Jugan Pavilion
190 Highland Ave.
Somerville, MA 02143
Mailing Address:
186 Highland Ave.
Somerville, MA 02143
Apartments for the Elderly 27
Residents 27
Total Staff 3

Jeanne Jugan Residence
186 Highland Ave.
Somerville, MA 02143
Tel: 617-776-4420; Fax: 617-623-0707
Rev. JOSEPH J. DOWNEY, Chap.
Senior Citizen Total in Residence 112
Total Staff 102
Little Sisters of the Poor 16
Residents 84

Southbridge
Diocese of Worcester

Providence House Nursing Home of Southbridge
84 Chapin St.
Southbridge, MA 01550
Tel: 508-765-9133
Member of Saint Vincent Healthcare System, Inc.
Beds 226

Springfield
Diocese of Springfield in Massachusetts

St. Michael's Residence
86 Wendover Rd.
Springfield, MA 01118
Tel: 413-783-6773
In res.,
Revs.:
LUKE T. FENNESSEY
THOMAS S. GREENE
MANUEL ROCHA
JOHN TOKARZ
JOHN J. SEXTON
Rev. Msgr. ROGER VIAU
Total Staff 2
Total in Residence 6

Taunton
Diocese of Fall River

Bethany House Adult Day Care
72 Church Green
Taunton, MA 02780
Tel: 508-822-9200

Marian Manor Inc.
33 Summer St.
Taunton, MA 02780
Tel: 508-822-4885
Mr. THOMAS F. HEALY, Admin.
Rev. HUGH J. MUNRO, Chap.
Sr. PAULINA CARDENAS, O.P., Dir. Pastoral Care
Dominican Sisters of Charity of the Presentation of the Blessed Virgin Mary 46
Total Staff 165
Guests 175

Waltham
Archdiocese of Boston

Maristhill Nursing Home
66 Newton St.
Waltham, MA 02154
Tel: 617-893-0240
JANET C. MURPHY, Admin.
Nursing Home sponsored by the Marist Missionary Sisters, offering skilled and rehabilitative nursing care.
Priests 2
Sisters 6
Residents 123
Total Staff 132

West Springfield
Diocese of Springfield in Massachusetts

The Brightside for Families & Children
Private, Non-Profit Agency.
2112 Riverdale St.
Springfield, MA 01089
Tel: 413-788-7366
Sisters of Providence.
Sr. KATHLEEN POPKO, S.P., Ph.D., Chm., Bd. of Trustees
RALPH B. SPERRY, Ph.D., Pres.
Children in Residence 125
Children in Day Treatment Program 55
Placement Services:
Children in Foster Homes 10
Adoption Services 25
Pregnant Parenting Youth Services 100
Outpatient Mental Health Clinic 6,000
Family Stabilization Team 100
Acute Residential Treatment 325

Whitinsville
Diocese of Worcester

St. Camillus Nursing Home Inc.
447 Hill St.
Whitinsville, MA 01588
Tel: 508-234-7306
Mr. DAVID C. TURNER
Bro. THOMAS FARRELL, O.S.Cam., Dir. Pastoral Care
Priests 1
Brothers 2
Beds 123
Patients assisted annually 43,070
St. Camillus Institute
497 Hill St.
Whitinsville, MA 01588
St. Camillus Rectory
495 Hill St.
Whitinsville, MA 01588
Rev. JACK GALLAGHER, O.S.Cam.

Worcester
Diocese of Worcester

Notre Dame Long Term Care Center
559 Plantation St.
Worcester, MA 01605
Tel: 508-852-3011; Fax: 508-852-0397
LINDA J. CRAGIN, Admin.
Beds 123
Employees 180
Total Assisted 166
Total Staff 277

Providence Extended Care Center
119 Providence St.
Worcester, MA 01604
Tel: 508-860-5000
Member of Saint Vincent Healthcare System, Inc.
Rev. THOMAS M. BARRY, Chap.
Beds 130
Patients assisted annually 1,000
Total Staff 270

Vianney House
222 June St.
Worcester, MA 01602
Tel: 508-791-0311
Retired Priests' Home.
Most Rev. BERNARD J. FLANAGAN
Rev. Msgr. THOMAS J. DALEY
Rev. Msgr. EDMOND G. HADDAD
Revs.:
WILLIAM W. MCGOVERN
CYRIL LEBEAU
RICHARD HANNIGAN
JOHN F. CAHILL, Admin.
JOSEPH ASH
Total Staff 3

MICHIGAN

Allen Park
Archdiocese of Detroit

Little Sisters of the Poor
P.O. Box 610
Allen Park, MI 48101
Sr. CHARLES MARIE, Supr.

Battle Creek
Diocese of Kalamazoo

Mercy Pavilion Skilled Nursing Home and Senior Care Residence
80 N. 20 St.
Battle Creek, MI 40915
Tel: 616-964-5400; Fax: 616-964-5559
Sub. of Battle Creek Health System.
Mr. MICHAEL C. RICHARDS, Admin.
Bed Capacity 77
Senior Care Residence Beds 64

Bloomfield Hills
Archdiocese of Detroit

St. Elizabeth's Briarbank
1315 N. Woodward Ave.
Bloomfield Hills, MI 48304
Tel: 810-644-1011
Daughters of Divine Charity.
Sr. M. PASCHAL, Admin.
Sisters 15
Aged Residents 44

Villa Francesca
565 W. Long Lake Rd.
Bloomfield Hills, MI 48302
Tel: 810-644-5390
Daughters of Divine Charity.
Sr. MARY AURELIA GEGUS, F.D.C., Admin.
Sisters 3
Lay Staff 2
Employees 2
Under Care 15

Dearborn Heights
Archdiocese of Detroit

Vista Maria
20651 W. Warren Ave.
Dearborn Heights, MI 48127
Tel: 313-271-3050
DIANE BOSTIC ROBINSON, Exec. Dir.
Residential treatment programs for adolescent girls in conflict. Sponsored by the Sisters of the Good Shepherd.
Sisters 3
Girls Residential 145
Lay Staff 221
S.F.C. 26
Independent Living 6

Detroit
Archdiocese of Detroit

Christ Child House
15751 Joy Rd.
Detroit, MI 48228
Tel: 313-584-6077; Fax: 313-584-1148
JOHN YABLONKY, ACSW, Exec. Dir.

Don Bosco Hall, Inc.
10001 Petosky
Detroit, MI 48204
Tel: 313-834-8677
CHARLES SMALL, Dir.
Residential treatment center for boys, ages 12-17, in need of care, guidance and therapy.
Lay Staff 41
Residents 23
Emergency Shelter Program 12
Transitional Services 180
Mentoring Program 155

St. Catherine's House
1641 Webb Ave.
Detroit, MI 48206
Tel: 313-868-4505
MARY CONNORS, Mgr.
For elderly-ambulatory & younger disabled ambulatory women.
Capacity 12

St. Joseph's Home
4800 Cadieux Rd.
Detroit, MI 48224
Tel: 313-882-3800; Fax: 313-882-6944
Carmelite Sisters of the Divine Heart of Jesus.
Sr. MARY MAGDALENE Admin.
Sisters 5
Lay Staff 68
Aged Residents 104

St. Mary's Residence
2120 Orleans St.
Detroit, MI 48207
Tel: 313-259-6874; 259-0459
Sr. M. FIDELIS, F.D.C., Admin.
Rev. WILLIAM LUNNON
A residence for women desiring home-like surroundings.
Daughters of Divine Charity.
Sisters 6
Residents 60

Dimondale
Diocese of Lansing

St. Lawrence Dimondale Center
4000 N. Michigan Rd. (M-99)

Dimondale, MI 48821
Tel: 517-646-6258
Rev. STANLEY CZARNOTA, Chap. in res., Tel: 517-646-0408; Fax: 517-646-7578
DIANNE WEAVER, Admin.
Sr. MARY KATHLEEN BOTSFORD, R.S.M., Pastoral Care Asst. Nursing Home
Nursing Home Residents 178
Total Staff 272
Total Assisted 177

Dowagiac
Diocese of Kalamazoo

Dowagiac Nursing Home
610 Uneta St.
Dowagiac, MI 49047
Tel: 616-782-3471
Sisters of St. Joseph 2
Bed Capacity 100

Escanaba
Diocese of Marquette

Bishop Noa Home for Senior Citizens
2900 3rd Ave., S.
Escanaba, MI 49829
Tel: 906-786-5810; Fax: 906-786-5372
Sisters of St. Paul de Chartres.
In res.,
Revs.:
EMIL J. BEYER, Assoc. Chap.
GILBERT N. NEUROHR, Chap.
Sisters of St. Paul de Chartres 5
Residents 123

Farmington Hills
Archdiocese of Detroit

Marillac Programs
A Division of St. Vincent and Sarah Fisher Center,
22255 Greenfield, Ste. 330
Southfield, MI 48334
Tel: 810-559-2272; Fax: 810-559-2226
JEAN VICKERS, Exec. Dir.
CHERYL BUKOFF, Dir.
Outreach case management and counseling services for pregnant and parenting teens in the tri-county area. Eight beds for the transitional housing of eight teen mothers 16-18 years of age and eight homeless babies 0-18 months of age.

Mercy Services for Aging
34605 Twelve Mile Rd.
Farmington Hills, MI 48331-3221
Tel: 810-305-7920
GERALD BRUEN, Pres.

St. Vincent and Sarah Fisher Center
27400 W. Twelve Mile Rd.
Farmington Hills, MI 48334
Tel: 313-538-6000; 810-626-7527
JEAN M. VICKERS, Exec. Dir.
Licensed capacity for: Residential care 60 (ages 4-15), Specialized Foster Care 120 (ages 0-17), Seton Preschool & Child Care Center 49 (ages 2 weeks-5 yrs.).
Pregnancy and Parenting For Teen Parents (Ages 16-19) Outreach Program:
Residential 41

Seton Nursery School and Infant-Toddler Child Care Center
29475 Inkster Rd.
Farmington Hills, MI 48018
Tel: 810-626-6990
ANN COYLE Dir.
Center licensed for 80 children, 8 weeks-5.5 years.
In Day Care 68
Legal Title: *Seton Nursery School and Infant-Toddler Child Care Center - St. Vincent Sara Fisher Center*

Flint
Diocese of Lansing

Marian Hall
529 Martin Luther King Ave.
Flint, MI 48502
Tel: 810-238-7646
SHARON DUCKWORTH, Admin.
Sisters of the Precious Blood 3
Residents 80

Grand Rapids
Diocese of Grand Rapids

Contemplative Sisters of the Good Shepherd
1355 Walker Ave., N.W.
Grand Rapids, MI 49504
Tel: 616-454-6268
Sr. HEART OF MARY FILLION, C.G.S., Supr.
Total Sisters 6
Sisters of the Good Shepherd
Sr. THERESA HILLARY, R.G.S., Coord.
Rev. Msgr. CHARLES D. BROPHY, Chap.
Res.,
1247 Rennslaer, N.W.
Grand Rapids, MI 49504
Sisters of the Good Shepherd 2

St. Ann's Home
2161 Leonard St., N.W.
Grand Rapids, MI 49504
Tel: 616-453-7715; Fax: 616-453-7359
Carmelite Sisters of the Divine Heart of Jesus.
Sr. MARY THERESE ESSELMAN, Carmel.D.C.J., Exec. Dir.
Sisters 5
Residents 135

Kalamazoo
Diocese of Kalamazoo

Borgess Nursing Home
537 Chicago Ave.
Kalamazoo, MI 49001
Tel: 616-382-2392; Fax: 616-382-0843
Mrs. RUTH M. OLECH, Admin.
Bed Capacity 121

Lake Orion
Archdiocese of Detroit

Guest House for Women Religious
1840 W. Scripps Rd., Box 68
Lake Orion, MI 48360
Tel: 248-391-3100
A state licensed and JCAHO accredited endorsed residential treatment center for Catholic sisters and women in formation.
Sr. MAE KIERANS, C.S.J., Prog. Dir.
Bed Capacity 20
Central Admissions Office, from U.S. & Canada call: 800-626-6910.
Office of Guest House, Inc. Management Services Offices
1601 Joslyn Rd., P.O. Box 420
Lake Orion, MI 48361
Tel: 248-391-4445

Livonia
Archdiocese of Detroit

Marybrook Manor
36975 W. Five Mile Rd.
Livonia, MI 48154
Tel: 313-464-9667
Sr. MARY MODESTA PIWOWAR, C.S.S.F., Pres.
Sr. MARY RENETTA, C.S.S.F., Exec. Vice Pres.
Sr. ELIZABETH ANN C.S.S.F., N.H.A., Admin.
Residents 29

Marycrest Manor
15475 Middlebelt Rd.
Livonia, MI 48154
Tel: 313-427-9175
Sr. M. INNOCENT, F.S.S.J., Admin. Skilled nursing facility
Ownership: Franciscan Sisters of St. Joseph.
Sisters 4
Residents 55
Served by Marianhill Fathers.

Marywood Nursing Care Center
36975 W. Five Mile Rd.
Livonia, MI 48154
Tel: 313-464-0600
Long-term care Facility.
Sr. MARY MODESTA PIWOWAR, C.S.S.F., Pres.
Sr. MARY RENETTA C.S.S.F., Exec. Vice Pres.
Sr. ELIZABETH ANN C.S.S.F., N.H.A., Admin.
Sisters 3
Capacity 91

Ryan Senior Residences of the Archdiocese of Detroit. Inc.
Central Office, 14469-C Levan Rd.
Livonia, MI 48154
Tel: 313-953-5873
Rev. Msgr. ROBERT V. MONTICELLO, Exec. Dir.
Madonna Villa
17825 Fifteen Mile Rd.
Clinton Township, MI 48035
Tel: 810-792-0358
Total Staff 18
Number of Units 90
Number of Persons Served in 12 Month Period 1,080
SUZANNE SZCZEPANSKI-WHITE, Admin.
Casa Maria
600 Maple Vista
Imlay City, MI 48444
Tel: 810-724-6300
Total Staff 16
Number of Units 90
Number of Persons Served in 12 Months Period 1,080
PAUL WALKER, Admin.
Villa Marie
15131 Newburgh
Livonia, MI 48154
Tel: 313-464-9494
Total Staff 15
Number of Units 90
Number of Persons Served in 12 Month Period 1,080
Sr. LUCILLE BLIZMAN, O.P., Admin.
Marian Place
408 W. Front St.
Monroe, MI 48161
Tel: 313-241-2414
Total Staff 11
Number of Units 53
Number of Persons Served in 12 Month Period 636
KAREN MORRIN, Admin.
Kundig Center
3300 Jeffries Fwy.
Detroit, MI 48208
Tel: 313-894-0555
Total Staff 18
Number of Units 160
Number of Persons Served in 12 Month Period 1,680
THOMAS MCCUISH, Admin.
Stapleton Center
9341 Agnes
Detroit, MI 48214
Tel: 313-822-0397
Total Staff 15
Number of Units 59
Number of Persons Served in 12 Month Period 708
JANNIE M. SCOTT, Admin.
Marian Oakland-West
29250 W. Ten Mile Rd.
Farmington Hills, MI 48336
Tel: 810-474-7204
Total Staff 14
Number of Units 90
Number of Persons Served in 12 Month Period 1,080
ELAINE MACDERMOTT, Admin.
Marydale Center
3147 Tenth Ave.
Port Huron, MI 48060
Tel: 810-985-9683
Total Staff 11
Number of Units 59
Number of Persons Served in 12 Month Period 708
Sr. ANN CHRISTINE CHARRON, Admin.
Maryhaven
11350 Reeck Road
Southgate, MI 48195
Tel: 313-287-2111
Total Staff 18
Number of Units 90
Number of Persons Served in 12 Month Period 1,080
Sr. PAULA COONEY, I.H.M., Admin.

Mount Clemens
Archdiocese of Detroit

St. Joseph Mercy Living Care Center
A Division of Mercy Mt. Clemens Corp.
37700 Harper
Mount Clemens, MI 48043
Tel: 810-468-0827
ROBERT L. BEYER, Pres.
Bed Capacity 264

Nazareth
Diocese of Kalamazoo

Dillon Complex for Independent Living, Inc.
Nazareth, MI 49074
Tel: 616-342-0263
Sponsored by the Sisters of St. Joseph.
Sr. LUCY SCHNEIDER, S.S.J., Mgr.
Residents 79

Northville
Archdiocese of Detroit

Our Lady of Providence Center
16115 Beck Rd.
Northville, MI 48167
Tel: 313-453-1300
Sr. THERESA TAMBURO, D.S.M.P., Supr., Admin.
Rev. STANISLAUS C. KUKULSKI, Chap.

Otsego
Diocese of Kalamazoo

Otsego Senior Apts., Inc.
Baraga Manor, 301 Washington St.

Otsego, MI 49078
Tel: 616-694-9711
Sr. JEAN KENNEDY, S.S.J., Res. Mgr.
Managed by Catholic Family Services, Diocese of Kalamazoo.
1819 Gull Rd.
Kalamazoo, MI 49001
Apartments 48

Saginaw
Diocese of Saginaw

St. Francis Nursing Home
915 N. River Rd.
Saginaw, MI 48609
Fax: 517-781-3791
Sr. JANE MARIE LEBIEDZINSKI, C.S.S.F., Admin.
Rev. EDWARD TROMBLEY, Chap.
Felician Sisters (Livonia, MI) 4
Residents 100

St. Vincent Home-Boysville of Michigan, Inc.
925 N. River Rd.
Saginaw, MI 48609
Tel: 517-781-2780; Fax: 517-781-5422
RICK BOONE, M.S.W., C.S.W., Regl. Dir.
Mr. JOE MARTINUS, Pastoral Min.
Youth 56
Residential and community based treatment programs for troubled youth and families with facilities located throughtout the state of Michigan and one in Ohio, under the auspices of the Brothers of the Holy Cross at Notre Dame.
Holland House
614 E. Holland Ave.
Saginaw, MI 48601
Tel: 517-755-5397
Boys 14
Boysville's Family & Community Support Program
925 N. River Rd.
Saginaw, MI 48609
Tel: 517-781-2780
Boys 32
Girls 24
Includes Specialized Foster Care, Supervised Independent Living, In-Home Treatment, Families First, and Nokomis Challenge.
Curtis House
P.O. Box 309
Frankenmuth, MI 48734
Tel: 517-652-3212
Boys 14

Southfield
Archdiocese of Detroit

Boysville of Michigan, Inc.
Community Resource Office, 17117 W. Nine Mile Rd., Ste. 445
Southfield, MI 48075
Tel: 810-569-6630; Fax: 810-569-8171
Residential and communtiy based treatment programs for troubled youth and families with facilities located throughout the state of Michigan and one in the state of Ohio under the auspices of the Brothers of Holy Cross at Notre Dame.
Bro. FRANCIS BOYLAN, C.S.C., Exec. Dir.
Associate Executive Directors:
EDWARD J. OVERSTREET
PAUL S. NEITMAN
Bowman House / Boysville of Michigan, Inc.
17200 Rowe St.
Detroit, MI 48205
Tel: 313-372-7320
Boysville's Family & Community Support Program
19403 W. Chicago
Detroit, MI 48228
Tel: 313-838-7500
Includes specialized foster care, supervised independent living, in-home family treatment, & Families First.
Bro. FRANCIS BOYLAN, C.S.C., Exec. Dir.
LYNNE ALEXANDER, Regl. Dir.
Cabrini Center / Boysville of Michigan, Inc.
23915 Elmira
Redford, MI 48239
Tel: 313-537-7868
Girls 14
Hitchcock Center / Boysville of Michigan, Inc.
5675 Larkins
Detroit, MI 48210
Tel: 313-895-5119
Boys 15
Holy Cross Center / Boysville of Michigan, Inc.
5690 Cecil
Detroit, MI 48210
Tel: 313-895-2200
Day treatment, education, recreation program for Detroit region.
Johnson House / Boysville of Michigan, Inc.
7798 W. Fort St.
Detroit, MI 48209
Tel: 313-554-1700
Boys 15
King House / Boysville of Michigan, Inc.
24455 Crocker Blvd.
Mt. Clemens, MI 48043
Tel: 810-463-7130
Boys 14
Moreau Center / Boysville of Michigan, Inc.
3500 Comboni Way
Monroe, MI 48162
Tel: 313-242-5898
Boys 67
GEORGE BIRKAM, Reg. Dir.
St. Cecilia House / Boysville of Michigan, Inc.
7001 Burlingame St.
Detroit, MI 48204
Tel: 313-372-7320
Boys 30
St. Thomas Assessment Center / Boysville of Michigan, Inc.
8333 Townsend
Detroit, MI 48213
Tel: 313-579-1600
Sisters 1
Boys 27
Xavier Center / Boysville of Michigan, Inc.
27652 W. Outer Dr.
Ecorse, MI 48229
Tel: 313-381-5845
Boys 14

St. Francis Family Services
17500 W. Eight Mile Rd.
Southfield, MI 48075
Tel: 810-552-0750
RITA MONTGOMERY GRZELIK, Exec. Dir.
Foster home respite & adoption services for infants through 17 years.

Sheltering Arms
18310 W. 12 Mile
Southfield, MI 48076
Tel: 810-557-7373
Adult day care for the elderly. A service of Catholic Social Services of Oakland County.
Lay Staff 8
Volunteers 50
Patients assisted annually 85

St. Clair Shores
Archdiocese of Detroit

Sisters of Bon Secours Nursing Care Center
26001 E. Jefferson
St. Clair Shores, MI 48081
Tel: 810-779-7000
HENRY DEVRIES, CEO
ANNE SADLER, Admin.
GARY JANKOWSKI, Chief Finance Officer
Sr. ANNE MARIE MACK, C.S.B., V.P., Mission Effectiveness
Sr. PATRICIA SALTSZ, I.H.M., Dir. Spiritual Care
Long Term Care Facility.
Sisters 3
Bed Capacity 195

Sisters of Bon Secours Nursing Care Center
26001 E. Jefferson
St. Clair Shores, MI 48081
Tel: 810-779-7000
ANNE SADLER, Admin.
A member of the Bon Secours of Michigan Healthcare Systems, Inc. operated by the Sisters of Bon Secours. The center provides short and long term nursing, residential care and rehabilitative services for older adults.
Bed Capacity 200

Warren
Archdiocese of Detroit

A Friends House Adult Day Care Center
28111 Imperial Dr.
Warren, MI 48093
Tel: 810-751-6260
Daytime care for older adults. Support services for care giving families. A service of Catholic Services of Macomb.
CAROL YEE, Dir.

Waterford
Archdiocese of Detroit

Fox Manor, Inc.
2350 Watkins Lake Rd.
Waterford, MI 48238
Tel: 810-674-9590
Dominican Sisters.
Residential facility for independent senior citizens of moderate or limited means.
Sr. VIRGINIA BERAK, Admin.

Lourdes Nursing Home
Dominican Sisters of Oxford, MI
2300 Watkins Lake Rd.
Waterford, MI 48328
Tel: 810-674-2241
Sr. SUSAN MCMAHON, O.P., Admin.
Rev. JEROME KRIEG, Res. Chap.
Skilled & basic nursing facility for men and women; 24 hour nursing care.
Residents 108

St. Jude Home, Inc.
2270 Marwood
Waterford, MI 48328
Tel: 810-673-5179
SAM YAKER, Pres.
Dominican Sisters residential facility for those over 60 years of age requiring supervisory care, but not skilled nursing.
Religious 1
Lay Staff 6
Residents 6
McFadden Home
2150 Watkins Lake Rd.
Waterford, MI 48328
Tel: 810-673-3347
Religious 2
Lay Staff 2
Residents 6

MINNESOTA

Albany
Diocese of St. Cloud

Mother of Mercy Nursing Home and Retirement Center
Box 676
Albany, MN 56307
Tel: 320-845-2195
BOB WIKAN, Admin.
Rev. JOHN EIDENSCHINK, O.S.B., Chap.
Guests 114

Austin
Diocese of Winona

Sacred Heart Hospice, Inc.
1200 Twelfth St., S.W.
Austin, MN 55912
Tel: 507-433-1808
REBECCA MATHEWS HALVERSON, Admin.
Rev. FRANK E. ENRIGHT, Chap.
Sisters of the Third Order of St. Francis of the Congregation of Our Lady of Lourdes 1
Bed Capacity 59
Residents 59
Adult Day Care (patient days) 5,244
Alzheimer's Day Program (patient days) 2,900

Breckenridge
Diocese of St. Cloud

St. Francis Home
Breckenridge, MN 56520
Tel: 218-643-7661
KALVIN G. MICHELS, Vice Pres. Admin.
Rev. STANLEY WIESER, Chap.
KAREN STOKES, Pastoral Care Dir.
Residents 124

Cold Spring
Diocese of St. Cloud

Assumption Court
615 1st St. N.
Cold Spring, MN 56320
Tel: 320-685-4110
Sr. MARY ROGER, O.S.B., Admin.
Rev. MARK SCHNEIDER, O.S.B., Chap.
Residents 34

Assumption Home
715 N. First St.
Cold Spring, MN 56320
Tel: 320-685-3693; Fax: 320-685-7044
Sr. MARY ROGER ANDERT, O.S.B., Admin.
Rev. MARK SCHNEIDER, O.S.B., Chap.
Sisters of St. Benedict 2
Residents 95

John Paul Apartments
200 Eighth Ave. N.
Cold Spring, MN 56320
Tel: 320-685-4429
Pioneer Housing Development, Inc.
Sr. MARY ROGER ANDERT, O.S.B., Admin.
Rev. MARK SCHNEIDER, O.S.B., Chap.

Apartments 67

Mother Teresa Home
101 Tenth Ave.
Cold Spring, MN 56320
Tel: 320-685-8626
Mr. Steven P. Bresnahan, Exec. Dir.
John Krueger, Dir. Residential Svcs.
Supervised Living Situation for Persons with Developed Mental Disabilities.
Residents 4

St. Ann's Home
103 10th Ave. N.
Cold Spring, MN 56320
Tel: 320-685-7898
Mr. Steven P. Bresnahan, Exec, Dir,
John Krueger, Dir. Residential Svcs.
Supervised Living Situation for Persons with Developed Mental Disabilities.
Residents 4

St. Luke's Home
411 Eighth Ave. N.
Cold Spring, MN 56320
Tel: 320-685-7750
Mr. Steven P. Bresnahan, Exec. Dir.
John Krueger, Dir. Residential Svcs.
Adults with mild to moderate developmental disabilities.
Residents 4

Cold Springs
Diocese of St. Cloud

Bethany Home
13 8th Ave. S.
Cold Springs, MN 56320
Tel: 320-685-7899
Mr. Steven P. Bresnahan, Exec. Dir,
John Krueger, Dir. Residential Svcs.
Supervised Living Situation for Persons with Developed Mental Disabilities.

Crookston
Diocese of Crookston

Villa St. Vincent
516 Walsh St.
Crookston, MN 56716
Mr. Michael D. Siekas, Admin.
Sisters of St. Benedict 3
Board and Care Beds 34
Assisted Living Beds 27
Skilled Nursing Beds 104
Residents 138

Detroit Lakes
Diocese of Crookston

St. Mary's Nursing Center
Detroit Lakes, MN 56501
Mr. Chuck Hofius, Admin.
Residents 139
Attended by Staff of St. Mary's Regional Health Center.

Duluth
Diocese of Duluth

Benedictine Health Center
(Sub. of Benedictine Health System)
935 Kenwood Ave.
Duluth, MN 55811
Tel: 218-723-6408; Fax: 218-723-6449
Rev. Bernard Brennan, Chap.
Sr. Mary Susan Dewitt, O.S.B., Dir. of Chaplaincy Svcs.
Rehabilitation services and respite care.
Permanent Guests 120
Day Care:
Adults 44
Children 89

St. Ann's Senior Residence
330 E. Third St.
Duluth, MN 55805
Tel: 218-727-8831; Fax: 218-727-8833
Mr. Frederick Olsen, Admin.
Rev. Robert Bester, Chap.
Sisters of St. Benedict 1
Residents 185

Fergus Falls
Diocese of St. Cloud

Catholic Charities Intensive Treatment Unit
Box 1006
Fergus Falls, MN 56538-1006
Tel: 218-739-9325; Fax: 218-739-2242
Mr. Steven Bresnahan, Exec. Dir. in St. Cloud
John Krueger, Dir. Residential Svc. in St. Cloud
Children 14

Hastings
Archdiocese of St. Paul and Minneapolis

Regina Convalescent and Nursing Care and Retirement Center
Hastings, MN 55033
Tel: 612-480-4333
Rev. James J. Dunne, S.S.C., Res. Chap.
Regina Healthcare
Number under care 74
(Convalescent and Nursing Care) 61
(Retirement Center) 42
(Boarding Care) 32
Total Staff 67

Little Falls
Diocese of St. Cloud

Alverna Apartments
300 Eighth Ave., S.E.
Little Falls, MN 56345
Tel: 320-632-1246
Bea Britz, Chap.
Residents 64

St. Camillus Place
1100 S.E. Fourth St.
Little Falls, MN 56345
Tel: 320-632-6894
Mary Cordts, Admin.
Randal Fossum, Dir.
Bea Britz, Chap.
Beds 14

St. Otto's Care Center
920 S.E. 4th St.
Little Falls, MN 56345
Tel: 320-632-9281; Fax: 320-632-1120
Cory Glad, Admin.
Bea Britz, Chap.
Residents 150

Minneapolis
Archdiocese of St. Paul and Minneapolis

St. Joseph's Home for Children
1121 E. 46th St.
Minneapolis, MN 55407
Tel: 612-827-6241
Mr. Douglas Goke, Admin.
In res.,
Rev. Msgr. J. Jerome Boxleitner
Intake; Emergency Shelter; Diagnostic and Assessment; Serving 3,821 Children Yearly; Residential Treatment (services 81); Day Treatment (services 49); Family Stability (outreach) Serving 120 Families Yearly; 3 Community Homes Serving 115 Yearly.
Lay persons 205

Morris
Diocese of St. Cloud

Villa of St. Francis Nursing Home
1001 Scott Ave.
Morris, MN 56267
Tel: 320-589-1133
Carol Abele, Admin.
Guests 138

Parkers Prairie
Diocese of St. Cloud

St. William's Living Center
P.O. Box 30
Parkers Prairie, MN 56361
Tel: 218-338-4671; Fax: 218-338-5917
Paul Baer, Admin.
Guests 90

Pierz
Diocese of St. Cloud

St. Mary's Villa Inc.
Pierz, MN 56364
Tel: 320-468-6405
Rev. Kenneth Brenny
Virginia M. Meyer, Admin.
Guests 101

Rochester
Diocese of Winona

Guest House
4800 48th St., N.E., P.O. Box 954
Rochester, MN 55903
Tel: 800-634-4155; 507-288-4693
William C. Morgan, Dir.
A State licensed, JCAHO accredited and ecclesiastically endorsed residential treatment center for priests, brothers, deacons and seminarians. (Corporate headquarters located in Lake Orion, MI 48361).
Bed Capacity 39

Madonna Towers of Rochester, Inc.
4001 19th Ave., N.W.
Rochester, MN 55901
Tel: 507-288-3911; Fax: 507-288-0393
Subsidiary of Benedictine Health System.
Mark Cairns, Admin.
Rev. Cathal J. Gallagher, S.S.C.
Guests 168
Chapel of the Immaculate Conception
Health Care Endowment Fund
4001 19th Ave., N.W.
Rochester, MN 55901

Sleepy Eye
Diocese of New Ulm

Divine Providence Community Home & Lake Villa Maria Senior Apts.
700 3rd Ave. N.W.
Sleepy Eye, MN 56085-1099
Tel: 507-794-3011;794-5333
Daughters of St. Mary of Providence.
Sr. Sharon Williams, D.S.M.P., Admin.
Sisters 4
Lay Workers 76
Aged Residents 58
Tenants 26

St. Cloud
Diocese of St. Cloud

Caritas Family Services, Catholic Charities Community Services
305 N. Seventh Ave.
St. Cloud, MN 56303
Tel: 320-252-4121; Fax: 320-259-8761
Mr. Steven P. Bresnahan, Exec. Dir.
Thomas Keaveny, L.I.C.S.W., Dir. Community Svcs.

Community Services of Catholic Charities
205 Seventh Ave. N.
St. Cloud, MN 56303
Tel: 320-259-8757; Fax: 320-240-3339
Community Service of Catholic Charities: SILS (Semi-Independent Living Skills), Personal Care Attendants, Community Support for Mentally Ill and Related Services to Persons with Disabilities.
Mr. Steven P. Bresnahan, Exec. Dir.
Thomas Keaveny, L.I.C.S.W., Dir. Community Svcs.

Day Treatment Services
1712 Seventh Ave. S.
St. Cloud, MN 56301
Tel: 320-251-3647
Mr. Steven P. Bresnahan, Exec. Dir.
John Krueger, Dir. Residential Svcs.
Students 24

In-Home Family Services, Catholic Charities Community Services
700 Mall Germain
St. Cloud, MN 56302
Tel: 320-251-1404; Fax: 320-252-8180
Mr. Steven P. Bresnahan, Exec. Dir.
Thomas Keaveny, L.I.C.S.W., Dir. Community Svcs.

LaPaz Community Inc.
1730 Seventh Ave., S.
St. Cloud, MN 56301
Tel: 320-253-9470
Mr. Steven P. Bresnahan, Exec. Dir.
Harvey Schmitt, Dir. Housing Svcs.

St. Benedict's Center
1810 Minnesota Blvd., S.E.
St. Cloud, MN 56304
Tel: 320-252-0010; Fax: 320-654-2351
Linda Doerr, Exec. Dir.
Robin Theis, Admin., Housing and Community Svcs.
Rev. Meinrad Dindorf, O.S.B., Chap.
Corporate Division of the St. Cloud Hospital. Operated under the auspices of the local Catholic Church of St. Cloud.
Residential Homes for residents with Alzheimers. All Benedict Homes are managed by St. Benedict's Center. A division of the St. Cloud Hospital. Operated under the auspices of the local Catholic Church of St. Cloud.
Residents 222
Benedict Village

2000 15th Ave., S.E.
St. Cloud, MN 56304
Tel: 320-252-4380
LINDA DOERR, Exec. Dir.
ROBIN THEIS, Admin., Housing and Community Svcs.
Rev. MEINRAD DINDORF, O.S.B., Chap.
Managed by St. Benedict's Center. A Division of the St. Cloud Hospital. Operated under the auspices of the local Catholic Church of St. Cloud.
Residents 115
Benedict Homes
Isaiah House
2052 15th Ave., S.E.
St. Cloud, MN 56304
Tel: 320-252-0010
Ruth House
1342 Minnesota Blvd., S.E.
St. Cloud, MN 56304
Tel: 320-252-0010
Rebekah House
1346 Minnesota Blvd., S.E.
St. Cloud, MN 56304
Tel: 320-252-0010
Sarah House
2060 15th Ave., S.E.
St. Cloud, MN 56304
Tel: 320-252-0010
Daniel House
1344 Minnesota Blvd., S.E.
St. Cloud, MN 56304
Tel: 320-252-0010
Timothy House
1348 Minnesota Blvd., S.E.
St. Cloud, MN 56304
Tel: 320-252-0010
Residential Homes for residents with Alzheimers. All Benedict Homes are managed by St. Benedict's Center. A division of the St. Cloud Hospital. Operated under the auspices of the local Catholic Church of St. Cloud.
Day Break
2056 15th Ave., S.E.
St. Cloud, MN 56304
Tel: 320-252-0010
Adult day care for individuals with memory loss located outside of Center but on Campus. Operated under the auspices of the local Catholic Church of St. Cloud.
Staff 2
Participants 10
Day Break II
2044 15th Ave., S.E.
St. Cloud, MN 56304
Tel: 320-252-0010
Adult day care for frail elderly in residential setting on campus. Operated under the auspices of the local Catholic Church of St. Cloud.
Staff 5
Participants 7
Benedict Court
1980 15 Ave., S.E.
St. Cloud, MN 56304
Tel: 320-252-0010
Assisted living apartments.
LINDA DOERR, Exec. Dir.
ROBIN THEIS, Admin., Housing and Community Svcs.
Sr. JUDITH SCHAFFER, Benedict Court Dir.
Rev. MEINRAD DINDORF, O.S.B., Chap.
Managed by St. Benedict's Center. A Division of the St. Cloud Hospital. Operated under the auspices of the local Catholic Church of St. Cloud.
Staff 12
Residents 31

**Benet Place*
1420 Minnesota Blvd., S.E.
St. Cloud, MN 56304
Tel: 320-252-2557
Subsidized apartments with supportive services for older adults only. Operated under the auspices of the local Catholic Church of St. Cloud.
Staff 4
Tenants 43

St. Cloud Children's Home of the Diocese of St. Cloud
1726 Seventh Ave. S.
St. Cloud, MN 56301
Tel: 320-251-8811; Fax: 320-251-3198
Mr. STEVEN P. BRESNAHAN, Exec. Dir.
JOHN KRUEGER, Dir. Residential Svcs.
Children 78
Youth Learning Center
374 Fourth Ave. S.
St. Cloud, MN 56301
Tel: 320-253-6614
Cottage 8 - St. Cloud Children's Home
1700 Seventh Ave. S.
St. Cloud, MN 56301
Tel: 320-251-9101

St. Elizabeth Home
306 15th Ave., N.
St. Cloud, MN 56301
Tel: 320-252-8350
Mr. STEVEN P. BRESNAHAN, Exec. Dir.
JOHN KRUEGER, Dir. of Residential Svcs.
Board and Lodging Home for Functionally Impaired Adults.
Residents 18

St. Paul
Archdiocese of St. Paul and Minneapolis

Bethany Convent for Retired Sisters
1870 Randolph
St. Paul, MN 55105
Tel: 612-690-7050
Sr. DOLORE ROCHON, Admin.
Sr. MARY CALDER, C.S.J., Dir. of Community
Sisters of St. Joseph of Carondelet.
Residents 150

Franciscan Health Community
1925 Norfolk Ave.
St. Paul MN 55116
Tel: 612-696-8400
JOSEPH STANISLAV, Pres. & CEO
Clergy:
Rev. Msgr. FRANCIS J. FLEMING
Revs.:
MARTIN M.P. FLEMING
JOHN R. FLEMING (NU)
Sisters 4
Aged Residents 223

Guild Supported Housing Services
289 E. Fifth St.
St. Paul, MN 55101
Tel: 612-291-0067
Programs owned by The Guild of Catholic Women. Supportive living environments for adults who have experienced serious and persistant mental illness. Apartments and group living available.
Capacity for clients:
St. Paul 160
Dakota County 75

Holy Family Residence
330 S. Exchange St.
St. Paul, MN 55102
Tel: 612-227-0336
Sr. MARGUERITE MC CARTHY, Supr.
Rev. ROBERT FITZGERALD, S.J., Chap.
Little Sisters of the Poor 12
Aged Residents 75
Apartments 32
Total Staff, all facilities 136

Our House of Minnesota, Inc. I
1846 Dayton Ave.
St. Paul, MN 55104
Tel: 612-644-6650
Office
Tel: 612-646-1104
DENNIS HOLMAN, Admin.
Staff 8
Mentally Handicapped Adults 6

Our House of Minnesota, Inc. II
1846 Portland
St. Paul, MN 55104
Tel: 612-644-2411
Office:
Tel: 612-646-1104
DENNIS HOLMAN, Admin.
Staff 14
Mentally Handicapped Adults 6

Our Lady of Good Counsel Home
2076 St. Anthony Ave.
St. Paul, MN 55104
Tel: 612-646-2797
Sisters of St. Dominic. Servants of Relief for Incurable Cancer.
Sr. M. JOSEPH, O.P., Supr.
Rev. JAMES W. JACKSON
Nursing Sisters 9
Bed capacity 40
Patients assisted annually 175
Total Assisted 175
Total Staff 35

Staples
Diocese of St. Cloud

Mary Rondorf Retirement Home of Sacred Heart Parish
Staples, MN 56479
Tel: 218-894-2124
Mrs. VIRGINIA ROLLINS, Admin.
Guests 45

Wabasha
Diocese of Winona

St. Elizabeth's Health Care Center
626 Shields Ave.
Wabasha, MN 55981
Tel: 612-565-4581
(Conducted in connection with St. Elizabeth's Hospital).
THOMAS CROWLEY, Admin.
Rev. JOSEPH R. MCGINNIS
Skilled Beds 100
Admissions 90
St. Elizabeth's Nursing Home
1200 5th Grant Blvd., W.
Wabasha, MN 55981
(Conducted in connection with St. Elizabeth's Hospital).
THOMAS CROWLEY, Pres.
Rev. JOSEPH MCGINNIS
Beds 50
Residents 50

Waite Park
Diocese of St. Cloud

St. Francis Home
25 Second St. N.
Waite Park, MN 56387
Tel: 320-251-7630
Supervised living situation for Persons with Developed Disabilities.
Mr. STEVEN P. BRESNAHAN, Exec. Dir.
JOHN KRUEGER, Dir. Residential Svcs.
Residents 4

Winona
Diocese of Winona

St. Anne Hospice, Inc.
1347 W. Broadway
Winona, MN 55987
Tel: 507-454-3621
RICHARD BOYD, Admin.
Rev. Msgr. J. RICHARD FEITEN, Chap.
Sisters of the Third Order of St. Francis of the Congregation of Our Lady of Lourdes 4
Bed Capacity 134
Residents 134
Adult Day Care (patient days) 873

St. Francis Community Programs of Minnesota, Inc.
725 W. Broadway
Winona, MN 55987
Tel: 507-454-7711
AAmethyst House
428 W. Broadway
Winona, MN 55987
Tel: 507-452-8877
A 14-bed transitional living adult alcohol and chemical abuse home in two locations.
Hiawatha Hall
725 W. Broadway
Winona, MN 55987
Tel: 507-454-7711
A 13-bed mental health residential treatment facility.
Wenonah Hall
221 E. Fourth St.
Winona, MN 55987
Tel: 507-452-1191
10-bed capacity for the mentally ill.
Carillian House
1623 Fourth St., N.W.
Rochester, MN 55901
Tel: 507-281-3000
An 18-bed transitional living alcohol and chemical abuse home for adults.

MISSISSIPPI

Bay St. Louis
Diocese of Biloxi

Notre Dame de la Mer Retirement Apartments
292 Hwy. 90
Bay St. Louis, MS 39520
Tel: 601-467-2885; Fax: 601-466-6300
PATTY ROBERTS, Mgr.
Total Staff 8
Total in Residence 62

Biloxi
Diocese of Biloxi

Gabriel Manor
2321 Atkinson Rd.
Biloxi, MS 39531
Tel: 601-388-1013
Ms. LOUISE CUMMINS, Res. Mgr.

Total Staff 6
Total in Residence 52

Santa Maria Retirement Apartments
674 Beach
Biloxi, MS 39530
Tel: 601-432-1289
Sr. PHYLLIS GOLAB, C.S.C., Res. Mgr.
Total Staff 6
Total in Residence 231

Jackson
Diocese of Jackson

D'Evereaux Hall Home, Inc.
P.O. Box 2248
Jackson, MS 39225
Tel: 601-355-8634
Mrs. LINDA RAFF

St. Mary Orphan Home, Inc.
P.O. Box 2248
Jackson, MS 39225
Tel: 601-355-8634
Mrs. LINDA RAFF

Ocean Springs
Diocese of Biloxi

Samaritan House
642 Jackson Ave.
Ocean Springs, MS 39564
JUDY HIGGINS, Mgr.
Total Staff 3
Total in Residence 52

Villa Maria Retirement Apartments
921 Porter Ave.
Ocean Springs, MS 39564
Tel: 601-875-8811
Mrs. CINDY A. LADNIER, Mgr.
Total Staff 15
Total in Residence 225

MISSOURI

Blue Springs
Diocese of Kansas City-St. Joseph

St. Mary's Manor
111 Mock Ave.
Blue Springs, MO 64014
Tel: 816-228-5655
PAT BAKER, Admin.
Rev. JOACHIM SCHIEBER, O.S.B., Chap.
Long term care facility with skilled nursing care and residential care.
Skilled care 132
Residential care 57

Columbia
Diocese of Jefferson City

Columbia Nursing Home Ministry
65202
P.O. Box 103-BC
Stoutsville, MO 65283
Tel: 573-672-3294
Rev. RICHARD C. HUNKINS, Dir.

Eureka
Archdiocese of St. Louis

Price Memorial
Forby Rd., P.O. Box 476
Eureka, MO 63025
Tel: 314-587-3200
Bro. JOHN SPILA, O.S.F., Admin.
A skilled nursing facility conducted by the Franciscan Missionary Brothers of St. Joseph's Hill Infirmary.
Brothers 3
Residents 120

St. Joseph Hill Infirmary, Inc.
St. Joseph Rd.
Eureka, MO 63025
Tel: 314-587-3661
Bro. BERNARDO TROSA, O.S.F., Admin.
A skilled nursing facility conducted by the Franciscan Missionary Brothers of the Sacred Heart of Jesus.
Brothers 11
Residents 127
Total Assisted 120
Total Staff 55

Florissant
Archdiocese of St. Louis

Father Dunne's News Boys Home
853 Dunn Rd.
Florissant, MO 63031
Tel: 314-837-0513
Corporate Title: Father Dunne's Newsboys' Home and Protectorate
WILLIAM J. DONLEY, Exec. Dir.
Emergency and long-term residential care to homeless, neglected and abused boys, status offenders and boys with family problems. Ages 12-21.
Children 30
Total in Residence 109
Total Staff 27

Marygrove Services, Inc.
2705 Mullanphy Ln.
Florissant, MO 63031
Tel: 314-837-1702; Fax: 314-837-5319
Owned and operated under the auspices of Catholic Charities.
Sr. HELEN NEGRI, D.C., Admin.
Residential treatment for emotionally disturbed males and females (ages 6-19). Special education, therapy and medical services. Overnight emergency care: males and females (Birth-18).
Bed Capacity 87
Sequoia House - Mullanphy
Group Home for Females Ages 17-21.
Beds 10
Sycamore House
Bed Capacity 3
Overnight Emergency Care: Bed Capacity 8

Jefferson City
Diocese of Jefferson City

St. Joseph's Home
1306 W. Main St.
Jefferson City, MO 65109
Tel: 573-635-0166
Conducted by the Carmelite Sisters of the Divine Heart of Jesus.
GRACE HOFFMANN, Admin.
Sr. LYDIA ANN BRAUN, Supr.
DENISE SOMMERER, Dir. Nurses
Rev. THOMAS MCGRATH, Chap.
Sisters 6
Residents 90

Villa Marie Skilled Nursing Facility
1030 Edmonds St.
Jefferson City, MO 65109
Tel: 573-761-6700
Owned and operated by St. Louis Health Care Network, a member of the SSM Health Care System.
JOHN H. SCHULTE, Admin.
Ms. BARBARA L. LOWRY, Dir. Nursing Svcs.
Rev. HUGH F. BEHAN, Chap.
Franciscan Sisters of Mary, St Louis 4
Bed Capacity 120

Kansas City
Diocese of Kansas City-St. Joseph

Brighton Place
2429 Brighton
Kansas City, MO 64127
Tel: 816-231-3211
MARY DAVIS, Mgr.

Cathedral Square Towers
444 W. 12th St.
Kansas City, MO 64105
Tel: 816-471-6555
Apartment Residence for the Elderly and Handicapped.
Mrs. SANDRA CARLSON, Mgr.
Ms. CATHERINE ANCONA, Asst. Mgr.
Mr. NEAL D. COLBY, JR., Diocesan Liaison
Units 156
Total in Residence 167
Total Staff 8

Columbus Park Plaza
801 Pacific
Kansas City, MO 64106
Tel: 816-472-0887
Mr. NEAL D. COLBY, Diocesan Liaison
Apartment residence for elderly and handicapped.
Units 56
Total in Residence 55
Total Staff 2

Jeanne Jugan Center
8745 James A. Reed Rd.
Kansas City, MO 64138
Tel: 816-761-4744; Fax: 816-761-4724
Legal Title: *Little Sisters of the Poor*
Little Sisters of the Poor
Sr. MAUREEN WEISS, Supr.
Rev. FRANCIS J. SCHUELE, Chap.
Sisters 14
Apartments 33
Beds 78
Total in Residence 121
Total Staff 90

Marlborough Manor
1818 E. 79th St.
Kansas City, MO 64132
Tel: 816-221-4377
Rental housing for low income.

Red Bridge Place
11300 Colorado
Kansas City, MO 64137
Tel: 816-761-4667
ANN SCOTT, Mgr.

Redemptorist Retirement Home
207 W. Linwood
Kansas City, MO 64111-1327
Tel: 816-561-3025
Sr. M. ANNETTE SCHORMAN, C.S.J., Dir.
Guests 19
Total Staff 6

Tremont Place
6161 N. Chatham
Kansas City, MO 64151
Tel: 816-587-7707
CAROL SINCLAIR, Mgr.

Kirkwood
Archdiocese of St. Louis

St. Agnes Home for the Elderly
10341 Manchester Rd.
Kirkwood, MO 63122
Tel: 314-965-7616; Fax: 314-965-3179
Sr. M. ANGELINA Finnel, Carmel.D.C.J., Admin.
Rev. Msgr. JOSEPH O'BRIEN
In res.,
His Eminence JOHN JOSEPH CARDINAL CARBERRY, Former Archbishop of St. Louis
Conducted for Elderly Ladies, Gentlemen and Couples by the Carmelite Sisters of the Divine Heart of Jesus.
Legal Title: *Carmelite Sisters of the Divine Heart of Jesus of Missouri*
Sisters 10
Guests 122
Total Staff 109

Liberty
Diocese of Kansas City-St. Joseph

Immacolata Manor Foundation
2101 Hughes Rd.
Liberty, MO 64068-9397
Tel: 816-781-4332; Fax: 816-781-8820
Residential Care Center for developmentally disabled women.
Sr. MARY IMELDA KOCH, O.S.B., Exec. Dir.
Sr. THERESE KOCH, O.S.B., Pres. (Foundation)
Operated by the Immacolata Board of Directors.
Residents 29
Total Staff 22

Our Lady of Mercy Country Home
2205 Hughes Rd.
Liberty, MO 64068
Tel: 816-781-5711
Mercedarian Missionaries of Berriz.
Sr. DELIA GOMEZ, M.M.B., Pres.
Guests 110
Sisters 33

Mehlville
Archdiocese of St. Louis

Nazareth Living Center
2 Nazareth Ln.
Mehlville, MO 63129
Tel: 314-487-3950
Residential and Skilled Nursing Care Facility.
Sisters of St. Joseph of Carondelet and General Public.
Sr. AUDREY OLSON, C.S.J., Supr.
Rev. THOMAS GRAHAM, Chap.
Total Assisted 288
Total Staff 250

Normandy
Archdiocese of St. Louis

Maria Droste Residence
7660 Natural Bridge Rd.
Normandy, MO 63121
Tel: 314-383-5553
Sisters of the Good Shepherd
For Women in Need.

Capacity 12

St. Vincent Home for Children
7401 Florissant Rd.
Normandy, MO 63121
Tel: 314-261-6011
Legal Title: *The German St. Vincent Orphan Association*
Sr. JOANN KELZER, S.C.C., Exec. Dir.
Sr. PAULINE SHAFER, Supr.
Rev. MARTIN MANNION, Chap.
Sisters of Christian Charity 6
Children 48
Chapel of the Sacred Heart.

Savannah
Diocese of Kansas City-St. Joseph

La Verna Heights Retirement Center, Inc.
104 E. Park Ave., P.O. Box 488
Savannah, MO 64485-0488
Tel: 816-324-3179
MICHAEL BURAK, Admin.
Sisters of St. Francis of Savannah.
Guest Capacity 39
Total Assisted 72
Total Staff 52

La Verna Village Apartments
1000-1005 Hall Ave.
Savannah, MO 64485
Tel: 816-324-3179
Sisters of St. Francis of Savannah.
Rev. WALTER HEENEY, O.S.B., Chap.
DOYLE MCCUSH, Mgr.
Apartments for the elderly and handicapped.
Units 20
Total in Residence 24

La Verna Village Nursing Home
904 Hall Ave., P.O. Box 279
Savannah, MO 64485
Tel: 816-324-3185; Fax: 816-324-4097
MICHAEL BURAK, Admin.
Sisters of St. Francis of Savannah.
Sr. M. MAGDALENE, O.S.F., Asst. Admin.
Guest Capacity 120
Total Assisted 161
Total Staff 124

Springfield
Diocese of Springfield-Cape Girardeau

St. John's Mercy Villa
1100 E. Montclair
Springfield, MO 65807
Tel: 417-888-8500; Fax: 417-888-8532
Sisters of Mercy Healthcare System (St. Louis).
Skilled Care of Long Term Nursing Home, for the Aged and Chronically Ill.
Mr. DON SWAFFORD, Admin.
Rev. WAYNE BARRON, C.M.F., Chap.
Sisters 2
Bed Capacity 150

St. Charles
Archdiocese of St. Louis

St. Joseph Carmelite Home
723 First Capitol Dr.
St. Charles, MO 63301
Tel: 314-946-4140
Rev. ALBERT F. DANTER, Chap.
Conducted by the Carmelite Sisters of the Divine Heart of Jesus.
Legal Title: *Carmelite Sisters of the Divine Heart of Jesus of Missouri*
Sisters 5
Guests 103

St. Louis
Archdiocese of St. Louis

Alexian Brothers Lansdowne Village
4624 Lansdowne
St. Louis, MO 63116
Tel: 314-351-6888; Fax: 314-351-5825
Total Assisted 435
Total Staff 150

Alexian Brothers Sherbrooke Village
4005 Ripa Ave.
St. Louis, MO 63125
Tel: 314-544-1111; Fax: 314-544-5134
C. MICHAEL ROTH, Pres.
Total in Residence (Assisted Living) 44
Total Assisted (Nursing Care) 114

Boys Hope/Girls Hope of St. Louis, Inc.
755 S. New Ballas Rd., Ste. 120
St. Louis, MO 63141
Tel: 314-692-7477; Fax: 314-692-7810
CAROLYN HENRY, Exec. Dir.
Residential Care for Adolescent Boys and Girls, Troubled by Family Disruptions, who are Capable of College Preparatory High School Work. Ages 7-18.
Total Assisted 55
Total Staff 13

Cardinal Glennon Children's Hospital
1465 S. Grand Blvd.
St. Louis, MO 63104
Tel: 314-577-5600; Fax: 314-268-6468
Mr. DOUGLAS A. RIES, Pres.
Sr. JUDITH CARRON, R.S.M., Dir. of Pastoral Care
A Member of the SSM Health Care System.
Sisters 4
Bed Capacity (for Children) 190
Patients assisted annually 164,573

Cathedral Tower
325 N. Newstead Ave.
St. Louis, MO 63108
Tel: 314-531-0511
Ms. RUTH RAITHEL, Admin.
Residence for Women, Men and Girls. Operated by Catholic Charities.
Sisters 11
Residents 124

Chariton Apartments
4249 Michigan Ave.
St. Louis, MO 63111
Tel: 314-352-7600
Retirement Home for the Elderly, Conducted by the Third Order of St. Francis, Franciscan Tertiary Province of Missouri, Inc.
Residents 136
Apartments 122

Father Dempsey's Hotel, Inc.
3427 Washington Ave.
St. Louis, MO 63103
Rev. Msgr. CHARLES A. MOTTIN, Dir.
Total in Residence 43
Total Staff 3

Father Jim's Home
3427 Washington Ave.
St. Louis, MO 63103
Tel: 314-535-7221
Rev. Msgr. CHARLES A. MOTTIN, Gen. Mgr.
Under Care 81
Total in Residence 44
Total Staff 4

Fusz Pavilion
3601 Lindell Blvd.
St. Louis, MO 63108
Tel: 314-534-1201
A Retirement Home for Jesuits.
Rev. PAUL C. PILGRAM, S.J., Rector
Bro. ROBERT L. AUG, S.J., Asst. Rector
Revs.:
JOHN R. ALLEN, S.J.
LAWRENCE E. BARRY, S.J.
CHRISTIAN L. BONNET, S.J.
JOHN C. CHOPPESKY, S.J.
DARYL G. CORNISH, S.J.
VINCENT F. DAUES, S.J.
ANDREW J. DEEMAN, S.J.
WILLIAM F. FERRELL, S.J.
JOSEPH P. FISHER, S.J.
JOHN G. FLANNIGAN, S.J.
LOUIS J. HANLON, S.J.
ROBERT J. HENLE, S.J.
FRANCIS R. LEIKER, S.J.
EDWARD P. MANHARD, S.J.
LEONARD M. MURRAY, S.J.
J. PAUL O'CONNOR, S.J.
JOHN R. PADBERG, S.J.
GEORGE M. PIEPER, S.J.
BERNARD C. SCHULTE, S.J.
EDWARD H. WINTERGALEN, S.J.
JEROME A. ZUMMACH, S.J.
Bros.:
PAUL M. HOFER, S.J.
ROBERT H. NILGES, S.J.
PHILIP G. MALONE, S.J.
JOHN J. SCHWENDEMANN, S.J.
Priests 22
Brothers 5
Total Assisted 26
Total Staff 25

Little Sisters of the Poor, Home for the Aged
3225 N. Florissant Ave.
St. Louis, MO 63107
Tel: 314-421-6022
Sr. MARY SYLVIA KARL, L.S.P., Supr.
Rev. JOSEPH GROBEN, M.S.F., Chap.
Sisters 14
Residents 110
Total assisted 79
Total Staff 127

Marian Hall Agencies
1340 Partridge Ave.
St. Louis, MO 63130
Tel: 314-726-3339
Sr. PATRICIA JOHNSON, C.S.J., Admin.
Residential Care to Homeless, Neglected and Abused Adolescent Girls (ages 12-18) with Emotional and/or Behavioral Problems.
Legal Title: *Managers of the Roman Catholic Orphan Asylums of St. Louis*
Sisters 2
Lay Staff 17
Capacity 24

Marian Hall Emergency Shelter
325 N. Newstead
St. Louis, MO 63108
Tel: 314-531-0511
Emergency Shelter in a Residential Setting for Runaway, Homeless or Abused Adolescent Girls (ages 12-18), with Emotional and/or Behavioral Problems.
Legal Title: *Managers of the Roman Catholic Orphan Asylums of St. Louis*
Lay Staff 11
Capacity 10
Total Assisted 281

Mary, Queen and Mother Nursing Center
7601 Watson Rd.
St. Louis, MO 63119
Rev. JOHN P. COMER
BETTY ETTE, Admin., Tel: 314-961-8485
Total Assisted 327
Total Staff 250

Mother of Good Counsel Home
6825 Natural Bridge Rd., (St. Louis Co.)
St. Louis, MO 63121
Tel: 314-383-4765
Sr. M. STEPHANIE BELGERI, O.S.F., Admin.
Rev. BERNARD F. HUHN, Chap.
Skilled Nursing Facility for Men and Women.
Conducted by Sisters of St. Francis of the Martyr St. George.
Sisters 10
Residents 114
Total Staff 156

Queen of Peace Center
325 N. Newstead Ave.
St. Louis, MO 63108
Tel: 314-531-0511
CONSTANCE S. NEUMANN, Admin.
Substance Abuse Treatment and Rehabilitation for Drug-Affected Women and their Children. Three levels of Care: Outpatient and Inpatient Residential, Medicaid Provider, Therapeutic Daycare and Nursery. Focus on High-Risk Pregnant Women. DMH certified.
Beds 42
Outpatient 150
Total Assisted 1,093
Total Staff 82

Regina Cleri Home
7850 Kenrick Rd.
St. Louis, MO 63119
Tel: 314-968-2240
A Retirement Home for Priests Conducted by the Archdiocese of St. Louis.
Sr. GERALDINE VOGEL, C.PP.S., Admin.
Sisters of the Most Precious Blood of O'Fallon, MO 4
Franciscan Sisters of Our Lady of Perpetual Help 1
Priests 34
Total Staff 24

Rosati Group Home, Inc.
4532 Lindell Blvd.
St. Louis, MO 63108
Tel: 314-367-5500
JOHN M. LALLY, Pres.
Group Home and Stabilization Center for homeless mentally ill adults.

Rosati Stabilization Center
4224 N. Grand Ave.
St. Louis, MO 63107
Tel: 314-534-6624
Residential Transitional Facility for Mentally Ill Homeless.
Managed by the St. Patrick Center.
Capacity 15
Total Assisted 72
Total Staff 9

St. Joseph's Home for Boys
4753 S. Grand Blvd.
St. Louis, MO 63111-1459
Tel: 314-481-9121; Fax: 314-481-5605
Sr. CECILIA LADDA, C.S.J., Exec. Dir.
JAMES M. SINCLAIR, SR., Prog. Dir.
Emergency and Long-Term Residential Treatment Center for Young Men (ages 6-14) with Moderate to Severe Behavioral, Emotional, Family, and/or Educational Problems. Majority are Survivors of Neglect and/or Abuse. Day Treatment Program for Grades 1-8, Residents and Day Students.
Legal Title: *Managers of the Roman Catholic Orphan Asylums of St. Louis*
Sisters of St. Joseph of Carondelet 3
Lay Staff 55
Residential 44
Day Treatment 30
Total Assisted 123

St. Martha's Hall
P.O. Box 4950
St. Louis, MO 63108
Tel: 314-533-1313
MICHELLE SCHILLER-BAKER, Dir.
Provides Shelter, Education, Counseling and Aid to Abused Women & their Children.
Capacity 25

St. Philippine Duchesne Shelter
1015 Goodfellow Blvd.
St. Louis, MO 63112
Tel: 314-454-1012
MARY CARROLL, M.S.W., Coord.
ARNETTA HARRIS, Dir.
Serves homeless families & their children.
Emergency Shelter:
Total Assisted 571
Total Staff 7

SSM Rehabilitation Institute
6420 Clayton Rd., #600
St. Louis, MO 63117
Tel: 314-768-5300; Fax: 314-768-5355
Owned & operated by St. Louis Health Care Network for the rehabilitation of pediatrics, adolescents & adults. A member of the SSM Health Care System.
MELINDA CLARK, Pres.
Bed capacity:
St. Mary's Health Center, St. Louis 60
St. Joseph Health Center, St. Charles 20
Outpatient Locations 13

Villa Maria Center
8351 Florissant Rd.
St. Louis, MO 63121
Tel: 314-521-2255
Ms. MARY PATTON, M.S.
Under the Auspices of Catholic Services for Children and Youth. Comprehensive Program for Unmarried Parents; Provides Individual and Group Counseling, Arranges Obstetrical and Pediatric Care, Provides Educational Services Including Academic and Personal Growth and Development, Training in Parenting and Living Skill.
Capacity 13
Total Assisted 49
Total Staff 13

NEBRASKA

Boys Town
Archdiocese of Omaha

**Father Flanagan's Boys' Home*
Boys Town, NE 68010
Tel: 402-498-1111
Rev. VALENTINE J. PETER, Exec. Dir.
Dr. PATRICK MCGINNIS, Dir. Education
Rev. EUGENE MCREYNOLDS, O.S.B.
High School:
Dr. RIHCARD LOHMEIER, Prin.
Teachers 29
Students 446
Grade School:
CATHY DESALVO, Prin.
Teachers 14
Students 111
Boys Town USA
DON WEBER, Special Deputy, Public Policy Advisor
Dr. DAVID COUGHLIN, Deputy Exec. Dir. Youth Care
DAVID SHANAHAN, Dir. Home Campus & Midwest Region
Boys Town National Research & Training Center
TOM DOWD, Dir.
MARK GRAHAM, Dir. of Operations
Managed Care Division
KAREN AUTHIER, Dir.
Boys Town Research Division
Dr. DAN DALY, Dir.
Boys Town National Research Hospital for Children
Dr. PATRICK BROOKHOUSER, Dir.
Father Flanagan High School
Dr. PATRICK MCGINNIS, Prin.
Boys Town Crisis Hotline
Tel: 800-448-3000
CONSTANCE GARRETT, Coord.
Boys Town Religious Education Program
TOM EVERSON, Dir.
KATHY SORENSEN, Assoc. Dir.

David City
Diocese of Lincoln

St. Joseph's Villa, Inc.
927 7th St.
David City, NE 68632
Tel: 402-367-3045; Fax: 402-367-3730
Sisters Adorers of the Blood of Christ (Wichita, KS).
JOYCE STEWART, Admin.
Residents 65

Kearney
Diocese of Grand Island

Mount Carmel Home-Keens' Memorial
412 W. 18th St.
Kearney, NE 68847
Tel: 308-237-2287
Sr. EMERANTIANA, O.Carm., Supr.
Carmelites 13
Guests 79

Lincoln
Diocese of Lincoln

Bonacum House
3301 Sheridan Blvd.
Lincoln, NE 68506
Residence for retired priests.
Rev. Msgr. WILLIAM J. REZABEK
Rev. Msgr. DENIS L. BARRY
Rev. Msgr. CHARLES J. KEENAN
Rev. Msgr. CLARENCE P. REISDORFF
Revs.:
ERNEST O. SLOUP
JOHN W. KELLY

Madonna Rehabilitation Hospital
5401 South St.
Lincoln, NE 68506
Tel: 402-489-7102
Physical Medicine and Rehabilitation, Outpatient Services, Long-Term Care, and Adult Day Care.
Rev. STANLEY REDMERSKI, Chap.
Sisters 9
Beds 252
Patients assisted annually 1,998

Norfolk
Archdiocese of Omaha

St. Joseph Nursing Home
401 N. 18th St.
Norfolk, NE 68701
Tel: 402-371-9404
JOYCE GIBBS, Interim Admin.
Rev. WILLIAM DEVINE, Chap.
Missionary Benedictine Sisters 3
Aged Residents 95

Omaha
Archdiocese of Omaha

**Alegent Health - Bergan Mercy Health System dba Alegent Health - Mercy Care Center*
1870 S. 75 St.
Omaha, NE 68124
Tel: 402-398-6800
Sisters of Mercy of the Americas.
MARY KEERES, Contact Person
S. DOTTIE BROWN, Svc. Leader
Subacute Care/Skilled Nursing Facility.
Beds 246
Average Daily Census 220

Mercy Villa
1845 S. 72 St.
Omaha, NE 68124
Retirement Home for the Sisters of Mercy of the Americas.
Sr. JOHNEEN OWENS, R.S.M., Administrator & Contact
Rev. Msgr. WILLIAM A. FOSTER, Chap.
Resident Sisters 36

New Cassel Retirement Center
900 N. 90 St.
Omaha, NE 68114
Tel: 402-393-2277
School Sisters of St. Francis.
Mr. JOSEPH H. SCHULTE, Dir.
Rev. JAMES R. TIEGS
MARY ANN KRESS, Dir. Pastoral Care
JOSEPH H. SCHULTE, Contact
Sisters 5
Aged Residents 165

West Point
Archdiocese of Omaha

Franciscan Care Services, Inc., (d.b.a. St. Joseph Retirement Community)
320 E. Decatur
West Point, NE 68788
Tel: 402-372-3477
Sr. ANGELINE HENSEN, Admin.
Franciscan Sisters of Christian Charity, Manitowoc, WI 7
Residents 61

NEW HAMPSHIRE

Allenstown
Diocese of Manchester

Pine Haven Boys Center
River Rd., P.O. Suncook
Allenstown, NH 03275
Somascan Fathers.
Revs.:
JOHN VITALI, C.R.S., M.Ed., Dir.
GIULIANO GEROSA, C.R.S., M.A., Supr.
PAOLO RIVA, C.R.S.
Total Staff 38
Children 20

Berlin
Diocese of Manchester

St. Vincent de Paul Nursing Home
29 Providence Ave.
Berlin, NH 03570
Tel: 603-752-1820
STEVEN WOODS, Admin.
Rev. JOSEPH A. COTE, Chap.
Sr. THERESA RICHARD, S.P.
Sisters of Charity of Providence 6
Aged residents 80

Dover
Diocese of Manchester

St. Ann
Dover, NH 03820
Tel: 603-742-2612; Fax: 603-743-3055
Sr. MARGARET THERESE, O.Carm., Admin.
Rev. FREDERICK J. PENNETT, Chap.
Sisters 5
Total Staff 87
Aged residents 54

Jaffrey
Diocese of Manchester

Good Shepherd Nursing Home
20 Plantation Dr.
Jaffrey, NH 03452
Tel: 603-532-8762
JUDITH A. LEBLANC, Admin.
Total Staff 126
Total Assisted 83

Laconia
Diocese of Manchester

Bishop Bradley Apartments
406 Court St.
Laconia, NH 03246
Total Staff 1
Aged residents 25
Apartments 25

St. Francis Home for the Aged
Laconia, NH 03246
Tel: 603-524-0466; Fax: 603-527-0884
Mrs. JULIEANN R. FAY, Admin.
Rev. RAYMOND A. DEMERS, Chap.
Total Staff 72
Aged residents 51

Manchester
Diocese of Manchester

Carpenter Center, Inc.
323 Franklin St.
Manchester, NH 03101
CAROL HAEBLER, Mgr.
Apartments 119

DBH Shelter, Inc.
DBH Shelter II, Inc.
Apartments 8
DBH Shelter III, Inc.
Apartments 28
DBH Management, Inc.
Total Staff 8
Total Assisted 155

Frances Warde House, Inc.
435 Union St.
Manchester, NH 03103
Residents 26

Mt. Carmel Nursing Home
235 Myrtle St.
Manchester, NH 03104
Tel: 603-627-3811
Carmelite Sisters for the Aged and Infirm.
Sr. JACINTA MARY, O.Carm., Supr. Admin.
Rev. ALBERT L. BOULANGER
Sisters 7
Total Staff 175
Aged residents 120
Total Assisted 145

St. Peter's Home
Manchester, NH 03102-3093
Tel: 603-625-9313; Fax: 603-625-1910
Sr. FLORENCE THERRIEN, S.C.S.H., Dir.
Mrs. DONNA M. VACHON, Asst. Dir.
Sr. RITA BEAULIEU, S.C.S.H., Treas.
Sisters of Charity (Grey Nuns) 4
Total Staff 70
Children 309

St. Teresas Manor & Bishop Primeau Apartments
519 Bridge St.
Manchester, NH 03104
Tel: 603-668-2373
STEPHEN V. FULCHINO, Admin.
LINDA ILLG, Apt. Mgr.
Rev. J. KIERAN O'CONNOR
Sisters 1
Aged Residents 51

Nashua
Diocese of Manchester

Marguerite's Place
120 Main St., Room 110
Nashua, NH 03060
Tel: 603-598-1582
Sr. MARY SHARON WALSH, G.N.S.H., CEO
Total Staff 13
Total in Residence 17

Rochester
Diocese of Manchester

St. Charles Children's Home
19 Grant St.
Rochester, NH 03867
Sisters of Charity of Our Lady, Mother of The Church.
Mother M. PAUL MARIE
Rev. MAURICE R. BOULANGER, Chap.
Sisters 6
Dependent Children 25

Windham
Diocese of Manchester

Warde Health Center
21 Searles Rd.
Windham, NH 03087
Fax: 603-890-1293
Sisters of Mercy
Ms. MONIQUE DOSOGNE, Admin.
Sisters 30
Total Staff 40
Total Assisted 40

NEW JERSEY

Cape May
Diocese of Camden

Victorian Towers Associates
608 Washington St.
Cape May, NJ 08204
Tel: 609-884-5883
Mr. EDWARD STAGEMYER, Supt.

Cherry Hill
Diocese of Camden

The Manor at St. Mary's
1743 Kresson Rd.
Cherry Hill, NJ 08003
Sr. VIRGINIA KUREK, L.S.I.C., Admin.

Marian Residence
1000 Cropwell Rd.
Cherry Hill, NJ 08003
Tel: 609-424-1131
Sr. M. MELCHIOR, L.S.I.C., Supvr.

St. Mary's Nursing Home
1730 Kresson Rd.
Cherry Hill, NJ 08003
Tel: 609-424-9521
Little Servant Sisters of the Immaculate Conception.
Sr. MARY FRANCES SZYMANSKA, Supr.
Sr. M. BEATRIX WIECZOREK, Admin.
Chaplains:
Rev. WILLIAM D. TITMAS
In res.,
Rev. Msgr. JOSEPH E. CONLON
Sisters 7
Residents 215

Village Apartments of Cherry Hill, NJ, Inc.
212 Lourdes Ct.
Cherry Hill, NJ 08003
Tel: 609-424-7913
Mr. MILTON BECK, Supt.

Denville
Diocese of Paterson

Franciscan Oaks Independent Living Units & Health Center
21 Pocono Rd.
Denville, NJ 07834
Staffed by Sisters of the Sorrowful Mother.

St. Francis Health Resort
Denville, NJ 07834
Fax: 201-625-9245
Rest and Residential Home.
Mr. WILLIAM MILIANES, Admin.
Rev. WILLIAM J. FREESWICK, Chap.
Sisters of the Sorrowful Mother 16
Bed Capacity 100
Apartments 63
Guests 150

Hoboken
Archdiocese of Newark

Good Counsel, Inc. (St. Francis Home)
303 Madison St.
Hoboken, NJ 07030
Tel: 201-798-9059; 795-0637; 800-723-8331 (Hotline); Fax: 201-795-0809
Rev. BENEDICT J. GROESCHEL, C.F.R., Chm.
CHRISTOPHER R. BELL, Exec. Dir.
Housing, counseling and referrals for single women who are pregnant or single mothers with children.
Good Counsel, Inc.
P.O. Box 6068
Hoboken, NJ 07030
Tel: 201-795-0637
Residences for single mothers and children.
Rev. BENEDICT J. GROESCHEL, C.F.R., Chm.
CHRISTOPHER R. BELL, Exec. Dir.

Hopewell
Diocese of Trenton

St. Michael's Orphanage and Industrial School
Mailing Address: c/o the Diocese of Trenton
701 Lawrenceville Rd.
Trenton, NJ 08648

Jersey City
Archdiocese of Newark

St. Ann's Home for the Aged
198 Old Bergen Rd.
Jersey City, NJ 07305
Tel: 201-433-0950
Sr. NORAH CLARKE, C.S.J.P., LNHA Admin.
HENRY WOJTOWICZ, Pastoral Care
Sisters of St. Joseph of Peace 5
Total Staff 166
Under Care 106

St. Joseph's Home
81 York St.
Jersey City, NJ 07302
Tel: 201-413-9280
Sr. KRISTIN FUNARI, C.S.J.P., Dir.
Total Staff 13
Total Assisted 111
Transitional housing for homeless women and children.

The Nurturing Place
Sr. BARBARA MORAN, C.S.J.P., Dir., Tel: 201-413-1982
Total Staff 19
Total Assisted 110
A developmental child care center for disadvantaged youngsters.

St. Joseph's Home for the Blind
537 Pavonia Ave.
Jersey City, NJ 07306
Tel: 201-653-8300
Sisters of St. Joseph of Peace.
Sr. TERESA CATHERINE CARBERRY, C.S.J.P., Admin.
Rev. ROBERT L. QUIGLEY, Chap.
Sisters 3
Nursing Home Patients 129
Residents 7

St. Mary's Residence for Business and Professional Women
240 Washington St.
Jersey City, NJ 07302
Tel: 201-432-6289
Sisters of St. Joseph of Peace.
Sr. MARY DONOHUE, C.S.J.P., Admin.
Total Staff 7
Total Assisted 40

Kearny
Archdiocese of Newark

New Jersey Boystown
499 Belgrove Dr.
Kearny, NJ 07032
Tel: 201-991-2850
Family Counseling Services.
Rev. FRANCIS T. MAIONE, Ed.S., Dir.
Pregnancy Counseling and Adoption.
Tel: 201-991-3770

Lawrenceville
Diocese of Trenton

Morris Hall-Saint Lawrence, Inc.
Morris Hall - St. Mary's Residence.
1 Bishop's Dr., P.O. Box 6498
Lawrenceville, NJ 08648-0498
Tel: 609-896-0006
Mr. CHARLES L. BRENNAN, CEO
Mrs. ROSALIE DANEK, R.N., Admin.
In res.,
Revs.:
EDWARD ALZERT
JUSTIN J. HERBST, Chap.
ROBERT MURRAY
EARL GANNON
EDWIN DZIENKIEWICZ
FRANCIS KAPICA
Rev. Msgr. JOHN O'BRIEN
Guests 180

Morris Hall / Saint Lawrence, Inc.
St. Lawrence Rehabilitation Center.
2381 Lawrenceville Rd.
Lawrenceville, NJ 08648
Tel: 609-896-9500
Mr. CHARLES L. BRENNAN, Admin.
Rev. JUSTIN J. HERBST, Chap.
Sr. CLAIRE DESTEFANO, S.S.J., Dir. Pastoral Care
Bed Capacity 116
Bed Licensure 116

Morris Hall / Saint Lawrence, Inc.
Morris Hall - St. Joseph's Nursing Center.
1 Bishop's Dr.
Lawrenceville, NJ 08648-0498
Tel: 609-896-0006
Mrs. ROSALIE DANEK, Admin.
Skilled Nursing Care Facility for the Chronically Ill.
Residences for Senior Citizens.
Bed Capacity 120
Licensed Beds 120
Total in Residence 50

Montclair
Archdiocese of Newark

Mother Seton Residence
51 Washington St.
Montclair, NJ 07042
Tel: 201-783-1400
Sisters of Charity of St. Elizabeth
Sr. ROSE VINCENT, Admin.
Residents 23

St. Vincent's Nursing Home
(Div. of St. Joseph's Hospital and Medical Center)
45 Elm St.
Montclair, NJ 07042
Tel: 201-754-4800; Fax: 201-746-2362

Conducted by Sisters of Charity of St. Elizabeth.
Mr. THOMAS P. SHEEHY, JR., Admin.
Sisters 5
Capacity: Long term care beds 141

Newark
Archdiocese of Newark

Queen of Peace
60 Jay St.
Newark, NJ 07103
Tel: 201-481-9056
Total Staff 4
Total Assisted 330
Missionary Sisters of Charity.

Newfield
Diocese of Camden

Mater Dei Nursing Home
176 Rte. 40
Newfield, NJ 08344
Tel: 609-358-2061
Marianites of Holy Cross.
Sr. ANNE EBERSOLD, Admin.
Rev. SEBASTIAN V. ANNINO, Chap.
Sisters 4
Bed Capacity 64
Residents assisted annually 64

North Plainfield
Diocese of Metuchen

Villa Maria Sanitarium
641 Somerset St.
North Plainfield, NJ 07060-4909
Tel: 908-757-3050; Fax: 908-754-9190
Home for the aged (with infirmary).
Sr. M. LUZIANA, O.S.F., Co-Admin.
KAREN UEBELC, Co-Admin.
Rev. CYPRIAN M. SULLIVAN, O.F.M.Conv., Chap., Tel: 908-756-4186
Patients and Residents 86

Paramus
Archdiocese of Newark

Mount St. Andrew Villa
55 W. Midland Ave.
Paramus, NJ 07652
Tel: 201-261-5950
Sr. JOANN BROMLEY, S.C.
Sisters of Charity of St. Elizabeth 2
Residents 55

Paterson
Diocese of Paterson

St. Joseph Rest Home for Aged Women
Conducted by Daughters of Charity of the Most Precious Blood.
46 Preakness Ave.
Paterson, NJ 07522
Sr. MARIA GORETTI CHALOUX, Supr.
Residents 25

Pleasantville
Diocese of Camden

Our Lady's Residence
1100 Clematis Ave.
Pleasantville, NJ 08232
Hospitaler Sisters of Mercy.
Sr. M. AURELIA Admin. & Supr.
Rev. LEONARD CARRIERI, M.SS.CC., Chap.
Sisters 7
Beds 214
Patients assisted annually 214

Red Bank
Diocese of Trenton

Collier Group Home
180 Spring St.
Red Bank, NJ 07701
Tel: 908-842-8337
Mr. PAUL DESANTIS, Dir.
24 hour program-Therapy and Educational Services. Provided Under the Supervision of the Sisters of the Good Shepherd.
Capacity 12

Saddle River
Archdiocese of Newark

Villa Marie Claire
12 W. Saddle River Rd.
Saddle River, NJ 07458
Residence for retired, independent men & women.
Sisters of St. Joseph of Peace 8
Residents 32

Somerset
Diocese of Metuchen

McCarrick Care Center
15 Dellwood Ln.
Somerset, NJ 08873
Tel: 732-545-4200
JAMES F. CARON, Admin.
Rev. MAURICE CARLTON, Chap.
In res.,
Rev. Msgr. JOSEPH R. BRZOZOWSKI
Sisters 2
Patients assisted annually 142

Totowa
Diocese of Paterson

St. Joseph's Home for the Elderly
140 Shepherd Ln.
Totowa, NJ 07512
Tel: 201-942-0300
Conducted by Little Sisters of the Poor.
Sr. JOSEPH GRENON, L.S.P., Supr.
Rev. RAYMOND BEACH, O.F.M., Chap.
Sisters 17
Residents 131

Trenton
Diocese of Trenton

Cathedral Square Housing, Inc.
26 W. Hanover Pl.
Trenton, NJ 08608
Tel: 609-392-1111
Most Rev. JOHN C. REISS, Dir.
Senior Citizen Housing Project.

Sister Georgine School
544 Chestnut Ave.
Trenton, NJ 08611
Tel: 609-396-5444
Sisters of St. Francis

Vineland
Diocese of Camden

Bishop McCarthy Residence
1045 E. Chestnut Ave.
Vineland, NJ 08360
Hospitaler Sisters of Mercy.
Mr. ROBERT W. DEATON, Admin.
Sr. ELETTA FELLI, Supr.
Rev. EDWARD P. SOMMERS, Chap.
Sisters 5
Beds 182
Patients assisted annually 182

Wickatunk
Diocese of Trenton

Collier Services
Conover Rd.
Wickatunk, NJ 07765
Tel: 908-946-4771
Ms. AIDEEN BUGLER, Program Dir.
Sr. ELLEN KELLY, Exec. Dir.
Adolescent Boys and Girls and their Families.
Capacity 136
Mrs. JOAN KEELER, Prog. Dir. of Kateri Center, Tel: 908-946-9694
Mrs. LYNDA SHERIDAN, Prog. Dir., Shepherd Center for Child Care, Tel: 908-946-4323
Day Care for children 6 weeks-6 years.
Capacity 82

Woodbridge
Diocese of Metuchen

St. Joseph Senior Residence
One St. Joseph Terr.
Woodbridge, NJ 07095
Tel: 732-634-0004
Sr. MARY LOUISE, L.S.I.C., Admin.
Rev. THADDEUS L. ZAORSKI (NEW) Chap.
Little Servant Sisters 17
Residents 60

NEW MEXICO

Albuquerque
Archdiocese of Santa Fe

Casa Angelica
5629 Isleta Blvd., S.W.
Albuquerque, NM 87105
Tel: 505-877-5763
The Daughters of Charity of Canossa Christo Rey Community.
Home for developmentally disabled children.
Sisters 2
Residents 16
Lay Staff 45

Good Shepherd Center, Inc.
218 Iron St., S.W., P.O. Box 749
Albuquerque, NM 87103
Tel: 505-243-2527
Direct Service Agency for the Homeless.
JACK CLIFFORD, Pres.
Total Staff 9

Good Shepherd Manor
10127 Guadalupe Tr., N.W., P.O. Box 10248
Albuquerque, NM 87184
Tel: 505-898-0177
Bro. SAVIO CHARRON, B.G.S., M.H.A., Admin.
Sponsored by Bro. Mathias Barrett, Inc. of New Mexico. Shelter Care Facility for aged adults.
Residents 40
Staff 21

Marie Amadea Shelter for Unwed Mothers
(Alternative to Abortion)
P.O. Box 708
Albuquerque, NM 87103
Tel: 505-242-1516
Mrs. DOROTHY WICKENS, Dir.
Home for unwed expectant women.
Total Assisted 20
Total Staff 8

Carlsbad
Diocese of Las Cruces

St. Mary's Health Care Center
(Sub. of St. Mary of the Plains Hospital)
2330 West Pierce
Carlsbad, NM 88220
Tel: 505-887-0516; Fax: 505-885-8239
ROBERT GOODE, Dir.

Hobbs
Diocese of Las Cruces

St. Mary Medical Center
(Sub. of St. Mary of the Plains Hospital)
2410 North Fowler
Hobbs, NM 88240
Tel: 505-392-5572; Fax: 505-392-4848
ROBERT GOODE, Dir.

St. Mary's Family Health Care Center
(Sub. of St. Mary of the Plains Hospital)
515 East Main
Hobbs, NM 88240
Tel: 505-393-1096; Fax: 505-393-3758
ROBERT GOODE, Dir.

Santa Fe
Archdiocese of Santa Fe

Villa Therese Catholic Clinic
219 Cathedral Pl.
Santa Fe, NM 87501
Tel: 505-983-8561
Sr. PATRICK MARIE BERNARD, S.C., Dir.
Sisters of Charity of Cincinnati, Ohio 1
Patients assisted annually 5,000

NEW YORK

Albany
Diocese of Albany

Arbor House
302 Western Ave.
Albany, NY 12203
Tel: 518-489-6030
Legal Title: *Arbor House, Inc.*

Bishop Broderick Apartments Housing Development Fund Co., Inc.
50 Prescott St.
Albany, NY 12205
Tel: 518-869-7441; Fax: 518-869-0443
Senior Citizen and Handicapped Housing.
JANE LAX, Dir.

C.S.C. Housing Development Fund Co., Inc., dba Sanderson Court Senior Apts.
6 Carondelet Dr.
Watervliet, NY 12189
Tel: 518-436-0156; 782-1123; Fax: 518-782-1125
MICHELE KRAMM, Dir.

DePaul Management Corp.
41 N. Main Ave.

Albany, NY 12203
Tel: 518-459-0183; Fax: 518-459-0202
Sr. GRACE R. DIAZ, S.N.J.M., Exec. Dir.
ROSALIE MACE, Assoc. Exec. Dir.
Managing diocesan sponsored housing for persons of low income who are elderly or mobility impaired.

LaSalle School, Inc.
391 Western Ave.
Albany, NY 12203
Tel: 518-242-4731; Fax: 518-242-4747
Brothers of the Christian Schools 9
Mr. WILLIAM WOLFF, Exec. Dir.
Residential and day programs, independent living program, sexual victim/offender program, licensed substance abuse treatment program, and preventative services for boys (ages 12-18) and their families in New York State. Registered New York State Junior and Senior High School and certified School of Special Education.
Prevention Families 40
Resident Students 100
Day Students 30
The La Salle School Foundation of Albany

Saint Anne Institute
160 N. Main Ave.
Albany, NY 12206
Tel: 518-437-6500
RALPH F. FEDULLO, Exec. Dir.
Residential and Community-based Preventive Service Center. Regents accredited and certified junior and senior H.S. for the emotionally handicapped and Preschool program for 3-4 year olds who are speech impaired and emotionally disturbed. Residential care and Day Treatment for young women ages 12-18. Family Services, Vocational Training, Sex Abuse Prevention and Juvenile Sex Offender Programs for male and female adolescents in crisis and their families.
Capacity:
Residential 124
Day Treatment 40
Juvenile Sex Offender & Sex Abuse Prevntion Families 90

Saint Catherine's Center for Children
40 N. Main Ave.
Albany, NY 12203
Tel: 518-453-6700; Fax: 518-453-6712
Ms. HELEN HAYES, Exec. Dir.
Residential and day treatment, group homes and foster family programs for children with special needs. Community based prevention programs; Parent aides; Parent Training; Transitional Program for Homeless Families.
Individuals assisted 1,250
The Foundation for St. Catherine's Center for Children

St. Vincent Apartments Housing Development Fund Co., Inc.
475 Yates St.
Albany, NY 12208
Tel: 518-482-8915; Fax: 518-489-1220
E. BYRL MOORE, Building Dir.

Teresian House (1974)
Washington Ave. Ext.
Albany, NY 12203
Tel: 518-456-2000
Corporate Title: Teresian House Nursing Home Co., Inc.
Carmelite Sisters for the Aged and Infirm.
Sr. JOSEPH MARY BRECANIER, O.Carm., Admin.
Rev. GERARD LEE, O.F.M., Chap.
Bed Capacity 300
Teresian House Foundation

Villa Mary Immaculate
301 Hackett Blvd.
Albany, NY 12208
Tel: 518-482-3363
S.N.F. and long term skilled care nursing home.
Franciscan Sisters of Allegany, NY
Allegany Health System
JAMES A. REYNOLDS, Pres. & CEO
Revs.:
JOHN F. FITZPATRICK
FRANCIS J. GILCHREST
Sr. MARY PATRICIA NERF, R.S.M.
Sr. BARBARA DUDLEY, R.S.M.
Sr. PATRICIA MILLS, S.N.J.M.
Sr. ROSE ANN FERRARA, S.N.J.M.
Sisters 4
Bed Capacity 160
Patients assisted annually 252

Altamont
Diocese of Albany

Bernard & Caroline Cobb Memorial School (1962)
Corporate Name: Cobb Memorial School and Preschool
Altamont, NY 12009
Tel: 518-861-6446
Conducted by Sisters of the Presentation of the B.V.M. for Handicapped Children 2 1/2 to 21 years.
Students 40

Amityville
Diocese of Rockville Centre

Dominican Village, Inc.
565 Albany Ave.
Amityville, NY 11701
Tel: 516-842-6091
Sr. HELEN BUTLER, Pres. & CEO
Sr. VIRGINIA MAGUIRE, Vice Pres.
Apartments 200
Staff 100

Amsterdam
Diocese of Albany

Mt. Loretto Nursing Home
302 Swart Hill Rd.
Amsterdam, NY 12010
Tel: 518-842-6790; Fax: 518-843-5993
Health Care Facility & 24 Hour Skilled Nursing Care. Conducted by the Sisters of the Resurrection.
Sr. PATRICIA ANNE CORBETT, C.R., Admin.
Sr. MARY LUCILLE BOROWSKI, C.R., Supr.
Rev. RAYMOND S. PIECHOCKI, Chap.
Capacity 120

Auburn
Diocese of Syracuse

Mercy Housing Development Fund Co., Inc.
Mercy Apartments, 1 Thornton Ave.
Auburn, NY 13021
Tel: 315-253-2015
40 one bedroom units for the elderly and handicapped.
Christopher Community, Inc., (Managing Agent).

Baldwinsville
Diocese of Syracuse

Smokey Hollow Housing Development Fund Company, Inc.
Mailing Address: St. Mary's Apartments, Baldwinsville
1654 W. Onondaga St.
Syracuse, NY 13204
Tel: 315-424-1821
Christopher Community, Inc., (Managing Agent).

Batavia
Diocese of Buffalo

St. Luke Manor
17 Wiard St.
Batavia, NY 14020
Tel: 716-343-8806
JOHN R. DURNO
Bed Capacity 20
Patients assisted annually 20

Bayside
Diocese of Brooklyn

Ozanam Hall of Queens Nursing Home, Inc.
42-41 201st St.
Bayside, NY 11361
Tel: 718-423-2000
Sr. M. PHILIP ANN, O.Carm., Admin.
Chaplains:
Revs.:
MARTIN J. O'SULLIVAN
DANIEL SHEEHAN
Carmelite Sisters for the Aged and Infirm.
Sisters 19
Residents 432

Blauvelt
Archdiocese of New York

St. Dominic Home
10913
Tel: 914-359-3400; Fax: 914-359-4253
Sr. JOSEPH MARY, O.P., Exec. Dir.
Capacity: Boys 12
Girls 12
In Foster Homes 670
Group Homes 57
Boys 26
Girls 31
AOBH Girls 6
Sisters 17
New York Offices
343 E. 137th St.
Bronx, NY 10454
Tel: 718-993-5765
Special education program for emotionally disturbed mentally ill children ages 6-15.
Capacity 72
Preschool ages 3-5
Capacity 48
Community residences for developmentally disabled.
Capacity 65
Community residences for emotionally handicapped.
Capacity 36
TORCH (To Reach Children)
2340 Andrews Ave.
Bronx, NY 10463
Tel: 718-365-7238

Brewerton
Diocese of Syracuse

Bartell Road Housing Development Fund Co., Inc.
Bartell Rd.
Brewerton, NY 13029
c/o Christopher Community
1654 W. Onondaga St.
Syracuse, NY 13204
20 units, one bedroom apartments. Christopher Community, Inc., (Managing Agent).

Bronx
Archdiocese of New York

Franciscan Health System of New York, Inc.
2975 Independence Ave.
Bronx, NY 10463-4699
Tel: 718-548-1700; Fax: 718-601-3384
JEANNE LEE, Pres. & CEO
Rev. ALBERT PELLICANE, C.P., Chap.
Legal Title: *Frances Schervier Home and Hospital*
Legal Title: *Frances Schervier Housing Development Fund Corporation*
Legal Title: *Frances Schervier Nutrition Services, Inc.*
Legal Title: *Frances Schervier Child Care and Learning Center*
Legal Title: *Frances Schervier Long Term Home Health Care Program*
Franciscan Sisters of the Poor Health System, Inc.
708 Third Ave., Ste. 200
New York, NY 10017
Tel: 212-818-1987; Fax: 212-808-0096
Franciscan Sisters of the Poor Foundation, Inc.
708 Third Ave., Ste. 200
New York, NY 10017
Tel: 212-818-1987; Fax: 212-808-0096
Total Assisted 523
Total Staff 456

Jeanne Jugan Residence
3200 Baychester Ave.
Bronx, NY 10475
Fax: 718-671-0305
Sr. PAUL L.S.P., Supr.
Little Sisters of the Poor 14
Bed Capacity 92
Adult Care 32
Nursing Home 60

Medical Missionaries of Mary
563 Minneford Ave.
Bronx, NY 10464-1118
Tel: 718-885-0945; Fax: 718-885-0010
Sr. PHILOMENA SHEERIN, M.M.M., Supr. Gen.
Sr. ANNE MARIE HUBBARD, M.M.M., Reg. Supr.

Providence Rest
3304 Waterbury Ave.
Bronx, NY 10465
Tel: 718-931-3000
Sr. SELINE MARY FLORES, Admin.
Sr. LUCILLE VERGA
Sisters of St. John the Baptist 20
Bed Capacity 200
Total Assisted 161
Total Staff 214

Saint Dominic's Home - Prevention Program (ASTAAN)
2345 University Ave.
Bronx, NY 10468
Tel: 718-584-4407
Parent Aide Counseling Advocacy Information and Referral.
Families 100
Families Served 200

St. Patrick's Home for the Aged and Infirm
66 Van Cortlandt Park S.
Bronx, NY 10463
Tel: 718-519-2800
Carmelite Sisters for the Aged and Infirm.

Sr. M. PATRICK MICHAEL, O.Carm., Admin.
Rev. GERARD ORLANDO, C.P., Dir. Pastoral Care
Sisters 16
Bed Capacity 264
Total Assisted 349
Total Staff 350

Brooklyn
Diocese of Brooklyn

Bishop Francis J. Mugavero Center for Geriatric Care, Inc.
155 Dean St.
Brooklyn, NY 11217
Tel: 718-694-6700
ANN C. CARROLL, Admin.
Affiliated with Catholic Medical Center.
Total Staff 340
Total Assisted 288

Holy Family Home
1740 84th St.
Brooklyn, NY 11214
Tel: 718-232-3666
Affiliated with Catholic Medical Center.
MARY ANNE ROSE, Admin.
Sr. ANNE SHEEHAN, C.S.J., Dir. Pastoral Care Office
Deacon FRANK ROSATI
Total Staff 224
Total Assisted 188

SS. Joachim & Anne Residence, Inc.
2720 Surf Ave.
Brooklyn, NY 11224
Tel: 718-714-4800
MARIE FERRARA, Admin.

Buffalo
Diocese of Buffalo

The Franciscan Center, Inc.
1910 Seneca St.
Buffalo, NY 14210-1842
Tel: 716-822-8017
Emergency & Transitional Shelters for Adolescent Males 16-20.
Rev. JOSEPH BAYNE, O.F.M.Conv., Exec. Dir. & Guardian
Total Assisted 120
Total Staff 14
St. Joseph, Foster Parent, Friary
Tel: 716-826-6714

German Roman Catholic Orphan Home
795 Main St.
Buffalo, NY 14203
Temporarily Inactive

Nazareth Nursing Home
291 North St.
Buffalo, NY 14201
Tel: 716-881-2323
Sr. M. BERNARD KEANE, O.S.F.
Mr. AUSTIN J. BARRETT, Admin.
Franciscan Sisters of the Immaculate Conception 9
Bed Capacity 125
Patients assisted annually 125
Total Staff 220
Legal Title: *Nazareth Nursing Home of the Franciscan Sisters of the Immaculate Conception*
Attended by Chapel attended by Oblate Fathers of Holy Angels Church.

St. Francis Geriatric & Healthcare Services, Inc.
(Formerly known as St. Francis Hospital).
2787 Main St.
Buffalo, NY 14214
Tel: 716-837-4200; Fax: 716-837-2924
Sr. JEANNE WEISBECK, O.S.F., CEO
Rev. JOSEPH MORENO, Chap.
Sisters of the Third Order of St. Francis 7
Patients assisted annually 3,000
Bed Capacity 120
Total Assisted 229
Total Staff 195

Castleton
Diocese of Albany

Resurrection Nursing Home
(Corporate Name: Resurrection Nursing Home, Inc.)
Castleton, NY 12033
Tel: 518-732-7617; Fax: 518-732-4211
Nursing Home (Established 1962).
Conducted by Sisters of Resurrection
Bed Capacity 80

Catskill
Diocese of Albany

St. Joseph's Villa
38 Prospect Ave.
Catskill, NY 12414
Tel: 518-943-5701
Sr. ROBERTA F. BRUNNER, O.S.F., Admin.
An Adult Care Facility for Men and Women.

Cicero
Diocese of Syracuse

Cicero Housing Development Fund Company Inc.
Mailing Address:
1654 W. Onondaga St.
Syracuse, NY 13204
Tel: 315-424-1821
Sacred Heart Apartments
Cicero, NY 13039
Christopher Community, Inc., (Managing Agent).

Clarence
Diocese of Buffalo

Brothers of Mercy Housing Co., Inc.
10500 Bergtold Rd.
Clarence, NY 14031
Tel: 716-795-2122
Ms. LENORE MAURER, Admin.
Bro. JUDE HOLZFOERSTER, Pres.
Bed Capacity 100
Total in Residence 117
Total Staff 4

Brothers of Mercy Nursing & Rehabilitation Center
10570 Bergtold Rd.
Clarence, NY 14031
Tel: 716-759-6985
Mr. DANIEL J. KENNY, Admin.
Bro. JUDE HOLZFOERSTER, F.M.M., Pres.
Rev. JOHN J. SARDINA, Chap.
In res.,
Bro. HUGH DENOMME, F.M.M., Dir. Pastoral Care
Bed Capacity 240

Brothers of Mercy Sacred Heart Home, Inc.
4520 Ransom Rd.
Clarence, NY 14031
Tel: 716-759-2644
Mr. MICHAEL J. MALONEY, Admin.
Bro. JUDE HOLZFOERSTER, F.M.M., Pres. of Board
Rev. JOHN J. SARDINA, Chap.
In res.,
Rev. PATRICK ROLAK, O.F.M.Conv.
Bed Capacity 80
Total in Residence 80
Total Staff 46

Clifton Park
Diocese of Albany

Halfmoon Housing Development Fund Co., Inc. dba Bishop Hubbard Senior Apartments / De Paul Management Corp.
54 Katherine Dr.
Clifton Park, NY 12065
Tel: 518-383-2705
MARILYN D. HAGGERTY, Dir.

Dobbs Ferry
Archdiocese of New York

St. Cabrini Nursing Home
115 Broadway
Dobbs Ferry, NY 10522
Tel: 914-693-6800
Sr. SUZANNE POULIN, C.N.D., Dir. Pastoral Care
Missionary Sisters of the Sacred Heart 5
Bed Capacity 304
Total Assisted 474
Total Staff 437

Dunkirk
Diocese of Buffalo

St. Vincent's Home for the Aged
319 Washington Ave.
Dunkirk, NY 14048
Tel: 716-366-2066; Fax: 716-366-0545
Catholic Charities of Buffalo, Inc.
ELAINE J. SZCZERBACKI, Admin.
Residents 40
Total Staff 25

Fayetteville
Diocese of Syracuse

Redfield South Housing Development Fund Co., Inc.
Redfield Village Apartments, 380 Salt Springs Rd.
Fayetteville, NY 13066
Tel: 315-637-8280
50 one bedroom units. Christopher Community, Inc., (Managing Agent).

Garrison
Archdiocese of New York

St. Christopher's Inn
P.O. Box 150
Garrison, NY 10524-0150
Tel: 914-424-3616
Temporary shelter for homeless men.
Atonement Friars.
Rev. BERNARD PALKA, S.A., Dir.
Total Assisted 3,281
Total Staff 35

Harrison
Archdiocese of New York

St. Vincent's Hospital and Medical Center of New York, Westchester Branch
275 North St.
Harrison, NY 10528
Tel: 914-967-6500; Fax: 914-967-1633
BRIAN L. FITZSIMMONS, Ph.D.
Psychiatric Hospital.
Capacity 133
Patients assisted annually 2,226
Sisters of Charity of St. Vincent de Paul 3
All outpatient program admissions 1,734
Partial Hospital 240
Methadone Maintenance Treatment Program 130

Hawthorne
Archdiocese of New York

Rosary Hill Home
Hawthorne, NY 10532
Tel: 914-769-0114
Legal Title: *The Servants of Relief for Incurable Cancer*
Free home for incurable cancer patients.
Sr. M. DOMINIC, Admin.
Sr. MIRIAM O.P., Supr.
Rev. JOHN PROPPE, O.F.M.Cap., Chap.
Professed Sisters of St. Dominic 25
Capacity 72
Patients assisted annually 401

Huntington
Diocese of Rockville Centre

St. Joseph's Guest Home for the Aged, Inc.
350 Cuba Hill Rd.
Huntington, NY 11743
Tel: 516-368-9528
Missionary Sisters of St. Benedict.
Sr. M. BOGUSLAWA KAPUSTA, O.S.B.
In res.,
Rev. THOMAS CURRY

Jamaica
Diocese of Brooklyn

Msgr. James H. Fitzpatrick Pavilion for Skilled Nursing Care
152-11 89th Ave.
Jamaica, NY 11432
Tel: 718-291-4300
Affiliated with Catholic Medical Center.
GREGORY BRADLEY, Admin.
Total Staff 109
Total Assisted 115
Residents 115

Kenmore
Diocese of Buffalo

KMH Homes, Inc.
Administrative Offices
2950 Elmwood Ave.
Kenmore, NY 14217
Residential Health Care Facility.
Sponsored by the Sisters of Mercy.
Bed Capacity 160
Total Assisted 160
Total Staff 152

Lackawanna
Diocese of Buffalo

Baker Victory Services
780 Ridge Rd.
Lackawanna, NY 14218
Tel: 716-828-9500
Rev. Msgr. ROBERT C. WURTZ, Pres. of the Board
JAMES J. CASION, C.E.O.
JOSEPH J. COZZO, C.O.O.
J. BRENT HERMAN, Personnel Dir.
Staff 800
Boys and Girls in Residence (Ages 10-22) 424
Boys and Girls in Educational Program 229

Teachers 41
Preventive and Outpatient Clinic Clients (Ages Birth-18) 700
Total Assisted 2,500

Our Lady of Victory Infant Home
790 Ridge Rd.
Lackawanna, NY 14218
Tel: 716-828-9500
Rev. Msgr. ROBERT C. WURTZ, P.A., Pres.
Sisters of St. Joseph 2
Children Assisted Annually 1,323
Care of physically and/or mentally handicapped children and prenatal and post-partum maternity services.
Choose Life Program
Tel: 716-824-4709
Prenatal and post-partum maternity residential and out patient services provided. Foster care and Adoption Placement Services; neighborhood group home for adolescent girls; Nursery School for emotionally disturbed preschoolers; respite care in the home for disabled children. Intermediate care facility providing residential care for severely developmentally disabled children and young adults.

Lake Placid
Diocese of Ogdensburg

St. Margaret Convent
420 Old Military Rd.
Lake Placid, NY 12946
Tel: 518-523-2929
Sisters of Mercy
Sr. M. CAMILLUS O'KEEFE, R.S.M., Supr.

Uihlein Mercy Center
420 Old Military Rd.
Lake Placid, NY 12946
Tel: 518-523-2464; Fax: 518-523-1401
Institute of the Sisters of Mercy of the Americas, Regional Community of New York.
DOUGLAS MENZIES, Admin.
Skilled Nursing Facility.
Sisters 3
Total Staff 220
Total Assisted 210

Lancaster
Diocese of Buffalo

St. Elizabeth's Home
5539 Broadway
Lancaster, NY 14086
Tel: 716-683-5150; Fax: 716-683-4049
CAROL A. WANTUCH, Admin.
Rev. WILLIAM J. ROCHE, Chap.
Sisters of the Third Order of St. Francis 1
Residents 117
Total Staff 56

Latham
Diocese of Albany

Our Lady of Hope Residence
Little Sisters of the Poor
Jeanne Jugan Ln.
Latham, NY 12110
Tel: 518-785-4551
Rev. FIRMIN FINN, O.F.M.Conv.
Nursing Facility 70
Adult Care 30
Apartments for the Elderly 17

Lincolndale
Archdiocese of New York

Lincoln Hall
P.O. Box 600
Lincolndale, NY 10540
Tel: 914-248-7474; Fax: 914-248-5173
KATHLEEN T. O'KULA, C.S.W., Exec. Dir.
City Office
220 E. 23rd St.
New York, NY 10010
Capacity Boys 207
Total Staff 287
Total Assisted 483

Lockport
Diocese of Buffalo

St. Clare Manor
543 Locust St.
Lockport, NY 14094
Fax: 716-434-5900
Conducted by Catholic Charites of the Diocese of Buffalo.
Mr. JOHN DURNO, Admin.
Residents 28

Middletown
Archdiocese of New York

St. Teresa's Nursing Home
120 Highland Ave.
Middletown, NY 10940
Tel: 914-342-1033; Fax: 914-344-5631
In res.,
Rev. RICHARD C. JOYCE
Bed Capacity 98
Total Assisted 98
Total Staff 122

Millbrook
Archdiocese of New York

Cardinal Hayes Home for Children
North Ave., P.O. Box CHHC
Millbrook, NY 12545
Tel: 914-677-6363; Fax: 914-677-6691
FRED APERS, Exec. Dir.
Residential care for developmentally disabled children and young adults.
Franciscan Missionaries of Mary 5
Capacity of residential facilities:
Millbrook Intermediate Care Facility 43
Community Intermediate Care Facilities 50
Total assisted 100
Total Staff 247
In-home Respite Services.

Montrose
Archdiocese of New York

Kolping-on-Hudson
95 Montrose Point Rd.
Montrose, NY 10548
Tel: 914-737-9547
(Catholic Kolping Society New York, Inc.)
Total Assisted 2,000
Total Staff 10

Nanuet
Archdiocese of New York

St. Agatha Home of the New York Foundling Hospital
135 Convent Rd.
Nanuet, NY 10954
Tel: 914-623-3461
(Residential.)
Sisters of Charity of St. Vincent de Paul of New York.
ROSEMARIE CRISTELLO, Dir.
Rev. MICHAEL F. GANNON, Chap.
Bed Capacity 126
Diagnostic Facilities 26
In Foster Homes 38
Group Homes 99
Non-secure Detention 8 beds
Adult Intermediate Care facilities 65 beds
Family Support/Respite 10 beds
Runaway Youth Program.
Refugee Assistance Program.
Ulster County Prevention.

Nesconset
Diocese of Rockville Centre

Cleary Deaf Child Center, Inc.
301 Smithtown Blvd.
Nesconset, NY 11767
Tel: 516-588-0530 (Voice and TTY); Fax: 516-588-0016
Directed by Catholic Charities.
Day School (Infants thru 21 years).
Sr. CATHERINE FITZGIBBON, C.S.J., Supt.
Students 75

New York
Archdiocese of New York

Calvary Hospital
1740 Eastchester Rd.
Bronx, NY 10461
Tel: 718-863-6900
For advanced cancer patients.
FRANK A. CALAMARI, Exec. Dir.
Rev. MICHAEL ALESSANDRO, Chap
MARY TERESA O'NEILL, Asst. Admin. & Dir. Pastoral Services
Pastoral Staff 16
Accommodations for 200
Patients assisted annually 3,300

Catholic Guardian Society
1011 First Ave.
New York, NY 10022
Tel: 212-371-1000
Mr. JOHN FREIN, Exec. Dir.
Intermediate care facilities, individual residential alternatives and family support programs for mentally retarded, developmentally disabled adults. Group home program for boys and girls, ages 13-21 years; agency operated boarding homes and adoption services for boys and girls ages 0-16; provides foster homes for boys and girls ages 0-21; and specialized foster homes for children with AIDS.
Total Assisted 1,075
Total Staff 506

Catholic Home Bureau
1011 First Ave.
New York, NY 10022
Tel: 212-371-1000
Sr. UNA MCCORMACK, O.P., Exec. Dir.
Placement of dependent and neglected boys and girls ages birth-18 in foster and adoptive homes and agency-operated boarding homes. Maternity-Birthcare Services Program provides free, confidential counseling, medical & shelter care to single and married parents seeking help in planning for their unborn children. Toll-free hotline 1-800-592-HELP.
Total Assisted 1,269
Total Staff 306

Cor Mariae
251 W. 14th St.
New York, NY 10011
Tel: 212-929-9837
Residence for formerly homeless senior women.
PATRICIA BYRON, Coord.
Total Assisted 25
Total Staff 6

Covenant House Under 21
460 W. 41st St.
New York, NY 10036
(Runaway and Homeless Youth.)
Sr. MARY ROSE MCGEADY, D.C., Pres.

The Dwelling Place
409 W. 40th St.
New York, NY 10018
Tel: 212-564-7887
For homeless women.
Sr. NANCY CHIARELLO, O.S.F., Admin.
Total Assisted 100
Total Staff 5

El Carmelo Residence
249 W. 14th St.
New York, NY 10011
Tel: 212-242-8224
Sr. MODESTA PEREZ, Supr.

Good Shepherd Services
305 7th Ave., 9th Floor
New York, NY 10001
Tel: 212-475-4245
Sr. PAULETTE LOMONACO, Exec. Dir.
Provides foster care and adoption services (formerly McMahon services for children) and five residential programs for troubled adolescents, a training program for social service workers and a comprehensive range of neighborhood family services to individuals and youth from the South Brooklyn community. These services include educational support, employment, counseling, crisis intervention, literacy, skills training and advocacy services.

Guild of the Infant Savior
1011 First Ave., Room 1116
New York, NY 10022
Tel: 212-371-1000, Ext. 2440

The Jeanne d'Arc Residence
253 W. 24th St.
New York, NY 10011
Tel: 212-989-5952
Women 18 to 40.
Sr. ROSE ANN MENKE, Admin.
Accommodations for 140
Sisters of Divine Providence 7

Kateri Residence
150 Riverside Dr.
New York, NY 10024
Tel: 212-769-0744; Fax: 212-873-0658
Skilled Nursing Care/Residential Health Care Facility for the Elderly.
LASCELLES L. BOND, Acting Admin.
Asst. Admins.:
ROBERT G. SUSSINGHAM
EILEEN DOLPHIN
DORIS HUNG, Controller
ROBERT R. MORGAN, M.D., Medical Dir.
SARAH A. JERRO, R.N., Dir. of Nursing Services
BARBARA A. GAUGHAN, R.N., Dir. of Admissions/RUGS
Sr. PATRICIA GEOGHEGAN, P.B.V.M., Dir. Pastoral Care

Sr. MIRIAM POVEDA, R.S.H.M., Pastoral Care Assoc.
Sr. PADRAIC MARY MCGUINNESS, O.P., Pastoral Care Assoc.
Sr. DOROTHY VOLIN, P.B.V.M., Dir. of Recreation and Volunteers
WILLIAM C. KELLY, Plant Coord.
Attended by Franciscan Friars from St. Francis of Assisi Friary.
In res.,
Rev. VINCENT MELE, O.F.M. (Immaculate Conception Prov.)
Rev. Msgr. ANTHONY LOFTUS
Rev. Msgr. JAMES HANLON
Rev. Msgr. OWEN J. MCENANEY
Bed Capacity 520
Total Assisted 752
Total Staff 623

Kennedy Child Study Center
151 E. 67th St.
New York, NY 10021
Tel: 212-988-9500
ANN WILLIAMS, Ph.D., Exec. Dir.
Preschool Special Education 125
Infant/Parent Services 50
Case Management Services
Family Support Services 40
Parent Program 60
Clinic Program 400
Bronx Site
1021 E. 178th St.
Bronx, NY 10460
Tel: 212-842-0200
Preschool Special Education 125
Infant/Parent Services 50
Case Management Services
Clinic Program 400
Family Support Services 40
Parent Program 60

Kolping Society of New York Men's Residence (Catholic Kolping Society New York, Inc.)
165 E. 88th St.
New York, NY 10128
Tel: 212-369-6647
For young Catholic men.
MARY MINARIK, Mgr.
Total in Residence 88
Total Staff 11

Kolping-on-Concourse
2916 Grand Concourse
Bronx, NY 10458
Tel: 212-733-6119
JORGE PARIS, Mgr.
(Catholic Kolping Society New York, Inc.)
Total in Residence 90
Total Staff 7

Lavelle School for the Blind
221st St. and Paulding Ave.
New York, NY 10469
Tel: 718-882-1212
Sisters of St. Dominic of Blauvelt.
Sr. LOUIS MARIE BAXTER, O.P., Supt.
Capacity 100

Leo House
332 W. 23rd St.
New York, NY 10011
Tel: 212-929-1010
For the Clergy, Sisters & Laity.
Dr. FRANCIS J. PILECKI, Exec. Dir.
Senior Citizens in Residence 10
Total Staff 35
Catholic Hotel for Travelers 9,000

Mary Manning Walsh Home
1339 York Ave.
New York, NY 10021
Tel: 212-628-2800
Carmelite Sisters for the Aged and Infirm.
Sr. M. KEVIN PATRICIA LYNCH, Admin.
Rev. Msgr. JAMES J. MURRAY, Chap.
Rev. RICHARD PEIRIS, Asst. Chap.
Total Staff 488
Total Assisted 362

Mission of the Immaculate Virgin
Mount Loretto
Staten Island, NY 10309
Tel: 718-317-2600
STEPHEN RYNN, Exec. Dir.
In res.,
Rev. Msgr. JOSEPH C. ANSALDI
Rev. Msgr. JAMES F. BOLGER
Legal Title: *Mission of the Immaculate Virgin for the Protection of Homeless and Destitute Children*
Intermediate Care Facility:
Capacity 12
Community Residence:
Capacity 4
Day Care Center:
Capacity 45
Individual Residential Alternatives:
St. Matthew Cottage:
Capacity 8
St. Patrick Cottage:
Capacity 8
108 Bedell St.:
Capacity 6
6532 Amboy Rd.:
Capacity 7
Residential & Day Care:
Total Assisted 70
Total Staff 93

New York Foundling Charitable Corp.
590 Avenue of the Americas
New York, NY 10011
Tel: 212-633-9300
Sr. ELIZABETH VERMAELEN, S.C., Pres.

New York Foundling Hospital for Pediatric, Medical and Rehabilitative Care, Inc., The
590 Avenue of the Americas
New York, NY 10011
Tel: 212-633-9300
Sr. HELEN MURPHY, Exec. Dir.
RUTH MULLER, Admin.
Sponsored by Sisters of Charity of St. Vincent de Paul of New York.
Children 136

New York Foundling Hospital, The
590 Avenue of the Americas
New York, NY 10011
Tel: 212-633-9300
(Children from Infancy to 21)
Sr. HELEN MURPHY, Exec. Dir.
Children cared for during the year:
In the institution 469
In foster homes 1,937
In adoptive homes 244
Mothers cared for in St. Mary's Maternity Residence 261
Group residences 308
Diagnostic reception centers 228
Sisters of Charity of St. Vincent de Paul of New York 18
Family day care 243 children
Group day care 101
Mother and abusing parent and child program: Families 301
Children 534
Mother and child program: 59 mothers and 59 babies
Community-based services:
Families 350
Children 1,000
Programs for handicapped children 120
Foster Boarding Home Program:
Children with AIDS 22
Total Assisted 6,300
Total Staff 1,200

Padre Pio Shelter for Homeless Men
419 E. 155th St.
Bronx, NY 10455
Tel: 718-292-3713
Total Assisted 18/night
Bro. FRANCOIS GARON, C.F.R., Dir.
Rev. DENIS ANTOINE LEVASQUE, C.F.R., Asst. Dir.

Pelletier School & Services
147 W. 70th St.
New York, NY 10023
MARY ELLEN MURPHY, Program Dir.
Day School-Day Treatment Program for girls and boys 13-17.
Bed Capacity 50

Pius XII Youth and Family Services
Office of the Pres., 866 Third Ave., 30th Floor
New York, NY 10022
Tel: 212-702-9850
Bro. ROBERT FONTAINE, C.S.C., Pres. & CEO
Executive Offices.
The Victor J. Riley Jr. Center for Human Services
188 W. 230th St.
Bronx, NY 10463
Tel: 718-561-2073
Provides residential, community, chemical dependency and corporate services to over 25,000 people in New York State.
Residential Services:
Chester Campus
Gibson Hill Rd.
Chester, NY 10918
Tel: 914-469-2121
Complete residential services for troubled adolescent males.
Capacity 114
Sugar Loaf Union Free School District
Special Act School for youngsters at Chester Campus.
Rhinecliff Campus
Morton Rd.
Rhinecliff, NY 12574
Tel: 914-876-4084
Complete residential services for troubled adolescent males.
Capacity 96
Rhinecliff Union Free School District
Special Act School for youngsters at Rhinecliff Campus.
Group Homes
c/o Chester Campus, Gibson Hill Rd.
Chester, NY 10918
Tel: 914-469-2121
Three group homes and one non-secure detention group home for adolescent males in Orange and Dutchess Counties.
Foster Boarding Homes & Adoption
188 W. 230th St.
Bronx, NY 10463
Tel: 718-562-7855
395 Ann St.
Newburgh, NY 12550
Tel: 914-565-4618
Placement for 550 infants, children and adolescents in New York City and the Hudson Valley. Offices provide services and medical care to natural families, children and foster parents and recruitment of new foster parents. Adoptive parents are sought for children freed for adoption.
Admission & Family Services
188 W. 230th St.
Bronx, NY 10463
Tel: 718-562-7855
Morton Rd.
Rhinecliff, NY 12574
Tel: 914-876-4084
Offices for referral contact and for services to the families of children in residential care. Includes aftercare and independent living services.
Community Services:
North Bronx Family Service Center
2190 University Ave.
Bronx, NY 10453
Tel: 718-365-1400
Preventive services center for local community.
Court Diversion Project
1967 Turnbull Ave.
Bronx, NY 10473
Tel: 718-931-2611
900 Sheridan Ave.
Bronx, NY 10473
Tel: 718-681-0056
Counseling services to youngsters and families when a PINS petition has been filed in family court to divert youngster from residential placement.
University Heights Day Care
2167 University Ave.
Bronx, NY 10453
Tel: 718-584-6400
On-site day care for preschool children and after-school care for school-age children. Office for family day care that provides in-home services for families.
Children 101
Goshen Day Care
59 St. John St.
Goshen, NY 10924
Tel: 914-294-7502
Montessori-based day care for 60 3- to 5-year-olds.
Employment Training and Job Placement
Snow House
135 Hall of Fame Terr.
Bronx, NY 10453
Tel: 718-365-7755
Training and placement in auto mechanics, word processing and secretarial skills. Special family support and resource program which coordinates job training with family services.
Young Adult Training Academy
320 E. 96th St.
New York, NY 10128
Educational opportunities for students in job training programs.
Student Services - Dropout Prevention
Theodore Roosevelt High School
500 E. Fordham Rd.
Bronx, NY 10458
Morris High School
166th St. & Boston Rd.
Bronx, NY 10456
South Bronx High School
701 St. Ann's Ave.
Bronx, NY 10455
I.S. 206B
2280 Aqueduct Ave.
Bronx, NY 10468

P.S. 79
125 E. 181st St.
Bronx, NY 10453
P.S. 279
2100 Walton Ave.
Bronx, NY 10453
Adlai Stevenson High School
1980 Lafayette Ave.
Bronx, NY 10473
Walton High School
West 196 St. & Reservoir Ave.
Bronx, NY 10468
Counseling services to identified population of students considered high risk for dropping out of school.
After School Programs
Family Service Center
2190 Unviersity Ave.
Bronx, NY 10453
Supervised Latch-key program of classes, workshops and recreation for 6-18 year olds. Teen Program for adolescents provides recreational program year round.
Beacon Program
Middle School 45, 2502 Lorillard Pl.
Bronx, NY 10458
Tel: 718-367-9577
Community Center serving youths, children and adults in educational, recreational and social services after school, evenings, and weekends.
P.S. 91
220 Aqueduct Ave.
Bronx, NY 10453
Tutoring for students 6-18 who are one year or more behind grade level. G.E.D. program for high school equivalency. English as a second language classes.
"Aimin' High" Family Service Center
2190 University Ave.
Bronx, NY 10453
One hundred at-risk teens involved in sports and education programs with added community service.
Chemical Dependency Services:
Chemical Dependency Clinics:
224 Main St.
Goshen, NY 10924
Tel: 914-294-5888
15 Lake St.
Newburgh, NY 12550
Tel: 914-562-8255
10 Orchard St.
Middletown, NY 10940
Tel: 914-343-7675
305 Rte. 17M
Monroe, NY 10950
Tel: 914-782-0295
140 Hammond St.
Port Jervis, NY 12771
Tel: 914-856-8635
Medically supervised outpatient clinics for chemically dependent adults and their families.
Alcohol Clinic
200 Rte. 17M
Monroe, NY 10950
Tel: 914-782-6600
Specialized clinic for the treatment of alcoholics and their families.
School-based Services
Alternatives
224 Main St.
Goshen, NY 10924
Tel: 914-294-8009
Chemical dependency awareness and prevention program. Taught to school districts in Orange County. Summer and year-round programs in chemical dependency, AIDS, coping with behavioral problems and others.
Student Assistance Services.
Gateway Center
46 Roe St.
Newburgh, NY 12550
Tel: 914-569-0034
Chemical dependency outpatient clinic for Newburgh high school students, located on school grounds.
Employee Assistance Services.
Employee Assistance Services Office
Main Office
339 Main St.
Goshen, NY 10924
Tel: 800-962-7487
Employee Assistance Programs for corporations, businesses, governments and groups. Provides confidential counseling, assessment and referral for employees on a self-initiated or supervisor-recommended basis. Training for supervisors and services provided in areas outside the office area.
Residential and Community Services:
Total Assisted 25,079
Total Staff 653

Sacred Heart Residence
432 W. 20th St.
New York, NY 10011
Tel: 212-929-5790
Congregation of Mothers of the Helpless
Working or studying young ladies ages 19-29.
Sr. GUADALUPE SORDO ECHEUERRIA, Admin.
Capacity 30

St. Agnes' Residence
237 W. 74th St.
New York, NY 10023
Tel: 212-874-1361
For students and working women under 40.
Sr. MAFY JOACHIM Admin.
Daughters of Mary of the Immaculate Conception 2
Accommodations for 99
Franciscan Fathers of St. Francis Monastery.

St. Joseph's Immigrant Home
425 W. 44th St.
New York, NY 10036
Tel: 212-246-5363
For students and working women.
Sr. MAEY CELINE, Admin.
Daughters of Mary of the Immaculate Conception 2
Accommodations for 94

St. Mary's Residence
225 E. 72nd St.
New York, NY 10021
Tel: 212-249-6850
For students and young working women.
Sr. M. PERPETUA KODBA, F.D.C., Admin.
Sr. M. VIRGINIA SKARUPA, F.D.C., Dir. of Admissions
Daughters of Divine Charity 5
Accommodations for 145

St. Rose's Home
71 Jackson St.
New York, NY 10002
Tel: 212-677-8132
Legal Title: *The Servants of Relief for Incurable Cancer*
Free home for incurable cancer patients.
Sr. M. KEVIN O.P., Supr.
Sr. M. DENISE O.P., Admin.
Rev. GERARD MULVEY, O.F.M.Cap., Chap.
Dominican Sisters of the Congregation of St. Rose of Lima 10
Bed Capacity 60
Patients assisted annually 160

St. Vincent dePaul Residence
900 Intervale Ave.
New York, NY 10459
Tel: 718-589-6965
Mr. JORGE VASQUEZ, Dir.

St. Zita's Home for Adults
143 W. 14th St.
New York, NY 10011
Tel: 212-243-7200
Home for Women.
Sr. MARY EDWARD, Supr.
Sisters of Reparation of the Congregation of Mary 12
Accommodations for 46 Women

Terence Cardinal Cooke Health Care Center
1249 Fifth Ave.
New York, NY 10029
Tel: 212-360-1000
Mr. JAMES D. CAMERON, Pres. & CEO
Hospital for developmentally disabled.
Bed Capacity 50
Developmental Disabilities Clinic
1249 Fifth Ave.
New York, NY 10029
Comprehensive Outpatient medical, therapeutic and educational services.
Patients assisted annually 46,000
Dialysis
1249 Fifth Ave.
New York, NY 10029
19 End State Renal Dialysis Stations
Patients assisted annually 22,000
(For information concerning nursing home see Homes for Aged category.)

Terence Cardinal Cooke Health Care Center
1249 Fifth Ave.
New York, NY 10029
Tel: 212-360-1000; Fax: 212-289-2739
JAMES D. CAMERON, Pres. & CEO
In res.,
Rev. KEITH GERARD FENNESSY
Skilled nursing facility.
Bed Capacity 517
Skilled Nursing Facility AIDS Program.
Bed Capacity 156
(See Special Hospitals Category for additional services offered from this Health Care Center.)

Thorpe Family Residence, Inc.
2252 Crotona Ave.
New York, NY 10457
Sr. BARBARA LENNIGER, O.P., Exec. Dir.
The Crotona-Thorpe Housing Development Fund Corporation (Sub of Thorpe Family Residence, Inc.),
2252 Crotona Ave.
New York, NY 10457
Sr. MARY MURRAY, O.P., Pres.

Niagara Falls
Diocese of Buffalo

Mount St. Mary's LTC Facility, Inc.
2600 Main St.
Niagara Falls, NY 14305
JOHN L. LOMEO, Admin.
Sponsored by the Sisters of St. Francis.
Bed Capacity 131

St. Mary's Manor
515 Sixth St.
Niagara Falls, NY 14301
JOHN M. DUNN, Admin.
Rev. ROBERT E. PRIESTER, Chap.
Bed Capacity 119
Total Assisted 43,109

North Greenbush
Diocese of Albany

S.J. Housing Development Fund Company, Inc. dba St. Jude's Apartments
50 Dana Ave.
Wynantskill, NY 12198
Tel: 518-283-5690; Fax: 518-283-5893
MELISSA GILL, Dir.
Nonprofit housing facility for elderly and handicapped persons of very low income.
Apartments 50

North Syracuse
Diocese of Syracuse

Pitcher Hill-Christopher Housing Development Fund Co., Inc.
114 Elbow Rd.
North Syracuse, NY 13212
Engaged in the construction and operation of nonprofit housing facilities for elderly and handicapped persons of low income. 100 units, one bedroom apartments. Christopher Community, Inc., (Managing Agent).

Ogdensburg
Diocese of Ogdensburg

St. Joseph's Home
420 Lafayette St.
Ogdensburg, NY 13669
Tel: 315-393-3780; Fax: 315-393-3847
WILLIAM L. O'REILLY, Admin.
Most Rev. PAUL S. LOVERDE, Chm.
Total Staff 95
Total Assisted 117

Olean
Diocese of Buffalo

St. Joseph Manor
2211 W. State St.
Olean, NY 14760
Fax: 716-373-4375
MARILYN J. GIBBIN, Admin.
Bed Capacity 22
Total Assisted 44
Total Staff 77

Orchard Park
Diocese of Buffalo

W.N.Y. Catholic LongTerm Care, Inc. dba Father Baker Manor
6400 Powers Rd.
Orchard Park, NY 14127
Tel: 716-667-0001
Nursing facility sponsored by Our Lady of Victory Hospital of Lackawanna, Mercy Hospital of Buffalo and St. Joseph Hospital of Cheektowaga.
Bed Capacity 160
Total Assisted 160
Total Staff 225

Ossining
Archdiocese of New York

The Cardinal McCloskey Emergency Residential School
155 N. Highland Ave.

Ossining, NY 10562
Mr. JOHN M. QUEENAN, Pres.

Oswego
Diocese of Syracuse

St. Luke's Housing Development Fund Co., Inc.
St. Luke's Apartments, W. First St.
Oswego, NY 13126
Engaged in the construction and operation of a non-profit housing facility for elderly and handicapped persons of low income. 100 units, one bedroom apartments. Christopher Community, Inc., (Managing Agent).

Saint Luke's Residential Health Care Facility Co., Inc.
299 E. First St.
Oswego, NY 13126
Tel: 315-342-3166
Mr. TERRENCE GORMAN, Admin.

Port Jefferson
Diocese of Rockville Centre

Maryhaven Center of Hope
Myrtle ave.
Port Jefferson, NY 11777
Tel: 516-474-4100; Fax: 516-474-4110
Mr. LEWIS GROSSMAN, CEO
Sheltered Workshop
Consumers 372
Staff 67
Day Programs
Consumers 824
Staff 324
Residential Programs
Consumers 282
Staff 392
Provides svcs. to multi-handicapped children & adults; Vocational & sheltered workshop prog. for adults; day treatment prog. for adults; community residence prog. for adults; residential-day school for the mentally retarded emotionally disturbed (5-21 yrs).

Queens Village
Diocese of Brooklyn

Queen of Peace Residence
110-30 221st St.
Queens Village, NY 11429
Tel: 718-464-1800
Legal Title: *Home for the Aged, Little Sisters of the Poor*
Sr. CECILIA MARY, L.S.P., Admin.
Rev. Msgr. WILLIAM J. RODGERS, Chap.
In res.,
Revs.:
PAUL McC. KLOHR
JOSEPH J. BIHLER
JOHN HUGHES
JAMES MEADE
ALFRED WEINLICH
JOHN STONEBRIDGE
Sisters 18

Rensselaer
Diocese of Albany

East Greenbush Housing Development Fund Co., Inc. dba Branson Manor Senior Apartment
3 Grandview Dr.
Rensselaer, NY 12144
Tel: 518-283-8280; Fax: 518-283-8292
GEORGETTE KNOTT-DEFOE, Exec. Dir.

Rhinebeck
Archdiocese of New York

Astor Home for Children, The
36 Mill St., P.O. Box 5005
Rhinebeck, NY 12572-5005
Tel: 914-876-4081; Fax: 914-876-2020
Sr. ROSE LOGAN, D.C., Exec. Dir.
Rev. GEORGE J. KUHN, Chap.
Daughters of Charity 4
Residential Treatment Facility: Severely emotionally disturbed-mentally ill boys and girls, 5-12 years of age:
Bed Capacity 20
Residential Treatment Center (Rhinebeck):
Bed Capacity 55
Therapeutic Foster Boarding Homes 8
Family-Based Treatment 10
Child Guidance Clinics: Rhinebeck, Poughkeepsie, Beacon, Bronx, ages birth-18,
Capacity: unlimited
Day treatment programs ages 5-12,
Capacity Dutchess Co. 56
Bronx 156
Therapeutic Nursery, Bronx 40
Intensive Parenting Program, Bronx, ages birth-18.
Capacity 53 families
Head Start-Day Care Centers: Poughkeepsie, Beacon, Red Hook, Millerton, Wingdale, ages 3-5.
Capacity 350
Day Care Centers: Beacon, Red Hook, Millerton,
Capacity 45
Special Education Nursery, Wingdale, ages 3-5.
Capacity 10
Parent/Child Program.
Capacity 85
Total Assisted 4,010
Total Staff 525

Astor Learning Center, The
36 Mill St., P.O. Box 5005
Rhinebeck, NY 12572-5005
Tel: 914-876-4081; Fax: 914-876-2020
Special Education Program for emotionally disturbed-mentally ill children ages 6-13 in the Residential Treatment Center and local community.
Capacity 75
Total Assisted 123
Total Staff 38

Ferncliff Nursing Home
52 River Rd.
Rhinebeck, NY 12572
Tel: 914-876-2011; Fax: 914-876-2019
Carmelite Sisters for the Aged and Infirm
Sr. M. BERNADETTE THERESE REILLY, Admin.
Rev. PETER SMITH, Chap.
Bed Capacity 328

Rochester
Diocese of Rochester

St. Ann's Home for the Aged
1500 Portland Ave.
Rochester, NY 14621
Tel: 716-342-1700
Sisters of St. Joseph
Sr. MARIE MICHELLE PEARTREE, Pres.
Rev. PETER T. BAYER, Dir. of Pastoral Care
In res.,
Rev. GEORGE VOGT
Rev. Msgr. LESLIE WHALEN
Rev. Msgr. CHARLES BOYLE
Residents 354

St. Ann's Nursing Home Co., Inc.
(The Heritage)
1450 Portland Ave.
Rochester, NY 14621
Sr. MARIE MICHELLE PEARTREE, Pres.
Residents 237

St. Joseph's Villa of Rochester
3300 Dewey Ave.
Rochester, NY 14616
Tel: 716-865-1550
ROGER C. BATTAGLIA, Pres. & C.E.O.
RICHARD PALERMO, Pres.

Rome
Diocese of Syracuse

C.N.C. Inc.
W. Thomas St.
Rome, NY 13440
Tel: 315-735-7545
Facility for ten deinstitutionalized chronically mentally ill individuals living in a group home.

Rome Mall Housing Development Fund Company, Inc.
Mailing Address:
1654 W. Onondaga St.
Syracuse, NY 13204
Tel: 315-424-1821
Rome Mall Apts.
Rome, NY 13440
40 one bedroom units for the elderly. Christopher Community, Inc., (Managing Agent).

Saranac Lake
Diocese of Ogdensburg

St. Joseph's Rehabilitation Center, Inc.
99 Glenwood Estates, P.O. Box 470
Saranac Lake, NY 12983
Tel: 518-891-3950; 891-4135 (Admissions); Fax: 518-891-3986
Alcoholism Rehab.
Revs.:
ARTHUR M. JOHNSON, S.A., Exec. Dir.
TIM SULLIVAN, S.A., Chap.
MARK TRAENKLE, S.A.
Bros.:
ALAN LEMAY, S.A.
DOMINIC MCDONNELL, S.A.
PASCHAL STEEN, S.A.
Franciscan Friars of the Atonement.
Priests 2
Brothers 2
Residents 62

Sayville
Diocese of Rockville Centre

Good Samaritan Nursing Home
Sayville, NY 11782
Tel: 516-244-2400
Sr. MARYAN E. RUSSO, C.I.J., Admin.
Chaplains:
Sr. ELIZABETH TOOHIG
Rev. FRANCIS B. NUSS
Total Assisted 100
Total Staff 145

Sea Cliff
Diocese of Rockville Centre

St. Christopher-Ottilie Corp.
101 Downing Ave.
Sea Cliff, NY 11579
Tel: 516-643-8800
Directed by Sisters of the Good Shepherd.
ROBERT J. MCMAHON, Acting Exec. Dir.
Residential Treatment Center, Bed Capacity 20, Day Treatment Program for Adolescent Girls, Capacity 20; Residential Treatment Facility, Capacity 14; Family Service Clinic providing Comprehensive Mental Health Counseling for local residents.
Community Programs:
Group Home
760 Conklin St.
Farmingdale, NY 11735
Bed Capacity 7
Rose Pelletier Center
81 E. 2nd St.
Deer Park, NY 11729
Indepedent Living Programs
Bed Capacity 7
Gatehouse
151 Burrs Lane
Dix Hills, NY 11746
Emergency Shelter for Adolescents
Capacity 5
Marydale
10 Reid Ave.
Babylon, NY 11702
Teen Parent Residence.
Bed Capacity 12
Peconic Heights
235 W. Main St.
Riverhead, NY 11901
Emergency Shelter for Homeless Women
Bed Capacity 10
Good Shepherd Residence
203 Roanoke Ave.
Riverhead, NY 11901
Emergency Shelter for Homeless Women
Bed Capacity 12
St. Joseph Residence
122 Vernon Valley Rd.
East Northport, NY 11731
Emergency Shelter for Homeless Women
Bed Capacity 10
Morning Star Community
151 Burrs Ln.
Dix Hills, NY 11746-9020
Alcoholism Halfway House
Bed Capacity 20

Silver Creek
Diocese of Buffalo

St. Columbans on the Lake, Home for the Aged
2546 Lake Rd.
Silver Creek, NY 14136
Tel: 716-934-4515
Sr. CORONA COLLEARY, Admin.
In res.,
Revs.:
PATRICK CASHMAN
RICHARD GRIMME
ANTHONY HASSETT
EDMUND BAHL, S.S.C.
FRANCIS MCCULLAGH
Columban Sisters 11
Aged Residents 50

Slingerlands
Diocese of Albany

Marie-Rose Manor HDFCI
100 Marquis Dr.
Slingerlands, NY 12159
Fax: 518-459-0204
GWEN FRIESEN, Dir.

Sloatsburg
Ukrainian Catholic Diocese of Stamford

St. Joseph's Home
125 Sisters Servants Ln., Box 25
Sloatsburg, NY 10974-0025
Tel: 914-753-2555
Sr. CHARLOTTE PIPPINA, Admin.
Sisters Servants of Mary Immaculate 10
Residents 27
Staff 12

Springfield Gardens
Diocese of Brooklyn

Martin De Porres Group Homes
136-25 218th St.
Springfield Gardens, NY 11413
Bro. PHILIP ROFRANO, F.S.C., Exec. Dir.
Sr. VIRGINIA LACKER, R.S.M., A.F.S.C., Coord. Youth Care

Staten Island
Archdiocese of New York

Carmel Richmond Nursing Home, Inc.
88 Old Town Rd.
Staten Island, NY 10304-4299
Tel: 718-979-5000
Carmelite Sisters for the Aged and Infirm.
Sr. M. STEPHEN MCBRIDE, O.Carm., Admin.
Rev. ERIC KYLE, O.F.M., Chap.
Bed Capacity 300
Friends of Carmel Richmond, Inc.
Rev. Msgr. MICHAEL F. O'DONNELL
Total Assisted 300
Total Staff 358

Syosset
Diocese of Rockville Centre

St. Mary's Children and Family Services
525 Convent Rd.
Syosset, NY 11791-3864
Tel: 516-921-0808
Under the sponsorship of the Sisters of Mercy.
LIZ GIORDANO, Exec. Dir.
Residential treatment center, non-secure detention, group homes, foster boarding homes, diagnostic assessment prog., preventive svc. prog. in Hempstead. Residential treatment facility for mentally ill children.

Syracuse
Diocese of Syracuse

Bernardine Apartments, Inc.
417 Churchill Ave.
Syracuse, NY 13205
Tel: 315-469-7786
Mr. JAMES INTRONE, Pres.
TIM CARROLL, Mgr.

Christopher Community, Inc.
1654 W. Onondaga St.
Syracuse, NY 13204
Tel: 315-424-1821
Professional management and consultants of housing programs for the elderly, families and special populations.
Mr. PETER WHITE, Exec. Dir.
FRED ZOLNA, Housing Devel. Specialist

Churchill Manor, Inc.
750 E. Brighton Ave.
Syracuse, NY 13205
Tel: 315-424-1821
A non-profit corporation founded to provide housing for low and moderate income families and individuals.

Hawley Winton Housing Development Fund, Inc.
Walter Ludovico Apts., 340 Winton St.
Syracuse, NY 13203
Tel: 315-422-0475
33 one bedroom units occupied. Christopher Community, (Managing Agent).

Loretto
700 E. Brighton Ave.
Syracuse, NY 13205
Tel: 315-469-5561
Legal Title: *Loretto Rest Nursing Home Company, Inc.*
Mr. PATRICK DEPTULA, Exec. Vice Pres.
Rev. WILBUR J. VOTRAW, Chap.

Loretto Geriatric Community Residences, Inc.
5018 S. Salina St.
Syracuse, NY 13205
Tel: 315-492-0896
4810 S. Salina St.
Syracuse, NY 13205
Tel: 315-469-8562
50 Syracuse St.
Baldwinsville, NY 13027
Tel: 315-635-1647
8659 Carpenter Rd.
Baldwinsville, NY 13027
Tel: 315-635-1763

Loretto Rest, Inc.
750 E. Brighton Ave.
Syracuse, NY 13205
Tel: 315-469-5061
Adult Home.
Mr. PATRICK DEPTULA, Exec. Vice Pres.
Rev. WILBUR J. VOTRAW, Chap.

Ludden Housing Development Fund Company, Inc.
1654 W. Onondaga St.
Syracuse, NY 13204
Tel: 315-424-1821
Fifty one bedroom apartments for the elderly and handicapped. Units opened in 1992 and are located on Fay Road, Town of Geddes. Christopher Community Inc., (Managing Agent).

Marcellus Apartments Housing Development Fund Company, Inc.
Mailing Address:
1654 W Onondaga St.
Syracuse, NY 13204
Tel: 315-424-1821
Christopher Community, Inc., (Managing Agent).

Miller Road Housing Development Co., Inc.
(Brewerton)
Mailing Address:
1654 W. Onondaga St.
Syracuse, NY 13204
Tel: 315-424-1821
Housing for well elderly.

Mother Marianne Cope Housing Development Fund Co., Inc.
1654 W. Onondaga St.
Syracuse, NY 13204
Tel: 315-424-1821
E. Fayette St.
Syracuse, NY,
24 Units for HIV+ patients.

Mount St. James Corporation
1654 W. Onondaga St.
Syracuse, NY 13204
Tel: 315-424-1821
Engaged in the operation of a non-profit housing facility known as Mount St. James Apartments, at 338 Jamesville Ave., for persons of low to moderate income. Christopher Community, Inc., (Managing Agents).

Pompei Housing Development Fund Company, Inc.
c/o Christopher Community, Inc.
1654 W. Onondaga St.
Syracuse, NY 13204
Tel: 315-424-1821
50 one bedroom apartments for the elderly and handicapped. Christopher Community, Inc., (Managing Agent).

Pond St. Housing Development Fund Co., Inc.
Bishop Harrison Apartments, Pond St.
Syracuse, NY 13208
Operation of 48 units, one bedroom apartments for the elderly and handicapped. Christopher Community Inc., (Managing Agent).

Providence House Apartments
1700 W. Onondaga St.
Syracuse, NY 13204
Tel: 315-471-8427
Senior citizen housing, 100 units. Christopher Community, (Managing Agent).

St. Camillus Health & Rehabilitation Center
813 Fay Rd.
Syracuse, NY 13219
Tel: 315-488-2951
Mrs. AILEEN M. BALITZ, Pres.
Mr. RICK KING, Dir. Social Svcs.
St. Camillus Foundation
813 Fay Rd.
Syracuse, NY 13219
Mr. MARTIN M. DUGGAN, Chm.
KAROLAN PIZIO-MUNRO, Pres.

St. Peter's Italian Church Housing Development Fund Co., Inc. Villa Scalabrini Apts.
709 James St.
Syracuse, NY 13203
RAYMOND A. BANACH, Vice Pres. & Treas.
MARIO ROSSI, Sec.
Operation of a non-profit housing facility for aged, well persons of low income at the 800 Block of E. Willow St. in Syracuse. 120 units, one-bedroom apartments. Christopher Community, Inc., (Managing Agent).

Stoneleigh Housing Development Fund Co., Inc.
Stoneleigh Apartments, 400 Lamb Ave., Canastota
Syracuse, NY 13032
Engaged in the construction and operation of a non-profit housing facility for elderly and handicapped persons of low income. 100 units, one bedroom apartments. Christopher Community, Inc., (Managing Agent).

Tyson Place Housing Development Fund Company, Inc.
Mailing Address: Blessed Sacrament Apartments
16544 W. Onondaga St.
Syracuse, NY 13204
Tel: 315-424-1821
Christopher Community, Inc., (Managing Agent).

Town of Gates
Diocese of Syracuse

Steger Housing Development Fund Co., Inc.
4100 Lydell Rd.
Town of Gates, NY,
1654 W. Onondaga St.
Syracuse, NY 13204
Tel: 315-424-1821
56 apartments for well elderly.

Troy
Diocese of Albany

St. Mary's Woodland Village, Inc.
Upper Tibbits Ave.
Troy, NY 12180
Tel: 518-273-2040
Mrs. ROBIN SAGE, Admin.
Bed Capacity 155

Tupper Lake
Diocese of Ogdensburg

Mercy Healthcare Center, Inc.
114 Wawbeek Ave.
Tupper Lake, NY 12986
Tel: 518-359-3355
PAUL M. SCARPINATO, Admin.
Skilled Nursing Facility.
Sisters of Mercy of the Americas (Dobbs Ferry) 1
Capacity 80 Beds

Tuxedo
Archdiocese of New York

Samaritan Manor at Tuxedo, Inc.
Meyers Rd.
Tuxedo, NY 10987
Sr. MARY MORLEY, Pres.
An adult care facility.

Uniondale
Diocese of Rockville Centre

Mercy Hospice
St. Pius X Service Center, 122o front St.
Uniondale, NY 11553
Tel: 516-485-3060
Total Annually Assisted 300
Staff 20
Volunteers 80

Utica
Diocese of Syracuse

Catherine St. Housing Development Fund Company, Inc.
Mailing Address: Mt. Carmel Apartments
1654 W. Onondaga St.
Syracuse, NY 13201-0511
Tel: 315-424-1821
Christopher Community, Inc., (Managing Agent).

St. Joseph Nursing Home
2535 Genesee St.
Utica, NY 13501
Tel: 315-797-1230
Sr. SEAN WILLIAM O'BRIEN, O.Carm., Admin.

Wading River
Diocese of Rockville Centre

Little Flower Children's Services
Wading River, NY 11792

Tel: 516-929-6200
Directed by the Diocese of Brooklyn. Foster care, adoption & post-adoption svcs., intermediate care facilities, residential treatment center, Special Act school district, family day care, family care for MR/DD clients, foster homes for teen mothers & their babies.
Rev. Msgr. JOHN T. FAGAN, Exec. Vice Pres. (CEO)
Mrs. MARY G. RYDER, Exec. Dir. (COO)
Sisters of the Holy Family of Nazareth
Sr. AGNESE PALCZYNSKI, C.S.F.N., Supr.

Warwick
Archdiocese of New York

Villa Frances at the Knolls
Franciscan System of Warwick, Inc.
20 Grand St.
Warwick, NY 10990
Tel: 914-986-2267
F. DENNIS HARRINGTON, Pres.
Rev. EDWARD SULLIVAN, Chap.
Capacity 120

Watervliet
Diocese of Albany

Delatour Housing
Delatour Housing Development Fund Company, Inc. dba, Carondelet Commons Senior Apartments.
2 Carondelet Dr.
Watervliet, NY 12189
Tel: 518-783-0444; Fax: 518-783-0456
DORIS SEIP, Building Dir.

Italian-American Housing Development Fund Co., Inc. dba Cabrini Acers Senior Apts.
4 Carondelet Dr.
Watervliet, NY 12189
Tel: 518-785-0050; Fax: 518-785-0110
DORIS SEIP, Building Dir.

St. Colman's Home
Watervliet, NY 12189
Tel: 518-273-4911; Fax: 518-273-3312
Sisters of the Presentation of the B.V.M.
Sr. M. VIRGINIA, P.B.V.M., Dir.
Rev. JOHN A. MOLYN, Chap.
Tel: 518-271-6784
Children 50

West Islip
Diocese of Rockville Centre

Good Samaritan Hospice
1000 Montauk Hwy.
West Islip, NY 11795
Tel: 516-376-4001
Admissions to Program 371

Our Lady of Consolation Geriatric Care Center
111 Beach Dr.
West Islip, NY 11795
Tel: 516-587-1600; Fax: 516-587-5960
Under the supervision of the Sisters of St. Dominic.
Sr. AUDREY HARSEN, O.P.
Rev. ROBERT A. HYATT, Chap.
Total Assisted 450
Total Staff 625

West Park
Archdiocese of New York

St. Cabrini Home
West Park, NY 12493
Tel: 914-384-6500; Fax: 914-384-6001
JAMES J. LAVELLE, Exec. Dir.
Children 80
In Foster Homes 32
Agency Operated Boarding Home 12
Group Homes 108
Missionary Sisters of Sacred Heart 5
Served by Redemptionist Fathers.
Cabrini-on-Hudson
An adult community.
Residents 60

White Plains
Archdiocese of New York

Cardinal McCloskey Services
Two Holland Ave.
White Plains, NY 10603
Tel: 914-997-8000
Mrs. MARJORIE MCLOUGHLIN, Exec. Dir.
Sisters 3
In Foster Homes 500
In Group Homes 46
In Family Day Care:
Site I Capacity 540
Site II Capacity 115
Site III Capacity 145
Cardinal McCloskey Emergency Residential School
155 N. Highland Ave.
White Plains, NY 10562
Capacity 20

Williamsville
Diocese of Buffalo

Holy Family Home
410 Mill St.
Williamsville, NY 14221
Tel: 716-634-5400
Sr. PAULA MARIE NOTARTHOMAS, O.S.F., CEO
Sisters of St. Francis of the Third Order Regular 7
Residents 85
Total Staff 53

St. Francis Home of Williamsville
147 Reist St.
Williamsville, NY 14221
Tel: 716-633-5400; Fax: 716-663-6404
Legal Title: *Catholic Charities of Buffalo, NY*
Skilled Nursing Facility.
JAMES A. WALSH, Ph.D., Admin.
Rev. Msgr. HENRY J. GUGINO
Residents 142
Total Assisted 194
Total Staff 200

Yonkers
Archdiocese of New York

St. Eleanora's Home for Convalescents
127 S. Broadway
Yonkers, NY 10701
Tel: 914-378-7000
Unit of St. Joseph's Nursing Home (Yonkers).

NORTH CAROLINA

Belmont
Diocese of Charlotte

**Holy Angels, Inc.*
P.O. Box 710
Belmont, NC 28012
Tel: 704-825-4161; Fax: 704-825-0553
Mrs. REGINA P. MOODY, M.Ed., Exec. Dir.
Mother MARY BENIGNUS HOBAN, R.S.M., Pres.
Sisters of Mercy 6
Capacity (All Programs) 174
Residential and developmental programs and services for children and adults with mental retardation and physical disabilities.
Holy Angels Specialized Community Residential Center (Children 0-20)
Little Angels Child Development Center
On-site integrated day care.
Great Adventures Social Club
Adults with mental retardation.
South Point
Children/Adult group home.
Belhaven
Adult group home.
Lakewood
Adult group home.
Fox Run ICF/MR Group Homes
Beds 18

Hayesville
Diocese of Charlotte

Good Shepherd Home Health & Hospice Agency, Inc.
P.O. Box 465
Hayesville, NC 28904
Tel: 704-389-6311; Fax: 704-389-9584
Mr. THOMAS J. TAAFFE, Exec. Dir
Home Health Care & Hospice.
Murphy Branch
104 E. Hwy. 64, W.
Murphy, NC 28906
Tel: 704-837-3430; Fax: 704-837-3485

High Point
Diocese of Charlotte

Maryfield Nursing Home
1315 Greensboro Rd.
High Point, NC 27260
Tel: 910-886-2444; Fax: 910-886-4036
Sr. LUCY HENNESSY, S.M.G., Admin.
Rev. JOHN MURPHY, O.S.F.S., Non-Res. Chap.
Poor Servants of the Mother of God 7
Beds 115

Rosman
Diocese of Charlotte

**Frances Warde Health Service*
Star Rte. 1, Box 581
Rosman, NC 28772
Tel: 704-884-7990; Fax: 704-966-9609
Sr. GRETCHEN HERMANNY, R.S.M., M.D., Medical Dir.
Sisters 4

NORTH DAKOTA

Bismarck
Diocese of Bismarck

Emmaus Place
1020 N. 26th St.
Bismarck, ND 58501
Tel: 701-258-2618
Priests retirement home.
Revs.:
CHARLES H. BACKES
JOSEPH H. ADKINS
JOHN H. KUHN
Rev. Msgr. GERALD J. WALSH
Revs.:
LADISLAUS BRYDL
WILLIAM A. RUSHFORD
Total Staff 4
Total in Residence 6

Marillac Manor
1016 N. 28th St.
Bismarck, ND 58501
Tel: 701-258-8702; Fax: 701-223-3127
ROBERT G. SUERTH, Admin.
Retirement Apartments 78
Total Staff 11
Total in Residence 90

St. Vincent's Care Center
1021 N. 26 St.
Bismarck, ND 58501-3199
Tel: 701-223-6888
TIMOTHY N. BURCHILL, Admin.
Sisters of St. Benedict 3
Total Staff 150
Resident Patients 101

Edgeley
Diocese of Fargo

Manor St. Joseph
404 Fourth Ave.
Edgeley, ND 58433
Tel: 701-493-2477
TAMMY JANGULA, Admin.
Sister Servants of Christ the King 2
Guests 40
Bed Capacity 40
Staff 33

Ellendale
Diocese of Fargo

Ellendale Nursing Center
201 8th St. N.
Ellendale, ND 58436
Tel: 701-349-3312; Fax: 701-349-3944
Operated by Benedictine Health System Long Term Care Inc.
Mr. TONY HANSON, Admin.
Bed Capacity 74
Staff 92

Fargo
Diocese of Fargo

Friendship, Inc. dba Villa Nazareth
3004 S. 11th St.
Fargo, ND 58103
Tel: 701-235-8217
Presentation Sisters (P.B.V.M.).
A community-based facility providing an array of educational, social and clinical services for children and adults with mental retardation and other developmental disabilities.

Riverview Place, Inc.
5300 12th St., S.
Fargo, ND 58103
Tel: 701-237-4700
THOMAS DONALDSON, CFO
Revs.:
JOHN STEARNS, (Retired)
VLADAS ALEKSONIS, (Retired)
PETER GRADY, (Retired)
JEROME FILTEAU, (Retired)
WILLIAM J. MEHOK, S.J., (Retired)
MAURICE MUELLER, (Retired)
JOHN MOORE, (Retired)
LAMBERT STUDZINSKI, (Retired)
Residents 180

Staff 60

Grand Forks
Diocese of Fargo

St. Anne's Guest Home
524 N. 17th St.
Grand Forks, ND 58203
Tel: 701-746-9401
Sr. ELAINE MARIE ROGGENBUCK, O.S.F.
Sr. REBECCA METZGER, Admin.
Sisters of St. Francis of the Immaculate Heart of Mary (Hankinson, ND) 11
Staff 36
Guests 86

Hankinson
Diocese of Fargo

St. Gerard Community Nursing Home
613 First Ave. S.W.
Hankinson, ND 58041
Tel: 701-242-7891
Rev. PAUL KOEHLER, Chap.
Sr. ROSE MARIE FREUND, O.S.F., Admin.
Sisters of St. Francis of the Immaculate Heart of Mary (Hankinson, ND) 2
Beds 37
Patients assisted annually 37
Independent Living Unit Beds 11
Staff 65

La Moure
Diocese of Fargo

La Moure Healthcare Manor
Hwy. 13, P.O. Box 627
La Moure, ND 58458
Tel: 701-883-5363; Fax: 701-883-5711
Operated by Benedictine Health System Long Term Care, Inc.
Mr. TONY HANSON, Admin.
Bed Capacity 60
Staff 60

Rolette
Diocese of Fargo

Presentation Care Center
304 John St.
Rolette, ND 58366
Tel: 701-246-3786
KIMBER WRAALSTAD, Pres. CEO
Beds 48
Patients Assisted 65
Staff 75

Sentinel Butte
Diocese of Bismarck

Home on the Range
HC 1, Box 41
Sentinel Butte, ND 58654
Tel: 701-872-3745; Fax: 701-872-3748
Mr. WINSTON SATRAN, Exec. Dir.
Rev. DAVID MORMAN, Chap.
Staff 90
Children 158

Wahpeton
Diocese of Fargo

Wahpeton Health Care Center
1307 N. Seventh St.
Wahpeton, ND 58075
Tel: 701-642-6667
Operated by Benedictine Health System Long Term Care, Inc.
KATHLEEN HOEFT, Admin.
Residents 181
Long-term Care Beds 166
Basic Care Beds 15
Staff 185

OHIO

Akron
Diocese of Cleveland

Francesca Residence
39 N. Portage Path
Akron, OH 44303
Tel: 330-867-6334
Sr. M. MARTIN GREEN, F.D.C., Admin.
Rev. THOMAS F. SULLIVAN, Chap.
Daughters of Divine Charity 8
Total Under Care 47
Total in Residence 40
Total Staff 12

Leonora Hall
39 N. Portage Path
Akron, OH 44303
Tel: 216-867-1752
Residence for Young Women.
Sr. M. ANTOINETTE, F.D.C., Admin.
Daughters of Divine Charity 2
Residents 20

Beachwood
Diocese of Cleveland

Villa Sancta Anna Home for the Aged, Inc.
25000 Chagrin Blvd.
Beachwood, OH 44122-5665
Tel: 216-464-9250
Sr. M. ELISABETH ANN RECHKA, V.S.C., Admin.
Rev. KENNETH J. KATRICAK, O.S.B., Chap. & Asst. Admin.
Vincentian Sisters of Charity (Bedford, Ohio) 4
Residents 68
Total Assisted 68
Total Staff 80

Bedford
Diocese of Cleveland

Light of Hearts Villa, Inc.
283 Union St.
Bedford, OH 44146
Tel: 216-232-1991
Sr. HELEN THERESE SCASNY, V.S.C., Exec. Dir.
Sr. KATHY THOMAS, C.S.J., Asst. Dir.
Total in Residence 83
Total Staff 46

Canton
Diocese of Youngstown

House of Loreto
2812 Harvard Ave., N.W.
Canton, OH 44709
Tel: 330-453-8137
Sr. GLADYS SPENGLER, C.D.S., Exec. Dir.
Sr. CLAIRE BATTERSON, C.D.S., Admin.
Rev. JOSEPH PHILLIPS, S.P., Chap.
In res.,
Rev. NORBERT R. WEST
Sisters of the Congregation of the Divine Spirit 15
Residents 93
Total Staff 82

Centerville
Archdiocese of Cincinnati

The Franciscan at St. Leonard
8100 Clyo Rd.
Centerville, OH 45458
Tel: 937-433-0480
A facility of the Franciscan Health System of Dayton, sponsored by the Franciscan Sisters of the Poor Health System, Inc. A residence for Senior Citizens.
Revs.:
JAMES VAN VURST, O.F.M., Dir. Pastoral Care
ANTHONY PERFETTO, S.M., Staff Chap.
SAMUEL ZEBRON, O.F.M., Moderator & Chap., Sunday Community
JUVENAL PFALZER, O.F.M., (Retired)
ROMAN PRALZER, O.F.M., (Retired)
Residents 600

Cincinnati
Archdiocese of Cincinnati

Archbishop Leibold Home for the Aged
476 Riddle Rd.
Cincinnati, OH 45220-2493
Tel: 513-281-8001
The Little Sisters of the Poor.
Revs.:
JOVIAN WEIGEL, O.F.M., Chap.
AUGUST J. KNIEPP
Sr. REGINA LOFTUS, L.S.P., Supr.
Sisters 14
Residents 115

The Franciscan at St. Clare
100 Compton Rd.
Cincinnati, OH 45215
Tel: 513-761-9036
A member of the Franciscan Health System of the Ohio valley.
R. CHEISOPHER WEST, Pres./CEO
SHARON K. THORNTON, Admin.
Pastoral Care Dept.:
Sr. ELLEN DURSO, S.F.P.
Residents 142
Retired Sisters 45
Retired Brothers 3
Retired Priests 5
Other Residents 116

The Franciscan at West Park
2950 West Park Dr.
Cincinnati, OH 45238
Tel: 937-451-8900
A Member of the Franciscan Health System of Cincinnati, Inc.
R. CHRISTOPHER WEST, Pres. & CEO
TIMOTHY C. DRESSMAN, Admin.
Sr. ARLENE MCGOWAN, Vice Pres. Mission
JOHNNY RILEY, Dir. Pastoral Care
Ms. ALBERTA UTRUP, Chaplain
Residents 310

Mercy St. Theresa Center
7010 Rowan Hill Dr., Ste. 200
Cincinnati, OH 45227
Tel: 513-271-7010; Fax: 513-527-0181
MARY F. YOUNG, Admin.
Rev. STEPHEN J. EMERICK, Chap.
Sisters 3
Permanent Residents 149

St. Aloysius Orphanage
4721 Reading Rd.
Cincinnati, OH 45237
Tel: 513-242-7600; Fax: 513-242-2845
For boys and girls ages 6-14.
Sisters of Notre Dame (Covington, KY).
DONNA SAUNDERS, Exec. Dir.
Mr. KEN GLASSMEYER, Prin.
Sisters 3
Children 36

St. Joseph Infant and Maternity Home dba St. Joseph Home
10722 Wyscarver Rd.
Cincinnati, OH 45241
Tel: 513-563-2520
Sisters of Charity of Cincinnati, OH.
Sr. MARIANNE VAN VURST, Admin.
Children and young adults with severe/profound mental and motor disabilities 47

St. Joseph Orphanage
Archdiocesan Children's Residential Center.
5400 Edalbert
Cincinnati, OH 45239
ROBERT J. WEHR, Ph.D., Exec. Dir.
A.C.T. Child Case Management
5400 Edalbert Dr.
Cincinnati, OH 54239
Tel: 513-245-9944; Fax: 513-245-9401
ROBERT J. WEHR, Ph.D., Exec. Dir.
Employees 53
St. Joseph Villa
5400 Edalbert
Cincinnati, OH 45239
Tel: 513-741-3100
Residential Treatment Children 6-18.
ROBERT J. WEHR, Ph.D., Exec. Dir.
Staff 70
Residents 35
Altercrest
274 Sutton Rd.
Cincinnati, OH 45230
Tel: 513-231-5010
Residential Treatment for Boys ages 12-18.
ROBERT J. WEHR, Ph.D., Exec. Dir.
Staff 42
Residents 36
C.A.R.E. Child Case Management
90 Lawn Ave.
Hamilton, OH 45013
Tel: 513-887-2100
ROBERT J. WEHR, Ph.D., Exec. Dir.
Staff 11
Family Ties Therapeutic Foster Care
5400 Edalbert
Cincinnati, OH 45239
Tel: 513-741-3100
ROBERT J. WEHR, Ph.D., Exec. Dir.
Staff 11
Individualized Services
411 Oak St.
Cincinnati, OH 45219
Tel: 513-281-3700
Dr. ROBERT J. WEHR, Ph.D., Exec. Dir.
Staff 52

St. Margaret Hall
1960 Madison Rd.
Cincinnati, OH 45206-1896
Tel: 513-751-5880; Fax: 513-751-9813
Sr. M. JOACHIM ANNE FERENCHAK, O.Carm., Admin.
Revs.:
JEROME A. SCHAEPER, Chap.
RODNEY MCDANIEL, Assoc. Chap.
In res.,
Rev. CORNELIUS C. BERNING

Carmelite Sisters for the Aged and Infirm 9
Residents 133

Sisters of Charity Senior Care Corp., dba Bayley Place
990 Bayley Place Dr.
Cincinnati, OH 45233
Tel: 513-347-5500; Fax: 513-347-5553
Sr. JEANNE ROACH, Admin.

Cleveland
Diocese of Cleveland

Christ Child - DePaul Day Care Center
2320 E. 24th St.
Cleveland, OH 44115
Tel: 216-687-0006; Fax: 216-687-0403
Day Care program co-sponsored by Catholic Social Services and Counseling of Cuyahoga County. Funded by United Way & Catholic Charities.
ELBERT W. CLARK, JR., M.A., L.S.W.

Holy Family Home
6707 State Rd.
Cleveland, OH 44134
Tel: 216-885-3100; Fax: 216-885-0644
Free nursing home for terminal cancer patients who are unable to pay.
Legal Title: *The Servants of Relief for Incurable Cancer*
Administered by Dominican Sisters of the Third Order, Congregation of St. Rose of Lima.
Sr. M. EDWIN, O.P., Supr.
Rev. JOSEPH F. CIOLEK, Chap., Tel: 216-842-1436
Sisters 9
Bed Capacity 50
Patients assisted annually 200

Jennings Hall Inc.
10204 Granger Rd.
Cleveland, OH 44125
Tel: 216-581-2900; Fax: 216-581-1517
Mrs. MARTHA M. KUTIK, Admin., Exec. Dir.
Rev. KESTUTIS ZEMAITIS (Vilnius) Chap., Tel: 216-581-2900
Residential Long-Term Care Facility. Under Diocesan Auspices.
Sisters 7
Residents 150
Total Assisted 150
Total Staff 190

Mount Alverna Home, Inc. & Mount Alverna Home Annex, Inc.
6765 State Rd.
Parma, OH 44134
Tel: 216-843-7800; Fax: 216-843-7107
ROBERT J. SHERRIN, Admin.
Rev. ERIC GAUCHAT, Cap. O.F.M.
Capacity 203
Residents 203
Total Assisted 203
Total Staff 313

Mount St. Joseph
21800 Chardon Rd.
Cleveland, OH 44117
Tel: 216-531-7426; Fax: 216-531-4033
Sr. M. MICHAEL SALVIANO, CNHA
Conducted by Sisters of St. Joseph of St. Mark - Mount St. Joseph.
Sisters 22
Bed Capacity 100
Residents 100
Total Assisted 100
Total Staff 150

Rose Mary, The Johanna Grasselli Rehabilitation and Education Center
19350 Euclid Ave.
Cleveland, OH 44117
Tel: 216-481-4823
Mrs. PATRICIA A. COLOMBO, Exec. Dir.
Sisters of the Humility of Mary 1
Children 40
Residents 84
Bed Capacity 86
Total Staff 250

St. Augustine Manor
7801 Detroit Ave.
Cleveland, OH 44102
Tel: 216-634-7400; Fax: 216-634-7483
Affiliated with Catholic Charities.
Mrs. MARY DOYLE, Chm., Board of Trustees
Mr. PATRICK GAREAU, Pres. & CEO
Rev. JOSEPH A. ROMANSKY, Residence Chap.
Bed Capacity 248
Patients assisted annually 650
Total in Residence 242
Total Staff 355
Coterie of St. Augustine Manor, The
7801 Detroit Ave.
Cleveland, OH 44102
Tel: 216-634-7400
(Operates the Coterie Boutique)
Mrs. MARGARET LYNCH, Pres.

Sts. Mary and Joseph Home for the Aged
4291 Richmond Rd.
Cleveland, OH 44122-6199
Tel: 216-464-1222
Little Sisters of the Poor
Mother CHANTEL I.S.P.
In res.,
Revs.:
THOMAS CAREY, S.M.
EDWARD CORRIGAN, S.M.
CLAUDE GAEBELEIN
JOHN J. GERRITY
PAUL DUZINSKI, O.F.M.Conv.
Sisters 13
Fraternity Members 2
Bed Capacity 125

Columbus
Diocese of Columbus

Nazareth Towers
300 E. Rich St.
Columbus, OH 43215
Tel: 614-464-4780; Fax: 614-464-1733
Sr. MARY LOIS SCHMELTZER, O.P., Admin.
Total Staff 7
Total in Residence 216

Rosemont Center
(House of the Good Shepherd)
2440 Dawnlight Ave.
Columbus, OH 43211
Tel: 614-471-2626
Sr. MONICA NOWAK, R.G.S., Exec. Dir.
Sisters of the Good Shepherd 10
Total Staff 125
Rosemont Center Endowment Fund

St. Raphael Home for the Aged, Inc.
1550 Roxbury Rd.
Columbus, OH 43212
Tel: 614-486-0436; Fax: 614-486-1640
Carmelite Sisters for Aged and Infirm.
Sr. MARY ROBERT ROMANO, O.Carm., Admin. & Supr.
Rev. LARRY NOLAN, Chap.
Residents 78
Total Assisted 70
Total Staff 110

St. Rita Home
880 Greenlawn Ave.
Columbus, OH 43223
Tel: 614-443-9433; Fax: 614-443-1196
Sr. M. JACQUELINE O.Carm., Supr. & Admin.
Rev. EDWIN J. MCNULTY, Chap.
Carmelite Sisters for Aged and Infirm 6
Total Staff 200
Guests 100
Total Assisted 140

Seton London, Inc.
350 Cambridge Dr.
London, OH 43140
Tel: 614-852-4233

Seton South Columbus, Inc.
155 Highview Blvd.
Columbus, OH 43207
Tel: 614-492-9944

Seton Square North
1776 Drew Ave.
Columbus, OH 43235
Tel: 614-451-1995
CINDY FISHER, Gen. Mgr. Seton Projects
Total in Residence 240
Total Staff 4

Seton Washington Court House, Inc.
400 N. Glenn Ave.
Washington Court House, OH 43160
Tel: 614-335-2292
Total in Residence 42
Total Staff 2

Coshocton
Diocese of Columbus

Seton Coshocton, Inc.
377 Clow Ln.
Coshocton, OH 43812
Tel: 614-451-1995
Apartments 40
Total Staff 3

Dayton
Archdiocese of Cincinnati

The Maria Joseph Living Care Center
4830 Salem Ave.
Dayton, OH 45416
Tel: 937-278-2692; Fax: 937-278-9016
Skilled Nursing-Intermediate Nursing; Independent Living.
BONNIE G. LANGDON, Pres. & CEO
Sr. BETTY MASSAREK, C.PP.S., Past. Care Coord.
Sr. ROSE MARTIN MORAND, S.C., Pastoral Care Coordinator
Rev. HARRY CAVANAUGH, C.PP.S., Chap.
Licensed/Certified Nursing Care 384
Independent Living 56

Mercy Siena Woods
235 W. Orchard Springs Dr.
Dayton, OH 45415
Tel: 937-278-8211; Fax: 937-278-8046
Nursing Home, nonsectarian. A member of The Mercy Health System. Specialized Alzheimer's Center. Sponsored by the Religious Sisters of Mercy. 53 years of ministry.
SUSAN M. HAYES, Admin. & CEO
Rev. FRANCIS MASSARELLA, Res. Chap.
Sisters 1
Residents 99

Siena Springs
6215 N. Main St.
Dayton, OH 45415
Tel: 937-274-4790
Apartments, Independent Living for the Elderly.
Sponsored by Sisters of Mercy.
Sr. PATRICIA CONNOLLY, R.S.M., Admin.,Mgr. & CEO
Residents 45

Dover
Diocese of Columbus

Seton Square Dover, I, Inc.
501 James St.
Dover, OH 44622
Tel: 330-343-3611
CHARLES ERBE, Co-Mgr.
MYRTLE ERBE, Co-Mgr.
Total Staff 3
Total in Residence 51

Seton Square Dover, II, Inc.
139 Fillmore St.
Dover, OH 44622
Tel: 330-343-3611
A retirement residence for the elderly.
Total Staff 3
Total in Residence 42

Fairlawn
Diocese of Cleveland

St. Edward Home dba The Village at Saint Edward Nursing Care and Assisted Living
3131 Smith Rd.
Fairlawn, OH 44333
Tel: 330-666-1183
JOHN J. HENNELLY, Pres. & CEO
Rev. JOHN F. WILSON, Chap.
Sisters 4
Nursing Care Residents 100
Assisted Living Residents 26
Total Staff 137
St. Edward Housing Corporation dba The Village at St. Edward Independent Living
3125 Smith Rd.
Fairlawn, OH 44333
Tel: 330-668-2828
JOHN J. HENNELLY, Pres. & CEO
Rev. JOHN F. WILSON, Chap.
Total in Residence 163
Total Staff 32

Green Springs
Diocese of Toledo

St. Francis Health Care Center, Rehab Hospital Section
401 N. Broadway St.
Green Springs, OH 44836
Tel: 419-639-2626; Fax: 419-639-3559
Owned by Franciscan Sisters of Our Lady of Perpetual Help (St. Louis, MO).
Operated by Franciscan Sisters of Our Lady of Perpetual Help of Ohio Corp.
GREGORY T. STORER, CEO
CHARLES HULL, M.D., Medical Dir.
Rev. DONALD R. MUELLER, Chap.
Sisters 6
Bed capacity 36

Total Assisted 439
Total Staff 133

St. Francis Health Care Centre (ICF & Skilled)
401 N. Broadway St.
Green Springs, OH 44836
Tel: 419-639-2626; Fax: 419-639-3559
Owned by Franciscan Sisters of Our Lady of Perpetual Help (St. Louis, MO).
Operated by Franciscan Sisters of Our Lady of Perpetual Help of Ohio Corp.
GREGORY T. STORER, CEO
CHARLES HULL, M.D., Medical Dir.
Rev. DONALD R. MUELLER
Sisters 6
Bed capacity 150
Total under care 147

Hamilton
Archdiocese of Cincinnati

The Franciscan at Schroder
1302 Millville Ave.
Hamilton, OH 45013
Tel: 513-867-1300; Fax: 513-867-1415
A Facility of the Franciscan Health System of the Ohio Valley. Sponsored by the Franciscan Sisters of the Poor Health System, Inc. Special unit for Alzheimer Treatment.
Ms. MARCY MORGAN, Exec. Dir.
Residents 132

Hubbard
Diocese of Youngstown

Villa Maria Teresa
50 Warner Rd.
Hubbard, OH 44425
Tel: 330-759-9329 (Villa); 875-4635 (Emmaus House)
Retired Priests' Residence.
Residents 5

Independence
Diocese of Cleveland

Marycrest
7800 Brookside Rd.
Independence, OH 44131
Tel: 216-524-5280; Fax: 216-524-2127
Residential treatment and transitional living for adolescent girls and adolescent mothers and babies.
Euphrasia Center
2320 E. 24th St.
Cleveland, OH 44115
Sisters 3
Total Assisted 70
Total Staff 130

Kenton
Diocese of Columbus

Seton Kenton, Inc.
699 Morningside Dr.
Kenton, OH 43326
Tel: 419-673-7202
MARY LOU SWEET, Mgmt. Rep.
DAVID MANNS, Maintenance
Total Staff 2
Total in Residence 53

Lancaster
Diocese of Columbus

Seton Lancaster, Inc.
232 Gay St.
Lancaster, OH 43130
Tel: 614-681-1403

Louisville
Diocese of Youngstown

Emmaus House
1515 California Ave.
Louisville, OH 44641
Tel: 330-875-4635
Rev. JOHN C. FINNIGAN, Admin.
Retired Priests' Residence.
Residents 6
Total Staff 4

St. Joseph Care Center
2308 Reno Dr.
Louisville, OH 44641
Tel: 330-875-5562
Sr. EDWARDINE BAZNIK, S.J.S.M., Admin.
Sisters of St. Joseph of St. Mark 4
Sisters of the Humility of Mary 1
Sisters of St. Francis of Mary Immaculate 1
(Nursing Home) 153
(Assisted Living) 52
Total Staff 143

Marion
Diocese of Columbus

Seton Square Marion, Inc.
255 Richland Rd.
Marion, OH 43302
Tel: 614-389-4746
DEBRA J. ERWIN, Office Mgr.
DON OSBORN, Maintenance
Total in Residence 107
Total Staff 3

North Lima
Diocese of Youngstown

The Assumption Village
9800 Market St.
North Lima, OH 44452
Tel: 330-549-0740; Fax: 330-549-0701
Sponsorship: Humility of Mary Health Care System
Member: HM Health Services.
Sr. ROSEMARY HAMMER, H.M., Pres & CEO
JOYCE DEPAOLA, Dir., Nursing
Special Care Unit for residents with Alzheimer's or Dementia.
Beds 150

The Assumption Village
9800 Market St.
North Lima, OH 44452
Tel: 330-549-0740; Fax: 330-549-0701
Sr. ROSEMARY HAMMER, H.M., Pres. & CEO
Rev. Msgr. ANDREW PROKOP
Vincentian Sisters of Charity 3
Residents 150
Total Staff 200

Oregon
Diocese of Toledo

Sacred Heart Home
4900 Navarre Ave.
Oregon, OH 43616-3599
Tel: 419-698-4331; Fax: 419-698-1109
Little Sisters of the Poor.
Sr. CHARLES MARIE, L.S.P., Supr.
Revs.:
JOVEN MALANYAON
FERNAN J. BRENNAN, O.S.F.S.
JOSEPH D. SHENK
Sisters 12
Aged Residents 119
Independent Living Apartments 20
Total Staff 165

Parma
Diocese of Cleveland

Parmadale
6753 State Rd.
Parma, OH 44134
Tel: 216-845-7700; Fax: 216-845-5910
MICHAEL J. HAGGERTY
THOMAS W. WOLL, Exec. Dir.
Rev. JOSEPH J. SEMINATORE, Chap.
In res.,
Rev. JAMES R. SEMONIN
Specialized Residential Services; Intensive Treatment Services; Partial Hospitalization; Community Flexible Clinical Response; Specialized Foster Care; Wrap-Around Services; Whole Family Treatment; In-Home Services; Outpatient Services; Transitional Independent Living; Day Care; Training and Consultation Services; and Volunteer Program.
Residential Capacity 128
Total Capacity 90
Total Staff 300

Reynoldsburg
Diocese of Columbus

Seton Square East, Inc.
1235 Briarcliff Rd.
Reynoldsburg, OH 43068
Tel: 614-861-4860

Richfield
Diocese of Cleveland

Regina Health Center
5232 Broadview Rd.
Richfield, OH 44286-9608
Tel: 216-659-4161; Fax: 216-659-3899
Sr. JUDITH ANN KARAM, C.S.A., Pres.
Sponsored by Sisters of Charity of St. Augustine.
Nursing Home Beds 81
Assisted Living Units 74
Total in Residence 65
Total Assisted 144
Total Staff 136

Springfield
Archdiocese of Cincinnati

Oakwood Village Retirement Community
1500 Villa Rd.
Springfield, OH 45503
Tel: 937-390-9000; Fax: 937-390-9333

Tiffin
Diocese of Toledo

St. Francis Home Inc.
182 St. Francis Ave.
Tiffin, OH 44883
Mr. ANGELO VIVINO Admin.
Mr. WILLIAM BOOTH, Chm., Board of Trustees
Rev. RUSSELL GILLIG, Chap.
Residents 173
Total Staff 230

Toledo
Diocese of Toledo

St. Anthony Villa / Boysville of Michigan, Inc.
2740 W. Central Ave.
Toledo, OH 43606
Tel: 419-473-1353; Fax: 419-473-2963
Residential and community-based treatment programs for troubled youth and families with facilities located throughout the state of Michigan and one facility in the state of Ohio under the auspices of the Brothers of Holy Cross at Notre Dame.
Bro. FRANCIS BOYLAN, C.S.C., Exec. Dir.
VICKY PRIMER, Ph.D., Reg. Dir.
Deacon JOHN ALGEE, Pastoral Min.
Sisters 2
Lay Staff 100
Residential 75

Urbana
Archdiocese of Cincinnati

Mercy McAuley Center-Mercy Health Systems
906 Scioto St.
Urbana, OH 43078
Tel: 937-653-5432; Fax: 937-652-2072
RICHARD ZECHIEL, Admin.
Residents 129

Warren
Metropolitan Archdiocese of Pittsburgh, Byzantine

Infant of Prague Manor
169 Kenmore, N.E.
Warren, OH 44483
Tel: 330-372-4700
Sr. MARGARET MARY, O.S.B., Admin.
Apartments 46
Staff 4
In Residence 41
Housing for the elderly.

Wellston
Diocese of Columbus

Seton Square Wellston, Inc.
570 W. First St.
Wellston, OH 45692
Tel: 614-384-6174

Zanesville
Diocese of Columbus

Seton Housing, Inc.
516 Sheridan St.
Zanesville, OH 43701
Tel: 614-453-4422
Total Staff 2
Total in Residence 45

OKLAHOMA

Broken Arrow
Diocese of Tulsa

Franciscan Villa
17110 E. 51st St., S.
Broken Arrow, OK 74012
Tel: 918-355-1596; Fax: 918-355-2954
Retirement Residence and Health Care Center for Intermediate Nursing Care.

Sisters of the Sorrowful Mother.
Mrs. IRENE HULSEY, R.N., Admin.
Rev. HARRY S. BARTNIK, Chap.
Beds 60
Apartments 66
Residents 128
Total Staff 75

Oklahoma City
Archdiocese of Oklahoma City

St. Ann's Home, Inc.
9400 St. Ann's Dr.
Oklahoma City, OK 73162
Tel: 405-728-7888; Fax: 405-728-1302
Mrs. JOY ECKER, Admin.
Rev. DONALD C. MOORE, Chap.
Sisters 4
Beds 120
Total assisted 113

Villa Isenbart, Inc.
c/o Associated Catholic Charities, 1501 Classen Blvd.
Oklahoma City, OK 73106
Mr. TIMOTHY O'CONNOR, Dir.
40 Apartment Residences for Low-Income Elderly, Under Construction. Completion due January, 1997.

Ponca City
Archdiocese of Oklahoma City

St. Mary's Housing Foundation
408 S. 8th St.
Ponca City, OK 74601
Rev. JOHN MICHALICKA, Pres.
Senior Citizens Residences 6

Westminster Village, Inc.
1601 Academy Rd.
Ponca City, OK 74604
Tel: 405-762-6641
Via Christi Health System.
PAULA BAKKE, Pres. & CEO
Nursing Care for Aged.
Residents 110

OREGON

Baker City
Diocese of Baker

St. Elizabeth Health Care Center
3985 Midway Dr.
Baker City, OR 97814
Tel: 541-523-4452; Fax: 541-523-8151
ERNEST WICK, Admin.
Sisters of St. Francis of Philadelphia 3
Licensed Beds 120

Beaverton
Archdiocese of Portland in Oregon

Maryville Nursing Home
14645 S.W. Farmington Rd.
Beaverton, OR 97007
Tel: 503-643-8626
Sr. GERALDINE BERNARDS, Admin.
SHARON FLAMAND, R.N., Dir. Nurses
Rev. JOHN M. DOMIN, Chap.
Sisters 8
Lay Workers 177
Guests 294
Little Flower Development Center
4415 S.W. 148th Ave.
Beaverton, OR 97007
Children 220

Mt. Angel
Archdiocese of Portland in Oregon

Benedictine Nursing Center
540 S. Main St.
Mt. Angel, OR 97362-9523
Tel: 503-845-6841
JOHN H. HOGAN, Admin.
Chaplains:
Sr. JOSEPH FENNIMORE
Revs.:
MARION DEL MONACO
KURT SMIDT-JERNSTROM, Pastor & Inter-faith Chap.
Home Health Agency
Staff 39
Patients assisted annually 544
Sisters 2
Patients assisted annually 445

North Bend
Archdiocese of Portland in Oregon

Evergreen Court for Retirement Living, Inc.
451 O'Connell St.
North Bend, OR 97459
Tel: 541-756-2545
WILLIAM J. HEALY, CEO

St. Catherine's Residence and Nursing Center
3959 Sheridan Ave.
North Bend, OR 97459
Tel: 541-756-4151; Fax: 541-756-1049
WILLIAM J. HEALY, Pres. & CEO
Sisters 11
Patients assisted annually 400
Bed Capacity 151

Portland
Archdiocese of Portland in Oregon

Mt. St. Joseph Residence and Extended Care Center
3060 S.E. Stark St.
Portland, OR 97214-3099
Tel: 503-232-6193; Fax: 503-235-2772
Operated by the Sisters of Mercy, Omaha Regional Community.
MARY KLEIN, Pres. & CEO & Contact Person
CATHY COLBY, Dir. Pastoral Care
Rev. STEPHEN STOBIE
Sisters 15
Residents 375

PENNSYLVANIA

Allison Park
Diocese of Pittsburgh

Providence Connections, Inc.
Corporate Office, 9000 Babcock Blvd.
Allison Park, PA 15101
Tel: 412-931-5241; Fax: 412-635-5416
Sr. DONNA MARIE GRIBSCHAW, C.D.P., Exec. Dir.
Providence Day Care Center, North
Total Assisted 24
Total Staff 9
Providence Child Care Center, South
Total Assisted 54
Total Staff 5
Providence Family Support Center
Total Assisted 60
Total Staff 9
Amelia House
Total Assisted 8
Total Staff 1
Purpose: To engage in educational activities and operation of day care centers and other related services to women and children.

Regency Hall Nursing Home, Inc.
9399 Babcock Blvd.
Allison Park, PA 15101
Tel: 412-366-8540; Fax: 412-369-9789
Vincentian Sisters of Charity.
Sr. DOROTHY DOLAK, V.S.C., Admin.
Rev. EDWARD MCSWEENEY
Beds 143
Total Staff 175

Ambler
Archdiocese of Philadelphia

St. Mary's Villa for Children
701 Bethlehem Pike, P.O. Box 388
Ambler, PA 19002-0388
Tel: 215-242-0376; 643-7676
Sr. M. EUNICE, C.S.F.N., D.S.W., Admin.
Provides services for dependent-neglected children with emotional problems 5-12 and their families.
Sisters of the Holy Family of Nazareth 10
Capacity 65
Total Staff 70
Total Assisted 89

Aston
Archdiocese of Philadelphia

Assisi House
600 Red Hill Rd.
Aston, PA 19014
Tel: 215-459-8990
Home for retired Sisters of St. Francis of Philadelphia.
Sr. BERNADETTE MCINNIS, O.S.F., L.N.H.A., Admin.
Rev. GERALD M. DOLAN, O.F.M., Chap.
Residents 140

Audubon
Archdiocese of Philadelphia

St. Gabriel's Hall
Box 7280
Audubon, PA 19407-7280
Tel: 215-247-2776 (Philadelphia); 610-666-7970 (Audubon)
Bros.:
ROBERT KINZLER, F.S.C., A.C.S.W., Exec. Dir.
JOSEPH F. MAHON, F.S.C., Dir.
Mr. JOHN GAYNOR, F.S.C., Prog. Dir.
Mr. ROBERT D. BURNS, JR., Asst. Dir. Education
Dr. NIAZ AMADYAR, Ph.D., Asst. Dir. Clinical Svcs.
Mr. MICHAEL PURCELL, Asst. Dir. Support
Offers residential treatment for court-committed delinquent boys, ages 12-18.
Capacity 201
Total Staff 230
Total Assisted 500

Baden
Diocese of Pittsburgh

**Villa St. Joseph of Baden, Inc.*
State St.
Baden, PA 15005
Tel: 412-869-2151
Sr. ANNA MARIE GAGLIA, C.S.J., Pres. & Contact Person

Bensalem
Archdiocese of Philadelphia

St. Francis Homes for Boys
857 Langstroth Ln.
Bensalem, PA 19020-5735
Tel: 215-638-9310
FRANCIS E. SWIACKI, JR., L.S.W., Admin.
Provides residential treatment in four campus-based group homes and seven community-based group homes for boys, ages 12 to 18; also Supervised Living for boys 17 and older.
Total Assisted 150
Capacity 100
Total Staff 110

Bethlehem
Diocese of Allentown

Grace Mansion Personal Care Residence of Holy Manor
1200 Spring St.
Bethlehem, PA 18018
Tel: 610-865-6748
Rev. Msgr. DENNIS A. RIGNEY, Pres. & CEO
KAREN ABRUZZESE, Admin.
Mr. JIM POLASKI, Diocesan Dir.
Personal care facility for 25 elderly.
Total in Residence 25
Total Staff 12

Holy Family Adult Day Care
1200 Spring St.
Bethlehem, PA 18018
Tel: 610-865-5595
BARBARA FAHRINGER, Dir.
Day care for elderly clients 22

Holy Family Apartments
330-338 13th Ave.
Bethlehem, PA 18018
Tel: 610-866-4603
Rev. Msgr. DENNIS A. RIGNEY, Pres.
RAY LAUDENSLAGER, Mgr.
Catholic housing for the elderly.
Apartments 50
Residents 52

Holy Family Manor
1200 Spring St.
Bethlehem, PA 18018
Tel: 610-865-5595; Fax: 610-865-5866
Rev. Msgr. DENNIS A. RIGNEY, M.Div., L.S.W., A.C.S.W., Pres. & CEO
Mrs. CONSTANCE C. STAIR, R.N., N.H.A., Admin.
Rev. JOSEPH A. ROCK, Th.F., Chap.
Nursing Care for the Aged, Chronically Ill, or Invalid.
Total Assisted 208
Total Staff 240
Skilled and intermediate care facility.
Capacity 208
Total Staff 240
Patients assisted annually 279

Trexler Pavilion, Personal Care Residence of Holy Family Manor
1220 Prospect Ave.
Bethlehem, PA 18018
Tel: 610-868-7776
Rev. Msgr. DENNIS A. RIGNEY, Pres. & CEO
KAREN ABRUZZESE, Admin.
Mr. JAMES POLASKI, Diocesan Dir.
Personal care facility for 23 elderly.

Total in Residence 21
Total Staff 12

Columbia
Diocese of Harrisburg

St. Anne's Home
3952 Columbia Ave.
Columbia, PA 17512-9715
Tel: 717-285-5443
Adorers of the Blood of Christ.
Sr. M. CARMELA GUITO, A.S.C., Admin.
Rev. JOHN HERBER, C.PP.S., Chap.
Sisters 19
Total Staff 190
Guests 121
Cottages 36
Residents in Retirement Village 43

Dallas
Diocese of Scranton

Mercy Center Nursing Unit, Inc.
Lake St., Box 370
Dallas, PA 18612
Tel: 717-675-2131; Fax: 717-674-5658
Sr. JAYNE PRUITT, R.S.M., Admin.
LOUISE CHRISTOFOR, R.N., Dir. of Nursing
Rev. FRANCIS G. KULIG, Chap.

Danville
Diocese of Harrisburg

Holy Family Convent and Infirmary
One Montour St.
Danville, PA 17821
Tel: 717-275-3141
Home for the Aged Sisters of Christian Charity.
Sr. GEMMA STREIT, S.C.C., Supr.
Rev. LEONARD CASEY, Chap., Tel: 717-275-0103
Sisters of Christian Charity 90

Maria Hall
Maria Hall Dr.
Danville, PA 17821
Tel: 717-275-1120
Home for retired Sisters of SS. Cyril and Methodius.
Sr. M. ROSAMUND, SS.C.M., Admin.
Rev. FREDERICK A. FARACE, Chap.
Sisters 84

Maria Joseph Manor
875 Montour Blvd.
Danville, PA 17821
Tel: 717-275-4221; Fax: 717-275-4711
Sr. M. JEANETTE, SS.C.M., Exec. Dir.
Sr. M. MARGUERITE, SS.C.M., Admin.
Rev. FRANCIS TAMBURRO Tel: 717-275-8740
Nursing Home Beds 60
Pers. Care Beds 37
Independent Living Units 100
Sisters 15
The Meadows at Maria Joseph Manor
875 Montour Blvd.
Danville, PA 17821
Tel: 717-271-1000; Fax: 717-275-4711
Sr. ELIZABETH ANN MATONAK, SS.C.M., Dir.

Darby
Archdiocese of Philadelphia

Little Flower Manor
1201 Springfield Rd.
Darby, PA 19023
Tel: 610-534-6000; Fax: 610-534-6039
Staffed by Sisters of the Divine Redeemer.
All Skilled Nursing Care.
Rev. EDWARD J. CASEY, Chap.
Total Staff 220
Patients assisted annually 159

St. Francis Country House
1412 Lansdowne Ave.
Darby, PA 19023-1218
Tel: 610-461-6510; Fax: 610-237-6558
Opened June 30, 1913.
Mrs. JUDITH P. HORVATH, Admin.
Rev. EDWARD J. KENNEDY, Chap.
Residents 273

Villa Saint Joseph
14th St. and Lansdowne Ave.
Darby, PA 19023
Tel: 215-586-8535
Home for aged, infirm and convalescent priests of the Archdiocese of Philadelphia.
Rev. Msgr. D. JAMES MCGETTIGAN, Rector
Rev. EDWARD J. CASEY, Asst. Rector
Sisters 1
Total Staff 43
Residents 50

Villa St. Teresa
1215 Springfield Rd.
Darby, PA 19023
Tel: 610-583-0700
Staffed by Sisters of the Divine Redeemer.
Residential.
Sr. M. ANNE ANGELCYK, S.D.R., Admin.
Sr. THOMAS MARNELL, S.D.R., Supr.
Total Staff 32
Residents 54

Downingtown
Archdiocese of Philadelphia

St. John Vianney Hospital
151 Woodbine Rd.
Downingtown, PA 19335
Tel: 610-269-2600
Center for Healing for Priests, Brothers, and Sisters.
LOUIS D. HORVATH, Admin.
Rev. CHARLES R. O'HARA, Chap.
Bed Capacity 54

St. Martha Manor
470 Manor Ave.
Downingtown, PA 19335
Tel: 610-873-8490
COLLEEN PATRICIA FRANKFIELD, N.H.A., Admin.
Capacity 120
Total Staff 188
Total Assisted 120

Du Bois
Diocese of Erie

Christ the King Manor, Inc.
1100 W. Long Ave.
Du Bois, PA 15801
Tel: 814-371-3180
Rev. MARK S. SWOGER, Chap.
Residents 160

Easton
Diocese of Allentown

Antonian Towers
2405 Hillside Ave.
Easton, PA 18042
Tel: 610-258-2033
Total in Residence 50
Total Staff 2
Rev. Msgr. DENNIS A. RIGNEY, Pres.
Mrs. JUDITH KERN, Mgr.
Catholic housing for the elderly.
Apartments 50

Elmhurst
Diocese of Scranton

St. Mary's Villa Nursing Home
Elmhurst, PA 18416
Tel: 717-842-7621; Fax: 717-842-2953
COLLEEN M. LANDO, N.H.A., Admin./CEO
Sr. MARIE CONCEPTA, C.J.C., Convent Supr., Tel: 717-842-7466
Rev. JOSEPH C. OSTROWSKI, Chap.
Poor Sisters of Jesus Crucified and the Sorrowful Mother 9
Residents 112
Total Staff 175

Elverson
Archdiocese of Philadelphia

St. Mary of Providence Center
227 Isabella Rd.
Elverson, PA 19520
Tel: 610-942-4166
Sr. BERNARDINE UGOLINI, D.S.M.P., Supr.
Rev. GERARD J. HOFFMAN, Chap.
Residence for Senior Citizens. Center of Spirituality, Retreats and Days of Recollection.
Sisters 4
Capacity 39
Overnight and day retreats 90
Total in Residence 52

Emsworth
Diocese of Pittsburgh

Holy Family Institute
8235 Ohio River Blvd.
Emsworth, PA 15202
Tel: 412-766-4030
Sisters of the Holy Family of Nazareth.
Sr. LINDA YANKOSKI, Exec. Dir.
Dedicated to helping children who are abandoned, abused or neglected, and to working with families in crisis. Teen parenting program, after school partial hospitalization program, special education services, and private counseling services.
Sisters 1
Total Assisted: Chidren 1,829
Families 537
Total Staff 285

Erie
Diocese of Erie

Bishop Michael J. Murphy Residence for Retired Priests
400 E. Gore Rd.
Erie, PA 16509
Tel: 814-825-0680
Rev. Msgr. ROBERT J. SMITH, J.C.L., Dir.

Community House Inc.
521 W. 7th St.
Erie, PA 16502
Tel: 814-459-5853
CARLEEN M. DAVIS, Exec. Dir.

Gannondale Residential Center for Girls
4635 E. Lake Rd.
Erie, PA 16511
Tel: 814-899-7659
North American Union of Sisters of Our Lady of Charity-Erie.
Sr. CAROL PREGNO, O.L.C., Supr.
Mr. LOUIS J. GRANDE, A.C.S.W., Exec. Dir.
Rev. Msgr. LAWRENCE E. BRANDT, J.C.D. Ph.D., Chap.
Residents 45

Mercy Center for Women
1039 E. 27th St.
Erie, PA 16504
Tel: 814-453-3668
TISH DONZE, Exec. Dir.

Mercy Terrace Apartments
430 E. Grandview Blvd.
Erie, PA 16504
Tel: 814-825-6791
Sr. M. FELICE DUSKA, R.S.M., Mgr.
Sisters of Mercy of Erie

St. Mary's Home of Erie
607 E. 26th St.
Erie, PA 16504
Tel: 814-459-0621; Fax: 814-454-0909
Sr. ANASTASIA VALIMONT, S.S.J., Admin.
Rev. Msgr. JOSEPH WARDANSKI, Chap.
Sisters 20
Residents 131
Patients-Nursing Home 228

St. Patrick Haven, Inc.
147 E. 12th St.
Erie, PA 16501
Tel: 814-454-7219; 814-838-5430
Sr. MARIE EILEEN MOYER, Admin.

Flourtown
Archdiocese of Philadelphia

Bethlehem Retirement Village
100 W. Wissahickon Ave.
Flourtown, PA 19031
Tel: 215-233-0998
Staffed by the Sisters of St. Joseph.
Sr. JOAN GRELIS, S.S.J., Mgr.
Apartments 100
Total Staff 4
Total in Residence 113

St. Joseph Villa
110 W. Wissahickon Ave.
Flourtown, PA 19031-1898
Tel: 215-836-4179
Chaplains:
Revs.:
GERARD M. DUFF, O.S.A.
GEORGE J. CALLAGHAN, O.S.A.
Sr. MARIE RUDEGEAIR, S.S.J., N.H.A., Admin.
Bed Capacity 324
Total Staff 300
Total Assisted 101,000

Sisters of St. Joseph of Philadelphia, St. Joseph Villa Staff
110 W. Wissahickon Ave.
Flourtown, PA 19031-1898
Sr. MARY SCHERR, S.S.J., Contact
Beds 108

Greensburg
Diocese of Greensburg

Neumann House
2900 Seminary Dr.

Greensburg, PA 15601
Fax: 412-834-7351
Residence for retired Priests.
In res.,
Rev. Msgr. JOHN L. GARRED Tel: 412-837-1472
Rev. Msgr. ROBERT A. HANICAK Tel: 412-834-7991
Revs.:
ALOYSIUS J. BAHLEDA Tel: 412-834-5953
LOUIS W. CHEATHAM Tel: 412-850-7619
EDWARD V. CURRY Tel: 412-850-7647
APOLINARY MURAWSKI Tel: 412-834-0458
FRANCIS M. OTT Tel: 412-832-8345
FRANCIS D. PIRULLI Tel: 412-836-3827
MICHAEL A. BIENIA Tel: 412-836-1017

St. Anne Home
685 Angela Dr.
Greensburg, PA 15601
Tel: 412-837-6070; Fax: 412-837-6099
Rev. EDWARD J. KRETZ, Chap.
Sr. BERNICE M. FIEDOR, C.S.S.F., Admin.
In res.,
Revs.:
EDWIN H. HIRT Tel: 412-837-9443
ANDREW J. CHARNOKI Tel: 412-853-8935
Felician Sisters 8
Capacity 125

Harborcreek
Diocese of Erie

**Benetwood Apartments for Persons Elderly and Handicapped*
641 Troupe Rd.
Harborcreek, PA 16421-1048
Tel: 814-899-0088
Sr. MARY THERESE WACKER, O.S.B., Mgr.
Benedictine Sisters of Erie.
Residents 81

Harborcreek Youth Services
5712 Iroquois Ave.
Harborcreek, PA 16421
Tel: 814-899-7664; Fax: 814-899-3075
Mr. JAMES E. HENRY, A.C.S.W., L.S.W., Dir.
Dr. DAVID SULLIVAN, Ph.D., Clinical Dir.
Children 190

Harrisburg
Diocese of Harrisburg

Villa Teresa Nursing Home
1051 Avila Rd.
Harrisburg, PA 17109
Tel: 717-652-5900; Fax: 717-652-5941
Carmelite Sisters
Sr. TIMOTHY ANNE, O.Carm., Admin.
Rev. WALTER A. SEMPKO, Chap.
Sisters 7
Bed Capacity 184
Total Staff 250

Hermitage
Diocese of Erie

John XXIII Home
2250 Shenango Fwy.
Hermitage, PA 16148
Tel: 412-981-3200
Miss ROBERTA T. LAMONT, Admin.
Rev. Msgr. HOMER DEWALT, Chap.
Residents 142

Holland
Archdiocese of Philadelphia

St. Joseph Home for the Aged
1182 Holland Rd.
Holland, PA 18966
Tel: 215-357-5511; Fax: 215-357-1701
Sisters of St. Casimir
Sr. M. LAWRENCE, Admin.
Rev. JOHN A. CANNON, Chap.
Residents 92

Hollidaysburg
Diocese of Altoona-Johnstown

Dmitri Manor Priests' Residence
St. Mary's Ln.
Hollidaysburg, PA 16648
Rev. Msgr. ROBERT J. SALY, Admin.
Aged Residents 7
Staff 2

Garvey Manor
Logan Blvd.
Hollidaysburg, PA 16648
Tel: 814-695-5571
Sr. M. VERONICA CIARLANTE, O.Carm., Supr. & Admin.
Carmelite Sisters for the Aged and Infirm 8
Aged Residents 150
Patients assisted annually 208
Total Staff 210

St. Leonard's Home, Inc.
601 N. Montgomery St.
Hollidaysburg, PA 16648
Tel: 814-695-9581; Fax: 814-695-2606
Legal Title: *St. Leonard's Home, Inc.*
Sr. DOROTHY M. PAWLUS, C.S.F.N., Admin.
Sisters of the Holy Family of Nazareth 3
Aged Residents 23
Total Staff 14

Huntingdon Valley
Archdiocese of Philadelphia

Redeemer Long Term Care & Elder Services
727 Welsh Rd.
Huntingdon Valley, PA 19006
Tel: 215-938-0180; Fax: 215-938-1237
Subsidiary of Holy Redeemer Health System, Inc.
Mailing Address: Communications Department c/o 1648 Huntingdon Pike
Meadowbrook, PA 19046
Sisters of the Holy Redeemer, C.S.R.
St. Joseph's Manor
1616 Huntingdon Pike
Meadowbrook, PA 19046
Tel: 215-938-4000
Rev. Msgr. CHARLES V. GALLEN, Chap.
Personal and Long-term Nursing Care; Provides a full range of therapies and support services; Medicare approved comprehensive outpatient rehabilitation facility. (CORF).
The Lafayette Redeemer
8580 Verree Rd.
Philadelphia, PA 19111
Tel: 215-214-2800
VIRGINIA A. THOMPSON, Pres. Long Term Care & Elder Svcs.
Independent living apartments, Personal care and long term nursing care.

Redeemer Village
1551 Huntingdon Pike
Huntingdon Valley, PA 19006
Tel: 215-947-8168
Mailing Address:—Communications Department Holy Redeemer Health System, c/o 1648 Huntingdon Pike
Meadowbrook, PA 19046
Subsidiary of Holy Redeemer Health System, Inc. Low income housing for the elderly or handicapped, subsidized by HUD.
Sisters of the Holy Redeemer, C.S.R.
FRANCIS G. HAMEL, Mgr., Redeemer Village
Apartments 151
Redeemer Village II
1551 Huntingdon Pike
Huntingdon Valley, PA 19006
Tel: 215-947-8168
Subsidiary of Holy Redeemer Health System, Inc. Low income housing for the elderly or handicapped, subsidized by HUD.
Sisters of the Holy Redeemer, C.S.R.
Apartments 49

Immaculata
Archdiocese of Philadelphia

Camilla Hall Nursing Home
P.O. Box 100
Immaculata, PA 19345-0100
Tel: 610-644-1152
Sisters, Servants of the Immaculate Heart of Mary
Sr. MARIE JEROME, I.H.M., Admin.
Mother MARIE GENEVIEVE, Supr.
Chaplains:
Rev. MICHAEL L. WALSH
Rev. Msgr. CHARLES V. GALLEN
Bed Capacity 248
Residents 210

Lansdale
Archdiocese of Philadelphia

St. Mary Manor
701 Lansdale Ave.
Lansdale, PA 19446
Tel: 215-368-0900; Fax: 215-362-2891
Immaculate Heart of Mary Sisters.
MAUREEN HUMPHREYS HECKLER, Admin.
Rev. JOSEPH F. MCCAFFERTY, Chap.
Total Staff 210
Residents 205

Lebanon
Diocese of Harrisburg

Villa Vianney
915 S. Lincoln Ave.
Lebanon, PA 17042
Tel: 717-273-1295
Home for Convalescent and Retired Priests of the Diocese of Harrisburg.
Very Rev. DAVID T. MCANDREW, V.F., Admin.
In res.,
Rev. Msgr. VINCENT J. TOPPER
Rev. Msgr. LEO A. BEIERSCHMITT
Rev. JOHN J. SUKNAIC
Residences 9
Total Staff 4
Residents 3

Merion Station
Archdiocese of Philadelphia

McAuley Convent
517 Montgomery Ave.
Merion Station, PA 19066
Tel: 610-667-2775
Infirmary for Religious Sisters of Mercy.
Sr. THERESA MONAGHAN, R.S.M., Supr.
Sr. MARY BONAVENTURE, R.S.M., Dir.
Total Staff 40
Total Assisted 36

Nanticoke
Diocese of Scranton

Mercy Health Care Center
(Skilled Care Nursing Facility)
Newport St.
Nanticoke, PA 18634
Tel: 717-735-7300
ROBERT D. WILLIAMS, Vice Pres. of Aging Svcs.
LAURA REIDER NOVAKOWSKI, Admin.
Rev. BERNARD A. TOLOCZKO, Chap.
Bed Capacity 110
Patients assisted annually 110

New Philadelphia
Diocese of Allentown

Holy Family Apartments
Valley St. & Clay St.
New Philadelphia, PA 17959
Tel: 717-429-0699
Rev. Msgr. DENNIS A. RIGNEY, Pres.
Mrs. JOANNE MCCANN, Mgr.
Catholic housing for the elderly.
Apartments 11
Total Staff 2

Orwigsburg
Diocese of Allentown

Holy Family Adult Day Care at St. Francis Center
900 W. Market St.
Orwigsburg, PA 17961
Tel: 717-366-2924
Rev. Msgr. DENNIS A. RIGNEY, Pres. & CEO
Mrs. LINDA HERB, Dir.
Day care for the elderly.
Clients 34

Holy Family Home Health and Hospice Care
Schuylkill County and Admin. Office, 900 W. Market St.
Orwigsburg, PA 17961
Tel: 717-366-0990; 800-726-8761
5 Hearthstone Ct., Ste. 201
Reading, PA 19606
Tel: 610-779-6432
ARLENE MONGRAIN, R.N., B.S., Exec. Dir.
Patients assisted annually 1,641

Holy Family Residence
900 W. Market St.
Orwigsburg, PA 17961
Tel: 717-366-2912
Rev. Msgr. DENNIS A. RIGNEY, Pres. & CEO
MARY LOUISE PAUL, Admin.
Mr. JAMES POLASKI, Diocesan Coord.
Personal care facility for 58 elderly of Holy Family Manor.
Total in Residence 49
Total Staff 22

Philadelphia
Archdiocese of Philadelphia

Catholic Home for Girls
(St. Joseph Catholic Home for Children)
5238 N. Broad St.
Philadelphia, PA 19141
Tel: 215-324-2610
Sr. LOUISE KANE, S.S.J., L.S.W., Admin.
Provides Therapeutic Group Home Care; Maternity Home Care; Mother/Baby Supervised Independent Living; Outreach School Social Work for Adolescent Girls. Mental Health services available on site

for all residents.
Sisters of St. Joseph 4
Sisters of Mercy 1
Capacity 60

Holy Family Home
5300 Chester Ave.
Philadelphia, PA 19143-4993
Tel: 215-729-5153
Little Sisters of the Poor.
Mother MARY VINCENT, L.S.P., Admin.
Rev. DOUGLAS M. MCKAY, Chap.
Total Staff 120
Residents 110

Immaculate Mary Home
2990 Holme Ave.
Philadelphia, PA 19136-1829
Tel: 215-335-2100; Fax: 215-331-1016
Opened March 1976.
Sr. CORDA MARIE O.S.F., N.H.A., Admin.
JUDITH A. PASSERINI, Acting Admin.
Total Staff 317
Total Assisted 296

Mount Nazareth
2755 Holme Ave.
Philadelphia, PA 19152
Tel: 215-338-8992
Sisters of the Holy Family Of Nazareth.
Home for retired and infirm sisters.
Sr. MARGARET MARY MACHOWSKI, C.S.F.N., Supr.
Rev. Msgr. CHARLES J. SCHAEFLEIN, Chap.
Resident Sisters 52
Total Staff 16
Total Assisted 42

Sacred Heart Free Home for Incurable Cancer
1315 W. Hunting Park Ave.
Philadelphia, PA 19140
Tel: 215-329-3222
Opened April 27, 1930.
Sisters of the Third Order of St. Dominic.
Sr. M. JUDE, O.P., Supr.
Sr. M. ANNETTE, O.P., Admin.
Legal Title: *The Servants of Relief for Incurable Cancer*
Bed Capacity 45
Total Staff 40
Patients assisted annually 103
Attended by Oblates of St. Francis de Sales.

Sacred Heart Manor
6445 Germantown Ave.
Philadelphia, PA 19119
Tel: 215-438-5268
Carmelite Sisters for the Aged and Infirm.
Sr. M. PATRICIA MICHAEL, O.Carm., Admin.
Rev. JOHN S. HEIM, Chap.
Nursing Care Residents 171
Independent Living Residents 72
Personal Care Boarding Home 24

St. Gabriel's System
Administrative Offices, 117 S. 17th St., Ste. 1701
Philadelphia, PA 19103
Tel: 215-665-8777; Fax: 215-665-8821
Bro. ROBERT J. KINZLER, F.S.C., A.C.S.W., Exec. Dir.
Administrative and Intake services for residential treatment; Group Home care and Day Treatment for Court-committed delinquent boys, ages 12-17. (See St. Gabriel's Hall, De LaSalle in Towne, De LaSalle Vocational and De LaSalle Aftercare).
Total Staff 420
Total Assisted 2,000

St. Ignatius Nursing Home
4401 Haverford Ave.
Philadelphia, PA 19104
Tel: 215-349-8800; Fax: 215-222-3078
Sr. MARY AGATHA CEBULA, C.S.S.F., N.H.A., Admin.
Attended from St. Ignatius Church.
Felician Sisters 6
Bed Capacity 176
Total Staff 185
Total in Residence 176

St. John Neumann Nursing Home
10400 Roosevelt Blvd.
Philadelphia, PA 19116
Tel: 215-698-5600
Sisters of the Holy Family of Nazareth.
Rev. L. JAMES MULLEN, Chap.
Beds 226
Total Staff 294

St. Joseph Housing Corporation
Mount St. Joseph Convent
Philadelphia, PA 19118-2694
Tel: 215-248-7200
Total Staff 4
Total in Residence 107
Staffed by the Sisters of St. Joseph.

St. Joseph's House for Boys
4010-4012 Ashburner St.
Philadelphia, PA 19136-2801
Tel: 215-332-3490
Rev. FRANCIS R. DUFFY, C.S.Sp., Ph.D., Dir.
Provides community-based group home residential treatment for boys 8-18.
Capacity 40
Total Staff 39
Total Assisted 56

St. Vincent's Orphanage Tacony
7201 Milnor St.
Philadelphia, PA 19135
Tel: 215-624-5601
Revs.:
ENGELBERT G. MICHEL, Pres., Bd. of Mgrs.
EDUARDO G. MONTERO, J.C.L., Chap.
Provides Family Oriented residential care for children 2-12 years of age.
Residential program, 84 boys and girls; comprehensive emergency shelter.
Capacity 84

Metropolitan Archdiocese of Philadelphia Ukrainian

Ascension Manor, Inc.
911 N. Franklin St.
Philadelphia, PA 19123
Tel: 215-922-1116
Most Rev. STEPHEN SULYK, D.D., S.T.L., Pres.
Revs.:
JAMES MELNIC, Exec. Vice Pres.
MICHAEL HUTSKO, Sec. & Treas.
Directors:
Most Rev. WALTER PASKA
Rev. JOHN FIELDS
MICHAEL SMYLIE
Dr. JAROSLAW JARYMOWYCH
JEANNE KARBIWNYK
IHOR SHUST
MARIE J. HANUSEY, Gen. Mgr.
Ascension Manor I
911 N. Franklin St.
Philadelphia, PA 19123
Tel: 215-922-1116
ANNA SIWAK, Mgr.
Ascension Manor II
970 N. Seventh St.
Philadelphia, PA 19123
Tel: 215-923-3907
EWHENIA NOWAKIWSKY, Mgr.

Home of Divine Providence
209 W. Chestnut Hill Ave.
Philadelphia, PA 19118
Tel: 215-247-7107
Sr. CECELIA SWORIN, S.S.M.I., Admin.
Rev. ANTHONY RADCHUK, Chap.
Home for the aged - personal care home.
Sisters 11
Residents 30

Pittsburgh
Diocese of Pittsburgh

Franciscan Child Day Care Center
1401 Hamilton Rd.
Pittsburgh, PA 15234-2399
Tel: 412-882-5085
CAROL UNRUE, Dir.
Sr. MARIAN BLODIS, O.S.F., Pres.
Total Assisted 100
Total Staff 30

Home for the Aged of the Little Sisters of the Poor
1028 Benton Ave.
Pittsburgh, PA 15212
Tel: 412-761-5373
Sr. MARGARET BANAR, Supr. & Admin.
Rev. JEROME A. DIXON, J.C.L.
Sisters 14
Total Staff 92
Residents 106

Marian Hall Home, Inc.
934 Forest Ave.
Pittsburgh, PA 15202
Tel: 412-761-1999; 761-2556
Personal care home for women.
Lay Staff 28
In Residence:
Sisters 22
Lay Women 24

Marian Manor Corp.
2695 Winchester Dr.
Pittsburgh, PA 15220-4099
Tel: 412-563-6866 (Admin.); 563-1244 (Nursing Service)
Sr. EILEEN CHLEBOWSKI, N.H.A., Admin.
Rev. HENRY SZARNICKI, Chap.
Sisters of the Holy Spirit 13
Total Staff 292
Residents 214

Mt. Alvernia Day Care & Learning Center, Kindergarten
146 Hawthorne Rd.
Pittsburgh, PA 15209
Total Assisted 80
Total Staff 13

Providence Child Care Center
400 Hoodridge Dr.
Pittsburgh, PA 15234
Tel: 412-562-3745
Sr. MARIA FEST, Contact Person
Purpose: to engage in educational activities and operation of a day care program.

St. Joseph Nursing and Health Care Center, Inc.
5324 Penn Ave.
Pittsburgh, PA 15224-1798
Tel: 412-665-5100
ARTHUR L. NANCE, N.H.A., Admin.
Rev. DAVID DIXON, Chap.
Beds 158
Patients assisted annually 158

St. Paul Manor
148 Monastery Ave.
Pittsburgh, PA 15203
Tel: 412-381-4744
GERTRUDE BUSCH, R.N., Admin.
Total Assisted 62
Total Staff 58

St. Pius X Residence, Inc.
2681 Waddington Ave.
Pittsburgh, PA 15226
Tel: 412-563-5040; Fax: 412-563-3776
MARY JO HUMMEL, Admin.
Rev. THOMAS M. MARPES, Chap.

**St. Francis Plaza, Inc.*
451 44th St.
Pittsburgh, PA 15201-1122
Tel: 412-683-6252; Fax: 412-683-4269
Sr. M. SYLVIA SCHULER, Chm.
Sisters 2
Residents 106

Villa De Marillac Nursing Home
5300 Stanton Ave.
Pittsburgh, PA 15206
Tel: 412-361-2833
Non-sectarian, skilled nursing home.
Sr. THERESA NOVAK, V.S.C., N.H.A., Contact
Rev. THOMAS MURPHY, Chap.
Vincentian Sisters of Charity 5
Total Staff 75
Bed Capacity 52
Total Assisted 75

Vincentian Child Care, Inc.
8200 McKnight Rd.
Pittsburgh, PA 15237
Tel: 412-366-8588
Sr. GEORGINE BIRES, V.S.C., Contact Person
Purpose: to engage in educational activities; operating a day care program; to perform any lawful acts to effectuate purposes of this corporation and in this pursuit to apply funds or incomes exclusively for charitable, religious, scientific, literary, and educational purposes.

Vincentian Home Inc.
111 Perrymont Rd.
Pittsburgh, PA 15237
Tel: 412-366-5600
Vincentian Sisters of Charity.
Sr. ANNE KULL, V.S.C., Admin.
Rev. ROBERT DRAKE, C.PP.S., Chap.
Sisters 9
Total Staff 250
Bed Capacity 221
Patients assisted annually 221

Pottsville
Diocese of Allentown

Queen of Peace Apartments
777 Water St.
Pottsville, PA 17901
Tel: 717-628-4504
Rev. Msgr. DENNIS A. RICHEY, Pres.
Mrs. MARY ANN STERNER, Mgr.

Catholic housing for the elderly.
Apartments 65
Total in Residence 65
Total Staff 1

Reading
Diocese of Allentown

Queen of Angels Apartment
22 Rothermel St., Hyde Park
Reading, PA 19605
Tel: 610-921-3115
Rev. Msgr. DENNIS A. RIGNEY, Pres.
Ms. VALERIE PHELPS, Mgr.
Catholic housing for the elderly.
Apartments 45
Total in Residence 45
Total Staff 2

Rosemont
Archdiocese of Philadelphia

St. Edmond's Home for Children
320 S. Roberts Rd.
Rosemont, PA 19010
Tel: 610-525-8800
Daughters of St. Mary of Providence.
MARK E. FITZGERALD, Admin.
Rev. Msgr. EDWARD P. CULLEN, V.G., Chap.
Licensed I.C.F./M.R. care for severly/profoundly impaired, physically handicapped boys and girls 1-16 years of age at admission.
Capacity 40

Saint Clair
Diocese of Allentown

Neumann Apartments
25 N. Nichols St.
Saint Clair, PA 17970
Tel: 717-429-0699
Mrs. MARY ANN STERNER
Catholic housing for the elderly.
Total in Residence 25
Total Staff 2
Apartments 25
Total in Residence 25
Total Staff 2

Scranton
Diocese of Scranton

Home for Aged of the Little Sisters of the Poor, Holy Family Residence
2500 Adams Ave.
Scranton, PA 18509
Tel: 717-343-4065; 346-5788; Fax: 717-347-1941
Sr. MONIQUE GALLAGHER, p.s.d.p., Supr. & Admin.
Rev. JOSEPH F. MEIGHAN, Chap.
Little Sisters of the Poor 16
Aged Residents 58
Residents in Independent Living Apts. 22

St. Joseph's Center
2010 Adams Ave.
Scranton, PA 18509
Tel: 717-342-8379; 961-1549
Sr. VINCENTIA DORSEY, I.H.M., Admin.
Rev. WILLIAM B. PICKARD, Chap.
Sisters, Servants of the Immaculate Heart of Mary 11
Bed Capacity 147
Patients assisted annually 158

Uniontown
Metropolitan Archdiocese of Pittsburgh, Byzantine

Mount Macrina Manor Nursing Home
520 W. Main St.
Uniontown, PA 15401
Tel: 412-437-1400; Fax: 412-430-1095
CELESTE L. GOLONSKI, N.H.A., Exec. Dir.
Sisters of St. Basil the Great 6
Beds 120

St. Basil's Home
530 W. Main St., Box 878
Uniontown, PA 15401
Tel: 412-437-7480; 437-5826
Sr. EVELYN SWEDA, O.S.B.M., Admin.
Sisters of St. Basil the Great 3
Residents 9

Ventnor
Archdiocese of Philadelphia

Villa St. Joseph by the Sea
114 S. Princeton Ave.
Ventnor, PA 08406
Tel: 609-822-7184
Summer residence for aged, infirm, and convalescent priests of the Archdiocese of Philadelphia.
Rev. Msgr. D. JAMES MCGETTIGAN, M.A., Rector
Rev. EDWARD J. CASEY, Asst. Rector

Warminster
Archdiocese of Philadelphia

Regina Coeli Residence for Priests
685 York Rd.
Warminster, PA 18974
Tel: 215-441-4642
Rev. JAMES D. BEISEL, Admin.
Home for retired priests of the Archdiocese of Philadelphia.
Total Staff 5
Total in Residence 12

Wilkes-Barre
Diocese of Scranton

Little Flower Manor of the Diocese of Scranton
200 S. Meade St.
Wilkes-Barre, PA 18702
Tel: 717-823-6131
Sr. M. JEANETTE LINDSAY, O.Carm., Supr. & Admin.
Rev. W. JEFFREY PAVLISH, Chap.
Conducted by the Carmelite Sisters for the Aged and Infirm.
Sisters 8
Aged Residents 133
Total Staff 190

Yardley
Archdiocese of Philadelphia

D'Youville Manor
1750 Quarry Rd.
Yardley, PA 19067
Tel: 215-579-1750
Operated by Grey Nuns of the Sacred Heart. Assisted living retirement residence for the elderly.
Sr. JACQUELINE WEIGLE, G.N.S.H., Dir.
Capacity 51
Total Staff 28
Total in Residence 50

York
Diocese of Harrisburg

Misericordia Convalescent Home
998 S. Russell St.
York, PA 17402
Tel: 717-755-1964
Daughters of Our Lady of Mercy.
Sr. CARMEL MARIE, D.M., Admin.
Sisters 6
Bed Capacity 55
Total Staff 45
Total Assisted 45

PUERTO RICO

Arecibo
Diocese of Arecibo, Puerto Rico

Hogar de Ancianos San Vicente
Mailing Address:
P.O. Box 4196
Vega Baja, P.R 00694
Bo. Almirante Sur-Carr 645 Km. 6.6
Vega Baja, PR 00763
Tel: 787-855-0487
Hermanas de la Presentacion 3
Guests 31

Hogar Sta. Maria Eufrasia
Calle Andres Garcia, No. 10
Arecibo, PR 00612
Tel: 809-878-5166
House for Unwed Mothers.
Good Shepherd Sisters 4
Unwed Mothers 12

La Milagrosa Home for Orphan Girls
Cotto Ave., No. 987
Arecibo, PR 00612
Tel: 809-878-6231
Sisters of Charity 7
Girls 20

San Rafael Home for Aged
00612
Hogar Geriatrico San Rafael
Calle Cervantes
Arecibo, P.R 00612
Tel: 787-878-3813
Sisters of Charity 5
Guests 37

Dorado
Archdiocese of San Juan, Puerto Rico

Santuario del Espiritu Santo
Box 187
Dorado, PR 00646-0187
Tel: 809-796-2798
Revs.:
CARLOS CONNORS, C.S.Sp., Supr. & Dir.
ROBERT GRAVES, C.S.Sp.
GERARDO A. SEIFRIED, C.S.Sp., (Retired)
JOSE WEHNING, C.S.Sp., (Retired)

Hato Rey
Archdiocese of San Juan, Puerto Rico

Jesuit Community - Casa Claver
398 Francisca Sein
Hato Rey, PR 00917
Mailing Address:
Apto. 22634 U.P.R. Sta.
San Juan, PR 00931-2634
Rev. FERNANDO PICO, S.J., Insular Supr.

Isabela
Diocese of Arecibo, Puerto Rico

Hogar Infantil Jesus Nazareno, Inc.
P.O. Box 1671
Isabela, PR 00662

Lares
Diocese of Arecibo, Puerto Rico

Fundacion Irma Fe
Calle Comerio No. 52
Lares, PR 00669
Tel: 787-897-6090
Charity Sisters of St. Joseph (Mexico) 6
Guests 25

Ponce
Diocese of Ponce, Puerto Rico

Home for Aged and Infirm
Barrio Sabenetas, P.O. Box 2127
Ponce, PR 00731
Tel: 787-840-7575
Sr. ANGELA ESTEVEZ, Supr.
Rev. PERFECTO ALVAREZ, O.S.A., Chap.
Total Staff 16
Residents 206

Puerta De Tierra
Archdiocese of San Juan, Puerto Rico

Asylum For The Aged and Infirm
Hogar de la Providencia, Stop 5, Box 5279
Puerta De Tierra, PR 00906
Tel: 809-722-1331
Sisters of the Poor
Sr. CELSA VASQUEZ, Supr.
Rev. OVIDIO ORTEGA, Chap.
Sisters 19
Patients assisted annually 275

Rio Piedras
Archdiocese of San Juan, Puerto Rico

Asylum For Orphan Girls
107 Jose de Diego St. S.
Rio Piedras, PR 00925
Tel: 809-765-6114
Daughters of Charity
Sr. VIRGINIA TORRES, H.C., Supr.
Rev. HIGINIO MADRAZO, C.M., Chap.
Sisters 15
Beds 70

Centro N. Sra. de la Providencia
Sisters of Notre Dame.
R.F.D. #2, Box 16T
Rio Piedras, PR 00928
Tel: 809-761-0273

Hogar Carmelitano
Julian Bengochea Final;
Urb. San Martin
Rio Piedras, PR 00924
Tel: 809-769-6510
Carmelite Sisters (Spain)
Sr. TERESA M. NEGRON, Supr.
Beds 3,200
Patients assisted annually 360

Hogar Santa Teresa Jornet for the Aged
Cupey Alto, Km. 3, Hm. 8, Box 21012

Rio Piedras, PR 00928
Tel: 809-761-5805
Sisters of the Poor
Sr. FELISA BRAVO, Supr.
Rev. CARLOS DIONISIO CRUZ DAVILA, Chap.
Sisters 18
Beds 210
Guests 220

RHODE ISLAND

Cumberland
Diocese of Providence

Mount St. Rita Health Centre
15 Sumner Brown Rd.
Cumberland, RI 02864
Tel: 401-333-6352
Legal Title: *Mount St. Rita Health Centre Inc.*
Licenced Nursing Home.
Sr. JOAN BAILEY, R.S.M., Admin.
Rev. RAYMOND E. DYER, Chap.
Residents 88

Newport
Diocese of Providence

St. Clare Home
309 Spring St.
Newport, RI 02840
Tel: 401-849-3204; Fax: 401-849-5780
Legal Title: *The Saint Clare Home*
Nursing Facility.
MARY ANN ALTRUI, Admin.
Rev. TIMOTHY L. GILLEN
In res.,
Rev. TIMOTHY J. SULLIVAN
Daughters of the Holy Spirit 1
R.N., Nursing Sisters 1
Lay Nurses 9
Lay Employees 61
Residents 46

North Kingstown
Diocese of Providence

Scalabrini Villa
860 N. Quidnessett Rd.
North Kingstown, RI 02852
Tel: 401-884-1802
Legal Title: *Scalabrini Villa Inc.*
Full Skilled Nursing Facility.
Rev. EDWARD J. MARINO, C.S., Admin., Tel: 401-884-1242
Sr. WILMA LOPEZI, F.A.S., Supr., Tel: 401-884-4594
In res.,
Rev. Msgr. OSCAR A. GUILBAULT Tel: 401-884-1426
Rev. GUIDO FERRONATO, C.S. Tel: 401-884-6072
Franciscan Apostolic Sisters 3
Residents 120

North Smithfield
Diocese of Providence

St. Antoine Residence
400 Mendon Rd.
North Smithfield, RI 02895
Tel: 401-767-3500
Legal Title: *Saint Antoine Residence*
MARY ANN ALTRUI, Admin.
Rev. DONAT A. BARRETTE, Chap.
In res.,
Rev. Msgr. EDMUND J. BROCK
Rev. Msgr. DONAT J. FAGNANT
Rev. WILLIAM F. PYNE
Residents 260

Pawtucket
Diocese of Providence

Jeanne Jugan Apartments
310 Sayles Ave.
Pawtucket, RI 02860
Apartments for elderly 27
Residents 33

Jeanne Jugan Residence
964 Main St.
Pawtucket, RI 02860
Tel: 401-723-4314; Fax: 401-727-2885
Legal Title: *Jeanne Jugan Residence of the Little Sisters of the Poor*
Rev. Msgr. WILLIAM I. VARSANYI, J.C.D., Chap.
In res.,
Rev. Msgr. PAUL A. LLOYD
Rev. OLIVA T. DOUCET
Little Sisters of the Poor 14
Residents 74

Providence
Diocese of Providence

St. Joseph Living Center
153 Dean St.
Providence, RI 02903
Tel: 401-272-3335
DIANE E. EVANS, R.N., B.S.N., Exec. Dir.
Assisted and independent living and respite care facility, a division of St. Joseph Health Services of Rhode Island.
Residents 60

Woonsocket
Diocese of Providence

Saint Francis House
167 Blackstone St.
Woonsocket, RI 02895
Tel: 401-762-5255
Legal Title: *Saint Francis House, Woonsocket RI*
HELEN STRADONE, Dir.
Rev. JOSEPH D. SHANLEY, Chap.
Residents 59

SOUTH CAROLINA

Charleston
Diocese of Charleston

Carter-May Home
1660 Ingram Rd.
Charleston, SC 29407
Tel: 803-556-8314
Mrs. JANINE N. BAUDER, Admin.
Residents 15

Myrtle Beach
Diocese of Charleston

Mercy Hospice of Horry County
P.O. Box 1409
Myrtle Beach, SC 29578
Tel: 803-236-2282
Owned and operated by SSM Health Care. A member of the SSM Health Care System.
Sr. CONSTANCE FAHEY, F.S.M., Exec. Dir.
Sisters 4
Lay Staff 23
Patients assisted annually 325

SOUTH DAKOTA

Aberdeen
Diocese of Sioux Falls

Aberdeen Living Center
(Operated by Benedictine Health System Long Term Care, Inc.)
1700 N. Hwy. 281
Aberdeen, SD 57401
Tel: 605-225-7315

Mother Joseph Manor, Nursing Care Facility
1002 N. Jay St.
Aberdeen, SD 57401
Tel: 605-229-0550
TOM SNYDER, Admin.
Rev. CHARLES EMEZIE (Nigeria)
Presentation Sisters of the B.V.M. (Aberdeen, SD) 2
Residents 81
Units for Apartment Living 57
Adult Day Care.
Community Outreach.
Respite Care.
Health Screening Clinics.
Family Support Council.

Milbank.
Diocese of Sioux Falls

St. William Home for the Aged
Milbank, SD 57252
Tel: 605-432-4538; Fax: 605-432-5412
Conducted by Daughters of St. Mary of Providence, Milbank.
Rev. RAY OHO, O.S.B.
Guests 60
Angela Hall Assisted Living Center
Guests 22
Sisters 5

Mitchell
Diocese of Sioux Falls

Brady Memorial Home
500 S. Ohlman, P.O. Box 430
Mitchell, SD 57301
Tel: 605-966-7701; Fax: 605-996-5726
Mrs. ROBERTA CLARK, Admin.
Rev. THOMAS MCPHILLIPS, Chap.
Presentation Sisters of the B.V.M. 4
Skilled Nursing Care Units 83
Senior Residences 9
Bishop Hoch Villa
Units for Congregate Living 6
Additional Senior Units 3
Brady Day Services Adult Day Care.
Respite Care Bed 1

Sioux Falls
Diocese of Sioux Falls

Prince of Peace Retirement Community, Inc.
4500 Prince of Peace Pl.
Sioux Falls, SD 57103
Tel: 605-371-0700
Mr. GARY TUSCHEN, Admin.
Presentation Sisters of B.V.M. 1
Nursing Home Beds 90
Congregate Apartments 74
Assisted Living Apartments 32

Sisseton
Diocese of Sioux Falls

Tekakwitha Nursing Center, Inc.
(sub. of Benedictine Health System)
6 E. Chestnut
Sisseton, SD 57262
Tel: 605-693-7693; Fax: 605-698-3091
Mr. ROBERT E. FAEHN, Admin.
Sr. COLETTA VAN HEEK, Dir. Pastoral Care
Residents 101
(Owned and operated by: Benedictine Health System).

TENNESSEE

Dyersburg
Diocese of Memphis

St. Joseph Manor
885 Hwy. 51, Byp. W., P.O. Box 151
Dyersburg, TN 38024
Tel: 901-285-8560
BEVERLY BATES, Acting Mgr.

The Village Apartments
Hwy. 51 Byp. W., P.O. Box 151
Dyersburg, TN 38024
Tel: 901-285-8560
BEVERLY BATES, Acting Mgr.

Westgate Apartments
1405-8 Meeks
Dyersburg, TN 38024
Tel: 901-286-4874
Ms. ANGELA HARRIS, Mgr.

Germantown
Diocese of Memphis

Madonna Learning Center for Retarded Children
7007 Poplar Ave.
Germantown, TN 38138
Tel: 901-752-5767
Sisters of St. Benedict (Ferdinand, IN).
Sr. MARY MARK GRAF, O.S.B.
Sisters 2
Lay Teachers 7
Students 45

Humboldt
Diocese of Memphis

St. Matthew Manor
2575 Viking Dr.
Humboldt, TN 38343
Tel: 901-784-7229
Ms. MARY FAULKNER, Mgr.

Jackson
Diocese of Memphis

St. Mary Manor
1771 Hwy. 45 By-Pass
Jackson, TN 38305
Tel: 901-668-5633
JOEL BIRDSONG, Mgr.

Knoxville
Diocese of Knoxville

Columbus Home, Inc.
119 Dameron Ave.
Knoxville, TN 37917

Tel: 423-971-3570; Fax: 423-546-0433
DAVID DOTSON, Exec. Dir.
Total Assisted 500
Total Staff 22

Memphis
Diocese of Memphis

DeNeuville Heights School for Girls (1875)
3060 Baskin St.
Memphis, TN 38127
Title of Incorporation: House of the Good Shepherd.
Sr. M. ROSALINDA SOBREMISANA, R.G.S., Admin.
Sisters 13
Lay Staff 52
Students 60

Diocese of Memphis Housing Corp.
P.O. Box 41705
Memphis, TN 38174-1705
Tel: 901-722-4761; 722-4772
Mr. DAVID FIELD, Dir. of Housing
Mrs. MICHELLE R. BURRELL, Asst. Dir. of Housing

Northwood Park Apartments
1130 N. Breedlove
Memphis, TN 38107
Tel: 901-522-9134
Mr. TYRONE KNOLLS, Mgr.

St. Peter Home for Children (1852)
1805 Poplar Ave.
Memphis, TN 38104
Tel: 901-725-8240

St. Peter Manor
108 N. Auburndale
Memphis, TN 38104
Tel: 901-278-8200
Sr. MARILYN TERWILLIGER, S.S.J., Mgr.
Rev. WILLIAM BURKE
St. Peter Chapel & Activity Center

St. Peter Villa
141 N. McLean
Memphis, TN 38104-2644
Tel: 901-276-2021
Diocesan Nursing Home.
LINDA WARF, Exec Dir.
Rev. WILLIAM BURKE, Chap., Tel: 901-276-2021

Moscow
Diocese of Memphis

St. Mark Village Apartments
85 St. Mark Cove
Moscow, TN 38057
Tel: 901-877-3456
Ms. GEORGIA LAUGHTER, Mgr.

Nashville
Diocese of Nashville

St. Bernard After School Program
2020 24th Ave. S.
Nashville, TN 37212
Tel: 615-298-1298
BRENDA DYE, Dir.
Lay Staff 10
Students 80

St. Mary Orphanage, Inc. dba St. Mary Villa
30 White Bridge Rd.
Nashville, TN 37205
Mr. DAVID GLASCOE, Admin.
Rev. Msgr. GEORGE W. ROHLING, V.G., Chap.

St. Mary Villa Child Development Center
30 White Bridge Rd.
Nashville, TN 37205
Tel: 615-356-6336
JOANNE CHASE, Prog. Dir.
Staff 30
Children 137

St. Mary Villa Retirement Community, Inc.
2400 21st Ave.
Nashville, TN 37212

**Villa Child Care, Inc.*
30 White Bridge Rd.
Nashville, TN 37205
Tel: 615-356-6111
JOANNE CHASE, Prog. Dir.
Staff 20
Children 90

Villa Maria Manor, Inc. dba Villa Maria Manor
32 White Bridge Rd.
Nashville, TN 37205
Tel: 615-352-3084
Mailing Address:
2400 21st Ave.
Nashville, TN 37212
Mr. WILLIAM P. SINCLAIR, Mng. Agent
Residents 211

Signal Mountain
Diocese of Knoxville

Alexian Village Health Care Center (1938)
100 James Blvd.
Signal Mountain, TN 37377
Tel: 423-886-0100
Licensed Skilled & Intermediate Care Nursing Home.
Bro. LARRY KRUEGER, C.F.A., Dir. Community
Rev. MARO CANNON, C.F.A., Chap.
Mr. DAN GRAY, CEO
Brothers 12
Bed Capacity 114
Patients assisted annually 105
Assisted Living 33

Alexian Village of Tennessee, Inc.
100 James Blvd.
Signal Mountain, TN 37377
Tel: 423-870-0101
Life Care Residences and Nursing Home.
Mr. DAN GRAY, Pres.
Life Care Units 277

TEXAS

Arlington
Diocese of Fort Worth

Nuestro Hogar, Inc. Catholic Charities
709 Magnolia St.
Arlington, TX 76012
Tel: 817-261-0608
65 unit apartment complex for the elderly and disabled.
Total in Residence 68
Total Staff 3

Brownsville
Diocese of Brownsville

Mother of Perpetual Help Home
519 E. Madison St.
Brownsville, TX 78520
Tel: 210-546-6745; 546-0711
Sisters of the Holy Spirit and Mary Immaculate.
Sr. JANE F. AMBROSE, S.H.Sp., Admin.
Sisters 3
Capacity 45
Chapel attended from Immaculate Conception Cathedral.

Corpus Christi
Diocese of Corpus Christi

Mount Carmel Home
4130 S. Alameda St.
Corpus Christi, TX 78411
Tel: 512-855-6243
Sr. MARY TERESA, Supr.
Rev. JOHN THOMAS KENNA, Chaplain
Sisters 9
Residents 92

Villa Maria, Inc.
3146 Saratoga Blvd.
Corpus Christi, TX 78415
Tel: 512-857-6171; Fax: 512-857-6173
Apartment complex for senior adults.
Total Staff 4
Total in Residence 62

Crowley
Diocese of Fort Worth

St. Francis Village, Inc.
1 Chapel Plaza
Crowley, TX 76036
Tel: 817-292-5786
(On shores of Lake Benbrook near Fort Worth)
Residence village for retirees and the elderly sponsored by Franciscan Tertiary Provinces Foundation & SFV, Inc. (Illinois).
Revs.:
J. MICHAEL EWERT, O.F.M., Dir.
ARMAND LUBANSKI, O.F.M., (Retired)
AUGUSTINE HEALY, O.C.D., (Retired)
CAL GIESEN, O.F.M., (Retired)
VINCENT ELSEN, O.F.M., Chap.
In res.,
Revs.:
RAY BOBBER, O.F.M., (Retired)
PETER FRITZ, O.F.M., (Retired)
RAYMOND NYTES, O.F.M.
DONALD WERR, O.F.M.
JOHN OSTDIEK, O.F.M.
RONALD J. AXEN
MATHIAS KIEMEN, O.F.M.
Residents 450
Franciscan Tertiary Provinces Foundation
1 Chapel Plaza
Crowley, TX 76036
Sponsor corporation of St. Francis Village (retirement village) in Crowley, TX.
Rev. J. MICHAEL EWERT, O.F.M., Pres.
Total in Residence 450
Total Staff 24

El Paso
Diocese of El Paso

Nazareth Hall
4614 Trowbridge
El Paso, TX 79903
Tel: 915-565-4677; Fax: 915-566-7530
Sr. ELISA RODRIGUEZ, Admin. Nursing Center

Villa Maria
920 S. Oregon St.
El Paso, TX 79901
Tel: 915-533-5152
Home for Aged Women and Men.
Sr. MARY ANN HAMOR, C.S.J., Dir.
Women Residents 16
Men Residents 7

Fort Worth
Diocese of Fort Worth

Casa del Cor, Inc.
2701 Burchill Rd., N.
Fort Worth, TX 76105
Tel: 817-534-0814; Fax: 817-535-8779

Casa, Inc. Housing for the Elderly and Handicapped
3201 Sondra Dr.
Fort Worth, TX 76107
Tel: 817-332-7276
Units 200
Total in Residence 197
Total Staff 7

Hillje
Diocese of Victoria in Texas

Czech Catholic Home For The Aged
Rte. 3, Box 40
El Campo, TX 77437
Tel: 409-648-2628

Houston
Diocese of Galveston—Houston

Casa de Esperanza, De Los Ninos, Inc.
Mailing Address: P.O. Box 66581
Houston, TX 77006
Tel: 713-529-0639
Homes for children in crisis situations.
Sr. KATHY FOSTER, S.S.M.N., Dir.
Mr. WILLIAM JONES, Asst. Dir.
Sisters 15
Served 600
Total Assisted 135
Total Staff 20

Casa Juan Diego
4818 Rose
Houston, TX 77007
Tel: 713-869-7376
Mr. MARK ZWICK, Dir.
Houses 16
Patients assisted annually 263,700

Casa Maria de Guadalupe Medical Clinic and Social Service Center
(Catholic Worker)
6101 Edgemoor
Houston, TX 77081
Tel: 713-995-9414
Mailing Address:
P.O. Box 70113
Houston, TX 77270
Patients assisted annually 229,300

Covenant House Texas
1111 Lovett Blvd.
Houston, TX 77006
Tel: 713-523-2231
Sr. MARY ROSE MCGEADY, Pres.
CAROLYN LARSEN, Exec. Dir.
ANDREA METZGER, Pastoral Min.

Served 4,200

Pope John XXIII Priest Residence
2407 E. Holcombe Blvd.
Houston, TX 77021-2023
Tel: 713-748-4608
Residents 14
Total Staff 2

St. Dominic Nursing Home
St. Dominic Center, 2409 E. Holcombe Blvd.
Houston, TX 77021-2023
Tel: 713-741-8701
Mrs. RUTH WHIGHAM, Admin.
Aged Residents 130

St. Dominic Residence Hall
St. Dominic Diocesan Center, 2401 E. Holcombe Blvd.
Houston, TX 77021-2023
Tel: 713-741-8700
Ms. BILLIE J. COKER, Admin.
Aged Residents 1,432
Total Staff 24

Santa Maria Hostel
807 Paschall St.
Houston, TX 77009
Tel: 713-228-0125
Intensive residential treatment (substance abuse) for women ages 18 and above.
Ms. CHERYL EMPEY, Exec. Dir.
Residents 20
Patients assisted annually 283
Total Staff 9

Kenedy
Archdiocese of San Antonio

John Paul II Nursing Home
215 Tilden, P.O. Box 359
Kenedy, TX 78119
Tel: 210-583-9841
Sr. MARIA LODZIANA, S.O.L.S., Admin.
Seraphic Sisters of Our Lady of Sorrows 5
Residents 63

Laredo
Diocese of Corpus Christi

Sacred Heart Children's Home
3310 S. Zapata Hwy.
Laredo, TX 78046
Tel: 210-723-3343
Servants of the Sacred Heart of Jesus and of the Poor.
Mother MARIA YOLANDA FERNANDEZ, S.S.H.P., Supr.
Rev. ANGEL VISCARRA
Sisters 15
Children 60

Panhandle
Diocese of Amarillo

St. Ann's Nursing Home
P.O. Box 1179
Panhandle, TX 79068
Tel: 806-537-3194
Rev. Msgr. MONROE J. MATTHIESEN, Dir.
JANA SCHICK, Admin.
School Sisters of St. Francis
Residents 56

St. Joseph's Home for Retired Priests
P.O. Box 1179
Panhandle, TX 79068
Pastor Emeriti:
Rev. Msgr. JAMES W. SONDERMAN
Rev. Msgr. CLIFTON J. CORCORAN
Rev. Msgr. MONROE J. MATTHIESEN, Dir.

San Antonio
Archdiocese of San Antonio

Casa De Padres
8520 Cross Mountain Tr.
San Antonio, TX 78255
Home for retired Priests of San Antonio.
Rev. Msgr. THOMAS J. COLLINS, No. 302, Dir., Tel: 210-698-0682
Rev. Msgr. ANTHONY J. COSTANTINO, No. 201
Rev. ROGELIO MARTINEZ, No. 1101, Tel: 210-698-2243
Rev. Msgr. J. LEROY MANNING, No. 1102, Tel: 210-698-3183
Rev. Msgr. ROY RIHN, No. 301, Tel: 210-431-9903
Rev. Msgr. BERNARD C. MULLANEY, No. 402, Tel: 210-698-3975
Rev. Msgr. ALOIS J. GOERTZ, No. 402, Tel: 210-698-9067
In res.,
Rev. Msgr. PATRICK J. MURRAY, No. 701, Tel: 210-698-0349

Father Flanagan's Boys' Town of San Antonio
503 Urban Loop
San Antonio, TX 78204
Tel: 210-271-1010
Ms. DEBORAH WILSON, Site Dir.
Staff 47
Bed Capacity 48
Children Under Care 41
Residential Center (For Children under 18)
8400, 8401, 8402, 8405, 8406 Flanagan St.
San Antonio, TX 78249
Tel: 210-271-1010
Staff 18
Bed Capacity 30
Youth Shelter
503 Urban Loop
San Antonio, TX 78204
Tel: 210-271-3131
Staff 16
Bed Capacity 18
Total Assisted 300
Common Sense Parenting
503 Urban Loop
San Antonio, TX 78204
Tel: 210-271-1010
Staff 4
Total Assisted 200
Family Preservation Services
503 Urban Loop
San Antonio, TX 78204
Tel: 210-271-1010
Staff 25
Families Assisted 50

Incarnate Word Motherhouse and Retirement Center
4707 Broadway
San Antonio, TX 78209
Tel: 210-829-7561
For lay persons also.
Mr. RICHARD BOYD, Exec. Dir.
Rev. Msgr. THOMAS A. FRENCH, Chap.
Total in Residence 203

Oblate Madonna Residence
5722 Blanco Rd.
San Antonio, TX 78216
Tel: 210-341-2350
Home for retired Priests and Brothers.
Missionary Oblates of Mary Immaculate.
Revs.:
CLIFFORD BLACKBURN, O.M.I., Dir.
DONALD STAVINOHA, O.M.I., Asst. Dir.
JOSE AZPIAZU, O.M.I.
ALAN BRELIVET, O.M.I.
JOHN BUSCH, O.M.I.
JOHN CLARKSON, O.M.I.
EDWARD J. CRONIN, O.M.I.
JAMES P. DELANEY, O.M.I.
LAURENT DUPUIS, O.M.I.
ALBERT FECCI, O.M.I.
MAXIMO FUENTE, O.M.I.
ANTHONY GOOSSENS, O.M.I.
JOSEPH HAMEL, O.M.I.
RICHARD HOULAHAN, O.M.I.
ROBERT KOERNER, O.M.I.
JOSEPH LYONS, O.M.I.
JEROME MEAGHER, O.M.I.
SEBASTIAN MOZOS, O.M.I.
PATRICK O'BRIEN, O.M.I.
GEORGE O'CONNELL, O.M.I.
RAYMOND POMAVILLE, O.M.I.
ALFRED PRADO, O.M.I.
MICHAEL SLATTERY, O.M.I.
ANTONIO STRANO, O.M.I.
ROGER TEMME, O.M.I.
Bros.:
EMMANUEL HOFFART, O.M.I.
JOSEPH PALAZZO, O.M.I.
ARTHUR TUCKER, O.M.I.
Priests 25
Brothers 3
Sisters of the Sacred Heart of Jesus 1

Padua Place
80 Peter Baque Rd.
San Antonio, TX 78209
Tel: 210-826-7721
Home for infirm and retired Priests.
Sr. ROSE MARY MARTINEZ, M.S.S.A., Admin.
In res.,
Revs.:
JAMES COLEMAN (SAN)
ULLRIC J. PROELLER (FAR)
ANDREW COELS, C.I.C.M.
PETER VERGAUWEN (SAN)
THEODORE CLERX, C.I.C.M.
FRANCIS MAAS, M.S.F.
EUGENE JANSON (VIC)
RUSSELL SCHULTZ (SAN)
FRANCIS NELAN, M.S.C.
CHARLES LARVE (SAN)
Rev. Msgr. ANTHONY COSTANTINO
Rev. Msgr. VICTOR SCHMIDTZINSKY (VIC)
Bro. EDWARD KINSLEY, M.S.F.
Priests 17
Brothers 1

Providence Home & Family Services, Inc.
(Foster Home and Childcare for HIV Positive Children).
2650 Castroville Rd.
San Antonio, TX 78237
Tel: 210-434-2111; Fax: 210-433-2806
PATRICIA N. KOZAR, Dir.
Sisters 4

St. Francis Nursing Home
630 W. Woodlawn
San Antonio, TX 78212
Tel: 210-736-3177
Home for the Aged and Convalescents.
Seraphic Sisters of Our Lady of Sorrows.
Sr. ALFONSA BOBEK, S.O.L.S., Pres. of Corp.
Sr. ELIZABETH DUBICKA, S.O.L.S., Admin.
Sisters 8
Bed Capacity 152

St. Joseph's Community
520 Fordham Ln.
San Antonio, TX 78228-4821
Tel: 210-436-3771
Home for Infirm Marianist Brothers and Priests.
Bro. JAMES JAECKLE, S.M., Dir.
Revs.:
RALPH J. DYER, S.M.
HERBERT KRAMER, S.M.
GEORGE H. SCHERRER, S.M.
RICHARD J. SCHNEIDER, S.M.
THOMAS M. SCHELBLE, S.M.
Infirm Brothers 19
Infirm Priests 5

St. Peter & Joseph Childrens Home
919 Mission Rd.
San Antonio, TX 78210
Tel: 210-533-1203
Rev. Msgr. MARVIN G. DOERFLER, LMSW-AP, Exec. Dir.
House Parent Staff 12
Administrative & Support Staff 20
Bed Capacity 60
Children Under Care (ages 2-18) 60

Seton Home for Homeless, Pregnant Young Women
1115 Mission Rd.
San Antonio, TX 78210
Tel: 210-533-3504
BRENDA L. TATRO, Exec. Dir.
Bed Capacity 16

Visitation Hospitality House of San Antonio, Texas and La Posada Transitional Housing
945 W. Huisache
San Antonio, TX 78201
Tel: 210-735-6910
A non-profit corporation chartered under the laws of the State of Texas.
Operated by the Sisters of Charity of the Incarnate Word of San Antonio, TX.
Sr. NEOMI HAYES, C.C.V.I., Program Coord.
Sr. YOLANDA TARANGO, C.C.V.I., Dir.
Provides human services for homeless women and children on a temporary basis.
La Posada Transitional Housing

San Juan
Diocese of Brownsville

San Juan Home Health and Hospice
400 N. Nebraska, P.O. Box 2359
San Juan, TX 78589
Tel: 210-782-0333; Fax: 210-782-0335
Mrs. OLGA NAVARRO, Admin.

San Juan Nursing Home
300 N. Nebraska, P.O. Box 1238
San Juan, TX 78589
Tel: 210-787-1771; Fax: 210-787-8091
Legal Title: *San Juan Nursing Home, Inc., of the Diocese of Brownsville, a Texas Non-Profit Corporation*
Most Rev. RAYMUNDO J. PENA, Chm.
Mrs. OLGA CORTEZ-NAVARRO, Admin.
NORMA PERALES, Asst.
Bed Capacity 127

Stephenville
Diocese of Fort Worth

CASA Brendan and CASA II, Inc. Catholic Charities
1300 Hyman

Stephenville, TX 76401
Tel: 817-965-6964
86 unit apartment complex for the elderly and handicapped.
Total in Residence 86
Total Staff 6

Waco
Diocese of Austin

DePaul Center
301 Londonderry Dr.
Waco, TX 76712
Tel: 817-776-5970; 1-800-777-5043
Psychiatric Hospital & Pastoral Care.
Sr. MARY ANN RYAN, Dir. Pastoral Care
Dr. KEITH M. HANKINS, Ed.D., Admin.
Daughters of Charity of St. Vincent de Paul.
Daughters of Charity 1
Bed Capacity 64
Patients assisted annually 1,900

The Regis Retirement Home and St. Elizabeth Nursing Home
400 Austin Ave., P.O. Box 1909
Waco, TX 76703
Tel: 817-756-5441; Fax: 817-754-0133
MICHAEL SIMS, Admin.
Rev. ALECK LAZEK, Chap.
Sisters of Charity of the Incarnate Word (Houston) 2
Residents 220

UTAH

Salt Lake City
Diocese of Salt Lake City

St. Joseph Villa
451 Bishop Federal Ln.
Salt Lake City, UT 84115-2295
Tel: 801-487-7557
Operated by Sisters of Charity of the Incarnate Word Health Care System.
GALEN K. EWER, Pres. & CEO
Residents 300
Total in Residence 287
Total Assisted 449
Total Staff 240

VERMONT

Burlington
Diocese of Burlington

St. Joseph's Group Home
c/o Vermont Catholic Charities, Inc., 351 North Ave.
Burlington, VT 05401
Tel: 802-862-2623
Diocesan institution under direction of Vermont Catholic Charities, Inc.
Youths 5

St. Joseph's Home for Aged
243 N. Prospect St.
Burlington, VT 05401
Tel: 802-864-0264
Operated by Vermont Catholic Charities.
Rev. ROLAND J. RIVARD, Dir.
ESTHER MACPHERSON, Admin.
Rev. Msgr. EDWARD J. GELINEAU
Revs.:
OMER L. DUFAULT
EDWARD J. HART
THOMAS BEARY
WALTER WELLS
Sisters 1
Guests 32

Derby Line
Diocese of Burlington

Michaud Memorial Manor
Derby Line, VT 05830
Tel: 802-873-3152
Conducted by Vermont Catholic Charities.
Rev. ROLAND J. RIVARD, Dir.
Mrs. THERESE FORTIN, Admin.
Guests 28

Rutland
Diocese of Burlington

Loretto Home for Aged
Rutland, VT 05701
Tel: 802-773-8840
Conducted by Vermont Catholic Charities.
Rev. ROLAND J. RIVARD, Dir.
TERRY DION CAVACAS, Admin.
Rev. JOHN GAGNON, Res. Chap.
Guests 57

St. Joseph Assisted Living Residence/Kervick Home
131 Convent Ave.
Rutland, VT 05701
Tel: 802-775-5133
Sr. MIRIAM FRANCIS PREDOM, S.S.J., Pres.
Sr. MARY POLWORTH, S.S.J., Vice. Pres.
Conducted by Covenant Health Systems, Inc.
Guests 26

VIRGINIA

Charlottesville
Diocese of Richmond

Our Lady of Peace
751 Hillsdale Dr.
Charlottesville, VA 22901
Tel: 804-973-1155
Mrs. PAMELA DOSHIER, Admin.
Nursing Bed Capacity 30
Independent Units 64
Assisted Units 36

Hampton
Diocese of Richmond

Seton Manor
215 Marcella Rd.
Hampton, VA 23666
Tel: 804-827-6512
Ms. TONYA CLARK, Mgr.
Residents 113

Lynchburg
Diocese of Richmond

McGurk House Apartments
2425 Tate Springs Rd.
Lynchburg, VA 24501
Independent Living for adults 62 yrs. or older, or mobility impaired.
Ms. MELISSA CROSIER, Property Mgr., Tel: 804-846-2425
Apartments 89

Nott Homes, Inc.
3009-3011 Roundelay Rd.
Lynchburg, VA 24502
CALVIN STATON, Dir., Tel: 804-239-0722

Newport News
Diocese of Richmond

St. Francis Nursing Center
4 Ridgewood Pkwy.
Newport News, VA 23602
PATRICIA N. MILLER, Admin., Tel: 757-886-6500
Total Assisted 115

Norfolk
Diocese of Richmond

Madonna Home
814 W. 37th St.
Norfolk, VA 23508
Tel: 757-623-6662
CHARLENE DAVIS, Dir.
Residents 14

St. Mary's Infant Home
317 Chapel St.
Norfolk, VA 23504
Tel: 804-622-2208
WILLIAM M. JOLLY, Admin.
Long term care for multiply handicapped children birth to eleven years old.
Daughters of Wisdom 2
Beds 88

Richmond
Diocese of Richmond

Marywood Apartments
1261 Marywood Ln.
Richmond, VA 23229
Tel: 804-740-5567
PATRICIA SCOTT, Res. Mgr.
Residents 126

Our Lady of Hope Health Center, Inc.
13700 N. Gayton Rd.
Richmond, VA 23233
WALT S. PITTS, Admin., Tel: 804-360-1960
Total Assisted 127

St. Francis Home, Inc.
2511 Wise St.
Richmond, VA 23225-3952
Tel: 804-231-1043; Fax: 804-231-1065
Mr. DAVID CRAN, Dir.
Bed Capacity 63

St. Joseph's Home for the Aged
1503 Michael Rd.
Richmond, VA 23229
Tel: 804-288-6245
Sr. EDWARD MARIE MCCARTHY, L.S.P., Supr.
Rev. THOMAS W. STUMPF, O.S.B., Chap.
Little Sisters of the Poor 12
Guests 72
Attended by Benedictine Fathers.

St. Joseph's Villa
8000 Brook Rd.
Richmond, VA 23227-1338
Tel: 804-553-3200; Fax: 804-553-3259
RAMON E. PARDUE, Exec. Dir.
Children in Res. 12
Children in Day Care 155
Children in Extended Day Services 24
Children in Special Education 50
Children in Alternative Education 30
Children in Transitional Housing 40

St. Joseph's Villa Housing Corp
8000 Brook Rd.
Richmond, VA 23227-1399
Tel: 804-553-3283; Fax: 804-553-3259
Mr. RAMON E. PARDUE, Exec Dir.
Apartments for Physically Challenged Adults.
Apartments 60
St. Joseph's Villa Housing Corp., II

St. Mary Wood's
1257 Marywood Ln.
Richmond, VA 23229
Tel: 804-741-8624
RANDY SCOTT, Admin.
Units 118

Roanoke
Diocese of Richmond

The Achievement Center-St. Vincent's Home, Inc.
Mailing Address:
P.O. Box 12368
Roanoke, VA 24025
Tel: 540-982-0128
615 N. Jefferson St.
Roanoke, VA 24016
BARBARA ANN WHITWELL, Dir.

De Paul Family Services, Inc.
4502 Starkey Rd., S.W.
Roanoke, VA 24014
Tel: 540-989-7355
Specialized Foster Care.
HERB BESKAR, Exec. Dir.

Our Lady of the Valley Retirement Community
650 N. Jefferson St.
Roanoke, VA 24016
Tel: 540-345-5111
Mr. MICHAEL BRUBAKEN, Admissions Counselor

Suffolk
Diocese of Richmond

Bon Secours-Maryview Nursing Care
4775 Bridge Rd.
Suffolk, VA 23435
Tel: 757-686-0488
Ms. EILEEN MALO, Admin.
Bed Capacity 120
Martha W. Davis Cancer Center
Maryview Employee Assistance Program
Maryview MedCare Centers (Urgent Care)
Maryview Wellspring Home Health Agency
Maryview Hospice Program

Virginia Beach
Diocese of Richmond

Marian Manor
5345 Marian Ln.
Virginia Beach, VA 23462
Tel: 804-456-5018
IRVIN LAND, Admin.
Units 100
Nursing Beds 30

Russell House
900 First Colonial Rd.
Virginia Beach, VA 23454
Tel: 804-481-0770
ELEANOR OLSEN, Admin.
Units 119

WASHINGTON

Bellevue
Archdiocese of Seattle

Champion House
1800 145th Pl. S.E.
Bellevue, WA 98007
Tel: 206-644-4477

Elbert House
16000 N.E. 8th St.
Bellevue, WA 98008
Tel: 206-747-5111

Halcyon
1200 134th Ave. N.E.
Bellevue, WA 98005
Tel: 206-643-780; Fax: 206-746-0438

Bellingham
Archdiocese of Seattle

The Martin Center
2806 Douglas
Bellingham, WA 98225
Tel: 206-733-5804
Children 26

Bothell
Archdiocese of Seattle

The Franciscan Healthcare Center at Bothell
10909 N.E. 185th St.
Bothell, WA 98011
Tel: 206-486-7174; 483-9905; Fax: 206-487-1313
Sisters of St. Francis of Philadelphia.
KEN BLOOMSTINE, Admin.
Beds 135

Chehalis
Archdiocese of Seattle

Providence Place
350 S.E. Washington Ave.
Chehalis, WA 98532
Tel: 360-740-8389

Chewelah
Diocese of Spokane

Dominicare
303 E. King St., P.O. Box 1070
Chewelah, WA 99109
Sr. SHARON STAMGLER, O.P., CEO
A home care/chore service in Stevens County.

Clarkston
Diocese of Spokane

Austen Manor
30 apartments for senior citizens and mobility handicapped.
1222 Chestnut St.
Clarkston, WA 99403
CHARLES GRASSESCKI, Mgr.

Lewis and Clark District Council of St. Vincent de Paul
Office:
604 Second St.
Clarkston, WA 99403
Tel: 509-758-7061; Fax: 509-758-9545
Stores:
609 Third St.
Clarkston, WA 99403
3138 5th St.
Lewiston, ID 83501

Colville
Diocese of Spokane

The Rhodena, A Washington Non-profit Organization
2305 Wynne St.
Colville, WA 99114
A six unit affordable housing complex for families living in Colville, WA.

Dayton
Diocese of Spokane

St. Vincent de Paul Store
257 E. Main St.
Dayton, WA 99328
Tel: 509-382-4146
Mailing Address:
112 S. First St.
Dayton, WA 99328-1307

Enumclaw
Archdiocese of Seattle

The Franciscan Healthcare Center at Enumclaw
2323 Jensen St.
Enumclaw, WA 98022
Tel: 360-825-2541; 825-9938; Fax: 360-825-7023
Sisters of St. Francis of Philadelphia.
MARY WILLIFORD, Admin.

Everett
Archdiocese of Seattle

Providence Home Care and Hospice of Snohomis County
2731 Wetmore Ave., #520
Everett, WA 98201
Tel: 206-261-4800

Issaquah
Archdiocese of Seattle

Marianwood
3725 Providence Point Dr., S.E.
Issaquah, WA 98027
Tel: 206-391-2800; Fax: 206-391-5440
Sisters of St. Joseph of Peace and PeaceHealth.
Ms. ANN E. HUGHES, Admin.
MARY GOULD, Pastoral Care Svcs.
Sisters 1
Bed Capacity 120

Manito Station
Diocese of Spokane

Spokane Boys' Ranch, Inc.
(aka Morning Star Boys' Ranch)
P.O. Box 8087
Manito Station, WA 99203
Tel: 509-448-1411
Rev. JOSEPH M. WEITENSTEINER, Dir.
Children in residence 16

Olympia
Archdiocese of Seattle

Providence Mother Joseph Care Center
3333 Ensign Rd., N.E.
Olympia, WA 98506
Tel: 360-493-4900
Mr. ROBERT WILDENHAUS, Admin.
Sr. ELLEN DUFFY, S.N.J.M., Pastoral Care

Providence SoundHomeCare and Hospice
3706 Griffin Ln., S.E.
Olympia, WA 98501
Tel: 800-869-7062; 360-459-8311

Pasco
Diocese of Spokane

St. Vincent de Paul Store
1120 W. Sylvester
Pasco, WA 99301
Tel: 509-547-2341; Fax: 509-547-7804

Pullman
Diocese of Spokane

Pioneer Square
S.E. 220 Kamiaken
Pullman, WA 99163
Bed Capacity 45

Redmond
Archdiocese of Seattle

Emma McRedmond Manor
7960 169th N.E.
Redmond, WA 98052
Tel: 206-869-2424

Seattle
Archdiocese of Seattle

Chancery Place
910 Marion
Seattle, WA 98104
Tel: 206-343-9415

The Franciscan
15237 21st Ave. S.W.
Seattle, WA 98166
Tel: 206-431-8001

The Josephinum
1902 2nd Ave.
Seattle, WA 98101
Tel: 206-448-8500

Providence Home Services
425 Pontius Ave., N., Ste. 300
Seattle, WA 98109
Tel: 206-320-4848

Providence Mount St. Vincent
4831 35th Ave. S.W.
Seattle, WA 98126
Tel: 206-937-3700; Fax: 206-938-8999
Legal Title: *Sisters of Providence in Washington*
Ms. CHARLENE BOYD, Admin.
Rev. BRIAN MCGOVERN, Chap.
Sisters 3
Bed Capacity 176
Apartments 111

Providence Mount St. Vincent
4831 35th Ave. S.
Seattle, WA 98126
Tel: 206-937-3700

Vincent House
1423 First Ave.
Seattle, WA 98101
Tel: 206-682-9307
Sponsored by the Sisters of Providence.

The Westlake
2008 Westlake Ave.
Seattle, WA 98121
Tel: 206-340-0410

Spokane
Diocese of Spokane

Cathedral Plaza Apartments
W. 1120 Sprague Ave.
Spokane, WA 99204
Bed Capacity 150

Catholic Charities, Inc.
W. 1023 Riverside Ave., P.O. Box 1453
Spokane, WA 99210-1453
Tel: 509-358-4250
Mrs. DONNA HANSON, Bishop's Sec. for Social Ministries

Catholic Family Service
W. 1023 Riverside Ave., P.O. Box 1453
Spokane, WA 99210-1453
Tel: 509-358-4260
MICHAEL T. RYAN, Dir.

The Delaney
W. 242 Riverside Ave.
Spokane, WA 99201
Bed Capacity 84

Fahy Garden Apartments
W. 1403 Dean Ave.
Spokane, WA 99201
Bed Capacity 31

Fahy West Apartments
W. 1523 Dean Ave.
Spokane, WA 99201
Bed Capacity 54

Guse Summit View
Housing for single parents with children.
820 N. Summit Blvd.
Spokane, WA 99201

House of Charity
Hospitality house for homeless men.
W. 9 Main Ave., P.O. Box 1453
Spokane, WA 99210-1453
Tel: 509-624-7821
ED MCCARRON, Dir.

Miryam's House
A long-term residence for women in transition.
W. 1805 Ninth St.
Spokane, WA 99204

The O'Malley
E. 707 Mission Ave.
Spokane, WA 99202
Bed Capacity 100

Rockwood Lane/Court
E. 221 Rockwood Blvd.
Spokane, WA 99202
KIM MOE, Property Mgr.
Bed Capacity 106
Residents 140

St. Anne's Children's Home
Therapeutic child care for abused/neglected children

and assistance to their parents through parent education and counseling.
N. 707 Cedar St.
Spokane, WA 99201-1999
Tel: 509-325-7672
PAT WOLF, Dir.

St. Joseph Care Center
W. 20 Ninth Ave.
Spokane, WA 99204
Tel: 509-838-6437
ALICE ANDERSON, Admin.
Sisters of Providence 3
Residents 103

St. Joseph dba St. Brendan Continuing Care Center
(A Non-profit Corporation)
E. 17 Eighth Ave.
Spokane, WA 99202
Tel: 509-624-1161
Sisters of Providence.
ALICE ANDERSON, Admin.
Beds 165

St. Joseph's Counseling Center
N. 1016 Superior St.
Spokane, WA 99202
Tel: 509-483-6495
Sr. CARMEL GREGG, O.S.F., Dir., St. Joseph Family Center
Sisters of St. Francis of Philadelphia 7

St. Margaret's Shelter
Emergency shelter for single women & children.
P.O. Box 1453
Spokane, WA 99210
Tel: 509-624-7624
STEPHANIE KENNEDY, Dir.

St. Vincent de Paul Parish Conference
St. Francis of Assisi Parish
4207 N. Jefferson
Spokane, WA 99205
Tel: 509-327-9149

St. Vincent de Paul Social Service Office
E. 2901 Trent Ave.
Spokane, WA 99202
Tel: 509-534-2824 (Social Svc.); 535-2491 (Main Store & Office)
SCOTT COOPER, Social Svc. Dir.
BRIAN TAYLOR, Mgr. Main Store & Business Office
Legal Title: *St. Vincent de Paul Social Service Office and Main Store St. Business Office*

St. Vincent de Paul Society
Spokane District Council
E. 2901 Trent Ave.
Spokane, WA 99202
Tel: 509-534-2824
Mr. GEORGE S. VASIL, Pres.

Senior Citizen Housing
W. 242 Riverside Ave.
Spokane, WA 99201
Tel: 509-624-6060
Mr. RICHARD CUNNINGHAM, Dir.

Transitional Living Center
3128 N. Hemlock
Spokane, WA 92204
HOLLY MILLAR
Housing for homeless families.

Women's Drop In Center
218 S. Howard
Spokane, WA 92204-1419
MONICA WALTERS
A safe place for women at risk.

Tacoma
Archdiocese of Seattle

The Franciscan Health Care Center at Tacoma
6220 S. Alaska
Tacoma, WA 98408
Tel: 206-473-2273
Sisters of St. Francis of Philadelphia.
LINDA LARSON, Admin.
Licensed skilled beds 123

The Franciscan Health Care Center at University Place
2901 Bridgeport Way W.
Tacoma, WA 98466
Tel: 206-564-1643; 564-1663; Fax: 206-565-5965
Sisters of St. Francis of Philadelphia.
Mr. JAMES EDWARDS, Admin.
Licensed skilled beds 70
Licensed assisted living beds 40

Norm Fournier Court
112 S. 127th
Tacoma, WA 98444
Tel: 206-531-5087

Tumwater
Archdiocese of Seattle

Tumwater Apartments
5701 6th Ave., S.W.
Tumwater, WA 98501
Tel: 206-352-4321

Walla Walla
Diocese of Spokane

Catholic Children and Family Services
5 W. Alder St., Ste. 333
Walla Walla, WA 99362
Tel: 509-525-0572; Fax: 509-525-0576
RICHARD A. GARCIA, M.S.W., Dir.

Garden Court Apartments
Sixth & Alder Sts.
Walla Walla, WA 99362
Bed Capacity 20

Mike Foye Apartments
Sixth & Alder Sts.
Walla Walla, WA 99362
Bed Capacity 27

St. Vincent de Paul Store
308 W. Main St.
Walla Walla, WA 99362
Tel: 509-525-3903 (Store); 529-6778 (Office)
TERRY ADAMS, Store Mgr.
ALBERT TORRETTA, Society Pres.

WEST VIRGINIA

Clarksburg
Diocese of Wheeling-Charleston

Madonna Day Care Center
444 E. Pike St.
Clarksburg, WV 26031
Tel: 304-622-4453

Wheeling
Diocese of Wheeling-Charleston

Good Shepherd Nursing Home
159 Edgington Ln.
Wheeling, WV 26003
Tel: 304-242-1093
Mr. DONALD R. KIRSCH, Admin.
Rev. JOHN WEIGLEIN, S.M., Chap.
Sisters 3
Bed Capacity 192

Holy Family Child Care Center
161 Edgington Ln.
Wheeling, WV 26003
Tel: 304-242-5222
CHARLOTTE P. MALONE, Dir.

St. John's Home for Children
141 Key Ave.
Wheeling, WV 26003-7412
Tel: 304-242-5633
TERENCE A. MCCORMICK, Exec. Dir.
Children 8

Welty Home for the Aged, Inc.
21 Washington Ave.
Wheeling, WV 26003-6261
Tel: 304-242-5233
Sr. SHEILA ROONEY, O.L.C., Dir.
Sisters 2
Residents 45
Welty Home Trust
Trustees:
Most Rev. BERNARD W. SCHMITT
Rev. ROBERT C. NASH
RICHARD G. HERNDON, ESQ.
Welty Retirement Apartments
1276 National Rd.
Wheeling, WV 26003
Tel: 304-242-5820

WISCONSIN

Appleton
Diocese of Green Bay

Franciscan Care Center, Inc.
2915 N. Meade St.
Appleton, WI 54911-1598
Tel: 414-731-3184; Fax: 414-731-3206
MARGE RANKIN, Vice Pres. Operations/Admin.
Sr. AGNES TERESE ECKELKAMP, O.S.F., Chap. Spiritual Svcs.
Total assisted 235

McKinnon Manor
2525 E. Lourdes Dr.
Appleton, WI 54915
Tel: 414-733-0234
DONALD VAN VREEDE, Dir.
Bed Capacity 12

Arcadia
Diocese of La Crosse

Franciscan Skemp Healthcare, Mayo Health System, Arcadia Campus Nursing Home
464 S. St. Joseph Ave.
Arcadia, WI 54612
Tel: 608-323-3341
Rev. ROBERT F. POLCYN, O.F.M. Cap., Chap., Tel: 608-539-3704
Bed Capacity 75

Baraboo
Diocese of Madison

St. Clare Meadows Care Center
1414 Jefferson St.
Baraboo, WI 53913
Tel: 608-356-4838; Fax: 608-356-5441
Owned and operated by SSM Health Care. A member of the SSM Health Care System.
Mr. CRAIG UBBELOHDE, Admin.

Eau Claire
Diocese of La Crosse

St. Francis Apartment
851 University Dr.
Eau Claire, WI 54701
Tel: 715-834-1388
DAVID B. FISH, Chm.
Legal Title: *Hospital Sisters Health Care-West, Inc.*
Units 60
Total in residence 65

Fond du Lac
Archdiocese of Milwaukee

St. Francis Home for Aged
365 Gillett St.
Fond du Lac, WI 54935
Tel: 414-923-7980; Fax: 414-923-7995
Sisters of St. Agnes, C.S.A.
Sr. M. IRENE KOHNE, C.S.A., Admin.
Rev. JOQUE CONSTANCE, O.F.M.Cap., Chap.
Sisters 2
Residents 70
St. Clare Terrace
Residents 34
Independent Elderly Apartments 30
Total Staff 3

Green Bay
Diocese of Green Bay

McClosky Program, Inc.
Our Lady of Charity Center, 2640 West Point Rd., P.O. Box 10357
Green Bay, WI 54307-0357
Tel: 414-494-8747
Sr. PATRICIA DOLAN, O.L.C., Dir.
A Community based residential facility for women 18 years old and over who are pregnant or in a crisis situation and in need of transitional supervision and guidance. Needs addressed are personal and family problems. Also, shelter offered during crisis or unemployment.
Total assisted 43

The McCormick Memorial Home for the Aged
212 Iroquois Ave.
Green Bay, WI 54301-1918
Tel: 414-437-0883
JAMES GENRICH, Admin.
Rev. THADDEUS J. KOSZAREK, Chap.
Sisters of St. Francis of the Holy Cross 1
Lay Helpers 28
Residents 62

Our Lady of Charity Center, Inc.
2640 West Point Rd., P.O. Box 10357
Green Bay, WI 54307-0357
Tel: 414-494-8747
Sr. BARBARA JEAN ARNSMEYER, O.L.C., Dir.
Total assisted 50

Greenfield
Archdiocese of Milwaukee

Clement Manor Health Center
3939 S. 92nd St.
Greenfield, WI 53228
Tel: 414-321-1800
Sponsored by School Sisters of St. Francis.
Corporate Title: Villa Clement, Inc.
WILLIAM H. LANGE, Pres. & CEO
Mr. DENNIS FERGER, Admin.
Rev. DANIEL T. MURPHY, Chap.
Sisters 2
Residents 168
Adult Day Care 50
Child Day Care 35

Clement Manor Retirement Community
9339-9405 W. Howard Ave.
Greenfield, WI 53228
Tel: 414-546-7375
Corporate Title: Villa Clement, Inc. Sponsored by the School Sisters of St. Francis.
Mr. DENNIS FERGER, Admin.
DANIEL T. MURPHY, Chap.
Sisters 2
Residents 235
Apartments 201

Hillsboro
Diocese of La Crosse

St. Joseph's Nursing Home
P.O. Box 527
Hillsboro, WI 54634
(See Hospital Listing.)

Janesville
Diocese of Madison

St. Elizabeth Home
502 St. Lawrence Ave.
Janesville, WI 53545
Tel: 608-752-6709
Rev. JAMES MATTUCCI, Chap.
Aged Residents 43

Kaukauna
Diocese of Green Bay

St. Paul Home, Inc.
1211 Oakridge Ave.
Kaukauna, WI 54130-9961
Tel: 414-766-6020; Fax: 414-766-9161
Sr. PATRICIA SEVCIK, Pastoral Care Dir.
JAMES J. FEH, Admin.
Rev. PAUL SCHULZE, S.D.S., Chap.
Skilled care nursing home; 24 hour nursing service.
St. Paul Manor
509 W. Wisconsin Ave.
Kaukauna, WI 54130-1999
Tel: 414-766-6027
Franciscan Sisters of Christian Charity 5
Total Assisted 27
JAMES J. FETT, Admin.
Sr. MARY HUGH KERKHOF, O.S.F., Manor Service Coord.
Community based residential facility (CBRF): assisted living for men, women, and couples with no age limit.
Franciscan Sisters of Christian Charity 4
Licensed Capacity 156
Total Assisted 129

Kenosha
Archdiocese of Milwaukee

St. Joseph's Adult Day Care Center, Inc.
9244 29th Ave.
Kenosha, WI 53144
Tel: 414-694-6000
Ms. JOYCE MITCHELL, Dir.
Sponsored by: Carmelite Sisters of the Divine Heart of Jesus.
Total Assisted 75
Total Staff 10

St. Joseph's Home for the Aged
9244 29th Ave.
Kenosha, WI 53143
Tel: 414-694-0080
Corporate Title: Carmelite Sisters of the Divine Heart of Jesus.
Sr. MARY EMMANUEL APANITES, D.C.J., Admin.
Sr. M. JACINTA CUSUMANO, D.C.J., Supr.
Rev. ANTHONY JELINEK (Hungary) Chap.
Sisters 5
Residents 93
Adult Day Care 45
Total Staff 150

St. Joseph's Villa, Independent living units
Apartments 44

La Crosse
Diocese of La Crosse

Bethany-St. Joseph Care Center
2501 Shelby Rd.
La Crosse, WI 54601
Tel: 608-788-5700
THOMAS RAND, Admin.
Rev. THOMAS J. SMITH, Chap., Tel: 608-788-4555
Bed Capacity 226
Patients assisted annually 205

Elder Care of North La Crosse, Inc. (Village Apts. of St. James)
800 St. James St.
La Crosse, WI 54603
Tel: 608-791-9784
Units 24

Franciscan Elder Care, Inc.
800 West Avenue S.
La Crosse, WI 54601-4796
Tel: 608-791-9774
JOANNE K. KELLY, Vice-Pres.

Franciscan Skemp Healthcare, Mayo Health System, La Crosse Campus Nursing Home
620 S. 11th St.
La Crosse, WI 54601
Tel: 608-791-9787
DEBRA J. HELDT, Admin.
Bed Capacity 95
Patients assisted annually 190

St. Joseph's Nursing Home
2902 East Ave., S.
La Crosse, WI 54601
Tel: 608-788-9870
Operated by Catholic Charities, Inc., Diocese of La Crosse.
JAMES S. BIALECKI, Admin.
Rev. THOMAS J. SMITH, Chap., Tel: 608-788-4555
Patients assisted annually 80
Units 80

Lomira
Archdiocese of Milwaukee

Hope Nursing Home, Inc.
438 Ashford Ave., P.O. Box 280
Lomira, WI 53048-0280
Tel: 414-269-4386; Fax: 414-269-4616
Sr. ANN JOSEPHA LENCIONI, Admin.
Sisters of Charity of St. Joan Antida 2
Patients assisted annually 42
Total Staff 48

Madison
Diocese of Madison

St. Marys Care Center
1347 Fish Hatchery Rd.
Madison, WI 53715
Tel: 608-257-0781
Owned and operated by SSM Health Care. A member of the SSM Health Care System.
WILLIAM BENDER, Admin.

Manitowoc
Diocese of Green Bay

Felician Village Inc.
1700 S. 18th St.
Manitowoc, WI 54220
Sr. MARY CLAUDE SZYPERSKI, C.S.S.F., Dir.
Apartments 134
Villagers 180

St. Mary's Home for the Aged
2005 Division St.
Manitowoc, WI 54220-5699
Tel: 414-684-7171; Fax: 414-684-0240
Sr. NOEL MARIE GABRIEL, C.S.S.F., Admin.
Rev. THOMAS WOJCIECHOWSKI, O.F.M., Chap.
Sisters 28
Aged Residents 297

Milwaukee
Archdiocese of Milwaukee

Alexian Village of Milwaukee, Inc.
7979 W. Glenbrook Rd.
Milwaukee, WI 53223
Tel: 414-355-9300
Congregation of Alexian Brothers, Immaculate Conception Province.
Mr. DANIEL C. KREJCI, Admin. & Pres.
Rev. JOE JAGODENSKY, S.D.S., Chap.
Nursing Home and Life Care Facility
Residents 341
Brothers 3
Total Staff 89

Catholic Charities Senior Daycare Center
4021 N. 90th St.
Milwaukee, WI 53222
Tel: 414-464-8004
Sponsored by Catholic Charities of the Archdiocese of Milwaukee.

Daystar, Inc.
P.O. Box 11709
Milwaukee, WI 53217
Tel: 414-228-8887
Transitional living program for battered women without children, for up to two years.
Residents 16
Total Staff 4

Marian Catholic Center, Inc.
3333 W. Highland Blvd.
Milwaukee, WI 53208
Tel: 414-344-8100
Corporate Title: Marian Catholic Center, Inc.
Sponsored by Franciscan Sisters, Daughters of the Sacred Hearts of Jesus and Mary, Wheaton, IL.
MICHAEL K. ZIMMERMAN, Admin.
Rev. ROBERT J. GLOUDEMAN, Chap.
Residents 290
Total Staff 380

Marian Franciscan Center, Inc.
9632 W. Appleton Ave.
Milwaukee, WI 53225
Tel: 414-461-8850
JAMES D. GRESHAM, Pres.
Franciscan Sisters, Daughters of the Sacred Hearts of Jesus and Mary, Wheaton, IL
Residents 330
Total Staff 430

**Milwaukee Catholic Home*
2462 N. Prospect Ave.
Milwaukee, WI 53211-4462
Tel: 414-224-9700
Mr. PAUL J. CONNOLLY, N.H.A., Exec. Dir.
Rev. CHARLES R. KEEFE, Dir. Pastoral Care
Corporate Title: Milwaukee Catholic Home, Inc.
Retirement Home Residents 127
Retirement Home Total Staff 92
Nursing Home Residents 51
Nursing Home Total Staff 45

Rosalie Manor, Inc.
4803 W. Burleigh St.
Milwaukee, WI 53210
Tel: 414-449-2868
ROSEMARIE FISHER, Dir.
Community Programs for Single and First-Time Parents.
Franciscan Sisters Daughters of the Sacred Hearts of Jesus & Mary of Wheaton, IL.
Total Assisted 2,000 families per year
Total Staff 62

Sacred Heart Rehabilitation Institute, Inc.
2350 N. Lake Dr.
Milwaukee, WI 53211
Tel: 414-298-6700
Daughters of Charity of St. Vincent de Paul.
WILLIAM H. LANGE, Adm.
Sr. MARGARET ANN ARNOLD, Chap.
Sisters 1
Bed Capacity 81
Patients assisted annually 14,000
Total Staff 300
Satellite Locations:
Sacred Heart Rehabilitation Institute
Lakeland Medical Center, Hwy. NN
Elkhorn, WI 53121
Sacred Heart Rehabilitation Institute
Memorial Hosp. at Oconomowoc, 791 E. Summit Ave.
Oconomowoc, WI 53066

St. Ann Rest Home
2020 S. Muskego Ave.
Milwaukee, WI 53204
Tel: 414-383-2630
Conducted by the Dominican Sisters (Congregation of the Immaculate Conception).
Sr. M. COLUMBA, O.P., Admin.
Sisters 7
Residents 54

St. Anne's Home for the Elderly
3800 N. 92nd St.

Milwaukee, WI 53222
Tel: 414-463-7570; Fax: 414-463-2311
Sisters of the Divine Savior
Mr. MICHAEL W. BERRY, Admin.
Rev. RUSSELL F. WITON, Chap.
Retired Priests 16
Terrace-Independent Living Apartments 16
Residents 106
Total Staff 159

St. Charles Youth and Family Services
151 S. 84th St., P.O. Box 14005
Milwaukee, WI 53214
Tel: 414-476-3710
Mr. JAMES M. SAMPSON, Pres.
Residents 78
Girls in Holy Cross Group Home 12
Total Assisted 750
Total Staff 200

St. Mary's Nursing Home
3516 W. Center St.
Milwaukee, WI 53210
Tel: 414-873-9250
Corporate Title: St. Mary's Nursing Home of Milwaukee, Inc.
Sisters of the Divine Savior
Mr. TIMOTHY J. CIMBALNIK
In res.,
Most Rev. ARNOLD COTY, S.D.S.
Rev. DANIEL CARROLL, S.D.S.
Residents 113
Total Staff 199

The Terrace at St. Francis, Inc.
3200 S. 20th St.
Milwaukee, WI 53215
Fax: 414-389-3300
Sponsored by the Congregation of the Sisters of St. Felix of Cantalice of the United States of America, Inc., Chicago Province. (Felician Sisters).
Skilled Nursing Facility for Transitional & Extended Subacute Care.
Sr. M. RAMONA DOMBROWSKI, C.S.S.F., Pres.
Beds 81

Villa St. Francis, Inc.
1910 W. Ohio Ave.
Milwaukee, WI 53215
Fax: 414-649-2880
Sr. MARY RAMONA DOMBROWSKI, C.S.S.F., Pres.
Sponsored by the Congregation of the Sisters of St. Felix of Cantalice of the United States of America, Inc. Chicago Province. (Felician Sisters).
Independent & Assisted Living Facility
Resident Apartments 142
Total Staff 63

Mount Calvary
Archdiocese of Milwaukee

Cristo Rey Ranch, Inc.
N8102 Calvary St.
Mount Calvary, WI 53057
Sister Servants of Christ the King
A group foster/respite home to provide treatment and care of children/adolescents.
Total Assisted 20
Total Staff 4

Villa Loretto Nursing Home
Mount Calvary, WI 53057
Tel: 414-753-3211
Sr. MARY ROSE, Supr.
Sisters 8
Residents 52
Total Assisted 49
Total Staff 90
Corporate Title: Sister Servants of Christ the King, Inc. dba Villa Loretto.

Neenah
Diocese of Green Bay

Assisi Homes of Neenah, Inc.
210 Byrd Ave.
Neenah, WI 54946
Tel: 414-821-0336
SHERRI BEYER, Mgr.
(An independent living community for Seniors.)
Total in residence 38

Villa Saint Clare, Inc.
130 Byrd Ave.
Neenah, WI 54952
SHERRI BEYER, Mgr.
Special care facility, affordable housing with supportive accommodations in an independent setting for seniors 55+.
Total in Residence 45

New London
Diocese of Green Bay

St. Joseph Residence, Inc., New London
107 E. Beckert Rd.
New London, WI 54961
Tel: 414-982-5354
Mr. DANIEL W. ORR, CEO
Residences for senior citizens 45
Staff 16
Nursing care:
Total assisted 107
Staff 152

Niagara
Diocese of Green Bay

Maryhill Manor Nursing Home (SNF)
501 Madison Ave.
Niagara, WI 54151
Tel: 715-251-3178; Fax: 715-251-1200
Sponsored by School Sisters of St. Francis, Milwaukee.
JOANNE D. WALL, Pres. & CEO
Elderly Residents 75

Onalaska
Diocese of La Crosse

Franciscan Skemp Healthcare, Mayo Health System, Onalaska Nursing Home
1600 Main St.
Onalaska, WI 54650
Tel: 608-783-4681
LARRY ALENS, Admin.
Beds 112
Patients assisted annually 224

Oshkosh
Diocese of Green Bay

The Convent Project, Inc.
435 High Ave.
Oshkosh, WI 54901
Tel: 414-235-6002
BARBARA BAKER, Sec.

Portage
Diocese of Madison

Divine Savior Nursing Home
715 W. Pleasant St.
Portage, WI 53901
Tel: 608-742-4131
(See Divine Savior Hospital, Portage.)
Aged Residents 124

Racine
Archdiocese of Milwaukee

Marian Housing Center, Inc
4105 Spring St.
Racine, WI 53405
Tel: 414-633-5807
STEVE KUKLIN, Pres.
Franciscan Sisters, Daughters of the Sacred Hearts of Jesus and Mary, Wheaton, IL.
HUD subsidized housing for the elderly
Residents 40

St. Monica's Senior Citizens Home, Inc.
3920 N. Green Bay Rd.
Racine, WI 53404
Tel: 414-639-5050
Non-Profit Corp.
Sr. IRENE HANIKA, O.S.A., Supr. and Admin.
Rev. RICHARD ZELONIS, S.C.J., Chap.
Sisters of St. Rita 6
Residents 124
Total Staff 45

South Milwaukee
Archdiocese of Milwaukee

Franciscan Villa
3601 S. Chicago Ave.
South Milwaukee, WI 53172
Tel: 414-764-4100
ROGER L. DEMARK
Catholic Health Corporation.
Residents 150
Adult Day Care 30
Child Day Care 22
Total Staff 154

Sparta
Diocese of La Crosse

Elder Care of Sparta, Inc.
622 S. Court
Sparta, WI 54656
Tel: 608-791-9774
Units 24

Franciscan Skemp Healthcare, Mayo Health System, Sparta Campus Nursing Home
310 W. Main St.
Sparta, WI 54656-2142
Tel: 608-269-2132
SUSAN STEIVANG, Admin.
Rev. MARK A. WALLJASPER, Chap.
Bed Capacity 30

St. Francis
Archdiocese of Milwaukee

Canticle Court, Inc.
3201 S. Lake Dr.
St. Francis, WI 53235
Tel: 414-744-9959; Fax: 414-744-7636
An Apartment building sponsored by the Sisters of St. Francis of Assisi funded by HUD for low income elderly persons who can live independently.
Units 48
Total in Residence 49
Total Staff 2

Juniper Court, Inc.
3209 S. Lake Dr.
St. Francis, WI 53235-3702
Tel: 414-744-5878; Fax: 414-744-7636
Sr. ANNE MARY RISCHAR, O.S.F., Pres.
An apartment building with congregate meal site for persons of low to moderate income who can live independently.
Sponsored by the Sisters of St. Francis of Assisi, St. Francis, Wisconsin.
Total in Residence 58
Total Units 53
Total Staff 2

St. Ann Adult Day Care, Inc.
3221 S. Lake Dr.
St. Francis, WI 53235
Tel: 414-482-1340
Sr. EDNA LONERGAN, O.S.F., Dir.
Sisters of St. Francis of Assisi, St. Francis, WI.
Total Assisted 150
Total Staff 120

Stoughton
Diocese of Madison

Nazareth House
814 Jackson St.
Stoughton, WI 53589
Tel: 608-873-6448; Fax: 608-873-0829
Poor Sisters of Nazareth.
Sr. ROSE HOYE, P.S.N., Supr.
Sisters 6
Aged Residents 99

Superior
Diocese of Superior

St. Francis Home, Inc.
1800 New York Ave.
Superior, WI 54880
Tel: 715-394-5591
KURT GRAVES, CEO
Deacon PHIL L. MARTINEAU, Supvr. Pastoral Care
Bed Capacity 192

Two Rivers
Diocese of Green Bay

Sisters Treatment Group Home
3904 Martin Ln.
Two Rivers, WI 54241
Tel: 414-794-1524
Co-Directors:
Sr. IRMINA BULA, S.S.J.-T.O.S.F.
Sr. EDMUND ANTONIEWICZ, S.S.J.-T.O.S.F.
For physically and mentally handicapped.
Children 6
Adults 2
Staff 5
Total assisted 8

Watertown
Diocese of Madison

St. Joseph's Home
705 Clyman St.
Watertown, WI 53094
Tel: 414-261-4283
Sisters of Charity of Our Lady, Mother of the Church.
Rev. RAYMOND ASHENBRENNER, O.P., Chap.
Sisters 4

Aged Residents 27

Wausau
Diocese of La Crosse

Marywood Convalescent Center
1821 N. 4th Ave.
Wausau, WI 54401
Tel: 715-675-9451
KATHRYN L. SPRAGUE, Admin.
Operated by Catholic Charities, Inc., Diocese of La Crosse.
Units 90
Patients assisted annually 131

Wauwatosa
Archdiocese of Milwaukee

St. Camillus Health Center, Inc.
10101 W. Wisconsin Ave.
Wauwatosa, WI 53226
Tel: 414-258-1814
Skilled Nursing Home.
Order of the Servants of the Sick (Order of St. Camillus).
DONALD G. KLEIN, Chief Exec. Officer
Very Rev. WILLIAM F. CRONIN, O.S.Cam., Pres.
RICK JOHNSON, CEO
Ms. KATHLEEN SULLIVAN, Dir. of Pastoral Care, C.P.E. Program Sup.
Chaplains:
Revs.:
CLAUDE PULVERMACHER, O.F.M.Cap.
CARLO NOTARO, O.S.Cam.
Ms. BARBARA BAUDHUIN
Ms. SALLY REDMOND
In res.,
Revs.:
GEORGE A. KOLANDA
JOHN O'BRIEN, S.J.
PETER T. AMRHEIN
LEON BRIELMAIER
WALTER GAWINEK
Patients assisted annually 360

San Camillo, Inc.
10200 W. Bluemound Rd.
Wauwatosa, WI 53226
Tel: 414-259-6300
Order of the Servants of the Sick (Order of St. Camillus).
Very Rev. WILLIAM CRONIN, O.S.Cam., Pres., Chap.
Rev. CARLO NOTARO, O.S.Cam., Chap.
Independent living facilities for older adults.
Residents 560

West Allis
Archdiocese of Milwaukee

St. Joan Antida Home, Inc.
6700 W. Beloit Rd.
West Allis, WI 53219
Tel: 414-541-6575; 541-9840; Fax: 414-541-8040
JULIE M. NICHOLAS, Admin.
Sr. MARY ALICE WILLEMS, O.S.M., Chap.
Sisters of Charity of St. Joan Antida 3
Residents 73
Total Staff 100

Villa Clement Health Center
9047 W. Greenfield Ave.
West Allis, WI 53214
Tel: 414-453-9290
Corporate Title: Villa Clement Health Center
WILLIAM LANGE, Pres. & CEO
GEORGINA DENNIK-CHAMPION, N.H.A., Admin.
Rev. LUIS PACHECO-SANCHEZ, Chap.
Skilled Nursing Home.
Sponsored by School Sisters of St. Francis.
Sisters 2
Residents 194

WYOMING

Casper
Diocese of Cheyenne

St. Anthony Manor
211 E. Sixth St.
Casper, WY 82601
Tel: 307-237-0844
Rev. Msgr. JAMES O'NEILL
Administrators:
PATRICIA JOHNSTON
LOU ANN TOOKER
Total Staff 6
Total in Residence 64

Cheyenne
Diocese of Cheyenne

Holy Trinity Manor
2516 E. 18th St.
Cheyenne, WY 82001
Tel: 307-778-8850
Sr. RUTH ANN HEHN, S.C.L., Admin.
Total Staff 1
Total in Residence 30

Torrington
Diocese of Cheyenne

St. Joseph's Children's Home
Box 1117
Torrington, WY 82240-1117
Tel: 307-532-4197; Fax: 307-532-8405
ROBERT C. MAYOR, Exec. Dir.
Children 62
Total Staff 127
Total Assisted 120

Diocesan Abbreviations

ARCHDIOCESES AND DIOCESES

(ALB) .... Albany (New York)
(ALN) .... Allentown (Pennsylvania)
(ALT) .... Altoona-Johnstown (Pennsylvania)
(ALX) .... Alexandria (Louisiana)
(AGN) .... Agana (Guam)
(AMA) .... Amarillo (Texas)
(ANC) .... Anchorage (Alaska)
(ARE) .... Arecibo (Puerto Rico)
(ARL) .... Arlington (Virginia)
(ARM) .... Armenian Catholic Exarchate (Pennsylvania)
(ATH) .... Apostolate To Hungarians (Washington, DC)
(ATL) .... Atlanta (Georgia)
(AUS) .... Austin (Texas)
(B) .... Boise (Idaho)
(BAK) .... Baker (Oregon)
(BAL) .... Baltimore (Maryland)
(BEA) .... Beaumont (Texas)
(BEL) .... Belleville (Illinois)
(BGP) .... Bridgeport (Connecticut)
(BIR) .... Birmingham (Alabama)
(BIS) .... Bismarck (North Dakota)
(BLX) .... Biloxi (Mississippi)
(BO) .... Boston (Massachusetts)
(BR) .... Baton Rouge (Louisiana)
(BRK) .... Brooklyn (New York)
(BUF) .... Buffalo (New York)
(BUR) .... Burlington (Vermont)
(BWN) .... Brownsville (Texas)
(CAM) .... Camden (New Jersey)
(CC) .... Corpus Christi (Texas)
(CGS) .... Caguas (Puerto Rico)
(CHI) .... Chicago (Illinois)
(CHK) .... Chalan Kanoa
(CHL) .... Charlotte (North Carolina)
(CHR) .... Charleston (South Carolina)
(CHY) .... Cheyenne (Wyoming)
(CI) .... Caroline Islands
(CIN) .... Cincinnati (Ohio)
(CLV) .... Cleveland (Ohio)
(COL) .... Columbus (Ohio)
(COS) .... Colorado Springs (Colorado)
(COV) .... Covington (Kentucky)
(CR) .... Crookston (Minnesota)
(DAL) .... Dallas (Texas)
(DAV) .... Davenport (Iowa)
(DEN) .... Denver (Colorado)
(DET) .... Detroit (Michigan)
(DM) .... Des Moines (Iowa)
(DOD) .... Dodge City (Kansas)
(DUB) .... Dubuque (Iowa)
(DUL) .... Duluth (Minnesota)
(E) .... Erie (Pennsylvania)
(ELP) .... El Paso (Texas)
(EST) .... Eparchy of Saint Thomas the Apostle
(EVN) .... Evansville (Indiana)
(FAR) .... Fargo (North Dakota)
(FBK) .... Fairbanks (Alaska)
(FgM) .... Foreign Mission Section
(FR) .... Fall River (Massachusetts)
(FRS) .... Fresno (California)
(FTW) .... Fort Wayne-South Bend (Indiana)
(FWT) .... Fort Worth (Texas)
(GAL) .... Galveston-Houston (Texas)
(GAY) .... Gaylord (Michigan)
(GB) .... Green Bay (Wisconsin)
(GBG) .... Greensburg (Pennsylvania)
(GF) .... Great Falls-Billings (Montana)
(GI) .... Grand Island (Nebraska)
(GLP) .... Gallup (New Mexico)
(GR) .... Grand Rapids (Michigan)
(GRY) .... Gary (Indiana)
(HBG) .... Harrisburg (Pennsylvania)
(HEL) .... Helena (Montana)
(HON) .... Honolulu (Hawaii)
(HRT) .... Hartford (Connecticut)
(HT) .... Houma-Thibodaux (Louisiana)
(IND) .... Indianapolis (Indiana)
(JC) .... Jefferson City (Missouri)
(JKS) .... Jackson (Mississippi)
(JOL) .... Joliet in Illinois
(JUN) .... Juneau (Alaska)
(KAL) .... Kalamazoo (Michigan)
(KC) .... Kansas City-St. Joseph (Missouri)
(KCK) .... Kansas City in Kansas
(KNX) .... Knoxville (Tennessee)
(L) .... Louisville (Kentucky)
(LA) .... Los Angeles (California)
(LAF) .... Lafayette (Louisiana)
(LAN) .... Lansing (Michigan)
(LC) .... La Crosse (Wisconsin)
(LEX) .... Lexington (Kentucky)
(LFT) .... Lafayette in Indiana
(LIN) .... Lincoln (Nebraska)
(LIT) .... Lithuanian Apostolate for Lithuanian Catholics
(LKC) .... Lake Charles (Louisiana)
(LR) .... Little Rock (Arkansas)
(LSC) .... Las Cruces (New Mexico)
(LUB) .... Lubbock (Texas)
(LAV) .... Las Vegas (Nevada)
(MAD) .... Madison (Wisconsin)
(MAN) .... Manchester (New Hampshire)
(MAR) .... Marquette (Michigan)
(MEM) .... Memphis (Tennessee)
(MET) .... Metuchen (New Jersey)
(MGZ) .... Mayaguez (Puerto Rico)
(MI) .... Marshall Islands
(MIA) .... Miami (Florida)
(MIL) .... Milwaukee (Wisconsin)
(MO) .... Military Services (Maryland)
(MOB) .... Mobile (Alabama)
(MRY) .... Monterey in California
(NEW) .... Newark (New Jersey)
(NO) .... New Orleans (Louisiana)
(NOR) .... Norwich (Connecticut)
(NSH) .... Nashville (Tennessee)
(NTN) .... Newton (Melkite, United States)
(NU) .... New Ulm (Minnesota)
(NY) .... New York (New York)
(OAK) .... Oakland (California)
(OG) .... Ogdensburg (New York)
(OKL) .... Oklahoma City (Oklahoma)
(OLD) .... Our Lady of Deliverance *Syriac* (Union City, New Jersey)
(OLL) .... Our Lady of Lebanon of Los Angeles (California)
(OM) .... Omaha (Nebraska)
(ORG) .... Orange in California
(ORL) .... Orlando (Florida)
(OWN) .... Owensboro (Kentucky)
(P) .... Portland in Oregon
(PAT) .... Paterson (New Jersey)
(PBL) .... Pueblo (Colorado)
(PBR) .... Pittsburgh *Byzantine* (Pennsylvania)
(PCE) .... Ponce (Puerto Rico)
(PEO) .... Peoria (Illinois)
(PH) .... Philadelphia (Pennsylvania)
(PHU) .... Philadelphia *Ukrainian* (Pennsylvania)
(PHX) .... Phoenix (Arizona)
(PIT) .... Pittsburgh (Pennsylvania)
(PMB) .... Palm Beach (Florida)
(PP) .... Personal Prelatures
(PRM) .... Parma *Byzantine* (Ohio)
(PRO) .... Providence (Rhode Island)
(PRT) .... Portland (Maine)
(PSC) .... Passaic *Byzantine* (New Jersey)
(PT) .... Pensacola-Tallahassee (Florida)
(R) .... Raleigh (North Carolina)
(RC) .... Rapid City (South Dakota)
(RCK) .... Rockford (Illinois)
(RIC) .... Richmond (Virginia)
(RNO) .... Reno (Nevada)
(ROC) .... Rochester (New York)
(ROM) .... Romanian (Byzantine) (Ohio)
(RVC) .... Rockville Centre (New York)
(SAC) .... Sacramento (California)
(SAG) .... Saginaw (Michigan)
(SAL) .... Salina (Kansas)
(SAM) .... St. Maron of Brooklyn (U.S.A.), Eparchy of
(SAN) .... San Angelo (Texas)
(SAT) .... San Antonio (Texas)
(SAV) .... Savannah (Georgia)
(SB) .... San Bernadino (California)
(SC) .... Sioux City (Iowa)
(SCL) .... St. Cloud (Minnesota)
(SCR) .... Scranton (Pennsylvania)
(SD) .... San Diego (California)
(SEA) .... Seattle (Washington)
(SFD) .... Springfield in Illinois
(SFE) .... Santa Fe (New Mexico)
(SFR) .... San Francisco (California)
(SFS) .... Sioux Falls (South Dakota)
(SHP) .... Shreveport (Louisiana)
(SJ) .... San Jose in California
(SJN) .... San Juan (Puerto Rico)
(SJP) .... St. Josaphat in Parma (Ohio)
(SLC) .... Salt Lake City (Utah)
(SP) .... St. Petersburg (Florida)
(SPC) .... Sprgfld-Cape Girardeau (Missouri)
(SPK) .... Spokane (Washington)
(SPP) .... Samoa-Pago Pago
(SPR) .... Springfield in Massachusetts
(SR) .... Santa Rosa in California
(STA) .... St. Augustine (Florida)
(STF) .... Stamford *Ukrainian* (Connecticut)
(STL) .... St. Louis (Missouri)
(STN) .... St. Nicholas in Chicago *Ukrainian*
(STO) .... Stockton (California)
(STP) .... St. Paul and Minneapolis (Minnesota)
(STU) .... Steubenville (Ohio)
(STV) .... St. Thomas, Virgin Islands
(SUP) .... Superior (Wisconsin)
(SY) .... Syracuse (New York)
(TLS) .... Tulsa (Oklahoma)
(TOL) .... Toledo (Ohio)
(TR) .... Trenton (New Jersey)
(TUC) .... Tucson (Arizona)
(TYL) .... Tyler (Texas)
(VEN) .... Venice (Florida)
(VIC) .... Victoria in Texas
(VNN) .... Van Nuys *Byzantine* (California)
(WCH) .... Wichita (Kansas)
(WDC) .... Washington (District of Columbia)
(WH) .... Wheeling-Charleston (West Virginia)
(WIL) .... Wilmington (Delaware)
(WIN) .... Winona (Minnesota)
(WOR) .... Worcester (Massachusetts)
(Y) .... Youngstown (Ohio)
(YAK) .... Yakima (Washington)

DIOCESAN & PRIESTS

An Alphabetical List of Diocesan and Religious Priests of the United States

REPORTED TO THE PUBLISHERS FOR THIS ISSUE
(Cardinals, Archbishops, Bishops, Archabbots and Abbots are listed in previous section)

ABBREVIATIONS

aa.a.	Assumptionists.
b.g.s.	Little Brothers of the Good Shepherd.
b.s.o.	Basilian Salvatorian Fathers.
c.f.a.	Alexian Brothers.
c.f.c.	Congregation of Christian Brothers.
c.f.m.m.	Brothers of the Poor of St. Francis.
c.f.p.	Brothers of the Poor of St. Francis.
c.f.r.	Franciscan Friars of the Renewal.
c.f.x.	Brothers of St. Francis Xavier.
c.i.c.m.	Missionhurst Congregation of the Immaculate Heart of Mary.
c.j.	Josephite Fathers.
c.j.m.	Congregation of Jesus and Mary, Eudist Fathers.
c.m.	Congregation of the Mission, Vincentian Fathers.
c.m.c.	Congregation of Mother Coredemptrix.
c.m.f.	Claretian Missionaries, Missionary Sons of the Immaculate Heart of Mary.
c.m.i.	Carmelites of Mary Immaculate.
c.m.m.	Congregation of Mariannhill Missionaries, Mariannhill Fathers and Brothers.
c.m.vd.	Mekhitarist Fathers.
c.o.	Oratorians.
c.p.	Congregation of the Passion, Passionist Fathers.
c.p.m.	Congregation of the Fathers of Mercy.
c.pp.s.	Society of the Precious Blood.
c.r.	Congregation of the Resurrection, Resurrectionist Fathers.
c.r.	Theatine Fathers.
c.r.i.c.	Canons Regular of the Immaculate Conception.
c.r.l.	Canons Regular of the Lateran.
c.r.m.	Adorno Fathers.
c.r.s.	Somascan Fathers, Order of St. Jerome Aemilian.
c.r.s.p.	Clerics Regular of St. Paul, Barnabite Fathers.
c.s.	Missionaries of St. Charles-Scalabrinians.
c.s.b.	Basilian Fathers.
c.s.c.	Priests and Brothers of the Congregation of Holy Cross.
c.s.j.	Congregation of St. Joseph.
c.s.p.	Paulist Fathers.
c.s.p.x.	Brothers of Saint Pius X.
c.s.s.	Stigmatine Fathers and Brothers, Congregation of the Sacred Stigmata.
c.s.sp.	Holy Ghost Fathers, Congregation of the Holy Ghost.
c.ss.r.	Redemptorist Fathers.
c.s.v.	Clerics of St. Viator, Viatorian Fathers.
d.l.p.	Diocesan Labor Priests.
er.cam.	Camaldolese Hermits of the Congregation of Monte Corona.
f.c.	Brothers of Charity.
f.d.p.	Sons of Divine Providence.
f.f.i.	Franciscan Friars of the Immaculate
f.f.s.c.	Franciscan Brothers of the Holy Cross.
f.i.c.	Brothers of Christian Instruction.
f.j.	Congregation of St. John.
f.m.j.	The Monastic Fraternity of Jerusalem.
f.m.m.	Brothers of Mercy.
f.m.s.	Marist Brothers.
f.m.s.i.	Sons of Mary Missionary Society.
f.s.c.	Brothers of the Christian Schools.
f.s.e.	Brothers of the Holy Eucharist.
f.s.p.	Brothers of St. Patrick.
f.s.r.	Brothers of the Congregation of Our Lady of the Holy Rosary.
glmy.	The Glenmary Home Missioners.
i.c.	Institute of Charity.
i.h.m.	Brothers of the Immaculate Heart of Mary.
i.m.c.	Consolata Missionaries.
l.b.s.f.	Little Brothers of Saint Francis.
l.c.	Legionaries of Christ.
m.afr.	Missionaries of Africa.
m.c.b.s.	Missionary Congregation of the Blessed Sacrament.
m.c.c.j.	Comboni Missionaries of the Heart of Jesus.
m.d.	Mercedarios Descalzos.
m.e.p.	Paris Foreign Mission Society.
m.g.	Guadalupe Missioners.
m.h.m.	Mill Hill Missionaries.
m.i.c.	Congregation of Marians of the Immaculate Conception.
m.j.	Missionaries of St. Joseph.
m.m.	Maryknoll Fathers, Catholic Foreign Mission Society of America.
m.s.	The Missionaries of Our Lady La Salette.
m.s.c.	Missionaries of the Sacred Heart.
m.s.c.	Missionary Servants of Christ.
m.s.f.	Congregation of the Missionaries of the Holy Family.
m.s.p.	Missionaries of St. Paul.
m.sp.s.	Missionaries of the Holy Spirit.
m.ss.a.	Missionaries of the Holy Apostles.
m.ss.cc.	Missionaries of the Sacred Hearts of Jesus and Mary.
o.a.r.	Order of the Augustinian Recollects.
o.carm.	Carmelite Fathers and Brothers.
o.cart.	Order of Carthusians.
o.c.d.	Discalced Carmelite Friars.
o.cist.	Cistercian Fathers.
o.c.s.o.	The Cistercians Order of the Strict Observance, Trappists.
o.de.m.	Order of Our Lady of Mercy.
o.f.m.	Franciscan Friars, Order of Friars Minor.
o.f.m.cap.	The Capuchin Friars, Franciscan Fathers.
o.f.m-.conv.	Conventual Franciscans, Friars Minor Conventual.
o.h.	Hospitaller Brothers of St. John of God.
o.i.c.	Order of the Imitation of Christ.
o.l.c.	Brothers of Our Lady of Providence.
o.m.	Minim Fathers.
o.mar.	Congregation of Maronite Monks.
o.m.i.	Oblates of Mary Immaculate.
o.m.v.	Oblates of the Virgin Mary.
o.p.	Order of Preachers, Dominican Fathers.
o.praem.	Canons Regular of Premontre, Premonstratensians, Norbertines.
o.r.c.	Operarios del Reina de Cristo.
o.s.a.	The Augustinians.
o.s.b.	Benedictine Monks, Olivetan Benedictines, Sylvestrine Benedictines.
o.s.b.cam.	Camaldolese Hermits.
o.s.b.m.	Order of St. Basil the Great.
o.s.c.	Canons Regular of the Order of the Holy Cross, Crosier Fathers.
o.s.cam.	Camillian Fathers and Brothers.
o.s.f.	Religious Brothers of the Third Order Regular of St. Francis.
o.s.f.	Franciscan Brothers of Christ the King.
o.s.f.	Franciscan Brothers of the Third Order Regular.
o.s.f.	Franciscan Missionary Brothers of the Sacred Heart of Jesus.
o.s.f.s.	Oblates of St. Francis de Sales.
o.s.j.	Oblates of St. Joseph.
o.s.m.	Servite Fathers.
o.s.p.p.e.	Pauline Fathers.
o.ss.s.	Brigittine Monks.
o.ss.t.	Order of the Most Holy Trinity, Trinitarian Fathers.
p.i.m.e.	Pontifical Institute for Foreign Missions.
r.c.j.	Rogationist Fathers.
s.a.	Franciscan Friars of the Atonement.
s.a.c.	Society of the Catholic Apostolate, Pallottine Fathers.
s.c.	Brothers of the Sacred Heart.
s.c.	Servants of Charity.
s.ch.	Society of Christ.
sch.p.	Piarist Fathers.
s.c.j.	Congregation of the Priests of the Sacred Heart of Jesus.
s.d.b.	Salesians of Don Bosco.
s.d.s.	Society of the Divine Savior.
s.d.v.	Vocationist Fathers, Society of the Divine Vocations.
s.f.	Sons of the Holy Family.
s.f.c.	Society of the Brothers of Charity.
s.f.m.	Scarboro Foreign Missions.
s.j.	Jesuit Fathers and Brothers, Society of Jesus.
s.l.t.	Servants of Our Lady of the Most Holy Trinity.
s.m.	Society of Mary, Marianists.
s.m.	Marist Fathers.
s.m.a.	Society of African Missions.
s.m.m.	Montfort Missionaries.
s.m.p.	Society of Our Mother of Peace.
s.o.cist.	Cistercian Monks of the Strict Observance.
s.o.l.t.	Society of Our Lady of the Most Holy Trinity.
s.p.	Servants of the Paraclete.
s.p.s.	St. Patrick's Missionary Society.
s.s.	Society of the Priest of Saint Sulpice, Sulpician Fathers.
s.s.c.	Society of St. Columban, St. Columban's Foreign Mission Society.
ss.cc.	Congregation of the Sacred Hearts of Jesus and Mary.
s.s.e.	Society of Saint Edmund.
s.s.j.	St. Joseph's Society of the Sacred Heart, Josephite Fathers.
s.s.p.	Pauline Fathers and Brothers, Society of St. Paul for the Apostolate of Communications.
s.s.s.	Congregation of the Blessed Sacrament.
s.s.t.	Missionary Society of St. Thomas the Apostle.
s.t.	Missionary Servants of the Most Holy Trinity.
s.v.d.	Society of the Divine Word.
s.x.	Xaverian Missionary Fathers, St. Francis Xavier Mission Society.
t.o.r.	Third Order Regular of Saint Francis.
v.c.	Vincentian Congregation.

The letters in parentheses designate the diocese. See the "Diocesan Abbreviations". Numbers in brackets designate the numerical order of the Church in cities in which there are four or more Catholic Churches listed. Letters in brackets designate categories in the Institution Section.

A

Aaron, Andrew '96 (BAL) Clarksville, MD St. Louis Church.

Aaron, James L. '54 (PIT) [78] Pittsburgh, PA Most Holy Name of Jesus Church.

Aaron, James R. '57 (SAN) Retired.

Aaron, Robert *o.m.i.* '72 (BEL) [G] Belleville, IL Missionary Oblates of Mary Immaculate - St. Henry's Oblate Residence; [K] Belleville, IL Oblate Preaching Team.

Abad, Msgr. Federico '46 (PCE) On Duty Outside the Diocese

Abad, Jose Antonio P. '82 (AGN) Tamuning, GU St. Anthony and St. Victor Church.

Abano, Edgardo D. '85 (MET) Piscataway, NJ St. Frances Cabrini Church.

Abara, Lawrence N. (LAF) [F] Lafayette, LA Our Lady of Lourdes Regional Medical Center, Inc.

Abarrategui, Leandro *o.f.m.* '54 (SJN) [3] Carolina, PR Santa Clara de Asis Church.

Abarratelegui, Leanardo (SJN) [3] Carolina, PR Santa Clara de Asis Church.

Abate, Anthony P. *o.f.m.* '56 (NY) [Z] Mount Vernon, NY St. Bernardine of Siena Friary.

Abaya, Francisco (NY) Manhattan, NY New York University Medical Center.

Abbass, Jobe *o.f.m.conv.* '85 (ALB) [A] Rensselaer, NY Conventual Franciscan Friars.

Abbaticchio, Damian *o.s.b.* '45 (RIC) [6] Virginia Beach, VA St. Gregory the Great Church; [L] Richmond, VA Ethnic and Special Ministries.

Abbatiello, Robert *o.f.m.cap.* '90 (NY) [Z] Garrison, NY

St. Francis Friary.
Abbott, Donald (BO) Wilmington, MA St. Dorothy Church.
Abbott, Donald S. '73 (CHR) On Duty Outside the Diocese.
Abbott, Eugene J. '57 (STP) Minneapolis, MN Minnesota Soldiers' Home; Special Assignment.
Abbott, Kerry M. *o.f.m.conv.* (BIS) [1] Minot, ND Minot Air Force Base Chapel.
Abbott, Walter M. *s.j.* '56 (BO) [W] Boston, MA Arrupe House.
Abbott, William M. *s.j.* '72 (NEW) [B] Jersey City, NJ Saint Peter's College; [N] Jersey City, NJ Jesuits of Saint Peter's College, Inc.
Abbruzzese, Msgr. John A. (BO) On Duty Outside the Archdiocese.
Abdella, Peter M. *c.s.p.* '85 (SD) [M] San Diego, CA University of California at San Diego (Campus Ministry).
Abdoo, Louis *i.m.c.* '73 (SB) [1] San Bernardino, CA Our Lady of the Rosary Cathedral.
Abdulmasih, Yousif '75 (OLD) [1] Newark, NJ Our Lady of Deliverance Church; Toronto, St. Joseph Church.
Abe, John Adam '84 (RIC) Staunton, VA St. Francis of Assisi Church.
Abel, Robert M. '73 (L) [22] Louisville, KY St. Elizabeth Ann Seton Church; [52] Louisville, KY St. Mary Church.
Abele, Alan Carl '73 (ANC) On Duty Outside Archdiocese.
Abele, Joseph P. '49 (GI) Retired.
Abell, Donald E. '76 (BEL) Eldorado, IL St. Mary Church.
Abell, Edward '67 (GAL) [A] Houston, TX St. Mary's Seminary.
Abella, Ray *o.s.f.s.* (STO) Jamestown, CA Sierra Conservation Center.
Abella, Ray G. *o.s.f.s.* '93 (TOL) [K] Toledo, OH Oblates of St. Francis de Sales.
Abercrombie, Jamie M. *c.s.b.* '73 (GAL) Rosenberg, TX Our Lady of Guadalupe Church.
Abernethy, David S. *c.o.* '94 (PIT) [N] Pittsburgh, PA Congregation of the Oratory of St. Philip Neri; [Q] Slippery Rock, PA Office for Campus Ministry.
Abert, Richard P. *s.j.* '76 (MIL) [64] Milwaukee, WI St. Patrick's Church; [P] Milwaukee, WI Jesuit Community at Marquette University.
Abeysekera, B. Stanley '63 (ALX) Winnfield, LA Our Lady of Lourdes Church.
Abi-Nadar, Maron '37 (SAM) Retired.
Abi-Sarkis, Elias '75 (SAM) Unassigned.
Ablahad, Najor '43 (EST) Retired.
Ablog, Frederico J. *s.s.s.* '90 (CLV) Highland Heights, OH St. Paschal Baylon Church; [P] Cleveland, OH Blessed Sacrament Community.
Aboody, Charles '62 (NTN) Retired.
Abosike, James O. '79 (DEN) [22] Denver, CO Presentation of Our Lady Church.
Abracinskas, Albert C. '40 (BO) Retired.
Abraham, Benedict *s.a.c.* '65 (VEN) [3] Sarasota, FL St. Martha Church.
Abraham, John J. '79 (BAL) [39] Baltimore, MD Immaculate Conception Church.
Abraham, John J. '79 (WIL) Perry Point, MD Veterans Admin.
Abraham, Thaddeus '90 (BRK) [178] Queens, NY Holy Family Church.
Abraham, Thomas J. '66 (LC) Hatley, WI St. Florian Church.
Abrahams, John '79 (BAL) Special Assignment.
Abramovic, Joseph M. *o.f.m.* '60 (STL) [44] St. Louis, MO St. Joseph Church.
Abramowicz, Richard B. '86 (MET) Retired.
Abramowicz, Msgr. Sylvester '46 (NEW) Retired.
Abrams, John L. '51 (BRK) Absent on Sick Leave.
Abranches, Keith *s.j.* '87 (CHI) [C] Chicago, IL Jesuit Community at Loyola University of Chicago.
Abreu, John E. '74 (PRO) [3] Central Falls, RI St. Matthew's Church.
Abreu, Jose *c.m.* (ARE) [3] Manati, PR Sagrada Familia Church.
Abruzzese, Joseph A. (PRO) Absent on Leave.
Abts, Cletus '44 (LC) Retired.
Abts, John *o.f.m.* '90 (SAT) [70] San Antonio, TX San Jose y San Miguel Church.
Abucewicz, Msgr. John A. '44 (BO) Retired.
Abugel, Alexander G. '80 (BRK) [184] Queens, NY St. Joan of Arc Church.
Acaba, Jose A. '82 (MGZ) Cabo Rojo, PR St. Michael Church.
Accardi, Joseph N. '90 (PH) Levittown, PA St. Michael the Archangel Church.
Acciarito, Anthony J. '78 (BRK) [97] Brooklyn, NY Our Lady of Guadalupe Church.
Acebo, Jeff (OAK) [3] Oakland, CA St. Anthony's Church.
Acerbi, Luigi *p.i.m.e.* '50 (PAT) [M] Wayne, NJ P.I.M.E. Missionaries Residence.
Aceto, Gabriel *o.f.m.* (BO) [W] Andover, MA St. Francis Friary.
Acevedo, Anthony '73 (MIA) [G] Miami, FL Mercy Hospital.
Acevedo, Bertulfo '55 (ARE) [4] Vega-Baja, PR Our Lady of Carmen-Playa Church.
Acevedo, Joaquin *o.f.m.* '60 (ELP) [B] El Paso, TX St. Anthony's School of Theology.
Acevedo, Luis H. '51 (ELP) Retired.
Acevedo, Natividad *o.p.* '86 (SJN) [8] Bayamon, PR Invencion de la Santa Cruz Church.
Achi, Stephen *m.s.p.* '86 (WDC) [B] Washington, DC St. Joseph's Seminary.
Achonwa, Aloysius (WDC) [31] Washington, DC Nigerian Catholic Community Church.
Acker, Karl H. '63 (MIL) Saukville, WI Immaculate Conception Church.
Acker, Thomas S. *s.j.* (DET) [K] Detroit, MI Jesuit Provincial Office-Detroit Province of the Society of Jesus
Acker, Thomas S. *s.j.* '63 (WH) [A] Wheeling, WV Wheeling Jesuit University.
Ackeret, Dennis R. '68 (MIL) [2] Wauwatosa, WI Christ King Church.
Ackerman, Donald K. '61 (EVN) [3] Vincennes, IN St. John the Baptist Church; [4] Vincennes, IN St. Thomas Church.
Ackerman, Phillip '78 (FAR) [2] Fargo, ND Holy Spirit Church; Fargo, ND Veterans Administration Facility.
Ackerman, Raymond J. '34 (CHI) Retired.
Ackerman, Raymond K. '91 (OKL) Special Assignment; [C] Oklahoma City, OK Mount St. Mary High School.
Ackerson, Msgr. Francis A. '46 (ALT) Retired.
Acklin, Thomas *o.s.b.* '80 (GBG) [A] Latrobe, PA St. Vincent Seminary; [H] Latrobe, PA Saint Vincent Archabbey.
Acosta, Carlos Lopez '60 (NY) [139] Bronx, NY St. Francis of Assisi Church.
Acosta, Edgardo '83 (MGZ) Rincon, PR St. Rose of Lima Church.
Acosta, Francisco '70 (BWN) [1] McAllen, TX Our Lady of Perpetual Help Church.
Acosta, Humberto J. '74 (BWN) Absent.
Acquarc, Philip *c.s.b.* '70 (PHX) Special Assignment.
Acquarc, Philip A. *c.s.b.* '70 (VNN) Gilbert, AZ St. Thomas the Apostle Church; [A] Phoenix, AZ Congregation of Saint Basil.
Acquavia, Msgr. Paschal L. '48 (BUF) [1] Batavia, NY St. Anthony Church.
Acrea, John W. '62 (DM) Creston, IA Holy Spirit Church.
Acri, John A. '65 (HBG) Enola, PA Our Lady of Lourdes Church.
Acton, Msgr. John '48 (LA) Glendora, CA St. Dorothy Church.
Acton, Thomas M. '57 (LA) Gardena, CA Maria Regina Church.
Adackapara, Matthew '60 (TR) Freehold, NJ St. Robert Bellarmine Church.
Adam, Charles A. '86 (DAV) [A] Davenport, IA St. Ambrose University Seminary; [B] Davenport, IA St. Ambrose University.
Adam, John *s.j.* (NY) [DD] Bronx, NY Saint Jutta Foundation, Inc.
Adam, Nicholas '76 (DAV) Mount Pleasant, IA St. Alphonsus Church.
Adam, Richard A. '88 (SC) Duncombe, IA St. Joseph's Church; [B] Fort Dodge, IA St. Edmond High School.
Adamcik, Bryan F.J. '96 (NEW) Emerson, NJ Church of the Assumption.
Adamczyk, Stanley J. '48 (NEW) Retired.
Adamec, Joseph *c.ss.r.* '52 (BO) [13] Boston, MA Basilica of Our Lady of Perpetual Help.
Adamiak, Msgr. Leo '46 (SJP) [11] Youngstown, OH Holy Trinity Church.
Adamiak, Stephen (SJP) Retired.
Adamich, Albert R. '48 (CHI) Evergreen Park, IL Most Holy Redeemer Church.
Adamich, Albert R. '88 (CHI) Retired.
Adamko, Cyril A. '53 (Y) Retired.
Adamo, Joseph A. '73 (WOR) [2] Worcester, MA Ascension Church.
Adamo, Joseph P. '42 (NY) Retired; [Z] New York, NY Our Lady of Consolation Residence.
Adamo, Msgr. Salvatore J. '45 (CAM) Haddon Township, NJ St. Vincent Pallotti Church; Retired.
Adams, Alvin J. '67 (PIT) [4] Munhall, PA St. Rita Church; [C] Pittsburgh, PA Canevin Catholic High School.
Adams, Archie H. '55 (MAD) Absent on Sick Leave.
Adams, Benedict *o.f.m.cap.* '57 (MAD) [M] Madison, WI San Damiano Friary.
Adams, Charles F. *o.f.m.* '40 (ROC) Fairport, NY Assumption of the Blessed Virgin Mary Church.
Adams, Cletus A. *t.o.r.* '41 (ALT) [F] Hollidaysburg, PA St. Joseph Friary.
Adams, Daniel '80 (P) On Duty Outside the Archdiocese.
Adams, Daniel '80 (SFR) [6] San Francisco, CA St. Benedict Parish at St. Francis Xavier Church; [47] San Francisco, CA Sacred Heart Church.
Adams, David A. '88 (TR) Mount Holly, NJ Sacred Heart Church.
Adams, David C. '61 (KAL) Benton Harbor, MI St. John-St. Bernard Church.
Adams, Edmond F. '52 (SC) Retired.
Adams, Msgr. George J. '50 (STU) Retired.
Adams, H. J., Jr. '68 (NO) [6] Metairie, LA St. Christopher the Martyr Church.
Adams, J.K. '95 (SPK) [E] Spokane, WA Gonzaga Preparatory School.
Adams, James P. '82 (ATL) Buford, GA Prince of Peace Church.
Adams, John '69 (WDC) [U] Washington, DC Community of Christ.
Adams, John *o.p.* '96 (ANC) [1] Anchorage, AK Holy Family Cathedral.
Adams, John E. '69 (WDC) Special Ministries.
Adams, Msgr. Michael '46 (CC) Retired.
Adams, Michael J. '59 (CHI) [131] Chicago, IL St. Mary, Star of the Sea Church.
Adams, Michael T. '68 (MRY) On Duty Outside the Diocese.
Adams, Msgr. Oliver E. '54 (MOB) [2] Mobile, AL St. Catherine of Siena Church.
Adams, Patrick *o.f.m.* '42 (SP) [O] St. Petersburg, FL St. Anthony Friary.
Adams, Msgr. Raymond A. '51 (BUR) Retired.
Adams, Richard T. '65 (NY) [109] New York, NY St. Rose of Lima Church; Goshen, NY St. John the Evangelist Church.
Adams, Msgr. Robert '45 (OAK) Retired.
Adams, Rodney '91 (STP) [C] St. Paul, MN College of St. Catherine.
Adams, Rodney T. *o.p.* '91 (STL) [P] St. Louis, MO St. Dominic Priory.
Adams, Scott '95 (OKL) Ponca City, OK Church of St. Mary.
Adams, Stephen E. '81 (DEN) Johnstown, CO St. John the Baptist Church; Windsor, CO Our Lady of the Valley Church.
Adams, T. Edmund *o.s.b.* '89 (PRO) [P] Portsmouth, RI Abbey of St. Gregory the Great.
Adams, Terrance *t.o.r.* '67 (ARL) Herndon, VA St. Joseph Church.
Adams, Thomas J. '64 (OM) [45] Omaha, NE St. Therese of the Child Jesus Church.
Adams, Walter C. '84 (NY) Military Chaplains.
Adams, William *s.v.d.* '45 (LA) [76] Los Angeles, CA St. Malachy Church.
Adams, William '78 (VEN) Arcadia, FL St. Paul Church.
Adamski, Donald J. *o.f.m.conv.* '75 (ELP) [17] El Paso, TX Our Lady of Mt. Carmel Church.
Adamski, John S. '71 (ATL) [12] Atlanta, GA Shrine of the Immaculate Conception Church.
Adamsky, Raymond J. '58 (MIL) Retired.
Adamson, Fred '95 (PHX) [24] Phoenix, AZ St. Theresa Church.
Adamson, Joseph J. '90 (CAM) Runnemede, NJ St. Maria Goretti Church.
Adamson, Milton N. *c.s.c.* '66 (PHX) [C] Phoenix, AZ St. Joseph's Hospital and Medical Center; [F] Phoenix, AZ Holy Cross Congregation of Casa Santa Cruz.
Adan, Aurelio '69 (CGS) [B] Aibonito, PR Casa Manresa.
Adarve, Hernan '61 (SJN) [12] Bayamon, PR Nuestra Senora de la Milagrosa Church.
Adcock, Basil W. '80 (NTN) Leave of Absence.
Addari, Enzo *s.c.* '76 (LAN) [E] Chelsea, MI St. Louis Center for Exceptional Children & Adults.
Adde-Nweah, John Benedict '87 (FTW) [7] Fort Wayne, IN St. John Baptist Church.
Adducci, Anthony J. '76 (CHI) [J] Chicago, IL St. Joseph Hospital.
Adejoh, Patrick '92 (LA) [80] Los Angeles, CA St. Mary Magdalen Church.
Adelman, Norbert '56 (ORL) Longwood, FL Church of the Nativity.
Adelman, Norbert *c.pp.s.* '56 (TOL) [M] Bellevue, OH Sorrowful Mother Shrine.
Adelmann, Edward *o.carm.* '75 (JOL) [J] Darien, IL Carmelite Fathers Provincial Office.
Adelmann, Frederick J. *s.j.* '47 (BO) [W] Weston, MA Campion Health Center, Inc.
Adessa, Msgr. Domenick J. '47 (RVC) [O] Amityville, NY Queen of the Rosary, Motherhouse.
Adessa, Msgr. Dominick J. *p.e.* '47 (BRK) [204] Queens, NY Nativity of the Blessed Virgin Mary Church; Retired.
Adeyanju, Henry M. (BO) [4] Waltham, MA St. Mary Church.
Adhana, Gabre-Tinsaye *s.t.l.* '47 (GAL) [52] Houston, TX St. Nicholas Church.
Adkins, Joseph H. '47 (BIS) Retired; [G] Bismarck, ND Emmaus Place.
Adkins, Patrick J. *o.s.c.* '50 (PHX) Phoenix, AZ Good Samaritan Medical Center; [F] Phoenix, AZ Crosier Community of Phoenix (Canons Regular of the Order of the Holy Cross).
Adogamhe, Paul '76 (NY) [191] Bronx, NY St. Thomas Aquinas Church.
Adolf, Gregory P. '91 (TUC) Sierra Vista, AZ St. Andrew Church.

Adolfo, Hermengildo '68 (FRS) Tehachapi, CA California Correctional Institution.
Adolfo, Neil '68 (FRS) Tehachapi, CA St. Malachy Church.
Adomaitis, John J. '44 (GAY) Mackinaw City, MI St. Anthony of Padua Church; Retired.
Adonizio, Joseph J. '56 (SCR) West Pittston, PA Immaculate Conception Church.
Adorno, Anibal '92 (DAL) [1] Dallas, TX Cathedral-Santuario de Guadalupe Church.
Adragna, Joseph J. '65 (STL) Gardenville, MO St. George Church.
Adrian, Stephen J. '39 (NU) Retired.
Adrian, Stephen J. '68 (STP) [29] St. Paul, MN St. Matthew Church.
Adrians, Thomas M. '67 (PBL) [2] Pueblo, CO Christ the King Church.
Adu, Martin K. '75 (MIA) [6] Fort Lauderdale, FL St. George Church.
Aduba, John '81 (LAN) Goodrich, MI St. Mark the Evangelist Church.
Adugu, Damain '70 (CHI) [57] Chicago, IL St. Felicitas Church.
Adversario, Efren F. '89 (AGN) Inarajan, GU St. Joseph Church.
Aelavanthara, Antony '68 (ALX) St. Joseph, LA St. Joseph Church.
Aerts, Daniel C. '77 (GR) Reed City, MI St. Philip Neri Church.
Afanador, Hernan '82 (ORL) [8] Orlando, FL St. Isaac Jogues Church.
Afangide, Anthony *m.s.p.* '86 (GAL) Barrett Station, TX St. Martin de Porres Church.
Afenugo, Emmanuel '83 (AMA) On Duty Outside the Diocese.
Affanoso, Joseph L. '56 (NEW) [1] East Orange, NJ Holy Name of Jesus Church; Montclair, NJ Mountainside Hospital.
Affelt, Francis *o.f.m.* '52 (FTW) [K] Mishawaka, IN St. Francis Provincialate.
Afful-Broni, Anthony '68 (NY) Cortlandt Manor, NY Holy Spirit Church.
Agambi, Isaac (NY) [63] New York, NY St. Joseph of the Holy Family Church; Mount Vernon, NY Mount Vernon Hospital.
Agan, Jose '70 (NEW) Glen Rock, NJ St. Catharine Church.
Agapito, John *c.p.m.* '89 (WH) [G] Morgantown, WV Our Lady of Good Counsel Franciscan Friary.
Agar, Bartholomew A. *o.praem.* '58 (GB) [I] De Pere, WI St. Norbert Abbey.
Agbaka, Desmond *c.s.sp.* '85 (MIA) North Miami, FL Holy Family Church.
Ager, Fay W. '79 (OG) Chateaugay, NY St. Patrick Church.
Agius, Grace '42 (DET) [51] Detroit, MI Most Holy Trinity Church.
Agliardo, Michael *s.j.* (NY) [CC] New York, NY University Apostolate.
Agliardo, Michael J. *s.j.* '94 (NY) [Z] New York, NY Jesuit Community at Fordham University.
Agnew, Francis H. *c.m.* '60 (STL) Sereno, MO Our Lady of Victory Church.
Agnew, John C. '90 (BO) [V] Cambridge, MA Opus Dei, Prelature of the Holy Cross and Opus Dei.
Agonis, Edwin *o.f.m.conv.* '41 (BGP) [1] Fairfield, CT St. Anthony of Padua Church.
Agostinelli, Gianni *c.s.* '86 (BRK) [71] Brooklyn, NY St. Joseph Patron of the Universal Church.
Agostino, Emil *o.carm.* '64 (NEW) Englewood, NJ St. Cecilia's Church.
Agostino, Joseph V. *c.m.* '83 (BRK) [66] Brooklyn, NY St. John the Baptist Church; [U] Brooklyn, NY St. John the Baptist Rectory.
Agostino, Sixtus *m.c.c.j.* '72 (CHI) [N] La Grange Park, IL Comboni Mission Center.
Agostino, Stephen J. *s.j.* '93 (CLV) [E] Cleveland, OH St. Ignatius High School.
Agresti, Albert A. *s.j.* '80 (BO) [W] Boston, MA The Society of Jesus of New England-Provincial Offices.
Agresti, Albert A. *s.j.* '80 (CHI) [C] Chicago, IL Jesuit Community at Loyola University of Chicago.
Agudo, Teodoro *o.f.m.cap.* '54 (NO) [61] New Orleans, LA St. Theresa Of Avila Church.
Aguggia, Steven J. '93 (BRK) [103] Brooklyn, NY Our Lady of Miracles Church.
Aguilar, Arturo *s.s.c.* '84 (OM) [K] St. Columbans, NE St. Columban's Foreign Mission Society.
Aguilar, Benjamin *o.carm.* '93 (LA) [F] Encino, CA Crespi Carmelite High School.
Aguilar, Genaro P. *c.s.c.* '83 (FR) [B] North Easton, MA Holy Cross Fathers Religious.
Aguilar, Jose A. *s.j.* '82 (OAK) [N] Berkeley, CA Jesuit Community at Jesuit School of Theology at Berkeley.
Aguilar, Jose M. (NY) [65] New York, NY St. Jude Church.
Aguilar, Jose Maria *sch.p.* '59 (LA) [75] Los Angeles, CA St. Lucy Church.
Aguilar, Ricardo '95 (AUS) Rogers, TX St. Matthew Church; Temple, TX Our Lady of Guadalupe Church.
Aguilar, Rogelio Mur *o.carm.* '56 (MGZ) Anasco, PR St. Anthony Abbot Church.
Aguilera, George '83 (LA) [39] Los Angeles, CA St. Aloysius Gonzaga Church.
Aguilera, Sal '84 (ELP) On Duty Outside of Diocese.
Aguirre, Ignacio *o.s.b.* '53 (CGS) Humacao, PR Maria Reina de la Paz Church.
Aguirre, Osmar R. '93 (YAK) Toppenish, WA St. Aloysius Church.
Aguirre, Robert G. '72 (CHI) Wauconda, IL Transfiguration Church.
Aguirre-Garza, Jesus *o.f.m.* '96 (SAT) [50] San Antonio, TX St. Leonard's Church; [B] San Antonio, TX Franciscan Formation Program in San Jose Friary (Casa Juan Diego).
Aguirre-Garza, Jesus M. *o.f.m.* '96 (SAT) [70] San Antonio, TX San Jose y San Miguel Church.
Agumanu, Benedict '66 (LA) Claremont, CA Our Lady of the Assumption Church.
Ahearn, Donald J. '51 (CHI) [112] Chicago, IL St. Juliana Church; Retired.
Ahearn, John S. *o.f.m.* '50 (PAT) [M] Butler, NJ St. Anthony Friary.
Ahearn, Kieran T. '64 (BGP) Leave of Absence.
Ahearn, Richard F. '60 (BO) Danvers, MA St. Mary of the Annunciation Church.
Ahern, Bernard '54 (ALB) Retired.
Ahern, Dennis P. *s.j.* '70 (CHI) [C] Chicago, IL Jesuit Community at Loyola University of Chicago.
Ahern, Jack '79 (BO) [4] Brookline, MA St. Mary of the Assumption Church.
Ahern, Msgr. John B. '54 (NY) [88] New York, NY Our Lady of Loreto Church; [I] New York, NY The Catholic Charities of the Archdiocese of New York.
Ahern, John J. '48 (CHI) Retired.
Ahern, John J. '49 (CHI) Retired.
Ahern, John S. '54 (HRT) Norfolk, CT Immaculate Conception Church.
Ahern, John V. '67 (SY) [2] Liverpool, NY Immaculate Heart of Mary Church.
Ahern, Richard *c.s.s.* '54 (BO) [Z] Waltham, MA Stigmatine Fathers and Brothers.
Ahern, Thomas '54 (SJ) Retired.
Ahern, Thomas '94 (BRK) [190] Queens, NY St. Leo Church.
Ahern, Thomas W. '48 (NOR) Chester, CT St. Joseph Church.
Aherne, Greg *s.j.* '60 (SFR) [48] San Francisco, CA Star of the Sea Church.
Aherne, Gregory D. *s.j.* '60 (SJ) [M] Los Gatos, CA Sacred Heart Jesuit Center.
Aherne, James *m.s.* '73 (HRT) [3] Hartford, CT Immaculate Conception Church; [7] Hartford, CT St. Anne Church.
Aherne, James J. *m.s.* '73 (HRT) [M] Hartford, CT Missionaries of LaSalette Provincial Secretary.
Aherne, John '57 (MOB) Semmes, AL Holy Name of Jesus Church.
Ahlbach, William J. '62 (SFR) [3] San Mateo, CA St. Matthew Church.
Ahlemeyer, Richard J. '77 (BRK) [227] Queens, NY St. Pius V Church.
Ahler, Richard H. *s.j.* '61 (MIL) [P] Milwaukee, WI Jesuit Community at Marquette University.
Ahles, Donald M. '71 (RCK) Cary, IL SS. Peter & Paul Church.
Ahles, Jerome *o.f.m.* '44 (MRY) [I] San Miguel, CA San Miguel Retreat House.
Ahles, Jerry *o.f.m.* (MRY) [G] San Miguel, CA Franciscan Friars, O.F.M.
Ahlin, Robert J. '71 (PIT) Brentwood, PA St. Sylvester Church.
Ahlstrom, Michael P. '69 (CHI) Rolling Meadows, IL St. Colette Church.
Ahn, Joseph S. '66 (BRK) [226] Queens, NY St. Paul Chong Ha-Sang Roman Catholic Chapel.
Ahn, Michael '79 (SEA) Special Assignment.
Aho, Charles A. (SY) Liverpool, NY Developmental Center; Special Assignment.
Ahrems, Noel G. *o.carm.* '53 (NOR) Middletown, CT Long Lane School.
Ahren, Noel G. *o.carm.* '46 (NOR) [D] Deep River, CT Mount St. John.
Ahrens, Giles *c.p.* '52 (BRK) [U] Jamaica, NY Immaculate Conception Monastery.
Ahrens, William B. '51 (STL) Concord Village, MO St. Simon the Apostle Church.
Ahrensfield, Michael E. '80 (ALN) [8] Reading, PA St. Margaret Church.
Ahumanda, Jose E. *c.s.c.* '83 (FTW) [J] South Bend, IN Congregation of Holy Cross Indiana Province Provincial House.
Ahurwendeire, Emiliano '82 (DET) [54] Detroit, MI Our Lady of Good Counsel Church.
Aichele, Raymond P. '58 (CIN) [B] Cincinnati, OH Mt. St. Mary's Seminary of the West.
Aiello, Anthony '69 (DM) [2] Des Moines, IA All Saints Church.
Aiello, John A. '85 (MEM) [10] Memphis, TN Holy Rosary Church.
Aiello, John D. '69 (MIL) Special Assignment.
Aiello, Louis F. '77 (SY) Tully, NY St. Leo Church.
Aigner, Edward M. '72 (WIL) Princess Anne, MD University of Maryland, Eastern Shore; [O] Newark, DE Univ. of Delaware Newman Center.
Aigner, Edward M., Jr. '72 (WIL) Westover, MD Eastern Correctional Institution.
Aiken, Lloyd E. '70 (BAL) Glyndon, MD Sacred Heart Church.
Aiken, Richard J. '70 (MIL) Greendale, WI St. Alphonsus Church.
Aiken, Msgr. Roy F. '46 (CHR) Retired.
Aineto, Luis *s.d.b.* '61 (PMB) Belle Glade, FL St. Philip Benizi Church.
Aita, Mark C. *s.j.* '83 (CAM) [4] Camden, NJ Holy Name Church; [R] Camden, NJ Saint Luke's Catholic Medical Services, Inc.
Aitcheson, William '88 (ARL) Colonial Beach, VA St. Elizabeth Church.
Aitcheson, William M. '88 (RNO) On Duty Outside the Diocese.
Aitesbaomo, Martin *o.p.* (CHI) [173] Chicago, IL St. Pius V Church.
Ajamie, Albert '50 (IND) Retired.
Ajayi, Vincent O. '94 (NY) [3] Mt. Vernon, NY Our Lady of Victory Church.
Ajuonu, Innocent '83 (MIA) [1] Miami, FL St. Mary's Cathedral.
Ajuria, Cruz *o.f.m.* '57 (SJN) [52] San Juan, PR Resurreccion del Senor Church.
Akalefu, Wisdom '83 (BRK) [153] Queens, NY Ascension Church.
Akano, Yoshi *c.s.s.r.* (NY) [150] Bronx, NY Immaculate Conception Church.
Akekee, Wlademer '49 (SAM) Retired.
Akers, Bert *s.j.* '61 (WIL) Ocean City, MD St. Mary, Star of the Sea Church.
Akhein, Florantinus '93 (CI) Tol, FM Assumption of the Blessed Virgin Mary Church.
Akian, Mikael '35 (ARM) [A] La Crescenta, CA Mekhitarist School.
Akiki, Joseph '87 (SAM) Orlando, FL St. Jude Mission Church; [E] Williston, VT Blessed Rafka Retreat Center.
Akiona, Lane *ss.cc.* (HON) [4] Honolulu, HI St. Augustine Church.
Akkin, Florentinus '93 (CI) Tol, FM Assumption of the Blessed Virgin Mary Church; Puluwat, FM Santiago Church.
Akordor, Edmund '80 (NO) [45] New Orleans, LA St. Matthias Church.
Akpabio, Felix '78 (BRK) [238] Queens, NY Sacred Heart Church.
Akpan, Msgr. Godwin *m.s.p.* '60 (WDC) [B] Washington, DC St. Joseph's Seminary.
Aksamit, Stanley J. '77 (SPR) Greenfield, MA Sacred Heart Church; Turners Falls, MA St. Mary's Church; Turners Falls, MA St. Anne Church.
Akwue, Francis *c.s.sp.* '71 (MIA) [17] Miami, FL St. Catherine of Siena Church.
Al-Badwi, Alfred '91 (OLL) Dayton, OH Saint Ignatius Mission Church.
Al-Nahal, Jean *m.l.m.* '93 (OLL) San Antonio, TX St. George Church.
Al-Nahal, John *m.l.m.* '93 (OLL) [A] San Antonio, TX The Congregation of Maronite Lebanese Missionaries.
Alabart, Francis X. '40 (FRS) Retired.
Alagia, Vincent *s.j.* '58 (CHL) Mars Hill, NC St. Andrew the Apostle Church.
Alagia, Vincent P. *s.j.* '58 (CHL) [J] Charlotte, NC Jesuit Community; [M] Hot Springs, NC Jesuit House of Prayer.
Alaharasan, V. Anthony J. '65 (NOR) Preston, CT St. Catherine of Siena Church.
Alamo, Emiliano '66 (PCE) Villalba, PR Our Lady of Mt. Carmel Church.
Alapatt, Mathew *m.s.f.s.* '62 (KAL) [1] Kalamazoo, MI St. Augustine Cathedral; [D] Kalamazoo, MI Borgess Medical Center.
Alarcon, Felix '63 (RVC) Priests Released from Diocesan Assignment.
Alarcon, Felix '63 (VEN) [L] Naples, FL Catholic Hispanic Center.
Alava, Andres *o.a.r.* '63 (LSC) Anthony, NM St. Anthony's Church.
Alayon, Hermenegildo '79 (CGS) Gurabo, PR San Jose Church.
Alba, Msgr. Jose M. '48 (NEW) [18] Jersey City, NJ St. Nicholas Church; Retired.
Alba, Ricardo de *m.sp.s.* '81 (LA) [3] Oxnard, CA Our Lady of Guadalupe Parish Church.
Albacete, Msgr. Lorenzo '73 (WDC) On Duty Outside the Archdiocese.
Albacete-Cintron, Msgr. Lorenzo M. *c.s.sp.* '73 (PCE) [B] Ponce, PR The Pontifical Catholic University of Puerto Rico.
Albaladejo, Juan A. '85 (MET) [3] New Brunswick, NJ Our Lady of Mt. Carmel Church.
Albamonti, Richard (NOR) Westbrook, CT St. Mark Church.
Albano, Arturo '74 (SFR) Colma, CA Holy Angels Church.

Albano, George M. '44 (TR) Retired.
Albano, Peter J. *c.m.* '68 (BRK) [D] Queens and Staten Island, NY St. John's University; [U] Jamaica, NY Vincentian Residence.
Albano, Vincent *s.o.l.t.* '72 (CC) Robstown, TX St. Anthony Church; [H] Robstown, TX Society of Our Lady of the Most Holy Trinity.
Albarano, Richard '68 (LA) Downey, CA St. Raymond Church.
Albee, Paul M. '84 (LA) Fillmore, CA St. Francis of Assisi Church.
Alber, Thomas L. '85 (JC) Milan, MO St. Mary Church.
Alberdi, Inmanol *c.p.* (SJN) [46] San Juan, PR Nuestra Senora de la Piedad Church.
Alberg, Leo W. '91 (LA) Rancho Palos Verdes, CA St. John Fisher Church.
Albero, Steven J. *o.praem.* '92 (PH) [D] Philadelphia, PA St. John Neumann High School; [Z] Philadelphia, PA St. Norbert Priory.
Albers, Austin *o.f.m.* '64 (SFD) [4] Quincy, IL St. Francis Solanus Church; [K] Quincy, IL St. Francis Solanus Friary.
Albers, Edwin O. *o.f.m.* '61 (SFD) Bishop Creek, IL St. Aloysius Church; Dieterich, IL Immaculate Conception Church; Island Grove, IL St. Joseph Church; [K] Teutopolis, IL St. Francis Assisi Friary.
Albers, George J. *c.pp.s.* '62 (CLV) [53] Cleveland, OH Our Lady of Good Counsel Church.
Albers, Paul C. '37 (DAV) Retired.
Albers, Robert J. *s.a.c.* '48 (MIL) [35] Milwaukee, WI Holy Cross Church; [S] Elkhorn, WI St. Vincent Pallotti Center.
Albers, Thomas L. *c.pp.s.* '67 (JC) Sedalia, MO St. Patrick Church.
Albert, Andrew R. *s.m.* '65 (BO) [59] Boston, MA Our Lady of Victories Church; [W] Boston, MA Marist Fathers of Our Lady of Victories (Boston Prov.).
Albert, Claude '64 (PRT) [3] Lewiston, ME Holy Family Church.
Albert, George S. *s.j.* '72 (BO) [W] Boston, MA The Society of Jesus of New England-Provincial Offices.
Albert, J. W. '83 (SHP) Retired.
Albert, James R. '86 (PRT) Eagle Lake, ME St. Mary's Church; Wallagrass, ME St. Joseph's Church.
Albert, Msgr. Louis W. '34 (WDC) Retired.
Albert, Patrick L. '92 (SCR) Dickson City, PA Visitation of the Blessed Virgin Mary Church.
Albert, Xavier R. '63 (STL) [1] St. Charles, MO St. Charles Borromeo Church.
Alberte, Carl P. '58 (MIL) Pewaukee, WI St. Mary's Church.
Alberth, Regis R. '80 (PIT) Beaver, PA SS. Peter and Paul Church.
Albertine, Richard *m.m.* '66 (WDC) [B] Washington, DC Maryknoll Fathers and Brothers.
Alberts, Edward T. '75 (NSH) Brentwood, TN Holy Family Church.
Alberts, Keith M. '94 (CLV) [1] Euclid, OH St. Christine Church.
Albertson, Clinton E. *s.j.* '49 (LA) [C] Los Angeles, CA Loyola Marymount University.
Albertson, Eric '86 (ARL) Military Chaplains.
Albertson, Lawrence '65 (KCK) [1] Overland Park, KS Church of the Ascension.
Albietz, Henry F. '74 (CIN) Bellefontaine, OH St. Patrick's Church.
Albino, Brian E. *s.j.* '79 (BO) [W] Boston, MA The Society of Jesus of New England-Provincial Offices.
Albino, Brian E. '79 (FR) [5] New Bedford, MA Our Lady of the Immaculate Conception Church.
Albino, John C. '90 (NY) [162] Bronx, NY St. Margaret Mary Church.
Albino, Ramon E. '84 (MGZ) Aguadilla, PR La Milagrosa Church.
Albosta, John T. '64 (SCR) Waymart, PA St. Mary's Church.
Albrecht, Craig '95 (SAG) Mount Pleasant, MI Sacred Heart Church.
Albrecht, G.R. Keith '77 (CIN) [51] Cincinnati, OH St. Jude the Apostle Church; Leave of Absence.
Albrecht, James W. '58 (NEW) [M] South Orange, NJ Opus Dei.
Albrecht, Louis Henry '86 (BAK) La Grande, OR Our Lady of the Valley Church.
Albrecht, Walter H. '43 (SAC) Retired and in Senior Ministry.
Albright, Charles W. *c.s.p.* '49 (NY) [Z] Scarsdale, NY Paulist Fathers Generalate.
Albright, R. Gerard *s.j.* '58 (DET) [K] Detroit, MI Jesuit Community at the University of Detroit.
Albright, Robert E. '72 (BAL) Special Assignment; [O] Baltimore, MD Archdiocesan Office-Newman Center; [O] Baltimore, MD Archdiocesan Office-Newman Center.
Alcantara, Miguel B. '65 (CHI) [134] Chicago, IL St. Matthias Church.
Alcazar, Emanuel '89 (ELP) [29] El Paso, TX St. Paul the Apostle Church.
Alciati, Paul J. '77 (SY) [6] Binghamton, NY St. John the Evangelist Church.
Alco, James J. '90 (SCR) [2] Hazleton, PA Church of the Most Precious Blood.
Alcocer, Jose '60 (ELP) [36] El Paso, TX San Jose Church.
Alcocer, Jose M. *m.ss.cc.* '64 (SJN) [1] Trujillo Alto, PR San Bartolome Church.
Alcoser, Michael E. *c.s.c.* '87 (FTW) [20] South Bend, IN St. Therese, Little Flower Church.
Aldana, Antonio '53 (NY) [169] Bronx, NY Our Lady of Angels Church.
Aldasoro, Msgr. Francisco '47 (SD) Retired.
Aldegunde, Jose R. '58 (BRK) [201] Queens, NY St. Michael Church.
Alder, Ronald J. '69 (DET) Dundee, MI St. Irene Church.
Alderson, George K. '71 (GBG) [1] Uniontown, PA St. John The Evangelist Church.
Alderson, John *o.f.m.* (NEW) Fair Lawn, NJ St. Anne's Church.
Aldrich, Ralph '53 (PEO) Retired.
Aldridge, William J. *o.p.* '46 (BR) [J] Ponchatoula, LA Rosaryville/Spirit Life Center.
Aldworth, Thomas '75 (CHI) [167] Chicago, IL St. Peter's Church; [N] Chicago, IL St. Peter's Friary.
Alecio, Freddy '91 (SJN) [11] Carolina, PR Jesus Mediador Church; [B] Rio Piedras, PR Seminario Menor San Jose.
Aleckna, John Mark *c.p.* '41 (HRT) [M] West Hartford, CT Holy Family Monastery/Retreat.
Alejunas, Richard *s.d.b.* '89 (COL) [H] Columbus, OH Salesian Center.
Aleksa, Thomas M. '75 (E) Bradford, PA St. Bernard Church.
Aleksonis, Vladas '34 (FAR) Retired; [E] Fargo, ND Riverview Place, Inc.
Aleman, Msgr. Vernon P. '35 (NO) [55] New Orleans, LA St. Raphael the Archangel Church; Retired.
Alenchery, Siby J. '87 (RVC) Coram, NY St. Frances Cabrini Church.
Alengadan, George '82 (OAK) [3] Walnut Creek, CA St. Mary's Church.
Alers, Juan M. '69 (LKC) Oakdale, LA Sacred Heart Church.
Alesandro, Msgr. John A. '66 (RVC) Garden City, NY St. Joseph's Church; East Meadow, NY Nassau County Police Department.
Alessandrini, Raniero *c.s.* '57 (CHI) [N] Chicago, IL Scalabrini House of Theology.
Alessandro, Michael J. '44 (NY) Bronx, NY Calvary Hospital; Retired; [T] New York, NY Calvary Hospital.
Alexander, Andrew *s.j.* '79 (OM) [K] Omaha, NE Jesuit Community At Creighton University.
Alexander, Anthony F. '45 (CLV) Perry, OH St. Cyprian Church; Retired.
Alexander, F. Leon '66 (WH) South Charleston, WV Blessed Sacrament Church.
Alexander, Fred *o.c.d.* '82 (MIL) Holy Hill, WI St. Mary of the Hill Church; [P] Holy Hill, WI Discalced Carmelite Monastery.
Alexander, Jim *s.c.j.* '44 (MIL) [P] Franklin, WI Villa Maria.
Alexander, John D. *s.j.* '54 (NY) [Z] New York, NY Jesuit Community at Fordham University; [DD] New York, NY Brooklyn Prep Alumni Association.
Alexander, Jon *o.p.* '85 (LSC) Silver City, NM St. Francis Newman Center Parish Church.
Alexander, Joseph J. '73 (LAF) Eunice, LA St. Anthony of Padua Church.
Alexander, Marc R. '85 (HON) [A] Kaneohe, HI St. Stephen's Diocesan Center.
Alexandrunas, Albert *o.f.m.cap.* '65 (WH) Belle, WV St. John Church; [N] Charleston, WV Capuchins-St. Anthony Friary.
Alfano, Jane (SD) [5] El Cajon, CA St. Luke Church.
Alfano, Michael A.J. (BO) Maynard, MA St. Bridget Church.
Alfaro, Juan '62 (SAT) [64] San Antonio, TX St. Rose of Lima Church.
Alfonso, Alexander '68 (SJ) [5] Sunnyvale, CA Church of The Resurrection.
Alfonso, Jairo *c.s.* (BRK) [71] Brooklyn, NY St. Joseph Patron of the Universal Church.
Alheim, Peter *o.f.m.* (NY) [146] Bronx, NY Holy Cross Church.
Alicea, Adrian *s.s.s.* '90 (CGS) [5] Caguas, PR Santisimo Sacramento Church.
Alicea, Msgr. Joaquin A. '71 (PCE) [B] Ponce, PR The Pontifical Catholic University of Puerto Rico.
Alicea, Luis Antonio '96 (CGS) Humacao, PR Dulce Nombre de Jesus Church.
Alimena, Leonard S. '57 (DEN) Retired.
Alisauskas, Peter J. '43 (SCR) Retired.
Alise, Mark A. '85 (BR) On Leave.
Alkire, Thomas J. *o.carm.* '63 (STO) [5] Stockton, CA St. Gertrude Church.
Alkire, Timothy M. '85 (LFT) [3] Lafayette, IN St. Boniface Church.
Allain, Thomas D. *c.s.p.* '94 (CHR) Clemson, SC St. Andrew Church.
Allaire, Barry J. '61 (BUF) [D] Olean, NY Archbishop Walsh High School.
Allaire, Barry J. '72 (BUF) Hinsdale, NY St. Helen Church.
Allaire, Robert A. '61 (PRO) Wakefield, RI St. Francis Church.
Allanach, Robert C. *o.m.i.* '80 (NO) [38] New Orleans, LA St. Joan Of Arc Church; [K] New Orleans, LA Boys Hope; [S] New Orleans, LA Jesuit Program for Living and Learning of New Orleans, Inc.
Allard, George L. '60 (PRO) [1] West Warwick, RI Christ the King Church.
Allard, Gilles *i.m.c.* '63 (SB) [H] San Bernardino, CA Newman Catholic Fellowship.
Allard, John C. '75 (PRO) [1] Woonsocket, RI St. Agatha's Church; [10] Woonsocket, RI Precious Blood Church.
Allard, Marcel M. '65 (MAN) Newton, NH Mary, Mother of the Church.
Allard, William '55 (OWN) [1] Owensboro, KY St. Stephen Cathedral.
Allega, Ernest P. '76 (WOR) Uxbridge, MA St. Mary's Church.
Allegra, Christopher '70 (L) [3] Springfield, KY Holy Trinity Church.
Allegretto, William M. *c.m.* '85 (MOB) Opelika, AL St. Mary of the Mission Church.
Alleman, Msgr. C. J. '49 (GAL) Retired.
Allen, A. Christopher '81 (PMB) Hobe Sound, FL St. Christopher Church.
Allen, Charles H. '73 (BGP) [A] Fairfield, CT Fairfield University; [O] Fairfield, CT The Fairfield Jesuit Community-Fairfield University.
Allen, David E. '78 (BR) Livonia, LA St. Frances Xavier Cabrini Church.
Allen, David G. *s.j.* '79 (BAL) [M] Baltimore, MD Jesuit Fathers and Brothers Maryland Provincial Curia.
Allen, David W. '95 (DEN) [2] Aurora, CO St. Michael the Archangel Church.
Allen, Francis *s.m.m.* '51 (FR) Dighton, MA St. Peter's Church.
Allen, Francis R. *s.j.* '56 (BGP) [O] Fairfield, CT The Fairfield Jesuit Community-Fairfield University.
Allen, Frederick *m.m.* '65 (SJ) [M] Los Altos, CA Maryknoll.
Allen, James *o.m.i.* '65 (CHI) [N] Chicago, IL The Oblate House of Theology.
Allen, John Andrew '90 (PRT) Biddeford, ME St. Mary's Church.
Allen, John G. '70 (HBG) [7] (Penbrook), PA St. Margaret Mary Alacoque Church.
Allen, John R. *s.j.* '42 (STL) [O] St. Louis, MO Fusz Pavilion.
Allen, Joseph (FAR) Langdon, ND St. Alphonsus Church.
Allen, Joseph A. '53 (BIS) On Duty Outside the Diocese.
Allen, Joseph A. '53 (GR) Retired.
Allen, Joseph C. '50 (BIR) Athens, AL St. Paul's Church.
Allen, Joseph P. *o.p.* '67 (HRT) [14] New Haven, CT St. Mary's Priory Church.
Allen, Joseph P. '91 (CHI) Lansing, IL St. Ann Church.
Allen, Loren '94 (SR) Eureka, CA St. Bernard Church; [B] Eureka, CA St. Bernard's High School.
Allen, Michael '71 (EVN) Jasper, IN St. Joseph Church.
Allen, Paul L. *s.j.* '38 (DET) [P] Clarkston, MI Colombiere Center.
Allen, Peter A. '71 (RVC) Cutchogue, NY Sacred Heart Church.
Allen, Philip J. '58 (WCH) Aleppo, KS Immaculate Conception Church; Garden Plain, KS St. Anthony Church.
Allen, Philip T. '59 (OG) Redford, NY Assumption of the B.V.M. Church.
Allen, Richard (SP) [4] Tampa, FL Good Shepherd Church.
Allen, Msgr. Richard F. '56 (CHL) [4] Charlotte, NC St. Ann Church.
Allen, Richard L. '61 (GB) Neenah, WI St. Gabriel the Archangel Church.
Allen, Richard T. *o.s.a.* '63 (JOL) New Lenox, IL St. Jude Church.
Allen, Terry E. '61 (ALX) Lecompte, LA St. Martin Church.
Allen, Thomas E. '48 (SPC) Lamar, MO St. Mary Church.
Allen, William F. '31 (SPR) Retired.
Allende, Santiago Rivera '83 (MGZ) Moca, PR Our Lady of Monserrate Church.
Allender, Raymond P. *s.j.* '75 (SJ) [D] San Jose, CA Bellarmine College Preparatory.
Allender, Thomas G. *s.j.* '71 (SJ) [M] Los Gatos, CA Sacred Heart Jesuit Center.
Aller, Domingo *o.s.a.* '61 (SJN) [15] Bayamon, PR Ntra. Sra. Monserrate Church.
Allessandro, Michael J. '44 (NY) [127] Bronx, NY St. Anthony Church.
Alletto, Nicholas P. '45 (ROC) Retired.
Alleyne, Msgr. Edward D. '60 (CAM) [6] Cherry Hill, NJ Queen of Heaven Church.
Alliata, Peter R. '61 (WDC) Mount Rainier, MD St. James Church.
Allie, Robert *o.m.i.* '51 (STP) [28] St. Paul, MN St.

Mary Church; St. Paul, MN St. Paul-Ramsey Hospital; St. Paul, MN Gillette Children's Hospital.
Allie, Stanley J. '58 (ALB) On Duty Outside the Diocese.
Allie, Stanley J. '58 (ANC) Wasilla, AK Sacred Heart Church.
Alliegro, Msgr. Michael J. '73 (MET) East Brunswick, NJ St. Bartholomew Church.
Allin, R. Benedict *o.s.b.* '67 (STL) [1] Creve Coeur, MO St. Anselm Church; [P] St. Louis, MO The Abbey of St. Mary and St. Louis.
Alling, James '92 (PHX) Kingman, AZ St. Mary's Church.
Allison, Msgr. Bruce '61 (E) [C] Erie, PA Cathedral Preparatory School; [C] Erie, PA Cathedral Preparatory School.
Allison, Jeffrey *c.s.c.* '96 (AUS) [13] Austin, TX St. Ignatius Martyr Church.
Allison, Joseph C. '56 (CIN) Morrow, OH St. Philip the Apostle Church.
Allison, Michael '91 (PMB) [B] West Palm Beach, FL Cardinal Newman High School.
Allman, Mark '96 (ALB) Guilderland, NY Christ the King Church.
Allman, Timothy J. '58 (SP) [2] Clearwater, FL Light of Christ Church; [F] Clearwater, FL Light of Christ Preschool.
Allmaras, Alfred '59 (FAR) Michigan, ND St. Lawrence O'Toole Church.
Allt, John F. '73 (TUC) [15] Tucson, AZ St. Joseph Church.
Allue, Emilio S. (BO) [4] Framingham, MA St. Stephen Church.
Almade, Frank D. '78 (PIT) [O] Allison Park, PA The Sisters of Divine Providence; [R] Wildwood, PA Christ Child Society of Pittsburgh.
Almango, R. Stephen *o.f.m.* '65 (PIT) [60] Pittsburgh, PA St. Pamphilus Church.
Almarza, Juan *o.a.r.* '65 (LSC) Anthony, NM St. Anthony's Church.
Almasy, Alcuin M. *o.s.b.* '60 (TUC) [F] St. David, AZ Holy Trinity Monastery.
Almazan, Jose A. *c.m.* '63 (CC) Premont, TX St. Theresa of the Infant Jesus Church.
Almazan, Nestor '75 (CLV) Wickliffe, OH Our Lady of Mount Carmel Church.
Almeida, George F. '65 (FR) East Taunton, MA Holy Family Church.
Almendariz, Jose (MGZ) San Sebastian, PR San Sebastian Martir Church.
Almendra, Leoncio T. '60 (NOR) Retired.
Almendras, Joel '75 (MRY) Soledad, CA Correctional Training Facility.
Alminde, Joseph M. *s.j.* '62 (BAL) [D] Baltimore, MD Loyola High School.
Almonte, Alfred P. *c.s.* '61 (PRO) [4] Johnston, RI St. Rocco Church.
Almyr, Augustin '74 (BRK) [109] Brooklyn, NY Our Lady of Refuge Church.
Alonso, Armando '90 (MIA) [27] Miami, FL St. Michael the Archangel Church.
Alonso, Ignacio *c.m.* '60 (PCE) [8] Ponce, PR La Milagrosa Church.
Alonso, Jose A. *l.c.* '64 (PRO) [T] Wakefield, RI "Mater Ecclesiae" International Formation Center.
Alonso, Msgr. Jose A. '68 (PAT) Absent on Leave.
Alonso, Jose Luis *o.p.* '61 (PCE) Yauco, PR Holy Rossary Church; [B] Ponce, PR The Pontifical Catholic University of Puerto Rico.
Alonso, Oscar *sch.p.* '68 (MIA) [C] Fort Lauderdale, FL Cardinal Gibbons High School.
Alonso, Santiago '50 (ELP) [35] El Paso, TX San Antonio Church.
Alookaran, Joy '80 (NEW) Scotch Plains, NJ St. Bartholomew Church.
Alphonse, Anthony '92 (TYL) Paris, TX Our Lady of Victory Church.
Alphonso, John '68 (DAL) [I] Dallas, TX St. Paul Medical Center.
Alrutz, Paul *s.m.a.* '75 (BO) [W] Dedham, MA African Mission House and African Cultural Center.
Alsola, Felix '86 (DET) [H] Southfield, MI Providence Hospital.
Alt, Clement B. *c.pp.s.* '51 (CIN) Rockford, OH St. Teresa Church.
Alt, Kenneth G. *c.pp.s.* '78 (FTW) [11] Fort Wayne, IN Most Precious Blood Church.
Altamira, Francisco *m.sp.s.* '39 (LA) [3] Oxnard, CA Our Lady of Guadalupe Parish Church.
Altavilla, Philip A. '92 (SCR) [21] Scranton, PA St. Patrick's Church.
Altavista, Salvatore D. *m.s.* '64 (HRT) [M] Hartford, CT Missionaries of LaSalette Provincial Secretary.
Altenbaugh, Richard L. '60 (PT) [9] Pensacola, FL St. John the Evangelist Church.
Altermatt, Gregory '76 (HRT) [I] Waterbury, CT St. Mary Hospital.
Althoff, Arthur J. '55 (STL) [5] Lemay, MO St. Martin of Tours Church.
Althoff, Gaudentius '38 (SFS) Retired.
Altier, Robert J. '89 (STP) [12] St. Paul, MN St. Agnes Church.
Altine, Richard L. '95 (KAL) Battle Creek, MI St. Philip Church.
Altman, David *o.c.s.o.* '79 (SLC) [F] Huntsville, UT Abbey of Our Lady of the Holy Trinity of the Order of Cistercians.
Altman, Joseph W. '76 (CHI) Harvey, IL Ascension-St. Susanna Church.
Altmann, George '44 (BAL) Retired.
Altmann, Robert T. '62 (LC) [5] Wausau, WI St. Matthew Church.
Alton, Ed (CHL) [L] Charlotte, NC Diocesan Office of Campus Ministry.
Altrui, Ronald P. '81 (NY) Beacon, NY St. Joachim Church.
Altstock, Edward '59 (P) Molalla, OR St. James Church.
Altuna, Javier *s.j.* '66 (LA) Inglewood, CA St. John Chrysostom Church.
Alvar, Zosimo, Jr. '89 (SFR) Burlingame, CA St. Catherine of Siena Church.
Alvarado, Felix E. '90 (PCE) Aguirre, PR Sacred Heart Church.
Alvarado, John P. '88 (MET) [3] Perth Amboy, NJ Holy Trinity Church.
Alvarado, Marco Antonio '83 (CHI) [82] Chicago, IL Holy Innocents Church.
Alvarado, Robert *c.m.f.* '39 (SAT) [12] San Antonio, TX Immaculate Heart of Mary Church.
Alvarado, Roberto '89 (ELP) [31] El Paso, TX St. Raphael Church.
Alvares, Augustine '50 (P) Retired.
Alvarez, Abel *o.s.a.* '58 (NY) [49] New York, NY Holy Rosary Church; Bronx, NY Lincoln Medical and Mental Health Center.
Alvarez, Anthony M. '93 (MET) On Duty Outside the Diocese.
Alvarez, Antonio '85 (ARE) On Duty Outside the Diocese.
Alvarez, Armando '72 (SJN) [45] San Juan, PR Ntra. Sra. del Perpetuo Socorro Church.
Alvarez, Eduardo *s.j.* '74 (MIA) [D] Miami, FL Belen Jesuit Preparatory School; [H] Miami, FL Jesuit Fathers of the Province of the Antilles, Inc.
Alvarez, Fred *s.a.* '61 (NY) [Z] Garrison, NY Franciscan Friars of the Atonement.
Alvarez, Isaias *o.s.a.* (SJN) [15] Bayamon, PR Ntra. Sra. Monserrate Church.
Alvarez, Javier *o.f.m.* '89 (LA) [72] Los Angeles, CA St. Joseph Church.
Alvarez, Jay '81 (PMB) [F] Delray Beach, FL Opus Dei.
Alvarez, Julio '75 (WDC) Hyattsville, MD St. Mark Church.
Alvarez, Manuel '44 (SFE) Retired.
Alvarez, Michael *s.d.b.* '79 (LA) [C] Rosemead, CA Don Bosco Technical Institute.
Alvarez, Miguel *c.s.* (CHI) [122] Chicago, IL Santa Maria Addolorata Church.
Alvarez, Miguel *sch.p.* '61 (PCE) [4] Ponce, PR Our Lady of Mt. Carmel Church; [B] Ponce, PR The Pontifical Catholic University of Puerto Rico.
Alvarez, Milton *c.m.f.* '77 (CHI) [N] Oak Park, IL Claretian Fathers Headquarters of U.S.A. Eastern Province.
Alvarez, Pablo *f.s.s.p.* '86 (SCR) [M] Elmhurst, PA Priestly Fraternity of St. Peter (F.S.S.P.).
Alvarez, Pablo D. *f.s.s.p.* '86 (LR) [L] Little Rock, AR Priestly Fraternity of St. Peter.
Alvarez, Pablo D. '86 (PCE) On Duty Outside the Diocese.
Alvarez, Perfecto *o.s.a.* '52 (PCE) [B] Ponce, PR The Pontifical Catholic University of Puerto Rico; [D] Ponce, PR Home for Aged and Infirm.
Alvarez, Pompilio '60 (NY) [130] Bronx, NY St. Athanasius Church.
Alvarez, Porfirio '69 (LA) Santa Fe Springs, CA St. Pius X Church.
Alvarez, Rafael *o.f.m.* '95 (LA) [68] Los Angeles, CA Santa Isabel Church.
Alvarez, Ramon (SJN) [F] Guaynabo, PR Opus Dei.
Alvarez, Ramon '82 (DAL) [16] Dallas, TX St. Edward Church.
Alvarez, Victor *s.s.p.* '83 (YAK) Toppenish, WA St. Aloysius Church.
Alvarez, Xavier '73 (AMA) Absent on Leave.
Alvernaz, Dennis M. '71 (FRS) Yosemite National Park, CA Our Lady of the Snows Church.
Alves, Eugene L. '61 (BO) [2] Gloucester, MA Our Lady of Good Voyage Church.
Alves, Francis *s.j.* '95 (WDC) [M] Washington, DC The Jesuit Community at Georgetown University.
Alves, Msgr. Joseph T. '53 (BO) Retired.
Alves, Ronald *c.m.f.* '72 (FRS) [8] Fresno, CA St. Anthony Claret Church.
Alvesteffer, Eugene '65 (GR) Retired.
Alvey, J. Paul '53 (SC) Retired.
Alvey, Leonard J. '58 (OWN) Non-Parochial Assignments; [A] Owensboro, KY Brescia College.
Alvez, Angel Oscar *l.d.* '96 (PCE) [18] Ponce, PR Church Santisimo Sacramento Church.
Alwell, Juniper *o.f.m.conv.* '56 (R) Burlington, NC Blessed Sacrament Church.
Alyward, James W. '64 (SFR) Burlingame, CA St. Catherine of Siena Church.
Alzate, Alberto '77 (LAV) [6] Las Vegas, NV St. Anne Church.
Alzert, Edward (TR) [L] Lawrenceville, NJ Morris Hall-Saint Lawrence, Inc.
Alzugaray, Msgr. Joseph '67 (SR) Petaluma, CA St. James Church.
Amabile, Patsy C. '73 (CAM) [5] Cherry Hill, NJ St. Thomas More Church.
Amachei, Jerome (SY) [1] Syracuse, NY The Cathedral of the Immaculate Conception.
Amadeo, Michael (DM) On Special Assignment.
Amador, Alfonso *c.ss.r.* (CGS) Fajardo, PR Santiago Apostol Church.
Amador, Alfonso *c.ss.r.* '58 (SJN) [2] San Juan, PR San Agustin Church.
Amaldoss, '78 (NO) [8] Metairie, LA St. Edward the Confessor Church.
Amalfitano, Joseph A. '63 (PH) Marcus Hook, PA Immaculate Conception Church.
Amalraj, Loyola '81 (MIL) Muskego, WI St. Leonard Congregation Church.
Amanchukwu, Emeka Godfrey '89 (NY) Ardsley, NY Our Lady of Perpetual Help Church.
Amandolare, Msgr. Ronald A. '61 (PAT) Chatham, NJ St. Patrick's Church.
Amann, John J. '66 (BRK) [161] Queens, NY St. Catherine of Sienna Church.
Amann, Msgr. Robert A. '50 (CIN) [33] Cincinnati, OH Holy Angels Church.
Amann, Steven J. '74 (MIL) New Berlin, WI St. Elizabeth Ann Seton Church.
Amann, William '54 (ROC) Hamlin, NY St. Elizabeth Ann Seton Church.
Amantegui, Carmelo *s.j.* (NY) [152] Bronx, NY St. Jerome's Church.
Amantia, Damian-Vincent *t.o.r.* '90 (FWT) [8] Fort Worth, TX St. Andrew Church.
Amanzeh, Augustine '74 (SAT) San Antonio, TX San Antonio State Hospital.
Amar, Joseph P. '74 (FTW) [B] Notre Dame, IN University of Notre Dame Du Lac.
Amar, Joseph P. '74 (SAM) On Duty Outside the Diocese.
Amar, Mubarak Anwar '91 (PEO) Elkhart, IL St. Patrick Church.
Amaral, Angelo (NEW) [17] Newark, NJ St. James Church.
Amaral, Stephen P. '78 (PRO) [N] Peace Dale, RI St. Dominic Savio Youth Center; [N] Peace Dale, RI Tower Hill Camp.
Amaraseka, Giles '73 (AUS) [14] Austin, TX St. John Neumann Church.
Amato, Antonio '61 (PRT) Dexter, ME St. Ann's Church.
Amato, Benet *o.s.b.* '79 (IND) Cannelton, IN St. Michael Church; Tell City, IN St. Paul Church; Troy, IN St. Pius Church; [J] St. Meinrad, IN St. Meinrad Archabbey.
Amato, Frank *s.a.c.* '88 (BRK) [110] Brooklyn, NY Our Lady of the Rosary of Pompeii Church.
Amato, Joseph '59 (ALB) Retired.
Amato, Joseph S. '59 (VEN) [3] Sarasota, FL St. Martha Church.
Amato, Msgr. Nicholas P. '70 (BAL) Parkton, MD Our Lady of Grace Church.
Amato, Salvatore '69 (BRK) [233] Queens, NY Resurrection-Ascension Church.
Amberger, Frank '96 (CIN) Coldwater, OH Holy Trinity Church.
Ambert, Jorge *s.j.* '66 (SJN) [22] San Juan, PR San Ignacio de Loyola Church; [C] Hato Rey, PR Renovacion Conyugal.
Ambosta, Dawson '75 (NY) Bronxville, NY St. Joseph Church.
Ambre, John T. '75 (GRY) [12] East Chicago, IN St. Patrick Church.
Ambrogi, James J. '64 (PH) Malvern, PA St. Patrick Church.
Ambros, Joseph M. '46 (WDC) [B] Washington, DC Diocesan Laborer Priests, House of Studies.
Ambrose, Thomas E. *s.j.* '47 (NY) [Z] New York, NY Murray-Weigel Hall.
Ambrosio, Joseph '74 (NEW) [28] Newark, NJ Our Lady of Mt. Carmel Church.
Ambrosy, David J. '85 (DUB) [11] Dubuque, IA St. Joseph the Worker Church.
Amedee, Msgr. Francis J. '48 (HT) [1] Thibodaux, LA St. Joseph Co-Cathedral; [E] Thibodaux, LA St. Joseph Manor.
Ameling, Richard H. '66 (GRY) [2] Michigan City, IN Notre Dame Church.
Amen, Maurice E. *c.s.c.* '61 (FTW) [J] South Bend, IN Congregation of Holy Cross Indiana Province Provincial House.
Amengual, Miguel '46 (LA) Torrance, CA Nativity Church.
Ament, Msgr. Ernest P. '29 (DUB) Bellevue, IA St.

Joseph's Church; Retired.
Ament, Richard J. '66 (DUB) Central City, IA St. Stephen's Church; Coggon, IA St. John the Evangelist Church; Prairieburg, IA St. Joseph's Church.
Ament, Robert J. '52 (DUB) Chester, IA St. Stephen's Church; Lourdes, IA Our Lady of Lourdes Church.
Amerando, Jerry '84 (FRS) Visalia, CA St. Mary Church.
Amershek, Charles M., Jr. '75 (ALT) [6] Johnstown, PA St. Rochus Church.
Ames, Gregory K. '86 (DEN) Greeley, CO St. Peter Church; [P] Greeley, CO University of Northern Colorado (Greeley).
Ames, John J. '82 (PH) Conshohocken, PA St. Matthew Church; [D] Springfield, PA Cardinal O'Hara High School.
Amesse, Michael J. *o.m.i.* '84 (HBG) Dallastown, PA St. Joseph Church.
Amey, Robert G. '69 (WDC) [4] Silver Spring, MD St. Catherine Laboure Church.
Amezaga, Louis D. '96 (LSC) [1] Las Cruces, NM Cathedral of Immaculate Heart of Mary.
Amezcua, Alfonso *o.r.c.* '87 (PCE) Adjuntas, PR St. Joachim Church; Castaner, PR Our Lady of the Miraculous Medal Church.
Amezcua, Pedro E. *o.r.c.* '86 (SB) Mecca, CA Our Lady of Guadalupe Shrine Church; [1] Riverside, CA Our Lady of Guadalupe Shrine Church; [E] Riverside, CA Operarios Del Reino De Cristo, O.R.C.
Amico, Alexander D. '73 (E) Coalport, PA St. Basil the Great Church.
Amico, Charles R. '52 (BUF) [A] East Aurora, NY Christ the King Seminary.
Amico, Francis A. *c.s.b.* '75 (GAL) [Q] Sugar Land, TX Basilian Mission Center.
Amico, Nicholas H. '51 (DET) Oak Park, MI Our Lady of Fatima Church.
Amico, Msgr. Richard S. '60 (BUF) [5] Niagara Falls, NY St. Joseph Church.
Amidon, Philip *s.j.* '74 (OM) [23] Omaha, NE St. John Church.
Amidon, Philip R. *s.j.* '74 (OM) [K] Omaha, NE Jesuit Community At Creighton University.
Amiot, Ronald J. *s.j.* (BO) [W] Weston, MA Campion Center; [Y] Weston, MA Campion Renewal Center.
Amiro, Raymond M. '43 (SFE) Retired.
Amirtharaj, Arokiyam *s.d.b.* (CIN) [54] Cincinnati, OH St. Louis Church.
Amissah, Kofi '79 (ALB) [6] Albany, NY St. George Church; Special Assignment.
Ammering, Bruce F. '54 (ROC) [8] Rochester, NY Blessed Sacrament Church.
Amo, Steven '92 (SPR) West Springfield, MA St. Thomas the Apostle Church.
Amodio, Francis *o.carm.* '82 (NY) [97] New York, NY Our Lady of the Scapular/St. Stephen Church.
Amora, Ben (TR) Tuckerton, NJ St. Teresa Church.
Amora, Edito '77 (TR) Brick Town, NJ Visitation Church.
Amore, Innocent *o.f.m.cap.* '34 (NY) [B] Beacon, NY St. Lawrence of Brindisi Friary.
Amoros, Juan Maria *o.carm.* '55 (MGZ) Anasco, PR St. Anthony Abbot Church.
Amos, Msgr. James '54 (PT) [3] Pensacola, FL Holy Spirit Church; [E] Tallahassee, FL Casa Calderon, Inc.
Amos, Msgr. John R. '73 (MOB) Mon Luis Island, AL St. Rose of Lima Church.
Amos, Martin J. '68 (CLV) Shaker Heights, OH St. Dominic Church.
Amrhein, Peter T. '48 (MIL) Retired; [N] Wauwatosa, WI St. Camillus Health Center, Inc.
Amrhein, Quentin *c.p.* '53 (HRT) [M] West Hartford, CT Holy Family Monastery/Retreat.
Amrhein, Raphael *c.p.* '62 (PMB) [G] North Palm Beach, FL Our Lady of Florida Spiritual Center.
Amrhein, Robert *o.f.m.conv.* '62 (SY) [2] Syracuse, NY Assumption B.V.M. Church; Syracuse, NY St. Joseph's Hospital Health Center; [O] Syracuse, NY St. Joseph's Hospital Health Center.
Amundarain, Atanasio *c.p.* (SJN) [9] Carolina, PR Santa Gema Galgani Church.
Amundsen, Robert L. '69 (DEN) [3] Fort Collins, CO John XXIII University Parish Church; [P] Fort Collins, CO Colorado State University (Fort Collins).
Amy, Msgr. Peter L. '64 (LA) Sylmar, CA St. Didacus Church.
Amyot, Andrew J. '64 (OG) Norfolk, NY Visitation of the B.V.M. Church.
An Ninh, Vincent Nguyen '71 (DET) Clawson, MI Guardian Angels Church.
Anable, Richard J. *s.j.* '45 (PAT) [I] Morristown, NJ Loyola House of Retreats.
Anadore, Charles E. '50 (BO) [1] Milton, MA St. Agatha Church; Retired.
Anania, Alexis *o.f.m.* (PIT) [N] McKeesport, PA Franciscan Friars.
Anastasia, Tom '91 (SP) Valrico, FL St. Stephen Church.
Anastasio, Thomas '58 (BRK) [115] Brooklyn, NY St. Patrick Church.
Ancharski, John J. '83 (TUC) Solomon, AZ Our Lady of Guadalupe Church; Safford, AZ Conservation Center; Fort Grant Rural Station, AZ Fort Grant Training Center; Solomon, AZ Our Lady of Guadalupe.
Ancheril, Jose '86 (BEL) St. Libory, IL St. Liborius Church.
Ancona, Msgr. Gaspar F. '63 (GR) Byron Center, MI St. Sebastian's Church.
Anctil, Leo '43 (SUP) Retired.
Anctil, Peter Claude *o.s.b.* '67 (BUR) [G] Weston, VT Priory of Benedictine Monks.
Andalikiewicz, Charles '58 (KCK) [6] Kansas City, KS Sacred Heart Church; [12] Kansas City, KS St. John the Evangelist Church.
Andary, Edward J. '69 (PBL) Aguilar, CO St. Anthony Church; Walsenburg, CO St. Mary Church.
Andary, John S. '51 (SAM) Retired.
Andary, Thomas M. '41 (MAR) Retired.
Andel, David '95 (SB) [6] Riverside, CA St. Catherine of Alexandria Church.
Anderl, Henry *o.s.b.* '45 (SCL) [I] Collegeville, MN St. John's Abbey, of the Order of St. Benedict.
Anderlonis, Joseph J. '69 (PH) [49] Philadelphia, PA St. George Church.
Anders, Arnold '50 (VIC) Ganado, TX Assumption of the B.V.M. Church.
Anderson, Alexander R. '75 (STL) Eureka, MO Sacred Heart Church.
Anderson, Andrew '74 (MIA) [1] Miami, FL St. Mary's Cathedral.
Anderson, Anthony *s.o.l.t.* '91 (CC) Robstown, TX St. Anthony Church; [H] Robstown, TX Society of Our Lady of the Most Holy Trinity.
Anderson, Arthur *o.f.m.* '83 (CHI) [N] Chicago, IL St. Joseph Friary.
Anderson, Arthur C. '62 (RVC) Brookville, NY St. Paul the Apostle Church.
Anderson, Arthur Edward '60 (SD) Retired.
Anderson, Arthur T. '58 (CAM) [9] Camden, NJ Sacred Heart Church; [G] Camden, NJ Our Lady of Lourdes Medical Center, Inc.
Anderson, B. Ernest '82 (B) Aberdeen, ID Blessed Sacrament Church; American Falls, ID St. Mary Church.
Anderson, Basil J. *o.s.b.* '54 (MIL) [P] Benet Lake, WI St. Benedict's Abbey.
Anderson, Bertil J. '74 (PRO) [8] Warwick, RI St. Rita's Church.
Anderson, Daniel J. *o.f.m.* '76 (CIN) [M] Cincinnati, OH Pleasant Street Friary.
Anderson, Edward C. *c.s.v.* '50 (LAV) [D] Las Vegas, NV Clerics of St. Viator Retirement Home.
Anderson, Emil '64 (E) Retired.
Anderson, Emil '64 (SEA) Kirkland, WA Holy Family Church.
Anderson, Gabriel C. '89 (DUB) Dyersville, IA Basilica of St. Francis Xavier.
Anderson, George M. *s.j.* '73 (NY) [80] New York, NY Nativity Church; [Z] New York, NY "America;" Residence and publication office of the America Press.
Anderson, Gregory H. *o.p.* '47 (SFR) [13] San Francisco, CA St. Dominic Church; [N] San Francisco, CA St. Dominic Priory.
Anderson, James B. '78 (GAL) [A] Houston, TX St. Mary's Seminary.
Anderson, John *c.ss.r.* '40 (BO) [13] Boston, MA Basilica of Our Lady of Perpetual Help.
Anderson, John C. '59 (PEO) Special Assignment; [M] Henry, IL King's House of Retreats - Diocese of Peoria.
Anderson, John C. '93 (SUP) [1] Superior, WI Cathedral of Christ the King.
Anderson, John D. '62 (FAR) Hankinson, ND St. Philip's Church.
Anderson, John E. '66 (LSC) [2] Las Cruces, NM Holy Cross Church.
Anderson, John F. '50 (CLV) Chesterland, OH St. Anselm Church; Retired.
Anderson, John R. '96 (ATL) Alpharetta, GA St. Thomas Aquinas Church.
Anderson, Msgr. John V. '52 (DEN) [1] Denver, CO Cathedral of the Immaculate Conception.
Anderson, Jordan S. *o.praem* '96 (ORG) [D] Siverado, CA St. Michael's College Preparatory High School; [H] Silverado, CA Norbertine Fathers.
Anderson, Joseph G. '63 (MIL) [2] South Milwaukee, WI St. John's Church.
Anderson, Joseph K. *o.s.b.* '54 (LSC) Deming, NM Holy Family Church.
Anderson, Joseph R. '48 (SFS) Retired.
Anderson, Joseph W. '62 (PEO) [2] La Salle, IL St. Hyacinth's Church.
Anderson, Jude *o.s.b.* '94 (B) [C] Jerome, ID Ascension Priory.
Anderson, Kenneth J. '87 (RCK) Fulton, IL Immaculate Conception Church.
Anderson, Kevin '83 (SCL) [10] St. Cloud, MN Christ Church; [L] St. Cloud, MN Newman Center, Inc.
Anderson, Knute *o.s.b.* '56 (SCL) [I] Collegeville, MN St. John's Abbey, of the Order of St. Benedict.
Anderson, Louis L. '63 (GR) [17] Grand Rapids, MI St. Mary Magdalen Church.
Anderson, Luke *s.o.cist.* '54 (ALN) [K] New Ringgold, PA Cistercian Conventual Priory, St. Mary's Priory.
Anderson, Msgr. Marcel '57 (ALX) Retired.
Anderson, Mark R. '86 (E) Morrisdale, PA St. Agnes Church.
Anderson, Michael F. '83 (STP) [16] St. Paul, MN St. Bernard Church.
Anderson, R. Bentley *s.j.* '96 (BO) [W] Chestnut Hill, MA The Jesuit Community at Boston College.
Anderson, Richard W. *s.j.* '66 (CHI) [C] Chicago, IL Jesuit Community at Loyola University of Chicago.
Anderson, Robert L. *s.j.* '50 (NO) [C] New Orleans, LA Loyola University.
Anderson, Robert M. *o.s.m.* '65 (ORG) [H] Buena Park, CA Servite Fathers And Brothers.
Anderson, Ronald '72 (DET) Milford, MI St. Mary, Our Lady of the Snows Church.
Anderson, Ronald *s.j.* '83 (BO) [W] Chestnut Hill, MA The Jesuit Community at Boston College.
Anderson, Ronald C. '66 (BWN) Absent.
Anderson, Stephen A. '59 (E) [B] Erie, PA Mercyhurst College.
Anderson, Stephen A. '79 (E) [P] Erie, PA Newman Centers and Campus Ministry.
Anderson, Terence '84 (SFS) Faulkton, SD St. Thomas the Apostle Church.
Anderson, William A. '63 (WH) Elkins, WV St. Brendan Church.
Anderson, William C. '52 (TR) Holmdel, NJ St. Benedict Church.
Anderson, William R. '42 (BO) Retired.
Andert, Thomas *o.s.b.* '75 (SCL) [I] Collegeville, MN St. John's Abbey, of the Order of St. Benedict.
Andicoechea, Anselmo *c.p.* (SJN) [9] Carolina, PR Santa Gema Galgani Church.
Andonian, Rafael *c.m.vd.* (BO) [5] Cambridge, MA Holy Cross Church.
Andonian, Raphael *o.m.ven.* '65 (ARM) Boston, MA Holy Cross Church.
Andracki, Jerome *c.r.* '42 (CHI) [D] Chicago, IL Weber High School; [J] Chicago, IL Our Lady of the Resurrection Medical Center.
Andrade, Anthony *o.s.b.* (STP) [27] St. Paul, MN St. Mark Church.
Andrade, Antonio L. (BO) Boston, MA Boston City Hospital.
Andrade, Bernardino '65 (OAK) Oakley, CA St. Anthony Church.
Andrade, David M. (FR) [22] Fall River, MA St. William's Church.
Andrade, Richard G. '83 (FR) [K] Fall River, MA St. John Vianney House.
Andrae, Henry C. '78 (E) Stoneboro, PA St. Columbkille Church.
Andraschko, Msgr. James F. '59 (SFS) [3] Sioux Falls, SD Holy Spirit Church.
Andre, Leonard J. '61 (MIL) Retired.
Andre, Ludwig M. '57 (SJ) Los Altos, CA St. Simon Church.
Andreatta, Msgr. Tullio '38 (SB) Retired.
Andree, Daniel *c.ss.r.* '80 (WCH) [14] Wichita, KS St. Joseph Church; [G] Wichita, KS Redemptorist Mission House.
Andree, John *c.ss.r.* '68 (CHI) [9] Chicago, IL St. Alphonsus Church; [136] Chicago, IL St. Michael Church.
Andres, Anthony G. '45 (CIN) [56] Cincinnati, OH St. Margaret Mary Church.
Andres, Edmundo *c.m.f.* '56 (CHI) [N] Oak Park, IL Claretian Fathers Headquarters of U.S.A. Eastern Province.
Andres, James R. *o.f.m.cap.* '63 (DET) [P] Washington, MI Capuchin Retreat.
Andres, Joseph P. '48 (CIN) Retired.
Andres, Timothy *o.carm.* '86 (JOL) [J] Joliet, IL St. Elias Carmelites.
Andreu, Ramon *s.j.* '55 (LA) [73] Los Angeles, CA St. Kevin Church.
Andrews, Alexander *o.s.b.* '69 (SCL) [I] Collegeville, MN St. John's Abbey, of the Order of St. Benedict.
Andrews, Dennis M. '65 (MIL) Brookfield, WI St. John Vianney Church.
Andrews, Dennis M. *c.s.b.* '70 (GAL) [Q] Houston, TX Residence of the Basilian Fathers of the University of St. Thomas.
Andrews, Edward *o.s.a.* '59 (CHI) [D] Chicago, IL St. Rita High School; [N] Chicago, IL St. Rita Monastery.
Andrews, Eric *c.s.p.* '95 (NY) [104] New York, NY St. Paul the Apostle Church.
Andrews, Gregory J. '76 (SP) [1] Clearwater, FL All Saints Church.
Andrews, John '96 (OM) On Duty Outside the Archdiocese.
Andrews, John F. '62 (FR) [19] Fall River, MA St. Patrick's Church.
Andrews, Lawrence W. '78 (OG) Absent on Leave.
Andrews, Mark J. *s.j.* (DET) [B] Berkley, MI Loyola House.
Andrews, Mark W. *s.j.* '92 (CHI) [D] Wilmette, IL

Loyola Academy.
Andrews, Peter J. '88 (PRO) [1] Providence, RI Cathedral of SS. Peter and Paul.
Andrews, Robert *o.s.a.* '55 (PH) Havertown, PA St. Denis Church.
Andrews, William L. '42 (CLV) [4] Lakewood, OH St. James Church; Retired.
Andrey, Robert '83 (SFR) [41] San Francisco, CA St. Patrick Church.
Andrie, Donald *c.s.p.* '94 (COL) [J] Columbus, OH Campus Ministry.
Andriekus, Leonard *o.f.m.* '40 (PRT) [I] Kennebunkport, ME St. Anthony's Friary.
Andries, John W. '96 (ALX) Plaucheville, LA Mater Dolorosa Church.
Andrus, Albin '73 (PRT) [1] Portland, ME Cathedral of the Immaculate Conception; Portland, ME Maine Medical Center.
Andrus, Albin A. '73 (PRT) [M] South Portland, ME Southern Maine Technical College.
Andrus, Charles *s.s.j.* '76 (LA) [51] Los Angeles, CA St. Brigid's Church.
Andrus, David L. *s.j.* '79 (LAF) [A] Grand Coteau, LA St. Charles College.
Andrus, Richard R. *s.v.d.* '83 (STL) [53] St. Louis, MO St. Nicholas Church.
Andrushkiw, Vladimir '36 (STF) Retired.
Anduaga, Francisco J. *c.r.l.* '67 (ARE) Corozal-Palmarito, PR La Milagrosa Church.
Andujar, J. Iriarte *o.p.* '86 (PRO) [P] Providence, RI St. Thomas Aquinas Priory at Providence College.
Angadiath, Jacob '72 (DAL) [25] Dallas, TX St. Pius X Church; [5] Garland, TX St. Thomas the Apostle Church.
Angelicchio, Paul F. '77 (SY) Fairmount, NY Holy Family Church.
Angelini, Joseph *o.f.m.conv.* '65 (NEW) [2] Hoboken, NJ St. Joseph's Church.
Angelini, Joseph *o.f.m.conv.* '65 (TR) Point Pleasant Beach, NJ St. Peter Church.
Angelini, Joseph '67 (MIA) [35] Miami, FL Visitation Church.
Angell, Charles *s.a.* '60 (NY) [Z] Garrison, NY Franciscan Friars of the Atonement; [Z] Garrison, NY St. Christopher's Friary.
Angella, Ludovico '47 (NY) Middletown, NY St. Joseph Church.
Angelle, Msgr. Robert G. '56 (LAF) [14] Lafayette, LA St. Mary, Mother of the Church.
Angelo, Girard F. '55 (SCR) Harleigh, PA Sacred Heart of Jesus Church.
Angelo, Thomas M. '85 (NOR) Military Chaplains.
Angeloni, Michael A. '75 (WIL) Milford, DE St. John the Apostle Church.
Angeloni, Owen *o.f.m.* '62 (ALB) [A] Catskill, NY St. Anthony Friary.
Angelov, Kiril '89 (STF) Ludlow, MA SS. Peter and Paul Church; South Deerfield, MA Holy Ghost Church.
Angelovic, Michael '65 (SEA) [21] Seattle, WA Assumption Church.
Angelucci, Patrick *s.d.b.* '74 (PAT) [D] Paterson, NJ Don Bosco Technical High School.
Anger, Raymond G. '57 (WOR) Retired.
Angers, Joseph *o.p.* '48 (NSH) [I] Nashville, TN St. Cecilia Convent.
Angert, James *t.o.r.* '71 (STU) [A] Steubenville, OH Franciscan University of Steubenville; [F] Steubenville, OH Holy Spirit Monastery.
Angilella, Joseph T. *s.j.* '65 (SFR) [N] San Francisco, CA Jesuit Community at University of San Francisco.
Anginoli, Joseph T. '75 (PAT) Green Pond, NJ St. Simon the Apostle Church.
Angkel, Julio '83 (CI) Moen, FM Immaculate Heart of Mary Cathedral; [C] Tunnuk, Chuuk, FM Vicariate Residence.
Angle, Camillus *t.o.r.* '54 (ALT) [F] Newry, PA St. Bernardine Monastery.
Angles, Sebastian '44 (BRK) Retired.
Angles, Sebastian '44 (ORL) Retired.
Anglim, Ronald H. '65 (CHI) Libertyville, IL St. Joseph Church.
Anglim, Thomas M. '54 (VEN) [5] Fort Myers, FL St. Francis Xavier Church; [F] Fort Myers, FL Villa Francisco; [K] Fort Myers, FL St. Francis Xavier School Foundation.
Anglin, John *o.f.m.* '81 (BO) [W] Boston, MA Ministry of the Word.
Angotti, Joseph A. (GRY) Highland, IN St. James the Less Church.
Anguiano, James '82 (LA) [D] Playa Del Rey, CA St. Bernard High School.
Anguiano, James '85 (LA) Graduate Studies.
Angulo, Raul '85 (MIA) [8] Miami, FL Mother of Christ Church.
Anh, Anthony Nguyen Phuoc '90 (RVC) Dix Hills, NY St. Matthew Church.
Anholzer, Daniel *o.f.m.cap.* '80 (SAG) [14] Saginaw, MI St. Joseph Church.
Aniban, Toribio Ives '66 (SJ) San Jose, CA O'Connor Hospital; [H] San Jose, CA O'Connor Hospital.
Anich, Kenneth *s.v.d.* '73 (DUB) [B] Epworth, IA Divine Word College.
Aniefuna, Clifford *o.carm.* '83 (WDC) [B] Washington, DC Whitefriars Hall.
Aniello, Frederick M. '79 (HRT) Wethersfield, CT Incarnation Church.
Anifer, Jeffrey '67 (DET) Ecorse, MI St. Francis Xavier Church.
Aniszczyk, Leon S. '73 (MET) Sayreville, NJ St. Stanislaus Kostka Church.
Anithottom, Joseph *c.m.i.* (BEA) Dayton, TX St. Joseph the Worker Church.
Ankenbrandt, Thomas F. *s.j.* '60 (DET) [P] Clarkston, MI Colombiere Center.
Ankenbrandt, Thomas W. '56 (TOL) Retired.
Annese, Joseph P. '62 (LAV) Boulder City, NV St. Andrew's Church.
Annese, Lucius *o.f.m.* (BO) [3] Cambridge, MA St. Francis of Assisi Church.
Annie, Frederick P. '78 (WH) [1] Huntington, WV St. Joseph's Church; [B] Huntington, WV St. Joseph Central Catholic High School.
Annino, Sebastian V. '61 (CAM) Rosenhayn, NJ St. Mary's Church; [H] Newfield, NJ Mater Dei Nursing Home.
Annunziato, Michael *ss.cc.* '53 (BWN) Edinburg, TX Sacred Heart Church.
Anoia, John '57 (SP) [4] Clearwater, FL St. Cecelia Church.
Anoia, John '57 (SPR) Retired.
Anosike, Donatus Ugochukwu *m.s.p.* '90 (LKC) Welsh, LA St. Joseph Church.
Ansaldi, Msgr. Joseph C. '62 (NY) [F] New York, NY St. Joseph by the Sea, High School; [G] New York, NY Seton Foundation for Learning, Inc.; [O] New York, NY Mission of the Immaculate Virgin.
Ansbro, Msgr. Francis J. '51 (NY) Peekskill, NY Assumption Church.
Anschutz, Larry '82 (SFD) Mount Olive, IL Ascension Church; Mount Olive, IL Holy Trinity Church.
Anselment, Joseph '61 (ALB) Queensbury, NY Our Lady of the Annunciation Church.
Anselmi, Albert J.B. '71 (ALT) On Duty Outside the Diocese.
Anselmi, Albert J.B. '71 (WH) Coalton, WV St. Patrick Church. Huttonsville, WV St. John Bosco Church.
Anselmi, Victor J. '74 (ALN) Ringtown, PA St. Mary Church. [7] Shenandoah, PA St. Stephen Church.
Anslow, Thomas C. *c.m.* '72 (LA) [R] Los Angeles, CA Vincentian Fathers and Brothers.
Anson, Cesar R. '77 (TR) Medford, NJ St. Mary of the Lakes Church.
Anstiss, Arthur '60 (SFE) Retired.
Anta, Antonio '55 (NEW) Retired.
Antal, Andras '68 (CLV) [21] Cleveland, OH St. Elizabeth Church.
Antall, Richard C. '80 (CLV) Painesville, OH St. Mary Church; [X] Cleveland, OH Diocesan Hispanic Office.
Antao, Msgr. John S. '60 (NEW) [15] Elizabeth, NJ Our Lady of Fatima Church.
Antczak, John '63 (JOL) Bradley, IL St. Joseph Church; Kankakee, IL Riverside Medical Center.
Antczak, Robert A. '64 (NEW) [15] Jersey City, NJ St. Mary's Church.
Antekeier, Charles R. '62 (GR) [6] Grand Rapids, MI St. Francis Xavier Church.
Anthamatten, Joseph *c.pp.s.* '43 (CIN) [B] Carthagena, OH St. Charles.
Anthony, Angelo P. *c.pp.s.* '89 (CIN) [23] Dayton, OH Precious Blood Church; [M] Dayton, OH Provincial House of the Cincinnati Province of the Society of the Precious Blood; [U] Dayton, OH Community Support Charitable Trust.
Anthony, Edd *o.f.m.* '77 (STL) [P] St. Louis, MO Franciscan Friary of St. Anthony of Padua.
Anthony, Howard A. '59 (OKL) Retired.
Anthony, John Francis (NY) Staten Island, NY Staten Island University Hospital South.
Anthony, Joseph L. '80 (LAV) [12] Las Vegas, NV St. Joseph, Husband of Mary Church.
Anthony, Julian K. '66 (PHU) [A] Washington, DC St. Josaphat Seminary.
Anthony, Walter *c.s.p.* '56 (NY) [Z] Scarsdale, NY Paulist Fathers Generalate.
Antinarelli, Ronald A. '73 (ROC) Penfield, NY Holy Spirit Church.
Antipas, Douglas *o.f.m.cap.* (AGN) [F] Agana Heights, GU St. Fidelis Friary.
Antiporek, James W. '81 (JOL) Bolingbrook, IL St. Dominic Church.
Antl, Louis *o.f.m.* '48 (STL) [P] St. Louis, MO Franciscan Friary of St. Anthony of Padua.
Antle, Nicholas C. '59 (GAL) Retired.
Antoine, James *o.f.m.cap.* '67 (GF) Lodge Grass, MT Our Lady of Loretto Church.
Antolini, Vincenzo *o.m.v.* '58 (BO) [B] Boston, MA Oblate Provincialate.
Anton, Luciano *o.m.i.* '47 (LA) Pacoima, CA Mary Immaculate Church.
Anton, Ronald J. *s.j.* '83 (BAL) [C] Baltimore, MD Loyola College; [M] Baltimore, MD Jesuit Community of Loyola College, Inc.
Antonanzas, Msgr. Jesus R. Diez '57 (PCE) [A] Ponce, PR Diocesan Seminary.
Antoncic, Msgr. John J. '68 (BRK) [176] Queens, NY Holy Child Jesus Church.
Antone, William *o.m.i.* '80 (OAK) [N] Oakland, CA Oblate Provincial House & Procure.
Antonelli, Msgr. Louis '49 (CHK) MP San Isidro Mission Parish Church.
Antonelli, Robert C. *c.s.c.* '65 (FTW) [J] South Bend, IN Congregation of Holy Cross Indiana Province Provincial House.
Antonellis, Joseph A. '72 (BO) [2] Revere, MA Immaculate Conception Church.
Antonicelli, Charles V. '93 (WDC) [1] Silver Spring, MD St. Andrew Apostle Church.
Antonio, William (WDC) [B] Washington, DC Oblate College/Oblate Center for Mission Studies.
Antonitti, A. Felix '52 (NEW) [25] Newark, NJ St. Michael's Church.
Antonucci, Richard J. *o.praem.* '72 (PH) [Z] Philadelphia, PA St. Norbert Priory.
Antony, Asir (RVC) Rockville Centre, NY Mercy Medical Center; [I] Rockville Centre, NY Mercy Medical Center.
Antony, Charles '70 (NY) Absent on Leave.
Antony, George Koyikara '80 (BRK) [217] Queens, NY Our Lady of Perpetual Help Church.
Antony, John Francis (NY) [221] Staten Island, NY Our Lady Star of the Sea Church.
Antony, John K. '96 (LR) [5] Little Rock, AR Christ the King Church.
Antos, Paul J. '54 (ALB) [2] Watervliet, NY Immaculate Conception Church.
Antoun, Bernard '95 (OLD) North Hollywood, CA Jesus Sacred Heart Church.
Antoun, Msgr. Elie '80 (SAM) Retired.
Antouni, Bernard '95 (LA) [1] North Hollywood, CA Jesus Sacred Heart Antiochene Syrian Catholic Mission Church.
Antram, Cormac *o.f.m.* '54 (GLP) St. Michaels, AZ St. Michael Church.
Antry, Theodore J. *o.praem.* '66 (PH) [B] Paoli, PA Daylesford Abbey; [Z] Paoli, PA Daylesford Abbey.
Antunez, Roy L. *s.j.* '71 (P) [L] Portland, OR Jesuit Provincial Office (Oregon Prov.).
Antus, Lawrence T. *o.m.i.* '53 (DUL) Cook, MN St. Mary's Church.
Antus, Lawrence T. *o.m.i.* '58 (DUL) Orr, MN Holy Cross Church.
Antus, Roland J. '62 (DUL) Brainerd, MN St. Francis Church.
Antweiler, Donald J. '73 (JC) St. Thomas, MO St. Thomas the Apostle Church.
Antwi-Bosiako, Dominic (L) [19] Louisville, KY Christ the King Church.
Anukam, Anselm '79 (LA) El Segundo, CA St. Anthony Church.
Anumudu, Alphonsus '73 (NY) [89] New York, NY Our Lady of Lourdes Church.
Anuszewski, Albert *o.ss.t.* '91 (BAL) [M] Baltimore, MD Holy Trinity Monastery.
Anuszewski, Albert M. *o.ss.t.* '91 (WDC) [M] Hyattsville, MD St. John de Matha Monastery, Order of Most Holy Trinity.
Anuszewski, Damian *o.ss.t.* '79 (BAL) [M] Baltimore, MD Holy Trinity Monastery.
Anyaka, Godfrey (NY) Bronx, NY St. Barnabas Hospital.
Anyanwu, Celestine '83 (BRK) [170] Queens, NY St. Gabriel Church.
Anyanwu, Chris '80 (NEW) Newark, NJ St. Michael Medical Center.
Anyanwu, Chris '85 (NEW) [14] Newark, NJ Queen of Angels Church.
Anyimaduwireko, Joseph (NY) Nanuet, NY St. Anthony Church.
Anziano, James J. '81 (PH) [21] Philadelphia, PA St. Bartholomew Church.
Anzoategui, Francisco J. *s.x.* '88 (BO) [3] Peabody, MA St. John the Baptist Church; [W] Holliston, MA Xaverian Missionaries.
Apassa, Cyril '71 (RNO) [6] Reno, NV St. Therese Church of the Little Flower.
Apel, John A. *s.j.* '69 (CHY) St. Stephens, WY St. Stephen's Church; [C] St. Stephens, WY St. Stephens Mission - Jesuit Community.
Apoldite, Dennis A. '78 (TR) [11] Trenton, NJ Sacred Heart Church.
Apolinares, Jaime G. '42 (NO) [43] New Orleans, LA St. Maria Goretti Church.
Aponte, Eliud '86 (PCE) On Duty Outside the Diocese.
Apostoli, Andrew D. *c.f.r.* '67 (NY) [18] Yonkers, NY Most Holy Trinity Church; [A] Yonkers, NY St. Joseph's Seminary; [Z] Yonkers, NY Saint Felix Friary.
Appel, George '57 (BIR) On Duty Outside the Diocese.
Appelby, Gerald J. '59 (ROC) Pittsford, NY Church of the Transfiguration.
Appelt, Francis '52 (GRY) [K] Cedar Lake, IN Our Lady of Lourdes Friary.
Appicci, Richard D. *o.s.a.* '60 (PH) [Z] Villanova, PA

Provincial Offices of the Order of St. Augustine, Province of St. Thomas of Villanova; [Z] Villanova, PA St. Thomas Monastery.
Applegate, Gary '81 (KCK) Olathe, KS St. Paul's Church.
Applegate, Msgr. P.A Bennett '45 (COL) Retired.
Appleyard, Msgr. George '68 (SJP) McKees Rocks, PA St. John the Baptist Church; Pittsburgh, PA St. George Church.
Appleyard, Joseph A. *s.j.* '62 (BO) [W] Chestnut Hill, MA The Jesuit Community at Boston College.
Aquila, Samuel '76 (DEN) [1] Denver, CO Cathedral of the Immaculate Conception.
Aquino, James J. '65 (WOR) [11] Worcester, MA Our Lady of Loreto Church.
Aquino, Joseph G. *m.s.* '69 (ATL) Cartersville, GA St. Francis of Assisi Church.
Aquino, Msgr. Oscar '64 (NY) [36] New York, NY St. Francis de Sales Church.
Aquino, Peter M. '69 (NEW) [13] Elizabeth, NJ SS. Peter and Paul's Church.
Aracich, Anthony S. *s.j.* '67 (NY) [80] New York, NY Nativity Church.
Aracil, Xaver *s.d.b.* (NEW) [3] Elizabeth, NJ St. Anthony's Church.
Arackal, Joseph J. *v.c.* '67 (STP) Vermillion, MN St. John the Baptist Church.
Arackal, Mathew '81 (BIS) Hazelton, ND St. Paul Church; Linton, ND St. Anthony Church.
Aragon, Ramon '50 (SFE) [8] Albuquerque, NM Our Lady of Guadalupe Church.
Aragon, Salvador *o.f.m.* '55 (SFE) [1] Santa Fe, NM The Cathedral of San Francisco de Asis.
Aramburo, Eugenio '88 (MRY) Greenfield, CA Holy Trinity Church.
Aramburu, Jose A. *m.m.* '84 (NY) [Z] Maryknoll, NY Maryknoll Fathers and Brothers.
Arana, Francisco '64 (SJN) [1] Toa Baja, PR Nuestra Senora de Covadonga Church.
Arango, Gilbert L. '93 (STO) Modesto, CA St. Stanislaus Church.
Aranha, George A. '75 (SJ) [16] San Jose, CA St. Martin of Tours Church.
Araque, Alvaro U. '72 (STO) [8] Stockton, CA St. Mary of the Assumption Church.
Arata, Miguel A. '95 (NEW) [1] Garfield, NJ Our Lady of Mt. Virgin Church.
Araujo, Manuel *c.m.* '54 (MGZ) [8] Mayaquez, PR San Vicente Church.
Araujo, Robert J. *s.j.* '93 (BO) [W] Boston, MA The Society of Jesus of New England-Provincial Offices.
Aravindassery, Anthony '75 (CHI) [165] Chicago, IL St. Patrick Church.
Aravjo, Robert J. *s.j.* '93 (SPK) [C] Spokane, WA Gonzaga University.
Araya-Morales, Reynord '89 (ORL) [4] Lakeland, FL St. Joseph's Church.
Arbanas, Harold P. '48 (GF) Retired.
Arbelaez, Ernesto (STO) Hughson, CA St. Anthony Church.
Arbizu, Juventino '44 (NO) Retired.
Arboleda, Vidal '55 (ORL) [9] Orlando, FL St. John Vianney Church; Retired.
Arcamo, Floro B. '65 (SFR) Belmont, CA St. Mark Church.
Arce, Aaron *o.p.* '80 (SAT) San Antonio, TX Methodist Hospital; [B] San Antonio, TX Dominican Priory of Juan Macias.
Arce, Robert P. '64 (NY) [162] Bronx, NY St. Margaret Mary Church.
Arceneaux, Chester '92 (LAF) Abbeville, LA St. Therese of the Child Jesus Church.
Arceneaux, Jules M. '90 (LAF) Eunice, LA St. Thomas More Church.
Arceneaux, Louis A. *c.m.* '66 (LAF) [A] Grand Coteau, LA St. Charles College.
Archambault, Donald '70 (DET) [27] Detroit, MI St. Gerard Church.
Archambault, Msgr. Henry N. '59 (NOR) Taftville, CT Sacred Heart Church.
Archambault, Paul A. '72 (PRO) Absent on Leave.
Archambault, Richard L. '55 (NOR) [G] Putnam, CT Holy Spirit Provincial House.
Archer, Arthur A. '80 (NOR) Niantic, CT St. Agnes Church.
Archer, Richard R. *o.p.* '58 (BR) Ponchatoula, LA St. Joseph Church.
Archer, Scott '90 (PEO) Fairbury, IL St. John the Baptist Church.
Archer, W. Donald '48 (CR) Retired.
Archey, Eugene C. '40 (WOR) Retired.
Archuleta, Marvin *s.f.* '70 (WDC) [B] Silver Spring, MD Holy Family Seminary.
Arciga, Michael '92 (KC) Leave of Absence.
Arcilesi, Leonard '89 (OWN) Cadiz, KY St. Stephen Church.
Arciszewski, Gilbert G. '59 (MIL) [60] Milwaukee, WI Our Lady, Queen of Peace Church.
Arcuri, Carmen '61 (COL) [30] Columbus, OH St. Mary Magdalene Church.
Arcuri, Frank A. *s.j.* '56 (MIL) [P] Milwaukee, WI Jesuit Community at Marquette University.
Ardagh, Brian '95 (CHI) Orland Hills, IL St. Elizabeth Seton Church.
Ardis, John B. *c.s.p.* '90 (NY) [104] New York, NY St. Paul the Apostle Church.
Ardolf, Edward J. '64 (NU) North Mankato, MN Holy Rosary Church.
Ardolf, Paul C. '49 (STP) Norwood, MN Ascension Church.
Ardos, Msgr. George A. '59 (TR) Washington Crossing, NJ St. George Church; Trenton, NJ Mercer County Correction Center.
Ardouin, Beaubrun '93 (NEW) Roselle, NJ Church of St. Joseph the Carpenter.
Arehambault, James H. '67 (HRT) Retired.
Arejola, Rodolfo '68 (AGN) Asan, GU Holy Family, Nino Perdido Church.
Arel, Donald *o.m.i.* '64 (OAK) [A] Berkeley, CA The Jesuit School of Theology at Berkeley.
Arella, Msgr. Gerard J. '54 (BRK) [79] Brooklyn, NY St. Mark's Church.
Arenas, Msgr. Francisco '50 (SJN) [17] San Juan, PR Francisca Javiera Cabrini Church.
Arenas, Joseph Victor '70 (NY) [199] Staten Island, NY Blessed Sacrament Church.
Arens, John F. (BO) Absent on Sick Leave.
Arens, John F. '74 (BO) [E] Needham, MA St. Sebastian's Country Day School, Inc.
Arentsen, Edwin F. '43 (BEL) Retired.
Arenz, James *s.j.* '65 (LA) [C] Los Angeles, CA Loyola Marymount University.
Ares, Francisco J. '83 (BRK) [162] Queens, NY Christ the King Church.
Aresseril, Xavier '64 (B) Weiser, ID St. Agnes Church.
Aresta, Frank *s.c.j.* '81 (MIL) [P] Franklin, WI Villa Maria.
Arevalo, Joseph '65 (RVC) Huntington Station, NY St. Hugh of Lincoln Church.
Argent, Robert W. '55 (STL) [16] St. Louis, MO Resurrection of Our Lord Church.
Argentino, Ralph '68 (SP) Pinellas Park, FL Sacred Heart Church.
Argue, Patrick *ss.cc.* '62 (LA) [D] Mission Hills, CA Alemany High School; [R] Mission Hills, CA Congregation of the Sacred Hearts.
Arguelles, Antonio G. (CC) Retired.
Arguelles, I. Anthony '74 (BLX) [5] Biloxi, MS St. John Church; [6] Biloxi, MS St. Louis Church.
Arguinzoniz, Francisco '54 (PCE) On Duty Outside the Diocese.
Argullo, Msgr. Michael A. '37 (CAM) Haddon Heights, NJ St. Rose's Church; Retired.
Argy, Msgr. William '40 (OG) Retired.
Argy, Msgr. William J. '40 (OG) [1] Ogdensburg, NY St. Mary's Cathedral; Lisbon, NY SS. Philip and James Church.
Ariano, Msgr. Joseph W. '51 (OM) Retired.
Arias, Ariel '85 (RNO) Carson City, NV Corpus Christi Church.
Arias, David *o.a.r.* '52 (NEW) West New York, NJ St. Joseph of the Palisades Church.
Arias, Guillermo *s.j.* '72 (SJN) [22] San Juan, PR San Ignacio de Loyola Church.
Arias, Guillermo '73 (NEW) [24] Jersey City, NJ St. Paul of the Cross Church.
Arias, Herman '85 (PAT) [2] Passaic, NJ St. Anthony of Padua Church.
Arias, Hernan (PAT) Paterson, NJ Passaic County Jail.
Arias, Jesus '92 (MIA) [33] Miami, FL St. Timothy Church.
Arias, Jose *o.a.r.* '60 (NEW) [N] West Orange, NJ Augustinian Recollects.
Arico, Carl '60 (NEW) [5] Bayonne, NJ St. Vincent de Paul Church.
Aridas, Christopher '73 (RVC) Selden, NY St. Margaret of Scotland Church.
Arimond, James C.L. *s.j.* '70 (CHI) [D] Chicago, IL St. Ignatius Jesuit Community.
Arimond, Vincent '55 (DUL) [2] Duluth, MN Good Shepherd Church.
Arista, Gregario *o.a.r.* '96 (NY) [BB] Bronx, NY St. Joseph's Center.
Ariza, Campo E. (ARE) On Duty Outside the Diocese.
Ariza, Campo Emilio (CGS) [14] Caguas, PR, PR Divino Nino Church.
Ariza, Vicente (SJN) [F] Guaynabo, PR Opus Dei.
Arizpe, Samuel '87 (BWN) San Carlos, TX St. Joseph the Worker Church.
Arizti, Fernando *s.j.* '71 (LA) [51] Los Angeles, CA St. Brigid's Church.
Arkins, Michael *s.s.s.* (SLC) Salt Lake City, UT County Youth Detention Center.
Arkins, Michael J. *s.s.s.* '73 (SLC) [7] Taylorsville, UT St. Martin de Porres Church.
Arko, Richard '90 (CLV) [4] Barberton, OH St. Mary's Church.
Arle, David '84 (VEN) [1] Fort Myers, FL St. Vincent de Paul Church.
Arledge, Thaddaeus R. *o.s.b.* '56 (SEA) [M] Lacey, WA St. Martin's Abbey.
Arlotta, Jack '92 (NY) Rye, NY Resurrection Church.
Armando, Fuoco '43 (SHP) Retired.
Armas, Calixto '43 (SFR) [48] San Francisco, CA Star of the Sea Church.
Armas, James '43 (SFR) Retired.
Armato, Robert J. '95 (BRK) [182] Queens, NY The Incarnation Church.
Armbrust, Leo F. '77 (PMB) Special Assignment.
Armbruster, Julius *o.s.b.* '42 (SFS) [F] Marvin, SD Blue Cloud Abbey.
Armell, Francisco *o.c.* '68 (SJN) [61] San Juan, PR Santa Teresita Del Nino Jesus Church.
Armenio, Peter V. '80 (CHI) [W] Chicago, IL Opus Dei.
Armey, Charles R. '80 (WOR) [3] Southbridge, MA Sacred Heart Church.
Arminio, Alfonse M. '61 (NEW) Military Chaplains.
Arminio, Thomas G. '81 (NEW) Woodcliff Lake, NJ Our Lady Mother of the Church.
Armistead, John M. '71 (STO) [4] Stockton, CA St. George Church.
Arms, Michael M. '68 (STP) Lake Elmo, MN Guardian Angels Church.
Armshaw, Joseph R. *c.ss.r.* (NO) [P] Lacombe, LA Redemptorist Fathers and Brothers - Holy Redeemer Mission Center.
Armshaw, Msgr. Patrick J. '62 (RVC) Greenlawn, NY St. Francis of Assisi Church; [L] Bethpage, NY Central Council.
Armstrong, Christopher R. (CIN) [89] Cincinnati, OH St. William Church.
Armstrong, Daniel F. (IND) Richmond, IN Holy Family Church; Richmond, IN St. Andrew Church; Richmond, IN St. Mary Church; [N] Richmond, IN Earlham College Newman Center.
Armstrong, Daniel F. '78 (IND) Retired.
Armstrong, James L. '77 (PIT) [3] Butler, PA St. Paul Church.
Armstrong, John F. *s.j.* '78 (NO) [C] New Orleans, LA Loyola University; [P] New Orleans, LA Jesuit Provincial Office.
Armstrong, Msgr. Peter G. '54 (SFR) Redwood City, CA St. Pius Church.
Armstrong, Regis *o.f.m.cap.* '67 (NY) [Z] White Plains, NY St. Conrad Friary.
Armstrong, Msgr. Robert A. '62 (BAL) [1] Baltimore, MD Cathedral of Mary Our Queen.
Armstrong, Rodney J. *s.s.j.* '91 (BEA) [3] Beaumont, TX Blessed Sacrament Church.
Armstrong, Steven A. *s.j.* '87 (SFR) [38] San Francisco, CA Our Lady of Fatima Byzantine Catholic Church; [N] San Francisco, CA Jesuit Community at University of San Francisco.
Arnao, Thomas V. '82 (RVC) Merrick, NY Cure of Ars Church.
Arnaud, Michael J. '75 (LAF) [13] Lafayette, LA St. Leo Church.
Arnberg, Todd '76 (LUB) O'Donnell, TX St. Pius X Church.
Arneson, James E. '67 (IND) Retired.
Arnheiter, Burkard *o.s.b.* '37 (SCL) [I] Collegeville, MN St. John's Abbey, of the Order of St. Benedict.
Arnhols, Msgr. Richard J. '73 (NEW) [10] Elizabeth, NJ St. Patrick's Church.
Arnholt, Joseph M. '73 (PH) Ardmore, PA St. Colman Church.
Arnister, Msgr. Edward A. '79 (TR) [4] Trenton, NJ Holy Cross Church.
Arnold, Andrew L. '59 (WH) Retired.
Arnold, Msgr. Daniel K. '75 (E) [2] Erie, PA Blessed Sacrament Church.
Arnold, Edward C. '57 (NSH) Franklin, TN St. Philip Church.
Arnold, Edward R. *m.m.* '63 (NY) [Z] Maryknoll, NY Maryknoll Fathers and Brothers.
Arnold, J. Ralph '41 (BEL) Retired.
Arnold, John D. *s.j.* '73 (STL) [P] St. Louis, MO De Smet Jesuit High School Community.
Arnold, Robert P. '75 (SCR) Luzerne, PA Sacred Heart Church.
Arnold, Roger S. *s.v.d.* '61 (CHI) [B] Techny, IL Divine Word Residence; [N] Chicago, IL Divine Word Theologate; [N] Techny, IL Society of the Divine Word, Provincial Headquarter-Chicago Prov.
Arnold, Stanley (SPR) [F] Springfield, MA Mercy Hospital.
Arnold, William L. '80 (COL) Dover, OH St. Joseph Church.
Arnoldt, David M. '68 (WIN) Military Chaplains.
Arnone, Leo F. '93 (ALT) [I] University Park, PA Penn State Catholic Community.
Arnott, John J. (BUR) Bethel, VT St. Anthony Church.
Arnott, John J. '74 (PIT) On Duty Outside the Diocese.
Arnout, Eric R., Jr. '96 (ALN) [11] Allentown, PA St. Thomas More Church.
Arnsparger, Roger K. '77 (LEX) Corbin, KY Sacred Heart Church.
Arnzen, Kenneth '57 (B) Nezperce, ID Holy Trinity Church.
Arocho, Jose A. '91 (CGS) Yabucoa, PR Santos Angeles Cutodios Church.
Arocho, Marcelino '88 (MGZ) San German, PR San German de Auxerre Church.

Arockiam, Michaelsami (CHI) [140] Chicago, IL St. Monica Church.
Arokiasamy, G. '79 (NEW) [34] Newark, NJ Sacred Heart Church.
Arokiasamy, Kulan Daisamy '71 (DET) Eastpointe, MI St. Veronica Church.
Arokiasamy, Kulandiasamy (PH) [T] Meadowbrook, PA Holy Redeemer Hospital and Medical Center.
Arong, Jose R. *o.m.i.* '66 (OAK) [21] Oakland, CA Sacred Heart Church.
Aronica, Paul *s.d.b.* '47 (NY) [Z] New Rochelle, NY Salesian Provincial House.
Aronyu, Cuthbert '72 (OAK) [5] Oakland, CA St. Benedict Church.
Arpie, Msgr. Robert A. '47 (NY) Retired.
Arpin, Fred *c.ss.r.* '81 (OAK) [N] Oakland, CA Redemptorists.
Arputham, Michael A. '78 (NY) [201] Staten Island, NY St. Christopher Church.
Arquitt, William A. (DUB) Retired.
Arraiza, Luis Gerardo *o.f.m.cap.* '88 (SAT) [13] San Antonio, TX Our Lady of the Angels Church; [M] San Antonio, TX Capuchin Franciscan Friars (Spain).
Arrambide, James C. *c.ss.r.* (GAL) [50] Houston, TX St. Raphael the Archangel Church.
Arrando, Angelo S. '71 (BGP) [1] Danbury, CT St. Gregory's Church.
Arredondo, Jesus *m.sp.s.* '52 (LA) Huntington Park, CA St. Martha Church.
Arregui Moso, Miguel '59 (CGS) Juncos, PR Inmaculada Concepcion Church.
Arresta, Frank *s.c.j.* '81 (MIL) [P] Hales Corners, WI Priests of the Sacred Heart.
Arriaga, Romeo Rojas *o.f.m.* '93 (ELP) [B] El Paso, TX Roger Bacon College.
Arriage, Martin *o.f.m.* '74 (ELP) [B] El Paso, TX St. Anthony's School of Theology.
Arribas, Santiago *c.m.* '58 (ARE) [1] Manati, PR La Candelaria Church.
Arrien, Mariano *c.p.* '32 (ARE) Lares, PR St. Joseph Church.
Arrieta, David '62 (SJN) [19] San Juan, PR San Francisco de Monte Alvernia Church.
Arrilucea, Jesus Maria P. *o.a.r.* '65 (ELP) [8] El Paso, TX Guardian Angel Church.
Arrizurieta, Candido *c.m.* '54 (NY) [Z] New York, NY Vincentian Fathers.
Arrizurieta, Candido *c.m.* '56 (NY) [44] New York, NY Holy Agony Church.
Arroyave, Jhon J. '95 (GAL) Conroe, TX Sacred Heart Church.
Arroygo, Peter '85 (BO) [69] Boston, MA Sacred Heart Church.
Arroyo, Brigido U. '61 (AGN) Tamuning, GU St. Anthony and St. Victor Church.
Arroyo, Edward B. *s.j.* '75 (NO) [C] New Orleans, LA Loyola University.
Arroyo, Joseph A. *s.j.* '62 (PH) [C] Philadelphia, PA St. Joseph's University; [Z] Philadelphia, PA Jesuit Community at St. Joseph's University.
Arroyo, Mario J. '77 (GAL) Pasadena, TX St. Pius the Fifth Church.
Arroyo, Ricardo *o.f.m.* (ELP) Presidio, TX Santa Teresa de Jesus Church.
Arruda, Henry S. '67 (FR) [6] New Bedford, MA Our Lady of Mt. Carmel Church.
Arsenault, Edward J. '91 (MAN) [2] Manchester, NH St. Anne Church.
Arsenault, James M. '89 (RIC) West Point, VA Our Lady of the Blessed Sacrament Church.
Arsenault, Joseph B. *m.m.* '59 (NY) [Z] Maryknoll, NY Maryknoll Fathers and Brothers.
Arsenault, Raymond J. *s.m.* '51 (BO) [Y] Framingham Centre, MA The Marist House.
Arseneau, Vernon '72 (JOL) West Chicago, IL St. Mary Church.
Arseneault, David J. (ALT) Bakerton, PA Sacred Heart Church; Elmora, PA St. Jude Church; Spangler, PA Holy Cross Church; Spangler, PA St. Patrick's Church.
Arter, Ronald '61 (COL) Lancaster, OH St. Mark Church.
Arthasseril, Jerome S. '66 (NEW) Verona, NJ Our Lady of the Lake Church.
Arthur, David J. *c.s.c.* '54 (FR) [B] North Easton, MA Stonehill College.
Arthur, E. Eugene *s.j.* '66 (KC) [B] Kansas City, MO Rockhurst College; [J] Kansas City, MO Rockhurst College - Jesuit Community.
Arthur, Msgr. E. Robert '38 (WDC) Hospital & Nursing Home Ministries; [L] Washington, DC Jeanne Jugan Residence-St. Joseph's Villa.
Arthur, Francis *o.f.m.* '79 (SAG) [9] Bay City, MI St. Stanislaus Church.
Artiga, Steven E. *s.j.* '94 (LA) [R] Culver City, CA Ignatius House, The Novitiate of the California Province, Society of Jesus.
Artim, Michael '63 (VNN) Retired.
Artis, George *s.v.d.* '62 (AUS) [4] Austin, TX Holy Cross Church.
Artis, George *s.v.d.* '62 (JKS) [6] Jackson, MS Holy Ghost Church; [G] Jackson, MS Tougaloo College Newman Center.
Artmann, Robert J. '64 (MIL) [K] Brookfield, WI Elmbrook Memorial Hospital, Inc.
Arts, Paul-Louis '64 (SC) [4] Sioux City, IA St. Casimir Church; [5] Sioux City, IA St. Francis of Assisi Church; [6] Sioux City, IA Immaculate Conception Church.
Arturi, Bradley K. '62 (NY) [EE] New Rochelle, NY Opus Dei (Prelature of the Holy Cross and Opus Dei).
Artuso, Grazioso '64 (BGP) [19] Bridgeport, CT St. Raphael's Church.
Artysiewicz, Chet '73 (WDC) [M] Washington, DC Glenmary House of Studies.
Artzer, James *s.v.d.* '50 (TR) [M] Bordentown, NJ Society of the Divine Word.
Arul, Arokisamy *c.s.c.* '81 (FTW) [A] Notre Dame, IN Moreau Seminary.
Arul, John '70 (MRY) San Luis Obispo, CA San Luis Obispo Church.
Arulappa, Devaraj '86 (TYL) Center, TX St. Therese Church; Nacogdoches, TX Sacred Heart Church.
Arvay, Alfred S. '58 (NEW) On Duty Outside the Archdiocese.
Asantey, Samuel (NY) Carmel, NY St. James the Apostle Church.
Asare-Dankwah, John '94 (NO) [45] New Orleans, LA St. Matthias Church.
Ascencio, Joseph A. '82 (COL) Special Assignment.
Aschenbrenner, George A. *s.j.* '65 (ALN) [A] Wernersville, PA Novitiate of St. Isaac Jogues; [N] Wernersville, PA Jesuit Center for Spiritual Growth.
Aschenbrenner, George F. '42 (CHI) [4] Lemont, IL St. James at Sag Bridge Church; Retired.
Aschenbrenner, Ralph L. '61 (SAL) Lincoln, KS St. Patrick's Church.
Ascherl, Vincent '81 (ELP) Retired.
Aschmann, Karl '50 (CHL) Concord, NC St. James Church.
Ascolese, Robert J. '89 (MET) [6] Perth Amboy, NJ Most Holy Rosary Church; Perth Amboy, NJ Raritan Bay Medical Center.
Asencios-Pablo, Maximo *m.ss.a.* (HRT) [2] Waterbury, CT Immaculate Conception Church.
Asenjo, Jose Maria '65 (GAL) South Houston, TX Our Lady of Grace Church.
Asghedom, Tesfaldet *m.c.c.j.* '85 (LA) Compton, CA St. Albert the Great Church.
Ash, Joseph '58 (WOR) [M] Worcester, MA Vianney House.
Ash, Joseph H. '58 (WOR) Retired.
Ashbaugh, William '93 (LAN) [3] Ann Arbor, MI St. Thomas the Apostle Church.
Ashbeck, David '68 (GB) Isaar, WI St. Sebastian Church.
Ashe, Brendan '59 (CC) Orange Grove, TX St. John of the Cross Church.
Ashe, John F. '63 (NOR) Portland, CT St. Mary Church.
Ashe, Joseph C. '76 (NOR) [2] Middletown, CT St. John Church.
Ashe, Kevin P. '63 (NEW) [3] Jersey City, NJ St. Anne's Church; Special Assignment; [S] Union City, NJ Park Performing Arts, Inc.
Ashenbrenner, Raymond *o.p.* '51 (MAD) [H] Watertown, WI St. Joseph's Home.
Ashenbrenner, Raymond N. *o.p.* '51 (CHI) [N] Chicago, IL Dominicans (Provincial Office).
Ashenbrenner, Robert D. *o.s.f.s.* '54 (PH) [Z] Philadelphia, PA Oblates of St. Francis De Sales.
Ashfeld, Bernard '82 (SFS) Sioux Falls, SD South Dakota State Penitentiary & Minnehaha County Jail.
Ashkar, Dominic F. '62 (SAM) Washington, DC Our Lady of Lebanon Church.
Ashley, Benedict M. *o.p.* '48 (STL) [P] St. Louis, MO Dominican Community of St. Louis.
Ashley, William F. *f.s.s.p.* '79 (PAT) Pequannock, NJ Our Lady of Fatima Chapel (Tridentine) Church.
Ashline, Alfred '49 (ALB) Retired.
Ashman, Robert F. '86 (NY) [190] Bronx, NY St. Theresa of the Infant Jesus Church.
Ashman, Robert S. (NY) Tuckahoe, NY Immaculate Conception Church.
Ashmore, Ronald (IND) [41] Indianapolis, IN St. Simon Church.
Ashton, John P. '55 (Y) Campbell, OH St. Lucy's Church.
Ashurst, Peter G. '92 (OKL) Frederick, OK St. Helen Church.
Ashwell, G. Barry '69 (SEA) Oak Harbor, WA St. Augustine Church.
Asip, Msgr. James W. '37 (BRK) [191] Queens, NY St. Luke Church; Retired; [L] Brooklyn, NY Catholic Charities.
Asir, Antony '82 (RVC) Lynbrook, NY Our Lady of Peace Church.
Asis, Alfonso '75 (AGN) Toto, GU Immaculate Heart of Mary Church.
Asma, Lawrence F. *c.m.* '83 (STL) [K] Bridgeton, MO De Paul Health Center; [P] St. Louis, MO Vincentian Bellerive Residence.
Asmar, Maroun '93 (SAM) Somerset, NJ St. Sharbel Church.
Aspinall, Campion W. *c.j.* '61 (LA) Santa Maria, CA St. Louis de Montfort Church.
Aspiras, Jose '47 (SEA) Retired.
Assenmacher, Hugh *o.s.b.* '58 (LR) [A] Subiaco, AR Subiaco Monastery.
Astruc, Rene *s.j.* '54 (ANC) [G] Anchorage, AK Jesuit House.
Astudillo, Antonio P. '73 (LA) [7] Long Beach, CA Holy Innocents Church.
Asturi, Bruno '76 (PBR) Upper St. Clair, PA St. Gregory Nazianzus Church.
Astuto, Lucian S. '57 (OM) [34] Omaha, NE St. Patrick Church.
Asuncion, Leo '79 (OAK) El Cerrito, CA St. John the Baptist Church.
Atanga, Joseph *s.j.* '87 (NY) [Z] New York, NY Jesuit Community at Fordham University.
Atcher, Joseph *o.carm.* '76 (NEW) Tenafly, NJ Our Lady of Mount Carmel Church.
Atchison, Donald W '57 (KAL) Retired.
Atchley, Jonathan M. '88 (LA) [39] Los Angeles, CA St. Aloysius Gonzaga Church; [2] Oxnard, CA Santa Clara Church.
Aten, Robert L. '79 (STL) Special Assignment; [P] Centerville, MO Contemplative Heart of Mary Hermitage.
Atkins, Daniel '87 (IND) Bloomington, IN St. Paul Catholic Center Church; [N] Bloomington, IN Indiana University, Bloomington Newman Center.
Atkins, James '72 (RVC) East Northport, NY St. Anthony of Padua Church.
Atkins, James '81 (SFR) Retired.
Atkins, James P. '75 (ATL) On Duty Outside the Archdiocese.
Atkinson, Anselm *o.s.b.* '82 (WOR) [N] Petersham, MA St. Mary's Monastery.
Atkinson, John V. '61 (MEM) [18] Memphis, TN St. Michael's Church.
Atkinson, Sean '69 (JKS) Leland, MS St. James Church.
Atkinson, William E. *o.s.a.* '74 (PH) [D] Drexel Hill, PA Monsignor Bonner High School.
Ato, Lorenzo *s.m.* '88 (NY) [95] New York, NY Our Lady Queen of Martyrs Church.
Atok, George L. *s.d.b.* '82 (NO) [D] Marrero, LA Archbishop Shaw High School.
Atonio, Falniko '92 (SPP) [5] (Leone), AS Church of the Holy Cross.
Atoyebi, John Bola '94 (CHI) Blue Island, IL St. Benedict Church.
Attak, Cyril '64 (PRM) Allen Park, MI St. Stephen Church.
Attanasio, Raymond V. '58 (MET) Laurence Harbor, NJ St. Lawrence Church.
Attanasio, Scott F. '95 (NEW) Kearny, NJ St. Stephen's Church.
Attea, Msgr. Antoine '58 (BUF) Jamestown, NY St. James Church.
Attridge, Terry '65 (NY) Dobbs Ferry, NY Sacred Heart Church.
Attumaly, Antony *m.ss.cc.* '88 (HBG) Blue Ridge Summit, PA St. Rita Church; Fairfield, PA Immaculate Conception of the Blessed Virgin Mary Church.
Atwater, John T. '63 (BO) Groton, MA St. James Church; Groton, MA Sacred Heart Church.
Atwill, Msgr. William H. '44 (LA) Retired.
Atwood, Ray E. '94 (DUB) [8] Dubuque, IA Holy Ghost Church.
Atwood, Ronald E. '84 (OAK) Richmond, CA St. David of Wales Church.
Atwood, Ronald J. '69 (COL) [43] Columbus, OH St. Thomas the Apostle Church.
Atwood, Wilbur J. *s.s.j.* '58 (NO) [P] New Orleans, LA Josephite Fathers and Brothers.
Atzert, Edward P. '37 (TR) Retired.
Au, John Truong '73 (GR) White Cloud, MI St. Joseph's Church.
Au, Thomas Y. '79 (LIN) Roseland, NE Sacred Heart Church.
Au, William A. '75 (BAL) [80] Baltimore, MD SS. Philip and James Church.
Aubespin, Francis Borgin *s.v.d.* '65 (LAF) [4] Lafayette, LA Immaculate Heart of Mary Church.
Aubin, Msgr. Joseph '55 (OG) Keeseville, NY Church of the Immaculate Conception; Keeseville, NY St. John the Baptist Church.
Aubin, Joseph '61 (LAN) Durand, MI St. Mary Church.
Aubin, Pierre *m.s.c.* (OG) [J] Watertown, NY Mission Project Service.
Aubin, Pierre *m.s.c.* '58 (OG) Evans Mills, NY St. Mary Church; [J] Watertown, NY Sacred Heart Foundation.
Aubin, Ronald B. '81 (SP) Land O'Lakes, FL Our Lady of the Rosary Church.
Auble, Theodore J. '75 (ROC) [M] Rochester, NY Diocesan Office of Campus Ministry.
Aubrey, Robert J. '71 (DM) Cumming, IA St. John Church.

Aubry, Donald W. '47 (NY) [Z] Maryknoll, NY Maryknoll Fathers and Brothers.
Aubry, Ronald J. '81 (COL) Millersburg, OH St. Peter Church.
Aubut, Charles E. '41 (BO) Retired.
Auby, John R. '94 (MAD) Middleton, WI St. Bernard Church.
Auchter, John A. '54 (ALN) Lake Harmony, PA St. Peter the Fisherman Church.
Aucoin, Msgr. Charles '47 (MOB) Retired.
Aucoin, Msgr. Robert H. '70 (OG) [A] Ogdensburg, NY Wadhams Hall.
Auda, Lawrence '60 (SFD) Benld, IL St. Joseph Church; Gillespie, IL SS. Simon and Jude Church.
Audet, Arthur J. '85 (HRT) Forestville, CT St. Matthew Church.
Audet, Dennis '78 (MAN) Rochester, NH Holy Rosary Church.
Audet, Joseph R. *m.s.f.* '73 (CC) [1] Beeville, TX Our Lady of Victory Church.
Audette, Albert D., Jr. '93 (BGP) Bethel, CT St. Mary's Church.
Audibert, John '67 (PRT) [7] Portland, ME Sacred Heart Church.
Auer, Benedict L. *o.s.b.* '80 (SEA) [M] Lacey, WA St. Martin's Abbey.
Auer, John '79 (COS) [13] Colorado Springs, CO Saint Paul Church.
Auer, John J. '57 (BAL) Millersville, MD Our Lady of the Fields Church.
Auer, Joseph E. '57 (CHI) [4] Oak Lawn, IL St. Linus Church.
Auer, Paul '45 (SEA) Retired.
Auer, Peter J. *s.o.l.t.* '93 (CC) [H] Robstown, TX Society of Our Lady of the Most Holy Trinity.
Auer, Robert F. '51 (DUB) Retired.
Aufdermauer, Joseph A. '68 (MIL) [75] Milwaukee, WI St. Stephen Church.
Aufieri, Robert J. (NY) [161] Bronx, NY St. Margaret of Cortona Church.
Aufiero, Louis D. '65 (BRK) [178] Queens, NY Holy Family Church.
Auger, Gaston E. '32 (PRT) Retired.
Auger, George *c.s.v.* '61 (CHI) [N] Arlington Heights, IL Viatorian Province Center-Clerics of St. Viator.
Auger, Gerald E. '55 (MAN) Retired.
Auger, Raymond D. '56 (PRT) Sanford, ME St. Ignatius Martyr Church.
Auguste, Jean-Miguel '93 (BRK) [139] Brooklyn, NY St. Therese of Lisieux Church.
Augustine, Emanuele '73 (NY) [138] Bronx, NY St. Dominic Church.
Augustine, Kenneth J. '77 (MIL) Franklin, WI St. James Church.
Augustine, Maria S. *s.j.* '90 (CHI) [C] Chicago, IL Jesuit Community at Loyola University of Chicago.
Augustine, Msgr. Roger J. '59 (SC) Moville, IA Immaculate Conception Church.
Augustine, Russell A. '89 (BGP) Brookfield, CT St. Joseph's Church.
Augustinowitz, Michael E. '75 (BUR) Greensboro Bend, VT St. Michael Church; Hardwick, VT St. Norbert Church.
Augustyn, Albert J. '47 (SCR) Inkerman, PA St. Mark's Church.
Augustyn, Andrew M. '47 (GI) Retired.
Augustyn, Cyril *o.f.m.conv.* '53 (FR) [1] Taunton, MA Our Lady of the Holy Rosary Church.
Augustyn, James M. '63 (BUF) [6] Lackawanna, NY St. Michael the Archangel Church.
Augustyn, Richard H. '76 (BUF) [34] Buffalo, NY Immaculate Heart of Mary Church; Buffalo, NY Buffalo General Hospital.
Aultz, Gary C. '69 (OKL) Absent on Leave.
Auman, Robert '47 (SFE) Retired.
Aumann, J. *o.p.* (WDC) [11] Washington, DC St. Dominic Church & Priory Church.
Aumann, Jordan *o.p.* '45 (CHI) [N] River Forest, IL St. Thomas Aquinas Priory.
Aurentz, John W. '50 (HBG) Retired.
Aurilia, John C. *o.f.m.cap.* '66 (CHL) Hendersonville, NC Immaculate Conception Church.
Ausenbaugh, Andy '95 (OWN) [1] Owensboro, KY St. Stephen Cathedral.
Ausperk, Michael D. '89 (CLV) [1] Elyria, OH St. Agnes Church.
Austgen, Robert *c.s.c.* '58 (FTW) [B] Notre Dame, IN University of Notre Dame Du Lac.
Austgen, Robert J. *c.s.c.* '58 (FTW) [J] Notre Dame, IN Holy Cross Community, Corby Hall, University of Notre Dame.
Austin, C. Gerard *o.p.* '59 (WDC) [C] Washington, DC Catholic University of America, The.
Austin, Joseph (ALB) [L] Saratoga Springs, NY St. John Neumann Residence.
Austin, Joseph *c.ss.r.* '39 (ALB) [L] Saratoga Springs, NY St. John Neumann Residence.
Austin, Stephen E. '84 (TLS) McAlester, OK St. John Church.
Austin, Walter J. '81 (NO) Chalmette, LA Prince of Peace Church.
Auth, James E. '61 (TOL) [13] Toledo, OH Regina Coeli Church.
Auth, William G. *o.s.f.s.* '69 (TOL) [K] Toledo, OH Oblates of St. Francis de Sales.
Auther, John *s.j.* (PHX) [7] Phoenix, AZ SS. Anthony and Pius X Church.
Auve, Msgr. Perron Joseph '62 (YAK) Ellensburg, WA St. Andrew's Church.
Avallone, Paul P. *s.d.b.* '50 (PAT) [D] Paterson, NJ Don Bosco Technical High School.
Avau, Felix A. *c.i.c.m.* '54 (SAT) Poteet, TX St. Philip Benizi Church.
Avella, Alberto '80 (GLP) Show Low, AZ St. Rita Church.
Avella, Robert E. '75 (ARL) Fairfax, VA St. Leo's Church.
Avella, Steven M. '79 (MIL) Special Assignment.
Avella, William '50 (RNO) Retired.
Avellaneda, J. Armando, P. *m.ss.a.* '56 (ARL) Dale City, VA Holy Family Church.
Avello, Vicente Salas *o.de.m.* '66 (PCE) [13] Ponce, PR Santuario San Judas Tadeo Church.
Avendano, Alvaro D. '91 (ATL) [2] Atlanta, GA Holy Cross Church.
Averamenko, Alexander '96 (STN) [1] Chicago, IL St. Nicholas Ukrainian Catholic Cathedral.
Averbeck, Ronald J. '61 (CIN) [83] Cincinnati, OH St. Stephen Church.
Averman, Melvin R. *o.f.m.cap.* '53 (WH) Point Pleasant, WV Sacred Heart Church; [N] Charleston, WV Capuchins-St. Anthony Friary.
Aversa, Alfred S. '88 (CAM) Paulsboro, NJ St. John's Church.
Aversa, Domenic R. *t.o.r.* '59 (ALT) [F] Hollidaysburg, PA St. Joseph Friary.
Avery, Edward V. '70 (PH) [74] Philadelphia, PA St. Jerome Church; [T] Philadelphia, PA Nazareth Hospital.
Avery, Joseph E. *m.m.* '49 (NY) [Z] Maryknoll, NY Maryknoll Fathers and Brothers.
Avery, Raymond '44 (MET) Retired; [H] Somerset, NJ Maria Regina Residence.
Avicolli, Maurice C. *o.praem.* '68 (PH) [Z] Paoli, PA Daylesford Abbey.
Avila, Daniel C. '87 (FRS) Hanford, CA St. Brigid Church.
Avila, Msgr. Lourenco '52 (SB) Ontario, CA St. Elizabeth Ann Seton Church.
Avila, Mark *o.m.v.* (SAC) [20] Sacramento, CA St. Robert Church.
Avila, Martin '57 (SFR) Novato, CA Our Lady of Loretto Church.
Aviles, Joe '90 (SAT) [56] San Antonio, TX St. Mary Magdalen Church.
Aviles, Victor (SJN) [8] Bayamon, PR Invencion de la Santa Cruz Church.
Avitabile, Camillo *m.s.* '53 (ORL) [2] Orlando, FL Blessed Trinity Church.
Avramenko, Alexander '96 (STN) [1] Chicago, IL St. Nicholas Ukrainian Catholic Cathedral; San Francisco, CA Immaculate Conception Church; Santa Clara, CA St. Vladimir Church.
Awad, Msgr. Assad '57 (SAM) Roanoke, VA St. Elias Church.
Awalt, Msgr. William J. '47 (WDC) [3] Washington, DC St. Ann Church.
Axe, Thomas R. '60 (CIN) [31] Cincinnati, OH Good Shepherd Church.
Axe, William J. *o.ss.t.* '74 (BAL) Jessup, MD St. Lawrence Church.
Axen, Ronald J. '40 (DUB) Retired.
Axen, Ronald J. '40 (FWT) [G] Crowley, TX St. Francis Village, Inc.
Axtmann, Joseph S. '44 (FAR) Munich, ND St. Mary's Church.
Ayala, Agustin Mateo (WDC) Mount Rainier, MD St. James Church.
Ayala, Marcos *o.f.m.conv.* (SAT) [B] San Antonio, TX San Damiano Friary.
Ayala, Richardo, III (BWN) On Leave.
Ayala, Saul '71 (SB) Mecca, CA Our Lady of Guadalupe Shrine Church.
Ayala-Rendon, Daniel '86 (HRT) [14] Waterbury, CT St. Margaret's Church.
Ayathupadam, Joseph '61 (CHL) Albemarle, NC Our Lady of the Annunciation Church.
Ayd, Joseph D. *s.j.* '54 (SCR) [C] Scranton, PA University of Scranton.
Aydt, Raymond A. '46 (BIS) Grenora, ND St. Boniface Church.
Ayers, Cameron *s.j.* '86 (SFR) [N] San Francisco, CA Jesuit Community at University of San Francisco.
Ayers, Fabian *c.r.* '59 (L) [K] Louisville, KY Nazareth Home.
Ayers, John J. '51 (SPR) Northfield, MA St. Patrick Church.
Aylward, Gerard J. *c.s.p.* '53 (CHR) Clemson, SC St. Andrew Church.
Aymanamkuzhy, Jacob '60 (PMB) Port St. Lucie, FL St. Lucie Church.
Aymanathil, Mathew '59 (NEW) Emerson, NJ Church of the Assumption.
Ayo, Nicholas *c.s.c.* '59 (FTW) [B] Notre Dame, IN University of Notre Dame Du Lac; [J] Notre Dame, IN Holy Cross Community, Corby Hall, University of Notre Dame.
Ayoob, John '65 (PIT) Moon Township, PA St. Margaret Mary Church.
Ayotte, David J. '92 (LA) Lancaster, CA Sacred Heart Church.
Ayoub, Fawaz '79 (BEA) [9] Port Arthur, TX St. Therese the Little Flower of Jesus Church.
Ayoub, Msgr. S. Paul '53 (BUF) [6] Cheektowaga, NY Mother of Divine Grace Church.
Ayoyu, Isaac '86 (CHK) Chalan Kanoa Village, MP Cathedral of Our Lady of Mt. Carmel.
Azadian, Joseph G. *s.j.* '52 (LA) El Segundo, CA St. Anthony Church.
Azar, Fahed F. '80 (SAM) Scranton, PA St. Ann Church.
Azar, John T., Jr. '88 (NTN) North Hollywood, CA St. Anne Church.
Azaro, Stanley R. *o.p.* '75 (PRO) [P] Providence, RI St. Thomas Aquinas Priory at Providence College.
Azcoiti, Vicente '56 (BWN) [2] Mission, TX Our Lady of the Holy Rosary Church.
Azcoitia, Florentino *s.j.* '52 (MIA) [H] Miami, FL Jesuit Fathers of the Province of the Antilles, Inc.
Azcona, Eric *o.f.m.cap.* '51 (FWT) [6] Fort Worth, TX Our Lady of Guadalupe Church.
Aziz, George *s.j.* '57 (SR) Sebastopol, CA St. Sebastian Church.
Aziz, Yousef *b.s.o.* '86 (NTN) [B] Methuen, MA Basilian Salvatorian Order.
Azizo, Thomas B. (OLD) Farmington Hills, MI St. Thomas Church.
Azoon, Philip '94 (NTN) Scranton, PA St. Joseph Church.
Azpiazu, Jose *o.m.i.* '28 (SAT) [K] San Antonio, TX Oblate Madonna Residence.
Azzarone, Daniel M. '78 (PRO) [5] Cranston, RI St. Mary Church.
Azzarto, Anthony J. *s.j.* '69 (NEW) [C] Jersey City, NJ St. Peter's Preparatory School.

B

Ba Do, Ai '51 (ALN) [3] Bethlehem, PA Holy Ghost Church.
Babalya, Michael T. '86 (TR) Willingboro, NJ Corpus Christi Church.
Babb, James C. *s.j.* '46 (ATL) [K] Atlanta, GA Ignatius House.
Babbitt, William T. '70 (FR) North Attleboro, MA St. Mary's Church; Retired.
Babcock, James K. '81 (NTN) Fullerton, CA Holy Cross Church; San Bernardino, CA St. Philip Church.
Babcock, Timothy F. '68 (DET) Rochester, MI St. Andrew Church.
Babeu, Gill C. '87 (BGP) [4] Bridgeport, CT St. Ann's Church.
Babich, Ronald J. '77 (DET) Fraser, MI Our Lady Queen of All Saints Church.
Babicz, Edmund A. '84 (MAN) Sanbornville, NH St. Anthony Church.
Babiczuk, Freddie, Jr. '86 (FR) Wareham, MA St. Patrick's Church.
Babin, Albert *c.ss.r.* '52 (BLX) [E] Biloxi, MS St. John Neumann Residence.
Babin, Patrick J. *o.m.i.* '40 (STP) [N] St. Paul, MN Oblate Residence.
Babineau, Alexis A. *a.a.* '45 (WOR) [N] Worcester, MA Assumptionists (Augustinians of the Assumption).
Babineau, William E. '68 (MAN) [4] Berlin, NH Guardian Angel Church.
Babinski, Donald E. '81 (RVC) Williston Park, NY St. Aidan's Church.
Babka, Robert H. '68 (STL) [7] St. Louis, MO Immaculate Heart of Mary Church.
Bablitch, Michael A. '37 (GB) Retired.
Babonas, Alphonse '62 (DET) [10] Detroit, MI St. Anthony Church.
Babowitch, John F. '96 (PH) [20] Philadelphia, PA St. Barnabas Church.
Babula, Benjamin S. '75 (GBG) [2] Connellsville, PA Holy Trinity Church.
Babulski, Robert E. '69 (NEW) Retired.
Bac, Isidore D.T. *c.m.c.* '70 (LIN) [3] Lincoln, NE Immaculate Heart of Mary Church.
Bac, Isidore M. *c.m.c.* '83 (STP) [28] Minneapolis, MN St. Joseph Hien Church.
Baca, Alfred S. '89 (ORG) [8] Santa Ana, CA St. Joseph's Church.
Baca, Paul M. '49 (SFE) [3] Albuquerque, NM Community of the Risen Saviour Church.
Bacalso, Felipe *s.j.* '90 (BO) [W] Chestnut Hill, MA The Jesuit Community at Boston College.
Baccaro, Gaetano T. '85 (SY) [3] Liverpool, NY St. John Church.
Baccellieri, Joseph '66 (P) [7] Portland, OR Assumption Church.
Bacchi, Lee F. '77 (JOL) Chebanse, IL SS. Mary and Joseph's Church; Clifton, IL St. Peter's Church.

Bacchi, Robert A. (CHI) Maywood, IL St. Eulalia Church.
Bacevice, Joseph A. '77 (CLV) [25] Cleveland, OH St. George Church.
Bacevicius, John A. '36 (FAR) Kintyre, ND St. Boniface's Church.
Bacevicius, John J. *o.f.m.* '62 (PRT) [I] Kennebunkport, ME St. Anthony's Friary.
Bach, Frank J. '56 (SPK) [15] Spokane, WA St. Mary Church.
Bach, James Nguyen '94 (NO) Belle Chasse, LA Our Lady of Perpetual Help Church.
Bach, John A. '71 (LFT) [D] Lafayette, IN St. Anthony Health Care; [F] Lafayette, IN Monastery of the Precious Blood.
Bach, Lester *o.f.m.cap.* '57 (GB) [M] Appleton, WI Monte Alverno Retreat Center.
Bachand, Joseph G. *m.s.* '76 (HRT) [M] Hartford, CT Missionaries of LaSalette Provincial Secretary.
Bacher, Anthony A. *c.s.sp.* '46 (VEN) [G] Sarasota, FL Congregation of the Holy Ghost.
Bacher, Arthur A. '54 (CLV) Richfield, OH St. Victor Church.
Bacher, Msgr. Robert E. '48 (CLV) Clinton, OH St. George Church.
Bachkay, John M. '83 (PIT) [31] Pittsburgh, PA St. Louise de Marillac Church.
Bachman, Michael J. '84 (BGP) [17] Bridgeport, CT St. Patrick Church.
Bachman, Paul B. '44 (SFS) Retired.
Bachmann, Leonard *s.t.* '55 (WDC) [B] Silver Spring, MD Holy Trinity Mission Seminary (1926); [M] University Park, MD Holy Trinity Missionary Cenacle.
Bachmeier, Benjamin '68 (SD) San Diego, CA Mercy Hospital; [F] San Diego, CA Mercy Hospital and Medical Center dba Mercy Healthcare San Diego.
Bachmeier, Bernard A. '68 (FAR) On Duty Outside the Diocese.
Bachmeier, Mark V. '89 (P) Astoria, OR St. Mary, Star of the Sea Church.
Bachnak, Francis J. '43 (KC) Retired.
Bachner, James M. '96 (PIT) West View, PA St. Athanasius Church.
Bacia, Eliot *o.f.m.* '62 (MIL) [P] Milwaukee, WI Francis and Clare House.
Bacik, James J. '62 (TOL) [5] Toledo, OH Corpus Christi, University of Toledo Church; [N] Toledo, OH University of Toledo Campus Ministry.
Bacik, Leonard M. '72 (CLV) [3] Lorain, OH Holy Trinity Church.
Bacino, Benjamin J. '75 (PBL) Gardner, CO Sacred Heart Church; Walsenburg, CO St. Mary Church.
Backes, Charles H. '48 (BIS) Retired; [G] Bismarck, ND Emmaus Place.
Backes, Hugo G. '36 (BIS) Retired.
Backes, John J. '73 (NY) Garnerville, NY St. Gregory Barbarigo Church.
Backiel, Bernard *m.i.c.* (DET) Detroit, MI Detroit Receiving Hospital.
Backiel, Bernard *m.i.c.* '60 (DET) [74] Detroit, MI Sweetest Heart of Mary Church; Detroit, MI Michigan Health Care Corporation.
Backiel, Bernard *m.i.c.* '60 (SPR) [I] Stockbridge, MA Congregation of Marians.
Backous, Timothy *o.s.b.* '86 (SCL) [B] Collegeville, MN St. John's University; [I] Collegeville, MN St. John's Abbey, of the Order of St. Benedict.
Bacleon, Misael '84 (NY) [52] New York, NY Immaculate Conception Church.
Bacon, Roger L. '60 (PRO) [2] Pawtucket, RI St. Cecilia's Church.
Bacovin, Ronald '66 (TR) Lakehurst, NJ St. John Church.
Badarzynski, Rembert *o.f.m.* '49 (PIT) [N] Ben Avon, PA St. Anthony Friary and Mission House.
Baddick, Thomas D. '81 (ALN) [7] Reading, PA St. Joseph Church.
Badding, Joseph P. '69 (BUF) [26] Buffalo, NY St. Gerard Church.
Badeaux, Kevin '84 (BEA) Special Assignment.
Badem, Wendel J. '48 (MIL) Retired.
Baden, Robert D. '77 (RC) Kadoka, SD Our Lady of Victory Church; Wall, SD St. Patrick's Church.
Bader, Edward '82 (NY) [153] Bronx, NY St. Joan of Arc Church.
Bader, Edward A. *c.s.b.* '63 (GAL) [C] Houston, TX University of St. Thomas; [Q] Houston, TX Residence of the Basilian Fathers of the University of St. Thomas.
Bader, Paul A. '61 (CIN) [69] Cincinnati, OH Our Lady of the Rosary Church.
Bader, Paul L. '58 (ALN) Coplay, PA St. Peter Church.
Badgely, Augustine T. '87 (NY) [4] New Rochelle, NY Holy Family Church.
Badger, Arthur '53 (TOL) Retired.
Badgerow, Rock J. '79 (GR) Evart, MI Sacred Heart Church; Marion, MI St. Agnes Church.
Badia, Leonard F. '60 (BRK) [168] Queens, NY St. Francis of Assisi Church.
Badillo, Robert *m.id.* '95 (NY) [180] Bronx, NY Santa Maria Church; [Z] Bronx, NY Idente Missionaries of Santa Maria Residence.
Badnerosky, Myron M. '56 (PSC) Levittown, PA Our Lady of Perpetual Help Church.
Bado, Walter *s.j.* '59 (LEX) [2] Lexington, KY The Newman Center, Holy Spirit Church; [L] Lexington, KY The Newman Center Holy Spirit Parish University of Kentucky.
Badovsky, Thomas '73 (PEO) Depue, IL St. Mary's Church.
Badurina, Gabriel *t.o.r.* (WDC) [9] Washington, DC St. Blaise Church.
Badurina, Gabriel *t.o.r.* '62 (PIT) [N] Pittsburgh, PA Croatian Commissariate, T.O.R.
Baehr, David J. '64 (SY) [4] Oswego, NY St. Mary Church.
Baek, Augustine *s.d.b.* '95 (BO) [N] Boston, MA Salesian Boys & Girls Club.
Baenziger, Edward J. *c.s.b.* '76 (GAL) [Q] Houston, TX Residence of the Basilian Fathers of the University of St. Thomas.
Baer, Campion *o.f.m.cap.* '56 (MIL) [B] Mount Calvary, WI St. Lawrence Seminary; [P] Mount Calvary, WI St. Lawrence Friary.
Baer, M. Stuart '92 (PEO) On Duty Outside the Diocese.
Baer, Robert W. *c.s.p.* '54 (NY) [Z] Scarsdale, NY Paulist Fathers Generalate.
Baer, Stuart (PAT) [J] Denville, NJ Sisters of the Sorrowful Mother Health Care Ministry Corp.
Baer, Timothy K. '96 (WDC) Hyattsville, MD St. Mark Church.
Baer, William '96 (STP) [8] St. Paul, MN The Nativity of Our Lord Church.
Baerwald, Jeffrey P. *s.j.* '89 (NY) [Z] New York, NY Jesuit Community at Fordham University.
Baeten, David '62 (GB) [11] Green Bay, WI St. Matthew Church.
Baeten, Lambert C. *o.praem.* '59 (GB) [I] De Pere, WI St. Norbert Abbey.
Bafaro, Michael P. '53 (WOR) [13] Worcester, MA Our Lady of Mt. Carmel and St. Ann Church.
Baffa, Robert J. '66 (BUR) North Bennington, VT St. John the Baptist Church.
Bagan, Francis *o.m.i.* '52 (PT) Perry, FL Immaculate Conception Church.
Bagatin, Tarcisio *c.s.* '58 (SY) [21] Syracuse, NY St. Peter Church.
Bagdanavicius, Vytautas *m.i.c.* '36 (CHI) [N] Chicago, IL Congregation of Marian Fathers of the Immaculate Conception.
Bagdonis, Raymond *o.carm.* '94 (NY) Middletown, NY Our Lady of Mt. Carmel Church.
Baggarly, John D. *s.j.* '60 (CHI) [C] Chicago, IL Jesuit Community at Loyola University of Chicago.
Baggerly, John D. *s.j.* '60 (CHI) [N] Chicago, IL Chicago Province of the Society of Jesus-Provincial Office.
Baggetta, Joseph J. '74 (BO) [31] Boston, MA St. James the Greater in Chinatown Church; Boston, MA Juvenile Detention and Treatment Facilities.
Baggio, Gianantonio '92 (SJ) [7] San Jose, CA Holy Cross Church.
Baggio, John A. '55 (BEL) West Frankfort, IL St. John the Baptist Church.
Bagienski, Ronald A. '69 (BUF) [28] Buffalo, NY Holy Apostles SS. Peter and Paul Church.
Baginskis, Boleslaus *m.i.c.* '42 (CHI) [162] Chicago, IL Our Lady of Aglona Church.
Bagley, Gary J. '72 (BUF) [P] Williamsville, NY Franciscan Missionary Sisters of the Divine Child, Inc.; [S] Allegany State Park, NY Camp Turner.
Bagley, John J. '60 (WOR) North Grafton, MA St. Mary's Church.
Bagley, Ronald M. *c.j.m.* '77 (BUF) [1] West Seneca, NY St. Bonaventure Church; [O] West Seneca, NY St. Bonaventure.
Baglio, Joseph L. '44 (STP) Retired.
Bagnato, James D. *o.praem.* '79 (WIL) [B] Claymont, DE Archmere Academy; [I] Claymont, DE Immaculate Conception Priory of the Canons Regular of Premontre.
Bahena, Jesus '95 (GAL) [23] Houston, TX St. Cyril of Alexandria Church.
Bahhuth, Albert '96 (LA) Whittier, CA St. Gregory the Great Church.
Bahl, Edmund *s.s.c.* '43 (BUF) [M] Silver Creek, NY St. Columbans on the Lake, Home for the Aged.
Bahleda, Aloysius J. '58 (GBG) Retired; [G] Greensburg, PA Neumann House.
Bahlinger, Donald G. *s.j.* '59 (GAL) [41] Houston, TX St. Joseph Church.
Bahning, Frederick C. '45 (DUB) Retired.
Bahr, Joseph E. '60 (DOD) Claflin, KS Immaculate Conception Church; Ellinwood, KS St. Joseph Church.
Baiardi, Sereno *o.f.m.* '66 (MIL) [P] Burlington, WI Queen of Peace Friary; [Y] Waterford, WI General Secretariat of the Franciscan Missions, Inc.
Baidoo, Joseph '85 (RVC) Deer Park, NY SS. Cyril and Methodius Church.
Baidoo, Raphael *o.ss.t.* '77 (VIC) Goliad, TX Immaculate Conception Church.
Baier, Donald E. '75 (VEN) Holmes Beach, FL St. Bernard's Church.
Baier, Donald M. '70 (RVC) Malverne, NY Our Lady of Lourdes Church.
Baier, William J. '82 (STL) Bridgeton, MO St. Mary Church.
Bailey, Casey *o.c.s.o.* '83 (P) [L] Lafayette, OR The Cistercian (Trappist) Abbey of Our Lady of Guadalupe.
Bailey, David P. '65 (BO) Sherborn, MA St. Theresa Church.
Bailey, Declan *o.f.m.* '44 (SP) [O] St. Petersburg, FL St. Anthony Friary.
Bailey, Douglas *s.d.s.* '77 (ORL) [E] Melbourne, FL Florida Institute of Technology Campus Ministry.
Bailey, Fred K. '83 (ORG) Yorba Linda, CA St. Martin Church.
Bailey, Msgr. John L. '41 (WDC) [14] Washington, DC St. Francis Xavier Church; Retired.
Bailey, Msgr. Joseph G. '43 (OG) Retired; [A] Ogdensburg, NY Wadhams Hall.
Bailey, Justin J. *o.f.m.* '60 (NY) [Z] New York, NY Franciscan Friars, Order of Friars Manor.
Bailey, Lawrence '86 (SEA) Military Chaplains.
Bailey, Paul F. '58 (BO) [4] Plymouth, MA St. Peter Church.
Bailey, Richard L. *s.j.* '58 (STL) [F] St. Louis, MO De Smet Jesuit High School; [P] St. Louis, MO De Smet Jesuit High School Community.
Bailey, Robert L. '93 (PRO) Riverside, RI St. Brendan Church.
Bailey, Scott *c.ss.r.* (BAL) [94] Baltimore, MD St. Wenceslaus Church.
Baillargeon, Albert G. '47 (MAN) Retired.
Bailleres, Anthony *l.c.* '81 (HRT) [V] Orange, CT Legion of Christ, Inc.
Bailon, Abelardo '58 (LA) Huntington Park, CA St. Matthias Church.
Baily, Harold E. '69 (PIT) Sewickley, PA St. James Church; Allegheny County, PA Sewickley Valley Hospital; [Q] Slippery Rock, PA Office for Campus Ministry.
Baima, Thomas A. '80 (CHI) Skokie, IL St. Peter Church.
Bain, Daniel '64 (RIC) Elkton, VA Holy Infant Church.
Bain, J.F. Michael '62 (PHX) Flagstaff, AZ Nativity of B.V.M. Church.
Bain, John K. '70 (RNO) Zephyr Cove, NV Our Lady of Tahoe Church.
Bain, Ken '90 (SFS) Clark, SD St. Michael Church.
Bain, Richard '80 (SFR) San Anselmo, CA St. Anselm Church; Special Assignment.
Bain, Thomas J. *s.j.* '56 (CLV) [E] Cleveland, OH St. Ignatius High School.
Baird, James '93 (DEN) Arvada, CO Spirit of Christ Parish Church.
Baird, Joseph A. *o.s.f.s.* '68 (WIL) [I] Childs, MD Oblates of St. Francis De Sales.
Baird, Msgr. Lawrence J. '69 (ORG) [1] Orange, CA Cathedral of the Holy Family.
Baistra, Jorge '74 (SAT) [71] San Antonio, TX San Juan Capistrano Church.
Bajek, Gerald (NEW) Closter, NJ St. Mary's Church.
Bajek, Mietek *o.m.i.* '81 (SFS) Sisseton, SD St. Catherine Church; Sisseton, SD St. Peter Church.
Bajkowski, Dennis (TR) [A] Lakewood, NJ Georgian Court College; [R] Princeton, NJ Campus Ministry for the Diocese of Trenton.
Bajkowski, Dennis W. '71 (CAM) Pine Hill, NJ St. Edward's Church.
Bajorek, James R. '80 (PH) [A] Wynnewood, PA Theological Seminary of St. Charles Borromeo, Overbrook.
Bajorek, Joseph S. *s.d.b.* '45 (NEW) Mahwah, NJ Immaculate Heart of Mary Church.
Bak, Bernard '88 (BAL) Cockeysville, MD St. Joseph Church.
Bakatuinamina, Sebastien *c.i.c.m.* (STP) Cedar Lake, MN St. Patrick Church.
Baker, Andrew R. '91 (ALN) Graduate Studies.
Baker, Bartley P. '93 (NEW) [20] Jersey City, NJ Our Lady of Mercy Church.
Baker, Donald C. '95 (NY) [141] Bronx, NY St. Frances de Chantal Church.
Baker, Donald H. '66 (WOR) [4] Gardner, MA Sacred Heart of Jesus Church.
Baker, Donald P. '80 (CHL) Absent On Leave.
Baker, George (NY) Manhattan, NY Mount Sinai Medical Center.
Baker, George E. '81 (NY) [76] New York, NY St. Monica Church.
Baker, Gerald H. '83 (OWN) Hopkinsville, KY SS. Peter and Paul Church.
Baker, Jack H. '93 (DET) [8] Dearborn, MI Sacred Heart Church.
Baker, James E. '63 (DOD) Burdett, KS Holy Rosary Church; Hanston, KS St. Anthony Church; Jetmore, KS St. Lawrence Church.
Baker, James H. *s.j.* '69 (BEL) [A] Cahokia, IL Parks College of Saint Louis University.
Baker, James H. *s.j.* '69 (STL) [C] St. Louis, MO Saint

Louis University; [P] St. Louis, MO Jesuit Community Corporation at St. Louis University - Jesuit Hall.
Baker, Jay '92 (HT) Larose, LA Our Lady of the Rosary Church.
Baker, John C. '82 (PRO) [1] Pawtucket, RI St. Anthony's Church.
Baker, John Sims '94 (NSH) [6] Nashville, TN St. Henry Church.
Baker, John W. '39 (SPC) Retired.
Baker, Joseph M. '85 (TUC) [3] Tucson, AZ Holy Family Church.
Baker, Msgr. Joseph W. '51 (STL) [37] St. Louis, MO St. Hedwig Church.
Baker, Joseph W. '69 (NY) [60] New York, NY St. John the Martyr Church.
Baker, Kenneth *s.j.* '62 (PAT) Pequannock, NJ Our Lady of Fatima Chapel (Tridentine) Church.
Baker, Kenneth R. '62 (CIN) [27] Dayton, OH St. Rita Church.
Baker, Kenneth W. *s.j.* '60 (P) [L] Portland, OR Jesuit Provincial Office (Oregon Prov.).
Baker, Msgr. Michael '74 (LA) [57] Los Angeles, CA St. Columbkille Church.
Baker, Nicholas J. '63 (LIN) Crete, NE Sacred Heart Church.
Baker, Richard D. '90 (NY) Graduate Studies; [Z] New York, NY St. John Neumann Residence.
Baker, Robert J. '70 (STA) [1] St. Augustine, FL Cathedral of St. Augustine; [L] St. Augustine, FL Flagler College Newman Center.
Baker, Thomas E. '89 (LA) [23] Los Angeles, CA Our Lady of Guadalupe Church.
Baker, W. Pierre '78 (MAN) Keene, NH St. Bernard Church.
Baker, William S. '55 (SY) Clayville, NY St. Patrick Church.
Baker, William T. '82 (ALN) On Duty Outside the Diocese.
Bakewell, Anderson E. *s.j.* '51 (P) [L] Portland, OR Jesuit Provincial Office (Oregon Prov.).
Bakewell, Anderson E. *s.j.* '51 (SFE) [K] Santa Fe, NM Discalced Carmelite Monastery.
Bakewell, Donald V. '66 (DUB) Preston, IA St. Joseph's Church; Sabula, IA St. Peter Church; Springbrook, IA SS. Peter and Paul Church; [D] Bellevue, IA Marquette High School; [F] Bellevue, IA Bellevue Area Catholic Elementary School.
Bakh, Antoine '88 (OLL) Fullerton, CA St. John Maron Mission Church.
Bakke, Lawrence M. '75 (MAD) Sun Prairie, WI St. Albert the Great Church.
Bakker, Richard T. '59 (BO) [2] Malden, MA St. Joseph Church.
Bakle, John L. *s.m.* '67 (CIN) [M] Dayton, OH Marianist Provincialate.
Bakle, John L. *s.m.* '67 (COL) [2] Columbus, OH St. Agatha Church; [39] Columbus, OH Saint Stephen the Martyr Church.
Bakos, Stephen '36 (Y) Retired.
Baky, Isidore '72 (MIA) [7] Fort Lauderdale, FL St. Helen Church.
Bakyil, Alphonsus *s.o.l.t.* '85 (GAL) [51] Houston, TX St. Monica Church.
Bala, Paul '69 (SAG) Wilmot, MI St. Michael Church.
Bala, Paul W. '69 (SAG) Cass City, MI St. Pancratius Church.
Balaban, Oryst (SJP) Retired.
Balado, Armando '49 (MIA) [29] Miami, FL St. Raymond Church.
Balagapo, Victorio (SFR) [11] San Francisco, CA St. Charles Borromeo Church.
Balagat, Arturo '75 (SB) Norco, CA St. Mel Church.
Balagtas, Rodel '91 (LA) Valinda, CA St. Martha Church.
Balas, Christopher *o.f.m.conv.* (R) [E] Wilmington, NC Conventual Franciscans O.F.M.Conv.
Balas, Christopher *o.f.m.conv.* '57 (R) Burgaw, NC St. Joseph Church.
Balas, David *o.cist.* '53 (DAL) [B] Irving, TX University of Dallas.
Balas, David *o.cist.* '54 (DAL) [M] Irving, TX Cistercian Abbey of Our Lady of Dallas.
Balash, Michael D. '87 (Y) Ashtabula, OH Our Lady of Mt. Carmel Church.
Balasko, George J. '67 (Y) East Liverpool, OH St. Ann's Church; Wellsville, OH Immaculate Conception Church.
Balaskus, Charles '65 (CHI) [4] Oak Lawn, IL St. Linus Church.
Balaun, George W. '72 (CLV) Brook Park, OH St. Peter the Apostle Church.
Balazs, Richard P. *c.r.* '65 (CHI) [D] Chicago, IL Weber High School; [N] Chicago, IL Provincial Office of the Congregation of the Resurrection.
Balazy, Edwin W. '62 (DET) [3] Dearborn Heights, MI St. John the Baptist Church.
Balbi-Port, Mario '47 (NEW) [3] Elizabeth, NJ St. Anthony's Church.
Balchunas, Henry A. '65 (HRT) Wolcott, CT St. Pius X Church.
Balcom, Gary E. '72 (BO) Absent on Sick Leave.
Balczeniuk, Mark G. '83 (SCR) [15] Wilkes-Barre, PA Maternity of the Blessed Virgin Mary Church.
Balczewski, Leslaw *s.j.* '59 (CHI) [N] Chicago, IL Sacred Heart Mission House; [N] Chicago, IL Sacred Heart Mission House.
Baldacchino, Peter '96 (NEW) Ridgewood, NJ Our Lady of Mount Carmel Church.
Balderas, Jose Luis '68 (SAT) La Pryor, TX St. Joseph Church.
Balderas, Msgr. Luis G. '44 (SD) Retired.
Balderrama, George *s.c.j.* '73 (MIL) [K] Milwaukee, WI St. Francis Hospital; [P] Hales Corners, WI Sacred Heart Monastery.
Baldonado, Angel *s.d.b.* '77 (OAK) [E] Richmond, CA Salesian High School.
Baldonado, Felipe *o.f.m.* '38 (ORG) [3] Huntington Beach, CA SS. Simon and Jude Church.
Baldonado, Luis *o.f.m.* '52 (PHX) [19] Phoenix, AZ St. Mary's Basilica; [23] Phoenix, AZ Sacred Heart Church.
Baldonieri, Thomas F. '90 (CHI) [198] Chicago, IL St. Tarcissus Church.
Baldovin, John F. *s.j.* '75 (OAK) [A] Berkeley, CA The Jesuit School of Theology at Berkeley; [N] Berkeley, CA Jesuit Community at Jesuit School of Theology at Berkeley.
Baldrick, James F. '63 (PH) [1] Norristown, PA Epiphany of Our Lord Church.
Balducelli, Roberto *o.s.f.s.* '36 (WIL) [3] Wilmington, DE St. Anthony of Padua Church.
Balduck, Walter *o.f.m.cap.* '73 (SAG) [9] Saginaw, MI St. Anthony of Padua Church; [G] Saginaw, MI Queen of Angels Friary and Retreat House.
Balduf, Raymond J. *s.j.* '51 (NEW) [C] Jersey City, NJ St. Peter's Preparatory School.
Baldus Leonard M. *o.m.i.* '42 (SPC) Mansfield, MO Immaculate Heart of Mary Church.
Baldwin, Bradley *t.o.r.* '94 (STP) Brooklyn Park, MN St. Gerard Church.
Baldwin, David E. '77 (CHI) [28] Chicago, IL St. Benedict the African (East) Church.
Baldwin, Msgr. Edward J. '55 (DET) Bloomfield Hills, MI St. Owen Church.
Baldwin, John F. '59 (CHI) Military Chaplains.
Baldwin, Michael E. '83 (WCH) [20] Wichita, KS St. Vincent de Paul Church.
Baldyga, William L. '69 (HRT) Suffield, CT St. Joseph's Church.
Bales, Robert J. '57 (MIL) Slinger, WI St. Peter's Church.
Bales, Thomas E. '74 (RCK) Sterling, IL St. Mary Church.
Balestino, Francis P. '60 (ALT) [15] Johnstown, PA St. Francis of Assisi Church.
Balestrieri, Edward '59 (BEL) Vienna, IL St. Paul Church.
Balinong, Alfredo *s.j.* '64 (NY) [18] New York, NY Blessed Sacrament Church.
Balint, R. James '61 (DAL) Plano, TX Prince of Peace Church.
Balint, Stephen J. '65 (BGP) [3] Norwalk, CT St. Ladislaus Church.
Balio, Paul '72 (SD) [1] San Diego, CA St. Joseph Cathedral; San Diego, CA UCSD Medical Center.
Balistreri, Anthony '93 (SJP) [9] Rossford, OH St. Michael Church.
Balizan, Daniel '89 (SFE) Clovis, NM Our Lady of Guadalupe Church.
Balkan Paschal *o.c.s.o.* '55 (ARL) [J] Berryville, VA Cistercian Abbey of Our Lady of the Holy Cross.
Balker, Msgr. Joseph W. '44 (FRS) Retired.
Ball, Bruce E. '78 (LC) Absent on Leave.
Ball, David '62 (CHI) Military Chaplains.
Ball, Edward *m.s.c.* '66 (RCK) [H] Aurora, IL Missionaries of the Sacred Heart Community.
Ball, Matthew J. '91 (RVC) Absent on Leave.
Ball, Raymond A. '87 (MAN) [11] Manchester, NH St. John the Baptist Church; [C] Manchester, NH Trinity High School.
Ball, Richard D. '77 (SC) Merrill, IA Assumption Church; [B] Le Mars, IA Gehlen Catholic School.
Ball, Thomas J. '66 (BUR) [1] Burlington, VT Cathedral of the Immaculate Conception.
Ball, Wayne L. '89 (RIC) Roanoke, VA St. Gerard Church; Salem, VA Salem VA Medical Center.
Ballard, Kevin *s.j.* '85 (SAC) [14] Sacramento, CA St. Ignatius Church.
Ballentine, Edgar S. '46 (NSH) Retired.
Ballester, Msgr. Buenaventura '43 (ARE) [2] Arecibo, PR Church of Sagrado Corazon de Jesus.
Ballester, Msgr. Pedro J. '58 (PCE) [6] Ponce, PR San Conrado Church.
Ballestrazzi, Libero *c.s.j.* '44 (CLV) [P] Avon, OH Congregation of St. Joseph.
Balleza, John '85 (SJ) [13] San Jose, CA St. Julie Church.
Ballman, Thomas J. '43 (CIN) [4] Dayton, OH St. Anthony of Padua Church; Retired.
Ballor, Milton A. *c.pp.s.* '55 (CIN) St. Wendelin, OH St. Wendelin Church; Sharpsburg, OH St. Paul Church.
Balluff, John '88 (JOL) Elmhurst, IL Immaculate Conception Church.
Ballweber, Eugene L. (CHI) Retired.
Ballweg, John M. '56 (NEW) Union, NJ Holy Spirit Church; [B] South Orange, NJ Seton Hall University.
Ballweg, Msgr. Lawrence '40 (RVC) Retired.
Balmeo, Simeon '65 (AGN) Maina, GU Our Lady of the Purification Church.
Balog, John '67 (PSC) Wilkes-Barre, PA St. John's Church.
Balog, Robert A. '72 (RCK) Johnsburg, IL St. John the Baptist Church.
Baloga, Herbert *o.f.m.conv.* '38 (SPR) [10] Chicopee, MA St. Stanislaus Basilica.
Baloga, Herbert C. *o.f.m.conv.* '38 (SPR) [F] Springfield, MA Mercy Hospital.
Balogh, Donald J. '49 (CLV) [5] Parma, OH St. Francis de Sales Church; Retired.
Balquin, Don M. '93 (FBK) Delta Junction, AK Our Lady of Sorrows Church.
Balsam, John B. *o.p.* '47 (DAL) [M] Irving, TX Dominican Priory of St. Albert the Great.
Balser, Edward '56 (JKS) Brandon, MS St. Paul Church.
Balser, Robert *c.ss.r.* '49 (GR) [3] Grand Rapids, MI St. Alphonsus Church.
Balta, Msgr. Raymond A. '69 (PBR) Johnstown, PA St. Mary's Church.
Baltazar, Ayala '43 (SJ) Retired.
Baltes, Gabriel *o.s.b.* '91 (JOL) Lisle, IL St. Joan of Arc Church; [J] Lisle, IL St. Procopius Abbey.
Baltes, Timothy '76 (SCL) [8] St. Cloud, MN St. Paul Church.
Baltrucki, Leon S. '40 (BRK) Retired.
Baltrusaitis, Gabriel *o.f.m.* '54 (PRT) [I] Kennebunkport, ME St. Anthony's Friary.
Baltrushunas, Anthony P. '37 (BO) Retired.
Baltz, Albert G. '70 (BUR) Bristol, VT St. Ambrose Church.
Baltz, David P. *m.c.c.j.* '67 (NEW) [N] Montclair, NJ Comboni Missionaries of the Heart of Jesus (Verona Fathers).
Baltz, John P., Jr. '43 (NSH) Centerville, TN Christ the Redeemer Church; Hohenwald, TN Holy Trinity Church; Waynesboro, TN St. Cecilia Church; Retired.
Balvo, Msgr. Charles D. '76 (NY) On Duty Outside the Archdiocese.
Balwinski, Gerald E. '69 (SAG) Standish, MI Resurrection of the Lord Church.
Balys, Thomas I. *o.c.d.* '63 (GRY) [K] Munster, IN Discalced Carmelite Fathers Monastery.
Balzer, Raymond J. '49 (FTW) Auburn, IN Immaculate Conception Church.
Bambenek, Oliver *o.f.m.cap.* '65 (MIL) [B] Mount Calvary, WI St. Lawrence Seminary; [P] Mount Calvary, WI St. Lawrence Friary.
Bamber, William J. *c.m.* '55 (MET) [H] Plainsboro, NJ Vincentian Residence.
Bambera, Joseph C. '83 (SCR) [8] Scranton, PA Holy Name Church.
Bamberg, Callistus M. *o.f.m.* '61 (ALB) [B] Loudonville, NY Siena College.
Bambir, Vjekoslav *o.f.m.* '40 (CHI) [N] Chicago, IL Croatian Franciscan Custody of the Holy Family.
Bambol, John *o.f.m.conv.* '41 (PRT) [4] Portland, ME St. Louis Church.
Bambrick, John P. (TR) Manalapan, NJ St. Thomas More Church.
Bambrick, John W. '70 (ALN) [3] Minersville, PA Our Lady of Mount Carmel Church.
Bambrick, Msgr. Kevin '47 (BLX) [6] Biloxi, MS St. Louis Church; Retired.
Banach, Henry S. '48 (WOR) Retired.
Banach, Joseph S. '56 (MET) Retired.
Banach, Michael '88 (WOR) On Special or Other (Arch)Diocesan Assignment.
Banach, Walter F. '39 (LIN) Retired.
Banaga, Gregg *c.m.* '79 (CLV) [30] Cleveland, OH Holy Rosary Church.
Banas, Leonard N. *c.s.c.* '57 (FTW) [B] Notre Dame, IN University of Notre Dame Du Lac; [J] Notre Dame, IN Holy Cross Community, Corby Hall, University of Notre Dame.
Banazak, Gregory '85 (DET) [A] Orchard Lake, MI SS. Cyril and Methodius Seminary.
Banden, Joseph W. '69 (STL) [11] Florissant, MO Transfiguration Church.
Bandiera, Colombo F. '52 (WH) Retired.
Bandle, Ronald J. '68 (MIL) Special Assignment.
Bandurski, Pawel *s.ch.* '92 (SJ) [1] Sunnyvale, CA St. Albert Chmielowski Polish Catholic Pastoral Mission Church; [3] Sunnyvale, CA St. Cyprian Church.
Bane, Msgr. Raymond T. '51 (NO) Retired.
Banet, Charles *c.pp.s.* (GAL) Retired.
Banet, Charles H. *c.pp.s.* '49 (GAL) [2] Galveston, TX Holy Rosary Church.
Banet, Charles H. *c.pp.s.* '49 (LFT) [A] Rensselaer, IN Saint Joseph's College.
Banet, Paul H. *s.s.j.* '55 (GAL) [2] Galveston, TX Holy Rosary Church.

Banet, Stephen J. '77 (IND) Columbus, IN St. Bartholomew Church.
Bang, Joseph '74 (GAL) [K] Houston, TX The Catholic Chaplain Corps.
Bang, Le Huy *c.ss.r.* '46 (LA) [R] Baldwin Park, CA Vietnamese Redemptorist Mission.
Baniak, Walter '41 (ALB) Retired.
Banick, Msgr. Thomas V. '63 (SCR) [14] Wilkes-Barre, PA St. Mary's Church of the Immaculate Conception.
Banigan, Herbert '46 (DEN) Retired.
Banken, Robert L. '68 (STL) Military Chaplains.
Banker, Richard '88 (STP) Prior Lake, MN St. Michael Church.
Banko, John M. '72 (MET) Hillsborough, NJ Mary, Mother of God Church.
Banks, Charles *o.m.i.* '66 (SAT) [M] San Antonio, TX Provincial Administration Office, Oblates of Mary Immaculate (Southern Prov.); [M] San Antonio, TX St. Anthony Catholic High School House.
Banks, David A. '73 (SP) Homosassa, FL St. Thomas the Apostle Church.
Banks, Edward J. *s.j.* '50 (BO) Dedham, MA St. Mary Church; [W] Boston, MA The Society of Jesus of New England-Provincial Offices; [W] Weston, MA Campion Center.
Banks, Evan *o.f.m.* '50 (NEW) Fair Lawn, NJ St. Anne's Church.
Banks, Gary Michael *s.t.* '76 (LA) [4] Los Angeles, CA Ascension Church.
Banks, Michael *o.f.m.cap.* '84 (NY) New Paltz, NY St. Joseph Church; [Z] New Paltz, NY St. Joseph Friary.
Banks, Peter *o.f.m.cap.* '73 (SFR) [N] Burlingame, CA Capuchin Provincial House.
Bannan, Louis I. *s.j.* '44 (SJ) [B] Santa Clara, CA Santa Clara University.
Bannan, Msgr. Martin '56 (BRK) [U] Brooklyn, NY St. Joseph's Priest Residence.
Bannan, Peter F. '67 (NY) Pelham, NY St. Catharine Church.
Bannantine, Thomas E. *s.j.* '65 (OM) [K] Omaha, NE Jesuit Community At Creighton University.
Banner, Russell J. '67 (CLV) [7] Cleveland, OH Annunciation Church.
Bannin, Eugene *s.j.* '50 (PMB) [3] West Palm Beach, FL St. Ann Church; [E] West Palm Beach, FL Noreen McKeen Residence for Geriatric Care.
Bannon, Anthony *l.c.* '75 (HRT) [V] Orange, CT Legion of Christ, Inc.
Banos, Felix '58 (ORL) Lake Wales, FL Holy Spirit Church.
Bantle, Charles *o.f.m.cap.* '48 (DET) [K] Detroit, MI St. Bonaventure Friary.
Bantz, William E. '60 (Y) Maximo, OH St. Joseph Church.
Banuelas, Msgr. Arturo '76 (ELP) [30] El Paso, TX St. Pius X Church.
Banzin, Robert S. '64 (CHI) Niles, IL St. John Brebeuf Church.
Bao, Tran Quoc *c.ss.r.* '90 (LA) [R] Baldwin Park, CA Vietnamese Redemptorist Mission.
Baptista, Diogo C. '69 (SR) Crescent City, CA St. Joseph Church.
Baptista, Michael *s.d.b.* '85 (LA) [F] Bellflower, CA St. John Bosco High School.
Baptiste, Chuck '96 (PIT) Center Township, PA St. Frances Cabrini Church.
Baptiste, Glen *c.r.* (CHI) [N] Chicago, IL Provincial Office of the Congregation of the Resurrection.
Barachini, Nello A. *c.m.* '86 (BGP) [2] Bridgeport, CT St. Ambrose Church; Bridgeport, CT Bridgeport Hospital.
Barajas, Abel '96 (MIA) Plantation, FL St. Gregory Church.
Barajas, Msgr. Ricardo '52 (FRS) Mendota, CA Our Lady of Guadalupe Church.
Barak, Christopher L. '87 (LIN) Aurora, NE St. Mary's Church; Cheney, NE St. Michael Church; Palmyra, NE St. Leo's Church.
Barakat, Jean Pierre '89 (OLL) Las Vegas, NV St. Sharbel Mission Church.
Baraki, Tesfamariam '75 (WDC) [15] Washington, DC St. Gabriel Church; [25] Washington, DC Kidane-Mehret Ge'ez Rite Catholic Church; [V] Washington, DC Ethiopian and Eritrean Catholic Mission, USA.
Baran, Blaise R. '82 (MET) Raritan, NJ St. Ann Church.
Baran, John P. '84 (BGP) [2] Fairfield, CT Assumption Church.
Baran, Joseph L. '47 (MIL) Retired.
Baran, Volodymyr *c.ss.r.* '85 (PHU) Newark, NJ St. John the Baptist Church.
Baranek, Raymond '76 (CLV) Absent on Leave.
Baraniak, James T. *o. praem.* '93 (GB) [5] De Pere, WI Our Lady of Lourdes Church; [A] De Pere, WI St. Norbert Abbey; [I] De Pere, WI St. Joseph Priory.
Baraniewicz, Joseph *o.s.f.s.* '57 (LAN) [H] Adrian, MI Motherhouse of the Sisters of St. Dominic.
Baranowski, Art '68 (DET) [T] Marysville, MI National Alliance of Parishes Restructuring into Communities.
Baranowski, Arthur R. '68 (DET) Marysville, MI St. Christopher Church.
Baranowski, David J. '73 (HRT) [7] Hamden, CT St. Stephen's Church.
Baranowski, Stanley A. '55 (MIL) Retired.
Baranowski, Xavier S. '34 (SPR) Retired.
Baransky, Francis J. '79 (ALN) Coaldale, PA SS. Cyril and Methodius Church; Coaldale, PA St. John the Baptist Church; Coaldale, PA St. Mary of the Assumption Church.
Barasinski, John B. '81 (GRY) [1] Michigan City, IN St. Mary of the Immaculate Conception Church.
Baraski, Andrew '92 (SY) Graduate Studies.
Baratelli, David J. '82 (NEW) [2] Jersey City, NJ St. Aloysius Church.
Barattini, John H. '44 (NO) Retired.
Barauskas, Peter *m.i.c.* '39 (NOR) [F] Thompson, CT Marian Fathers.
Barbato, Robert A. *o.f.m.cap.* '87 (OAK) [N] Berkeley, CA Capuchin Franciscan Order, House of Studies.
Barbella, John J. '87 (MET) Flemington, NJ St. Magdalen de Pazzi Church.
Barber, Bradley A. M. (CC) [5] Corpus Christi, TX Most Precious Blood Church.
Barber, Hal L. '61 (SFS) Dell Rapids, SD St. Mary's Church.
Barber, Michael *s.m.* '90 (STL) [P] St. Louis, MO Provincialate of the Society of Mary, Province of St. Louis.
Barber, Michael D. *s.j.* '79 (STL) [C] St. Louis, MO Saint Louis University; [P] St. Louis, MO Leo Brown Jesuit Community.
Barber, Michael L. *s.j.* '75 (PH) [Z] Philadelphia, PA Jesuit Community at St. Joseph's University.
Barber, Robert *o.f.m.* '84 (PRT) [I] Kennebunkport, ME St. Anthony's Friary.
Barbernitz, John '50 (MOB) Camden, AL St. Joseph Church; Orrville, AL Immaculate Conception Church.
Barbernitz, John P. '50 (BAL) [5] Baltimore, MD St. Alphonsus Church; Retired.
Barbetta, Philip '72 (BRK) Absent on Leave.
Barbian, Leonard M. '65 (MIL) Special Assignment.
Barbone, Joseph F. '72 (NEW) Plainfield, NJ St. Bernard's Church.
Barbour, Hugh C. *o.praem* '90 (ORG) [A] Silverado, CA St. Michael's Norbertine Postulancy, Novitiate and Juniorate; [H] Silverado, CA Norbertine Fathers.
Barcellona, Thomas J. '95 (CAM) Bridgeton, NJ Immaculate Conception Church.
Barcelo, Jose '53 (BRK) [116] Brooklyn, NY St. Peter-St. Paul-Our Lady of Pilar Church; [W] Brooklyn, NY Centro Evangelizacion San Vicente de Paul.
Barch, Howard C. '93 (PEO) Penfield, IL St. Lawrence's Church.
Barcio, Robert '47 (E) [1] Erie, PA St. Peter Cathedral.
Barcio, Robert G. '47 (E) Retired.
Barclay, Robert F. '75 (BRK) [170] Queens, NY St. Gabriel Church.
Barclift, Richard '66 (PEO) Moline, IL Christ the King Church.
Barcome, Earl W. '52 (GB) Retired.
Barczak, Rene *o.f.m.* '64 (PH) [D] Philadelphia, PA Archbishop Ryan High School; [Z] Philadelphia, PA St. Pius X Friary.
Bardes, Msgr. George F. '44 (NY) Retired; [E] White Plains, NY Archbishop Stepinac High School.
Bardino, Jose '62 (MIA) [3] Hialeah, FL St. Benedict Church.
Bardon, John Brent '68 (TUC) [18] Tucson, AZ Saint Odilia Church.
Barett, Robert '46 (SY) [S] Syracuse, NY St. Pius X Home, Inc.
Barfield, Daniel R. *s.j.* '67 (LSC) Alamogordo, NM St. Jude Church.
Barfknecht, David *o.s.b.* '89 (HON) [H] Waialua, Oahu, HI Benedictine Monastery of Hawaii.
Barga, Louis J. *c.pp.s.* '54 (CIN) Philothea, OH St. Mary's Church.
Bargielski, John C. '45 (GRY) Retired.
Baribeau, Donald G. *m.s.* '75 (R) Washington, NC Mother of Mercy Church.
Baril, Gerald *m.s.* '59 (FR) [K] Attleboro, MA La Salette Provincial House.
Barile, Ralph '82 (BRK) [200] Queens, NY St. Mel Church.
Barile, Ralph E. '82 (TR) On Duty Outside the Diocese.
Barille, Nicholas *s.t.* '95 (LA) Compton, CA Our Lady of Victory Church.
Baris, Bernard *m.s.* '69 (MAN) Lebanon, NH Sacred Heart Church.
Barius, Placid *o.f.m.* '43 (PRT) [I] Kennebunkport, ME St. Anthony's Friary.
Barjacoba, Peter '60 (NY) Absent on Leave.
Barkemeyer, John H. '90 (CHI) [A] Mundelein, IL University of St. Mary of the Lake-Mundelein Seminary.
Barkenquest, Lehr *o.s.f.s.* '64 (LAN) Clarklake, MI St. Rita Church.
Barker, Barnabas *t.o.r.* '58 (DAV) Mount Pleasant, IA Mental Health Institute, St. Dymphna Chapel.
Barker, Brian '94 (BEL) Herrin, IL Our Lady of Mount Carmel Church.
Barker, Msgr. Harry O. '57 (SHP) [5] Shreveport, LA Sacred Heart of Jesus Church.
Barker, Jack D. '92 (SB) La Quinta, CA St. Francis of Assisi Church.
Barker, James '80 (BAL) Special Assignment; [Q] Baltimore, MD Serra Club.
Barker, James M. '80 (BAL) [61] Baltimore, MD St. Michael Church.
Barker, John A. '59 (L) Brandenburg, KY St. John the Apostle Church.
Barker, Joseph F. '53 (ALB) Johnstown, NY St. Patrick Church.
Barker, Richard '92 (GAL) [77] Houston, TX St. Vincent de Paul Church.
Barker, Ronald A. '75 (BO) [2] Revere, MA Immaculate Conception Church.
Barker, Virgil M. '88 (LFT) Peru, IN St. Charles Borromeo Church.
Barkett, James S. '91 (ARL) Dale City, VA Holy Family Church.
Barkey, Patrick C. '90 (PIT) Scott Township, PA SS. Simon and Jude Church.
Barkin, Martin F. '77 (PIT) Unity, PA St. John the Baptist Church.
Barletta, Michael G. '66 (E) [27] Erie, PA St. Patrick/St. Hedwig Church.
Barley, Tom '91 (SAN) St. Lawrence, TX St. Lawrence Church; Stanton, TX St. Joseph's Church.
Barlog, Raymond M. '55 (CHI) [209] Chicago, IL St. Turibius Church.
Barlow, James P. '73 (SAT) Military Chaplains.
Barlowski, Joseph R. '41 (HRT) Retired.
Barman, William '81 (ORG) [4] Santa Ana, CA Our Lady of Lourdes Church.
Barmasse, Gerald R. *c.s.c.* '76 (FTW) [J] South Bend, IN Congregation of Holy Cross Indiana Province Provincial House.
Barnd, Donald *s.c.j.* '78 (MIL) [P] Franklin, WI Villa Maria.
Barnes, Bernard M. *o.s.m.* '48 (CHI) [N] Chicago, IL Servite Friars - Eastern Province.
Barnes, Gavin *o.s.b.* '52 (IND) [B] St. Meinrad, IN St. Meinrad Seminary-College of Liberal Arts; [J] St. Meinrad, IN St. Meinrad Archabbey.
Barnes, Gerard J. '62 (PH) Retired.
Barnes, James H. '69 (LA) [70] Los Angeles, CA St. Joan of Arc Church.
Barnes, John E. '55 (LR) Retired; [H] Little Rock, AR St. John Manor.
Barnes, John G. '52 (DUB) Retired.
Barnes, Joseph A. '57 (ALN) Birdsboro, PA Immaculate Conception Church.
Barnes, Msgr. Joseph C. '58 (FRS) Tehachapi, CA St. Malachy Church.
Barnes, Robert *o.c.s.o.* '70 (ARL) [J] Berryville, VA Cistercian Abbey of Our Lady of the Holy Cross.
Barnes, Robert W. '80 (NOR) Occum, CT St. Joseph Church.
Barnes, Thomas C. '87 (COV) [6] Covington, KY Holy Cross Church.
Barnett, Fred J. '52 (JC) Laurie, MO Shrine of St. Patrick Church.
Barnett, James Q. *o.p.* '65 (CHI) [N] Chicago, IL Dominicans (Provincial Office).
Barnett, Larry *o.s.b.* '76 (SFS) [F] Marvin, SD Blue Cloud Abbey.
Barnett, Msgr. Stephen T. '70 (SFS) [1] Sioux Falls, SD St. Joseph Cathedral.
Barnhardt, Bruno *o.s.b.cam.* '66 (MRY) [G] Big Sur, CA New Camaldoli Hermitage.
Barnhart, Victor A. '90 (STL) Pagedale, MO St. Catherine of Siena Church.
Barnhill, Robert K. '85 (LIN) [8] Lincoln, NE St. Mary Church.
Barnickel, William *o.f.m.* (SFD) [K] Sherman, IL Our Lady of Angels Friary.
Barnufsky, Stephen C. *o.f.m.* '76 (SPK) [11] Spokane, WA St. Francis of Assisi, Friars Church.
Barnum, Martin '74 (CHI) On Duty Outside the Archdiocese.
Barnum, Martin '74 (MIL) [B] Hales Corners, WI Sacred Heart School of Theology.
Barnwell, Gerald P. '77 (FR) [2] Fall River, MA Blessed Sacrament Church.
Baron, Jody (PSC) Absent on Sick Leave.
Baron, John B. '73 (NEW) Lodi, NJ St. Francis de Sales Church; [Q] Teaneck, NJ Fairleigh Dickinson Univ.-Teaneck Campus.
Barona, German *m.s.c.* '86 (RCK) [H] Aurora, IL Missionaries of the Sacred Heart Community.
Barone, Frank '67 (BUF) Perrysburg, NY Wende Correctional Facility.
Barone, Frank E. '67 (BUF) [2] Lackawanna, NY St. Anthony Church.
Barone, Michael J. '75 (DAL) Duncanville, TX Holy Spirit Church.
Barone, Robert J. '67 (SCR) [3] Scranton, PA St. Anthony of Padua Church; [A] Dalton, PA Saint Pius X Seminary; [O] Scranton, PA Immaculate Heart of Mary Center, Marywood.
Baroni, Barry J. '79 (ALT) [19] Johnstown, PA St.

Andrew's Church.
Baronti, David '73 (SPK) On Duty Outside the Diocese.
Baroody, Sami W. '94 (NTN) West Paterson, NJ St. Ann's Church.
Barousse, Raphael *o.s.b.* '55 (NO) [P] St. Benedict, LA St. Joseph Abbey.
Barozzi, Italo '65 (BRK) [33] Brooklyn, NY St. Dominic Church.
Barr, Brian Patrick '93 (RVC) West Hempstead, NY St. Thomas, the Apostle Church.
Barr, Eric R. '84 (RCK) [3] Aurora, IL St. Joseph Church.
Barr, Francis *o.s.a.* '87 (NY) [168] Bronx, NY St. Nicholas of Tolentine Church.
Barr, Frederick *c.s.c.* (P) [L] Portland, OR Holy Cross Father & Brother, C.S.C. - University of Portland.
Barr, Frederick *c.s.c.* '54 (P) [B] Portland, OR University of Portland.
Barr, Frederick L. (BO) Awaiting Assignment.
Barr, Joseph F. '78 (BAL) Davidsonville, MD Holy Family Church.
Barr, Liam M. '74 (LIN) Valparaiso, NE Sts. Mary and Joseph's Church.
Barr, Philip R. '48 (PH) Retired.
Barr, Pierre J. '51 (CHI) [145] Chicago, IL Our Lady of Fatima Church; Retired.
Barr, Stanley J. '57 (CAM) Longport, NJ Epiphany Church.
Barr, Walter M. '59 (BEL) Christopher, IL St. Andrew Church.
Barrand, James '89 (VNN) On Leave.
Barranger, Richard J. *o.p.* '87 (PRO) [B] Providence, RI Providence College; [P] Providence, RI St. Thomas Aquinas Priory at Providence College.
Barrango, Rogelio *s.d.b.* (SJN) [37] San Juan, PR Maria Auxiliadora Church.
Barras, Greg '84 (BLX) [7] Biloxi, MS St. Mary Church.
Barras, Michael J. '73 (LKC) [1] Lake Charles, LA Immaculate Conception Cathedral.
Barras, Robert S. '80 (GAL) [16] Houston, TX St. Catherine of Siena Church.
Barre, Michael L. *s.s.* '70 (BAL) [A] Baltimore, MD St. Mary's Seminary and University.
Barreda, Giles *o.f.m.* '61 (NY) [Z] New York, NY Franciscan Province of the Immaculate Conception.
Barreneche, Franco *o.c.* '44 (SJN) [61] San Juan, PR Santa Teresita Del Nino Jesus Church.
Barrera, Albino F. *o.p.* '93 (PRO) [P] Providence, RI St. Thomas Aquinas Priory at Providence College.
Barrera, Gustavo '79 (BWN) [10] Brownsville, TX Saint Mary, Mother of the Church.
Barres, John O. '89 (WIL) On Duty Outside the Diocese.
Barret, Kevin S. '92 (PCE) On Duty Outside the Diocese.
Barrett, Charles J. *s.m.* '42 (WDC) [M] Washington, DC Marist Provincial House.
Barrett, D. Oliver *c.s.sp.* '48 (PT) [7] Pensacola, FL St. Anne Church.
Barrett, Daniel J. (BO) Retired.
Barrett, David S. '64 (GB) Keshena, WI St. Michael Church; South Branch, WI St. Joseph of the Lake Church.
Barrett, Edward F. '61 (SCR) [10] Scranton, PA Immaculate Conception Church.
Barrett, Edward J. (LA) West Los Angeles, CA Veterans Administration Wadsworth Hospital Center; Military and VA Chaplains.
Barrett, Edward J. '57 (HBG) On Duty Outside the Diocese.
Barrett, Edward J. '75 (CHI) [1] Des Plaines, IL St. Mary Church.
Barrett, Emmett A. *o.f.m.* '55 (PAT) [M] Butler, NJ St. Anthony Friary.
Barrett, Msgr. Francis X. '55 (ALN) [5] Reading, PA Holy Guardian Angels Church.
Barrett, Gerard *o.m.i.* '64 (SAT) Del Rio, TX Sacred Heart Church.
Barrett, Msgr. Harry C. '73 (NY) On Special or Other (Arch)Diocesan Assignment.
Barrett, James L. '56 (KAL) Marshall, MI St. Mary Church.
Barrett, James L. '82 (CHI) Skokie, IL St. Joan of Arc Church.
Barrett, John (JOL) Elmhurst, IL Mary, Queen of Heaven Church.
Barrett, John '78 (RVC) Setauket, NY St. James Church.
Barrett, Kevin J. *m.afr.* '70 (SP) [O] St. Petersburg, FL Missionaries of Africa.
Barrett, M. Stephen *s.s.* '79 (BAL) [M] Baltimore, MD Sulpician Provincial House.
Barrett, M. Stephen *s.s.* '79 (BGP) On Duty Outside the Diocese.
Barrett, Michael '84 (PH) [135] Philadelphia, PA St. Peter the Apostle Church.
Barrett, Michael *o.f.m.* '90 (SFD) [4] Quincy, IL St. Francis Solanus Church; [K] Quincy, IL St. Francis Solanus Friary.
Barrett, Michael D. '84 (MAN) On Duty Outside the Diocese.
Barrett, Michael F. '57 (HBG) [5] Lancaster, PA St. Joseph Church.
Barrett, Michael G. '76 (MIL) Grafton, WI St. Joseph's Church.
Barrett, Michael J. '85 (GAL) [P] Houston, TX Opus Dei.
Barrett, Miles J. '82 (SC) On Duty Outside the Diocese.
Barrett, Patrick H. '57 (MET) [4] Carteret, NJ St. Elizabeth of Hungary Church.
Barrett, Patrick J. '52 (PRT) [1] Portland, ME Cathedral of the Immaculate Conception; Retired.
Barrett, Patrick J. '59 (GAY) Mapleton, MI St. Joseph Church.
Barrett, Robert E. (BO) Permanent Disability.
Barrett, Robert P. '48 (Y) Retired.
Barrett, Thomas '88 (ORL) [7] Orlando, FL St. Charles Borromeo Church; Special Assignment.
Barrett, Thomas '93 (PMB) [B] West Palm Beach, FL Cardinal Newman High School.
Barrett, Thomas J. *c.ss.r.* '67 (TOL) [2] Lima, OH St. Gerard Church.
Barrett, Thomas M. '71 (BEL) New Baden, IL St. George Church.
Barrett, Tom '88 (ORL) [A] Orlando, FL Bishop Moore High School.
Barrett, Walter C. '75 (RIC) [5] Norfolk, VA Basilica of St. Mary.
Barrett, William M. '59 (ROC) Lyons, NY St. Michael Church.
Barretta, Msgr. Anthony J. '47 (BRK) [212] Queens, NY Our Lady of Hope Church; Retired; [Y] Brooklyn, NY Holy Cross.
Barrette, Dacian '75 (Y) Brewster, OH St. Therese Church; Retired.
Barrette, Donat A. '54 (PRO) [M] North Smithfield, RI St. Antoine Residence.
Barrette, Eugene *m.s.* '67 (ORL) [3] Orlando, FL Good Shepherd Church.
Barricks, Robert '94 (P) [16] Portland, OR Holy Family Church.
Barrientos, Gustavo '87 (OM) [32] Omaha, NE Our Lady of Guadalupe Church.
Barrientos, Jesus H. *o.c.d.* '46 (CGS) [2] Caguas, PR San Jose Church.
Barrios, Diego *c.m.f.* '42 (LA) [R] Rancho Dominguez, CA Dominguez Seminary Inc.
Barron, Cecil *c.m.f.* '42 (FRS) [8] Fresno, CA St. Anthony Claret Church.
Barron, Clemente *c.p.* '70 (CHI) [N] Chicago, IL Passionist Provincial Office.
Barron, Clemente *c.p.* '70 (SAT) [M] San Antonio, TX Casa Pasionista Guadalupe.
Barron, Daniel *o.m.v.* '96 (SFD) [2] Alton, IL Immaculate Conception-St. Mary's Church; [3] Alton, IL St. Patrick Church.
Barron, Donald L. '71 (SPR) Lenox, MA St. Ann's Church.
Barron, Edward M. '38 (CHI) Retired.
Barron, Gerald *o.f.m.* (SFR) [N] Burlingame, CA Capuchin Provincial House.
Barron, Gerald *o.f.m.cap.* '66 (LA) [B] Santa Ynez, CA San Lorenzo Novitiate and Seminary.
Barron, Harold R. *o.p.* '43 (PRO) [P] Providence, RI St. Thomas Aquinas Priory at Providence College.
Barron, Henry T. '88 (CHR) [11] Charleston, SC Church of the Nativity.
Barron, James W.C. *o.p.* '83 (PRO) [P] Providence, RI St. Thomas Aquinas Priory at Providence College.
Barron, John P. *s.j.* '82 (ALN) [A] Wernersville, PA Novitiate of St. Isaac Jogues; [N] Wernersville, PA Jesuit Center for Spiritual Growth.
Barron, Robert E. '86 (CHI) [A] Mundelein, IL University of St. Mary of the Lake-Mundelein Seminary.
Barron, Stanley C. '74 (PAT) Ogdensburg, NJ St. Thomas of Aquin Church.
Barron, Wayne J. *c.m.f.* '58 (SPC) [D] Springfield, MO St. John's Mercy Villa; [E] Springfield, MO Claretians Missionaries' Residence-Villa Claret.
Barrons, Brian *m.m.* '84 (NY) [Z] Maryknoll, NY Maryknoll Fathers and Brothers; [Z] Maryknoll, NY Maryknoll Fathers and Brothers.
Barrow, John '80 (PMB) [4] Delray Beach, FL St. Vincent Ferrer Church.
Barrow, Joseph A. '96 (NEW) [3] Newark, NJ Blessed Sacrament Church.
Barruetabena, Esteban *c.p.* '54 (SJN) [46] San Juan, PR Nuestra Senora de la Piedad Church.
Barruetabena, Felix *c.p.* (SJN) [9] Carolina, PR Santa Gema Galgani Church.
Barrus, Paul W. '78 (DAL) Richardson, TX St. Paul the Apostle Church.
Barry, Bernard J. '39 (SPK) Retired.
Barry, David E. *s.j.* '78 (R) [1] Durham, NC Holy Cross Church; [E] Durham, NC Jesuit Community; [H] Durham, NC North Carolina Central University.
Barry, Msgr. Denis L. '35 (LIN) Retired; [E] Lincoln, NE Bonacum House.
Barry, Donald M. *s.j.* '66 (BGP) [D] Fairfield, CT Fairfield College Preparatory School; [O] Fairfield, CT The Fairfield Jesuit Community-Fairfield University.
Barry, Edward '73 (NY) Dover Plains, NY St. Charles Borromeo Church.
Barry, Edward F. '43 (HRT) [M] Hartford, CT Missionaries of LaSalette Provincial Secretary.
Barry, Francis (SAV) Retired.
Barry, George F. *s.j.* '54 (BO) [W] Weston, MA Campion Health Center, Inc.
Barry, Gerard D. '50 (BO) [1] Newton, MA St. Bernard Church.
Barry, Henry F. '41 (BO) Rockland, MA Holy Family Church; Retired.
Barry, James '59 (NEW) [N] Cliffside Park, NJ St. Patrick's Missionary Society.
Barry, James *c.p.* '69 (CHI) [N] Chicago, IL Passionist Community-CTU.
Barry, James D. (NU) Jessenland, MN St. Thomas (Mission) Church.
Barry, James D. '61 (NU) Arlington, MN St. Mary Church; Henderson, MN St. Joseph Church.
Barry, James F. '67 (CAM) Clayton, NJ St. Catherine's Church.
Barry, James H. *s.j.* '40 (BO) [W] Weston, MA Campion Health Center, Inc.
Barry, James J. '69 (BO) [4] Chelsea, MA Our Lady of Grace Church.
Barry, Msgr. John F. '61 (LA) Manhattan Beach, CA American Martyrs Church.
Barry, John M. '88 (WDC) Laurel, MD St. Nicholas Church.
Barry, Joseph A. '35 (STA) Retired.
Barry, Lawrence E. *s.j.* '58 (STL) [O] St. Louis, MO Fusz Pavilion.
Barry, Leo '51 (WOR) Retired.
Barry, Maurice J. '67 (HRT) Windsor, CT St. Gertrude's Church.
Barry, Msgr. Patrick J. '54 (NY) [6] Mt. Vernon, NY SS. Peter and Paul Church.
Barry, Paul '48 (WDC) Retired.
Barry, Raymond J. '65 (HRT) Branford, CT St. Therese Church.
Barry, Robert *o.p.* '73 (PEO) [2] Champaign, IL St. John's Catholic Chapel; [O] Champaign, IL St. John's Catholic Student Chapel and Newman Foundation, University of Illinois.
Barry, Robert L. *o.p.* '73 (CHI) [N] River Forest, IL St. Thomas Aquinas Priory.
Barry, Ronald (RVC) Retired.
Barry, Thomas J. '67 (HRT) Glastonbury, CT St. Dunstan Church; Special and other (Arch)Diocesan Assignment.
Barry, Thomas M. '61 (WOR) [28] Worcester, MA St. Stephen's Church; [K] Worcester, MA Providence Extended Care Center.
Barry, Msgr. Thomas P. '39 (DEN) [1] Englewood, CO All Souls Church; Retired.
Barry, Msgr. Wiliam J. '44 (LA) Retired.
Barry, William A. *s.j.* '62 (BO) [W] Boston, MA The Society of Jesus of New England-Provincial Offices; [W] Boston, MA The Society of Jesus of New England-Provincial Offices.
Barsen, Msgr. Herman J. '40 (LAF) Retired.
Barszcz, Benedict *s.a.c.* '89 (BRK) [79] Brooklyn, NY St. Mark's Church.
Barszcz, Benedict *s.a.c.* '90 (BUF) [O] North Tonawanda, NY Society of the Catholic Apostolate.
Barszczewski, Francis A. '68 (PH) Clifton Heights, PA Sacred Heart Church.
Barta, Ardel H. '63 (DUB) On Leave of Absence.
Barta, Msgr. James O. (DUB) On Special or Other (Arch)Diocesan Assignment.
Barta, Wayne J. '60 (MIL) Ashford, WI St. Martin's Church; St. Kilian, WI St. Kilian's Church.
Bartak, James J. '89 (OM) Newcastle, NE St. Peter Church; Ponca, NE St. Joseph Church.
Bartchak, Mark L. '81 (E) [29] Erie, PA St. Stanislaus Church.
Bartczyszyn, Steve *c.r.* '86 (CHI) [D] Chicago, IL Weber High School.
Bartek, James F. '53 (OM) Retired.
Bartek, Valerian '82 (LIN) Grant, NE Mother of Sorrows Church.
Bartek, William C. '61 (OM) Retired.
Bartel, Franklin L. '70 (PHX) Litchfield Park, AZ St. Thomas Aquinas Church.
Bartel, Leo J. '58 (RCK) Morrison, IL St. Mary Church.
Bartel, Martin R. *o.s.b.* '85 (GBG) [B] Latrobe, PA St. Vincent College; [H] Latrobe, PA Saint Vincent Archabbey.
Bartell, Ernest J. *c.s.c.* '61 (FTW) [B] Notre Dame, IN University of Notre Dame Du Lac; [J] Notre Dame, IN Holy Cross Community, Corby Hall, University of Notre Dame.
Bartelme, James P. '82 (SUP) Gilman, WI SS. Peter and Paul Church; Lublin, WI St. Stanislaus Church.
Barter, Robert J. '61 (PRM) Detroit, MI St. Nicholas Church.
Barth, Camillus *c.p.* '34 (HRT) [M] West Hartford, CT Holy Family Monastery/Retreat.
Barth, Msgr. Charles P. '56 (CAM) Merchantville, NJ St. Peter's Church.
Barth, J. Robert *s.j.* '61 (BO) [C] Chestnut Hill, MA

Boston College; [W] Chestnut Hill, MA The Jesuit Community at Boston College.
Barth, Michael *s.t.* '79 (CLV) [P] Cleveland, OH Missionary Servants of the Most Holy Trinity.
Barth, Michael '94 (COV) [B] Alexandria, KY Bishop Brossart High School.
Barth, Michael D. '94 (COV) Alexandria, KY St. Mary of the Assumption Church.
Barth, Michael K. *s.t.* '79 (CLV) [3] Cleveland, OH St. Agnes - Our Lady of Fatima Church.
Barth, Raymond J. '85 (KAL) Bridgman, MI Our Lady Queen of Peace Church.
Barthel, Charles W. '82 (STL) [2] St. Louis, MO Epiphany of Our Lord Church.
Barthelme, Frederick J. '34 (STP) Retired.
Bartko, Gerald *o.s.f.s.* '66 (BUF) [5] Lockport, NY St. Patrick Church.
Bartko, Louis *o.f.m.* '90 (IND) Batesville, IN St. Louis Church.
Bartkus, Msgr. Algimantas A. '65 (ALN) On Duty Outside the Diocese.
Bartlett, Albert P. *s.j.* '54 (NY) [145] Bronx, NY St. Helena Church; [Z] New York, NY Jesuit Community at Fordham University.
Bartlett, H. James *s.m.* '69 (CIN) [M] Dayton, OH Marianist Provincialate.
Bartlett, James *s.m.* '69 (CIN) [24] Dayton, OH Queen of Apostles Church.
Bartlett, Lee F. '72 (WOR) [16] Worcester, MA Sacred Heart Church.
Bartlett, Richard *c.m.f.* '50 (CHI) [163] Chicago, IL St. Pancratius Church; [N] Oak Park, IL Claretian Fathers Headquarters of U.S.A. Eastern Province.
Bartley, David J. '70 (BO) [2] Lynn, MA St. Jean Baptiste Church.
Bartley, Denis *s.s.c.* '51 (LA) [R] Los Angeles, CA Columban Fathers, Procure House.
Bartley, Vincent '69 (NY) [223] Staten Island, NY St. Paul Church.
Bartley, William J. '37 (BRK) Retired.
Bartman, Roch *o.f.m.conv.* '31 (MRY) [G] Arroyo Grande, CA St. Joseph's Cupertino Novitiate.
Bartnik, Harry S. '56 (TLS) Retired; [F] Broken Arrow, OK Franciscan Villa.
Bartnik, James T. '75 (BUF) [18] Buffalo, NY St. Casimir Church.
Bartnikowski, Raymond B. '63 (CLV) Maple Heights, OH St. Wenceslas Church.
Bartniski, William D. '67 (GAL) [5] Galveston, TX St. Peter the Apostle Church.
Bartok, Msgr. Charles '47 (ORL) Retired.
Bartollotta, Victor W., Jr. '90 (ROC) On Duty Outside the Diocese.
Bartolo, Salvador *o.carm.* '52 (JOL) [J] Darien, IL Carmelite Fathers Provincial Office.
Barton, Raymond A. '66 (RIC) Charlottesville, VA Church of the Holy Comforter.
Bartone, Donald E. '48 (DET) Retired.
Bartos, Francis J. '54 (PH) East Greenville, PA St. Philip Neri Church.
Bartos, Msgr. John V. '52 (PH) Warminster, PA Nativity of Our Lord Church.
Bartos, Kris '85 (MIA) [15] Miami, FL St. Agatha Church.
Bartos, Kris A. '85 (DET) On Duty Outside the Archdiocese.
Bartosic, Mark '94 (CHI) [5] Chicago, IL St. Agnes of Bohemia Church.
Bartoszek, Richard J. '89 (DET) Woodhaven, MI Our Lady of the Woods Church; Detroit, MI Heritage Hospital.
Bartoszewski, Leszek (OAK) [3] San Leandro, CA St. Felicitas Church.
Bartoul, William '77 (SAM) On Duty Outside the Diocese.
Bartruff, Louis B. '45 (BRK) Retired; [U] Douglaston, NY Bishop Mugavero Residence.
Bartsch, Edward C. '49 (VIC) High Hill, TX Nativity of the Blessed Virgin Mary Church; Praha, TX St. Mary's Church.
Bartsch, Ken *o.f.m. conv.* '75 (STP) Bloomington, MN St. Bonaventure Church.
Bartz, Richard B. (CHI) [J] Chicago, IL Columbus Hospital.
Barusefski, Ronald '89 (PSC) North Fort Myers, FL All Saints Byzantine Catholic Church.
Barwig, Regis N. '59 (GB) [I] Oshkosh, WI Community of Our Lady.
Barwin, John G. '80 (E) Mount Jewett, PA St. Joseph Church; Bradford, PA Federal Correction Institution.
Baryski, Wojciech *s.ch.* (DET) Hamtramck, MI St. Florian Church.
Barzyk, Andrew A. '94 (CHI) Niles, IL St. John Brebeuf Church.
Barzyk, Msgr. Robert R. '58 (GAL) Retired.
Basa, Francis J. '71 (CLV) [4] Akron, OH Christ the King Church.
Basarab, John G. '79 (PSC) Annandale, VA Epiphany of Our Lord Church.
Baseford, Paul '57 (SB) Retired.
Baseheart, Edward H. '42 (CHI) [73] Chicago, IL St. Gregory Church; Retired.
Basetti-Sani, Giulio F. *o.f.m.* '35 (PAT) [M] Butler, NJ St. Anthony Friary.
Bash, Cletus '56 (OKL) Special Assignment; [E] Oklahoma City, OK Mercy Health Center.
Basil, John E. '62 (NEW) Hohokus, NJ St. Luke's Church.
Basile, Gioacchino '95 (NEW) West New York, NJ St. Joseph of the Palisades Church.
Basile, Nicholas F. '49 (NY) [174] Bronx, NY Our Lady of Mt. Carmel Church; Retired.
Baskara Tulus Wardaya, Francis Xavier *s.j.* '92 (MIL) [P] Milwaukee, WI Jesuit Community at Marquette University.
Basler, Msgr. Howard B. '58 (BRK) [L] Brooklyn, NY Catholic Charities; [U] Brooklyn, NY St. Joseph's Priest Residence.
Basols, Jose Andres *sch.p.* '68 (SJN) [58] San Juan, PR Santisimo Salvador Church.
Basquel, Thomas *c.s.sp.* (NY) [195] Staten Island, NY St. Ann Church.
Bass, Francis E. '48 (DAV) Iowa City, IA Veteran's Administration Hospital; Retired; [J] Iowa City, IA Mercy Hospital.
Bass, Michael E. '87 (LR) Pocahontas, AR St. Paul the Apostle Church.
Bass, Msgr Ricardo E. '74 (DET) [4] St. Clair Shores, MI St. Joan of Arc Church.
Bassano, Michael '75 (SY) On Duty Outside the Diocese.
Basso, Anthony *s.d.v.* '93 (NEW) Palisades Park, NJ St. Nicholas Church.
Basso, Richard '62 (SEA) [C] Bellevue, WA Eastside Catholic High School.
Basso, Settimo *c.s.* '41 (PRO) [4] Johnston, RI St. Rocco Church.
Bastia, Raymond B. '75 (PRO) [2] Johnston, RI Our Lady of Grace Church.
Bastian, Robert J. '43 (CIN) Retired.
Bastianelli, Dan *s.s.j.* '64 (BEA) [3] Beaumont, TX Blessed Sacrament Church.
Bastides, Alexis '84 (NY) [18] New York, NY Blessed Sacrament Church.
Bastien, James R. '95 (BUF) Williamsville, NY St. Gregory the Great Church.
Bastos, Luiz '95 (ORL) Kissimmee, FL Holy Redeemer Church.
Bastress, Msgr. Arthur '51 (BAL) [46] Baltimore, MD St. Jerome Church; [78] Baltimore, MD St. Peter the Apostle Church.
Basznianin, Richard '84 (TR) Brick Town, NJ St. Dominic Church.
Batch, Thomas A. '76 (SAC) Knights Landing, CA St. Paul Church.
Batcha, James '85 (PRM) Lorain, OH St. Michael Church; Lorain, OH St. Nicholas Church.
Batcheldor, C. Joseph '57 (L) Shelbyville, KY Annunciation of the Blessed Virgin Mary Church.
Batcho, Michael '73 (PHU) Absent on Leave.
Batcho, Robert J. '88 (STF) [2] Ansonia, CT SS. Peter and Paul Church.
Bateman, John '96 (HBG) [3] Harrisburg, PA St. Francis of Assisi Church.
Bates, Donald J. *o.s.a.* '60 (CHI) [N] Olympia Fields, IL Austin Friary.
Bates, James R. '63 (LFT) Noblesville, IN Our Lady of Grace Church.
Bates, Urban M. *o.p.* '53 (ANC) [1] Anchorage, AK Holy Family Cathedral.
Bath, Winston L. '72 (ALB) Hudson, NY Church of St. Mary.
Bathke, Joseph *c.pp.s.* '78 (KC) [3] St. Joseph, MO St. Francis Xavier Church.
Batista, George L. '83 (NEW) On Duty Outside the Archdiocese.
Batista, George L. '83 (PMB) Lake Worth, FL St. Luke Church.
Batkiewicz, Joseph '71 (CLV) Berea, OH St. Adalbert Church.
Batkiewicz, Joseph J. '35 (ALB) Retired.
Batory, Stephen '47 (P) Retired.
Batson, Msgr. John R. '57 (MEM) Retired.
Batt, Dacian *o.f.m.* '58 (PEO) Metamora, IL St. Mary's Church; Washburn, IL St. Elizabeth Church.
Battafarano, Gregory *o.carm.* '67 (WDC) [B] Washington, DC Whitefriars Hall.
Battaglia, Ignatius *c.s.* '59 (PRO) [15] Providence, RI Holy Ghost Church.
Batterberry, Michael J. '70 (SEA) [B] Seattle, WA John F. Kennedy Memorial High School.
Battiato, Patrick W. '76 (COS) Security, CO Holy Family Church.
Battiato, Ronald '61 (OM) Clarkson, NE SS. Cyril and Methodius Church.
Battirossi, Bartholomew *m.c.c.j.* '42 (LA) [11] Los Angeles, CA Holy Cross Church.
Battista, Msgr. Leo '48 (WOR) Retired.
Battisti, Lewis A. '62 (CAM) Margate, NJ Blessed Sacrament Church.
Battle, Lawrence '49 (SB) Retired.
Battocletti, Richard '53 (STU) [7] Steubenville, OH St. Peter's Church; [9] Steubenville, OH St. Stanislaus Church.
Batts, Peter M. *o.p.* '81 (WDC) [B] Washington, DC Dominican House of Studies.
Batule, Robert J. '85 (RVC) Mineola, NY Corpus Christi Church.
Batykefer, John J. '90 (PIT) Natrona Heights, PA Our Lady of the Most Blessed Sacrament Church.
Batza, Msgr. Joseph '41 (PHU) Retired.
Bau, Chau Xuan *c.ss.r.* '62 (LA) [R] Baldwin Park, CA Vietnamese Redemptorist Mission; [CC] Baldwin Park, CA The Redemptorist Vietnamese Mission Corporation.
Bau, Mark *c.m.c.* '77 (FWT) [15] Fort Worth, TX St. Rita Church.
Baudone, Louis '59 (GR) Retired.
Bauer, Carl E. '63 (WH) Star City, WV St. Mary's Church.
Bauer, Charles A. '78 (MEM) [7] Memphis, TN Blessed Sacrament Church.
Bauer, Donald J. '48 (SY) [10] Utica, NY St. Joseph and St. Patrick Church; Retired.
Bauer, Erwin J. '75 (DET) Harsens Island, MI St. Mark Church; Retired.
Bauer, Francis '41 (EVN) Retired.
Bauer, Msgr. Henry '48 (KC) Retired.
Bauer, Jacob F. '48 (GI) Retired.
Bauer, John '73 (PIT) [6] Ambridge, PA Good Samaritan Church.
Bauer, John F. '65 (E) Sheffield, PA St. Anthony Church; Warren, PA Warren State Hospital.
Bauer, John M. '79 (STP) Deephaven, MN St. Therese Church.
Bauer, Joseph O. '53 (SAG) Retired.
Bauer, Karl A. '67 (NY) [142] Bronx, NY St. Frances of Rome Church.
Bauer, Lawrence T. *c.s.c.* '35 (FTW) [J] South Bend, IN Congregation of Holy Cross Indiana Province Provincial House.
Bauer, Msgr. Leonard A. '37 (BEL) [F] Belleville, IL Meredith Memorial Home; [K] Belleville, IL Serra Club of St. Clair County.
Bauer, Mark F. '86 (GR) Coopersville, MI St. Michael's Church; [K] Coopersville, MI Grand Valley State University Catholic Campus Ministry.
Bauer, Paul '91 (SD) [3] Chula Vista, CA St. Pius X Church.
Bauer, Ralph '47 (LR) Retired.
Bauer, Robert *s.d.b.* '71 (COL) [H] Columbus, OH Salesian Center.
Bauer, Robert A. '87 (DET) Carleton, MI St. Patrick Church.
Bauer, Robert J. *s.d.b.* '71 (COL) [A] Columbus, OH Pontifical College Josephinum.
Bauer, Roy R. '59 (SFD) [8] Quincy, IL St. Peter Church.
Bauer, Stephan *o.s.c.* '92 (CHI) [N] Chicago, IL Crosier Community of Chicago.
Bauer, Stephen F. '77 (STL) Dutzow, MO St. Vincent de Paul Church.
Bauer, Steven *o.s.c.* '88 (CHI) [170] Chicago, IL SS. Peter and Paul Church.
Bauer, Sylvester W. '42 (SPC) Retired.
Bauer, William M. '73 (ALB) Greenville, NY St. John the Baptist Church.
Bauerle, Bernhard *o.carm.* '64 (JOL) [C] Joliet, IL Joliet Catholic Academy; [J] Joliet, IL St. Elias Carmelites.
Bauernfeind, Thomas '63 (BAL) [5] Baltimore, MD St. Alphonsus Church.
Baugh, David G. '57 (CLV) [6] Euclid, OH St. William Church.
Bauhoff, Msgr. Richard C. '73 (RVC) Roslyn, NY St. Mary's Church.
Bauhs, Eugene J. '48 (MAD) Retired.
Bauler, Msgr. Gary P. '67 (LA) Pasadena, CA St. Philip the Apostle Church.
Bauler, Robert J. '57 (BIR) Retired.
Baum, Boniface '46 (CHI) [N] Chicago, IL St. Peter's Friary.
Baum, Msgr. Charles J. '34 (CHR) Greenville, SC St. Mary's Church; Retired.
Baum, Dennis *o.f.m.* (NY) [13] New York, NY St. Anthony of Padua Church.
Baum, Jerome '47 (CHI) [N] Chicago, IL St. Peter's Friary.
Baum, Terrence A. *s.j.* '81 (NY) [F] New York, NY Xavier High School.
Bauman, Dale '82 (FTW) Albion, IN Blessed Sacrament Church; Ligonier, IN St. Patrick Church.
Bauman, John F. '69 (NEW) [25] Jersey City, NJ St. Paul's Church.
Bauman, Rodger R. '82 (STP) Richfield, MN St. Peter Church.
Bauman, William A. '60 (KC) [40] Kansas City, MO St. Thomas More Church.
Baumann, Anthony *o.f.m.* '44 (SFR) [5] San Francisco, CA St. Anthony Church; [J] San Francisco, CA St. Mary's Medical Center.
Baumann, Charles R. *s.j.* '80 (RC) White River, SD St. Ignatius Church; White River, SD Sacred Heart

Church; St. Francis, SD Rosebud Reservation Church.
Baumann, Gregory R. *s.j.* '93 (LA) [10] Los Angeles, CA Dolores Mission Church.
Baumann, Hugh *o.s.b.* '41 (NO) [P] St. Benedict, LA St. Joseph Abbey.
Baumann, John A. *s.j.* '69 (OAK) [N] Oakland, CA Murray Residence Community; [R] Oakland, CA Pacific Institute for Community Organization.
Baumann, Lawrence '64 (PHX) [4] Phoenix, AZ Immaculate Heart of Mary Church.
Baumann, Richard *o.f.m.* '46 (GLP) Houck, AZ St. John Church.
Baumann, Richard J. *s.j.* '75 (CHI) [89] Chicago, IL St. Ignatius Church.
Baumann, Silas '51 (GB) [I] Appleton, WI St. Fidelis Friary.
Baumann, Steve '92 (ORL) Ormond Beach, FL St. Brendan Church.
Baumann, Theodore J. '67 (BEL) Bartelso, IL St. Cecilia Church.
Baumberger, Richard '89 (SFS) Ramona, SD St. William of Vercelli Church.
Baumberger, Rudolph *o.s.b.* '43 (SCL) [I] Collegeville, MN St. John's Abbey, of the Order of St. Benedict.
Baumbusch, Steven *p.i.m.e.* '83 (DET) [K] Detroit, MI P.I.M.E. Missionaries of SS. Peter and Paul.
Baumert, Frank J. '78 (OM) Neligh, NE St. Francis Church.
Baumgaertner, Msgr. William L. '46 (STP) Retired.
Baumgartel, David A. '73 (WIL) Liftwood, DE Immaculate Heart of Mary Church; Wilmington, DE A.I. du Pont Institute.
Baumgartner, Msgr. A. Thomas '58 (BAL) [91] Baltimore, MD St. Ursula Church.
Baumgartner, Andrew *o.s.b.* '60 (B) [C] Jerome, ID Ascension Priory.
Baumgartner, Bernard *c.ss.r.* '44 (BAL) Annapolis, MD St. Mary Church; [M] Annapolis, MD Saint Mary Rectory.
Baumgartner, David '90 (CR) [1] Crookston, MN Cathedral of the Immaculate Conception.
Baumgartner, John '43 (BAK) Retired.
Baumgartner, John H. '63 (MIL) [56] Milwaukee, WI Mother of Perpetual Help Church; [76] Milwaukee, WI St. Stephen, Martyr Church.
Baumhart, Raymond C. *s.j.* '57 (CHI) [C] Chicago, IL Jesuit Community at Loyola University of Chicago.
Baumiller, Robert C. *s.j.* '65 (CIN) [M] Cincinnati, OH Jesuit Community at Xavier Unversity.
Baumstein, Paschal M. *o.s.b.* '79 (CHL) [J] Belmont, NC Belmont Abbey.
Baur, Edward *s.v.d.* '55 (GAL) [1] Galveston, TX St. Mary's Cathedral Basilica; [K] Houston, TX The Catholic Chaplain Corps.
Baur, Joseph *o.f.m.* (OAK) [R] Berkley, CA Multicultural Institute.
Baur, Joseph A. *o.f.m.* '52 (PHX) Guadalupe, AZ Our Lady of Guadalupe Church.
Baures, Steven H. '83 (LC) New Lisbon, WI St. Paul Church.
Baures, Steven M. '83 (LC) Germantown, WI Our Lady of the Lake Church.
Bausch, Michael A. '79 (ROC) Henrietta, NY Church of the Good Shepherd.
Bausch, William (TR) Retired.
Bauschka, Joseph C. '55 (GB) Elcho, WI Holy Family Church.
Bauta, Krzysztof T. '86 (CC) On Duty Outside the Diocese.
Bautch, Richard J. *s.j.* '94 (CHI) [N] Chicago, IL Chicago Province of the Society of Jesus-Provincial Office.
Bautista, Gaspar '75 (LA) San Gabriel, CA St. Anthony Church.
Bautista, Javier *m.s.c.* '95 (RCK) [H] Aurora, IL Missionaries of the Sacred Heart Community.
Bautista, Jose '91 (ORL) Melbourne, FL Our Lady of Lourdes Church.
Bauwens, Joseph P. *o.c.s.o.* '56 (DUB) [K] Peosta, IA New Melleray Abbey, Order of Cistercians of the Strict Observance.
Bauwens, Thomas E. '87 (OM) Walthill, NE St. Joseph Church; Winnebago, NE St. Augustine's Church; [O] Winnebago, NE St. Augustine's Indian Mission.
Bava, David '73 (WDC) [18] Washington, DC Holy Redeemer Church.
Bavaro, John D. *o.f.m.* '63 (BO) [P] Andover, MA Franciscan Center; [W] Andover, MA St. Francis Friary; [Y] Andover, MA Franciscan Center - Retreat House.
Baver, John J. (PIT) [4] New Castle, PA St. Vitus Church.
Baver, Msgr. William F. '81 (ALN) [10] Allentown, PA St. Stephen of Hungary Church.
Bavero, Benvenute *o.f.m.* '44 (LA) [4] Santa Barbara, CA St. Barbara Church; [R] Santa Barbara, CA Franciscan Friary, Order of Friars Minor (Old Mission).
Bavinger, R. Bruce *s.j.* '78 (WDC) [E] North Bethesda, MD Georgetown Preparatory School.
Bawiec, Edward J. '54 (PEO) Peru, IL St. Valentine's Church.
Bawyn, Anthony '82 (SEA) Special Assignment.
Baxa, Henry R. '90 (SAL) Beloit, KS St. John the Baptist Church.
Baxer, Joseph *m.s.* '71 (WDC) [M] Washington, DC La Salette Community.
Baxter, Gregory P. '88 (OM) Verdigre, NE St. Wenceslaus Church.
Baxter, Michael *c.s.c.* (FTW) [B] Notre Dame, IN University of Notre Dame Du Lac.
Baxter, Stephen R. '81 (WCH) Fredonia, KS Sacred Heart Church; Neodesha, KS St. Ignatius Church.
Baxter, Thomas *o.s.b.* '79 (CHI) [N] Chicago, IL Monastery of the Holy Cross.
Baxter, Thomas F. '76 (MAD) Lancaster, WI St. Clement Church.
Bay, Joseph N. '94 (COL) Graduate Studies.
Bayard, Nicholas R. '46 (CHR) Greer, SC Blessed Trinity Church.
Baybay, Felicito S. '74 (ORL) St. Cloud, FL St. Thomas Aquinas Church.
Bayer, Edward J. '56 (BAL) Randallstown, MD Holy Family Church; [Q] Baltimore, MD Cursillo Movement.
Bayer, Lawrence J. '58 (CLV) [2] Parma, OH St. Bridget Church.
Bayer, Leonard '51 (SFE) Retired.
Bayer, Peter T. '71 (ROC) Rochester, NY St. Ann's Home/Heritage; [E] Rochester, NY St. Ann's Home for the Aged.
Bayer, Walter C. '42 (STA) Korona, FL St. Mary's Church.
Bayhi, M. Jeffrey '79 (BR) [2] Baton Rouge, LA St. Agnes Church.
Bayhi, W. Peter *s.j.* '66 (NO) [8] New Orleans, LA Holy Name of Jesus Church.
Baylis, Thomas J. '59 (HRT) [2] Milford, CT St. Ann's Church.
Bayne, David C. *s.j.* '52 (DET) [K] Detroit, MI Jesuit Provincial Office-Detroit Province of the Society of Jesus.
Bayne, Joseph *o.f.m.conv.* '85 (BUF) [J] Buffalo, NY The Franciscan Center, Inc.
Baysinger, Leo A. *s.d.b.* '67 (AUS) [6] Waco, TX St. Louis Church; [B] Waco, TX Reicher Catholic High School; [H] Waco, TX Salesians of Don Bosco.
Baz, Louis '81 (OLL) Cincinnati, OH St. Anthony of Padua Church.
Bazan, Arnaldo '58 (MIA) Coral Gables, FL Little Flower Church.
Bazan, Msgr. Joaquin (SFE) [21] Albuquerque, NM St. Anne Church.
Bazan, Msgr. Joaquin '62 (WDC) On Duty Outside the Archdiocese.
Bazan, Michael J. '84 (ARL) Warrenton, VA St. John the Evangelist Church.
Bazina, Basile (BO) Burlington, MA St. Margaret Church.
Bazton, Jose M. Garcia *m.ss.cc.* '62 (SJN) [10] Bayamon, PR San Juan Bautista de la Salle Church.
Bazzi, Michael J. '64 (EST) El Cajon, CA St. Peter Chaldean Parish Church.
Bazzi, Michael J. '64 (SD) El Cajon, CA St. Peter Church.
Bazzoli, Bob *o.s.f.s.* '88 (CHL) [4] Greensboro, NC St. Paul the Apostle Church.
Beach, Francis W. '76 (PH) [70] Philadelphia, PA Immaculate Heart of Mary Church; [D] Philadelphia, PA Roman Catholic High School for Boys.
Beach, Raymond *o.f.m.* '48 (PAT) [K] Totowa, NJ St. Joseph's Home for the Elderly.
Beach, Robert '50 (SFE) Retired.
Beachum, Edwin (MOB) [1] Montgomery, AL St. Peter Church.
Beacom, John F. '37 (OM) Retired.
Beacom, Vincent L. '44 (SC) Retired.
Beain, Victorio *o.f.m.* '42 (SJN) [52] San Juan, PR Resurreccion del Senor Church.
Beal, John P. '74 (E) On Duty Outside Diocese.
Beal, John P. '74 (WDC) [C] Washington, DC Catholic University of America, The.
Beale, Kenneth R. '92 (NEW) Military Chaplains.
Beale, Robert P. (BO) Norfolk County, MA Dedham.
Bean, Charles S. '62 (CAM) On Sick Leave; [L] Cherry Hill, NJ Vianney Villa.
Bean, Donald '63 (BUR) Unassigned.
Beane, Raymond A. *o.f.m.* '38 (NY) [Z] New York, NY Franciscan Friars, Order of Friars Manor.
Beans, Elmer (FBK) Mountain Village, AK St. Lawrence Church.
Beard, Msgr. Raymond '41 (BAK) Retired.
Bearden, Clark '89 (BLX) Lumberton, MS Our Lady of Perpetual Help Church; [G] Lumberton, MS Pearl River Junior College, St. Joseph Catholic Center.
Beardsley, Frederick '60 (RIC) Retired.
Beary, Thomas J. '62 (BUR) Retired; [F] Burlington, VT St. Joseph's Home for Aged.
Beasley, Msgr. Thomas J. '53 (BUF) [1] Orchard Park, NY Nativity Church.
Beat, Jerome A. (WCH) [9] Wichita, KS Our Lady of Perpetual Help Church.
Beat, Jerome A. '63 (WCH) [17] Wichita, KS St. Patrick Church.
Beath, James D. '79 (CHI) Skokie, IL St. Peter Church.
Beaton, Angus *c.j.m.* '56 (SD) [M] San Diego, CA San Diego State University Newman Center.
Beaton, Kevin '87 (SAM) Wilkes-Barre, PA St. George Church.
Beattie, Msgr. James T. '61 (WDC) [1] Bethesda, MD St. Bartholomew Church.
Beattie, John A. *o.s.f.s.* '65 (VEN) [A] Fort Myers, FL Bishop Verot High School.
Beattie, Msgr. John A. '66 (LA) [41] Los Angeles, CA St. Ambrose Church.
Beattie, Joseph A. *o.s.f.s.* '65 (VEN) [A] Fort Myers, FL Bishop Verot High School.
Beattie, Thomas '93 (SEA) Sequim, WA St. Joseph Church.
Beatty, James H. '74 (CLV) Avon Lake, OH Holy Spirit Church.
Beatty, John '50 (SD) Retired.
Beatty, Michael D. '64 (CIN) [82] Cincinnati, OH St. Simon the Apostle Church.
Beaubien, David W. '93 (WDC) [3] Washington, DC St. Ann Church.
Beauchamp, E. William *c.s.c.* '82 (FTW) [B] Notre Dame, IN University of Notre Dame Du Lac; [B] Notre Dame, IN University of Notre Dame Du Lac; [J] Notre Dame, IN Holy Cross Community, Corby Hall, University of Notre Dame.
Beauchemin, Ronald *m.s.* '68 (FR) [K] Attleboro, MA La Salette Provincial House.
Beauclair, Stephen G. *o.s.b.* '67 (STP) Hastings, MN St. Elizabeth Ann Seton Church.
Beaudet, Eugene J. '53 (OG) Essex, NY St. Joseph Church; Willsboro, NY St. Philip of Jesus Church.
Beaudet, George W. '75 (PRT) East Millinocket, ME St. Peter's Church.
Beaudin, William *o.f.m.* '81 (BO) [BB] Boston, MA St. Anthony Shrine.
Beaudin, William R. '82 (BUR) Marshfield, VT North American Martyrs Church; [J] Burlington, VT University of Vermont-The Catholic Center at UVM.
Beaudoin, Andrew *s.s.s.* '54 (CLV) [P] Cleveland, OH Congregation of the Blessed Sacrament Provincial House.
Beaudoin, Andrew *s.s.s.* '54 (SP) Spring Hill, FL St. Frances Xavier Cabrini Church.
Beaudoin, Hubert N. *o.praem.* '56 (PH) [D] Philadelphia, PA St. John Neumann High School; [Z] Philadelphia, PA St. Norbert Priory.
Beaudry, David '82 (GB) Alverno, WI St. Joseph Church; Northeim, WI St. Casimir Church.
Beaulieu, Earl '60 (SHP) Retired.
Beaulieu, Kerry '74 (ORG) [1] Huntington Beach, CA St. Bonaventure Church.
Beaulieu, Peter R. '83 (WOR) [3] Worcester, MA Blessed Sacrament Church; Worcester, MA ADCARE Hospital of Worcester; On Special or Other (Arch)Diocesan Assignment.
Beaulieu, Peter R. '93 (WOR) Worcester, MA Memorial Hospital.
Beaulieu, Raymond '42 (PRO) Retired.
Beaulieu, Richard C. '76 (BO) Beverly, MA St. Mary Star of the Sea Church.
Beaulieu, Richard W. '71 (FR) [6] Fall River, MA Notre Dame de Lourdes Church.
Beaulieu, Robert J. '57 (HEL) Bozeman, MT Holy Rosary Church.
Beaumont, Gregory J. '96 (FRS) Clovis, CA Our Lady of Perpetual Help Church.
Beaumont, Msgr. Joachim B. '59 (NY) [31] New York, NY St. Elizabeth Church.
Beaumont, Joseph '48 (VEN) Retired.
Beaumont, Richard '58 (FWT) [9] Fort Worth, TX St. Bartholomew Church.
Beaupre, R. Bradley *c.s.c.* '68 (BGP) [O] Bridgeport, CT Provincial Offices of the Priests and Brothers of Holy Cross, Eastern Province.
Beauregard, David *o.m.v.* '80 (BO) [W] Milton, MA House of Theological Studies and Provincialate.
Beauregard, James E. '70 (BUR) Readsboro, VT St. Joachim Church.
Beauregard, Paul W. *o.m.i.* '61 (BO) [9] Lowell, MA St. Marie Church.
Beauregard, Thomas '51 (TOL) Retired.
Beausang, Msgr. Charles C. '46 (CAM) Retired.
Beausoleil, Charles *o.m.i.* (HRT) [M] Hamden, CT Oblates of Mary Immaculate.
Beausoleil, Charles *o.m.i.* '56 (NY) [BB] Newburgh, NY Our Lady of Hope Center.
Beauvais, David E. '62 (RCK) [6] Rockford, IL St. James Church.
Beauvais, Leon F. '58 (BO) [69] Boston, MA Sacred Heart Church.
Beaven, Robert W. '68 (CHI) Grayslake, IL St. Gilbert Church.
Beaver, Nelson '76 (TOL) Norwalk, OH St. Mary, Mother of the Redeemer Church; Peru, OH St. Alphonsus Liguori Church.
Beaver, Reinard W. '56 (SPK) Retired.

Beaver, William A. *o.s.b.* '85 (GBG) Jeannette, PA Sacred Heart Church.
Beavers, Carl A. '68 (CHY) [1] Cheyenne, WY St. Mary's Cathedral; Cheyenne, WY U.S. Veterans Administration Hospital 1.
Bebak, Brian '86 (WCH) Fort Scott, KS Mary Queen of Angels Church.
Bebedik, Hilarion *o.s.b.m.* '48 (RVC) [N] Glen Cove, NY St. Josaphatis Monastery, Novitiate and Retreat House.
Bebek, Dominic L. '53 (LA) Sick Leave.
Bebel, Alfred J. '58 (SY) [8] Syracuse, NY Our Lady of Solace Church; Syracuse, NY University Hospital; Special Assignment.
Becera, Rafael *c.s.* '95 (GAL) [43] Houston, TX St. Leo the Great Church.
Becerra, Alfred '44 (FRS) Faculties Only.
Becerra, Robert '89 (NEW) [1] Elizabeth, NJ St. Mary of the Assumption Church; Elizabeth, NJ Elizabeth General Medical Center.
Bechamps, Vincent *o.ss.t.* '66 (NO) [16] New Orleans, LA Our Lady Of Good Counsel Church; New Orleans, LA University Hospital.
Bechard, Bernard J. *s.s.e.* '49 (BUR) Sheldon Springs, VT St. Anthony Church.
Bechard, Dean P. *s.j.* '91 (BGP) [O] Fairfield, CT The Fairfield Jesuit Community-Fairfield University.
Bechard, Gerard V. '80 (DET) [5] Westland, MI SS. Simon and Jude Church.
Becherer, David '48 (MOB) On Duty Outside the Archdiocese.
Becherer, James R. '54 (CLV) Retired.
Becht, James '53 (RC) Bonesteel, SD Immaculate Conception Church.
Bechtel, Francis '43 (PHX) Retired.
Bechtel, James C. '71 (ALN) Gordon, PA Our Lady of Good Counsel Church.
Bechtold, Paul I. *c.p.* '41 (CHI) [N] Chicago, IL Immaculate Conception Monastery.
Beck, Aelred J. *o.s.b.* '48 (GBG) Youngstown, PA Sacred Heart Church; [H] Latrobe, PA Saint Vincent Archabbey.
Beck, Msgr. Albert J. '49 (GAL) [32] Houston, TX Holy Cross Chapel; On Special Assignment.
Beck, Charles L. '45 (MAD) Retired.
Beck, David J. '67 (TOL) Bluffton, OH St. Mary Church; [3] Lima, OH St. John the Evangelist Church.
Beck, Edward *c.p.* '85 (NY) [DD] New York, NY Passionist Residence.
Beck, Erwin G. *s.j.* '60 (NEW) [C] Jersey City, NJ St. Peter's Preparatory School.
Beck, Msgr. George A. '41 (GAL) [32] Houston, TX Holy Cross Chapel; Retired.
Beck, Henry *o.f.m.* (CIN) [M] Cincinnati, OH St. Francis Seraph Friary.
Beck, Joseph C. '84 (PIT) [5] Pittsburgh, PA St. Bede Church; Allegheny County, PA Forbes Health Center/ Center for Gerontology/Hospice; Allegheny County, PA Kane Regional Center - Glen Hazel; Allegheny County, PA Woodhaven Convalescent Center.
Beck, Lawrence J. '88 (LA) Montebello, CA Our Lady of the Miraculous Medal Church.
Beck, Leo J. '37 (PIT) Retired; [N] Pittsburgh, PA St. John Vianney Manor.
Beck, Richard *o.m.i.* '67 (SAT) Eagle Pass, TX Our Lady of Refuge Church.
Beck, Richard P. '55 (MIL) Retired.
Beck, Richard W. '74 (SCR) Pleasant Mount, PA St. James Church.
Beck, Robert '66 (DUB) [L] Dubuque, IA Visitation Convent.
Beck, Robert P. '76 (BEA) Military Chaplains.
Beck, Robert R. '66 (DUB) [C] Dubuque, IA Loras College.
Becker, Anthony J. '47 (RCK) Retired.
Becker, Arthur J. '73 (ALB) [1] Cohoes, NY St. Agnes-St. Patrick Church; [4] Cohoes, NY St. Marie Church.
Becker, Bruno *o.s.b.* '51 (P) [L] St. Benedict, OR Mt. Angel Abbey.
Becker, Charles J. *s.s.* '53 (CAM) [6] Camden, NJ St. Joseph's Church; Retired.
Becker, Charles P. '86 (CHI) Other Assignments.
Becker, David R. '66 (ALT) Shade Gap, PA St. Mary's Church; Huntingdon, PA State Correctional Institution.
Becker, Dennis E. '62 (NU) Hutchinson, MN Church of St. Anastasia.
Becker, Donald W. '67 (BUF) [3] Batavia, NY St. Mary Church.
Becker, Franklyn W. '64 (MIL) On Leave.
Becker, Frederick J. '59 (NY) [159] Bronx, NY St. Lucy Church; Bronx, NY Our Lady of Mercy Medical Center; [S] New York, NY Our Lady of Mercy Medical Center.
Becker, George A. '53 (LC) Elmwood, WI Sacred Heart Church; Spring Valley, WI Sacred Heart of Jesus Church.
Becker, John J. '72 (GB) [1] Oshkosh, WI St. Peter Church.
Becker, John R. *s.j.* '56 (PHX) [B] Phoenix, AZ Brophy College Preparatory.
Becker, Joseph M. *s.j.* '39 (CIN) [M] Cincinnati, OH Faber Jesuit Community.
Becker, Joseph P. *o.s.f.s.* '69 (ALN) Allentown, PA Lehigh Valley Hospital at Cedar Crest; [K] Center Valley, PA Oblates of St. Francis de Sales.
Becker, Luke *o.s.b.* '34 (KC) [J] Conception, MO Conception Abbey.
Becker, Michael A. '75 (ALT) [12] Altoona, PA St. Rose of Lima Church.
Becker, Nicholas J. '38 (SC) Retired.
Becker, Paul D. '73 (BIS) Foxholm, ND St. Mary Church; [D] Minot, ND St. Joseph's Hospital dba UniMed Medical Center.
Becker, Richard F. '72 (PBL) [12] Pueblo, CO St. Joseph Church; Vineland, CO St. Therese Church.
Becker, Robert '79 (AUS) [9] Austin, TX Sacred Heart Church.
Becker, Robert T. '64 (SFD) [5] Springfield, IL St. Agnes Church.
Becker, Ronald '72 (TR) [13] Trenton, NJ St. Francis of Assisium Church.
Becker, Russell C. *o.f.m.* '72 (HON) [1] Honolulu, HI Cathedral of Our Lady of Peace.
Becker, Thomas G. '80 (SCL) Glenwood, MN Sacred Heart Church.
Becker, Valentine A. *s.m.* '42 (WDC) [M] Washington, DC Marist Provincial House.
Becker, Vincent J. '62 (BUF) [46] Buffalo, NY St. Martin Church.
Becker, William M. '88 (WIN) [A] Winona, MN Immaculate Heart of Mary Seminary, Saint Mary's University of MN #43.
Beckers, Msgr. Henry F. '47 (ALX) Retired.
Beckfelt, John W. '74 (LC) Big River, WI Nativity of the Blessed Virgin Mary Church.
Beckman, David '92 (DUB) [G] Mason City, IA Newman Catholic.
Beckman, David M. '90 (DUB) Mason City, IA Holy Family Church.
Beckman, Msgr. Donald M. '70 (RVC) Uniondale, NY St. Martha Church.
Beckman, Gary L. '95 (DAV) Bettendorf, IA Our Lady of Lourdes Church.
Beckman, John J. *s.j.* '54 (CIN) [F] Cincinnati, OH St. Xavier High School.
Beckman, John J. *s.j.* '65 (CIN) [M] Cincinnati, OH Faber Jesuit Community.
Beckman, Joseph '54 (CIN) [B] Cincinnati, OH Mt. St. Mary's Seminary of the West.
Beckman, Joseph F. '54 (CIN) Retired.
Beckman, Mark '90 (NSH) Springfield, TN Our Lady of Lourdes Church.
Beckman, Martin A. '58 (STP) South St. Paul, MN St. John Vianney Church.
Beckman, Peter *o.s.b.* '36 (KCK) [H] Atchison, KS St. Benedict's Abbey.
Beckman, Richard J. '56 (OKL) Newkirk, OK St. Francis of Assisi Church.
Beckman, Robert E. *s.j.* '56 (CHI) [N] Chicago, IL Chicago Province of the Society of Jesus-Provincial Office.
Beckmann, Msgr. Donald M. *d.min.* '70 (RVC) [2] Rockville Centre, NY Campus Parish of Long Island Church; Davis Park, NY Most Precious Blood Church; [Q] Rockville Centre, NY The Campus Parish of Long Island.
Becnel, Msgr. Terry B. '64 (NO) Buras, LA Our Lady of Good Harbor Church.
Becquet, Paul *c.pp.s.* '56 (SAL) Washington, KS St. Augustine's Church.
Bedard, Andre L. '57 (MAN) Bennington, NH St. Patrick Church.
Bedard, J. Raymond '53 (WOR) Retired.
Bedard, Paul *s.d.b.* '68 (NEW) [3] Elizabeth, NJ St. Anthony's Church.
Bedard, Roland *m.s.* '46 (TUC) Tucson, AZ U.S. Veterans Hospital.
Bedenikovic, Stephen *o.f.m.* '85 (MIL) [72] Milwaukee, WI Sacred Heart Church.
Bedessem, Henry W. '59 (GB) Retired.
Bedillion, James R. '75 (PIT) [O] Bellevue, PA Mount Assisi Convent.
Bednar, Dwayne '91 (CLV) Cleveland, OH Cleveland Clinic Hospital.
Bednar, Dwayne A. '91 (CLV) [3] Parma, OH St. Charles Borromeo Church.
Bednar, Francis M. '74 (CLV) [69] Cleveland, OH Sacred Heart of Jesus Church.
Bednar, Gerald J. '83 (CLV) [A] Wickliffe, OH St. Mary Seminary.
Bednar, Martin *o.f.m.* '64 (SP) [O] Belleair Bluffs, FL St. James Friary.
Bednar, Merrick J. '90 (BUF) [4] Tonawanda, NY St. Francis of Assisi Church; [D] Tonawanda, NY Cardinal O'Hara High School.
Bednar, Thomas V. *c.s.c.* '85 (FTW) [J] South Bend, IN Congregation of Holy Cross Indiana Province Provincial House.
Bednarik, John *o.f.m.cap.* '68 (SJN) [B] Rio Piedras, PR Fraternidad Santa Maria de Los Angeles; [G] Rio Piedras, PR The Viceprovince of Saint John the Baptist, Puerto Rico, of the Order Friars Minor Capuchins.
Bednarik, Juan *o.f.m.cap.* '68 (SJN) [18] San Juan, PR San Francisco de Asis Church.
Bednark, Walter '47 (SCL) Retired.
Bednarski, Mitchell J. '44 (LAN) Retired.
Bednartz, Msgr. August C. '52 (BRK) Retired; [B] Elmhurst, NY Cathedral Preparatory Seminary of the Immaculate Conception; [Y] Farmingdale, NY St. Charles.
Bednarz, Jan '72 (SLC) Vernal, UT St. James the Greater Church.
Bednarz, Matt A. '42 (CHI) [78] Chicago, IL St. Hilary Church; [201] Chicago, IL St. Thecla Church; Retired; [U] Chicago, IL Catholic League for Religious Assistance to Poland.
Bedoya, Carlos '90 (ORL) [9] Orlando, FL St. John Vianney Church.
Bedoya, Guillermo L. Corrales '89 (PRO) [6] Providence, RI Assumption of the Blessed Virgin Mary Church.
Bedoya, Hugo *c.m.* '56 (BRK) [243] Queens, NY St. Teresa Church.
Beebe, Msgr. Charles J. '70 (PEO) [9] Peoria, IL St. Jude's Church.
Beebe, David E. '61 (CAM) [N] Blackwood, NJ St. Pius X Spiritual Life Center.
Beechem, Joseph '40 (IND) Retired.
Beeching, Roy T. '74 (GRY) [6] Hammond, IN St. Joseph Church.
Beeda, Msgr. Francis J. '61 (SCR) [6] Hazleton, PA St. Joseph's Church.
Beeman, James W. '53 (HBG) Retired.
Beemster, John *s.v.d.* '40 (MIL) [P] East Troy, WI Divine Word Seminary.
Beerman, Andrew J. '96 (WIN) On Duty Outside the Diocese.
Beerntsen, Harold A. '61 (GB) Lena, WI Holy Cross Church.
Beers, J. Michael '79 (BAL) [A] Emmitsburg, MD Mount St. Mary's Seminary.
Beers, John Michael *s.s.l.* '79 (ALN) On Duty Outside the Diocese.
Beeson, Msgr. Lawrence A. (DM) On Special Assignment.
Beever, Carlton '74 (IND) [37] Indianapolis, IN St. Philip Neri Church.
Beez, John E. *s.j.* '61 (COL) [25] Columbus, OH Community of Holy Rosary and St. John Church.
Beezer, Arnold R. *s.j.* '64 (P) [L] Portland, OR Jesuit Provincial Office (Oregon Prov.).
Befort, Daryl '95 (WCH) [13] Wichita, KS St. Francis of Assisi Church.
Befort, Earl J. *o.f.m.cap.* '69 (SAL) Catharine, KS St. Catherine's Church; [D] Hays, KS St. Bonaventure's Friary; [H] Hays, KS Comeau Catholic Campus Center at Fort Hays State University.
Begay, Joseph N. *s.s.j.* '59 (WDC) [27] Washington, DC St. Luke Church.
Begg, Christopher T. '77 (WDC) [24] Washington, DC St. Joseph on Capitol Hill Church; Special Ministries; [C] Washington, DC Catholic University of America, The.
Beggane, Thomas P. '78 (LSC) [1] Las Cruces, NM Cathedral of Immaculate Heart of Mary.
Beggans, Msgr. Joseph A. '43 (NEW) [12] Jersey City, NJ St. John the Baptist Church; Retired; [N] Rutherford, NJ St. John Vianney Residence for Priests.
Beggiani, Seely '61 (SAM) [A] Washington, DC Our Lady of Lebanon Maronite Seminary.
Beggiani, Seely '61 (WDC) [C] Washington, DC Catholic University of America, The.
Beggin, Thomas M. '79 (GF) Retired.
Begin, Daniel L. '75 (CLV) [16] Cleveland, OH St. Cecilia Church; [23] Cleveland, OH Epiphany Church.
Begin, Msgr. Raymond F. '52 (PRT) Gray, ME St. Gregory Church.
Begin, Robert T. '64 (CLV) [17] Cleveland, OH St. Colman Church; Avon, OH Our Lady of the Wayside.
Begley, James J. '82 (RIC) Bedford, VA Holy Name of Mary Church.
Begley, John J. *s.j.* '62 (BO) [W] Boston, MA The Society of Jesus of New England-Provincial Offices.
Begley, John J. *s.j.* '62 (SCR) [C] Scranton, PA University of Scranton.
Begley, Patrick J. '63 (BAL) Retired.
Begley, Paul '55 (OM) [11] Omaha, NE St. Bridget Church; Retired.
Begley, Thomas B. '60 (SPR) Cheshire, MA St. Mary of the Assumption Church.
Begley, Thomas M. '89 (STL) Valley Park, MO Sacred Heart Church.
Begly, Mark S. '84 (ALT) New Baltimore, PA St. John the Baptist Church.
Begnaud, Adam *o.s.b.* '96 (NO) [A] St. Benedict, LA St. Joseph's Seminary College; [P] St. Benedict, LA St. Joseph Abbey.
Begolly, Michael J. '81 (GBG) Indiana, PA St. Thomas

More University Parish Church.
Begue, Joseph E. *c.m.* '55 (STL) [P] St. Louis, MO Vincentian Henrietta Residence; [W] St. Louis, MO The Vincentian Press Religious Supply.
Behan, George P. '56 (PRO) Lincoln, RI St. Jude Church.
Behan, Harry P. '73 (NU) St. Peter, MN St. Peter Church.
Behan, Hugh F. '64 (JC) Jefferson City, MO Renz Correctional Facility; Jefferson City, MO Central Missouri Correctional Center; Special Assignments; [D] Jefferson City, MO Villa Marie Skilled Nursing Facility.
Behan, Jim *o.s.f.s.* '73 (R) Carolina Beach, NC Immaculate Conception Church.
Behan, Msgr. Philip A. '70 (SB) Hesperia, CA Holy Family Church.
Behan, Thomas W. *o.s.a.* '58 (OAK) Castro Valley, CA Our Lady of Grace Church.
Behen, John M. *c.pp.s.* '46 (JC) Sedalia, MO St. Patrick Church.
Behl, Msgr. Richard A. '66 (MET) [1] Metuchen, NJ Cathedral of St. Francis.
Behler, Donald '47 (CIN) Retired.
Behman, Toma A. '54 (DET) [2] Southfield, MI St. Bede Church.
Behnen, Robert *o.f.m.* '60 (STL) Oakville, MO St. Francis of Assisi Church.
Behnke, John J. *c,s.p.* '76 (STP) [29] Minneapolis, MN St. Lawrence Church; [N] Minneapolis, MN Paulist Fathers.
Behnke, Robert C. '73 (CHI) [19] Chicago, IL Assumption of the B.V.M./St. Catherine of Genoa Church; [169] Chicago, IL SS. Peter and Paul Church.
Behnke, Thomas *o.c.d.* '48 (LR) [A] Little Rock, AR Marylake - Carmelite Novitiate.
Behon, Sebastian Mongo '90 (WDC) [36] Washington, DC St. Patrick Church.
Behrens, Msgr. A.W. '45 (SC) Retired.
Behrens, Herman *s.c.j.* '70 (PH) [46] Philadelphia, PA St. Francis de Sales Church.
Behringer, William R. *s.m.* '60 (CIN) [M] Dayton, OH Marianist Provincialate.
Behrmann, Msgr. Elmer H. '38 (STL) Retired.
Beichner, Paul E. *c.s.c.* '39 (FTW) [J] South Bend, IN Congregation of Holy Cross Indiana Province Provincial House.
Beierschmitt, Msgr. Leo A. (HBG) [G] Lebanon, PA Villa Vianney.
Beigel, Gerard '86 (OAK) [5] Fremont, CA St. Leonard Church.
Beighlie, James T. *c.m.* '79 (STL) [P] St. Louis, MO Vincentian Bellerive Residence.
Beilman, J. Brian '86 (OM) Humphrey, NE St. Francis Church.
Beining, Paul R. *s.j.* '55 (SCR) [C] Scranton, PA University of Scranton.
Beinlich, James P. *o.s.a.* '72 (OG) Carthage, NY St. James Minor Church; Deferiet, NY St. Rita Church.
Beirne, Charles J. *s.j.* '69 (NY) [Z] New York, NY Jesuit Provincial's Office.
Beirne, Gerald E. '62 (PRO) Greenville, RI St. Philip's Church.
Beirne, M. Christen '69 (NEW) Mahwah, NJ Immaculate Conception Church.
Beirne, Robert M. '63 (PRO) [1] Central Falls, RI Holy Trinity Church.
Beischel, Richard L. *c.pp.s.* '56 (CIN) [M] Dayton, OH Provincial House of the Cincinnati Province of the Society of the Precious Blood.
Beischel, Thomas *c.pp.s.* '58 (CIN) [K] Dayton, OH St. Elizabeth Medical Center, Inc.
Beischel, Thomas J. *c.pp.s.* '58 (CIN) [U] Dayton, OH Community Support Charitable Trust.
Beisel, James D. '80 (PH) [D] Warminster, PA Archbishop Wood Catholic High School; [U] Warminster, PA Regina Coeli Residence for Priests.
Beitans, John '73 (IND) Starlight, IN St. John the Baptist Church.
Beiter, Eugene J. '64 (LAN) Leslie, MI SS. Cornelius and Cyprian Church.
Beiter, Msgr. Lambert M. '37 (ALT) Retired.
Beiter, Robert G. '64 (BUF) Brocton, NY St. Patrick Church.
Beiting, Msgr. Ralph '49 (LEX) Louisa, KY St. Jude Church.
Beitzinger, George J. '45 (MIL) Retired.
Bejgrowicz, Joseph S. '70 (NEW) Kenilworth, NJ St. Theresa's Church.
Bek, Robert *c.ss.r.* '64 (GAL) [33] Houston, TX Holy Ghost Church.
Bek, Viktor '92 (PHU) Millville, NJ St. Nicholas Church.
Beksha, Francis W. '46 (BO) Franklin, MA St. Mary Church; Retired.
Belair, Eugene '53 (SCL) Ogilvie, MN St. Kathryn's Church.
Belair, Eugene G. '53 (SCL) Mora, MN St. Mary's Church.
Belanger, Gerald R. '75 (MAN) Portsmouth, NH St. James Church.
Belanger, Leo J. *s.j.* '32 (DET) [P] Clarkston, MI Colombiere Center.
Belanger, Rene A. *s.s.s.* '50 (CLV) [P] Cleveland, OH Congregation of the Blessed Sacrament Provincial House.
Belanggoy, Plutarco A. *c.i.c.m.* '96 (BWN) Alamo, TX Resurrection Church.
Belanich, Giordano '75 (NEW) Fairview, NJ St. John the Baptist Church.
Belanich, Giordano '75 (PAT) On Duty Outside the Diocese.
Belauskas, August J. '68 (CHI) [A] Mundelein, IL University of St. Mary of the Lake-Mundelein Seminary.
Belcher, Paul F. *s.j.* '63 (SAC) [14] Sacramento, CA St. Ignatius Church.
Belchez, Caesae A. '95 (HBG) Gettysburg, PA St. Francis Xavier's Church.
Belczak, Edward A. '72 (DET) [1] Troy, MI St. Thomas More Church.
Belczak, Thomas A. '80 (DET) [4] Redford, MI St. Valentine Church.
Belda, Leo W. '42 (MIL) Retired.
Belen, Germain *o.f.m.conv.* (SAV) St. Simons Island, GA St. Williams Church.
Belfield, John '58 (STU) Retired.
Belford, Msgr. William J. '74 (NY) Blauvelt, NY St. Catharine Church.
Belgarde, George H. *s.j.* '88 (NY) [Z] New York, NY Jesuit Provincial's Office.
Belgarde, George H. '88 (OG) [J] Hogansburg, NY St. Regis Mission.
Belhumeur, Paul *m.s.* '61 (FR) [K] Attleboro, MA La Salette Provincial House.
Belhumeur, Roger E. '61 (PRO) Retired.
Beligotti, Richard J. '68 (ROC) Leicester, NY St. Thomas Aquinas Church.
Beligotti, Robert L. '68 (ROC) [7] Auburn, NY St. Francis of Assisi Church.
Belinski, Michael *c.s.c.* '89 (FTW) [9] South Bend, IN Holy Cross Church.
Belisch, Carl L. *c.s.b.* '65 (GAL) [F] Houston, TX St. Thomas High School.
Belisle, Ronald H. '62 (SEA) Camas, WA St. Thomas Church.
Belitz, Justin *o.f.m.* '61 (IND) [13] Indianapolis, IN Sacred Heart of Jesus Church.
Belitz, Ronald C. '79 (GB) [8] Green Bay, WI St. Jude Church.
Beliveau, Richard '60 (BRK) Absent on Leave.
Belizario, Nelson '68 (L) [A] Louisville, KY Bellarmine College; [B] Louisville, KY St. Francis DeSales High School.
Bell, Arthur J. '56 (DET) Retired.
Bell, Brian T. '70 (TUC) On Duty Outside the Diocese.
Bell, Msgr. Carl F. '66 (LA) Encino, CA St. Cyril Church.
Bell, Edward H. '77 (PH) [124] Philadelphia, PA Our Lady of Mt. Carmel Church.
Bell, Edward M. '64 (WH) Parkersburg, WV St. Margaret Mary Church.
Bell, Gerard L. '73 (L) Shepherdsville, KY St. Aloysius Church.
Bell, Gerard P. *s.j.* (WDC) [V] Silver Spring, MD Apostleship of Prayer.
Bell, Gerard P. *s.j.* '57 (NY) [Z] New York, NY Jesuit Provincial's Office.
Bell, Ira J. '52 (STL) Retired.
Bell, Joseph W. '74 (SPK) [2] Spokane, WA Assumption of the Blessed Virgin Mary Church.
Bell, Michael J. '79 (SAG) Caro, MI Sacred Heart Church.
Bell, Michael T. '61 (MRY) San Luis Obispo, CA California Men's Colony West.
Bell, Milford C. '49 (FTW) Retired.
Bell, Milford C. '49 (WH) Retired.
Bell, Richard A. *m.m.* '57 (NY) [Z] Maryknoll, NY Maryknoll Fathers and Brothers.
Bellagamba, Anthony *i.m.c.* '52 (MET) [H] Somerset, NJ Consolata Society for Foreign Missions.
Belland, David '87 (SCL) Absent on Leave.
Bellantonio, Albert '69 (BRK) [111] Brooklyn, NY Our Lady of Solace Church.
Bellavista, Jose '35 (LA) Retired.
Bellavista, Jose '36 (LA) Los Nietos, CA Our Lady of Perpetual Help Church.
Bellefeuille, Albert A. '54 (MAN) Colebrook, NH St. Brendan Church.
Bellenoit, George C. '72 (FR) Mansfield, MA St. Mary's Church.
Belleque, Thomas A. '85 (SEA) Sumner, WA St. Andrew Church; Orting, WA U.S. Soldiers' Home.
Beller, Frederic J. *o.s.b.* '43 (JOL) [J] Lisle, IL St. Procopius Abbey.
Beller, Joseph '58 (Y) Retired.
Bellesorte, Anthony R. *o.c.s.o.* '69 (SAC) [A] Vina, CA Abbey of New Clairvaux, Trappist Seminary; [H] Vina, CA Abbey of New Clairvaux, Trappist.
Bellester, Msgr. Pedro J. '58 (PCE) Special Assignment.
Belletty, Emile '78 (LA) [12] Los Angeles, CA Holy Name of Jesus Church; [48] Los Angeles, CA St. Bernadette Church; [97] Los Angeles, CA Transfiguration Church.
Bellew, Msgr. Francis P. '66 (NY) Wappingers Falls, NY St. Mary Church.
Bellew, Lawrence *c.p.* '53 (BRK) [U] Jamaica, NY Immaculate Conception Monastery.
Bellew, Lawrence *c.p.* '53 (RVC) West Islip, NY Good Samaritan Hospital; [I] West Islip, NY The Samaritan Corporation.
Bellinghausen, David *o.s.b.* '86 (FWT) Muenster, TX Sacred Heart Church.
Bellino, Samuel P. *s.j.* '88 (SFR) [E] San Francisco, CA St. Ignatius College Preparatory (Coed); [N] San Francisco, CA Jesuit Community at St. Ignatius College Preparatory.
Bellisario, Andrew E. *c.m.* '84 (STO) Patterson, CA Sacred Heart Church.
Bellittiere, David A. '89 (BUF) Snyder, NY Christ the King Church.
Belliveau, Gary J. '85 (MAN) Hudson, NH St. Kathryn Church.
Bello, David *o.p.* '81 (OAK) [N] Oakland, CA Western Dominican Province.
Bello, Giles *o.f.m.* '55 (BO) [BB] Boston, MA St. Anthony Shrine.
Bellon, John E. *c.ss.r.* '41 (DET) [34] Detroit, MI Holy Redeemer Church.
Bellopede, Louis P. '91 (PH) [3] Norristown, PA Holy Saviour Church.
Bellow, Richard M. *o.f.m.conv.* '70 (CHL) [6] Charlotte, NC St. John Neumann Church.
Belluomini, Msgr. Ralph '60 (FRS) [2] Bakersfield, CA Our Lady of Perpetual Help Church.
Belmonte, John M. *s.j.* (MIL) [P] Milwaukee, WI Jesuit Provincial Office, Wisconsin Province.
Belogi, James '81 (ALB) Guilderland, NY St. Madeleine Sophie Church.
Beloin, Robert L. '73 (HRT) [R] New Haven, CT Yale University-St. Thomas More Catholic Center and Chapel.
Belschner, Wayne '95 (BO) [3] Woburn, MA St. Charles Church.
Belsole, Kurt J. *o.s.b.* '78 (GBG) [H] Latrobe, PA Saint Vincent Archabbey.
Belsome, Garland T. '90 (BR) [6] Baton Rouge, LA Christ the King Church; [K] Baton Rouge, LA Christ the King Parish and Catholic Student Center.
Belt, David D. '90 (OM) Wisner, NE St. Joseph Church.
Beltrami, Robert *o.f.m.* '62 (P) [25] Portland, OR Our Lady of Sorrows Church.
Beltran, Esteban *ss.cc.* '56 (SJN) [8] Guaynabo, PR Nuestra Senora de la Paz Church.
Beltran, Justo '69 (BRK) [143] Brooklyn, NY St. Vincent de Paul Church.
Beltran, Rafael *c.m.f.* '78 (SJN) [2] Bayamon, PR San Antonio Maria Claret Church.
Beltran Regado, Justo R. '69 (BRK) Brooklyn, NY Wyckoff Heights Hospital.
Beltzner, Lucian W. *o.carm.* '63 (NY) Middletown, NY Our Lady of Mt. Carmel Church.
Belzer, Msgr. Paul J. '54 (BUF) Pendleton, NY Good Shepherd Church.
Benacchio, Onorio *c.s.* '50 (VEN) Immokalee, FL Our Lady of Guadalupe Church.
Benack, Henry I. '51 (RVC) Glen Cove, NY St. Patrick's Church; Glen Cove, NY North Shore Community Hospital at Glen Cove.
Benak, Wes *o.s.a.* '92 (CHI) [N] Chicago, IL St. John Stone Friary.
Benakovic, Benedict *o.f.m.conv.* '49 (GRY) [12] Gary, IN St. Joseph The Worker Church.
Benas, Randy '85 (SJ) Los Altos, CA St. Simon Church.
Benassu, Greg '95 (ATL) Kennesaw, GA St. Catherine of Siena Church.
Benavente, James L.G. '94 (AGN) [1] Agana, GU Dulce Nombre de Maria Cathedral - Basilica; [A] Agana, GU Father Duenas Minor Seminary.
Benbenek, Gerald J. '66 (PEO) Farmer City, IL Sacred Heart Church.
Bench, John F. '64 (CHR) Absent On Leave.
Benda, Dennis '83 (SFS) On Leave of Absence.
Benda, Frank M. '57 (DUB) Earlville, IA St. Joseph's Church; Greeley, IA St. Joseph's Church.
Benda, Frederick J. *s.j.* '72 (CLV) [C] Cleveland, OH John Carroll Jesuit Community.
Benda, M. Eugene '60 (DAV) Tipton, IA St. Mary's Church.
Bendel, Eugene '57 (STL) [4] University City, MO St. Patrick Church.
Benden, Stephen *c.ss.r.* '89 (OM) [19] Omaha, NE Holy Name Church.
Bender, Arthur C. *s.j.* '78 (NY) [F] New York, NY Regis High School; [Z] New York, NY St. Ignatius Loyola Residence.
Bender, James W. *c.pp.s.* '52 (CIN) [M] Dayton, OH Provincial House of the Cincinnati Province of the Society of the Precious Blood.
Bender, Joseph J. '57 (ALT) Retired.
Bender, Lawrence *s.s.* '51 (WDC) On Duty Outside the Archdiocese.
Bender, Lawrence A. *s.s.* '51 (BAL) [K] Baltimore, MD

St. Charles Villa; [M] Baltimore, MD St. Charles Villa.
Bender, Philip M. '64 (ALT) State College, PA Good Shepherd Church.
Bender, Reginald G. *o.s.b.* '59 (GBG) [H] Latrobe, PA Saint Vincent Archabbey.
Bender, Msgr. Thomas G. '56 (COL) Powell, OH St. Joan of Arc Church.
Bender, Thomas J. '61 (ALN) Unassigned.
Bendernagel, Cajetan *c.p.* '52 (HRT) [M] West Hartford, CT Holy Family Monastery/Retreat.
Benderof, Richard *o.f.m.* '87 (SFD) [B] Quincy, IL Quincy University.
Bendik, Msgr. John J. '67 (SCR) [4] Pittston, PA St. John the Evangelist Church.
Bendixen, Arthur (ORL) Sabbatical.
Bendorf, Richard *o.f.m.* '87 (SFD) [1] Quincy, IL St. Anthony of Padua Church; [6] Quincy, IL St. Joseph Church.
Bendyk, Marian '82 (CLV) [35] Cleveland, OH Immaculate Heart of Mary Church.
Bendzella, Sylvester J. '59 (ALT) Clarence, PA St. Michael's Church; Snow Shoe, PA St. Mary's Church.
Bene, Philip '94 (STL) Mehlville, MO St. Margaret Mary Alacoque Church.
Benecki, Stanley '84 (COL) [7] Columbus, OH Sts. Augustine and Gabriel Church.
Benedett, Edmund *s.j.* '50 (TUC) [3] Tucson, AZ Holy Family Church.
Benedict, Francis *o.s.b.* '76 (LA) [W] Valyermo, CA St. Andrew's Abbey Retreat House (All Groups).
Benedict, Msgr. Michael J. '43 (LAF) Retired.
Benedicto, Benjamin '62 (ORG) Newport Beach, CA Our Lady Queen of Angels Church.
Benedik, Hilarion *o.s.b.m.* '48 (STF) [B] Glen Cove, NY Basilian Fathers Novitiate of the Order of St. Basil the Great.
Benefiel, Msgr. Harry E. '60 (LAF) Retired.
Benelli, Charles *i.m.c.* '69 (MET) [H] Somerset, NJ Consolata Society for Foreign Missions.
Benestad, Msgr. Thomas J. '70 (ALN) On Duty Outside the Diocese.
Benestad, Msgr. Thomas J. '70 (PH) [A] Wynnewood, PA Theological Seminary of St. Charles Borromeo, Overbrook.
Bengert, Anthony L. '65 (ELP) Absent on Leave.
Bengford, Ronald J. '94 (PRO) [7] Cranston, RI St. Paul Church.
Bengochea, Gerardo *s.j.* '63 (NY) [50] New York, NY Holy Trinity Church.
Benguria, Juan B. (SJN) [46] San Juan, PR Nuestra Senora de la Piedad Church.
Benguria, Juan Bautista '57 (SJN) [46] San Juan, PR Nuestra Senora de la Piedad Church.
Benham, Michael C. '76 (MIL) Burlington, WI St. Charles Church.
Benhen, Robert *o.f.m.* '60 (STL) [P] Oakville, MO St. Francis Friary.
Benicewicz, Joseph *ofm conv.* '88 (BUF) [D] Athol Springs, NY St. Francis High School; [O] Athol Springs, NY St. Francis of Assisi Friary.
Benintende, Joseph '70 (ALB) Ilion, NY Annunciation Church.
Benischeck, Bernard J. '53 (PH) [39] Philadelphia, PA St. Dominic Church.
Benish, William '72 (AUS) Leander, TX St. Margaret Mary Church.
Benitez, Andres '40 (MIA) [H] Miami, FL Jesuit Fathers of the Province of the Antilles, Inc.
Benitez, Andres *s.j.* '44 (MIA) [D] Miami, FL Belen Jesuit Preparatory School.
Benitez, Eduardo '66 (ORL) Retired.
Benito, Daniel G. '51 (ELP) [14] El Paso, TX Our Lady of Assumption Church.
Benjamin, Don Carlos *o.carm.* '67 (JOL) [J] Darien, IL Carmelite Fathers Provincial Office.
Benjamin, John '93 (SB) [2] Corona, CA St. Edward Church.
Benkowski, Gregory '84 (OM) [18] Omaha, NE Holy Ghost Church.
Benkowski, Gregory *s.m.* '84 (STL) [P] St. Louis, MO Provincialate of the Society of Mary, Province of St. Louis.
Benliro, Fernando C. '58 (OM) [29] Omaha, NE St. Mary Magdalene Church.
Benn, Walter J. '77 (PH) Downingtown, PA St. Joseph Church.
Bennet, Gregory '92 (BAL) [9] Baltimore, MD Annunciation Church.
Bennett, Msgr. Austin P. '49 (BRK) [U] Brooklyn, NY Curial Residence.
Bennett, Christopher '90 (SJ) [11] San Jose, CA St. Christopher Church.
Bennett, Msgr. Donald T. '67 (RVC) Garden City, NY St. Joseph's Church.
Bennett, Gordon D. *s.j.* '75 (LA) [F] Los Angeles, CA Loyola High School.
Bennett, John E. *s.j.* '53 (PH) [C] Philadelphia, PA St. Joseph's University; [Z] Philadelphia, PA Jesuit Community at St. Joseph's University.
Bennett, Msgr. John F. '71 (RVC) Baldwin, NY St. Christopher Church.
Bennett, Joseph R. '66 (CHI) [145] Chicago, IL Our Lady of Fatima Church.
Bennett, Joseph T. *s.j.* '57 (BO) [E] Boston, MA Boston College High School & Jesuit Community.
Bennett, Melvin J. '69 (LFT) Crawfordsville, IN St. Bernard Church.
Bennett, Michael X. '71 (HBG) Absent on Leave.
Bennett, Noel I. '59 (MIA) [2] Miami Beach, FL St. Joseph Church.
Bennett, Norman S. *c.ss.r.* '71 (BRK) [107] Brooklyn, NY Our Lady of Perpetual Help Basilica.
Bennett, Owen *o.f.m.conv.* '40 (ALB) [A] Rensselaer, NY Conventual Franciscan Friars.
Bennett, Richard L. '72 (JOL) [5] Joliet, IL Sacred Heart Church.
Bennett, Richard S. *c.ss.r.* '96 (PH) [25] Philadelphia, PA St. Boniface Church.
Bennett, Rolland *o.m.i.* '61 (PMB) Riviera Beach, FL St. Francis of Assisi Church.
Bennett, Msgr. Thomas '57 (COL) [22] Columbus, OH Immaculate Conception Church.
Bennett, Thomas F. '68 (HRT) Washington Depot, CT Our Lady of Perpetual Help Church.
Bennett, Msgr. Thomas M. '57 (COL) [C] Columbus, OH St. Charles Preparatory School.
Bennington, Msgr. J. Clement '45 (PH) Abington, PA Our Lady Help of Christians Church; Retired.
Beno, Brian M. '76 (MIL) Awaiting Assignment.
Beno, John R. '59 (PBL) Retired.
Beno, Joseph '57 (P) Retired.
Benoit, Adrian J. '65 (SPR) [7] Springfield, MA Immaculate Conception Church.
Benoit, Lloyd F. '90 (LAF) Cecilia, LA St. Joseph Church.
Benoit, Louis R. '79 (RIC) Christiansburg, VA Holy Spirit Catholic Church; Pearisburg, VA Holy Family Church.
Benoit, Raymond (BO) [1] Weymouth, MA St. Albert the Great Church.
Benoit, Ronald H. '55 (BUR) Richmond, VT Our Lady of the Holy Rosary Church.
Benoit, Vincent *o.p.* '78 (P) [6] Eugene, OR St. Thomas More Church.
Benoit, Vincent *o.p.* '84 (P) [D] Eugene, OR Marist High School.
Benonis, Richard R. '58 (PH) On Duty Outside the Archdiocese.
Benonis, William J. '52 (PH) Swarthmore, PA Notre Dame de Lourdes Church.
Bensman, Gerald E. '64 (CIN) McCartyville, OH Sacred Heart of Jesus Church.
Bensman, John L. '56 (CIN) Chickasaw, OH Most Precious Blood Church; St. Sebastian, OH St. Sebastian Church.
Benson, Gerard *o.carm.* '42 (VEN) [G] Venice, FL Carmel in Venice.
Benson, James A. *s.j.* '56 (BO) [3] Newton, MA St. Ignatius Church.
Benson, Msgr. John D. '47 (WDC) Retired.
Benson, Joseph A. '84 (NO) [4] Slidell, LA St. Margaret Mary Church; Slidell, LA Greenbriar Nursing & Convalescent Home; Slidell, LA Guest House of Slidell Nursing Home; Slidell, LA Greenery Neurologic Rehabilitation Center at Slidell.
Benson, Pierre *m.afr.* '70 (WDC) [M] Washington, DC Missionaries of Africa.
Benson, Richard *c.m.* '78 (LA) [A] Camarillo, CA St. John's Seminary; [A] Camarillo, CA St. John's Seminary.
Bentivegna, Salvatore A. *o.s.j.* '63 (SCR) White Haven, PA St. Patrick's Church.
Bentivoglio, Louis '53 (VEN) Retired.
Bentley, David '75 (ALB) On Duty Outside the Diocese.
Benton, James F. '73 (LIN) Seward, NE St. Vincent de Paul Church.
Bentz, John '66 (COL) Marysville, OH Our Lady of Lourdes Church; Marysville, OH Ohio Reformatory for Women.
Benvegnu, Msgr. Mark O. '41 (SLC) Retired.
Benwell, Msgr. William '80 (MET) Warren, NJ Our Lady of the Mount Church; [N] Metuchen, NJ The Catholic Lawyers Guild of the Diocese of Metuchen, Inc.
Benya, Edward G. *s.j.* '84 (NO) [P] New Orleans, LA Jesuit Provincial Office.
Benz, David H. '75 (PH) Military Chaplains.
Benz, James J. '74 (STL) Richmond Heights, MO Little Flower, St. Teresa of the Infant Jesus Church.
Benz, Walter J. '50 (PIT) Glenshaw, PA St. Mary Church.
Benzinger, Oscar L. *s.j.* '67 (MIL) [P] Milwaukee, WI Jesuit Provincial Office, Wisconsin Province.
Benzoni, Martin *o.praem.* '81 (ORG) [H] Silverado, CA Norbertine Fathers.
Berancourt, Homero *s.d.b.* (SJN) Catano, PR San Francisco de Sales Church.
Berard, Aram J. *s.j.* '66 (BO) [W] Boston, MA Loyola House.
Berardi, Msgr. Ferdinando D. '77 (NY) [76] New York, NY St. Monica Church; [DD] New York, NY Catholic Medical Mission Board, Inc.
Berardi, James J. '59 (CLV) [1] Akron, OH Annunciation Church; Akron, OH Akron City Hospital.
Berardi, Thomas F. '76 (ALB) Cobleskill, NY St. Vincent de Paul Church; [B] Albany, NY Maria College.
Berbena, Christopher '80 (OAK) [2] Walnut Creek, CA St. John Vianney Church.
Berberian, David '74 (ALB) [9] Troy, NY Our Lady of Victory Church.
Berberich, Peter K. '47 (CHR) Retired.
Berberich, Thomas E. '59 (HRT) [6] New Britain, CT St. Francis of Assisi Church.
Berbig, Steven A. '87 (RVC) Mastic Beach, NY St. Jude Church.
Berbusse, Edward J. *s.j.* '45 (NY) [Z] New York, NY Murray-Weigel Hall.
Berchmanz, Anthony '67 (NEW) Military Chaplains.
Bercier, Barry *a.a.* '85 (WOR) [N] Worcester, MA Assumptionists of Assumption College.
Bercik, G. Michael *o.f.m.* '79 (BO) [1] Marlboro, MA St. Ann Church.
Berding, Richard P. '84 (L) [47] Louisville, KY St. Luke Church.
Berdis, Donald E. '63 (E) [2] Farrell, PA Our Lady of Fatima Church.
Berdugo, Hernan '82 (SJN) Rio Grande, PR San Francisco de Asis Church.
Berean, Christopher H. '87 (NY) Saugerties, NY St. Mary of the Snow Church.
Bereda, Stanislaw J. '65 (GAY) Posen, MI St. Casimir Church.
Berehout, Paul A. '96 (ARL) Manassas, VA All Saints Church.
Berendt, Msgr. James '55 (COL) [18] Columbus, OH Holy Cross Church.
Berens, Cyprian E. *o.f.m.* '51 (MAR) Calumet, MI St. Paul the Apostle Church.
Beretta, John W. *o.s.a.* '45 (CHI) [N] Olympia Fields, IL The Augustinian Provincialate Tolentine Center.
Bereza, Stepan '93 (STF) [7] New Britain, CT St. Josaphat Church.
Berg, Msgr. Arnold J. '33 (NU) Retired.
Berg, Donald M. '47 (LC) Pittsville, WI St. Joachim Church; Spaulding-City Point, WI North American Martyrs Church.
Berg, John Leonard '83 (NU) Absent on Leave.
Berg, Paul '48 (DET) Retired.
Berg, Peter M. '71 (OG) Dannemora, NY St. Joseph Church; Dannemora, NY Clinton Correctional Facility.
Berg, Ralph *c.m.f.* '64 (LA) [R] Los Angeles, CA Missionary Sons of the Immaculate Heart of Mary; [R] Los Angeles, CA Claretian Retreat Center Community.
Berg, Ramon A. '82 (CHL) Retired.
Berg, Richard F. *c.s.c.* '63 (P) [38] Portland, OR St. Vincent de Paul Church; [B] Portland, OR University of Portland; [L] Portland, OR Holy Cross Father & Brother, C.S.C. - University of Portland.
Berg, Msgr. S. Theodore '61 (BUF) [63] Buffalo, NY St. Teresa Church.
Berg, Timothy (SEA) Toledo, WA St. Francis Xavier Church.
Berg, Timothy '79 (SEA) Winlock, WA Sacred Heart Church; [G] Centralia, WA Providence Centralia Hospital.
Berg, Timothy '79 (SFE) On Duty Outside the Archdiocese.
Bergamo, John A. '65 (SCR) East Stroudsburg, PA St. Matthew's Church.
Bergbower, Daniel J. '88 (SFD) Effingham, IL Sacred Heart Church.
Berge, Frank J. '78 (DET) Macomb, MI St. Isidore Church.
Bergedick, Charles T. *s.m.* '57 (CIN) [M] Dayton, OH Marianist Provincialate.
Bergen, William J. *s.j.* '55 (NY) [51] New York, NY St. Ignatius Loyola Church.
Bergen, William J. *s.j.* '65 (NY) [Z] New York, NY St. Ignatius Loyola Residence.
Berger, Bernard M. '64 (GI) North Platte, NE St. Patrick Church.
Berger, John G. '67 (NU) Gibbon, MN St. Willibrord Church.
Berger, Joseph *s.l.t.* '59 (CC) Retired.
Berger, Lawrence B. '66 (LC) [4] La Crosse, WI Holy Trinity Church.
Berger, Michel R. *f.s.s.p.* '94 (SCR) [M] Elmhurst, PA Priestly Fraternity of St. Peter (F.S.S.P.).
Berger, Robert F. '62 (HBG) Myerstown, PA Mary, Gate of Heaven Church.
Bergeron, Albert G. '62 (HT) On Leave.
Bergeron, Marc H. '70 (FR) [12] Fall River, MA St. Anne's Church.
Bergeron, Michael A. '96 (HT) [1] Thibodaux, LA St. Joseph Co-Cathedral.
Bergeron, Robert E. '52 (BO) Dracut, MA St. Therese Church.
Bergeur, John '45 (NEW) [N] Rutherford, NJ St. John Vianney Residence for Priests.

Bergeur, John X. '45 (NEW) Retired.
Bergewisch, Fred F. *s.j.* '55 (CHI) [C] Chicago, IL Jesuit Community at Loyola University of Chicago; [N] Chicago, IL Chicago Province of the Society of Jesus-Provincial Office.
Berggreen, Msgr. Robert H. '64 (BR) [2] Baton Rouge, LA St. Agnes Church.
Berghammer, Robert J. '49 (MIL) Le Roy, WI St. Andrew's Church.
Bergin, Msgr. Clifford E. (CHI) Retired.
Bergin, James *s.v.d.* '69 (CHI) [B] Techny, IL Divine Word Residence.
Bergin, John J. *s.v.d.* '67 (BO) [W] Duxbury, MA Society of the Divine Word.
Bergin, John J. *s.j.* '67 (STL) [P] St. Louis, MO De Smet Jesuit High School Community.
Bergin, Pascal (CC) On Duty Outside the Diocese.
Bergin, Paschal '57 (SAT) Runge, TX St. Anthony's Church.
Bergin, Patrick A. *m.m.* '59 (NY) [Z] Maryknoll, NY Maryknoll Fathers and Brothers.
Bergin, Patrick A. *m.m.* '59 (RVC) Hampton Bays, NY St. Rosalie's Church.
Bergin, Patrick P. '57 (SAT) Kenedy, TX Our Lady of Peace Church.
Bergin, Robert D. '62 (HRT) Special and other (Arch-)Diocesan Assignment; [N] West Hartford, CT Mercyknoll, Incorporated.
Bergin, Msgr. Thomas '61 (NY) [E] New York, NY Cathedral High School.
Bergin, Msgr. Thomas J. '61 (NY) [58] New York, NY St. John the Evangelist Church; [D] New York, NY Department of Education.
Bergin, Thomas J. '62 (ORL) New Smyrna Beach, FL Our Lady Star of the Sea Church.
Bergin, Msgr. William A. '42 (SD) Retired.
Bergman, Charles B. '58 (PIT) Zelienople, PA St. Gregory Church.
Bergman, Richard L. '55 (DM) Stuart, IA All Saints Church.
Bergman, Msgr. Robert '71 (KCK) Shawnee, KS St. Joseph's Church.
Bergner, David J. *s.d.s.* '76 (RIC) [K] Richmond, VA Commonwealth Catholic Charities.
Bergquist, Patrick '90 (BAL) Special Assignment.
Bergquist, Patrick '90 (FBK) [1] Fairbanks, AK Sacred Heart Cathedral.
Bergs, David J. '76 (LSC) Carrizozo, NM St. Rita Church.
Bergsbaken, Dennis L. '78 (GB) Hortonville, WI SS. Peter and Paul Church.
Bergstadt, John P. '67 (GB) [5] Green Bay, WI St. Bernard Church.
Bergthold, LeRoy J. '44 (DAV) Retired; [M] Davenport, IA St. Vincent Center.
Bergwall, John E. *m.m.* '59 (NY) [Z] Maryknoll, NY Maryknoll Fathers and Brothers.
Berinti, Ben *c.pp.s.* '85 (ORL) [6] Orlando, FL St. Andrew Church.
Berinti, Benjamin J. *c.pp.s.* '85 (CIN) [M] Dayton, OH Provincial House of the Cincinnati Province of the Society of the Precious Blood.
Beristain, Juan M. '71 (SJN) [6] Toa Baja, PR Santisima Trinidad Church.
Berk, Aloysius '67 (PIT) [7] Pittsburgh, PA St. Catherine of Siena Church.
Berkemeier, Charles A. '58 (IND) Retired.
Berkhout, Frans (ALN) [C] Ashland, PA Cardinal Brennan Jr./Sr. High School.
Berkhout, Frans J. (ALN) Ashland, PA St. Joseph Church; Ashland, PA St. Mauritius Church.
Berko, Matthew '62 (SJP) Apopka, FL St. Mary's Church; Spring Hill, FL St. Andrew Church.
Berkov, Matthew '62 (SJP) St. Petersburg, FL Epiphany of Our Lord Church.
Berland, Mark '74 (SAL) Grainfield, KS St. Agnes Church; Park, KS Sacred Heart Church.
Berling, Alban *o.s.b.* '45 (IND) [J] St. Meinrad, IN St. Meinrad Archabbey.
Berlo, Benedict *c.p.* '40 (NY) [BB] New York, NY Cardinal Spellman Retreat House.
Berlo, Benedict *c.p.* '57 (NY) [Z] New York, NY Passionist Spiritual Center.
Berlowski, Michael Peter '95 (GAL) [28] Houston, TX St. Francis de Sales Church.
Bermingham, Msgr. Charles E. '23 (RVC) Retired.
Bermingham, Msgr. Charles E. '32 (RVC) Williston Park, NY St. Aidan's Church.
Bermingham, Thomas V. *s.j.* '49 (NY) [Z] New York, NY Jesuit Community at Fordham University.
Bermudez, Alberto '86 (NO) [1] Marrero, LA Immaculate Conception Church.
Bermudez, Jose '80 (SPR) On Duty Outside the Diocese.
Bernacki, William J. *o.p.* '56 (CHI) [D] Oak Park, IL Fenwick High School; [N] River Forest, IL St. Thomas Aquinas Priory.
Bernadicou, Paul J. *s.j.* '65 (SFR) [N] San Francisco, CA Jesuit Community at University of San Francisco.
Bernal, Edward M. '87 (SAT) [43] San Antonio, TX St. John Berchmans Church.
Bernans, Arvids '64 (COL) Military Chaplains.
Bernans, Arvids '76 (TUC) Fort Huchuca, AZ Fort Huchuca Army Post.
Bernard, Andre '71 (WOR) Absent on Leave.
Bernard, Andre '73 (SR) Scotia, CA St. Patrick Church.
Bernard, George C. *c.s.c.* '49 (P) [B] Portland, OR University of Portland; [L] Portland, OR Holy Cross Father & Brother, C.S.C. - University of Portland.
Bernard, Gerard *m.s.c.* '53 (PRO) Cranston, RI Rhode Island State Institutions.
Bernard, John P. '62 (BUF) Batavia, NY Veterans Hospital.
Bernard, John P. '62 (CAM) Retired.
Bernard, Msgr. M. J. '52 (LKC) Creole, LA Sacred Heart of Jesus Church.
Bernard, Paul J. '41 (SPR) Retired.
Bernardi, Peter J. *s.j.* (DET) [K] Detroit, MI Jesuit Provincial Office-Detroit Province of the Society of Jesus.
Bernardin, Paul A. *o.p.* '61 (HRT) [14] New Haven, CT St. Mary's Priory Church.
Bernardo, Emilio A. '42 (LA) Retired.
Bernardy, Patrick A. '60 (GB) Niagara, WI St. Anthony Church; Pembine, WI St. Margaret Church.
Bernas, Casimir *o.c.s.o.* '58 (SLC) [F] Huntsville, UT Abbey of Our Lady of the Holy Trinity of the Order of Cistercians.
Bernas, Elwood S. '84 (STU) Absent on Leave.
Bernas, Eugene '66 (NEW) Belleville, NJ St. Anthony's Church.
Bernas, Thomas A. '94 (CHI) [197] Chicago, IL St. Symphorosa and Seven Sons Church.
Bernasconi, Gino '50 (VIC) Retired.
Bernatonis, John F. '45 (BO) Retired.
Bernauer, Edmund G. '61 (NEW) [D] Summit, NJ The Oratory Catholic Preparatory School.
Bernauer, James '52 (CR) Retired.
Bernauer, James W. *s.j.* '75 (BO) [W] Chestnut Hill, MA The Jesuit Community at Boston College.
Bernbrock, John *s.j.* '56 (PHX) [2] Scottsdale, AZ Our Lady of Perpetual Help Church.
Bernbrock, John E. *s.j.* '56 (MIL) [P] Milwaukee, WI Jesuit Provincial Office, Wisconsin Province.
Berndt, Rudolph C. '76 (DAV) Blue Grass, IA St. Andrew Church; Buffalo, IA St. Peter's Church.
Bernelli, Matthew '64 (BGP) [13] Bridgeport, CT St. Mary's Church.
Bernemann, Timothy C. '85 (DAV) Absent on Leave.
Berner, Albert J. '68 (NEW) [3] Bayonne, NJ St. Henry's Church; [Q] Upper Montclair, NJ Montclair State University.
Berner, Francis '70 (NO) [63] New Orleans, LA St. Thomas The Apostle Church; New Orleans, LA Delgado College; New Orleans, LA Southern University in New Orleans; New Orleans, LA University of New Orleans.
Berner, Michael '86 (DM) Earling, IA St. Joseph Church.
Bernier, Daniel L. '93 (MAN) [7] Nashua, NH St. Joseph Church.
Bernier, Lawrence J. '63 (SPR) East Longmeadow, MA St. Michael's Church.
Bernier, Paul *s.s.s.* (NY) [CC] New York, NY University Apostolate.
Bernier, Roland *m.s.* '57 (LKC) De Ridder, LA St. Joseph's Church.
Berning, Cornelius C. '31 (CIN) Retired; [L] Cincinnati, OH St. Margaret Hall.
Berning, James C. '91 (WIN) [3] Rochester, MN Resurrection Church.
Berning, John B. '34 (CIN) Retired.
Bernotas, Robert J. '83 (LFT) Earl Park, IN St. John the Baptist Church; Goodland, IN SS. Peter and Paul Church; Kentland, IN St. Joseph Church.
Bernott, Albert R. '43 (GR) Retired.
Bernott, Ernest J. '48 (GR) Retired.
Berns, Eric R. '96 (LC) Graduate Studies.
Berny, Paul W. '72 (ATL) Fayetteville, GA St. Gabriel Church.
Berran, Donald M. '60 (BRK) [158] Queens, NY Blessed Virgin Mary, Help of Christians Church.
Berres, Peregrin *o.s.b.* '57 (SCL) [I] Collegeville, MN St. John's Abbey, of the Order of St. Benedict.
Berret, Anthony J. *s.j.* '71 (PH) [C] Philadelphia, PA St. Joseph's University; [Z] Philadelphia, PA Jesuit Community at St. Joseph's University; [Z] Philadelphia, PA St. Alphonsus House.
Berrigan, Daniel J. *s.j.* '52 (NY) [Z] New York, NY West Side Jesuit Community.
Berrio, Augusto *s.j.* '63 (SD) [12] San Diego, CA Our Lady of Guadalupe Church.
Berrios, George '89 (BRK) [165] Queens, NY Corpus Christi Church.
Berrueta, Jose *s.d.b.* '62 (NY) [72] New York, NY Mary Help of Christians Church.
Berruete, Joseph *s.d.b.* '62 (NY) [3] Port Chester, NY Our Lady of the Rosary Church.
Berry, Dennis *s.t.* (PAT) [P] Stirling, NJ Father Judge Apostolic Center.
Berry, James A. '75 (HON) Holualoa, HI St. Michael The Archangel Church.
Berry, William F. '66 (WDC) College Park, MD Holy Redeemer Church.
Berryman, Harold '58 (GB) [1] Appleton, WI St. Bernadette Church.
Berschied, Paul L. '86 (COV) Independence, KY St. Cecilia Church.
Bershara, Msgr. Ronald (PMB) [D] West Palm Beach, FL St. Mary's Hospital, Inc.
Berson, Bob *glmy.* '49 (CIN) [M] Fairfield, OH Headquarters of Glenmary Home Missioners.
Berson, Robert *glmy.* '53 (CIN) West Union, OH Holy Trinity Church.
Berson, Robert C. '53 (CIN) [U] Fairfield, OH Glenmary Home Missioners Charitable Trust.
Bertasius, Anthony '37 (ELP) Retired.
Bertasius, Msgr. Anthony '37 (PAT) [6] Paterson, NJ St. Casimir's Church.
Bertelli, Very James '59 (BO) Sudbury, MA St. Anselm Church.
Bertels, George '55 (KCK) Beattie, KS St. Malachy's Church; Marysville, KS St. Gregory's Church.
Bertels, Henry J. *s.j.* '62 (NY) [Z] New York, NY Jesuit Provincial's Office.
Berten, Gerald L. '89 (WOR) [Q] Worcester, MA Campus Ministry.
Bertha, Joseph '80 (PSC) Amherst, NY St. Stephen's Church.
Bertha, Joseph W. (BUF) Amherst, NY Millard Fillmore Surburban Hospital.
Berthelette, Ernest H. '74 (PRO) On Duty Outside the Diocese.
Berther, Patrick *o.f.m.cap.* '34 (GF) Retired.
Berthiaume, Eugene F. '58 (WOR) Brookfield, MA St. Mary's Church.
Berthiaume, Gary D. '68 (CLV) Released from Diocesan Assignment.
Berthoumieux, Jean Markelor '94 (NEW) Hillside, NJ Christ the King Church.
Bertin, Gerard '89 (WOR) [3] Gardner, MA Our Lady of the Holy Rosary Church.
Bertini, Angelo '73 (AUS) [7] Waco, TX St. Mary of the Assumption Church.
Bertino, Dominic V. '75 (GRY) Hobart, IN St. Bridget Church.
Bertioni, Albert *s.m.* '79 (RVC) [D] Uniondale, NY Kellenberg Memorial High School.
Bertiz, Santos '93 (NEW) Fairfield, NJ St. Thomas More Church.
Bertke, Erwin J. (CIN) Retired.
Bertke, Erwin J. '43 (CIN) [52] Cincinnati, OH St. Lawrence Church.
Bertocchi, Luigi *o.s.b.* '70 (SCL) [I] Collegeville, MN St. John's Abbey, of the Order of St. Benedict.
Bertogli, John O. '77 (DM) Churchville, IA Assumption of the Blessed Virgin Mary Church; Irish Settlement, IA St. Patrick Church; St. Marys, IA Immaculate Conception Church.
Bertolina, Thomas J. '58 (GBG) North Huntingdon, PA St. Agnes Church.
Bertolotti, David P. '91 (BRK) [11] Brooklyn, NY St. Anthony of Padua-St. Alphonsus Church.
Bertolucci, John '65 (ALB) Latham, NY St. Ambrose Church; Albany, NY Albany Medical Center Hospital.
Berton, Joseph F. *c.ss.r.* '40 (PH) [135] Philadelphia, PA St. Peter the Apostle Church.
Bertoniere, Gabriel *o.c.s.o.* '58 (WOR) [N] Spencer, MA St. Joseph's Abbey.
Bertram, Michael *o.f.m.cap.* '88 (DET) Hazel Park, MI St. Mary Magdalen Church.
Bertrand, Aloysius J. '43 (PBL) [D] Grand Junction, CO St. Mary Hospital and Medical Center.
Bertrand, Armand J. '89 (SC) Fonda, IA Our Lady of Good Counsel Church; Varina, IA St. Columbkille's Church.
Bertrand, C. Conley '59 (LAF) Rynella, LA St. Marcellus Church.
Bertrand, Emmanuel *o.p.* '58 (NY) [AA] Sparkill, NY Dominican Convent of Our Lady of the Rosary.
Bertrand, Joseph '60 (BEA) [C] Beaumont, TX St. Elizabeth Hospital of Beaumont.
Bertrand, Richard D. *s.j.* '79 (BO) [W] Boston, MA The Society of Jesus of New England-Provincial Offices.
Bertrand, Richard D. *s.j.* '79 (PRT) Auburn, ME St. Louis Church; [4] Lewiston, ME St. Mary's Church.
Bertrand, Victor E. *c.s.v.* (LR) [11] Little Rock, AR Our Lady of the Holy Souls Church; North Little Rock, AR U.S. Veterans Administration Hospital.
Bertrand, Victor E. '62 (CHI) [N] Arlington Heights, IL Viatorian Province Center-Clerics of St. Viator.
Bertrand, Vincent E. '87 (SPC) Marshfield, MO Holy Trinity Church.
Bertsche, Conrad J. '45 (BEL) Retired.
Berube, John J. '48 (BO) Retired.
Berube, Louis '47 (PRT) Retired.
Berube, Msgr. Louis D. '30 (OG) Retired.
Berube, Paul W. '60 (BO) Wayland, MA St. Zepherin Church.
Berube, Richard N. *s.s.e.* '70 (BUR) [G] Colchester, VT Society of St. Edmund.
Berube, Theodore E. '41 (NOR) Wauregan, CT Sacred Heart Church; Retired.

Beseau, Steven '95 (KCK) Prairie Village, KS St. Ann's Church.
Besendorfer, Ralph L. *j.c.d.* '59 (STA) Callahan, FL Our Lady of Consolation Church.
Beshara, Msgr. Ronald N. '71 (PMB) [D] West Palm Beach, FL St. Mary's Hospital, Inc.
Beshara, Msgr. Ronald N. '71 (SAM) West Palm Beach, FL Mary Mother of Light Maronite Mission Church.
Beshoner, Sebastian *o.s.b.* '55 (LR) Paris, AR St. Joseph's Church.
Besinga, Dionisio '82 (LAV) [4] Las Vegas, NV Our Lady of Las Vegas Church.
Besse, Joseph A. '45 (PRO) Retired.
Bessert, James W. '80 (SAG) [2] Bay City, MI St. Boniface Church.
Bessette, Ernest '38 (FR) Retired.
Best, Richard '61 (JOL) Absent on Sick Leave.
Best, Russell W. '86 (BO) [60] Boston, MA St. Patrick Church.
Best, Russell W.M., Jr. '86 (BO) [36] Boston, MA St. Joseph Church.
Bester, Robert '79 (CR) On Duty Outside the Diocese.
Bester, Robert '79 (DUL) [D] Duluth, MN St. Ann's Senior Residence.
Bestler, Joseph '57 (GB) Stephensville, WI St. Patrick Church; Retired.
Bestler, Joseph L. '57 (GB) Shiocton, WI St. Denis Church.
Beston, William J. *c.s.c.* '48 (FR) [B] North Easton, MA Holy Cross Fathers Religious; [P] Taunton, MA Paul A. Dever State School (For Retarded) Newman Center.
Betancur, Nelson '75 (PAT) [8] Passaic, NJ Our Lady of Fatima Church.
Betancurt, Rigoberto *o.s.m.* '83 (SHP) [4] Monroe, LA St. Joseph Church.
Betchel, James (ALN) [C] Ashland, PA Cardinal Brennan Jr./Sr. High School.
Betit, John D. '94 (SPR) East Longmeadow, MA St. Michael's Church.
Betley, Michael E. '80 (GB) Plainfield, WI St. Paul Church.
Betoni, John P. *o.s.a.* '62 (PH) [C] Villanova, PA Villanova University; [Z] Villanova, PA St. Thomas Monastery.
Betowski, E. Paul *s.j.* '49 (BAL) [M] Baltimore, MD Jesuit Fathers and Brothers Maryland Provincial Curia.
Betrozoff, Larry '73 (MRY) San Luis Obispo, CA San Luis Obispo Church.
Bettendorf, James B. '59 (LAN) [8] Flint, MI St. Leo the Great Church.
Betti, Frederick G. *s.j.* '90 (ROC) [B] Rochester, NY McQuaid Jesuit High School.
Betti, Jose (ARE) Retired.
Betti, Mark J. '96 (R) New Bern, NC St. Paul Church.
Bettinger, Eugene *o.carm.* '76 (NEW) Demarest, NJ St. Joseph's Church.
Bettinger, Mark T. '93 (PBL) Grand Junction, CO St. Joseph Church.
Bettley, Emil L. '83 (NY) [99] New York, NY Our Lady of Victory Church.
Betts, John C. '68 (P) Albany, OR Our Lady of Perpetual Help Church.
Betz, James '71 (CAM) Military Chaplains.
Betz, James S. '89 (WDC) [1] Bowie, MD Ascension Church.
Betz, Kenneth '65 (EVN) Ireland, IN Annunciation of the Blessed Virgin Mary Church.
Betz, Robert L. '73 (MIL) [70] Milwaukee, WI St. Roman Church.
Betz, Thomas *o.f.m.cap.* '91 (PH) [79] Philadelphia, PA St. John the Evangelist Church.
Betzen, James G. *c.pp.s.* '81 (KC) [30] Kansas City, MO Sacred Heart-Guadalupe Church; [A] Kansas City, MO Precious Blood Mission House.
Beunen, Emmanuel *o.f.m.* '70 (CLV) Warrensville Heights, OH St. Jude Church; Cleveland, OH Cleveland House of Correction; Cleveland, OH Cuyahoga Hills Boys School; Cleveland, OH Dept. of Youth Services; Cleveland, OH Sunny Acres Skilled Nursing Facility; [P] Cleveland, OH St. Jude Friary.
Beuth, William J. *c.pp.s.* '59 (CIN) [M] Dayton, OH Provincial House of the Cincinnati Province of the Society of the Precious Blood.
Beuther, Richard J. '96 (BRK) [199] Queens, NY St. Matthias Church.
Beutner, Edward F. '65 (SUP) On Leave.
Beuzer, Vincent J. *s.j.* '58 (ANC) [G] Anchorage, AK Holy Spirit Retreat House; [I] Anchorage, AK Holy Spirit Retreat House.
Bevan, James J., Jr. '75 (LAV) [9] Las Vegas, NV St. Francis de Sales Church.
Bevan, Norman *c.s.sp.* '70 (CHI) [B] Chicago, IL The Catholic Theological Union at Chicago.
Bevan, Thomas R. '63 (BAL) Special Assignment.
Bevans, Stephan *s.v.d.* '71 (CHI) [N] Techny, IL Society of the Divine Word, Provincial Headquarter-Chicago Prov.
Bevans, Stephen B. *s.v.d.* '71 (CHI) [B] Chicago, IL The Catholic Theological Union at Chicago; [N] Chicago, IL Divine Word Theologate.
Bevard, Herbert A. '72 (PH) [17] Philadelphia, PA St. Athanasius Church.
Bevenour, Richard F. '57 (DAV) On Duty Outside the Diocese.
Bevens, Stephen *s.v.d.* '71 (CHI) [B] Techny, IL Divine Word Residence.
Beveridge, John P. '72 (SFD) [5] Quincy, IL St. John the Baptist Church.
Bevilacqua, Jerome *o.s.a.* '65 (SD) [B] San Diego, CA Austin House - House of Formation; [H] San Diego, CA Augustinian Community.
Bevington, William S. '51 (NSH) Hendersonville, TN Our Lady of the Lake Church; [L] Hendersonville, TN Legion of Mary; [L] Hendersonville, TN Priests Eucharistic League.
Bevins, John J. '58 (HRT) [2] Waterbury, CT Immaculate Conception Church.
Beyenka, John T. '37 (CHI) [140] Chicago, IL St. Monica Church; Retired.
Beyer, Baldwin *o.f.m.cap.* (SB) Twentynine Palms, CA Blessed Sacrament Church.
Beyer, Emil J. '40 (MAR) Retired; [D] Escanaba, MI Bishop Noa Home for Senior Citizens.
Beyer, Gregory *o.f.m.cap.* '62 (DEN) [3] Denver, CO Annunciation Church; Northglenn, CO Immaculate Heart of Mary Church; [M] Denver, CO Annunciation Friary.
Beyer, Lawrence A. '96 (DAL) Plano, TX Prince of Peace Church.
Beyer, Leroy O. '66 (WH) Retired.
Beyer, Richard J. '81 (DAV) On Duty Outside the Diocese.
Beyette, Paul V. '50 (OG) Retired.
Bezdicek, Valerian V. '39 (GF) Retired.
Bezunartea, Herman O. '58 (FRS) Bass Lake, CA St. Dominic Savio Church.
Bezuszka, Stanley J. *s.j.* '46 (BO) [W] Chestnut Hill, MA The Jesuit Community at Boston College.
Bezzina, Benjamin '77 (GLP) On Duty Outside of Diocese.
Biagi, Vincent L. *s.j.* '78 (NY) [F] New York, NY Regis High School; [Z] New York, NY St. Ignatius Loyola Residence.
Biain, Jose *o.f.m.* '48 (MIA) Special Assignment; [H] Miami, FL Franciscan Fathers' Residence.
Bialas, Andrew A. *c.s.v.* '44 (JOL) [2] Kankakee, IL St. Patrick Church; Kankakee, IL Shapiro Development Center.
Bialkowski, David W. (BUF) [3] Cheektowaga, NY St. John Gualbert Church.
Bialkowski, Henry A. '49 (NOR) Retired.
Bialkowski, Jacek '96 (SCR) [3] Williamsport, PA St. Boniface's Church.
Bialoncik, Emmanuel *o.f.m.* '73 (BWN) Elsa, TX Sacred Heart Church.
Biancalana, Angelo *m.c.c.j.* '58 (CHI) [N] La Grange Park, IL Comboni Mission Center.
Biancalana, Angelo *m.c.c.j.* '58 (CIN) [V] Cincinnati, OH The Comboni Lay Missionaries Association.
Bianchi, Paul '64 (DM) Portsmouth, IA St. Mary Church.
Bianchi, Raymond S. '52 (TR) [1] Trenton, NJ St. Mary Cathedral.
Bianco, Anthony M. *c.r.s.p.* '51 (ALN) [K] Bethlehem, PA The Barnabite Fathers Barnabite Spiritual Center.
Bianco, Hamilcar '35 (P) Retired.
Biase, Justin *o.f.m.conv.* '70 (TR) Riverside, NJ St. Peter Church.
Biase, Justin A. *o.f.m.conv.* '70 (NY) [B] New York, NY St. Francis Novitiate.
Biasio, Mariano *c.s.j.* '54 (LA) Lancaster, CA Blessed Junipero Serra Church.
Biasiol, Virgilio *o.f.m.* '42 (LA) [R] Santa Barbara, CA Franciscan Friary, Order of Friars Minor (Old Mission).
Biasiotto, Richard P. *o.f.m.* '64 (PAT) [M] Butler, NJ St. Anthony Friary.
Bibeault, Norbert P. *c.s.v.* '56 (LAV) [A] Las Vegas, NV Bishop Gorman High School; [D] Las Vegas, NV Clerics of St. Viator Retirement Home.
Biber, J. Morton '85 (RIC) Powhatan, VA St. John Neumann Church.
Bich, Tran Ngoc *c.ss.r.* '52 (LA) [R] Baldwin Park, CA Vietnamese Redemptorist Mission.
Bichl, William M. *s.j.* '67 (CLV) [C] Cleveland, OH John Carroll University; [C] Cleveland, OH John Carroll Jesuit Community.
Bichsel, William J. *s.j.* '59 (P) [L] Portland, OR Jesuit Provincial Office (Oregon Prov.).
Bickel, Timothy C. '92 (MIL) New Berlin, WI Holy Apostles Church.
Bickerstaff, Albert C. *o.s.b.* '67 (GBG) [H] Latrobe, PA Saint Vincent Archabbey.
Bickett, Tony '83 (OWN) Hawesville, KY Immaculate Conception Church; Lewisport, KY St. Columba Church.
Bickford, Robert M. *s.j.* '41 (SPK) [C] Spokane, WA Gonzaga University.
Bickle, John *o.f.m.* (NY) Manhattan, NY St. Vincent Hospital.
Bickle, John *o.f.m.conv.* '84 (NEW) [2] Hoboken, NJ St. Joseph's Church.
Bico, Antonio '93 (NEW) Harrison, NJ Holy Cross Church.
Bicomong, Sergio '79 (TR) On Duty Outside the Diocese.
Bicsey, John B. '55 (E) Grove City, PA Beloved Disciple Church.
Bicsko, Stephen C. *c.m.* '70 (BRK) [D] Queens and Staten Island, NY St. John's University; [U] Queens Village, NY DePaul Residence.
Bicz, Marian '88 (RVC) Franklin Square, NY St. Catherine of Sienna Church.
Biczak, Arkad '63 (SFE) [26] Albuquerque, NM St. John the Apostle Church.
Bida, John A. '73 (NY) Brewster, NY St. Lawrence O'Toole Church.
Bidawid, Kamal Warda '68 (EST) Turlock, CA St. Thomas Assyrian-Chaldean Parish Church.
Bidinger, Bruce M. *s.j.* '86 (PH) [Z] Philadelphia, PA Jesuit Community at St. Joseph's University.
Bidinger, Bruce M. *s.j.* '86 (SCR) [C] Scranton, PA University of Scranton.
Bidwell, Michael L. '89 (CIN) [37] Cincinnati, OH Holy Trinity Church.
Bidwill, Joseph E. *o.p.* '55 (STP) [15] Minneapolis, MN St. Albert the Great Church.
Bie, Paul R. '83 (RVC) Riverhead, NY St. John the Evangelist Church.
Biebel, Msgr. William E. '62 (E) [1] Erie, PA St. Peter Cathedral.
Bieberle, Victor '51 (WCH) Retired.
Biecker, Thomas C. *s.j.* '40 (DET) [P] Clarkston, MI Colombiere Center.
Biedermann, Msgr. Arnold '45 (LA) Ventura, CA Sacred Heart Church.
Biedermann, Msgr. Arnold '49 (LA) Retired.
Bieganowski, Ronald R. *s.j.* '72 (MIL) [P] Milwaukee, WI Jesuit Community at Marquette University.
Biegler, Steven '93 (RC) McIntosh, SD St. Bonaventure's Church; McLaughlin, SD St. Bernard Church.
Bielanski, Joseph J. '80 (STU) Absent on Leave.
Bielawa, Thomas G. *s.d.s.* '72 (PHX) Cashion, AZ St. William Church.
Bielby, Donald J. *c.s.c.* (FTW) [16] South Bend, IN St. Patrick Church.
Bielecki, Michael *o.s.a.* '83 (PH) Villanova, PA St. Thomas of Villanova Parish Community Church.
Bielek, Robert M. '74 (CLV) [9] Lorain, OH Nativity of the Blessed Virgin Mary Church.
Bielen, Msgr. Stephen A. '45 (MET) Hackettstown, NJ Assumption of the Blessed Virgin Mary Church.
Bielonko, Joseph '59 (WOR) Dudley, MA St. Andrew Bobola Church.
Bielskas, Edward J. '41 (GR) Retired.
Bielski, Francis V. '57 (PH) Willow Grove, PA St. David Church.
Bieluch, Chester A. '48 (HRT) [3] Torrington, CT St. Mary's Church.
Bien, Francis P. '58 (BRK) [186] Queens, NY St. Josaphat Church.
Bien Quang Do, Joseph '64 (SD) [2] El Cajon, CA Our Lady of Grace Church.
Bienia, Michael A. '58 (GBG) Retired; [G] Greensburg, PA Neumann House.
Bieniek, Stanislaus (GAL) [76] Houston, TX St. Thomas More Church.
Bienvenu, Emmett M. *s.j.* '44 (NO) [C] New Orleans, LA Loyola University; [P] New Orleans, LA Ignatius Residence.
Bienvenu, Kenneth '60 (LAF) St. Martinville, LA St. Martin of Tours Church.
Bienvenu, Paul G. '92 (LAF) Berwick, LA St. Stephen Church.
Bier, Joseph V. '36 (MIL) Retired.
Bier, Louis C. '76 (PH) Springfield, PA St. Francis of Assisi Church.
Biergans, Kent *o.f.m.conv.* '67 (IND) [I] Mount Saint Francis, IN Mount Saint Francis Friary and Retreat Center; [J] Mount Saint Francis, IN Provincial Headquarters for the Conventual Franciscan Province.
Bierie, Elwyn L. '38 (DUB) Retired.
Bierman, Earl C. '57 (COV) Retired.
Biermann, John G. *s.a.c.* '69 (WDC) [B] West Hyattsville, MD Pallottine Seminary at Green Hill.
Biernacki, Jacob S. '67 (SPC) Sarcoxie, MO St. Agnes Church.
Biernat, Leon J. '92 (BUF) [1] Tonawanda, NY St. Amelia Church.
Biersack, Thomas E. '81 (MIL) New Munster, WI St. Alphonsus Church.
Bierschenk, Stephen W. '76 (DAL) [27] Dallas, TX St. Thomas Aquinas Church.
Bierster, Msgr. Leo N. '52 (HBG) Hershey, PA St. Joan of Arc Church.
Biesiada, Msgr. Louis W. (PAT) Retired.
Biesinger, Robert J. '56 (BUF) Absent on Leave; [O] Buffalo, NY Sheehan Residence for Priests.

Bietighofer, Alfred J. '65 (BGP) [4] Norwalk, CT St. Mary's Church.

Biffar, Cornelius *ss.cc.* '51 (FR) [K] Fairhaven, MA Sacred Hearts Provincial House.

Biffar, William *c.ss.r.* '47 (ORL) New Smyrna Beach, FL Sacred Heart Church.

Bigelow, William R. '67 (BUF) [30] Buffalo, NY Holy Family Church.

Biggers, Clarence J. *o.c.s.o.* '50 (ATL) [I] Conyers, GA The Monastery of the Holy Spirit.

Biggs, Anselm G. *o.s.b.* '40 (CHL) [J] Belmont, NC Belmont Abbey.

Bigley, Michael *s.d.s.* '87 (NSH) Cookeville, TN St. Thomas Aquinas Church; Sparta, TN St. Andrew Church.

Biglin, Martin J. '67 (NY) [5] New Rochelle, NY Holy Name of Jesus Church.

Bignall, Douglas J. '93 (DET) Farmington, MI Our Lady of Sorrows Church.

Bigot, Ross G. '48 (STP) Retired.

Bihler, Joseph J. '46 (BRK) Retired; [R] Queens Village, NY Queen of Peace Residence.

Bihr, Msgr. Louis J. '68 (PAT) [3] Wayne, NJ Immaculate Heart of Mary Church.

Bihuniak, Michael J. '89 (MET) Fords, NJ Our Lady of Peace Church.

Bik, Michael *o.s.b.* '93 (SCL) [I] Collegeville, MN St. John's Abbey, of the Order of St. Benedict.

Bikoma, Msgr. Edward J. '51 (EST) Chicago, IL St. Ephrem's Church; Chicago, IL Mart Mariam Parish Church.

Bilanych, Msgr. John '40 (PHU) [8] Philadelphia, PA Christ the King Church.

Bilicky, Louis S. '49 (BO) Maynard, MA St. Casimir Church.

Bilinsky, William (CHI) [J] Chicago, IL Resurrection Medical Center.

Bilinsky, Msgr. William M. (STN) Chicago, IL Resurrection and Our Lady of Resurrection.

Bill, J. Armand '56 (PRT) Retired.

Bill, Msgr. Ronald '57 (SY) Cicero, NY Sacred Heart Church.

Bill, Thomas *c.s.c.* (P) [L] Portland, OR Holy Cross Father & Brother, C.S.C. - University of Portland.

Bill, Thomas *c.s.c.* '55 (P) [B] Portland, OR University of Portland.

Billac, Christopher A. *s.j.* '65 (GAL) [F] Houston, TX Strake, Jesuit College Preparatory Inc.

Biller, Harold N. '70 (ALT) [8] Johnstown, PA St. Patrick's Church.

Biller, Thomas P. '57 (TLS) [9] Tulsa, OK The Madalene Church.

Billett, Robert *c.m.f.* '57 (LA) [R] Los Angeles, CA Claretian Retreat Center Community; [W] Los Angeles, CA Claretian Retreat Center (All Groups).

Billian, Michael R. '84 (TOL) [B] Toledo, OH Central Catholic High School.

Billiard, Donald *o.f.m.* '83 (SFE) [4] Albuquerque, NM Holy Family Church; [J] Albuquerque, NM San Antonio Provincial Friary Franciscan Friars.

Billig, Cloud *o.f.m.* (SFD) [K] Sherman, IL Our Lady of Angels Friary.

Billig, Maynard *o.f.m.* '39 (STL) [P] St. Louis, MO Franciscan Friary of St. Anthony of Padua.

Billimek, Alvin O. *c.ss.r.* '38 (STL) [P] Liguori, MO St. Clement Health Care Center.

Billing, Jerome D. '71 (STL) Union, MO Immaculate Conception Church.

Billinger, James J. '83 (WCH) [12] Wichita, KS St. Elizabeth Ann Seton Church.

Billings, George K. *c.m.* '80 (STL) Perryville, MO St. Vincent De Paul Church.

Billman, George B. '72 (FAR) Fessenden, ND St. Augustine's Church.

Billotte, Philip J. '66 (ROC) Naples, NY St. Januarius Church.

Billotti, Joseph E. *s.j.* '63 (CI) [B] Pohnpei, FM PATS (Pohnpei Agriculture and Trade School).

Billy, Dennis *c.ss.r.* '80 (WDC) [M] Washington, DC Holy Redeemer College.

Billy, George '48 (PSC) Retired.

Bilodeau, Florent R. '57 (MAN) Hampstead, NH St. Anne Church.

Bilodeau, Leopold J. '73 (BUR) Burlington, VT Fletcher Allen Health Care.

Bilodeau, Roger '65 (MAN) Lincoln, NH St. Joseph Church.

Bilos, Leo '37 (STN) [6] Palatine, IL Immaculate Conception Church; Retired.

Bilot, James '92 (DET) Bloomfield Hills, MI St. Hugo of the Hills Church.

Bilotta, Anthony J. '45 (BUF) Retired.

Bilski, Harry '58 (AUS) Temple, TX V.A. Hospital.

Bilskie, Msgr. Maurilius '43 (EVN) [7] Evansville, IN Holy Rosary Church; Retired.

Bily, Msgr. Edward '51 (SAT) New Braunfels, TX SS. Peter and Paul Church.

Bily, John C. '58 (VIC) Weimar, TX St. Michael Church.

Bily, Lambert S. '63 (SAT) [20] San Antonio, TX Our Lady of Sorrows Church.

Binder, Albert H. '51 (FAR) Mooreton, ND St. Anthony's Church.

Binder, Mark J. '71 (SPC) Kennett, MO St. Cecilia Church.

Bindner, Charles J. '58 (L) [30] Louisville, KY St. Helen Church.

Binh, John Phan Cong '51 (SHP) Retired.

Biniek Joseph P. '78 (ARL) Dale City, VA Holy Family Church.

Biniszkiewicz, Msgr. Leonard E. '63 (BUF) [14] Niagara Falls, NY St. Teresa of the Infant Jesus Church.

Binkowski, Msgr. George '72 (STF) Brooklyn, NY Holy Ghost Church.

Binkowski, James P. '56 (LC) Eau Galle, WI St. Henry Church.

Binsfeld, Msgr. Michael A. '67 (RCK) Special Assignment.

Binsfeld, Steven '79 (SCL) [1] St. Cloud, MN St. Mary's Cathedral of St. Cloud.

Binz, Stephen J. '81 (LR) [10] Little Rock, AR Our Lady of Good Counsel Church; Malvern, AR St. John the Baptist Church.

Binzer, Joseph R. '94 (CIN) [25] Cincinnati, OH St. Dominic Church.

Bionda, Bonaventure *o.f.m.* (ALB) [3] Watervliet, NY Our Lady of Mt. Carmel Church.

Biondi, Lawrence H. *s.j.* '70 (STL) [C] St. Louis, MO Saint Louis University; [P] St. Louis, MO Jesuit Community Corporation at St. Louis University - Jesuit Hall.

Biondi, Nicholas A. '38 (PIT) Retired; [N] Pittsburgh, PA St. John Vianney Manor.

Biondino, Joseph P. '55 (ALB) [10] Schenectady, NY St. Joseph Church.

Biondino, Joseph P. '55 (BGP) Leave of Absence.

Biondolillo, Gabriel *o.m.i.* '56 (BEL) [G] Belleville, IL Shrine of Our Lady of the Snows.

Bir, Stanley *o.f.m.* '52 (CIN) [M] Cincinnati, OH St. Clement Friary.

Birarelli, Carl A. '58 (CIN) Retired.

Birarelli, Carl A. '58 (VEN) [2] Sarasota, FL Our Lady Queen of Martyrs Church.

Birch, Donald G. '67 (PH) [90] Philadelphia, PA St. Madeleine Sophie Church.

Birch, Keith L. '71 (DUB) Tama-Toledo, IA St. Patrick's Church.

Birch, Msgr. Thomas J. '59 (ALN) Shillington, PA St. John Baptist de la Salle Church; Retired.

Birchmeyer, Robert J. '73 (SY) Solvay, NY St. Cecilia Church.

Bircumshaw, Colin F. (SLC) [C] Ogden, UT St. Joseph Regional School.

Bircumshaw, Colin F. '75 (SLC) [3] Ogden, UT St. Joseph's Church.

Bird, James F. '91 (E) Hermitage, PA Church of Notre Dame; [C] Du Bois, PA Du Bois Area Catholic Schools.

Bird, Stephen J. '76 (OKL) [15] Oklahoma City, OK St. Patrick's Church; Special Assignment.

Birdsall, Anthony J. '60 (GB) Sturgeon Bay, WI Corpus Christi Church.

Birdsall, Hugh G. *s.d.s.* '62 (MIL) Greendale, WI St. Alphonsus Church; [B] Hales Corners, WI Sacred Heart School of Theology.

Birdsall, John M. '56 (RC) Retired.

Birdsall, Richard W. '45 (SC) Retired.

Bireley Robert L. *s.j.* '64 (CHI) [C] Chicago, IL Jesuit Community at Loyola University of Chicago.

Birge, George D. '56 (BGP) Newtown, CT St. Rose of Lima Church.

Biriruka, Ernest '81 (MIA) [1] Hialeah, FL Immaculate Conception Church.

Birk, John '61 (CHI) Brookfield, IL St. Barbara Church.

Birk, John '63 (SPK) Special Ministry; [G] Pasco, WA Our Lady of Lourdes Health Center.

Birk, John G. '63 (CHI) Chicago, IL Hines V.A. Hospital.

Birk, John W. '70 (L) [33] Louisville, KY Holy Name Church.

Birkel, John B. '96 (LIN) [8] Lincoln, NE St. Mary Church.

Birkel, Richard C. (WDC) [G] Washington, DC Lt. Joseph P. Kennedy, Jr., Institute.

Birkel, Robert C. '49 (L) Retired.

Birkenfeld, Darryl '88 (AMA) On Duty Outside the Diocese.

Birkenhauer, Henry F. *s.j.* '45 (CLV) [E] Cleveland, OH St. Ignatius High School; [U] Cleveland, OH Jesuit Retreat House.

Birket, Dwight '72 (WCH) [16] Wichita, KS St. Margaret Mary Church.

Birkhead, Henry G. '56 (PH) [34] Philadelphia, PA Christ the King Church.

Birkle, Walter A. '58 (NY) [172] Bronx, NY Our Lady of Grace Church; [M] Bronx, NY District Council of the Bronx.

Birkmaier, James E. '68 (GF) [G] Great Falls, MT Benefis Health Care.

Birkmeyer, John R. *c.s.c.* '57 (AUS) [H] Austin, TX Congregation of Holy Cross - Southern Province.

Birmingham, Robert F. '93 (HRT) Middlebury, CT St. John of the Cross Church.

Biron, Gerald R. *m.s.* '60 (SPR) [1] Westfield, MA Holy Trinity Church.

Biron, Robert G. '74 (MAN) Somersworth, NH St. Martin Church.

Biroschak, Robert V. '93 (LA) Ventura, CA Our Lady of the Assumption Church.

Birringer, Raphael *s.d.s.* '51 (MIL) [P] Milwaukee, WI Salvatorian Provincial Residence.

Birzer, W. L. '39 (DOD) Retired.

Bisaillon, Rene '59 (HON) Waipahu, HI St. Joseph Church.

Bisbal, Pedro J. Silva *o.m.* '75 (CGS) Cayey, PR Nuestra Senora de la Asuncion Church.

Bisbee, Burnell B. *s.j.* '75 (OM) [C] Omaha, NE Creighton Preparatory School.

Bischko, Kenneth *t.o.r.* '64 (SP) [4] Clearwater, FL St. Cecelia Church.

Bischof, Donald R. '83 (PIT) Monroeville, PA North American Martyrs Church.

Bischof, Simon *o.s.b.* '55 (SCL) [5] St. Cloud, MN St. Augustine Church.

Bischoff, Albert J. *s.j.* '56 (IND) [D] Indianapolis, IN Brebeuf Jesuit Preparatory School, Inc.

Bischoff, Msgr. Francis J. (PAT) Retired.

Bisenius, Thomas R. '54 (DUB) Garryowen, IA St. Patrick's Church.

Bisgrove, Charles *s.c.j.* '90 (MIL) Franklin, WI Sacred Hearts of Jesus and Mary Church; St. Martins, WI Holy Assumption Church.

Bishara, Boctor '51 (LA) [K] Lynwood, CA St. Francis Medical Center.

Bisharat, George Said '92 (NTN) North Hollywood, CA St. Anne Church.

Bishop, Benedict *o.c.d.* '54 (BO) [W] Brighton, MA Carmelite Monastery.

Bishop, E. Louis *s.j.* '64 (PHX) [B] Phoenix, AZ Brophy College Preparatory.

Bishop, Joseph E. '58 (SAC) Yuba City, CA St. Isidore Church.

Bishop, Patrick A. '74 (ATL) [4] Marietta, GA Church of the Transfiguration.

Bishop, Patrick J. *s.m.* '45 (OAK) San Lorenzo, CA St. John the Baptist Church.

Bishop, Robert *c.m.f.* '71 (LA) [R] Los Angeles, CA Claretian Retreat Center Community; [R] Rancho Dominguez, CA Dominguez Seminary Inc.

Bishop, Thomas A. '75 (CHI) Buffalo Grove, IL St. Mary Church.

Bishop, Thomas G. '70 (Y) [4] Canton, OH St. Anthony's Church.

Bisignano, Joseph J. '81 (NY) Beacon, NY St. John Evangelist Church.

Bismonte, Honesto '54 (LA) Gardena, CA St. Anthony of Padua Church.

Bisoffi, Joseph L. *o.s.cam.* '72 (MIL) [K] Milwaukee, WI St. Francis Hospital; [P] Wauwatosa, WI St. Camillus Community House.

Bispels, William J. '61 (PH) [74] Philadelphia, PA St. Jerome Church.

Bisson, Andrew R. '93 (PRT) [I] Kennebunkport, ME St. Anthony's Friary.

Bisson, Eddy N. '68 (MAN) Laconia, NH Sacred Heart Church.

Bisson, Roger *m.afr.* '55 (WDC) [M] Washington, DC Missionaries of Africa.

Bissonette, James '88 (DUL) Carlton, MN St. Francis Church.

Bissot, Robert H. '57 (GAY) Cadillac, MI St. Ann Church; Harietta, MI St. Edward Church.

Bistany, Msgr. Joseph '37 (SAM) Retired.

Bistricky, Frederick J. '65 (MIL) Retired.

Biszek, Robert J. '65 (ALN) [4] Bethlehem, PA Holy Infancy Church.

Bitanga, Msgr. Fred A. '64 (SFR) [41] San Francisco, CA St. Patrick Church.

Bitangjol, Albert P. '56 (SFR) Retired.

Bitsko, Daniel J. '65 (PSC) Smithtown, NY Resurrection Church.

Bittel, Patrick M. '82 (OWN) Morganfield, KY St. Ann's Church.

Bittenz, Francis A. *s.j.* '36 (DET) [P] Clarkston, MI Colombiere Center.

Bitterman, John L. *s.s.* '69 (BAL) [M] Baltimore, MD Sulpician Provincial House.

Bittmenn, David J. '94 (SLC) [1] Salt Lake City, UT Cathedral of the Madeleine; [B] Salt Lake City, UT Judge Memorial Catholic High School.

Bittner, Gregory T. '85 (BIR) Pell City, AL Our Lady of the Lake Church.

Bittner, Wayne W. '64 (MIL) Plymouth, WI St. John the Baptist's Church.

Bitz, Al '69 (FAR) Casselton, ND St. Leo Church.

Biven, Louis Russell '57 (MOB) [17] Mobile, AL Our Savior Church.

Bixenman, Joe '72 (AMA) Canadian, TX Sacred Heart Church.

Bixenman, Joseph E. '72 (AMA) Pampa, TX St. Vincent de Paul Church.

Bizaca, Mate '73 (LA) San Pedro, CA Mary, Star of the Sea Church.

Bizkarra, Juan *s.j.* '35 (CI) Angaur, FM Holy Rosary Church.
Bjorklund, Brian '66 (DET) Military Chaplains.
Bjorum, James L. '76 (DET) [1] St. Clair Shores, MI St. Germaine Church.
Blacet, Msgr. William J. '46 (KC) [28] Kansas City, MO Our Lady of Good Counsel Church.
Black, Alvin *o.f.m.* '60 (SCR) [12] Wilkes-Barre, PA St. Joseph Church; [M] Wilkes-Barre, PA St. Joseph's Friary.
Black, James P. '88 (COL) [1] Columbus, OH St. Joseph Cathedral.
Black, Joseph '56 (P) Junction City, OR St. Helen Church; Monroe, OR St. Rose Church; Veneta, OR St. Catherine of Siena Church.
Blackall, John C. '51 (HRT) [9] Waterbury, CT St. Cecilia's Church; [T] Waterbury, CT Spanish-Speaking Center.
Blackall, L. Randall '54 (HRT) Glastonbury, CT St. Paul's Church.
Blackburn, Clifford *o.m.i.* '47 (SAT) [K] San Antonio, TX Oblate Madonna Residence; [M] San Antonio, TX Provincial Administration Office, Oblates of Mary Immaculate (Southern Prov.).
Blackburn, David *o.c.s.o.* '54 (SPC) [E] Ava, MO Assumption Abbey (Trappist).
Blackburn, Michael *o.f.m.* '86 (LAV) [10] Las Vegas, NV St. James the Apostle Church.
Blackowski, Theodore A. *o.f.m.* '45 (SP) [O] St. Petersburg, FL St. Anthony Friary.
Blackwell, Edward '76 (HBG) On Duty Outside the Diocese.
Blackwell, Edward A. '76 (MIA) [B] Opa Locka, FL St. Thomas University.
Blackwell, Maurice J. '74 (BAL) [29] Baltimore, MD St. Edward Church.
Blackwell, Michael J. '73 (WDC) Landover Hills, MD St. Mary's Catholic Church.
Blackwood, Wallace E. (BO) [2] Peabody, MA St. Ann Church.
Bladt, Joel S. *s.t.* '61 (SAV) Bainbridge, GA St. Joseph's Church.
Blaes, James F. *c.s.c.* '55 (FTW) [17] South Bend, IN Faith & Hope & Charity Chapel; [J] South Bend, IN Congregation of Holy Cross Indiana Province Provincial House.
Blaes, Paul '51 (KC) Retired.
Blaeser, Alfred A. '32 (BRK) Retired.
Blaeser, Donald P. *o.f.m.* '70 (GRY) [K] Cedar Lake, IN San Damiano Friary.
Blaetter, James R. *s.j.* '80 (BGP) [O] Fairfield, CT The Fairfield Jesuit Community-Fairfield University.
Blaettler, James R. *s.j.* '80 (BGP) [A] Fairfield, CT Fairfield University.
Blaha, John F. '75 (GB) [7] Green Bay, WI St. Joseph Church.
Blain, Lionel A. '54 (PRO) [7] Woonsocket, RI St. Joseph's Church.
Blaine, James E. (SLC) Draper, UT State Penitentiary.
Blaine, James E. '77 (SLC) American Fork, UT St. Peter's Church.
Blaine, Michael '87 (PH) [D] Philadelphia, PA St. Maria Goretti High School.
Blaine, Michael J. '91 (PH) [84] Philadelphia, PA King of Peace Church.
Blair, Guy *s.c.j.* '82 (MIL) [P] Hales Corners, WI Sacred Heart Monastery.
Blair, Guy A. *s.c.j.* '82 (MAD) [9] Madison, WI Saint Joseph Church.
Blair, John C. (MAN) [I] Nashua, NH St. Joseph Hospital.
Blair, Msgr. Raymond O. '60 (MAN) On Duty Outside the Diocese.
Blair, Stephen N. '73 (LA) Military and VA Chaplains.
Blais, Denis *c.p.m.* '93 (LAF) Iota, LA St. Joseph Church.
Blais, George P. '90 (ORG) El Toro, CA Santiago de Compostela Church.
Blais, Jean *s.d.s.* '64 (MIL) [P] Milwaukee, WI Salvatorian Provincial Residence.
Blais, Melvin J. '42 (STP) Retired.
Blais, Robert L. '63 (PRO) Absent on Leave.
Blais, Robert R. *o.p.* '68 (L) [46] Louisville, KY St. Louis Bertrand Church.
Blais, Roger '50 (KC) On Duty Outside the Diocese.
Blais, Roger H. '50 (TLS) Hartshorne, OK Holy Rosary Church.
Blais, Roland O. '44 (MAN) [9] Manchester, NH St. George Church; Retired.
Blake, Andrew P. '63 (RVC) Sag Harbor, NY St. Andrew's Church.
Blake, Carlyle *c.ss.r.* (OAK) [N] Oakland, CA Redemptorists.
Blake, David *o.f.m.* (BUF) [R] Williamsville, NY Newman Club Chaplains; [R] Williamsville, NY Newman Club Chaplains.
Blake, David D. *o.f.m.* '95 (BUF) [O] St. Bonaventure, NY St. Bonaventure Friary.
Blake, John Vincent *o.p.* '51 (SFE) [29] Albuquerque, NM St. Thomas Aquinas University Parish Church.
Blake, Peter M. '84 (STL) Union, MO Immaculate Conception Church.
Blake, Philip C. *s.j.* '61 (SJ) [L] Los Altos, CA Jesuit Retreat House.
Blake, Richard *s.j.* '69 (BO) [W] Chestnut Hill, MA The Jesuit Community at Boston College.
Blake, Robert '77 (SR) Cloverdale, CA St. Peter's Church.
Blake, William *s.v.d.* '90 (CHI) [B] Techny, IL Divine Word Residence.
Blake, William B. '63 (SCR) Jessup, PA St. Michael's Church.
Blakely, Leonard J. '80 (WIL) Chestertown, MD Sacred Heart Church; Chestertown, MD Washington College; [O] Chestertown, MD Washington College Newman Center; [O] Newark, DE Univ. of Delaware Newman Center.
Blakely, Paige '84 (ORL) Special Assignment.
Blakely, Paige A. '84 (ORL) DeBary, FL St. Ann's Church
Blaker, John (OAK) Dublin, CA St. Raymond Church.
Blanch, Jose Maria *s.f.* '51 (SFE) Santa Cruz, NM Holy Cross Church.
Blanchard, David *o.carm.* '87 (WDC) [B] Washington, DC Whitefriars Hall.
Blanchard, Donald V. '69 (BR) [12] Baton Rouge, LA St. Jean Vianney Church.
Blanchard, John L. *s.j.* '48 (DET) [P] Clarkston, MI Colombiere Center.
Blanchard, Peter *s.m.* '67 (NO) [F] Covington, LA The St. Paul's School.
Blanchet, Leo (MOB) Whistler, AL St. Bridget Church.
Blanchett, Conrad *m.s.* '43 (TUC) Pirtleville, AZ St. Bernard's Church.
Blanchette, Brian D. '85 (PRT) Calais, ME Immaculate Conception Church.
Blanchette, Melvin C. *s.s.* '46 (BAL) [M] Baltimore, MD Sulpician Provincial House.
Blanchette, Michael '84 (JOL) Absent on Leave.
Blanchette, Oliver R. *a.a.* '44 (WOR) Fiskdale, MA St. Anne's and St. Patrick's Church.
Blanchette, Roger E. *s.j.* '64 (HEL) [5] Missoula, MT St. Francis Xavier Church; [E] Missoula, MT St. Patrick Hospital Corporation.
Blanchfield, David W. '82 (BGP) [1] Norwalk, CT St. Jerome Church.
Blanchfield, John P. '50 (HRT) Plantsville, CT St. Aloysius Church.
Blanchfield, Joseph J. '41 (PH) Norwood, PA St. Gabriel Church; Retired.
Blanco, Adalberto '77 (LA) Santa Monica, CA St. Anne Church.
Blanco, Gonzalo *o.s.b.* '92 (BIS) [A] Richardton, ND Assumption Abbey.
Blanco, Ignacio *c.m.f.* '51 (SAT) [12] San Antonio, TX Immaculate Heart of Mary Church.
Blanco, John *s.d.b.* '64 (NY) [2] Port Chester, NY Corpus Christi Church.
Blanco, Joseph J. '84 (DEN) Roggen, CO Sacred Heart Church.
Blanco, Telesforo R. *o.s.a.* '60 (BEA) [1] Port Arthur, TX Our Lady of Guadalupe Church.
Blanda, William C. '91 (LAF) Kaplan, LA Our Lady of the Holy Rosary Church.
Blandford, James T. '38 (LEX) Retired.
Blandino, Salvatore '53 (SJ) [4] Sunnyvale, CA St. Martin Church.
Blaney, Dennis J. '58 (GRY) [5] Michigan City, IN Sacred Heart Church.
Blaney, Jim *o.m.i.* '65 (JUN) Craig, AK St. John by the Sea Church.
Blaney, Philip L. '45 (HRT) Harwinton, CT Immaculate Heart of Mary Church; Retired.
Blaney, Robert M. '92 (BO) [3] Peabody, MA St. John the Baptist Church.
Blangiardi, B. Jeffrey *s.j.* '86 (BO) [W] Boston, MA The Society of Jesus of New England-Provincial Offices.
Blank, Godfrey *o.f.m.* '45 (SFE) [1] Santa Fe, NM The Cathedral of San Francisco de Asis.
Blank, Severius '58 (FWT) Burkburnett, TX St. Jude Thaddeus Church.
Blank, William H. '87 (NO) Franklinton, LA Holy Family Church.
Blankenship, John P. '63 (RIC) Colonial Heights, VA St. Ann Church; Petersburg, VA Federal Correctional Institution.
Blankinship, Calvin, Jr. '96 (B) Idaho Falls, ID Holy Rosary Church.
Blantz, James *c.s.c.* '56 (LA) [P] Chatsworth, CA Rancho San Antonio.
Blantz, Thomas E. *c.s.c.* '60 (FTW) [B] Notre Dame, IN University of Notre Dame Du Lac; [J] Notre Dame, IN Holy Cross Community, Corby Hall, University of Notre Dame.
Blaschko, Harvey *o.p.* '81 (CHI) [13] Chicago, IL Angel Guardian Croatian Catholic Mission Church; [N] Chicago, IL Croatian Dominican Fathers.
Blasco, Ignacio '62 (MIA) [24] Miami, FL St. Kevin Church.
Blascovich, Joseph D. '75 (HBG) Elizabethtown, PA St. Peter Church; [K] Harrisburg, PA Catholic Campus Ministry.
Blaser, John R. '64 (TOL) [41] Toledo, OH St. Thomas Aquinas Church.
Blasich, Bernard (CHI) Evergreen Park, IL St. Bernadette Church.
Blaska, John A. '53 (DET) Clawson, MI Guardian Angels Church; Retired.
Blaski, Henry *c.r.* '50 (CHI) [D] Chicago, IL Weber High School.
Blastic, Michael *o.f.m.conv.* '73 (BUF) [O] St. Bonaventure, NY St. Bonaventure Friary.
Blaszczak, Gerald R. *s.j.* '79 (SY) [A] Syracuse, NY Saint Andrew Hall.
Blaszczyk, Thaddeus J. '53 (DET) [2] Troy, MI St. Alan Church.
Blattner, Joseph H. '58 (PRT) Benedicta, ME St. Benedict's Church; Island Falls, ME St. Agnes Church.
Blattner, Joseph H. '58 (STL) On Duty Outside the Archdiocese.
Blaufuss, Tony '58 (KCK) Ottawa, KS Sacred Heart Church.
Blauvelt, Robert W. '59 (BRK) [233] Queens, NY Resurrection-Ascension Church.
Blay, Roberto Garcia '86 (PCE) [3] Ponce, PR Church of the Resurrection.
Blazak, Camillus W. '51 (BIR) Scottsboro, AL St. Jude Church.
Blazejewski, Richard J. '74 (BUF) Perry, NY St. Stanislaus Kostka Church.
Blazejewski, Richard W. '74 (BUF) Perry, NY St. Joseph Church.
Blazek, Eugene E. '76 (HON) Military Chaplains.
Blazek, James F. '79 (CHI) [94] Chicago, IL Immaculate Heart of Mary Church.
Blazek, John *c.s.c.* '58 (CLV) [E] Gates Mills, OH Gilmour Academy.
Blazewicz, William J. '59 (LC) Mondovi, WI Sacred Heart of Jesus Church.
Blazine, James A. '62 (BEL) [7] Belleville, IL St. Mary Church; Fayetteville, IL St. Pancratius Church.
Blazquez, Marcelo '60 (ALB) Retired.
Bleaux, Floyd J., Jr. '73 (OG) [1] Plattsburgh, NY Our Lady of Victory Church.
Blecha, Charles A. '40 (LC) Retired.
Blecha, Jordan R. *o.praem.* '39 (GB) [I] De Pere, WI St. Norbert Abbey.
Blee, Edward C. *s.m.* '55 (HON) [15] Honolulu, HI Star of the Sea Church.
Blee, Michael J. *s.j.* '37 (PH) [Z] Philadelphia, PA Jesuit Community at St. Joseph's University.
Blehl, Vincent F. *s.j.* '52 (NY) [Z] New York, NY Jesuit Provincial's Office.
Bleich, Msgr. Russell M. '60 (DUB) [4] Waterloo, IA St. Edward's Church; [D] Waterloo, IA Columbus High School.
Bleichner, Howard P. '67 (PIT) On Duty Outside the Diocese.
Bleichner, Howard P. *s.s.* '67 (WDC) [C] Washington, DC Catholic University of America, The.
Bleichner, Howard P. *s.s.* '72 (WDC) [A] Washington, DC Theological College of the Catholic University of America.
Bleiler, William C. '82 (CHR) Garden City, SC St. Michael Church.
Bleiler, William J. '66 (CAM) Mullica Hill, NJ Holy Name of Jesus Church.
Bleilevens, Charles A. '50 (BRK) [153] Queens, NY Ascension Church.
Blenker, Ambrose J. '62 (LC) Plum City, WI St. John the Baptist Church.
Blenkle, Joseph A. '90 (NY) Cortlandt Manor, NY St. Columbanus Church.
Blesnuk, Donald J. (BUF) On Duty Outside the Diocese.
Blessin, Thomas '63 (NEW) [B] Jersey City, NJ Saint Peter's College.
Blessin, Thomas C. *s.j.* '63 (NEW) [N] Jersey City, NJ Jesuits of Saint Peter's College, Inc.
Blessing, Howard '76 (LAF) [14] Lafayette, LA St. Mary, Mother of the Church.
Blessing, Loren *o.f.m.* '81 (FRS) [G] Three Rivers, CA St. Anthony's Retreat House.
Blessinger, James C. '64 (EVN) [1] Vincennes, IN Sacred Heart Church.
Blessington, Msgr. William H. '43 (DUB) Retired.
Blewett, John E. *s.j.* '53 (MIL) [P] Milwaukee, WI Jesuit Provincial Office, Wisconsin Province.
Blewett, John E. *s.j.* '53 (STL) [P] St. Louis, MO Jesuit Community Corporation at St. Louis University - Jesuit Hall.
Blicharski, Michael *s.o.cist.* '93 (CHI) [N] Willow Springs, IL Cistercian Fathers.
Blick, Ned '92 (WCH) [19] Wichita, KS St. Thomas Aquinas Church.
Blickhan, Donald '74 (SFD) Military Chaplains.
Blighton, Francis E. '74 (ROC) [12] Rochester, NY St. Charles Borromeo Church.
Blind, Thomas '81 (NEW) Summit, NJ St. Teresa's Church.
Blinn, Mark R. '43 (CLV) [3] Garfield Heights, OH St. Therese Church; Retired.

Blinn, Richard J. *s.j.* '69 (SAC) Davis, CA St. James Church.
Bliss, Michael '91 (PEO) [J] Peoria, IL St. Francis' Medical Center.
Bliszcz, Michael '87 (SJP) Pittsburgh, PA St. George Church.
Bliven, Edmond '50 (P) Retired.
Bliven, Lance R. *c.s.sp.* '74 (SB) Hemet, CA Our Lady of the Valley Church.
Bliven, Robert *o.s.c.* '56 (PHX) [4] Glendale, AZ St. Louis The King Church.
Bliven, Robert J. *o.s.c.* '56 (PHX) [F] Phoenix, AZ Crosier Community of Phoenix (Canons Regular of the Order of the Holy Cross).
Blizard, David '70 (WOR) Absent on Leave.
Blocher, James *c.s.b.* (VIC) Wharton, TX Our Lady of Mt. Carmel Church.
Blocher, James F. *c.s.b.* '75 (GAL) Angleton, TX St. Basil Church.
Block, John G. '63 (PMB) Boynton Beach, FL St. Mark Church.
Blockley, Matthew '96 (CHK) San Jose Village, District 7, MP San Jose Parish Church.
Blocklinger, James L. '66 (DUB) [2] Cedar Rapids, IA All Saints Church.
Bloh, John F. '64 (CAM) Swedesboro, NJ St. Joseph's Church.
Bloh, Stephen R. '81 (PH) Absent on Sick Leave.
Blom, Gerald '79 (NY) Middletown, NY St. Joseph Church.
Blomberg, John F. '59 (STL) Overland, MO All Souls Church.
Blong, Delbert F. '52 (PBL) Retired.
Blonigen, Aloysius *c.m.m.* '65 (DET) [K] Dearborn Heights, MI Our Lady of Grace Monastery.
Blonski, Joachim '92 (GLP) Farmington, NM Sacred Heart Church.
Blood, Bernard M. *s.m.m.* '50 (RVC) West Islip, NY Good Samaritan Hospital; [I] West Islip, NY The Samaritan Corporation; [N] Bay Shore, NY Montfort Missionaries.
Blood, Francis X. '79 (STL) [30] St. Louis, MO St. Cecilia Church; [W] St. Louis, MO Hispanic Ministry of the Archdiocese of St. Louis.
Bloom, Phillip '71 (SEA) [24] Seattle, WA Holy Family Church.
Bloom, R. Frederick '52 (WDC) Retired.
Blostic, Leonard *t.o.r.* '63 (ALT) [10] Johnstown, PA St. Anthony's Church; [D] Johnstown, PA Good Samaritan Medical Center.
Blotsky, Hugo L. *o.s.b.* '88 (BIS) Mandan, ND Christ the King Church; [A] Richardton, ND Assumption Abbey.
Blottman, William P. '65 (FR) [2] Taunton, MA Our Lady of the Immaculate Conception Church.
Blough, E. C. '33 (PEO) Retired.
Blough, E. C. '37 (PEO) [L] Peoria, IL St. Augustine Manor.
Blough, William G. '58 (PIT) Oakmont, PA St. Irenaeus Church.
Blout, Daniel L. '86 (GBG) [4] Greensburg, PA St. Paul Church; [C] Greensburg, PA Greensburg Central Catholic High School.
Blow, Thomas *o.f.m.conv.* '87 (BUF) [O] St. Bonaventure, NY St. Bonaventure Friary.
Blow, Thomas A. *o.f.m.conv.* '87 (CHI) [N] Chicago, IL Franciscan House of Studies.
Blowers, Leslie F. *m.m.* '63 (CIN) [M] Cincinnati, OH The Catholic Foreign Mission Society of America, Inc.; [V] Cincinnati, OH St. Andrew Kim Korean Catholic Society.
Blubaugh, Homer '69 (COL) Westerville, OH St. Paul the Apostle Church.
Bludnicki, Dennis G. '75 (BGP) [2] Bridgeport, CT St. Ambrose Church.
Blue, Peter W. *o.s.b.* (PAT) [M] Newton, NJ St. Paul's Abbey.
Blue Jacket, David S. '88 (DEN) [20] Denver, CO Our Lady of Lourdes Church.
Bluett, Anthony '69 (ORL) Winter Haven, FL St. Joseph's Church.
Bluett, James K. '67 (PT) Military Chaplains.
Bluett, John J. '63 (ORL) Winter Springs, FL St. Stephen Church.
Blum, John J. '96 (SP) Tarpon Springs, FL St. Ignatius Church.
Blum, Msgr. Orville '62 (AMA) Hereford, TX St. Anthony's Church.
Blum, Owen *o.f.m.* (SFD) [K] Sherman, IL Our Lady of Angels Friary.
Blum, Stephen J. '76 (TOL) Vermilion, OH St. Mary Church.
Blum, William G. *c.s.c.* '65 (FTW) [L] Notre Dame, IN Holy Cross Mission House.
Bluma, Dacian *o.f.m.* '49 (MIL) [P] Burlington, WI Queen of Peace Friary.
Blumenfeld, Donald '79 (NEW) [D] Scotch Plains, NJ Union Catholic Regional High School.
Blumeyer, A. James *s.j.* '63 (STL) [C] St. Louis, MO Saint Louis University; [P] St. Louis, MO Jesuit Community Corporation at St. Louis University - Jesuit Hall.
Blumm, John L. *m.s.* '45 (LKC) De Quincy, LA Our Lady of La Salette Church.
Blute, Robert H. '56 (BO) [1] Peabody, MA St. Adelaide Church.
Bly, Walter J. '64 (FTW) [7] South Bend, IN Corpus Christi Church; [C] South Bend, IN Saint Joseph's High School.
Blyman, Robert '52 (RVC) [N] Uniondale, NY St. Pius X Residence.
Blyman, Robert '71 (RVC) [N] Uniondale, NY St. Pius X Residence.
Blyskosz, Joseph J. '95 (FR) South Yarmouth, MA St. Pius Tenth Church.
Boackle, H. Paul '89 (SAM) Dover, NH St. George Church.
Boadt, Lawrence *c.s.p.* '69 (NEW) [S] Mahwah, NJ Paulist Press.
Boadt, Lawrence E. *c.s.p.* '69 (NY) [41] New York, NY Good Shepherd Church.
Boadt, Lawrence E. *c.s.p.* '69 (WDC) [B] Washington, DC St. Paul's College.
Boarman, Leon J. *c.s.c.* (AUS) [H] Austin, TX St. Joseph Hall.
Boarman, Leon J. *c.s.c.* '37 (AUS) [H] Austin, TX Congregation of Holy Cross - Southern Province.
Boateng-Mensah, John '73 (PT) [1] Tallahassee, FL Co-Cathedral of St. Thomas More.
Bobal, Msgr. Joseph K. '63 (E) Houtzdale, PA Christ the King Church; Osceola Mills, PA Immaculate Conception Church.
Boban, Dujo *o.f.m.* (SJ) [26] San Jose, CA St. Mary of the Assumption Church.
Bobber, Ray *o.f.m.* '57 (FWT) [G] Crowley, TX St. Francis Village, Inc.
Bobber, Raymar *o.f.m.* '57 (FWT) [H] Crowley, TX St. Maximilian Kolbe Friary.
Bober, Bernard '62 (STU) Retired.
Bober, Charles S. '72 (PIT) [54] Pittsburgh, PA St. John Vianney Church.
Bober, Francis J. '69 (WDC) Retired.
Bober, Marjan L. '63 (CAM) Collings Lakes, NJ Our Lady of the Lakes Church.
Bober, Richard J. '57 (CLV) [2] Euclid, OH St. Felicitas Church.
Boberek, Aurelius *o.s.b.* '57 (IND) [A] St. Meinrad, IN St. Meinrad Seminary; [J] St. Meinrad, IN St. Meinrad Archabbey.
Bobersky, Michael '35 (STN) Retired.
Bobrek, Edwin *o.f.m.* '51 (NY) [Z] New York, NY Franciscan Province of the Immaculate Conception.
Bocad, Deo '74 (NEW) East Orange, NJ East Orange Hospital; Orange, NJ Hospital Center at Orange.
Boccaccio, Michael A. '71 (BGP) [6] Norwalk, CT St. Philip Church.
Boccali, Ronnie *p.i.m.e.* '60 (COL) [H] Newark, OH P.I.M.E. Mission & Prayer Center.
Boccardi, Raymond C. '52 (PIT) Coylesville, PA St. John Church.
Bocciarelli, John *c.s.* '45 (BO) [2] Somerville, MA St. Anthony Church.
Boccieri, Ronald J. *m.m.* '62 (ALB) [S] Saratoga, NY Skidmore College.
Boccieri, Ronald J. *m.m.* '62 (NY) [Z] Maryknoll, NY Maryknoll Fathers and Brothers.
Boccio, Msgr. Charles P. '61 (BRK) [181] Queens, NY Immaculate Conception Church.
Boccio, Msgr. Charles P. '61 (NY) Bronx, NY Veterans Administration Hospital.
Bochenek, Joseph G. '71 (BAL) [19] Baltimore, MD St. Brigid Church.
Bochenski, Joseph *c.m.f.* (LAV) Pahrump, NV Our Lady of the Valley Church.
Bochicchio, Paul L. '71 (NEW) [1] Garfield, NJ Our Lady of Mt. Virgin Church.
Bochinski, Mark J. '58 (SCR) Avoca, PA SS. Peter and Paul Church.
Bochnak, Zenon A. '85 (MET) On Duty Outside the Diocese.
Bocian, Ronald C. '72 (ALN) Cumbola, PA St. Anthony of Padua Church; [C] Pottsville, PA Nativity B.V.M. High School.
Bocianowski, Thaddeus Nicholas (BUF) [2] Buffalo, NY St. Adalbert's Basilica.
Bocianski, Andrew B. '26 (SCR) Retired.
Bock, Lawrence R. '62 (HRT) Simsbury, CT St. Mary's Church.
Bockenfeld, Elgar *o.f.m.* '44 (STP) St. Benedict, MN St. Benedict Church; Union Hill, MN St. John the Evangelist Church.
Bocklage, Richard F. *s.j.* '55 (DEN) [M] Denver, CO Xavier Jesuit Center.
Bockskopf, Richard J. '70 (STL) [34] St. Louis, MO St. Francis de Sales Church; Maryland Heights, MO St. Blaise Church.
Bocod, Dioscoro P. (NEW) [2] Orange, NJ Our Lady of the Valley Church.
Bodah, Henry J. '78 (PRO) [4] Warwick, RI St. Francis of Assisi Church.
Bodart, William D. '61 (TOL) Kirby, OH St. Mary Church; Upper Sandusky, OH St. Peter Church.
Bodde, Frederick A. '53 (DET) Port Huron, MI St. Stephen Church.
Bodden, Charles J. *o.s.a.* '78 (CHI) [N] Olympia Fields, IL The Augustinian Provincialate Tolentine Center.
Bodden, Clarence *c.ss.r.* '49 (LA) Whittier, CA St. Mary of the Assumption Church; [R] Whittier, CA Redemptorist Fathers Mission House.
Boddie, James R., Jr. '78 (STA) [19] Jacksonville, FL St. Pius the Fifth Church.
Bodenschatz, Ronald *t.o.r.* '49 (ALT) [F] Loretto, PA Mount Assisi Monastery.
Bodenstedt, James A. *m.m.* '56 (SJ) [M] Los Altos, CA Maryknoll.
Bodensteiner, Peter C. '45 (DUB) Retired.
Bodero, Fortunato *o.p.* '66 (PCE) Yauco, PR Holy Rossary Church.
Bodnar, Edward W. *s.j.* '52 (WDC) [M] Washington, DC The Jesuit Community at Georgetown University.
Bodo, Murray L. *o.f.m.* '64 (CIN) [M] Cincinnati, OH Pleasant Street Friary.
Bodziak, Charles F. '67 (ALT) [2] Barnesboro, PA St. Stanislaus Kostka Church; [4] Barnesboro, PA Christ the King Church.
Bodziony, Ralph A. '58 (CLV) [37] Cleveland, OH St. John Cantius Church.
Boeckman, Floyd B. *o.m.i.* '55 (BEL) [G] Belleville, IL Shrine of Our Lady of the Snows; [K] Belleville, IL Missionary Association of Mary Immaculate-Mission Oblates of Mary Immaculate.
Boeckman, John R. '84 (E) Greenville, PA St. Michael Church.
Boeding, Damian '52 (SPC) Retired.
Boedy, Thomas G. *s.j.* '70 (STP) Delano, MN St. Joseph Church; Delano, MN St. Peter Church; [N] Minneapolis, MN La Storta Jesuit Community.
Boeff, Dismas *o.s.b.* '76 (CLV) Brook Park, OH St. Peter the Apostle Church; Cleveland, OH SouthWest General Hospital; [P] Cleveland, OH Benedictine Order of Cleveland.
Boegel, Joseph L. *c.m.* '49 (PH) [Z] Philadelphia, PA Congregation of the Mission.
Boeglin, John '78 (EVN) Jasper, IN Holy Family Church.
Boehm, Claude L. *c.s.c.* '35 (FTW) [J] South Bend, IN Congregation of Holy Cross Indiana Province Provincial House.
Boehm, Msgr. James A. '58 (STU) Wintersville, OH Blessed Sacrament Church.
Boehm, Michael J. (CHI) [4] Waukegan, IL Holy Family Church.
Boehm, Michael P. '94 (STL) Kirkwood, MO St. Peter Church.
Boehman, John R. *o.f.m.* (CIN) [M] Cincinnati, OH St. Francis Seraph Friary.
Boehme, Arnold *o.c.d.* '68 (MIL) [P] Milwaukee, WI Provincial Offices - Discalced Carmelites.
Boehme, Walter E. *s.j.* '70 (OM) [7] Omaha, NE St. Benedict the Moor Church; [K] Omaha, NE Jesuit Community At Creighton University.
Boehmicke, Roger A. '38 (L) [65] Louisville, KY St. Pius X Church; Louisville, KY Audubon Regional Medical Center; Retired.
Boehning, John A. '62 (NY) [118] New York, NY St. Thomas More Church.
Boeke, Aloysius B. '41 (CIN) Fort Loramie, OH St. Michael's Church; Retired.
Boeke, Anselm F. '43 (CIN) Piqua, OH St. Mary Church; Retired.
Boekelman, Timothy J. '77 (SC) Neptune, IA St. Joseph's Church; Struble, IA St. Joseph's Church; [B] Le Mars, IA Gehlen Catholic School.
Boel, Joseph H. *s.j.* (DET) [B] Berkley, MI Loyola House.
Boensch, Gregory A. '94 (CC) Freer, TX St. Mary Church.
Boenzi, Joseph *s.d.b.* '79 (OAK) [A] Berkeley, CA Dominican School of Philosophy and Theology; [N] Berkeley, CA Salesian Community.
Boes, Clair L. '65 (SC) Storm Lake, IA St. Mary's Church.
Boes, Marvin J. '62 (SC) [3] Sioux City, IA St. Boniface Church.
Boes, Steven E. '85 (OM) Battle Creek, NE St. Patrick's Church.
Boesche, Walfrid *o.f.m.* (SFD) [K] Sherman, IL Our Lady of Angels Friary.
Boesel, Msgr. James E. '54 (RVC) Hicksville, NY Our Lady of Mercy Church.
Boeshans, Msgr. Francis G. '48 (NO) Lacombe, LA St. John of the Cross Church.
Boessen, Msgr. Bernard H. '50 (STL) Retired.
Boettcher, John '91 (SR) On Duty Outside the Diocese.
Boettner, David '94 (KNX) [2] Chattanooga, TN Our Lady of Perpetual Help Church.
Boever, Richard A. *c.ss.r.* '73 (CHI) [29] Chicago, IL Blessed Sacrament Church.
Bofenkamp, Andrew H. '45 (LC) Retired.
Boff, Bernard J. '61 (TOL) [1] Toledo, OH Queen of the Most Holy Rosary Cathedral; [L] Toledo, OH Ursuline Convent of the Sacred Heart; [O] Toledo, OH

Office of Global Concerns.
Boffa, William L. '75 (FR) [3] Attleboro, MA St. Stephen's Church.
Bofto, Robert C. '63 (GF) Retired.
Bogardus, Thomas D. *o.s.a.* '64 (BO) [C] North Andover, MA Merrimack College.
Bogda, Dennis M.J. '67 (PBR) Lyndora, PA St. John the Baptist Church.
Bogdan, Msgr. Henry S. '48 (TR) [6] Trenton, NJ Incarnation Church; Retired.
Bogdan, Leonard A. '60 (KAL) Special Assignment.
Bogdan, Palka *s.d.s.* '92 (NEW) [N] Verona, NJ The Salvatorian Fathers.
Bogdziewicz, Msgr. Anthony F. '49 (NEW) Summit, NJ St. Teresa's Church; Retired; [N] Rutherford, NJ St. John Vianney Residence for Priests.
Bogel, William A. *c.m.* '68 (STL) [P] St. Louis, MO Vincentian-St. Lazare Residence; [R] Normandy, MO Marillac Provincial House.
Bogert, James (RVC) Priests Released from Diocesan Assignment.
Bogetto, Clarence J. *c.m.* '45 (STL) [P] Perryville, MO Congregation of The Mission.
Boggs, Msgr. Dennis R. '86 (ALT) On Special Assignment.
Bognacki, Edward R. '91 (NEW) Roseland, NJ Our Lady of the Blessed Sacrament Church.
Bognanno, Msgr. Frank E. '65 (DM) [7] Des Moines, IA St. Augustin's Church.
Bogniak, Msgr. Casimir A. '57 (E) Meadville, PA St. Mary Church.
Bogolin, Leonard *o.f.m.* '34 (CHI) [N] Lemont, IL The Slovene Franciscan Fathers, Order of Friars Minor, Commissariat of the Holy Cross.
Bogovich, Msgr. Paul P. '41 (GRY) [2] East Chicago, IN Holy Trinity Church.
Boguslawski, Steven C. *o.p.* '87 (WDC) [B] Washington, DC Dominican House of Studies.
Bogusz, Dennis A. '79 (GBG) Point Marion, PA St. Hubert Church.
Bogusz, Joseph G. '75 (BO) Awaiting Assignment.
Bohan, Philip F. *o.f.m.cap.* '67 (NY) [83] New York, NY Our Lady Queen of Angels Church.
Bohl, Ronald *o.f.m.conv.* '80 (IND) [I] Mount Saint Francis, IN Mount Saint Francis Friary and Retreat Center.
Bohlinger, Kenneth '76 (LFT) Leave of Absence.
Bohn, Raymond G. '43 (BUF) Retired; [O] Buffalo, NY Sheehan Residence for Priests.
Boholnick, Theodore '53 (PHU) Simpson, PA SS. Peter and Paul Church.
Bohr, Msgr. David A. '71 (SCR) [A] Dalton, PA Saint Pius X Seminary.
Bohr, Luke *o.s.b.* '48 (RCK) [H] Aurora, IL Marmion Abbey-St. Augustine's Abbey.
Bohrer, John D. '78 (CAM) Glassboro, NJ Our Lady of Lourdes Church.
Bohula, Edwin V. '55 (CHI) [4] Lemont, IL St. James at Sag Bridge Church.
Boiko, John G. (AUS) Elgin, TX Sacred Heart Church.
Boileau, David '56 (NO) [A] New Orleans, LA Notre Dame Seminary Graduate School of Theology.
Boileau, David A. '56 (NO) [15] New Orleans, LA Mater Dolorosa Church; [C] New Orleans, LA Loyola University.
Boisaubin, Robert D. '69 (STL) O'Fallon, MO Assumption Church.
Boisselle, Aime A. '59 (MAN) [3] Concord, NH Sacred Heart Church.
Boisvert, Gilbert O. '71 (OG) Altona, NY Holy Angels Church; Sciota, NY St. Louis Church.
Boisvert, Gregory *a.a.* '51 (BO) [W] Brighton, MA Assumptionist Center.
Boisvert, Gregory *a.a.* '51 (KNX) [1] Knoxville, TN Cathedral of the Sacred Heart of Jesus.
Boisvert, Keith W. (BAL) Educational Sabbatical.
Boisvert, Marc '84 (ORG) El Toro, CA El Toro Marine Base.
Boisvert, Robert G. '58 (MAN) [15] Manchester, NH St. Pius X Church.
Boisvert, Russel L. '64 (NOR) Montville, CT St. John Church.
Boivin, Henry P. '57 (BO) Whitman, MA Holy Ghost Church.
Boivin, John '76 (CHI) [1] Chicago, IL Cathedral of the Holy Name.
Boivin, Louis R. '48 (FR) [15] Fall River, MA St. Jean Baptiste Church; Retired.
Bojczuk, Thaddeus J. '73 (CHI) Summit, IL St. Joseph Church.
Bojek, Gerald '69 (NEW) Paramus, NJ Bergen Pines County Hospital.
Boji, Manuel Y. '68 (EST) Southfield, MI Our Lady of Chaldeans Cathedral, Mother of God Chaldean Parish Church.
Bok, James *o.f.m.* '74 (CIN) [M] Cincinnati, OH St. Francis Seraph Friary; [M] Cincinnati, OH St. Clare Friary.
Bok, James M. *o.f.m.* (CIN) [O] Cincinnati, OH Friars Club.
Bok, John *o.f.m.* '62 (CIN) [M] Cincinnati, OH St. Francis Seraph Friary.
Bokenkotter, Thomas '50 (CIN) [12] Cincinnati, OH Assumption of the Blessed Virgin Mary Church.
Bokinskie, Richard '79 (SAG) Marlette, MI St. Elizabeth Church; Mayville, MI St. Joseph Church.
Bokota, Marek '81 (NEW) Wallington, NJ Most Sacred Heart of Jesus Church.
Boks, Lawrence E. '66 (GAY) Harrisville, MI St. Anne Church; Mikado, MI St. Raphael Church.
Bolan, John E. *c.pp.s.* '53 (CIN) [M] Dayton, OH Provincial House of the Cincinnati Province of the Society of the Precious Blood.
Bolan, John E. *c.pp.s.* '53 (CLV) Cleveland, OH Veterans Administration Hospitals, Brecksville V.A.
Boland, Eamonn '69 (DUL) Eveleth, MN Resurrection Church.
Boland, Edward F. '44 (PRO) Retired; [P] Providence, RI St. John Vianney Residence.
Boland, Edward G. '51 (PH) Retired.
Boland, Msgr. Eugene M. '63 (PAT) Totowa Borough, NJ St. James of the Marches Church.
Boland, Jeremiah M. '81 (CHI) Deerfield, IL Holy Cross Church.
Boland, John '75 (GLP) Seboyeta, NM Our Lady of Sorrows Church.
Boland, John A. *s.j.* '58 (SY) [S] Syracuse, NY Jesuits at LeMoyne, Inc.
Boland, John P. '55 (PH) North Wales, PA St. Rose of Lima Church.
Boland, Msgr. John V. '65 (PAT) McAfee, NJ St. Francis de Sales Church.
Boland, Joseph B. (JC) Retired.
Boland, Michael M. '86 (CHI) River Forest, IL St. Luke Church; [G] Chicago, IL Catholic Charities of the Archdiocese of Chicago-Archdiocesan Offices.
Boland, Patrick *t.o.r.* '41 (ARL) [J] Winchester, VA Sacred Heart Friary.
Boland, Steve *m.s.c.* '86 (RCK) [H] Aurora, IL Missionaries of the Sacred Heart Community.
Boland, Thomas L. '65 (L) [34] Louisville, KY Holy Spirit Church.
Bolcar, Andrew J. '65 (CAM) Westville, NJ St. Anne's Church.
Bolderson, John D. '81 (STL) Apple Creek, MO St. Joseph's Church.
Bolds, Bernard L. '41 (LR) Retired.
Boldt, William J. '49 (NY) [230] Staten Island, NY St. Teresa Church.
Bolduc, Marcel *o.m.i.* '39 (PRT) [I] Augusta, ME St. Paul Retreat House and Cursillo Center; [L] Augusta, ME St. Paul Retreat House and Cursillo Center.
Bolduc, Msgr. Norman, Jr. '79 (MAN) Auburn, NH St. Peter Church.
Bolduc, Paul (BO) Boston, MA Deaconess Hospital.
Bolduc, Paul '58 (BO) [72] Boston, MA St. Thomas Aquinas Church.
Boler, Martin *o.s.b.* '60 (ROC) [I] Pine City, NY Mount Saviour Monastery.
Bolerasky, Msgr. Peter E. '55 (PEO) [4] Streator, IL St. Stephen's Church.
Boles, John P. '63 (BO) [26] Boston, MA St. Gregory Church.
Boles, Joseph M. *v.f.* '65 (SCR) Dalton, PA Our Lady of the Abingtons Church.
Bolesta, Michael C. '89 (PH) [AA] Huntingdon Valley, PA Sisters of the Holy Redeemer Provincialate.
Boley, Edward J. '44 (GBG) On Duty Outside the Diocese.
Boley, Robert *o.carm.* '75 (JOL) [J] Darien, IL Carmelite Fathers Provincial Office.
Bolez, Edward C. '74 (ALN) [5] Bethlehem, PA St. John Capistrano Church.
Bolger, Anthony J. '69 (HON) Kailua, HI St. Anthony Church.
Bolger, Msgr. James '74 (NY) [F] New York, NY St. Joseph by the Sea, High School.
Bolger, Msgr. James F. (NY) [O] New York, NY Mission of the Immaculate Virgin.
Bolger, Msgr. James F. '74 (NY) [L] New York, NY Catholic Youth Organization of the Archdiocese of New York Inc.
Bolger, John '50 (SP) [9] St. Petersburg, FL Transfiguration Church.
Bolger, Michael J. (RCK) [B] Freeport, IL Aquin Central Catholic Junior-Senior High School.
Bolger, Michael J. '92 (RCK) [2] Freeport, IL St. Joseph Church.
Bolger, Richard T. '66 (PH) Willow Grove, PA St. David Church.
Bolger, Msgr. William '53 (SD) Retired.
Bolha, Jeremy *o.s.b.* '59 (E) St. Marys, PA Queen of the World Church.
Bolieau, Henry G. '72 (NOR) Absent on Leave.
Bolin, John *s.m.* '55 (HON) [D] Honolulu, HI St. Louis School.
Bolin, John F. *s.m.* '55 (HON) [H] Honolulu, HI Marianist Hall Community; [J] Honolulu, HI Aina Kupaa O Maili.
Boll, John E. '70 (SAC) Woodland, CA Holy Rosary Church.
Boll, John J. *o.p.* '82 (NO) [25] New Orleans, LA St. Anthony Of Padua Church; [64] New Orleans, LA St. Thomas More Church; New Orleans, LA Tulane-Newcomb.
Bollea, Richard C. '62 (HRT) [7] Waterbury, CT Sacred Heart Church; Waterbury, CT Waterbury Hospital.
Boller, Kenneth J. *s.j.* '75 (NY) [F] New York, NY Xavier High School.
Boller, Robert J. '91 (STP) Watertown, MN Immaculate Conception Church.
Bolling, Joseph M. '91 (MOB) [13] Mobile, AL St. Matthew Church.
Bollman, Richard W. *s.j.* '69 (CIN) [78] Cincinnati, OH St. Robert Bellarmine Church; [D] Cincinnati, OH Xavier University; [M] Cincinnati, OH Jesuit Community at Xavier University.
Bolman, Anthony P. '60 (SFE) [2] Albuquerque, NM Ascension Church.
Bologna, Anthony F. '43 (DET) [25] Detroit, MI St. Gabriel Church; Retired.
Bolser, Charles G. *c.s.v.* '73 (CHI) [D] Arlington Heights, IL St. Viator High School.
Bolser, Robert T. *c.s.v.* '95 (CHI) [210] Chicago, IL St. Viator Church.
Bolster, M. Thomas '82 (GR) [1] Grand Rapids, MI Cathedral of St. Andrew.
Bolte, George '38 (FAR) Retired.
Bolte, Richard '83 (COV) [1] Newport, KY Corpus Christi Church; [B] Newport, KY Newport Central Catholic High School.
Bolte, Thomas L. '80 (CIN) [38] Cincinnati, OH St. Ignatius Loyola Church.
Bolton, Bill *s.d.b.* '87 (LA) [B] Bellflower, CA De Sales Hall.
Bolton, Donald *c.ss.r.* '52 (ORL) [F] New Smyrna Beach, FL St. Alphonsus Villa-Redemptorist Fathers and Brothers.
Bolton, Norman B. '83 (SPR) [P] Amherst, MA University of Massachusetts and Amherst College, Newman Center.
Bolton, Paul J. '62 (PRO) On Duty Outside the Diocese.
Bolts, T. William *s.m.* (SJ) [20] San Jose, CA Queen of Apostles Church.
Bolvary, Paul L. '47 (PIT) Retired.
Boly, S.J., Craig '74 (SEA) [11] Seattle, WA St. Joseph Church.
Bomar, Msgr. Fred '60 (AUS) [19] Austin, TX St. Peter the Apostle Church.
Bomba, Paul M. '77 (WOR) Military Chaplains.
Bombardier, Dennis P. '68 (SPR) Millers Falls, MA St. John's Church.
Bombardier, Gerald W. '73 (BUR) Winooski, VT St. Francis Xavier Church.
Bombardier, Paul A. '82 (SPR) Ware, MA Our Lady of Mt. Carmel Church.
Bombardier, Wilfrid F. '43 (MAN) Retired.
Bombera, Alex *t.o.r.* '46 (SFS) Plankinton, SD St. John Church; Plankinton, SD State Training School.
Bomberger, Ray *s.s.j.* '71 (BEA) [7] Beaumont, TX Our Mother of Mercy Church.
Bommarito, Vincent '77 (STL) [10] Florissant, MO St. Thomas the Apostle Church.
Bona, Joseph F. *s.j.* '72 (DEN) [M] Denver, CO Xavier Jesuit Center.
Bonacci, (Eugene) Thomas P. '72 (OAK) [3] Concord, CA St. Francis of Assisi Church.
Bonacci, Louis *s.j.* '62 (CIN) [Q] Cincinnati, OH Xavier University Campus Ministry.
Bonacci, Louis A. *s.j.* '73 (CIN) [M] Cincinnati, OH Jesuit Community at Xavier University.
Bonaccorsi, Salvatore S. *o.s.a.* '57 (BO) [C] North Andover, MA Merrimack College.
Bonacum, Thomas '79 (SB) Retired.
Bonadies, Kenneth P. '65 (HRT) [4] Hamden, CT St. Ann's Church.
Bonadio, Joseph *s.s.* '64 (BAL) [32] Baltimore, MD St. Francis of Assisi Church.
Bonadio, Joseph J. *s.s.* '64 (BAL) [M] Baltimore, MD Sulpician Provincial House.
Bonafed, Joseph E. '92 (GBG) [4] Uniontown, PA St. Therese, the Little Flower of Jesus Church.
Bonano, Salvatore *c.m.f.* '84 (LA) [R] Rancho Dominguez, CA Dominguez Seminary Inc.
Bonanti, Thomas A. '85 (PT) [8] Pensacola, FL St. Anthony of Padua Church; [10] Pensacola, FL St. Joseph Church.
Bonar, Clyde A. '84 (ORL) Apopka, FL St. Francis of Assisi Church.
Bonarrigo, David *t.o.r.* '78 (ARL) Herndon, VA St. Joseph Church.
Bonavia, Sebastian *o.f.m.cap.* '44 (NO) [3] New Orleans, LA Annunciation Church.
Bonavitacola, John M. '88 (PH) [131] Philadelphia, PA Our Mother of Mercy Prison Chaplaincy Church; [139] Philadelphia, PA St. Raymond of Penafort Church; Philadelphia, PA Philadelphia Prison System.
Bonczewski, Msgr. William D. '76 (OLL) [C] North Jackson, OH National Shrine of Our Lady of Lebanon.
Bond, B. Daniel '84 (RIC) Mathews, VA Church of

Francis de Sales; Middlesex County, VA Church of the Visitation.
Bond, Ernest W. '88 (COS) Bailey, CO St. Mary's of the Rockies Church.
Bond, Robert *glmy.* '60 (TLS) Hugo, OK Immaculate Conception Church.
Bond, Robert E. *o.p.* '55 (PRO) [B] Providence, RI Providence College; [P] Providence, RI St. Thomas Aquinas Priory at Providence College.
Bond, Thomas Aquinas *o.c.s.o.* '39 (ROC) [I] Piffard, NY Abbey of the Genesee.
Bonderenko, Thomas '80 (BAL) Special Assignment.
Bondi, Paul (ALB) Retired.
Bondi, Richard A. '74 (SPR) [11] Springfield, MA Our Lady of the Sacred Heart Church.
Bondi, Steven '86 (JOL) Wheaton, IL St. Michael Church.
Bondy, Alberto P. '86 (DET) [6] Livonia, MI St. Michael Church.
Boneck, Norman D. '62 (LC) [1] Wausau, WI Holy Name of Jesus Church.
Boned, Enrique '57 (MIA) [1] Hialeah, FL Immaculate Conception Church.
Bonelli, Msgr. Theodore V. '61 (NEW) Retired.
Bones, James J. '64 (PH) Levittown, PA Immaculate Conception B.V.M. Church.
Boney, Vincent *c.p.* '57 (SCR) [M] Scranton, PA Saint Ann's Passionist Monastery.
Bonfadini, Leo '74 (PBL) Absent on Leave.
Bonfigilo, Anthony J. '48 (WDC) Retired.
Bonfiglio, David G. '63 (BO) [14] Cambridge, MA Sacred Heart of Jesus Church; Boston, MA Cambridge Hospital; Boston, MA Mount Auburn Hospital.
Bonfiglio, Gregory R. *s.j.* '93 (LA) [10] Los Angeles, CA Dolores Mission Church.
Bonfilgio, David G. (BO) Retired.
Bongard, Joseph W. '86 (PH) [6] Norristown, PA St. Titus Church; [D] Norristown, PA Kennedy-Kenrick Catholic High School.
Bonghanoy, Edgardo '80 (HON) [3] Honolulu, HI St. Anthony Church.
Bongiorno, Angelo *s.d.b.* '42 (BO) [E] Boston, MA Don Bosco Preparatory School of Technology.
Bonham, Ray O. '94 (OM) Heun, NE Holy Trinity Church.
Bonhert, Edward A. '85 (SFR) [53] San Francisco, CA St. Vincent de Paul Church.
Bonian, Stephen J. *s.j.* '82 (BO) [W] Boston, MA The Society of Jesus of New England-Provincial Offices.
Bonian, Steve *s.j.* '82 (TLS) [6] Tulsa, OK St. Francis Xavier-Our Lady of Guadalupe Church.
Boniface, Jeyarah *s.j.* '87 (BO) [W] Chestnut Hill, MA The Jesuit Community at Boston College.
Bonifas, Casper *c.pp.s.* '43 (CIN) [B] Carthagena, OH St. Charles.
Bonifas, Roger D. '45 (TOL) Ottoville, OH Immaculate Conception Church; Retired.
Bonifazi, Flavian *s.a.c.* '43 (BAL) [52] Baltimore, MD St. Leo Church.
Bonikowski, Leon V. *o.s.f.s.* '65 (PH) [Z] Philadelphia, PA Oblates of St. Francis De Sales.
Bonin, David L. '74 (ROC) Odessa, NY St. Benedict Church; Watkins Glen, NY St. Mary of the Lake Church.
Bonin, Harold A. '65 (CHI) [100] Chicago, IL St. Jerome Church.
Bonin, Raymond *o.carm.* '82 (PHX) [6] Phoenix, AZ St. Agnes Church.
Bonin, Richard G. '46 (NU) Gaylord, MN St. Michael Church; Winthrop, MN St. Francis de Sales Church.
Bonjean, Jerry *s.d.b.* '67 (LA) [B] Bellflower, CA De Sales Hall.
Bonjean, Richard '76 (MRY) Retired.
Bonk, Carl *s.j.* '82 (CLV) [E] Cleveland, OH St. Ignatius High School; [U] Cleveland, OH Jesuit Retreat House.
Bonk, Matthew *o.s.b.* '42 (CLV) [P] Cleveland, OH Benedictine Order of Cleveland.
Bonke, James (IND) Greenwood, IN Our Lady of the Greenwood Church.
Bonke, James R. '70 (IND) [1] Indianapolis, IN SS. Peter and Paul Cathedral.
Bonn, Ferdinand C. '49 (JC) Retired.
Bonnar, David J. '88 (PIT) Bethel Park, PA St. Thomas More Church.
Bonneau, Roger *o.carm.* '60 (JOL) [J] Darien, IL Carmelite Fathers Provincial Office.
Bonnell, Robert A. '49 (CLV) Oberlin, OH Sacred Heart Church; Retired.
Bonnell, Victor G. '60 (SLC) Layton, UT St. Rose of Lima Church.
Bonner, Charles E. '65 (PH) Yeadon, PA St. Louis Church.
Bonner, Dismas *o.f.m.* '58 (STL) [T] Dittmer, MO Il Ritiro-The Little Retreat.
Bonner, Joseph P. '53 (SCR) Weston, PA Sacred Heart Church.
Bonner, Michael J. *s.v.d.* '66 (CHI) [32] Chicago, IL St. Bronislava Church; [B] Techny, IL Divine Word Residence.
Bonner, Patrick J. *o.s.b.* '59 (PAT) [M] Newton, NJ St. Paul's Abbey.
Bonner, W. Richard '61 (NY) [Z] Esopus, NY Redemptorist Priests and Brothers C.Ss.R. (Province of Baltimore).
Bonner, William J. *s.v.d.* '67 (LA) [76] Los Angeles, CA St. Malachy Church.
Bonnet, Christian L. *s.j.* '38 (STL) [O] St. Louis, MO Fusz Pavilion.
Bonneville, Lionel E. '63 (SPR) [3] Ludlow, MA St. John the Baptist Church.
Bonnici, John S. '91 (NY) [34] New York, NY Epiphany Church; [D] New York, NY Department of Education.
Bonnici, William (DET) [5] Roseville, MI Sacred Heart Church.
Bonnot, Bernard R. '67 (BRK) [14] Brooklyn, NY St. Augustine Church.
Bonnot, Bernard R. '67 (Y) On Duty Outside the Diocese.
Bono, Vincent *s.c.* '81 (NO) [P] New Orleans, LA Brothers of the Sacred Heart; [R] New Orleans, LA Center of Jesus the Lord; [R] Ponchatoula, LA Magnificat Center of the Holy Spirit.
Bonomo, James H. '70 (RIC) [E] Richmond, VA St. Mary's Hospital.
Bonsignore, Dennis '81 (ROC) [11] Rochester, NY St. Cecilia Church.
Bonsignore, Mark '95 (HRT) [I] Hartford, CT Saint Francis Hospital and Medical Center.
Bonsignore, Mark J. '67 (HRT) Wallingford, CT Resurrection Church.
Bonski, Eugene *m.s.s.a.* (HRT) New Haven, CT Connecticut Correctional Institution.
Bonsor, Jack '74 (SFR) Special Assignment; [A] Menlo Park, CA St. Patrick Seminary; [A] Menlo Park, CA St. Patrick Seminary.
Bonvouloir, Philip *a.a.* '57 (NY) [87] New York, NY Our Lady of Guadalupe Church.
Bonzagni, John J. '80 (SPR) Lenox Dale, MA St. Vincent de Paul's Church; [C] Pittsfield, MA St. Joseph Central High School.
Book, Msgr. A. Joseph '63 (E) Greenville, PA St. Michael Church.
Boone, Kirby *c.f.x.* (FBK) Tanana, AK St. Aloysius Church.
Boone, Thomas A. '61 (CLV) Brook Park, OH Assumption of Mary Church.
Boor, Colin J. '50 (WCH) Hutchinson, KS Our Lady of Guadalupe Church; Hutchinson, KS Kansas State Industrial Reformatory.
Booth, Earl J. '44 (LR) Retired.
Booth, Earl J. '60 (LR) [H] Little Rock, AR St. John Manor.
Booth, Edward N. '74 (STA) [1] St. Augustine, FL Cathedral of St. Augustine.
Booth, John (SY) Binghamton, NY Binghamton Psychiatric Hospital.
Booth, John A. '82 (SY) Deposit, NY St. Joseph Church.
Booth, Mark Thomas *ofm conv.* '85 (BUF) [D] Athol Springs, NY St. Francis High School; [O] Athol Springs, NY St. Francis of Assisi Friary.
Booth, Michael A. '89 (SD) Valley Center, CA St. Stephen Church.
Booth, Raymond '57 (ROC) Webster, NY St. Paul Church.
Booth, Stephen R. *m.m.* '86 (NY) [Z] Maryknoll, NY Maryknoll Fathers and Brothers.
Boothali, Anthony '89 (SCR) [3] Williamsport, PA St. Boniface's Church.
Bootkoski, Msgr. Paul G. '66 (NEW) Saddle River Borough, NJ St. Gabriel the Archangel Church.
Boquet, Gregory M. *o.s.b.* '88 (NO) [A] St. Benedict, LA St. Joseph's Seminary College; [P] St. Benedict, LA St. Joseph Abbey.
Boquet, Shenan J. '93 (HT) Lockport, LA Holy Savior Church.
Boracco, John B. *p.i.m.e.* '30 (DET) [K] Detroit, MI P.I.M.E. Missionaries of SS. Peter and Paul.
Boras, Kurt D. '86 (CHI) [A] Mundelein, IL University of St. Mary of the Lake-Mundelein Seminary.
Borawski, Gerald J. '72 (LFT) Frankfort, IN St. Mary Church.
Borbely, James A. *s.j.* '76 (PH) [Z] Philadelphia, PA Jesuit Community at St. Joseph's University.
Borbridge, David *s.j.* (MOB) [B] Mobile, AL Spring Hill College.
Borbridge, David C. *s.j.* '63 (NO) [P] New Orleans, LA Jesuit Provincial Office.
Borchardt, Edward '96 (SPK) [15] Spokane, WA St. Mary Church.
Borcherding, Martin '73 (LAF) [3] Lafayette, LA Holy Cross Church.
Borcic, John J. '76 (STL) Webster Groves, MO Mary, Queen of Peace Church.
Borcz, Casimir Adalbert *o.c.d.* '45 (GRY) [K] Munster, IN Discalced Carmelite Fathers Monastery.
Borda, Peter Paul '42 (SD) Retired.
Bordages, Msgr. Martin '41 (BEA) [5] Port Arthur, TX St. James Church; Retired.
Bordeaux, Henry *o.c.d.* '62 (LR) [A] Little Rock, AR Marylake - Carmelite Novitiate.
Bordeleau, Normand G. '85 (BRK) Released from Diocesan Assignment.
Bordeleau, Normand G. '85 (MAN) Concord, NH N.H. State Hospital.
Bordelon, H. Gerald '56 (ALX) [2] Alexandria, LA Our Lady of Prompt Succor Church.
Bordelon, Lloyd '91 (LAF) Cow Island, LA St. Anne Church.
Bordelon, Msgr. Roland '50 (ALX) On Duty Outside the Diocese.
Borden, Wilfred F. *o.m.i.* '63 (LA) [C] Santa Paula, CA Thomas Aquinas College.
Bordenca, Charles '55 (BIR) Retired.
Bordenkircher, Robert *o.p.* '54 (BR) Ponchatoula, LA St. Joseph Church.
Bordignon, Angelo *c.s.* '51 (LA) [87] Los Angeles, CA St. Peter Church.
Bordignon, Narciso *c.r.s.* '67 (GAL) [11] Houston, TX Assumption Church.
Bordonaro, Joseph C. '89 (PH) Primos, PA St. Eugene Church; [D] Springfield, PA Cardinal O'Hara High School.
Boreczky, John V. '48 (CHI) Retired.
Borel, Albert W. '81 (LKC) Graduate Studies.
Boren, Edward Daniel *o.f.m.* '64 (VIC) Bay City, TX Our Lady of Guadalupe Church.
Borer, Gerard J. *s.j.* '59 (COS) [8] Colorado Springs, CO Our Lady of the Pines-Black Forest Church.
Borer, Robert D. '76 (STU) Cambridge, OH St. Benedict Church.
Boretto, Christopher '87 (SY) [9] Binghamton, NY St. Patrick Church; Binghamton, NY Our Lady of Lourdes Memorial Hospital.
Borg, Manuel *c.ss.r.* '89 (CHI) [9] Chicago, IL St. Alphonsus Church.
Borg, Marcellinus *o.f.m.* '59 (NY) [Z] New York, NY Franciscan Province of the Immaculate Conception.
Borg, Ron *c.s.b.* (DET) [44] Detroit, MI St. Louis the King Church.
Borgelt, Daniel E. '93 (TOL) [4] Fremont, OH St. Joseph Church.
Borger, Theodore R. '83 (DAV) Military Chaplains.
Borgerding, John *o.s.b.* '66 (LA) [R] Valyermo, CA St. Andrew's Abbey.
Borgers, Charles *o.m.i.* '41 (SAT) [M] San Antonio, TX Oblate Benson Residence (Southern Prov.).
Borges, Jose Angel *s.j.* '69 (SJN) [22] San Juan, PR San Ignacio de Loyola Church.
Borges, Laurence '59 (BO) [1] Weymouth, MA St. Albert the Great Church.
Borges, Mario L. '82 (OAK) [7] Oakland, CA St. Columba's Church.
Borgesen, Kenneth *o.ss.t.* '87 (NO) [16] New Orleans, LA Our Lady Of Good Counsel Church.
Borgia, Anthony A. '84 (TOL) Galion, OH St. Joseph Church.
Borgmeyer, Dean G. '81 (WH) Dunbar, WV Christ the King Church; Nitro, WV Holy Trinity Church.
Borgo, John V. *s.j.* '57 (BGP) [I] Bridgeport, CT St. Vincent's Medical Center; [O] Fairfield, CT The Fairfield Jesuit Community-Fairfield University.
Borgo, John V. *s.j.* '57 (BO) [W] Boston, MA The Society of Jesus of New England-Provincial Offices.
Borgognoni, Msgr. Charles L. '48 (SY) Retired.
Borgola, Bonaventure *o.f.m.* '39 (ALT) [17] Johnstown, PA St. Therese of the Child Jesus Church.
Borgonovo, Mario (MGZ) Aguadilla, PR San Jose Obrero Church.
Borho, Charles D. '57 (P) St. Paul, OR St. Paul Church.
Borino, David J. '86 (HRT) [1] Meriden, CT Our Lady of Mount Carmel Church.
Bork, Vincent '95 (DOD) Great Bend, KS St. Rose of Lima Church.
Borkowski, Aloysius J. '39 (GBG) Retired.
Borkowski, Edward *s.v.d.* '44 (CHI) [B] Techny, IL Divine Word Residence.
Borkowski, Francis '77 (NY) Military Chaplains.
Borkowski, John A. '49 (PRO) Retired.
Borkowski, Mark A. '96 (DET) [6] St. Clair Shores, MI St. Margaret Church.
Borkowski, Raymond *o.f.m.conv.* '61 (NOR) Cromwell, CT St. John Church.
Borkowski, Thomas *o.carm.* '81 (JOL) [J] Darien, IL Carmelite Fathers Provincial Office.
Borkowski, Walter '85 (OAK) [2] Concord, CA St. Bonaventure Church.
Borlang, Stephan (SAC) Quincy, CA St. John Church.
Borman, Ron *o.f.m.conv.* '92 (IND) [3] Terre Haute, IN St. Benedict Church.
Bormann, Charles '58 (PHX) On Duty Outside the Diocese.
Bormann, Paul D. '85 (SC) Wesley, IA St. Joseph's Church.
Bornbach, Raymond H. '41 (LC) Retired.
Borntrager, Conrad M. *o.s.m.* '60 (CHI) [15] Chicago, IL Annunciata Church; [N] Chicago, IL Servite Friars - Eastern Province; [N] Chicago, IL Servite Friars - Eastern Province.
Borocz, Isaac *o.s.b.* '82 (WDC) [M] Washington, DC St. Anselm's Abbey.
Borodach, John J. '57 (PBR) Clairton, PA Ascension of

Our Lord Church.
Borodach, Joseph '60 (PBR) Bradenville, PA St. Mary's Church.
Boronat, Francis *sch.p.* '54 (LA) [21] Los Angeles, CA Our Lady Help of Christians (Maria Auxiliadora) Church; [D] Playa Del Rey, CA St. Bernard High School; [R] Los Angeles, CA Piarist Fathers.
Borosh, Carl '68 (STU) Retired.
Boroughs, Philip *s.j.* '78 (SEA) [A] Seattle, WA Seattle University.
Borowczyk, Martin R. '42 (CHI) [45] Chicago, IL St. Constance Church; [64] Chicago, IL St. Francis Borgia Church; Retired.
Borowiak, David J. '71 (BUF) [3] Depew, NY St. James Church.
Borowiak, Henry M. '44 (BUF) [3] Depew, NY St. James Church; Retired.
Borowiak, Kenneth A. '87 (LIN) Dwight, NE Assumption Church.
Borowik, John (NEW) Lyndhurst, NJ St. Michael's Church.
Borowski, Charles E.J. '66 (WOR) West Warren, MA St. Stanislaus Church.
Borowski, Ladislaus '48 (DET) Retired.
Borowski, Paul J. *c.ss.r.* '87 (BRK) [C] Whitestone, NY St. Alphonsus Formation Residence.
Borre, Robert J. (CHI) Chicago, IL V.A. Lakeside Medical Center.
Borrelli, Msgr. Anthony '54 (COL) [28] Columbus, OH St. Margaret of Cortona Church.
Borrero, Victor R. *s.e.m.v.* '89 (ARE) Hatillo, PR Our Lady of Guadalupe Church.
Borsa, Msgr. Anthony '32 (PHU) Retired.
Borsari, John Peter (GAL) [11] Houston, TX Assumption Church.
Borski, Charles *o.m.i.* '70 (GAL) [36] Houston, TX Immaculate Conception Church.
Borski, Msgr. Chester L. '67 (GAL) [A] Houston, TX St. Mary's Seminary.
Borski, Jerome *o.s.b.* '92 (PAT) [M] Morristown, NJ St. Mary's Abbey.
Borstelmann, James E. '67 (NY) Croton Falls, NY St. Joseph Church.
Borsuk, Msgr. Alan J. '59 (PSC) Hillsborough Township, NJ St. Mary's Church.
Borsuk, Ronald W. '58 (PBR) Conemaugh, PA Holy Trinity Church.
Bortolazzo, Peter *c.s.* '39 (BO) [67] Boston, MA Sacred Heart Church.
Borucki, Wallace T. '65 (BUF) Cattaraugus, NY St. Mary's Church; East Otto, NY St. Isidore Church; Little Valley, NY St. Mary Church.
Boruszewski, Msgr. Joseph A. '53 (BUF) Varysburg, NY St. Joseph Church.
Boruta, Alexander *o.f.m.* '60 (GAY) Skidway Lake, MI St. Stephen of Hungary Church.
Borycz, Edmund S. '69 (DET) Military Chaplains.
Borzaga, Reynold *f.s.c.a.* '47 (NY) [Z] New York, NY Brothers of the Christian Schools of Manhattan College, Inc.
Borzaga, Rinaldo '47 (BRK) Retired.
Borzuchowski, John W. '68 (NY) [2] Kingston, NY Immaculate Conception Church; Castle Point, NY Veterans Administration Medical Center.
Borzych, Alexander J. '80 (GI) Military Chaplains.
Bosack, Albert J. '43 (BUF) Lyndonville, NY St. Joseph Church; Retired.
Bosarge, Lee '95 (BLX) Bay St. Louis, MS Our Lady of the Gulf Church.
Bosarge, Manuel Leon, IV '95 (BLX) [1] Biloxi, MS Cathedral of the Nativity of the Blessed Virgin Mary.
Bosch, John *c.pp.s.* '52 (CIN) [B] Carthagena, OH St. Charles.
Bosch, Stanley *s.t.* '86 (ORG) [A] Santa Ana, CA Trinity Missions House of Studies; [H] Santa Ana, CA Trinitarian Missionaries/Missionary Servants of the Most Holy Trinity.
Bosch, William J. *s.j.* '60 (SY) [S] Syracuse, NY Jesuits at LeMoyne, Inc.
Boschert, Hubert G. *s.j.* '68 (MIL) [P] Milwaukee, WI Jesuit Provincial Office, Wisconsin Province.
Boschert, Joseph N. '60 (COV) California, KY Sts. Peter and Paul Church.
Boschetto, Danilo *s.x.* '70 (PAT) [M] Wayne, NJ Xaverian Missionary Fathers.
Bosco, John M. '71 (LAN) Milan, MI Immaculate Conception Church.
Bosco, Pudhota J., Jr. '86 (OKL) Norman, OK St. Thomas More University Parish Church; [K] Norman, OK Campus Ministry for the Archdiocese of Oklahoma City.
Boscoe, John L. *c.s.b.* '72 (GAL) [Q] Sugar Land, TX Basilian Mission Center.
Boscutti, Darrio L. '86 (CHI) [176] Chicago, IL St. Priscilla Church.
Bose, Raja '63 (BGP) Newtown, CT St. Rose of Lima Church.
Bosio, August P. *s.d.b.* '46 (SP) [E] Tampa, FL Mary Help of Christians School.
Boskamp, Charles '41 (MIL) [T] Waukesha, WI Secular Institute of Schoenstatt Fathers.
Bosken, Robert E. *s.j.* '56 (STL) [P] St. Louis, MO De Smet Jesuit High School Community.
Boslett, Donald E. '59 (ALT) Renovo, PA St. Joseph's Church; Altoona, PA Altoona Hospital.
Bosnich, David A. '95 (PBR) Sheffield, PA St. Michael Church.
Bossa, Barry *s.a.c.* '81 (NY) [13] Yonkers, NY Our Lady of Mt. Carmel Church.
Bosse, Dennis *o.f.m.* '90 (CIN) [E] Cincinnati, OH Roger Bacon High School.
Bosse, Dennis *o.f.m.* '91 (CIN) [C] Cincinnati, OH St. Anthony Shrine, Francisan Candidacy.
Bosse, Roger *o.f.m.* '83 (CIN) [E] Cincinnati, OH Roger Bacon High School; [U] Cincinnati, OH Community Support Charitable Trust; [U] Cincinnati, OH Roger Bacon High School Endowment.
Bosse, Roger T. *o.f.m.* '83 (CIN) [M] Cincinnati, OH St. Clement Friary.
Bossi, Paul R. '69 (BUF) [14] Buffalo, NY Blessed Sacrament Church.
Bossi, Stephen E. *c.s.p.* '86 (P) [Q] Portland, OR Paulist Fathers Catholic Center for Evangelization.
Bossi, Stephen E.M. *c.s.p.* '85 (P) [28] Portland, OR St. Philip Neri Church.
Bossie, Robert *s.c.j.* '75 (MIL) [P] Hales Corners, WI Priests of the Sacred Heart.
Bossie, Robert W. *s.c.j.* '75 (CHI) [N] Chicago, IL Priests of the Sacred Heart.
Bossman, David M. *o.f.m.* '65 (NY) [Z] New York, NY Franciscan Friars, Order of Friars Manor.
Bosso, Stephen '78 (PMB) [A] Boynton Beach, FL St. Vincent de Paul Regional Seminary.
Bosso, Stephen C. '78 (PT) On Duty Outside the Diocese.
Bostwick, John '69 (RIC) On Duty Outside the Diocese.
Bostwick, John *o.praem.* '76 (GB) [I] De Pere, WI St. Joseph Priory.
Botean, John Michael '86 (ROM) Canton, OH St. George Cathedral.
Boteju, Bernard '85 (TYL) Longview, TX St. Mary Church.
Botia, Omar '90 (RNO) [6] Reno, NV St. Therese Church of the Little Flower.
Botik, Msgr. William A. '44 (DAL) [3] Dallas, TX Blessed Sacrament Church.
Botkin, Edward A. '73 (DAV) Delmar, IA St. Patrick's Church; Petersville, IA Immaculate Conception Church; Welton, IA St. Anne Church; [B] Davenport, IA St. Ambrose University.
Botsko, Jerome '82 (PBR) Brownsville, PA St. Nicholas Church.
Bottazo, Alex '43 (LAN) Retired.
Botte, Gregory *o.f.m.* '68 (NY) [Z] New York, NY Franciscan Province of the Immaculate Conception.
Botthof, Robert J. *o.p.* '87 (CHI) River Forest, IL St. Vincent Ferrer Priory Church.
Bottino, Msgr. Dominic J. '78 (CAM) Somerdale, NJ Our Lady of Grace Church.
Bottino, Msgr. Edward J. '52 (BRK) [197] Queens, NY Mary's Nativity Church.
Botton, Pierre A. '56 (BGP) Westport, CT St. Luke Church.
Botz, Lawrence '40 (SCL) Retired.
Botz, Paschal *o.s.b.* '31 (SCL) [I] Collegeville, MN St. John's Abbey, of the Order of St. Benedict.
Botz, Roger *o.s.b.* '60 (SCL) [G] St. Cloud, MN St. Cloud Hospital.
Botzum, William A. *c.s.c.* '43 (FTW) [17] South Bend, IN Faith & Hope & Charity Chapel; [B] Notre Dame, IN University of Notre Dame Du Lac; [J] Notre Dame, IN Holy Cross Community, Corby Hall, University of Notre Dame.
Bou, Pedro L. *s.v.d.* '74 (TR) Lakewood, NJ St. Anthony Claret Church.
Bou-Mehri, Gebran (SLC) Salt Lake City, UT Veterans Administration Hospital.
Bou-Merhi, Gebran '88 (OLL) Murray, UT Saint Jude Church.
Bou-Merhi, Gebran '88 (SLC) [5] Murray, UT St. Jude Church.
Bouchard, Charles E. *o.p.* '79 (STL) [B] St. Louis, MO Aquinas Institute of Theology; [P] St. Louis, MO Dominican Community of St. Louis.
Bouchard, Marcel H. '72 (FR) Sandwich, MA Corpus Christi Church.
Bouchard, Norman '88 (PBL) Absent on Leave.
Bouchard, Msgr. Paul L. '72 (MAN) [7] Manchester, NH St. Edmond Church.
Bouchard, Robert '84 (PRT) [7] Portland, ME Sacred Heart Church; [8] Portland, ME St. Christopher's Church.
Bouchard, Thomas '53 (DUL) Retired.
Bouchea, M. Lawrence *o.s.b.* '89 (BIR) [E] Cullman, AL St. Bernard Abbey.
Boucher, Clarence R. '40 (BO) Retired.
Boucher, Edward '60 (SAG) Military Chaplains.
Boucher, Gerard A. '53 (MAN) Plaistow, NH Holy Angels Church.
Boucher, Gilmond *o.m.i.* '58 (MAN) Claremont, NH St. Mary Church.
Boucher, Kevin J. '91 (FAR) Bottineau, ND St. Mark's Church; [I] Bottineau, ND Minot State University-Bottineau.
Boucher, Maurice U. *s.s.e.* '48 (BUR) Alburg, VT St. Amadeus Church; [K] Isle La Motte, VT St. Anne's Shrine.
Boucher, Nelson '53 (MAN) Laconia, NH Sacred Heart Church; Retired.
Boucher, Raymond J. *o.f.m.* '64 (OAK) [P] Danville, CA San Damiano Retreat.
Boucher, Richard R. *m.s.* '60 (HRT) [M] Hartford, CT Missionaries of LaSalette Provincial Secretary.
Boucher, Roger R. '73 (WOR) Military Chaplains.
Boucrees, Thaddeus *s.v.d.* '52 (BLX) [A] Bay St. Louis, MS St. Augustine's.
Boudoin, Burt '82 (SD) [2] El Cajon, CA Our Lady of Grace Church.
Boudreau, George *o.p.* '83 (MIA) [18] Miami, FL St. Dominic Church; [B] Miami, FL Barry University.
Boudreau, Paul '83 (NOR) Coventry, CT St. Mary Church.
Boudreau, Thomas '56 (LA) [9] Los Angeles, CA Divine Saviour Church.
Boudreau, Thomas C. '95 (BO) [2] Woburn, MA St. Barbara Church.
Boudreaux, Claude P. *s.j.* '50 (NO) [F] New Orleans, LA Jesuit High School.
Boudreaux, Msgr. Edward L. '42 (NO) [19] New Orleans, LA Our Lady Of The Rosary Church; Retired.
Boudreaux, John S. '73 (LAF) On Duty Outside the Diocese.
Boudreaux, John S. '73 (MOB) [3] Mobile, AL Corpus Christi Church.
Boudreaux, Msgr. Roland J. '42 (HT) Retired; [E] Thibodaux, LA The Diocese of Houma-Thibodaux Historical Research Center.
Bouffard, Msgr. James F. '70 (NEW) Haworth, NJ Sacred Heart Church.
Bouffier, Robert *s.m.* '74 (BO) [11] Boston, MA St. Anthony Church.
Bouffier, Robert J. *s.m.* '74 (CIN) [M] Dayton, OH Marianist Provincialate.
Boufford, Thomas F. '81 (GR) Lake Odessa, MI St. Edward's Church.
Boughton, Michael *s.j.* '79 (BGP) [D] Fairfield, CT Fairfield College Preparatory School; [O] Fairfield, CT The Fairfield Jesuit Community-Fairfield University.
Bouhall, William G. '94 (CLV) [1] Parma, OH St. Anthony of Padua Church.
Boul, Walter '41 (STL) Retired.
Boulanger, Albert L. (MAN) [J] Manchester, NH Mt. Carmel Nursing Home.
Boulanger, Albert L. '62 (MAN) Manchester, NH Nursing Homes.
Boulanger, Andre '65 (PHX) Unassigned.
Boulanger, Gerard J. *m.s.* '73 (NOR) Brooklyn, CT Our Lady of La Salette Church.
Boulanger, Maurice R. '47 (MAN) [H] Rochester, NH St. Charles Children's Home.
Boulanger, Raymond *s.m.* '51 (BO) [Y] Framingham Centre, MA The Marist House.
Boulden, Garry '77 (SPK) Absent on Leave.
Boule, Roland B. '32 (FR) Retired.
Boulet, Marshall '71 (LKC) Elton, LA St. Paul's Church.
Boulet, Norman J. '69 (FR) Absent on Leave; [K] Fall River, MA Priests' Hostel.
Boulette, Michael J. '76 (SAT) Kerrville, TX Notre Dame Church.
Bouley, Allan *o.s.b.* '62 (SCL) [I] Collegeville, MN St. John's Abbey, of the Order of St. Benedict.
Boulos, Peter '93 (SAM) Atlanta, GA St. Joseph's Maronite Church; Lawrence, MA St. Anthony Church.
Boulton, David G. *s.j.* '61 (BO) [W] Boston, MA The Society of Jesus of New England-Provincial Offices; [W] Weston, MA Campion Center.
Boumans, Albert J. '52 (LAF) [2] New Iberia, LA Nativity of Our Lady Church.
Bourassa, Msgr. Stanley C. '55 (CR) Barnesville, MN Assumption Church.
Bourbon, Arthur '77 (PHX) Retired.
Bourbon, Frank C. *s.j.* '65 (WH) [A] Wheeling, WV Wheeling Jesuit University.
Bourcy, Robert Scott (ROC) Macedon, NY St. Patrick Church.
Bourdeau, Leo *s.m.* '42 (BO) [4] Methuen, MA St. Theresa Church.
Bourdon, Norman W. '73 (PRO) Cumberland, RI St. Joan's Church.
Bourek, David F. '79 (LIN) Hastings, NE St. Michael's Church; [K] Hastings, NE St. Cecilia High School Endowment Fund.
Bouressa, Donald J. '61 (PRO) Point Judith, RI St. Mary, Star of the Sea Church.
Bourg, Edwin (LAF) [13] Lafayette, LA St. Leo Church; Retired.
Bourg, Rodney P. '78 (NO) Reserve, LA St. Peter Church.
Bourgault, Ronald L. '63 (BO) [5] Quincy, MA St. Mary Church.

Bourgea, Roger J. *s.m.* '59 (BO) [59] Boston, MA Our Lady of Victories Church; Boston, MA University Hospital; [W] Boston, MA Marist Fathers of Our Lady of Victories (Boston Prov.).
Bourgeois, Bernard W. '95 (BUR) Barre, VT St. Monica Church.
Bourgeois, Donald E. '85 (SY) Bainbridge, NY St. John the Evangelist Church.
Bourgeois, Francis L. '61 (LAF) Robert's Cove, LA St. Leo IV Church.
Bourgeois, Francois A. *m.s.* '54 (HON) Kekaha, HI St. Theresa Church.
Bourgeois, Henry *c.s.c.* '62 (BO) [X] Framingham, MA Fontbonne Hall.
Bourgeois, Msgr. Joseph E. '58 (NO) [3] Metairie, LA St. Ann Church and Shrine Church; Metairie, LA St. Ann Shrine Church.
Bourgeois, Msgr. Lloyd V. '57 (SD) [38] San Diego, CA San Rafael Church.
Bourgeois, Louis D. '59 (BO) Hamilton, MA St. Paul Church.
Bourgeois, Richard J. *o.s.b.* '76 (BO) [W] Hingham, MA Glastonbury Abbey.
Bourgeois, Roger *s.s.s.* '57 (SFE) [23] Albuquerque, NM St. Charles Borromeo Church.
Bourgeois, Roy L. *m.m.* '72 (NY) [Z] Maryknoll, NY Maryknoll Fathers and Brothers.
Bourget, Laurence *o.c.s.o.* '42 (WOR) [N] Spencer, MA St. Joseph's Abbey.
Bourke, Albert *o.c.d.* '39 (BO) [W] Brighton, MA Carmelite Monastery.
Bourke, Charles E., Jr. '70 (BO) Military & VA Chaplains.
Bourke, Msgr. Daniel J. '34 (SAV) [4] Savannah, GA Most Blessed Sacrament Church; Retired.
Bourke, John F. '60 (CAM) Berlin, NJ Our Lady of Mt. Carmel Church.
Bourke, Martin *s.s.c.* '74 (ORG) [G] Westminster, CA Korean Catholic Ministry; [H] Westminster, CA Columban Fathers.
Bourke, Michael J. '60 (CAM) Washington Township, NJ SS. Peter and Paul Church.
Bourke, Msgr. Myles M. '42 (NY) [28] New York, NY Corpus Christi Church; Retired.
Bourke, Nathaniel J. '59 (GF) [7] Billings, MT St. Thomas the Apostle Church.
Bourke, Ulick *s.m.a.* '68 (NEW) [N] Tenafly, NJ Society of African Missions, Provincialate, S.M.A. Fathers.
Bourne, Peter '61 (B) Salmon, ID St. Charles Church; [C] Lemhi, ID Hermitage of St. Joseph.
Bourque, Charles J. (BO) Boston, MA The Arbour Hospital.
Bourque, Charles J. '62 (BO) [56] Boston, MA Our Lady of Lourdes Church.
Bourque, John R. '48 (SPR) Retired.
Bourque, Msgr. Joseph A. '55 (LKC) Westlake, LA St. John Bosco Church.
Bourque, Real *o.m.i.* '54 (MAN) [K] Hudson, NH Missionary Oblates of Mary Immaculate.
Bourque, Thomas *t.o.r.* '82 (ALT) [A] Loretto, PA St. Francis College.
Bourque, Thomas G. '82 (ALT) [F] Loretto, PA Mount Assisi Monastery.
Bourret, Philip L. *s.j.* '41 (SJ) [M] Los Gatos, CA California Province of the Society of Jesus, Jesuit Provincial Office; [M] Los Gatos, CA Sacred Heart Jesuit Center.
Bouska, Jerome A. '56 (LA) South Gate, CA St. Helen Church.
Bousquet, Roland *s.t.l.* '54 (FR) [20] New Bedford, MA St. Theresa Church.
Bouterie, Thomas R. '80 (HT) [7] Houma, LA St. Louis Church.
Boutin, Emile R. (BO) [1] Norwood, MA St. Catherine of Siena Church.
Bouton, Thomas F. '83 (BO) Absent on Leave.
Boutot, Michel *c.s.sp.* '93 (NO) [7] New Orleans, LA Holy Ghost Church.
Bouzigard, Michael *s.j.* (SAT) [17] San Antonio, TX Our Lady of Guadalupe Church.
Bova, Eugene R. '57 (BIS) Retired.
Bova Conte, Michael J. '71 (BO) Sudbury, MA Our Lady of Fatima Church.
Bovankovich, John '28 (PSC) Retired.
Bovankovich, John '28 (VNN) Phoenix, AZ St. Stephen Church.
Bovard, William R. '64 (PIT) Franklin Park Borough, PA St. John Neumann Church.
Bove, Ralph A. *c.s.* '78 (NY) [94] New York, NY Our Lady of Pompeii Church.
Bovenzi, Robert *c.p.* '85 (SAT) [32] San Antonio, TX St. Cecilia Church; [M] San Antonio, TX Casa Pasionista Guadalupe.
Bowab, Michael L. '60 (BO) Permanent Disability.
Bowden, John V. '62 (TR) Brick Town, NJ Epiphany Church.
Bowden, Lloyd '49 (JOL) Retired.
Bowe, John C. *c.r.* '68 (PBL) Pagosa Springs, CO Immaculate Heart of Mary Church.
Bowe, John F. '73 (PH) Sellersville, PA St. Agnes Church.
Bowe, Msgr. Martin (RVC) Riverhead, NY St. John the Evangelist Church.
Bowen, Daniel T. '56 (HBG) [H] Ephrata, PA St. Clement's Mission House.
Bowen, Donald J. '64 (FR) Special Assignment.
Bowen, Gerard J. '77 (BAL) [13] Baltimore, MD St. Augustine Church.
Bowen, Henry G. '56 (WOR) [21] Worcester, MA St. Charles Borromeo Church.
Bowen, John W. *s.s.* '49 (BAL) [A] Baltimore, MD St. Mary's Seminary and University; [K] Baltimore, MD St. Charles Villa; [M] Baltimore, MD St. Charles Villa.
Bowen, Joseph D. '57 (PH) Abington, PA Our Lady Help of Christians Church.
Bowen, Robert *s.s.j.* '59 (NO) [P] New Orleans, LA Josephite Fathers and Brothers.
Bowens, Lorin M. '74 (MAD) Lime Ridge, WI St. Boniface Church.
Bower, Alan E. '89 (STA) [14] Jacksonville, FL Sacred Heart Church.
Bower, Lawrence C. '88 (BAK) Vale, OR St. Patrick's Church.
Bower, Robert F. '59 (E) Cambridge Springs, PA St. Anthony Church.
Bowering, Gerhard H. *s.j.* '70 (BGP) [O] Fairfield, CT The Fairfield Jesuit Community-Fairfield University.
Bowers, Phillip T. '64 (LFT) Fishers, IN Holy Spirit Church.
Bowers, Robert J. (BO) [1] Milton, MA St. Agatha Church.
Bowers, Ronald '64 (STP) [A] St. Paul, MN The Saint Paul Seminary; [C] St. Paul, MN University of St. Thomas.
Bowers, Vernon J. '39 (RIC) Retired.
Bowes, Bruce O. '92 (NY) Hopewell Junction, NY St. Columba Church.
Bowes, Charles '71 (CIN) [43] Cincinnati, OH St. John the Baptist Church.
Bowes, David '46 (KNX) Retired.
Bowes, John C. *c.m.* '85 (BUF) [C] Niagara University, NY Niagara University; [O] Niagara University, NY Vincentian Community at Niagara University.
Bowes, Vincent *o.c.d.* '61 (BO) [W] Brighton, MA Carmelite Monastery.
Bowes, Vincent *o.c.d.* '61 (MIL) [P] Milwaukee, WI Provincial Offices - Discalced Carmelites.
Bowker, Jeffrey *l.c.* '94 (HRT) [V] Orange, CT Legion of Christ, Inc.
Bowlds, Robert Kent '93 (JKS) Madison, MS St. Francis of Assisi Church.
Bowler, James M. *s.j.* '74 (BO) [W] Boston, MA The Society of Jesus of New England-Provincial Offices.
Bowler, Joseph D. *o.s.f.s.* '45 (WIL) [I] Wilmington, DE DeSales House.
Bowler, Michael '57 (CHI) [209] Chicago, IL St. Turibius Church.
Bowles, Richard J. '61 (PT) [12] Pensacola, FL St. Michael Church.
Bowles, William H. '91 (NU) Nicollet, MN St. Paul Church.
Bowling, Frederick T. '64 (BAL) Retired.
Bowling, George K. '47 (L) Retired.
Bowling, Robert A. '54 (RNO) [6] Reno, NV St. Therese Church of the Little Flower.
Bowman, James (RVC) Priests Released from Diocesan Assignment.
Bowman, James C. '65 (RVC) Military Chaplains.
Bowman, John '65 (SEA) Mercer Island, WA St. Monica Church
Bowman, R. Peter '55 (CHI) [199] Chicago, IL St. Teresa Church.
Bowman, Ronald P. '82 (ALN) [4] Pottsville, PA St. Patrick Church; Frackville, PA State Prison.
Bowski, Eugene (GLP) Chinle, AZ Our Lady of Fatima, Indian Mission Church.
Boxleitner, Msgr. J. Jerome '56 (STP) Lino Lakes, MN Minnesota Correctional Facility; [I] Minneapolis, MN St. Joseph's Home for Children.
Boyack, Kenneth G. *c.s.p.* '79 (WDC) [B] Washington, DC St. Paul's College; [V] Washington, DC Paulist National Catholic Evangelization Assoc.
Boyce, Edmund J. *o.s.b.* '62 (MIL) [P] Benet Lake, WI St. Benedict's Abbey.
Boyce, James J. *o.carm.* '77 (NEW) Cresskill, NJ St. Therese of Lisieux Church.
Boyce, Thomas '66 (JKS) Batesville, MS St. Mary Church.
Boyd, C. Morris '78 (CHL) Asheville, NC St. Joan of Arc Church.
Boyd, Douglas A. '79 (PIT) [54] Pittsburgh, PA St. John Vianney Church.
Boyd, James A. '63 (BRK) Military Chaplains.
Boyd, John D. *s.j.* '47 (NY) [Z] New York, NY Jesuit Community at Fordham University.
Boyd, Joseph '50 (NY) Larchmont, NY SS. John and Paul Church.
Boyd, Norman *s.a.* '65 (NY) [Z] Garrison, NY Franciscan Friars of the Atonement.
Boyd, Richard '79 (CR) Park Rapids, MN St. Peter's Church.
Boyd, Rick *o.m.i.* '79 (CR) Two Inlets, MN St. Mary's Church.
Boyd, Theophane *o.c.s.o.* '55 (DEN) [M] Snowmass, CO St. Benedict's Monastery.
Boyea, Earl '78 (DET) [A] Detroit, MI Sacred Heart Major Seminary, Inc.
Boyea, Ivan G. '69 (OG) [4] Watertown, NY St. Patrick Church.
Boyer, Msgr. Leland '49 (LA) La Canada Flintridge, CA St. Bede the Venerable Church.
Boyer, Msgr. Leland J. (LA) Retired.
Boyer, Mark G. '76 (SPC) Special Assignment.
Boyer, Millard G. (LAF) On Special Assignment.
Boyer, Thomas J. '68 (OKL) [1] Oklahoma City, OK Cathedral of Our Lady of Perpetual Help.
Boyer, Wayne M. '87 (JC) Martinsburg, MO St. Joseph Church; Wellsville, MO Resurrection Church.
Boyhan, J. Patrick '77 (NOR) [F] Cromwell, CT Missionaries of the Holy Apostles.
Boylan, Colman *o.f.m.cap.* '49 (NOR) [4] Middletown, CT St. Pius X Church.
Boylan, Dennis '74 (AMA) Childress, TX Holy Angels Church.
Boylan, John J. '56 (BRK) [176] Queens, NY Holy Child Jesus Church.
Boylan, Martin M. '80 (SCR) Gouldsboro, PA St. Rita Church.
Boyle, Andrew J. *o.s.a.* '54 (PH) [Z] Villanova, PA St. Thomas Monastery.
Boyle, Msgr. Charles '40 (ROC) [E] Rochester, NY St. Ann's Home for the Aged.
Boyle, Msgr. Charles V. '40 (ROC) Retired.
Boyle, Daniel J. '78 (SPR) Adams, MA Notre Dame des Sept Douleurs Church; Adams, MA St. Thomas Aquinas Church.
Boyle, Dennis P. '73 (PH) Military Chaplains.
Boyle, Edward F. *s.j.* '69 (BO) [E] Boston, MA Boston College High School & Jesuit Community.
Boyle, Eugene '36 (SJ) [3] Palo Alto, CA St. Ann Chapel.
Boyle, Eugene J. '46 (SJ) Special Assignment; Retired.
Boyle, Msgr. Francis V. '55 (NY) [199] Staten Island, NY Blessed Sacrament Church.
Boyle, George J. '52 (PH) Manoa, PA Sacred Heart Church.
Boyle, Gregory J. *s.j.* '84 (LA) [10] Los Angeles, CA Dolores Mission Church.
Boyle, Howard (BAL) Retired.
Boyle, J. Leo (BO) Retired.
Boyle, James '61 (SEA) Puyallup, WA All Saints Church; Buckley, WA Rainier School.
Boyle, James A. '49 (FWT) Retired.
Boyle, James E. '66 (ROC) Fairport, NY St. John of Rochester Church.
Boyle, James F. *c.s.c.* '57 (SCR) [4] Wilkes-Barre, PA St. Casimir's Church.
Boyle, James M. '56 (HRT) Retired.
Boyle, John *s.j.* '60 (LA) [BB] Los Angeles, CA Archdiocesan Office for Campus Ministry.
Boyle, John '83 (NY) [226] Staten Island, NY St. Roch Church.
Boyle, John B. *v.f.* '76 (SCR) Tobyhanna, PA St. Ann Church.
Boyle, John J. (ALT) Retired.
Boyle, John L. *s.j.* '60 (LA) [C] Los Angeles, CA Loyola Marymount University.
Boyle, John P. '56 (DAV) [C] Iowa City, IA Catholic Chair of Religion.
Boyle, John T. '69 (CHI) [57] Chicago, IL St. Felicitas Church.
Boyle, Msgr. Lawrence P. '62 (CAM) Brigantine, NJ St. Thomas Church.
Boyle, Leo A. '44 (KC) Retired.
Boyle, Michael G. '95 (RVC) Baldwin, NY St. Christopher Church.
Boyle, Michael J. *c.m.* '59 (PHX) [26] Phoenix, AZ St. Vincent de Paul Church.
Boyle, Patrick *o.f.m.* (NY) Dobbs Ferry, NY St. Cabrini Nursing Home.
Boyle, Patrick *o.s.m.* '56 (ORG) [H] Buena Park, CA Servite Fathers And Brothers.
Boyle, Patrick *o.c.s.o.* '67 (SLC) [F] Huntsville, UT Abbey of Our Lady of the Holy Trinity of the Order of Cistercians.
Boyle, Patrick D. *o.f.m.* '80 (NY) [Z] Mount Vernon, NY St. Bernardine of Siena Friary.
Boyle, Patrick J. *s.j.* '63 (CHI) [A] Mundelein, IL University of St. Mary of the Lake-Mundelein Seminary.
Boyle, Msgr. Patrick J. '65 (NY) [135] Bronx, NY St. Brendan Church.
Boyle, Msgr. Raymond J. '56 (PEO) Seneca, IL St. Patrick's Church.
Boyle, Richard *o.s.m.* '84 (P) [31] Portland, OR St. Rita Church.
Boyle, Richard M. *o.s.m.* '84 (P) [L] Portland, OR The Grotto, The National Sanctuary of Our Sorrowful Mother.
Boyle, Richard P. *s.j.* '75 (BO) [W] Boston, MA The Society of Jesus of New England-Provincial Offices.
Boyle, Richard P. *s.j.* '75 (TUC) [F] Tucson, AZ Jesuit Community of the Vatican Observatory.

Boyle, Robert J. *s.j.* '50 (BUF) [50] Buffalo, NY St. Michael Church.
Boyle, Robert J. '51 (BO) Acton, MA St. Elizabeth of Hungary Church; [D] Brighton, MA Archdiocesan Central High Schools, Inc.
Boyle, Robert J. '63 (PIT) Bellevue, PA Assumption of the Blessed Virgin Mary on the Beautiful River Church.
Boyle, Robert R. *s.j.* '50 (MIL) [P] Wauwatosa, WI Jesuit Community at St. Camillus.
Boyle, Stephen M. *o.praem.* '90 (ORG) [H] Silverado, CA Norbertine Fathers.
Boyle, Stephen M. *o.praem.* '92 (ORG) [D] Siverado, CA St. Michael's College Preparatory High School.
Boyle, Sylvan *o.carm.* '48 (GAL) [3] Houston, TX St. Albert of Trapani Church.
Boyle, Thomas '56 (PHX) Retired.
Boyle, Thomas '64 (ALB) Gloversville, NY Sacred Heart Church.
Boyle, Thomas S. '41 (CHI) [57] Chicago, IL St. Felicitas Church; Retired.
Boyle, Valentine L. *o.carm.* '46 (PHX) [16] Phoenix, AZ St. Luke Church; [F] Phoenix, AZ Carmelite Community.
Boyle, Victor J. '60 (BRK) Absent on Leave.
Boyle, William E. *s.j.* '45 (NY) [Z] New York, NY Jesuit Community at Fordham University.
Boyle, William M. '56 (ORL) [1] Orlando, FL Mary Queen of the Universe Shrine Church.
Boymer, Lloyd J. '43 (CLV) Macedonia, OH Our Lady of Guadalupe Church; Retired.
Boysak, Basil '35 (PSC) Retired.
Bozada, Mark N. *o.p.* (STL) On Duty Outside the Archdiocese.
Bozanic, Anton (BRK) [T] Brooklyn, NY Catholic Migration & Refugee Office, Catholic Migration Services, Inc.
Bozanic, Anton '77 (BRK) [203] Queens, NY Most Precious Blood Church.
Bozek, Robert J. '78 (WDC) [5] Silver Spring, MD Christ the King Church; Pastoral Center Special Ministries.
Bozel, Msgr. Robert A. '48 (BAL) Retired; [K] Baltimore, MD Stella Maris Operating Corporation.
Boznar, Joseph P. '70 (CLV) [76] Cleveland, OH St. Vitus Church.
Bozung, James M. '61 (GR) Belmont, MI Assumption of the Blessed Virgin Mary Church.
Bozza, Nicholas G. '77 (PAT) [7] Paterson, NJ St. George Church.
Bozzelli, Joseph V. '67 (WIL) Bear, DE St. Elizabeth Ann Seton Church.
Bozzelli, Richard '94 (BAL) [53] Baltimore, MD Little Flower, Shrine of Church.
Bozzo, Kenneth J. '80 (FRS) Kingsburg, CA Holy Family Church.
Braak, Thomas E. '59 (DUB) Marshalltown, IA St. Henry's Church; [F] Marshalltown, IA Marshalltown Area Consolidated Catholic School.
Braakhuis, Frits J. *c.m.* '49 (CHY) Riverton, WY St. Margaret's Church.
Braaten, James B. '89 (BIS) Mohall, ND St. Jerome Church.
Braband, James *s.v.d.* '80 (CHI) [B] Techny, IL Divine Word Residence; [N] Techny, IL Society of the Divine Word, Provincial Headquarter-Chicago Prov.
Bracci, Carlos A. '77 (NEW) Harrison, NJ Holy Cross Church.
Bracco, Theodore *o.f.m.* (SFD) [K] Teutopolis, IL St. Francis Assisi Friary.
Bracht, Donald F. *s.m.* '43 (SJ) [M] Cupertino, CA The Marianist Mission.
Bracikowski, Felix *ofm conv.* '38 (BUF) [D] Athol Springs, NY St. Francis High School; [O] Athol Springs, NY St. Francis of Assisi Friary.
Bracke, James A. *c.s.c.* '80 (COS) [9] Colorado Springs, CO Sacred Heart Church.
Bracken, Jerome *c.p.* '68 (BRK) [U] Jamaica, NY Immaculate Conception Monastery.
Bracken, Msgr. John J. '67 (BRK) [233] Queens, NY Resurrection-Ascension Church.
Bracken, Joseph A. *s.j.* '62 (CIN) [D] Cincinnati, OH Xavier University; [M] Cincinnati, OH Jesuit Community at Xavier Unversity.
Bracken, W. Jerome *c.p.* '68 (NEW) [A] South Orange, NJ Immaculate Conception Seminary; [B] South Orange, NJ Seton Hall University.
Bracken, Walter *s.v.d.* '71 (CHI) [B] Techny, IL Divine Word Residence; [N] Techny, IL Society of the Divine Word, Provincial Headquarter-Chicago Prov.
Brackenridge, David F. '52 (PH) Upper Darby, PA St. Alice Church.
Bracket, Louis P. '47 (MAR) Retired.
Brackett, Anthony H. '59 (BUR) Retired.
Brackett, Christopher *l.c.* '93 (HRT) [B] Cheshire, CT Novitiate of the Legion of Christ.
Brackett, Joseph '57 (GLP) Retired.
Brackett, Richard M. *s.j.* '55 (BO) [W] Weston, MA Campion Health Center, Inc.
Brackin, Msgr. Francis A. '37 (CHI) Retired.
Brackin, James *s.c.j.* '75 (MIL) [P] Hales Corners, WI Sacred Heart Monastery.
Brackin, James D. *s.c.j.* '75 (MIL) [B] Hales Corners, WI Sacred Heart School of Theology.
Brackley, J. Dean *s.j.* '76 (NY) [Z] New York, NY Jesuit Provincial's Office.
Bracq, Edward E. '50 (MAN) Retired.
Bradbury, Henry M. '59 (BRK) [U] Jamaica, NY Vincentian Residence.
Braden, Msgr. Leroy H. '53 (GAL) Pearland, TX St. Helen Church.
Braden, Patrick O. *c.s.b.* '52 (GAL) [Q] Houston, TX Residence of the Basilian Fathers of the University of St. Thomas.
Bradican, Msgr. Francis L. '36 (ARL) Annandale, VA Holy Spirit Church; Retired.
Bradler, Robert '62 (ROC) [L] Rochester, NY Holy Childhood Association.
Bradler, Robert C. '62 (ROC) [59] Rochester, NY St. Thomas the Apostle Church.
Bradley, Alfred *c.ss.r.* '88 (STV) [2] Christiansted, VI Church of the Holy Cross; [B] St. Thomas, VI Miscellaneous Organizations.
Bradley, Allan P. '72 (SUP) New Richmond, WI Immaculate Conception Church.
Bradley, Allan W. '70 (COV) Ludlow, KY Sts. Boniface and James Church.
Bradley, Bruce A. '78 (DAL) Allen, TX St. Jude Church.
Bradley, Charles (PAT) Absent on Leave.
Bradley, Daniel *m.s.* '94 (ATL) Smyrna, GA St. Thomas the Apostle Church.
Bradley, Denis J.M. '70 (WDC) Special Ministries.
Bradley, Dennis J. '77 (PIT) Midland, PA St. Blaise Church.
Bradley, Edward C. *s.j.* '79 (PH) [Z] Philadelphia, PA Jesuit Community at St. Joseph's University.
Bradley, Edward G. '66 (NEW) [1] Orange, NJ St. John's Church; [C] West Orange, NJ Seton Hall Preparatory School.
Bradley, Gary *s.j.* '75 (CHK) Garapan Village, District 11, MP Kristo Rai Parish Church.
Bradley, H. Cornell *s.j.* '69 (PH) [C] Philadelphia, PA St. Joseph's University; [Z] Philadelphia, PA Jesuit Community at St. Joseph's University.
Bradley, Harold C. (STL) [P] St. Louis, MO Jesuit Community Corporation at St. Louis University - Jesuit Hall.
Bradley, Hugh J. '89 (CAM) [3] Vineland, NJ St. Francis of Assisi Church.
Bradley, J. Edward '75 (OWN) Henderson, KY Holy Name of Jesus Church.
Bradley, J. Richard '81 (TLS) Muskogee, OK Saint Joseph Church.
Bradley, James F. '43 (PH) Media, PA Nativity of the Blessed Virgin Mary Church; Retired.
Bradley, James F. *o.s.f.s.* '61 (DET) [D] Southgate, MI Aquinas High School.
Bradley, James F. *o.s.f.s.* '61 (TOL) [K] Toledo, OH Oblates of St. Francis de Sales.
Bradley, James J. (PH) [1] Drexel Hill, PA St. Andrew Church.
Bradley, James P. *s.j.* '58 (WDC) [M] Washington, DC Carroll House.
Bradley, James P. *s.j.* '67 (NO) [P] New Orleans, LA Jesuit Provincial Office.
Bradley, James P. '73 (BRK) [208] Queens, NY Our Lady of the Cenacle Church.
Bradley, John A. '65 (ORG) Capistrano Beach, CA San Felipe de Jesus Church.
Bradley, John J. (PH) [7] Philadelphia, PA St. Aloysius Church.
Bradley, Msgr. John J. '42 (SB) Retired.
Bradley, John J. '48 (PH) [3] Drexel Hill, PA St. Charles Borromeo Church; Retired.
Bradley, John J. '67 (ALB) [3] Albany, NY Blessed Sacrament Church.
Bradley, John Paul '44 (CHL) Absent On Leave.
Bradley, Joseph (SFR) Special Assignment.
Bradley, Joseph '91 (SFR) San Francisco, CA Serra Club of San Francisco (Downtown).
Bradley, Msgr. Joseph P. '38 (BAL) Retired.
Bradley, Joseph P. '91 (SFR) [4] San Francisco, CA St. Anne Church.
Bradley, Jude C. *o.s.b.* '47 (PAT) [M] Newton, NJ St. Paul's Abbey.
Bradley, Matthew '72 (BO) [Y] Scituate, MA Foyer of Charity.
Bradley, Michael J. '78 (CHI) [1] Cicero, IL St. Anthony Church.
Bradley, Msgr. Paul F. '41 (TR) Retired.
Bradley, Paul J. '71 (PIT) Ross Township, PA St. Sebastian Church.
Bradley, Randall '81 (WCH) Leave of Absence.
Bradley, Richard S. *s.j.* '49 (P) [L] Portland, OR Jesuit Provincial Office (Oregon Prov.).
Bradley, Richard S. *s.j.* '49 (SB) [E] Morongo Valley, CA St. Michael's of Morongo Valley, Inc.
Bradley, Richard W. *o.carm.* '59 (NEW) Paramus, NJ Carmelite Chapel of St. Therese.
Bradley, Robert *s.j.* (AUS) [9] Austin, TX Sacred Heart Church.
Bradley, Robert '73 (CC) Retired.
Bradley, Robert I. *s.j.* '55 (ARL) [6] Alexandria, VA St. Louis Church.
Bradley, Robert M. '57 (LA) Retired.
Bradley, Theodore F.X. '58 (SPK) Retired.
Bradley, Thomas J. '93 (CHI) [179] Chicago, IL Queen of All Saints Basilica.
Bradley, Msgr. William J. '57 (NY) [1] New Rochelle, NY Blessed Sacrament Church.
Bradly, Michael '91 (TUC) Globe, AZ Holy Angels Church.
Bradower, Theodore J. *t.o.r.* '50 (FWT) [8] Fort Worth, TX St. Andrew Church.
Bradshaw, Alexander H. '85 (ROC) [23] Rochester, NY Holy Ghost Church.
Bradshaw, Jordan *o.p.* (SEA) [P] Seattle, WA Office of Campus and Young Adult Ministry.
Bradshaw, Joseph *o.p.* '92 (SEA) [22] Seattle, WA Blessed Sacrament Church.
Bradshaw, Paul F. '70 (FTW) [B] Notre Dame, IN University of Notre Dame Du Lac.
Bradshaw, Terry L. '80 (L) [11] Louisville, KY St. Bartholomew Church.
Bradt, Kevin M. *s.j.* '79 (OAK) [N] Berkeley, CA Jesuit Community at Jesuit School of Theology at Berkeley.
Bradtke, Thomas A. '62 (DEN) Absent on Leave.
Bradunas, John J. *o.s.f.s.* '73 (WIL) [3] Wilmington, DE St. Anthony of Padua Church.
Brady, Andrew J. *s.j.* '45 (NY) [Z] New York, NY Murray-Weigel Hall.
Brady, Charles '55 (SAC) [3] Sacramento, CA Holy Spirit Church.
Brady, Coman V. '59 (BRK) [144] Brooklyn, NY St. Vincent Ferrer Church.
Brady, Daniel J. '42 (NY) Armonk, NY St. Patrick Church; Retired.
Brady, Daniel J. '61 (CHI) [1] Mt. Prospect, IL St. Cecilia Church.
Brady, Daniel O. '84 (RIC) Pocahontas, VA St. Elizabeth Church; Tazewell, VA St. Theresa Church.
Brady, Daniel P. *o.p.* '48 (DAL) [M] Irving, TX Dominican Priory of St. Albert the Great.
Brady, Edmund P. '59 (BRK) [193] Queens, NY St. Margaret Mary Church; [216] Queens, NY Our Lady of Mount Carmel Church.
Brady, Edward E. (PH) Hilltown, PA Our Lady of the Sacred Heart Church.
Brady, Msgr. Frank J. '46 (SC) Retired.
Brady, G. James *c.s.c.* (P) [L] Portland, OR Holy Cross Father & Brother, C.S.C. - University of Portland.
Brady, Gerald '83 (SPR) Hatfield, MA Holy Trinity Church.
Brady, Msgr. Gerard J. '59 (SR) Napa, CA St. Thomas Aquinas Church.
Brady, James *s.m.m.* '92 (BRK) [195] Queens, NY St. Mary Gate of Heaven Church.
Brady, James H.T. *s.o.l.t.* '89 (CC) [H] Robstown, TX Society of Our Lady of the Most Holy Trinity.
Brady, James H.T. *s.o.l.t.* '89 (WH) Grant Town, WV St. Anthony's Church.
Brady, James J. '53 (MIL) Hales Corners, WI St. Mary's Church.
Brady, James J. '72 (TR) Bradley Beach, NJ Ascension Church.
Brady, James R. '57 (ALN) Tremont, PA Immaculate Conception Church.
Brady, Jeremiah D. *s.s.j.* (BAL) [M] Baltimore, MD St. Joseph's Manor.
Brady, John '49 (LA) Van Nuys, CA St. Elisabeth Church.
Brady, John '55 (SFS) Retired.
Brady, Msgr. John B. '55 (WDC) Avenue, MD Holy Angels Church; [V] Pomfret, MD Ministr-O-Media, Inc.
Brady, John F. *s.j.* '48 (DEN) [30] Denver, CO St. Ignatius Loyola Church; [M] Denver, CO Loyola Parish - Jesuit Community.
Brady, Msgr. Joseph '89 (SD) Poway, CA St. Gabriel Church.
Brady, Jude W. *o.s.b.* '80 (E) St. Marys, PA St. Mary Church.
Brady, Jules M. *s.j.* '53 (KC) [B] Kansas City, MO Rockhurst College; [J] Kansas City, MO Rockhurst College - Jesuit Community.
Brady, Martin D. *t.o.r.* '56 (WH) Stonewood, WV Our Lady of Perpetual Help Church.
Brady, Mel P. *o.f.m.* '50 (DET) [3] Detroit, MI St. Aloysius Church.
Brady, Patrick *o.m.i.* '48 (NY) [BB] Newburgh, NY Our Lady of Hope Center.
Brady, Patrick A. '61 (WIL) Rehoboth, DE St. Edmond Church; Retired.
Brady, Patrick J. '64 (CAM) [5] Atlantic City, NJ Our Lady Star of the Sea Church.
Brady, Philip W. '43 (BGP) Retired.
Brady, Reginald '93 (DET) Royal Oak, MI Shrine of the Little Flower Church.
Brady, Richard J. '59 (BO) [5] Lawrence, MA St. Francis Church.
Brady, Msgr. Roger J. (BO) Belmont, MA St. Luke Church.
Brady, Severin *o.f.m.* '66 (PRO) [P] Providence, RI St.

Francis Friary.
Brady, Theodore E.A. *s.j.* '61 (BAL) [I] Baltimore, MD Mercy Medical Center, Inc.; [M] Baltimore, MD Ferdinand Wheeler House.
Brady, Msgr. Thomas C. '54 (RCK) South Beloit, IL St. Peter Church.
Brady, Thomas E. *s.j.* '47 (ALB) [O] Auriesville, NY Jesuit Retreat House for Priests, Religious and Lay People.
Brady, Msgr. Thomas F. '59 (BRK) [50] Brooklyn, NY Good Shepherd Church.
Brady, Vincent '67 (SAC) [1] Sacramento, CA Cathedral of the Blessed Sacrament.
Brady, Vincent '95 (PSC) Wilkes-Barre, PA St. Mary's Church.
Brady, William J. *o.p.* '42 (NO) [30] New Orleans, LA St. Dominic Church.
Brady, William J. '80 (SFR) [28] San Francisco, CA St. John of God Church; [S] San Francisco, CA Newman Center, University of California Medical Center.
Braganza, Joe '81 (NY) [1] Port Chester, NY Our Lady of Mercy Church.
Bragotti, Joseph *m.c.c.j.* '62 (CIN) [M] Cincinnati, OH Comboni Missionaries (Verona Fathers)-Comboni Mission Center.
Brague, Robert J. '70 (VEN) Palmetto, FL Holy Cross Church.
Brahill, John *o.s.b.* '82 (RCK) [H] Aurora, IL Marmion Abbey-St. Augustine's Abbey.
Brahm, Harvey W. '51 (MIL) Brookfield, WI St. Luke Church.
Braida, Ernest E. '64 (DAV) Newton, IA Sacred Heart Church.
Brainard, Arthur *s.d.b.* '53 (OAK) [E] Richmond, CA Salesian High School.
Brainard, Ernest '45 (OAK) [2] Oakland, CA St. Andrew-St. Joseph Church.
Brainard, Ernest B. '45 (OAK) Retired.
Brainerd, Winthrop J. '87 (WDC) [36] Washington, DC St. Patrick Church.
Brajkovich, Thomas R. '61 (PEO) Wyoming, IL St. Dominic's Church.
Brakora, Anthony '35 (LAN) Retired.
Braley, James P. '75 (BO) [1] Norwood, MA St. Catherine of Siena Church.
Braman, Dennis J. '96 (ALT) [12] Altoona, PA St. Rose of Lima Church.
Brambilla, Charles A. '71 (STP) Lindstrom, MN St. Bridget of Sweden Church.
Brambilla, Sigmund *o.f.m.* (SPR) Northampton, MA Veterans Administration Hospital.
Brambilla, Sigmund *o.f.m.* '55 (NY) [Z] New York, NY Franciscan Province of the Immaculate Conception.
Bramble, Donald *o.p.* '76 (SB) [10] Riverside, CA St. Andrew's Newman Center Church; [E] Riverside, CA St. Vincent Ferrer House; [H] Riverside, CA St. Andrews Newman Center.
Bramble, Donald J. *o.p.* '76 (OAK) [N] Oakland, CA Western Dominican Province.
Brambora, Jeffrey S. '93 (LFT) [1] Lafayette, IN St. Mary Cathedral.
Bramlage, Gregory '96 (IND) Richmond, IN Holy Family Church; Richmond, IN St. Andrew Church; Richmond, IN St. Mary Church; [N] Richmond, IN Earlham College Newman Center.
Bramlage, James A. '64 (CIN) [1] Cincinnati, OH St. Peter in Chains Cathedral.
Bramlage, Vincent J. '43 (CIN) Retired.
Bramwell, Bevil *o.m.i.* '85 (MAN) [K] Hudson, NH Missionary Oblates of Mary Immaculate.
Branagan, Henry *f.m.s.i.* '63 (BO) [B] Framingham, MA Sylva Maria.
Brancaccio, Alberto A. *s.o.l.t.* '93 (CC) [H] Robstown, TX Society of Our Lady of the Most Holy Trinity.
Branch, Edward '74 (ATL) [L] Atlanta, GA Campus Ministry.
Branch, Edward B. '74 (L) On Duty Outside the Archdiocese.
Branch, Leslie '71 (WDC) Retired; [D] Washington, DC Archbishop Carroll High School.
Branche, John S. '54 (OG) Retired.
Branconnier, Gerard '78 (WOR) Absent on Leave.
Brand, Edmund H. *o.c.s.o.* '54 (ATL) [I] Conyers, GA The Monastery of the Holy Spirit.
Brand, Leo A. *c.pp.s.* '63 (JC) Pilot Grove, MO St. Joseph Church.
Brand, Michael *c.s.b.* '73 (LAN) [F] Ann Arbor, MI St. Joseph Mercy Hospital.
Brand, William *o.f.m.* '74 (LA) [P] Los Angeles, CA St. Anne's.
Brande, Edward W. *s.j.* '63 (NEW) [B] Jersey City, NJ Saint Peter's College; [N] Jersey City, NJ Jesuits of Saint Peter's College, Inc.
Brandenberger, Robert J. *c.m.* '52 (PH) [B] Philadelphia, PA St. Vincent's Seminary; [Z] Philadelphia, PA Congregation of the Mission.
Brandenhoff, Peter B. '70 (WIN) On Duty Outside the Diocese.
Brandes, John F. '51 (NU) On Duty Outside the Diocese.
Brandes, John F. '51 (STP) On Duty Outside the Archdiocese.
Brandmeyer, William H. '37 (BEL) Retired.
Brando, Joseph J. '72 (KNX) Alcoa, TN Our Lady of Fatima Church.
Brandow, Stephen J. '96 (ALX) [6] Alexandria, LA St. Rita Church.
Brandstrader, Frederick L. '68 (CHI) Wheeling, IL St. Joseph the Worker Church.
Brandt, Joseph D. '83 (PH) West Chester, PA St. Agnes Church; [D] West Chester, PA Bishop Shanahan High School.
Brandt, Msgr. Lawrence E. '69 (E) [H] Erie, PA Gannondale Residential Center for Girls.
Brandt, Paul C. '84 (PH) Roslyn, PA St. John of the Cross Church; [D] Wyncote, PA Bishop McDevitt High School.
Branigan, Francis H. '37 (GR) Retired.
Branigan, Patrick G. '43 (RVC) Retired.
Brankin, Anthony J. '75 (CHI) [206] Chicago, IL St. Thomas More Church.
Brankin, Patrick '79 (TLS) Collinsville, OK St. Therese Church.
Brankin, Patrick M. '79 (CHI) On Duty Outside the Archdiocese.
Brannen, Brett A. '91 (SAV) Macon, GA St. Joseph's Church.
Brannen, Charles J. *s.j.* '52 (CHI) [C] Chicago, IL Jesuit Community at Loyola University of Chicago.
Brannigan, Joseph E. *m.m.* '46 (NY) [Z] Maryknoll, NY Maryknoll Fathers and Brothers.
Brannon, Bernard I. *s.j.* '53 (SJ) [M] Los Gatos, CA California Province of the Society of Jesus, Jesuit Provincial Office.
Brannon, Robert F. '58 (GBG) West Newton, PA Holy Family Church.
Branon, Philip J. '51 (BUR) South Hero, VT St. Rose of Lima Church.
Bransfield, J. Brian '94 (PH) Newtown, PA St. Andrew Church.
Bransfield, Msgr. Michael J. '71 (PH) On Duty Outside the Archdiocese.
Bransfield, Msgr. Michael J. '71 (WDC) [Q] Washington, DC Basilica of the National Shrine of the Immaculate Conception.
Bransfield, Thomas A. '64 (BUR) Orleans, VT St. Theresa of Child Jesus Church.
Branson, Bernard E. '59 (KC) Smithville, MO Church of the Good Shepherd.
Brant, Paul W. *s.j.* (R) Kinston, NC Holy Trinity-Our Lady of the Atonement Church.
Brantley Charles (CHL) Statesville, NC St. Philip the Apostle Church.
Brantman, Thomas E. '75 (RCK) Hampshire, IL St. Charles Borromeo Church.
Brantome, Oscar '88 (MIA) Absent on Sick Leave.
Braquet, David J. (ALX) Powhatan, LA St. Francis Church.
Braquet, David Jude '94 (ALX) Natchitoches, LA Immaculate Conception Church.
Brashears, William '82 (AMA) [10] Amarillo, TX St. Mary's Church.
Brasher, C. John '75 (SFE) Springer, NM St. Joseph Church.
Brasley, Msgr. Lucian R. (CC) Retired.
Brassard, Leo *a.a.* '69 (BO) [W] Brighton, MA Assumptionist Center.
Brassard, Ronald E. '74 (PRO) [3] Cranston, RI Immaculate Conception Church.
Brassil, James A. '62 (RVC) Seaford, NY Maria Regina Church.
Brassil, Kevin J. '58 (PRO) Portsmouth, RI St. Barnabas Church.
Bratek, Martin *c.r.* '72 (PT) Panama City, FL St. John the Evangelist Church.
Brath, John A. '68 (SPC) Kimberling City, MO Our Lady of the Cove Church.
Bratko, Kenneth R. *c.r.* '64 (CHI) Schaumburg, IL St. Matthew Church.
Bratkowski, Allen *o.s.cam.* '89 (MIL) [K] Milwaukee, WI St. Mary's Hospital of Milwaukee; [P] Wauwatosa, WI St. Camillus Community House.
Bratus, Walter N. '56 (GBG) Retired.
Braud, Dominic *o.s.b.* '61 (NO) [P] St. Benedict, LA St. Joseph Abbey.
Braud, Dominic R. *o.s.b.* '61 (NO) [A] St. Benedict, LA St. Joseph's Seminary College.
Braud, Edmond P. '83 (BR) Retired.
Braud, Ronald J. '64 (NO) Gretna, LA St. Joseph Church.
Braudis, Joseph M. '77 (ALN) Hamburg, PA St. Mary Church.
Brauer, Frank J. '86 (BAL) Cumberland, MD St. Patrick Church.
Brauer, Mark S. '92 (DET) [17] Detroit, MI St. Christine Church; [26] Detroit, MI St. Gemma Galgani Church.
Braukman, Donald '86 (CR) Florian, MN Assumption Church, Greenbush, MN Blessed Sacrament Church.
Brault, Bernard *s.m.m.* '68 (BRK) [195] Queens, NY St. Mary Gate of Heaven Church.
Brault, Gilles '71 (MAR) Champion, MI Sacred Heart Church; Republic, MI St. Augustine Church; Marquette, MI Marquette General Hospital.
Brault, Gilles R. '76 (STA) Military Chaplains.
Brault, Laurence V. '77 (WOR) Upton, MA Holy Angels Church.
Brault, Y. David '77 (WDC) Poolesville, MD Our Lady of the Presentation Church.
Braun, Brian *o.f.m.cap.* '60 (CHI) [146] Chicago, IL Our Lady Gate of Heaven Church.
Braun, David F. '54 (CHI) Retired.
Braun, David J. '55 (MIL) Lake Geneva, WI St. Francis de Sales Church.
Braun, David L. '81 (BEL) Wendelin, IL Holy Cross Church.
Braun, Dean '69 (BEL) Lively Grove, IL St. Anthony Church.
Braun, Donald B. '57 (MIL) Fox Lake, WI Immaculate Conception - St. Mary Church; Lost Lake, WI St. Mary's Church; Randolph, WI St. Gabriel Church.
Braun, Edgar F. '40 (MIL) Retired.
Braun, Msgr. Francis '54 (BUF) [45] Buffalo, NY St. Mark Church.
Braun, Gary G. '77 (STL) [V] St. Louis, MO Washington University Newman Centers.
Braun, Gerard E. *s.j.* '46 (NY) [Z] New York, NY St. Ignatius Loyola Residence; [Z] New York, NY Jesuit Seminary and Mission Bureau, Inc. (Jesuit Deferred Funds); [DD] New York, NY Jesuit Seminary and Mission Bureau, Inc.
Braun, H. Gerard '85 (FAR) [4] Grand Forks, ND St. Thomas Aquinas Parish, UND Church; [H] Grand Forks, ND Univ. of North Dakota Newman Center.
Braun, John S. '87 (SPC) Monett, MO St. Lawrence Church.
Braun, Michael C. '61 (LC) Black River Falls, WI St. Joseph Church.
Braun, Msgr. Michael R. '67 (FRS) [2] Bakersfield, CA Our Lady of Perpetual Help Church; [H] Bakersfield, CA Bakersfield College Newman Center.
Braun, Norbert L. '57 (CIN) Retired.
Braun, Robert *o.m.i.* '51 (BEL) [G] Belleville, IL Shrine of Our Lady of the Snows.
Braun, Robert G. '59 (MIL) Eden, WI St. Mary's Church.
Braun, Serran R. '55 (SAN) Retired.
Braun, Virgil '60 (SCL) Eden Valley, MN The Church of the Assumption.
Braun, Virgil R. '60 (NU) Eden Valley, MN St. Peter Church.
Braun, Warren '52 (Y) Retired.
Braunreuther, Robert J. *s.j.* '65 (BO) [W] Chestnut Hill, MA The Jesuit Community at Boston College.
Bravo, Enrique *c.s.b.* '96 (SFE) [14] Albuquerque, NM Sacred Heart Church.
Bravo, Gregorio (SJN) [36] San Juan, PR Maria Madre de La Iglesia Church.
Bravo, Joseph A. '77 (SFR) Olema, CA Sacred Heart Church.
Bray, Kevin '67 (FRS) Absent on Sick Leave.
Bray, Kevin '67 (LA) Retired.
Bray, Kevin M. *o.s.b.* '51 (PAT) [M] Morristown, NJ St. Mary's Abbey.
Bray, William A. '54 (HRT) East Haven, CT St. Clare Church.
Brazaskas, Robert '66 (TUC) Green Valley, AZ Our Lady of the Valley Church.
Brazil, Sean *s.s.c.* (ORG) Special Assignment; [G] Westminster, CA Korean Catholic Ministry; [H] Westminster, CA Columban Fathers.
Brazynetz, Alex E. '78 (CLV) [13] Cleveland, OH St. Boniface Church.
Breaker, Donald J. '64 (CIN) Military Chaplains.
Bream, James I. '64 (SFS) Yankton, SD Sacred Heart Church.
Breau, Paschal *s.a.* '79 (NY) [Z] Garrison, NY Generalate of the Franciscan Friars of the Atonement-St. James Friary.
Breault, Charles *o.m.i.* '59 (BO) [W] Lowell, MA Missionary Oblates of Mary Immaculate.
Breault, Charles *o.m.i.* '59 (MAN) [K] Hudson, NH Missionary Oblates of Mary Immaculate.
Breault, William F. *s.j.* '62 (SAC) [H] Carmichael, CA Jesuit High School Community of Sacramento.
Breaux, Duane L. '90 (BR) Pierre Part, LA St. Joseph the Worker Church.
Breaux, Louis Allen '81 (LAF) Catahoula, LA St. Rita Church.
Breaux, O. Joseph '68 (LAF) Duson, LA St. Theresa of the Child Jesus Church; [K] Opelousas, LA Cursillo Center.
Brecht, David L. *o.s.a.* '65 (CHI) [N] Olympia Fields, IL The Augustinian Provincialate Tolentine Center; [N] Olympia Fields, IL Tolentine Monastery at Tolentine Center.
Brechtl, Joseph A. '44 (MAD) Retired.
Breckensiek, Marne *o.f.m.* '65 (PEO) [3] Peoria, IL Sacred Heart Church.
Bredeck, Martin J. *s.j.* '64 (KC) [B] Kansas City, MO Rockhurst College; [J] Kansas City, MO Rockhurst College - Jesuit Community.

Bredemann, George '83 (PHX) Unassigned.
Bredeweg, Frank H. *c.s.b.* '64 (DET) [E] Redford, MI Catholic Central High School.
Breedlove, Lawrence '56 (FWT) [4] Fort Worth, TX Holy Name of Jesus Church.
Breen, Bernard J. '72 (L) [48] Louisville, KY St. Margaret Mary Church.
Breen, Brendan *c.p.* '50 (BO) [24] Boston, MA St. Gabriel's Church; [W] Brighton, MA St. Gabriel's Passionist Community.
Breen, Msgr. Edward J. '58 (BRK) [210] Queens, NY Our Lady of Fatima Church.
Breen, James '80 (BGP) Wilton, CT Our Lady of Fatima Church.
Breen, John (NY) West Nyack, NY St. Francis of Assisi Church.
Breen, John F. '47 (NY) Retired.
Breen, Joseph P. '61 (NSH) [5] Nashville, TN St. Edward's Church.
Breen, Kenneth *o.de.m.* '85 (CLV) [67] Cleveland, OH St. Rocco Church; Cleveland, OH Cuyahoga County Jail.
Breen, Michael *s.s.c.* '47 (BO) [W] Quincy, MA St. Columban's Foreign Mission Society.
Breen, Michael J. '82 (SY) [4] Liverpool, NY St. Joseph the Worker Church.
Breen, Philip M. '65 (NSH) [2] Nashville, TN St. Ann Church.
Breen, Robert H. '57 (PH) Riegelsville, PA St. Lawrence Church.
Breen, Stephen B. (WIL) Retired.
Breen, Stephen P. '55 (WIL) Garfield Park, DE Holy Spirit Church.
Breen, Msgr. Vincent D. '62 (BRK) [81] Brooklyn, NY St. Mary Mother of Jesus Church.
Brehob, Keith *s.j.* '96 (LA) [BB] Los Angeles, CA Archdiocesan Office for Campus Ministry.
Breidenbach, John '87 (EVN) [4] Evansville, IN Corpus Christi Church.
Breier, Donald P. '69 (PIT) Castle Shannon, PA St. Anne Church.
Breier, Henry J. '94 (STL) Oakville, MO Queen of All Saints Church.
Breig, Gary R. '76 (STL) Military Chaplains.
Breighner, Joseph F. '71 (BAL) [1] Baltimore, MD Cathedral of Mary Our Queen; Special Assignment.
Breit, Melvin P. '62 (MIL) [37] Milwaukee, WI Holy Rosary Church; [68] Milwaukee, WI St. Rita's Church.
Breitbach, Richard C. '61 (MIL) [C] Milwaukee, WI Cardinal Stritch College.
Breitenstein, Stephen '42 (P) Roy, OR St. Francis of Assisi Church.
Breitnauer, James L. '59 (BUF) [4] West Seneca, NY St. William Church.
Brelivet, Alan *o.m.i.* '31 (SAT) [K] San Antonio, TX Oblate Madonna Residence.
Brelsford, William J. '70 (LA) [94] Los Angeles, CA St. Timothy Church.
Brembos, Msgr. George M. '56 (MET) Far Hills, NJ St. Elizabeth Church; [N] Peapack, NJ Everitt Academy.
Brenberger, Thomas R. *c.pp.s.* '66 (CIN) Egypt, OH St. Joseph Church; Minster, OH St. Augustine's Church; [U] Dayton, OH Community Support Charitable Trust.
Brenda, William H. *o.p.* '49 (GAL) [35] Houston, TX Holy Rosary Church.
Brendel, John A. '39 (RVC) West Islip, NY Our Lady of Lourdes Church; Retired.
Brenes-Chavez, Fabio R. '85 (NEW) [5] Elizabeth, NJ Immaculate Conception Church.
Brengartner, Robert E. '42 (Y) [4] Massillon, OH St. Mary's Church; Retired.
Brenk, Frederick E. *s.j.* '63 (MIL) [P] Milwaukee, WI Jesuit Provincial Office, Wisconsin Province.
Brenkert, Edward J. '72 (BRK) [164] Queens, NY St. Clement Pope Church.
Brenkle, Msgr. John J. '58 (SR) Saint Helena, CA St. Helena Church.
Brennan, Bernard '61 (SFR) Special Assignment; Military Chaplains.
Brennan, Bernard '65 (DUL) [D] Duluth, MN Benedictine Health Center.
Brennan, Bernard F. (OAK) Military Chaplains.
Brennan, Brian C. '79 (NY) [1] New York, NY Cathedral of St. Patrick.
Brennan, C. John '54 (SC) Retired.
Brennan, Cathal '52 (P) [9] Portland, OR Blessed Sacrament Church; [15] Portland, OR Holy Cross Church.
Brennan, Charles M. *o.s.m.* '48 (CHI) [N] Chicago, IL Servite Friars - Eastern Province.
Brennan, Msgr. Daniel H. '43 (ORG) Costa Mesa, CA St. John the Baptist Church.
Brennan, Denis J. '63 (ALB) Rotterdam Junction, NY St. Margaret of Cortona Church.
Brennan, Dennis '74 (LA) On Duty Outside the Archdiocese.
Brennan, Msgr. Dermot R. '56 (NY) Yorktown Heights, NY St. Patrick Church.
Brennan, Donald *o.s.a.* '68 (FWT) Pilot Point, TX St. Thomas Aquinas Church.
Brennan, Edmund J. '82 (ALN) Emmaus, PA St. Ann Church.
Brennan, Edward C. '63 (BRK) Released from Diocesan Assignment.
Brennan, Elmer F. '42 (CIN) Retired.
Brennan, Eugene P. '70 (STL) Warrenton, MO Holy Rosary Church.
Brennan, Eugene P. *m.s.* '80 (HRT) [M] Hartford, CT Missionaries of LaSalette Provincial Secretary.
Brennan, Fernan J. *o.s.f.s.* '41 (TOL) [J] Oregon, OH Sacred Heart Home; [K] Toledo, OH Oblates of St. Francis de Sales.
Brennan, Msgr. Francis M. (NY) [204] Staten Island, NY Holy Child Church; Retired.
Brennan, Msgr. Francis P. (NY) Retired.
Brennan, George *m.s.* '75 (FR) [K] Attleboro, MA La Salette Shrine.
Brennan, George '87 (VEN) [5] Sarasota, FL St. Patrick Church.
Brennan, Msgr. George J. (BUF) Retired.
Brennan, George P. '68 (STL) [5] St. Louis, MO Holy Innocents Church.
Brennan, Gerald H. *o.f.m.* '46 (PRO) [F] Providence, RI St. Francis Friary.
Brennan, Gerard M. (BO) Retired.
Brennan, J. Gregory *o.f.m.* '79 (BUF) Humphrey, NY St. Pacificus, Mission of St. Bonaventure University Friary Church; [O] St. Bonaventure, NY St. Bonaventure Friary.
Brennan, James '85 (DEN) [35] Denver, CO St. Rose of Lima Church.
Brennan, James F. '55 (BO) Permanent Disability.
Brennan, James H. *s.s.* '31 (BAL) [K] Baltimore, MD St. Charles Villa; [M] Baltimore, MD St. Charles Villa.
Brennan, James J. '89 (PH) Absent on Leave; [L] Springfield, PA Divine Providence Village.
Brennan, James P. *c.ss.r.* '64 (NY) [23] New York, NY St. Cecilia Church.
Brennan, Msgr. John '55 (TYL) [A] Tyler, TX Trinity Mother Frances Health System.
Brennan, John D. '70 (PIT) Kennedy Township, PA St. Malachy Church.
Brennan, John J. *s.j.* '46 (LA) [6] Los Angeles, CA Blessed Sacrament Church.
Brennan, John J. '78 (SPR) [3] Westfield, MA St. Casimir's Church; [5] Westfield, MA St. Peter's Church.
Brennan, John P. *s.m.a.* '64 (LA) [A] Camarillo, CA St. John's Seminary.
Brennan, John W. *o.s.f.s.* '65 (WIL) [I] Childs, MD Oblates of St. Francis De Sales.
Brennan, Joseph *o.s.c.* '45 (SCL) [I] Onamia, MN Crosier Monastery.
Brennan, Joseph (Dennis) *o.s.b.* '74 (LA) [R] Valyermo, CA St. Andrew's Abbey.
Brennan, Msgr. Joseph F. (LA) Retired.
Brennan, Msgr. Joseph F. '56 (SD) Retired.
Brennan, Joseph L. *c.m.* '43 (LA) [95] Los Angeles, CA St. Vincent De Paul Church.
Brennan, Joseph P. '54 (ROC) Retired.
Brennan, Joseph T. *s.j.* '69 (CHI) [D] Chicago, IL St. Ignatius College Prep; [D] Chicago, IL St. Ignatius Jesuit Community.
Brennan, Joseph V. '80 (LA) Norwalk, CA St. Linus Church.
Brennan, Keith *s.d.s.* '70 (MIL) [5] Wauwatosa, WI St. Pius X Church.
Brennan, Keith R. '84 (STA) Special Assignment.
Brennan, Lawrence C. '76 (STL) [3] University City, MO Our Lady of Lourdes Church; [A] St. Louis, MO Kenrick-Glennon Seminary.
Brennan, Mark E. '76 (WDC) Pastoral Center Special Ministries.
Brennan, Matthew F. '62 (BIR) [5] Birmingham, AL Blessed Sacrament Church.
Brennan, Michael *c.p.* (SAC) [G] Redding, CA Mercy Medical Center.
Brennan, Michael *c.p.* '53 (MET) [H] South River, NJ Passionist Provincial Office.
Brennan, Michael J. '71 (BRK) [86] Brooklyn, NY St. Michael's Church.
Brennan, Patrick *c.p.* '73 (LA) [R] Pasadena, CA Passionist Community; [W] Sierra Madre, CA Mater Dolorosa Retreat Center.
Brennan, Patrick '77 (P) Special Assignment; [A] St. Benedict, OR Mount Angel Seminary.
Brennan, Patrick A. *o.s.a.* '63 (ORG) Buena Park, CA St. Pius V Church.
Brennan, Patrick J. '73 (CHI) Inverness, IL Holy Family Church.
Brennan, Paul '59 (ROC) [2] Auburn, NY Sacred Heart Church.
Brennan, Philip M. *o.s.m.* '41 (P) [L] Portland, OR The Grotto, The National Sanctuary of Our Sorrowful Mother.
Brennan, Pierce A. *s.j.* '76 (NY) [F] New York, NY Fordham Preparatory School; [Z] New York, NY Jesuit Community at Fordham University.
Brennan, Pierce A. *s.j.* '76 (RVC) Oceanside, NY St. Anthony Church.
Brennan, Msgr. Ralph A. '57 (AUS) Brenham, TX St. Mary of the Immaculate Conception Church; [M] Brenham, TX Blinn College Catholic Student Union.
Brennan, Robert (NY) Castle Point, NY Veterans Administration Medical Center.
Brennan, Robert '51 (CLV) Retired.
Brennan, Robert E. '45 (SY) [17] Syracuse, NY St. John the Baptist Church; Retired.
Brennan, Robert E. '65 (PH) [6] Norristown, PA St. Titus Church.
Brennan, Robert F. '51 (CLV) [64] Cleveland, OH SS. Philip and James Church.
Brennan, Robert J. '47 (NY) New York, NY Marine and Aviation Department.
Brennan, Robert J. '49 (NY) Retired.
Brennan, Robert J. *c.s.c.* '68 (ORL) [F] Cocoa Beach, FL Holy Cross Fathers, Eastern Priests Province.
Brennan, Msgr. Robert J. '89 (RVC) [1] Rockville Centre, NY St. Agnes Cathedral.
Brennan, Robert L. '64 (PH) [140] Philadelphia, PA Resurrection of Our Lord Church.
Brennan, Msgr. Robert M. '65 (NEW) [1] Hackensack, NJ Holy Trinity Church.
Brennan, Robert O. *s.j.* '53 (NY) [Z] New York, NY Murray-Weigel Hall.
Brennan, Roderick *o.f.m.cap.* '45 (NY) [Z] Garrison, NY St. Francis Friary.
Brennan, Ronan P. '50 (SAC) Sutter Creek, CA Immaculate Conception Church; Retired and in Senior Ministry.
Brennan, Msgr. Seamus F. '72 (MET) Edison, NJ St. Matthew Church.
Brennan, Terrence M. *s.j.* '76 (MIL) [E] Milwaukee, WI Marquette University High School; [P] Milwaukee, WI Pere Marquette House Jesuit Community.
Brennan, Thomas *s.j.* '63 (BO) [W] Chestnut Hill, MA The Jesuit Community at Boston College.
Brennan, Thomas '66 (TR) Bay Head, NJ Sacred Heart Church.
Brennan, Thomas *s.d.b.* '82 (NY) [72] New York, NY Mary Help of Christians Church.
Brennan, Thomas '89 (LAN) Retired.
Brennan, Thomas N. *s.j.* '67 (MIL) [P] Milwaukee, WI Arrupe House Jesuit Community.
Brennan, Timothy J. *o.s.b.* '78 (PAT) [M] Morristown, NJ St. Mary's Abbey.
Brennan, Walter M. *o.s.m.* '61 (CHI) [N] Chicago, IL Servite Friars - Eastern Province.
Brennan, William B. '53 (DET) [8] Dearborn Heights, MI St. Sebastian Church.
Brennan, William J. '42 (SPK) Retired.
Brennan, William J. '49 (L) Retired.
Brennan, William J. *s.j.* '51 (LUB) Spur, TX St. Mary Church.
Brennan, William J. *s.j.* '51 (MIL) [P] Milwaukee, WI Jesuit Provincial Office, Wisconsin Province.
Brennan, William P. '63 (CAM) [4] Cherry Hill, NJ St. Pius X Church.
Brennan, William V. *c.m.* '41 (CHI) [C] Chicago, IL Vincentian Community at DePaul University.
Brennell, John J. '78 (STL) Kirkwood, MO St. Peter Church.
Brenner, Raymond A. '69 (EVN) [10] Evansville, IN Resurrection Church.
Brenner, Msgr. Thomas R. (HBG) [K] Harrisburg, PA Catholic Campus Ministry.
Brenner, Msgr. Thomas R. '61 (HBG) Chambersburg, PA Corpus Christi Church.
Brennick, Stephen '59 (BO) [6] Somerville, MA Patronage of St. Joseph Church.
Brennock, Michael *o.s.a.* '70 (ORG) Buena Park, CA St. Pius V Church.
Brenny, Kenneth '63 (SCL) Pierz, MN St. Joseph's Church; [E] Pierz, MN Holy Trinity School; [H] Pierz, MN St. Mary's Villa Inc.
Brenon, Terence '91 (SAN) [4] San Angelo, TX St. Mary's Church.
Brenon, Terry (SAN) Carlsbad, TX St. Therese of the Child Jesus Church.
Brensinger, Richard C. '92 (ALN) Sinking Spring, PA St. Ignatius Loyola Church.
Brentrup, Bruce *s.d.s.* '59 (MIL) [P] Milwaukee, WI Salvatorian Provincial Residence.
Brenza, William J. '70 (HRT) [9] New Haven, CT St. Francis Church.
Breski, Martin *o.f.m.conv.* '69 (BAL) [M] Ellicott City, MD Order of Friars Minor Conventual.
Breslawski, William G. '79 (RVC) Nesconset, NY Church of the Holy Cross.
Bresler, C. John '75 (SFE) Cimarron, NM Immaculate Conception Church.
Breslin, J. Michael '65 (RIC) Cape Charles, VA St. Charles Church.
Breslin, John *s.m.m.* '56 (BRK) [U] Ozone Park, NY Montfort Missionaries Provincialate.
Breslin, John B. *s.j.* '73 (SY) [S] Syracuse, NY Jesuits at LeMoyne, Inc.
Breslin, John B. *s.j.* '73 (WDC) [C] Washington, DC Georgetown University.
Breslin, Msgr. John E. '61 (PH) [35] Philadelphia, PA St. Christopher Church.

Breslin, John S. '85 (CHI) [6] Chicago, IL St. Ailbe Church.
Breslin, Joseph W. '39 (SCR) Retired; [N] Dunmore, PA Villa St. Joseph.
Breslin, Msgr. Lawrence K. '57 (CIN) [7] Dayton, OH St. Charles Borromeo Church.
Breslin, William E. '74 (DEN) [1] Aurora, CO Queen of Peace Church.
Bresnahan, James F. *s.j.* '59 (BO) [W] Boston, MA The Society of Jesus of New England-Provincial Offices.
Bresnahan, James F. *s.j.* '59 (CHI) [N] Chicago, IL Chicago Province of the Society of Jesus-Provincial Office.
Bresnahan, John E. *o.s.a.* '36 (PH) [Z] Villanova, PA St. Thomas Monastery.
Bresnahan, John J. '60 (CHI) Schiller Park, IL St. Beatrice Church.
Bresnahan, Richard F. '58 (PEO) Coal Valley, IL St. Maria Goretti Church.
Bresnahan, Thomas J. '40 (DET) Retired; [Q] Troy, MI Gabriel Richard Institute.
Bresnahan, Thomas J. '60 (MAN) Londonderry, NH St. Mark the Evangelist Church.
Bresnehan, Msgr. Paul M. '54 (BUR) Proctor, VT St. Dominic Church.
Brestel, Msgr. Joseph R. (PAT) [P] Paterson, NJ Riese Corporation.
Brestel, Msgr. Joseph R. '38 (PAT) Hawthorne, NJ St. Anthony's Church.
Brethour, Gary G. '89 (LIN) Curtis, NE St. James Church.
Bretl, James J. *s.d.s.* '65 (NSH) McMinnville, TN St. Catherine Church; Smithville, TN St. Gregory Church.
Breton, Albert E. '54 (SPR) Agawam, MA St. Theresa of the Child Jesus Church.
Breton, Denis R. '76 (BUR) Hyde Park, VT St. Teresa Church; Morrisville, VT Holy Cross Church.
Breton, Raymond G. '68 (OAK) [10] Oakland, CA St. Jarlath's Church.
Bretone, Richard (BRK) [175] Queens, NY St. Helen Church.
Brett, Frank X. '59 (KNX) Norris, TN St. Joseph Church.
Brett, James D. '41 (CHI) Lake Forest, IL St. Mary Church; Retired.
Brett, James G. '44 (JKS) Meridian, MS St. Patrick Church; Retired.
Brett, Stephen F. *s.s.j.* '76 (WDC) [27] Washington, DC St. Luke Church.
Bretz, Msgr. John W. '41 (SFD) Retired; [J] Springfield, IL St. Joseph's Home.
Bretzke, James T. *s.j.* '81 (MIL) [P] Milwaukee, WI Jesuit Provincial Office, Wisconsin Province.
Bretzke, James T. *s.j.* '81 (OAK) [A] Berkeley, CA The Jesuit School of Theology at Berkeley; [N] Berkeley, CA Jesuit Community at Jesuit School of Theology at Berkeley.
Breu, David L. '73 (NU) Ivanhoe, MN SS. Peter & Paul Church; Wilno, MN St. John Cantius Church.
Breulmann, Hermann '77 (NY) [Z] New York, NY Jesuit Provincial's Office.
Breunig, Robert L. '51 (DEN) Retired.
Breunig, Rudy *s.t.* '65 (ORG) [A] Santa Ana, CA Trinity Missions House of Studies; [H] Santa Ana, CA Trinitarian Missionaries/Missionary Servants of the Most Holy Trinity.
Breuning, Walter A. '54 (PEO) Henry, IL St. Joseph's Church; Henry, IL St. Mary's Church.
Brevetti, Adrian '42 (BRK) Retired.
Brew, Frederick A. *s.j.* '43 (ALN) [A] Wernersville, PA Novitiate of St. Isaac Jogues.
Brewczynski, Jacek '96 (DET) Waterford, MI Our Lady of the Lakes Church.
Brewer, Dexter S. '89 (NSH) Decherd, TN Good Shepherd Church.
Brewer, Gervase '43 (MAR) Retired.
Brewer, James P. '77 (PRT) Bangor, ME St. John's Church; [G] Bangor, ME St. Xavier's Home.
Brewer, Martin L. *s.j.* '54 (LA) [2] Santa Barbara, CA Our Lady of Sorrows Church.
Brewer, Timothy M. '79 (WOR) [1] Worcester, MA St. Paul's Cathedral; [Q] Worcester, MA Campus Ministry.
Brewerton, Peter H. '40 (HT) Retired.
Brey, Floyd A. *s.j.* '35 (OM) [C] Omaha, NE Creighton Preparatory School.
Brey, Lawrence S. '53 (MIL) Retired.
Breza, Paul J. '63 (WIN) Hokah, MN St. Peter's Church.
Brezik, Victor B. *c.s.b.* '40 (GAL) [Q] Houston, TX Residence of the Basilian Fathers of the University of St. Thomas.
Brezinski, Blaine *c.p.* (RVC) Shelter Island, NY Our Lady of the Isle Church; [P] Shelter Island Heights, NY St. Gabriel's Youth House.
Breznikar, Victor '40 (SPK) Retired.
Brezovec, John F. '66 (ALT) [1] Johnstown, PA St. John Gualbert Cathedral; Johnstown, PA Memorial Hospital; Johnstown, PA Lee Hospital.
Brian, Bertrand J. '50 (L) Retired.
Brice, Donald '58 (WDC) [4] Washington, DC Annunciation Church.
Brice, Frederick J. '69 (MIA) Lighthouse Point, FL St. Paul the Apostle Church.
Brice, Steven J. '82 (LC) [2] Wausau, WI St. Anne Church.
Briceland, W. Alan *s.j.* '65 (NY) [Z] New York, NY West Side Jesuit Community.
Briceno, Joseph '81 (PHX) Unassigned.
Brichetto, James M. *s.j.* '63 (CIN) [11] Cincinnati, OH St. Antoninus Church; [M] Cincinnati, OH Faber Jesuit Community.
Brick, Daniel F. '42 (OM) [28] Omaha, NE St. Mary Church.
Brick, Maurice J. *o.f.m.* '45 (NY) [146] Bronx, NY Holy Cross Church.
Brick, Paul T. *s.d.s.* '63 (SAV) [4] Columbus, GA St. Benedict the Moor Church.
Bricker, Brian *o.p.* '89 (MAD) [J] Sinsinawa, WI Dominican Motherhouse.
Bricker, Brian *o.p.* '90 (DUB) [I] Dubuque, IA St. Dominic Villa.
Brickl, Joseph M. '37 (MAD) Retired.
Brickler, R. Richard '61 (ROC) [9] Rochester, NY St. Boniface Church.
Brickley, John J. '35 (DUB) Retired.
Brickman, Donald P. '81 (CLV) [1] Cleveland, OH Cathedral of St. John the Evangelist.
Brickner, Charles W. '75 (RIC) Woodlawn, VA St. Joseph's Church.
Brickner, Ronald J. (TOL) On Duty Outside the Diocese.
Bride, Harry *c.s.c.* (P) [L] Portland, OR Holy Cross Father & Brother, C.S.C. - University of Portland.
Bride, Harry *c.s.c.* '49 (P) [B] Portland, OR University of Portland.
Bride, Msgr. Thomas R. '67 (NOR) New London, CT St. Mary, Star of the Sea Church; On Special or Other (Arch)Diocesan Assignment.
Bridge, George H. *c.ss.r.* '48 (VEN) Wauchula, FL St. Michael Church.
Bridge, Raphael G. *o.s.b.* '50 (CHL) [J] Belmont, NC Belmont Abbey.
Bridge, Robert E. '72 (CHI) [168] Chicago, IL St. Peter Canisius Church.
Bridges, Clarence S. '88 (ALT) [1] Johnstown, PA St. John Gualbert Cathedral; Altoona, PA Altoona Hospital.
Bridges, Geoffrey *o.f.m.* (OAK) [R] Oakland, CA Missionaries of the Kingship of Christ.
Bridges, JAmes P. '62 (SAN) [4] Midland, TX St. Stephen's Church.
Bridgman, Mark '96 (OM) [16] Omaha, NE Holy Cross Church.
Bried, William '79 (TR) Brant Beach, NJ St. Francis of Assisi Church.
Brieffies, John *m.s.f.* '56 (RIC) [L] Richmond, VA Ethnic and Special Ministries; [M] West Point, VA Missionaries of the Holy Family, General Mission Office—M.S.F. Inc.
Brielmaier, Leon '77 (MIL) [N] Wauwatosa, WI St. Camillus Health Center, Inc.
Brielmaier, Leon J. '77 (MIL) Retired.
Brien, Paul *m.m.* '60 (DET) [K] Detroit, MI Maryknoll Fathers and Brothers.
Brien, Peter C. *m.m.* '60 (WDC) [B] Washington, DC Maryknoll Fathers and Brothers.
Brienz, Edward R. '96 (Y) [4] Massillon, OH St. Mary's Church.
Bries, Marvin J. '73 (DUB) Britt, IA St. Patrick's Church; Corwith, IA St. Mary's Church; Woden, IA Sacred Heart Church.
Briese, Dominic *o.p.* '96 (PHX) [5] Phoenix, AZ Most Holy Trinity Church.
Brietbach, Richard C. '61 (MIL) Whitefish Bay, WI St. Monica's Church.
Brietske, Richard C. '62 (TR) Willingboro, NJ Corpus Christi Church.
Briffa, Philip '60 (DET) [3] Warren, MI St. Cletus Church.
Briffa, Salvino (DET) Allenton, MI St. John the Evangelist Church.
Brigandi, Msgr. Paul A. (SY) [W] Oswego, NY St. Peter & St. Paul.
Brigandi, Msgr. Paul A. '54 (SY) [8] Binghamton, NY St. Mary of the Assumption Church.
Briganti, Philip J. '73 (PAT) Military Chaplains.
Briggman, Michael J. '68 (ALN) Bally, PA Most Blessed Sacrament Church.
Briggs, Everett F. '33 (WH) Retired.
Brigham, Kenneth M. '61 (CHI) [150] Chicago, IL Our Lady Help of Christians Church.
Brighenti, Kenneth D. '88 (MET) Parlin, NJ St. Bernadette Church.
Brignac, Horace L., Jr. '83 (NO) [55] New Orleans, LA St. Raphael the Archangel Church.
Brill, Robert D. (WOR) [B] Worcester, MA Assumption College.
Brimley, Wilfred *c.s.p.* '62 (NY) [Z] Scarsdale, NY Paulist Fathers Generalate.
Brimley, Wilfred A. *c.s.p.* (STP) [29] Minneapolis, MN St. Lawrence Church; [N] Minneapolis, MN Paulist Fathers.
Brincat, George R. '57 (LA) Tujunga, CA Our Lady of Lourdes Church.
Brindamour, Albert H. (PRO) [10] Woonsocket, RI Precious Blood Church.
Brindamour, Albert H. '46 (PRO) Retired.
Brindamour, Maurice L. '74 (PRO) [7] Woonsocket, RI St. Joseph's Church.
Brink, Joseph C. '63 (COV) Alexandria, KY St. Mary of the Assumption Church.
Brinker, Brian J. '88 (RVC) North Merrick, NY Sacred Heart Church; East Meadow, NY Nassau County Medical Center.
Brinker, Louis B. '50 (COV) Cynthiana, KY St. Edward Church.
Brinker, Maurice J. '54 (LEX) Retired; [F] Versailles, KY Taylor Manor Nursing Home.
Brinker, Paul '36 (COV) Dayton, KY St. Bernard Church.
Brinker, Paul J. '36 (COV) Retired.
Brinker, William *c.s.c.* '46 (CHI) [D] Niles, IL Notre Dame High School.
Brinkman, Barry '91 (SAL) Concordia, KS Our Lady of Perpetual Help Church.
Brinkman, Charles J. '77 (PH) [3] Philadelphia, PA St. Agatha-St. James Church; [DD] Philadelphia, PA Newman Apostolate.
Brinkman, Don G. '67 (STL) Absent on Sick Leave.
Brinkman, Frederick C. *c.ss.r.* '75 (ROC) [K] Canandaigua, NY Notre Dame Retreat House.
Brinkman, Gabriel *o.f.m.* '51 (SFD) [H] Effingham, IL St. Anthony's Memorial Hospital; [K] Teutopolis, IL St. Francis Assisi Friary.
Brinkman, James J. '81 (SUP) Farmington, WI Assumption of the Blessed Virgin Mary Church; Somerset, WI St. Anne Church.
Brinkman, John T. *m.m.* '71 (NY) [Z] Maryknoll, NY Maryknoll Fathers and Brothers.
Brinkman, Michael (PMB) Belle Glade, FL St. Philip Benizi Church.
Brinkman, Norbert C. '45 (CIN) Retired.
Brinkman, Terence *s.t.d.* '73 (GAL) Kingwood, TX St. Martha Church.
Brinkmann, Frederick C. *c.ss.r.* '75 (NY) [DD] Esopus, NY Holy Shroud Guild; [DD] Esopus, NY Holy Shroud Guild.
Brinkmann, Gerard *c.ss.r.* '61 (PH) [25] Philadelphia, PA St. Boniface Church.
Brinkmoeller, David E. '71 (CIN) [5] Dayton, OH Ascension Church.
Brinn, Adrian '68 (SB) Palm Springs, CA Our Lady of Solitude Church.
Brinn, John J. '62 (NY) [2] Poughkeepsie, NY St. Mary Church.
Brinsmade, John F. '81 (HRT) [2] West Haven, CT St. John Vianney Church.
Briody, Hugh J. '63 (SUP) On Duty Outside the Diocese.
Briody, Msgr. Thomas '39 (SD) Retired.
Brioschi, Thomas H. '86 (STP) [30] St. Paul, MN St. Pascal Baylon Church.
Brioso, Luis Renier *c.m.* (SJN) Loiza, PR Santiago Apostol, El Mayor Church.
Briscoe, Orville '84 (NSH) Retired.
Briseno, Miguel *o.f.m.conv.* (SAT) [B] San Antonio, TX San Damiano Friary; [C] San Antonio, TX St. Mary's University of San Antonio, Texas; [M] San Antonio, TX San Damiano Friary.
Briseno, Pedro '81 (BWN) [9] Brownsville, TX St. Luke Church; [I] Harlingen, TX KMBH-TV 60/KHID-FM 88.1/KMBH-FM 88.9.
Brisk, Ralph *c.p.* '29 (CHI) [N] Chicago, IL Immaculate Conception Monastery; [N] Chicago, IL Daneo Hall.
Briske, Larry F. '64 (MIL) Retired.
Brisotti, William F. '68 (RVC) Central Islip, NY St. John of God Church.
Brissette, Eugene C. *s.j.* '51 (BO) [W] Weston, MA Campion Health Center, Inc.
Brissette, Reginald R. '63 (PRT) Biddeford, ME St. Andre's Church.
Brisson, Robert A. '85 (NY) [EE] New Rochelle, NY Opus Dei (Prelature of the Holy Cross and Opus Dei).
Brito, Cristiano *o.s.b.* '91 (GBG) [H] Latrobe, PA Saint Vincent Archabbey.
Britt, Jerome C. '82 (COV) Burlington, KY Immaculate Heart of Mary Church.
Britt, William J. '53 (STL) Retired.
Brittain, Gerald W. '62 (MIL) West Bend, WI Holy Angels Church.
Britto, Federico A. '82 (PH) [67] Philadelphia, PA St. Ignatius of Loyola Church.
Britz, Francis '55 (SCL) Mayhew Lake, MN Annunciation Church.
Britz, Gerald F. '48 (DET) Retired.
Brixius, Hilary R. '68 (WIN) St. James, MN St. James Church.
Brizzolara, Andrew *c.s.* '75 (NY) [64] New York, NY St. Joseph Church.
Broach, Richard H. '77 (MIL) [10] Milwaukee, WI St. Barbara's Church.

Broadhurst, T. Paul *c.s.b.* '60 (ROC) [I] Rochester, NY Basilian Residence.
Brobst, James P. *o.m.i.* '90 (SFD) [1] Alton, IL SS. Peter and Paul Church.
Brobst, Richard A. '65 (Y) [9] Youngstown, OH St. Brendan's Church.
Brocato, Francis W. *o.p.* '90 (PRO) [P] Providence, RI St. Thomas Aquinas Priory at Providence College.
Brocato, Robert S. '95 (SJ) [22] San Jose, CA Sacred Heart of Jesus Church.
Broccolo, Gerard T. '65 (CHI) On Duty Outside the Archdiocese.
Brochtrup, Eugene '48 (MIL) [P] Milwaukee, WI Salvatorians - Jordan Hall.
Brochu, Albert E. *a.a.* '43 (NY) [87] New York, NY Our Lady of Guadalupe Church.
Brochu, Gerard H. '50 (BUR) Retired.
Brock, Msgr. Edmund J. '36 (PRO) Retired; [M] North Smithfield, RI St. Antoine Residence.
Brock, Herald *c.f.r.* '94 (NY) [Z] Yonkers, NY Saint Felix Friary; [Z] New York, NY St. Joseph's Friary.
Brock, John '62 (JKS) Natchez, MS Assumption of the B.V.M. Church.
Brockel, Kenneth E. '69 (JC) Perry, MO St. William Church.
Brockett, Norman L. (HRT) Cheshire, CT Church of the Epiphany.
Brockhaus, Msgr. Edward F. '64 (SD) [30] San Diego, CA St. Jude Church.
Brockhaus, Thomas Aq. *o.s.b.* '39 (P) [L] St. Benedict, OR Mt. Angel Abbey.
Brockland, John '91 (STL) Hazelwood, MO St. Martin de Porres Church.
Brockland, Robert J. *c.m.* '74 (STL) [P] Perryville, MO Congregation of The Mission.
Brockman, Blaise '77 (LA) Tujunga, CA Our Lady of Lourdes Church.
Brockman, David D. '90 (R) [6] Raleigh, NC St. Luke the Evangelist Church.
Brockman, Leon *o.c.s.o.* '55 (SPC) [E] Ava, MO Assumption Abbey (Trappist).
Brockman, Norbert C. *s.m.* '73 (CIN) [M] Dayton, OH Marianist Provincialate.
Brockman, Norbert C. *s.m.* '73 (SAT) [C] San Antonio, TX St. Mary's University of San Antonio, Texas; [M] San Antonio, TX Casa Maria Marianist Community.
Brockson, Scott D. '96 (PH) [32] Philadelphia, PA St. Cecilia Church.
Broderick, Francis *o.s.b.* '36 (KCK) Seneca, KS SS. Peter and Paul's Church.
Broderick, Msgr. Gerard W. '42 (BAL) Retired.
Broderick, James M. '60 (BO) [1] Haverhill, MA St. George Church.
Broderick, John '89 (SY) Vestal, NY Our Lady of Sorrows Church.
Broderick, John A. '44 (BO) Retired.
Broderick, John D. '63 (PRO) [2] Newport, RI Jesus Saviour Church.
Broderick, John F. *s.j.* '45 (BO) [W] Weston, MA Campion Center.
Broderick, Msgr. Kilian J. '67 (DAL) Coppell, TX St. Ann Church; [J] Dallas, TX Catholic Charities; [J] Dallas, TX St. Stephen, Inc.
Broderick, Leo P. '56 (DET) Algonac, MI St. Catherine Church.
Broderick, Michael '87 (WOR) Whitinsville, MA St. Patrick's Church.
Broderick, Richard '70 (ALB) Crescent, NY St. Mary Church.
Broderick, William '49 (SAC) Carmichael, CA Our Lady of the Assumption Church; Retired and in Senior Ministry.
Brodersen, Charles F. '48 (OM) Retired.
Brodersen, Steven W. '85 (SC) Algona, IA St. Cecelia Church.
Broderson, Donald '68 (OAK) Retired.
Brodeur, Dennis A. '77 (PRO) On Duty Outside the Diocese.
Brodeur, Henry *m.s.* '66 (MAN) Lebanon, NH Sacred Heart Church.
Brodeur, Scott N. *s.j.* '90 (BO) [W] Boston, MA The Society of Jesus of New England-Provincial Offices.
Brodeur, Theodore J. '66 (MAR) Sault Sainte Marie, MI Holy Name of Mary Church.
Brodfuehrer, Robert S. (CHI) Retired.
Brodfuehrer, Robert S. '45 (CHI) [46] Chicago, IL St. Cornelius Church; [64] Chicago, IL St. Francis Borgia Church.
Brodie, Paul S. *o.f.m.cap.* '67 (SJN) [4] San Juan, PR San Antonio Church.
Brodie, Thomas *o.p.* '58 (BO) [W] Cambridge, MA Faber House.
Brodnick, Edward J. '76 (COV) Union, KY St. Timothy Church.
Brodnick, Joseph '69 (CLV) Absent on Leave.
Brody, Donald '47 (GB) [I] Appleton, WI St. Fidelis Friary.
Brodzeller, Robert E. *s.j.* '63 (OM) [C] Omaha, NE Creighton Preparatory School; [G] Omaha, NE Alegent Health - Bergan Mercy Health System dba Algent Health - Bergan Mercy Medical Center.
Broering, Joseph '53 (COV) [I] Covington, KY Madonna Manor, Inc.
Broering, Raymond L. '53 (COV) Retired.
Broering, Victor F. '42 (CIN) Retired.
Brogan, Edward P. '44 (NY) Retired; [Z] New York, NY Our Lady of Consolation Residence.
Brogan, Hugh T. '69 (WDC) Retired.
Brogan, John F. '75 (BRK) [80] Brooklyn, NY St. Martin of Tours-Fourteen Holy Martyrs Church; [T] Brooklyn, NY Catholic Migration & Refugee Office, Catholic Migration Services, Inc.
Brogan, John J. '75 (BRK) [Y] Douglaston, NY Society of the Immaculate Conception of Brooklyn.
Brogan, Leo T. '67 (PHX) On Duty Outside the Diocese.
Brogan, Neal E. '66 (TLS) Henryetta, OK St. Michael Church.
Brogan, Paul '94 (LA) Woodland Hills, CA St. Mel Church.
Brogan, William '64 (NY) Absent on Leave.
Brogley, Charles F. *s.m.* '44 (WDC) [M] Washington, DC Marist Provincial House.
Broglio, Msgr. Timothy '77 (CLV) Released from Diocesan Assignment.
Brogus, Albert G. '45 (SCR) Retired.
Brohead, Martin *t.o.r.* '42 (ARL) [J] Winchester, VA Sacred Heart Friary.
Broker, John A. *c.ss.r.* '44 (MIL) [S] Oconomowoc, WI Perpetual Help Retreat Center.
Broker, Ralph H. '36 (STP) Retired.
Broker, William *c.ss.r.* '49 (MIL) [S] Oconomowoc, WI Perpetual Help Retreat Center.
Bromenshenkel, Fintan *o.s.b.* '45 (SCL) [I] Collegeville, MN St. John's Abbey, of the Order of St. Benedict.
Bromenshenkel, Silvan *o.s.b.* '47 (SCL) [I] Collegeville, MN St. John's Abbey, of the Order of St. Benedict.
Bromham, Frederick *o.f.m.* '33 (LA) [R] Santa Barbara, CA Franciscan Friary, Order of Friars Minor (Old Mission).
Bromley, Vincent M. '65 (SUP) Gordon, WI St. Anthony of Padua Church; Minong, WI St. Mary Church; Solon Springs, WI St. Pius X Church; Superior, WI Middle River Center.
Bromschwig, Arthur F. '50 (STL) [5] St. Charles, MO St. Peter Church.
Bronder, Joseph P. *o.s.b.* '69 (GBG) [H] Latrobe, PA Saint Vincent Archabbey.
Broniak, Leonard *c.ss.r.* '79 (SAT) [M] San Antonio, TX Redemptorists of Texas-Redemptorist Community at St. Gerard.
Broniszewski, Leo *o.carm.* '56 (NY) Tarrytown, NY Transfiguration Church.
Bronk, Philip *s.t.* '51 (SD) La Mesa, CA Little Flower Haven; [G] La Mesa, CA Little Flower Haven.
Bronkiewicz, Msgr. Laurence R. '73 (BGP) Westport, CT Assumption Church.
Brooks, Bryan V. '93 (TLS) Okmulgee, OK St. Anthony's Church.
Brooks, Charles '65 (GB) Mackville, WI St. Edward Church.
Brooks, David R. *s.j.* '78 (CAM) [4] Camden, NJ Holy Name Church; [S] Camden, NJ Camden Center for Law and Social Justice, Inc.
Brooks, Donald W. '61 (TLS) [1] Tulsa, OK Holy Family Cathedral; Special Assignment.
Brooks, Edwin J. *s.j.* '39 (NY) [Z] New York, NY St. Ignatius Loyola Residence.
Brooks, Jeddie P. '77 (SPR) Monson, MA St. Patrick's Church.
Brooks, John E. *s.j.* '59 (WOR) [N] Worcester, MA Jesuits of Holy Cross College, Inc.
Brooks, Msgr. John N. '49 (NY) Retired.
Brooks, Michael J. *ss.cc.* '61 (SB) Cathedral City, CA St. Louis Church.
Brooks, Robert '95 (SAC) Roseville, CA St. Rose Church.
Brooks, Robert C. '61 (ARL) Leesburg, VA St. John the Apostle Church.
Brooks, Thomas M. '78 (E) [11] Erie, PA Sacred Heart Church.
Brooks, William C. '76 (AUS) [3] Waco, TX St. Jerome Church.
Broom, Edward *o.m.v.* '86 (LA) Hawaiian Gardens, CA St. Peter Chanel Church.
Broome, Robert C. *s.j.* '43 (DET) [P] Clarkston, MI Colombiere Center.
Brophy, Msgr. Charles D. '39 (GR) Retired; [F] Grand Rapids, MI Contemplative Sisters of the Good Shepherd.
Brophy, Edward G. '93 (BRK) [163] Queens, NY St. Clare Church.
Brophy, John L. '69 (MIL) Kewaskum, WI Holy Trinity Church; Wayne, WI St. Bridget Church.
Brophy, Peter *o.f.m.* '85 (NY) [35] New York, NY St. Francis of Assisi Church.
Brophy, Peter V. *o.f.m.* '85 (NY) [Z] New York, NY The Franciscan Vocation Ministry of Holy Name Province.
Brophy, R. Michael *s.j.* '69 (CIN) [P] Milford, OH Milford Spiritual Center.
Brosius, Alfred G. (DUB) Retired.
Brosk, Steven J. '90 (NEW) Military Chaplains.
Broski, Mark *o.s.b.* '91 (ARL) [K] Bristow, VA St. Benedict Monastery.
Broski, Mark *o.s.b.* '91 (KCK) [A] Atchison, KS Benedictine College; [H] Atchison, KS St. Benedict's Abbey.
Brosmer, Donald '59 (EVN) Retired.
Brosmer, Thomas J. '69 (COL) Hilliard, OH St. Brendan Church.
Brosnan, Msgr. Dermot N. '57 (SAT) [T] San Antonio, TX The Patrician Movement.
Brosnan, Msgr. John R. '37 (LA) [43] Los Angeles, CA St. Ann Church; Retired.
Brosnan, Msgr. Liam P. '59 (SAT) [63] San Antonio, TX St. Pius X Church.
Brosnan, Thomas F. '81 (BRK) [226] Queens, NY St. Paul Chong Ha-Sang Roman Catholic Chapel; [T] Brooklyn, NY Catholic Migration & Refugee Office, Catholic Migration Services, Inc.
Brost, Frederick '56 (SUP) Stetsonville, WI Sacred Heart of Jesus Church.
Brothersen, Maynard J. '48 (DAV) Retired; [M] Davenport, IA St. Vincent Center.
Brou, Francis R. *s.j.* '61 (BR) [11] Baton Rouge, LA Immaculate Conception Church; [K] Baton Rouge, LA Martin Luther King, Jr. Student Center.
Brou, Hubert J. '56 (BR) [3] Baton Rouge, LA St. Aloysius Church.
Brouchoud, Earl R. '46 (GB) Retired.
Broudou, Joseph '96 (OM) [22] Omaha, NE St. Joan of Arc Church.
Broughan, Leonard *o'carm.* '55 (JOL) [J] Darien, IL Carmelite Fathers Provincial Office.
Brougher, Douglas C. '62 (NO) [37] New Orleans, LA St. James Major Church; New Orleans, LA Touro Infirmary.
Brouillard, Donald *s.s.s.* '50 (NY) [55] New York, NY St. Jean Baptiste Church.
Brouillard, John '56 (P) Retired.
Brouillard, Louis A. (AGN) Retired.
Brouillette, Thomas S. '96 (LIN) [11] Lincoln, NE St. Teresa's Church.
Brouke, Gabriel Vanden *ss.cc.* '48 (HON) [H] Honolulu, HI St. Patrick's Monastery.
Broussard, A. Rex '66 (LAF) Church Point, LA Our Lady of the Sacred Heart Church.
Broussard, Dennis A. '91 (MAN) [1] Concord, NH St. John the Evangelist Church.
Broussard, F. David '93 (LAF) [2] Opelousas, LA Our Lady of Mercy Church.
Broussard, Henry J. '72 (LAF) Judice, LA St. Basil Church.
Broussard, Hubert C. '52 (HT) Retired.
Broussard, John S. *c.s.b.* '48 (GAL) Manvel, TX Sacred Heart of Jesus Church.
Broussard, Kenneth M. (LAF) Absent on Leave.
Broussard, Oris '60 (LKC) Jennings, LA Immaculate Conception Church; [C] Lake Charles, LA Holy City Community.
Broussard, Paul (LAF) Absent on Sick Leave.
Broussard, Ronald *v.g.* '88 (LAF) Duson, LA St. Benedict the Moor Church.
Broussard, Warren *s.j.* '88 (LAF) Grand Coteau, LA St. Charles Borromeo Church.
Broussard, Msgr. William L. '56 (AUS) [N] Austin, TX Texas Conference of Catholic Health Facilities.
Broussard, Msgr. William L. '56 (GAL) On Duty Outside the Diocese.
Brouwers, Hans A.L. '78 (PH) [C] Immaculata, PA Immaculata College.
Brovey, Steven L. '91 (CHR) Georgetown, SC St. Mary's Church; Georgetown, SC St. Cyprian Church.
Brown, Msgr. Anthony M. '49 (HEL) Retired.
Brown, Arnold *o.f.m.* '49 (SP) [O] St. Petersburg, FL St. Anthony Friary.
Brown, Arthur A. '57 (BO) [1] Norwood, MA St. Catherine of Siena Church.
Brown, Benedict J. '74 (L) Military Chaplains.
Brown, Bonaventure *o.f.m.* '41 (PAT) [M] Ringwood, NJ Holy Name Friary.
Brown, Bruce '63 (P) Milwaukie, OR St. John the Baptist Church.
Brown, Charles (PSC) Retired.
Brown, Charles '89 (NY) On Duty Outside the Archdiocese.
Brown, Charles C. '58 (SFE) Los Alamos, NM Immaculate Heart of Mary Church.
Brown, Charles E. '71 (WDC) Burtonsville, MD Resurrection Parish Church.
Brown, Charles L. '73 (BRK) Absent on Leave.
Brown, Charles L., III '67 (WIL) Salisbury, MD St. Francis De Sales Church.
Brown, David *o.s.m.* (CHI) [159] Chicago, IL Our Lady of Sorrows, Basilica of.
Brown, David G. *o.s.b.* '75 (CHL) [J] Belmont, NC Belmont Abbey.
Brown, David O. *o.s.m.* '48 (CHI) [N] Chicago, IL Servite Friars - Eastern Province.
Brown, Edward J. *m.s.* '81 (RVC) [Q] Rockville Centre, NY The Campus Parish of Long Island.
Brown, Eugene M. '60 (NU) [2] New Ulm, MN St. Mary Church.
Brown, Everett *s.m.m.* '61 (BRK) [U] Ozone Park, NY

Montfort Missionaries Provincialate.
Brown, Ferdinand L. *c.s.c.* '42 (FTW) [J] South Bend, IN Congregation of Holy Cross Indiana Province Provincial House.
Brown, Francis '43 (STU) Retired.
Brown, Francis E. '62 (BO) On Duty Outside the Archdiocese.
Brown, George *o.m.i.* '64 (MAN) [K] Hudson, NH Missionary Oblates of Mary Immaculate.
Brown, Gerald L. *s.s.* '64 (BAL) [M] Baltimore, MD Sulpician Provincial House.
Brown, Gerard J. '46 (TR) Leave of Absence.
Brown, Harold C. *c.pp.s.* '59 (TOL) Glandorf, OH St. John the Baptist Church.
Brown, Henry '51 (IND) [29] Indianapolis, IN St. Lawrence Church; Indianapolis, IN Community Hospital North; Indianapolis, IN Winona Medical Center.
Brown, Isaac Jogues *o.s.b.* '84 (P) [L] St. Benedict, OR Mt. Angel Abbey; [N] St. Benedict, OR Mount Angel Abbey Retreat House.
Brown, James '62 (BWN) Pharr, TX St. Margaret Mary Church.
Brown, James E. '72 (TOL) Marblehead, OH St. Joseph Church.
Brown, James J. '62 (L) On Duty Outside the Archdiocese.
Brown, James V. *o.a.r.* '46 (OM) [21] Omaha, NE St. James Church.
Brown, John J. '83 (BRK) [120] Brooklyn, NY Queen of All Saints Church.
Brown, John T. '48 (STP) Retired.
Brown, John T. *glmy.* '84 (TLS) Idabel, OK St. Francis De Sales Church.
Brown, Joseph A. *s.j.* '72 (MIL) [P] Milwaukee, WI Jesuit Provincial Office, Wisconsin Province.
Brown, Joseph E. *s.j.* '56 (STL) [C] St. Louis, MO Saint Louis University; [P] St. Louis, MO Jesuit Community Corporation at St. Louis University - Jesuit Hall.
Brown, Justin *o.s.b.* '90 (NO) [P] St. Benedict, LA St. Joseph Abbey.
Brown, Justin G. *o.s.b.* '90 (HT) [5] Thibodaux, LA St. John The Evangelist Church.
Brown, Kenneth '77 (STL) [47] St. Louis, MO St. Margaret of Scotland Church.
Brown, Konstantin K. '88 (ROM) Special Assignment.
Brown, Leonard J. *c.m.f.* '82 (MET) [4] Perth Amboy, NJ Our Lady of Fatima Church.
Brown, Lewis E. '67 (ROC) Military Chaplains.
Brown, Mark *o.f.m.* (PRT) [6] Portland, ME St. Peter's Church; [6] Portland, ME St. Peter's Church.
Brown, Matthew F. '63 (SY) Vestal, NY Our Lady of Sorrows Church; Vestal, NY Binghamton Nursing Homes; Special Assignment.
Brown, Matthew J. *o.s.b.* '49 (OKL) Wewoka, OK St. Joseph Church; [I] Shawnee, OK St. Gregory's Abbey.
Brown, Matthew J. *o.s.b.* '49 (TLS) Holdenville, OK St. Stephen's Church.
Brown, Michael '74 (TOL) Military Chaplains.
Brown, Michael *o.carm.* '93 (JOL) [J] Darien, IL Carmelite Fathers Provincial Office.
Brown, Michael R. (ROC) Corning, NY St. Mary Church; Corning, NY St. Patrick Church; Corning, NY St. Vincent de Paul Church; Painted Post, NY Immaculate Heart of Mary Church.
Brown, Michael R. '89 (ROC) [3] Elmira, NY St. Mary Church.
Brown, Nicholas *s.c.j.* '76 (SAT) San Antonio, TX St. Luke's Baptist Hospital; University Hospital; [M] San Antonio, TX Harcar House; [M] San Antonio, TX Priests of the Sacred Heart-House of Formation.
Brown, Patrick '66 (PAT) On Duty Outside the Diocese.
Brown, Patrick *o.c.s.o.* '74 (WOR) [N] Spencer, MA St. Joseph's Abbey.
Brown, Patrick E. '78 (PAT) Stirling, NJ St. Vincent de Paul Church; Morristown, NJ Morris County Jail.
Brown, Patrick M. *o.f.m.* '59 (PAT) [M] Butler, NJ St. Anthony Friary.
Brown, Phillip J. '89 (BIS) Graduate Studies.
Brown, Raymond E. *s.s.* '53 (MIA) Miami Shores, FL St. Rose of Lima Church.
Brown, Raymond E. *s.s.* '53 (STA) On Duty Outside the Diocese.
Brown, Richard '80 (DAL) Absent on Leave.
Brown, Richard *s.p.* '80 (STL) [P] St. Louis, MO Servants of the Paraclete; [T] Dittmer, MO Vianney Renewal Center.
Brown, Richard H. *s.j.* '58 (SD) [12] San Diego, CA Our Lady of Guadalupe Church.
Brown, Robert '63 (SC) Maple River, IA St. Francis of Assisi Church; Mount Carmel, IA Our Lady of Mt. Carmel Church.
Brown, Robert A. '42 (L) Howardstown, KY St. Ann Church; Retired.
Brown, Robert A. *o.s.f.s.* '67 (ARL) Reston, VA St. John Neumann Church.
Brown, Msgr. Robert L. '69 (NOR) Montville, CT St. John Church; On Special or Other (Arch)Diocesan Assignment.
Brown, Robert W. '66 (ORL) [10] Orlando, FL St. Joseph Church.
Brown, Roderick M. *o.p.* '79 (BUF) [19] Buffalo, NY SS. Columba & Brigid Church; [49] Buffalo, NY St. Martin de Porres Church.
Brown, Roderick M. *o.p.* '79 (CHI) [N] Chicago, IL Dominicans (Provincial Office).
Brown, Shaun (NTN) Military Chaplains.
Brown, Stephen *s.v.d.* '93 (LA) [71] Los Angeles, CA St. John, The Evangelist Church.
Brown, Sylvester F. '56 (WIN) Janesville, MN St. Ann's Church.
Brown, Theophile *o.s.b.* '56 (SCL) [I] Collegeville, MN St. John's Abbey, of the Order of St. Benedict.
Brown, Theophile W. *o.s.b.* '50 (RIC) [M] Richmond, VA Mary Mother of the Church Abbey.
Brown, Thomas E. '78 (E) Galeton, PA St. Bibiana Church.
Brown, Timothy B. *s.j.* '86 (BAL) [C] Baltimore, MD Loyola College; [M] Baltimore, MD Jesuit Community of Loyola College, Inc.
Brown, Victor *o.p.* '63 (NO) [30] New Orleans, LA St. Dominic Church.
Brown, Vincent A. '34 (BRK) [206] Queens, NY Our Lady of the Angelus Church; Retired.
Brown, Vincent A. '57 (HRT) Branford, CT St. Mary Church.
Brown, W. P. '80 (PT) Bayou George, FL Our Lady of the Rosary Church.
Brown, W.T. St. John '92 (CC) [13] Corpus Christi, TX St. Anselm Anglican Use Community Church.
Brown, Walter William '94 (JKS) Meridian, MS St. Patrick Church.
Brown, Warren *o.m.i.* '82 (SAT) [B] San Antonio, TX Joseph Gerard House of Studies; [C] San Antonio, TX Oblate School of Theology.
Brown, Wayland Y. '77 (SAV) Special Assignment.
Brown, William *o.m.v.* '94 (SFD) [2] Alton, IL Immaculate Conception-St. Mary's Church; [3] Alton, IL St. Patrick Church.
Brown, William A. '94 (STP) Edina, MN St. Patrick Church.
Brown, William E. '88 (SFR) Redwood City, CA St. Pius Church.
Brown, William J. '55 (SY) Fulton, NY Immaculate Conception Church.
Brown, William P. '80 (PT) Fountain, FL Our Lady Queen of Peace Mission Church.
Browne, Msgr. Edward P. '51 (ARL) Annandale, VA St. Michael's Church.
Browne, Egbert J. '62 (PH) [69] Philadelphia, PA Immaculate Conception Church.
Browne, Francis J. *c.ss.r.* '68 (HRT) [5] Enfield, CT St. Patrick's Church.
Browne, George E. *c.m.* '46 (PH) [Z] Philadelphia, PA Congregation of the Mission.
Browne, George T. '55 (DET) [1] Roseville, MI St. Angela Church.
Browne, Gerald '81 (MET) [3] Carteret, NJ Sacred Heart Church.
Browne, J. Patrick '67 (SJ) [1] San Jose, CA St. Joseph Cathedral.
Browne, John T. *o.s.b.* '56 (NEW) Maplewood, NJ St. Joseph's Church; [N] Newark, NJ Newark Abbey.
Browne, Joseph *c.s.c.* (P) [L] Portland, OR Holy Cross Father & Brother, C.S.C. - University of Portland.
Browne, Joseph P. *c.s.c.* '55 (P) [8] Portland, OR St. Birgitta Church.
Browne, Joseph T. *s.j.* '56 (NY) [BB] Staten Island, NY Mount Manresa Jesuit Retreat House.
Browne, Michael E. *s.j.* '71 (NEW) [C] Jersey City, NJ St. Peter's Preparatory School.
Browne, Robert M. '61 (BO) Wilmington, MA St. Thomas of Villanova Church.
Browne, Ronald '88 (DET) Graduate Studies.
Browne, Stanley T. '81 (GB) [7] Green Bay, WI St. Joseph Church.
Browne, Vincent T. '54 (MAD) Military Chaplains.
Brownell, Patrick P. '94 (KNX) [6] Knoxville, TN St. John Neumann Church.
Brownell, Robert A. '69 (RIC) [15] Richmond, VA St. Peter Church.
Brownfield, David (DAV) DeWitt, IA St. Joseph's Church.
Brownfield, David L. '90 (DAV) Grand Mound, IA Church of St. Philip and James.
Brownfield, Frowin '56 (SPC) Retired.
Brownfield, Robert L. '92 (DAV) Retired; [M] Iowa City, IA O'Keefe Hall.
Brownholtz, George J. *o.s.f.s.* '69 (WIL) [I] Childs, MD Oblates of St. Francis De Sales.
Browning, John E. *s.j.* '59 (NEW) [C] Jersey City, NJ St. Peter's Preparatory School.
Browning, Joseph E. *s.j.* '54 (NO) [P] New Orleans, LA Ignatius Residence.
Browning, Lawrence *c.p.* '55 (CHI) [N] Chicago, IL Immaculate Conception Monastery.
Browning, William *c.p.* '49 (L) [2] Louisville, KY St. Agnes Church; [L] Louisville, KY Sacred Heart Retreat.
Brownsey, Brian K. '96 (PEO) Moline, IL Sacred Heart Church.
Brownstein, Donald '81 (COS) [12] Colorado Springs, CO St. Patrick's Church.
Broxmeyer, Dominic *o.s.b.* '45 (P) [L] St. Benedict, OR Mt. Angel Abbey.
Brozat, Charles *s.a.* '57 (NY) [Z] Garrison, NY Generalate of the Franciscan Friars of the Atonement-St. James Friary.
Brozena, Joseph M. '58 (SCR) [3] Old Forge, PA St. Michael's Church.
Brozonowicz, Gregorz P. '96 (NOR) Moosup, CT All-Hallows Church.
Brubaker, Claude E. '55 (VEN) [4] Sarasota, FL St. Michael the Archangel Church.
Brubaker, George J. '80 (WIL) Baltimore, MD Delaware Air National Guard; On Duty Outside the Diocese.
Brubaker, Scott '82 (PHX) [22] Phoenix, AZ Our Lady of the Valley Church.
Bruce, Joseph J. *s.j.* '81 (BO) [W] Boston, MA Loyola House; [W] Boston, MA The Society of Jesus of New England-Provincial Offices.
Bruce, Raymond '58 (GR) Caledonia, MI Holy Family Church.
Bruce, Robert '64 (Y) [12] Canton, OH St. Peter's Church.
Bruce, Robert J. '64 (Y) Retired.
Bruce, Terry '67 (KC) [1] Independence, MO St. Ann's Church.
Bruch, James A. '65 (SC) [10] Sioux City, IA Sacred Heart Church.
Bruch, Lynn '86 (SC) St. Benedict, IA St. Benedict's Church.
Bruch, Walter L. '50 (SC) Odebolt, IA St. Martin's Church; Retired.
Bruck, Donald '68 (DM) Hamburg, IA St. Mary Church.
Bruck, Donald '82 (DM) Shenandoah, IA St. Mary Church.
Brucker, G. Fredrick '76 (GR) [1] Muskegon, MI Our Lady of Grace Church; On Duty Outside the Diocese.
Brucker, George W. '56 (ALB) [16] Schenectady, NY St. Paul the Apostle Church.
Bruckner, Ronald L. '65 (SFE) [1] Albuquerque, NM Annunciation Church.
Brucksch, James L. '69 (GAY) Oscoda, MI Sacred Heart Church.
Brucz, James M. *c.s.p.* '74 (CHR) Clemson, SC St. Andrew Church; [H] Clemson, SC Clemson University.
Bruder, John W. *o.c.s.o.* '56 (BUR) Other Residence.
Brudzynski, Peter F. (BO) Retired.
Brudzynski, Peter F. '50 (VEN) [1] Venice, FL Epiphany Cathedral.
Bruecken, Albert *o.s.b.* '77 (KC) [A] Conception, MO Conception Seminary College; [J] Conception, MO Conception Abbey; [O] Conception, MO Conception Benedictine Trust.
Bruemmer, Joseph A. '48 (CIN) Retired.
Bruemmer, Joseph J. *o.s.c.* '47 (PHX) [F] Phoenix, AZ Crosier Community of Phoenix (Canons Regular of the Order of the Holy Cross).
Bruening, Allen '51 (CLV) Retired.
Bruening, Bernard H. '59 (CIN) Miamisburg, OH Our Lady of Good Hope Church.
Bruening, Joseph B. '53 (CIN) Franklin, OH St. Mary's Church.
Bruetsch, Joseph '70 (LFT) [1] Lafayette, IN St. Mary Cathedral.
Brug, Theodore R. '56 (STL) [4] University City, MO St. Patrick Church.
Bruggeman, Donald R. '62 (DUB) [3] Cedar Rapids, IA St. Jude Church; [D] Cedar Rapids, IA LaSalle High School; [D] Cedar Rapids, IA Regis High School.
Bruggeman, Gerald H. '49 (COS) Retired; [B] Colorado Springs, CO Penrose-St. Francis Health Services.
Brugger, Craig F. '73 (PH) [54] Philadelphia, PA St. Helena Church.
Brugger, Donald E. *s.j.* '70 (CHI) [C] Chicago, IL Jesuit Community at Loyola University of Chicago.
Brugger, Msgr. Robert L. '68 (E) Meadville, PA St. Brigid Church.
Brugli, Msgr. Angelo '52 (BRK) [97] Brooklyn, NY Our Lady of Guadalupe Church.
Brum, David *j.c.l.* '81 (FRS) [6] Fresno, CA St. Alphonsus Church.
Brum, Louis '74 (BWN) On Assignment Outside the Diocese.
Brum, Louis L. '74 (PRO) Bristol, RI St. Elizabeth's Church.
Brumleu, Ernest J. '47 (GAL) Retired.
Brumleve, Matthew '88 (KC) [6] St. Joseph, MO St. Patrick's Church; Easton, MO St. Joseph's Church; [3] Independence, MO St. Mark Church.
Brummel, Mark J. *c.m.f.* '60 (CHI) [149] Chicago, IL Our Lady of Guadalupe Church; [N] Chicago, IL Claretian Missionaries, St. Jude League, Inc.; [N] Oak Park, IL Claretian Fathers Headquarters of U.S.A. Eastern Province.
Brummel, Thomas *c.m.f.* '59 (CHI) [N] Oak Park, IL Claretian Fathers Headquarters of U.S.A. Eastern Province.
Brummer, Lawrence *o.f.m.* '58 (SAT) [46] San Antonio, TX St. Joseph Church.

Brundage, John L. '70 (MET) Bridgewater, NJ St. Bernard Church.
Brundage, Thomas T. '88 (MIL) Special Assignment; [B] Hales Corners, WI Sacred Heart School of Theology.
Brune, James '48 (EVN) Retired.
Brune, Meinrad *o.s.b.* '61 (IND) [J] St. Meinrad, IN St. Meinrad Archabbey.
Brune, Theodore *o.s.b.* '75 (IND) [J] St. Meinrad, IN St. Meinrad Archabbey.
Brunelle, Richard *a.a.* '63 (BO) [W] Brighton, MA Assumptionist Center.
Brunet, Msgr. Frederic J. '60 (HT) Chauvin, LA St. Joseph Church.
Brunet, Gerald O. *o.m.i.* '57 (SEA) Forks, WA St. Anne Parish Church.
Brunet, Jules A. '55 (BR) White Castle, LA Our Lady of Prompt Succor Church.
Brunett, John L. *s.j.* '55 (BAL) [C] Baltimore, MD Loyola College; [M] Baltimore, MD Jesuit Community of Loyola College, Inc.
Brunette, Bernard M. *o.praem.* '51 (MAD) [9] Madison, WI Saint Joseph Church.
Bruney, J. Lawrence '84 (PIT) [4] New Castle, PA St. Vitus Church.
Brungardt, Aloysius B. '71 (SAL) Plainville, KS Sacred Heart Church; Zurich, KS St. Ann's Church.
Brungs, Robert A. *s.j.* '64 (STL) [C] St. Louis, MO Saint Louis University; [P] St. Louis, MO Jesuit Community Corporation at St. Louis University - Jesuit Hall; [W] St. Louis, MO Institute for Theological Encounter with Science & Technology (ITEST).
Bruni, John E. '76 (CAM) Blackwood, NJ St. Agnes Church.
Brunick, Charles *c.s.p.* '70 (CHI) [125] Chicago, IL Old St. Mary Church.
Bruning, David R. '78 (TOL) Bascom, OH St. Patrick Church; Liberty, OH St. Andrew Church.
Bruning, William '93 (KCK) [4] Topeka, KS Most Pure Heart of Mary Church; [B] Topeka, KS Hayden High School.
Brunkan, Msgr. Walter L. '56 (DUB) Greene, IA St. Mary's Church; Roseville, IA St. Mary Church.
Brunner, Frank J. '55 (WH) Retired.
Brunner, Msgr. James C. *v.g.* '54 (VIC) Bay City, TX Holy Cross Church.
Brunner, John H. '62 (NU) Fairfax, MN St. Andrew Church; Franklin, MN Sacred Heart Church.
Brunner, Thomas J. '74 (CIN) Troy, OH St. Patrick Church.
Brunner, William M. *s.s.c.* '62 (SB) Needles, CA St. Ann Church.
Brunnert, Edward J. *m.s.* '63 (STL) [P] St. Louis, MO La Salette Missionaries; [P] St. Louis, MO La Salette Missionaries.
Brunnert, Jude *m.s.* '64 (LKC) De Quincy, LA Our Lady of La Salette Church; Dequincy, LA Phelps Correctional Center.
Brunnert, Theodore J. '54 (STL) Sullivan, MO St. Anthony Church.
Bruno, Anthony J. '68 (HRT) [2] Enfield, CT St. Adalbert's Church; Enfield, CT Connecticut Correctional Institution.
Bruno, John *r.c.j.* '74 (FRS) Del Rey, CA St. Katherine Church; Sanger, CA St. Mary Church.
Brunovsky, Michael *o.s.b.* '93 (CLV) [E] Cleveland, OH Benedictine High School; [P] Cleveland, OH Benedictine Order of Cleveland.
Brunovsky, Steven K. '92 (CLV) [14] Akron, OH St. Paul Church.
Bruns, J. Edgar '48 (NO) Retired; [A] New Orleans, LA Notre Dame Seminary Graduate School of Theology.
Bruns, Wilbert H. *c.m.* '51 (STL) [P] St. Louis, MO Vincentian Henrietta Residence.
Brunskill, Richard W. '83 (PEO) Chatsworth, IL SS. Peter and Paul Church; Cullom, IL St. John's Church.
Brunton, Daniel B. '60 (SPR) Lenox, MA St. Ann's Church; Lenox Dale, MA St. Vincent de Paul's Church.
Brusato, Martin '89 (SAC) [1] Sacramento, CA Cathedral of the Blessed Sacrament; Galt, CA St. Christopher Church.
Brusatti, Louis T. *c.m.* '75 (GAL) [A] Houston, TX St. Mary's Seminary; [C] Houston, TX University of St. Thomas.
Bruse, James C. '84 (ARL) Kilmarnock, VA St. Francis de Sales Church.
Bruso, Robert D. '93 (WOR) Clinton, MA St. John the Evangelist Church.
Brutus, Ferry '80 (MIA) North Miami, FL Holy Family Church.
Bryan, Dunstan *o.f.m.conv.* '37 (IND) [I] Mount Saint Francis, IN Mount Saint Francis Friary and Retreat Center.
Bryan, Francis E. '62 (IND) [B] Indianapolis, IN Marian College.
Bryan, Kevin J. '76 (L) [66] Louisville, KY St. Raphael the Archangel Church.
Bryan, Paul *c.ss.r.* '59 (PH) [135] Philadelphia, PA St. Peter the Apostle Church.
Bryant, F. Michael '69 (WDC) [16] Washington, DC Holy Comforter—St. Cyprian Church; [V] Washington, DC District of Columbia Detention Facility.
Bryant, James M. '85 (STU) Chesapeake, OH St. Ann Church
Bryant, Michael '69 (WDC) Special Ministries; [V] Hyattsville, MD Prison Outreach Ministry.
Bryant, Michael M. '78 (SCR) [C] Dallas, PA College Misericordia.
Bryce, Ambrose S. '61 (CAM) Waterford, NJ St. Anthony Church.
Bryce, Edward M. '60 (PIT) [5] Pittsburgh, PA St. Bede Church.
Bryce, Vincent *o.p.* '57 (GR) Edmore, MI St. Margaret Mary Church; Stanton, MI St. Bernadette of Lourdes Church.
Bryce, Vincent W. *o.p.* '57 (CHI) [N] Chicago, IL Dominicans (Provincial Office).
Bryda, Ronald J. '66 (CLV) Litchfield, OH Our Lady Help of Christians Parish Church.
Brydl, Ladislaus C. '31 (BIS) Retired; [G] Bismarck, ND Emmaus Place.
Bryerton, Robert R. '74 (TUC) Sierra Vista, AZ Our Lady of the Mountains Church.
Bryk, John J. '53 (CLV) [3] Lakewood, OH St. Hedwig Church.
Bryl, Thaddeus '66 (LIN) Grafton, NE St. Helena's Church; Sutton, NE St. Mary's Church.
Bryl, Thaddeus J. '66 (MIL) On Duty Outside the Archdiocese.
Brylinski, Bruce '83 (COV) Vanceburg, KY Holy Redeemer Church.
Brylinski, Bruce C. *glmy.* '83 (LEX) Grayson, KY Ss. John & Elizabeth Church.
Brylinski, Bruce C. '83 (PIT) On Duty Outside the Diocese.
Brylka, Vincent R. '65 (OAK) Martinez, CA St. Catherine of Siena Church.
Brynda, Msgr. Gerald J. '57 (TUC) Yuma, AZ Immaculate Conception Church.
Bryon, Paul J. (R) Retired.
Bryon, Thomas C. '63 (STL) [49] St. Louis, MO St. Mary Magdalen Church.
Bryson, John *s.m.* '53 (DET) [E] Harper Woods, MI Notre Dame High School.
Bryson, John H. '50 (MAN) West Swanzey, NH St. Anthony Church.
Bryson, Robert C. (BO) Hingham, MA Resurrection of Our Lord and Saviour Jesus Christ Church; Retired.
Brzakowski, Jerome *s.v.d.* '45 (TR) [M] Bordentown, NJ Society of the Divine Word.
Brzek, Jon J. '83 (PIT) Military Chaplains.
Brzezicki, Zbigniew '88 (STF) Fall River, MA St. John-the-Baptist Church; Woonsocket, RI St. Michael Church.
Brzezinski, Hilary *o.f.m.* '76 (JKS) Greenwood, MS St. Francis of Assisi Church.
Brzezinski, Jerome A. '69 (DET) Auburn Hills, MI St. John Fisher Chapel University Parish Church; [S] Auburn Hills, MI St. John Fisher Chapel University Parish; [T] Warren, MI Catholic Campus Ministers Association.
Brzezniak, Aurelian W. *ofm conv.* '45 (BUF) [D] Athol Springs, NY St. Francis High School; [O] Athol Springs, NY St. Francis of Assisi Friary.
Brzoska, Anthony B. *s.j.* '59 (LA) [C] Los Angeles, CA Loyola Marymount University.
Brzostowski, Hilary *o.f.m.conv.* '69 (NOR) Cromwell, CT St. John Church.
Brzozowski, Edward J. '44 (CHI) [143] Chicago, IL St. Nicholas of Tolentine Church; Retired.
Brzozowski, Msgr. Joseph R. '37 (MET) Retired; [G] Somerset, NJ McCarrick Care Center.
Brzozowski, Simon *m.s.f.* (CC) [1] Beeville, TX Our Lady of Victory Church.
Brzozowski, Simon P. *m.s.f.* '73 (CC) [2] Beeville, TX Sacred Heart Mission Church.
Buatava, Vitori *s.m.* '83 (BO) [W] Boston, MA Marist Fathers of Our Lady of Victories (Boston Prov.).
Buby, Bertrand A. *s.m.* '64 (CIN) [D] Dayton, OH The University of Dayton; [M] Dayton, OH Marianist Provincialate.
Bucaria, James A. '72 (SP) Masaryktown, FL St. Mary, Our Lady of Sorrows Church.
Bucaro, Michael '80 (SB) Chino, CA Southern Conservation Center.
Buccafurni, Ferdinand '58 (PH) [40] Philadelphia, PA St. Donato Church; [112] Philadelphia, PA Our Lady of Angels Church.
Buccellato, Sebastian *o.f.m.* '51 (NY) [142] Bronx, NY St. Frances of Rome Church; [Z] New York, NY Franciscan Province of the Immaculate Conception; [Z] New York, NY St. Clare Friary.
Bucchen, Vincenzo *r.c.j.* '79 (LA) [R] North Hills, CA Rogationist Fathers.
Bucchino, John *o.f.m.* '73 (NY) [Z] New York, NY Franciscan Province of the Immaculate Conception.
Bucci, Evan *o.f.m.conv.* '57 (ALB) [12] Albany, NY Our Lady of Angels Church.
Bucci, Michael J. '62 (GBG) Retired.
Bucci, Richard A. '73 (PRO) [9] West Warwick, RI SS. Peter and Paul Church.
Bucciantini, Charles '72 (JKS) Cleveland, MS Our Lady of Victories Church; Rosedale, MS Sacred Heart Church; [G] Cleveland, MS Delta State University Newman Center.
Bucciarelli, Michael R. '75 (TUC) San Manuel, AZ St. Bartholomew Church.
Bucciarelli, Robert P. '60 (MIL) [O] Brookfield, WI Opus Dei-Prelature of the Holy Cross and Opus Dei.
Bucciferro, Eugene '63 (JOL) [17] Joliet, IL St. Patrick Church.
Bucciferro, William *s.d.b.* '83 (COL) [H] Columbus, OH Salesian Center.
Bucek, Timothy P. '76 (GAL) Pattison/Brookshire, TX Sacred Heart Church.
Buchanan, David (BIR) Eutaw, AL St. Mary Church; Livingston, AL St. Francis of Assisi Church.
Buchanan, David '93 (BIR) Tuscaloosa, AL Holy Spirit Church.
Buchanan, Donald '45 (SD) Lemon Grove, CA St. John of the Cross Church; Retired.
Buchanan, Donald E. '65 (IND) Military Chaplains.
Buchanan, John J. '36 (STP) Retired.
Buchanan, Robert '68 (SB) On Duty Outside the Diocese.
Buchanan, Robert E. '68 (RNO) [2] Reno, NV Our Lady of the Snows Church.
Bucher, Mel '61 (SD) [H] San Luis Rey, CA San Luis Rey; [K] San Luis Rey, CA Mission San Luis Rey Retreat.
Bucher, Otto N. *o.f.m.cap.* '59 (MIL) [B] Hales Corners, WI Sacred Heart School of Theology; [P] Milwaukee, WI St. Conrad House.
Bucher, Msgr. Philip A. '61 (SPC) Branson, MO Our Lady of the Lake Church.
Bucher, Vitus *o.s.b.* '41 (SCL) [I] Collegeville, MN St. John's Abbey, of the Order of St. Benedict.
Buchette, Anthony L. (BO) Awaiting Assignment.
Buchheit, Msgr. Jerome J. '51 (STL) Ballwin, MO Holy Infant Church.
Buchheit, Richard A. '63 (STL) [11] St. Louis, MO Most Holy Trinity Church; [29] St. Louis, MO St. Bridget of Erin Church.
Buchholz, Athanasius *o.s.b.* '54 (P) [L] St. Benedict, OR Mt. Angel Abbey.
Buchignani, Peter P. '65 (MEM) [8] Memphis, TN St. Francis of Assisi Church.
Buchignani, Richard G. '62 (NSH) Lawrenceburg, TN Sacred Heart Church; [L] Nashville, TN Diocesan Council of Catholic Women.
Buchleitner, Donald N. '70 (PIT) [50] Pittsburgh, PA Holy Innocents Church.
Buchman, Joel '91 (TOL) [14] Toledo, OH Sacred Heart of Jesus Church; Toledo, OH St. Vincent Medical Center; [H] Toledo, OH St. Vincent Medical Center.
Buchmeier, Robert P. '91 (WDC) Clinton, MD Church of St. John the Evangelist.
Buchmiller, Ronald J. '69 (SD) Military Chaplains.
Bucia, Msgr. Edward H. '62 (CAM) [6] Camden, NJ St. Joseph's Church.
Buck, Daniel P. (CHI) [2] Cicero, IL St. Frances of Rome Church.
Buck, Francis C. *s.j.* '46 (BO) [W] Boston, MA The Society of Jesus of New England-Provincial Offices.
Buck, Francis C. *s.j.* '46 (GLP) Church Rock, NM St. Philip Benizi Church; Fort Wingate, NM St. Eleanor Church.
Buck, Franklin G. '85 (ORL) [4] Lakeland, FL St. Joseph's Church.
Buck, James '41 (SEA) Retired.
Buckalew, Jack '74 (SEA) Bremerton, WA Holy Trinity Church.
Bucke, Gerald L. '43 (BO) [35] Boston, MA St. Joseph Church.
Buckel, John J. '80 (IND) [A] St. Meinrad, IN St. Meinrad Seminary.
Bucki, John P. *s.j.* '79 (NY) [37] New York, NY St. Francis Xavier Church; [Z] New York, NY Jesuit Provincial's Office; [Z] New York, NY Xavier Jesuit Community.
Bucki, Peter *o.f.m.conv.* '39 (BAL) [M] Ellicott City, MD Order of Friars Minor Conventual.
Buckius, Walter A. *s.j.* '52 (WH) [A] Wheeling, WV Wheeling Jesuit University.
Buckles, David '88 (LFT) Special Assignment; [H] West Lafayette, IN St. Thomas Aquinas Parish and Foundation for Catholic Students attending Purdue Univ.
Buckles, Luke D. *o.p.* '78 (OAK) [A] Berkeley, CA Dominican School of Philosophy and Theology; [N] Oakland, CA Dominican Order (Western Province), St. Albert's Priory; [N] Oakland, CA Western Dominican Province.
Buckley, Brendan P. *o.f.m.cap.* '81 (BRK) [87] Brooklyn, NY St. Michael's Church; [U] Brooklyn, NY St. Michael's Friary.
Buckley, Charles *o.s.b.* '70 (OKL) [I] Shawnee, OK St. Gregory's Abbey.
Buckley, Cornelius M. *s.j.* '62 (SFR) [N] San Francisco, CA Jesuit Community at University of San Francisco.
Buckley, Msgr. Edwin T. '41 (BUR) Retired.

Buckley, Francis *s.j.* '58 (OAK) [A] Oakland, CA Graduate School of Theology, School of Applied Theology.
Buckley, Francis J. *s.j.* '58 (SFR) [N] San Francisco, CA Jesuit Community at University of San Francisco.
Buckley, Frederick J. '45 (BO) Retired.
Buckley, George M. *m.m.* '39 (SJ) [M] Los Altos, CA Maryknoll.
Buckley, George P. *o.m.i.* '40 (BO) [Z] Tewksbury, MA Immaculate Heart of Mary Novitiate-Infirmary.
Buckley, Gerald Albert *o.p.* '57 (P) [18] Portland, OR Holy Rosary Parish & Dominican Priory Church.
Buckley, Gerald J. '57 (SY) [1] Binghamton, NY St. Andrew Church; Binghamton, NY Binghamton Psychiatric Hospital.
Buckley, Harold P. '53 (RVC) Retired.
Buckley, James *o.c.d.* '60 (SR) [M] Oakville, CA Carmelite House of Prayer.
Buckley, James '82 (GLP) Absent on Leave.
Buckley, James B. *f.s.s.p.* '65 (SCR) [M] Elmhurst, PA Priestly Fraternity of St. Peter (F.S.S.P.).
Buckley, James C. *c.s.c.* '51 (OAK) [3] Hayward, CA St. Clement Church.
Buckley, James F. '59 (FR) Chatham, MA Holy Redeemer Church.
Buckley, James M. '90 (OM) Plainview, NE St. Paul Church.
Buckley, John E. '59 (BO) Burlington, MA St. Margaret Church.
Buckley, John J. *c.m.* '57 (PH) [Z] Philadelphia, PA Congregation of the Mission.
Buckley, John K. '47 (BO) Retired.
Buckley, John M. *s.j.* '56 (NEW) [B] Jersey City, NJ Saint Peter's College; [N] Jersey City, NJ Jesuits of Saint Peter's College, Inc.
Buckley, Joseph F. '43 (BRK) [28] Brooklyn, NY St. Cecilia Church; Retired.
Buckley, Lawrence J. *c.ss.r.* '49 (BO) [13] Boston, MA Basilica of Our Lady of Perpetual Help.
Buckley, Michael *o.c.d.* '47 (SJ) [M] San Jose, CA Carmelite Monastery, Novitiate.
Buckley, Michael *s.j.* '62 (BO) [W] Chestnut Hill, MA The Jesuit Community at Boston College.
Buckley, Michael D. (LA) Sick Leave.
Buckley, Ramon J. '77 (STP) Clearwater, MN St. Luke Church.
Buckley, Robert G. '58 (BO) [2] Methuen, MA St. Monica Church.
Buckley, Robert L. '57 (ALB) Schuylerville, NY Notre Dame-Visitation Church.
Buckley, Thomas E. *s.j.* '70 (LA) [C] Los Angeles, CA Loyola Marymount University.
Buckley, Thomas J. (BO) Amesbury, MA Sacred Heart Church.
Buckley, Thomas J. *s.j.* '70 (OAK) [N] Berkeley, CA Jesuit Community at Jesuit School of Theology at Berkeley.
Buckley, Thomas J. *s.j.* '74 (WDC) [M] Washington, DC The Jesuit Community at Georgetown University.
Buckley, Thomas R. '76 (ALN) Limeport, PA St. Joseph Church.
Buckley, Thomas W. '55 (BO) Essex, MA St. John the Baptist Church.
Buckley, Timothy J. '92 (PH) Brookline, PA Annunciation B.V.M. Church.
Buckman, Franklin J. '63 (BAK) Klamath Falls, OR St. Pius Xth Church.
Buckman, Franklin J. '63 (ORG) On Duty Outside the Diocese.
Buckner, Christopher M. '80 (ARL) Fredericksburg, VA St. Mary Church.
Bucko, Raymond A. *s.j.* '83 (SY) [S] Syracuse, NY Jesuits at LeMoyne, Inc.
Buckon, Neal J. '95 (CLV) South Euclid, OH St. Margaret Mary Church.
Buckson, John R. '92 (OM) [15] Omaha, NE St. Francis Assisi Church; [32] Omaha, NE Our Lady of Guadalupe Church.
Bucmys, Cornelius *o.f.m.* '62 (BRK) [U] Brooklyn, NY St. Casimir's Monastery, Printing Plant and Cultural Center.
Bucolo, Joseph W. '54 (SCR) Pardeesville, PA St. Nazarius Church.
Bucon, Raymond H. '79 (DET) Wayne, MI St. Mary Church.
Buczyna, Andrew '87 (JOL) Westmont, IL Holy Trinity Church.
Buczynski, Edward '61 (DUL) Hill City, MN St. John Church.
Budai, Frank A. '88 (GLP) Retired.
Budde, John G. '77 (DET) Novi, MI Holy Family Church.
Budden, William A. '68 (RCK) Oregon, IL St. Mary Church.
Buddendorff, Kenneth A. *s.j.* '61 (DAL) [D] Dallas, TX Jesuit College Preparatory School.
Budi, Hartono *s.j.* '94 (OAK) [N] Berkeley, CA Jesuit Community at Jesuit School of Theology at Berkeley.
Budka, Dennis G. '84 (MIL) [3] Waukesha, WI St. John Neumann Church.
Budnar, Randy J. '88 (MAD) Waunakee, WI St. John the Baptist Church.
Budney, Msgr. David F. '57 (CAM) [5] Cherry Hill, NJ St. Thomas More Church.
Budnick, Austin J. *o.f.m.* '51 (ROC) [I] Watkins Glen, NY St. Anthony of Padua Friary.
Budovic, Francis X. *s.j.* '38 (DET) [62] Detroit, MI SS. Peter and Paul Jesuit Church.
Budwick, Msgr. John J. '64 (NY) [1] Newburgh, NY St. Patrick Church.
Budzikowski, Kenneth A. '80 (CHI) Park Ridge, IL St. Paul of the Cross Church.
Budzynski, Daniel A. '56 (MIL) Retired.
Buebendorf, Victor J. '64 (NY) [213] Staten Island, NY St. Mary Church.
Bueche, Charles C. *c.ss.r.* '53 (STL) [P] Liguori, MO Liguori Mission House/Redemptorists.
Bueche, Gary '70 (DET) Allen Park, MI St. Frances Cabrini Church.
Bueche, Walter *c.ss.r.* '38 (ORL) [F] New Smyrna Beach, FL St. Alphonsus Villa-Redemptorist Fathers and Brothers.
Bueche, William *c.ss.r.* '78 (CHI) [N] Bangkok, Thailand.
Buechele, Andrew C. *sch.p.* '69 (WDC) [B] Washington, DC Queen of Pious Schools House of Studies-Piarist Fathers; [C] Washington, DC Catholic University of America, The.
Buehler, John A. '74 (SY) [9] Utica, NY St. John Church.
Buehler, Paul A. *c.pp.s.* '44 (CIN) [M] Dayton, OH Provincial House of the Cincinnati Province of the Society of the Precious Blood.
Buenaventura, Cesar (OAK) Military Chaplains.
Buenger, Edward A. *c.s.c.* '53 (FTW) [J] South Bend, IN Congregation of Holy Cross Indiana Province Provincial House.
Buening, Robert B. '58 (CIN) [41] Cincinnati, OH St. James Church.
Buening, Ulric *o.f.m.cap.* '53 (MIL) [25] Milwaukee, WI St. Francis of Assisi Church; [Y] Milwaukee, WI Capuchin Franciscan Tertiary Province of St. Joseph of Wisconsin, Inc.
Buenzli, August H. '53 (MAD) Briggsville, WI St. Mary Help of Christians Church.
Buerger, Francis J. '44 (CIN) Retired.
Buermann, Eric R. *o.s.b.* '45 (CGS) Humacao, PR Maria Reina de la Paz Church.
Buersmeyer, David A. '80 (DET) Lincoln Park, MI Christ the Good Shepherd Church.
Buerster, James A. '79 (BEL) Murphysboro, IL St. Andrew Church.
Buescher, David G. '71 (JC) Absent on Leave.
Bueter, Paul '59 (FTW) Goshen, IN St. John the Evangelist Church; Milford, IN Our Lady of Guadalupe Church.
Bueter, Robert J. *s.j.* '73 (LEX) [A] Lexington, KY Lexington Catholic High School.
Buetow, Harold A. '44 (BRK) Retired; [U] Douglaston, NY Bishop Mugavero Residence.
Buettner, George '52 (BAL) Retired.
Buffardi, Joseph G. '76 (PAT) [10] Paterson, NJ St. Mary's Church.
Buffer, Thomas '91 (COL) [5] Columbus, OH St. Andrew Church.
Buffington, Jon '81 (EST) On Assignment Outside the Diocese
Buffington, Jon '81 (P) [J] Portland, OR Providence Portland Medical Center.
Bugarin, Fred '75 (ANC) Kodiak, AK St. Mary's of Kodiak and the Islands Church.
Bugarin, Michael '91 (DET) Special Assignment.
Bugay, Stephen R. '84 (GBG) Clymer, PA Church of the Resurrection.
Bugayong, Demetrio '70 (LA) Carson, CA St. Philomena Church.
Buggert, Donald W. *o.carm.* '66 (WDC) [B] Washington, DC Whitefriars Hall.
Buggy, Leon *s.t.* '60 (WDC) [B] Silver Spring, MD Holy Trinity Mission Seminary (1926).
Bugler, Henry J. '75 (NO) [57] New Orleans, LA St. Rita Church.
Bugler, Msgr. Joseph T. '38 (JC) Retired.
Bugliosi, Mario *o.s.f.s.* '43 (WIL) [3] Wilmington, DE St. Anthony of Padua Church; [G] Wilmington, DE The Antonian.
Bugman, Msgr. John H. '52 (BUF) Retired.
Bugno, Krzysztof *s.d.s.* '85 (BRK) [187] Queens, NY St. Joseph Church.
Bugno, Krzysztof *s.d.s.* '85 (NEW) [N] Verona, NJ The Salvatorian Fathers.
Buhl, Wilbert L. '60 (GB) Maplewood, WI St. Mary Church.
Buhler, Richard O. *s.j.* '70 (COS) [E] Sedalia, CO Sacred Heart Retreat House - Jesuit Community; [G] Sedalia, CO Sacred Heart Jesuit Retreat House.
Buhman, Leo T. '48 (JC) Retired.
Buholzer, Robert E. '56 (MAD) Palmyra, WI St. Mary Church.
Buhr, Donald L. '66 (STL) [9] Florissant, MO St. Sabina Church.
Buhr, Eugene '54 (LA) Hawthorne, CA St. Joseph Church.
Buhrfeind, William J. '38 (CHI) [3] Mt. Prospect, IL St. Raymond de Penafort Church; [2] Oak Lawn, IL St. Gerald Church; Retired.
Buhrman, Donald A. '86 (GI) Lexington, NE St. Ann's Church.
Bui, Francis '90 (HT) Amelia, LA Thanh Gia Church.
Bui, Francis T. '75 (LA) [9] Long Beach, CA St. Lucy Church.
Bui, Marion Joseph *o.c.d.* '95 (OKL) [14] Oklahoma City, OK Our Lady of Mount Carmel and St. Therese Little Flower Church.
Bui, Peter *s.d.b.* '90 (LA) [C] Rosemead, CA Don Bosco Technical Institute; [D] Rosemead, CA Don Bosco Technical Institute.
Bui, Tin Mahn '75 (SFE) [9] Albuquerque, NM Our Lady of Lavang Church.
Bui, Vincent Doan '95 (LAN) Flushing, MI St. Robert Church.
Bui Anh Tuan, Athanasius M. *c.m.c.* '81 (SB) [E] Corona, CA Congregation of the Mother Coredemptrix.
Bui-Trang-Nghiem, Joseph '73 (WDC) [L] Washington, DC Cardinal O'Boyle Residence for Priests.
Buitrago, Luis '67 (DAL) Plano, TX St. Mark the Evangelist Church.
Buitrago, Tarsicio '64 (ARL) [1] Alexandria, VA Blessed Sacrament Church.
Bujnak, George A. '65 (PSC) Nesquehoning, PA St. Mary's Church.
Bukala, Casimir R. *s.j.* '66 (CLV) [C] Cleveland, OH John Carroll Jesuit Community.
Bukase, Joseph *c.i.c.m.* '84 (BWN) Hidalgo, TX Sacred Heart Church.
Bukaty, Lawrence J. '76 (ALN) [3] Mahanoy City, PA St. Casimir Church; [C] Ashland, PA Cardinal Brennan Jr./Sr. High School.
Bukauskas, Anthony '46 (STL) Retired.
Bukofsky, James W. '71 (BRK) [181] Queens, NY Immaculate Conception Church.
Bukoski, Joseph, III *ss.cc.* '79 (HON) [H] Kaneohe, HI Congregation of the Sacred Hearts of Jesus and Mary (Hawaii Province SS.CC.); [H] Kaneohe, HI Sacred Hearts Center.
Bukowski, Vincent J. '42 (NEW) Retired.
Bulfer, Stephen C. '73 (FRS) Mariposa, CA St. Joseph Church.
Bulger, Albion F. '56 (MAN) [9] Nashua, NH Resurrection Church.
Bulger, John '64 (SEA) Marysville, WA St. Mary's Church.
Bull, Albert D. '41 (CHI) Retired.
Bullene, Richard *c.s.c.* '83 (FTW) [J] Notre Dame, IN Holy Cross Community, Corby Hall, University of Notre Dame.
Bullene, Richard S. *c.s.c.* '83 (FTW) [B] Notre Dame, IN University of Notre Dame Du Lac.
Bullock, Gabriel G. *o.s.b.* '61 (PEO) [A] Peru, IL St. Bede Abbey and Academy.
Bullock, Myron F. '53 (BO) [4] Gloucester, MA Sacred Heart Church.
Bullock, Robert W. '56 (BO) Sharon, MA Our Lady of Sorrows Church.
Bullock, Scott E. '91 (DUB) Graduate Studies.
Bullwinkel, W. Andrew '78 (SEA) [23] Seattle, WA Christ the King Church.
Bulman, Msgr. Robert T. '40 (TR) Sea Girt, NJ St. Mark Church; Retired.
Bulovas, Msgr. Francis J. '43 (BRK) [247] Queens, NY Transfiguration Church; Retired.
Bultman, Robert S. '67 (EVN) Celestine, IN St. Celestine Church.
Bulwith, Richard E. '67 (CHI) [30] Chicago, IL St. Bonaventure Church; [G] Chicago, IL Catholic Charities of the Archdiocese of Chicago-Archdiocesan Offices.
Bumbar, Philip '68 (SJP) Lyndora, PA St. Michael Church.
Bumbarger, Bruce *m.ss.cc.* '92 (CAM) [8] Camden, NJ Our Lady of Fatima and Mount Carmel Church.
Bump, James F. '78 (GBG) Sutersville, PA St. Charles Borromeo Church.
Bumpus, Harold '63 (SP) Citrus Springs, FL St. Elizabeth Ann Seton Church.
Bumstead, Msgr. John J. '55 (BGP) [5] Danbury, CT St. Peter's Church.
Bunch, Timothy S. '79 (CIN) Fort Loramie, OH St. Michael's Church.
Bunchek, Edward P. '65 (PIT) [3] West Mifflin, PA Holy Trinity Church.
Bunda, Roland *s.m.* (MRY) [G] Santa Cruz, CA Society of Mary, Marianists.
Bunda, Roland *s.m.* '78 (MRY) [J] Monterey, CA Department of Campus Ministry; [J] Monterey, CA Department of Campus Ministry.
Bundz, Michael '81 (STF) Rome, NY St. Michael Church; Utica, NY St. Volodymyr the Great Church.
Bungay, Eugene L. '58 (BEL) Retired.
Bunger, Kevin J. '83 (SY) [2] Binghamton, NY St. Ann Church; Sanitaria Springs, NY St. Joseph Church.

Bungo, Samuel '77 (E) Frenchville, PA St. Mary of the Assumption Church.
Buni, Leon (TR) Lakewood, NJ St. Mary of the Lake Church.
Bunn, James F. '64 (ALT) Ashville, PA St. Thomas Aquinas Church; Fallentimber, PA St. Mary Magdalen's Church; Fallentimber, PA St. Joan of Arc Church.
Bunnell, Adam E. *o.f.m.conv.* '74 (WDC) [B] Washington, DC St. Bonaventure Friary.
Bunnell, Thomas J. *s.j.* '74 (P) [L] Portland, OR Jesuit Provincial Office (Oregon Prov.).
Bunny, Msgr. Michael '65 (LA) Newbury Park, CA St. Julie Billiart Church.
Bunofsky, Walter *s.v.d.* '60 (DUB) [B] Epworth, IA Divine Word College.
Bunse, Gerald L. '83 (SFD) Edwardsville, IL St. Mary Church.
Bunsic, Albert *o.c.d.* '67 (SJ) [M] San Jose, CA Carmelite Monastery, Novitiate.
Buntel, Richard A. (BO) Awaiting Assignment.
Bunyk, Vasyl '93 (PHU) Passaic, NJ St. Nicholas Church.
Buonanno, Vito A. *m.div.* '81 (BRK) [211] Queens, NY Our Lady of Grace Church.
Buongirno, Richard T. '84 (NOR) [1] Middletown, CT St. Francis Church.
Buono, Joseph *c.ss.r.* '43 (BRK) [107] Brooklyn, NY Our Lady of Perpetual Help Basilica.
Buote, Martin L. '60 (FR) [9] New Bedford, MA St. Anne Church.
Bur, George *s.j.* '72 (PH) [H] Philadelphia, PA The Gesu School; [Z] Philadelphia, PA Gesu School Jesuit Community and Outreach Center(S.J.).
Bur, George W. *s.j.* '72 (PH) [BB] Philadelphia, PA Urban House of Prayer.
Bur, Stanislaus '50 (SAG) Retired.
Bura, Msgr. John '71 (PHU) [A] Washington, DC St. Josaphat Seminary.
Burak, Alex '62 (PHU) Edwardsville, PA St. Vladimir's Church; Wilkes-Barre, PA SS. Peter and Paul Church.
Burak, Paul '72 (CHI) Chicago Ridge, IL Our Lady of the Ridge Church.
Burakowski, Anthony E. '36 (HBG) Retired.
Burakowski, Wieslaw '92 (NSH) Clarksville, TN Immaculate Conception Church.
Buranosky, Dennis M. '72 (PIT) Imperial, PA St. Columbkille Church.
Burba, Edward A. '75 (CLV) Bedford, OH St. Mary Church.
Burbach, Jude *o.s.b.* '53 (KCK) Blaine, KS St. Columbkille Church; Lillis, KS St. Joseph's Church; Onaga, KS St. Vincent de Paul Church.
Burbach, Richard C. *s.j.* '88 (MIL) [P] Milwaukee, WI Jesuit Provincial Office, Wisconsin Province.
Burbach, Richard C. *s.j.* '88 (WDC) [M] Washington, DC Leonard Neale House.
Burbank, F. James *c.s.c.* '57 (FR) [B] North Easton, MA Stonehill College.
Burbank, Robert J. '86 (HRT) East Haven, CT St. Vincent de Paul's Church.
Burbank, William '62 (HRT) [17] New Haven, CT St. Rose of Lima Church.
Burbidge, Michael F. '84 (PH) [AA] Merion, PA Religious Sisters of Mercy Convent.
Burch, Francis F. *s.j.* '63 (PH) [C] Philadelphia, PA St. Joseph's University; [Z] Philadelphia, PA Jesuit Community at St. Joseph's University.
Burch, Thaddeus J. *s.j.* '61 (MIL) [C] Milwaukee, WI Marquette University; [P] Milwaukee, WI Jesuit Community at Marquette University.
Burchell, Richard '75 (CLV) [1] Barberton, OH St. Augustine Church.
Burchfield, Michael '93 (FRS) Merced, CA Our Lady of Mercy/St. Patricks Church.
Burchianti, Leo R. '64 (PIT) Retired; [N] Pittsburgh, PA St. John Vianney Manor.
Burchill, John *o.p.* '65 (MAN) [L] Pittsfield, NH Berakah.
Burchill, John Patrick *o.p.* (NY) [Z] New York, NY St. Vincent Ferrer Priory.
Burckhard, Leonard '73 (FAR) [5] Fargo, ND St. Anthony of Padua Church.
Burckhart, William C. '53 (BO) Belmont, MA St. Joseph Church.
Burden, George W. *s.s.j.* '91 (NO) Reserve, LA Our Lady of Grace Church.
Burdess, James J. '88 (ALN) Orefield, PA St. Joseph The Worker Church.
Burdick, Thomas J. '84 (SB) [6] Riverside, CA St. Catherine of Alexandria Church.
Burdiek, Fabian F. *o.f.m.* '74 (STP) [10] St. Paul, MN Sacred Heart Church; St. Paul, MN St. John's Hospital.
Burdt, Eric *o.ss.t.* '65 (MEM) [C] Memphis, TN Christian Brothers High School.
Burdt, Eric T. *o.ss.t.* '65 (BAL) [M] Baltimore, MD Holy Trinity Monastery.
Burdt, Eric T. *o.ss.t.* '65 (MEM) [J] Memphis, TN Order of The Holy Trinity.
Bureau, Germain H. '53 (PRT) Oakland, ME St. Theresa Church.
Burek, Frank J. '71 (CHI) Burbank, IL St. Albert the Great Church.
Burg, Thomas R. '64 (CLV) Absent on Leave.
Burgaleta, Claudio *s.j.* '92 (BO) [W] Chestnut Hill, MA The Jesuit Community at Boston College.
Burgaleta, Claudio M. *s.j.* '92 (NEW) [N] Jersey City, NJ Jesuits of Saint Peter's College, Inc.
Burgard, David G. '94 (DET) Clawson, MI Guardian Angels Church.
Burgdorf, Joseph H. *c.p.m.* '52 (OWN) [F] South Union, KY Fathers of Mercy.
Burge, Robert A. '71 (CLV) Litchfield, OH Our Lady Help of Christians Parish Church.
Burger, Edward K. *s.j.* '70 (KC) [B] Kansas City, MO Rockhurst College; [J] Kansas City, MO Rockhurst College - Jesuit Community.
Burger, Frank '69 (KCK) Olathe, KS Prince of Peace Church.
Burger, Frank J. '38 (KAL) Retired.
Burger, Herman N. '73 (CAM) Ventnor, NJ St. James Church.
Burger, Joseph W. '54 (OKL) Blackwell, OK St. Joseph's Church; Tonkawa, OK St. Joseph's Church; [K] Norman, OK Campus Ministry for the Archdiocese of Oklahoma City.
Burger, Mark '80 (CIN) [63] Cincinnati, OH St. Michael Church
Burger, Mark J. '80 (CIN) [35] Cincinnati, OH Holy Family Church.
Burger, Matthias *o.s.b.* '47 (P) [2] Portland, OR St. Agatha Church; [L] St. Benedict, OR Mt. Angel Abbey.
Burger, Philip G. *v.f.* '83 (HBG) Coal Township, PA Our Lady of Hope Church; Trevorton, PA St. Patrick Church
Burger, Raymond '60 (KCK) Lenexa, KS Holy Trinity Church
Burger, Raymond O. *s.j.* '48 (LC) Prairie du Chien, WI St. John Nepomucene Church.
Burger, Robert '48 (KCK) Lenexa, KS Holy Trinity Church, Retired.
Burget, Joel *o.f.m.conv.* '66 (BEL) [E] Centralia, IL St. Mary's Hospital.
Burghardt, Walter J. *s.j.* '41 (WDC) [E] Washington, DC Gonzaga College High School; [V] Washington, DC Woodstock Theological Center.
Burghoff, Theodore '55 (STL) Kirkwood, MO St. Peter Church.
Burgoon, Charles E. '64 (STL) [36] St. Louis, MO St. Gabriel the Archangel Church.
Burgos, Adnel '88 (BRK) [243] Queens, NY St. Teresa Church.
Burgos, Juan *o.p.* (SJN) [6] Bayamon, PR Santo Domingo de Guzman Church.
Burgoyne, Sidney C. '54 (PH) Boothwyn, PA St. John Fisher Church.
Burian, Edward P. '65 (SFS) Ipswich, SD Holy Cross Church; Leola, SD Our Lady of Perpetual Help Church.
Burk, Bill *s.d.b.* '93 (NY) [3] Port Chester, NY Our Lady of the Rosary Church.
Burkard, Msgr. Paul J.E. '69 (BUF) [3] Orchard Park, NY Our Lady of the Sacred Heart Church.
Burkardt. Msgr. Harold J. '47 (ALT) Newry, PA St. Patrick's Church; Retired.
Burkart, Donald R. '58 (GB) Crivitz, WI St. Mary Church.
Burkart, James M. (GAL) [75] Houston, TX St. Theresa Church.
Burkauskas, Peter M. '79 (PH) [10] Philadelphia, PA St. Andrew Church.
Burke, Alfred '69 (NEW) Berkeley Heights, NJ Church of the Little Flower.
Burke, Alfred M. *o.s.a.* '57 (CHI) [N] Olympia Fields, IL The Augustinian Provincialate Tolentine Center.
Burke, Amadeus *o.f.m.* '35 (BO) [Z] Boston, MA Saint Anthony Residence.
Burke, Msgr. Ambrose J. '21 (DAV) Retired.
Burke, Christopher R. '86 (PBR) Trauger, PA St. Mary's Church.
Burke, Clement '61 (DUB) On Duty Outside the Archdiocese.
Burke, Clement J. '61 (STP) Minneapolis, MN Abbott-Northwestern Hospital.
Burke, David M. '42 (BO) [4] Milton, MA St. Pius Tenth Church.
Burke, Dennis M. *o.praem.* '29 (GB) [E] De Pere, WI St. Norbert College; [I] De Pere, WI St. Joseph Priory.
Burke, Donal (SFR) [B] San Francisco, CA Capuchi House of Studies.
Burke, Donald J. '49 (STL) Bel-Ridge, MO St. Thomas More Church.
Burke, Edmund M. '77 (NY) [1] Kingston, NY Holy Name of Jesus Church; [4] Kingston, NY St. Mary Church.
Burke, Edward *o.f.m.* (NY) Callicoon, NY Community General Hospital.
Burke, Edward *o.f.m.* '62 (SP) [O] St. Petersburg, FL St. Anthony Friary.
Burke, Edward J. *c.m.* '41 (BUF) [C] Niagara University, NY Niagara University; [O] Niagara University, NY Vincentian Community at Niagara University.
Burke, Edward P. '73 (PH) [5] Philadelphia, PA All Saints Church.
Burke, Msgr. Edward T. '35 (BRK) Retired; [V] Brooklyn, NY Monastery of the Sisters Adorers of the Precious Blood.
Burke, Edward T. *s.j.* '56 (SJ) [M] Los Gatos, CA California Province of the Society of Jesus, Jesuit Provincial Office; [M] Los Gatos, CA Sacred Heart Jesuit Center.
Burke, Edward W. *s.j.* '46 (CIN) [M] Cincinnati, OH Faber Jesuit Community.
Burke, Edwin F. '62 (BGP) [3] Norwalk, CT St. Ladislaus Church.
Burke, Eugene A. *c.s.c.* '53 (PHX) [F] Phoenix, AZ Holy Cross Congregation of Casa Santa Cruz.
Burke, Francis J. *s.j.* '60 (STP) [N] Minneapolis, MN La Storta Jesuit Community.
Burke, Geoffrey D. '79 (ALB) Special Assignment; [M] Latham, NY Provincial House of the Sisters of St. Joseph of Carondelet (Albany Province).
Burke, Gilbert J. *o.s.b.* '62 (GBG) [H] Latrobe, PA Saint Vincent Archabbey.
Burke, Gregory '51 (HEL) [6] Butte, MT St. Ann Church.
Burke, Harry '63 (NY) [E] New York, NY Cardinal Hayes High School.
Burke, Henry J. '45 (CHR) Retired.
Burke, James *o.p.* (R) [E] Raleigh, NC De Porres House.
Burke, James *o.p.* '49 (R) [E] Raleigh, NC Dominican Community.
Burke, Msgr. James '64 (PMB) Palm Beach, FL St. Edward Church.
Burke, Msgr. James A. '56 (NEW) Westfield, NJ St. Helen Church.
Burke, James C. '64 (ROC) Avon, NY St. Agnes Church.
Burke, James E. '58 (NY) [227] Staten Island, NY Sacred Heart Church.
Burke, James F. *c.s.sp.* '52 (GAL) Plantersville, TX St. Mary Church.
Burke, James G. '77 (BO) Littleton, MA St. Anne Church.
Burke, James J. *c.ss.r.* '56 (VEN) Wauchula, FL St. Michael Church.
Burke, John C. *c.s.c.* '40 (FTW) [J] South Bend, IN Congregation of Holy Cross Indiana Province Provincial House.
Burke, Msgr. John D. '56 (NY) [204] Staten Island, NY Holy Child Church.
Burke, Msgr. John F. '46 (MAN) [13] Manchester, NH Our Lady of Perpetual Help Church; Retired.
Burke, John F. '55 (WOR) West Boylston, MA Our Lady of Good Counsel Church.
Burke, John R. '54 (E) On Duty Outside Diocese.
Burke, John R. '72 (L) [19] Louisville, KY Christ the King Church.
Burke, John W. *o.p.* '60 (WDC) [B] Washington, DC Dominican House of Studies.
Burke, Joseph A. *s.j.* '51 (WH) [A] Wheeling, WV Wheeling Jesuit University.
Burke, Joseph D. *c.s.c.* '65 (LA) Pacific Palisades, CA Corpus Christi Church.
Burke, Joseph F. *s.j.* '78 (NY) [5] New York, NY St. Aloysius Church.
Burke, Kevin F. *s.j.* '86 (BO) [W] Cambridge, MA Faber House; [W] Cambridge, MA Weston Jesuit Community.
Burke, Lawrence *o.f.m.* '41 (PAT) [N] Ringwood, NJ Mt. St. Francis.
Burke, Leonard J. '42 (BO) Retired.
Burke, Mark J. *s.j.* '93 (BGP) [O] Fairfield, CT The Fairfield Jesuit Community-Fairfield University.
Burke, Michael '50 (CC) Retired.
Burke, Michael *s.c.j.* '63 (CHI) [N] Chicago, IL Priests of the Sacred Heart.
Burke, Michael *s.c.j.* '63 (MIL) [P] Hales Corners, WI Priests of the Sacred Heart.
Burke, Michael J. '62 (PH) [60] Philadelphia, PA Holy Innocents Church.
Burke, Michael J. '76 (PAT) Unassigned.
Burke, Michael L. (MAD) [10] Madison, WI St. Maria Goretti Church.
Burke, Michael M. *o.p.* (R) [E] Raleigh, NC De Porres House.
Burke, Michael M. '50 (NY) Mt. Kisco, NY St. Francis of Assisi Church.
Burke, Michael M. *o.p.* '68 (R) [E] Raleigh, NC Dominican Community.
Burke, Paul A. '96 (ATL) [3] Marietta, GA St. Joseph Church.
Burke, Paul E. *o.s.f.s.* '54 (WIL) [B] Wilmington, DE Salesianum School.
Burke, Peter D. '65 (PH) East Lansdowne, PA St. Cyril of Alexandria Church.
Burke, Richard *c.p.* '76 (MET) [H] South River, NJ Passionist Provincial Office.
Burke, Richard *c.p.* '76 (SCR) [M] Scranton, PA Saint Ann's Passionist Monastery.
Burke. Msgr. Richard J. '51 (ARL) Retired.

Burke, Richard P. (WOR) [B] Worcester, MA Assumption College.
Burke, Richard P. *s.j.* '51 (WOR) [N] Worcester, MA Jesuits of Holy Cross College, Inc.
Burke, Robert E. '47 (DET) [2] Birmingham, MI Holy Name Church.
Burke, Robert M. *o.s.a.* '55 (BO) [C] North Andover, MA Merrimack College.
Burke, Robert R. *s.j.* '64 (BO) [W] Boston, MA The Society of Jesus of New England-Provincial Offices.
Burke, Robert R. *s.j.* '64 (KC) [J] Kansas City, MO Rockhurst College - Jesuit Community.
Burke, Robert R. *s.j.* '65 (KC) [B] Kansas City, MO Rockhurst College.
Burke, Ronald A. '54 (SFR) San Bruno, CA St. Bruno Church.
Burke, Ronald J. '72 (HON) Waipahu, HI Resurrection of the Lord Church.
Burke, Terence '75 (AMA) [E] Amarillo, TX Catholic Family Service, Inc.
Burke, Thomas *c.ss.r.* '81 (ATL) Griffin, GA Sacred Heart Church.
Burke, Thomas J. *o.ss.t.* '78 (BAL) [A] Baltimore, MD St. Mary's Seminary and University; [M] Baltimore, MD Holy Trinity Monastery; [Q] Baltimore, MD Trinitarian Counseling Services, Inc.
Burke, Msgr. Thomas P. '53 (CHL) Retired.
Burke, Vincent de Paul *o.s.f.s.* '57 (WIL) [B] Wilmington, DE Salesianum School.
Burke, Walter C. *o.p.* '40 (PRO) [P] Providence, RI St. Thomas Aquinas Priory at Providence College.
Burke, Walter Dev (SAC) Redding, CA Our Lady of Mercy Church.
Burke, Walter E. '47 (DET) Retired.
Burke, Walter J. *o.praem.* '44 (PH) Paoli, PA St. Norbert Church.
Burke, William '75 (MEM) [I] Memphis, TN St. Peter Manor; [I] Memphis, TN St. Peter Villa.
Burke, William A. '66 (CHI) Lansing, IL St. Ann Church.
Burke, Msgr. William F. '43 (BRK) Retired.
Burke, Msgr. William F. '59 (BAL) [32] Baltimore, MD St. Francis of Assisi Church.
Burke, William P. (RVC) Absent on Leave.
Burke, William T. *s.j.* '69 (ANC) [G] Anchorage, AK Holy Spirit Retreat House.
Burkemper, Robert W. '81 (STL) [5] Florissant, MO St. Dismas Church.
Burkert, Gerald F. (IND) Beech Grove, IN Holy Name Church.
Burkett, William C. '71 (MIL) Brookfield, WI St. John Vianney Church.
Burkey, Blaine E. *o.f.m.cap.* '61 (SAL) [D] Hays, KS St. Bonaventure's Friary; [H] Hays, KS Comeau Catholic Campus Center at Fort Hays State University.
Burkhalter, Ross C. '94 (OM) [30] Omaha, NE Mary Our Queen Church.
Burkhard, John D. *o.f.m.conv.* '67 (WDC) [B] Washington, DC St. Bonaventure Friary.
Burkhardt, Alan T. '86 (LC) [3] Stevens Point, WI St. Joseph Church.
Burkhardt, Godfrey F. *o.s.b.* '45 (GBG) [H] Latrobe, PA Saint Vincent Archabbey.
Burkhardt, Odilo *o.s.b.* '50 (SFS) [F] Marvin, SD Blue Cloud Abbey.
Burkhart, John J. *o.s.a.* '56 (DET) Grosse Pointe Park, MI St. Clare of Montefalco Church.
Burkhart, Roy *c.s.sp.* '44 (FRS) [C] Bakersfield, CA Mercy Healthcare Bakersfield.
Burkholder, Robert '47 (DET) Retired.
Burkle, Raymond A. '90 (DUB) [4] Waterloo, IA St. Edward's Church.
Burkley, John T. '70 (CLV) [5] Euclid, OH St. Robert Bellarmine Church; [AA] Euclid, OH St. Robert's Holy Name Society Boosters.
Burks, William P. '86 (L) Pleasure Ridge Park, KY St. Polycarp Church.
Burkus, John '40 (ELP) Retired.
Burla, Francis J. '63 (NEW) Montclair, NJ Immaculate Conception Church.
Burlas, Anthony J. *o.s.b.* '58 (GBG) Forbes Road, PA St. Mary Church; [H] Latrobe, PA Saint Vincent Archabbey.
Burlton, Msgr. Francis H. '54 (BEA) [6] Beaumont, TX Our Lady of the Assumption Church.
Burmester, Edwin J. '40 (STL) [36] St. Louis, MO St. Gabriel the Archangel Church; Retired.
Burn, William C. '56 (CHR) Retired.
Burnell, George F. *o.s.a.* '45 (PH) [C] Villanova, PA Villanova University; [Z] Villanova, PA St. Thomas Monastery.
Burnell, Robert J. '70 (CHI) Morton Grove, IL St. Martha Church.
Burnet, Donald *o.m.i.* '66 (SAT) [M] San Antonio, TX Provincial Administration Office, Oblates of Mary Immaculate (Southern Prov.).
Burnet, Jerome *o.m.i.* (SAT) [M] San Antonio, TX Provincial Administration Office, Oblates of Mary Immaculate (Southern Prov.); [S] San Antonio, TX Missionary Oblates of Mary Immaculate of Texas Continuing Care Foundation.
Burnet, Jerome C. *o.m.i.* (SAT) [B] San Antonio, TX George Sexton House of Studies.
Burnett, Eugene David *o.f.m.* '54 (LA) [72] Los Angeles, CA St. Joseph Church.
Burnett, Eugene David *o.f.m.* '54 (ORG) [C] Santa Ana, CA Mater Dei High School; [H] Santa Ana, CA Franciscan Fathers.
Burnett, George P. '61 (HRT) [1] Ansonia, CT Assumption Church.
Burnett, James '68 (JOL) [2] Naperville, IL Sts. Peter and Paul Church.
Burnett, James E. '74 (DAV) Military Chaplains.
Burnett, John C. '85 (SFD) [2] Springfield, IL Blessed Sacrament Church.
Burnett, Robert E. '55 (SCR) Plains, PA Sacred Heart Church.
Burnett, Timothy J. *o.s.b.* '80 (NO) [A] St. Benedict, LA St. Joseph's Seminary College; [P] St. Benedict, LA St. Joseph Abbey.
Burnette, Kurt '89 (SB) [5] Fontana, CA St. Nicholas Church.
Burnette, Kurt '89 (VNN) Fontana, CA St. Nicholas Church.
Burnham, Alfred S. '76 (LA) Culver City, CA St. Augustine Church.
Burnia, Scott '88 (SD) Jamul, CA St. Pius X Church.
Burnie, James H. *c.s.sp.* '93 (SB) Hemet, CA Our Lady of the Valley Church.
Burns, Msgr. A. Francis '63 (NY) [7] Mt. Vernon, NY St. Ursula Church.
Burns, Msgr. Bernard '38 (SFE) Retired.
Burns, Bernard J. '53 (SAC) Portola, CA Holy Family Church.
Burns, Charles D. *s.v.d.* '62 (OAK) [20] Oakland, CA St. Patrick's Church.
Burns, Charles E. '58 (GAL) Retired.
Burns, Charles F. *s.j.* '72 (STP) [6] St. Paul, MN The Immaculate Heart of Mary Church.
Burns, Clement *o.p.* '54 (CIN) [30] Cincinnati, OH St. Gertrude Church; [M] Cincinnati, OH St. Gertrude Priory.
Burns, Cyril J. '56 (SPR) South Hadley, MA St. Theresa of the Infant Jesus Church.
Burns, David E. '61 (GAL) Retired.
Burns, Dennis J. '50 (BO) Marblehead, MA Our Lady, Star of the Sea Church.
Burns, Donald W. '50 (STP) Retired.
Burns, Edward J. *o.s.a.* '40 (PH) [Z] Villanova, PA St. Thomas Monastery.
Burns, Edward J. '54 (FR) Retired.
Burns, Edward J. '83 (PIT) [A] Pittsburgh, PA Saint Paul Seminary.
Burns, Ernest '51 (HEL) Retired.
Burns, Eugene P. '55 (CHI) Retired.
Burns, Francis H. '48 (DET) Retired.
Burns, Msgr. G. Thomas '57 (NEW) Livingston, NJ St. Raphael Church.
Burns, Gerald H. '69 (BR) Napoleonville, LA St. Anne Church; Plattenville, LA Assumption of the Blessed Virgin Mary Church.
Burns, Msgr. Gerald J. '50 (SCR) Retired; [N] Dunmore, PA Villa St. Joseph.
Burns, Hugh D. *o.p.* '82 (NEW) [27] Jersey City, NJ Sacred Heart Church.
Burns, James '62 (GLP) Retired.
Burns, James P. '93 (STP) [20] St. Paul, MN St. Francis De Sales Church.
Burns, John '90 (PEO) Kewanee, IL St. Francis of Assisi Church.
Burns, John '95 (MRY) [4] Salinas, CA Madonna Del Sasso Church.
Burns, John A. *c.s.sp.* '42 (ALX) [F] Natchitoches, LA Holy Ghost Fathers Home, Maison Brothier.
Burns, John A. '48 (BRK) [83] Brooklyn, NY Mary Queen of Heaven Church.
Burns, John F. '48 (BO) Retired.
Burns, John M. '82 (STP) [O] Lake Elmo, MN Carmel of Our Lady of Divine Providence; [T] Lake Elmo, MN Hermits of the Most Blessed Virgin Mary of Mount Carmel.
Burns, John R. '65 (ALB) South Kortright, NY Church of the Most Precious Blood of Jesus.
Burns, John R. '90 (PEO) Walnut, IL St. John's Church.
Burns, John T. '58 (CIN) Retired.
Burns, Joseph '55 (JOL) Steger, IL St. Liborius Church.
Burns, Joseph H. '60 (CAM) Hammonton, NJ St. Anthony of Padua Church.
Burns, Msgr. Lawrence E. '56 (MAN) Portsmouth, NH St. Catherine of Siena Church.
Burns, Lawrence E. '62 (BUF) Blasdell, NY Our Mother of Good Counsel Church.
Burns, Lawrence J. *m.m.* (BO) Wakefield, MA St. Joseph Church.
Burns, Lawrence J. '64 (SC) Carroll, IA St. Lawrence Church.
Burns, Leo J. *s.j.* '36 (MIL) [P] Wauwatosa, WI Jesuit Community at St. Camillus.
Burns, Malcolm J. (GAL) On Duty Outside the Diocese.
Burns, Malcolm J. '85 (RVC) Oyster Bay, NY St. Dominic's Church.
Burns, Michael '83 (LA) Venice, CA St. Mark Church.
Burns, Michael J. '58 (SJ) Los Altos, CA St. William Church.
Burns, Michael J. '73 (TR) Bordentown, NJ St. Mary Church.
Burns, Norbert C. *s.m.* '53 (CIN) [D] Dayton, OH The University of Dayton; [M] Dayton, OH Marianist Provincialate.
Burns, Patrick *m.c.c.j.* '82 (CHI) Blue Island, IL St. Donatus Church.
Burns, Patrick G. '92 (BRK) [157] Queens, NY Blessed Sacrament Church.
Burns, Patrick J. *s.j.* '50 (MIL) [C] Milwaukee, WI Marquette University.
Burns, Patrick J. *s.j.* '63 (MIL) [P] Milwaukee, WI Jesuit Community at Marquette University.
Burns, Paul D. *c.s.s.* '62 (WOR) Milford, MA Sacred Heart Church.
Burns, Peter *s.j.* '92 (LA) [C] Los Angeles, CA Loyola Marymount University.
Burns, Robert A. *o.p.* '61 (TUC) [I] Tucson, AZ University of Arizona.
Burns, Robert E. '44 (CHI) [31] Chicago, IL St. Bride Church; Retired.
Burns, Robert I. *s.j.* '52 (LA) [C] Los Angeles, CA Loyola Marymount University.
Burns, Robert O. *s.j.* '57 (OM) [K] Omaha, NE Jesuit Community At Creighton University.
Burns, T. Lee '56 (PRT) Retired.
Burns, Thomas '44 (SFS) Retired.
Burns, Thomas *m.s.c.* '64 (RCK) [H] Aurora, IL Missionaries of the Sacred Heart Community.
Burns, Thomas E. (CAM) Retired.
Burns, Thomas J. '54 (SFR) Retired.
Burns, Thomas L. *s.c.j.* '65 (JKS) Booneville, MS St. Francis of Assisi Church; Corinth, MS St. James Church.
Burns, Timothy L. '76 (BIR) [5] Huntsville, AL Our Lady Queen of the Universe Church.
Burns, Tom *m.s.c.* '65 (SB) Upland, CA St. Joseph Church.
Burns, Msgr. Vincent L. '56 (PH) [1] Drexel Hill, PA St. Andrew Church.
Burns, Vincent M. *s.j.* '57 (BGP) [A] Fairfield, CT Fairfield University; [O] Fairfield, CT The Fairfield Jesuit Community-Fairfield University.
Burns, Vincent P. '67 (PH) Military Chaplains.
Burns, William A. '33 (ROC) Waverly, NY St. James Church; Retired.
Burns, William J. '53 (BO) Walpole, MA St. Mary Church.
Burns, William L. '85 (HRT) Naugatuck, CT St. Francis of Assisi Church.
Burr, Jeremiah R. *m.m.* '67 (NY) [Z] Maryknoll, NY Maryknoll Fathers and Brothers.
Burr, Thomas E. '74 (RCK) McHenry, IL St. Mary Church.
Burr, Thomas W. '61 (ROC) Horseheads, NY St. Mary Our Mother Church.
Burrascano, Anthony P. *o.s.a.* '79 (PH) Bryn Mawr, PA Our Mother of Good Counsel Church; [Z] Villanova, PA Provincial Offices of the Order of St. Augustine, Province of St. Thomas of Villanova.
Burrell, David B. *c.s.c.* '59 (FTW) [B] Notre Dame, IN University of Notre Dame Du Lac; [J] Notre Dame, IN Holy Cross Community, Corby Hall, University of Notre Dame.
Burrows, Michael *o.s.b.* '80 (RCK) [H] Aurora, IL Marmion Abbey-St. Augustine's Abbey.
Burruano, Albert J. (PH) [88] Philadelphia, PA St. Lucy Church.
Burrus, Barry '93 (LEX) Pikeville, KY St. Francis of Assisi Church.
Burshek, James J. *s.j.* '75 (OAK) [N] Berkeley, CA Jesuit Community at Jesuit School of Theology at Berkeley.
Burshnick, Francis J. *s.c.j.* '70 (JKS) Southhaven, MS Christ the King Church; Walls, MS Sacred Heart Church; [E] Nesbit, MS St. Michael Community House.
Burson, James *c.j.m.* '63 (SD) [3] San Diego, CA Blessed Sacrament Church; San Diego, CA Alvarado, Grossmont and Kaiser Hospitals.
Burt, Donald X. *o.s.a.* '55 (PH) [C] Villanova, PA Villanova University; [Z] Villanova, PA St. Thomas Monastery.
Burt, Julian F. *o.s.b.* '41 (GBG) [H] Latrobe, PA Saint Vincent Archabbey.
Burtchaell, James T. *c.s.c.* '53 (TR) [N] Princeton, NJ Our Lady of Princeton.
Burtchaell, James T. *c.s.c.* '60 (FTW) [J] South Bend, IN Congregation of Holy Cross Indiana Province Provincial House.
Burton, C. Jeffries *s.j.* '67 (CAM) Pleasantville, NJ St. Peter's Church; [Q] Mays Landing, NJ Atlantic Community College; [Q] Pomona, NJ Richard Stockton College of New Jersey.
Burton, Charles '80 (KNX) Kingsport, TN St. Dominic Church; Sneedville, TN St. James the Apostle Church.
Burton, John F.X. *s.j.* '54 (DEN) [2] Lakewood, CO Christ on the Mountain Parish Church.

Burton, John H. '72 (CAM) Villas, NJ St. Raymond Church.
Burton, Msgr. Richard '63 (WDC) [5] Washington, DC St. Anthony Church.
Burton, William *o.f.m.* '89 (SFD) [B] Quincy, IL Quincy University.
Burtschi, J. Richard *s.j.* '71 (STL) [P] St. Louis, MO Jesuit Community Corporation at St. Louis University - Jesuit Hall.
Burwinkel, Elmer J. '84 (IND) Retired.
Bury, Harold J. '55 (STP) On Duty Outside the Archdiocese.
Buryska, James '65 (WIN) [G] Rochester, MN General Motherhouse of the Sisters of the Third Order Regular of St. Francis of the Congregation of Our.
Burzynski, Michael H. '89 (BUF) [3] Kenmore, NY St. John the Baptist Church.
Burzynski, Regis *o.f.m.* '55 (GAY) Whittemore, MI St. James Church.
Bus, Anthony *c.r.* '84 (CHI) [193] Chicago, IL St. Stanislaus Kostka Church.
Busca, Salvatore L. *s.p.* '55 (SB) [G] Cherry Valley, CA Servants of the Paraclete Guadalupe Retreat Center.
Busch, Msgr. Aloysius J. '52 (PAT) Highland Lakes, NJ Our Lady of Fatima Church.
Busch, Arthur A. '58 (WCH) [2] Wichita, KS All Saints Church.
Busch, August '56 (EVN) Retired.
Busch, James *c.p.* '42 (SAC) [H] Citrus Heights, CA Christ the King Retreat.
Busch, Jan H. *o.s.a.* '49 (PH) [C] Villanova, PA Villanova University; [Z] Villanova, PA St. Thomas Monastery.
Busch, John *o.m.i.* '40 (SAT) [K] San Antonio, TX Oblate Madonna Residence.
Busch, Joseph '80 (ALB) [1] Watervliet, NY St. Brigid Church.
Busch, Peter *t.o.r.* '45 (SP) Pinellas Park, FL Sacred Heart Church.
Busch, Robert '93 (AMA) [11] Amarillo, TX St. Thomas the Apostle Church; [K] Canyon, TX Catholic Student Center at West Texas A & M University.
Busch, Vernon *o.f.m.cap.* '60 (BAL) Cumberland, MD SS. Peter and Paul Church; [M] Cumberland, MD SS. Peter and Paul Friary.
Buscher, Adelbert *o.s.b.* '41 (IND) [J] St. Meinrad, IN St. Meinrad Archabbey.
Buscher, Adelbert *o.s.b.* '41 (VEN) [2] Fort Myers, FL Church Of The Resurrection Of Our Lord.
Buschmiller, Robert J. '44 (CIN) [20] Cincinnati, OH St. Cecilia Church; Retired.
Busco, Msgr. John J. '40 (PH) [3] Norristown, PA Holy Saviour Church; Retired.
Buse, Harold J. '77 (OM) Norfolk, NE Sacred Heart Church.
Busemeyer, Louis E. *s.j.* '70 (CHI) [D] Chicago, IL St. Ignatius Jesuit Community.
Bush, Bernard J. *s.j.* '65 (SJ) [L] Los Altos, CA Jesuit Retreat House.
Bush, Edward E. '57 (PEO) Colona, IL St. Patrick's Church.
Bush, Frederick W. '51 (ROC) Penfield, NY Holy Spirit Church.
Bush, John H. '39 (LAN) Retired.
Bush, Robert '69 (SAN) [1] Abilene, TX Sacred Heart Church.
Bush, Scott '92 (HON) Hilo, HI St. Joseph Church.
Bush, William C. '62 (LEX) Nicholasville, KY St. Luke Church.
Bushee, Richard J. '88 (PRO) [12] Providence, RI St. Edward's Church.
Bushell, Ralph *c.pp.s.* '49 (KC) [J] Liberty, MO Precious Blood Center.
Busher, Robert J. '76 (DAV) Oskaloosa, IA St. Mary's Church.
Bushinski, Edward A. *c.s.sp.* '50 (PIT) [B] Pittsburgh, PA Duquesne University of the Holy Ghost.
Bushy, Timothy F. '83 (CR) [1] Crookston, MN Cathedral of the Immaculate Conception ; [B] Crookston, MN Cathedral - Religious Education/Faith Formation.
Bushy, Timothy F. '83 (FAR) On Duty Outside the Diocese.
Bussen, Robert J. '71 (SLC) Park City, UT St. Mary of the Assumption Church.
Bustamante, Arturo *o.f.m.* '81 (ELP) Presidio, TX Santa Teresa de Jesus Church.
Bustamante, Francisco '83 (NY) [Z] New York, NY Jesuit Provincial's Office.
Busteed, Francis '51 (SAT) Absent on Sick Leave.
Busteed, Robert T. '69 (SCR) Bastress, PA Immaculate Conception Church.
Bustinza, Pedro *o.ss.t.* '63 (ARE) Isabela, PR St. Anthony Church.
Butcavage, Leonard M. '72 (SCR) [5] Hazleton, PA Holy Trinity Church.
Butch, Ananius G. *o.s.b.* '93 (E) St. Marys, PA Sacred Heart of Jesus Church.
Butch, Brian (TR) Princeton, NJ St. Paul Church.
Butera, George J. '68 (BO) Beverly, MA St. John the Evangelist Church.
Butkowski, Alto *o.s.b.* '41 (SCL) [I] Collegeville, MN St. John's Abbey, of the Order of St. Benedict.
Butkus, Casimir '46 (DET) Retired.
Butler, Allan L.W. '67 (BO) Abington, MA St. Bridget Church.
Butler, Arthur *o.f.m.* '43 (PAT) [M] Ringwood, NJ Holy Name Friary.
Butler, B. '44 (STA) [F] Jacksonville, FL All Saints Home.
Butler, Bede J. *o.s.b.* '51 (PBL) [E] Canon City, CO Holy Cross Abbey.
Butler, Daniel J. '66 (PT) Niceville, FL Holy Name of Jesus Church.
Butler, David A. *o.p.* '57 (L) [4] Springfield, KY St. Rose Church.
Butler, Francis *s.s.j.* '85 (LAF) Church Point, LA Our Mother of Mercy Church.
Butler, Francis T. '54 (HRT) Canaan, CT St. Joseph's Church.
Butler, Henry J. *s.j.* '40 (BO) [W] Weston, MA Campion Health Center, Inc.
Butler, James F. '69 (R) Southern Pines, NC St. Anthony of Padua Church.
Butler, Msgr. James M. '52 (ALN) [4] Bethlehem, PA Holy Infancy Church.
Butler, James P. (BO) Absent on Sick Leave.
Butler, John '60 (HON) On Duty Outside the Diocese.
Butler, John J. '54 (L) [C] Louisville, KY Sacred Heart Academy; [M] Louisville, KY Ursuline Motherhouse of the Immaculate Conception.
Butler, John M. '72 (GBG) [3] Connellsville, PA St. John the Evangelist Church.
Butler, John R. '57 (MET) Colonia, NJ St. John Vianney Church.
Butler, Michael '85 (R) Absent on Leave.
Butler, Michael C. '84 (COS) [3] Colorado Springs, CO Divine Redeemer Church.
Butler, Michael T. '89 (STL) [A] St. Louis, MO Kenrick-Glennon Seminary.
Butler, Norman O. *m.s.* '62 (HRT) [M] Hartford, CT Missionaries of LaSalette Provincial Secretary.
Butler, Patrick J. '82 (ALB) Guilderland, NY Christ the King Church.
Butler, Paul '94 (FTW) [10] South Bend, IN Holy Family Church.
Butler, Paul F. '87 (RVC) Oyster Bay, NY St. Dominic's Church.
Butler, Rene J. *m.s.* '73 (SPR) [1] Westfield, MA Holy Trinity Church.
Butler, Richard (BO) [4] Norwood, MA St. Timothy Church.
Butler, Robert E. *s.j.* '58 (LA) Alhambra, CA St. Thomas More Church.
Butler, Robert J. '62 (BO) Pepperell, MA St. Joseph Church.
Butler, Robert R. *m.s.* '69 (HRT) [M] Hartford, CT Missionaries of LaSalette Provincial Secretary.
Butler, Thomas *o.carm.* '50 (L) [59] Louisville, KY Our Lady of Mount Carmel Church.
Butler, Thomas J. *c.m.* '77 (PH) [B] Philadelphia, PA DePaul Novitiate; [Z] Philadelphia, PA Congregation of the Mission.
Butler, Thomas W. '82 (LAN) Hillsdale, MI St. Anthony Church.
Butler, Timothy A. '88 (BO) Military & VA Chaplains.
Butler, Victor *s.v.d.* '64 (TR) [M] Bordentown, NJ Society of the Divine Word.
Butler, Vincent E. *s.j.* '63 (NY) [F] New York, NY Xavier High School.
Butler, William *c.s.sp.* '44 (STA) Orange Park, FL St. Catherine's Church.
Butler, William L. '61 (BO) [4] Revere, MA St. Mary of the Assumption Church.
Butler, Xavier *s.a.* '47 (NY) [Z] Garrison, NY Franciscan Friars of the Atonement.
Butori, Harry '52 (HEL) [1] Butte, MT Butte Catholic Community North Church; [9] Butte, MT St. Joseph Church.
Butrie, Matthew Peter '95 (PSC) New York, NY St. Mary's Church.
Butryn, Msgr. Richard E. '58 (E) Meadville, PA St. Brigid Church; Meadville, PA Crawford Country Home.
Butsch, Matthew *o.s.b.* '43 (P) [L] St. Benedict, OR Mt. Angel Abbey.
Butters, Craig '83 (ORG) [2] Anaheim, CA St. Boniface Church.
Butters, Joseph E. '65 (JOL) Mokena, IL St. Mary Church.
Buttimer, Joseph J. '63 (SD) Leave of Absence.
Buttimer, Maurice L. *s.j.* '43 (BO) [W] Weston, MA Campion Health Center, Inc.
Buttinelli, Anthony '38 (NY) Retired.
Buttini, Mario S. *o.s.j.* '39 (SCR) [B] Pittston, PA St. Joseph's Oblate Seminary; [M] Pittston, PA Eastern Province of the Oblates of St. Joseph.
Buttner, Michael '78 (CHL) Lenoir, NC St. Francis of Assisi Church.
Buttner, Michael T. '75 (BAL) [51] Baltimore, MD St. Lawrence Church.
Buttomer, Jeremiah R. *c.s.c.* '43 (AUS) [H] Austin, TX Congregation of Holy Cross - Southern Province.
Buttomer, Jeremiah R. *c.s.c.* '43 (FTW) [J] South Bend, IN Congregation of Holy Cross Indiana Province Provincial House.
Buttrick, Dean T. '63 (SUP) [3] Superior, WI St. Anthony Church; Lake Nebagamon, WI St. Anthony Church.
Butz, Crispin *o.f.m.* '50 (SFE) [J] Albuquerque, NM San Antonio Provincial Friary Franciscan Friars.
Buu, Francis X. '74 (NY) [52] New York, NY Immaculate Conception Church.
Buvala, Andrew *o.f.m.* '47 (GAY) Peshabestown, MI Blessed Kateri Tekakwitha Church.
Buvala, Medard *o.f.m.* '43 (JOL) [11] Joliet, IL St. John the Baptist Church; [J] Joliet, IL St. John the Baptist Friary.
Buvens, Edward P. *s.j.* '69 (NO) [F] New Orleans, LA Jesuit High School.
Buvens, Msgr. Norman '64 (SHP) Bossier City, LA Christ the King Church.
Buxkemper, Msgr. Roland '65 (LUB) [8] Lubbock, TX St. Theresa's Church; Shallowater, TX St. Phillip Benizi Church.
Buxman, Donald R. '70 (P) Oregon City, OR St. John the Apostle Church.
Buyansky, Timothy *o.s.b.* '69 (CLV) [E] Cleveland, OH Benedictine High School; [P] Cleveland, OH Benedictine Order of Cleveland.
Buzek, Joseph J. '42 (ORL) Retired.
Buzek, Joseph L. '42 (COL) Retired.
Buzga, John *glmy.* (TLS) Idabel, OK St. Francis De Sales Church.
Buzynski, Laurin *o.f.m.* (SFD) [K] Sherman, IL Our Lady of Angels Friary.
Buzzelli, Aaron N. *o.s.b.* '77 (GBG) [H] Latrobe, PA Saint Vincent Archabbey.
Buzzerio, Joseph E. '77 (NEW) Hackensack, NJ Bergen County Sheriff Detention Center.
Buzzerio, Joseph R. (NEW) Paramus, NJ Bergen County Youth Detention Center.
Byabato, Deus-Dedit (NOR) Willimantic, CT St. Joseph Church.
Byaruhanga, Frederick '89 (LA) [70] Los Angeles, CA St. Joan of Arc Church.
Bydlon, Msgr. Adam J. '46 (PH) [78] Philadelphia, PA St. John Cantius Church; Retired.
Byer, James M. '81 (CHL) Maggie Valley, NC St. Margaret Church.
Byerley, E. Joseph '93 (CAM) Woodbury, NJ St. Patrick's Church.
Byerley, Timothy E. '85 (CAM) [4] Cherry Hill, NJ St. Pius X Church.
Byers, Dohrman W. (CIN) Arnheim, OH St. Mary Church; Sardinia, OH St. Elizabeth Parish Church.
Byers, John A. '95 (LAN) [1] Ann Arbor, MI St. Francis of Assisi Church.
Byington, Edward J. '70 (FR) Hyannis, MA St. Francis Xavier's Church.
Bykowski, Norbert H. '56 (CHI) Military Chaplains.
Bynon, Msgr. Joseph P. '56 (BRK) [233] Queens, NY Resurrection-Ascension Church.
Byrd, Freddie '88 (IND) [B] St. Meinrad, IN St. Meinrad Seminary-College of Liberal Arts.
Byrd, Freddie '88 (OWN) On Duty Outside the Diocese.
Byrd, Howard W. *s.s.j.* '75 (NO) [4] New Orleans, LA Blessed Sacrament Church.
Byrd, Thomas J. '50 (BAL) Retired; [C] Emmitsburg, MD Mount Saint Mary's College.
Byrider, Charles L. '41 (CLV) [5] Akron, OH St. Francis de Sales Church; [17] Akron, OH St. Sebastian Church; Retired.
Byrne, Albert F. '47 (STP) North St. Paul, MN St. Peter Church.
Byrne, Albert J. '79 (ALN) Frackville, PA St. Joseph Church; Maizeville, PA Our Lady of Siluva Church.
Byrne, Alexius W. *s.j.* '53 (SEA) [A] Seattle, WA Seattle University.
Byrne, Basil *o.c.s.o.* '76 (WOR) [N] Spencer, MA St. Joseph's Abbey.
Byrne, David J. '78 (CHI) Evergreen Park, IL St. Bernadette Church.
Byrne, Edward *c.ss.r.* '44 (BRK) [107] Brooklyn, NY Our Lady of Perpetual Help Basilica.
Byrne, Edward G. '64 (NY) Ossining, NY St. Ann Church.
Byrne, Francis A. *c.m.* '62 (STL) [P] Perryville, MO Congregation of The Mission.
Byrne, Frederick *o.s.b.* '82 (ALT) [I] University Park, PA Penn State Catholic Community.
Byrne, Gary '87 (MRY) Hollister, CA Sacred Heart Church; Tres Pinos, CA Immaculate Conception Church.
Byrne, George '69 (SD) Del Mar, CA St. William of York Church.
Byrne, Glen F. (BO) [11] Boston, MA St. Anthony Church.
Byrne, Glenn '75 (BAL) Special Assignment; Educational Sabbatical.
Byrne, Msgr. Harry J. '46 (NY) Retired.
Byrne, Harry M. *o.p.* '78 (STL) [B] St. Louis, MO Aquinas Institute of Theology.

Byrne, Msgr. Henry L. '37 (STL) Retired.
Byrne, Hugh A. '62 (BRK) [246] Queens, NY St. Thomas More-St. Edmund Church.
Byrne, J. Patrick '55 (COL) On Duty Outside the Diocese.
Byrne, James A.P. *s.j.* '47 (WDC) [E] North Bethesda, MD Georgetown Preparatory School.
Byrne, James F. '52 (IND) Retired.
Byrne, James O. '37 (CIN) St. Marys, OH Holy Rosary Church; Retired.
Byrne, James P. *o.s.f.s.* '60 (ALN) Robesonia, PA St. Francis de Sales Church.
Byrne, Joel *o.f.m.* '51 (SAN) Big Lake, TX St. Margaret of Cortona Church.
Byrne, John F. *s.s.j.* '66 (BAL) [M] Baltimore, MD St. Joseph Society of the Sacred Heart House of Central Administration; [M] Baltimore, MD St. Joseph's Manor.
Byrne, John H. '44 (STL) Retired.
Byrne, John J. '25 (RVC) Retired; [N] Uniondale, NY St. Pius X Residence.
Byrne, Msgr. John T. '45 (STL) Retired.
Byrne, Joseph F. '69 (BO) [5] Waltham, MA Our Lady, Comforter of the Afflicted Church.
Byrne, Joseph L. '54 (HEL) Townsend, MT Holy Cross Church.
Byrne, Msgr. Laserian '48 (FRS) [7] Fresno, CA St. Anthony of Padua Church.
Byrne, Laurence *s.d.b.* '53 (OAK) [E] Richmond, CA Salesian High School.
Byrne, Luke J. *s.j.* '65 (STL) [P] St. Louis, MO White House Retreat Jesuit Community; [T] St. Louis, MO White House Retreat.
Byrne, Mel *c.p.* '64 (LA) Monrovia, CA Immaculate Conception Church.
Byrne, Paul '51 (SEA) Retired.
Byrne, Peter J. '84 (NY) [191] Bronx, NY St. Thomas Aquinas Church; [207] Staten Island, NY Immaculate Conception Church; [208] Staten Island, NY St. John the Baptist de La Salle Church.
Byrne, Pierce D. '53 (NEW) [2] Linden, NJ Holy Family Church.
Byrne, Raymond J. '57 (NY) Irvington-on-the-Hudson, NY Immaculate Conception Church.
Byrne, Robert '44 (KC) Retired.
Byrne, Robert H. '75 (SAG) Shields, MI Holy Spirit Church.
Byrne, Robert P. '50 (LA) Retired.
Byrne, Thomas C. *o.s.b.* '49 (RIC) [M] Richmond, VA Mary Mother of the Church Abbey.
Byrne, Thomas H. *s.j.* '53 (SJ) [D] San Jose, CA Bellarmine College Preparatory.
Byrne, Thomas J. *s.j.* '53 (SJ) San Jose, CA Agnews State Hospital.
Byrne, Thomas R. '58 (DET) [1] Monroe, MI St. Anne Church; Special Assignment.
Byrne, Tom *c.s.sp.* '64 (GAL) [67] Houston, TX St. Philip Neri Church.
Byrne, W. Gordon '32 (NEW) Retired.
Byrne, William D. '94 (WDC) [2] Rockville, MD Shrine of St. Jude Church.
Byrnes, Donald M. '55 (NO) St. Bernard, LA St. Bernard Church.
Byrnes, Edward M. '80 (MEM) [11] Memphis, TN Holy Spirit Church.
Byrnes, Francis J. '51 (BRK) Absent on Sick Leave; Retired.
Byrnes, James J. '80 (STL) Chesterfield, MO Incarnate Word Church.
Byrnes, James T. '86 (NY) [E] New York, NY Cardinal Hayes High School.
Byrnes, John D. '94 (ALT) [13] Johnstown, PA Our Mother of Sorrows Church; [B] Johnstown, PA Bishop McCort High School.
Byrnes, John J. *o.s.a.* '55 (ALB) Waterford, NY St. Mary of the Assumption Church.
Byrnes, John J. '66 (CAM) Bellmawr, NJ Mary, Mother of the Church; [A] Haddonfield, NJ Paul VI High School.
Byrnes, John J. '94 (ALT) [11] Johnstown, PA St. Michael's Church.
Byrnes, John P. '45 (TR) Retired.
Byrnes, John W. '47 (BRK) [183] Queens, NY SS. Joachim and Anne Church.
Byrnes, Michael J. '96 (DET) [4] St. Clair Shores, MI St. Joan of Arc Church.
Byrnes, Paul A. (BAL) Frostburg, MD St. Michael Church.
Byrnes, Robert R. '67 (GBG) Leechburg, PA Church of the Assumption.
Byrnes, Timothy '52 (LAN) [3] Lansing, MI Holy Cross Church.
Byrns, Joseph P. '69 (BRK) [127] Brooklyn, NY St. Rose of Lima Church.
Byrolly, Bruce '58 (WIL) Cambridge, MD St. Mary Refuge of Sinners Church.
Byron, J. Michael (STP) [C] St. Paul, MN University of St. Thomas.
Byron, J. Michael '89 (STP) Graduate Studies.
Byron, Joseph F. '53 (WDC) Potomac, MD Our Lady of Mercy Church; Retired.
Byron, Patrick J. '58 (YAK) Retired.
Byron, William '62 (YAK) Roslyn, WA Immaculate Conception Church.
Byron, William J. *s.j.* '61 (WDC) [M] Washington, DC The Jesuit Community at Georgetown University.
Byrth, Peter *o.carm.* '59 (JOL) [J] Darien, IL Carmelite Community; [M] Darien, IL Provincial Office of Lay Carmelites and Scapular Confraternity.
Bzdyra, Stephen '79 (HRT) Wallingford, CT SS. Peter and Paul Church.

C

Caamano, Raphael '78 (BO) [V] Chestnut Hill, MA Opus Dei.
Cabala, Thomas S. '79 (CHI) South Holland, IL St. Jude the Apostle Church.
Caballe, Peter *c.m.f.* '36 (SAT) [12] San Antonio, TX Immaculate Heart of Mary Church.
Caballero, Francisco (SB) Ontario, CA Our Lady of Guadalupe Church.
Caballero, Francisco '53 (TOL) Retired.
Caballero, Lloyd C. '40 (BR) Retired.
Cabanas, R. Jaime '55 (BWN) [1] Harlingen, TX Our Lady of the Assumption Church.
Cabaong, Honorato '60 (HEL) Deer Lodge, MT Montana State Prison; Warm Springs, MT Warm Springs State Hospital.
Cabasino, Philip *c.ss.r.* '47 (BO) [13] Boston, MA Basilica of Our Lady of Perpetual Help.
Cabasino, Philip A. *c.ss.r.* '47 (BO) Boston, MA Massachusetts Mental Health Center; Boston, MA V.A. Medical Centers.
Cabazi, Ruta A. '65 (IND) [F] Beech Grove, IN St. Francis Hospital and Health Centers.
Cabell, Barry *c.s.c.* '89 (AUS) [13] Austin, TX St. Ignatius Martyr Church; Austin, TX Brown School; Austin, TX School for the Deaf.
Caboboy, Juan '76 (ORG) Laguna Hills, CA St. Nicholas Church.
Cabral, Clifford J. '79 (PRO) Pascoag, RI St. Joseph's Church.
Cabral, Kenneth J. '50 (OAK) Retired.
Cabrera, Sergio '73 (MIA) [29] Miami, FL St. Raymond Church.
Cabrerizo, Juan L. *sch.p.* '77 (PCE) [C] Coto Laurel, PR Colegio Ponceno.
Cabrita, Paul *s.m.* '86 (BR) [7] Baton Rouge, LA St. Francis De Sales Parish Church; Gramercy, LA Most Sacred Heart of Jesus Church.
Caccavale, Charles '91 (BRK) [230] Queens, NY Queen of Angels Church.
Caccavalle, Paschal *o.f.m.cap.* '35 (NY) [151] Bronx, NY Immaculate Conception Church.
Caccavalle, Paschal *o.f.m.cap.* '46 (PAT) [12] Paterson, NJ Our Lady of Lourdes Church.
Caccavalle, Pius *o.f.m.cap.* '47 (NY) [Z] New York, NY Immaculate Conception Friary.
Cacciapuoti, Antonio '90 (LA) Goleta, CA St. Raphael Church.
Caceres, Alonso '59 (ORG) [2] Santa Ana, CA Our Lady of Guadalupe Church.
Caceres, Marco *c.ss.r.* (TR) Hightstown, NJ St. Anthony of Padua Church.
Cach, Mark '83 (P) Medford, OR Sacred Heart of Jesus Church.
Cadarso, Carmelo '59 (VEN) Bradenton, FL St. Joseph Church.
Cadden, Donald R. *s.j.* '58 (SPK) [G] Spokane, WA Sacred Heart Medical Center.
Cadden, Thomas J. '55 (COL) [35] Columbus, OH Our Lady of Victory Church.
Caddy, James L. '64 (CLV) Gates Mills, OH St. Francis of Assisi Church.
Cadena, Enrique '84 (ROC) [14] Rochester, NY Corpus Christi Church.
Cadera, James R. '57 (MRY) On Duty Outside the Diocese.
Cadigan, Timothy J. *s.j.* '91 (WDC) [M] Washington, DC The Jesuit Community at Georgetown University.
Cadorette, Curtis R. *m.m.* '77 (NY) [Z] Maryknoll, NY Maryknoll Fathers and Brothers.
Cadran, Raymond G. '78 (WDC) [B] Washington, DC LaSalette Novitiate; [M] Washington, DC La Salette Community.
Cadusale, Jose '60 (BRK) Queens, NY Queens Hospital Center—Pastoral Care Office; [U] Jamaica, NY Parsons Manor.
Cadwallader, George B. '92 (PH) [94] Philadelphia, PA St. Martin of Tours Church.
Cady, Frank G. '81 (TUC) Rio Rico, AZ Nativity of Our Lord Jesus Christ Church.
Caesar, Floyd '75 (ALN) Ashland, PA St. Joseph Church; Ashland, PA St. Mauritius Church.
Caesar, Roger J. *s.s.j.* '76 (BAL) [M] Baltimore, MD St. Joseph Society of the Sacred Heart House of Central Administration.
Cafarelli, Aquinas F. *o.s.b.* '65 (MAN) [K] Manchester, NH St. Anselm Abbey.
Caffarelli, Theodore *s.s.c.* '49 (BUF) [3] West Seneca, NY Fourteen Holy Helpers Church.
Caffe, John I. '62 (STL) St. Ann, MO St. Gregory Church.
Caffery, James *m.s.* '60 (ATL) Smyrna, GA St. Thomas the Apostle Church.
Caffrey, Benet W. *o.s.b.* '58 (PAT) [M] Morristown, NJ St. Mary's Abbey.
Caffrey, Edward F. '57 (SPK) Clayton, WA St. Joseph Church; Deer Park, WA St. Mary's Presentation Church.
Caffrey, Gerald *c.m.f.* '80 (PHX) Prescott, AZ United States Veterans Hospital (Prescott).
Caffrey, Joseph P. '63 (PT) Panama City, FL St. Dominic Church.
Caffrey, William J. *s.v.d.* '59 (LA) Lancaster, CA Sacred Heart Church; [D] Lancaster, CA Paraclete High School.
Cafiero, Johnpaul *o.f.m.* (CHI) [D] Chicago, IL Hales Franciscan High School, Inc.
Cafone, James M. '65 (NEW) [B] South Orange, NJ Seton Hall University.
Caforio, Stephen *o.f.m.* '49 (NY) [Z] New York, NY St. Clare Friary.
Caggiano, Frank '87 (BRK) [72] Brooklyn, NY Shrine Church of St. Jude.
Caggiano, Kyrin *o.carm.* '62 (L) [B] Louisville, KY St. Francis DeSales High School.
Cagney, John M. *o.praem.* '48 (PH) [D] Philadelphia, PA St. John Neumann High School; [Z] Philadelphia, PA St. Norbert Priory.
Cahalan, Patrick J. *s.j.* '65 (LA) [F] Los Angeles, CA Loyola High School.
Cahalane, Msgr. Thomas P. '63 (TUC) [8] Tucson, AZ Our Mother of Sorrows Church.
Cahalane, Timothy *m.s.c.* '59 (LA) [50] Los Angeles, CA St. Brendan Church; Graduate Studies.
Cahill, Brendan J. '90 (GAL) On Duty Outside the Diocese.
Cahill, Clemente *c.ss.r.* '51 (CGS) [1] Caguas, PR Cathedral Dulce Nombre de Jesus Church.
Cahill, Daniel '73 (TR) Keansburg, NJ St. Ann Church.
Cahill, Msgr. Daniel R. '43 (SFR) Retired.
Cahill, Dennis H. '77 (DUB) Osage, IA Sacred Heart Church.
Cahill, Donald C. '67 (CHI) Tinley Park, IL St. George Church.
Cahill, Edward B. '60 (PH) Springfield, PA Holy Cross Church.
Cahill, Frank '68 (MIA) Retired.
Cahill, J. Donald *s.m.* (STL) [4] Creve Coeur, MO Our Lady of the Pillar Church; [F] Kirkwood, MO Vianney High School.
Cahill, James P. '61 (CHL) Sylva, NC St. Mary Church.
Cahill, John F. '51 (WOR) [M] Worcester, MA Vianney House.
Cahill, John W. '63 (RCK) [2] Freeport, IL St. Joseph Church.
Cahill, John W. '73 (COV) [1] Covington, KY Cathedral, Basilica of the Assumption.
Cahill, Joseph W. '76 (PRT) Bar Harbor, ME Holy Redeemer Church; Northeast Harbor, ME St. Ignatius Church.
Cahill, Neil *s.j.* '56 (OM) [K] Omaha, NE Jesuit Community At Creighton University.
Cahill, Patrick *c.s.v.* '62 (SFD) Rochester, IL Church of St. Jude.
Cahill, Msgr. Paul J. '35 (PH) Lansdale, PA St. Stanislaus Church; Retired.
Cahill, Msgr. Richard (NY) New York, NY National Catholic Community Service.
Cahill, Msgr. Richard M. '58 (BUF) Grand Island, NY St. Stephen Church.
Cahill, Thomas *m.j.* '88 (PCE) [7] Ponce, PR Santa Maria Church; On Duty Outside the Diocese.
Cahill, William C. (SY) Special Assignment.
Cahill, William C. '61 (SY) [5] Rome, NY Transfiguration Church; Mohawk, NY Oneida Correctional Facility I.
Cahoon, John E. '89 (GAL) [18] Houston, TX St. Charles Borromeo Church.
Cai, Xavier *s.j.* '40 (BRK) [209] Queens, NY Our Lady of China Chapel.
Caiazzo, Gregory G. *c.s.p.* '76 (NY) [Z] Scarsdale, NY Paulist Fathers Generalate; [Z] Scarsdale, NY Paulist Fathers Generalate.
Caiazzo, Nicholas '92 (NOR) On Duty Outside the Diocese.
Caimi, Luke A. '58 (WDC) Retired.
Cain, Dennis R. '79 (DUB) Maquoketa, IA Sacred Heart Church.
Cain, Frederick L. '70 (PIT) [2] Bridgeville, PA Holy Child Church.
Cain, Gervase *t.o.r.* '57 (ARL) Luray, VA Our Lady of the Valley Church.
Cain, Harry J. *s.j.* '63 (BO) [W] Weston, MA Campion Center.
Cain, James R. '56 (OM) Springfield, NE St. Joseph Church.
Cain, John C. '58 (CHI) Harwood Heights, IL St. Rosalie Church.
Cain, John F. '56 (SC) Retired.
Cain, John N. '47 (NSH) Retired.

Cain, John T. '44 (SPR) West Springfield, MA St. Thomas the Apostle Church.
Cain, Joseph P. *o.s.c.* '44 (PHX) [F] Phoenix, AZ Crosier Community of Phoenix (Canons Regular of the Order of the Holy Cross).
Cain, Randy '88 (CC) [12] Laredo, TX St. John Neumann Church.
Cain, Robert K.C. '95 (TLS) Bartlesville, OK St. John's Church.
Cain, Thomas *m.s.c.* '65 (RCK) [H] Aurora, IL Missionaries of the Sacred Heart Community.
Cain, Thomas M. *o.p.* '37 (DAL) [M] Irving, TX Dominican Priory of St. Albert the Great.
Cain, Urban A. *o.f.m.* '48 (BO) [Z] Boston, MA Saint Anthony Residence.
Cain, William F. *s.j.* '69 (LA) [C] Los Angeles, CA Loyola Marymount University.
Cain, William P. *s.j.* '76 (NY) [Z] New York, NY Jesuit Provincial's Office; [Z] New York, NY Xavier Jesuit Community.
Caine, John W. *c.m.* '55 (PH) [Z] Philadelphia, PA Congregation of the Mission.
Caine, Msgr. Martin J. '46 (BUF) Retired.
Cairns, James E. *c.m.* '69 (FRS) [C] Fresno, CA Saint Agnes' Medical Center.
Cairns, John L. '63 (ALB) Clifton Park, NY St. Edward the Confessor Church.
Cairns, Stephen P. '68 (TOL) Swanton, OH St. Richard Church.
Cairns, Thomas '63 (BIR) Absent on Leave.
Cairone, A. Robert '64 (CAM) Magnolia, NJ St. Gregory's Church.
Cajes, Prisco (OAK) [3] Oakland, CA St. Anthony's Church.
Calabrese, Charles L. '72 (FWT) [M] Fort Worth, TX Texas Christian University Catholic Community.
Calabrese, Charles L. '72 (STU) On Duty Outside the Diocese.
Calabrese, Daniel '87 (NY) Absent on Leave.
Calabrese, Peter M. *c.r.s.p.* (ALN) [K] Bethlehem, PA The Barnabite Fathers Barnabite Spiritual Center.
Calabrese, Robert *o.f.m.cap.* '83 (NY) [151] Bronx, NY Immaculate Conception Church.
Calabro, John E. '73 (PH) [44] Philadelphia, PA Epiphany of Our Lord Church.
Calabro, Nicholas J. '66 (BGP) [4] Greenwich, CT St. Roch Church.
Calais, Floyd J. (LAF) Retired.
Calais, Tommy '83 (LAF) Four Corners, LA St. Peter the Apostle Church.
Calamari, Joseph M. *s.s.j.* (BLX) Pass Christian, MS Our Mother of Mercy Church.
Calamari, Paul '80 (NO) Absent on Leave.
Calarco, Dominic *s.x.* '55 (BO) [W] Holliston, MA Xaverian Missionaries.
Calcagno, Jerome *c.m.* '49 (NO) [60] New Orleans, LA St. Stephen Church.
Caldara, John N. '46 (ALB) Retired.
Caldarella, James J. '71 (WOR) Princeton, MA Prince of Peace Church.
Caldas, Msgr. Constantino R. '51 (BGP) [15] Bridgeport, CT Our Lady of Fatima Church; Retired.
Calder, Kenneth J. '60 (BRK) [91] Brooklyn, NY Our Lady of Angels Church.
Calderon, Francisco '50 (MIA) [16] Miami, FL St. Brendan Church.
Calderon, Gerardo *f.m.m.* '92 (MIA) [2] Pompano Beach, FL San Isidro Church.
Calderon, Vicente, Jr. '63 (ELP) [31] El Paso, TX St. Raphael Church.
Calderwood, Vincent T. '44 (BRK) Retired.
Calderwood, Vincent T. '44 (MET) [H] Somerset, NJ Maria Regina Residence.
Caldognetto, Dominic *s.x.* '66 (MIL) [B] Franklin, WI Xaverian Missionary Fathers College Seminary.
Caldwell, Dorothy (NY) [S] New York, NY Saint Vincent's Medical Center of Richmond.
Caldwell, Msgr. Frank J. '81 (RVC) [1] Rockville Centre, NY St. Agnes Cathedral.
Caldwell, H. Fred '95 (DAL) [15] Dallas, TX St. Cecilia Church.
Caldwell, J. Ripley '54 (SJ) [M] Los Gatos, CA Sacred Heart Jesuit Center.
Caldwell, James V. '60 (SD) [28] San Diego, CA St. Jerome Church; Chula Vista, CA South Bay Detention Facility.
Caldwell, John A. '70 (L) Campbellsville, KY Our Lady of Perpetual Help Church; Finley, KY Our Lady of the Hills Church; Greensburg, KY Holy Redeemer Church.
Caldwell, Joseph R. *s.j.* '54 (SJ) [M] Los Gatos, CA California Province of the Society of Jesus, Jesuit Provincial Office.
Caldwell, Thomas A. *s.j.* '56 (MIL) [P] Milwaukee, WI Jesuit Community at Marquette University.
Caldwell, William '68 (KC) Excelsior Springs, MO St. Ann Church.
Caldwell, William T. '44 (L) Retired.
Calegari, Leonard J. '63 (SFR) Pacifica, CA St. Peter Church.
Calero, Luis F. *s.j.* '83 (SJ) [B] Santa Clara, CA Santa Clara University.
Calero Gomez, Nomar '91 (MGZ) Moca, PR Our Lady of Monserrate Church.
Calhoun, C. John '64 (NY) Absent on Leave.
Calhoun, George *o.c.s.o.* '40 (WOR) [N] Spencer, MA St. Joseph's Abbey.
Calhoun, Gerald '61 (OWN) Bowling Green, KY Holy Spirit Church.
Calhoun, Ronald G. '72 (BO) Middleboro, MA Sacred Heart Church.
Calhoun, William '63 (ATL) Retired.
Calicchio, Isaac J. *o.f.m.* '56 (ALB) [1] Troy, NY St. Anthony of Padua Church.
Calicott, John W. '74 (CHI) [79] Chicago, IL Holy Angels Church.
Caligiuri, Msgr. Angelo M. '58 (BUF) [2] Cheektowaga, NY Infant of Prague Church.
Caligiuri, Msgr. Anthony J. '49 (BUF) Lewiston, NY St. Peter Church.
Calik, Joseph *s.ch.* '60 (SEA) [13] Seattle, WA St. Margaret of Scotland Church.
Calimeri, Anthony F. '47 (ROC) Retired.
Calise, Joseph '80 (BRK) [B] Elmhurst, NY Cathedral Preparatory Seminary of the Immaculate Conception.
Calkins, Arthur B. '70 (NO) On Duty Outside the Archdiocese.
Calkins, Frank M. *o.s.m.* '30 (CHI) [N] Chicago, IL Servite Friars - Eastern Province.
Calkins, Gerard M. *o.s.m.* '45 (ORG) [H] Orange, CA Servite Fathers and Brothers.
Calkins, Msgr. Howard W. '67 (NY) [63] New York, NY St. Joseph of the Holy Family Church; [DD] Bronx, NY Abraham House, Inc.
Calkins, John J. '49 (RCK) Loves Park, IL St. Bridget Church; Retired.
Calkins, Lawrence (Leroy) M. *o.s.m.* '35 (CHI) [N] Chicago, IL Servite Friars - Eastern Province.
Calkins, Leroy *o.s.m.* '35 (P) Roseburg, OR U.S. Veterans Administration Hospital.
Calkins, Martin J. *s.j.* (DET) [K] Detroit, MI Jesuit Provincial Office-Detroit Province of the Society of Jesus.
Calkins, Martin J. *s.j.* '94 (WDC) [M] Washington, DC The Jesuit Community at Georgetown University.
Calkins, Raymond J. '46 (SC) Retired.
Calkins, Ronald L. '78 (NO) Mandeville, LA Mary Queen of Peace Church.
Callaghan, Msgr. Aloysius R. '71 (ALN) On Duty Outside the Diocese.
Callaghan, George J. *o.s.a.* '56 (PH) [U] Flourtown, PA St. Joseph Villa; [Z] Villanova, PA St. Thomas Monastery.
Callaghan, Michael '90 (BAL) [75] Baltimore, MD Our Lady of Victory Church; [D] Severn, MD Archbishop Spalding High School.
Callaghan, Michael J. *c.m.* '76 (BRK) [D] Queens and Staten Island, NY St. John's University.
Callaghan, Patrick C. *o.f.m.* '46 (NY) [Z] New York, NY Franciscan Friars, Order of Friars Manor.
Callaghan, Philip P. *s.j.* '60 (SAC) [J] Applegate, CA Our Lady of the Oaks Villa.
Callaghan, Philip P. *s.j.* '60 (SFR) [C] San Francisco, CA University of San Francisco.
Callahan, Msgr. Brian F. '65 (BRK) [141] Brooklyn, NY St. Thomas Aquinas Church.
Callahan, Daniel *s.a.* (NY) [Z] Garrison, NY Franciscan Friars of the Atonement.
Callahan, David P. '87 (BO) Melrose, MA St. Mary of the Annunciation Church.
Callahan, Dennis D. '62 (MIL) Pell Lake, WI St. Mary's Church.
Callahan, Edward M. '59 (SPR) [12] Springfield, MA Sacred Heart Church; Springfield, MA Wesson Memorial Hospital Unit; Springfield, MA Municipal Hospital.
Callahan, Edward R. *s.j.* '49 (BO) [W] Chestnut Hill, MA The Jesuit Community at Boston College.
Callahan, Francis F. *s.j.* '43 (BO) [W] Weston, MA Campion Health Center, Inc.
Callahan, Msgr. Francis J. *v.f.* '72 (SCR) [20] Wilkes-Barre, PA St. Therese's Church.
Callahan, Francis X. '49 (HRT) Woodmont, CT St. Agnes Church.
Callahan, Francis X. '63 (BAL) Bel Air, MD St. Margaret Church.
Callahan, James '44 (NEW) Retired.
Callahan, James A. '73 (PH) [153] Philadelphia, PA Transfiguration of Our Lord Church.
Callahan, James F. *s.m.a.* (WIN) [5] Rochester, MN St. Francis of Assisi Church.
Callahan, James F. *s.m.a.* '75 (BO) [W] Dedham, MA African Mission House and African Cultural Center.
Callahan, James P. '74 (STL) [2] St. Charles, MO St. Cletus Church.
Callahan, Jerome *o.carm.* '52 (JOL) [J] Darien, IL Carmelite Fathers Provincial Office.
Callahan, Jerome *o.carm.* '52 (VEN) [6] Sarasota, FL St. Thomas More Church.
Callahan, John J. *s.j.* '70 (DEN) [M] Denver, CO Regis Jesuit Community (The Jesuits at Regis University).
Callahan, Joseph F. *c.s.c.* '70 (SCR) [4] Wilkes-Barre, PA St. Casimir's Church.
Callahan, Joseph H. '86 (CLV) El Salvador, C.A., OH Parroquial de Nuestra Senora de Guadalupe.
Callahan, Joseph W. '66 (PH) [152] Philadelphia, PA St. Timothy Church.
Callahan, Kevin G. '84 (STL) [9] Florissant, MO St. Sabina Church.
Callahan, L. Jacqueline (TR) Middletown, NJ St. Catherine Church.
Callahan, Leonard F. '69 (COV) On Duty Outside the Diocese.
Callahan, Michael J. '76 (BRK) [U] Jamaica, NY Vincentian Residence.
Callahan, Nelson J. '53 (CLV) Bay Village, OH St. Raphael Church.
Callahan, Raymond J. '48 (MIL) Retired.
Callahan, Raymond J. *s.j.* '69 (BO) [H] Boston, MA Nativity Preparatory School; [W] Boston, MA The Society of Jesus of New England-Provincial Offices.
Callahan, Raymond J. *s.j.* '69 (CHI) [D] Wilmette, IL Loyola Academy.
Callahan, Richard B. *m.m.* '64 (NY) [Z] Maryknoll, NY Maryknoll Fathers and Brothers; [Z] Maryknoll, NY M.M.A.F. Charitable Trust; [AA] Maryknoll, NY Maryknoll Sisters Charitable Trust.
Callahan, Msgr. Richard J. '51 (CAM) Haddon Heights, NJ St. Rose's Church.
Callahan, Ronan *c.p.* '51 (HRT) [M] West Hartford, CT Holy Family Monastery/Retreat.
Callahan, Ronan P. *c.p.* (NOR) [A] Cromwell, CT Holy Apostles College and Seminary.
Callahan, Msgr. Steven '87 (SD) [A] San Diego, CA St. Francis Seminary.
Callahan, Vincent '75 (CHI) [N] Chicago, IL St. Peter's Friary.
Callahan, William J. *s.j.* '72 (MIL) [P] Milwaukee, WI Jesuit Provincial Office, Wisconsin Province.
Callahan, William P. *o.f.m.conv.* '77 (MIL) [45] Milwaukee, WI Basilica of St. Josaphat.
Callahan, Zachary '58 (RVC) Uniondale, NY St. Martha Church.
Callan, James B. '74 (ROC) [14] Rochester, NY Corpus Christi Church.
Callan, John '82 (MIA) [C] Fort Lauderdale, FL Cardinal Gibbons High School.
Callan, L. James '45 (ROC) Retired.
Callan, Patrick J. '61 (RVC) Bridgehampton, NY Queen of the Most Holy Rosary Church.
Callanan, Edward E. *s.j.* '58 (PHX) [11] Phoenix, AZ St. Francis Xavier Church.
Callanan, Jonas *i.c.* (PEO) Pontiac, IL Illinois State Penitentiary.
Callanan, Michael G. *m.m.* '60 (LA) [R] Los Angeles, CA Maryknoll Fathers and Brothers.
Callari, William P. '79 (MAR) Houghton, MI St. Albert the Great University Parish Church; South Range, MI Holy Family Church; [G] Houghton, MI St. Albert the Great, University Parish.
Calle, Juan de la '54 (PMB) Retired.
Calleja, Msgr. Guido '53 (MOB) Magnolia Springs, AL St. John the Baptist Church.
Callery, Peter *s.j.* '72 (NO) [F] New Orleans, LA Jesuit High School.
Calles, Msgr. Robert S. '63 (ELP) [13] El Paso, TX Most Holy Trinity Church.
Callipare, Joseph '85 (PT) [13] Pensacola, FL St. Paul Church.
Callis, Elbert '76 (MEM) Dyersburg, TN Holy Angels Church.
Callone, Ivan *i.m.c.* '53 (CAM) Egg Harbor City, NJ St. Nicholas Church.
Callone, Ivan *i.m.c.* '53 (MET) [H] Somerset, NJ Consolata Society for Foreign Missions.
Calme, Stephen J. '54 (CIN) Retired.
Caloca-Rivas, Rigoberto *o.f.m.* '82 (OAK) [A] Berkeley, CA Franciscan School of Theology; [N] Oakland, CA Franciscan Friars.
Calovini, Msgr. Gerald E. '73 (STU) Wintersville, OH Blessed Sacrament Church; Wintersville, OH Our Lady of Lourdes Church; [J] Steubenville, OH Campaign for Human Development.
Calpin, Thomas J. '54 (PH) Morrisville, PA Holy Trinity Church.
Calter, Arthur M. '56 (BO) Hingham, MA Resurrection of Our Lord and Saviour Jesus Christ Church.
Caluda, Charles J. '62 (NO) Garyville, LA St. Hubert Church.
Calumba, Faron P. '79 (HRT) Newington, CT Holy Spirit Church.
Calvert, Roland *o.s.f.s.* '65 (LAN) [H] Adrian, MI Motherhouse of the Sisters of St. Dominic.
Calvo, Gabriel '52 (WDC) [B] Washington, DC Diocesan Laborer Priests, House of Studies.
Calvo, Msgr. Oscar (AGN) Retired.
Calvo, Randolph R. '77 (SFR) [1] South San Francisco, CA All Souls Church; Special Assignment.
Calvo Muniain, Jose M. '59 (CGS) Juncos, PR Inmaculada Concepcion Church.
Camacho, Enrique '81 (YAK) Retired.
Camacho, Gilbert '47 (ELP) Retired.

Camacho, Henry *o.p.* '60 (PRO) [27] Providence, RI St. Pius V Church.
Camacho, Henry A. *o.p.* (PRO) [P] Providence, RI St. Pius Priory.
Camacho, Jesus '75 (B) Jerome, ID St. Jerome's Church.
Camacho, Jose Fco. Baez '87 (MGZ) [3] Mayaquez, Mayaguez Ascension Church.
Camacho, Juan L.G. '55 (AGN) Tumon Bay, GU Blessed Diego Luis de San Vitores Church.
Camacho, Robert '79 (RCK) Carpentersville, IL St. Monica Church.
Camacho, Msgr. Zoilo L.G. '54 (AGN) Dededo, GU Santa Barbara Church.
Camadella, Christian F. *o.f.m.* '56 (NY) [35] New York, NY St. Francis of Assisi Church.
Camara, Michael M. *o.f.m.* '89 (FR) [18] Fall River, MA St. Michael's Church.
Camarda, Ronald A. '90 (STA) Military Chaplains.
Camarena, Miguel *c.s.* '90 (LA) Sun Valley, CA Our Lady of the Holy Rosary Church.
Cambra, Dan *m.i.c.* '86 (MIL) [9] Kenosha, WI St. Peter's Church.
Cambra, Raymond '77 (FR) [14] Fall River, MA St. Elizabeth's Church.
Cameli, Louis J. *s.t.d.* (CHI) [52] Chicago, IL St. Edward Church; [A] Mundelein, IL University of St. Mary of the Lake-Mundelein Seminary.
Camera, Bede G. *o.s.b.* '88 (MAN) [16] Manchester, NH St. Raphael Church; [K] Manchester, NH St. Anselm Abbey.
Cameron, Albert S. '57 (MAN) Retired.
Cameron, Hilary J. '64 (PRT) Berwick, ME Our Lady of Peace Church.
Cameron, Kevin '84 (DM) [13] Des Moines, IA Visitation Church.
Cameron, Peter John *o.p.* '86 (NY) [A] Yonkers, NY St. Joseph's Seminary; [Z] New York, NY St. Vincent Ferrer Priory.
Cameron, Robert '59 (KC) Special Assignment.
Cameron, Robert V. *glmy.* '66 (RIC) Gate City, VA St. Bernard Church.
Cameron-Mowat, Andrew *s.j.* '92 (OAK) [N] Berkeley, CA Jesuit Community at Jesuit School of Theology at Berkeley.
Camille, Edward J. '58 (CLV) Brecksville, OH St. Basil the Great Church; Retired.
Camilleri, Emanuel M. *o.p.* '37 (NO) [P] New Orleans, LA Dominican Fathers & Brothers, Southern Dominican Province.
Camilleri, Emmanuel '66 (HBG) [F] Lancaster, PA St. Joseph Hospital.
Camilleri, Joseph M. '74 (BR) Bayou Pigeon, LA St. Joan of Arc Church.
Camilli, E. Michael *m.s.c.* '60 (ALN) [A] Center Valley, PA Missionaries of the Sacred Heart.
Camilli, E. Michael *m.s.c.* '60 (BAL) [A] Baltimore, MD St. Mary's Seminary and University.
Camire, Bernard J. *s.s.s.* '66 (NY) [55] New York, NY St. Jean Baptiste Church; [DD] New York, NY Nocturnal Adoration Society of the United States.
Cammayo, Ruben '80 (NY) [131] Bronx, NY St. Augustine Church; Bronx, NY Bronx-Lebanon Hospital Center.
Cammisa, James N. '49 (TR) Retired.
Camp, Alfred L. '57 (JKS) Natchez, MS St. Mary Church.
Camp, Steven '87 (RVC) Mastic Beach, NY St. Jude Church.
Campagna, Robert M. *o.f.m.* '77 (NY) [Z] New York, NY Franciscan Province of the Immaculate Conception; [DD] Mount Vernon, NY Franciscan Mission Associates; [DD] Mount Vernon, NY St. Dymphna Devotion.
Campagnone, Msgr. Francis '48 (ORL) New Smyrna Beach, FL Our Lady Star of the Sea Church; Retired.
Campagnone, Msgr. Francis A. '48 (BGP) Retired.
Campagnone, Nicholas '65 (ALB) Retired.
Campana, Pedro '56 (SJN) [19] Bayamon, PR Santa Rosa de Lima Church.
Campana, Thomas J. '80 (CHI) [4] Oak Park, IL St. Giles Church.
Campbell, Andrew S. *o.s.b.* '81 (GBG) [H] Latrobe, PA Saint Vincent Archabbey.
Campbell, Bernard *c.s.p.* '68 (AUS) [11] Austin, TX St. Austin's Church; [M] Austin, TX University Catholic Center.
Campbell, Bernard *o.f.m.cap.* '68 (MAN) [5] Manchester, NH Blessed Sacrament Church.
Campbell, Bernard '89 (STV) [1] Barrenspot, VI Church St. Ann Church.
Campbell, Colm '60 (BRK) [243] Queens, NY St. Teresa Church.
Campbell, Colm '63 (BRK) [T] Brooklyn, NY Catholic Migration & Refugee Office, Catholic Migration Services, Inc.
Campbell, Donald C. *c.s.p.* '62 (NY) [104] New York, NY St. Paul the Apostle Church.
Campbell, Douglas '76 (WCH) Lindsborg, KS St. Bridget of Sweden Church; McPherson, KS St. Joseph Church.
Campbell, Dwight P. '91 (PEO) Nauvoo, IL SS. Peter and Paul's Church.
Campbell, Francis *o.m.i.* '42 (BO) [Z] Tewksbury, MA Immaculate Heart of Mary Novitiate-Infirmary.
Campbell, Msgr. Frank '53 (P) North Plains, OR St. Edward Church.
Campbell, Frederick F. '80 (STP) West St. Paul, MN St. Joseph Church.
Campbell, Gerard J. *s.j.* '51 (WDC) [20] Washington, DC Holy Trinity Church.
Campbell, Gerardo *c.ss.r.* '67 (CGS) [1] Caguas, PR Cathedral Dulce Nombre de Jesus Church.
Campbell, Howard W. '61 (PIT) [5] Munhall, PA St. Theresa of Lisieux Church.
Campbell, Hugh P. '61 (PH) Westtown, PA St. Maximilian Kolbe Church.
Campbell, James *m.s.c.* '72 (RCK) [H] Aurora, IL Missionaries of the Sacred Heart Community.
Campbell, James D. *o.p.* '62 (R) [E] Raleigh, NC Dominican Community; [E] Raleigh, NC De Porres House.
Campbell, James F. '57 (PEO) [N] Peoria, IL Immaculate Conception Convent.
Campbell, Msgr. James F. '64 (BUF) [5] West Seneca, NY Queen of Heaven Church.
Campbell, Joel A. *o.f.m.* '50 (BUF) [O] St. Bonaventure, NY St. Bonaventure Friary.
Campbell, John '50 (SFD) Retired.
Campbell, Msgr. John '55 (ORG) San Juan Capistrano, CA (Old Mission) Church.
Campbell, John D. *s.j.* '76 (MIL) [29] Milwaukee, WI Gesu Parish Church.
Campbell, John J. *s.j.* '50 (DEN) [M] Denver, CO Xavier Jesuit Center.
Campbell, Msgr. John Michael '71 (STU) Minerva, OH St. Gabriel the Archangel Church.
Campbell, John P. *c.s.p.* '69 (BO) [P] Boston, MA Paulist Center; [W] Boston, MA Paulist Fathers Residence.
Campbell, John R. '58 (STL) Retired.
Campbell, Msgr. John S. '66 (ALN) [5] Minersville, PA St. Vincent de Paul Church.
Campbell, Joseph (SPC) Poplar Bluff, MO Sacred Heart Church.
Campbell, Joseph *c.ss.r.* '41 (DEN) [32] Denver, CO St. Joseph's Church.
Campbell, Joseph '60 (FAR) Retired.
Campbell, Louis J. (SCR) [19] Scranton, PA St. Michael's Church; [M] Elmhurst, PA Priestly Fraternity of St. Peter (F.S.S.P.).
Campbell, Michael '79 (STL) [14] St. Louis, MO Our Lady of Sorrows Church.
Campbell, Michael J. '93 (ATL) Lilburn, GA St. John Neumann Church.
Campbell, Norbert J. '60 (PIT) [3] New Castle, PA St. Joseph the Worker Church.
Campbell, Paul B. *s.j.* '88 (SY) [S] Syracuse, NY Jesuits at LeMoyne, Inc.
Campbell, Paul F. '65 (WOR) Dudley, MA St. Anthony's Church.
Campbell, Paul J. *o.s.f.s.* '82 (WIL) [B] Wilmington, DE Salesianum School.
Campbell, Peter A. *c.m.* '85 (PH) [B] Philadelphia, PA DePaul Novitiate.
Campbell, Peter E. *m.s.c.* '60 (RCK) [H] Aurora, IL Missionaries of the Sacred Heart Community.
Campbell, Ralph C. *s.j.* '59 (ALN) [A] Wernersville, PA Novitiate of St. Isaac Jogues.
Campbell, Robert *o.p.* '57 (SD) [1] San Diego, CA St. Joseph Cathedral.
Campbell, Robert I. *o.p.* '56 (CHI) [N] River Forest, IL St. Thomas Aquinas Priory.
Campbell, Robert J. *m.s.* '58 (BUR) Windsor, VT St. Francis of Assisi Church.
Campbell, Stephen *s.j.* '85 (MOB) [B] Mobile, AL Spring Hill College.
Campbell, Theodore C. '72 (STP) Golden Valley, MN Good Shepherd Church.
Campbell, Thomas E. '80 (SAV) [4] Savannah, GA Most Blessed Sacrament Church.
Campbell, Thomas L. *c.s.c.* '48 (FR) [K] North Dartmouth, MA Holy Cross Mission House.
Campbell, Msgr. Thomas P. '17 (BRK) [168] Queens, NY St. Francis of Assisi Church.
Campbell, Msgr. Thomas P. '43 (BRK) Retired.
Campbell, Wayne '86 (OAK) [3] San Leandro, CA St. Felicitas Church.
Campbell, William D. '58 (SCR) [10] Scranton, PA Immaculate Conception Church.
Campbell, William G. '63 (FR) Marion, MA St. Rita's Church.
Campbell, William J. '43 (TR) Retired.
Campbell, William W. (BO) Retired.
Campechano, Francisco Javier '95 (STO) Modesto, CA Our Lady of Fatima Church.
Campellone, Joseph G. *o.s.f.s.* '96 (PH) [Z] Philadelphia, PA Father Judge Faculty House.
Campi, Vincent L. '45 (WH) Retired.
Campion, Msgr. John J. '51 (SD) Retired.
Campion, John R. '48 (HBG) Chambersburg, PA Corpus Christi Church; Doylesburg, PA Our Lady of Refuge Mission Church.
Campion, Joseph J. '73 (ALN) Catasauqua, PA St. Lawrence Church.
Campion, Joseph J. *s.s.j.* '91 (LAF) Rayne, LA Shrine of Our Mother of Mercy Church.
Campion, Owen F. '66 (NSH) On Duty Outside the Diocese.
Campion, Thomas B. '52 (HRT) Wethersfield, CT Corpus Christi Church; Wethersfield, CT Sacred Heart Church.
Campion, Thomas F. '57 (MAD) [G] Monroe, WI St. Clare Hospital.
Campion, William T. '77 (ALN) [2] Mahanoy City, PA St. Canicus Church; [4] Mahanoy City, PA St. Fidelis Church.
Campo, Arturo Miguel O *o.f.m.* '85 (SAT) [70] San Antonio, TX San Jose y San Miguel Church.
Campo, Lance J. (NO) [1] Metairie, LA Our Lady of Divine Providence Church.
Campo, Richard W. '85 (ALN) [7] Bethlehem, PA Notre Dame of Bethlehem Church.
Campobello, Mark A. '91 (RCK) [1] Rockford, IL St. Peter Cathedral; [2] Aurora, IL Holy Angels Church.
Campoli, John F. (TR) On Duty Outside the Diocese.
Campoli, Timothy J. '74 (SPR) Greenfield, MA Blessed Sacrament Church.
Campos, Miguel *sch.p.* '96 (LA) [75] Los Angeles, CA St. Lucy Church.
Campuzano, J. Eduardo '46 (CAM) Retired.
Camuso, Robert '92 (SEA) [3] Seattle, WA St. Anne Church; [13] Seattle, WA St. Margaret of Scotland Church.
Can, Anselm Dinh Vuong *c.m.c.* '77 (GAL) [Q] Houston, TX Congregation of the Mother Coredemptrix.
Canaan, Timothy '92 (OG) [2] Plattsburgh, NY St. John the Baptist Church.
Canal, Manuel '58 (MRY) [1] Salinas, CA Christ the King Church.
Canary, John F. '69 (CHI) [A] Mundelein, IL University of St. Mary of the Lake-Mundelein Seminary.
Canas, Eugene *o.m.i.* '64 (SAT) [M] San Antonio, TX Oblate Benson Residence (Southern Prov.); [M] San Antonio, TX Provincial Administration Office, Oblates of Mary Immaculate (Southern Prov.).
Canavan, Francis P. *s.j.* '50 (NY) [Z] New York, NY Jesuit Community at Fordham University.
Canavan, Gerald D. '69 (PH) [124] Philadelphia, PA Our Lady of Mt. Carmel Church.
Canavan, John D. '55 (DET) [2] Taylor, MI St. Constance Church.
Canavan, Mark P. '71 (CHI) [2] Cicero, IL St. Frances of Rome Church.
Canavan, Msgr. Martin '68 (PHU) Absent on Leave.
Canavera, Lawrence J. '67 (GB) [14] Green Bay, WI St. Philip the Apostle Church.
Cancro, Francis T. '81 (CHL) Asheville, NC St. Eugene Church.
Candelaria, Ernest *c.s.j.* '58 (LA) Lancaster, CA Blessed Junipero Serra Church; [D] Lancaster, CA Paraclete High School.
Candelas, Rafael '59 (SJN) [56] San Juan, PR Sagrado Corazon de Jesus Church.
Candreva, Thomas '63 (RVC) Great Neck, NY St. Aloysius Church.
Cane, Pere '93 (MIL) [Y] Racine, WI Missionary Community of St. Paul the Apostle and Mary, Mother of the Church, Inc.
Cane-Gombau, Pere '93 (MIL) [5] Kenosha, WI St. Mark's Church.
Canepa, Jorge A. *c.s.c.* '56 (FTW) [J] South Bend, IN Congregation of Holy Cross Indiana Province Provincial House.
Canez, Jorge '79 (PHX) [3] Phoenix, AZ Holy Family Church; [10] Phoenix, AZ St. Edward Confessor Church.
Canfield, Francis E. *s.j.* '67 (TOL) [C] Toledo, OH St. John's Jesuit High School.
Canfield, Msgr. Francis X. '45 (DET) Retired; [T] Grosse Pointe Farms, MI American Friends of the Vatican Library.
Canfield, Joseph '58 (SUP) Retired.
Cangemi, Dominic *s.t.* '44 (BLX) Pearlington, MS St. Joseph Church.
Canino, Louis *o.f.m.* '69 (CHL) [5] Greensboro, NC St. Pius X Church.
Canjar, John A. '49 (DEN) Retired.
Cann, Hilarion V. (WH) Retired.
Cann, Leslie '58 (PMB) Hobe Sound, FL St. Christopher Church.
Cann, Luke W. (NY) [C] Poughkeepsie, NY Marist College.
Canna, Joseph '70 (LA) [1] Long Beach, CA St. Anthony Church.
Cannan, Walter F. '68 (SY) Oriskany, NY St. Stephen, Protomartyr Church.
Cannariato, Paul A. '83 (NEW) [12] Jersey City, NJ St. John the Baptist Church.
Canniff, James B. '60 (BO) [46] Boston, MA St. Mary Church.
Canning, John *o.carm.* '55 (NY) [97] New York, NY Our Lady of the Scapular/St. Stephen Church.
Canning, John W. (OG) Retired.

Canning, Wilfred S. *c.s.b.* '55 (GAL) [Q] Houston, TX Dominican Fathers and Brothers, St. Mark Priory, Inc.; [Q] Houston, TX Dillon House.
Cannon, Hugh D. '66 (RVC) Plainview, NY St. Pius X Church.
Cannon, James *c.ss.r.* (ALB) Saratoga Springs, NY St. Clement Church.
Cannon, John A. '48 (PH) [G] Holland, PA Villa Joseph Marie High School for Girls; [X] Holland, PA St. Joseph Home for the Aged; [AA] Holland, PA Villa Joseph Marie.
Cannon, Maro *c.f.a.* '85 (KNX) [C] Signal Mountain, TN Alexian Village Health Care Center; [F] Signal Mountain, TN Alexian Brothers.
Cannon, Michael J. '81 (ORL) Altamonte Springs, FL Annunciation Church.
Cannon, Richard F. (BO) [73] Boston, MA St. Vincent de Paul Church.
Cannon, Robert R. '78 (VEN) [2] Venice, FL Our Lady of Lourdes Church.
Cannon, Msgr. Thomas (CAM) Retired.
Cannon, Msgr. Thomas *s.j.* '55 (ORL) De Land, FL St. Peter's Church.
Cannon, William B. '54 (CAM) [4] Cherry Hill, NJ St. Pius X Church.
Canny, Michael (SAC) Redding, CA Our Lady of Mercy Church.
Canny, Stephen J. '61 (SR) Cotati, CA St. Joseph Church.
Cano, Emilio '37 (PCE) Retired.
Canonici, Msgr. Paul '57 (JKS) [A] Jackson, MS St. Joseph Catholic School.
Canterbury, Keith (SAC) Weaverville, CA St. Patrick Church.
Canterna, Charles J. '76 (BAL) [93] Baltimore, MD St. Vincent de Paul Church; Baltimore, MD Maryland Correctional Adjustment Center; Special Assignment.
Cantillon, Joseph '76 (OAK) [5] Fremont, CA St. Leonard Church.
Cantley, Msgr. Michael J. '55 (BRK) [149] Queens, NY St. Anastasia Church.
Cantones, Joel P. '81 (NO) [24] New Orleans, LA St. Andrew the Apostle Church.
Cantore, John *c.m.* '63 (SPC) [C] Cape Girardeau, MO St. Francis' Medical Center.
Cantu, Oscar '94 (GAL) [17] Houston, TX St. Cecilia Church.
Cantwell, Edward F. '58 (ALB) Hudson, NY Church of St. Mary; Special Assignment.
Cantwell, James *o.f.m.conv.* '61 (L) [6] Louisville, KY St. Anthony Church.
Cantwell, James S. *o.f.m.conv.* (IND) Indianapolis, IN Veterans' Administration Hospital.
Cantwell, John '69 (SAC) Citrus Heights, CA Holy Family Church.
Cantwell, Stephen F. *c.m.* '82 (PH) [69] Philadelphia, PA Immaculate Conception Church.
Cantwell, William J. *c.s.p.* '56 (NY) [Z] Scarsdale, NY Paulist Fathers Generalate.
Cantwell, William J. *c.s.p.* '56 (PMB) [G] Vero Beach, FL Paulist Fathers Retirement Home.
Canty, Richard J. '85 (SAV) Special Assignment.
Canuel, Paul E. '66 (FR) [2] New Bedford, MA Nuestra Senora de Guadalupe Church; [13] New Bedford, MA St. Hedwig Church; [15] New Bedford, MA St. John the Baptist Church; [N] Fall River, MA Special Apostolates, Department of.
Canzano, Ettore *c.s.s.* '47 (BO) [Z] Waltham, MA Stigmatine Fathers and Brothers.
Canzio, Celestino *o.f.m.* '73 (NY) [Z] New York, NY Franciscan Province of the Immaculate Conception.
Cao, John '89 (HT) On Duty Outside the Diocese.
Cao Phuong Ky, Joseph *s.s.* (SPC) [E] Carthage, MO Congregation of the Mother Co-Redemptrix, United States Assumption Province.
Cao Xuan Canh, Joseph M. *c.m.c.* (SPC) [E] Carthage, MO Congregation of the Mother Co-Redemptrix, United States Assumption Province.
Capacetti, Luis O. '87 (SJN) [5] Guaynabo, PR Maria Madre de la Misericordia Church.
Capacillo, Euben *o.a.r.* '75 (ORG) [5] Santa Ana, CA Our Lady of the Pillar Church.
Capalbo, Kenneth *o.f.m.* '74 (SFD) [B] Quincy, IL Quincy University.
Capato, Justino *o.s.b.* '80 (PAT) [M] Morristown, NJ St. Mary's Abbey.
Capdepon, Federico '83 (MIA) [9] Miami, FL Mother of Our Redeemer Church.
Capdeville, Henri *o.s.b.* '93 (TUC) [F] St. David, AZ Holy Trinity Monastery.
Capella, Joseph *s.a.c.* '90 (CAM) [C] Pennsauken, NJ Bishop Eustace Prep School.
Capelle, John J. *s.j.* '47 (NO) [F] New Orleans, LA Jesuit High School.
Capellupo, Frank '76 (BRK) [100] Brooklyn, NY Our Lady of Lourdes Church.
Capen, George G. *o.m.i.* '59 (MAN) [K] Hudson, NH Missionary Oblates of Mary Immaculate.
Capetillo, Modesto '48 (SD) Retired.
Capewell, Timothy J. '83 (TR) West Windsor, NJ Church of St. David the King.
Capik, Msgr. William J. '55 (MET) Basking Ridge, NJ St. James Church.
Capillo, John E. '69 (BRK) [64] Brooklyn, NY Immaculate Heart of Mary Church.
Capitani, Msgr. Anthony L. '46 (TR) Retired.
Capitani, Sylvan P. '64 (HBG) New Freedom, PA St. John the Baptist Church.
Capitolo, Mario L. *s.j.* '59 (SJ) [D] San Jose, CA Bellarmine College Preparatory.
Capitolo, Paul F. *s.j.* '69 (SFR) [E] San Francisco, CA St. Ignatius College Preparatory (Coed); [N] San Francisco, CA Jesuit Community at St. Ignatius College Preparatory.
Capizzi, Simeon *o.f.m.* '53 (SP) [O] St. Petersburg, FL St. Anthony Friary.
Caplice, Richard I. *s.j.* '64 (NEW) [26] Jersey City, NJ St. Peter's Church.
Caplis, Roger J. '58 (CHI) Blue Island, IL St. Benedict Church.
Capo, Msgr. Jaime '49 (SJN) [5] Guaynabo, PR Maria Madre de la Misericordia Church.
Capolarello, Salvatore L. '78 (BRK) [235] Queens, NY St. Robert Bellarmine Church.
Capone, Albert J. (BO) [10] Lowell, MA St. Michael Church.
Caponi, Jerome '60 (VIC) Retired.
Caporali, Paul M. *s.d.b.* '54 (LA) Bellflower, CA St. Dominic Savio Church.
Capozzelli, Anthony M. '73 (E) Retired; [O] Erie, PA Theophilus.
Capozzelli, Msgr. Emmanuel '49 (NEW) Retired.
Cappelletti, Edward *s.d.b.* '50 (NY) [Z] New Rochelle, NY Salesian Provincial House.
Cappelletti, Joseph '82 (CLV) Lyndhurst, OH St. Clare Church.
Cappelli, Msgr. Angelo J. '48 (STU) Retired.
Cappelloni, David P. '86 (SCR) Dallas, PA Gate of Heaven Church.
Cappelloni, Thomas A. '76 (SCR) Jackson, PA St. Martin of Tours Church.
Cappiello, Luis Rios '81 (ARE) [4] Arecibo, PR Santa Ana Church.
Cappo, Louis C. '46 (MAR) [1] Marquette, MI St. Peter Cathedral.
Cappucci, Chester *o.m.i.* '63 (GB) Baileys Harbor, WI St. Mary of the Lake Church; Sister Bay, WI St. Rosalia Church.
Cappuccino, Gregory J. '73 (RVC) Valley Stream, NY Blessed Sacrament Church.
Caprio, Albert A. *o.p.* '66 (MET) [H] New Brunswick, NJ De Porres House; [M] New Brunswick, NJ Catholic Center at Rutgers University.
Caprio, Robert J. *o.f.m.* '63 (BO) [P] Andover, MA Franciscan Center; [W] Andover, MA St. Francis Friary; [Y] Andover, MA Franciscan Center - Retreat House.
Capriolo, Victor R. '71 (MIL) [1] Wauwatosa, WI St. Bernard's Church.
Capua, Msgr. Nicholas J. '56 (BRK) [191] Queens, NY St. Luke Church.
Capuano, John J. '40 (WOR) Retired.
Capuci, John M. '90 (BO) [D] Braintree, MA Archbishop Williams' High School.
Caputo, Louis *s.d.v.* '67 (NEW) [25] Newark, NJ St. Michael's Church.
Caputo, Ralph J. '75 (BRK) [231] Queens, NY Queen of Peace Church.
Capyak, Michael S. '84 (MAR) Leave of Absence.
Caraballo, Antonio '80 (ARE) Quebradillas, PR Sacred Heart Church.
Caraballo, Msgr. Benito '40 (HON) Retired.
Carabello, Francis J. '68 (NO) Gretna, LA St. Joseph Church.
Caracci, Christopher P. '94 (ORL) Altamonte Springs, FL Annunciation Church.
Carapella, Thomas *t.o.r.* '92 (ALT) [A] Loretto, PA St. Francis College; [F] Loretto, PA St. Francis Friary, Third Order Regular of St. Francis of Penance; [H] Huntingdon, PA Juniata College.
Carathers, Patrick '81 (AMA) [7] Amarillo, TX St. Hyacinth's Church; Vega, TX Immaculate Conception Church.
Carbajales, Ignacio '60 (MIA) On Duty Outside the Archdiocese.
Carberry, John '81 (SFD) [2] Quincy, IL St. Boniface Church.
Carbine, Francis A. '62 (PH) [1] Bensalem, PA St. Charles Borromeo Church.
Carbo, Eugene J. '62 (PH) Strafford, PA Our Lady of the Assumption Church.
Carbonaro, Dennis J. '81 (PH) [A] Wynnewood, PA Theological Seminary of St. Charles Borromeo, Overbrook.
Carbone, Angelo *c.s.* '56 (KC) [18] Kansas City, MO Holy Rosary Church.
Carbone, Anthony J. '93 (GBG) New Kensington, PA St. Joseph Church.
Carbone, Joseph M. *o.s.m.* '59 (DEN) [21] Denver, CO Our Lady of Mt. Carmel Church.
Carbone, Roland *o.s.b.* '56 (KC) [A] Conception, MO Conception Seminary College.
Carbone, Vito J. '62 (PH) [120] Philadelphia, PA Our Lady of Loreto Church.
Carbonneau, Robert *c.p.* '78 (CHI) [N] Chicago, IL Passionist Community-CTU.
Carboy, Daniel J. *c.ss.r.* '66 (CHL) Concord, NC St. James Church.
Carcerano, Michael J. '76 (LA) Gardena, CA Maria Regina Church; Simi Valley, CA St. Rose of Lima Church.
Carchidi, Rudolph V. *c.s.c.* '55 (FR) [B] North Easton, MA Stonehill College.
Carcich, G. John '45 (R) Retired.
Cardelli, Daniel E. '57 (OAK) Danville, CA St. Isidore's Church; [R] Oakland, CA Italian Catholic Federation.
Carden, Robert F. '56 (PBL) Vineland, CO St. Therese Church.
Carden, Robert J. '57 (NY) Absent on Leave.
Carden, Robert J. '57 (PBL) [12] Pueblo, CO St. Joseph Church.
Cardenas, David J. '61 (GAL) [71] Houston, TX Resurrection Church.
Cardenas, Eugenio *m.sp.s.* '82 (LA) Huntington Park, CA St. Martha Church.
Cardenas, Jader de Jesus (GAL) [21] Houston, TX St. Christopher Church.
Cardenas, Marco *c.m.f.* (CHI) [166] Chicago, IL St. Paul Church.
Cardente, Edward S. '74 (PRO) [1] North Providence, RI St. Anthony's Church.
Cardenzana, Philip A. '65 (DAV) Newton, IA Sacred Heart Church.
Cardiff, Msgr. John I. '45 (CHI) [4] Oak Lawn, IL St. Linus Church; Retired.
Cardillo, Clement (NEW) [S] South Orange, NJ Salesians of Don Bosco, S.D.B.
Cardinal, Maurice '50 (SB) Apple Valley, CA Our Lady of the Desert Church.
Cardinali, Fred '38 (FTW) Retired.
Cardona, George '53 (MIA) [5] Hialeah, FL St. John the Apostle Church; Retired.
Cardone, Joseph P. '87 (TOL) Fostoria, OH St. Wendelin Church.
Cardone, Thomas A. *s.m.* '85 (RVC) [D] Uniondale, NY Kellenberg Memorial High School; [N] Mineola, NY Provincial Residence and Novitiate.
Cardoni, Albert A. *s.j.* '60 (BGP) [A] Fairfield, CT Fairfield University; [O] Fairfield, CT The Fairfield Jesuit Community-Fairfield University.
Cardoso, Luis A. '58 (FR) [18] Fall River, MA St. Michael's Church.
Cardoso, Reinaldo M. '60 (PRO) [4] West Warwick, RI St. Anthony Church.
Cardoza, Timothy N. '83 (FRS) Tulare, CA St. Rita Church.
Cardy, William E. *o.f.m.* '72 (FBK) Aniak, AK St. Theresa Church; Holy Cross, AK Holy Cross Church.
Carek, Peter P. '60 (MIL) [4] Wauwatosa, WI St. Jude the Apostle Church.
Carel, William L. '41 (SC) Retired.
Carelli, Msgr. Richard J. '53 (WOR) Retired.
Carew, Cyprian E. *o.c.s.o.* '47 (ATL) [I] Conyers, GA The Monastery of the Holy Spirit.
Carew, Lawrence F. '66 (BGP) [4] Danbury, CT St. Joseph's Church.
Carey, Brian *c.s.sp.* '58 (STA) [3] Jacksonville, FL Christ the King Church.
Carey, Charles M. *c.s.c.* '35 (FTW) [B] Notre Dame, IN University of Notre Dame Du Lac; [J] Notre Dame, IN Holy Cross Community, Corby Hall, University of Notre Dame.
Carey, David M. '62 (BAL) Special Assignment; [N] Baltimore, MD The School Sisters of Notre Dame in the City of Baltimore (Baltimore Prov.).
Carey, Donald D. '96 (STL) [5] St. Charles, MO St. Peter Church.
Carey, J. Peter *s.j.* '64 (CIN) [M] Cincinnati, OH Faber Jesuit Community.
Carey, James H. '66 (SY) [14] Syracuse, NY St. Charles Church.
Carey, John *o.f.m.cap.* '53 (GBG) Export, PA St. Mary Church.
Carey, Joseph H. *c.s.c.* '69 (FTW) [B] Notre Dame, IN University of Notre Dame Du Lac; [J] Notre Dame, IN Holy Cross Community, Corby Hall, University of Notre Dame.
Carey, Msgr. Leo P. '51 (PAT) Retired; [P] Chester, NJ Nazareth Village.
Carey, Michael *o.p.* '77 (OAK) [B] Moraga, CA Saint Mary's College; [N] Moraga, CA Dominican Community; [Q] Moraga, CA St. Mary's College Campus Ministry.
Carey, Paul J. '42 (PH) New Hope, PA St. Martin of Tours Church; Retired.
Carey, Paul V. '71 (SY) Pompey, NY Immaculate Conception Church.
Carey, Raymond '70 (P) Special Assignment.
Carey, Richard '55 (LA) Pomona, CA St. Joseph Church.
Carey, Richard T. '65 (WOR) North Brookfield, MA St.

Joseph's Church.
Carey, Robert *c.s.v.* '57 (SJ) San Jose, CA O'Connor Hospital.
Carey, Robert H. *c.s.v.* '58 (CHI) [N] Arlington Heights, IL Viatorian Province Center-Clerics of St. Viator.
Carey, Stephen '62 (CAM) Sea Isle City, NJ St. Joseph's Church.
Carey, Thomas *s.m.* '49 (CLV) [N] Cleveland, OH Sts. Mary and Joseph Home for the Aged.
Carey, Thomas '49 (NEW) Retired.
Carey, Thomas F. '37 (PIT) Whitehall, PA St. Gabriel of the Sorrowful Virgin Church; Allegheny County, PA Leader - Bethel Park; Allegheny County, PA Leader - Greentree; Allegheny County, PA Mt. Lebanon Manor Convalescent Center; Allegheny County, PA Southwestern Nursing and Rehabilitation Center; Retired.
Carey, Thomas G. *s.m.* '49 (WDC) [M] Washington, DC Marist Provincial House.
Carey, Thomas P. '34 (IND) Retired.
Carey, William F. '67 (BGP) Military Chaplains.
Carey, William G. '81 (BGP) [3] Stamford, CT St. Cecilia's Church.
Carey, William H. '59 (SHP) Many, LA St. John the Baptist Church.
Carey, Msgr. William J. '43 (PRO) Retired.
Carey, William V. '44 (PEO) Wenona, IL St. Mary's Church.
Carfagna, Frank A. '67 (Y) [8] Canton, OH St. Joseph's Church.
Carges, Bernard L. '60 (ROC) Ithaca, NY Immaculate Conception Church.
Cargill, Msgr. Eugene '59 (GAL) League City, TX St. Mary Church.
Cargo, Thomas H. *c.m.* '78 (LA) [95] Los Angeles, CA St. Vincent De Paul Church.
Caridi, Michael A. '94 (PIT) Monroeville, PA St. Bernadette Church.
Carie, Giles *o.f.m.conv.* '61 (LSC) Mesilla Park, NM Shrine and Parish of Our Lady of Guadalupe Church.
Cariglio, Michael J. '70 (Y) [6] Youngstown, OH Our Lady of Mt. Carmel Church.
Carignan, Raymond P. *s.s.j.* '61 (LAF) Crowley, LA St. Theresa Church.
Carignan, Ronald *o.m.i.* '59 (BEL) [G] Belleville, IL Missionary Oblates of Mary Immaculate - St. Henry's Oblate Residence.
Carillo, J.M. *m.c.c.j.* '40 (NEW) [N] Montclair, NJ Comboni Missionaries of the Heart of Jesus (Verona Fathers).
Carina, Chester H. '85 (MET) Bernardsville, NJ Our Lady of Perpetual Help Church; [K] Bernardsville, NJ Sacred Heart Chapel.
Carini, James P. '65 (NOR) Tolland, CT St. Matthew Church.
Carkenord, David '62 (FTW) Waterloo, IN St. Michael the Archangel Church.
Carkhuff, Thomas *o.s.c.* '76 (STP) [N] Shoreview, MN Crosier Community of Shoreview.
Carl, Kenneth '46 (OM) Olean, NE Sacred Heart Church.
Carles, Alexander J. '88 (MET) Clinton, NJ Immaculate Conception Church.
Carleton, Robert J. *m.m.* '64 (NY) [Z] Maryknoll, NY Maryknoll Fathers and Brothers.
Carley, Edward B. '48 (WIL) Retired.
Carley, Patrick F. '69 (SLC) [2] Salt Lake City, UT Our Lady of Guadalupe Church.
Carlin, Bernie *c.ss.r.* '78 (GR) [3] Grand Rapids, MI St. Alphonsus Church.
Carlin, George *s.o.l.t.* '84 (CC) [H] Robstown, TX Society of Our Lady of the Most Holy Trinity.
Carlin, Harry V. *s.j.* '48 (SFR) [E] San Francisco, CA St. Ignatius College Preparatory (Coed); [N] San Francisco, CA Jesuit Community at St. Ignatius College Preparatory.
Carlin, Msgr. John A. '39 (NY) [16] Yonkers, NY St. Peter Church; Retired.
Carlin, John T. '76 (CLV) [3] Parma, OH St. Charles Borromeo Church.
Carlin, Thomas F. *s.j.* '76 (FBK) St. Michael, AK St. Michael Church; Stebbins, AK St. Bernard Church; Unalakleet, AK Church of the Holy Angels.
Carlin, Warren *o.carm.* '58 (JOL) [J] Darien, IL Carmelite Fathers Provincial Office.
Carlino, Richard A. '79 (ALB) [2] Schenectady, NY St. Anthony Church; [13] Schenectady, NY Our Lady of the Assumption Church.
Carlo, Joseph C. '63 (BUF) [1] Niagara Falls, NY St. Charles Church.
Carlo, Raymond (RVC) Priests Released from Diocesan Assignment.
Carlo, Raymond J. '87 (STA) Orange Park, FL St. Catherine's Church.
Carlone, Carmen A. '69 (CAM) Williamstown, NJ St. Mary's Church.
Carlos, Joseph '75 (STL) [P] St. Louis, MO Franciscan Friary of St. Anthony of Padua.
Carlos, Miguel '95 (LAN) [4] Jackson, MI Queen of the Miraculous Medal Church.
Carlsen, Jeffrey '72 (BAL) Jessup, MD Maryland House of Correction & Annex; Special Assignment.
Carlson, Curtis *o.f.m.cap.* '95 (SAL) Hays, KS St. Joseph's Church; [D] Hays, KS St. Joseph's Friary.
Carlson, Edward A. '83 (CHI) [52] Chicago, IL St. Edward Church.
Carlson, George F. '66 (BO) [10] Lawrence, MA St. Patrick Church.
Carlson, Gerald J. '62 (GI) Kearney, NE Prince of Peace Church.
Carlson, J. Arnold (AMA) Retired.
Carlson, James R. '73 (SAG) Munger, MI St. Norbert Church; Reese, MI St. Elizabeth Church.
Carlson, Richard D. '69 (NEW) Hillside, NJ Christ the King Church.
Carlson, Robert D. '63 (GAL) Galena Park, TX Our Lady of Fatima Church.
Carlson, Steven '96 (R) Clinton, NC Immaculate Conception Church.
Carlton, Maurice T. '68 (MET) South River, NJ Corpus Christi Church; [G] Somerset, NJ McCarrick Care Center.
Carlucci, F. Antonio *r.c.j.* (LA) [R] Oxnard, CA Rogationist Fathers.
Carmichael, Eugene J. *s.j.* '73 (CIN) [M] Cincinnati, OH Jesuit Community at Xavier Unversity.
Carmody, Emeric *o.carm.* '54 (NEW) Teaneck, NJ St. Anastasia's Church.
Carmody, Francis R. *s.j.* '55 (BAL) [M] Baltimore, MD Ferdinand Wheeler House; [Q] Baltimore, MD Jesuit Seminary Guild & Jesuit Mission Bureau, Maryland Province, Inc.
Carmody, James F. '70 (WOR) [17] Worcester, MA St. Andrew the Apostle Church.
Carmody, James P. '63 (RVC) New Hyde Park, NY Notre Dame Church.
Carmody, Lawrence W. '90 (COS) [2] Colorado Springs, CO Corpus Christi Church.
Carmody, Michael J. '83 (GAL) Brazoria, TX St. Joseph Church.
Carmody, Stephen F. *o.p.* '81 (PH) [61] Philadelphia, PA Holy Name of Jesus Church; [Z] Philadelphia, PA Holy Name Priory, Dominican Friars.
Carmola, Michael J. '64 (SY) Special Assignment; [U] Syracuse, NY Christ the King Retreat House.
Carmon, Dominic '60 (NO) [31] New Orleans, LA St. Frances Xavier Cabrini Church.
Carmona, Eduardo '83 (LA) [15] Los Angeles, CA Immaculate Conception Church.
Carmona, Henry '78 (B) Rupert, ID St. Nicholas Church.
Carmona, Hugo '85 (PRO) [24] Providence, RI Our Lady of Mt. Carmel Church.
Carmone, Anthony F. '47 (PRO) Retired.
Carnago, William J. '88 (DET) [36] Detroit, MI Immaculate Heart of Mary Church; Special Assignment.
Carne Joseph D. '71 (MAR) Bessemer, MI St. Sebastian Church.
Carnero, Denis '68 (CHI) [161] Chicago, IL Our Lady of Victory Church.
Carnevale, John *o.f.m.* '66 (PAT) Pompton Lakes, NJ Our Lady of the Assumption Church.
Carnevale, Thomas J. '61 (PRO) Retired.
Carney, Aloysius S. '60 (NEW) Plainfield, NJ St. Mary Church; Plainfield, NJ Muhlenberg Medical Center.
Carney, Angus N. *o.s.a.* '43 (PH) [Z] Villanova, PA St. Thomas Monastery.
Carney, Christopher M. '71 (BAL) [61] Baltimore, MD St. Michael Church.
Carney, Edward '63 (PEO) Special Residence.
Carney, J. Michael '70 (SY) Clark Mills, NY Church of the Annunciation.
Carney, James R. *s.j.* '56 (NY) [F] New York, NY Regis High School; [Z] New York, NY St. Ignatius Loyola Residence.
Carney, John '70 (BAL) Retired.
Carney, John F. '91 (SFE) Tijeras, NM Holy Child Church.
Carney, Joseph T. '68 (MIA) Miami Springs, FL Blessed Trinity Church.
Carney, Msgr. Patrick J. '55 (NY) [28] New York, NY Corpus Christi Church.
Carney, Ralph *o.f.m.* '53 (SEA) [4] Tacoma, WA St. John Bosco Church.
Carney, Richard F. '55 (KC) [33] Kansas City, MO Our Lady of Sorrows Church.
Carney, Robert *s.a.c.* '66 (MIL) [P] Milwaukee, WI St. Vincent Community.
Carney, Robert E. (TUC) Douglas, AZ St. Luke Church; Pirtleville, AZ St. Bernard's Church.
Carney, Robert V. *s.a.c.* '66 (MIL) [D] Milwaukee, WI Pius XI High School; [P] Milwaukee, WI Pallotti House; [Y] Milwaukee, WI Pallottine Fathers and Brothers, Inc., Disability Trust; [Y] Milwaukee, WI Pallottine Fathers and Brothers, Inc., Educational and Apostolic Ministry Trust.
Carney, Thomas *m.s.c.* '54 (RCK) [H] Aurora, IL Missionaries of the Sacred Heart Community.
Carnicelli, Xavier *o.f.m.* '57 (NY) [Z] New York, NY Franciscan Province of the Immaculate Conception.
Caro, Ernesto (CIN) [14] Dayton, OH Holy Family Church.
Caro, Jorge '89 (MGZ) Lajas, PR De la Merced Parish Church.
Caro, Robert *s.j.* '70 (BO) [W] Chestnut Hill, MA The Jesuit Community at Boston College.
Caro, Robert V. *s.j.* '70 (LA) [C] Los Angeles, CA Loyola Marymount University.
Carod, Rogelio '35 (SJN) [17] San Juan, PR Francisca Javiera Cabrini Church.
Carolan, Charles *s.s.c.* '60 (LA) [66] Los Angeles, CA St. Gregory Nazianzen Church.
Carolan, Charles B. '55 (VIC) Flatonia, TX Sacred Heart Church.
Carolan, Craig G. '91 (BWN) Progreso, TX Holy Spirit Church.
Carolan, Emmit (SAT) [41] San Antonio, TX St. James the Apostle Church.
Carolan, J. Lawrence '69 (SR) Calistoga, CA Our Lady of Perpetual Help Church.
Carolan, John J. '51 (CHI) [2] Oak Park, IL St. Catherine of Siena-St. Lucy Church; Retired.
Carolan, Thomas *o.f.m.* '58 (CLV) Warrensville Heights, OH St. Jude Church; [P] Cleveland, OH St. Jude Friary.
Carolin, Joeseph C. '66 (HBG) South Mountain, PA Restoration Center.
Carolin, William, J. '45 (LAN) Retired.
Carolin, William J. '45 (LAN) Brighton, MI St. Patrick Church.
Caroluzza, Thomas J. '58 (RIC) [5] Virginia Beach, VA Holy Spirit Church.
Caron, Antonin R. '69 (PRT) Sabbatical.
Caron, David '89 (SPR) Graduate Studies.
Caron, Donald R. '89 (ATL) Lawrenceville, GA St. Marguerite D'Youville Church.
Caron, Gerard *s.m.* '54 (BO) [W] Boston, MA Marist Fathers Lourdes Residence; [BB] Boston, MA Chapel of Our Lady of Lourdes.
Caron, Gerard J. '94 (PRO) [1] Woonsocket, RI St. Agatha's Church; [10] Woonsocket, RI Precious Blood Church.
Caron, Marc '89 (PRT) Sabbatical.
Caron, Paul A. (FR) Acushnet, MA St. Francis Xavier's Church.
Caronan, John E. *o.praem.* '94 (ORG) [A] Silverado, CA St. Michael's Norbertine Postulancy, Novitiate and Juniorate; [H] Silverado, CA Norbertine Fathers.
Carosella, Jerome A. '63 (VEN) Boca Grande, FL Our Lady of Mercy Church.
Carotenuto, Anthony M. '68 (TR) New Egypt, NJ Assumption Church.
Carpanese, Mario *s.d.b.* '46 (BO) [E] Boston, MA Don Bosco Preparatory School of Technology.
Carpena, Octavio R. '84 (MET) On Duty Outside the Diocese.
Carpender, John W. '53 (DUB) Monti, IA St. Patrick's Church; Ryan, IA St. Patrick's Church.
Carpender, Thomas J. '48 (DUB) Retired.
Carpenter, Christopher '95 (PHX) [1] Phoenix, AZ SS. Simon and Jude Cathedral.
Carpenter, Edward C., Jr. '95 (ELP) Pecos, TX Santa Rosa Church.
Carpenter, Edward V. '43 (SC) Retired.
Carpenter, Ralph *c.s.p.* '44 (SFR) [K] San Francisco, CA Home for the Aged of the Little Sisters of the Poor.
Carpenter, Ralph T. *c.s.p.* '44 (NY) [Z] Scarsdale, NY Paulist Fathers Generalate.
Carpenter, William L. *c.s.v.* '77 (CHI) [210] Chicago, IL St. Viator Church.
Carpentier, Normand E. '71 (PRT) Old Orchard Beach, ME St. Margaret's Church.
Carpentier, Robert A. '67 (PRO) Absent on Leave.
Carpine, Eric *o.f.m.* '75 (NY) [35] New York, NY St. Francis of Assisi Church.
Carpinelli, Vincent G. '71 (CAM) Glassboro, NJ St. Bridget's Church.
Carqueijo Se, Luiz Antonio *o.s.b.* '92 (GBG) [H] Latrobe, PA Saint Vincent Archabbey.
Carr, Alton T. *c.ss.r.* '60 (GAL) [33] Houston, TX Holy Ghost Church.
Carr, Andrew *c.ss.r.* '92 (BAL) [60] Baltimore, MD St. Michael Church.
Carr, Bernard '76 (LFT) On Duty Outside the Diocese.
Carr, Bernard J. '76 (SB) Anza, CA Sacred Heart Church.
Carr, Brendan T. '72 (BAL) Glen Burnie, MD Church of the Crucifixion.
Carr, Charles T. '80 (BGP) [3] Bridgeport, CT St. Andrew Church; Leave of Absence.
Carr, Cornelius *s.j.* (GB) [M] Oshkosh, WI Jesuit Retreat House.
Carr, David '80 (PMB) [B] West Palm Beach, FL Cardinal Newman High School.
Carr, David W. '80 (WOR) On Duty Outside the Diocese.
Carr, Ephrem *o.s.b.* '67 (IND) [J] St. Meinrad, IN St. Meinrad Archabbey.
Carr, Eugene R. '63 (SCR) [13] Scranton, PA St. John the Evangelist Church.
Carr, Gary M. '82 (SPC) Houston, MO St. Mark Church.
Carr, Gerald F. *o.f.m.* '56 (NY) [35] New York, NY St.

Francis of Assisi Church.
Carr, Msgr. James A. (CAM) Retired.
Carr, James M. '34 (ALN) Retired; [J] Bethlehem, PA Holy Family Villa.
Carr, James P. *s.j.* '92 (BO) [E] Boston, MA Boston College High School & Jesuit Community.
Carr, James V. '69 (RIC) Portsmouth, VA Church of the Resurrection.
Carr, John A. *c.s.p.* (NY) [Z] Scarsdale, NY Paulist Fathers Generalate.
Carr, John A. *c.s.p.* '40 (SFR) [31] San Francisco, CA Old St. Mary's Cathedral.
Carr, John F. '47 (BO) Retired.
Carr, Mark V. '52 (BO) Abington, MA St. Nicholas Church.
Carr, Martin P. '74 (GB) Special Assignment.
Carr, Michael '68 (CHY) [3] Cheyenne, WY St. Joseph's Church.
Carr, Paul *f.s.s.p.* '92 (SCR) [E] Moscow, PA St. Gregory's Academy.
Carr, Paul S. *f.s.s.p.* '92 (SCR) [M] Elmhurst, PA Priestly Fraternity of St. Peter (F.S.S.P.).
Carr, Peter *o.f.m.* '39 (SP) [O] St. Petersburg, FL St. Anthony Friary.
Carr, Raymond *s.m.* '63 (NO) [9] New Orleans, LA Holy Name Of Mary (Algiers) Church.
Carr, Walter F. '92 (AUS) Andice, TX Santa Rosa Church; Georgetown, TX St. Helen's Church.
Carr, William F. *s.j.* '56 (BGP) [A] Fairfield, CT Fairfield University; [O] Fairfield, CT The Fairfield Jesuit Community-Fairfield University.
Carr, William H. '69 (RIC) Williamsburg, VA St. Bede's Church.
Carr, William M. '59 (WCH) [1] Wichita, KS Cathedral of the Immaculate Conception.
Carranco, Juan '50 (SJ) [5] Santa Clara, CA Our Lady of Peace Church.
Carrano, Michael A. '70 (BRK) [12] Brooklyn, NY Assumption of the Blessed Virgin Mary Church; [E] Brooklyn, NY Office of Religious Education: Evangelization and Catholic Formation.
Carranza, Fernando '95 (NEW) [1] Newark, NJ Cathedral of the Sacred Heart Basilica.
Carranza, Riz. J. '80 (LA) Carson, CA St. Philomena Church.
Carrara, Christopher '94 (OG) Saranac Lake, NY St. Bernard Church.
Carraro, Francesco '95 (NEW) Bergenfield, NJ St. John the Evangelist Church.
Carreira, Emmanuel M. *s.j.* '60 (CLV) [C] Cleveland, OH John Carroll Jesuit Community.
Carreiro, Walter A. (BO) [1] Cambridge, MA St. Anthony Church.
Carrella, Eugene J. '84 (NY) Crestwood, NY Church of the Annunciation.
Carreon, Albert S. '51 (GAL) Retired.
Carreras, Carlos *s.j.* '76 (ATL) [4] Atlanta, GA Immaculate Heart of Mary Church.
Carrero, Dario *o.f.m.* '95 (SJN) [4] Toa Baja, PR Jose Obrero Church.
Carrero, Jesse *c.m.f.* '65 (CHI) [N] Oak Park, IL Claretian Fathers Headquarters of U.S.A. Eastern Province.
Carrero, Jesse *c.m.f.* '65 (MET) [4] Perth Amboy, NJ Our Lady of Fatima Church.
Carrico, Rui M. '87 (HRT) [4] Hartford, CT Our Lady of Fatima Church.
Carrier, Herve G. '47 (PRT) Retired.
Carrier, J. Victor '69 (SPR) [4] Chicopee, MA St. Anne's Church.
Carrier, Joseph S. '33 (PRT) Retired.
Carrier, Michael J. '95 (WIL) Elkton, MD Immaculate Conception Church.
Carrier, Paul E. *s.j.* '77 (BGP) [A] Fairfield, CT Fairfield University; [O] Fairfield, CT The Fairfield Jesuit Community-Fairfield University; [V] Bridgeport, CT Newman Centers.
Carriere, David *o.f.m.* '63 (LA) [R] Santa Barbara, CA Franciscan Friary, Order of Friars Minor (Old Mission).
Carriere, Henry G. '46 (CR) Retired.
Carrieri, Leonard *m.ss.cc.* '36 (CAM) [H] Pleasantville, NJ Our Lady's Residence; [L] Linwood, NJ Villa Pieta.
Carriero, John P. *s.j.* '63 (ROC) [B] Rochester, NY McQuaid Jesuit High School.
Carrigan, Fredrick '61 (PRT) On Duty Outside the Diocese.
Carrigan, John T. *o.p.* '38 (SPR) [J] West Springfield, MA Monastery of the Mother of God, Dominican Nuns (Contemplative).
Carrigan, Thomas '60 (SAC) Westwood, CA Our Lady of the Snows Church.
Carrigg, George A. '57 (BO) [19] Boston, MA St. Christopher Church.
Carrigg, William J. '56 (PRT) Fort Fairfield, ME St. Denis Church; Limestone, ME St. Louis Church.
Carrillo, Arhtur *c.p.* '70 (CHI) [N] Chicago, IL Passionist Provincial Office.
Carrillo, Msgr. Arsenio S. *v.g.* '56 (TUC) [1] Tucson, AZ St. Augustine's Cathedral; Special Assignment.
Carrillo, Eon *s.f.* '74 (SFE) Santa Cruz, NM Holy Cross Church.
Carrillo, Sergio '82 (MIA) [3] Miami, FL Corpus Christi Church.
Carrillo, Victor '87 (SAT) Floresville, TX Sacred Heart Church.
Carrington, Richard J. '76 (NEW) [1] Hoboken, NJ Our Lady of Grace Church.
Carrion, Jose A. *o.f.m.cap.* '92 (ARE) [1] Utuado, PR San Miquel Church.
Carrion, Michael W. '77 (BAL) [24] Baltimore, MD St. Clare Church.
Carrion, Patrick '82 (BAL) Special Assignment.
Carrion-Parroco, Jose Antonio (SJN) [1] Toa Alta, PR San Esteban, Protomartir Church.
Carrola, Rudolph T., Jr. '88 (SAT) Macdona, TX Our Lady Queen of Heaven Church; Von Ormy, TX Sacred Heart Church.
Carroll, Msgr. Aidan M. '63 (LA) Valinda, CA St. Martha Church; [D] La Puente, CA Bishop Amat Memorial High School.
Carroll, Brian '62 (JKS) Clarksdale, MS St. Elizabeth Church; Clarksdale, MS Immaculate Conception Church.
Carroll, Brian *o.f.m.* '86 (NY) [35] New York, NY St. Francis of Assisi Church.
Carroll, Clement D. '60 (CHI) Other Assignments.
Carroll, Msgr. Daniel '37 (CHY) Retired.
Carroll, Daniel *s.d.s.* '44 (MIL) [N] Milwaukee, WI St. Mary's Nursing Home.
Carroll, Daniel *o.carm.* '60 (CHI) [D] Chicago, IL Mt. Carmel High School; [N] Chicago, IL Carmelite Priory of St. Cyril.
Carroll, Msgr. Donald M. '34 (CHI) Retired.
Carroll, Eamon R. *o.carm.* '46 (CHI) [N] Chicago, IL Brandsma House.
Carroll, Edmund F. *t.o.r.* '57 (PIT) [N] Pittsburgh, PA Franciscan Friars, T.O.R.; [N] Pittsburgh, PA Third Order Regular of Saint Francis - Province of the Most Sacred Heart of Jesus.
Carroll, Edward E. '50 (MIL) Retired.
Carroll, Edward G. '67 (BO) [2] Woburn, MA St. Barbara Church.
Carroll, Emmett *o.f.m.conv.* '54 (TR) Seaside Park, NJ St. Catharine of Siena Church.
Carroll, Emmett H. *s.j.* '62 (SEA) [A] Seattle, WA Seattle University.
Carroll, Francis B. *o.f.m.* '36 (BO) [Z] Boston, MA Saint Anthony Residence.
Carroll, George A. *s.j.* '58 (SD) Jacumba, CA St. Mary Magdalene Church.
Carroll, Gilbert A. '41 (CHI) [207] Chicago, IL St. Timothy Church; Retired.
Carroll, Howard '54 (SFS) Retired; [I] Sioux Falls, SD The Berakkah House.
Carroll, J. Alfred *s.j.* '59 (SPK) [C] Spokane, WA Gonzaga University.
Carroll, Msgr. James '45 (COL) Retired.
Carroll, James '49 (JKS) Shelby, MS St. Mary Church; Parchman, MS Mississippi State Penitentiary.
Carroll, James *o.f.m.* '79 (PSC) [B] Sybertsville, PA Holy Dormition Monastery.
Carroll, James J. '56 (NEW) Fairview, NJ St. John the Baptist Church.
Carroll, James M. '68 (BO) [6] Haverhill, MA St. Rita Church.
Carroll, John *t.o.r.* '38 (WDC) [M] Washington, DC St. Louis Friary.
Carroll, John A. *s.s.j.* '66 (ARL) [4] Alexandria, VA St. Joseph's Church.
Carroll, John A. *s.s.j.* '66 (WDC) [B] Washington, DC St. Joseph's Seminary.
Carroll, John D. '51 (CHI) Chicago, IL West Side V.A. Hospital.
Carroll, Msgr. John J. '66 (PAT) Kinnelon, NJ Our Lady of the Magnificat Church.
Carroll, Msgr. John P. '42 (BO) Retired.
Carroll, John P. '53 (BO) [6] Quincy, MA Most Blessed Sacrament Church.
Carroll, John R. (BO) Boston, MA Beth Israel Hospital.
Carroll, Joseph *s.j.* '42 (OAK) [17] Oakland, CA St. Mary, Immaculate Conception-St. Francis de Sales Church.
Carroll, Msgr. Joseph A. '31 (NEW) Kearny, NJ St. Cecilia's Church; Retired.
Carroll, Msgr. Joseph A. '74 (SD) [35] San Diego, CA St. Rita Church; [J] San Diego, CA St. Vincent de Paul Village; [N] San Diego, CA Catholic Committee on Scouting.
Carroll, Joseph D. '41 (ALN) Retired; [J] Bethlehem, PA Holy Family Villa.
Carroll, Joseph P. *s.j.* '41 (OAK) [N] Berkeley, CA Jesuit Community at Jesuit School of Theology at Berkeley.
Carroll, L. Patrick *s.j.* (SPK) [6] Spokane, WA St. Aloysius Church.
Carroll, Lawrence J. '81 (BGP) [2] Stratford, CT St. James Church; [C] Fairfield, CT Notre Dame Catholic High School.
Carroll, Maurice E. (NY) [122] New York, NY St. Vincent de Paul Church.
Carroll, Michael (SAC) [7] Sacramento, CA Presentation of the Blessed Virgin Mary Church.
Carroll, Michael '67 (LA) Temple City, CA St. Luke the Evangelist Church.
Carroll, Michael A. '85 (RVC) East Rockaway, NY St. Raymond's Church.
Carroll, Msgr. Michael J. '61 (PH) Rydal, PA St. Hilary of Poitiers Church.
Carroll, Michael J. *c.m.* '77 (BRK) [D] Queens and Staten Island, NY St. John's University; [U] Jamaica, NY Vincentian Residence.
Carroll, Michael R. '70 (GB) Marion, WI St. Mary Church; Tigerton, WI St. Anthony Church.
Carroll, Norman P. '93 (WIL) [6] Wilmington, DE St. Hedwig Church.
Carroll, Owen '73 (NTN) Oakland, CA St. John The Theologian Church.
Carroll, Owen '73 (OAK) [A] Berkeley, CA Dominican School of Philosophy and Theology; [B] Moraga, CA Saint Mary's College.
Carroll, Patrick *c.s.sp.* '66 (STA) Elkton, FL St. Ambrose Church.
Carroll, Patrick A. '43 (OM) Retired.
Carroll, Patrick C. *s.j.* '66 (YAK) [4] Yakima, WA St. Joseph's Church.
Carroll, Patrick J. '53 (NY) [88] New York, NY Our Lady of Loreto Church.
Carroll, Patrick J. '54 (ORL) Barefoot Bay, FL St. Luke Church.
Carroll, Patrick M. '71 (NY) [10] Yonkers, NY St. Joseph Church; [E] White Plains, NY Archbishop Stepinac High School.
Carroll, Msgr. Ralph E. '58 (NO) [7] Metairie, LA St. Clement of Rome Church.
Carroll, Msgr. Richard L. '59 (NO) [4] Slidell, LA St. Margaret Mary Church; Slidell, LA Greenbriar Nursing & Convalescent Home; Slidell, LA Guest House of Slidell Nursing Home; Slidell, LA Greenery Neurologic Rehabilitation Center at Slidell.
Carroll, Robert *o.carm.* '71 (CHI) [D] Mundelein, IL Carmel High School; [N] Mundelein, IL Carmelite Monastery.
Carroll, Msgr. Robert B. '63 (PAT) [1] Passaic, NJ St. Nicholas Church.
Carroll, Robert J. '75 (PH) [A] Wynnewood, PA Theological Seminary of St. Charles Borromeo, Overbrook.
Carroll, Roger F. '63 (STP) [14] St. Paul, MN St. Andrew Church.
Carroll, Thomas F. *o.p.* '58 (CIN) [30] Cincinnati, OH St. Gertrude Church; [M] Cincinnati, OH St. Gertrude Priory.
Carroll, Thomas J. *m.s.* '54 (ATL) Snellville, GA St. Oliver Plunkett Church.
Carroll, Thomas J. *s.j.* '84 (LA) [F] Los Angeles, CA Loyola High School.
Carroll, Thomas R. *sch.p.* '70 (LEX) [B] Martin, KY The Piarist School; [G] Prestonsburg, KY Piarist Fathers.
Carroll, Tom (SJ) [P] Mountain View, CA Mountain View Serra Club.
Carroll, Vincent *o.f.m.* '62 (BO) [BB] Boston, MA St. Anthony Shrine.
Carroll, W. Russell *o.f.m.* '40 (NY) [Z] New York, NY Franciscan Friars, Order of Friars Manor.
Carroll, William '50 (B) Retired.
Carroll, William C. *s.j.* '69 (BUF) [O] Buffalo, NY Canisius Jesuit Community.
Carroll, William R. '70 (BO) [1] Arlington, MA St. Agnes Church.
Carron, J. Walter '37 (ROC) Geneseo, NY St. Mary Church; Retired.
Carron, Malcolm *s.j.* '51 (DET) [K] Detroit, MI Jesuit Community at the University of Detroit.
Carrozza, Andrew P. '90 (NY) Mahopac, NY St. John the Evangelist Church.
Carrozzo, Anthony M. *o.f.m., d.min.* (BUF) [C] St. Bonaventure, NY St. Bonaventure University; [C] St. Bonaventure, NY St. Bonaventure University.
Carrozzo, Anthony M. *o.f.m.* '64 (BUF) [O] St. Bonaventure, NY St. Bonaventure Friary.
Carscallen, Edward C. '47 (TUC) Special Assignment; Retired.
Carson, David L. *o.f.m.* '84 (NY) On Duty Outside the Archdiocese.
Carson, John '64 (NY) [3] Yonkers, NY St. Ann Church.
Carson, Paul C. '83 (KC) Retired.
Carson, Robert E. *o.praem.* '46 (GB) [I] De Pere, WI St. Norbert Abbey; [I] De Pere, WI St. Norbert Abbey.
Carson, Msgr. Stanley B. '79 (ALT) [4] Altoona, PA Sacred Heart Church.
Carta, Umberto '35 (CAM) Retired.
Cartagena, Antonio '85 (CGS) [11] Barrio Rio Canas, PR San Juan Apostol y Evangelista Church.
Cartaya, Pedro *s.j.* '67 (MIA) [D] Miami, FL Belen Jesuit Preparatory School; [H] Miami, FL Villa Arrieta.
Carten, Thomas F. *c.s.c.* '79 (SCR) [C] Wilkes-Barre, PA Kings College.
Carter, Augustine W. *o.carm.* '51 (LA) [R] Los Angeles, CA Mount Carmel Priory, Carmelite Fathers and Brothers.
Carter, Daniel E. '79 (SFR) [26] San Francisco, CA St.

James Church; San Francisco, CA Youth Guidance Center.
Carter, Edward W. *s.j.* '62 (CIN) [M] Cincinnati, OH Faber Jesuit Community.
Carter, Eli K., Jr. '75 (HON) Ewa, HI Immaculate Conception Church.
Carter, Francis T. '86 (HRT) [10] New Britain, CT St. Mary's Church.
Carter, Msgr. James A. '66 (CHR) [17] Charleston, SC Christ Our King Church.
Carter, James C. *s.j.* '58 (NO) [C] New Orleans, LA Loyola University.
Carter, John T. '49 (E) [16] Erie, PA St. George Church.
Carter, John T. '70 (BAL) Military Chaplains.
Carter, Kevin E. '86 (NEW) Hillsdale, NJ St. John the Baptist Church.
Carter, Leo J. *o.s.b.* '53 (BIR) Cullman, AL Sacred Heart Church; [E] Cullman, AL St. Bernard Abbey.
Carter, Mark *o.f.m.cap.* '92 (PIT) Conway, PA Our Lady of Peace Church; [N] Rochester, PA St. Cecilia Friary.
Carter, Martin J. *s.a.* '75 (BRK) [113] Brooklyn, NY Our Lady of Victory Church; [T] Brooklyn, NY Catholic Migration & Refugee Office, Catholic Migration Services, Inc.
Carter, Raymond '49 (COL) Retired.
Carter, Robert E. *s.j.* '63 (NY) [Z] New York, NY West Side Jesuit Community.
Carter, Stephen *o.f.m.cap.* '82 (WDC) [39] Washington, DC Shrine of the Sacred Heart Church.
Carter, William H. '75 (ALN) Lost Creek, PA St. Mary Magdalen Church; [1] Shenandoah, PA Annunciation Church.
Carton, A. Richard '93 (PAT) Mountain Lakes, NJ St. Catherine of Siena Church.
Carton, Msgr. George A. '44 (PEO) Retired; [L] Peoria, IL St. Joseph's Home of Peoria.
Carton, Leo F. '43 (CHI) Skokie, IL St. Peter Church; Retired.
Carton, William J. '59 (TR) Sea Girt, NJ St. Mark Church.
Cartwright, Christopher M. *s.j.* '80 (SAC) [14] Sacramento, CA St. Ignatius Church.
Carty, John T. '50 (PRO) Retired.
Carty, Robert E. '54 (MAN) Retired.
Caruana, Alfred E. *s.j.* '71 (NY) [Z] New York, NY Jesuit Provincial's Office; [Z] New York, NY Xavier Jesuit Community; [DD] New York, NY Xavier Society for the Blind.
Carucci, David (MOB) [K] Montgomery, AL Alabama State University Newman Center; [L] Montgomery, AL St. John's Soup Kitchen, Inc.
Carucci, David '95 (MOB) [5] Montgomery, AL St. John the Baptist Church.
Caruso, Carmen A. '66 (JOL) On Duty Outside the Diocese.
Caruso, Carmen A. '66 (VEN) Sanibel, FL St. Isabel Church.
Caruso, Daniel M. '94 (SY) Johnson City, NY St. James Church.
Caruso, Gerardo M. '78 (PH) Norwood, PA St. Gabriel Church.
Caruso, Lawrence '51 (LA) [1] Long Beach, CA St. Anthony Church.
Caruso, Michael P. *s.j.* '82 (KC) [B] Kansas City, MO Rockhurst College; [J] Kansas City, MO Rockhurst College - Jesuit Community.
Caruso, Philip J. '78 (NY) [172] Bronx, NY Our Lady of Grace Church.
Caruso, Robert '80 (PHX) [1] Mesa, AZ All Saints Church.
Caruso, Vincent *o.de.m.* '27 (CLV) [57] Cleveland, OH Our Lady of Mount Carmel Church; [P] Cleveland, OH Mercedarians.
Carvajal, Damian '53 (SJN) [12] San Juan, PR Cristo Redentor Church.
Carvajal, Msgr. Felipe N. '68 (PAT) Dover, NJ Our Lady Queen of the Most Holy Rosary Church.
Carvajal, Raul H. '65 (MRY) Watsonville, CA Assumption Church.
Carvalho, David *o.s.b.* '57 (SD) [H] Oceanside, CA Prince of Peace Abbey, Benet Hill.
Carvalho, Gordian J., Jr. '85 (HON) Kalaheo, HI Holy Cross Church.
Carven, John W. *c.m.* '60 (BAL) [M] Emmitsburg, MD Vincentian House.
Carven, John W. *c.m.* '60 (PH) [Z] Philadelphia, PA Congregation of the Mission.
Carver, Dennis '94 (BLX) Pass Christian, MS Sacred Heart Church.
Carvill, Michael '82 (FR) [P] North Dartmouth, MA University of Massachusetts Dartmouth Catholic Campus Ministry.
Carvill, Michael '90 (FR) [17] Fall River, MA St. Louis Church; [Q] Fall River, MA Priestly Fraternity of the Missionaries of St. Charles Borromeo, Inc.
Carville, John *s.t.d.* '63 (BR) [21] Baton Rouge, LA St. Thomas More Church.
Cary, Liam '92 (P) [M] Beaverton, OR St. Mary of the Valley Convent.
Cary, Robert '57 (SJ) [H] San Jose, CA O'Connor Hospital.
Cary, William J. '58 (SUP) Retired.
Carzon, Thomas *o.m.v.* '96 (BO) [BB] Boston, MA St. Francis Chapel.
Casabon, Luis '61 (MIA) [5] Hialeah, FL St. John the Apostle Church.
Casaclang, Joseph D. '64 (RVC) Manhasset, NY St. Mary's Church.
Casagram, Michael *o.c.s.o.* '82 (L) [L] Trappist, KY Abbey of Our Lady of Gethsemani, of the Order of Cistercians of the Strict Observance.
Casale, Charles B. '69 (FRS) Wofford Heights, CA St. Jude Church.
Casale, Msgr. Franklyn M. '67 (NEW) On Duty Outside the Archdiocese.
Casaleggio, Dave '81 (LAV) [4] Las Vegas, NV Our Lady of Las Vegas Church.
Casaliggi, John R. '36 (GBG) Retired.
Casares, Benigno Palomo *o.s.a.* '66 (SJN) [1] Bayamon, PR San Agustin Church.
Casari, Michael T. '95 (WIL) Fairfax, DE St. Mary Magdalen Church.
Casarotto, Secondo *c.s.* '66 (BUF) [9] Buffalo, NY St. Anthony of Padua Church.
Casaus, Vicente *sch.p.* '52 (LA) [75] Los Angeles, CA St. Lucy Church.
Casavantes, Carlos *f.s.p.* '86 (CC) [18] Corpus Christi, TX St. Paul the Apostle Church; [A] Corpus Christi, TX Corpus Christi Academy.
Casavantes, Carlos S. *f.s.s.p.* '85 (SCR) [M] Elmhurst, PA Priestly Fraternity of St. Peter (F.S.S.P.).
Casavantes, Carlos S. *f.s.p.* '86 (CC) [16] Corpus Christi, TX St. Michael the Archangel Latin Mass Community Church.
Casazza, Msgr. David J. '43 (NEW) River Edge, NJ St. Peter the Apostle Church; Retired.
Cascelli, Msgr. George J. (NY) [59] New York, NY St. John Nepomucene Church; [A] Yonkers, NY St. Joseph's Seminary; [E] New York, NY Cathedral High School.
Cascia, Philip J. '77 (HRT) Prospect, CT St. Anthony's Church.
Cascino, Marion *o.f.m.* '49 (NY) [1] New York, NY Cathedral of St. Patrick; [Z] New York, NY Padua Friary.
Cascione, James R. *c.ss.r.* '83 (STV) [2] Christiansted, VI Church of the Holy Cross; [B] St. Thomas, VI Miscellaneous Organizations.
Casciotti, James A. *s.j.* '78 (BAL) [M] Baltimore, MD Jesuit Fathers and Brothers Maryland Provincial Curia.
Casco, Jose M. '54 (ARE) [13] Arecibo, PR Church of Santa Cecilia.
Case, Francis J. '66 (SY) New Berlin, NY St. Theresa of the Infant Jesus Church.
Case, Frank E. *s.j.* '69 (P) [L] Portland, OR Jesuit Provincial Office (Oregon Prov.).
Case, Lowell D. *s.s.j.* '80 (WDC) [23] Washington, DC Incarnation Church.
Case, Richard D. *s.j.* '75 (FBK) Pilot Station, AK St. Charles Spinola Church; St. Marys, AK Church of the Nativity; [E] St. Marys, AK Brother Joe Prince Jesuit Community.
Case, Msgr. Vincent T. '58 (NY) [4] Yonkers, NY St. Bartholomew Church.
Casella, David P. '75 (NY) [169] Bronx, NY Our Lady of Angels Church.
Casella, Thomas A. *c.m.* '71 (MET) [J] Plainsboro, NJ Vincentian Renewal Center.
Caserta, Angelo C. '45 (CIN) Piqua, OH St. Boniface Church; Retired.
Caserta, Charles W. (CIN) Retired.
Caserta, Thomas G. '79 (BRK) [B] Douglaston, NY Cathedral Residence of the Immaculate Conception.
Casey, Msgr. A. Robert '43 (SY) [S] East Syracuse, NY Bishop Grimes Priests Residence.
Casey, Anthony C. '58 (BRK) [30] Brooklyn, NY St. Columba Church.
Casey, Daniel *o.p.* '38 (DET) [21] Detroit, MI St. Dominic Church.
Casey, Daniel J. '58 (SAC) Roseville, CA St. Rose Church.
Casey, David J. *s.j.* '69 (NY) [Z] New York, NY Jesuit Community at Fordham University.
Casey, Denis '56 (TLS) [E] Tulsa, OK Saint Francis Hospital, Inc.
Casey, Diarmuid *c.s.sp.* '69 (SJ) Mountain View, CA St. Athanasius Church.
Casey, Donald A. (SB) Retired.
Casey, Edward J. '79 (PH) [U] Darby, PA Villa Saint Joseph; [U] Ventnor, PA Villa St. Joseph by the Sea; [X] Darby, PA Little Flower Manor.
Casey, Francis M. '64 (RVC) Seaford, NY Maria Regina Church; Retired.
Casey, Msgr. George T. '37 (SCR) Retired.
Casey, James E. '69 (WDC) Retired.
Casey, John *s.a.c.* '67 (LUB) Brownfield, TX St. Anthony's Church.
Casey, John D. '55 (HRT) [5] New Haven, CT St. Boniface's Church; [7] New Haven, CT St. Casimir's Church.
Casey, John F. *o.s.a.* '39 (PH) [Z] Villanova, PA St. Thomas Monastery.
Casey, Msgr. John F. '54 (BRK) [182] Queens, NY The Incarnation Church.
Casey, Msgr. John H. '57 (CAM) Haddon Township, NJ St. Vincent Pallotti Church.
Casey, John J. '32 (LA) [R] Los Angeles, CA Amat House; [W] Montebello, CA DePaul Center.
Casey, John J. '84 (MET) North Plainfield, NJ St. Joseph Church.
Casey, John V. *o.s.a.* '39 (BO) [C] North Andover, MA Merrimack College.
Casey, John W. '45 (SCR) Retired.
Casey, Joseph H. *s.j.* '49 (BO) [W] Weston, MA Campion Center.
Casey, Joseph M. '66 (PAT) Morristown, NJ Assumption of the Blessed Virgin Mary Church; Morristown, NJ Morristown Memorial Hospital.
Casey, Kevin *c.p.* '67 (MET) [H] South River, NJ Passionist Provincial Office.
Casey, Kevin M. *c.p.* '56 (MET) Old Bridge, NJ St. Thomas the Apostle Church.
Casey, Leonard '52 (HBG) [G] Danville, PA Holy Family Convent and Infirmary.
Casey, Liam C. '62 (ALB) On Duty Outside the Diocese.
Casey, Liam C. '93 (HRT) [I] Hartford, CT Saint Francis Hospital and Medical Center.
Casey, M. Joseph *s.j.* '67 (CHI) [D] Chicago, IL St. Ignatius Jesuit Community.
Casey, Marion G. '34 (NU) Ivanhoe, MN Divine Providence Hospital & Home; Retired; [B] Ivanhoe, MN Divine Providence Health Center.
Casey, Martin J. *s.j.* '43 (WDC) [M] Washington, DC The Jesuit Community at Georgetown University.
Casey, Matthew *o.m.i.* '47 (HBG) Dallastown, PA St. Joseph Church.
Casey, Noah *o.s.b.* '76 (IND) [18] Indianapolis, IN St. Bernadette Church; [J] St. Meinrad, IN St. Meinrad Archabbey.
Casey, Patrick L. '65 (NU) Olivia, MN St. Aloysius Church; Renville, MN Holy Redeemer Church.
Casey, Patrick T. '80 (STP) [17] St. Paul, MN St. Casimir Church.
Casey, Paul E. *s.s.c.* '54 (OM) [K] St. Columbans, NE St. Columban's Foreign Mission Society.
Casey, Peter J. '68 (BO) [1] Somerville, MA St. Ann Church.
Casey, Richard L. '65 (BO) Foxboro, MA St. Mary Church.
Casey, Robert A. (SY) Special Assignment.
Casey, Msgr. Robert A. '43 (SY) Retired.
Casey, Robert E. (BO) Amesbury, MA Sacred Heart Church.
Casey, Robert G. '94 (CHI) [96] Chicago, IL Saint Ita Church.
Casey, Thomas J. *o.s.a.* (BO) [6] Lawrence, MA Holy Rosary Church.
Casey, Thomas J. *s.j.* '62 (KC) [B] Kansas City, MO Rockhurst College; [J] Kansas City, MO Rockhurst College - Jesuit Community.
Casey, Thomas M. *o.s.a.* '65 (BO) [C] North Andover, MA Merrimack College.
Casey, Thomas M. *o.s.a.* '65 (PH) [C] Villanova, PA Villanova University.
Casey, Walter E. (BO) Retired.
Casey, William *c.p.m.* '90 (OWN) [F] South Union, KY Fathers of Mercy.
Casey, William C. '69 (KNX) [6] Knoxville, TN St. John Neumann Church.
Casey, William J. *c.m.* '43 (PH) [Z] Philadelphia, PA Congregation of the Mission.
Cash, Msgr. Richard L. '89 (OWN) Aurora, KY St. Henry Church.
Cashel, Richard '54 (SFS) Dimock, SD SS. Peter and Paul Church.
Cashen, Michael '91 (RCK) [H] McHenry, IL Villa Desiderata Retreat House.
Cashen, Michael '92 (TLS) On Duty Outside the Diocese.
Cashin, James '65 (SAT) Brackettville, TX St. Mary Magdalen Church.
Cashioli, Lawrence J. '82 (MET) Retired.
Cashman, Ambrose *c.p.* '67 (MET) [H] South River, NJ Passionist Provincial Office.
Cashman, Christopher '77 (BRK) [240] Queens, NY St. Sebastian Church.
Cashman, James *o.s.c.* '48 (SCL) Foreston, MN St. Louis Bertrand Church; [I] Onamia, MN Crosier Monastery.
Cashman, Jeremiah '55 (LC) Cornell, WI Holy Cross Church; Jim Falls, WI Sacred Heart Church.
Cashman, Joseph C. '60 (WIN) Absent on Leave.
Cashman, Msgr. Michael J. '75 (MET) Woodbridge, NJ St. James Church.
Cashman, Patrick '42 (BUF) [M] Silver Creek, NY St. Columbans on the Lake, Home for the Aged.
Cashnelli, Toni (CIN) [M] Cincinnati, OH St. Francis Seraph Friary.
Casillas, Rafael '72 (LA) [35] Los Angeles, CA Resurrection Church.
Casimano, Santino '75 (GLP) On Duty Outside of Diocese.

Casio, Efrin (OAK) Pleasanton, CA Federal Correctional Institution.
Casjar, Julian '77 (RVC) Hicksville, NY Holy Family Church.
Caskey, John '82 (SCL) Pearl Lake, MN Holy Cross Church; St. Nicholas, MN St. Nicholas Church.
Caskey, John U. (L) [55] Louisville, KY Most Blessed Sacrament Church.
Caskey, John V. *c.ss.r.* '44 (CGS) Aguas Buenas, PR Church of Tres Santos Reyes.
Caskin, John J. *s.j.* '60 (BO) [W] Boston, MA The Society of Jesus of New England-Provincial Offices.
Caskins, John J. *s.j.* '60 (PRT) Perry, ME St. Ann Church.
Caslin, Msgr. Peter C. '41 (LA) [4] Long Beach, CA St. Bartholomew Church; Retired.
Casper, Christian J. *o.s.b.* '57 (PAT) [M] Morristown, NJ St. Mary's Abbey.
Casper, Kenneth R. *o.f.m.cap.* '80 (MIL) [B] Mount Calvary, WI St. Felix Friary.
Casper, Paul *s.c.j.* '57 (JKS) Holly Springs, MS St. Joseph Church; [G] Holly Springs, MS Rust College Newman Center.
Casper, Robert '44 (MIL) [P] Milwaukee, WI Salvatorians - Jordan Hall.
Caspers, William A. (CHY) Thermopolis, WY St. Francis Church.
Cassar, Edward A. '69 (BRK) [126] Brooklyn, NY St. Rosalia-Regina Pacis Church.
Cassato, Msgr. David L. '72 (BRK) [105] Brooklyn, NY Shrine of Our Lady of Mount Carmel Church.
Cassel, Harry A. *o.s.a.* '50 (PH) Bryn Mawr, PA Our Mother of Good Counsel Church.
Cassella, John J. '58 (PIT) [4] Swissvale, PA Madonna del Castello Church.
Cassem, Ned H. *s.j.* '70 (BO) [W] Weston, MA Campion Center.
Cassem, Ned H. *s.j.* '70 (MIL) [P] Milwaukee, WI Jesuit Provincial Office, Wisconsin Province.
Casserly, Eugene D. '69 (PT) [11] Pensacola, FL St. Mary Church.
Cassese, Anthony '77 (CLV) [36] Cleveland, OH St. Jerome Church.
Cassese, John-Marie *o.f.m.* '50 (NY) [Z] New York, NY Padua Friary.
Cassidy, Bernard F. *s.j.* '63 (HON) [7] Honolulu, HI Newman Center at the University of Hawaii, Holy Spirit Parish Church; [H] Honolulu, HI Jesuit Fathers House.
Cassidy, Msgr. Charles C. (PAT) Retired.
Cassidy, Daniel '78 (CHI) [151] Chicago, IL Our Lady of Lourdes Church.
Cassidy, Daniel H. *s.s.j.* '43 (BAL) [M] Baltimore, MD St. Joseph's Manor.
Cassidy, Daniel J. *o.p.* '57 (PRO) [P] Providence, RI St. Thomas Aquinas Priory at Providence College.
Cassidy, Dominic J. '74 (DAV) On Duty Outside the Diocese.
Cassidy, Dominic J. '74 (RCK) [D] Elgin, IL St. Joseph Hospital.
Cassidy, Felix F. *o.p.* '54 (SFR) [13] San Francisco, CA St. Dominic Church; [N] San Francisco, CA St. Dominic Priory.
Cassidy, Francis '59 (LA) Monrovia, CA Immaculate Conception Church.
Cassidy, Francis P. '57 (CHI) [143] Chicago, IL St. Nicholas of Tolentine Church.
Cassidy, James (STP) Minneapolis, MN Metropolitan Medical Center.
Cassidy, James E. *o.s.f.s.* '55 (CAM) [L] Pittsgrove, NJ Villa St. Joseph.
Cassidy, James E. *o.s.f.s.* '55 (WIL) [I] Childs, MD Oblates of St. Francis De Sales.
Cassidy, James G. *o.s.b.* '84 (MAN) [K] Manchester, NH St. Anselm Abbey.
Cassidy, James M. '61 (CLV) Ashland, OH St. Edward Church.
Cassidy, Msgr. James P. '51 (NY) Cortlandt Manor, NY Holy Spirit Church; [DD] New York, NY Catholic Foundation for the Dominican Republic.
Cassidy, John M. '58 (CHI) [48] Chicago, IL St. Daniel the Prophet Church.
Cassidy, John T. '79 (PT) [15] Pensacola, FL St. Thomas More Church.
Cassidy, John V. '69 (LC) Eastman, WI St. Wenceslaus Church.
Cassidy, Joseph A. '59 (PAT) Budd Lake, NJ St. Jude Church.
Cassidy, Joseph L. '46 (NEW) Rutherford, NJ St. Mary's Church.
Cassidy, Kevin W. '60 (MAD) Wisconsin Dells, WI St. Cecilia Church.
Cassidy, Laurence L. *s.j.* '61 (NEW) [B] Jersey City, NJ Saint Peter's College; [N] Jersey City, NJ Jesuits of Saint Peter's College, Inc.
Cassidy, Martin J. '57 (MIA) [1] Pompano Beach, FL Assumption Church.
Cassidy, Patrick '47 (RIC) Retired.
Cassidy, Richard '67 (BUF) [A] East Aurora, NY Christ the King Seminary.
Cassidy, Richard '67 (DET) On Duty Outside the Archdiocese.
Cassidy, Robert T. '58 (STP) Edina, MN Our Lady of Grace Church.
Cassidy, Terry '67 (PEO) Chenoa, IL St. Joseph's Church.
Cassidy, Theodore K. *s.m.* '68 (CIN) [C] Dayton, OH Marianist Novitiate; [M] Dayton OH Marianist Provincialate.
Cassidy, Msgr. Thomas J. '57 (ARL) [3] Arlington, VA St. Ann Church.
Cassiere, Achilles *o.f.m.cap.* '52 (NEW) [4] Orange, NJ Mt. Carmel Church; [N] Union City, NJ Capuchin Friars - Prov. Stigmata of St. Francis.
Cassiero, Daniel '68 (NY) Absent on Leave.
Cassin, Msgr. Andrew J. '54 (WDC) Waldorf, MD St. Peter Church.
Cassion, Kieran *o.f.m.* '45 (NEW) East Rutherford, NJ St. Joseph's Church.
Cassista, Fern *m.s.* (FR) [M] Attleboro, MA La Salette Center for Christian Living.
Castaldi, Joseph '63 (NOR) New London, CT St. Joseph Church.
Castaldo, Edward *c.ss.r.* '62 (CHI) [9] Chicago, IL St. Alphonsus Church.
Castaldo, John '87 (BGP) New Fairfield, CT St. Edward the Confessor Church.
Castaneda, Heibar '94 (MRY) Arroyo Grande, CA St. Patrick Church.
Castaneda, Mario '95 (STO) Tracy, CA St. Bernard's Church.
Castaneda, Oscar '87 (MIA) Opa Locka, FL Our Lady of Perpetual Help Church.
Castaneda, Severiano '71 (LA) [57] Los Angeles, CA St. Columbkille Church.
Casteel, Michael J. '84 (SPC) Leave of Absence.
Casteig, Alfonso *o.f.m.cap.* '56 (DAL) [8] Dallas, TX Our Lady of Lourdes Church.
Castellani, John J. '48 (HRT) Retired.
Castellani, Paul A. '96 (PH) [60] Philadelphia, PA Holy Innocents Church.
Castellano, Francis J. *v.f.* '60 (SCR) [5] Williamsport, PA Mater Dolorosa Church; [6] Williamsport, PA St. Ann's Church.
Castellanos, Ricardo C. '70 (MIA) [2] Pompano Beach, FL San Isidro Church.
Castellino, Albert *c.ss.r.* '61 (CHI) [136] Chicago, IL St. Michael Church.
Castelot, John '42 (DET) [3] Livonia, MI St. Edith Church; Retired.
Castelow, Ralph T. '89 (WIL) Dover, DE Holy Cross Church.
Caster, Gary '92 (PEO) [B] Peoria, IL Notre Dame High School.
Caster, Kevin (L) [3] Louisville, KY St. Albert the Great Church; [B] Louisville, KY Trinity High School.
Castilejos, Jorge '89 (SJN) [4] Carolina, PR Santo Cristo de la Agonia Church.
Castillo, Carlos '83 (OKL) Edmond, OK St. Monica Church.
Castillo, Carlos C. *c.m.f.* '73 (LA) [K] Los Angeles, CA Queen of Angels-Hollywood Presbyterian Medical Center; [R] Los Angeles, CA Claretian Retreat Center Community.
Castillo, Domingo '91 (AMA) Hereford, TX San Jose Church.
Castillo, Francisco '67 (BWN) Weslaco, TX St. Joan of Arc Church.
Castillo, Jose '80 (SD) National City, CA St. Mary Church.
Castillo, Richard S. '83 (PT) Quincy, FL St. Thomas the Apostle Church; Tallahassee, FL Federal Correctional Institution.
Castillo, Rolando J. '94 (MIA) [3] Miami, FL Corpus Christi Church.
Castillo, Rolo '92 (RIC) [5] Virginia Beach, VA Holy Spirit Church.
Castle, Nathan *o.p.* '76 (PHX) [H] Phoenix, AZ Office of Youth and Young Adult Ministries.
Castle, Nathan G. *o.p.* '85 (PHX) [F] Tempe, AZ Dominicans (Dominican Community-Jordan House).
Castles, Patrick J. '69 (TR) Hightstown, NJ St. Anthony of Padua Church.
Castrillo, Jesus '49 (LA) El Monte, CA Our Lady of Guadalupe Church.
Castrillo, Jesus Saez *o.de.m.* '69 (CGS) Cayey, PR Nuestra Senora de la Merced Church.
Castrillon, Heriberto Mejias '84 (CGS) Las Piedras, PR Inmaculada Concepcion Church.
Castro, Anthony A. '84 (GAL) Deer Park, TX St. Hyacinth Church; Katy, TX Epiphany of the Lord Church.
Castro, John G. *o.m.i.* '62 (BWN) [8] Brownsville, TX St. Joseph Church.
Castro, Patrick *o.f.m.cap.* '88 (AGN) Yona, GU San Francisco d'Assisi Church.
Castro, Reinel '96 (ORL) Haines City, FL St. Ann Church.
Castro, Robert '85 (SR) Napa, CA St. John the Baptist Church.
Castronovo, Edmund A. '76 (SY) Sherburne, NY St. Malachy Church; Georgetown, NY Camp Georgetown; South Plymouth, NY Camp Pharsalia.
Caswell, Thomas C. '66 (SPK) Pullman, WA Sacred Heart Church.
Catagnus, James N. '70 (PH) [9] Philadelphia, PA St. Ambrose Church.
Catala, Felix E. *c.ss.r.* '75 (MGZ) [2] Mayaquez, PR Our Lady of Mt. Carmel Church.
Catalana, Mark '91 (SJ) Cupertino, CA St. Joseph of Cupertino Church.
Catalano, James *o.s.j.* '63 (FRS) [1] Bakersfield, CA Our Lady of Guadalupe Church.
Catalano, James A. *s.j.* '95 (NY) [Z] New York, NY Xavier Jesuit Community.
Catallo, Sylvester *o.f.m.cap.* '54 (NY) [B] Beacon, NY St. Lawrence of Brindisi Friary.
Catanach, Richard '88 (LSC) Ruidoso, NM St. Eleanor Church.
Catanello, Ignatius '66 (BRK) [178] Queens, NY Holy Family Church.
Catania, Thomas M. '73 (BRK) [158] Queens, NY Blessed Virgin Mary, Help of Christians Church; Released from Diocesan Assignment.
Catanzaro, Albert *c.p.* '45 (BRK) [U] Jamaica, NY Immaculate Conception Monastery.
Catarise, Joseph '82 (ROC) [M] Rochester, NY Diocesan Office of Campus Ministry.
Catellani, Remus A. *m.c.c.j.* '47 (NEW) [N] Montclair, NJ Comboni Missionaries of the Heart of Jesus (Verona Fathers).
Catoir, John T. (PAT) [3] Passaic, NJ Assumption of the Blessed Virgin Mary Church; [P] Passaic, NJ St. Jude Media Ministries.
Cattaert, Michael *c.i.c.m.* '37 (SAT) [M] San Antonio, TX Missionhurst Community Residence.
Catucci, Thomas F. (SY) Kirkwood, NY St. Mary Church; Special Assignment.
Catullo, Pasquale R. '63 (PH) [12] Philadelphia, PA Annunciation B.V.M. Church; Center Square, PA St. Helena Church; Retired.
Catuso, Orville J. *s.j.* (GB) [M] Oshkosh, WI Jesuit Retreat House.
Catuso, Orville J. *s.j.* '53 (GB) [2] Appleton, WI St. Bernard Church.
Caul, Robert F. '61 (PRO) [R] Narragansett, RI Our Lady of Peace Spiritual Life Center.
Cauley, Robert W. '42 (CLV) Retired.
Cauley, Thomas F. '81 (PMB) Port St. Lucie, FL Holy Family Church.
Caulfield, John '59 (ORL) [4] Lakeland, FL St. Joseph's Church.
Caulfield, John F. *s.j.* '44 (BO) [W] Chestnut Hill, MA The Jesuit Community at Boston College.
Caulfield, Msgr. John J. '48 (PH) Exton, PA SS. Philip and James Church.
Caulfield, Sean '49 (B) Lewiston, ID St. Stanislaus Church; [F] Lewiston, ID Lewis and Clark State College.
Cautela, Mauro '74 (PIT) Ellwood City, PA Purification of the Blessed Virgin Mary Church.
Cauterucci, Francis J. '90 (PH) [3] Drexel Hill, PA St. Charles Borromeo Church.
Cavagnaro, John A. '75 (CAM) Sea Isle City, NJ St. Joseph's Church.
Cavagnaro, Mark R. '70 (CAM) Marmora, NJ The Church of the Resurrection.
Cavagnuolo, Salvatore F. '67 (HRT) Yalesville, CT Our Lady of Fatima Church.
Cavalconte, Charles C. *o.p.* '80 (BO) [W] Dover, MA St. Stephen Priory.
Cavalier, Robert C. '72 (NO) [4] Kenner, LA St. Jerome Church.
Cavalier, Wayne *o.p.* '93 (NO) [25] New Orleans, LA St. Anthony Of Padua Church; [P] New Orleans, LA Dominican Fathers & Brothers, Southern Dominican Province.
Cavallaro, Msgr. Galliano J. '42 (PRO) Retired.
Cavalli, Victor *o.p.* '48 (OAK) [4] Berkeley, CA St. Mary Magdalen Church.
Cavalluzzi, Kevin P. '93 (BRK) [155] Queens, NY St. Benedict Joseph Labre Church.
Cavanagh, Brian '58 (LA) Covina, CA Sacred Heart Church.
Cavanagh, David '85 (BO) Boston, MA Massachusetts General Hospital; [V] Chestnut Hill, MA Opus Dei.
Cavanagh, Gerald F. *s.j.* '64 (DET) [C] Detroit, MI University of Detroit Mercy; [K] Detroit, MI Jesuit Community at the University of Detroit.
Cavanagh, Msgr. James M. '52 (BRK) [91] Brooklyn, NY Our Lady of Angels Church.
Cavanagh, Michael J. '59 (PBL) Retired.
Cavanaugh, Brian *t.o.r.* '82 (STU) [A] Steubenville, OH Franciscan University of Steubenville; [F] Steubenville, OH Holy Spirit Monastery.
Cavanaugh, Daniel J. (BO) [52] Boston, MA Most Precious Blood Church; Boston, MA Newton-Wellesley Hospital.
Cavanaugh, Daniel J. '66 (PH) Ridley Park, PA St. Madeline Church.
Cavanaugh, Harry *c.pp.s.* '54 (CIN) [L] Dayton, OH The Maria Joseph Living Care Center.

Cavanaugh, James K. '51 (Y) Retired.
Cavanaugh, John *c.ss.r.* '46 (ORL) New Smyrna Beach, FL Sacred Heart Church.
Cavanaugh, John '90 (FAR) West Fargo, ND Blessed Sacrament Church.
Cavanaugh, John L. '51 (NY) Retired; [E] White Plains, NY Archbishop Stepinac High School.
Cavanaugh, John L. '56 (CIN) [84] Cincinnati, OH St. Teresa Church; Retired.
Cavanaugh, John R. (ROC) [I] Rochester, NY Basilian Residence.
Cavanaugh, Joseph A. *s.j.* '62 (ALB) [O] Auriesville, NY Jesuit Retreat House for Priests, Religious and Lay People.
Cavanaugh, Kevin P. '86 (HRT) Military Chaplains.
Cavanaugh, Michael *o.s.f.s.* (ARL) [D] Fairfax, VA Paul VI High School; [J] Fairfax, VA Oblates of St. Francis de Sales Residence.
Cavanaugh, Michael *o.s.f.s.* (WDC) [B] Washington, DC Oblates of St. Francis de Sales House of Studies.
Cavanaugh, Paul K. *c.m.* (BRK) [Y] Jamaica, NY Vincentian Service Corps.-East Inc.
Cavanaugh, Peter M. '66 (PRO) [7] Warwick, RI St. Peter's Church.
Cavanaugh, Theodore *o.f.m.* '48 (NEW) Elmwood Park, NJ St. Leo's Church.
Cavazos, Gilberto *o.f.m.* '85 (STL) [P] St. Louis, MO Franciscan Friary of St. Anthony of Padua.
Caveglia, Patrick *o.s.b.* '94 (KC) [A] Conception, MO Conception Seminary College; [J] Conception, MO Conception Abbey.
Cavell, Lawrence '89 (HT) Montegut, LA Sacred Heart Church.
Cavellier, Richard (DET) [6] Clinton Twp., MI St. Valerie of Ravenna Church.
Caverly, J. Bernard '65 (SP) [8] St. Petersburg, FL St. Raphael Church.
Caverly, Patrick J. '61 (ORL) Altamonte Springs, FL Annunciation Church.
Caverte, Rolando '62 (SFR) [17] San Francisco, CA Church of the Epiphany.
Cavey, Donald J. '76 (RIC) Hampton, VA VA Medical Center.
Caviglia, Caesar '55 (LAV) Retired.
Cavoto, Joseph F. *s.a.* '80 (NY) Harrison, NY St. Vincent Hospital and Medical Center of New York; [Z] New York, NY Atonement Friars.
Cawley, Joseph A. *s.j.* '45 (ALN) [A] Wernersville, PA Novitiate of St. Isaac Jogues.
Cawley, Martin *o.c.s.o.* '61 (P) [L] Lafayette, OR The Cistercian (Trappist) Abbey of Our Lady of Guadalupe.
Cawley, Patrick '70 (GR) Retired.
Cawley, Thomas *c.m.* '57 (KC) [J] Kansas City, MO Vincentian Parish Mission Center.
Cawley, Thomas *c.m.* '57 (KCK) Nortonville, KS St. Joseph's Church.
Cawley, Msgr. Thomas J. '36 (SCR) Retired; [N] Dunmore, PA Villa St. Joseph.
Cawley, William '73 (GF) On Duty Outside of the Diocese.
Cawley, William M. '73 (HBG) [3] York, PA St. Patrick Church; [A] York, PA York Catholic High School.
Cayer, John B. '96 (PT) Panama City, FL St. Dominic Church.
Caylor, Dennis J. '75 (CIN) Mount Carmel, OH St. Veronica Church.
Cazayoux, Clair M. *s.j.* '62 (NO) [P] New Orleans, LA Ignatius Residence.
Cazenavette, John J. *s.j.* '53 (SP) [C] Tampa, FL Jesuit High School.
Cebula, Joseph S. '75 (ALB) Stamford, NY Sacred Heart Church.
Cebula, Richard S. *o.s.b.* '41 (SEA) [6] Tacoma, WA St. Joseph's Church; [13] Tacoma, WA Holy Rosary Church; [M] Lacey, WA St. Martin's Abbey.
Cebula, Thomas '68 (Y) [1] Massillon, OH St. Barbara's Church.
Cebulka, Peter R. '93 (MET) East Brunswick, NJ St. Bartholomew Church.
Cecchini, Franco *c.r.s.* '70 (HRT) [6] Hartford, CT Sacred Heart Church.
Cecere, Michael *c.m.f.* '43 (SAT) [12] San Antonio, TX Immaculate Heart of Mary Church.
Cecero, John J. *s.j.* '89 (BAL) [M] Baltimore, MD Jesuit Fathers and Brothers Maryland Provincial Curia.
Cecero, John J. *s.j.* '89 (BGP) [O] Fairfield, CT The Fairfield Jesuit Community-Fairfield University.
Cecil, Bruce *c.s.c.* '92 (PHX) Tolleson, AZ Blessed Sacrament Church.
Cecil, Ivo E. (L) Retired.
Cecil, Patrick G. '78 (CHI) Wadsworth, IL St. Patrick Church.
Ceckowski, Robert J. '55 (SPR) Three Rivers, MA SS. Peter and Paul Church.
Cedillo, Bruno (BWN) [7] Brownsville, TX St. Eugene De Mazenod Church.
Cedolia, Robert J. '78 (PIT) Holiday Park, PA Our Lady of Joy Church.
Cedrone, Laurence C. (BO) Retired.
Cefai, John M. '35 (TLS) Retired.
Cegielka, Francis A. *s.a.c.* '31 (BUF) [O] North Tonawanda, NY Society of the Catholic Apostolate.
Ceja, Miguel '90 (SB) Palm Springs, CA Our Lady of Solitude Church.
Cejudo, Serafin '56 (GAL) [4] Galveston, TX St. Patrick Church.
Cekovsky, Andrew B. '41 (ALB) Retired.
Cekovsky, Andrew B. '41 (SPR) [H] Holyoke, MA Sisters of Providence Care Centers, Inc.
Celano, Freddy '87 (CGS) Naranjito, PR San Miguel Arcangel Church.
Celano, Joseph G. '87 (MET) [1] New Brunswick, NJ St. Peter Apostle Church; [M] New Brunswick, NJ Catholic Center at Rutgers University.
Celano, Leo J. *o.praem.* '72 (ORG) [H] Silverado, CA Norbertine Fathers.
Celano, Leo John *o.praem.* (LA) Norwalk, CA California Youth Authority.
Celeste, Charles R. '80 (ALB) [4] Little Falls, NY Holy Family Church.
Celia, Joseph A. '67 (HBG) Selinsgrove, PA St. Pius X Church; Selinsgrove, PA Selinsgrove Center; [K] Harrisburg, PA Catholic Campus Ministry.
Celiano, Alfred V. '53 (NEW) [B] South Orange, NJ Seton Hall University.
Celichowski, John *o.f.m.cap.* '93 (CHI) [146] Chicago, IL Our Lady Gate of Heaven Church.
Celino, Juventino C. '82 (ELP) [32] El Paso, TX St. Stephen, Deacon and Martyr Church.
Cell, Robert *m.s.c.* '47 (RCK) [H] Aurora, IL Missionaries of the Sacred Heart Community.
Cellini, Ronald R. '79 (CHR) Beaufort, SC St. Peter's Church; [H] Beaufort, SC University of South Carolina, Beaufort Extension Newman Center.
Cellini, Ronald R. '79 (PIT) On Duty Outside the Diocese.
Cellucci, Carl D. '53 (PH) Retired.
Celso, Thomas B. '79 (ROC) On Duty Outside the Diocese.
Cembor, Thomas M. '79 (NEW) [2] Irvington, NJ St. Leo's Church.
Cencula, Leonard '63 (STU) Dillonvale, OH St. Adalbert Church.
Cendejas, Rafael *o.a.r.* '96 (LA) [4] Oxnard, CA Mary Star of the Sea Church.
Cenefeldt, Harry E. '54 (TR) [8] Trenton, NJ Our Lady of Good Counsel Church.
Cenerini, Michael '87 (PHX) [C] Phoenix, AZ St. Joseph's Hospital and Medical Center.
Cenkner, William *o.p.* '58 (WDC) [C] Washington, DC Catholic University of America, The.
Centala, Theodore *o.c.d.* '65 (WDC) [B] Washington, DC Monastery of Our Lady of Mount Carmel.
Centino, Rustico '73 (SAC) Vallejo, CA St. Basil Church.
Centner, David *o.c.d.* '71 (OAK) [N] Berkeley, CA Carmelite (Discalced) House of Studies.
Centrella, Msgr. Arthur J. '54 (PH) [3] Norristown, PA Holy Saviour Church.
Centrella, Dismas *o.f.m.* (BO) [42] Boston, MA St. Leonard of Port Maurice Church.
Cepeda, Abraham *s.d.b.* (SJN) Catano, PR San Francisco de Sales Church.
Cepeda, Jose Arturo '96 (SAT) [1] San Antonio, TX Cathedral of San Fernando.
Cepeda, Ray '79 (AGN) On Duty Outside the Archdiocese.
Ceperley, Eugene F. '55 (SC) Moorland, IA Our Lady of Good Counsel Church.
Ceplecha, Christian W. *o.s.b.* '53 (JOL) [A] Lisle, IL Benedictine University; [J] Lisle, IL St. Procopius Abbey.
Cepress, Adalbert J. '44 (NU) Retired.
Cera, James B. '64 (MIL) Kansasville, WI St. Mary's-Dover Church.
Cera, Raymond M. *c.pp.s.* '46 (LFT) [A] Rensselaer, IN Saint Joseph's College.
Cerank, Gerald A. '72 (OG) Mooers, NY St. Joseph Church; Mooers Forks, NY St. Ann Church.
Ceranowski, Albert B. '64 (TOL) Oregon, OH St. Ignatius Church.
Ceranowski, Gerald L. '67 (TOL) [26] Toledo, OH St. Joan of Arc Church.
Cerbin, Walter A. *s.s.j.* '55 (BR) Donaldsonville, LA St. Catherine of Siena Church.
Cerbone, James '80 (NY) [3] Poughkeepsie, NY Holy Trinity Church.
Cercone, Raymond A. '48 (PIT) Retired.
Ceresatto, John *c.s.s.* '40 (BO) [W] Waltham, MA Stigmatine Fathers & Brothers Provincial House.
Ceresko, Anthony R. *o.s.f.s.* '70 (TOL) [K] Toledo, OH Oblates of St. Francis de Sales.
Cerezo, Alberto F. (YAK) On Duty Outside the Diocese.
Cerezo, Alfonso '43 (SB) Rancho Cucamonga, CA Our Lady of Mount Carmel Church.
Ceriello, Joseph A. '78 (BRK) Military Chaplains.
Cerio, Frank '86 (ORL) [7] Orlando, FL St. Charles Borromeo Church.
Cerkas, John W. '70 (GB) Laona, WI St. Leonard Church; Long Lake, WI St. Norbert Church.
Cernaj, Emil *s.v.d.* '51 (CHI) [N] Techny, IL Society of the Divine Word, Provincial Headquarter-Chicago Prov.
Cernauskas, Daniel '54 (MIA) Tamarac, FL St. Malachy Church.
Cerne, Joze '92 (CLV) [47] Cleveland, OH St. Mary Church.
Cernich, Joseph '83 (SFD) Absent on Leave.
Cerniglia, Francis J. '53 (CHI) Elk Grove Village, IL Queen of the Rosary Church; Retired.
Cerniglia, George J. *s.m.* '69 (BAL) [M] Baltimore, MD Marianists Community (New York Province); [Q] Baltimore, MD Marianist Conference.
Cernoch, Gerard '64 (VIC) Shiner, TX SS. Cyril and Methodius Church.
Cerny, George F. '64 (CHI) [23] Chicago, IL St. Bartholomew Church.
Cerpich, Richard J. '61 (MIL) Adell, WI St. Patrick Church; Cascade, WI St. Mary's Church; Dacada, WI St. Nicholas Church; Mitchell, WI St. Michael Church; Random Lake, WI St. Mary's Church.
Cerretto, Michael P. *c.s.b.* '69 (GAL) [F] Houston, TX St. Thomas High School.
Cerretto, Michael P. *c.s.b.* '69 (GRY) [K] Merrillville, IN Basilian Fathers Residence.
Cerrito, Msgr. Albert J. '51 (PRO) Retired.
Cerrone, Michael J. *u.s.a.* '81 (SAV) Military Chaplains.
Cerullo, Fritz J. *o.s.a.* '71 (BO) Andover, MA St. Augustine Church.
Cerulo, Thomas N. *o.ss.t.* '78 (WDC) [M] Hyattsville, MD St. John de Matha Monastery, Order of Most Holy Trinity.
Cervantes, Fidel '55 (ELP) [13] El Paso, TX Most Holy Trinity Church.
Cervantes, Leo '62 (RIC) Emporia, VA St. Richard Church; Emporia, VA St. Peter the Apostle Church.
Cervantes, Lucius F. *s.j.* '46 (STL) [P] St. Louis, MO Jesuit Community Corporation at St. Louis University - Jesuit Hall.
Cervantes, Rhenne A. '92 (NO) [3] Slidell, LA St. Luke the Evangelist Church.
Cervella, Albert T. '79 (ALN) [J] Bethlehem, PA Holy Family Villa.
Cervenak, Andrew '78 (TR) Retired.
Cervera, Pascual '87 (NY) [149] Bronx, NY Holy Spirit Church.
Cervero, Joseph '89 (BGP) Darien, CT St. John Church.
Cervini, John I. '68 (RVC) Wyandanch, NY Our Lady of the Miraculous Medal Church.
Cervinski, Paul L. '61 (BIS) [5] Minot, ND St. Theresa, the Little Flower Church.
Cervoni, Stephen F. '67 (CAM) Woodstown, NJ St. Joseph's Church.
Cerwonka, Clarence G. '61 (PBL) Military Chaplains.
Cerwonka, Clarence J. '61 (SY) [8] Binghamton, NY St. Mary of the Assumption Church.
Cesanek, Damian *o.f.m.* '69 (PEO) [2] Bloomington, IL St. Mary's Church.
Cesario, Victor *o.f.m.* '39 (NY) [Z] New York, NY Franciscan Province of the Immaculate Conception.
Cesaro, Nicholas J. '54 (HRT) [8] Hartford, CT St. Augustine Church.
Cesarone, Jeffrey T. *o.praem.* '94 (PH) [Z] Paoli, PA Daylesford Abbey.
Cesarone, Jeffrey T. *o.praem.* '94 (WIL) [B] Claymont, DE Archmere Academy; [I] Claymont, DE Immaculate Conception Priory of the Canons Regular of Premontre.
Cessario, Romanus *o.p.* (BO) [A] Boston, MA St. John's Seminary.
Cesta, James M. (SY) [2] Oswego, NY St. Joseph Church.
Cestare, Gerald '95 (RVC) West Babylon, NY Our Lady of Grace Church.
Cestaro, Joseph A. '62 (BRK) [94] Brooklyn, NY Our Lady of Czestochowa-St. Casimir Church.
Cestaro, Joseph J. '46 (NEW) Belleville, NJ St. Anthony's Church; Retired; [N] Rutherford, NJ St. John Vianney Residence for Priests.
Cestero, Luis '36 (CGS) [2] Caguas, PR San Jose Church.
Ch'e, James '54 (AGN) Tamuning, GU St. Anthony and St. Victor Church.
Chaanine, George '96 (OLL) Awaiting Assignment.
Chaback, Msgr. Michael J. *s.t.d.* (ALN) [A] Northampton, PA Mary Immaculate Seminary.
Chaback, Msgr. Michael J. '70 (ALN) [2] Bethlehem, PA SS. Cyril and Methodius Church.
Chabak, Robert M. *v.f.* '72 (NEW) [4] Hoboken, NJ SS. Peter and Paul's Church.
Chabala, Brian J. '77 (DET) Farmington Hills, MI St. Fabian Church.
Chabot, Bertrand R. '46 (FR) Retired.
Chabot, Peter L. *m.m.* '65 (NY) [Z] Maryknoll, NY Maryknoll Fathers and Brothers.
Chabot, Robert *s.s.s.* '66 (SFE) [23] Albuquerque, NM St. Charles Borromeo Church.
Chabot, Roger P. '65 (PRT) Auburn, ME St. Philip's Church.
Chachlowski, Marek '82 (NEW) [4] Linden, NJ St. Theresa of the Child Jesus Church.
Chacko, Joy T. '92 (TR) [2] Trenton, NJ Blessed

Sacrament Church.
Chacko, Sebastian '76 (SPP) [2] Pago Pago, AS Co-Cathedral of St. Joseph the Worker.
Chacon, Frank '89 (GLP) Concho, AZ San Rafael Church; St. Johns, AZ St. John the Baptist Church.
Chacon, Gilbert M. *s.j.* '73 (SJ) [M] Los Gatos, CA California Province of the Society of Jesus, Jesuit Provincial Office.
Chacon, Jorge '74 (NEW) North Bergen, NJ St. Brigid Church.
Chadwick, John '95 (NEW) Cedar Grove, NJ St. Catherine of Siena Church.
Chadwick, Lawrence A. '75 (RVC) Dix Hills, NY St. Matthew Church.
Chagas, Virgilio P. '67 (NEW) Elizabeth, NJ St. Elizabeth Hospital; [G] Elizabeth, NJ St. Elizabeth Hospital.
Chagnon, Robert J. '40 (HRT) Retired.
Chaguaceda, Juan Manuel *o.s.a.* '53 (NY) [49] New York, NY Holy Rosary Church.
Chaisson, John C. '66 (BO) [1] Peabody, MA St. Adelaide Church.
Chaisson, Louis '65 (HT) On Leave.
Chalany, Robert J. *o.s.b.* '52 (BRK) Brooklyn, NY Veterans Administration Medical Center.
Chalany, Robert J. *o.s.b.* '52 (PAT) [M] Newton, NJ St. Paul's Abbey.
Chalek, Kazimierz *m.i.c.* '87 (SPR) [I] Stockbridge, MA Congregation of Marians.
Chalhoub, Maximos '39 (NTN) Retired.
Chalifour, Gerald F. '52 (MAN) Retired.
Chalkey, Andrew G. *o.m.i.* '56 (BEL) [F] Belleville, IL Our Lady of the Snows Apartment Community Retirement Home; [G] Belleville, IL Missionary Oblates of Mary Immaculate - St. Henry's Oblate Residence.
Challancin, James '68 (LFT) [A] Rensselaer, IN Saint Joseph's College.
Challancin, James '68 (MAR) On Duty Outside the Diocese.
Challinor, Michael '91 (NY) Stony Point, NY Immaculate Conception Church.
Challman, Stephen G. '96 (NY) [206] Staten Island, NY Holy Rosary Church.
Chalmers, H. Edward '79 (WOR) East Douglas, MA St. Denis Church; [2] Fitchburg, MA St. Bernard's Church.
Chaloult, Msgr. Gilman '47 (PRT) Caribou, ME Holy Rosary Church; Retired.
Chaloux, Joseph '94 (ATL) Athens, GA St. Joseph's Church.
Chalupa, Fred '73 (AUS) On Duty Outside the Diocese.
Chamberlain, Charles M. *o.s.f.s.* '93 (WIL) [B] Wilmington, DE Salesianum School.
Chamberlain, Henry T. *s.j.* '61 (CHI) [N] Chicago, IL Chicago Province of the Society of Jesus-Provincial Office.
Chamberlain, Msgr. Michael J. '66 (DEN) [16] Denver, CO Mother of God Church.
Chamberlain, Robert '54 (Y) Retired.
Chamberlain, Robert F. '57 (GI) Retired.
Chamberlain, Msgr. Robert J. '64 (DM) [9] Des Moines, IA St. Joseph's Church.
Chamberlain, Thomas '70 (AUS) On Duty Outside the Diocese.
Chamberlin, Gregory D. *o.s.b.* '65 (EVN) [14] Evansville, IN St. Benedict Church.
Chamberlin, Gregory D. *o.s.b.* '65 (IND) [J] St. Meinrad, IN St. Meinrad Archabbey.
Chamberlin, Mark '68 (CC) [22] Corpus Christi, TX St. Theresa Church.
Chambers, Francis E. *o.s.a.* '78 (PH) [Z] Villanova, PA St. John Stone Friary.
Chambers, Henry C. '65 (BO) Millis, MA St. Thomas the Apostle Church.
Chambers, James *s.j.* '55 (IND) [25] Indianapolis, IN St. Joan of Arc Church.
Chambers, Leonard R. '65 (SPC) Joplin, MO St. Peter Church.
Chambers, Thomas E. *c.s.c.* '61 (NO) [22] New Orleans, LA Sacred Heart Of Jesus Church; [C] New Orleans, LA Our Lady of Holy Cross College.
Chamblain, Joseph M. *o.s.m.* '84 (CHI) [N] Chicago, IL Servite Friars - Eastern Province; [N] Chicago, IL Servite Friars - Eastern Province.
Champagn, Robert *s.m.* (BO) Boston, MA Metro West Medical Center.
Champagne, Dennis V. '71 (SEA) Snohomish, WA St. Michael's Church.
Champagne, Michael '94 (LAF) [M] Lafayette, LA Community of Jesus Crucified.
Champagne, Rene *c.p.* '49 (DET) [K] Detroit, MI St. Paul of the Cross Community, Congregation of the Passion; [P] Detroit, MI St. Paul of the Cross Retreat Center.
Champagne, Robert E. *s.m.* '51 (BO) [Y] Framingham Centre, MA The Marist House.
Champigny, Richard *o.carm.* '65 (SPR) [K] Williamstown, MA Mount Carmel Retreat Center.
Champigny, Roger G. '60 (PRO) [2] Warwick, RI St. Catherine Church.
Champigny, Thomas R. '81 (SPR) Easthampton, MA Our Lady of Good Counsel Church.
Champion, James D. '76 (WOR) Blackstone, MA St. Paul's Church.
Champlin, Msgr. Joseph M. '56 (SY) [1] Syracuse, NY The Cathedral of the Immaculate Conception.
Champlin, Michael A. *o.p.* '66 (SUP) [I] Webster, WI Thomas More Center for Preaching and Prayer, Inc.
Champlin, William E. '93 (WOR) [8] Worcester, MA Our Lady of the Angels Church.
Champoux, Thomas C. '67 (YAK) Richland, WA Christ the King Church.
Chan, Albert *s.j.* '47 (SFR) [N] San Francisco, CA Jesuit Community at University of San Francisco; [U] San Francisco, CA The Ricci Institute for Chinese-Western Cultural History at the Center for the Pacific Rim.
Chan, Paul '50 (NY) [DD] New York, NY Chinese Catholic Information Center.
Chan-Kyu, Simeon Je '50 (JOL) Itasca, IL St. Andrew Kim Church.
Chancler, Joseph A. *t.o.r.* '83 (ALT) [A] Loretto, PA St. Francis College; [A] Loretto, PA St. Francis College; [F] Loretto, PA St. Francis Friary, Third Order Regular of St. Francis of Penance.
Chancy, Richard F. '91 (BO) [CC] Dorchester, MA University of Massachusetts at Boston Campus Ministry.
Chandler, Anthony L. '89 (L) [32] Louisville, KY Holy Family Church.
Chandler, John W. *s.j.* '64 (LA) [R] Culver City, CA Ignatius House, The Novitiate of the California Province, Society of Jesus.
Chandonnet, A. J. *c.ss.r.* '50 (GAL) [33] Houston, TX Holy Ghost Church; Retired.
Chandrankunnel, Mathew '64 (NEW) Dumont, NJ St. Mary's Church; Englewood, NJ Englewood Hospital.
Chane, Lawrence J. '62 (BO) Dracut, MA St. Therese Church.
Chaney, Robert E. '88 (SAV) [2] Savannah, GA St. Anthony's Church.
Chang, Benedict '63 (SFR) [48] San Francisco, CA Star of the Sea Church.
Chang, Cornelius P. *o.s.b.* '62 (GBG) [H] Latrobe, PA Saint Vincent Archabbey.
Chang, Gordon '84 (LA) Hacienda Heights, CA St. John Vianney Church.
Chang, Joseph *o.s.b.* '57 (JOL) [J] Lisle, IL St. Procopius Abbey.
Chang, Simeon '49 (SFR) [34] San Francisco, CA St. Monica Church; Retired.
Chang-Lei, Francis X. *s.j.* '49 (GAL) [10] Houston, TX Ascension Chinese Mission Church.
Chant, William S. '88 (BUR) Graniteville, VT St. Sylvester Church.
Chao, Joseph '48 (P) Retired.
Chao, Joseph '61 (NY) [54] New York, NY St. James Church.
Chapdelaine, Gerard E. *s.j.* '66 (SEA) [C] Tacoma, WA Bellarmine Preparatory School.
Chapeau, Mary Paul *o.cart.* '45 (BUR) [G] Arlington, VT Carthusian Foundation, Charterhouse of the Transfiguration.
Chapel, Joseph R. '92 (NEW) [B] South Orange, NJ Seton Hall University.
Chapell, Norbert A. '48 (CHI) Hickory Hills, IL St. Patricia Church; Retired.
Chapin, Daniel L. '72 (OG) Clayton, NY St. Mary of Clayton Church; Lafargeville, NY St. John the Evangelist Church.
Chaplin, John *c.s.c.* '68 (P) [B] Portland, OR University of Portland.
Chaplin, John G. *c.s.c.* '68 (E) Houtzdale, PA Christ the King Church.
Chapman, A. James '39 (PH) [72] Philadelphia, PA Saint Irenaeus Church; Retired.
Chapman, Gerard C. '91 (PH) [102] Philadelphia, PA St. Matthew Church.
Chapman, Lawrence J. '77 (MIL) [D] Burlington, WI Catholic Central High School.
Chapman, Michael A. '82 (PH) [154] Philadelphia, PA St. Veronica Church.
Chapman, Michael L. '69 (OKL) Weatherford, OK St. Eugene's Church; [K] Norman, OK Campus Ministry for the Archdiocese of Oklahoma City.
Chapman, Robert J. '67 (PH) Lansdowne, PA St. Philomena Church.
Chappell, Arthur B. *o.s.a.* '69 (PH) [C] Villanova, PA Villanova University.
Chappell, James T. '67 (DUB) [7] Dubuque, IA Sacred Heart Church.
Chappetto, Raymond F. *v.e.* '71 (BRK) [2] Brooklyn, NY St. Agatha's Church.
Charankat, Peter '59 (OAK) [3] Walnut Creek, CA St. Mary's Church; Walnut Creek, CA Kaiser-Permanente Medical Center.
Charbonneau, Damian M. *o.s.m.* '50 (CHI) [N] Chicago, IL Servite Friars - Eastern Province.
Charbonneau, Roger L. '71 (BUR) Colchester, VT Holy Cross Church.
Charbonneau, William R. (HRT) On Duty Outside the Archdiocese.
Charest, Anthony *s.m.* '40 (BO) [10] Cambridge, MA Our Lady of Pity Church.
Charest, Roger M. *s.m.m.* '42 (RVC) [N] Bay Shore, NY Montfort Missionaries.
Charipar, Henry W. '68 (DUB) Dorchester, IA St. Mary's Church; Hanover, IA St. Mary's Church; New Albin, IA St. Joseph's Church.
Charland, George A. '60 (WOR) Baldwinville, MA St. Vincent De Paul Church.
Charland, Paul A. '71 (PRO) Foster, RI St. Paul the Apostle Church.
Charlebois, Msgr. John J. '54 (GRY) Valparaiso, IN St. Paul Church.
Charlebois, Msgr. Robert L. '57 (GRY) On Duty Outside the Diocese.
Charles, Frank A. *s.v.d.* '67 (LAF) [8] Lafayette, LA St. Anthony Church.
Charles, Henry '71 (WDC) Takoma Park, MD Our Lady of Sorrows Church.
Charlot, Lucien '61 (BRK) Brooklyn, NY Kings County Hospital Center.
Charlton, Robert *ss.cc.* '88 (FR) Fairhaven, MA St. Mary's Church; [K] Fairhaven, MA Sacred Hearts Provincial House.
Charm, Robert W. '77 (OAK) [11] Oakland, CA St. Lawrence O'Toole Church.
Charman, Eugene J. '71 (HRT) Southington, CT Immaculate Conception Church; Special and other (Arch)Diocesan Assignment.
Charnley, George '76 (DET) Canton, MI Saint John Neumann Church.
Charnoki, Andrew J. '43 (GBG) Retired; [G] Greensburg, PA St. Anne Home.
Charnoki, John J. '45 (PIT) [35] Pittsburgh, PA St. Raphael Church; Retired.
Charnoki, Msgr. William G. *j.c.l.* '65 (GBG) Indiana, PA St. Bernard Church.
Charpentier, Dale '83 (HT) On Leave.
Charters, Thomas S. '75 (OWN) Elkton, KY St. Susan Church; Guthrie, KY Sts. Mary & James Church.
Chase, Chan '62 (R) Retired.
Chase, Charles E. '79 (OG) Copenhagen, NY St. Mary Church.
Chase, Kenneth M. '84 (DET) [31] Detroit, MI St. Hedwig Church.
Chase, Lee P. (ROC) Penfield, NY St. Joseph Church.
Chase, Martin L. *s.j.* (DET) [K] Detroit, MI Jesuit Provincial Office-Detroit Province of the Society of Jesus.
Chase, Maurice '53 (SD) Retired.
Chase, P. Geoffrey *o.s.b.* '59 (PRO) [P] Portsmouth, RI Abbey of St. Gregory the Great.
Chase, Raymond '78 (BAL) Special Assignment; [H] Timonium, MD Villa Maria, A Residential Treatment Center.
Chase, Terrence R. '84 (GRY) Schererville, IN St. Michael Church.
Chassaniol, Warren F. '65 (HT) Grand Isle, LA Our Lady of the Isle Church.
Chasse, Joseph S. *s.m.* '52 (PRT) Hamlin, ME St. Joseph Church; Van Buren, ME St. Bruno - St. Remi Church.
Chasse, Lucien *s.m.* '43 (BO) [59] Boston, MA Our Lady of Victories Church; [W] Boston, MA Marist Fathers of Our Lady of Victories (Boston Prov.).
Chateau, Paul F. '66 (DET) Oak Park, MI Our Lady of Fatima Church.
Chatham, Msgr. Donald '65 (AUS) On Duty Outside the Diocese.
Chatigny, Donat W. *m.m.* '34 (NY) [Z] Maryknoll, NY Maryknoll Fathers and Brothers.
Chau, Peter Do Quang '73 (NSH) Ashland City, TN St. Martha Church.
Chaumont, James '77 (SAN) [3] San Angelo, TX St. Margaret Church.
Chaupetta, Victor W. '70 (BO) [W] Ipswich, MA Missionaries of Our Lady of LaSalette Corp.
Chauvin, David M. '64 (BR) Vacherie, LA St. Philip Church.
Chavarin, Jose '79 (SFR) [44] San Francisco, CA St. Peter Church.
Chavarria, Horacio '66 (BWN) [3] Brownsville, TX Church of the Good Shepherd.
Chavarriq, Jerome *c.ss.r.* '84 (ATL) Griffin, GA Sacred Heart Church.
Chaves, David *l.c.* '74 (PRO) [E] Greenville, RI Immaculate Conception Academy; [G] Warwick, RI Overbrook Academy at Our Lady of Providence Center.
Chavez, Msgr. Adolphus '56 (SB) [5] San Bernardino, CA Our Lady of Guadalupe Church; Loma Linda, CA Jerry Pettis Memorial Hospital.
Chavez, Msgr. Albert '47 (LSC) Retired.
Chavez, Arturo G. '91 (SB) Blythe, CA St. Joan of Arc Church.
Chavez, Carlos '84 (SFE) Clovis, NM Sacred Heart Church.
Chavez, Don J. '89 (SFE) Abiquiu, NM St. Thomas Apostle Church.

Chavez, Frank '76 (SAN) [1] Odessa, TX Holy Redeemer Church.
Chavez, Gerald F. '73 (FRS) Bishop, CA Our Lady of Perpetual Help Church.
Chavez, Johnny Lee '76 (SFE) Pecos, NM St. Anthony Church.
Chavez, Jose *c.ss.r.* '84 (SAT) [M] San Antonio, TX Redemptorists of Texas-Redemptorist Community at St. Gerard.
Chavez, Jose '96 (MRY) Nipomo, CA St. Joseph Church.
Chavez, Luis N. '91 (TUC) Douglas, AZ Immaculate Conception Church.
Chavez, Manuel '96 (SR) Cloverdale, CA St. Peter's Church.
Chavez, Patrick J. '68 (SFE) El Rito, NM San Juan Nepomuceno Church.
Chavez, Phillip *s.o.l.t.* '93 (CC) [H] Robstown, TX Society of Our Lady of the Most Holy Trinity.
Chavez, Vincent P. '91 (SFE) Arroyo Seco, NM Holy Trinity Church.
Cheah, Joseph P. *o.s.m.* '92 (ORG) Fullerton, CA St. Juliana Falconieri Church; [L] Fullerton, CA California State University Fullerton, Newman Center.
Cheatham, Louis W. '45 (GBG) Retired; [G] Greensburg, PA Neumann House.
Checchio, James F. (CAM) On Duty Outside the Diocese.
Checon, Amarilho '57 (BRK) [T] Brooklyn, NY Catholic Migration & Refugee Office, Catholic Migration Services, Inc.
Cheeramkuzhy, Matthew *c.m.i.* '75 (NSH) Loretto, TN Sacred Heart Church; Saint Joseph, TN St. Joseph Church; [K] Liberty, TN Carmelites of Mary Immaculate Center of Spirituality.
Cheesman, Robert *c.ss.r.* '57 (NY) [AA] Hastings-on-Hudson, NY Sisters of St. Francis.
Cheetham, William J. '46 (PIT) [36] Pittsburgh, PA St. Regis Church.
Cheikho, John Hanna '68 (EST) West Bloomfield, MI St. Thomas Chaldean Catholic Parish Church.
Chelena, Thomas '68 (PRM) Absent on Leave.
Chelick, James A. '76 (GR) [23] Grand Rapids, MI St. Thomas the Apostle Church.
Cheline, Paschal *o.s.b.* '64 (P) [L] St. Benedict, OR Mt. Angel Abbey.
Chemazar, Blase *o.f.m.* '53 (CHI) [194] Chicago, IL St. Stephen Church; [N] Lemont, IL The Slovene Franciscan Fathers, Order of Friars Minor, Commissariat of the Holy Cross.
Chembakassery, Vincent '80 (BIS) Stanley, ND Queen of the Most Holy Rosary Church.
Chemino, Stephen Scott '93 (ALX) Plaucheville, LA Mater Dolorosa Church.
Chen, Anthony K. '52 (CHI) Schiller Park, IL St. Maria Goretti Church; Retired.
Chen, John '86 (DAL) Richardson, TX Mission of the Sacred Heart of Jesus Church.
Chen, Raphael '52 (AMA) Retired.
Chen, Vincent P. '57 (MET) Phillipsburg, NJ SS. Philip and James Church; Phillipsburg, NJ Warren Hospital.
Chenevey, Anthony L. *s.s.p.* '58 (Y) [A] Canfield, OH Society of St. Paul.
Cheney, Edmund K. *s.j.* '42 (WOR) [N] Worcester, MA Jesuits of Holy Cross College, Inc.
Cheney, James '95 (FAR) Devils Lake, ND St. Joseph's Church.
Cheney, Jesse C. '43 (LR) Retired; [H] Little Rock, AR St. John Manor.
Cheng, Joseph *s.d.b.* '59 (LA) [52] Los Angeles, CA St. Bridget's Chinese Catholic Center Church.
Chengazhacheril, George '86 (SAN) On Duty Outside the Diocese.
Chengazhacheril, George S. '86 (AUS) Moody, TX Our Lady of San Juan Church.
Chenot, Paul *c.p.* '51 (BRK) Queens, NY Creedmoor Psychiatric Center; [U] Jamaica, NY Immaculate Conception Monastery.
Chenoweth, Robert '63 (JC) Retired.
Chenoweth, Robert J. '63 (STL) [K] St. Louis, MO Saint Louis University Hospital.
Cheol Kim, Edward Eui '85 (LA) [47] Los Angeles, CA St. Basil's Church.
Cheol Lee, Adrian Jae '88 (COS) [6] Colorado Springs, CO Korean Catholic Community Church.
Cheol Soo Lee, Stephanus (SFR) [32] San Francisco, CA St. Michael Korean Church.
Chepaitis, Peter S. '72 (NY) [Z] New York, NY Franciscan Friars, Order of Friars Manor.
Chepanis, Anthony J. '48 (PMB) Highland Beach, FL St. Lucy Church; Retired.
Cheplic, Msgr. Peter A. '72 (NEW) [2] Jersey City, NJ St. Aloysius Church.
Chepponis, James '85 (PIT) Kennedy Township, PA St. Malachy Church.
Cheri, Fernand J. *o.f.m.* '78 (NSH) [13] Nashville, TN St. Vincent de Paul Church.
Cherry, Athanasius C. *o.s.b.* '68 (GBG) [H] Latrobe, PA Saint Vincent Archabbey.
Cherubini, Perry A. '85 (CAM) Northfield, NJ St. Bernadette Church.
Cherukarakunnel, Alexander J. '63 (HRT) North Haven, CT St. Therese's Church.
Cherup, Michael A. '81 (PT) [1] Pensacola, FL Cathedral of the Sacred Heart.
Cheruparambil, Francis '82 (TR) Union Beach, NJ Holy Family Church.
Chervenak, Gregory *o.f.m.cap.* '79 (PIT) [N] Pittsburgh, PA St. Augustine Friary.
Chervenak, Stephen M. '60 (PIT) White Oak Boro, PA St. Angela Church.
Chesebrough, Charles S. '67 (IND) Bloomington, IN St. Charles Borromeo Church.
Chesney, Michael E. *s.j.* '91 (SP) [C] Tampa, FL Jesuit High School.
Chess, Msgr. Edwin R. '37 (CHI) Retired.
Chester, Thomas '93 (TR) On Duty Outside the Diocese.
Chethipuzha, Varghese '69 (NY) [125] Bronx, NY St. Ann Church; Bronx, NY North Central Bronx Hospital.
Chetock, James J. '93 (WH) Weirton, WV St. Joseph the Worker Church.
Chetwynd, Clyde H. '80 (BO) Medway, MA St. Joseph Church.
Chevalier, Martin G. '83 (DM) Adel, IA St. John Church.
Chevalier, Thomas H. '80 (ALB) [10] Albany, NY St. Margaret Mary Church.
Chevedden, James N., S.J. '78 (SJ) [M] Los Gatos, CA California Province of the Society of Jesus, Jesuit Provincial Office.
Chew, Randolph G. '71 (PRO) [11] Warwick, RI St. William's Church.
Chi, Msgr. John '42 (SEA) [31] Seattle, WA Our Lady of Mount Virgin Church.
Chi, Paul Chu Van '75 (ORG) Garden Grove, CA St. Callistus Church.
Chia, Luis '59 (GAL) Highlands, TX St. Jude Thaddeus Church.
Chiang, John B. '53 (NY) [116] New York, NY St. Teresa Church; On Duty Outside the Archdiocese.
Chiang, Joseph S. '59 (NEW) Paramus, NJ Our Lady of the Visitation Church.
Chiang, Joseph S. '59 (NY) [DD] New York, NY Chinese Clergy & Religious Association in North America.
Chiara, Msgr. Peter A. '48 (RVC) East Islip, NY St. Mary's Church; Retired.
Chiaramonte, Anthony '65 (ALB) Special Assignment.
Chiaravalle, Dominic M. '65 (PH) [44] Philadelphia, PA Epiphany of Our Lord Church.
Chiarilli, Msgr. Patrick S. '61 (CAM) [3] Vineland, NJ St. Francis of Assisi Church.
Chiasson, Arthur B. *m.afr.* '38 (LR) St. Vincent, AR St. Mary Church.
Chiasson, Ron *o.m.i.* '76 (SD) San Diego, CA R.J. Donovan Correctional Facility.
Chiavello, Donald C. '59 (CAM) Minotola, NJ St. Michael's Church.
Chichetto, James W. *c.s.c.* '68 (FR) [B] North Easton, MA Stonehill College.
Chicoine, Msgr. George D. '41 (MAN) Retired.
Chidiac, Bakhos '91 (OLL) St. Paul, MN Holy Family Church.
Chieffo, Ralph J. '75 (PH) [84] Philadelphia, PA King of Peace Church.
Chiffriller, Edward J. *s.s.j.* '74 (BAL) [M] Baltimore, MD St. Joseph Society of the Sacred Heart House of Central Administration.
Chihak, Msgr. John P. '36 (DUB) Retired.
Child, John F. '59 (DET) [7] Dearborn, MI St. Martha Church.
Chilen, Michael D. '69 (CC) Military Chaplains.
Chiles, Richard P. *o.praem.* '87 (JKS) [2] Jackson, MS St. Mary Church; [7] Jackson, MS Christ the King Church; [E] Jackson, MS Priory of St. Moses the Black; [G] Jackson, MS Jackson State University Newman Center.
Chillog, Thomas A. '84 (STU) Lore City, OH SS. Peter and Paul Church.
Chilmark, Richard J. '60 (NEW) Roseland, NJ Our Lady of the Blessed Sacrament Church.
Chilson, Elbert V. '78 (DEN) [4] Fort Collins, CO St. Elizabeth Ann Seton Church.
Chilton, Michael '74 (HEL) Retired.
Chimera, Angelo M. '69 (BUF) [52] Buffalo, NY The Nativity of the Blessed Virgin Church.
Chimiak, Karl A. '80 (WDC) Ridge, MD St. Michael Church.
Chimiak, Mark W. '95 (WDC) [3] Bethesda, MD Little Flower Church.
Chin, Peter *c.ss.r.* '75 (BAL) [66] Baltimore, MD Our Lady of Fatima Church.
Chinchar, Gerald T. *s.m.* '82 (CIN) [D] Dayton, OH The University of Dayton; [M] Dayton, OH Marianist Provincialate.
Chinchilla, Jose '48 (SR) Special Assignment.
Ching, Herbert '47 (HON) Retired.
Chinh, Ngo Anthony *s.x.* '94 (MIL) [B] Franklin, WI Xaverian Missionary Fathers College Seminary.
Chinh, Peter '50 (ORG) Retired.
Chini, Silvio *o.s.j.* (SCR) Exeter, PA St. Anthony of Padua Church; [M] Pittston, PA Eastern Province of the Oblates of St. Joseph.
Chinnici, Joseph *o.f.m.prov.* '72 (LA) [CC] Los Angeles, CA St. Francis Center.
Chinnici, Joseph P. *o.f.m.* '72 (OAK) [A] Berkeley, CA Franciscan School of Theology; [N] Oakland, CA Franciscan Friars Provincial Office, Province of St. Barbara; [N] Oakland, CA Franciscan Friars Provincial Office, Province of St. Barbara.
Chiodini, Msgr. Jasper J. '42 (STL) Retired.
Chiodo, Msgr. Frank E. '76 (DM) [8] Des Moines, IA Basilica of Saint John; [I] Des Moines, IA Society of St. John (Brothers of Saint Benedict).
Chiodo, Peter *c.pp.s.* '60 (Y) Niles, OH Our Lady of Mt. Carmel Church.
Chiosso, James *s.d.b.* '49 (NY) [Z] New Rochelle, NY Salesian Provincial House.
Chirapurathel, Felix *o.praem.* (TYL) Trinity, TX Most Holy Trinity Church.
Chirayath, Chummar *o.s.j.* '78 (FRS) [1] Bakersfield, CA Our Lady of Guadalupe Church.
Chirayil, Joseph T. '61 (NY) [194] Staten Island, NY St. Adalbert Church.
Chircop, Joseph *s.s.p.* '58 (DET) [K] Detroit, MI Society of St. Paul.
Chirdon, Howard *c.p.* '50 (ALT) [J] Bedford, PA St. Mary's House of Greater Solitude.
Chiriaco, William J. '86 (PH) [D] Philadelphia, PA West Philadelphia Catholic High School.
Chiriboga, Emiliano *s.d.b.* '63 (NY) [3] Port Chester, NY Our Lady of the Rosary Church.
Chirichiello, Richard *o.s.b.* '95 (GBG) [H] Latrobe, PA Saint Vincent Archabbey.
Chirico, Peter F. *s.s.* '56 (CAM) On Duty Outside the Diocese.
Chirico, Peter F. *s.s.* '56 (SEA) [1] Seattle, WA St. James Cathedral.
Chisek, Anthony S. '43 (CHI) Retired.
Chisholm, Gregory *s.j.* '93 (DET) [K] Detroit, MI Jesuit Community at the University of Detroit.
Chisholm, Gregory C. *s.j.* '93 (BO) [W] Boston, MA The Society of Jesus of New England-Provincial Offices.
Chisholm, Thomas *o.s.b.* '89 (JOL) [J] Lisle, IL St. Procopius Abbey.
Chitwood, Dennis '84 (STL) [W] St. Louis, MO St. Louis Catholic Charismatic Renewal.
Chizmar, Msgr. John G. '75 (ALN) Jim Thorpe, PA Immaculate Conception Church.
Chladek, Melchior *o.cist.* '55 (DAL) [M] Irving, TX Cistercian Abbey of Our Lady of Dallas.
Chlebo, John C. '80 (CLV) [1] Parma, OH St. Anthony of Padua Church.
Chleborad, Gerald (CHY) [3] Cheyenne, WY St. Joseph's Church.
Chlopecki, Robert J. '74 (BEL) Leave of Absence.
Chmely, Edward V. '41 (CHR) Retired.
Chmiel, Bronislaus '69 (CHI) [75] Chicago, IL St. Helen Church.
Chmiel, Gerald J. '70 (TOL) [2] Fremont, OH St. Ann Church.
Chmielewski, Francis J. '73 (BUF) [13] Buffalo, NY St. Bernard Church.
Chmielewski, Msgr. Joseph '37 (CAM) Retired.
Chmielewski, Philip J. *s.j.* '81 (CHI) [N] Chicago, IL Chicago Province of the Society of Jesus-Provincial Office.
Chmil, John J. '95 (SCR) [16] Wilkes-Barre, PA St. Nicholas Church.
Chmura, Gary D. '78 (CLV) [58] Cleveland, OH Our Lady of Peace Church.
Chmura, Julian '64 (DET) [4] Detroit, MI St. Andrew Church.
Chmura, Stanislaus '70 (RIC) Retired.
Chmurski, Marek '95 (FR) Centerville, MA Our Lady of Victory Church.
Chmylar, Gregory *o.s.b.m.* '44 (STF) Long Island City, NY Holy Cross Church.
Cho, Laurentius '88 (ORG) Special Assignment.
Cho, Laurentius '90 (ORG) [G] Anaheim, CA St. Thomas Korean Catholic Center.
Cho, Paul H. '81 (PH) [56] Philadelphia, PA Holy Angels Church.
Choate, Lawrence M. *o.s.m.* '78 (CHI) [159] Chicago, IL Our Lady of Sorrows, Basilica of; [N] Chicago, IL Servite Friars - Eastern Province.
Choate, Norman *c.r.* '63 (MOB) [8] Montgomery, AL Resurrection Catholic Church.
Choby, David R. '74 (NSH) Gallatin, TN St. John Vianney Church.
Choc, Pedro *o.s.b.* '90 (SFS) [F] Marvin, SD Blue Cloud Abbey.
Chochol, Ronald C. '64 (STL) Sabbatical.
Chodacki, Jeremy *o.f.m.conv.* '29 (SPR) [A] Granby, MA St. Hyacinth College and Seminary.
Choi, Jun Gui (Michael) '91 (WDC) College Park, MD St. Andrew Kim Church.
Choi, Mark '94 (LA) Lomita, CA St. Margaret Mary Alacoque Church.
Choi, Peter (TR) Browns Mills, NJ The Church of the Korean Martyrs.
Chojnacki, David '69 (CLV) Absent on Leave.

Chojnacki, Gerald J. *s.j.* '73 (NY) [Z] New York, NY Jesuit Provincial's Office.
Cholette, John B. '36 (NY) Retired.
Cholewa, Gregory *o.m.i.* '76 (CHI) [174] Chicago, IL Precious Blood Church.
Cholij, Roman '83 (STF) Fresh Meadows, NY Annunciation of the B.V.M. Church.
Choma, James S. '86 (NEW) [B] South Orange, NJ Seton Hall University.
Chomko, Stephen '46 (PHU) Berwick, PA SS. Cyril and Methodius Church.
Chomko, Stephen '46 (STF) Retired.
Chonko, Michael J. '43 (Y) Retired.
Chontos, Joseph E. '82 (KCK) [5] Topeka, KS Our Lady of Guadalupe Church.
Choo, Mary Joseph (OKL) [9] Oklahoma City, OK St. Paul, Apostle Church.
Choo, Thomas *ss.cc.* '69 (HON) [4] Honolulu, HI St. Augustine Church.
Choong, Norbert '84 (AMA) Retired.
Choorackunnel, John Vianney *c.m.i.* '64 (LAF) Loreauville, LA Our Lady of Victory Church.
Choppesky, John C. *s.j.* '44 (STL) [O] St. Louis, MO Fusz Pavilion.
Choquet, Robert M. '83 (CHL) Absent On Leave.
Choquette, Paul A. '56 (WOR) Retired.
Chorikavunkal, Joseph Augustine '75 (LUB) Muleshoe, TX Immaculate Conception Church.
Chornyak, Joseph '53 (PBR) New Salem, PA St. Mary's Church.
Choromanski, Zbigniew '81 (NEW) [10] Newark, NJ St. Casimir's Church.
Chorpenning, Joseph *o.s.f.s.* '79 (PH) [C] Philadelphia, PA St. Joseph's University.
Chorpenning, Joseph *o.s.f.s.* '79 (WIL) [I] Wilmington, DE Oblates of St. Francis De Sales.
Chortos, Donald '66 (PIT) Tarentum, PA Holy Martyrs Church.
Chotin, Msgr. Joseph L. '64 (NO) Mandeville, LA Our Lady of the Lake Church.
Chouinard, Lionel G. '65 (PRT) Augusta, ME St. Augustine's Church.
Chouinard, Marcel G. '56 (PRT) Skowhegan, ME Notre Dame De Lourdes Church.
Chouter, Oleksa '91 (STF) Spring Valley, NY SS. Peter and Paul Church.
Chovanec, Paul R. '72 (GAL) [21] Houston, TX St. Christopher Church.
Chow, Luke L. '54 (PH) Levittown, PA St. Michael the Archangel Church.
Chowning, Daniel *o.c.d.* '88 (MIL) [P] Milwaukee, WI Provincial Offices - Discalced Carmelites; [P] Holy Hill, WI Discalced Carmelite Monastery.
Chowning, Michael *o.f.m.* '68 (LEX) Hazard, KY Mother of Good Counsel Church; Jackson, KY Holy Cross Church; [K] Hazard, KY Father Farrell Spiritual Life Center.
Chrepta, Msgr. Stephen J. '45 (STF) Retired.
Chretien, Richard L. '67 (FR) Westport, MA Our Lady of Grace Church.
Christ, John P. *o.s.c.* '65 (DET) Royal Oak, MI St. Dennis Church; [K] Riverview, MI Crosier Community of Riverview.
Christ, Raymond J. *o.s.f.s.* '51 (HBG) Manheim, PA St. Richard Church.
Christancho, Jorge '78 (ATL) Gainesville, GA St. Michael's Church.
Christen, Charles L. '89 (PIT) [70] Pittsburgh, PA St. Cyril of Alexandria Church; Allegheny County, PA Allegheny General Hospital.
Christensen, Donald L. '59 (SAG) [8] Saginaw, MI St. Andrew Church.
Christensen, Lawrence P. *c.m.* '84 (DEN) Longmont, CO St. John the Baptist Church.
Christensen, Michael R. '79 (LIN) [10] Lincoln, NE St. Peter Church.
Christensen, Peter F. '85 (STP) [A] St. Paul, MN St. John Vianney Seminary; [C] St. Paul, MN University of St. Thomas.
Christensen, William A. *s.m.* '73 (STL) [P] St. Louis, MO Provincialate of the Society of Mary, Province of St. Louis.
Christi, Frank *o.s.m.* '56 (ORG) [H] Buena Park, CA Servite Fathers And Brothers.
Christian, George G. *o.p.* '55 (L) [46] Louisville, KY St. Louis Bertrand Church.
Christian, John S. '84 (TR) Leave of Absence.
Christian, Lawrence *c.m.f.* '83 (SAT) [B] San Antonio, TX Immaculate Heart Claretian Seminary.
Christian, Norman H. '67 (STL) Leave of Absence.
Christiana, Nicholas M. '78 (ALT) Absent on Leave.
Christiansen, Andrew J. *s.j.* '72 (WDC) [M] Washington, DC Leonard Neale House.
Christiansen, J. Richard (WOR) [B] Worcester, MA Assumption College.
Christie, Maria Joseph *s.j.* '88 (STL) [P] St. Louis, MO Jesuit Community Corporation at St. Louis University - Jesuit Hall.
Christman, Msgr. Bernard E. '59 (OG) Lyon Mountain, NY St. Bernard Church; Lyon Mountain, NY Lyon Mountain Correctional Facility.
Christman, Ralph '56 (HON) Waianae, HI Sacred Heart Church; [H] Honolulu, HI Maryknoll Fathers House.
Christman, Robert '79 (MIA) Absent on Leave.
Christof, Francis T. *o.s.f.s.* '82 (WIL) [I] Childs, MD Oblates of St. Francis De Sales.
Christoffersen, Hans *o.f.m.conv.* '87 (STL) [P] St. Louis, MO St. Bonaventure Friary (Province of Our Lady of Consolation).
Christopher, Charles A. *c.s.b.* '60 (GAL) [7] Houston, TX St. Anne Church.
Christopher, Mark '57 (PMB) Fort Pierce, FL St. Anastasia Church.
Christopher, Patrick '91 (STL) [4] St. Charles, MO Sts. Joachim and Ann Church.
Christy, Timothy A. '92 (MET) [1] New Brunswick, NJ St. Peter Apostle Church.
Chrobak, Lyle *o.f.m.* '62 (GB) [I] Pulaski, WI Assumption of B.V.M. Friary.
Chrobot, Leonard F. '64 (FTW) [8] South Bend, IN St. Hedwig Church.
Chrusciel, Bogumil '68 (NEW) [35] Newark, NJ St. Stanislaus Church.
Chrysostom, Francis X. '60 (LA) [K] Inglewood, CA Daniel Freeman Memorial Hospital.
Chryst, Robert D. '68 (SY) [12] Syracuse, NY St. Anthony of Padua Church; Special Assignment.
Chrzastek, Brian *o.p.* '92 (PRO) [P] Providence, RI St. Thomas Aquinas Priory at Providence College.
Chu, Bernard M.C. *s.j.* '60 (OAK) [N] Oakland, CA Murray Residence Community; [R] Berkeley, CA Inter-Friendship House Association, Friendship Center.
Chu, Peter *s.j.* '68 (LA) [R] Los Angeles, CA Columbiere House.
Chu, Peter Thanh Ngoc '55 (GAL) [78] Houston, TX Vietnamese Martyrs Church.
Chu, Quang Vinh '91 (ORG) [2] Anaheim, CA St. Boniface Church.
Chubirko, Michael *s.d.b.* '60 (PSC) Elizabeth, NJ SS. Peter and Paul Church.
Chudzinski, Frederick V. *s.s.* '36 (BAL) [K] Baltimore, MD St. Charles Villa; [M] Baltimore, MD St. Charles Villa.
Chukwu, Christopher '80 (DET) Walled Lake, MI St. William Church.
Chun, Francis '63 (P) Absent on Leave.
Chung, Alex '88 (LA) Paramount, CA Our Lady of the Rosary Church.
Chung, Anthony '83 (SFR) Redwood City, CA St. Pius Church; San Francisco, CA Kaiser Hospital Redwood City; San Francisco, CA Sequoia Hospital; Special Assignment.
Chung, Francis K. *s.j.* (SFR) [2] San Francisco, CA St. Agnes Church.
Chuong, Matthias *c.m.c.* (STP) [28] Minneapolis, MN St. Joseph Hien Church.
Chupela, Msgr. Andrew A. '55 (GBG) [3] Uniontown, PA Nativity of the Blessed Virgin Mary Church.
Chura, Andrew '58 (PBR) Toronto, OH St. Joseph Church.
Church, Msgr. James F. '58 (SAC) [19] Sacramento, CA St. Philomene Church.
Church, Tim '95 (DAL) Coppell, TX St. Ann Church.
Church, Wenceslaus '59 (CHI) [N] Chicago, IL St. Peter's Friary.
Churchill, Raymond '54 (HON) Retired.
Churchwell, Stephen T. '76 (ATL) [8] Atlanta, GA Sacred Heart of Jesus Church.
Chwakek, Kazimierz *m.i.c.* '87 (SPR) [I] Stockbridge, MA Congregation of Marians.
Chwalek, John C. '48 (SPR) Adams, MA St. Stanislaus Kostka Church.
Chwalinski, Stanley R. '67 (BUF) Attica, NY St. Vincent de Paul Church.
Chwaliszewski, Roman *o.f.m.conv.* '60 (FR) [7] New Bedford, MA Our Lady of Perpetual Help Church.
Chwieroth, Edward J. '50 (PH) [56] Philadelphia, PA Holy Angels Church; Cheltenham, PA St. Joseph Church.
Chycinski, Gregory A. '71 (MIL) [61] Milwaukee, WI Our Lady of Sorrows Church.
Chylewski, Msgr. Anthony '52 (SD) [37] San Diego, CA St. Vincent de Paul Church.
Chylko, Gerard *c.ss.r.* '79 (BAL) [66] Baltimore, MD Our Lady of Fatima Church.
Ciaiola, Joseph A. '47 (E) Brookville, PA Immaculate Conception Church.
Cialene, Donald '75 (NEW) Montclair, NJ Our Lady of Mt. Carmel Church.
Ciambella, Perry A. '92 (BUF) Blossom, NY St. Gabriel Church.
Ciambelli, Blase A. '64 (WOR) On Special or Other (Arch)Diocesan Assignment.
Ciampaglio, Msgr. Joseph A. '62 (PAT) Rockaway Township, NJ St. Clement, Pope and Martyr Church.
Ciancimino, David S. *s.j.* '88 (BUF) [D] Buffalo, NY Canisius High School; [O] Buffalo, NY Canisius Jesuit Community.
Ciandella, Roch *o.f.m.* '72 (NY) [BB] Wappingers Falls, NY Mt. Alvernia Retreat House.
Ciani, Francis P. '39 (ALB) Retired.
Ciano, Kenneth J. '95 (IND) [30] Indianapolis, IN St. Luke Church.
Ciaramitaro, James *o.f.m.conv.* '88 (PEO) [2] Peoria, IL Holy Family Church.
Ciaramitaro, Victor P. '72 (MEM) Paris, TN Holy Cross Church.
Ciaravolo, Ronald '58 (NY) Absent on Leave.
Ciardiello, Bruno *o.f.m.* '45 (BRK) [106] Brooklyn, NY Our Lady of Peace Church.
Ciaudelli, Louis P. '61 (PH) [115] Philadelphia, PA Our Lady of Consolation Church.
Ciavaglia, Julio M. *c.r.s.p.* '66 (BUF) [B] Youngstown, NY St. Anthony Zaccaria Seminary.
Ciba, Thomas J. '74 (NEW) [2] Bayonne, NJ St. Andrew's Church.
Cibulskis, Pete *m.i.c.* '53 (MIL) [9] Kenosha, WI St. Peter's Church.
Cicale, Henry *f.m.s.i.* '70 (BO) [B] Framingham, MA Sylva Maria.
Ciccarino, Christopher M. '96 (NEW) On Duty Outside the Archdiocese.
Ciccolini, Samuel R. '69 (CLV) [8] Akron, OH Immaculate Conception Church; [V] Akron, OH Interval Brotherhood Home Alcohol-Drug Rehabilitation Center.
Ciccone, Joseph A. *c.s.p.* '89 (DEN) [4] Boulder, CO St. Thomas Aquinas University Parish Church; [P] Boulder, CO University of Colorado (Boulder).
Ciccone, Mark K. *s.j.* '85 (LA) [F] Los Angeles, CA Loyola High School.
Ciccone, Michael *o.p.* '75 (WDC) [B] Washington, DC Dominican House of Studies.
Ciccone, Nicholas C., Jr. '84 (BO) Natick, MA St. Patrick Church.
Cicerale, Charles W. '75 (MET) Raritan, NJ St. Joseph Church.
Cichanowicz, Casimir *s.s.e.* '43 (VEN) [G] Englewood, FL Society of St. Edmund Residence.
Cichon, Michael W. '85 (NY) [202] Staten Island, NY St. Clare Church.
Cici, William '59 (E) Retired.
Cicinato, Michael '76 (MRY) San Luis Obispo, CA Nativity of Our Lady Church.
Cicola, Alfred C. '67 (PIT) Harwick, PA Our Lady of Victory Church.
Cid, Manuel *o.de.m.* '45 (SJN) [40] San Juan, PR Nuestra Senora de la Merced Church.
Cieciorka, Josef '30 (MAD) Retired.
Ciemiega, Ernest '57 (CHI) [33] Chicago, IL St. Bruno Church.
Cieniewicz, Donald W. '83 (ALN) [9] Reading, PA St. Mary Church; [C] Reading, PA Reading Central Catholic High School (Monsignor Bornemann Memorial).
Cienik, Kenneth *s.a.* '77 (R) Apex, NC St. Andrew the Apostle Church.
Cieri, Domenic L. '81 (BAL) Severn, MD St. Bernadette Church.
Ciesielski, Heinc '46 (PEO) Retired.
Ciesla, Fred *c.r.* '49 (CHI) [D] Chicago, IL Weber High School.
Ciesla, Walter M. '81 (GRY) Kingsford Heights, IN Immaculate Heart of Mary Church; Westville, IN Westville Correctional Center.
Cieslak, William M. *o.f.m.cap.* '73 (OAK) [A] Berkeley, CA Franciscan School of Theology; [A] Berkeley, CA Franciscan School of Theology; [N] Oakland, CA Franciscan Friars Provincial Office, Province of St. Barbara.
Cieslik, Eugene (SFD) [11] Springfield, IL Sacred Heart of Jesus Church.
Cieslik, R. Dale '82 (L) [27] Louisville, KY St. Gabriel the Archangel Church.
Cieslikowski, Thomas J. '88 (HRT) Yalesville, CT Our Lady of Fatima Church.
Cieslinski, Robert '43 (P) Retired.
Ciesniewski, Richard P. '57 (DET) Retired.
Ciesniewski, Richard P. '57 (PHX) Sun City, AZ St. Elizabeth Seton Church.
Ciferni, Andrew *o.praem.* (WDC) [B] Washington, DC Washington Theological Union.
Ciferni, Andrew D. *o.praem.* '66 (PH) [Z] Paoli, PA Daylesford Abbey.
Cigan, John J. '74 (PSC) Binghamton, NY Holy Spirit Church.
Cigolini, Santo *c.s.* (VEN) Clewiston, FL St. Margaret Church.
Cikovic, Charles '86 (VEN) Absent on Leave.
Cilia, Francis V. '79 (SJ) [8] San Jose, CA Holy Family Church.
Cilia, Joseph *o.carm.* '68 (JOL) [J] Darien, IL Carmelite Fathers Provincial Office.
Cilinski, Msgr. John T. '48 (ARL) Woodbridge, VA Our Lady of Angels Church.
Cilinski, Julius J. '45 (ARL) Clifton, VA St. Andrew the Apostle Church; Retired.
Cilinski, Robert '79 (ARL) [M] Fairfax, VA George Mason University, Catholic Campus Ministry House.
Cilinski, Robert C. '79 (ARL) Special Assignment; [M]

Fairfax, VA George Mason University, Catholic Campus Ministry House.
Cillo, David M. '85 (PIT) [31] Pittsburgh, PA St. Louise de Marillac Church.
Cilwick, Theodore T. '43 (CHR) Retired.
Cima, Jose Maria '58 (SB) Redlands, CA St. Mary Church.
Cima, Thomas E. '67 (CHI) Calumet City, IL St. Victor Church.
Cimarrusti, Francis A. '64 (CHI) [134] Chicago, IL St. Matthias Church; [G] Chicago, IL Catholic Charities of the Archdiocese of Chicago-Archdiocesan Offices.
Cimbala, Edward G. '88 (PSC) Jessup, PA Holy Ghost Church.
Cimino, John V. *o.praem.* '61 (PH) [Z] Paoli, PA Daylesford Abbey.
Cimino, Michael '86 (SFE) [10] Albuquerque, NM Our Lady of the Assumption Church.
Cimmarrusti, Francis A. '64 (CHI) [59] Chicago, IL St. Fidelis Church.
Cimperman, Victor J. '43 (CLV) [4] Akron, OH Christ the King Church; Retired.
Cimpl, Charles L. '78 (SFS) [8] Sioux Falls, SD St. Therese Church.
Cincinnati, Anthony '87 (WH) Follansbee, WV St. Anthony's Church.
Cincoski, Edward E. *s.j.* '50 (DET) [P] Clarkston, MI Colombiere Center.
Cincotta, Anthony '74 (SY) On Duty Outside the Diocese.
Cindric, John R. '74 (GBG) Belle Vernon, PA St. Sebastian Church.
Cinesi, Joseph '80 (MIA) [8] Fort Lauderdale, FL St. Jerome Church.
Cingle, Martin A. '73 (ALT) [16] Johnstown, PA Visitation of the B.V.M. Church.
Cingolani, Gabriele *c.p.* '59 (MET) [H] South River, NJ Passionist Provincial Office.
Cini, Msgr. J. Thomas '68 (WIL) Liftwood, DE Immaculate Heart of Mary Church.
Cini, Robert *m.s.s.p.* '53 (DET) [3] Dearborn, MI St. Bernadette Church.
Cinque, Frank *o.m.v.* '88 (BO) [B] Boston, MA Oblate Provincialate.
Cinque, Ralph G. *o.s.b.* '55 (MAN) [K] Manchester, NH St. Anselm Abbey.
Cinque, Stephen J. '81 (NEW) Maywood, NJ Our Lady Queen of Peace Church.
Cinque, Thomas *o.m.v.* '91 (BO) [B] Boston, MA Oblate Provincialate.
Cinquegrani, David *c.p.* '96 (HRT) [C] West Hartford, CT Saint Joseph College; [M] West Hartford, CT Holy Family Monastery/Retreat; [Q] Farmington, CT Holy Family Retreat House.
Cinquegrani, R. Bruce '79 (MEM) [2] (Bartlett), TN St. Ann Church.
Cinson, Victor, Jr. '74 (STU) Harriettsville, OH St. Henry Church; Lowell, OH Our Lady of Mercy Church.
Cintolo, Antonio A. '45 (BO) Retired.
Cintron, Angel Luis '91 (CGS) Aibonito, PR Church of St. Joseph.
Cintron, Freddy '87 (BRK) [39] Brooklyn, NY St. Fortunata Church; [39] Brooklyn, NY St. Fortunata Church.
Cintron, Segismundo '89 (PCE) Penuelas, PR St. Joseph Church; [B] Ponce, PR The Pontifical Catholic University of Puerto Rico.
Cintula, Francis M. '65 (CHL) North Wilkesboro, NC St. John Baptist de LaSalle Church.
Cio, Robert '74 (NEW) New Providence, NJ Our Lady of Peace Church.
Cioffi, Alfred '85 (MIA) [24] Miami, FL St. Kevin Church.
Cioffi, Paul L. *s.j.* '59 (WDC) [M] Washington, DC The Jesuit Community at Georgetown University; [V] Washington, DC Institute for Pastoral Renewal, Inc.
Cioffi, Phillip F. '81 (CHI) Forest Park, IL St. Bernardine Church.
Cioffi, Ronald J. '69 (TR) Keyport, NJ St. Joseph Church.
Ciolek, Msgr. Casimir S. '46 (CLV) [37] Cleveland, OH St. John Cantius Church; [2] Garfield Heights, OH SS. Peter and Paul Church; Retired; [V] Cleveland, OH Society of St. Vincent de Paul, Diocesan Central Council.
Ciolek, Joseph F. '47 (CLV) [L] Cleveland, OH Holy Family Home.
Cioppa, Philip '83 (ALB) On Duty Outside the Diocese.
Cioppa, Philip M. '83 (YAK) Sunnyside, WA St. Joseph's Church.
Cioppi, Martin T. '81 (PH) Upper Gwynedd, PA Corpus Christi Church; [F] Lansdale, PA Lansdale Catholic High School.
Ciordia, Pedro Ma. '61 (LA) El Monte, CA Our Lady of Guadalupe Church.
Ciorra, Anthony '73 (NEW) Livingston, NJ St. Raphael Church.
Ciorra, Anthony *o.f.m.cap.* '73 (NY) [Z] White Plains, NY St. Conrad Friary.
Ciorra, Anthony J. *o.f.m.cap.* '73 (PAT) [B] Morristown, NJ College of Saint Elizabeth; [O] Convent Station, NJ College of St. Elizabeth Newman Center.
Ciotola, Msgr. Romano '65 (COL) Grove City, OH Our Lady of Perpetual Help Church.
Ciotoli, Vincent J. '76 (ALB) Ravena, NY St. Patrick Church.
Cipar, Daniel *m.s.c.* '61 (Y) East Palestine, OH Our Lady of Lourdes Church; [A] Youngstown, OH Sacred Heart Retreat House & Renewal Center.
Cipolla, Richard G. '84 (BGP) [D] Fairfield, CT Fairfield College Preparatory School; [S] Darien, CT Convent of St. Birgitta.
Cippel, John A. '60 (SP) Spring Hill, FL St. Frances Xavier Cabrini Church.
Ciprian, Carl A. '76 (CLV) [3] Barberton, OH Holy Trinity Church.
Cipriano, Joseph F. '59 (SCR) [2] Old Forge, PA St. Mary's Church.
Cipriano, Robert '87 (SFR) [2] San Mateo, CA St. Gregory Church.
Ciranni, Salvatore *r.c.j.* '55 (FRS) Sanger, CA St. Mary Church.
Cirba, Richard J. '89 (SCR) Carbondale, PA St. Rose of Lima Church.
Cirignani, Anthony *o.f.m.* '83 (CHI) [111] Chicago, IL St. Joseph Church.
Cirilli, Matthew R. '64 (PIT) [2] Butler, PA St. Michael the Archangel Church.
Cirino, Andre *o.f.m.* '67 (NY) [BB] Wappingers Falls, NY Mt. Alvernia Retreat House.
Ciriza, Jesus M. '59 (SJN) Rio Grande, PR Nuestra Senora del Carmen Church.
Cirone, John *c.m.f.* '96 (CHI) [80] Chicago, IL Holy Cross/Immaculate Heart of Mary Church.
Cirone, Theodore Salvatore *c.m.f.* '55 (CHI) [N] Chicago, IL Claretian Missionaries, St. Jude League, Inc.; [N] Oak Park, IL Claretian Fathers Headquarters of U.S.A. Eastern Province; [N] Oak Park, IL Claretian Fathers Headquarters of U.S.A. Eastern Province.
Cirrincione, Msgr. Joseph A. '34 (ROC) Retired; [L] Rochester, NY Family Rosary For Peace, Inc.
Cis, James '38 (FTW) Retired.
Ciscar, Tomas *o.c.* '78 (SJN) [61] San Juan, PR Santa Teresita Del Nino Jesus Church.
Cisco, Bede *o.s.b.* '78 (IND) [B] St. Meinrad, IN St. Meinrad Seminary-College of Liberal Arts; [J] St. Meinrad, IN St. Meinrad Archabbey.
Cisdyn, Myroslaw (SJP) St. Petersburg, FL Epiphany of Our Lord Church.
Cisetti, Joseph '91 (KC) [39] (Kansas City North), MO St. Therese Parish Church.
Cisewski, John '71 (NO) [45] New Orleans, LA St. Matthias Church.
Cislo, Robert (DET) Canton, MI Saint John Neumann Church.
Cisneros, Hilario *m.sp.s.* '92 (LA) Huntington Park, CA St. Martha Church.
Cisneros, Msgr. Octavio '71 (BRK) [U] Brooklyn, NY Curial Residence.
Cisneros, Msgr. Octavio '71 (NY) [DD] New York, NY Felix Varela Foundation, Inc., The.
Cistone, Joseph R. '75 (PH) [11] Philadelphia, PA St. Anne Church.
Citino, Angelo R. '77 (PH) [110] Philadelphia, PA Nativity of the Blessed Virgin Mary Church.
Citro, Anthony M. '94 (GAY) Cheboygan, MI St. Mary-St. Charles Church.
Ciuba, Msgr. Edward J. '59 (NEW) North Caldwell, NJ Notre Dame Church.
Ciuffoletti, Angelo G. '64 (GBG) Youngwood, PA Holy Cross Church.
Ciulek, Joseph '43 (ALB) Retired.
Ciullo, Michael '75 (MAN) Milford, NH St. Patrick Church.
Ciullo, Michael *o.c.d.* '75 (MIL) [P] Milwaukee, WI Provincial Offices - Discalced Carmelites.
Ciungu, John '42 (ROM) Mission Hills, CA St. Mary Romanian Catholic Mission Church; Retired.
Ciupek, James (BUF) Williamsville, NY St. Gregory the Great Church.
Ciurej, Richard S. '54 (OM) Retired.
Ciurpita, John N. '89 (PHU) Hazleton, PA St. Michael's Church; McAdoo, PA St. Mary's Church; Shenandoah, PA St. Michael's Church.
Civiello, John D. '68 (PRT) [5] Portland, ME St. Patrick's Church.
Civille, John R. '66 (CIN) Middletown, OH Holy Family Church.
Civzelis, Victor *m.i.c.* '64 (CHI) [162] Chicago, IL Our Lady of Aglona Church.
Cizik, Ladis J. '87 (PIT) Washington County, PA Canonsburg Hospital.
Cizur, Ignacio *o.f.m.cap.* '72 (DAL) [9] Dallas, TX Our Lady of Perpetual Help Church.
Claassen, Richard *o.c.d.* '93 (TUC) [21] Tucson, AZ Santa Cruz Church.
Claerr, Francis *c.m.m.* '48 (DET) [K] Dearborn Heights, MI Our Lady of Grace Monastery.
Claffey, James E. *c.m.* '72 (RVC) [H] Hicksville, NY Catholic Charities Central Administration.
Clagett, Carl P. '55 (COL) [33] Columbus, OH Our Lady of the Miraculous Medal Church.
Clair, John J. '82 (CHI) [A] Chicago, IL St. Joseph Seminary.
Clancey, Msgr. Thomas C. '45 (BRK) [19] Brooklyn, NY St. Bernard's Church.
Clancy, Bernard *o.m.i.* '41 (MIA) [2] Miami, FL Christ the King Church.
Clancy, Douglas P. '71 (HRT) [4] Manchester, CT St. James Church.
Clancy, Frank *s.c.j.* '74 (BWN) Harlingen, TX Valley Baptist Medical Center; [E] Harlingen, TX Priests of the Sacred Heart.
Clancy, Frederick J. '45 (TR) Retired.
Clancy, Patrick M.J. *o.p.* '39 (CHI) [N] Chicago, IL Dominicans (Provincial Office).
Clancy, Rafael '74 (AUS) [16] Austin, TX St. Louis Church.
Clancy, Rian *c.p.* '53 (CHI) [N] Chicago, IL Immaculate Conception Monastery.
Clancy, Robert E. '74 (CLV) [16] Akron, OH Sacred Heart of Jesus Church; Akron, OH Akron General Hospital.
Clancy, Thomas *s.j.* '55 (NO) [C] New Orleans, LA Loyola University; [S] New Orleans, LA Jesuit Seminary and Mission Bureau.
Clancy, Msgr. Thomas C. '45 (BRK) Retired; [V] Queens Village, NY St. Ann's Novitiate, Little Sisters of the Poor.
Clancy, Timothy R. *s.j.* '89 (CHI) [C] Chicago, IL Jesuit Community at Loyola University of Chicago.
Clancy, Timothy R. *s.j.* '89 (P) [L] Portland, OR Jesuit Provincial Office (Oregon Prov.).
Claney, Richard (BO) [C] Boston, MA Emmanuel College.
Clanton, Bruce *s.d.s.* '78 (MIL) [P] Milwaukee, WI Salvatorian Provincial Residence.
Clapham, Bruce '95 (CHY) Rock Springs, WY Our Lady of Sorrows Church; Rock Springs, WY SS. Cyril and Methodius Church; Rock Springs, WY Our Lady of Sorrows/Sts. Cyril & Methodius Church.
Clapp, Kenneth A. '90 (MIL) On Duty Outside the Archdiocese.
Clapsaddle, Harlan B. '77 (RCK) Dixon, IL St. Anne Church.
Clarahan, Eugene F. '52 (WIL) Retired.
Clarahan, Michael '58 (CHI) [N] Chicago, IL St. Peter's Friary.
Clark, Andrew '83 (NY) Absent on Leave.
Clark, Anthony '79 (LSC) Hobbs, NM Our Lady of Guadalupe Church.
Clark, Anthony *s.v.d.* '85 (IND) [39] Indianapolis, IN St. Rita Church.
Clark, Benjamin *o.c.s.o.* '50 (CHR) [E] Moncks Corner, SC Mepkin Abbey.
Clark, C. Thomas '49 (L) Retired.
Clark, Curtis L. '84 (ARL) [2] Arlington, VA St. Agnes Church.
Clark, Curtis L. '84 (PH) [A] Wynnewood, PA Theological Seminary of St. Charles Borromeo, Overbrook.
Clark, Curtis L., Jr. '84 (ARL) On Duty Outside the Diocese.
Clark, Daniel C. '80 (L) On Special Assignment.
Clark, David L. '84 (P) Estacada, OR St. Aloysius Church.
Clark, Msgr. Dennis R. '66 (SD) Rancho Santa Fe, CA Church of the Nativity.
Clark, Douglas K. '76 (SAV) [1] Savannah, GA Cathedral of St. John the Baptist.
Clark, Edward F. *s.j.* '45 (NY) [Z] New York, NY Jesuit Community at Fordham University.
Clark, Edward Wm. '72 (LA) [A] Camarillo, CA St. John's Seminary College of the Archdiocese of Los Angeles.
Clark, Emmanuel W. *o.s.b.* '61 (P) Mt. Angel, OR St. Mary Church; [L] St. Benedict, OR Mt. Angel Abbey.
Clark, Msgr. Eugene V. (NY) [DD] New York, NY Friends of American Art in Religion, Inc.
Clark, Msgr. Eugene V. '51 (NY) [2] New York, NY St. Agnes Church; [DD] New York, NY Patrons of the Arts in the Vatican Museums; [DD] New York, NY Vatican Museums, Information Office of the.
Clark, Gerard J. '40 (MIL) Retired.
Clark, H. Robert '51 (CHI) [179] Chicago, IL Queen of All Saints Basilica; Retired.
Clark, Howard T. '57 (WIL) [5] Wilmington, DE St. Elizabeth Church; Newark, DE Medical Center of Delaware.
Clark, J. Donald *s.j.* '48 (SY) [S] Syracuse, NY Jesuits at LeMoyne, Inc.
Clark, James E. '96 (ALB) Middleburgh, NY St. Catherine Church.
Clark, James M. '72 (TR) Lincroft, NJ St. Leo the Great Church.
Clark, James P. '52 (NY) [2] Mt. Vernon, NY St. Francis of Assisi Church.
Clark, James W. '56 (FR) Retired.
Clark, James W. '84 (GBG) Monessen, PA The Epiphany of Our Lord Church.
Clark, John '66 (SEA) Unassigned.
Clark, John F. *c.m.* '70 (STL) [A] St. Louis, MO

Kenrick-Glennon Seminary; [P] St. Louis, MO Vincentian-St. Lazare Residence.
Clark, Msgr. John J. (CAM) Retired.
Clark, John R. '96 (WDC) [8] Silver Spring, MD St. Michael Church.
Clark, John W. *s.j.* '59 (SFR) [C] San Francisco, CA University of San Francisco; [N] San Francisco, CA Jesuit Community at University of San Francisco.
Clark, Joseph J. '96 (ARL) Annandale, VA Holy Spirit Church.
Clark, Joseph L. '76 (RIC) Fort Monroe, VA St. Mary Star of the Sea Church.
Clark, Keith *o.f.m.cap.* '65 (MIL) [B] Mount Calvary, WI St. Lawrence Seminary; [P] Mount Calvary, WI St. Lawrence Friary.
Clark, Kevin *o.s.b.* '76 (NO) Bogalusa, LA Annunciation B.V.M. Church; [P] St. Benedict, LA St. Joseph Abbey.
Clark, Msgr. Laurence E. '54 (LA) Retired.
Clark, Lucian *c.p.* '65 (MET) [H] South River, NJ Passionist Provincial Office.
Clark, Matthew R. *o.s.b.* '87 (NO) [A] St. Benedict, LA St. Joseph's Seminary College; [P] St. Benedict, LA St. Joseph Abbey.
Clark, Michael *o.m.i.* '60 (BEL) [G] Belleville, IL Missionary Oblates of Mary Immaculate - St. Henry's Oblate Residence.
Clark, Michael '95 (OWN) [1] Paducah, KY St. Francis de Sales Church; [2] Paducah, KY Rosary Chapel.
Clark, Patrick S. '61 (SEA) Issaquah, WA St. Joseph Church.
Clark, Peter A. *s.j.* '92 (PH) [Z] Philadelphia, PA Jesuit Community at St. Joseph's University.
Clark, Ray '91 (OWN) Mayfield, KY St. Joseph Church.
Clark, Richard D. '63 (ALT) Conemaugh, PA Sacred Heart Church.
Clark, Richard D. '93 (MRY) Carmel, CA San Carlos Borromeo Basilica.
Clark, Msgr. Robert '53 (CC) Retired.
Clark, Robert *s.s.c.* '65 (OM) [K] St. Columbans, NE St. Columban's Foreign Mission Society.
Clark, Robert P. '84 (NU) Kandiyohi, MN St. Patrick Church; Lake Lillian, MN St. Thomas More Church.
Clark, Steven E. '90 (NY) Peekskill, NY Assumption Church.
Clark, Thomas F. *s.j.* '81 (BO) [22] Boston, MA St. Francis de Sales-St. Philip Church; [W] Boston, MA Loyola House; [W] Boston, MA The Society of Jesus of New England-Provincial Offices.
Clark, Thomas R. '62 (L) [2] Valley Station, KY Our Lady Help of Christians Church; [4] Valley Station, KY St. Timothy Church.
Clark, Timothy *o.c.s.o.* '80 (P) [L] Lafayette, OR The Cistercian (Trappist) Abbey of Our Lady of Guadalupe.
Clark, Tom '55 (OWN) Cloverport, KY St. Rose Church.
Clark, Vernon F. '80 (CHY) Buffalo, WY St. John the Baptist Church.
Clark, William P. *o.m.i.* '55 (BEL) [G] Belleville, IL Shrine of Our Lady of the Snows; [K] Belleville, IL Our Lady of the Snows Layman's Association.
Clarke, Arthur A. *s.j.* '47 (NY) [Z] New York, NY Jesuit Provincial's Office.
Clarke, Arthur A. *s.j.* '50 (SJN) [22] San Juan, PR San Ignacio de Loyola Church.
Clarke, Daniel J. '54 (DM) Perry, IA St. Patrick Church.
Clarke, David M. *s.j.* '64 (DEN) [B] Denver, CO Regis University; [M] Denver, CO Regis Jesuit Community (The Jesuits at Regis University).
Clarke, Fergus '73 (ORG) Placentia, CA St. Joseph Church.
Clarke, Gerardo R. *o.s.f.s.* '57 (CHL) Albemarle, NC Our Lady of the Annunciation Church.
Clarke, Msgr. Hugh (CC) Retired.
Clarke, James A. '70 (Y) Salem, OH St. Paul's Church.
Clarke, James B. '95 (BO) [51] Boston, MA Most Holy Redeemer Church.
Clarke, Msgr. James T. '38 (SCR) Retired; [N] Dunmore, PA Villa St. Joseph.
Clarke, Jim '80 (LA) Redondo Beach, CA St. James Church.
Clarke, John A. '59 (CAM) Washington Township, NJ SS. Peter and Paul Church.
Clarke, John W. '45 (DM) Imogene, IA St. Patrick Church.
Clarke, Kevin T. *s.j.* '73 (HEL) [5] Missoula, MT St. Francis Xavier Church.
Clarke, Noel '78 (NY) [193] Bronx, NY Visitation Church.
Clarke, Peter '63 (CHR) Murphy Village, SC St. Edward Church.
Clarke, Robert J. '73 (PIT) [47] Pittsburgh, PA Guardian Angels Church.
Clarke, Thomas E. *s.j.* '50 (NY) [Z] New York, NY Jesuit Provincial's Office; [Z] New York, NY Xavier Jesuit Community; [AA] Highland Mills, NY Religious of Jesus and Mary; [BB] Highland Mills, NY Bethany Retreat House.
Clarke, Msgr. Thomas J. '34 (EVN) Retired.
Clarke, W. Norris *s.j.* '45 (NY) [Z] New York, NY Jesuit Community at Fordham University.
Clarkin, Herbert '45 (HRT) [K] West Hartford, CT Saint Mary Home.
Clarkson, John *o.m.i.* '55 (SAT) [K] San Antonio, TX Oblate Madonna Residence.
Clarkson, Theodore J. *s.j.* '44 (SY) [S] Syracuse, NY Jesuits at LeMoyne, Inc.
Clarkson, William J. *m.s.c.* '69 (SAT) [M] San Antonio, TX Missionaries of the Sacred Heart.
Claro, Mario R. '67 (WH) Morgantown, WV St. Theresa's Church.
Clary, Michael O. '77 (KC) Blue Springs, MO St. John La Lande Church.
Clasen, Leonard '40 (WIN) Retired.
Class, Michael D. *s.j.* '90 (CHI) [D] Chicago, IL St. Ignatius Jesuit Community.
Classick, Bede E. *o.s.b.* '67 (PAT) [M] Newton, NJ St. Paul's Abbey.
Clauder, J. Gibbs '73 (MAD) Leave of Absence.
Clausen, Kenneth J. '53 (GF) Retired; [K] Billings, MT Ministry to Nursing Homes.
Clausen, William J. '62 (RCK) Maple Park, IL St. Mary Church.
Clauss, Joseph '56 (EVN) Retired.
Clavelle, Richard F. *o.s.b.* '60 (MAN) [K] Manchester, NH St. Anselm Abbey.
Clavenna, Msgr. Charles G. '56 (STL) Augusta, MO Immaculate Conception Church.
Claver, Karl *f.s.s.p.* '79 (SCR) [M] Elmhurst, PA Priestly Fraternity of St. Peter (F.S.S.P.).
Clavero, Jose M. *sch.p.* '64 (NY) [12] New York, NY Annunciation Church; [Z] New York, NY Calasanzian Fathers (Piarists).
Clavin, M. Oliver '70 (SPC) Kelso, MO St. Augustine Church.
Clavin, Nicholas P. '73 (SD) [37] San Diego, CA St. Vincent de Paul Church.
Clay, Frederick L. *c.s.b.* '83 (GAL) Missouri City, TX Holy Family Church; [Q] Sugar Land, TX Basilian Mission Center.
Clay, John C. '51 (STP) [33] St. Paul, MN St. Stanislaus Church.
Clay, Michael G. '80 (R) Chapel Hill, NC St. Thomas More Church.
Clayton, Msgr. C. Murray '56 (SHP) [5] Shreveport, LA Sacred Heart of Jesus Church.
Clayton, Daniel J. '68 (DAL) Rowlett, TX Sacred Heart Church.
Cleare, Rudi '83 (ORL) Special Assignment.
Cleary, Christopher *c.p.* '86 (WOR) [N] Shrewsbury, MA Passionist Fathers of Shrewsbury, Inc., Calvary Retreat Center; [P] Shrewsbury, MA Calvary Retreat Center, Passionist Community.
Cleary, Dennis *m.m.* '77 (STA) [H] Jacksonville, FL Maryknoll Fathers & Brothers.
Cleary, Donald '68 (KC) Odessa, MO St. George Church.
Cleary, Donald M. '71 (OM) Wayne, NE St. Mary Church; [G] Wayne, NE Providence Medical Center.
Cleary, Edward J. '40 (MEM) Retired.
Cleary, Edward L. *o.p.* '57 (CHI) [N] River Forest, IL St. Thomas Aquinas Priory.
Cleary, Edward L. *o.p.* '57 (PRO) [P] Providence, RI St. Thomas Aquinas Priory at Providence College.
Cleary, Edward M. '56 (SFR) Daly City, CA Our Lady of Mercy Church; Retired.
Cleary, Francis X. *s.j.* '63 (STL) [C] St. Louis, MO Saint Louis University; [P] St. Louis, MO Jesuit Community Corporation at St. Louis University - Jesuit Hall.
Cleary, Gerard '61 (BLX) Pascagoula, MS Our Lady of Victories Church.
Cleary, Herbert J. *s.j.* (BO) [U] Boston, MA Marian Manor.
Cleary, Herbert J. *s.j.* '68 (BO) [W] Boston, MA Loyola House.
Cleary, Hugh W. *c.s.c.* '73 (ALB) [T] Albany, NY The Family Rosary Worldwide Office; [T] Albany, NY The Family Rosary Worldwide Office.
Cleary, Hugh W. *c.s.c.* '73 (BGP) [O] Bridgeport, CT Provincial Offices of the Priests and Brothers of Holy Cross, Eastern Province.
Cleary, Hugh W. *c.s.c.* '73 (LA) [CC] Hollywood, CA Family Theater Productions.
Cleary, James *t.o.r.* '41 (ARL) [J] Winchester, VA Sacred Heart Friary.
Cleary, James L. *o.f.m.cap.* '70 (LA) [74] Los Angeles, CA St. Lawrence of Brindisi Church
Cleary, Msgr. Kevin '48 (FRS) Ridgecrest, CA St. Ann Church.
Cleary, Michael J. '53 (SR) Napa, CA St. Apollinaris Church.
Cleary, Patrick J. '78 (BO) [70] Boston, MA St. Stephen Church; Society of St. James the Apostle; [W] Boston, MA The Society of St. James the Apostle, Inc.
Cleary, Paul '74 (SAT) [34] San Antonio, TX St. Dominic Church.
Cleary, Philip C. '79 (CHI) Missionary Work.
Cleary, Richard E. *o.s.f.s.* '59 (R) [2] Durham, NC Holy Infant Church.
Cleary, Richard J. *o.s.b.* '55 (KC) [J] Conception, MO Conception Abbey.
Cleary, Richard T. *s.j.* '66 (BO) [W] Chestnut Hill, MA The Jesuit Community at Boston College; [CC] Chestnut Hill, MA Boston College University Chaplaincy.
Cleary, William *c.ss.r.* '62 (CHI) [N] Bangkok, Thailand; [N] Parana, Brazil Rua Consulheiro Sinimbu.
Cleary, William *c.ss.r.* '62 (DEN) [M] Denver, CO The Redemptorists/Denver Province.
Cleary, William D. '55 (IND) Retired.
Cleary, William J. *o.s.f.s.* '52 (PH) [Z] Philadelphia, PA Oblates of St. Francis De Sales.
Cleary, William M. *o.s.a.* '61 (WDC) [B] Silver Spring, MD Austin Friars Hall, Order of St. Augustine.
Cleaton, C. Thomas '75 (CLV) Bay Village, OH St. Raphael Church.
Cleator, Gerard B. *o.p.* '65 (CHI) [N] Chicago, IL Dominicans (Provincial Office).
Clegg, Thomas '90 (IND) [4] Indianapolis, IN Good Shepherd Church; [7] Indianapolis, IN Holy Rosary Church.
Clegg, Timothy '71 (LFT) On Duty Outside the Diocese.
Clemens, John W. '72 (CHI) [73] Chicago, IL St. Gregory Church; [X] Chicago, IL The Aquin Guild.
Clemens, Norbert H. *c.s.b.* '41 (GAL) Retired; [Q] Houston, TX Dillon House.
Clemens, Thomas Kirk *s.m.* '42 (B) Nampa, ID St. Paul's Church.
Clement, James P. '45 (BR) Retired.
Clement, Richard H. '85 (ALN) [3] Reading, PA St. Catharine of Siena Church.
Clement, Thomas '79 (DEN) Akron, CO St. Joseph Church.
Clement, Thomas '95 (SFS) Aberdeen, SD Sacred Heart Church.
Clemente, Joseph J. '81 (SY) [1] Rome, NY St. John the Baptist Church.
Clemente, Michael '55 (ALB) Retired.
Clemente, Oscar '80 (FR) West Harwich, MA Holy Trinity Church.
Clemente, Vincent L. '76 (VEN) [3] Sarasota, FL St. Martha Church.
Clementi, Innocent *s.d.b.* '49 (MIA) [25] Miami, FL St. Kieran Church.
Clementi, Innocent *s.d.b.* '51 (PAT) [N] Haledon, NJ Institute of the Daughters of Mary Help of Christians.
Clementich, LeRoy *c.s.c.* (ANC) [G] Anchorage, AK Fathers and Brothers of Holy Cross.
Clementich, LeRoy E. *c.s.c.* '57 (FTW) [J] South Bend, IN Congregation of Holy Cross Indiana Province Provincial House.
Clements, Charles '62 (MIA) Special Assignment.
Clements, Daniel A. '54 (NSH) Retired.
Clements, George H. '57 (CHI) On Duty Outside the Archdiocese.
Clements, Richard '46 (OWN) Retired.
Clements, Robert '90 (PHX) [12] Phoenix, AZ St. Gregory Church; Special Assignment.
Clements, Seamus *c.s.sp.* '47 (NEW) [22] Jersey City, NJ Our Lady of Victories Church.
Clements, Thomas P. '55 (CHL) Salisbury, NC Sacred Heart Church.
Clemins, Msgr. Francis J. '50 (PH) Trooper, PA Visitation B.V.M. Church.
Clemo, Ronald M. *s.j.* '67 (SJ) [D] San Jose, CA Bellarmine College Preparatory.
Clemons, Delma '66 (OWN) Fancy Farm, KY St. Jerome Church.
Clenaghan, Gerard *o.m.i.* '47 (SEA) [4] Seattle, WA St. Benedict Church.
Clennon, Raymond J. *o.carm.* '67 (JOL) [I] Darien, IL Carmelite Carefree Retirement Village; [J] Darien, IL Carmelite Community; [M] Darien, IL Office of the Carmelite Midwest Commissary Provincial.
Clerkin, Robert J. '80 (RVC) Garden City, NY St. Joseph's Church.
Clerkin, Thomas *c.s.p.* '85 (AUS) [11] Austin, TX St. Austin's Church.
Clermont, John *o.f.m.cap.* '53 (NY) [57] New York, NY St. John the Baptist Church.
Clerx, Theodore *c.i.c.m.* '57 (SAT) [K] San Antonio, TX Padua Place.
Cletus, Sales T. (Ranjan) *i.m.s.* '84 (TYL) Crockett, TX St. Francis of the Tejas Church.
Cleu, Paul E. '74 (OAK) [3] Fremont, CA St. James The Apostle Church.
Cleveland, S. Gregory *o.m.v.* '95 (MET) Avenel, NJ St. Andrew Church.
Cleves, Simeon *o.f.m.* '55 (L) [42] Louisville, KY St. Joseph Church.
Cleves, William F. '78 (COV) [A] Covington, KY Thomas More College.
Click, Patrick R. '71 (LFT) West Lafayette, IN St. Thomas Aquinas Church; [H] West Lafayette, IN St. Thomas Aquinas Parish and Foundation for Catholic Students attending Purdue Univ.
Cliff, Joseph '39 (MIA) Retired.
Clifford, David K. '91 (NY) [133] Bronx, NY St. Benedict Church.
Clifford, Donald G. '43 (BO) Retired.
Clifford, Donald G. *s.j.* '62 (PH) [C] Philadelphia, PA St.

Joseph's University; [Z] Philadelphia, PA Jesuit Community at St. Joseph's University.
Clifford, Donald P. '61 (BO) Marshfield, MA Our Lady of the Assumption Church.
Clifford, James *o.s.a.* '72 (P) Central Point, OR Shepherd of the Valley Church; [L] Gold Hill, OR Augustinian Community.
Clifford, James J. '45 (WOR) Retired.
Clifford, Jerome *s.c.j.* '61 (MIL) [P] Hales Corners, WI Priests of the Sacred Heart.
Clifford, Jerome A. *s.j.* '49 (DET) [P] Clarkston, MI Colombiere Center.
Clifford, Joseph '89 (VEN) [1] Sarasota, FL Incarnation Church.
Clifford, Leo *o.f.m.* '45 (NY) [115] New York, NY St. Stephen of Hungary Church.
Clifford, Marc J. *o.s.f.s.* '69 (OKL) Duncan, OK Assumption Church.
Clifford, Michael J. '60 (GB) Coleman, WI Ss. Francis of Assisi and Wenceslaus Church.
Clifford, Paul T. '92 (BO) Wakefield, MA St. Joseph Church.
Clifford, Peter C. '76 (ROC) Newark, NY St. Michael Church.
Clifford, Philip M. *c.s.v.* '45 (CHI) [N] Arlington Heights, IL Viatorian Province Center-Clerics of St. Viator.
Clifford, Richard J. *s.j.* '66 (BO) [W] Cambridge, MA Weston Jesuit Community.
Clifford, Thomas *s.j.* '81 (WDC) [E] Washington, DC Gonzaga College High School.
Clifford, Thomas A. *o.p.* '60 (NO) [25] New Orleans, LA St. Anthony Of Padua Church.
Clifford, Thomas F. *s.j.* '81 (SCR) [C] Scranton, PA University of Scranton.
Clift, James C. '57 (OAK) Point Richmond, CA Our Lady of Mercy Church.
Clifton, James F. '88 (OM) [K] Omaha, NE Jesuit Community At Creighton University.
Clinch, Kevin D. '90 (TUC) Kearny, AZ Infant Jesus of Prague Church.
Clines, Paul J. '44 (CLV) [1] Barberton, OH St. Augustine Church; Retired.
Clinet, Mircea '51 (ROM) Dearborn, MI St. Mary Church.
Clinton, Donald E. (MAN) Wilton, NH Sacred Heart Church.
Clinton, Donald E. '90 (MAN) Greenville, NH Sacred Heart Church.
Clinton, Kenneth J. '48 (WIN) Retired.
Clinton, Kevin I. '74 (STP) Mendota, MN St. Peter Church.
Clisch, Norman A. '65 (MAR) Crystal Falls, MI Guardian Angels Church.
Clody, Msgr. Albert W. '65 (BUF) [5] Buffalo, NY All Saints Church.
Clogher, Msgr. John J. '31 (OAK) Retired.
Cloherty, Francis J. '62 (BO) [7] Brockton, MA St. Patrick Church.
Cloherty, John J. '60 (SFR) Colma, CA Holy Angels Church.
Cloherty, Thomas '74 (DAL) Irving, TX Chapel of the Incarnation; [O] Irving, TX Diocese of Dallas Campus Ministry.
Cloherty, Thomas '82 (DAL) [B] Irving, TX University of Dallas.
Cloherty, Thomas P. *k.c.h.s.* '74 (DAL) [P] Irving, TX Diocesan Historian.
Clohessy, Kevin P. '85 (JC) Taos, MO St. Francis Xavier Church.
Cloney, Michael '68 (SR) Eureka, CA St. Bernard Church.
Cloney, Robert D. *s.j.* '60 (NY) [Z] New York, NY Jesuit Community at Fordham University.
Cloonan, Joseph F. '44 (ROC) Retired.
Clooney, David '64 (PHU) Chester, PA Holy Ghost Church.
Clooney, Francis X. *s.j.* '78 (BO) [W] Chestnut Hill, MA The Jesuit Community at Boston College.
Cloquet, Victor '50 (SEA) Retired.
Clore, Victor '65 (DET) [18] Detroit, MI Christ the King Church.
Close, James J. '63 (CHI) [H] Chicago, IL Mission of Our Lady of Mercy-Mercy Home for Boys and Girls.
Close, John L. '82 (ALB) [16] Albany, NY St. Teresa of Avila Church; Special Assignment.
Cloud, Charles W. '89 (TUC) [13] Tucson, AZ St. Francis de Sales Church.
Clough, Wulfstan F. *o.s.b.* '96 (GBG) [H] Latrobe, PA Saint Vincent Archabbey.
Clougherty, Paul L. '60 (BO) Holbrook, MA St. Joseph Church.
Cloutier, Edmond '46 (OAK) [M] Oakland, CA Bishop Begin Villa.
Cloutier, Roland C. '66 (NOR) Hebron, CT The Church of the Holy Family.
Cloutier, Ronald F. '72 (GAL) [2] Houston, TX All Saints Church; Houston, TX Harris County Jail.
Cloutier, Wilbur G. '58 (ALX) Retired.
Clovis, Stephen M. '89 (P) Scappoose, OR St. Wenceslaus Church; [C] Portland, OR Central Catholic High School.
Clubb, Ronald E. '86 (STP) [7] Minneapolis, MN Holy Name Church.
Clunan, Msgr. Paul W. '43 (MEM) Retired.
Clune, Gerald F. '40 (ALB) Retired.
Clune, Gerald F. '40 (SB) [E] Morongo Valley, CA St. Michael's of Morongo Valley, Inc.
Clune, Malaky *o.p.* '60 (SJN) Catano, PR Nuestra Senora del Carmen Church.
Clyde, George A. '42 (NEW) Retired.
Clyne, Msgr. James B. '47 (LA) Retired.
Clyne, Msgr. Vincent F. '45 (NY) [195] Staten Island, NY St. Ann Church; Retired.
Coady, Edward L. (BAL) Retired.
Coady, Francis '76 (SAL) Clyde, KS St. John the Baptist's Church.
Coady, John '59 (GF) Retired.
Coakley, John P. *s.j.* '70 (CHI) [D] Chicago, IL St. Ignatius Jesuit Community; [J] Maywood, IL Foster G. McGaw Hospital of Loyola University of Chicago.
Coakley, Lawrence R. '76 (HBG) New Cumberland, PA St. Theresa of the Infant Jesus Church.
Coakley, Paul S. '83 (WCH) [6] Wichita, KS Church of the Resurrection.
Coakley, Richard J. *s.j.* '37 (BO) [W] Weston, MA Campion Health Center, Inc.
Coates, John T. '45 (PH) Center Square, PA St. Helena Church; Retired.
Coates, Roderick J.D. *s.s.j.* '89 (WDC) [8] Washington, DC St. Benedict the Moor Church.
Cobb, Daniel *o.s.b.* '44 (NO) Mandeville, LA St. Tammany Parish Prison; [P] St. Benedict, LA St. Joseph Abbey.
Cobb, Gerald T. *s.j.* '81 (SEA) [A] Seattle, WA Seattle University.
Cobb, Richard E. *s.j.* '62 (LA) [F] Los Angeles, CA Loyola High School.
Cobeaga Msgr. Victorino '54 (ARE) [6] Vega-Baja, PR Our Lady of Lourdes Church.
Cobel, Lawrence F. '73 (BUF) [4] Lackawanna, NY St. Barbara Church.
Coble, Scott W. *s.j.* '79 (SPK) [C] Spokane, WA Gonzaga University.
Coble, Timothy *o.cist.* '86 (DAL) [M] Irving, TX Cistercian Abbey of Our Lady of Dallas.
Coburn, Albert J. *o.p.* '48 (NO) [P] New Orleans, LA Dominican Fathers & Brothers, Southern Dominican Province.
Coburn, Msgr. Vincent P. '41 (NEW) Bloomfield, NJ Church of St. Thomas the Apostle; Short Hills, NJ St. Rose of Lima Church; Retired.
Coby, Thomas W. '73 (RVC) Greenlawn, NY St. Francis of Assisi Church.
Cocca, Stephen M. '96 (WDC) [3] Rockville, MD St. Mary Church.
Cocciardi, Donato *o.f.m.conv.* '37 (ALB) [A] Rensselaer, NY Conventual Franciscan Friars.
Cochran George L. *o.p.* '62 (PRO) [P] Providence, RI St. Thomas Aquinas Priory at Providence College.
Cochran Paul *s.j.* '94 (FBK) Chefornak, AK St. Catherine Church; Newtok, AK Holy Family Church; Toksook Bay, AK St. Peter the Fisherman Church.
Cochran Steve (EVN) [J] Vincennes, IN Old Cathedral Library & Museum, Inc.
Cochrane, Richard J. *o.s.a.* '73 (PH) [G] Malvern, PA Malvern Preparatory School for Boys.
Cocio, Carlos '83 (TUC) Absent on Leave; [F] Tucson, AZ Regina Cleri Center.
Cockayne, John E. '85 (HRT) Thomaston, CT St. Thomas Church.
Coco, Francis J. *s.j.* '51 (LAF) [J] Grand Coteau, LA Our Lady of the Oaks Retreat House.
Cocozza, Dennis '75 (NEW) Belleville, NJ St. Anthony's Church.
Cocucci, Joseph M.P.R. '96 (WIL) Middletown, DE St. Joseph Church.
Cocuzzi, Bruno *o.c.d.* '56 (MAN) [M] Peterborough, NH The Common-St. Joseph Monastery.
Cocuzzi, Msgr. George A. '49 (NY) [185] Bronx, NY St. Raymond Church.
Cocuzzi, Msgr. George A. '49 (ROC) Retired.
Coda, Joseph '63 (NEW) [N] Rutherford, NJ St. John Vianney Residence for Priests.
Coda, Joseph F. '63 (NEW) Oradell, NJ St. Joseph's Church; Retired.
Codd, Kevin '79 (SPK) Oroville, WA Immaculate Conception Church; Tonasket, WA Holy Rosary Church.
Coddaire, Louis *o.s.b.cam.* '78 (MRY) [G] Big Sur, CA New Camaldoli Hermitage.
Code, Sean K. '93 (ALT) [2] Altoona, PA Immaculate Conception Church; [B] Altoona, PA Bishop Guilfoyle High School.
Cody, Aelred *o.s.b.* '57 (IND) [J] St. Meinrad, IN St. Meinrad Archabbey.
Cody, Daniel '62 (STA) [15] Jacksonville, FL St. Joseph's Church.
Cody, Henry P. '58 (HRT) [7] West Hartford, CT St. Timothy's Church.
Cody, John *c.ss.r.* '81 (SAT) [M] San Antonio, TX Redemptorists of Texas-Redemptorist Community at St. Gerard.
Cody, John F. '49 (WIN) Retired.
Cody, Msgr. John K. '73 (COL) [15] Columbus, OH St. Francis of Assisi Church; [44] Columbus, OH Korean Catholic Community Church.
Cody, John R. *c.ss.r.* '81 (SAT) [19] San Antonio, TX Our Lady Of Perpetual Help Church.
Cody, Kevin W. '93 (MAN) Military Chaplains.
Cody, Michael '58 (SEA) Retired.
Cody, Michael F. *s.s.c.* '73 (BO) [W] Quincy, MA St. Columban's Foreign Mission Society.
Cody, Nicholas A. '54 (STP) Retired.
Cody, Thomas '68 (STA) [13] Jacksonville, FL Resurrection Church.
Coelho, Gabriel Prashant *o.f.m.cap.* (DET) [K] Detroit, MI St. Bonaventure Friary.
Coello, Demetrio *s.d.b.* '60 (SJN) Catano, PR San Francisco de Sales Church.
Coels, Andrew *c.i.c.m.* '48 (SAT) [K] San Antonio, TX Padua Place.
Coen, Alphonsus *c.p.* '77 (SCR) [2] Scranton, PA St. Ann's Church.
Coen, Charles P. '68 (NY) Red Hook, NY St. Christopher Church.
Coen, James *c.ss.r.* '53 (WDC) [M] Washington, DC Holy Redeemer College.
Coen, John *s.a.c.* '62 (RNO) Sparks, NV Immaculate Conception Church; [B] Reno, NV St. Mary's Regional Medical Center.
Coen, Mark '90 (DUL) Brainerd, MN St. Francis Church.
Coen, William R. (BO) [2] Milton, MA St. Elizabeth Church; Boston, MA Massachusetts Hospital School; Retired.
Coenen, Tom '77 (DM) Clarinda, IA St. Clare Church.
Coens, Frank *o.f.m.* '73 (MEM) [5] Memphis, TN St. Augustine Church; [J] Memphis, TN Franciscan Friars (Sacred Heart Prov.) of Memphis.
Coerber, Joseph H. '66 (MIL) Marytown, WI St. Mary Church.
Coerver, Richard V. '76 (STL) Pacific, MO St. Bridget Church.
Coerver, Robert F. *c.m.* '41 (STL) [A] St. Louis, MO Kenrick-Glennon Seminary.
Cofenas, Robert G. '73 (ALN) [5] Allentown, PA Our Lady Help of Christians Church.
Coffey, Msgr. Andrew V. '47 (SAC) Davis, CA St. James Church; Retired and in Senior Ministry.
Coffey, Charles J. *c.s.sp.* '50 (GAL) [1] Galveston, TX St. Mary's Cathedral Basilica.
Coffey, Edward N. '37 (CHI) [4] Cicero, IL Mary, Queen of Heaven Church; Retired.
Coffey, Msgr. James F. '31 (RVC) Bay Shore, NY St. Patrick's Church; Retired.
Coffey, James H. '45 (BO) [1] Brookline, MA St. Aidan Church; Retired.
Coffey, John P. '73 (CHR) Camden, SC Our Lady of Perpetual Help Church.
Coffey, Joseph L. '96 (PH) [83] Philadelphia, PA St. Katherine of Siena Church.
Coffey, Michael '91 (CAM) Atco, NJ Assumption Church.
Coffey, Peter *s.d.s.* '68 (NSH) Cookeville, TN St. Thomas Aquinas Church; Sparta, TN St. Andrew Church.
Coffey, Msgr. Thomas A. '48 (TR) Retired; [M] Trenton, NJ Villa Neumann.
Coffey, William H. '45 (OG) Retired.
Coffield, Msgr. John V. '41 (ORG) Capistrano Beach, CA San Felipe de Jesus Church; Retired.
Cogan, Patrick *s.a.* '77 (WDC) [B] Washington, DC Atonement Seminary-Franciscan Friars of the Atonement.
Cogan, William B. *s.j.* '55 (ALB) [O] Auriesville, NY Jesuit Retreat House for Priests, Religious and Lay People.
Cogan, William B. *s.j.* '55 (NY) [BB] Staten Island, NY Mount Manresa Jesuit Retreat House.
Coghill, Elstan *o.f.m.* '48 (GAY) Indian River, MI Cross in the Woods Catholic Shrine Church.
Coghlan, Msgr. Brian '63 (ORG) Seal Beach, CA Holy Family Church.
Coghlan, John '74 (MOB) Citronelle, AL St. Thomas Church; Mount Vernon, AL St. Cecilia Church.
Coghlan, John A. '44 (STO) Retired.
Coghlan, John C. '43 (CIN) Retired.
Cogo, Joseph A. *c.s.* '59 (BO) [67] Boston, MA Sacred Heart Church.
Cohalan, Msgr. Florence '38 (NY) [2] New York, NY St. Agnes Church; Retired.
Cohan, Dennis '74 (NEW) Glen Rock, NJ St. Catharine Church.
Cohan, Francis J. '46 (P) Retired.
Cohan, Msgr. Robert W. '55 (E) [18] Erie, PA St. James Church.
Cohea, Victor H. '80 (NO) [33] New Orleans, LA St. Francis De Sales Church.
Cohelo, Gabriel *o.f.m.cap.* (DET) Detroit, MI Harper Hospital and Rehabilitation Center.
Cohen, Gerald P. *c.s.c.* '63 (NOR) [K] Willimantic, CT Campus Ministry.

Cohen, Harold F. *s.j.* '58 (NO) [C] New Orleans, LA Loyola University.
Coine, Robert E. '76 (WIL) Ridgely, MD St. Benedict Church.
Coiro, Gregory *o.f.m.cap.* '82 (LA) [F] La Canada Flintridge, CA St. Francis High School.
Coiro, Mark J. '84 (BO) Billerica, MA St. Theresa Church.
Coke, James E. '53 (GAY) Elk Rapids, MI Sacred Heart Church.
Coke, James E. '53 (LC) Retired.
Cokus, Msgr. Joseph J. '58 (LA) Sierra Madre, CA St. Rita Church.
Colacicco, Frank '79 (SAN) Absent on Leave.
Colacicco, Frank L. (OAK) Danville, CA St. Isidore's Church.
Colagreco, Michael A. '77 (PH) Newtown Square, PA St. Anastasia Church.
Colaiacovo, Arthur J. '92 (PAT) Stirling, NJ St. Vincent de Paul Church.
Colaj, Rene Otzoy *o.s.b.* '82 (RCK) [H] Aurora, IL Marmion Abbey-St. Augustine's Abbey.
Colamarino, Dennis '73 (PIT) Duquesne, PA Christ the Light of the World Church.
Colankin, Dimitrij '76 (AUS) Caldwell, TX St. Mary's Church.
Colapietro, Peter M. '76 (NY) [45] New York, NY Holy Cross Church.
Colaresi, Robert E. *o.carm.* '67 (JOL) [J] Darien, IL Carmelite Community; [L] Darien, IL Carmelite Spiritual Center; [M] Darien, IL Society of the Little Flower.
Colasurdo, Peter '77 (STA) [4] St. Augustine, FL San Sebastian Church.
Colautti, John *o.s.b.* '55 (DET) [K] Detroit, MI St. Sylvester Monastery.
Colavecchio, John A. '39 (SFD) Retired.
Colavechio, Francis D. '50 (LR) Fairfield Bay, AR St. Francis Assisi Church.
Colavechio, Xavier G. *o.praem.* '55 (JKS) [E] Jackson, MS Priory of St. Moses the Black.
Colberg, Msgr. James P. '55 (LA) Santa Maria, CA St. Mary of the Assumption Church.
Colbert, Arthur T. *s.s.j.* '64 (BAL) [M] Baltimore, MD St. Joseph's Manor.
Colbert, C. F. '41 (WCH) Retired.
Colbert, John '96 (BEA) [8] Beaumont, TX St. Pius X Church.
Colbert, Joseph D. '59 (BRK) [222] Queens, NY St. Pancras Church.
Colbert, Richard *s.m.* '64 (SP) [7] Tampa, FL Our Lady of Perpetual Help Church; [B] Tampa, FL Tampa Catholic High School.
Colbert, Richard A. *c.pp.s.* '69 (JC) Fayette, MO St. Joseph Church; [F] Fayette, MO Central Methodist College.
Colborn, Francis R. '64 (LA) [12] Los Angeles, CA Holy Name of Jesus Church.
Colburn, Harold '40 (ALB) Retired.
Colchin, Stephen E. '84 (FTW) Bluffton, IN St. Joseph Church.
Cole, Barry '82 (CHI) [W] Oak Park, IL Oak Park Study Center.
Cole, Basil B. *o.p.* '66 (OAK) [N] Oakland, CA Dominican Order (Western Province), St. Albert's Priory; [N] Oakland, CA Western Dominican Province.
Cole, Edwin '64 (JC) Columbia, MO Sacred Heart Church.
Cole, Edwin J. '64 (JC) Columbia, MO University Hospital & Clinics.
Cole, J. Gerard '39 (WDC) Retired; [L] Washington, DC Cardinal O'Boyle Residence for Priests.
Cole, James J. '71 (BGP) Brookfield, CT St. Marguerite Bourgeoys Church.
Cole, Raymond L. '72 (MET) East Millstone, NJ St. Joseph Church.
Cole, Robert F. '72 (MAN) Plymouth, NH St. Matthew Church; [N] Plymouth, NH Plymouth State College Campus Ministry.
Cole, Robert J. '72 (CLV) Olmsted Falls, OH St. Mary of the Falls Church.
Cole, Russan *o.f.m.conv.* '51 (MIL) Brandon, WI St. Brendan Church; Springvale, WI St. Mary Church; Waupun, WI St. Joseph's Church.
Colella, David L. *o.ss.t.* '57 (DAL) [28] Dallas, TX Santa Clara Church.
Coleman, Msgr. Brian P. '63 (GB) [1] De Pere, WI St. Francis Xavier Church; Special Assignment.
Coleman, C. Michael '67 (KC) Special Assignment.
Coleman, Christopher *m.s.c.* '65 (SAN) Big Spring, TX Immaculate Heart of Mary Church.
Coleman, Christopher L. '94 (BRK) [236] Queens, NY St. Rose of Lima Church.
Coleman, Dave '81 (KCK) Horton, KS St. Leo's Church; Purcell, KS St. Mary's Church.
Coleman, Donald E. '74 (SD) Carlsbad, CA St. Elizabeth Seton Church.
Coleman, Ed *o.m.i.* '56 (PHX) Sun City, AZ St. Clement of Rome Church.
Coleman, Ed '83 (P) Silverton, OR St. Paul Church.
Coleman, Edward C. *o.m.i.* '56 (STP) [N] St. Paul, MN Oblate Provincial Offices; [N] St. Paul, MN Oblate Residence.
Coleman, Edward W. '70 (ALN) Nesquehoning, PA Sacred Heart Church.
Coleman, Msgr. George W. '64 (FR) [16] Fall River, MA St. Joseph's Church.
Coleman, Gerald D. *s.s.* '68 (SFR) [A] Menlo Park, CA St. Patrick Seminary; [A] Menlo Park, CA St. Patrick Seminary; [U] Mountain View, CA Hospital and Health Services Liaison.
Coleman, Gerald J. '78 (TLS) [16] Tulsa, OK St. Thomas More Church.
Coleman, James '46 (SAN) Retired.
Coleman, James '46 (SAT) [K] San Antonio, TX Padua Place.
Coleman, James '73 (P) On Duty Outside the Archdiocese.
Coleman, James *p.i.m.e.* '76 (COL) [H] Newark, OH P.I.M.E. Mission & Prayer Center.
Coleman, James F. *s.j.* '56 (NY) [Z] New York, NY Murray-Weigel Hall.
Coleman, Msgr. James G. '62 (HRT) Guilford, CT St. George Church.
Coleman, James G. '77 (TUC) [19] Tucson, AZ St. Pius X Church.
Coleman, John '54 (NY) Absent on Sick leave.
Coleman, John '71 (SFR) On Duty Outside the Archdiocese.
Coleman, John *o.carm.* '78 (LA) [F] Encino, CA Crespi Carmelite High School.
Coleman, John '88 (PHX) [2] Mesa, AZ Christ the King Church.
Coleman, John A. *s.j.* '67 (OAK) [A] Berkeley, CA The Jesuit School of Theology at Berkeley; [N] Oakland, CA Murray Residence Community; [N] Berkeley, CA Jesuit Community at Jesuit School of Theology at Berkeley.
Coleman, John P. '50 (KC) [7] Kansas City, MO St. Catherine of Siena Church; Retired.
Coleman, John R. '50 (SJ) Alviso, CA Our Lady, Star of the Sea Church.
Coleman, Joseph (BO) Boston, MA St. John of God Hospital.
Coleman, Joseph K. '81 (BO) [R] Brighton, MA St. John of God Hospital.
Coleman, Michael *ss.cc.* '58 (FR) [K] Fairhaven, MA Sacred Hearts Provincial House.
Coleman, Michael '81 (JC) Osage Bend, MO St. Margaret Church; Wardsville, MO St. Stanislaus Church.
Coleman, Robert '78 (NEW) [1] Newark, NJ Cathedral of the Sacred Heart Basilica.
Coleman, Robert '87 (JOL) Bloomingdale, IL St. Isidore Church.
Coleman, Msgr. Robert F. '78 (NEW) [A] South Orange, NJ Immaculate Conception Seminary; [B] South Orange, NJ Seton Hall University.
Coleman, Robert P. '78 (CHI) [172] Chicago, IL St. Philomena Church.
Coleman, Thomas '87 (GLP) Quemado, NM Sacred Heart Church.
Coleman, W. Philip '59 (BGP) Retired.
Coleman, William J. *m.m.* '39 (NY) [Z] Maryknoll, NY Maryknoll Fathers and Brothers.
Colendrino, J. Rudolpho (CHK) San Antonio Village, District 6, MP San Antonio De Padua Parish Church.
Colendrino, Jose Rudolpho (CHK) Saipan, MP San Jude Parish Church.
Coles, Edward T. *s.j.* '59 (DAL) [26] Dallas, TX St. Rita Church.
Coles, Edward T. *s.j.* '59 (GAL) [F] Houston, TX Strake, Jesuit College Preparatory Inc.
Coless, Gabriel M. *o.s.b.* '57 (PAT) [M] Morristown, NJ St. Mary's Abbey.
Coletta, Carmen J. *o.s.a.* '38 (BO) [C] North Andover, MA Merrimack College.
Coletta, Ralph V. '61 (CLV) [9] Akron, OH St. John the Baptist Church.
Coletta, Msgr. Thomas J. '63 (PAT) [14] Paterson, NJ Our Lady of Victories Church.
Coletti, Arnold F. '62 (BO) Lexington, MA Sacred Heart Church.
Coley, James E. '47 (TR) Washington Crossing, NJ St. George Church; Retired.
Colfer, Robert *o.m.i.* '40 (PMB) Riviera Beach, FL St. Francis of Assisi Church.
Colgan, John '48 (SP) Retired.
Colgan, Marvin '40 (PEO) Retired.
Colgan, Myles *o.carm.* '48 (JOL) [J] Darien, IL Carmelite Fathers Provincial Office.
Colgan, Richard J. *s.j.* '55 (BAL) [Q] Baltimore, MD Jesuit Seminary Guild & Jesuit Mission Bureau, Maryland Province, Inc.
Colgan, Richard J. *s.j.* '55 (PH) [Z] Philadelphia, PA Jesuit Community at St. Joseph's University.
Colgan, Richard J. *c.s.p.* '79 (BO) [P] Boston, MA Paulist Center; [BB] Boston, MA Chapel of the Holy Spirit.
Colgan, Thomas A. *s.j.* '75 (SPK) [E] Spokane, WA Gonzaga Preparatory School; [O] Spokane, WA Kateri Northwest Ministry Institute.
Colgan, Thomas J. '49 (RVC) Northport, NY St. Philip Neri Church.
Colgan, Tobias *o.s.b.* '82 (IND) [J] St. Meinrad, IN St. Meinrad Archabbey.
Colhour, David *c.p.* '94 (GAL) [S] Houston, TX Holy Name Retreat Center.
Colibraro, Daniel '56 (CHY) Casper, WY Our Lady of Fatima Church.
Colibraro, Philip '57 (CHY) Casper, WY Our Lady of Fatima Church.
Colicchio, Damian *o.f.m.cap.* '62 (NEW) [B] Lodi, NJ Felician College; [O] Lodi, NJ Immaculate Conception Convent.
Colicchio, Ralph M. '67 (HRT) [7] New Haven, CT St. Casimir's Church; New Haven, CT Yale-New Haven Hospital.
Coll, Eduardo *i.v.e.* (FR) [17] New Bedford, MA St. Kilian Church; [Q] New Bedford, MA The Institute of the Incarnate Word, Inc.
Coll, Eduardo '88 (BRK) [48] Brooklyn, NY St. Gabriel The Archangel Church.
Coll, Jerome B. *s.j.* '59 (PH) [C] Philadelphia, PA St. Joseph's University; [Z] Philadelphia, PA Jesuit Community at St. Joseph's University.
Coll, John J. *s.j.* '56 (PIT) [1] Pittsburgh, PA St. Paul Cathedral.
Coll, Msgr. Robert J. '59 (ALN) Retired.
Collard, Bruce W. '80 (MAN) [3] Nashua, NH St. Christopher Church; [N] Durham, NH Campus Ministries.
Colleary, Patrick O. '74 (PHX) [1] Glendale, AZ Our Lady of Perpetual Help Church.
Colleoni, Xavier *m.c.c.j.* '52 (LA) [11] Los Angeles, CA Holy Cross Church.
Coller, Jerome *o.s.b.* '59 (SCL) [I] Collegeville, MN St. John's Abbey, of the Order of St. Benedict.
Colleran, Desmond '56 (ORG) Inactive Leave.
Colleran, James A. '63 (CHI) Missionary Work.
Colleran, Msgr. Kevin J. '72 (NY) [183] Bronx, NY St. Philip Neri Church.
Collet, John *o.m.i.* (AUS) [H] Austin, TX St. Edward's University.
Collet, John '67 (DAL) [A] Irving, TX Holy Trinity Seminary.
Collette, Msgr. Richard E. '52 (WOR) [5] Fitchburg, MA Immaculate Conception Church.
Colletti, Joseph A. '71 (LFT) Unassigned.
Colletti, Peter '84 (CLV) [10] Akron, OH St. Martha Church.
Colletti, Richard M. '78 (WIN) [3] Mankato, MN St. John the Baptist's Church.
Collier, Joseph Mel '58 (SD) [33] San Diego, CA St. Michael Church.
Colligan, Flavian *o.f.m.* '39 (PAT) [M] Butler, NJ St. Anthony Friary.
Colligan, Msgr. Joseph F. '50 (RVC) Centerport, NY Our Lady Queen of Martyrs Church; Retired.
Colligan, Owen *o.f.m.* '39 (NY) [Z] New York, NY Franciscan Friars, Order of Friars Manor.
Collignon, James A. *m.m.* '53 (NY) [34] New York, NY Epiphany Church; [Z] Maryknoll, NY Maryknoll Fathers and Brothers.
Colling, Paul J. '87 (GI) Scottsbluff, NE Our Lady of Guadalupe Church.
Collini, Msgr. Celsus '47 (BRK) [185] Queens, NY St. John Vianney Church; [231] Queens, NY Queen of Peace Church.
Collins, Austin I. *c.s.c.* '82 (FTW) [B] Notre Dame, IN University of Notre Dame Du Lac; [J] Notre Dame, IN Holy Cross Community, Corby Hall, University of Notre Dame.
Collins, Msgr. Bernard G. '37 (DUB) Retired.
Collins, Carl P. '91 (HT) Theriot, LA St. Eloi Church.
Collins, Charles E. '72 (BO) [8] Cambridge, MA St. John the Evangelist Church.
Collins, Charles I. '82 (WIN) Byron, MN Christ the King Church; Kasson, MN Holy Family Church.
Collins, Corwin *o.s.b.* '57 (SCL) Albany, MN Seven Dolors Church.
Collins, Daniel J. '58 (CHI) [128] Chicago, IL St. Mary of the Lake Church; [J] Evanston, IL Saint Francis Hospital of Evanston.
Collins, Denis E. *s.j.* '69 (SFR) [N] San Francisco, CA Jesuit Community at University of San Francisco.
Collins, Edward A. '68 (PAT) Pequannock, NJ Holy Spirit Church.
Collins, Edward F. '35 (DAV) Retired.
Collins, Edward F. '35 (SAC) Fair Oaks, CA St. Mel Church.
Collins, Edwin (RVC) Retired.
Collins, Edwin J. '54 (RVC) Malverne, NY Our Lady of Lourdes Church.
Collins, Msgr. Fachtna P. '50 (LA) Retired.
Collins, Frederick J. '55 (BO) Georgetown, MA St. Mary Church.
Collins, James *s.d.b.* '39 (SFR) [N] San Francisco, CA Salesian Provincial Residence.
Collins, Msgr. James E. '39 (RVC) Oyster Bay, NY St. Dominic's Church; Retired.
Collins, James J. '64 (PH) [C] Philadelphia, PA Holy Family College.

Collins, James M. *s.j.* '58 (BO) [W] Chestnut Hill, MA The Jesuit Community at Boston College; [W] Cohasset, MA Bellarmine House.
Collins, James M. '95 (CHL) Franklin, NC St. Francis of Assisi Church.
Collins, James P. '69 (BRK) [30] Brooklyn, NY St. Columba Church; [G] Brooklyn, NY Bishop Kearney.
Collins, James R. '68 (CIN) [25] Cincinnati, OH St. Dominic Church.
Collins, James R. '81 (PRO) [3] Pawtucket, RI St. Edward's Church.
Collins, John E. *c.s.p.* '74 (NY) [104] New York, NY St. Paul the Apostle Church.
Collins, John J.L. *s.j.* '44 (BO) [W] Chestnut Hill, MA The Jesuit Community at Boston College.
Collins, John M. '69 (LA) Military and VA Chaplains.
Collins, John M. '79 (CHI) [200] Chicago, IL St. Thaddeus Church.
Collins, John P. '72 (PH) Upper Darby, PA St. Alice Church; [D] Springfield, PA Cardinal O'Hara High School.
Collins, Joseph I. '40 (BO) Retired.
Collins, Kevin *o.m.i.* '82 (SAT) [C] San Antonio, TX Oblate School of Theology; [O] San Antonio, TX Oblate Renewal Center.
Collins, Kevin *c.m.* '85 (CHI) [C] Chicago, IL Vincentian Community at DePaul University.
Collins, Laurence '77 (CHI) [J] Evergreen Park, IL Little Company of Mary Hospital and Health Care Centers.
Collins, Leonard J. *c.s.c.* '69 (AUS) [H] Austin, TX Congregation of Holy Cross - Southern Province.
Collins, Michael (ORL) Sabbatical.
Collins, Msgr. Michael '43 (ORG) Seal Beach, CA St. Anne's Church; Retired.
Collins, Michael J. *o.s.b.* '37 (PAT) [M] Morristown, NJ St. Mary's Abbey.
Collins, Michael J. '67 (BR) [13] Baton Rouge, LA St. Jude the Apostle Church.
Collins, Michael J. '85 (JOL) Absent on Leave.
Collins, Michael T. *o.praem.* (WIL) [B] Claymont, DE Archmere Academy; [I] Claymont, DE Immaculate Conception Priory of the Canons Regular of Premontre.
Collins, Neil J. '58 (NEW) Belleville, NJ St. Anthony's Church.
Collins, Patrick W. '64 (PEO) Absent on Leave.
Collins, Raymond *c.ss.r.* '70 (RVC) Bethpage, NY St. Martin of Tours Church.
Collins, Raymond F. '59 (PRO) On Duty Outside the Diocese.
Collins, Raymond F. *s.t.d.* '59 (WDC) [C] Washington, DC Catholic University of America, The; [C] Washington, DC Catholic University of America, The.
Collins, Raymond G. *o.s.f.s.* '59 (ARL) Vienna, VA Our Lady of Good Counsel Church.
Collins, Raymond T.A. *o.p.* '45 (PRO) [P] Providence, RI St. Thomas Aquinas Priory at Providence College.
Collins, Robert '81 (AUS) Retired.
Collins, Robert C. *s.j.* '67 (NY) [Z] New York, NY "America;" Residence and publication office of the America Press; [DD] New York, NY America Press, Inc., The.
Collins, Robert L. '66 (ROC) [60] Rochester, NY St. Thomas More Church.
Collins, Msgr. Russell J. '37 (BO) Retired.
Collins, Seamus *o.p.* '58 (SP) Hudson, FL St. Michael Church.
Collins, Stephen L., III '83 (E) On Leave of Absence.
Collins, T. Byron *s.j.* '52 (WDC) [M] Washington, DC The Jesuit Community at Georgetown University.
Collins, Terrence '71 (R) Kill Devil Hills, NC Holy Redeemer Church.
Collins, Thomas E. '92 (NY) [E] White Plains, NY Archbishop Stepinac High School.
Collins, Msgr. Thomas J. '48 (SAT) Retired; [K] San Antonio, TX Casa De Padres.
Collins, Thomas R. '72 (RIC) Richlands, VA St. Mary Church.
Collins, Thomas S. '92 (PT) [1] Tallahassee, FL Co-Cathedral of St. Thomas More.
Collins, Timothy '54 (BAK) Retired.
Collins, Msgr. Timothy S. '58 (NY) [96] New York, NY Our Lady of the Rosary Church.
Collins, William '33 (ALB) Retired.
Collins, William *c.ss.r.* '49 (TR) [Q] Long Branch, NJ San Alfonso Retreat House.
Collins, William A. '61 (BAL) Randallstown, MD Holy Family Church; Special Assignment.
Collins, William B. '74 (PAT) Hamburg, NJ St. Jude the Apostle Church.
Collins, William F. '65 (CAM) Franklinville, NJ Nativity Church.
Collins, Msgr. William J. '60 (NY) [5] Kingston, NY St. Peter Church.
Collins, William J. *m.s.c.* '67 (SAT) [28] San Antonio, TX St. Anthony of Padua Church.
Collins, William P. '56 (RCK) [7] Rockford, IL St. Mary Church; [J] Rockford, IL Martin House.
Collins, Wm. Emmett *c.ss.r.* '52 (STL) [B] St. Louis, MO St. John Neumann House.
Collison, Craig A. '78 (SC) Willey, IA St. Mary's Church; [B] Carroll, IA Kuemper Catholic High School.
Collogan, Robert '82 (JOL) Graduate Studies.
Collopy John C. (BAL) Special Assignment; Retired; [K] Baltimore, MD Stella Maris Operating Corporation.
Colloton, Paul *o.p.* '90 (GR) [I] Grand Rapids, MI Motherhouse of the Dominican Sisters.
Colloton, Paul H. *o.p.* '90 (CHI) [N] Chicago, IL Dominicans (Provincial Office).
Colloty, Ronald *o.f.m.* '37 (ORG) [3] Huntington Beach, CA SS. Simon and Jude Church.
Collova, S. Joseph '76 (MIL) On Leave.
Collucci, Bennett '57 (SAL) Hays, KS St. Joseph's Church; [D] Hays, KS St. Joseph's Friary.
Collum, Patrick '92 (NO) [21] New Orleans, LA The Resurrection Of Our Lord Church.
Colnaghi, Andrew *o.s.b.cam.* '79 (MRY) [G] Big Sur, CA New Camaldoli Hermitage.
Colnaghi, Andrew '79 (OAK) [R] Berkeley, CA Incarnation Monastery, Camaldolese Benedictines.
Colohan, Edward A. '61 (BGP) [3] Trumbull, CT St. Stephen Church.
Colomb, Jackson '90 (CHI) Evanston, IL St. Mary Church.
Colombo, Ronald A. '72 (GB) Cooperstown, WI St. James Church; Kellnersville, WI St. Joseph Church.
Colon, Angel Molina '94 (CGS) Naranjito, PR San Miguel Arcangel Church.
Colon, Hector *c.ss.r.* '76 (PCE) Guayama, PR St. Anthony of Padua Church.
Colon, Msgr. Jose '61 (PCE) Retired.
Colon, Jose E. '63 (PCE) On Duty Outside the Diocese.
Colon, Jose E. '63 (SJN) [D] San Juan, PR VA Medical Center.
Colon, Juan Jose '95 (CGS) Naguabo, PR Nuestra Senora del Rosario Church.
Colon, Timothy *o.s.c.* '79 (NY) [S] New York, NY St. Vincent's Hospital and Medical Center of New York.
Colon, Vincent A. '50 (STP) Retired.
Colonnese, Louis M. '57 (DAV) On Duty Outside the Diocese; [P] Davenport, IA Commitment.
Colopy, James L. '86 (COL) Zaleski, OH St. Sylvester Church.
Colosimo, Eugene *s.j.* '43 (SJ) [M] Los Gatos, CA California Province of the Society of Jesus, Jesuit Provincial Office.
Colosimo, Eugene J. '43 (SJ) [M] Los Gatos, CA Sacred Heart Jesuit Center.
Colosimo, Felix R. '65 (SY) [6] Utica, NY St. Anthony of Padua Church.
Colpitts, Albert B. '73 (PRT) Westbrook, ME St. Edmund Church.
Colter, Dennis J. '66 (DUB) [A] Dubuque, IA Seminary of St. Pius X; [C] Dubuque, IA Loras College; [L] Dubuque, IA Mt. St. Francis.
Colton, Bernard '50 (PHX) Retired.
Colton, Bradford '45 (HRT) Wethersfield, CT Corpus Christi Church; Retired.
Colton, Cyril *s.a.* '52 (NY) [Z] Garrison, NY Generalate of the Franciscan Friars of the Atonement-St. James Friary.
Colton, Gary '68 (HON) Haiku, HI St. Rita Church; Paia, HI Holy Rosary Church.
Colucci, Gregory (PAT) [9] Paterson, NJ St. Joseph's Church.
Colwell Michael '94 (AMA) On Duty Outside the Diocese.
Comandini, Glenn J. '86 (MET) South River, NJ St. Stephen Protomartyr Church.
Comber, Thomas E. *c.s.p.* '55 (NY) [Z] Scarsdale, NY Paulist Fathers Generalate.
Comber, Thomas E. *c.s.p.* '55 (WDC) [B] Washington, DC St. Paul's College; [V] Washington, DC Paulist National Catholic Evangelization Assoc.
Comboy, Richard J. *s.j.* '69 (SPK) [B] Spokane, WA St. Michael's Institute.
Combs, Gordon *o.f.m.cap.* '64 (AGN) [F] Agana Heights, GU St. Fidelis Friary.
Combs, Gordon *o.f.m.cap.* '64 (HON) Aiea, HI St. Elizabeth Church; [F] Honolulu, HI St. Francis Healthcare System of Hawaii.
Combs, J. Derran *o.f.m.* '94 (NSH) [13] Nashville, TN St. Vincent de Paul Church.
Combs, Regis V. '46 (LA) Retired.
Comeau, Gerard *m.s.* '61 (FR) [K] Attleboro, MA La Salette Provincial House.
Comeau, Ronald R. '71 (LFT) On Duty Outside the Diocese.
Comer, John P. '64 (STL) [34] St. Louis, MO St. Francis de Sales Church; [O] St. Louis, MO Mary, Queen and Mother Nursing Center.
Comer, Michael E. '80 (COV) Dayton, KY St. Bernard Church.
Comerford, Aidan '81 (LA) [89] Los Angeles, CA St. Sebastian Church.
Comerford, Christopher '96 (SFD) [2] Springfield, IL Blessed Sacrament Church.
Comerford, John J. *o.carm.* '77 (CHI) [N] Mundelein, IL Carmelite Monastery.
Comerford, Patrick '69 (LA) [K] Santa Monica, CA Saint John's Hospital and Health Center.
Comeskey, Edwin T. '55 (SY) Vernon, NY Holy Family Church.
Comey, John M. *s.j.* '44 (PH) [Z] Philadelphia, PA Jesuit Community at St. Joseph's University.
Comiskey, Msgr. James A. '50 (LUB) [1] Lubbock, TX Cathedral Christ the King Church.
Comiskey, John P. '60 (NY) [E] New York, NY Monsignor Farrell High School.
Comisky, Ben *o.s.b.* '90 (TYL) Jefferson, TX Immaculate Conception Church.
Commane, William J. (BO) Retired.
Commons, Patrick M. '51 (IND) Retired.
Commons, Thomas *s.v.d.* '47 (CHI) [B] Techny, IL Divine Word Residence.
Commyn, James E. '86 (DET) Richmond, MI St. Augustine Church.
Como, Denis R. *s.j.* '66 (BO) [W] Boston, MA Jesuit Urban Center & Immaculate Conception Community.
Compaired, Fernando '63 (MIA) [9] Miami, FL Mother of Our Redeemer Church.
Compentente, Virgilio '67 (NY) [9] Yonkers, NY Immaculate Conception Church.
Complo, Daniel C. '54 (DET) Harper Woods, MI Our Lady Queen of Peace Church.
Comstock, Douglas G. '67 (OG) Sackets Harbor, NY St. Andrew Church.
Comstock, Eliot *o.f.m.conv.* '69 (IND) [I] Mount Saint Francis, IN Mount Saint Francis Friary and Retreat Center.
Comtois, Norman *o.m.i.* '73 (MAN) [K] Hudson, NH Missionary Oblates of Mary Immaculate.
Comtois, Roger M. '55 (NOR) Rockville, CT St. Bernard Church.
Conaboy, Conan *c.p.* '47 (MET) [H] South River, NJ Passionist Provincial Office.
Conaboy, Conan *c.p.* '47 (SCR) [15] Scranton, PA St. Joseph's Church; [M] Scranton, PA Saint Ann's Passionist Monastery.
Conahan, John J. '62 (PH) Jenkintown, PA Immaculate Conception Church.
Conan, Constantine J. *c.s.sp.* '48 (VEN) [G] Sarasota, FL Congregation of the Holy Ghost.
Conard, Raymond J. '55 (GB) On Duty Outside the Diocese.
Conaty, Charles '88 (CAM) Wildwood, NJ St. Ann's Church; [B] Wildwood, NJ Wildwood Catholic High School.
Conaty, Peter *c.s.sp.* '83 (OAK) [1] Hayward, CA All Saints Church.
Conboy, Joseph T. '53 (SCR) Retired; [N] Dunmore, PA Villa St. Joseph.
Conboy, Michael F. '74 (ROC) Corning, NY St. Mary Church; Corning, NY St. Patrick Church; Corning, NY St. Vincent de Paul Church; Painted Post, NY Immaculate Heart of Mary Church.
Conboy, Richard L. *s.t.l.* '60 (PIT) Allegheny County, PA Kane Regional Center - Scott; [O] Coraopolis, PA Our Lady of the Sacred Heart Convent.
Concagh, Thomas V. *c.m.* '52 (BRK) [D] Queens and Staten Island, NY St. John's University; [U] Jamaica, NY Vincentian Residence.
Concannon, Stephen F. '64 (PRT) Scarborough, ME St. Maximilian Kolbe Church.
Concepcion, Francisco '65 (ARE) Vega-Alta, PR Immaculate Conception of Blessed Virgin Mary Church.
Concha, Alfonso J. '76 (PH) Military Chaplains.
Concha, Antonio *s.j.* '63 (ELP) [21] El Paso, TX Sacred Heart Church.
Concha, Sergio E. *c.s.c.* '63 (FTW) [J] South Bend, IN Congregation of Holy Cross Indiana Province Provincial House.
Concordia, George Lawrence *o.p.* '58 (NY) [22] New York, NY St. Catherine of Siena Church; [Z] New York, NY St. Catherine of Siena Priory; [DD] New York, NY Dominican Shrine of St. Jude, Inc.
Conde, Jose Maria *s.f.* (SFE) Chimayo, NM Holy Family Church.
Conde, Norberto '89 (GAL) [59] Houston, TX Our Lady of Sorrows Church.
Conde, Thomas P. '87 (CHI) Sauk Village, IL St. James Church.
Condon, Daniel J. '81 (ROC) Mount Morris, NY St. Patrick Church; Nunda, NY Holy Angels Church.
Condon, Denis '78 (CHI) [2] Mt. Prospect, IL St. Emily Church.
Condon, Edwin D., Jr. '61 (BO) Military & VA Chaplains.
Condon, Eugene L. '56 (CHR) Absent On Leave.
Condon, Gerald A. '56 (DUB) Dumont, IA St. Francis Church; Hampton, IA St. Patrick's Church.
Condon, Gerald W. '55 (BAK) Heppner, OR St. Patrick's Church; Ione, OR St. William Church.
Condon, John F.X. *s.j.* '55 (NY) [Z] New York, NY Murray-Weigel Hall.
Condon, Msgr. John J. '56 (BRK) [155] Queens, NY St. Benedict Joseph Labre Church.
Condon, Liam '63 (ALB) Salem, NY Holy Cross Church.
Condon, Louis M. '48 (PEO) Retired.
Condon, Msgr. Michael J. '41 (LA) [1] Oxnard, CA St.

Anthony Church; Retired.
Condon, Msgr. Robert F. '54 (LA) [70] Los Angeles, CA St. Joan of Arc Church; Retired.
Condon, Robert M. '56 (SC) [A] Sioux City, IA Briar Cliff College.
Condon, T. Mark (PAT) [5] Clifton, NJ SS. Cyril and Methodius Church.
Condon, Thomas M. *o.p.* '88 (STL) [P] St. Louis, MO St. Dominic Priory.
Condon, William F. '54 (RIC) Colonial Heights, VA St. Ann Church.
Condren, William '73 (PT) Gulf Breeze, FL St. Ann Church.
Condron, Patrick A. '76 (WH) On Duty Outside the Diocese.
Condron, Robert F. '69 (HRT) [1] Ansonia, CT Assumption Church.
Condry, John T. *s.j.* '49 (LAF) [J] Grand Coteau, LA Our Lady of the Oaks Retreat House.
Coneglio, Andrew '36 (CHI) Retired.
Conen, Paul F. *s.j.* '57 (DET) [K] Detroit, MI Jesuit Community at the University of Detroit.
Conesa, Msgr. Diego '57 (SP) Sun City Center, FL Prince of Peace Church.
Conesa, Msgr. Diego '57 (STA) On Duty Outside the Diocese.
Confer, Bernard T. *o.p.* '73 (HRT) [14] New Haven, CT St. Mary's Priory Church.
Confer, Thomas B. *o.p.* (HRT) [N] North Guilford, CT Monastery of Our Lady of Grace; [N] North Guilford, CT Monastery of Our Lady of Grace.
Confroy, Mark W. *o.s.b.* '42 (PAT) [M] Morristown, NJ St. Mary's Abbey; [N] Convent Station, NJ St. Anne Villa.
Confroy, Thomas J. *o.s.b.* '58 (PAT) [M] Morristown, NJ St. Mary's Abbey.
Cong, Joseph Chu '87 (WOR) [A] Spencer, MA St. Joseph's Abbey School of Theology and Institute of Monastic Studies; [N] Spencer, MA St. Joseph's Abbey.
Congdon, Robert J. '87 (BO) Graduate Studies.
Congdon, Stephen H. '62 (MET) Cranbury, NJ Nativity of Our Lord Church.
Congro, Basil P. '78 (CHR) Yonges Island, SC St. Mary Church.
Conheeney, Thomas P. '55 (NEW) [1] Bayonne, NJ St. Mary Star of the Sea Church.
Conklin, Christopher J. (SAL) Retired.
Conlan, Msgr. F. Allan (SCR) Elmhurst, PA St. Eulalia Church.
Conlan, Msgr. James S. '53 (NY) Pine Bush, NY The Infant Saviour Church; Absent on Sick leave; [Z] Suffern, NY Parish Mission Team Res.
Conlan, Timothy *o.p.* '67 (SFR) [13] San Francisco, CA St. Dominic Church; [N] San Francisco, CA St. Dominic Priory.
Conlan, Walter *s.j.* '76 (BO) [W] Chestnut Hill, MA The Jesuit Community at Boston College.
Conlan, William J. *o.p.* '48 (WDC) [B] Washington, DC Dominican House of Studies; [C] Washington, DC Catholic University of America, The.
Conley, Charles E. '74 (MIL) Union Grove, WI St. Robert Bellarmine Church.
Conley, Edward W. *o.p.* '43 (NO) [30] New Orleans, LA St. Dominic Church.
Conley, James '85 (WCH) On Duty Outside the Diocese.
Conley, John E. *c.s.c.* '79 (FTW) [A] Notre Dame, IN Moreau Seminary; [B] Notre Dame, IN University of Notre Dame Du Lac; [J] Notre Dame, IN Holy Cross Community, Corby Hall, University of Notre Dame.
Conley, John J. *s.j.* '83 (NY) [Z] New York, NY Jesuit Community at Fordham University.
Conley, John P. *c.p.* '76 (GAL) [S] Houston, TX Holy Name Retreat Center.
Conley, John P. '93 (SFR) [1] San Mateo, CA St. Bartholomew Church.
Conley, Joseph J. '44 (MIL) Retired.
Conley, Lawrence J. '67 (PRT) Norway, ME St. Catherine of Sienna Church.
Conley, Martin P. '57 (OM) Tekamah, NE St. Patrick Church.
Conley, Martin R. '83 (PIT) [1] Pittsburgh, PA St. Paul Cathedral.
Conley, Nancy (HON) [J] Honolulu, HI Spiritual Life Center.
Conley, Peter V. '64 (BO) [2] Brookline, MA Infant Jesus Church; [P] Boston, MA Archdiocesan Information Center.
Conley, Philip P. '62 (Y) Poland, OH Holy Family Church.
Conley, Msgr. Raymond J. '36 (DM) Retired.
Conley, Robert '55 (LA) [56] Los Angeles, CA St. Columban Church.
Conley, Rory T. '89 (WDC) [4] Silver Spring, MD St. Catherine Laboure Church.
Conley, Roy H. '61 (PIT) Pleasant Hills, PA St. Elizabeth Church.
Conley, Seraphin *t.o.r.* '61 (ORL) [D] Winter Park, FL San Pedro Spiritual Development Center; [F] Winter Park, FL San Pedro Center, Third Order Regular of St. Francis; [F] Winter Park, FL Franciscan Friars, T.O.R., Provincial Residence, San Pedro Friary.
Conley, Thomas P. '47 (CHI) [4] Des Plaines, IL St. Zachary Church; Stickney, IL St. Pius X Church; Retired.
Conlin, Bernard J. '40 (WOR) [12] Worcester, MA Our Lady of Lourdes Church; Retired.
Conlin, Daniel C. '90 (STP) Graduate Studies.
Conlin, Edward F. *s.s.e.* '46 (MOB) [H] Selma, AL Edmundite Fathers.
Conlin, Edwin J. '42 (NY) [52] New York, NY Immaculate Conception Church; Manhattan, NY Beth Israel Medical Center.
Conlin, James J. *s.j.* '54 (SCR) [C] Scranton, PA University of Scranton.
Conlin, John A. *s.j.* '54 (WDC) [2] Washington, DC St. Aloysius Church; [E] Washington, DC Gonzaga College High School.
Conlin, Leo *c.s.p.* '46 (SFR) [31] San Francisco, CA Old St. Mary's Cathedral.
Conlin, Leo E. *c.s.p.* '46 (NY) [Z] Scarsdale, NY Paulist Fathers Generalate.
Conlin, Raymond E. '80 (PAT) [8] Clifton, NJ St. Philip the Apostle Church.
Conlin, Robert *t.o.r.* '56 (STU) [A] Steubenville, OH Franciscan University of Steubenville.
Conlin, Robert P. '56 (BUF) Pavilion, NY St. Mary Church.
Conlon, Anthony J. '62 (WH) Vienna, WV St. Michael's Church.
Conlon, Arthur F. '54 (TR) [24] Trenton, NJ St. Vincent de Paul Church.
Conlon, Christopher W. *s.m.* '66 (CIN) [D] Dayton, OH The University of Dayton; [M] Dayton, OH Marianist Provincialate; [Q] Dayton, OH University of Dayton Campus Ministry.
Conlon, Colm '59 (ORG) Irvine, CA St. John Neumann Church.
Conlon, Edward F. '56 (CIN) On Duty Outside the Archdiocese.
Conlon, James '64 (OAK) [B] Oakland, CA Holy Names College.
Conlon, John J. *s.s.j.* '40 (BAL) [M] Baltimore, MD St. Joseph Society of the Sacred Heart House of Central Administration.
Conlon, Msgr. Joseph E. '47 (CAM) Retired; [H] Cherry Hill, NJ St. Mary's Nursing Home.
Conlon, Matthew T. *o.f.m.* '45 (ALB) [B] Loudonville, NY Siena College.
Conlon, Philip J. '55 (MAD) Retired.
Conlon, R. Daniel '77 (CIN) New Bremen, OH Holy Redeemer Church.
Conlon, Richard W. '90 (BRK) [28] Brooklyn, NY St. Cecilia Church.
Conlon, Timothy C. *o.s.c.* '79 (NY) [4] New York, NY All Saints Church; [Z] New Rochelle, NY Crosier (Canons Regular of the Order of the Holy Cross).
Conmy, John J. *o.s.f.s.* '36 (WIL) [I] Childs, MD Oblates of St. Francis De Sales.
Conmy, Thomas M. *c.s.c.* '57 (SP) Dunedin, FL Our Lady of Lourdes Church.
Conn, James J. *s.j.* '74 (BAL) [A] Baltimore, MD St. Mary's Seminary and University; [A] Baltimore, MD St. Mary's Seminary and University; [M] Baltimore, MD Jesuit Fathers and Brothers Maryland Provincial Curia.
Conn, Thomas V. *s.j.* '61 (LA) [C] Santa Paula, CA Thomas Aquinas College.
Connaghan, Daniel H. '90 (HRT) [3] Bristol, CT St. Gregory's Church.
Connall, Darrin '92 (SPK) Colville, WA Immaculate Conception Church; Kettle Falls, WA Sacred Heart Church; Northport, WA Pure Heart of Mary Church.
Connaughton, James '50 (MIA) Deerfield Beach, FL St. Ambrose Church; Retired.
Connaughton, Msgr. Lawrence M. '70 (NY) [62] New York, NY St. Joseph Church.
Conneally, J. Philip *s.j.* '44 (LA) [F] Los Angeles, CA Loyola High School.
Connealy, Gerald A. '87 (OM) Petersburg, NE St. John the Baptist Church; Raeville, NE St. Bonaventure Church.
Conneely, Sean *s.s.c.* '69 (CHI) [N] Chicago, IL Columban Fathers Mission Center.
Conneen, Laurence J. *o.s.a.* '37 (PH) [Z] Villanova, PA St. Thomas Monastery.
Connell, Msgr. Andrew F. *k.j.* '51 (BO) [73] Boston, MA St. Vincent de Paul Church; [BB] Boston, MA St. Thomas More Chapel; [FF] Boston, MA Propagation of the Faith and Holy Childhood Association & Society of St. Peter the Apostle.
Connell, James C. '44 (SJ) [M] Los Altos, CA Maryknoll.
Connell, James E. '87 (MIL) [1] Milwaukee, WI St. John Cathedral; Special Assignment.
Connell, John Andrew '81 (PAT) Morris Plains, NJ St. Virgilius Church.
Connell, John F. '62 (WOR) Northbridge, MA St. Peter Church.
Connell, John K. (BO) Awaiting Assignment.
Connell, John M. '85 (LR) [13] Little Rock, AR St. Theresa's Church.
Connell, John R. *c.ss.r.* '26 (ALB) [L] Saratoga Springs, NY St. John Neumann Residence.
Connell, Kevin G. *s.j.* '94 (P) [D] Portland, OR Jesuit High School.
Connell, Loren *o.f.m.* '76 (GAL) [Q] Houston, TX Franciscan Friars; [U] Houston, TX Kolbe Project, Inc.
Connell, Mark J. '86 (NY) [E] Somers, NY John F. Kennedy High School.
Connell, Martin *s.j.* '94 (CLV) [E] Cleveland, OH St. Ignatius High School.
Connell, Patrick J. '92 (DET) [4] Birmingham, MI St. Regis Church.
Connell, Stephen J. '62 (WIL) Greenville, DE St. Joseph on the Brandywine Church.
Connell, William J. '76 (Y) [1] Youngstown, OH Cathedral of St. Columba.
Connell, William R. '75 (MAD) [2] Beloit, WI St. Jude Church.
Connellan, Thomas J. *c.s.p.* '56 (PAT) [A] Oak Ridge, NJ Paulist Novitiate.
Connelly, Brennan *o.f.m.* (NEW) Fair Lawn, NJ St. Anne's Church.
Connelly, Christian T. '96 (ARL) [1] Arlington, VA Cathedral of St. Thomas More.
Connelly, Christopher D. '93 (SPR) [6] Springfield, MA Holy Name Church.
Connelly, Donald C. '57 (PH) [BB] Malvern, PA St. Joseph's in the Hills.
Connelly, Donald F. '58 (WIN) Plainview, MN St. Joachim's Church.
Connelly, Edward C. '65 (BAL) Crofton, MD St. Elizabeth Ann Seton Church.
Connelly, George R. '45 (TUC) Retired.
Connelly, James *c.s.c.* '64 (P) [B] Portland, OR University of Portland; [B] Portland, OR University of Portland; [L] Portland, OR Holy Cross Father & Brother, C.S.C. - University of Portland.
Connelly, Msgr. James A. '47 (HRT) Retired.
Connelly, Msgr. James F. '55 (PH) [147] Philadelphia, PA Stella Maris Church.
Connelly, Msgr. James N. '49 (BUF) Retired; [O] Tonawanda, NY O'Hara Residence.
Connelly, John J. '50 (BO) [8] Newton, MA Sacred Heart Church.
Connelly, Kevin S.D. (NY) [D] New York, NY Department of Education.
Connelly, Laurence '59 (GAL) [49] Houston, TX St. Michael Church.
Connelly, Mark J. *s.j.* (PH) [C] Philadelphia, PA St. Joseph's University; [Z] Philadelphia, PA Jesuit Community at St. Joseph's University.
Connelly, Msgr. Michael J. '60 (BRK) [246] Queens, NY St. Thomas More-St. Edmund Church.
Connelly, Norbert '56 (STU) Martins Ferry, OH St. Mary Church.
Connelly, Msgr. Paul J. (DM) Retired.
Connelly, Peter *o.s.b.* '87 (WOR) [N] Still River, MA Benedictine Monks, St. Benedict Abbey.
Connelly, Robert J. '49 (SAC) Retired and in Senior Ministry.
Connelly, William P. '45 (RIC) Retired.
Connelly, Xavier *o.s.b.* '89 (WOR) [N] Still River, MA Benedictine Monks, St. Benedict Abbey.
Conner, Glenn T. '50 (PIT) [N] Pittsburgh, PA St. John Vianney Manor.
Conner, Glenn T. '52 (PIT) Retired.
Conner, Herbert K. *s.j.* '61 (CHR) Simpsonville, SC St. Mary Magdalene Church.
Conner, John *o.f.m.cap.* '84 (NY) [57] New York, NY St. John the Baptist Church.
Conner, Michael P. '85 (GAY) Onekama, MI St. Joseph Church.
Conner, Paul *o.p.* '67 (SFR) [N] San Francisco, CA St. Dominic Priory.
Conner, Paul M. *o.p.* '67 (PRO) [P] Providence, RI St. Thomas Aquinas Priory at Providence College.
Conner, Robert J. '49 (PH) Penndel, PA Our Lady of Grace Church.
Conner, Steven '94 (NEW) Lyndhurst, NJ Sacred Heart Church.
Conners, Quinn R. *o.carm.* '71 (CHI) [N] Chicago, IL Carmelite Fathers Residence.
Connerton, Barry R.L. '70 (PRO) [7] Providence, RI St. Augustine's Church.
Connery, J. Thomas '63 (ALB) Glenville, NY Immaculate Conception Church.
Connery, John P. *o.s.f.s.* '69 (WIL) Elsmere, DE Veteran's Hospital; [B] Wilmington, DE Salesianum School.
Connery, Thomas '83 (ORL) [A] Daytona Beach, FL Father Lopez High School.
Connery, Thomas J. *s.d.b.* '83 (ORL) Daytona Beach, FL Our Lady of Lourdes Church.
Connick, Alfred J. (BO) Retired.
Conniff, Msgr. John J. (BUF) [S] Angola, NY St. Vincent de Paul Camp; [T] Buffalo, NY Good Counsel Apartments; [T] Buffalo, NY Timon Towers Housing Development Fund Company, Inc.
Conniff, Msgr. John J. '49 (BUF) Retired.

Connoe, William K. '66 (PBL) Cortez, CO St. Margaret Mary Church.
Connole, Marlin '68 (SEA) Bellevue, WA Sacred Heart Church.
Connolly, Andrew (RVC) Sick Leave.
Connolly, Brian W. '55 (PIT) On Duty Outside the Diocese.
Connolly, Charles B. *s.j.* '74 (BO) [W] Boston, MA Jesuit Urban Center & Immaculate Conception Community.
Connolly, Msgr. Clement J. '64 (LA) South Pasadena, CA Holy Family Church.
Connolly, Edward B. '66 (ALN) Mount Carbon, PA St. Francis de Sales Church; [2] Pottsville, PA St. Joseph Church.
Connolly, Edward J. '49 (SB) [4] Riverside, CA Sacred Heart Church.
Connolly, Eugene G. '54 (NY) [1] New York, NY Cathedral of St. Patrick.
Connolly, Fidelis *c.p.* '50 (PH) [Z] Philadelphia, PA St. Michael's Passionist Residence.
Connolly, Francis T. '59 (CHL) [5] Greensboro, NC St. Pius X Church.
Connolly, Gerard M. *t.o.r.* '69 (ALT) [1] Barnesboro, PA St. John the Baptist's Church; [3] Barnesboro, PA Our Lady of Mt. Carmel Church.
Connolly, James H. '48 (BO) Bellingham, MA St. Blaise Church.
Connolly, Msgr. James M. '56 (NY) Bronxville, NY St. Joseph Church.
Connolly, James M. '78 (ALN) Military Chaplains.
Connolly, James P. '54 (NY) [58] New York, NY St. John the Evangelist Church.
Connolly, Jerry P. '67 (GF) Plentywood, MT St. Joseph's Church.
Connolly, John '64 (ALB) Delanson, NY Our Lady of Fatima Church.
Connolly, John *s.d.b.* '81 (NEW) Bloomfield, NJ Church of St. Thomas the Apostle.
Connolly, John G. '63 (BO) Wrentham, MA St. Mary Church.
Connolly, John J. (GAL) Port Bolivar, TX Our Mother of Mercy Church.
Connolly, John J., Jr. '94 (BO) [44] Boston, MA St. Mark Church.
Connolly, John P. *o.s.f.s.* '57 (CAM) [L] Pittsgrove, NJ Villa St. Joseph.
Connolly, John T. '78 (PAT) [15] Paterson, NJ St. Stephen's Church.
Connolly, Joseph *s.v.d.* '60 (BO) [W] Boston, MA Divine Word Missionaries.
Connolly, Joseph *t.o.r.* '68 (VEN) [2] Sarasota, FL Our Lady Queen of Martyrs Church.
Connolly, Joseph A. *o.s.f.s.* '52 (CAM) [L] Pittsgrove, NJ Villa St. Joseph.
Connolly, Kevin '85 (WIN) Pipestone, MN St. Leo's Church.
Connolly, Larkin '47 (PMB) Lake Worth, FL St. Luke Church; Retired.
Connolly, Leo L. '81 (COL) [38] Columbus, OH St. Philip The Apostle Church.
Connolly, Leon L. '58 (DUB) On Duty Outside the Archdiocese.
Connolly, Luke *c.p.* '52 (CHI) [N] Chicago, IL Passionist Provincial Office; [N] Chicago, IL Immaculate Conception Monastery.
Connolly, Mark '57 (BGP) [2] Greenwich, CT St. Michael the Archangel Church; [W] Greenwich, CT Clemons Productions, Inc.
Connolly, Martin '45 (NY) [Z] New York, NY Pope John Paul II Residence.
Connolly, Martin '49 (PAT) [P] Chester, NJ Nazareth Village.
Connolly, Martin C. '49 (PAT) Retired.
Connolly, Martin J. '46 (NY) Retired.
Connolly, Matthew J. '53 (ORL) [2] Orlando, FL Blessed Trinity Church; Special Assignment.
Connolly, Maurice V. (BO) [3] Salem, MA St. James Church; Retired.
Connolly, Michael *o.f.m.cap.* '78 (NY) Valhalla, NY Westchester County Medical Center; [Z] White Plains, NY St. Conrad Friary.
Connolly, Michael C. *o.s.f.s.* '74 (ARL) Reston, VA St. John Neumann Church.
Connolly, Michael J. *s.j.* '68 (BO) [W] Boston, MA The Society of Jesus of New England-Provincial Offices.
Connolly, Michael J. *s.j.* '68 (SPK) [C] Spokane, WA Gonzaga University.
Connolly, Msgr. Neil A. '58 (NY) [70] New York, NY St. Mary Church.
Connolly, Patrick *s.j.* '66 (LA) [R] Los Angeles, CA Columbiere House.
Connolly, Patrick Francis *o.p.* '52 (NY) [22] New York, NY St. Catherine of Siena Church; [Z] New York, NY St. Catherine of Siena Priory.
Connolly, Patrick J. *s.j.* '66 (MIL) [P] Milwaukee, WI Jesuit Provincial Office, Wisconsin Province.
Connolly, Patrick J. '67 (GRY) Schererville, IN St. Michael Church.
Connolly, Paul E. '83 (DAV) East Pleasant Plain, IA St. Joseph's Church; Richland, IA St. Frances Xavier Cabrini Church; [E] Davenport, IA Assumption High School.
Connolly, Peter *c.ss.r.* '77 (MIL) [S] Oconomowoc, WI Perpetual Help Retreat Center.
Connolly, Robert P. '79 (PIT) [A] Pittsburgh, PA Saint Paul Seminary.
Connolly, Robert V. '45 (LC) Retired; [I] La Crosse, WI Holy Cross (Seminary) Diocesan Center.
Connolly, Scott '95 (SEA) Aberdeen, WA St. Mary's Church; Aberdeen, WA SS. Peter and Paul Church; Hoquiam, WA Our Lady of Good Help Church; Ocean Shores, WA St. Jerome Church.
Connolly, T. Gerard *s.j.* '58 (NY) [Z] New York, NY Jesuit Community at Fordham University.
Connolly, Thomas '52 (SFS) Retired.
Connolly, Thomas *s.j.* '63 (B) DeSmet, ID Sacred Heart Church.
Connolly, Thomas J. (P) [Q] Portland, OR Oregon Catholic Conference.
Connolly, William J. *s.j.* (BO) [W] Boston, MA The Society of Jesus of New England-Provincial Offices; [W] Cambridge, MA Weston Jesuit Community.
Connor, Adrian J. *o.praem.* '95 (ORG) [D] Siverado, CA St. Michael's College Preparatory High School; [H] Silverado, CA Norbertine Fathers.
Connor, Brian P. '89 (LIN) David City, NE St. Francis Church; [C] David City, NE Aquinas/St. Mary's Schools; [K] David City, NE Aquinas High School Endowment Fund.
Connor, Charles P. '90 (SCR) [21] Scranton, PA St. Patrick's Church.
Connor, Francis J. '40 (STU) Retired.
Connor, Gerald T. '54 (ROC) [52] Rochester, NY St. Pius Tenth Church.
Connor, J. Patrick '61 (NSH) Columbia, TN St. Catherine Church.
Connor, James *s.j.* '59 (WDC) [M] Washington, DC Woodstock Jesuit Community.
Connor, James '78 (HEL) Kalispell, MT Risen Christ Church.
Connor, James E. '60 (PRT) [J] Saco, ME Bay View Community.
Connor, James L. *s.j.* '59 (WDC) [V] Washington, DC Woodstock Theological Center.
Connor, John *c.s.c.* (SB) Thermal, CA San Felipe de Jesus Church.
Connor, John *c.p.* '84 (SCR) [M] Scranton, PA Saint Ann's Passionist Monastery.
Connor, John E. '32 (BO) Retired.
Connor, John P. '62 (CAM) Bridgeton, NJ Immaculate Conception Church.
Connor, John S. *c.s.c.* '70 (SB) Coachella, CA Our Lady of Soledad Church.
Connor, John V. '46 (WDC) Retired.
Connor, Joseph J. *s.j.* '42 (BO) [W] Chestnut Hill, MA The Jesuit Community at Boston College; [W] Weston, MA Campion Health Center, Inc.
Connor, Kevin (STP) [C] St. Paul, MN University of St. Thomas.
Connor, Kevin T. '87 (MAN) On Duty Outside the Diocese.
Connor, Martin P. '64 (BO) [A] Boston, MA St. John's Seminary School of Theology; [FF] Boston, MA League of Catholic Women of the Archdiocese of Boston.
Connor, Patrick *s.v.d.* '57 (TR) [M] Bordentown, NJ Society of the Divine Word.
Connor, Patrick L. '83 (ROC) [1] Elmira, NY Sts. Peter and Paul of Eastside Catholic Parish Church; [4] Elmira, NY St. John the Baptist of Eastside Catholic Parish Church; [6] Elmira, NY St. Cecilia of Eastside Catholic Parish Church.
Connor, Robert A. '64 (NY) [EE] New Rochelle, NY Opus Dei (Prelature of the Holy Cross and Opus Dei).
Connor, Robert M. '58 (BO) Norfolk, MA St. Jude Church.
Connor, Steven J. *c.s.p.* '89 (NY) [104] New York, NY St. Paul the Apostle Church.
Connor, Vincent '71 (SB) Chino, CA California Youth Authority.
Connor, William *m.s.c.* '57 (OG) [2] Watertown, NY Our Lady of the Sacred Heart, Missionaries of the Sacred Heart Church; Watertown, NY Watertown Correctional Facility.
Connor, William J. '46 (COL) Retired.
Connor, William J. '66 (LA) [65] Los Angeles, CA St. Gerard Majella Church.
Connor, William K. '66 (PBL) Mancos, CO St. Rita Church.
Connors, Albert *c.m.f.* '73 (LA) [R] Rancho Dominguez, CA Dominguez Seminary Inc.
Connors, Brocard *o.carm.* '57 (NY) [Z] Tappan, NY St. Eliseus Priory.
Connors, Carlos *c.s.sp.* '37 (SJN) [E] Dorado, PR Santuario del Espiritu Santo.
Connors, Cletus *o.s.b.* '72 (SCL) [I] Collegeville, MN St. John's Abbey, of the Order of St. Benedict.
Connors, Edmund P. '66 (NY) [195] Staten Island, NY St. Ann Church; [E] New York, NY Moore Catholic High School.
Connors, Msgr. Edward M. '47 (NY) Retired; [E] White Plains, NY Archbishop Stepinac High School.
Connors, Edward P. '36 (CHI) Blue Island, IL St. Benedict Church; Retired.
Connors, Francis B. '50 (FR) Retired.
Connors, Francis E. '73 (BUR) Burlington, VT Fletcher Allen Health Care.
Connors, James V. *c.m.* '40 (STO) Patterson, CA Sacred Heart Church.
Connors, Joseph *s.v.d.* '52 (CHI) [B] Techny, IL Divine Word Residence.
Connors, Michael E. *c.s.c.* '84 (FTW) [B] Notre Dame, IN University of Notre Dame Du Lac; [J] Notre Dame, IN Holy Cross Community, Corby Hall, University of Notre Dame; [M] Notre Dame, IN Our Lady of Fatima Retreat Center.
Connors, Paul *s.v.d.* '63 (CHI) [B] Techny, IL Divine Word Residence; [N] Techny, IL Society of the Divine Word, Provincial Headquarter-Chicago Prov.
Connors, Richard (MAN) [E] Salem, NH St. Joseph Regional School.
Connors, Richard P. '79 (PH) Absent on Sick Leave.
Connors, Richard W. '69 (MAN) Salem, NH St. Joseph Church.
Connors, Robert A. '55 (NEW) Oakland, NJ Our Lady of Perpetual Help Church.
Connors, Robert L. '71 (BO) Newburyport, MA Immaculate Conception Church.
Connors, Terrence L. '75 (MAD) Jefferson, WI St. John the Baptist Church.
Conole, Robert W. '91 (BO) [2] Methuen, MA St. Monica Church.
Conoscenti, Frederick M. '65 (BUF) On Duty Outside the Diocese.
Conover, James A. '78 (TR) Keyport, NJ St. Joseph Church.
Conover, Sylvan J. *o.f.m.cap.* '49 (NY) Wassaic, NY Wassaic Development Center; [Z] Yonkers, NY St. Clare Friary.
Conrad, Anthony J. '49 (DAV) Retired; [M] Davenport, IA St. Vincent Center.
Conrad, Arthur Dennis '77 (RIC) [3] Richmond, VA Holy Rosary Church; [13] Richmond, VA St. Patrick Church.
Conrad, Brian '81 (HBG) [K] Harrisburg, PA Catholic Campus Ministry.
Conrad, Brian P. '76 (HBG) Bonneauville, PA St. Joseph Church.
Conrad, James H. '64 (ALT) [2] Windber, PA SS. Cyril and Methodius Church.
Conrad, John F. '63 (GB) Clarks Mills, WI Immaculate Conception Church.
Conrad, Robert '70 (SY) New Hartford, NY St. Thomas Church.
Conrad, Simon *o.f.m.* '62 (GLP) St. Michaels, AZ St. Michael Church.
Conrad, Simon R. *o.f.m.cap.* '46 (STL) [54] St. Louis, MO St. Patrick Church; [P] St. Louis, MO St. Patrick Friary.
Conrad, Stanley '38 (AUS) Retired.
Conrad, Sylvester A. '52 (DAV) Lovilia, IA St. Peter's Church; Knoxville, IA Veteran's Administration Hospital.
Conro, Ronald J. '65 (RCK) Elizabeth, IL St. Mary Church; Scales Mound, IL Holy Trinity Church.
Conroy, Cyril J. '52 (BO) Beverly, MA St. Margaret Church.
Conroy, Donald B. '64 (GBG) On Duty Outside the Diocese.
Conroy, Donald B. '64 (WDC) [B] Washington, DC Marian Fathers Scholasticate; [V] Washington, DC National Institute for the Family, Inc.
Conroy, Edward G. '45 (BRK) Retired.
Conroy, Edward M. '49 (NY) [185] Bronx, NY St. Raymond Church.
Conroy, Francis M. '64 (BO) [1] Newton, MA St. Bernard Church.
Conroy, Francis X. '72 (BEA) Orange, TX St. Francis of Assisi Church.
Conroy, Gerard D. '42 (PH) [Z] Philadelphia, PA Congregation of the Mission.
Conroy, J. Peter *s.j.* '71 (BUF) [O] Buffalo, NY Canisius Jesuit Community.
Conroy, James P. '53 (DAV) [5] Davenport, IA St. Anthony's Church.
Conroy, James R. *s.j.* '78 (BAL) [M] Baltimore, MD Ferdinand Wheeler House; [Q] Baltimore, MD Ignatian Lay Volunteer Corps.
Conroy, Jerome *o.p.* (NY) Manhattan, NY Memorial Sloan Kettering Cancer Center.
Conroy, John Jerome *o.p.* '49 (NY) [22] New York, NY St. Catherine of Siena Church; [Z] New York, NY St. Catherine of Siena Priory.
Conroy, Kevin M. '82 (CLV) Wooster, OH St. Mary of the Immaculate Conception Church.
Conroy, Martin J. *c.s.sp.* '54 (DET) [48] Detroit, MI St. Mary Church.
Conroy, Michael F. *s.p.s.* '65 (CHI) Park Ridge, IL Mary, Seat of Wisdom Church.
Conroy, Patrick J. '83 (SEA) [A] Seattle, WA Seattle University.
Conroy, Phillip M. (BO) Boston, MA St. Elizabeth's

Medical Center.
Conroy, Thomas J. '48 (STP) Retired; [C] St. Paul, MN University of St. Thomas.
Conroy, Msgr. Walter R. '28 (BGP) Retired; [O] Stamford, CT Our Lady Queen of the Clergy Home.
Conry, Austin (MOB) [11] Mobile, AL Little Flower Church.
Conry, James A. '53 (CLV) Wadsworth, OH Sacred Heart Church.
Conry, Roy *o.carm.* '56 (TUC) [A] Tucson, AZ Salpointe Catholic High School; [F] Tucson, AZ Carmelite Priory.
Conry, Thomas P. *s.j.* '43 (DET) [P] Clarkston, MI Colombiere Center.
Consalvi, Mark *ss.cc.* '43 (HON) [5] Honolulu, HI Blessed Sacrament Church.
Consani, Robert E. '63 (KAL) [4] Kalamazoo, MI St. Monica Church.
Consentine, Rocco *c.pp.s.* (TOL) [M] Bellevue, OH Sorrowful Mother Shrine.
Conserva, Stephen *o.m.i.* '74 (SFD) [A] Godfrey, IL Immaculate Heart of Mary Novitiate.
Considine, Msgr. John J. '36 (NY) [132] Bronx, NY St. Barnabas Church; Retired; [E] New York, NY Cardinal Spellman High School.
Considine, Matthew J. *s.m.m.* '77 (BRK) [195] Queens, NY St. Mary Gate of Heaven Church; [U] Ozone Park, NY Montfort Missionaries Provincialate.
Consla, Federico J. *c.ss.r.* '70 (CGS) San Lorenzo, PR Nuestra Senora de la Mercedes Church.
Constance, Jogues *o.f.m.cap.* (MIL) [N] Fond du Lac, WI St. Francis Home for Aged.
Constance, Jogues '53 (MIL) [P] Mount Calvary, WI St. Lawrence Friary.
Constance, Msgr. Samuel C. '55 (TR) Retired.
Constant, Van '93 (HT) Bourg, LA St. Ann Church.
Constantine, Bennett '58 (LAN) Eaton Rapids, MI St. Peter Church.
Constantine, Cyprian *o.s.b.* '77 (DEN) [N] Boulder, CO Abbey of St. Walburga.
Constantine, Cyprian G. *o.s.b.* '77 (GBG) [H] Latrobe, PA Saint Vincent Archabbey.
Constantino, Joseph S. *s.j.* '87 (NY) [Z] New York, NY Jesuit Provincial's Office.
Contadino, Eugene J. *s.m.* '70 (CIN) [D] Dayton, OH The University of Dayton; [M] Dayton, OH Marianist Provincialate.
Contant, Msgr. Robert W. '46 (FTW) Hessen Cassel, IN St. Joseph Church.
Contardi, Michael *o.de.m.* '60 (CLV) [67] Cleveland, OH St. Rocco Church.
Conte, Denis A. '75 (BO) Absent on Sick Leave.
Conte, James W. '48 (NY) Absent on Sick leave.
Conte, John P. '58 (ALN) Unassigned.
Conte, John P. '64 (HRT) Special and other (Arch)Diocesan Assignment; [A] Bloomfield, CT St. Thomas Seminary.
Conterno, Austin *s.d.b.* '48 (SFR) [45] San Francisco, CA SS. Peter and Paul Church.
Conti, Cornelius *o.f.m.* '62 (HRT) [14] Hartford, CT St. Patrick-St. Anthony Church.
Conti, Hilary *o.s.b.* '50 (NY) [DD] Esopus, NY Holy Shroud Guild.
Conti, Hilary *o.s.b.* '50 (PAT) [M] Clifton, NJ Holy Face of Jesus Monastery.
Conti, John P. '46 (NY) Retired.
Conti, Joseph A. (OG) [1] Plattsburgh, NY Our Lady of Victory Church; [C] Plattsburgh, NY Seton Catholic Central.
Conti, Msgr. Leo J. '50 (EVN) Retired.
Continillo, Msgr. Rocco A. '56 (CAM) Carneys Point, NJ Corpus Christi Church.
Contons, Albert J. '48 (BO) [63] Boston, MA St. Peter Church.
Contran, Sergio *m.c.c.j.* '50 (CIN) [M] Cincinnati, OH Comboni Missionaries (Verona Fathers)-Comboni Mission Center.
Contreras, David '93 (AMA) Stratford, TX St. Joseph's Church.
Conva, Matthias T. '62 (NEW) [8] Newark, NJ St. Benedict's Church.
Converse, Brian J. '91 (NOR) Taftville, CT Sacred Heart Church.
Converset, John *m.c.c.j.* '71 (CIN) [M] Cincinnati, OH Comboni Missionaries (Verona Fathers)-Comboni Mission Center.
Convertino, David I. *o.f.m.* '77 (PRO) [P] Providence, RI St. Francis Friary.
Convery, Paul C. '84 (PH) [47] Philadelphia, PA St. Francis Xavier Church; [Z] Philadelphia, PA Archdiocesan Oratory of St. Philip Neri (C.O.).
Convery, Thomas L. *s.s.c.* '40 (PRO) [P] Bristol, RI St. Columban's Retirement House.
Convey, Edwin H. *s.j.* '53 (BAL) [C] Baltimore, MD Loyola College; [M] Baltimore, MD Jesuit Community of Loyola College, Inc.
Conway, David '52 (WDC) [29] Washington, DC St. Mary, Mother of God Church.
Conway, Edwin M. '60 (CHI) [G] Chicago, IL Catholic Charities of the Archdiocese of Chicago-Archdiocesan Offices.
Conway, Gerald W. '56 (WIN) Wabasha, MN St. Felix Church.
Conway, James '85 (SAT) [59] San Antonio, TX St. Patrick Church.
Conway, Msgr. Jeffrey '73 (NY) [221] Staten Island, NY Our Lady Star of the Sea Church.
Conway, John '62 (FAR) Retired.
Conway, John E. *m.m.* '73 (NY) [Z] Maryknoll, NY Maryknoll Fathers and Brothers.
Conway, John J. *c.m.* '45 (BRK) [U] Queens Village, NY DePaul Residence.
Conway, John J. *c.m.* '45 (PH) [Z] Philadelphia, PA Congregation of the Mission.
Conway, Msgr. John L. '56 (GBG) Irwin, PA Immaculate Conception Church.
Conway, John R. '69 (SFE) [27] Albuquerque, NM St. Jude Thaddeus Church.
Conway, John T. '77 (PH) [29] Philadelphia, PA St. Carthage Church.
Conway, Msgr. Joseph P. '45 (ALB) Menands, NY Church of St. Joan of Arc; Retired.
Conway, Laurence J. '59 (MIA) [3] Miami Beach, FL St. Mary Magdalen Church.
Conway, Malachy (SAC) Red Bluff, CA Sacred Heart Church.
Conway, Msgr. Michael (PAT) On Duty Outside the Diocese.
Conway, Msgr. Michael '60 (MIA) Davie, FL St. David Church.
Conway, Michael *s.d.b.* '92 (NO) [D] Marrero, LA Archbishop Shaw High School.
Conway, Michael J. *o.ss.t.* '73 (NY) [20] New York, NY St. Brigid Church.
Conway, Neil '63 (CLV) Retired.
Conway, Patrick F. *c.s.sp.* '47 (SFR) [K] San Rafael, CA Nazareth House.
Conway, Pierre H. *o.p.* '41 (WDC) [B] Washington, DC Dominican House of Studies.
Conway, Richard C. '63 (BO) Randolph, MA St. Bernadette Church.
Conway, Richard J. '45 (BAK) Retired.
Conway, Richard T. '83 (BO) Reading, MA St. Athanasius Church.
Conway, Robert *c.pp.s.* '53 (CIN) [B] Carthagena, OH St. Charles.
Conway, Thomas '86 (BLX) Columbia, MS Industrial and Training School.
Conway, Thomas A. *c.pp.s.* '57 (KC) Kearney, MO Church of the Annunciation; [J] Liberty, MO Precious Blood Center.
Conway, Thomas D. '60 (BO) [43] Boston, MA St. Margaret Church.
Conway, Tommy '86 (BLX) Columbia, MS Most Holy Trinity Church.
Conway, Msgr. Walter J. '48 (PH) [157] Philadelphia, PA St. William Church; Retired.
Conway, William '77 (JOL) Bensenville, IL St. Alexis Church.
Conwill, Giles A. '73 (SD) Leave of Absence.
Conyard, James R. *s.j.* '62 (P) [L] Portland, OR Jesuit Provincial Office (Oregon Prov.).
Conyard, Joseph W. *s.j.* '59 (P) [L] Portland, OR Jesuit Provincial Office (Oregon Prov.).
Conyers, Richard *c.s.c.* '69 (FTW) [9] South Bend, IN Holy Cross Church.
Coogan, Roch A. *o.f.m.* '54 (SP) [O] St. Petersburg, FL St. Anthony Friary.
Cook, Adrian L. '72 (MOB) Brewton, AL St. Maurice Church.
Cook, Blaine '44 (BIS) Retired.
Cook, Brian '85 (WDC) Absent On Leave.
Cook, Daniel '90 (GR) On Duty Outside the Diocese.
Cook, Daniel '90 (STU) [J] Steubenville, OH The Fraternity of Priests, Inc.
Cook, Douglas '94 (ORG) Costa Mesa, CA St. Joachim Church.
Cook, Edward J. '67 (MIL) [30] Milwaukee, WI Congregation of the Great Spirit Church.
Cook, John B. '49 (TR) Retired.
Cook, John J. '45 (HRT) Cheshire, CT St. Bridget's Church.
Cook, John N. '56 (GI) Retired.
Cook, Joseph T. '86 (CHI) [126] Chicago, IL St. Mary Church.
Cook, Louis G. '58 (WIN) St. Charles, MN St. Charles Borromeo Church.
Cook, Michael J. '73 (WIL) Woodcrest, DE St. Matthew Church.
Cook, Michael L. *s.j.* '66 (SPK) [C] Spokane, WA Gonzaga University.
Cook, Millard *o.s.b.* '92 (NY) [133] Bronx, NY St. Benedict Church.
Cook, Millard S. *o.s.b.* '92 (GBG) [H] Latrobe, PA Saint Vincent Archabbey.
Cook, Msgr. Paul G. '59 (BAL) Cockeysville, MD St. Joseph Church.
Cook, Robert J. '65 (LC) [1] La Crosse, WI St. Joseph the Workman Cathedral.
Cook, Ronald '93 (B) Buhl, ID Immaculate Conception Church.
Cook, Thomas R. *o.s.a.* '57 (MIA) [H] Miami, FL Casa San Lorenzo.
Cook, Thomas S. '88 (LA) La Puente, CA St. Louis of France Church.
Cook, Tim (CR) [C] Detroit Lakes, MN St. Mary's Regional Health Center.
Cook, Timothy R. '83 (STL) [1] St. Louis, MO St. Louis Cathedral.
Cook, Walter A. *s.j.* '52 (WDC) [M] Washington, DC The Jesuit Community at Georgetown University.
Cook, William G. '88 (NEW) [6] Bayonne, NJ Mt. Carmel Church.
Cook, William R. '71 (CLV) Retired.
Cooke, Colman M. '65 (SP) Holiday, FL St. Vincent De Paul Church.
Cooke, Msgr. John F. (CAM) Pitman, NJ Our Lady Queen of Peace Church.
Cooke, Kevin '78 (BIR) Gadsden, AL St. James Church.
Cooke, Patrick M. *c.s.sp.* '63 (PIT) Sharpsburg, PA St. Mary Church.
Cooke, Vincent M. *s.j.* '67 (BUF) [C] Buffalo, NY Canisius College; [O] Buffalo, NY Canisius Jesuit Community.
Cooke, Vincent M. *s.j.* '67 (NY) [DD] New York, NY Catholic Medical Mission Board, Inc.
Cooke, Msgr. Vincent W. '30 (CHI) Retired; [G] Chicago, IL Catholic Charities of the Archdiocese of Chicago-Archdiocesan Offices.
Cool, Brian C. '93 (ROC) Canandaigua, NY St. Mary Church; [M] Rochester, NY Diocesan Office of Campus Ministry.
Cooley, George J. '76 (CIN) Leave of Absence.
Cooley, John E. '48 (LA) Retired.
Cooley, Stephen *o.carm.* '69 (JOL) [J] Darien, IL Carmelite Fathers Provincial Office.
Cooley, Stephen V. *o.carm.* '67 (GAL) [49] Houston, TX St. Michael Church.
Coombs, James R. *s.s.e.* '52 (BUR) [G] Colchester, VT Society of St. Edmund.
Coomes, J. Eugene *s.j.* '48 (STL) [P] St. Louis, MO Jesuit Community Corporation at St. Louis University - Jesuit Hall.
Coon, David N. '93 (SPC) [3] Springfield, MO Immaculate Conception Church.
Coonan, James J. (PH) [87] Philadelphia, PA St. Leo Church.
Coonan, Joseph A. '89 (WOR) [25] Worcester, MA St. John's Church.
Coonan, Robert J. '65 (SPR) Hatfield, MA St. Joseph's Church.
Cooney, Art *o.f.m.cap.* '76 (SAG) [9] Saginaw, MI St. Anthony of Padua Church.
Cooney, Camillus '56 (LR) [A] Subiaco, AR Subiaco Monastery.
Cooney, David *s.d.s.* '67 (PHX) [17] Phoenix, AZ St. Mark Church.
Cooney, Dennis '74 (VEN) Bradenton, FL SS. Peter and Paul the Apostles Church.
Cooney, Francis C. *m.s.* '69 (HRT) [5] Hartford, CT Our Lady of Sorrows Church; [M] Hartford, CT Missionaries of LaSalette Provincial Secretary.
Cooney, Gerald (FWT) Retired.
Cooney, Msgr. James '64 (BRK) [163] Queens, NY St. Clare Church.
Cooney, John M. '62 (HRT) Watertown, CT St. John the Evangelist Church.
Cooney, Msgr. Joseph P. '42 (PH) Wayne, PA St. Katharine of Siena Church; Retired.
Cooney, Michael N. '75 (DET) Mount Clemens, MI St. Peter Church.
Cooney, Patrick *o.s.b.* '91 (IND) [J] St. Meinrad, IN St. Meinrad Archabbey.
Cooney, Robert F. *c.s.v.* '57 (LAV) [D] Las Vegas, NV Clerics of St. Viator Retirement Home.
Cooney, Roger P. '70 (COL) [A] Columbus, OH Pontifical College Josephinum.
Cooney, Roger P. '70 (COV) On Duty Outside the Diocese.
Cooney, Romaeus *o.carm.* '58 (ALB) [4] Troy, NY Holy Trinity Church; [5] Troy, NY St. Joseph Church.
Cooney, Sean K. '59 (ORL) Goldenrod, FL Saints Peter and Paul Church.
Cooney, Stephen A. '76 (LIN) Brainard, NE Holy Trinity Church.
Cooney, Theophane *c.p.* '52 (BRK) [180] Queens, NY Immaculate Conception Church; [U] Jamaica, NY Immaculate Conception Monastery.
Cooney, Xavier *s.v.d.* '83 (WH) Webster Springs, WV St. Anne's Church.
Coons, David F. '83 (IND) [38] Indianapolis, IN St. Pius X Church; [C] Indianapolis, IN Bishop Chatard High School.
Cooper, Angus *o.f.m.* '61 (OAK) [N] Oakland, CA Franciscan Friars Provincial Office, Province of St. Barbara.
Cooper, Angus C. *o.f.m.* '61 (LA) [72] Los Angeles, CA St. Joseph Church.
Cooper, Craig D. (BAL) Absent on Leave.
Cooper, David E. '70 (MIL) [3] West Allis, WI Holy Assumption Church.
Cooper, Donald A. '53 (NEW) Washington Township,

NJ Our Lady of Good Counsel Church.
Cooper, Donald J. '63 (E) Force, PA St. Joseph Church.
Cooper, Harold L. *s.j.* '49 (NO) [P] New Orleans, LA Ignatius Residence.
Cooper, Harold V. '49 (SC) Retired.
Cooper, James W. '80 (LIN) Friend, NE St. Joseph's Church.
Cooper, Jeffrey A. *c.s.c.* '94 (FTW) [J] South Bend, IN Congregation of Holy Cross Indiana Province Provincial House.
Cooper, John A. '80 (LIN) Tecumseh, NE St. Andrew's Church.
Cooper, Joseph M. *o.f.m.cap.* '95 (MAN) [2] Manchester, NH St. Anne Church.
Cooper, L. Damian '86 (RVC) Huntington Station, NY St. Hugh of Lincoln Church.
Cooper, Leo (KCK) Special Assignment.
Cooper, Mark A. *o.s.b.* '76 (MAN) [K] Manchester, NH St. Anselm Abbey.
Cooper, Michael W. *s.j.* '73 (CHI) [C] Chicago, IL Jesuit Community at Loyola University of Chicago.
Cooper, Patrick E. '91 (CHR) Cheraw, SC St. Peter's Church.
Cooper, R. John '83 (CLV) Released from Diocesan Assignment.
Cooper, Ronald C. '83 (CIN) Greenfield, OH St. Benignus Church; New Vienna, OH St. Michael Church.
Cooper, Thomas T. '55 (STL) Retired.
Cooper, Warren L. '71 (NO) Chalmette, LA Our Lady of Prompt Succor Church.
Coopmans, Joseph R. *o.praem.* '81 (GB) [4] Green Bay, WI Annunciation of the Blessed Virgin Mary Church.
Coover, Thomas (OLL) Leave of Absence.
Copeland, Leonard R. *o.c.d.* '67 (MIL) [24] Milwaukee, WI St. Florian's Church.
Copenhaver, John L. '88 (LIN) Shelby, NE Sacred Heart Church.
Copp, Rodney J. '73 (BO) Watertown, MA St. Patrick Church.
Coppenrath, Leonard A. '53 (BO) [1] Brookline, MA St. Aidan Church.
Copper, Stephen G. '95 (WOR) [23] Worcester, MA St. George Church.
Coppinger, Edmund T. '59 (WIL) Wilmington Manor, DE Our Lady of Fatima Church.
Coppinger, John *s.a.* '72 (NY) [4] Yonkers, NY St. Bartholomew Church.
Coppola, David L. '86 (PAT) Kinnelon, NJ Our Lady of the Magnificat Church; [C] Wayne, NJ De Paul High School.
Coppola, Paul R. '51 (BUF) Retired.
Cops, Augustine *o.f.m.cap.* (DET) [16] Detroit, MI St. Charles Borromeo Church; [58] Detroit, MI Our Lady of Sorrows Church.
Cops, Peter *s.s.s.* '52 (CLV) [P] Cleveland, OH Congregation of the Blessed Sacrament Provincial House.
Cops, Peter E. *s.s.s.* '52 (LIN) [F] Waverly, NE Our Lady of Good Counsel Retreat House.
Copsey, Robert *s.o.l.t.* '94 (CC) Robstown, TX St. Anthony Church; [H] Robstown, TX Society of Our Lady of the Most Holy Trinity.
Copsey, Robert A. '78 (SAC) [15] Sacramento, CA St. Joseph's Church.
Corali, Serafino A. '47 (RVC) Retired; [N] Uniondale, NY St. Pius X Residence.
Corapi, John *s.o.l.t.* '91 (CC) [H] Robstown, TX Society of Our Lady of the Most Holy Trinity.
Corbally, Christopher *s.j.* '76 (TUC) [F] Tucson, AZ Kino House.
Corbellini, Peter *c.s.* '82 (CHI) [17] Chicago, IL St. Anthony Church.
Corbett, Carlos *c.ss.r.* '53 (CGS) Aguas Buenas, PR Church of Tres Santos Reyes.
Corbett, Eugene J. *s.j.* '62 (SJ) Santa Clara, CA Santa Clara Valley Medical Center; [D] San Jose, CA Bellarmine College Preparatory.
Corbett, George J. *c.ss.r.* '43 (STL) [P] Liguori, MO St. Clement Health Care Center.
Corbett, James B. *c.s.p.* '35 (NY) [Z] Scarsdale, NY Paulist Fathers Generalate.
Corbett, James B. *c.s.p.* '35 (STP) [29] Minneapolis, MN St. Lawrence Church; [N] Minneapolis, MN Paulist Fathers.
Corbett, John '95 (NEW) [1] Jersey City, NJ St. Aedan's Church.
Corbett, John B. '56 (PIT) [50] Pittsburgh, PA Holy Innocents Church.
Corbett, John D. *o.p.* '80 (COL) [A] Columbus, OH Pontifical College Josephinum.
Corbett, John V. *c.ss.r.* '46 (SPR) [8] Springfield, MA Our Lady of Hope Church.
Corbett, Michael E. '54 (PBL) Retired.
Corbett, Richard '95 (NEW) Secaucus, NJ Immaculate Conception Church.
Corbett, Robert '51 (STL) Manchester, MO Christ, Prince of Peace Church.
Corbett, W. Joseph '95 (ATL) Dunwoody, GA All Saints Catholic Church.
Corbin, Don '70 (TOL) [H] Oregon, OH St. Charles Hospital.
Corbino, Thomas A. '72 (JOL) Warrenville, IL St. Irene Church.
Corbley, Timothy L. '93 (STP) Inver Grove Heights, MN St. Patrick Church.
Corbo, Alfred P. '56 (CHI) Franklin Park, IL St. Gertrude Church.
Corces, Pedro '88 (MIA) Coral Gables, FL St. Augustine Church.
Corciulo, Msgr. Cosimo '56 (SB) Norco, CA California Rehabilitation Center.
Corcoran, Albert C. *s.j.* '36 (SFR) [N] San Francisco, CA Jesuit Community at University of San Francisco.
Corcoran, Brian M. '72 (SD) [1] El Cajon, CA Holy Trinity Church.
Corcoran, Msgr. Clifton J. '54 (AMA) Retired; [D] Panhandle, TX St. Joseph's Home for Retired Priests.
Corcoran, D. Stanley '90 (DAL) Commerce, TX St. Joseph Church; [O] Irving, TX Diocese of Dallas Campus Ministry.
Corcoran, Edward *o.s.f.s.* '41 (ARL) Vienna, VA Our Lady of Good Counsel Church.
Corcoran, Edward G. '56 (CHI) Berwyn, IL St. Leonard Church.
Corcoran, Frank '54 (JKS) Crystal Springs, MS St. John Church.
Corcoran, Harry T. *s.j.* '43 (OAK) [A] Berkeley, CA The Jesuit School of Theology at Berkeley; [N] Berkeley, CA Jesuit Community at Jesuit School of Theology at Berkeley.
Corcoran, John J. '55 (RVC) Center Moriches, NY St. John the Evangelist Church.
Corcoran, John W. '53 (BO) East Bridgewater, MA St. John Church.
Corcoran, Kevin '88 (SY) [3] Syracuse, NY Blessed Sacrament Church.
Corcoran, Lawrence E. *s.j.* '63 (BO) [W] Weston, MA Campion Center.
Corcoran, Msgr. Lawrence J. '43 (COL) [18] Columbus, OH Holy Cross Church; Retired.
Corcoran, Mel M. *o.s.m.* '44 (ORG) [H] Anaheim, CA Servite Fathers and Brothers.
Corcoran, Michael *s.j.* '88 (NY) [F] New York, NY Xavier High School.
Corcoran, Sean *c.s.s.p.* '55 (SFR) [49] San Francisco, CA St. Stephen Church.
Corcoran, William D. '86 (BUR) Barre, VT St. Monica Church.
Corcoran, William T. '81 (CHI) [37] Chicago, IL Christ the King Church; [A] Chicago, IL Archbishop Quigley Preparatory Seminary.
Corcuera, Manuel R. '76 (CHK) MP San Francisco de Borja Parish Church.
Cordano, Virgil *o.f.m.* '45 (LA) [R] Santa Barbara, CA Franciscan Friary, Order of Friars Minor (Old Mission).
Cordaro, Frank '85 (DM) Lacona, IA Holy Trinity Church of Southeast Warren County.
Cordeiro, Anthony G. *o.p.* '67 (OAK) [N] Oakland, CA Western Dominican Province; [N] Oakland, CA Dominican Order, Siena House.
Cordero, Faustino '71 (BRK) [125] Brooklyn, NY St. Rocco's Church.
Cordero, Mamerto '74 (NEW) [18] Jersey City, NJ St. Nicholas Church; Jersey City, NJ Christ Hospital.
Cordery, Robert J. '80 (BO) [E] Boston, MA Catholic Memorial High School and Lower School.
Cordes, Christopher '95 (JC) [1] Jefferson City, MO St. Joseph Cathedral.
Cordier, Leonard *c.ss.r.* '38 (ORL) [F] New Smyrna Beach, FL St. Alphonsus Villa-Redemptorist Fathers and Brothers.
Cordileone, Salvatore '82 (SD) On Duty Outside the Diocese.
Cordisco, Philip *o.ss.t.* '60 (NY) [218] Staten Island, NY Our Lady of Mt. Carmel-St. Benedicta Church.
Cordova, Hugo *o.f.m.* '91 (ELP) [B] El Paso, TX St. Anthony's School of Theology.
Cordy Robert J. '38 (MAR) Retired.
Coreas, Edwin '92 (GAL) [18] Houston, TX St. Charles Borromeo Church.
Corena, Pedro *o.ss.t.* '66 (SJN) [14] Bayamon, PR Espiritu Santo Church.
Coric, Christopher *o.f.m.conv.* '71 (BUF) [7] Lackawanna, NY Our Lady of Bistrica Church.
Coric, Doiminik '40 (CHI) [N] Chicago, IL Croatian Franciscan Custody of the Holy Family.
Coriden, James A. '57 (GRY) On Duty Outside the Diocese.
Corigliano, Anthony *c.s.s.* '55 (BO) [W] Waltham, MA Stigmatine Fathers & Brothers Provincial House.
Corkery, Daniel '55 (ALX) Cloutierville, LA St. John the Baptist Church.
Corkery, Raymond *o.carm.* '59 (JOL) [4] Joliet, IL Mount Carmel Church.
Corl, Ronald *c.p.* '66 (DET) [K] Detroit, MI St. Paul of the Cross Community, Congregation of the Passion; [P] Detroit, MI St. Paul of the Cross Retreat Center.
Corley, Joseph M. '75 (PH) [107] Philadelphia, PA Most Blessed Sacrament Church; [D] Philadelphia, PA John W. Hallahan Catholic Girls High School.
Corley, Malachy *o.c.s.o.* '55 (ATL) [I] Conyers, GA The Monastery of the Holy Spirit.
Corley, Theodosius *o.f.m.cap.* '74 (PRT) [3] Portland, ME St. Joseph's Church; [J] Portland, ME Motherhouse of the Sisters of Mercy of the Americas; [M] Portland, ME Westbrook College.
Corley, Thomas '85 (JOL) Coal City, IL Assumption Church.
Cormack, James B. *c.m.* '76 (STL) [65] St. Louis, MO St. Vincent de Paul Church.
Cormack, Michael J. '54 (SAC) Roseville, CA St. Rose Church; Retired and in Senior Ministry.
Cormier, Allen L. *c.s.c.* '46 (AUS) [H] Austin, TX Congregation of Holy Cross - Southern Province.
Cormier, Allen L. *c.s.c.* '46 (FTW) [J] South Bend, IN Congregation of Holy Cross Indiana Province Provincial House.
Cormier, Gregory P. '83 (LAF) Parks, LA St. Joseph Church.
Cormier, Joseph '52 (P) Retired.
Cormier, Leo G. (BO) Retired.
Cormier, Norman R. '59 (PRT) Retired.
Cormier, Roger C. '61 (BO) [4] Everett, MA St. Therese Church.
Cormier, William '71 (WOR) Spencer, MA Mary, Queen of the Rosary Church.
Corneille, Cecil (STV) [2] Estate Elizabeth, VI Our Lady of Perpetual Help Church.
Corneille, Cecil '95 (STV) [1] St. Thomas, VI Cathedral of Sts. Peter and Paul.
Cornejo, Quirino H. '91 (SAN) Junction, TX St. Theresa of the Child Jesus Church; Menard, TX Sacred Heart Church.
Cornejo, Vincent C. '56 (MET) Woodbridge, NJ Our Lady of Mt. Carmel Church.
Cornelius, Leonard *o.f.m.* '69 (AUS) Old Washington-on-the Brazos, TX Blessed Virgin Mary Church; [H] Brenham, TX Order of Friars Minor; [I] Brenham, TX Monastery of St. Clare.
Cornelius, Msgr. William R. '58 (STU) [8] Steubenville, OH St. Pius X Church.
Cornell, Robert J. *o.praem.* (GB) [B] De Pere, WI St. Norbert College; [I] De Pere, WI St. Joseph Priory.
Cornelli, Leo *o.s.b.* '35 (DET) [K] Detroit, MI St. Sylvester Monastery.
Cornelli, Neil '37 (LAN) Retired.
Cornelli, Neil '37 (STA) Fernandina Beach, FL St. Michael's Church.
Cornely, Francis J. '48 (PH) Essington, PA St. Margaret Mary Alacoque Church; Retired.
Cornely, Joseph *s.t.* '60 (WDC) [M] Adelphi, MD Missionary Servants of the Most Holy Trinity.
Corniel, Rafael G. '75 (NY) [103] New York, NY St. Paul Church.
Cornish, Daryl G. *s.j.* '82 (STL) [O] St. Louis, MO Fusz Pavilion.
Cornish, Ronald '68 (KCK) Holton, KS St. Dominic's Church; Mayetta, KS St. Francis Xavier Church.
Cornwell, Malcolm *c.p.* '69 (RVC) Shelter Island, NY Our Lady of the Isle Church.
Corominas, John *c.m.f.* '49 (LA) [R] Rancho Dominguez, CA Dominguez Seminary Inc.
Corona, Andrew (GRY) [2] Hammond, IN Our Lady of Perpetual Help Church.
Corona, Andrew '93 (GRY) [B] Hammond, IN Bishop Noll Institute.
Corona, John J. '71 (RNO) Gardnerville, NV St. Gall Church.
Corona, Msgr. Michael J. '68 (MET) Phillipsburg, NJ SS. Philip and James Church.
Coronado, Genero '51 (LA) Retired.
Coronel, Juan S. '32 (LA) Retired.
Corpora, Joseph V. *c.s.c.* (PHX) [J] Goodyear, AZ St. John Vianney School Development Fund.
Corpora, Joseph V. *c.s.c.* '84 (PHX) Goodyear, AZ Saint John Vianney Church.
Corr, Msgr. John F. (PAT) Retired.
Corr, John Raymond *o.p.* '56 (SAN) [5] San Angelo, TX St. Joseph Church.
Corradi, Frank *s.c.* '85 (LC) [5] Eau Claire, WI St. Olaf Church.
Corradin, Gina *c.s.* '58 (CHI) [N] Stone Park, IL Scalabrini Mission Center.
Corrado, Dennis M. *c.o.* '70 (BRK) [22] Brooklyn, NY St. Boniface Church; [U] Brooklyn, NY Oratory of Saint Philip Neri, Congregation Pontifical Right.
Corral, Jose '79 (TOL) Findlay, OH St. Michael Church.
Corral, Jose C. *s.j.* (BO) [27] Boston, MA Holy Family Church.
Corral, Jose C. *s.j.* '66 (BO) [E] Boston, MA Boston College High School & Jesuit Community.
Corral, Roberto *o.p.* '88 (SFR) [13] San Francisco, CA St. Dominic Church; [N] San Francisco, CA St. Dominic Priory.
Corrao, John A. *c.s.* '56 (PRO) [4] Johnston, RI St. Rocco Church.
Correa, Adrian R. (BWN) Graduate Studies.
Correa, Gino *o.f.m.* '76 (CHI) [N] Chicago, IL St. Joseph Friary.
Correa, Gino *o.f.m.* '76 (SFE) Jemez Pueblo, NM San Diego Indian Missions Church.
Corredato, John *c.s.v.* '68 (SFD) Edwardsville, IL St.

Boniface Church.
Correia, Edward E. '68 (FR) [14] New Bedford, MA St. James Church.
Correlo, Bruce '85 (LA) [81] Los Angeles, CA St. Michael Church.
Correnti, Joseph M. '72 (LR) Springdale, AR St. Raphael's Church; Tontitown, AR St. Joseph's Church.
Corriere, Basil *e.c.* '87 (STU) [F] Bloomingdale, OH Holy Family Hermitage.
Corrigan, Allen F. '82 (CLV) Maple Heights, OH St. Martin of Tours Church.
Corrigan, Austin B. '43 (SUP) Retired.
Corrigan, Msgr. Bernard '47 (NY) Warwick, NY St. Stephen Church.
Corrigan, Edward *s.m.* '43 (CLV) [N] Cleveland, OH Sts. Mary and Joseph Home for the Aged.
Corrigan, Edward J. *s.m.* '43 (WDC) [M] Washington, DC Marist Provincial House.
Corrigan, F. J. '38 (SFD) Retired.
Corrigan, Gregory M. '86 (WIL) Claymont, DE Holy Rosary Church; [A] Wilmington, DE St. Mark's High School.
Corrigan, Msgr. Hugh J. '63 (NY) [9] Yonkers, NY Immaculate Conception Church.
Corrigan, James B. *s.j.* '49 (MIL) [P] Wauwatosa, WI Jesuit Community at St. Camillus.
Corrigan, James J. '56 (NY) [E] New York, NY Cardinal Spellman High School.
Corrigan, James V. *o.s.a.* '66 (CHI) [N] Olympia Fields, IL The Augustinian Provincialate Tolentine Center.
Corrigan, James V. *o.s.a.* '66 (SD) San Diego, CA Sharp Memorial Hospital.
Corrigan, Kevin B. *c.s.sp.* '60 (SJ) Mountain View, CA St. Athanasius Church.
Corrigan, Michael T. '75 (CHR) Florence, SC St. Ann Church; [H] Florence, SC Francis Marion University Newman Center.
Corrigan, Michael T. '75 (GAL) On Duty Outside the Diocese.
Corriveau, Ernest J. *m.s.* '64 (FR) [K] Attleboro, MA La Salette Shrine.
Corriveau, Kip '95 (ROC) Absent on Leave.
Corriveau, Raymond *o.p.* '55 (PRT) [I] Lewiston, ME SS. Peter and Paul Priory.
Corriveau, Roger R. *a.a.* '74 (WOR) [N] Worcester, MA Assumptionists of Assumption College.
Corriveau, Ronald E. '71 (MAN) Epping, NH St. Joseph Church.
Corry, Francis J. '74 (NY) [E] New York, NY Cardinal Spellman High School.
Corry, James J. *c.s.sp.* '57 (STA) [18] Jacksonville, FL St. Paul's Church.
Corry, John J. '52 (RC) Retired.
Corso, Charles *c.s.c.* '75 (P) [B] Portland, OR University of Portland.
Corso, Charles W. *c.s.c.* (FTW) [J] South Bend, IN Congregation of Holy Cross Indiana Province Provincial House.
Cortelyou, John R. *c.m.* '40 (CHI) [C] Chicago, IL Vincentian Community at DePaul University.
Cortes, Antonio '96 (MRY) [2] Salinas, CA Sacred Heart Church.
Cortes, Jesse '62 (LAV) [6] Las Vegas, NV St. Anne Church.
Cortes, Raul '62 (LA) Reseda, CA St. Catherine of Siena Church.
Cortese, Francis X. *o.praem.* '62 (PH) [48] Philadelphia, PA St. Gabriel Church.
Cortese, Patrick S. '48 (SCR) Retired.
Cortese, Richard '82 (MEM) [16] Memphis, TN St. Louis Church.
Cortesi, David J. '63 (CHI) [58] Chicago, IL St. Ferdinand Church.
Cortez, Fernando (OAK) [3] Oakland, CA St. Anthony's Church.
Cortez, Jose '73 (ARE) [5] Utuado, PR Our Lady of Sorrows Church.
Cortez, Ramiro *o.m.i.* '70 (SAT) Eagle Pass, TX Sacred Heart Church.
Corti, Claudio *p.i.m.e.* '92 (DET) [K] Detroit, MI P.I.M.E. College Community.
Corti, Claudio *p.i.m.e.* '92 (PAT) [M] Wayne, NJ P.I.M.E. Missionaries Residence.
Cortney, Edward P. '63 (GI) Chadron, NE St. Patrick's Church.
Cortney, Kevin J. '50 (GI) Retired.
Cortney, Louis M. *o.s.m.* '39 (CHI) [N] Chicago, IL Servite Friars - Eastern Province.
Coruna, Roberto D. '77 (MET) Piscataway, NJ Our Lady of Fatima Church.
Coryer, Francis J. '82 (OG) De Kalb Junction, NY St. Henry Church; Edwards, NY Sacred Heart Church.
Cosby, R. Roy '54 (ARL) Falls Church, VA St. James Church.
Coschignano, Joseph C. '69 (RVC) Rocky Point, NY St. Anthony of Padua Church.
Cosellas, Ramon J. (SJN) [B] Rio Piedras, PR Fraternidad Santa Maria de Los Angeles.
Cosentino, Jack A. '70 (FAR) On Duty Outside the Diocese.
Coseo, Msgr. F. Gordon '38 (OG) Malone, NY Notre Dame Church; Retired.
Cosgayon, Gerard *o.a.r.* '88 (NY) [154] Bronx, NY St. John's Church.
Cosgrove, Edward C. *c.ss.r.* '55 (BLX) [E] Biloxi, MS St. John Neumann Residence.
Cosgrove, Francis J. *s.j.* '48 (NY) [Z] New York, NY St. Ignatius Loyola Residence.
Cosgrove, Francis J. '65 (JKS) Madison, MS St. Francis of Assisi Church.
Cosgrove, Msgr. Henry P. '41 (BRK) Retired; [U] Douglaston, NY Bishop Mugavero Residence.
Cosgrove, J. Kelly '43 (LC) Retired.
Cosgrove, J. Kelly '43 (ORL) Retired.
Cosgrove, James R. '51 (ROC) Waterloo, NY St. Mary Church.
Cosgrove, Jerome P. '63 (SC) Le Mars, IA St. Joseph's Church.
Cosgrove, Joseph '60 (LA) Moorpark, CA Holy Cross Church.
Cosgrove, Joseph J. '92 (BAL) Severna Park, MD St. John the Evangelist Church.
Cosgrove, Thomas *c.ss.r.* '45 (STL) [P] Liguori, MO Liguori Mission House/Redemptorists.
Cosgrove, William B. '74 (NY) Hopewell Junction, NY St. Denis Church; [DD] Scarsdale, NY Catholic Charismatic Renewal Office.
Cosgrove, William J. '55 (ROC) Shortsville, NY St. Dominic Church.
Coskren, Thomas M. *o.p.* '54 (PRO) [F] Providence, RI St. Thomas Aquinas Priory at Providence College.
Coslowsky, Marion '42 (SB) Retired.
Cosmic, John J. '90 (OG) Chaumont, NY All Saints Church.
Cosmos, George (RIC) [9] Richmond, VA St. Edward The Confessor Church.
Coss, John *f.m.s.i.* '56 (BO) [B] Framingham, MA Sylva Maria.
Cossavella, Anthony J. '81 (PH) [3] Norristown, PA Holy Saviour Church.
Cossette, Raymond '55 (DUL) Retired.
Costa, Anthony J. '90 (PH) [11] Philadelphia, PA St. Anne Church.
Costa, Caetano F.X. '64 (RVC) Ronkonkoma, NY St. Joseph's Church.
Costa, David '85 (FR) North Dighton, MA St. Joseph's Church.
Costa, Eriberto '81 (SC) [1] Sioux City, IA Cathedral of the Epiphany.
Costa, Eugene *o.de.m.* '74 (CLV) [57] Cleveland, OH Our Lady of Mount Carmel Church; [P] Cleveland, OH Mercedarians.
Costa, Eugene A. '74 (CLV) Cleveland, OH Lutheran Medical Center.
Costa, Eugene E. '76 (SFD) Athens, IL Holy Family Church; Sherman, IL St. John Vianney Church.
Costa, Gabriel B. '79 (NEW) [B] South Orange, NJ Seton Hall University.
Costa, Joseph M. *s.j.* '54 (SJ) [M] Los Gatos, CA California Province of the Society of Jesus, Jesuit Provincial Office; [M] Los Gatos, CA Sacred Heart Jesuit Center.
Costa, Joseph M. '77 (FR) [F] Fall River, MA St. Vincent's Home Corp.
Costa, Mario '53 (RVC) Brookville, NY St. Paul the Apostle Church.
Costa, Salvatore *o.m.i.* '42 (BO) [Z] Tewksbury, MA Immaculate Heart of Mary Novitiate-Infirmary.
Costa, Thomas C. '78 (RVC) Westbury, NY St. Brigid Church.
Costabile, George '58 (FRS) Retired.
Costantino, Msgr. Anthony J. '44 (SAT) Retired; [K] San Antonio, TX Casa De Padres; [K] San Antonio, TX Padua Place.
Costantino, Joseph S. '87 (NY) [Z] New York, NY St. Ignatius Loyola Residence.
Costanzo, John J. '64 (PBL) Fruita, CO Sacred Heart Church; Grand Junction, CO St. Joseph Church.
Costello, Andrew *c.ss.r.* '65 (TOL) [2] Lima, OH St. Gerard Church.
Costello, Aquinas *o.p.* '68 (LA) [59] Los Angeles, CA St. Dominic Church.
Costello, Bernard B. '63 (PIT) On Duty Outside the Diocese.
Costello, Charles P. *s.j.* '60 (BAL) [M] Baltimore, MD Ferdinand Wheeler House; [Q] Baltimore, MD Ignatian Lay Volunteer Corps.
Costello, Daniel T. *s.j.* '54 (STL) [P] St. Louis, MO Jesuit Community Corporation at St. Louis University - Jesuit Hall.
Costello, Edward *o.f.m.conv.* '61 (MET) [I] Watchung, NJ McAuley Hall Inc.
Costello, Msgr. Francis M. '45 (NY) Retired.
Costello, Frank B. *s.j.* '52 (SPK) [C] Spokane, WA Gonzaga University.
Costello, James J. *s.j.* '66 (COS) [E] Sedalia, CO Sacred Heart Retreat House - Jesuit Community; [G] Sedalia, CO Sacred Heart Jesuit Retreat House.
Costello, James P. '60 (CLV) [6] Parma, OH Holy Family Church.
Costello, John '89 (BRK) [T] Brooklyn, NY Catholic Migration & Refugee Office, Catholic Migration Services, Inc.
Costello, John F. *s.j.* '83 (CHI) [N] Chicago, IL Chicago Province of the Society of Jesus-Provincial Office; [N] Chicago, IL Chicago Province of the Society of Jesus-Provincial Office.
Costello, John F. '96 (VEN) [4] Naples, FL St. William Church.
Costello, John J. (BRK) [Y] Brooklyn, NY Pro Sanctity Movement.
Costello, John J. '53 (SY) Sherrill, NY St. Helena Church.
Costello, John J. '89 (BRK) [150] Queens, NY St. Andrew Avellino Church.
Costello, John M. '72 (STL) Washington, MO St. Francis Borgia Church.
Costello, John M. *s.j.* '84 (ROC) [B] Rochester, NY McQuaid Jesuit High School.
Costello, Joseph J. '60 (CLV) Hudson, OH St. Mary Church.
Costello, Msgr. Lawrence D. '64 (RVC) Mineola, NY Corpus Christi Church; Retired.
Costello, Mark J. *o.f.m.cap.* '91 (CHI) [N] Chicago, IL St. Clare Friary.
Costello, Paul *o.m.i.* '77 (WDC) [B] Washington, DC Oblate College/Oblate Center for Mission Studies.
Costello, Raymond *m.s.c.* '45 (ALN) [A] Center Valley, PA Missionaries of the Sacred Heart.
Costello, Richard D. *s.j.* '53 (BGP) [O] Fairfield, CT The Fairfield Jesuit Community-Fairfield University.
Costello, Robert B. '53 (BO) Abington, MA St. Nicholas Church.
Costello, Robert T. *s.j.* '63 (STL) [F] St. Louis, MO St. Louis University High School, George H. Backer Memorial; [P] St. Louis, MO St. Louis University High School Jesuit Community.
Costello, Theodore (SP) Palm Harbor, FL St. Luke the Evangelist Church.
Costello, Thomas J. (SY) Special Assignment; [W] Syracuse, NY David W. Barry Foundation.
Costello, Timon *o.f.m.cap.* '58 (GB) [M] Appleton, WI Monte Alverno Retreat Center.
Costello, Vincent F. '76 (CHI) Arlington Heights, IL Our Lady of the Wayside Church.
Costello, Msgr. William '52 (RVC) Franklin Square, NY St. Catherine of Sienna Church.
Costello, William J. '64 (CHI) Antioch, IL St. Peter Church.
Costello, William M. '74 (FR) [8] Taunton, MA St. Mary's Church.
Costelloe, M. Joseph *s.j.* '46 (MIL) [P] Wauwatosa, WI Jesuit Community at St. Camillus.
Costelloe, M. Joseph *s.j.* '46 (OM) [K] Omaha, NE Jesuit Community at Creighton University.
Coster, Henry G. *s.j.* '65 (SCR) [C] Scranton, PA University of Scranton.
Costigan, George (PAT) Retired.
Costigan, P. James '68 (SAV) [3] Augusta, GA St. Mary on the Hill Church.
Costigan, Richard F. *s.j.* '64 (CHI) [C] Chicago, IL Jesuit Community at Loyola University of Chicago.
Costigan, Richard J. '50 (TUC) Retired.
Cote, David P. '68 (PRT) Military Chaplains.
Cote, Donald J. '49 (FAR) Retired.
Cote, Duaine M. '62 (FAR) Edgeley, ND Transfiguration Church.
Cote, E. Joseph '69 (BAL) [22] Baltimore, MD St. Charles Borromeo Church.
Cote, Gerald M. '56 (TUC) Retired.
Cote, Joseph A. *o.p.* (WDC) [11] Washington, DC St. Dominic Church & Priory Church.
Cote, Joseph A. '51 (MAN) [J] Berlin, NH St. Vincent de Paul Nursing Home.
Cote, Normand C. '58 (OG) Coopersville, NY St. Joseph Church.
Cote, Paul E. '71 (PRT) Oquossoc, ME Our Lady of the Lakes Church.
Cote, Roland P. '71 (MAN) [1] Nashua, NH St. Aloysius Church.
Cotone, Michael *o.s.c.* '74 (DUL) Grand Rapids, MN St. Joseph's Church.
Cotta, Myron '87 (FRS) Gustine, CA Our Lady of Miracles Church.
Cotter, Charles B. '50 (OG) Retired.
Cotter, David W. *o.s.b.* '79 (MAN) [K] Manchester, NH St. Anselm Abbey.
Cotter, Eugene J. '56 (NEW) [B] South Orange, NJ Seton Hall University.
Cotter, Francis Xavier *o.c.d.* '89 (MIL) [P] Holy Hill, WI Discalced Carmelite Monastery.
Cotter, George G. *m.m.* '60 (NY) [Z] Maryknoll, NY Maryknoll Fathers and Brothers.
Cotter, John F. '80 (SAG) Beal City, MI St. Joseph the Worker Church.
Cotter, Lawrence E. '52 (OG) Colton, NY St. Patrick Church.
Cotter, Patrick John '57 (LA) Retired.
Cotter, Pius *o.f.m.cap.* '88 (GB) Brussels, WI St. Francis and St. Mary Parish Church.
Cotter, Raymond C. '86 (GAY) Absent on Leave.
Cotter, Robert L. '47 (OG) Star Lake, NY St. Hubert Church.

Cotter, Vince '83 (OAK) Antioch, CA St. Ignatius Church.
Cottingham, David T. *c.s.sp.* '75 (PIT) [B] Pittsburgh, PA Duquesne University of the Holy Ghost.
Cotton, Charles '73 (COL) [30] Columbus, OH St. Mary Magdalene Church.
Cottone, Paul P. '49 (SCR) [16] Scranton, PA St. Lucy's Church.
Cottrell, Frank '50 (SJ) Retired.
Cottrell, James '68 (SP) Retired.
Cotugno, Joseph '64 (ALB) Rensselaer, NY St. John Church.
Coucelo, Andres '68 (MIA) Hollywood, FL Nativity Church.
Couch, Edward W. *o.m.i.* '61 (GAL) [S] Dickinson, TX Christian Renewal Center.
Coughlan, Msgr. Michael J. '52 (SD) Retired.
Coughlan, R. E. '90 (SFE) [4] Santa Fe, NM St. Anne's Church.
Coughlin, Bernard J. *s.j.* '55 (SPK) [C] Spokane, WA Gonzaga University.
Coughlin, Charles T. *s.s.j.* '45 (WDC) [8] Washington, DC St. Benedict the Moor Church.
Coughlin, Conall R. *o.s.b.* '58 (PAT) [M] Morristown, NJ St. Mary's Abbey.
Coughlin, Daniel C. *c.s.c.* '50 (FTW) [18] South Bend, IN St. Stanislaus Church.
Coughlin, Daniel P. '60 (CHI) [41] Chicago, IL St. Clement Church.
Coughlin, Howard L. '53 (CHR) Mauldin, SC St. Elizabeth Ann Seton Church.
Coughlin, John '83 (NY) [A] Yonkers, NY St. Joseph's Seminary; [Z] New York, NY Franciscan Friars, Order of Friars Manor.
Coughlin, Joseph '45 (ALB) [L] Saratoga Springs, NY St. John Neumann Residence.
Coughlin, Msgr. Joseph F. '44 (BUF) Retired.
Coughlin, Kenneth F. '90 (LAN) Pinckney, MI St. Mary Church.
Coughlin, Leo '56 (LAV) [2] Las Vegas, NV Christ the King Church.
Coughlin, Paul (BO) [1] Medford, MA St. Francis of Assisi Church.
Coughlin, Paul E. '66 (PRT) South Portland, ME Church of the Holy Cross; South Portland, ME St. John the Evangelist Church.
Coughlin, Richard '53 (ORG) Inactive Leave.
Coughlin, Roger J. '51 (CHI) Retired; [G] Chicago, IL Catholic Charities of the Archdiocese of Chicago-Archdiocesan Offices.
Coughlin, Thomas '77 (HON) On Duty Outside the Diocese.
Coughlin, Thomas G. *o.m.i.* (BO) [12] Lowell, MA Nuestra Senora del Carmen 1990 Church.
Coughlin, William D. '66 (BO) Wakefield, MA Most Blessed Sacrament Church.
Coughlin, William E. *c.s.b.* (GAL) Missouri City, TX Holy Family Church.
Couhig, Michael D. *c.s.c.* '80 (LA) Burbank, CA St. Francis Xavier Church.
Coulombe, Dale '79 (ORG) Inactive Leave.
Coulter, Lawrence W. '86 (GI) Anselmo, NE St. Anselm's Church.
Coulthard, Gregory *s.d.s.* '67 (BIR) [3] Huntsville, AL St. Joseph's Church.
Coulthardt, Gregory *s.d.s.* '67 (GB) [I] New Holstein, WI Salvatorian Center Residence.
Counce, Paul D. '79 (BR) Special Assignment.
Countie, Charles G. *o.carm.* '78 (STO) [5] Stockton, CA St. Gertrude Church.
Coupar, David A. (LAF) Absent on Leave.
Cour, Raymond *c.s.c.* '41 (FTW) [17] South Bend, IN Faith & Hope & Charity Chapel.
Cour, Raymond F. *c.s.c.* '41 (FTW) [B] Notre Dame, IN University of Notre Dame Du Lac; [J] Notre Dame, IN Holy Cross Community, Corby Hall, University of Notre Dame.
Courcy, Leo J. '62 (BUR) On Duty Outside the Diocese.
Courcy, Timothy *o.s.b.* '62 (ROC) [I] Pine City, NY Mount Saviour Monastery.
Courier, Rick L. '85 (MAR) Menominee, MI Holy Redeemer Church.
Cournoyer, Alfred '85 (SPR) On Duty Outside the Diocese.
Cournoyer, Napoleon '34 (PRT) Retired.
Courtemanche, Normand L. '65 (PRO) [10] Pawtucket, RI Our Lady of Consolation Church.
Courtney, Edward '55 (HEL) [8] Butte, MT St. John the Evangelist Church.
Courtney, Humphrey J. '51 (HEL) Retired; [B] Helena, MT Carroll College.
Courtney, Joseph B. *c.s.b.* '56 (GAL) [Q] Houston, TX Dominican Fathers and Brothers, St. Mark Priory, Inc.; [Q] Houston, TX Dillon House.
Courtney, Patrick E. '87 (LFT) Unassigned.
Courtney, Paul J. '43 (IND) Retired.
Courtney, Thomas M. '51 (SPR) [18] Springfield, MA St. Patrick's Church.
Courtney, Thomas M. '59 (ALN) Catasauqua, PA Annunciation B.V.M. - St. Mary's Church.
Courtright, Lawrence P. '61 (TLS) [E] Tulsa, OK St. John Medical Center, Inc.
Courtright, Raymond '92 (FAR) Enderlin, ND St. Patrick's Church.
Courville, J. Douglas '76 (LAF) Erath, LA Our Lady of Lourdes Church.
Courville, James '79 (BEA) Absent On Leave.
Courville, Robert W. '63 (LAF) Krotz Springs, LA St. Anthony Church.
Coury, Philip J. *c.m.* '71 (PBL) Las Animas, CO St. Mary Church.
Cousens, Dennis '77 (L) [50] Louisville, KY St. Martin Church.
Cousineau, Robert H. *s.j.* (CHY) Guernsey, WY St. Anthony's Church.
Cousins, John P. *o.f.m.cap.* '76 (DEN) [3] Denver, CO Annunciation Church; [7] Denver, CO Cure D'Ars Church; [M] Denver, CO Annunciation Friary.
Coutinha, Paul *s.a.c.* '82 (MIL) [35] Milwaukee, WI Holy Cross Church; [P] Milwaukee, WI Pallotti House.
Coutinho, Absalom '72 (PAT) [1] Wayne, NJ Annunciation Church.
Couto, Robert '96 (MAN) [5] Nashua, NH Immaculate Conception Church.
Coutu, Joseph '81 (GLP) On Duty Outside of Diocese.
Couture, Bernard G. '50 (BUR) Retired.
Couture, Fernand '43 (STA) Retired.
Couture, Fernand '70 (SFE) [J] Jemez Springs, NM The Jemez Program, Our Lady of Lourdes Novitiate.
Couture, Paul E. *s.s.e.* '56 (BUR) [G] Colchester, VT Society of St. Edmund.
Couture, Roger *o.m.i.* '55 (MAN) [M] Hudson, NH Oblates of Mary Immaculate Retreat House.
Couture, Roland '53 (BO) [W] Lowell, MA Missionary Oblates of Mary Immaculate.
Couturier, Albert '88 (GAY) St. Helen, MI St. Helen Church.
Couturier, David *o.f.m.cap.* '79 (NY) [Z] Garrison, NY St. Francis Friary.
Couturier, George M. '81 (HRT) [R] New Britain, CT Central Connecticut State University Newman House.
Covarrubias, Raul R. '83 (B) Glenns Ferry, ID Our Lady of Limerick Church; Mountain Home, ID Our Lady of Good Counsel Church.
Covarrubias, Salomon P. '91 (YAK) Royal City, WA St. Michael the Archangel Church.
Covas, Peter '57 (SB) Alta Loma, CA St. Peter & St. Paul Church.
Coveney, James B. '64 (ALT) Colver, PA Holy Family Church.
Coveny, Richard C. '56 (BUF) Colden, NY Our Lady of the Sacred Heart Church.
Cover, Phillip B. '70 (LFT) On Duty Outside the Diocese.
Covert, James A. '76 (L) On Special Assignment.
Covertino, David I. *o.f.m.* (PRO) [N] Providence, RI St. Francis Chapel & City Ministry Center.
Covington, Larry '85 (AUS) [16] Austin, TX St. Louis Church; Austin, TX School for the Blind.
Cowan, Anthony '95 (SAT) [52] San Antonio, TX St. Margaret Mary Church.
Cowan, George R. '65 (BRK) [200] Queens, NY St. Mel Church.
Cowan, Vincent '43 (MRY) Retired.
Cowan, Vincent '43 (SAN) Retired.
Coward, Robert *c.p.* '68 (CHI) [N] Chicago, IL Passionist Provincial Office.
Cowart, Conrad (STA) [14] Jacksonville, FL Sacred Heart Church.
Cowden, David '82 (ANC) Palmer, AK St. Michael Church.
Cowden, David '82 (OKL) On Duty Outside the Archdiocese.
Cowell, Raymond '56 (CHI) Missionary Work.
Cower, D. Craig '54 (RC) Retired; [D] Rapid City, SD Priest Retirement and Aid Association.
Cowgill, Msgr. Francis A. '52 (ANC) [2] Anchorage, AK St. Anthony Church.
Cowhig, Edward D. '45 (BO) Danvers, MA St. Alphonsus Church; Retired.
Cowie, Donald *s.m.* '61 (SAT) [F] San Antonio, TX Central Catholic High School; [M] San Antonio, TX Central Catholic Marianist Community; [M] San Antonio, TX Central Catholic Marianist Community.
Cowles, James M. '86 (RIC) Blacksburg, VA St. Mary & Newman Community Church.
Cox, Alan '76 (LFT) On Duty Outside the Diocese.
Cox, Bernard '91 (IND) Bedford, IN St. Vincent de Paul Church; Mitchell, IN St. Mary/Assumption Church.
Cox, Brian M. (BAL) Unassigned.
Cox, Msgr. Craig A. '78 (LA) Encino, CA Our Lady of Grace Church.
Cox, David D. '81 (JC) Canton, MO St. Joseph Church; [A] Hannibal, MO St. Thomas Aquinas Seminary.
Cox, Francis '50 (WCH) Arkansas City, KS Sacred Heart Church.
Cox, Msgr. Gregory A. '76 (LA) [42] Los Angeles, CA St. Anastasia Church; [Y] Los Angeles, CA Catholic Charities of Los Angeles, Inc.
Cox, Msgr. Gregory A. '76 (SAC) [P] Sacramento, CA Catholic Charities of California, Inc.
Cox, James *t.o.r.* '47 (ALT) [F] Newry, PA St. Bernardine Monastery.
Cox, Msgr. James F. '51 (NY) Washingtonville, NY St. Mary Church.
Cox, Jesse deP. *o.p.* '87 (CHI) [24] Chicago, IL St. Basil/Visitation Church; [N] Chicago, IL Dominicans (Provincial Office).
Cox, Msgr. John F. '36 (PRO) [7] Warwick, RI St. Peter's Church; Retired.
Cox, John J. '53 (PH) [36] Philadelphia, PA St. Clement Church.
Cox, John Paul '91 (PEO) Annawan, IL Sacred Heart Church.
Cox, Joseph C. '46 (MAD) Pardeeville, WI St. Mary Church.
Cox, Michael J. *m.s.* '37 (HRT) [M] Hartford, CT Missionaries of LaSalette Provincial Secretary.
Cox, Noel *c.s.sp.* '55 (STA) High Springs, FL St. Madeleine Church.
Cox, Paul '54 (ALB) Lake George, NY Sacred Heart Church.
Cox, Robert M. '80 (DAL) Greenville, TX St. William Church; [P] Dallas, TX White Rose Women's Center.
Cox, William E. '42 (MIL) Retired.
Cox, William J. '56 (PH) Honey Brook, PA St. Peter Church.
Coxen, Gervis J. *m.m.* '37 (NY) [Z] Maryknoll, NY Maryknoll Fathers and Brothers.
Coyle, Alcuin *o.f.m.* '54 (NY) [35] New York, NY St. Francis of Assisi Church.
Coyle, Arthur M. '77 (BO) [13] Lowell, MA St. Patrick Church.
Coyle, Charles G. *s.j.* '65 (FWT) [J] Lake Dallas, TX Montserrat Jesuit Retreat House.
Coyle, Dan '89 (FRS) [3] Bakersfield, CA Sacred Heart Church; Oildale, CA Christ the King Church.
Coyle, Edward J. '80 (ALN) Special Assignment.
Coyle, Eugene P. '54 (BRK) [18] Brooklyn, NY St. Bernadette Church.
Coyle, James '83 (ORL) Sabbatical.
Coyle, Msgr. James A. '32 (PH) Levittown, PA Queen of the Universe Church; Valley Forge, PA St. Teresa of Avila Church; Retired.
Coyle, Patrick *s.m.* '45 (SFR) [B] San Francisco, CA St. Peter Chanel Seminary.
Coyle, Patrick '60 (DUL) Aitkin, MN St. James Church.
Coyle, Patrick J. *s.m.* '45 (SFR) [N] San Francisco, CA Provincial Residence.
Coyle, Robert J. '91 (RVC) Glen Cove, NY St. Patrick's Church.
Coyle, T. William *c.ss.r.* '44 (CHI) [N] Bangkok, Thailand; [N] Parana, Brazil Rua Consulheiro Sinimbu.
Coyle, T. William *c.ss.r.* '44 (DEN) [M] Denver, CO The Redemptorists/Denver Province.
Coyle, T. William *c.ss.r.* '44 (FAR) Special Assignment.
Coyle, Thomas J. '70 (MAD) Darlington, WI Holy Rosary Church.
Coyne, Edwin J. '62 (BGP) Retired.
Coyne, Msgr. George R. '59 (STU) Tiltonsville, OH St. Joseph Church.
Coyne, George V. *s.j.* '65 (BAL) [M] Baltimore, MD Jesuit Fathers and Brothers Maryland Provincial Curia.
Coyne, George V. *s.j.* '65 (TUC) [F] Tucson, AZ Jesuit Community of the Vatican Observatory.
Coyne, Gregory J. '89 (STL) [Q] Kirkwood, MO Opus Dei.
Coyne, James F. '56 (NY) Absent on Sick leave.
Coyne, James P. '75 (SEA) [3] Tacoma, WA St. Frances Cabrini Church.
Coyne, Joseph '72 (HT) On Leave.
Coyne, Msgr. Joseph B. '45 (WDC) [3] Bethesda, MD Little Flower Church; Retired.
Coyne, Joseph C. '69 (HBG) Quarryville, PA St. Catherine of Siena Church.
Coyne, Msgr. Michael J. '55 (CAM) Absecon, NJ St. Elizabeth Ann Seton Church.
Coyne, Patrick J. '51 (BAL) Retired.
Coyne, Robert R. '76 (PIT) Franklin Park Borough, PA St. John Neumann Church.
Coyne, Ronald D. (BO) Absent on Sick Leave.
Coyte, Thomas '74 (DEN) [10] Denver, CO Holy Cross Church.
Coz, Richard T. *s.j.* '58 (PHX) [B] Phoenix, AZ Brophy College Preparatory.
Cozzens, Donald B. '65 (CLV) Cleveland Heights, OH St. Ann Church; [A] Wickliffe, OH St. Mary Seminary; [AA] Wickliffe, OH Center for Pastoral Leadership Services, Inc.
Cozzini, Robert P. '60 (NEW) Cliffside Park, NJ Epiphany Church.
Cozzubbo, Gregory P. *c.m.* '84 (PH) [155] Philadelphia, PA St. Vincent de Paul Church.
Crabb, John T. *s.j.* (BO) [Q] Methuen, MA Holy Family Hospital and Medical Center; [W] Boston, MA Loyola House.
Crable, John M. '53 (OG) [2] Plattsburgh, NY St. John the Baptist Church; Plattsburgh, NY Champlain Valley Physicians Hospital Medical Center.
Crafts, George W. '65 (GAL) [P] Houston, TX Opus Dei.
Crager, Richard *s.d.b.* '85 (NY) [BB] West Haverstraw,

NY Don Bosco Retreat Center and Marian Shrine; [BB] West Haverstraw, NY Marian Shrine.
Craig, Bruce *s.d.b.* '74 (PAT) [3] Paterson, NJ St. Anthony's Church.
Craig, Christopher A. '93 (IND) Columbus, IN St. Bartholomew Church.
Craig, Donald '74 (CHI) [J] Chicago, IL St. Anthony Hospital.
Craig, John V. *s.j.* '77 (STL) [P] St. Louis, MO De Smet Jesuit High School Community.
Craig, Lawrence *ss.cc.* '41 (FR) [K] Fairhaven, MA Sacred Hearts Provincial House.
Craig, Lawrence J. '73 (CHI) [20] Chicago, IL Assumption Church; [20] Chicago, IL Assumption Church; [X] Chicago, IL Kolbe House.
Craig, Richard J. '61 (BO) Chelmsford, MA St. John the Evangelist Church.
Craig, Richard T. '88 (MAR) Leave of Absence.
Craig, Robert *o.f.m.cap.* '67 (PIT) Allegheny County, PA St. Francis Medical Center; [J] Pittsburgh, PA St. Francis Medical Center; [N] Pittsburgh, PA St. Augustine Friary.
Craig, Robert G. '64 (E) Cambridge Springs, PA St. Anthony Church; Cambridge Springs, PA Cambridge Springs Correction Institution.
Craig, Rod '77 (FRS) On Special Assignment.
Craig, Samuel L. '76 (WDC) [5] Washington, DC St. Anthony Church.
Craig, Thomas J. '82 (FWT) Carrollton, TX St. Catherine of Siena Church.
Craig, William (PH) [T] Philadelphia, PA Mercy Catholic Medical Center.
Craig, William R. (BAL) Grantsville, MD St. Ann Church; Mount Savage, MD St. Patrick Church.
Craig, William R. *o.praem.* '55 (PH) [T] Darby, PA Mercy Catholic Medical Center; [Z] Paoli, PA Daylesford Abbey.
Crain, George L. *s.j.* '51 (LA) [C] Los Angeles, CA Loyola Marymount University.
Cramblitt, Richard E. '72 (BAL) [87] Baltimore, MD Shrine of the Sacred Heart Church.
Cramer, David W. '91 (SCR) Kingston, PA St. Ignatius Church.
Cramer, Harry N. '84 (WH) Bridgeport, WV All Saints Church.
Cramer, Joe '77 (KCK) Osawatomie, KS St. Philip Neri Church.
Cramer, John R. '90 (SY) [7] Syracuse, NY Our Lady of Pompei Church.
Cramer, Joseph '77 (KCK) Mound City, KS Sacred Heart Shrine to St. Philippine Duchesne Church.
Cramer, William '77 (PAT) [J] Paterson, NJ St. Joseph's Hospital and Medical Center.
Cramer, William N. (PAT) Paterson, NJ St. Joseph Hospital.
Crandall, Thom A. '81 (PT) Port St. Joe, FL St. Joseph Church.
Crandall, William W. '48 (ALB) Worcester, NY St. Joseph Church.
Crane, Jeff '89 (SAT) On Leave.
Crane, Msgr. Thomas E. '57 (BUF) [3] North Tonawanda, NY St. Joseph Church.
Crane, William H. *m.s.* '41 (HRT) [M] Hartford, CT Missionaries of LaSalette Provincial Secretary.
Crangle, Thomas *o.f.m.cap.* '89 (CHL) [10] Charlotte, NC St. Thomas Aquinas Church.
Crangle, Thomas *o.f.m.cap.* '89 (NEW) [N] Union City, NJ Capuchin Friars - Prov. Stigmata of St. Francis.
Cranor, Bernard *o.s.b.* '62 (SFE) [J] Abiquiu, NM Monastery of Christ in the Desert.
Craven, Msgr. Thomas P. '56 (PH) West Chester, PA St. Agnes Church.
Crawford, Brian *o.s.j.* (SAC) [A] Loomis, CA Mount St. Joseph Novitiate and Seminary.
Crawford, C. Slade '65 (PT) [2] Pensacola, FL Little Flower Church.
Crawford, Canice *t.o.r.* '55 (PIT) [N] Pittsburgh, PA Franciscan Friars, T.O.R.
Crawford, John G. '63 (CLV) South Euclid, OH St. Gregory the Great Church.
Crawford, Larry P. '66 (IND) [41] Indianapolis, IN St. Simon Church.
Crawford, Richard E. '75 (PEO) Retired.
Crawford, Robert P. *c.m.* '47 (PH) [Z] Philadelphia, PA Congregation of the Mission.
Cray, David G. *s.s.e.* (MOB) [A] Selma, AL Edmundite House of Formation.
Cray, David G. *s.s.e.* '72 (MOB) [H] Selma, AL Edmundite Fathers.
Cray, Kevin *s.d.s.* '49 (E) Retired.
Craycraft, Duane M. '67 (LFT) Marion, IN St. Paul Church.
Craycroft, B. Leo '57 (L) Radcliff, KY St. Christopher Church.
Craycroft, George P. '58 (L) Retired; [M] St. Catharine, KY Sansbury Memorial Infirmary.
Creagan, Daniel A. *s.j.* '58 (NO) [8] New Orleans, LA Holy Name of Jesus Church.
Creagan, Robert F. '88 (KAL) Coldwater, MI St. Charles Church; Coldwater, MI Florence Crane Correctional Facility for Women; Coldwater, MI Florence Crane Annex; Coldwater, MI Lakeland Correctional Facility for Men.
Creager, Robert J. '54 (PEO) [4] Ottawa, IL St. Patrick's Church.
Creagh, Kevin *c.m.* '96 (BUF) [R] Williamsville, NY Newman Club Chaplains.
Creagh, Kevin G. *c.m.* '96 (BUF) [C] Niagara University, NY Niagara University; [O] Niagara University, NY Vincentian Community at Niagara University.
Creagh, Richard C. '76 (CHI) [84] Chicago, IL Holy Rosary Church.
Creagh, Thomas P. '67 (L) [36] Louisville, KY St. Ignatius Church.
Crean, Hugh F. '62 (SPR) [6] Springfield, MA Holy Name Church.
Crean, Msgr. Timothy J. '33 (LA) Pasadena, CA Assumption of the Blessed Virgin Mary Church; Retired.
Creane, Anthony J. '56 (SPR) [4] Westfield, MA St. Mary's Church.
Creary, J. Edwin '73 (MEM) [28] Memphis, TN St. William Church.
Creason, Hubert E. '58 (STL) Catawissa, MO St. James Church.
Creason, Richard H. '67 (STL) [11] St. Louis, MO Most Holy Trinity Church.
Creaven, John *c.ss.r.* '49 (HBG) Lititz, PA St. James Church.
Creaven, John J. *c.ss.r.* '49 (HBG) [H] Ephrata, PA St. Clement's Mission House.
Creed, C. Patrick '51 (L) [M] Nazareth, KY Generalate, Motherhouse and Novitiate of the Sisters of Charity of Nazareth.
Creed, C. Patrick '96 (L) Retired.
Creed, Peter M. '67 (SY) [5] Syracuse, NY Most Holy Rosary Church.
Creed, William E. *s.j.* '71 (GRY) [K] East Chicago, IN Roque Gonzalez Residence-Jesuit Fathers; [P] Hammond, IN Seimetz Center; [P] Hammond, IN Spiritual Life Center.
Creeden, Patrick D. *o.s.b.* '78 (CHI) [N] Chicago, IL Monastery of the Holy Cross.
Creedon, Gerard '68 (ARL) [4] Arlington, VA St. Charles Borromeo Church.
Creedon, James J. *m.ss.a.* '79 (WH) Franklin, WV St. Elizabeth Ann Seton Church; Petersburg, WV St. Mary's Church.
Creedon, Joseph D. '68 (PRO) Kingston, RI Christ the King Church; [S] Kingston, RI University of Rhode Island Catholic Center.
Creel, Jesse (R) Retired.
Cregan, Francis A. *o.a.r.* '95 (NY) [B] Suffern, NY Tagaste Monastery; [S] Suffern, NY Good Samaritan Hospital of Suffern.
Cregan, James F. '63 (PT) [2] Tallahassee, FL Blessed Sacrament Church; Lanark Village, FL Sacred Heart of Jesus Church.
Cregan, John C. '87 (ARL) [1] Alexandria, VA Blessed Sacrament Church.
Cregan, John J. '61 (CLV) [52] Cleveland, OH Our Lady of Angels Church.
Cregan, Mark T. *c.s.c.* '83 (NY) [188] Bronx, NY Sacred Heart Church.
Cregan, Robert G. *s.j.* '67 (NEW) [C] Jersey City, NJ St. Peter's Preparatory School.
Cregon, Frank *o.a.r.* (NY) Suffern, NY Good Samaritan Hospital.
Crehan, Joseph L. *s.s.c.* '54 (BO) [2] Everett, MA Immaculate Conception Church; [W] Quincy, MA St. Columban's Foreign Mission Society.
Crehan, Lawrence F. '74 (PH) West Chester, PA St. Agnes Church.
Crehan, Mathias J. *o.f.m.* (IND) Indianapolis, IN Veterans' Administration Hospital.
Crehan, Matthias *o.f.m.* '75 (GLP) Laguna, NM St. Joseph Church.
Creider, Philip B. '77 (OKL) Military Chaplains.
Creighton, Bernard R. *o.f.m.* '67 (PAT) [M] Butler, NJ St. Anthony Friary.
Creighton, Msgr. Edward '47 (SD) Retired.
Creighton, Gerard E. '51 (BO) Retired.
Creighton, Henry *ss.cc.* '49 (FR) [K] Fairhaven, MA Sacred Hearts Provincial House.
Creighton, James J. *s.j.* '60 (CHI) [D] Chicago, IL St. Ignatius Jesuit Community; [J] Maywood, IL Foster G. McGaw Hospital of Loyola University of Chicago.
Creighton, Matthew E. *s.j.* '57 (CHI) [C] Chicago, IL Jesuit Community at Loyola University of Chicago.
Crema, Peter *c.s.j.* '57 (LA) San Pedro, CA St. Peter Church.
Cremaldi, Angelo '60 (LAF) [3] Opelousas, LA Our Lady Queen of Angels Church.
Cremer, Matthias P. *s.c.j.* '44 (MIL) [B] Hales Corners, WI Sacred Heart School of Theology.
Cremer, Patrick M. *s.c.j.* '44 (MIL) [P] Franklin, WI Villa Maria; [Q] Milwaukee, WI Ancilla Convent.
Cremins, John J. '69 (BRK) [12] Brooklyn, NY Assumption of the Blessed Virgin Mary Church; Released from Diocesan Assignment.
Cremonie, Louis D. '72 (HRT) [4] Manchester, CT St. James Church.
Crenner, William A. '52 (KAL) Delton, MI St. Ambrose Church.
Crepaz, Ilario '56 (NEW) [4] Union City, NJ St. Anthony of Padua Church.
Crepeau, John J. '72 (DET) Absent on Leave.
Crescenzi, Rocco *f.d.p.* '43 (BO) [U] Boston, MA Don Orione Nursing Home.
Creson, Mike '87 (KNX) South Pittsburg, TN Our Lady of Lourdes Church.
Crespin, George E. (OAK) [R] Berkley, CA Multicultural Institute.
Crespin, George E. '62 (OAK) [3] Berkeley, CA St. Joseph The Worker Church.
Cressman, Richard *s.d.b.* '80 (BO) [N] Boston, MA Salesian Boys & Girls Club.
Cretella, Biagio '49 (HRT) Retired.
Crevani, Decimo *c.s.* '61 (NEW) [12] Newark, NJ St. Columba's Church.
Crewe, Ronald O. '63 (MIL) Whitewater, WI St. Patrick's Church.
Crews, Clyde F. '73 (L) [A] Louisville, KY Bellarmine College.
Crews, John S. '71 (SR) [H] Sonoma, CA Hanna Boys Center.
Cribben, Andrew *o.praem.* '94 (JKS) [2] Jackson, MS St. Mary Church; [7] Jackson, MS Christ the King Church; [E] Jackson, MS Priory of St. Moses the Black; [G] Jackson, MS Jackson State University Newman Center.
Cribben, Msgr. Philip J. '62 (PH) [76] Philadelphia, PA St. Joan of Arc Church.
Cribbin, Austin J. '56 (BAK) Retired.
Cribbin, James '85 (SD) On Duty Outside the Diocese.
Cribbin, Msgr. Thomas F. (BRK) [L] Brooklyn, NY Catholic Charities; [L] Brooklyn, NY Catholic Charities; [L] Brooklyn, NY Catholic Charities.
Cribbin, Msgr. Thomas F. '42 (BRK) Retired; [L] Brooklyn, NY Catholic Charities; [U] Brooklyn, NY St. Joseph's Priest Residence.
Cribbs, James '90 (ALB) Hancock, NY St. Paul the Apostle Church.
Cricchio, Santo *o.f.m.conv.* '91 (BAL) [26] Baltimore, MD St. Clement Mary Hofbauer Church.
Cricchio, Santo *o.f.m.conv.* '91 (BRK) [61] Brooklyn, NY Most Holy Trinity Church.
Crider, Robert E. '53 (KC) Plattsburg, MO St. Ann's Church.
Crifasi, Peter D. '49 (BR) Baton Rouge, LA Nursing Homes not under Catholic auspices.
Crilly, James *c.s.v.* '56 (LAV) [1] Las Vegas, NV Guardian Angel Cathedral.
Crilly, Marc *o.s.b.* '93 (WOR) [N] Still River, MA Benedictine Monks, St. Benedict Abbey.
Crilly, Patrick *o.s.a.* '50 (ORG) Buena Park, CA St. Pius V Church.
Crimmins, Michael C. '70 (NY) [68] New York, NY St. Malachy's Church; [D] New York, NY Department of Education; [CC] New York, NY University Apostolate.
Crimmins, Thomas *o.f.m.conv.* (ALB) [A] Rensselaer, NY Conventual Franciscan Friars.
Crino, Patrick M. '88 (TUC) [20] Tucson, AZ Saints Peter and Paul Church.
Criqui, Kenneth '63 (KC) Carrollton, MO St. Mary's Church.
Criscitelli, Anthony *t.o.r.* '80 (STP) Brooklyn Park, MN St. Gerard Church.
Criscuolo, Salvatore A. '78 (WDC) Fort Washington, MD St. Ignatius Church; Special Ministries.
Crisologo, Aurelio P. '59 (SD) San Marcos, CA St. Mark Church.
Crisostomo, Michael C. '96 (AGN) Yigo, GU Our Lady of Lourdes Church.
Crisp, Robert '75 (DAL) [P] Dallas, TX Commission on Ecumenism.
Crisp, Robert R. '75 (DAL) [1] Garland, TX Good Shepherd Church.
Crispo, John R. '50 (BO) Burlington, MA St. Margaret Church.
Crispo, Roderick A. *o.f.m.* '55 (BRK) [106] Brooklyn, NY Our Lady of Peace Church.
Cristancho, Francisco '85 (ARL) [2] Alexandria, VA Good Shepherd Church.
Cristobal, Adrian F. '89 (AGN) Barrigada, GU San Vicente Ferrer Church.
Cristobal, Adrian L.F. '89 (AGN) [A] Agana, GU Father Duenas Minor Seminary.
Cristobal, Daniel *o.f.m.cap.* '59 (AGN) Chalan Pago, GU Nuestra Senora de la Paz y Buen Viaje Church; [H] Agana, GU Secular Franciscans.
Critchlow, Donald E. '82 (CC) [16] Laredo, TX St. Peter the Apostle Church.
Crivello, Peter '93 (MRY) Santa Cruz, CA Holy Cross Church.
Crkva, Odilo *o.s.b.* '53 (JOL) [A] Lisle, IL Benedictine University; [J] Lisle, IL St. Procopius Abbey.
Croak, David P. '66 (DEN) [4] Aurora, CO St. Therese Church.
Croak, Thomas *c.m.* '65 (CHI) [N] Chicago, IL Vincentian Community, Congregation of the Mission, Midwest Province.

Croal, James '96 (ORG) La Habra, CA Our Lady of Guadalupe Church.
Croal, Thomas '58 (ORG) Absent on Sick Leave.
Croce, Albert J. *c.s.c.* '50 (FR) [B] North Easton, MA Holy Cross Fathers Religious.
Croce, Angelus '58 (PAT) Newton, NJ St. Joseph's Church.
Crocenzi, George *c.s.sp.* '49 (CIN) [16] Dayton, OH St. James Church.
Crochet, Barry F. '93 (LAF) Kaplan, LA Our Lady of the Holy Rosary Church.
Crofut, Robert J. '72 (BGP) Huntington, CT St. Lawrence Church.
Croghan, James P. *s.j.* '85 (MI) Ebeye, MH Queen of Peace Church.
Croghan, John P. (SY) Special Assignment.
Croghan, John P. '75 (SY) Clinton, NY St. Mary Church; [V] Clinton, NY Hamilton College Newman Center.
Croghan, Joseph F. *m.m.* '62 (NY) [Z] Maryknoll, NY Maryknoll Fathers and Brothers.
Croglio, James (BUF) [D] Buffalo, NY St. Joseph's Collegiate Institute.
Croisetiere, David N. '77 (SD) [24] San Diego, CA St. Charles Borromeo Church.
Croke, Alfred M. '63 (NY) Livingston Manor, NY St. Aloysius Church.
Crombie, Francis H. '68 (SPR) [19] Springfield, MA St. Paul Church.
Cron, Steven D. '78 (GR) [11] Grand Rapids, MI St. James Church.
Cron, Walter '59 (NEW) [O] Englewood Cliffs, NJ St. Michael Villa.
Cronauer, David W. '73 (ALT) Cresson, PA St. Francis Xavier Church.
Cronauer, Patrick T. *o.s.b.* '84 (GBG) [H] Latrobe, PA Saint Vincent Archabbey.
Crone, Patrick H. '71 (CIN) Bethel, OH St. Mary Church; Felicity, OH Our Mother of Good Counsel Church.
Cronin, Blaise *o.f.m.* '44 (PHX) [19] Phoenix, AZ St. Mary's Basilica; [A] Phoenix, AZ St. Mary's High School.
Cronin, Boniface D. *o.s.b.* '40 (PAT) [M] Newton, NJ St. Paul's Abbey.
Cronin, Brian '74 (ALB) Unassigned.
Cronin, Daniel C. '55 (NOR) Columbia, CT St. Columba Church.
Cronin, Daniel F. '46 (BO) Westford, MA St. Catherine Church.
Cronin, Daniel V. '53 (PMB) Lake Worth, FL St. Luke Church.
Cronin, David '48 (VEN) Retired.
Cronin, Edward '25 (SB) Retired.
Cronin, Edward J. *o.m.i.* '54 (SAT) [K] San Antonio, TX Oblate Madonna Residence; [T] San Antonio, TX Oblate Missions.
Cronin, Edward J. '80 (CHI) [A] Mundelein, IL University of St. Mary of the Lake-Mundelein Seminary.
Cronin, Msgr. Edward T. '50 (SB) [8] Riverside, CA St. John the Evangelist Church.
Cronin, Frank C. '58 (STU) On Duty Outside the Diocese.
Cronin, Harry *c.s.c.* '62 (LA) Venice, CA St. Mark Church.
Cronin, James (SFE) [C] Santa Fe, NM College of Santa Fe.
Cronin, James *o.s.b.* '54 (ROC) [I] Pine City, NY Mount Saviour Monastery.
Cronin, James D. '76 (JUN) Retired.
Cronin, James E. '47 (SPR) Retired.
Cronin, Msgr. James J. '45 (BAL) [41] Baltimore, MD St. Isaac Jogues Church; Aberdeen, MD St. Joan of Arc Church; Retired.
Cronin, James J. '62 (HRT) [4] Milford, CT St. Mary's Church.
Cronin, John F. '47 (BRK) Retired; [U] Douglaston, NY Bishop Mugavero Residence.
Cronin, John P. '57 (FR) [K] Fall River, MA St. John Vianney House.
Cronin, Kean D. '63 (DET) [4] Livonia, MI St. Genevieve Church.
Cronin, Kevin *o.f.m.* '74 (NEW) [N] Hohokus, NJ St. Anthony of Padua.
Cronin, Michael J. '95 (WIN) [7] Rochester, MN St. Pius X Church.
Cronin, Patrick '67 (SAT) [21] San Antonio, TX Prince of Peace Church.
Cronin, Msgr. Paul T. '56 (BUF) Retired; [O] Buffalo, NY Sheehan Residence for Priests.
Cronin, Peadar *ss.cc.* '72 (LA) [D] La Verne, CA Damien Boys High School; [R] La Verne, CA Congregation of the Sacred Hearts.
Cronin, Peter C. '81 (WDC) [8] Silver Spring, MD St. Michael Church.
Cronin, Peter F. '50 (PH) [3] Drexel Hill, PA St. Charles Borromeo Church.
Cronin, Peter J. *s.s.c.* (BUF) [5] West Seneca, NY Queen of Heaven Church.
Cronin, Richard '60 (JC) Loose Creek, MO Immaculate Conception Church.
Cronin, Richard J. *o.s.b.* '66 (PAT) [M] Morristown, NJ St. Mary's Abbey.
Cronin, Robert *s.o.l.t.* '83 (CC) [H] Robstown, TX Society of Our Lady of the Most Holy Trinity.
Cronin, Robert J. *s.o.l.t.* (FAR) Turtle Mountain Reservation, ND (Chippewa Indians) Church; Turtle Mountain Reservation, ND (Chippewa Indians) Church.
Cronin, Robert J. *s.o.l.t.* '83 (FAR) Belcourt, ND St. Ann Church.
Cronin, Sean '73 (LA) Lomita, CA St. Margaret Mary Alacoque Church; [C] Rancho Palos Verdes, CA Marymount College, Palos Verdes, California; [BB] Los Angeles, CA Archdiocesan Office for Campus Ministry.
Cronin, Sylvester J. '88 (MET) Highland Park, NJ St. Paul the Apostle Church.
Cronin, Terence *o.f.m.* '30 (SFR) [7] San Francisco, CA St. Boniface Church.
Cronin, Thomas '69 (KC) Blue Springs, MO St. Robert Bellarmine Church; On Duty Outside the Diocese.
Cronin, Thomas J. *s.j.* '53 (BR) [J] Convent, LA Manresa, House of Retreats.
Cronin, Timothy F. *s.j.* '62 (SPK) [C] Spokane, WA Gonzaga University.
Cronin, Timothy P. '85 (STL) Cottleville, MO St. Joseph Church.
Cronin, Tom '69 (RNO) [6] Reno, NV St. Therese Church of the Little Flower.
Cronin, Vincent I. '57 (ALN) Palmerton, PA Sacred Heart Church.
Cronin, W. Vincent '43 (HRT) Retired.
Cronin, William *o.s.cam.* '76 (MIL) [N] Wauwatosa, WI San Camillo, Inc.
Cronin, William F. *o.s.cam.* (WOR) [R] Whitinsville, MA St. Camillus Institute, Inc.
Cronin, William F. *o.s.cam.* '76 (MIL) [N] Wauwatosa, WI St. Camillus Health Center, Inc.; [P] Wauwatosa, WI St. Camillus Provincialate; [Y] Wauwatosa, WI St. Camillus Institute, Inc.; [Y] Wauwatosa, WI St. Camillus Communities, Inc.; [Y] Wauwatosa, WI St. Camillus Ministries, Inc.
Cronk, James F. '69 (DET) Novi, MI St. James Church.
Cronkleton, Thomas E., Jr. '86 (CHY) Pine Bluffs, WY St. Paul's Church.
Cronogue, Michael P. *s.s.e.* '77 (BUR) [A] Colchester, VT St. Michael's College; [G] Colchester, VT Society of St. Edmund.
Crook, David G. '81 (BEL) Leave of Absence.
Crooker, Robert W. *c.s.b.* '53 (GAL) [Q] Houston, TX Residence of the Basilian Fathers of the University of St. Thomas.
Crookes, Brian '53 (VIC) St. John, TX St. John the Baptist Church.
Crookston, James F. '71 (ALT) Lock Haven, PA Immaculate Conception Church.
Crookston, Michael J. '80 (GBG) North Huntingdon, PA St. Elizabeth Ann Seton Church.
Crosby, Msgr. Charles E. '56 (MAN) [1] Manchester, NH St. Joseph Cathedral.
Crosby, Daniel *o.f.m.cap.* '64 (GF) Lame Deer, MT Blessed Sacrament Church.
Crosby, Donald *s.j.* '68 (OAK) [1] Concord, CA St. Agnes Church.
Crosby, Donald F. *s.j.* '68 (OAK) [N] Berkeley, CA Jesuit Community at Jesuit School of Theology at Berkeley.
Crosby, Donald W. (JC) Absent on Leave.
Crosby, John M. '52 (CHI) Palos Heights, IL St. Alexander Church.
Crosby, Michael *o.f.m.* '64 (STL) [P] St. Louis, MO Franciscan Friary of St. Anthony of Padua; [T] Dittmer, MO Il Ritiro-The Little Retreat.
Crosby, Michael *o.f.m.cap.* '66 (MIL) [11] Milwaukee, WI St. Benedict the Moor Church.
Crosby, Neil A. '81 (CLV) Wadsworth, OH Sacred Heart Church.
Crosby, Vincent de Paul *o.s.b.* '72 (GBG) [H] Latrobe, PA Saint Vincent Archabbey.
Crosier, Raymond '75 (AMA) Groom, TX Immaculate Heart of Mary Church.
Cross, Charles V. '60 (BIR) [5] Birmingham, AL Blessed Sacrament Church.
Cross, Msgr. Michael L. '62 (MRY) Felton, CA St. John Church.
Cross, Peter '60 (DAV) Retired.
Cross, Robert A. '52 (CHI) Retired.
Cross, Vern F. '31 (DUB) Retired.
Cross, William D. '85 (STU) Wintersville, OH Blessed Sacrament Church; Wintersville, OH Our Lady of Lourdes Church.
Cross, William H. '74 (CIN) [47] Cincinnati, OH St. John Vianney Church.
Crossan, Seamus S. '83 (PHX) Williams, AZ St. Joseph's Church.
Crosse, Charles '53 (SEA) Retired.
Crosser, Raymond G. (ALT) Retired.
Crossin, John *o.s.f.s.* '76 (WDC) [B] Washington, DC Cluster of Independent Theological School, The.
Crossin, John W. *o.s.f.s.* '76 (WDC) [B] Washington, DC DeSales School of Theology; [B] Washington, DC Deshairs Community-Oblates of St. Francis de Sales Residence.
Crossman, James (DUL) [1] Duluth, MN Cathedral of Our Lady of the Rosary.
Crossmeyer, Robert *c.p.* '88 (BIR) [7] Birmingham, AL Holy Family Church.
Crosthwait, Msgr. Joseph H. (GAL) Retired.
Croston, John *c.s.c.* '62 (PHX) [F] Phoenix, AZ Holy Cross Congregation of Casa Santa Cruz.
Croteau, Fernand A. '57 (MAN) Hooksett, NH Holy Rosary Church.
Croteau, Francois A. '42 (HRT) Retired.
Croteau, Roger H. '67 (MAN) Absent on Leave.
Crotti, Msgr. William A. '25 (SCR) Retired; [N] Dunmore, PA Villa St. Joseph.
Crotty, Columban *ss.cc.* '58 (FR) [K] Fairhaven, MA Sacred Hearts Provincial House.
Crotty, Desmond G. '72 (NO) [32] New Orleans, LA St. Francis Of Assisi Church.
Crotty, John C. *s.s.j.* '55 (BAL) [81] Baltimore, MD St. Pius V Church.
Crotty, John M. '47 (NY) Retired.
Crotty, Msgr. Matthew M. '44 (BAK) Special Assignment.
Crotty, Thomas M. *o.s.m.* '60 (CHI) [N] Chicago, IL Servite Friars - Eastern Province.
Crotty, Vincent *c.ss.r.* '49 (RVC) Bethpage, NY St. Martin of Tours Church.
Crouse, Thomas *o.s.b.* '82 (IND) [B] St. Meinrad, IN St. Meinrad Seminary-College of Liberal Arts; [J] St. Meinrad, IN St. Meinrad Archabbey.
Crouse, William S. '59 (ALT) Penns Valley, PA Blessed Kateri Tekakwitha Church; Bellefonte, PA State Correctional Institution.
Crowe, Francis R. *o.p.* '47 (AMA) [9] Amarillo, TX St. Martin De Porres Mission Church.
Crowe, Francis R. *o.p.* '47 (CHI) [N] Chicago, IL Dominicans (Provincial Office).
Crowe, George W. '65 (PH) [121] Philadelphia, PA Our Lady of Lourdes Church.
Crowe, Hugh '58 (LA) [43] Los Angeles, CA St. Ann Church.
Crowe, Martin *c.ss.r.* '40 (BRK) [107] Brooklyn, NY Our Lady of Perpetual Help Basilica.
Crowe, Raymond *o.m.i.* '54 (MIA) [2] Miami, FL Christ the King Church.
Crowe, Msgr. William A. '47 (PT) Panama City, FL St. Dominic Church.
Crowley, Alan N. *o.carm.* '41 (BO) [P] Peabody, MA Catholic Information Center; [BB] Peabody, MA St. Theresa Carmelite Chapel.
Crowley, Bonaventure '47 (LAN) [3] Lansing, MI Holy Cross Church.
Crowley, Cale J. *s.s.* '69 (BAL) [M] Baltimore, MD Sulpician Provincial House.
Crowley, Charles '77 (TOL) Retired.
Crowley, Charles G. *s.j.* '51 (BO) [W] Boston, MA Loyola House.
Crowley, Charles J. '53 (KAL) Retired.
Crowley, Daniel B. *o.p.* '51 (NEW) [27] Jersey City, NJ Sacred Heart Church.
Crowley, Daniel J. '68 (BO) [9] Quincy, MA Star of the Sea Church.
Crowley, Dennis '89 (PAT) [5] Wayne, NJ Our Lady of the Valley Church.
Crowley, Edmund G. '70 (MAN) Military Chaplains.
Crowley, Edward T. *c.s.sp.* '50 (LR) Conway, AR St. Joseph's Church.
Crowley, Francis *c.m.* '57 (KC) [J] Kansas City, MO Vincentian Parish Mission Center.
Crowley, Francis J. '53 (BO) Military & VA Chaplains.
Crowley, Francis J. '53 (PRO) Providence, RI Veterans Administration Hospital.
Crowley, J. David '54 (PIT) [49] Pittsburgh, PA Holy Angels Church.
Crowley, James M. *o.m.i.* '87 (CHR) Joanna, SC St. Boniface Church; Newberry, SC St. Mark Church; [H] Clinton, SC Presbyterian College Newman Center; [H] Newberry, SC Newberry College Newman Center.
Crowley, John A. '61 (PMB) Vero Beach, FL St. John of the Cross Church.
Crowley, John D. '70 (BO) [9] Cambridge, MA St. Mary of the Annunciation Church.
Crowley, Kenan *o.f.m.cap.* '44 (PIT) [29] Pittsburgh, PA Our Lady of the Angels Church; Allegheny County, PA Kane Regional Center - McKeesport.
Crowley, Kevin J. '64 (BO) Medfield, MA St. Edward the Confessor Church.
Crowley, Patrick J. *ss.cc.* '72 (OAK) [3] Alameda, CA St. Joseph Basilica.
Crowley, Paul *s.j.* '92 (BO) [W] Chestnut Hill, MA The Jesuit Community at Boston College.
Crowley, Paul G. *s.j.* '58 (SJ) [B] Santa Clara, CA Santa Clara University.
Crowley, R. Kevin '68 (MET) Edison, NJ Guardian Angels Church.
Crowley, Richard P. '64 (BO) Braintree, MA St. Francis of Assisi Church.
Crowley, Stephen L. '55 (HRT) Retired.
Crowley, Thomas F. '56 (LC) Cadott, WI St. Rose of Lima Church; Drywood, WI St. Anthony Church.

Crowley, Thomas F. '76 (WDC) Greenbelt, MD St. Hugh Church.
Crowley, Thomas G. '87 (DM) Defiance, IA St. Peter Church; Westphalia, IA St. Boniface Church.
Crowley, Timothy '76 (ANC) [6] Anchorage, AK Our Lady of Guadalupe Church.
Crowley, Timothy '76 (LAN) On Duty Outside the Diocese.
Crowley, William *c.s.sp.* '50 (PIT) [B] Pittsburgh, PA Duquesne University of the Holy Ghost.
Crowley, William C. '74 (B) Lewiston, ID St. James Church.
Crowley, William P. *c.s.sp.* '60 (SFR) [8] San Francisco, CA St. Brendan Church.
Crum, Thomas '75 (Y) Absent on Leave.
Crum, William '76 (NEW) [1] Elizabeth, NJ St. Mary of the Assumption Church.
Crumbley, Charles W. '67 (Y) [4] Warren, OH St. James Church.
Crumley, William *c.s.c.* '64 (LAF) Charenton, LA Immaculate Conception Church.
Crumlish, John C. '58 (OAK) Castro Valley, CA Transfiguration Church.
Crumlish, Msgr. Richard C. '45 (BUF) [63] Buffalo, NY St. Teresa Church; Retired.
Crummy, Michael E. '86 (MET) Milford, NJ St. Edward the Confessor Church.
Crunican, James '63 (P) Grand Ronde, OR St. Michael Church; Sheridan, OR Good Shepherd Church.
Crupi, Msgr. Francis J. '52 (MET) [7] New Brunswick, NJ St. Mary of Mount Virgin Church.
Cruz, Carlos Dionisio '80 (SJN) [14] San Juan, PR Nuestra Senora de la Esperanza Church.
Cruz, David '86 (LUB) On Duty Outside the Diocese.
Cruz, David R. '86 (SAT) [A] San Antonio, TX The Assumption-St. John's Seminary.
Cruz, Domingo '73 (HT) Kraemer, LA St. Lawrence the Martyr Church.
Cruz, Faustino *s.m.* '88 (BO) [W] Boston, MA Marist Fathers and Brothers Provincial House.
Cruz, Gilbert J. '81 (LA) [17] Los Angeles, CA Mother of Sorrows Church; [81] Los Angeles, CA St. Michael Church.
Cruz, Gilbert J. '81 (SJN) Retired.
Cruz, Gustavo '74 (LAV) Overton, NV St. John, the Evangelist Church.
Cruz, Gustavo '74 (LSC) Special Assignment.
Cruz, Hector J. *s.m.* '77 (ELP) [39] El Paso, TX Santa Lucia Church.
Cruz, Luciano (PAT) [2] Paterson, NJ St. Agnes Church.
Cruz, Manuel '80 (NEW) [1] Newark, NJ Cathedral of the Sacred Heart Basilica; Newark, NJ St. Michael Medical Center.
Cruz, Michael *o.f.m.cap.* (AGN) [F] Agana Heights, GU St. Fidelis Friary.
Cruz, Msgr. Remberto '50 (SJN) Retired.
Cruz, Renato B. '81 (NY) [204] Staten Island, NY Holy Child Church.
Cruz, Robert-Joel '96 (HT) [5] Houma, LA St. Bernadette Church.
Cruz, Tito *s.m.* (BO) [59] Boston, MA Our Lady of Victories Church.
Cryan, James F. *o.s.f.s.* '65 (TOL) [K] Toledo, OH Oblates of St. Francis de Sales.
Cryan, John J. '81 (NEW) [20] Jersey City, NJ Our Lady of Mercy Church.
Cryans, Andrew W. '75 (MAN) Milford, NH St. Patrick Church.
Crynes, J. Peter '67 (SCR) Shavertown, PA St. Therese Church.
Cser, Ladislaus *s.j.* '45 (RVC) St. James, NY SS. Philip and James Church; Retired.
Csete, Ivan '81 (NY) Military Chaplains.
Csizmar, Richard A. '68 (BUF) Albion, NY St. Mary Assumption Church; Albion, NY St. Joseph Church.
Csizmazia, Placid *o.cist.* '40 (DAL) [B] Irving, TX University of Dallas; [M] Irving, TX Cistercian Abbey of Our Lady of Dallas.
Csorba, Dominic *o.f.m.* '62 (NY) [115] New York, NY St. Stephen of Hungary Church.
Csorba, Dominic L. *o.f.m.* (NY) [DD] New York, NY Hungarian Catholic League of America, Inc.
Cuadrado, Angel *o.de.m.* '86 (CGS) Cayey, PR Nuestra Senora de la Merced Church.
Cuadros, Jesus '66 (BRK) [157] Queens, NY Blessed Sacrament Church.
Cubells, Joseph *s.f.* '26 (WDC) [B] Silver Spring, MD Holy Family Seminary.
Cuccaro, John '79 (PBR) Homer City, PA Holy Protection of Mary, The Mother of God Church.
Cuccia, Salvatore H. *o.praem.* '66 (BAL) [74] Baltimore, MD Our Lady, Queen of Peace Church.
Cuccia, Salvatore H. *o.praem.* '66 (PH) [Z] Paoli, PA Daylesford Abbey.
Cuddigan, John D. *s.j.* '62 (SD) Lemon Grove, CA St. John of the Cross Church.
Cuddihy, Msgr. William '56 (SD) [22] San Diego, CA St. Catherine Laboure Church.
Cuddy, John '53 (SAV) Macon, GA St. Joseph's Church.
Cuddy, William F., Jr. '79 (BO) Military & VA Chaplains.
Cude, Stephen D. '69 (OKL) Elk City, OK St. Matthew's Church.
Cudemo, Nicholas V. '63 (PH) Retired.
Cudinach, Salvadore *sch.p.* '53 (LA) [92] Los Angeles, CA Santa Teresita Church.
Cudnik, Chester C. '48 (CLV) [10] Cleveland, OH St. Barbara Church.
Cuenin, Walter H. (BO) [4] Newton, MA St. John the Evangelist Church.
Cuenin, Walter H. '70 (BO) [6] Newton, MA Our Lady Help of Christians Church.
Cuesta, Benedicto '51 (SFE) Retired.
Cuevas, Geronimo '86 (MRY) [3] Salinas, CA St. Mary of the Nativity Church.
Cuevas, Randy M. '82 (BR) Donaldsonville, LA Ascension of Our Lord Jesus Christ Church.
Cuevas, Wilson '81 (ELP) [1] El Paso, TX St. Patrick's Cathedral; [6] El Paso, TX Corpus Christi Church; El Paso, TX El Paso County Jail.
Cuff, Thomas E. '83 (SPR) [1] Northampton, MA Annunciation Church; Absent on Leave.
Cugnidoro, Angelo *c.s.* '63 (CIN) [80] Cincinnati, OH Sacred Heart Church.
Culhane, Alberic *o.s.b.* '57 (SCL) [B] Collegeville, MN St. John's University; [I] Collegeville, MN St. John's Abbey, of the Order of St. Benedict.
Culhane, Eugene J. *s.j.* '45 (NEW) [B] Jersey City, NJ Saint Peter's College.
Culhane, Eugene K. *s.j.* '45 (NEW) [N] Jersey City, NJ Jesuits of Saint Peter's College, Inc.
Culhane, Thomas '47 (KCK) Prairie Village, KS St. Ann's Church.
Culkin, Msgr. Francis J. '44 (SY) Lee Center, NY St. Joseph Church; Retired.
Culkin, Harry M. '42 (BRK) [U] Douglaston, NY Bishop Mugavero Residence.
Culkin, J. Stewart '71 (ARL) Vienna, VA St. Mark's Church.
Culkin, Michael '78 (WDC) On Duty Outside the Archdiocese.
Cull, Lawrence W. '69 (NEW) Cranford, NJ St. Michael's Church.
Cull, Paul J. '45 (CHI) [3] Waukegan, IL St. Dismas Church; Retired.
Cullen, Bernard J. *o.c.s.o.* '48 (DUB) [K] Peosta, IA New Melleray Abbey, Order of Cistercians of the Strict Observance.
Cullen, Christopher M. *s.j.* '94 (WDC) [M] Washington, DC Carroll House.
Cullen, Daniel *s.m.a.* '47 (NEW) [N] Tenafly, NJ Society of African Missions, Provincialate, S.M.A. Fathers.
Cullen, Donald '71 (KCK) Roeland Park, KS St. Agnes Church.
Cullen, Msgr. Edward P. '62 (PH) [M] Rosemont, PA St. Edmond's Home for Children.
Cullen, Francis J. '54 (LA) [73] Los Angeles, CA St. Kevin Church; Sick Leave.
Cullen, George H. '48 (CHI) Retired.
Cullen, Msgr. J. Peter '67 (BGP) New Canaan, CT St. Aloysius Church.
Cullen, John F. '41 (PH) Wyndmoor, PA Seven Dolors Church; Retired.
Cullen, Martin T. '57 (FAR) Retired.
Cullen, Michael D. (SUP) Chelsea, WI Assumption of the Blessed Virgin Mary Church.
Cullen, Patrick *s.p.s.* '52 (PAT) [2] Clifton, NJ St. Andrew the Apostle Church.
Cullen, Patrick P. '68 (BIR) [1] Birmingham, AL St. Paul's Cathedral.
Cullen, Paul M. *o.s.m.* '65 (CHI) [18] Chicago, IL Assumption of the Blessed Virgin Mary Church; [N] Chicago, IL Servite Friars - Eastern Province.
Cullen, Robert B. *s.j.* '58 (BAL) [D] Baltimore, MD Loyola High School.
Cullen, Robert B. *s.j.* '58 (PIT) [R] Pittsburgh, PA Jesuit Community of Pittsburgh.
Cullen, Sean '62 (CHI) [N] Chicago, IL St. Patrick's Missionary Society.
Cullen, Thomas F. '53 (CLV) Westlake, OH St. Ladislas Church; Retired.
Cullen, Msgr. Thomas J. '52 (GAL) Texas City, TX St. Mary Church.
Cullen, Msgr. Thomas J. '52 (MOB) On Leave from the Archdiocese.
Cullen, William '48 (JOL) Retired.
Cullen, William '83 (JKS) Pearl, MS St. Jude Church.
Cullen, William J. *s.j.* '65 (BO) [H] Boston, MA Nativity Preparatory School; [W] Boston, MA Loyola House.
Culleton, James P. '46 (PEO) Retired.
Culleton, Thomas L. '91 (SLC) Roosevelt, UT St. Helen's Church.
Culley, Brian *c.m.f.* '84 (AUS) San Marcos, TX St. John the Evangelist Church; Uhland, TX St. Michael's Church.
Culley, Brian *c.m.f.* '84 (LA) San Gabriel, CA San Gabriel Church; [R] San Gabriel, CA Claretian Missionaries (Missionary Sons of the Immaculate Heart of Mary).
Culley, Thomas *s.j.* (BO) Concord, MA St. Bernard Church.
Culligan, Kevin *o.c.d.* (CHI) [N] Chicago, IL Edith Stein House of Studies.
Culligan, Kevin *o.c.d.* (WH) [N] Hinton, WV Monastery of Christ on the Mountain.
Culligan, Martin J. *c.m.* '57 (CHI) [C] Chicago, IL Vincentian Community at DePaul University.
Culligan, Michael A. '59 (SR) Petaluma, CA St. James Church.
Cullinan, John '46 (PHX) [14] Phoenix, AZ St. Joan of Arc Church.
Cullinan, John F. '46 (PHX) Retired.
Cullinane, Brian P. *o.f.m.* '71 (NEW) Elmwood Park, NJ St. Leo's Church.
Cullinane, Jeremiah J. (DAL) [O] Irving, TX Diocese of Dallas Campus Ministry.
Cullinane, Jeremiah J. '59 (FTW) [B] Fort Wayne, IN Saint Francis College of Fort Wayne, Inc.
Cullinane, Jeremiah J. '59 (WH) On Duty Outside the Diocese.
Cullinane, John '56 (BRK) [171] Queens, NY St. Genevieve Church.
Cullinen, James L. '87 (CHI) Oak Forest, IL St. Damian Church.
Cullings, David Ronald '67 (P) [5] Eugene, OR St. Peter Church.
Culliton, Leo J. '50 (VEN) Lake Placid, FL St. James Church.
Culloty, John P. '72 (BO) [16] Boston, MA St. Brigid Church.
Culnane, William R. '60 (SCR) [5] Wilkes-Barre, PA St. Dominic Church.
Culotta, Joachim *o.p.* '64 (MEM) [23] Memphis, TN St. Peter's Church; [J] Memphis, TN Order Of Preachers (Southern Dominican Prov.).
Culotta, Joseph '83 (BIR) Decatur, AL St. Ann's Church; [I] Decatur, AL St. Ann's Educational Foundation.
Culotta, Salvador J. '53 (BEA) [8] Beaumont, TX St. Pius X Church.
Culotta, Thomas C. '61 (HRT) East Berlin, CT Sacred Heart Church.
Culver, Garry (DM) On Special Assignment.
Culver, James A. '55 (SY) [4] Rome, NY St. Peter Church.
Culver, Richard '85 (OAK) Pittsburg, CA Our Lady Queen of the World Church.
Culver, Msgr. T. Joseph '63 (GAL) La Marque, TX Our Lady Queen of Peace Church.
Cumberland, Matthew T. '92 (LA) South El Monte, CA Epiphany Church.
Cumella, Anthony N. '66 (ALX) Retired.
Cumiskey, Thomas M. *o.p.* '55 (DAL) [M] Irving, TX Dominican Priory of St. Albert the Great.
Cummings, Brian J. *s.s.e.* '96 (BUR) [G] Colchester, VT Society of St. Edmund.
Cummings, Carl '75 (BAL) Military Chaplains.
Cummings, Charles *o.c.s.o.* '71 (SLC) [F] Huntsville, UT Abbey of Our Lady of the Holy Trinity of the Order of Cistercians.
Cummings, Charles J. '68 (SCR) Lords Valley, PA St. John Neumann Church.
Cummings, Frederick F. '41 (SY) Retired.
Cummings, Gabriel '84 (SAV) [5] Savannah, GA Most Pure Heart of Mary Church.
Cummings, Msgr. George '43 (SP) Citrus Springs, FL St. Elizabeth Ann Seton Church; Retired.
Cummings, James '61 (OAK) [6] Fremont, CA Santa Paula Church.
Cummings, James M. *s.m.* '43 (ATL) [C] Atlanta, GA Marist School.
Cummings, Jerome '64 (LA) La Canada Flintridge, CA St. Bede the Venerable Church; [F] La Canada Flintridge, CA St. Francis High School.
Cummings, John J. '88 (LFT) Leave of Absence.
Cummings, Jose *c.m.* '77 (PCE) [14] Ponce, PR San Vicente-Cantera Church.
Cummings, Leo B. *m.s.* '66 (ATL) Calhoun, GA St. Clements Church.
Cummings, Leo P. '64 (SCR) [I] Carbondale, PA Marian Community Hospital.
Cummings, Maurice *o.carm.* '71 (SPR) [K] Williamstown, MA Mount Carmel Retreat Center.
Cummings, Patrick John '78 (GAL) [72] Houston, TX St. Rose of Lima Church.
Cummings, Paul '55 (LAN) Retired.
Cummings, Thomas W. *s.j.* '69 (DEN) [M] Denver, CO Regis Jesuit Community (The Jesuits at Regis University).
Cummins, Anthony O. '65 (SAT) Boerne, TX St. Peter the Apostle Church.
Cummins, Charles '94 (SLC) [B] Ogden, UT St. Joseph Catholic High School.
Cummins, Charles E. '68 (SLC) [3] Ogden, UT St. Joseph's Church; [C] Ogden, UT St. Joseph Regional School.
Cummins, Charles T. '68 (LA) On Duty Outside the Archdiocese.
Cummins, Charles T. '68 (SLC) [H] Ogden, UT Weber State University, Newman Center.

Cummins, Michael E. '95 (KNX) [2] Knoxville, TN All Saints Catholic Church.
Cummins, Michael J. *c.m.* '77 (BRK) [D] Queens and Staten Island, NY St. John's University.
Cummins, Michael J. *c.m.* '77 (NY) [CC] New York, NY University Apostolate.
Cummins, Robert L. '86 (RIC) [12] Virginia Beach, VA Star of the Sea Church.
Cummins, Timothy '45 (FRS) Retired.
Cuneo, James J. '63 (DEN) Arvada, CO Spirit of Christ Parish Church.
Cuneo, Msgr. James J. '67 (BGP) [1] Stratford, CT Holy Name of Jesus Church.
Cung, Ephrem Vu Khiem *c.m.c.* (BO) [62] Boston, MA St. Peter Church.
Cunha, Domingos da '71 (PRO) [25] Providence, RI Our Lady of the Rosary Church.
Cunha, Eginor '92 (NEW) Kearny, NJ St. Cecilia's Church.
Cunnane, Michael A. '61 (SD) Santee, CA Guardian Angels Church.
Cunneen, Sean Raymond '67 (NEW) [4] Elizabeth, NJ Blessed Sacrament Church.
Cunney, Henry M. '59 (BO) Merrimac, MA Nativity Church.
Cunniff, Charles E. *c.s.p.* '83 (BO) [P] Boston, MA Paulist Center; [W] Boston, MA Paulist Fathers Residence; [CC] Boston, MA Newman House Catholic Center at Boston University.
Cunniff, Declan J. '68 (NEW) [B] South Orange, NJ Seton Hall University; [N] Newark, NJ Newark Abbey.
Cunniff, Hubert F. *s.j.* '38 (BO) [W] Weston, MA Campion Health Center, Inc.
Cunniff, Vincent '53 (P) Retired.
Cunniffe, James A. *s.c.j.* '57 (JKS) Hernando, MS Holy Spirit Church; Senatobia, MS St. Gregory the Great Church; [E] Nesbit, MS St. Michael Community House; [G] Senatobia, MS Northwest Mississippi Community College Newman Center.
Cunningham, Ambrose '50 (PEO) [2] Rock Island, IL Sacred Heart Church.
Cunningham, Augustine W. *o.s.b.* '61 (RIC) [M] Richmond, VA Mary Mother of the Church Abbey.
Cunningham, Christopher '90 (LA) Palmdale, CA St. Mary Church.
Cunningham, Don *s.j.* '64 (JOL) Winfield, IL St. John the Baptist Church.
Cunningham, Douglas '87 (SY) Norwich, NY St. Paul Church.
Cunningham, Edward *o.m.i.* '58 (WIN) Minnesota City, MN St. Paul's Church.
Cunningham, Gerard M. '93 (WDC) Military Chaplains.
Cunningham, James *c.s.s.* '50 (BO) Boston, MA Waltham-Weston Hospital & Medical Center; [Z] Waltham, MA Stigmatine Fathers and Brothers.
Cunningham, James '61 (NY) [164] Bronx, NY St. Mary Church.
Cunningham, James B. '87 (BUF) [9] Cheektowaga, NY St. Philip the Apostle Church.
Cunningham, James J. '61 (NY) Bronx, NY Bronx Psychiatric Center.
Cunningham, James K. '95 (BRK) [50] Brooklyn, NY Good Shepherd Church.
Cunningham, John (TLS) Bartlesville, OK St. John's Church.
Cunningham, John '91 (PMB) [1] West Palm Beach, FL Holy Name of Jesus Church.
Cunningham, John E. '51 (DM) Retired.
Cunningham, John F. *o.p.* '53 (PRO) [P] Providence, RI St. Thomas Aquinas Priory at Providence College.
Cunningham, John F. '56 (LA) [70] Los Angeles, CA St. Joan of Arc Church; Retired.
Cunningham, John F. '74 (PHX) [5] Mesa, AZ St. Bridget Church.
Cunningham, John H. '65 (ALX) Jena, LA St. Mary Church.
Cunningham, John J. '56 (CHI) [176] Chicago, IL St. Priscilla Church.
Cunningham, John P. '79 (BAL) [90] Baltimore, MD St. Thomas More Church.
Cunningham, Msgr. Joseph C. '71 (PH) Wayne, PA St. Isaac Jogues Church.
Cunningham, Joseph L. '56 (MIL) [7] West Allis, WI St. Mary, Help of Christians Church.
Cunningham, Joseph L. '63 (BRK) [174] Queens, NY St. Gregory the Great Church.
Cunningham, Kieran P. *o.s.b.* '62 (SEA) [G] Olympia, WA Providence St. Peter Hospital; [M] Lacey, WA St. Martin's Abbey.
Cunningham, Leonard A. *o.c.s.o.* '50 (CHR) [E] Moncks Corner, SC Mepkin Abbey.
Cunningham, Lloyd Thomas *s.v.d.* (LA) [R] Los Angeles, CA Casa Guadalupe.
Cunningham, Michael '86 (OAK) [4] Concord, CA Queen of All Saints Church.
Cunningham, Nicholas J. '79 (TOL) Kelley's Island, OH St. Michael Church; Put-In-Bay, OH Mother of Sorrows Church.
Cunningham, Msgr. Patrick '41 (PT) Retired.
Cunningham, Peter J. '56 (MOB) [16] Mobile, AL Our Lady of Lourdes Church.
Cunningham, Philip *c.s.p.* '56 (SFR) [31] San Francisco, CA Old St. Mary's Cathedral.
Cunningham, Phillip J. *c.s.p.* '56 (NY) [Z] Scarsdale, NY Paulist Fathers Generalate.
Cunningham, Richard G. '57 (BO) [A] Boston, MA St. John's Seminary School of Theology.
Cunningham, Msgr. Robert J. '69 (BUF) [O] Buffalo, NY Bishop's Residence; [T] Buffalo, NY Monsignor Adamski Village Housing Development Fund Company, Inc.; [T] Buffalo, NY Good Counsel Apartments.
Cunningham, Sam *s.v.d.* '81 (LA) [R] Los Angeles, CA Casa Guadalupe.
Cunningham, Sebastian *o.f.m.conv.* '60 (LSC) Carlsbad, NM St. Edward Church.
Cunningham, Vianney *t.o.r.* '70 (ORL) [2] Lakeland, FL St. Anthony's Church; [A] Lakeland, FL Santa Fe Catholic High School; [E] Lakeland, FL Florida Southern College Newman Center.
Cunningham, Vincent P. *s.m.m.* '60 (RVC) West Islip, NY Good Samaritan Hospital; [I] West Islip, NY The Samaritan Corporation; [I] West Islip, NY The Samaritan Corporation; [N] Bay Shore, NY Montfort Missionaries.
Cunningham, W. A. *s.j.* '48 (PH) [Z] Philadelphia, PA Jesuit Community at St. Joseph's University.
Cunningham, William T. '55 (DET) [46] Detroit, MI Madonna Church.
Cunnion, Theodore J. *s.j.* '43 (NY) [Z] New York, NY Murray-Weigel Hall.
Cuny, W. Timothy *o.s.a.* '70 (CHI) [N] Olympia Fields, IL The Augustinian Provincialate Tolentine Center; [N] Olympia Fields, IL Tolentine Monastery at Tolentine Center.
Cuomo, Rocco A. '64 (TR) Bayville, NJ St. Barnabas Church.
Cupich, Msgr. Blase J. '75 (COL) [A] Columbus, OH Pontifical College Josephinum.
Cupich, Msgr. Blase J. '75 (OM) On Duty Outside the Archdiocese.
Cupp, Edwin '69 (WH) Absent on Sick Leave.
Cupple, Gerald J. '85 (DET) Lincoln Park, MI St. Henry Church.
Curalli, Joseph *c.ss.r.* '78 (SEA) [32] Seattle, WA Sacred Heart of Jesus Church.
Curci, Richard G. '72 (GBG) Arnold, PA All Saints Church; New Kensington, PA Mt. St. Peter Church.
Curcio, Ralph V. '61 (NY) [109] New York, NY St. Rose of Lima Church; [1] Port Chester, NY Our Lady of Mercy Church.
Cure, Laverne J. '41 (CHI) Ingleside, IL St. Bede Church.
Curesky, Mark L. *o.f.m.conv.* '75 (BAL) [M] Ellicott City, MD Order of Friars Minor Conventual.
Curiel, James A. *o.c.d.* '99 (SAT) [18] San Antonio, TX Our Lady of Mt. Carmel and St. Therese, Discalced Carmelite Fathers Church.
Curiel, James Anthony *o.c.d.* (SAT) [M] San Antonio, TX Discalced Carmelites (Prov. of St. Therese).
Curley, Augustine J. *o.s.b.* '88 (NEW) [N] Newark, NJ Newark Abbey.
Curley, Frank *o.m.i.* '47 (PMB) [4] West Palm Beach, FL St. John Fisher Church.
Curley, John H. *s.j.* (BO) Dedham, MA St. Mary Church; Boston, MA St. Elizabeth's Medical Center; Absent on Sick Leave.
Curley, Msgr. Joseph K. '62 (RVC) Centereach, NY Assumption of the Blessed Virgin Mary Church.
Curley, Martin W. '56 (RVC) Bayville, NY St. Gertrude's Church.
Curley, Patrick J. '53 (JKS) Retired.
Curley, Patrick J. '70 (JKS) Yazoo City, MS St. Mary Church; Yazoo City, MS St. Francis Church.
Curley, Robert (RVC) Retired.
Curley, Terence P. '72 (BO) Dedham, MA St. Susanna Church.
Curley, Thomas J. '39 (CHI) [206] Chicago, IL St. Thomas More Church; Wauconda, IL Transfiguration Church; Retired.
Curley, Thomas J. '70 (NY) Chester, NY St. Columba Church.
Curnutte, William G. (SLC) Retired.
Curran, Anthony '72 (ALB) [9] Schenectady, NY St. John the Evangelist Church.
Curran, Anthony T. '67 (ATL) Lawrenceville, GA St. Lawrence Church.
Curran, Charles E. '58 (ROC) On Duty Outside the Diocese.
Curran, Francis D. '50 (CLV) Willoughby, OH Immaculate Conception Church.
Curran, Msgr. Francis L. '38 (MAN) Retired.
Curran, Francis T. '69 (GI) Kimball, NE St. Joseph's Church.
Curran, George A. *s.j.* '51 (DET) [P] Clarkston, MI Colombiere Center.
Curran, Gerald X. '48 (Y) Retired.
Curran, Msgr. Hugh D. '54 (NY) Pelham Manor, NY Our Lady of Perpetual Help Church.
Curran, Hugh J. *c.s.b.* '51 (GAL) Missouri City, TX Holy Family Church.
Curran, James *c.m.f.* '83 (CHI) [N] Oak Park, IL Claretian Fathers Headquarters of U.S.A. Eastern Province.
Curran, James B. *s.d.b.* '51 (MIA) [25] Miami, FL St. Kieran Church.
Curran, James P. '63 (CAM) Glassboro, NJ Our Lady of Lourdes Church.
Curran, John *l.c.* '96 (HRT) [V] Orange, CT Legion of Christ, Inc.
Curran, John F. '46 (HRT) [1] West Haven, CT Our Lady of Victory Church; Retired.
Curran, John F. *s.j.* '59 (CI) [C] Tunnuk, Chuuk, FM Vicariate Residence.
Curran, John J. '54 (WCH) Aleppo, KS Immaculate Conception Church; Garden Plain, KS St. Anthony Church.
Curran, John W. '57 (CHI) Homewood, IL St. Joseph Church.
Curran, John W. *o.f.m.conv.* '71 (LSC) Artesia, NM Our Lady of Grace Church.
Curran, Joseph B. '45 (PH) Springfield, PA Holy Cross Church; Retired.
Curran, Joseph F. *s.j.* '56 (BAL) [M] Baltimore, MD Jesuit Fathers and Brothers Maryland Provincial Curia.
Curran, Joseph L. '76 (BO) Watertown, MA Sacred Heart Church.
Curran, Juan *o.m.i.* (SJN) [24] Bayamon, PR Santa Teresa de Avila Church.
Curran, Juan *o.m.i.* '78 (SJN) [7] San Juan, PR Ntr. Sra. de la Caridad del Cobre Church.
Curran, Michael J. '81 (BRK) Released from Diocesan Assignment.
Curran, Michael J. '81 (RVC) [A] Huntington, NY Diocesan Seminary of the Immaculate Conception.
Curran, Oliver '76 (GLP) Pinetop, AZ St. Mary of the Angels Church.
Curran, Patrick J. '55 (HRT) [6] West Hartford, CT St. Thomas the Apostle Church.
Curran, Patrick J. '55 (SLC) On Duty Outside the Diocese.
Curran, Paul F. (BO) Canton, MA St. Gerard Majella Church.
Curran, Msgr. Paul F. '57 (PH) Huntingdon Valley, PA St. Albert the Great Church.
Curran, R. Emmett *s.j.* '68 (WDC) [M] Washington, DC The Jesuit Community at Georgetown University.
Curran, Richard G. (BO) Awaiting Assignment.
Curran, Robert F. *s.j.* '74 (SFR) [C] San Francisco, CA University of San Francisco; [N] San Francisco, CA Jesuit Community at University of San Francisco.
Curran, Thomas B. *o.s.f.s* '84 (PH) [D] Philadelphia, PA Northeast Catholic High School for Boys; [Z] Philadelphia, PA Oblates of St. Francis De Sales.
Curran, Thomas M. (BO) Hudson, MA St. Michael Church.
Curran, William J. '69 (CHI) Berwyn, IL St. Leonard Church.
Currans, Clem '74 (SC) [B] Granville, IA Spalding Catholic High School.
Currans, Clem W. '74 (SC) Granville, IA St. Joseph Church.
Current, Maurice H. '80 (LIN) Beaver Crossing, NE Sacred Heart Church.
Currie, Charles L. *s.j.* '63 (PH) [C] Philadelphia, PA St. Joseph's University; [Z] Philadelphia, PA Jesuit Community at St. Joseph's University.
Currie, Donald '79 (SAT) On Leave.
Currie, Joseph A. *s.j.* '68 (NO) [C] New Orleans, LA Loyola University.
Currier, Thomas F. '50 (DUB) Belmond, IA St. Francis Xavier Church; Retired.
Curry, Edward V. '47 (GBG) Retired; [G] Greensburg, PA Neumann House.
Curry, Frederic F. '49 (TUC) [15] Tucson, AZ St. Joseph Church; Retired.
Curry, James '94 (CHI) Tinley Park, IL Saint Julie Billiart Church.
Curry, James J. *s.j.* '74 (NY) [F] New York, NY Loyola School; [Z] New York, NY St. Ignatius Loyola Residence.
Curry, Joseph M. '86 (MET) [1] New Brunswick, NJ St. Peter Apostle Church.
Curry, Robert *s.j.* '64 (R) [E] Durham, NC Jesuit Community.
Curry, Robert O. *c.ss.r.* '73 (BR) [H] Baton Rouge, LA Redemptorist Fathers Vice Provincialate.
Curry, Robert S. *s.j.* '64 (R) [7] Raleigh, NC St. Raphael Church.
Curry, Terrence M. *s.j.* '94 (DET) [K] Detroit, MI Jesuit Community at the University of Detroit.
Curry, Terrence W. *s.j.* '77 (WDC) [K] Washington, DC Georgetown University Hospital.
Curry, Terrence W. *s.j.* '77 (WOR) [N] Worcester, MA Jesuits of Holy Cross College, Inc.
Curry, Thomas P. '51 (RVC) Retired; [J] Huntington, NY St. Joseph's Guest Home for the Aged, Inc.; [N] Uniondale, NY St. Pius X Residence.
Curso, Manuel '72 (SFR) Daly City, CA Our Lady of Mercy Church.
Curtin, Clifford J. '51 (NOR) Retired.

Curtin, Eugene P. '56 (BO) Lexington, MA St. Brigid Church.
Curtin, Gregory F. *s.j.* '65 (NO) [C] New Orleans, LA Loyola University.
Curtin, James (JOL) Coal City, IL Assumption Church; St. Anne, IL St. Anne Church.
Curtin, James E. '52 (DET) Melvindale, MI St. Mary Magdalen Church.
Curtin, James F. '51 (BO) [7] Quincy, MA Our Lady of Good Counsel Church.
Curtin, L. Michael '61 (WDC) [T] Washington, DC Opus Dei; [V] Washington, DC Catholic Information Center.
Curtin, Martin *o.f.m.cap.* '90 (NY) [83] New York, NY Our Lady Queen of Angels Church.
Curtin, Paul J. *s.j.* '53 (NY) [Z] New York, NY Murray-Weigel Hall.
Curtin, Msgr. Richard B. '42 (NY) Retired.
Curtin, Timothy *s.j.* '52 (BGP) [Q] Bridgeport, CT The Society of Our Lady of the Way.
Curtin, Timothy A. *s.j.* '52 (RVC) [P] Manhasset, NY St. Ignatius Retreat House, Inisfada.
Curtin, Vincent C. *s.j.* '68 (BAL) [M] Baltimore, MD Jesuit Fathers and Brothers Maryland Provincial Curia.
Curtis, Howard *o.c.s.o.* '57 (P) [L] Lafayette, OR The Cistercian (Trappist) Abbey of Our Lady of Guadalupe.
Curtis, John C. '84 (LEX) Berea, KY St. Clare Church; Mt. Vernon, KY Our Lady of Mt. Vernon Church; [L] Berea, KY St. Clare Church-Berea College.
Curtis, Joseph C. '69 (CHI) Zion-Beach Park, IL Our Lady of Humility Church.
Curtis, Martin *o.carm.* '75 (CHI) [68] Chicago, IL St. Gelasius Church.
Curtis, Patrick *o.f.m.* '51 (SFD) Teutopolis, IL St. Francis of Assisi Church; [K] Teutopolis, IL St. Francis Assisi Friary.
Curtis, Robert J. '36 (TOL) Retired.
Curtis, Robert P. *c.s.p.* '71 (LA) [86] Los Angeles, CA St. Paul the Apostle Church.
Curtis, Robert P. *c.s.p.* '71 (NY) [Z] Scarsdale, NY Paulist Fathers Generalate.
Curtis, Msgr. Walter W. '37 (BGP) Retired.
Curtis, William D. '47 (WIN) Retired.
Curtiss, Donald J. '71 (ROC) Rochester, NY Strong Memorial Hospital; [J] Rochester, NY St. Joseph Convent Infirmary.
Curtiss, John B. '57 (LC) Retired.
Curtsinger, George (FWT) Retired.
Curzydlo, Ignatius *s.a.c.* '39 (BUF) [O] North Tonawanda, NY Society of the Catholic Apostolate.
Cusack, Msgr. Andrew T. '60 (BGP) On Duty Outside the Diocese.
Cusack, Msgr. Andrew T. '60 (NEW) [A] South Orange, NJ Immaculate Conception Seminary; [B] South Orange, NJ Seton Hall University; [B] South Orange, NJ Seton Hall University.
Cusack, Donald E. '59 (CHI) [J] Waukegan, IL Saint Therese Medical Center.
Cusack, Francis V. '54 (MOB) Orange Beach, AL St. Thomas by the Sea Church.
Cusack, Francis W. *c.p.* '58 (L) [L] Louisville, KY Sacred Heart Retreat.
Cusack, James C. '56 (GR) Retired.
Cusack, John J. *c.m.* '45 (PH) [Z] Philadelphia, PA Congregation of the Mission.
Cusack, John J. '71 (PAT) Military Chaplains.
Cusack, Paul *c.p.* '59 (MET) [H] South River, NJ Passionist Provincial Office.
Cusack, Thomas *s.s.c.* '62 (LA) [R] Los Angeles, CA Columban Fathers, Procure House.
Cusatis, Girard J. '63 (PH) [1] Drexel Hill, PA St. Andrew Church.
Cusato, Michael *o.f.m.* (STP) [10] St. Paul, MN Sacred Heart Church.
Cuschieri, Msgr. Albert A. '61 (DAL) [7] Dallas, TX Mary Immaculate Church.
Cushing, Alan '57 (SFE) Retired.
Cushing, Charles B. '54 (BRK) Absent on Sick Leave.
Cushing, Robert A. '78 (SAV) Special Assignment.
Cushing, Vincent de P. *o.f.m.* '63 (WDC) [B] Washington, DC Washington Theological Union.
Cushing, Vincent de Paul *o.f.m.* (WDC) [M] Silver Spring, MD Gemelli House.
Cushing, Walter F. '56 (ROC) [11] Rochester, NY St. Cecilia Church.
Cusick, Eugene G. '64 (PH) Holland, PA St. Bede the Venerable Church.
Cusick, John C. '70 (CHI) [165] Chicago, IL St. Patrick Church.
Cusick, Kevin M. '92 (WDC) Military Chaplains.
Cusick, Thomas H. '64 (DET) Belleville, MI St. Anthony Church.
Cusick, William F. '55 (SCR) Dallas, PA Gate of Heaven Church.
Cusimano, Salvatore J. '49 (BUF) [11] Niagara Falls, NY Prince of Peace Church; Retired.
Cusma, Joseph S. '53 (NY) Retired.
Cusmano, John '64 (DET) [8] Dearborn Heights, MI St. Sebastian Church.
Custer, Edward O. *m.m.* '72 (CHI) [N] Chicago, IL Maryknoll Fathers & Brothers.
Custer, John S. '83 (PBR) [A] Pittsburgh, PA Byzantine Catholic Seminary of SS. Cyril and Methodius.
Custer, John S. '83 (PSC) On Duty Outside Diocese.
Custer, Michael H. *o.s.b.* '41 (MAN) [K] Manchester, NH St. Anselm Abbey.
Custodio, Rinaldo B. '62 (STP) Savage, MN St. John the Baptist Church.
Cutajar, Alfred *s.j.* '69 (BAL) [I] Cumberland, MD Sacred Heart Hospital.
Cutie, Albert R. '95 (MIA) [5] Fort Lauderdale, FL St. Clement Church.
Cutler, S Oley *s.j.* '55 (NY) [Z] New York, NY Murray-Weigel Hall.
Cutrara, Vincent *c.s.* '57 (CHI) Melrose Park, IL Our Lady of Mount Carmel Church.
Cutrone, Dominick F. '55 (BRK) [96] Brooklyn, NY Our Lady of Grace Church.
Cvelbar, Joseph '32 (PIT) Retired; [N] Pittsburgh, PA St. John Vianney Manor.
Cwalina, Msgr. John F. '38 (RVC) Cutchogue, NY Our Lady of Ostrabrama Church; Retired.
Cwiekowski, Bruce '75 (P) [G] Portland, OR Catholic Charities of the Archdiocese of Portland in Oregon.
Cwiekowski, Frederick J. *s.s.* '62 (HRT) On Duty Outside the Archdiocese.
Cwiekowski, Frederick J. *s.s.* '62 (SFR) [A] Menlo Park, CA St. Patrick Seminary.
Cwik, Patrick '74 (LAN) [4] Lansing, MI Immaculate Heart of Mary Church.
Cwynar, Paul '87 (PIT) [2] Swissvale, PA Word of God Church.
Cylwicki, Albert W. *c.s.b.* '60 (ROC) [I] Rochester, NY Basilian Residence.
Cymbor, Msgr. John A. '50 (STU) Flushing, OH St. Paul's Church.
Cymbrowski, Martin *c.m.* '30 (HRT) [M] Manchester, CT DePaul Provincial Residence.
Cymerman, Alex B. *o.f.m.conv.* '65 (PAT) [6] Clifton, NJ St. John Kanty Church.
Cyprys, Ronald '69 (DET) [6] Dearborn Heights, MI Our Lady of Grace Church.
Cyr, Guy *s.m.* (BO) [10] Cambridge, MA Our Lady of Pity Church.
Cyr, Joel '71 (PRT) Sabbatical.
Cyr, Lawrence S. *c.pp.s.* '44 (SAN) Coleman, TX Sacred Heart Church.
Cyr, Myles *o.m.i.* (PRT) Brownville Junction, ME St. Francis Xavier Church.
Cyr, Myles *o.m.i.* '54 (MAN) [K] Colebrook, NH Shrine of Our Lady of Grace.
Cyr, Philip '69 (PRT) Houlton, ME St. Mary's Church.
Cyr, Richard E. '60 (DET) [6] Sterling Heights, MI St. Matthias Church.
Cyr, Roger '59 (PRT) Lincoln, ME St. Mary Church.
Cyr, Terrence *o.carm.* '75 (KCK) [1] Leavenworth, KS Immaculate Conception Church; [4] Leavenworth, KS St. Joseph's Church.
Cyr, William F. '71 (SPR) Williamstown, MA St. Patrick's Church; Williamstown, MA St. Raphael's Church.
Cyscon, Peter J. '73 (CHI) Berwyn, IL St. Odilo Church.
Cyscon, Philip E. '84 (CHI) [44] Chicago, IL St. Columbanus Church.
Cyvas, Matthew '41 (ALB) Retired.
Czachor, Christopher '51 (PSC) Absent on Sick Leave.
Czachor, Richard E. '77 (SCR) West Hazleton, PA Transfiguration Church.
Czachorowski, Richard S. '65 (NEW) Lyndhurst, NJ St. Michael's Church.
Czahur, John P. '77 (TR) Riverton, NJ Sacred Heart Church.
Czaja, Blaise *c.p.* '64 (CHI) [N] Chicago, IL Passionist Provincial Office.
Czaja, Joseph S. '46 (Y) Retired.
Czajka, Norman M. '61 (CHI) [36] Chicago, IL St. Camillus Church.
Czajkowski, Andrew A. '74 (LAN) Davison, MI St. John Church.
Czapiewski, Stanislaus *s.j.* '40 (DET) Hamtramck, MI St. Ladislaus Church; [P] Clarkston, MI Colombiere Center.
Czapinski, Richard J. '58 (PIT) Penn Hills, PA St. Gerard Majella Church.
Czapla, Bruce *o.f.m.* '89 (MAN) Derry, NH St. Thomas Aquinas Church.
Czarcinski, Edward A. '88 (MET) Milltown, NJ Our Lady of Lourdes Church.
Czarkowski, Joseph '74 (E) Johnsonburg, PA Holy Rosary Church; Wilcox, PA St. Anne Church.
Czarnecki, Anthony '66 (WOR) Webster, MA St. Joseph's Church.
Czarnecki, Edmund S. '64 (ORL) Cocoa, FL Blessed Sacrament Church.
Czarnecki, Edward R. '66 (BUF) Blasdell, NY Our Mother of Good Counsel Church.
Czarnecki, Ervin J. *s.j.* '52 (OM) [K] Omaha, NE Jesuit Community At Creighton University.
Czarnecki, Ervin J. *s.j.* '52 (WIN) [1] Mankato, MN SS. Peter and Paul's Church.
Czarnota, Reynold A. '53 (PH) Retired.
Czarnota, Stanley '56 (LAN) [F] Lansing, MI St. Lawrence Hospital and Healthcare Services; [G] Dimondale, MI St. Lawrence Dimondale Center.
Czartorynski, David F. '84 (ALN) Military Chaplains.
Czaster, Herman '65 (HRT) Kensington, CT St. Paul's Church.
Czaus, Joseph C. '89 (ALN) Unassigned.
Czech, Edmund *o.f.m.* '44 (MIL) [P] Burlington, WI Queen of Peace Friary.
Czech, Edward M. '73 (CLV) Military Chaplains.
Czechowicz, Bernard J. '54 (BUF) Retired.
Czechowicz, Walter '51 (ALB) [8] Amsterdam, NY St. Stanislaus Church.
Czekala, Henry *c.m.* '44 (SY) [S] Utica, NY St. Vincent's Mission House.
Czelusniak, Donald '78 (ALB) Gloversville, NY St. Mary of Mt. Carmel Church.
Czerkies, Joseph '62 (PAT) [6] Passaic, NJ St. Joseph's Church.
Czerwien, Richard *ss.cc.* '83 (BWN) Edinburg, TX Sacred Heart Church.
Czerwinski, James W. *o.f.m.* '77 (NEW) Wood-Ridge, NJ Our Lady of the Assumption Church.
Czerwionka, Frank *c.s.v.* '59 (JOL) [I] Bourbonnais, IL Our Lady of Victory Nursing Home.
Czuba, Flavius *o.f.m.* '47 (GAY) Indian River, MI Cross in the Woods Catholic Shrine Church.
Czywil, Valerian *o.f.m.conv.* (BO) [7] Lawrence, MA Holy Trinity Church.
Czyzynski, John *s.c.j.* '63 (MIL) [P] Franklin, WI St. Francis Residence; [P] Hales Corners, WI Priests of the Sacred Heart; [P] Hales Corners, WI Priests of the Sacred Heart.

D

D'Abele, Peter *s.m.m.* '75 (BRK) [U] Ozone Park, NY Montfort Missionaries Provincialate.
D'Addezio, Msgr. Louis A. '61 (PH) [137] Philadelphia, PA St. Philip Neri Church.
D'Agostini, Mario *s.p.* '65 (STL) [P] St. Louis, MO Servants of the Paraclete.
D'Agostino, Carl L. '59 (CLV) Independence, OH St. Michael Church.
D'Agostino, Joseph '41 (ALB) Retired.
D'Agostino, Lorenzo *s.s.e.* '42 (BUR) [G] Colchester, VT Society of St. Edmund.
D'Agostino, Rodolfo *r.c.j.* '64 (LA) [R] North Hills, CA Rogationist Fathers.
D'Albro, Thomas G. '71 (BRK) Released from Diocesan Assignment.
D'Alessandro, Benedict *o.f.m.* '66 (NY) [5] Mt. Vernon, NY Our Lady of Mount Carmel Church.
D'Alessandro, Francis X. *o.f.m.* '53 (NY) [Z] New York, NY Padua Friary.
D'Alessandro, Peter P. *s.j.* '66 (PH) [G] Philadelphia, PA St. Joseph's Preparatory School; [Z] Philadelphia, PA St. Joseph's Preparatory School Jesuit Community, Arrupe House.
D'Alessandro, Salvatore '39 (SY) Retired.
D'Alonges, John P. '71 (HRT) [4] Torrington, CT St. Peter's Church.
D'Alonzo, Alfred F. *c.s.c.* '53 (FTW) [B] Notre Dame, IN University of Notre Dame Du Lac; [J] Notre Dame, IN Holy Cross Community, Corby Hall, University of Notre Dame.
D'Amato, James J. '49 (BRK) Retired.
D'Ambrosi, Girolamo *s.a.c.* '39 (NY) [91] New York, NY Our Lady of Mt. Carmel Church; [Z] New York, NY Pallottine Fathers.
D'Ambrosia, Peter *s.m.* '85 (BO) [Y] Framingham Centre, MA The Marist House.
D'Amico, Carducci S. '64 (BGP) [19] Bridgeport, CT St. Raphael's Church.
D'Amico, Carmen A. '82 (PIT) [6] Pittsburgh, PA St. Benedict the Moor Church.
D'Amico, Frank (STL) Overland, MO All Souls Church.
D'Amico, Joseph A. '95 (NEW) Verona, NJ Our Lady of the Lake Church.
D'Amico, Michael H. '64 (CAM) Ocean City, NJ St. Frances Cabrini Church.
D'Anca, Msgr. Achille '45 (BRK) Retired.
D'Andrea, Edward R. '73 (RVC) East Northport, NY St. Anthony of Padua Church.
D'Angelis, Henry *o.f.m.cap.* '41 (NY) [B] Beacon, NY St. Lawrence of Brindisi Friary.
D'Angelo, Anthony '74 (SP) Spring Hill, FL Saint Joan of Arc Church.
D'Angelo, Benedict *c.pp.s.* '42 (CIN) [B] Carthagena, OH St. Charles.
D'Angelo, Donald S. '68 (SFR) [3] Menlo Park, CA The Church of the Nativity.
D'Angelo, Joseph J. (RVC) Garden City, NY St. Anne Church; East Meadow, NY Nassau County Police Department; [Q] Rockville Centre, NY The Campus Parish of Long Island.
D'Angelo, Rocco '56 (SP) Retired.
D'Angelo, Thomas P. '84 (NY) [2] Mt. Vernon, NY St. Francis of Assisi Church; Bronx, NY Our Lady of Mercy Medical Center; [E] New York, NY Cardinal

Spellman High School; [S] New York, NY Our Lady of Mercy Medical Center.
d'Anjou, Henry G. (NY) [4] Port Chester, NY Sacred Heart of Jesus Church; Retired; [E] White Plains, NY Archbishop Stepinac High School.
d'Anjou, John R. *s.j.* '72 (BO) [W] Boston, MA Jesuit Urban Center & Immaculate Conception Community.
D'Antonio, Anthony '39 (NY) [174] Bronx, NY Our Lady of Mt. Carmel Church; Retired.
D'Antonio, John A. *o.praem.* '73 (PH) [Z] Paoli, PA Daylesford Abbey.
D'Antonio, Ronald M. '77 (BRK) [167] Queens, NY St. Fidelis Church.
D'Arcy, William *o.f.m.conv.* '37 (TR) Point Pleasant Beach, NJ St. Peter Church.
D'Arcy, William '73 (AGN) On Duty Outside the Archdiocese.
D'Argenio, Herbert F. '59 (NY) [159] Bronx, NY St. Lucy Church.
D'Artiaga, Jose '63 (SJN) [53] San Juan, PR Santa Rosa de Lima Church.
d'Auby, Phillip *s.m.* '61 (SFR) [37] San Francisco, CA Notre Dame des Victoires Church.
D'Auriol, Vincent '60 (NY) Retired.
D'Aurizio, Joseph F. '56 (ROC) [30] Rochester, NY St. John Evangelist Church.
D'Aurora, Joseph '73 (RIC) Military Chaplains.
D'Aversa, Robert J. *t.o.r.* '73 (ORL) [D] Winter Park, FL San Pedro Spiritual Development Center; [F] Winter Park, FL San Pedro Center, Third Order Regular of St. Francis; [F] Winter Park, FL Franciscan Friars, T.O.R., Provincial Residence, San Pedro Friary.
D'Cruz, Ferreolus '59 (ALX) Echo, LA St. Francis de Sales Church; [C] Alexandria, LA St. Frances Cabrini Hospital.
D'Cruz, Michael *o.f.m.* '57 (NY) [Z] New York, NY Franciscan Province of the Immaculate Conception.
D'Elia, Michael A. '54 (BGP) [19] Bridgeport, CT St. Raphael's Church; Bridgeport, CT Bridgeport Health Care.
D'Emma, Gregory J. '70 (NEW) Military Chaplains.
d'Entremont, Clarence J. '36 (FR) Retired.
D'Eon, Earl '89 (PHX) Sun City, AZ St. Clement of Rome Church.
D'heedene, Walter O. *c.i.c.m.* '67 (SAT) [23] San Antonio, TX Sacred Heart Church.
D'Incecco, Alfred '75 (NY) [E] New York, NY Cardinal Hayes High School.
D'Ippolito, Donald *o.f.m.* (BO) [57] Boston, MA Our Lady of Mt. Carmel Church.
D'Mello, Lawrence '73 (SAN) On Duty Outside the Diocese.
D'Mello, Olympio '81 (LA) Canoga Park, CA Our Lady of the Valley Church.
D'Onofrio, Ernest *o.f.m.* '43 (NY) County, NY Dutchess County Jail; [BB] Wappingers Falls, NY Mt. Alvernia Retreat House.
D'Ostilio, Silvio *c.s.sp.* '54 (SB) Hemet, CA Holy Spirit Parish Church.
D'Silva, Aloysius J. '61 (CHL) Spruce Pine, NC St. Lucien Church.
D'Silva, Joseph (TR) Little Silver, NJ Fort Monmouth.
D'Silva, Percival L. '64 (WDC) [10] Washington, DC Blessed Sacrament, Shrine of the Most Church.
D'Souza, Claude J. '65 (RVC) Westbury, NY St. Brigid Church.
D'Souza, Gilbert '73 (BGP) Riverside, CT St. Catherine of Siena Church.
Da Costa, Joseph Dinis *o.f.m.* (FRS) Faculties Only.
Da Cunha, Edgar *s.d.v.* '83 (PAT) [I] Florham Park, NJ Vocationist Fathers Retreat Center; [M] Florham Park, NJ Father Justin Vocationary.
Da Custa, Leonard '58 (NY) [6] Mt. Vernon, NY SS. Peter and Paul Church.
Da Prato, Felix *o.c.d.* '40 (LR) [A] Little Rock, AR Marylake - Carmelite Novitiate.
Da Roza, George *s.s.c.* '85 (OM) [K] St. Columbans, NE St. Columban's Foreign Mission Society.
da Silva, Antonio L. *s.d.v.* '83 (NEW) Palisades Park, NJ St. Nicholas Church.
da Silva, Jorge '71 (SJ) [M] Cupertino, CA Marianist Provincial Residence; [M] Los Gatos, CA Marianists.
da Silva, Joseph '72 (B) [5] Boise, ID Risen Christ Catholic Community Church.
Dabash, G. Adrian *o.p.* '71 (PRO) [P] Providence, RI St. Thomas Aquinas Priory at Providence College.
Dabbene, Bernard J. *s.d.b.* '66 (SFR) [12] San Francisco, CA Corpus Christi Church.
Dabcosky, Edward J. '56 (ALT) [5] Altoona, PA Holy Rosary Church; Altoona, PA Veterans Medical Center.
Dabney, Philip *c.ss.r.* '78 (WDC) [M] Washington, DC Holy Redeemer College.
Dabovich, Louis '46 (OAK) Pittsburg, CA Good Shepherd Church.
Dabria, Jerry J. '55 (NO) Retired.
Dabrowski, George *c.m.* '58 (HRT) [18] New Haven, CT St. Stanislaus Church.
Dabrowski, Hyacinth M. *o.f.m.cap.* '32 (MET) Manville, NJ Sacred Heart of Jesus Church.
Dabrowski, Hyacinth M. *o.f.m.cap.* '32 (PAT) [M] Oak Ridge-Milton, NJ St. Stanislaus B. M. Friary.
Dabrowski, James O. '84 (CAM) Mount Ephraim, NJ Sacred Heart Church.
Dabruzzi, James S. '53 (SUP) Retired.
Dacechen, Mario *o.s.b.m.* '88 (STN) Detroit, MI St. John the Baptist Church.
Dacey, Donald '53 (DET) Retired.
Dacey, Martin J. '44 (SCR) Retired; [N] Dunmore, PA Villa St. Joseph.
Dachauer, Andrew C. *s.j.* '64 (STO) Mammoth Lakes, CA St. Joseph Church.
Dachille, Arnold V. '59 (DET) [4] Dearborn, MI St. Clement Church.
Dacier, Gerard A. (BO) Retired.
DaCorte, Allan *o.f.m.* '77 (STL) [P] St. Louis, MO Franciscan Friary of St. Anthony of Padua.
DaCosta, Lee '73 (BWN) Grulla, TX Holy Family Church; Rio Grande City, TX Immaculate Conception Church.
Dadey, Neil (ALT) [H] Huntingdon, PA Juniata College.
Dadey, Neil R. '81 (ALT) Lock Haven, PA St. Agnes Church.
Daenen, Arsene *ss.cc.* (HON) Kalaupapa, HI St. Francis Church; [G] Kalaupapa, Molokai, HI Kalaupapa Settlement.
Dafonte, Gregorio '57 (CGS) Cayey, PR Nuestra Senora de la Merced Church.
Dagelen, Anthony L. *s.j.* '65 (MIL) [P] Wauwatosa, WI Jesuit Community at St. Camillus.
Dagher, George '43 (NTN) Retired.
Dagit, Rick D. '86 (DUB) Ackley, IA St. Mary's Church; Eldora, IA St. Mary's Church.
Dagle, Harold F. '59 (ALN) [3] Allentown, PA Immaculate Conception Church.
Dagnoli, Albert *ss.cc.* '68 (FR) [K] Fairhaven, MA Sacred Hearts Provincial House.
Dagwell, Robert A. '54 (LR) Retired.
Dahl, Henry J. '96 (FR) Sandwich, MA Corpus Christi Church.
Dahlberg, Daniel J. '67 (SUP) Balsam Lake, WI Our Lady of the Pines Church; Centuria, WI St. Patrick Church; Osceola, WI St. Joseph Church.
Dahlby, Charles G. '77 (SFD) Kincaid, IL St. Rita Church; Pawnee, IL St. Mary Church.
Dahlheimer, Cosmas *o.s.b.* '36 (SCL) [I] Collegeville, MN St. John's Abbey, of the Order of St. Benedict.
Dahlheimer, Ronald W. '59 (STP) Kilkenny, MN St. Canice Church.
Dahlinger, James H. *s.j.* '91 (NEW) [B] Jersey City, NJ Saint Peter's College; [N] Jersey City, NJ Jesuits of Saint Peter's College, Inc.
Dahlinger, James H. *s.j.* '91 (NY) [Z] New York, NY Jesuit Provincial's Office.
Dahlke, Robert W. *s.j.* '65 (RVC) Syosset, NY St. Edward Confessor Church.
Dahlquist, Thomas S. '96 (YAK) White Salmon, WA St. Joseph Church.
Dahm, Charles W. *o.p.* '64 (CHI) [86] Chicago, IL Holy Trinity Church; [173] Chicago, IL St. Pius V Church; [N] Chicago, IL Dominicans (Provincial Office); [N] Chicago, IL Dominican Community.
Dahm, Paul '62 (RVC) [I] West Islip, NY The Samaritan Corporation; [I] West Islip, NY The Samaritan Corporation.
Dahm, Paul J. '62 (RVC) West Islip, NY Good Samaritan Hospital.
Dahmen, Vernon (MOB) On Leave from the Archdiocese.
Dahms, Paul G. '58 (RC) Deadwood, SD St. Ambrose Church.
Dahms, Williams *s.s.s.* '43 (NY) [55] New York, NY St. Jean Baptiste Church.
Daiber, Msgr. Sean J. '67 (CAM) On Duty Outside the Diocese.
Daigle, Christopher P. '78 (TLS) [4] Tulsa, OK St. Catherine Church.
Daigle, Donald R. '68 (PRT) North Vassalboro, ME St. Bridget's Church.
Daigle, Eugene *c.ss.r.* '72 (ORL) New Smyrna Beach, FL Sacred Heart Church.
Daigle, Gregory J. '93 (BR) [3] Baton Rouge, LA St. Aloysius Church.
Daigle, H.C. Paul '46 (HT) Retired.
Daigle, Msgr. Jules O. '25 (LKC) Retired.
Daigle, Robert E. '63 (GAL) Retired.
Daigle, Steven '89 (DUL) Chisholm, MN St. Joseph's Church.
Dailey, Gary M. '85 (SPR) Lee, MA St. Mary's Church.
Dailey, Joseph E. '77 (DET) Orion Township, MI Christ the Redeemer Church.
Dailey, Joseph W. '49 (ROC) Retired.
Dailey, Robert H. *s.j.* '43 (SJ) [M] Los Gatos, CA Sacred Heart Jesuit Center.
Dailey, Ronald G. '41 (PRO) Retired.
Dailey, Thomas F. *o.s.f.s.* '87 (ALN) [B] Center Valley, PA Allentown College of St. Francis de Sales; [K] Center Valley, PA Oblates of St. Francis de Sales.
Dailey, William '59 (RVC) Northport, NY St. Philip Neri Church.
Dailey, Msgr. William J. '57 (TR) [18] Trenton, NJ St. Joseph Church; Trenton, NJ Helene Fuld Hospital.
Daily, Leo J. '44 (HRT) Yalesville, CT Our Lady of Fatima Church; Retired.
Daily, Vincent E. '59 (BO) [3] Lawrence, MA Assumption of the Blessed Virgin Mary Church; [2] Milton, MA St. Elizabeth Church.
Dair, Richard J. '80 (ARL) Retired.
Dakes, John T. '87 (WDC) Suitland, MD St. Bernardine Church.
Dakin, Kenneth M. '88 (SAT) Uvalde, TX Sacred Heart Church.
Dalbec, John *s.c.j.* '41 (MIL) [P] Franklin, WI Villa Maria.
Dalbec, Paul *m.s.* '53 (FR) [K] Attleboro, MA La Salette Shrine.
Dalbelo, Americo *c.ss.r.* (CHI) [9] Chicago, IL St. Alphonsus Church.
Dalbon, Luis *s.d.b.* '47 (ARE) Orocovis, PR San Juan Bautista Church.
Dale, J. Douglas '88 (ORG) [3] Anaheim, CA St. Justin Martyr Church.
Dale, James E. '39 (NY) Retired.
Dale, Williams J. '74 (RIC) [7] Norfolk, VA St. Pius X Church.
Daleiden, Francis *o.s.b.* '57 (RCK) Amboy, IL St. Patrick Church; [H] Aurora, IL Marmion Abbey-St. Augustine's Abbey.
Daleke, Don (DM) Retired.
Daleo, Joseph '71 (BEA) Special Assignment.
Daleo, Paul *o.f.m.cap.* '77 (NEW) [N] Union City, NJ Capuchin Friars - Prov. Stigmata of St. Francis.
Daley, Brian *s.j.* (FTW) [B] Notre Dame, IN University of Notre Dame Du Lac.
Daley, Brian E. *s.j.* '70 (NY) [Z] New York, NY Jesuit Provincial's Office.
Daley, Daniel P. '70 (BUR) On Duty Outside the Diocese.
Daley, Daniel P. '70 (GLP) Blanco, NM St. Rose Church; Bloomfield, NM St. Mary Church.
Daley, Msgr. Ernest J. '55 (E) [10] Erie, PA Our Lady of Peace Church.
Daley, Francis E. '63 (BO) [3] Arlington, MA St. James the Apostle Church.
Daley, Frederick (SY) Utica, NY Mohawk Valley Psychiatric Center.
Daley, Frederick D. '74 (SY) [7] Utica, NY St. Francis de Sales Church.
Daley, Jacques de Paul *o.s.b.* '71 (GBG) Greensburg, PA Westmoreland Hospital; [H] Latrobe, PA Saint Vincent Archabbey.
Daley, James D. '54 (ALB) Delmar, NY St. Thomas the Apostle Church.
Daley, James J. '93 (BO) Acton, MA St. Elizabeth of Hungary Church.
Daley, James M. '42 (BUF) Retired.
Daley, John A. '56 (BO) [2] Malden, MA St. Joseph Church.
Daley, John J. '46 (SY) Fulton, NY Holy Family Church; Retired.
Daley, John T. '43 (RVC) New Hyde Park, NY Holy Spirit Church; Retired.
Daley, Joseph A. '68 (CHY) Cody, WY St. Anthony Church.
Daley, Joseph D. '37 (BO) Retired.
Daley, Neil '55 (ANC) Retired.
Daley, Owen W. *s.j.* '60 (NY) [Z] New York, NY West Side Jesuit Community.
Daley, Raymond *o.p.* '52 (NY) Pleasantville, NY Holy Innocents Church.
Daley, Msgr. Thomas J. '38 (WOR) Retired; [M] Worcester, MA Vianney House.
Daley, Timothy J. '87 (TLS) Claremore, OK St. Cecilia Church.
Daley, Wallace '55 (ORG) On Duty Outside the Diocese.
Dall, Msgr. Norbert P. '45 (LC) Retired.
Dall'Agnese, Sergio *c.s.* '79 (MIA) Lighthouse Point, FL St. Paul the Apostle Church.
Dalla Villa, Msgr. Anthony '64 (NY) [1] New York, NY Cathedral of St. Patrick.
Dallen, James '69 (SAL) On Duty Outside the Diocese.
Dallen, James '69 (SPK) [7] Spokane, WA St. Ann Church.
Dallmeier, Michael *o.f.m.* '63 (TUC) [4] Tucson, AZ Mission San Xavier del Bac Church.
Dallo, Victor *c.m.* '57 (BRK) [W] Brooklyn, NY Centro Evangelizacion San Vicente de Paul.
Dally, Peter F. '85 (TLS) Skiatook, OK Sacred Heart Church.
DalMaso, John *s.d.b.* '37 (LA) [F] Bellflower, CA St. John Bosco High School.
Dalpiaz, Gino *c.s.* '51 (CHI) [N] Stone Park, IL Scalabrini Mission Center.
Dalseth, Gerald '64 (SCL) Morris, MN Assumption of the Blessed Virgin Mary Church.
Dalton, Brendan '69 (MIA) Hollywood, FL St. Bernadette Church.
Dalton, Donald T. '60 (STL) Special Assignment.
Dalton, George R. '84 (PIT) Graduate Studies.
Dalton, Howard '68 (NY) Absent on Leave.
Dalton, J. Paul '78 (SEA) Issaquah, WA Mary, Queen of Peace Church.

Dalton, James E. *o.s.f.s.* '72 (PH) [Z] Philadelphia, PA Father Judge Faculty House.
Dalton, James L. '68 (SEA) Kirkland, WA Holy Family Church.
Dalton, James P. '68 (SAV) Albany, GA St. Teresa Church.
Dalton, John '48 (CLV) Retired.
Dalton, John '81 (AMA) [J] Channing, TX Disciples of the Lord Jesus Christ.
Dalton, John A. '55 (L) [66] Louisville, KY St. Raphael the Archangel Church.
Dalton, John Bryan '70 (MIA) Deerfield Beach, FL St. Ambrose Church.
Dalton, John C. '48 (CLV) [28] Cleveland, OH Holy Name Church.
Dalton, Msgr. John W. '58 (DUB) Retired.
Dalton, Michel W. *o.f.m.cap.* '78 (AGN) Agana Heights, GU Our Lady of the Blessed Sacrament Church; [F] Agana Heights, GU St. Fidelis Friary.
Dalton, Peadar (MOB) On Leave from the Archdiocese.
Dalton, Robert A. '62 (BIR) Russellville, AL Good Shepherd Church.
Dalton, William P. '56 (NY) Katonah, NY St. Mary of the Assumption Church.
Dalupang, Arturo O. '95 (CHR) Kingstree, SC St. Ann's Church; Lake City, SC St. Philip's Church.
DaLuz, Marcelo *o.f.m.conv.* (WDC) [B] Washington, DC St. Bonaventure Friary.
Daly, Albert *o.carm.* (NY) Montrose, NY Franklin D. Roosevelt Hospital.
Daly, Albert *o.carm.* '33 (NY) [Z] Middletown, NY St. Albert's Priory.
Daly, Anthony C. *s.j.* '72 (STL) [C] St. Louis, MO Saint Louis University; [P] St. Louis, MO Jesuit Community Corporation at St. Louis University - Jesuit Hall.
Daly, Bartholomew *m.h.m.* '62 (NY) [93] New York, NY Our Lady of Peace Church.
Daly, Msgr. Charles W. '51 (HRT) [12] Hartford, CT St. Luke Church; Retired.
Daly, Christopher H. '60 (NY) [2] White Plains, NY St. John the Evangelist Church.
Daly, Denis E. *s.j.* '64 (STL) [C] St. Louis, MO Saint Louis University; [P] St. Louis, MO Jesuit Community Corporation at St. Louis University - Jesuit Hall.
Daly, Desmond '66 (SP) Hudson, FL St. Michael Church.
Daly, Earnest *l.c.* '91 (HRT) [B] Cheshire, CT Novitiate of the Legion of Christ.
Daly, Francis J. *s.j.* '72 (CHI) [D] Chicago, IL St. Ignatius Jesuit Community; [N] Chicago, IL Chicago Province of the Society of Jesus-Provincial Office.
Daly, Frederick T. *s.j.* '44 (DEN) [M] Denver, CO Xavier Jesuit Center.
Daly, George '47 (OAK) Retired.
Daly, J. Daniel *s.j.* '92 (DET) [E] Detroit, MI University of Detroit Jesuit High School and Academy.
Daly, James A. *s.j.* '56 (NY) [Z] New York, NY Murray-Weigel Hall.
Daly, James F. *c.s.sp.* '63 (MIA) [9] Fort Lauderdale, FL St. John the Baptist Church.
Daly, James J. '44 (BO) Retired.
Daly, James P. '39 (PH) [132] Philadelphia, PA Our Mother of Sorrows Church; Retired.
Daly, Jerome R. '87 (ARL) McLean, VA St. John's Church.
Daly, Msgr. John '36 (NY) Retired.
Daly, John '59 (LA) [14] Los Angeles, CA Holy Trinity Church.
Daly, John J. '46 (PH) Retired.
Daly, John J. '58 (HRT) North Haven, CT St. Barnabas Church.
Daly, Msgr. John K. '36 (NY) [5] White Plains, NY Our Lady of Sorrows Church.
Daly, John P. *s.j.* '56 (LA) [C] Los Angeles, CA Loyola Marymount University.
Daly, John R. *s.j.* '63 (STL) [P] St. Louis, MO The Jesuits of the Missouri Province.
Daly, Joseph *c.m.* '60 (BRK) [U] Jamaica, NY St. Vincent's House.
Daly, Joseph F. '42 (BRK) [192] Queens, NY St. Margaret's Church; Retired.
Daly, Joseph V. *c.m.* '60 (BRK) [D] Queens and Staten Island, NY St. John's University.
Daly, Kevin *o.f.m.* '80 (ALB) [B] Loudonville, NY Siena College; [S] Loudonville, NY Siena College.
Daly, Leo J. *s.j.* '61 (RVC) [P] Manhasset, NY St. Ignatius Retreat House, Inisfada.
Daly, Lowrie *s.j.* '45 (STL) [K] Creve Coeur, MO St. John's Mercy Medical Center.
Daly, Lowrie J. *s.j.* '45 (STL) [P] St. Louis, MO Jesuit Community Corporation at St. Louis University - Jesuit Hall.
Daly, M. Paul '71 (PAT) [C] Sparta, NJ Pope John XXIII High School.
Daly, Michael '75 (DET) [L] Livonia, MI Provincial House and Novitiate of the Sisters of St. Felix.
Daly, Peter J. '86 (WDC) Prince Frederick, MD St. John Vianney Church; [C] Washington, DC Catholic University of America, The.
Daly, Richard L. '58 (BEL) Du Quoin, IL Sacred Heart of Jesus Church.
Daly, Robert J. *s.j.* '63 (BO) [W] Chestnut Hill, MA The Jesuit Community at Boston College.
Daly, Robert L. '41 (NEW) Hillside, NJ St. Catherine of Siena Church; Retired.
Daly, Shawn T. '95 (HRT) Branford, CT St. Mary Church.
Daly, Simeon *o.s.b.* '48 (IND) [A] St. Meinrad, IN St. Meinrad Seminary; [B] St. Meinrad, IN St. Meinrad Seminary-College of Liberal Arts; [J] St. Meinrad, IN St. Meinrad Archabbey.
Daly, Thomas A. '87 (SFR) Lagunitas, CA St. Cecilia Church; San Francisco, CA San Francisco Police Department; Special Assignment; [D] Kentfield, CA Marin Catholic College Preparatory (Coed).
Daly, Thomas J. (BO) On Special or Other Diocesan Assignment.
Daly, Timothy (ORL) [9] Orlando, FL St. John Vianney Church.
Daly, Vincent M. '71 (BRK) [244] Queens, NY St. Teresa of Avila Church.
Daly, Msgr. William J. '46 (NEW) Livingston, NJ St. Philomena Church; West Orange, NJ St. Joseph's Church; Retired.
Dalzell, James P. '49 (FR) Retired.
Dambrauskas, Stephen '48 (SP) Retired.
Damhorst, Joseph *s.j.* '68 (RC) Kyle, SD Our Lady of Sorrows Church; Wanblee, SD Ignatius Loyola Church; Pine Ridge, SD Holy Rosary Church; [B] Pine Ridge, SD Jesuit Community of Holy Rosary Mission.
Damian, Lawrence P. '71 (BUF) Collins Center, NY St. Frances Cabrini Church; Eden, NY St. Mary of Immaculate Conception Church; Langford, NY St. Martin Church.
Damian, Ronald '88 (WOR) Uxbridge, MA St. Mary's Church.
Damico, Rodney M. '92 (COL) Marion, OH St. Mary Church.
Damis, Frank J. '84 (NY) [3] Kingston, NY St. Joseph Church.
Damjanov, Zvonimir '37 (SFD) Pana, IL St. Patrick Church; Retired.
Dammeir, James L. '79 (MIL) [52] Milwaukee, WI St. Matthew's Church.
Damoah, Augustine Ansu '90 (NY) Cortlandt Manor, NY St. Columbanus Church.
Damond, Patrick J. '96 (E) [3] Sharon, PA St. Joseph Church.
Damron, Robert '83 (LEX) Jellico, KY St. Boniface Church; Williamsburg, KY Our Lady of Perpetual Help Church.
Damroth, William '93 (NY) [6] Yonkers, NY Christ the King Church.
Danagher, Edward F. *c.m.* '46 (LA) [R] Los Angeles, CA Vincentian Fathers and Brothers.
Danaher, Msgr. Mortimer '53 (STA) [3] Jacksonville, FL Christ the King Church.
Danaher, Philip M. *s.v.d.* '83 (CHI) [58] Chicago, IL St. Ferdinand Church; [B] Techny, IL Divine Word Residence.
Danaher, Philip M. *s.v.d.* '83 (JOL) Addison, IL St. Philip The Apostle Church.
Danaher, Msgr. T. Leo '55 (STA) Ponte Vedra Beach, FL Our Lady Star of the Sea Church.
Danber, Bernard *o.s.a.* '86 (PRM) Akron, OH St. Michael the Archangel Church; Akron, OH Dormition of Virgin Mary Church.
Danber, Bernard R. *o.s.a.* '86 (CHI) [N] Olympia Fields, IL The Augustinian Provincialate Tolentine Center.
Danczyk, Mark J. '92 (MIL) [6] Kenosha, WI St. Mary's Church.
Dandelet, James D. '54 (WIN) Retired.
Dandry, Anthony M. '89 (MET) South Plainfield, NJ Sacred Heart Church.
Dandurand, Douglas E. (STP) [C] St. Paul, MN University of St. Thomas.
Dandurand, Douglas E. '82 (SC) On Duty Outside the Diocese.
Dandurand, Douglas E. '82 (STP) [A] St. Paul, MN The Saint Paul Seminary.
Dane, James E. '83 (MOB) Bay Minette, AL St. Agatha Church; [K] Bay Minette, AL Faulkner State Jr. College Newman Center.
Dane, John '91 (LEX) Middlesboro, KY St. Julian Church.
Daneault, Paul W. '66 (MAN) Absent on Sick Leave.
Danek, Michael E. *c.r.* '86 (CHI) [74] Chicago, IL St. Hedwig Church.
Danel, Joseph B. *s.j.* '52 (P) [L] Portland, OR Jesuit Provincial Office (Oregon Prov.).
Danen, Lyle '85 (ORL) Sabbatical.
Danforth, Clarence E. '81 (GRY) Graduate Studies.
Dang, Chin Van '83 (ORG) El Toro, CA El Toro Marine Base.
Dang, Chin Van '83 (RIC) Military Chaplains.
Dang, Francis Hoang '95 (LA) El Monte, CA Nativity Church.
Dang, Joseph *s.v.d.* '93 (DUB) [B] Epworth, IA Divine Word College.
Dang, Thien *o.s.b.* '93 (P) [L] St. Benedict, OR Mt. Angel Abbey.
Dang, Vincent '95 (SCR) [14] Wilkes-Barre, PA St. Mary's Church of the Immaculate Conception.
Dang Nguyen, Joseph Kim '93 (LA) [3] Long Beach, CA St. Barnabas Church.
Danhauer, Richard T. '57 (OWN) Princeton, KY St. Paul Church.
Daniel, Bruno *o.s.b.* (PAT) [M] Clifton, NJ Holy Face of Jesus Monastery.
Daniel, John C. '92 (SFE) Tucumcari, NM St. Anne Church.
Daniel, Joseph A. '52 (PH) [2] Phoenixville, PA Holy Trinity Church.
Daniel, Michael *s.a.* '57 (MRY) Seaside, CA St. Francis Xavier Church.
Daniele, Anthony J. (BO) Retired.
Danielewicz, Noel *o.f.m.conv.* '76 (BIR) Bessemer, AL St. Francis of Assisi Church.
Daniels, Eugene '84 (NY) Milton, NY St. James Church.
Daniels, John W. '36 (GRY) Retired.
Daniels, Joseph E. '90 (PRT) [3] Lewiston, ME Holy Family Church.
Daniels, Lawrence *o.c.d.* '65 (MIL) [P] Milwaukee, WI Provincial Offices - Discalced Carmelites.
Daniels, Leo Francis *c.o.* '65 (BWN) Pharr, TX St. Jude Thaddeus Church; [E] Pharr, TX Oratory of St. Philip Neri, of Pontifical Right.
Daniels, Paul A. '57 (MIL) [2] Menomonee Falls, WI Good Shepherd Church.
Danielsen, Thomas *c.ss.r.* '64 (TUC) [H] Tucson, AZ Redemptorist Picture Rocks Retreat.
Danielson, Charles R. '92 (BUR) Montpelier, VT St. Augustine Church.
Danielson, Daniel E. '63 (OAK) Pleasanton, CA St. Augustine Church.
Danielson, Harold *s.d.b.* '66 (LA) Bellflower, CA St. Dominic Savio Church.
Danik, Daniel A. '48 (NEW) Retired.
Danilak, John '61 (PSC) Retired.
Daniszewski, Msgr. Alfred '45 (MAN) [10] Manchester, NH St. Hedwig Church.
Daniszewski, Msgr. John D. '43 (E) Retired.
Danko, Michael S. '52 (LIN) Retired.
Danks, Arthur J. '43 (GB) Retired.
Danna, Msgr. Anthony S. '67 (BRK) [131] Brooklyn, NY Sacred Hearts of Jesus and Mary and St. Stephen Church.
Danneker, David L. '82 (HBG) [4] Lancaster, PA St. John Neumann Church.
Danneker, Edward A. '64 (ATL) Dahlonega, GA St. Luke Catholic Church; [L] Atlanta, GA Campus Ministry.
Dannenfelser, Lambert R. *o.f.m.* '40 (CIN) [P] Cincinnati, OH Friarhurst Retreat Center.
Danner, Brian '95 (SC) Fort Dodge, IA Corpus Christi Church.
Danner, James L. '74 (MEM) Military Chaplains.
Danner, Michael A. '65 (GR) On Special Assignment; [A] Grand Rapids, MI Christopher House-College Department of St. Joseph's Seminary.
Danos, Dean F. '80 (HT) Larose, LA Our Lady of the Rosary Church.
Danowski, Alexander J. '59 (PBL) Retired.
Danquah, Anankwah '86 (BRK) [54] Brooklyn, NY Holy Family Church.
Dansak, Thomas E. '73 (PIT) Military Chaplains.
Dant, Nicholas '75 (IND) Graduate Studies.
Dante, Neil F. '64 (CAM) Westville Grove, NJ Most Holy Redeemer Church.
Danter, Albert F. '43 (STL) [O] St. Charles, MO St. Joseph Carmelite Home.
Dantinne, Gary J. '68 (GB) Little Suamico, WI St. Pius Church; Suamico, WI St. Benedict Church.
Danylo, Bohdan '96 (STF) [6] Hartford, CT St. Michael Church; Syracuse, NY St. John the Baptist Church.
Dao, Anthony Chinh Quang *o.p.* '82 (GAL) [56] Houston, TX Our Lady of Lavang Church; [A] Houston, TX St. Mary's Seminary.
Dao, Ngo Van *c.ss.r.* '86 (LA) [R] Baldwin Park, CA Vietnamese Redemptorist Mission.
Dao, Nhoung V. (LA) Retired.
Daoust, Joseph P. *s.j.* '69 (DET) [K] Detroit, MI Jesuit Community at the University of Detroit.
DaPonte, Paul J. '93 (PRO) [7] Warwick, RI St. Peter's Church.
DaPonte, Robert (HON) [2] Honolulu, HI Co-Cathedral of St. Theresa of the Child Jesus.
Daprile, James '76 (Y) On Duty Outside the Diocese.
Daprile, James M. '76 (CIN) [B] Cincinnati, OH Mt. St. Mary's Seminary of the West.
Darbouze, Gerard '55 (MIA) [20] Miami, FL St. James Church.
Darbouze, Msgr. Rollin J. '69 (BRK) [53] Brooklyn, NY Holy Cross Church.
Darby, Bernard M. '49 (CAM) Retired.
Darby, Thomas J. '47 (NY) Retired; [Z] New York, NY Pope John Paul II Residence.
Darcy, Brendan *s.m.a.* (WDC) [M] Takoma Park, MD Society of African Missions (S.M.A.).

Darcy, Daivd M. '94 (SPR) Greenfield, MA Sacred Heart Church.
Darcy, David M. '94 (SPR) Turners Falls, MA St. Mary's Church; Turners Falls, MA St. Anne Church.
Darcy, Msgr. Harold P. '54 (NEW) [B] South Orange, NJ Seton Hall University; [B] South Orange, NJ Seton Hall University.
Darcy, John J. '79 (PRO) On Duty Outside the Diocese.
Dardis, Hugh A. '49 (NY) Wurtsboro, NY St. Joseph Church.
Dare, Glenn '74 (P) On Duty Outside the Archdiocese.
Dare, Glenn '74 (SAC) Auburn, CA St. Joseph Church.
Dargan, Peter S. '61 (HRT) Orange, CT Holy Infant Church.
Dargis, Andre E. *a.a.* '67 (WOR) [N] Worcester, MA Assumptionists (Augustinians of the Assumption).
Daries, Joseph *c.m.f.* '56 (LA) [R] Rancho Dominguez, CA Dominguez Seminary Inc.
Darilek, Dennis '73 (SAT) [60] San Antonio, TX St. Paul Church.
Darin, David M. '91 (BEL) New Athens, IL St. Agatha Church.
Darkowski, Msgr. Leon S. '43 (PIT) Retired.
Darling, Franklin A. '58 (SPR) Greenfield, MA Holy Trinity Church.
Darling, George E. '84 (GR) Belding, MI St. Joseph's Church; Miriam, MI St. Mary's Church.
Darling, William G. '73 (ROC) [55] Rochester, NY St. Salome Church.
Darling, Willis F. *c.m.* '32 (STL) [P] Perryville, MO Congregation of The Mission.
Darnall, Thomas W. '52 (OKL) [17] Oklahoma City, OK Sacred Heart Church; Retired.
Darnell, Lawrence T. *o.m.v.* '82 (LA) Hawaiian Gardens, CA St. Peter Chanel Church.
Darnieder, Donald A. '55 (MIL) Retired.
Darow, Robert G. '63 (CHI) [78] Chicago, IL St. Hilary Church.
Darragh, John '68 (HEL) [1] Helena, MT Cathedral of St. Helena.
Das Neves, Antonio '61 (SB) Adelanto, CA Christ the Good Shepherd Church.
Dascenzo, Joseph J. '58 (PIT) Baden, PA St. John the Baptist Church.
Daschbach, Edwin *s.v.d.* '66 (WH) Glenville, WV Good Shepherd Church.
Dash, Alan J. '67 (R) [2] Raleigh, NC Catholic Student Center, North Carolina State University Church; [H] Raleigh, NC Catholic Student Center.
Dash, George *o.f.m.cap.* (NY) State, NY St. Clare's Secure Unit; State, NY Taconic Correctional Facility; City, NY Anna M. Kross Center.
Dash, George *o.f.m.cap.* '92 (BRK) [87] Brooklyn, NY St. Michael's Church.
Dash, George J. *o.f.m.cap.* (NY) State, NY Bayview Correctional Facility.
DaSilva, Anthony '88 (NEW) [8] Newark, NJ St. Benedict's Church.
DaSilva, Joseph '72 (B) [E] Boise, ID Nazareth.
DaSilva, Joseph '72 (BRK) Released from Diocesan Assignment.
daSilva, Marcos '88 (BO) [2] Somerville, MA St. Anthony Church.
Dasseville, Armand *o.f.m.cap.* '49 (NY) [57] New York, NY St. John the Baptist Church.
Datko, James L. *o.m.i.* '51 (STP) [N] St. Paul, MN Oblate Residence; [Q] Buffalo, MN Christ the King Retreat Center.
Datko, Jerome *o.m.i.* '56 (DUL) Sandstone, MN St. Luke's Church.
Dattilo, Anthony M. '84 (CIN) [21] Dayton, OH Our Lady of the Rosary Church; [28] Dayton, OH St. Stephen Church.
Dattilo, Theophane *o.f.m.* '44 (DET) [5] Southfield, MI St. Michael Church.
Dattilo, Tony '90 (STL) [6] St. Charles, MO St. Robert Bellarmine Church.
Datty, Edward *s.a.* '49 (NY) [207] Staten Island, NY Immaculate Conception Church.
Datty, Edward J. *s.a.* (NY) Staten Island, NY Bayley Seton Hospital.
Datty, Edward J. *s.a.* '49 (NY) [S] New York, NY Bayley Seton Hospital.
Datzman, Harold L. *o.s.b.* '65 (PEO) Ladd, IL St. Benedict's Church; [A] Peru, IL St. Bede Abbey and Academy.
Dauenhauer, John (PAT) Absent on Leave.
Daues, Mark J. *s.j.* '94 (KC) [D] Kansas City, MO Rockhurst High School.
Daues, Vincent F. *s.j.* '48 (STL) [O] St. Louis, MO Fusz Pavilion.
Daugherty, Daniel L. '94 (TYL) Whitehouse, TX Prince of Peace Church.
Daugherty, Scott '83 (FRS) Porterville, CA St. Anne Church.
Daum, John J. '45 (Y) [6] Canton, OH St. Joan of Arc Church; Retired.
Dauphinais, Gerard V. (MAN) On Duty Outside the Diocese.
Dauphinais, Henry *m.s.* '55 (TUC) Tucson, AZ U.S. Veterans Hospital.
Dauphinais, Louis Marie *o.m.a.r.* '70 (SAM) [C] Bethlehem, SD Holy Nativity Monastery.
Dauses, Jeffrey '90 (BAL) Clarksville, MD St. Louis Church.
Dauss, Francis (SP) Retired.
Dautremont, Charles R. '60 (GR) [14] Grand Rapids, MI St. Dominic Church.
Davadilla, Patrick Joel *s.v.d.* (FRS) [7] Fresno, CA St. Anthony of Padua Church.
Davalos, Carlos '78 (SAT) Pleasanton, TX St. Andrew Church.
Davantes, Charles B. '79 (TR) [17] Trenton, NJ St. Joachim Church.
Davenport, Bernard F. '74 (WOR) [17] Worcester, MA St. Andrew the Apostle Church; Worcester, MA University of Mass Medical Center; On Special or Other (Arch)Diocesan Assignment.
Davenport, Christopher M. '61 (PRO) [7] Pawtucket, RI St. Leo's Church.
Davenport, Clement A. '48 (SFR) [3] Menlo Park, CA The Church of the Nativity.
Davenport, Thomas J. '42 (SFD) Retired.
Davern, Raymond J. '58 (KCK) [3] Kansas City, KS Christ the King Church.
Davern, Msgr. Robert B. '51 (SY) Syracuse, NY Van Duyn Home & Hospital; Special Assignment; [S] Syracuse, NY St. Pius X Home, Inc.
Davern Timothy '78 (PHX) [2] Tempe, AZ Our Lady of Mt. Carmel Church.
Davern Timothy R. '78 (PHX) [2] Tempe, AZ Our Lady of Mt. Carmel Church.
Davey, Edward M. '53 (PAT) Newton, NJ St. Joseph's Church.
Davey, John J. (PRO) [4] Providence, RI St. Ann's Church.
Davey, John J. '52 (PRO) Retired.
Davey, Philip D. *o.s.b.* '75 (PEO) [A] Peru, IL St. Bede Abbey and Academy; [A] Peru, IL St. Bede Abbey and Academy.
Davey, Robert W. '62 (SAG) Bridgeport, MI St. Christopher Church.
Davich, George F. '62 (SLC) [10] Salt Lake City, UT St. Vincent de Paul Church.
David, Basilio '50 (DET) Retired.
David, Craig '96 (ATL) Lilburn, GA St. John Neumann Church.
David, George '71 (ROM) Roebling, NJ St. Mary Church; Trenton, NJ St. Basil Church.
David, Joseh '93 (SAM) New Castle, PA St. John the Baptist Church.
David, Raymond J. '45 (RVC) Retired; [N] Uniondale, NY St. Pius X Residence.
Davidowich, Glenn M. '89 (PSC) Trumbull, CT St. John the Baptist Church.
Davids, John J. '76 (PH) Doylestown, PA Our Lady of Mount Carmel Church.
Davidson, Carl J. '64 (NO) [A] New Orleans, LA Notre Dame Seminary Graduate School of Theology.
Davidson, John '64 (EVN) [13] Evansville, IN St. Anthony Church.
Davidson, William '51 (DET) Retired.
Davidson, William B. '51 (DET) [3] Troy, MI St. Anastasia Church.
Davied, Frank L. *o.f.m.* '76 (PBL) [3] Pueblo, CO Holy Family Church.
Davies, Brian *o.p.* '82 (NY) [Z] New York, NY Jesuit Community at Fordham University.
Davies, Daniel T. *o.p.* '58 (NY) Hawthorne, NY Holy Rosary Church.
Davies, Julian A. *o.f.m.* '60 (ALB) [B] Loudonville, NY Siena College.
Davies, Steven E. '77 (SFR) [52] San Francisco, CA St. Thomas More Church; San Francisco, CA Kaiser Hospital San Francisco; Special Assignment.
Davignon, Charles P. '56 (BUR) Essex Junction, VT Holy Family Church.
Davignon, Philip A. '62 (FR) Raynham, MA St. Ann Church.
Davila, Andres (ARE) On Duty Outside the Diocese.
Davila, Carlos Dionisio Cruz '80 (SJN) [E] Rio Piedras, PR Hogar Santa Teresa Jornet for the Aged.
Davila, Johnny '84 (SAT) On Leave.
Davila, Rafael R. *m.m.* '58 (GAL) [Q] Houston, TX Maryknoll Fathers and Brothers.
Davila, Reinaldo *o.f.m.* '90 (SFE) Albuquerque, NM Presbyterian Hospital; Albuquerque, NM University Hospital.
Davin, Neil *c.p.* '52 (BRK) [U] Jamaica, NY Immaculate Conception Monastery.
Davin, Neil W. *c.p.* '52 (MET) Edison, NJ St. Matthew Church; [H] South River, NJ Passionist Provincial Office.
Davin, William *c.p.* '56 (WH) Kingwood, WV St. Sebastian's Church; Masontown, WV St. Zita's Church.
Davino, Louis *o.f.m.* '72 (JOL) [11] Joliet, IL St. John the Baptist Church; [J] Joliet, IL St. John the Baptist Friary.
Davino, Michael J. '86 (CHR) [4] Charleston, SC Sacred Heart Church; [16] Charleston, SC Christ the Divine Teacher Church; [H] Charleston, SC The Citadel.
Davis, Alexander *o.f.m.cap.* '64 (NEW) [4] Orange, NJ Mt. Carmel Church; East Orange, NJ Veterans Administration Hospital.
Davis, Augustine *o.s.b.* '59 (IND) [J] St. Meinrad, IN St. Meinrad Archabbey.
Davis, Charles J. (CAM) On Duty Outside the Diocese.
Davis, Christopher *o.s.b.* (FWT) [M] Wichita Falls, TX Catholic Campus Ministry.
Davis, Christopher *o.s.b.* '58 (PRO) [P] Portsmouth, RI Abbey of St. Gregory the Great.
Davis, Clement T. '70 (IND) [35] Indianapolis, IN St. Monica Church.
Davis, Clyde F. *m.m.* '63 (SJ) [M] Los Altos, CA Maryknoll.
Davis, Cyprian *o.s.b.* '56 (IND) [A] St. Meinrad, IN St. Meinrad Seminary; [J] St. Meinrad, IN St. Meinrad Archabbey.
Davis, Daniel C. *o.p.* '94 (CHI) [D] Oak Park, IL Fenwick High School; [N] Chicago, IL Dominicans (Provincial Office).
Davis, Edward J. '49 (NOR) Retired.
Davis, Edward V. *m.m.* '61 (NY) [Z] Maryknoll, NY Maryknoll Fathers and Brothers.
Davis, Eugene V. '35 (TR) Retired; [M] Trenton, NJ Villa Neumann.
Davis, F. Hampton '90 (LAF) [L] Lafayette, LA Our Lady of Wisdom Catholic Student Center.
Davis, Francis R. (ROC) Corning, NY St. Mary Church; Retired.
Davis, Frank Hampton '90 (LAF) [6] Lafayette, LA Our Lady of Wisdom, University of Southwestern Louisiana Church.
Davis, Gary G. '75 (L) [10] Louisville, KY St. Barnabas Church.
Davis, Henry J. *s.s.j.* '93 (NO) [56] New Orleans, LA St. Raymond Church.
Davis, James J. *o.p.* '53 (PRO) [P] Providence, RI St. Thomas Aquinas Priory at Providence College.
Davis, John E. '69 (FAR) On Duty Outside the Diocese.
Davis, John P. '63 (PRT) Retired.
Davis, Joseph E. '76 (PRO) Valley Falls, RI St. Patrick Church.
Davis, Joseph P. '72 (PAT) Succasunna, NJ St. Therese Church.
Davis, Kenneth *o.f.m.conv.* '65 (SAT) [B] San Antonio, TX San Damiano Friary.
Davis, Kenneth *o.f.m.conv.* '86 (SAT) [M] San Antonio, TX San Damiano Friary.
Davis, Kenneth G. *o.f.m.conv.* '86 (SAT) [C] San Antonio, TX Oblate School of Theology.
Davis, Mark E. '96 (TOL) Sandusky, OH SS. Peter and Paul Church.
Davis, Michael '87 (PH) West Chester, PA SS. Simon and Jude Church.
Davis, Michael '90 (MIA) Hollywood, FL Nativity Church; [C] Fort Lauderdale, FL St. Thomas Aquinas High School.
Davis, Raymond '84 (JOL) Bensenville, IL St. Alexis Church; Retired.
Davis, Richard *t.o.r.* '80 (STU) [A] Steubenville, OH Franciscan University of Steubenville; [F] Steubenville, OH Holy Spirit Monastery.
Davis, Richard P. '63 (LR) Adona, AR St. Elizabeth's Church; Bigelow, AR St. Boniface's Church.
Davis, Royden B. *s.j.* '59 (SCR) [C] Scranton, PA University of Scranton; [E] Scranton, PA Scranton Preparatory School.
Davis, Terrence '69 (SJ) [3] Santa Clara, CA St. Justin Church.
Davis, Thomas A. '68 (CC) [6] Laredo, TX San Augustine Church; [15] Laredo, TX St. Patrick Church; [J] Laredo, TX San Augustin Historical Preservation & Restoration Society, Inc.
Davis, Thomas E. '49 (NEW) Retired.
Davis, Thomas R. (R) Elizabeth City, NC Holy Family Church.
Davis, W. E. *o.s.f.s.* '82 (PH) [Z] Philadelphia, PA Oblates of St. Francis De Sales.
Davis, Msgr. Wilbur '64 (ORG) [2] Anaheim, CA St. Boniface Church.
Davis, William *o.m.i.* (AUS) [H] Austin, TX St. Edward's University.
Davis, William *ss.cc.* '44 (FR) [K] Fairhaven, MA Sacred Hearts Provincial House.
Davis, William *o.m.i.* '57 (GAL) [37] Houston, TX Immaculate Heart of Mary Church.
Davis, William E. *o.s.f.s.* (PH) [D] Philadelphia, PA Northeast Catholic High School for Boys.
Davis, William F. *o.s.f.s.* (WDC) [B] Washington, DC Oblates of St. Francis de Sales House of Studies.
Davis, Msgr. William F. '56 (MEM) Retired.
Davis, William J. '43 (BRK) Retired.
Davis, William T. '43 (BRK) [215] Queens, NY Our Lady of the Miraculous Medal Church.
Davish, William M. *s.j.* '46 (BAL) [C] Baltimore, MD Loyola College; [M] Baltimore, MD Jesuit Community of Loyola College, Inc.
Davison, Ben '92 (SD) Lakeside, CA Our Lady of Perpetual Help Church.
Davison, Timothy L. '85 (TLS) [6] Tulsa, OK St. Francis Xavier-Our Lady of Guadalupe Church; [I] Tulsa, OK

University of Tulsa Newman Center.
Davitt, James P. (CHI) [4] Lemont, IL St. James at Sag Bridge Church.
Davitt, James P. '55 (CHI) Retired.
Davitt, Liam '67 (B) Cottonwood, ID Monastery of St. Gertrude; [B] Cottonwood, ID St. Mary's Hospital.
Davitt, Patrick (DM) Harlan, IA St. Michael Church.
DaVola, F. Robert '67 (BWN) [4] Mission, TX St. Paul Church.
Davoren, Stephen V. '96 (LA) Downey, CA St. Raymond Church.
Daw, Timothy M. '91 (CLV) [33] Cleveland, OH St. Ignatius Church.
Dawber, Stephen F. *s.j.* '69 (BO) [E] Boston, MA Boston College High School & Jesuit Community.
Dawes, Timothy '86 (PIT) Coraopolis, PA St. Joseph Church.
Dawidziak, Msgr. Stanley J. (BUF) Retired.
Dawis, Ralph '54 (NY) Staten Island, NY St. Vincent's Medical Center of Richmond; [S] New York, NY Saint Vincent's Medical Center of Richmond.
Daws, Dominic '55 (B) Retired.
Dawson, Cletus *c.p.* '43 (ALT) [J] Bedford, PA St. Mary's House of Greater Solitude.
Dawson, Ivan *c.ss.r* (P) [17] Portland, OR Holy Redeemer Church.
Dawson, Msgr. James D. '54 (LIN) [1] Lincoln, NE Cathedral of the Risen Christ.
Dawson, John H. '67 (LA) Sick Leave.
Dawson, Msgr. Joseph '51 (STA) Retired.
Dawson, Joseph I. '62 (L) Calvary, KY Holy Name of Mary Church.
Dawson, Richard E. '81 (PT) Cantonment, FL St. Jude Thaddeus Church.
Dawson, William *s.j.* (BAL) Hickory, MD St. Ignatius Church.
Dawson, William A. *s.j.* '58 (BAL) [M] Baltimore, MD Jesuit Fathers and Brothers Maryland Provincial Curia.
Dawson, William F. '54 (DAV) [B] Davenport, IA St. Ambrose University.
Dawson-Amoah, Jude *o.p.* '87 (HBG) Chambersburg, PA Corpus Christi Church.
Day, Charles J. '81 (CHR) Greenville, SC Our Lady of the Rosary Church.
Day, Dennis '76 (B) Priest River, ID St. Catherine's Church.
Day, Dennis C. '76 (B) Sandpoint, ID St. Joseph's Church.
Day, Edward E. '52 (BWN) Raymondville, TX St. Anthony Church.
Day, Edward E. '52 (ELP) On Duty Outside of Diocese.
Day, Edward R. '91 (PIT) Aliquippa, PA St. Titus Church; Elizabeth, PA St. Michael Church.
Day, James R. *o.ss.t.* '72 (PH) Bristol, PA St. Ann Church.
Day, James Richard '96 (NO) [13] Metairie, LA St. Philip Neri Church.
Day, Jerome J. *o.s.b.* '95 (MAN) [K] Manchester, NH St. Anselm Abbey.
Day, Msgr. John D. '39 (BO) [52] Boston, MA Most Precious Blood Church; Retired.
Day, John Patrick *c.p.* '72 (BEL) Cahokia, IL St. Catherine Laboure Church.
Day, John Patrick *c.p.* '72 (CHI) [N] Chicago, IL Passionist Provincial Office.
Day, L. Dudley *o.s.a.* '53 (CHI) [X] Chicago, IL The Institute on Religious Life.
Day, Lenox C. *s.j.* '63 (SJ) Santa Clara, CA Santa Clara Valley Medical Center; [D] San Jose, CA Bellarmine College Preparatory.
Day, Martin *o.f.m.conv.* '91 (IND) [4] Terre Haute, IN St. Joseph Church.
Day, Wilfred E. '67 (IND) [1] New Albany, IN Holy Family Church.
Day, William '86 (GLP) Milan, NM St. Vivian Church; San Mateo, NM San Mateo Church; San Rafael, NM San Rafael Church.
Daya, John *o.f.m.cap.* '78 (HBG) [2] York, PA St. Joseph Church.
Daz, Rudolph A. '54 (SLC) Bountiful, UT St. Olaf Church.
De Adder, James W. '55 (BO) [A] Weston, MA Pope John XXIII National Seminary.
De Agostini, Claudio *c.s.j.* '58 (LA) San Pedro, CA St. Peter Church.
De Angelis, Sante *o.f.m.* '62 (MIL) [P] Burlington, WI Queen of Peace Friary; [Y] Waterford, WI General Secretariat of the Franciscan Missions, Inc.
De Angelo, Jude *o.f.m.conv.* '84 (ALB) [A] Rensselaer, NY Conventual Franciscan Friars.
De Angelo, Jude *o.f.m. conv.* '84 (TR) Seaside Heights, NJ Our Lady of Perpetual Help Church.
de Armas, Alexio *o.c.d.* '58 (PCE) [12] Ponce, PR San Jose Church.
de Armas, Alexio Jose *o.c.d.* '58 (PCE) [B] Ponce, PR The Pontifical Catholic University of Puerto Rico.
de Azevedo, Antonio Carvalho '62 (BGP) [2] Danbury, CT Immaculate Heart of Mary Church.
de Blas, Alonso *o.f.m.* '64 (PHX) [G] Scottsdale, AZ Franciscan Renewal Center, Inc. (Casa de Paz Y Bien).
De Brito Alves, Joseph '67 (BGP) [15] Bridgeport, CT Our Lady of Fatima Church.
De Caprio, John '49 (ALB) Retired.
De Carlo, Philip J. '55 (PIT) Monaca, PA St. John the Baptist Church.
De Celles, John C. '96 (ARL) [1] Alexandria, VA Blessed Sacrament Church.
De Clerk, Msgr. Rainer J. '34 (LR) Retired.
De Costa, George '64 (HON) Keaukaha, Hilo, HI Malia Puka'O Kalani (Mary Gate of Heaven) Church.
De Cristobal, Ferdinand '65 (GRY) [4] Gary, IN Holy Rosary Church.
De Crits, Albert *c.i.c.m.* '40 (ARL) [J] Arlington, VA Missionhurst, C.I.C.M.-Central House and Provincialate.
de Dios, Alfredo *o.a.r.* '60 (LA) [82] Los Angeles, CA San Miguel Church.
de Dios, Francisco Mendez '60 (ARL) [4] Arlington, VA St. Charles Borromeo Church.
De Dominici, Lorenzo '46 (LA) San Pedro, CA Mary, Star of the Sea Church.
De Francisco, Joseph '75 (DAV) [B] Davenport, IA St. Ambrose University.
De Ganck, Roger *o.c.s.o.* '35 (SR) [N] Whitethorn, CA Our Lady of the Redwoods Abbey.
De Garis, Herbert P. '91 (NY) Garnerville, NY St. Gregory Barbarigo Church.
De Groot, Ambrose '45 (GB) [I] Appleton, WI St. Fidelis Friary.
De Guzman, Dennis '91 (OM) [40] Omaha, NE St. Robert Bellarmine Church.
De Hondt, Ronald '73 (DET) [A] Detroit, MI Sacred Heart Major Seminary, Inc.
de jesus, Carmelo *o.c.d.* '47 (PCE) [B] Ponce, PR The Pontifical Catholic University of Puerto Rico.
de Jesus, Msgr. Herminio '69 (PCE) Juana Diaz, PR Nuestra Senora de Lourdes Church; [B] Ponce, PR The Pontifical Catholic University of Puerto Rico.
de Jesus, Rafael Alvarado '94 (PCE) Patillas, PR Inmaculado Corazon de Maria Church.
de la Calle, Juan '54 (PMB) Indiantown, FL Holy Cross Church.
de la Cruz, Carlos E. *s.j.* '75 (NO) [P] New Orleans, LA Jesuit Provincial Office.
De La Cruz, Jenaro *o.c.d.* '66 (OKL) [14] Oklahoma City, OK Our Lady of Mount Carmel and St. Therese Little Flower Church.
de la Cruz, Juan '57 (ATL) [1] Marietta, GA Holy Family Church.
de la Cruz, Luis Maria *s.e.m.v.* '81 (ARE) Hatillo, PR Our Lady of Guadalupe Church.
De La Garza, Joseph G. '51 (SAT) Stonewall, TX St. Francis Xavier Church.
de la Iglesia, Celestino *c.m.f.* '31 (LA) [R] Rancho Dominguez, CA Dominguez Seminary Inc.
De La Pena, Richard (NY) Castle Point, NY Veterans Administration Medical Center.
De La Pena, Rick (NY) Fishkill, NY Church of St. Mary, Mother of the Church.
De La Pinera, Fernando '51 (NO) Retired.
de la Puebla, Tomas *c.m.* '49 (PCE) [8] Ponce, PR La Milagrosa Church.
De la Rosa, Frank '78 (SJN) [6] Carolina, PR Epifania Del Senor Church.
De La Rosa, Jose Luis '84 (SAT) [68] San Antonio, TX St. Vincent de Paul Church.
De La Rosa, Vincent '55 (SAT) On Leave.
de la Torre, Bartholomew *o.p.* '67 (LA) [C] Santa Paula, CA Thomas Aquinas College.
de la Torre, Mario '86 (LA) Canoga Park, CA Our Lady of the Valley Church.
de la Vega, Francis *o.a.r.* '43 (NEW) [N] West Orange, NJ Augustinian Recollects.
De Laura, Felice J. '63 (BRK) [245] Queens, NY St. Thomas Apostle Church.
De Lazzer, Dorino '59 (DEN) [2] Aurora, CO St. Michael the Archangel Church.
de Leon, Edward T. *o.m.i.* (BWN) San Juan, TX Virgen de San Juan del Valle Shrine Church.
De Leon, Jose A. '81 (CGS) Las Piedras, PR Inmaculada Concepcion Church.
De Leon, Juancho '94 (NEW) Lyndhurst, NJ Sacred Heart Church.
de Leon, Robert *c.s.c.* '85 (ALB) [T] Albany, NY The Family Rosary Worldwide Office.
de Leon, Robert E. *c.s.c* '85 (BGP) [O] Bridgeport, CT Provincial Offices of the Priests and Brothers of Holy Cross, Eastern Province.
De Leonardis, Gerard *o.f.m.cap.* '49 (NY) [B] Beacon, NY St. Lawrence of Brindisi Friary.
De Lillio, Richard R. *o.s.f.s.* '66 (WIL) [I] Wilmington, DE Oblates of St. Francis De Sales.
de Llano, Domingo '66 (CC) [9] Laredo, TX San Martin De Porres Church.
de los Reyes, Joel '75 (AGN) Barrigada, GU San Vicente Ferrer Church.
de M. Pereira, Luciano J. '54 (FR) Somerset, MA St. John of God Church.
De Man, Thomas *o.p.* '62 (SEA) [P] Seattle, WA Office of Campus and Young Adult Ministry; [P] Seattle, WA Office of Campus and Young Adult Ministry.
De Marcellis, Evasio '60 (TR) Princeton, NJ St. Paul Church.
De Mayo, John B. '61 (PH) Penn Valley, PA St. Justin Martyr Church.
De Meersman, Clement *c.i.c.m.* '52 (SAT) Devine, TX St. Joseph's Church.
de Mello, Arthur T. '34 (FR) Absent on Sick Leave.
De Mesa, Juan Perez '94 (NEW) [3] Jersey City, NJ St. Anne's Church.
de Miguel, Juan Pascual (VEN) Arcadia, FL St. Paul Church.
de Morchoven, Werner Papeians *o.s.b.* '38 (LA) [R] Valyermo, CA St. Andrew's Abbey.
De Nard, Silvio *s.c.* '79 (PH) [B] Springfield, PA Don Guanella House of Formation.
De Noble, Augustine *o.s.b.* '55 (P) [L] St. Benedict, OR Mt. Angel Abbey.
De Pasquale, Daniel '61 (ALB) Retired.
De Paula, Aderbal T. '83 (NY) [19] Yonkers, NY Our Lady of Fatima Church.
De Peaux, Rowland C. *o.praem.* '51 (GB) [I] De Pere, WI St. Joseph Priory.
de Ramos, Fidel '64 (WDC) Oxon Hill, MD St. Columba Church.
de Ranitz, Richard *o.p.* '70 (CHI) [N] Chicago, IL Dominicans (Provincial Office).
De Rosa, Arnold P. '63 (NEW) [B] South Orange, NJ Seton Hall University.
de Rossi, G. B. '46 (CLV) [P] Cleveland, OH Congregation of the Blessed Sacrament Provincial House.
De Runtz, Msgr. Clarence '45 (KCK) On Duty Outside the Archdiocese.
De Sanctis, Peter '79 (BRK) [208] Queens, NY Our Lady of the Cenacle Church.
De Santi, Bruno *c.s.j.* '51 (LA) San Pedro, CA St. Peter Church.
De Santis, Linus *o.f.m.conv.* (ATL) [L] Atlanta, GA Campus Ministry; [L] Atlanta, GA Campus Ministry.
de Serpa, Roberto '46 (PRO) Retired.
de Silva, Lionel A. *c.s.p.* '59 (NY) [41] New York, NY Good Shepherd Church.
De Simone, David A. (NY) Port Jervis, NY Most Sacred Heart Church.
De Simone, Bartholomew *o.f.m.* '44 (NY) [Z] New York, NY Franciscan Province of the Immaculate Conception.
De Souza, Carl '66 (RIC) Franklin, VA St. Jude Church.
de Souza, Owen '70 (LA) Carson, CA St. Philomena Church.
De Tommaso, Louis *o.f.m.* '54 (NY) [Z] New York, NY Franciscan Province of the Immaculate Conception.
de Verteuil, Jack '89 (FBK) Healy, AK Holy Mary of Guadalupe Church.
de Vianney Guerra, Jesus *o.p.* '57 (NO) [P] New Orleans, LA Dominican Fathers & Brothers, Southern Dominican Province.
De Vita, James C. '57 (RVC) Retired.
de Vlamm, Jozef *o.p.* '53 (PCE) Yauco, PR Holy Rossary Church.
de Water, Joseph M. '67 (NO) [12] New Orleans, LA Immaculate Heart Of Mary Church.
De'Tomasi, Francisco *o.s.m.* '53 (ELP) [24] El Paso, TX St. Ignatius of Loyola Church.
Deaconson, James '85 (VIC) Vanderbilt, TX St. John Bosco Church.
DeAlwis, Rohan '82 (FTW) [16] Fort Wayne, IN Queen of Angels Church.
DeAmato, Norbert *o.f.m.* (BO) [3] Cambridge, MA St. Francis of Assisi Church.
Dean, Alfred A. *s.s.j.* '89 (JKS) Fayette, MS St. Anne Church; Natchez, MS Holy Family Church.
Dean, Frederic D. '65 (PRO) [2] Woonsocket, RI St. Aloysius Church.
Dean, Harry F., Jr. (AUS) [12] Austin, TX St. Catherine of Siena Church.
Dean, James N. '91 (MOB) Auburn, AL St. Michael Church; [K] Auburn, AL Auburn University Newman Center.
Dean, John T. '72 (SPR) [5] Westfield, MA St. Peter's Church; [P] Amherst, MA University of Massachusetts and Amherst College, Newman Center.
Dean, Joseph *glmy.* '45 (CIN) [M] Fairfield, OH Headquarters of Glenmary Home Missioners.
Dean, Joseph *glmy.* '45 (TLS) Idabel, OK St. Francis De Sales Church.
Dean, Joseph *s.c.j.* '84 (GB) [M] Baileys Harbor, WI St. Joseph Retreat Center.
Dean, Martin J. *m.s.c.* '76 (CHI) [N] Chicago, IL Institute for Spiritual Leadership.
Dean, Walter R. *o.s.f.s.* '49 (WIL) [I] Wilmington, DE Oblates of St. Francis De Sales.
Dean, William E. '76 (PH) [144] Philadelphia, PA Sacred Heart of Jesus Church.
DeAndrea, Msgr. Joseph A. '53 (GBG) On Duty Outside the Diocese.
Deane, Declan '72 (OAK) [2] Fremont, CA Holy Spirit Church; [N] Berkeley, CA Jesuit Community at Jesuit School of Theology at Berkeley.
Deane, Edwin *o.f.m.* '44 (HT) [4] Houma, LA Our Lady

of the Most Holy Rosary Church.
Deane, Gregory S. '54 (CC) Port Aransas, TX St. Joseph Church.
Deane, J. Peter *s.j.* '66 (TOL) [K] Toledo, OH St. Mary's Jesuit Community.
Deane, Msgr. Joseph '59 (SAT) [32] San Antonio, TX St. Cecilia Church.
DeAngelis, Antonio *c.s.* '81 (SJ) [7] San Jose, CA Holy Cross Church.
DeAngelis, Mark J. (BO) Military & VA Chaplains.
DeAngelis, William *o.s.b.* '50 (CC) Retired; [H] Sandia, TX Corpus Christi Abbey.
DeAngelo, Jude *o.f.m.conv.* '84 (ALB) [L] Rensselaer, NY Provincialate, Immaculate Conception Friary - Order of Friars Minor Conventual; [L] Rensselaer, NY Provincialate, Immaculate Conception Friary - Order of Friars Minor Conventual.
DeAntoniis, Paul J. *o.praem.* '63 (WIL) [B] Claymont, DE Archmere Academy; [I] Claymont, DE Immaculate Conception Priory of the Canons Regular of Premontre.
DeAntonio, Michael R. '71 (CHR) Spartanburg, SC St. Paul the Apostle Church; Spartanburg, SC St. Joseph's Church; [H] Spartanburg, SC Converse College, Wofford College, Spartanburg Methodist College Newman Center.
Deardorff, Joseph F. *c.pp.s.* '82 (CIN) [M] Dayton, OH Provincial House of the Cincinnati Province of the Society of the Precious Blood.
Dearhammer, John W. '91 (CHI) [135] Chicago, IL St. Maurice Church.
Dearing, Arnold *o.f.m.conv.* '51 (IND) Clarksville, IN St. Anthony of Padua Church.
Deary, John F. *o.s.a.* '66 (VEN) Cape Coral, FL Blessed Katharine Drexel Church.
Deas, Msgr. George T. '51 (BRK) [207] Queens, NY Our Lady of the Blessed Sacrament Church.
Dease, Dennis J. '69 (STP) [C] St. Paul, MN University of St. Thomas.
Deasio, August J. '75 (STU) Retired.
Deast, Ken '87 (LA) [37] Los Angeles, CA St. Agatha Church.
Deasy, Edward '62 (ALX) Retired.
Deasy, Jerry '67 (BIR) [21] Birmingham, AL Prince of Peace Church.
Deasy, Msgr. Timothy '58 (MOB) Daphne, AL Christ the King Church.
Deasy, Wayman P. *m.m.* '59 (NY) [Z] Maryknoll, NY Maryknoll Fathers and Brothers.
Deatrick, John D. '66 (L) [49] Louisville, KY St. Martha Church.
Deaver, Stephen F. '59 (GI) Mitchell, NE St. Theresa's Church.
DeAvila, Rafael *m.g.* '74 (LA) [85] Los Angeles, CA St. Paul Church.
DeBacker, Thomas '54 (OM) Pierce, NE St. Joseph Church.
Debaenst, Emmanuel '34 (SFE) Retired.
DeBellis, John A. '85 (NY) [219] Staten Island, NY Our Lady, Queen of Peace Church.
DeBenedetto, David J. '94 (BR) On Leave.
DeBenedictis, Salvatore *o.f.m.* '44 (NY) [Z] New York, NY Franciscan Province of the Immaculate Conception.
DeBiase, William *o.f.m.* '66 (ALB) [B] Loudonville, NY Siena College.
Debicki, John P. '64 (CHI) [127] Chicago, IL St. Mary of the Angels Church.
DeBisschop, James P. '88 (PEO) Rapids City, IL St. John the Baptist Church.
Debitetto, Ronald E. '63 (WOR) Retired.
DeBlanc, Msgr. Irving A. '38 (LKC) [8] Lake Charles, LA Our Lady Queen of Heaven Church; Retired; [E] Lake Charles, LA Our Lady Queen of Heaven Manor.
DeBlanc, Jefferson J. '77 (LAF) Henderson, LA Our Lady of Mercy Church.
Deblasio, Dominck A. '40 (PIT) Retired.
Deblasio, Ernie '88 (MEM) [8] Memphis, TN St. Francis of Assisi Church.
Debo, William D. '95 (JC) Columbia, MO Our Lady of Lourdes Church; Columbia, MO University Hospital & Clinics.
DeBock, William A. '49 (MAD) East Bristol, WI St. Joseph Church.
DeBoe, Stanley W. *o.ss.t.* '83 (BAL) Jessup, MD St. Lawrence Church.
Debold, Walter A. '42 (NEW) Retired; [B] South Orange, NJ Seton Hall University.
DeBona, Guerric *o.s.b.* '86 (IND) [B] St. Meinrad, IN St. Meinrad Seminary-College of Liberal Arts; [J] St. Meinrad, IN St. Meinrad Archabbey.
DeBruin, Edward *s.d.s.* '53 (MIL) [P] Milwaukee, WI Salvatorians - Jordan Hall.
DeBruycker, James '82 (STP) [30] Minneapolis, MN St. Leonard of Port Maurice Church.
DeBruycker, James R. '82 (STP) Minneapolis, MN Hennepin County Medical Center.
Debski, John '37 (TUC) Retired.
Debski, Joseph E. '64 (MIL) Delavan, WI St. Andrew's Church.
Decal, Wilfredo G. '77 (HT) [6] Houma, LA St. Gregory Barbarigo Church.
DeCarlo, Thomas M. '69 (DM) [D] Johnston, IA Bishop Drumm Retirement Center.
DeCarolis, Joseph R. '59 (HRT) Prospect, CT St. Anthony's Church.
DeCarolis, Vito C. '54 (HRT) [4] Milford, CT St. Mary's Church.
Decell, Stephen '87 (HT) On Leave.
Decewicz, Michael W. '78 (PIT) Monroeville, PA St. Bernadette Church.
Dechant, Leo *c.s.j.* '80 (CLV) [D] Lorain, OH Lorain Catholic High School; [P] Avon, OH Congregation of St. Joseph.
Dechant, Paul *c.s.p.* (MEM) [20] Memphis, TN St. Patrick's Church; [J] Memphis, TN Paulist Fathers (New York); [M] Memphis, TN St. Patrick's Center.
Dechering, Anton '62 (SP) [2] St. Petersburg, FL Blessed Trinity Church.
DeCiccio, Ernesto *c.s.p.* '88 (KNX) [4] Knoxville, TN John XXIII Catholic Center Church; [J] Knoxville, TN UT-Knoxville, Newman Foundation, Inc.
DeCicco Pascal A. *o.s.a.* '52 (PH) [18] Philadelphia, PA St. Augustine Church.
Deck, Alcuin *o.s.b.* '39 (RCK) [H] Aurora, IL Marmion Abbey-St. Augustine's Abbey.
Deck, Allan F. *s.j.* '76 (LA) [R] Los Angeles, CA Columbiere House.
Deck, Marion *t.o.r.* '69 (ARL) [J] Winchester, VA Sacred Heart Friary.
Decker, Douglas '78 (GF) Special Assignment.
Decker, Douglas '78 (OG) Potsdam, NY St. Mary Church.
Decker, James D. '85 (MAN) Military Chaplains.
Decker, Lawrence J. '84 (ALB) [3] Amsterdam, NY St. Joseph-St. Michael-Our Lady of Mount Carmel Church.
Decker, Maurice C. '50 (DET) Retired.
Decker, Neil F. *s.j.* '58 (BO) [R] Cambridge, MA Youville Hospital & Rehabilitation Center, Inc.; [U] Cambridge, MA Youville Healthcare Center, Inc.; [W] Cambridge, MA Faber House; [W] Cambridge, MA Weston Jesuit Community; [FF] Cambridge, MA The Youville House, Inc.
Decker, Raymond G. '58 (SFR) Retired.
Decker, Robert L. '83 (OG) Long Lake, NY St. Henry Church; Newcomb, NY St. Therese Church.
Decker, William Jonathan '76 (OLL) Portland, OR Saint Sharbel Church; Portland, OR Saint Sharbel Church.
Deckman, Peter '64 (ROC) Penn Yan, NY St. Michael Church; [M] Rochester, NY Diocesan Office of Campus Ministry; [M] Penn Yan, NY St. Michael's Church.
DeClippel, Ludo *c.j.* '68 (LA) [1] Santa Barbara, CA Holy Cross Church.
DeCneudt, Msgr. Ferdinand '39 (DET) Retired.
DeCock, Robert *i.s.s.s.* '96 (CC) [14] Corpus Christi, TX SS. Cyril and Methodius Church.
DeCock, Robert *c.c.* '96 (MIL) [T] Waukesha, WI Secular Institute of Schoenstatt Fathers.
DeCola, Vincent P. *s.j.* '88 (WDC) [M] Washington, DC The Jesuit Community at Georgetown University.
DeConcilis, Anthony J. *c.s.c.* '67 (FR) [B] North Easton, MA Stonehill College.
DeCondorpusa, Alfonso '95 (NEW) [1] Hackensack, NJ Holy Trinity Church.
DeCosta George D. '64 (HON) Papaaloa, HI St. Anthony Church.
DeCosta Joseph F. '90 (NOR) New London, CT St. Joseph Church.
Decoteau, Joseph A. *m.s.* '40 (LKC) [2] Sulphur, LA Our Lady of LaSalette Church.
Decoteau, Vernon '75 (SPR) Belchertown, MA St. Francis of Assisi Church.
Decowski, Frank J. '59 (STP) Retired.
DeCrans, Joseph '84 (CR) Frazee, MN Sacred Heart Church.
Deddens Norbert J. (L) Retired.
Deddens Norbert J. '51 (BWN) San Benito, TX Our Lady, Queen of the Universe Church.
Dede, James R. '51 (IND) Retired.
Dede, John F. '47 (IND) [5] Terre Haute, IN St. Margaret Mary Church.
Dede, Paul M. '64 (IND) Spencer, IN St. Jude the Apostle Church.
Dedek, John F. '55 (CHI) Elk Grove Village, IL St. Julian Eymard Church.
Dedera, Philip (JOL) [I] Naperville, IL St. Patrick's Residence.
DeDomenico, Msgr. Francis A. '56 (NEW) Hasbrouck Heights, NJ Corpus Christi Church.
DeDominici, Lorenzo '46 (LA) Retired.
DeDominicis, Daniels *c.s.sp.* '49 (PIT) [P] Bethel Park, PA Holy Ghost Animation Center.
Dee, Damian '56 (SP) Indian Rocks Beach, FL St. Jerome Church.
Dee, Neal '64 (AMA) [8] Amarillo, TX St. Joseph's Church.
Deegan, James D. *o.m.i.* '70 (STP) [Q] Buffalo, MN Christ the King Retreat Center.
Deegan, John E. *o.s.a.* '61 (PH) [C] Villanova, PA Villanova University; [Z] Villanova, PA Provincial Offices of the Order of St. Augustine, Province of St. Thomas of Villanova; [Z] Villanova, PA St. John Stone Friary.
Deegan, Ronan J. *t.o.r.* '58 (WH) Moundsville, WV St. Francis Xavier's Church.
Deehan, Robert J. '89 (BO) [7] Lynn, MA St. Pius the Fifth Church.
Deehr, Anselm *s.t.* '90 (LA) Compton, CA Our Lady of Victory Church.
Deeker, Geoffrey J. *c.s.s.* '60 (SPR) [3] Pittsfield, MA Our Lady of Mt. Carmel Church.
Deeley, Kevin J. (BO) Military & VA Chaplains.
Deeley, Msgr. Robert P. '73 (BO) Lexington, MA St. Brigid Church; [X] Lexington, MA Grey Nuns Provincial House.
Deeman, Andrew J. *s.j.* '41 (STL) [O] St. Louis, MO Fusz Pavilion.
Deeney, Aloysius *o.c.d.* '74 (LR) [A] Little Rock, AR Marylake - Carmelite Novitiate.
Deeney, Charles J. *o.m.i.* '71 (ORL) Altamonte Springs, FL Annunciation Church.
Deere, Msgr. Gerald '38 (DM) Retired.
Deering, Msgr. Mark '53 (AUS) [6] Waco, TX St. Louis Church.
Deering, William '41 (EVN) St. Bernard, IN St. Bernard Church.
Deering, William '56 (EVN) Special Assignment.
Deery, Lawrence P. *o.m.i.* '41 (BO) [3] Lowell, MA Immaculate Conception Church.
Deeter, Timothy '81 (BEA) Absent On Leave.
Deeves, John F. *s.j.* '58 (DAL) [D] Dallas, TX Jesuit College Preparatory School.
Deevy, Edward '62 (ALX) Absent on Leave.
Defayette, Jeffrey M. '88 (WDC) Germantown, MD Mother Seton Parish Church.
DeFazio, Crescenzio '57 (BIR) [13] Birmingham, AL St. Mark's Church.
Defazio, Vincent G. '92 (SFE) Las Vegas, NM Our Lady of Sorrows Church.
DeFelice, Jonathan P. *o.s.b.* '74 (MAN) [A] Manchester, NH St. Anselm Abbey Seminary; [B] Manchester, NH Saint Anselm College; [K] Manchester, NH St. Anselm Abbey.
Deffenbaugh, Joseph T. '79 (Y) On Duty Outside the Diocese.
Deffenbaugh, Terry A. *o.s.a.* '75 (CHI) [N] Olympia Fields, IL Austin Friary.
DeFilippis, Anthony '60 (JOL) Absent on Sick Leave.
DeFillippes, Gerardo (NY) Suffern, NY Good Samaritan Hospital.
Defler, Herman J. *m.s.f.* '38 (BWN) Donna, TX St. Joseph Church.
DeFolco, Joseph '85 (SEA) Kirkland, WA St. John Mary Vianney Church.
DeForge, Michael W. '79 (BUR) [J] Burlington, VT University of Vermont-The Catholic Center at UVM; [J] Burlington, VT University of Vermont-The Catholic Center at UVM.
DeForke, John C. '59 (GAL) Hitchcock, TX Our Lady of Lourdes Church.
DeFour, Reginald *c.s.sp.* '64 (PIT) [B] Pittsburgh, PA Duquesne University of the Holy Ghost.
DeFrancesco, Albert J. '43 (CIN) Retired.
DeFrancisco, Joseph '75 (BEA) On Duty Outside the Diocese.
DeFranco, Anthony '38 (ALB) [2] Schenectady, NY St. Anthony Church; [9] Schenectady, NY St. John the Evangelist Church; Retired.
DeFrange, Jonathan M. *o.s.b.* '78 (NO) Folsom, LA St. John the Baptist Church; [A] St. Benedict, LA St. Joseph's Seminary College; [P] St. Benedict, LA St. Joseph Abbey.
DeFronzo, Anthony R. (HRT) Rocky Hill, CT St. James Church.
DeFronzo, Anthony R. '81 (PSC) On Duty Outside Diocese.
DeGaetano, Louis J. '79 (BRK) [91] Brooklyn, NY Our Lady of Angels Church.
Degagne, Richard E. '82 (FR) North Attleboro, MA Sacred Heart Church.
Degan, Bernard P. *c.m.* '43 (NO) [P] New Orleans, LA Vincentian Fathers.
Degan, Bernard P. *c.m.* '43 (SAN) Sweetwater, TX Holy Family Church.
Degan, Siro Dal *o.s.j.* '60 (MRY) Davenport, CA St. Vincent De Paul Church; [G] Santa Cruz, CA Oblates of St. Joseph Provincial House and Shrine.
DeGante, Adalberto '79 (DEN) Fort Morgan, CO St. Helena Church; Iliff, CO St. Catherine of Siena Church; Peetz, CO Sacred Heart Church; Sterling, CO St. Anthony Church.
DeGante, Adalberto '79 (GLP) On Duty Outside of Diocese.
Degen, Jerome A. '59 (SC) Manson, IA St. Thomas Church.
Degenhardt, Gervase *o.f.m.cap.* '58 (PIT) [29] Pittsburgh, PA Our Lady of the Angels Church.
DeGeorge, Salvatore F. *o.m.i.* '65 (GAL) [63] Houston, TX St. Patrick Church.
DeGerolami, Michael '74 (SAT) [60] San Antonio, TX

St. Paul Church.
Degeyter, Edward '70 (LAF) Jeanerette, LA St. John the Evangelist Church.
DeGiorgio, John M. '80 (RIC) Mechanicsville, VA Church of the Redeemer.
DeGiovine, Christopher '77 (ALB) Special Assignment; [B] Albany, NY The College of Saint Rose; [M] Albany, NY Convent of the Sacred Heart.
Deglaire, Pierre *c.s.sp.* '70 (SB) Colton, CA San Salvador Church.
Degnan, Daniel A. *s.j.* '66 (NY) [Z] New York, NY Jesuit Community at Fordham University.
Degnan, Henry B. '48 (PH) [5] Norristown, PA St. Paul Church; Retired.
Degnan, James F. '55 (BO) Hopkinton, MA St. John the Evangelist Church.
Degnan, John F. '51 (JC) St. Elizabeth, MO St. Lawrence Church.
Degnan, Msgr. Paul '32 (SAC) Oroville, CA St. Thomas the Apostle Church; Retired and in Senior Ministry.
DeGrandis, Robert *s.s.j.* '60 (GAL) [2] Galveston, TX Holy Rosary Church.
DeGrocco, Joseph '88 (RVC) Wantagh, NY St. Frances de Chantal Church.
DeGroot, Francis J. '93 (MAR) Rudyard, MI St. Joseph Church.
DeGroot, Ignatius *o.f.m.* '64 (OAK) [9] Oakland, CA St. Elizabeth's Church; [N] Oakland, CA Franciscan Friars.
DeGroot, Kenneth J. *o.praem.* '61 (GB) [17] Green Bay, WI St. Willebrord Church.
Degutis, George D. '38 (PH) [10] Philadelphia, PA St. Andrew Church; Retired.
Dehetre, Mark '93 (LAN) Grand Blanc, MI Holy Family Church.
Dehler, William A. *s.j.* '44 (CHI) [C] Chicago, IL Jesuit Community at Loyola University of Chicago.
Dehne, Carl L. *s.j.* '70 (CHI) [C] Chicago, IL Jesuit Community at Loyola University of Chicago.
Dehner, Eugene *o.s.b.* '40 (KCK) [A] Atchison, KS Benedictine College; [H] Atchison, KS St. Benedict's Abbey.
Dehner, Philip R. *o.c.s.o.* '53 (ATL) [I] Conyers, GA The Monastery of the Holy Spirit.
DeHondt, Ronald J. '73 (DET) [29] Detroit, MI St. Gregory Church.
Deibel, David (OAK) [B] Moraga, CA Saint Mary's College; [Q] Moraga, CA St. Mary's College Campus Ministry.
Deibel, David L. '83 (SR) [M] Napa, CA Provincialate Community.
Deichert, Joseph '84 (BIS) On Duty Outside the Diocese.
DeIelse, Salvatore L. '66 (CAM) [2] Vineland, NJ Sacred Heart Church.
Deig, Robert A. '50 (EVN) [17] Evansville, IN St. John the Evangelist Church.
Deikel, Jeffrey J. '76 (LA) Santa Clarita, CA Our Lady of Perpetual Help Church.
Deiker, James P. '93 (DOD) LaCrosse, KS St. Michael Church.
Deimeke, L. Edward '75 (ALB) [7] Schenectady, NY Immaculate Conception Church.
Deimel, George *c.ss.r.* '37 (BAL) [94] Baltimore, MD St. Wenceslaus Church.
Deis, Dennis L. *o.m.i.* '65 (STP) [Q] Buffalo, MN Christ the King Retreat Center.
Deis, Michael S. *o.m.i.* '47 (BEL) [G] Belleville, IL Missionary Oblates of Mary Immaculate - St. Henry's Oblate Residence.
Deisch, Raymond '62 (RC) [D] Rapid City, SD Priest Retirement and Aid Association.
Deister, Charles C. '63 (STL) [3] Creve Coeur, MO St. Monica Church.
Deitch, Richard S. '86 (SFR) [1] San Francisco, CA Cathedral of St. Mary (Assumption).
Deitchman, Carl '84 (HEL) Kalispell, MT St. Matthew Church.
Deitelhoff, Bernard H. '57 (MAD) Argyle, WI St. Joseph Church.
Deiters, James E. '91 (BEL) O'Fallon, IL St. Clare Church.
Deitzer, Gerald E. *c.m.* '55 (PH) [Z] Philadelphia, PA Congregation of the Mission; [Z] Philadelphia, PA Congregation of the Mission.
DeJardin, Joseph R. *s.j.* '61 (P) [D] Portland, OR Jesuit High School.
DeJonghe, Harold J. '57 (LA) Retired.
DeJulio, David T. '90 (SP) [1] St. Petersburg, FL Cathedral of St. Jude the Apostle.
DeJulio, Robert J. '72 (NY) Brewster, NY St. Lawrence O'Toole Church.
Deka, John S. '58 (CLV) [32] Cleveland, OH St. Hyacinth Church.
Dekat, Carl M. '53 (KCK) Emmett, KS Holy Cross Church; Rossville, KS St, Stanislaus Church; St. Marys, KS Immaculate Conception Church.
Dekat, Earl '66 (KCK) Paola, KS Holy Trinity Church.
Deken, John C. '72 (STL) Military Chaplains.
Del, Curtis Van *s.j.* '65 (COS) [8] Colorado Springs, CO Our Lady of the Pines-Black Forest Church.
del Burgo, Lucio *o.c.d.* '73 (MIA) [M] Miami, FL Discalced Carmelite Friars of Miami, Inc.
del Cerro, Helios *c.m.* '61 (LA) [29] Los Angeles, CA Our Lady of the Rosary of Talpa Church.
del Cura, Felix Martinez *o.p.* '54 (PCE) Yauco, PR Holy Rossary Church.
del Cura, Felix Martinez *o.p.* '54 (SJN) [3] Bayamon, PR Catalina de Siena Church.
Del Giudice, Carl '81 (CHL) Brevard, NC Sacred Heart Church.
Del Monaco, Marion '66 (P) [K] Mt. Angel, OR Benedictine Nursing Center.
del Nino Jesus, Rene A. Maria *s.e.m.v.* '83 (ARE) Hatillo, PR Our Lady of Guadalupe Church.
Del Priore, Kenneth '83 (SD) [11] San Diego, CA Our Lady of Angels Church.
del Riego, Rutilio J. '65 (WDC) [B] Washington, DC Diocesan Laborer Priests, House of Studies.
Del Toro, Alfredo *m.c.c.j.* '86 (CHI) [139] Chicago, IL St. Michael the Archangel Church.
Del Toro, Jose *t.o.r.* '95 (STU) [A] Steubenville, OH Franciscan University of Steubenville; [F] Steubenville, OH Holy Spirit Monastery.
del Val, Feliciano '36 (GAL) Retired.
Del Valle, Jorge *m.sp.s.* (LA) [A] Camarillo, CA St. John's Seminary.
Del Valle, Tomas '79 (SJN) On Duty Outside the Archdiocese.
Del Vecchio, Joseph F. '72 (WDC) [44] Washington, DC St. Vincent De Paul Church.
Dela Cruz, Erwin *m.s.* '92 (HON) Waipahu, HI St. Joseph Church.
Dela Cruz, Vicente '90 (HT) Morgan City, LA Holy Cross Church.
deLadurantaye, Paul F. '88 (ARL) [1] Arlington, VA Cathedral of St. Thomas More.
Delahanty, Patrick D. '87 (L) [63] Louisville, KY St. Peter Claver Church.
Delahunty, Richard A. '65 (ORG) Yorba Linda, CA St. Martin Church.
Delahunty, Thomas '54 (SEA) Retired.
Delahunty, Thomas P. '55 (SAC) Retired and in Senior Ministry.
DeLand, Robert J. '73 (SAG) [15] Saginaw, MI SS. Peter and Paul Church.
Delaney, Brian '75 (LA) Montebello, CA Our Lady of the Miraculous Medal Church.
Delaney, Charles A. *c.s.c.* '49 (FTW) [J] South Bend, IN Congregation of Holy Cross Indiana Province Provincial House.
Delaney, David F. '61 (BO) Melrose, MA Incarnation Church.
Delaney, Msgr. Dennis M. '76 (STL) [7] St. Louis, MO Immaculate Heart of Mary Church.
Delaney, Donald M. *s.d.b.* '76 (NY) [F] New Rochelle, NY Salesian High School.
Delaney, Francis H. (BO) Retired.
Delaney, Msgr. Howard L. '40 (PBL) Retired.
Delaney, J. Joseph '48 (ALB) Clinton Heights, NY St. Mary Church.
Delaney, James P. *o.m.i.* '36 (SAT) [K] San Antonio, TX Oblate Madonna Residence.
Delaney, James T. '61 (BAL) [C] Emmitsburg, MD Mount Saint Mary's College.
Delaney, James T. '61 (WIL) On Duty Outside the Diocese.
Delaney, Msgr. John '64 (MIA) Sabbatical.
Delaney, John '81 (FTW) [15] Fort Wayne, IN St. Peter Church.
Delaney, John H. '81 (FTW) [2] Fort Wayne, IN St. Andrew Church.
Delaney, John J. '62 (NY) [52] New York, NY Immaculate Conception Church.
Delaney, John W. '95 (BO) Needham, MA St. Joseph Church.
Delaney, Larry '90 (CR) East Grand Forks, MN Sacred Heart Church.
Delaney, Lawrence '67 (LAN) [I] De Witt, MI St. Francis Retreat Center.
Delaney, Matthew S. '51 (LA) Retired.
Delaney, Michael J. '85 (SCR) [1] Hazleton, PA St. Gabriel's Church.
DeLaney, Michael M. *c.s.c.* '87 (P) [B] Portland, OR University of Portland; [L] Portland, OR Holy Cross Father & Brother, C.S.C. - University of Portland.
Delaney, Michael V. *s.j.* '85 (DEN) [1] Fort Collins, CO St. Joseph Church.
Delaney, Ralph B. *s.j.* '43 (BO) [W] Weston, MA Campion Health Center, Inc.
Delaney, Richard F. '62 (RVC) Garden City, NY St. Joseph's Church.
Delaney, T. Timothy '79 (SCR) [3] Wilkes-Barre, PA St. Boniface Church.
Delaney, Thomas '57 (JKS) Grenada, MS St. Peter Church.
Delaney, Thomas P. *s.j.* '61 (LA) [2] Santa Barbara, CA Our Lady of Sorrows Church.
Delaney, Msgr. William '44 (CHY) [2] Cheyenne, WY Holy Trinity Church; Retired.
Delaney, William *c.pp.s.* '63 (LA) [38] Los Angeles, CA St. Agnes Church.
Delaney, Msgr. William B. '42 (NY) [2] White Plains, NY St. John the Evangelist Church; Retired.
Delaney, William I. '61 (RVC) Retired.
Delaney, William J. '54 (NY) [47] New York, NY Holy Innocents Church.
Delaney, William K. *s.j.* '85 (LA) [C] Los Angeles, CA Loyola Marymount University.
Delano, Kenneth J. '60 (FR) [10] Fall River, MA Our Lady of the Immaculate Conception Church.
Delany, John M. '40 (LA) Retired.
Delargy, Torlach C. '66 (SFR) [T] San Francisco, CA Opus Dei.
DeLarue, Louis '75 (BEA) Mauriceville, TX St. Maurice Church.
deLaunay, Herbert '75 (LAF) Carencro, LA St. Peter Church.
DeLay, Dominic *o.p.* '93 (SAC) Benicia, CA St. Dominic Church.
Delay, Donald R. (BO) Awaiting Assignment.
Delbel, James A. '81 (OG) Hopkinton, NY Church of the Holy Cross; Saint Regis Falls, NY St. Ann Church.
Delclos, John L. '71 (BAL) Special Assignment.
DelConte, Eugene A. *o.s.a.* '55 (OG) Carthage, NY St. James Minor Church; Deferiet, NY St. Rita Church.
DelDuca, John A. '68 (CAM) Hammonton, NJ St. Martin de Porres Church.
DeLeers, Stephen V. (MIL) [A] Milwaukee, WI Saint Francis Seminary.
DeLeers, Vincent J. *o.praem.* '46 (SFE) [J] Albuquerque, NM Santa Maria de la Vid Priory.
DeLeeuw, John '44 (LAF) Retired.
Delehanty, Thomas F. '41 (SPR) Retired.
DeLellis, Francis V. '49 (PRO) Retired.
Delendick, John '77 (BRK) [3] Brooklyn, NY St. Agnes Church.
DeLeo, Roy James '69 (NEW) [6] Elizabeth, NJ St. Genevieve's Church.
DeLeon, Benedict '80 (SAC) Vacaville, CA St. Mary Church.
DeLeon, Eddie *c.m.f.* '91 (SPC) [E] Springfield, MO Claretians Missionaries' Residence-Villa Claret; [I] Springfield, MO The Nancy McGregor House, Southwest MO State University, Drury College, Ozark Technical College.
DeLeon, Edward T. *o.m.i.* '80 (BWN) [I] San Juan, TX Virgen de San Juan del Valle Shrine.
DeLeon, Emmanuel *s.v.d.* '89 (CHI) [B] Techny, IL Divine Word Residence.
DeLeon, Michael *o.s.b.* '95 (CC) [H] Sandia, TX Corpus Christi Abbey.
DeLeon, Michael A. *o.s.b.* '95 (CC) [4] Beeville, TX St. Joseph Church.
Delgado, Enrique '96 (MIA) Key Biscayne, FL St. Agnes Church.
Delgado, Joseph '95 (SJ) [12] San Jose, CA St. John Vianney Church.
Delgado, Julio *c.ss.r.* (CGS) Fajardo, PR Santiago Apostol Church.
Delgado, Leo *c.m.f.* '55 (PHX) [G] Phoenix, AZ Mt. Claret Retreat Center.
Delgado, Leslie N. '55 (LA) [96] Los Angeles, CA Sanctuary of Our Lady of Guadalupe Church.
Delgado, Rodolfo '96 (SAC) [5] Sacramento, CA Our Lady of Guadalupe Shrine Church.
Delgado, Ruben '81 (BWN) [5] Brownsville, TX Our Lady of Good Counsel Church.
Delich, David L. *o.p.* '63 (CHI) [N] Chicago, IL Dominicans (Provincial Office); [N] Chicago, IL Dominicans (Provincial Office).
Deliman, Msgr. Edward M. '73 (PH) [156] Philadelphia, PA Visitation B.V.M. Church.
Delis, Robert *s.d.b.* '79 (SFR) [N] San Francisco, CA Salesian Provincial Residence.
Delisi, Anthony *o.c.s.o.* '54 (ATL) [I] Conyers, GA The Monastery of the Holy Spirit.
DeLisle, Henri A. *o.m.i.* '58 (NOR) [F] Willimantic, CT Oblates of Mary Immaculate; [I] Willimantic, CT Immaculata Retreat House.
Delisle, Richard *m.s.* '59 (FR) [K] Attleboro, MA La Salette Shrine.
Dell, Robert *c.o.* '90 (SEA) [1] Vancouver, WA Our Lady of Lourdes Church; [Q] Vancouver, WA Vancouver Oratorian Community.
Dell, Robert S. *c.o.* '90 (CHR) [E] Rock Hill, SC Oratory of St. Philip Neri, Congregation of the Oratory of Pontifical Rite.
Dell'Anno, Anthony V. '69 (BRK) [147] Queens, NY St. Aloysius Church.
Dell'Oro, Italo *c.r.s.* '82 (GAL) [11] Houston, TX Assumption Church.
Della Neve, Louis F. '52 (BUF) [1] Lockport, NY St. Anthony Church.
Della Penna, Marshall *o.f.m.* '60 (NY) [35] New York, NY St. Francis of Assisi Church.
Della Penta, Joseph C. *o.p.* '35 (CHI) [N] River Forest, IL St. Thomas Aquinas Priory.
della Picca, Angelo A. '45 (CIN) [D] Cincinnati, OH College of Mount St. Joseph.
della Picca, Msgr. Paul B. '59 (ALN) [9] Bethlehem, PA Our Lady of Pompeii Church.
Della Pietra, Douglas '96 (ROC) [12] Rochester, NY St.

Charles Borromeo Church.
DellaBadia, Leonard *c.s.s.* '35 (NY) [4] White Plains, NY Our Lady of Mt. Carmel Church.
Dellaporte, Dominic (TR) Manasquan, NJ St. Denis Church.
DellaVecchia, Carol *c.pp.s.* '48 (Y) Niles, OH Our Lady of Mt. Carmel Church.
DelliCarpini, John J. '76 (PH) [A] Wynnewood, PA Theological Seminary of St. Charles Borromeo, Overbrook.
Dello Russo, John F. *o.s.a.* '87 (NY) [168] Bronx, NY St. Nicholas of Tolentine Church.
Dellos, Richard '68 (SY) Greene, NY Immaculate Conception Church.
Delmonte, Albert L. '64 (ROC) East Rochester, NY St. Jerome Church.
Delmonte, Richard F. (HRT) Permanent Deacons.
Delmore, Eugene *s.j.* '69 (FBK) Kotlik, AK St. Joseph Church; Mountain Village, AK St. Lawrence Church.
DeLong, Allen *s.m.* '45 (LA) [F] Chatsworth, CA Chaminade College Preparatory.
Delonnay, Lawrence '75 (DET) Waterford, MI Our Lady of the Lakes Church.
DeLora, John P. '94 (NY) [5] New Rochelle, NY Holy Name of Jesus Church.
DeLorenzo, Francis Solanus *o.f.m.* '47 (ALB) [A] Catskill, NY St. Anthony Friary.
DeLorenzo, John R. '76 (SY) [17] Syracuse, NY St. John the Baptist Church.
DeLorenzo, Vincent '65 (LAN) Burton, MI Holy Redeemer Church.
DeLorme, R. Daniel '57 (SY) Homer, NY St. Margaret Church.
Delort, Norbert E. *c.ss.r.* '62 (STL) [P] Liguori, MO St. Clement Health Care Center.
Delos, Bernard M. '45 (ALB) Retired.
DelPrete, Frank G. '77 (NEW) Edgewater, NJ Holy Rosary Church.
DeLuca, Albert J. '57 (NY) [111] New York, NY Sacred Hearts of Jesus and Mary Church; Manhattan, NY New York University Medical Center.
DeLuca, Anthony G. '53 (PIT) Monroeville, PA North American Martyrs Church.
DeLuca, David *m.s.c.* '66 (RCK) [H] Aurora, IL Missionaries of the Sacred Heart Community.
DeLuca, Francis G. '58 (WIL) Retired.
DeLuca, Paul F. '81 (CIN) [10] Dayton, OH St. Helen Church.
DeLuca, Stephen J. '65 (BGP) [5] Greenwich, CT St. Agnes Church.
DeLucci, Thomas '85 (NY) [136] Bronx, NY St. Clare of Assisi Church.
DeLucia, Gerald M. '78 (Y) Lowellville, OH Our Lady of the Holy Rosary Church.
DeLucia, Vincent *o.p.* '94 (PRO) [P] Providence, RI St. Thomas Aquinas Priory at Providence College.
Deluney, Gerald C. '69 (SB) [1] Corona, CA Corpus Christi Church.
DelValle, Tomas '80 (NY) [110] New York, NY Sacred Heart of Jesus Church.
DelVecchio, Msgr. Michael E. '54 (BUF) [24] Buffalo, NY St. Francis of Assisi Church.
Delzell, David G. (TR) Retired.
Delzingaro, Dick M. *c.r.s.p.* '96 (ALN) [K] Bethlehem, PA The Barnabite Fathers Barnabite Spiritual Center.
DeMaio, Joseph *o.carm.* '65 (ROC) [B] Rochester, NY McQuaid Jesuit High School; [I] Rochester, NY Whitefriars Priory.
DeManuele, James *c.p.* '78 (L) [L] Louisville, KY Sacred Heart Retreat.
Demarais, Garvin J. '81 (OG) West Chazy, NY St. Joseph Church.
DeMarco, Nathan I. '79 (CAM) West Collingswood, NJ Transfiguration Church.
DeMarco, Peter A. '60 (BGP) [4] Trumbull, CT St. Theresa's Church.
DeMaria, Herculan F.X. *o.f.m.cap.* '50 (BR) Gonzales, LA St. Mark Church.
DeMaria, Lawrence '51 (NO) New Orleans, LA Veterans Affairs Medical Center.
deMaria, Lawrence A. '51 (NO) [11] Metairie, LA St. Louis King of France Church.
DeMarinis, John H. '62 (Y) [8] Youngstown, OH St. Anthony's Church.
DeMartini, Rodney J. *s.m.* '75 (SR) [O] Sebastopol, CA National Catholic AIDS Network.
DeMartinis, Michael G. (E) Du Bois, PA St. Michael Church.
DeMartinis, O. Robert '86 (ALB) Frankfort, NY Our Lady Queen of Apostles Church.
DeMartino, Robert J '92 (ARL) Clifton, VA St. Andrew the Apostle Church.
Demasi, Michael A. '43 (BUR) East Dorset, VT St. Jerome Church; Retired.
DeMattia, John '68 (PAT) Whippany, NJ Our Lady of Mercy Church.
Dembow, Leonard '65 (NEW) Nutley, NJ St. Mary's Church.
Demeck, Norman *c.p.* '52 (MET) [H] South River, NJ Passionist Provincial Office.
Demeck, Norman *c.p.* '52 (TR) [A] Lakewood, NJ Georgian Court College.
DeMeester, Peter '28 (WH) Retired.
Demek, Martin H. '75 (BAL) [95] Baltimore, MD St. William of York Church.
Demers, Bertrand '48 (KNX) [B] Knoxville, TN St. Mary's Medical Center, Inc.
Demers, Francis *o.m.i.* '55 (BO) [W] Lowell, MA Missionary Oblates of Mary Immaculate.
Demers, Francis *o.m.i.* '55 (CHI) [N] Chicago, IL The Oblate House of Theology.
Demers, Gerard A. *s.m.* '59 (BO) [12] Lawrence, MA Sacred Heart Church.
Demers, Normand J. '58 (PRO) [2] East Providence, RI St. Martha Church.
Demers, Paul R. *s.c.* '81 (MAN) [B] Nashua, NH Rivier College.
Demers, Raymond A. '55 (MAN) [J] Laconia, NH St. Francis Home for the Aged.
Demers, Richard D. '83 (OG) Military Chaplains.
Demers, Thomas *o.p.* '39 (PRT) [I] Lewiston, ME SS. Peter and Paul Priory.
Demers, Wilfred G. '59 (MAN) Windham, NH St. Matthew Church.
Demetzky, Alex D. '53 (CLV) [7] Lorain, OH St. Ladislaus Church; Retired.
DeMeulemeester, Patrick '95 (PEO) Lincoln, IL Holy Family Church.
DeMeulenaere, Martin *o.s.b.* '73 (KC) [10] Kansas City, MO St. Elizabeth's Church; [J] Conception, MO Conception Abbey.
DeMeules, Donald H. '83 (JKS) Retired.
Deming, Robert N. '58 (KC) Unassigned.
Demko, Dennis *c.ss.r.* '80 (CGS) San Lorenzo, PR Nuestra Senora de la Mercedes Church.
Demko, James '82 (PSC) Freeland, PA St. Mary's Church.
Demkovich, Msgr. John J. '65 (PAT) [3] Passaic, NJ Assumption of the Blessed Virgin Mary Church.
Demkovich, Michael T. *o.p.* '81 (SFE) [29] Albuquerque, NM St. Thomas Aquinas University Parish Church; [N] Albuquerque, NM Dominican Ecclesial Institute.
Deml, Frank '57 (DEN) [1] Lakewood, CO St. Bernadette Church.
Demmer, Donald '73 (DET) Garden City, MI St. Dunstan Church.
Demo, John M. (OG) [2] Ogdensburg, NY Notre Dame Church.
DeMott, Lester *c.m.* '55 (STA) [E] Jacksonville, FL St. Vincent's Medical Center, Inc.
DeMott, Lester T. *c.m.* '51 (PH) [Z] Philadelphia, PA Congregation of the Mission.
DeMott, Stephen T. *m.m.* '76 (NY) [Z] Maryknoll, NY Maryknoll Fathers and Brothers.
Dempsey, Dennis K. '80 (STP) On Duty Outside the Archdiocese.
Dempsey, Edward M. '67 (NOR) Absent on Leave.
Dempsey, J. Richard *s.j.* '51 (DET) [P] Clarkston, MI Colombiere Center.
Dempsey, James '56 (BEA) [C] Beaumont, TX St. Elizabeth Hospital of Beaumont.
Dempsey, John G. (STL) [39] St. Louis, MO St. Joan of Arc Church.
Dempsey, Msgr. Michael J. '58 (BRK) [218] Queens, NY Our Lady, Queen of Martyrs Church.
Dempsey, Nicholas '71 (SD) [19] San Diego, CA St. Agnes Church.
Dempsey, Richard J. '58 (CHI) Evergreen Park, IL Most Holy Redeemer Church.
Dempsey, Robert J. '80 (CHI) On Duty Outside the Archdiocese.
Dempsey, Terrence E. *s.j.* '85 (STL) [C] St. Louis, MO Saint Louis University; [P] St. Louis, MO Jesuit Community Corporation at St. Louis University - Jesuit Hall.
Dempsey, Thomas J. '39 (PH) Lansdowne, PA St. Philomena Church; Retired.
Dempsey, Thomas J. '61 (RCK) [3] Elgin, IL St. Mary Church.
Dempsey, Msgr. Thomas J. '62 (STL) Mattese, MO Assumption Church.
Dempski, Daniel *o.s.b.* '80 (WDC) [B] Washington, DC Dominican House of Studies.
Dempski, Daniel G. *o.s.b.* '79 (MAN) [K] Manchester, NH St. Anselm Abbey.
Dempster, A. Patrick '51 (Y) Retired.
Dempster, Douglas W. '62 (WIL) Retired.
Dempsy, Thomas F. '65 (BO) Retired.
Demse, Thomas (MIL) [H] Waukesha, WI Waukesha Catholic School System, Inc.
Demse, Thomas P. '76 (MIL) Hartland, WI St. Charles Church.
Demski, Msgr. Arthur A. '54 (BRK) [186] Queens, NY St. Josaphat Church; Absent on Sick Leave.
DeMuro, S. Patrick '85 (HRT) Retired.
Demuth, Msgr. George R. '46 (SCR) Retired.
Demuth, Paul E. '68 (GB) [15] Green Bay, WI Resurrection Church.
Denapoli, Ettore J. '49 (PIT) Retired.
DeNardi, Charles A. '36 (OWN) Retired.
Denault, Paul *o.carm.* '80 (NY) [Z] Middletown, NY St. Albert's Priory; [Z] Middletown, NY Brandsma Priory.
Denburger, John J. *o.c.s.o.* '63 (ROC) [I] Piffard, NY Abbey of the Genesee.
Dendinger, Robert L. '75 (TOL) Napoleon, OH St. Augustine Church.
Dendinger, William J. '65 (OM) Military Chaplains.
Dene, Charles J. '58 (ALN) Lost Creek, PA St. Mary Magdalen Church; Minersville, PA FCI-Schuylkill, Federal Correctional Institute.
Dene, Joseph '62 (WH) Retired.
Deneault, Normand J. '45 (PRO) Retired; [P] Providence, RI St. John Vianney Residence.
Denehy, Msgr. John '45 (ORL) Retired.
Denehy, John F. '56 (FR) Retired.
Denesha, J. Everett '50 (OG) Raymondville, NY St. Raymond Church.
Dengl, Nicholas *o.f.m.* '56 (Y) [J] Youngstown, OH Mt. Alvernia Friary.
Denha, Suleiman '59 (EST) Oak Park, MI Mar Addai Chaldean Parish Church.
Denham, Jim (AUS) [F] Austin, TX Seton Medical Center.
Denig, Philip '85 (DEN) On Duty Outside the Archdiocese.
Denig, Stephen J. *c.m.* '75 (BRK) [D] Queens and Staten Island, NY St. John's University; [U] Jamaica, NY Vincentian Residence.
Deniger, Joseph *c.s.sp.* '58 (LR) Conway, AR St. Joseph's Church.
DeNinno, Dale E. '78 (PIT) [16] Pittsburgh, PA Immaculate Conception Church; [20] Pittsburgh, PA St. Joseph Church.
Deninno, Louis '76 (PIT) [7] Pittsburgh, PA St. Catherine of Siena Church.
Denison, Frederick J. '73 (IND) Frenchtown, IN St. Bernard Church.
Denman, Donald '42 (P) Retired.
Denn, James J. *c.s.c.* '61 (WDC) [K] Washington, DC Georgetown University Hospital.
Dennehy, John D. '81 (NEW) Verona, NJ Our Lady of the Lake Church; [Q] Newark, NJ Essex County College, Rutgers University/Newark, NJIT.
Dennehy, Mark M. *o.s.m.* '46 (CHI) [15] Chicago, IL Annunciata Church; [N] Chicago, IL Servite Friars - Eastern Province.
Dennehy, Martin J. '51 (BGP) Retired.
Dennehy, Thomas '58 (MIA) Retired.
Dennemann, Thomas J. '73 (CIN) Mount Repose, OH St. Elizabeth Ann Seton Church.
Dennen, Gerard F. '41 (BRK) Retired.
Dennerlein, Arno A. '69 (JOL) Lombard, IL Sacred Heart Church.
Dennerlein, John L. '74 (JOL) [3] Joliet, IL Holy Family Church.
Dennett, John A. '62 (GI) Retired.
Dennigan, Patrick J. '62 (BUR) Retired.
Denning, John *c.s.c.* '87 (FR) [C] Taunton, MA Coyle and Cassidy High School.
Denning, John F. *c.s.c.* '87 (FR) [B] North Easton, MA Holy Cross Fathers Religious.
Denning, Joseph B. '60 (DAV) [8] Davenport, IA St. Paul the Apostle Church.
Dennis, Allan J. *m.m.* '32 (NY) [Z] Maryknoll, NY Maryknoll Fathers and Brothers.
Dennis, Clay '52 (SFE) Retired.
Dennis, George T. *s.j.* '54 (WDC) [C] Washington, DC Catholic University of America, The; [M] Washington, DC Leonard Neale House.
Dennis, James J. '42 (BGP) Retired.
Dennis, John J. *o.s.f.s.* '45 (PH) [D] Philadelphia, PA Father Judge High School for Boys; [Z] Philadelphia, PA Father Judge Faculty House.
Dennis, John M. *s.j.* '86 (CHI) [D] Chicago, IL St. Ignatius Jesuit Community.
Dennis, Patrick '74 (TUC) Tucson, AZ Metropolitan Correctional Complex.
Dennis, Patrick '78 (B) On Duty Outside the Diocese.
Dennis, Samuel *o.s.b.* '57 (SFE) [L] Pecos, NM Our Lady of Guadalupe Benedictine Abbey.
Dennis, Thomas J. '92 (SFD) [1] Springfield, IL Cathedral of the Immaculate Conception.
Dennison, Arthur '73 (MIA) Coral Springs, FL St. Andrew Church.
Denniston, John '79 (RVC) Huntington, NY St. Patrick's Church.
Denny, Charles '27 (TOL) Bono, OH Our Lady of Mt. Carmel Church.
Denny, Charles '69 (TOL) Mansfield, OH St. Charles Hospital; [H] Oregon, OH St. Charles Hospital.
Denny, David '80 (PBL) [I] Crestone, CO Spiritual Life Institute of America, Inc.
Denny, John T. *o.s.a.* '90 (PH) [D] Drexel Hill, PA Monsignor Bonner High School.
Denny, Joseph P. '67 (PH) [21] Philadelphia, PA St. Bartholomew Church.
Denny, Thomas *s.j.* '68 (NEW) [C] Jersey City, NJ St. Peter's Preparatory School.
Deno, Msgr. Lawrence M. (OG) Hammond, NY St. Peter Church.
Denomme, Msgr. George E. '48 (WOR) [3] Leominster, MA St. Cecilia's Church.

Densmore, Robert J. '61 (MAN) [2] Manchester, NH St. Anne Church; Manchester, NH Elliott Hospital.
Dente, Thomas A. '93 (NEW) Wyckoff, NJ St. Elizabeth Church.
Denti, Msgr. Carl J. '42 (SY) Retired.
Dentici, Thomas '53 (DEN) Minturn, CO St. Patrick's Church.
Dentinger, Roy E. '50 (L) Retired.
Dentinger, Vincent P. (L) Raywick, KY St. Francis Xavier Church; St. Mary, KY St. Charles Church.
Dentzman, Robert *o.f.m.* '48 (GAY) Petoskey, MI St. Francis Xavier Church.
Denys, Charles *c.i.c.m.* '44 (ARL) [J] Arlington, VA Missionhurst, C.I.C.M.-Central House and Provincialate.
Denzel, F. William *o.m.i.* '55 (BO) [Z] Tewksbury, MA Immaculate Heart of Mary Novitiate-Infirmary.
Denzer, Joseph W. '68 (BRK) [77] Brooklyn, NY St. Malachy's Church; Absent on Sick Leave.
Denzer, Thomas F. *s.j.* '61 (KC) [B] Kansas City, MO Rockhurst College; [J] Kansas City, MO Rockhurst College - Jesuit Community.
DeOtero, Roberto '77 (HON) On Duty Outside the Diocese.
DePascale, Albert *c.pp.s.* '62 (Y) Niles, OH Our Lady of Mt. Carmel Church.
DePasquale, Dominic '61 (SB) Retired.
Depatie, Donald L. '78 (PRO) Cumberland, RI St. Aidan Church.
DePaul, Genska *o.f.m.* (CHI) [B] Chicago, IL The Catholic Theological Union at Chicago.
Depeaux, Bernard F. '50 (BUR) Retired.
DePetris, Joseph J. (BAL) Absent on Leave.
DePew, Daniel R. '85 (GR) On Special Assignment; [A] Grand Rapids, MI Christopher House-College Department of St. Joseph's Seminary.
DePietro, Arthur J. '37 (BO) On Special or Other Diocesan Assignment.
Depinet, Robert L. *m.m.* '61 (CLV) [P] Cleveland, OH Maryknoll Fathers.
DePinto, Basil '58 (OAK) Piedmont, CA Corpus Christi Church; Oakland, CA Kaiser-Permanente Medical Center.
Depman, Francis J. '81 (PH) West Grove, PA Assumption B.V.M. Church.
Deponai, Joseph J. '83 (NY) Military Chaplains.
DePorter, Arnold W. '63 (WDC) Issue, MD Holy Ghost Church.
DePra, Italo '51 (P) Retired.
DePriest, Ellis L. *s.m.* '53 (NO) New Orleans, LA Byzantine Catholic Mission Church; [A] New Orleans, LA Notre Dame Seminary Graduate School of Theology.
DeProfio, Msgr. Louis A. '56 (BGP) [4] Trumbull, CT St. Theresa's Church.
DeProspero, Nicholas '70 (PSC) Pottstown, PA St. John the Baptist Church.
Deptula, Jan '81 (NY) [99] New York, NY Our Lady of Victory Church.
Deptula, Michael '84 (PHX) Lake Havasu City, AZ Our Lady of the Lake Church.
Deptula, Rick *o.f.m.conv.* (BAL) [B] Ellicott City, MD Friary of St. Joseph Cupertino; [M] Ellicott City, MD St. Joseph Cupertino Friary, Friars Minor Conventual of St. Francis of Assisi.
Deptula, Stanley L. '96 (PEO) Moline, IL Sacred Heart Church.
Derasmo, John M. '81 (RVC) Massapequa, NY St. Rose of Lima Church.
Derbes, Louis J. *c.m.* '51 (STL) [P] Perryville, MO Congregation of The Mission.
Derbish, Michael *o.f.m.* '62 (SJP) Aliquippa, PA Ss. Peter and Paul Church.
Derbyshire, Joseph J. '36 (NEW) Garwood, NJ Church of St. Anne.
Derbyshire, Joseph V. '46 (NEW) Retired.
DeRea, Philip *m.s.c.* '68 (ALN) [K] Reading, PA Missionaries of the Sacred Heart.
DeRea, Philip *m.s.c.* '68 (WDC) [V] Washington, DC Missionary Vehicle Association, Inc.
DeRego, Frank '87 (LFT) West Lafayette, IN St. Thomas Aquinas Church; [H] West Lafayette, IN St. Thomas Aquinas Parish and Foundation for Catholic Students attending Purdue Univ.
Deresienski, Stanely M. *s.s.e.* '78 (NOR) [A] Enders Island, CT St. Edmund's Novitiate.
Deresienski, Stanley M. *s.s.e.* '78 (NOR) [F] Mystic, CT Society of St. Edmund; [I] Enders Island, CT Edmundite Apostolate Center.
Derfus, Kenneth J. '55 (MIL) East Troy, WI St. Peter's Church.
Dericks, Msgr. John H. '41 (PAT) Retired.
DeRitis, Gilbert J. *m.m.* '54 (SJ) [M] Los Altos, CA Maryknoll.
Derivan, Thomas B. '72 (NY) [145] Bronx, NY St. Helena Church.
Derivaux, Donald F. '55 (JKS) McComb, MS St. Alphonsus Church.
Derks, Joel *o.s.b.* '63 (SPC) [6] Springfield, MO St. Joseph's Church.
Dermody, Ralph '43 (COL) Retired.
Dermody, Thomas '62 (SAC) On Duty Outside the Diocese.
Dermody, Thomas '62 (SD) San Diego, CA Calipatria State Prison.
Dermond, Msgr. John K. '68 (TR) [13] Trenton, NJ St. Francis of Assisium Church.
Dermott, William R. '82 (ALN) [1] Bethlehem, PA St. Anne Church.
Dernbach, Arthur P. '53 (P) [37] Portland, OR St. Thomas More Church.
Dernek, Daniel R. '62 (STP) Marysburg, MN Immaculate Conception Church.
Dernek, Daniel R. '62 (WIN) On Duty Outside the Diocese.
Dernek, Richard J. '70 (WIN) Blooming Prairie, MN St. Columbanus Church; Geneva, MN St. Mary Church.
DeRoche, Wilfred '65 (OG) Rouses Point, NY St. Patrick Church.
DeRoeck, Walter G. '71 (CHI) Elmwood Park, IL St. Celestine Church.
DeRose, Martin '88 (ALB) Schenectady, NY Ellis Hospital; Special Assignment.
Derosier, Edmond '73 (BO) Shirley, MA St. Anthony Church.
DeRouen, Keith '83 (LAF) St. Martinville, LA St. Martin of Tours Church.
DeRouen, Robert R. *s.j.* '54 (DEN) [M] Denver, CO Xavier Jesuit Center.
Derrane, Mark G. '95 (BO) [4] Medford, MA St. Raphael Church.
Derrenbacher, James W. '45 (NY) Centerville, NY St. John the Evangelist Church; Retired.
Derrera, Ferdinand *s.j.* '61 (GAL) [41] Houston, TX St. Joseph Church.
Derrig, Joseph M. '63 (PH) [4] Norristown, PA St. Patrick Church.
Derrig, Philip T. *s.j.* '44 (STL) [P] St. Louis, MO Jesuit Community Corporation at St. Louis University - Jesuit Hall.
Derringer, James N. '58 (P) [P] Portland, OR University of Portland.
Derry, Daniel '63 (SJ) Gilroy, CA St. Mary Church.
Dersinner, Joseph L. *s.j.* '57 (B) DeSmet, ID Sacred Heart Church.
DeRuntz, Msgr. Clarence M. '45 (COL) [A] Columbus, OH Pontifical College Josephinum.
DeRussy, Edward '57 (SP) Zephyrhills, FL St. Joseph Church.
Derwinski, Victor A. '44 (LIN) Retired.
Dery, Dominic '71 (PIT) [78] Pittsburgh, PA Most Holy Name of Jesus Church.
Dery, Henry R. '48 (HRT) Retired.
Dery, John P. '76 (PRO) Nasonville, RI St. Theresa of the Child Jesus Church.
Derylo, Walter W. '68 (GAY) [4] Alpena, MI St. Mary Church.
Derzack, Thomas A. '76 (ALN) Lansford, PA St. Michael Church.
Des Roches, Robert *o.f.m.* '87 (PRT) [I] Kennebunkport, ME St. Anthony's Friary.
Des Rosiers, Denis A. '69 (OAK) [10] Oakland, CA St. Jarlath's Church.
DeSalvo, Donald D. '69 (RCK) Somonauk, IL St. John the Baptist Church.
DeSalvo, Raphael *o.s.b.* '45 (LR) Scranton, AR St. Ignatius Church.
DeSalvo, William '88 (JOL) Elmhurst, IL Visitation Church.
DeSanctis, Albert M. '80 (SAL) Junction City, KS St. Francis Xavier's Church.
DeSanre, John G. '64 (TR) Deal, NJ St. Mary of the Assumption Church.
DeSante, Paul J. '59 (E) [B] Erie, PA Gannon University.
DeSantis, Joseph A. '75 (ALN) West Bangor, PA St. Roch Church; [C] Bangor, PA Pius X High School.
DeSantis, Linus *o.f.m.conv.* '71 (ATL) Lithia Springs, GA St. John Vianney Church.
DeSanto, Joseph A. '54 (NY) Larchmont, NY St. Augustine Church.
Desaulniers, Richard P. '70 (PRO) Manville, RI St. James Church.
Desautels, Alfred R. *s.j.* '50 (WOR) [N] Worcester, MA Jesuits of Holy Cross College, Inc.
Desch, Paul *o.f.m.* '56 (CIN) [26] Cincinnati, OH St. Francis Seraph Church; [M] Cincinnati, OH St. Francis Seraph Friary.
Deschamps, Wilfred H. '90 (MAN) Gorham, NH Holy Family Church.
DeSciose, Michael C. '75 (PBL) [D] Pueblo, CO St. Mary-Corwin Hospital.
Deshotel, J. Douglas '78 (DAL) Irving, TX St. Luke Church.
Deshotels, James M. *s.j.* '93 (NO) [P] New Orleans, LA Ignatius Residence.
DeSiano, Francis P. *c.s.p.* '72 (NY) [Z] Scarsdale, NY Paulist Fathers Generalate.
Desiderio, Frank R. *c.s.p.* '82 (WDC) [B] Washington, DC St. Paul's College.
Desilets, Donald A. '52 (SPR) Retired.
Desilets, Viateur '46 (LAF) [1] Opelousas, LA St. Landry Church; Retired.
DeSilva, Gregory Bede '82 (FRS) Kerman, CA St. Patrick Church; Tranquillity, CA St. Paul Church.
DeSilva, Praxid '69 (NY) Manhattan, NY St. Vincent Hospital; [S] New York, NY St. Vincent's Hospital and Medical Center of New York.
DeSimone, Russell J. *o.s.a.* '51 (PH) [Z] Villanova, PA St. Thomas Monastery.
Desjardins, Msgr. Dominique '38 (SFR) Redwood City, CA Our Lady of Mount Carmel Church.
Desjardins, George A. '59 (MAN) [9] Manchester, NH St. George Church.
Desjardins, Lionel '46 (BO) [W] Lowell, MA Missionary Oblates of Mary Immaculate.
Desjardins, Raymond S. '42 (MAN) Retired.
DesLauriers, Matthias *o.carm.* '60 (NY) [Z] Middletown, NY St. Albert's Priory; [Z] Middletown, NY St. Albert's Priory; [BB] Middletown, NY National Shrine of Our Lady of Mount Carmel.
DeSloover, A. Robert '74 (TOL) Miller City, OH St. Nicholas Church; New Cleveland, OH Holy Family Church.
Desmarais, Gerard R. '75 (MAN) [7] Nashua, NH St. Joseph Church.
Desmarais, Paul E. '79 (PRO) [A] Providence, RI Seminary of Our Lady of Providence.
Desmarais, Rene '63 (DET) Port Huron, MI St. Joseph Church.
Desmarais, Rene L. '63 (DET) [S] Port Huron, MI John Courtney Murray Newman Center.
Desmond, Barry '59 (MOB) Retired.
Desmond, Donald J. '64 (RVC) East Hampton, NY Most Holy Trinity Church.
Desmond, Hubert E. '58 (BO) [1] Woburn, MA St. Anthony Church.
Desmond, Msgr. Joseph E. '47 (MAN) Hudson, NH St. John the Evangelist Church; Retired.
Desmond, Joseph L. '74 (MET) On Duty Outside the Diocese.
Desmond, Michael Finbar '40 (MOB) [F] Mobile, AL Little Sisters of the Poor, Home For the Aged, Inc.
Desmond, Michael J. '71 (NEW) Kearny, NJ St. Stephen's Church.
Desmond, Nicholas R. '84 (CHI) [63] Chicago, IL St. Francis of Assisi/Our Lady of the Angels Church.
DeSocio, John A. '78 (ROC) [I] Rochester, NY Becket Hall.
Desormeaux, Roland *c.s.* '82 (PMB) [2] Delray Beach, FL Our Lady of Perpetual Help Mission Church.
Desormeaux, Scott '91 (LKC) Jennings, LA Our Lady of Perpetual Help Church; Jennings, LA American Legion Hospital.
Desrochers, Timothy H. '64 (MAR) [F] Garden, MI Marygrove Retreat Center.
Desrosiers, Alfred A. '61 (PRO) Absent on Leave.
DesRosiers, Denis '69 (SPR) On Duty Outside the Diocese.
DesRosiers, N. Wilfrid *s.s.j.* '55 (BAL) [M] Baltimore, MD St. Joseph Society of the Sacred Heart House of Central Administration.
Desrosiers, Paul H. '75 (NO) Lacombe, LA Sacred Heart Church.
DesRosiers, Philip J. '66 (BO) [3] Everett, MA St. Joseph Church.
DesRuisseaux, Charles E. '60 (MAN) [3] Manchester, NH St. Anthony of Padua Church.
Desruisseaux, G. Frantz '78 (BGP) [2] Norwalk, CT St. Joseph's Church.
Dessert, Msgr. James A. '34 (LA) Retired.
Desso, Leo C. '79 (ANC) Eagle River, AK St. Andrew Church.
DeStefano, Neal J. *s.j.* '79 (BO) [W] Boston, MA The Society of Jesus of New England-Provincial Offices.
DeStefano, Richard '62 (BEA) [9] Beaumont, TX St. Jude Thaddeus Church.
DeStephano, Mark T. *s.j.* '88 (NEW) [B] Jersey City, NJ Saint Peter's College; [N] Jersey City, NJ Jesuits of Saint Peter's College, Inc.
DeSutter, Gilbert J. '54 (STP) Retired.
DeSutter, Mark '82 (PEO) [O] Macomb, IL St. Francis of Assisi Newman Center.
Detaege, Paul *o.f.m.cap.* (DET) [K] Detroit, MI St. Mary's Friary.
DeTemple, Michael *o.p.* (PRO) [P] Providence, RI St. Pius Priory.
DeTemple, Michael *o.p.* '81 (BO) [W] Dover, MA St. Stephen Priory; [Y] Dover, MA St. Stephen Priory Spiritual Life Center.
DeTemple, Michael *o.p.* '81 (PRO) [27] Providence, RI St. Pius V Church.
Determan, Joseph *o.p.* '51 (SAT) [B] San Antonio, TX Dominican Priory of Juan Macias.
Deters, Frederick J. *s.j.* '67 (IND) [D] Indianapolis, IN Brebeuf Jesuit Preparatory School, Inc.; [F] Beech Grove, IN St. Francis Hospital and Health Centers.
Deters, Gregory J. '87 (DET) Temperance, MI St. Anthony Church.
Deters, Richard T. *s.j.* '39 (CIN) [M] Cincinnati, OH Faber Jesuit Community.
Detig, Joseph E. *s.v.d.* '62 (LAF) Jeanerette, LA Our Lady of the Rosary Church.

Detisch, John J. '88 (E) [2] Erie, PA Blessed Sacrament Church.
Detisch, Scott P. '87 (E) [B] Erie, PA Gannon University.
Detloff, Edward X. '57 (CHI) [198] Chicago, IL St. Tarcissus Church.
DeTomasi, Gerardo *m.c.c.j.* '63 (LA) [11] Los Angeles, CA Holy Cross Church.
DeTommaso, Louis *o.f.m.* '54 (SP) Tarpon Springs, FL St. Ignatius Church.
DeTore, Richard *c.m.f.* '64 (SAT) [B] San Antonio, TX Immaculate Heart Claretian Seminary; [D] San Antonio, TX Antonian College Preparatory High School.
Dettenwanger, Dennis '64 (CIN) [1] Hamilton, OH St. Ann's Church; [2] Hamilton, OH St. Joseph's Church.
Dettling, William *o.p.* '59 (COL) [A] Columbus, OH Pontifical College Josephinum.
Dettmer, Alfred J. '56 (GRY) Dyer, IN St. Maria Goretti Church; [3] Michigan City, IN Queen of All Saints Church.
Dettmer, David J. '80 (BRK) [18] Brooklyn, NY St. Bernadette Church; [36] Brooklyn, NY St. Ephrem's Church; [G] Brooklyn, NY Xaverian.
Deutsch, Bernard F. '51 (STL) Retired.
Deutsch, Daniel J. '94 (RCK) Loves Park, IL St. Bridget Church.
Deutsch, George E. '57 (TR) Forked River, NJ St. Pius X Church.
Deutsch, Paul *s.j.* '90 (DAL) [D] Dallas, TX Jesuit College Preparatory School.
Deutsch, Timothy (DUL) [1] Duluth, MN Cathedral of Our Lady of the Rosary.
Deutschmann, Msgr. Edward J. '52 (STL) [38] St. Louis, MO St. James the Greater Church.
Devan, Msgr. Clarence M. (OG) Hogansburg, NY St. Patrick Church; Retired.
Devane, John F. *s.j.* '52 (BO) [W] Chestnut Hill, MA The Jesuit Community at Boston College.
Devaney, Michael J. *o.m.i.* '57 (COL) West Jefferson, OH SS. Simon and Jude Church; [H] West Jefferson, OH SS. Simon and Jude.
Devaney, Roy J. '52 (WOR) Retired.
Devany, John *c.p.* '45 (DET) [K] Detroit, MI St. Paul of the Cross Community, Congregation of the Passion.
Devaraj, Arulappa '86 (TYL) Center, TX St. Therese Church.
Devasagayam, Arulanandam '90 (NY) [99] New York, NY Our Lady of Victory Church.
Deveau, Adhemar *o.m.i.* '52 (BO) [FF] Lowell, MA Oblate Ministry Development Service.
Deveau, Adhemar *o.m.i.* '52 (MAN) [K] Hudson, NH Missionary Oblates of Mary Immaculate.
Deveau, Daniel R. '75 (MAN) Groveton, NH St. Francis Xavier Church; North Stratford, NH Sacred Heart Church.
DeVeer, Richard S. '65 (BO) [2] Quincy, MA St. Boniface Church.
Devenney, Timothy L. '93 (DUB) On Leave of Absence.
Devenny, Joseph A. *s.j.* '37 (BO) [W] Weston, MA Campion Health Center, Inc.
Dever, Msgr. Daniel J. '52 (HON) [A] Kaneohe, HI St. Stephen's Diocesan Center.
Dever, Dennis A. '60 (BO) [5] Somerville, MA St. Clement Church.
Dever, Gerard V. '71 (BO) [1] Quincy, MA St. Ann Church.
Dever, James *o.f.s.f.* (TR) [R] Princeton, NJ Campus Ministry for the Diocese of Trenton.
Dever, Msgr. William '65 (MIA) [7] Fort Lauderdale, FL St. Helen Church.
Devereaux, Martin C. '66 (PMB) Special Assignment.
Devereaux, Thomas W. '68 (SR) Healdsburg, CA St. John the Baptist Church.
Devereux, James A. *s.j.* '58 (CHL) [9] Charlotte, NC St. Peter Church; [J] Charlotte, NC Jesuit Community.
Devereux, Raymond P. '68 (CHI) [7] Chicago, IL All Saints-St. Anthony Church.
Devereux, Thomas W. *o.s.b.* '59 (GBG) [H] Latrobe, PA Saint Vincent Archabbey.
deVerteuil, Jack '89 (FBK) Nenana, AK St. Theresa Church.
Devery, Thomas P. '77 (NY) [Z] Suffern, NY Parish Mission Team Res.
DeVille, George T. (PIT) [2] Bridgeville, PA Holy Child Church; Allegheny County, PA Mayview State Hospital.
DeVille, William H. '62 (COL) [41] Columbus, OH Sacred Heart Church.
Devillers, Arnaud J. *f.s.s.p.* '85 (SCR) [M] Elmhurst, PA Priestly Fraternity of St. Peter (F.S.S.P.).
Devin, John *c.ss.r.* '49 (BO) [13] Boston, MA Basilica of Our Lady of Perpetual Help.
Devine, Arthur '57 (TUC) [20] Tucson, AZ Saints Peter and Paul Church.
Devine, Charles '65 (SB) San Jacinto, CA St. Anthony Church.
Devine, Daniel P. '65 (PH) Feasterville, PA Assumption B.V.M. Church.
Devine, Donald G. *s.j.* '65 (PAT) [I] Morristown, NJ Loyola House of Retreats.
Devine, Finbarr *ss.cc.* '70 (LA) South Pasadena, CA Holy Family Church.
Devine, Frank J. *s.j.* '54 (BO) [W] Cambridge, MA Weston Jesuit Community.
Devine, J. Donald *s.s.c.* '54 (OM) [K] St. Columbans, NE St. Columban's Foreign Mission Society.
Devine, James T. '60 (BRK) [217] Queens, NY Our Lady of Perpetual Help Church; [219] Queens, NY Our Lady of the Skies Chapel; Queens, NY Veterans Affairs Extended Care Center, St. Albans, NY.
Devine, Msgr. Joseph A. '49 (HRT) [4] Waterbury, CT Our Lady of Loreto Church.
Devine, Joseph T. '80 (HRT) Military Chaplains.
Devine, Kevin A. *c.s.p.* '56 (NY) [41] New York, NY Good Shepherd Church.
Devine, Michael '57 (SP) Port Richey, FL St. James the Apostle Church.
Devine, Patrick A. '69 (HBG) Bloomsburg, PA St. Columba Church.
Devine, Patrick T. '61 (LC) Retired; [I] La Crosse, WI Holy Cross (Seminary) Diocesan Center.
Devine, Richard J. *c.m.* '55 (BRK) [D] Queens and Staten Island, NY St. John's University; [U] Queens Village, NY DePaul Residence.
Devine, Stephen M. '64 (FRS) Huron, CA St. Frances Cabrini Church.
Devine, Terry '85 (OWN) Henshaw, KY St. Ambrose Church; Marion, KY St. William Church; Sturgis, KY St. Francis Borgia Church.
Devine, Thomas '68 (ELP) [8] El Paso, TX Guardian Angel Church.
Devine, Msgr. Thomas F. '45 (SPR) Longmeadow, MA St. Mary's Church.
Devine, Msgr. W. J. '31 (DM) Retired.
Devine, William (OM) [H] Norfolk, NE St. Joseph Nursing Home.
Devine, William B. '58 (SC) On Duty Outside the Diocese.
Devine, William D. '73 (BO) Military & VA Chaplains.
Devine, William G. *s.j.* '57 (BO) [Y] Gloucester, MA Eastern Point Retreat House.
Devine, William J. (CHI) Retired.
Devine, Msgr. William P. '50 (NEW) Short Hills, NJ St. Rose of Lima Church.
Devine, William P. '52 (DUB) Retired.
Devine, Wm. Denis '45 (MIL) [P] Franklin, WI Villa Maria.
Deviney, Raymond L. '59 (SCR) Blakeslee, PA Christ the King Church.
Devino, Terrence P. *s.j.* '87 (BO) [E] Boston, MA Boston College High School & Jesuit Community; [W] Boston MA Arrupe House.
Devino, Terrence P. *s.j.* '87 (SPR) On Duty Outside the Diocese.
DeVita, Thomas F. '78 (KAL) New Buffalo, MI St. Mary of the Lake Church.
DeVita, Thomas F. '78 (RVC) Priests Released from Diocesan Assignment.
Devito, Darius *o.f.m.cap.* '57 (NY) [Z] Yonkers, NY St. Clare Friary.
DeVito, Michael C. '76 (HRT) [10] Hartford, CT St. Justin Church.
DeVliegher, Joseph *c.s.c.* '68 (AUS) Betram, TX Holy Cross Church; Burnet, TX Our Mother of Sorrows Church; [H] Austin, TX Congregation of Holy Cross - Southern Province.
Devlin, Chester J. '71 (WOR) Northboro, MA St. Bernadette Church.
Devlin, David J. *o.s.f.s.* '77 (VEN) [3] Fort Myers, FL St. Cecilia Church.
Devlin, Eoghan *l.c.* '94 (HRT) [B] Cheshire, CT Novitiate of the Legion of Christ.
Devlin, Eugene J. *s.j.* '51 (NEW) [B] Jersey City, NJ Saint Peter's College; [N] Jersey City, NJ Jesuits of Saint Peter's College, Inc.
Devlin, Francis X. *o.s.a.* '73 (PH) [D] Drexel Hill, PA Monsignor Bonner High School.
Devlin, James E. '72 (BRK) [167] Queens, NY St. Fidelis Church.
Devlin, Joseph D. *s.j.* '66 (BGP) [O] Fairfield, CT The Fairfield Jesuit Community-Fairfield University.
Devlin, Joseph D. *s.j.* '66 (BO) [W] Boston, MA The Society of Jesus of New England-Provincial Offices.
Devlin, Joseph F. '48 (PH) Glenolden, PA St. George Church; Retired.
Devlin, Msgr. Joseph M. '36 (NY) [141] Bronx, NY St. Frances de Chantal Church; Retired.
Devlin, Joseph P. '91 (PH) Willow Grove, PA St. David Church; [D] Warminster, PA Archbishop Wood Catholic High School.
Devlin, Msgr. Joseph W. '56 (CAM) [L] Cherry Hill, NJ Vianney Villa.
Devlin, Kevin '54 (OKL) Perry, OK St. Rose of Lima Church.
Devlin, Mark *s.d.b.* '79 (NO) [D] Marrero, LA Archbishop Shaw High School.
Devlin, Michael H. '68 (SPR) [1] Chicopee, MA Assumption Church; Springfield, MA Baystate Medical Center, Springfield Hospital Unit; Springfield, MA Wesson-Women's Hospital Unit.
Devlin, Philip T. *c.s.c.* '56 (FTW) [J] South Bend, IN Congregation of Holy Cross Indiana Province Provincial House.
Devlin, Raymond A. *s.j.* '55 (SJ) [M] Los Gatos, CA California Province of the Society of Jesus, Jesuit Provincial Office.
Devlin, Raymond D. *s.j.* '55 (STO) [1] Stockton, CA Cathedral of the Annunciation.
Devlin, Vianney M. *o.f.m.* '55 (NY) [115] New York, NY St. Stephen of Hungary Church.
Devold, Cyprian '84 (NO) [21] New Orleans, LA The Resurrection Of Our Lord Church.
DeVolder, Philip '80 (FTW) Decatur, IN St. Mary Church.
Devorak, James W. '72 (NU) Hutchinson, MN Church of St. Anastasia.
Devorak, James W. '73 (NU) Stewart, MN Church of St. Boniface.
DeVore, David G. '88 (CIN) On Special and Diocesan Assignment.
Devore, Gerald T. '62 (BGP) [4] Stamford, CT St. Maurice Church.
DeVries, Gary '85 (DUB) [H] Cedar Rapids, IA Mercy Medical Center, Cedar Rapids, Iowa.
DeVries, Thomas D. '89 (MIL) On Duty Outside the Archdiocese.
DeVries, William J. '90 (MEM) Covington, TN St. Alphonsus Church.
Dewaele, Joseph *c.i.c.m.* '49 (ARL) [J] Arlington, VA Missionhurst, C.I.C.M.-Central House and Provincialate.
DeWalt, Msgr. Homer '50 (E) [K] Hermitage, PA John XXIII Home.
Dewan, Wilfred *c.s.p.* '53 (BRK) [150] Queens, NY St. Andrew Avellino Church.
Dewan, Wilfred *c.s.p.* '53 (NY) [Z] Scarsdale, NY Paulist Fathers Generalate.
Dewan, William '86 (JOL) Bloomingdale, IL St. Isidore Church.
Dewane, Daniel '71 (GB) Kewaunee, WI Holy Rosary Church.
Dewane, Msgr. Frank J. '88 (GB) On Duty Outside the Diocese.
Dewane, John B. '54 (GB) [O] Green Bay, WI Sacred Heart Seminary, Inc.
Dewane, John B. '62 (GB) Special Assignment.
deWasseige, Eric *o.p.* '65 (CHI) [N] Chicago, IL Dominicans (Provincial Office).
Dewes, John W. '65 (CHI) Barrington, IL St. Anne Church.
Dewig, Eugene '50 (EVN) [11] Evansville, IN Sacred Heart Church.
DeWitt, David D. '84 (PIT) Bethel Park, PA St. Valentine Church.
DeWitt, Robert A. '60 (L) [M] Nazareth, KY Generalate, Motherhouse and Novitiate of the Sisters of Charity of Nazareth.
DeWolf, Paul *c.i.c.m.* '50 (ARL) [J] Arlington, VA Missionhurst, C.I.C.M.-Central House and Provincialate.
Dewson, Msgr. John H. '47 (WIL) Liftwood, DE Immaculate Heart of Mary Church; Retired.
Deye, Anthony H. '37 (COV) Erlanger, KY St. Henry Church; Retired.
Deye, Walter C. *s.j.* '75 (IND) [D] Indianapolis, IN Brebeuf Jesuit Preparatory School, Inc.
Deyo, Paul *ss.cc.* '61 (MIA) Hallandale, FL St. Matthew Church.
Deyo, Paul A. '76 (DAV) [2] Iowa City, IA St. Patrick's Church; [F] Iowa City, IA The Regina Catholic Education Center.
DeYoung, Thomas J. '83 (GR) [2] Grand Rapids, MI Basilica of St. Adalbert.
Deziel, Rudolph *s.m.* '37 (BO) [59] Boston, MA Our Lady of Victories Church; Boston, MA Massachusetts General Hospital; [W] Boston, MA Marist Fathers of Our Lady of Victories (Boston Prov.).
Dharmaraj, Anthony *m.s.f.s.* (ALX) Vidalia, LA Our Lady of Lourdes Church.
Dharmaraj, Anthony *m.s.f.s.* '92 (ALX) Ferriday, LA St. Patrick Church.
Dhm, Edward U. '92 (PEO) [4] Streator, IL St. Stephen's Church.
Dhondt, Edward F. '69 (LFT) Anderson, IN St. Ambrose Church.
Di Cerbo, Almerico F. '46 (ALB) Retired.
Di Falco, Anthony F. *s.d.b.* '44 (SFR) [45] San Francisco, CA SS. Peter and Paul Church.
Di Giovanni, Algonso '96 (NEW) Paramus, NJ Our Lady of the Visitation Church.
Di Giralamo, Gerald F. *s.a.* '81 (RVC) Central Islip, NY St. John of God Church.
Di Gregorio, Michael F. *o.s.a.* '73 (PH) [142] Philadelphia, PA St. Rita of Cascia Church.
Di Lella, Alexander A. *o.f.m.* '55 (WDC) [C] Washington, DC Catholic University of America, The.
Di Lella, Mario *o.f.m.* '53 (ATL) [L] Atlanta, GA Campus Ministry.
Di Marco, Abel A. '56 (PCE) [B] Ponce, PR The Pontifical Catholic University of Puerto Rico.
Di Maria, Matthew *c.m.f.* '63 (LA) Arcadia, CA Annunciation Church.

Di Marzio, Msgr. Nicholas '70 (NEW) [G] Newark, NJ Catholic Community Services (C.C.S.) Mt. Carmel Guild Hospital.
Di Mauro, Joseph *s.a.* '78 (BO) [W] Brockton, MA Chapel of Our Saviour; [BB] Brockton, MA Chapel of Our Saviour.
di Miglio, Isidoro *o.f.m.* '47 (NY) [Z] New York, NY Franciscan Province of the Immaculate Conception.
Di Pasquale, Donald '62 (NEW) [7] Bayonne, NJ Our Lady of the Assumption Church.
Di Pasquale, Ralph *o.f.m.* '56 (NY) [Z] New York, NY Franciscan Province of the Immaculate Conception.
Di Peri, Joseph B. '56 (NEW) Retired.
Di Senso, Gerard J. '53 (NY) Otisville, NY Holy Name Church.
Diab, Thomas (LUB) Military Chaplains.
Diab, Thomas '71 (SAN) Military Chaplains.
Diacetis, Anthony C. '69 (ALB) Ballston Lake, NY Our Lady of Grace Church.
Diachek, Robert M. '71 (PAT) Morris Plains, NJ Greystone Park Psychiatric Hospital; [P] Morristown, NJ Priests Residence.
Diadia, Chester '58 (RVC) Floral Park, NY St. Hedwig's Church.
Diaferio, Vincent F. '58 (FR) [9] Fall River, MA Our Lady of the Holy Rosary Church.
Diamond, David E. '83 (PH) Center Square, PA St. Helena Church.
Diamond, Joseph A. *s.j.* '60 (PH) [Z] Philadelphia, PA Jesuit Community at St. Joseph's University.
Diamond, Matthew J. '71 (BRK) [150] Queens, NY St. Andrew Avellino Church.
Dianda, Carl F. '59 (WDC) [13] Washington, DC St. Francis de Sales Church.
Dias, Frank '71 (NY) [A] New York, NY Cathedral Preparatory Seminary.
Dias, John *c.s.c.* (NY) Manhattan, NY Cabrini Medical Center.
Dias, John F. *c.s.c.* '63 (FR) [K] North Dartmouth, MA Holy Cross Mission House.
Dias, Orsete '94 (RVC) Levittown, NY St. Bernard Church.
Diaz, Alberto '85 (ARE) [3] Arecibo, PR Nuestra Senora del Carmen Church.
Diaz, Alvaro *o.f.m.* (CAM) [4] Vineland, NJ St. Isidore Church.
Diaz, Alvaro '45 (SJN) Retired.
Diaz, Alvaro '73 (CAM) [O] Vineland, NJ Spanish Catholic Center.
Diaz, Angel '76 (ARE) [2] Vega-Baja, PR N.S. de la Providencia Church.
Diaz, Angel R. '85 (ARE) Lares, PR St. Judas Tadeos Church.
Diaz, Erno B. '69 (NY) [34] New York, NY Epiphany Church.
Diaz, Msgr. Felipe C. '46 (BRK) Brooklyn, NY Woodhull Medical & Mental Health Center.
Diaz, Francisco '77 (MIA) [14] Miami, FL Prince of Peace Church.
Diaz, Francisco Restrepo (DET) [3] St. Clair Shores, MI St. Isaac Jogues Church.
Diaz, Gilbert M. '94 (KNX) [3] Chattanooga, TN St. Jude Church.
Diaz, Gonzalo '63 (MGZ) On Special Assignment.
Diaz, Gonzalo '63 (SJN) [F] Guaynabo, PR Opus Dei.
Diaz, Hernan Quintero '80 (BWN) [4] Harlingen, TX St. Anthony Church.
Diaz, Hernando '71 (SLC) Tooele, UT St. Marguerite's Church.
Diaz, Jesus '54 (ARE) Vega-Alta, PR Santa Ana Church.
Diaz, Msgr. Jesus R. (PCE) [B] Ponce, PR The Pontifical Catholic University of Puerto Rico.
Diaz, Jose Matias '89 (NEW) [A] Kearny, NJ Redemptoris Mater.
Diaz, Kevin '84 (PHX) Flagstaff, AZ Our Lady of Guadalupe Church.
Diaz, Martin *o.p.* '78 (LA) [59] Los Angeles, CA St. Dominic Church; [BB] Los Angeles, CA Archdiocesan Office for Campus Ministry.
Diaz, Michael '73 (SD) Military Chaplains.
Diaz, Miguel Gil '86 (CGS) Cidra, PR Nuestra Senora del Carmen Church.
Diaz, Oscar '94 (SR) Saint Helena, CA St. Helena Church.
Diaz, Robert '79 (BWN) Retired.
Diaz, Thomas K. '81 (SR) Fort Bragg, CA Our Lady of Good Counsel Church.
Diaz Vilar, Juan '68 (NEW) [B] Jersey City, NJ Saint Peter's College.
DiBacco, John V., Jr. '67 (WH) Martinsburg, WV St. Joseph's Church.
DiBardino, Anthony '76 (CAM) Pennsauken, NJ St. Cecilia's Church.
Dibb, William C. *s.j.* '60 (FBK) [C] Fairbanks, AK Jesuit Residence.
Dibble, Michael B. (NY) [105] New York, NY St. Peter Church.
Dibble, Romuald '47 (MIL) [P] Milwaukee, WI Salvatorians - Jordan Hall.
DiBlasi, Msgr. Augustine J. '45 (NY) Retired; [E] White Plains, NY Archbishop Stepinac High School.
DiBuo, Roger (WIL) Dover, DE Holy Cross Church.
DiBuono, Msgr. Pasquale M. '44 (CAM) Hammonton, NJ St. Martin de Porres Church; Retired.
DiCesare, Giosue Scotto *s.d.v.* '52 (NEW) [25] Newark, NJ St. Michael's Church.
Dicharry, Harold E. *c.m.* '42 (NO) [60] New Orleans, LA St. Stephen Church.
Dicharry, Warren F. *c.m.* '45 (DAL) [6] Dallas, TX Holy Trinity Church.
Dick, Firmus '54 (EVN) Schnellville, IN Sacred Heart Church.
Dick, Gregory M. *o.praem* '96 (ORG) [A] Silverado, CA St. Michael's Norbertine Postulancy, Novitiate and Juniorate; [H] Silverado, CA Norbertine Fathers.
Dick, John '96 (DAL) Ennis, TX St. John Nepomucene Church.
Dickes, Jerome H. '48 (OM) Retired.
Dickey, Merrell '94 (SP) Spring Hill, FL St. Frances Xavier Cabrini Church.
Dickie, Msgr. John A. '56 (SD) [31] San Diego, CA St. Mary Magdalene Church.
Dickinson, Stephen '58 (FAR) Retired.
Dickinson, William R. '89 (CLV) Hudson, OH St. Mary Church.
Dickman, John W. '48 (L) Pewee Valley, KY St. Aloysius Church; Retired.
Dickman, Richard C. '93 (LC) Alma, WI St. Lawrence Church.
Dickmann, Louis H. '59 (COV) Falmouth, KY St. Francis Xavier Church.
Dickrell, Cyril *s.d.s.* '53 (GB) School Hill, WI Holy Trinity Church.
Dicks, Thomas K. '87 (NY) [138] Bronx, NY St. Dominic Church.
Dickson, Henry E. *s.s.j.* (MOB) Chastang, AL St. Peter the Apostle Church.
Dickson, Henry E. *s.s.j.* '60 (MOB) Prichard, AL St. James Major Church.
Dickson, Norman J. *s.j.* (DET) [B] Berkley, MI Loyola House; [K] Detroit, MI Jesuit Provincial Office-Detroit Province of the Society of Jesus; [T] Detroit, MI Jesuit Seminary Association.
DiCristina, Frank A. (PAT) On Duty Outside the Diocese.
Dicristina, Frank T. '86 (SB) Redlands, CA Sacred Heart Church.
Didas, James F. *s.s.j.* '33 (BAL) [M] Baltimore, MD St. Joseph's Manor.
Didier, Jacques R. *m.e.p.* '53 (SFR) [N] San Francisco, CA Paris Foreign Mission Society Residence.
DiDone, Matthew *c.s.* '67 (PMB) [3] Delray Beach, FL Our Lady Queen of Peace Church.
Diebel, Thomas '79 (LUB) Special Assignment.
Dieckhaus, Anthony W. '62 (PH) [152] Philadelphia, PA St. Timothy Church.
Dieckhaus, Joseph C. '74 (PH) [AA] Philadelphia, PA Sister Servants of the Holy Spirit of Perpetual Adoration (S.Sp.S.A.P.).
Dieckman Vincent A. *o.f.m.* '38 (CIN) [M] Cincinnati, OH St. Clement Friary.
Dieckmann, Michael E. '74 (STL) Hillsboro, MO Church of the Good Shepherd.
Diederich, Donald '58 (RVC) Setauket, NY St. James Church.
Diederich, Everett A. *s.j.* '52 (STL) [P] St. Louis, MO Jesuit Community Corporation at St. Louis University - Jesuit Hall.
Diederichs, Michael F. '42 (PHX) Retired.
Diedrick, Charles T. '78 (CLV) Northfield, OH St. Barnabas Church.
Diefenbach, Gabriel *o.f.m.cap.* '36 (GB) [M] Appleton, WI Monte Alverno Retreat Center.
Diegel, Ron '75 (TYL) Marshall, TX St. Joseph Church.
Diegelman, Clarence L. '43 (CIN) Retired; [B] Carthagena, OH St. Charles.
Diegelman, Robert '93 (R) Wendell, NC St. Eugene Church.
Diehl, Dennis P. '74 (BAL) Fulton, MD St. Francis of Assisi Mission Church.
Diehl, Michael C. '55 (TUC) Retired.
Diehl, Thomas J. *s.j.* '50 (CIN) [28] Cincinnati, OH St. Francis Xavier Church; [P] Milford, OH Milford Spiritual Center.
DieKemper, Barnabas '65 (CHI) [N] Chicago, IL St. Peter's Friary.
Dieker, James P. '93 (DOD) Liebenthal, KS St. Joseph Church.
Diekhoff, Bernard *c.pp.s.* '47 (KC) [3] St. Joseph, MO St. Francis Xavier Church.
Diekmann, Godfrey *o.s.b.* '31 (SCL) [I] Collegeville, MN St. John's Abbey, of the Order of St. Benedict.
Diele, Joseph '85 (BRK) [8] Brooklyn, NY St. Ann-St. George Church.
Diels, Gaston *ss.cc.* '47 (HON) [H] Kaneohe, HI Sacred Hearts Center.
Diem, Joseph (BO) Hopkinton, MA St. John the Evangelist Church.
Diemand, James E. '68 (SPR) Orange, MA St. Mary Church.
Diemer, Charles J. '38 (CHI) Retired.
Diemer, Joseph *o.s.b.cam.* '49 (MRY) [G] Big Sur, CA New Camaldoli Hermitage.
Dien, Vincent '46 (SB) Retired.
Dienert, Robert T. '62 (LR) Searcy, AR St. James Church.
Dieninis, Lionginas '38 (GAY) Retired.
Dierker, Louis P. '40 (STL) [4] Florissant, MO St. Christopher Church; Retired.
Dierkes, Richard '81 (KC) [1] St. Joseph, MO St. Joseph's Co-Cathedral.
Diermeier, Joseph *o.f.m.cap.* '78 (LC) Cassel, WI Sacred Heart Church; Halder, WI St. Patrick Church; Marathon City, WI Nativity of the Blessed Virgin Mary Church.
Diersen, William M. '50 (L) Retired.
Diersing, Leo '39 (SAN) Retired.
Diesbourg, Raymond *m.s.c.* '74 (RCK) [H] Aurora, IL Missionaries of the Sacred Heart Community.
Dieter, Thomas '83 (JOL) On Duty Outside the Diocese.
Dieter, Thomas M. '83 (SP) [1] Largo, FL St. Catherine of Siena Church.
Dieter, Xavier L. *o.c.s.o.* '58 (DUB) [K] Peosta, IA New Melleray Abbey, Order of Cistercians of the Strict Observance.
Dietlein, Damian *o.s.b.* '57 (BIS) [A] Richardton, ND Assumption Abbey.
Dietlein, Damian *o.s.b.* '57 (IND) [A] St. Meinrad, IN St. Meinrad Seminary.
Dietlein, Raymond *o.s.b.* '54 (BIS) [A] Richardton, ND Assumption Abbey.
Dietrich, Christopher *o.f.m.cap.* '59 (NY) [17] Yonkers, NY Sacred Heart Church.
Dietrich, Douglas D. '96 (LIN) [1] Lincoln, NE Cathedral of the Risen Christ.
Dietrich, Edward (SB) Retired.
Dietrich, John J. '93 (HRT) Special and other (Arch)Diocesan Assignment; [A] Bloomfield, CT St. Thomas Seminary.
Dietrich, Michael A. '65 (SY) [17] Syracuse, NY St. John the Baptist Church; Syracuse, NY Hutchings Psychiatric Center; Special Assignment.
Dietsch, William '71 (EVN) Poseyville, IN St. Francis Xavier Church.
Dietz, Conrad R. '57 (BRK) [B] Douglaston, NY Cathedral Residence of the Immaculate Conception.
Dietz, Conrad R. '57 (RVC) Oceanside, NY St. Anthony Church.
Dietz, Donald *o.m.i.* '57 (YAK) Bridgeport, WA St. Anne's Church; Chelan, WA St. Francis de Sales Church.
Dietz, Donald L. '57 (STP) [N] St. Paul, MN Oblate Residence.
Dietz, Francis '40 (DET) Retired.
Dietz, Joseph S. '87 (NY) Scarsdale, NY Immaculate Heart of Mary Church.
Dietz, Msgr. Norbert J. '49 (STL) [3] University City, MO Our Lady of Lourdes Church.
Dietz, Xavier Ortiz '77 (SAT) On Leave.
Dietzel, Elmer J. '51 (MAD) Brodhead, WI St. Rose Church.
Dietzen, John J. '54 (PEO) [1] Bloomington, IL Holy Trinity Church.
Dietzen, Vincent E. '53 (PEO) [3] Bloomington, IL St. Patrick's Church; Retired.
Dietzenbach, John '80 (BAL) Libertytown, MD St. Peter Church.
Dietzler, William J. '69 (MIL) [K] Racine, WI St. Mary's Medical Center.
Diez, A. Oscar '68 (DAL) [13] Dallas, TX St. Augustine Church.
Diez, Alvaro '68 (YAK) East Wenatchee, WA Holy Apostles Church.
Diez, Antonio '59 (SP) Riverview, FL Resurrection Church.
Diez, Jose L. *o.s.a.* '72 (MGZ) San German, PR St. Rose of Lima Church.
Diez, Toribio Pascual *o.s.b.* '40 (MGZ) [6] Mayaquez, PR Sacred Heart Church.
Diezel, Joseph J. '62 (SB) Retired.
Diezeman, Andrew S. '45 (IND) Retired.
DiFabio, Mark '95 (SPR) West Springfield, MA St. Thomas the Apostle Church.
DiFede, Thomas V. *o.p.* '59 (COL) Zanesville, OH St. Thomas Aquinas Church.
DiFederico, Gabriel '78 (MEM) [10] Memphis, TN Holy Rosary Church.
Diffley, Francis A. *m.m.* '50 (HON) [13] Honolulu, HI Sacred Heart Church; [H] Honolulu, HI Maryknoll Fathers House.
Diffley, Jerome E. '45 (SP) [4] St. Petersburg, FL Holy Family Church; Retired.
Diffley, Patrick J. '63 (BRK) Released from Diocesan Assignment.
DiFilippo, John V. *o.s.f.s.* '45 (PH) [Z] Philadelphia, PA Oblates of St. Francis De Sales.
DiFolco, Thomas P. '83 (CIN) [59] Cincinnati, OH St. Martin De Porres Church.
DiFrancesco, Walter L. '59 (SAV) [4] Augusta, GA St. Teresa of Avila Church.
DiFruscio, John A. '69 (BO) On Special or Other Diocesan Assignment; Absent on Sick Leave.

Digal, Danilo C. '78 (NO) [1] Kenner, LA Nativity of Our Lord Church.
DiGeronimo, Michael A. '76 (WOR) Leicester, MA St. Joseph's Church; Leicester, MA St. Pius X Church.
DiGeronimo, Richard '73 (LFT) Unassigned.
Diggins, John Martin *o.p.* '94 (PRO) [P] Providence, RI St. Thomas Aquinas Priory at Providence College.
DiGiacobbe, Albert C. '66 (PH) [54] Philadelphia, PA St. Helena Church.
DiGiacomo, James J. *s.j.* '56 (NY) [F] New York, NY Regis High School; [Z] New York, NY "America;" Residence and publication office of the America Press.
DiGiovanni, Stephen M. '77 (BGP) [O] Stamford, CT St. John Fisher Seminary Residence.
DiGiralamo, Gerald (RVC) Northport, NY Veteran's Hospital.
DiGirolamo, Dante M. '48 (NEW) Special Assignment; [R] Kearny, NJ Eucharistic Shrine of the Adorable Face of Jesus.
DiGirolamo, Paul A. '83 (PH) [23] Philadelphia, PA St. Bernard Church.
DiGiulio, Anthony '55 (MAN) [L] West Franklin, NH Our Lady of the Sacred Heart Convent.
DiGiulio, Richard S. '69 (BUF) [1] Cheektowaga, NY St. Aloysius Gonzaga Church.
Dignan, Eamon '59 (WDC) Waldorf, MD Our Lady Help of Christians Church.
Dignan, Thomas '57 (BIS) Tioga, ND St. Thomas Church.
DiGregorio, Joseph L. '66 (PH) Military Chaplains.
DiGuardo, Domenic *s.d.b.* '37 (NY) [BB] West Haverstraw, NY Don Bosco Retreat Center and Marian Shrine; [BB] West Haverstraw, NY Marian Shrine.
DiIanni, Albert *s.m.* '60 (BO) [59] Boston, MA Our Lady of Victories Church; [W] Boston, MA Marist Fathers of Our Lady of Victories (Boston Prov.).
DiIenno, Nicholas C. *o.s.f.s.* '43 (CAM) [L] Pittsgrove, NJ Villa St. Joseph.
DiIorio, Michael C. '77 (PH) King of Prussia, PA Mother of Divine Providence Church.
DiLella, Christopher C. '79 (PAT) Madison, NJ St. Vincent Martyr Church.
DiLeo, Anthony M. '64 (SB) Temecula, CA St. Catherine Church.
DiLeo, Richard *s.c.j.* (GAL) [26] Houston, TX St. Elizabeth Ann Seton Church.
DiLeonardi, Rocco *o.carm.* '56 (JOL) [J] Joliet, IL St. Elias Carmelites.
Dilettuso, Joseph (BLX) Special Assignment.
Dilg, Donald W. *c.s.c.* '75 (FTW) [12] South Bend, IN St. Joseph Church.
Dilgen, William M. *s.m.m.* '47 (RVC) [N] Bay Shore, NY Montfort Missionaries.
Dilger, Basil *o.s.b.* '61 (SFS) [F] Marvin, SD Blue Cloud Abbey.
Dilger, Donald '59 (EVN) Retired.
Diliberto, Peter J. '43 (LA) [R] Los Angeles, CA Amat House; [W] Montebello, CA DePaul Center.
Dilion, Joseph A. '46 (HRT) Retired.
Dilipy, Basilio '94 (CI) Dublon, FM St. Anthony's Church; Dublon, FM St. Anthony's Church.
Dill, Edwin *s.t.* '59 (BIR) Demopolis, AL St. Leo Church.
Dilla, Francis E. (CHI) Retired.
Dillabough, Msgr. Daniel J. '74 (SD) [8] San Diego, CA Immaculata Church.
Dillane, Maurice '63 (SAT) On Duty Outside the Archdiocese.
Dillard, Msgr. Russell L. '78 (WDC) [7] Washington, DC St. Augustine Church.
Dillard, Steven *s.j.* '86 (SPK) [E] Spokane, WA Gonzaga Preparatory School.
Dillemuth, Frederick J. *s.j.* '54 (NY) [Z] New York, NY Jesuit Community at Fordham University.
Diller, Harold *c.pp.s.* '34 (CIN) [B] Carthagena, OH St. Charles.
Dilley, Gary D. '72 (CHR) Absent On Leave.
Dillinger, Joseph Andrew '96 (SC) [2] Sioux City, IA Blessed Sacrament Church.
Dillingham, Charles C. '73 (WIL) Fairfax, DE St. Mary Magdalen Church.
Dillmann, Alan M. '59 (ATL) [12] Atlanta, GA Shrine of the Immaculate Conception Church.
Dillon, Arthur J. '45 (CHI) Barrington, IL St. Anne Church; Retired.
Dillon, Charles P. *s.s.* '39 (BAL) [K] Baltimore, MD St. Charles Villa; [M] Baltimore, MD St. Charles Villa.
Dillon, Ciarian *o.m.i.* '54 (OAK) Crockett, CA St. Rose of Lima Church.
Dillon, David *o.carm.* '65 (JOL) Glendale Heights, IL St. Matthew Church.
Dillon, Msgr. David A. '42 (STP) Retired.
Dillon, Dennis *s.j.* '69 (CLV) [E] Cleveland, OH St. Ignatius High School; [U] Cleveland, OH Jesuit Retreat House.
Dillon, Msgr. Desmond P. '41 (YAK) Kennewick, WA St. Joseph's Church; Retired.
Dillon, Msgr. Edward J. (ATL) [M] Atlanta, GA Carlow College Bicentennial Fund, Inc.
Dillon, Edward J. *o.f.m.* '55 (NY) [Z] New York, NY Franciscan Friars, Order of Friars Manor.
Dillon, Edward J. '60 (ROC) Clifton Springs, NY St. Felix Church; Clifton Springs, NY St. Felix / St. Francis Parish Cluster Church; Phelps, NY St. Francis Church.
Dillon, Msgr. Edward J. '67 (ATL) [3] Atlanta, GA Holy Spirit Church.
Dillon, Edward J. '88 (PAT) [C] Madison, NJ Bayley-Ellard High School.
Dillon, Geoffrey R. *s.j.* '83 (SFR) [N] San Francisco, CA Jesuit Community at University of San Francisco.
Dillon, Gerald F. *c.s.b.* '62 (GAL) Angleton, TX St. Basil Church.
Dillon, James P. '73 (BRK) Military Chaplains.
Dillon, Jeffry T. '81 (BRK) [U] Douglaston, NY Bishop Mugavero Residence.
Dillon, Jerome V. '77 (OM) Military Chaplains.
Dillon, John (RVC) Absent on Leave.
Dillon, John D. '59 (ROC) Auburn, NY Auburn Correctional Facility.
Dillon, John J. '85 (RVC) Valley Stream, NY Blessed Sacrament Church.
Dillon, John T. *s.j.* '63 (CHI) [C] Chicago, IL Jesuit Community at Loyola University of Chicago.
Dillon, Michael J. '60 (SAC) Rocklin, CA SS. Peter and Paul Church.
Dillon, Richard J. '61 (NY) On Duty Outside the Archdiocese.
Dillon, Robert '65 (RIC) Appomattox, VA Our Lady of Peace Church; Buckingham, VA Church of the Nativity.
Dillon, Msgr. Robert E. '36 (SY) [3] Syracuse, NY Blessed Sacrament Church; Retired.
Dillon, Robert E. '65 (RIC) Quinque, VA Shepherd of the Hills Church.
Dillon, Thomas J. *o.s.a.* '57 (PH) [130] Philadelphia, PA Our Mother of Consolation Church.
Dillon, Thomas J. '59 (GI) Sutherland, NE Sacred Heart Church.
Dillon, William *s.a.* '69 (NY) [Z] Garrison, NY Generalate of the Franciscan Friars of the Atonement-St. James Friary.
DiLorenzo, Francis X. '68 (HON) [J] Honolulu, HI Aina Kupaa O Maili.
DiLorenzo, Thomas (BO) Winthrop, MA Holy Rosary Church.
DiLoreto, Anthony '54 (B) Salmon, ID St. Charles Church.
DiLuzio, James *c.s.p.* '93 (LA) [86] Los Angeles, CA St. Paul the Apostle Church.
Dilworth, Kevin *s.j.* '84 (PHX) [B] Phoenix, AZ Brophy College Preparatory.
DiMaggio, Joseph F. '55 (ALB) Johnstown, NY Immaculate Conception Church.
Dimapilis, Jose Rizal *o.p.* '67 (NOR) Middletown, CT Connecticut Valley Hospital.
DiMaria, Peter J. '93 (PH) Media, PA Nativity of the Blessed Virgin Mary Church.
DiMarzio, Nicholas A. '70 (NEW) [28] Newark, NJ Our Lady of Mt. Carmel Church.
DiMarzio, Vito *r.c.j.* '75 (LA) [R] Oxnard, CA Rogationist Fathers.
DiMascola, Charles J. '81 (SPR) Turners Falls, MA Our Lady of Czestochowa Church.
DiMattei, Robert A. '91 (BAL) Pasadena, MD St. Jane Frances de Chantal Church.
DiMatteo, John *o.ss.t.* '36 (PH) Bristol, PA St. Ann Church.
DiMauro, John C. *o.f.m.* '56 (BO) [P] Andover, MA Franciscan Center; [W] Andover, MA St. Francis Friary; [Y] Andover, MA Franciscan Center - Retreat House.
DiMauro, Joseph *s.a.* '78 (BO) [P] Brockton, MA Chapel of Our Savior-Catholic Pastoral and Information Center.
DiMauro, Joseph A. *o.s.f.s.* '73 (PH) [D] Philadelphia, PA Father Judge High School for Boys; [Z] Philadelphia, PA Oblates of St. Francis De Sales.
DiMauro, Msgr. Joseph V. '67 (CAM) Blackwood, NJ St. Agnes Church.
Dimengo, Michael G. '77 (CLV) [1] Cleveland, OH Cathedral of St. John the Evangelist.
Dimic, Milan *s.d.b.* '85 (BGP) [4] Fairfield, CT Holy Cross Church.
Dimler, G. Richard *s.j.* '63 (NY) [Z] New York, NY Jesuit Community at Fordham University.
Dimock, Giles *o.p.* '66 (STU) [A] Steubenville, OH Franciscan University of Steubenville; [F] Steubenville, OH Holy Spirit Monastery.
Dimond, Arthur '51 (COL) [29] Columbus, OH St. Mary Church; Retired.
Dinan, Dennis '92 (NY) Blauvelt, NY St. Catharine Church.
Dinan, John '58 (WCH) Retired.
Dinan, Paul '37 (JOL) Retired.
DiNardo, Daniel A. '66 (CAM) Bridgeton, NJ St. Teresa of Avila Church.
DiNardo, Msgr. Daniel N. '77 (PIT) Franklin Park Borough, PA Saints John and Paul Church.
DiNardo, Hector *c.r.m.* '56 (NEW) Lodi, NJ St. Joseph's Church.
DiNardo, Lawrence A. *m.ch.a.* '74 (PIT) [73] Pittsburgh, PA Holy Wisdom Church.
DiNardo, Mark A. '58 (CLV) [60] Cleveland, OH St. Patrick Church.
DiNardo, Msgr. Ramon A. '50 (WDC) Retired.
DiNardo, Salvatore *o.p.* '31 (SFR) [N] San Francisco, CA St. Dominic Priory.
DiNardo, Salvatore M. *o.p.* '54 (SJ) [D] Mountain View, CA St. Francis High School; [K] Mountain View, CA Villa Siena.
Dinda, John J. '62 (PH) Spring City, PA St. Joseph Church.
Dindorf, Meinrad *o.s.b.* '58 (SCL) [H] St. Cloud, MN St. Benedict's Center; [H] St. Cloud, MN St. Benedict's Center; [H] St. Cloud, MN St. Benedict's Center.
Dindorf, Meinrad *o.s.b.* '58 (STP) Minneapolis, MN University of Minnesota Hospitals.
Dineen, Michael P. '49 (MIL) Kenosha, WI Kenosha Hospital and Medical Center.
Dineen, William *c.pp.s.* '66 (KC) Liberty, MO St. James Church; [A] Liberty, MO Society of the Precious Blood Provincial Offices; [J] Liberty, MO Precious Blood Society Provincial Office.
Dinelli, William J. '56 (SAC) Sacramento, CA University of California, Davis Medical Center.
Dinello, John E. '85 (PIT) [2] Bridgeville, PA Holy Child Church.
Dineros, Santiago '55 (RVC) Ronkonkoma, NY St. Joseph's Church.
Dinga, William '75 (RIC) Retired.
Dinger, Clair M. '53 (LAN) Milan, MI Immaculate Conception Church.
Dinger, Clair M. '53 (STU) On Duty Outside the Diocese.
Dinges, Anthony '57 (RIC) Retired.
Dinh, Dominic (DAV) Retired.
Dinh, Dominic Do van '72 (SJ) [21] San Jose, CA Our Lady Queen of Martyrs, Vietnamese Mission Church.
Dinh, Hai *c.ss.r.* '91 (DAL) [2] Garland, TX Mother of Perpetual Help Church.
Dinh, Hao '93 (SJ) [4] Santa Clara, CA St. Lawrence the Martyr Church.
Dinh, Nghia Huu '96 (HT) Golden Meadow, LA Our Lady of Prompt Succor Church.
Dinh, Tran Thuc '61 (OAK) [3] San Leandro, CA St. Felicitas Church.
Dinh Tuan Ngan, Joseph (SPC) [E] Carthage, MO Congregation of the Mother Co-Redemptrix, United States Assumption Province.
Dinh Viet Luan, Felix M. (SPC) [E] Carthage, MO Congregation of the Mother Co-Redemptrix, United States Assumption Province.
Dinh Vuong Can, Anselm M. *c.m.c.* (SPC) [E] Carthage, MO Congregation of the Mother Co-Redemptrix, United States Assumption Province.
Dinh-Van-Thiep, Philip '83 (GB) Wautoma, WI St. Joseph Church.
DinhShea, Quang Duc *s.v.d.* '92 (DUB) [B] Epworth, IA Divine Word College.
Dinicco, Henry P. '58 (GBG) Mount Pleasant, PA St. Pius X Church.
Dininni, Nicholas J. *o.s.j.* '93 (SCR) [8] Pittston, PA St. Rocco Church.
Dinio, Miguel *o.p.* (SAN) Carlsbad, TX St. Therese of the Child Jesus Church.
Dinkel, Emil *c.pp.s.* '52 (DOD) Hugoton, KS St. Helen Church; Satanta, KS St. Alphonsus Church.
Dinkel, Harvey P. *o.f.m.cap.* '61 (DEN) [M] Denver, CO St. Francis of Assisi Friary.
Dinkins, Msgr. Jack M. '63 (GAL) Katy, TX Epiphany of the Lord Church.
Dinneen, James J. *s.j.* '62 (RVC) [P] Manhasset, NY St. Ignatius Retreat House, Inisfada.
Dinneen, John A. *s.j.* '60 (BO) [W] Chestnut Hill, MA The Jesuit Community at Boston College.
Dino, Gerald *o.e.s.l.* '65 (PSC) Linden, NJ St. George's Church.
DiNoia, Joseph Augustine *o.p.* '70 (WDC) [B] Washington, DC Dominican House of Studies.
DiNola, Leonard J. '58 (NY) Buchanan, NY St. Christopher Church.
DiNorcin, Americo '59 (WDC) Retired.
Diogo, Louis M. '46 (PRO) Retired.
Diomartich, Msgr. Felix S. '37 (LA) [45] Los Angeles, CA St. Anthony Church; Retired.
Dion, Gerald '51 (WOR) Webster, MA St. Louis Church.
Dion, Gerard J. '92 (MAN) Manchester, NH Nursing Homes; Goffstown, NH Hillsborough County Nursing Home.
Dion, Louis F. *a.a.* '40 (WOR) [B] Worcester, MA Assumption College; [N] Worcester, MA Assumptionists (Augustinians of the Assumption).
Dion, Maurice B. '44 (SAL) Retired.
Dionne, Adrian L. *o.p.* '49 (COL) Somerset, OH St. Joseph's Church; Somerset, OH Holy Trinity Church; [H] Somerset, OH St. Joseph's Rectory.
Dionne, Earl J. '58 (MIL) Retired.
Dionne, Francis '81 (SP) [5] Clearwater, FL St. Michael The Archangel Church.
Dionne, Leo *o.m.i.* '59 (MIA) [2] Miami, FL Christ the King Church.
Dionne, Martin *o.p.* '49 (PRT) [I] Lewiston, ME SS.

Peter and Paul Priory.
DiOrio, Ralph A. '57 (WOR) On Special or Other (Arch)Diocesan Assignment.
DiPaul, Lawrence M. '73 (PH) Absent on Leave.
DiPerri, James (BO) [17] Boston, MA St. Catherine of Siena Church.
Diphe, Juan '76 (HEL) Military Chaplains.
DiPietro, Leroy A. '70 (PIT) Brentwood, PA St. Sylvester Church.
DiPietro, Rodric J. '76 (COL) [16] Columbus, OH St. Elizabeth Church.
Dippre, Mark '92 (PHX) [6] Mesa, AZ St. Timothy Church.
Dipre, Gilio L. '55 (E) [B] Erie, PA Gannon University.
DiPucchio, Anthony F.X. '52 (WOR) Retired.
DiRaffaele, William F. (NY) [6] Yonkers, NY Christ the King Church.
Direnzo, Michael J. '70 (STU) On Duty Outside the Diocese.
Dirig, Walter F. *c.m.* '39 (PH) [Z] Philadelphia, PA Congregation of the Mission.
Dirkx, Dennis A. '72 (MIL) [A] Milwaukee, WI Saint Francis Seminary.
DiRuscio, Romano *s.c.* '51 (PH) [L] Springfield, PA Don Guanella School for Retarded Boys; [L] Springfield, PA Cardinal Krol Center; [Z] Springfield, PA Servants of Charity (S.C.).
DiRusso, Anthony '63 (MAN) North Walpole, NH St. Peter Church.
DiSano, Frank E. '84 (ROC) Absent on Leave.
Disch, Msgr. John H. '39 (LAF) [1] New Iberia, LA St. Peter Church; Retired.
Dischler, Raymond J. '73 (MAD) Poynette, WI St. Thomas Church.
DiSciacca, Joseph V. '73 (HRT) Bloomfield, CT Sacred Heart Church.
Dishaw, Conrad J. '48 (MAR) Retired.
Diskin, Francis X. *c.s.p.* '46 (NY) [104] New York, NY St. Paul the Apostle Church; [Z] Scarsdale, NY Paulist Fathers Generalate.
Diskin, John J. *s.j.* '63 (BO) [W] Weston, MA Campion Center.
Diskin, Michael L. '77 (PHX) [24] Phoenix, AZ St. Theresa Church; Special Assignment.
Diskin, Miles Eric '75 (PIT) [38] Pittsburgh, PA Sacred Heart Church.
Dismachek, Francis M. '34 (PIT) Retired; [N] Pittsburgh, PA St. John Vianney Manor.
DiSpigno, Francis *o.f.m.* '96 (TR) Brant Beach, NJ St. Francis of Assisi Church.
DiSpigno, Gennaro '81 (RVC) Baldwin, NY St. Christopher Church.
Dissek, Jerome M. '69 (BUF) Cuba, NY Our Lady of Angels Church; Friendship, NY Sacred Heart Church.
DiStefano, John '52 (BEA) Retired.
DiStefano, Joseph '84 (ORG) Absent on Sick Leave.
Distefano, Simeon *o.f.m.* '63 (NY) [Z] New York, NY Franciscan Province of the Immaculate Conception.
Dister, John E. *s.j.* '62 (DET) [K] Detroit, MI Jesuit Provincial Office-Detroit Province of the Society of Jesus; [K] Detroit, MI Jesuit Community at the University of Detroit.
DiTaddeo, Alessandro '54 (CC) [11] Laredo, TX St. Frances Cabrini Church.
Ditch, Robert G. '56 (STL) [1] Florissant, MO North American Martyrs Church.
Ditenhofer, John A. '61 (STL) [2] University City, MO Christ the King Church.
Ditillo, James J. *s.j.* '74 (BAL) Glyndon, MD Sacred Heart Church; [M] Baltimore, MD Jesuit Fathers and Brothers Maryland Provincial Curia.
Ditta, Angelo '86 (RVC) Ronkonkoma, NY St. Joseph's Church.
Ditta, Angelo '96 (RVC) [B] Patchogue, NY St. Joseph's College.
Dittami, Mark A. *o.carm.* '65 (BO) [P] Peabody, MA Catholic Information Center.
Dittberner, Arnold *o.s.b.* '33 (SCL) [I] Collegeville, MN St. John's Abbey, of the Order of St. Benedict.
Dittberner, Jerome M. '64 (STP) [A] St. Paul, MN The Saint Paul Seminary; [C] St. Paul, MN University of St. Thomas.
Dittman, Bernard F. '55 (RCK) Menominee, IL Nativity of the Blessed Virgin Mary Church.
Dittman, Bernard F. '55 (VEN) Retired.
Dittman, Msgr. Harold J. '48 (WIN) Retired.
Dittmeier, Charles (NY) [DD] Maryknoll, NY Maryknoll Mission Association of the Faithful.
Dittmeier, Charles R. '70 (L) On Duty Outside the Archdiocese.
Ditto, Anthony W. '90 (GBG) Herminie, PA St. Edward Church.
Dittoe, Msgr. John T. '45 (COL) Retired.
Ditty, James '89 (RIC) Retired.
DiTullio, Peter S. *s.c.* '68 (PRO) [4] East Providence, RI Sacred Heart Church.
DiUlio, Albert J. *s.j.* '74 (MIL) [P] Milwaukee, WI Jesuit Community at Marquette University.
Diurczak, Eugene '68 (NEW) [6] Bayonne, NJ Mt. Carmel Church.
Divan, Anthony L. '65 (PEO) Retired.
Diver, Patrick *s.d.b.* '74 (PAT) [D] Paterson, NJ Don Bosco Technical High School.
Divine, Kevin J. (BO) Absent on Leave.
Diviney, Andrew *s.j.* '61 (LA) Northridge, CA Our Lady of Lourdes Church.
Diviney, Msgr. Charles E. '31 (BRK) [29] Brooklyn, NY St. Charles Borromeo Church; Retired.
Divis, Daniel O. '79 (CLV) [8] Lorain, OH St. Mary Church.
Divis, James '76 (LIN) McCool Junction, NE St. Patrick's Church; York, NE St. Joseph's Church.
DiVito, John *c.s.* (CHI) [M] Northlake, IL Villa Scalabrini Home for the Aged.
Divizia, John *s.d.b.* '35 (NY) [BB] West Haverstraw, NY Don Bosco Retreat Center and Marian Shrine; [BB] West Haverstraw, NY Marian Shrine.
Dixey, Edward J. *o.s.a.* '57 (PH) [Z] Villanova, PA St. Thomas Monastery.
Dixon, Alvin '69 (NO) [B] New Orleans, LA Divine Word Missionaries, Augustine Tolton House of Studies.
Dixon, Daniel B. '56 (PIT) Beaver, PA SS. Peter and Paul Church; Center Township, PA St. Frances Cabrini Church.
Dixon, David '57 (PIT) [L] Pittsburgh, PA St. Joseph Nursing and Health Care Center, Inc.
Dixon, Francis '76 (MEM) [A] Memphis, TN Christian Brothers University.
Dixon, J. Isidore '64 (WDC) Rosaryville, MD Church of the Most Holy Rosary.
Dixon, James M. *s.j.* '73 (CHI) [N] Chicago, IL Chicago Province of the Society of Jesus-Provincial Office.
Dixon, James R. '70 (BEL) [K] Belleville, IL Scott Air Force Base.
Dixon, James R. '70 (NO) Military Chaplains.
Dixon, Jerome A. '57 (PIT) [L] Pittsburgh, PA Home for the Aged of the Little Sisters of the Poor.
Dlabal, Norbert F. '72 (SAL) Tipton, KS St. Boniface's Church.
Dluge, James A. '70 (SUP) Frederic, WI St. Dominic Church; Grantsburg, WI Immaculate Conception Church.
Dlugos, Raymond *o.s.a.* '83 (ALB) [10] Albany, NY St. Margaret Mary Church.
Dmoch, Paul '76 (NY) Rosendale, NY St. Peter Church.
Do, Vien Van '90 (PEO) Bement, IL St. Michael Church; Monticello, IL St. Philomena Church.
Do Binh Dinh, Luke M. *c.m.c.* '77 (NO) [B] Metairie, LA Congregation of the Mother Coredemptrix Formation House.
Do Cao Tung, Francis Xavier M. *c.m.c.* (SPC) [E] Carthage, MO Congregation of the Mother Co-Redemptrix, United States Assumption Province.
Do Quang Chinh, Michael M. *c.m.c.* '93 (SPC) [E] Carthage, MO Congregation of the Mother Co-Redemptrix, United States Assumption Province.
Dobbin, Edmund J. *o.s.a.* '62 (PH) [C] Villanova, PA Villanova University; [Z] Villanova, PA St. Thomas Monastery.
Dobbin, Jay D. '64 (GF) On Duty Outside of the Diocese.
Dobbins, Robert R. *s.j.* '67 (NY) [Z] New York, NY Jesuit Community at Fordham University.
Dober, Edward J. '76 (LA) Paramount, CA Our Lady of the Rosary Church.
Dobes, Msgr. George E. '68 (CHI) Military Chaplains.
Dobihal, Robert F. '50 (STP) Retired.
Dobitz, Roger '85 (SFS) On Leave of Absence.
Dobkiewicz, Stanley '43 (PH) [D] Philadelphia, PA Father Judge High School for Boys.
Dobkowski, Msgr. Paulin J. '54 (BEL) Johnston City, IL St. Paul Church; Johnston City, IL St. Paul Church.
Dobnikar, Ivan *o.s.b.* '49 (JOL) [J] Lisle, IL St. Procopius Abbey.
Dobo, Leo '46 (ORL) Lake Wales, FL Holy Spirit Church; Retired.
Dobosiewicz, Leon W. '46 (Y) Retired.
Dobosiewicz, Stephen J. '42 (E) Retired.
Dobosz, Emil J. '49 (WH) Retired.
Dobosz, Eugeniusz '85 (TYL) Sulphur Springs, TX St. James Church.
Dobosz, Jerry '95 (TYL) Texarkana, TX Sacred Heart Church.
Dobranski, John '89 (BAL) Westminster, MD St. John Church.
Dobrosky, John M. '83 (TR) Highlands, NJ Our Lady of Perpetual Help Church.
Dobrowolski, Thomas (STN) Lincoln, NE St. George's Church; Omaha, NE Assumption of B.V.M. Church.
Dobrowski, Klemens '87 (PHX) [24] Phoenix, AZ St. Theresa Church.
Dobrowski, Peter P. '71 (PHX) Bullhead City, AZ St. Margaret Mary Church.
Dobry, Jerome *o.s.b.* '44 (JOL) [J] Lisle, IL St. Procopius Abbey.
Dobrzenski, Francis G. '77 (MAR) Ewen, MI Sacred Heart Church; Watersmeet, MI Immaculate Conception Church.
Dobrzynski, Martin J. '84 (GRY) New Chicago, IN Assumption of the Blessed Virgin Mary Church.
Dobson, Christopher *t.o.r.* '78 (ARL) Herndon, VA St. Joseph Church.
Dobson, Christopher J. *t.o.r.* (ALT) [F] Loretto, PA St. Bonaventure Friary.
Dobson, Gregory J. '83 (BUF) [3] Orchard Park, NY Our Lady of the Sacred Heart Church; [D] Buffalo, NY Villa Maria Academy.
Dochstader, Richard '75 (JOL) [4] Naperville, IL St. Margaret Mary Church.
Dockendorf, Ronald '82 (SCL) Buckman, MN St. Michael's Church.
Dockendorff, Carl J. '45 (LC) Retired.
Dockerill, Walter '60 (PMB) [J] West Palm Beach, FL Our Lady Queen of Peace Catholic Cemetery, Inc.
Dockerill, Walter J. '60 (PMB) Wellington, FL St. Rita Church.
Dockers, Anthony '45 (OKL) Retired.
Doctor, John *o.f.m.* '76 (STL) [P] St. Louis, MO Franciscan Friary of St. Anthony of Padua.
Doda, Eugene J., Jr. '77 (MIL) [3] Menomonee Falls, WI St. James Church.
Dodaro, Robert J. *o.s.a.* '82 (CHI) [N] Olympia Fields, IL The Augustinian Provincialate Tolentine Center.
Dodd, Anthony J. '61 (CLV) Brook Park, OH Assumption of Mary Church; Retired.
Dodd, Michael *o.c.d.* '79 (BO) [W] Brighton, MA Carmelite Monastery.
Dodd, Msgr. Richard F. '48 (COL) Junction City, OH St. Patrick's Church.
Dodds, Michael *o.p.* '77 (OAK) [A] Berkeley, CA Dominican School of Philosophy and Theology; [N] Oakland, CA Dominican Order (Western Province), St. Albert's Priory.
Dodds, Michael J. *o.p.* '77 (OAK) [N] Oakland, CA Western Dominican Province.
Dodds, Perry W. '54 (B) Retired.
Dodge, Erwin J. *o.s.a.* (CHI) [J] Chicago, IL Holy Cross Hospital.
Dodge, Linus '50 (L) [L] Trappist, KY Abbey of Our Lady of Gethsemani, of the Order of Cistercians of the Strict Observance.
Dodgson, William '50 (B) Retired.
Doerfler, John '91 (GB) On Duty Outside the Diocese.
Doerfler, John '91 (WDC) [B] Washington, DC St. Joseph's Seminary.
Doerfler, Joseph *o.f.m.cap.* '55 (MAD) [M] Madison, WI San Damiano Friary.
Doerfler, Msgr. Marvin G. '59 (SAT) [I] San Antonio, TX St. Peter & Joseph Childrens Home.
Doerger, Berard *o.f.m.* '61 (GLP) [A] Gallup, NM Diocesan Diaconate Formation Program.
Doerger, Stanley D. '58 (CIN) Xenia, OH St. Brigid Church.
Doerhoff, Dennis E. '76 (STL) [49] St. Louis, MO St. Mary Magdalen Church.
Doerner, David L. *s.a.* '60 (LA) [R] Los Angeles, CA Atonement Friars.
Doerr, Richard J. '93 (LFT) Carmel, IN Our Lady of Mount Carmel Church; Muncie, IN St. Francis of Assisi Church.
Doerre, Edmund J. '63 (LC) Chippewa Falls, WI Holy Ghost Church; Springfield, WI St. Bridget Church.
Doersam, Carl G. '45 (NY) Retired.
Doersching, Lawrence *s.m.* '73 (SFR) [N] San Francisco, CA Marianist Community.
Doersching, Lawrence *s.m.* '73 (STL) [P] St. Louis, MO Provincialate of the Society of Mary, Province of St. Louis.
Doffing, Gordon M. '60 (STP) [4] St. Paul, MN Holy Childhood Church.
Dofner, Andrew J. *s.j.* '67 (P) [L] Portland, OR Jesuit Provincial Office (Oregon Prov.).
Doga, Msgr. Al R. '49 (GAL) [2] Spring, TX St. Edward Church.
Dogali, Michael F. '92 (BGP) [1] Greenwich, CT St. Mary's Church; [1] Stamford, CT St. John's Church.
Dohar, William J. *c.s.c.* '73 (OAK) [N] Berkeley, CA Holy Cross Fathers-Holy Cross Center.
Dohar, William J. *c.s.c.* '80 (FTW) [B] Notre Dame, IN University of Notre Dame Du Lac.
Doheny, Luke (ALB) [L] Saratoga Springs, NY St. John Neumann Residence.
Doheny, Richard '48 (SAC) Fair Oaks, CA St. Mel Church.
Doheny, Thomas R. '58 (MAD) [4] Beloit, WI St. Thomas the Apostle Church.
Doherty, Charles '58 (CC) Aransas Pass, TX St. Mary, Star of the Sea Church.
Doherty, Daniel C. *s.j.* '76 (BAL) [M] Baltimore, MD Jesuit Fathers and Brothers Maryland Provincial Curia.
Doherty, Daniel J. '94 (SCR) [18] Wilkes-Barre, PA Sacred Heart of Jesus Church.
Doherty, Desmond '75 (LA) Claremont, CA Our Lady of the Assumption Church.
Doherty, Donald J. *m.m.* '62 (NY) [Z] Maryknoll, NY Maryknoll Fathers and Brothers.
Doherty, Duane *o.f.m.conv.* '63 (DET) [4] Birmingham, MI St. Regis Church.
Doherty, Duane *o.f.m.conv.* '63 (IND) [J] Mount Saint Francis, IN Provincial Headquarters for the Conventual Franciscan Province.
Doherty, Edward C. *m.ss.a.* '68 (BGP) [K] Bridgeport,

CT Roncalli Apartments; [K] Bridgeport, CT Roncalli Charities Inc.
Doherty, Eugene '39 (JOL) Retired; [I] Naperville, IL St. John Vianney Villa.
Doherty, Francis *ss.cc.* '71 (OAK) [3] Alameda, CA St. Joseph Basilica.
Doherty, Msgr. Francis E. '41 (MAD) Retired.
Doherty, George E. '50 (NEW) Retired.
Doherty, Glennon '78 (STL) Grantwood, MO Our Lady of Providence Church.
Doherty, Glennon C. '78 (STL) [A] St. Louis, MO Kenrick-Glennon Seminary.
Doherty, Henry F. '56 (BO) Hanover, MA St. Mary of the Sacred Heart Church.
Doherty, James J. *c.s.c.* '78 (SCR) [C] Wilkes-Barre, PA Kings College.
Doherty, Msgr. John B. '39 (LA) Retired.
Doherty, John B. '80 (NY) Absent on Leave.
Doherty, John E. *c.ss.r.* '38 (BO) [13] Boston, MA Basilica of Our Lady of Perpetual Help; Boston, MA Dana Farber Cancer Institute.
Doherty, John R. '64 (NEW) [2] Bayonne, NJ St. Andrew's Church.
Doherty, Msgr. John T. '45 (NY) [144] Bronx, NY St. Gabriel Church; Retired; [E] White Plains, NY Archbishop Stepinac High School.
Doherty, Joseph M. *c.s.c.* '41 (FTW) [J] South Bend, IN Congregation of Holy Cross Indiana Province Provincial House.
Doherty, Louis *c.p.* '57 (CHI) [N] Chicago, IL Immaculate Conception Monastery.
Doherty, Michael *o.f.m.* '76 (OAK) [N] Oakland, CA Franciscan Friars Provincial Office, Province of St. Barbara.
Doherty, Neil '69 (MIA) Margate, FL St. Vincent Church.
Doherty, Patrick A. '56 (ORG) Newport Beach, CA Our Lady of Mount Carmel Church.
Doherty, Patrick D. *s.j.* '65 (SJ) [M] Los Gatos, CA California Province of the Society of Jesus, Jesuit Provincial Office.
Doherty, Msgr. Patrick G. '45 (FRS) Retired.
Doherty, Msgr. Patrick J. '55 (BWN) [6] Brownsville, TX Our Lady of Guadalupe Church.
Doherty, Patrick J. '59 (MAD) Absent on Sick Leave.
Doherty, Paul '95 (WOR) Whitinsville, MA St. Patrick's Church.
Doherty, Raymond J. *s.s.e.* '58 (BUR) [G] Colchester, VT Society of St. Edmund.
Doherty, Robert G. *s.j.* '60 (BO) [W] Weston, MA Campion Center.
Doherty, Robert J. '70 (BO) [5] Medford, MA Sacred Heart Church.
Doherty, Timothy '76 (RCK) [1] Rockford, IL St. Peter Cathedral.
Doherty, William J. '55 (SPR) [4] Holyoke, MA Immaculate Conception Church; [F] Springfield, MA Mercy Hospital.
Dohle, Benedict *o.s.b.* '54 (OM) [K] Elkhorn, NE Mount Michael Abbey.
Dohman, William *j.c.l.* '73 (B) Grangeville, ID SS. Peter and Paul Church; Grangeville, ID SS. Peter and Paul Church.
Dohner, Stephen J. '76 (CLV) Cleveland Heights, OH St. Louis Church.
Dohogne, David J. '92 (SPC) Doniphan, MO St. Benedict Church.
Doiron, David E. '69 (WOR) [1] Worcester, MA St. Paul's Cathedral; On Special or Other (Arch)Diocesan Assignment.
Dokupil, Edward J. '64 (AUS) Bastrop, TX Ascension Church.
Dolak, Mark J. '79 (MET) [J] Little York, NJ Bethany Ridge.
Dolan, Bernard M. '66 (BGP) [1] Trumbull, CT Christ the King Church.
Dolan, Charles *c.s.s.* '58 (BO) [W] Waltham, MA Stigmatine Fathers & Brothers Provincial House.
Dolan, Charles F.X. *s.j.* '46 (NEW) [C] Jersey City, NJ St. Peter's Preparatory School.
Dolan, Charles F.X. *s.j.* '46 (TR) Manasquan, NJ St. Denis Church.
Dolan, Daniel *m.m.* '54 (WDC) [B] Washington, DC Maryknoll Fathers and Brothers.
Dolan, Edward *s.s.c.* '58 (OM) [K] St. Columbans, NE St. Columban's Foreign Mission Society.
Dolan, Frank *o.m.i.* '73 (BO) [U] Lowell, MA D'Youville Manor.
Dolan, Gerald M. *o.f.m.* '56 (NY) [Z] New York, NY Franciscan Friars, Order of Friars Manor.
Dolan, Gerald M. *o.f.m.* '56 (PH) [U] Aston, PA Assisi House.
Dolan, Hugh '57 (PT) Marianna, FL St. Anne Church.
Dolan, James '54 (NEW) [B] Jersey City, NJ Saint Peter's College.
Dolan, James F. *s.j.* '51 (NEW) [N] Jersey City, NJ Jesuits of Saint Peter's College, Inc.
Dolan, James J. '49 (RVC) Retired.
Dolan, James Linus *o.p.* '60 (NO) [P] New Orleans, LA Dominican Fathers & Brothers, Southern Dominican Province.
Dolan, James R. *s.j.* '70 (ROC) [B] Rochester, NY McQuaid Jesuit High School.
Dolan, James W. '75 (PIT) [59] Pittsburgh, PA Our Lady of Loreto Church.
Dolan, John *o.s.f.s.* '95 (ARL) [J] Alexandria, VA Oblates of St. Francis de Sales Residence.
Dolan, John J. *o.s.f.s.* '95 (ARL) [D] Alexandria, VA Bishop Ireton High School.
Dolan, John P. '89 (SD) Oceanside, CA St. Mary Star of the Sea Church.
Dolan, John R. *m.s.* '68 (BO) [BB] Ipswich, MA National Shrine of Our Lady of La Salette.
Dolan, John R. '79 (BO) [W] Ipswich, MA Missionaries of Our Lady of LaSalette Corp.
Dolan, John R. '79 (HRT) [M] Hartford, CT Missionaries of LaSalette Provincial Secretary.
Dolan, Joseph M. '92 (WOR) [4] Leominster, MA St. Leo's Church.
Dolan, Joseph V. *s.j.* '52 (NY) [Z] New York, NY Jesuit Community at Fordham University.
Dolan, Laurence P. *o.f.m.* '65 (ORG) [3] Huntington Beach, CA SS. Simon and Jude Church.
Dolan, Lawrence *c.ss.r.* '42 (ORL) [F] New Smyrna Beach, FL St. Alphonsus Villa-Redemptorist Fathers and Brothers.
Dolan, Leo A. '52 (STP) Retired.
Dolan, Leo M. '60 (SAT) [39] San Antonio, TX St. Helena Church.
Dolan, Louis F. *c.s.sp.* '50 (VEN) [G] Sarasota, FL Congregation of the Holy Ghost.
Dolan, Luis M. *c.p.* '45 (NY) [33] New York, NY St. Emeric Church.
Dolan, Mark A. '76 (STL) Bissell Hills, MO St. Jerome Church.
Dolan, Michael J. '96 (HRT) Guilford, CT St. George Church.
Dolan, Msgr. Neal T. '64 (SD) Lakeside, CA Our Lady of Perpetual Help Church.
Dolan, Patrick '95 (DEN) [4] Englewood, CO St. Thomas More Church.
Dolan, Patrick G. '71 (JC) Salisbury, MO St. Joseph Church.
Dolan, Patrick J. (BO) Awaiting Assignment.
Dolan, Patrick J. '78 (L) [2] Springfield, KY Holy Rosary Church.
Dolan, Paul A. '84 (RVC) Kings Park, NY St. Joseph's Church.
Dolan, Paul F. '45 (BAL) Taneytown, MD St. Joseph Church; Retired; [K] Baltimore, MD Stella Maris Operating Corporation.
Dolan, Peter C. '54 (PMB) Port St. Lucie, FL St. Lucie Church; Retired.
Dolan, Raymond '56 (B) On Duty Outside the Diocese.
Dolan, Robert G. *s.j.* '76 (SAC) [H] Carmichael, CA Jesuit High School Community of Sacramento.
Dolan, Robert L. *s.j.* '73 (CHI) [C] Chicago, IL Jesuit Community at Loyola University of Chicago.
Dolan, Thomas D. '51 (BRK) [166] Queens, NY St. Elizabeth's Church; Retired.
Dolan, Thomas P. '45 (RCK) Harmon, IL St. Flannen Church; Maytown, IL St. Patrick Church; Walton, IL St. Mary Church.
Dolan, Timothy '83 (STP) Long Lake, MN St. George Church.
Dolan, Msgr. Timothy M. '76 (STL) On Duty Outside the Archdiocese.
Dolan, Walter *o.f.m.* '60 (CLV) [P] Cleveland, OH Padua Franciscan Friary.
Dolan, Walter *o.f.m.* '61 (CLV) [E] Cleveland, OH Padua Franciscan High School.
Dolan, William S. *s.j.* '82 (SY) [S] Syracuse, NY Jesuits at LeMoyne, Inc.
Dolandson, Richard *o.f.m.cap.* (NOR) Middletown, CT Middlesex Memorial Hospital.
Dolbec, Jacques *s.o.l.t.* '95 (CC) [H] Robstown, TX Society of Our Lady of the Most Holy Trinity.
Dolbec, Jacques *s.o.l.t.* '95 (FAR) Belcourt, ND St. Ann Church; Turtle Mountain Reservation, ND (Chippewa Indians) Church; Turtle Mountain Reservation, ND (Chippewa Indians) Church.
Dolciamore, John V. '52 (CHI) Retired; [A] Mundelein, IL University of St. Mary of the Lake-Mundelein Seminary.
Dold, John F. '73 (DEN) Absent on Leave.
Dolehide, John R. *o.p.* '47 (CHI) [1] Oak Lawn, IL St. Catherine of Alexandria Church; [N] Chicago, IL Dominicans (Provincial Office).
Dolezal, Richard R. '76 (MIL) On Duty Outside the Archdiocese.
Dolezal, Thomas H. '70 (KCK) Axtell, KS St. Michael's Church; Summerfield, KS Holy Family Church.
Dolinic, Louis S. '66 (BUF) [5] Depew, NY Our Lady of the Blessed Sacrament Church.
Doll, Donald A. *s.j.* '68 (OM) [K] Omaha, NE Jesuit Community At Creighton University.
Doll, William P. '50 (PBL) Holly, CO St. Frances of Rome Church.
Dollar, Robert J. '60 (BEL) Retired.
Dollard, John J. '45 (OAK) Retired.
Dollard, Mark E. (MAN) Lisbon, NH St. Catherine of Siena Church.
Dollard, Mark E. '91 (MAN) Woodsville, NH St. Joseph Church.
Dollard, Richard D. '58 (RIC) Tappahannock, VA St. Timothy Church.
Dollen, Bernard '53 (ROC) [M] Rochester, NY Diocesan Office of Campus Ministry.
Dollen, Bernard F. '53 (ROC) North Chili, NY St. Christopher Church.
Dollen, Msgr. Charles '54 (SD) Retired.
Dollinger, Cletus *o.c.s.o.* '50 (SLC) [F] Huntsville, UT Abbey of Our Lady of the Holy Trinity of the Order of Cistercians.
Dollinger, Msgr. John M. '57 (E) [17] Erie, PA St. Hedwig/St. Patrick Church; Erie, PA Erie County Prison.
Dollinger, Robert J. '54 (L) Retired.
Dols, Francisco *t.o.r.* '47 (NEW) [14] Elizabeth, NJ Immaculate Heart of Mary Church.
Dolsina, Stanley '46 (DUL) Retired.
Dolski, V. Anthony '59 (GB) [1] De Pere, WI St. Francis Xavier Church.
Domaica, Jose Luis *o.a.r.* '64 (NY) [154] Bronx, NY St. John's Church.
Domandich, Anthony '58 (SEA) Retired.
Domas, John Robert '50 (SB) Beaumont, CA San Gorgonio Church.
Domaszewicz, Chester '78 (VEN) [1] Venice, FL Epiphany Cathedral.
Dombroski, Dean H. '64 (GB) Humboldt, WI Our Lady Queen of Peace Church.
Dombroski, Dean W. '64 (GB) Eaton, WI SS. Cyril and Methodius Church.
Dombrow, William A. '70 (PH) [68] Philadelphia, PA Immaculate Conception Church.
Dombrowski, Francis J. *o.f.m.cap.* '59 (MIL) [S] Milwaukee, WI The Dwelling Place.
Dombrowski, John *o.f.m.* '84 (STP) [10] St. Paul, MN Sacred Heart Church.
Dombrowski, Robert J. '60 (FTW) Bremen, IN St. Dominic Church.
Dombrowski, Ronald J. '72 (SAG) Port Sanilac, MI St. Mary Church.
Dombrowski, Stanley J. *o.s.f.s.* '83 (WIL) [I] Wilmington, DE Oblates of St. Francis De Sales.
Dombrowski, Steven '89 (CHI) [3] Mt. Prospect, IL St. Raymond de Penafort Church.
Dombrowski, Timothy '73 (LAN) [F] Ann Arbor, MI St. Joseph Mercy Hospital.
Domec, Msgr. Charles C. '56 (GAL) The Woodlands, TX Sts. Simon and Jude Church.
Domeck, Casimiro '73 (ARE) Florida, PR Our Lady of Mercy Church.
Domhoff, Ronald J. '72 (L) [B] Louisville, KY Trinity High School.
Domin, Edward '88 (ALN) [3] Easton, PA St. Jane Frances de Chantal Church.
Domin, John M. '50 (P) Retired; [K] Beaverton, OR Maryville Nursing Home.
Domingo, Alberto *c.m.f.* '79 (LA) [20] Los Angeles, CA Our Lady of Solitude Church.
Domingo, Santiago '65 (CC) [14] Laredo, TX St. Jude Church.
Domingue, Kenneth '91 (LAF) Basile, LA St. Augustine Church.
Dominguez, Baltasar '81 (NEW) West New York, NJ St. Joseph of the Palisades Church.
Dominguez, Francisco *a.a.* '56 (BO) [W] Brighton, MA Assumptionist Center.
Dominguez, Jorge L. (SJN) [F] Guaynabo, PR Opus Dei.
Dominguez, Julio Fernandez *o.m.* '48 (SJN) [16] San Juan, PR Ntra. Sra. de Fatima Church.
Dominguez, M. Marciano *c.s.b.* '90 (GAL) [Q] Sugar Land, TX Basilian Mission Center.
Dominguez, Patricio *o.m.i.* '60 (SAT) Eagle Pass, TX Our Lady of Refuge Church.
Dominiak, Gerald J. '59 (MIL) Thiensville, WI St. Cecilia's Church.
Dominiak, Thomas M. '61 (GAY) Rogers City, MI St. Ignatius Church.
Dominic, Abraham B. '87 (NY) [217] Staten Island, NY Our Lady Help of Christians Church.
Dominic, Francis J. '52 (MAD) Retired.
Dominic, Joseph A. '39 (SEA) Aberdeen, WA SS. Peter and Paul Church; Retired.
Dominicis, Severino *s.a.c.* '39 (NY) [91] New York, NY Our Lady of Mt. Carmel Church; [Z] New York, NY Pallottine Fathers.
Dominik, Kevin J. '88 (PIT) Unity, PA St. John the Baptist Church.
Dominik, Stanley J. '58 (GRY) [5] Hammond, IN St. John Bosco Church.
Dominique, Todd '94 (TOL) Delphos, OH St. John the Evangelist Church.
Dommer, Ian *o.s.b.* '79 (SCL) [I] Collegeville, MN St. John's Abbey, of the Order of St. Benedict.
Domnick, Alphonsus *t.o.r.* '44 (SCR) Retired.
Domnick, Alphonsus M. *t.o.r.* '44 (SCR) [N] Dunmore, PA Villa St. Joseph.
Dompka, John A. '49 (PIT) Retired.
Dompke, Ramon *c.ss.r.* '64 (CHI) [152] Chicago, IL Our

Lady of Lourdes Church.
Domurat, Thomas S. (BO) Society of St. James the Apostle.
Dona, Thomas M. '65 (DEN) [14] Denver, CO Montbello Catholic Parish-Church of the Ascension; Byers, CO Our Lady of the Plains Church.
Donachie, Joseph J. '45 (NY) Retired.
Donadio, Vincent J. '73 (TR) Point Pleasant, NJ St. Martha Church.
Donaghey, Bernard *s.v.d.* '57 (SB) [D] San Bernardino, CA St. Bernardine Medical Center.
Donaghey, John *s.v.d.* '54 (CHI) [B] Techny, IL Divine Word Residence; [N] Techny, IL Society of the Divine Word, Provincial Headquarter-Chicago Prov.
Donaghey, Patrick H. '85 (ATL) Lilburn, GA St. John Neumann Church.
Donaghy, Harry '67 (ALB) [7] Troy, NY St. Mary Church.
Donaghy, Thomas J. '79 (BAL) Ellicott City, MD St. Paul Church.
Donahoe, James H. *s.j.* '51 (BAL) [M] Baltimore, MD Jesuit Fathers and Brothers Maryland Provincial Curia.
Donahoe, Patrick *t.o.r.* '74 (PIT) [N] Pittsburgh, PA Franciscan Friars, T.O.R.; [N] Pittsburgh, PA Franciscan Friars, T.O.R.
Donahoe, Msgr. Thomas M. '54 (SC) Graettinger, IA Immaculate Conception Church.
Donahue, Aidan N. '86 (HRT) [A] Bloomfield, CT St. Thomas Seminary.
Donahue, Anthony *o.f.m.cap.* (NY) Wingdale, NY Harlem Valley Psychiatric Center.
Donahue, Anthony *o.f.m.cap.* '51 (MAN) [5] Manchester, NH Blessed Sacrament Church.
Donahue, Bernard F. *o.s.f.s.* '58 (ALN) [B] Center Valley, PA Allentown College of St. Francis de Sales; [K] Center Valley, PA Oblates of St. Francis de Sales.
Donahue, Brian G. '83 (FAR) Special Assignment; [A] Fargo, ND Cardinal Muench Seminary.
Donahue, Cecil J. *o.s.b.* '54 (MAN) [K] Manchester, NH St. Anselm Abbey; [N] Durham, NH Campus Ministries.
Donahue, Daniel J. (BO) Awaiting Assignment.
Donahue, Dennis M. '90 (ARL) Falls Church, VA St. Anthony's Church.
Donahue, Edward J. *c.ss.r.* '42 (PH) [135] Philadelphia, PA St. Peter the Apostle Church.
Donahue, Edward J. *o.f.m.* '56 (NEW) East Rutherford, NJ St. Joseph's Church.
Donahue, Edward J. '80 (ALN) Orefield, PA St. Joseph The Worker Church; On Duty Outside the Diocese.
Donahue, Eugene L. *s.j.* '70 (DET) [K] Detroit, MI Jesuit Community at the University of Detroit.
Donahue, Eugene L. *s.j.* '70 (OM) [K] Omaha, NE Jesuit Community At Creighton University.
Donahue, J. Christopher *s.j.* '90 (LA) [10] Los Angeles, CA Dolores Mission Church.
Donahue, John *s.j.* '64 (OAK) [A] Berkeley, CA The Jesuit School of Theology at Berkeley.
Donahue, John '73 (NEW) Belleville, NJ Clara Maass Hospital.
Donahue, John G. '60 (STP) [7] St. Paul, MN Maternity of the Blessed Virgin Church.
Donahue, John J. *c.s.c.* '70 (NY) Manhattan, NY St. Clare's Hospital & Health Center; [S] New York, NY St. Clare's Hospital and Health Center.
Donahue, John P. *c.s.p.* '57 (NY) [Z] Scarsdale, NY Paulist Fathers Generalate.
Donahue, John P. *c.s.p.* '57 (WDC) [B] Washington, DC St. Paul's College.
Donahue, John R. *s.j.* '64 (OAK) [N] Berkeley, CA Jesuit Community at Jesuit School of Theology at Berkeley.
Donahue, Joseph '70 (NY) Absent on Leave.
Donahue, Joseph P. '45 (HRT) Naugatuck, CT St. Francis of Assisi Church; Retired.
Donahue, L. Scott '82 (CHI) [112] Chicago, IL St. Juliana Church; [H] Chicago, IL Mission of Our Lady of Mercy-Mercy Home for Boys and Girls.
Donahue, Martin P. '61 (WOR) [22] Worcester, MA St. Christopher Church.
Donahue, Michael E. *s.j.* '80 (NY) [Z] New York, NY Jesuit Provincial's Office; [Z] New York, NY Xavier Jesuit Community.
Donahue, Paul H. '49 (DAV) Retired; [M] Davenport, IA St. Vincent Center.
Donahue, Richard (BO) On Duty Outside the Archdiocese.
Donahue, Stephen '86 (IND) Charlestown, IN St. Michael Church; Henryville,, IN St. Francis Xavier Church.
Donahue, Thomas J. '62 (LR) Retired.
Donahue, Tom '62 (LR) [H] Little Rock, AR St. John Manor.
Donahue, William '86 (SR) [4] Santa Rosa, CA Resurrection Church.
Donahue, William H. *c.s.c.* '49 (AUS) Copperas Cove, TX Holy Family Church.
Donahue, William P. '70 (GBG) [4] Latrobe, PA St. Rose Church.
Donahugh, Donald E. '62 (BEA) [C] Port Arthur, TX St. Mary Hospital.
Donahugh, Donald E. '62 (RCK) Active Outside the Diocese.
Donajkowski, Charles G. '91 (GAY) Gills Pier, MI St. Wenceslaus Church; Lake Leelanau, MI St. Mary Church.
Donald, Michael (STL) [W] St. Louis, MO Archdiocesan Stewardship Education Committee.
Donald, Michael L. '72 (STL) Crystal City, MO Sacred Heart Church.
Donaldson, Richard *o.f.m.cap.* '57 (NOR) [4] Middletown, CT St. Pius X Church.
Donaldson, Thomas *c.ss.r.* '77 (STP) Brooklyn Center, MN St. Alphonsus Church.
Donaldson, Thomas J. '68 (LC) Ellsworth, WI St. Francis of Assisi Church.
Donarski, Richard *o.c.s.o.* '86 (ATL) [I] Conyers, GA The Monastery of the Holy Spirit.
Donat, Robert J. '66 (SB) Montclair, CA Our Lady of Lourdes Church.
Donatelli, Gino *s.j.* '82 (LEX) [1] Lexington, KY Cathedral of Christ the King.
Donatelli, Philip J. '67 (PIT) Peters Township, PA St. Benedict the Abbot Church.
Donato, Gaudelio (HON) Kahului, HI Christ the King Church.
Donato, John J. *c.s.c.* '91 (FTW) [9] South Bend, IN Holy Cross Church; [J] South Bend, IN Congregation of Holy Cross Indiana Province Provincial House.
Donato, Msgr. Thomas A. '65 (NEW) Ramsey, NJ St. Paul Church.
Dondanville, Joseph '95 (PEO) Mendota, IL Holy Cross Church.
Dondero, Joseph L. *s.j.* '46 (SJ) [M] Los Gatos, CA California Province of the Society of Jesus, Jesuit Provincial Office; [M] Los Gatos, CA Sacred Heart Jesuit Center.
Donders, Sjef *m.afr.* '57 (WDC) [M] Washington, DC Missionaries of Africa.
Dondzila, Henry J. '56 (GR) Lakewood Club, MI St. Mary of the Woods Church.
Donegan, Augustine *t.o.r.* '46 (STU) [A] Steubenville, OH Franciscan University of Steubenville; [F] Steubenville, OH Holy Spirit Monastery.
Donegan, Msgr. James F. '35 (BRK) [184] Queens, NY St. Joan of Arc Church; Retired.
Donegan, William *ss.cc.* '65 (FR) [K] Fairhaven, MA Sacred Hearts Provincial House.
Donehue, Ambrose *o.f.m.* '51 (WDC) [3] Silver Spring, MD St. Camillus Church.
Donelin, John M. '40 (BO) Retired.
Donellan, Msgr. Thomas J. '56 (BAL) Hunt Valley, MD St. Francis Xavier Church.
Doner, Roy R. '81 (SAC) Chico, CA Our Divine Savior Church.
Dong, Quang Minh '91 (OAK) Pinole, CA St. Joseph's Church.
Donini, Augustin *o.f.m.* '44 (NY) [Z] New York, NY Franciscan Province of the Immaculate Conception.
Donini, Leone '95 (NEW) [4] Union City, NJ St. Anthony of Padua Church.
Donio, Frank *s.a.c.* '94 (CAM) [C] Pennsauken, NJ Bishop Eustace Prep School.
Donio, Thomas S. '95 (CAM) Absecon, NJ St. Elizabeth Ann Seton Church.
Donish, Peter '70 (PSC) Beaver Meadows, PA SS. Peter and Paul Church.
Donlan, Francis *c.ss.r.* '45 (ORL) [F] New Smyrna Beach, FL St. Alphonsus Villa-Redemptorist Fathers and Brothers.
Donlan, Paul A. '62 (SFR) [T] San Francisco, CA Opus Dei.
Donlan, Robert R. '67 (SP) Brooksville, FL St. Anthony Church.
Donlan, Thomas *o.p.* '44 (NY) [2] New York, NY St. Agnes Church; [DD] New York, NY Catholic Actors Guild of America, Inc., The.
Donlan, Thomas C. *o.p.* '44 (CHI) [N] Chicago, IL Dominicans (Provincial Office).
Donlon, Aidan *s.a.c.* '55 (FWT) Wichita Falls, TX State Hospital; [F] Wichita Falls, TX Bethania Regional Health Care Center.
Donlon, James I. '75 (ALB) Lake George, NY Sacred Heart Church; [4] Watervliet, NY St. Patrick Church; Special Assignment.
Donlon, James W. '65 (PH) Conshohocken, PA St. Matthew Church.
Donlon, William J. '37 (BO) Natick, MA Sacred Heart Church; Retired.
Donnay, Raymond N. '50 (SCL) Sobieski, MN St. Stanislaus Church.
Donnellan, Francis A. *s.s.e.* '45 (MOB) [H] Selma, AL Edmundite Fathers.
Donnelly, Brendan '52 (ORL) Retired.
Donnelly, Brendan P. *o.s.b.* '46 (MAN) [K] Manchester, NH St. Anselm Abbey.
Donnelly, Eamonn *s.v.d.* '70 (LA) [25] Los Angeles, CA Our Lady of Loretto Church; [R] Los Angeles, CA Society of the Divine Word Western Province.
Donnelly, Msgr. Edward J. '54 (RVC) Hicksville, NY Holy Family Church.
Donnelly, Elmer '33 (ALB) Retired.
Donnelly, Eugene F. '48 (BRK) [210] Queens, NY Our Lady of Fatima Church; Retired.
Donnelly, Msgr. Felix G. '45 (SAV) [1] Savannah, GA Cathedral of St. John the Baptist; Retired.
Donnelly, Gerard J. *o.s.b.* '46 (MAN) [K] Manchester, NH St. Anselm Abbey.
Donnelly, James '48 (PAT) [15] Paterson, NJ St. Stephen's Church.
Donnelly, Jeffrey *o.f.m.* '39 (JOL) [J] Joliet, IL St. John the Baptist Friary.
Donnelly, Jeffry *o.f.m.* '66 (JOL) [11] Joliet, IL St. John the Baptist Church.
Donnelly, Msgr. John '58 (SPK) [8] Spokane, WA St. Anthony Church.
Donnelly, John P. *s.j.* '65 (MIL) [P] Milwaukee, WI Jesuit Community at Marquette University.
Donnelly, Joseph T. '71 (HRT) [3] Manchester, CT St. Bridget's Church.
Donnelly, Joseph-Benedict *o.c.s.o.* '43 (P) [L] Lafayette, OR The Cistercian (Trappist) Abbey of Our Lady of Guadalupe.
Donnelly, Msgr. Lawrence E. '49 (LA) Retired.
Donnelly, Lucien R. *o.s.b.* '48 (NEW) [N] Newark, NJ Newark Abbey.
Donnelly, Michael *s.s.c.* '63 (OM) [K] St. Columbans, NE St. Columban's Foreign Mission Society.
Donnelly, P. Martin '64 (TOL) [31] Toledo, OH St. Martin de Porres Church.
Donnelly, Paul J. '58 (BIR) Guntersville, AL St. William's Church.
Donnelly, Paul V. '88 (STA) [1] Gainesville, FL St. Patrick's Church.
Donnelly, Richard A. '62 (PRO) [4] Cranston, RI St. Mark Church.
Donnelly, Robert *m.m.* '59 (HON) Honaunau, HI St. Benedict Church.
Donnelly, Robert J. '91 (ALB) Fort Ann, NY St. Ann Church.
Donnelly, Robert W. '57 (TOL) [1] Toledo, OH Queen of the Most Holy Rosary Cathedral.
Donnelly, Robert W. *m.m.* '59 (HON) [H] Honolulu, HI Maryknoll Fathers House.
Donnelly, Russell '75 (PH) [2] Chester, PA Blessed Katharine Drexel Church.
Donnelly, Sean '54 (SPK) Retired.
Donnelly, Sean J. '82 (CLV) Parma Heights, OH St. John Bosco Church.
Donnelly, Thomas '61 (RNO) [5] Reno, NV St. Rose of Lima Church.
Donnelly, Thomas F. *m.m.* '57 (HON) [13] Honolulu, HI Sacred Heart Church; [H] Honolulu, HI Maryknoll Fathers House.
Donnelly, Thomas F. *m.m.* '57 (NY) [Z] Maryknoll, NY Maryknoll Fathers and Brothers.
Donnelly, Timothy *o.s.b.* '65 (LR) [A] Subiaco, AR Subiaco Monastery; [C] Subiaco, AR Subiaco Academy.
Donnelly, Timothy M. *s.v.d.* '88 (TR) [7] Trenton, NJ Our Lady of the Divine Shepherd Church.
Donnelly, William '64 (ROC) [3] Elmira, NY St. Mary Church.
Donnelly, William E. '71 (JOL) [3] Naperville, IL St. Raphael Church.
Donnelly, William F. *s.j.* '63 (SJ) [B] Santa Clara, CA Santa Clara University.
Donnelly, William J. *o.s.a.* '67 (PH) Havertown, PA St. Denis Church.
Donnelly, William P. '64 (PH) Upper Darby, PA St. Alice Church.
Donnelly, William S. *m.m.* '65 (NY) [Z] Maryknoll, NY Maryknoll Fathers and Brothers.
Donner, Jeffrey '78 (SAG) Mount Pleasant, MI St. Mary University Parish Church.
Donner, Randall '92 (OM) [27] Omaha, NE St. Margaret Mary Church.
Donnoonny, George '91 (NY) Graduate Studies.
Dono, Abram E. '64 (TUC) [2] Tucson, AZ Blessed Kateri Tekakwitha Church; [J] Tucson, AZ St. Nicholas Indian Center.
Donofrio, Michael J. '76 (PH) On Duty Outside the Archdiocese.
Donoghue, Harry T. *o.p.* '57 (NY) Pleasantville, NY Holy Innocents Church.
Donoghue, Henry A. '64 (WOR) [23] Worcester, MA St. George Church.
Donoghue, John F. '54 (B) [2] Boise, ID St. Mark's Church.
Donoghue, Kelly C. '94 (OG) Absent on Leave.
Donoghue, Paul *s.m.* '68 (STL) [P] St. Louis, MO Provincialate of the Society of Mary, Province of St. Louis.
Donoher, Edward *c.s.b.* '49 (DET) [E] Redford, MI Catholic Central High School.
Donohie, John M. '65 (PH) [54] Philadelphia, PA St. Helena Church.
Donohoe, Edward '50 (STO) Retired.
Donohoe, John P. '45 (SEA) Retired.
Donohoe, Patrick K. '82 (CC) Taft, TX Holy Family Church; Taft, TX Immaculate Conception Church.
Donohoe, Peter J. '50 (SFD) Brighton, IL St. Alphonsus Church.

Donohoe, Philip M. '53 (OKL) El Reno, OK Sacred Heart Church.
Donohoe, Richard E. '84 (BIR) Anniston, AL Sacred Heart of Jesus Church.
Donohoe, Msgr. Robert J. '37 (PHX) Retired.
Donohoe, Robert W. '50 (CLV) Peninsula, OH Mother of Sorrows Church.
Donohoe, Stephen S. '92 (BO) [10] Lawrence, MA St. Patrick Church.
Donohoe, Thomas C. *s.j.* '41 (OM) [C] Omaha, NE Creighton Preparatory School.
Donohoe, Thomas E. '62 (RVC) Long Beach, NY St. Mary of the Isle Church.
Donohoe, Thomas M. *s.j.* '43 (SJ) [M] Los Gatos, CA California Province of the Society of Jesus, Jesuit Provincial Office; [M] Los Gatos, CA Sacred Heart Jesuit Center.
Donohoe, Thomas P. '52 (BO) Carlisle, MA St. Irene Church.
Donohoe, William *c.pp.s.* '48 (CIN) [B] Carthagena, OH St. Charles.
Donohoo, Daniel B. (IND) Bloomington, IN St. John the Apostle Church.
Donohoo, Lawrence J. *o.p.* '85 (WDC) [B] Washington, DC Dominican House of Studies.
Donohue, Aidan N. '86 (HRT) Special and other (Arch)Diocesan Assignment.
Donohue, Edward J. '36 (JC) Retired.
Donohue, James *c.r.* (BAL) [C] Emmitsburg, MD Mount Saint Mary's College.
Donohue, John F. *o.carm.* '48 (JOL) [J] Darien, IL Carmelite Fathers Provincial Office.
Donohue, John J. '48 (CHI) [52] Chicago, IL St. Edward Church; Retired.
Donohue, John J. '73 (NEW) Bloomfield, NJ St. Valentine Church.
Donohue, John W. *s.j.* '50 (NY) [Z] New York, NY "America;" Residence and publication office of the America Press.
Donohue, Michael T. '75 (NOR) East Lyme, CT St. Matthias Church.
Donohue, Patrick W. '75 (NEW) [34] Newark, NJ Sacred Heart Church.
Donohue, Peter *c.s.c.* '56 (ORL) Retired; [F] Cocoa Beach, FL Holy Cross Fathers, Eastern Priests Province.
Donohue, Peter M. *o.s.a.* '79 (PH) [C] Villanova, PA Villanova University.
Donohue, Raymond '51 (R) Retired.
Donohue, Raymond A.J. '75 (BUF) Mayville, NY St. Mary Church; Sherman, NY St. Isaac Jogues Church.
Donohue, Robert W. '50 (CLV) Retired.
Donohue, Thomas '41 (L) [1] Valley Station, KY St. Clement Church.
Donohue, Thomas E. '41 (L) Retired.
Donohue, Timothy C. *o.carm.* '51 (NY) [Z] Scarborough, NY Carmelite Fathers, NY Prov. of St. Elias.
Donoso, Fermin J. *c.s.c.* '67 (FTW) [J] South Bend, IN Congregation of Holy Cross Indiana Province Provincial House.
Donovan, Charles A. *c.s.p.* '40 (NY) [Z] Scarsdale, NY Paulist Fathers Generalate.
Donovan, Charles A. *c.s.p.* '40 (SFR) [31] San Francisco, CA Old St. Mary's Cathedral.
Donovan, Charles F. *s.j.* '43 (BO) [W] Chestnut Hill, MA The Jesuit Community at Boston College.
Donovan, Daniel E. '49 (ALN) Bangor, PA Our Lady of Good Counsel Church.
Donovan, David I. *s.j.* '68 (BO) [W] Boston, MA Jesuit Urban Center & Immaculate Conception Community.
Donovan, Dennis *s.d.b.* '83 (NY) [Z] New Rochelle, NY Salesian Provincial House.
Donovan, Edmund J. '41 (E) Retired.
Donovan, Edward *c.s.p.* '59 (LA) Carpinteria, CA St. Joseph Church.
Donovan, Msgr. Edward J. '54 (NY) State, NY Green Haven Correctional Facility.
Donovan, Edward R. *c.s.p.* '59 (NY) [Z] Scarsdale, NY Paulist Fathers Generalate.
Donovan, J. *o.p.* '39 (PRT) [G] Lewiston, ME Marcotte Nursing Home - D'Youville Pavilion.
Donovan, J. Michael '65 (SY) Marcellus, NY St. Francis Xavier Church.
Donovan, J. Paul '58 (TLS) Owasso, OK St. Henry Church.
Donovan, James *o.m.i.* '51 (BEL) [I] Belleville, IL Retreat and Renewal Center.
Donovan, James *o.p.* '55 (PRT) [I] Lewiston, ME SS. Peter and Paul Priory.
Donovan, James J. '87 (CHI) Niles, IL Our Lady of Ransom Church.
Donovan, James W. *c.s.p.* '68 (CHI) [125] Chicago, IL Old St. Mary Church.
Donovan, John L. (BO) Retired.
Donovan, John P. '86 (SY) Special Assignment; [V] Hamilton, NY Catholic Newman Community of Colgate University.
Donovan, Msgr. John T. '44 (MIL) Retired.
Donovan, Joseph D. '40 (ROC) Retired.
Donovan, Joseph F. '53 (BO) [4] Brockton, MA St. Margaret Church.
Donovan, Msgr. Joseph J. '51 (NEW) Bergenfield, NJ St. John the Evangelist Church; Retired.
Donovan, Joseph J. *m.m.* '79 (SFR) [N] San Francisco, CA Maryknoll Fathers and Brothers, Catholic Foreign Mission Society of America, Inc.
Donovan, Kevin G. '88 (HRT) Avon, CT St. Ann's Church.
Donovan, Michael A. '62 (DET) [3] Roseville, MI St. Donald Church.
Donovan, Michael B. *o.s.f.s.* '67 (WIL) [I] Childs, MD Oblates of St. Francis De Sales.
Donovan, Patrick *o.s.m.* '55 (OAK) [N] Berkeley, CA Servite Community, Sarpi Priory.
Donovan, Patrick *o.s.m.* '55 (ORG) Fullerton, CA St. Philip Benizi Church.
Donovan, Paul A. *s.j.* '56 (SD) [B] San Diego, CA University of San Diego.
Donovan, Richard *o.f.m.* (BO) [1] Marlboro, MA St. Ann Church.
Donovan, Richard R. '58 (RVC) Garden City, NY St. Anne Church.
Donovan, Robert '53 (ROC) [3] Rochester, NY St. Andrew Church.
Donovan, Robert '54 (ROC) Retired.
Donovan, Robert C. '70 (FR) Pocasset, MA St. John the Evangelist Church.
Donovan, Msgr. Thomas A. '50 (GAL) [76] Houston, TX St. Thomas More Church; Retired.
Donovan, Msgr. Thomas F. '57 (BRK) [237] Queens, NY Sacred Heart of Jesus Church.
Donovan, Thomas P. *s.j.* '44 (BO) [W] Weston, MA Campion Center.
Donovan, Victor *c.p.* '36 (HRT) [M] West Hartford, CT Holy Family Monastery/Retreat.
Donovan, Vincent J. *c.s.sp.* '52 (CHL) Monroe, NC Our Lady of Lourdes Church.
Donovan, Msgr. Walter J. '44 (ATL) [8] Atlanta, GA Sacred Heart of Jesus Church; Retired.
Donovan, Msgr. William (SY) [W] Utica, NY Calvary.
Donovan, William D. '61 (BGP) [5] Fairfield, CT Holy Family Church.
Donovan, William G. '94 (PH) Collingdale, PA St. Joseph Church.
Donovan, Msgr. William J. '50 (SY) [3] Utica, NY Our Lady of Lourdes Church.
Donovan, Msgr. William L. '43 (SCR) Retired; [N] Dunmore, PA Villa St. Joseph.
Donton, Joseph P. '91 (PEO) [12] Peoria, IL St. Peter's Church.
Doocey, Michael F. (BO) Retired.
Doody Cyril J. '56 (BRK) [79] Brooklyn, NY St. Mark's Church.
Doody Michael J. *s.j.* '78 (BO) [W] Boston, MA The Society of Jesus of New England-Provincial Offices.
Doody Michael J. *s.j.* '78 (STL) [C] St. Louis, MO Saint Louis University; [P] St. Louis, MO Jesuit Community Corporation at St. Louis University - Jesuit Hall.
Doody Patrick *c.s.sp.* (RIC) [E] Norfolk, VA Bon Secours - De Paul Medical Center, Inc.
Doody Peter J. '71 (PAT) [8] Clifton, NJ St. Philip the Apostle Church.
Doody Msgr. Timothy F. '42 (GRY) Retired.
Doogan, Msgr. John P. '46 (SEA) Retired.
Doogan, Joseph H. '48 (SEA) [27] Seattle, WA Our Lady of Fatima Church; Retired.
Dooher, John A. '69 (BO) [BB] Boston, MA Our Lady of Good Voyage Chapel; [FF] Braintree, MA Our Lady of Kazan Russian Greek Catholic Mission.
Dooher, John J. (BO) Dedham, MA St. Mary Church.
Doolan, Ailbe *o.c.d.* '53 (SJ) [M] San Jose, CA Carmelite Monastery, Novitiate.
Doolan, John M. *s.j.* '63 (ALB) [O] Auriesville, NY Shrine of Our Lady of Martyrs.
Doolan, Vincent P. '74 (BO) [D] Cambridge, MA Matignon High School.
Doolan, Vincent P. '80 (BO) Marshfield, MA St. Christine Church.
Dooley, Bernard J. *s.j.* '55 (BAL) [M] Baltimore, MD Jesuit Fathers and Brothers Maryland Provincial Curia.
Dooley, Daniel M. '61 (PH) Norwood, PA St. Gabriel Church.
Dooley, Francis B. '45 (IND) Retired.
Dooley, Harry J. *c.s.p.* '58 (NY) [Z] Scarsdale, NY Paulist Fathers Generalate.
Dooley, Msgr. Joseph P. '56 (ALN) Martins Creek, PA St. Rocco Church.
Dooley, Joseph W. '44 (IND) Retired; [O] Indianapolis, IN International Catholic Deaf Association (Chapter No. 38).
Dooley, Kevin F. '84 (MAD) Platteville, WI St. Mary Church.
Dooley, Malachy R. *o.p.* '49 (CHI) [D] Oak Park, IL Fenwick High School; [N] River Forest, IL St. Thomas Aquinas Priory.
Dooley, Michael D. *s.j.* '85 (DAL) [D] Dallas, TX Jesuit College Preparatory School.
Dooley, Peter C. '76 (RVC) Bellmore, NY St. Barnabas the Apostle Church.
Dooley, Msgr. R. Joseph '69 (WDC) Retired.
Dooley, Thomas V. '91 (DM) Leon, IA St. Brendan Church; Maloy, IA Immaculate Conception Church.
Dooley, William E. *s.j.* '46 (MIL) [P] Milwaukee, WI Jesuit Community at Marquette University.
Doolin, William *c.s.sp.* '37 (SFR) Millbrae, CA St. Dunstan Church.
Doolin, Msgr. William A. '45 (PH) [13] Philadelphia, PA St. Anselm Church; Upper Darby, PA St. Alice Church; Retired.
Dooling, Patrick '82 (MRY) Capitola, CA St. Joseph Church.
Dooling, Stuart *o.s.f.s.* '40 (CAM) [L] Pittsgrove, NJ Villa St. Joseph.
Doonan, John A. '52 (BO) Retired.
Dooner, William B. '70 (PH) Oxford, PA Sacred Heart Church; [DD] Philadelphia, PA Newman Apostolate.
Dora, Msgr. Peter A. '72 (ATL) Athens, GA St. Joseph's Church.
Dora, Msgr. Peter P. '67 (BGP) [1] Stratford, CT Holy Name of Jesus Church.
Dorais, Gerald A. '55 (WOR) [4] Fitchburg, MA St. Francis of Assisi Church.
Doran, Austin '78 (LA) [A] Camarillo, CA St. John's Seminary; [A] Camarillo, CA St. John's Seminary.
Doran, Brian '71 (LA) Vernon, CA Holy Angels Parish of the Deaf Church.
Doran, Edward *o.s.a.* '61 (PH) [111] Philadelphia, PA St. Nicholas of Tolentine Church.
Doran, Edward P. '84 (BRK) [47] Brooklyn, NY St. Francis Xavier Church.
Doran, John '45 (PHX) Retired.
Doran, John E. '66 (WOR) [4] Leominster, MA St. Leo's Church.
Doran, Msgr. John E. '72 (NEW) Upper Montclair, NJ St. Cassian Church.
Doran, Joseph *s.d.b.* '66 (BO) [Y] Ipswich, MA Sacred Heart Retreat Center.
Doran, Matthew J. '44 (SY) Retired.
Doran, Msgr. Thomas M. '47 (SY) Whitesboro, NY St. Anne Church; Retired.
Doran, William '58 (VIC) Meyersville, TX SS. Peter & Paul Church.
Doran, William J. *s.j.* '55 (OM) [C] Omaha, NE Creighton Preparatory School.
Dorcy, Roger P. '80 (PBL) [7] Pueblo, CO Our Lady of the Meadows Church.
Dore, Denis ' 4 (BRK) Retired.
Dore, Denis M. '44 (BRK) [228] Queens, NY St. Pius X Church.
Dore, James *o.s.m.* '58 (ORL) Palm Bay, FL Our Lady of Grace Church.
Dore, James M. *o.s.m.* '58 (CHI) [N] Chicago, IL Servite Friars - Eastern Province; [N] Chicago, IL Servite Friars - Eastern Province.
Dore, Robert '89 (JKS) Chatawa, MS St. Teresa Church.
Dore, Thomas M. '61 (CHI) [4] Oak Park, IL St. Giles Church.
Dorenbusch, Thomas A. '57 (CIN) Tipp City, OH St. John the Baptist Church.
Dorenkemper, Mark *c.pp.s.* '48 (CIN) [B] Carthagena, OH St. Charles.
Dorff, Francis *o.praem* '60 (SFE) [J] Albuquerque, NM Santa Maria de la Vid Priory.
Dorff, John J. *c.ss.r.* '69 (HBG) Ephrata, PA Mother of Perpetual Help Church; [H] Ephrata, PA St. Clement's Mission House.
Dorgan, Gerard L. '58 (BO) Danvers, MA St. Mary of the Annunciation Church.
Dorgan, John J. '65 (RIC) [4] Norfolk, VA Sacred Heart Church.
Dorgan, Joseph A. *s.j.* '56 (NY) [F] New York, NY Regis High School; [Z] New York, NY St. Ignatius Loyola Residence.
Dorhauer, C. Robert '63 (STL) [5] Creve Coeur, MO St. Richard Church.
Dorian, Brendan '58 (YAK) On Duty Outside the Diocese.
Dorian, L. Brendon '58 (PHX) [21] Phoenix, AZ St. Paul Church.
Dorich, John '61 (VNN) Phoenix, AZ St. Stephen Church.
Dorin, Robert R. *s.j.* '67 (BO) [W] Boston, MA The Society of Jesus of New England-Provincial Offices.
Dorin, Robert R. *s.j.* '67 (SPK) [C] Spokane, WA Gonzaga University.
Doriot, Thomas E. '49 (FTW) On Special Assignment.
Doris, Andrew T. '47 (SAV) Retired.
Doris, Andrew T. '57 (SAV) [1] Augusta, GA Church of the Most Holy Trinity.
Doris, John A. '75 (SCR) [5] Dunmore, PA St. Mary of Mount Carmel Church.
Dormer, David J. '77 (SCR) Military Chaplains.
Dorn, George *c.ss.r.* '50 (ORL) [F] New Smyrna Beach, FL St. Alphonsus Villa-Redemptorist Fathers and Brothers.
Dorn, Jerry *glmy.* '78 (CIN) [M] Fairfield, OH Headquarters of Glenmary Home Missioners.
Dorn, Jim Van *o.f.m.conv.* '67 (IND) [I] Mount Saint

Francis, IN Mount Saint Francis Friary and Retreat Center.
Dorn, John *o.ss.t.* '81 (BAL) [M] Baltimore, MD Holy Trinity Monastery.
Dorn, Louis E. '72 (JC) Marshall, MO St. Peter Church; Marshall, MO Marshall State School-Hospital.
Dorn, Rupert *o.f.m.cap* '51 (MAD) [M] Madison, WI San Damiano Friary.
Dornak, Melvin '92 (AUS) West, TX Assumption Church.
Dornbos, William '68 (HEL) Special Assignments.
Dorner, Joseph E. '95 (GB) [13] Green Bay, WI SS. Peter and Paul Church.
Dorney, Msgr. Dennis C. '67 (TLS) [10] Tulsa, OK St. Mary Church.
Dorney, Msgr. James J. '58 (NY) [224] Staten Island, NY St. Peter Church.
Dorniak, Joseph *o.f.m.conv.* '79 (BGP) [6] Danbury, CT Sacred Heart Church.
Dorniak, Joseph *o.f.m.conv.* '79 (PMB) [B] Fort Pierce, FL John Carroll High School.
Dornier, Russell L. *s.j.* '44 (NO) [P] New Orleans, LA Ignatius Residence.
Doro, Michael J. '72 (MAD) [2] Janesville, WI St. John Vianney Church.
Doroin, Elias E. '64 (GAL) [K] Houston, TX The Catholic Chaplain Corps.
Dorr, James *c.m.* '44 (BRK) [U] Jamaica, NY Vincentian Residence.
Dorr, James F. *c.m.* '58 (BRK) [D] Queens and Staten Island, NY St. John's University.
Dorr, Richard J. '55 (DET) Retired.
Dorrill, James F. '60 (MOB) [1] Mobile, AL Cathedral of the Immaculate Conception; [K] Mobile, AL University of South Alabama Catholic Student Center.
Dorrity, Daniel '69 (MIA) Special Assignment.
Dorrler, Michael E. *s.j.* '83 (CHI) [T] Barrington, IL Bellarmine Hall.
Dorrmann, William J. '55 (CIN) Shandon, OH St. Aloysius Church.
Dorsch, Henry L. '68 (SPR) [8] Pittsfield, MA St. Mark's Church.
Dorsch, Larry W. '75 (WH) [1] Wheeling, WV St. Joseph's Cathedral.
Dorsel, John F. (R) Absent on Leave.
Dorsey, Daniel *glmy.* '78 (LR) Monticello, AR St. Mark Church.
Dorsey, Garret D. '59 (PIT) Allison Park, PA St. Ursula Church.
Dorsey, Joseph A. *c.s.c.* '57 (FTW) [J] South Bend, IN Congregation of Holy Cross Indiana Province Provincial House.
Dorsey, Lawrence J. '59 (OM) Ralston, NE St. Gerald Church.
Dorsey, Patrick J. *s.j.* '96 (MIL) [P] Milwaukee, WI Jesuit Community at Marquette University.
Dorson, James E. '77 (RIC) [12] Virginia Beach, VA Star of the Sea Church.
Dorta, Juan Manuel *s.j.* '55 (MIA) [D] Miami, FL Belen Jesuit Preparatory School; [H] Miami, FL Villa Arrieta.
Dorton, John '70 (DM) [11] Des Moines, IA St. Peter's Church.
Dorwart, William *c.s.c.* '80 (COS) [E] Cascade, CO Holy Cross Novitiate.
Dorwart, William D. *c.s.c.* '80 (FTW) [J] South Bend, IN Congregation of Holy Cross Indiana Province Provincial House.
Dory, Michael '76 (GB) Military Chaplains.
Dos Reis, Jose Q. '64 (PRO) Providence, RI Rhode Island Hospital; [C] Warwick, RI Bishop Hendricken High School.
dos Remedios, Francis *o.s.b.* '82 (BIS) Hebron, ND St. Ann Church; [A] Richardton, ND Assumption Abbey.
Dos Santos, Jose '68 (ALN) [4] Bethlehem, PA Holy Infancy Church.
dos Santos, Jose A.F. '53 (FR) [8] Fall River, MA Our Lady of Health Church.
Doscher, Joseph *s.c.j.* (SP) [O] Pinellas Park, FL Priests of the Sacred Heart.
Doscher, Joseph *s.c.j.* '73 (MIL) [P] Hales Corners, WI Priests of the Sacred Heart.
Dosen, Anthony J. '82 (CHI) [N] Chicago, IL Vincentian Community, Congregation of the Mission, Midwest Province.
Doser, Edward A. *c.s.b.* '55 (GAL) [F] Houston, TX St. Thomas High School.
Dosh, Mark B. '58 (STP) On Duty Outside the Archdiocese.
Doskey, Msgr. Clinton J. '54 (NO) [54] New Orleans, LA St. Pius X Church.
Dostie, Benoit C. *m.s.c.* '40 (OG) [2] Watertown, NY Our Lady of the Sacred Heart, Missionaries of the Sacred Heart Church.
Dotson, Msgr. Paul T. '68 (LA) Woodland Hills, CA St. Bernardine of Siena Church.
Doub, Nicholas *o.s.b.* '87 (SCL) [I] Collegeville, MN St. John's Abbey, of the Order of St. Benedict.
Doucet, Camille *m.s.* '68 (FR) [K] Attleboro, MA La Salette Provincial House.
Doucet, David A. '69 (BO) [3] Somerville, MA St. Benedict Church.
Doucet, Ovila T. (PRO) [M] Pawtucket, RI Jeanne Jugan Residence.
Doucet, Ovila T. '53 (PRO) Retired.
Doucette, Michael L. '75 (PRT) Madawaska, ME St. Thomas Aquinas Church.
Doudican, James '48 (CHY) [2] Cheyenne, WY Holy Trinity Church; Retired.
Doueihi, Hector Y. '55 (SAM) Brooklyn, NY Cathedral of Our Lady of Lebanon.
Dougher, John L. '64 (PRT) Westbrook, ME St. Mary's Church.
Dougherty, C. Peter '61 (LAN) Special Assignment.
Dougherty, Charles *c.p.* '68 (RVC) Shelter Island, NY Our Lady of the Isle Church.
Dougherty, Charles F. '63 (SJ) Milpitas, CA St. John the Baptist Church.
Dougherty, Damien '75 (STL) [T] Dittmer, MO Il Ritiro-The Little Retreat.
Dougherty, Daniel J. '70 (PH) Kennett Square, PA St. Patrick Church.
Dougherty, David *c.pp.s.* '49 (KC) [J] Liberty, MO Precious Blood Center.
Dougherty, Msgr. David T. '50 (BRK) [13] Brooklyn, NY St. Athanasius Church.
Dougherty, Denis *o.s.b.* '56 (KC) [13] Kansas City, MO St. Gabriel Archangel Church; [O] Kansas City, MO Benedictine Counseling and Consulting Institute.
Dougherty, Msgr. Denis R. '48 (WCH) Colwich, KS Sacred Heart Church.
Dougherty, Edward *m.m.* (NY) [101] New York, NY Our Saviour Church.
Dougherty, Edward (TR) Washington Crossing, NJ St. George Church; [M] Trenton, NJ Villa Neumann.
Dougherty, Edward J. '53 (TR) Retired.
Dougherty, Edward J. *s.j.* '70 (NO) [P] New Orleans, LA Jesuit Provincial Office.
Dougherty, Edward M. *m.m.* '79 (NY) [Z] Maryknoll, NY Maryknoll Fathers and Brothers.
Dougherty, Eugene J. '53 (PIT) [73] Pittsburgh, PA Holy Wisdom Church.
Dougherty, Francis D. *o.s.f.s.* '38 (WIL) [B] Wilmington, DE Salesianum School.
Dougherty, George Patrick '67 (GAL) Retired.
Dougherty, Henry E. '41 (PH) Levittown, PA Queen of the Universe Church; Retired.
Dougherty, Hugh J. (PH) South Coventry, PA St. Thomas More Church.
Dougherty, James '67 (JOL) [18] Joliet IL St. Paul the Apostle Church.
Dougherty, James J. *s.j.* '59 (STL) [P] St. Louis, MO Hallahan House.
Dougherty, James R. '68 (BEL) Centralia, IL St. Mary Church.
Dougherty, John C. '45 (PH) [21] Philadelphia, PA St. Bartholomew Church; Retired.
Dougherty, John J. *c.s.c.* '93 (PHX) [J] Phoenix, AZ Andre House of Arizona.
Dougherty, Joseph A. *o.s.f.s.* '61 (PH) [D] Philadelphia, PA Father Judge High School for Boys; [Z] Philadelphia, PA Father Judge Faculty House.
Dougherty, Joseph D. '48 (PH) Hatboro, PA St. John Bosco Church; [DD] Philadelphia, PA Newman Apostolate.
Dougherty, Luke *o.s.b.* '55 (SD) [H] Oceanside, CA Prince of Peace Abbey, Benet Hill.
Dougherty, Matthew C. '60 (MIL) Retired.
Dougherty, Owen *c.p.* '91 (CHI) [N] Chicago, IL Passionist Community-CTU.
Dougherty, Paul V. '80 (PH) Warminster, PA Nativity of Our Lord Church; [R] Philadelphia, PA Catholic Center for the Deaf and Hard of Hearing.
Dougherty, Peter C. '61 (LAN) East Lansing, MI St. John the Evangelist, Student Parish Church.
Dougherty, Philip J. *s.j.* '41 (OM) [C] Omaha, NE Creighton Preparatory School.
Dougherty, Robert G. *s.j.* '60 (BO) [Y] Weston, MA Campion Renewal Center.
Dougherty, Stephen J. '73 (PH) Narberth, PA St. Margaret Church; [A] Wynnewood, PA Theological Seminary of St. Charles Borromeo, Overbrook.
Dougherty, Terrence *o.c.d.* '63 (MAN) [M] Peterborough, NH The Common-St. Joseph Monastery.
Dougherty, William *c.pp.s.* '46 (CIN) [B] Carthagena, OH St. Charles.
Dougherty, William J. *o.s.f.s.* '59 (WIL) [3] Wilmington, DE St. Anthony of Padua Church; Elsmere, DE Veteran's Hospital.
Dougherty, William J. *c.s.p.* '63 (TUC) [11] Tucson, AZ St. Cyril of Alexandria Church.
Dougherty, William J. '69 (PH) Doylestown, PA Our Lady of Mount Carmel Church; Absent on Sick Leave.
Dougherty, William N. *o.s.f.s.* '65 (ARL) Reston, VA St. John Neumann Church.
Doughty, Edward '95 (BO) Danvers, MA St. Richard Church.
Doughty, Rees '94 (NY) [82] New York, NY Notre Dame Church; [CC] New York, NY University Apostolate.
Douglas, David M. '65 (LFT) West Lafayette, IN Blessed Sacrament Church.
Douglas, Gordon '68 (SEA) [16] Seattle, WA St. Matthew Church; [B] Seattle, WA Blanchet High School.
Douglas, John *c.p.* '81 (BRK) [U] Jamaica, NY Immaculate Conception Monastery.
Douglas, Louis '58 (ALB) Retired.
Douglas, Marian *o.f.m.* '57 (MAR) Calumet, MI Sacred Heart Church.
Douglas, Michael W. '75 (WDC) [8] Silver Spring, MD St. Michael Church; Pastoral Center Special Ministries.
Douglas, Norman K. '74 (CLV) [10] Akron, OH St. Martha Church.
Douglass, Vincent J. *c.ss.r.* '66 (ATL) Hapeville, GA St. John the Evangelist Church.
Dousdebes, Rene *s.j.* '66 (NY) [Z] New York, NY Jesuit Provincial's Office.
Doussan, Msgr. Douglas A. '60 (NO) [34] New Orleans, LA St. Gabriel the Archangel Church.
Dove, Thomas J. *c.s.p.* (SFR) [31] San Francisco, CA Old St. Mary's Cathedral.
Dover, Edward R. '85 (LA) Monterey Park, CA St. Thomas Aquinas Church.
Dovick, Robert E. '54 (CHI) Palos Heights, IL Incarnation Church.
Dowalgo, Mitchell G. *c.s.b.* '82 (LSC) [4] Las Cruces, NM St. Albert the Great Newman Parish Church; [B] Las Cruces, NM Basilian Fathers.
Dowbush, Yaroslaw '86 (STN) Tucson, AZ St. Michael Church.
Dowd, Barry '82 (ORL) [1] Orlando, FL Mary Queen of the Universe Shrine Church.
Dowd, Barry G. '84 (BUR) On Duty Outside the Diocese.
Dowd, Brian P. '91 (BRK) [34] Brooklyn, NY St. Edmund's Church; [217] Queens, NY Our Lady of Perpetual Help Church.
Dowd, James '56 (P) Cottage Grove, OR Our Lady of Perpetual Help Church.
Dowd, John *c.ss.r.* (CHI) [9] Chicago, IL St. Alphonsus Church.
Dowd, John M. *o.s.m.* '59 (ORG) [H] Buena Park, CA Servite Fathers And Brothers.
Dowd, John R. '63 (MAD) Green Lake, WI Our Lady of the Lake Church.
Dowd, Karl E. '60 (MAN) [3] Nashua, NH St. Christopher Church.
Dowd, Patrick A. '59 (MIL) Retired.
Dowd, Robert A. *c.s.c.* '94 (FTW) [J] Notre Dame, IN Holy Cross Community, Corby Hall, University of Notre Dame; [J] South Bend, IN Congregation of Holy Cross Indiana Province Provincial House.
Dowd, Robert A. *c.s.c.* '94 (LA) Santa Monica, CA St. Monica Church.
Dowd, Thomas M. '54 (GI) Retired.
Dowdel, Lawrence J., Jr. '91 (LA) Ventura, CA Our Lady of the Assumption Church.
Dowdell, Aaron M. *o.ss.t.* '74 (BAL) [M] Baltimore, MD Holy Trinity Monastery.
Dowdell, Aaron M. *o.ss.t.* '74 (NY) [20] New York, NY St. Brigid Church.
Dowdell, Msgr. Joseph M. '63 (BUF) Lakewood, NY Sacred Heart Church.
Dowdell, Thomas R. '71 (OKL) Enid, OK St. Gregory the Great Church.
Dowdle, David P. '79 (CHI) [67] Chicago, IL St. Gall Church.
Dowds, James *c.ss.r.* '85 (WDC) [M] Washington, DC Holy Redeemer College.
Dowdy, James H. '69 (BAL) Absent on Leave.
Dowell, William J. '45 (DET) Retired.
Dower, Douglas '87 (RVC) Elmont, NY St. Boniface Church.
Dowling, Edward T. *s.j.* '69 (NY) [Z] New York, NY Jesuit Community at Fordham University.
Dowling, Edwin A. '77 (CLV) Loudonville, OH St. Peter Church; [Y] Cleveland, OH Office of Newman Campus Ministry.
Dowling, Finbarr *o.s.b.* (STL) Concord Hill, MO St. Ignatius Church.
Dowling, Jack *o.s.a.* '68 (FWT) Gainesville, TX St. Mary Church.
Dowling, John *m.s.f.* '74 (SAT) [M] San Antonio, TX MSF Center & Provincialate.
Dowling, John C. '51 (NEW) Retired.
Dowling, John R. '83 (KNX) [5] Knoxville, TN Holy Ghost Church; Tazewell, TN Christ The King Church.
Dowling, Joseph Kevin '80 (NSH) McEwen, TN St. Patrick Church; Tennessee Ridge, TN St. Elizabeth Ann Seton Church.
Dowling, Jude '54 (HRT) [M] West Hartford, CT Holy Family Monastery/Retreat.
Dowling, Lawrence R. '91 (CHI) [50] Chicago, IL St. Denis Church; Arlington Heights, IL St. James Church.
Dowling, Michael J. '56 (NEW) Retired.
Dowling, P. Finbarr *o.s.b.* '68 (STL) [P] St. Louis, MO The Abbey of St. Mary and St. Louis.
Dowling, Patrick '87 (JC) Missionary Assignment in Peru.
Dowling, Msgr. Philip J. '56 (PH) [133] Philadelphia, PA St. Patrick Church.

Dowling, Raymond (DAL) Seagoville, TX Federal Correctional Institution.
Dowling, Raymond G. '61 (GB) On Duty Outside the Diocese.
Dowling, Msgr. Thomas C. '55 (NO) Retired.
Dowling, Timothy '92 (PAT) Kinnelon, NJ Our Lady of the Magnificat Church.
Dowling, William '94 (LA) El Monte, CA Nativity Church.
Dowling, William P. '54 (SAV) Retired.
Downes, Msgr. Stephen N. '66 (LA) Goleta, CA St. Raphael Church.
Downes, Thomas J. '51 (CHI) Retired.
Downey, Alvin T. *o.s.b.* '70 (GBG) [H] Latrobe, PA Saint Vincent Archabbey.
Downey, James *o.s.b.* '46 (KCK) [H] Atchison, KS St. Benedict's Abbey.
Downey, Joseph F. *s.j.* (DET) [K] Detroit, MI Jesuit Provincial Office-Detroit Province of the Society of Jesus.
Downey, Joseph F. *s.j.* '48 (CHI) [N] Evanston, IL Canisius House.
Downey, Joseph J. '43 (BO) Retired; [U] Somerville, MA Jeanne Jugan Residence.
Downey, Kevin *o.f.m.* (PAT) Pompton Lakes, NJ Our Lady of the Assumption Church.
Downey, Michael '73 (SAC) Fairfield, CA Holy Spirit Church.
Downey, Patrick M. '80 (DOD) Great Bend, KS St. Patrick Church.
Downey, Robert '64 (SB) Retired.
Downey, Timothy M. '38 (TOL) Retired.
Downie, Arley '88 (GLP) Waterflow, NM Sacred Heart Church.
Downing, Brendan W. '79 (BRK) [173] Queens, NY St. Gertrude Church.
Downing, Charles H. '65 (PRO) [7] West Warwick, RI St. Joseph's Church.
Downing, Msgr. Joseph C. '62 (CAM) Pennsauken, NJ St. Stephen Church.
Downs, Bruce '94 (PHX) [3] Tempe, AZ Resurrection Church.
Downs, Gregory Todd '91 (LAF) Carencro, LA St. Peter Church.
Downs, James A. '70 (PIT) Bessemer, PA St. Anthony Church; Hillsville, PA St. Lawrence Church; Lawrence County, PA Lawrence County Jail.
Downs, John L. '55 (OG) Massena, NY St. Joseph Church.
Downs, L. James '66 (WDC) Clinton, MD Church of St. John the Evangelist.
Downs, Leroy J. '43 (WCH) Retired.
Downs, Richard J. '45 (ALB) Retired.
Downs, Robert J. '51 (ROC) Moravia, NY St. Patrick Church; Scipio Center, NY St. Bernard Church.
Downs, Walter J. *m.s.c.* '58 (Y) [A] Youngstown, OH Sacred Heart Retreat House & Renewal Center; [N] Youngstown, OH Sacred Heart Retreat and Renewal Center.
Doyen, Mitchell '91 (STL) [14] St. Louis, MO Our Lady of Sorrows Church; [E] St. Louis, MO Saint Mary's High School.
Doyle, Brendan '63 (JC) Linn, MO St. George Church; [B] Jefferson City, MO Helias High School.
Doyle, Brendan '89 (ATL) Blue Ridge, GA St. Anthony's Church.
Doyle, Charles E. '53 (GRY) Beverly Shores, IN St. Ann Church.
Doyle, Dan F. *s.m.* (MIA) Special Assignment.
Doyle, Daniel E. *o.s.a.* (PH) [B] Villanova, PA St. Augustine Friary.
Doyle, Daniel E. *o.s.a.* '86 (PH) [C] Villanova, PA Villanova University.
Doyle, Daniel F. *s.m.* (BAL) [M] Baltimore, MD Marianists Community (New York Province).
Doyle, Daniel J. '48 (BO) [2] Salem, MA Immaculate Conception Church.
Doyle, Denis '70 (SR) Ferndale, CA Church of the Assumption.
Doyle, Dennis J. '65 (STL) [4] St. Charles, MO Sts. Joachim and Ann Church.
Doyle, Dennis M. '92 (STL) [3] Creve Coeur, MO St. Monica Church.
Doyle, Donald E. '53 (ALB) Windham, NY St. Theresa of Child Jesus Church.
Doyle, Donald L. *c.m.* '48 (MET) [H] Plainsboro, NJ Vincentian Residence.
Doyle, Edward A. '64 (JC) Absent on Leave.
Doyle, Edward P. *o.p.* '39 (PRO) Providence, RI Summit Medical Center; [P] Providence, RI St. Thomas Aquinas Priory at Providence College.
Doyle, Eugene '76 (SCL) Sauk Rapids, MN Sacred Heart Church.
Doyle, Francis J. *o.s.a.* '70 (WDC) [B] Washington, DC Augustinian College, Order of St. Augustine.
Doyle, Gerald '73 (GLP) Retired.
Doyle, Msgr. James '59 (NY) Pearl River, NY St. Margaret Church.
Doyle, James '61 (LKC) [6] Lake Charles, LA St. Theodore's Church.
Doyle, James F. '49 (ROC) Lima, NY St. Rose Church.
Doyle, Msgr. James J. '35 (PAT) Netcong, NJ St. Michael's Church; Retired.
Doyle, James J. *c.s.c.* '50 (SCR) [C] Wilkes-Barre, PA Kings College.
Doyle, James Michael '57 (SFS) [6] Sioux Falls, SD St. Mary Church.
Doyle, James P. '57 (CHI) Volo, IL St. Peter Church.
Doyle, Jerald A. '69 (BGP) [4] Stratford, CT Our Lady of Grace Church.
Doyle, John '52 (DUL) Floodwood, MN St. Louis Church.
Doyle, John '58 (JOL) Joliet, IL Joliet Correctional Depot.
Doyle, John A. *c.m.* '48 (ALB) [L] Albany, NY Vincentian Fathers Residence.
Doyle, John F. '59 (NEW) Retired.
Doyle, John J. '58 (JOL) [7] Joliet, IL St. Anne Church.
Doyle, Msgr. John J. '70 (CHI) Evergreen Park, IL Queen of Martyrs Church.
Doyle, John J. *o.f.m.* '75 (PAT) Butler, NJ St. Anthony Church.
Doyle, John L. '52 (BO) [62] Boston, MA St. Peter Church.
Doyle, John T. *o.s.f.s.* '52 (VEN) [3] Fort Myers, FL St. Cecilia Church.
Doyle, John V. '41 (PRO) Retired.
Doyle, Joseph *s.j.* '70 (SP) [C] Tampa, FL Jesuit High School.
Doyle, Joseph C. '72 (NEW) Ridgefield Park, NJ St. Francis of Assisi Church.
Doyle, Joseph M. '40 (NEW) Retired.
Doyle, Joseph M. *s.s.j.* '68 (NO) [F] New Orleans, LA St. Augustine High School; [H] New Orleans, LA St. Augustine High School; [P] New Orleans, LA Josephite Fathers and Brothers; [S] New Orleans, LA Pierre Toussaint Foundation of New Orleans, Inc.
Doyle, Kennth '66 (ALB) [5] Albany, NY St. Catherine of Siena Church.
Doyle, Lawrence J. '45 (BO) [10] Lawrence, MA St. Patrick Church; Retired.
Doyle, Lawrence Michael *o.s.m.* '65 (CHI) [N] Chicago, IL Servite Friars - Eastern Province.
Doyle, Mark A. '58 (LC) [1] Wisconsin Rapids, WI Our Lady, Queen of Heaven Church.
Doyle, Martin *s.j.* '91 (NY) [Z] New York, NY Jesuit Provincial's Office.
Doyle, Mathias F. '62 (BUF) [O] St. Bonaventure, NY St. Bonaventure Friary.
Doyle, Michael '59 (CAM) [9] Camden, NJ Sacred Heart Church.
Doyle, Michael '94 (TYL) [D] Tyler, TX Tyler Junior College and The University of Texas at Tyler Newman Center.
Doyle, Michael J. '67 (SPR) [3] Springfield, MA Blessed Sacrament Church; [M] Springfield, MA Casa Cristo Rey.
Doyle, Michael J. '85 (BO) Sudbury, MA Our Lady of Fatima Church.
Doyle, Michael L. *o.s.m.* '65 (DEN) [21] Denver, CO Our Lady of Mt. Carmel Church.
Doyle, Michael M. '89 (NU) Lake Benton, MN St. Genevieve Church; Tyler, MN St. Dionysius Church.
Doyle, Patrick A. '75 (IND) [25] Indianapolis, IN St. Joan of Arc Church.
Doyle, Paul F. *c.s.c.* '77 (FTW) [B] Notre Dame, IN University of Notre Dame Du Lac; [J] Notre Dame, IN Holy Cross Community, Corby Hall, University of Notre Dame.
Doyle, Philip R. '48 (NY) Retired.
Doyle, Richard J. '54 (ALB) Athens, NY St. Patrick Church.
Doyle, Robert A. '61 (NEW) [20] Jersey City, NJ Our Lady of Mercy Church.
Doyle, Robert A. *s.j.* '62 (STL) [P] St. Louis, MO White House Retreat Jesuit Community; [T] St. Louis, MO White House Retreat.
Doyle, Robert M. '49 (BO) [7] Somerville, MA St. Polycarp Church.
Doyle, Seamus '56 (MIA) Miami Shores, FL St. Rose of Lima Church.
Doyle, Stephen *o.f.m.* '62 (BO) [BB] Boston, MA St. Anthony Shrine.
Doyle, Msgr. Thomas '54 (LA) La Crescenta, CA St. James the Less Church.
Doyle, Thomas *s.s.* '60 (BAL) [M] Baltimore, MD Sulpician Provincial House.
Doyle, Thomas '84 (BRK) [U] Brooklyn, NY Curial Residence.
Doyle, Thomas A. '40 (TUC) Retired.
Doyle, Thomas D. (BUF) Oakfield, NY St. Cecilia Church.
Doyle, Thomas F. '66 (PH) Royersford, PA Sacred Heart Church.
Doyle, Thomas J. *s.j.* '46 (PH) [Z] Philadelphia, PA Jesuit Community at St. Joseph's University.
Doyle, Thomas R. '62 (DAV) Albia, IA St. Mary's Church.
Doyle, Msgr. Timothy '48 (ORG) Retired.
Doyle, Msgr. Vincent J. '65 (NEW) Union, NJ Holy Spirit Church.
Doyle, Msgr. Walter H. '43 (STO) Retired.
Doyle, William *s.j.* (BO) Boston, MA Spaulding Rehabilitation Hospital.
Doyle, William F. *s.j.* '53 (BO) [W] Boston, MA Loyola House.
Doyon, Bernard *o.m.i.* '48 (BWN) San Juan, TX Virgen de San Juan del Valle Shrine Church; [I] San Juan, TX Virgen de San Juan del Valle Shrine.
Drab, John (RVC) Retired.
Drab, Stephen J. '37 (GBG) Retired.
Drabek, Howard '91 (GAL) [77] Houston, TX St. Vincent de Paul Church.
Drabik, Richard J. *m.i.c.* '60 (SFE) [J] Bernalillo, NM Southwest Marian Divine Mercy Center.
Drabik, Richard J. *m.i.c.* '60 (SPR) [I] Stockbridge, MA Congregation of Marians.
Drabiska, Frank J. '76 (PIT) [2] Swissvale, PA Word of God Church.
Drag, Roderick *o.f.m.* '49 (PH) [D] Philadelphia, PA Archbishop Ryan High School; [Z] Philadelphia, PA St. Pius X Friary.
Dragga, Thomas (CLV) [A] Wickliffe, OH St. Mary Seminary.
Dragga, Thomas M. (CLV) Willoughby Hills, OH St. Noel Church; [A] Wickliffe, OH Borromeo Seminary.
Drago, Caridade *s.j.* '75 (CHI) [C] Chicago, IL Jesuit Community at Loyola University of Chicago.
Dragon, Joseph W. '78 (PH) East Goshen, PA SS. Peter and Paul Church.
Draim, David *o.s.b.* '73 (SP) [O] St. Leo, FL St. Leo Abbey.
Drain, William A. '74 (CIN) [62] Cincinnati, OH St. Matthias Church.
Drake, Carl '64 (COL) Leave of Absence.
Drake, Robert *c.pp.s.* '30 (PIT) [K] Pittsburgh, PA Vincentian Home Inc.
Drake, Robert J. '64 (PIT) [R] Pittsburgh, PA St. Joseph's House of Hospitality, Inc.
Drake, Roy A. *s.j.* '63 (NY) [Z] New York, NY Murray-Weigel Hall.
Drake, Sebastian *o.f.m.* '45 (SPK) [11] Spokane, WA St. Francis of Assisi, Friars Church.
Drake, Timothy A. '71 (RIC) [10] Virginia Beach, VA St. Matthew Church.
Drance, George *s.j.* '95 (NY) [82] New York, NY Notre Dame Church.
Drance, George W. *s.j.* '95 (MIL) [P] Milwaukee, WI Jesuit Provincial Office, Wisconsin Province.
Drance, George W. '95 (NY) [Z] New York, NY Jesuit Provincial's Office.
Drapeau, Benoit J. *c.j.m.* '59 (BUF) [1] West Seneca, NY St. Bonaventure Church; [O] West Seneca, NY St. Bonaventure.
Draper, Andrew *t.o.r.* '88 (ARL) Luray, VA Our Lady of the Valley Church.
Drapp, Alfred E. (CIN) Retired.
Drass, Damian P. *t.o.r.* '60 (WH) Philippi, WV St. Elizabeth Parish and Newman Center Church; [Q] Philippi, WV Newman Center Alderson-Broaddus College.
Draude, Frank C. '49 (RCK) Retired.
Draugialis, Josef '63 (LA) Los Nietos, CA Our Lady of Perpetual Help Church.
Dravecky, Msgr. Michael A. '33 (PIT) Retired.
Draves-Arpaia, Neil '79 (PHX) On Duty Outside the Diocese.
Dreasen, John R. '79 (RVC) Elmont, NY St. Boniface Church.
Dreckman, Philip *s.j.* '62 (STP) [6] St. Paul, MN The Immaculate Heart of Mary Church.
Dreckman, Philip F. *s.j.* '62 (MIL) [P] Milwaukee, WI Jesuit Community at Marquette University.
Dreese, Msgr. John J. '59 (COL) New Lexington, OH St. Rose of Lima Church.
Dreffein, Larry *o.f.m.* '76 (JOL) [I] Oak Brook, IL Mayslake Village.
Dreger, Msgr. Francis X. '51 (PH) [32] Philadelphia, PA St. Cecilia Church.
Dreher, Ernest O. '48 (MIL) Retired.
Dreher, Jacob J. '43 (DOD) Retired.
Dreher, John D. '64 (PRO) Coventry, RI Our Lady of Czenstochowa Church.
Dreici, Pascal *c.ss.r.* '44 (CHI) [N] Bangkok, Thailand; [N] Parana, Brazil Rua Consulheiro Sinimbu.
Dreici, Pascal *c.ss.r.* '44 (DEN) [M] Denver, CO The Redemptorists/Denver Province.
Dreier, Bruce A. '78 (SFR) [17] San Francisco, CA Church of the Epiphany.
Dreiling, Augustine *o.s.b.* '58 (KC) Conception Junction, MO St. Columba Church.
Dreiling, Gerald G. *c.pp.s.* '58 (CIN) [M] Dayton, OH Provincial House of the Cincinnati Province of the Society of the Precious Blood.
Dreiling, Kilian *c.pp.s.* '36 (CIN) [B] Carthagena, OH St. Charles.
Dreiling, Msgr. Raymond C. '75 (FRS) Clovis, CA Our Lady of Perpetual Help Church; [J] Clovis, CA Catholic Professional & Business Breakfast Club of the Fresno Diocese.
Dreisbach, Charles V. '59 (BAK) Klamath Falls, OR Sacred Heart Church.
Dreisoerner, Msgr. John H. '38 (JC) Retired.

Drendel, Ralph J. *s.j.* '53 (SJ) [D] San Jose, CA Bellarmine College Preparatory.
Drennan, Jimmy D. '96 (SAT) [60] San Antonio, TX St. Paul Church.
Drennan, Lawrence J. '61 (BO) Lincoln, MA St. Joseph Church.
Drennan, Msgr. William A. '55 (STL) [58] St. Louis, MO St. Raphael The Archangel Church.
Drennen, Christopher J. *o.s.a.* '83 (ALB) Mechanicville, NY Assumption-St. Paul Church.
Drenzek, Peter C. '69 (MIL) [3] Fond du Lac, WI St. Mary's Church.
Dresen, Arthur G. '44 (COS) Retired.
Dressel, Willard J. *s.j.* '54 (OM) [C] Omaha, NE Creighton Preparatory School.
Dressell, Stephen G. *m.s.* '47 (HRT) [5] Hartford, CT Our Lady of Sorrows Church; [M] Hartford, CT Missionaries of LaSalette Provincial Secretary.
Dressen, Nicholas '79 (SCL) Big Lake, MN Our Lady of the Lake Church.
Dressler, Philip J. '61 (CHI) [112] Chicago, IL St. Juliana Church.
Dressler, Robert A. '59 (ALN) Kelayres, PA Immaculate Conception Church.
Dressman, Richard E. '72 (CIN) [51] Cincinnati, OH St. Jude the Apostle Church; [V] Cincinnati, OH Catholic Charismatic Renewal Liaison.
Dressman, Robert *s.j.* (CIN) [M] Cincinnati, OH Faber Jesuit Community.
Dreves, Mark D. '95 (LEX) [3] Lexington, KY Mary, Queen of the Holy Rosary Church.
Drew, Andrew *o.f.m.cap.* '61 (SPR) [L] Springfield, MA St. Francis of Assisi Chapel and Catholic Information Center.
Drew, George W. *c.ss.r.* '50 (BO) [13] Boston, MA Basilica of Our Lady of Perpetual Help.
Drew, James F. '74 (HON) On Duty Outside the Diocese.
Drew, James F. '74 (RVC) North Merrick, NY Sacred Heart Church.
Drew, John J. *m.m.* '42 (SJ) [M] Los Altos, CA Maryknoll.
Drewelow, David C. '80 (SPC) On Duty Outside the Diocese.
Drewniak, Stanley '78 (CHI) [36] Chicago, IL St. Camillus Church.
Drexler, Charles H. '69 (E) [B] Erie, PA Gannon University.
Drexler, George D. '39 (NEW) Retired.
Drexler, Harold J. '55 (DUB) Hopkinton, IA St. Luke's Church; Sand Springs, IA Immaculate Conception Church.
Drieci, Pat *c.ss.r.* (FRS) Faculties Only.
Driesch, Albert *t.o.r.* '46 (WH) Moundsville, WV St. Francis Xavier's Church.
Driesch, David A. '82 (PIT) Neshannock, PA St. Camillus Church; [Q] Slippery Rock, PA Office for Campus Ministry.
Drilling, Peter '67 (BUF) [A] East Aurora, NY Christ the King Seminary.
Drinan, Daniel *c.m.f.* '77 (CHI) [N] Oak Park, IL Claretian Fathers Headquarters of U.S.A. Eastern Province.
Drinan, Robert F. *s.j.* '53 (BO) [W] Boston, MA The Society of Jesus of New England-Provincial Offices.
Drinan, Robert F. *s.j.* '53 (WDC) [M] Washington, DC The Jesuit Community at Georgetown University.
Drinkwater, Warren *c.ss.r.* '62 (BLX) [E] Biloxi, MS St. John Neumann Residence.
Driscoll, Arthur J. '52 (BO) Andover, MA St. Robert Bellarmine Church.
Driscoll, Brian J. '96 (JC) [2] Jefferson City, MO St. Peter Church; [B] Jefferson City, MO Helias High School.
Driscoll, Daniel *s.v.d.* '38 (CHI) [B] Techny, IL Divine Word Residence.
Driscoll, Daniel '76 (HEL) [4] Anaconda, MT Anaconda Catholic Community Church.
Driscoll, Donald D. *s.j.* '65 (OM) [K] Omaha, NE Jesuit Community At Creighton University.
Driscoll, Donald T. (NY) Orangeburg, NY Rockland Psychiatric Center.
Driscoll, Eugene '70 (LUB) [4] Lubbock, TX St. Elizabeth University Parish Church.
Driscoll, George F. '61 (NY) [Z] New York, NY Jesuit Community at Fordham University.
Driscoll, James '55 (OAK) Retired.
Driscoll, James A. *o.p.* '54 (PRO) [B] Providence, RI Providence College; [P] Providence, RI St. Thomas Aquinas Priory at Providence College.
Driscoll, James E. '55 (OAK) Danville, CA St. Isidore's Church.
Driscoll, James J. '43 (NEW) Retired.
Driscoll, Jeremy *o.s.b.* '81 (P) [L] St. Benedict, OR Mt. Angel Abbey.
Driscoll, John M. *o.s.a.* '51 (PH) [C] Villanova, PA Villanova University; [Z] Villanova, PA St. Thomas Monastery.
Driscoll, John P. '47 (FR) [18] New Bedford, MA St. Lawrence Martyr Church.
Driscoll, John P. *s.j.* '52 (NO) [P] New Orleans, LA Ignatius Residence.
Driscoll, John P. '54 (JOL) Herscher, IL St. Margaret Mary Church; Irwin, IL St. James The Apostle Church.
Driscoll, Joseph J. (BO) On Duty Outside the Archdiocese.
Driscoll, Joseph J. '79 (MIL) [Y] Milwaukee, WI National Association of Catholic Chaplains.
Driscoll, Msgr. Maurice F. '42 (BEL) Retired.
Driscoll, Michael *o.carm.* '67 (PMB) [5] Boca Raton, FL St. Jude Church.
Driscoll, Michael '76 (FTW) [B] Notre Dame, IN University of Notre Dame Du Lac.
Driscoll, Michael '77 (HEL) On Duty Outside the Diocese.
Driscoll, Michael '92 (PEO) Tiskilwa, IL St. Mary's Church.
Driscoll, Michael A. '68 (MET) Belvidere, NJ St. Patrick Church.
Driscoll, Michael J. '92 (PEO) Camp Grove, IL St. Patrick Church.
Driscoll, Nicholas J. (BO) Awaiting Assignment.
Driscoll, Paul G. '64 (RVC) Levittown, NY St. Bernard Church.
Driscoll, Richard *s.d.s.* '65 (MIL) [P] Milwaukee, WI Salvatorian Provincial Residence.
Driscoll, Richard A. '55 (BO) Topsfield, MA St. Rose of Lima Church.
Driscoll, Thomas F. '60 (OG) Alexandria Bay, NY St. Cyril of Alexandria Church; Redwood, NY St. Francis Xavier Church.
Driscoll, Msgr. Thomas J. '61 (BGP) [5] Stratford, CT Our Lady of Peace Church.
Driscoll, Walter L. '57 (BO) Permanent Disability.
Driscoll, William J. *o.mar.* '63 (SAM) [C] Petersham, MA Most Holy Trinity Monastery.
Driscoll, William J. '65 (E) Linesville, PA St. Philip Church.
Driscoll, William M. *s.j.* '51 (BAL) [C] Baltimore, MD Loyola College; [K] Baltimore, MD Stella Maris Operating Corporation.
Drobach, William F. *s.a.* '88 (LA) [83] Los Angeles, CA St. Odilia Church.
Drobel, William F. '32 (PH) [83] Philadelphia, PA St. Katherine of Siena Church; Retired.
Drobin, Paul J. '66 (SY) New Hartford, NY St. John the Evangelist Church.
Drobinski, Joseph J. '75 (WIL) Newark, DE Parish of the Resurrection Church.
Droessler, Joseph '95 (ORG) San Juan Capistrano, CA (Old Mission) Church.
Droessler, Wayne J. '69 (DUB) Clarion, IA St. John's Church; Eagle Grove, IA Sacred Heart Church.
Drogon, Greg '82 (PAT) [11] Paterson, NJ St. Michael the Archangel Church.
Drogowski, Joseph '49 (DET) Retired; [H] Southfield, MI Providence Hospital.
Drohan, James J. *s.j.* '43 (WOR) [N] Worcester, MA Jesuits of Holy Cross College, Inc.
Drolet, Francis K. *s.j.* '47 (NY) [Z] New York, NY St. Ignatius Loyola Residence.
Drolet, Roger C. *c.s.v.* '33 (CHI) [N] Arlington Heights, IL Viatorian Province Center-Clerics of St. Viator.
Droll, Msgr. Larry J. '73 (SAN) Wall, TX St. Ambrose Church.
Droll, Louis J. '68 (SAN) Retired.
Drone, Msgr. Raphael E. '43 (BEL) Retired.
Drongowski, Stanley *o.p.* (MAD) [3] Madison, WI Blessed Sacrament Church.
Drongowski, Stanley A. *o.p.* '79 (STL) [P] St. Louis, MO Dominican Community of St. Louis.
Droski, Norman P. '64 (GR) Muskegon Heights, MI Sacred Heart Church.
Drouin, Marc B. '90 (MAN) Belmont, NH St. Joseph Church.
Drouncheck, Anthony M. '89 (ALN) [3] Reading, PA St. Catharine of Siena Church.
Drozd, Henry J. '62 (DAL) On Duty Outside the Diocese.
Drozdzik, Roch T. (R) Pinehurst, NC Sacred Heart Church.
Droze, D. Anthony '85 (CHR) Greenville, SC St. Mary's Church.
Druding, John C. '76 (ATL) Roswell, GA St. Andrew Church.
Druggan, Dennis *o.f.m.cap.* '84 (MIL) [B] Mount Calvary, WI St. Lawrence Seminary; [P] Mount Calvary, WI St. Lawrence Friary.
Drummond, Alexander '94 (ARL) Chantilly, VA St. Timothy Church.
Drummond, Eslyn Joseph '54 (NOR) Voluntown, CT St. Thomas Apostle Church.
Drummond, Robert T. *o.s.a.* (NY) [216] Staten Island, NY Our Lady of Good Counsel Church.
Drummy, John A. '71 (SUP) Amery, WI St. Joseph Church; Georgetown, WI Our Lady of the Holy Rosary Church.
Drupieski, Stanley R. *o.s.f.s.* '64 (WIL) [B] Wilmington, DE Salesianum School.
Drury, Dennis G. '82 (GB) Rosiere, WI St. Peter and St. Hubert Church.
Drury, George L. *s.j.* '52 (BO) [W] Cambridge, MA Weston Jesuit Community.
Drury, Michael J. '71 (PAT) Long Valley, NJ St. Luke Church.
Drury, Michael P. '84 (MRY) [G] Monterey, CA Oratorian Community-Congregation of the Oratory of Pontifical Right.
Drury, Robert '79 (OWN) Curdsville, KY St. Elizabeth Church; St. Joseph, KY St. Alphonsus Church.
Drutowski, Robert J. '79 (MIL) Mukwonago, WI St. James Church.
Dryden, Alex *s.a.c.* '54 (CAM) [C] Pennsauken, NJ Bishop Eustace Prep School.
Dryden, John D. *s.j.* '53 (LA) [R] Los Angeles, CA Columbiere House.
Drzaic, Francis *s.v.d.* '62 (BLX) [A] Bay St. Louis, MS St. Augustine's.
Drzaic, Frank *s.v.d.* (CHI) [32] Chicago, IL St. Bronislava Church.
Drzal, Stanislaw *s.ch.* '73 (PAT) [6] Passaic, NJ St. Joseph's Church.
Dtonne, J. Joseph *c.ss.r.* '80 (PCE) Guayama, PR St. Anthony of Padua Church.
Du, Luke Pham Anh '54 (BRK) [147] Queens, NY St. Aloysius Church; [T] Brooklyn, NY Catholic Migration & Refugee Office, Catholic Migration Services, Inc.
Du Buisson, William *o.m.i.* '55 (SAN) Ozona, TX Our Lady of Perpetual Help Church; Sonora, TX St. Ann's Church.
Du Charme, Paul E. '55 (GB) [14] Green Bay, WI St. Philip the Apostle Church.
Du Four, Rene P. *o.m.i.* '54 (BEL) [F] Belleville, IL Our Lady of the Snows Apartment Community Retirement Home.
Duaime, Jeffrey T. *c.s.sp.* '86 (ARL) [7] Arlington, VA Our Lady, Queen of Peace Church.
Duane, Robert J. '53 (NY) Ardsley, NY Our Lady of Perpetual Help Church.
Duane, Thomas J. '71 (PH) [124] Philadelphia, PA Our Lady of Mt. Carmel Church; Roslyn, PA St. John of the Cross Church.
Dubay, Thomas E. *s.m.* '50 (WDC) [M] Washington, DC Marist Provincial House.
Dube, Andre R. '85 (BGP) [4] Stamford, CT St. Clement's Church.
Dube, Donald V. '61 (SPR) Absent on Leave.
Dube, George *m.s.* '48 (FR) [K] Attleboro, MA La Salette Provincial House.
Dube, Marcel *o.carm.* '54 (JOL) [J] Darien, IL Carmelite Fathers Provincial Office.
Dube, Stephen D. '78 (WH) Weirton, WV St. Joseph the Worker Church.
Dubel, Edward A. *c.r.* '57 (SB) Rialto, CA St. Thomas More Church.
Dubell, Msgr. James H. '65 (TR) Burlington, NJ St. Paul Church.
Dubi, Leonard A. '68 (CHI) Hazel Crest, IL St. Anne Church.
Dubitsky, Roman '65 (PHU) Perth Amboy, NJ Assumption of B.V.M. Church; Toms River, NJ St. Stephen's Church.
Dublinski, Steven L. '85 (SPK) [10] Spokane, WA St. Charles Church.
Dubois, Andrew '95 (PRT) [5] Lewiston, ME St. Patrick's Church; [6] Lewiston, ME SS. Peter and Paul Church.
DuBois, Msgr. Charles J. '64 (LKC) Lake Arthur, LA Our Lady of the Lake Church.
DuBois, David J. '80 (GAL) Tomball, TX St. Anne Church.
DuBois, Francis J. '70 (ALB) Latham, NY St. Ambrose Church.
Dubois, Raymond J. *s.s.s.* '49 (CLV) [P] Cleveland, OH Blessed Sacrament Community.
DuBois, Msgr. William '48 (SP) Retired.
Dubois, Yvon *a.a.* '53 (BO) Boston, MA V.A. Medical Centers; [W] Brighton, MA Assumptionist Center.
Dubovici, Mihail '93 (STF) Auburn, NY SS. Peter and Paul Church.
Dubowski, George *o.f.m.* '41 (FTW) [K] Mishawaka, IN St. Francis Provincialate.
Dubowski, George *o.f.m.* '42 (GRY) [K] Cedar Lake, IN Our Lady of Lourdes Friary.
Dubre, Sinclair '86 (BEA) [5] Port Arthur, TX St. James Church.
Dubriske, Edward J. *s.s.e.* '64 (BUR) [G] Colchester, VT Society of St. Edmund.
Duc, Dominic Tran Minh '90 (PH) Highland Park, PA St. Laurence Church.
Duc Hau, Joseph Nguyen *s.e.* '69 (P) [1] Portland, OR Southeast Asian Vicariate Church.
Duc Tien, Msgr. Peter '60 (ORG) Special Assignment.
Duc-Minh, Joseph '61 (LA) [A] Camarillo, CA St. John's Seminary College of the Archdiocese of Los Angeles.
Duca, Michael '78 (DAL) [A] Irving, TX Holy Trinity Seminary.
Ducaji, John '54 (JOL) Wheaton, IL St. Mark Church.
Ducate, Richard '67 (KC) Butler, MO St. Patrick's Church.

Ducci, Alex '61 (STA) Orange Park, FL St. Catherine's Church.
Ducette, Msgr. John I. '62 (BUF) [5] Tonawanda, NY St. Timothy Church.
Ducey, William *ss.cc.* '55 (FR) [K] Fairhaven, MA Sacred Hearts Provincial House.
Duch, Robert G. '64 (PIT) Aspinwall, PA St. Scholastica Church.
Duchaine, R. Mark '78 (SC) Holstein, IA Our Lady of Good Counsel Church.
Duchala, Francis *o.f.m.* '36 (PBR) Girard, PA SS. Cyril and Methodius Church.
DuCharme, Lawrence M. '61 (DET) Absent on Sick Leave.
Duchene, Joseph A. *c.s.sp.* '52 (PIT) [B] Pittsburgh, PA Duquesne University of the Holy Ghost.
DuChez, Daniel B. *o.s.* '56 (PCE) On Duty Outside the Diocese.
DuChez, Daniel B. *o.s.* '86 (LC) Chippewa Falls, WI St. Charles Borromeo Church.
Duchschere, Paul '90 (FAR) [6] Fargo, ND St. Paul Newman Center, N.D.S.U. Church; [H] Fargo, ND St. Paul's Catholic Chapel.
Ducre, Kennon Y. *s.t.l.* '83 (ELP) [2] El Paso, TX All Saints Church.
Ducthllan, Polycarp *c.m.c.* '91 (AMA) [5] Amarillo, TX Our Lady of Vietnam Church.
Duda, Francis *m.i.c.* '43 (SPR) [I] Stockbridge, MA Congregation of Marians.
Duda, Robert '84 (JOL) Elmhurst, IL Immaculate Conception Church.
Duda, Stanislaus J. '42 (FAR) Retired.
Dudack, William E. '55 (HRT) Simsbury, CT St. Mary's Church.
Dudak, Msgr. George A. '56 (PAT) Schooley's Mountain, NJ Our Lady of the Mountain Church.
Dudash, Derrick F. '74 (GRY) Hebron, IN St. Helen Church.
Duddy, Patrick A. '39 (PH) Stowe, PA St. Gabriel Church; Retired.
Dudek, Anthony *m.s.* '37 (MIL) [P] Milwaukee, WI La Salette Fathers.
Dudek, Bernard *o.f.m.conv.* '60 (BAL) [20] Baltimore, MD St. Casimir Church.
Dudek, Ladislaus '40 (SFS) Salem, SD St. Mary Church; Retired.
Dudek, Ladislaus J. '66 (ALN) [8] Allentown, PA SS. Peter and Paul Church.
Dudek, Stephen S. '84 (GR) Holland, MI St. Francis de Sales Church; On Special Assignment.
Dudink, Edward *s.v.d.* '46 (BO) [W] Duxbury, MA Society of the Divine Word.
Dudkiewicz, Stanley '52 (SY) [9] Syracuse, NY Sacred Heart Church.
Dudley, Francis R. '46 (STP) [7] St. Paul, MN Maternity of the Blessed Virgin Church; Retired.
Dudley, James *m.s.c.* '56 (SAT) Sabinal, TX St. Patrick's Church.
Dudziak, Paul M. '69 (WDC) Dunkirk, MD Jesus the Good Shepherd Church.
Dudzik, Dariusz K. '95 (NOR) Pawcatuck, CT St. Michael Church.
Dudzinski, Anthony J. '96 (FAR) [3] Grand Forks, ND St. Michael's Church.
Dudzinski, Edward F., Jr. '78 (WIL) Absent on Sick Leave.
Dudzinski, Paul L. '86 (ARL) Falls Church, VA St. James Church.
Dudzinski, Sylvester W. '39 (CHI) Blue Island, IL St. Isidore Church; Retired.
Duell, James S. '82 (CIN) Bradford, OH Immaculate Conception Church; Covington, OH St. Teresa Church.
Duellman, Virgil S. '60 (WIN) Austin, MN Queen of Angels Church.
Duenas, Jaime H. '50 (NY) [167] Bronx, NY Nativity of Our Blessed Lady Church.
Duenas, Jose Luis *o.a.r.* '59 (NY) [126] Bronx, NY St. Anselm Church.
Duerr, Gregory *o.s.b.* '64 (P) [A] St. Benedict, OR Mount Angel Seminary; [L] St. Benedict, OR Mt. Angel Abbey.
Dues, Mark J. *s.j.* '94 (KC) [J] Kansas City, MO Rockhurst High School - Jesuit Community.
Duesdieker, Robert W. '80 (JC) Bourbon, MO St. Francis Church; Cuba, MO Holy Cross Church; Steelville, MO St. Michael Church.
Duesman, Msgr. Jerome P. '68 (DAL) Irving, TX Holy Family of Nazareth Church.
Duesman, Msgr. Leon '65 (DAL) [4] Garland, TX St. Michael the Archangel Church.
Duet, Wayne J. '75 (LAF) [12] Lafayette, LA St. Jules Church.
Dueweke, Donald G. '66 (SAG) Maple Grove, MI St. Michael Church.
Dufault, Andrew J. *m.afr.* '39 (LR) [F] Hot Springs National Park, AR Monastery of Our Lady of Charity of Refuge (Good Shepherd).
Dufault, Omer L. '42 (BUR) Retired; [F] Burlington, VT St. Joseph's Home for Aged.
Dufault, Wilfrid J. *a.a.* '34 (WOR) [B] Worcester, MA Assumption College; [N] Worcester, MA Assumptionists of Assumption College.
Duff, Gerard M. *o.s.a.* '59 (PH) [U] Flourtown, PA St. Joseph Villa; [Z] Villanova, PA St. Thomas Monastery.
Duff, John J. '77 (NY) Pawling, NY St. John the Evangelist Church.
Duff, Paul J. *c.s.c.* '55 (FR) [B] North Easton, MA Holy Cross Fathers Religious.
Duff, Thomas M. *o.s.m.* '49 (CHI) [N] Chicago, IL Servite Friars - Eastern Province.
Duff, William '63 (LAV) Retired.
Duffe, Stephen J. '96 (NEW) Washington Township, NJ Our Lady of Good Counsel Church.
Duffell, John P. '69 (NY) [14] New York, NY Ascension Church.
Duffey, Joseph A. *o.s.a.* '52 (PH) Flourtown, PA St. Genevieve Church; [Z] Flourtown, PA Augustinians (O.S.A.).
Duffey, Thomas J. '49 (DET) [61] Detroit, MI St. Patrick Church; [Q] Detroit, MI St. Patrick's Senior Center, Inc.
Duffey, William R. *s.j.* '51 (MIL) [P] Milwaukee, WI Jesuit Provincial Office, Wisconsin Province.
Dufficy, Edward C. '50 (CHI) [3] Oak Park, IL St. Edmund Church; Retired.
Duffin, Stephen '91 (ORG) Laguna Beach, CA St. Catherine of Siena Church.
Duffner, Paul A. *o.p.* '40 (P) [18] Portland, OR Holy Rosary Parish & Dominican Priory Church.
Duffner, Ralph J. '56 (SPC) New Hamburg, MO St. Lawrence Church.
Dufford, Robert *s.j.* '73 (GB) [M] Oshkosh, WI Jesuit Retreat House.
Duffy, Aidan *o.f.m.* '56 (BO) [BB] Boston, MA St. Anthony Shrine.
Duffy, Andrew F. *c.s.sp.* '58 (MET) Edison, NJ John F. Kennedy Medical Center; [H] Metuchen, NJ Libermann House.
Duffy, David J. *o.s.a.* '57 (PH) [G] Malvern, PA Malvern Preparatory School for Boys.
Duffy, Donald '59 (NO) Edgard, LA St. John the Baptist Church.
Duffy, Donald J. '43 (CHI) Buffalo Grove, IL St. Mary Church; Retired.
Duffy, Edward *o.carm.* '82 (NY) Middletown, NY Our Lady of Mt. Carmel Church.
Duffy, Edward V. '52 (NEW) Harrington Park, NJ Our Lady of Victories Church.
Duffy, Edwin '42 (NY) Retired.
Duffy, Edwin J. '61 (HON) Retired.
Duffy, Emmanuel *o.f.m.* '30 (PAT) [M] Butler, NJ St. Anthony Friary.
Duffy, Eugene J. '50 (LA) Retired.
Duffy, Francis C. *o.p.* '60 (WDC) [11] Washington, DC St. Dominic Church & Priory Church.
Duffy, Francis J. '70 (PAT) Morristown, NJ St. Margaret's Church.
Duffy, Francis L. *s.j.* '58 (BAL) [I] Baltimore, MD Mercy Medical Center, Inc.
Duffy, Francis R. *c.s.sp.* '41 (PH) [K] Philadelphia, PA St. Joseph's House for Boys; [Z] Philadelphia, PA Holy Ghost Fathers.
Duffy, Msgr. Francis X. '49 (NY) Retired; [DD] New York, NY St. Paul's Guild, Inc.
Duffy, G. Ralph '65 (WDC) [2] Rockville, MD Shrine of St. Jude Church.
Duffy, Gabriel '58 (WDC) [12] Washington, DC Epiphany Church.
Duffy, George '63 (MIA) [6] Pompano Beach, FL St. Henry Church.
Duffy, George A. *s.j.* '55 (BO) [E] Boston, MA Boston College High School & Jesuit Community.
Duffy, Hugh '66 (PMB) Okeechobee, FL Sacred Heart Church.
Duffy, Hugh E. *o.s.f.s.* '60 (WIL) [I] Childs, MD Oblates of St. Francis De Sales.
Duffy, James '55 (JOL) Villa Park, IL St. John the Apostle Church.
Duffy, James D. *s.m.* '79 (STP) [25] St. Paul, MN St. Louis King of France Church.
Duffy, James H. '56 (MIL) Special Assignment.
Duffy, John *c.s.p.* '75 (AUS) [11] Austin, TX St. Austin's Church.
Duffy, Msgr. John F. '45 (ROC) Retired.
Duffy, John J. '52 (PH) [2] Bensalem, PA St. Elizabeth Ann Seton Church; Retired.
Duffy, Msgr. John R. '45 (SY) [S] Syracuse, NY St. Pius X Home, Inc.
Duffy, Joseph P. *s.j.* '57 (BO) [W] Chestnut Hill, MA The Jesuit Community at Boston College.
Duffy, Jude *o.f.m.cap.* '58 (SP) [6] Tampa, FL Most Holy Redeemer Church.
Duffy, Michael '76 (RIC) Hopewell, VA St. James Church.
Duffy, Michael A. *o.f.m.* '71 (PH) [V] Philadelphia, PA St. Francis Inn; [Z] Philadelphia, PA Order of Friars Minor, Holy Name Province.
Duffy, Patrick '46 (FAR) Retired.
Duffy, Patrick *o.c.s.o.* '81 (ATL) [I] Conyers, GA The Monastery of the Holy Spirit.
Duffy, Patrick P. '74 (CIN) [71] Cincinnati, OH Our Lady of Victory Church.
Duffy, Patrick S. *o.c.s.o.* '81 (SFE) Anton Chico, NM San Jose Church.
Duffy, Paul J. *s.j.* '67 (STL) [C] St. Louis, MO Saint Louis University; [P] St. Louis, MO Jesuit Community Corporation at St. Louis University - Jesuit Hall.
Duffy, Paul J. *m.m.* '79 (NY) [Z] Maryknoll, NY Maryknoll Fathers and Brothers.
Duffy, Raymond J. '68 (FRS) Riverdale, CA St. Ann Church.
Duffy, Regis A. *o.f.m.* '61 (BUF) [O] St. Bonaventure, NY St. Bonaventure Friary.
Duffy, Msgr. Robert E. '48 (NEW) [24] Jersey City, NJ St. Paul of the Cross Church.
Duffy, Robert M. '42 (CHI) Tinley Park, IL Saint Julie Billiart Church; Retired.
Duffy, Robert P. '40 (OM) Retired.
Duffy, Roger K. *c.s.sp.* '60 (GAL) Bellville, TX SS. Peter & Paul Church.
Duffy, Stephen '57 (NO) Unassigned; [C] New Orleans, LA Loyola University.
Duffy, Stephen F. '65 (NEW) [25] Jersey City, NJ St. Paul's Church.
Duffy, Stephen V. *s.j.* '43 (NY) [F] New York, NY Regis High School; [Z] New York, NY St. Ignatius Loyola Residence.
Duffy, Thomas J. '66 (PH) Linfield, PA St. Clare Church.
Duffy, Msgr. Thomas M. '53 (WDC) [10] Washington, DC Blessed Sacrament, Shrine of the Most Church.
Duffy, Msgr. Thomas R. '58 (CHR) Florence, SC St. Anthony's All Souls Memorial Church.
Duffy, Vincent *s.d.b.* '48 (PAT) [3] Paterson, NJ St. Anthony's Church.
Duffy, William J. *s.j.* '31 (BO) [W] Weston, MA Campion Health Center, Inc.
Dufner, Andrew J. *s.j.* '67 (P) [N] Pacific City, OR Nestucca Sanctuary.
Dufner, Daniel G. '96 (YAK) Kennewick, WA St. Joseph's Church.
Dufner, Thomas W. '83 (STP) St. Louis Park, MN Holy Family Church.
Dufour, Clement E. '58 (FR) [8] New Bedford, MA Sacred Heart Church.
Dufour, David '94 (NO) [7] Metairie, LA St. Clement of Rome Church.
Dufour, George J. '70 (BO) [1] Salem, MA St. Anne Church.
Dufour, Louis C. '58 (BO) Absent on Sick Leave.
DuFour, Rene *o.m.i.* '54 (BEL) [G] Belleville, IL Missionary Oblates of Mary Immaculate - St. Henry's Oblate Residence.
Dufresne, Oliver J. '45 (STP) Retired.
Dufresne, Vincent J. '83 (BR) Labadieville, LA St. Philomena Church.
Dugal, James H. *c.pp.s.* '56 (COL) [23] Columbus, OH St. James the Less Church.
Dugal, William '76 (JOL) [C] Addison, IL Driscoll Catholic High School.
Dugan, Msgr. Edward T. '45 (NY) Marlboro, NY St. Mary Church; Retired.
Dugan, J. Thomas '70 (E) Fairview, PA Holy Cross Church.
Dugan, James L. *s.j.* '73 (BUF) [O] Buffalo, NY Canisius Jesuit Community.
Dugan, James M. '89 (ALT) [22] Johnstown, PA St. Benedict's Church.
Dugan, Paul J. *s.j.* '56 (BUF) [O] Buffalo, NY Canisius Jesuit Community.
Dugan, T. Michael '88 (DAL) [17] Dallas, TX St. Elizabeth Church.
Dugan, Thomas P. *c.s.b.* '60 (GAL) [Q] Sugar Land, TX Basilian Mission Center.
Dugan, William M. '49 (SPK) Retired.
Dugandzic, Nicholas *o.p.* '65 (CHI) [N] Chicago, IL Croatian Dominican Fathers.
Dugandzic, Peter '95 (RVC) Seaford, NY St. William, the Abbot Church.
Dugas, Jerome A. '62 (BR) Plaquemine, LA St. Clement of Rome Church.
Dugas, Scott '77 (HT) Schriever, LA St. Bridget Church.
Dugas, Willard (LAF) On Special Assignment.
Duggan, Brendan *c.s.s.p.* (TR) Freehold, NJ St. Robert Bellarmine Church.
Duggan, Charles T. '44 (BO) [4] Medford, MA St. Raphael Church; Retired.
Duggan, Dennis D. '80 (DET) [53] Detroit, MI Our Lady Gate of Heaven Church; [73] Detroit, MI St. Suzanne Church.
Duggan, Eugene F. '46 (SFR) Sausalito, CA St. Mary Star of the Sea Church; Retired.
Duggan, J. Edward '50 (CHI) [23] Chicago, IL St. Bartholomew Church; Retired.
Duggan, Jeremiah C. '55 (CHI) [25] Chicago, IL St. Bede the Venerable Church.
Duggan, John H. *s.j.* '57 (SCR) [C] Scranton, PA University of Scranton.
Duggan, Msgr. John J. '33 (BAL) [80] Baltimore, MD SS. Philip and James Church.
Duggan, Msgr. John M. '43 (BUF) Retired.

Duggan, John P. '34 (BUF) [7] Niagara Falls, NY St. Mary of the Cataract Church.
Duggan, Joseph P. '64 (VEN) Retired.
Duggan, Kevin P. '87 (MET) South River, NJ Corpus Christi Church.
Duggan, Michael A. *m.m.* '59 (NY) [Z] Maryknoll, NY Maryknoll Fathers and Brothers.
Duggan, Nicholas '62 (SAC) [17] Sacramento, CA St. Paul Church.
Duggan, Oliver F. '71 (SEA) Bothell, WA St. Elizabeth Ann Seton Church.
Duggan, Paul '71 (PAT) New Vernon, NJ Christ the King Church.
Duggan, Paul E. '48 (SFR) Retired.
Duggan, Peter J. '55 (SEA) Kent, WA Holy Spirit Parish Church.
Duggan, Robert D. '69 (WDC) Gaithersburg, MD St. Rose of Lima Church.
Duggan, Robert J. *c.s.b.* '64 (DET) [7] Detroit, MI Ste. Anne Church.
Duggan, Sean B. *o.s.b.* '88 (NO) [A] St. Benedict, LA St. Joseph's Seminary College; [P] St. Benedict, LA St. Joseph Abbey.
Duggan, Thomas '47 (JC) Brookfield, MO Immaculate Conception Church.
Duggan, Thomas *c.ss.r.* '53 (STL) [P] Liguori, MO Liguori Mission House/Redemptorists.
Duggan, William E. '53 (SFR) [8] San Francisco, CA St. Brendan Church; San Francisco, CA St. Thomas More Society; Special Assignment.
Duggins, Dominic *glmy.* '74 (CIN) [M] Fairfield, OH Headquarters of Glenmary Home Missioners.
Dugue, Nerva W. '93 (NEW) [2] East Orange, NJ Holy Spirit-Our Lady Help of Christians Church.
Duhaime, James H. '61 (PRO) [6] Woonsocket, RI Holy Family Church.
Duhaime, John N. '71 (WH) Hinton, WV St. Patrick Church.
Duhart, Clarence *c.ss.r.* '37 (DEN) [M] Denver, CO The Redemptorists/Denver Province.
Duhart, Maurice J. *m.e.p.* '48 (SFR) [N] San Francisco, CA Paris Foreign Mission Society Residence.
Duhe, Thomas P. '78 (BR) Greenwell Springs, LA St. Alphonsus Liguori Church.
Duignan, Andrew '58 (CAM) North Cape May, NJ St. John of God Church.
Duignan, Msgr. Kevin F. '52 (MOB) [1] Montgomery, AL St. Peter Church.
Dukart, George A. '59 (BIS) [3] Dickinson, ND St. Patrick Church.
Dukart, Norman J. '67 (BIS) Williston, ND St. Joseph Church.
Duke, Msgr. Charles J. '47 (NO) Retired.
Duke, Jerome J. '68 (CLV) [2] Lakewood, OH SS. Cyril and Methodius Church.
Duke, Joseph A. *s.j.* '46 (PH) [Z] Philadelphia, PA Jesuit Community at St. Joseph's University; [AA] Philadelphia, PA Monastery of the Visitation Nuns.
Dukehart, Claude H. *s.s.* '43 (BAL) [K] Baltimore, MD St. Charles Villa; [M] Baltimore, MD St. Charles Villa.
Duker, Msgr. Russell A. *s.e.o.d.* '70 (PBR) [1] Pittsburgh, PA Holy Spirit Church.
DuLac, Msgr. Henri J. '45 (STP) Retired.
Dulaney, William R. '73 (BRK) [192] Queens, NY St. Margaret's Church; [B] Elmhurst, NY Cathedral Preparatory Seminary of the Immaculate Conception.
Dulanto, Angel *o.s.a.* '51 (NY) [49] New York, NY Holy Rosary Church.
Dulberg, Albert V. '36 (B) Retired.
Dulek, Lawrence V. (MIL) [A] Milwaukee, WI Saint Francis Seminary.
Dulek, Lawrence V. '73 (MIL) [7] Milwaukee, WI St. Anthony's Church.
Dullea, Charles W. *s.j.* '47 (SFR) [C] San Francisco, CA University of San Francisco; [N] San Francisco, CA Jesuit Community at University of San Francisco.
Dullea, John F. *s.j.* '59 (SJ) [D] San Jose, CA Bellarmine College Preparatory.
Dulles, Avery *s.j.* '56 (NY) [A] Yonkers, NY St. Joseph's Seminary; [Z] New York, NY Jesuit Community at Fordham University.
Dulock, Vincent *c.s.b.* '69 (GAL) Angleton, TX St. Basil Church.
Dulzer, Kenan '48 (CHI) [N] Chicago, IL St. Peter's Friary.
Duma, Gregory '64 (ROM) Canton, OH St. Theodore Church; Canton, OH St. George Cathedral.
Dumais, George J. *s.j.* '71 (HEL) Special Assignments.
Dumais, George J. *s.j.* '71 (P) [L] Portland, OR Jesuit Provincial Office (Oregon Prov.).
Dumais, Steven *s.d.b.* '78 (NO) [D] Marrero, LA Archbishop Shaw High School; [G] Marrero, LA Archbishop Shaw Junior High School.
Duman, Charles J. '52 (SFS) Retired.
Dumas, Msgr. Alfred J. '31 (MAN) Retired.
Dumas, Msgr. Edmund H. '36 (OG) Tupper Lake, NY St. Alphonsus Church; Retired.
Dumas, Emile E. *m.m.* '67 (NY) [Z] Maryknoll, NY Maryknoll Fathers and Brothers.
Dumas, Salvador '74 (CHK) San Jose Village, MP San Jose Church.
Dumas, Terrence J. '88 (LAN) [2] Ann Arbor, MI St. Patrick Church.
Duminiak, John J. '60 (ALN) Beaver Meadows, PA St. Mary Church.
Duminuco, Vincent J. *s.j.* '64 (NY) [Z] New York, NY "America;" Residence and publication office of the America Press; [Z] New York, NY Jesuit Provincial's Office.
Dumm, Demetrius R. *o.s.b.* '47 (GBG) [H] Latrobe, PA Saint Vincent Archabbey.
Dumm, Wilfred M. *o.s.b.* '45 (SAV) [E] Savannah, GA Benedictine Military School; [F] Savannah, GA The Benedictine Priory.
Dummer, Anthony *o.m.i.* (LA) San Fernando, CA St. Ferdinand Church.
Dummer, Leo *o.m.i.* '59 (OAK) [N] Oakland, CA Oblate Provincial House & Procure.
Dumminger, Urban *c.pp.s.* '51 (CIN) [B] Carthagena, OH St. Charles.
Dumont, C. Peter '71 (MAN) Suncook, NH St. John the Baptist Church.
Dumont, Gerald '80 (BRK) [27] Brooklyn, NY St. Catherine of Genoa Church.
DuMouchel, Raymond E. '56 (CHR) Summerton, SC St. Mary's Church; Summerton, SC St. Mary's Church.
Dumoulin, Marcel L. '61 (PRT) Fairfield, ME Immaculate Heart of Mary Church.
Dumphrey, Joseph C. *o.s.f.s.* '64 (BUF) [2] Lockport, NY St. John the Baptist Church; [5] Lockport, NY St. Patrick Church.
Dumphy, Charles J. '55 (WOR) [3] Worcester, MA Blessed Sacrament Church.
Dumpson, Roland '83 (NY) Absent on Leave.
Dunbar, Francis '55 (ALB) Johnstown, NY St. Anthony Church.
Duncan, Andrew '93 (CHY) Gillette, WY St. Matthew's Church.
Duncan, Msgr. Arthur L. '47 (CHL) Retired.
Duncan, Msgr. Edward J. '41 (PEO) [2] Champaign, IL St. John's Catholic Chapel; [O] Champaign, IL St. John's Catholic Student Chapel and Newman Foundation, University of Illinois.
Duncan, Msgr. John C. '60 (LFT) Carmel, IN Our Lady of Mount Carmel Church; [I] Mt. Carmel, IN Our Lady of Mount Carmel Parochial School Trust.
Duncan, Joseph '89 (PH) Manoa, PA Sacred Heart Church.
Duncan, William H. '90 (GR) Holland, MI Our Lady of the Lake Church.
Duncanson, Msgr. Richard F. '71 (SD) [4] Chula Vista, CA St. Rose of Lima Church.
Dunckel, Michael G. '92 (SAG) Helena, MI St. Anthony Church; Parisville, MI St. Mary Church.
Duncklee, Lawrence T. '80 (RVC) Centereach, NY Assumption of the Blessed Virgin Mary Church.
Dundon, Raymond J. '36 (BRK) [144] Brooklyn, NY St. Vincent Ferrer Church; Retired.
Dundon, Robert W. *s.j.* '69 (MIL) [P] Milwaukee, WI Jesuit Provincial Office, Wisconsin Province.
Dunegan, Bertrand H. *o.s.b.* '57 (GBG) [H] Latrobe, PA Saint Vincent Archabbey.
Dunfee, James M. '84 (STU) Burkhart, OH St. Joseph's Church; Miltonsburg, OH St. John the Baptist Church; Woodsfield, OH St. Sylvester Church; Sardis, OH St. John Bosco Mission Church.
Dunfey, Ronald K. '52 (JUN) Retired.
Dungan, Cormac *o.f.m.* '41 (BO) [Z] Boston, MA Saint Anthony Residence.
Dunghe, Adelmo P. *s.j.* '95 (STL) [P] St. Louis, MO Jesuit Community Corporation at St. Louis University - Jesuit Hall.
Dunham, Larry *o.f.m.* '74 (GAL) [4] Galveston, TX St. Patrick Church.
Dunkel, Henry N. '45 (DUB) Retired.
Dunklee, Lawrence G. '78 (LC) De Soto, WI Sacred Heart Church; Genoa, WI St. Charles Borromeo Church.
Dunkley, George '77 (WOR) Absent on Leave.
Dunkley, George A. '70 (SD) Vista, CA St. Francis Church.
Dunlap, William M. '74 (TR) Brick Town, NJ Visitation Church.
Dunleavy, Francis J. '40 (MIA) [1] Miami Beach, FL St. Francis de Sales Church; Retired.
Dunleavy, Msgr. Joseph J. '41 (MAR) Retired.
Dunleavy, Steven '84 (SD) Leave of Absence.
Dunleavy, Thomas J. '75 (PH) [23] Philadelphia, PA St. Bernard Church.
Dunleavy, Thomas P. '34 (MAR) Retired.
Dunmyer, Raymond A. '76 (BIR) Tuscaloosa, AL St. Francis of Assisi University Parish Church; [H] Tuscaloosa, AL Diocesan Campus Ministry Office; [H] Tuscaloosa, AL University of Alabama in Tuscaloosa.
Dunn, Charles J. *s.j.* '55 (WOR) [N] Worcester, MA Jesuits of Holy Cross College, Inc.
Dunn, Didacus *o.f.m.cap.* '56 (STL) [P] St. Louis, MO St. Patrick Friary.
Dunn, Donald F. '61 (COS) [7] Colorado Springs, CO Our Lady of Guadalupe Church.
Dunn, Edmond J. '72 (DAV) [A] Davenport, IA St. Ambrose University Seminary; [B] Davenport, IA St. Ambrose University.
Dunn, Msgr. Edward C. '43 (TOL) Tiffin, OH St. Joseph Church; Retired.
Dunn, Edward T. *s.j.* '56 (BUF) [O] Buffalo, NY Canisius Jesuit Community.
Dunn, Gerald R. '57 (MAN) Dover, NH St. Mary Church.
Dunn, Harold F. *m.ss.a.* '78 (WH) Rainelle, WV Sacred Heart Church.
Dunn, Jerome *o.f.m.cap.* '68 (PIT) [N] Pittsburgh, PA St. Augustine Friary.
Dunn, John '54 (DET) Retired.
Dunn, John J. *s.j.* '49 (P) [L] Portland, OR Jesuit Provincial Office (Oregon Prov.).
Dunn, John P. '49 (STP) Retired.
Dunn, Joseph T. *o.s.f.s.* '41 (WIL) [I] Childs, MD Oblates of St. Francis De Sales.
Dunn, Laurence J. '68 (CHI) Northfield, IL St. Philip the Apostle Church.
Dunn, Lawrence E. '61 (DET) Yale, MI Sacred Heart Church.
Dunn, Lawrence P. *m.i.c.* '87 (WDC) [B] Washington, DC Marian Fathers Scholasticate.
Dunn, Leo F. *c.ss.r.* '44 (ROC) [K] Canandaigua, NY Notre Dame Retreat House.
Dunn, Msgr. Louis W. '47 (PRO) Retired; [P] Providence, RI St. John Vianney Residence.
Dunn, Msgr. Meinrad M. '45 (BEL) Retired.
Dunn, Michael Lawrence '94 (BGP) [2] Trumbull, CT St. Catherine of Siena Church.
Dunn, Ralph F. *c.s.c.* '60 (FTW) [J] South Bend, IN Congregation of Holy Cross Indiana Province Provincial House.
Dunn, Raymond V. *s.j.* '57 (BO) [W] Boston, MA The Society of Jesus of New England-Provincial Offices.
Dunn, Richard '80 (SY) Military Chaplains.
Dunn, Richard C. '45 (TOL) Retired.
Dunn, Msgr. Richard F. '58 (BRK) [165] Queens, NY Corpus Christi Church.
Dunn, Richard R. '33 (BGP) Retired.
Dunn, Robert '85 (CC) Gregory, TX Immaculate Conception Church.
Dunn, Robert M. '92 (NY) [53] New York, NY Incarnation Church.
Dunn, Robert T. '44 (NY) Retired.
Dunn, Stephen *c.p.* '64 (MET) [H] South River, NJ Passionist Provincial Office.
Dunn, Stephen '69 (OWN) Absent on Leave.
Dunn, Stephen '71 (SD) [B] San Diego, CA University of San Diego.
Dunn, Thomas E. (WOR) [B] Worcester, MA Assumption College.
Dunn, William A. '65 (COL) [32] Columbus, OH St. Michael Church.
Dunn, William J. '51 (OAK) San Lorenzo, CA St. John the Baptist Church.
Dunne, Andrew J. *o.s.f.s.* '59 (LAN) Michigan Center, MI Our Lady of Fatima Church.
Dunne, Dennis T. (STP) [N] Minneapolis, MN Maryknoll Fathers and Brothers, Catholic Foreign Mission Society of America.
Dunne, Edward *c.ss.r.* '49 (BRK) [107] Brooklyn, NY Our Lady of Perpetual Help Basilica.
Dunne, George H. *s.j.* '36 (LA) [C] Los Angeles, CA Loyola Marymount University.
Dunne, Gerald M. *o.s.f.s.* '77 (PH) [D] Philadelphia, PA Father Judge High School for Boys; [Z] Philadelphia, PA Father Judge Faculty House.
Dunne, James J. *s.s.c.* '47 (STP) [J] Hastings, MN Regina Medical Center; [M] Hastings, MN Regina Convalescent and Nursing Care and Retirement Center.
Dunne, James M. '61 (BRK) [160] Queens, NY St. Camillus Church.
Dunne, John S. *c.s.c.* '54 (FTW) [B] Notre Dame, IN University of Notre Dame Du Lac; [J] Notre Dame, IN Holy Cross Community, Corby Hall, University of Notre Dame.
Dunne, Msgr. Joseph A. '42 (NY) Retired.
Dunne, P. Gerard *s.s.c.* '69 (OM) [K] St. Columbans, NE St. Columban's Foreign Mission Society.
Dunne, Patrick J. '70 (NY) [5] White Plains, NY Our Lady of Sorrows Church; White Plains, NY Burke Rehabilitation Center.
Dunne, Peter '50 (OM) [M] Omaha, NE Institute of the Apostolic Oblates.
Dunne, Msgr. Peter F. '44 (OM) Boys Town, NE Immaculate Conception B.V.M. Church; Retired.
Dunne, Peter J. '54 (PH) Retired.
Dunne, Raymond A. *s.j.* '50 (CHI) Prospect Heights, IL St. Alphonsus Liguori Church; [D] Wilmette, IL Loyola Academy.
Dunne, Richard J. '60 (BRK) Released from Diocesan Assignment.
Dunne, Thomas *s.d.b.* '72 (BO) [E] Boston, MA Don Bosco Preparatory School of Technology.
Dunnigan, Daniel D. *s.j.* '63 (CLV) [E] Cuyahoga Falls, OH Walsh Jesuit High School.
Dunning, James P. '63 (ORG) Mission Viejo, CA St.

Kilian Church.
Dunphy, James R. *m.s.* '57 (STL) [P] St. Louis, MO La Salette Missionaries.
Dunphy, Richard W. *s.j.* '73 (STL) [C] St. Louis, MO Saint Louis University; [P] St. Louis, MO Jesuit Community Corporation at St. Louis University - Jesuit Hall.
Dunphy, Robert J. '65 (CAM) Mount Ephraim, NJ Sacred Heart Church.
Dunphy, Thomas R. '58 (CLV) Valley City, OH St. Martin of Tours Church.
Dunson, Donald '94 (CLV) [A] Wickliffe, OH St. Mary Seminary.
Duoba, Jonas *m.i.c.* '46 (CHI) [N] Chicago, IL Congregation of Marian Fathers of the Immaculate Conception.
Duong, Cu Minh (MOB) [14] Mobile, AL St. Monica Church.
Duong, Paul '74 (SJ) Saratoga, CA Church of the Ascension.
Duong Binh Minh, Thomas '90 (OAK) Pittsburg, CA Our Lady Queen of the World Church.
DuPerry, Irenee *s.m.* '69 (BO) [4] Methuen, MA St. Theresa Church.
Duplessis, Donald M. *o.s.m.* '61 (ORG) Fullerton, CA St. Juliana Falconieri Church.
DuPont, Arthur J. '54 (HRT) Plantsville, CT Mary Our Queen Church; [V] Hartford, CT Catholic Cemeteries Association of the Archdiocese of Hartford, Inc.
Dupont, George '43 (BO) [W] Lowell, MA Missionary Oblates of Mary Immaculate.
Dupont, Guy B. *o.p* '68 (WDC) [11] Washington, DC St. Dominic Church & Priory Church.
Duprey, Msgr. Dennis J. '70 (OG) [2] Ogdensburg, NY Notre Dame Church; Ogdensburg, NY Riverview Correctional Facility.
Dupuis, George H. '50 (BUR) Arlington, VT St. Margaret Mary Church.
Dupuis, Laurent *o.m.i.* '36 (SAT) [K] San Antonio, TX Oblate Madonna Residence.
Dupuis, Philip '51 (LAN) Chelsea, MI St. Mary Church; [L] Lansing, MI Diocesan Service Committee.
Dupuis, Wayne *c.s.v.* '70 (LAV) [15] Las Vegas, NV St. Viator Church.
Duquesnay, Damian *o.s.b.* '46 (SP) [O] St. Leo, FL St. Leo Abbey.
Duquet, Heribert *m.e.p.* '39 (SFR) [10] San Francisco, CA St. Cecilia Church.
Duquette, Delphis O. '46 (BO) Retired.
Duquette, Don Bosco *o.f.m.cap.* '64 (PRT) [3] Portland, ME St. Joseph's Church; [M] Portland, ME Westbrook College.
Duquette, Lucien G. '56 (BUR) Retired.
Duquette, Roy H. '58 (SPR) [1] Northampton, MA Annunciation Church.
Dura, Eduardo '77 (SFR) [2] South San Francisco, CA Mater Dolorosa Church.
Duraczynski, Msgr. Jerome A. '42 (SFS) Retired.
Duraczynski, Msgr. Jerry '42 (PH) [2] Norristown, PA St. Francis of Assisi Church.
Duraczynski, Walter (PH) [5] Norristown, PA St. Paul Church.
Duraczynski, Walter '57 (SFS) Retired.
Duran, Alfonso M. *m.j.* '56 (PCE) On Duty Outside the Diocese.
Duran, Ernesto '42 (BRK) Retired.
Duran, Msgr. George '52 (LA) Maywood, CA St. Rose of Lima Church.
Duran, Jorge '75 (SAT) On Leave.
Duran, Said '95 (TYL) Nacogdoches, TX Sacred Heart Church.
Durand, Donald A. '58 (P) [12] Portland, OR St. Clare Church.
Durand, Henri *m.s.* '42 (SPR) [4] Holyoke, MA Immaculate Conception Church.
Durant, Thomas P. '76 (SY) Morrisville, NY St. Joan of Arc Church; Munnsville, NY St. Therese of the Infant Jesus Church.
Durante, Charles '93 (RNO) Carson City, NV St. Teresa's of Avila Church.
Durbin, Clarence R. *c.s.c.* '45 (FTW) [B] Notre Dame, IN University of Notre Dame Du Lac; [J] Notre Dame, IN Holy Cross Community, Corby Hall, University of Notre Dame.
Durbin, Clement B. '54 (COL) Retired.
Durbin, John G. *s.t.l.* '79 (R) Fayetteville, NC St. Patrick Church.
Durchholz, Jack J. '95 (EVN) Ferdinand, IN St. Ferdinand Church.
Durette, Constant H. *m.afr.* '43 (SP) [O] St. Petersburg, FL Missionaries of Africa.
Durette, Mathias D. *o.s.b.* '93 (MAN) [K] Manchester, NH St. Anselm Abbey.
Durham, J. Charles '90 (BUR) Rutland, VT Christ the King Church.
Durham, Neal *s.d.s.* '82 (MIL) [K] Milwaukee, WI St. Joseph's Hospital of Franciscan Sisters, Milwaukee, Inc.
Durham, Neil *s.d.s.* (MIL) [P] Milwaukee, WI Salvatorian Provincial Residence.
Durig, D. Kent '93 (WH) Fort Ashby, WV Annunciation of the Lord Church; Ridgeley, WV St. Anthony Church.
Duris, Lawrence M. '69 (CHI) [156] Chicago, IL Our Lady of Peace Church; [171] Chicago, IL St. Philip Neri Church.
Duritsa, George M. '53 (Y) [15] Youngstown, OH St. Elizabeth's Church; Retired.
Durkee, David R. '80 (CLV) Chardon, OH St. Mary Church.
Durkee, John E. *c.s.v.* '43 (CHI) [N] Olympia Fields, IL Viatorian Residence.
Durken, Daniel *o.s.b.* '56 (SCL) [I] Collegeville, MN St. John's Abbey, of the Order of St. Benedict.
Durkin, Msgr. Charles J. '55 (SFR) [48] San Francisco, CA Star of the Sea Church.
Durkin, Charles T. '79 (CHI) Other Assignments.
Durkin, Daniel '73 (FTW) Avilla, IN St. Mary of the Assumption Church.
Durkin, Edward J. *s.j.* '75 (NY) [5] New York, NY St. Aloysius Church.
Durkin, Eugene F. '49 (CHI) [1] Chicago, IL Cathedral of the Holy Name; Retired.
Durkin, Gregory *c.p.* '51 (HRT) [M] West Hartford, CT Holy Family Monastery/Retreat.
Durkin, James J. '68 (CAM) [1] Vineland, NJ Our Lady of Pompeii Church.
Durkin, John L. '67 (NY) Amenia, NY Immaculate Conception Church.
Durkin, John R. '42 (DAV) Retired.
Durkin, Joseph T. *s.j.* '33 (WDC) [M] Washington, DC The Jesuit Community at Georgetown University.
Durney, Charles W. '63 (PH) Absent on Sick Leave.
Durocher, Alain '92 (OAK) [N] Berkeley, CA St. Thomas Aquinas House.
Durr, Edmund J. '65 (SY) [4] Syracuse, NY Holy Trinity Church.
Durrie, Robert L. '54 (DEN) Retired.
Durso, Michael H. *s.j.* '66 (STL) [P] St. Louis, MO De Smet Jesuit High School Community.
Durst, Msgr. Gerald F. '44 (COL) [A] Columbus, OH Pontifical College Josephinum.
Durst, Msgr. Gerald F. '44 (SUP) On Duty Outside the Diocese.
DuRussel, Henry P. '45 (SAG) Midland, MI Assumption Blessed Virgin Mary Church.
Duscher, Romuald *o.s.b.cam.* '76 (MAN) [M] New Boston, NH Epiphany Monastery.
Duscher, Romuald *o.s.b.cam.* '76 (MRY) [G] Big Sur, CA New Camaldoli Hermitage.
Duschinsky, Vitus J. *o.f.m.* '42 (SFD) Teutopolis, IL St. Francis of Assisi Church; [K] Teutopolis, IL St. Francis Assisi Friary.
Duschl, Frederick J. '65 (TOL) Blakeslee, OH St. Joseph Church; Montpelier, OH Sacred Heart Church.
Dusecina, Regis '73 (PBR) Greensburg, PA St. Nicholas of Myra Church.
Dushack, Douglas L. '72 (MAD) [8] Madison, WI St. James Church.
Dusheck, Leo *s.v.d.* '61 (CHI) [B] Techny, IL Divine Word Residence.
Dusheck, Leo *s.v.d.* '61 (PIT) [N] Pittsburgh, PA Society of The Divine Word.
Dussan, Louis *c.m.f.* '49 (LUB) Petersburg, TX Sacred Heart Church.
Dusseau, Martin *o.s.b.* '55 (IND) [J] St. Meinrad, IN St. Meinrad Archabbey.
Dusseault, Emile *m.s.* '54 (R) Swansboro, NC St. Mildred Church.
Duster, James J. '59 (DUB) Mount Vernon, IA St. John's the Baptist Church.
Duston, Thomas Lierre '92 (MAN) Marlborough, NH Sacred Heart Church; Troy, NH Immaculate Conception Church.
Dusza, Donald W. '83 (ALT) [11] Johnstown, PA St. Michael's Church; [13] Johnstown, PA Our Mother of Sorrows Church.
Dutchoff, C. Robert '56 (MAD) Absent on Sick Leave.
Dutel, Gilbert J. '70 (LAF) Ville Platte, LA Our Lady Queen of All Saints Church.
Dutkiewicz, Eugene M. *s.j.* '61 (MIL) [P] Milwaukee, WI Arrupe House Jesuit Community; [P] Milwaukee, WI Jesuit Provincial Office, Wisconsin Province; [Y] Milwaukee, WI The Jesuit Partnership.
Dutkiewicz, Eugene M. *s.j.* '61 (NO) [P] New Orleans, LA Jesuit Provincial Office.
Dutkiewicz, Thomas A. '56 (PIT) [N] Pittsburgh, PA St. Francis Friary.
Dutra, Luiz C. '55 (LAF) On Special Assignment; [H] Lafayette, LA De La Salle Christian Brothers.
Dutram, Charles J. '58 (WOR) Retired.
Duvall, Justin *o.s.b.* '78 (IND) [A] St. Meinrad, IN St. Meinrad Seminary; [J] St. Meinrad, IN St. Meinrad Archabbey.
Duvelius, Dennis *f.s.s.p.* '96 (SCR) [M] Elmhurst, PA Priestly Fraternity of St. Peter (F.S.S.P.).
Duvelsdorf, Peter *s.d.b.* '58 (PMB) North Palm Beach, FL St. Paul of the Cross Church.
Duvelsdorf, Peter L. '58 (RVC) Priests Released from Diocesan Assignment.
Dux, James M. '48 (PH) Retired.
Dux, John H. '73 (STA) Military Chaplains.
Duykim Tran, Joseph M. '90 (NEW) Roselle Park, NJ The Assumption Church.
Duyshart, Edwin C. '84 (LA) Azusa, CA St. Frances of Rome Church.
Duzinski, Paul *o.f.m.conv.* '81 (BAL) [M] Ellicott City, MD Order of Friars Minor Conventual.
Duzinski, Paul *o.f.m.conv.* '81 (CLV) [N] Cleveland, OH Sts. Mary and Joseph Home for the Aged.
Dvorak, Donald T. *o.p.* '63 (NO) [25] New Orleans, LA St. Anthony Of Padua Church.
Dvorak, Franklin A. '70 (OM) [48] Douglas Co., NE St. Wenceslaus Church.
Dvorak, Gerald L. '79 (STP) West St. Paul, MN St. Michael Church.
Dvorscak, James '76 (JOL) Lombard, IL Christ the King Church.
Dwomoh, Charles '86 (VIC) [1] Victoria, TX Our Lady of Victory Cathedral.
Dworak, Joseph J. '65 (ALB) Special Assignment; [H] Amsterdam, NY St. Mary's Hospital.
Dworak, Walter W. '72 (PIT) O'Hara Township, PA St. Joseph Church.
Dwulit, Andrij Taras '90 (STN) Houston, TX Protection of the Mother of God Church.
Dwyer, Msgr. Adrian I. '36 (STL) [59] St. Louis, MO St. Roch Church; Retired.
Dwyer, Albert D. '58 (SAL) Beloit, KS St. John the Baptist Church.
Dwyer, Arthur J. *m.m.* '49 (HON) [13] Honolulu, HI Sacred Heart Church; [H] Honolulu, HI Maryknoll Fathers House; [H] Honolulu, HI Maryknoll Fathers House.
Dwyer, Daniel P. *o.f.m.* '88 (ALB) [B] Loudonville, NY Siena College.
Dwyer, David F. '54 (GF) Retired.
Dwyer, Dennis E. '66 (COS) Parker, CO Ave Maria Church.
Dwyer, Dermot '62 (SAC) Colfax, CA St. Dominic Church.
Dwyer, Donald M. (NY) [170] Bronx, NY Our Lady of the Assumption Church.
Dwyer, Eugene F. *s.j.* '59 (CHI) [C] Chicago, IL Jesuit Community at Loyola University of Chicago.
Dwyer, J. Floyd '48 (LC) Retired; [I] La Crosse, WI Holy Cross (Seminary) Diocesan Center.
Dwyer, John '92 (TR) [21] Trenton, NJ St. Raphael Church.
Dwyer, John A. '74 (WOR) [8] Fitchburg, MA Sacred Heart of Jesus Church.
Dwyer, John F. '56 (NY) Tappan, NY Our Lady of the Sacred Heart Church; Bronx, NY U.S.V.A. Medical Center.
Dwyer, Msgr. John R. '67 (BRK) [206] Queens, NY Our Lady of the Angelus Church.
Dwyer, John T. '60 (NY) Piermont, NY St. John Church.
Dwyer, Kevin F. *o.s.a.* '62 (BO) [C] North Andover, MA Merrimack College; [C] North Andover, MA Merrimack College.
Dwyer, Kevin F. *o.s.a.* '62 (PH) [C] Villanova, PA Villanova University.
Dwyer, Msgr. M. Shields '32 (SY) Retired.
Dwyer, Michael *m.s.c.* '46 (BEA) Cleveland, TX St. Mary Church.
Dwyer, Msgr. Michael F. '38 (NY) Retired.
Dwyer, Msgr. Morris L. (OG) [5] Plattsburgh, NY St. Peter Church; Retired.
Dwyer, Morris R. '55 (ALB) Morris, NY Holy Cross Church.
Dwyer, Timothy *s.m.* '68 (STL) [P] St. Louis, MO Provincialate of the Society of Mary, Province of St. Louis.
Dwyer, Vincent *o.c.s.o.* '61 (WOR) [N] Spencer, MA St. Joseph's Abbey.
Dwyer, William M. '38 (SY) Retired.
Dybas, Richard W. '59 (ALB) [5] Cohoes, NY St. Michael Church.
Dych, William V. *s.j.* '63 (NY) [Z] New York, NY Jesuit Community at Fordham University.
Dye, David M. '92 (ATL) Dunwoody, GA All Saints Catholic Church.
Dye, Gerald B. '57 (B) New Plymouth, ID St. Aloysius Church; Payette, ID Holy Family Church.
Dye, Robert M. '91 (TLS) [14] Tulsa, OK St. Pius X Church.
Dyer, Donald L. '57 (STL) [4] Florissant, MO St. Christopher Church.
Dyer, Edward J. '41 (WOR) Retired.
Dyer, Eugene J. '85 (CHI) [1] Des Plaines, IL St. Mary Church.
Dyer, Francis X. *o.p.* '69 (CHI) [N] Chicago, IL Dominicans (Provincial Office).
Dyer, George *o.p.* '61 (KNX) Lenoir City, TN St. Thomas the Apostle Church.
Dyer, George A. '36 (HRT) Retired.
Dyer, George J. '53 (CHI) Wadsworth, IL St. Patrick Church; Retired; [X] Mundelein, IL Civitas Dei Foundation.
Dyer, Joseph '74 (JKS) [5] Jackson, MS Holy Family Church.
Dyer, Ralph J. *s.m.* '47 (SAT) [K] San Antonio, TX St.

Joseph's Community.
Dyer, Raymond E. '46 (PRO) Retired; [M] Cumberland, RI Mount St. Rita Health Centre.
Dyer, Thomas P. '69 (Y) [6] Canton, OH St. Joan of Arc Church.
Dyer, Msgr. Timothy '74 (LA) [57] Los Angeles, CA St. Columbkille Church.
Dyer, Msgr. Timothy J. '74 (LA) [18] Los Angeles, CA Nativity Church.
Dyer, William *m.afr.* '70 (WDC) [M] Washington, DC Missionaries of Africa.
Dyjak, Luke *o.f.m.conv.* '48 (BAL) [M] Ellicott City, MD Order of Friars Minor Conventual.
Dykas, Benjamin (ALT) [4] Johnstown, PA St. Columba's Church.
Dylag, Michael R. (DET) [T] Detroit, MI Pope John Paul II Cultural Foundation, Inc.
Dylag, Michael R. '65 (GBG) On Duty Outside the Diocese.
Dymowski, Thomas *o.ss.t.* '85 (VIC) [F] Victoria, TX Trinity House.
Dymski, J. Daniel '60 (VEN) Marco Island, FL San Marco Church.
Dynak, Waldemar '80 (CHI) [3] Cicero, IL St. Mary of Czestochowa Church.
Dynch, William *s.j.* '63 (BO) [W] Chestnut Hill, MA The Jesuit Community at Boston College.
Dynes, Leo J. '54 (STP) Retired.
Dysinger, Luke *o.s.b.* '86 (LA) [R] Valyermo, CA St. Andrew's Abbey.
Dytkowski, Louis M. '60 (BGP) [4] Fairfield, CT Holy Cross Church.
Dzermejko, David F. '74 (PIT) [3] Charleroi, PA Mary Mother of the Church.
Dziadosz, Edward T. '55 (PH) Retired.
Dziadosz, Msgr. Henry J. '49 (NOR) Moodus, CT St. Bridget Church.
Dziak, Theodore *s.j.* '83 (BO) [W] Chestnut Hill, MA The Jesuit Community at Boston College.
Dziedzic, Gerald H. '74 (HRT) Terryville, CT Immaculate Conception Church.
Dziedziech, Wiktor '82 (SP) [7] St. Petersburg, FL St. Paul Church.
Dziedziejko, Edwin F. *o.f.m.cap.* '79 (MIL) [B] Mount Calvary, WI St. Lawrence Seminary; [P] Mount Calvary, WI St. Lawrence Friary.
Dzieglewicz, John T. *s.j.* '83 (NY) [Z] New York, NY Jesuit Community at Fordham University.
Dziekan, Wayne H. '94 (GAY) [1] Gaylord, MI St. Mary Cathedral.
Dzielak, Msgr. Thomas L. '63 (RCK) Rock Falls, IL St. Andrew Church.
Dzien, Joseph Duc '83 (NO) Chalmette, LA Our Lady of Prompt Succor Church.
Dzienkiewicz, Edwin (TR) [L] Lawrenceville, NJ Morris Hall-Saint Lawrence, Inc.
Dzienkiewicz, Edwin '64 (PT) Retired.
Dzierzek, Zygmunt *o.m.i.* '42 (BEL) [G] Belleville, IL Shrine of Our Lady of the Snows.
Dzieszko, Tadeucz (CHI) [58] Chicago, IL St. Ferdinand Church.
Dzikowski, Piotr *s.ch.* '87 (SEA) [10] Tacoma, WA SS. Peter & Paul Church.
Dziob, Msgr. Michael W. '42 (PRO) Retired; [P] Providence, RI St. John Vianney Residence.
Dziordz, Walter *m.i.c.* '84 (SPR) [I] Stockbridge, MA Congregation of Marians; [I] Stockbridge, MA Congregation of Marians.
Dziorek, Anthony *c.r.* '75 (CHI) [192] Chicago, IL St. Stanislaus, Bishop and Martyr Church.
Dzuban, Giles *o.c.d.* '44 (BO) [W] Brighton, MA Carmelite Monastery.
Dzurenda, Thomas J. '65 (MET) Watchung, NJ St. Mary Church.

E

Eades, B. G. '73 (DAL) Special Assignment.
Eagan, Henry J. *o.s.a.* '42 (PH) [Z] Villanova, PA St. Thomas Monastery.
Eagan, Joseph *s.j.* '53 (SFR) Larkspur, CA St. Patrick Church.
Eagan, Joseph F. *s.j.* '53 (MIL) [P] Milwaukee, WI Jesuit Provincial Office, Wisconsin Province.
Eagan, William J. *s.j.* '75 (BGP) [D] Fairfield, CT Fairfield College Preparatory School.
Eagen, Msgr. Brent I. '56 (SD) Special Assignment; [B] San Diego, CA University of San Diego.
Eagle, Raphael *t.o.r.* (FWT) [12] Fort Worth, TX St. Mary of the Assumption Church.
Eagleson, Donald W. '85 (SR) Eureka, CA Sacred Heart Church.
Eakin, Daniel '85 (LR) Absent on Leave.
Earl, John P. '94 (RCK) [1] Elgin, IL St. Joseph Church.
Earl, Marcellus R. *o.c.s.o.* '63 (ROC) [I] Piffard, NY Abbey of the Genesee.
Earl, Patrick F. *s.j.* '74 (BAL) [C] Baltimore, MD Loyola College; [C] Baltimore, MD Loyola College; [M] Baltimore, MD Jesuit Community of Loyola College, Inc.
Earley, Daniel J. *o.s.f.s.* '48 (TOL) [C] Toledo, OH St. Francis de Sales High School; [K] Toledo, OH Oblates of St. Francis de Sales.
Earley, Jerome *o.c.d.* '95 (NO) [B] New Orleans, LA St. John of the Cross, Discalced Carmelite House of Studies.
Earley, Kiernan *c.p.* '57 (HRT) [M] West Hartford, CT Holy Family Monastery/Retreat.
Earley, Philip B. '74 (BO) [1] Arlington, MA St. Agnes Church.
Earls, John Patrick *o.s.b.* '65 (SCL) [I] Collegeville, MN St. John's Abbey, of the Order of St. Benedict.
Early, Francis J. '85 (WDC) Bushwood, MD Sacred Heart Church.
Early, Joseph E. *m.m.* '39 (SJ) [M] Los Altos, CA Maryknoll.
Early, Msgr. Thomas C. '51 (ALX) Retired.
Early, William F. '68 (BRK) Absent on Sick Leave.
Earner, Thomas F. '62 (SP) New Port Richey, FL St. Thomas Aquinas Church; [F] New Port Richey, FL St. Thomas Aquinas Early Childhood Center.
Earps, James D. *s.j.* (SFR) [U] Los Angeles, CA Christian Live Communities (Sodalities).
East, Msgr. Raymond '81 (WDC) [41] Washington, DC St. Teresa of Avila Church.
Easterling, William T. '82 (LA) Valinda, CA St. Martha Church.
Eastman, Patrick W. '84 (TLS) [3] Tulsa, OK St. Bernard of Clairvaux Church.
Easton, Frederick C. '66 (IND) [23] Indianapolis, IN St. Gabriel the Archangel Church.
Easton, Msgr. William M. '70 (DET) Royal Oak, MI Shrine of the Little Flower Church.
Eaton, John *o.f.m.* '78 (LR) McGehee, AR St. Mary Church.
Eaton, Vincent M. *s.s.* '41 (BAL) [K] Baltimore, MD St. Charles Villa; [M] Baltimore, MD St. Charles Villa.
Ebach, Aloys *c.pp.s.* '74 (SUP) Fifield, WI St. Francis of Assisi Church; Park Falls, WI St. Anthony Church.
Ebacher, Jerome *o.c.s.o.* '49 (P) [L] Lafayette, OR The Cistercian (Trappist) Abbey of Our Lady of Guadalupe.
Ebarb, Walter E. '62 (SHP) On Leave.
Ebbesmier, John (PHX) [A] Phoenix, AZ Bourgade Catholic High School.
Ebbesmier, John '78 (PHX) [8] Phoenix, AZ St. Augustine Church.
Ebeicbe, Isacc '87 (CIN) [7] Dayton, OH St. Charles Borromeo Church.
Ebejer, George '47 (BRK) [125] Brooklyn, NY St. Rocco's Church; Retired.
Ebejer, Lino P. '91 (WH) Thomas, WV St. Thomas Aquinas Church.
Ebel, Stephen P. '70 (DAV) Long Grove, IA St. Ann's Church.
Ebenhoeh, John *o.s.f.s.* '64 (TOL) [C] Toledo, OH St. Francis de Sales High School.
Ebenhoeh, John O. '64 (TOL) [K] Toledo, OH Oblates of St. Francis de Sales.
Eberhardt, Norbert C. *s.j.* '52 (MIL) [P] Wauwatosa, WI Jesuit Community at St. Camillus.
Eberhardy, William '77 (GB) Absent on Leave.
Ebert, Mark S. '76 (STL) [4] Lemay, MO St. Bernadette Church.
Eberz, Ambrose G. *o.s.b.* '40 (GBG) [H] Latrobe, PA Saint Vincent Archabbey.
Ebey, Carl F. *c.s.c.* '72 (FTW) [J] South Bend, IN Congregation of Holy Cross Indiana Province Provincial House.
Eblen, James '64 (SEA) [17] Seattle, WA St. Patrick Church; Special Assignment.
Ebner, Frank '47 (SCL) Retired.
Ebrom, Robert '71 (CHI) [7] Chicago, IL All Saints-St. Anthony Church.
Ebuk, Lawrence A. *m.s.p.* '88 (GAL) McNair, TX Holy Family Church.
Eburn, Brian '66 (STA) Crescent City, FL St. John the Baptist Church.
Eccleston, John '55 (SCL) Special Assignment; [J] Little Falls, MN St. Francis Convent.
Echave, Jose Ignacio '54 (ELP) [37] El Paso, TX San Juan Bautista Church.
Echert, John '87 (STP) [A] St. Paul, MN The Saint Paul Seminary; [C] St. Paul, MN University of St. Thomas.
Echevarria, Wilfredo *o.ss.t.* '81 (ARE) Isabela, PR St. Anthony Church.
Echeverria, Miguel *o.a.r.* (LSC) Anthony, NM St. Anthony's Church.
Echeverria, Ramon J. '96 (PMB) Vero Beach, FL St. Helen Church.
Echle, Msgr. Edward V. '35 (BAL) Retired.
Echle, Msgr. Edward V. '43 (BAL) Frederick, MD St. John the Evangelist Church.
Echle, Msgr. Harry A. '42 (WDC) [35] Washington, DC Our Lady of Victory Church; Retired.
Eck, Ivan C. '51 (WCH) Mount Vernon, KS St. Rose Church; Ost, KS St. Joseph Church; Waterloo, KS St. Louis Church.
Eck, John E. *c.s.v.* '63 (SFD) [9] Springfield, IL St. Patrick Church; [11] Springfield, IL Sacred Heart of Jesus Church.
Eck, Reinhard C. '50 (WCH) Andale, KS St. Joseph Church.
Eckart, Frank E. '69 (TOL) [14] Toledo, OH Sacred Heart of Jesus Church.
Eckart, Placidus *o.s.b.* '49 (LR) Fort Smith, AR St. Boniface Church.
Eckart, Stephen '54 (LR) [A] Subiaco, AR Subiaco Monastery.
Eckelkamp, David *o.f.m.* '53 (STL) [P] St. Louis, MO Franciscan Friary of St. Anthony of Padua.
Eckelkamp, Ianatius *o.f.m.* (SFD) [K] Sherman, IL Our Lady of Angels Friary.
Eckenrod, Edward L. '78 (ALT) [11] Altoona, PA Our Lady of Lourdes Church; [D] Altoona, PA Mercy Regional Health System.
Ecker, George *c.s.s.* '36 (BO) [Z] Waltham, MA Stigmatine Fathers and Brothers.
Ecker, George *c.s.s.* '36 (SPR) [9] Springfield, MA Our Lady of Mt. Carmel Church.
Ecker, Msgr. John A. '58 (YAK) [1] Yakima, WA St. Paul Cathedral.
Ecker, Msgr. Robert J. '51 (BRK) Released from Diocesan Assignment.
Eckermann, Msgr. Charles H. '56 (SY) Manlius, NY St. Ann Church.
Eckert, Carl '54 (LFT) Retired.
Eckert, Sidney J. '66 (DET) [30] Detroit, MI Guardian Angels Church.
Eckert, William F. '64 (CAM) Retired.
Eckhard, John L. '88 (STL) Riverview Gardens, MO St. Catherine of Alexandria Church.
Eckhoff, Evan *o.f.m.* '57 (KNX) [F] Mountain City, TN Franciscan Friars.
Eckinger, Joseph Ambrose *o.p.* '81 (CIN) [30] Cincinnati, OH St. Gertrude Church; [C] Cincinnati, OH Dominican Novitiate; [M] Cincinnati, OH St. Gertrude Priory.
Eckley, Michael P. '91 (OM) Fremont, NE St. Patrick Church.
Eckman, Mark A. '85 (PIT) [54] Pittsburgh, PA St. John Vianney Church; [C] Mt. Lebanon, PA Seton-LaSalle Catholic High School.
Eckrich, James P. '53 (WIL) Centreville, MD Mother of Sorrows Church.
Eckroth, Leonard A. '58 (BIS) Hague, ND St. Mary Church; Strasburg, ND Sts. Peter and Paul Church.
Eckroth, Richard *o.s.b.* '52 (SCL) [I] Collegeville, MN St. John's Abbey, of the Order of St. Benedict.
Eckstein, Francis '58 (IND) New Marion, IN St. Magdalen Church; Osgood, IN St. John Church.
Eckstein, Frank '58 (IND) Millhousen, IN Immaculate Conception Church.
Eco, Roy '80 (OAK) Union City, CA Our Lady of the Rosary Church.
Eco, Roy V. '80 (OAK) [K] Hayward, CA St. Rose Hospital; [O] Hayward, CA Sisters of St. Joseph of Wichita, KS.
Edamattam, Thomas '66 (RVC) Huntington, NY St. Patrick's Church.
Edapaddy, Thomas *c.m.i.* '64 (LAF) Coteau Holmes, LA St. Elizabeth Church.
Edathiparampil, Simon (CHI) [94] Chicago, IL Immaculate Heart of Mary Church; Chicago, IL Knanite Syro-Malabar Catholic Mission of the Archdiocese of Chicago Church.
Eddy, William A. '75 (CHI) Chicago Heights, IL St. Kieran Church.
Edelen, Luke A. *o.s.b.* '80 (NEW) [N] Newark, NJ Newark Abbey.
Edelen, Richard D. '75 (LEX) Beattyville, KY Queen of All Saints Church.
Edelin, Richard A. '79 (GAL) Military Chaplains.
Eden, Timothy *s.m.* '77 (SJ) [M] San Jose, CA Marianist Community.
Edens, William *c.s.p.* '81 (LA) [86] Los Angeles, CA St. Paul the Apostle Church.
Eder, Donald '54 (LAN) Retired.
Eder, Donald J. '60 (LFT) Fishers, IN St. Louis de Montfort Church.
Ederer, John F. '77 (SAG) Ithaca, MI St. Paul the Apostle Church.
Edgerly, Leo, Jr. '84 (OAK) Antioch, CA St. Ignatius Church.
Ediza, Manuel '79 (SD) [29] San Diego, CA St. John the Evangelist Church; San Diego, CA Children's Hospital; San Diego, CA Sharp Memorial Hospital.
Edmunds, John *s.t.* '76 (NEW) [10] Jersey City, NJ Christ, the King Church.
Edogwo, Linus V. '86 (NEW) [23] Newark, NJ St. Mary's Church.
Edokwe, Hyacinth *c.s.sp.* '91 (MIA) [2] Pompano Beach, FL San Isidro Church.
Edomobi, Eustace '75 (NEW) [5] Newark, NJ St. Antoninus Church; Newark, NJ University of Medicine & Dentistry.
Edrich, Paul J. '54 (CIN) [47] Cincinnati, OH St. John Vianney Church.
Eduvala, Andre *o.f.m.cap.* (AGN) [F] Agana Heights, GU St. Fidelis Friary.
Edwards, Bill '85 (OG) Burke, NY St. George Church; Altona, NY Altona Correctional Facility.

Edwards, Brice *c.p.* '70 (HRT) [M] West Hartford, CT Holy Family Monastery/Retreat.
Edwards, Byron H. '87 (SPC) Retired.
Edwards, Charles A. '86 (SFD) Carrollton, IL St. John the Evangelist Church; White Hall, IL All Saints Church.
Edwards, Cyril D. '84 (SCR) [1] Freeland, PA St. Ann's Church; [Q] Scranton, PA Catholic Youth Center.
Edwards, Edward M. *o.s.m.* '83 (CHI) [N] Chicago, IL Servite Friars - Eastern Province.
Edwards, Edward M. *o.s.m.* '83 (MET) [I] Watchung, NJ Mount St. Mary.
Edwards, J. Daniel '94 (LAF) Richard, LA St. Edward Church.
Edwards, James F. '61 (ORL) Retired.
Edwards, James T. '76 (STL) Normandy, MO St. Ann Church.
Edwards, John *s.j.* '54 (PMB) [3] West Palm Beach, FL St. Ann Church.
Edwards, John F. '55 (HRT) Wethersfield, CT Incarnation Church.
Edwards, John G. '50 (BO) Retired.
Edwards, John J. *s.j.* (PMB) [J] West Palm Beach, FL Emmaus Residence.
Edwards, Lawrence A. '39 (DET) Retired.
Edwards, Michael '79 (PMB) [5] West Palm Beach, FL St. Juliana Church; [J] West Palm Beach, FL Our Lady Queen of Peace Catholic Cemetery, Inc.
Edwards, Philip *o.s.b.* '67 (LA) [R] Valyermo, CA St. Andrew's Abbey; [W] Valyermo, CA St. Andrew's Abbey Retreat House (All Groups).
Edwards, Robert '81 (Y) Lisbon, OH St. George Church.
Edwards, Robert D. '83 (FWT) Cisco, TX Holy Rosary Church; Ranger, TX St. Rita Church.
Edwards, Robert Dale '83 (FWT) Eastland, TX St. Francis Xavier Church; Strawn, TX St. John Church.
Edwards, Roy D. '46 (LAF) Retired.
Edwards, Thomas *t.o.r.* '40 (ALT) [F] Loretto, PA Mount Assisi Monastery.
Edwards, Thomas '90 (OAK) [2] Oakland, CA St. Andrew-St. Joseph Church.
Edwards, Thomas L. '58 (ALN) Retired.
Edwin, Rex '95 (CI) Seinwar, FM Most Pure Heart of Mary Church.
Edyk, Msgr. Eugene (DET) [3] Clinton Twp., MI St. Paul of Tarsus Church.
Edyvean, Msgr. Walter J. (BO) On Duty Outside the Archdiocese.
Eeles, Justin *o.f.m.* '39 (PAT) [M] Ringwood, NJ Holy Name Friary.
Eelman, William C. '53 (TR) Retired.
Eftink, Msgr. Edward M. '66 (SPC) Jackson, MO Immaculate Conception Church.
Eftink, Glenn A. '93 (SPC) [1] Cape Girardeau, MO Cathedral of St. Mary.
Egan, Arthur B. '57 (CLV) Avon, OH St. Mary of the Immaculate Conception Church.
Egan, Bartholemew *c.s.sp.* '69 (BRK) [91] Brooklyn, NY Our Lady of Angels Church.
Egan, Brennan *o.f.m.* '65 (NY) [Z] New York, NY Franciscan Province of the Immaculate Conception; [Z] New York, NY Franciscan Province of the Immaculate Conception.
Egan, Brian J. '50 (BIR) [4] Birmingham, AL St. Bernard's Church; [I] Birmingham, AL Catholic Housing of Birmingham, Inc.
Egan, Brian J. '87 (WCH) Hutchinson, KS Holy Cross Church.
Egan, Charles *c.s.s.* '46 (BO) [Z] Waltham, MA Stigmatine Fathers and Brothers.
Egan, Daniel *s.a.* '45 (NY) [K] Barryville, NY New Hope Manor; [Z] Garrison, NY Franciscan Friars of the Atonement; [DD] Barryville, NY New Hope Manor.
Egan, Msgr. Edward F. '41 (PRO) Retired; [P] Providence, RI St. John Vianney Residence.
Egan, Eugene E. '54 (WIN) Fulda, MN St. Gabriel's Church.
Egan, Francis M. '45 (PH) Absent on Leave.
Egan, George A. *m.m.* '55 (NY) [Z] Maryknoll, NY Maryknoll Fathers and Brothers.
Egan, Gerard P. '65 (CHI) Other Assignments.
Egan, Harvey D. *s.j.* '69 (BO) [W] Chestnut Hill, MA The Jesuit Community at Boston College.
Egan, Harvey F. '41 (STP) Retired.
Egan, James A. *s.j.* '65 (OM) [K] Omaha, NE Jesuit Community At Creighton University.
Egan, Msgr. John J. '43 (CHI) [1] Chicago, IL Cathedral of the Holy Name; Retired; [C] Chicago, IL De Paul University.
Egan, John J. '59 (NEW) Retired.
Egan, John Martin *o.p.* '56 (WDC) [B] Washington, DC Dominican House of Studies.
Egan, John P. *s.j.* '63 (MIL) [P] Milwaukee, WI Jesuit Provincial Office, Wisconsin Province.
Egan, Joseph *s.a.* '50 (NY) [Z] Garrison, NY Franciscan Friars of the Atonement.
Egan, Joseph Anthony *o.f.m.cap.* '65 (NY) [Z] White Plains, NY St. Conrad Friary.
Egan, Joseph M. '42 (ROC) Retired.
Egan, Philip '82 (KC) [2] Kansas City, MO St. Monica Parish Church; [23] Kansas City, MO New Catholic Community Church.
Egan, Robert J. *s.j.* '73 (SPK) [C] Spokane, WA Gonzaga University.
Egan, Robert M. '54 (ROC) Groton, NY St. Anthony Church.
Egan, Robert M. *c.s.v.* '78 (CHI) [N] Arlington Heights, IL Clerics of St. Viator-Provincial Residence.
Egan, Msgr. Robert P. '43 (NEW) Retired.
Egan, Thomas *c.ss.r.* '33 (ALB) [L] Saratoga Springs, NY St. John Neumann Residence.
Egan, Thomas F. '75 (WOR) [2] Leominster, MA Holy Family of Nazareth Church.
Egan, Msgr. Thomas J. '36 (SD) Retired.
Egbers, James B. '65 (COV) Cold Spring, KY St. Joseph Church.
Egbule, Joseph (SY) Camillus, NY St. Joseph Church.
Egbulem, Christian Nwaka *o.p.* '76 (WDC) [13] Washington, DC St. Francis de Sales Church.
Egert, Clifford A. '38 (DAV) Retired; [M] Davenport, IA St. Vincent Center.
Eggerling, Milton '54 (BO) [70] Boston, MA St. Stephen Church; [W] Boston, MA The Society of St. James the Apostle, Inc.
Eggerling, Milton '54 (OAK) Retired.
Eggert, Charles M. '38 (STP) Retired.
Eggert, Francis T. '58 (SFE) [7] Albuquerque, NM Our Lady of Fatima Church.
Egging, Martin L. '93 (GI) [2] Grand Island, NE Blessed Sacrament Church; [A] Grand Island, NE Central Catholic Junior Senior High School.
Eggleston, Earl Edward '96 (SD) [5] San Diego, CA Good Shepherd Church.
Eggleston, William J. *m.m.* '47 (NY) [Z] Maryknoll, NY Maryknoll Fathers and Brothers.
Eggleton, Christopher T. *o.p.* '88 (MIA) [18] Miami, FL St. Dominic Church.
Egierd, Henry A. '80 (MET) Retired.
Egitto, Philip J. '88 (ORL) Daytona Beach, FL Our Lady of Lourdes Church.
Egloff, Adolph '40 (EVN) Retired.
Eglsaer, Harry *s.j.* '51 (OM) [C] Omaha, NE Creighton Preparatory School; [G] Omaha, NE Alegent Health - Bergan Mercy Health System dba Algent Health - Bergan Mercy Medical Center.
Ego, Anthony M. '85 (PEO) Chillicothe, IL St. Edward's Church.
Egurrola, Vicente (SJN) Retired.
Ehler, Gerard *o.p.* '63 (OAK) [N] Oakland, CA Dominican Order (Western Province), St. Albert's Priory.
Ehlinger, Andrew *o.f.m.conv.* '33 (ALB) [A] Rensselaer, NY Conventual Franciscan Friars.
Ehmann, Benedict A. '29 (ROC) Retired; [L] Rochester, NY Censores Librorum.
Ehr, Donald J. *s.v.d.* '55 (CHI) [53] Chicago, IL St. Elizabeth Church.
Ehrens, Richard J. '58 (CHI) Harwood Heights, IL St. Rosalie Church; [S] Chicago, IL Kolping Center.
Ehrhart, Charles (RVC) Priests Released from Diocesan Assignment.
Ehrman, Dale *o.s.c.* '90 (STP) [N] Shoreview, MN Crosier Community of Shoreview.
Ehrne, Robert *c.p.* '53 (HRT) [M] West Hartford, CT Holy Family Monastery/Retreat.
Ehwald, Joseph A. '62 (COL) Reynoldsburg, OH St. Pius X Church.
Eiardi, Anthony J. *s.j.* '41 (BGP) [O] Fairfield, CT The Fairfield Jesuit Community-Fairfield University.
Eichenberger, Thomas P. '76 (MIL) Cudahy, WI Holy Family Church.
Eichenseer, Donald W. '61 (BEL) [8] Belleville, IL St. Teresa of the Child Jesus Church.
Eichhoff, William M. '64 (OKL) [8] Oklahoma City, OK St. Francis of Assisi Church; [K] Norman, OK Campus Ministry for the Archdiocese of Oklahoma City.
Eichhorst, Franklin *o.f.m.cap.* '57 (LSC) Lovington, NM St. Thomas Aquinas Church.
Eichman, Dominic P. '43 (LC) Retired; [I] La Crosse, WI Holy Cross (Seminary) Diocesan Center.
Eichner, Philip K. *s.m.* '66 (RVC) [D] Uniondale, NY Kellenberg Memorial High School; [N] Mineola, NY Provincial Residence and Novitiate.
Eichoff, Paul E. '70 (TLS) Vinita, OK Holy Ghost Church.
Eichor, Msgr. Edward C. '59 (STL) [4] Lemay, MO St. Bernadette Church.
Eichorn, Harry B. *c.s.c.* '57 (FR) [B] North Easton, MA Stonehill College.
Eickhoff, Jeffrey '95 (LIN) [7] Lincoln, NE St. Joseph Church.
Eickhoff, Matthew F. '89 (LIN) Nebraska City, NE St. Mary's Church; [C] Nebraska City, NE Lourdes Junior-Senior High School; [K] Nebraska City, NE Lourdes Central High School Endowment Fund.
Eickholt, Henry C. '44 (SAG) Retired.
Eid, Frederick M. '47 (NEW) [1] Hoboken, NJ Our Lady of Grace Church; Retired.
Eidenschink, John *o.s.b.* '41 (SCL) [H] Albany, MN Mother of Mercy Nursing Home and Retirement Center.
Eifler, John G. '61 (L) [25] Louisville, KY St. Frances of Rome Church.
Eigo, Francis A. *o.s.a.* '64 (PH) [C] Villanova, PA Villanova University; [Z] Villanova, PA St. Thomas Monastery.
Eikens, Leroy F. '62 (WIN) Retired.
Eikmeier, Msgr. Bernard J. '51 (HON) Kailua, HI St. Anthony Church; Retired.
Eilerman, Craig R. '87 (COL) Lancaster, OH St. Mary Church.
Eilerman, William *c.pp.s.* '51 (CIN) [B] Carthagena, OH St. Charles.
Eilers, Joseph B. '49 (STL) Biehle, MO St. Maurus Church.
Eilert, Msgr. Edward J. '64 (NEW) Livingston, NJ St. Philomena Church.
Eimer, Frank J. '58 (L) Jeffersontown, KY St. Edward Church.
Eimer, Robert *o.m.i.* '53 (BEL) [G] Belleville, IL Shrine of Our Lady of the Snows.
Einck, Gregory J. '44 (DUB) Retired.
Einhaus, Henry *m.s.c.* '60 (RCK) [H] Aurora, IL Missionaries of the Sacred Heart Community.
Eiroa, Andres '88 (PCE) [G] Alhambra, Ponce, PR Prelature of the Holy Cross and Opus Dei.
Eis, Charles '66 (SPK) Military Chaplains.
Eisel, Howard P. *s.s.c.* '54 (DUL) Crosby, MN St. Joseph's Church.
Eisele, Francis X. '66 (RVC) West Islip, NY Our Lady of Lourdes Church.
Eisele, James F. '88 (LAN) Deerfield, MI St. Alphonsus Church.
Eisele, Paul F. '68 (SC) St. Joseph, IA St. Joseph's Church.
Eisemann, Frederick F. '53 (ROC) [21] Rochester, NY Holy Cross Church.
Eisler, Rudolph J. '63 (NY) Spring Valley, NY St. Joseph Church.
Eisweirth, Thomas '74 (Y) [7] Youngstown, OH Sacred Heart of Jesus Church.
Eivers, Michael '55 (MIA) Pembroke Pines, FL St. Edward Church.
Ejimadu, Festus '93 (DET) Inkster, MI Holy Family Parish Church; Inkster, MI St. Kevin and St. Norbert Church.
Ekanem, Anthony *m.s.p.* '89 (BEA) [3] Port Arthur, TX Sacred Heart Church.
Ekdahl, Kenneth W. '91 (TR) Maple Shade, NJ Our Lady of Perpetual Help Church; [B] Delran, NJ Holy Cross High School.
Ekenachi, Donatus I. '83 (LA) [69] Los Angeles, CA St. Jerome Church.
Ekman, Robert '57 (SCL) Retired.
Ekpo, Joseph (CHI) [D] Oak Park, IL Fenwick High School.
Ekpo, Joseph '86 (CHI) Bellwood, IL St. Simeon Church.
Eksterowicz, Francis C. '85 (BUR) Richford, VT All Saints Church.
Ekweariri, Joseph '77 (OWN) [D] Paducah, KY Lourdes Hospital.
Ekwueme, Clifford C. '83 (NY) [159] Bronx, NY St. Lucy Church.
Ekwuribe, Matthew '67 (PIT) [74] Pittsburgh, PA Incarnation of the Lord Church.
El-Bacha, Assaad *m.l.m.* '92 (OLL) San Antonio, TX St. George Church; [A] San Antonio, TX The Congregation of Maronite Lebanese Missionaries.
El-Hayek, Nehmatallah '62 (SAM) On Duty Outside the Diocese.
El-Hayek, Nehmatallah '62 (SP) Inverness, FL Our Lady of Fatima Church.
El-Khalli, Msgr. Georges '81 (SAM) Williamsville, NY St. John Maron Church.
Elam, Ray *o.s.a.* '70 (P) Roseburg, OR St. Joseph Church.
Elambassery, Xavier '66 (SJP) Latrobe, PA Assumption of B.V.M. Church.
Elanjileth, John M. '45 (ROM) McKeesport, PA St. Mary Church.
Elanjileth, John M. '50 (PIT) Allegheny County, PA McKeesport Hospital.
Elder, Jerome C. '57 (LA) [4] Long Beach, CA St. Bartholomew Church.
Elder, John W. *s.j.* '65 (BGP) [A] Fairfield, CT Fairfield University; [O] Fairfield, CT The Fairfield Jesuit Community-Fairfield University.
Elder, Leonard *s.c.j.* (GAL) [26] Houston, TX St. Elizabeth Ann Seton Church.
Elder, William S. '81 (NY) [62] New York, NY St. Joseph Church.
Eldredge, Richard *t.o.r.* '78 (FWT) [4] Arlington, TX St. Maria Goretti Church.
Eldridge, Louis J. '85 (MET) Dunellen, NJ St. John the Evangelist Church.
Eldringhoff, John '68 (KC) Raytown, MO Our Lady of Lourdes Church.
Eleanya, Conleth '88 (CAM) Williamstown, NJ St. Mary's Church.
Elejalde, Manuel *c.p.* '26 (ARE) Lares, PR St. Joseph Church.
Elekwachi, Martin '80 (BRK) [245] Queens, NY St.

Thomas Apostle Church.
Eles, Joseph '65 (PSC) Retired.
Elewaut, Thomas J. *c.j.* '86 (LA) [B] Santa Maria, CA St. Joseph Seminary (Josephite Fathers' Novitiate); [D] Santa Maria, CA St. Joseph High School.
Elford, Ricardo *c.ss.r.* '64 (CHI) [N] Bangkok, Thailand; [N] Parana, Brazil Rua Consulheiro Sinimbu.
Elford, Ricardo *c.ss.r.* '64 (DEN) [M] Denver, CO The Redemptorists/Denver Province.
Eli, Jude *o.p.* '76 (LA) [59] Los Angeles, CA St. Dominic Church.
Elia, Faouzi Y. '77 (OLL) Peoria, IL St. Sharbel Church.
Elias, Woodrow '43 (DM) Retired.
Elis, Patrick H. '69 (BUF) Cassadaga, NY Immaculate Conception Church; Sinclairville, NY St. John the Evangelist Church.
Elizondo, Virgil '63 (SAT) [64] San Antonio, TX St. Rose of Lima Church.
Elkin, Fredic F. '77 (SY) Military Chaplains.
Elko, Joseph M. '70 (HRT) [13] New Haven, CT Saint Martin de Porres Church.
Eller, Hugh *o.f.m.* '53 (PRO) [P] Providence, RI St. Francis Friary.
Ellerbrock, Timothy '80 (BWN) Absent.
Ellerman, Thomas *s.m.* '61 (NO) [C] New Orleans, LA Our Lady of Holy Cross College.
Ellias, John P. '64 (ALT) St. Michael, PA St. Michael's Church.
Ellifritz, R. Michael '67 (COL) [10] Columbus, OH Christ the King Church.
Ellinghausen, Jude T. '58 (DET) North Branch, MI SS. Peter and Paul Church.
Elliot, James *o.f.m.conv.* (BAL) [B] Ellicott City, MD Friary of St. Joseph Cupertino.
Elliott, Edward C. '44 (MEM) Retired.
Elliott, James *o.f.m.conv.* (BAL) [M] Ellicott City, MD St. Joseph Cupertino Friary, Friars Minor Conventual of St. Francis of Assisi.
Elliott, Joseph *c.ss.r.* '49 (LA) Whittier, CA St. Mary of the Assumption Church; [R] Whittier, CA Redemptorist Fathers Mission House.
Elliott, Joseph W. '71 (OG) Brownville, NY Immaculate Conception of the B.V.M. Church.
Elliott, Msgr. Peter J. '73 (WDC) [V] Silver Spring, MD Catholics Committed to Support the Pope.
Elliott, Roger *c.p.* '58 (SCR) [2] Scranton, PA St. Ann's Church.
Elliott, Msgr. Ron (KC) Higginsville, MO St. Mary's Church.
Elliott, Thomas *c.s.c.* '67 (BGP) [I] Bridgeport, CT St. Vincent's Medical Center.
Elliott, Thomas *c.s.c.* '67 (FTW) [J] South Bend, IN Congregation of Holy Cross Indiana Province Provincial House.
Elliott, Timothy P. '82 (STL) [3] St. Charles, MO St. Elizabeth Ann Seton Church.
Elliott, Trumie Culpepper '88 (L) Samuels, KY St. Gregory Church.
Elliott, William *o.m.i.* (AUS) [6] Austin, TX Our Lady of Guadalupe Church.
Elliott, Msgr. William E. '60 (SD) [14] San Diego, CA Our Lady of Refuge Church.
Elliott, William J. *s.j.* '61 (WDC) [E] North Bethesda, MD Georgetown Preparatory School.
Ellis, Alfred J. *o.s.a.* '63 (BO) Andover, MA St. Augustine Church.
Ellis, Kail C. *o.s.a.* '67 (PH) [C] Villanova, PA Villanova University; [Z] Villanova, PA St. John Stone Friary.
Ellis, Matthew '88 (DET) [5] Dearborn, MI Divine Child Church.
Ellison, Joseph *c.ss.r.* '39 (ORL) [F] New Smyrna Beach, FL St. Alphonsus Villa-Redemptorist Fathers and Brothers.
Ellos, William *s.j.* '68 (SAT) [C] San Antonio, TX St. Mary's University of San Antonio, Texas.
Ellos, William J. *s.j.* '68 (MIL) [P] Milwaukee, WI Jesuit Provincial Office, Wisconsin Province.
Ellspermann, Camillus *o.s.b.* '50 (EVN) St. Henry, IN St. Henry Church.
Ellspermann, Camillus *o.s.b.* '50 (IND) [J] St. Meinrad, IN St. Meinrad Archabbey.
Ellspermann, Gerard *o.s.b.* '39 (IND) [J] St. Meinrad, IN St. Meinrad Archabbey.
Elmer, Msgr. Charles '52 (AUS) On Duty Outside the Diocese.
Elmer, Gregory *o.s.b.* '76 (LA) [R] Valyermo, CA St. Andrew's Abbey.
Elmer, John *o.f.m.conv.* (DUB) Ames, IA St. Cecilia Church; Gilbert, IA SS. Peter and Paul Church.
Elmer, Richard J. *c.s.b.* '57 (DET) [E] Redford, MI Catholic Central High School.
Elmer, Timothy '73 (SY) Chittenango, NY St. Patrick Church.
Elmlinger, Msgr. Herbert '42 (FRS) Retired.
Elmo, Francis E. '63 (NY) Absent on Leave.
Elo, Richard *c.pp.s.* '63 (CIN) [B] Carthagena, OH St. Charles.
Elorriaga, Javier *o.ss.t.* '68 (SJN) [13] Bayamon, PR Ascension Del Senor Church.
Elsasser, Thomas G. '88 (CLV) Middleburg Heights, OH St. Bartholomew Church.
Elsbernd, Alphonse *s.v.d.* '29 (CHI) [B] Techny, IL Divine Word Residence.
Elsemann, Frederick F. '53 (ROC) Retired.
Elsen, Vincent *o.f.m.* '47 (FWT) [G] Crowley, TX St. Francis Village, Inc.; [H] Crowley, TX St. Maximilian Kolbe Friary.
Elser, William '86 (LR) Barling, AR Sacred Heart of Mary Church.
Elshoff, Matthew *o.f.m.cap.* '52 (LA) [F] La Canada Flintridge, CA St. Francis High School.
Elshoff, Matthew *o.f.m.cap.* '82 (LA) [F] La Canada Flintridge, CA St. Francis High School.
Elsinghorst, Francis X. *s.j.* '54 (NY) [32] New York, NY St. Elizabeth of Hungary Church.
Elskamp, Frederick J. '62 (JC) Holts Summit, MO St. Andrew Church.
Elsner, Martin L. *s.j.* '62 (SAT) [17] San Antonio, TX Our Lady of Guadalupe Church.
Elston, Joseph '85 (SCR) [1] Williamsport, PA Annunciation Church.
Elverman, Donald A. '54 (MIL) Retired.
Elworthy, Joseph *c.ss.r.* '39 (BLX) [E] Biloxi, MS St. John Neumann Residence.
Ely, Peter B. *s.j.* '69 (KC) [B] Kansas City, MO Rockhurst College; [J] Kansas City, MO Rockhurst College - Jesuit Community.
Emanuel, John F. '92 (TUC) Clifton, AZ Sacred Heart Church.
Emanuel, Steve '93 (OM) [G] West Point, NE Franciscan Care Services, Inc., (d.b.a. St. Francis Memorial Hospital.
Emanuel, Steven '93 (OM) West Point, NE Assumption B.V.M. Church.
Emechete, Innocent '72 (SAC) Vacaville, CA California Medical Facility, Solano Co.
Emerick, David *s.c.j.* '86 (MIL) [P] Hales Corners, WI Priests of the Sacred Heart.
Emerick, Stephen J. '58 (CIN) [L] Cincinnati, OH Mercy St. Theresa Center.
Emerling, James R. '53 (HRT) New Hartford, CT Immaculate Conception Church.
Emerson, George F. '56 (BO) [4] Framingham, MA St. Stephen Church.
Emerson, Richard A. '78 (GRY) Munster, IN St. Thomas More Church.
Emerson, Robert F. '55 (JOL) Gilman, IL Immaculate Conception Church.
Emery, Robert E. '87 (NEW) Belleville, NJ St. Peter's Church.
Emezie, Charles '83 (SFS) [D] Aberdeen, SD St. Luke's Midland Regional Medical Center; [E] Aberdeen, SD Mother Joseph Manor, Nursing Care Facility.
Emge, John P. '50 (EVN) Retired.
Emling, Bertin L. *o.s.b.* '35 (GBG) [H] Latrobe, PA Saint Vincent Archabbey.
Emling, Marion J. *o.s.b.* '78 (GBG) [H] Latrobe, PA Saint Vincent Archabbey.
Emmenegger, Msgr. Joseph E. '42 (MIL) Retired.
Emmons, Rayford E. '74 (PH) [3] Philadelphia, PA St. Agatha-St. James Church.
Emo, Eugene '61 (ROC) Unassigned.
Emon, Neil *o.s.c.* '67 (DET) [1] Taylor, MI St. Alfred Church.
Emon, Neil J. *o.s.c.* '67 (DET) Riverview, MI St. Cyprian Church; [K] Riverview, MI Crosier Community of Riverview.
Empereur, James L. *s.j.* '65 (MIL) [P] Milwaukee, WI Jesuit Provincial Office, Wisconsin Province.
Emperur, James L. *s.j.* '65 (SAT) [1] San Antonio, TX Cathedral of San Fernando.
Emrisek, Gene J. *o.f.m.cap.* '68 (DEN) [3] Denver, CO Annunciation Church; [M] Denver, CO Annunciation Friary.
Encinas, Andrew G. '90 (LA) Culver City, CA St. Augustine Church.
Encisco, Jesus A. (NEW) Lodi, NJ St. Francis de Sales Church.
Enciso, Herman '81 (MRY) Absent on Sick Leave.
Endebrock, Msgr. Donald M. '51 (MET) [1] Carteret, NJ St. Joseph Church; Retired.
Endebrock, Msgr. John J. '38 (TR) Avon, NJ St. Elizabeth Church; Retired.
Endejan, John H. '57 (MIL) [1] Milwaukee, WI St. John Cathedral; [H] Milwaukee, WI All Saints Catholic East School System, Inc.
Enderle, Gilbert A. *c.ss.r.* '62 (CHI) [N] Chicago, IL Redemptorist Theology Residence.
Enderle, Msgr. M.N. '46 (BEA) Groves, TX St. Peter the Apostle Church.
Enderle, Msgr. Martin N. '46 (BEA) Retired.
Enderle, Msgr. Marvin F. '61 (BEA) Orange, TX St. Mary Church.
Enderlin, Joseph J. '46 (LR) Bella Vista, AR St. Bernard Church.
Enderlin, Ronald E. '69 (PEO) Lacon, IL Immaculate Conception Church.
Enders, Robert F. '39 (MIL) Retired.
Endres, Gilbert J. '52 (STP) Retired.
Endres, James F. '82 (PH) Warminster, PA Nativity of Our Lord Church; [D] Warminster, PA Archbishop Wood Catholic High School.
Endres, John C. *s.j.* '76 (OAK) [A] Berkeley, CA The Jesuit School of Theology at Berkeley; [N] Berkeley, CA Jesuit Community at Jesuit School of Theology at Berkeley.
Endres, William '82 (ROC) Rochester, NY Rochester General Hospital.
Endress, James R. '60 (EVN) Special Assignment.
Endslow, Bartholomew S. *s.s.j.* '49 (LAF) Lebeau, LA Immaculate Conception Church.
Enette, Rawlin *s.s.j.* '59 (NO) [2] New Orleans, LA All Saints Church.
Engbarth, David R. '76 (RCK) [4] Aurora, IL St. Mary Church; [5] Aurora, IL St. Nicholas Church.
Engbers, Thomas J. '67 (MIA) Miami Shores, FL St. Martha Church.
Engbers, William J. '39 (IND) St. Nicholas, IN St. Nicholas Church; Retired.
Engel, John '54 (P) Retired.
Engel, Paul *o.f.m.cap.* '64 (NY) [Z] Garrison, NY St. Francis Friary.
Engel, Ronald G. '77 (MIL) [3] South Milwaukee, WI St. Mary's Church.
Engelbrecht, Henry H. '68 (NO) [36] New Orleans, LA St. Henry Church.
Engelen, R. J. '30 (ALX) Retired.
Engelhardt, Adam J. '42 (FAR) Retired.
Engelhardt, Charles F. *o.s.f.s.* '77 (PH) [D] Philadelphia, PA Father Judge High School for Boys; [Z] Philadelphia, PA Father Judge Faculty House.
Engelhart, Henry Ray '63 (BEL) Shawneetown, IL St. Mary Church.
Engelhart, William '70 (JKS) Retired.
Engels, Eugene R. '63 (BR) Plaquemine, LA St. John the Evangelist Church.
Engels, Francis C. '62 (PEO) Absent on Leave.
Engels, Richard J. '60 (WIN) Mazeppa, MN SS. Peter and Paul Church.
Engen, Bruce '89 (DUL) Walker, MN St. Agnes Church; Duluth, MN Indian Missions Church.
Engh, Michael *s.j.* '81 (LA) [C] Los Angeles, CA Loyola Marymount University.
Engh, Michael E. *s.j.* '81 (LA) [C] Los Angeles, CA Loyola Marymount University.
England, Barry '68 (FTW) [3] South Bend, IN St. Anthony de Padua Church.
England, Robert '77 (SD) Absent on Sick Leave.
Engle, James C. '63 (BEA) Special Assignment.
Engle, Richard F. '56 (COL) Chillicothe, OH Veteran's Administration Medical Center; Retired.
Englehardt, Msgr. Herbert G. '40 (BUF) Retired.
Engler, Ernest J. '51 (DUB) Retired.
Engler, Msgr. Francis V. '46 (BUF) [60] Buffalo, NY St. Rose of Lima Church.
Engler, Simon *t.o.r.* '49 (CLV) [26] Cleveland, OH St. Henry Church.
Engler, Simon M. *t.o.r.* '49 (SFS) Armour, SD St. Paul the Apostle Church.
Englert, Anthony A. '87 (CHI) [A] Chicago, IL St. Joseph Seminary.
Englert, James O.J. '78 (SFS) Wakonda, SD St. Patrick Church; [H] Vermillion, SD St. Thomas More Catholic Newman Center.
Englert, Michael *o.f.m.conv.* '89 (BUF) Athol Springs, NY St. Francis of Assisi Church.
Englert, Wilfred '86 (EVN) [18] Evansville, IN St. Joseph Church.
Englert, William J. '53 (CLV) Fairport Harbor, OH St. Anthony of Padua Church; Retired.
English, Joseph *o.f.m.cap.* '90 (AGN) Mangilao, GU Santa Teresita Church.
English, Paul F. '85 (ROC) [I] Rochester, NY Basilian Residence; [M] Rochester, NY Diocesan Office of Campus Ministry.
English, Richard P. *s.j.* '51 (NY) [Z] New York, NY Murray-Weigel Hall.
English, Robert K. '89 (OM) Spencer, NE St. Mary Church.
English, Msgr. Tobias P. '63 (LA) Pasadena, CA St. Andrew Church.
English, William J. '60 (BO) [6] Quincy, MA Most Blessed Sacrament Church.
English, Msgr. William J. '69 (WDC) Pastoral Center Special Ministries; [N] Kensington, MD St. John Vianney House.
Enke, Msgr. Paul P. '72 (COL) Dublin, OH St. Brigid of Kildare Church.
Enlow, Leo J. '75 (SFD) Effingham, IL St. Anthony of Padua Church.
Enman, Frederick M. *s.j.* '88 (WOR) [N] Worcester, MA Jesuits of Holy Cross College, Inc.
Enneking, Marvin '91 (SCL) Rice, MN Immaculate Conception Church.
Enneking, Thomas *o.s.c.* '84 (CHI) [N] Chicago, IL Crosier Community of Chicago.
Enneking, Tom *o.s.c.* '84 (CHI) [80] Chicago, IL Holy Cross/Immaculate Heart of Mary Church.
Ennis, James E. '50 (LC) Hillsboro, WI St. Aloysius Church; [E] Hillsboro, WI St. Joseph's Memorial Hospital, Inc.
Ennis, William '64 (ORL) [5] Orlando, FL Holy Family Church.

Eno, Robert B. *s.s.* '63 (HRT) On Duty Outside the Archdiocese.
Eno, Robert B. *s.s.* '63 (WDC) [A] Washington, DC Theological College of the Catholic University of America; [C] Washington, DC Catholic University of America, The.
Enojo, Jesus P. '67 (NY) [54] New York, NY St. James Church.
Enright, Columba J. *t.o.r.* '56 (WDC) [B] Wheaton, MD St. Thomas More Friary, Third Order Regular of St. Francis; [C] Washington, DC Catholic University of America, The; [Q] Washington, DC Basilica of the National Shrine of the Immaculate Conception.
Enright, Edward J. *o.s.a.* '73 (PH) [C] Villanova, PA Villanova University.
Enright, Frank E. '43 (WIN) Retired; [F] Austin, MN Sacred Heart Hospice, Inc.
Enright, James C. '69 (BUF) On Duty Outside the Diocese.
Enright, James C. '69 (ROC) [3] Auburn, NY St. Mary Church; Auburn, NY Auburn Correctional Facility.
Enright, John P. '53 (CHI) Palatine, IL Santa Teresita Vicariate Church.
Enright, John S. *s.j.* '55 (SJ) [M] Los Gatos, CA Sacred Heart Jesuit Center.
Enright, Michael P. '84 (CHI) [93] Chicago, IL Immaculate Conception of the Blessed Virgin Mary Church.
Enright, Thomas M. '66 (CHI) Wauconda, IL Transfiguration Church.
Enright, Timothy *c.s.sp.* (SFR) San Francisco, CA Laguna Honda Home.
Enright, Msgr. Vincent L. '47 (E) Retired.
Enriquez, Alex '85 (TR) Red Bank, NJ St. James Church.
Enriquez, Juan '80 (LA) Pacoima, CA Guardian Angel Church.
Ensman, Raymond '66 (TOL) Port Clinton, OH Immaculate Conception Church.
Enweiler, Donald A. (COV) [9] Covington, KY Church of Our Savior.
Enyan-Boadu, Peter '84 (ROC) [21] Rochester, NY Holy Cross Church.
Enzler, Msgr. John J. '73 (WDC) Potomac, MD Our Lady of Mercy Church.
Enzman, David L. '83 (CLV) Willowick, OH St. Mary Magdalene Church.
Enzweiler, Donald A. '87 (COV) [5] Covington, KY St. Benedict Church; [B] Erlanger, KY St. Henry District High School.
Eppenbrock, Donald J. '60 (SAG) Lexington, MI St. Denis Church.
Epperley, Wayne T. *c.s.sp.* '82 (SB) Idyllwild, CA Queen of Angels Church.
Epping, Robert L. *c.s.c.* '70 (FTW) [J] South Bend, IN Congregation of Holy Cross Indiana Province Provincial House.
Eraly, Matthew (NY) Manhattan, NY Mount Sinai Medical Center.
Erat, William G. (PH) [EE] Glenside, PA Counseling Center at St. Luke's.
Erb, Charles *s.v.d.* '33 (TR) [M] Bordentown, NJ Society of the Divine Word.
Erb, Francis J. '54 (ROC) Retired.
Erb, Vincent I. '50 (CHL) Retired.
Erbacher, Joseph F. '72 (EVN) St. Anthony, IN St. Anthony Church.
Erbacher, William J. '87 (ARL) Manassas, VA Sacred Heart Church.
Erbe, Edward J. '51 (MAD) Evansville, WI St. Paul Church.
Erbrick, Thomas J. *o.s.f.s.* (PH) [D] Philadelphia, PA Father Judge High School for Boys.
Erbrick, Thomas J. *o.s.f.s.* (WDC) [B] Washington, DC Deshairs Community-Oblates of St. Francis de Sales Residence.
Ercolano, Anthony S. '73 (BRK) [148] Queens, NY American Martyrs Church; [G] Middle Village, NY Christ the King.
Erdei, Joseph J. *o.s.b.m.* '58 (PSC) [B] Matawan, NJ Basilian Fathers of Mariapoch.
Erdeljac, Frank '83 (PIT) [O] Villa Maria, PA Sisters of the Humility of Mary.
Erdeljac, Frank G. '83 (PIT) Lawrence County, PA Jameson Memorial Hospital; [J] New Castle, PA St. Francis Hospital of New Castle.
Erdle, Thomas M. '55 (ROC) [44] Rochester, NY St. Mark Church.
Erdlen, Harry J. *o.s.a.* '57 (PH) [G] Malvern, PA Malvern Preparatory School for Boys; [Z] Malvern, PA Augustinians (O.S.A.).
Eremito, Anthony '67 (NY) Absent on Leave.
Erestain, Alfonso E. '64 (RNO) Fallon, NV Fallon Naval Air Station Base Chapel.
Erhart, Charles M. '60 (RVC) Military Chaplains.
Erhart, Henry *s.j.* '55 (BAL) [D] Baltimore, MD Loyola High School.
Erhueh, Msgr. Anthony O. '66 (NY) [229] Staten Island, NY St. Sylvester Church.
Ericksen, William L. '95 (MIL) New Berlin, WI Holy Apostles Church.
Erickson, John '66 (KCK) [6] Topeka, KS Sacred Heart Church.
Erickson, John R. *o.s.b.* '50 (GBG) [H] Latrobe, PA Saint Vincent Archabbey.
Erickson, Matthew *o.p.* '90 (Y) [13] Youngstown, OH St. Dominic's Church.
Erickson, Philip L. '95 (L) [66] Louisville, KY St. Raphael the Archangel Church.
Erickson, Robert *s.j.* '74 (SPK) Keller, WA St. Rose of Lima Church; Nespelem, WA Sacred Heart Mission Church; Omak, WA St. Mary Mission Church; Omak, WA St. Joseph Church.
Erickson, Robert E. *c.s.v.* '67 (CHI) [N] Arlington Heights, IL Clerics of St. Viator-Provincial Residence; [N] Arlington Heights, IL Viatorian Province Center-Clerics of St. Viator.
Erickson, Robert J. '58 (SB) Lake Arrowhead, CA Our Lady of the Lake Church.
Erikson, Richard M. '85 (BO) [A] Boston, MA St. John's Seminary.
Erkens, William J. '40 (PIT) Retired.
Erlenheim, Adrian *o.f.m.* '37 (LA) [R] Santa Barbara, CA Franciscan Friary, Order of Friars Minor (Old Mission).
Ermer, James '78 (FAR) On Duty Outside the Diocese; [A] Fargo, ND Cardinal Muench Seminary.
Ermis, Norman '83 (SAT) [A] San Antonio, TX The Assumption-St. John's Seminary.
Ernest, Bryan D. '82 (GI) Alliance, NE Holy Rosary Church.
Ernest, Francis P. *s.j.* '57 (BAL) [37] Baltimore, MD St. Ignatius Church.
Ernest, Stephen *s.v.d.* (OAK) [A] Berkeley, CA Dominican School of Philosophy and Theology.
Ernest, Stephen *s.v.d.* '67 (OAK) [6] Oakland, CA St. Bernard's Church.
Ernst, Albert C. '53 (NO) [3] Kenner, LA St. Elizabeth Ann Seton Church.
Ernst, Jeffrey *o.f.m.cap.* '96 (DEN) [3] Denver, CO Annunciation Church.
Ernst, Norbert A. '72 (STL) House Springs, MO Our Lady, Queen of Peace Church.
Ernst, Stephen *s.t.* '86 (WDC) [M] Adelphi, MD Father Thomas O'Keeffe Missionary Cenacle.
Ernst, William W. '64 (IND) [4] New Albany, IN St. Mary Church.
Ernster, James M. '55 (MIL) Retired.
Ernster, Milo L. '55 (WIN) Dodge Center, MN St. John Baptist de La Salle Church.
Ernstmann, Mark C. '51 (SPC) Forsyth, MO Our Lady of the Ozarks Church.
Erpelding, Edward '66 (FTW) Syracuse, IN St. Martin de Porres Church.
Erpelding, Michael J. '89 (SC) Storm Lake, IA St. Mary's Church.
Erpen, Msgr. B. A. '47 (AMA) Retired.
Erps, Jim *s.j.* '80 (LA) [BB] Los Angeles, CA Archdiocesan Office for Campus Ministry.
Errecalde, Javier *o.de.m.* '54 (PCE) [13] Ponce, PR Santuario San Judas Tadeo Church.
Erro, Sabino *o.f.m.* '54 (DAL) [9] Dallas, TX Our Lady of Perpetual Help Church.
Erstad, William D. '56 (SB) Perris, CA St. James Church.
Ertle, Thomas J. *o.p.* '56 (COL) Zanesville, OH St. Thomas Aquinas Church.
Ertzbischoff, Edmond L. '76 (LAN) [2] Ypsilanti, MI St. John Church.
Ervin, Mark W. '90 (WDC) Piscataway, MD St. Mary Church.
Ervin, Thomas '74 (SFR) Absent on Leave.
Erwin, James M. *o.p.* '45 (CHI) [N] River Forest, IL St. Thomas Aquinas Priory.
Erwin, Patrick O. '91 (PAT) Unassigned.
Esbind, Jace '87 (LKC) Graduate Studies.
Escalante, Agustin M. '88 (SFR) [1] South San Francisco CA All Souls Church.
Escalante, Peter '78 (SD) [21] San Diego, CA St. Brigid Church.
Escalante, Ronald '95 (ARL) [5] Alexandria, VA St. Lawrence Church.
Esch, Eugene *o.s.b.* '54 (B) Glenns Ferry, ID Our Lady of Limerick Church; [C] Jerome, ID Ascension Priory.
Eschbach, Victor J. '72 (PH) Parkesburg, PA Our Lady of Consolation Church.
Eschbacher, Jerome J. '56 (SPC) Retired.
Eschweiler, Edward R. '48 (MIL) Retired.
Eschweiler, Francis L. '35 (MIL) Retired.
Escobar, Agustin '87 (ORG) Westminster, CA Blessed Sacrament Church.
Escobar, Joseph A. *o.p.* '88 (PRO) Bristol, RI St. Elizabeth's Church.
Escobar, Octavio '67 (STO) Ceres, CA St. Jude Church.
Escobedo, Armando '64 (BWN) Mercedes, TX Our Lady of Mercy Church.
Escobedo, Jaime '93 (SD) [A] San Diego, CA St. Francis Seminary.
Escribano, Peter E. '88 (MET) On Duty Outside the Diocese.
Esenther, Keith *s.j.* '71 (DET) [E] Detroit, MI University of Detroit Jesuit High School and Academy.
Esenther, Keith J. *s.j.* '71 (DET) [K] Detroit, MI Jesuit Provincial Office-Detroit Province of the Society of Jesus.
Esguerra, Bernardino C. (TR) Atlantic Highlands, NJ St. Agnes Church.
Eshiowu, Evaristus M. (LA) [67] Los Angeles, CA St. Ignatius of Loyola Church.
Esmilla, Efren V. '93 (PH) Wallingford, PA St. John Chrysostom Church.
Esmond, William '55 (ALB) Whitehall, NY Our Lady of Angels Church.
Esmurdoc, F. Christopher '96 (CLV) Strongsville, OH St. John Neumann Church.
Esparza, Javier *ss.cc.* '58 (SJN) [8] Guaynabo, PR Nuestra Senora de la Paz Church.
Esparza, Luis *o.f.m.cap.* (ARE) Retired.
Espejel, Rene J. *c.s.b.* '87 (GAL) [Q] Sugar Land, TX Basilian Mission Center.
Espelage, Thomas R. '70 (CIN) St. Paris, OH Sacred Heart Church; Urbana, OH St. Mary Church; [Q] Urbana, OH Urbana University Campus Ministry.
Espenshade, William T. '68 (CHY) Riverton, WY St. Margaret's Church.
Esper, Abraham L. '85 (SY) Whitesboro, NY St. Paul Church.
Esper, Jerome *c.s.c.* (CHI) [D] Niles, IL Notre Dame High School.
Esper, Jerome *c.s.c.* '61 (CHI) [D] Niles, IL Notre Dame High School.
Esper, John (DET) [A] Detroit, MI Sacred Heart Major Seminary, Inc.; [T] Eastpointe, MI Detroit Catholic Charismatic Renewal.
Esper, Joseph M. '82 (DET) [3] Redford, MI Our Lady of Loretto Church.
Esper, Thomas '51 (DET) Retired.
Espin, Orlando O. '72 (SD) [B] San Diego, CA University of San Diego.
Espin, Orlando O. '72 (VEN) Absent on Leave.
Espineda, Cesar Ching *s.v.d.* '84 (NY) [17] New York, NY St. Bernard Church.
Espinel, Marcos Luis *o.p.* '59 (SJN) [3] Bayamon, PR Catalina de Siena Church.
Espino, Jose '83 (MIA) Homestead, FL Sacred Heart Church.
Espinosa, Anthony '96 (OM) Columbus, NE St. Bonaventure Church.
Espinosa, Boris '78 (CGS) Maunabo, PR San Isidor Labrador Church.
Espinosa, Donald B. *a.a.* '71 (WOR) Fiskdale, MA St. Anne's and St. Patrick's Church.
Espinosa, Jesus *o.a.r.* (LSC) [6] Las Cruces, NM Santa Rosa de Lima Church.
Espinoza, Galo *o.a.r.* '92 (NEW) [N] West Orange, NJ Augustinian Recollects.
Espitia, David '94 (SAN) Absent on Leave.
Espona, Msgr. Juan '82 (PCE) Special Assignment.
Esposito, Anthony '56 (Y) Absent on Leave.
Esposito, Augustine M. *o.s.a.* '79 (PH) [A] Wynnewood, PA Theological Seminary of St. Charles Borromeo, Overbrook; [D] Drexel Hill, PA Monsignor Bonner High School.
Esposito, Ernest T. '67 (BGP) [2] Fairfield, CT Assumption Church; [G] Bridgeport, CT Catholic Charities of Fairfield County.
Esposito, Joseph J. '54 (BRK) Absent on Sick Leave.
Esposito, Lawrence J. '76 (WOR) Berlin, MA St. Joseph the Good Provider Church.
Esposito, Louis '64 (BAL) [72] Baltimore, MD Our Lady of Pompei Church.
Esposito, Mario *o.carm.* '77 (ALB) [M] Germantown, NY St. Teresa's Motherhouse.
Esposito, Mario *o. carm.* '77 (NY) Middletown, NY Our Lady of Mt. Carmel Church; [Z] Middletown, NY St. Albert's Priory.
Esposito, Ralph '67 (LR) Van Buren, AR St. Michael's Church.
Esposito, Samuel J. '78 (PIT) Allegheny County, PA Eye and Ear Hospital; Allegheny County, PA Montefiore Hospital; Allegheny County, PA Presbyterian-University Hospital.
Esposito, William C. '58 (SY) Cleveland, NY St. Mary of the Assumption Church.
Esquivel, Msgr. John '68 (FRS) Fowler, CA St. Lucy Church; Selma, CA St. Joseph Church.
Esquivez, Miguel '82 (SAN) On Duty Outside the Diocese.
Ess, Thomas '66 (CHI) [N] Chicago, IL St. Peter's Friary.
Esseff, Msgr. John A. '53 (SCR) [A] Dalton, PA Saint Pius X Seminary.
Esselman, Thomas *c.m.* '80 (STL) [B] St. Louis, MO Aquinas Institute of Theology.
Esselman, Thomas E. *c.m.* '80 (STL) [P] St. Louis, MO Vincentian-St. Lazare Residence.
Esser, James J. *o.f.m.* '67 (GB) Krakow, WI St. Casimir Church.
Esser, Paul M. '57 (MIL) [7] Racine, WI St. Paul the Apostle Church.
Essex, Msgr. Donald S. '73 (WDC) [2] Bethesda, MD St. Jane Frances de Chantal Church.

Essig, Edward J. '94 (ALN) [4] Pottsville, PA St. Patrick Church.
Essig, Herbert '74 (JOL) Lombard, IL St. Pius X Church.
Essig, Robert G. '38 (SJ) [6] San Jose, CA St. Frances Cabrini Church; Retired.
Essling, Harold '78 (AUS) [13] Austin, TX St. Ignatius Martyr Church.
Essman, Charles P. '56 (COL) Retired.
Essman, Ronald J. '76 (DET) [4] Troy, MI St. Elizabeth Ann Seton Church.
Estabrook, Joseph '69 (ALB) Military Chaplains.
Estensoro, Jose '60 (ARE) Hatillo, PR Perpetual Help Church.
Estepa, Francisco *s.v.d.* '83 (WDC) [M] Washington, DC Divine Word College.
Estephan, Andre S. *m.l.m.* '90 (OLL) Lewisville, TX Our Lady of Lebanon Mission Church; [A] San Antonio, TX The Congregation of Maronite Lebanese Missionaries.
Esterka, Msgr. Peter '63 (ORG) [3] Orange, CA St. Norbert Church.
Esteve, Alfonso '47 (SJN) On Duty Outside the Archdiocese.
Estevez, Felipe '70 (MIA) [15] Miami, FL St. Agatha Church.
Esti, Giovanni *m.c.c.j.* '91 (LA) [R] Azusa, CA Casa Comboni Mission Seminary.
Estibalez, Inocencio '52 (SP) Retired.
Estilette, Grady J. '63 (LAF) Gueydan, LA St. Peter Church.
Estok, Edward T. '85 (CLV) [6] Euclid, OH St. William Church.
Estrada, Enrique '93 (MIA) Higher Studies.
Estrada, Hector Diaz (SJN) [D] San Juan, PR VA Medical Center.
Estrada, Manuel '86 (SFR) [17] San Francisco, CA Church of the Epiphany.
Estrada, Miguel *c.m.f.* '60 (CHI) [80] Chicago, IL Holy Cross/Immaculate Heart of Mary Church.
Estrada, Sabino '72 (BRK) [240] Queens, NY St. Sebastian Church.
Estrem, John '86 (STP) [1] St. Paul, MN Cathedral of St. Paul.
Esty, Gregory L. '75 (STP) Richfield, MN St. Richard Church; [H] Richfield, MN Blessed Trinity Catholic School of Richfield, Minnesota.
Esutin, Msgr. Charles E. '43 (LA) Retired.
Etchingham, Msgr. Lawrence '56 (CHY) [2] Cheyenne, WY Holy Trinity Church; Retired.
Ethen, Jeff '88 (SCL) Belle River, MN St. Nicholas Church; Parkers Prairie, MN Church of St. William; Urbank, MN Sacred Heart Church.
Etheredge, F. William '75 (RCK) [B] Rockford, IL Boylan Central Catholic High School.
Ethier, Raymond '85 (ALB) Philmont, NY Sacred Heart Church.
Ethier, Robert D. '45 (PRO) [10] Pawtucket, RI Our Lady of Consolation Church; Retired.
Etienne, Bernard '93 (EVN) Princeton, IN St. Joseph Church.
Etienne, Clifton *s.v.d.* '79 (SB) [A] Riverside, CA Divine Word Seminary.
Etienne, Paul '92 (IND) [3] Indianapolis, IN Christ The King Church.
Etlinger, Peter J. *c.s.b.* '47 (ROC) [I] Rochester, NY Residence of Basilian Fathers-The Aquinas Institute.
Ettel, Dale *o.s.c.* '82 (STP) Anoka, MN St. Stephen Church; [N] Anoka, MN Crosier Community of Anoka.
Ettensohn, John *o.m.i.* '89 (BEL) [G] Belleville, IL Missionary Oblates of Mary Immaculate - St. Henry's Oblate Residence; [K] Belleville, IL Oblate Preaching Team.
Ettlinger, Gerard H. *s.j.* '66 (NY) [Z] New York, NY Jesuit Provincial's Office.
Ettner, Wilhelm J. '93 (ARL) [2] Arlington, VA St. Agnes Church.
Ettorre, George P. '62 (PH) [2] Norristown, PA St. Francis of Assisi Church.
Etuale, Etuale '77 (HON) [10] Honolulu, HI Our Lady of the Mount Church.
Etuale, Viane '90 (SPP) [1] Pago Pago, AS Cathedral of the Holy Family.
Etzel, George A. '42 (MIL) Retired.
Etzel, Peter J. *s.j.* '94 (MIL) [P] Milwaukee, WI Arrupe House Jesuit Community.
Etzel, Raymond A. '50 (TOL) Retired.
Euk, Vincent T. (NY) [E] New York, NY Cardinal Spellman High School.
Euker, John T. '74 (GBG) Perryopolis, PA St. John the Baptist Church.
Euresti, Jesse '65 (AUS) Luling, TX St. John the Evangelist Church.
Euresti, Jesse '65 (VIC) On Duty Outside the Diocese.
Euteneur, Thomas '88 (PMB) Indiantown, FL Holy Cross Church.
Euvrad, Scott '93 (BO) [7] Lynn, MA St. Pius the Fifth Church.
Evancho, George '64 (PBR) East Pittsburgh, PA St. Mary's Church; Rankin, PA St. John's Church.
Evancho, Robert '79 (PSC) St. Petersburg, FL St. Therese Church.
Evangelista, Humberto *c.m.f.* '61 (CGS) [8] Barrio Rio Canas, PR Immaculado Corozon de Maria Church.
Evangelista, Humberto *c.m.f.* '61 (SJN) [27] San Juan, PR San Jose Obrero Church.
Evangelisto, Louis Anthony '54 (HRT) [8] New Haven, CT St. Donato's Church; [R] Hamden, CT Catholic Community at Quinnipac College.
Evanick, Michael '60 (PRM) Merrillville, IN St. Michael Church.
Evanish, Robin S. '83 (PIT) [16] Pittsburgh, PA Immaculate Conception Church; [20] Pittsburgh, PA St. Joseph Church.
Evanko, Joseph J. '91 (SCR) Mountaintop, PA St. Jude's Church.
Evanofski, Bernard P. '86 (SCR) Larksville, PA St. Anthony of Padua Church.
Evans, Alan Augustine *o.p.* '61 (NY) [Z] New York, NY St. Vincent Ferrer Priory.
Evans, Albert *ss.cc.* '48 (FR) [K] Fairhaven, MA Sacred Hearts Provincial House.
Evans, Edward '80 (WDC) Cheverly, MD St. Ambrose Church; Retired.
Evans, Eldridge T. '65 (CAM) [1] Atlantic City, NJ Holy Spirit Church.
Evans, Msgr. Ferdinand A. '34 (CIN) Retired.
Evans, Msgr. Ferdinand A. '34 (VEN) Englewood, FL St. Raphael Church.
Evans, Msgr. Francis J. '57 (BRK) [211] Queens, NY Our Lady of Grace Church.
Evans, G. William '78 (TR) Beverly, NJ St. Joseph Church.
Evans, George *s.s.s.* '57 (CLV) [P] Cleveland, OH Congregation of the Blessed Sacrament Provincial House; [P] Cleveland, OH Blessed Sacrament Community.
Evans, George *o.c.s.o.* '61 (SAT) San Antonio, TX Audie Murphy VA Hospital.
Evans, George J. *o.c.s.o.* '61 (ATL) [I] Conyers, GA The Monastery of the Holy Spirit.
Evans, George P. '77 (BO) [A] Boston, MA St. John's Seminary School of Theology; [A] Boston, MA St. John's Seminary.
Evans, James L. '94 (AUS) Dripping Springs, TX St. Martin de Porres Church.
Evans, John L., II '80 (FAR) Lisbon, ND St. Aloysius Church; Lisbon, ND Soldier's Home.
Evans, John Whitney '57 (DUL) Special Assignment.
Evans, Ken '86 (NEW) Scotch Plains, NJ Immaculate Heart of Mary Church.
Evans, Michael A. *s.j.* '83 (DET) [E] Detroit, MI Loyola High School.
Evans, Michael J. '92 (LA) Manhattan Beach, CA American Martyrs Church.
Evans, Paul J. '42 (DUB) Retired.
Evans, Richard A. '82 (CLV) [3] Parma, OH St. Charles Borromeo Church.
Evans, Richard D. '80 (CLV) [76] Cleveland, OH St. Vitus Church.
Evans, Msgr. Robert C. '73 (PRO) Cumberland, RI St. Joan's Church.
Evans, Tim '93 (DEN) [3] Lakewood, CO Our Lady of Fatima Church.
Evans, Timothy '94 (MOB) Daphne, AL Christ the King Church.
Evans, Timothy G. '73 (PIT) Elizabeth, PA St. Michael Church.
Evans, Wilfred F. '68 (SY) [10] Syracuse, NY St. Andrew the Apostle Church; Syracuse, NY Veterans Administration Hospital; Special Assignment.
Evans, William M. '81 (CHL) Absent On Leave.
Evard, Paul A. '61 (IND) On Duty Outside the Archdiocese.
Evatt, Thomas A. '76 (CHR) Aiken, SC St. Mary, Help of Christians Church; [H] Aiken, SC University of South Carolina, Aiken Extension Newman Center.
Eve, Paul W. '82 (L) Leave of Absence.
Evenson, Dennis D. '67 (STP) Northfield, MN St. Dominic Church.
Evenson, Robert L. '91 (SEA) Castle Rock, WA St. Mary Church; Kelso, WA St. Mary Church.
Everding, Richard F. '66 (STL) Fenton, MO St. Paul Church.
Everett, Willis E. '90 (COL) [32] Columbus, OH St. Michael Church.
Everitt, Edward *o.p.* '68 (MEM) [J] Memphis, TN Order Of Preachers (Southern Dominican Prov.).
Everling, Robert M. (SCR) Retired; [N] Dunmore, PA Villa St. Joseph.
Evernden, Michael E. *c.s.p.* '74 (WH) Morgantown, WV St. John's University Parish, Newman Hall Church.
Evers, Gerard A. '40 (CIN) [62] Cincinnati, OH St. Matthias Church; Retired.
Evers, Leonard M. '68 (GB) Cecil, WI St. Martin Church; Shawano, WI Sacred Heart Church.
Evers, Linus *c.pp.s.* '71 (SUP) Butternut, WI Immaculate Conception Church; Clam Lake, WI St. George Church; Glidden, WI Most Precious Blood Church.
Evers, Paul '80 (HON) Military Chaplains.
Evers, Paul C. '54 (WIN) Currie, MN Immaculate Heart of Mary Church.
Evers, Robert B. '60 (GRY) Lake Station, IN St. Francis Xavier Church.
Eversole, Paul M. '95 (ARL) Woodbridge, VA Our Lady of Angels Church.
Everts, Donald '95 (GB) [1] Marinette, WI Holy Family Church.
Every, Robert L. *o.p.* '55 (NO) [25] New Orleans, LA St. Anthony Of Padua Church.
Eves, John A. '41 (LA) Retired.
Evett, Lester J. *s.j.* '38 (DET) [P] Clarkston, MI Colombiere Center.
Evgler, Ernest '51 (DUB) Mount Vernon, IA St. John's the Baptist Church.
Evich, Paul J. *o.s.b.* '51 (BO) [W] Hingham, MA Glastonbury Abbey.
Evoy, John J. *s.j.* '43 (SPK) [C] Spokane, WA Gonzaga University.
Evrard, Donald J. '56 (IND) [F] Indianapolis, IN St. Vincent Hospital and Health Care Center, Inc.
Ewald, Daniel M.J. '86 (PCE) On Duty Outside the Diocese.
Ewen, Kurt '93 (ORL) Winter Park, FL St. Margaret Mary Church.
Ewen, Sharbel *o.s.b.* '88 (SD) [H] Oceanside, CA Prince of Peace Abbey, Benet Hill; [K] Oceanside, CA Prince of Peace Retreat Center.
Ewens, James M. *s.j.* '70 (MIL) [P] Milwaukee, WI Jesuit Community at Marquette University.
Ewert, J. Michael *o.f.m.* '59 (CHI) [X] Chicago, IL S.F.V., Inc.
Ewert, J. Michael *o.f.m.* '59 (FWT) [G] Crowley, TX St. Francis Village, Inc.; [G] Crowley, TX St. Francis Village, Inc.
Ewert, J. Michael *o.f.m.* '59 (IND) [40] Indianapolis, IN St. Roch Church.
Ewing, Matt J. *o.carm.* '54 (LA) [R] Los Angeles, CA Mount Carmel Priory, Carmelite Fathers and Brothers.
Ewing, Richard A. '46 (MET) Annandale, NJ Mountainview Youth Correctional Facility; Retired.
Exley, Thomas G. '46 (NU) Retired.
Extejt, John I. *o.s.f.s.* '85 (TOL) [C] Toledo, OH St. Francis de Sales High School; [K] Toledo, OH Oblates of St. Francis de Sales.
Extejt, Thomas J. '73 (TOL) [20] Toledo, OH St. Charles Borromeo Church.
Eyerman, Matthew S. '95 (CHI) [4] Chicago, IL St. Agatha Church.
Eylar, William D. '53 (CLV) [43] Cleveland, OH St. Leo the Great Church; Retired.
Eyman, Bryan R. '85 (PRM) Fairport Harbor, OH St. Michael Church; Mentor-on-the-Lake, OH St. Andrew the Apostle Church.
Ezaki, Bernard J. '88 (ALN) [7] Bethlehem, PA Notre Dame of Bethlehem Church; [C] Bethlehem, PA Bethlehem Catholic High School.
Eze, Anthony '78 (LA) [89] Los Angeles, CA St. Sebastian Church.
Eze, Cyprian '88 (LKC) Westlake, LA St. John Bosco Church.
Ezeibekwe, Samuel (FAR) [1] Grand Forks, ND Holy Family Church.
Ezerskis, Charles E. '61 (CHI) [5] Cicero, IL Our Lady of Charity Church.
Ezharath, Joseph (WH) Paden City, WV Mater Dolorosa Church; Sistersville, WV Holy Rosary Church.
Ezpericueta, Lucas '79 (FRS) Arvin, CA St. Thomas Church.

F

Faase, Albert A. '37 (CHR) Retired.
Faber, Emmett N. '55 (AUS) Bastrop, TX Federal Correctional Institute.
Faber, Emmett N. '55 (LC) On Duty Outside the Diocese.
Faber, Msgr. William '36 (FTW) Retired.
Fabian, Cyril *o.p.* '56 (WIN) [1] Winona, MN Cathedral of the Sacred Heart.
Fabian, Jack '68 (DET) [T] Detroit, MI Clergy Health Plan; [T] Newport, MI Companions of Christ the Lamb.
Fabian, John C. *o.p.* '59 (CHI) [N] Chicago, IL Dominicans (Provincial Office).
Fabian, John L. '48 (SCR) [3] Plymouth, PA St. Stephen's Church.
Fabiano, Philip F. *o.f.m.cap.* '64 (BRK) [87] Brooklyn, NY St. Michael's Church; [U] Brooklyn, NY St. Michael's Friary.
Fabing, Charles '39 (HEL) Retired; [B] Helena, MT Carroll College.
Fabing, Robert J. *s.j.* '74 (OAK) [N] Berkeley, CA Jesuit Community at Jesuit School of Theology at Berkeley.
Fabing, Robert J. *s.j.* '74 (SJ) [L] Los Altos, CA Jesuit Retreat House; [P] Los Altos, CA Jesuit Institute for Family Life.
Fabish, Rapael A. *o.p.* '53 (CHI) [N] Chicago, IL Dominicans (Provincial Office).
Fabish, Raphael '42 (PEO) [K] Rock Island, IL St. Anthony's Continuing Care Center; [N] Rock Island, IL St. Mary of the Angels Convent.

Fabisiak, Chester *s.j.* '39 (SFD) [2] Springfield, IL Blessed Sacrament Church.
Fabisinski, Msgr. Edmund J. '36 (NY) [194] Staten Island, NY St. Adalbert Church.
Fabj, Frank T. '84 (GAL) [6] Galveston, TX Sacred Heart Church.
Fabre, Richard '73 (LAF) Bayou Vista, LA St. Bernadette Church.
Fabre, Shelton J. '89 (BR) Grosse Tete, LA St. Joseph Church; Maringouin, LA Immaculate Heart of Mary Church.
Fabrizio, Henry E. '50 (Y) Retired.
Fabula, Vincent J. *o.c.s.o.* '68 (DAV) Sugar Creek, IA Sts. Mary and Joseph Church; [O] Wheatland, IA Our Lady of the Prairie Retreat.
Facci, John *s.a.c.* '71 (ALB) [6] Cohoes, NY St. Rita-Sacred Heart Church.
Facura, Joseph C. '68 (RIC) Norton, VA St. Anthony Church.
Fadallan, Elbert '80 (LUB) Plainview, TX Sacred Heart Church.
Fadden, Msgr. Joseph A. '54 (SCR) [11] Scranton, PA St. Clare Church.
Faddish, Alvin V. *o.f.m.* '63 (PAT) [5] Paterson, NJ St. Bonaventure Church.
Fader, John J. '47 (LA) On Duty Outside the Archdiocese.
Fador, Francis R. '96 (HRT) Madison, CT St. Margaret Church.
Fadrowski, Stanislaus '39 (SCL) Retired.
Fadrowski, William J. '87 (NEW) North Arlington, NJ Queen of Peace Church.
Faesser, Arthur A. '76 (GI) Kearney, NE Youth Development Center; [D] Kearney, NE University of Nebraska at Kearney Newman Apostolate.
Fafinski, Donald S. '66 (BUF) Jamestown, NY St. John Church.
Fagan, Arthur J. '67 (CHI) Elk Grove Village, IL Queen of the Rosary Church.
Fagan, Bernard D. *s.j.* '52 (RC) [4] Rapid City, SD St. Isaac Jogues Church; [B] Howes, SD Kino Jesuit Community.
Fagan, Msgr. Daniel E. '61 (RVC) Valley Stream, NY Holy Name of Mary Church.
Fagan, Edward J. *o.a.r.* '63 (NY) [154] Bronx, NY St. John's Church.
Fagan, Msgr. Emmet (BRK) [L] Brooklyn, NY Catholic Charities.
Fagan, George V., Jr. '69 (COS) [F] Colorado Springs, CO Mount St. Francis.
Fagan, Gerard F. *s.j.* '47 (NY) [Z] New York, NY Jesuit Community at Fordham University.
Fagan, Harry J. '51 (CLV) Madison, OH Immaculate Conception Church; Retired.
Fagan, John E. *s.j.* '83 (BO) [47] Boston, MA St. Mary of the Angels Church; [W] Boston, MA Loyola House; [W] Boston, MA The Society of Jesus of New England-Provincial Offices.
Fagan, Msgr. John T. '52 (BRK) [O] Brooklyn, NY Little Flower Children's Services.
Fagan, Msgr. John T. '52 (RVC) [G] Wading River, NY Little Flower Children's Services.
Fagan, Joseph K. '67 (BO) Stoughton, MA Immaculate Conception Church.
Fagan, Joseph P. '37 (NEW) Retired.
Fagan, Kevin '81 (FWT) Knox City, TX Santa Rosa Church; Rhineland, TX St. Joseph Church.
Fagan, Paul *c.p.* '86 (MET) [H] South River, NJ Passionist Provincial Office.
Fagan, Paul *c.p.* '86 (NY) [DD] New York, NY Passionist Residence.
Fagan, Msgr. Robert Emmet '55 (RVC) Bay Shore, NY St. Patrick's Church.
Fagan, Robert R. '58 (ALN) Tamaqua, PA St. Jerome Church.
Faggioni, Ernest *s.d.b.* '47 (NO) [2] Harvey, LA St. John Bosco Church.
Fagin, Gerald M. *s.j.* '69 (NO) [C] New Orleans, LA Loyola University.
Fagnani, Anthony G. '48 (NY) Retired.
Fagnant, Msgr. Donat J. '28 (PRO) Retired; [M] North Smithfield, RI St. Antoine Residence.
Fagone, Benedict *o.f.m.conv.* (HRT) [M] New Britain, CT Conventual Franciscans.
Fagot, Hacker J. *s.j.* '57 (BR) [J] Convent, LA Manresa, House of Retreats.
Faherty, William B. *s.j.* '44 (STL) [P] St. Louis, MO Jesuit Community Corporation at St. Louis University - Jesuit Hall; [P] St. Louis, MO The Jesuits of the Missouri Province; [W] St. Louis, MO The Museum of Western Jesuit Missions.
Fahey, Msgr. Charles J. '59 (BRK) [L] Brooklyn, NY Catholic Charities.
Fahey, Msgr. Charles J. '59 (NY) [Z] New York, NY Jesuit Community at Fordham University.
Fahey, Msgr. Charles J. '59 (SY) [19] Syracuse, NY St. Lucy Church; On Duty Outside the Diocese.
Fahey, Edward J., Jr. (TR) Leave of Absence.
Fahey, Edward J., Jr. (WIL) [5] Wilmington, DE St. Elizabeth Church.
Fahey, George *s.m.* '46 (MRY) [G] Santa Cruz, CA Society of Mary, Marists.
Fahey, Msgr. Gerard '51 (SR) [5] Santa Rosa, CA Star of the Valley Church.
Fahey, James *c.s.c.* '56 (FTW) [2] South Bend, IN St. Adalbert Church.
Fahey, James W. '70 (FR) Military Chaplains.
Fahey, John H. '61 (WH) Lubeck, WV St. Monica's Church; Ravenswood, WV St. Matthew Church.
Fahey, John K. *s.j.* '45 (NY) [Z] New York, NY Murray-Weigel Hall.
Fahey, John M. '54 (TUC) [3] Tucson, AZ Holy Family Church; Retired.
Fahey, John P. '84 (LA) [K] Los Angeles, CA St. Vincent Medical Center.
Fahey, John P. *c.ss.r.* '96 (DEN) [32] Denver, CO St. Joseph's Church.
Fahey, Joseph R. *s.j.* '68 (BO) [E] Boston, MA Boston College High School & Jesuit Community.
Fahey, Kevin '53 (R) Laurinburg, NC St. Mary Church.
Fahey, Michael A. *s.j.* '64 (BO) [W] Boston, MA The Society of Jesus of New England-Provincial Offices.
Fahey, Michael A. *s.j.* '64 (WDC) [V] Washington, DC Theological Studies, Inc.
Fahey, Robert *s.m.* '53 (SP) [7] Tampa, FL Our Lady of Perpetual Help Church.
Fahey, Thomas C. *o.f.m.* '47 (CHY) Retired.
Fahey, Thomas C. *o.f.m.* '47 (FTW) [K] Huntington, IN Victory Noll—Motherhouse of Our Lady of Victory Missionary Sisters.
Fahey, William M. '54 (PH) Eddystone, PA St. Rose of Lima Church.
Fahnbulleh, Augustine L. '78 (RVC) Mineola, NY Winthrop Hospital; [I] Port Jefferson, NY The St. Charles Corporation.
Fahnestock, John '71 (SB) Victorville, CA St. Joan of Arc Church.
Fahnlander, William J. '46 (BIS) Mandan, ND Christ the King Church; Retired.
Fahrbach, Paul '84 (TOL) Custar, OH St. Louis Church; Deshler, OH Immaculate Conception Church.
Fahy, Msgr. Francis J. '61 (BRK) [122] Brooklyn, NY Resurrection Church.
Fahy, Msgr. John J. '42 (NEW) [1] Orange, NJ St. John's Church; Retired; [N] Rutherford, NJ St. John Vianney Residence for Priests.
Fahy, Joseph A. *c.p.* '56 (ATL) [11] Atlanta, GA St. Paul of the Cross Church.
Fahy, Murty M. *o.s.f.s.* '58 (STO) Lodi, CA St. Anne Church.
Fahy, Thomas *o.s.b.* '57 (WDC) [M] Washington, DC St. Anselm's Abbey.
Faiella, William W. *c.s.c.* '79 (FTW) [J] South Bend, IN Congregation of Holy Cross Indiana Province Provincial House.
Failla, Anthony J. '56 (BRK) [38] Brooklyn, NY St. Finbar's Church; [L] Brooklyn, NY Catholic Charities.
Faiola, Msgr. Samuel J. '49 (BUF) Retired.
Faiola, Thomas *o.f.m.cap.* '85 (NY) [57] New York, NY St. John the Baptist Church.
Fairbairn, Frank E. (BO) Society of St. James the Apostle.
Fairbanks, Florian *o.s.b.* '39 (BIS) St. Anthony, ND St. Anthony Church; [A] Richardton, ND Assumption Abbey.
Fairbanks, Gregory J. '90 (PH) [34] Philadelphia, PA Christ the King Church.
Fairchild, Msgr. Edward J. '59 (COL) Westerville, OH St. Paul the Apostle Church.
Fairfield, Jeffry L. *o.carm.* '46 (STO) [5] Stockton, CA St. Gertrude Church.
Fairman, Timothy J. '88 (CHI) Arlington Heights, IL St. James Church.
Faistl, Clement '37 (COL) [10] Columbus, OH Christ the King Church; Retired.
Fait, Thomas G. '74 (MIL) Paris, WI St. John the Baptist Church.
Faith, Rudolph '41 (DUL) Retired.
Fajardo, Ricardo (NY) [65] New York, NY St. Jude Church.
Fajella, Francis J. *m.ss.a.* '82 (NY) Scarsdale, NY St. Pius X Church.
Fala, John G. '65 (PH) Ambler, PA St. Joseph Church; Absent on Sick Leave.
Falaniko, Mikaele '86 (SPP) [5] (Leone), AS Church of the Holy Cross.
Falardeau, Ernest *s.s.s.* '56 (SFE) [23] Albuquerque, NM St. Charles Borromeo Church.
Falardeau, Normand R. *s.s.s.* '52 (SFE) [23] Albuquerque, NM St. Charles Borromeo Church.
Falbo, Samuel J. '60 (SFE) [D] Albuquerque, NM St. Pius X High School.
Falco, Frank M. *o.s.m.* '67 (CHI) Hillside, IL St. Domitilla Church; [N] Chicago, IL Servite Friars - Eastern Province.
Falco, Ronald G. '81 (WOR) [1] Leominster, MA St. Anna's Church.
Falcone, Emillo '57 (RCK) Active Outside the Diocese.
Falduti, James *o.f.m.* '94 (R) [4] Raleigh, NC St. Francis of Assisi Church.
Faletoi Konelio '92 (HON) Papaikou, HI Immaculate Heart of Mary Church.
Faletta, Joseph '72 (ALB) Stuyvesant Falls, NY St. Mary Church.
Faletti, Stephen L. '83 (JC) Absent on Leave.
Faley, Roland *t.o.r.* '56 (RVC) [A] Huntington, NY Diocesan Seminary of the Immaculate Conception.
Faliskie, Edmund *c.ss.r.* '89 (BRK) [C] Whitestone, NY St. Alphonsus Formation Residence.
Falk, Conrad *o.s.b.* '52 (KC) [J] Conception, MO Conception Abbey.
Falk, Msgr. Dennis G. '57 (B) On Special Assignment.
Falk, Gerald R. '59 (GB) [8] Appleton, WI St. Thomas More Church.
Falkenhan, Pierce M. '80 (PIT) [2] Bridgeville, PA Holy Child Church.
Falkenthal, Thomas W. '75 (CHI) Military Chaplains.
Falla, Gustavo Adolfo '96 (BGP) [7] Bridgeport, CT St. Charles Church.
Faller, Henry E. '47 (KC) Retired.
Falletta, Frank J. '66 (ROC) [41] Rochester, NY St. Lawrence Church.
Falletta, Joseph '72 (ALB) Stuyvesant, NY Nativity of the Blessed Virgin Mary Church.
Fallon, Daniel R. '76 (CHI) [154] Chicago, IL Our Lady, Mother of the Church.
Fallon, David F. '70 (CLV) [70] Cleveland, OH San Juan Bautista Church; [X] Cleveland, OH Diocesan Hispanic Office.
Fallon, Francis H. *s.s.j.* '45 (BAL) [M] Baltimore, MD St. Joseph Society of the Sacred Heart House of Central Administration.
Fallon, James J. '62 (SY) Johnson City, NY St. James Church; Absent on Sick Leave.
Fallon, Msgr. James L. '43 (PAT) Morris Plains, NJ St. Virgilius Church; Retired.
Fallon, John '55 (OG) Absent on Sick Leave.
Fallon, John '69 (BIR) Tuscaloosa, AL Holy Spirit Church.
Fallon, John '95 (FAR) Pisek, ND St. John Nepomucene Church.
Fallon, John C.K. '71 (ATL) [9] Atlanta, GA St. Anthony of Padua Church; Atlanta, GA U.S. Penitentiary.
Fallon, John F.X. '61 (BO) Boston, MA V.A. Medical Centers; Awaiting Assignment.
Fallon, John J. '46 (BO) Ayer, MA St. Mary Church; Retired.
Fallon, John J. '52 (LA) Retired.
Fallon, John P. *o.s.f.s.* '60 (STO) [A] Stockton, CA St. Mary's High School.
Fallon, Joseph *s.j.* '53 (BO) [W] Chestnut Hill, MA The Jesuit Community at Boston College.
Fallon, Joseph P. '96 (NY) Middletown, NY St. Joseph Church.
Fallon, Marc *c.s.c.* '91 (BRK) [95] Brooklyn, NY Our Lady of Good Counsel Church.
Fallon, William J. '64 (CAM) Paulsboro, NJ St. John's Church.
Falls, Msgr. Thomas B. '32 (PH) Manoa, PA Sacred Heart Church; Retired.
Falotico, Ronald S. '69 (CAM) Pleasantville, NJ St. Peter's Church.
Falsetto, Francis J. *s.j.* '48 (SPK) [C] Spokane, WA Gonzaga University.
Falsey, James E. '70 (SAG) On Duty Outside the Diocese.
Falsey, James E. '72 (FBK) Koyukuk, AK St. Patrick Church; Nulato, AK Our Lady of the Snows Church.
Falsina, Vittorio *s.x.* '88 (CHI) [N] Chicago, IL Xaverian Missionaries (S.X.).
Falteisek, Edwin F. *s.j.* '57 (MIL) [P] Milwaukee, WI Jesuit Provincial Office, Wisconsin Province; [P] Milwaukee, WI Jesuit Community at Marquette University.
Falter, John F. *c.pp.s.* '61 (CIN) [M] Dayton, OH Provincial House of the Cincinnati Province of the Society of the Precious Blood.
Faluszczak, James G. '96 (E) Du Bois, PA St. Catherine Church.
Falvella, Richard J. '41 (BUR) Retired.
Falvey, Edmund F. '61 (WOR) [18] Worcester, MA St. Bernard Church.
Falvey, Jeremiah A. *c.s.sp.* '55 (PH) [Z] Bensalem, PA Congregation of the Holy Ghost Fathers and Brothers.
Falvey, Msgr. Sinon '45 (ORG) Retired.
Fama, Benjamin '83 (ORG) Fountain Valley, CA Holy Spirit Church.
Fama, Lawrence J. '92 (NEW) Livingston, NJ St. Philomena Church.
Fambrini, Robert A. *s.j.* '79 (LA) [R] Culver City, CA Ignatius House, The Novitiate of the California Province, Society of Jesus.
Fanale, James F. *c.s.v.* '69 (CHI) [N] Arlington Heights, IL Clerics of St. Viator-Provincial Residence; [N] Arlington Heights, IL Viatorian Province Center-Clerics of St. Viator.
Fane, Kevin R. *o.p.* '69 (CHI) [J] Evanston, IL Saint Francis Hospital of Evanston; [N] Chicago, IL Dominicans (Provincial Office).
Fanelli, Charles V. '71 (CHI) Northlake, IL St. John Baptist Vianney, Cure of Ars Church; [X] Northlake,

IL Italian Catholic Federation.
Fanelli, Msgr. Eugene A. '40 (NEW) [28] Newark, NJ Our Lady of Mt. Carmel Church; Fort Lee, NJ Madonna Church; Retired.
Fanelli, James G. '56 (HRT) [3] East Hartford, CT St. Christopher Church.
Faneman, Thomas M. '92 (OM) Norfolk, NE Sacred Heart Church.
Faneye, Benedict *o.p.* '94 (WDC) Washington, DC St. Elizabeth's Hospital (Government Operated).
Fangman, Frederick '63 (DUB) [H] Oelwein, IA Mercy Hospital of Franciscan Sisters.
Fangman, James E. '63 (SC) Kingsley, IA St. Michael's Church.
Fangman, Paul J. '49 (OM) Retired.
Fangman, Robert M. '54 (SC) Coon Rapids, IA Annunciation Church.
Fangman, Wilfred *o.s.b.* '49 (KCK) [9] Kansas City, KS SS. Cyril and Methodius Church; [13] Kansas City, KS St. Joseph and St. Benedict Church.
Fangmann, Frederick C. '63 (DUB) Oelwein, IA Sacred Heart Church.
Fangmeyer, Leroy J. '89 (WDC) [2] Rockville, MD Shrine of St. Jude Church; Pastoral Center Special Ministries.
Fanning, Gerard F. '38 (LAV) Retired.
Fanning, Gerard F. '38 (RNO) Retired.
Fanning, John E. '68 (NY) [99] New York, NY Our Lady of Victory Church.
Fanning, Leo M. '54 (ORL) Retired.
Fanning, Leo M. '54 (PAT) Retired.
Fanning, Patrick *ss.cc.* '83 (FR) [K] Fairhaven, MA Sacred Hearts Provincial House.
Fannon, Noel '61 (BLX) Waveland, MS St. Clare Church.
Fannon, Msgr. Robert C. '46 (Y) Retired.
Fannon, Thomas J. '41 (BAL) Retired.
Fanrak, James M. '71 (LR) Eureka Springs, AR St. Elizabeth's Church.
Fanta, Thomas G. '88 (CLV) Rocky River, OH St. Christopher Church.
Fanti, Joseph J. '90 (ALN) On Duty Outside the Diocese.
Fanti, Joseph J. '90 (SCR) [16] Scranton, PA St. Lucy's Church.
Fanucci, Santino J. '58 (SCR) [3] Nanticoke, PA St. Francis of Assisi Church.
Faour, George '91 (NEW) [4] Hoboken, NJ SS. Peter and Paul's Church.
Farabaugh, Kenneth '68 (BAL) Hickory, MD St. Ignatius Church.
Farace, Frederick A. (HBG) [G] Danville, PA Maria Hall; [I] Danville, PA Villa Sacred Heart.
Farace, Frederick A. '55 (HBG) Retired.
Faraci, Douglas F. '69 (BUF) Buffalo, NY Buffalo General Hospital; Buffalo, NY Roswell Park Memorial Institute.
Faraci, Francis '59 (LAN) [10] Flint, MI St. Mary Church.
Faraj, John *b.s.o.* '78 (NTN) Brooklyn, NY Church of the Virgin Mary.
Farana, Mario P. '71 (SFR) [42] San Francisco, CA St. Paul Church.
Farana, Nicholas E. '44 (SJ) [5] Sunnyvale, CA Church of The Resurrection; Retired.
Farano, Michael A. '68 (ALB) Loudonville, NY St. Pius X Church; Special Assignment.
Farao, John B. *o.f.m.conv.* '88 (FRS) Coalinga, CA St. Paul The Apostle Church.
Faraone, David J. '85 (ROC) Sodus, NY Epiphany Church.
Faraone, Emmanuel *o.f.m.* '41 (NY) [Z] New York, NY Padua Friary.
Faraone, Joseph J. '72 (NY) Carmel, NY St. James the Apostle Church.
Farbolin, Alberic *o.c.s.o.* '93 (ATL) [I] Conyers, GA The Monastery of the Holy Spirit.
Fardellone, Emil *s.d.b.* '42 (BO) [E] Boston, MA Don Bosco Preparatory School of Technology.
Fares, Lawrence T. '50 (DET) [4] Clinton Twp., MI St. Ronald Church.
Fareta, Albert M. '86 (BO) Hingham, MA St. Paul Church.
Faria, Andre H. '93 (FR) Centerville, MA Our Lady of Victory Church; [O] Fall River, MA Diocesean Catholic Youth Organization.
Faria, Carl M.D. '88 (MRY) Marina, CA St. Jude Parish Community Church; [J] Monterey, CA Department of Campus Ministry.
Faria, Manuel T. '38 (FR) [18] Fall River, MA St. Michael's Church.
Farias, Jorge '81 (BWN) Absent.
Farias, Joseph A. *s.d.b.* '64 (CC) [7] Laredo, TX San Luis Rey Church.
Farias, Joseph G. '75 (PAT) Mount Hope, NJ St. Bernard's Church; [O] Madison, NJ Drew University Catholic Campus Ministry; [O] Madison, NJ Fairleigh Dickinson University and Drew University.
Faricy, Robert L. *s.j.* '62 (MIL) [P] Milwaukee, WI Jesuit Provincial Office, Wisconsin Province.
Farin, Paul W. '88 (BRK) [47] Brooklyn, NY St. Francis Xavier Church; [F] Brooklyn, NY Bishop Loughlin Memorial High School.
Farina, Carlo A. *s.j.* '64 (SJ) [B] Santa Clara, CA Santa Clara University.
Farina, Edward '43 (PIT) Retired.
Farina, Msgr. Michael diTeccia '54 (WDC) [36] Washington, DC St. Patrick Church; [V] Washington, DC Paul VI Institute for the Arts.
Farina, Msgr. Michael F. '54 (WDC) Retired.
Farinango, Alberto *o.p.* (BRK) [11] Brooklyn, NY St. Anthony of Padua-St. Alphonsus Church.
Faris, John D. '76 (SAM) [D] Staten Island, NY Pastoral Center.
Farkas, Paul *o.f.m.cap.* '51 (PIT) [N] Pittsburgh, PA St. Augustine Friary.
Farke, Rodney '72 (SFS) Yankton, SD St. Benedict Church; [I] Yankton, SD The House of Mary Shrine, Inc.
Farland, David '74 (SPR) Absent on Leave.
Farland, George A. '68 (SPR) [12] Springfield, MA Sacred Heart Church.
Farland, Norman '66 (ORL) Bartow, FL St. Thomas Aquinas Church.
Farland, Roch *o.f.m.* '54 (DET) [5] Southfield, MI St. Michael Church.
Farleo, Brennan-Joseph *o.f.m.conv.* '86 (SY) [5] Binghamton, NY SS. Cyril and Method Church.
Farley, Bernard C. '68 (PH) Absent on Sick Leave.
Farley, David G. '52 (RVC) Wantagh, NY St. Frances de Chantal Church; Retired.
Farley, James V. '65 (PRO) Ashaway, RI Our Lady of Victory Church; Bradford, RI St. Vincent de Paul Church.
Farley, John B. '93 (PBL) Grand Junction, CO Immaculate Heart of Mary Church.
Farley, Msgr. John J. '62 (NY) [A] Yonkers, NY St. Joseph's Seminary.
Farley, Laurence F. '54 (RIC) Retired.
Farley, Leo O. '54 (NEW) Livingston, NJ St. Barnabas Medical Center.
Farley, Leslie A. '93 (LR) Engelberg, AR St. John the Baptist Church; Walnut Ridge, AR Immaculate Heart of Mary Church.
Farley, Thomas '79 (P) [P] Portland, OR University of Portland.
Farley, Thomas B. '79 (P) McMinnville, OR St. James Church.
Farmer, Bruce '81 (TOL) Marygrove, OH Immaculate Conception Church.
Farmer, Bruce L. '81 (TOL) [20] Toledo, OH St. Charles Borromeo Church; Richfield Center, OH St. Elizabeth of Hungary Church.
Farmer, J. Kevin '93 (BAL) Frederick, MD St. John the Evangelist Church.
Farmer, James '79 (BAL) [89] Baltimore, MD St. Thomas Aquinas Church.
Farmer, Matthew P. '81 (LEX) Special Assignment.
Farmer, Michael '95 (MOB) [3] Montgomery, AL St. Bede Church.
Farmer, Regis M. '73 (PIT) Wildwood, PA St. Catherine of Sweden Church.
Farmer, Richard R. *o.p.* '55 (CHI) [N] River Forest, IL St. Thomas Aquinas Priory.
Farnan, Donald '87 (KC) [24] Kansas City, MO St. Louis Church; [38] Kansas City, MO St. Therese Little Flower Church.
Farnik, John M. *c.ss.r.* '62 (GAL) [33] Houston, TX Holy Ghost Church.
Farragher, Leo J. *s.s.j.* '37 (BAL) [I] Baltimore, MD St. Joseph Medical Center.
Farrand, John L. *s.j.* '53 (NY) [F] New York, NY Loyola School; [Z] New York, NY St. Ignatius Loyola Residence.
Farre, Ramon '53 (LA) Ventura, CA Sacred Heart Church; [A] Camarillo, CA St. John's Seminary College of the Archdiocese of Los Angeles.
Farre, Raymond P. '41 (TR) Retired.
Farrel, Patrick J. *o.c.d.* '62 (MIL) [P] Holy Hill, WI Discalced Carmelite Monastery.
Farrell, Anthony G. '64 (DAV) Grinnell, IA St. Mary's Church.
Farrell, Bernard '65 (BLX) Ocean Springs, MS St. Alphonsus Church.
Farrell, Charles D. *o.p.* '54 (DET) [21] Detroit, MI St. Dominic Church.
Farrell, Dennis J. '73 (BRK) [58] Brooklyn, NY Holy Name Church.
Farrell, Donald J. '54 (PH) East Lansdowne, PA St. Cyril of Alexandria Church; Retired.
Farrell, Edmund J. '43 (GR) Retired.
Farrell, Emmet L. '65 (SD) San Ysidro, CA Our Lady of Mt. Carmel Church.
Farrell, Emmett L. '65 (SC) On Duty Outside the Diocese.
Farrell, Msgr. Francis '55 (BLX) [2] Biloxi, MS Our Lady of Fatima Church; Biloxi, MS V.A. Center.
Farrell, George A. '96 (MET) Somerset, NJ St. Matthias Church.
Farrell, Gerard *o.s.b.* '46 (SCL) [I] Collegeville, MN St. John's Abbey, of the Order of St. Benedict.
Farrell, J. Aloysius *c.s.p.* '43 (NY) [Z] Scarsdale, NY Paulist Fathers Generalate.
Farrell, James *s.j.* '46 (CLV) [E] Cleveland, OH St. Ignatius High School; [U] Cleveland, OH Jesuit Retreat House.
Farrell, James '56 (OAK) [N] Oakland, CA Redemptorists.
Farrell, Jeremiah *s.s.* '87 (SFR) [U] Menlo Park, CA Vatican II Institute for Clergy Formation.
Farrell, John *c.ss.r.* '48 (BAL) [85] Baltimore, MD Sacred Heart of Jesus Church.
Farrell, John E. '62 (BO) Lynnfield, MA Our Lady of the Assumption Church.
Farrell, John F. '47 (PRO) Retired.
Farrell, Msgr. John J. '34 (CHI) Berwyn, IL St. Leonard Church; Retired.
Farrell, John J. *o.s.a.* '59 (PH) [C] Villanova, PA Villanova University; [Z] Villanova, PA St. Thomas Monastery.
Farrell, John P. *o.p.* '39 (NY) [AA] Blauvelt, NY Congregation of St. Dominic General Motherhouse of the Sisters of St. Dominic of Blauvelt.
Farrell, Joseph '74 (TR) Tabernacle, NJ Holy Eucharist Church.
Farrell, Joseph L. *o.s.a.* '91 (BO) [CC] North Andover, MA Merrimack College Campus Ministry Center.
Farrell, Joseph L. '95 (PH) Upper Gwynedd, PA Corpus Christi Church.
Farrell, Msgr. Kevin J. '78 (WDC) Pastoral Center Special Ministries.
Farrell, Kevin R. '65 (JOL) Wood Dale, IL Holy Ghost Church.
Farrell, Lawrence *o.p.* '71 (SB) [E] Riverside, CA St. Vincent Ferrer House.
Farrell, Martin *o.s.d.* '78 (OG) Bombay, NY St. Joseph Church; Fort Covington, NY St. Mary Church.
Farrell, Michael A. '70 (ORL) Palm Bay, FL St. Joseph Church.
Farrell, Michael J. *s.s.j.* '60 (GAL) [8] Houston, TX St. Anne de Beaupre Church.
Farrell, Patrick '60 (JKS) Greenville, MS St. Joseph Church.
Farrell, Patrick E. '61 (VEN) Holmes Beach, FL St. Bernard's Church.
Farrell, Paul *c.ss.r.* '52 (STL) [P] Liguori, MO Liguori Mission House/Redemptorists.
Farrell, Philip N. '93 (PIT) Green Tree, PA St. Margaret Church.
Farrell, Richard T. '84 (ROC) Elmira, NY St. Joseph Hospital.
Farrell, Robert *s.j.* '64 (BO) [W] Chestnut Hill, MA The Jesuit Community at Boston College.
Farrell, Robert J. '80 (CIN) [67] Cincinnati, OH Nativity of Our Lord Church.
Farrell, Seamus J. '67 (OAK) [2] Hayward, CA St. Bede Church.
Farrell, Thomas '82 (LEX) Carlisle, KY Shrine of Our Lady of Guadalupe Church.
Farrell, Thomas '92 (GB) [2] Appleton, WI St. Bernard Church.
Farrell, Thomas F. '43 (HRT) Windsor Locks, CT St. Robert Bellarmine Church.
Farrell, Thomas P. '82 (LEX) Paris, KY Annunciation of the Blessed Virgin Mary Church.
Farrell, Timothy '89 (GLP) Farmington, NM Sacred Heart Church.
Farrell, Walter L. *s.j.* '47 (DET) [K] Detroit, MI Jesuit Provincial Office-Detroit Province of the Society of Jesus.
Farrell, William '78 (CHL) On Duty Outside the Diocese.
Farrell, William J. '47 (MIL) Retired.
Farrell, William J. *s.j.* '52 (NY) [Z] New York, NY Murray-Weigel Hall; [Z] New York, NY St. Ignatius Loyola Residence.
Farrelly, John *o.s.b.* '55 (WDC) [M] Washington, DC St. Anselm's Abbey.
Farrelly, John P. '84 (ATL) Carrollton, GA Church of Our Lady of Perpetual Help; [L] Atlanta, GA Campus Ministry.
Farrelly, Matthew *c.s.sp.* '42 (NY) [2] New York, NY St. Agnes Church.
Farrelly, Peter T. *s.j.* '53 (BO) [W] Weston, MA Campion Health Center, Inc.
Farrelly, Msgr. Terence J. '50 (ORL) Rockledge, FL St. Mary's Church; Retired.
Farrelly, Thomas '61 (NY) [134] Bronx, NY Blessed Sacrament Church.
Farren, Edward J. *s.j.* '62 (PH) [Z] Philadelphia, PA Jesuit Community at St. Joseph's University.
Farren, John Aquinas *o.p.* (NY) [Z] New York, NY St. Vincent Ferrer Priory.
Farrera, Rafael *s.m.* '70 (ELP) [11] El Paso, TX La Purisima Church.
Farricker, William J. *s.j.* '43 (NY) [Z] New York, NY Murray-Weigel Hall.
Farris, Daniel L. '67 (SFE) [19] Albuquerque, NM Santuario San Martin de Porres Church.
Farris, James M. '76 (ORG) Inactive Leave.
Farris, John V. *c.m.* (STL) [P] St. Louis, MO Vincentian Bellerive Residence.
Farris, Msgr. Semaan '54 (ORL) Retired.

Farris, William J. *o.f.m.* '77 (IND) Batesville, IN St. Louis Church; St. Peter, IN St. Peter Church.
Farrugia, David *o.p.* '60 (SB) [E] Riverside, CA St. Vincent Ferrer House; [H] Riverside, CA St. Andrews Newman Center.
Farrugia, David *o.p.* '90 (SB) [10] Riverside, CA St. Andrew's Newman Center Church.
Farrugia, Edwin W. '60 (SFR) [15] San Francisco, CA St. Elizabeth Church.
Farry, John A. '65 (CHI) [204] Chicago, IL St. Thomas Apostle Church.
Farry, John J. '67 (PH) [87] Philadelphia, PA St. Leo Church.
Farsaci, Francis A. *o.s.a.* '64 (PH) [C] Villanova, PA Villanova University; [Z] Villanova, PA St. Thomas Monastery.
Farwell, Richard B. '81 (CHL) Lincolnton, NC St. Dorothy Church.
Fasano, Jerome '77 (ARL) Great Falls, VA St. Catherine of Siena Church.
Faschan, Matthew '46 (BR) Retired.
Fasching, Felix J. '45 (NU) Regal, MN St. Anthony (Mission) Church; Spicer, MN Our Lady of the Lakes Church.
Fasciglione, Max S. '74 (CAM) Cape May Court House, NJ Our Lady of the Angels Church.
Fasline, Anthony '62 (Y) Retired.
Faso, Charles '67 (CHI) [N] Chicago, IL St. Peter's Friary.
Fassbender, Anthony D. *c.m.* '38 (NO) [P] New Orleans, LA Vincentian Fathers.
Fassbinder, Richard W. '53 (CHI) Lake Villa, IL Prince of Peace Church.
Fassero, Jonathan *o.s.b.* '78 (IND) [B] St. Meinrad, IN St. Meinrad Seminary-College of Liberal Arts; [J] St. Meinrad, IN St. Meinrad Archabbey.
Fassett, Edward S. *s.j.* '88 (SFR) [E] San Francisco, CA St. Ignatius College Preparatory (Coed); [N] San Francisco, CA Jesuit Community at St. Ignatius College Preparatory.
Fata, Joseph A. '68 (Y) Boardman, OH St. Luke Church.
Fater, Douglas '70 (SAT) [10] San Antonio, TX Holy Trinity Church.
Fath, Gerald *o.p.* '71 (NO) [P] New Orleans, LA Dominican Fathers & Brothers, Southern Dominican Province.
Fath, Howard *m.s.c.* '61 (RCK) [H] Aurora, IL Missionaries of the Sacred Heart Community.
Fath, Robert *c.m.f.* '79 (CHI) [N] Chicago, IL Claretian Missionaries, St. Jude League, Inc.; [N] Oak Park, IL Claretian Fathers Headquarters of U.S.A. Eastern Province.
Fatooh, Charles G. '85 (MRY) Seaside, CA St. Francis Xavier Church; Special Assignment.
Fatora, Joachim R. *o.s.b.* '54 (ALT) Hastings, PA St. Bernard Church.
Faucher, Eugene J. '51 (CHI) Arlington Heights, IL St. Edna Church; Retired.
Faucher, Henry '52 (SR) Cloverdale, CA St. Peter's Church.
Faucher, W. Thomas '71 (B) On Duty Outside the Diocese.
Faucher, W. Thomas '71 (BAK) Sisters, OR St. Edward Church.
Faugno, Valerian *o.f.m.* (BO) [W] Brighton, MA St. Bonaventure Friary, Franciscan Friars.
Faul, Charles '80 (RIC) [2] Virginia Beach, VA Church of the Holy Apostles.
Faulhaber, Gregory *s.t.d.* '79 (BUF) [A] East Aurora, NY Christ the King Seminary; [A] East Aurora, NY Christ the King Seminary.
Faulkner, Matthew *o.carm.* '89 (BRK) [140] Brooklyn, NY St. Thomas Aquinas Church.
Faure, Dominique '90 (PEO) [O] Peoria, IL Newman Foundation at Bradley University & Illinois Central College.
Fauser, Arthur W. (DET) Farmington, MI Our Lady of Sorrows Church.
Fauser, Arthur W. '50 (DET) Retired.
Faust, Gary J. '78 (STL) Richmond Heights, MO Immacolata Church.
Faust, Louis J. '74 (WDC) Baden, MD St. Michael Church.
Faust, William (RNO) [B] Reno, NV St. Mary's Regional Medical Center.
Faustina, John '47 (PHX) Prescott, AZ Sacred Heart Church.
Faustina, John M. '47 (PHX) Retired.
Faustner, William J. '76 (COL) Kenton, OH Immaculate Conception Church.
Fausz, Kevin P. *c.m.* '91 (STL) Perryville, MO St. Vincent De Paul Church; Silver Lake, MO St. Rose of Lima Church; [W] St. Louis, MO St. Vincent de Paul Educational Foundation.
Favalora, John Clement '61 (MIA) [B] Opa Locka, FL St. Thomas University.
Favara, Joseph F. '41 (SAG) Mount Pleasant, MI Sacred Heart Church; Retired.
Favreau, Bruce T. '80 (OG) Lake Clear, NY St. John in the Wilderness Church.
Favret, J. Raymond '48 (CIN) West Chester, OH St. John Church.
Fawcett, Msgr. Henry F. '64 (SD) [13] San Diego, CA Our Lady of Mt. Carmel Church.
Fawls, Msgr. Daniel J. (BUF) Harris Hill, NY Nativity of the Blessed Virgin Mary Church.
Fay, David E. '64 (CIN) [29] Cincinnati, OH St. Gabriel Church.
Fay, Gregory J. '76 (STA) Switzerland, FL San Juan Del Rio Church.
Fay, John F. *m.m.* '52 (NY) [Z] Maryknoll, NY Maryknoll Fathers and Brothers.
Fay, Michael Jude '78 (BGP) Darien, CT St. John Church.
Fay, Robert D. '67 (BO) Absent on Sick Leave.
Fay, William J. '64 (GBG) [A] Latrobe, PA St. Vincent Seminary.
Fay, William J. '64 (PIT) On Duty Outside the Diocese.
Fay, William P. (BO) On Duty Outside the Archdiocese.
Fayad, Samuel J. *c.s.s.* '48 (NY) [4] White Plains, NY Our Lady of Mt. Carmel Church.
Fayad, Samuel J. *c.s.s.* '48 (WOR) Milford, MA Sacred Heart Church.
Fayle, Vaughn J. *o.m.i.* '87 (SAT) [B] San Antonio, TX George Sexton House of Studies; [C] San Antonio, TX Oblate School of Theology.
Fazio, Carmine *o.f.m.cap.* '75 (PAT) Denville, NJ St. Clare Hospital; [J] Denville, NJ Sisters of the Sorrowful Mother Health Care Ministry Corp.
Fazio, Cosimo '48 (NY) [3] New Rochelle, NY St. Joseph Church.
Fazio, Paul *o.f.m.conv.* (MRY) [G] Arroyo Grande, CA St. Joseph Cupertino Province, Provincial Center.
Fazio, Paul *o.f.m.conv.* '74 (OAK) San Pablo, CA St. Paul Church; [N] San Pablo, CA Franciscans, Conventual of California.
Fazzalaro, Msgr. Francis J. '45 (MIA) [5] Pompano Beach, FL St. Gabriel Church.
Fealey, Edward J. '86 (CHI) Western Springs, IL St. John of the Cross Church.
Fearon, John F. '51 (CHI) Forest Park, IL St. Bernardine Church; Retired.
Fecci, Albert *o.m.i.* '46 (SAT) [K] San Antonio, TX Oblate Madonna Residence.
Feccia, Augusto *c.s.* '62 (LA) [Q] Sun Valley, CA Villa Scalabrini.
Fecher, Msgr. Vincent '50 (SAT) Hondo, TX St. John the Evangelist Church.
Fechhelm, Richard A. '48 (MIL) Retired.
Fechner, Erich A. '92 (STL) Cottleville, MO St. Joseph Church.
Fecht, Geoffrey *o.s.b.* '76 (SCL) [I] Collegeville, MN St. John's Abbey, of the Order of St. Benedict.
Fecko, Leonard '89 (CIN) [Q] Cincinnati, OH University of Cincinnati Newman Center.
Fecko, Leonard J. '89 (CIN) [65] Cincinnati, OH St. Monica-St. George Parish Newman Center Church.
Fecteau, Raymond L. '72 (WDC) Darnestown, MD Our Lady of the Visitation Church.
Fedders, Albert V. *m.m.* '37 (NY) [Z] Maryknoll, NY Maryknoll Fathers and Brothers.
Fedders, William J. '68 (LEX) Paintsville, KY St. Michael Catholic Church.
Feddish, Msgr. Basil '31 (STF) Retired.
Fedell, Anthony *o.f.m.* '66 (NY) [35] New York, NY St. Francis of Assisi Church.
Federici, Martin J. '66 (BGP) [1] Bridgeport, CT St. Augustine Cathedral; Leave of Absence.
Federico, Cesidio J. '57 (WH) Clarksburg, WV Immaculate Conception Church.
Federico, Ralph P. '52 (BUF) Bemus Point, NY Our Lady of Lourdes Church.
Federline, Thomas A. '85 (GBG) Brady's Bend, PA St. Patrick Church; Parker, PA St. Mary, Our Lady of the Snows Church.
Fedewa, Eugene F. '36 (DET) Harper Woods, MI Our Lady Queen of Peace Church; Retired.
Fedewa, Matthew J. '58 (LAN) Morrice, MI St. Mary Church.
Fedewa, Sylvester L. '54 (LAN) [6] Lansing, MI St. Gerard Church.
Fedigan, F. Terrence '74 (PIT) South Park Township, PA Nativity Church.
Fedigan, James J. *s.j.* '65 (NY) [Z] New York, NY Murray-Weigel Hall.
Fedor, Gregory '83 (Y) Boardman, OH St. Luke Church; [C] Youngstown, OH Cardinal Mooney High School.
Fedor, Lawrence M. *o.s.b.* (LC) [E] Marshfield, WI St. Joseph's Hospital.
Fedor, Lawrence M. *o.s.b.* '76 (TUC) [F] St. David, AZ Holy Trinity Monastery.
Fedor, Mark Q. '72 (CLV) [13] Cleveland, OH St. Boniface Church.
Fedor, Robert P. '61 (E) Conneautville, PA St. Peter Church.
Fedora, Joseph *m.m.* '84 (NY) [Z] Maryknoll, NY Maryknoll Fathers and Brothers.
Fedorek, Msgr. Joseph J. '53 (PHU) Elizabeth, NJ St. Vladimir's Church.
Fedorowich, Msgr. Michael '55 (PHU) Shamokin, PA Transfiguration of Our Lord Church.
Fedyk, Msgr. Jaroslaw (SJP) Retired.
Fee, Msgr. John B. '37 (PH) [23] Philadelphia, PA St. Bernard Church; Retired.
Fee, John M. *ss.cc.* '56 (DET) Harper Woods, MI Our Lady Queen of Peace Church.
Fee, Pat '61 (ORG) Laguna Hills, CA St. Nicholas Church.
Fee, Msgr. Paul A. '40 (BEA) Retired.
Feehan, Stephen S. '62 (NEW) Bloomfield, NJ Church of St. Thomas the Apostle.
Feehily, John W. '73 (OKL) [16] (Midwest City), OK St. Philip Neri Church.
Feela, Paul F. '78 (STP) [A] St. Paul, MN The Saint Paul Seminary; [C] St. Paul, MN University of St. Thomas.
Feeley, Sylvester E. *c.ss.r.* '48 (BRK) [107] Brooklyn, NY Our Lady of Perpetual Help Basilica.
Feeley, Thomas M. *c.s.c.* '55 (FR) [B] North Easton, MA Stonehill College; [P] Norton, MA Wheaton College Newman Center.
Feely, Msgr. James B. '58 (GB) [6] Green Bay, WI St. John Church; [M] Chambers Island, WI Holy Name Retreat House.
Feely, Thomas H. *s.j.* '75 (NY) [F] New York, NY Regis High School; [Z] New York, NY St. Ignatius Loyola Residence.
Feenan, Msgr. J. Francis '53 (PAT) Convent Station, NJ St. Thomas More Church.
Feeney, Bernard (PAT) Retired.
Feeney, Edward '37 (E) [13] Erie, PA St. Ann Church.
Feeney, Francis M. '33 (ROC) Penfield, NY Holy Spirit Church; Retired.
Feeney, J. Edward '37 (E) Retired.
Feeney, John *s.m.a.* '41 (NEW) [N] Tenafly, NJ Society of African Missions, Provincialate, S.M.A. Fathers.
Feeney, John J. '54 (PRT) Cape Elizabeth, ME St. Bartholomew Church.
Feeney, John J. '55 (LA) Retired.
Feeney, John P. '52 (GB) Retired.
Feeney, Joseph J. *s.j.* '65 (PH) [C] Philadelphia, PA St. Joseph's University; [Z] Philadelphia, PA Jesuit Community at St. Joseph's University; [Z] Philadelphia, PA St. Alphonsus House.
Feeney, Kevin J. '77 (CHI) [196] Chicago, IL St. Sylvester Church.
Feeney, Msgr. Leo J. '66 (DAV) [M] Davenport, IA St. Vincent Center.
Feeney, Michael *o.s.b.* '46 (SEA) [G] Tacoma, WA St. Joseph Medical Center; [M] Lacey, WA St. Martin's Abbey.
Feeney, Michael *o.f.m.* '48 (BO) [BB] Boston, MA St. Anthony Shrine.
Feeney, Robert E. '56 (BIS) Mandan, ND St. Joseph Church.
Feeney, Robert E. '56 (GBG) Ford City, PA Holy Trinity Church.
Feeney, Robert J. '51 (LA) Retired.
Feeney, Robert T. '86 (PH) [77] Philadelphia, PA St. John the Baptist Church.
Feeney, Thomas '79 (CC) Refugio, TX Our Lady of Refuge Church.
Feeney, Thomas M. '48 (PH) Retired.
Feeney, Thomas P. '79 (CC) Refugio, TX St. James the Apostle Church.
Feeney, William P. '72 (PIT) Monongahela, PA Transfiguration Church.
Feeser, William '77 (SAC) [7] Sacramento, CA Presentation of the Blessed Virgin Mary Church.
Fegan, William P. '75 (CHI) Berwyn, IL St. Odilo Church.
Fehlner, Peter Damian Mary of the Sacred *f.f.i.* '57 (FR) [K] New Bedford, MA Marian Friary of Our Lady, Queen of the Seraphic Order.
Fehn, Jerome W. '78 (STP) Edina, MN Our Lady of Grace Church; Edina, MN Fairview-Southdale Hospital; St. Louis Park, MN Methodist Hospital.
Fehrenbach, Charles (ALB) [L] Saratoga Springs, NY St. John Neumann Residence.
Fehrenbach, Charles G. *c.ss.r.* '35 (PH) [135] Philadelphia, PA St. Peter the Apostle Church.
Fehrenbach, James *o.f.m.* '71 (CIN) [M] Cincinnati, OH St. Francis Seraph Friary.
Fehring, Fabian *o.f.m.cap.* '53 (GF) Hardin, MT St. Joseph's Church.
Feicht, Donald L. '70 (Y) Alliance, OH St. Joseph's Church.
Feichter, Paul *o.f.m.* '47 (SP) [O] St. Petersburg, FL St. Anthony Friary.
Feierfeil, Gerald F. '67 (SC) Boone, IA Sacred Heart Church; [B] Algona, IA Bishop Garrigan Catholic High School.
Feifel, Eugene '27 (LA) Retired.
Feigh, Conan E. *o.s.b.* '57 (ALT) [I] University Park, PA Penn State Catholic Community.
Feil, Carl *o.s.m.* (SFE) Tome, NM Immaculate Conception Church.
Feil, Carl M. *o.s.m.* '61 (CHI) [N] Chicago, IL Servite Friars - Eastern Province.
Feild, Martin Eugene '59 (BAL) Taneytown, MD St. Joseph Church.

Feiss, Hugh *o.s.b.* '66 (B) [C] Jerome, ID Ascension Priory.
Feiss, Hugh *o.s.b.* '66 (P) [L] St. Benedict, OR Mt. Angel Abbey.
Feit, Matthias '56 (PHX) Retired.
Feiten, Msgr. J. Richard '48 (WIN) [F] Winona, MN St. Anne Hospice, Inc.
Fekete, George J. '65 (GR) Lowell, MI St. Mary's Church.
Feketie, Michael J. '57 (NEW) Rahway, NJ St. Mary's Church.
Felczak, Leonard J. '44 (CHI) [198] Chicago, IL St. Tarcissus Church; Retired.
Feld, Norbert F. *s.s.c.* '49 (PRO) [P] Bristol, RI St. Columban's Retirement House.
Feldbrugge, Theo M. *m.h.m.* '54 (LA) [R] Los Angeles, CA Mill Hill Missionaries Procure.
Feldcamp, William J. '65 (SCR) Carbondale, PA St. Rose of Lima Church.
Feldhaus, Msgr. Eugene A. '46 (BRK) [172] Queens, NY St. Gerard Majella Church; Retired.
Feldhaus, Thomas F. '76 (CIN) Ripley, OH St. Michael Church.
Feldkamp, Angelo J. *o.praem.* '68 (GB) [I] De Pere, WI St. Norbert Abbey.
Feldman, George J. *o.praem.* '43 (GB) [I] De Pere, WI St. Joseph Priory.
Feldmann, Jerome W. '58 (BEL) Marydale, IL St. Teresa of Avila Church.
Feldmeier, Peter E. '87 (STP) [A] St. Paul, MN The Saint Paul Seminary; [C] St. Paul, MN University of St. Thomas.
Feldner, William *s.v.d.* '74 (NO) [50] New Orleans, LA St. Paul the Apostle Church.
Felice, John M. *o.f.m.* (NY) [35] New York, NY St. Francis of Assisi Church; [Z] New York, NY Franciscan Friars, Order of Friars Manor; [DD] New York, NY Shrine of St. Jude, Inc.
Felice-Pace, Albert *o.p.* '60 (TUC) [I] Tucson, AZ University of Arizona.
Felices, Fernando '82 (SJN) [B] Rio Piedras, PR Seminario Mayor Interdiocesano Santa Maria de los Angeles.
Felion, Jerome '47 (CR) Retired.
Felix, Bernard J. '37 (CIN) Retired.
Felix, Paul '90 (GAL) [2] Spring, TX St. Edward Church.
Felix, William P. '81 (LC) Chippewa Falls, WI St. Charles Borromeo Church; Cooks Valley, WI St. John the Baptist Church; Tilden, WI St. Peter Church; [N] Tilden, WI Institute of St. Joseph.
Feliz, Normando '75 (VEN) LaBelle, FL Our Lady Queen of Heaven Church.
Felker, Joseph F. '73 (SB) Redlands, CA Sacred Heart Church.
Fell, Arnold A. *c.s.c.* '43 (FTW) [L] Notre Dame, IN Holy Cross Mission House.
Fell, Gall *o.s.b.* '33 (SCL) [I] Collegeville, MN St. John's Abbey, of the Order of St. Benedict.
Fell, John N. '88 (MET) Whitehouse Station, NJ Our Lady of Lourdes Church.
Feller, Donald J. '46 (GB) Retired.
Feller, Richard J. '53 (CHI) South Holland, IL Holy Ghost Church.
Fellner, Msgr. John V. '49 (BEL) Retired.
Fellrath, Frank W. '89 (MET) Fords, NJ Our Lady of Peace Church.
Felock, Michael '52 (PRM) Barberton, OH St. Nicholas Church.
Felsecker, Henry J. *m.m.* '31 (SJ) [M] Los Altos, CA Maryknoll.
Felt, James W. *s.j.* '56 (SJ) [B] Santa Clara, CA Santa Clara University.
Felt, Richard '69 (PHX) [3] Scottsdale, AZ St. Bernadette Church.
Felten, John N. *s.j.* (CIN) [M] Cincinnati, OH Faber Jesuit Community.
Feltis, Jerome '79 (FAR) Absent on Leave.
Feltman, Harold R. '55 (GR) Retired.
Feltman, Philip S. '66 (TOL) Sandusky, OH St. Mary Church.
Felton, Daniel J. '81 (GB) [7] Oshkosh, WI St. Raphael the Archangel Church.
Feltz, John G. '73 (BUR) Fairfax, VT St. Luke Church.
Feltz, Joseph E. '79 (PIT) [3] Charleroi, PA Mary Mother of the Church.
Feltz, Thomas F. '85 (LA) Bellflower, CA St. Bernard Church.
Femenia, Nicholas '25 (SAN) Retired.
Femenia, Nicholas '25 (SAT) Retired.
Feminelli, John '87 (CC) On Special Assignment.
Feminelli, John J. '87 (CC) Tivoli, TX Our Lady of Guadalupe Church.
Femminineo, Joseph P. '58 (DET) Retired.
Fenech, Francis '50 (PMB) Retired.
Fenech, Francis X. '50 (PMB) Lake Worth, FL Sacred Heart Church.
Fenelon, David (DM) Retired.
Fenger, Guy '77 (MIA) Sunrise, FL All Saints Church; [C] Fort Lauderdale, FL St. Thomas Aquinas High School.
Fenili, J. Robert *c.ss.r.* '62 (DEN) [M] Denver, CO The Redemptorists/Denver Province.
Fenlon, John (SY) [W] Cortland, NY St. Mary.
Fenlon, John P. '70 (SY) Cortland, NY St. Mary Church.
Fenlon, Thomas B. '61 (NY) [89] New York, NY Our Lady of Lourdes Church.
Fenlon, Thomas J. '42 (HEL) Helmville, MT St. Thomas Church; Retired.
Fenn, William (SEA) Bellevue, WA St. Louise Church.
Fennell, Joseph G. *s.j.* '45 (BO) [W] Weston, MA Campion Health Center, Inc.
Fennell, Patrick A. *o.s.b.* '89 (PEO) [A] Peru, IL St. Bede Abbey and Academy.
Fenner, Charles J. *c.s.sp.* '54 (PIT) [B] Pittsburgh, PA Duquesne University of the Holy Ghost.
Fenner, Eric *o.f.m.conv.* '46 (TR) Seaside Park, NJ St. Catharine of Siena Church.
Fennessey, Luke T. '42 (SPR) Retired; [H] Springfield, MA St. Michael's Residence.
Fennessy, James J. '68 (ATL) Lilburn, GA St. John Neumann Church.
Fennessy, Joseph H. '56 (HBG) Berwick, PA Immaculate Conception of the Blessed Virgin Mary Church.
Fennessy, Keith '84 (NY) Manhattan, NY Terence Cardinal Cooke Health Care Center.
Fennessy, Keith Gerard '84 (NY) [V] New York, NY Terence Cardinal Cooke Health Care Center.
Fennessy, Peter *s.j.* '70 (CLV) [C] Cleveland, OH John Carroll University.
Fennessy, Peter J. *s.j.* '70 (BO) [W] Boston, MA The Society of Jesus of New England-Provincial Offices.
Fennessy, Peter J. *s.j.* '70 (CLV) [C] Cleveland, OH John Carroll Jesuit Community.
Fenske, Donald J. '58 (CHI) Calumet City, IL Our Lady of Knock Church.
Fenstermaker, James E. *c.s.c.* '84 (BRK) [95] Brooklyn, NY Our Lady of Good Counsel Church.
Fenton, Cornelius *c.pp.s.* '49 (CIN) [B] Carthagena, OH St. Charles.
Fenton, Joseph D. *s.m.* '72 (WDC) [M] Washington, DC Marist Provincial House.
Fenton, Lawrence E. '63 (GI) On Duty Outside the Diocese.
Fenton, Lawrence E. '63 (PMB) [1] West Palm Beach, FL Holy Name of Jesus Church.
Fenton, Norman H. *o.p.* '62 (WDC) [B] Washington, DC Dominican House of Studies.
Fenton, Patrick J. *s.s.s.* '50 (CLV) [P] Cleveland, OH Blessed Sacrament Community.
Fenton, William *o.c.d.* '48 (LA) Alhambra, CA St. Therese Church.
Fenzl, Roderick R. *o.praem.* '55 (GB) [I] De Pere, WI St. Norbert Abbey.
Ferenczy, George *o.cist.* '44 (DAL) [M] Irving, TX Cistercian Abbey of Our Lady of Dallas.
Ferens, Boniface D. '59 (BUF) Sardinia, NY St. Jude Church.
Ferens, Joseph F. '53 (DET) Retired.
Fergus, Edward L. *s.j.* '53 (DET) [P] Clarkston, MI Colombiere Center.
Fergus, Thomas K. *o.p.* '65 (PRO) [P] Providence, RI St. Thomas Aquinas Priory at Providence College.
Ferguson, Carlos '77 (GAL) Retired.
Ferguson, Gary M. '71 (TOL) Archbold, OH St. Peter Church; Stryker, OH St. John the Evangelist Church.
Ferguson, James A. '85 (ALX) Marksville, LA St. Joseph's Church.
Ferguson, John *s.j.* '54 (SLC) [4] Ogden, UT St. Mary's Church.
Ferguson, Peter (GAL) The Woodlands, TX Sts. Simon and Jude Church.
Ferguson, Ronald J. *s.j.* '65 (CHI) [C] Chicago, IL Jesuit Community at Loyola University of Chicago.
Ferhatian, Basil *c.m.vd.* '32 (ARM) Los Angeles, CA Our Lady Queen of Martyrs Church.
Ferhatian, Basil *c.m.vd.* '32 (LA) [30] Los Angeles, CA Our Lady Queen of Martyrs Church.
Ferigle, Salvador M. '57 (BO) [V] Cambridge, MA Opus Dei, Prelature of the Holy Cross and Opus Dei.
Ferland, Martin '95 (RC) [B] Bethlehem, SD Holy Nativity Monastery.
Ferland, Msgr. Oscar R. '44 (PRO) Retired.
Ferland, Thomas J. '87 (PRO) [1] East Providence, RI St. Francis Xavier Church.
Ferlisi, Paschal A. *o.s.b.* '71 (BIR) [16] Birmingham, AL Our Lady of Sorrows Church; [E] Cullman, AL St. Bernard Abbey.
Ferlita, Ernest *s.j.* '62 (NO) [C] New Orleans, LA Loyola University.
Fermeglia, Charles '88 (BRK) [64] Brooklyn, NY Immaculate Heart of Mary Church.
Fernan, Matthew '89 (NY) [E] New York, NY Cardinal Hayes High School.
Fernandes, Anthony *s.d.b.* '77 (OAK) [N] Berkeley, CA Salesian Community.
Fernandes, Babasino (FTW) Monroeville, IN St. Rose of Lima Church.
Fernandes, Herondi *s.x.* '76 (PAT) [M] Wayne, NJ Xaverian Missionary Fathers.
Fernandes, John '77 (OAK) [8] Oakland, CA St. Cyril Church.
Fernandes, Jose Manuel '59 (NEW) [26] Newark, NJ Our Lady of Fatima Church.
Fernandes, Lucian '67 (RVC) East Islip, NY St. Mary's Church.
Fernandes, Mauro de Souza *o.s.b.* '84 (GBG) [H] Latrobe, PA Saint Vincent Archabbey.
Fernandes, Patricio *s.j.* '89 (BAL) [37] Baltimore, MD St. Ignatius Church.
Fernandes, Rogue '69 (LA) Azusa, CA St. Frances of Rome Church.
Fernandes, Roque '64 (BRK) [154] Queens, NY St. Bartholomew's Church.
Fernandes, Stephen A. '76 (FR) [20] Fall River, MA SS. Peter and Paul Church.
Fernandes, Sydney '79 (HON) Hawi, HI Sacred Heart Church.
Fernandez, Cesar A. '95 (LA) Norwalk, CA St. John of God Church.
Fernandez, Daniel '95 (ARE) On Duty Outside the Diocese.
Fernandez, Eduardo *s.j.* '92 (ELP) [21] El Paso, TX Sacred Heart Church.
Fernandez, Edward P. '70 (DAL) Retired.
Fernandez, Elias *c.ss.t.* '69 (ARE) Isabela, PR Our Lady of Mount Carmel Church.
Fernandez, Emmanuel '79 (LAF) Lydia, LA St. Nicholas Church.
Fernandez, Epifanio *o.ss.t.* '59 (SJN) [13] Bayamon, PR Ascension Del Senor Church.
Fernandez, Fausto '61 (MIA) Absent on Leave.
Fernandez, Fidel *o.de.m.* (SJN) [40] San Juan, PR Nuestra Senora de la Merced Church.
Fernandez, Fidel *o.m.* '74 (CGS) Cayey, PR Nuestra Senora de la Asuncion Church.
Fernandez, Francisco X. *o.f.m.cap.* '58 (FWT) [5] Fort Worth, TX Immaculate Heart of Mary Church.
Fernandez, Frank '79 (PHX) [15] Phoenix, AZ St. Joseph Church.
Fernandez, Isidro '40 (CGS) [C] Aibonito, PR Casa Salesiana de Retiros.
Fernandez, Jose A. '60 (BGP) Retired.
Fernandez, Jose Luis *o.ss.t.* '69 (PCE) [10] Ponce, PR La Santisima Trinidad Church.
Fernandez, Jose Maria '59 (GAL) [19] Houston, TX Christ the King Church.
Fernandez, Jose Ramon '59 (SJN) [4] Trujillo Alto, PR Bienveturada Virgen Maria de Lourdes Church.
Fernandez, Luis J. '71 (NO) On Duty Outside the Archdiocese.
Fernandez, Manuel '59 (TR) [3] Long Branch, NJ St. John the Baptist Church.
Fernandez, Manuel '62 (ORL) Eustis, FL St. Mary of the Lakes Church.
Fernandez, Manuel *s.d.b.* '69 (LA) Bellflower, CA St. Dominic Savio Church.
Fernandez, Marcellus '68 (STA) On Duty Outside the Diocese.
Fernandez, Michael *c.m.f.* '53 (CHI) [149] Chicago, IL Our Lady of Guadalupe Church.
Fernandez, Miguel A. '50 (MIA) Retired.
Fernandez, Nelson '56 (MIA) Special Assignment.
Fernandez, Nobincio *ss.cc.* '65 (HON) [H] Kaneohe, HI Sacred Hearts Center.
Fernandez, Msgr. Orlando '49 (MIA) Retired.
Fernandez, Romualdo *c.m.f.* (SJN) [23] Bayamon, PR Santa Maria Church.
Fernandez, Serapio *o.f.m.* (PCE) [B] Ponce, PR The Pontifical Catholic University of Puerto Rico.
Fernandez, Serapio '50 (ARE) [5] Arecibo, PR Church of Christ the King.
Fernandez, Severiano *o.s.a.* '64 (BEA) Vidor, TX Our Lady of Lourdes Church.
Fernandez, Vincente '82 (SJN) [5] Guaynabo, PR Maria Madre de la Misericordia Church.
Fernandez Cartagena, Elias '88 (PCE) On Duty Outside the Diocese.
Fernando, Augustine '64 (RVC) Elmont, NY St. Vincent de Paul Church.
Fernando, Bernard '65 (NEW) Hackensack, NJ Hackensack Medical Center.
Fernando, Damian '70 (LA) San Pedro, CA Holy Trinity Church.
Fernando, Gamini E. '72 (NY) [3] Poughkeepsie, NY Holy Trinity Church; State, NY Green Haven Correctional Facility.
Fernando, J. Paul '62 (LA) [K] Lynwood, CA St. Francis Medical Center.
Fernando, Joachim '62 (BRK) [228] Queens, NY St. Pius X Church.
Fernando, Nimal George '89 (FTW) [4] Fort Wayne, IN St. Elizabeth Ann Seton Church.
Fernando, Simon '60 (RVC) Commack, NY Christ the King Church.
Fernando, Stan '78 (JOL) Elmhurst, IL Visitation Church.
Fernando, Susil (FTW) Decatur, IN St. Mary Church.
Fernando, Venantius M. '61 (NEW) [4] Irvington, NJ St. Paul the Apostle Church.
Fernando, Walter '73 (LA) Pasadena, CA Assumption of the Blessed Virgin Mary Church.
Fernando, Wellington *s.j.* '89 (BO) [W] Chestnut Hill,

MA The Jesuit Community at Boston College.
Fernz, John (BO) Boston, MA Carney Hospital; Boston, MA Wrentham State School.
Fernz, John E. '62 (BO) Wrentham, MA St. Mary Church.
Ferone, John M. *s.j.* '83 (CIN) [M] Cincinnati, OH Faber Jesuit Community.
Ferracino, Placido *o.m.v.* '86 (BO) [B] Boston, MA Oblate Provincialate.
Ferraioli, Msgr. Frank B. '61 (PAT) Parsippany, NJ St. Christopher Church.
Ferraioli, Joseph *o.m.i.* '77 (GR) [9] Grand Rapids, MI Immaculate Heart of Mary Church.
Ferran, Michael *i.c.* '43 (SP) Seminole, FL Blessed Sacrament Church.
Ferrante, Frank J. *c.m.f.* '70 (LA) [R] Los Angeles, CA Claretian Retreat Center Community; [W] Los Angeles, CA Claretian Retreat Center (All Groups).
Ferrante, Msgr. Joseph L. '74 (TR) [12] Trenton, NJ St. Anthony Church.
Ferrara, Angelus P. *o.s.p.p.e.* '90 (PH) [Z] Doylestown, PA Pauline Fathers Monastery, Shrine of Our Lady of Czestochowa.
Ferrara, Bede *o.f.m.* '50 (BO) [W] Lynn, MA Franciscan Community (Province of Immaculate Conception).
Ferrara, Charles F. *s.j.* '90 (STL) [P] St. Louis, MO De Smet Jesuit High School Community.
Ferrara, Francis '53 (SP) Spring Hill, FL St. Theresa Church.
Ferrara, John *o.m.v.* '82 (BO) [B] Boston, MA Oblate Provincialate.
Ferrara, Joseph J. '42 (SCR) [4] Hazleton, PA Holy Trinity Church; Retired.
Ferrara, Joseph R. '77 (CAM) Woodstown, NJ St. Joseph's Church; [A] Carneys Point, NJ St. James High School.
Ferrara, Pasquale '37 (DAV) [L] Davenport, IA Kahl Home for the Aged and Infirm.
Ferrara, Pasquale L. '37 (DAV) Retired.
Ferrarese, Fernando A. *m.div.* '77 (BRK) [13] Brooklyn, NY St. Athanasius Church.
Ferrari, Steven A. '80 (BRK) [73] Brooklyn, NY St. Laurence Church.
Ferraro, Joseph A. '90 (NEW) [11] Jersey City, NJ Holy Rosary Church.
Ferraro, Michael M. '68 (BO) [4] Lynn, MA St. Mary Church.
Ferraro, Patrick B. '92 (Y) [11] Youngstown, OH St. Christine's Church.
Ferraro, Romano J. '60 (BRK) Absent on Leave; [U] Jamaica, NY Parsons Manor.
Ferraro, Ronald A. '60 (HRT) [5] Waterbury, CT Our Lady of Lourdes Church.
Ferraro, Vincent J. '70 (BUF) [1] Kenmore, NY St. Andrew Church; [K] Kenmore, NY Kenmore Mercy Hospital.
Ferrazoli, Henry R. '61 (NEW) Retired.
Ferre, Antonio '53 (PCE) [17] Ponce, PR Our Lady of Mt. Carmel Church.
Ferreira, Alfonse *o.f.m.* '72 (BO) [W] Lynn, MA Franciscan Community (Province of Immaculate Conception); [W] Lynn, MA Franciscan Community (Province of Immaculate Conception).
Ferreira, Jose S. (BO) [1] Cambridge, MA St. Anthony Church.
Ferreira, Joseph A. '59 (OAK) [2] San Leandro, CA St. Alphonsus Liguori Church.
Ferreira, Manuel P. '60 (FR) [5] Taunton, MA St. Anthony's Church.
Ferrell, William F. *s.j.* '36 (STL) [O] St. Louis, MO Fusz Pavilion.
Ferrence, John J. *o.s.a.* '52 (PH) [D] Drexel Hill, PA Monsignor Bonner High School.
Ferrer, Anthony P. *t.o.r.* '56 (AUS) [2] Waco, TX St. Francis on the Brazos Church.
Ferrer, Charles M. (CHI) [127] Chicago, IL St. Mary of the Angels Church; [W] Chicago, IL Midtown Center.
Ferrer, Gonzalo *t.o.r.* '81 (SHP) [B] Shreveport, LA Schumpert Medical Center.
Ferrer, Guillermo Casa *t.c.* (BAL) Odenton, MD St. Joseph Church.
Ferrer, Jorge *s.j.* '77 (SJN) [22] San Juan, PR San Ignacio de Loyola Church.
Ferrer, Miguel '67 (SJN) [15] Carolina, PR Ntra. Sra. Reina de la Paz Church.
Ferrer, Peter '61 (LA) Artesia, CA Holy Family Church.
Ferrero, Anthony T. '81 (SB) Chino, CA Our Lady of Guadalupe Church.
Ferrero, Bartolomeo Santino '60 (DET) [56] Detroit, MI Our Lady of Mt. Carmel Church.
Ferrett, Walter L. '66 (SCR) [24] Scranton, PA Sacred Hearts of Jesus and Mary Church.
Ferrick, Mortimer A. *c.s.c.* '57 (FR) [K] North Dartmouth, MA Holy Cross Mission House.
Ferrick, Raymond J. '77 (PRO) [6] Cranston, RI St. Matthew Church; Georgiaville, RI St. Michael's Church.
Ferrick, Robert T. *s.j.* '57 (BO) [U] Framingham, MA St. Patrick's Manor, Inc.; [W] Weston, MA Campion Center.
Ferrie, Francis '65 (NO) [13] New Orleans, LA Incarnate Word Church.
Ferrier, Francis *s.j.* '61 (BR) [F] Baton Rouge, LA Our Lady of the Lake Regional Medical Center.
Ferrier, Francis V. *s.j.* '61 (BR) [20] Baton Rouge, LA Sacred Heart of Jesus Church.
Ferrier, Ronald J. '68 (PH) [AA] Philadelphia, PA Provincial House of the Sisters of the Holy Family of Nazareth.
Ferrigan, Robert E. '61 (CHI) Winnetka, IL Sacred Heart Church.
Ferrigno, Denis P. '50 (HRT) Retired.
Ferring, Msgr. Robert L. '50 (DUB) Retired.
Ferris, Carl A. '55 (GI) Retired.
Ferris, James (ALB) [L] Saratoga Springs, NY St. John Neumann Residence.
Ferris, James *c.ss.r.* '35 (NY) [92] New York, NY Our Lady of Perpetual Help Church.
Ferris, James *c.ss.r.* '50 (ALB) [L] Saratoga Springs, NY St. John Neumann Residence.
Ferris, Msgr. Norman J. '53 (SAM) Fall River, MA St. Anthony of the Desert Church.
Ferris, Thomas B. '63 (PIT) [70] Pittsburgh, PA St. Cyril of Alexandria Church.
Ferrito, Msgr. Joseph L. (PAT) Retired.
Ferro, Ralph '71 (RVC) Roosevelt, NY Queen of the Most Holy Rosary Church.
Ferro, Robert A. '73 (BRK) Absent on Leave.
Ferron, Joseph B. '45 (LC) Retired.
Ferronato, Guido *c.s.* '38 (PRO) [M] North Kingstown, RI Scalabrini Villa.
Ferruzzi, William '76 (NEW) [N] South Orange, NJ Salesian Residence.
Ferry, James '84 (FR) [3] Fall River, MA Espirito Santo Church.
Fertal, Joseph *s.v.d.* '59 (SB) [A] Riverside, CA Divine Word Seminary.
Feser, Victor *o.s.b.* '64 (BIS) [A] Richardton, ND Assumption Abbey; [B] Bismarck, ND University of Mary.
Fessard, Gerald B. *j.c.l.* '72 (LA) On Special or Other (Arch)Diocesan Assignment.
Fessio, Joseph D. *s.j.* '72 (SFR) [N] San Francisco, CA Jesuit Community at University of San Francisco.
Fest, Donald M. *s.s.j.* '76 (BAL) [92] Baltimore, MD St. Veronica Church.
Festle, Robert H. (CHI) Retired.
Festle, Robert H. '55 (CHI) [X] Wilmette, IL Musica Pacis.
Fetcho, John E. '64 (SY) Lakeland, NY Our Lady of Peace Church.
Fete, Msgr. Joseph N. '74 (COL) [1] Columbus, OH St. Joseph Cathedral.
Fete, Kevin L. '85 (Y) Middlebranch, OH St. Therese Little Flower Church.
Fetscher, James F. '68 (MIA) [26] Miami, FL St. Louis Church.
Fetterer, Raymond A. '35 (MIL) Retired.
Fetters, Donald G. *c.s.c.* '76 (OAK) [N] Berkeley, CA Holy Cross Fathers-Holy Cross Center.
Feucht, Urban *o.s.b.* '55 (SEA) [G] Olympia, WA Providence St. Peter Hospital; [M] Lacey, WA St. Martin's Abbey.
Feudjio, Jerome '90 (STV) [1] St. Thomas, VI Cathedral of Sts. Peter and Paul.
Feuerbacher, Edward F. '57 (STL) Affton, MO St. Dominic Savio Church.
Feusahrens, Frederick J. '72 (RIC) [14] Richmond, VA St. Paul Church.
Fewing, Ross '77 (SEA) [Q] Seattle, WA Catholic Hospital Ministries.
Fey, Albert J. *c.pp.s.* '46 (KCK) Baileyville, KS Sacred Heart Church.
Fey, Christian *o.f.m.cap.* '45 (STL) [P] St. Louis, MO St. Crispin's Friary.
Fey, George *c.pp.s.* '43 (SAN) [4] San Angelo, TX St. Mary's Church.
Fey, Joseph '51 (FTW) [J] Notre Dame, IN Holy Cross Community, Corby Hall, University of Notre Dame.
Fey, Thomas J. '70 (ALX) Military Chaplains.
Fiala, John M. '84 (OM) Absent on Leave.
Fiala, Timothy R. (CHI) Northfield, IL St. Philip the Apostle Church.
Fialkowski, Edward '78 (CHI) La Grange, IL St. Cletus Church.
Fialkowski, Thomas M. '66 (E) [9] Erie, PA Our Lady of Mt. Carmel Church; Erie, PA Veterans Administration Hospital.
Fiandaca, Charles *t.o.r.* (ORL) [E] Orlando, FL University of Central Florida Newman Center.
Fiano, Guy *o.carm.* '83 (PMB) [G] Boca Raton, FL St. Elias Priory-Order of Carmelites, NY.
Fiano, Guy *o.carm.* '85 (PMB) [B] Boca Raton, FL Pope John Paul II High School.
Fice, Joseph J. *s.j.* '72 (PHX) [B] Phoenix, AZ Brophy College Preparatory.
Ficenec, Leonard C. '57 (OM) Tarnov, NE St. Michael Church; Retired.
Fichtenman, William L. '81 (L) Elizabethtown, KY St. James Church; White Mills, KY St. Ignatius Church.
Fichtner, Joseph '43 (PHX) [25] Phoenix, AZ St. Thomas the Apostle Church.
Fichtner, Joseph A. *o.s.c.* '43 (PHX) [F] Phoenix, AZ Crosier Community of Phoenix (Canons Regular of the Order of the Holy Cross).
Fichtner, Robert C. '55 (BO) Watertown, MA St. Patrick Church.
Fick, David J. '88 (ALN) West Reading, PA Sacred Heart Church.
Fickel, William F. *s.s.s.* '81 (CLV) [P] Cleveland, OH Blessed Sacrament Community.
Fickes, Daniel R. '91 (CLV) Olmsted Falls, OH St. Mary of the Falls Church.
Ficko, Anthony D. '56 (GRY) [1] Whiting, IN Immaculate Conception Church.
Ficorilli, Chad R. *o.s.b.* '79 (E) St. Marys, PA Sacred Heart of Jesus Church.
Fictum, Robert *s.d.s.* '78 (MIL) [3] Wauwatosa, WI St. Joseph Congregation Church.
Fidalgo, Federico '63 (CC) Retired.
Fidalgo, Manuel Garcia '47 (MIA) [A] Miami, FL St. John Vianney College Seminary.
Fider, William P. '66 (DUL) [14] Duluth, MN St. Michael's Church.
Fidler, W. Larch, IV '87 (PRT) [M] Brunswick, ME Bowdoin College; [M] Lewiston, ME Bates College.
Fidler, W. Larch, IV '87 (STL) On Duty Outside the Archdiocese.
Fiedler, Donald J. '59 (DOD) On Duty Outside the Diocese.
Fiedler, Donald J. '59 (TUC) [20] Tucson, AZ Saints Peter and Paul Church.
Fiedler, Msgr. Ernest J. '52 (KC) [1] Kansas City, MO Cathedral of Immaculate Conception; [27] Kansas City, MO Old St. Patrick's Church.
Fiedler, Kenneth J. '71 (MAD) [6] Madison, WI Our Lady, Queen of Peace Church.
Fiedorczyk, Henry P. '42 (HRT) [2] New Britain, CT Holy Cross Church; Retired.
Fiedorowicz, Joseph '75 (KNX) Athens, TN St. Mary Church.
Fiedurek, Jan *s.ch.* '79 (MIA) Hallandale, FL St. Charles Borromeo Church.
Field, Eugene Joseph '94 (NEW) [2] Bayonne, NJ St. Andrew's Church.
Field, James A. (BO) [4] Norwood, MA St. Timothy Church.
Field, Michael J. '82 (CAM) [3] Cherry Hill, NJ St. Peter Celestine Church.
Field, Raymund J. *c.s.v.* '48 (SJ) [3] Sunnyvale, CA St. Cyprian Church.
Field, Thomas E. *glmy.* '78 (CHL) Bryson City, NC St. Joseph Church.
Field, Msgr. William N. '40 (NEW) [B] South Orange, NJ Seton Hall University.
Fields, John '86 (PHU) Lansdale, PA Presentation of Our Lord Church; Warrington, PA St. Anne's Church; [D] Philadelphia, PA Ascension Manor, Inc.
Fields, Robert H. '82 (JC) Centralia, MO Holy Spirit Church; Columbia, MO University Hospital & Clinics.
Fields, Stephen M. *s.j.* '52 (WDC) [M] Washington, DC The Jesuit Community at Georgetown University.
Fields, William F. '91 (MOB) [1] Mobile, AL Cathedral of the Immaculate Conception.
Fierro, Msgr. David G. '76 (ELP) [1] El Paso, TX St. Patrick's Cathedral; [9] El Paso, TX Holy Family Church.
Fierro, Paul *s.d.s.* '75 (MIL) [P] Milwaukee, WI Salvatorians - Jordan Hall.
Fierros, Rick '78 (FRS) Delano, CA St. Mary's of the Miraculous Medal Church.
Fifagrowicz, Joseph G. '62 (BUF) Lyndonville, NY St. Joseph Church; Medina, NY Sacred Heart Church.
Figaro, Egbert J. *c.s.sp.* (CHI) [129] Chicago, IL St. Mary Magdalene Church.
Figel, Terence J. *o.m.i.* '64 (BEL) [K] Belleville, IL Scott Air Force Base.
Figel, Terence J. *o.m.i.* '64 (STP) [N] St. Paul, MN Oblate Provincial Offices; [N] St. Paul, MN Oblate Residence.
Figge, Edwin H. '41 (STL) Retired.
Figge, Glennon E. *c.m.* '55 (EVN) [F] Evansville, IN Seton Residence.
Figge, Glennon E. *c.m.* '55 (STL) [P] St. Louis, MO Vincentian Residence.
Figlia, Sidney *s.d.b.* '68 (NO) [2] Harvey, LA St. John Bosco Church.
Figliola, Nicholas J. '64 (RVC) Coram, NY St. Frances Cabrini Church.
Figliozzi, Richard '79 (RVC) Freeport, NY Our Holy Redeemer Church.
Figol, Volodymyr (STF) Retired.
Figueiredo, Anthony J. '94 (NEW) Higher Studies.
Figueredo, Sergio *s.j.* '60 (MIA) [5] Miami, FL Gesu Church.
Figueroa, Alberto *o.f.m.,cap.* '90 (ARE) [1] Utuado, PR San Miquel Church.
Figueroa, Angel '86 (SJN) [2] Toa Alta, PR San Fernando Church.
Figueroa, Domingo *c.r.l.* '96 (ARE) Corozal-Palmarito, PR La Milagrosa Church.
Figueroa, Gregory *s.a.* '43 (NY) [Z] Garrison, NY

Franciscan Friars of the Atonement.

Figueroa, Marcos A. *o.f.m.* '93 (OAK) [N] Oakland, CA Franciscan Friars Provincial Office, Province of St. Barbara.

Figueroa, Ruben *o.f.m.* '75 (TYL) Diboll, TX Our Lady of Guadalupe Church.

Figuerola, Adrian '71 (IND) [H] Indianapolis, IN St. Augustine Home, Little Sisters of the Poor.

Figurelle, Elwood F. (ALT) Mount Union, PA St. Catherine's Church.

Figurelli, Nicholas '82 (NEW) [C] West Orange, NJ Seton Hall Preparatory School.

Figurelli, Nicholas G. '82 (NEW) Westfield, NJ Holy Trinity Church.

Filacchione, Msgr. Marc A. '80 (NY) [74] New York, NY St. Michael Church.

Filardi, Edward J. '94 (WDC) Gaithersburg, MD St. Martin Church.

Filary, Richard M. '82 (SAG) [3] Bay City, MI St. Hedwig Church.

Filiatreau, Hilary *o.s.b.* '49 (LR) Altus, AR St. Mary Church.

Filice, Francis (SFR) [27] San Francisco, CA St. John the Evangelist Church.

Filice, Peter F. *s.j.* '71 (SJ) [B] Santa Clara, CA Santa Clara University.

Filice, Richard '76 (CC) [12] Corpus Christi, TX Saint Andrew By the Sea Parish Church.

Filip, Francis B. '36 (PIT) Retired.

Filip, John T. '44 (ROM) Retired.

Filipetto, Silvano '86 (CHI) On Duty Outside the Archdiocese.

Filipich, Nicholas '53 (BLX) Retired.

Filipkowski, Peter '86 (PAT) Parsippany, NJ St. Peter the Apostle Church.

Filipowicz, Stefan *s.j.* '61 (CHI) [N] Chicago, IL Sacred Heart Mission House.

Filippelli, John L.M. *s.s.j.* (WDC) [B] Washington, DC St. Joseph's Seminary.

Filippi, Alan (COS) [B] Colorado Springs, CO Penrose-St. Francis Health Services.

Filippine, John E. '58 (CIN) [88] Cincinnati, OH St. Vivian Church.

Filips, Mark D. '89 (OM) [41] Omaha, NE St. Rose Church.

Filipski, Raymond R. '75 (NEW) Bergenfield, NJ St. John the Evangelist Church.

Fillion, Normand A. *o.m.i.* '50 (MAN) [3] Manchester, NH St. Anthony of Padua Church.

Fillion, Stephen J. '79 (SAG) Harrison, MI St. Athanasius Church.

Fillman, G. Allan '77 (TOL) Tiffin, OH St. Mary Church; [B] Tiffin, OH Calvert High School; [L] Tiffin, OH St. Francis Convent.

Filmanski, Francis E. '53 (RVC) Floral Park, NY St. Hedwig's Church.

Filmyer, Bernard G. *s.j.* '52 (BAL) [M] Baltimore, MD Jesuit Fathers and Brothers Maryland Provincial Curia.

Filteau, Jerome E. '41 (FAR) Retired; [E] Fargo, ND Riverview Place, Inc.

Filut, David C. '68 (MIL) [4] Waukesha, WI St. William Church.

Fimbel, Duane G. (BUF) [2] North Tonawanda, NY St. Albert the Great Church; North Tonawanda, NY DeGraff Memorial Hospital.

Fimiani, Msgr. Louis F. '60 (NEW) Nutley, NJ Holy Family Church.

Fin, Robert G. '43 (E) Retired; [B] Erie, PA Gannon University.

Finamore, Robert A. '70 (WDC) College Park, MD Holy Redeemer Church.

Finan, James A. '59 (BAL) [Q] Upper Marlboro, MD Knights of Columbus.

Finan, James A. '59 (WDC) Absent On Leave.

Finch, G. William '89 (WDC) Cheverly, MD St. Ambrose Church.

Finch, Joseph E. '58 (ALB) [M] Germantown, NY St. Teresa's Motherhouse.

Finch, Joseph E. '58 (OM) Absent on Sick Leave

Finch, Raymond J. *m.m.* '76 (NY) [Z] Maryknoll, NY Maryknoll Fathers and Brothers.

Fincutter, John F. *s.v.d.* '50 (MIL) [P] East Troy, WI Divine Word Seminary.

Finder, James L. '91 (JC) Rich Fountain, MO Sacred Heart Church.

Findlan, Msgr. Joseph G. '38 (PIT) Retired; [N] Pittsburgh, PA St. John Vianney Manor.

Findlay, David '67 (E) [11] Erie, PA Sacred Heart Church.

Finegan, Gerard '67 (VEN) [1] Sarasota, FL Incarnation Church.

Finegan, Paul J. '70 (BO) Chelmsford, MA St. Mary Church.

Finelli, Jay A. '92 (PRO) [1] East Providence, RI St. Francis Xavier Church.

Finelli, Victor F. '89 (ALN) Whitehall, PA St. Elizabeth Church.

Fineran, A. Gerard *s.j.* '50 (NO) [P] New Orleans, LA Jesuit Provincial Office.

Finerty, Bernard *o.f.m.cap.* '61 (PIT) Conway, PA Our Lady of Peace Church; [N] Rochester, PA St. Cecilia Friary.

Finerty, D. Bryan '59 (PRO) [5] Woonsocket, RI St. Charles Church.

Finerty, Raymond *o.p.* '71 (P) Ashland, OR Our Lady of the Mountain Church; [P] Portland, OR University of Portland.

Fingerle, Fred G. '63 (BUF) Andover, NY Blessed Sacrament Church; Whitesville, NY St. John of the Cross Church.

Finis, John '40 (EVN) Retired.

Fink, Msgr. Charles R. '76 (RVC) Hewlett, NY St. Joseph's Church.

Fink, Daniel *o.f.m.conv.* (BO) [7] Lawrence, MA Holy Trinity Church.

Fink, Frederick T. '61 (NU) Darwin, MN St. John Church; Forest City, MN St. Gertrude Church.

Fink, John L. '69 (IND) [3] New Albany, IN Our Lady of Perpetual Help Church.

Fink, Joseph P. '83 (STP) [23] St. Paul, MN St. John of St. Paul Church.

Fink, Karel '91 (AUS) Llano, TX Holy Trinity Church; Mason, TX St. Joseph's Church.

Fink, Peter E. *s.j.* '69 (BO) [W] Cambridge, MA Weston Jesuit Community.

Fink, Philip *o.f.m.cap.* '77 (PIT) [N] Pittsburgh, PA St. Patrick Friary.

Finlan, Robert T. '94 (ALN) [C] Reading, PA Holy Name High School.

Finlan, Robert T., Jr. '94 (ALN) Shillington, PA St. John Baptist de la Salle Church.

Finlay, Joseph F. '57 (STA) Palatka, FL St. Monica's Church; Palatka, FL St. Monica's Church.

Finley, James F. '63 (BRK) Released from Diocesan Assignment.

Finley, James F. '63 (TR) Lakehurst, NJ U.S. Naval Air Warfare Center.

Finley, Msgr. James J. '49 (STL) Retired.

Finley, James J. *s.j.* '52 (NY) [Z] New York, NY Murray-Weigel Hall.

Finley, Jeffrey *c.pp.s.* '90 (OAK) Newark, CA St. Edward's Church; Fremont, CA Washington Hospital.

Finley, Phillip Mark '85 (B) Eagle, ID St. Matthew Church.

Finley, Thomas (LAF) [6] Lafayette, LA Our Lady of Wisdom, University of Southwestern Louisiana Church.

Finley, Thomas M. *c.m.* '54 (PH) [Z] Philadelphia, PA Congregation of the Mission.

Finley, William '81 (ORL) Sabbatical.

Finm, Seamus *o.m.i.* '76 (WDC) [B] Washington, DC Oblate College/Oblate Center for Mission Studies.

Finn, Alfred E. '65 (BO) Permanent Disability.

Finn, Arthur *c.ss.r.* '29 (ALB) [L] Saratoga Springs, NY St. John Neumann Residence.

Finn, Msgr. Cecil E. '37 (TLS) Retired.

Finn, Daniel J. '72 (BO) [44] Boston, MA St. Mark Church.

Finn, Dominick *o.s.f.s.* '56 (PH) Norristown, PA Norristown State Hospital.

Finn, Dominick F. *o.s.f.s.* '56 (PH) [2] Norristown, PA St. Francis of Assisi Church.

Finn, Edward S. *c.ss.r.* '52 (BRK) Brooklyn, NY Veterans Administration Medical Center.

Finn, Edward S. *c.ss.r.* '52 (SCR) Special Assignment.

Finn, Firmin *o.f.m.conv.* (ALB) [J] Latham, NY Our Lady of Hope Residence.

Finn, Firmin *o.f.m.conv.* '55 (SY) [2] Syracuse, NY Assumption B.V.M. Church; Syracuse, NY St. Joseph's Hospital Health Center; [O] Syracuse, NY St. Joseph's Hospital Health Center.

Finn, Francis J. '39 (NEW) Retired.

Finn, Gregory T. *o.s.j.* '89 (SCR) [B] Pittston, PA St. Joseph's Oblate Seminary.

Finn, John *o.s.f.s.* '62 (WIL) Newark, DE Medical Center of Delaware.

Finn, John *m.s.c.* '84 (SAT) [M] San Antonio, TX Missionaries of the Sacred Heart.

Finn, John A. *o.s.f.s.* '62 (WIL) [I] Wilmington, DE DeSales House.

Finn, John P. '81 (NO) Luling, LA Holy Family Church.

Finn, Michael E. '77 (SCR) Moscow, PA St. Catherine of Siena Church.

Finn, Msgr. Peter G. '65 (NY) [211] Staten Island, NY St. Joseph, St. Thomas Church; [I] New York, NY The Catholic Charities of the Archdiocese of New York.

Finn, Raymond C. *o.p.* '70 (NO) [P] New Orleans, LA Dominican Fathers & Brothers, Southern Dominican Province.

Finn, Robert E. *s.j.* '91 (CHI) [N] Chicago, IL Chicago Province of the Society of Jesus-Provincial Office.

Finn, Seamus *o.m.i.* '76 (WDC) [V] Silver Spring, MD Oblate Conference.

Finn, Msgr. Thomas B. '37 (COV) Retired.

Finn, William '73 (JUN) On Duty Outside the Diocese.

Finn, William P. '48 (PH) [Z] Philadelphia, PA Congregation of the Mission.

Finnane, Daniel P. '63 (MAD) De Forest, WI St. Olaf Church.

Finnegan, Ambrose *o.f.m.conv.* '26 (STP) [Q] Prior Lake, MN Franciscan Retreat House.

Finnegan, Charles V. *o.f.m.* '58 (PH) [Z] Philadelphia, PA Order of Friars Minor, Holy Name Province.

Finnegan, Corentine J. *o.c.s.o.* '47 (ATL) [I] Conyers, GA The Monastery of the Holy Spirit.

Finnegan, Gerald F. *s.j.* '67 (BO) [W] Boston, MA The Society of Jesus of New England-Provincial Offices.

Finnegan, Gerald F. *s.j.* '67 (PH) [C] Philadelphia, PA St. Joseph's University; [Z] Philadelphia, PA Jesuit Community at St. Joseph's University.

Finnegan, J. Kevin '96 (STP) Bloomington, MN St. Edward Church.

Finnegan, James P. *o.s.f.s.* '58 (ALN) Colesville, PA Assumption B.V.M. Church; [B] Center Valley, PA Allentown College of St. Francis de Sales; [K] Center Valley, PA Oblates of St. Francis de Sales.

Finnegan, John P. '54 (CHI) Vernon Hills, IL St. Mary of Vernon Church.

Finnegan, John S. '56 (SY) Camillus, NY St. Joseph Church.

Finnegan, John T. (BO) Retired.

Finnegan, Joseph '65 (HEL) Special Assignments.

Finnegan, Kevin '90 (GLP) Absent on Leave.

Finnegan, Lawrence J. '70 (SFR) San Anselmo, CA St. Anselm Church.

Finnegan, Michael '45 (HT) Retired.

Finnegan, Michael J. '74 (SP) [1] Largo, FL St. Catherine of Siena Church.

Finnegan, Peter J. '42 (WCH) Retired.

Finnegan, Robert K. *o.praem.* '52 (GB) [A] De Pere, WI St. Norbert Abbey; [I] De Pere, WI St. Norbert Abbey; [O] De Pere, WI Canons Regular of Magnovarad, Ltd.; [O] De Pere, WI NORBERT & CO.; [O] De Pere, WI Norbertine Generalate, Inc.

Finnegan, Roscoe L. '47 (SCL) Retired.

Finnegan, Msgr. Thomas J. (BO) Retired.

Finnegan, William J. '57 (CHI) Orland Park, IL Our Lady of the Woods Church.

Finnell, Eugene L. '56 (PEO) Morton, IL Blessed Sacrament Church.

Finnell, John H. '78 (WH) Absent on Sick Leave; [F] Wheeling, WV Paul VI Pastoral Center.

Finneran, Michael '42 (BIR) Retired.

Finnerty, Msgr. D. Joseph '63 (BRK) [240] Queens, NY St. Sebastian Church.

Finnerty, Msgr. Edward G. '37 (NY) Retired.

Finnerty, Msgr. James J. '55 (NEW) [15] Jersey City, NJ St. Mary's Church.

Finnerty, Joseph G. '61 (NOR) [4] Norwich, CT St. Mary Church; [J] Uncasville, CT Emmaus-Diocesan Spiritual Life Center.

Finnerty, Msgr. Joseph L. '57 (SD) Poway, CA St. Michael Church.

Finnerty, Peter F. '71 (CAM) Pomona, NJ Assumption Church.

Finnerty, Vincent H. *c.m.* (CHL) [3] Greensboro, NC St. Mary Church; [O] Charlotte, NC Centro Catolico Hispano.

Finnerty, William A. '55 (KCK) [3] Overland Park, KS Holy Spirit Church.

Finnestad, Jerald L.C. '80 (FAR) [2] Grand Forks, ND St. Mary's Church.

Finney, Donald *m.i.c.* '94 (NOR) [C] Thompson, CT Marianapolis Preparatory School; [F] Thompson, CT Marian Fathers.

Finnigan, Francis *c.p.* '68 (PMB) [G] North Palm Beach, FL Our Lady of Florida Spiritual Center.

Finnigan, John B. '61 (MAN) Newmarket, NH St. Mary Church.

Finnigan, John C. '59 (Y) [1] Canton, OH All Saints Church; [12] Canton, OH St. Peter's Church; [I] Louisville, OH Emmaus House.

Finnigan, Msgr. Thomas J. '55 (DET) [15] Detroit, MI St. Cecilia Church.

Finno, James P. '72 (CHI) Matteson, IL St. Lawrence O'Toole Church.

Finochietto, Arnold '36 (ELP) Retired.

Finsterbach, Thomas P. *s.j.* '76 (SJ) [M] Los Gatos, CA California Province of the Society of Jesus, Jesuit Provincial Office.

Finucan, J. Thomas '55 (LC) Fountain City, WI Immaculate Conception Church.

Finucan, Msgr. James P. '47 (LC) Retired; [I] La Crosse, WI Holy Cross (Seminary) Diocesan Center.

Finucane, Joseph F. '59 (E) Corry, PA St. Elizabeth Church.

Finucane, Robert '54 (B) Genesee, ID St. Mary Church.

Fior, Ubaldo M. *c.r.s.p.* '51 (BUF) Lewiston, NY Holy Family Church; [B] Youngstown, NY St. Anthony Zaccaria Seminary.

Fiore, Arthur B. '75 (WIL) New Castle, DE St. Peter Church.

Fiore, Benjamin *s.j.* '74 (BUF) [O] Buffalo, NY Canisius Jesuit Community.

Fiore, James '72 (PMB) Lantana, FL Holy Spirit Church.

Fiore, John J. *c.s.b.* '57 (GRY) [B] Merrillville, IN Andrean High School; [K] Merrillville, IN Basilian Fathers Residence.

Fiore, Joseph A. (BUF) Darien Center, NY Our Lady of

Good Counsel Church.
Fiore, Joseph A. '70 (BUF) Bennington Center, NY Sacred Heart of Jesus Church.
Fiore, Peter A. *o.f.m.* '55 (ALB) [B] Loudonville, NY Siena College.
Fiore, Salvatore *s.j.* '45 (NY) North Tarrytown, NY Immaculate Conception Church.
Fiorelli, Lewis S. *o.s.f.s.* '70 (ARL) Reston, VA St. John Neumann Church.
Fiorentin, Francis *c.s.* '51 (PRO) [8] Providence, RI St. Bartholomew's Church.
Fioretti, Jerome '32 (PRO) Retired.
Fiorillo, Antimo '43 (NY) [180] Bronx, NY Santa Maria Church; Retired.
Fiorino, Alfred *s.j.* '60 (SD) La Jolla, CA Veterans Administration Hospital.
Fiorino, Alfred L. *s.j.* '60 (NY) [Z] New York, NY Jesuit Provincial's Office.
Fiorino, D. Joseph '61 (NEW) [1] Elizabeth, NJ St. Mary of the Assumption Church.
Fiorino, Joseph '61 (NEW) Elizabeth, NJ St. Elizabeth Hospital; [G] Elizabeth, NJ St. Elizabeth Hospital.
Firko, Frank A. *s.t.l.* '77 (PBR) Hermitage, PA St. Michael Church.
Firneno, Ralph *s.a.c.* '57 (CAM) [C] Pennsauken, NJ Bishop Eustace Prep School.
Firpo, John A. (ROC) [19] Rochester, NY St. Helen Church.
Fisch, Gerald M. '57 (SC) Ida Grove, IA Sacred Heart Church.
Fischer, Adrian *o.f.m.* '75 (SHP) Grambling, LA St. Benedict the Black Church; West Monroe, LA St. Paschal Church; [G] Grambling, LA Student Center.
Fischer, Andrew C. '82 (PIT) Sharpsburg, PA St. John Cantius Church; Sharpsburg, PA Madonna of Jerusalem Church.
Fischer, Anthony W. '29 (LC) Retired.
Fischer, Barry J. *c.pp.s.* '73 (CIN) [M] Dayton, OH Provincial House of the Cincinnati Province of the Society of the Precious Blood.
Fischer, Brian J. '79 (CHI) [A] Mundelein, IL University of St. Mary of the Lake-Mundelein Seminary.
Fischer, Charles G. '50 (OWN) Clarkson, KY St. Elizabeth of Hungary Church; St. Paul, KY St. Paul Church.
Fischer, Charles H. '71 (KAL) Hastings, MI St. Rose of Lima Church.
Fischer, Msgr. Don L. '67 (DAL) Richardson, TX St. Joseph Church.
Fischer, Emil William '66 (PIT) [N] Pittsburgh, PA St. Francis Friary.
Fischer, Eugene '65 (SD) Retired.
Fischer, G. William *o.s.f.s.* (E) Special or Diocesan Assignment; On Duty Outside Diocese.
Fischer, G. Wm. *o.s.f.s.* '69 (TOL) [K] Toledo, OH Oblates of St. Francis de Sales.
Fischer, Henry J. '71 (BEL) Freeburg, IL St. Joseph Church.
Fischer, Hilary *m.s.c.* '57 (RCK) [H] Aurora, IL Missionaries of the Sacred Heart Community.
Fischer, James A. *c.m.* '43 (STL) [P] Perryville, MO Congregation of The Mission.
Fischer, James J. *s.j.* '55 (ROC) [B] Rochester, NY McQuaid Jesuit High School.
Fischer, John '86 (SFS) Redfield, SD St. Bernard Church.
Fischer, John M. '63 (E) Albion, PA St. Lawrence Church.
Fischer, John P. '76 (CIN) Withamsville, OH St. Thomas More Church.
Fischer, Joseph A. '40 (MIL) Retired.
Fischer, Kenneth J. '71 (CHI) [51] Chicago, IL St. Dorothy Church.
Fischer, Louis A. '63 (SLC) On Duty Outside the Diocese; Retired.
Fischer, Lowell '54 (JOL) Retired; [K] Frankfort, IL Motherhouse, Novitiate, Sacred Heart Residence, Portiuncula, Center for Prayer.
Fischer, Mark *f.s.s.p.* '95 (SCR) [M] Elmhurst, PA Priestly Fraternity of St. Peter (F.S.S.P.).
Fischer, Mark F. *f.s.s.p.* (ATL) [M] Alpharetta, GA St. Francis de Sales Latin Mass Community - Pastoral Center.
Fischer, Philip C. *s.j.* '61 (MIL) [P] Milwaukee, WI Jesuit Provincial Office, Wisconsin Province.
Fischer, Philip C. *s.j.* '61 (STL) [P] St. Louis, MO Jesuit Community Corporation at St. Louis University - Jesuit Hall.
Fischer, Richard O. '76 (BAK) Arlington, OR St. Francis Church; Condon, OR St. John's Church.
Fischer, Tarsicius '46 (CHI) [N] Chicago, IL St. Peter's Friary.
Fischer, William '69 (E) [C] Erie, PA Cathedral Preparatory School.
Fischer, William J. *o.praem.* '78 (GB) [I] De Pere, WI St. Norbert Abbey.
Fischer, William J. *o.praem.* '78 (PH) [Z] Paoli, PA Daylesford Abbey.
Fischler, James P. *c.i.c.m.* '76 (BWN) [2] Brownsville, TX Christ the King Church.
Fisette, Kevin R. '81 (PRO) [5] West Warwick, RI St. James Church; [C] Warwick, RI Bishop Hendricken High School.
Fish, Alfred H. '77 (OG) West Leyden, NY St. Mary's Nativity Church.
Fishel, Gregory *s.d.b.* '89 (NO) [4] Harvey, LA St. Rosalie Church.
Fisher, A. J. (BAK) Retired.
Fisher, Albert '81 (BIR) Jasper, AL St. Cecilia Church.
Fisher, Bernard '45 (MIL) [P] East Troy, WI Divine Word Seminary.
Fisher, Charles '90 (FAR) Drayton, ND St. Edward's Church.
Fisher, Charles M. '74 (RIC) Sabbatical.
Fisher, Clarence L. '61 (HON) Wahiawa, HI Our Lady of Sorrows Church.
Fisher, Craig B. '79 (PH) Feasterville, PA Assumption B.V.M. Church.
Fisher, D. Theodore *s.j.* '53 (LA) [C] Los Angeles, CA Loyola Marymount University.
Fisher, David (OLL) Graduate Studies.
Fisher, David E. '86 (LAN) Owosso, MI St. Joseph Church.
Fisher, Msgr. David L. '56 (GBG) Penn, PA St. Boniface Church.
Fisher, Donald C. '61 (PIT) Slippery Rock, PA St. Peter Church.
Fisher, Donald J. '54 (L) [72] Louisville, KY St. Thomas More Church.
Fisher, Edward K. '92 (MEM) [2] (Bartlett), TN St. Ann Church.
Fisher, Msgr. Edward T. '49 (BUF) [2] North Tonawanda, NY St. Albert the Great Church.
Fisher, Frederick J. '42 (CHI) Retired.
Fisher, Gerald E. '51 (LC) [4] Stevens Point, WI St. Peter Church.
Fisher, Harry W. '64 (FWT) Valley View, TX St. John Church.
Fisher, James *c.s.p.* '59 (MEM) [J] Memphis, TN Paulist Fathers (New York).
Fisher, James F. *c.s.p.* '59 (MEM) [20] Memphis, TN St. Patrick's Church.
Fisher, James F. *c.s.p.* '59 (NY) [Z] Scarsdale, NY Paulist Fathers Generalate.
Fisher, John J. *o.s.f.s.* '88 (WIL) [B] Wilmington, DE Salesianum School.
Fisher, Joseph P. *s.j.* '43 (STL) [O] St. Louis, MO Fusz Pavilion.
Fisher, Kyle *c.ss.r.* '63 (DEN) Greeley, CO Our Lady of Peace Church.
Fisher, Martin '51 (GF) Retired; [G] Billings, MT Saint Vincent Hospital and Health Center.
Fisher, Martin '86 (ALB) Glens Falls, NY St. Mary Church; [C] Glens Falls, NY St. Mary-St. Alphonsus Regional Catholic School.
Fisher, Michael W. '90 (WDC) Hillcrest Heights, MD Holy Family Church.
Fisher, Paul R. *o.praem.* '95 (PH) Paoli, PA St. Norbert Church.
Fisher, Raymond A. '71 (TOL) [21] Toledo, OH St. Clement Church.
Fisher, Robert '92 (DET) Plymouth, MI Our Lady of Good Counsel Church.
Fisher, Robert B. *s.v.d.* '65 (GAL) [T] Prairie View, TX Prairie View A & M University Catholic Center.
Fisher, Robert D. '80 (DEN) Greeley, CO St. Mary Church.
Fisher, Robert J. '80 (TOL) [33] Toledo, OH St. Michael Church.
Fisher, Robert J. '92 (DET) Special Assignment.
Fisher, Terry A. '85 (FTW) Warsaw, IN Sacred Heart Church.
Fisher, William '93 (KCK) Leawood, KS Cure of Ars Church.
Fisher, William F. *o.s.f.s.* '61 (DET) [3] Monroe, MI St. Joseph's Church.
Fisherkeller, William P. *c.s.v.* '60 (SFD) Granite City, IL Holy Family Church.
Fishwick, Joseph '75 (MIA) Special Assignment.
Fiske, Jack J. *c.ss.r.* '80 (ORL) [F] New Smyrna Beach, FL Redemptorist Fathers of the Vice Province of Richmond.
Fister, Anselm *o.s.b.* '82 (BAK) Dufur, OR St. Alphonsus Church; Wasco, OR St. Mary's Church.
Fister, Anselm *o.s.b.* '82 (SD) [H] Oceanside, CA Prince of Peace Abbey, Benet Hill.
Fister, Jerome '57 (JUN) Retired.
Fitch, David *s.j.* '54 (SJ) [2] Santa Clara, CA St. Clare Church.
Fitterer, L. Paul *s.j.* '63 (P) [L] Portland, OR Jesuit Provincial Office (Oregon Prov.).
Fittin, Edward Seton *o.s.b.* (PAT) [D] Morristown, NJ Delbarton School.
Fittin, Edward Seton J. *o.s.b.* '93 (PAT) [M] Morristown, NJ St. Mary's Abbey.
Fitz, James F. *s.m.* '74 (CIN) [M] Dayton, OH Marianist Provincialate; [M] Dayton, OH Marianist Provincialate.
Fitz-Henry, Edward '85 (MRY) San Juan Bautista, CA San Juan Bautista Church.
Fitz-Patrick, David M. '79 (WDC) Military Chaplains.
Fitzgerald, Alfred J. '66 (STL) Absent on Sick Leave.
Fitzgerald, Allan D. *o.s.a.* '67 (PH) [B] Villanova, PA St. Augustine Friary; [C] Villanova, PA Villanova University.
FitzGerald, Bernard *c.m.* '39 (STL) [P] Perryville, MO Congregation of The Mission.
Fitzgerald, Brennan *o.f.m.* '61 (NY) [35] New York, NY St. Francis of Assisi Church.
Fitzgerald, Christopher *i.c.* '58 (SP) Seffner, FL St. Francis of Assisi Church.
Fitzgerald, Cornelius (ATL) Canton, GA St. Michael the Archangel Church.
Fitzgerald, David *s.a.* '65 (NY) [Z] Garrison, NY Generalate of the Franciscan Friars of the Atonement-St. James Friary.
Fitzgerald, Denis *s.t.* '45 (WDC) [M] Adelphi, MD Missionary Servants of the Most Holy Trinity.
Fitzgerald, Donald J. '55 (BUF) Retired.
Fitzgerald, Edmund H. '57 (PRO) Misquamicut, RI Church of St. Clare.
Fitzgerald, Edmund J. '68 (FR) Westport, MA St. John the Baptist Church.
Fitzgerald, Edward P. '40 (CHI) Retired.
Fitzgerald, Edward T. '59 (SPR) Ware, MA All Saints Church.
Fitzgerald, Edward W. '95 (CHR) Aiken, SC St. Mary, Help of Christians Church.
Fitzgerald, Garrett J. *s.j.* '55 (NY) [Z] New York, NY Jesuit Community at Fordham University.
Fitzgerald, George R. *c.s.p.* '65 (DEN) [4] Boulder, CO St. Thomas Aquinas University Parish Church; [P] Boulder, CO University of Colorado (Boulder).
Fitzgerald, Howard '78 (DM) Dunlap, IA St. Patrick Church; Woodbine, IA Sacred Heart Church.
Fitzgerald, Hugh V. '53 (NEW) [16] Jersey City, NJ St. Michael's Church.
Fitzgerald, James '64 (JOL) Downers Grove, IL St. Joseph Church.
Fitzgerald, James C. '43 (LAN) Retired.
Fitzgerald, James E. *s.j.* '61 (MIL) [P] Milwaukee, WI Jesuit Community at Marquette University.
Fitzgerald, James E. '67 (BUF) Brant, NY Our Lady of Mt. Carmel Church.
Fitzgerald, John (PIT) Robinson Township, PA Holy Trinity Church.
Fitzgerald, John '58 (RVC) Setauket, NY St. James Church; [Q] Rockville Centre, NY The Campus Parish of Long Island.
Fitzgerald, John '63 (STO) Twain Harte, CA All Saints Church.
Fitzgerald, John B. '55 (LA) [10] Long Beach, CA St. Maria Goretti Church.
Fitzgerald, John B. *c.m.* '61 (ALN) Bangor, PA Our Lady of Good Counsel Church.
Fitzgerald, John E. '57 (PH) Narberth, PA St. Margaret Church.
Fitzgerald, John F. *o.s.b.* '50 (PEO) [A] Peru, IL St. Bede Abbey and Academy.
Fitzgerald, John G. '62 (LA) Lompoc, CA Our Lady Queen of Angels Church.
Fitzgerald, John J. *o.s.a.* '41 (PH) [Z] Villanova, PA St. Thomas Monastery.
Fitzgerald, John L. '67 (BAL) Military Chaplains.
Fitzgerald, John W. '53 (SFE) Retired.
Fitzgerald, Joseph *o.carm.* (LA) [F] Encino, CA Crespi Carmelite High School.
Fitzgerald, Msgr. Joseph M. '58 (BGP) Huntington, CT St. Lawrence Church.
FitzGerald, Kevin T. *s.j.* '88 (CHI) [C] Chicago, IL Jesuit Community at Loyola University of Chicago.
Fitzgerald, M. Durkin *c.ss.r.* '49 (SEA) [32] Seattle, WA Sacred Heart of Jesus Church.
Fitzgerald, Mark J. *c.s.c.* '40 (FTW) [B] Notre Dame, IN University of Notre Dame Du Lac; [J] Notre Dame, IN Holy Cross Community, Corby Hall, University of Notre Dame.
Fitzgerald, Michael C. '78 (DUB) Bluffton, IA St. Bridget Church; Cresco, IA Assumption of the Blessed Virgin Mary Church; Cresco, IA St. Joseph's Church; Plymouth Rock, IA St. Agnes Church; [F] Cresco, IA Notre Dame System of Education.
Fitzgerald, Michael J. '80 (PH) [151] Philadelphia, PA St. Thomas Aquinas Church.
Fitzgerald, Neil F. '54 (HRT) [3] Hamden, CT Our Lady of Mt. Carmel Church.
Fitzgerald, P. Timothy '75 (DM) On Duty Outside the Diocese.
Fitzgerald, Patrick '39 (KCK) Retired.
Fitzgerald, Patrick Timothy '75 (FTW) [B] Notre Dame, IN University of Notre Dame Du Lac.
Fitzgerald, Peter A. *c.m.* '46 (BUF) [O] Niagara University, NY Vincentian Community at Niagara University.
Fitzgerald, R. Martin '89 (R) On Duty Outside the Diocese.
Fitzgerald, Raymond R. *s.j.* '91 (NO) [F] New Orleans, LA Jesuit High School.
Fitzgerald, Robert H. *s.j.* '66 (STP) [M] St. Paul, MN Holy Family Residence; [N] Minneapolis, MN La Storta Jesuit Community.
Fitzgerald, Msgr. Stephen J. '41 (NY) Pocantico Hills, NY The Magdalene Church; Retired.

Fitzgerald, Thomas '68 (MAD) Portage, WI St. Mary Church.

Fitzgerald, Thomas J. *s.s.j.* '31 (BAL) [M] Baltimore, MD St. Joseph's Manor.

Fitzgerald, Thomas J. '42 (CHI) [204] Chicago, IL St. Thomas Apostle Church; Retired.

Fitzgerald, Thomas J. *s.s.s.* '64 (SAT) [45] San Antonio, TX St. Joseph Church.

Fitzgerald, Thomas J. '75 (PAT) [4] Clifton, NJ St. Clare's Church.

Fitzgerald, Thomas P. '66 (STP) Cottage Grove, MN St. Rita Church.

Fitzgerald, Thomas R. *s.j.* '52 (BAL) [M] Baltimore, MD Jesuit Fathers and Brothers Maryland Provincial Curia.

Fitzgerald, Timothy *c.p.* '56 (PIT) [N] Pittsburgh, PA St. Paul of the Cross Monastery.

Fitzgerald, Timothy J. (SC) Gilmore City, IA St. John's Church; Rolfe, IA St. Margaret's Church.

Fitzgerald, Vincent *o.m.i.* '50 (BEL) [G] Belleville, IL Missionary Oblates of Mary Immaculate - St. Henry's Oblate Residence.

Fitzgerald, William *c.ss.r.* '43 (CHI) [N] Bangkok, Thailand; [N] Parana, Brazil Rua Consulheiro Sinimbu.

Fitzgerald, William *c.ss.r.* '43 (DEN) [M] Denver, CO The Redemptorists/Denver Province.

FitzGerald, William '44 (BAL) Retired.

Fitzgerald, William F. (OM) Retired.

Fitzgerald, Msgr. William F. '50 (TR) [8] Trenton, NJ Our Lady of Good Counsel Church.

Fitzgerald, William H. *s.j.* '51 (WOR) [N] Worcester, MA Jesuits of Holy Cross College, Inc.

Fitzgerald, William J. '57 (KAL) Battle Creek, MI St. Philip Church.

Fitzgibbon, Edmond J. '59 (STL) Shrewsbury, MO St. Michael Church.

Fitzgibbons, Al L. '54 (RCK) On Disability Leave.

Fitzgibbons, John A. '68 (PH) Sharon Hill, PA Holy Spirit Church.

Fitzgibbons, John P. *s.j.* '85 (OM) [K] Omaha, NE Campion House.

Fitzgibbons, Paul L. '84 (CHL) Statesville, NC St. Philip the Apostle Church.

Fitzgibbons, Peter L. '84 (CHL) Military Chaplains.

Fitzhenry, John Stephen *o.p.* '58 (NEW) [27] Jersey City, NJ Sacred Heart Church.

Fitzhugh, David '88 (STN) [1] Chicago, IL St. Nicholas Ukrainian Catholic Cathedral; San Diego, CA Our Lady of Perpetual Help Church.

Fitzmaurice, Msgr. Francis J. '48 (PH) Retired.

Fitzmaurice, James *o.f.m.* '84 (BO) [5] Newton, MA Mary Immaculate of Lourdes Church; [W] Boston, MA Ministry of the Word.

Fitzmaurice, Terence *o.s.b.* '63 (JOL) [J] Lisle, IL St. Procopius Abbey.

Fitzmaurice, Terence *o.s.b.* '63 (SUP) Phillips, WI Our Lady of the North Church.

Fitzmaurice, V. Paul '73 (GBG) Harrison City, PA St. Barbara Church.

Fitzmyer, Joseph A. *s.j.* '51 (WDC) [C] Washington, DC Catholic University of America, The; [M] Washington, DC The Jesuit Community at Georgetown University.

Fitzpatrick, Daniel J. *s.j.* '55 (NY) [Z] New York, NY Jesuit Community at Fordham University.

Fitzpatrick, Donnelly J. '63 (PEO) Atkinson, IL St. Anthony's Church.

Fitzpatrick, Edmund J. '42 (CHI) Retired.

Fitzpatrick, Edmund J. '47 (CHI) [164] Chicago, IL St. Pascal Church.

Fitzpatrick, Edward '58 (ALB) Ushers, NY Corpus Christi Church.

Fitzpatrick, Edward '68 (RVC) Uniondale, NY St. Martha Church.

Fitzpatrick, Edward J. '58 (ALB) Special Assignment.

Fitzpatrick, Edward J. '70 (DAV) [H] Iowa City, IA Newman Catholic Student Center; [M] Iowa City, IA O'Keefe Hall.

Fitzpatrick, Edward T. *o.s.f.s.* '74 (WIL) [I] Wilmington, DE Oblates of St. Francis De Sales.

FitzPatrick, Emmett J. '58 (PHX) Sun Lakes, AZ St. Steven Church.

Fitzpatrick, Msgr. Franklin E. '47 (BRK) Retired.

Fitzpatrick, James '71 (SAG) [10] Bay City, MI St. Vincent de Paul Church.

Fitzpatrick, James F. '95 (BRK) [21] Brooklyn, NY Blessed Sacrament Church.

Fitzpatrick, James M. '84 (FR) Hyannis, MA St. Francis Xavier's Church.

Fitzpatrick, Jerold F. '62 (MAD) Gratiot, WI St. Joseph Church.

Fitzpatrick, Jerome B. *o.s.b.* '43 (PAT) [M] Morristown, NJ St. Mary's Abbey.

Fitzpatrick, John '64 (ALB) [10] Albany, NY St. Margaret Mary Church; Special Assignment.

Fitzpatrick, Msgr. John E. '70 (PAT) Oak Ridge, NJ St. Thomas, the Apostle Church.

Fitzpatrick, John F. '64 (ALB) [J] Albany, NY Villa Mary Immaculate.

Fitzpatrick, John J. '60 (SAV) Tybee Island, GA St. Michael's Church.

Fitzpatrick, John P. '52 (STP) Retired.

Fitzpatrick, John P. '60 (BO) On Special or Other Diocesan Assignment.

Fitzpatrick, Msgr. Joseph A. '31 (SFR) Retired.

Fitzpatrick, Joseph F. *s.j.* '65 (NY) Greenwood Lake, NY Holy Rosary Church.

Fitzpatrick, Kevin *o.s.m.* '54 (P) Milwaukie, OR Christ the King Church.

Fitzpatrick, Mallick J. *s.j.* '60 (NY) [F] New York, NY Fordham Preparatory School; [Z] New York, NY Jesuit Community at Fordham University.

Fitzpatrick, Michael J. *s.j.* '77 (BAK) Pendleton, OR St. Andrew's Indian Mission Church.

Fitzpatrick, Michael J. '83 (PH) [D] Drexel Hill, PA Archbishop Prendergast High School.

Fitzpatrick, Patrick F.X. '39 (NEW) Retired.

Fitzpatrick, Patrick G. '62 (TR) Union Beach, NJ Holy Family Church.

Fitzpatrick, Msgr. Peter A. '45 (PH) [133] Philadelphia, PA St. Patrick Church; Retired.

Fitzpatrick, R. Michael '71 (OM) [1] Omaha, NE St. Cecilia's Cathedral.

Fitzpatrick, Robert J. '54 (CHI) Ingleside, IL St. Bede Church; Round Lake, IL St. Joseph Church; Retired.

Fitzpatrick, Robert J. '73 (STP) Little Canada, MN St. John the Evangelist Church.

Fitzpatrick, Thomas J. *o.s.f.s.* '61 (CHL) Kernersville, NC Holy Cross Church.

Fitzpatrick, Thomas P. '61 (SY) [6] Syracuse, NY Our Lady of Lourdes Church.

Fitzpatrick, Vincent *s.t.* '44 (PAT) [M] Stirling, NJ Holy Spirit Missionary Cenacle.

Fitzpatrick, Vincent '92 (FAR) Wales, ND St. Michael's Church.

Fitzsimmons, Donald J. *c.s.v.* '60 (CHI) [N] Arlington Heights, IL Clerics of St. Viator-Provincial Residence.

Fitzsimmons, Msgr. Eugene J. '60 (CAM) Gibbstown, NJ St. Michael's Church.

Fitzsimmons, Francis *m.s.* '68 (LKC) [4] Sulphur, LA St. Theresa Church.

Fitzsimmons, Francis *m.s.* '69 (GAL) Friendswood, TX Mary, Queen Church.

Fitzsimmons, Gerald J. *s.m.m.* '75 (BRK) [U] Ozone Park, NY Montfort Missionaries Provincialate.

Fitzsimmons, Richard '56 (PEO) Peterstown, IL SS. Peter and Paul Church.

Fitzsimmons, Msgr. Richard G. '56 (PEO) Mendota, IL Holy Cross Church.

Fitzsimmons, Robert Philip *o.p.* '55 (NY) [22] New York, NY St. Catherine of Siena Church, Manhattan, NY New York Hospital; [Z] New York, NY St. Catherine of Siena Priory.

Fitzsimmons, Thomas B. '62 (CAM) Stratford, NJ St. Luke's Church.

Fitzsimmons, Thomas B. '62 (CIN) [41] Cincinnati, OH St. James Church.

Fitzsimons, Philip '81 (SEA) Monroe, WA St. Mary of the Valley Church.

Fitzwilliam, Ivan '48 (SB) Retired.

Fiut, Casimiro *c.ss.r.* '88 (RCK) DeKalb, IL St. Mary Church.

Fives, Carl J. '42 (BAL) [C] Emmitsburg, MD Mount Saint Mary's College.

Fives, Carl J. '42 (SCR) On Duty Outside the Diocese.

Fix, Donald P. '80 (PIT) Military Chaplains.

Fix, Joseph J. '68 (GR) Baldwin, MI St. Ann's Church.

Fix, Robert H. '53 (CHR) [4] Columbia, SC Our Lady of the Hills Church.

Fizcaya, Natividad Acevedo *o.p.* (SJN) [B] Toa Alta, PR Santo Domingo de Guzman Priory.

Flaat, Bart A. *c.i.c.m.* '63 (BWN) [4] McAllen, TX St. Joseph the Worker Church.

Flach, Carl J. '58 (P) Hillsboro, OR St. Matthew Church.

Flach, James A. '86 (SFD) Bethalto, IL Our Lady Queen of Peace Church; Grantfork, IL St. Gertrude Church; Marine, IL St. Elizabeth Church; St. Jacob, IL St. James Church.

Flach, Thomas D. '71 (BEL) Caseyville, IL St. Stephen Church.

Flack, LaVern *o.s.a.* '55 (JOL) [J] New Lenox, IL Augustinian Friary.

Flack, Robert S. *s.j.* '74 (CHI) [N] Chicago, IL Chicago Province of the Society of Jesus-Provincial Office.

Fladung, Charles '92 (DAV) Knoxville, IA St. Anthony's Church; Melcher, IA Sacred Heart Church; Pella, IA St. Mary's Church.

Flagg, Robert W. '65 (BO) On Special or Other Diocesan Assignment; [A] Boston, MA St. John's Seminary.

Flagg, Wayne N. '88 (VIC) Frelsburg, TX SS. Peter and Paul Church; Mentz, TX St. Roch Church.

Flagor, David A. '91 (DOD) Ashland, KS Holy Spirit Church; Ashland, KS St. Joseph Church; Greensburg, KS St. Joseph Church.

Flahavan, Edward J. '57 (STP) St. Paul, MN Ramsey County Correctional Facilities; Special Assignment.

Flahavan, Robert J. *s.j.* '50 (MIL) [P] Wauwatosa, WI Jesuit Community at St. Camillus.

Flaherty, Charles B. *s.s.c.* '50 (BO) [34] Boston, MA St. John Chrysostom Church; [W] Quincy, MA St. Columban's Foreign Mission Society.

Flaherty, Daniel E. '70 (BO) [1] Waltham, MA St. Charles Borromeo Church.

Flaherty, Daniel J. '54 (DEN) Longmont, CO Spirit of Peace Parish Church.

Flaherty, Daniel L. *s.j.* '60 (CHI) [N] Chicago, IL Chicago Province of the Society of Jesus-Provincial Office; [N] Evanston, IL Canisius House.

Flaherty, Edward F. *s.j.* '65 (DEN) [M] Denver, CO Xavier Jesuit Center.

Flaherty, Francis T. '62 (WDC) Retired.

Flaherty, Frederick R. *m.s.* '57 (R) Havelock, NC Annunciation Church.

Flaherty, Msgr. J. Francis *p.a.* '55 (CAM) Somerdale, NJ Our Lady of Grace Church; Retired.

Flaherty, James J. '80 (PT) De Funiak Springs, FL St. Margaret Church; Freeport, FL Christ the King Mission Church.

Flaherty, James P. *s.j.* '92 (MIL) [P] Milwaukee, WI Jesuit Provincial Office, Wisconsin Province.

Flaherty, James P. '92 (NY) [Z] New York, NY Jesuit Provincial's Office; [Z] New York, NY Xavier Jesuit Community.

Flaherty, Jay '85 (KNX) Gatlinburg, TN St. Mary Church.

Flaherty, Jay M. '85 (NSH) On Duty Outside the Diocese.

Flaherty, John '90 (DUB) [D] Gilbertville, IA Don Bosco High School.

Flaherty, John J. *o.s.a.* '55 (CHI) [N] Olympia Fields, IL Tolentine Monastery at Tolentine Center.

Flaherty, John R. '90 (DUB) Raymond, IA St. Joseph's Church.

Flaherty, Kevin H. *s.j.* '83 (CHI) [N] Chicago, IL Chicago Province of the Society of Jesus-Provincial Office.

Flaherty, Kevin S. (RVC) Absent on Leave.

Flaherty, Leon J. *c.pp.s.* '61 (COL) [23] Columbus, OH St. James the Less Church.

Flaherty, Malachy *o.f.m.cap.* (RVC) Retired.

Flaherty, Malachy *o.c.s.o.* '60 (SLC) [F] Huntsville, UT Abbey of Our Lady of the Holy Trinity of the Order of Cistercians.

Flaherty, Malachy C. *o.f.m.cap.* '42 (RVC) Greenlawn, NY St. Francis of Assisi Church; Melville, NY Long Island Developmental Center.

Flaherty, Michael T. '73 (CIN) [55] Cincinnati, OH St. Margaret of Cortona Church.

Flaherty, Richard C. *o.f.m.* '82 (BUF) [O] St. Bonaventure, NY St. Bonaventure Friary.

Flaherty, Thomas *o.s.b.* '48 (KCK) [H] Atchison, KS St. Benedict's Abbey.

Flaherty, William '52 (CHI) Winnetka, IL SS. Faith, Hope and Charity Church.

Flaherty, William H. '33 (RVC) Retired.

Flaherty, William J. '52 (CHI) Flossmoor, IL Infant Jesus of Prague Church; Retired.

Flahive, James J. '48 (SPR) [2] Chicopee, MA Holy Name of Jesus Church.

Flajole, John *o.f.m.* '64 (LA) [R] Santa Barbara, CA Franciscan Friary, Order of Friars Minor (Old Mission).

Flammia, Paul (BO) Saugus, MA Blessed Sacrament Church.

Flanagan, Austin E. '66 (SCR) [2] Hazleton, PA Church of the Most Precious Blood; [I] Hazleton, PA Hazleton-Saint Joseph Medical Center.

Flanagan, Bernard A. '82 (ALN) [4] Saint Clair, PA St. Mary Church; [C] Pottsville, PA Nativity B.V.M. High School.

Flanagan, Brian '63 (PAT) [7] Clifton, NJ St. Paul Church.

Flanagan, Bruce G. (BO) Hanover, MA St. Mary of the Sacred Heart Church.

Flanagan, Damian '91 (MIA) [6] Miami, FL Good Shepherd Church.

Flanagan, David J. '87 (MAD) Sun Prairie, WI Sacred Hearts of Jesus and Mary Church.

Flanagan, Edward *o.f.m.* '64 (SP) [O] Belleair Bluffs, FL St. James Friary.

Flanagan, Edward R. '88 (MET) Spotswood, NJ Immaculate Conception Church.

Flanagan, Francis A. *c.ss.r.* '42 (STL) [P] Liguori, MO St. Clement Health Care Center.

Flanagan, Msgr. Francis B. '32 (BUR) Retired.

Flanagan, Francis D. *o.m.i.* '36 (BO) [Z] Tewksbury, MA Immaculate Heart of Mary Novitiate-Infirmary.

Flanagan, James (BO) On Duty Outside the Archdiocese.

Flanagan, James *s.o.l.t.* '52 (CC) Robstown, TX St. Anthony Church; [H] Robstown, TX Society of Our Lady of the Most Holy Trinity.

Flanagan, James D. '71 (NY) [147] Bronx, NY Holy Family Church.

Flanagan, James E. *c.s.s.* '50 (SPR) [9] Springfield, MA Our Lady of Mt. Carmel Church.

Flanagan, James W. '61 (CLV) [Y] Cleveland, OH Office of Newman Campus Ministry.

Flanagan, James W. '61 (DUB) On Duty Outside the Archdiocese.

Flanagan, John '59 (SY) [4] Utica, NY Sacred Heart Church.
Flanagan, John *m.s.f.* '74 (SAT) Kenedy, TX Our Lady of Peace Church; Runge, TX St. Anthony's Church.
Flanagan, John D. '73 (NY) [96] New York, NY Our Lady of the Rosary Church.
Flanagan, Joseph F. X. *s.j.* '59 (BO) [W] Chestnut Hill, MA The Jesuit Community at Boston College.
Flanagan, Lawrence W. *s.j.* '52 (OM) [K] Omaha, NE Jesuit Community At Creighton University.
Flanagan, Michael J. *m.s.* '60 (ATL) Snellville, GA St. Oliver Plunkett Church.
Flanagan, Michael T. '65 (JC) Columbia, MO Our Lady of Lourdes Church.
Flanagan, Msgr. P. Kevin '59 (PAT) Chester, NJ St. Lawrence the Martyr Church.
Flanagan, Patrick *c.m.* (BUF) [R] Williamsville, NY Newman Club Chaplains.
Flanagan, Msgr. Patrick J. '56 (SAT) Converse, TX St. Monica Church.
Flanagan, Patrick S. *c.m.* '92 (BUF) [C] Niagara University, NY Niagara University.
Flanagan, Patrick S.L. *c.m.* '92 (BUF) [O] Niagara University, NY Vincentian Community at Niagara University.
Flanagan, Sean B. '59 (LA) Reseda, CA St. Catherine of Siena Church.
Flanagan, Thomas '56 (SAT) [31] San Antonio, TX St. Brigid Church.
Flanagan, Msgr. Thomas J. '49 (BRK) Retired.
Flanagan, Thomas J. '74 (SC) On Duty Outside the Diocese.
Flanagan, Thomas P. '69 (PH) Upper Gwynedd, PA Corpus Christi Church.
Flanagan, William '64 (JC) Monroe City, MO Holy Rosary Church.
Flanagan, William J. '28 (SFR) Belmont, CA St. Mark Church.
Flanagan, William J. '46 (SFR) Retired.
Flanary, Michael '89 (GB) Algoma, WI St. Mary Church.
Flanery, Joseph-Mary *o.c.d.* '55 (MIL) [P] Holy Hill, WI Discalced Carmelite Monastery.
Flanigan, Msgr. Gerald A. '51 (DET) Retired.
Flanigan, James F. *c.s.c.* '62 (FTW) [B] Notre Dame, IN University of Notre Dame Du Lac; [J] Notre Dame, IN Holy Cross Community, Corby Hall, University of Notre Dame.
Flanigan, Thomas K. '50 (ALB) [12] Troy, NY St. Peter Church.
Flanik, Rudolph *o.carm.* '42 (JOL) [J] Darien, IL Carmelite Fathers Provincial Office.
Flannery, Edward H. '37 (PRO) Georgiaville, RI St. Michael's Church.
Flannery, Edward M. '35 (CHI) [182] Chicago, IL St. Rene Goupil Church; Retired.
Flannery, Gerald K. '59 (DET) [1] Livonia, MI St. Aidan Church.
Flannery, Joseph D. '53 (SCR) Taylor, PA Immaculate Conception Church.
Flannery, Kevin L. *s.j.* '87 (DET) [K] Detroit, MI Jesuit Provincial Office-Detroit Province of the Society of Jesus.
Flannery, Michael '50 (NY) Retired.
Flannery, Michael '64 (JKS) [1] Jackson, MS St. Peter Cathedral.
Flannery, Robert B. '73 (BEL) Trenton, IL St. Mary Church.
Flannigan, John G. *s.j.* '43 (STL) [O] St. Louis, MO Fusz Pavilion.
Flannigan, Patrick *o.f.m.* '90 (WDC) [M] Washington, DC Commissariat of the Holy Land, Franciscan Monastery - Mount St. Sepulchre.
Flaska, John '68 (SFE) Military Chaplains.
Flater, Gerald *o.m.i.* '57 (BO) Tewksbury, MA St. William Church.
Flatley, Brian M. '66 (BO) [1] Arlington, MA St. Agnes Church; On Special or Other Diocesan Assignment.
Flatley, Eugene T. '46 (GB) Retired.
Flattery, John J. '55 (PEO) Retired.
Flavin, Daniel F. '45 (BIS) Retired.
Flavin, James *o.m.i.* '63 (MIA) Miramar, FL St. Stephen Church.
Flavin, James A. '87 (BO) [2] Brockton, MA St. Colman of Cloyne Church.
Flavin, John E. '61 (CHI) Glenview, IL Our Lady of Perpetual Help Church; [M] Glenview, IL Maryhaven Inc.
Flecce, William '60 (SLC) Provo, UT St. Francis of Assisi Church.
Fleck, David '75 (EVN) St. Philip, IN St. Philip's Church.
Fleck, John '59 (TOL) Spencerville, OH St. Patrick Church.
Fleck, John W. '59 (TOL) Landeck, OH St. John Baptist Church.
Fleck, Kenneth J. '76 (CHI) Other Assignments.
Fleck, Richard A. *o.p.* '55 (BO) [W] Dover, MA St. Stephen Priory; [Y] Dover, MA St. Stephen Priory Spiritual Life Center.
Flecky, Michael J. *s.j.* '77 (OM) [K] Omaha, NE Jesuit Community At Creighton University.
Fleischhacker, John J. *o.s.c.* '61 (DUL) McGregor, MN Holy Family Church.
Fleischhacker, John J. *o.s.c.* '61 (SCL) [I] Onamia, MN Crosier Monastery.
Fleischman, Richard J. '68 (MIL) [2] Sheboygan, WI SS. Cyril and Methodius Church; [Y] Sheboygan, WI St. Thomas High School, Inc.
Fleischmann, George R. '56 (MIL) Retired.
Fleishaker, Joseph *s.v.d.* '47 (TR) [M] Bordentown, NJ Society of the Divine Word.
Fleiter, Robert F. '61 (STL) Herculaneum, MO Church of the Assumption of B.V.M.
Flek, Msgr. Ladis Laus J. (PAT) Retired.
Fleming, Austin H. '73 (BO) Concord, MA Our Lady Help of Christians Church.
Fleming, Daniel J. '96 (ATL) Duluth, GA St. Benedict Church.
Fleming, David *o.f.m.* '43 (BO) [Z] Boston, MA Saint Anthony Residence.
Fleming, David *s.m.* '69 (STL) [P] St. Louis, MO Provincialate of the Society of Mary, Province of St. Louis.
Fleming, David '90 (DM) On Special Assignment.
Fleming, David L. (STL) [P] St. Louis, MO Jesuit Community Corporation at St. Louis University - Jesuit Hall.
Fleming, Msgr. Edward J. '44 (NEW) Retired; [B] South Orange, NJ Seton Hall University.
Fleming, Msgr. Francis J. '39 (STP) [M] St. Paul, MN Franciscan Health Community.
Fleming, Msgr. Francis J. '42 (STP) Retired.
Fleming, George '94 (ALB) [9] Schenectady, NY St. John the Evangelist Church.
Fleming, J. Brendan '52 (P) Sutherlin, OR St. Francis Xavier Church.
Fleming, J.J. '85 (SAG) Carrollton, MI St. John the Baptist Church.
Fleming, James *s.j.* '95 (SFR) [24] San Francisco, CA St. Ignatius Church.
Fleming, James J. *s.j.* '95 (BO) [W] Boston, MA The Society of Jesus of New England-Provincial Offices.
Fleming, James J. *s.j.* '95 (SFR) [N] San Francisco, CA Jesuit Community at University of San Francisco.
Fleming, Jeffrey '92 (HEL) [1] Helena, MT Cathedral of St. Helena.
Fleming, John F. '49 (NY) Retired.
Fleming, John M. '61 (CAM) Hammonton, NJ St. Anthony of Padua Church.
Fleming, John R. '42 (NU) Retired.
Fleming, John R. '42 (STP) [M] St. Paul, MN Franciscan Health Community.
Fleming, John W. '96 (MAN) [3] Nashua, NH St. Christopher Church.
Fleming, Msgr. Joseph H. '43 (ALT) Retired.
Fleming, Joseph W. '74 (ALT) St. Augustine, PA St. Augustine Church.
Fleming, Martin M.P. '52 (STP) Special Assignment; [M] St. Paul, MN Franciscan Health Community.
Fleming, Patrick J. *c.m.* '43 (PH) [Z] Philadelphia, PA Congregation of the Mission.
Fleming, Msgr. Patrick V. '48 (ALT) Retired.
Fleming, R. Maurus *o.s.b.* '53 (PRO) [P] Portsmouth, RI Abbey of St. Gregory the Great.
Fleming, Raymond H. '82 (ROC) [46] Rochester, NY Emmanuel Church of the Deaf of the Diocese of Rochester; [48] Rochester, NY St. Monica Church; [L] Rochester, NY St. Francis de Sales Deaf Assn.
Fleming, Terence K. '67 (ROC) On Duty Outside the Diocese.
Fleming, Msgr. Terrance '73 (LA) [1] Los Angeles, CA Cathedral of Our Lady of the Angels.
Fleming, Thomas '55 (JOL) South Wilmington, IL St. Lawrence Church.
Fleming, Thomas B. '76 (WOR) [1] Leominster, MA St. Anna's Church.
Fleming, Thomas E. *s.j.* '50 (BUF) [O] Buffalo, NY Canisius Jesuit Community.
Fleming, Thomas F. *s.j.* '42 (BO) [W] Chestnut Hill, MA The Jesuit Community at Boston College.
Fleming, Thomas J. '59 (BO) [3] Gloucester, MA St. Peter Church.
Fleming, Thomas J. '85 (SAG) Zilwaukee, MI St. Matthew Church.
Fleming, Msgr. Vincent A. '44 (SR) Retired.
Fleming, Msgr. W. Stanley '52 (COV) Retired.
Fleming, Msgr. William J. '48 (SCR) [1] Williamsport, PA Annunciation Church.
Fleming, William J. '58 (NSH) [1] Nashville, TN Cathedral of the Incarnation.
Flemming, James '86 (VEN) Lehigh Acres, FL St. Raphael Church.
Flens, Daniel A. '89 (CHI) Chicago Heights, IL St. Kieran Church.
Flesey, Msgr. John W. '69 (NEW) [A] South Orange, NJ Immaculate Conception Seminary; [B] South Orange, NJ Seton Hall University.
Fletcher, Emeric *o.s.b.* '60 (KCK) [H] Atchison, KS St. Benedict's Abbey.
Fletcher, Patrick '85 (PCE) On Duty Outside the Diocese.
Fleury, Joseph M. '84 (WDC) [M] Washington, DC Marist Provincial House.
Flickinger, Don '64 (SJ) [6] San Jose, CA St. Frances Cabrini Church.
Flickinger, Don D. '64 (FRS) On Duty Outside the Diocese.
Flickinger, Robert E. '75 (KAL) Paw Paw, MI St. Mary Church.
Flinn, Msgr. George B. '66 (ALT) [1] Johnstown, PA St. John Gualbert Cathedral.
Flint, Edward A. *s.j.* (DET) [K] Detroit, MI Jesuit Provincial Office-Detroit Province of the Society of Jesus.
Flint, James *o.s.b.* '83 (JOL) [A] Lisle, IL Benedictine University; [J] Lisle, IL St. Procopius Abbey.
Flint, Kenneth '42 (NOR) Retired.
Flis, Stanislaw '69 (DET) [A] Orchard Lake, MI SS. Cyril and Methodius Seminary.
Flisiak, Stefan '32 (OM) Retired.
Fliss, James W. '75 (BUF) [3] Buffalo, NY St. Agatha Church.
Fliss, Paul J. '92 (MIL) [6] Sheboygan, WI St. Peter Claver Church.
Fliss, Richard L. '66 (LC) [10] La Crosse, WI St. Thomas More Church.
Floch, W. Roy '77 (SPK) Military Chaplains.
Flock, Robert H. '82 (LC) Foreign Missions.
Flohr, Gregory J. '64 (GBG) Saltsburg, PA St. Matthew Church.
Flood, Augustine '64 (GBG) Crabtree, PA St. Bartholomew Church.
Flood, Charles J. *o.ss.t.* '90 (BAL) [M] Baltimore, MD Holy Trinity Monastery.
Flood, Francis A. *o.s.b.* '93 (SP) [O] St. Leo, FL St. Leo Abbey.
Flood, J. Michael '68 (PH) Glenside, PA St. Luke the Evangelist Church; [DD] Philadelphia, PA Newman Apostolate; [EE] Glenside, PA Counseling Center at St. Luke's.
Flood, James F. '62 (CLV) Stow, OH Holy Family Church.
Flood, Msgr. James J. '58 (PH) Narberth, PA St. Margaret Church.
Flood, Joseph *c.s.s.* '49 (BO) [W] Waltham, MA Stigmatine House.
Flood, Matthew C. *s.j.* '61 (NY) [F] New York, NY Fordham Preparatory School; [Z] New York, NY Jesuit Community at Fordham University.
Flood, Maurice *o.c.s.o.* '91 (ARL) [J] Berryville, VA Cistercian Abbey of Our Lady of the Holy Cross; [L] Berryville, VA Retreat House, Holy Cross Abbey.
Flood, Msgr. Patrick '45 (FRS) Retired.
Flood, Paul A. '90 (ATL) Toccoa, GA St. Mary's Church.
Flood, Peter J. '69 (TR) Military Chaplains.
Flood, Msgr. William '57 (BRK) [211] Queens, NY Our Lady of Grace Church.
Flora, Carmel *o.f.m.cap.* '53 (DET) [K] Detroit, MI St. Bonaventure Friary.
Florczyk, Walter '62 (SY) Absent on Sick Leave.
Florek, Msgr. Frederick J. '64 (SD) [36] San Diego, CA St. Therese Church.
Florek, Richard *o.f.m.conv.* '72 (BAL) [26] Baltimore, MD St. Clement Mary Hofbauer Church.
Florek, Thomas W. *s.j.* '86 (CHI) [N] Chicago, IL Chicago Province of the Society of Jesus-Provincial Office.
Flores, Arthur *o.m.i.* '92 (SAT) [M] San Antonio, TX De Mazenod House.
Flores, Cirilo '91 (ORG) Costa Mesa, CA St. Joachim Church.
Flores, Msgr. Daniel '88 (CC) On Special Assignment; [A] Corpus Christi, TX Corpus Christi Academy.
Flores, Florentino '68 (ARE) [2] Camuy, PR Our Lady of the Miraculous Medal Church.
Flores, Jose '73 (CGS) Caguas, P.R. Hospital Hima; [E] Caguas, PR Movimiento Juan XXIII.
Flores, Jose A. (ARE) On Duty Outside the Diocese.
Flores, Lee '85 (GAL) [38] Houston, TX St. Jerome Church.
Flores, Ramiro '95 (OAK) Pinole, CA St. Joseph's Church.
Flores, Richard '74 (FWT) [15] Fort Worth, TX St. Rita Church.
Floretta, Edward A. '60 (BRK) [133] Brooklyn, NY SS. Simon and Jude Church.
Florez, Laurence A. '59 (PHX) Retired.
Florez, Luis '59 (STA) [1] Jacksonville, FL Assumption Church.
Florez, Virgilio (LSC) Lordsburg, NM St. Joseph Church.
Flori, David J. '86 (DAL) [24] Dallas, TX St. Philip Church.
Florido, Msgr. Raphael A. '45 (BRK) [55] Brooklyn, NY Holy Family Church; Retired.
Florido, Vicente '70 (NY) [163] Bronx, NY St. Martin of Tours Church.
Florio, Anselmo M. *o.cist.* '54 (TR) Mount Laurel, NJ St. John Neumann Church; [M] Mount Laurel, NJ Cistercian Monastery of Our Lady of Fatima.
Flour, Anton '35 (SPK) Retired.
Flower, Thomas A. '65 (HRT) Tariffville, CT St.

Bernard's Church.
Flowers, Thomas A. '77 (WIL) Middletown, DE St. Joseph Church.
Fluet, Gregoire J. '82 (NOR) North Grosvenordale, CT St. Joseph Church.
Fluetsch, John '91 (FRS) [7] Fresno, CA St. Anthony of Padua Church.
Flusche, David '46 (LR) [A] Subiaco, AR Subiaco Monastery.
Flusche, Ernest A. '54 (OKL) Norman, OK St. Joseph's Church.
Flusche, Vincent '90 (LR) [6] Little Rock, AR St. Edward Church.
Flusk, Msgr. Joseph F. '53 (NEW) Hohokus, NJ St. Luke's Church.
Flynn, Anthony G. '66 (PH) [102] Philadelphia, PA St. Matthew Church; Chester Heights, PA St. Thomas the Apostle Church.
Flynn, Arthur C. '52 (BO) Reading, MA St. Agnes Church.
Flynn, Brian *o.f.m.* '60 (OAK) [P] Danville, CA San Damiano Retreat.
Flynn, Charles '69 (DUL) [2] Duluth, MN Good Shepherd Church; [8] West Duluth, MN St. James Church.
Flynn, Charles L. (WOR) [B] Worcester, MA Assumption College.
Flynn, Charles R. *o.s.a.* '43 (PH) [Z] Villanova, PA St. Thomas Monastery.
Flynn, D. Michael *s.j.* '73 (NY) [80] New York, NY Nativity Church.
Flynn, Msgr. Daniel V. '48 (NY) Harrison, NY St. Gregory the Great Church.
Flynn, Dennis *s.v.d.* (SB) San Bernardino, CA San Bernardino County Medical Center.
Flynn, Edmund *o.c.s.o.* '70 (ARL) [J] Berryville, VA Cistercian Abbey of Our Lady of the Holy Cross.
Flynn, Edward J. '44 (RVC) Retired; [N] Uniondale, NY St. Pius X Residence.
Flynn, Edward R. '54 (SD) On Duty Outside the Diocese.
Flynn, Fabian A. *o.f.m.* '51 (NY) Obernburg, NY St. Mary Church.
Flynn, Francis '67 (PMB) Lake Worth, FL Sacred Heart Church.
Flynn, Francis J. (BRK) Absent on Sick Leave; Retired.
Flynn, Francis J. '37 (GR) Retired.
Flynn, Francis J. '37 (KAL) Retired.
Flynn, Francis J. '69 (OG) Potsdam, NY St. Mary Church; Potsdam, NY St. Francis of Assisi Campus Parish (Newman Center) Church.
Flynn, Francis J. *m.m.* '76 (NY) [Z] Maryknoll, NY Maryknoll Fathers and Brothers.
Flynn, George '41 (JOL) Retired.
Flynn, George R. (BO) Society of St. James the Apostle.
Flynn, J. Joseph *o.f.m.cap.* (NY) [CC] New York, NY University Apostolate.
Flynn, J. Michael *s.j.* '96 (R) [7] Raleigh, NC St. Raphael Church.
Flynn, James '55 (L) [51] Louisville, KY St. Martin de Porres Church.
Flynn, James '73 (SD) [A] San Diego, CA St. Francis Seminary.
Flynn, James A. '39 (STL) Retired.
Flynn, Msgr. James B. '48 (SFR) Redwood City, CA St. Matthias Church.
Flynn, James B. '64 (WOR) Southborough, MA St. Matthew Church; [C] Worcester, MA Holy Name Central Catholic High School.
Flynn, James E. '67 (CHI) [83] Chicago, IL Holy Name of Mary Church.
Flynn, James P. '36 (BUF) Retired.
Flynn, James P. '47 (NY) Patterson, NY Sacred Heart Church.
Flynn, James R. *o.s.a.* '72 (PH) [G] Malvern, PA Malvern Preparatory School for Boys.
Flynn, John *o.s.a.* '53 (CHI) [40] Chicago, IL St. Clare of Montefalco Church.
Flynn, Msgr. John A. (OM) [O] Omaha, NE The Omaha Archdiocesan Community Foundation and Donor Directed Depository.
Flynn, John A. '54 (OM) [2] Omaha, NE St. Adalbert Church; [O] Omaha, NE Omaha Archdiocesan Educational Foundation, Inc.
Flynn, John C. '55 (NY) [163] Bronx, NY St. Martin of Tours Church.
Flynn, Msgr. John F. '52 (SAT) [57] San Antonio, TX St. Matthew's Church.
Flynn, John F. *s.m.a.* '56 (PMB) Vero Beach, FL St. Helen Church.
Flynn, John H. (BO) Retired.
Flynn, John J. (NY) Retired.
Flynn, John J. *s.j.* '69 (LA) [C] Los Angeles, CA Loyola Marymount University.
Flynn, John L. *s.j.* '64 (SJ) [D] San Jose, CA Bellarmine College Preparatory.
Flynn, John R. *o.s.a.* '71 (ORL) Casselberry, FL St. Augustine Church.
Flynn, Joseph A. '47 (HRT) Retired.
Flynn, Joseph D. '62 (BO) Walpole, MA Blessed Sacrament Church.
Flynn, Joseph Leo *c.p.* '33 (HRT) [M] West Hartford, CT Holy Family Monastery/Retreat.
Flynn, Joseph P. *c.s.p.* '44 (NY) [104] New York, NY St. Paul the Apostle Church; [Z] Scarsdale, NY Paulist Fathers Generalate.
Flynn, Mark F. '72 (HRT) Southbury, CT Sacred Heart Church.
Flynn, Msgr. Martin J. '30 (RVC) Huntington, NY St. Patrick's Church; Retired.
Flynn, Matthew *o.c.s.o.* '58 (WOR) [N] Spencer, MA St. Joseph's Abbey.
Flynn, Michael *o.carm.* '60 (CHI) [142] Chicago, IL Nativity of Our Lord Church.
Flynn, Michael *o.carm.* '61 (JOL) [J] Darien, IL Carmelite Fathers Provincial Office
Flynn, Michael '71 (RVC) Copiague, NY Our Lady of the Assumption Church.
Flynn, Michael E. '77 (CHI) Hickory Hills, IL St. Patricia Church.
Flynn, Michael F. '91 (BGP) [7] Norwalk, CT St. Thomas the Apostle Church.
Flynn, Michael J. '94 (PT) [4] Pensacola, FL Nativity of Our Lord Church.
Flynn, Michael J. *s.j.* '96 (R) [E] Durham, NC Jesuit Community.
Flynn, Patrick *c.ss.r.* '69 (BAL) Annapolis, MD St. Mary Church. [M] Annapolis, MD Saint Mary Rectory.
Flynn, Robert G. '53 (BO) Retired.
Flynn, Robert V. '56 (Y) Streetsboro, OH St. Joan of Arc Church
Flynn, Msgr. Sean P. '75 (TR) [1] Toms River, NJ St. Joseph Church.
Flynn, Stephen F.X. '58 (ALN) Coplay, PA St. Peter Church; Retired.
Flynn, Thomas '61 (HEL) On Duty Outside the Diocese.
Flynn, Thomas A. '60 (CLV) North Olmsted, OH St. Clarence Church.
Flynn, Thomas J. *c.s.sp.* '53 (SHP) Rayville, LA Sacred Heart Church.
Flynn, Thomas M. '58 (CAM) Oaklyn, NJ St. Aloysius Church.
Flynn, Thomas P. '60 (DET) Grosse Ile, MI Sacred Heart Church.
Flynn, Thomas V. *o.p.* '46 (DEN) [28] Denver, CO St. Dominic's Church.
Flynn, Vincent J. '45 (HRT) Retired.
Flynn, William J. *s.s.* '59 (SCR) Montdale, PA Corpus Christi Church.
Flynn, William J. '64 (NOR) [E] Windham, CT St. Joseph Living Center.
Flynt, James M. '85 (MIL) [16] Milwaukee, WI St. Casimir's Church; [50] Milwaukee, WI St. Mary of Czestochowa Church.
Fobare, Scott D. '87 (OG) [1] Watertown, NY Holy Family Church.
Fodor, Nicholas Vitez *sch.p.* '49 (BUF) [O] Derby, NY Piarist Fathers.
Foeckler, Christopher *m.j.* '86 (PCE) [7] Ponce, PR Santa Maria Church.
Foelker, James *o.m.i.* '55 (CC) [4] Kingsville, TX St. Martin Church.
Foeller, Msgr. Charles J. '50 (COL) Cardington, OH Sacred Hearts Church.
Foerch, Benjamin J. *o.f.m.* '65 (SCR) [12] Wilkes-Barre, PA St. Joseph Church; Wilkes-Barre, PA Veteran's Administration Hospital; [M] Wilkes-Barre, PA St. Joseph's Friary.
Foerstler, Robert V. *o.p.* '57 (OAK) [N] Oakland, CA Western Dominican Province.
Fogal, Joseph B. '75 (WIN) Fairmont, MN St. John Vianney Church.
Fogarty, Austin '81 (ATL) Lithonia, GA Christ Our Hope Church.
Fogarty, Daniel '49 (NY) Retired.
Fogarty, Declan (Finbarr) *o.s.a.* '59 (ORG) Buena Park, CA St. Pius V Church.
Fogarty, Msgr. Edmund F. '45 (NY) Shrub Oak, NY Saint Elizabeth Ann Seton Church.
Fogarty, Msgr. George V. '46 (BRK) [189] Queens, NY St. Kevin Church; Retired; [U] Douglaston, NY Bishop Mugavero Residence.
Fogarty, Gerald J. *o.m.i.* '59 (NO) [R] Marrero, LA Ave Maria Retreat House.
Fogarty, Gerald P. *s.j.* '70 (WDC) [M] Washington, DC The Jesuit Community at Georgetown University.
Fogarty, James (SLC) Retired.
Fogarty, John *o.carm.* '50 (TUC) [9] Tucson, AZ Sacred Heart Church.
Fogarty, Joseph *o.p.* '59 (MAD) [J] Sinsinawa, WI Dominican Motherhouse.
Fogarty, Joseph *o.p.* '94 (DUB) [I] Dubuque, IA St. Dominic Villa.
Fogarty, Msgr. Noel '57 (MIA) Plantation, FL St. Gregory Church.
Fogarty, Paul '67 (ATL) [2] Atlanta, GA Holy Cross Church.
Fogarty, Stephen R. *o.s.a.* '34 (PH) [Z] Villanova, PA St. Thomas Monastery.
Fogarty, Thomas *s.s.p.* '57 (Y) [A] Canfield, OH Society of St. Paul.
Fogle, Bruce '83 (OWN) Axtel, KY St. Anthony Church; McQuady, KY St. Mary-of-the-Woods Church.
Foglio, John '61 (LAN) Retired.
Fohlin, Paul *o.c.d.* '81 (MIL) [P] Holy Hill, WI Discalced Carmelite Monastery.
Foisy, Leonard R. '57 (MAN) [11] Manchester, NH St. John the Baptist Church; Absent on Sick Leave.
Foix, Evarist V. *o.c.d.* '28 (LR) [A] Little Rock, AR Marylake - Carmelite Novitiate.
Foken, Herman J. '43 (TLS) Retired.
Folbrecht, Robert '75 (LA) Chatsworth, CA St. John Eudes Church.
Folchetti, John T. '74 (BRK) Released from Diocesan Assignment.
Folda, John T. '89 (LIN) Palmyra, NE St. Leo's Church.
Foley, Msgr. Andrew E. '54 (SFS) Retired.
Foley, Augustine E. *o.s.b.* '89 (NO) [A] St. Benedict, LA St. Joseph's Seminary College; [P] St. Benedict, LA St. Joseph Abbey.
Foley, Brendan P. '55 (HT) Lockport, LA Holy Savior Church.
Foley, Daniel *s.j.* (CIN) [M] Cincinnati, OH Faber Jesuit Community.
Foley, Msgr. Daniel J. '40 (BGP) Retired; [J] Danbury, CT The Pope John Paul II Center for Health Care, Inc.
Foley, Daniel R. '60 (SPR) [10] Holyoke, MA St. Jerome's Church.
Foley, David E. '56 (BIR) [1] Birmingham, AL St. Paul's Cathedral.
Foley, David M. '72 (MEM) [27] Memphis, TN St. Therese of the Infant Jesus Church.
Foley, Dennis *c.ss.r.* '61 (TR) [Q] Long Branch, NJ San Alfonso Retreat House.
Foley, Edward *o.f.m.cap.* '75 (CHI) [B] Chicago, IL The Catholic Theological Union at Chicago.
Foley, Eugene *o.carm.* '86 (PMB) [5] Boca Raton, FL St. Jude Church.
Foley, Francis P. *c.h.c.* '75 (SB) Military Chaplains.
Foley, Francis P. '84 (PH) Military Chaplains.
Foley, Gerald J. '48 (BO) Saugus, MA Blessed Sacrament Church.
Foley, Gerald J. '59 (GB) [2] Manitowoc, WI Holy Innocents Church.
Foley, Gerald K. '61 (CR) Special Assignment.
Foley, Gerald K. '61 (STP) St. Paul, MN HealthEast, Inc.
Foley, Gerard M. '56 (ALX) Tioga, LA Immaculate Heart of Mary Church.
Foley, Ignatius L. *c.m.* '41 (NO) [P] New Orleans, LA Vincentian Fathers.
Foley, J. Patrick '73 (SD) On Duty Outside the Diocese.
Foley, James D. (BO) [6] Salem, MA St. Joseph Church.
Foley, James F. '36 (NEW) Retired.
Foley, James F. '49 (BUR) Retired.
Foley, James J. '66 (PH) East Goshen, PA SS. Peter and Paul Church.
Foley, James J. '78 (BO) Beverly, MA St. Mary Star of the Sea Church; [Q] Brighton, MA St. Elizabeth's Hospital of Boston.
Foley, Msgr. James S. '32 (TR) Bordentown, NJ St. Mary Church; Retired.
Foley, James S. *s.j.* '52 (NEW) [C] Jersey City, NJ St. Peter's Preparatory School.
Foley, Jerome '84 (SFR) Special Assignment.
Foley, Jerome P. '80 (SFR) [S] San Francisco, CA Newman Center, San Francisco State University.
Foley, Jerome P. '84 (SFR) [52] San Francisco, CA St. Thomas More Church.
Foley, John *o.s.f.s.* '59 (STO) Sonora, CA St. Patrick Church.
Foley, John B. *s.j.* '72 (STL) [C] St. Louis, MO Saint Louis University; [P] St. Louis, MO Jesuit Community Corporation at St. Louis University - Jesuit Hall.
Foley, John E. '40 (BO) Retired.
Foley, John F. *s.j.* '58 (BO) [W] Weston, MA Campion Center; [Y] Weston, MA Campion Renewal Center.
Foley, John I. '41 (BO) Retired.
Foley, John J. (BO) Retired.
Foley, John J. '31 (WOR) Retired.
Foley, John J. '50 (NY) [6] Yonkers, NY Christ the King Church; Yonkers, NY Yonkers Police Department.
Foley, John J. *c.s.p.* '67 (SFR) [31] San Francisco, CA Old St. Mary's Cathedral.
Foley, John J. '74 (WOR) [4] Worcester, MA Christ the King Church.
Foley, John K. '59 (LA) Montrose, CA Holy Redeemer Church.
Foley, John L. '33 (DET) Retired.
Foley, John P. *s.j.* '67 (CHI) [177] Chicago, IL St. Procopius Church; [D] Chicago, IL Cristo Rey Jesuit High School, Inc.
Foley, John T. '58 (BO) Permanent Disability.
Foley, Joseph P. *c.m.* '68 (BRK) [D] Queens and Staten Island, NY St. John's University; [U] Jamaica, NY St. Vincent's House.
Foley, Leo *s.m.* '43 (WDC) [C] Washington, DC Catholic University of America, The; [M] Washington, DC Marist Provincial House.
Foley, Louis *o.f.m.* '41 (SP) [O] St. Petersburg, FL St. Anthony Friary.

Foley, Marc *o.c.d.* (CHI) [N] Chicago, IL Edith Stein House of Studies.
Foley, Matthew '89 (CHI) Missionary Work.
Foley, Msgr. Matthew F. '56 (BRK) [37] Brooklyn, NY Epiphany Church.
Foley, Msgr. Maurice D. '34 (LFT) Retired.
Foley, Michael '70 (PT) [3] Tallahassee, FL Good Shepherd Church.
Foley, Michael *s.p.* '73 (STL) [P] St. Louis, MO Servants of the Paraclete.
Foley, Michael '74 (JOL) Morris, IL Immaculate Conception of the Blessed Virgin Mary Church.
Foley, Michael G. '70 (WOR) Milford, MA St. Mary of the Assumption Church.
Foley, Michael G. '86 (CHI) [105] Chicago, IL St. John Berchmans Church; [A] Chicago, IL Archbishop Quigley Preparatory Seminary.
Foley, Msgr. Noel '63 (JKS) [1] Jackson, MS St. Peter Cathedral; Jackson, MS University of Mississippi Medical Center; [G] Jackson, MS Belhaven College Newman Center; [G] Jackson, MS Millsaps College Newman Center; [G] Jackson, MS University of Mississippi Medical Center - Newman Center.
Foley, Odoric *o.f.m.conv.* '54 (SY) [5] Endicott, NY St. Joseph Church.
Foley, Patrick *c.s.c.* '56 (SAT) [M] San Antonio, TX Holy Cross Community.
Foley, Patrick H. '72 (STA) Special Assignment.
Foley, Paul T. '55 (WOR) Retired.
Foley, Peter J. '67 (PH) Darby, PA Blessed Virgin Mary Church.
Foley, Richard L. *o.s.a.* '60 (BO) Andover, MA St. Augustine Church.
Foley, Stephen C. '67 (HRT) [A] Bloomfield, CT St. Thomas Seminary.
Foley, Thomas C. '57 (BO) [3] Milton, MA St. Mary of the Hills Church.
Foley, Thomas F. *m.m.* '48 (SJ) [M] Los Altos, CA Maryknoll.
Foley, Thomas S. '86 (BO) Winchester, MA St. Mary Church.
Foley, Timothy M. '65 (STL) Ferguson, MO Sts. John and James Church.
Foley, Walter W. '20 (ATL) Hartwell, GA Sacred Heart of Jesus Church.
Foley, William (STL) [P] St. Louis, MO Jesuit Community Corporation at St. Louis University - Jesuit Hall.
Foley, William *s.m.* '48 (BO) [W] Boston, MA Marist Fathers and Brothers Provincial House.
Foley, William A. *s.m.* '48 (ORL) Retired.
Foley, William B. *s.j.* '77 (BO) [W] Boston, MA The Society of Jesus of New England-Provincial Offices.
Foley, William E. '79 (WDC) [35] Washington, DC Our Lady of Victory Church.
Foley, Msgr. William J. '67 (NY) New City, NY St. Augustine Church.
Foley, William P. '74 (BAL) [9] Baltimore, MD Annunciation Church.
Folger, Ronald H. '67 (CHI) Libertyville, IL St. Joseph Church.
Follen, George R. *s.j.* '49 (DET) [62] Detroit, MI SS. Peter and Paul Jesuit Church.
Folliard, Msgr. John '50 (LA) [5] Long Beach, CA St. Cornelius Church.
Folliard, Msgr. John P. '50 (LA) Retired.
Follmann, Roland F. *o.s.a.* '60 (JOL) [C] New Lenox, IL Providence Catholic High School; [J] New Lenox, IL Augustinian Friary.
Follmar, A. Joseph '59 (LC) Greenwood, WI St. Mary Help of Christians Church; Willard, WI Holy Family Church.
Folmer, John '68 (SAC) Rancho Cordova, CA St. John Vianney Church.
Folsey, William David *o.p.* '60 (PRO) [P] Providence, RI St. Thomas Aquinas Priory at Providence College.
Folsom, Cassian *o.s.b.* '84 (IND) [J] St. Meinrad, IN St. Meinrad Archabbey.
Folsom, Paul '65 (SCL) Battle Lake, MN Our Lady of the Lake Church; Maine, MN Church of Saint James at Maine.
Folsom, William (MOB) [8] Mobile, AL St. Joan of Arc Church.
Foltyn, Msgr. Emilian '64 (AUS) Dime Box, TX St. Joseph's Church.
Foltz, Charles '68 (B) Caldwell, ID St. Mary Church.
Foltz, Michael H. '89 (CR) Argyle, MN St. Rose Church.
Folzenlogan, Joseph D. *s.j.* '71 (IND) [D] Indianapolis, IN Brebeuf Jesuit Preparatory School, Inc.
Folzenlogen, John N. *s.j.* '65 (GAL) [F] Houston, TX Strake, Jesuit College Preparatory Inc.
Fonck, Benet A. *o.f.m.* '72 (STL) [25] St. Louis, MO St. Anthony of Padua Church; [P] St. Louis, MO Franciscan Friary of St. Anthony of Padua.
Fondevila, Perfecto '62 (SJN) [20] San Juan, PR San Francisco Javier Church.
Fondriest, James '72 (Y) Absent on Leave.
Fones, Michael S. '92 (SLC) [H] Salt Lake City, UT University of Utah, Newman Center.
Fonse, Michael S. *o.p.* '92 (SLC) [7] Salt Lake City, UT St. Catherine of Siena Church.
Fonseca, Erwin A. *c.s.c.* '91 (FTW) [J] South Bend, IN Congregation of Holy Cross Indiana Province Provincial House.
Fonseca, Harvey '92 (FRS) Livingston, CA St. Jude Thaddeus Church.
Fonseca, John '50 (BGP) Retired.
Fonseka, Matthew '69 (NEW) Saddle Brook, NJ St. Philip the Apostle Church.
Fonsela, Rolando '94 (SB) [A] Riverside, CA Blessed Junipero Serra House of Formation.
Fontaine, David *o.carm.* '79 (JOL) [J] Darien, IL Carmelite Fathers Provincial Office.
Fontaine, Edouard '43 (LAF) Retired.
Fontaine, John-Paul '52 (WOR) Retired.
Fontana, Charles S. '69 (DET) Trenton, MI St. Timothy Church.
Fontana, Diana (SPR) West Springfield, MA St. Thomas the Apostle Church.
Fontana, Glenn J. '92 (PEO) Carthage, IL Immaculate Conception Church.
Fontana, John *o.s.m.* '78 (STL) Affton, MO Seven Holy Founders Church.
Fontana, John M. *o.s.m.* '78 (CHI) [N] Chicago, IL Servite Friars - Eastern Province.
Fontanella, Andrew J. '56 (HBG) Carlisle, PA St. Patrick Church.
Fontanez, Msgr. Rafael '57 (SJN) [26] San Juan, PR San Jose Church.
Fonte, Martin Mary of the Crucified Jesus *f.f.i.* '94 (FR) [K] New Bedford, MA Marian Friary of Our Lady, Queen of the Seraphic Order.
Fontenot, Bryan J. *o.p.* '81 (NO) [25] New Orleans, LA St. Anthony Of Padua Church; [C] New Orleans, LA Xavier University of Louisiana; [P] New Orleans, LA Dominican Fathers & Brothers, Southern Dominican Province.
Fonti, Joseph G. '92 (BRK) [34] Brooklyn, NY St. Edmund's Church; [141] Brooklyn, NY St. Thomas Aquinas Church; [141] Brooklyn, NY St. Thomas Aquinas Church.
Foppe, Cyril *o.m.i.* '49 (CR) Baudette, MN Sacred Heart Church.
Foran, Edward R. '60 (HRT) Retired.
Foran, Martin J. '62 (NEW) [B] South Orange, NJ Seton Hall University; [C] West Orange, NJ Seton Hall Preparatory School.
Foran, Peter '22 (LA) [6] Long Beach, CA St. Cyprian Church.
Forand, Clarence W. '45 (SPR) Retired.
Forbes, Eric *o.f.m.cap.* '90 (AGN) [F] Agana Heights, GU St. Fidelis Friary.
Forbes, Msgr. Eugene A. '41 (SAG) Fisherville, MI St. Anthony Church.
Forbes, John J. '91 (R) Sanford, NC St. Stephen Church.
Forbes, Richard L. '67 (CAM) Somerdale, NJ Our Lady of Grace Church.
Forbes, Wayne A. '61 (P) [21] Portland, OR St. John Fisher Church.
Forbidussi, John E. '94 (PIT) Peters Township, PA St. Benedict the Abbot Church.
Forcano, Benito *sch.p.* '66 (PCE) [C] Coto Laurel, PR Colegio Ponceno.
Forcelle, Joseph '80 (SFS) [5] Sioux Falls, SD St. Lambert Church.
Forcier, Richard-Jacob *o.f.m.conv.* '86 (NOR) Stafford Springs, CT St. Edward Church.
Ford, David R. '86 (CHI) Graduate Studies.
Ford, Harold L. '49 (LA) [8] Long Beach, CA St. Joseph Church.
Ford, J. Joseph '67 (PRT) Wells, ME St. Mary Church; [G] Waterville, ME Seton Village Inc.
Ford, James M. '66 (LA) [5] Santa Barbara, CA San Roque Church.
Ford, John *c.s.s.* '56 (BO) [W] Waltham, MA Stigmatine Fathers & Brothers Provincial House.
Ford, John *s.t.* '74 (CLV) [P] Cleveland, OH Missionary Servants of the Most Holy Trinity.
Ford, John T. *c.s.c.* '59 (FTW) [J] South Bend, IN Congregation of Holy Cross Indiana Province Provincial House.
Ford, John T. *c.s.c.* '59 (WDC) [C] Washington, DC Catholic University of America, The.
Ford, Lawrence D. *o.f.m.* '96 (BO) [BB] Boston, MA St. Anthony Shrine.
Ford, Mark *c.m.* '92 (GLP) Page, AZ Immaculate Heart of Mary Church; Tuba City, AZ St. Jude Church.
Ford, Matthew M. *o.s.m.* '48 (CHI) [N] Chicago, IL Servite Friars - Eastern Province.
Ford, Michael F. *s.j.* '75 (WOR) [N] Worcester, MA Jesuits of Holy Cross College, Inc.; [Q] Worcester, MA Campus Ministry.
Ford, Nevin *o.f.m.* '54 (LA) [R] Santa Barbara, CA St. Anthony's Seminary.
Ford, Patrick J. *s.j.* '74 (SPK) [C] Spokane, WA Gonzaga University.
Ford, Richard J. '60 (ALN) [5] Reading, PA Holy Guardian Angels Church.
Ford, Msgr. Robert A. (NY) [E] White Plains, NY Archbishop Stepinac High School.
Ford, William A. '82 (STO) Retired.
Fording, John D. '42 (PIT) Retired; [N] Pittsburgh, PA St. John Vianney Manor.
Forest, Gerald *m.s.* '49 (FR) [K] Attleboro, MA La Salette Shrine.
Forester, Raymond L. '66 (WIL) Perryville, MD Church of the Good Shepherd.
Forgach, Carl J. '60 (Y) [5] Canton, OH St. Benedict Church.
Forgit, Ambrose R. *ss.cc.* '55 (WDC) [B] Cheverly, MD Damien House.
Foriadori, V. David '86 (E) Tidioute, PA St. John Church.
Forintos, Bradley '91 (DET) New Baltimore, MI St. Mary Church.
Forish, Andrew '42 (DET) Retired.
Foriska, John M. '70 (GBG) Calumet, PA St. Stanislaus Church; United, PA St. Florian Church.
Forkin, Gerald *o.m.i.* (BO) [16] Lowell, MA Sacred Heart Church.
Forliti, John E. '62 (STP) [31] Minneapolis, MN St. Olaf Church.
Forman, Bruce H. '74 (STL) [55] St. Louis, MO SS. Peter and Paul Church.
Forman, Patrick J. '89 (BUR) Brattleboro, VT St. Michael Church.
Formusa, Salvatore '35 (JOL) Retired.
Fornasari, Archimedes *m.c.c.j.* '50 (CHI) [B] Chicago, IL The Catholic Theological Union at Chicago.
Forner, Craig '75 (SFR) [16] San Francisco, CA St. Emydius Church.
Forni, John V. '77 (ROC) Wolcott, NY St. Thomas the Apostle Church; Wolcott, NY St. Mary Magdalene Church.
Forno, R. Adam '87 (ALB) Rensselaer, NY St. Joseph Church.
Forrest, Thomas *c.ss.r.* '54 (WDC) [M] Washington, DC Holy Redeemer College.
Forrester, Donal F. *c.s.p.* '34 (NY) [104] New York, NY St. Paul the Apostle Church; [Z] Scarsdale, NY Paulist Fathers Generalate.
Forrey, William C. '90 (HBG) [K] Harrisburg, PA Catholic Campus Ministry.
Forry, Thomas P. (BO) Waltham, MA Coordinator of Prison Ministry.
Forsen, James R. '79 (LA) Baldwin Park, CA St. John the Baptist Church.
Forsmann, Leonard '76 (SPK) Clarkston, WA Holy Family Church.
Forst, Aloysius A. '49 (STL) Berkeley, MO Holy Ghost Church.
Forst, Msgr. Charles '45 (STL) [2] Lemay, MO Most Precious Blood Church.
Forst, Msgr. Robert M. '51 (ALN) [7] Allentown, PA St. Paul Church.
Forst, William '54 (JC) Retired.
Forster, Andrew A. *s.s.* '39 (BAL) [K] Baltimore, MD St. Charles Villa; [M] Baltimore, MD St. Charles Villa.
Forster, Francis P. *o.s.b.* '64 (CHL) [J] Belmont, NC Belmont Abbey.
Forster, Msgr. William J. '54 (BO) [4] Everett, MA St. Therese Church.
Forsthoefel, Paulinus F. *s.j.* '47 (DET) [K] Detroit, MI Jesuit Community at the University of Detroit.
Forsyth, George W. '46 (BRK) Retired.
Forsyth, Kevin J. '86 (HRT) Watertown, CT St. John the Evangelist Church.
Forte, Anthony '91 (NEW) [22] Newark, NJ St. Lucy's Church.
Forte, Anthony J. *s.j.* '83 (BO) [W] Boston, MA The Society of Jesus of New England-Provincial Offices.
Forte', John Paul *o.p.* '93 (SJ) [O] Palo Alto, CA Newman Center, Catholic Community at Stanford.
Fortenbaugh, Msgr. Francis W. '47 (BAL) [3] Baltimore, MD St. Agnes Church; Retired.
Fortenberry, Jerome D. *c.m.* '55 (BEL) Cairo, IL St. Patrick Church.
Fortener, Kenneth R. '69 (L) [5] Louisville, KY St. Ann Church; [28] Louisville, KY St. George Church.
Fortier, Msgr. Charles '45 (LA) [9] Los Angeles, CA Divine Saviour Church.
Fortier, Harvey J. '55 (ALX) Evergreen, LA Little Flower Church.
Fortier, Joel F. '69 (JOL) Bloomingdale, IL St. Isidore Church.
Fortier, Joseph C. *s.j.* '90 (P) [L] Portland, OR Jesuit Provincial Office (Oregon Prov.).
Fortier, Roger A. '80 (MAN) Farmington, NH St. Peter Church.
Fortier, Theodore L. *a.a.* '53 (BO) [3] Quincy, MA St. John the Baptist Church; Boston, MA Quincy Hospital; [W] Brighton, MA Assumptionist Center.
Fortin, Bernard *o.p.* (PRT) [I] Lewiston, ME SS. Peter and Paul Priory.
Fortin, Ernest *a.a.* '49 (BO) [W] Brighton, MA Assumptionist Center.
Fortin, John R. *o.s.b.* '76 (MAN) [K] Manchester, NH St. Anselm Abbey.
Fortin, Richard A. '62 (WOR) Millbury, MA Assumption Church.
Fortin, Robert *a.a.* '58 (BO) [W] Brighton, MA Assumptionist Center.

Fortin, Roger M. '65 (PRO) [5] Warwick, RI St. Gregory the Great Church.
Fortner, Douglas F. '70 (COV) Edgewood, KY St. Pius X Church.
Fortney, Kenneth E. '79 (HEL) Harlowton, MT St. Joseph Church.
Fortuna, George B. '57 (DET) Retired.
Fortuna, Joseph J. '80 (CLV) [8] Cleveland, OH Ascension Church.
Fortuna, Stanley *c.f.r.* '90 (NY) [Z] New York, NY St. Crispin Friary.
Fortunato, Anthony M. *o.de.m.* '67 (CLV) [57] Cleveland, OH Our Lady of Mount Carmel Church; [P] Cleveland, OH Mercedarians.
Fortunato, Vincent *o.f.m.cap.* '80 (NEW) [N] Union City, NJ Capuchin Friars - Prov. Stigmata of St. Francis.
Fortunato, Vincent *o.f.m.cap.* '80 (WDC) [B] Washington, DC St. Francis Friary-Capuchin College.
Fortune, William J. (DEN) [B] Denver, CO Regis University.
Fortunio, Carlo *o.p.* '85 (NEW) West New York, NJ St. Mary Help of Christians Church.
Foshage, Nathanael *o.s.b.* '68 (OM) [K] Elkhorn, NE Mount Michael Abbey.
Foshage, Nathanael *o.s.b.* '68 (PBL) Ouray, CO St. Daniel the Prophet Church; Silverton, CO St. Patrick Church.
Foshage, Ronald *m.s.* '75 (BEA) Jasper, TX St. Michael Church.
Fosnot, James '94 (RIC) Clarksville, VA St. Catherine of Siena Church; South Hill, VA Good Shepherd Church.
Fosselman, Albert '60 (RNO) Retired.
Fosselman, David H. *c.s.c.* '83 (FTW) [J] South Bend, IN Congregation of Holy Cross Indiana Province Provincial House.
Fosselman, Msgr. John '42 (LA) Downey, CA St. Raymond Church; Downey, CA Rancho Los Amigos Medical Center, L.A. County Facility.
Fosselman, Robert J. '42 (LFT) Retired.
Fossier, Msgr. Emile '43 (HT) [1] Houma, LA Cathedral of St. Francis De Sales; Retired.
Fossier, Ignatius *o.s.b.* '44 (NO) [P] St. Benedict, LA St. Joseph Abbey.
Foster, Clyde K. '75 (CLV) Solon, OH St. Rita Church.
Foster, Msgr. Edward C. '51 (BUR) Retired.
Foster, Edward M. '51 (DUL) Pine River, MN Our Lady of Lourdes Church.
Foster, James A. '72 (ALX) Colfax, LA St. Joseph Church.
Foster, James J. '80 (STL) [1] Jennings, MO Corpus Christi/St.Lucy Church; [3] Jennings, MO St. Louise de Marillac Church.
Foster, James K. *c.s.c.* '95 (FTW) [J] South Bend, IN Congregation of Holy Cross Indiana Province Provincial House.
Foster, James M. '85 (ALT) Bellefonte, PA St. John the Evangelist's Church; Altoona, PA Altoona Hospital.
Foster, John '91 (STO) Manteca, CA St. Anthony Church.
Foster, John F. *s.j.* '68 (SEA) [A] Seattle, WA Seattle University.
Foster, John J. '51 (PH) Fallsington, PA St. Joseph the Worker Church.
Foster, Jonathan D. *o.f.m.* '60 (JOL) [L] Downers Grove, IL Mayslake Marmion Ministries, Inc.
Foster, Joseph R. (BO) Marblehead, MA Our Lady, Star of the Sea Church.
Foster, Msgr. Michael (BO) [4] Newton, MA St. John the Evangelist Church.
Foster, Patrick '56 (EVN) Jasper, IN St. Joseph Church.
Foster, Raymond *o.carm.* '73 (JOL) [J] Joliet, IL St. Elias Carmelites.
Foster, Reginald *o.c.d.* '66 (MIL) [P] Milwaukee, WI Provincial Offices - Discalced Carmelites.
Foster, Robert *c.s.v.* '60 (TUC) [E] Tucson, AZ Carondelet Health Care Corporation of Arizona, Inc.
Foster, Robert L. '47 (GI) Retired.
Foster, Tom *s.j.* '72 (MRY) Capitola, CA St. Joseph Church.
Foster, William '85 (TOL) [H] Toledo, OH St. Vincent Medical Center.
Foster, William A. '43 (OM) Retired; [H] Omaha, NE Mercy Villa.
Fostner, Jay *o.praem.* '88 (CHI) [N] Chicago, IL Premonstratensian Fathers and Brothers (Norbertines).
Foudy, Denis D. '46 (SFR) Retired.
Foudy, Msgr. John T. '40 (SFR) [10] San Francisco, CA St. Cecilia Church; Retired.
Foudy, Msgr. Robert E. '43 (SPR) [4] Springfield, MA Holy Cross Church; Retired.
Foudy, Thomas F. '67 (MIA) [3] Pompano Beach, FL St. Coleman Church.
Fountain, Dennis *o.f.m.* '81 (LSC) Roswell, NM St. Peter Church; Roswell, NM St. John's Church.
Fountain, Robert J. '55 (BO) [3] Medford, MA St. Joseph Church.
Fournier, Denis *o.s.b.* '60 (BIS) [A] Richardton, ND Assumption Abbey; [B] Bismarck, ND University of Mary.
Fournier, Raymond *s.m.* (BO) [12] Lawrence, MA Sacred Heart Church.
Fournier, Raymond J. *o.c.s.o.* '81 (ROC) [I] Piffard, NY Abbey of the Genesee.
Fournier, W. Donald '53 (SPR) Retired.
Fournier, William '73 (DUL) [11] Duluth, MN St. Lawrence's Church.
Fouser, Otto *o.f.m.conv.* '55 (NEW) [2] Hoboken, NJ St. Joseph's Church; [3] Hoboken, NJ St. Francis Church.
Foutts, Patrick *o.praem.* '93 (ORG) [H] Silverado, CA Norbertine Fathers.
Fowerbaugh, Msgr. F. Raymond '55 (GRY) [2] Whiting, IN Sacred Heart Church.
Fowler, Msgr. Eugene A. '48 (NY) Retired.
Fowler, John W. '53 (DAL) Irving, TX St. Luke Church.
Fowler, Joseph M. '73 (L) [35] Louisville, KY Holy Trinity Church.
Fowler, Richard A. '88 (BUR) Island Pond, VT St. James the Greater Church.
Fowler, Terence L. '88 (BWN) [2] Harlingen, TX Immaculate Heart of Mary Church.
Fowlkes, Eric L. '89 (NSH) Clarksville, TN Immaculate Conception Church.
Fox, Arnold J. *o.s.b.* '34 (SEA) [M] Lacey, WA St. Martin's Abbey.
Fox, Brian *s.s.j.* '91 (GAL) [30] Houston, TX St. Francis Xavier Church.
Fox, Daniel *o.f.m.cap.* '75 (DET) [K] Detroit, MI St. Bonaventure Friary; [K] Detroit, MI St. Bonaventure Friary.
Fox, Daniel '82 (LA) Bellflower, CA St. Bernard Church.
Fox, Donal R. *o.s.b.* '66 (NEW) [1] Linden, NJ St. Elizabeth's Church.
Fox, Donal R. *o.s.b.* '66 (PAT) [M] Morristown, NJ St. Mary's Abbey.
Fox, Francis E. '58 (PH) [101] Philadelphia, PA Maternity B.V.M. Church.
Fox, Francis J. '42 (ALN) Retired.
Fox, Fredrick '52 (DUL) Retired.
Fox, Gabriel '74 (GAY) Manistee, MI St. Mary of Mt. Carmel Shrine Church.
Fox, George W. '61 (MAD) Doylestown, WI St. Patrick Church.
Fox, James E. '74 (DEN) Longmont, CO St. John the Baptist Church.
Fox, James F. *s.j.* '71 (NY) [Z] New York, NY West Side Jesuit Community.
Fox, James F. *s.j.* '71 (WDC) [V] Washington, DC Jesuit Secondary Education Association.
Fox, James R. '90 (DEN) Westminster, CO St. Mark Church.
Fox, John J. '60 (BUF) Getzville, NY St. Pius X Church; Retired.
Fox, Joseph *o.p.* (NY) [Z] New York, NY St. Vincent Ferrer Priory.
Fox, Joseph F. '43 (SCR) Retired.
Fox, Leo '56 (SFS) Retired.
Fox, Leonard D. '55 (SFS) Vermillion, SD St. Agnes Church.
Fox, Martin '65 (GB) [6] Oshkosh, WI Sacred Heart Church.
Fox, Melvin E. '63 (GR) North Muskegon, MI Prince of Peace Church.
Fox, Msgr. Michael D. '50 (NOR) [1] Middletown, CT St. Francis Church.
Fox, Msgr. Patrick '52 (SD) La Jolla, CA All Hallows Church.
Fox, Peter D. *s.j.* '66 (CHI) [C] Chicago, IL Jesuit Community at Loyola University of Chicago.
Fox, Richard *o.c.s.o.* '59 (SPC) [E] Ava, MO Assumption Abbey (Trappist).
Fox, Richard '85 (SFS) Mitchell, SD Holy Spirit Church.
Fox, Richard E. '92 (SCR) [10] Scranton, PA Immaculate Conception Church.
Fox, Robert J. '55 (SFS) Alexandria, SD St. Mary of Mercy Church; [I] Alexandria, SD Fatima Family Apostolate.
Fox, Robert J. '59 (GF) Retired.
Fox, Sean P. '53 (SEA) Mountlake Terrace, WA St. Pius X Church.
Fox, Thomas *o.f.m.* '62 (IND) [36] Indianapolis, IN St. Patrick Church.
Fox, Thomas E. '59 (BRK) [54] Brooklyn, NY Holy Family Church.
Fox, Thomas E. '60 (LFT) Remington, IN Sacred Heart Church.
Foxen, David K. *m.s.c.* (TOL) Mansfield, OH Ohio State Reformatory.
Foxhoven, Msgr. Omer V. '44 (DEN) Retired.
Foy, Edward J. '45 (ROC) Elmira Heights, NY St. Charles Borromeo Church; Retired.
Foy, Felican *o.f.m.* (NEW) Fair Lawn, NJ St. Anne's Church.
Foy, Felician *o.f.m.* (PAT) Paterson, NJ St. Joseph Hospital.
Foy, Felician A. *o.f.m.* '47 (PAT) [P] Paterson, NJ St. Anthony's Guild.
Foye, Harold J. *c.s.p.* '46 (BO) [P] Boston, MA Paulist Center; [W] Boston, MA Paulist Fathers Residence.
Foye, Harold J. *c.s.p.* '46 (NY) [Z] Scarsdale, NY Paulist Fathers Generalate.
Foye, Thomas M. '55 (NEW) [3] Bayonne, NJ St. Henry's Church.
Foynes, Aiden '33 (SP) [F] Clearwater, FL Little Nazareth Early Childhood Center.
Foynes, Aiden '61 (SP) [4] Clearwater, FL St. Cecelia Church.
Foyo, Alexis *o.s.b.* '83 (SD) [H] Oceanside, CA Prince of Peace Abbey, Benet Hill.
Foys, Msgr. Roger J. '73 (STU) Toronto, OH St. Francis of Assisi Church; Toronto, OH St. Joseph's Church; Toronto, OH Servants of Christ the King Church; [B] Steubenville, OH Catholic Central High School; [J] Toronto, OH Charismatic Renewal; [J] Steubenville, OH Diocesan Committee of Administrative Review; [J] Steubenville, OH Lay Employees Pension Plan; [J] Steubenville, OH Synod Committee.
Fraats, Ralph J. '60 (ROC) [59] Rochester, NY St. Thomas the Apostle Church.
Fraber, Joseph (DEN) [34] Denver, CO St. Mary Magdalene's Church.
Fracaro, Mark '67 (JOL) Manteno, IL St. Joseph Church.
Fradet, Msgr. W. John '50 (BUR) [2] Burlington, VT St. Anthony's Church; [3] Burlington, VT Christ the King Church.
Fraenzle, Wilfred J. '64 (LEX) [5] Lexington, KY St. Elizabeth Ann Seton Church.
Fraga, Bento R. *v.f.* '56 (FR) [9] Taunton, MA St. Paul's Church.
Fragomeni, Richard '75 (ALB) On Duty Outside the Diocese.
Fragomeni, Richard '75 (CHI) [B] Chicago, IL The Catholic Theological Union at Chicago.
Fraher, Joseph P. '50 (CHY) Retired.
Fraher, Kevin *c.ss.r.* (CHI) [N] Glenview, IL The Redemptorists of Glenview, Illinois; [T] Glenview, IL Villa Redeemer.
Fraher, Leonard W. (SUP) Retired.
Fraile, Mariano *o.c.d.* '47 (PCE) [12] Ponce, PR San Jose Church.
Fraile, Tomas *c.r.* '63 (DEN) [26] Denver, CO St. Cajetan's Church.
Frain, Msgr. Thomas J. '48 (TR) Retired.
Frambes, John C. *o.f.m.* '79 (ALB) [B] Loudonville, NY Siena College.
Frana, Clarence L. '51 (DUB) Retired.
Francavilla, Joseph F. '68 (NTN) McLean, VA Holy Transfiguration Church.
France-Kelly, Kenneth A. *o.p.* '81 (COL) [36] Columbus, OH St. Patrick Church; [42] Columbus, OH Shrine of Blessed Margaret of Castello Church; [L] Columbus, OH Blessed Margaret Guild, Inc.
Franceschini, Mark *o.s.m.* '59 (DEN) Westminster, CO Holy Trinity Church.
Franceschini, Msgr. Philip J. '66 (NY) [220] Staten Island, NY Our Lady of Pity Church.
Francesco, Richard G. '87 (NEW) Montclair, NJ Immaculate Conception Church.
Francik, Gerard '87 (BAL) Special Assignment; [C] Emmitsburg, MD Mount Saint Mary's College.
Francis, A. Edwin (CIN) Retired.
Francis, Bernard C. '69 (NO) Hahnville, LA Our Lady of the Holy Rosary Church.
Francis, Daniel *c.ss.r.* '91 (NY) [23] New York, NY St. Cecilia Church; [150] Bronx, NY Immaculate Conception Church.
Francis, Msgr. Eugene G. '52 (GAL) [39] Houston, TX St. John Neumann Church.
Francis, Msgr. George J. '37 (OAK) [2] Hayward, CA St. Bede Church; Retired.
Francis, Mark R. *c.s.v.* '82 (CHI) [B] Chicago, IL The Catholic Theological Union at Chicago; [N] Chicago, IL Viatorian Residence.
Francis, Paul R. '41 (BO) Retired.
Francis, Ray A. '63 (NEW) [37] Newark, NJ St. Thomas Aquinas Church.
Francis, William C. '58 (BO) [27] Boston, MA Holy Family Church.
Francisco, Alexander M. '79 (HT) [7] Thibodaux, LA St. Thomas Aquinas Church; Thibodaux, LA Nicholls State University; Thibodaux, LA Thibodaux General Hospital.
Francisco, Joaquim P. *c.s.sp.* '68 (PRO) [4] Pawtucket, RI Immaculate Heart of Mary Church.
Franciscus, Thomas *c.ss.r.* '65 (CHI) [N] Bangkok, Thailand.
Francisko, Gary '82 (PRM) Absent on Leave.
Franck, James E. *c.pp.s.* '64 (OAK) [N] San Leandro, CA Society of the Precious Blood.
Franck, John *c.pp.s.* '67 (LA) [38] Los Angeles, CA St. Agnes Church.
Franck, John L. *a.a.* '77 (BO) [W] Brighton, MA Assumptionist Center.
Franck, Marc E. '53 (PRT) Retired.
Franck, Mark '53 (PRT) [I] Waterville, ME Mt. St. Joseph Priest Retirement Home.
Franco, Andres Balvanera *c.c.r.* '86 (JOL) Bensenville,

IL St. Alexis Church.
Franco, David *o.s.f.s.* '76 (LAN) [6] Ypsilanti, MI Transfiguration Catholic Church.
Franco, Federico *o.s.m.* '91 (ELP) [24] El Paso, TX St. Ignatius of Loyola Church.
Franco, Geraldo Ildeo (BO) [2] Marlboro, MA Immaculate Conception Church.
Franco, Msgr. Hilary (NY) Ossining, NY St. Augustine Church.
Franco, Robert J. '82 (CLV) Strongsville, OH St. John Neumann Church.
Franco, Robert M. *m.ch.a.* '73 (PIT) Forest Hills, PA St. Maurice Church.
Franco, Ronald A. *c.s.p.* '95 (NY) [Z] Scarsdale, NY Paulist Fathers Generalate.
Franco, Salvator V. '53 (BRK) Absent on Sick Leave.
Franco, Victor *l.c.* '81 (HRT) [B] Cheshire, CT Novitiate of the Legion of Christ.
Francois, Jean-Augustin '90 (BRK) [238] Queens, NY Sacred Heart Church.
Francois, Theodore V. *s.j.* '70 (NY) [Z] New York, NY Jesuit Provincial's Office; [Z] New York, NY West Side Jesuit Community.
Franczek, August '48 (MAR) On Duty Outside the Diocese.
Franczek, J. August '48 (GAY) Hale, MI St. Pius X Church.
Franczek, Walter '41 (ORL) Retired.
Franczek, Walter J. '41 (MAR) Retired.
Franer, Msgr. William J. (CIN) Retired.
Franey, John A. '63 (PH) Collegeville, PA St. Eleanor Church; [DD] Philadelphia, PA Newman Apostolate.
Frank, Alfred E. (PAT) Permanent Deacons.
Frank, Edward R. '57 (SAV) Moultrie, GA Immaculate Conception Church.
Frank, Emmeran *o.f.m.* '56 (BR) [H] Baton Rouge, LA Franciscan Residence.
Frank, Eugene G. '57 (BIS) Retired.
Frank, Gerald W. '70 (BWN) [5] McAllen, TX Holy Spirit Church.
Frank, Joseph A. '49 (NEW) Retired.
Frank, Paul *o.m.i.* '50 (MIA) [2] Miami, FL Christ the King Church.
Frank, Richard W. '72 (JC) Freeburg, MO Holy Family Church.
Frank, Thomas R. *s.s.j.* '78 (NO) [B] New Orleans, LA Josephite House of Studies.
Frank, Thomas R. *s.s.j.* '78 (WDC) [32] Washington, DC Our Lady of Perpetual Help Church.
Frank, Tom '70 (AUS) Pflugerville, TX St. Elizabeth Church.
Franken, William F. '88 (BAL) [75] Baltimore, MD Our Lady of Victory Church.
Frankenberger, William J. *c.s.b.* '73 (GAL) [Q] Sugar Land, TX Basilian Mission Center.
Frankey, Charles M. '57 (STL) Ellisville, MO St. Clare of Assisi Church.
Frankhauser, William *s.j.* '29 (BUF) [7] Buffalo, NY St. Ann Church.
Franklin, David W. '85 (BGP) [4] Stamford, CT St. Clement's Church; [2] Stamford, CT St. Leo's Church.
Franklin, Edward L. '62 (OG) Absent on Sick Leave.
Franklin, Edward L. '62 (SB) Lake Tamarisk, CA St. Augustine Church.
Franklin, George '86 (STV) [3] Estate Tutu, VI Holy Family Parish Church.
Frankman, Gregory '81 (SFS) Florence, SD Blessed Sacrament Church.
Franko, George M. '50 (Y) Retired.
Franko, Jack *o.m.i.* '67 (BWN) Port Isabel, TX Our Lady Star of the Sea Church.
Frankovich, Frank '68 (SB) On Duty Outside the Diocese.
Frankovich, Lawrence *o.f.m.* '66 (MIL) [2] West Allis, WI St. Augustine's Church.
Franks, Becket *o.s.b.* '86 (JOL) [J] Lisle, IL St. Procopius Abbey.
Franks, Donald E. '79 (COL) Chillicothe, OH St. Mary Church.
Fransco, Peter J. '58 (SC) Mallard, IA St. Mary's Church.
Fransiscus, Thomas *c.ss.r.* '44 (DEN) [M] Denver, CO The Redemptorists/Denver Province.
Fransiscus, Thomas *c.ss.r.* '65 (CHI) [N] Parana, Brazil Rua Consulheiro Sinimbu.
Fransiscus, Thomas J. *c.ss.r.* (FRS) Planada, CA Sacred Heart Church.
Fransolin, Roberto *s.x.* '83 (PAT) [M] Wayne, NJ Xaverian Missionary Fathers.
Frantz, Henry L. *c.pp.s.* '54 (ORL) Longwood, FL Church of the Nativity.
Franz, Louis *c.m.* '57 (GLP) Page, AZ Immaculate Heart of Mary Church.
Franz, Paul R. '54 (BO) [2] Medford, MA St. James Church.
Franz, S. Michael '69 (CLV) [72] Cleveland, OH St. Stephen Church.
Franzen, Robert B. '53 (SFD) Chatham, IL St. Joseph Church.
Franzinell, Benjamin '75 (LAV) Retired.
Franzman, Thomas R. '70 (CHI) [138] Chicago, IL St. Michael Church.
Frapaul, Sam *o.f.m.cap.* (PAT) [7] Passaic, NJ Mt. Carmel Church.
Frappier, Msgr. George L. '56 (PRO) [4] Woonsocket, RI St. Anthony's Church.
Fraraccio, Ugo *s.d.v.* (PAT) [M] Florham Park, NJ Father Justin Vocationary.
Frascati, Marino *o.de.m.* '51 (BUF) [O] LeRoy, NY Order of the BVM of Mercy/Mercedarian Friars.
Fraser, Donald D. '74 (B) Homedale, ID St. Hubert Church; Parma, ID Sacred Hearts of Jesus and Mary Church.
Fraser, Gerald C. (BO) Priestly Renewal.
Fraser, Gerald D. '38 (CHI) Retired.
Fraser, James F. '65 (BRK) [179] Queens, NY Holy Trinity Church.
Fraser, John F. '96 (NY) [1] Yonkers, NY St. Anthony Church.
Fraser, Michael B. '75 (NO) [5] Marrero, LA The Visitation of Our Lady Church.
Fraser, Thomas '35 (DET) Retired.
Fratic, Joseph P. '64 (BO) Dover, MA Most Precious Blood Church.
Fratus, James F. (BO) [1] Chelsea, MA Our Lady of the Assumption Church; [2] Chelsea, MA St. Rose Church; Boston, MA Juvenile Court Chaplains.
Fratus, Thomas *o.f.m.* '52 (CHI) [167] Chicago, IL St. Peter's Church; [N] Chicago, IL St. Peter's Friary.
Frausto, Jorge *o.f.m.* '86 (ELP) [15] El Paso, TX Our Lady of Guadalupe Church.
Frawley, Brian *o.s.a.* '86 (WDC) [B] Washington, DC Augustinian College, Order of St. Augustine.
Frawley, Gerard *s.a.c.* '68 (DET) [3] Wyandotte, MI St. Joseph Church.
Frawley, John P. '44 (CHI) [206] Chicago, IL St. Thomas More Church; Retired.
Frawley, Patrick J. '78 (BRK) [210] Queens, NY Our Lady of Fatima Church.
Frayne, Thomas M. '88 (CHI) [97] Chicago, IL St. James Church.
Frazer, Edward J. *s.s.* '61 (BAL) [M] Baltimore, MD Sulpician Provincial House.
Frazer, J. Francis '75 (PIT) Beaver Falls, PA St. Philomena Church.
Frazer, Joseph H. '84 (AUS) [17] Austin, TX St. Margaret of Scotland Church.
Frazier, Lawrence K. (BAL) Educational Sabbatical.
Frazier, Richard W. '96 (COV) Fort Thomas, KY St. Thomas Church.
Frazier, William B. *m.m.* '56 (NY) [Z] Maryknoll, NY Maryknoll Fathers and Brothers.
Frazzitta, Barry W. '59 (BRK) [64] Brooklyn, NY Immaculate Heart of Mary Church; [96] Brooklyn, NY Our Lady of Grace Church; Brooklyn, NY The Brooklyn-Caledonian Hospital.
Frechette, Leo L. '55 (MAN) Retired.
Frechette, Leonard A. '52 (PRT) Retired.
Frechette, Paul G. '78 (NTN) Worcester, MA Our Lady of Perpetual Help Church.
Frechette, Thomas A. '86 (FR) Attleboro Falls, MA St. Mark's Church; [C] Attleboro, MA Bishop Feehan High School.
Frecker, Msgr. A. Anthony '72 (COL) Chillicothe, OH St. Peter Church.
Fredeman, Felix '57 (LR) [A] Subiaco, AR Subiaco Monastery.
Frederick, Curt J. '75 (MIL) Brookfield, WI St. Dominic Church.
Frederick, Joseph B. '56 (MIL) [79] Milwaukee, WI St. Veronica's Church.
Frederick, Lawrence A. '66 (LR) [11] Little Rock, AR Our Lady of the Holy Souls Church; [B] Little Rock, AR Catholic High School.
Frederick, Ronald P. '69 (ROC) Unassigned.
Fredericks, James L. '77 (SFR) On Duty Outside the Archdiocese.
Fredericks, Michael '87 (SB) [8] Riverside, CA St. John the Evangelist Church.
Fredette, Albert *m.s.* '52 (FR) [K] Attleboro, MA La Salette Shrine.
Fredette, Joseph *m.s.* '57 (FR) [K] Attleboro, MA La Salette Shrine.
Free, Daniel *c.p.* '52 (BAL) [I] Baltimore, MD St. Agnes HealthCare, Inc.; [M] Baltimore, MD St. Joseph's Passionist Community.
Free, Harold J. *s.j.* '53 (LA) [K] Burbank, CA Providence Saint Joseph Medical Center.
Free, Harold J. *s.j.* '53 (P) [L] Portland, OR Jesuit Provincial Office (Oregon Prov.).
Freed, Eric *s.d.b.* '90 (OAK) [N] Berkeley, CA Salesian Community.
Freed, Robert '83 (WCH) Retired.
Freedman, Mark *o.f.m.cap.* (DET) [K] Detroit, MI St. Mary's Friary.
Freegard, Charles E. '35 (SLC) Retired.
Freeh, Vincent T. *m.s.c.* '59 (OG) [2] Watertown, NY Our Lady of the Sacred Heart, Missionaries of the Sacred Heart Church.
Freel, Frank J. *c.ss.r.* '46 (NY) [92] New York, NY Our Lady of Perpetual Help Church.
Freeman, George J. '65 (STP) Faribault, MN Immaculate Conception Church.
Freeman, Hilary J. *o.p.* '52 (CHI) [N] River Forest, IL St. Thomas Aquinas Priory.
Freeman, James '65 (DM) On Duty Outside the Diocese.
Freeman, James A. '65 (TUC) [15] Tucson, AZ St. Joseph Church; [E] Tucson, AZ Carondelet Health Care Corporation of Arizona, Inc.
Freeman, John A. '73 (PH) Media, PA St. Mary Magdalen Church; [DD] Philadelphia, PA Newman Apostolate; [DD] Philadelphia, PA Newman Apostolate.
Freeman, Joseph M. *s.j.* '44 (KC) [B] Kansas City, MO Rockhurst College; [J] Kansas City, MO Rockhurst College - Jesuit Community.
Freeman, Lawrence '69 (DEN) [5] Denver, CO Blessed Sacrament Church.
Freeman, Lawrence M. '69 (DEN) [G] Denver, CO Religious Education-Pastoral Care of Developmentally Disabled Persons.
Freeman, Msgr. Robert E. '57 (CC) [17] Corpus Christi, TX St. Patrick Church.
Freeman, Roland '67 (DEN) [5] Denver, CO Blessed Sacrament Church.
Freemesser, Paul J. '59 (ROC) [4] Auburn, NY St. Alphonsus Church; Auburn, NY Mercy Health and Rehabilitation Center.
Freeswick, William J. '69 (PAT) [K] Denville, NJ St. Francis Health Resort.
Freeze, J. Donald *s.j.* '63 (WDC) [P] Faulkner, MD Loyola on the Potomac Retreat House.
Frega, John *o.f.m.cap.* '56 (NY) [B] Beacon, NY St. Lawrence of Brindisi Friary.
Fregapane, Msgr. Mercurio A. '51 (HBG) [2] Lebanon, PA St. Benedict the Abbot Church.
Fregault, Roland A. *o.f.m.* '43 (NEW) Elmwood Park, NJ St. Leo's Church.
Fregeau, Guido Anthony '95 (GAL) [17] Houston, TX St. Cecilia Church.
Frego, Max '63 (SAG) Retired.
Freidel, John J. '86 (SPC) [I] Cape Girardeau, MO Southeast Missouri State University, Newman Center.
Freidel, Lawrence *s.v.d.* '28 (CHI) [B] Techny, IL Divine Word Residence.
Freiermuth, Harry '59 (MRY) Retired.
Freire, Gerardo *s.j.* '56 (MIA) [H] Miami, FL Villa Arrieta.
Freishyn-Chirovsky, John M. '90 (SJP) [3] Parma, OH Pokrova Ukrainian Catholic Parish Church.
Freitag, Patrick '96 (SEA) Everett, WA St. Mary Magdalen Church.
Freitas, Daniel L. '49 (FR) Retired.
Freitas, Fernando P. '48 (PRO) Retired.
Freitas, Patrick '65 (HON) [12] Honolulu, HI St. Philomena Church.
Freitas, Robert E. '72 (OAK) [11] Oakland, CA St. Lawrence O'Toole Church.
Fremgen, Edward '92 (LA) Lakewood, CA St. Pancratius Church.
Fremont-Smith, Peter *s.o.l.t.* '92 (CC) [H] Robstown, TX Society of Our Lady of the Most Holy Trinity.
French, D. James *s.j.* '74 (NEW) [26] Jersey City, NJ St. Peter's Church; [C] Jersey City, NJ St. Peter's Preparatory School.
French, Donald J. '76 (HRT) [6] New Haven, CT St. Brendan's Church.
French, Jim R. '78 (STL) St. Louis County, MO St. Sebastian Church.
French, John F. '54 (ALB) Ballston Spa, NY St. Mary Church; Retired.
French, Michael D. *s.j.* '75 (BAL) [C] Baltimore, MD Loyola College; [M] Baltimore, MD Jesuit Community of Loyola College, Inc.
French, Raymond *c.s.sp.* '91 (PIT) [B] Pittsburgh, PA Duquesne University of the Holy Ghost.
French, Raymond D. *c.s.sp.* (PIT) [Q] Slippery Rock, PA Office for Campus Ministry.
French, Robert E. '63 (RIC) [1] Hampton, VA Immaculate Conception Church.
French, Msgr. Thomas A. '49 (SAT) [K] San Antonio, TX Incarnate Word Motherhouse and Retirement Center; [N] San Antonio, TX Incarnate Word Motherhouse and Retirement Community.
French, Walter V. '65 (NEW) Retired.
Frenier, Steven *o.f.m.conv.* '82 (SPR) [10] Chicopee, MA St. Stanislaus Basilica.
Frenoy, Fortune *s.m.* '55 (ORL) [1] Orlando, FL Mary Queen of the Universe Shrine Church.
Freret, Warren '88 (RNO) Hawthorne, NV Our Lady of Perpetual Help Church.
Freret, Warren Joseph (GAL) Retired.
Frerker, Jack W. '63 (BEL) Special Assignment.
Frerker, Jack W. '63 (SEA) [P] Seattle, WA Office of Campus and Young Adult Ministry.
Frerkes, James J. '62 (MRY) Nipomo, CA St. Joseph Church.
Frese, Joseph R. *s.j.* '44 (NY) [Z] New York, NY Jesuit Community at Fordham University.
Fresno, Leonidas *o.s.a.* '64 (SAT) [47] San Antonio, TX St. Jude Church.

Freson, Kenan *o.f.m.* '67 (CIN) [C] Cincinnati, OH St. Anthony Shrine, Franciscan Candidacy; [M] Cincinnati, OH St. Francis Seraph Friary; [U] Cincinnati, OH Community Support Charitable Trust.
Freund, John B. *c.m.* '65 (BRK) [D] Queens and Staten Island, NY St. John's University; [U] Jamaica, NY St. Vincent's House.
Freund, Joseph *c.ss.r.* (BAL) [85] Baltimore, MD Sacred Heart of Jesus Church.
Freund, Melchior *o.s.b.* '57 (SCL) [I] Collegeville, MN St. John's Abbey, of the Order of St. Benedict.
Frey, Msgr. Andrew F. '48 (BR) Retired.
Frey, Francis '58 (SAN) [5] Odessa, TX St. Mary's Church.
Frey, Frank D. *o.f.m.* '43 (CIN) [M] Cincinnati, OH St. Clement Friary.
Frey, Jerome '50 (LAF) [M] Lafayette, LA Community of Jesus Crucified.
Frey, John T. '70 (CAM) [4] Vineland, NJ St. Isidore Church.
Frey, Ross *b.s.o.* (NTN) On Duty Outside the Eparchy.
Freyaldenhoven, George P. '48 (LR) Retired.
Freyer, Timothy '89 (ORG) San Clemente, CA Our Lady of Fatima Church.
Freymuth, Michael '79 (STL) [3] St. Louis, MO Holy Family Church.
Freyne, Barry '60 (SJ) [1] Palo Alto, CA St. Thomas Aquinas Church.
Frias, Msgr. Carlos G. '67 (ELP) [14] El Paso, TX Our Lady of Assumption Church.
Frias, Ramon *o.f.m.cap.* '72 (NY) [57] New York, NY St. John the Baptist Church.
Frias, Msgr. Santiago C. '59 (RIC) [3] Norfolk, VA Holy Trinity Church.
Friberg, Daniel W. '62 (STP) Hugo, MN St. John the Baptist Church.
Friday, Robert M. '61 (PIT) On Duty Outside the Diocese.
Friday, Robert M. '61 (WDC) [C] Washington, DC Catholic University of America, The; [C] Washington, DC Catholic University of America, The.
Fride, Edward O. '86 (LAN) [L] Ann Arbor, MI Christ the King Catholic Center.
Fridgen, Joseph '50 (SCL) Retired.
Friebel, Rick *c.pp.s.* '78 (ORL) [6] Orlando, FL St. Andrew Church.
Fried, Francis L. '68 (STP) [23] Minneapolis, MN SS. Cyril & Methodius Church.
Friedel, James *o.s.a.* '65 (CHI) [N] Olympia Fields, IL Tolentine Monastery at Tolentine Center.
Friedel, John (J.) F. '86 (SPC) Special Assignment.
Friedel, Robert E. '57 (CLV) Twinsburg, OH SS. Cosmas and Damian Church.
Friedell, John C. '54 (DUB) [C] Dubuque, IA Loras College.
Friedell, Ronald G. '66 (DUB) State Center, IA St. Joseph's Church; Marshalltown, IA Veterans' Home.
Friederick, John J. '65 (DUB) Colesburg, IA St. Patrick's Church; Edgewood, IA St. Mark's Church.
Friedl, Bernard *o.s.b.* '92 (CR) Lake Park, MN St. Francis Xavier's Church.
Friedl, Bernard *o.s.b.* '92 (SCL) [I] Collegeville, MN St. John's Abbey, of the Order of St. Benedict.
Friedl, Erwin J. '71 (CHI) [46] Chicago, IL St. Cornelius Church.
Friedl, Msgr. Francis P. '43 (DUB) Retired.
Friedman, Cecil H. '50 (SC) Retired.
Friedman, Daniel L. '72 (BEL) Aviston, IL St. Francis of Assisi Church.
Friedman, Robert '89 (Y) Hubbard, OH St. Patrick's Church.
Friedrich, Aloys *c.pp.s.* '36 (CIN) [B] Carthagena, OH St. Charles.
Friedrich, Jim D. '89 (SFS) Herreid, SD St. Michael Church.
Friedrich, Lawrence '47 (SFS) Retired.
Friedrich, Ralph '43 (Y) Retired.
Friedrichs, Paul L. '78 (CIN) [4] Cincinnati, OH St. Aloysius Gonzaga Church; On Special and Diocesan Assignment.
Friedrichs, Richard M. '70 (PRO) [R] Narragansett, RI Our Lady of Peace Spiritual Life Center.
Friedrichsen, Timothy A. (SC) Special Assignment; [A] Sioux City, IA Briar Cliff College.
Friel, Edward J. *o.s.f.s.* '41 (CAM) [L] Pittsgrove, NJ Villa St. Joseph.
Friel, Edward M. '89 (CAM) Berlin, NJ Our Lady of Mt. Carmel Church.
Friel, James E. '52 (PBL) [9] Pueblo, CO St. Anne Church.
Friel, John F. *o.s.f.s.* '70 (WIL) [I] Wilmington, DE Oblates of St. Francis De Sales.
Friel, Lee *o.f.m.cap.* '56 (AGN) [F] Agana Heights, GU St. Fidelis Friary.
Friel, Mark M. '63 (BUF) [7] Niagara Falls, NY St. Mary of the Cataract Church; Niagara Falls, NY Niagara Falls Memorial Medical Centers.
Friend, R. Scott '87 (LR) De Queen, AR St. Barbara's Church.
Frient, Lawrence '84 (Y) Andover, OH Our Lady of Victory Church.
Fries, Msgr. Francis A. '35 (HRT) Retired.
Fries, Richard R. *m.m.* '76 (LA) [R] Los Angeles, CA Maryknoll Fathers and Brothers.
Frigault, Edward F. '49 (NOR) Willimantic, CT St. Joseph Church.
Frigo, Martin A. *o.praem.* '49 (PH) [Z] Paoli, PA Daylesford Abbey.
Frigo, William *o.f.m.cap.* '63 (GB) [3] Appleton, WI St. Joseph Church.
Frilot, Msgr. Eugene '55 (LA) Glendale, CA Church of the Incarnation.
Frimtong-Manso, Robert (CC) [E] Corpus Christi, TX Spohn Hospital.
Frink, John A. '87 (ALN) [8] Bethlehem, PA Our Lady of Perpetual Help Church.
Frinsko, Donald '79 (ORL) [2] Lakeland, FL St. Anthony's Church.
Frisbie, Kenneth J. '48 (HRT) Cheshire, CT St. Thomas Becket Church.
Frisch, Joseph C. '45 (WIN) Dakota, MN Holy Cross Church.
Frisch, Kenneth J. '78 (MAD) Highland, WI SS. Anthony and Philip Church.
Frisch, Ralph *s.t.* '59 (PAT) [M] Stirling, NJ Holy Spirit Missionary Cenacle.
Frisch, Ralph *s.t.* '59 (WDC) [B] Silver Spring, MD Holy Trinity Mission Seminary (1926).
Frische, Emile *m.h.m.* '70 (NY) [Z] Hartsdale, NY Mill Hill Fathers Residence.
Friske, Joseph P. '62 (SAG) On Duty Outside the Diocese.
Frisoli, John B. *o.f.m.* '48 (BO) [W] Brighton, MA St. Bonaventure Friary, Franciscan Friars.
Frison, Basil *c.m.f.* '36 (LA) [R] Rancho Dominguez, CA Dominguez Seminary Inc.
Frison, Ted (P) Salem, OR Youth Correctional Facility.
Frison, Ted '72 (P) Woodburn, OR MacLaren Youth Correctional Facility.
Fritsch, Albert J. *s.j.* '67 (LEX) [J] Livingston, KY Appalachia Science in the Public Interest.
Fritsch, Michael C. '85 (IND) Greencastle, IN St. Paul the Apostle Church; Putnamville, IN Indiana State Farm; [N] Greencastle, IN DePauw Catholic Campus Ministry.
Fritz, Francis E. '45 (CIN) Withamsville, OH St. Thomas More Church; Retired.
Fritz, Germain L. *o.s.b.* '61 (PAT) [M] Morristown, NJ St. Mary's Abbey.
Fritz, Henry H. *o.s.b.* '52 (PEO) Peru, IL St. Joseph's Church; [A] Peru, IL St. Bede Abbey and Academy.
Fritz, Norbert '42 (P) Retired.
Fritz, Peter *o.f.m.* '50 (FWT) [G] Crowley, TX St. Francis Village, Inc.; [H] Crowley, TX St. Maximilian Kolbe Friary.
Fritz, Richard A. '75 (KAL) Bronson, MI St. Mary's Church.
Fritz, Robert '75 (CAM) [2] Cherry Hill, NJ Holy Rosary Church.
Fritzen, James C. (SY) [W] Syracuse, NY St. Mary-St. Agnes.
Fritzen, James C. '69 (SY) Phoenix, NY St. Stephen Church.
Fritzen, Michael J. *s.v.d.* '69 (GAL) [46] Houston, TX St. Mary of the Purification Church.
Frizelle, Msgr. John D. '51 (AUS) Copperas Cove, TX Holy Family Church; Retired.
Frizzell, Edward *s.d.b.* '75 (NY) [Z] New Rochelle, NY Salesian Provincial House.
Frizzell, Lawrence E. '62 (NEW) [B] South Orange, NJ Seton Hall University.
Froehle, Charles L. '63 (STP) Buffalo, MN St. Francis Xavier Church.
Froehlich, Canice *o.f.m.cap.* '47 (STL) [P] St. Louis, MO St. Patrick Friary.
Froehlich, James *o.f.m.cap.* '82 (WDC) [B] Washington, DC St. Francis Friary-Capuchin College.
Froehlich, Msgr. Mark J. '69 (STU) Bridgeport, OH St. Joseph Church; [J] Steubenville, OH Holy Name Society.
Froehlich, Raymond '67 (PIT) Sewickley, PA St. James Church.
Froelich, Canice *o.f.m.cap.* '47 (STL) [54] St. Louis, MO St. Patrick Church.
Froelich, James E. *c.pp.s.* '55 (LFT) [A] Rensselaer, IN Saint Joseph's College.
Froeschl, Msgr. Martin H. '49 (KC) Retired.
Froidurot, Michel '78 (SD) [24] San Diego, CA St. Charles Borromeo Church.
Fromholzer, Francis J. '58 (ALN) [7] Allentown, PA St. Paul Church.
Frommelt, Robert M. *s.j.* '38 (MIL) [P] Wauwatosa, WI Jesuit Community at St. Camillus.
Frommeyer, James F. '45 (CIN) Retired.
Frommholz, Anthony F. *c.s.sp.* '44 (ALX) [F] Natchitoches, LA Holy Ghost Fathers Home, Maison Brothier.
Fron, Raymond S. '64 (SAG) [6] Bay City, MI St. Joseph Church.
Fronckewicz, Stephen *o.s.b.* '57 (NOR) [E] Willimantic, CT Holy Family Home and Shelter, Inc.
Fronckowiak, Dennis F. '77 (BUF) [4] North Tonawanda, NY Our Lady of Czestochowa Church.
Fronczak, Dennis A. '75 (BUF) Grand Island, NY St. Stephen Church.
Fronczek, Louis *o.f.m.* '59 (GB) [J] Manitowoc, WI Holy Family Convent of Franciscan Sisters of Christian Charity.
Fronske, Edward *o.f.m.* '67 (GLP) Whiteriver, AZ St. Francis Apache Indian Church.
Frontiero, Anthony R. '91 (MAN) [6] Manchester, NH St. Catherine Church.
Frost, James I.J. '76 (BRK) [232] Queens, NY St. Raphael Church.
Frost, John M. '87 (DM) Grand River, IA St. Patrick Church; Osceola, IA St. Bernard Church.
Frost, Peter J. '70 (BO) Absent on Sick Leave.
Frost, Stephen '84 (FRS) [10] Fresno, CA St. Helen Church.
Frost, Stephen '84 (ORG) Inactive Leave.
Frost, Stephen '84 (SR) [K] Penngrove, CA Newman Hall, Sonoma State University, Intercollegiate Catholic Ministries.
Frost, Stephen A. '77 (FRS) On Special Assignment; [J] Fresno, CA Catholic Truth International.
Frost, Thomas *o.f.m.* '60 (TUC) Topawa, AZ San Solano Missions - Tohono O'odham Indian Reservation Church.
Frost, William P. '58 (CIN) [D] Dayton, OH The University of Dayton.
Frozena, Kenneth R. '60 (GB) Sherwood/St. John, WI St. John-Sacred Heart Church.
Frueh, David P. *s.s.j.* '71 (BLX) Pascagoula, MS St. Peter the Apostle Church.
Frueh, Robert '63 (BRK) Brooklyn, NY Kingsboro Psychiatric Center; [U] Brooklyn, NY St. Joseph's Priest Residence.
Fruge, Msgr. Donald J. '72 (AUS) Special Assignments.
Fruge, Msgr. Donald J. '72 (GAL) On Duty Outside the Diocese.
Frugoli, A. Francis *s.j.* '45 (SFR) [E] San Francisco, CA St. Ignatius College Preparatory (Coed); [N] San Francisco, CA Jesuit Community at St. Ignatius College Preparatory.
Frundt, Oscar H. '56 (WIL) Brandywood, DE Church of the Holy Child; Retired.
Fruth, Paul '74 (DUL) Crosslake, MN Immaculate Heart Church.
Fry, James Q. '79 (ORG) Military Chaplains.
Fry, Richard C. '58 (SJ) [13] San Jose, CA St. Julie Church.
Fry, Timothy *o.s.b.* '41 (KCK) [H] Atchison, KS St. Benedict's Abbey.
Fryar, Thomas S. '78 (DEN) [1] Englewood, CO All Souls Church.
Fryberger, Paul *c.s.c.* (P) [L] Portland, OR Holy Cross Father & Brother, C.S.C. - University of Portland.
Fryberger, Paul *c.s.c.* '36 (P) [B] Portland, OR University of Portland.
Frydrych, Jerzy *s.ch.* '85 (GAL) [54] Houston, TX Our Lady of Czestochowa Church.
Frye, Kenneth *c.p.m.* '90 (L) Glasgow, KY St. Helen Church.
Fryer, Patrick L. '73 (WH) On Duty Outside the Diocese.
Frysiak, Msgr. Chester S. '54 (BUF) [58] Buffalo, NY Queen of Peace Church.
Fu, Bartholomew Paul *o.p.* (NY) [Z] New York, NY St. Catherine of Siena Priory.
Fu, John *s.v.d.* '30 (CHI) [N] Techny, IL Society of the Divine Word, Provincial Headquarter-Chicago Prov.; [S] Chicago, IL Catholic Chinese Cultural Center.
Fu, Joseph '60 (NEW) [1] Garfield, NJ Our Lady of Mt. Virgin Church.
Fu, Paul B. *o.p.* '46 (NY) [22] New York, NY St. Catherine of Siena Church; Manhattan, NY New York Hospital.
Fuccile, Dominic G. '66 (NEW) Maplewood, NJ Immaculate Heart of Mary Church.
Fucheck, Robert '66 (ORL) Lady Lake, FL St. Timothy Church.
Fuchs, Athanase *o.s.b.* '41 (DUL) Ball Club, MN St. Joseph's Church; Duluth, MN Indian Missions Church.
Fuchs, John D. *s.j.* '75 (SEA) [7] Tacoma, WA St. Leo the Great Church.
Fuchs, Moritz A. '55 (SY) Hannibal, NY Our Lady of the Rosary Church.
Fuchs, Msgr. Robert A. '41 (AUS) Retired.
Fuchs, Ronald G., Jr. '90 (ATL) Blairsville, GA St. Francis of Assisi Church.
Fuchs, Msgr. Sylvester (AUS) Retired.
Fuchs, Msgr. Sylvester '49 (GAL) Retired.
Fucinaro, Thomas J. '89 (LIN) On Duty Outside the Diocese.
Fuemmeler, James R. '58 (JC) Camdenton, MO St. Anthony Church.
Fuente, Maximo *o.m.i.* '31 (SAT) [K] San Antonio, TX Oblate Madonna Residence.
Fuentes, Rodolfo Godinez '91 (STA) [20] Jacksonville, FL San Jose Church.
Fuentes, Theo *c.m.f.* '51 (PHX) [G] Phoenix, AZ Mt. Claret Retreat Center.

Fuentez, Trinidad '78 (ELP) [20] El Paso, TX Queen of Peace Church.
Fugee, Michael Charles '94 (NEW) Short Hills, NJ St. Rose of Lima Church.
Fugini, Francis *o.f.m.cap.* '54 (PIT) [N] Pittsburgh, PA St. Augustine Friary.
Fuhrman, Nicholas *o.s.b.* '54 (LR) [E] Jonesboro, AR St. Bernard's Regional Medical Center; [I] Jonesboro, AR Holy Angels Convent-Motherhouse.
Fuhrman, Msgr. Robert J. (NEW) [A] South Orange, NJ Seton Hall University College Seminary; [B] South Orange, NJ Seton Hall University; [B] South Orange, NJ Seton Hall University.
Fuhrman, Robert J. (NY) [DD] New York, NY Catholic Medical Mission Board, Inc.
Fuhrmann, Nicholas *o.s.b.* '54 (LR) Weiner, AR St. Anthony's Church.
Fuino, Crispin *o.f.m.conv.* '48 (TR) Riverside, NJ St. Peter Church.
Fuino, Michael A. '42 (NEW) [15] Newark, NJ St. Francis Xavier Church; Newark, NJ United Hospitals Of Newark.
Fujihara, Fidelis *s.a.* '65 (NY) [Z] Garrison, NY Generalate of the Franciscan Friars of the Atonement-St. James Friary.
Fukes, Gary M. '88 (SY) Dewitt, NY Holy Cross Church.
Fulcher, John M. '56 (COL) Crooksville, OH Church of the Atonement.
Fulco, William J. *s.j.* '66 (LA) [C] Los Angeles, CA Loyola Marymount University.
Fuld, Charles '86 (SD) Escondido, CA Church of the Resurrection.
Fulgenzi, Mario A. *o.s.b.* '68 (GBG) [2] Latrobe, PA St. Vincent Basilica; [H] Latrobe, PA Saint Vincent Archabbey.
Fullam, Paul Joseph *c.p.* '53 (BRK) [U] Jamaica, NY Immaculate Conception Monastery.
Fullam, Todd Dominick '94 (BLX) [2] Gulfport, MS St. James Church.
Fullam, Msgr. Vincent F. *j.d.* '65 (RVC) [A] Huntington, NY Diocesan Seminary of the Immaculate Conception.
Fullen, John N. '95 (BAL) Hagerstown, MD St. Mary Church.
Fullenkamp, Leonard *c.pp.s.* '39 (CIN) [B] Carthagena, OH St. Charles.
Fuller, Donald F. '58 (GB) Darboy, WI Holy Angels Church.
Fuller, Gerald *o.m.i.* '55 (SPC) Mansfield, MO Immaculate Heart of Mary Church.
Fuller, Jon D. *s.j.* '90 (BO) [W] Boston, MA Jesuit Urban Center & Immaculate Conception Community.
Fuller, Leigh *s.j.* '66 (CHL) [5] Charlotte, NC St. Gabriel Church; [J] Charlotte, NC Jesuit Community.
Fuller, Mark '88 (NSH) Lafayette, TN Holy Family Church; Lebanon, TN St. Frances Cabrini Church.
Fuller, Mark L. '79 (STL) Webster Groves, MO Holy Redeemer Church; Kirkwood, MO St. Joseph Hospital; [K] Kirkwood, MO St. Joseph Hospital of Kirkwood.
Fuller, Neil D. *s.v.d.* '69 (SB) Frontera, CA California Institute for Women; [A] Riverside, CA Divine Word Seminary.
Fuller, Msgr. Robert D. '56 (TUC) [12] Tucson, AZ St. Frances Cabrini Church.
Fuller, Roger J. '84 (DEN) Absent on Leave.
Fuller, Timothy M. '93 (OKL) [7] Oklahoma City, OK St. Eugene's Church.
Fullmer, Hugh '72 (JOL) [4] Lockport, IL St. Joseph Church.
Fullum, John J. '67 (BRK) [222] Queens, NY St. Pancras Church.
Fulton, David I. '67 (MET) Baptistown, NJ Our Lady of Victories Church.
Fulton, Eugene '67 (NY) [D] New York, NY Department of Education; [BB] Larchmont, NY Trinity Retreat.
Fulton, Eugene '67 (PSC) On Duty Outside Diocese.
Fulton, Joseph *o.p.* '42 (SEA) [22] Seattle, WA Blessed Sacrament Church.
Fulton, Kenneth S. '50 (TLS) Sand Springs, OK St. Patrick's Church.
Fulton, Malachy *o.s.b.* '43 (IND) [J] St. Meinrad, IN St. Meinrad Archabbey.
Fulton, Robert '62 (MOB) Greenville, AL St. Elizabeth Church.
Fulton, Robert G. '80 (RVC) [C] West Islip, NY St. John the Baptist; [N] Uniondale, NY St. Pius X Residence.
Fulton, Robert W. '62 (MOB) Andalusia, AL Christ the King Church.
Fulton, Terry A. '94 (SAC) [19] Sacramento, CA St. Philomene Church.
Fumo, Harold '55 (ORG) San Juan Capistrano, CA (Old Mission) Church; Absent on Sick Leave.
Funaro, Msgr. Joseph (BRK) [L] Brooklyn, NY Catholic Charities.
Funaro, Msgr. Joseph A. '65 (BRK) [12] Brooklyn, NY Assumption of the Blessed Virgin Mary Church.
Funcheon, Gerald A. '65 (LFT) Retired.
Funesti, Peter K. '88 (NEW) Bloomfield, NJ Church of St. Thomas the Apostle.
Fung, Joseph M. *s.j.* '86 (CHI) [N] Chicago, IL Chicago Province of the Society of Jesus-Provincial Office.
Funk, C. Alan '91 (LFT) Marion, IN St. Paul Church.
Funk, David J. *o.f.m.cap.* '68 (GB) [F] Oshkosh, WI Mercy Medical Center.
Funk, Msgr. David R. '74 (COL) [2] Columbus, OH St. Agatha Church.
Funk, Louis F. '44 (CIN) [1] Cincinnati, OH St. Peter in Chains Cathedral; Retired.
Funk, Peter C. '64 (PH) [44] Philadelphia, PA Epiphany of Our Lord Church.
Funk, Virgil C. '63 (RIC) On Duty Outside the Diocese.
Funk, Wayne G. '62 (BAL) Frederick, MD St. John the Evangelist Church.
Funk, Wiatt A. '68 (NSH) Murfreesboro, TN St. Rose of Lima Church.
Funke, Gerald J. '80 (B) Idaho Falls, ID Holy Rosary Church.
Funke, Msgr. Richard P. '60 (DUB) [3] Dubuque, IA St. Columbkille's Church.
Funke, Ronald R. *s.j.* '68 (P) [L] Portland, OR Jesuit Provincial Office (Oregon Prov.).
Funke, Ronald R. *s.j.* '68 (SEA) [A] Seattle, WA Seattle University.
Funtilla, Aloysius M. *c.i.c.m.* (CHI) [12] Chicago, IL St. Angela Church.
Furdek, John M. '84 (JOL) Villa Park, IL St. Alexander Church.
Furey, Frederick *ss.cc.* '46 (COL) Marion, OH St. Mary Church; Marion, OH Marion Correctional Institution.
Furey, J. Barry '71 (BGP) [3] Bridgeport, CT St. Andrew Church.
Furey, John *c.ss.r.* '60 (BO) [13] Boston, MA Basilica of Our Lady of Perpetual Help.
Furey, Thomas J. '73 (PH) Holland, PA St. Bede the Venerable Church.
Furfaro, Msgr. Francis J. '41 (SY) Oswego, NY Oswego County Jail; Retired.
Furfaro, Virgil (SFE) Moriarty, NM Estancia Valley Catholic Parish Church.
Furlan, Gerard *s.x.* '58 (PAT) [M] Wayne, NJ Xaverian Missionary Fathers.
Furlan, Michael J. '75 (CHI) [117] Chicago, IL St. Leo The Great Church.
Furlan, William '48 (SCL) Retired.
Furlong, Aidan M. *a.a.* '53 (WOR) Fiskdale, MA St. Anne's and St. Patrick's Church.
Furlong, J. Daryl '66 (MAD) [3] Janesville, WI St. Patrick Church.
Furlong, James '84 (LUB) Special Assignment; [B] Lubbock, TX St. Mary of the Plains Hospital.
Furlong, Jude *l.c.* '74 (PRO) [T] Wakefield, RI "Mater Ecclesiae" International Formation Center.
Furlong, Thomas D. '60 (OM) [24] Omaha, NE St. John Vianney Church.
Furman, Laurie *s.j.* (MOB) [B] Mobile, AL Spring Hill College.
Furmanski, Leonard A. '59 (PH) [81] Philadelphia, PA St. Josaphat Church.
Furnari, Casper '68 (BRK) [220] Queens, NY Our Lady of the Snows Church.
Furrevig, Edward G. '67 (NEW) Union, NJ Holy Spirit Church.
Furtado, Alwyn *c.s.sp.* '65 (SFR) Millbrae, CA St. Dunstan Church.
Furtado, Steven R. (FR) [3] Fall River, MA Espirito Santo Church.
Furtmann, John A. '57 (MIL) Hubertus, WI St. Hubert's Church.
Fus, Msgr. Edward A. '43 (BRK) [177] Queens, NY Holy Cross Church; Retired.
Fusare, Francis '96 (ROC) [1] Rochester, NY Sacred Heart Cathedral.
Fusco, Albin *o.f.m.* '61 (NY) [Z] New York, NY Padua Friary.
Fusco, Blaise J. *o.f.m.cap.* '41 (PIT) [N] Pittsburgh, PA St. Conrad Friary; [O] Pittsburgh, PA Motherhouse and Novitiate of the Vincentian Sisters of Charity.
Fusco, Frederick *o.f.m.* '42 (ALB) [A] Catskill, NY St. Anthony Friary.
Fusco, Philip N. '46 (GRY) Retired.
Fusco, Thomas M. '85 (RVC) West Hempstead, NY St. Thomas, the Apostle Church; [A] Huntington, NY Diocesan Seminary of the Immaculate Conception.
Fuselier, Karl '94 (LKC) [2] Lake Charles, LA Immaculate Heart of Mary Church.
Fushek, Dale J. '78 (PHX) [6] Mesa, AZ St. Timothy Church.
Fuss, Edward F. *s.m.* '89 (BR) Gramercy, LA Most Sacred Heart of Jesus Church.
Fussner, Donald T. (NY) [105] New York, NY St. Peter Church.
Futie, Richard F. '82 (BGP) [3] Stamford, CT St. Mary's Church.
Futo, Ignatius *s.j.* '81 (STL) [C] St. Louis, MO Saint Louis University; [P] St. Louis, MO Jesuit Community Corporation at St. Louis University - Jesuit Hall.
Futrell, John C. *s.j.* '58 (DEN) [M] Denver, CO Xavier Jesuit Center.
Futter, Volker *o.s.b.* '69 (OM) [K] Schuyler, NE Benedictine Mission House.
Fuytinck, Albert A. *c.ss.r.* '42 (STL) [P] Liguori, MO St. Clement Health Care Center.
Fye, Lawrence C. '59 (Y) [1] Youngstown, OH Cathedral of St. Columba.

G

Gaalaas, Patrick J. '72 (TLS) Broken Arrow, OK St. Benedict Church.
Gabadian, Msgr. Sarkis '52 (ARM) Philadelphia, PA St. Mark's Armenian Catholic Church.
Gabalski, Msgr. John R. '48 (BUF) [61] Buffalo, NY St. Stanislaus Church; [T] Buffalo, NY Monsignor Adamski Village, Inc.
Gabel, Garold L. '79 (LIN) [4] Lincoln, NE North American Martyrs Church.
Gabel, Manuel '57 (DEN) [3] Boulder, CO St. Martin de Porres Church.
Gabel, Martin '68 (JOL) Wheaton, IL St. Michael Church.
Gabel, Robert *o.f.m.* '51 (PAT) [M] Ringwood, NJ Holy Name Friary.
Gaber, Francis '51 (DUL) Retired.
Gaberle, Jiri P. '89 (MIL) On Duty Outside the Archdiocese.
Gabin, John D. '75 (PH) Richboro, PA St. Vincent de Paul Church.
Gabino, Pedro '91 (STO) Absent on Leave.
Gabriel, Astrik L. '31 (FTW) [B] Notre Dame, IN University of Notre Dame Du Lac.
Gabriel, Eduardo *o.p.* (AUS) [H] Austin, TX Dominican Fathers; [H] Austin, TX St. Joseph Hall.
Gabriel, Eduardo *o.p.* '92 (DAL) [M] Irving, TX Dominican Priory of St. Albert the Great.
Gabriel, John *m.s.* '91 (MIL) [P] Twin Lakes, WI La Salette Missionaries Shrine.
Gabriel, John D. '87 (NEW) Bloomfield, NJ Church of St. Thomas the Apostle.
Gabriel, Michael A. '84 (CHI) Lansing, IL St. Ann Church.
Gabriel, Vicente S. '40 (LA) Retired.
Gabriele, John J. '68 (RVC) Absent on Leave.
Gabrus, Alois *o.f.m.* '72 (STP) [10] St. Paul, MN Sacred Heart Church.
Gabuzda, Richard J. '81 (SCR) On Duty Outside the Diocese.
Gacki, Peter '51 (CHI) [48] Chicago, IL St. Daniel the Prophet Church.
Gacki, Peter *o.f.m.cap.* '51 (PAT) [M] Oak Ridge-Milton, NJ St. Stanislaus B. M. Friary.
Gadarowski, Msgr. Bronislaw A. '43 (NOR) Retired.
Gaddy, Msgr. James '65 (LKC) Kinder, LA St. Philip Neri Church.
Gaddy, Kenneth *c.ss.r.* '88 (STV) [3] Frederiksted, VI Church of St. Patrick; [B] St. Thomas, VI Miscellaneous Organizations.
Gadenz, Pablo '96 (TR) Keansburg, NJ St. Ann Church.
Gadient, Peter J. '45 (LIN) Osceola, NE St. Vincent's Church.
Gadziala, Timothy A. '94 (ATL) [1] Marietta, GA Holy Family Church.
Gadzinski, Mark '82 (STU) Absent on Leave.
Gaebelein, Claude '46 (CLV) [N] Cleveland, OH Sts. Mary and Joseph Home for the Aged.
Gaebelein, Claude J. '46 (CLV) [4] Barberton, OH St. Mary's Church; Retired.
Gaeke, Thomas M. '75 (CIN) [14] Dayton, OH Holy Family Church; [18] Dayton, OH St. Mary's Church.
Gaelens, Albert R. *c.s.b.* '60 (ROC) [B] Rochester, NY The Aquinas Institute; [I] Rochester, NY Residence of Basilian Fathers-The Aquinas Institute.
Gaertner, Robert *c.pp.s.* '43 (CIN) [B] Carthagena, OH St. Charles.
Gaesser, Ronald E. '61 (ROC) Ithaca, NY St. Catherine of Siena Church; Lansing, NY All Saints Church.
Gaeta, Bernard N. '73 (Y) Ashtabula, OH Mother of Sorrows Church.
Gaeta, David (TR) McGuire Air Force Base, NJ McGuire Air Force Base.
Gaeta, David R. '80 (SLC) On Duty Outside the Diocese.
Gaeta, Francis X. '63 (RVC) Westbury, NY St. Brigid Church.
Gaetano, Francis *s.a.c.* '48 (CAM) [L] Camden, NJ Dominican Sisters of the Perpetual Rosary Chaplain's Residence.
Gaetano, Francis *s.a.c.* '48 (NEW) Fairview, NJ Our Lady of Grace Church.
Gaetano, Msgr. Lewis F. '73 (STU) Mingo Junction, OH Annunciation Church; Mingo Junction, OH St. Agnes Church.
Gaffey, Eugene F. '69 (PRT) Whitefield, ME St. Denis Church.
Gaffey, Msgr. James P. '60 (SR) [1] Santa Rosa, CA Cathedral of St. Eugene.
Gaffey, Kevin P. '57 (SFR) Novato, CA St. Anthony of Padua Church.

Gaffigan, Charles A. '62 (ALB) Lake Luzerne, NY Holy Infancy Church.
Gaffigan, William J. '64 (ALB) Canajoharie, NY St. Peter's and Paul's Church.
Gaffney, Edward M. *o.p.* '49 (BAL) [A] Emmitsburg, MD Mount St. Mary's Seminary.
Gaffney, Francis P. '64 (CAM) Bellmawr, NJ Mary, Mother of the Church.
Gaffney, J. Michael '73 (OG) Lake Placid, NY St. Agnes Church.
Gaffney, J. Patrick *s.m.m.* '54 (RVC) [N] Bay Shore, NY Montfort Missionaries.
Gaffney, J. Patrick *s.m.m.* '54 (STL) [W] Arnold, MO AJT, Inc.
Gaffney, James '52 (MEM) Retired.
Gaffney, James F. '85 (ALN) [1] Shenandoah, PA Annunciation Church.
Gaffney, Msgr. James J. (CAM) Retired.
Gaffney, Msgr. James J. '50 (CAM) Glassboro, NJ Our Lady of Lourdes Church.
Gaffney, John H. *o.s.a.* '45 (TLS) [B] Tulsa, OK Cascia Hall Preparatory School.
Gaffney, Joseph '67 (LA) Thousand Oaks, CA St. Paschal Baylon Church.
Gaffney, Michael *o.f.m.cap.* (DET) [K] Detroit, MI St. Mary's Friary.
Gaffney, Patrick *c.s.c.* '74 (FTW) [B] Notre Dame, IN University of Notre Dame Du Lac; [J] Notre Dame, IN Holy Cross Community, Corby Hall, University of Notre Dame.
Gaffney, Patrick W. *c.ss.r.* '81 (WIL) Seaford, DE Our Lady of Lourdes Church.
Gaffney, Thomas F. '58 (HRT) [9] New Britain, CT St. Joseph's Church.
Gaffney, Msgr. Thomas J. '50 (NY) [200] Staten Island, NY St. Charles Church.
Gaffney, William *c.s.s.r.* (NY) [150] Bronx, NY Immaculate Conception Church.
Gaffney, William *c.ss.r.* '60 (PH) [135] Philadelphia, PA St. Peter the Apostle Church.
Gagala, John '58 (DET) [1] Southfield, MI St. Beatrice Church; [H] Southfield, MI Providence Hospital.
Gagan, Charles R. '68 (SFR) [24] San Francisco, CA St. Ignatius Church; [N] San Francisco, CA Jesuit Community at University of San Francisco.
Gagan, Philip R. (STA) Absent on Sick Leave.
Gage, George D. '79 (ROM) Youngstown, OH St. Mary Church; Sharon, PA St. John Church.
Gage, Gregory A. '67 (P) Newberg, OR St. Peter Church.
Gage, Philip S. *s.m.* '69 (WDC) [M] Washington, DC Marist Provincial House.
Gaglia, Fred R. '63 (SB) Rancho Cucamonga, CA Sacred Heart Church.
Gagliano, Philip J. '76 (NY) Harrison, NY St. Gregory the Great Church; [1] Yonkers, NY St. Anthony Church.
Gagliardi, Carmelo *o.f.m.cap.* '73 (BRK) [105] Brooklyn, NY Shrine of Our Lady of Mount Carmel Church.
Gagliardi, Richard '62 (OAK) El Sobrante, CA St. Callistus Church.
Gagliardo, Anthony F. '61 (BUF) Retired.
Gaglione, John R. '76 (BUF) [10] Niagara Falls, NY Our Lady of the Rosary Church.
Gaglione, Joseph *c.s.sp.* '64 (SAT) [O] New Braunfels, TX Spiritan Renewal Center.
Gagnard, Louis '52 (ALX) Retired.
Gagne, Donald *s.m.* '59 (BO) [Y] Framingham Centre, MA The Marist House.
Gagne, Marc R. '85 (MAN) [4] Concord, NH Immaculate Heart of Mary Church.
Gagne, Rene E. '51 (PRO) Retired; [P] Providence, RI St. John Vianney Residence.
Gagne, Roger C. '75 (PRO) [20] Providence, RI St. Mary's Church.
Gagne, Ron *m.s.* '71 (ATL) [2] Marietta, GA Church of St. Ann.
Gagne, Ronald '66 (DUL) Keewatin, MN St. Mary's Church; Nashwauk, MN St. Cecilia's Church; Duluth, MN Indian Missions Church.
Gagne, Walter *s.a.* '71 (NY) [Z] Garrison, NY Generalate of the Franciscan Friars of the Atonement-St. James Friary.
Gagnepain, John F. *c.m.* '62 (STL) [P] St. Louis, MO Vincentian Residence.
Gagnier, John '78 (ROC) Newark, NY St. Michael Church.
Gagnon, Adelard J. '56 (BO) [53] Boston, MA Our Lady of the Assumption Church.
Gagnon, Andre J. '57 (MAN) Manchester, NH Nursing Homes; [L] Manchester, NH St. George Manor.
Gagnon, George C. '55 (ALB) Whitehall, NY Notre Dame des Victoires Church; Special Assignment.
Gagnon, Henry W. '64 (BO) Bedford, MA St. Michael Church.
Gagnon, Herve *o.m.i.* '45 (BO) [W] Lowell, MA Missionary Oblates of Mary Immaculate.
Gagnon, Jean Paul '82 (WOR) Millville, MA St. Augustine's Church.
Gagnon, John '49 (BUR) Retired; [F] Rutland, VT Loretto Home for Aged.
Gagnon, Joseph A. '61 (DET) Melvindale, MI St. Conrad Church.
Gagnon, Leo G. '72 (MAN) Portsmouth, NH Immaculate Conception Church.
Gagnon, Michel *o.f.m.* '57 (SD) San Luis Rey, CA Mission San Luis Rey de Francia Church; [H] San Luis Rey, CA San Luis Rey.
Gagnon, Raymond E. '72 (MAN) [6] Nashua, NH Infant Jesus Church.
Gagnon, Richard *s.d.s.* '65 (NSH) Smyrna, TN St. Luke Church.
Gagnon, Ronald P. '56 (TUC) [5] Tucson, AZ Most Holy Trinity Church.
Gahagan, William H. '70 (KNX) Johnson City, TN St. Mary Church; [J] Johnson City, TN ETSU-Catholic Center; [K] Knoxville, TN Diocesan Council of Catholic Women.
Gahan, James L. '68 (STL) [4] St. Charles, MO Sts. Joachim and Ann Church; [E] St. Charles, MO Duchesne High School.
Gaiardo, Martin J. '70 (SCR) Retired.
Gailiusis, George S. *o.f.m.* '40 (PRT) [I] Kennebunkport, ME St. Anthony's Friary.
Gainer, Msgr. Ronald W. '73 (ALN) Whitehall, PA Holy Trinity Church.
Gainer, Msgr. Ronald W. *j.c.l.* '73 (PH) [A] Wynnewood, PA Theological Seminary of St. Charles Borromeo, Overbrook.
Gaines, G. Timothy '87 (DEN) Frederick, CO St. Theresa Church.
Gaines, Michael T. '87 (E) North East, PA St. Gregory Thaumaturgus Church.
Gaitan, Ramon *o.a.r.* '60 (KCK) [K] Kansas City, KS Casa Juan Diego Centro de Evangelization.
Gaiter, Chester E. *s.j.* '76 (STL) [P] St. Louis, MO Jesuit Community Corporation at St. Louis University - Jesuit Hall.
Gaj, Zygmut '41 (GAY) Retired.
Gajdos, Thomas '70 (MIL) Cedarburg, WI Divine Word Catholic Church.
Gajdzinski, Norman A. '63 (CLV) [3] Garfield Heights, OH St. Therese Church.
Gajere, James D. '88 (BRK) [181] Queens, NY Immaculate Conception Church.
Gajewski, Msgr. Chester A. '50 (SCR) Unassigned or Leave of Absence.
Gal, Gedeon *o.f.m.* '29 (BUF) [O] St. Bonaventure, NY St. Bonaventure Friary.
Galambos, Stephen *o.f.m.* '96 (MET) [6] New Brunswick, NJ St. Ladislaus Church.
Galan, Jose M. '65 (PCE) [15] Ponce, PR Church of the Sacred Heart.
Galan, Juan Cerro '88 (SP) On Duty Outside the Diocese.
Galanaugh, Joseph T. '79 (PH) Absent on Leave.
Galang, Jose '78 (SJ) [3] Santa Clara, CA St. Justin Church.
Galarza, Tomas '86 (CGS) Las Piedras, PR San Juan Bautista Church.
Galas, Daniel E '57 (OM) Snyder, NE St. Leo Church.
Galas, Daniel E. '57 (OM) North Bend, NE St. Charles Borromeo Church.
Galasso, Michael S. '71 (HRT) [15] Hartford, CT St. Peter Church.
Galaz, Jesse C. '81 (LA) [40] Los Angeles, CA St. Alphonsus Church.
Galban, Antonio M. *o.s.b.* '63 (MGZ) [6] Mayaquez, PR Sacred Heart Church.
Galchus, Robert *o.m.* (STA) [E] Jacksonville, FL St. Vincent's Medical Center, Inc.
Galchus, Robert P. *c.m.* '49 (PH) [Z] Philadelphia, PA Congregation of the Mission.
Galdon, Peter P. '68 (NEW) [18] Jersey City, NJ St. Nicholas Church.
Galdon, Richard M. '59 (NEW) Retired.
Gale, Robert '68 (BO) Awaiting Assignment.
Galea, John '62 (STU) [5] Steubenville, OH Our Lady of North America Martyrs Church.
Galea, Michael A. '80 (BR) Donaldsonville, LA St. Francis of Assisi Church.
Galek, Peter '84 (CHI) [184] Chicago, IL St. Richard Church.
Galens, Jeffrey '90 (NY) [E] New York, NY Cardinal Hayes High School.
Galeon, Arnelo A. '91 (NEW) [3] Jersey City, NJ St. Anne's Church.
Galeone, Msgr. Victor B. '60 (BAL) [3] Baltimore, MD St. Agnes Church; [Q] Baltimore, MD Ladies of Charity.
Galetto, Paul W. '82 (CAM) [C] Richland, NJ St. Augustine Preparatory School.
Galiardi, Roman *o.s.b.* '57 (JOL) [J] Lisle, IL St. Procopius Abbey.
Galiardi, Roman S. *o.s.b.* '57 (JOL) Lisle, IL St. Joan of Arc Church.
Galic, Bernard J. '70 (FTW) [10] South Bend, IN Holy Family Church.
Galic, Joseph *o.f.m.* (DET) [5] Troy, MI St. Lucy Church.
Galinac, Robert *o.f.m.* '69 (ALN) [6] Bethlehem, PA St. Joseph Church.
Galinada, Michael *s.m.* '17 (OAK) [N] Berkeley, CA Marist Fathers and Brothers.
Galindo, Msgr. Rudolph '54 (SD) Retired.
Galipeau, Roland J. '64 (SPR) [2] Holyoke, MA Holy Cross Church.
Galivan, James F. '81 (CHI) Lyons, IL St. Hugh Church.
Galka, Paul *o.f.m.conv.* '80 (ALB) [A] Rensselaer, NY Conventual Franciscan Friars.
Galko, Joseph '80 (ALN) Unassigned.
Gall, Florian J. '61 (MET) Whitehouse Station, NJ Our Lady of Lourdes Church.
Gall, Jacob M. '62 (FTW) Kendallville, IN Immaculate Conception Church.
Gall, Sylvester '38 (SCL) Retired.
Gall, Thomas S. '92 (OM) [44] Omaha, NE St. Stephen the Martyr Church.
Gallagher, Adrian *ofm conv.* '92 (BUF) [D] Athol Springs, NY St. Francis High School; [O] Athol Springs, NY St. Francis of Assisi Friary.
Gallagher, Andrew J. '46 (RVC) Point Lookout, NY Our Lady of the Miraculous Medal Church; Retired.
Gallagher, Brian *s.s.c.* '52 (PRO) [P] Bristol, RI St. Columban's Retirement House.
Gallagher, Brian T. '60 (YAK) On Duty Outside the Diocese.
Gallagher, Cathal J. *s.s.c.* (WIN) [F] Rochester, MN Madonna Towers of Rochester, Inc.
Gallagher, Charles '44 (CHI) La Grange, IL St. Cletus Church.
Gallagher, Charles A. *s.j.* '58 (NEW) [B] Jersey City, NJ Saint Peter's College; [N] Jersey City, NJ Jesuits of Saint Peter's College, Inc.
Gallagher, Charles G. '44 (CHI) Retired.
Gallagher, Chester G. '50 (WIN) Absent on Leave.
Gallagher, Cornelius F. '42 (STU) Retired.
Gallagher, Cyrus *o.f.m.cap.* '65 (DEN) [3] Denver, CO Annunciation Church; [M] Denver, CO Annunciation Friary.
Gallagher, Daniel '65 (JKS) [1] Jackson, MS St. Peter Cathedral; Jackson, MS Veterans Administration Hospital.
Gallagher, Daniel J. '51 (PH) Doylestown, PA Our Lady of Mount Carmel Church.
Gallagher, David F. *c.s.s.* '59 (BO) [W] Waltham, MA Stigmatine House.
Gallagher, Dennis *a.a.* '78 (BO) [W] Brighton, MA Assumptionist Center.
Gallagher, Dennis J. *o.s.a.* '65 (PH) [C] Villanova, PA Villanova University; [Z] Villanova, PA St. Thomas Monastery.
Gallagher, E. Henry *o.p.* '36 (BO) [W] Dover, MA St. Stephen Priory.
Gallagher, Edward *s.a.* '71 (R) Apex, NC St. Andrew the Apostle Church.
Gallagher, Edward F. '46 (SCR) Retired; [N] Dunmore, PA Villa St. Joseph.
Gallagher, Edward L. '53 (BO) Carver, MA Our Lady of Lourdes Church.
Gallagher, Msgr. Eugene A. '43 (SFR) Retired.
Gallagher, Eugene P. '38 (NY) Retired.
Gallagher, F. Anthony '61 (TOL) Providence, OH St. Patrick Church.
Gallagher, Msgr. Francis J. '47 (FRS) Retired.
Gallagher, Francis J. '73 (PH) Jenkintown, PA Immaculate Conception Church.
Gallagher, Francis L. '48 (BO) Billerica, MA St. Andrew Church; Retired.
Gallagher, Francis M. '64 (PH) Croydon, PA St. Thomas Aquinas Church.
Gallagher, Francis M. '87 (PEO) [4] Rock Island, IL St. Pius X Church.
Gallagher, J. Gerald '57 (CAM) Woodbury, NJ St. Patrick's Church.
Gallagher, Jack *o.s.cam.* '81 (WOR) [K] Whitinsville, MA St. Camillus Nursing Home Inc.
Gallagher, Msgr. James '44 (PT) [3] Pensacola, FL Holy Spirit Church; Retired.
Gallagher, James '65 (CHI) [J] Evergreen Park, IL Little Company of Mary Hospital and Health Care Centers.
Gallagher, James E. '87 (RIC) New Bohemia, VA Church of the Sacred Heart.
Gallagher, John *o.f.m.cap.* (NEW) [N] Orange, NJ St. Veronica Giuliani Friary, Capuchin Franciscan Friars.
Gallagher, John (PIT) [J] Cranberry Township, PA St. Francis Nursing Center-North.
Gallagher, John *o.s.cam.* (WOR) [N] Whitinsville, MA St. Camillus Community.
Gallagher, Msgr. John A. '55 (NY) [15] Yonkers, NY St. Paul the Apostle Church.
Gallagher, John C. *c.s.b.* '60 (GAL) [Q] Houston, TX Residence of the Basilian Fathers of the University of St. Thomas.
Gallagher, John E. '59 (BO) [7] Lowell, MA St. Louis de France Church.
Gallagher, John J. *o.s.a.* '45 (PH) [Z] Villanova, PA St. Thomas Monastery.

Gallagher, John M. '71 (GB) Gillett, WI St. John Church.
Gallagher, Msgr. John P. '51 (SCR) [2] Dunmore, PA Christ the King Church.
Gallagher, John P. '57 (PH) Gladwyne, PA St. John Baptist Vianney Church.
Gallagher, John P. '68 (PIT) Cranberry Township, PA St. Ferdinand Church.
Gallagher, John P. '80 (DAV) Riverside, IA St. Mary of the Assumption Church.
Gallagher, John R. '55 (DUB) [H] Cedar Rapids, IA Mercy Medical Center, Cedar Rapids, Iowa.
Gallagher, John R. '93 (WH) [1] Wheeling, WV St. Joseph's Cathedral.
Gallagher, Joseph J. '55 (BAL) Retired.
Gallagher, Joseph J. '63 (PH) [141] Philadelphia, PA St. Richard Church.
Gallagher, Joseph P. '73 (PH) West Chester, PA St. Agnes Church; Absent on Sick Leave.
Gallagher, Joseph T. '42 (PRO) Retired.
Gallagher, Joseph W. *c.s.p.* '61 (GR) Grand Rapids, MI Chapel of St. Paul-Catholic Information Center.
Gallagher, Kevin E. *s.j.* '61 (CHI) [N] Chicago, IL Chicago Province of the Society of Jesus-Provincial Office.
Gallagher, Kevin P. '83 (ALN) [5] Reading, PA Holy Guardian Angels Church.
Gallagher, Maurice O. '50 (PBL) Avondale, CO Sacred Heart Church.
Gallagher, Michael *s.j.* '84 (ELP) [21] El Paso, TX Sacred Heart Church.
Gallagher, Michael F. '68 (NY) Military Chaplains.
Gallagher, Msgr. Michael J. '66 (SD) [2] El Cajon, CA Our Lady of Grace Church.
Gallagher, Michael J. '69 (WIL) On Duty Outside the Diocese.
Gallagher, Otmar *o.f.m.cap.* '48 (VEN) [D] Port Charlotte, FL Bon Secours-St. Joseph Hospital.
Gallagher, Patrick *o.f.m.conv.* '65 (ALB) Fonda, NY St. Cecilia Church.
Gallagher, Msgr. Patrick J. (MOB) [K] Dothan, AL Wallace Community College Newman Center.
Gallagher, Msgr. Patrick J. '66 (LA) San Pedro, CA Mary, Star of the Sea Church; [CC] San Pedro, CA Apostleship of the Sea, Catholic Maritime Ministry.
Gallagher, Patrick J. '70 (MOB) Dothan, AL St. Columba Church.
Gallagher, Paul *o.f.m.* (GAL) [T] Houston, TX University of Houston Central Campus Catholic Newman Association.
Gallagher, Paul V. '63 (RIC) Retired.
Gallagher, Peter (IND) [C] Indianapolis, IN Father Thomas Scecina Memorial High School.
Gallagher, Peter '92 (IND) [8] Indianapolis, IN Holy Spirit Church.
Gallagher, Philip P. '77 (LAN) Fowler, MI Most Holy Trinity Church.
Gallagher, Raymond '90 (SAN) Ozona, TX Our Lady of Perpetual Help Church; Sonora, TX St. Ann's Church.
Gallagher, Richard (TR) Leave of Absence.
Gallagher, Msgr. Richard J. '49 (STL) [64] St. Louis, MO St. Thomas of Aquin Church.
Gallagher, Richard J. '60 (SEA) Pe Ell, WA St. Joseph's Church; Raymond, WA St. Lawrence Church; Seaview, WA St. Mary Church.
Gallagher, Robert '73 (LA) Norwalk, CA St. John of God Church.
Gallagher, Robert A. '77 (STU) On Duty Outside the Diocese.
Gallagher, Robert J. '73 (LA) [D] Santa Fe Springs, CA St. Paul High School.
Gallagher, Roger P. '54 (WDC) Retired; [L] Washington, DC Cardinal O'Boyle Residence for Priests.
Gallagher, Simeon *o.f.m.cap.* '71 (STL) [54] St. Louis, MO St. Patrick Church; [P] St. Louis, MO St. Patrick Friary.
Gallagher, Simon P. *o.s.b.* '73 (PAT) [M] Morristown, NJ St. Mary's Abbey.
Gallagher, Thomas *s.p.s.* '49 (NO) [4] Slidell, LA St. Margaret Mary Church; Slidell, LA Greenbriar Nursing & Convalescent Home; Slidell, LA Guest House of Slidell Nursing Home; Slidell, LA Greenery Neurologic Rehabilitation Center at Slidell.
Gallagher, Thomas *s.j.* '61 (ANC) [G] Anchorage, AK Jesuit Residence.
Gallagher, Thomas '61 (CLV) Cleveland, OH Cleveland Psychiatric; Cleveland, OH Veterans Administration Hospitals, Brecksville V.A.
Gallagher, Thomas *s.j.* '61 (FBK) McGrath, AK St. Michael Church.
Gallagher, Thomas B. '56 (OAK) Retired; [M] Oakland, CA Bishop Begin Villa.
Gallagher, Thomas G. '68 (RVC) North Merrick, NY Sacred Heart Church.
Gallagher, Thomas J. *s.j.* '70 (BO) [W] Boston, MA Jesuit Urban Center & Immaculate Conception Community.
Gallagher, Thomas M. *o.f.m.* '82 (PAT) Little Falls, NJ Our Lady of the Holy Angels Church.
Gallagher, Thomas P. *o.s.f.s.* '67 (PH) [D] Philadelphia, PA Father Judge High School for Boys; [Z] Philadelphia, PA Father Judge Faculty House.
Gallagher, Msgr. Thomas V. '45 (NY) Retired; [Z] New York, NY Our Lady of Consolation Residence.
Gallagher, Timothy *o.m.v.* '79 (BO) [B] Boston, MA Oblate Provincialate; [W] Milton, MA House of Theological Studies and Provincialate.
Gallagher, William '88 (ORL) On Duty Outside the Diocese.
Gallagher, William '88 (YAK) [1] Yakima, WA St. Paul Cathedral.
Gallagher, William E. '46 (SEA) Retired.
Gallagher, William G. '53 (RVC) Priests Released from Diocesan Assignment.
Gallagher, William J. '47 (WOR) Retired.
Gallagher, Msgr. William J. '69 (BUF) [1] Buffalo, NY St. Joseph's Cathedral.
Gallagher, William M. '53 (PRO) On Duty Outside the Diocese.
Gallagher, William P. '65 (BUR) Woodstock, VT Our Lady of the Snows Church.
Gallant Fernard J. *s.m.* '44 (BO) [Y] Framingham Centre, MA The Marist House.
Gallant John P. '60 (NY) Pine Plains, NY St. Anthony Church.
Gallant, Jon-Paul '78 (FR) [4] Taunton, MA Sacred Heart Church.
Gallant, Rodrigue J. '47 (MAN) Retired.
Gallardo, David F. '84 (LA) [24] Los Angeles, CA Our Lady of Guadalupe Church.
Gallardo, Joseph J. *o.a.r.* (ORG) Fullerton, CA St. Mary's Church.
Gallarelli, George A. *s.j.* '62 (BGP) [D] Fairfield, CT Fairfield College Preparatory School; [O] Fairfield, CT The Fairfield Jesuit Community-Fairfield University.
Gallaro, George D. '72 (NTN) Warren, MI Our Lady of Redemption Church.
Gallas, James R. *s.j.* '52 (LA) [6] Los Angeles, CA Blessed Sacrament Church.
Gallatin, Paul H. '58 (OKL) [3] Oklahoma City, OK St. Charles Borromeo Church.
Gallego, Eduardo '71 (SJN) [19] Carolina, PR Ntra. Sra. de Fatima Church.
Gallego, Jose M. *o.m.* '57 (SJN) [16] San Juan, PR Ntra. Sra. de Fatima Church.
Gallegos, Albert *o.s.m.* '64 (SFE) Peralta, NM Our Lady of Guadalupe Church.
Gallegos, Albert M. *o.s.m.* '64 (CHI) [N] Chicago, IL Servite Friars - Eastern Province.
Gallegos, David *o.s.m.* (SFE) Belen, NM Our Lady of Belen Church.
Gallegos, David M. *o.s.m.* '66 (CHI) [N] Chicago, IL Servite Friars - Eastern Province.
Gallegos, Joseph *c.r.* '69 (PBL) Durango, CO Sacred Heart Church.
Gallemore, Timothy A. '92 (FRS) Laton, CA Shrine of Our Lady of Fatima Church.
Gallen, Msgr. Charles V. '47 (PH) [U] Immaculata, PA Camilla Hall Nursing Home; [X] Huntingdon Valley, PA Redeemer Long Term Care & Elder Services.
Gallen, Msgr. F. Thomas '47 (COL) [C] Columbus, OH St. Charles Preparatory School.
Gallen, Francis H. '47 (PH) Bridgeport, PA St. Augustine Church; Retired.
Gallen, John A. '69 (HT) Morgan City, LA Sacred Heart of Jesus Church.
Gallenbach, Thomas '58 (SFD) Military Chaplains.
Gallenbach, Thomas E. '58 (LAV) [12] Las Vegas, NV St. Joseph, Husband of Mary Church.
Gallenstein, Joseph '90 (COV) Florence, KY St. Paul Church.
Gallenstein, Stephen '76 (LEX) Morehead, KY Church of Jesus Our Savior; [L] Morehead, KY Catholic Student Center-Morehead State University.
Gallerani, Philip G. '62 (SPR) Springfield, MA Wesson-Women's Hospital Unit; Absent on Leave.
Galles, Msgr. Francis A. '52 (WIN) Preston, MN St. Columban Church.
Galli, Clarence '53 (SFE) Retired.
Gallia, Andrew R. '62 (SCR) Jessup, PA St. Mary's Assumption Church.
Galligan, Charles H. '87 (PRO) [12] Pawtucket, RI St. Teresa Church.
Galligan, Eymard *s.s.e.* '47 (BUR) [G] Colchester, VT Society of St. Edmund.
Galligan, Richard H. *s.j.* '70 (BUF) [O] Buffalo, NY Canisius Jesuit Community.
Galligan, Richard R. *s.j.* (BUF) [R] Williamsville, NY Newman Club Chaplains.
Galligan, Richard R. *s.j.* '70 (NY) [Z] New York, NY Jesuit Provincial's Office.
Gallina, Leo J. '65 (E) [14] Erie, PA St. Boniface Church.
Gallinger, Carl J. '89 (CHY) Laramie, WY St. Paul's Newman Center Church.
Gallipoli, Mario *c.p.* '61 (BRK) [U] Jamaica, NY Immaculate Conception Monastery.
Gallivan, Msgr. David M. '66 (BUF) Williamsville, NY SS. Peter and Paul Church.
Gallo, David M. *a.a.* '88 (WOR) [N] Worcester, MA Assumptionists of Assumption College.
Gallo, Msgr. Joseph J. '46 (PAT) Retired; [P] Chester, NJ Nazareth Village.
Gallo, Msgr. Louis J. '48 (PAT) Retired; [P] Chester, NJ Nazareth Village.
Gallo, Regis *o.f.m.* (FR) [K] Onset, MA St. Joseph Novitiate-Franciscan Friars.
Gallo, Regis *o.f.m.* '62 (BO) [W] Boston, MA St. Christopher Friary.
Gallo, Vincent J. '60 (BRK) [19] Brooklyn, NY St. Bernard's Church.
Gallogly, Francis X. *o.s.a.* '65 (ALB) Mechanicville, NY Assumption-St. Paul Church.
Galluppi, Louis M. '83 (NOR) Ellington, CT St. Luke Church.
Gallus, David E. *o.s.c.* '66 (STP) Anoka, MN St. Stephen Church; [N] Anoka, MN Crosier Community of Anoka; [W] Shoreview, MN Crosier Missions.
Galluzzo, James (P) Aloha, OR St. Elizabeth Ann Seton Church.
Galonek, David B. '96 (WOR) Milford, MA St. Mary of the Assumption Church.
Galour, Joseph L. '38 (GF) Retired.
Galovich, George '71 (STL) Potosi, MO St. James Church.
Galuszka, Thaddeus *m.s.* '51 (MIL) [P] Twin Lakes, WI La Salette Missionaries Shrine.
Galuszka, Msgr. Walter C. '38 (BRK) [67] Brooklyn, NY St. John Cantius Church; Retired.
Galvan, Alfred '65 (ELP) Absent on Leave.
Galvan, Alfred '65 (LSC) Deming, NM St. Ann's Church.
Galvan, P. Michael (OAK) Pinole, CA St. Joseph's Church.
Galvez, Salvador '87 (NO) [41] New Orleans, LA St. Julian Eymard Church.
Galvin, Aloysius C. *s.j.* '57 (WDC) [E] North Bethesda, MD Georgetown Preparatory School.
Galvin, Bartholomew J. *m.m.* '53 (NY) [Z] Maryknoll, NY Maryknoll Fathers and Brothers.
Galvin, Bartholomew J. *m.m.* '53 (RVC) Bohemia, NY St. John Nepomucene Church.
Galvin, Edward *s.m.a.* '62 (NEW) [N] Tenafly, NJ Society of African Missions, Provincialate, S.M.A. Fathers.
Galvin, Edward *s.m.a.* '62 (WDC) [V] Washington, DC S.M.A. Social Concerns Department.
Galvin, Edward J. *s.m.a.* (NEW) Newark, NJ Essex County Jail.
Galvin, Edward J. *s.m.a.* '62 (NEW) [11] Newark, NJ St. Charles Borromeo's Church.
Galvin, Gregory P. '94 (NOR) Willimantic, CT St. Joseph Church.
Galvin, James *c.m.* '51 (LA) [W] Santa Barbara, CA St. Mary's Seminary Center.
Galvin, James G. '93 (SAT) [57] San Antonio, TX St. Matthew's Church.
Galvin, James M. *c.m.* (LA) [CC] Santa Barbara, CA World Wide Marriage Encounter.
Galvin, John P. '68 (BO) On Duty Outside the Archdiocese.
Galvin, John P. '68 (WDC) [C] Washington, DC Catholic University of America, The.
Galvin, Richard *o.s.b.* '48 (P) [L] St. Benedict, OR Mt. Angel Abbey.
Galvin, Thomas J. '82 (PIT) Penn Hills, PA St. Bartholomew Church.
Galvin, William J. *m.m.* '56 (NY) [Z] Maryknoll, NY Maryknoll Fathers and Brothers.
Galyo, Msgr. John M. '54 (PH) [4] Phoenixville, PA Sacred Heart Church; Pottstown, PA Holy Trinity Church.
Gamache, Barry J. '81 (PRO) [9] Woonsocket, RI Our Lady, Queen of Martyrs Church.
Gamache, Daniel '45 (FR) [6] Fall River, MA Notre Dame de Lourdes Church; Retired.
Gamache, Roland L. '67 (WOR) Winchendon, MA Immaculate Heart of Mary Church.
Gamallo, Edito '75 (NEW) [1] Jersey City, NJ St. Aedan's Church.
Gamarra, Manuel (SJN) [5] San Juan, PR Asuncion de La Virgen Church.
Gamba, John J. '42 (COL) Retired.
Gamba, Jose '86 (NEW) [25] Jersey City, NJ St. Paul's Church.
Gambatese, Angelus P. *o.f.m.* '59 (PAT) [5] Paterson, NJ St. Bonaventure Church.
Gamber, Matthew T. *s.j.* '95 (CHI) [D] Chicago, IL St. Ignatius Jesuit Community.
Gamber, William K. '64 (STP) Minneapolis, MN Veterans Administration Medical Center; Special Assignment; Retired.
Gambet, Daniel G. *o.s.f.s.* '57 (ALN) [B] Center Valley, PA Allentown College of St. Francis de Sales; [K] Center Valley, PA Oblates of St. Francis de Sales.
Gambino, Msgr. Anthony J. (MET) [8] Perth Amboy, NJ La Asuncion Church.
Gambino, Msgr. Anthony J. '69 (MET) [6] Perth Amboy, NJ Most Holy Rosary Church.
Gamble, Anthony *c.pp.s.* '42 (CIN) [B] Carthagena, OH St. Charles.
Gamboa, Damian *o.f.m.* '64 (SJ) [18] San Jose, CA Our

Lady of Guadalupe Church.
Gambon, John A. '49 (STL) Retired.
Gambone, Michael J. '56 (PH) [134] Philadelphia, PA St. Paul Church.
Gambro, John M. *o.p.* '57 (CHI) [D] Oak Park, IL Fenwick High School; [N] River Forest, IL St. Thomas Aquinas Priory.
Gamel, Robert E. (FRS) Boron, CA St. Joseph Church.
Gameros, L. Ignacio '81 (TUC) Marana, AZ St. Christopher's Church.
Gamm, David B. '72 (COV) [7] Covington, KY St. John Church.
Gamm, Joseph M. *c.m.f.* '45 (LA) [28] Los Angeles, CA Our Lady Queen of the Angels Church.
Gamrot, Jaroslaw *m.i.c.* '91 (WDC) [B] Washington, DC Marian Fathers Scholasticate.
Gamulani, Abdon *m.afr.* '72 (CHI) [124] Chicago, IL St. Martin De Porres Church; [N] Chicago, IL Missionaries of Africa.
Gana, Stanley M. '70 (PH) Absent on Sick Leave.
Ganahl, James '56 (SB) Retired.
Gandolfi, Louis *c.s.* (CHI) [122] Chicago, IL Santa Maria Addolorata Church.
Gandolfo, Kenneth '82 (BO) Dedham, MA St. Susanna Church.
Gandrau, James '58 (SEA) [2] Seattle, WA St. Alphonsus Church.
Ganiel, Joseph F. '83 (CAM) Salem, NJ St. Mary's Church.
Ganley, Charles '52 (SAG) Retired.
Ganley, Thomas R. '85 (MET) Piscataway, NJ Our Lady of Fatima Church.
Ganly, John C. *m.m.* '59 (NEW) [N] South Orange, NJ Maryknoll Fathers.
Gann, Sean J. '94 (RVC) Sayville, NY St. Lawrence the Martyr Church.
Gannon, Bernard J. '71 (CAM) Brigantine, NJ St. Thomas Church.
Gannon, Charles E. '43 (DAV) Retired; [M] Davenport, IA St. Vincent Center.
Gannon, Clair F. *o.s.b.* '41 (GBG) [H] Latrobe, PA Saint Vincent Archabbey.
Gannon, Daniel J. *s.j.* '68 (CHY) St. Stephens, WY St. Stephen's Church; [C] St. Stephens, WY St. Stephens Mission - Jesuit Community.
Gannon, Dismas *o.c.s.o.* '50 (P) [L] Lafayette, OR The Cistercian (Trappist) Abbey of Our Lady of Guadalupe.
Gannon, Donald C. *s.j.* '76 (NY) [80] New York, NY Nativity Church; [Z] New York, NY Jesuit Provincial's Office; [Z] New York, NY Xavier Jesuit Community.
Gannon, Earl A. '45 (TR) Retired; [L] Lawrenceville, NJ Morris Hall-Saint Lawrence, Inc.
Gannon, Gerard M. '56 (SCR) Archbald, PA St. Thomas Aquinas Church.
Gannon, James *o.f.m.* '87 (PH) [Z] Philadelphia, PA St. Pius X Friary.
Gannon, Msgr. James J. '42 (E) Retired.
Gannon, Msgr. John M. '41 (E) [20] Erie, PA St. Joseph Church; Retired.
Gannon, Joseph T. '75 (STP) Retired.
Gannon, Michael F. '65 (NY) [I] New York, NY The Catholic Charities of the Archdiocese of New York; [N] Nanuet, NY St. Agatha Home of the New York Foundling Hospital.
Gannon, Patrick '76 (NO) Luling, LA St. Anthony of Padua Church.
Gannon, Patrick J. '60 (LA) La Mirada, CA St. Paul of the Cross Church.
Gannon, Robert I. '60 (NY) [219] Staten Island, NY Our Lady, Queen of Peace Church; [E] New York, NY Moore Catholic High School.
Gannon, Roger *c.p.* (NEW) [N] Union City, NJ Congregation of the Passion (Passionists)-St. Michael's Residence.
Gannon, Roger *c.p.* '47 (MET) [H] South River, NJ Passionist Provincial Office.
Gannon, Msgr. Rowland '42 (STL) [2] Creve Coeur, MO St. John Bosco Church.
Gannon, Msgr. Rowland E. '41 (STL) Retired.
Gannon, Thomas M. *s.j.* '67 (GRY) [K] East Chicago, IN Roque Gonzalez Residence-Jesuit Fathers; [P] Hammond, IN Heartland Center.
Gannon, William Robert *o.p.* '53 (NY) Manhattan, NY Memorial Sloan Kettering Cancer Center; [Z] New York, NY St. Vincent Ferrer Priory.
Ganshert, Daniel T. '74 (MAD) [11] Madison, WI St. Patrick Church.
Ganss, George E. *s.j.* '37 (STL) [P] St. Louis, MO Jesuit Community Corporation at St. Louis University - Jesuit Hall.
Ganss, Karl P. '68 (RCK) DeKalb, IL St. Mary Church.
Ganssle, Joseph *o.f.m.* '58 (NY) [Z] New York, NY Franciscan Friars, Order of Friars Manor.
Gantert, Richard M. '75 (MEM) [26] Memphis, TN Our Lady of Sorrows Church.
Gantley, Donald M. *o.s.m.* '59 (CHI) Hillside, IL St. Domitilla Church; [N] Chicago, IL Servite Friars - Eastern Province.
Gantley, Mark J. '91 (SY) [15] Syracuse, NY St. Daniel Church
Ganucheau, William R. (LAF) Absent on Leave.
Ganuza, Felix *sch.p.* '20 (NY) [Z] New York, NY Calasanzian Fathers (Piarists).
Ganuza, Felix '76 (NY) [12] New York, NY Annunciation Church.
Ganzy, F. Alexander (SJP) Ambridge, PA Ss. Peter and Paul Church.
Gara, Msgr. Robert '45 (LA) Sierra Madre, CA St. Rita Church; Retired.
Garamendi, Martin *o.m.* '52 (SJN) [16] San Juan, PR Ntra. Sra. de Fatima Church.
Garanzini, Michael J. *s.j.* '80 (STL) [C] St. Louis, MO Saint Louis University; [C] St. Louis, MO Saint Louis University; [P] St. Louis, MC Jesuit Community Corporation at St. Louis University - Jesuit Hall.
Garatea, Juan Maria '59 (B) Burley, ID St. Theresa Church.
Garavaglia, Henry J. '64 (STL) [11] Florissant, MO Transfiguration Church.
Garavel, Andrew J. *s.j.* '92 (BGP) [O] Fairfield, CT The Fairfield Jesuit Community-Fairfield University.
Garaventa, Louis T. *s.j.* '76 (BUF) [D] Buffalo, NY Canisius High School; [O] Buffalo, NY Canisius Jesuit Community.
Garay, Edward W. '66 (CAM) Cape May, NJ Our Lady Star of the Sea Church.
Garbacik, Louis S. '54 (SCR) [10] Hazleton, PA St. Stanislaus Church.
Garbacz, Kazimerz *s.v.d.* '69 (CHI) [B] Techny, IL Divine Word Residence.
Garbacz, Kazimerz *s.v.d.* '70 (CHI) [N] Techny, IL Society of the Divine Word, Provincial Headquarter-Chicago Prov.; [N] Techny, IL Society of the Divine Word, Provincial Headquarter-Chicago Prov.
Garbarino, Joseph J. '83 (PAT) Montville, NJ St. Pius X Church.
Garber, Andrew V. *o.s.b.* '56 (MIL) Bristol, WI St. Scholastica Church.
Garber, Stephen A. *s.j.* '54 (PH) [G] Philadelphia, PA St. Joseph's Preparatory School; [Z] Philadelphia, PA Jesuit Community at St. Joseph's University.
Garbin, Arthur L. '41 (PIT) [O] Coraopolis, PA Our Lady of the Sacred Heart Convent.
Garbin, Raymond P. '63 (JOL) Addison, IL St. Philip The Apostle Church.
Garceau, James G. *c.r.i.c.* '84 (LA) [64] Los Angeles, CA St. Francis of Assisi Church; [B] Los Angeles, CA Canons Regular of the Immaculate Conception-Novitiate; [R] Los Angeles, CA Canons Regular of the Immaculate Conception.
Garced, Wilberto Reyes '29 (NY) [DD] New York, NY Lumen Dei.
Garces, Francis *o.f.m.cap.* '66 (FWT) [5] Fort Worth, TX Immaculate Heart of Mary Church.
Garces-Henao, Carlos '95 (HRT) [17] New Haven, CT St. Rose of Lima Church.
Garcia, Albert *ss.cc.* '69 (HON) Waialua, HI St. Michael Church.
Garcia, Alfredo *ss.cc.* '63 (BWN) Santa Rosa, TX St. Mary Church.
Garcia, Antonio (LA) [34] Los Angeles, CA Presentation of the B.V.M. Church.
Garcia, Antonio *o.dem.* '67 (PCE) [9] Ponce, PR La Merced Church.
Garcia, Antonio '81 (SJN) [14] Carolina, PR Ntra. Sra. Del Carmen Church.
Garcia, Avelino '68 (BAL) [15] Baltimore, MD St. Benedict Church.
Garcia, Avelino '68 (SP) On Duty Outside the Diocese.
Garcia, Daniel '88 (AUS) [23] Austin, TX St. Vincent de Paul Church.
Garcia, David *c.o.* (BWN) [E] Pharr, TX Oratory of St. Philip Neri, of Pontifical Right.
Garcia, David '75 (SAT) [1] San Antonio, TX Cathedral of San Fernando.
Garcia, E. Roberto '82 (PCE) On Duty Outside the Diocese.
Garcia, Edgar *o.m.i.* '85 (LA) San Fernando, CA Santa Rosa Church.
Garcia, Eduardo *o.s.* '93 (PCE) [11] Ponce, PR San Jose Obrero Church.
Garcia, Eduardo H. '90 (CC) [6] Corpus Christi, TX Our Lady of Guadalupe Church.
Garcia, Eliseo *o.s.a.* '59 (SJN) [1] Bayamon, PR San Agustin Church.
Garcia, Emilio G. '57 (ORL) Dunnellon, FL St. John the Baptist Church.
Garcia, Esau N. *c.p.* '87 (ORL) Sanford, FL All Souls Church.
Garcia, Francisco *o.f.m.cap.* '78 (PCE) [5] Ponce, PR Santa Teresita Church; [E] Ponce, PR Residencia Asis; [H] Ponce, PR Albergue La Providencia, Inc.
Garcia, George '73 (MIA) Coconut Grove, FL St. Hugh Church.
Garcia, Gerardo *o.s.a.* (CHI) [4] Waukegan, IL Holy Family Church.
Garcia, Gilcardo '85 (NEW) Fairview, NJ St. John the Baptist Church.
Garcia, Guillermo C. *c.j.* '75 (LA) [3] Santa Barbara, CA Our Lady of Guadalupe Church.
Garcia, Hector *c.ss.r.* (CGS) Fajardo, PR Santiago Apostol Church.
Garcia, Isidoro *c.m.f.* '54 (SAT) [N] San Antonio, TX Cordi-Marian Missionary Sisters.
Garcia, James L. '70 (SFR) [1] Menlo Park, CA St. Anthony Church.
Garcia, Jesus Alberto '94 (SJN) [2] Toa Alta, PR San Fernando Church.
Garcia, John G. '47 (OAK) Brentwood, CA Immaculate Heart of Mary Church.
Garcia, Jose '52 (MIA) [24] Miami, FL St. Kevin Church.
Garcia, Jose Isidore *o.m.i.* '64 (GAL) [15] Houston, TX Church of the Blessed Sacrament.
Garcia, Jose L. (ARE) On Duty Outside the Diocese.
Garcia, Jose L. *o.m.* '63 (CGS) Cayey, PR Nuestra Senora de la Asuncion Church.
Garcia, Jose Ma. *ss.cc.* (SJN) [9] Guaynabo, PR Sagrados Corazones Church.
Garcia, Juan '70 (ELP) [A] El Paso, TX St. Charles Seminary College Program.
Garcia, Juan A. *f.m.m.* (BEA) [4] Beaumont, TX Cristo Rey Church.
Garcia, Juan F. *c.r.i.c.* '67 (SPR) [3] Springfield, MA Blessed Sacrament Church; [M] Springfield, MA Casa Cristo Rey.
Garcia, Juan Jose '96 (HRT) [B] Cheshire, CT Novitiate of the Legion of Christ.
Garcia, Louis '93 (STO) Absent on Leave.
Garcia, Luis '50 (LA) Lynwood, CA St. Emydius Church.
Garcia, Luis J. *j.c.l.* '76 (GLP) Aztec, NM St. Joseph Church; Flora Vista, NM Holy Trinity Church.
Garcia, Manuel (SJN) [D] San Juan, PR Centro Medico de P.R.
Garcia, Manuel '75 (SJN) Dorado, PR Ntra. Sra. de La Salud Church.
Garcia, Marcelino *s.j.* '70 (MIA) [D] Miami, FL Belen Jesuit Preparatory School; [H] Miami, FL Jesuit Fathers of the Province of the Antilles, Inc.
Garcia, Michael A. *o.p.* '81 (CHI) [N] Chicago, IL Dominicans (Provincial Office).
Garcia, Millan J. '62 (SFE) Albuquerque, NM University Hospital.
Garcia, Nicolas '48 (STO) Newman, CA St. Joachim Church.
Garcia, Msgr. Otto L. *j.c.d.* '73 (BRK) [1] Brooklyn, NY The Cathedral-Basilica of St. James.
Garcia, Patrick Kenny Q. '68 (AGN) Mongmong, GU Nuestra Senora de Las Aquas Church.
Garcia, Paul '93 (ELP) [31] El Paso, TX St. Raphael Church.
Garcia, Pedro '64 (MIA) Naranja, FL St. Ann Mission Church.
Garcia, Pedro '92 (AUS) Taylor, TX Our Lady of Guadalupe Church.
Garcia, Pedro V. '65 (GR) [13] Grand Rapids, MI St. Joseph The Worker Church.
Garcia, Rafael *s.j.* '93 (ELP) [21] El Paso, TX Sacred Heart Church.
Garcia, Rafael E. '85 (FRS) Goshen, CA St. Thomas the Apostle Church; Visalia, CA Holy Family Church.
Garcia, Msgr. Raymond '55 (SAT) Retired.
Garcia, Reynaldo *s.j.* '76 (NO) [P] New Orleans, LA Jesuit Provincial Office.
Garcia, Ricardo '88 (ORG) Placentia, CA St. Joseph Church.
Garcia, Ricardo '92 (BWN) [3] Mission, TX Our Lady of St. John of the Fields Church.
Garcia, Richard J. '73 (SJ) [14] San Jose, CA St. Leo the Great Church; Special Assignment.
Garcia, Roberto *o.s.a.* '48 (MGZ) San German, PR St. Rose of Lima Church.
Garcia, Roberto *o.f.m.cap.* '59 (DAL) [8] Dallas, TX Our Lady of Lourdes Church.
Garcia, Roberto '82 (SJN) [3] Toa Baja, PR Espiritu Santo Church.
Garcia, Msgr. Roberto '86 (PCE) [B] Ponce, PR The Pontifical Catholic University of Puerto Rico.
Garcia, Rolando '86 (MIA) Leisure City, FL St. Martin de Porres Church.
Garcia, Salvador '52 (PCE) On Duty Outside the Diocese.
Garcia, Sergio *c.r.i.c.* '94 (LA) [B] Los Angeles, CA Canons Regular of the Immaculate Conception-Novitiate; [R] Los Angeles, CA Canons Regular of the Immaculate Conception.
Garcia, Severiano *c.m.* '50 (CGS) [8] Barrio Rio Canas, PR Immaculado Corozon de Maria Church.
Garcia R., Juan F. '96 (SHP) [1] Shreveport, LA St. John Berchmans Cathedral.
Garcia-Cardona, Carlos '92 (LKC) Iowa, LA St. Raphael Church.
Garcia-Miro, Sergio '78 (MIA) North Miami Beach, FL St. Lawrence Church.
Gard, Charles '87 (LA) Diamond Bar, CA St. Denis Church; Glendale, CA Holy Family Church.
Gardella, Robert *o.s.a.* '66 (DET) Grosse Pointe Park, MI St. Clare of Montefalco Church.

Gardin, Msgr. Vernon E. (STL) [5] Creve Coeur, MO St. Richard Church.
Gardin, Msgr. Vernon E. '71 (STL) [H] St. Louis, MO Catholic Guidance Center; [H] St. Louis, MO St. Mary's Special School for Exceptional Children.
Gardiner, Christopher B. '68 (MAR) Gladstone, MI Holy Family Church.
Gardiner, James J. *s.a.* '69 (NY) [Z] New York, NY Atonement Friars.
Gardiner, James K. '69 (GAY) Traverse City, MI St. Francis of Assisi Church.
Gardiner, Richard E. '67 (WDC) Solomons, MD Our Lady Star of the Sea Church.
Garding, William '82 (SCL) Special Assignment.
Gardner, Clarence W. '42 (ROC) [4] Auburn, NY St. Alphonsus Church; Retired.
Gardner, Clement '67 (ALT) Hollidaysburg, PA St. Michael's Church.
Gardner, Daniel L. '78 (KCK) [5] Topeka, KS Our Lady of Guadalupe Church.
Gardner, George C. *c.ss.r.* (BO) Boston, MA Children's Hospital.
Gardner, George C. *c.ss.r.* '47 (BO) [13] Boston, MA Basilica of Our Lady of Perpetual Help.
Gardner, Harold B. *c.s.b.* '59 (DET) [E] Redford, MI Catholic Central High School.
Gardner, Jerome '79 (CIN) Fairfield, OH Sacred Heart of Jesus Church.
Gardner, Msgr. Laurence R. '36 (MAN) [1] Manchester, NH St. Joseph Cathedral; Retired.
Gardner, Louis C. '54 (OG) Chazy, NY Sacred Heart Church.
Gardner, Maurice '52 (KCK) Retired.
Gardner, Royal J. '51 (SPR) [4] Pittsfield, MA Sacred Heart Church.
Gardner, Simeon '54 (SP) Retired.
Gardner, Thomas *o.f.m.* '79 (STL) [P] St. Louis, MO Franciscan Friary of St. Anthony of Padua.
Gardner, William M. '92 (PEO) Lostant, IL St. John the Baptist's Church; Wenona, IL St. Mary's Church.
Gardner, William P. '62 (TR) [1] Toms River, NJ St. Joseph Church.
Gardocki, Thomas F. '65 (WIL) Retired.
Gardon, Emmanuel H. *c.p.* '50 (OAK) [1] Hayward, CA All Saints Church.
Gardzalla, Leo M. '45 (SCR) [4] Nanticoke, PA St. Joseph's Church.
Gareau, Timothy W. '88 (CLV) Fairview Park, OH St. Angela Merici Church.
Gargani, Francis J. *c.ss.r.* '71 (NY) [Z] Esopus, NY Redemptorist Priests and Brothers C.Ss.R. (Province of Baltimore); [BB] Esopus, NY Mount St. Alphonsus Redemptorist Retreat Center.
Gargantiel, Isidro T. '68 (GR) Free Soil, MI St. John Cantius Church; Scottville, MI St. Jerome Church; [K] Edmore, MI Montcalm Community College Newman Center.
Garibaldi, Anthony *o.f.m.* '76 (LA) [W] Malibu, CA Serra Retreat.
Gariboldi, Ronald J. '61 (BO) Rockport, MA St. Joachim Church.
Gariepy, Andre M. '58 (WOR) [1] Gardner, MA Holy Spirit Church.
Gariepy, Robert E. '63 (WOR) Retired.
Gariepy, Thomas P. *c.s.c.* '74 (FR) [B] North Easton, MA Stonehill College.
Gariolo, Joseph M. *c.r.s.p.* '50 (BUF) [B] Youngstown, NY St. Anthony Zaccaria Seminary.
Garisto, James '77 (NY) [219] Staten Island, NY Our Lady, Queen of Peace Church; [F] New York, NY St. Joseph by the Sea, High School.
Garity, Linus J. '33 (BEL) [F] Belleville, IL Our Lady of the Snows Apartment Community Retirement Home.
Garity, Linus J. '33 (MIL) Retired.
Garkowski, John J. '66 (BRK) [154] Queens, NY St. Bartholomew's Church; [T] Astoria-Long Island City, NY Regional Service Centers.
Garland, Reynolds *o.f.m.* '61 (BR) Carville, LA National Hansen's Disease Center.
Garland, Msgr. Robert P. '53 (PIT) Cecil, PA St. Mary Church.
Garland, William T. '62 (FR) [P] Fall River, MA Diocesan Education Center.
Garlick, Thomas B. (WOR) [21] Worcester, MA St. Charles Borromeo Church; On Special or Other (Arch)Diocesan Assignment.
Garneau, James F. (R) Graduate Studies.
Garner, Joel *o.praem.* (SFE) [N] Albuquerque, NM Norbertine Community of New Mexico, Inc.
Garner, Joel P. *o.praem.* '65 (SFE) [11] Albuquerque, NM Our Lady of Most Holy Rosary Church; [J] Albuquerque, NM Santa Maria de la Vid Priory.
Garner, Kirby D. '77 (AUS) [25] Austin, TX San Jose Church.
Garofalo, Kenneth *o.f.m.* '55 (BO) [57] Boston, MA Our Lady of Mt. Carmel Church.
Garoffolo, Vincent '41 (NEW) Retired.
Garone, Thomas *o.f.m.* '73 (MAN) Derry, NH St. Thomas Aquinas Church.
Garrahy, Michael '51 (WCH) Retired.
Garramone, Dominic M. *o.s.b.* '92 (PEO) [A] Peru, IL St. Bede Abbey and Academy; [C] Peru, IL St. Bede Academy.
Garred, Msgr. John L. '52 (GBG) Retired; [G] Greensburg, PA Neumann House.
Garret, Sean '64 (SAT) On Duty Outside the Archdiocese.
Garrett, Mark A. *o.s.a.* '70 (SAT) Spring Branch, TX St. Joseph Church; [C] San Antonio, TX Oblate School of Theology.
Garrett, Sean '64 (PT) Fort Walton Beach, FL St. Mary Church.
Garrett, Thomas P. *o.s.a.* '39 (SD) [H] San Diego, CA Augustinian Community.
Garrick, David A. *c.s.c.* '76 (FTW) [B] Notre Dame, IN University of Notre Dame Du Lac; [J] Notre Dame, IN Holy Cross Community, Corby Hall, University of Notre Dame.
Garrido, Alejandro '92 (CHI) [5] Chicago, IL St. Agnes of Bohemia Church.
Garrigan, Gerard *o.s.b.* '89 (STL) [1] Creve Coeur, MO St. Anselm Church; [P] St. Louis, MO The Abbey of St. Mary and St. Louis.
Garrity, Francis A. '41 (CHI) Park Forest, IL St. Irenaeus Church; Retired.
Garrity, Francis D. '56 (BO) Needham, MA St. Bartholomew Church.
Garrity, John M. '58 (CLV) Berea, OH St. Mary's Church.
Garrity, Patrick '76 (KNX) Seymour, TN Holy Family Church; [A] Knoxville, TN Knoxville Catholic High School.
Garrity, Paul V. '73 (BO) [4] Lynn, MA St. Mary Church; [6] Lynn, MA St. Patrick Church.
Garrity, Robert M. '81 (RCK) Huntley, IL St. Mary Church.
Garrity, Stephen M. *s.j.* '70 (WDC) [P] Faulkner, MD Loyola on the Potomac Retreat House.
Garrote, Sancho E. '76 (NY) [143] Bronx, NY St. Francis Xavier Church.
Garrote, Sancho G. '76 (NY) Bronx, NY Bronx Municipal Hospital Center, Abraham Jacobi Hospital, Nathan B. VanEtten Hospital.
Garrott, William P. *o.p.* '94 (COL) Zanesville, OH St. Thomas Aquinas Church.
Garrow, Mark *m.i.c.* '84 (SPR) [I] Stockbridge, MA Congregation of Marians.
Garry, Brian *s.j.* '82 (SP) [C] Tampa, FL Jesuit High School.
Garry, Gerald *s.v.d.* '59 (CHI) [B] Techny, IL Divine Word Residence.
Garry, Peter '68 (RVC) Seaford, NY St. William, the Abbot Church.
Garry, Ronald B. '83 (RC) Lemmon, SD St. Mary's Church.
Garst, Charles C. *o.s.f.s.* '83 (PH) [D] Philadelphia, PA Father Judge High School for Boys.
Garst, Charles C. *o.s.f.s.* '83 (WIL) [3] Wilmington, DE St. Anthony of Padua Church.
Garthwaite, Thomas F. '55 (LC) Retired.
Gartland, Daniel B. '82 (LFT) [4] Lafayette, IN St. Lawrence Church.
Gartland, James G. *s.j.* '93 (CHI) [177] Chicago, IL St. Procopius Church.
Gartland, R. Vincent '81 (TR) Lawrenceville, NJ St. Ann Church.
Gartland, Msgr. Thomas A. '49 (NY) Bedford, NY St. Patrick Church.
Gartner, Charles A. '58 (RVC) Hicksville, NY Our Lady of Mercy Church; Retired.
Gartner, Edward J. *s.s.j.* '49 (BAL) [M] Baltimore, MD St. Joseph Society of the Sacred Heart House of Central Administration.
Gartner, John *s.s.s.* '53 (CLV) [P] Cleveland, OH Congregation of the Blessed Sacrament Provincial House; [P] Cleveland, OH Blessed Sacrament Community.
Gartner, Joseph *glmy.* '40 (CIN) [M] Fairfield, OH Headquarters of Glenmary Home Missioners.
Gartska, Joseph A. '39 (GB) Retired.
Garvey, Charles J. '47 (COV) [6] Covington, KY Holy Cross Church; Retired.
Garvey, Francis J. '59 (NU) Manannah, MN Church of Our Lady; Willmar, MN Regional Treatment Center; [F] Willmar, MN Willmar Regional Treatment Center.
Garvey, James W. '76 (PIT) [8] Pittsburgh, PA St. Charles Lwanga Church.
Garvey, John *glmy.* '57 (CIN) [M] Fairfield, OH Headquarters of Glenmary Home Missioners.
Garvey, John *glmy.* '57 (RIC) Gate City, VA St. Bernard Church.
Garvey, John F. *s.j.* '74 (NY) [F] New York, NY Xavier High School.
Garvey, John J. *s.j.* '50 (BUF) [O] Buffalo, NY Canisius Jesuit Community.
Garvey, John M. *m.s.* '53 (HRT) [M] Hartford, CT Missionaries of LaSalette Provincial Secretary.
Garvey, John M. *m.s.* '53 (STL) [P] St. Louis, MO La Salette Missionaries.
Garvey, John M. '58 (SFS) Webster, SD Christ the King Church.
Garvey, Justin *c.p.* '43 (BRK) [U] Jamaica, NY Immaculate Conception Monastery.
Garvey, Michael '71 (Y) Military Chaplains.
Garvey, Thomas *s.c.j.* '58 (MIL) [P] Hales Corners, WI Sacred Heart Monastery.
Garvey, Thomas J. '57 (STP) Retired.
Garvin, Msgr. Joseph P. '73 (PH) Highland Park, PA St. Laurence Church; [J] Philadelphia, PA The Catholic Social Services of the Archdiocese of Philadelphia.
Garvin, Thomas R. *s.j.* '58 (SEA) Friday Harbor, WA St. Francis Church; [A] Seattle, WA Seattle University.
Garvy, John '83 (ORL) Retired.
Gary, Paul Q. '84 (CHL) [1] Charlotte, NC St. Patrick Cathedral.
Garza, Amador '85 (BWN) On Assignment Outside the Diocese.
Garza, Amador '85 (IND) [A] St. Meinrad, IN St. Meinrad Seminary.
Garza, Carlos '90 (BWN) Weslaco, TX San Martin de Porres Church.
Garza, Jesus '79 (CHI) On Duty Outside the Archdiocese.
Garza, Roberto '96 (MIA) Key West, FL St. Mary, Star of the Sea Church.
Garzarelli, Santo R. '61 (PH) On Duty Outside the Archdiocese.
Garzon-Blanco, Armando '95 (TUC) Absent on Leave; [F] Tucson, AZ Regina Cleri Center.
Gasbarre, Msgr. Francis E. '41 (CLV) Bedford, OH St. Mary Church; Retired.
Gasbarri, Italo *o.ss.t.* '48 (BAL) [M] Baltimore, MD Holy Trinity Monastery.
Gasiunas, John '28 (BEL) Retired.
Gaska, Henry *s.v.d.* '88 (WDC) [M] Washington, DC Divine Word College.
Gaske, Bartholomew *o.f.m.conv.* '40 (SY) [2] Syracuse, NY Assumption B.V.M. Church.
Gaskin, Matthew L. *o.f.m.* '50 (PAT) [M] Butler, NJ St. Anthony Friary.
Gasnick, Roy *o.f.m.* '60 (SP) [O] St. Petersburg, FL St. Anthony Friary.
Gaspar, Joseph W. *m.s.c.* '41 (ALN) [K] Reading, PA Missionaries of the Sacred Heart.
Gasparik, Francis *o.f.m.cap.* '86 (NY) [57] New York, NY St. John the Baptist Church.
Gasparin, Giampietro *c.s.j.* '79 (CLV) [D] Lorain, OH Lorain Catholic High School; [P] Avon, OH Congregation of St. Joseph.
Gasparin, Giampietro *c.s.j.* '79 (LA) [R] Los Angeles, CA Congregation of St. Joseph Casa Nazareth.
Gasparro, Anthony *o.s.a.* '41 (PH) [111] Philadelphia, PA St. Nicholas of Tolentine Church.
Gaspeny, Peter J. '83 (SAG) [5] Bay City, MI St. James Church.
Gass, Michael W. '77 (DEN) [4] Lakewood, CO St. Jude Church.
Gass, Robert J. '53 (OM) [12] Omaha, NE Christ the King Church; [L] Omaha, NE Sisters of the Annunciation of the Archdiocese of Omaha.
Gass, Msgr. Sylvester F. '39 (MIL) Retired.
Gassert, Adelbert '48 (CLV) Northfield, OH Western Reserve Psychiatric Habilitation Center; Retired.
Gassert, Adelbert J. '48 (CLV) Independence, OH St. Michael Church.
Gastalver, Alfredo (SJN) [F] Guaynabo, PR Opus Dei.
Gaston, James T. '70 (GBG) [3] Greensburg, PA Our Lady of Grace Church.
Gaston, Juan Cruz *o.f.m.cap.* '67 (DAL) [9] Dallas, TX Our Lady of Perpetual Help Church; [10] Dallas, TX Our Lady of San Juan De Los Lagos and St. Theresa Church; [M] Dallas, TX Capuchin Franciscan Friars, Vice Province of Texas.
Gately, Alfred A. *o.p.* '41 (NY) [121] New York, NY St. Vincent Ferrer Church.
Gately, R. Troy '89 (GAL) [19] Houston, TX Christ the King Church; On Special Assignment.
Gately, Robert '52 (SP) [1] St. Petersburg, FL Cathedral of St. Jude the Apostle.
Gately, Robert E. '52 (COL) Retired.
Gates, Gabriel *o.c.d.* '42 (MIL) [P] Milwaukee, WI Provincial Offices - Discalced Carmelites.
Gathen, Anthony *c.m.m.* '71 (DET) [K] Dearborn Heights, MI Our Lady of Grace Monastery.
Gatlin, Bernerd (LA) Wilmington, CA Holy Family Church.
Gatlin, Larry B. '67 (OKL) [12] Oklahoma City, OK St. James Church.
Gatman, Ronald P. *o.s.b.* '79 (SAV) [B] Savannah, GA Benedictine Military School; [F] Savannah, GA The Benedictine Priory.
Gato, Reynold J. *s.j.* '68 (SAC) [C] Sacramento, CA Jesuit High School.
Gatschet, Fred '93 (SAL) [1] Salina, KS Cathedral of the Sacred Heart.
Gattari, Valentine A. '54 (DET) [8] Detroit, MI Annunciation Church.
Gatti, Daniel J. *s.j.* '72 (NY) [F] New York, NY Xavier High School.
Gatto, Dennis J. *s.m.* '81 (CIN) [M] Dayton, OH Marianist Provincialate.
Gatto, Joseph '83 (BUF) [A] East Aurora, NY Christ the

King Seminary.
Gatto, Joseph C. (BUF) [A] Buffalo, NY Pope John II Residence.
Gatto, Joseph C. *s.t.d.* '83 (BUF) [A] East Aurora, NY Christ the King Seminary.
Gatto, Reynold J. *s.j.* '68 (SAC) [H] Carmichael, CA Jesuit High School Community of Sacramento.
Gatto, Msgr. Vincent S. '55 (WDC) Garrett Park, MD Holy Cross Church.
Gatzak, John P. '75 (HRT) Special and other (Arch)Diocesan Assignment; [V] Hartford, CT Counterpoint Communications, Inc.
Gau, David *s.j.* '62 (RC) St. Francis, SD St. Charles Church; St. Francis, SD Rosebud Reservation Church.
Gau, Guy *o.s.b.* '62 (SFS) [F] Marvin, SD Blue Cloud Abbey.
Gauchat, Eric *cap. o.f.m.* (CLV) [N] Cleveland, OH Mount Alverna Home, Inc. & Mount Alverna Home Annex, Inc.
Gaudet, Msgr. Joseph A. '52 (BO) [7] Brockton, MA St. Patrick Church.
Gaudet, Roger B. '89 (IND) Fortville, IN St. Thomas Church.
Gaudette, Edward J. '52 (BO) [6] Revere, MA St. Theresa Church.
Gaudin, Rene *ss.cc.* '57 (FR) [K] Fairhaven, MA Sacred Hearts Provincial House.
Gaudio, Robert '74 (ROC) Palmyra, NY St. Anne Church.
Gaudio, Robert '93 (ROC) Marion, NY St. Gregory Church.
Gaudreau, Bernard E. '75 (BUR) Montpelier, VT St. Augustine Church.
Gaudreau, James E. '69 (BO) [3] Lynn, MA St. Joseph Church.
Gaudreau, Walter *s.m.* (BO) [4] Methuen, MA St. Theresa Church.
Gaughan, Msgr. Francis J. '36 (PH) [102] Philadelphia, PA St. Matthew Church; Retired.
Gaughan, James '74 (MIA) [B] Opa Locka, FL St. Thomas University.
Gaughan, James M. '74 (OM) Absent on Leave.
Gaughan, Joseph '94 (FTW) [3] South Bend, IN St. Anthony de Padua Church.
Gaughan, Msgr. Patrick E. '68 (STU) Athens, OH St. Paul's Church.
Gaughan, Paul '52 (RIC) Retired.
Gaughan, Thomas E. *c.s.c.* '87 (FTW) [B] Notre Dame, IN University of Notre Dame Du Lac; [J] Notre Dame, IN Holy Cross Community, Corby Hall, University of Notre Dame.
Gaughran, John '53 (PEO) Retired.
Gaugler, Robert *c.ss.r.* '39 (SJN) [2] San Juan, PR San Agustin Church.
Gaul, Cornelius '45 (DM) Retired.
Gaul, Richard G. '68 (DUB) Garber, IA St. Michael's Church; Garnavillo, IA St. Joseph's Church.
Gaul, Thomas J. '73 (R) Hope Mills, NC Good Shepherd Church.
Gaulin, Frederick J. *c.m.* '50 (PH) [Z] Philadelphia, PA Congregation of the Mission.
Gaulin, Roger '65 (NOR) Absent on Leave.
Gaulrapp, Leo *c.pp.s.* '46 (CIN) [B] Carthagena, OH St. Charles.
Gaumond, Normand R. '73 (WOR) Harvard, MA St. Theresa's Church.
Gaumond, Paul J. '74 (NOR) Wauregan, CT Sacred Heart Church.
Gaunt, James J. *c.s.b.* '64 (GAL) Manvel, TX Sacred Heart of Jesus Church; [Q] Manvel, TX The Basilian Fathers' Monastery of Citeaux.
Gaunt, Thomas P. *s.j.* '81 (BAL) [M] Baltimore, MD Jesuit Fathers and Brothers Maryland Provincial Curia; [M] Baltimore, MD Ferdinand Wheeler House.
Gaunt, Thomas P. *s.j.* '81 (NY) [Z] New York, NY Jesuit Provincial's Office.
Gaus, Msgr. Arnold L. '59 (ALT) Ebensburg, PA Holy Name Church.
Gausch, Joseph P. '45 (PH) [51] Philadelphia, PA Good Shepherd Church; Retired.
Gauthier, Donald F., Jr. '75 (MAN) Goffstown, NH St. Lawrence Church.
Gauthier, Ernest L. '62 (KC) Holden, MO St. Patrick's Church.
Gauthier, John '65 (PHX) On Leave.
Gauthier, Joseph D. *s.j.* '44 (BO) [W] Chestnut Hill, MA The Jesuit Community at Boston College.
Gauthier, Lawrence T. '55 (MAR) Retired.
Gauthier, Rene G. '48 (FR) [15] Fall River, MA St. Jean Baptiste Church.
Gauthreaux, Msgr. L. Earl '56 (NO) [43] New Orleans, LA St. Maria Goretti Church.
Gautreau, Evan B. *c.ss.r.* '38 (STL) [P] Liguori, MO St. Clement Health Care Center.
Gautreau, Henry W. '79 (BR) [14] Baton Rouge, LA St. Louis, King of France Church.
Gauvin, Leo *o.m.i.* '50 (BWN) San Juan, TX Virgen de San Juan del Valle Shrine Church; [I] San Juan, TX Virgen de San Juan del Valle Shrine.
Gauvin, Maurice O. '86 (FR) [23] Fall River, MA Santo Christo Church.
Gauvreau, Thomas H. '48 (SPR) Retired.
Gavaler, Campion P. *o.s.b.* '59 (GBG) [H] Latrobe, PA Saint Vincent Archabbey.
Gavigan, P. Patrick '53 (CHL) Retired.
Gavigan, Peter '62 (NY) [178] Bronx, NY Our Lady of Victory Church.
Gavigan, Thomas J. *c.ss.r.* '60 (PCE) Guayama, PR St. Anthony of Padua Church.
Gavigan, Tomas *c.ss.r.* '60 (SJN) [2] San Juan, PR San Agustin Church.
Gavin, Carney E. '65 (BO) [21] Boston, MA St. Columbkille Church; On Special or Other Diocesan Assignment; On Duty Outside the Archdiocese.
Gavin, Emmett *o.carm.* '87 (CHI) [N] Chicago, IL Carmelite Fathers Residence.
Gavin, Francis T. '47 (NEW) Retired; [B] South Orange, NJ Seton Hall University.
Gavin, Harold E. '51 (WIN) Kellogg, MN St. Agnes Church
Gavin, James M. '51 (LA) [R] Los Angeles, CA Amat House.
Gavin, James P. *o.f.m.cap.* '65 (NY) [Z] Garrison, NY St. Francis Friary.
Gavin, John *o.s.a.* '48 (STL) [6] St. Louis, MO Immaculate Conception-St. Henry Church.
Gavin, John T. *o.s.f.s.* '60 (R) Goldsboro, NC St. Mary Church.
Gavin, Kenneth J. *s.j.* '75 (NY) [Z] New York, NY Jesuit Provincial's Office; [Z] New York, NY St. Ignatius Loyola Residence.
Gavin, Robert A. *o.f.m.* '59 (NY) [35] New York, NY St. Francis of Assisi Church.
Gavin, Robert V. *s.s.* '61 (SFR) [A] Menlo Park, CA St. Patrick Seminary.
Gavin, Russell *o.carm.* '47 (JOL) Darien, IL Our Lady of Mount Carmel Church.
Gavin, William F. *s.j.* '62 (ALN) [A] Wernersville, PA Novitiate of St. Isaac Jogues.
Gavit, James F. '54 (SAG) [7] Bay City, MI St. Maria Goretti Church.
Gavitt, J. Duane '84 (SCR) [17] Wilkes-Barre, PA St. Patrick's Church.
Gavotto, Robert W. *o.s.a.* '64 (OAK) Castro Valley, CA Our Lady of Grace Church.
Gawin, George *s.a.c.* '56 (MIL) [P] Milwaukee, WI St. Vincent Community.
Gawinek, Walter '35 (MIL) [N] Wauwatosa, WI St. Camillus Health Center, Inc.
Gawlik, Gilbert *s.v.d.* '54 (CHI) [B] Techny, IL Divine Word Residence; [N] Techny, IL Society of the Divine Word, Provincial Headquarter-Chicago Prov.
Gawronski, Chester J. '76 (E) [13] Erie, PA St. Ann Church.
Gawronski, Mark '91 (DET) [72] Detroit, MI St. Stephen-Mary Mother of the Church.
Gawronski, Raymond T. *s.j.* '86 (MIL) [P] Milwaukee, WI Jesuit Community at Marquette University.
Gay, James A. '59 (BGP) Military Chaplains.
Gay, John Curry '56 (HRT) [2] Waterbury, CT Immaculate Conception Church.
Gayarre, Domingo *s.s.s.* '52 (CGS) [5] Caguas, PR Santisimo Sacramento Church.
Gayarre, Eugenio '61 (ARE) Corozal, PR Holy Family Church.
Gaydos, Anthony M. *o.s.m.* '48 (CHI) [N] Chicago, IL Servite Friars - Eastern Province.
Gaydos, Anthony M. *o.s.m.* '48 (SPC) Ironton, MO Ste. Marie Du Lac Church; [C] Pilot Knob, MO Arcadia Valley Hospital.
Gaydos, Msgr. John R. '68 (STL) [36] St. Louis, MO St. Gabriel the Archangel Church.
Gaydos, Robert M. *c.ss.r.* '44 (STL) [P] Liguori, MO St. Clement Health Care Center.
Gaydosik, David L. '87 (STU) Carrollton, OH Our Lady of Mercy Church; Morges, OH St. Mary Church.
Gaynard, Thomas P. '65 (PH) King of Prussia, PA Mother of Divine Providence Church.
Gaynor, James E. *c.pp.s.* '67 (CIN) [M] Dayton, OH Provincial House of the Cincinnati Province of the Society of the Precious Blood.
Gaynor, Joseph T. '45 (ROC) [4] Auburn, NY St. Alphonsus Church; Retired.
Gaynor, William J. '35 (ROC) [4] Auburn, NY St. Alphonsus Church; Retired.
Gayso, Edward V. '50 (IND) Retired.
Gaytan, Alfredo *s.o.l.t.* (CC) Robstown, TX St. Anthony Church.
Gaytan, Alfredo *s.o.l.t.* '82 (CC) [H] Robstown, TX Society of Our Lady of the Most Holy Trinity.
Gayton, John J. *m.i.c.* '86 (SPR) [I] Stockbridge, MA Congregation of Marians.
Gaza, J. Patrick '68 (GRY) [16] Gary, IN SS. Monica-St. Luke Church.
Gazarkiewicz, Joseph F. '85 (GRY) Schererville, IN St. Michael Church.
Gazin, Mark R. *c.s.b.* '90 (GAL) [C] Houston, TX University of St. Thomas; [Q] Houston, TX Residence of the Basilian Fathers of the University of St. Thomas; [T] Houston, TX University of St. Thomas Campus Ministry.
Gaztelu, Msgr. Angel '38 (MIA) [22] Miami, FL St. John Bosco Church.
Geaney, Gregory *o.carm.* '59 (JOL) [J] Darien, IL Carmelite Fathers Provincial Office.
Geaney, John *c.s.p.* '64 (WDC) [V] Washington, DC ITP Paulist Communications.
Geaney, John J. *c.s.p.* '64 (WDC) [B] Washington, DC St. Paul's College.
Geany, Nash P. (NY) West Point, NY Stewart Field.
Gearhart, Edwin F. '73 (CIN) [53] Cincinnati, OH St. Leo the Great Church; [54] Cincinnati, OH St. Louis Church.
Gearheard, William J. '94 (LAF) Eunice, LA St. Anthony of Padua Church.
Gearing, Msgr. Daniel A. '38 (PIT) Baldwin Boro, PA St. Albert the Great Church; Retired.
Gearing, Edward P. '44 (GBG) Retired.
Geary, Edward A. *s.j.* '62 (PH) [Z] Philadelphia, PA Jesuit Community at St. Joseph's University.
Geary, Edward P. '64 (BO) Littleton, MA St. Anne Church.
Geary, John *s.j.* '47 (FRS) Bakersfield, CA Kern Medical Center, Bakersfield Memorial Hospital & San Joaquin Community Hospital.
Geary, Mark *o.p.* (NSH) [F] Nashville, TN St. Thomas Hospital; [H] Nashville, TN Dominican Friars.
Geary, Patrick G. '56 (DUB) [6] Waterloo, IA Blessed Sacrament Church.
Gebbia, Gregory V. *o.f.m.* '86 (NY) [115] New York, NY St. Stephen of Hungary Church.
Gebelein, Gary '74 (STL) [6] Florissant, MO St. Ferdinand Church.
Gebhard, Robert L. '87 (BUF) [35] Buffalo, NY St. James Church.
Gebhardt, Joseph M. '50 (B) Retired.
Gebhardt, Paul L. (CIN) Middletown, OH Holy Family Church.
Gebhardt, Paul L. '91 (CIN) [E] Middletown, OH Fenwick High School.
Gedeon, Thomas W. *s.j.* '56 (DET) [K] Detroit, MI Jesuit Provincial Office-Detroit Province of the Society of Jesus.
Geders, Joseph C. *c.m.* '84 (CHI) [C] Chicago, IL Vincentian Community at DePaul University; [N] Chicago, IL Vincentian Community, Congregation of the Mission, Midwest Province.
Geditz, Roger '69 (SFS) Watertown, SD Immaculate Conception Church.
Gedvila, Izidorius '48 (GF) Retired.
Gee, Daniel N. '95 (ARL) Manassas, VA All Saints Church.
Gee, John F. '53 (WOR) Auburn, MA North American Martyrs Church.
Gee, Peter *f.s.s.p.* (KCK) [D] Spring Hill, MO Our Lady of Compassion.
Gee, Peter J. *f.s.s.p.* '95 (SCR) [M] Elmhurst, PA Priestly Fraternity of St. Peter (F.S.S.P.).
Geelan, Thomas E. '62 (SC) [2] Sioux City, IA Blessed Sacrament Church.
Geenen, Roy J. '68 (GB) Menasha, WI St. Patrick Church.
Geers, Carl J. '43 (CIN) [1] Cincinnati, OH St. Peter in Chains Cathedral; Retired.
Geers, Frank *o.f.m.* '58 (CIN) [C] Cincinnati, OH St. Anthony Shrine, Francisan Candidacy.
Gefell, Msgr. Gerard J. '41 (OG) Retired.
Gefell, Msgr. Gerard J. '41 (ROC) Retired.
Gefell, Msgr. Joseph G. '41 (OG) Retired.
Gefell, Msgr. Joseph G. '41 (ROC) Retired.
Gegotek, Tadeusz '91 (BEL) Military Chaplains.
Gehant, Rembert *o.s.b.* '44 (IND) [J] St. Meinrad, IN St. Meinrad Archabbey.
Gehl, James C. '74 (LA) Canoga Park, CA St. Joseph the Worker Church.
Gehl, James E. '69 (SY) Dewitt, NY Holy Cross Church.
Gehl, Walter N. '44 (MIL) Retired.
Gehlen, Elzear *s.v.d.* '44 (CHI) [1] Mt. Prospect, IL St. Cecilia Church; [B] Techny, IL Divine Word Residence.
Gehling, Kenneth B. '62 (DUB) [H] Mason City, IA North Iowa Mercy Health Center.
Gehring, Fredric P. *c.m.* '30 (PH) [Z] Philadelphia, PA Congregation of the Mission.
Gehring, Robert P. (GRY) [O] Gary, IN Indiana University Northwest.
Gehring, Robert P. '66 (GRY) [14] Gary, IN St. Mark Church.
Geib, David W. *o.p.* '67 (P) [N] McKenzie Bridge, OR St. Benedict Lodge-Dominican Retreat & Conference Center.
Geib, Harry F. *s.j.* '92 (BAL) [M] Baltimore, MD Jesuit Fathers and Brothers Maryland Provincial Curia.
Geigel, Francis G. '38 (GB) Retired.
Geiger, Bernard M. *o.f.m.conv.* '59 (CHI) [Q] Libertyville, IL Marytown, U.S. National Center of the Militia of the Immaculata Movement.
Geiger, Damon *o.ss.t.* '71 (BAL) [M] Baltimore, MD Holy Trinity Monastery.
Geiger, Eugene E. '47 (NEW) [2] Irvington, NJ St. Leo's Church.
Geiger, James A. '50 (COL) Sugar Grove, OH St. Joseph Church.

Geiger, James H. *c.ss.r.* (SP) [9] Tampa, FL St. Joseph Church.
Geiger, William *c.ss.r.* '54 (HBG) [2] Lancaster, PA St. Anthony of Padua Church.
Geilenkirchen, Jude '74 (DEN) [16] Denver, CO Mother of God Church.
Geinzer, Eugene M. *s.j.* '74 (CHI) [C] Chicago, IL Jesuit Community at Loyola University of Chicago.
Geinzer, John A. '67 (PIT) Turtle Creek, PA St. Colman Church.
Geinzer, Patrick *c.p.* '95 (SCR) [2] Scranton, PA St. Ann's Church.
Geis, John F. '64 (IND) St. Mary-of-the-Knobs, IN St. Mary-of-the-Knobs Church.
Geiselhart, Charles T. '86 (PIT) [2] Swissvale, PA Word of God Church.
Geisen, Bernard S. '44 (GF) Retired.
Geiser, Allen '90 (GB) Askeaton, WI St. Patrick Church.
Geisinger, Robert *s.j.* '91 (CHI) [89] Chicago, IL St. Ignatius Church.
Geisser, Raymond E. *o.s.a.* '60 (MIA) [B] Opa Locka, FL St. Thomas University; [H] Miami, FL Casa San Lorenzo.
Geissler, Lloyd F. '42 (LC) Retired.
Geissler, Ralph J. '38 (LC) Retired.
Geissler, Msgr. Robert '47 (NY) Retired.
Geiszel, John I. *s.j.* '57 (LA) [F] Los Angeles, CA Loyola High School.
Gelati, Dario '53 (PIT) Retired.
Gelencser, Paul L. *o.praem.* '41 (ORG) [H] Silverado, CA Norbertine Fathers.
Gelfenbien, Gary Paul '71 (ALB) Chatham, NY St. James Church.
Gelin, Henry C. *s.j.* '51 (DET) [P] Clarkston, MI Colombiere Center.
Gelinas, Rene *m.s.* '60 (FR) [K] Attleboro, MA La Salette Shrine.
Gelinas, Rene '60 (STL) [P] St. Louis, MO La Salette Missionaries.
Gelineau, Msgr. Edward J. '42 (BUR) Retired; [F] Burlington, VT St. Joseph's Home for Aged.
Gelineau, H. Raymond '69 (WOR) Absent on Leave.
Gelis, Mark *m.j.* '94 (PCE) On Duty Outside the Diocese.
Gellel, Lawrence *s.j.* '54 (BRK) [221] Queens, NY Our Lady of Sorrows Church.
Geller, Charles '73 (SAN) Fort Stockton, TX St. Agnes Church.
Geller, Charles H. '73 (BEL) Special Assignment.
Gelpi, Donald L. *s.j.* '64 (OAK) [A] Berkeley, CA The Jesuit School of Theology at Berkeley; [N] Berkeley, CA Jesuit Community at Jesuit School of Theology at Berkeley.
Gelsomino, Peter A. '55 (NY) Shrub Oak, NY Saint Elizabeth Ann Seton Church.
Gelthaus, Harry J. '85 (L) [1] Valley Station, KY St. Clement Church.
Gelthaus, Lawrence J. '88 (L) Albany, KY Emmanuel Catholic Church.
Gembala, Joseph J. '87 (DET) [5] Sterling Heights, MI St. Malachy Church.
Gemperline, Joachim *c.p.* '53 (L) [L] Louisville, KY Sacred Heart Retreat.
Gemskie, Charles A. '77 (JOL) Carol Stream, IL Corpus Christi Church.
Gemuend, Msgr. David W. (GAY) Frankfort, MI St. Ann Church.
Gemza, Richard J. '95 (BGP) [1] Bridgeport, CT St. Augustine Cathedral.
Gendelmann, Clemens J. '85 (PH) [DD] Philadelphia, PA Newman Apostolate.
Gendreau, Claude R. '93 (PRT) Waterville, ME Holy Spirit Church.
Gendreau, Michael P. '90 (PRT) St. Agatha, ME St. Agatha's Church; Sinclair, ME St. Joseph Church.
Gendreau, Richard R. '69 (FR) [3] Swansea, MA St. Michael's Church.
Gendron, Charles A. *m.s.* '44 (LKC) [3] Sulphur, LA Our Lady of Prompt Succor Church.
Gendron, Michael E. '95 (MAN) [12] Manchester, NH St. Marie Church; [17] Manchester, NH Sacred Heart of Jesus Church.
Gendusa, Anthony *m.s.c.* '40 (RCK) [H] Aurora, IL Missionaries of the Sacred Heart Community.
Genello, Patrick J. '83 (SCR) [3] Hazleton, PA Holy Rosary Church.
Genest, Gilles *m.s.* '62 (FR) [K] Attleboro, MA La Salette Provincial House; [K] Attleboro, MA La Salette Missionary Association.
Genevive, Frank M. *o.f.m.* '83 (NY) [Z] Mount Vernon, NY St. Bernardine of Siena Friary.
Geng, Dennis *o.c.d.* '89 (MIL) [P] Milwaukee, WI Provincial Offices - Discalced Carmelites.
Gengaro, Nicholas S. '81 (NEW) [B] South Orange, NJ Seton Hall University.
Gengras, Joseph C. '49 (HRT) Bloomfield, CT Sacred Heart Church.
Geniesse, Joseph '57 (AUS) [F] Austin, TX Seton Medical Center.
Genito, Joseph A. *o.s.a.* '75 (ORL) Casselberry, FL St. Augustine Church.
Gennardo, Vincent J. *c.s.* '64 (CHI) Melrose Park, IL Our Lady of Mount Carmel Church.
Genovese, Seamus D. '75 (OAK) [18] Oakland, CA Our Lady of Lourdes Church.
Genovesi, James W. (LC) Norwalk, WI St. Augustine of Hippo Church.
Genovesi, James W. '71 (MAR) On Duty Outside the Diocese.
Genovesi, Vincent J. *s.j.* '69 (PH) [C] Philadelphia, PA St. Joseph's University; [Z] Philadelphia, PA Jesuit Community at St. Joseph's University.
Gensert, Bernon *o.f.m.* '47 (STL) [P] St. Louis, MO Franciscan Friary of St. Anthony of Padua.
Genska, Depaul A. *o.f.m.* '58 (NY) [Z] New York, NY Franciscan Friars, Order of Friars Manor.
Gensler, George D. '70 (BR) On Leave.
Gensler, Thomas W. *s.j.* (DET) [K] Detroit, MI Jesuit Provincial Office-Detroit Province of the Society of Jesus.
Gentile, Carl J. '60 (PIT) Churchill Borough, PA St. John Fisher Church.
Gentile, Emile A. *t.o.r.* '64 (ORL) Mount Dora, FL St. Patrick's Church; Special Assignment.
Gentile, Gennaro L. '71 (NY) Croton-on-Hudson, NY Holy Name of Mary Church.
Gentile, Gilbert J. *s.j.* '78 (SD) [4] San Diego, CA Christ the King Church.
Gentile, Henry S. *c.s.* '59 (NY) [205] Staten Island, NY Holy Family Church; [Z] Staten Island, NY Scalabrinian Missionaries.
Gentile, Thomas E. '73 (L) [30] Louisville, KY St. Helen Church.
Gentili, Joseph P. '87 (PH) [1] Norristown, PA Epiphany of Our Lord Church; Graduate Studies.
Gentleman, John W. '87 (BO) Chelmsford, MA St. John the Evangelist Church.
Gentner, John F. '64 (SAG) Essexville, MI St. John the Evangelist Church.
Genua, Ronald L. '65 (HRT) [2] Ansonia, CT Holy Rosary Church.
Genuardi, Gasper A. '68 (PH) Conshohocken, PA SS. Cosmas and Damian Church.
Genuario, Msgr. William A. '56 (BGP) Riverside, CT St. Catherine of Siena Church.
Genz, William J. '65 (PH) Absent on Leave.
Genzlinger, Walter L. '49 (NEW) [17] Jersey City, NJ Mt. Carmel Church; Retired.
Geogan, Philip J. '79 (NOR) Stonington, CT St. Mary Church.
Geoghan, John J. (BO) Absent on Sick Leave.
Geoghan, John J. '62 (BO) [Z] Boston, MA Regina Cleri, Inc.
Geoghegan, Msgr. Arthur T. '41 (PRO) Retired.
Geohegan, James *o.c.d.* '60 (SR) [L] Oakville, CA Carmelite House of Prayer.
George, Alexander '65 (LA) [7] Los Angeles, CA Christ the King Church.
George, Dale '58 (SC) Rock Valley, IA St. Mary's Church.
George, Msgr. David M. '76 (BO) [9] Brockton, MA St. Theresa Church.
George, Msgr. David M. '76 (SAM) Brockton, MA St. Theresa Church.
George, Francis E. *o.m.i.* (P) [Q] Portland, OR Oregon Catholic Conference.
George, Francis M. '87 (LAN) Fowlerville, MI St. Agnes Church.
George, Frederick *o.s.b.* '75 (CHL) [A] Belmont, NC Belmont Abbey College; [L] Charlotte, NC Diocesan Office of Campus Ministry.
George, George C. '86 (AUS) McGregor, TX St. Eugene Church.
George, Jose '77 (BRK) [43] Brooklyn, NY St. Frances de Chantal Church.
George, Msgr. Joseph S. '62 (LA) Thousand Oaks, CA St. Paschal Baylon Church.
George, Lloyd D. *s.j.* '73 (BAL) [D] Baltimore, MD Loyola High School.
George, Patrick *t.o.r.* (PIT) Allegheny County, PA Eye and Ear Hospital; Allegheny County, PA Montefiore Hospital; Allegheny County, PA Presbyterian-University Hospital.
George, Patrick *t.o.r.* '55 (PIT) [N] Pittsburgh, PA Franciscan Friars, T.O.R.
George, Richard E. '95 (PMB) [2] Boca Raton, FL Our Lady of Lourdes Church.
George, Robert J. '76 (PIT) [O] Pittsburgh, PA Convent of Mercy.
George, Robert P. '95 (ALN) Emmaus, PA St. Ann Church.
George, W. Frederick *o.s.b.* '75 (CHL) [J] Belmont, NC Belmont Abbey.
George, Walter *c.ss.r.* (CHI) [9] Chicago, IL St. Alphonsus Church.
George, William L. *s.j.* '73 (WDC) [M] Washington, DC The Jesuit Community at Georgetown University.
Georgia, John J. '75 (HRT) North Haven, CT St. Frances Cabrini Church.
Gephart, John B. '46 (L) Louisville, KY Jewish Hospital; Louisville, KY Kosair-Children's Hospital; Louisville, KY Norton Hospital; Retired; [L] Louisville, KY Bishop David Apartments.
Gera, Francis T. '64 (PSC) Hazleton, PA St. Mary's Church.
Geracci, John R. *c.s.c.* '92 (SCR) [C] Wilkes-Barre, PA Kings College.
Geraci, Anthony J. '75 (CIN) Russells Point, OH St. Mary of the Woods Church.
Geraghty, James '68 (NY) Absent on Leave.
Geraghty, Msgr. Martin T. '64 (BRK) [169] Queens, NY St. Francis de Sales Church.
Geraghty, Paul *o.s.b.* '86 (ROC) [I] Pine City, NY Mount Saviour Monastery.
Geraghty, Thomas *f.s.c.* (JKS) Greenville, MS St. Joseph Church.
Geraghty, Walter F. '48 (HRT) Southington, CT St. Dominic Church.
Gerardo, John A. '76 (WOR) On Duty Outside the Diocese.
Gerathy, Msgr. Kenneth A. '54 (NY) [201] Staten Island, NY St. Christopher Church.
Geraughty, Michael '84 (ORG) Inactive Leave.
Gerber, Francis J., Jr. '84 (DEN) Grand Lake, CO St. Anne Church.
Gerbino, A. Richard '52 (CAM) On Sick Leave; [L] Cherry Hill, NJ Vianney Villa.
Gerdelman, Clemens J. '85 (PH) [2] Chester, PA Blessed Katharine Drexel Church.
Gerdes, Harry J. '62 (CIN) [50] Cincinnati, OH St. Joseph Church.
Gerena, Luis Ricardo '85 (SJN) [25] San Juan, PR San Jorge Church.
Gerend, Lawrence S. '76 (GB) Norman, WI St. Joseph Church.
Gerety, Msgr. John L. '57 (MET) Retired.
Gerg, Joseph *o.s.b.* '65 (ALT) Patton, PA Our Lady of Perpetual Help Church; Patton, PA Queen of Peace Church; St. Lawrence, PA St. Lawrence's Church.
Gergel, Stephen J. '62 (ALT) Military Chaplains.
Gergen, Charles L. '48 (LIN) York, NE St. Joseph's Church.
Gergen, Michael *s.d.b.* '79 (LA) [C] Rosemead, CA Don Bosco Technical Institute; [D] Rosemead, CA Don Bosco Technical Institute.
Gerhard, John J. *s.j.* '49 (NY) [Z] New York, NY Jesuit Provincial's Office.
Gerhard, John P. *o.p.* '53 (NY) [121] New York, NY St. Vincent Ferrer Church.
Gerhard, John Peter *o.p.* '53 (NY) [Z] New York, NY St. Vincent Ferrer Priory.
Gerhardt, Msgr. Bernard C. '53 (WDC) [1] Washington, DC St. Matthew Cathedral; Pastoral Center Special Ministries.
Gericke, Timothy F. '65 (MAD) Markesan, WI St. Joseph Church.
Gering, Kenneth *o.f.m.conv.* '58 (IND) [I] Mount Saint Francis, IN Mount Saint Francis Friary and Retreat Center.
Gerken, Theodore '57 (ALB) Germantown, NY Resurrection Church.
Gerl, Robert '79 (LAN) On Duty Outside the Diocese.
Gerlach, Dominic B. *c.pp.s.* '50 (LFT) [A] Rensselaer, IN Saint Joseph's College.
Gerlach, John H. *o.p.* '63 (SFD) [L] Springfield, IL Convent of Our Lady of the Sacred Heart.
Gerlach, Matthew J. '96 (TLS) Broken Arrow, OK St. Benedict Church.
Gerlach, Michael J. '82 (PH) Chalfont, PA St. Jude Church; [DD] Philadelphia, PA Newman Apostolate.
Gerlich, Robert S. *s.j.* '73 (NO) [C] New Orleans, LA Loyola University.
Gerlock, Stanley (SY) Binghamton, NY Broome County Jail.
Gerlock, Stanley J. '60 (SY) Chenango Forks, NY St. Rita Church.
Gerloff, Charles W. '45 (ARL) Retired.
Germain, Jean '47 (SHP) Retired.
Germaine, Kenneth *s.d.b.* '67 (SP) [E] Tampa, FL Mary Help of Christians School.
German, Ambrose *o.f.m.* '53 (JC) Hermann, MO St. George Church.
German, Gary *o.f.m.* '88 (SAT) [33] San Antonio, TX St. Clare Church.
German, Kenneth N. (BO) [10] Lawrence, MA St. Patrick Church; Awaiting Assignment.
German, Michael J. '68 (NEW) River Edge, NJ St. Peter the Apostle Church.
German, Timothy J. '73 (ORG) Inactive Leave.
Germann, Daniel V. *s.j.* '63 (SJ) [B] Santa Clara, CA Santa Clara University.
Germann, Lauren A. '78 (SCL) Staples, MN Sacred Heart Church.
Germovnik, Francis *c.m.* '41 (STL) [P] Perryville, MO Congregation of The Mission.
Gernatt, Msgr. David A. '47 (BUF) Retired.
Gerosa, Giuliano *c.r.s.* '78 (MAN) [H] Allenstown, NH Pine Haven Boys Center.
Gerres, Daniel W. '66 (WIL) Liftwood, DE Immaculate Heart of Mary Church; Wilmington, DE Delaware Army National Guard; Wilmington, DE Gander Hill Correctional Center.
Gerrety, James P. '57 (COV) Erlanger, KY Mary, Queen

of Heaven Church; Retired.
Gerritts, John R. '63 (SUP) Rhinelander, WI St. Joseph's Church.
Gerrity, John J. '35 (CLV) Maple Heights, OH St. Martin of Tours Church; Retired.
Gerrity, John J. '58 (CLV) [N] Cleveland, OH Sts. Mary and Joseph Home for the Aged.
Gerrity, Raymond J. '45 (CHI) [145] Chicago, IL Our Lady of Fatima Church; Retired.
Gersbach, Karl A. *o.s.a.* (CHI) [N] Olympia Fields, IL The Augustinian Provincialate Tolentine Center.
Gersbach, Karl A. *o.s.a.* '61 (PH) [Z] Villanova, PA St. Thomas Monastery.
Gerst, Lawrence G. '87 (STL) Retired.
Gerstenkorn, Msgr. Joseph J. '34 (WCH) Retired
Gerstle, Fabian *o.f.m.* '48 (PEO) [3] Peoria, IL Sacred Heart Church.
Gerth, John '93 (SP) [8] St. Petersburg, FL St. Raphael Church.
Gerth, Kenneth *m.c.c.j.* '65 (CIN) [M] Cincinnati, OH Comboni Missionaries (Verona Fathers)-Comboni Mission Center.
Gerum, Jerome G. '50 (LC) Retired.
Gerut, William F. *s.j.* '67 (LC) Prairie du Chien, WI St. Gabriel Church; Prairie du Chien, WI St. John Nepomucene Church.
Gervacio, Adrian R. '67 (HON) Military Chaplains.
Gervais, Bernard *o.s.b.* '44 (PBL) [D] Canon City, CO St. Thomas More Hospital and Progressive Care Center.
Gervais, Bernard P. *o.s.b.* '44 (PBL) [E] Canon City, CO Holy Cross Abbey.
Gervasio, Thomas N. '82 (TR) [17] Trenton, NJ St. Joachim Church.
Gerwronka, Francis *c.s.v.* (JOL) [2] Kankakee, IL St. Patrick Church.
Gese, David '78 (SEA) [16] Tacoma, WA Visitation Church.
Gessner, Henry E. '47 (STP) Retired.
Gessner, Kurt *o.f.m.cap.* '57 (GB) [3] Appleton, WI St. Joseph Church; [I] Appleton, WI St. Joseph Friary.
Gesy, Lawrence '75 (BAL) Brunswick, MD St. Francis of Assisi Church.
Getchel, Richard '76 (GB) [3] Green Bay, WI St. Agnes Church.
Getlik, Stephen J. '37 (TR) Retired.
Getreu, David E. '94 (COL) Gahanna, OH St. Matthew Church.
Getsinger, Ronald A. '68 (WH) New Cumberland, WV Immaculate Conception Church.
Getsy, John *o.f.m.cap.* '66 (PIT) [29] Pittsburgh, PA Our Lady of the Angels Church.
Getting, Diego J. *c.pp.s.* '71 (GRY) [5] East Chicago, IN Our Lady of Guadalupe Church.
Gettinger, Robert J. '64 (STL) [27] St. Louis, MO St. Augustine Church.
Gettlefinger, Robert (CHL) [5] Charlotte, NC St. Gabriel Church.
Getty, Roy G. '39 (PIT) Retired.
Getz, Joseph J. *o.s.a.* '51 (ALB) Cambridge, NY St. Patrick Church.
Getz, Msgr. Robert '61 (LSC) Roswell, NM Assumption of the Blessed Virgin Mary Church.
Geurtz, Gary '81 (FWT) [9] Fort Worth, TX St. Bartholomew Church.
Geusic, Stephen *m.s.c.* '43 (ALN) [A] Center Valley, PA Missionaries of the Sacred Heart.
Geyer, Kenneth A. *o.s.b.* '53 (CHL) [J] Belmont, NC Belmont Abbey; [J] Belmont, NC Belmont Abbey.
Geyer, Raymond J. *o.s.b.* '49 (CHL) [J] Belmont, NC Belmont Abbey.
Geyman, Donald R. '96 (GAY) Cheboygan, MI St. Mary-St. Charles Church.
Geysen, Clement *ss.cc.* (HON) [H] Honolulu, HI St. Patrick's Monastery.
Gfroerer, Gerard J. '51 (RVC) Retired; [N] Uniondale, NY St. Pius X Residence.
Ghanoum, Gabriel *b.s.o.* '93 (NTN) Miami, FL St. Jude Church; Delray Beach, FL St. Nicholas Church.
Ghazal, Edmond J. *b.c.o.* '58 (NTN) Plymouth, MI St. Michael Church; Warren, MI Our Lady of Redemption Church.
Ghebrecristos, Tesfamariam *m.c.c.j.* '79 (LA) Compton, CA St. Albert the Great Church.
Ghezzi, Luciano *p.i.m.e.* '74 (DET) [K] Detroit, MI P.I.M.E. Missionaries of SS. Peter and Paul.
Ghezzi, Richard G. '86 (SCR) Bentley Creek, PA St. Ann's Church.
Ghiloni, Mark '83 (COL) Portsmouth, OH Holy Redeemer Church.
Ghio, John J. '80 (STL) [41] St. Louis, MO St. John the Baptist Church.
Ghiorso, David A. '81 (SFR) Special Assignment; [R] San Francisco, CA Catholic Youth Organization of the Archdiocese of San Francisco; [U] San Rafael, CA Catholic Scouting.
Ghirlando, Gabriel *s.j.* '66 (BO) [W] Weston, MA Campion Center.
Ghisalberti, Giacomo G. '70 (R) Riegelwood, NC Christ the King Church.
Ghyselinck, Mark R. *c.s.c.* '88 (FTW) [B] Notre Dame, IN University of Notre Dame Du Lac; [J] Notre Dame, IN Holy Cross Community, Corby Hall, University of Notre Dame.
Giachino, Valeriano *s.s.p.* '57 (LA) [R] Los Angeles, CA Society of St. Paul.
Giacomini, Antonio *o.f.m.cap.* (R) Retired.
Giacomini, Salvatore *s.d.b.* '51 (SFR) [12] San Francisco, CA Corpus Christi Church; [45] San Francisco, CA SS. Peter and Paul Church.
Giacopelli, John A. '59 (KC) Retired.
Giacosa, Charley '62 (NSH) Dickson, TN St. Christopher Church.
Giammarino, George '41 (NY) Retired.
Giammarino, Msgr. Vincent J. '43 (CAM) Retired.
Giammona, Msgr. John J. '59 (GR) Weare Twp., MI St. Joseph's Church.
Giampietro, Anthony *c.s.b.* (NY) [174] Bronx, NY Our Lady of Mt. Carmel Church.
Giandurco, Joseph R. '87 (NY) [A] Yonkers, NY St. Joseph's Seminary.
Gianelli, Gene '70 (HRT) Woodbridge, CT Church of the Assumption.
Giangiacomo, Tosello *c.s.sp.* '48 (ARE) Orocovis, PR Our Lady of Fatima Church.
Giangiacomo, Tosello *c.s.sp.* '48 (PCE) [B] Ponce, PR The Pontifical Catholic University of Puerto Rico.
Giannamore, Msgr. Anthony J. '56 (STU) Retired.
Giannamore, Msgr. Anthony J. '58 (CIN) [V] Centerville, OH St. Leonard Faith Community.
Giannamore, Peter A. '95 (WH) [10] Wheeling, WV St. Michael's Church.
Gianni, Vincent J. (BO) [5] Revere, MA Our Lady of Lourdes Church.
Giannini, Stephen W. '93 (IND) [15] Indianapolis, IN St. Ann Church.
Giannini, Steve '93 (IND) [C] Indianapolis, IN Roncalli High School.
Giannitelli, Michael C. '91 (NOR) Colchester, CT St. Andrew Church.
Giannone, Ronald *o.f.m.cap.* '90 (WIL) [F] Wilmington, DE Ministry of Caring, Inc.; [I] Wilmington, DE St. Felix Friary; [J] Wilmington, DE Monastery of St. Veronica Giuliani.
Gianola, William '62 (CHY) Retired.
Giaquinto, Albert C. *s.s.* '48 (WDC) [A] Washington, DC Theological College of the Catholic University of America; [C] Washington, DC Catholic University of America, The.
Giaquinto, Albert G. '48 (NOR) On Duty Outside the Diocese; Retired.
Giardina, Robert J. '76 (PRO) [3] West Warwick, RI Sacred Heart Church.
Giardino, Andrew *o.f.m.* '86 (HRT) [14] Hartford, CT St. Patrick-St. Anthony Church.
Giardino, Louis '75 (BIR) [4] Huntsville, AL Holy Spirit Church.
Gibas, John J. '43 (PH) Retired.
Gibas, Robert G. '62 (Y) Navarre, OH St. Clement's Church.
Gibbeaut, Wayne *o.f.m.* '83 (SFE) [1] Santa Fe, NM The Cathedral of San Francisco de Asis.
Gibbons, Charles (DEN) Retired.
Gibbons, Christopher W. *m.m.* '45 (NY) [Z] Maryknoll, NY Maryknoll Fathers and Brothers.
Gibbons, Francis X. '83 (ORG) Inactive Leave.
Gibbons, George J. '45 (MIL) Retired.
Gibbons, James M. '52 (BO) Scituate, MA St. Frances Xavier Cabrini Church.
Gibbons, John '56 (DEN) [34] Denver, CO St. Mary Magdalene's Church.
Gibbons, John J. '58 (NEW) Fairview, NJ St. John the Baptist Church.
Gibbons, Msgr. John J. '60 (TR) Brick Town, NJ St. Dominic Church.
Gibbons, John M. '89 (ALN) [11] Reading, PA St. Peter Church.
Gibbons, Robert C. (SP) [7] St. Petersburg, FL St. Paul Church.
Gibbons, Thomas F. *m.m.* '48 (PH) [59] Philadelphia, PA Holy Family Church.
Gibbons, Thomas J. *s.j.* '60 (BO) [W] Boston, MA The Society of Jesus of New England-Provincial Offices; [W] Boston, MA The Society of Jesus of New England-Provincial Offices.
Gibbons, William F. '57 (CLV) Independence, OH St. Michael Church; Retired.
Gibbons, Williams F. '57 (CLV) [6] Lorain, OH St. Joseph Church.
Gibbs, John (DUL) [C] Duluth, MN St Mary's Medical Center.
Gibbs, Phillip G. '94 (DUB) Marion, IA St. Joseph's Church; Springville, IA St. Isidore's Church.
Gibino, Joseph R. '81 (BRK) [1] Brooklyn, NY The Cathedral-Basilica of St. James; [E] Brooklyn, NY Office of Religious Education: Evangelization and Catholic Formation.
Gibino, Joseph R. '81 (RVC) [A] Huntington, NY Diocesan Seminary of the Immaculate Conception.
Giblin, Berard A. *o.f.m.* '43 (ALB) [B] Loudonville, NY Siena College.
Giblin, C. Homer *s.j.* '58 (NY) [Z] New York, NY Jesuit Community at Fordham University.
Giblin, Msgr. Lawrence E. '44 (SY) [12] Binghamton, NY St. Thomas Aquinas Church; Retired.
Giblin, Richard J. '66 (SY) [1] Endicott, NY Our Lady of Good Counsel Church.
Giblin, William M. '59 (NEW) Secaucus, NJ Immaculate Conception Church.
Gibney, Laurence H. '54 (NY) New Windsor, NY St. Joseph Church.
Gibney, Robert G '54 (NEW) Ridgewood, NJ Our Lady of Mount Carmel Church.
Gibowski, Boguslaw T. '69 (PRO) [12] Woonsocket, RI St. Stanislaus Church.
Gibson, Beryl '96 (SAL) Junction City, KS St. Francis Xavier's Church.
Gibson, Bruno *o.p.* '60 (OAK) [4] Berkeley, CA St. Mary Magdalen Church.
Gibson, Christopher *c.p.* '75 (CHI) [N] Chicago, IL Immaculate Conception Monastery.
Gibson, James *c.r.* '79 (CHI) [N] Chicago, IL Provincial Office of the Congregation of the Resurrection.
Gibson, Jay L. *c.m.* '93 (COS) Burlington, CO St. Catherine of Siena Church; Stratton, CO St. Charles Borromeo Church.
Gibson, John '88 (NY) [52] New York, NY Immaculate Conception Church; Manhattan, NY New York University Medical Center.
Gibson, John W. '45 (PIT) Retired.
Gibson, Msgr. Lawrence J. '55 (LA) San Marino, CA Saints Felicitas and Perpetua Church.
Gibson, Michael P. '48 (STL) Retired.
Gibson, Robert J. '58 (SCR) Kingston, PA St. Ignatius Church.
Gibson, Stephen C. *c.s.c.* '70 (FTW) [L] Notre Dame, IN Holy Cross Mission House; [M] Notre Dame, IN Our Lady of Fatima Retreat Center.
Gibson, Stephen G. '81 (GRY) [11] East Chicago, IN St. Mary Church.
Gibson, Thomas F. '93 (PEO) [14] Peoria, IL St. Thomas Church.
Gick, Francois *s.j.* '80 (BO) [W] Boston, MA The Society of Jesus of New England-Provincial Offices.
Gidaro, Joseph C. *o.ss.t.* '87 (BAL) [M] Baltimore, MD Holy Trinity Monastery.
Gidaro, Joseph C. *o.ss.t.* '87 (NY) [20] New York, NY St. Brigid Church.
Gideon, Peter M. '76 (COL) New Boston, OH St. Monica Church; Wheelersburg, OH St. Peter Church.
Gidley, Lawrence *o.s.b.* '40 (KC) [J] Conception, MO Conception Abbey.
Giebel, Alfred W. '72 (ANC) [3] Anchorage, AK St. Benedict Church.
Giedgaudas, Francis *o.f.m.* '47 (BRK) [U] Brooklyn, NY St. Casimir's Monastery, Printing Plant and Cultural Center.
Giel, John C. '78 (ORL) Leesburg, FL St. Paul's Church.
Gielow, Richard *c.m.* '70 (KC) [J] Kansas City, MO Vincentian Parish Mission Center.
Gienko, Marion *c.r.* '48 (CHI) [D] Chicago, IL Gordon Technical High School.
Gier, Gregory A. '67 (TLS) Bartlesville, OK St. John's Church; Dewey, OK Our Lady of Guadalupe Church.
Gier, Thomas P. *s.o.l.t.* '62 (CC) [H] Robstown, TX Society of Our Lady of the Most Holy Trinity.
Gieranowski, William '49 (FTW) Retired.
Giermek, Joachin *o.f.m.conv.* '69 (BAL) [M] Ellicott City, MD Order of Friars Minor Conventual.
Gierut, Casimir '49 (SFD) Retired.
Gierut, Joseph A. '32 (DET) Retired.
Gies, Norman J. '49 (BAL) Retired.
Gies, William *m.s.c.* '53 (ALN) [K] Reading, PA Missionaries of the Sacred Heart.
Giese, Samuel C. '85 (WDC) [2] Silver Spring, MD St. Bernadette Church.
Giese, Vincent J. '65 (CHI) Retired.
Giesen, Cal *o.f.m.* '47 (FWT) [G] Crowley, TX St. Francis Village, Inc.; [H] Crowley, TX St. Maximilian Kolbe Friary.
Giesing, Msgr. Anthony A. '55 (SD) [29] San Diego, CA St. John the Evangelist Church.
Giesler, Linus T. '41 (L) Retired; [K] Louisville, KY Nazareth Home.
Giesler, Michael E. '79 (STL) [Q] Kirkwood, MO Opus Dei.
Gietl, Joseph A. '73 (GAL) [5] Houston, TX St. Ambrose Church.
Gietzen, Albin J. '56 (GAY) Hannah, MI St. Mary Church.
Gigante, Louis R. '59 (NY) [130] Bronx, NY St. Athanasius Church.
Gigantiello, Jamie J. '95 (BRK) [115] Brooklyn, NY St. Patrick Church.
Giganto, Jose A. *o.s.a.* '65 (SAT) [47] San Antonio, TX St. Jude Church.
Giggi, J. Robert '53 (BO) Natick, MA St. Linus Church.
Giglio, Msgr. Charles J. '58 (CAM) [1] Camden, NJ Immaculate Conception Cathedral.
Giglio, Michael E. '94 (ORL) [5] Orlando, FL Holy Family Church.
Gigliotti, James *t.o.r.* '80 (FWT) [4] Arlington, TX St.

Maria Goretti Church.
Gigliotti, Vincent J. '76 (GBG) Brownsville, PA St. Peter Church.
Gignac, Francis T. *s.j.* (DET) [K] Detroit, MI Jesuit Provincial Office-Detroit Province of the Society of Jesus.
Gignac, Francis T. *s.j.* '67 (WDC) [C] Washington, DC Catholic University of America, The; [M] Washington, DC Carroll House.
Gil, Fernando '88 (ORL) Poinciana, FL St. Rose of Lima Church.
Gil, Rudi '78 (SB) On Leave.
Gilardi, Ron *o.f.m.cap.* '88 (SAL) [G] Victoria, KS Capuchin Center for Spiritual Life.
Gilardi, Ronald *o.f.m.cap.* '88 (SAL) [D] Victoria, KS St. Fidelis Friary.
Gilb, Msgr. Eugene A. '57 (LA) Rancho Palos Verdes, CA St. John Fisher Church.
Gilberg, William J. (NY) [BB] New York, NY Cardinal Spellman Retreat House.
Gilbert, Dennis '71 (MRY) [2] Salinas, CA Sacred Heart Church.
Gilbert, Msgr. Donald J. '68 (MAN) Candia, NH St. Paul Church.
Gilbert, Douglas B. *s.m.a.* '83 (NEW) [N] Tenafly, NJ Society of African Missions, Provincialate, S.M.A. Fathers.
Gilbert, John R. '56 (STP) Marystown, MN St. Mary of the Purification Church.
Gilbert, Joseph T. '79 (SCR) Swoyersville, PA St. Mary of Czestochowa Church.
Gilbert, Maurice L. '66 (WOR) [2] Southbridge, MA Notre Dame Church.
Gilbert, Philip F. *c.pp.s.* '60 (LFT) [A] Rensselaer, IN Saint Joseph's College.
Gilbert, Valmont R. '57 (PRT) Rockland, ME St. Bernard's Church.
Gilberto, Fernandez '59 (MIA) [A] Miami, FL St. John Vianney College Seminary.
Gilbertson, C. Lee '86 (SPR) [1] Holyoke, MA Blessed Sacrament Church.
Gilbertson, Lee '86 (SPR) [P] Amherst, MA University of Massachusetts and Amherst College, Newman Center.
Gilbo, Roberto M. *c.s.c.* '67 (FTW) [J] South Bend, IN Congregation of Holy Cross Indiana Province Provincial House.
Gilborges, Anthony A. *o.s.f.s.* '89 (WIL) [B] Wilmington, DE Salesianum School.
Gilbride, Thomas '57 (NO) Unassigned.
Gilchrest, Francis J. '45 (ALB) [J] Albany, NY Villa Mary Immaculate.
Gilchrest, Frank '45 (ALB) [4] Albany, NY St. Casimir Church; [1] Amsterdam, NY St. Casimir Church.
Gilchrist, Msgr. John J. '57 (NEW) Harrison, NJ Holy Cross Church.
Gilday, Francis J. *s.j.* '38 (BO) [W] Weston, MA Campion Health Center, Inc.
Gilday, Robert J. '75 (IND) [21] (Speedway City), IN St. Christopher Church.
Gildea, Arthur P. *c.ss.r.* '67 (HBG) Ephrata, PA Mother of Perpetual Help Church; [H] Ephrata, PA St. Clement's Mission House.
Gildea, Joseph J. *o.s.a.* '39 (PH) [Z] Villanova, PA St. Thomas Monastery.
Gildner, Leo H. '53 (PEO) [2] Ottawa, IL St. Francis of Assisi Church.
Gile, Joseph M. '88 (WCH) [1] Wichita, KS Cathedral of the Immaculate Conception; [I] Wichita, KS Spiritual Life Center.
Giles, Dominic *s.d.s.* '46 (BIR) [2] Huntsville, AL St. Mary of the Visitation Church.
Giles, Gabriel *o.f.m.cap.* '35 (GBG) Export, PA St. Mary Church.
Giles, John H., Jr. '87 (LKC) [8] Lake Charles, LA Our Lady Queen of Heaven Church; [A] Lake Charles, LA St. Louis High School.
Gilette, Randall *c.p.* '71 (HRT) [M] West Hartford, CT Holy Family Monastery/Retreat.
Gilfether, Francis *s.m.a.* '60 (NEW) [N] Tenafly, NJ Society of African Missions, Provincialate, S.M.A. Fathers.
Gilfillan, Msgr. James M. '47 (SD) La Jolla, CA Mary, Star of the Sea Church; Retired.
Gilg, James E. '66 (OM) [48] Douglas Co., NE St. Wenceslaus Church; [B] Omaha, NE V.J. & Angela Skutt Catholic High School of Omaha.
Gilgun, Bernard E. '54 (WOR) On Special or Other (Arch)Diocesan Assignment.
Gilhooley, James '55 (NY) [C] Newburgh, NY Mt. St. Mary College; [CC] New York, NY University Apostolate.
Gilhooley, Msgr. John P. '57 (BRK) Military Chaplains.
Giliberti, Francis A. '70 (PH) Media, PA Nativity of the Blessed Virgin Mary Church.
Gill, Cecil J. '44 (MOB) Retired.
Gill, David H. *s.j.* '67 (BO) [W] Chestnut Hill, MA The Jesuit Community at Boston College.
Gill, Desmond '46 (SP) Inverness, FL Our Lady of Fatima Church; Retired.
Gill, Edward B. '41 (OM) St. Edward, NE St. Edward Church.
Gill, Gerald Dennis '83 (PH) Southampton, PA Our Lady of Good Counsel Church.
Gill, James J. *s.j.* '57 (BO) [FF] Brighton, MA The Christian Institute for the Study of Human Sexuality; [FF] Brighton, MA The Jesuit Educational Center for Human Development.
Gill, Joseph C. *s.j.* '59 (RC) [4] Rapid City, SD St. Isaac Jogues Church; [B] Howes, SD Kino Jesuit Community.
Gill, Michael J. '66 (NOR) Oakdale, CT Our Lady of the Lakes Church.
Gill, Nicolas *c.p.* '40 (SCR) [M] Scranton, PA Saint Ann's Passionist Monastery.
Gill, Paul R. '66 (SB) Loma Linda, CA St. Joseph the Worker Church.
Gill, Richard *l.c.* '91 (WDC) [M] Potomac, MD Legionaries of Christ; [V] Bethesda, MD Alpha Omege, Inc. The Legion of Christ Inc.
Gill, Msgr. Richard J. '56 (BUF) Silver Creek, NY Our Lady of Mt. Carmel Church.
Gill, William J. '55 (RVC) Hampton Bays, NY St. Rosalie's Church.
Gillan, C.H. '85 (BAK) Enterprise, OR St. Katherine's Church.
Gillece, Alfred F. (GAL) Retired.
Gilleece, Msgr. Thomas E. '68 (NY) Congers, NY St. Paul Church.
Gillelan, Robert M. '89 (HBG) Hanover, PA St. Joseph Church.
Gillen, Edward B. *s.j.* '51 (NEW) [B] Jersey City, NJ Saint Peter's College; [N] Jersey City, NJ Jesuits of Saint Peter's College, Inc.
Gillen, Francis '64 (BRK) [97] Brooklyn, NY Our Lady of Guadalupe Church.
Gillen, George D. '71 (NEW) Roselle, NJ Church of St. Joseph the Carpenter.
Gillen, Msgr. James G. '52 (WDC) On Duty Outside the Archdiocese.
Gillen, Msgr. John J. '45 (NY) Retired; [Z] New York, NY St. John Neumann Residence.
Gillen, Niles J. *o.carm.* '56 (L) [59] Louisville, KY Our Lady of Mount Carmel Church.
Gillen, Paul T. *c.ss.r.* '46 (ORL) [F] New Smyrna Beach, FL St. Alphonsus Villa-Redemptorist Fathers and Brothers.
Gillen, Peter D. '78 (BRK) [236] Queens, NY St. Rose of Lima Church.
Gillen, Timothy L. '42 (PRO) Retired; [M] Newport, RI St. Clare Home.
Giller, Roderic *o.s.b.* '62 (KCK) Seneca, KS SS. Peter and Paul's Church.
Gilles, Charles W. *o.m.i.* '38 (WDC) [B] Washington, DC Oblate College/Oblate Center for Mission Studies.
Gilles, Eugene *s.a.c.* '58 (FAR) Ligderwood, ND St. Boniface's Church.
Gilles, Richard W. '94 (LC) Chippewa Falls, WI Notre Dame Church; [C] Chippewa Falls, WI McDonell Central Catholic High School.
Gilles, Robert F. '57 (PEO) Minonk, IL St. Patrick's Church.
Gilles, Thomas C. '67 (CLV) Chardon, OH St. Mary Church.
Gillespie, Anthony '82 (FTW) New Haven, IN St. John the Baptist Church; [C] Fort Wayne, IN Bishop Luers High School.
Gillespie, Barnabas *o.s.b.* '80 (IND) St. Mark, IN St. Mark Church; [J] St. Meinrad, IN St. Meinrad Archabbey.
Gillespie, Barnabus *o.s.b.* '80 (IND) Leopold, IN St. Augustine Church.
Gillespie, C. Kevin *s.j.* (BAL) [C] Baltimore, MD Loyola College; [M] Baltimore, MD Jesuit Community of Loyola College, Inc.
Gillespie, Edward F. '57 (RCK) [6] Aurora, IL Our Lady of Good Counsel Church.
Gillespie, Francis J. *s.j.* '72 (CHL) [2] Charlotte, NC Our Lady of the Assumption Church; [J] Charlotte, NC Jesuit Community.
Gillespie, Francis T. '59 (ALN) [8] Reading, PA St. Margaret Church.
Gillespie, Jerome F. '82 (BO) [8] Lynn, MA Sacred Heart Church.
Gillespie, John D. '72 (STA) [4] Gainesville, FL St. Augustine Church; [L] Gainesville, FL University of Florida-St. Augustine Parish and Student Center.
Gillespie, Msgr. John E. '53 (PH) [114] Philadelphia, PA Our Lady of Calvary Church.
Gillespie, John L. '95 (R) Chapel Hill, NC St. Thomas More Church.
Gillespie, Joseph '50 (PHX) Sun City, AZ St. Elizabeth Seton Church.
Gillespie, Joseph P. *o.p.* '70 (STL) [B] St. Louis, MO Aquinas Institute of Theology; [P] St. Louis, MO Dominican Community of St. Louis.
Gillespie, Paul G. *o.s.f.s.* (TOL) [C] Toledo, OH St. Francis de Sales High School.
Gillespie, Paul G. *o.s.f.s.* '56 (TOL) [K] Toledo, OH Oblates of St. Francis de Sales.
Gillespie, Robert B. '43 (GR) Retired.
Gillespie, Thomas E. '72 (MAD) Jefferson, WI St. Lawrence Church; [K] Jefferson, WI St. Coletta School for Exceptional Children.
Gillespie, Thomas F. '61 (SB) Chino, CA St. Margaret Mary Church.
Gillespie, Thomas M. *o.s.f.s.* '56 (PH) [Z] Philadelphia, PA Oblates of St. Francis De Sales.
Gillespie, Thomas M. '68 (BO) North Reading, MA St. Theresa Church.
Gillespie, Victor *o.s.b.* '56 (LR) Clarksville, AR Holy Redeemer Church.
Gillette, Theodore M. '78 (OG) Black River, NY St. Paul Church.
Gilley, Charles F. *s.j.* '96 (NY) [F] New York, NY Regis High School; [Z] New York, NY St. Ignatius Loyola Residence.
Gillgannon, Francis G. '54 (JC) California, MO Annunciation Church.
Gillgannon, Michael '58 (KC) Mission Duty.
Gillgannon, Patrick (GAL) Retired.
Gillick, Lawrence E. *s.j.* '72 (OM) [K] Omaha, NE Campion House.
Gillick, Thomas A. '37 (NEW) Retired; [N] Rutherford, NJ St. John Vianney Residence for Priests.
Gillig, John '57 (FTW) Retired.
Gillig, Russell F. '36 (TOL) Retired; [J] Tiffin, OH St. Francis Home Inc.
Gilligan, Adrian *o.s.a.* (PH) [Z] Bryn Mawr, PA Augustinians Brothers (O.S.A.).
Gilligan, Adrian *o.s.a.* '68 (PH) Bryn Mawr, PA Our Mother of Good Counsel Church.
Gilligan, Msgr. Francis J. '24 (STP) Retired.
Gilligan, Michael J. '69 (CHI) Other Assignments.
Gillin, Thomas M. *s.j.* '52 (CHR) Aiken, SC St. Gerard's Church.
Gillin, Thomas P. '74 (PH) Downingtown, PA St. Joseph Church; [G] Bryn Mawr, PA Country Day School of the Sacred Heart.
Gillis, David C. '79 (ALN) Shillington, PA St. John Baptist de la Salle Church.
Gillis, Edward F. '46 (BO) Retired.
Gillis, Francis B. *s.m.a.* '52 (BO) [W] Dedham, MA African Mission House and African Cultural Center.
Gillis, James *c.s.c.* (LA) [S] Ventura, CA Sisters of the Holy Cross.
Gillis, Ralph J. '59 (GB) Argonne, WI St. Mary Church; Crandon, WI St. Joseph Church.
Gillis, Roger S. *s.j.* '78 (SEA) [A] Seattle, WA Seattle University.
Gillis, Ronald '67 (WDC) [T] Washington, DC Opus Dei.
Gillon, James A. *s.j.* '74 (BO) [W] Boston, MA Arrupe House.
Gillooly, Patrick J. '53 (WH) Retired.
Gills, Thomas '86 (BAL) Millersville, MD Our Lady of the Fields Church.
Gillum, William *o.f.m.cap.* '76 (PIT) Rochester, PA St. Cecilia Church; [N] Rochester, PA St. Cecilia Friary.
Gilmartin, Daniel J. (BO) Bellingham, MA Assumption Church; Retired.
Gilmartin, Gregory J. *m.m.* '48 (NY) [Z] Maryknoll, NY Maryknoll Fathers and Brothers.
Gilmartin, Msgr. John D. '72 (RVC) Wyandanch, NY Our Lady of the Miraculous Medal Church; [H] Hicksville, NY Catholic Charities Central Administration.
Gilmartin, Msgr. John E. '56 (BGP) [5] Stratford, CT Our Lady of Peace Church.
Gilmartin, Paul P. *s.j.* '62 (BO) [A] Weston, MA Pope John XXIII National Seminary; [W] Boston, MA The Society of Jesus of New England-Provincial Offices; [W] Chestnut Hill, MA The Jesuit Community at Boston College.
Gilmore, Alan *o.c.s.o.* '70 (L) [L] Trappist, KY Abbey of Our Lady of Gethsemani, of the Order of Cistercians of the Strict Observance.
Gilmore, Brendan *o.carm.* '35 (NEW) Englewood, NJ St. Cecilia's Church.
Gilmore, Raymond '62 (HEL) Hamilton, MT St. Francis Church.
Gilmore, Ronald M. '69 (WCH) [F] Wichita, KS Catholic Care Center, Inc.
Gilmore, Vincent M. *o.praem.* '90 (ORG) [D] Siverado, CA St. Michael's College Preparatory High School; [H] Silverado, CA Norbertine Fathers.
Gilmour, James W. *c.ss.r.* '72 (BRK) [C] Whitestone, NY St. Alphonsus Formation Residence.
Gilroy, Gregory J. *o.f.m.conv.* '88 (LA) Hermosa Beach, CA Our Lady of Guadalupe Church.
Gilroy, Thomas *s.m.* '41 (ATL) [C] Atlanta, GA Marist School.
Gilsdorf, Daniel C. '60 (GB) [7] Appleton, WI St. Therese Church.
Gilsdorf, Gordon J. '49 (GB) Special Assignment.
Gilsdorf, Richard W. '56 (GB) Casco, WI Holy Trinity Church.
Gilsenan, John P. '56 (WCH) [3] Wichita, KS Blessed Sacrament Church.
Gilsoul, James M. '86 (GB) [F] Appleton, WI St. Elizabeth Hospital.
Gilvary, Paul J. *s.j.* '51 (PH) [Z] Philadelphia, PA Jesuit Community at St. Joseph's University.

Gilvey, John A. *o.s.f.s.* '79 (CHL) [4] Greensboro, NC St. Paul the Apostle Church; [L] Charlotte, NC Diocesan Office of Campus Ministry.
Gimbrone, Richard J. '85 (BUF) Retired.
Gimeno, Fabian G. '60 (ORL) St. Cloud, FL St. Thomas Aquinas Church.
Gimpl, Carl '55 (P) Salem, OR St. Joseph Church; [P] Portland, OR University of Portland.
Ginart, Arthur J. '66 (NO) [48] New Orleans, LA St. Nicholas Of Myra Church.
Ginchereau, Dolor *s.m.* '38 (BO) [Y] Framingham Centre, MA The Marist House.
Ginel, Robert J. '78 (NY) Ellenville, NY St. Mary and St. Andrew Church.
Gingras, Dennis C. '90 (HRT) [3] Enfield, CT St. Bernard's Church.
Gingras, Jerome *o.f.m.conv.* '78 (ALB) Glenville, NY Immaculate Conception Church.
Gini, John *o.f.m.* '63 (TUC) [4] Tucson, AZ Mission San Xavier del Bac Church.
Gini, John E. '63 (PBL) On Duty Outside the Diocese.
Ginn, Roman *o.c.s.o.* '53 (L) [L] Trappist, KY Abbey of Our Lady of Gethsemani, of the Order of Cistercians of the Strict Observance.
Gins, Paul *o.s.m.* '75 (ORG) [D] Anaheim, CA Servite High School; Servite High School Development Fund; [H] Anaheim, CA Servite Fathers and Brothers.
Gins, Paul M. *o.s.m.* '75 (CHI) [N] Chicago, IL Servite Friars - Eastern Province.
Ginsterblum, John M. *s.j.* '53 (STP) [N] Minneapolis, MN La Storta Jesuit Community.
Ginter, Michael '79 (JOL) Peotone, IL St. Paul the Apostle Church.
Ginther, Benjamin H. '41 (KAL) Retired.
Ginther, Lawrence P. '46 (WIN) Retired.
Ginther, Richard M. '83 (IND) [1] Indianapolis, IN SS. Peter and Paul Cathedral.
Gintoli, Msgr. Blase M. '69 (BGP) [2] Fairfield, CT Assumption Church.
Ginty, Msgr. Thomas M. '85 (HRT) Special and other (Arch)Diocesan Assignment.
Gionet, Urbain J. '51 (WOR) Retired.
Giorda, Adolph *o.f.m.* '48 (NY) [Z] New York, NY Franciscan Province of the Immaculate Conception.
Giordani, Msgr. Mark J. '69 (PAT) [1] Paterson, NJ Cathedral of St. John the Baptist; Paterson, NJ Passaic County Jail.
Giordano, John C. '67 (MET) North Plainfield, NJ St. Luke Church.
Giordano, Joseph *c.i.c.m.* (BRK) [36] Brooklyn, NY St. Ephrem's Church.
Giorgi, Daniel *o.ss.t.* '41 (VIC) Cuero, TX Our Lady of Guadalupe Church.
Giorgio, Amy (JKS) Bruce, MS Catholic Community of Calhoun County Church.
Gipson, Msgr. Robert W. '62 (LA) Downey, CA St. Raymond Church.
Gira, Stephen *c.r.* '77 (STL) Spanish Lake, MO Our Lady of Loretto Church.
Girard, Msgr. Armand '45 (SAL) Manhattan, KS St. Isidore Church; Retired; [H] Manhattan, KS St. Isidore's Catholic Student Center.
Girard, Charles A. '66 (WDC) [M] Washington, DC Marist Provincial House.
Girard, Cosmas *o.f.m.* '35 (PAT) [M] Ringwood, NJ Holy Name Friary.
Girard, Peter M. *o.p.* '92 (HRT) [14] New Haven, CT St. Mary's Priory Church.
Girard, Steven P. '74 (BAL) [25] Baltimore, MD St. Clement Church.
Girardeau, Robert A. '93 (SAV) [8] Savannah, GA St. James Church.
Girardin, Peter T. '60 (BO) Military & VA Chaplains.
Girdis, Joseph C. (PIT) [5] Munhall, PA St. Theresa of Lisieux Church; Retired.
Girnius, Charles F. *m.m.* '44 (NY) [Z] Maryknoll, NY Maryknoll Fathers and Brothers.
Giroir, Frank J. '81 (NO) Harahan, LA St. Rita Church.
Girolami, Dante L. *o.s.a.* '41 (PH) [Z] Villanova, PA St. Thomas Monastery.
Girone, Joseph D. '83 (NEW) [1] Elizabeth, NJ St. Mary of the Assumption Church.
Girouard, Robert J. '59 (PRT) Sabbatical.
Giroux, Armand *m.s.* '58 (FR) [K] Attleboro, MA La Salette Shrine.
Giroux, Garry B. '76 (OG) Constable, NY St. Francis of Assisi Church; Trout River, NY St. Bridget Church.
Giroux, Harry E. '76 (OG) Canton, NY St. Thomas More Church.
Giroux, Raymond A. '63 (BUR) South Burlington, VT St. John Vianney Church.
Giroux, Regis J. '70 (SPR) [2] Springfield, MA All Souls Church.
Giroux, Richard M. '69 (MAN) Keene, NH St. Margaret Mary Church.
Giroux, Msgr. Robert J. (OG) [2] Ogdensburg, NY Notre Dame Church; Retired.
Giroux, William P. '80 (BUR) Chester, VT St. Joseph Church.
Girres, Edward M. '79 (SC) [1] Sioux City, IA Cathedral of the Epiphany; [B] Sioux City, IA Bishop Heelan Catholic High School.
Girse, Milton *c.ss.r.* '40 (CHI) [136] Chicago, IL St. Michael Ministry.
Girzone, Joseph '55 (ALB) Retired.
Gits, Douglas J. '53 (WIN) Hayfield, MN Sacred Heart Church.
Gitter, Aloysius A. '28 (GB) Retired.
Gitter, Aloysius A. '28 (SAT) Retired.
Gitter, Paul R. '93 (LC) Augusta, WI St. Anthony de Padua Church; Brackett, WI Holy Guardian Angels Church; Fall Creek, WI St. John the Apostle Church.
Gittins, Anthony *c.s.sp.* '67 (CHI) [B] Chicago, IL The Catholic Theological Union at Chicago.
Gittins, Gordon '68 (DM) Harlan, IA St. Michael Church.
Gitzen, Blase *o.f.m.cap.* '46 (DET) [K] Detroit, MI St. Bonaventure Friary.
Gitzen, Patrick *o.m.i.* '75 (SAT) [F] San Antonio, TX St. Anthony Catholic High School; [M] San Antonio, TX St. Anthony Catholic High School House.
Giudice, Anthony R. *o.f.m.cap.* '54 (ARL) Purcellville, VA St. Francis de Sales Church.
Giudice, Francis J. '56 (PRO) [1] Providence, RI Cathedral of SS. Peter and Paul.
Giuliani, John B. '60 (BGP) [N] West Redding, CT The Benedictine Grange.
Giuliani, John P. *c.o.* '80 (CHR) Rock Hill, SC St. Anne's Church; [E] Rock Hill, SC Oratory of St. Philip Neri, Congregation of the Oratory of Pontifical Rite.
Giuliano, Anthony J. '84 (NY) [2] Mt. Vernon, NY St. Francis of Assisi Church.
Giuliano, Carmen *s.a.* '61 (NY) [14] Yonkers, NY Our Lady of the Rosary Church.
Giuliano, Carmen *s.a.* '61 (WDC) [B] Washington, DC Atonement Seminary-Francisan Friars of the Atonement.
Giuliano, Louis A. '44 (BRK) Retired.
Giuliano, Steven B. '80 (WIL) Elsmere, DE Corpus Christi Church.
Giulietti, Julio *s.j.* '72 (BO) [W] Boston, MA The Society of Jesus of New England-Provincial Offices.
Giulietti, Julio *s.j.* '72 (WDC) [M] Washington, DC The Jesuit Community at Georgetown University.
Giunta, S. C. '54 (JOL) Wilton Center, IL St. Patrick Church.
Giuntini, Robert '76 (RVC) Bay Shore, NY St. Patrick's Church.
Giusani, Augustine H. '47 (HRT) [1] New Britain, CT All Saints Church; [5] New Britain, CT St. Ann Church.
Giusta, Frank '63 (ATL) [7] Atlanta, GA Our Lady of Lourdes Church.
Giusti, David (SEA) Vashon, WA St. John Vianney Church.
Givey, David W. '71 (PH) Milmont Park, PA Our Lady of Peace Church.
Glab, Joseph J. *c.r.* '75 (CHI) [D] Chicago, IL Gordon Technical High School.
Glackin, Thomas J. '68 (VEN) [2] Naples, FL St. John the Evangelist Church.
Glade, Albert G. *o.p.* '72 (STL) [B] St. Louis, MO Aquinas Institute of Theology; [P] St. Louis, MO St. Dominic Priory.
Gladstone, James J. *s.j.* '66 (OM) [K] Omaha, NE Jesuit Community At Creighton University.
Glahn, Carl J. '52 (OWN) Providence, KY Holy Cross Church; Sebree, KY St. Michael Church.
Glancy, Alfred '55 (NY) [3] Kingston, NY St. Joseph Church.
Glancy, Christopher J. *c.s.v.* '93 (CHI) [N] Arlington Heights, IL Viatorian Province Center-Clerics of St. Viator.
Glancy, Joseph *t.o.r.* '59 (SFS) Wagner, SD St. John the Baptist Church.
Glanzmann, Edward J. *o.s.b.* '79 (CHI) [J] Blue Island, IL St. Francis Hospital and Health Center; [N] Chicago, IL Monastery of the Holy Cross.
Glapiak, Edward '61 (WIL) [6] Wilmington, DE St. Hedwig Church.
Glaser, Lawrence A. *o.c.s.o.* '58 (SAC) [A] Vina, CA Abbey of New Clairvaux, Trappist Seminary; [H] Vina, CA Abbey of New Clairvaux, Trappist.
Glasgow, Mark W. '62 (PIT) [2] Munhall, PA St. Maximilian Kolbe Church; Allegheny County, PA Veterans Administration - Oakland.
Glasgow, Robert K. '85 (MAN) Military Chaplains.
Glasgow, Thomas G. '69 (NO) [27] New Orleans, LA St. Brigid Church.
Glasl, Simon J. *c.ss.r.* '30 (ALB) [L] Saratoga Springs, NY St. John Neumann Residence.
Glasnovic, Serafin '45 (ALX) Retired.
Glass, Gerald J. '56 (PHX) Retired.
Glass, Robert H. *c.s.b.* '74 (OAK) [C] Oakland, CA Bishop O'Dowd High School.
Glass, Rolland T. '43 (MIL) Retired.
Glass, Senan *o.f.m.cap.* '57 (CLV) [31] Cleveland, OH Holy Trinity - St. Edward Church; [P] Cleveland, OH St. Paul Friary.
Glass, Senan *o.f.m.cap.* '66 (CLV) [18] Cleveland, OH Conversion of St. Paul Church.
Glassman, Douglas R. *o.f.m.* '89 (NY) [Z] New York, NY Franciscan Friars, Order of Friars Manor.
Glassmire, David R. (BUF) Lancaster, NY St. Mary of the Assumption Church.
Glastetter, Donald A. '65 (STL) Wentzville, MO St. Patrick Church.
Glatt, Eugene '59 (SPK) Oakesdale, WA St. Catherine of Alexandria Church; Rosalia, WA Holy Rosary Church; St. John, WA Our Lady of Perpetual Help Church; Tekoa, WA Sacred Heart Church.
Glatts, Joseph M. '66 (PH) Military Chaplains.
Glaub, Eugene *o.m.i.* '55 (BEL) [G] Belleville, IL Missionary Oblates of Mary Immaculate - St. Henry's Oblate Residence.
Glaves, John J. '56 (LIN) Exeter, NE St. Stephen's Church.
Glavin, Msgr. Edward R. '35 (ALB) [7] Amsterdam, NY St. Mary Church; Retired.
Glavin, Joseph A. *s.j.* '48 (BO) [W] Chestnut Hill, MA The Jesuit Community at Boston College.
Glavin, Leonard *o.f.m.cap.* '54 (NY) [57] New York, NY St. John the Baptist Church.
Glavin, Patrick *o.f.m.cap.* '59 (PRT) [3] Portland, ME St. Joseph's Church; [M] Portland, ME Westbrook College.
Glavina, Carmelo '54 (NY) Dobbs Ferry, NY Our Lady of Pompeii Church.
Gleason, Jack A. '95 (TLS) [10] Tulsa, OK St. Mary Church.
Gleason, James *c.ss.r.* '49 (CHI) [9] Chicago, IL St. Alphonsus Church.
Gleason, James '67 (LA) Palmdale, CA St. Mary Church.
Gleason, John L. '46 (NU) Retired.
Gleason, Joseph F. '87 (PH) [19] Philadelphia, PA St. Barbara Church; [D] Philadelphia, PA Roman Catholic High School for Boys.
Gleason, Laurence J. '96 (PH) [126] Philadelphia, PA Our Lady of Ransom Church.
Gleason, Msgr. Paul D. '47 (PRT) Retired.
Gleason, Terence *c.o.* '80 (BRK) [22] Brooklyn, NY St. Boniface Church.
Gleason, William J. *s.j.* '36 (NY) [Z] New York, NY Murray-Weigel Hall.
Gleba, Peter W. '53 (SY) [9] Syracuse, NY Sacred Heart Church; [22] Syracuse, NY St. Stephen Church.
Gleba, William P. '58 (SY) [5] Rome, NY Transfiguration Church.
Glebe, Edward *c.ss.r.* '57 (GAL) [33] Houston, TX Holy Ghost Church.
Gleeson, Edward D. '69 (CHI) Other Assignments.
Gleeson, Emmet *o.carm.* '44 (JOL) [J] Joliet, IL St. Elias Carmelites.
Gleeson, John P. '75 (STO) Retired.
Gleeson, Joseph '65 (BRK) Queens, NY Veterans Affairs Extended Care Center, St. Albans, NY.
Gleeson, Michael '75 (LA) San Gabriel, CA St. Anthony Church.
Gleeson, Patrick '52 (JOL) [I] Joliet, IL Our Lady of Angels Retirement Home; [J] Darien, IL Carmelite Fathers Provincial Office.
Gleeson, Stephen J. '63 (BGP) [3] Trumbull, CT St. Stephen Church.
Gleeson, Terence P. *c.o.* '80 (BRK) [U] Brooklyn, NY Oratory of Saint Philip Neri, Congregation Pontifical Right.
Gleeson, Thomas F. *s.j.* '68 (WDC) [M] Washington, DC Leonard Neale House.
Gleeson, William T. '66 (PBL) Capulin, CO St. Joseph Church.
Gleissner, Leopold *o.f.m.cap.* '52 (MAD) Hollandale, WI St. Patrick Church.
Gleixner, Joseph *m.s.c.* '65 (RCK) [H] Aurora, IL Missionaries of the Sacred Heart Community.
Glenn, Msgr. Francis A. '38 (PIT) [26] Pittsburgh, PA St. Mary of Mercy Church; Retired.
Glennon, James G. *o.s.a.* '52 (MIA) Dania, FL Church of the Resurrection.
Glennon, Thomas G. *s.s.c.* '79 (CHI) [N] Chicago, IL Columban Fathers Mission Center.
Glennon, William P. '54 (PAT) Morristown, NJ Assumption of the Blessed Virgin Mary Church.
Glentzer, Harold M. *o.s.b.* '35 (PBL) [E] Canon City, CO Holy Cross Abbey.
Glepko, Robert J. '76 (CLV) Cleveland Heights, OH St. Ann Church.
Gliatta, Ronald *o.f.m.* '77 (HRT) [15] Waterbury, CT St. Michael Church; [19] Waterbury, CT St. Thomas Church.
Glick, George W. '63 (BAL) Hancock, MD St. Peter's Church.
Glimm, Msgr. Francis X. '35 (RVC) Retired.
Glinkowski, Raphael *o.s.p.p.e.* '62 (GBG) Kittanning, PA Armstrong County Hospital.
Glinkowski, Raphael K. *o.s.p.p.e.* '62 (GBG) [H] Kittanning, PA Pauline Fathers Monastery.
Glisson, Nicholas J. '79 (STA) Graduate Studies.
Glockner, David *glmy.* '66 (CIN) Manchester, OH St. Mary Church; Peebles, OH St. Mary Queen of Heaven Church; West Union, OH Holy Trinity Church.
Glockner, Michael W. *c.s.c.* '70 (KAL) Albion, MI St.

John the Evangelist Church.
Glogowski, John F. '71 (SFR) Daly City, CA Our Lady of Mercy Church.
Glogowski, John J. '62 (ROC) Hilton, NY St. Leo Church.
Gloisten, Robert '54 (RIC) [1] Virginia Beach, VA Church of the Ascension.
Gloninger, Hugh M. '56 (PIT) [3] Butler, PA St. Paul Church; Butler County, PA Butler County Jail.
Gloria de la Inmaculada, Alberto Jesus *s.e.m.v.* '94 (ARE) Hatillo, PR Our Lady of Guadalupe Church.
Glorie, Msgr. John W. '60 (MIA) [4] Pompano Beach, FL St. Elizabeth of Hungary Catholic Church.
Glorioso, Charles '95 (SHP) [1] Shreveport, LA St. John Berchmans Cathedral.
Glosser, William F. '84 (ALN) Schuylkill Haven, PA St. Ambrose Church; [M] Orwigsburg, PA St. Francis Center.
Gloudeman, Francis *o.praem.* (LA) Wilmington, CA SS. Peter and Paul's Church.
Gloudeman, Francis M. *o.praem.* '91 (ORG) [H] Silverado, CA Norbertine Fathers.
Gloudeman, Robert J. '64 (MIL) [N] Milwaukee, WI Marian Catholic Center, Inc.
Glover, George *o.s.b.* '88 (RCK) [H] Aurora, IL Marmion Abbey-St. Augustine's Abbey.
Glovik, Karl L. '61 (DUB) [1] Cedar Rapids, IA Immaculate Conception Church; [8] Cedar Rapids, IA St. Wenceslaus Church.
Gluc, Vincent *o.f.m.conv.* '79 (BAL) [M] Ellicott City, MD Order of Friars Minor Conventual.
Gluekert, Leopold G. *o.carm.* '68 (CHI) [N] Chicago, IL Brandsma House.
Gluszek, Msgr. Joseph '35 (GF) [2] Great Falls, MT Eastside Catholic Communities Church; Retired.
Gluszek, W. Adalbert '22 (SFR) Retired; [K] San Francisco, CA Home for the Aged of the Little Sisters of the Poor.
Glynn, Edward *s.j.* '67 (SPK) [C] Spokane, WA Gonzaga University.
Glynn, Msgr. Francis J. '37 (NY) [205] Staten Island, NY Holy Family Church; Retired.
Glynn, Francis M. '51 (WIN) Retired.
Glynn, Francis M. '70 (BO) [1] Lowell, MA St. Anthony Church.
Glynn, Msgr. Gerard N. '41 (STL) Retired.
Glynn, John F. *o.s.a.* '39 (LA) [F] Ojai, CA Villanova Preparatory School.
Glynn, John P. '48 (PH) Retired.
Glynn, Martin G. '78 (PAT) Franklin, NJ Immaculate Conception Church.
Glynn, Msgr. Michael '46 (JKS) [3] Jackson, MS St. Richard Church; Retired.
Glynn, Robert J. *s.j.* '91 (PHX) [B] Phoenix, AZ Brophy College Preparatory.
Glynn, Seamus A. '58 (ORG) [4] Anaheim, CA San Antonio Church.
Glynn, Thomas J. '54 (LA) San Pedro, CA Holy Trinity Church.
Glynn, Thomas L. '64 (STN) [2] Chicago, IL St. Joseph Church.
Glynn, Msgr. William F. '47 (BO) Duxbury, MA Holy Family Church.
Gmerek, Ronald E. (E) [B] Erie, PA Gannon University.
Gmerek, Ronald E. '71 (E) Houtzdale, PA Christ the King Church; On Duty Outside Diocese.
Gnall, Julian M. *o.s.b.* '55 (PBR) Retired.
Gnarackatt, Joseph '67 (TR) [10] Trenton, NJ Our Lady of Sorrows Church.
Gniewyk, Eugene G. '90 (NEW) Upper Montclair, NJ St. Cassian Church.
Gnirk, Lloyd A. '78 (OM) [38] Omaha, NE St. Pius X Church.
Gobbo, Paolo '94 (BO) [W] Holliston, MA Xaverian Missionaries.
Gobitas, Msgr. Gerald (ALN) [3] Easton, PA St. Jane Frances de Chantal Church.
Goblirsch, Robert P. '60 (NU) Dawson, MN St. James Church; Madison, MN St. Michael Church.
Goce, Lauro '37 (SD) Retired.
Goda, Paul J. *s.j.* '66 (SJ) [B] Santa Clara, CA Santa Clara University.
Godecker, Jeffery H. '69 (IND) [10] Indianapolis, IN Immaculate Heart of Mary Church.
Godenciuc, Vasile '81 (STF) Rochester, NY Epiphany of Our Lord Church.
Godfrey, Joseph J. *s.j.* '69 (PH) [C] Philadelphia, PA St. Joseph's University; [Z] Philadelphia, PA Jesuit Community at St. Joseph's University; [Z] Philadelphia, PA St. Alphonsus House.
Godfrey, Kevin *o.f.m.conv.* '84 (IND) [I] Mount Saint Francis, IN Mount Saint Francis Friary and Retreat Center.
Godfrey, Timothy S. *s.j.* '85 (STL) [P] St. Louis, MO Leo Brown Jesuit Community.
Godic, Frank G. '73 (CLV) [42] Cleveland, OH St. Lawrence Church.
Godin, James M. '79 (MIL) [X] Milwaukee, WI Milwaukee Archdiocesan Campus Ministry.
Godin, Norman J. '73 (PRO) [3] Providence, RI St. Agnes Church.
Godinez, J. Jesus (GAL) [31] Houston, TX St. Gregory the Great Church.
Godley, Msgr. James '40 (CHY) Retired.
Godley, Patrick '53 (SEA) Bainbridge Island, WA St. Cecilia's Church.
Goebel, Bernard M. '29 (SAT) Retired; [N] San Antonio, TX Our Lady of Czestochowa.
Goebel, Joseph A. '50 (CLV) Twinsburg, OH SS. Cosmas and Damian Church; Retired.
Goebel, Nicholas L. '58 (MIL) Auburn, WI St. Matthias Church; [Q] Campbellsport, WI St. Joseph Convent.
Goebel, Robert A. *s.j.* '63 (SPK) [E] Spokane, WA Gonzaga Preparatory School.
Goebel, Robert W. '74 (CIN) [81] Cincinnati, OH St. Saviour Church.
Goeckner, Jeffrey W. '95 (SFD) [2] Decatur, IL Our Lady of Lourdes Church.
Goedde, Bernard C., Jr. '72 (BEL) Millstadt, IL St. James Church.
Goedert, Edmund N. *c.s.c.* '43 (FTW) [B] Notre Dame, IN University of Notre Dame Du Lac; [G] Notre Dame, IN University Health Services; [J] Notre Dame, IN Holy Cross Community, Corby Hall, University of Notre Dame.
Goedert, Robert A. *o.p.* '51 (CHI) [N] Chicago, IL Dominicans (Provincial Office).
Goedert, William O. '55 (CHI) [3] Oak Lawn, IL St. Germaine Church; [3] Oak Lawn, IL St. Germaine Church; Retired.
Goedken, James J. '66 (DUB) Key West, IA St. Joseph's Church.
Goedken, Nestor B. '43 (DUB) Retired.
Goehring, Raymond '64 (LAN) [4] Lansing, MI Immaculate Heart of Mary Church; On Duty Outside the Diocese.
Goeke, James F. *s.j.* '88 (KC) [12] Kansas City, MO St. Francis Xavier Church; [J] Kansas City, MO St. Francis Xavier - Jesuit Community.
Goeke, John W. '59 (COV) Leave of Absence.
Goekler, Thomas F. '67 (HRT) On Duty Outside the Archdiocese.
Goellner, Glennon '50 (STL) [6] Florissant, MO St. Ferdinand Church.
Goentges, Charles J. '40 (DET) Retired.
Goergan, Michael A. '62 (CHI) [186] Chicago, IL St. Robert Bellarmine Church.
Goergen, David J. *m.afr.* '69 (WDC) [M] Washington, DC Missionaries of Africa.
Goergen, Donald *o.p.* '75 (STL) [B] St. Louis, MO Aquinas Institute of Theology.
Goerner, Basil S. '93 (MAR) Ironwood, MI Our Lady of Peace Church.
Goerner, James E. '93 (PH) Horsham, PA St. Catherine of Siena Church.
Goertz, Msgr. Alois J. '48 (SAT) Retired; [K] San Antonio, TX Casa De Padres.
Goertz, Bernard C. '52 (AUS) [10] Austin, TX Santa Barbara Church; Special Assignments.
Goertz, Howard '77 (AUS) Kyle, TX St. Anthony Marie De Claret Church; Stony Point, TX Father Joel Atwood Catholic Community Center Church.
Goertz, Victor '52 (AUS) Special Assignments.
Goethals, Gregory M. *s.j.* '88 (SFR) [E] San Francisco, CA St. Ignatius College Preparatory (Coed); [N] San Francisco, CA Jesuit Community at St. Ignatius College Preparatory.
Goettemoeller, L. H. *c.pp.s.* '49 (DAV) Bloomfield, IA St. Mary Magdalen Church; Eldon, IA St. Aloysius Church.
Goetz, Donald R. '68 (L) [16] Louisville, KY St. Brigid Church; [39] Louisville, KY St. James Church.
Goetz, Donatus *o.f.m.cap.* '45 (NY) [Z] Yonkers, NY St. Clare Friary.
Goetz, Gerald E. *s.j.* '73 (STP) [Q] Lake Elmo, MN Jesuit Retreat House.
Goetz, J. Raymond '81 (OWN) [I] Murray, KY Murray State University Newman House.
Goetz, Joseph W. '60 (CIN) Yellow Springs, OH St. Paul Church; [Q] Yellow Springs, OH Antioch College Campus Ministry.
Goetz, Martin G. '92 (DAV) [2] Davenport, IA Our Lady of Victory Church.
Goetz, Ray '81 (OWN) Murray, KY St. Leo Church.
Goff, William P. *c.m.* (BAL) Emmitsburg, MD St. Joseph Church; [M] Emmitsburg, MD Vincentian House.
Gogel, Odo *o.s.b.* '50 (SFS) [F] Marvin, SD Blue Cloud Abbey.
Goggin, Cornelius J. '56 (MAN) Bedford, NH St. Elizabeth Seton Church.
Goggin, Gerald *c.s.s.* '46 (BO) [W] Waltham, MA Stigmatine House; [Z] Waltham, MA Stigmatine Fathers and Brothers.
Goggin, John T. '64 (NU) On Duty Outside the Diocese.
Goggin, Msgr. Leo J. '39 (RVC) Dix Hills, NY St. Matthew Church; Retired.
Goggin, Thomas J. '57 (VEN) Fort Myers Beach, FL Ascension Church.
Goggins, James K. '94 (DEN) [1] Denver, CO Cathedral of the Immaculate Conception.
Goguen, Francis T. '66 (WOR) [3] Leominster, MA St. Cecilia's Church.
Gohm, Robert '75 (SAG) [1] Saginaw, MI St. Mary Cathedral; [2] Saginaw, MI Holy Family Church.
Gohmann, Myron *c.p.* '55 (CHI) [N] Chicago, IL Immaculate Conception Monastery.
Gohring, William '84 (ORL) De Land, FL St. Peter's Church.
Goiburu, Ignacio *c.p.* '43 (ARE) Lares, PR St. Joseph Church.
Goicoechea, Gregorio J. *o.f.m.cap.* '45 (SAT) [13] San Antonio, TX Our Lady of the Angels Church; [M] San Antonio, TX Capuchin Franciscan Friars (Spain); [T] San Antonio, TX Secular Franciscan Order.
Goicoechea, Javier *sch.p.* '54 (SJN) [58] San Juan, PR Santisimo Salvador Church.
Going, Joseph G. *o.p.* '49 (PT) [9] Pensacola, FL St. John the Evangelist Church.
Goins, James '92 (OKL) [K] Norman, OK Campus Ministry for the Archdiocese of Oklahoma City.
Goins, James A. '92 (OKL) Lawton, OK Holy Family Church.
Golas, Eugene S. '55 (GR) On Special Assignment.
Golas, John S. '81 (HRT) [1] Manchester, CT Assumption Church.
Golasinski, Donald J. '62 (BEA) Groves, TX Immaculate Conception Church.
Golasinski, Msgr. James L. '58 (GAL) [9] Houston, TX Annunciation Church.
Gold, William F. '65 (SD) Oceanside, CA St. Margaret Church.
Goldasich, Mark '81 (KCK) Tonganoxie, KS Sacred Heart Church.
Goldbach, Peter D. *c.m.* '44 (BRK) [D] Queens and Staten Island, NY St. John's University; [U] Jamaica, NY Vincentian Residence.
Goldback, Edmund *o.f.m.conv.* '65 (TOL) Carey, OH Our Lady of Consolation, Basilica-National Shrine Church.
Goldberg, James M. '76 (GBG) Lucernemines, PA St. Louis Church.
Golden, Edward '61 (ROC) Fairport, NY Assumption of the Blessed Virgin Mary Church.
Golden, Francis P. *s.j.* '71 (NY) [Z] New York, NY Jesuit Provincial's Office.
Golden, Frank *s.j.* '71 (SJN) [22] San Juan, PR San Ignacio de Loyola Church.
Golden, George E. '76 (WDC) Forestville, MD Mt. Calvary Church.
Golden, James '48 (DUL) Retired.
Golden, Patrick '96 (RIC) Williamsburg, VA St. Bede's Church.
Golden, Paul L. *c.m.* '65 (BUF) [C] Niagara University, NY Niagara University; [O] Niagara University, NY Vincentian Community at Niagara University.
Golden, Paul L. *c.m.* '65 (CHI) [C] Chicago, IL De Paul University; [C] Chicago, IL De Paul University.
Golden, R. Thomas '63 (GB) Menasha, WI St. John Church.
Goldian, Edward R. *s.j.* '69 (STL) [41] St. Louis, MO St. John the Baptist Church.
Goldikovskis, Msgr. Alexander I. '41 (CLV) [39] Cleveland, OH St. Josaphat Church; Retired.
Golding, Edward '88 (ALB) Summit, NY St. Anna Church; [S] Cobleskill, NY State University of New York College of Agricultural & Technology at Cobleskill.
Goldrick, Timothy J. '72 (FR) Assonet, MA St. Bernard's Church.
Gole, Joseph '43 (MIL) [B] Hales Corners, WI Sacred Heart School of Theology; [P] Hales Corners, WI Sacred Heart Monastery.
Golemba, Msgr. Roman '75 (STF) Rochester, NY St. Josaphat Church.
Golenski, John D. *s.j.* '80 (BO) [W] Boston, MA The Society of Jesus of New England-Provincial Offices.
Golias, Andrew J. '70 (PH) [A] Wynnewood, PA Theological Seminary of St. Charles Borromeo, Overbrook.
Golik, Stanislaus '39 (OM) [46] Omaha, NE St. Thomas More Church; Retired.
Golini, Ronald (NTN) Leave of Absence.
Golino, Arthur A. '80 (NY) [199] Staten Island, NY Blessed Sacrament Church.
Golka, James R. '94 (GI) Kearney, NE St. James Church.
Gollapalli, Alphonse '89 (OKL) Woodward, OK St. Peter's Church.
Gollatz, Ronald J. '72 (CHI) Lake Zurich, IL St. Francis de Sales Church.
Gollinge, Donald '58 (NY) Absent on Leave.
Gollob, Timothy A. '58 (DAL) [5] Dallas, TX Holy Cross Church; Dallas, TX Veterans Administration Hospital.
Golobich, John '48 (DUL) Retired.
Golombek, Msgr. Robert K. '65 (BUF) [2] Kenmore, NY Blessed Sacrament Church.
Goltz, William A. '50 (DUB) Retired.
Golueke, Thomas J. '77 (BAL) [82] Baltimore, MD St. Pius X Church.
Goman, Ralph J. '64 (STP) [31] Minneapolis, MN St. Olaf Church.

Gomes, Herman *ss.cc.* (HON) Makawao, HI St. Joseph Church.
Gomes, John (CHI) [J] Chicago, IL St. Joseph Hospital.
Gomes, John A. '69 (FR) [3] Taunton, MA Our Lady of Lourdes Church.
Gomes, John Stanley '95 (NEW) [4] Elizabeth, NJ Blessed Sacrament Church.
Gomes, Martin *ss.cc.* '69 (FR) [K] Fairhaven, MA Sacred Hearts Provincial House.
Gomes, Martin *ss.cc.* '69 (WDC) Seat Pleasant, MD St. Margaret Church.
Gomes, Robert M. '66 (CAM) Oaklyn, NJ St. Aloysius Church.
Gomes, Ronald A. (BO) Absent on Leave.
Gomes, William '69 (RVC) Point Lookout, NY Our Lady of the Miraculous Medal Church.
Gomes-Kelly, John R. '62 (SD) Unassigned.
Gomez, Msgr. Antonio '51 (SJN) [13] San Juan, PR Cristo Rey Church.
Gomez, Arturo S. *c.m.f.* '80 (FRS) [8] Fresno, CA St. Anthony Claret Church.
Gomez, Daniel A. '84 (MET) Iselin, NJ St. Cecelia Church.
Gomez, Edmund '93 (SB) [4] San Bernardino, CA Our Lady of Fatima Church; [8] San Bernardino, CA St. Bernardine Church.
Gomez, Edmundo '69 (NY) [145] Bronx, NY St. Helena Church.
Gomez, Emerito *o.f.m.* '82 (FRS) Delano, CA Our Lady of Guadalupe Church.
Gomez, Enrique '77 (CGS) Vieques, PR Inmaculada Concepcion Church.
Gomez, Eusebio *o.c.d.* '70 (MIA) [M] Miami, FL Discalced Carmelite Friars of Miami, Inc.
Gomez, Francisco (SLC) [2] Kearns, UT St. Francis Xavier Church; [4] Midvale, UT St. Therese of the Child Jesus Church; [C] Kearns, UT St. Francis Xavier Regional School.
Gomez, Francisco *o.f.m.conv.* '76 (STP) [Q] Prior Lake, MN Franciscan Retreat House.
Gomez, Frank '61 (BWN) Retired.
Gomez, Msgr. Henry '58 (LA) Bell Gardens, CA St. Gertrude Church.
Gomez, Humberto '88 (SAC) [15] Sacramento, CA St. Joseph's Church.
Gomez, Jose '78 (GAL) [P] Houston, TX Opus Dei.
Gomez, Jose '78 (SAT) [R] San Antonio, TX Opus Dei (Prelature of the Holy Cross and Opus Dei).
Gomez, Jose '95 (AMA) Borger, TX St. John the Evangelist Church.
Gomez, Jose H. (GAL) [U] Houston, TX Asociacion Nacional de Sacerdotes Hispanos.
Gomez, Jose L. *s.d.b.* '60 (ARE) Orocovis, PR San Juan Bautista Church.
Gomez, Msgr. Leo '63 (GLP) [1] Gallup, NM Cathedral of the Sacred Heart.
Gomez, Lorenzo (DET) [T] Bloomfield Hills, MI The Legion of Christ, Inc.; [T] Bloomfield Hills, MI Opdyke, Inc.; [T] Bloomfield Hills, MI Logos, Inc. (Michigan).
Gomez, Miguel '81 (MIA) [6] Miami, FL Good Shepherd Church.
Gomez, Orlando De Jesus '86 (CGS) [7] Caguas, PR El Salvador Church.
Gomez, Ramon J. '85 (OAK) Union City, CA St. Anne Church.
Gomez, Raul *s.d.s.* '87 (MIL) [B] Hales Corners, WI Sacred Heart School of Theology.
Gomez, Raul *s.d.s.* '87 (WDC) [B] Silver Spring, MD Salvatorian Community.
Gomez, Rene '63 (SFR) [3] San Rafael, CA St. Raphael Church.
Gomez, Vicente '61 (LA) Retired.
Gomez, Walter (ARE) On Duty Outside the Diocese.
Gomez, Walter '80 (SJ) [18] San Jose, CA Our Lady of Guadalupe Church.
Gomide, Tomaz '71 (RVC) Mineola, NY Corpus Christi Church.
Gomolski, Joseph T. '81 (WIL) Retired.
Gomulka, Eugene T. '74 (ALT) Military Chaplains.
Gomulka, Henry J. '42 (GB) Retired.
Gonda, Andrew (GI) Retired.
Gonda, Gerard *o.s.b.* '80 (CLV) [E] Cleveland, OH Benedictine High School; [P] Cleveland, OH Benedictine Order of Cleveland.
Gondek, Albert *o.s.f.s.* '66 (R) Whiteville, NC Sacred Heart Church.
Gondek, Joseph A. '37 (MAR) Retired.
Gonder, David *s.d.b.* '81 (NY) [Z] New Rochelle, NY Salesian Provincial House.
Gonderinger, Gerald E. '74 (OM) [44] Omaha, NE St. Stephen the Martyr Church.
Gondra, Tomas '58 (SJN) [52] San Juan, PR Resurreccion del Senor Church.
Gonet, Charles F. '58 (SPR) [14] Springfield, MA St. Catherine of Siena Church.
Gongora, Luis '65 (DAL) [7] Dallas, TX Mary Immaculate Church.
Goni, Joachim *o.a.r.* '40 (ORG) [5] Santa Ana, CA Our Lady of the Pillar Church.
Goni, Paul *o.a.r.* '51 (LA) [4] Oxnard, CA Mary Star of the Sea Church.
Gonia, Raymond L. '90 (SUP) Military Chaplains.
Gonnelly, Theophane *o.s.b.* '47 (SFS) [F] Marvin, SD Blue Cloud Abbey.
Gonsalves, Lino S. (RVC) Manorhaven, NY Our Lady of Fatima Church.
Gonser, Richard A. '62 (CLV) North Ridgeville, OH St. Julie Billiart Church.
Gonsorcik, Joseph '38 (MET) Retired.
Gonsorcik, Pat *s.c.j.* '70 (MIL) [P] Hales Corners, WI Priests of the Sacred Heart.
Gonter, Louis J. '49 (BUF) Retired.
Gonter, Louis J. '49 (ORL) Lady Lake, FL St. Timothy Church; Retired.
Gonthier, Armand *m.s.* '40 (FR) [K] Attleboro, MA La Salette Shrine.
Gonyo, Lance M. '93 (ROC) [52] Rochester, NY St. Pius Tenth Church; [3] Elmira, NY St. Mary Church.
Gonyo, Roland G. '73 (OG) [2] Ogdensburg, NY Notre Dame Church.
Gonzales, Msgr. Antonio '62 (LUB) [7] Lubbock, TX St. Patrick Church.
Gonzales, Emilio '88 (SEA) Unassigned.
Gonzales, Gabriel '39 (NO) Retired.
Gonzales, Gabriel '84 (LA) [36] Los Angeles, CA Sacred Heart Church.
Gonzales, George '79 (ORG) Dana Point, CA St. Edward Church; Absent on Sick Leave.
Gonzales, Ignacio (BWN) [1] Harlingen, TX Our Lady of the Assumption Church.
Gonzales, Loren M. *o.s.m.* '89 (TUC) Miami, AZ Our Lady of the Blessed Sacrament Church.
Gonzales, Loreto '78 (LA) Artesia, CA Holy Family Church; [CC] Los Angeles, CA Filipino Pastoral Ministry.
Gonzales, Orestes '86 (NY) [EE] New Rochelle, NY Opus Dei (Prelature of the Holy Cross and Opus Dei).
Gonzales, Robert A. '78 (COL) [A] Columbus, OH Pontifical College Josephinum.
Gonzales, Robert A. '78 (TUC) On Duty Outside the Diocese.
Gonzales, Roberto Solivan '81 (CGS) [9] Barrio Rio Canas, PR San Pablo Apostol Church.
Gonzalez, Angel *s.p.* '52 (FRS) Reedley, CA St. Anthony Church.
Gonzalez, Anthoney '92 (LA) [5] Los Angeles, CA Assumption Church.
Gonzalez, Antonio '50 (FRS) Hanford, CA Immaculate Heart Church.
Gonzalez, Msgr. Antonio '62 (LUB) [A] Lubbock, TX Christian Renewal Center.
Gonzalez, Arnold *c.m.f.* '58 (LA) [20] Los Angeles, CA Our Lady of Solitude Church.
Gonzalez, Carmelo Arroyo *o.a.r.* '73 (NY) [Z] New York, NY Augustinian Recollects Provincial Residence, Province of St. Nicholas of Tolentine.
Gonzalez, Charles G. *s.j.* '67 (CAM) [9] Camden, NJ Sacred Heart Church.
Gonzalez, Daniel (TYL) Sulphur Springs, TX St. James Church; Sulphur Springs, TX St. James Church.
Gonzalez, Domingo '64 (ORL) Bartow, FL St. Thomas Aquinas Church.
Gonzalez, Eduardo *s.d.b.* '81 (DAL) Ennis, TX St. John Nepomucene Church; [P] Ferris, TX Holy Name Society.
Gonzalez, Felix J. '81 (NY) [172] Bronx, NY Our Lady of Grace Church.
Gonzalez, Flavio '77 (CHI) [1] Des Plaines, IL St. Mary Church.
Gonzalez, Francisco *s.f.* '64 (WDC) Takoma Park, MD Our Lady of Sorrows Church; [B] Silver Spring, MD Holy Family Seminary.
Gonzalez, George (SAV) [2] Columbus, GA Our Lady of Lourdes Church.
Gonzalez, George '71 (SB) Lake Elsinore, CA St. Frances of Rome Church.
Gonzalez, George G. '67 (SAT) Military Chaplains.
Gonzalez, Gonzalo *o.s.a.* '49 (SJN) [1] Bayamon, PR San Agustin Church.
Gonzalez, Hector '79 (VEN) [7] Fort Myers, FL Hispanic Missions of Fort Myers Church.
Gonzalez, Hernan (BWN) [I] San Juan, TX Virgen de San Juan del Valle Shrine.
Gonzalez, Hilario Rivera '74 (SJN) [9] San Juan, PR Santa Catalina Laboure Church.
Gonzalez, Hugo '89 (PHX) Buckeye, AZ Saint Henry Church.
Gonzalez, Jorge A. '87 (BWN) San Benito, TX Our Lady, Queen of the Universe Church.
Gonzalez, Jose (VEN) [L] Lake Placid, FL Comunidad Catolica Hispana Santiago Apostol Mission.
Gonzalez, Jose '54 (SP) [8] St. Petersburg, FL St. Raphael Church.
Gonzalez, Jose '69 (SR) Healdsburg, CA St. John the Baptist Church.
Gonzalez, Jose '91 (VEN) Lake Placid, FL Comunidad Catolica Hispana Santiago Apostol Mission Church.
Gonzalez, Juan *c.pp.s.* '76 (GRY) [5] East Chicago, IN Our Lady of Guadalupe Church.
Gonzalez, Luis P. '94 (NEW) [A] Kearny, NJ Redemptoris Mater.
Gonzalez, Marcos '94 (LA) Camarillo, CA St. Mary Magdalen Church.
Gonzalez, Mario '55 (VEN) Retired.
Gonzalez, Mario *o.s.a.* '58 (SJN) [18] Bayamon, PR Santa Rita de Casia Church.
Gonzalez, Rafael *c.r.l.* '93 (ARE) Corozal-Palos Blancos, PR Christ the King Church.
Gonzalez, Msgr. Ricardo '57 (NEW) [8] Jersey City, NJ St. Boniface's Church.
Gonzalez, Romualdo M. *sch.p.* '71 (LA) [75] Los Angeles, CA St. Lucy Church.
Gonzalez, Ruben *c.m.f.* (SJN) [27] San Juan, PR San Jose Obrero Church.
Gonzalez, Rudolph F. '87 (NY) [31] New York, NY St. Elizabeth Church; [1] Port Chester, NY Our Lady of Mercy Church.
Gonzalez, Silvino *o.de.m.* '41 (PCE) [9] Ponce, PR La Merced Church.
Gonzalez-Abreu, Hector '79 (MIA) On Duty Outside the Archdiocese.
Gonzalez-Buelta, Benjamin '70 (MIA) [D] Miami, FL Belen Jesuit Preparatory School.
Gonzalez-Chao, Luis '58 (SJN) [3] Toa Baja, PR Espiritu Santo Church.
Gonzalez-Florez, Jose D. '96 (ATL) [4] Atlanta, GA Immaculate Heart of Mary Church.
Good, Clarence P. '46 (STL) Shrewsbury, MO Cure of Ars Church.
Good, John B. *m.s.* '44 (HRT) [M] Hartford, CT Missionaries of LaSalette Provincial Secretary.
Goodavish, Michael J. *o.f.m.conv.* '87 (IND) [4] Terre Haute, IN St. Joseph Church; [N] Terre Haute, IN Indiana State University, Rose Hulman Institute Newman Center.
Goodbout, George E. '63 (BR) [F] Baton Rouge, LA Our Lady of the Lake Regional Medical Center.
Goodbout, George E. '63 (STU) On Duty Outside the Diocese.
Goode, Francis '87 (SB) [10] Riverside, CA St. Andrew's Newman Center Church; [E] Riverside, CA St. Vincent Ferrer House.
Goode, James E. *o.f.m.* '72 (NY) [Z] New York, NY St. Clare Friary.
Goode, Joseph J. '73 (PAT) Rockaway, NJ Sacred Heart Church.
Goode, Lawrence C. '64 (SFR) [18] San Francisco, CA St. Finn Barr Church; [U] San Francisco, CA Legion of Mary.
Goode, Michael *c.pp.s.* '79 (SAN) Sweetwater, TX Holy Family Church.
Goode, William F. '60 (WDC) Indian Head, MD St. Mary Star of the Sea Church.
Goodill, Msgr. Robert D. '38 (E) [23] Erie, PA St. Luke Church; Retired.
Goodly, Timothy '93 (LKC) [4] Lake Charles, LA St. Henry Church.
Goodman, Fidelis C. *m.m.* '49 (NY) [Z] Maryknoll, NY Maryknoll Fathers and Brothers.
Goodman, Frank '59 (ORL) Retired.
Goodman, Frank '59 (SP) Retired.
Goodman, Julian B. '66 (RIC) [1] Norfolk, VA Blessed Sacrament Church.
Goodman, Leo M., III '91 (HBG) [4] York, PA St. Rose of Lima Church.
Goodman, Msgr. Norman D. '60 (PEO) Lincoln, IL Holy Family Church.
Goodrow, Robert '62 (DET) Military Chaplains.
Goodrum, James R. '57 (LFT) Monticello, IN Our Lady of the Lakes Church.
Goodwin, Calvin M. *s.j.* '79 (PRT) [C] Portland, ME Cheverus High School; [I] Portland, ME St. Ignatius Residence.
Goodwin, Henry D. *o.carm.* '34 (BO) [P] Peabody, MA Catholic Information Center.
Goodwin, James P. *s.j.* '43 (SPK) [K] Spokane, WA Regis Community.
Goodwin, Owen *ss.cc.* '54 (FR) [K] Fairhaven, MA Sacred Hearts Provincial House.
Goodwin, Owen F. *ss.cc.* '54 (PRO) [P] Narragansett, RI Christian Brothers' Center.
Goodwin, Patrick A. '69 (OAK) Dublin, CA St. Raymond Church.
Goodwin, Raymond M., Jr. '69 (WOR) Hopedale, MA Sacred Heart of Jesus Church.
Goodwin, Robert T. '57 (MAN) Absent on Sick Leave.
Goodwin, Thomas L. '86 (CC) Alice, TX Our Lady of Guadalupe Church.
Goodwine, Msgr. John J. '38 (NY) Retired.
Goodwine, Msgr. Joseph G. '39 (NY) Retired.
Goodyear, Robert *s.t.* '75 (JKS) Magee, MS St. Stephen Church; Sanatorium, MS Boswell Retardation Center.
Gooley, Laurence L. *s.j.* '65 (P) [L] Portland, OR Jesuit Provincial Office (Oregon Prov.).
Goolsby, Gregory D. '93 (ATL) Duluth, GA St. Benedict Church.
Goossens, Anthony *o.m.i.* '39 (SAT) [K] San Antonio, TX Oblate Madonna Residence.
Goossens, Hippolyte L. *c.j.* '56 (LA) Camarillo, CA Camarillo State Hospital-Development Center.
Gootee, Stanley J. *s.v.d.* '44 (GAL) [46] Houston, TX St.

Mary of the Purification Church.
Goraieb, Charles '91 (PHX) Peoria, AZ St. Charles Borromeo Church.
Gorak, Stanley C. '38 (GI) Retired.
Goralka, Albert A. '45 (PIT) Retired.
Gorczyca, Andrzej '74 (BRK) [241] Queens, NY St. Stanislaus Bishop and Martyr Church.
Gorczyca, Benvenute *o.f.m.conv.* '33 (BUF) [21] Buffalo, NY Corpus Christi Church.
Gordan, Msgr. John '38 (NY) [212] Staten Island, NY St. Margaret Mary Church.
Gordinier, William '58 (ROC) Geneseo, NY St. Mary Church.
Gordon, Charles B. *c.s.c.* '87 (FTW) [A] Notre Dame, IN Moreau Seminary; [J] South Bend, IN Congregation of Holy Cross Indiana Province Provincial House.
Gordon, Emmanuel *c.p.* '50 (MET) [H] South River, NJ Passionist Provincial Office.
Gordon, Gerald R. *s.j.* '60 (SPK) [C] Spokane, WA Gonzaga University; [G] Spokane, WA Sacred Heart Medical Center.
Gordon, Gerard A. '88 (RVC) Hicksville, NY St. Ignatius Loyola Church.
Gordon, Gregory (LAV) North Las Vegas, NV St. Christopher Church.
Gordon, James *i.c.* '69 (SP) Seminole, FL Blessed Sacrament Church.
Gordon, James E. '81 (RIC) Portsmouth, VA Holy Angels Church.
Gordon, Msgr. John '39 (NY) Retired.
Gordon, Msgr. John '47 (DET) Special Assignment.
Gordon, John B. '85 (MET) On Duty Outside the Diocese.
Gordon, John F. '88 (NEW) Rochelle Park, NJ Sacred Heart Church; [D] Montvale, NJ St. Joseph Regional High School.
Gordon, John T. '47 (DET) Harper Woods, MI Our Lady Queen of Peace Church.
Gordon, Joseph A. '71 (SFR) East Palo Alto, CA St. Francis of Assisi Church.
Gordon, Kevin M. '83 (SUP) Rice Lake, WI St. Joseph Church.
Gordon, L. William '65 (OG) Port Henry, NY St. Patrick Church.
Gordon, M. Gerald *t.o.r.* '69 (PH) [Z] Fairless Hills, PA St. Anthony Friary.
Gordon, Robert J. '73 (PAT) [8] Clifton, NJ St. Philip the Apostle Church.
Gore, Robert D. '65 (BEL) [8] Belleville, IL St. Teresa of the Child Jesus Church.
Gore, William R. *o.s.f.s.* '69 (PHU) Wilmington, DE St. Nicholas Church.
Gore, William R. *o.s.f.s.* '69 (WIL) [I] Wilmington, DE DeSales House.
Gorena, Pedro '66 (SJN) [13] Bayamon, PR Ascension Del Senor Church.
Gorges, Bernard X. '95 (WCH) [2] Wichita, KS All Saints Church.
Gorges, Peter '68 (JUN) [1] Juneau, AK Cathedral of the Nativity of The Blessed Virgin Mary.
Gorgis, Noel (EST) Scottsdale, AZ Mar Auraha Chaldean Catholic Parish Church.
Gorgon, Richard P. (NY) [Z] New York, NY Jesuit Provincial's Office.
Gorham, Francis X. *o.m.i.* '58 (BO) [3] Lowell, MA Immaculate Conception Church; Boston, MA Saints Memorial Medical Center.
Gorham, Peter P. '53 (PRT) Retired.
Gori, Peter G. *o.s.a.* '79 (BO) [4] Lawrence, MA St. Augustine Church.
Gorinas, Vytautas '70 (RCK) South Beloit, IL St. Peter Church; Retired.
Gorman, Charles L. '54 (GF) Retired.
Gorman, Cyril *o.s.b.* '90 (SCL) [I] Collegeville, MN St. John's Abbey, of the Order of St. Benedict.
Gorman, Francis A. *o.f.m.* '39 (CHR) Greenville, SC St. Anthony of Padua Church.
Gorman, Francis P. '59 (NY) North Tarrytown, NY St. Teresa of Avila Church; North Tarrytown, NY Holy Cross Church.
Gorman, George F. '36 (PRO) Retired; [P] Providence, RI St. John Vianney Residence.
Gorman, James (STP) Burnsville, MN Church of the Risen Savior.
Gorman, James P. '73 (PH) [36] Philadelphia, PA St. Clement Church.
Gorman, James T. '57 (NY) [1] Port Chester, NY Our Lady of Mercy Church; State, NY Bedford Hills Correctional Facility.
Gorman, Msgr. John '34 (DM) Retired.
Gorman, John '58 (SB) San Bernardino, CA San Bernardino Community Hospital.
Gorman, John E. *s.d.s.* '69 (WDC) [B] Silver Spring, MD Salvatorian Community.
Gorman, John F. '29 (CHI) Riverdale, IL Queen of Apostles Church; Retired.
Gorman, John J. '45 (RVC) Babylon, NY St. Joseph's Church; Retired.
Gorman, Joseph F. '55 (HRT) [12] Waterbury, CT St. Leo the Great Church; [D] Waterbury, CT Sacred Heart High School.
Gorman, Joseph P. '56 (NY) [38] New York, NY St. Frances Xavier Cabrini Church.
Gorman, Kevin *o.s.b.* '51 (PEO) Arlington, IL St. Patrick's Church; Cherry, IL Holy Trinity Church.
Gorman, Kevin D. *o.s.b.* '51 (PEO) [A] Peru, IL St. Bede Abbey and Academy.
Gorman, Lawrence J. (CHI) Retired.
Gorman, Leo J. *c.p.* '57 (NY) [Z] Pelham Manor, NY St. Vincent's Residence; [DD] Pelham, NY Passionist Communications, Inc.
Gorman, Michael J. (BAL) [A] Baltimore, MD St. Mary's Seminary and University.
Gorman, Michael J. '80 (LC) Special Assignment; [A] La Crosse, WI Holy Cross Seminary House of Formation; [I] La Crosse, WI Holy Cross (Seminary) Diocesan Center.
Gorman, Patrick J. '59 (LA) [48] Los Angeles, CA St. Bernadette Church.
Gorman, Paul J. '40 (NU) Retired.
Gorman, Richard F. '82 (NY) [E] New York, NY Cardinal Spellman High School.
Gorman, Robert G. '80 (MET) [7] Perth Amboy, NJ Holy Spirit Church.
Gorman, Rody I. '55 (LA) Huntington Park, CA St. Matthias Church.
Gorman, Thomas (TOL) Delphos, OH St. John the Evangelist Church.
Gorman, William '73 (ALB) Unassigned.
Gorman, William N. '76 (MOB) Heron Bay, AL St. Michael the Archangel Church.
Gormley, Charles E. '51 (PH) Bala-Cynwyd, PA St. Matthias Church.
Gormley, George J. '45 (RIC) Retired.
Gormley, Gerard '85 (SR) [3] Santa Rosa, CA St. Rose of Lima Church.
Gormley, James J. *s.j.* '54 (WH) [A] Wheeling, WV Wheeling Jesuit University.
Gormley, James W. '54 (PH) Stowe, PA St. Gabriel Church.
Gormley, Kevin '64 (JC) Absent on Leave.
Gormley, Michael *s.a.c.* '41 (DET) Allen Park, MI St. Frances Cabrini Church; Detroit, MI Oakwood Hospital.
Gormley, Raymond P. '92 (CAM) [2] Vineland, NJ Sacred Heart Church.
Gormley, William J. *c.m.* '49 (PH) [Z] Philadelphia, PA Congregation of the Mission.
Gormley, William J. *c.m.* '49 (RVC) [Q] Rockville Centre, NY The Campus Parish of Long Island.
Gorney, Msgr. Francis L. '40 (ALT) Retired.
Gorney, Joseph *c.ss.r.* '51 (SP) [9] Tampa, FL St. Joseph Church.
Gornick, Thomas (WH) Retired.
Gorny, Edward V. *glmy.* '68 (SAV) Sylvania, GA Our Lady of the Assumption Church; [I] Sylvania, GA Catholic Cemetery.
Gorospe, Paterno '66 (NEW) Teaneck, NJ Holy Name Hospital; [G] Teaneck, NJ Holy Name Hospital.
Gorowski, Roman *c.m.* '72 (BRK) [134] Brooklyn, NY St. Stanislaus Kostka Church.
Gorr, Benjamin '79 (VEN) Retired.
Gorra, Edward M. '55 (LAN) [11] Flint, MI St. Matthew Church.
Gorrell, Paul '91 (PAT) Chatham Township, NJ Corpus Christi Church; Absent on Leave.
Gorski, Alex F. '43 (WIL) Retired.
Gorski, Chris '88 (TYL) Longview, TX St. Mary Church.
Gorski, Eugene F. *c.s.c.* '60 (SCR) [C] Wilkes-Barre, PA Kings College.
Gorski, J. Donald '59 (CHR) On Duty Outside the Diocese.
Gorski, John J. '64 (CLV) Avon, OH Holy Trinity Church.
Gorski, Lawrence E. '75 (CHI) [148] Chicago, IL Our Lady of Grace Church.
Gorski, Robert E. '80 (MAN) Merrimack, NH St. John Neumann Church.
Gorski, Terrence *o.f.m.* '75 (BWN) Rio Hondo, TX St. Helen Church.
Gorski, Msgr. Walter J. '53 (NEW) Wallington, NJ Most Sacred Heart of Jesus Church.
Gorsuch, Joseph G. '62 (TUC) Eloy, AZ St. Helen Church.
Gorton, Timothy J. '82 (PRO) [4] Warren, RI St. Mary of the Bay Church; [S] Bristol, RI Roger Williams University.
Gosche, Msgr. Joseph E. '55 (SPC) Fredericktown, MO St. Michael Church.
Goscinak, Darius '92 (HRT) [2] New Britain, CT Holy Cross Church.
Gosma, Robert D. '59 (MIL) Genesee Depot, WI St. Paul Church.
Gosnell, David H. '65 (GRY) [2] Merrillville, IN St. Andrew Church.
Gosnell, Stephen D. '78 (BAL) Edgewood, MD Prince of Peace Church.
Goss, Francis G. '47 (BO) [5] Brockton, MA Our Lady of Lourdes Church; Retired.
Goss, Joseph *o.p.* '55 (BR) Donaldsonville, LA Ascension of Our Lord Jesus Christ Church.
Gosselin, Andre *s.m.* '64 (BO) [3] Methuen, MA Our Lady of Mount Carmel Church.
Gosselin, Fernand L. *m.m.* '70 (BO) [W] East Walpole, MA Maryknoll Department of Development.
Gosselin, Gerard G. '85 (PRT) Camden, ME Our Lady of Good Hope Church.
Gosselin, Homer P. '69 (SPR) [3] Ludlow, MA St. John the Baptist Church.
Gosselin, Joseph P. *m.s.* '65 (FR) [K] Attleboro, MA La Salette Shrine.
Gosselin, Lawrence '76 (NTN) Military Chaplains.
Gosselin, Michael H. '73 (HRT) [12] New Britain, CT St. Peter's Church.
Gosselin, Richard '58 (BO) Ayer, MA St. Mary Church.
Gosselin, Robert H. '56 (BO) Groveland, MA St. Patrick Church.
Gossman, John A. '71 (DUB) Hiawatha, IA St. Elizabeth Ann Seton Parish Church.
Goswitz, Leonard '90 (LA) Artesia, CA Holy Family Church.
Gosz, Isadore M. *o.praem.* '46 (GB) [I] De Pere, WI St. Norbert Abbey.
Gotay, Tarcisio *o.c.* '73 (SJN) [61] San Juan, PR Santa Teresita Del Nino Jesus Church.
Goth, Dennis J. '84 (LFT) Dunkirk, IN St. Mary Church; Union City, IN St. Mary Church.
Gothe, Marcus '59 (P) Retired.
Gothie, George J. '67 (PAT) Hopatcong, NJ St. Jude's Church.
Gothing, Donald B. (WOR) On Special or Other (Arch)Diocesan Assignment.
Gothman, August '93 (CR) Moorhead, MN St. Joseph's Church; [F] Moorhead, MN St. Thomas Newman Center.
Gotimer, Msgr. James E. '53 (BRK) [154] Queens, NY St. Bartholomew's Church.
Gott, Harold P. *o.f.m.conv.* '60 (IND) [J] Mount Saint Francis, IN Provincial Headquarters for the Conventual Franciscan Province.
Gottbrath, Hilary *o.f.m.conv.* '41 (IND) [I] Mount Saint Francis, IN Mount Saint Francis Friary and Retreat Center.
Gottemoeller, Mark '76 (IND) Martinsville, IN St. Martin of Tours Church.
Gottemoller, Bartholomew *o.c.s.o.* '42 (SLC) [F] Huntsville, UT Abbey of Our Lady of the Holy Trinity of the Order of Cistercians.
Gottin, Pio *o.f.m.cap.* '48 (BO) [60] Boston, MA St. Patrick Church.
Gottschalk, David *o.f.m.cap.* '69 (DEN) [M] Denver, CO St. Francis of Assisi Friary.
Gottschalk, Matthew *o.f.m.cap.* '53 (MIL) [Y] Milwaukee, WI House of Peace.
Gotwalt, Joseph F. '65 (HBG) [1] Harrisburg, PA Cathedral Parish of St. Patrick Church; [K] Harrisburg, PA Catholic Campus Ministry.
Goudreau, George W. '48 (PRT) Retired.
Goudreau, Joseph L. '63 (PRT) Military Chaplains.
Goudreau, Paul '60 (SP) Hudson, FL St. Michael Church.
Goudreau, Remy A. *o.f.m.* '39 (BO) [Z] Boston, MA Saint Anthony Residence.
Gough, James F. '40 (PH) [102] Philadelphia, PA St. Matthew Church; Retired.
Gough, Joseph E. *s.j.* '43 (KC) [B] Kansas City, MO Rockhurst College; [J] Kansas City, MO Rockhurst College - Jesuit Community.
Gough, Peter *o.f.m.conv.* '43 (TOL) Carey, OH Our Lady of Consolation, Basilica-National Shrine Church.
Gouin, Joseph O. '65 (MAR) Kingsford, MI American Martyrs Church.
Gould, Clayton '81 (LR) Batesville, AR St. Mary's Church; Newport, AR St. Cecilia's Church.
Gould, Eugene '44 (PEO) Retired.
Gould, Msgr. James C. *s.j.* '74 (MI) Majuro, MH Cathedral of the Assumption; Ebeye, MH Queen of Peace Church; MH Outer Island Parish Church.
Gould, James R. '81 (ARL) [2] Arlington, VA St. Agnes Church.
Gould, Lawrence *s.a.c.* '76 (FWT) Glen Rose, TX St. Rose of Lima Church; Granbury, TX St. Frances Cabrini Church.
Gould, Louis J. '62 (WOR) [10] Worcester, MA Our Lady of Fatima Church; Worcester, MA Memorial Hospital.
Gould, William '65 (B) Post Falls, ID St. George's Church.
Goulding, Laurence B. *glmy.* '62 (SAV) Claxton, GA St. Christopher Church.
Gouldrick, John W. *c.m.* '69 (PH) [69] Philadelphia, PA Immaculate Conception Church; [B] Philadelphia, PA St. Vincent's Seminary; [Z] Philadelphia, PA Congregation of the Mission.
Goulet, Raymond O. (BO) Absent on Sick Leave.
Goulet, Wayne F. '74 (PHX) Special Assignment.
Goulet, Xavier G. *o.f.m. conv.* '70 (SAG) Oakley, MI St. Michael Church.
Gourley, Marshall *c.r.* '82 (DEN) [19] Denver, CO Our Lady of Guadalupe Church.
Gouthier, Nolan '84 (BEA) Bridge City, TX St. Henry Church; [E] Beaumont, TX Lamar University-Catholic Student Center.

Gouthro, Arthur *s.a.* '69 (NY) [Z] Garrison, NY Generalate of the Franciscan Friars of the Atonement-St. James Friary.
Goveas, Benedict *o.f.m.* '53 (NY) [Z] New York, NY Franciscan Province of the Immaculate Conception.
Govern, William H. '34 (RVC) Retired.
Govorchin, Vincent '55 (SLC) On Duty Outside the Diocese.
Gowen, Daniel F. '89 (TR) [12] Trenton, NJ St. Anthony Church.
Gower, James M. '53 (PRT) Retired.
Gower, Peter J. '84 (PRO) [28] Providence, RI St. Raymond's Church; Providence, RI Miriam Hospital.
Gowin, Wladyslaw *s.chr.* '54 (CHI) [87] Chicago, IL Holy Trinity Mission Church.
Gowing, Thomas '69 (SR) Garberville, CA Our Lady of the Redwoods Church.
Goyette, Giles R. *o.mar.* '82 (SAM) [C] Petersham, MA Most Holy Trinity Monastery.
Gozaloff, Msgr. Paul J. '56 (WDC) Mechanicsville, MD Immaculate Conception Church.
Graap, Augustine *o.carm.* '66 (NY) State, NY Mid-Orange Correctional Facility; State, NY Otisville Correctional Facility; [Z] Middletown, NY St. Albert's Priory.
Grab, Michael J. '77 (HBG) [1] York, PA Immaculate Conception of the Blessed Virgin Mary Church; [A] York, PA York Catholic High School.
Grabarz, Casimir *c.s.c.* '39 (FTW) [L] Notre Dame, IN Holy Cross Mission House.
Grabert, Colman *o.s.b.* '65 (IND) [J] St. Meinrad, IN St. Meinrad Archabbey.
Grabish, John J. '72 (ALN) [2] Easton, PA St. Bernard Church; [5] Easton, PA St. Michael Church.
Grabner, Donald *o.s.b.* '54 (KC) [A] Conception, MO Conception Seminary College; [J] Conception, MO Conception Abbey.
Grabner, Eugene *o.s.b.* (WCH) [E] Fort Scott, KS Mercy Hospital.
Grabner, Kenneth *c.s.c.* '60 (FTW) [J] Notre Dame, IN Holy Cross Brother Center.
Grabovsky, Justin *o.f.m.conv.* '36 (TR) Seaside Park, NJ St. Catharine of Siena Church.
Grabowski, Dennis '76 (Y) Absent on Leave.
Grabowski, Eugene M. '89 (R) Edenton, NC St. Anne Church.
Grabowski, Fidelis *m.i.c.* '45 (SPR) [I] Stockbridge, MA Congregation of Marians.
Grabowski, Francis E. (MET) Piscataway, NJ St. Frances Cabrini Church; Retired; [H] Somerset, NJ Maria Regina Residence.
Grabowski, Walter '81 (BUF) [10] Cheektowaga, NY Queen of Martyrs Church.
Grabowsky, Msgr. Myron '67 (PHU) Bristol, PA St. Mary's Church.
Grabrian, Dennis '70 (COS) On Duty Outside Diocese.
Grabrian, John J. '70 (DEN) Loveland, CO St. John the Evangelist Church.
Grabys, Joseph J. '49 (ALB) [1] Amsterdam, NY St. Casimir Church.
Grace, Edward D. '67 (CHI) Skokie, IL St. Peter Church.
Grace, Edward G. *o.s.a.* '41 (CHI) [N] Olympia Fields, IL The Augustinian Provincialate Tolentine Center.
Grace, Gerald '65 (PMB) Highland Beach, FL St. Lucy Church.
Grace, Gerald *m.s.c.* '87 (SAT) [M] San Antonio, TX Missionaries of the Sacred Heart.
Grace, Gerald P. *s.j.* '54 (CHI) [N] Chicago, IL Chicago Province of the Society of Jesus-Provincial Office; [N] Chicago, IL Chicago Province of the Society of Jesus-Provincial Office; [X] Chicago, IL Jesuit International Missions, Inc.
Grace, Hugh R. '64 (NY) Saugerties, NY St. Mary of the Snow Church.
Grace, James N. '59 (CHI) Military Chaplains.
Grace, Msgr. James P. '61 (BRK) [150] Queens, NY St. Andrew Avellino Church.
Grace, John '37 (NY) Retired.
Grace, John '88 (MAN) [12] Manchester, NH St. Marie Church.
Grace, John A. '79 (RIC) Harrisonburg, VA Blessed Sacrament Church.
Grace, John J. '48 (SAC) South Lake Tahoe, CA St. Theresa Church; Retired and in Senior Ministry.
Grace, John J. '50 (CHI) [198] Chicago, IL St. Tarcissus Church.
Grace, Joseph W. '53 (LFT) Portland, IN Immaculate Conception Church; Marion, IN U.S. Veteran's Hospital.
Grace, Patrick J. '49 (ROC) Retired.
Grace, Peter A. *c.p.* '72 (SCR) [M] Scranton, PA Saint Ann's Passionist Monastery; [R] Scranton, PA Saint Ann's Media, Inc.
Grace, Robert S. '55 (WDC) North Beach, MD St. Anthony Church.
Grace, Thomas A. *c.m.* '64 (CHI) [G] Chicago, IL Catholic Charities of the Archdiocese of Chicago-Archdiocesan Offices; [N] Chicago, IL Vincentian Community, Congregation of the Mission, Midwest Province.
Gracey, John '93 (FRS) [6] Bakersfield, CA St. Philip the Apostle Church.
Gracias, Urbano '52 (NO) [46] New Orleans, LA St. Maurice Church.
Gracz, Msgr. Henry C. (ATL) McDonough, GA St. James The Apostle Church.
Graczyk, Carl *o.f.m.* '73 (PH) [D] Philadelphia, PA Archbishop Ryan High School; [Z] Philadelphia, PA St. Pius X Friary.
Graczyk, Glen G. '81 (MIL) Caledonia, WI St. Louis Church.
Graczyk, Randolph *o.f.m.cap.* '68 (GF) Pryor, MT St. Charles Borromeo Mission Church.
Grad, Malcolm '58 (CIN) On Special and Diocesan Assignment.
Gradeck, A. Edward '28 (HRT) Retired.
Graden, John L. *o.s.f.s.* '76 (TOL) [37] Toledo, OH St. Pius X Church; [K] Toledo, OH Oblates of St. Francis de Sales.
Gradillas, Arnulfo *c.s.sp.* '78 (AMA) [2] Amarillo, TX St. Laurence Cathedral; [L] Amarillo, TX Marriage Encounter.
Gradilone, Msgr. Thomas J. '50 (BRK) [218] Queens, NY Our Lady, Queen of Martyrs Church.
Grady, Bernard C. '68 (DUB) On Duty Outside the Archdiocese.
Grady, Donald F. *s.j.* '44 (BO) [W] Boston, MA The Society of Jesus of New England-Provincial Offices.
Grady, Donald F. *s.j.* '44 (CHR) Gaffney, SC Sacred Heart Church; [H] Gaffney, SC Limestone College Newman Center.
Grady, Francis J. *s.s.c.* '63 (CHI) Forest Park, IL St. Bernardine Church.
Grady, James P. '77 (STL) Elsberry, MO Sacred Heart Church.
Grady, L. Augustine *s.j.* '46 (NY) [Z] New York, NY Jesuit Community at Fordham University.
Grady, Michael '94 (MIA) Plantation, FL St. Gregory Church; [C] Fort Lauderdale, FL St. Thomas Aquinas High School.
Grady, Peter W. '53 (FAR) Retired; [E] Fargo, ND Riverview Place, Inc.
Grady, William R. '55 (LFT) Muncie, IN St. Mary Church.
Graeber, Msgr. Richard A. '53 (BUF) [1] Kenmore, NY St. Andrew Church.
Graef, Msgr. Franz '57 (NO) [A] New Orleans, LA Notre Dame Seminary Graduate School of Theology.
Graef, Msgr. Franz '57 (SHP) On Duty Outside the Diocese.
Graehler, Kenneth '63 (EVN) Sullivan, IN St. Mary Church.
Graf, Gary M. '84 (CHI) [4] Waukegan, IL Holy Family Church.
Graf, Harold '68 (PHX) Sun City West, AZ Our Lady of Lourdes Church.
Graf, Henry C. '49 (PH) Quakertown, PA St. Isidore Church.
Graf, Herbert *o.f.m.conv.* '59 (SAV) Hazlehurst, GA Good Shepherd Church.
Graf, James W. '72 (L) [61] Louisville, KY St. Patrick Church; Louisville, KY Central State Hospital.
Graf, John H. '46 (COL) Retired.
Graf, John W. '74 (PH) West Grove, PA Assumption B.V.M. Church.
Graf, Paul '82 (LFT) [C] Lafayette, IN St. Elizabeth Hospital Medical Center.
Graf, William E. '60 (ROC) [54] Rochester, NY Most Precious Blood Church; [L] Rochester, NY Archivist; [L] Rochester, NY Censores Librorum.
Graff, Ed '55 (AMA) Tulia, TX Church of the Holy Spirit.
Graff, Edward R. '55 (ALN) Retired.
Graff, Francis C. '65 (PIT) Neshannock, PA St. Camillus Church; Lawrence County, PA Almira Home; Lawrence County, PA Belvedere Retirement Home; Lawrence County, PA Golden Hill Nursing Home; Lawrence County, PA Haven Convalescent Home; Lawrence County, PA Highland Hall Care Center; Lawrence County, PA Hill View Manor; Lawrence County, PA Indian Creek Nursing Center; Lawrence County, PA Jack Rees Nursing and Rehabilitation Services Lawrence County, PA The Overlook Medical Clinic.
Graff, J. Austin '36 (CHI) Retired.
Graff, Joseph P. '76 (GAY) [2] Alpena, MI St. Bernard Church.
Graff, Robert L. '52 (TUC) Retired.
Graff, Timothy G. '85 (NEW) Saddle River Borough, NJ St. Gabriel the Archangel Church.
Graffis, Joseph T. '71 (L) [9] Louisville, KY St. Augustine Church.
Graffius, Peregrine *o.s.m.* '59 (ORG) [G] Orange, CA St. Vincent de Paul Society.
Graffius, Peregrine M. *o.s.m.* '59 (ORG) Fullerton, CA St. Philip Benizi Church; [H] Buena Park, CA Servite Fathers And Brothers.
Grafsky, George J. '71 (STP) Montgomery, MN Holy Redeemer Church; Shieldsville, MN St. Patrick Church.
Graham, Alfred '60 (MEM) [18] Memphis, TN St. Michael's Church.
Graham, Clifford *o.m.v.* '81 (BO) [B] Boston, MA Oblate Provincialate.
Graham, Edgar B. *s.j.* '54 (BAL) [C] Baltimore, MD Loyola College; [C] Baltimore, MD Loyola College; [M] Baltimore, MD Jesuit Community of Loyola College, Inc.
Graham, Msgr. George P. '52 (RVC) Levittown, NY St. Bernard Church.
Graham, Gilbert J. *o.p.* '49 (CHI) [N] River Forest, IL St. Thomas Aquinas Priory.
Graham, Gilbert J. *o.p.* '49 (DAL) [19] Dallas, TX St. Jude Chapel and Information Center Church.
Graham, J. David '91 (MEM) [2] (Bartlett), TN St. Ann Church; [M] Cordova, TN Serra Club.
Graham, James '85 (SPR) Absent on Leave.
Graham, James G. '66 (PIT) [22] Pittsburgh, PA St. Lawrence O'Toole Church.
Graham, Msgr. James J. '73 (PH) North Wales, PA St. Rose of Lima Church; [A] Wynnewood, PA Theological Seminary of St. Charles Borromeo, Overbrook.
Graham, James K. '93 (NTN) Fremont, CA St. Elias Church.
Graham, James P. *c.m.* '37 (STL) [P] Earth City, MO Congregation of the Mission Midwest Province (Vincentians); [P] Perryville, MO Congregation of The Mission.
Graham, John E. '44 (DAV) Retired.
Graham, John J. '90 (BO) [69] Boston, MA Sacred Heart Church.
Graham, Msgr. John K. *c.ss.r.* (NY) [23] New York, NY St. Cecilia Church; [E] New York, NY Cardinal Hayes High School.
Graham, Joseph B. '63 (PH) [74] Philadelphia, PA St. Jerome Church.
Graham, Michael *s.a.* '69 (NY) [Z] Garrison, NY Generalate of the Franciscan Friars of the Atonement-St. James Friary.
Graham, Michael J. *s.j.* '88 (CIN) [D] Cincinnati, OH Xavier University; [M] Cincinnati, OH Jesuit Community at Xavier Unversity.
Graham, Msgr. Neil J. '59 (NY) [50] New York, NY Holy Trinity Church.
Graham, Raymond *s.m.m.* '47 (RVC) [N] Eastport, NY Shrine of Our Lady of the Island.
Graham, Robert *s.m.* '50 (BO) [4] Haverhill, MA St. Joseph's Church.
Graham, Robert A. *s.j.* '41 (SJ) [M] Los Gatos, CA California Province of the Society of Jesus, Jesuit Provincial Office.
Graham, Thomas '60 (STL) [O] Mehlville, MO Nazareth Living Center.
Graham, Msgr. Thomas A. '62 (BRK) [228] Queens, NY St. Pius X Church.
Graham, Thomas D. '48 (PH) [102] Philadelphia, PA St. Matthew Church.
Graham, Walter F. *c.m.* '49 (MET) [H] Plainsboro, NJ Vincentian Residence.
Graham, William '65 (CAM) Millville, NJ St. John Bosco Church.
Graham, William *o.f.m.cap.* '72 (PIT) [N] Pittsburgh, PA St. Patrick Friary.
Graham, William C. '76 (DUL) On Duty Outside the Diocese.
Graham, William C. '76 (NY) [4] New York, NY All Saints Church.
Graham, William F. *s.j.* '42 (ALN) [A] Wernersville, PA Novitiate of St. Isaac Jogues.
Grailey, Joseph P. '80 (PH) [74] Philadelphia, PA St. Jerome Church.
Grajek, Lawrence F. '57 (SB) Big Bear Lake, CA St. Joseph Church.
Grala, Paul *s.o.l.t.* (CC) Robstown, TX St. Anthony Church; [H] Robstown, TX Society of Our Lady of the Most Holy Trinity.
Gralapp, Robert W. '64 (SC) Manilla, IA Sacred Heart Church.
Gralinski, Thomas J. '41 (HBG) [3] Lancaster, PA Assumption of the Blessed Virgin Mary Church.
Gramaje, Art *c.m.f.* (AUS) [M] San Marcos, TX Catholic Student Center.
Gramaje, Art *c.m.f.* '94 (AUS) San Marcos, TX St. John the Evangelist Church.
Gramajo, Rodolfo '93 (SR) Ukiah, CA St. Mary of the Angels Church.
Gramata, Raymond '70 (E) Erie, PA St. Vincent's Health Center; [G] Erie, PA Saint Vincent Health Center.
Grambow, Arnold J. '69 (MAR) Gladstone, MI All Saints Church.
Gramigna, Francis J. '64 (CAM) Wildwood Crest, NJ Assumption B.V.M. Church.
Gramkee, David '66 (ROC) Seneca Falls, NY St. Patrick Church.
Grammond, Maurice '50 (P) Retired.
Grams, Douglas L. '87 (NU) Tracy, MN St. Mary Church; Tracy, MN St. Mary Church; Walnut Grove, MN St. Paul Church.
Gramza, Ronald J. '73 (MIL) [1] Waukesha, WI St. Joseph's Church.
Gran, Thomas '50 (PBR) Retired.

Granadino, David '81 (LA) Sepulveda, CA Our Lady of Peace Church.
Granados, Carlos E. '88 (ARE) Hatillo, PR Our Lady of Mt. Carmel Church.
Granahan, Gerard '66 (ORL) Sabbatical.
Granata, Joseph P. '75 (RVC) Central Islip, NY St. John of God Church.
Granato, Anthony F. '56 (NEW) East Newark, NJ St. Anthony's Church.
Granato, Msgr. Joseph J. '55 (NEW) [22] Newark, NJ St. Lucy's Church.
Granato, Marius *o.c.s.o.* '64 (WOR) [N] Spencer, MA St. Joseph's Abbey.
Grancini, Steven M. *c.r.s.p.* '57 (SD) [15] San Diego, CA Our Lady of the Rosary Church.
Grande, Alphonsus *c.p.* '42 (HRT) [M] West Hartford, CT Holy Family Monastery/Retreat.
Grande, Bernardine *c.p.* '45 (BRK) [U] Jamaica, NY Immaculate Conception Monastery.
Grande, Kenneth J. '78 (BRK) [240] Queens, NY St. Sebastian Church.
Grandillo, James J. '54 (CLV) [1] Cleveland, OH Cathedral of St. John the Evangelist; [29] Cleveland, OH Holy Redeemer Church; Retired.
Grandpre, Louis E. '61 (DET) [3] Clinton Twp., MI St. Paul of Tarsus Church.
Graner, Thomas '94 (FAR) Rolette, ND Sacred Heart Church.
Graney, William F. '71 (WIL) Fairfax, DE St. Mary Magdalen Church.
Granfield, David *o.s.b.* '52 (WDC) [M] Washington, DC St. Anselm's Abbey.
Granfield, Patrick *o.s.b.* '57 (WDC) [C] Washington, DC Catholic University of America, The; [M] Washington, DC St. Anselm's Abbey.
Grange, John '66 (NY) [152] Bronx, NY St. Jerome's Church.
Granich, Msgr. Bernard E. '53 (STL) [40] St. Louis, MO St. John the Apostle and Evangelist Church.
Grankowski, Zbigniew W. '83 (DET) [2] Dearborn, MI St. Barbara Church.
Granstrand, Charles P. '66 (NEW) Park Ridge, NJ Our Lady of Mercy Church.
Grant, Douglas '80 (PRO) North Kingstown, RI St. Francis De Sales Church.
Grant, Frederick A. (BO) Retired.
Grant, James '56 (SPK) Retired.
Grant, James A. '66 (PH) Warrington, PA St. Joseph Church.
Grant, Jeffery A. '82 (SFD) Casey, IL St. Charles Borromeo Church; Greenup, IL Christ the King Church; Marshall, IL St. Mary Church.
Grant, Matthew M. '65 (BRK) Absent on Sick Leave.
Grant, Robert '84 (DM) On Duty Outside the Diocese.
Grant, Robert H. '49 (B) Retired.
Grant, Robert L. '80 (DAV) [B] Davenport, IA St. Ambrose University.
Grant, William David '86 (LIN) Fairbury, NE St. Michael's Church.
Grant, Zachary *o.f.m.cap.* '56 (SPR) [L] Springfield, MA St. Francis of Assisi Chapel and Catholic Information Center.
Grantz, Leon *c.p.* '46 (CHI) [J] Chicago, IL Our Lady of the Resurrection Medical Center; [N] Chicago, IL Immaculate Conception Monastery.
Granville, Msgr. William A. '43 (BO) Retired.
Granzotto, Peter *s.d.b.* '57 (NY) [2] Port Chester, NY Corpus Christi Church.
Grappolli, Frank *s.x.* (PAT) [M] Wayne, NJ Xaverian Missionary Fathers.
Grasha, Donald F. '84 (LA) Ventura, CA Sacred Heart Church.
Grasher, Albert, Jr. '86 (SPK) Chewelah, WA St. Mary of the Rosary Church; Springdale, WA Sacred Heart Church; Valley, WA Holy Ghost Church.
Grasing, John A. '88 (WIL) Newark, DE St. John the Baptist-Holy Angels Church.
Graskow, Paul '43 (STF) Retired.
Grass, Aloysius P. *c.m.* '51 (PH) [Z] Philadelphia, PA Congregation of the Mission; [Z] Philadelphia, PA Congregation of the Mission.
Grass, Msgr. Don C. '61 (GRY) Crown Point, IN St. Mary Church.
Grass, Kenneth E. *c.m.* '56 (STL) [P] Perryville, MO Congregation of The Mission.
Grasselli, Renato '94 (NEW) [A] Kearny, NJ Redemptoris Mater.
Grassi, Dominic J. '73 (CHI) [109] Chicago, IL St. Josaphat Church.
Grassl, Joseph A. '50 (LC) Knowlton, WI St. Francis Xavier Church; Peplin, WI St. John the Baptist Church.
Grasso, Aldo *o.s.j.* '44 (MRY) [G] Santa Cruz, CA Oblates of St. Joseph Provincial House and Shrine.
Grasso, Anthony R. *c.s.c.* '78 (SCR) [C] Wilkes-Barre, PA Kings College.
Grasso, Philip A. '43 (MAD) Retired.
Grasso, Raymond '57 (JOL) [5] Naperville, IL St. Thomas the Apostle Church; Naperville, IL Edward Hospital.
Grasso, Richard '63 (PAT) On Duty Outside the Diocese.
Grasso, Richard E. '63 (ORL) Retired.
Grathwohl, John M. '55 (KAL) Retired.
Gratkowski, Eugene W. '67 (CHI) [69] Chicago, IL St. Genevieve Church.
Gratsch, Edward J. '48 (CIN) Retired; [B] Cincinnati, OH Mt. St. Mary's Seminary of the West.
Grattan, Bernard V. (ALT) [16] Johnstown, PA Visitation of the B.V.M. Church; [D] Johnstown, PA Good Samaritan Medical Center.
Grattaroti, Robert A. '62 (WOR) Charlton City, MA St. Joseph's Church.
Gratto, Stephen H. '73 (OG) Morrisonville, NY St. Alexander Church; [3] Plattsburgh, NY St. Joseph Church.
Grauel, Frank B. '84 (L) [34] Louisville, KY Holy Spirit Church; Retired.
Grauls, Paul *s.d.b.* '62 (NY) [117] New York, NY St. Thomas the Apostle Church.
Gravel, Claude *o.ss.t.* '81 (BAL) [M] Baltimore, MD Holy Trinity Monastery.
Gravel, Claude J. *o.ss.t.* '81 (WDC) [M] Hyattsville, MD St. John de Matha Monastery, Order of Most Holy Trinity.
Graven, John P. '57 (FAR) On Duty Outside the Diocese.
Graven, John P. '57 (ORG) Stanton, CA St. Polycarp Church.
Graven, Thomas J. '68 (STU) Fairpoint, OH St. Joseph Church; Maynard, OH St. Stanislaus Church.
Graves, Alfred C. '67 (SPR) Absent on Leave.
Graves, C. Edwin, III '92 (LR) Helena, AR St. Mary's Church.
Graves, Joseph A. '56 (PEO) Retired.
Graves, Robert *c.s.sp.* '50 (SJN) [E] Dorado, PR Santuario del Espiritu Santo.
Graves, W. Robert *c.s.sp.* '50 (VEN) [G] Sarasota, FL Congregation of the Holy Ghost.
Gray, Brian M. '86 (BGP) [5] Stamford, CT St. Gabriel Church; Stamford, CT Stamford Hospital.
Gray, Daniel J. '76 (PRO) [3] Warwick, RI St. Clement's Church.
Gray, Edward J. *c.ss.r.* '58 (ORL) [F] New Smyrna Beach, FL Redemptorist Fathers of the Vice Province of Richmond.
Gray, Francis Jerome '49 (CHI) [N] Chicago, IL St. Peter's Friary.
Gray, Howard *s.j.* '61 (BO) [W] Chestnut Hill, MA The Jesuit Community at Boston College.
Gray, Howard J. *s.j.* (DET) [K] Detroit, MI Jesuit Provincial Office-Detroit Province of the Society of Jesus.
Gray, John F. '86 (PT) [6] Pensacola, FL St. Anne Church.
Gray, John H. *s.j.* '55 (BAL) [C] Baltimore, MD Loyola College; [C] Baltimore, MD Loyola College; [M] Baltimore, MD Jesuit Community of Loyola College, Inc.
Gray, John W. '58 (PRO) [11] Providence, RI St. Charles Borromeo Church.
Gray, Jude J. *o.s.b.* '68 (MAN) [K] Manchester, NH St. Anselm Abbey.
Gray, Kevin J. '84 (HRT) [14] Waterbury, CT St. Margaret's Church.
Gray, Paul '85 (DAL) [2] Dallas, TX All Saints Church.
Gray, Msgr. Philip A. '60 (SCR) [5] Scranton, PA St. Francis Church.
Gray, Robert '88 (SJ) [5] San Jose, CA Five Wounds Portuguese National Church; Special Assignment.
Gray, Robert B. '57 (L) [23] Louisville, KY St. Elizabeth of Hungary Church; [71] Louisville, KY St. Therese Church.
Gray, Ronald *o.carm.* '43 (NEW) Leonia, NJ St. John the Evangelist's Church.
Gray, Sherman W., Jr. '70 (BGP) [6] Stamford, CT Holy Name of Jesus Church.
Gray, Teodoro '49 (SJN) [59] San Juan, PR Stella Maris Church.
Gray, Timothy *s.c.j.* '78 (GAL) [68] Houston, TX St. Philip of Jesus Church.
Graystone, Geoffrey *s.m.* '46 (NO) [A] New Orleans, LA Notre Dame Seminary Graduate School of Theology.
Graziadio, Domenick T. '66 (RVC) Glen Cove, NY St. Rocco Church.
Graziani, Joseph A. '45 (HRT) Retired.
Graziano, Damien '67 (JOL) Oakbrook Terrace, IL Ascension of Our Lord Church.
Graziano, Msgr. Domenick T. '66 (RVC) Glen Cove, NY St. Rocco Church.
Graziano, Gerard J. '61 (NEW) Northvale, NJ St. Anthony's Church.
Graziano, Peter N. '63 (FR) Attleboro Falls, MA St. Mark's Church.
Grealish, James '69 (RIC) Radford, VA St. Jude Church.
Greaney, Francis M. (BO) Retired.
Greaney, John F. '55 (HBG) Marysville, PA Our Lady of Good Counsel Church.
Greaney, Thomas M. *o.s.m.* '70 (CHI) [N] Chicago, IL Service Friars - Eastern Province.
Greany, Brendan *c.ss.r.* '63 (WIL) Chester, Kent Island, MD St. Christopher Church.
Greatorex, Robert W. '57 (LC) [E] Stevens Point, WI St. Michael's Hospital and School for Med. Technology; [J] Stevens Point, WI St. Joseph Congregational Home.
Greaves, Gerald F. '74 (NEW) Edgewater, NJ Holy Rosary Church.
Greaves, John G. '58 (PRO) [1] Cranston, RI St. Ann Church.
Greb, Michael *o.f.m.cap.* (CLV) [A] Wickliffe, OH Borromeo Seminary.
Grebasch, Richard L. '58 (MIL) Lake Five, WI St. Columba Church; Monches, WI St. John's Church.
Grecco, Robert J. '93 (PIT) Aliquippa, PA St. Titus Church.
Grech, Joseph '52 (MRY) Santa Margarita, CA Holy Angels Church.
Greco, Anthony F. '79 (WIL) Georgetown, DE St. Michael the Archangel Church.
Greco, Evan J. *o.f.m.* '58 (NY) Yulan, NY St. Anthony of Padua Church.
Greco, Ray *o.s.b.* '63 (PHX) Litchfield Park, AZ St. Thomas Aquinas Church.
Greco, Raymond *o.s.b.* '63 (MRY) [G] San Luis Obispo, CA Monastery of the Risen Christ.
Greco, Robert *o.carm.* '55 (NY) [97] New York, NY Our Lady of the Scapular/St. Stephen Church; Manhattan, NY Bellevue Hospital.
Greeley, Andrew M. '54 (CHI) Other Assignments.
Greeley, Msgr. Joseph F. '74 (LA) South El Monte, CA Epiphany Church; Wilmington, CA Holy Family Church.
Green, Austin E. *o.p.* '53 (DAL) [M] Irving, TX Dominican Priory of St. Albert the Great.
Green, Bernard *s.d.s.* '73 (GLP) Cibecue, AZ St. Catherine Church.
Green, David E. '88 (PRO) [10] Warwick, RI St. Timothy's Church.
Green, Francis J. *o.s.f.s.* '48 (PH) [Z] Philadelphia, PA Father Judge Faculty House.
Green, Msgr. Gerard A. '40 (NY) Retired.
Green, Msgr. Gerard L. '56 (BUF) Hamburg, NY SS. Peter and Paul Church.
Green, Gregory A. *c.s.c.* '62 (FTW) [B] Notre Dame, IN University of Notre Dame Du Lac; [J] Notre Dame, IN Holy Cross Community, Corby Hall, University of Notre Dame.
Green, Msgr. James P. '76 (PH) On Duty Outside the Archdiocese.
Green, Lacy '51 (JKS) Retired.
Green, Michael R. *o.s.b.* '70 (DET) [B] Oxford, MI St. Benedict Monastery.
Green, Romuald *o.f.m.* '55 (BUF) [O] St. Bonaventure, NY St. Bonaventure Friary.
Green, Ronald (NY) Manhattan, NY Terence Cardinal Cooke Health Care Center.
Green, Ronald '96 (MRY) Hollister, CA Sacred Heart Church; Tres Pinos, CA Immaculate Conception Church.
Green, Ronald L. *m.m.* '85 (NY) [Z] Maryknoll, NY Maryknoll Fathers and Brothers.
Green, Thomas J. '63 (BGP) On Duty Outside the Diocese.
Green, Thomas J. '63 (WDC) [C] Washington, DC Catholic University of America, The.
Green, Thomas P. *s.j.* '61 (NY) [5] New York, NY St. Aloysius Church.
Green, William H. '63 (SUP) Cable, WI St. Ann Church; Hayward, WI St. Joseph's Church.
Green, William L. *c.m.* '55 (BUF) [C] Niagara University, NY Niagara University; [O] Niagara University, NY Vincentian Community at Niagara University.
Greenburg, Alcuin E. '55 (GAL) [K] Houston, TX The Catholic Chaplain Corps; [K] Houston, TX The Catholic Chaplain Corps.
Greene, Daniel P. '58 (YAK) Military Chaplains.
Greene, Edward *o.f.m.* '45 (NY) Jeffersonville, NY St. George Church; Youngsville, NY St. Francis of Assisi Church.
Greene, Frank '48 (PH) [D] Philadelphia, PA Father Judge High School for Boys.
Greene, Gordon L. '94 (KAL) Byron Center, MI St. Mary's Visitation Church.
Greene, J. Gerard *m.m.* '43 (NY) [Z] Maryknoll, NY Maryknoll Fathers and Brothers.
Greene, James F. '61 (FR) [4] New Bedford, MA Our Lady of Fatima Church.
Greene, John C. '85 (GAY) [1] Alpena, MI St. Anne Church.
Greene, John L. '76 (SFR) [49] San Francisco, CA St. Stephen Church; San Francisco, CA San Francisco Fire Department.
Greene, Michael *c.p.* '82 (ATL) [11] Atlanta, GA St. Paul of the Cross Church.
Greene, Michael M. '79 (BRK) [24] Brooklyn, NY St. Brigid Church.
Greene, Richard R. '65 (LAF) [5] Lafayette, LA Our Lady of Fatima Church.
Greene, Robert W. *m.m.* '37 (CIN) [M] Cincinnati, OH The Catholic Foreign Mission Society of America, Inc.

Greene, Thomas S. '55 (SPR) Retired; [H] Springfield, MA St. Michael's Residence.
Greene, Msgr. William L. '50 (BR) St. Francisville, LA Our Lady of Mount Carmel Church.
Greenfield, James J. *o.s.f.s.* '90 (WDC) [S] Washington, DC Archdiocesan Campus Ministry.
Greenhalgh, Donald C. '84 (ARL) Fairfax, VA St. Mary of Sorrows Church.
Greenlaw, Martin F. '68 (SFR) Retired.
Greenleaf, Daniel P. '95 (PRT) Bangor, ME St. John's Church.
Greenough, Patrick *o.f.m.conv.* (CHI) [N] Libertyville, IL Marytown, Our Lady of Fatima Friary; [Q] Libertyville, IL Marytown, U.S. National Center of the Militia of the Immaculata Movement.
Greenslade, Robert J. '54 (DEN) [11] Denver, CO Holy Family Church; [34] Denver, CO St. Mary Magdalene's Church.
Greenwald, Alfred F. '58 (GAL) Retired.
Greenway, George G. '87 (SPR) Special Assignment.
Greenwell, Charles C. '82 (SAN) [2] San Angelo, TX Holy Angels Church.
Greenwell, Joseph *c.ss.r.* '48 (LAF) Crowley, LA Immaculate Heart of Mary Church.
Greenwell, Michael A. *o.carm.* '79 (L) [B] Louisville, KY St. Francis DeSales High School.
Greenwood, Kevin L. '90 (STU) On Duty Outside the Diocese.
Greer, G. Michael '81 (COV) Erlanger, KY St. Barbara Church.
Greer, Michael '75 (MIA) [6] Miami, FL Good Shepherd Church.
Greerough, Patrick W. *o.f.m.conv.* (CHI) [N] Chicago, IL Franciscan House of Studies.
Grega, Bernard F. '62 (ALT) Conemaugh, PA Assumption of B.V.M. Church.
Gregoire, Jocelyn *c.s.sp.* (PIT) [Q] Slippery Rock, PA Office for Campus Ministry.
Gregoire, Paul L. '55 (MAN) Dover, NH St. Charles Church.
Gregoire, Wilfrid G. '56 (PRO) Westerly, RI Immaculate Conception Church.
Gregorek, Joseph C. '65 (E) [B] Erie, PA Gannon University.
Gregorek, Stan M. '66 (PIT) Natrona Heights, PA Our Lady of the Most Blessed Sacrament Church.
Gregori, Anthony F. '53 (GF) Retired.
Gregori, Emidio O. '58 (BGP) [2] Stratford, CT St. James Church.
Gregorie, Jocelyn *c.s.sp.* '86 (PIT) [B] Pittsburgh, PA Duquesne University of the Holy Ghost.
Gregorio, Robert J. '68 (CAM) Pine Hill, NJ St. Edward's Church.
Gregory, Joseph F. *s.j.* '47 (FAR) Veseleyville, ND St. Luke Church; Warsaw, ND St. Stanislaus Church; Retired.
Gregory, Joseph F. *s.j.* '47 (MIL) [P] Milwaukee, WI Jesuit Provincial Office, Wisconsin Province.
Gregory, Kenneth '73 (ALB) Grafton, NY St. John Francis Regis Church; Albany, NY Albany Medical Center Hospital; Special Assignment.
Gregory, Peter A. '73 (SPR) [5] Pittsfield, MA St. Charles Church.
Gregory, Robert S. '69 (KC) [10] Kansas City, MO St. Elizabeth's Church.
Gregovich, Lawrence E. '72 (SPC) On Duty Outside the Diocese.
Grehl, Paul F. *o.s.f.s.* '60 (LAN) [B] Jackson, MI Lumen Christi High School.
Greig, Msgr. Harry D., II '76 (LKC) [1] Lake Charles, LA Immaculate Conception Cathedral.
Greig, Msgr. Kenneth R. '67 (BEA) Groves, TX St. Peter the Apostle Church.
Grein, Blane *o.f.m.* '62 (GLP) Chinle, AZ Our Lady of Fatima, Indian Mission Church; [A] Chinle, AZ Native American Lay Ministry and Diaconate Program.
Greinader, Msgr. Linford F. '43 (ALT) Retired.
Greiner, James A. '63 (OKL) Mustang, OK Church of the Holy Spirit.
Greiner, Kenneth A. '53 (ALT) Retired.
Greiner, Lawrence (SB) Retired.
Greiner, Lawrence '37 (SAG) Retired.
Greiner, Robert M. '93 (BAK) Nyssa, OR St. Bridget of Kildare Church.
Greisen, Thomas '82 (KC) [A] Conception, MO Conception Seminary College.
Greisen, Thomas A. '82 (OM) On Duty Outside the Archdiocese.
Greiten, Gregory J. '92 (MIL) Hales Corners, WI St. Mary's Church.
Grek, Richard *c.r.* '67 (RCK) [A] Woodstock, IL Resurrection Center Retreat House.
Greka, David '62 (AMA) On Duty Outside the Diocese.
Grelak, Andrezj (BO) [3] Chelsea, MA St. Stanislaus Church.
Grell, Loras K. '96 (LIN) [12] Lincoln, NE St. Thomas Aquinas Church; [I] Lincoln, NE University of Nebraska, Newman Club.
Grellinger, R. Michael '62 (MIL) Pewaukee, WI SS. Peter and Paul Church.
Grembla, Joseph P. '57 (CHI) [33] Chicago, IL St. Bruno Church.
Grembocki, Joseph L. '71 (ALN) [1] McAdoo, PA St. Kunegunda Church.
Gremillion, Msgr. John E. '41 (LAF) Retired.
Gremillion, Msgr. John E. '41 (ORL) Retired.
Gremmels, John '91 (FWT) Keller, TX St. Elizabeth Ann Seton Church.
Grenache, Claude L. *a.a.* '66 (WOR) [B] Worcester, MA Assumption College; [Q] Worcester, MA Campus Ministry.
Grendler, Albert O. '59 (SC) Spirit Lake, IA St. Mary's Church.
Grenham, John Patrick '80 (NO) Florissant, LA San Pedro Pescador Church.
Grenham, Thomas *s.p.s.* (BO) [18] Boston, MA St. Cecilia Church.
Grennan, James P. '51 (SAL) Logan, KS St. John's Church; Stockton, KS St. Thomas Church.
Grennan, Lawrence E. '66 (SAL) Manhattan, KS Seven Dolors Church.
Grennan, Thomas J. '48 (NO) On Duty Outside the Archdiocese; Retired.
Grenon, Paul R. '78 (PRO) [1] Warwick, RI St. Benedict Church
Gres-Gayer, Jacques '69 (WDC) [C] Washington, DC Catholic University of America, The.
Greskiewicz, Joseph A. '69 (SCR) Plains, PA SS. Peter and Paul Church.
Greskoviak, Neri *o.f.m.* '63 (PEO) Benson, IL St. John Church; Roanoke, IL St. Joseph Church.
Greskowiak, Stephen '89 (VNN) Anchorage, AK Saint Nicholas of Myra Church.
Gresock, Thomas G. '85 (BUF) Absent on Leave.
Gress, Armand E. *o.s.b.* '37 (CLV) [P] Cleveland, OH Benedictine Order of Cleveland.
Gress, Warren (RVC) Absent on Leave.
Gretchko, A. Edward (PBR) Ashtabula, OH St. Nicholas Church.
Gretchko, Andrew Edward '72 (Y) Conneaut, OH St. Frances Cabrini Church.
Gretz, James R., Jr. '94 (PIT) Glenshaw, PA St. Bonaventure Church.
Grevatch, William N. '64 (LC) [6] Wausau, WI St. Michael Church.
Grevencamp, Raymond *c.pp.s.* '49 (CIN) [B] Carthagena, OH St. Charles.
Greving, Louis H. '46 (SC) Retired.
Grewe, Michael W. '79 (OM) [21] Omaha, NE St. James Church.
Grey, Michael *c.s.sp.* '79 (PIT) [B] Pittsburgh, PA Duquesne University of the Holy Ghost.
Grey, Thomas J. *s.j.* '51 (BO) [W] Chestnut Hill, MA The Jesuit Community at Boston College.
Greytak, William '56 (HEL) Boulder, MT St. Catherine Church; Boulder, MT Boulder River School and Hospital; [B] Helena, MT Carroll College.
Grib, Philip J. *s.j.* '72 (CHI) [45] Chicago, IL St. Constance Church.
Grib, Phillip J. *s.j.* '72 (CHI) [D] Chicago, IL St. Ignatius Jesuit Community.
Grib, Robert I. *s.j.* '77 (IND) [D] Indianapolis, IN Brebeuf Jesuit Preparatory School, Inc.
Gribbin, Msgr. Robert C. '47 (HBG) Hanover, PA St. Joseph Church.
Gribble, G. Michael '81 (COL) Granville, OH St. Edward the Confessor Church.
Gribble, Richard E. *c.s.c.* '89 (FR) [B] North Easton, MA Stonehill College.
Gribbon, John J. '50 (BRK) [149] Queens, NY St. Anastasia Church.
Gribbon, Joseph A. *c.ss.r.* '56 (RIC) [O] Hampton, VA Holy Family Retreat House.
Gribbon, Michael C. '81 (BRK) [10] Brooklyn, NY St. Anselm's Church.
Gribik, John '89 (SJP) Wheeling, WV St. Mary Church.
Grice, Edward M. '80 (NO) Arabi, LA St. Louise De Marillac Church.
Grieco, Charles '68 (PAT) Retired; [P] Chester, NJ Nazareth Village.
Grieco, Michael '83 (LA) [97] Los Angeles, CA Transfiguration Church.
Grieco, Msgr. Nicholas V. '59 (BGP) Weston, CT St. Francis of Assisi Church.
Grieman, Gerald G. '79 (STP) [21] St. Paul, MN St. Gregory the Great Church; [24] St. Paul, MN St. Leo Church; [34] St. Paul, MN Highland Catholic Community Church.
Griener, George E. *s.j.* '73 (OAK) [A] Berkeley, CA The Jesuit School of Theology at Berkeley; [A] Berkeley, CA The Jesuit School of Theology at Berkeley; [N] Berkeley, CA Jesuit Community at Jesuit School of Theology at Berkeley.
Gries, Andrew *o.c.s.o.* '59 (ARL) [J] Berryville, VA Cistercian Abbey of Our Lady of the Holy Cross.
Gries, Eugene E. *o.praem.* '68 (GB) [A] De Pere, WI St. Norbert Abbey; [I] De Pere, WI St. Norbert Abbey; [O] De Pere, WI NORBERT & CO.
Griesbach, John '76 (FRS) Kerman, CA St. Patrick Church; Tranquillity, CA St. Paul Church.
Griese, Celsus *o.f.m.* '55 (CIN) [M] Cincinnati, OH St. Francis Center.
Griese, Roger E. '42 (CIN) Retired.
Griesedieck, Msgr. Edmund O. '65 (STL) Glencoe, MO St. Alban Roe Church.
Griesemer, Edward *s.c.j.* '57 (MIL) [7] Milwaukee, WI St. Anthony's Church; [P] Hales Corners, WI Sacred Heart Monastery.
Griffey, Brendan M. '74 (JC) Missionary Assignment in Peru.
Griffin, Barry *s.d.s.* '64 (MIL) [P] Milwaukee, WI Salvatorian Provincial Residence.
Griffin, Bertram F. '57 (P) [24] Portland, OR Church of St. Michael, the Archangel.
Griffin, Charles R. '56 (COL) Chillicothe, OH St. Peter Church; Chillicothe, OH Chillicothe Correctional Institution; Chillicothe, OH Ross Correctional Institution and Honor Camp.
Griffin, Msgr. Charles T. '58 (BUF) [32] Buffalo, NY Holy Spirit Church.
Griffin, David G. '66 (BUF) [6] Niagara Falls, NY St. Leo Church.
Griffin, David R. *o.s.b.* '76 (GBG) [H] Latrobe, PA Saint Vincent Archabbey.
Griffin, Devin *o.carm.* '64 (JOL) [J] Darien, IL Carmelite Fathers Provincial Office.
Griffin, Edward J. *o.s.a.* '49 (PH) [142] Philadelphia, PA St. Rita of Cascia Church.
Griffin, Francis J. *s.j.* '39 (BO) [W] Weston, MA Campion Center.
Griffin, George J. '73 (ARL) [2] Alexandria, VA Good Shepherd Church.
Griffin, James C. '82 (RIC) Chesapeake, VA St. Therese of Lisieux Church.
Griffin, James P. '49 (NY) [8] Yonkers, NY St. Eugene Church.
Griffin, John '72 (SR) Rohnert Park, CA St. Elizabeth Seton Church.
Griffin, John A. '38 (PH) [4] Bensalem, PA Our Lady of Fatima Church; Retired.
Griffin, John Cullen '77 (MRY) Corralitos, CA Holy Eucharist Church.
Griffin, Joseph F. '47 (DUB) Retired.
Griffin, Joseph J. *o.s.f.s.* '56 (PH) [Z] Philadelphia, PA Oblates of St. Francis De Sales.
Griffin, Joseph M. '82 (SAG) Chesaning, MI Our Lady of Perpetual Help Church.
Griffin, Joseph T. *c.s.p.* '46 (BO) [P] Boston, MA Paulist Center; [W] Boston, MA Paulist Fathers Residence.
Griffin, Joseph T. *c.s.p.* '46 (NY) [Z] Scarsdale, NY Paulist Fathers Generalate.
Griffin, Michael *o.c.d.* '50 (MIL) [P] Holy Hill, WI Discalced Carmelite Monastery.
Griffin, Michael '90 (SFS) White, SD St. Paul Attended Church; [H] Brookings, SD Pius XII Student Center.
Griffin, Michael J. '49 (MAN) Hampton, NH Our Lady of the Miraculous Medal Church.
Griffin, Noel '64 (LA) Sick Leave.
Griffin, Msgr. Patrick '45 (COL) Retired.
Griffin, Patrick E. '67 (STP) [33] Minneapolis, MN St. Stephen Church.
Griffin, Patrick J. *c.m.* '79 (PH) [Z] Philadelphia, PA Congregation of the Mission.
Griffin, Richard J. '42 (PH) [4] Bensalem, PA Our Lady of Fatima Church; Retired.
Griffin, Robert *s.j.* '61 (LA) [K] Duarte, CA Santa Teresita Hospital.
Griffin, Robert E. *s.j.* '61 (LA) [R] Los Angeles, CA Columbiere House.
Griffin, Robert E. *s.j.* '61 (SJ) [M] Los Gatos, CA Sacred Heart Jesuit Center.
Griffin, Robert F. '49 (MAN) Retired.
Griffin, Thomas *o.s.a.* (CHI) [J] Chicago, IL Holy Cross Hospital.
Griffin, Thomas A. *s.j.* '58 (MIA) [5] Miami, FL Gesu Church.
Griffith, Edwin '64 (LSC) Retired.
Griffith, Gavin *o.f.m.* '65 (STL) [T] Dittmer, MO Il Ritiro-The Little Retreat.
Griffith, John O. '39 (PIT) Retired.
Griffith, Sidney H. *s.t.* '65 (WDC) [C] Washington, DC Catholic University of America, The; [M] Riverdale, MD Holy Spirit Missionary Cenacle.
Griffith, Thomas *s.v.d.* (CHI) [B] Techny, IL Divine Word Residence; [N] Techny, IL Society of the Divine Word, Provincial Headquarter-Chicago Prov.; [N] Techny, IL Society of the Divine Word, Provincial Headquarter-Chicago Prov.; [X] Techny, IL Blessed Arnold Religious Charitable Trust.
Griffiths, James '56 (SJP) Retired.
Griffiths, John M. '76 (CHI) Graduate Studies.
Griffiths, Thomas *c.p.* '57 (BRK) [U] Jamaica, NY Immaculate Conception Monastery.
Grifone, Fabian *o.f.m.* '54 (NY) [79] New York, NY Most Precious Blood Church.
Grigassy, Daniel P. *o.f.m.* '77 (WDC) [B] Silver Spring, MD Holy Name College.
Grigus, Paschal *o.f.m.* '50 (CHI) [111] Chicago, IL St. Joseph Church.
Grile, Harry A. *c.ss.r.* '68 (CHI) [N] Chicago, IL Redemptorist Theology Residence.
Grile, Patrick *c.ss.r.* '73 (GR) [3] Grand Rapids, MI St.

Alphonsus Church.
Grill, Msgr. Philip L. '43 (LA) [5] Santa Barbara, CA San Roque Church; Retired.
Grilliot, Thomas J. '76 (CIN) West Milton, OH Transfiguration Church.
Grillo, Anthony '38 (BRK) Retired.
Grimaldi, Joseph R. '83 (BRK) [212] Queens, NY Our Lady of Hope Church.
Grimalia, Msgr. Vincent J. '68 (SCR) [1] Plymouth, PA Nativity of the Blessed Virgin Mary Church.
Grimes, Donald J. *c.s.c.* '73 (SCR) [C] Wilkes-Barre, PA Kings College; [M] Wilkes-Barre, PA Moreau House.
Grimes, Edwin T. *o.s.a.* '36 (PH) Havertown, PA St. Denis Church.
Grimes, J. Colby '78 (COL) [21] Columbus, OH Holy Spirit Church.
Grimes, John J. (BO) Society of St. James the Apostle.
Grimes, Jordan K. *c.p.* '49 (ORL) [F] Orlando, FL Bethany House of Beutel.
Grimes, Msgr. Kenneth F. '57 (COL) [34] Columbus, OH Our Lady of Peace Church.
Grimes, Mark E. '64 (BGP) New Fairfield, CT St. Edward the Confessor Church.
Grimes, Price D., Jr. (OKL) Absent on Sick Leave.
Grimes, Raymond P. '55 (PBL) Lamar, CO St. Francis De Sales-Our Lady of Guadalupe Church.
Grimes, Robert R. *s.j.* '84 (NY) [Z] New York, NY Jesuit Community at Fordham University.
Grimm, Robert B. *s.j.* '76 (P) [L] Portland, OR Jesuit Provincial Office (Oregon Prov.).
Grimme, D. Timothy '77 (ALT) Bellefonte, PA St. John the Evangelist's Church.
Grimme, Richard '40 (BUF) [M] Silver Creek, NY St. Columbans on the Lake, Home for the Aged.
Grimmer, James A. '54 (BUF) East Eden, NY St. Mary Church.
Grimmond, Christopher J. '87 (OM) Fordyce, NE St. John the Baptist Church; Menominee, NE St. Boniface Church.
Grinena, Agustin '46 (PCE) Penuelas, PR Sacred Heart Church.
Griner, William S. '61 (L) Jeffersontown, KY St. Michael Church.
Grinis, Bruno B. '40 (CHI) [169] Chicago, IL SS. Peter and Paul Church; Retired.
Grinis, Julian G. '39 (CHI) [1] Lemont, IL St. Alphonsus Church; Retired.
Grinko, Frank *o.f.m.cap.* '81 (SAL) [C] Victoria, KS St. John's Rest Home.
Grinko, Frank X. *o.f.m.cap.* '81 (SAL) Victoria, KS St. Fidelis Church; Vincent, KS St. Boniface Church; [D] Victoria, KS St. Fidelis Friary.
Grinnell, Horace H. '74 (ARL) Falls Church, VA St. Anthony's Church.
Grinsell, John *s.d.b.* '71 (NEW) [C] Ramsey, NJ Don Bosco Preparatory High School for Boys.
Grippe, Louis A. '69 (SCR) Harveys Lake, PA Our Lady of Victory Church.
Grippo, Robert F. '72 (NY) [190] Bronx, NY St. Theresa of the Infant Jesus Church.
Gripshover, Ronald J., Jr. '96 (ARL) Lake Ridge, VA St. Elizabeth Seton Church.
Grisaitis, Joseph N. '64 (BRK) [151] Queens, NY St. Ann's Church.
Grise, J. Clifford '45 (BGP) Retired.
Grismer, Raymond J. '33 (CLV) Sheffield, OH St. Teresa Church; Retired.
Griswold, Edward J. '73 (TR) Colts Neck, NJ St. Mary Church.
Grix, Robert *o.f.m.cap.* (NY) [Z] New York, NY Immaculate Conception Friary.
Grix, Robert *o.f.m.cap.* '78 (NEW) [N] Union City, NJ Capuchin Friars - Prov. Stigmata of St. Francis.
Grizzelle-Reid, Paul *s.c.j.* '72 (MIL) [B] Hales Corners, WI Sacred Heart School of Theology.
Groarke, Francis P. '73 (PH) [41] Philadelphia, PA St. Edmond Church.
Grob, Jeffrey '92 (CHI) Winnetka, IL SS. Faith, Hope and Charity Church.
Groben, Joseph *m.s.f.* '36 (STL) [O] St. Louis, MO Little Sisters of the Poor, Home for the Aged.
Grochowski, Bernard (LAV) Military Chaplains.
Grochowski, Bernard J. '63 (WOR) Military Chaplains.
Grodavent, Msgr. Thomas J. '45 (WDC) Retired.
Grodecki, Henry W. *c.m.* '75 (DEN) [12] Denver, CO Holy Ghost Church.
Groden, Michael F. '65 (BO) [18] Boston, MA St. Cecilia Church.
Grodnicki, Robert *o.s.a.* '88 (NY) [168] Bronx, NY St. Nicholas of Tolentine Church.
Groeller, David J. '92 (IND) Jeffersonville, IN Sacred Heart Church.
Groenewold, Robert E. *s.j.* '62 (NY) [BB] Staten Island, NY Mount Manresa Jesuit Retreat House.
Groenewold, Thomas W. '87 (RVC) [1] Rockville Centre, NY St. Agnes Cathedral.
Groesch, Edward '51 (SFD) Greenfield, IL St. Michael Church; Hagaman, IL St. Catherine Church.
Groeschel, Benedict J. *c.f.r.* '59 (BRK) [O] Brooklyn, NY St. Francis Home for Boys.
Groeschel, Benedict J. *c.f.r.* '59 (NEW) [K] Hoboken, NJ Good Counsel, Inc. (St. Francis Home); [K] Hoboken, NJ Good Counsel, Inc. (St. Francis Home).
Groeschel, Benedict J. *c.f.r.* '59 (NY) [A] Yonkers, NY St. Joseph's Seminary; [D] New York, NY Department of Education; [K] Staten Island, NY Good Counsel; [Z] New York, NY St. Crispin Friary; [BB] Larchmont, NY Trinity Retreat.
Groescher, Larry *o.f.m.cap.* (DET) [K] Detroit, MI St. Mary's Friary.
Grogan, Brendan '61 (MIA) Absent on Leave.
Grogan, Francis E. *c.s.c.* '55 (FR) South Easton, MA Holy Cross Church.
Grogan, Gerald P. '60 (VEN) Avon Park, FL Our Lady of Grace Church.
Grogan, James Clyde '68 (BEL) [4] East St. Louis, IL St. Patrick Church.
Grogan, James M. '95 (STP) New Brighton, MN St. John the Baptist Church.
Grogan, Patrick '40 (ORL) Rockledge, FL St. Mary's Church; Retired.
Grogan, Richard P. '37 (IND) Retired.
Grogan, Thomas A. '68 (NEW) Scotch Plains, NJ St. Bartholomew Church.
Grogan, Todd '90 (CIN) Englewood, OH St. Paul's Church.
Grogan, Vincent B. *o.f.m.* '63 (NY) [35] New York, NY St. Francis of Assisi Church.
Grogan, William E. '83 (PH) Kimberton, PA St. Basil the Great Church.
Grogan, William P. '76 (CHI) [100] Chicago, IL St. Jerome Church.
Groh, Christopher '79 (JOL) [16] Joliet, IL St. Mary Nativity Church.
Grohe, Eugene J. *c.ss.r.* (NY) Port Ewen, NY Presentation of the Virgin Mary Church; [Z] Esopus, NY Redemptorist Priests and Brothers C.Ss.R. (Province of Baltimore).
Groher, Robert C. '66 (GB) Special Assignment.
Grollig, Francis X. *s.j.* '53 (DET) [P] Clarkston, MI Colombiere Center.
Grollmes, Eugene E. *s.j.* '64 (STL) [C] St. Louis, MO Saint Louis University; [P] St. Louis, MO Jesuit Community Corporation at St. Louis University - Jesuit Hall.
Gromadzki, Stanley G. '89 (MET) Manville, NJ Sacred Heart of Jesus Church.
Gron, Stanislaw *s.j.* '86 (CHI) [N] Chicago, IL Sacred Heart Mission House.
Groncki, Msgr. Richard (NEW) [1] Newark, NJ Cathedral of the Sacred Heart Basilica.
Grondalski, Thaddeus J. '41 (WH) Retired.
Groner, John W. '71 (JC) Hannibal, MO Holy Family Church.
Gronert, Stephen (WCH) Marion, KS Holy Family Church.
Gronifillo, Alejandro A. '74 (TR) [2] Toms River, NJ St. Justin Church.
Gronowski, Ronald V. '69 (GAY) East Tawas, MI St. Joseph Church; Tawas City, MI Immaculate Heart of Mary Church.
Gronski, Peter '71 (STF) Yonkers, NY St. Michael Church.
Groody, Daniel G. *c.s.c.* '92 (OAK) [N] Berkeley, CA Holy Cross Fathers-Holy Cross Center.
Groover, Henry B. *o.p.* '92 (MIA) [18] Miami, FL St. Dominic Church.
Groover, Henry B. *o.p.* '92 (NO) [P] New Orleans, LA Dominican Fathers & Brothers, Southern Dominican Province.
Grosch, Robert D. '74 (GF) Havre, MT St. Jude Thaddeus Church.
Groshek, Richard J. '62 (LAN) [13] Flint, MI St. Pius X Church.
Grosko, Joseph P. (PIT) [64] Pittsburgh, PA Resurrection Church.
Gross, Barry '75 (LFT) On Duty Outside the Diocese.
Gross, Barry R. '75 (WDC) [E] Wheaton, MD Good Counsel High School.
Gross, Donald L. '59 (LFT) Logansport, IN All Saints Church; Lucerne, IN St. Elizabeth Church.
Gross, Francis *o.s.f.s.* (BUF) [7] Niagara Falls, NY St. Mary of the Cataract Church.
Gross, Gary L. '83 (LIN) Wahoo, NE St. Wenceslaus Church; [C] Wahoo, NE Neumann High School; [K] Wahoo, NE Bishop Neumann High School Endowment Fund.
Gross, Gerard *c.ss.r.* '78 (ATL) [I] Conyers, GA The Monastery of the Holy Spirit.
Gross, Joseph J. *o.ss.t.* '70 (TR) Asbury Park, NJ Our Lady of Mt. Carmel Church.
Gross, Justin *s.c.j.* '41 (MIL) [P] Milwaukee, WI St. Joseph House of Formation.
Gross, Kenneth A. '71 (DM) [1] Council Bluffs, IA Holy Family Church.
Gross, Lawrence C. '53 (HBG) Danville, PA St. Joseph Church.
Gross, Lee W. '87 (ARL) [4] Arlington, VA St. Charles Borromeo Church; On Duty Outside the Diocese.
Gross, Lee W. '87 (BAL) [A] Emmitsburg, MD Mount St. Mary's Seminary; [A] Emmitsburg, MD Mount St. Mary's Seminary.
Gross, Matthew *o.f.m.cap.* '61 (DEN) [3] Denver, CO Annunciation Church; [M] Denver, CO Annunciation Friary.
Gross, Ralph C. '70 (MIL) [48] Milwaukee, WI St. Margaret Mary Church.
Gross, Richard C. '62 (NU) Watkins, MN Church of St. Anthony.
Gross, Richard J. '63 (FAR) Special Assignment.
Gross, Richard K. *s.j.* '76 (NOR) Storrs, CT St. Thomas Aquinas Church; [K] Willimantic, CT Campus Ministry.
Gross, Stephen F. '66 (LC) [3] Wausau, WI St. James the Greater Church; [4] Wausau, WI St. Mary (Immaculate Conception) Church.
Gross, Stephen R. *o.f.m.conv.* '69 (MRY) [G] Arroyo Grande, CA St. Joseph Cupertino Province, Provincial Center.
Gross, Thomas L. '75 (HON) Kailua, HI St. John Vianney Church.
Gross, Val '63 (FAR) [4] Fargo, ND SS. Anne & Joachim Church.
Grosser, Msgr. Elmer J. '46 (COV) Southgate, KY St. Therese of the Infant Jesus Church; Retired.
Grosskopf, Albert A. *s.j.* '83 (SFR) [N] San Francisco, CA Jesuit Community at University of San Francisco.
Grosso, James D. '79 (BGP) [4] Danbury, CT St. Joseph's Church.
Grosso, Lucius *o.f.m.* '64 (PHX) [19] Phoenix, AZ St. Mary's Basilica.
Grosz, Edward M. (BUF) [13] Niagara Falls, NY St. Stanislaus Kostka Church.
Grote, Alan W. '82 (GBG) [1] Latrobe, PA Holy Family Church.
Groth, Msgr. Ronald C. '69 (LKC) [2] Lake Charles, LA Immaculate Heart of Mary Church.
Grothjan, James K. *c.pp.s.* '51 (CIN) [M] Dayton, OH Provincial House of the Cincinnati Province of the Society of the Precious Blood.
Grotovsky, Edward '94 (JOL) Downers Grove, IL St. Joseph Church.
Grotzinger, Alfred L. *o.s.b.* '41 (GBG) [H] Latrobe, PA Saint Vincent Archabbey.
Groucutt, George L. '46 (E) Retired.
Grous, Albin J. '87 (DET) [A] Orchard Lake, MI SS. Cyril and Methodius Seminary.
Grous, Albin J. '87 (PH) On Duty Outside the Archdiocese.
Grover, David A. '83 (CAM) [1] Cherry Hill, NJ St. Mary's Church.
Grover, Peter *o.m.v.* (BO) [BB] Boston, MA St. Clement's Archdiocesan Eucharistic Shrine.
Groves, Edmund '49 (PHX) Retired.
Groves, William '80 (PBL) Absent on Leave.
Grozio, Stephen M. *c.m.* '78 (BRK) [66] Brooklyn, NY St. John the Baptist Church; [U] Brooklyn, NY St. John the Baptist Rectory.
Grubb, James E. '55 (DAV) Eddyville, IA St. Mary's Church; Ottumwa, IA Sacred Heart Church.
Grubba, Dale W. '66 (MAD) Princeton, WI St. John the Baptist Church.
Gruben, John *o.a.r.* '74 (LA) [R] Oxnard, CA St. Augustine Priory O.A.R.
Gruber, Aloys Conrad '67 (STO) Oakdale, CA St. Mary of the Annunciation Church.
Gruber, Anthony '70 (NOR) Moosup, CT All-Hallows Church.
Gruber, Eric J. '91 (ALN) Schuylkill Haven, PA St. Ambrose Church; [O] Kutztown, PA Christopher House.
Gruber, J. Paul '45 (CIN) [38] Cincinnati, OH St. Ignatius Loyola Church; Retired.
Gruber, Kevin W. '80 (RVC) Center Moriches, NY St. John the Evangelist Church.
Gruber, Mark F.X. *o.s.b.* '83 (GBG) [H] Latrobe, PA Saint Vincent Archabbey.
Gruber, Robert L. '53 (COV) Southgate, KY St. Therese of the Infant Jesus Church.
Grubisch, Donald W. '53 (WIN) La Crescent, MN The Crucifixion Church.
Gruchot, Stanley J. '45 (CHI) Retired.
Gruden, Msgr. William J. '79 (SAG) Argyle, MI St. Joseph Church.
Grudowski, Msgr. Robert J. (PH) Conshohocken, PA St. Mary Church.
Gruenbauer, Hans H. '76 (CIN) Amelia, OH St. Bernadette's Church.
Gruhn, Raymond C. '66 (BRK) [137] Brooklyn, NY St. Sylvester Church.
Grumm, Thomas J. '75 (PH) [77] Philadelphia, PA St. John the Baptist Church.
Grummer, James E. *s.j.* (MIL) [P] Milwaukee, WI Jesuit Provincial Office, Wisconsin Province; [P] Milwaukee, WI Jesuit Community at Marquette University.
Grumsey, David *o.f.m.conv.* '86 (HBG) [5] Shamokin, PA Mother Cabrini Church.
Grundhaus, Msgr. Roger L. '66 (CR) [1] Crookston, MN Cathedral of the Immaculate Conception; [E] Crookston, MN Marywood Residential Community.
Grundowski, Francis M. '71 (ALN) Brockton, PA St.

Bartholomew Church; Tuscarora, PA St. Bertha Church.
Grunebach, Paul '76 (PIT) Glenshaw, PA St. Mary Church.
Grunewald, Bernard *er. o.l.s.* '77 (OLL) [D] Philippi, WV Our Lady of Solitude Hermitage.
Grunloh, Donatus *o.f.m.* '49 (SHP) West Monroe, LA St. Paschal Church.
Grupa, Henry '54 (FRS) Retired.
Grupczynski, Gerald *s.ch.* '88 (DET) [K] Sterling Heights, MI Society of Christ Provincial Home
Grupczynski, Gerald R. *s.ch.* '88 (TOL) [15] Toledo, OH St. Adalbert Church.
Gruss, Robert D. '94 (DAV) [8] Davenport, IA St. Paul the Apostle Church.
Gruszczyk, Jerome H. '47 (NEW) [B] Jersey City, NJ Saint Peter's College; [N] Jersey City, NJ Jesuits of Saint Peter's College, Inc.
Gruver, David '85 (ORG) Laguna Niguel, CA St. Timothy Church.
Gruver, Peter *o.m.v.* '90 (BO) [B] Boston, MA Our Lady of Grace Seminary.
Gryga, S. '37 (JOL) Retired.
Gryga, Theodore '64 (SY) Military Chaplains.
Grzankowski, Ted *o.f.m.conv.* (BAL) [M] Ellicott City, MD St. Joseph Cupertino Friary, Friars Minor Conventual of St. Francis of Assisi.
Grzechowiak, Francis *c.r.* '46 (CHI) [192] Chicago, IL St. Stanislaus, Bishop and Martyr Church.
Grzegorzewski, Thomas *s.d.b.* '85 (OAK) [N] Berkeley, CA Salesian Community.
Grzela, Andrew S. '91 (CHI) [184] Chicago, IL St. Richard Church.
Grzela, Marek '92 (CHI) Tinley Park, IL St. George Church.
Grzela, Wieslaw '89 (RCK) Algonquin, IL St. Margaret Mary Church.
Grzeskowiak, Edward S. '36 (STP) Retired.
Grzybowski, Joseph *o.f.m.conv.* '49 (FR) [1] Taunton, MA Our Lady of the Holy Rosary Church.
Grzybowski, Robert M. *o.f.m.conv.* '53 (ROC) [6] Auburn, NY St. Hyacinth Church.
Grzymski, Donald *o.f.m.conv.* '80 (BAL) [D] Baltimore, MD Archbishop Curley High School; [M] Baltimore, MD Immaculate Heart of Mary Friary.
Gschwend, James P. *s.j.* '65 (CHI) [N] Chicago, IL Chicago Province of the Society of Jesus-Provincial Office.
Gschwind, Fred H. '52 (LFT) Tipton, IN St. John the Baptist Church.
Gsell, John W. '36 (PH) [59] Philadelphia, PA Holy Family Church; Retired.
Guagliardo, Salvatore J. '59 (RCK) Lena, IL St. Joseph Church.
Guajardo, Hilario '89 (AUS) Gatesville, TX Our Lady of Lourdes Church.
Gualderon, Msgr. Ernest J. '45 (LA) [1] Long Beach, CA St. Anthony Church; Retired.
Gualtieri, Ray A. '64 (PIT) Scott Township, PA Our Lady of Grace Church.
Guandalini, Julius S. '44 (HRT) Retired.
Guarcello, Russell V. '43 (BO) Retired.
Guarino, Msgr. Charles A. '67 (RVC) St. James, NY SS. Philip and James Church.
Guarino, R. Michael (BO) Graduate Studies.
Guarino, Thomas G. '77 (NEW) [A] South Orange, NJ Immaculate Conception Seminary; [B] South Orange, NJ Seton Hall University.
Guarnieri, Richard '71 (NY) [136] Bronx, NY St. Clare of Assisi Church.
Guarracino, Ralph '54 (BRK) [Y] Middle Village, NY St. John's.
Guastella, Luke *o.f.m.cap.* '41 (PAT) Passaic, NJ St. Mary Hospital.
Guastella, Msgr. Richard J. '72 (NY) [206] Staten Island, NY Holy Rosary Church.
Guay, Robert F. '73 (PIT) On Duty Outside the Diocese.
Guba, Michael '65 (NEW) [3] Garfield, NJ Church of Our Lady of Sorrows.
Gubanich, Michael T. '47 (PIT) Retired.
Gubbels, Joyce (OM) [D] Omaha, NE St. Pius X-St. Leo School.
Gubbels, Richard '65 (DM) Atlantic, IA SS. Peter and Paul Church.
Gubbels, Wayne '71 (DM) Neola, IA St. Patrick Church; Weston, IA St. Columbanus Church.
Gubbins, John '70 (MIA) Military Chaplains.
Gubbins, John F. '50 (LA) Retired.
Gubbins, William B. '55 (CHI) [105] Chicago, IL St. John Berchmans Church.
Gubernat, Michael E. '77 (NEW) [6] Jersey City, NJ St. Anthony of Padua Church.
Gubser, John H. '62 (Y) Niles, OH St. Stephen's Church.
Gubser, Paul L. '67 (Y) Dungannon, OH St. Philip Neri Church; Salineville, OH St. Patrick's Church; Summitville, OH St. John's Church.
Guckert, William T. '66 (SY) Brewerton, NY St. Agnes Church.
Gude, George W. '32 (CIN) Retired.
Gude, Thomas A. '66 (WDC) Lexington Park, MD Immaculate Heart of Mary Church.
Gudewicz, John '70 (PIT) Finleyville, PA St. Francis of Assisi Church.
Gudime, Devasahayam '90 (KAL) St. Joseph, MI St. Joseph Church.
Gudino, Eduardo '94 (SD) El Centro, CA Our Lady of Guadalupe Church.
Guenette, J. Andre '69 (WOR) [3] Gardner, MA Our Lady of the Holy Rosary Church.
Guenter, Frank '66 (GAL) On Duty Outside the Diocese.
Guenther, Bernard *c.ss.r.* '31 (CHI) [9] Chicago, IL St. Alphonsus Church.
Guenther, Daniel C. '82 (SC) Grand Junction, IA St. Brigid's Church; Jefferson, IA St. Joseph's Church.
Guenther, Msgr. Donald E. '62 (NEW) West Orange, NJ St. Joseph's Church.
Guenther, George J. *s.j.* '45 (MIL) [P] Wauwatosa, WI Jesuit Community at St. Camillus.
Guenther, Msgr. Thomas A. '64 (CAM) West Collingswood, NJ Transfiguration Church.
Guentner, Francis J. *s.j.* '47 (STL) [F] St. Louis, MO Jesuit Community Corporation at St. Louis University - Jesuit Hall.
Guentner, Hugh *o.s.m.* '91 (DEN) [4] Denver, CO Assumption Church.
Guerdet, Randy J. '89 (SC) [1] Sioux City, IA Cathedral of the Epiphany.
Guerette, William J. (BO) Retired.
Guerin, Msgr. Eugene E. '25 (SPR) Retired.
Guerin, Louis T. '87 (PMB) Highland Beach, FL St. Lucy Church.
Guerin, Peter J. *o.s.b.* '63 (MAN) [K] Manchester, NH St. Anselm Abbey.
Guerin, Philip X. '42 (CHI) [11] Chicago, IL St. Andrew Church; Retired.
Guerin, William A. *o.s.f.s.* '57 (WIL) [I] Wilmington, DE DeSales House.
Guerini, Ademir *c.s.* '89 (WDC) [33] Washington, DC Our Lady Queen of the Americas Church; [38] Washington, DC Portuguese Catholic Community Church.
Guerlin, Msgr. Eugene '25 (SPR) [H] Holyoke, MA Mont Marie Health Care Center, Inc.
Guerra, Aroldo *sch.p.* '54 (NY) [12] New York, NY Annunciation Church; [Z] New York, NY Calasanzian Fathers (Piarists).
Guerra, Juan Gabriel *l.c.* '91 (MAD) [I] Edgerton, WI Legion of Christ, Inc.; [M] Edgerton, WI Oaklawn Incorporated.
Guerra, Richard *o.m.i.* '78 (BWN) San Benito, TX St. Benedict Church.
Guerreiro, Clarence L. *ss.cc.* '70 (HON) Kaneohe, HI St. Ann Church.
Guerreiro, Clyde *ss.cc.* '76 (HON) Lihue, HI Immaculate Conception Church.
Guerrera, Vittorio '91 (HRT) Wolcott, CT St. Pius X Church.
Guerrero, Msgr. Andres '57 (PCE) Coamo, PR St. Blase Church.
Guerrero, Demetrio Santana '88 (PCE) [2] Ponce, PR Christ the King Church.
Guerrero, Felixberto Leon *o.f.m.cap.* '36 (AGN) Sinajana, GU Saint Jude Thaddeus Church.
Guerrero, Jose C. '72 (ELP) [16] El Paso, TX Our Lady of the Light Church.
Guerrero, Jose Ma. (ARE) On Duty Outside the Diocese.
Guerrero, Lawrence M. '83 (STO) [6] Stockton, CA St. Linus Church.
Guerrero, Robert '92 (SB) Hesperia, CA Holy Family Church.
Guerrero, Toby '96 (SAT) [30] San Antonio, TX St. Bonaventure Church.
Guerrini, Roderic M. '63 (LA) Venice, CA St. Mark Church.
Guertin, Donald F. *c.s.c.* '61 (SB) Coachella, CA Our Lady of Soledad Church.
Guesnier, Rene *o.s.b.* '61 (DOD) St. John, KS St. John the Apostle Church; Seward, KS St. Francis Xavier Church.
Guessetto, Robert J. *o.s.a.* '79 (PH) [130] Philadelphia, PA Our Mother of Consolation Church; [Z] Villanova, PA Provincial Offices of the Order of St. Augustine, Province of St. Thomas of Villanova.
Guest, Francis *o.f.m.* '41 (TUC) [4] Tucson, AZ Mission San Xavier del Bac Church.
Guest, Richard '94 (ARL) Stafford, VA St. William of York Church.
Guetter, Michael A. '41 (NU) Retired.
Guevara, Alfonso M. '77 (BWN) [2] Brownsville, TX Christ the King Church.
Guevara, Msgr. Jose Maria '68 (SAT) Crystal City, TX Sacred Heart Church.
Guevara, Miguel H. '67 (GI) Retired.
Guevin, Benedict M. *o.s.b.* '85 (MAN) [K] Manchester, NH St. Anselm Abbey.
Guffey, David L. *c.s.c.* '91 (FTW) [A] Notre Dame, IN Moreau Seminary; [J] South Bend, IN Congregation of Holy Cross Indiana Province Provincial House.
Guggenbiller, Michael J. '95 (CLV) Concord Twp., OH St. Gabriel Church.
Gugino, Msgr. Henry J. (BUF) [H] Buffalo, NY The Catholic Charities of the Diocese of Buffalo; [M] Williamsville, NY St. Francis Home of Williamsville; [T] Buffalo, NY Good Counsel Apartments; [T] Buffalo, NY Monsignor Kirby Apartments Housing Development Fund Company, Inc.; [T] Buffalo, NY St. Timothy's Park Villa Housing Development Fund Company, Inc.; [T] Buffalo, NY La Casa Del Tainos Housing Development Fund Company, Inc.
Guglielmelli, Michael V. *o.f.m.conv.* '70 (NEW) [3] Hoboken, NJ St. Francis Church.
Guglielmi, Donald A. '84 (BGP) Huntington, CT St. Lawrence Church; Graduate Studies.
Guglielmo, Allen '68 (NEW) [G] Hoboken, NJ St. Mary Hospital.
Guglielmone, Robert E. '78 (RVC) Wantagh, NY St. Frances de Chantal Church.
Gugliemelli, Neil O. '54 (SCR) [7] Hazleton, PA Our Lady of Grace Church.
Gugliotta, Francis *s.x.* '52 (PAT) [M] Wayne, NJ Xaverian Missionary Fathers.
Gugliotta, Kevin A. '96 (NEW) Short Hills, NJ St. Rose of Lima Church.
Guichard, Alvaro '69 (MIA) [1] Miami Beach, FL St. Francis de Sales Church.
Guido, Msgr. John L. '42 (NY) [190] Bronx, NY St. Theresa of the Infant Jesus Church.
Guido, Joseph J. *o.p.* '81 (PRO) [P] Providence, RI St. Thomas Aquinas Priory at Providence College.
Guido, Paul R. *o.f.m.* '66 (ALB) Palenville, NY Sacred Heart Church.
Guido, Thomas '87 (PT) [3] Tallahassee, FL Good Shepherd Church.
Guido, Msgr. William F. '44 (NY) Retired.
Guidon, Patrick '50 (SAT) [B] San Antonio, TX Joseph Gerard House of Studies.
Guidry, Dale '82 (AMA) Dalhart, TX St. Anthony's Church.
Guidry, Joseph I. *s.v.d.* '57 (BR) [18] Baton Rouge, LA St. Paul the Apostle Church.
Guidry, Michael S. '71 (LAF) Patterson, LA St. Joseph Church.
Guidry, Raymond *s.v.d.* '57 (LAF) [4] Opelousas, LA Holy Ghost Church.
Guiglielmo, Alan '68 (NEW) Hoboken, NJ St. Mary's Hospital.
Guijarro de Corzo, Mario A. '78 (SJN) [6] Guaynabo, PR San Pedro Martir de Verona Church.
Guilbault, Msgr. Oscar A. '31 (PRO) Retired; [M] North Kingstown, RI Scalabrini Villa.
Guilbeau, Aubrey V. '82 (LKC) Iowa, LA St. Raphael Church.
Guillaume, Lionel A. '46 (ALB) Retired.
Guillemette, Arthur T. '39 (NU) Retired.
Guillemette, Joseph H. '23 (STP) Retired.
Guillemette, Marc (MAN) Bedford, NH St. Elizabeth Seton Church.
Guillen, Juan '74 (TUC) Yuma, AZ Immaculate Conception Church.
Guillen, Manuel R. '62 (SB) Retired.
Guillen, Patricio '57 (SB) Retired.
Guillen, Randy A. '96 (NEW) [4] Union City, NJ St. Anthony of Padua Church.
Guillen, Robert T. '70 (WDC) [13] Washington, DC St. Francis de Sales Church.
Guillermo, Rodrigo J. (GAL) Retired.
Guillet, Bernard L. *a.a.* '44 (NY) [87] New York, NY Our Lady of Guadalupe Church.
Guillette, Ronald '65 (GB) Reedsville/Maple Grove, WI St. Mary-St. Patrick Church.
Guillot, Msgr. Leo '56 (BR) Albany, LA St. Margaret Queen of Scotland Church.
Guilmain, Roland O. *a.a.* '53 (WOR) [N] Worcester, MA Assumptionists (Augustinians of the Assumption).
Guilmette, Emile *s.m.* '57 (BO) [4] Haverhill, MA St. Joseph's Church.
Guiltnane, Justin *s.c.j.* '53 (MIL) [P] Hales Corners, WI Sacred Heart Monastery; [Y] Franklin, WI Congregation of the Priests of the Sacred Heart Support and Maintenance Trust.
Guimon, Michael M. *o.s.m.* '70 (CHI) Hillside, IL St. Domitilla Church; [N] Chicago, IL Servite Friars - Eastern Province; [N] Chicago, IL Servite Friars - Eastern Province.
Guimond, John *o.f.m.cap.* '82 (LC) [I] Marathon City, WI St. Anthony Retreat Center.
Guinan, Frank '66 (PMB) Juno Beach, FL St. Patrick Church.
Guinan, Michael '53 (GF) Retired.
Guinan, Michael D. *o.f.m.* '63 (OAK) [A] Berkeley, CA Franciscan School of Theology.
Guinan, Msgr. Thomas P. '45 (BGP) Retired.
Guindon, William G. *s.j.* '50 (BO) [W] Boston, MA Loyola House.
Guiney, John *s.m.a.* '61 (JOL) Roselle, IL St. Walter Church.
Guiney, John E. '47 (BO) Retired.
Guiniven, John *c.ss.r.* '37 (ALB) [L] Saratoga Springs, NY St. John Neumann Residence.
Guirsch, Bernard G. '40 (CHI) Chicago Heights, IL St.

Paul Church; Retired.
Guischard, John A. '68 (BUR) Rutland, VT St. Peter Church; Retired.
Guise, Cyril *o.c.d.* '59 (MIL) [P] Holy Hill, WI Discalced Carmelite Monastery.
Guiterrez, Michael D. '93 (LA) [36] Los Angeles, CA Sacred Heart Church.
Guitierrez, Jeronimo '81 (SJ) Gilroy, CA St. Mary Church.
Guitron, Steven J. '94 (LA) Alhambra, CA All Souls Church.
Gula, Richard *s.s.* '73 (OAK) [A] Berkeley, CA Franciscan School of Theology.
Gulas, William E. *o.f.m.* '61 (CLV) [71] Cleveland, OH St. Stanislaus Church; [P] Cleveland, OH St. Stanislaus Friary.
Gulash, George M. '92 (ALT) [1] Altoona, PA Cathedral of the Blessed Sacrament.
Gulczynski, Msgr. John T. '36 (DAL) [27] Dallas, TX St. Thomas Aquinas Church.
Gulig, Msgr. Robert F. '61 (GB) Denmark, WI All Saints Church.
Guljas, Andrew *c.s.c.* '68 (FTW) [A] Notre Dame, IN Moreau Seminary.
Gulley, Anthony D. '56 (ALB) [3] Albany, NY Blessed Sacrament Church; Special Assignment; [B] Albany, NY The College of Saint Rose.
Gulley, James '81 (ALB) [7] Amsterdam, NY St. Mary Church.
Gullickson, Msgr. Thomas E. '76 (SFS) On Duty Outside the Diocese.
Gullo, Joseph A. '85 (BUF) [1] Orchard Park, NY Nativity Church.
Gully, Bernard L. '62 (SAN) Andrews, TX Our Lady of Lourdes Church.
Gumapo, Polycarpo '70 (SAC) [2] Sacramento, CA All Hallows Church.
Gumataotao, Augustin *o.f.m.cap.* '73 (AGN) Agat, GU Our Lady of Mount Carmel Church.
Gumbert, Kenneth R. *o.p.* '85 (PRO) [P] Providence, RI St. Thomas Aquinas Priory at Providence College.
Guminga, Theodore C. '59 (STP) [25] Minneapolis, MN St. Hedwig Church.
Gummersheimer, Gary P. '79 (BEL) Tipton, IL St. Patrick Church; [B] Waterloo, IL Gibault Catholic High School.
Gumpai, Domingo B. '80 (SFE) Socorro, NM San Miguel Church.
Gumprecht, Thomas *s.a.* '68 (NY) [Z] Garrison, NY Generalate of the Franciscan Friars of the Atonement-St. James Friary.
Gunderman, Richard J. *s.a.c.* '50 (MIL) [D] Milwaukee, WI Pius XI High School; [P] Milwaukee, WI St. Vincent Community.
Gunderson, Gerald T. '76 (CHI) Riverside, IL St. Mary Church.
Gundrum, Alfredo *o.f.m.cap.* (CHI) [113] Chicago, IL St. Kevin Church; [146] Chicago, IL Our Lady Gate of Heaven Church.
Gunia, Edward S. '49 (CHI) Retired.
Gunn, Francis X. *o.f.m.* (ALB) [B] Loudonville, NY Siena College.
Gunn, Francis X. *o.f.m.* '81 (ALB) [B] Loudonville, NY Siena College; [S] Loudonville, NY Siena College.
Gunn, James L. '77 (MAD) Dickeyville, WI Holy Ghost Church.
Gunning, Eugene L. '55 (SCR) [26] Scranton, PA St. Vincent de Paul Church.
Gunning, Joseph *s.v.d.* '47 (TR) [M] Bordentown, NJ Society of the Divine Word.
Gunnoud, James B. '59 (HRT) Cheshire, CT St. Bridget's Church.
Gunshinan, James *c.s.c.* '89 (FTW) [12] South Bend, IN St. Joseph Church.
Gunther, William '60 (MIA) Retired.
Gunti, Charles E. *o.f.m.* '68 (STL) [P] St. Louis, MO Franciscan Friary of St. Anthony of Padua.
Gunti, Frederick W. '64 (LR) On Duty Outside the Diocese.
Gunti, Frederick W. '64 (MOB) [B] Mobile, AL Spring Hill College.
Guntzelman, Louis J. '57 (CIN) On Special and Diocesan Assignment.
Gunville, Gary M. '83 (GF) Absent on Leave.
Gunzel, Ray *s.p.* '69 (SFE) [J] Jemez Springs, NM The Jemez Program, Our Lady of Lourdes Novitiate.
Guoan, Paul '87 (LAN) Clio, MI SS. Charles and Helena Church.
Guppenberger, August *glmy.* '61 (CIN) [M] Fairfield, OH Headquarters of Glenmary Home Missioners.
Gural, Marion A. '56 (BRK) Absent on Sick Leave.
Gurath, Guy G. '64 (MIL) Juneau, WI Immaculate Conception Church.
Gurath, Msgr. Guy J. '64 (MIL) Clyman, WI St. John's Church.
Gurdak, Joseph R. *o.f.m.cap* '70 (ORL) Lake Wales, FL Holy Spirit Church.
Guredet, Randy J. '89 (SC) Special Assignment.
Gurka, Gerald J. '80 (SCR) Wanamie, PA St. Mary's Church.
Gurkis, Albin *m.i.c.* '43 (NOR) [C] Thompson, CT Marianapolis Preparatory School; [F] Thompson, CT Marian Fathers.
Gurley, Francis P. (WOR) [B] Worcester, MA Assumption College.
Gurnell, Anthony '64 (SAC) Retired and in Senior Ministry.
Gurnell, Anthony '69 (MRY) Cayucos, CA St. Joseph Church.
Gurovich, Daniel '74 (PHU) Bethlehem, PA St. Josaphat's Church.
Gurrieri, John A. '67 (BRK) [67] Brooklyn, NY St. John Cantius Church.
Gurski, John K. '64 (NEW) [3] Garfield, NJ Church of Our Lady of Sorrows.
Gurtler, Gary *s.j.* '79 (BO) [W] Chestnut Hill, MA The Jesuit Community at Boston College.
Guschwan, George M. '72 (CLV) [5] Elyria, OH Sacred Heart of Jesus Church.
Gusiora Alphonsus '83 (PCE) On Duty Outside the Diocese.
Gusmer Msgr. Charles W. '66 (NEW) Cedar Grove, NJ St. Catherine of Siena Church.
Gussoni, Lino '44 (NY) Retired.
Gustafson, Christopher E. (CHI) [39] Chicago, IL St. Christina Church.
Gustafson, George C. '76 (MAR) Manistique, MI St. Francis de Sales Church.
Gustafson, Gilbert J. '77 (STP) Mendota, MN St. Peter Church.
Gustas, Bernard J. '60 (ALB) [10] Schenectady, NY St. Joseph Church.
Guste, Placid *s.m.p.* '61 (SPC) [E] Marionville, MO The Society of Our Mother of Peace, Sons of Our Mother of Peace.
Guste, Placid *s.m.p.* '61 (STL) [P] High Ridge, MO Society of Our Mother of Peace; [T] High Ridge, MO Society of Our Mother of Peace-Maria Fonte Solitude.
Guste, Robert I. '50 (NO) Chalmette, LA Prince of Peace Church.
Gustin, Clement *o.s.c.* '55 (DUL) Chisholm, MN St. Joseph's Church.
Gustin, Clement N. *o.s.c.* '55 (SCL) [I] Onamia, MN Crosier Monastery.
Gustin, Theodore F. '57 (BIS) Wilton, ND Sacred Heart Church.
Gutauskas, Vaclovas *s.j.* '45 (CHI) [N] Chicago, IL Lithuanian American Jesuits.
Gutekunst, John P. '80 (PH) [T] Philadelphia, PA St. Agnes Medical Center.
Guter, Lawrence '45 (DUB) Retired.
Gutgsell, Michael F. '74 (OM) [40] Omaha, NE St. Robert Bellarmine Church.
Gutgsell, Stephen J. '84 (OM) Aloys, NE St. Aloysius Church; Monterey, NE St. Boniface Church; St. Charles, NE St. Anthony Church.
Guth, Edward L. *s.j.* '60 (ALB) [O] Auriesville, NY Gonzaga Jesuit Community.
Guth, Edward L. *s.j.* '60 (BUF) [50] Buffalo, NY St. Michael Church.
Guthman, William (KCK) Topeka, KS Kansas Neurological Institute and Kansas Reception and Diagnostic Center.
Guthneck, Peter E. '71 (GF) Big Sandy, MT St. Margaret Mary Church.
Guthrie, Alfred R. '55 (BRK) [57] Brooklyn, NY Holy Innocents Church.
Guthrie, Eric D. *o.s.b.* '81 (BIR) [E] Cullman, AL St. Bernard Abbey.
Guthrie, Frederick '62 (BO) [1] Gloucester, MA St. Ann Church.
Guthrie, John G. '90 (BIS) Belfield, ND St. Bernard Church.
Guthrie, Milton J. '57 (MEM) [22] Memphis, TN Our Lady Of Perpetual Help Church.
Guthrie, Paul *o.f.m.* '53 (PSC) [B] Sybertsville, PA Holy Dormition Monastery.
Guthrie, Raymond '84 (JOL) Glen Ellyn, IL St. James the Apostle Church.
Guthrie, Raymond P. '84 (PEO) On Duty Outside the Diocese.
Gutierrez, Alvin '61 (PIT) Bobtown, PA St. Ignatius of Antioch Church.
Gutierrez, Celestino '64 (VEN) [3] Sarasota, FL St. Martha Church.
Gutierrez, Dionisio *o.a.r.* '63 (NY) [126] Bronx, NY St. Anselm Church.
Gutierrez, Edgardo '94 (BGP) [2] Norwalk, CT St. Joseph's Church.
Gutierrez, Felipe Fernandez *o.s.a.* '71 (MGZ) Aguada, PR St. Francis of Assisi Church.
Gutierrez, Msgr. Fernando '66 (SD) [22] San Diego, CA St. Catherine Laboure Church.
Gutierrez, Franco '65 (SJN) [3] San Juan, PR Nuestra Senora de la Altagracia Church.
Gutierrez, Gilberto '73 (PAT) [1] Paterson, NJ Cathedral of St. John the Baptist.
Gutierrez, Javier *o.m.* '71 (SJN) [16] San Juan, PR Ntra. Sra. de Fatima Church.
Gutierrez, Javier '83 (JUN) On Duty Outside the Diocese.
Gutierrez, Jose '73 (STP) [16] St. Paul, MN St. Bernard Church.
Gutierrez, Jose M. '76 (CC) [11] Corpus Christi, TX Sacred Heart Church; On Special Assignment; [E] Corpus Christi, TX Spohn Hospital.
Gutierrez, Julio '49 (CGS) Retired.
Gutierrez, Larry A. *s.s.j.* '85 (GAL) [66] Houston, TX St. Peter Claver Church.
Gutierrez, Vicente *m.sp.s.* '73 (LA) Huntington Park, CA St. Martha Church.
Gutman, Msgr. Gordon G. '33 (Y) Retired.
Gutmann, David '83 (P) Forest Grove, OR St. Anthony Church; Yamhill, OR St. John Church; [P] Portland, OR University of Portland.
Gutmann, Donald K. '91 (P) Florence, OR St. Mary, Our Lady of the Dunes Church.
Gutowski, Edmund *c.m.* '60 (BRK) [134] Brooklyn, NY St. Stanislaus Kostka Church.
Gutowski, Matthew J. '88 (OM) [L] Omaha, NE Sisters of the Annunciation of the Archdiocese of Omaha.
Guttenberger, Xavier '35 (AUS) Retired.
Guttendorf, James R. '65 (RIC) Highland Springs, VA St. John Church.
Gutting, James G. '75 (E) Titusville, PA St. Titus Church.
Gutting, John C. '54 (LA) [2] Long Beach, CA St. Athanasius Church.
Guyder, Thomas F. '40 (SY) Retired; [S] Syracuse, NY St. Pius X Home, Inc.
Guyer, James B. *s.j.* '72 (DEN) [M] Denver, CO Regis Jesuit Community (The Jesuits at Regis University).
Guyon, Guy E. *o.praem* '40 (GB) [I] De Pere, WI St. Norbert Abbey.
Guyot, Gilmore H. *c.m.* '34 (STL) [P] Perryville, MO Congregation of The Mission.
Guz, Edmund F. '55 (CHI) Burnham, IL Mother of God Church.
Guz, Leonard '55 (JOL) Downers Grove, IL Divine Savior Church.
Guzik, Stanley *o.m.i.* '46 (GAL) Alvin, TX St. John the Baptist Church.
Guzikowski, Msgr. Gerard '43 (GAY) Manistee, MI Guardian Angels Church.
Guzinski, Joseph D. *c.p.* '51 (BRK) [U] Jamaica, NY Immaculate Conception Monastery.
Guzman, Alfonso *o.f.m.* '71 (SJN) [4] Toa Baja, PR Jose Obrero Church.
Guzman, Alfonso D. *o.f.m.* '71 (NY) [Z] New York, NY Franciscan Friars, Order of Friars Manor.
Guzman, Alfredo *s.j.* (ARE) Special Assignment.
Guzman, Alfredo *s.j.* (SJN) [22] San Juan, PR San Ignacio de Loyola Church.
Guzman, Alfredo *s.j.* '83 (ARE) [A] Arecibo, PR Pontificia Universidad Catholica de Puerto Rico, Recinto de Arecibo.
Guzman, Baudilio *s.j.* '91 (SJN) [22] San Juan, PR San Ignacio de Loyola Church; [C] Rio Piedras, PR Centro Universitario Catolico.
Guzman, Julian *s.d.s.* '68 (MIL) [P] Milwaukee, WI Salvatorian Provincial Residence.
Guzman, Marco (GAL) Dickinson, TX Shrine of the True Cross Church.
Guzman, Msgr. Raul '62 (PAT) [8] Passaic, NJ Our Lady of Fatima Church.
Guzman-Chavez, Erasto '79 (P) Cornelius, OR St. Alexander Church.
Gwale, Ralph (BO) [11] Boston, MA St. Anthony Church.
Gwaltney, Wally '77 (P) [J] Roseburg, OR Mercy Medical Center, Inc.
Gwiazda, Francis A. '69 (PH) [86] Philadelphia, PA St. Laurentius Church.
Gwinner, David '84 (COL) Reynoldsburg, OH St. Pius X Church.
Gwozdz, John P. '86 (HRT) Glastonbury, CT St. Paul's Church.
Gwozdz, Thomas *o.f.m.conv.* '53 (BAL) [M] Ellicott City, MD Order of Friars Minor Conventual.
Gwozdz, Thomas L. *s.d.b.* '75 (COL) [A] Columbus, OH Pontifical College Josephinum; [H] Columbus, OH Salesian Center.
Gwudz, John S. '72 (NOR) Military Chaplains.
Gyamfi, Paul Miki (NY) [183] Bronx, NY St. Philip Neri Church.
Gyan, Eric V. '86 (BR) Brusly, LA St. John the Baptist Church.
Gyhra, Lawrence J. '66 (LIN) Wahoo, NE St. Wenceslaus Church.
Gyure, William '91 (NEW) [2] Jersey City, NJ St. Aloysius Church; Kearny, NJ Hudson County Correctional Center.

H

Ha, Alexander H. '93 (ORG) Los Alamitos, CA St. Hedwig Church.
Ha, Thomas (ORG) Stanton, CA St. Polycarp Church.
Ha, Vinh '93 (CHI) [96] Chicago, IL Saint Ita Church.
Ha Pham, Louis M. *c.m.c.* '94 (DEN) Wheat Ridge, CO Queen of Vietnamese Martyrs Church.
Haag, Msgr. Christian D. '38 (PAT) Morristown, NJ St. Margaret's Church; Retired.

Haake, Thomas *o.m.v.* '81 (BO) [B] Boston, MA Oblate Provincialate.
Haaland, Byron *s.c.j.* '77 (GB) [M] Baileys Harbor, WI St. Joseph Retreat Center.
Haar, George B. '51 (STL) Retired.
Haas, Dietrich A. '67 (MIL) [T] Waukesha, WI Secular Institute of Schoenstatt Fathers.
Haas, Francis '64 (E) On Leave of Absence.
Haas, John '47 (SEA) Gig Harbor, WA Washington Corrections Center for Women.
Haas, John M. '80 (BO) [FF] Braintree, MA Pope John Center.
Haas, Joseph H. '59 (MIL) Port Washington, WI St. Peter of Alcantara Church.
Haas, Julian *o.f.m.cap.* '65 (STL) [P] St. Louis, MO St. Crispin's Friary.
Haas, Lawrence '63 (FAR) Carrington, ND Sacred Heart Church.
Haas, Melvin B. '54 (BEL) Breese, IL St. Augustine Church.
Haas, Msgr. Murray V. '37 (PEO) Retired.
Haas, Ralph L. '55 (BEL) Hecker, IL St. Augustine of Canterbury Church; Chester, IL Chester Mental Health Center.
Haas, Robert '62 (TOL) New London, OH Our Lady of Lourdes Church.
Haas, Roger *ofm conv.* '69 (BUF) [D] Athol Springs, NY St. Francis High School; [O] Athol Springs, NY St. Francis of Assisi Friary.
Haas, Roger M. *o.f.m.conv.* '69 (BAL) [M] Ellicott City, MD Order of Friars Minor Conventual.
Haas, Roger M. *o.f.m. conv.* '69 (BUF) [A] East Aurora, NY Christ the King Seminary.
Haas, Theodore A. '44 (COS) [1] Colorado Springs, CO St. Mary's Cathedral.
Haase, Albert '83 (STL) [P] St. Louis, MO Franciscan Friary of St. Anthony of Padua.
Haase, Howard G. '83 (MIL) [6] Kenosha, WI St. Mary's Church.
Haasl, Edgar '58 (OAK) [13] Oakland, CA St. Louis Bertrand Church.
Hababag, Jimmy B. (GAL) Kingwood, TX St. Martha Church.
Habe, Robert W. '62 (PIT) Russellton, PA Transfiguration Church.
Habenicht, James F. *m.m.* '50 (SJ) [M] Los Altos, CA Maryknoll.
Haber, Edward A. '58 (NEW) Nutley, NJ Our Lady of Mount Carmel Church.
Haberek, Jerome A. '77 (PRO) On Duty Outside the Diocese.
Haberkern, Thomas A. '93 (STL) Leave of Absence.
Haberkorn, Timothy '92 (KCK) [1] Kansas City, KS Cathedral of St. Peter the Apostle; [B] Kansas City, KS Bishop Ward High School.
Haberman, C. Robert '75 (PBL) On Duty Outside the Diocese.
Haberman, Clayton J. '50 (WIN) Retired.
Haberman, Lawrence R. '68 (DAL) Retired.
Haberman, Robert '75 (SFR) Special Assignment.
Haberthier, John A. (DOD) Retired.
Habiger, Msgr. James D. '51 (WIN) Retired.
Habiger, Matthew *o.s.b.* '68 (KCK) [H] Atchison, KS St. Benedict's Abbey.
Habing, Paul '80 (SFD) On Duty Outside the Diocese.
Hablewitz, James A. '67 (GB) [2] Green Bay, WI Nativity of Our Lord Church.
Haby, Gerald *s.m.* '69 (TYL) Mount Pleasant, TX St. Michael Church.
Haby, Gerald C. *s.m.* '69 (STL) [P] St. Louis, MO Provincialate of the Society of Mary, Province of St. Louis.
Hacala, Joseph R. *s.j.* '75 (CHI) [C] Chicago, IL Jesuit Community at Loyola University of Chicago.
Hachey, Paul J. *s.m.* '84 (ATL) [C] Atlanta, GA Marist School.
Hack, Michael A. '70 (CHI) Flossmoor, IL Infant Jesus of Prague Church.
Hack, Thomas J. '55 (GR) [6] Muskegon, MI St. Michael's Church.
Hackel, Robert *s.m.* '65 (FWT) [A] Fort Worth, TX Nolan Catholic High School.
Hackenmueller, Jerome B. '69 (STP) [31] St. Paul, MN St. Patrick Church.
Hacker, George *s.d.b.* '38 (SFR) [N] San Francisco, CA Salesian Provincial Residence.
Hacker, Jack *c.ss.r.* '59 (STL) [B] St. Louis, MO St. John Neumann House.
Hacker, Leonard G. *s.j.* '47 (MI) Ebeye, MH Queen of Peace Church.
Hacker, Louis-Marie *o.s.b.* '85 (CC) [H] Sandia, TX Corpus Christi Abbey.
Hackert, Eugene C. '51 (NU) Clements, MN St. Joseph Church; Morgan, MN St. Michael Church.
Hackett, Denis *o.f.m.conv.* '74 (R) Jacksonville, NC Shrine of the Infant of Prague, Church of the Holy Spirit.
Hackett, James F. '68 (L) [45] Louisville, KY St. Leonard Church.
Hackett, John P. '46 (BUR) Retired.
Hackman, Marvin R. '71 (CIN) [K] Springfield, OH Mercy Medical Center; [Q] Springfield, OH Mercy Medical Center, Wittenberg University Campus Ministry.
Hackman, Paul W. '52 (CLV) West Salem, OH St. Stephen Church; Retired.
Hadad, Gerard '69 (DET) [2] Roseville, MI St. Athanasius Church.
Hadalski, Andrew *s.v.d.* '59 (TR) Yardville, NJ Garden State Correctional Center; [M] Bordentown, NJ Society of the Divine Word.
Hadberg, Dennis C. '72 (E) Clearfield, PA St. Francis Church.
Haddad, Msgr. Edmond G. '46 (WOR) Retired; [M] Worcester, MA Vianney House.
Haddad, James J. '58 (BO) Needham, MA St. Joseph Church.
Haddad, John W. *b.s.o.* '43 (NTN) Miami, FL St. Jude Church.
Haddad, Norman A. *o.p.* '61 (BO) [W] Dover, MA St. Stephen Priory; [Y] Dover, MA St. Stephen Priory Spiritual Life Center.
Haddad, William F. *b.s.o.* '42 (NTN) Atlanta, GA St. John Church.
Hadden, Thomas P. '58 (R) Wilmington, NC St. Mary Church.
Hadel, Richard E. *s.j.* '65 (STL) [F] St. Louis, MO St. Louis University High School, George H. Backer Memorial; [P] St. Louis, MO St. Louis University High School Jesuit Community.
Hadgkiss, Joseph *s.o.l.t.* '93 (CC) [H] Robstown, TX Society of Our Lady of the Most Holy Trinity.
Hadnagy, John Raphael *o.f.m. conv.* '90 (GR) [4] Grand Rapids, MI St. Anthony of Padua Church.
Hadusek, Paul J. '69 (NU) Appleton, MN St. John Church.
Hadyka, Richard J. '67 (CAM) Salem, NJ St. Mary's Church.
Haefeli, Joaquin (LA) Wilmington, CA SS. Peter and Paul's Church.
Haefling, Maurice *o.s.b.* '94 (KCK) [H] Atchison, KS St. Benedict's Abbey.
Haefner, Charles '32 (SUP) Retired.
Haefner, Douglas J. '83 (MET) Somerset, NJ St. Matthias Church.
Haegelin, William M. '76 (KCK) [2] Leavenworth, KS Sacred Heart of Jesus Church; [3] Leavenworth, KS St. Casimir's Church.
Haemmerle, Gerald R. '67 (CIN) [73] Cincinnati, OH Our Lord, Christ the King Church.
Haen, Edmund H. '40 (MIL) Retired.
Haener, Robert W. '57 (DET) Retired.
Haenke, Roger '91 (FAR) Absent on Leave.
Haesaert, William *c.s.v.* '80 (LAV) [15] Las Vegas, NV St. Viator Church.
Hafeman, Harry G. '76 (GB) Gresham, WI St. Francis Solanus Church; Leopolis, WI St. Mary Church.
Haffey, Thomas P. '69 (HEL) Conrad, MT St. Michael Church; Dutton, MT St. William Church.
Hafner, Walter *s.v.d.* '37 (CHI) [B] Techny, IL Divine Word Residence.
Hagan, Aelred *o.c.s.o.* '89 (CHR) [E] Moncks Corner, SC Mepkin Abbey.
Hagan, Barry J. *c.s.c.* '60 (P) [E] Portland, OR University of Portland; [L] Portland, OR Holy Cross Father & Brother, C.S.C. - University of Portland.
Hagan, Charles H. '70 (PH) On Duty Outside the Archdiocese.
Hagan, David I. *o.s.f.s.* '66 (PH) [Z] Philadelphia, PA Inner City House.
Hagan, Harry *o.s.b.* '86 (IND) [A] St. Meinrad, IN St. Meinrad Seminary; [J] St. Meinrad, IN St. Meinrad Archabbey.
Hagan, James '69 (SFR) On Duty Outside the Archdiocese.
Hagan, Martin *s.j.* '50 (STL) [F] St. Louis, MO St. Louis University High School, George H. Backer Memorial; [P] St. Louis, MO Jesuit Community Corporation at St. Louis University - Jesuit Hall.
Hagan, Paul '82 (LFT) Unassigned.
Hagan, Robert A. *s.j.* '72 (PBL) Trinidad, CO Most Holy Trinity, Trinidad Area Catholic Community (Trinidad Cluster) Church; Trinidad, CO Our Lady of Mt. Carmel, Trinidad Area Catholic Community (Trinidad Cluster) Church; Trinidad, CO St. Joseph, Trinidad Area Catholic Community (Trinidad Cluster) Church; [E] Trinidad, CO Trinidad Area Catholic Community.
Hagan, Thomas C. '61 (PH) Hatfield, PA St. Maria Goretti Church.
Hagan, Vincent (RVC) Sick Leave.
Hagan, William *o.m.i.* '61 (GB) Egg Harbor, WI St. John the Baptist Church; Fish Creek, WI St. Paul Church; Jacksonport, WI St. Michael Church.
Hagarman, Vincent A. *s.j.* '54 (CLV) [U] Akron, OH Loyola of the Lakes Jesuit Retreat House.
Hage, Simon '39 (NTN) Retired.
Hageder, James S. '94 (GBG) [1] Greensburg, PA Blessed Sacrament Cathedral.
Hagedorn, Robert L. '44 (CIN) Retired.
Hagedorn, Thomas J. '71 (CLV) [61] Cleveland, OH St. Patrick Church.
Hagee, Robert J. *s.j.* '61 (CIN) [M] Cincinnati, OH Faber Jesuit Community.
Hagemann, John *o.s.b.* '75 (OM) [C] Elkhorn, NE Mount Michael High School; [K] Elkhorn, NE Mount Michael Abbey.
Hagen, Gerald '91 (SUP) Highbridge, WI St. Anthony Church; Mellen, WI Holy Rosary Church.
Hagen, John J. *o.s.a.* '57 (PH) [C] Villanova, PA Villanova University; [Z] Villanova, PA St. Thomas Monastery.
Hagen, Joseph B. *o.f.m.* '46 (SHP) Hodge, LA St. Lucy Church.
Hagenbach, George G. '54 (PH) Berwyn, PA St. Monica Church.
Hagendorf, Thomas A. *o.praem.* '63 (BAL) [74] Baltimore, MD Our Lady, Queen of Peace Church.
Hagendorf, Thomas A. *o.praem.* '63 (PH) [Z] Paoli, PA Daylesford Abbey.
Hager, Carl G. *c.s.c.* '39 (FTW) [B] Notre Dame, IN University of Notre Dame Du Lac; [J] Notre Dame, IN Holy Cross Community, Corby Hall, University of Notre Dame.
Hagerman, James W. '86 (MET) Bridgewater, NJ St. Bernard Church.
Hagerty, Charles B. '59 (HRT) [2] Waterbury, CT Immaculate Conception Church.
Hagerty, Francis O. *s.j.* '49 (BO) [E] Boston, MA Boston College High School & Jesuit Community.
Hagerty, Msgr. John B. '55 (E) Corry, PA St. Thomas The Apostle Church.
Haggarty, Msgr. James J. '45 (BRK) Retired.
Haggarty, Msgr. James J. '45 (SFR) Redwood City, CA St. Pius Church.
Haggerty, Charles J. *o.carm.* '56 (NY) [Z] Middletown, NY St. Albert's Priory.
Haggerty, Colman *c.p.* '46 (BRK) [U] Jamaica, NY Immaculate Conception Monastery.
Haggerty, Donald (NY) On Duty Outside the Archdiocese.
Haggerty, Donald F. '89 (BAL) [A] Emmitsburg, MD Mount St. Mary's Seminary.
Haggerty, Edward '57 (CIN) [14] Dayton, OH Holy Family Church; [M] Fairfield, OH Headquarters of Glenmary Home Missioners.
Haggerty, Msgr. James J. '50 (BRK) Retired.
Haggerty, John *o.carm.* (NY) New Hampton, NY MID Hudson Psychiatric Center.
Haggerty, John J. '61 (NY) [145] Bronx, NY St. Helena Church.
Haggerty, Thomas J. '79 (RVC) East Meadow, NY St. Raphael Church.
Haggerty, Thomas M. '64 (BRK) [137] Brooklyn, NY St. Sylvester Church.
Haggins, Martin *o.f.m.cap.* '65 (SFR) Burlingame, CA Our Lady of Angels Church.
Haglof, Anthony *o.c.d.* '71 (BO) [W] Brighton, MA Carmelite Monastery.
Hagman, William J. '55 (OWN) Retired.
Hagmann, James J. '58 (LC) Blair, WI St. Ansgar Church; Whitehall, WI St. John the Apostle Church.
Hagstrom, Thomas J. '93 (SFD) [5] Springfield, IL St. Agnes Church; [H] Springfield, IL St. John's Hospital.
Hahn, Bernadine *o.f.m.* '43 (STL) [P] St. Louis, MO Franciscan Friary of St. Anthony of Padua.
Hahn, Dominic D. *o.s.b.* '80 (SEA) Shelton, WA St. Edward's Church; [M] Lacey, WA St. Martin's Abbey.
Hahn, Gerald '79 (NEW) Upper Saddle River, NJ Church of the Presentation.
Hahn, James Cornelius *o.p.* (MAD) [3] Madison, WI Blessed Sacrament Church.
Hahn, James David '61 (SCL) Cambridge, MN Christ the King Church.
Hahn, Raymond W. '74 (E) [14] Erie, PA St. Boniface Church; [C] Erie, PA Cathedral Preparatory School.
Hai, Dinh Minh *c.ss.r.* '96 (LA) [R] Baldwin Park, CA Vietnamese Redemptorist Mission.
Haig, Frank R. *s.j.* '60 (BAL) [C] Baltimore, MD Loyola College; [M] Baltimore, MD Jesuit Community of Loyola College, Inc.
Haigerty, Leo J. '57 (LFT) Logansport, IN All Saints Church.
Haight, Mark '76 (ALB) Glens Falls, NY St. Mary Church; Glens Falls, NY Glens Falls Hospital.
Haight, Roger D. *s.j.* '67 (BO) [W] Cambridge, MA Weston Jesuit Community.
Haikhana, Hilary Nguyen (BO) [62] Boston, MA St. Peter Church.
Hain, Msgr. Raymond B. '48 (LIN) Manley, NE St. Patrick's Church.
Hainen, Philip *o.f.m.cap.* '93 (WH) [N] Charleston, WV Capuchins-St. Anthony Friary.
Haines, Jeffrey R. '85 (MIL) West Bend, WI St. Frances Cabrini Church.
Haines, Kevin J. '87 (LFT) Carmel, IN Our Lady of Mount Carmel Church.
Haiss, Maurice (MOB) Holy Trinity, AL St. Joseph Church.
Hajduch, Joseph *c.pp.s.* '47 (CIN) [B] Carthagena, OH St. Charles.
Hajduk, Msgr. Edward J. '53 (NEW) [3] Bayonne, NJ

St. Henry's Church.
Hajduk, Kent *o.f.m.* '62 (DET) [H] Southfield, MI Providence Hospital.
Hajkowski, Stanislaw *s.ch.* '82 (WDC) [V] Silver Spring, MD Friends of John Paul II Foundation.
Hajtas, Francis '46 (NO) Retired.
Hakala, Thomas *o.carm.* (BO) [P] Peabody, MA Catholic Information Center.
Hakala, Thomas *o.carm.* '78 (JOL) [J] Darien, IL Carmelite Fathers Provincial Office.
Hake, Msgr. James E. '60 (SAL) Aurora, KS St. Peter's Church; Minneapolis, KS Immaculate Conception of the Blessed Virgin Mary Church; [I] Salina, KS Marymount Diocesan Activities Center, Inc.
Hakewerth, Quentin *s.m.* '60 (STL) [P] St. Louis, MO Provincialate of the Society of Mary, Province of St. Louis.
Halabura, Stephen J. '61 (ALN) Lansford, PA St. Ann Church; Lansford, PA SS. Peter and Paul Church.
Halaburda, Walter A. '59 (HBG) [1] Lebanon, PA Assumption of the Blessed Virgin Mary Church.
Haladus, Victorian *o.f.m.* '61 (CHI) Oak Forest, IL Oak Forest Hospital; [N] Oak Forest, IL St. Roch Friary-Franciscan Fathers.
Halaiko, David J. '67 (CLV) [13] Akron, OH Nativity Of the Lord Jesus Church.
Halata, William '53 (VIC) St. John, TX St. John the Baptist Church; Retired.
Halbach, Msgr. A. A. '32 (DUB) Retired.
Halbert, John K. *m.m.* '59 (NY) [Z] Maryknoll, NY Maryknoll Fathers and Brothers.
Halbing, William '82 (NEW) [24] Jersey City, NJ St. Paul of the Cross Church.
Halborg, John E. '80 (NY) [118] New York, NY St. Thomas More Church; [DD] New York, NY St. Ansgar Scandinavian Catholic League.
Haldane, Richard S. '92 (B) Salmon, ID St. Charles Church.
Hale, Francis A. '57 (HRT) Retired.
Hale, Msgr. Harry L. '52 (BGP) Retired.
Hale, Robert *o.s.b.cam.* '66 (MRY) [G] Big Sur, CA New Camaldoli Hermitage; [I] Big Sur, CA New Camaldoli Hermitage.
Hale, Robert B. *c.s.b.* '70 (ROC) [13] Rochester, NY Christ the King Church.
Haley, James A. *c.s.p.* '68 (WH) Morgantown, WV St. John's University Parish, Newman Hall Church.
Haley, James R. '87 (ARL) McLean, VA St. John's Church.
Haley, Joseph '60 (GAL) [K] Houston, TX The Catholic Chaplain Corps.
Haley, Joseph V. *c.m.* '54 (SJ) [N] Los Altos Hills, CA Daughters of Charity of St. Vincent de Paul (Laboure Residence), Seton Provincialate.
Haley, Thomas J. '78 (STL) Crestwood, MO St. Elizabeth of Hungary Church.
Haley, William J. '52 (BO) Holliston, MA St. Mary Church.
Halfacre, Philip '91 (PEO) [B] Ottawa, IL Marquette High School.
Halfacre, Philip D. '91 (PEO) Utica, IL St. Mary Church.
Halfmann, Msgr. Curtis T. '59 (LUB) [5] Lubbock, TX St. John Neumann Church.
Halfpenny, Patrick F. '75 (DET) Pontiac, MI St. Joseph Church; [A] Detroit, MI Sacred Heart Major Seminary, Inc.
Halkovic, Thomas M. *c.s.c.* '71 (FR) [B] North Easton, MA Stonehill College.
Hall, Adrian B. '64 (NO) [3] Slidell, LA St. Luke the Evangelist Church; Slidell, LA North Shore Living Center; Slidell, LA North Shore Regional Medical Center.
Hall, Alan *o.m.v.* '88 (LA) Hawaiian Gardens, CA St. Peter Chanel Church.
Hall, Bernard '77 (GR) Retired.
Hall, Charles D. '79 (GR) Ionia, MI SS. Peter and Paul Church.
Hall, Daniel *c.s.v.* '88 (CHI) [N] Arlington Heights, IL Viatorian Province Center-Clerics of St. Viator.
Hall, Douglas C. '79 (OM) Military Chaplains.
Hall, Eric *o.f.m.cap.* '96 (NY) [Z] New York, NY Immaculate Conception Friary.
Hall, Finbar '55 (LA) West Los Angeles, CA Veterans Administration Wadsworth Hospital Center; Military and VA Chaplains.
Hall, Francis J. '33 (BUF) Retired; [O] Buffalo, NY Sheehan Residence for Priests.
Hall, Henry '48 (MRY) Retired.
Hall, Howard *o.f.m.* '53 (LA) [W] Malibu, CA Serra Retreat.
Hall, Howard B. '62 (BR) St. James, LA St. James Church.
Hall, James W. '70 (ELP) [33] El Paso, TX St. Thomas Aquinas Church.
Hall, Jerome M. *s.j.* '77 (WDC) [M] Washington, DC Carroll House.
Hall, John '82 (PHX) Special Assignment.
Hall, John F. '55 (DET) [2] Westland, MI St. Damian Church; [4] Westland, MI St. Richard Church.
Hall, John M. '80 (IND) French Lick, IN Our Lady of the Springs Church; Paoli, IN Our Lord Jesus Christ the King Church.
Hall, John R. '80 (CHI) Niles, IL Our Lady of Ransom Church.
Hall, Joseph S. '85 (L) Clementsville, KY St. Bernard Church.
Hall, Martin (RVC) Retired.
Hall, Martin J. '52 (RVC) Levittown, NY St. Bernard Church.
Hall, Michael *o.s.b.* '65 (WDC) [M] Washington, DC St. Anselm's Abbey.
Hall, Ralph T. *o.p.* '55 (PRO) [P] Providence, RI St. Thomas Aquinas Priory at Providence College.
Hall, Richard *o.m.i.* '93 (SAT) [F] San Antonio, TX St. Anthony Catholic High School; [M] San Antonio, TX St. Anthony Catholic High School House.
Hall, Robert '85 (HEL) Bozeman, MT Resurrection Church; [H] Bozeman, MT Montana State University.
Hall, Robert C. '79 (ALT) [11] Altoona, PA Our Lady of Lourdes Church.
Hall, Robert E. '42 (SY) Retired.
Hall, Rodney L. '91 (SAC) Alturas, CA Sacred Heart Church.
Hall, Sidney Peter '57 (SAC) [18] Sacramento, CA St. Peter Church.
Hall, Thomas P. *c.s.p.* '77 (NY) [Z] Scarsdale, NY Paulist Fathers Generalate.
Hall, Thomas P. *c.s.p.* '77 (ORG) El Toro, CA El Toro Marine Base.
Hall, Walter J. '49 (ALN) Heckscherville, PA St. Kieran Church.
Hallahan, Kenneth P. '75 (CAM) [7] Camden, NJ St. Joseph's Pro-Cathedral.
Hallahan, Timothy J. '57 (SPR) Southwick, MA Our Lady of the Lake Church.
Hallahan, William *o.m.i.* '59 (SEA) [28] Seattle, WA Our Lady of Guadalupe Church.
Hallaran, John O. *s.s.j.* '85 (NO) [4] New Orleans, LA Blessed Sacrament Church.
Hallemann, John L. '55 (STL) Oakville, MO Queen of All Saints Church.
Haller, James W. '62 (MAN) Auburn, NH St. Peter Church.
Haller, Joseph A. *s.j.* '55 (WDC) [M] Washington, DC The Jesuit Community at Georgetown University.
Haller, Robert R. *o.p.* '69 (WDC) [11] Washington, DC St. Dominic Church & Priory Church.
Halleran, Thomas P. *s.v.d.* '44 (BO) [6] Somerville, MA Patronage of St. Joseph Church.
Hallett, Garth L. *s.j.* '59 (STL) [C] St. Louis, MO Saint Louis University; [P] St. Louis, MO Jesuit Community Corporation at St. Louis University - Jesuit Hall.
Halley, Kirino '92 (CI) Ulul, FM Sacred Heart Church.
Halley, Kirino B. '92 (CI) Fefan, FM Sacred Heart Church; Fefan, FM Sacred Heart Church.
Halley, Thomas A. *s.j.* '48 (OM) [23] Omaha, NE St. John Church; [K] Omaha, NE Jesuit Community At Creighton University.
Halligan, James '43 (LIN) Retired.
Halligan, James J. (NY) [105] New York, NY St. Peter Church.
Halligan, John J. *s.j.* '61 (NY) [Z] New York, NY Jesuit Provincial's Office.
Halligan, Nicholas Francis *o.p.* '43 (NY) [Z] New York, NY St Vincent Ferrer Priory.
Halligan, Raymond Ferrer *o.p.* '60 (NY) [Z] New York, NY St Vincent Ferrer Priory.
Hallin, Msgr. Albert W. '61 (PEO) [1] Ottawa, IL St. Columba Church.
Hallinan, Edward J. '83 (PH) [119] Philadelphia, PA Our Lady of Hope Church.
Hallinan, Mark *s.j.* '95 (NY) [Z] New York, NY St. Ignatius Loyola Residence.
Hallinan, Mark C. *s.j.* '95 (NY) [51] New York, NY St. Ignatius Loyola Church.
Hallissey, Msgr. James T. '40 (B) Retired.
Hallissey, LaSalle *o.p.* '79 (ANC) [1] Anchorage, AK Holy Family Cathedral.
Hallisy, Peter *c.p.* '51 (HRT) [M] West Hartford, CT Holy Family Monastery/Retreat.
Halliwell, Raymond *m.ss.a.* '93 (NOR) [A] Cromwell, CT Holy Apostles College and Seminary; [F] Cromwell, CT Missionaries of the Holy Apostles.
Halliwell, Robert J. '57 (NEW) Northvale, NJ St. Anthony's Church.
Hallock, Addison *m.ss.a.* '74 (NOR) [A] Cromwell, CT Holy Apostles College and Seminary; [F] Cromwell, CT Missionaries of the Holy Apostles.
Halloran, Msgr. Edward D. '35 (BGP) Retired; [O] Stamford, CT Our Lady Queen of the Clergy Home.
Halloran, Emmet '50 (ROC) Retired.
Halloran, James F. '43 (COS) Calhan, CO St. Michael's Church.
Halloran, Jerome D. '54 (WIN) Retired.
Halloran, John '48 (HON) On Duty Outside the Diocese.
Halloran, John '48 (LA) Lompoc, CA La Purisima Concepcion Church.
Halloran, John C. '62 (PRO) [5] Warwick, RI St. Gregory the Great Church.
Halloran, Joseph '53 (ALB) New Lebanon, NY Immaculate Conception Church.
Halloran, Joseph H. '47 (COS) Retired.
Halloran, Paul F. '53 (WIN) Retired.
Halloran, Walter *s.j.* '54 (SD) [38] San Diego, CA San Rafael Church.
Halloran, Walter H. *s.j.* '54 (MIL) [P] Milwaukee, WI Jesuit Provincial Office, Wisconsin Province.
Hallsten, Thomas J. *o.s.b.* '90 (STP) Lake St. Croix Beach, MN St. Francis Of Assisi Church.
Halmo, John F. '58 (MIL) Retired.
Halovatch, Paul J. '70 (HRT) [17] Waterbury, CT SS. Peter and Paul Church.
Halphen, Jude A. '93 (LAF) Cankton, LA St. John Berchmans Church.
Halphen, Marshall J. *o.s.a.* '63 (ALB) Waterford, NY St. Mary of the Assumption Church.
Halpin, John P. '54 (RVC) Central Islip, NY St. John of God Church; Central Islip, NY Central Islip State Hospital; West Brentwood, NY Pilgrim Psychiatric Center.
Halpin, Joseph '79 (TR) [2] Toms River, NJ St. Justin Church.
Halpin, Leo F. '42 (NY) Retired.
Halpin, Raymond J. '32 (ALB) Retired.
Halpin, Thomas A. *m.h.m.* '40 (NY) [Z] Hartsdale, NY Mill Hill Fathers Residence.
Halpine, Msgr. James F. '52 (TLS) [1] Tulsa, OK Holy Family Cathedral.
Halstead, James *o.s.a.* (CHI) Evanston, IL St. Nicholas Church.
Halstead, Philip '62 (PT) Retired.
Halter, Robert *o.s.b.* '60 (OM) [C] Elkhorn, NE Mount Michael High School; [K] Elkhorn, NE Mount Michael Abbey.
Halter, Robert *c.ss.r.* '70 (DET) [34] Detroit, MI Holy Redeemer Church.
Halton, Thomas P. '50 (WDC) [C] Washington, DC Catholic University of America, The.
Halus, Robert '82 (PBR) Pleasant City, OH St. Michael Church.
Haluska, Charles A. '51 (COL) Retired.
Halvey, William *s.v.d.* '76 (BLX) [A] Bay St. Louis, MS St. Augustine's.
Ham, George E. '67 (MAN) Hampton, NH Our Lady of the Miraculous Medal Church.
Ham, Jerome '68 (PEO) [2] Streator, IL St. Anthony of Padua Church.
Hamaday, Ronald A. *o.s.a.* '78 (PH) [G] Malvern, PA Malvern Preparatory School for Boys.
Hamaday, Ronald A. *o.s.a.* '78 (WDC) [B] Washington, DC Augustinian College, Order of St. Augustine.
Hamak, William L. '92 (SFS) Eden, SD Sacred Heart Church.
Hamame, Jaime (SB) Alta Loma, CA St. Peter & St. Paul Church.
Hambrough, Patrick K. '85 (STL) [15] St. Louis, MO Our Lady of the Holy Cross Church.
Hamburger, Msgr. Donald C. '46 (CHR) Retired.
Hamel, Edward L. *o.s.a.* (PH) [Z] Willowburn, PA Order of St. Augustine.
Hamel, Edward L. *o.s.a.* '54 (KAL) Douglas, MI St. Peter Church; [E] Douglas, MI Order of St. Augustine.
Hamel, J. Thomas *s.j.* '58 (WOR) [N] Worcester, MA Jesuits of Holy Cross College, Inc.
Hamel, James A. '92 (NEW) Maywood, NJ Our Lady Queen of Peace Church.
Hamel, Joseph *o.m.i.* '32 (SAT) [K] San Antonio, TX Oblate Madonna Residence.
Hamel, Philip N. '85 (FR) Absent on Leave.
Hamel, Robert F. '83 (STP) Retired.
Hamel, Roland M. *o.m.i.* '53 (MAN) [K] Colebrook, NH Shrine of Our Lady of Grace.
Hamernick, Joseph M. *s.j.* '62 (SCR) [C] Scranton, PA University of Scranton.
Hamill, Francis J. *s.j.* '61 (NEW) [C] Jersey City, NJ St. Peter's Preparatory School.
Hamill, William A. *o.s.a.* '72 (TLS) [B] Tulsa, OK Cascia Hall Preparatory School.
Hamilton, Daniel E. '72 (ARL) Lake Ridge, VA St. Elizabeth Seton Church.
Hamilton, Msgr. Daniel S. '58 (RVC) Lindenhurst, NY Our Lady of Perpetual Help Church.
Hamilton, Donald Joseph *o.c.s.o.* '46 (SPC) [E] Ava, MO Assumption Abbey (Trappist).
Hamilton, Edward A. '59 (ORL) Palm Bay, FL St. Joseph Church; Retired.
Hamilton, James '36 (SEA) Retired.
Hamilton, James '58 (CC) Aransas Pass, TX St. Mary, Star of the Sea Church; On Special Assignment.
Hamilton, James J. '53 (PRO) [10] Warwick, RI St. Timothy's Church.
Hamilton, John W. '70 (BUR) Shelburne, VT St. Catherine of Siena Church.
Hamilton, Joseph K. '54 (L) Retired.
Hamilton, Kenneth *s.v.d.* '95 (IND) [39] Indianapolis, IN St. Rita Church.
Hamilton, Lamont R. '79 (NY) [148] Bronx, NY Holy Rosary Church.

Hamilton, Mark M. '94 (L) [10] Louisville, KY St. Barnabas Church.
Hamilton, Philip A. '44 (DUB) Retired.
Hamilton, Terence J. '73 (CIN) [86] Cincinnati, OH St. Vincent Ferrer Church.
Hamilton, Thomas M. *s.m.* '88 (OAK) [N] Berkeley, CA Marist Fathers and Brothers.
Hamilton, William J. *s.j.* '63 (BO) [E] Boston, MA Boston College High School & Jesuit Community; [W] Boston, MA The Society of Jesus of New England-Provincial Offices.
Hamilton, William J. *s.j.* '63 (MAN) [3] Manchester, NH St. Anthony of Padua Church.
Hamilton, William J. '80 (SPR) [2] Holyoke, MA Holy Cross Church.
Hamlet, Ralph '62 (RIC) Scottsville, VA St. George Church.
Hamlett, Christopher (E) [B] Erie, PA Gannon University.
Hamlin, Raymond G. '91 (CLV) Cuyahoga Falls, OH St. Joseph Church.
Hamm, David A. *s.t.* '75 (JKS) Philadelphia, MS Holy Rosary Church.
Hamm, M. Dennis *s.j.* '70 (OM) [K] Omaha, NE Jesuit Community At Creighton University.
Hammeke, Gerald A. '52 (DOD) St. Mary, KS St. Mary Church; Spearville, KS St. John the Baptist Church; Windthorst, KS Immaculate Heart of Mary Church.
Hammel, Gerald *s.m.* '78 (SAT) Helotes, TX Our Lady of Guadalupe Church.
Hammelman, William *o.s.b.* '71 (P) [A] St. Benedict, OR Mount Angel Seminary; [L] St. Benedict, OR Mt. Angel Abbey.
Hammer, Msgr. Edmond '42 (NY) Retired.
Hammer, James *o.f.m.cap.* '65 (NOR) [4] Middletown, CT St. Pius X Church.
Hammer, Jefferson '60 (NY) Manhattan, NY St. Vincent Hospital; [S] New York, NY St. Vincent's Hospital and Medical Center of New York.
Hammer, John E. '79 (SAG) St. Louis, MI St. Joseph Church.
Hammer, Michael J. '69 (MIL) Special Assignment.
Hammer, William D. '80 (L) [27] Louisville, KY St. Gabriel the Archangel Church.
Hammerl, Msgr. Leo E. '44 (BUF) Retired; [O] Tonawanda, NY O'Hara Residence.
Hammerschmitt, Clemens '73 (PMB) Lake Worth, FL St. Matthew Church.
Hammerstein, Harold *o.s.b.* '48 (IND) [J] St. Meinrad, IN St. Meinrad Archabbey.
Hammett, Peter *o.s.b.* '72 (NO) [P] St. Benedict, LA St. Joseph Abbey.
Hammett, Peter E. *o.s.b.* '72 (NO) [A] St. Benedict, LA St. Joseph's Seminary College.
Hammon, Nevin *o.f.m.conv.* '63 (SY) Minoa, NY St. Mary Church.
Hammond, Charles *o.m.i.* '76 (LUB) Lamesa, TX St. Margaret Mary Church.
Hammond, Henry E. '40 (ARL) Retired.
Hammond, John *o.s.b.* '50 (BUR) [G] Weston, VT Priory of Benedictine Monks.
Hammond, Mark '89 (COL) [5] Columbus, OH St. Andrew Church.
Hammond, Martin '73 (BAL) [41] Baltimore, MD St. Isaac Jogues Church.
Hammond, Robert J. '52 (FTW) North Manchester, IN St. Robert Bellarmine Church.
Hammond, Robert W. '67 (ROC) Bath, NY St. Mary Church.
Hampe, Ray '76 (STL) [K] St. Charles, MO St. Joseph Health Center.
Hampe, Msgr. Raymond A. '54 (STL) [5] St. Charles, MO St. Peter Church; St. Charles, MO St. Joseph Health Center.
Hamperzonian, Jerry '70 (PSC) On Duty Outside Diocese.
Hamperzonian, Jerry '70 (SD) [3] San Diego, CA Blessed Sacrament Church; La Jolla, CA Veterans Administration Hospital.
Hampsch, John *c.m.f.* '52 (LA) [R] Los Angeles, CA Claretian Retreat Center Community.
Hampton, James J. '88 (MIA) [12] Fort Lauderdale, FL St. Pius X Church.
Han, Andrew '48 (LA) Retired.
Hanacsek, John '49 (TOL) Retired.
Hanafin, William '45 (BEA) Retired.
Hanauska, Joseph F. '40 (MIL) Retired.
Hanbury, Kevin M. '72 (NEW) [B] South Orange, NJ Seton Hall University.
Hanchak, Augustine *c.pp.s.* '52 (CIN) [B] Carthagena, OH St. Charles.
Hanchon, Donald F. '74 (DET) [25] Detroit, MI St. Gabriel Church.
Hancock, Msgr. George H. '47 (OWN) Grand Rivers, KY St. Anthony of Padua Church.
Hancock, Walter '47 (OWN) Retired.
Hand, Chester, Jr. '86 (AUS) Retired.
Hand, Dennis M. '75 (GRY) On Duty Outside the Diocese.
Hand, Kenneth J. '72 (BRK) [237] Queens, NY Sacred Heart of Jesus Church.
Hand, Msgr. Kevin '52 (AMA) White Deer, TX Sacred Heart Church.
Hand, Raymond *o.f.m.cap.* '62 (SPR) [L] Springfield, MA St. Francis of Assisi Chapel and Catholic Information Center.
Handges, Msgr. William E. '64 (ALN) [1] Easton, PA St. Anthony of Padua Church.
Handley, Robert '47 (LAN) Retired.
Handrahan, John B. *s.j.* '58 (BO) [W] Boston, MA The Society of Jesus of New England-Provincial Offices.
Hands, Michael '93 (RVC) West Islip, NY Our Lady of Lourdes Church.
Handwerker, Valentine '74 (MEM) Lexington, TN St. Andrew Church.
Hane, Howard S. (BO) Retired.
Hanefeldt, Joseph G. '84 (OM) [13] Omaha, NE St. Elizabeth Ann Church.
Hanel, Charles T. '83 (MIL) [73] Milwaukee, WI St. Sebastian's Church.
Hanem, Morgan P. *c.p.* '52 (NEW) [N] Union City, NJ Congregation of the Passion (Passionists)-St. Michael's Residence.
Haney, Bill *o.f.m.* '84 (MRY) Jolon, CA San Antonio Mission Church; San Miguel, CA San Miguel Church.
Haney, John R. '61 (PIT) Whitehall, PA St. Gabriel of the Sorrowful Virgin Church.
Haney, Michael *o.f.m.* '74 (SAT) [46] San Antonio, TX St. Joseph Church; [50] San Antonio, TX St. Leonard's Church.
Haney, Richard M. '35 (DET) Retired.
Haney, Thomas R. '58 (HBG) New Cumberland, PA St. Theresa of the Infant Jesus Church.
Hanh, Joseph Phan Trong '70 (KC) [17] Kansas City, MO Church of the Holy Martyrs.
Hanhauser, Martin A. '42 (SP) [O] St. Petersburg, FL St. Anthony Friary.
Hanic, John D. '83 (CHL) [4] Charlotte, NC St. Ann Church.
Hanicak, Msgr. Robert A. '36 (GBG) Retired; [G] Greensburg, PA Neumann House.
Hanifin, Michael '87 (ORG) [1] Huntington Beach, CA St. Bonaventure Church.
Hankiewicz, Edward A. '79 (GR) [21] Grand Rapids, MI Sacred Heart Church.
Hankinson, Aloysius *t.o.r.* '50 (ALT) [F] Hollidaysburg, PA St. Joseph Friary.
Hankinson, Aquin *o.f.m.conv.* '50 (NEW) [2] Hoboken, NJ St. Joseph's Church.
Hanks, Joseph H. '81 (NOR) Old Saybrook, CT St. John Church.
Hankus, David '84 (JOL) Lombard, IL Christ the King Church.
Hanley, Msgr. Andrew W. '40 (SD) Retired.
Hanley, Boniface F. *o.f.m.* '50 (PAT) West Milford Township, NJ St. Joseph Church.
Hanley, Dennis '81 (CHY) Cheyenne, WY U.S. Veterans Administration Hospital 1.
Hanley, Dennis P. '81 (HRT) Military Chaplains.
Hanley, Foster *o.carm.* '63 (TUC) [A] Tucson, AZ Salpointe Catholic High School; [F] Tucson, AZ Carmelite Priory.
Hanley, Francis X. *c.s.sp.* '59 (PIT) [P] Bethel Park, PA Holy Ghost Animation Center.
Hanley, Gerald T. '73 (RNO) Carson City, NV St. Teresa's of Avila Church.
Hanley, James F. *s.j.* '47 (MIL) [P] Milwaukee, WI Jesuit Provincial Office, Wisconsin Province.
Hanley, Msgr. James P. '51 (COL) Retired.
Hanley, James R. *s.j.* '58 (SJ) [L] Los Altos, CA Jesuit Retreat House.
Hanley, James T. '62 (PAT) Retired.
Hanley, John '56 (PHX) [1] Tempe, AZ Holy Spirit Church.
Hanley, John *o.s.f.s.* '86 (ALN) [B] Center Valley, PA Allentown College of St. Francis de Sales; [O] Kutztown, PA Christopher House.
Hanley, John A. *o.s.f.s.* '86 (ALN) [K] Center Valley, PA Oblates of St. Francis de Sales.
Hanley, John G. '50 (NEW) Retired.
Hanley, John P. (MIL) Retired.
Hanley, John P. '94 (PAT) Mendham, NJ St. Joseph's Church.
Hanley, John W. *o.m.i.* '70 (BO) [16] Lowell, MA Sacred Heart Church.
Hanley, Joseph F. '68 (CHR) [7] Charleston, SC Blessed Sacrament Church.
Hanley, Lawrence F. '52 (CHI) Antioch, IL St. Peter Church.
Hanley, Thomas E. '65 (WIL) Dover, DE Holy Cross Church.
Hanley, William '45 (SPK) Retired.
Hanlon, Andrew J. '68 (PH) Brookhaven, PA Our Lady of Charity Church.
Hanlon, Capistran J. *o.f.m.* '60 (ALB) [B] Loudonville, NY Siena College.
Hanlon, Edward J. '86 (WOR) [2] Southbridge, MA Notre Dame Church.
Hanlon, Francis J. *o.s.f.s.* '76 (WIL) [I] Wilmington, DE Oblates of St. Francis De Sales.
Hanlon, Msgr. James J. '38 (NY) Retired; [V] New York, NY Kateri Residence.
Hanlon, John R. '55 (BO) Retired.
Hanlon, Louis J. *s.j.* '39 (STL) [O] St. Louis, MO Fusz Pavilion.
Hanlon, Morgan *c.p.* '52 (NEW) [N] Union City, NJ Congregation of the Passion (Passionists)-St. Michael's Residence.
Hanlon, Robert M. *s.j.* '64 (BO) [E] Boston, MA Boston College High School & Jesuit Community; [W] Boston, MA The Society of Jesus of New England-Provincial Offices.
Hanlon, Robert M. *s.j.* '64 (MIA) [G] Fort Lauderdale, FL Holy Cross Hospital.
Hanlon, Robert P. *o.s.f.s.* '57 (PH) [Z] Philadelphia, PA Oblates of St. Francis De Sales.
Hanlon, Thomas C. '38 (CHI) Retired.
Hanly, John J. '50 (LA) Retired.
Hanly, Joseph M. *c.s.p.* '53 (NY) [Z] Scarsdale, NY Paulist Fathers Generalate.
Hanly, Joseph M. *c.s.p.* '53 (SFR) [31] San Francisco, CA Old St. Mary's Cathedral.
Hanly, Michael A. '67 (NEW) Verona, NJ Our Lady of the Lake Church.
Hanly, Thomas '62 (MIA) Hollywood, FL Little Flower Church; Retired.
Hanna, Austin B. '36 (ROC) Retired.
Hanna, Don Michael '64 (RIC) Yorktown, VA St. Joan of Arc Church.
Hanna, Msgr. Francis J. '42 (BUF) Retired.
Hanna, George *s.d.b.* '66 (NY) [117] New York, NY St. Thomas the Apostle Church; [DD] New York, NY Don Bosco Harlem Association, Inc.
Hanna, Jack H. *c.s.b.* '74 (GAL) [F] Houston, TX St. Thomas High School.
Hanna, Yousef '80 (OLD) Syriac Catholic Mission Church.
Hannafey, Francis T. *s.j.* '93 (BGP) [O] Fairfield, CT The Fairfield Jesuit Community-Fairfield University.
Hannahs, Norman G. *c.s.sp.* '56 (DET) [48] Detroit, MI St. Mary Church.
Hannan, Gabriel *s.t.* '55 (WDC) [M] Adelphi, MD Missionary Servants of the Most Holy Trinity.
Hannan, Msgr. Herbert J. '37 (OG) Retired.
Hannan, Msgr. Herbert J. '39 (OG) Brasher Falls, NY St. Patrick Church.
Hannan, James E. *o.s.a.* '44 (SD) [H] San Diego, CA Augustinian Community.
Hannan, James G. '81 (BRK) [14] Brooklyn, NY St. Augustine Church.
Hannan, John '55 (SAC) Weed, CA Holy Family Church.
Hannan, Msgr. John P. '47 (ARL) Clifton, VA St. Andrew the Apostle Church.
Hannappel, Joseph A. '84 (GI) Chappell, NE St. Joseph's Church.
Hannaway, Arthur '85 (VEN) Bokeelia, FL Our Lady of the Miraculous Medal Church.
Hanneke, Richard E. '76 (STL) Ellisville, MO St. Clare of Assisi Church; [W] St. Louis, MO Archdiocesan Charitable Bequest Council.
Hanneman, Dennis A. '72 (OM) [47] Omaha, NE St. Vincent de Paul Church.
Hannes, David A. '83 (PRM) Flushing, MI St. Michael Church.
Hannick, Anthony S. '58 (OAK) [1] Walnut Creek, CA St. Anne Church; Military Chaplains.
Hannick, Anthony S. '58 (YAK) Retired.
Hannifin, Francis M. '45 (L) Retired.
Hannigan, John T. '76 (CHI) Other Assignments.
Hannigan, John T. '76 (SFD) Morrisonville, IL St. Maurice Church.
Hannigan, Raymond J. '91 (HEL) Libby, MT St. Joseph Church.
Hannigan, Richard '59 (WOR) [M] Worcester, MA Vianney House.
Hannigan, Thomas J. '49 (MAN) [6] Manchester, NH St. Catherine Church.
Hannon, Msgr. James J. '45 (BLX) Retired.
Hannon, James J. '57 (RVC) Brentwood, NY St. Anne's Church.
Hannon, James W. '88 (BAL) Westernport, MD St. Peter Church.
Hannon, John Mark (BO) Hanson, MA St. Joseph the Worker Church.
Hannon, John P. '76 (HRT) [10] Hartford, CT St. Justin Church; Retired.
Hannon, Joseph (OG) Watertown, NY U.S. Army Headquarters Fort Drum.
Hannon, Ken *o.m.i.* '72 (SAT) [C] San Antonio, TX Oblate School of Theology; [M] San Antonio, TX De Mazenod House.
Hannon, Kevin E. '75 (SY) Mattydale, NY St. Margaret Church.
Hannon, Michael '47 (ORL) Retired.
Hannon, Richard T. '93 (GAY) Elmira, MI St. Thomas Aquinas Church; Vanderbilt, MI Holy Redeemer Church.
Hannon, Robert E. '54 (HON) Retired.
Hannon, Robert J. '79 (Y) Masury, OH St. Bernadette Church.
Hannon, Timothy G. '62 (MIA) [3] Fort Lauderdale, FL St. Anthony Church.

Hannon, W. Patrick *c.s.c.* '89 (P) [B] Portland, OR University of Portland; [L] Portland, OR Holy Cross Father & Brother, C.S.C. - University of Portland.
Hanouille, Roger *o.s.a.* '59 (ALB) Cambridge, NY St. Patrick Church.
Hanowsky, Andrew '88 (SJP) [1] Parma, OH St. Josaphat Cathedral.
Hanrahan, Denis G. '59 (OKL) Guthrie, OK St. Mary's Church.
Hanrahan, Edward J. *s.j.* '61 (BO) [W] Chestnut Hill, MA The Jesuit Community at Boston College.
Hanrahan, John A. '46 (GF) Retired.
Hanrahan, John A. *s.j.* '66 (BO) [W] Boston, MA The Society of Jesus of New England-Provincial Offices.
Hanrahan, John W. '55 (L) [60] Louisville, KY Our Mother of Sorrows Church.
Hanrahan, Michael '59 (ORL) Deltona, FL Our Lady of the Lakes Church.
Hanrahan, Michael '71 (COL) Absent on Sick Leave.
Hanrahan, William (LAV) Military Chaplains.
Hanrahan, William P. '69 (NEW) Military Chaplains.
Hanratty, Brendan '45 (SR) Retired.
Hanratty, Brendan *o.c.s.o.* '58 (SLC) [F] Huntsville, UT Abbey of Our Lady of the Holy Trinity of the Order of Cistercians.
Hansen, Albert M. '65 (BUF) West Falls, NY St. George Church.
Hansen, Howard *o.f.m.conv.* '57 (STP) [Q] Prior Lake, MN Franciscan Retreat House.
Hansen, John R. *s.m.p.* '81 (SPC) [E] Marionville, MO The Society of Our Mother of Peace, Sons of Our Mother of Peace.
Hansen, Lawrence H. '68 (NU) On Duty Outside the Diocese.
Hansen, Lawrence H. '68 (PH) [T] Philadelphia, PA Mercy Catholic Medical Center; [T] Darby, PA Mercy Catholic Medical Center.
Hansen, Michael H. '67 (NEW) West Orange, NJ Our Lady of Lourdes Church.
Hansen, Norbert P. *o.carm.* '54 (NY) [Z] Middletown, NY St. Albert's Priory.
Hansen, Robert H. '40 (LC) Retired; [I] La Crosse, WI Holy Cross (Seminary) Diocesan Center.
Hansen, Thomas J. *s.j.* (MIL) [P] Milwaukee, WI Jesuit Provincial Office, Wisconsin Province.
Hansen, Thomas J. *s.j.* '96 (OM) [K] Omaha, NE Jesuit Community At Creighton University.
Hanser, David J. '58 (MIL) [K] Milwaukee, WI St. Joseph's Hospital of Franciscan Sisters, Milwaukee, Inc.
Hanser, F. Patrick *c.m.* '70 (DAL) [I] Dallas, TX St. Paul Medical Center.
Hansmann, Joseph D. '62 (BEL) Paderborn, IL St. Michael Church.
Hanson, Christopher *o.s.b.* '96 (STL) [F] Creve Coeur, MO St. Louis Priory School; [P] St. Louis, MO The Abbey of St. Mary and St. Louis.
Hanson, Donald M. '71 (RVC) Priests Released from Diocesan Assignment.
Hanson, Msgr. James E. '61 (STL) Zell, MO St. Joseph Church.
Hanson, Kirby C. '70 (SFR) [51] San Francisco, CA St. Thomas, The Apostle Church.
Hanson, Richard N. '75 (CHL) [11] Charlotte, NC St. Vincent de Paul Church.
Hanson, William A. '72 (RVC) Port Jefferson, NY St. Gerard Majella Church.
Hanudel, Francis *o.f.m.* '72 (NY) [Z] New York, NY Franciscan Province of the Immaculate Conception.
Hanudel, Francis *o.f.m.* '72 (PAT) Paterson, NJ St. Joseph Hospital; [J] Paterson, NJ St. Joseph's Hospital and Medical Center.
Hanus, Thomas J. '66 (AUS) Cameron, TX St. Monica's Church.
Hanwell, John J. *s.j.* '91 (PRT) [C] Portland, ME Cheverus High School; [I] Portland, ME St. Ignatius Residence.
Hanzely, Joseph B. *s.j.* '48 (ALN) [A] Wernersville, PA Novitiate of St. Isaac Jogues.
Hanzo, Robert '56 (CLV) Retired.
Hapanowicz, Arthur R. '56 (SY) [2] Utica, NY Holy Trinity Church; [W] Utica, NY Holy Trinity.
Hapka, Jerome A. *s.a.c.* '55 (MIL) Wauwatosa, WI Milwaukee Regional Medical Center; [P] Milwaukee, WI Pallotti House.
Happel, Stephen P. '70 (IND) On Duty Outside the Archdiocese.
Happel, Stephen W. '70 (WDC) [C] Washington, DC Catholic University of America, The.
Harahan, Msgr. Robert E. '69 (NEW) Summit, NJ St. Teresa's Church.
Harak, G. Simon *s.j.* '79 (BGP) [A] Fairfield, CT Fairfield University; [O] Fairfield, CT The Fairfield Jesuit Community-Fairfield University.
Haran, Ignatius '59 (SAC) Folsom, CA St. John the Baptist Church.
Haran, James E. '44 (BUF) Retired.
Harasim, Edward A. '78 (CHI) [77] Chicago, IL St. Henry Church.
Harbaugh, James M. *s.j.* '78 (SEA) [A] Seattle, WA Seattle University.
Harbaugh, Paul E. '74 (BEL) Leave of Absence.
Harbert, William S. '62 (PEO) Absent on Leave.
Harbison, William *c.ss.r.* (BO) [13] Boston, MA Basilica of Our Lady of Perpetual Help.
Harbison, William *c.ss.r.* '66 (BAL) [85] Baltimore, MD Sacred Heart of Jesus Church.
Harbour, Gerald G. '73 (PRO) Providence, RI Rhode Island Hospital.
Harbour, Linn S. '86 (OM) Military Chaplains.
Harcar, Anthony '69 (OAK) Retired.
Harcarik, Bernard M. '63 (PIT) [63] Pittsburgh, PA Prince of Peace Church.
Harder, Ken '96 (TLS) [5] Tulsa, OK Christ the King Church.
Harder, William '86 (NY) [214] Staten Island, NY St. Mary of the Assumption Church.
Harder, William G. '86 (NY) [160] Bronx, NY St. Luke Church.
Hardesty, Ernest L. *v.f.* '75 (LR) Russellville, AR St. John's Church.
Hardesty, Leo '31 (OKL) Retired.
Hardick, Richard *o.s.a.* '66 (SD) [H] San Diego, CA Augustinian Community.
Hardiman, Msgr. James C. '39 (CHI) Retired.
Hardiman, John J. '49 (ALB) Latham, NY Our Lady of the Assumption Church.
Hardiman, Michael J. '78 (BRK) Special Assignment.
Hardin, Boniface *o.s.b.* '59 (IND) [J] St. Meinrad, IN St. Meinrad Archabbey.
Hardin, John S. *o.f.m.* '86 (OAK) [N] Oakland, CA Franciscan Friars Provincial Office, Province of St. Barbara; [N] Oakland, CA Franciscan Friars Provincial Office, Province of St. Barbara.
Hardin, Roy '64 (CAM) On Sick Leave.
Harding, Bernard '47 (BAL) [M] Baltimore, MD Holy Trinity Monastery.
Harding, Pius X. *o.s.b.* '93 (P) [L] St. Benedict, OR Mt. Angel Abbey.
Hardman, John E. *s.s.j.* '44 (GAL) [61] Houston, TX Our Mother of Mercy Church.
Hardon, John *s.j.* '47 (WDC) [V] Kensington, MD Inter Mirifica.
Hardy, John J. '38 (DET) Retired.
Hardy, Laurence A. *o.f.m.* '46 (SP) [O] St. Petersburg, FL St. Anthony Friary.
Hare, Robert '70 (NSH) [L] Nashville, TN Glenmary Department of Pastoral Services.
Haren, Donald J. *m.m.* '47 (SJ) [M] Los Altos, CA Maryknoll.
Haren, Thomas A. '73 (CLV) [36] Cleveland, OH St. Jerome Church.
Harer, Eric K. '84 (SY) [5] Oswego, NY St. Paul Church.
Harfmann, John G. *s.s.j.* '62 (WDC) [B] Washington, DC Josephite Pastoral Center; [B] Washington, DC St. Joseph's Seminary.
Hargadon, James E. '55 (L) Mount Washington, KY St. Francis Xavier Church.
Hargarten, Joseph F. '41 (GI) Retired.
Hargesheimer, Thomas J. '68 (WIN) Owatonna, MN St. Joseph's Church.
Hargreaves, Henry *s.j.* '47 (FBK) Nightmute, AK Our Lady of Perpetual Help Church; Toksook Bay, AK St. Peter the Fisherman Church; Tununak, AK St. Joseph Church.
Hargrove, Gerard (WDC) [S] Washington, DC Archdiocesan Campus Ministry.
Hargrove, Jerry E. '76 (WDC) Special Ministries.
Harguindeguy, Msgr. John '67 (FRS) [1] Fresno, CA St. John Cathedral.
Harhager, John H. *s.m.* '79 (WDC) [M] Washington, DC Marist Provincial House.
Harkabus, Donald W. *o.s.a.* '58 (CHI) [N] Olympia Fields, IL The Augustinian Provincialate Tolentine Center.
Harkins, Bernard K. *o.p.* '67 (WDC) [C] Washington, DC Catholic University of America, The.
Harkins, Conrad *o.f.m.* '61 (STU) [A] Steubenville, OH Franciscan University of Steubenville; [F] Steubenville, OH Holy Spirit Monastery.
Harkins, Frederick A. *s.j.* '39 (BO) [W] Weston, MA Campion Health Center, Inc.
Harkins, John M. '65 (PH) [103] Philadelphia, PA St. Michael Church.
Harkins, Kenneth *o.p.* '67 (WDC) [B] Washington, DC Dominican House of Studies.
Harkins, Michael J. '79 (BO) Chelmsford, MA St. Mary Church.
Harkins, Msgr. Thaddeus '55 (JKS) Greenwood, MS Immaculate Heart of Mary Church.
Harkins, Thomas A. '71 (CAM) [1] Camden, NJ Immaculate Conception Cathedral.
Harkrader, Edward O. '69 (PEO) Princeton, IL St. Louis Church.
Harlan, Michael J. *o.f.m.* (ALB) [S] Loudonville, NY Siena College.
Harland, Norman E. *s.j.* '67 (CHI) [D] Wilmette, IL Loyola Academy.
Harley, Ronald P. '67 (ROC) Geneva, NY St. Francis de Sales Church.
Harlow, Denis '58 (BLX) [4] Biloxi, MS Sacred Heart Church; Biloxi, MS Biloxi Regional Hospital, Gulf Coast Community Hospital.
Harlow, Francis G. '88 (B) On Duty Outside the Diocese.
Harlow, Lance '93 (BUR) Gilman, VT St. Theresa Church; St. Johnsbury, VT St. John the Evangelist Church.
Harlow, Sean *o.carm.* '69 (NY) Middletown, NY Our Lady of Mt. Carmel Church; [Z] Middletown, NY Brandsma Priory.
Harman, Charles W. '54 (LA) Retired.
Harman, Paul F. *s.j.* '68 (BO) [W] Boston, MA The Society of Jesus of New England-Provincial Offices.
Harman, Paul F. *s.j.* '68 (CHI) [C] Chicago, IL Jesuit Community at Loyola University of Chicago.
Harmening, Adrian W. *o.s.b.* (RIC) [7] Richmond, VA St. Benedict Church.
Harmening, Adrian W. *o.s.b.* '55 (RIC) [B] Richmond, VA Benedictine High School; [L] Richmond, VA Ethnic and Special Ministries; [M] Richmond, VA Mary Mother of the Church Abbey.
Harmless, J. William *s.j.* '87 (MOB) [B] Mobile, AL Spring Hill College.
Harmon, Alban *c.p.* '58 (R) Greenville, NC St. Peter's Church.
Harmon, Barry '90 (SFD) [3] Springfield, IL Christ The King Church.
Harmon, John (DM) Logan, IA St. Anne Church.
Harms, Msgr. William C. '65 (NEW) [B] South Orange, NJ Seton Hall University; [B] South Orange, NJ Seton Hall University.
Harnan, James *m.s.c.* '64 (AUS) Blanco, TX St. Ferdinand's Church.
Harnan, James *m.s.c.* '64 (SAT) [M] San Antonio, TX Missionaries of the Sacred Heart.
Harness, H. Robert '82 (DAV) DeWitt, IA St. Joseph's Church.
Harnett, Edward F. '58 (CHI) Wilmette, IL St. Francis Xavier Church.
Harnett, Msgr. Timothy '56 (SD) Encinitas, CA St. John the Evangelist Church.
Harney, Kenneth '89 (NO) [6] Metairie, LA St. Christopher the Martyr Church.
Harney, Peter '53 (WIL) Retired.
Harney, Thomas C. '62 (GF) Columbus, MT St. Mary's Church; Laurel, MT St. Anthony's Church.
Harnischfeger, William '93 (PHX) Sun City, AZ St. Elizabeth Seton Church.
Harnish, Lionel '54 (GAY) Retired.
Harold, Thomas J. '91 (RVC) Williston Park, NY St. Aidan's Church.
Harpe, David L. '94 (GR) Ada, MI St. Robert Church.
Harpel, John *s.v.d.* '44 (DUB) [H] New Hampton, IA St. Joseph Community Hospital.
Harper, Henry *s.s.j.* '50 (BAL) [79] Baltimore, MD St. Peter Claver Church.
Harper, Msgr. James J. '49 (KC) Retired.
Harper, John '47 (R) Retired.
Harper, John H. '87 (GB) [2] De Pere, WI St. Mary Church.
Harr, Gerald J. '62 (GI) Gering, NE Christ the King Church.
Harren, Robert C. '66 (SCL) [4] St. Cloud, MN St. Anthony of Padua Church.
Harrer, Frederic J. '45 (RVC) Hicksville, NY St. Ignatius Loyola Church; Retired.
Harrer, Ronald *o.m.i.* '70 (SFS) Rosholt, SD St. John the Baptist Church.
Harrigan, Philip K. *s.j.* '56 (BO) [12] Boston, MA St. Augustine Church; [E] Boston, MA Boston College High School & Jesuit Community; [W] Boston, MA The Society of Jesus of New England-Provincial Offices.
Harriman, Michael D. '68 (SFR) [10] San Francisco, CA St. Cecilia Church.
Harrington, Ashley *o.carm.* '67 (NEW) Tenafly, NJ Our Lady of Mount Carmel Church.
Harrington, Brian J. '67 (FR) North Dartmouth, MA St. Julie Billiart Church.
Harrington, Cornelius '41 (SEA) Retired.
Harrington, Msgr. D. B. '32 (HEL) Retired.
Harrington, Daniel J. *s.j.* '71 (BO) [W] Cambridge, MA Weston Jesuit Community.
Harrington, Donald J. *c.m.* '73 (BRK) [D] Queens and Staten Island, NY St. John's University; [U] Jamaica, NY St. Vincent's House.
Harrington, Donald J. *c.m.* '73 (NY) [C] Staten Island, NY St. John's University Staten Island Campus.
Harrington, Emmet '49 (P) Retired.
Harrington, Eugene J. *s.j.* '45 (WOR) [N] Worcester, MA Jesuits of Holy Cross College, Inc.
Harrington, Ignatius '82 (NTN) Columbus, OH Holy Resurrection Church; Zanesville, OH Holy Trinity Church.
Harrington, James J. '53 (BO) Manchester, MA Sacred Heart Church.
Harrington, Jay M. *o.p.* '85 (STP) [15] Minneapolis, MN St. Albert the Great Church; [C] St. Paul, MN University of St. Thomas; [N] Minneapolis, MN St. Albert the Great Priory.
Harrington, Jeremy *o.f.m.* '59 (CIN) [24] Cincinnati,

OH Corpus Christi Church.
Harrington, John D. '56 (BO) [E] Reading, MA Austin Preparatory School.
Harrington, Msgr. John F. '35 (SPR) [2] Holyoke, MA Holy Cross Church; Retired.
Harrington, Msgr. John M. '45 (NY) Retired.
Harrington, Joseph D. '56 (HEL) [B] Helena, MT Carroll College.
Harrington, Kevin J. '75 (FR) [2] Attleboro, MA St. Joseph's Church.
Harrington, Mark E. '79 (SC) Sac City, IA St. Mary's Church.
Harrington, Maurice D. '96 (LA) Norwalk, CA St. John of God Church.
Harrington, Richard L. '66 (BO) Randolph, MA St. Mary Church.
Harrington, Msgr. Robert J. '71 (NEW) [1] Elizabeth, NJ St. Mary of the Assumption Church.
Harrington, Russel J. '79 (LAF) [1] Lafayette, LA St. John the Evangelist Cathedral.
Harrington, Msgr. Thomas J. '64 (FR) [1] New Bedford, MA Holy Name Church.
Harris, Alfred J. '94 (WDC) Norbeck, MD St. Patrick Church.
Harris, Andrew *o.m.i.* '53 (P) Sweet Home, OR St. Helen Church.
Harris, Anton T. *s.j.* '75 (P) [D] Portland, OR Jesuit High School.
Harris, Daniel *c.m.* (LA) [A] Camarillo, CA St. John's Seminary.
Harris, Daniel E. *c.m.* '74 (STL) [P] St. Louis, MO Vincentian Residence.
Harris, David T. (MAR) Retired.
Harris, Edward *s.j.* '45 (FRS) Faculties Only.
Harris, Edwin B. *s.j.* '75 (SAC) [C] Sacramento, CA Jesuit High School; [H] Carmichael, CA Jesuit High School Community of Sacramento.
Harris, George E. '65 (BWN) Los Fresnos, TX St. Cecilia Church.
Harris, George G. *c.s.v.* '63 (CHI) [D] Arlington Heights, IL St. Viator High School.
Harris, Gerald P. '79 (SUP) River Falls, WI St. Bridget Church.
Harris, Glenn H. '92 (PEO) [3] Bloomington, IL St. Patrick's Church.
Harris, Jack D. '74 (LR) Jonesboro, AR Blessed Sacrament Church; [J] Little Rock, AR Catholic Campus Ministries.
Harris, James (CC) [2] Laredo, TX Christ the King Church.
Harris, James M. '48 (P) Retired.
Harris, John F. '84 (PRT) Sabattus, ME Our Lady of the Rosary Church.
Harris, Julian '91 (PMB) Wellington, FL St. Rita Church.
Harris, Msgr. Martin P. '55 (WDC) Hollywood, MD St. John Church.
Harris, Msgr. Michael '72 (ORG) Inactive Leave.
Harris, Michael B. '92 (SCR) [5] Dunmore, PA St. Mary of Mount Carmel Church.
Harris, Raymond Lee '94 (BAL) [10] Baltimore, MD St. Anthony of Padua Church.
Harris, Richard D. (CHR) [3] Charleston, SC St. Patrick's Church; [5] Charleston, SC Our Lady of Mercy Church.
Harris, Msgr. Robert M. '59 (BRK) [207] Queens, NY Our Lady of the Blessed Sacrament Church; [O] Brooklyn, NY St. Vincent's Services, Inc.
Harris, Scott T. *m.m.* '78 (NY) [Z] Maryknoll, NY Maryknoll Fathers and Brothers.
Harris, Steven *c.s.p.* (NY) [41] New York, NY Good Shepherd Church.
Harris, Steven J. '80 (PH) [150] Philadelphia, PA St. Therese of the Child Jesus Church.
Harris, Msgr. Wallace A. '72 (NY) [24] New York, NY St. Charles Borromeo Church; [M] New York, NY Society of St. Vincent De Paul, Archdiocesan Central Council of New York.
Harris, Whitney G. '80 (LKC) On Special Assignment.
Harris, William R. '78 (SEA) Anacortes, WA St. Mary's Church.
Harris, Xavier J. *o.f.m.* '48 (OAK) [A] Berkeley, CA Franciscan School of Theology.
Harrison, Arthur '56 (SJ) Retired.
Harrison, Brian *o.s.* (PCE) [11] Ponce, PR San Jose Obrero Church.
Harrison, Brian W. *o.s.* (PCE) [B] Ponce, PR The Pontifical Catholic University of Puerto Rico; [H] Ponce, PR Oblates of Wisdom.
Harrison, Craig F. '87 (FRS) Firebaugh, CA St. Joseph Church.
Harrison, Cyprian *o.c.s.o.* '57 (SPC) [A] Ava, MO Assumption Novitiate (Trappists).
Harrison, George E. '68 (FR) Seekonk, MA Our Lady of Mt. Carmel Church.
Harrison, James '55 (ATL) [1] Atlanta, GA Cathedral of Christ the King.
Harrison, Jeffrey D. *s.j.* '82 (STL) [52] St. Louis, MO St. Matthew, Apostle Church.
Harrison, Jeffrey D. '87 (STL) [F] St. Louis, MO St. Louis University High School, George H. Backer Memorial; [P] St. Louis, MO St. Matthew Jesuit Community.
Harrison, John B. *c.ss.r.* '67 (BAL) Edenton, MD St. Joseph Church.
Harrison, Michael *s.s.c.* '48 (PRO) [P] Bristol, RI St. Columban's Retirement House.
Harrison, Patrick '91 (OM) On Duty Outside the Archdiocese.
Harrison, Robert '64 (NY) [E] New York, NY Cardinal Hayes High School.
Harrison, Timothy '75 (ALB) [1] Watervliet, NY St. Brigid Church; [H] Troy, NY Seton Health System, Inc.
Harrison, Timothy J. '91 (BO) Belmont, MA St. Joseph Church.
Harrison, Todd *s.j.* (BAL) [M] Baltimore, MD Ferdinand Wheeler House.
Harrison, Todd W. *s.j.* (MIL) [P] Milwaukee, WI Jesuit Provincial Office, Wisconsin Province.
Harrison, William S. '72 (PH) [45] Philadelphia, PA St. Francis of Assisi Church.
Harrity, Msgr. Dennis '60 (DET) Grosse Pointe, MI Our Lady Star of the Sea Church.
Harrity, Francis P. '33 (WOR) Retired.
Harrity, Patrick *c.m.* '68 (EVN) [H] Evansville, IN Daughters of Charity of St. Vincent de Paul of Indiana, Inc.
Harrold, John '73 (SY) On Duty Outside the Diocese.
Harrold, John J. '92 (GBG) [1] Uniontown, PA St. John The Evangelist Church.
Harrold, Michael '50 (VIC) [1] Victoria, TX Our Lady of Victory Cathedral.
Harry, William J. *o.carm.* '83 (CHI) [D] Mundelein, IL Carmel High School; [N] Mundelein, IL Carmelite Monastery.
Harshaw, Albert E. '73 (CAM) Blue Anchor, NJ St. Lucy's Church; Ancora, NJ New Jersey State Mental Hospital.
Hart, Brian '63 (SEA) Special Assignment.
Hart, Charles *o.f.m.* (DET) Detroit, MI Henry Ford Hospital; [K] Detroit, MI St. Bonaventure Friary.
Hart, E. James '96 (FWT) Bedford, TX St. Michael Church.
Hart, Edward J. '55 (BUR) Retired; [F] Burlington, VT St. Joseph's Home for Aged.
Hart, Edward James '96 (FWT) [17] Fort Worth, TX St. Thomas More Church.
Hart, Gene *s.o.l.t.* '90 (CC) [H] Robstown, TX Society of Our Lady of the Most Holy Trinity.
Hart, Gregory G. '84 (LR) Mountain Home, AR St. Peter the Fisherman Church.
Hart, Harry J. '44 (SAG) Retired.
Hart, J. Joseph, Jr. '84 (BAL) Absent on Leave.
Hart, James (RVC) Absent on Leave.
Hart, Msgr. James '40 (ALB) [8] Albany, NY St. James Church; Retired.
Hart, James '65 (KC) [39] (Kansas City North), MO St. Therese Parish Church.
Hart, James P. '41 (BO) Retired.
Hart, John B. '60 (SLC) [8] West Jordan, UT St. Joseph the Worker Church.
Hart, Msgr. John E. '81 (PAT) Rockaway, NJ St. Cecilia's Church.
Hart, Joseph A. '73 (ROC) [38] Rochester, NY Our Lady Queen of Peace Church; [L] Rochester, NY Censores Librorum.
Hart, Joseph L. *s.s.e.* '55 (BUR) [G] Colchester, VT Society of St. Edmund.
Hart, Joseph L. *s.s.e.* '55 (NOR) [A] Mystic, CT Edmundite Seminary Guild.
Hart, Kevin '74 (WDC) Piscataway, MD St. Mary Church
Hart, Paul S. '89 (NO) [3] Kenner, LA St. Elizabeth Ann Seton Church.
Hart, Msgr. Peter F. '36 (BO) [7] Lynn, MA St. Pius the Fifth Church; Retired.
Hart, Philip *c.s.p.* '73 (LAN) [E] Clinton, MI Boysville of Michigan, Inc.
Hart, Philip W. *c.s.p.* '83 (NY) [Z] Scarsdale, NY Paulist Fathers Generalate.
Hart, Richard *o.f.m.cap.* '55 (MIL) [P] Milwaukee, WI St. Conrad House.
Hart, Robert A. '75 (GR) [5] Grand Rapids, MI Blessed Sacrament Church.
Hart, Robert P. *s.j.* '62 (OM) [K] Omaha, NE Jesuit Community At Creighton University.
Hart, Rolland A. '64 (OG) Heuvelton, NY St. Raphael's Church, Gouverneur, NY Gouverneur Correctional Facility
Hart, Ronald '71 (JOL) Bradley, IL St. Joseph Church.
Hart, Thomas '80 (NEW) New Providence, NJ Our Lady of Peace Church.
Hart, Thomas B. '44 (PRO) Retired.
Hart, Thomas J. '74 (SC) Breda, IA St. Bernard's Church
Hart, Thomas M. *o.s.b.* '88 (GBG) [H] Latrobe, PA Saint Vincent Archabbey.
Hart, William (GLP) Retired.
Hart, William C. '58 (CAM) [5] Cherry Hill, NJ St. Thomas More Church; [A] Cherry Hill, NJ Camden Catholic High School.
Hart, William M. '47 (ROC) Webster, NY Holy Trinity Church; Retired.
Hart, William T. '80 (NEW) Berkeley Heights, NJ Runnells County Hospital.
Harte, Al F. '64 (RCK) Woodstock, IL St. Mary Church; Woodstock, IL St. Mary Church.
Harte, F. Joseph '61 (ORL) [1] Orlando, FL Mary Queen of the Universe Shrine Church.
Harte, Paul D. '76 (CAM) Haddonfield, NJ Christ the King Regional School Church.
Hartel, Edward T. '62 (WDC) Retired.
Harten, Dennis J. *o.s.a.* '75 (PH) Villanova, PA St. Thomas of Villanova Parish Community Church.
Hartenbach, William E. *c.m.* '64 (STL) [P] Earth City, MO Congregation of the Mission Midwest Province (Vincentians).
Harter, Benedict W. '46 (SPC) Joplin, MO Joplin Hospital Ministry; [C] Joplin, MO St. John's Regional Medical Center; Mercy Lifecare Systems, Inc.
Harter, Leon A. *m.m.* '39 (SJ) [M] Los Altos, CA Maryknoll.
Harter, Michael G. *s.j.* '74 (STP) [B] St. Paul, MN Jesuit Novitiate.
Hartford, Msgr. Dixon '61 (ELP) [28] El Paso, TX St. Matthew Church.
Hartgen, Dennis T. '73 (ALN) Mohnton, PA St. Benedict's Church.
Hartgen, William E. *s.s.* '76 (BAL) [M] Baltimore, MD Sulpician Provincial House.
Harth, Charles F. '36 (BRK) [39] Brooklyn, NY St. Fortunata Church; Retired.
Harth, John M. '87 (SPC) Neosho, MO St. Canera Church; Seneca, MO St. Mary Church.
Hartigan, Daniel *o.s.a.* '45 (CHI) [40] Chicago, IL St. Clare of Montefalco Church.
Hartigan, Dennis P. '80 (TOL) [4] Fremont, OH St. Joseph Church; [B] Fremont, OH St. Joseph Central Catholic High School.
Hartigan, Robert R. *s.j.* '83 (DET) [62] Detroit, MI SS. Peter and Paul Jesuit Church; [T] Detroit, MI SS. Peter & Paul Jesuit Church Historical Fund.
Hartke, Florian *c.pp.s.* '35 (CIN) [B] Carthagena, OH St. Charles.
Hartlage, Albert J. '56 (L) Fairfield, KY St. Michael Church.
Hartlage, William C. '41 (L) Retired; [L] Louisville, KY Bishop David Apartments.
Hartle, Thomas *o.f.m.* (PAT) Pompton Lakes, NJ Our Lady of the Assumption Church.
Hartlein, Jerome D. '58 (BEL) Mascoutah, IL Holy Childhood of Jesus Church.
Hartley, Christopher (NY) [77] New York, NY Most Holy Crucifix Church.
Hartley, Gregory C. *s.j.* '86 (BAL) [D] Baltimore, MD Loyola High School.
Hartley, Paul M. '81 (JC) Belle, MO St. Alexander Church; Owensville, MO Immaculate Conception Church.
Hartling, Charles W. '79 (NEW) Wyckoff, NJ St. Elizabeth Church.
Hartman, Augustine *o.p.* '66 (SEA) [G] Seattle, WA Providence Seattle Medical Center.
Hartman, Donald '50 (MAR) Retired.
Hartman, Glenn R. '76 (CAM) Merchantville, NJ St. Peter's Church.
Hartman, Joseph F. *o.s.a.* '47 (DET) Grosse Pointe Park, MI St. Clare of Montefalco Church.
Hartman, Msgr. Joseph W. '52 (WDC) [8] Silver Spring, MD St. Michael Church; Retired; [L] Washington, DC Cardinal O'Boyle Residence for Priests.
Hartman, Ralph C. '59 (COV) Erlanger, KY St. Henry Church.
Hartman, Raymond S. '68 (COV) Crescent Springs, KY St. Joseph Church.
Hartman, Msgr. Thomas J. '71 (RVC) [C] Hicksville, NY Holy Trinity.
Hartmann, Cletus F. *s.j.* '46 (DET) [P] Clarkston, MI Colombiere Center.
Hartmann, Edward '76 (NY) On Duty Outside the Archdiocese.
Hartmann, Edward J. '76 (FBK) Galena, AK St. John Berchman Church.
Hartmann, Jerome J. '47 (CHI) Glenview, IL Our Lady of Perpetual Help Church.
Hartmann, Msgr. John F. '53 (BRK) [239] Queens, NY Sacred Heart Church.
Hartmann, Joseph A. '78 (DEN) Lafayette, CO Immaculate Conception Church.
Hartmann, Paul B. R. '94 (MIL) [2] Wauwatosa, WI Christ King Church.
Hartmann, Richard A. '73 (DET) [19] Detroit, MI St. Christopher Church.
Hartmann, Robert J. '85 (WCH) Anthony, KS Sacred Heart Church; Danville, KS Immaculate Conception Church; Harper, KS St. Patrick Church.
Hartmayer, Gregory J. *o.f.m.conv.* '79 (ATL) Jonesboro, GA St. Philip Benizi Church.
Hartmire, Chris (SAC) [P] Sacramento, CA Loaves & Fishes.
Hartnett, Daniel F. *s.j.* '74 (CHI) [N] Chicago, IL

Chicago Province of the Society of Jesus-Provincial Office.
Hartnett, Msgr. Donald '39 (FWT) Retired.
Hartnett, George '74 (SY) Syracuse, NY Crouse Irving Memorial Hospital.
Hartnett, George F. '74 (SY) Mattydale, NY St. Margaret Church; Special Assignment.
Hartnett, James '72 (ORG) Westminster, CA Blessed Sacrament Church.
Hartnett, James L. *s.m.* '55 (ATL) [C] Atlanta, GA Marist School.
Hartnett, Msgr. James R. '38 (STL) Retired.
Hartnett, Richard G. *s.j.* '43 (SP) [C] Tampa, FL Jesuit High School.
Hartnett, Robert L. '79 (BAL) [70] Baltimore, MD Our Lady of Mount Carmel Church.
Hartnett, Walter J. '45 (PH) Retired.
Hartrich, Kurt *o.f.m.* '66 (STL) [P] St. Louis, MO Franciscan Friary of St. Anthony of Padua.
Hartshorn, Christopher '94 (DM) West Des Moines, IA Sacred Heart Church.
Hartwig, Lawrence N. '67 (GR) On Duty Outside the Diocese.
Hartz, Gerald '59 (SC) [F] Sioux City, IA Monastery of the Discalced Carmelite Nuns.
Hartzer, John '54 (IND) Lawrenceburg, IN St. Lawrence Church.
Hartzler, Joseph *s.m.* '87 (HON) [H] Wailuku, Maui, HI Wailuku Marianist Community.
Harvan, Msgr. Michael S. '33 (SCR) Retired.
Harvey, Arthur S. *c.s.c.* '51 (FTW) [J] South Bend, IN Congregation of Holy Cross Indiana Province Provincial House.
Harvey, Charles K. '52 (WCH) Retired.
Harvey, David W. '68 (LAN) Fenton, MI St. John Church.
Harvey, George F. '55 (MAN) Tilton, NH St. Mary of the Assumption Church.
Harvey, James '86 (ORG) Inactive Leave.
Harvey, Msgr. James M. '75 (MIL) On Duty Outside the Archdiocese.
Harvey, James P. *o.s.f.s.* '60 (PH) [Z] Philadelphia, PA Oblates of St. Francis De Sales.
Harvey, James Phillip, II '96 (KNX) Greeneville, TN Notre Dame Church; Newport, TN Good Shepherd Church; Rogersville, TN St. Henry Church.
Harvey, Jeff *c.m.* '93 (FRS) [3] Fresno, CA The Catholic Community of Mt. Carmel/St. Alphonsus Church.
Harvey, John A. '66 (PIT) Bethel Park, PA St. Valentine Church.
Harvey, John D. *o.f.m.cap.* '72 (BAL) [56] Baltimore, MD St. Martin Church.
Harvey, John F. *o.s.f.s.* '44 (ALN) [B] Center Valley, PA Allentown College of St. Francis de Sales; [K] Center Valley, PA Oblates of St. Francis de Sales.
Harvey, John F. *o.s.f.s.* '44 (NY) [74] New York, NY St. Michael Church; [DD] New York, NY Courage.
Harvey, John L. '86 (CHI) [27] Chicago, IL St. Benedict the African (West) Church.
Harvey, L. Warren '88 (LR) [3] Little Rock, AR St. Augustine Church; [10] Little Rock, AR Our Lady of Good Counsel Church.
Harvey, Richard R. '51 (PRT) Retired.
Harvey, Wilfred *o.m.i.* '63 (MAN) [K] Hudson, NH Missionary Oblates of Mary Immaculate.
Harvey, Msgr. William R. '41 (ORG) Newport Beach, CA Our Lady Queen of Angels Church; Retired.
Hary, Melvin J. '54 (OAK) Rodeo, CA St. Patrick's Church.
Haryasz, Msgr. Francis S. '58 (STA) Retired.
Hasbrouck, John-Baptist *o.c.s.o.* '54 (P) [L] Lafayette, OR The Cistercian (Trappist) Abbey of Our Lady of Guadalupe.
Hascall, John S. *o.f.m.cap.* '67 (MAR) Assinins, MI The Most Holy Name of Jesus-Blessed Kateri Tekakwitha Church; Assinins, MI The Most Holy Name of Jesus-Blessed Kateri Tekakwitha Church.
Haschka, David J. *s.j.* '75 (STP) [6] St. Paul, MN The Immaculate Heart of Mary Church; [26] St. Paul, MN St. Luke Church.
Haschka, Jonathan *s.j.* '75 (MIL) [P] Milwaukee, WI Jesuit Provincial Office, Wisconsin Province.
Haselbauer, Joseph *s.c.j.* '55 (SFS) [B] Chamberlain, SD St. Joseph Indian School; [F] Chamberlain, SD Priests of the Sacred Heart.
Haselhorst, Vincent A. '57 (BEL) Germantown, IL St. Boniface Church.
Hasenberg, Aloysius J. '49 (MAR) Iron River, MI St. Agnes Church.
Hasenfuss, Louis B. *o.s.b.* '61 (TUC) [F] St. David, AZ Holy Trinity Monastery.
Hasenkamp, Robert '63 (KCK) Mission, KS St. Pius X Church.
Hasenoehrl, Daniel *o.s.b.* '60 (P) [L] St. Benedict, OR Mt. Angel Abbey.
Hasey, Adam J. '50 (FAR) Oakes, ND St. Charles Borromeo Church.
Hasieber, Joseph S. '73 (ALX) Pineville, LA Central Louisiana State Hospital.
Haskamp, Edward F. '50 (CIN) [37] Cincinnati, OH Holy Trinity Church; Retired.
Haskamp, Greg '93 (KC) [41] Kansas City, MO Visitation of the Blessed Virgin Church.
Haske, Henry B. *s.j.* '57 (WDC) [E] Washington, DC Gonzaga College High School.
Haskin, Jay C. '67 (BUR) Winooski, VT St. Stephen Church.
Haskins, Robert J. *s.j.* '54 (NY) [Z] New York, NY Murray-Weigel Hall.
Haslach, Stephen *c.p.* '54 (NY) [Z] Pelham Manor, NY St. Vincent's Residence; [DD] Pelham, NY Passionist Communications, Inc.
Haslam, Richard *o.m.i.* '50 (OAK) [N] Oakland, CA Oblate Provincial House & Procure.
Hasler, Clifford *m.s.* '71 (ATL) Snellville, GA St. Oliver Plunkett Church.
Haslinger, Philip S. '72 (LFT) Alexandria, IN St. Mary Church.
Haspedis, George '56 (SPK) [5] Spokane, WA Sacred Heart Church.
Hasse, James *s.j.* '69 (COL) [25] Columbus, OH Community of Holy Rosary and St. John Church.
Hasselhoff, Robert W. '59 (CIN) [14] Cincinnati, OH St. Bartholomew Church.
Hassett, Anthony '53 (BUF) [M] Silver Creek, NY St. Columbans on the Lake, Home for the Aged.
Hassett, James F. '75 (BUF) Barker, NY St. Patrick Church; Olcott, NY St. Charles Borromeo Church.
Hassett, Roy *o.f.m.* (SFD) [K] Sherman, IL Our Lady of Angels Friary.
Hassey, Athanase '50 (NTN) Retired.
Hasso, Bede J. *o.s.b.* '57 (GBG) [H] Latrobe, PA Saint Vincent Archabbey.
Hast, James *o.f.m.cap.* '77 (DET) [K] Detroit, MI St. Bonaventure Friary.
Hastillo, Stanley E. '42 (HRT) Retired.
Hastings, Edward T. *o.s.a.* (PH) [Z] Villanova, PA Fray de Leon Community.
Hastings, Edward T. *o.s.a.* '83 (PH) [C] Villanova, PA Villanova University.
Hastings, James J. *s.s.c.* '72 (OM) [K] St. Columbans, NE St. Columban's Foreign Mission Society.
Hastings, William J. '73 (CHI) [66] Chicago, IL St. Gabriel Church.
Hastrich, George '50 (RCK) [N] St. Charles, IL Queen of Americas Guild.
Hastrich, George M. '50 (MAD) Argyle, WI St. Joseph Church; [K] Madison, WI Saint Martin House.
Hatcher, John E. *s.j.* '74 (RC) [B] Howes, SD Kino Jesuit Community; [D] Howes, SD The Diocese of Rapid City Mahpiya na Maka Okoigna.
Hatcher, Msgr. William C. '71 (NEW) Bloomfield, NJ Church of St. Thomas the Apostle.
Hater, Robert J. '59 (CIN) [22] Cincinnati, OH St. Clare Church; [D] Dayton, OH The University of Dayton.
Hatfield, Placid W. *o.s.b.* '58 (PEO) Dalzell, IL St. Thomas More Church; [A] Peru, IL St. Bede Abbey and Academy.
Hathaway, Edward C. '91 (ARL) Clifton, VA St. Andrew the Apostle Church.
Hatrick, Brian M. '79 (BUF) North Evans, NY St. Vincent Church.
Hatton, Ronald '95 (PSC) Williamsburg, VA Ascension of Our Lord Church.
Hatton, Seamus *c.ss.r.* '62 (SP) Plant City, FL St. Clement Church.
Hattrup, Theobald *o.f.m.* '56 (CIN) [M] Cincinnati, OH St. Francis Seraph Friary.
Hauber, Douglas '89 (JOL) Bradley, IL St. Joseph Church.
Hauck, Bolivar *m.s.* '58 (STL) [P] St. Louis, MO La Salette Missionaries.
Hauck, Herbert C. '64 (STL) Kirkwood, MO St. Gerard Majella Church.
Hauer, Joseph L. '81 (DUB) Placid, IA St. John's Church.
Hauer, Maurus *o.f.m.conv.* '45 (LSC) Hobbs, NM St. Helena Church.
Hauf, Edward *o.m.i.* '66 (PT) Perry, FL Immaculate Conception Church.
Haugen, John S. '84 (DUB) [N] Cedar Falls, IA St. Stephen the Witness Catholic Student Center, University of Northern Iowa.
Haughey, John C. *s.j.* '61 (CHI) [C] Chicago, IL Jesuit Community at Loyola University of Chicago.
Haughney, Msgr. William J. '47 (MET) Cranbury, NJ Nativity of Our Lord Church; Retired.
Haungs, Edwin C. *s.j.* '39 (NY) [Z] New York, NY Murray-Weigel Hall.
Haupt, Lloyd '54 (SCL) Retired.
Haus, Robert A. *s.j.* '55 (BUF) [O] Buffalo, NY Canisius Jesuit Community.
Hausen, C. William '65 (PIT) Bairdford, PA St. Victor Church.
Hauser, Albert *o.s.b.* '60 (KCK) [3] Overland Park, KS Holy Spirit Church.
Hauser, Albert J. '81 (OG) [A] Ogdensburg, NY Wadhams Hall.
Hauser, Gerald B. '45 (MIL) Retired.
Hauser, John G. '71 (BRK) [133] Brooklyn, NY SS. Simon and Jude Church.
Hauser, Nathanael *o.s.b.* '83 (SCL) [I] Collegeville, MN St. John's Abbey, of the Order of St. Benedict.
Hauser, Richard J. *s.j.* '68 (OM) [K] Omaha, NE Jesuit Community At Creighton University.
Hausfeld, Bruce *o.f.m.* '61 (LSC) Alamogordo, NM Immaculate Conception Church.
Hausfeld, Bryant *o.f.m.* '65 (LSC) Alamogordo, NM Immaculate Conception Church.
Hausmann, Leo '92 (RC) Bison, SD Blessed Sacrament Church; Buffalo, SD St. Anthony Church; [D] Rapid City, SD Priest Retirement and Aid Association.
Hausmann, William C. *s.j.* '66 (P) [L] Portland, OR Jesuit Provincial Office (Oregon Prov.).
Haut, Msgr. Vincent J. '68 (STA) Orange Park, FL St. Catherine's Church.
Hauth, Msgr. Arthur W. '56 (NO) [52] New Orleans, LA SS. Peter and Paul Church; Retired.
Hautz, Roland *glmy.* '53 (CHL) Jefferson, NC St. Francis of Assisi Church.
Havel, Elias '95 (RC) [B] Bethlehem, SD Holy Nativity Monastery.
Havel, Gregory G. '90 (WIN) Harmony, MN The Nativity of the Blessed Virgin Church.
Havener, J. Riley *o.s.a.* '55 (ALB) Waterford, NY St. Mary of the Assumption Church.
Havens, James '79 (MOB) Grove Hill, AL Sacred Heart Church.
Haviland, William T. '62 (HBG) Sunbury, PA St. Monica Church.
Havron, Daniel *o.f.m.* '77 (DET) Special Assignment; [B] Detroit, MI Duns Scotus.
Hawes, Msgr. Cletus J. '52 (DUB) Evansdale, IA St. Nicholas Church.
Hawes, Donald J. '53 (DUB) [1] Waterloo, IA St. Joseph's Church; [2] Waterloo, IA St. Mary's Church.
Hawk, Pat *c.ss.r.* '69 (AMA) [H] Amarillo, TX Bishop DeFalco Retreat Center.
Hawken, Michael '94 (KCK) [2] Overland Park, KS Holy Cross Church.
Hawker, James (CHL) [L] Charlotte, NC Diocesan Office of Campus Ministry.
Hawker, James F. '60 (BO) On Duty Outside the Archdiocese.
Hawker, James F. '63 (BO) [8] Quincy, MA Sacred Heart Church.
Hawkins, Allan R.G. '94 (FWT) [1] Arlington, TX Church of St. Mary the Virgin.
Hawkins, Charles '78 (PMB) Jupiter, FL St. Peter Church.
Hawkins, Donald A. *s.j.* '76 (NO) [F] New Orleans, LA Jesuit High School.
Hawkins, Douglas W. *c.s.c.* '57 (BUR) Brandon, VT St. Mary's Church.
Hawkins, John *o.s.c.* '66 (LIN) Kenesaw, NE Sacred Heart Church.
Hawkins, John G. *o.s.c.* '66 (LIN) Doniphan, NE St. Ann's Church; [A] Hastings, NE Crosier Monastery.
Hawkins, Robert '65 (BAL) Special Assignment.
Hawkins, Robert '95 (BAL) [N] Baltimore, MD Little Sisters of the Poor-Provincial Residence.
Hawkins, Robert F. '75 (PRO) [6] Warwick, RI St. Kevin Church.
Hawkins, Robert G. '65 (BAL) [K] Baltimore, MD St. Martin's Home for Aged, Little Sisters of the Poor.
Hawkins, Stephen B. '75 (COL) Pickerington, OH Seton Parish Church.
Hawkins, Thomas '70 (KC) Weston, MO Holy Trinity Church.
Hawley, Benjamin B. *s.j.* (DET) [K] Detroit, MI Jesuit Community at the University of Detroit.
Haworth, Marcus A. *s.j.* '46 (STL) [P] St. Louis, MO Jesuit Community Corporation at St. Louis University - Jesuit Hall.
Hawthorne, Patrick J. '82 (WOR) [26] Worcester, MA St. Margaret Mary Church.
Hay, Francis J. '42 (WCH) Retired.
Hay, Theodore H. '55 (MOB) Retired.
Hay, W. Michael '92 (CIN) [72] Cincinnati, OH Our Lady of Visitation Church.
Hayatsu, Richard '65 (SEA) Renton, WA St. Anthony's Church.
Hayburn, Edmund L. '45 (OAK) Retired; [M] Oakland, CA Bishop Begin Villa.
Haycock, Anthony J. '72 (SEA) [15] Seattle, WA St. Mary Church; [L] Seattle, WA Catholic Seamen's Club.
Haycock, Donald J. *c.s.c.* '58 (ROC) [41] Rochester, NY St. Lawrence Church.
Hayda, Pavlo '92 (STN) [2] Chicago, IL St. Joseph Church.
Hayde, Msgr. Ronald E. '81 (RVC) [1] Rockville Centre, NY St. Agnes Cathedral; Ocean Beach, NY Our Lady of the Magnificat Church.
Haydel, Chris M. '75 (BR) [5] Baton Rouge, LA St. Charles Borromeo Church.
Hayden, Msgr. Ambrose V. '44 (STP) Retired.
Hayden, Msgr. Carl T. '45 (GI) Retired.
Hayden, Donald *o.ss.t.* '81 (BAL) [M] Baltimore, MD Holy Trinity Monastery.
Hayden, Donald C. '81 (RVC) Deer Park, NY SS. Cyril and Methodius Church.
Hayden, Eamonn *s.p.s.* '62 (SJ) [M] Saratoga, CA St.

Patrick's Missionary Society.
Hayden, Guy B. (SJ) Retired; [K] Mountain View, CA Villa Siena.
Hayden, Hilary *o.s.b.* '56 (WDC) [M] Washington, DC St. Anselm's Abbey.
Hayden, James P. '91 (GAY) Special Assignment.
Hayden, Johnrose H. '95 (LUB) Rotan, TX St. Joseph Church.
Hayden, Joseph F. '63 (L) On Duty Outside the Archdiocese.
Hayden, Joseph J. *s.j.* '70 (WH) [A] Wheeling, WV Wheeling Jesuit University.
Hayden, Joseph M. '48 (CAM) Retired.
Hayden, Joseph M. '48 (ORL) [2] Lakeland, FL St. Anthony's Church.
Hayden, Joseph Mark '48 (ORL) Retired.
Hayden, Lucian P. '49 (OWN) Russellville, KY Sacred Heart Church.
Hayden, Michael M. *o.c.s.o.* '54 (ROC) [I] Piffard, NY Abbey of the Genesee.
Hayden, Michael T. '85 (SUP) Pelican Lake, WI St. John Church; Rhinelander, WI Immaculate Conception Church.
Hayden, Patrick T. '90 (STL) On Duty Outside the Archdiocese.
Hayden, Ralph W. '64 (NU) Retired.
Hayden, Terence '77 (NO) Crown Point, LA St. Pius X Church.
Hayden, Thomas E. *s.m.a.* '58 (BO) [W] Dedham, MA African Mission House and African Cultural Center.
Haydinger, Christian '76 (RIC) Chesapeake, VA Prince of Peace Church.
Haydock, Kenneth '80 (SEA) Edmonds, WA Holy Rosary Church.
Hayduk, Michael '77 (PRM) Cleveland, OH St. Mary Church.
Hayek, Msgr. Sami '59 (SAM) Easton, PA Our Lady of Lebanon Church.
Hayek, Msgr. Stanley J. '59 (DUB) Charles City, IA Immaculate Conception Church.
Hayer, James '89 (PSC) East Brunswick, NJ Nativity of Our Lord Church.
Hayes, Bonaventure F. *o.f.m.* '67 (BUF) [A] East Aurora, NY Christ the King Seminary.
Hayes, Brian '92 (SD) [17] San Diego, CA Our Mother of Confidence Church.
Hayes, Canisius *s.t.* '46 (B) Ferdinand, ID Assumption Church; Greencreek, ID St. Anthony's Church.
Hayes, Charles V. *o.f.m.* '46 (PAT) [M] Butler, NJ St. Anthony Friary.
Hayes, Msgr. Denis A. '37 (PAT) Retired.
Hayes, Dennis J. '76 (SY) South Onondaga, NY Corpus Christi Church.
Hayes, Dennis J., III '86 (NO) Avondale, LA St. Bonaventure Church; [A] New Orleans, LA Notre Dame Seminary Graduate School of Theology.
Hayes, Donald J. *s.j.* '56 (CHI) [T] Barrington, IL Bellarmine Hall.
Hayes, Edward A. *m.m.* '59 (NY) [Z] Maryknoll, NY Maryknoll Fathers and Brothers.
Hayes, Edward J. '41 (NEW) Retired.
Hayes, Edward J. '57 (SY) Chadwicks, NY St. Anthony of Padua Church.
Hayes, Edwin *o.m.i.* '52 (MIA) [2] Miami, FL Christ the King Church.
Hayes, Finbarr *o.p.* '59 (OAK) [N] Oakland, CA Dominican Order (Western Province), St. Albert's Priory.
Hayes, Francis R. '39 (STP) Retired.
Hayes, Gary '85 (OWN) Peonia, KY St. Anthony's Church.
Hayes, Gary '90 (OWN) Grayson Springs, KY St. Augustine Church; Wax, KY St. Benedict Church.
Hayes, Gerard C. '60 (HT) Bayou Black, LA St. Anthony Church.
Hayes, Giles P. *o.s.b.* '65 (PAT) [D] Morristown, NJ Delbarton School; [M] Morristown, NJ St. Mary's Abbey.
Hayes, Msgr. J. Wayne '59 (FRS) [4] Fresno, CA Our Lady of Victory Church; Los Banos, CA St. Joseph Church.
Hayes, James '66 (ALB) Comstock, NY Great Meadows Correctional Institution; Special Assignment.
Hayes, James *s.s.s.* '77 (NY) [8] New York, NY St. Andrew Church.
Hayes, James A. *m.s.c.* '50 (CC) Agua Dulce, TX St. Frances of Rome Church.
Hayes, James A. *s.s.j.* '55 (WDC) [B] Washington, DC St. Joseph's Seminary.
Hayes, James C. (SY) Special Assignment.
Hayes, James C. '65 (SY) Onondaga Hill, NY St. Michael Church; Syracuse, NY Community General Hospital.
Hayes, James E. '36 (FTW) Retired.
Hayes, James E. '89 (DUB) [1] Dubuque, IA St. Raphael's Cathedral; [D] Dubuque, IA Wahlert High School.
Hayes, James L. '38 (DET) Retired.
Hayes, James M. *s.j.* '85 (WOR) [N] Worcester, MA Jesuits of Holy Cross College, Inc.; [Q] Worcester, MA Campus Ministry.
Hayes, James P. (NY) [8] New York, NY St. Andrew Church.
Hayes, John E. '33 (CHI) Zion-Beach Park, IL Our Lady of Humility Church; Retired.
Hayes, John H. (ROC) Dryden, NY Holy Cross Church.
Hayes, John J. '60 (CLV) [34] Cleveland, OH Immaculate Conception Church; Cleveland, OH University Hospitals.
Hayes, Msgr. John M. '30 (CHI) [54] Chicago, IL Epiphany Church; Retired.
Hayes, John S. '40 (ROC) Retired.
Hayes, Joseph '79 (MIA) Absent on Leave.
Hayes, Lawrence J. *o.f.m.* '89 (WIL) [10] Wilmington, DE St. Paul's Church.
Hayes, Leo J. '61 (BEL) Ava, IL St. Elizabeth Church; Menard, IL Menard Correctional Center.
Hayes, Martin '84 (OWN) Knottsville, KY St. William Church.
Hayes, Martin E. '84 (OWN) Philpot, KY St. Lawrence Church.
Hayes, Maurice *o.f.m.conv.* (IND) St. Mary-of-the-Woods, IN St. Mary Church.
Hayes, Maurice *o.f.m.conv.* '69 (IND) West Terre Haute, IN St. Leonard of Port Maurice Church; Terre Haute, IN Regional Hospital; Terre Haute, IN Union Hospital.
Hayes, Michael T. '60 (DUL) Moose Lake, MN Holy Angels Church; Moose Lake, MN Moose Lake State Hospital.
Hayes, Patrick E. '71 (BLX) Moss Point, MS St. Joseph Church.
Hayes, Patrick J. *c.s.v.* '43 (LAV) [D] Las Vegas, NV Clerics of St. Viator Retirement Home.
Hayes, Msgr. Paul J. '48 (NEW) New Providence, NJ Our Lady of Peace Church; Retired.
Hayes, Peter F. '38 (CHI) [154] Chicago, IL Our Lady, Mother of the Church; Retired.
Hayes, Robert E. '71 (SJ) [10] San Jose, CA St. Anthony Church.
Hayes, Sam '83 (CHY) Jackson, WY Our Lady of the Mountains Church.
Hayes, Stephen D. *o.p.* '88 (COL) [36] Columbus, OH St. Patrick Church.
Hayes, Terrence M. '72 (STP) [14] Minneapolis, MN Our Lady of Victory Church.
Hayes, Msgr. Thomas G. '46 (LA) Retired.
Hayes, Msgr. Thomas J. '35 (SY) New Hartford, NY St. John the Evangelist Church; Retired.
Hayes, Thomas J. *o.p.* '59 (OAK) [N] Oakland, CA Western Dominican Province.
Hayes, Thomas J. *o.p.* '59 (SFR) [13] San Francisco, CA St. Dominic Church; [N] San Francisco, CA St. Dominic Priory; [U] San Francisco, CA Shrine of St. Jude Thaddeus.
Hayes, Thomas J. *o.m.i.* '64 (SFR) [35] San Francisco, CA Most Holy Redeemer Church.
Hayes, Thomas J. *o.m.i.* '64 (STP) [N] St. Paul, MN Oblate Provincial Offices; [N] St. Paul, MN Oblate Residence.
Hayes, Thomas J. '73 (ALB) [15] Albany, NY Sacred Heart of Jesus Church.
Hayes, Thomas P. '94 (STO) Lodi, CA St. Anne Church.
Hayes, Timothy '96 (SPK) Walla Walla, WA St. Francis of Assisi Church; Walla Walla, WA St. Patrick Church.
Hayes, Timothy M. '85 (COL) Newark, OH Church of the Blessed Sacrament.
Hayes, William E. *s.j.* '58 (P) [D] Portland, OR Jesuit High School.
Hayes, William J. '42 (HRT) Retired.
Hayes, Xavier *c.p.* '59 (WOR) [N] Shrewsbury, MA Passionist Fathers of Shrewsbury, Inc., Calvary Retreat Center; [P] Shrewsbury, MA Calvary Retreat Center, Passionist Community.
Hayes, Zachary *o.f.m.* '59 (CHI) [B] Chicago, IL The Catholic Theological Union at Chicago; [N] Chicago, IL St. Joseph Friary.
Hayman, Robert W. '66 (PRO) [9] Providence, RI Blessed Sacrament Church.
Hayn, Carl H. *s.j.* '47 (SJ) [B] Santa Clara, CA Santa Clara University.
Haynes, Mark J. '85 (PH) Southampton, PA Our Lady of Good Counsel Church.
Haynes, Stephen S. *c.ss.r.* '88 (TOL) [2] Lima, OH St. Gerard Church.
Hays, Edward M. '58 (KCK) [K] Easton, KS Shantivanam Archdiocesan House of Prayer.
Hays, Henry Bryan *o.s.b.* '62 (SCL) [I] Collegeville, MN St. John's Abbey, of the Order of St. Benedict.
Hays, John '93 (SP) Zephyrhills, FL St. Joseph Church.
Hays, Joseph C. '51 (BEL) Retired.
Hays, Kevin W. '77 (CHI) [54] Chicago, IL Epiphany Church.
Hays, R. Rex *c.m.* '93 (LR) Huntsville, AR St. John's Church.
Hayward, William *m.i.c.* '89 (JOL) Darien, IL Our Lady of Peace Church.
Hazard, Michael D. '72 (KAL) [2] Kalamazoo, MI St. Joseph Church.
Hazebrouck, Maurice L. '45 (PRO) Retired.
Hazel, Robert L. '66 (STP) [4] Minneapolis, MN Ascension Church.
Hazel, Terrence J. '75 (Y) [C] Louisville, OH St. Thomas Aquinas High School; [P] Louisville, OH St. Thomas Aquinas High School Endowment Fund.
Hazelton, James '61 (HEL); On Duty Outside the Diocese.
Hazewski, Eugene J. '59 (NEW) Emerson, NJ Church of the Assumption.
Hazler, George '67 (DET) [H] Southfield, MI Providence Hospital.
Hazler, George F. (DET) [T] Waterford, MI Voluntas Dei Institute.
Hazlett, Canisius W. *c.p.* '36 (BO) Boston, MA Franciscan Children's Hospital; [W] Brighton, MA St. Gabriel's Residence.
Hazzard, William M. '63 (WIL) Woodcrest, DE St. Matthew Church.
Hazzouri, Alex J. '57 (SCR) Special Assignment.
Head, Bernard '53 (IND) [K] Saint Mary-of-the-Woods, IN Sisters of Providence General Administration.
Headley, Donald J. '58 (CHI) [153] Chicago, IL Our Lady of Mercy Church.
Headley, William R. *c.s.sp.* '64 (PIT) [B] Pittsburgh, PA Duquesne University of the Holy Ghost.
Heagerty, John J. '54 (SY) East Syracuse, NY St. Matthew Church.
Heagle, John L. '65 (LC) On Duty Outside the Diocese.
Healey, Andrew *ss.cc.* '59 (FR) [K] Fairhaven, MA Sacred Hearts Provincial House.
Healey, Bernard A. '95 (PRO) [7] Providence, RI St. Augustine's Church.
Healey, Charles J. *s.j.* '65 (BO) [A] Weston, MA Pope John XXIII National Seminary; [W] Boston, MA The Society of Jesus of New England-Provincial Offices; [W] Chestnut Hill, MA The Jesuit Community at Boston College.
Healey, Msgr. Edward '43 (COL) Retired.
Healey, Edward J. (FR) Mashpee, MA Christ The King Church.
Healey, Fergus *o.f.m.* '54 (BO) [BB] Boston, MA St. Anthony Shrine.
Healey, James F.X. *s.j.* '59 (R) Ahoskie, NC St. Charles Borromeo Church; [E] Durham, NC Jesuit Community.
Healey, John C. *s.s.c.* '39 (PRO) [P] Bristol, RI St. Columban's Retirement House.
Healey, John E. '70 (MAN) [6] Nashua, NH Infant Jesus Church; Nashua, NH Nursing Homes and Memorial Hospital.
Healey, Msgr. Joseph T. '31 (RCK) Retired.
Healey, Kenneth *s.m.* '70 (BO) [E] Reading, MA Austin Preparatory School.
Healey, Patrick D. '51 (SCR) [17] Scranton, PA St. Mary of the Assumption Church.
Healey, Timothy A. *s.j.* '61 (NY) Manhattan, NY Goldwater Memorial Hospital; [Z] New York, NY St. Ignatius Loyola Residence.
Healey, William B. '55 (SCR) Hawley, PA Blessed Virgin Mary, Queen of Peace Church.
Healy, Augustine *o.c.d.* '49 (FWT) [G] Crowley, TX St. Francis Village, Inc.
Healy, Clement '45 (SP) [O] St. Petersburg, FL St. Anthony Friary.
Healy, Cletus J. *s.j.* '51 (MIL) [P] Wauwatosa, WI Jesuit Community at St. Camillus.
Healy, Cornelius '66 (SFR) Fairfax, CA St. Rita Church.
Healy, Gabriel *ss.cc.* '57 (FR) [K] Fairhaven, MA Sacred Hearts Provincial House.
Healy, George F. *c.s.sp.* '53 (SAT) San Antonio, TX St. Luke's Baptist Hospital; University Hospital; [M] San Antonio, TX Harcar House.
Healy, Gerard M. '61 (MAD) Stoughton, WI St. Ann Church.
Healy, Jack *o.carm.* '70 (ROC) [B] Rochester, NY McQuaid Jesuit High School; [I] Rochester, NY Whitefriars Priory.
Healy, James E. '72 (KC) [3] Independence, MO St. Mark Church.
Healy, James F. (NY) Mamaroneck, NY St. Vito Church.
Healy, James J. *s.s.* '46 (BAL) [K] Baltimore, MD St. Charles Villa; [M] Baltimore, MD St. Charles Villa.
Healy, John '41 (SR) Retired.
Healy, John C. *s.s.c.* '39 (BUF) [P] Silver Creek, NY Missionary Sisters of St. Columbans, St. Columban's on the Lake.
Healy, John J. (SAC) [G] Sacramento, CA Mercy General Hospital.
Healy, Kieran J. *o.p.* '61 (OAK) [N] Oakland, CA Western Dominican Province.
Healy, Kilian *o.carm.* '37 (BO) [P] Peabody, MA Catholic Information Center; [BB] Peabody, MA St. Theresa Carmelite Chapel.
Healy, Michael J. '70 (SFR) [46] San Francisco, CA St. Philip the Apostle Church.
Healy, Patrick F. *o.m.i.* '47 (BO) [Z] Tewksbury, MA Immaculate Heart of Mary Novitiate-Infirmary.
Healy, Patrick J. '66 (E) Mercer, PA State Correctional Facility.
Healy, Msgr. Peter '53 (LA) Burbank, CA St. Robert

Bellarmine Church.
Healy, Robert *glmy.* '46 (CIN) [M] Fairfield, OH Headquarters of Glenmary Home Missioners.
Healy, Robert *glmy.* '46 (SAV) Claxton, GA St. Christopher Church.
Healy, Stephen M. '85 (BO) Marshfield, MA St. Ann's by the Sea Church.
Healy, Terence P. '62 (ALB) West Winfield, NY St. Joseph Church.
Healy, Thomas '67 (SAV) On Duty Outside the Diocese.
Healy, Thomas C. '95 (BO) [3] Weymouth, MA Immaculate Conception Church.
Healy, Thomas F. *s.j.* '65 (HEL) [5] Missoula, MT St. Francis Xavier Church.
Healy, Thomas I. '52 (CHI) [155] Chicago, IL Our Lady of Mount Carmel Church.
Healy, Thomas J. '66 (BRK) [221] Queens, NY Our Lady of Sorrows Church.
Healy, Msgr. Thomas P. '59 (SD) San Marcos, CA St. Mark Church.
Healy, William *o.c.d.* '46 (MIL) [24] Milwaukee, WI St. Florian's Church.
Healy, William P. '66 (PHX) [2] Scottsdale, AZ Our Lady of Perpetual Help Church.
Heaney, John F. '57 (PRO) Carolina, RI St. Mary's Church.
Heaney, John J. *s.j.* '52 (FWT) [J] Lake Dallas, TX Montserrat Jesuit Retreat House.
Heaney, Msgr. John P. '53 (SFR) San Francisco, CA San Francisco Police Department; Special Assignment.
Heaney, Joseph P. '53 (PRO) [1] Woonsocket, RI St. Agatha's Church; Retired.
Heanue, William *c.ss.r.* '47 (NY) [92] New York, NY Our Lady of Perpetual Help Church.
Hearn, Edward C. '31 (SY) Retired.
Hearn, Philip A. '66 (SY) [4] Rome, NY St. Peter Church.
Hearns, Joseph A. '40 (NEW) Retired.
Hearns, Joseph A. '40 (PAT) Paterson, NJ St. Joseph Hospital.
Heath, Christopher '88 (ORG) Tustin, CA St. Cecilia Church.
Heath, Mark *o.p.* '47 (WDC) [B] Washington, DC Dominican House of Studies.
Heavey, Edward J. *s.j.* '60 (NEW) [B] Jersey City, NJ Saint Peter's College; [N] Jersey City, NJ Jesuits of Saint Peter's College, Inc.
Hebda, Bernard A. (PIT) On Duty Outside the Diocese.
Hebda, Martin J. '67 (CHI) [J] Chicago, IL Mercy Hospital and Medical Center.
Hebein, James M. '57 (MAR) Retired.
Heberle, Frederick L. '56 (SPR) Sheffield, MA Our Lady of the Valley Church.
Heberlein, Kenneth '71 (TLS) [E] Tulsa, OK St. John Medical Center, Inc.
Heberlein, Msgr. Louis '51 (E) Brandy Camp, PA Holy Cross Church.
Heberlein, Msgr. Louis J. '51 (E) Brockway, PA St. Tobias Church.
Hebert, Albert *s.m.* '54 (BR) Convent, LA St. Michael the Archangel Church.
Hebert, Daniel J. '79 (ANC) [4] Anchorage, AK St. Elizabeth Ann Seton Church.
Hebert, Donald J. '68 (LAF) Mire, LA Assumption of the Blessed Virgin Mary Church.
Hebert, Donald J. '68 (SY) Utica, NY St. Luke; Special Assignment.
Hebert, Earl '52 (SPR) [2] Pittsfield, MA Notre Dame Church.
Hebert, Francis '60 (B) Retired.
Hebert, Gerard A. '81 (FR) Westport, MA St. George's Church.
Hebert, Msgr. J. Gaston '60 (LR) [5] Little Rock, AR Christ the King Church.
Hebert, John M. '51 (LIN) Retired.
Hebert, John M. '51 (OM) Retired.
Hebert, Lloyd P. (LAF) Absent on Leave.
Hebert, Mark '92 (PHX) [25] Phoenix, AZ St. Thomas the Apostle Church.
Hebert, Marvin A. '51 (GAL) Retired.
Hebert, Oliver J. *t.o.r.* '71 (ALT) [A] Loretto, PA St. Francis College.
Hebert, Paul L. '59 (NOR) Pomfret, CT Most Holy Trinity Church.
Hebert, Msgr. Ray P. '52 (NO) [1] Marrero, LA Immaculate Conception Church.
Hebert, Raymond L. '44 (WOR) Retired.
Hebert, Roger '49 (PAT) [3] Wayne, NJ Immaculate Heart of Mary Church; Retired.
Hebert, Roland G. '47 (WOR) Retired.
Hebert, Ronald '65 (SD) [18] San Diego, CA Sacred Heart Church.
Hebert, T. J. '49 (LAF) Retired.
Hebl, John H. '61 (MAD) Sullivan, WI St. Mary Help of Christians Church.
Hechenberger, Gerald R. '96 (BEL) Olney, IL St. Joseph Church.
Hecht, F. Torrens *s.j.* '46 (CHI) [C] Chicago, IL Jesuit Community at Loyola University of Chicago.
Heck, Roger C. '51 (MIL) [77] Milwaukee, WI St. Therese Church.
Heck, Theodore *o.s.b.* '29 (IND) [B] St. Meinrad, IN St. Meinrad Seminary-College of Liberal Arts; [J] St. Meinrad, IN St. Meinrad Archabbey.
Heck, Thomas A. '76 (SFS) Brookings, SD St. Thomas More Church.
Heck, Msgr. Thomas W. '57 (NEW) [2] Union City, NJ St. Augustine's Church.
Heckathorne, Brad *ofm conv.* '81 (BUF) [D] Athol Springs, NY St. Francis High School; [O] Athol Springs, NY St. Francis of Assisi Friary.
Heckel, Guerric Frederick A. '66 (CHR) [E] Moncks Corner, SC Mepkin Abbey.
Heckel, John F. *o.s.f.s.* '44 (WIL) [B] Wilmington, DE Salesianum School.
Hecker Msgr. Adolph J. '40 (SAL) Retired.
Hedberg, Earl M. '62 (AUS) Goldthwaite, TX St. Peter's Church; San Saba, TX St. Mary's Church.
Hedderman, Augustine Mary *m.f.v.a.* '95 (BIR) [E] Birmingham, AL Franciscan Missionaries of the Eternal Word, A Public Association of the Christian Faithful.
Hedderman, Msgr. John J. '60 (SLC) [5] Salt Lake City, UT St. Ambrose Church.
Hederman, Kevin F. '75 (STL) [1] Florissant, MO North American Martyrs Church.
Hedges, John P. '87 (DET) [6] Wyandotte, MI St. Stanislaus Kostka Church.
Hedges, L. John '43 (ROC) Penfield, NY St. Joseph Church; Retired.
Hedrick, John H. '70 (MAD) [1] Janesville, WI Nativity of St. Mary Church.
Hedrick, Kenneth J. '73 (NO) [1] New Orleans, LA St. Louis Cathedral.
Heeg, Lawrence S. '57 (GRY) Chesterton, IN St. Patrick Church.
Heekin, John M. '63 (PAT) [2] Wayne, NJ Holy Cross Church.
Heelan, Patrick A. *s.j.* '58 (WDC) [M] Washington, DC The Jesuit Community at Georgetown University.
Heemrood, Jan *o.m.i.* '45 (SAT) [C] San Antonio, TX Oblate School of Theology; [M] San Antonio, TX De Mazenod House.
Heenan, Michael F. '55 (RVC) Absent on Leave.
Heenan, Patrick F. '55 (MEM) [13] Memphis, TN St. James Church.
Heeney, Walter *o.s.b.* '43 (KC) [I] Savannah, MO La Verna Village Apartments; [K] Savannah, MO La Verna Heights Provincial House.
Heerdink, Eugene '51 (EVN) Dale, IN St. Joseph Church.
Heerey, John J. '55 (BRK) Released from Diocesan Assignment.
Heerey, John J. '55 (STA) Interlachen, FL St. John's Mission Church.
Heery, William *o.carm.* '42 (LA) [F] Encino, CA Crespi Carmelite High School.
Heese, Henry '61 (AUS) Kovar, TX Sts. Peter and Paul Church; Smithville, TX St. Paul the Apostle Church.
Heet, Alan *o.f.m.* '46 (L) [42] Louisville, KY St. Joseph Church.
Heet, Donald *o.s.f.s.* (WDC) [B] Washington, DC Oblates of St. Francis de Sales House of Studies.
Hefferan, John E. '56 (CHI) [2] Oak Lawn, IL St. Gerald Church.
Heffern, Colman *o.s.b.* '76 (SFE) [L] Pecos, NM Our Lady of Guadalupe Benedictine Abbey.
Heffernan, Enda *o.f.m.cap.* '73 (MRY) [I] Soquel, CA St. Clare's Retreat House.
Heffernan, Enda *o.f.m.cap.* '73 (SFR) [B] San Francisco, CA Capuchi House of Studies.
Heffernan, Henry G. *s.j.* '62 (WDC) [E] Washington, DC Gonzaga College High School.
Heffernan, James F. '50 (BRK) Released from Diocesan Assignment.
Heffernan, John J. *o.f.m.* '32 (CHI) Markham, IL St. Gerard Majella Church; Retired.
Heffernan, John J. *o.f.m.* '32 (R) [3] Durham, NC Immaculate Conception Church.
Heffernan, Raymond J. '57 (SEA) Port Townsend, WA St. Mary's, Star of the Sea Church.
Heffernan, Robert G. '63 (HRT) [5] Hamden, CT St. Joan of Arc Church.
Heffernan, Thomas A. '61 (BRK) Released from Diocesan Assignment.
Heffernan, Thomas A. '61 (PAT) Denville, NJ St. Clare Hospital; [J] Denville, NJ Sisters of the Sorrowful Mother Health Care Ministry Corp.
Heffner, Carroll E. '61 (NO) [4] Metairie, LA St. Benilde Church.
Heffner, George *s.v.d.* '57 (LAF) Mowata, LA St. Lawrence Church.
Heffner, Msgr. Helmut (LA) [A] Camarillo, CA St. John's Seminary.
Heffron, William *ss.cc.* '68 (FR) Fairhaven, MA St. Joseph's Church.
Heffron, William M. '53 (MIL) St. Peter, WI St. Peter Church.
Heft, James L. *s.m.* '73 (CIN) [D] Dayton, OH The University of Dayton; [D] Dayton, OH The University of Dayton; [M] Dayton, OH Marianist Provincialate.
Hegarty, Daniel P. '63 (BO) [11] Boston, MA St. Anthony Church.
Hegarty, John C. *c.s.sp.* '53 (NO) Diamond, LA St. Jude Church.
Hegarty, Michael P. '95 (CAM) Collingswood, NJ St. John's Church.
Hegarty, William '67 (CHI) [16] Chicago, IL St. Anselm Church.
Hegenauer, Msgr. John V. '40 (COV) Retired.
Hegenbarth, Robert S. '56 (LC) Bangor, WI St. Mary Church; West Salem, WI St. Leo the Great Church.
Hegener, Wilbert *o.f.m.* '36 (GAY) Petoskey, MI St. Francis Xavier Church.
Hegyi, Martin A. *s.j.* '63 (NY) [Z] New York, NY Jesuit Community at Fordham University.
Heher, Michael '78 (ORG) Cypress, CA St. Irenaeus Church.
Hehir, J. Bryan '66 (BAL) Ellicott City, MD Resurrection Church.
Hehir, J. Bryan '66 (BO) On Duty Outside the Archdiocese; [CC] Cambridge, MA Harvard-Radcliffe Catholic Student Center.
Hehman, Lawrence W. '65 (LEX) [4] Lexington, KY Pax Christi Catholic Church.
Hehn, Robert E. '63 (DEN) Rifle, CO St. Mary's Church.
Hehr, Horst '67 (DAV) [J] Clinton, IA Samaritan Health System, Inc.
Heiar, James *s.v.d.* '70 (DUB) [B] Epworth, IA Divine Word College.
Heid, Clement J. *o.s.b.* '44 (GBG) [H] Latrobe, PA Saint Vincent Archabbey.
Heid, Richard '47 (SCL) Retired.
Heid, Roland L. *o.s.b.* '41 (GBG) [H] Latrobe, PA Saint Vincent Archabbey.
Heide, Msgr. Herman L. '41 (NY) Retired; [E] White Plains, NY Archbishop Stepinac High School.
Heidecke, Albert *c.p.m.* (LAF) Iota, LA St. Joseph Church.
Heidelberger, Ronald '46 (DET) Retired; [H] Southfield, MI Providence Hospital.
Heidenreich, Robert A. '69 (CHI) [26] Chicago, IL St. Benedict Church.
Heidlage, Benno *o.f.m.* '48 (PEO) Metamora, IL St. Mary's Church; Washburn, IL St. Elizabeth Church.
Heidt, Charles A. '59 (BIS) [5] Bismarck, ND St. Mary Church.
Heidt, William G. *o.s.b.* '40 (SCL) [I] Collegeville, MN St. John's Abbey, of the Order of St. Benedict.
Heier, Thomas *c.m.m.* '58 (DET) [K] Dearborn Heights, MI Our Lady of Grace Monastery.
Heier, Vergil *c.m.m.* '63 (DET) [K] Dearborn Heights, MI Our Lady of Grace Monastery.
Heier, Vincent A. '77 (STL) [5] St. Louis, MO Holy Innocents Church.
Heikkala, Gregory R. '91 (MAR) Trenary, MI St. Rita Church.
Heil, John P. '74 (STL) Grantwood, MO Our Lady of Providence Church; [A] St. Louis, MO Kenrick-Glennon Seminary.
Heile, Edwin B. '60 (COV) Walton, KY All Saints Church.
Heille, Gregory J. *o.p.* '75 (STL) [B] St. Louis, MO Aquinas Institute of Theology; [P] St. Louis, MO St. Dominic Priory.
Heilman, Thomas O'Connor '39 (LFT) Retired.
Heim, Edward L. '71 (STL) Imperial, MO St. John Church.
Heim, Gerald *c.ss.r.* '51 (DAV) [4] Davenport, IA St. Alphonsus Church.
Heim, Hilary *o.s.b.* '49 (KCK) [H] Atchison, KS St. Benedict's Abbey.
Heim, Howard J. *s.j.* '53 (PH) [C] Philadelphia, PA St. Joseph's University; [Z] Philadelphia, PA Jesuit Community at St. Joseph's University.
Heim, John P. *s.j.* '65 (CIN) [M] Cincinnati, OH Faber Jesuit Community.
Heim, John S. '51 (PH) [90] Philadelphia, PA St. Madeleine Sophie Church; [X] Philadelphia, PA Sacred Heart Manor.
Heim, Michael J. '82 (PH) [76] Philadelphia, PA St. Joan of Arc Church.
Heiman, Harold *o.s.b.* '39 (LR) Ratcliff, AR St. Anthony Church; [A] Subiaco, AR Subiaco Monastery.
Heiman, Lawrence F. *c.pp.s.* '43 (LFT) [A] Rensselaer, IN Saint Joseph's College.
Heimann, Ambrose *c.pp.s.* '40 (CIN) [B] Carthagena, OH St. Charles.
Heimer, Michael G. '71 (GRY) Fish Lake, IN St. Anthony Church.
Heimerman, Francis D. '44 (DUB) Retired.
Heimos, Robert L. '67 (STL) Washington, MO Our Lady of Lourdes Church.
Hein, George J. '54 (RVC) Commack, NY Christ the King Church.
Hein, Joachim Le Quang '74 (SPK) On Duty Outside the Diocese.
Hein, John L. *s.j.* '51 (NO) [R] Metairie, LA Cenacle Retreat House.
Hein, Kenneth C. *o.s.b.* '69 (PBL) [E] Canon City, CO Holy Cross Abbey.

Heina, Steven C. '82 (SAL) Colby, KS Sacred Heart Church.
Heindel, Harold J. '66 (RVC) Centerport, NY Our Lady Queen of Martyrs Church.
Heindl, Arthur W. '40 (MAD) Retired.
Heindl, Elmer W. '36 (ROC) [12] Rochester, NY St. Charles Borromeo Church; Retired.
Heine, Michael *o.f.m.conv.* '90 (BAL) [D] Baltimore, MD Archbishop Curley High School; [M] Baltimore, MD Immaculate Heart of Mary Friary.
Heine, Simeon *s.a.* '48 (NY) [Z] Garrison, NY Franciscan Friars of the Atonement.
Heinecke, Gary *c.ss.r.* '73 (CHI) [N] Glenview, IL The Redemptorists of Glenview, Illinois.
Heineman, Msgr. Donald P. '47 (DUB) Retired.
Heinen, Francis A. '59 (NEW) Nutley, NJ Holy Family Church.
Heinen, Gerald *o.carm.* '50 (NEW) Teaneck, NJ St. Anastasia's Church.
Heinen, Miles *c.m.* '82 (LR) Huntsville, AR St. John's Church.
Heinen, Msgr. Paul '29 (SFD) Retired.
Heinen, Virgil O. '60 (SUP) Lake Tomahawk, WI St. John Vianney Church.
Heines, Timothy '94 (DAL) Plano, TX St. Elizabeth Ann Seton Church.
Heiney, Lawrence W. '75 (CHL) Tryon, NC St. John the Baptist Church.
Heinl, David A. '57 (CIN) St. Marys, OH Holy Rosary Church.
Heinlein, Anthony J. '65 (NY) Massapequa Park, NY Our Lady of Lourdes Church.
Heinlein, Anthony J. '65 (RVC) Massapequa Park, NY Our Lady of Lourdes Church.
Heinlein, Egbert *c.m.m.* '38 (DET) [K] Dearborn Heights, MI Our Lady of Grace Monastery.
Heinlein, Msgr. John T. '61 (RVC) New Hyde Park, NY Holy Spirit Church.
Heinrich, Harold D. '56 (HRT) [8] New Britain, CT St. John the Evangelist Church.
Heinsch, James *o.f.m.* '67 (PIT) [N] Ben Avon, PA St. Anthony Friary and Mission House.
Heintschel, Msgr. Donald '51 (TOL) [L] Sylvania, OH Sisters of St. Francis of the Congregation of Our Lady of Lourdes.
Heintz, Daniel W. '54 (ROC) Canisteo, NY St. Joachim Church; Rexville, NY St. Mary Church.
Heintz, Daniel W. '54 (SY) On Duty Outside the Diocese.
Heintz, Michael '93 (FTW) [3] Fort Wayne, IN St. Charles Borromeo Church.
Heintz, Robert L. '49 (SFD) Retired.
Heintzelman, Edward F. '84 (CAM) Westmont, NJ Holy Saviour Church.
Heintzelman, Gerard '79 (SR) [G] Napa, CA Queen of the Valley Hospital of Napa.
Heinz, David C. '77 (PEO) [5] Peoria, IL St. Bernard's Church.
Heinz, John R. *o.f.m.conv.* '93 (SB) [11] Riverside, CA St. Thomas the Apostle Church.
Heinz, Martin G. '94 (RCK) [1] Rockford, IL St. Peter Cathedral.
Heinz, Robert P. '80 (CHI) Prospect Heights, IL St. Alphonsus Liguori Church.
Heinz, Walter E. '62 (STU) Pomeroy, OH Sacred Heart Church.
Heinze, Arthur G. '68 (MIL) Hales Corners, WI St. Mary's Church.
Heinzel, Thomas R. '75 (HON) Kula, HI Our Lady Queen of the Angels Church.
Heis, Clarence G. '82 (CIN) Mechanicsburg, OH St. Michael's Church; North Lewisburg, OH Immaculate Conception Church.
Heise, Bert *o.f.m.* '57 (CIN) [M] Cincinnati, OH St. Francis Seraph Friary.
Heisel, Raymond G. '35 (ROC) [40] Rochester, NY Our Mother of Sorrows Church; Retired.
Heiser, Basil *o.f.m.conv.* '32 (IND) [J] Mount Saint Francis, IN Provincial Headquarters for the Conventual Franciscan Province.
Heiser, W. Charles *s.j.* '53 (STL) [C] St. Louis, MO Saint Louis University; [P] St. Louis, MO Jesuit Community Corporation at St. Louis University - Jesuit Hall.
Heisig, Kazimierz '78 (HRT) [9] Hartford, CT SS. Cyril and Methodius Church.
Heisler, James M. *s.a.c.* '70 (MIL) [8] Milwaukee, WI St. Anthony of Padua Church.
Heisse, John R. *m.m.* '85 (CHI) [N] Chicago, IL Maryknoll Fathers & Brothers.
Heithoff, James H. '77 (GI) North Platte, NE Holy Spirit Church.
Heiting, Paul '87 (WIN) Luverne, MN St. Catherine's Church.
Heitkamp, Samuel '67 (SAT) Poth, TX Blessed Sacrament Church.
Heitke, Lawrence R. '67 (MAD) Madison, WI Veterans' Administration Hospital.
Heitz, Louis S. '57 (LFT) Winchester, IN St. Joseph Church.
Heitz, Warren *o.s.b.* '66 (IND) [J] St. Meinrad, IN St. Meinrad Archabbey.
Heitzman, Clarence J. '56 (COV) Southgate, KY St. Therese of the Infant Jesus Church.
Heizman, Leo J. '69 (SY) East Syracuse, NY St. Matthew Church.
Helbing, Brendan *o.s.b.* '65 (LA) Montebello, CA St. Benedict Church.
Held, Aloys *o.f.m.* '43 (CIN) [M] Cincinnati, OH St. Francis Center.
Helduser, Msgr. Frederick J. '60 (PH) [4] Drexel Hill, PA St. Dorothy Church.
Heles, Msgr. Frederic G. '44 (DUB) Retired.
Helfenstein, Maurice R. '27 (SPK) Retired.
Helfrey, Donald C. '68 (KC) [5] Kansas City, MO St. Bernadette's Church.
Helfrich, Emil G. *o.m.i.* '49 (SFD) Green Creek, IL St. Mary Help of Christians Church; Lillyville, IL Sacred Heart of Jesus Church.
Helfrich, Frederick '71 (ROC) [48] Rochester, NY St. Monica Church; Rochester, NY St. Mary's Hospital; [H] Rochester, NY St. Mary's Hospital.
Helfrich, George J. '54 (CHI) [56] Chicago, IL St. Eugene Church; Retired.
Helfrich, P. Jeremiah *s.j.* '68 (LA) [2] Santa Barbara, CA Our Lady of Sorrows Church.
Helfrich, Thomas J. *o.s.f.s.* '78 (LAN) [B] Jackson, MI Lumen Christi High School.
Helfrich, Thomas J. *o.s.f.s.* '78 (TOL) [K] Toledo, OH Oblates of St. Francis de Sales.
Helget, Venard *o.s.b.* '40 (KCK) [H] Atchison, KS St. Benedict's Abbey.
Helldorfer, J. Nicholas *c.ss.r.* '36 (RIC) [2] Hampton, VA St. Joseph Church.
Hellenberg, Antony *o.s.b.* '66 (SCL) [I] Collegeville, MN St. John's Abbey, of the Order of St. Benedict.
Heller, Christopher J. '79 (RVC) Port Jefferson, NY St. Gerard Majella Church.
Heller, James '68 (SAG) [8] Bay City, MI St. Mary Church.
Hellman, Michael P. '83 (CHY) Green River, WY Immaculate Conception Church.
Hellmann, David E. '73 (LFT) Kokomo, IN St. Joan of Arc Church.
Hellmann, Msgr. Donald F. '53 (COV) [2] Covington, KY St. Agnes Church.
Hellmann, Wayne *o.f.m.conv.* '67 (STL) [P] St. Louis, MO St. Bonaventure Friary (Province of Our Lady of Consolation).
Hellstrom, R. Christopher '88 (DEN) [36] Denver, CO St. Vincent De Paul Church.
Hellwig, Lee W. '86 (HRT) [3] Ansonia, CT St. Anthony's Church.
Helm, Edward J. '66 (WDC) Special Ministries; [V] Landover Hills, MD Catholic Deaf Center.
Helm, John B. '77 (L) [7] Louisville, KY Ascension of Our Lord Church.
Helman, Bradford N. '68 (Y) [10] Canton, OH St. Michael the Archangel Church.
Helmich, George F. *c.s.p.* '57 (NY) [Z] Scarsdale, NY Paulist Fathers Generalate.
Helmich, George F. *c.s.p.* '57 (PMB) [G] Vero Beach, FL Paulist Fathers Retirement Home.
Helmick, Raymond F. *s.j.* (BO) [71] Boston, MA St. Theresa Church.
Helmick, Raymond G. *s.j.* '63 (BO) [W] Chestnut Hill, MA The Jesuit Community at Boston College.
Helmick, William M. '62 (BO) [71] Boston, MA St. Theresa Church.
Helmin, Virgil A. '75 (SCL) [3] St. Cloud, MN Holy Spirit Church.
Helms, Michael '90 (DOD) Leoti, KS St. Anthony of Padua Church; Marienthal, KS St. Mary Church; Tribune, KS St. Joseph Church.
Helms, Walter B. '69 (DAV) Muscatine, IA St. Mary's Church.
Helmueller, Lawrence C. *s.j.* '42 (OM) [K] Omaha, NE Jesuit Community At Creighton University.
Heltemes, Alfred J. '54 (SCL) Foley, MN St. John's Church.
Helwig, Alan R. '58 (WDC) [2] Bethesda, MD St. Jane Frances de Chantal Church.
Helwig, Paul C. '74 (HBG) [5] Steelton, PA Prince of Peace Church.
Heman, Richard J. '67 (STL) Affton, MO St. Dominic Savio Church.
Hemann, David A. '85 (SC) Sanborn, IA St. Cecilia's Church.
Hemann, Everett '71 (DUB) Ames, IA St. Thomas Aquinas Church (and Catholic Student Center) Church; [N] Ames, IA St. Thomas Aquinas Church and Catholic Student Center (Iowa State University).
Hemann, John W. '60 (DUB) Duncan, IA St. Wenceslaus Church; Garner, IA St. Boniface Church.
Hemann, Melvin D. '59 (DUB) Balltown, IA St. Francis of Assisi Church; Rickardsville, IA St. Joseph's Church; Sherrill, IA SS. Peter and Paul Church; [F] Balltown, IA Balltown-Sherrill Catholic School.
Hemauer, Gilbert *o.f.m.cap.* '64 (GF) Forsyth, MT Immaculate Conception Church.
Hemauer, William G. '36 (GB) Retired.
Hemberger, Kent A. '88 (WCH) [10] Wichita, KS St. Anne Church.
Hemberger, Robert E. '70 (WCH) [H] Wichita, KS Mt. St. Mary Convent, Motherhouse and Novitiate of the Sisters of St. Joseph.
Hembrow, William '60 (SFD) Fieldon, IL St. Mary Church; Jerseyville, IL Holy Ghost Church.
Hemenway, Richard '87 (SPK) Absent on Leave.
Hemkens, Edward B. '54 (STL) St. Louis, MO Lammert International Airport.
Hemler, Edward '64 (BAL) Fallston, MD St. Mark Church.
Hemler, Lawrence J. '88 (HBG) [1] York, PA Immaculate Conception of the Blessed Virgin Mary Church.
Hemler, Thomas J. '56 (HBG) Waynesboro, PA St. Andrew Church.
Hemm, Thomas *c.pp.s.* '78 (TOL) Ottawa, OH SS. Peter and Paul Church.
Hemm, Thomas W. *c.pp.s.* '76 (CIN) [M] Dayton, OH Provincial House of the Cincinnati Province of the Society of the Precious Blood.
Hemmer, Joseph *o.f.m.* '54 (FBK) Kaltag, AK St. Teresas Church; Ruby, AK St. Peter-in-Chains Church.
Hemmerle, R. Joseph '67 (L) [11] Louisville, KY St. Bartholomew Church; [B] Louisville, KY Trinity High School.
Hemmerling, Henry L. '66 (MET) Old Bridge, NJ Most Holy Redeemer Church.
Hemmersbach, Alfred F. '45 (LC) Retired; [I] La Crosse, WI Holy Cross (Seminary) Diocesan Center.
Hemming, Philip M. '67 (P) Keizer, OR St. Edward Church.
Hemp, Lawrence A. '67 (LUB) Post, TX Holy Cross Church; Slaton, TX Our Lady of Guadalupe Church.
Hempel, John L. '54 (ROC) Retired.
Hemphill, Anthony T. *s.v.d.* '58 (LR) [4] Little Rock, AR St. Bartholomew's Church.
Hemrick, Eugene (WDC) [C] Washington, DC Catholic University of America, The.
Hemrick, Eugene F. '63 (JOL) On Duty Outside the Diocese.
Hemsing, John D. '88 (MIL) Wind Lake, WI St. Clare Church.
Hemstreet, John G. '64 (TOL) Absent on Leave.
Henahan, Msgr. Thomas '30 (BGP) [K] Trumbull, CT St. Joseph's Manor.
Henahan, Msgr. Thomas F. '30 (BGP) Retired.
Henandez, Baltazar Nunez '88 (CGS) Cidra, PR Nuestra Senora del Carmen Church.
Henao, Alfonso '79 (NY) [1] Newburgh, NY St. Patrick Church.
Henao, Luis Emilio '74 (NO) [4] Kenner, LA St. Jerome Church.
Henault, James *m.s.* '80 (ORL) [2] Orlando, FL Blessed Trinity Church.
Henchal, Michael J. '73 (PRT) Special or Other Diocesan Assignment; [G] Portland, ME St. Joseph's Manor.
Henchey, Joseph C. *c.s.c.* '56 (NOR) [A] Cromwell, CT Holy Apostles College and Seminary.
Hencier, Jack *c.m.f.* '72 (LA) [R] Rancho Dominguez, CA Dominguez Seminary Inc.
Hendel, Lawrence '77 (SJ) [12] San Jose, CA St. John Vianney Church; Military Chaplains.
Hendel, Msgr. Richard P. '48 (RVC) Bay Shore, NY St. Patrick's Church; Retired.
Hendel, Msgr. Thomas W. '45 (BRK) [155] Queens, NY St. Benedict Joseph Labre Church; Retired.
Henden, Brian H. *o.carm.* '93 (NEW) Cresskill, NJ St. Therese of Lisieux Church.
Henderson, Christopher J. '94 (SAM) Uniontown, PA St. George Church.
Henderson, Donald R. '70 (PEO) [3] Spring Valley, IL St. Anthony's Church; [4] Spring Valley, IL SS. Peter and Paul's Church.
Henderson, James B. *o.c.s.o.* '60 (DUB) [K] Peosta, IA New Melleray Abbey, Order of Cistercians of the Strict Observance.
Henderson, John *o.f.m.conv.* '84 (P) Tillamook, OR Sacred Heart Church.
Henderson, John H. '87 (JC) Folk, MO St. Anthony of Padua Church; Jefferson City, MO Jefferson City Correctional Center; Booneville, MO Boonville Correctional Center.
Henderson, Robert J. '65 (COV) Cold Spring, KY St. Joseph Church.
Hendren, Lucian C. '63 (SFE) Corrales, NM San Ysidro Church.
Hendrick, Msgr. Frank J. '54 (ARL) Retired.
Hendrick, Matthew D. '85 (R) Wilmington, NC St. Mark Church.
Hendricks, Clare (GRY) On Duty Outside the Diocese.
Hendricks, Msgr. Donald W. '55 (NY) Buchanan, NY St. Christopher Church.
Hendricks, Edward S. '77 (BAL) Special Assignment; [O] Baltimore, MD Archdiocesan Office-Newman Center.
Hendricks, James P. '60 (L) [12] Louisville, KY St. Basil Church; [21] Louisville, KY St. Denis Church.
Hendricks, John J. '52 (TR) On Duty Outside the Diocese.
Hendricks, Joseph *ss.cc.* '48 (HON) Lahaina, HI Maria

Lanakila Church.
Hendricks, Msgr. Joseph '72 (COL) Dublin, OH St. Brigid of Kildare Church.
Hendricks, Scott B. '86 (BO) Stoneham, MA St. Patrick Church.
Hendricks, Theodore J. '65 (GB) Francis Creek, WI St. Anne Church; Kossuth, WI St. Augustine Church.
Hendricks, William J. *s.j.* '64 (SJN) [22] San Juan, PR San Ignacio de Loyola Church.
Hendrickson, W. Frederick '56 (L) [29] Louisville, KY Guardian Angels Church; [A] Louisville, KY Bellarmine College.
Hendriks, Boniface '45 (SFE) Retired.
Hendry, Gerald '85 (SP) Gulfport, FL Most Holy Name of Jesus Church; [B] St. Petersburg, FL St. Petersburg Catholic High School.
Hendry, Msgr. Owen J. '60 (NEW) Franklin Lakes, NJ Most Blessed Sacrament Church.
Hendry, Simon J. *s.j.* '77 (OAK) [N] Berkeley, CA Jesuit Community at Jesuit School of Theology at Berkeley.
Heneghan, James P. '83 (CHI) [30] Chicago, IL St. Bonaventure Church.
Heneghan, John F. '55 (YAK) Retired.
Heneghan, Jorlath '55 (SEA) Retired.
Heneghan, Sean '53 (SEA) Retired.
Heneghan, Msgr. Thomas F. '51 (NY) [101] New York, NY Our Saviour Church.
Henehan, Thomas P. *m.m.* '65 (NY) [Z] Maryknoll, NY Maryknoll Fathers and Brothers.
Henery, Ronald *o.p.* '50 (HT) [2] Houma, LA Annunziata Church.
Henery, Ronald *o.p.* '78 (NY) [Z] New York, NY St. Vincent Ferrer Priory.
Henesy, William '51 (RVC) Freeport, NY Our Holy Redeemer Church; Retired.
Heney, David '78 (LA) Santa Monica, CA St. Monica Church.
Heney, Frederick J. *s.j.* '63 (LA) West Hollywood, CA St. Victor Church; [R] Los Angeles, CA Columbiere House.
Hengel, Warren, Jr. '92 (FRS) Tipton, CA St. John Church.
Henger, Alcuin J. *o.m.i.* '55 (CR) Blackduck, MN St. Ann's Church.
Henger, Alcuin J. *o.m.i* '55 (DUL) Northome, MN St. Michael's Church.
Hengesbach, Julius L. '53 (KAL) Retired.
Hengle, John R. '68 (CLV) Tallmadge, OH Our Lady of Victory Church.
Henke, Donald E. '93 (STL) [1] St. Charles, MO St. Charles Borromeo Church; [E] St. Charles, MO Duchesne High School.
Henke, Msgr. James '66 (SAT) [35] San Antonio, TX St. Francis of Assisi Church.
Henkel, Albert J. '43 (KNX) [5] Knoxville, TN Holy Ghost Church; [K] Knoxville, TN Ladies of Charity.
Henkel, William M. '55 (CHI) Midlothian, IL St. Christopher Church; Westchester, IL Divine Infant Church; Retired.
Henkels, Edmund *o.s.b.* '59 (WDC) [M] Washington, DC St. Anselm's Abbey.
Henkels, Joseph *s.v.d.* '28 (CHI) [B] Techny, IL Divine Word Residence.
Henkes, Donald E. '66 (MEM) On Duty Outside the Diocese.
Henkes, Donald E. '66 (SAG) Mount Pleasant, MI Sacred Heart Church.
Henle, Robert J. *s.j.* '40 (STL) [O] St. Louis, MO Fusz Pavilion.
Henley, Earl *m.s.c.* (Y) [A] Youngstown, OH Sacred Heart Retreat House & Renewal Center.
Henley, Fred M. *s.j.* '58 (DET) [K] Detroit, MI Jesuit Provincial Office-Detroit Province of the Society of Jesus.
Henley, Fred M. *s.j.* '58 (OAK) [N] Berkeley, CA Jesuit Community at Jesuit School of Theology at Berkeley.
Henley, John R. '75 (ATL) Monroe, GA St. Anna's Church.
Henn, Joseph *s.d.s.* '78 (MIL) [P] Milwaukee, WI Salvatorian Provincial Residence.
Henne, Paul '56 (PIT) Ellwood City, PA St. Agatha Church; Lawrence County, PA Ellwood City Hospital.
Hennelly, Alfred T. *s.j.* '60 (NY) [Z] New York, NY Jesuit Community at Fordham University.
Hennelly, Michael F. '91 (PH) [1] Bensalem, PA St. Charles Borromeo Church.
Hennes, Paul R. '35 (DET) Retired.
Hennes, Paul R. '35 (ORL) Retired.
Hennessey, James J. *s.j.* '57 (SY) [S] Syracuse, NY Jesuits at LeMoyne, Inc.
Hennessey, John E. '67 (CHI) Niles, IL St. Isaac Jogues Church.
Hennessey, John P. '47 (BUF) Retired.
Hennessey, Joseph '91 (BO) [8] Boston, MA St. Ann Church.
Hennessey, Lawrence R. '71 (CHI) [A] Mundelein, IL University of St. Mary of the Lake-Mundelein Seminary.
Hennessey, Robert F. '78 (BO) [51] Boston, MA Most Holy Redeemer Church; [BB] East Boston, MA Our Lady of the Airways Chapel.
Hennessey, Robert J. *o.p.* '56 (PRO) [B] Providence, RI Providence College; [P] Providence, RI St. Thomas Aquinas Priory at Providence College.
Hennessey, Msgr. William *v.g.* '61 (MIA) [B] Opa Locka, FL St. Thomas University.
Hennessy, Douglas J. '63 (PEO) Danville, IL St. Paul's Church.
Hennessy, James W. '61 (WIN) Lewiston, MN St. Rose of Lima Church.
Hennessy, John '78 (FWT) Burleson, TX St. Ann Church.
Hennessy, John A. *s.j.* '52 (RC) St. Francis, SD Rosebud Reservation Church.
Hennessy, John J. *c.ss.r.* '53 (BO) [13] Boston, MA Basilica of Our Lady of Perpetual Help.
Hennessy, John J. *s.j.* '69 (RC) Martin, SD Our Lady of the Sacred Heart Church.
Hennessy, John P. *o.s.a.* '44 (PH) Flourtown, PA St. Genevieve Church; [Z] Flourtown, PA Augustinians (O.S.A.).
Hennessy, John V. *s.j.* '72 (P) [L] Portland, OR Jesuit Provincial Office (Oregon Prov.).
Hennessy, Joseph I. '63 (PHX) Chandler, AZ St. Andrew the Apostle Church.
Hennessy, Joseph P. '75 (PIT) Military Chaplains.
Hennessy, Patrick '71 (NY) [137] Bronx, NY Christ the King Church.
Hennessy, Thomas '96 (ATL) [3] Atlanta, GA Holy Spirit Church.
Hennessy, Thomas C. *s.j.* '47 (NY) [Z] New York, NY Jesuit Community at Fordham University.
Henning, David K. '82 (TOL) Absent on Leave.
Henning, Edward *o.f.m.cap.* '96 (NEW) [4] Orange, NJ Mt. Carmel Church.
Henning, Michael L. '74 (STL) St. Peters, MO All Saints Church; [W] St. Louis, MO Archdiocesan Stewardship Education Committee.
Henning, Phillip D. '93 (SAT) Fredericksburg, TX St. Mary's Church.
Henning, Richard G. '92 (RVC) Port Washington, NY St. Peter of Alcantara Church.
Henninger, George '85 (VIC) On Duty Outside the Diocese.
Henninger, Mark G. *s.j.* (DET) [K] Detroit, MI Jesuit Provincial Office-Detroit Province of the Society of Jesus
Hennington, Bruce M. '68 (MAD) Waunakee, WI St. John the Baptist Church.
Henrich, Steven *o.s.c.* '74 (DET) [K] Riverview, MI Crosier Community of Riverview.
Henrick, Eugene '63 (WDC) [24] Washington, DC St. Joseph on Capitol Hill Church.
Henrick, John C. '62 (NSH) Antioch, TN St. Ignatius of Antioch Church.
Henricksen, Francis C. '55 (DAV) Bettendorf, IA St. John Vianney Church.
Henritzy, Curtis E. *o.p.* '92 (PRO) [P] Providence, RI St. Thomas Aquinas Priory at Providence College.
Henry, Carol Ann *r.s.m.* (TR) [S] Asbury Park, NJ Mercy Center, Inc.
Henry, Charles W. *o.s.b.* '53 (IND) [F] Indianapolis, IN St. Vincent Hospital and Health Care Center, Inc.; [J] Indianapolis, IN St. Maur Priory.
Henry, Charles W. *o.s.b.* '53 (NEW) [N] Newark, NJ Newark Abbey.
Henry, Donald H. '71 (ALN) On Duty Outside the Diocese.
Henry, Donald H. '71 (VEN) [2] Naples, FL St. John the Evangelist Church.
Henry, Earl J. *o.s.b.* '64 (GBG) [H] Latrobe, PA Saint Vincent Archabbey.
Henry, Msgr. Edward C. '37 (TR) Retired.
Henry, James *s.v.d.* '59 (LA) [D] Lakewood, CA Saint Joseph High School.
Henry, James '71 (MRY) Arroyo Grande, CA St. Patrick Church.
Henry, James T. '64 (PH) [34] Philadelphia, PA Christ the King Church.
Henry, John P. '52 (RVC) Cutchogue, NY Sacred Heart Church; Retired.
Henry, Joseph A. '43 (PH) Riegelsville, PA St. Lawrence Church; Retired.
Henry, Joseph E. *s.j.* '60 (TUC) [F] Tucson, AZ Jesuit Community of the Vatican Observatory.
Henry, Joseph L. '36 (MAD) Retired.
Henry, Joseph P. '58 (PRO) Coventry, RI SS. John and Paul Church.
Henry, Larry *c.s.c.* '61 (GRY) [G] Michigan City, IN St. Anthony Hospital and Health Centers.
Henry, Leo G. '55 (PIT) Retired; [N] Pittsburgh, PA St. John Vianney Manor.
Henry, Patrick '81 (CLV) [10] Lorain, OH St. Peter Church.
Henry, Patrick '93 (SAC) Tulelake, CA Holy Cross Church.
Henry, Patrick J. '81 (CHI) [39] Chicago, IL St. Christina Church.
Henry, Patrick J. '81 (OM) Absent on Leave.
Henry, Paul J. '68 (ORL) [9] Orlando, FL St. John Vianney Church.
Henry, Paul J. '70 (BAL) Havre de Grace, MD St. Patrick's Church.
Henry, Perry F. *c.m.* '83 (NO) [40] New Orleans, LA St. Joseph Church; [60] New Orleans, LA St. Stephen Church.
Henry, Peter '68 (ORL) On Duty Outside the Diocese.
Henry, Robert P. '79 (NY) Nyack, NY St. Ann Church.
Henry, Thomas '44 (RIC) Retired.
Henry, Thomas J. '53 (NEW) [3] Linden, NJ St. John the Apostle Church.
Henseler, J. Thomas '63 (PEO) On Duty Outside the Diocese.
Henseler, Joseph N. '52 (LC) Chili, WI St. Stephen Church; Neillsville, WI St. Mary Church.
Henseler, Michael *s.d.s.* '77 (MIL) [P] Milwaukee, WI Salvatorian Provincial Residence.
Henseler, Thomas '63 (SFD) Mount Sterling, IL Holy Family Church.
Hensell, Eugene *o.s.b.* '69 (IND) [A] St. Meinrad, IN St. Meinrad Seminary; [B] St. Meinrad, IN St. Meinrad Seminary-College of Liberal Arts; [J] St. Meinrad, IN St. Meinrad Archabbey.
Hensgen, John A. *c.ss.r.* '36 (BLX) [E] Biloxi, MS St. John Neumann Residence.
Henson, Jerome M. '77 (ORG) Costa Mesa, CA St. John the Baptist Church.
Henson, Joel '93 (LA) Diamond Bar, CA St. Denis Church.
Hensy, Patrick E. *c.s.p.* '78 (AUS) [11] Austin, TX St. Austin's Church; [M] Austin, TX University Catholic Center.
Hentges, James E. *o.s.c.* '76 (NY) [Z] New Rochelle, NY Crosier (Canons Regular of the Order of the Holy Cross); [CC] New York, NY University Apostolate.
Hentschel, Cletus B. '51 (BEL) Retired.
Hentz, Otto H. *s.j.* '68 (WDC) [M] Washington, DC The Jesuit Community at Georgetown University.
Hentzner, John T. '45 (MIL) Retired.
Henz, Kenneth W. '51 (CIN) Retired.
Heon, Paul J. *m.afr.* '41 (SP) [O] St. Petersburg, FL Missionaries of Africa.
Hepburn, Timothy M. '94 (ATL) Fort Oglethorpe, GA St. Gerard's Church; [M] Atlanta, GA The Catholic Charismatic Renewal in Atlanta.
Hephner, John J. '59 (GB) Kaukauna, WI St. Aloysius Church.
Hepnar, Bede *o.f.m.* '57 (GRY) [K] Cedar Lake, IN Our Lady of Lourdes Friary.
Hepner, Ernest C. '61 (CLV) Bedford Heights, OH Holy Trinity Church.
Heppe, Patrick E. '77 (MIL) [1] Fond du Lac, WI St. Joseph's Church.
Heppen, Michael J. *c.s.c.* '63 (DET) [3] Birmingham, MI Our Lady Queen of Martyrs Church; Special Assignment.
Heppen, Michael J. *c.s.c.* '63 (FTW) [B] Notre Dame, IN University of Notre Dame Du Lac; [J] Notre Dame, IN Holy Cross Community, Corby Hall, University of Notre Dame.
Heppler, Richard Leo *o.f.m.* '38 (PAT) [M] Ringwood, NJ Holy Name Friary.
Heppner, Sylvester *o.f.m.* '59 (IND) Oldenburg, IN Holy Family Church; [K] Oldenburg, IN Motherhouse of the Congregation of the Sisters of the Third Order of St. Francis.
Hept, Wilfrid *o.f.m.* '44 (BO) [BB] Boston, MA St. Anthony Shrine.
Herald, Robert P. '89 (AUS) Frenstat, TX Holy Rosary Church; On Duty Outside the Diocese.
Heramb, James '68 (JOL) Paxton, IL St. Mary Church.
Herard, Msgr. Joseph P. '55 (DUB) [6] Dubuque, IA Church of the Resurrection.
Heras, Msgr. Michael '84 (CC) [8] Corpus Christi, TX Our Lady of Perpetual Help Church.
Heraty, John T. '67 (RCK) Mooseheart, IL School of the Loyal Order of Moose.
Herba, Stanislaw '64 (SLC) [4] Midvale, UT St. Therese of the Child Jesus Church.
Herbe, Donnan *o.f.m.* '45 (SFE) Cerrillos, NM St. Joseph Church.
Herbein, John J. '74 (E) Franklin, PA St. Patrick Church.
Herbek, Msgr. Adrian F. '59 (LIN) David City, NE St. Mary's Church.
Herber, Alvin L. *c.pp.s.* '50 (KC) Cameron, MO St. Munchin Church.
Herber, John *c.pp.s.* (HBG) [G] Columbia, PA St. Anne's Home.
Herber, Leo *c.pp.s.* '57 (CIN) [B] Carthagena, OH St. Charles.
Herber, Melvin J. '75 (FTW) Columbia City, IN St. Paul of the Cross Church.
Herber, Stanley J. '64 (IND) Connersville, IN St. Gabriel Church; Knightstown, IN St. Rose Church; New Castle, IN St. Anne Church.
Herberger, Roy T. '68 (BUF) Darien Center, NY Our Lady of Good Counsel Church; West Seneca, NY Wyoming Correctional Facility; [T] Buffalo, NY Hope of Buffalo, Inc.
Herbert, Eugene '81 (LA) Covina, CA St. Louise de Marillac Church.
Herbert, G. Paul '86 (WDC) [1] Washington, DC St.

Matthew Cathedral; Pastoral Center Special Ministries.
Herbert, J. Marc '50 (FR) [K] North Dartmouth, MA Holy Cross Mission House.
Herbert, John J. '83 (BUR) Rutland, VT St. Peter Church.
Herbert, Joseph L. *s.j.* '47 (STL) [P] St. Louis, MO The Jesuits of the Missouri Province.
Herbert, Leo P. '67 (ATL) Newnan, GA St. George's Church.
Herbert, Michael '92 (LAF) Port Barre, LA Sacred Heart of Jesus Church.
Herbert, Oliver *t.o.r.* '71 (ALT) [F] Loretto, PA St. Francis Friary, Third Order Regular of St. Francis of Penance.
Herbst, Charles T. *c.m.* '50 (STL) [P] Perryville, MO Congregation of The Mission.
Herbst, Justin J. '58 (TR) [J] Lawrenceville, NJ Morris Hall/Saint Lawrence, Inc.; [L] Lawrenceville, NJ Morris Hall-Saint Lawrence, Inc.; [O] Lawrenceville, NJ Our Lady of the Rosary Chapel; [S] Lawrenceville, NJ Morris Hall/St. Lawrence, Inc.
Herbst, Robert M. *o.f.m.conv.* '91 (SB) [11] Riverside, CA St. Thomas the Apostle Church; [11] Riverside, CA St. Thomas the Apostle Church.
Herbst, Thomas *o.f.m.* '91 (LSC) Mescalero, NM St. Joseph Church.
Herbster, Kenneth '63 (NEW) Union, NJ St. Michael's Church.
Hercek, Joseph R. '72 (MRY) Atascadero, CA St. William's Church.
Hercik, Terry A. '80 (GBG) Ford City, PA St. Mary Church.
Herda, Jerome G. '90 (MIL) [E] Milwaukee, WI Divine Savior Holy Angels High School.
Herdegen, Msgr. Anthony (FRS) Retired.
Heredia, Agnel Jose de (SFR) Half Moon Bay, CA Our Lady of the Pillar Church.
Heredia, Juan Victor '91 (BWN) Escobares, TX Sacred Heart Church.
Hereford, Thomas D. '56 (JC) On Duty Outside the Diocese.
Herek, Daniel P. '71 (OM) [39] Omaha, NE St. Richard Church.
Hereley, Peter J. *o.p.* '63 (CHI) [N] River Forest, IL St. Thomas Aquinas Priory; [U] River Forest, IL American Friends of the Ecole Biblique.
Heretick, Joseph S. '47 (GF) Retired.
Hergenrother, John C. '66 (CHI) La Grange Park, IL St. Louise de Marillac Church.
Herhenreader, Peter V. '59 (SCR) Royal, PA St. Pius X Church.
Heria, Fernando '96 (MIA) [32] Miami, FL St. Thomas the Apostle Church.
Herian, Kenneth J. *s.j.* '55 (MIL) [29] Milwaukee, WI Gesu Parish Church.
Heric, William '81 (SEA) [9] Seattle, WA St. George Church; [18] Seattle, WA St. Paul Church.
Herkowski, Arthur M. '54 (MIL) Retired.
Herkowski, Arthur M. '54 (RNO) Retired.
Herledan, John '55 (AUS) Retired.
Herlihy, Charles E. '94 (BO) [1] Arlington, MA St. Agnes Church.
Herlihy, Daniel J. '67 (MET) South Bound Brook, NJ Our Lady of Mercy Church.
Herlihy, Jude M. *o.s.m.* '56 (ORG) Fullerton, CA St. Juliana Falconieri Church.
Herlong, Theophilus L. '58 (LKC) Retired.
Herman, Gerard *o.f.m.conv.* '57 (SAV) Hinesville, GA St. Stephen, First Martyr Church.
Herman, Jerome A. '43 (DET) Retired.
Herman, John A. *c.s.c.* '95 (PHX) Goodyear, AZ Saint John Vianney Church.
Herman, Michael T. '89 (CHI) [144] Chicago, IL Notre Dame Church.
Herman, Robert D. '60 (WIN) Medford, MN Christ the King Church.
Hermann, Msgr. Carlton P. '52 (SFS) Lesterville, SD St. John the Baptist Church; Tabor, SD St. Wenceslaus Church.
Hermann, Cyril *o.f.m.* '38 (CIN) [M] Cincinnati, OH St. Clement Friary.
Hermann, Robert J. '63 (STL) Chesterfield, MO Incarnate Word Church.
Hermanns, Harold T. '54 (NEW) Retired; [N] Rutherford, NJ St. John Vianney Residence for Priests.
Hermanns, Mel *o.f.m.cap* '64 (GB) [M] Appleton, WI Monte Alverno Retreat Center.
Hermansen, Douglas V. '79 (TR) Avon, NJ St. Elizabeth Church; Neptune, NJ Jersey Shore Medical Center.
Hermes, Msgr. Daniel J. '69 (RCK) [5] Rockford, IL Holy Family Church.
Hermes, Eustace A. '41 (VIC) Retired.
Hermes, Michael '91 (KCK) [13] Kansas City, KS St. Joseph and St. Benedict Church.
Hermes, Roger J. '53 (STP) Retired.
Hermes, Thomas W. '82 (KC) Clinton, MO Holy Rosary Church.
Hermoso, Joseph '57 (ELP) [25] El Paso, TX St. Joseph's Church.
Hermoso, Msgr. Seth '67 (GAL) [12] Houston, TX St. Augustine Church.
Hernadez, Enrico A. '96 (SJ) Morgan Hill, CA St. Catherine of Alexandria Church.
Hernady, Martin '48 (TOL) Retired.
Hernandez, Alberto *o.f.m.* '70 (ELP) [B] El Paso, TX Roger Bacon College.
Hernandez, Msgr. Alfred '55 (LA) [67] Los Angeles, CA St. Ignatius of Loyola Church.
Hernandez, Alfred '82 (LA) [26] Los Angeles, CA Our Lady of Lourdes Church.
Hernandez, Alfred Ricardo '66 (SAT) Military Chaplains.
Hernandez, Alfredo '92 (PMB) On Duty Outside the Diocese.
Hernandez, Angelo J. '93 (PH) [154] Philadelphia, PA St. Veronica Church.
Hernandez, Anthony '95 (BRK) [198] Queens, NY St. Mary Star of the Sea Church.
Hernandez, Antonio *s.t.* '57 (SJN) Loiza, PR San Patricio Church.
Hernandez, Antonio *c.ss.r.* '67 (PCE) Guayama, PR St. Anthony of Padua Church.
Hernandez, Antonio '92 (SAT) [5] San Antonio, TX Holy Family Church.
Hernandez, Antonio A. *c.ss.r.* (PCE) [B] Ponce, PR The Pontifical Catholic University of Puerto Rico.
Hernandez, Apolinar '90 (SR) Petaluma, CA St. Vincent de Paul Church.
Hernandez, Bernardo '63 (SJN) [62] San Juan, PR San Vicente de Paul Church.
Hernandez, Blas '69 (LA) Hawthorne, CA St. Joseph Church.
Hernandez, Eliseo (SB) [5] Riverside, CA St. Anthony Church.
Hernandez, Esteban *m.s.f.* '87 (BWN) Edinburg, TX Holy Family Church.
Hernandez, Fernando A. '90 (NY) [191] Bronx, NY St. Thomas Aquinas Church.
Hernandez, Francis G. *s.j.* '63 (SAC) [C] Sacramento, CA Jesuit High School; [H] Carmichael, CA Jesuit High School Community of Sacramento.
Hernandez, Francisco '94 (MIA) [4] Miami, FL Epiphany Church.
Hernandez, Msgr. Gonzalo Diaz '63 (MGZ) Hormigueros, PR Shrine of Our Lady of Monserrate Church.
Hernandez, Javier '74 (CGS) Yabucoa, PR Santos Angeles Cutodios Church.
Hernandez, Jesus '66 (DAL) [15] Dallas, TX St. Cecilia Church.
Hernandez, Jesus Gomez '52 (SJN) [45] San Juan, PR Ntra. Sra. del Perpetuo Socorro Church.
Hernandez, Jimmy '83 (ARE) On Duty Outside the Diocese.
Hernandez, Jose '60 (SFE) [24] Albuquerque, NM St. Edwin Church.
Hernandez, Jose Estanislao *s.s.p.* '65 (LA) [R] Los Angeles, CA Society of St. Paul.
Hernandez, Jose Guillermo '89 (SJN) [43] San Juan, PR San Pablo Church.
Hernandez, Joseph F. '81 (LA) Pomona, CA Sacred Heart Church.
Hernandez, Juan Ramon *c.ss.r.* '80 (CGS) [1] Caguas, PR Cathedral Dulce Nombre de Jesus Church.
Hernandez, Lawrence C. *o.ss.t.* '78 (BAL) [M] Baltimore, MD Holy Trinity Monastery.
Hernandez, Lawrence C. *o.ss.t.* '78 (WDC) [M] Hyattsville, MD St. John de Matha Monastery, Order of Most Holy Trinity.
Hernandez, Manuel, Jr. '96 (CC) [17] Corpus Christi, TX St. Patrick Church.
Hernandez, Marco A. *c.s.b.* '87 (GAL) [Q] Sugar Land, TX Basilian Mission Center.
Hernandez, Martin A. '81 (BR) Prairieville, LA St. John the Evangelist Church.
Hernandez, Pedro '89 (ARE) Corozal, PR Holy Family Church.
Hernandez, Ramon '73 (SP) [14] Tampa, FL St. Paul Church.
Hernandez, Rene Javier '95 (MGZ) Lajas, PR Our Lady of the Purification Church.
Hernandez, Stephen C. '82 (LA) [53] Los Angeles, CA St. Camillus De Lellis Church; Los Angeles, CA L.A. County/University of Southern California Hospitals.
Hernandez, Victor M. *s.j.* '76 (MIA) [D] Miami, FL Belen Jesuit Preparatory School; [H] Miami, FL Jesuit Fathers of the Province of the Antilles, Inc.
Hernandez-Gonzalez, Francisco '90 (YAK) Mattawa, WA Our Lady of the Desert Church.
Hernandez-Tovar, Francisco '80 (SAC) Truckee, CA Assumption of the Blessed Virgin Mary Church.
Hernando, Henry L. (LA) [16] Los Angeles, CA Immaculate Heart of Mary Church.
Hernando, Jose L. '62 (MIA) Key Biscayne, FL St. Agnes Church.
Herne, Robert G. '47 (CHI) Northbrook, IL Our Lady of the Brook Church; Palos Hills, IL Sacred Heart Church; Retired.
Hernes, Thomas (KC) [O] Kansas City, MO Catholic Woman's Club.
Hernik, Jan *o.f.m.conv.* (BO) [7] Lawrence, MA Holy Trinity Church.
Herold, Anthony J. '79 (DAV) Ottumwa, IA St. Patrick's Church.
Herold, Carl A. '35 (IND) Retired.
Heron, J. Thomas '78 (PH) East Lansdowne, PA St. Cyril of Alexandria Church; [A] Wynnewood, PA Theological Seminary of St. Charles Borromeo, Overbrook.
Herp, Joseph T. '64 (L) [38] Louisville, KY Incarnation Church.
Herpin, Msgr. L. Michael '66 (LAF) Broussard, LA Sacred Heart of Jesus Church.
Herpin, Wayne *s.j.* '74 (PMB) [3] West Palm Beach, FL St. Ann Church.
Herr, Charles W.A. '48 (NEW) [4] Hoboken, NJ SS. Peter and Paul's Church.
Herr, Kenneth '68 (EVN) [16] Evansville, IN St. John Church; Special Assignment; [A] Evansville, IN Reitz Memorial High School.
Herrador, Blas P. '52 (GAL) [71] Houston, TX Resurrection Church.
Herrera, Anthony W. '91 (OAK) Pleasanton, CA St. Augustine Church.
Herrera, David Lee '89 (SAN) [2] Odessa, TX St. Anthony Church; [4] Odessa, TX St. Joseph Church.
Herrera, Edward '91 (LSC) Sunland Park, NM St. Martin de Porres Church.
Herrera, Emigdio '77 (LA) Santa Maria, CA St. John Neumann Church.
Herrera, Francisco '67 (ELP) [25] El Paso, TX St. Joseph's Church.
Herrera, Henry *c.m.f.* '42 (PHX) Seligman, AZ St. Francis Church.
Herrera, Jesus Enrique '96 (MRY) Watsonville, CA St. Patrick Church.
Herrera, Jose '88 (BRK) [24] Brooklyn, NY St. Brigid Church.
Herrera, Lawrence *s.j.* '81 (LA) [A] Camarillo, CA St. John's Seminary College of the Archdiocese of Los Angeles.
Herrera, Pedro E. *c.s.v.* '80 (CHI) [N] Arlington Heights, IL Viatorian Province Center-Clerics of St. Viator.
Herrera, Rosendo '96 (AMA) Pampa, TX St. Vincent de Paul Church.
Herrero, Jose *o.s.a.* '51 (NY) [67] New York, NY St. Lucy Church.
Herrero, Jose M. '52 (PCE) [3] Ponce, PR Church of the Resurrection; [B] Ponce, PR The Pontifical Catholic University of Puerto Rico.
Herrero, Msgr. Nicolas '59 (FRS) Exeter, CA Sacred Heart Church.
Herres, Msgr. Joseph W. '72 (LA) [46] Los Angeles, CA San Antonio de Padua Church; La Puente, CA St. Joseph Church.
Herrgott, George V. *s.s.c.* '79 (BO) [W] Quincy, MA St. Columban's Foreign Mission Society.
Herrgott, George V. *s.s.c.* '79 (OM) [K] St. Columbans, NE St. Columban's Foreign Mission Society.
Herrick, Marion L. *o.f.m.* '67 (GBG) Uniontown, PA Uniontown Hospital.
Herrlich, Neale W. *s.j.* '52 (SLC) [4] Ogden, UT St. Mary's Church.
Herrman, Gilbert P. '49 (DOD) Lakin, KS St. Anthony Church; Syracuse, KS St. Raphael Church.
Herrmann, Austin C. *c.pp.s.* '48 (SAN) Coleman, TX Sacred Heart Church.
Herrmann, Frank *s.j.* '74 (BO) [W] Chestnut Hill, MA The Jesuit Community at Boston College.
Herrmann, Richard J. '44 (LC) Retired.
Herrmann, Robert W. '58 (PIT) Robinson Township, PA Holy Trinity Church.
Herron, Bernard J. '54 (PH) [20] Philadelphia, PA St. Barnabas Church; [97] Philadelphia, PA St. Mary of Czestochowa Church.
Herron, Denis '73 (BRK) [213] Queens, NY Our Lady of Lourdes Church.
Herron, Francis X. '55 (PH) Trooper, PA Visitation B.V.M. Church.
Herron, Jack B. '74 (FAR) Military Chaplains.
Herron, Msgr. Joseph P. '62 (CAM) Ocean City, NJ St. Frances Cabrini Church; [F] Camden, NJ The Frank J. and Rosina W. Suttill Catholic Foundation.
Herron, Msgr. Thomas J. '73 (PH) Highland Park, PA St. Laurence Church; [A] Wynnewood, PA Theological Seminary of St. Charles Borromeo, Overbrook.
Hertel, Msgr. Herbert N. '42 (WCH) Retired.
Hertel, James R. '65 (PAT) [4] Wayne, NJ Our Lady of Consolation Church.
Hertel, John *o.carm.* '53 (JOL) [J] Darien, IL Carmelite Fathers Provincial Office.
Hertel, Joseph M. *o.f.m.* '66 (NY) [35] New York, NY St. Francis of Assisi Church.
Hertel, Joseph M. *o.f.m.* '66 (PAT) [P] Paterson, NJ St. Anthony's Guild.
Herttna, Matthew M. '45 (Y) [2] Massillon, OH National Shrine of St. Dymphna Church; Retired.
Hertweck, Robert W. *s.m.* '64 (CIN) [M] Dayton, OH Marianist Provincialate.
Heruday, Msgr. Joseph C. '41 (CLV) [AA] Cleveland, OH Catholic Tours of Ohio, Inc.
Heruday, Msgr. Joseph C. '43 (CLV) Maple Heights,

OH St. Wenceslas Church; Retired.
Hervey, Paul '95 (SP) [5] Tampa, FL Incarnation Church.
Herzing, James '95 (SCL) Sauk Rapids, MN Sacred Heart Church.
Herzog, John M. '56 (DUB) Colo, IA St. Mary's Church; Nevada, IA St. Patrick's Church.
Herzog, Lawrence A. '80 (STL) [59] St. Louis, MO St. Roch Church.
Herzog, Mark J. '79 (TOL) [1] Fremont, OH Sacred Heart Church.
Herzog, Msgr. Ronald P. '68 (BLX) Pass Christian, MS St. Paul Church.
Hesburgh, Theodore M. *c.s.c.* '43 (FTW) [B] Notre Dame, IN University of Notre Dame Du Lac; [J] Notre Dame, IN Holy Cross Community, Corby Hall, University of Notre Dame.
Heskamp, Charles *s.v.d.* '58 (LAF) [4] Lafayette, LA Immaculate Heart of Mary Church.
Heskamp, Joseph C. '48 (CIN) [86] Cincinnati, OH St. Vincent Ferrer Church; Retired.
Hesketh, John E. *o.s.b.* '94 (PAT) [M] Morristown, NJ St. Mary's Abbey.
Heskin, Thomas M. *o.s.m.* '55 (CHI) [J] Maywood, IL Foster G. McGaw Hospital of Loyola University of Chicago; [N] Chicago, IL Servite Friars - Eastern Province.
Hesler, Raymond F. *s.s.* '35 (BAL) [K] Baltimore, MD St. Charles Villa; [M] Baltimore, MD St. Charles Villa.
Heslin, Msgr. James J. '54 (STA) [7] Jacksonville, FL Holy Spirit Church.
Heslin, Philip J. '57 (SUP) On Special or Other (Arch)Diocesan Assignment.
Heslin, Sean '67 (ORL) [1] Orlando, FL St. James Cathedral.
Hess, Charles *o.p.* '47 (OAK) [A] Berkeley, CA Dominican School of Philosophy and Theology; [N] Oakland, CA Dominican Order (Western Province), St. Albert's Priory.
Hess, James D. *o.carm.* '76 (BRK) [140] Brooklyn, NY St. Thomas Aquinas Church.
Hess, James W. '53 (MIL) Retired.
Hess, John Paul '83 (STL) [7] Florissant, MO Sacred Heart Church.
Hess, Larry J. '79 (ALN) [O] Kutztown, PA Christopher House; [O] Kutztown, PA Christopher House.
Hess, Msgr. Michael N. '71 (DM) [A] West Des Moines, IA St. Joseph Educational Center; [B] West Des Moines, IA Dowling High School; [I] Des Moines, IA Dowling-St. Joseph Alumni Foundation.
Hess, Norbert *c.s.c.* '53 (CHI) [D] Niles, IL Notre Dame High School.
Hess, Richard J. '60 (DUB) St. Anthony, IA Sacred Heart Church; St. Anthony, IA Sacred Heart Church; Zearing, IA St. Gabriel Church; Zearing, IA St. Gabriel Church.
Hess, Robert *s.c.j.* '67 (JKS) [E] Nesbit, MS St. Michael Community House; [H] Walls, MS Sacred Heart League.
Hess, Stephen M. *s.j.* '95 (P) [19] Portland, OR St. Ignatius Church.
Hesse, Harold W. '38 (NU) Retired.
Hesse, Paul A '91 (CC) Odem, TX Sacred Heart Church.
Hesse, Peter *o.f.m.cap.* '43 (LC) [I] Marathon City, WI St. Anthony Retreat Center.
Hesse, Simon *o.f.m.cap.* '40 (DET) [P] Washington, MI Capuchin Retreat.
Hesse, Thomas N. '63 (KCK) Flush, KS St. Joseph's Church; Wamego, KS St. Bernard's Church.
Hessel, Gerald J. '67 (MIL) [5] Kenosha, WI St. Mark's Church; [Y] Kenosha, WI St. Mark Latin American Center.
Hesseldenz, Msgr. Clarence H. '44 (STL) Retired.
Hessian, Msgr. Patrick J. '53 (STP) Retired.
Hessian, Roger J. '61 (STP) Cannon Falls, MN St. Pius V Church.
Hession, Msgr. Edward I. '41 (FTW) [3] Fort Wayne, IN St. Charles Borromeo Church; Retired.
Hession, James J. (BO) Absent on Sick Leave.
Hession, Mark R. '84 (FR) [P] Fall River, MA Diocesan Education Center.
Hessling, Ambrose B. *o.s.b.* '57 (PEO) [A] Peru, IL St. Bede Abbey and Academy.
Hestasusilo, Anton *c.i.c.m.* '96 (BWN) [3] Mission, TX Our Lady of St. John of the Fields Church.
Hester, John '59 (SJ) [3] Palo Alto, CA St. Ann Chapel; Milpitas, CA Stanford Medical Center.
Heter, Bernard P. '74 (NY) Cornwall-on-Hudson, NY St. Thomas of Canterbury Church.
Hetteberg, Marcan *o.f.m.* '54 (CIN) [M] Cincinnati, OH St. Francis Center.
Hetternan, A. Joseph '65 (FRS) [4] Bakersfield, CA St. Francis Church.
Hettinger, Msgr. Clarence J. '42 (PEO) [15] Peoria, IL St. Vincent De Paul Church; Special Assignment; Retired.
Hettinger, Paul W. '39 (PEO) Retired.
Hetzler, Leo A. *c.s.b.* '55 (ROC) [I] Rochester, NY Basilian Residence.
Heuberger, Joseph '70 (P) Verboort, OR Visitation B.V.M. Church.
Heuberger, Mark '80 (PMB) [A] Boynton Beach, FL St. Vincent de Paul Regional Seminary; [A] Boynton Beach, FL St. Vincent de Paul Regional Seminary.
Heuberger, Mark '80 (VEN) On Duty Outside the Diocese.
Heuring, Msgr. Alvan P. '44 (DUB) Retired.
Heuring, Msgr. Alvan P. '44 (SFR) Retired.
Heuschkel, Robert R. '50 (Y) [13] Youngstown, OH St. Dominic's Church.
Heuser, Frederick A. '55 (MIL) [4] Kenosha, WI St. James Church.
Heuser, James *s.d.b.* '87 (BO) [E] Boston, MA Don Bosco Preparatory School of Technology.
Heusser, John F. '51 (PAT) [14] Paterson, NJ Our Lady of Victories Church.
Heuvel, Jeffrey Vanden '86 (GB) [N] Green Bay, WI University of Wisconsin Ecumenical Center.
Hever, John J. '52 (BO) Foxboro, MA St. Mary Church; Boston, MA Medfield State Hospital.
Hever, Thomas F. '62 (PHX) [3] Tempe, AZ Resurrection Church.
Hevern, Vincent W. *s.j.* '76 (SY) [S] Syracuse, NY Jesuits at LeMoyne, Inc.
Hevia, Todd O. '67 (PT) Milton, FL St. Rose of Lima Church.
Hewes, James E. '74 (ROC) [M] Rochester, NY Diocesan Office of Campus Ministry.
Hewes, Robert S. '78 (RVC) Hicksville, NY Our Lady of Mercy Church.
Hewett, Alfred J. '56 (CAM) Haddon Heights, NJ St. Rose's Church; Retired.
Hewitt, Msgr. Bernard P. '47 (CAM) Retired.
Hewitt, Charles L. '31 (BGP) [K] Trumbull, CT St. Joseph's Manor.
Hewitt, Charles L. '31 (HRT) Retired.
Hewitt, Kenneth R. '77 (PAT) Dover, NJ St. Mary's Church.
Hewitt, Thomas E. *c.s.c.* '39 (FTW) [J] South Bend, IN Congregation of Holy Cross Indiana Province Provincial House.
Hewitt, William J. '57 (MET) Hampton, NJ St. Ann Church.
Hewson, William J. '40 (BR) Retired.
Heyburn, Msgr. Kevin J. '48 (SAN) Olfen, TX St. Boniface Church; Rowena, TX St. Joseph's Church.
Heyburn, Theodore *c.ss.r.* '60 (WIL) Chester, Kent Island, MD St. Christopher Church.
Heyd, Joseph J. *o.s.b.* '56 (PEO) Peru, IL St. Joseph's Church; [A] Peru, IL St. Bede Abbey and Academy.
Heydens, Donald J. '70 (GR) On Special Assignment.
Heyman, George (ROC) Webster, NY Holy Trinity Church.
Heyman, Jerome M. *o.s.a.* '61 (KAL) Allegan, MI Blessed Sacrament Church.
Heymer, Richard H. '56 (GB) Whitelaw, WI St. Michael Church.
Heymer, Msgr. Edward D. '45 (MEM) Retired.
Heyndricks, Eugene P. '81 (NEW) Park Ridge, NJ Our Lady of Mercy Church.
Hezel, Francis X. *s.j.* '69 (CI) [A] Pohnpei, FM Micronesia Seminar; [C] Kolonia, Pohnpei, FM Jesuit House.
Hezel, Kenneth J. *s.j.* '66 (AGN) [H] Mangilao, GU Campus Ministry, Newman Center, University of Guam.
Hibner, Cyprian *o.carm.* '61 (PHX) [5] Glendale, AZ St. Raphael Church.
Hibner, Jerome H. '64 (BEL) Radom, IL St. Michael Church.
Hicarte, Mateo '53 (LA) [16] Los Angeles, CA Immaculate Heart of Mary Church.
Hickel, Msgr. John J. (STL) St. Paul, MO St. Paul Church.
Hickens, William F. *c.s.c.* '46 (FTW) [J] South Bend, IN Congregation of Holy Cross Indiana Province Provincial House.
Hickerson, Don '67 (RC) [1] Rapid City, SD Cathedral of Our Lady of Perpetual Help.
Hickey, Christopher J. (BO) Dedham, MA St. Mary Church.
Hickey, Daniel J. '59 (BO) [3] Malden, MA Sacred Hearts Church.
Hickey, Dennis W. *c.s.p.* '76 (NY) [Z] Scarsdale, NY Paulist Fathers Generalate.
Hickey, Msgr. Edward T. '45 (COV) Retired.
Hickey, George J. *i.m.c.* '80 (MET) [H] Somerset, NJ Consolata Society for Foreign Missions.
Hickey, George W. '73 (PRT) Hampden, ME St. Matthew Church; Winterport, ME St. Gabriel Church.
Hickey, Gerlad J. (BO) Awaiting Assignment.
Hickey, Gregory J. '79 (PH) [117] Philadelphia, PA Our Lady Help of Christians Church; [D] Norristown, PA Kennedy-Kenrick Catholic High School.
Hickey, James F. '68 (BO) Rockland, MA Holy Family Church.
Hickey, James V. '64 (HRT) Farmington, CT St. Patrick's Church.
Hickey, Jerome J. *o.c.s.o.* '59 (ATL) [I] Conyers, GA The Monastery of the Holy Spirit.
Hickey, John *c.m.* '49 (CHI) [C] Chicago, IL Vincentian Community at DePaul University.
Hickey, John '96 (AMA) Happy, TX Holy Name of Jesus Church; Nazareth, TX Holy Family Church.
Hickey, John P. '86 (PIT) Bellevue, PA Assumption of the Blessed Virgin Mary on the Beautiful River Church.
Hickey, Joseph M. '68 (RVC) Elmont, NY St. Vincent de Paul Church.
Hickey, Joseph W. '56 (NY) [143] Bronx, NY St. Francis Xavier Church.
Hickey, Kieran *o.f.m.cap.* '49 (GB) [F] Manitowoc, WI Holy Family Memorial, Inc.
Hickey, Meidon *o.f.m.* '43 (GLP) Fort Defiance, AZ Our Lady of Blessed Sacrament Church.
Hickey, Meldon *o.f.m.* '51 (GLP) [A] Gallup, NM Diocesan Diaconate Formation Program.
Hickey, Michael '62 (VEN) [5] Sarasota, FL St. Patrick Church.
Hickey, Peter D. *s.j.* '76 (BO) [E] Boston, MA Boston College High School & Jesuit Community.
Hickey, Regis *o.s.b.* '50 (KCK) [H] Atchison, KS St. Benedict's Abbey.
Hickey, Msgr. Robert P. '65 (NY) Ellenville, NY St. Mary and St. Andrew Church.
Hickey, Robert P. *o.s.a.* '92 (WDC) [B] Silver Spring, MD Austin Friars Hall, Order of St. Augustine.
Hickey, Thomas D. '49 (MIL) Retired.
Hickey, Thomas E. '70 (CHI) [41] Chicago, IL St. Clement Church.
Hickey, Thomas F. *c.ss.r.* '54 (BRK) [107] Brooklyn, NY Our Lady of Perpetual Help Basilica.
Hickey, William M. '86 (ATL) [10] Atlanta, GA St. Jude Church.
Hickey, Msgr. William T. '47 (BRK) [206] Queens, NY Our Lady of the Angelus Church; Retired.
Hickie, J. Noel '67 (BAK) On Duty Outside the Diocese.
Hickie, J. Noel '67 (P) [J] Eugene, OR Sacred Heart Medical Center.
Hickman, J. Stephen '82 (RIC) Military Chaplains.
Hicks, Alfred J. *s.j.* '66 (BO) [H] Boston, MA Nativity Preparatory School; [W] Boston, MA The Society of Jesus of New England-Provincial Offices.
Hicks, Msgr. Harold E. '43 (NY) Hyde Park, NY Regina Coeli Church.
Hicks, Ronald A. '94 (CHI) Orland Hills, IL St. Elizabeth Seton Church.
Hicks, Steven '82 (SAN) Military Chaplains.
Hidalgo, Juan Vincente *f.m.m.* '95 (WIL) [I] Seaford, DE Missionary Fraternity of Mary, USA, Ltd.
Hidding, Thomas *s.j.* '86 (SP) [8] Tampa, FL Sacred Heart Church; [S] Tampa, FL University of Tampa.
Hidgon, C. Paul '46 (DET) Port Huron, MI St. Stephen Church.
Hiebl, Charles J. '62 (LC) Southeastern Portage County, WI St. Maximilian Maria Kolbe Church.
Hien, John '63 (RVC) Seaford, NY St. William, the Abbot Church.
Hien, Joseph '64 (NY) [27] New York, NY St. Columba Church.
Hietpas, Raymond W. '35 (GB) Retired.
Higdon, C. Paul '46 (DET) Retired; [H] Port Huron, MI Mercy Hospital of Port Huron.
Higdon, Francis B. *m.m.* '67 (DEN) [M] Denver, CO Maryknoll Fathers, Catholic Foreign Mission Society of America (Legal Title).
Higginbotham, Matthew '94 (LAF) Scott, LA SS. Peter and Paul Church.
Higginbotham, Robert '75 (BLX) Military Chaplains.
Higgins, Charles J. '75 (BO) Danvers, MA St. Richard Church; [2] Haverhill, MA St. James Church.
Higgins, Msgr. Cornelius P. '44 (SAC) [7] Sacramento, CA Presentation of the Blessed Virgin Mary Church; Knights Landing, CA St. Paul Church; Retired and in Senior Ministry.
Higgins, Donald *c.s.s.* '64 (BO) [W] Waltham, MA Stigmatine House.
Higgins, E. E. '57 (PEO) Pontiac, IL St. Mary's Church.
Higgins, Edward '76 (PSC) Mahanoy City, PA St. Mary's Church.
Higgins, Edward F. '54 (GBG) Retired.
Higgins, Eugene F. *m.m.* '30 (NY) [Z] Maryknoll, NY Maryknoll Fathers and Brothers.
Higgins, Francis C. '68 (SAV) Thunderbolt, GA Nativity of Our Lord Church.
Higgins, Francis E. (SC) On Duty Outside the Diocese.
Higgins, Msgr. George C. '40 (CHI) Retired.
Higgins, Msgr. George G. '40 (WDC) [C] Washington, DC Catholic University of America, The.
Higgins, Msgr. J. Grant '38 (BUF) Angola, NY Most Precious Blood Church.
Higgins, James J. *c.ss.r.* '37 (STL) [P] Liguori, MO Liguori Mission House/Redemptorists.
Higgins, James P. *s.j.* '85 (BUF) [C] Buffalo, NY Canisius College; [O] Buffalo, NY Canisius Jesuit Community.
Higgins, Jerome *o.f.m.cap.* '54 (MIL) [B] Hales Corners, WI Sacred Heart School of Theology; [P] Milwaukee, WI St. Conrad House.
Higgins, John '81 (LA) [70] Los Angeles, CA St. Joan of Arc Church.
Higgins, John F. *m.s.* '72 (HRT) [M] Hartford, CT

Missionaries of LaSalette Provincial Secretary.
Higgins, John J. '52 (WDC) Retired.
Higgins, John J. *s.j.* '66 (WOR) [N] Worcester, MA Jesuits of Holy Cross College, Inc.
Higgins, John J. '96 (NY) [148] Bronx, NY Holy Rosary Church.
Higgins, Joseph P. '57 (MAD) Middleton, WI St. Bernard Church.
Higgins, Msgr. Laurence E. '53 (SP) [10] Tampa, FL St. Lawrence Church.
Higgins, Leonard H. '82 (TLS) Pawhuska, OK Immaculate Conception Church.
Higgins, Michael *o.carm.* '68 (LA) [3] North Hollywood, CA St. Jane Frances de Chantal Church.
Higgins, Michael *c.p.* '70 (CHI) [N] Chicago, IL Passionist Provincial Office.
Higgins, Michael *c.p.* '70 (DET) [K] Detroit, MI St. Paul of the Cross Community, Congregation of the Passion; [P] Detroit, MI St. Paul of the Cross Retreat Center.
Higgins, Michael *t.o.r.* '85 (ALT) [A] Loretto, PA St. Francis College.
Higgins, Michael J. '62 (BO) Wakefield, MA St. Florence Church.
Higgins, Msgr. Michael K. '64 (SD) Unassigned.
Higgins, Msgr. Patrick '54 (CC) [3] Corpus Christi, TX Holy Cross Church.
Higgins, Patrick O. '47 (SFD) Retired.
Higgins, Peter '56 (VIC) Blessing, TX St. Peter's Church.
Higgins, Philip A. *c.s.c.* '55 (MET) [7] New Brunswick, NJ St. Mary of Mount Virgin Church.
Higgins, Raymond '93 (DM) [6] Des Moines, IA St. Anthony's Church.
Higgins, Richard B. '68 (SAC) Military Chaplains.
Higgins, Robert J. *s.j.* '50 (BO) [E] Boston, MA Boston College High School & Jesuit Community.
Higgins, Suzanne (BO) [Q] Brockton, MA Good Samaritan Medical Center.
Higgins, Thomas C. *m.m.* '50 (NY) [Z] Maryknoll, NY Maryknoll Fathers and Brothers.
Higgins, Thomas M. '85 (PH) [129] Philadelphia, PA Our Lady of Victory Church.
Higgins, Thomas P. *s.j.* '64 (LA) [C] Los Angeles, CA Loyola Marymount University; [BB] Los Angeles, CA Archdiocesan Office for Campus Ministry.
Higgins, Msgr. William '43 (NY) Retired; [Z] New York, NY Our Lady of Consolation Residence.
Higgs, Donald X. '88 (WH) Farmington, WV St. Peters Church; Mannington, WV St. Patrick's Church.
Highberger, Donald E. *s.j.* '81 (SPK) [C] Spokane, WA Gonzaga University.
Highberger, George E. '61 (PHX) Chandler, AZ St. Mary's Church.
Highfill, H. Brian '74 (NO) Military Chaplains.
Highland, Msgr. Charles F. '50 (STU) Churchtown, OH St. John the Baptist Church; [I] Beverly, OH Washington Technical College; [J] Marietta, OH Search.
Highland, Terence *o.s.a.* (BO) Andover, MA St. Augustine Church.
Hight, Michael '82 (RC) Presho, SD Christ the King Church.
Hightower, O. Lee. '61 (HEL) Military Chaplains.
Higley, Gregory L. '81 (JC) Mexico, MO St. Brendan Church.
Higson, John '80 (LA) Santa Maria, CA St. John Neumann Church.
Higuera, Federico '82 (BEL) Cobden, IL St. Joseph Church.
Higuera, Julio '78 (PHX) Gilbert, AZ St. Anne Church.
Higuero, Francisco J. '68 (BRK) Released from Diocesan Assignment.
Hiland, George '58 (PEO) Retired.
Hiland, Gerard '85 (CIN) [51] Cincinnati, OH St. Jude the Apostle Church.
Hilbert, J. Robert *s.j.* '56 (MIL) [P] Milwaukee, WI Arrupe House Jesuit Community; [P] Milwaukee, WI Jesuit Provincial Office, Wisconsin Province.
Hilbert, John J. '60 (E) [24] Erie, PA St. Mark the Evangelist Church.
Hilbert, Joseph C. '52 (HBG) Gettysburg, PA St. Francis Xavier's Church.
Hilbert, Michael P. *s.j.* '83 (NY) [Z] New York, NY Jesuit Provincial's Office.
Hildebrand, Thomas M. '75 (TLS) [14] Tulsa, OK St. Pius X Church.
Hildebrandt, Henry F. '87 (DOD) Liberal, KS St. Anthony Church.
Hilderbrand, H. Michael '76 (IND) Jeffersonville, IN Sacred Heart Church; [C] Clarksville, IN Our Lady of Providence.
Hile, Donald E. '60 (WH) Salem, WV Sacred Heart Church; West Union, WV St. Patrick's Church.
Hilferty, John G. '78 (ALN) Jim Thorpe, PA St. Joseph Church.
Hilferty, Msgr. Thomas J. '52 (PH) Ardsley, PA Queen of Peace Church.
Hilfiker, Robert G. '87 (NY) Goshen, NY St. John the Evangelist Church; Ossining, NY St. Augustine Church.
Hilgartner, Richard B., Jr. '95 (BAL) Severna Park, MD St. John the Evangelist Church.
Hilgeman, Edward J. '52 (STL) [3] Lemay, MO St. Andrew Church.
Hilgert, E. John *c.p.* '75 (BIR) [7] Birmingham, AL Holy Family Church; Fairfield, AL St. Mary Church.
Hilinski, Joseph T. '76 (CLV) [55] Cleveland, OH Our Lady of Mercy Church.
Hilkert, John J. '43 (CLV) [11] Akron, OH St. Mary Church.
Hilkert, Robert C. '42 (CLV) Brunswick, OH St. Ambrose Church.
Hill, Allan J. '83 (HRT) Harwinton, CT Immaculate Heart of Mary Church; Kent, CT Sacred Heart Church.
Hill, Benet *o.s.b.* '85 (WDC) [M] Washington, DC St. Anselm's Abbey.
Hill, Msgr. Charles E. '64 (LA) Panorama City, CA St. Genevieve Church.
Hill, Donald '67 (BIS) On Duty Outside the Diocese.
Hill, Donald M. '94 (L) [26] Louisville, KY St. Francis of Assisi Church.
Hill, Edward T. '60 (BAL) Military Chaplains.
Hill, Frederick *o.f.m.cap.* '67 (RVC) Smithtown, NY St. John's Episcopal Hospital.
Hill, George H. '68 (WOR) On Duty Outside the Diocese.
Hill, J. Clifton *c.s.sp.* '65 (PIT) [B] Pittsburgh, PA Duquesne University of the Holy Ghost.
Hill, James B. *s.m.a.* '45 (BO) [W] Dedham, MA African Mission House and African Cultural Center.
Hill, John H. '49 (SY) Manlius, NY St. Ann Church; Retired.
Hill, Lawrence B. *s.j.* '46 (NY) [Z] New York, NY Murray-Weigel Hall.
Hill, Lawrence H. *o.s.b.* '65 (GBG) [H] Latrobe, PA Saint Vincent Archabbey.
Hill, Michael *o.f.m.* '77 (STL) [P] St. Louis, MO Franciscan Friary of St. Anthony of Padua.
Hill, Michael W. *o.f.m.* (HON) Makawao, HI St. Joseph Church.
Hill, Patrick J. '68 (LA) [49] Los Angeles, CA St. Bernard Church.
Hill, Paul J. *m.s.c.* '50 (Y) [A] Youngstown, OH Sacred Heart Retreat House & Renewal Center.
Hill, Msgr. Peter J. '36 (SFE) Retired; [A] Santa Fe, NM Immaculate Heart of Mary Seminary.
Hill, Philip '71 (NY) Military Chaplains.
Hill, R. Cary '66 (WDC) Pastoral Center Special Ministries.
Hill, Richard A. *s.j.* '58 (OAK) [A] Berkeley, CA The Jesuit School of Theology at Berkeley.
Hill, Richard A. *s.j.* '58 (SFR) [N] San Francisco, CA Jesuit Community at University of San Francisco.
Hill, Robert '57 (Y) Retired.
Hill, Robert Cary '66 (WDC) Beltsville, MD St. Joseph Church.
Hill, Timothy '59 (BIR) [23] Birmingham, AL St. Stanislaus Church.
Hill, W. Paul '64 (WDC) [4] Bowie, MD St. Pius X Church.
Hill, William B. *s.j.* '45 (SCR) [C] Scranton, PA University of Scranton.
Hill, William J. *o.p.* '50 (WDC) [B] Washington, DC Dominican House of Studies; [C] Washington, DC Catholic University of America, The.
Hillard, Matthew J. *o.s.f.s.* '91 (ARL) [J] Fairfax, VA Oblates of St. Francis de Sales Residence.
Hillebrand, Albert J. '53 (DET) Retired.
Hillen, Daniel P. '69 (HEL) [B] Helena, MT Carroll College.
Hillenbrand, John T. '70 (CHI) [168] Chicago, IL St. Peter Canisius Church.
Hiller, Everett J. '54 (RCK) Apple River, IL St. Joseph Church; Warren, IL St. Ann Church.
Hillesheim, Gerald A. '68 (NU) Ghent, MN St. Eloi Church; Minneota, MN St. Edward Church; Taunton, MN SS. Cyril and Methodius Church.
Hilley, Stephen '79 (MIA) Coconut Creek, FL St. Luke Church.
Hilliard, William J. '62 (HRT) Poquonock, CT St. Joseph's Church.
Hillier, David A. (TR) Leave of Absence.
Hillier, John G. '88 (WOR) On Special or Other (Arch)Diocesan Assignment.
Hillman, Eugene L. *c.s.sp.* '50 (PRO) [B] Newport, RI Salve Regina University.
Hills, Richard L. '32 (CHI) Flossmoor, IL Infant Jesus of Prague Church; Retired.
Hillyard, Matthew J. *o.s.f.s.* '91 (ARL) [D] Fairfax, VA Paul VI High School.
Hilmer, Robert E. '86 (DUB) [1] Waterloo, IA St. Joseph's Church; [2] Waterloo, IA St. Mary's Church.
Hils, Damien (FAR) [5] Fargo, ND St. Anthony of Padua Church.
Hilton, Francis G. *s.j.* '92 (BAL) [C] Baltimore, MD Loyola College.
Hilton, John '82 (DEN) Wheat Ridge, CO SS. Peter and Paul Church.
Hiltz, John T. '59 (ORG) Yorba Linda, CA St. Martin Church.
Hiltz, John T. '59 (TOL) On Duty Outside the Diocese.
Hiltz, Peter M. '59 (BAL) Brunswick, MD St. Francis of Assisi Church; Retired.
Hilz, Robert *t.o.r.* '70 (STU) [A] Steubenville, OH Franciscan University of Steubenville; [F] Steubenville, OH Holy Spirit Monastery.
Himes, Kenneth R. *o.f.m.* '76 (NY) [146] Bronx, NY Holy Cross Church.
Himes, Kenneth R. *o.f.m.* '76 (WDC) [M] Silver Spring, MD Gemelli House.
Himes, Michael J. '72 (BRK) Released from Diocesan Assignment.
Himes, Robert P. '58 (YAK) Grandview, WA Blessed Sacrament Church.
Himmelsbach, James R. '77 (STP) Military Chaplains.
Himsworth, Raymond J. (PH) [DD] Philadelphia, PA Newman Apostolate.
Himsworth, Raymond J. '62 (PH) Elkins Park, PA St. James Church.
Hinch, Msgr. Lawrence E. '59 (BRK) [243] Queens, NY St. Teresa Church.
Hinckley, Christopher '39 (FTW) Retired.
Hinde, Peter *o.carm.* '52 (JOL) [J] Darien, IL Carmelite Fathers Provincial Office.
Hindel, Richard *o.s.b.* '47 (IND) [J] St. Meinrad, IN St. Meinrad Archabbey.
Hindelang, Joseph *s.m.* '78 (BO) [W] Boston, MA Marist Fathers and Brothers Provincial House; [W] Boston, MA Marist Fathers of Our Lady of Victories (Boston Prov.).
Hindelang, Michael L. *s.j.* '38 (OM) [C] Omaha, NE Creighton Preparatory School.
Hindman, Gerald *o.s.b.* '45 (NO) [P] St. Benedict, LA St. Joseph Abbey.
Hindman, John R. '75 (SB) Crestline, CA St. Frances Xavier Cabrini Church.
Hinds, Edward J. '74 (PAT) Boonton, NJ Our Lady of Mount Carmel Church.
Hinds, William H. '87 (COV) Maysville, KY St. Patrick Church; [B] Maysville, KY St. Patrick High School.
Hindsley, Leonard P. *o.p.* '84 (PRO) [P] Providence, RI St. Thomas Aquinas Priory at Providence College.
Hines, Bartholomew F. *s.s.j.* '48 (BAL) [M] Baltimore, MD St. Joseph's Manor.
Hines, Bede F. *t.o.r.* '47 (ALT) [A] Loretto, PA St. Francis College; [F] Loretto, PA St. Francis Friary, Third Order Regular of St. Francis of Penance.
Hines, Christopher J. '92 (NEW) [B] South Orange, NJ Seton Hall University.
Hines, Hugh *o.f.m.* '60 (BO) [BB] Boston, MA St. Anthony Shrine.
Hines, J. William '72 (WDC) Military Chaplains.
Hines, Msgr. Leo F. (MAN) Retired.
Hines, William F. '47 (SCR) Retired.
Hiney, Thomas J. '56 (ALB) Rensselaer, NY St. John Church; Special Assignment.
Hinken, Michael *s.o.l.t.* '96 (BEA) Liberty, TX Immaculate Conception Church.
Hinkes, Gabriel A. *o.praem.* '37 (GB) [I] De Pere, WI St. Norbert Abbey.
Hinkle, Ignatius *o.f.m.conv.* '59 (OAK) San Pablo, CA St. Paul Church.
Hinkley, Michael F.X. '91 (HRT) Windsor, CT St. Gabriel's Church.
Hinnebusch, John Frederick *o.p.* '50 (WDC) [B] Washington, DC Dominican House of Studies; [C] Washington, DC Catholic University of America, The.
Hinnebusch, Paul G. *o.p.* '44 (DAL) [M] Irving, TX Dominican Priory of St. Albert the Great.
Hinnen, James W. '71 (MAD) Sun Prairie, WI Sacred Hearts of Jesus and Mary Church.
Hinni, Thomas R. *c.m.* '63 (PBL) La Junta, CO La Junta Catholic Parish Church.
Hinojal, Ricardo *o.a.r.* '62 (LSC) San Miguel, NM San Miguel Church; [B] Mesilla, NM Augustinian Recollects Fathers.
Hinojosa, Pedro Nolasco, Jr. '96 (CC) [1] Laredo, TX Blessed Sacrament Church.
Hinrichsen, Msgr. Carl D. '55 (NEW) Franklin Lakes, NJ Most Blessed Sacrament Church; Park Ridge, NJ Our Lady of Mercy Church; Retired.
Hinsvark, John '66 (FBK) Nome, AK St. Joseph Church; Teller, AK St. Ann Church.
Hinton, James *c.pp.s.* '43 (CIN) [B] Carthagena, OH St. Charles.
Hinton, John T. '73 (NO) Port Sulphur, LA St. Patrick Church.
Hintz, David R. '86 (LIN) [9] Lincoln, NE St. Patrick's Church; [K] Lincoln, NE Calvary Cemetery and Mausoleum Association.
Hippee, Michael E. '73 (MAD) [2] Madison, WI St. Bernard Church.
Hipsley, Milton A. '70 (BAL) Cumberland, MD St. Mary Church.
Hipwell, Patrick J. '77 (STP) Minnetonka, MN Immaculate Heart of Mary Church.
Hiramatsu, Joseph *s.a.* '82 (NY) [Z] Garrison, NY Generalate of the Franciscan Friars of the Atonement-St. James Friary.
Hire, Richard P. '70 (FTW) Elkhart, IN St. Thomas the Apostle Church.
Hirsch, Msgr. Clinton F. '45 (EVN) Retired.

Hirsch, Harold L. '53 (MET) Spotswood, NJ Immaculate Conception Church.
Hirsch, Joseph W. '86 (LC) Altdorf, WI St. Joseph Church; [2] Wisconsin Rapids, WI St. Lawrence Church; [C] Wisconsin Rapids, WI Assumption High School.
Hirsch, Robert *c.ss.r.* '46 (DET) [34] Detroit, MI Holy Redeemer Church.
Hirsch, Robert M. '47 (DUB) Calmar, IA St. Aloysius Church; [F] Calmar, IA Calmar-Festina-Spillville (CFS) Catholic Elementary School.
Hirt, Alan (CIN) [65] Cincinnati, OH St. Monica-St. George Parish Newman Center Church.
Hirt, Alan *o.f.m.* '77 (CIN) [M] Cincinnati, OH St. Francis Seraph Friary; [Q] Cincinnati, OH University of Cincinnati Newman Center.
Hirt, Edwin H. '39 (GBG) Retired; [G] Greensburg, PA St. Anne Home.
Hirt, Raymond E. *o.f.m.* '62 (TR) Brant Beach, NJ St. Francis of Assisi Church.
Hirt, William '70 (BAL) Absent on Leave.
Hirten, Timothy J. '93 (BRK) [184] Queens, NY St. Joan of Arc Church.
Hirtz, Daniel J. '73 (SPC) Pierce City, MO St. Mary Church.
Hisky, William G. '59 (BAL) Havre de Grace, MD St. Patrick's Church; On Duty Outside the Archdiocese.
Hislop, Edward J. '73 (HEL) [2] Helena, MT St. Mary Church.
Hissey, L. Pierce '66 (PHX) [13] Phoenix, AZ St. Jerome Church.
Hissrich, John E. '86 (PIT) [54] Pittsburgh, PA St. John Vianney Church.
Hitch, David F. '68 (DAV) [3] Iowa City, IA St. Thomas More Church.
Hitchcock, Msgr. James R. '46 (NSH) Joelton, TN St. Lawrence's Church.
Hitchcock, Martin B. '51 (BGP) Retired.
Hitchens, Robert '94 (PHU) Elizabeth, NJ St. Vladimir's Church.
Hitchko, Daniel D. '61 (SCR) Exeter, PA St. John the Baptist Church.
Hitchko, Daniel D. *v.f.* '64 (SCR) Exeter, PA St. Cecilia Church.
Hite, Gregory R. '81 (TOL) Mansfield, OH St. Mary Church.
Hite, James C. '73 (OWN) Retired.
Hite, Jordan *t.o.r.* '70 (SFS) Wagner, SD St. John the Baptist Church.
Hite, Richard B. *m.ss.a.* '70 (WH) [G] Old Fields, WV Holy Spirit Hermitage.
Hitpas, Joseph *o.m.i.* '65 (STP) [28] St. Paul, MN St. Mary Church.
Hitpas, William J. '67 (BEL) O'Fallon, IL St. Nicholas Church.
Hitt, Tobin '96 (SFE) Las Vegas, NM Our Lady of Sorrows Church.
Hitti, Michael '38 (OLL) Retired.
Hitti, Michael '38 (SAM) Retired.
Hladky, Sylvester '36 (PBR) Warren, OH SS. Peter and Paul's Church.
Hladni, Mirko '71 (CLV) [62] Cleveland, OH St. Paul Church.
Hlavacek, John F. '55 (LR) Retired; [H] Little Rock, AR St. John Manor.
Hlebs, Milan '51 (SJ) Retired.
Hlond, Waclaw *c.m.* '55 (HRT) [18] New Haven, CT St. Stanislaus Church.
Hlopko, John J. '36 (SCR) Retired.
Hmircik, Donald A. '56 (MIL) Retired.
Hnatyshyn, Robert '64 (SJP) McKeesport, PA St. John the Baptist Church.
Ho, Khanh '90 (BEA) [5] Beaumont, TX St. Joseph Church.
Ho, Mathias '55 (ORG) Retired.
Hoa, Bartholomew Do Thai *c.m.c.* '77 (DEN) Wheat Ridge, CO Queen of Vietnamese Martyrs Church.
Hoa, Trinh Duc *c.ss.r.* '93 (LA) [R] Baldwin Park, CA Vietnamese Redemptorist Mission.
Hoag, Michael R. *s.j.* '71 (NEW) [C] Jersey City, NJ St. Peter's Preparatory School.
Hoag, Timothy '95 (RC) [1] Rapid City, SD Cathedral of Our Lady of Perpetual Help.
Hoagland, James N. '57 (WCH) Little River, KS Holy Trinity Church; Lyons, KS St. Paul Church.
Hoagland, Victor *c.p.* '59 (MET) [H] South River, NJ Passionist Provincial Office.
Hoagland, Victor *c.p.* '59 (NEW) [N] Union City, NJ Congregation of the Passion (Passionists)-St. Michael's Residence.
Hoak, Jack *o.f.m.* '75 (NY) [Z] New York, NY Franciscan Province of the Immaculate Conception.
Hoan, Basil '77 (TYL) Center, TX St. Therese Church; Center, TX St. Therese Church.
Hoan, Joseph '73 (FRS) [10] Fresno, CA St. Helen Church.
Hoan, Joseph Cong '73 (FRS) [1] Fresno, CA St. John Cathedral.
Hoan, Michael '72 (ORG) Westminster, CA Blessed Sacrament Church.
Hoang, Joseph Vien *s.d.b.* '83 (NO) [D] Marrero, LA Archbishop Shaw High School.
Hoang, Joseph Viet '94 (SD) Spring Valley, CA Santa Sophia Church.
Hoang, Khanh San '94 (COS) Parker, CO Ave Maria Church.
Hoang, Louis Trung '95 (DOD) Garden City, KS St. Dominic Church; Ingalls, KS St. Stanislaus Church.
Hoang, Petrus Binh '96 (P) Salem, OR St. Joseph Church.
Hoang, Phuong '89 (SEA) Auburn, WA Holy Family Church.
Hoang-Anh-Thang, Francis *c.m.c.* '93 (SB) [E] Corona, CA Congregation of the Mother Coredemptrix.
Hoar, Leo James '66 (SPR) [5] Northampton, MA St. Mary of the Assumption Church; [P] Amherst, MA University of Massachusetts and Amherst College, Newman Center.
Hoar, Richard J. *s.j.* '56 (BUF) [O] Buffalo, NY Canisius Jesuit Community.
Hoar, Thomas F.X. *s.s.e.* '72 (NOR) [I] Enders Island, CT Edmundite Apostolate Center.
Hoar, Thomas F.X. *s.s.e.* '78 (NOR) [A] Enders Island, CT St. Edmund's Novitiate; [A] Mystic, CT Edmundite Seminary Guild; [F] Mystic, CT Society of St. Edmund.
Hoare, Liam *s.p.* '68 (SFE) Jemez Springs, NM Our Lady of the Assumption Church; [J] Jemez Springs, NM The Jemez Program, Our Lady of Lourdes Novitiate.
Hoat, Rochus Vu Dihn (BAL) [57] Baltimore, MD St. Mary of the Assumption Church.
Hoat, Rochus Vu Dinh (BAL) Retired.
Hoban, Alphonsus *s.a.* '38 (NY) [Z] Garrison, NY Franciscan Friars of the Atonement.
Hoban, Robert L. '79 (CLV) [5] Parma, OH St. Francis de Sales Church.
Hoban, Msgr. Thomas E. '60 (ALN) Emmaus, PA St. Ann Church.
Hobbes, Thomas F. '56 (SY) Endwell, NY Christ the King Church.
Hobbs, Msgr. James V. '57 (BAL) [2] Baltimore, MD Basilica of the National Shrine of the Assumption of the Blessed Virgin Mary.
Hobert, James M., Jr. '85 (TUC) Douglas, AZ St. Luke Church; Pirtleville, AZ St. Bernard's Church; [I] Douglas, AZ Cochise Community College.
Hobson, J. Mark '86 (CLV) Solon, OH Resurrection of Our Lord Church.
Hobt, Phillip '92 (DM) [A] Council Bluffs, IA Council Bluffs Area Catholic Education Systems, Inc.
Hoch, George B. *s.j.* '44 (NY) [Z] New York, NY Jesuit Community at Fordham University.
Hochhalter, Lester '91 (JOL) Lombard, IL St. Pius X Church.
Hochheim, William A. '60 (STA) Starke, FL St. Edward's Church.
Hochman, Richard C. *c.s.c.* '80 (FR) South Easton, MA Holy Cross Church.
Hochreiter, Robert S. '68 (SCR) Military Chaplains.
Hock, G. Harry *s.j.* '64 (WDC) [E] Washington, DC Gonzaga College High School.
Hock, William T. '48 (CHI) [198] Chicago, IL St. Tarcissus Church; Franklin Park, IL St. Gertrude Church; Retired.
Hocking, Harold J. *s.j.* '52 (ALN) [A] Wernersville, PA Novitiate of St. Isaac Jogues.
Hoctor, Thomas D. '57 (ROC) Rochester, NY Rochester Psychiatric Center.
Hoctor, Thomas J. '57 (ROC) [4] Rochester, NY St. Anne Church.
Hodapp, Timothy L. '85 (STP) Golden Valley, MN St. Margaret Mary Church.
Hodapp, Timothy L. '85 (WIN) On Duty Outside the Diocese.
Hodde, William G. '52 (FTW) Yoder, IN St. Aloysius Church.
Hoder, James A. '75 (CHI) Other Assignments.
Hoderny, Thomas S. '79 (E) Crown, PA St. Mary Church.
Hodge, William A. '74 (CAM) Penns Grove, NJ St. James Church.
Hodges, Henry D. '56 (PHX) Retired.
Hodges, Leo '86 (ORL) Ormond Beach, FL Prince of Peace Church; [E] Daytona Beach, FL Embry-Riddle Aeronautical University.
Hodges, Robert S. *o.praem.* '74 (ORG) [C] Santa Ana, CA Mater Dei High School; [H] Silverado, CA Norbertine Fathers.
Hodgson, John *c.ss.r.* (BAL) Ellicott City, MD Our Lady of Perpetual Help Church.
Hodgson, William M. '79 (SPC) Caruthersville, MO Sacred Heart Church.
Hodnett, John J. *c.m.* '59 (PH) [Z] Philadelphia, PA Congregation of the Mission.
Hoebing, Philibert *o.f.m.* '50 (SFD) [B] Quincy, IL Quincy University.
Hoedebeck, Paul *o.s.b.* '43 (LR) Shoal Creek, AR St. Scholastica's Church; [A] Subiaco, AR Subiaco Monastery.
Hoeffner, Robert '73 (ORL) [8] Orlando, FL St. Isaac Jogues Church.
Hoefgen, Francis *o.s.b.* '79 (SCL) [I] Collegeville, MN St. John's Abbey, of the Order of St. Benedict.
Hoefgen, Raymond J. '63 (MAR) Rapid River, MI St. Charles Borromeo Church.
Hoefler, Alexander *s.v.d.* '50 (LA) Torrance, CA Nativity Church.
Hoefler, Robert A. '85 (DM) [12] Des Moines, IA St. Theresa of the Child Jesus Church.
Hoegerl, Carl W. *c.ss.r.* '50 (BRK) [U] Brooklyn, NY Our Lady of Good Counsel Residence.
Hoek, John F. *s.j.* '44 (NY) [Z] New York, NY Murray-Weigel Hall.
Hoelck, Frank '59 (GI) Spalding, NE St. Michael's Church.
Hoelle, Philip C. *s.m.* '42 (CIN) [M] Dayton, OH Marianist Provincialate.
Hoelscher, James '58 (SAT) Pleasanton, TX St. Luke-Loire Church.
Hoelsken, Mark A. *s.j.* '91 (P) [L] Portland, OR Jesuit Provincial Office (Oregon Prov.).
Hoene, Robert E. *s.j.* '53 (OM) [K] Omaha, NE Jesuit Community At Creighton University.
Hoenig, George B. '65 (DAV) Muscatine, IA St. Mathias Church.
Hoenig, Gerald A. '52 (DAV) Montrose, IA St. Joseph's Church; Fort Madison, IA Iowa State Penitentiary.
Hoenisch, Richard '80 (SFR) Absent on Leave.
Hoeper, Robert J. *s.m.* '51 (CIN) [M] Huntsville, OH St. George Chapel of Marianist Community.
Hoeppner, Michael J. '75 (WIN) [2] Winona, MN St. Casimir's Church.
Hoerburger, Henry R. '43 (LC) Elk Mound, WI St. Joseph Church.
Hoernig, Alphonse X. *c.m.* '56 (STL) [P] Perryville, MO Congregation of The Mission.
Hoerning, Richard P. '73 (RVC) East Northport, NY St. Anthony of Padua Church.
Hoeser, Jerome G. '63 (LC) Mosinee, WI St. Paul Church.
Hoeshmann, George '92 (NY) Absent on Leave.
Hoesli, Frederick Damien *o.p.* '64 (NY) [121] New York, NY St. Vincent Ferrer Church; [Z] New York, NY St. Vincent Ferrer Priory.
Hoevel, Robert J. '42 (FTW) Retired.
Hoewischer, Harry E. *s.j.* '57 (DEN) [M] Denver, CO Xavier Jesuit Center.
Hoey, James F. '65 (WOR) Spencer, MA Mary, Queen of the Rosary Church.
Hoey, Robert F. *s.j.* '54 (BO) [W] Boston, MA Loyola House.
Hoff, Alphonse *o.f.m.* '44 (IND) Batesville, IN St. Louis Church.
Hoff, James E. *s.j.* '65 (CIN) [D] Cincinnati, OH Xavier University; [M] Cincinnati, OH Jesuit Community at Xavier Unversity.
Hoffay, Thomas '74 (NY) Absent on Leave.
Hoffen, Henry A. *s.j.* '53 (NY) [Z] New York, NY Xavier Jesuit Community.
Hoffenkamp, Robert A. '89 (JOL) Wood Dale, IL Holy Ghost Church.
Hoffer, Charles '46 (COV) [6] Covington, KY Holy Cross Church; Retired.
Hoffman, Charles A. *s.j.* '66 (SFR) [E] San Francisco, CA St. Ignatius College Preparatory (Coed).
Hoffman, David '75 (BAL) On Duty Outside the Archdiocese.
Hoffman, David '96 (GB) Kaukauna, WI Holy Cross Church.
Hoffman, Dennis H. '70 (DUL) Ely, MN St. Anthony's Church; [F] Duluth, MN University of MN-Duluth.
Hoffman, Dennis L. '90 (DAV) Keokuk, IA All Saints Church.
Hoffman, Dominic *o.p.* '41 (P) [18] Portland, OR Holy Rosary Parish & Dominican Priory Church.
Hoffman, Donald J. '54 (STL) Crestwood, MO St. Elizabeth of Hungary Church; St. Louis, MO St. Anthony Medical Center.
Hoffman, Edward '61 (PIT) [J] Pittsburgh, PA St. Francis Nursing Center-East.
Hoffman, Emmett G. '53 (GF) Retired.
Hoffman, Francis J. '92 (PIT) [M] Pittsburgh, PA Opus Dei.
Hoffman, Frank '71 (RNO) [F] Reno, NV University of Nevada, Newman Club.
Hoffman, Gerard J. '73 (PH) [D] Philadelphia, PA Roman Catholic High School for Boys; [X] Elverson, PA St. Mary of Providence Center.
Hoffman, James *o.f.m.* '67 (CHI) [N] Countryside, IL St. Gratian Friary, Franciscan Friars.
Hoffman, James A. '67 (SUP) Woodruff, WI Our Lady Queen of the Universe Church.
Hoffman, James R. '57 (TOL) [1] Toledo, OH Queen of the Most Holy Rosary Cathedral.
Hoffman, John R. '75 (CHI) [199] Chicago, IL St. Teresa Church.
Hoffman, Joseph M. '79 (BRK) [80] Brooklyn, NY St. Martin of Tours-Fourteen Holy Martyrs Church.
Hoffman, Mark '91 (E) [C] Saint Marys, PA Elk County Christian High School.
Hoffman, Mark A. '90 (E) St. Marys, PA Sacred Heart of Jesus Church.

Hoffman, Matthias H. '40 (CHI) Flossmoor, IL Infant Jesus of Prague Church; Retired.
Hoffman, Michael *s.d.s.* '82 (MIL) [P] Milwaukee, WI Salvatorian Provincial Residence.
Hoffman, Patrick '78 (AMA) [2] Amarillo, TX St. Laurence Cathedral.
Hoffman, Raniero *o.s.b.cam.* '75 (MRY) [G] Big Sur, CA New Camaldoli Hermitage.
Hoffman, Richard L. '50 (EVN) Retired.
Hoffman, Robert B. '69 (RCK) St. Charles, IL St. John Neumann Church.
Hoffman, Msgr. Robert F. '44 (DEN) [1] Aurora, CO Queen of Peace Church; Retired.
Hoffman, Thomas '80 (CHI) [214] Chicago, IL St. William Church.
Hoffman, Thomas A. *s.j.* '56 (OM) [K] Omaha, NE Jesuit Community At Creighton University.
Hoffman, Thomas D. *s.j.* '94 (CHI) [177] Chicago, IL St. Procopius Church.
Hoffman, Thomas W. *s.j.* '76 (NO) [F] New Orleans, LA Jesuit High School.
Hoffman, William G. '61 (ATL) Gainesville, GA St. Michael's Church; [L] Atlanta, GA Campus Ministry.
Hoffmann, Andrew W. '74 (SC) Denison, IA St. Rose of Lima Church.
Hoffmann, Charles G. '63 (GB) Antigo, WI St. John Church.
Hoffmann, Chris (ORL) [E] De Land, FL Stetson University Catholic Campus Ministry.
Hoffmann, Christopher A. '87 (ORL) Deltona, FL St. Clare Church.
Hoffmann, Edward D. '44 (SC) Retired.
Hoffmann, Edward M. '72 (DEN) [23] Denver, CO Church of the Risen Christ.
Hoffmann, Emmett G. '53 (GF) [K] Ashland, MT St. Labre Indian School Educational Association.
Hoffmann, Francis T. '89 (BGP) Bethel, CT St. Mary's Church.
Hoffmann, Frank '71 (RNO) [3] Reno, NV Our Lady of Wisdom Church.
Hoffmann, Lawrence R. '71 (DM) [6] Des Moines, IA St. Anthony's Church.
Hoffmann, Philip A. '64 (GB) Special Assignment.
Hoffmann, Msgr. Ralph G. '37 (GRY) Retired.
Hoffmann, Robert G. '69 (PAT) Netcong, NJ St. Michael's Church; Morris Plains, NJ Morris County Youth Center; Newton, NJ Sussex County Jail.
Hoffmann, Robert H. '56 (PEO) Clinton, IL St. John the Baptist's Church; Wapella, IL St. Patrick's Church.
Hoffmann, William A. '80 (GB) On Duty Outside the Diocese.
Hoffmaster, Harry '70 (DET) Retired.
Hoffner, Carlos *m.s.* '92 (MIL) [P] Milwaukee, WI La Salette Fathers.
Hoffner, Carlos *m.s.* '92 (RCK) Sterling, IL St. Mary Church.
Hofmann, Arthur '44 (SJ) Retired.
Hofmann, Charles A. *s.j.* '66 (SFR) [N] San Francisco, CA Jesuit Community at St. Ignatius College Preparatory.
Hofmann, Raymond *c.r.* '56 (L) [67] Louisville, KY Resurrection D.N.J.C. Church.
Hofmann, Stephen *o.s.b.* '41 (P) [L] St. Benedict, OR Mt. Angel Abbey.
Hofmann, Thomas X. '77 (CHR) Moncks Corner, SC St. Philip Benizi Church.
Hofschulte, Charles *c.j.* '71 (LA) [D] Santa Barbara, CA Bishop Garcia Diego High School.
Hofstede, John M. '75 (STP) [5] Minneapolis, MN Christ the King Church.
Hofstee, Gerard *s.v.d.* '35 (CHI) [B] Techny, IL Divine Word Residence.
Hofstetter, Robert J. '54 (KNX) [3] Chattanooga, TN St. Jude Church; [K] Knoxville, TN Diocesan Council of Catholic Women.
Hogan, Benedict *o.carm.* '59 (JOL) [J] Darien, IL Carmelite Fathers Provincial Office.
Hogan, Cornelius J. '38 (BO) Retired.
Hogan, Daniel M. '53 (STL) O'Fallon, MO St. Barnabas Church.
Hogan, David '55 (SC) Anthon, IA St. Joseph's Church; Danbury, IA St. Mary's Church.
Hogan, Dennis J. '73 (PAT) Lincoln Park, NJ St. Joseph's Church.
Hogan, Edward P. '46 (BRK) Retired.
Hogan, Edward T. *s.j.* '85 (WDC) [E] Washington, DC Gonzaga College High School.
Hogan, Francis E. *s.j.* '47 (MIL) [P] Milwaukee, WI Jesuit Provincial Office, Wisconsin Province.
Hogan, Francis T. '46 (BUF) Retired.
Hogan, Francis X. *c.m.f.* '49 (LA) [R] Rancho Dominguez, CA Dominguez Seminary Inc.
Hogan, Gary *c.r.* '86 (CHI) [74] Chicago, IL St. Hedwig Church.
Hogan, George C. '73 (BO) North Andover, MA St. Michael Church.
Hogan, James J. '61 (HEL) [1] Missoula, MT Christ the King Church; [H] Missoula, MT University of Montana.
Hogan, John *s.s.c.* '62 (DAL) [11] Dallas, TX St. Andrew Kim Church.
Hogan, Msgr. John F. '63 (WDC) [2] Bowie, MD Sacred Heart Church.
Hogan, John F., Jr. '88 (SY) Lacona, NY St. Frances Xavier Cabrini Church; Pulaski, NY St. John the Evangelist Church.
Hogan, John J. *o.m.i.* '65 (BO) [3] Lowell, MA Immaculate Conception Church; Boston, MA Saints Memorial Medical Center.
Hogan, John P. '73 (LC) Rudolph, WI St. Philip Church; [2] Wisconsin Rapids, WI St. Lawrence Church.
Hogan, John P. *o.f.m.* '75 (BO) [BB] Boston, MA St. Anthony Shrine.
Hogan, Joseph F. '88 (MET) Hillsborough, NJ Mary, Mother of God Church.
Hogan, Joseph T. '88 (PEO) [2] Champaign, IL St. John's Catholic Chapel; [O] Champaign, IL St. John's Catholic Student Chapel and Newman Foundation, University of Illinois.
Hogan, Leroy '57 (GB) Retired.
Hogan, Msgr. Michael '39 (DUL) Retired.
Hogan, Michael '65 (ALB) [3] Schenectady, NY Sacred Heart-St. Columba Church; Special Assignment; [B] Albany, NY Maria College.
Hogan, Michael C. '51 (ROC) Fairport, NY St. John of Rochester Church; Retired.
Hogan, Michael P. '67 (ATL) [10] Atlanta, GA St. Jude Church; [J] Snellville, GA Monastery of the Visitation.
Hogan, Peter E. *s.s.j.* '46 (BAL) [M] Baltimore, MD St. Joseph Society of the Sacred Heart House of Central Administration.
Hogan, Phil D. *o.f.m.* '62 (CHI) [D] Chicago, IL Hales Franciscan High School, Inc.
Hogan, Ralph R. '52 (PRO) Narragansett, RI St. Thomas More Church.
Hogan, Richard '86 (DET) Absent on Leave.
Hogan, Richard M. '81 (STP) [23] St. Paul, MN St. John of St. Paul Church.
Hogan, Robert E. *s.m.* '83 (CIN) [M] Dayton, OH Marianist Provincialate.
Hogan, Robert E. *s.m.* '83 (SAT) [C] San Antonio, TX St. Mary's University of San Antonio, Texas; [M] San Antonio, TX Marianist Residence.
Hogan, Msgr. Robert G. '59 (DUB) [5] Cedar Rapids, IA St. Matthew's Church; [D] Cedar Rapids, IA Regis LaSalle Foundation.
Hogan, Msgr. Robert J. '51 (BUF) [4] Niagara Falls, NY St. John de La Salle Church.
Hogan, Sean M. *c.s.sp.* '69 (PIT) [B] Pittsburgh, PA Duquesne University of the Holy Ghost.
Hogan, Terence '80 (MIA) Coral Gables, FL St. Augustine Church.
Hogan, Thomas *s.m.* '46 (HON) Wailuku, HI St. Anthony Church.
Hogan, Thomas B. *s.m.* '45 (WH) Buckhannon, WV Holy Rosary Church.
Hogan, Thomas J. *s.j.* '65 (STL) [P] St. Louis, MO Hallahan House.
Hogan, Thomas W. *s.m.* '46 (HON) [H] Wailuku, Maui, HI Wailuku Marianist Community.
Hogan, Timothy A. (L) On Special Assignment.
Hogan, Timothy D. '82 (DET) Military Chaplains.
Hogan, Timothy J. '82 (SC) Ashton, IA Our Lady of Perpetual Help Church; Sibley, IA St. Andrew's Church.
Hogan, Verne F. '57 (COV) Flemingsburg, KY St. Charles Church; May's Lick, KY St. Rose of Lima Church.
Hogan, Msgr. Vincent '44 (WCH) Erie, KS St. Ambrose Church; St. Paul, KS St. Francis Church.
Hogan, William *c.ss.r.* '48 (STL) [P] Liguori, MO Liguori Mission House/Redemptorists.
Hogan, William A. '66 (GF) [1] Great Falls, MT St. Ann's Cathedral.
Hogan, William D. *s.s.j.* '51 (MOB) Tuskegee Institute, AL St. Joseph Church; [K] Tuskegee Institute, AL Tuskegee University Newman Center.
Hogan, William E. '38 (L) Retired.
Hogan, Msgr. William F. '46 (NEW) Retired; [N] Rutherford, NJ St. John Vianney Residence for Priests.
Hogan, William H. *s.j.* '60 (CHI) [C] Chicago, IL Jesuit Community at Loyola University of Chicago.
Hogan, William T. *s.j.* '54 (NY) [Z] New York, NY Jesuit Community at Fordham University.
Hogarty, Paul '48 (PT) Retired.
Hoge, James *o.s.b.* '43 (SP) [O] St. Leo, FL St. Leo Abbey.
Hogenkamp, Leon J. *s.j.* '70 (ROC) [B] Rochester, NY McQuaid Jesuit High School.
Hoghstatter, Theodore (PEO) Absent on Leave.
Hohenbrink, Michael G. '74 (TOL) [19] Toledo, OH St. Catherine of Siena Church.
Hohenstein, Robert J. '68 (ALB) [13] Albany, NY Our Lady Help of Christians Church.
Hohenwarter, Norman C., Jr. '96 (HBG) Hanover, PA St. Joseph Church.
Hohl, Alan *o.c.s.o.* '63 (SLC) [F] Huntsville, UT Abbey of Our Lady of the Holy Trinity of the Order of Cistercians.
Hohlfeld, Raymond C. *m.m.* '34 (NY) [Z] Maryknoll, NY Maryknoll Fathers and Brothers.
Hohlmayer, Louis R. '53 (CIN) Lebanon, OH St. Francis de Sales Church; [S] Cincinnati, OH Archdiocesan Central Council of Cincinnati.
Hohman, Andrew *o.f.m.cap.* '54 (CLV) [18] Cleveland, OH Conversion of St. Paul Church; [P] Cleveland, OH St. Paul Friary.
Hohman, George R. *s.j.* '58 (WH) [A] Wheeling, WV Wheeling Jesuit University.
Hoi, Joseph '77 (JC) St. James, MO Missouri Veterans' Home.
Hoi, Joseph '84 (JC) Rosati, MO St. Anthony Church; St. James, MO Immaculate Conception Church.
Hoisington, Thomas '95 (WCH) [13] Wichita, KS St. Francis of Assisi Church.
Hojsik, Ambrose *o.f.m.conv.* '36 (ALB) [A] Rensselaer, NY Conventual Franciscan Friars.
Hokanson, Richard P. '74 (CHL) Newton, NC St. Joseph Church.
Hokanson, Richard P. '74 (WOR) On Duty Outside the Diocese.
Hoke, John D. '76 (HBG) Annville, PA St. Paul the Apostle Church; [K] Harrisburg, PA Catholic Campus Ministry.
Hoke, Thomas J. '67 (HBG) [4] York, PA St. Rose of Lima Church.
Holachek, Terence A. *o.p.* '57 (CC) [E] Corpus Christi, TX Spohn Hospital.
Holachek, Terence A. *o.p.* '57 (GAL) [Q] Houston, TX Dominican Fathers and Brothers, St. Mark Priory, Inc.
Holahan, Thomas J. *c.s.p.* '77 (BO) [CC] Cambridge, MA Massachusetts Institute of Technology Catholic Community.
Holahan, Thomas P. *c.s.p.* '77 (BO) [W] Boston, MA Paulist Fathers Residence.
Holanhaw, Thomas J. *c.s.p.* '77 (BO) [P] Boston, MA Paulist Center.
Holberton, William B. '61 (ROC) Retired.
Holbrook, Harold M. '57 (BGP) On Duty Outside the Diocese.
Holbrook, John G. *s.j.* '52 (OM) [K] Omaha, NE Jesuit Community At Creighton University.
Holbrook, William M. '70 (LFT) On Duty Outside the Diocese.
Holbus, Brian T. '81 (MIL) [10] Kenosha, WI St. Therese Church.
Holcomb, Joseph T. '80 (BRK) [120] Brooklyn, NY Queen of All Saints Church; [W] Astoria, NY St. Paul Center.
Hold, William '77 (SAC) Yreka, CA St. Joseph Church.
Holden, Edgar *o.f.m.conv.* '45 (CHL) Winston-Salem, NC Our Lady of Mercy Church.
Holden, James '62 (MOB) [6] Montgomery, AL St. Jude Church.
Holden, Paul '57 (WDC) Retired.
Holden, Peter *s.t.* '58 (WDC) [M] Adelphi, MD Missionary Servants of the Most Holy Trinity.
Holden, Robert A. '62 (TOL) Wauseon, OH St. Caspar Church.
Holder, Thomas '95 (KC) Blue Springs, MO St. John La Lande Church.
Holderied, Kurt *o.carm.* '59 (NEW) [P] Mahwah, NJ Carmel Retreat House.
Holdren, John C. '71 (RCK) On Health Leave.
Holguin, Jose R. '75 (LA) Burbank, CA St. Finbar Church.
Holhmann, George '92 (NY) Absent on Leave.
Holian, John P. '63 (NEW) Summit, NJ Overlook Hospital.
Holick, Robert *m.h.m.* '69 (NY) [143] Bronx, NY St. Francis Xavier Church; Bronx, NY Bronx Municipal Hospital Center, Abraham Jacobi Hospital, Nathan B. VanEtten Hospital.
Holicky, Gregory '72 (GRY) [G] Hammond, IN St. Margaret Mercy Healthcare Centers - North Campus.
Holihan, Daniel M. '57 (CHI) [G] Chicago, IL Catholic Charities of the Archdiocese of Chicago-Archdiocesan Offices.
Holihan, John W. '49 (NY) Retired.
Holinga, Thomas P. '74 (SFD) Petersburg, IL St. Peter Church.
Holko, Robert J. *s.c.j.* '71 (MEM) [14] Memphis, TN St. John's Church.
Holl, James E. '48 (STP) Hazelwood, MN Annunciation of the B.V.M. Church.
Holland, Cajetan *c.s.c.* '79 (ORL) [F] Cocoa Beach, FL Holy Cross Fathers, Eastern Priests Province.
Holland, Daniel F. '65 (ROC) [57] Rochester, NY St. Theodore Church.
Holland, Francis M. '52 (BUR) Retired.
Holland, George G. '55 (WOR) Retired.
Holland, Msgr. George T. '48 (PBL) Retired.
Holland, Msgr. Ian E. '58 (LA) Culver City, CA St. Augustine Church; Retired.
Holland, J Michael '63 (SEA) Burlington, WA St. Charles Church.
Holland, Msgr. James J. '52 (STL) [14] St. Louis, MO Our Lady of Sorrows Church; Retired.
Holland, Jeremiah *ss.cc.* '67 (OAK) [3] Alameda, CA St.

Joseph Basilica.
Holland, Jerome *c.ss.r.* '56 (NY) [78] New York, NY Most Holy Redeemer Church.
Holland, Msgr. John P. '48 (STL) Warson Woods, MO Ste. Genevieve Du Bois Church; Retired.
Holland, Joseph I. *s.j.* (BO) [W] Weston, MA Campion Center.
Holland, Kilian '56 (SD) Retired.
Holland, Kirk *o.f.m.conv.* '69 (ALB) [A] Rensselaer, NY Conventual Franciscan Friars.
Holland, Patrick F. *c.s.sp.* '51 (MET) Edison, NJ John F. Kennedy Medical Center; [H] Metuchen, NJ Libermann House.
Holland, Patrick F. *c.s.sp.* '51 (RVC) Westhampton Beach, NY Immaculate Conception Church.
Holland, Paul *s.j.* '80 (NOR) Storrs, CT St. Thomas Aquinas Church; [K] Willimantic, CT Campus Ministry.
Holland, Stanley *t.o.r.* '96 (STU) [A] Steubenville, OH Franciscan University of Steubenville; [F] Steubenville, OH Holy Spirit Monastery.
Holland, Thomas D. '55 (SC) On Duty Outside the Diocese.
Hollas, Eric *o.s.b.* '75 (SCL) [B] Collegeville, MN St. John's University; [I] Collegeville, MN St. John's Abbey, of the Order of St. Benedict.
Hollenbach, David *s.j.* '71 (BO) [W] Chestnut Hill, MA The Jesuit Community at Boston College.
Hollenbach, Frank A. '49 (MAR) Retired.
Holler, Martin J. '66 (STU) Athens, OH Christ the King University Parish Church; [I] Athens, OH Christ the King University Parish - Ohio University.
Holleran, Edward J. *o.f.m.* '44 (PAT) [M] Ringwood, NJ Holy Name Friary.
Holleran, Msgr. J. Warren '52 (SFR) Special Assignment; [A] Menlo Park, CA St. Patrick Seminary.
Holleran, Leo C. *m.s.* (ATL) Fairburn, GA St. Matthew's Church.
Holleran, Michael K. '79 (NY) [61] New York, NY St. Joseph Church.
Holley, Martin '87 (PT) [13] Pensacola, FL St. Paul Church.
Hollfelder, Eugene F. '68 (MAD) Ashton, WI St. Peter's Church.
Hollick, Leonard '61 (PSC) McAdoo, PA St. Michael Church.
Holliday, David D. (PAT) Absent on Leave.
Hollis, Mark L. '72 (CLV) Medina, OH St. Francis Xavier Church.
Holloran, Michael J. '82 (CIN) [1] Dayton, OH St. Adalbert's Church; [13] Dayton, OH Holy Cross Church.
Holloway, Alvin J. *s.j.* '56 (NO) [C] New Orleans, LA Loyola University.
Holloway, David L. '82 (KC) On Duty Outside the Diocese.
Holloway, James '70 (WDC) Chillum, MD St. John Baptist de la Salle Church.
Holly, Dennis Leo '64 (NSH) [L] Nashville, TN Glenmary Department of Pastoral Services.
Holly, John *o.f.m.cap.* '80 (GB) [3] Appleton, WI St. Joseph Church; [I] Appleton, WI St. Joseph Friary.
Holly, Walter J. *o.f.m.* '51 (TUC) San Carlos, AZ San Carlos Catholic Mission Church.
Hollywood, Patrick J. *o.m.i.* '60 (BO) [W] Tewksbury, MA Oblate Fathers-Office of the Provincial Treasurer; [Z] Tewksbury, MA Immaculate Heart of Mary Novitiate-Infirmary.
Holmer, James J. '76 (TOL) Fayette, OH Our Lady of Mercy Church; Lyons, OH Our Lady of Fatima Church.
Holmes, Albert '93 (SCL) Bertha, MN St. Joseph's Church; Henning, MN Church of St. Edward of Henning.
Holmes, Bernard G. *o.s.b.* '39 (MAN) [K] Manchester, NH St. Anselm Abbey.
Holmes, Del *glmy.* '63 (CIN) [M] Fairfield, OH Headquarters of Glenmary Home Missioners.
Holmes, Dennis '72 (BAK) Absent on Leave.
Holmes, Emmett P. *s.j.* '59 (CLV) [E] Cuyahoga Falls, OH Walsh Jesuit High School.
Holmes, John '69 (STU) Absent on Leave.
Holmes, Kevin D. '84 (MAD) [4] Madison, WI Holy Redeemer Church.
Holmes, Paul A. '81 (NEW) [B] South Orange, NJ Seton Hall University.
Holmes, Raymond M. '65 (NEW) Hasbrouck Heights, NJ Corpus Christi Church.
Holmes, Msgr. Richard J. '44 (NEW) Glen Rock, NJ St. Catharine Church; Hohokus, NJ St. Luke's Church; Retired.
Holmes, Robert L. *s.j.* '70 (STL) [P] St. Louis, MO White House Retreat Jesuit Community; [T] St. Louis, MO White House Retreat.
Holmes, Thomas '91 (ALB) Glens Falls, NY St. Mary Church; Special Assignment.
Holmgren, Raymond O. '53 (RCK) East Dubuque, IL St. Mary Church.
Holohan, Patrick *c.s.sp.* '56 (BRK) [U] Long Island City, NY Holy Ghost Fathers of Ireland.
Holoman, Msgr. Thomas L. '55 (LIN) Denton, NE St. Mary's Church; Denton, NE U.S. Veterans' Hospital.
Holoubek, Roger '69 (MIA) North Miami Beach, FL St. Lawrence Church.
Holpp, Lawrence V. '62 (PIT) Coraopolis, PA St. Joseph Church.
Holquin, Arthur '74 (ORG) [1] Orange, CA Cathedral of the Holy Family.
Holroyd, Patrick '74 (ARL) Reston, VA St. Thomas a Becket Church.
Holscher, Frank *c.i.c.m.* '56 (ARL) [J] Arlington, VA Missionhurst, C.I.C.M.-Central House and Provincialate.
Holt, Paul '72 (DM) Des Moines, IA United States Veterans Hospital.
Holt, Paul-Stephen '72 (WDC) On Duty Outside the Archdiocese.
Holt, Thomas G. '81 (MIL) On Leave.
Holt, William A. *o.p.* '76 (CIN) [30] Cincinnati, OH St. Gertrude Church; [M] Cincinnati, OH St. Gertrude Priory.
Holtel, Melvin *o.f.m.* (CIN) [M] Cincinnati, OH St. Francis Center.
Holterhoff, Edward G. '70 (PAT) On Duty Outside the Diocese.
Holterman, Herbert J. '51 (SPC) Retired.
Holtey, Gary M. '84 (SD) [26] San Diego, CA St. Didacus Church; San Diego, CA Alvarado, Grossmont and Kaiser Hospitals.
Holtgrewe, Don *o.f.m.* '63 (CIN) [24] Cincinnati, OH Corpus Christi Church.
Holthaus, Paul (BAL) Awaiting Assignment.
Holtman, Msgr. Clyde '49 (AUS) Rockne, TX Sacred Heart Church; String Prairie, TX St. Mary's of the Assumption Church.
Holtman, Elmer E. '64 (AUS) [21] Austin, TX St. Thomas More Church.
Holtman, W. Jeffrey '85 (SFD) Neoga, IL St. Mary of the Assumption Church; Sigel, IL St. Michael the Archangel Church.
Holtz, Albert T. *o.s.b.* '69 (NEW) [N] Newark, NJ Newark Abbey.
Holtz, Arthur *o.s.b.* '54 (GBG) New Derry, PA St. Martin Church.
Holtz, Brian '95 (EVN) [7] Evansville, IN Holy Rosary Church.
Holtz, James A. '74 (GAY) Fife Lake, MI St. Aloysius Church; Kalkaska, MI St. Mary of the Woods Church.
Holtz, Louis J. '58 (COV) Retired.
Holtz, Raymond C. '58 (COV) [8] Covington, KY Mother of God Church.
Holtz, Vernon A. *o.s.b.* '42 (GBG) [H] Latrobe, PA Saint Vincent Archabbey.
Holtzman, Jerome J. '57 (SFS) Watertown, SD Holy Name Church.
Holubowicz, Vincent B. '89 (MIL) Lomira, WI St. Mary Church.
Holup, James '59 (JOL) Ashkum, IL Assumption of the Blessed Virgin Mary Church.
Holup, Joseph M. '60 (MET) Warren, NJ Our Lady of the Mount Church.
Holwell, Harry '89 (B) [B] Lewiston, ID St. Joseph Regional Medical Center.
Holzer, Ambrose W. '45 (MAD) Retired.
Holzer, Paul A. '41 (PIT) [16] Pittsburgh, PA Immaculate Conception Church; [20] Pittsburgh, PA St. Joseph Church; Retired.
Holzer, Wm. '51 (DUB) Retired.
Holzhauser, Joseph '82 (SFS) Kimball, SD St. Margaret Church.
Holzmann, Michael F. '88 (RVC) Medford, NY St. Sylvester Church.
Homa, Joseph '56 (PSC) New Brunswick, NJ St. Joseph Church.
Homa, Richard M. '73 (CHI) Tinley Park, IL Saint Julie Billiart Church.
Homa, Thomas D. '57 (PH) [4] Bensalem, PA Our Lady of Fatima Church.
Homan, Daniel J. *o.s.b.* '69 (DET) [B] Oxford, MI St. Benedict Monastery.
Homann, Frederick A. *s.j.* '62 (PH) [C] Philadelphia, PA St. Joseph's University; [Z] Philadelphia, PA Jesuit Community at St. Joseph's University.
Homar, Anthony *c.r.* '40 (NY) Plattekill, NY Our Lady of Fatima Church.
Hombach, Leo J. *s.j.* '61 (SJ) [M] Los Gatos, CA California Province of the Society of Jesus, Jesuit Provincial Office.
Homco, Edward C. *c.pp.s.* '43 (GRY) [4] Whiting, IN St. John the Baptist Church.
Homer, P. Lawrence '59 (SCR) [18] Scranton, PA St. Mary's Church.
Homes, Ronald G. '93 (LIN) Prague, NE St. John's Church.
Homets, Frank S. '92 (SCR) [4] Pittston, PA St. John the Evangelist Church; [D] Pittston, PA Seton Catholic High School.
Hommel, George W. '66 (NY) West Hurley-Woodstock, NY St. John Church.
Hommrich, Thomas A. '64 (L) Holy Cross, KY Holy Cross Church; St. Francis, KY St. Francis of Assisi Church.
Homola, Michael E. '49 (HBG) Millersville, PA St. Philip the Apostle Church.
Homola, William B. '50 (SFE) Retired.
Homolak, William J. '59 (GBG) Avonmore, PA St. Ambrose Church.
Homsey, Sam F. *c.pp.s.* '36 (SAN) Winters, TX Our Lady of Mt. Carmel Church.
Honan, Eugene D. '67 (SPR) [5] Northampton, MA St. Mary of the Assumption Church.
Honea, Lonnie '96 (DAL) [2] Dallas, TX All Saints Church.
Honeygosky, Stephen R. *o.s.b.* '75 (GBG) Marguerite, PA St. Benedict Church.
Hong-Phuc, John B. *c.ss.r.* '48 (P) [1] Portland, OR Southeast Asian Vicariate Church.
Honhart, Mark A. '80 (KC) Richmond, MO Immaculate Conception Church.
Honkomp, Clinton P. *o.p.* '87 (CHI) [D] Oak Park, IL Fenwick High School; [N] River Forest, IL St. Thomas Aquinas Priory.
Honma, Kenji *ss.cc.* '89 (FR) [K] Fairhaven, MA Sacred Hearts Provincial House.
Honner, Paschal D. *o.s.b.* '56 (JOL) [A] Lisle, IL Benedictine University; [J] Lisle, IL St. Procopius Abbey.
Honore, Lionel P. *s.j.* '68 (WOR) [N] Worcester, MA Jesuits of Holy Cross College, Inc.
Hont, Leon *o.s.b.* '80 (E) St. Marys, PA Queen of the World Church.
Hood, Carl J. '86 (MEM) Bolivar, TN St. Mary Church; Selmer, TN St. Jude Church; [M] Memphis, TN St. Vincent DePaul Society.
Hood, Mervin J. '54 (SC) Early, IA Sacred Heart Church.
Hood-Rosales, Cris *s.d.b.* '88 (LA) [B] Bellflower, CA De Sales Hall.
Hoog, Eric *c.ss.r.* (BAL) Annapolis, MD St. Mary Church.
Hoogterp, John P. '49 (SAG) Retired.
Hoogterp, M. James '48 (GR) Retired.
Hoolahan, Michael J. *c.p.* '61 (CHI) [91] Chicago, IL Immaculate Conception Church; [N] Chicago, IL Immaculate Conception Monastery.
Hooper, J. Leon *s.j.* '75 (WDC) [M] Washington, DC Woodstock Jesuit Community; [V] Washington, DC Woodstock Theological Center.
Hooper, Robert K. '70 (PAT) [7] Clifton, NJ St. Paul Church.
Hoops, William (LA) Lompoc, CA Federal Correction Institution.
Hoorman, Albert F.H. '67 (PHX) [2] Phoenix, AZ Corpus Christi Church.
Hoormann, Harry H. *s.j.* '58 (PBL) Trinidad, CO Most Holy Trinity, Trinidad Area Catholic Community (Trinidad Cluster) Church; Trinidad, CO Our Lady of Mt. Carmel, Trinidad Area Catholic Community (Trinidad Cluster) Church; Trinidad, CO St. Joseph, Trinidad Area Catholic Community (Trinidad Cluster) Church; [E] Trinidad, CO Trinidad Area Catholic Community.
Hoover, Conrad '89 (CHL) Boone, NC St. Elizabeth Church.
Hoover, Edward F. '72 (CHI) Evanston, IL St. Mary Church.
Hoover, Gary *o.s.b.* '83 (CLV) [E] Cleveland, OH Benedictine High School; [P] Cleveland, OH Benedictine Order of Cleveland.
Hoover, James F. '60 (SAL) Oberlin, KS Sacred Heart Church; Selden, KS Sacred Heart Church.
Hoover, John P. '76 (CHL) Special Assignment.
Hoover, Matthew N. '95 (COL) New Albany, OH Church of the Resurrection.
Hopcus, Daniel R. '64 (ORG) Los Alamitos, CA St. Hedwig Church.
Hope, Abbott J. '54 (CAM) Malaga, NJ St. Mary's Church.
Hope, Donald E. '76 (SLC) [2] Ogden, UT St. James Church.
Hopefl, Gregory J. '76 (SUP) New Post, WI St. Ignatius Church; Reserve, WI St. Francis of Solanus Church; Stone Lake, WI St. Philip Church.
Hopf, George S. '49 (MIL) Retired.
Hopkins, John *l.c.* (ATL) [I] Dunwoody, GA Legionaries of Christ.
Hopkins, John P. '78 (WIL) Special Assignment.
Hopkins, Michael *c.ss.r.* (BO) [13] Boston, MA Basilica of Our Lady of Perpetual Help.
Hopkins, Michael *c.ss.r.* (STV) [3] Frederiksted, VI Church of St. Patrick.
Hopkins, Peter *l.c.* '91 (NY) [Z] Rye, NY Legionaries of Christ.
Hopkins, Richard J. '44 (GF) [1] Billings, MT St. Patrick's Co-Cathedral; Retired.
Hopkins, Robert (BAL) Retired.
Hopmeir, Ronald J. '91 (STL) De Soto, MO St. Rose of Lima Church.
Hopp, Raymond '65 (BAK) Lakeview, OR St. Patrick's Church.
Hopp, Thomas R. '66 (CIN) [25] Dayton, OH Queen of

Martyrs Church.
Hoppe, Arthur H. '47 (SCL) St. Rosa, MN St. Rose of Lima Church.
Hoppe, Lawrence L. '60 (GBG) Ford City, PA St. Francis of Paola Church.
Hoppe, Leslie J. *o.f.m.* '71 (CHI) [B] Chicago, IL The Catholic Theological Union at Chicago; [N] Chicago, IL Holy Name Friary-Franciscan House of Formation.
Hoppe, Msgr. Ronald C. '58 (ALX) [3] Alexandria, LA St. Frances Xavier Cabrini Church; Glenmora, LA St. Louis Church.
Hoppe, Sean *o.s.b.* '82 (IND) Fulda, IN St. Boniface Church; Siberia, IN St. Martin of Tours Church; [J] St. Meinrad, IN St. Meinrad Archabbey.
Hoppe, Sylvester J. '46 (KC) Retired.
Hoppe, William M. '78 (BRK) [139] Brooklyn, NY St. Therese of Lisieux Church.
Hoppenjans, Terence E. '55 (LEX) Pikeville, KY St. Francis of Assisi Church.
Hopping, John-Paul '85 (ORG) [3] Orange, CA St. Norbert Church.
Hoppough, Gregory J. *c.s.s.* (BO) [6] Waltham, MA Sacred Heart Church.
Hopwood, Msgr. Frederick J. '51 (CHR) Retired.
Hora, Robert J. '83 (BUF) [31] Buffalo, NY Holy Name of Jesus Church.
Horacek, Mark '43 (ALX) Retired.
Horacek, Mark '43 (GAL) Retired.
Horak, Msgr. Donald E. '63 (STU) Athens, OH Christ the King University Parish Church; [I] Athens, OH Christ the King University Parish - Ohio University.
Horak, Mark F. *s.j.* '94 (BAL) [M] Baltimore, MD Ferdinand Wheeler House; [Q] Baltimore, MD Catholic Community at Relay.
Horan, Denis F. '48 (MAN) [5] Nashua, NH Immaculate Conception Church.
Horan, Edward *s.o.l.t.* '87 (CC) [H] Robstown, TX Society of Our Lady of the Most Holy Trinity.
Horan, George '72 (LA) [36] Los Angeles, CA Sacred Heart Church; Los Angeles, CA Los Angeles County Jails in the City of Los Angeles, Adult Facilities.
Horan, Gerald M. *o.s.m.* '82 (ORG) [D] Anaheim, CA Servite High School; Servite High School Development Fund; [H] Anaheim, CA Servite Fathers and Brothers; [H] Buena Park, CA Servite Fathers And Brothers.
Horan, Jay *s.d.b.* '82 (NY) [BB] West Haverstraw, NY Don Bosco Retreat Center and Marian Shrine; [BB] West Haverstraw, NY Marian Shrine.
Horan, John '46 (SEA) Mercer Island, WA St. Monica Church; Retired.
Horan, John C. '51 (MAN) Hudson, NH St. John the Evangelist Church.
Horan, John F. *o.carm.* '84 (PMB) [B] Boca Raton, FL Pope John Paul II High School; [G] Boca Raton, FL St. Elias Priory-Order of Carmelites, NY.
Horan, Joseph '58 (NOR) Retired.
Horan, Mike '80 (SAT) Castroville, TX St. Louis Church.
Horan, Terence J. '68 (SFR) [3] San Mateo, CA St. Matthew Church.
Horan, Thomas *o.m.i.* '94 (MAN) [M] Hudson, NH Oblates of Mary Immaculate Retreat House.
Horan, Thomas A. '62 (ALN) Retired.
Horan, Msgr. Thomas C. '35 (SCR) Retired.
Horan, Timothy (ROC) [53] Rochester, NY St. Philip Neri Church.
Horan, Timothy E. '79 (ROC) [3] Rochester, NY St. Andrew Church.
Horanzy, Joseph M. '59 (SCR) [19] Wilkes-Barre, PA St. Stanislaus Kostka Church.
Horath, George B. '63 (MAD) Fennimore, WI St. Mary Church.
Horath, James R. '73 (SUP) Merrill, WI St. Francis Xavier Church.
Horath, William G. '75 (SUP) Three Lakes, WI St. Theresa Church.
Horejsi, Jeffrey P. '91 (NU) Willmar, MN St. Mary Church.
Horgan, Gerald B. '48 (BO) Georgetown, MA St. Mary Church; Retired.
Horgan, John A. '36 (HRT) Retired.
Horgan, John E. '72 (WOR) Sutton, MA St. Mark Church.
Horgan, Msgr. John V. '40 (BGP) Retired; [O] Stamford, CT Our Lady Queen of the Clergy Home.
Horgan, Joseph *m.s.* '44 (ALB) [A] Altamont, NY LaSalette Shrine and Seminary.
Horgan, Joseph C. '41 (WIL) Retired.
Horgan, Joseph E. '53 (PRO) Retired.
Horgan, Joseph J. *m.s.* '44 (HRT) [M] Hartford, CT Missionaries of LaSalette Provincial Secretary.
Horgan, Paul L. *s.j.* '68 (CI) [B] Pohnpei, FM PATS (Pohnpei Agriculture and Trade School).
Horgan, Sean *c.ss.r.* '53 (MOB) Monroeville, AL Annunciation Church; [K] Monroeville, AL Alabama Southern Community College Newman Center.
Horgan, Timothy J. '55 (NEW) Ridgefield, NJ St. Matthew's Church.
Horgan, Msgr. William '38 (SAC) Fair Oaks, CA St. Mel Church; Retired and in Senior Ministry.
Horgas, Robert '91 (E) Ridgway, PA St. Leo the Great Church.
Horkan, Msgr. Vincent J. '41 (DET) Retired; [L] Livonia, MI Provincial House and Novitiate of the Sisters of St. Felix.
Horley, Ray J. '58 (CLV) [49] Cleveland, OH St. Mel Church.
Horn, Augustine S. *o.s.b.* '45 (OKL) [I] Shawnee, OK St. Gregory's Abbey.
Horn, Francis J. *o.s.a.* '75 (WDC) [B] Washington, DC Augustinian College, Order of St. Augustine.
Horn, Joseph K. *o.praem.* '81 (ORG) [C] Santa Ana, CA Mater Dei High School; [H] Silverado, CA Norbertine Fathers.
Horn, Stephen R. '73 (GAL) [44] Houston, TX St. Luke the Evangelist Church.
Hornacek, Joseph F. '66 (MIL) [10] Racine, WI Sacred Heart Church.
Hornat, Stephen W. *s.s.e.* '76 (MOB) [A] Selma, AL Edmundite House of Formation; [H] Selma, AL Edmundite Fathers.
Horner, Arnold *c.p.* '34 (BRK) [U] Jamaica, NY Immaculate Conception Monastery.
Horner, Thomas J. '43 (PIT) Retired; [N] Pittsburgh, PA St. John Vianney Manor.
Horner, Thomas P. '55 (PH) [96] Philadelphia, PA St. Mary of the Assumption Church.
Horner, Timothy *o.s.b.* '53 (STL) [P] St. Louis, MO The Abbey of St. Mary and St. Louis.
Hornick, J. Michael '69 (ANC) [G] Anchorage, AK Holy Spirit Retreat House.
Hornstein, Eugene *o.s.b.* '46 (BIS) [A] Richardton, ND Assumption Abbey.
Horoshko, Michael '37 (PHU) Retired.
Horrigan, Msgr. Alfred F. '40 (L) [39] Louisville, KY St. James Church; Retired.
Horrigan, Finnbar *c.s.sp.* '55 (SFR) Millbrae, CA St. Dunstan Church.
Horrigan, Kevin D. '53 (STL) [R] Ladue, MO Carmel of St. Joseph.
Horrigan, Kevin P. '70 (BO) Newburyport, MA Immaculate Conception Church.
Horrigan, Leo R. '59 (DEN) [17] Denver, CO Notre Dame Church.
Horrigan, Sean *c.s.sp.* '49 (NY) [183] Bronx, NY St. Philip Neri Church.
Horst, Bernard L. *s.m.* '45 (KAL) [E] Portage, MI Society of Mary.
Horst, Kenneth '95 (NY) Absent on Leave.
Horstman, Keith L. '95 (LAN) Brighton, MI St. Patrick Church.
Hortiguela, Fernando *o.f.m.* '75 (SJN) [3] Carolina, PR Santa Clara de Asis Church.
Horton, John C. '66 (PEO) Mahomet, IL Our Lady of the Lake Church.
Horton, Joseph *o.m.i.* '69 (MAN) [K] Hudson, NH Missionary Oblates of Mary Immaculate.
Horton, Joseph *o.m.i.* '69 (NOR) [F] Willimantic, CT Oblates of Mary Immaculate.
Horton, W. Peter '79 (PIT) Allegheny County, PA Passavant Hospital; [B] Pittsburgh, PA La Roche College; [Q] Slippery Rock, PA Office for Campus Ministry.
Horvat, Francis '58 (KCK) [10] Kansas City, KS St. John the Baptist Church.
Horvath, Andrew B. '42 (GBG) Retired.
Horvath, Benedict *o.praem.* '40 (ORG) [H] Silverado, CA Norbertine Fathers.
Horvath, Bert '70 (AMA) [7] Amarillo, TX St. Hyacinth's Church; Vega, TX Immaculate Conception Church; [J] Amarillo, TX St. Francis Convent, Novitiate and U.S. Provincial House.
Horvath, Gerlac A. *o.praem.* '46 (ORG) [H] Silverado, CA Norbertine Fathers.
Horvath, Joseph P. '37 (FTW) Retired.
Horvath, Martin A. '43 (FTW) Goshen, IN St. John the Evangelist Church; Retired.
Horvath, Pius L. *o.s.b.* '53 (SFR) [N] Portola Valley, CA Woodside Priory.
Horvath, Richard E. '57 (PEO) [4] Peoria, IL St. Ann Church.
Horvath, Stephen '50 (Y) Retired.
Horvath, Stephen G. '40 (TR) Retired.
Horzen, Bernard A. *o.s.b.* '53 (PEO) [A] Peru, IL St. Bede Abbey and Academy.
Hosak, Peter J. '83 (ALN) [C] Allentown, PA Allentown Central Catholic High School.
Hosak, Peter J. '83 (PSC) Allentown, PA St. Andrew the Apostle Church; Allentown, PA St. Michael Church; Palmerton, PA SS. Peter and Paul Church.
Hose, Samuel L. '91 (AUS) College Station, TX St. Thomas Aquinas Church.
Hosey, Keith P. '56 (LFT) [G] Hartford City, IN John XXIII Center.
Hoshock, Richard '40 (TOL) Retired.
Hosie, James J. *s.j.* '65 (BO) [E] Boston, MA Boston College High School & Jesuit Community.
Hosie, Stanley W. *s.m.* '46 (WDC) [M] Washington, DC Marist Provincial House.
Hosinski, Albin L. *c.s.c.* '43 (FTW) [J] South Bend, IN Congregation of Holy Cross Indiana Province Provincial House.
Hosinski, Thomas *c.s.c.* '73 (P) [B] Portland, OR University of Portland; [L] Portland, OR Holy Cross Father & Brother, C.S.C. - University of Portland.
Hosko, George H. *c.s.b.* '68 (GAL) Retired; [Q] Houston, TX Dillon House.
Hosler, Paul E. '86 (KCK) Easton, KS St. Lawrence's Church; [5] Leavenworth, KS St. Joseph of the Valley Church; Mooney Creek, KS Corpus Christi Church.
Hospodar, Robert J. *j.c.l.* '78 (PSC) White Plains, NY St. Nicholas of Myra Church; Yonkers, NY St. Nicholas of Myra Church.
Hossan, John B. '53 (BGP) Redding, CT St. Patrick Church.
Host, Dick '74 (GR) [16] Grand Rapids, MI St. Mary's Church.
Hostetter, Laurence '87 (OWN) Studying Outside the Diocese.
Hostettler, Paul A. '50 (KNX) Copperhill, TN St. Catherine Church; Retired; [K] Knoxville, TN Diocesan Council of Catholic Women.
Hostia de la Purisima, Anibal Jesus *s.e.m.v.* '91 (ARE) Hatillo, PR Our Lady of Guadalupe Church.
Hosty, Edward '30 (CHI) Retired.
Hosty, Thomas J. '35 (CHI) Retired.
Hotard, Msgr. Howard H. '55 (NO) [1] Slidell, LA Our Lady of Lourdes Church.
Hotchkin, John F. '60 (CHI) On Duty Outside the Archdiocese.
Hotchkiss, Msgr. Eugene '48 (GB) Retired.
Hotovy, Dennis W. '57 (LIN) Wymore, NE St. Mary's Church.
Hottinger, Paul '75 (JOL) Bolingbrook, IL St. Francis of Assisi Church.
Hottinger, Theodore *s.j.* '63 (WIN) [1] Mankato, MN SS. Peter and Paul's Church.
Hottle, Maximilian *o.f.m.* '61 (TUC) Topawa, AZ San Solano Missions - Tohono O'odham Indian Reservation Church.
Hotz, Ernest *c.p.* '45 (BRK) [U] Jamaica, NY Immaculate Conception Monastery.
Hotz, Robert V. *s.j.* '86 (OM) [C] Omaha, NE Creighton Preparatory School.
Hotze, John '93 (WCH) On Duty Outside the Diocese.
Hotze, John '93 (WDC) [2] Bethesda, MD St. Jane Frances de Chantal Church.
Hotze, Leo *s.v.d.* '43 (CHI) [B] Techny, IL Divine Word Residence.
Houck, Gregory *o.carm.* '92 (NEW) Leonia, NJ St. John the Evangelist's Church.
Houck, Peter '46 (ANC) Retired.
Houck, Richard '65 (SD) Retired.
Houde, Arthur O. '48 (MAN) Retired.
Houde, Daniel *o.s.s.t.* '87 (PH) Bristol, PA St. Ann Church.
Houde, Paul C. '96 (BUR) [5] Burlington, VT St. Mark's Church.
Houdek, Francis J. *s.j.* '65 (DET) [K] Detroit, MI Jesuit Provincial Office-Detroit Province of the Society of Jesus.
Houdek, Francis J. *s.j.* '65 (OAK) Lafayette, CA St. Perpetua Church; [A] Oakland, CA Graduate School of Theology, School of Applied Theology; [A] Berkeley, CA The Jesuit School of Theology at Berkeley; [N] Berkeley, CA Jesuit Community at Jesuit School of Theology at Berkeley.
Hough, Roger W. '64 (SAL) Osborne, KS St. Aloysius Church.
Houghton, Msgr. Francis J. '51 (NEW) Retired.
Houghton, Timothy '91 (RVC) Absent on Leave.
Houlahan, Richard A. *o.m.i.* '58 (SAT) [K] San Antonio, TX Oblate Madonna Residence; [T] San Antonio, TX Oblate Missions; [T] San Antonio, TX Oblate Lourdes Grotto Shrine of the Southwest.
Houle, Andre L. *o.m.i.* '52 (PRT) Howland, ME St. Leo Church.
Houle, Cecil T. '38 (STP) Retired.
Houle, John A. *s.j.* '45 (LA) [R] Los Angeles, CA Columbiere House.
Houle, Michael R. '79 (STA) [A] Jacksonville, FL Bishop Kenny High School.
Houle, Norman H. *s.j.* '76 (BO) [W] Boston, MA Loyola House.
Houle, Roger A. '77 (PRO) [3] Woonsocket, RI St. Ann's Church; [8] Woonsocket, RI Our Lady of Victories Church.
Houle, Thomas *o.f.m.cap.* (NY) City, NY Anna M. Kross Center.
Houle, Thomas *o.f.m.cap.* '78 (NY) [57] New York, NY St. John the Baptist Church; City, NY James A. Thomas Center.
Houle, Thomas *o.f.m.cap.* '81 (RVC) Kings Park, NY Kings Park State Hospital.
Houle, Wilfred Andre '74 (BUR) Rutland, VT St. Peter Church.
Houlihan, John J. '64 (GF) [1] Billings, MT St. Patrick's Co-Cathedral; [2] Billings, MT Holy Rosary Church.
Houlihan, Michael K. '79 (LIN) [2] Lincoln, NE Blessed Sacrament Church.
Houlihan, Ralph D. *s.j.* '65 (STL) [P] St. Louis, MO St.

Louis University High School Jesuit Community.
Houlihan, Robert F. *s.j.* '57 (COS) [E] Sedalia, CO Sacred Heart Retreat House - Jesuit Community; [G] Sedalia, CO Sacred Heart Jesuit Retreat House.
Houndjame, Felicien K. '85 (STA) Orange Park, FL St. Catherine's Church.
Houran, J. William '52 (SFD) Retired.
Hourigan, Michael '66 (MIA) Sunrise, FL St. Bernard Church.
Hourihan, Brendan *o.carm.* '39 (NY) [Z] Middletown, NY St. Albert's Priory.
Hourihan, Msgr. James '31 (LA) Retired.
Hourihan, Msgr. John P. '49 (NEW) [18] Newark, NJ St. John's Church.
Hourihan, Raymond B. '87 (CHL) Waynesville, NC St. John the Evangelist Church.
Hourihane, Francis (RVC) Retired.
House, Richard Mel '92 (YAK) Ephrata, WA St. Rose of Lima Church.
Householder, Paul C. '73 (PIT) [3] McKees Rocks, PA St. John of God Church.
Houseknecht, Eric '95 (CHL) Maggie Valley, NC St. Margaret Church.
Houser, Joseph F. *c.s.c.* '35 (AUS) [H] Austin, TX Congregation of Holy Cross - Southern Province.
Houser, Joseph F. *c.s.c.* '35 (FTW) [J] South Bend, IN Congregation of Holy Cross Indiana Province Provincial House.
Houser, Samuel E. '76 (HBG) [5] Steelton, PA Prince of Peace Church.
Housey, Walter L. *c.m.* '56 (PHX) [26] Phoenix, AZ St. Vincent de Paul Church.
Houston, James A. '68 (WOR) Northboro, MA St. Rose of Lima Church.
Houston, Joseph F. '64 (SCR) [4] Plymouth, PA St. Vincent de Paul Church.
Hovald, Regis R. *o.p.* '64 (CHI) [N] Chicago, IL Dominicans (Provincial Office).
Hovey, Adrian *o.s.b.* '91 (NO) [P] St. Benedict, LA St. Joseph Abbey.
Hovley, Vincent E. *s.j.* '69 (COS) [E] Sedalia, CO Sacred Heart Retreat House - Jesuit Community; [G] Sedalia, CO Sacred Heart Jesuit Retreat House.
Howaniec, Henry *o.f.m.* '56 (GB) [I] Pulaski, WI Assumption of B.V.M. Friary.
Howard, Anthony '37 (L) Retired.
Howard, Anthony *o.f.m.conv.* '84 (SB) [3] Riverside, CA Queen of Angels Church.
Howard, C. Donald *s.a.* '72 (ARL) Sterling, VA Christ the Redeemer Church.
Howard, Clarence J. '61 (L) New Haven, KY St. Catherine Church; New Hope, KY St. Vincent de Paul Church.
Howard, Donald E. *c.s.p.* '58 (NY) [Z] Scarsdale, NY Paulist Fathers Generalate.
Howard, Edward *s.j.* '66 (NOR) [5] Norwich, CT SS. Peter and Paul Church.
Howard, Evan *o.f.m.* '55 (PHX) [19] Phoenix, AZ St. Mary's Basilica.
Howard, James '86 (ALB) [13] Troy, NY Sacred Heart Church.
Howard, Msgr. James J. '52 (PH) [1] Philadelphia, PA Cathedral Basilica of SS. Peter and Paul.
Howard, John *c.j.m.* '67 (SD) Solana Beach, CA St. James Church; Special Assignment.
Howard, John W. *s.j.* '68 (BO) [W] Chestnut Hill, MA The Jesuit Community at Boston College.
Howard, Joseph C., Jr. '89 (SHP) [9] Shreveport, LA St. Mary of the Pines Church; [A] Shreveport, LA Loyola College Prep.
Howard, Kenneth J. *s.s.j.* '87 (GAL) [61] Houston, TX Our Mother of Mercy Church.
Howard, Philip *c.s.sp.* (CHI) [129] Chicago, IL St. Mary Magdalene Church.
Howard, Msgr. Robert E. '62 (LA) [97] Los Angeles, CA Transfiguration Church.
Howard, T. Cyril '49 (SAG) Retired.
Howard, Theodore J. '65 (RVC) Shoreham, NY St. Mark Church.
Howard, Timothy J. *s.j.* '63 (MIL) [P] Milwaukee, WI Jesuit Provincial Office, Wisconsin Province.
Howard, Timothy J. *s.j.* '63 (TUC) [23] Tucson, AZ St. Thomas the Apostle Church.
Howard, Msgr. Vincent '47 (LAN) Retired.
Howarth, Joseph A. '90 (PRO) [1] Providence, RI Cathedral of SS. Peter and Paul.
Howarth, Joseph E. '80 (PH) [3] Bensalem, PA Saint Ephrem Church.
Howarth, Theodore J. *o.s.b.* '49 (NEW) [N] Newark, NJ Newark Abbey.
Howe, J. Norbert '56 (TOL) [4] Lima, OH St. Rose Church.
Howe, John H. '39 (LIN) Retired.
Howe, Robert J. '94 (SAG) Midland, MI Blessed Sacrament Church.
Howell, David '78 (LAN) Brighton, MI St. Mary Magdalen Church.
Howell, David W. '65 (BGP) [2] Norwalk, CT St. Joseph's Church.
Howell, Joseph W. '53 (TLS) [E] Tulsa, OK Saint Francis Hospital, Inc.
Howell, Michael '74 (CC) On Duty Outside the Diocese.
Howell, Michael '74 (GAL) [A] Houston, TX St. Mary's Seminary.
Howell, Michael J. '69 (KAL) [G] Nazareth, MI Motherhouse and Novitiate of the Sisters of St. Joseph.
Howell, Patrick J. *s.j.* '72 (SEA) [A] Seattle, WA Seattle University.
Howell, Rennyson (NY) [101] New York, NY Our Saviour Church.
Howell, Stephen H. '74 (SFR) Special Assignment; [D] San Mateo, CA Junipero Serra High School (Boys).
Hower, William J. '64 (MAD) Columbus, WI St. Jerome Church.
Howlahan, Brian F. (CLV) [AA] Wickliffe, OH Center for Pastoral Leadership Services, Inc.
Howley, Edward J. '47 (BGP) Darien, CT St. Thomas More Church.
Howley, Leo W. '36 (STP) Retired.
Howlin, Carroll '61 (JOL) On Duty Outside the Diocese.
Howlin, Carroll '61 (LEX) Whitley City, KY Good Shepherd Chapel.
Howren, John T. '96 (ATL) McDonough, GA St. James The Apostle Church.
Howscher, Franz *c.i.c.m.* '56 (ARL) [3] Alexandria, VA Queen of Apostles Church.
Howze, Joseph Lawson '59 (BLX) [H] Biloxi, MS Gabriel Manor II, Inc.
Hoy, Daniel J. '48 (PH) Strafford, PA Our Lady of the Assumption Church.
Hoye, Msgr. Daniel F. '72 (FR) [1] Attleboro, MA St. John the Evangelist Church.
Hoye, Ronald *c.m.* '91 (CHI) [N] Chicago, IL Vincentian Community, Congregation of the Mission, Midwest Province.
Hoyer, Michael '80 (MIA) [2] Fort Lauderdale, FL Our Lady Queen of Martyrs Church.
Hoying, David A. *c.pp.s.* '83 (CIN) Carthagena, OH St. Aloysius Church; Cranberry Prairie, OH St. Francis Church.
Hoying, John *c.pp.s.* '62 (TOL) Cuba, OH St. Isidore Church; Kalida, OH St. Michael Church.
Hoying, Leo A. '56 (CIN) Frenchtown, OH Holy Family Church; Versailles, OH St. Denis Church.
Hoying, Mark *c.pp.s.* '85 (CIN) [23] Dayton, OH Precious Blood Church.
Hoying, Vincent '58 (TOL) [H] Toledo, OH Mercy Hospital.
Hoynes, Richard '88 (LA) San Pedro, CA Holy Trinity Church.
Hoyng, William *c.pp.s.* '54 (TOL) Bismark, OH St. Sebastian Church; Marywood, OH St. Michael's Church; Reed, OH Assumption Church.
Hoyos, Jose E. '84 (ARL) Falls Church, VA St. Anthony's Church.
Hoyt, Stephen *o.f.m. cap.* '92 (CHL) [8] Charlotte, NC St. Matthew Church; [D] Charlotte, NC Mecklenburg Area Catholic Schools (M.A.C.S.).
Hoza, Rudolph *s.s.c.* '42 (PRO) [P] Bristol, RI St. Columban's Retirement House.
Hratz, Joseph A. '42 (DAV) Retired; [L] Davenport, IA Kahl Home for the Aged and Infirm.
Hrboka, Romildo *t.o.r.* '45 (PIT) [5] Millvale, PA St. Nicholas Church; [N] Pittsburgh, PA Croatian Commissariate, T.O.R.
Hrdlicka, Lambert A. '50 (STL) Retired.
Hrebic, Alban *o.s.b.* '52 (JOL) [J] Lisle, IL St. Procopius Abbey.
Hreha, James D. '87 (WIL) Dover, DE Holy Cross Church; Smyrna, MD Delaware Correctional Center.
Hren, Joseph I. *o.p.* '47 (CHI) [N] River Forest, IL St. Thomas Aquinas Priory.
Hren, Joseph I. *o.p.* '51 (CHI) [D] Oak Park, IL Fenwick High School.
Hribsek, Aloysius J. '49 (BGP) Retired; [U] North Stamford, CT Villa Maria Retreat House.
Hricko, Michael A. *s.j.* '73 (PH) [C] Philadelphia, PA St. Joseph's University.
Hricko, Michael A. *s.j.* '73 (SCR) [E] Scranton, PA Scranton Preparatory School.
Hrisko, Zachary *o.s.b.* '57 (JOL) [J] Lisle, IL St. Procopius Abbey.
Hritz, Paul '53 (CLV) [A] Wickliffe, OH St. Mary Seminary.
Hritz, Paul J. '53 (CLV) [44] Cleveland, OH Community of St. Malachi Church; [45] Cleveland, OH St. Malachi Church; Retired.
Hritzko, John '81 (FTW) [5] Mishawaka, IN St. Michael's Byzantine Ukrainian Catholic Church.
Hritzko, John '89 (STN) Mishawaka, IN St. Michael Church; Munster, IN St. Josaphat Church.
Hrubiak, Dennis M. '70 (PRM) Parma, OH Holy Spirit Church.
Hruby, Paul '82 (LA) [18] Los Angeles, CA Nativity Church.
Hruska, Eugene P. '58 (GF) Fort Shaw, MT St. Ann Church.
Hruska, Timothy W. '96 (MAR) Awaiting Assignment.
Hrydziuszko, Michael '95 (DET) [5] Clinton Twp., MI St. Thecla Church.
Hrynkiw, Wasyl '91 (STF) Lackawanna, NY Our Lady of Perpetual Help Church.
Hrynuck, Stephen '38 (PHU) Olyphant, PA SS. Cyril and Methodius Church.
Hsu, Peter '57 (BEL) Royalton, IL St. Aloysius Church.
Huan, Joseph Van Tran '73 (RIC) Military Chaplains.
Huar, Ralph F. '81 (STP) Rush City, MN Sacred Heart Church.
Huard, Jeffrey H. '94 (STP) Lakeville, MN All Saints Church.
Huard, Leo *o.carm.* '65 (JOL) [J] Darien, IL Carmelite Fathers Provincial Office.
Hubba, David C. '74 (NEW) Palisades Park, NJ St. Michael's Church.
Hubbard, J. Randall '90 (L) [34] Louisville, KY Holy Spirit Church.
Hubbard, John (LA) [K] Los Angeles, CA Queen of Angels-Hollywood Presbyterian Medical Center.
Hubbard, Lawrence E. '68 (STP) [33] Minneapolis, MN St. Stephen Church; Special Assignment.
Hubbert, Joseph G. *c.m.* '77 (BUF) [C] Niagara University, NY Niagara University; [O] Niagara University, NY Vincentian Community at Niagara University.
Hubble, Karl D. '39 (DET) Retired.
Hubbs, Timothy '84 (CAM) Somerdale, NJ Our Lady of Grace Church; [A] Haddonfield, NJ Paul VI High School.
Huber, Clarence W. '69 (LUB) Littlefield, TX Sacred Heart Church.
Huber, Daniel R. '50 (PBL) Canon City, CO St. Michael Church.
Huber, David W. '86 (RCK) Geneva, IL St. Peter Church.
Huber, George L. '48 (MIL) Retired.
Huber, J. William '59 (PBL) [16] Pueblo, CO St. Pius X Church.
Huber, John *c.s.b.* '92 (OAK) [C] Oakland, CA Bishop O'Dowd High School.
Huber, John R. '68 (PIT) Wireton, PA St. Catherine of Siena Church.
Huber, Justin *o.f.m.* '70 (KNX) [F] Mountain City, TN Franciscan Friars.
Huber, Kevin R. '91 (GRY) Saint John, IN St. John Evangelist Church.
Huber, Larry T., Jr. '95 (STL) House Springs, MO Our Lady, Queen of Peace Church.
Huber, Leo R. '67 (STP) Retired.
Huber, Mark D. '94 (LIN) [1] Lincoln, NE Cathedral of the Risen Christ.
Huber, Matthew '87 (HEL) [2] Missoula, MT Holy Family Church.
Huber, Paul A. *s.j.* '45 (CIN) [28] Cincinnati, OH St. Francis Xavier Church; [V] Cincinnati, OH Apostleship of Prayer.
Huber, Richard *m.s.c.* '59 (OG) [2] Watertown, NY Our Lady of the Sacred Heart, Missionaries of the Sacred Heart Church.
Huber, Richard '89 (STP) Minnetonka, MN Immaculate Heart of Mary Church.
Huber, Robert L. '56 (L) [8] Louisville, KY St. Athanasius Church.
Huber, Vincent J. '64 (STU) Toronto, OH St. Francis of Assisi Church; Toronto, OH St. Joseph's Church.
Huber, Walter *s.m.b.* '46 (DEN) [17] Denver, CO Notre Dame Church.
Huber, William D. '55 (COL) [26] Columbus, OH St. Ladislas Church.
Hubert, James *c.i.c.m.* '51 (SAT) [G] San Antonio, TX Mount Sacred Heart School.
Hubert, Raymond '58 (PMB) [1] Delray Beach, FL Emmanuel Church.
Hubertus, Albert '50 (SAT) [27] San Antonio, TX St. Anthony Mary Claret Church.
Hubertus, Gerald '64 (SAT) Seguin, TX St. James Church.
Huberty, Mark A. '96 (STP) [21] Minneapolis, MN St. Charles Borromeo Church.
Huberty, Ronald V. '90 (NU) [1] New Ulm, MN Cathedral of The Holy Trinity; Benson, MN St. Francis Church; Clontarf, MN St. Malachy Church; Danvers, MN Church of the Visitation; De Graff, MN St. Bridget Church; Murdock, MN Church of the Sacred Heart.
Hubler, Tony '92 (IND) Navilleton, IN St. Mary Church.
Hubmann, William *c.pp.s.* '79 (KC) [20] Kansas City, MO St. James Church; [A] Kansas City, MO Precious Blood Mission House.
Huck, Joseph '69 (MIA) North Lauderdale, FL Our Lady Queen of Heaven Church.
Hudak, Cyril '53 (MIA) Retired.
Hudak, Msgr. Francis J. '55 (HBG) New Oxford, PA Immaculate Conception of the Blessed Virgin Mary Church.
Hudak, Ralph G. '77 (CLV) [61] Cleveland, OH St. Patrick Church.
Hudak, Richard E. '68 (CLV) Fairview Park, OH St. Angela Merici Church.
Hudak, Thomas R. '73 (SCR) Lake Silkworth, PA Our Lady of Mount Carmel Church.
Hudanish, Jeffrey A. '93 (BGP) Darien, CT St. Thomas More Church; [C] Stamford, CT Trinity Catholic High School.

Hudepohl, Al D. *o.f.m.* '56 (CIN) [23] Cincinnati, OH St. Clement Church; [M] Cincinnati, OH St. Clement Friary.
Hudert, John P. *m.m.* '62 (NY) [Z] Maryknoll, NY Maryknoll Fathers and Brothers.
Hudgin, Christopher J. *o.s.f.s.* '81 (VEN) [A] Fort Myers, FL Bishop Verot High School; [K] Fort Myers, FL The Bishop Verot High School Foundation.
Hudock, Barry (E) [1] Erie, PA St. Peter Cathedral.
Hudson, Charles '62 (NEW) Roselle, NJ Center for Hope Hospice.
Hudson, Francis X. '74 (CAM) Millville, NJ St. John Bosco Church.
Hudson, Frank X. '74 (CAM) [P] Newfield, NJ Catholic Social Services Regional Counseling Center.
Hudson, Gerald F. *s.j.* '81 (SFR) [E] San Francisco, CA St. Ignatius College Preparatory (Coed); [N] San Francisco, CA Jesuit Community at St. Ignatius College Preparatory.
Hudson, Richard Reginald '96 (AUS) [14] Austin, TX St. John Neumann Church.
Hudziak, Jerome M. '64 (MIL) [3] Wauwatosa, WI St. Joseph Congregation Church.
Hudzik, Msgr. Leo A. '34 (CAM) Retired.
Huebner, Donald C. '54 (CIN) [1] Springfield, OH St. Bernard Church.
Huebner, Terrance J. '74 (MIL) Elkhorn, WI St. Patrick's Church.
Huebsch, Joseph R. '50 (FAR) Retired.
Huegelmeyer, Charles T. *m.m.* '51 (NY) [Z] Maryknoll, NY Maryknoll Fathers and Brothers.
Huehlefeld, Matthew '96 (VIC) Port Lavaca, TX Our Lady of the Gulf Church.
Hueller, Francis T. *s.a.c.* '48 (MIL) [P] Milwaukee, WI Pallotti House.
Huels, John M. *o.s.m.* '76 (CHI) [N] Chicago, IL Servite Friars - Eastern Province.
Huels, Vincent P. '42 (STL) Retired.
Huelsing, Justin *o.m.i.* (SPC) Mountain Grove, MO Sacred Heart Church.
Huelsman, Richard *s.j.* '54 (COL) [31] Columbus, OH St. Matthias Church.
Huerga, Alvaro *o.p.* '50 (PCE) [B] Ponce, PR The Pontifical Catholic University of Puerto Rico.
Huerta, Enrique *s.v.d.* (LA) [76] Los Angeles, CA St. Malachy Church.
Huertas, Ivan '93 (SJN) [B] Rio Piedras, PR Seminario Mayor Interdiocesano Santa Maria de los Angeles.
Huesca, Omar A. '81 (MIA) [31] Miami, FL St. Robert Bellarmine Church.
Huesing, Paul D. *c.s.p.* '82 (WDC) [B] Washington, DC St. Paul's College.
Huesman, E. Gerard '41 (BAL) Baltimore, MD Franklin Square Hospital.
Huesman, John E. *s.j.* '49 (OAK) [A] Berkeley, CA The Jesuit School of Theology at Berkeley; [N] Berkeley, CA Jesuit Community at Jesuit School of Theology at Berkeley.
Huete, Francis W. *s.j.* '82 (LAF) [A] Grand Coteau, LA St. Charles College.
Huffman, David L. '72 (STU) Belpre, OH St. Ambrose Church; [J] Belpre, OH Boy Scouts; [J] Steubenville, OH Ohio Conference Advisory Council.
Huffman, Timothy '93 (RIC) Roanoke, VA Our Lady of Nazareth Church.
Huffman, Timothy '93 (STU) Absent on Leave.
Huffstetter, Stephen *s.c.j.* '89 (CHI) [N] Chicago, IL Priests of the Sacred Heart.
Hug, Frederick I. '48 (TOL) Retired.
Hug, James E. *s.j.* '72 (MIL) [P] Milwaukee, WI Jesuit Provincial Office, Wisconsin Province.
Hug, James E. *s.j.* '72 (WDC) [M] Washington, DC K Street Jesuit Community; [V] Washington, DC Center of Concern.
Huggins, Michael L. '89 (SD) Leave of Absence.
Huggins, Williams A. '67 (SPC) Leopold, MO St. John Church.
Hughes, Albert C. '57 (BO) [2] Framingham, MA St. George Church.
Hughes, Brian C. '81 (SC) [A] Sioux City, IA Briar Cliff College.
Hughes, Charles (SAV) Dublin, GA Immaculate Conception Church.
Hughes, Charles *glmy.* '54 (CIN) [M] Fairfield, OH Headquarters of Glenmary Home Missioners.
Hughes, Charles J. '74 (BO) [4] Lynn, MA St. Mary Church.
Hughes, Dennis E. (SP) San Antonio, FL St. Anthony of Padua Church.
Hughes, Derek '86 (MRY) Cambria, CA Santa Rosa Church.
Hughes, Donald R. '52 (BUF) Retired.
Hughes, Edward J. '51 (CHI) Schaumburg, IL St. Matthew Church.
Hughes, Edward R. '58 (RCK) Sublette, IL Our Lady of Perpetual Help Church; West Brooklyn, IL St. Mary Church.
Hughes, Eugene *s.m.* '57 (ATL) [6] Atlanta, GA Our Lady of the Assumption Church.
Hughes, F. Rodger '64 (WH) Chester, WV Sacred Heart Church.
Hughes, Francis *s.v.d.* '52 (CHI) [B] Techny, IL Divine Word Residence.
Hughes, Francis J. '45 (Y) Retired.
Hughes, Francis J. '80 (BRK) [175] Queens, NY St. Helen Church.
Hughes, Msgr. Gerald '58 (DAL) Retired.
Hughes, Gerald *s.j.* '85 (DAL) [26] Dallas, TX St. Rita Church.
Hughes, Henry J. (BAL) [Q] Baltimore, MD Catholic Daughters of the Americas.
Hughes, James '80 (BRK) [206] Queens, NY Our Lady of the Angelus Church.
Hughes, James F. '52 (PH) Media, PA St. Mary Magdalen Church.
Hughes, James J. '45 (SFD) Retired.
Hughes, John *m.s.* (WOR) [6] Fitchburg, MA St. Joseph's Church.
Hughes, John '94 (BEA) [9] Beaumont, TX St. Jude Thaddeus Church.
Hughes, Msgr. John C. '49 (LA) Camarillo, CA St. Mary Magdalen Church.
Hughes, John F. '37 (BRK) Retired; [R] Queens Village, NY Queen of Peace Residence.
Hughes, John J. '54 (ARL) Springfield, VA St. Bernadette's Church.
Hughes, John Jay '54 (STL) [2] University City, MO Christ the King Church.
Hughes, Joseph '96 (KC) [10] Kansas City, MO St. Elizabeth's Church.
Hughes, Joseph A. '32 (DUL) [9] Duluth, MN St. John's Church; Retired.
Hughes, Joseph B. (BAL) Retired.
Hughes, Joseph W. '70 (TR) Rumson, NJ Holy Cross Church.
Hughes, Kenneth J. *s.j.* '66 (BO) [W] Cambridge, MA Faber House; [W] Cambridge, MA Weston Jesuit Community.
Hughes, Lawrence J. '64 (MAN) Retired.
Hughes, M. Curtis '45 (ALB) South Glens Falls, NY St. Michael the Archangel Church; Retired.
Hughes, Mark F. '82 (WDC) Fort Washington, MD St. Ignatius Church.
Hughes, Martin F. '44 (B) Retired.
Hughes, Matthew '96 (JOL) Hinsdale, IL St. Isaac Jogues Church.
Hughes, Msgr. Michael '45 (LA) Ventura, CA San Buenaventura Mission Church.
Hughes, Msgr. Michael '45 (ORG) Retired.
Hughes, Michael '54 (OKL) Medford, OK St. Mary's Church.
Hughes, Michael J. *o.s.a.* '75 (MIA) Dania, FL Church of the Resurrection.
Hughes, Msgr. Nicholas V. '44 (B) Retired.
Hughes, Pablo *o.m.i.* '73 (SJN) [7] San Juan, PR Ntr. Sra. de la Caridad del Cobre Church.
Hughes, Patrick M. '56 (LA) Irwindale, CA Our Lady of Guadalupe Church.
Hughes, Pete '81 (OWN) Hardinsburg, KY St. Romuald Church; Irvington, KY Holy Guardian Angels Church.
Hughes, Peter *c.s.sp.* '61 (FAR) [1] Fargo, ND St. Mary's Cathedral.
Hughes, Ray *c.r.* (SP) St. Pete Beach, FL St. John Church.
Hughes, Msgr. Richard A. '52 (WDC) Upper Marlboro, MD Saint Mary of the Assumption Church.
Hughes, Robert *s.m.* '59 (SJ) [M] Cupertino, CA Marianist Provincial Residence.
Hughes, Robert E. '90 (CAM) Barrington, NJ St. Francis de Sales Church; [A] Haddonfield, NJ Paul VI High School.
Hughes, Robert T. '54 (PEO) Retired.
Hughes, Robert W. '68 (MAD) Military Chaplains.
Hughes, Ronald J. '82 (SCR) Towanda, PA SS. Peter and Paul Church.
Hughes, Royce '64 (GAL) On Duty Outside the Diocese.
Hughes, Vincent *o.f.m.* '85 (SD) San Luis Rey, CA Mission San Luis Rey de Francia Church; [H] San Luis Rey, CA San Luis Rey.
Hughes, William C. '47 (STO) Retired.
Hughson, D. Thomas *s.j.* '71 (MIL) [P] Milwaukee, WI Arrupe House Jesuit Community.
Hughson, Robert S. '79 (BUF) [9] Niagara Falls, NY Our Lady of Mount Carmel Church; [D] Niagara Falls, NY Niagara Catholic Junior-Senior School.
Hugli, Richard *o.s.b.* '95 (SP) [O] St. Leo, FL St. Leo Abbey.
Hugo, William *o.f.m.cap.* '80 (BRK) [U] Brooklyn, NY St. Michael's Friary.
Hugo, William *o.f.m.cap.* '81 (BRK) [87] Brooklyn, NY St. Michael's Church.
Huguet, Francisco '75 (BRK) [71] Brooklyn, NY St. Joseph Patron of the Universal Church.
Huguley, Vernon '93 (BIR) [18] Birmingham, AL Our Lady Queen of the Universe Church; [22] Birmingham, AL Sacred Heart Church.
Huhmann, Msgr. John F. '50 (KC) Retired.
Huhn, Bernard F. '52 (STL) [O] St. Louis, MO Mother of Good Counsel Home.
Huhn, Donald W. '49 (STL) Retired.
Huhn, Thomas J. '69 (BEA) Jasper, TX St. Michael Church.
Huhtanen, Andrew *o.m.v.* '83 (MET) [H] Asbury, NJ Lanteri House.
Huitrado, Juan J. '80 (CHI) [187] Chicago, IL St. Roman Church.
Hulko, Joseph D. '67 (ALN) [1] Easton, PA St. Anthony of Padua Church.
Hull, Daniel L. (MIL) Lyons, WI St. Joseph's Church.
Hull, Francis M. *s.s.j.* '57 (NO) [29] New Orleans, LA St. David Church.
Hull, Michael '93 (NY) Graduate Studies.
Huller, Karl '54 (SPR) [1] Springfield, MA St. Michael's Cathedral.
Hullings, Clifford '61 (SPK) Retired.
Hulscher, Alfred J. *o.s.b.* '60 (SEA) [M] Lacey, WA St. Martin's Abbey; [M] Lacey, WA St. Martin's Abbey.
Hulshof, David F. '82 (SPC) [1] Springfield, MO Cathedral of St. Agnes; Special Assignment.
Hulsman, Msgr. Francis J. '34 (OM) Retired.
Hultberg, William J. *o.s.f.s.* '62 (WIL) [I] Wilmington, DE Oblates of St. Francis De Sales.
Hultquist, Thomas H. '76 (WOR) Barre, MA St. Joseph's Church.
Hum Na, Jin '82 (COL) [44] Columbus, OH Korean Catholic Community Church.
Humanitzki, Theodore '60 (STF) Retired.
Humbert, Robert G. *s.j.* '53 (CHI) [D] Wilmette, IL Loyola Academy.
Humbrecht, T. Allen '72 (KNX) [2] Chattanooga, TN Our Lady of Perpetual Help Church; [J] Chattanooga, TN Newman Foundation of Chattanooga, Inc.
Hume, Jorge '93 (SR) Graduate Studies.
Hume, Kenneth '63 (P) Retired.
Hume, Robert B. '43 (BRK) [57] Brooklyn, NY Holy Innocents Church; Retired.
Humenay, Robert '69 (E) On Duty Outside Diocese.
Huminski, Gregory J. '80 (BGP) [5] Norwalk, CT St. Matthew Church.
Humitz, Msgr. Robert S. '60 (DET) Clarkston, MI St. Daniel Church.
Humm, Alfred A. *o.s.b.* '35 (PAT) [M] Newton, NJ St. Paul's Abbey.
Hummel, Donald K. '78 (NEW) [D] Paramus, NJ Paramus Catholic High School.
Hummel, John D. *c.m.* '44 (PH) [Z] Philadelphia, PA Congregation of the Mission.
Hummell, Donald K. '78 (NEW) Paramus, NJ Our Lady of the Visitation Church.
Hummell, John F. '65 (PH) [28] Philadelphia, PA St. Callistus Church.
Hummer, Lawrence L. '73 (COL) Military Chaplains.
Humphrey, Arthur Frank *s.t.m., m.a.* '75 (NEW) [15] Newark, NJ St. Francis Xavier Church.
Humphrey, Stephen J. '67 (BEL) Columbia, IL Immaculate Conception of the B.V.M. Church.
Humphrys, Richard '57 (SB) Bloomington, CA St. Charles Borromeo Church.
Hunckler, Martin '80 (COS) [4] Colorado Springs, CO Holy Apostles Church.
Hund, Francis '82 (KCK) Meriden, KS St. Aloysius Church; Perry, KS St. Theresa's Church.
Hund, William *c.s.c.* (P) [L] Portland, OR Holy Cross Father & Brother, C.S.C. - University of Portland.
Hund, William *c.s.c.* '60 (P) [B] Portland, OR University of Portland.
Hundt, George F. '81 (PAT) [8] Paterson, NJ St. Gerard Majella Church.
Hundt, Robert P. '61 (LC) Middle Ridge, WI St. Peter Church; Saint Joseph Ridge, WI St. Joseph Church.
Huneger, Richard J. '73 (P) [32] Portland, OR St. Rose of Lima Church.
Huneke, Robert D. '69 (RVC) Absent on Leave.
Hung, Joseph '70 (SFR) [3] San Rafael, CA St. Raphael Church.
Hung, Joseph K. '68 (ORG) On Duty Outside the Diocese.
Hung, Pham Quoc *c.ss.r.* '94 (LA) [R] Baldwin Park, CA Vietnamese Redemptorist Mission.
Hung, Trinh Peter '79 (CHI) [205] Chicago, IL St. Thomas of Canterbury Church; [V] Chicago, IL Ministry in Higher Education.
Hung Hoang, Dominic '90 (OKL) Chandler, OK Our Lady of Sorrows Church.
Hunke, Norman F. '73 (OM) [1] Omaha, NE St. Cecilia's Cathedral.
Hunkeler, Edward J. '44 (OM) Retired.
Hunkins, Richard C. '56 (JC) Special Assignments; [D] Columbia, MO Columbia Nursing Home Ministry.
Hunkler, Cyril '83 (HEL) Plains, MT St. James Church; Thompson Falls, MT St. William Church.
Hunkler, Jerome '83 (FAR) New Rockford, ND St. John's Church.
Hunko, Gerard A. '91 (GAY) North Port, MI St. Gertrude Church; Suttons Bay, MI St. Michael the Archangel Church.
Hunstiger, Thomas P. '63 (STP) [21] St. Paul, MN St. Gregory the Great Church; [24] St. Paul, MN St. Leo Church; [34] St. Paul, MN Highland Catholic Community Church.
Hunt, Brendan *o.m.i.* '42 (BUF) [27] Buffalo, NY Holy Angels Church.
Hunt, Daniel J. *c.p.* '38 (BO) [W] Brighton, MA St.

Gabriel's Residence.
Hunt, Dennis '81 (LIN) Lawrence, NE Sacred Heart Church.
Hunt, Desmund *s.m.* '56 (CLV) Bedford, OH St. Pius X Church.
Hunt, Doug *c.r.* (PBL) Ignacio, CO St. Ignatius Parish Church.
Hunt, George W. *s.j.* '67 (NY) [Z] New York, NY "America;" Residence and publication office of the America Press; [DD] New York, NY America Press, Inc., The.
Hunt, Msgr. James A. '55 (BRK) [99] Brooklyn, NY Our Lady of Loreto Church; [108] Brooklyn, NY Our Lady of the Presentation Church.
Hunt, James M. '83 (GI) Ainsworth, NE St. Pius X Church.
Hunt, John M. '69 (OG) [2] Ogdensburg, NY Notre Dame Church.
Hunt, John W. '68 (PRO) Ashton, RI St. Joseph's Church.
Hunt, Kevin *o.c.s.o.* '79 (WOR) [N] Spencer, MA St. Joseph's Abbey.
Hunt, Lawrence J. *s.j.* '57 (CHL) Winston-Salem, NC St. Benedict the Moor Church; [J] Charlotte, NC Jesuit Community.
Hunt, Msgr. Luke '67 (PT) Gulf Breeze, FL St. Ann Church.
Hunt, Mark J. '85 (PH) Yardley, PA St. Ignatius of Antioch Church; Graduate Studies.
Hunt, Michael J. '41 (BRK) [43] Brooklyn, NY St. Frances de Chantal Church; Retired.
Hunt, Michael J. *c.s.p.* '67 (BO) [CC] Medford, MA Tufts University Catholic Center.
Hunt, Patrick J. '39 (PRO) Retired.
Hunt, Richard *s.j.* (SY) Vestal, NY St. Vincent de Paul Church.
Hunt, Robert W. *c.pp.s.* '54 (CIN) [M] Dayton, OH Provincial House of the Cincinnati Province of the Society of the Precious Blood.
Hunt, Ted '54 (SFE) Retired.
Hunt, Thomas *s.c.j.* '55 (MIL) [P] Franklin, WI Villa Maria.
Hunt Diaz, Kevin '84 (PHX) Unassigned.
Hunter, Alan '77 (SFD) Assumption, IL Assumption B.V.M. Church; Macon, IL St. Stanislaus Church; Moweaqua, IL St. Frances de Sales Church.
Hunter, Alcuin *o.f.m.conv.* (LSC) [D] Mesilla Park, NM Holy Cross Retreat and Friary.
Hunter, Eric '72 (SP) [5] Tampa, FL Incarnation Church.
Hunter, John J. '86 (NY) [2] Poughkeepsie, NY St. Mary Church.
Hunter, William R. (LA) Retired.
Hunthausen, John F. '52 (HEL) Dillon, MT St. Rose of Lima Church; [H] Dillon, MT Western Montana College.
Huntimer, Donald W. *c.s.v.* '59 (CHI) [N] Arlington Heights, IL Viatorian Province Center-Clerics of St. Viator.
Huntington, Msgr. Christopher '52 (RVC) East Hampton, NY Most Holy Trinity Church; Retired.
Huntzinger, Msgr. Ralph '50 (COL) Retired.
Huon, Phan Phat *c.ss.r.* '53 (LA) [R] Baldwin Park, CA Vietnamese Redemptorist Mission.
Huong, Joseph '85 (SAC) Yuba City, CA St. Isidore Church.
Huot, Leopold J. '45 (PRT) Retired.
Hupp, Msgr. Robert P. '40 (OM) Retired.
Huppenbauer, Walter '75 (CHI) [M] Chicago, IL Little Sisters of the Poor Center for the Aging.
Hurd, Timothy C. '92 (SHP) [1] Monroe, LA Jesus the Good Shepherd Church.
Hurkes, Charles F. *o.m.i.* '58 (SFD) Beltrees, IL St. Michael Church; Grafton, IL St. Patrick Church.
Hurley, Brendan *s.j.* '93 (WDC) [M] Washington, DC The Jesuit Community at Georgetown University.
Hurley, Cornelius P. *s.j.* '59 (NY) [Z] New York, NY Murray-Weigel Hall.
Hurley, Daniel *o.f.m.* '45 (BUF) [Q] West Clarksville, NY Mount Irenaeus, Franciscan Mountain Retreat & Holy Peace Friary; [R] Williamsville, NY Newman Club Chaplains.
Hurley, Msgr. Daniel J. '59 (RVC) Massapequa, NY St. Rose of Lima Church.
Hurley, Msgr. Edward '70 (DM) Urbandale, IA St. Pius X Church.
Hurley, Francis J. *c.s.c.* '53 (FR) [B] North Easton, MA Stonehill College.
Hurley, George '55 (JOL) Retired.
Hurley, Gerard '76 (JKS) Columbus, MS Annunciation Church; [G] Columbus, MS Mississippi State University for Women Student Center.
Hurley, J. Patrick *s.j.* '57 (P) [L] Portland, OR Jesuit Provincial Office (Oregon Prov.).
Hurley, James *s.d.b.* '76 (COL) [H] Columbus, OH Salesian Center.
Hurley, James P. *s.j.* '40 (SPK) [K] Spokane, WA Regis Community.
Hurley, James P. *m.s.* '48 (ATL) [2] Marietta, GA Church of St. Ann.
Hurley, Jerome M. *o.s.m.* '38 (CHI) [N] Chicago, IL Servite Friars - Eastern Province.
Hurley, John D. '42 (ROC) Retired.
Hurley, John F. *s.j.* '45 (SPK) [K] Spokane, WA Regis Community.
Hurley, John J. '56 (CHI) Arlington Heights, IL St. Edna Church.
Hurley, John J. *o.s.f.s.* '68 (WIL) [I] Wilmington, DE DeSales House.
Hurley, John J. '82 (WDC) [6] Silver Spring, MD St. John the Baptist Church.
Hurley, John W. '74 (CHI) Other Assignments.
Hurley, Joseph J. *c.ss.r.* '50 (CHI) [N] Glenview, IL The Redemptorists of Glenview, Illinois.
Hurley, Msgr. Leonard F. (WDC) [V] Washington, DC Carroll Manor Nursing & Rehabilitation Center.
Hurley, Leonard F. '58 (WDC) Hospital & Nursing Home Ministries; [L] Washington, DC Cardinal O'Boyle Residence for Priests.
Hurley, Msgr. Leonard F. '68 (WDC) [K] Washington, DC Providence Hospital.
Hurley, Michael F. '43 (PHX) Cottonwood, AZ Immaculate Conception Church.
Hurley, Patrick M. *o.s.b.* '76 (NEW) [1] Linden, NJ St. Elizabeth's Church.
Hurley, Patrick M. *o.s.b.* '76 (PAT) [M] Morristown, NJ St. Mary's Abbey.
Hurley, Paul Kevin (BO) Hanson, MA St. Joseph the Worker Church.
Hurley, Paul T. '82 (PRO) Slatersville, RI St. John the Evangelist Church.
Hurley, Paul W. '70 (BO) [2] Cambridge, MA Blessed Sacrament Church.
Hurley, Stephen *s.j.* (PHX) [B] Phoenix, AZ Brophy College Preparatory.
Hurley, Thomas J., Sr. (CHI) [34] Chicago, IL St. Cajetan Church.
Hurley, Msgr. Walter A. '65 (DET) Farmington, MI Our Lady of Sorrows Church.
Hurst, H. David *o.s.b.* '46 (PRO) [P] Portsmouth, RI Abbey of St. Gregory the Great.
Hurst, Mark *o.f.m.* '80 (WDC) [M] Washington, DC Commissariat of the Holy Land, Franciscan Monastery - Mount St. Sepulchre.
Hurst, Maynard E. '79 (BR) [14] Baton Rouge, LA St. Louis, King of France Church.
Hurst, Paul F. '77 (CIN) Germantown, OH St. Augustine Church.
Hurst, Thomas R. *s.s.* '73 (WDC) [A] Washington, DC Theological College of the Catholic University of America; [C] Washington, DC Catholic University of America, The.
Hurtado-Badillo, Domingo '93 (CHI) [123] Chicago, IL St. Mark Church.
Hurtuk, Joseph C. *s.m.* '74 (WDC) [M] Washington, DC Marist Provincial House.
Husain, Nicholas F. '85 (NO) New Orleans, LA Memorial Medical Center; New Orleans, LA Memorial Medical Center.
Huse, Ralph G. *s.j.* '75 (STL) [P] St. Louis, MO Bellarmine House of Studies.
Huse, Robert *o.a.r.* '56 (ORG) [5] Santa Ana, CA Our Lady of the Pillar Church.
Hushen, Mark A. *o.s.f.s.* '91 (WIL) [3] Wilmington, DE St. Anthony of Padua Church.
Huske, Leonard G. (CHI) Retired.
Hussack, Emil M. '49 (SCR) [24] Scranton, PA Sacred Hearts of Jesus and Mary Church.
Husselbeck, Francis E. '58 (ALB) Richfield Springs, NY St. Joseph Church.
Hussey, Daniel '85 (GLP) On Duty Outside of Diocese.
Hussey, Dennis R. '45 (HRT) East Haven, CT Our Lady of Pompeii Church.
Hussey, Gerald W. '78 (PRO) Little Compton, RI St. Catherine of Siena Church.
Hussey, M. Edmund '58 (CIN) [4] Springfield, OH St. Raphael Church.
Hussey, Michael J. *o.m.i.* '60 (CHR) Ridgeland, SC St. Anthony's Church.
Hussey, Michael J. *o.m.i.* '60 (STP) [N] St. Paul, MN Oblate Provincial Offices; [N] St. Paul, MN Oblate Residence.
Hussey, Patrick F. *s.j.* '68 (TOL) [K] Toledo, OH St. Mary's Jesuit Community.
Hussey, Thomas F. *s.j.* '43 (BO) [W] Boston, MA Jesuit Urban Center & Immaculate Conception Community.
Hussli, Edward J. '67 (MIL) Elba, WI St. Columbkille Church; Reeseville, WI Holy Family Church.
Hussmann, John R. '54 (DUB) Retired.
Husted, Richard S. *o.f.m.* '66 (NEW) East Rutherford, NJ St. Joseph's Church.
Hustedde, Edwin H. '56 (BEL) Valmeyer, IL Seven Dolors of the B.V.M. Church; [B] Waterloo, IL Gibault Catholic High School.
Huston, Richard E. '95 (SD) [36] San Diego, CA St. Therese Church.
Huszti, Michael J. '76 (PRM) Burton, OH Church of Weeping Madonna; Solon, OH St. John the Baptist Church; [B] Burton, OH Shrine of the Weeping Madonna of Mariapoch.
Hut, Clemens '36 (EVN) Retired.
Hutchins, H. James '67 (PH) [58] Philadelphia, PA Holy Cross Church.
Hutchins, Michael *s.v.d.* '75 (DUB) [B] Epworth, IA Divine Word College.
Hutchinson, Ronald '94 (GR) [2] Muskegon, MI St. Francis de Sales Church.
Hutchinson, William J. *s.j.* '66 (WDC) [M] Washington, DC Leonard Neale House; [V] Washington, DC Jesuit Social Ministries-National Office.
Huth, James *o.praem.* '88 (SFE) Albuquerque, NM St. Joseph Medical Center; [J] Albuquerque, NM Santa Maria de la Vid Priory.
Hutmacher, Robert '79 (CHI) [N] Chicago, IL St. Peter's Friary.
Hutnik, William J. '44 (PIT) Retired.
Hutsko, Basil J. '79 (PRM) Sterling Heights, MI St. Basils Church.
Hutsko, Joseph '79 (VNN) Denver, CO Holy Protection of the Mother of God Church.
Hutsko, Michael '84 (PHU) Middleport, PA Nativity of B.V.M. Church; Minersville, PA St. Nicholas Church; [D] Philadelphia, PA Ascension Manor, Inc.
Hutt, David *o.f.m.conv.* '49 (L) Pleasure Ridge Park, KY St. Paul Church.
Hutter, Eugene M. '88 (PSC) Philadelphia, PA Holy Ghost Church.
Hutter, John P. '92 (PH) [114] Philadelphia, PA Our Lady of Calvary Church.
Hutton, Leon '80 (LA) [A] Camarillo, CA St. John's Seminary; [A] Camarillo, CA St. John's Seminary.
Hutzler, James '80 (AMA) Umbarger, TX St. Mary's Church.
Huvane, James H. *m.m.* '70 (CLV) [P] Cleveland, OH Maryknoll Fathers.
Huy, Dominic Trinh The *o.p.* '75 (GAL) [38] Houston, TX St. Jerome Church; [73] Houston, TX Our Lady of Lourdes Church.
Huy Quyen, Nguyen '73 (JOL) Glen Ellyn, IL Queenship of Mary Church; Glen Ellyn, IL St. Petronille Church.
Huyett, Gerald T. *s.j.* '73 (NY) [Z] New York, NY West Side Jesuit Community.
Huyguet, Dean M. '85 (PEO) Westville, IL St. Mary's Church.
Huynh, Joseph Dinh C. '67 (PH) [151] Philadelphia, PA St. Thomas Aquinas Church.
Huynh, Viet '93 (PT) [2] Pensacola, FL Little Flower Church.
Huynh Tan Cong, Simon (SPC) [E] Carthage, MO Congregation of the Mother Co-Redemptrix, United States Assumption Province.
Hvozdovic, Andrew S. '87 (SCR) [6] Hazleton, PA St. Joseph's Church.
Hwan Jeong, Peter Sung '91 (P) [11] Portland, OR Church of Korean Martyrs.
Hwang, Bernard *o.s.b.* (P) Retired.
Hy, Hilary Tran-Khac '57 (WDC) [5] Bethesda, MD Our Lady of Vietnam Church.
Hyatt, Donald F. *c.s.b.* '68 (SFE) [D] Albuquerque, NM St. Pius X High School.
Hyatt, John R. *s.j.* '77 (BRK) [62] Brooklyn, NY St. Ignatius Church.
Hyatt, Martin *b.s.o.* '84 (NTN) [B] Methuen, MA Basilian Salvatorian Order.
Hyatt, Robert A. '63 (RVC) Amityville, NY Brunswick Hospital; Amityville, NY South Oaks Psychiatric Hospital; West Islip, NY Consolation Nursing Home; [J] West Islip, NY Our Lady of Consolation Geriatric Care Center.
Hybner, Joseph '63 (VIC) [5] Victoria, TX St. Mary's Church.
Hyclak, Walter J. '69 (CLV) [U] Cleveland, OH St. Joseph Christian Life Center.
Hyde, Mark *s.d.b.* '81 (BO) [N] Boston, MA Salesian Boys & Girls Club.
Hyde, Robert '88 (SY) Camillus, NY St. Joseph Church.
Hyde, Robert L. *o.praem.* '43 (GB) [I] De Pere, WI St. Norbert Abbey.
Hydo, Emerick J. *c.m.* '50 (ALN) Bangor, PA Our Lady of Good Counsel Church.
Hying, Donald J. '89 (MIL) On Duty Outside the Archdiocese.
Hykawy, Roman *o.s.b.m.* (STN) Warren, MI St. Josaphat Church.
Hyl, Robert J. '63 (BGP) Easton, CT Notre Dame of Easton Church.
Hyland, Msgr. Charles H. '29 (BO) Retired.
Hyland, Edward F. '67 (HRT) [17] Waterbury, CT SS. Peter and Paul Church.
Hyland, James G. '42 (BRK) Retired.
Hyland, James M. '81 (CHI) [147] Chicago, IL Our Lady of Good Counsel Church.
Hyland, John M. '68 (DAV) Burlington, IA St. John's Church; Burlington, IA St. Paul's Church.
Hyland, Sean '84 (MIA) [12] Miami, FL Our Lady of the Holy Rosary Church.
Hyland, Terrance W. *o.s.a.* '71 (BO) [C] North Andover, MA Merrimack College.
Hyland, Thomas J. '63 (CLV) North Ridgeville, OH St. Peter Church.
Hyman, David L. *o.f.m.* '60 (CHR) Anderson, SC St.

Mary of the Angels Church.
Hyman, Robert A. '61 (TUC) Tubac, AZ St. Ann Church.
Hymel, Ray '87 (NO) Destrehan, LA St. Charles Borromeo Church.
Hymel, Stephen J. '90 (BR) Greenwell Springs, LA St. Alphonsus Liguori Church.
Hyndman, Ernest R., Jr. (MOB) [6] Mobile, AL Holy Family Church.
Hynes, Aidan '81 (PMB) Hobe Sound, FL St. Christopher Church.
Hynes, Gerald *c.p.* '51 (BAL) [91] Baltimore, MD St. Ursula Church.
Hynes, Gerald *c.p.* '51 (MET) [H] South River, NJ Passionist Provincial Office.
Hynes, James B. '94 (NY) New City, NY St. Augustine Church.
Hynes, James F. *o.f.m.* '80 (NY) [48] New York, NY Holy Name of Jesus Church.
Hynes, James M. '73 (SAT) [43] San Antonio, TX St. John Berchmans Church.
Hynes, James P. '49 (PRO) [5] West Warwick, RI St. James Church.
Hynes, John F. '55 (DAV) Le Claire-Princeton, IA Our Lady of the River Church.
Hynes, John J. '54 (NY) [194] Staten Island, NY St. Adalbert Church.
Hynes, John M. '65 (WIL) Wilmington, DE St. Catherine of Siena Church.
Hynes, Joseph P. '55 (PRO) [12] Pawtucket, RI St. Teresa Church.
Hynes, Patrick '85 (PIT) Canonsburg, PA St. Patrick Church.
Hynes, Richard P. (CHI) Western Springs, IL St. John of the Cross Church.
Hynes, Thomas J. *c.m.* '59 (PH) [Z] Philadelphia, PA Congregation of the Mission.
Hynes, Msgr. William '49 (SR) Sebastopol, CA St. Sebastian Church.
Hynous, David M. *o.p.* '59 (CHI) [N] Chicago, IL Dominicans (Provincial Office).
Hypolite, Douglas J. *s.j.* '80 (GAL) [F] Houston, TX Strake, Jesuit College Preparatory Inc.

I

Iacovacci, Nicholas J. '51 (PRO) [20] Providence, RI St. Mary's Church; Retired.
Iaia, Paul P. '56 (BAL) Buckeystown, MD St. Joseph-on-Carrollton Manor Church.
Ianieri, Stanley A. '89 (WIL) Sherwood Park, DE St. John the Beloved Church.
Iannarella, James M. '96 (PH) Aston, PA St. Joseph Church.
Iannetti, Lawrence '85 (WOR) Absent on Leave.
Iannone, Raphael *o.f.m.cap.* '64 (BRK) [U] Brooklyn, NY St. Michael's Friary.
Iannoni, Raphael *o.f.m.cap.* '64 (BRK) [87] Brooklyn, NY St. Michael's Church.
Iannotti, Pascal A. '61 (ALB) St. Johnsville, NY St. Patrick Church.
Iannuzzi, William (CAM) [3] Cherry Hill, NJ St. Peter Celestine Church.
Iantosca, August J. '77 (BRK) [200] Queens, NY St. Mel Church; Queens, NY Creedmoor Psychiatric Center.
Ianucci, Thomas A. '94 (RIC) Bristol, VA St. Anne Church.
Iaquinta, Patsy '70 (WH) Bluefield, WV Sacred Heart Church.
Iaquinto, Richard *o.s.b.* '68 (BUR) [G] Weston, VT Priory of Benedictine Monks.
Iaquinto, Robert M. '81 (NEW) [11] Jersey City, NJ Holy Rosary Church.
Iasiello, Louis V. *o.f.m.* '78 (NY) [Z] New York, NY Franciscan Friars, Order of Friars Manor.
Iavarone, Armand *o.ss.t.* '43 (BAL) [M] Baltimore, MD Holy Trinity Monastery.
Iavarone, Armand *o.ss.t.* '43 (NY) Spring Valley, NY St. Joseph Church.
Iazzetta, Frank J. (TR) Leave of Absence.
Ibach, Michael J. '73 (YAK) Selah, WA Our Lady of Lourdes Church.
Ibach, William D. *s.j.* '59 (BO) [W] Boston, MA Loyola House.
Ibanez, Armando *o.p.* '93 (LA) [S] Los Angeles, CA Monastery of the Angels (Contemplative).
Ibanez, Rodolfo '51 (BR) Retired.
Ibarra, Genaro (BWN) Rio Hondo, TX St. Helen Church.
Ibrahim, Ibrahim *b.s.o.* '87 (NTN) Brooklyn, OH St. Elias Church.
Ide, Harold J. '52 (MIL) Retired.
Idranyi, Edmund M. '54 (VNN) San Luis Obispo, CA Saint Anne Church.
Idsert, Beltran '51 (SJN) [8] Bayamon, PR Invencion de la Santa Cruz Church.
Idzik, George '74 (NEW) [5] Jersey City, NJ St. Ann's Church.
Iffert, Wilbert J. '52 (BEL) Retired.
Ifkovits, Edward M. *s.j.* '86 (CHL) Mars Hill, NC St. Andrew the Apostle Church; [J] Charlotte, NC Jesuit Community.
Igle, Edward A. '74 (CAM) Newfield, NJ St. Rose of Lima Church.
Iglesias, Clement M. '58 (BEA) Fannett, TX St. Mary Church.
Iglesias, Etelvino *o.a.r.* '61 (ORG) [3] Santa Ana, CA Our Lady of Guadalupe Church.
Iglesias, Fernando '56 (LA) Pico Rivera, CA St. Marianne de Paredes Church.
Iglesias, Luis Fernando '53 (CC) Retired.
Ignacio, Alex C. '74 (FRS) Lindsay, CA Sacred Heart Church.
Ignacio, Roberto '74 (TR) [1] Toms River, NJ St. Joseph Church.
Ignacio, Vimencio '89 (SB) Apple Valley, CA Our Lady of the Desert Church.
Ignaszak, Michael '84 (MIL) New Berlin, WI St. Elizabeth Ann Seton Church.
Igo, James P. '54 (OG) Retired.
Igoe, John T. '56 (BIR) [10] Birmingham, AL St. Joseph's Church.
Igoe, Martin S. '62 (BGP) [6] Greenwich, CT Sacred Heart Church.
Iheaka, Emmanuel '90 (LR) [7] Little Rock, AR Immaculate Conception Church.
Ihenacho, David '87 (MIL) [63] Milwaukee, WI All Saints Church.
Iheoha, Bernard (NY) [142] Bronx, NY St. Frances of Rome Church; Bronx, NY Our Lady of Mercy Medical Center; [S] New York, NY Our Lady of Mercy Medical Center.
Iheonunekwu, Alexander '77 (NY) [131] Bronx, NY St. Augustine Church.
Ihnatowicz, Janusz '62 (GAL) [Q] Houston, TX Residence of the Basilian Fathers of the University of St. Thomas.
Ihrie, Bernard R., Jr. '55 (WDC) Camp Springs, MD St. Philip the Apostle Church.
Ilano, J. Ven '96 (RIC) [3] Newport News, VA St. Jerome Church.
Ilicki, Theodosius *o.s.b.m.* '88 (STF) [B] Glen Cove, NY Basilian Fathers Novitiate of the Order of St. Basil the Great.
Ililau, John Paul '90 (CI) Babeldaob, FM Catholic Churches.
Illies, Wilfred '50 (SCL) Retired.
Illig, A. Mark '85 (BUF) Eggertsville, NY St. Benedict Church; [R] Williamsville, NY Newman Club Chaplains.
Illikattil, Mathew K. '71 (KAL) Three Rivers, MI Immaculate Conception Church.
Illo, Joseph '91 (STO) Hughson, CA St. Anthony Church.
Ilmberger, Clement F. '46 (SPC) Retired.
Ilnicki, Theodosius *o.s.b.m.* '88 (RVC) [N] Glen Cove, NY St. Josaphatis Monastery, Novitiate and Retreat House.
Im, Andrew Yong Min '89 (SAT) San Antonio, TX Korean Catholic Community Church.
Imbelli, Robert '66 (NY) On Duty Outside the Archdiocese.
Imberi, Anthony '62 (SFS) Military Chaplains.
Imfeld, Thomas '59 (LEX) Corbin, KY Sacred Heart Church.
Imfield, Thomas J. '59 (LEX) Retired.
Imgrund, Norman P. (ALT) Tyrone, PA St. Matthew's Church.
Imhof, James A. *s.m.* '51 (PCE) Villalba, PR Our Lady Mother of Divine Providence Church.
Imholte, Otto *s.s.c.* '63 (OM) [K] St. Columbans, NE St. Columban's Foreign Mission Society; [O] Omaha, NE Marriage Encounter.
Immegart, Placid *o.s.b.* '41 (KC) [J] Conception, MO Conception Abbey.
Immel, Joseph '49 (LAN) Retired.
Immel, William A. '53 (DET) Retired.
Imming, David B. '65 (OKL) Alva, OK Sacred Heart Church; Cherokee, OK St. Cornelius Church; [K] Norman, OK Campus Ministry for the Archdiocese of Oklahoma City.
Imming, Donald R. '60 (SFS) Platte, SD St. Peter the Apostle Church.
Imokhai, Charles '68 (NY) [1] New Rochelle, NY Blessed Sacrament Church.
Imperial, Francisco '59 (NY) [177] Bronx, NY Our Lady of Solace Church.
Imperiale, Roger A. *o.f.m.* '33 (NY) [Z] Mount Vernon, NY St. Bernardine of Siena Friary.
Imse, James L. '75 (SUP) Birchwood, WI St. John Evangelist Church; Dobie, WI Our Lady of Lourdes Church; Haugen, WI Holy Trinity Church.
Imse, James L. '75 (WOR) On Duty Outside the Diocese.
In Hwang, Dominic Hwa '87 (RIC) [11] Richmond, VA St. Kim Taegon Church; [L] Richmond, VA Ethnic and Special Ministries.
Inametti, Vincent B. *m.s.p.* '86 (FWT) [7] Fort Worth, TX Our Mother of Mercy Church.
Ince, Michael W. '64 (STP) Elysian, MN St. Andrew Holy Trinity, Waterville, MN Church; Waterville, MN Holy Trinity Church.
India, Stephen J. *c.m.* '49 (ALB) [L] Albany, NY Vincentian Fathers Residence.
Infante, Richard A. '92 (PIT) Monroeville, PA St. Bernadette Church.
Infantini, Joseph Xavier '76 (TR) [10] Trenton, NJ Our Lady of Sorrows Church.
Infiesta, Ramon Alvarez '80 (MGZ) [C] Mayaguez, PR Opus Dei (Prelature of the Holy Cross and Opus Dei).
Infuhr, Frank J. '49 (LA) Retired.
Ingalls, Fred D. '74 (BUF) Alden, NY St. John the Baptist Church.
Ingebretsen, Edward J. *s.j.* '81 (WDC) [M] Washington, DC The Jesuit Community at Georgetown University.
Ingels, Gregory '74 (SFR) Special Assignment.
Ingemie, Dominic '67 (ALB) [8] Albany, NY St. James Church.
Ingham, G. Nicholas *o.p.* '81 (PRO) [P] Providence, RI St. Thomas Aquinas Priory at Providence College.
Ingham, Jeffrey A. '75 (R) [3] Raleigh, NC Our Lady of Lourdes Church.
Inghilterra, Vincent J. '72 (TR) Military Chaplains.
Inglot, Mark '81 (LAN) [4] Jackson, MI Queen of the Miraculous Medal Church.
Ingnacio, Roberto '74 (SCR) Montgomery, PA Allenwood Prison.
Ingram, Brian '90 (RVC) Bellmore, NY St. Barnabas the Apostle Church.
Ingram, James A. '85 (ORL) On Duty Outside the Diocese.
Ingram, James A. '85 (SR) Petaluma, CA U.S. Coast Guard Training Center.
Inigo, Javier *c.m.* '61 (PCE) [8] Ponce, PR La Milagrosa Church.
Inigo, Juan J. *c.m.* (PCE) [B] Ponce, PR The Pontifical Catholic University of Puerto Rico.
Inkel, Roland '47 (BIR) Retired.
Inman, Leonard T. '61 (ALT) Retired.
Innes, Ben *o.f.m.* '84 (OAK) [A] Berkeley, CA Franciscan School of Theology Student Residence.
Innocenzi, James G. '76 (TR) [19] Trenton, NJ St. Michael Church.
Inoue, Jun *s.v.d.* '88 (WDC) [M] Washington, DC Divine Word College.
Inselvini, Sante *s.m.* '70 (BRK) [45] Brooklyn, NY St. Francis of Assisi-St. Blaise Church.
Inserra, Ceaser *o.f.m.conv.* '47 (LA) [R] Torrance, CA Franciscan Friars, St. Bonaventure Friary.
Intranuovo, Ralph *s.c.j.* '83 (SAT) [M] San Antonio, TX Priests of the Sacred Heart-House of Formation.
Introini, Msgr. Elso C. (PAT) Hawthorne, NJ St. Anthony's Church.
Introvigne, Raymond D. '64 (NOR) Taftville, CT Sacred Heart Church.
Inverardi, Luigi *i.m.c.* '70 (SB) [1] San Bernardino, CA Our Lady of the Rosary Cathedral.
Inverso, Leon J '85 (TR) Atlantic Highlands, NJ St. Agnes Church.
Inwanyanwu, Linus '83 (NY) [28] New York, NY Corpus Christi Church.
Inzeo, Lawrence C. '78 (NY) [1] White Plains, NY St. Anthony Church.
Inzina, Joseph Robert '60 (SHP) [3] Monroe, LA Our Lady of Fatima Church; Monroe, LA Louisiana Training Institute; Monroe, LA E.A. Conway Memorial Hospital; [G] Monroe, LA Catholic Campus Ministry at Northeast Louisiana University.
Iocco, Vincent V. '92 (WIL) New Castle, DE St. Peter Church.
Iorio, Peter '93 (KNX) [4] Chattanooga, TN St. Stephen Church.
Iott, Martin J. *o.p.* '70 (R) [E] Raleigh, NC Dominican Community; [E] Raleigh, NC De Porres House.
Iovino, Paul '61 (PAT) Totowa Borough, NJ St. James of the Marches Church.
Ipolito, Pascal D. '70 (BUF) [2] West Seneca, NY St. Catherine of Siena Church.
Irace, Dominic P. '75 (ARL) [1] Arlington, VA Cathedral of St. Thomas More.
Iraly, Matthew (NY) [195] Staten Island, NY St. Ann Church.
Ireland, Dave R. '83 (CLV) Wickliffe, OH Our Lady of Mount Carmel Church.
Ireland, Donald '63 (MIA) Retired.
Iriondo, Josu *c.r.l.* '62 (NY) [129] Bronx, NY St. Anthony of Padua Church; [DD] New York, NY Centro Carismatico Catolico Hispano De La Arquidiocesis De Nueva York; [DD] New York, NY Hispanic Catholic Charismatic Center of the Archdiocese of New York.
Irish, Robert L. '92 (LAN) [5] Ypsilanti, MI Holy Trinity Student Chapel; [J] Ypsilanti, MI Holy Trinity Student Chapel.
Irizarry, Alan '83 (ARE) [4] Utuado, PR Nuestra Senora del Monte Carmelo Church.
Irizarry, Rafael (ARE) On Duty Outside the Diocese.
Irizarry, Msgr. Raul '41 (PCE) Retired.
Iroz, Anthony *o.a.r.* '36 (LA) [8] Los Angeles, CA Cristo Rey Church.
Irrgang, Kenneth E. '68 (NU) Retired.
Irudayaraj, Savarimuthu '85 (WIL) [13] Wilmington,

DE St. Thomas Church; Newark, DE Medical Center of Delaware.
Irvin, Charles E. '67 (LAN) [1] Ann Arbor, MI St. Francis of Assisi Church.
Irving, Peter '83 (LA) Wilmington, CA SS. Peter and Paul's Church.
Irwin, Francis X. (BO) [4] Peabody, MA St. Joseph Church.
Irwin, James W. *c.s.c.* '65 (FTW) [J] South Bend, IN Congregation of Holy Cross Indiana Province Provincial House.
Irwin, Joseph F. '62 (NY) Mamaroneck, NY Holy Trinity Church.
Irwin, Kevin W. '71 (NY) On Duty Outside the Archdiocese.
Irwin, Kevin W. '71 (WDC) [C] Washington, DC Catholic University of America, The.
Irwin, Michael T. *f.s.s.p.* '64 (SCR) [M] Elmhurst, PA Priestly Fraternity of St. Peter (F.S.S.P.).
Irwin, Patrick '69 (SP) Valrico, FL St. Stephen Church.
Irwin, Patrick F. '59 (MAN) Durham, NH St. Thomas More Church.
Irwin, Robert C. (BAK) Pendleton, OR St. Mary's Church.
Irwin, Robert P. '78 (OM) Elkhorn, NE St. Patrick Church.
Irwin, William E. '64 (WIL) Ogletown, DE Holy Family Church.
Isacsson, Alfred J. *o.carm.* '58 (NY) Tarrytown, NY Transfiguration Church.
Ischay, Matthew A. '75 (CLV) [12] Cleveland, OH Blessed Sacrament Church.
Ischler, Paul *o.m.i.* '39 (STP) [N] St. Paul, MN Oblate Residence.
Isenecker, Lawrence E. *s.j.* '57 (DET) [P] Clarkston, MI Colombiere Center.
Isermann, William D. '56 (PEO) Retired.
Isern, Fernando '93 (MIA) [4] Pompano Beach, FL St. Elizabeth of Hungary Catholic Church.
Isho, Emanuel Hana '84 (EST) North Hollywood, CA St. Paul Assyrian-Chaldean Catholic Parish Church.
Isichei, Patrick '66 (LAN) [14] Flint, MI Sacred Heart Church.
Iskandar, Sabin '68 (EST) Southfield, MI Our Lady of Chaldeans Cathedral, Mother of God Chaldean Parish Church.
Isla, Elias *sch.p.* (NY) [65] New York, NY St. Jude Church.
Islas, Mario '70 (ELP) On Duty Outside of Diocese.
Isopo, Dominic '80 (ALB) [11] Schenectady, NY St. Luke Church.
Issac, Jose P. '75 (SB) [7] Riverside, CA St. Francis de Sales Church.
Issing, Daniel J. *c.s.c.* '90 (FR) [B] North Easton, MA Stonehill College.
Istok, Adolph *c.r.* '44 (CHI) [D] Chicago, IL Weber High School.
Isvanca, Alois '89 (ROM) Astoria, NY St. Mary Romanian Catholic Mission Church.
Iszczuk, Cyril *o.s.b.m.* '89 (STF) Long Island City, NY Holy Cross Church.
Itodo, Pius (LA) [65] Los Angeles, CA St. Gerard Majella Church.
Ittiyappara, Mathew '67 (SR) Yountville, CA St. Joan of Arc Church.
Iturbe, Rene *s.m.* '54 (MRY) [G] Santa Cruz, CA Society of Mary, Marists.
Iturbe, Rene *s.m.* '74 (MRY) Santa Cruz, CA Star of the Sea Church.
Iturraran, Jose Luis *o.de.m.* '63 (PCE) [9] Ponce, PR La Merced Church.
Itzaina, John *s.d.b.* '74 (OAK) [E] Richmond, CA Salesian High School.
Ivan, Nicholas '56 (PRM) Livonia, MI Sacred Heart Church.
Ivanauskas, Balys C. '39 (CLV) [25] Cleveland, OH St. George Church; Retired.
Ivans, Joseph *o.c.d.* '53 (GRY) [K] Munster, IN Discalced Carmelite Fathers Monastery.
Ivers, Msgr. Leslie J. '79 (NY) [148] Bronx, NY Holy Rosary Church.
Ivers, Michael T. '74 (CHI) [4] Chicago, IL St. Agatha Church.
Ivers, Victor J. '45 (CHI) Libertyville, IL St. Joseph Church; Retired.
Iverson, Msgr. Stanley J. '49 (NO) Retired.
Ivory, Msgr. Thomas P. '64 (NEW) New Milford, NJ Ascension Church.
Iwan, Januscz '76 (DET) Eastpointe, MI St. Veronica Church.
Iwaniec, Wieslaw '86 (SAT) Stockdale, TX St. Mary Church.
Iwanowski, Thomas B. '75 (NEW) [19] Jersey City, NJ Our Lady of Czestochowa Church.
Iwasiw, Nestor '93 (PHU) [1] Philadelphia, PA Immaculate Conception of Blessed Virgin Mary, Cathedral.
Iwele, Gode *o.m.i.* '88 (WDC) [B] Washington, DC Oblate College/Oblate Center for Mission Studies.
Iwuagwu, Nicholas '80 (NY) [182] Bronx, NY SS. Philip and James Church.
Iwuanyanwu, Linus (NY) Manhattan, NY Columbia Presbyterian Medical Center.
Iwuc, Anthony D. '53 (PRO) [2] Central Falls, RI St. Joseph's Church.
Iwuji, Matthew C. '74 (GRY) [1] Gary, IN Cathedral of Holy Angels.
Izac, Andre C. '64 (R) Buxton, NC Our Lady of the Seas Church.
Izac, Andre C. '64 (WDC) On Duty Outside the Archdiocese.
Izer, Wesley W. *s.d.b.* '77 (VNN) Phoenix, AZ St. Stephen Church; [A] Phoenix, AZ Salesians of Don Bosco
Izguierdo, William *l.c.* '94 (WDC) [M] Potomac, MD Legionaries of Christ.
Izquierdo, Jose Maria '53 (MIA) [D] Miami, FL Belen Jesuit Preparatory School; [H] Miami, FL Jesuit Fathers of the Province of the Antilles, Inc.
Izral, John '56 (BLX) Retired.
Izyk, Andrew (CHI) [45] Chicago, IL St. Constance Church.
Izzo, Januarius *o.f.m.* (TR) Roebling, NJ Holy Assumption Church.
Izzo, John *s.j.* '80 (BO) [W] Chestnut Hill, MA The Jesuit Community at Boston College.

J

Jablinske, Raymond D. '68 (WH) [5] (Mt. Olivet), WV Our Lady of Peace Church.
Jablonovsky, John Cyril *c.p.* '40 (CHI) [N] Chicago, IL Immaculate Conception Monastery.
Jablonowski, Anthony *c.m.m.i.* '70 (CHY) On Duty Outside the Diocese.
Jablonowski, Anthony *c.m.m.i.* '70 (TUC) Patagonia, AZ St. Theresa Church.
Jablonowski, James N. '68 (MIL) [32] Milwaukee, WI St. Hedwig Church.
Jablonske, William J. '61 (LC) Weston, WI St. Agnes Church.
Jablonski, Edward J. '96 (PH) [2] Philadelphia, PA St. Adalbert Church.
Jablonski, Joseph *m.s.c.* '76 (RCK) [H] Aurora, IL Missionaries of the Sacred Heart Community.
Jablonski, Msgr. Stanislaus '41 (NY) [192] Bronx, NY St. Valentine Church; Retired.
Jablonski, Msgr. William W. '63 (RVC) East Rockaway, NY St. Raymond's Church.
Jabo, Scott W. '90 (E) St. Marys, PA Sacred Heart of Jesus Church; [C] Saint Marys, PA Elk County Christian High School.
Jabusch, Willard F. '56 (CHI) [V] Chicago, IL Ministry in Higher Education; [X] Wilmette, IL Musica Pacis.
Jach, Edward M. *s.m.* '64 (CIN) [27] Cincinnati, OH St. Francis de Sales Church; [M] Cincinnati, OH Marianist Community.
Jach, Edward M. *s.m.* '64 (STL) [P] St. Louis, MO Provincialate of the Society of Mary, Province of St. Louis
Jack, Cuthbert A. *o.s.b.* '90 (GBG) [H] Latrobe, PA Saint Vincent Archabbey.
Jack, Duane C. '67 (PEO) Kewanee, IL St. Mary's Catholic Church.
Jack, John Robert '92 (CIN) [13] Cincinnati, OH Assumption Church.
Jackanich, Msgr. Joseph '26 (PSC) Retired.
Jackels, Michael O. '81 (LIN) [1] Lincoln, NE Cathedral of the Risen Christ.
Jackiewicz, F. W. (TR) [R] Princeton, NJ Campus Ministry for the Diocese of Trenton.
Jackiewicz, Frederick W. '71 (TR) West Long Branch, NJ St. Jerome Church.
Jackovic, George V. '46 (PIT) Retired.
Jackson, Charles '55 (MIA) Retired.
Jackson, Charles A. '60 (COL) [A] Columbus, OH Pontifical College Josephinum.
Jackson, David *s.c.j.* '66 (BWN) Lyford, TX Prince of Peace Church.
Jackson, Donald F. '59 (TUC) San Manuel, AZ St. Bartholomew Church.
Jackson, Edward W. *c.ss.r.* '49 (HBG) Ephrata, PA Mother of Perpetual Help Church; [H] Ephrata, PA St. Clement's Mission House.
Jackson, James '60 (STP) Minneapolis, MN Hennepin County Courts; Special Assignment.
Jackson, James '85 (WCH) On Duty Outside the Diocese.
Jackson, James A. *m.m.* '48 (SJ) [M] Los Altos, CA Maryknoll.
Jackson, James J. '72 (SUP) Spooner, WI St. Francis De Sales Church.
Jackson, James M. '75 (WIL) Claymont, DE Holy Rosary Church.
Jackson, James W. '60 (STP) [K] St. Paul, MN Our Lady of Good Counsel Home.
Jackson, James W. *f.s.s.p.* '85 (SCR) [M] Elmhurst, PA Priestly Fraternity of St. Peter (F.S.S.P.).
Jackson, Joseph M. '74 (CHI) Palatine, IL St. Thomas of Villanova Church.
Jackson, Lawrence J. '60 (DET) [7] Sterling Heights, MI St. Michael Church.
Jackson, Owen R. *o.s.a.* '65 (PH) [C] Villanova, PA Villanova University.
Jackson, Raymond A. *c.s.b.* '58 (VIC) Wharton, TX Our Lady of Mt. Carmel Church.
Jackson, Robert '54 (RCK) [D] Belvidere, IL Saint Joseph Hospital.
Jackson, Robert H. '84 (CLV) Brunswick, OH St. Ambrose Church.
Jackson, Thomas *o.p.* '92 (CHI) [24] Chicago, IL St. Basil/Visitation Church.
Jackson, William J. *c.s.sp.* '58 (VEN) [G] Sarasota, FL Congregation of the Holy Ghost.
Jacmierski, Jan '60 (NY) [5] Poughkeepsie, NY St. Joseph Church.
Jacob, Anthony J. *o.s.b.* '65 (JOL) [C] Lisle, IL Benet Academy; [J] Lisle, IL St. Procopius Abbey.
Jacob, William *c.ss.r.* '46 (NY) [23] New York, NY St. Cecilia Church.
Jacobberger, Joseph '65 (P) [1] Portland, OR Cathedral of the Immaculate Conception.
Jacobi, Arthur H., Jr. '81 (DET) Centerline, MI St. Clement Church.
Jacobi, Donald (DM) Harlan, IA St. Michael Church.
Jacobi, Joseph A. '91 (OKL) Guymon, OK St. Peter's Church; [K] Norman, OK Campus Ministry for the Archdiocese of Oklahoma City.
Jacobowski, Raymond G. '61 (PEO) On Duty Outside the Diocese.
Jacobs, Allen A. '66 (R) Retired.
Jacobs, Charles E. '39 (LAN) Flushing, MI St. Robert Church; Retired.
Jacobs, Charles E. '86 (HRT) [8] Hartford, CT St. Augustine Church.
Jacobs, David E. '75 (LR) Texarkana, AR St. Edward's Church.
Jacobs, Eugene S. '46 (WH) Retired.
Jacobs, Gilbert H. *o.praem.* '55 (GB) Cleveland, WI St. Wendel Church.
Jacobs, Harry W. '73 (WDC) [42] Washington, DC St. Thomas Apostle Church.
Jacobs, James J. '74 (SCR) [4] Plymouth, PA St. Vincent de Paul Church; [R] Plymouth, PA Emmaus Spirituality Program for Priests.
Jacobs, James T. '43 (GB) Retired.
Jacobs, Joseph A. '40 (FTW) Retired.
Jacobs, Peter '55 (WDC) On Duty Outside the Archdiocese.
Jacobs, Philip '74 (COL) On Duty Outside the Diocese.
Jacobs, Pierre P. *s.j.* '44 (SFR) [N] San Francisco, CA Jesuit Community at University of San Francisco.
Jacobs, Richard A. (PAT) Retired.
Jacobs, Richard M. *o.s.a.* '83 (CHI) [N] Olympia Fields, IL The Augustinian Provincialate Tolentine Center.
Jacobs, Timothy *ss.cc.* '35 (HON) [H] Honolulu, HI St. Patrick's Monastery.
Jacobsen, James E. *s.j.* '59 (P) [L] Portland, OR Jesuit Provincial Office (Oregon Prov.).
Jacobsmeyer, Gregory H. *s.j.* '46 (STL) [P] St. Louis, MO Hallahan House.
Jacobson, Clifford '96 (CHY) Casper, WY St. Anthony of Padua Church.
Jacobson, Gary '65 (P) [1] Portland, OR Cathedral of the Immaculate Conception.
Jacobson, James *s.j.* '59 (P) Salem, OR Oregon State Penitentiary; Salem, OR Santiam Correctional Institution; Salem, OR Mill Creek Correctional Facility.
Jacolino, Dominic '41 (NY) Retired; [Z] New York, NY Pope John Paul II Residence.
Jacquel, John B. '83 (E) Edinboro, PA Our Lady of the Lake Church.
Jacquemin, George P. '72 (CIN) [10] Cincinnati, OH St. Anthony Church.
Jacquemin, John M. '39 (CIN) Retired; [B] Cincinnati, OH Mt. St. Mary's Seminary of the West.
Jacques, Alfred '60 (PRT) Rumford, ME St. Athanasius-St. John Church.
Jacques, Donald W. '53 (PRT) Brunswick, ME St. Charles Church.
Jacques, E. J. *s.j.* '66 (MOB) [9] Mobile, AL St. Joseph Church.
Jacques, Eugene F. '80 (NO) [20] New Orleans, LA Our Lady Star Of The Sea Church.
Jacques, Kenneth *o.s.b.* '67 (P) Gervais, OR Sacred Heart-St. Louis Church; [L] St. Benedict, OR Mt. Angel Abbey.
Jacques, Michael P. *s.s.e.* '82 (NO) [51] New Orleans, LA St. Peter Claver Church; [53] New Orleans, LA St. Philip the Apostle Church.
Jacques, Roger N. '78 (BO) [2] Waltham, MA St. Joseph Church.
Jacubco, Bernard *m.s.c.* '64 (OG) Glenfield, NY St. Mary Church.
Jacunski, Robert D. '56 (NEW) Caldwell, NJ St. Aloysius Church.
Jadaa, John '46 (NTN) Retired.
Jadgchew, John *c.pp.s.* '75 (CIN) [B] Carthagena, OH St. Charles.
Jadin, Samuel D. *o.praem.* '55 (GB) [J] Manitowoc, WI Holy Family Convent of Franciscan Sisters of Christian Charity.
Jadwisiak, Edmund '79 (PRM) Parma, OH Saint John the Baptist, Cathedral.
Jaeb, Maurus P. *o.s.b.* '95 (LA) Montebello, CA St.

Benedict Church.
Jaeb, Maurus P. *o.s.b.* '95 (OKL) [I] Shawnee, OK St. Gregory's Abbey.
Jaeger, David '69 (SEA) Special Assignment.
Jaeger, David '86 (AUS) [16] Austin, TX St. Louis Church.
Jaeger, James '86 (ROC) Hornell, NY St. Ann Church.
Jaeger, Louis M. '73 (DUB) Epworth, IA St. Patrick's Church.
Jaeger, Robert E. '90 (COS) Monument, CO St. Peter Church.
Jaekle, Lawrence E. '38 (CIN) Retired.
Jaenicke, Alfred J. '54 (HRT) [13] Hartford, CT St. Michael Church.
Jagdfeld, Laurence '75 (CHI) [N] Chicago, IL The Holy Evangelists Friary.
Jagielski, James '77 (DET) Military Chaplains.
Jagodensky, Joe *s.d.s.* '80 (MIL) [N] Milwaukee, WI Alexian Village of Milwaukee, Inc.
Jagodzinski, Charles *ofm conv.* '68 (BUF) [D] Athol Springs, NY St. Francis High School; [O] Athol Springs, NY St. Francis of Assisi Friary.
Jagodzinski, Chester C. '45 (PEO) Retired.
Jagodzinski, Msgr. Jan '54 (DET) [A] Orchard Lake, MI SS. Cyril and Methodius Seminary.
Jagodzinski, Msgr. John J. '62 (PH) Wayne, PA St. Katharine of Siena Church.
Jagoe, Bede R. *o.p.* '60 (CHI) [N] Chicago, IL Dominicans (Provincial Office).
Jagosz, Mitchell '86 (ORG) Inactive Leave.
Jahner, Anton P. *s.j.* '67 (SPK) [K] Spokane, WA Regis Community.
Jakanovich, Roberto *o.m.v.* '87 (BO) [B] Boston, MA Oblate Provincialate.
Jakel, Pat G. '85 (SFD) Nokomis, IL St. Louis Church; Witt, IL St. Barbara Church.
Jakobiak, Arthur '56 (SFE) Santa Fe, NM St. Vincent's Hospital.
Jakows, Ronald M. '90 (PH) [2] Philadelphia, PA St. Adalbert Church; [58] Philadelphia, PA Holy Cross Church; [D] Philadelphia, PA Roman Catholic High School for Boys.
Jaksina, Edward S. '55 (HRT) Seymour, CT Good Shepherd Church.
Jakubco, Bernard '64 (OG) Houseville, NY St. Hedwig Church; Lowville, NY St. Peter Church.
Jakubek, Eugene *s.j.* '54 (OM) [C] Omaha, NE Creighton Preparatory School.
Jakubiec, Bronislaw *s.d.s.* '81 (GRY) [K] Merrillville, IN Salvatorian Fathers (Society of the Divine Savior).
Jakubik, Emil (SY) Retired.
Jakubik, Richard J. '93 (CHI) Glenview, IL Our Lady of Perpetual Help Church.
Jakubowski, Allen F. '75 (LC) Abbotsford, WI St. Bernard Church; Owen, WI Holy Rosary Church.
Jakubowski, Joseph J. '40 (KC) Retired.
Jakubowski, Kenneth J. '91 (CLV) [5] Lakewood, OH St. Luke Church.
Jalbert, Edward *c.j.* '87 (LA) [B] Santa Maria, CA St. Joseph Seminary (Josephite Fathers' Novitiate); [D] Santa Maria, CA St. Joseph High School.
Jalbert, Marcel '38 (SB) Retired.
Jallas, Robert J. '84 (SFD) [4] Alton, IL St. Matthew Church.
Jamail, Msgr. James A. '68 (GAL) [77] Houston, TX St. Vincent de Paul Church.
Jamail, Michael A. '60 (BEA) [2] Beaumont, TX St. Anne Church.
James, Albert *s.m.a.* '73 (NEW) [N] Tenafly, NJ Society of African Missions, Provincialate, S.M.A. Fathers.
James, David J. '91 (SY) Cicero, NY Sacred Heart Church.
James, David L. '96 (ALN) [1] Allentown, PA Cathedral of St. Catharine of Siena.
James, Frank *s.p.* '69 (SB) [G] Cherry Valley, CA Servants of the Paraclete Guadalupe Retreat Center.
James, Joseph '94 (Y) [16] Youngstown, OH St. Joseph Church.
James, Msgr. Joseph W. '57 (LUB) Idalou, TX St. Philip Benizi Church; [C] Slaton, TX Our Lady of Mercy Retreat Center.
James, Melvin P. *s.v.d.* '75 (LA) [71] Los Angeles, CA St. John, The Evangelist Church.
James, Peter Paul *o.f.m.* '51 (CIN) [M] Cincinnati, OH St. Francis Seraph Friary.
James, Msgr. R. Joseph '61 (STA) [9] Jacksonville, FL Mary Queen of Heaven Church.
James, Thomas *s.v.d.* '69 (LAF) [4] New Iberia, LA St. Edward Church.
James, Thomas *s.v.d.* '96 (BLX) [E] Bay St. Louis, MS Southern Province of St. Augustine - Provincial Residence.
James, V. Warwick '80 (SJ) [4] Santa Clara, CA St. Lawrence the Martyr Church.
James, Msgr. William R. '54 (MOB) Robertsdale, AL St. Patrick Church.
Jameson, Msgr. W. Ronald '68 (WDC) [1] Washington, DC St. Matthew Cathedral.
Jamieson, Andrew *o.f.m.cap.* '88 (NEW) [5] Hoboken, NJ St. Ann's Church.
Jamison, Dale *o.f.m.* '74 (GLP) Zuni, NM St. Anthony Indian Mission, Our Lady of Guadalupe Church.
Jamme, Albert *m.afr.* '41 (WDC) [M] Washington, DC Missionaries of Africa.
Jammes, Jean Marie (LAF) Retired.
Jammes, Jean Marie '43 (LAF) St. Martinville, LA St. Martin of Tours Church.
Jammo, Sarhad '64 (EST) Troy, MI St. Joseph Chaldean Parish Church.
Jamnicky, John A. '72 (CHI) Chicago, IL Chicago O'Hare International Airport; [X] Chicago, IL Catholic Chaplaincy at O'Hare.
Jamros, Daniel P. *s.j.* '76 (BO) [W] Boston, MA The Society of Jesus of New England-Provincial Offices.
Jamros, Daniel P. *s.j.* '76 (BUF) [O] Buffalo, NY Canisius Jesuit Community.
Jamroz, Waclaw *s.d.s.* '90 (GRY) [K] Merrillville, IN Salvatorian Fathers (Society of the Divine Savior).
Jamula, Joseph M. '42 (WH) Retired.
Janacek, Msgr. Balthasar J. '50 (SAT) [1] San Antonio, TX Cathedral of San Fernando; San Antonio, TX Old Spanish Missions Church; [S] San Antonio, TX National Foundation for Mexican-American Vocations.
Janaczek, Joseph J. '71 (BUF) [1] Dunkirk, NY St. Hedwig Church.
Janaites, Stanley '55 (BAL) Sykesville, MD Springfield Hospital Center; Special Assignment.
Janak, Gary W. *j.c.l.* '88 (VIC) Yoakum, TX St. Joseph Church.
Janasik, Basil *o.f.m.* '45 (MIL) [P] Burlington, WI Queen of Peace Friary.
Jancarz, Janusz *s.ch.* '83 (VEN) Parrish, FL St. Francis Xavier Cabrini Church.
Jancius, John *m.i.c.* '34 (CHI) [N] Chicago, IL Congregation of Marian Fathers of the Immaculate Conception.
Janczukowicz, Msgr. Chester '48 (WOR) Webster, MA St. Joseph's Church.
Janda, James A.. '72 (SLC) [3] Salt Lake City, UT Our Lady of Lourdes Church.
Jandernoa, Ronald J. '94 (MET) Sayreville, NJ Our Lady of Victories Church; [A] South Amboy, NJ St. Mary Regional High School.
Janecek, James E. '95 (CC) [4] Corpus Christi, TX Holy Family Church; Alice, TX St. Joseph Church.
Janeck, Thomas More *o.f.m.cap.* '46 (DEN) [M] Denver, CO St. Francis of Assisi Friary; [N] Denver, CO Monastery of Our Lady of Light (Capuchin Poor Clares).
Janeczek, Vladimir '59 (GRY) [3] Hammond, IN St. Casimir Church.
Janelli, Msgr. Anthony '64 (FRS) Dinuba, CA St. Catherine Church.
Janer, Walter *s.j.* (SJN) [22] San Juan, PR San Ignacio de Loyola Church.
Janes, David A. '83 (SFS) De Smet, SD St. Thomas Aquinas Church.
Janesko, Francis J. (LR) Retired.
Janesko, John A. '52 (LR) Stuttgart, AR Holy Rosary Church; [L] Stuttgart, AR Holy Rosary Catholic School "Vision 2000" Educational Trust Fund.
Janette, Paul D. '63 (MIL) Special Assignment.
Janezic, Lawrence *o.f.m.* '78 (SAT) [69] San Antonio, TX San Francisco de la Espada Church.
Janiak, Anthony J. '42 (CHI) Retired.
Janicki, Carl F. '94 (PH) [21] Philadelphia, PA St. Bartholomew Church.
Janicki, Joseph A. '64 (MIL) [4] Menomonee Falls, WI St. Mary's Church.
Janicki, Laurian *o.f.m.* '64 (JOL) Wayne, IL Resurrection Church.
Janiga, Bruce G. '83 (NEW) [C] West Orange, NJ Seton Hall Preparatory School.
Janiga, Joseph '45 (DET) Retired.
Janik, Anthony F. *o.f.m.* '70 (GRY) [G] Crown Point, IN St. Anthony Medical Center, Inc.; [I] Crown Point, IN St. Anthony Home, Inc.; [K] Cedar Lake, IN Our Lady of Lourdes Friary.
Janik, Bruno '66 (CHI) Burbank, IL St. Albert the Great Church.
Janik, Leszek T. '92 (NOR) Old Lyme, CT Christ the King Church.
Janish, James '69 (SAT) Spring Branch, TX St. Joseph Church.
Janiszeski, Joseph *t.o.r.* '78 (FWT) [8] Fort Worth, TX St. Andrew Church.
Janiunas, Albin F. (BO) Retired.
Jankaitis, Ronald V. '79 (ALN) [2] Saint Clair, PA St. Casimir Church; [C] Pottsville, PA Nativity B.V.M. High School.
Janko, Jack *s.d.b.* '78 (BO) [N] Boston, MA Salesian Boys & Girls Club.
Jankowiak, Patrick '92 (SAG) [17] Saginaw, MI St. Stephen Church.
Jankowiak, Valentine A. '38 (ROC) [56] Rochester, NY St. Stanislaus Church; Retired.
Jankowski, Daniel C. '73 (CHI) [G] Chicago, IL Catholic Charities of the Archdiocese of Chicago-Archdiocesan Offices.
Jankowski, Marcellus A. (KC) Special Assignment.
Jankowski, Peter '96 (JOL) West Chicago, IL St. Mary Church.
Jankowski, Richard '92 (SP) [3] St. Petersburg, FL Holy Cross Church.
Jankowski, Valentine *o.f.m.conv.* '61 (LSC) Hobbs, NM St. Helena Church; Jal, NM St. Cecilia Church.
Jann, Francis J. '47 (BUF) Belfast, NY St. Patrick Church; Rushford, NY St. Mark Church.
Jannetta, Frank *o.f.m.* '79 (NY) [Z] New York, NY Franciscan Province of the Immaculate Conception.
Janning, Timothy J. '82 (CIN) Military Chaplains.
Janning, Timothy J. '82 (ORG) Tustin, CA Marine Corps Air Station.
Janocha, Carl W. '91 (OKL) Watonga, OK St. Rose of Lima Church.
Janoski, Steven A. '88 (SFD) Troy, IL St. Jerome Church.
Janovec, James J. '64 (GI) Valentine, NE St. Nicholas Church.
Janowiak, Paul A. *s.j.* '84 (SEA) [A] Seattle, WA Seattle University.
Janowicz, Barney '57 (SAG) Pigeon, MI St. Francis Borgia Church.
Janowicz, Richard '80 (STN) Springfield, OR Nativity of the Mother of God Church.
Janowski, Rock '64 (LA) Simi Valley, CA St. Peter Claver Church.
Janowski, Stanley *o.f.m.* '66 (CHI) [N] Chicago, IL Holy Name Friary-Franciscan House of Formation.
Janowski, Wieslaw *c.r.* (CHI) [88] Chicago, IL St. Hyacinth Church.
Jansch, Ronald *o.f.m.cap.* '50 (MIL) [P] Mount Calvary, WI St. Lawrence Friary.
Jansen, James H. '55 (BEL) Fairview Heights, IL Our Lady of the Assumption Church.
Janski, Jerome J. '50 (STP) Retired.
Janson, Eugene '76 (SAT) [K] San Antonio, TX Padua Place.
Janson, Eugene '76 (VIC) Retired.
Janson, Leo F. '45 (GF) Retired.
Janson, Richard J. *c.m.* '77 (STL) [P] St. Louis, MO Vincentian-St. Lazare Residence.
Jansonis, Alphonse B. '45 (BO) Permanent Disability.
Janssen, Henri *o.m.i.* '48 (BWN) San Juan, TX Virgen de San Juan del Valle Shrine Church; [I] San Juan, TX Virgen de San Juan del Valle Shrine.
Janssen, James M. '48 (DAV) Retired; [M] Davenport, IA St. Vincent Center.
Janssen, Orville H. '52 (GB) [2] Appleton, WI St. Bernard Church; Retired.
Jansze, Neville '86 (STO) Modesto, CA St. Joseph Church.
Janton, Anthony W. '77 (PH) [46] Philadelphia, PA St. Francis de Sales Church.
Janus, Mark-David *c.s.p.* '79 (NY) [Z] Scarsdale, NY Paulist Fathers Generalate.
Januszkiewicz, Henry '62 (WDC) Retired.
Janze, John E. '73 (ORG) Irvine, CA St. Thomas More Church.
Jaquemine, George P. '72 (CIN) [2] Cincinnati, OH St. Agnes Church.
Jaramillo, Cesar *c.ss.r.* '41 (MGZ) Aguadilla, PR St. Charles Borromeo Church.
Jaramillo, Fabio E. '81 (NY) [89] New York, NY Our Lady of Lourdes Church.
Jaramillo, Luis '95 (HRT) [5] Meriden, CT St. Rose of Lima Church.
Jaramillo, Luis D. '60 (SFE) [10] Albuquerque, NM Our Lady of the Assumption Church.
Jaramillo, Oscar '90 (B) On Duty Outside the Diocese.
Jaramillo, Peter '81 (AMA) Absent on Leave.
Jaramillo, Roberto '93 (SAC) [5] Sacramento, CA Our Lady of Guadalupe Shrine Church.
Jaranilla, Roberto F., Jr. '96 (LA) [7] Los Angeles, CA Christ the King Church.
Jarboe, J. Bruce '86 (BAL) Special Assignment.
Jarboe, W. Raymond '89 (BAK) Ontario, OR Blessed Sacrament Church.
Jarco, Emil *s.d.s.* '74 (GRY) [K] Merrillville, IN Salvatorian Fathers (Society of the Divine Savior).
Jarcynski, Eugene T. *c.s.c.* '55 (RVC) Northport, NY Veteran's Hospital.
Jardiniano, Rolly '84 (LA) Whittier, CA St. Gregory the Great Church.
Jarecki, Michael S. '44 (OG) Brushton, NY St. Mary Church; Retired.
Jarecki, Reynold *o.f.m.* '55 (MIL) [P] Burlington, WI Queen of Peace Friary.
Jarema, William '83 (COS) [3] Colorado Springs, CO Divine Redeemer Church.
Jarema, William '88 (COS) [H] Colorado Springs, CO Catholic Charismatic Renewal Services.
Jarka, Thomas H. '59 (CAM) [6] Cherry Hill, NJ Queen of Heaven Church.
Jarmak, Claude *o.f.m.conv.* '54 (SPR) [A] Granby, MA St. Hyacinth College and Seminary.
Jarmoluk, Joseph F. '84 (RCK) Mount Carroll, IL SS. John and Catherine Church; Savanna, IL St. John the Baptist Church.
Jarnot, Clement *o.f.m.conv.* '65 (BAL) [M] Ellicott City, MD Order of Friars Minor Conventual.

Jarnot, Clement *o.f.m.conv.* '65 (NOR) [3] Middletown, CT St. Mary of Czestochowa Church.
Jarosch, Eugene H. *s.a.c.* '51 (MIL) [P] Milwaukee, WI Pallotti House.
Jarosewic, Daniel F. '71 (CHI) [1] Oak Lawn, IL St. Catherine of Alexandria Church.
Jarosz, Joseph B. '62 (PH) [146] Philadelphia, PA St. Stanislaus Church.
Jarosz, Peter '89 (JOL) Roselle, IL St. Walter Church.
Jarosz, Stanley '65 (MET) Helmetta, NJ Holy Trinity Church.
Jaroszeski, Paul A. '76 (STP) [18] St. Paul, MN St. Cecilia Church.
Jarreau, Martin V. *s.j.* '36 (NO) [F] New Orleans, LA Jesuit High School.
Jarreau, Martin V. *s.j.* '49 (NO) [S] New Orleans, LA Jesuit Seminary and Mission Bureau.
Jarrell, Stephen '73 (IND) Greenwood, IN SS. Francis and Clare of Assisi Church.
Jarret, Peter A. *c.s.c.* '91 (FTW) Granger, IN St. Pius X Church.
Jarumbo, James J. '66 (MIL) [3] Sheboygan, WI St. Dominic Church.
Jarvais, Msgr. Walter G. '30 (NEW) Retired; [A] South Orange, NJ Seton Hall University College Seminary; [B] South Orange, NJ Seton Hall University; [N] Rutherford, NJ St. John Vianney Residence for Priests.
Jarvis, Edward A. *s.j.* '54 (PH) [82] Philadelphia, PA Old St. Joseph's Church.
Jarzombek, Casey '60 (VIC) Palacios, TX St. Anthony's Church.
Jarzombek, Dennis A. '79 (SAT) [56] San Antonio, TX St. Mary Magdalen Church.
Jarzynski, Edward A. (CHI) Retired.
Jasaitis, Raymond J. '62 (PAT) Retired; [P] Chester, NJ Nazareth Village.
Jasany, Robert J. '79 (CLV) [1] Lakewood, OH St. Clement Church.
Jasinski, Msgr. Anthony J. '49 (BUF) [9] Cheektowaga, NY St. Philip the Apostle Church; Retired.
Jasinski, John B. (SB) Military Chaplains.
Jasinski, Kazimierz '78 (DET) [H] Livonia, MI St. Mary Hospital.
Jasinski, Paul F. *c.s.v.* '46 (JOL) Goodrich, IL Sacred Heart Church.
Jasinski, Raymond J. (CHI) Retired.
Jaskula, Edward J. *c.r.* '55 (CHI) [D] Chicago, IL Gordon Technical High School.
Jaskulski, Bronislaus *o.f.m.* '46 (GRY) [K] Cedar Lake, IN Our Lady of Lourdes Friary.
Jaskulski, George *o.f.m.* '55 (CLV) [P] Cleveland, OH St. Stanislaus Friary; [Q] Cleveland, OH Marymount Congregational Home.
Jasper, Frank *o.f.m.* '73 (IND) [13] Indianapolis, IN Sacred Heart of Jesus Church.
Jasper, Louis H. '51 (COV) Retired.
Jaspers, J. Dennis '66 (CIN) [3] Cincinnati, OH All Saints Church.
Jaspers, Louis *c.i.c.m.* '52 (SAT) [36] San Antonio, TX St. Gabriel Church.
Jasso, Stephen *t.o.r.* '65 (FWT) [2] Fort Worth, TX All Saints Church.
Jastrab, David J. '75 (PIT) [63] Pittsburgh, PA Prince of Peace Church.
Jastrzebski, Edmund *c.r.* '74 (CHI) [192] Chicago, IL St. Stanislaus, Bishop and Martyr Church.
Jaszovsky, Joseph '31 (SFR) Retired; [K] San Francisco, CA Home for the Aged of the Little Sisters of the Poor.
Jatsiv, Myroslav '94 (STF) West Islip, NY Holy Family Church.
Jaume, John *c.r.* '66 (NY) Plattekill, NY Our Lady of Fatima Church.
Jautz, Martin L. '44 (MIL) Retired.
Java, Michael '73 (LA) Baldwin Park, CA St. John the Baptist Church.
Javor, Egon J. *o.s.b.* '41 (SFR) San Francisco, CA Knights of Malta; [N] Portola Valley, CA Woodside Priory.
Jawidzik, Edward M. '81 (TR) Belmar, NJ St. Rose Church.
Jaworowski, Msgr. Anthony E. '44 (PH) [2] Philadelphia, PA St. Adalbert Church; Swedesburg, PA Sacred Heart Church; Retired.
Jaworowski, Leon E. '43 (PH) Retired.
Jaworski, Sylvester *s.v.d.* '47 (MIL) [P] East Troy, WI Divine Word Seminary.
Jayachandra, Hermanagild '68 (DEN) [8] Denver, CO Church of the Good Shepherd.
Jayaraj, M. Jones '83 (TR) Brick Town, NJ St. Dominic Church.
Jayme, Eduardo *o.f.m.* '81 (CC) Hebbronville, TX Our Lady of Guadalupe Church.
Jazbec, Stanley '44 (SB) Retired.
Jazmines, Vincente '79 (OG) Gouverneur, NY St. James Church.
Jazowski, Msgr. John F. '48 (BGP) [2] Stamford, CT St. Bridget Church; Retired.
Jazwiecki, John *s.m.* (CLV) Bedford, OH St. Pius X Church.
Jean, Agapit H., Jr. '95 (MAN) Exeter, NH St. Michael Church.
Jean, Franky '93 (MIA) Miramar, FL St. Bartholomew Church.
Jean, Raymond J. '57 (NOR) Absent on Leave.
Jeanfreau, James J., Jr. '92 (NO) [5] Metairie, LA St. Catherine of Siena Church.
Jeannot, Leandre '70 (BO) [41] Boston, MA St. Leo Church.
Jecewiz, Jerome T. '75 (BRK) [60] Brooklyn, NY Holy Spirit Church.
Jedrychowski, Janus '95 (STF) Rochester, NY St. Josaphat Church.
Jedrzejewski, Richard A. '74 (BUF) [3] Dunkirk, NY St. Hyacinth Church.
Jeffers, Brian E. '92 (ROC) Geneva, NY St. Stephen Church.
Jeffers, Robert A. '54 (NY) [162] Bronx, NY St. Margaret Mary Church; Bronx, NY Bronx-Lebanon Hospital Center.
Jeffers, Msgr. Vincent W. '31 (NY) Retired; [E] White Plains, NY Archbishop Stepinac High School.
Jeffrey, C. James '59 (FAR) Cavalier, ND St. Bridget's Church.
Jeffrey, Donald *m.s.* '64 (MAN) West Lebanon, NH Holy Redeemer Church.
Jeffrey, George A. '65 (SCR) [20] Wilkes-Barre, PA St. Therese's Church.
Jeffries, Brian E. '73 (HRT) Seymour, CT St. Augustine's Church.
Jelenek, Matthew M. '96 (NY) Beacon, NY St. John Evangelist Church.
Jelinek, Anthony (MIL) [N] Kenosha, WI St. Joseph's Home for the Aged.
Jelinek, John P. *s.j.* '47 (OM) [K] Omaha, NE Jesuit Community At Creighton University.
Jelly, Frederick M. *o.p.* '56 (BAL) [A] Emmitsburg, MD Mount St. Mary's Seminary.
Jendersyk, Mark (JOL) Coal City, IL Assumption Church.
Jendrek, Michael J. '87 (BAL) [40] Baltimore, MD Immaculate Heart of Mary Church.
Jendzura, John M. '47 (PIT) [P] Bethel Park, PA Holy Ghost Animation Center.
Jenemann, Albert H. *s.j.* '60 (PH) [C] Philadelphia, PA St. Joseph's University; [Z] Philadelphia, PA Jesuit Community at St. Joseph's University.
Jenik, Msgr. John J. '70 (NY) [176] Bronx, NY Our Lady of Refuge Church.
Jenkins, Floyd A. *s.j.* '48 (LA) [C] Los Angeles, CA Loyola Marymount University.
Jenkins, J. Michael '79 (SFD) Collinsville, IL SS. Peter and Paul Church.
Jenkins, J. Wayne '72 (L) [34] Louisville, KY Holy Spirit Church; [35] Louisville, KY Holy Trinity Church.
Jenkins, John *c.s.c.* '83 (FTW) [A] Notre Dame, IN Moreau Seminary; [B] Notre Dame, IN University of Notre Dame Du Lac.
Jenkins, John M. '60 (CLV) [14] Akron, OH St. Paul Church.
Jenkins, Joseph A. '86 (WDC) Upper Marlboro, MD Saint Mary of the Assumption Church.
Jenkins, Paul D. '59 (RIC) Hopewell, VA St. James Church; Retired.
Jenkins, Ronnie (AUS) On Duty Outside the Diocese.
Jenkins, Wayne *s.c.j.* '77 (MIL) [P] Hales Corners, WI Sacred Heart Monastery.
Jenkinson, William R. '57 (PRO) Barrington, RI St. Luke's Church.
Jenko, Aloysius '35 (NY) Retired.
Jenks, Francis C. '70 (CHI) [1] Oak Park, IL Ascension Church.
Jenky, Daniel R. *c.s.c.* '74 (FTW) [B] Notre Dame, IN University of Notre Dame Du Lac; [J] Notre Dame, IN Holy Cross Community, Corby Hall, University of Notre Dame.
Jenne, Walter H. '70 (CLV) [15] Cleveland, OH St. Catherine Church; Brecksville, OH St. Basil the Great Church.
Jenner, David C. '66 (MAR) Gwinn, MI St. Anthony Church.
Jenner, James S. *o.p.* '51 (SFR) [N] San Francisco, CA St. Dominic Priory.
Jennett, Michael '74 (LA) Carpinteria, CA St. Joseph Church.
Jenniges, Leonard J. '48 (NU) Retired.
Jenniges, Leonard J. '48 (STP) Retired.
Jennings, Bernard J. '41 (LA) Altadena, CA St. Elizabeth of Hungary Church; Retired.
Jennings, Francis *c.ss.r.* '48 (ORL) Retired.
Jennings, Henry J. '62 (BO) [6] Somerville, MA Patronage of St. Joseph Church.
Jennings, John A. '50 (SEA) Retired; [N] Seattle, WA St. Joseph's Residence.
Jennings, John J. '49 (BO) [44] Boston, MA St. Mark Church; Retired; [U] Boston, MA St. Joseph Nursing Care Center.
Jennings, John P. '41 (CIN) Retired.
Jennings, Msgr. Joseph '43 (MOB) Retired.
Jennings, Kenneth E. '93 (NEW) [2] Jersey City, NJ St. Aloysius Church.
Jennings, Michael T. '69 (KNX) Harriman, TN Blessed Sacrament Church; Lancing, TN St. Ann Church.
Jennings, Oliver '72 (CHI) [104] Chicago, IL St. John de la Salle Church.
Jennings, Paul F., Jr. '74 (WIL) Easton, MD SS. Peter and Paul Church.
Jennings, Thomas J. '69 (WIN) Owatonna, MN Sacred Heart Church.
Jennings, Tommie '88 (SD) Military Chaplains.
Jennings, William E. '40 (WIL) Retired.
Jenniskens, Thomas J. *s.j.* '56 (LAF) [A] Grand Coteau, LA St. Charles College.
Jennrich, Michael J. *o.f.m.* '87 (NO) [P] New Orleans, LA Franciscan Fraternity.
Jensen, Benjamin E. '88 (SC) Charter Oak, IA St. Boniface Church; Dow City, IA St. Mary's Church.
Jensen, Daniel P. *m.m.* '62 (NY) [Z] Maryknoll, NY Maryknoll Fathers and Brothers.
Jensen, Joseph *o.s.b.* '54 (WDC) [C] Washington, DC Catholic University of America, The; [M] Washington, DC St. Anselm's Abbey; [V] Washington, DC Catholic Biblical Association.
Jensen, Larry '88 (SAM) Fayetteville, NC Archangel Michael Church.
Jenson, Glen T. '95 (STP) Montgomery, MN Holy Redeemer Church.
Jeon, Simon '92 (PHX) [5] Scottsdale, AZ St. Daniel the Prophet Church.
Jeong, John Hee-Wan '93 (SAC) [17] Sacramento, CA St. Paul Church; Rancho Cordova, CA St. John Vianney Church.
Jerabeck, Joseph '48 (COL) Westerville, OH St. Paul the Apostle Church; Retired.
Jerek, John M. '88 (Y) Kent, OH Immaculate Heart of Mary Church; [O] Kent, OH Kent State University Newman Center.
Jerge, Joseph W. '51 (E) Retired.
Jerge, Lawrence *c.s.c.* '68 (FR) [K] North Dartmouth, MA St. Joseph's Hall.
Jernejcic, Timothy '92 (SB) [2] Corona, CA St. Edward Church.
Jerome, Albert L. '59 (BEL) Nashville, IL St. Ann Church.
Jerome, Louis (NY) Yorktown Heights, NY St. Patrick Church.
Jerome, Marc-Arthur '90 (PRO) [16] Providence, RI Holy Name Church.
Jerome, Patrick '91 (KCK) Bonner Springs, KS Sacred Heart Church.
Jeronimo, Adalberto '90 (LA) [15] Los Angeles, CA Immaculate Conception Church.
Jerse, William M. '80 (CLV) [4] Euclid, OH St. Paul Church.
Jerus, Manuel '73 (AGN) Dededo, GU Santa Barbara Church.
Jeruzal, Joseph *o.f.m.cap.* '88 (LC) Halder, WI St. Patrick Church.
Jeruzal, Joseph B. *o.f.m.cap.* '88 (LC) Cassel, WI Sacred Heart Church; Marathon City, WI Nativity of the Blessed Virgin Mary Church.
Jervis, Paul W. '83 (BRK) [225] Queens, NY St. Paul the Apostle Church.
Jeselnick, Stephen '77 (E) On Duty Outside Diocese.
Jesiolowski, Sylvester E. '41 (PEO) Retired.
Jesionowski, Richard A. '68 (BUF) [13] Niagara Falls, NY St. Stanislaus Kostka Church.
Jeske, Richard M. *o.f.m.* '59 (SFD) Quincy, IL Illinois Veterans' Home; [B] Quincy, IL Quincy University.
Jesselli, Kenneth A. '84 (NY) [143] Bronx, NY St. Francis Xavier Church.
Jette, Donald J. *s.s.s.* '53 (GAL) [24] Houston, TX Corpus Christi Church.
Jette, Mark R. '72 (HRT) [2] Meriden, CT St. Joseph Church; [4] Meriden, CT St. Mary Church.
Jeub, Richard H. '66 (STP) Mendota, MN St. Peter Church; Special Assignment.
Jewison, Harry P. '54 (WIN) Retired.
Jewitt, Bernard C. '59 (TLS) [3] Tulsa, OK St. Bernard of Clairvaux Church.
Jezak, Thomas M. '66 (ALX) [2] Alexandria, LA Our Lady of Prompt Succor Church; Glenmora, LA St. Louis Church.
Jezeski, Henry '51 (CLV) Retired.
Jezierski, Zbigniew J. '61 (CAM) Lindenwold, NJ St. Lawrence's Church.
Jezowski, Anthony C. (BO) Awaiting Assignment.
Jicha, John J. '95 (BAL) Timonium, MD Church of the Nativity.
Jillisky, William F. '56 (ALB) Menands, NY Church of St. Joan of Arc.
Jimenez, Adrian '87 (ARE) [1] Camuy, PR St. Joseph Church.
Jimenez, Msgr. Armando '46 (WDC) Retired; [L] Washington, DC Cardinal O'Boyle Residence for Priests.
Jimenez, David J. '95 (YAK) Wapato, WA St. Peter Claver Church; White Swan, WA St. Mary's Church.
Jimenez, Eduardo '82 (MIA) [12] Miami, FL Our Lady of the Holy Rosary Church.
Jimenez, Felix *sch.p.* '26 (NY) [Z] New York, NY Calasanzian Fathers (Piarists).

Jimenez, Felix '70 (NY) [12] New York, NY Annunciation Church.
Jimenez, Francisco '65 (SJN) [2] Guaynabo, PR El Buen Pastor Church.
Jimenez, Francisco '88 (ARE) [7] Vega-Baja, PR Our Lady of Mt. Carmel Church.
Jimenez, Jose Luis *o.a.r.* '59 (LA) [8] Los Angeles, CA Cristo Rey Church.
Jimenez, Leonardo Rodriguez (SJN) [38] San Juan, PR Santa Maria de Los Angeles Church.
Jimenez, Rafael (DET) [72] Detroit, MI St. Stephen-Mary Mother of the Church.
Jiminez, P. Victorino (ARE) On Duty Outside the Diocese.
Jindra, Frank E. '84 (OM) Atkinson, NE St. Joseph Church; Stuart, NE St. Boniface Church.
Jirik, Charles C. '35 (STP) Retired.
Jiru, Richard A. '65 (MAD) Cuba City, WI St. Rose of Lima Church.
Joaquin, M. Joseph '81 (BGP) Georgetown, CT Sacred Heart Church.
Jocco, Joseph P. *o.s.f.s.* '84 (WIL) [I] Wilmington, DE Oblates of St. Francis De Sales.
Jocson, Salvador '57 (SFR) On Duty Outside the Archdiocese.
Jocys, Leonard '51 (GAY) Mackinaw City, MI St. Anthony of Padua Church; Riggsville, MI Sacred Heart Church.
Joda, Robert J. *s.j.* '58 (MIL) [P] Milwaukee, WI Jesuit Community at Marquette University.
Jodoin, Charles A. '93 (FR) [19] New Bedford, MA St. Mary's Church.
Joensen, William '89 (DUB) Graduate Studies.
Joerger, Jacob *o.p.* '48 (RCK) [N] St. Charles, IL Queen of Americas Guild.
Joerger, Robert *c.p.* '77 (MET) [H] South River, NJ Passionist Provincial Office.
Joffe, William I. '57 (RCK) On Disability Leave.
Johanek, John G. '43 (GB) Retired.
Johannes, Nicholas A. '70 (GB) Maple Grove, WI St. Patrick Church.
John, Andrew Peter '64 (LAF) Lawtell, LA Holy Family Church; Mallet, LA St. Ann Church.
John, Reginald (NY) City, NY MTF.
John, Richard *o.s.c.* '46 (SCL) Milaca, MN St. Mary's Church.
John, Richard T. *o.s.c.* '41 (SCL) [I] Onamia, MN Crosier Monastery.
Johns, Thomas W. '78 (CLV) Mentor, OH St. John Vianney Church.
Johnson, Andrew *o.c.s.o.* '91 (WOR) [N] Spencer, MA St. Joseph's Abbey.
Johnson, Arte (NY) [K] Barryville, NY New Hope Manor; [DD] Barryville, NY New Hope Manor.
Johnson, Arthur M. *s.a.* '77 (OG) [E] Saranac Lake, NY St. Joseph's Rehabilitation Center, Inc.; [F] Saranac Lake, NY Atonement Friars.
Johnson, Bartolome *o.s.b.* '93 (TUC) [F] St. David, AZ Holy Trinity Monastery.
Johnson, Bede L. *c.j.* '39 (LA) [B] Santa Maria, CA St. Joseph Seminary (Josephite Fathers' Novitiate).
Johnson, Bernard *o.praem.* '81 (ORG) [H] Silverado, CA Norbertine Fathers.
Johnson, Brian *c.ss.r.* '86 (OM) [19] Omaha, NE Holy Name Church.
Johnson, Carl '77 (LEX) Special Assignment.
Johnson, Carl D. '78 (NY) Monroe, NY Sacred Heart Church.
Johnson, Msgr. Charles B. '60 (HRT) [1] West Hartford, CT St. Brigid's Church; Special and other (Arch)Diocesan Assignment.
Johnson, Christopher *o.p.* '60 (NY) [22] New York, NY St. Catherine of Siena Church; [DD] New York, NY Dominican Shrine of St. Jude, Inc.
Johnson, Christopher P. *c.s.c.* '93 (FTW) [J] South Bend, IN Congregation of Holy Cross Indiana Province Provincial House.
Johnson, Cristopher *o.p.* (NY) [Z] New York, NY St. Catherine of Siena Priory.
Johnson, Daniel '54 (ORG) [2] Huntington Beach, CA St. Mary's by the Sea Church.
Johnson, Daniel E. '51 (HRT) Wallingford, CT Resurrection Church.
Johnson, Dave '89 (OWN) Leitchfield, KY St. Joseph's Church; Sunfish, KY St. John the Evangelist Church.
Johnson, David *o.f.m.* '84 (FRS) [G] Three Rivers, CA St. Anthony's Retreat House.
Johnson, David R. '80 (BR) Denham Springs, LA Immaculate Conception Church.
Johnson, David R. '80 (PIT) On Duty Outside the Diocese; Military Chaplains.
Johnson, David W. *s.j.* '69 (WDC) [C] Washington, DC Catholic University of America, The.
Johnson, Donald '55 (NY) Manhattan, NY Columbia Presbyterian Medical Center.
Johnson, Douglas '83 (SFS) On Leave of Absence.
Johnson, Earl *s.j.* '58 (LR) Cherokee Village, AR St. Michael's Church.
Johnson, Edward D. '55 (PRO) Portsmouth, RI St. Anthony's Church.
Johnson, Edward J. '58 (LA) [66] Los Angeles, CA St. Gregory Nazianzen Church.
Johnson, Edwin (LA) [F] Chatsworth, CA Chaminade College Preparatory.
Johnson, Msgr. Edwin '42 (DAL) Retired.
Johnson, Francis D. *s.j.* '53 (CIN) [M] Cincinnati, OH Jesuit Community at Xavier University.
Johnson, Francis P. '60 (HRT) [2] West Hartford, CT St. Helena Church.
Johnson, Msgr. Gregory '47 (BLX) Retired.
Johnson, H. Thomas '78 (DET) Shelby Twp., MI St. Kieran Church.
Johnson, Harold J. '49 (BO) Retired.
Johnson, Henry J. (LA) Retired.
Johnson, Howard '60 (JKS) On Duty Outside the Diocese.
Johnson, Howard '60 (WDC) [B] Washington, DC St. Joseph's Seminary.
Johnson, Howard J. '54 (MIL) Retired.
Johnson, J. Raymond '65 (NY) [Z] New York, NY Jesuit Community at Fordham University; [Z] New York, NY Jesuit Provincial's Office.
Johnson, James (SP) [R] St. Petersburg, FL Our Lady of Good Counsel Camp.
Johnson, Msgr. James '42 (NEW) Ridgefield, NJ St. Matthew's Church; Retired.
Johnson, James *s.p.* '60 (Y) Hubbard, OH St. Patrick's Church.
Johnson, James *o.f.m.cap.* '68 (OAK) [N] Berkeley, CA Capuchin Franciscan Order, House of Studies.
Johnson, James B. '80 (SP) Inverness, FL Our Lady of Fatima Church.
Johnson, Jef '86 (JUN) [2] Juneau, AK St. Paul The Apostle Church.
Johnson, Jeff '92 (MAR) Sugar Island, MI Sacred Heart Church.
Johnson, Jeff G. '92 (MAR) Brimley, MI St. Francis Xavier Church; Bay Mills, MI Blessed Kateri Tekakwitha Church; Sault Sainte Marie, MI St. Isaac Jogues Church.
Johnson, Jeffrey *s.o.l.t.* '91 (CC) [H] Robstown, TX Society of Our Lady of the Most Holy Trinity.
Johnson, Jerome A. '86 (MET) [5] New Brunswick, NJ Sacred Heart Church.
Johnson, John A. '88 (GR) [4] Muskegon, MI St. Joseph's Church; [5] Muskegon, MI St. Mary's Church.
Johnson, Msgr. John G. '74 (COL) [37] Columbus, OH St. Peter Church.
Johnson, John J. '48 (SPR) West Springfield, MA Immaculate Conception Church; [G] Springfield, MA Marriage Counseling Service.
Johnson, John J. '66 (STL) Ste. Genevieve, MO Ste. Genevieve's Church.
Johnson, John R. '72 (SAG) Midland, MI Blessed Sacrament Church.
Johnson, Msgr. Joseph I. '32 (SPR) [8] Pittsfield, MA St. Mark's Church; Retired.
Johnson, Joseph P. *s.j.* '60 (LSC) Artesia, NM St. Anthony Church.
Johnson, Ken *s.m.* (MRY) Santa Cruz, CA Star of the Sea Church.
Johnson, Kevin '87 (PT) [2] Tallahassee, FL Blessed Sacrament Church.
Johnson, Kirk '90 (DUB) [H] Mason City, IA North Iowa Mercy Health Center.
Johnson, L. Bede *c.j.* '39 (LA) Santa Maria, CA St. Louis de Montfort Church.
Johnson, Lawrence *o.praem.* '94 (ORG) [H] Silverado, CA Norbertine Fathers.
Johnson, Lawrence M. '83 (BAL) Special Assignment; [K] Baltimore, MD The Cardinal Shehan Center, Inc.; [K] Baltimore, MD Stella Maris Operating Corporation.
Johnson, Lawrence P. '76 (DUL) On Duty Outside the Diocese.
Johnson, Lawrence R. '75 (STP) Special Assignment.
Johnson, Lyle M. '76 (LIN) On Duty Outside the Diocese.
Johnson, Malcolm D. *c.s.c.* '59 (FTW) [J] South Bend, IN Congregation of Holy Cross Indiana Province Provincial House.
Johnson, O. Kenneth *s.j.* '92 (NO) [P] New Orleans, LA Jesuit Provincial Office.
Johnson, Oliver F. '62 (AUS) [12] Austin, TX St. Catherine of Siena Church.
Johnson, Patrick D. *c.s.p.* '74 (NY) [Z] Scarsdale, NY Paulist Fathers Generalate.
Johnson, Paul J. *o.p.* '59 (STP) [15] Minneapolis, MN St. Albert the Great Church.
Johnson, Peter '91 (CHY) Greybull, WY Sacred Heart Church; Lovell, WY St. Joseph's Church.
Johnson, Philip L. '64 (FWT) [6] Arlington, TX St. Vincent de Paul Church.
Johnson, Richard *c.p.* '51 (CHI) [N] Chicago, IL Passionist Provincial Office.
Johnson, Msgr. Richard E. '60 (DAL) [22] Dallas, TX St. Patrick Church.
Johnson, Richard G. '47 (BO) Beverly, MA St. Mary Star of the Sea Church.
Johnson, Msgr. Robert (DAL) [P] Commerce, TX Apostleship of Prayer.
Johnson, Robert E. '76 (STP) Bloomington, MN Nativity of the Blessed Virgin Mary Church.
Johnson, Robert F. '71 (SAT) Retired.
Johnson, Robert K. '90 (WOR) [1] Worcester, MA St. Paul's Cathedral.
Johnson, Stephen D. '72 (WOR) Athol, MA Our Lady Immaculate Church.
Johnson, Terrence M. '94 (CHI) Midlothian, IL St. Christopher Church.
Johnson, Tim '91 (SC) [B] Granville, IA Spalding Catholic High School.
Johnson, Timothy *o.carm.* '83 (PMB) [5] Boca Raton, FL St. Jude Church.
Johnson, Timothy K. '71 (OAK) [12] Oakland, CA St. Leo's Church.
Johnson, Walter *m.m.* (SJ) [H] Morgan Hill, CA O'Connor Hospital dba Saint Louise Hospital & Health Center.
Johnson, Walter W. '53 (SJ) [M] Los Altos, CA Maryknoll.
Johnson, William '58 (P) Retired.
Johnson, William J. '50 (CLV) Newbury, OH St. Helen Church; Retired.
Johnson, William T. *s.j.* '91 (MIL) [G] Milwaukee, WI Nativity Jesuit Middle School, Inc.; [P] Milwaukee, WI Jesuit Community at Marquette University.
Johnston, Donald '55 (NY) [95] New York, NY Our Lady Queen of Martyrs Church.
Johnston, Henry P. '76 (STO) Angels Camp, CA St. Patrick Church.
Johnston, J. Vann, Jr. *j.c.l.* '90 (KNX) [5] Knoxville, TN Holy Ghost Church.
Johnston, Jeffrey W. '86 (RVC) Hicksville, NY Holy Family Church.
Johnston, John F. '64 (BRK) Released from Diocesan Assignment.
Johnston, John F. '64 (NEW) [D] Summit, NJ The Oratory Catholic Preparatory School.
Johnston, Kenneth J. '68 (CAM) Deptford, NJ St. John Vianney Church; [B] Gloucester, NJ Gloucester Catholic High School.
Johnston, Michael '96 (P) Special Assignment.
Johnston, Michael O. '70 (NSH) [6] Nashville, TN St. Henry Church.
Johnston, Richard *s.c.j.* '58 (GAL) [47] Houston, TX St. Matthew the Evangelist Church.
Johnston, Richard *s.c.j.* '58 (MIL) [P] Hales Corners, WI Priests of the Sacred Heart.
Johnston, Robert A. *s.j.* '39 (MIL) [P] Wauwatosa, WI Jesuit Community at St. Camillus.
Johnston, Robert F. '62 (STL) Grantwood, MO Our Lady of Providence Church.
Johnston, Thomas J. *o.p.* '86 (DET) [2] St. Clair Shores, MI St. Gertrude Church.
Jolicoeur, Fabian A. *o.praem.* '39 (GB) [I] De Pere, WI St. Norbert Abbey.
Jollet, Robert (OG) Lake Pleasant, NY St. James, Major Church; Wells, NY St. Anne Church.
Jolley, Msgr. Edward W. '38 (BRK) Retired; [U] Douglaston, NY Bishop Mugavero Residence.
Jolly, George *c.ss.r.* '46 (DET) [34] Detroit, MI Holy Redeemer Church.
Joly, Henry L. (ALT) Retired.
Joly, Michael D. '94 (PAT) [1] Clifton, NJ Sacred Heart Church.
Jonaitis, Peter '44 (ALB) Retired.
Jonas, Lawrence A. *s.j.* '59 (MIL) [P] Milwaukee, WI Jesuit Provincial Office, Wisconsin Province.
Jonas, Lawrence A. *s.j.* '59 (SFS) Canton, SD St. Dominic Church.
Joncas, Jan Michael '69 (STP) [C] St. Paul, MN University of St. Thomas.
Jones, Augustine *o.s.b.* '53 (RCK) [H] Aurora, IL Marmion Abbey-St. Augustine's Abbey.
Jones, Bernard '45 (COL) Retired.
Jones, C. Gregory *c.s.v.* '96 (CHI) [210] Chicago, IL St. Viator Church.
Jones, Carleton Parker '87 (HRT) [14] New Haven, CT St. Mary's Priory Church.
Jones, Charles '45 (DEN) Retired.
Jones, Charles F. '63 (KC) [4] Independence, MO St. Mary's Church.
Jones, Clarence *c.o.* '94 (SEA) [1] Vancouver, WA Our Lady of Lourdes Church; [Q] Vancouver, WA Vancouver Oratorian Community.
Jones, Clarence Edward *c.o.* '94 (CHR) [E] Rock Hill, SC Oratory of St. Philip Neri, Congregation of the Oratory of Pontifical Rite.
Jones, David A. '89 (CHI) [10] Chicago, IL St. Ambrose Church.
Jones, David J. *m.m.* '62 (NY) [Z] Maryknoll, NY Maryknoll Fathers and Brothers.
Jones, Frank W. (GAL) Magnolia, TX St. Matthias the Apostle Church.
Jones, Herbert *o.carm.* '60 (JOL) [J] Darien, IL Carmelite Fathers Provincial Office.
Jones, Herbert *o.f.m.* '77 (SAT) [70] San Antonio, TX San Jose y San Miguel Church; [B] San Antonio, TX Franciscan Formation Program in San Jose Friary (Casa Juan Diego).
Jones, J. Overton '64 (CAM) [3] Atlantic City, NJ St.

Monica's Church.
Jones, James *o.s.b.* '48 (KC) [A] Conception, MO Conception Seminary College.
Jones, Msgr. James '57 (R) Retired.
Jones, James *o.f.m.* '76 (SP) [O] St. Petersburg, FL St. Anthony Friary.
Jones, James *o.f.m.cap.* '77 (NY) [Z] White Plains, NY St. Conrad Friary.
Jones, James W. '69 (COL) [41] Columbus, OH Sacred Heart Church.
Jones, Msgr. John B. '48 (GAL) Retired.
Jones, John E. '59 (L) On Special Assignment.
Jones, John L. '45 (ALB) [16] Albany, NY St. Teresa of Avila Church; Retired.
Jones, Joseph R. *c.p.* '65 (R) Greenville, NC St. Peter's Church.
Jones, Kenneth '69 (NEW) Plainfield, NJ St. Mary Church.
Jones, Mark R. '92 (MIL) Brookfield, WI St. Dominic Church.
Jones, Martin W. '94 (NOR) Willimantic, CT St. Mary Church.
Jones, Michael K. '92 (BGP) [7] Fairfield, CT St. Thomas Aquinas Church.
Jones, Michael T. '85 (WDC) Kensington, MD Holy Redeemer Church; Special Ministries; [E] Wheaton, MD Good Counsel High School.
Jones, Neil G. *m.s.* '72 (ATL) Canton, GA Our Lady of LaSalette Church.
Jones, Patrick F. '56 (PIT) Retired.
Jones, Raymond '36 (DET) Retired.
Jones, Raymond '36 (VEN) Lake Placid, FL St. James Church; Lake Placid, FL St. James Church.
Jones, Raymond A. *s.v.d.* '67 (LKC) [3] Lake Charles, LA Sacred Heart of Jesus Church.
Jones, Msgr. Raymond N. '59 (DEN) [1] Denver, CO Cathedral of the Immaculate Conception.
Jones, Richard T. *s.j.* '46 (RC) St. Francis, SD Rosebud Reservation Church.
Jones, Rick L. '90 (SPC) Webb City, MO Sacred Heart Church.
Jones, Robert *s.v.d.* '68 (BO) [W] Duxbury, MA Society of the Divine Word.
Jones, Robert C. *c.ss.r.* '78 (BAL) [91] Baltimore, MD St. Ursula Church.
Jones, Robert J. '69 (LA) [R] Los Angeles, CA Amat House; [W] Montebello, CA DePaul Center.
Jones, Robert J. *s.j.* '70 (P) [L] Portland, OR Jesuit Provincial Office (Oregon Prov.).
Jones, Robert M. '68 (BO) [Y] Duxbury, MA Miramar Retreat Center.
Jones, Robert W. '92 (RCK) St. Charles, IL St. John Neumann Church.
Jones, Ronald A. '92 (RCK) [8] Rockford, IL St. Patrick Church.
Jones, Thomas *o.f.m.* '59 (NY) Narrowsburg, NY St. Francis Xavier Church.
Jones, Thomas '70 (RVC) Port Jefferson, NY Mather Memorial Hospital; Port Jefferson, NY St. Charles Hospital, Port Jefferson, New York.
Jones, Thomas J. *c.s.c.* '72 (FTW) [6] South Bend, IN Christ the King Church.
Jones, Thomas W. *c.s.p.* '82 (NY) [Z] Scarsdale, NY Paulist Fathers Generalate.
Jones, Tony '89 (OWN) Brown's Valley, KY St. Anthony Church; [B] Owensboro, KY Owensboro Catholic High School.
Jones, W. Paul '96 (JC) Awaiting Assignment.
Jones, W. Thomas *s.m.* '47 (P) Jordan, OR Our Lady of Lourdes Church.
Jones, Msgr. William E. '60 (ALN) [4] Pottsville, PA St. Patrick Church.
Jones, Msgr. William H. '47 (DEN) Retired.
Jones, William P. '69 (ALN) Retired; [J] Bethlehem, PA Holy Family Villa.
Jones, William R. '67 (SY) [8] Syracuse, NY Our Lady of Solace Church.
Jonientz, Bernard '63 (SEA) Unassigned.
Jooji, Innocent (PIT) South Park Township, PA Nativity Church.
Joos, Justin *o.f.m.cap.* '36 (NY) [57] New York, NY St. John the Baptist Church.
Joppe, Stan N. *o.praem.* '55 (SFE) [J] Albuquerque, NM Santa Maria de la Vid Priory.
Joppe, Stanislaus N. *o.praem* '55 (GB) [I] De Pere, WI St. Norbert Abbey.
Jordan, Collins P. '85 (RC) Retired.
Jordan, Msgr. Edward F. '62 (AUS) [20] Austin, TX St. Theresa Church.
Jordan, Francis (DOD) [A] Garden City, KS St. Catherine Hospital.
Jordan, Francis W. '50 (MIL) Retired.
Jordan, Msgr. Harold F. '49 (STA) [1] St. Augustine, FL Cathedral of St. Augustine; [2] St. Augustine, FL Mission of Nombre de Dios and Shrine of Our Lady of La Leche Church.
Jordan, Harry J. '61 (CAM) Gloucester, NJ St. Mary's Church.
Jordan, John M. '83 (PIT) Allegheny County, PA West Penn Hospital.
Jordan, Msgr. John W. '69 (SCR) On Duty Outside the Diocese.
Jordan, Joseph A. *o.s.a.* '58 (PH) [Z] Villanova, PA Provincial Offices of the Order of St. Augustine, Province of St. Thomas of Villanova; [Z] Villanova, PA St. Thomas Monastery.
Jordan, Lawrence E. *s.m.* '34 (STL) [P] St. Louis, MO Provincialate of the Society of Mary, Province of St. Louis.
Jordan, Maryon *o.s.b.* '83 (CC) [H] Sandia, TX Corpus Christi Abbey.
Jordan, Maryon C. *o.s.b.* (LC) Coon Valley, WI St. Mary Church.
Jordan, Michael *s.o.l.t.* '83 (CC) [H] Robstown, TX Society of Our Lady of the Most Holy Trinity.
Jordan, Michael H. *s.j.* '55 (R) [E] Durham, NC Jesuit Community.
Jordan, Milton E. '72 (WDC) Germantown, MD Mother Seton Parish Church.
Jordan, Patrick (ORL) Retired.
Jordan, Patrick J. '78 (NY) Absent on Sick leave.
Jordan, Phelim *s.v.d.* '81 (CHI) [B] Techny, IL Divine Word Residence; [N] Chicago, IL Divine Word Theologate; [N] Techny, IL Society of the Divine Word, Provincial Headquarter-Chicago Prov.
Jordan, Regis *o.c.d.* '64 (WDC) [V] Washington, DC Institute of Carmelite Studies and ICS Publications.
Jordan, Regis *o.c.d.* '64 (WH) [N] Hinton, WV Monastery of Christ on the Mountain.
Jordan, Salvador *s.j.* (WDC) Chapel Point, MD St. Ignatius Church.
Jorden, James A. '83 (PT) On Leave of Absence.
Jordon, Thomas *o.carm.* '70 (JOL) [J] Darien, IL Carmelite Fathers Provincial Office.
Jorge, Francisco '56 (NY) [19] Yonkers, NY Our Lady of Fatima Church.
Jorgensen, Kenneth J. *s.j.* '75 (P) [L] Portland, OR Jesuit Provincial Office (Oregon Prov.).
Jorgensen, Kenneth J. *s.j.* '79 (BGP) [O] Fairfield, CT The Fairfield Jesuit Community-Fairfield University.
Jorgenson, James '69 (DET) [A] Detroit, MI Sacred Heart Major Seminary, Inc.
Jose, Carlos San *m.des.* '69 (ELP) Fabens, TX Our Lady of Guadalupe Church.
Joseph, Benedict *o.p.* '49 (COL) [I] Columbus, OH St. Mary of the Springs.
Joseph, Jean-Ronald '93 (VEN) [5] Fort Myers, FL St. Francis Xavier Church.
Joseph, John K. *c.m.i.* '77 (TOL) Leipsic, OH St. Mary Church.
Joseph, Msgr. Joseph D. '47 (BUF) Retired.
Joseph, Msgr. Joseph D. '47 (SAM) Retired.
Joseph, Karunei '72 (MIA) Coral Springs, FL St. Andrew Church.
Joseph, Louis '55 (CC) Retired.
Joseph, Louis '60 (FR) Retired.
Joseph, Msgr. Milam '64 (DAL) [B] Irving, TX University of Dallas.
Joseph, Msgr. Milam '64 (TYL) Special Assignment.
Joseph, Moussa '83 (SAM) Danbury, CT St. Anthony Church.
Joseph, Ramon '65 (RVC) Centereach, NY Assumption of the Blessed Virgin Mary Church.
Joseph, William '62 (PT) Retired.
Joseph, William T. '66 (PH) [2] Bensalem, PA St. Elizabeth Ann Seton Church; Glenolden, PA St. George Church.
Joslin, James R. '74 (ALB) Albany, NY Capital District Psychiatric Center; Special Assignment.
Joslyn, James W. '73 (CHI) Military Chaplains.
Josoma Stephen S. (BO) Awaiting Assignment.
Jost, Aloys *o.f.m.* '80 (STL) Oakville, MO St. Francis of Assisi Church.
Jost, C Thomas *s.j.* '68 (KC) [14] Kansas City, MO Guardian Angels Church; [J] Kansas City, MO Arrupe Jesuit Community.
Jost, Edward F. '96 (BUF) Springbrook, NY St. Vincent Church.
Josten, Paul T. '87 (SFS) Bowdle, SD St. Augustine Church; Roscoe, SD St. Thomas Apostle Church.
Jotting, Paul J. '66 (DUB) [8] Dubuque, IA Holy Ghost Church.
Joubert, Gerard *o.p.* (GAL) Retired.
Jovanovic, Msgr. Robert P. '61 (STL) Oakville, MO Queen of All Saints Church.
Jovellar, Lorenzo *s.j.* '46 (CGS) Caguas, PR Government Regional Hospital; [B] Juncos, PR Casa Cursillos de Cristiandad of Caguas.
Jowdy, Albert W. '84 (ATL) Alpharetta, GA St. Thomas Aquinas Church.
Joy, Msgr. James B. '61 (WDC) On Sick Leave.
Joy, Laurence '60 (LA) On Duty Outside the Archdiocese.
Joy, William '72 (BO) [6] Boston, MA St. Angela Church.
Joyal, Gerald F. '45 (MAN) Retired.
Joyal, Rene J (BO) Retired.
Joyce, Brian T. '63 (OAK) Pleasant Hill, CA Christ the King Church.
Joyce, David J. '68 (SPR) [8] Springfield, MA Our Lady of Hope Church.
Joyce, Donald *o.m.i.* '58 (WDC) [B] Washington, DC Oblate College/Oblate Center for Mission Studies.
Joyce, Edmund P. *c.s.c.* '49 (FTW) [B] Notre Dame, IN University of Notre Dame Du Lac; [J] Notre Dame, IN Holy Cross Community, Corby Hall, University of Notre Dame.
Joyce, Edwin (JOL) Absent on Sick Leave.
Joyce, Fabian *o.f.m.* '43 (BO) [Z] Boston, MA Saint Anthony Residence.
Joyce, George V. '43 (SPR) [8] Springfield, MA Our Lady of Hope Church.
Joyce, George V. '43 (WDC) Retired.
Joyce, Gerald P. '61 (CHI) Westchester, IL Divine Infant Church.
Joyce, James E. *c.s.p.* '38 (NY) [Z] Scarsdale, NY Paulist Fathers Generalate.
Joyce, James E. *c.s.p.* '38 (PMB) [G] Vero Beach, FL Paulist Fathers Retirement Home.
Joyce, James F. *s.j.* '75 (NY) [80] New York, NY Nativity Church; [Z] New York, NY Jesuit Provincial's Office.
Joyce, James K. '72 (SPR) [4] Pittsfield, MA Sacred Heart Church.
Joyce, James M. '48 (SFS) Brandon, SD Risen Savior Church.
Joyce, John E. '44 (STP) Retired.
Joyce, John J. '89 (BEL) Modoc, IL St. Leo Church; Ruma, IL St. Patrick Church; [H] Ruma, IL Provincial House, Adorers of the Blood of Christ, Province of Ruma.
Joyce, John M. '54 (ORG) [3] Orange, CA St. Norbert Church.
Joyce, Joseph *o.carm.* '71 (GAL) [14] Houston, TX St. Bernadette Soubirous Church.
Joyce, Kevin '80 (SJ) [15] San Jose, CA St. Maria Goretti Church.
Joyce, Michael '67 (OAK) Livermore, CA St. Michael's Church.
Joyce, Michael *o.f.m.cap.* '85 (PIT) [29] Pittsburgh, PA Our Lady of the Angels Church.
Joyce, Michael P. *c.m.* '76 (STL) [P] Earth City, MO Congregation of the Mission Midwest Province (Vincentians); [P] St. Louis, MO Vincentian Residence.
Joyce, Peter J. '83 (WOR) [4] Southbridge, MA St. Mary's Church.
Joyce, Peter M. '92 (CAM) Stratford, NJ St. Luke's Church.
Joyce, Pierce J. '34 (CHI) La Grange, IL St. Francis Xavier Church; Retired.
Joyce, Randal *c.p.* '50 (DET) [K] Detroit, MI St. Paul of the Cross Community, Congregation of the Passion.
Joyce, Raymond '62 (WCH) On Duty Outside the Diocese.
Joyce, Richard C. '48 (NY) Patterson, NY Sacred Heart Church; Retired; [V] Middletown, NY St. Teresa's Nursing Home.
Joyce, Stephen G. '78 (STL) Normandy, MO Ascension-St. Paul Church.
Joyce, Thomas (WH) Montgomery, WV Immaculate Conception Church.
Joyce, Thomas *c.p.* '69 (BRK) [180] Queens, NY Immaculate Conception Church; [U] Jamaica, NY Immaculate Conception Monastery.
Joyce, Thomas J. '68 (DOD) On Duty Outside the Diocese.
Joyce, Thomas J. '91 (NY) [2] White Plains, NY St. John the Evangelist Church.
Joyce, Timothy J. '59 (BO) [W] Hingham, MA Glastonbury Abbey.
Joyce, Tom *c.m.f.* '59 (CHI) [80] Chicago, IL Holy Cross/Immaculate Heart of Mary Church.
Joyce, William F. '60 (BO) [9] Boston, MA St. Anne Church.
Joyce, William J. *c.s.sp.* '59 (PIT) [P] Bethel Park, PA Holy Ghost Animation Center.
Joynes, Msgr. Joseph P. '64 (CAM) Washington Township, NJ Holy Family Church.
Jozefiak, Gregory '92 (PEO) [2] Champaign, IL St. John's Catholic Chapel; [O] Champaign, IL St. John's Catholic Student Chapel and Newman Foundation, University of Illinois.
Jozefiak, Matthew W. *c.pp.s.* '87 (GRY) [4] Whiting, IN St. John the Baptist Church.
Jozwiak, Lawrence '87 (GAL) [1] Houston, TX Sacred Heart Co-Cathedral.
Jozwiak, Richard E. '59 (SAG) Carrollton, MI St. Josaphat Church.
Jozwiak, Richard M. (CHI) Retired.
Jozwiak, Richard M. '48 (CHI) [3] Lemont, IL SS. Cyril and Methodius Church.
Jozwiak, Ronald J. '79 (DET) [40] Detroit, MI St. Josaphat Church; Special Assignment.
Jozwiak, Stanislaus J. '45 (PIT) Retired.
Jozwiak, Zygmunt '53 (SP) Retired.
Jozwicki, Stephen J. '53 (BRK) [94] Brooklyn, NY Our Lady of Czestochowa-St. Casimir Church.
Juaire, Joseph *o.m.i.* '49 (MAN) [K] Hudson, NH Missionary Oblates of Mary Immaculate.
Juan, Francisco *s.d.b.* (SJN) [37] San Juan, PR Maria Auxiliadora Church.
Juan, Marcial D. '66 (LA) [2] Los Angeles, CA Cathedral Chapel.

Juarez, Alejandro *o.f.m.* '88 (ELP) [B] El Paso, TX St. Anthony's School of Theology.
Juarez, Lucio '91 (LA) Huntington Park, CA St. Matthias Church.
Juarez, Rene *o.f.m.* '70 (LA) Santa Paula, CA Our Lady of Guadalupe Church.
Juarez, Robert '80 (LA) [23] Los Angeles, CA Our Lady of Guadalupe Church.
Juarez, Rudolph T. '80 (DAV) [7] Davenport, IA St. Mary's Church.
Juarez, Thomas *s.d.b.* '66 (CC) [7] Laredo, TX San Luis Rey Church.
Juchcinski, Clarence J. '48 (CHI) Harvey, IL St. John the Baptist Church; Retired.
Juchniewicz, Leon '80 (SAC) Marysville, CA St. Joseph Church.
Juchnowski, Msgr. Francis B. '56 (BUF) [13] Buffalo, NY St. Bernard Church.
Juda, Stephen *c.r.* '42 (CHI) [D] Chicago, IL Gordon Technical High School.
Judd, Augustine *o.p.* '96 (WDC) [B] Washington, DC Dominican House of Studies.
Judd, Stephen P. *m.m.* '78 (NY) [Z] Maryknoll, NY Maryknoll Fathers and Brothers.
Jude, Robert J. '49 (STP) Retired.
Jude, Msgr. Walter F. '45 (GR) Retired.
Judge, Anthony *c.ss.r.* '79 (DEN) [32] Denver, CO St. Joseph's Church.
Judge, James G. '72 (BUF) [8] Buffalo, NY Annunciation Church.
Judge, John G. '69 (NEW) Washington Township, NJ Our Lady of Good Counsel Church; Ridgewood, NJ Valley Hospital; Westwood, NJ Pascack Valley Hospital.
Judge, Michael *o.f.m.* '61 (NY) [35] New York, NY St. Francis of Assisi Church.
Judge, Philip G. *s.j.* '93 (NY) [F] New York, NY Regis High School; [Z] New York, NY St. Ignatius Loyola Residence.
Judge, Robert K. *s.j.* '65 (BAL) [C] Baltimore, MD Loyola College; [M] Baltimore, MD Jesuit Community of Loyola College, Inc.
Judge, Russell R. '78 (JC) Macon, MO Immaculate Conception Church.
Judge, Timothy M. '79 (PH) [AA] Huntingdon Valley, PA Sisters of the Holy Redeemer Provincialate.
Judie, John T. '87 (L) [56] Louisville, KY Mother of Good Counsel Church.
Judy, Albert *o.p.* '59 (CHI) [176] Chicago, IL St. Priscilla Church.
Judy, Albert *o.p.* '62 (CHI) [N] River Forest, IL St. Thomas Aquinas Priory.
Judy, Edward *o.f.m.cap.* '68 (DEN) [3] Denver, CO Annunciation Church; [M] Denver, CO Annunciation Friary.
Judy, Myron *o.carm.* '63 (JOL) [J] Darien, IL Carmelite Fathers Provincial Office.
Juelfs, Daniel '73 (RC) [3] Rapid City, SD St. Therese the Little Flower Church.
Juenker, Msgr. Paul R. '45 (BUF) Retired; [O] Tonawanda, NY O'Hara Residence.
Juergens, William H. *o.s.f.s.* '57 (WIL) [I] Wilmington, DE DeSales House.
Juettner, Mark R. '79 (STP) Crystal, MN St. Raphael Church.
Jugan, Joseph '58 (PBR) Canonsburg, PA St. Michael Church.
Jugenheimer, James R. '87 (PH) [D] Wyncote, PA Bishop McDevitt High School.
Jugis, Peter J. '83 (CHL) Belmont, NC Queen of the Apostles Church.
Juhas, John S. '75 (CLV) Brooklyn, OH St. Thomas More Church.
Juhasz, Ladislaus F. *s.j.* '54 (BUF) [O] Buffalo, NY Canisius Jesuit Community.
Juhl, Dennis '73 (DUB) Hazleton, IA St. Mary's Church; Lamont, IA St. Mary's Church; Strawberry Point, IA St. Mary's Church.
Juknialis, Joseph J. '69 (MIL) [3] Menomonee Falls, WI St. James Church; [A] Milwaukee, WI Saint Francis Seminary.
Juleen, Stuart '77 (SAT) Karnes City, TX St. Cornelius Church.
Julian, Mario *o.f.m.* '80 (BO) [W] Andover, MA St. Francis Friary.
Julien, Jean Ridly '96 (BGP) Awaiting Assignment.
Julien, Roland M. '65 (STA) [1] Gainesville, FL St. Patrick's Church.
Julius, James A. '65 (STL) Retired.
Julius, Joseph W. '45 (KNX) Alcoa, TN Our Lady of Fatima Church; Townsend, TN St. Francis of Assisi Church.
Julius, Joseph W. '45 (NSH) Retired.
Jung, Dennet *o.f.m.* '63 (LAF) [2] Lafayette, LA St. Paul The Apostle Church.
Jung, Eugene *m.s.c.* '50 (ALN) [K] Reading, PA Missionaries of the Sacred Heart.
Jung, Jay *c.m.* '77 (CHI) [C] Chicago, IL Vincentian Community at DePaul University.
Jung, Michael *o.s.b.* '63 (BR) Plaquemine, LA St. Clement of Rome Church; Baton Rouge, LA Baton Rouge General Medical Center.
Jung, Michael *o.s.b.* '63 (NO) [P] St. Benedict, LA St. Joseph Abbey.
Jung, Pius-Bio (ALB) [11] Albany, NY St. Mary Church.
Jung, Thomas U. '47 (BRK) [226] Queens, NY St. Paul Chong Ha-Sang Roman Catholic Chapel; [U] Douglaston, NY Bishop Mugavero Residence.
Jungbluth, Henry *s.v.d.* '30 (CHI) [B] Techny, IL Divine Word Residence.
Junge, Heiko T. '96 (P) [29] Portland, OR St. Pius X Church.
Jungers, Christopher J. '86 (PH) Absent on Leave.
Jungwirth, Alphonse *c.pp.s.* '43 (CIN) [B] Carthagena, OH St. Charles.
Juniet, Paul *o.f.m.* '66 (SFE) [4] Albuquerque, NM Holy Family Church; [12] Albuquerque, NM Queen of Angels Native American Center and Archdiocesan Shrine to Kateri Tekakwitha Church.
Junio, Joven '86 (HON) [3] Honolulu, HI St. Anthony Church.
Junod, Louis J. '65 (KNX) Retired; [B] Chattanooga, TN Memorial Hospital; [K] Chattanooga, TN Ladies of Charity.
Jupin, Alan D. '62 (ALB) [14] Schenectady, NY Our Lady of Fatima Church.
Juracek, Joseph *o.f.m.* '83 (NY) [35] New York, NY St. Francis of Assisi Church.
Juran, Michael P. '76 (BUF) Salamanca, NY St. Patrick Church.
Juras, Callistus *o.f.m.conv.* '54 (ROC) [6] Auburn, NY St. Hyacinth Church.
Jurasko, Joseph J. *o.p.* '40 (WDC) [11] Washington, DC St. Dominic Church & Priory Church.
Jurcak, Lawrence '81 (CLV) [1] Cleveland, OH Cathedral of St. John the Evangelist.
Jurcik, Peter '93 (ALN) Fountain Hill, PA St. Ursula Church.
Jurek, Daniel J. '73 (BEL) Dubois, IL St. Charles Borromeo Church; Tamaroa, IL Immaculate Conception Church.
Jurewich, Henry A. *s.j.* '54 (BO) [W] Weston, MA Campion Health Center, Inc.
Jurewicz, Francis Z. '59 (PIT) Richeyville, PA St. Agnes Church.
Jurgelaitis, Anthony A. *o.p.* '44 (PRO) [P] Providence, RI St. Thomas Aquinas Priory at Providence College.
Jurgelonis, Joseph J. '73 (WOR) Ashburnham, MA St. Denis Church; South Ashburnham, MA St. Anne Church.
Jurgensen, John J. '51 (BRK) [155] Queens, NY St. Benedict Joseph Labre Church.
Jurgensen, John W. '51 (BRK) Retired.
Jurgensmeier, Charles L. *s.j.* '88 (LA) [C] Los Angeles, CA Loyola Marymount University.
Jurich, James P. *s.j.* '67 (NY) [Z] New York, NY Jesuit Provincial's Office; [Z] New York, NY Xavier Jesuit Community; [DD] New York, NY Xavier Society for the Blind.
Jurisich, Melvin A. *o.f.m.* '70 (OAK) [N] Oakland, CA Franciscan Friars Provincial Office, Province of St. Barbara; [N] Oakland, CA Franciscan Friars Provincial Office, Province of St. Barbara.
Jurkowski, Victor J. *o.f.m.cap.* '58 (CAM) Gibbstown, NJ St. Michael's Church.
Jurkus, Alan F. '70 (MIL) Whitefish Bay, WI St. Monica's Church.
Jussaume, Andre P. '52 (FR) Retired.
Jussaume, Lucien '41 (FR) Retired.
Jusseaume, John E. (BO) Plainville, MA St. Martha Church; Retired.
Justi, Marvin *o.f.m.cap.* '58 (PIT) Rochester, PA St. Cecilia Church; Beaver County, PA Medical Center, Beaver Inc.; [N] Rochester, PA St. Cecilia Friary.
Justice, Joseph C. '75 (ORG) [6] Santa Ana, CA St. Anne's Church.
Justice, William J. '68 (SFR) [1] South San Francisco, CA All Souls Church.
Jutt, Anthony J. '51 (SPR) Housatonic, MA Corpus Christi Church; Housatonic, MA All Saints Church.
Jutt, Julius A. '51 (SPR) South Deerfield, MA St. James Church.
Jutte, Edgar *c.pp.s.* '62 (CIN) [B] Carthagena, OH St. Charles.
Jutton, David J. '66 (SY) Truxton, NY St. Patrick Church.
Juya, Filemon '81 (CHR) Batesburg, SC St. John of the Cross Church.
Juza, Philip J. '95 (SUP) Flambeau, WI St. Francis of Assisi Church; Jump River, WI St. Michael Church; Sheldon, WI St. John the Apostle Church.
Juzix, Richard *o.f.m.* '75 (SAC) [13] Sacramento, CA St. Francis of Assisi Church.

K

Kaack, John *s.j.* '74 (SP) [C] Tampa, FL Jesuit High School.
Kabat, Daniel *o.f.m.cap.* (DET) [K] Detroit, MI St. Mary's Friary.
Kabat, Daniel *o.f.m.cap.* (MAD) [4] Madison, WI Holy Redeemer Church.
Kabat, Robert J. '79 (GB) Greenleaf, WI St. Mary Church.
Kabura, Paschal (PIT) South Park Township, PA Nativity Church.
Kacerguis, Edward '71 (ALB) Special Assignment; [S] Troy, NY Rensselaer Polytechnic Institute.
Kachel, C. Leon '57 (PRO) [K] Providence, RI St. Joseph Health Services of Rhode Island - St. Joseph Hospital for Specialty Care.
Kachel, Steven J. '95 (LC) Polonia, WI Sacred Heart Church; [C] Stevens Point, WI Pacelli High School; [D] Stevens Point, WI Stevens Point Area Catholic Schools.
Kachmar, Msgr. Walter '43 (SJP) Retired.
Kachuba, John S. *m.a.* '74 (PRM) Euclid, OH St. Stephens Church.
Kachurka, Edward M. '89 (BRK) [204] Queens, NY Nativity of the Blessed Virgin Mary Church.
Kacinko, Elmer A. '61 (GBG) Coral, PA St. Francis Church.
Kacir, Marian '89 (NY) [59] New York, NY St. John Nepomucene Church.
Kacirk, Raymond J. *s.m.* '59 (CIN) [M] Dayton, OH Marianist Provincialate.
Kacprowicz, Joseph A. '36 (E) Retired.
Kacprzak, Stanley G. '85 (ROC) [30] Rochester, NY St. John Evangelist Church; [35] Rochester, NY Our Lady of Mercy Church.
Kaczkowski, Conrad J. *s.m.* '68 (SAT) [C] San Antonio, TX St. Mary's University of San Antonio, Texas; [M] San Antonio, TX Chaminade Community House.
Kaczkowski, Leon '34 (BAL) Retired; [K] Baltimore, MD Stella Maris Operating Corporation.
Kaczmarek, James '69 (MAR) Military Chaplains.
Kaczmarek, Peter '69 (RVC) Bayville, NY St. Gertrude's Church.
Kaczmarek, Thaddeus J. '71 (GBG) New Kensington, PA St. Mary of Czestochowa Church.
Kaczorek, Placid *o.f.m.conv.* '64 (SPR) [10] Chicopee, MA St. Stanislaus Basilica.
Kaczorowski, Edward J. '58 (WIL) [12] Wilmington, DE St. Stanislaus Kostka Church.
Kaczorowski, James '73 (CHI) [2] Chicago, IL St. Adalbert Church.
Kadamala, Abraham Samuel '75 (DAL) [3] Garland, TX St. Mary Malankara Church.
Kaddo, Msgr. Joseph F. '72 (SAM) Waterbury, CT Our Lady of Lebanon Church.
Kadera, Thomas '87 (CHY) Saratoga, WY St. Ann's Church.
Kadlec, Josef *s.j.* '77 (WDC) [M] Washington, DC The Jesuit Community at Georgetown University.
Kadzielawski, Edwin J. *c.s.c.* '49 (AUS) Marble Falls, TX St. John the Evangelist Church.
Kaeding, Robert F. '73 (TR) Wayside, NJ St. Anselm Church; Monmouth, NJ Monmouth County Jail.
Kaelin, Dennis '76 (NEW) [10] Elizabeth, NJ St. Patrick's Church; [N] East Orange, NJ Congregation of Christian Brothers.
Kaelin, Walter *c.p.* '42 (CHI) [N] Chicago, IL Passionist Provincial Office.
Kaelin, Walter *c.p.* '42 (L) [L] Louisville, KY Sacred Heart Retreat.
Kafer, Gerald *o.f.m.cap.* '76 (MIL) [B] Mount Calvary, WI St. Lawrence Seminary; [P] Mount Calvary, WI St. Lawrence Friary.
Kafka, Matthew S. (FTW) [13] Fort Wayne, IN St. Patrick Church; [F] Fort Wayne, IN St. Joseph Medical Center.
Kagan, Msgr. David D. '75 (RCK) Special Assignment.
Kahle, George G. *c.s.c.* '53 (FTW) [J] South Bend, IN Congregation of Holy Cross Indiana Province Provincial House.
Kahlhamer, Bernard '59 (SCL) Sauk Centre, MN Our Lady of the Angels Church.
Kahlich, Daniel P. '66 (VIC) Columbus, TX St. Anthony's Church.
Kahn, Eric *o.f.m.* '55 (SPC) [G] Republic, MO Cordis House.
Kahn, Eric *o.f.m.* '55 (STL) [P] St. Louis, MO Franciscan Friary of St. Anthony of Padua.
Kahrs, Lee J. '65 (GB) Osman, WI St. Isidore Church.
Kaicher, Edward '80 (SD) Fallbrook, CA St. Peter Church.
Kaifer, William J. *s.j.* '53 (WDC) [M] Washington, DC The Jesuit Community at Georgetown University.
Kail, Msgr. Michael J. '74 (OLL) Columbus, OH Maronite Catholic Community Church; Fairlawn, OH Our Lady of the Cedars of Mt. Lebanon Church.
Kaimann, Gerald J. '70 (JC) Jonesburg, MO St. Patrick Church; Montgomery City, MO Immaculate Conception Church.
Kain, Msgr. Peter V. '65 (BRK) [213] Queens, NY Our Lady of Lourdes Church.
Kain, Stephan *o.f.m.* '74 (SFR) [7] San Francisco, CA St. Boniface Church.
Kaiser, Msgr. Charles '32 (EVN) Fort Branch, IN Holy Cross Church; Retired.
Kaiser, Cletus H. '56 (MIL) Retired.
Kaiser, Joseph A. (BAL) Retired.

Kaiser, Joseph W. '55 (RCK) Richmond, IL St. Joseph Church.
Kaiser, Lawrence '64 (DET) [1] Dearborn Heights, MI St. Albert the Great Church.
Kaiser, Lawrence B. '73 (DEN) Fort Morgan, CO St. Helena Church.
Kaiser, Leonard G. '58 (LC) Independence, WI SS. Peter and Paul Church; North Creek, WI St. Michael Church.
Kaiser, Ralph L. '54 (KC) Buckner, MO Church of the Santa Fe.
Kaiser, Roman F. '58 (LC) Loyal, WI St. Anthony of Padua Church.
Kaiser, Thomas A '83 (GAY) Absent on Leave.
Kaiser, Thomas J. '49 (SLC) [10] Salt Lake City, UT St. Vincent de Paul Church; Retired.
Kaising, John J. '62 (CIN) Military Chaplains.
Kaithackal, Sebastian *c.m.i.* '81 (MET) [I] Flemington, NJ The Carmel of Mary Immaculate and St. Mary Magdalen.
Kakalec, Joseph M. *s.j.* '67 (PH) [C] Philadelphia, PA St. Joseph's University; [Z] Philadelphia, PA Jesuit Community at St. Joseph's University; [Z] Philadelphia, PA St. Alphonsus House.
Kakareka, Joseph R. '72 (SCR) [6] Nanticoke, PA St. Stanislaus Church.
Kakascik, Msgr. Edward '55 (STU) Marietta, OH St. Mary's Church; [I] Marietta, OH Marietta College.
Kakaty, Edward G. (BO) [10] Boston, MA Annunciation Cathedral.
Kakizaki, John T. '42 (BRK) Retired.
Kalabat, Frank Y. '95 (EST) Southfield, MI Our Lady of Chaldeans Cathedral, Mother of God Chaldean Parish Church.
Kalafsky, Andrew J. '43 (ROC) Bradford, NY St. Stanislaus Church; Retired.
Kalajian, Msgr. Joseph '31 (ARM) Detroit, MI St. Vartan's Church.
Kalamaja, Theodore M. *s.j.* '67 (MIL) [P] Milwaukee, WI Jesuit Provincial Office, Wisconsin Province.
Kalamaja, Theodore M. *s.j.* '67 (NO) New Orleans, LA Orleans Parish Correctional Center; [C] New Orleans, LA Loyola University.
Kalapurackal, Thomas *s.d.b.* '83 (OAK) Pinole, CA St. Joseph's Church; Rodeo, CA St. Patrick's Church.
Kalapurra, George *c.m.i.* '64 (BEA) [8] Port Arthur, TX St. Mary Church.
Kalapurra, George *c.m.i.* '64 (NY) Haverstraw, NY St. Peter Church.
Kalarickal, Thomas *c.m.i.* '55 (NY) [2] White Plains, NY St. John the Evangelist Church.
Kalariparampil, Joseph '53 (MIA) [7] Fort Lauderdale, FL St. Helen Church.
Kalas, Ronald N. '59 (CHI) Park Ridge, IL Mary, Seat of Wisdom Church.
Kalb, Bertram J. '44 (DUB) Retired.
Kalb, Howard E. *s.j.* '54 (OM) [K] Omaha, NE Jesuit Community At Creighton University.
Kalcic, Dismas *o.s.b.* '61 (JOL) [J] Lisle, IL St. Procopius Abbey.
Kalcic, Dismas B. *o.s.b.* '61 (SUP) Catawba, WI St. Paul the Apostle Church; Prentice, WI St. John Church.
Kalck, Michael V. '74 (CHI) [170] Chicago, IL SS. Peter and Paul Church.
Kalemeera, Augustine (LA) El Segundo, CA St. Anthony Church.
Kalenty, Adalbert *o.f.m.* '53 (GB) [I] Pulaski, WI Assumption of B.V.M. Friary.
Kaler, Adolph *o.m.i.* '57 (GAL) [37] Houston, TX Immaculate Heart of Mary Church.
Kalert, David A. *o.m.i.* '64 (STP) [N] St. Paul, MN Oblate Provincial Offices; [N] St. Paul, MN Oblate Residence; [W] St. Paul, MN Oblate Media and Communication Corporation.
Kaley, Richard *o.f.m.conv.* '75 (IND) St. Joseph Hill, IN St. Joseph Church; [I] Mount Saint Francis, IN Mount Saint Francis Friary and Retreat Center; [J] Mount Saint Francis, IN Provincial Headquarters for the Conventual Franciscan Province.
Kalich, Patrick J. '94 (GRY) Crown Point, IN St. Mary Church.
Kalicky, John E. *c.pp.s.* '61 (GRY) [4] Whiting, IN St. John the Baptist Church.
Kalil, Gordon *o.p.* '94 (LA) [59] Los Angeles, CA St. Dominic Church.
Kalin, Msgr. Leonard I. '56 (LIN) [12] Lincoln, NE St. Thomas Aquinas Church; [I] Lincoln, NE University of Nebraska, Newman Club.
Kalin, William A. '59 (LIN) On Duty Outside the Diocese.
Kalina, Isaac *o.s.b.* '89 (LA) [R] Valyermo, CA St. Andrew's Abbey; [W] Valyermo, CA St. Andrew's Abbey Retreat House (All Groups).
Kalinowski, Joseph J. '79 (E) East Brady, PA St. Eusebius Church.
Kalinowski, Loren M. '75 (SAG) [9] Bay City, MI St. Stanislaus Church.
Kalinowski, Ryszard *s.v.d.* '74 (LAF) [4] New Iberia, LA St. Edward Church.
Kalinowski, Stainslaus J. '45 (SCR) Retired.
Kalinski, Eugene E. '60 (GB) [I] Oshkosh, WI Community of Our Lady.
Kalita, Thomas M. '74 (WDC) Olney, MD St. Peter Church.
Kalkman, Richard '56 (SCL) On Duty Outside the Diocese.
Kalkman, Richard '56 (SFR) [4] South San Francisco, CA St. Veronica Church.
Kall, Anthony *o.f.m.conv.* '71 (ALB) [A] Rensselaer, NY Conventual Franciscan Friars; [L] Rensselaer, NY Provincialate, Immaculate Conception Friary - Order of Friars Minor Conventual; [T] Rensselaer, NY Order of Friars Minor Conventual Immaculate Conception Province Charitable Trust.
Kallabat, Stephen '66 (EST) Oak Park, MI Mar Addai Chaldean Parish Church.
Kalladan, Joseph K. '69 (GAL) New Waverly, TX St. Joseph Church.
Kallaher, Timothy S. '72 (CIN) [19] Dayton, OH Our Lady of the Immaculate Conception Church.
Kallanchira, Joseph *s.v.d.* '87 (MIL) [P] East Troy, WI Divine Word Seminary.
Kallarackal, Abraham *c.m.i.* '83 (ALX) Dupont, LA Immaculate Conception Church.
Kallarackal, Sebastian *c.m.i.* '77 (TYL) Jacksonville, TX Our Lady of Sorrows Church; Rusk, TX Rusk State Hospital and Skyview Unit, Texas Dept. of Corrections.
Kallatil, John '79 (BGP) Wilton, CT Our Lady of Fatima Church.
Kallattil, John *v.c.* (BGP) [5] Danbury, CT St. Peter's Church.
Kallock, Michael J. *c.s.p.* '73 (BO) [P] Boston, MA Paulist Center; [W] Boston, MA Paulist Fathers Residence; [BB] Boston, MA Chapel of the Holy Spirit.
Kallookalam, Joseph *c.m.i.* '71 (TYL) Gun Barrel City, TX St. Jude Church.
Kallor, John '73 (PH) [71] Philadelphia, PA Incarnation of Our Lord Church.
Kallumady, Thomas '73 (BRK) [18] Brooklyn, NY St. Bernadette Church.
Kalonga, Simon '84 (DEN) [3] Englewood, CO St. Louis Church.
Kalousieh, Georges '81 (ARM) Paterson, NJ Sacred Heart Church.
Kalscheuer, Henry N. '59 (MAD) Dodgeville, WI St. Joseph Church.
Kalscheuer, Roger *s.j.* '85 (OM) [14] Omaha, NE St. Frances Cabrini Church.
Kaltenbach, Victor J. '94 (SFD) Greenville, IL St. Lawrence Church.
Kaltreider, Msgr. Carl E. '79 (CHL) Shelby, NC St. Mary's Church.
Kalu, Clement '84 (LR) [2] Little Rock, AR St. Anne Church; [9] Little Rock, AR St. Mary Church; [12] Little Rock, AR St. Patrick's Church.
Kalu, Martin Ralph '89 (ATL) [1] Atlanta, GA Cathedral of Christ the King.
Kamas, John *s.s.s.* '75 (NY) [55] New York, NY St. Jean Baptiste Church.
Kamber, Kenneth L. '53 (L) Lebanon Junction, KY St. Benedict Church.
Kambitsch, Lawrence J. '69 (MRY) King City, CA St. John the Baptist Church.
Kamenski, Thomas *o.f.m.* (LAF) [F] Lafayette, LA Our Lady of Lourdes Regional Medical Center, Inc.
Kamide, Paul T. '63 (ORL) Port Orange, FL Epiphany Church.
Kamienski, Luciano *s.d.b.* '66 (LA) Inglewood, CA St. John Chrysostom Church.
Kamiensky, Joseph J. *s.j.* '77 (BUF) [D] Buffalo, NY Canisius High School; [O] Buffalo, NY Canisius Jesuit Community.
Kaminski, Frank T. *s.j.* '76 (CAM) [4] Camden, NJ Holy Name Church.
Kaminski, George '85 (FTW) [19] Fort Wayne, IN St. Vincent de Paul Church.
Kaminski, Henry T. '53 (NEW) Plainfield, NJ St. Mary Church; Plainfield, NJ St. Stanislaus Kostka Church.
Kaminski, Joseph M. '51 (GF) Retired.
Kaminski, Kevin A. '78 (MET) Raritan, NJ St. Joseph Church.
Kaminski, Louis T. '77 (SCR) Lake Winola, PA St. Mary of the Lake Church.
Kaminski, Neal *o.f.m.* '56 (RCK) [I] Rockford, IL The Poor Clares of Rockford.
Kaminski, Stephen J. '91 (CLV) [3] Garfield Heights, OH St. Therese Church.
Kaminski, Sy '53 (Y) [10] Youngstown, OH St. Casimir's Church.
Kaminski, Thomas J. '66 (CHI) [108] Chicago, IL St. John Fisher Church.
Kaminski, Walter '54 (HRT) [6] Meriden, CT St. Stanislaus Church.
Kaminsky, Joseph T. '61 (HRT) New Milford, CT St. Francis Xavier's Church.
Kamis, Robert '65 (CHI) [N] Chicago, IL St. Peter's Friary.
Kamla, Jerome J. '42 (LC) Retired.
Kamlage, Herman '57 (COV) Retired.
Kammer, Fred *s.j.* '76 (WDC) [M] Washington, DC K Street Jesuit Community.
Kammerer, Raymond (CIN) Waynesville, OH St. Augustine Church.
Kammerer, Richard F. '80 (RVC) Lindenhurst, NY Our Lady of Perpetual Help Church.
Kamp, Francis J. *s.v.d.* '47 (CHI) [B] Techny, IL Divine Word Residence; [N] Techny, IL Society of the Divine Word, Provincial Headquarter-Chicago Prov.; [U] Techny, IL S.V.D., Catholic Universities, Inc.; [U] Techny, IL Divine Word Missionaries, Inc., Divine Word Funds, Inc.
Kampa, Dennis C. '68 (STP) Kenyon, MN St. Michael Church; Pine Island, MN St. Michael Church.
Kampfer, Gerald D. '67 (ALB) Wilton, NY Wilton Developmental Center.
Kampher, Gerald D. '67 (ALB) Special Assignment.
Kampschneider, Daniel J. '79 (OM) On Duty Outside the Archdiocese.
Kampsen, Frederick '39 (SCL) Retired.
Kana, Steven '95 (AUS) Bryan, TX St. Anthony's Church; Temple, TX St. Luke's Church.
Kanar, Richard '94 (PSC) Annandale, VA Epiphany of Our Lord Church; Absent on Sick Leave.
Kanat, Kurian '58 (LAF) [1] Lafayette, LA St. John the Evangelist Cathedral.
Kanda, Francis P. '53 (PRO) Tiverton, RI St. Christopher Church.
Kanda, John R. *c.s.sp.* '42 (VEN) [G] Sarasota, FL Congregation of the Holy Ghost.
Kandathiduky, Joseph (CHI) Northlake, IL Syro-Malabar Catholic Mission of the Archdiocese of Chicago Church.
Kandathinkara, John J. *v.c.* '84 (BAL) Bradshaw, MD St. Stephen Church.
Kandathiparampil, Joseph '63 (WIL) Sherwood Park, DE St. John the Beloved Church; Wilmington, DE Bissell Hospital.
Kandel, Timothy (ORL) On Duty Outside the Diocese.
Kandrac, Antone *o.f.m.conv.* '57 (ALB) Nassau, NY St. Mary Church.
Kandt, Gregory '90 (RIC) Salem, VA Our Lady of Perpetual Help Church.
Kandula, Charles R. '76 (TR) [12] Trenton, NJ St. Anthony Church.
Kane, Aloysius T. '38 (PH) Retired.
Kane, Msgr. Arthur J. '36 (RVC) Retired.
Kane, Msgr. Bartholomew '37 (DM) Retired.
Kane, Brian E. '60 (LA) On Duty Outside the Archdiocese.
Kane, Cornelius T. *o.p.* '52 (WDC) [11] Washington, DC St. Dominic Church & Priory Church.
Kane, Dennis C. *o.p.* '46 (PRO) [P] Providence, RI St. Thomas Aquinas Priory at Providence College.
Kane, Edward *c.ss.r.* '47 (KC) [32] Kansas City, MO Our Lady of Perpetual Help Church; [J] Kansas City, MO Redemptorists of Kansas City.
Kane, Edward R. '78 (BRK) [34] Brooklyn, NY St. Edmund's Church.
Kane, Eugene '54 (PEO) Retired.
Kane, Farrell J. *o.carm.* '65 (CHI) Gurnee, IL St. Paul the Apostle Church.
Kane, Msgr. Francis A. '35 (SCR) Retired.
Kane, Francis J. '53 (PRT) Togus, ME Dept. of Veteran Affairs.
Kane, Francis J. '69 (CHI) Wilmette, IL St. Joseph Church.
Kane, George J. '51 (CHI) Schaumburg, IL Church of the Holy Spirit; Retired.
Kane, Herbert T. *s.j.* '52 (NY) [Z] Cornwall, NY Jogues Retreat.
Kane, Ignatius B. *o.s.b.* '61 (BIR) [E] Cullman, AL St. Bernard Abbey.
Kane, Msgr. James D. '58 (SY) Johnson City, NY Blessed Sacrament Church.
Kane, James J. '71 (ALB) [5] Schenectady, NY St. Helen Church; Special Assignment.
Kane, John '69 (SP) On Duty Outside the Diocese.
Kane, John J. '66 (PH) Springfield, PA St. Kevin Church.
Kane, Msgr. John T. '63 (LA) Hacienda Heights, CA St. John Vianney Church.
Kane, John W. *c.ss.r.* '44 (TUC) [F] Cortaro, AZ Desert House of Prayer.
Kane, Joseph E. '67 (EVN) Jasper, IN Precious Blood Church.
Kane, Msgr. Joseph F. '38 (PBL) Retired.
Kane, Joseph F. '46 (SY) [10] Syracuse, NY St. Andrew the Apostle Church.
Kane, Joseph M. '70 (BO) [U] Boston, MA Marian Manor.
Kane, Joseph P. *s.j.* '68 (NY) City, NY George M. Motchan Detention Center; City, NY George Viero Center; City, NY Rose M. Singer Center; [Z] New York, NY Jesuit Provincial's Office.
Kane, Joseph T. '62 (PH) Warrington, PA St. Robert Bellarmine Church.
Kane, Justin J. '44 (DUB) Retired.
Kane, Michael N. '80 (PSC) Coconut Creek, FL Our Lady of the Sign Church.
Kane, Paul *s.j.* (SPK) [E] Spokane, WA Gonzaga Preparatory School.

Kane, Paul '96 (MIA) Hollywood, FL Little Flower Church.
Kane, Philip M. '88 (JC) Glasgow, MO St. Mary Church; Slater, MO St. Joseph Church.
Kane, Terence '68 (ATL) Kennesaw, GA St. Catherine of Siena Church.
Kane, Thomas '69 (WOR) Absent on Leave.
Kane, Thomas A. '44 (PH) Bala-Cynwyd, PA St. Matthias Church; Retired.
Kane, Msgr. Thomas A. '52 (WDC) Norbeck, MD St. Patrick Church.
Kane, Thomas A. *c.s.p.* '75 (NY) [Z] Scarsdale, NY Paulist Fathers Generalate.
Kane, Thomas C. *o.p.* '52 (WDC) [C] Washington, DC Catholic University of America, The.
Kane, Thomas S. '67 (RVC) Riverhead, NY St. John the Evangelist Church.
Kane, Timothy '82 (DET) [68] Detroit, MI St. Rita Church.
Kane, Walter J. *s.j.* '68 (BO) [W] Boston, MA The Society of Jesus of New England-Provincial Offices.
Kane, William *s.v.d.* '47 (BO) [W] Boston, MA Divine Word Missionaries.
Kane, William '55 (LR) Retired.
Kane, William J. *s.j.* '48 (BEL) [E] Red Bud, IL St. Clement Health Services.
Kane, William J. *s.j.* '48 (STL) [P] St. Louis, MO The Jesuits of the Missouri Province.
Kane, Msgr. William J. '60 (WDC) [3] Bethesda, MD Little Flower Church; Pastoral Center Special Ministries.
Kang, John '59 (HON) [13] Honolulu, HI Sacred Heart Church.
Kang, Paul '91 (NEW) [6] Orange, NJ St. Andrew Kim Church.
Kang, Paul '91 (NY) On Duty Outside the Archdiocese.
Kangley, Bernard *o.carm.* '44 (LA) [R] Los Angeles, CA Mount Carmel Priory, Carmelite Fathers and Brothers.
Kania, Wojciech M. *s.chr.* '41 (LA) [22] Los Angeles, CA Our Lady of the Bright Mount Church.
Kanicki, Philip A. '85 (RIC) Military Chaplains.
Kanjiramkuzhy, John '64 (LAF) Mamou, LA St. Ann Church.
Kanka, Robert '56 (ROC) Retired.
Kannanaickal, Raphael *c.m.i.* '71 (PH) [9] Philadelphia, PA St. Ambrose Church.
Kannitzer, Columbian '50 (LR) [A] Subiaco, AR Subiaco Monastery.
Kanonik, Stephen F. '82 (CHI) [115] Chicago, IL St. Ladislaus Church.
Kanono, Joseph *m.s.c.* '76 (MI) Ebeye, MH Queen of Peace Church.
Kantner, William R. '75 (MEM) [12] Memphis, TN Incarnation Church.
Kantor, Msgr. Adolph A. '43 (SY) Retired.
Kanzic, Gerald B. '92 (PAT) Ringwood, NJ St. Catherine of Bologna Church.
Kao, Paulus '59 (LSC) Bayard, NM Our Lady of Fatima Church.
Kapalczynski, Msgr. Eugene J. '40 (MIL) Retired.
Kaparich, Albert N. '45 (HEL) Retired.
Kapfer, Lee *s.j.* '53 (SEA) [11] Seattle, WA St. Joseph Church.
Kapica, Francis A. '35 (MET) Retired.
Kapica, Francis A. '35 (TR) [L] Lawrenceville, NJ Morris Hall-Saint Lawrence, Inc.
Kapinus, Augustine *o.f.m.conv.* '58 (ALB) Northville, NY St. Francis of Assisi Church.
Kapitan, John *o.f.m.* '95 (PSC) [B] Sybertsville, PA Holy Dormition Monastery.
Kapitz, Donald '73 (SFE) Retired.
Kaplinski, Peter (VIC) [2] Victoria, TX Holy Family of Joseph, Mary & Jesus Church.
Kapoun, Robert E. '64 (STP) Special Assignment.
Kappalumakkel, Mathew '89 (HRT) [1] West Haven, CT Our Lady of Victory Church.
Kappe, John H. '71 (GAL) [22] Houston, TX St. Clare of Assisi Church.
Kappes, Joseph B. *s.j.* (DET) [K] Detroit, MI Jesuit Provincial Office-Detroit Province of the Society of Jesus.
Kapphahn, Leo W. *o.s.c.* '39 (PHX) [F] Phoenix, AZ Crosier Community of Phoenix (Canons Regular of the Order of the Holy Cross).
Kappler, Stephan '93 (OAK) Livermore, CA St. Michael's Church.
Kapral, Richard J. '70 (SY) Waterville, NY St. Bernard Church.
Kapron, Alan '94 (PSC) New Britain, CT Holy Trinity Church; South Hadley, MA St. Michael's Church.
Kapushion, Marvin J. '56 (PBL) [3] Pueblo, CO Holy Family Church.
Kapusnak, Joseph '66 (PBR) [2] Youngstown, OH St. Nicholas Church.
Karabin, Joseph D. '74 (PIT) Braddock, PA Good Shepherd Church; Allegheny County, PA Braddock General Hospital.
Karachira, Thomas '90 (WH) Harrisville, WV Christ Our Hope Church; St. Marys, WV St. John Church.
Karaffa, James G. *c.s.c.* (FTW) Granger, IN St. Pius X Church.
Karal, John W. '53 (DUB) Retired.
Karam, Peter '88 (OLL) Millbrae, CA Our Lady of Lebanon Church; Stockton, CA Maronite Catholic Community Church.
Karam, Peter '88 (SFR) [2] San Mateo, CA St. Gregory Church.
Karamitis, Dennis R. *s.j.* '75 (STP) [N] Minneapolis, MN La Storta Jesuit Community.
Karas, Boudau '84 (STF) Retired.
Karas, Stephen C. '65 (Y) Struthers, OH Holy Trinity Church.
Karasek, Edward '87 (AUS) West, TX Assumption Church.
Karath, William E. '71 (P) Bandon, OR Holy Trinity Church.
Karava, Norbert '80 (TLS) Durant, OK St. William Church.
Karban, Roger R. '64 (BEL) Renault, IL Our Lady of Good Counsel Church; [B] Waterloo, IL Gibault Catholic High School.
Karcher, Jerome '83 (ORG) [4] Huntington Beach, CA St. Vincent de Paul Church.
Karcsinski, Joseph J. '79 (BGP) [13] Bridgeport, CT St. Mary's Church.
Karcz, Lawrence *o.f.m.* (GB) [I] Green Bay, WI St. Mary of the Angels Friary.
Karczewski, Julian K. '74 (CAM) [5] Vineland, NJ St. Mary's Church.
Kardas, Thaddeus '70 (WOR) Absent on Leave.
Kardian, Richard S. *m.m.* '56 (BUF) [O] Buffalo, NY Maryknoll House.
Kardian, Richard S. *m.m.* '56 (CLV) [P] Cleveland, OH Maryknoll Fathers.
Kardian, Richard S. *m.m.* '56 (NY) [Z] Maryknoll, NY Maryknoll Fathers and Brothers.
Kardon, John A. *s.j.* (DET) [28] Detroit, MI Gesu Church.
Kardong, Terrence *o.s.b.* '63 (BIS) [A] Richardton, ND Assumption Abbey.
Kardos, Blase *o.f.m.conv.* '43 (NY) [B] New York, NY St. Francis Novitiate.
Kardos, Blase B. *o.f.m.conv.* (NY) Staten Island, NY Seaview Hospital and Home.
Kardzis, Krzysztof '84 (TOL) Norwalk, OH St. Paul Church.
Karels, Agdus S. '44 (NU) Retired.
Karels, Agdus S. '44 (STP) Retired.
Karels, Ambrose G. '59 (KC) Special Assignment.
Karenbauer, Richard P. '70 (GBG) Leechburg, PA St. Martha Church.
Karepin, James M. *o.p.* '90 (CHI) [N] Chicago, IL Dominicans (Provincial Office).
Karepin, James M. *o.p.* '90 (STF) Syracuse, NY St. John the Baptist Church.
Kareta, Gregory *o.f.m. con.* '56 (FRS) Avenal, CA St. Joseph Church.
Karg, Msgr. Andrew H. '64 (E) [10] Erie, PA Our Lady of Peace Church.
Karg, Msgr. William C. '57 (E) [3] Sharon, PA St. Joseph Church.
Karg, William D. '64 (CLV) [17] Akron, OH St. Sebastian Church.
Kari, Arnold A. '77 (RC) Philip, SD Sacred Heart Church.
Kariamadam, Joseph *c.m.i.* '74 (LKC) [4] Lake Charles, LA St. Henry Church.
Karier, Raymond *s.s.c.* '52 (OM) [K] St. Columbans, NE St. Columban's Foreign Mission Society.
Karikattil, Jose (SAC) Citrus Heights, CA Holy Family Church.
Karisa, Nathaniel (ROC) [I] Rochester, NY Basilian Residence.
Kariuki, Joseph '79 (PIT) Duquesne, PA St. Joseph Church.
Karl, Charles '57 (PEO) Retired.
Karl, Edward B. '57 (BGP) Bethel, CT St. Mary's Church.
Karl, Kevin '80 (OWN) [7] Owensboro, KY SS. Joseph and Paul Church.
Karle, William J. '72 (SCR) Sayre, PA Church of the Epiphany.
Karlen, Donald H. '64 (SY) [8] Utica, NY St. George Church; [10] Utica, NY St. Joseph and St. Patrick Church; [W] Whitesboro, NY Mount Olivet.
Karlin, Paulinus I. *o.f.m.cap.* '43 (SAL) Hays, KS St. Joseph's Church; [D] Hays, KS St. Joseph's Friary.
Karlowicz, Edwin *c.r.* (CHI) [107] Chicago, IL St. John Cantius Church.
Karls, Victor *c.ss.r.* '70 (STL) [P] Liguori, MO Liguori Mission House/Redemptorists.
Karmanocky, Bernard *o.f.m.* '73 (ALT) [17] Johnstown, PA St. Therese of the Child Jesus Church.
Karnik, George W. '58 (DUB) [5] Waterloo, IA St. John's Church.
Karnish, Robert A. '66 (GI) Gordon, NE St. Leo's Church.
Karns, David W. '74 (ALN) [3] McAdoo, PA St. Patrick Church.
Karoblis, Andrew K. '54 (LC) [4] Wisconsin Rapids, WI SS. Peter and Paul Church.
Karol, Msgr. Bernard A. '36 (MAR) Retired.
Karoor, Isaac '69 (BAL) Westminster, MD St. John Church.
Karp, Joseph A. '67 (ORG) Special Assignment; [G] Yorba Linda, CA Polish Center.
Karpiel, Peter '86 (RVC) Copiague, NY Our Lady of the Assumption Church.
Karpiey, Daniel J. '59 (HRT) Terryville, CT St. Casimir Church.
Karpinski, Robert D. '93 (BGP) [2] Trumbull, CT St. Catherine of Siena Church; [C] Trumbull, CT St. Joseph High School.
Karpyn, Gregory R. '87 (ALN) [C] Allentown, PA Allentown Central Catholic High School.
Karr, Raymond E. '59 (ALT) Meyersdale, PA SS. Philip and James Church; Absent on Leave.
Karrer, Walter *c.ss.r.* '47 (WCH) [14] Wichita, KS St. Joseph Church; [G] Wichita, KS Redemptorist Mission House.
Karris, Robert J. *o.f.m.* '65 (STL) [P] St. Louis, MO Franciscan Friary of St. Anthony of Padua.
Karssen, John H. *c.m.* '46 (DEN) [M] Denver, CO Congregation of the Mission Midwest Province: De Paul House.
Karuhn, Robert J. '65 (GB) Sturgeon Bay, WI St. Joseph Church.
Karvelis, Msgr. Bryan J. '56 (BRK) [142] Brooklyn, NY Transfiguration Church.
Karvelis, Francis V. '49 (HRT) [11] Waterbury, CT St. Joseph Church.
Karwacki, Bart *o.f.m.conv.* (BAL) [B] Ellicott City, MD Friary of St. Joseph Cupertino; [M] Ellicott City, MD St. Joseph Cupertino Friary, Friars Minor Conventual of St. Francis of Assisi.
Karwacki, Francis J. '83 (HBG) Lykens, PA Our Lady Help of Christians Church; Williamstown, PA Sacred Heart of Jesus Church.
Karwacki, Marion T. '36 (ORL) Retired.
Karwel, Henry *o.f.m.conv.* '57 (BAL) [M] Ellicott City, MD Order of Friars Minor Conventual.
Karwel, Henry *o.f.m.conv.* '57 (SPR) Ware, MA St. Mary's Church.
Karwin, John J. *s.j.* '67 (BO) [W] Boston, MA The Society of Jesus of New England-Provincial Offices.
Karwin, John J. *s.j.* '67 (WH) [A] Wheeling, WV Wheeling Jesuit University.
Karwowski, Edmund K '87 (HRT) Plainville, CT Our Lady of Mercy Church.
Kasak, Andrew *o.f.m.conv.* '45 (BAL) [88] Baltimore, MD St. Stanislaus Kostka Church.
Kasarda, John '61 (PBR) Mingo Junction, OH St. John the Baptist Church.
Kasch, John R. '54 (SFS) Howard, SD St. Agatha Church.
Kaschenbach, Msgr. Arthur J. '51 (SCR) Mount Pocono, PA St. Mary of the Mount Church.
Kasel, Joseph M. '48 (NU) Retired.
Kaserow, John M. *m.m.* '69 (CHI) [B] Chicago, IL The Catholic Theological Union at Chicago.
Kaserow, John M. *m.m.* '69 (NY) [Z] Maryknoll, NY Maryknoll Fathers and Brothers.
Kaseta, Peter *o.f.m.cap.* '67 (NY) [57] New York, NY St. John the Baptist Church.
Kash, Robert J. '52 (CHI) Retired.
Kashmer, George B. '58 (GRY) Retired.
Kasinskas, Clement *c.p.* (BO) [6] Cambridge, MA Immaculate Conception Church.
Kasinski, James J. '66 (BUF) [12] Niagara Falls, NY Sacred Heart Church.
Kaska, E. William '69 (DAV) [2] Davenport, IA Our Lady of Victory Church.
Kaskie, Brian '92 (JKS) [4] Jackson, MS St. Therese Church.
Kaslyn, Robert *s.j.* '85 (BO) [W] Cambridge, MA Faber House; [W] Cambridge, MA Weston Jesuit Community.
Kasny, Jiri *s.d.b.* '87 (COL) [A] Columbus, OH Pontifical College Josephinum; [H] Columbus, OH Salesian Center.
Kasparek, John *s.c.j.* '69 (MIL) [P] Hales Corners, WI Priests of the Sacred Heart.
Kasparek, John *s.c.j.* '69 (PMB) Stuart, FL St. Joseph Church.
Kasper, Eugene J. '59 (NEW) Rahway, NJ St. Mark's Church.
Kasper, John *o.s.f.s.* '79 (OAK) Piedmont, CA Corpus Christi Church.
Kasperek, David D. '63 (GB) Flintville, WI SS. Edward and Isidore Church.
Kasprick, Roger *o.s.b.* '59 (SCL) [I] Collegeville, MN St. John's Abbey, of the Order of St. Benedict.
Kasprzak, John F. '75 (BUF) Woodlawn, NY Our Lady of Grace Church.
Kasprzyk, James H. '65 (BUF) [8] Cheektowaga, NY Our Lady of Czestochowa Church; Retired.
Kasprzyk, Leon J. '61 (MET) Lambertville, NJ St. John the Evangelist Church.
Kasputis, Thomas R. '76 (CHI) Riverside, IL St. Mary Church.
Kass, George '43 (LA) Retired.

Kass, Thomas G. *c.s.v.* '77 (CHI) [N] Arlington Heights, IL Viatorian Province Center-Clerics of St. Viator.
Kassian, Jeffrey '96 (STN) [1] Chicago, IL St. Nicholas Ukrainian Catholic Cathedral.
Kassis, Daniel '81 (GLP) Absent on Leave.
Kasteel, Ben *s.m.* '64 (LUB) Plainview, TX Our Lady of Guadalupe Church.
Kasten, Edward F. '54 (MIL) Retired.
Kastenholz, John P. *o.praem.* '65 (GB) Navarino, WI St. Lawrence Church; [B] De Pere, WI St. Norbert College; [I] De Pere, WI St. Norbert Abbey.
Kaster, Alfred D. '60 (DUL) On Duty Outside the Diocese.
Kaster, Alfred D. '60 (SAC) Grass Valley, CA St. Patrick Church.
Kastigar, James J. '82 (CHI) [1] Cicero, IL St. Anthony Church.
Kastigar, John J. '52 (CHI) Military Chaplains.
Kastner, Edwin H. '51 (BEL) Retired.
Kastner, James A. '59 (OKL) [4] Oklahoma City, OK Christ the King Church.
Kasun, Stanley L. '94 (OM) Norfolk, NE Sacred Heart Church.
Kasza, John '93 (DET) Graduate Studies.
Kaszak, Edward '55 (DET) [13] Detroit, MI St. Bartholomew Church.
Kasznel, Richard C. '65 (STL) St. Mary's, MO Immaculate Conception Church.
Kaszynski, Robert S. '60 (FR) [21] Fall River, MA St. Stanislaus Church.
Katcher, Eugene T. '93 (DET) [5] Warren, MI St. Edmund Church.
Kathol, Quentin *o.s.b.* '63 (KC) Tarkio, MO St. Paul the Apostle Church; [J] Conception, MO Conception Abbey.
Kato, Stephen M. '48 (PIT) Retired.
Katorski, Robert H. '63 (MIL) [13] Milwaukee, WI Blessed Sacrament Church.
Katoski, Eugene *o.f.m.* '45 (CLV) [P] Cleveland, OH Padua Franciscan Friary; [Q] Cleveland, OH Monastery of the Poor Clares.
Katricak, Kenneth J. *o.s.b.* '83 (CLV) [N] Beachwood, OH Villa Sancta Anna Home for the Aged, Inc.; [P] Cleveland, OH Benedictine Order of Cleveland.
Katrij, Julian *o.s.b.m.* '40 (RVC) [N] Glen Cove, NY St. Josaphatis Monastery, Novitiate and Retreat House.
Katrij, Julian *o.s.b.m.* '40 (STF) [B] Glen Cove, NY Basilian Fathers Novitiate of the Order of St. Basil the Great.
Katsuno, Peter *s.a.* '40 (NY) [Z] Garrison, NY Generalate of the Franciscan Friars of the Atonement-St. James Friary.
Kattady, Augustine '71 (TUC) Superior, AZ St. Francis of Assisi Parish Church.
Katz, Jerome A. '71 (SY) Cortland, NY St. Anthony Church.
Katz, Roger L. '89 (DUB) Rockford, IA Holy Name Church; [H] Mason City, IA North Iowa Mercy Health Center.
Katziner, Stephen F. '74 (PH) [32] Philadelphia, PA St. Cecilia Church.
Kauchak, Justin R. *o.p.* '66 (BR) Hammond, LA Holy Ghost Church.
Kaucheck, Kenneth R. '76 (DET) [3] Troy, MI St. Anastasia Church.
Kaucky, Francis '59 (CHI) Oak Forest, IL St. Damian Church.
Kauffman, Dennis J. *c.s.b.* '79 (ROC) [B] Rochester, NY The Aquinas Institute; [I] Rochester, NY Residence of Basilian Fathers-The Aquinas Institute.
Kauffman, John '75 (DEN) Kremmling, CO St. Peter Church.
Kauffman, Niles *o.f.m.cap.* '58 (MIL) [25] Milwaukee, WI St. Francis of Assisi Church.
Kauffman, William B. '90 (WIL) [1] Wilmington, DE Cathedral of St. Peter; Apostleship of the Sea.
Kauffmann, James F. '75 (RIC) Ladysmith, VA St. Mary of the Annunciation Church.
Kaufman, Kent R. '93 (TOL) [27] Toledo, OH St. John the Baptist Church.
Kaufman, Philip *o.s.b.* '45 (SCL) [I] Collegeville, MN St. John's Abbey, of the Order of St. Benedict.
Kaufman, William C. '74 (PH) [15] Philadelphia, PA Ascension of Our Lord Church.
Kaufmann, Leo B. *s.j.* '51 (SPK) [K] Spokane, WA Regis Community.
Kaukus, Edwin J. '57 (BUF) Retired.
Kaul, John '75 (DET) Military Chaplains.
Kaunas, Bronius *o.s.j.* '42 (MRY) [G] Santa Cruz, CA Oblates of St. Joseph Provincial House and Shrine.
Kaut, Msgr. Bernd (WDC) [V] Washington, DC Nativity of the Blessed Virgin (German Mission).
Kauta, John B. '67 (NY) Bedford, NY St. Patrick Church.
Kautzky, Jon '62 (DM) Red Oak, IA St. Mary Church.
Kautzman, Jerome G. '59 (BIS) [1] Dickinson, ND Queen of Peace Church.
Kauzlarich, John R. '55 (CHI) Glenwood, IL St. John Church.
Kavanagh, Aelred M. *o.s.b.* '93 (NO) [A] St. Benedict, LA St. Joseph's Seminary College.
Kavanagh, Aidan *o.s.b.* '57 (IND) [J] St. Meinrad, IN St. Meinrad Archabbey.
Kavanagh, Charles J. *s.j.* '44 (LA) [C] Los Angeles, CA Loyola Marymount University.
Kavanagh, Msgr. Charles M. '63 (NY) [185] Bronx, NY St. Raymond Church; [DD] New York, NY Alfred E. Smith Memorial Foundation, Inc., The.
Kavanagh, Dermot *c.s.sp.* '60 (SR) Napa, CA St. Apollinaris Church.
Kavanagh, Donald '72 (BRK) [213] Queens, NY Our Lady of Lourdes Church.
Kavanagh, Msgr. Edward J. '48 (SAC) [21] Sacramento, CA St. Rose Church; [E] Sacramento, CA St. Patrick Children's Home, Inc.
Kavanagh, Francis X. *o.c.s.o.* '38 (ATL) [I] Conyers, GA The Monastery of the Holy Spirit.
Kavanagh, Henry '75 (PIT) [N] Pittsburgh, PA St. Paul of the Cross Monastery.
Kavanagh, James F. '64 (LA) [69] Los Angeles, CA St. Jerome Church.
Kavanagh, Msgr. John C. '42 (PH) Wynnewood, PA Presentation B.V.M. Church.
Kavanagh, Joseph J. *s.j.* '46 (NY) [80] New York, NY Nativity Church.
Kavanagh, Kevin J. '83 (COL) Delaware, OH St. Mary Church.
Kavanagh, Morgan '55 (BLX) Retired.
Kavanagh, Msgr. Richard T. '36 (IND) Retired.
Kavanagh, Aelred *o.s.b.* '94 (NO) [P] St. Benedict, LA St. Joseph Abbey.
Kavanagh, Msgr. Charles M. '63 (NY) [DD] New York, NY Partnership for Quality Education, Inc.
Kavanagh, Henry *c.p.* '75 (SCR) [M] Scranton, PA Saint Ann's Passionist Monastery.
Kavanagh, Msgr. John C. '42 (PH) Retired.
Kavanagh, John F. *s.j.* '71 (STL) [C] St. Louis, MO Saint Louis University; [P] St. Louis, MO Jesuit Community Corporation at St. Louis University - Jesuit Hall.
Kavanaugh, John J. '57 (WIL) Sherwood Park, DE St. John the Beloved Church.
Kavanaugh, John P. '48 (SFR) Redwood City, CA Our Lady of Mount Carmel Church; San Francisco, CA Knights of Malta.
Kavanaugh, Kieran *o.c.d.* '55 (WDC) [B] Washington, DC Monastery of Our Lady of Mount Carmel; [V] Washington, DC Institute of Carmelite Studies and ICS Publications.
Kavanaugh, Michael J. '85 (SAV) Port Wentworth, GA Our Lady of Lourdes Church.
Kavanaugh, Philip M. '73 (LA) [33] Los Angeles, CA Precious Blood Church.
Kavanaugh, Thomas *c.m.* '41 (SAT) [16] San Antonio, TX Our Lady of Grace Church.
Kavaney, C. Robert '85 (BIS) [2] Dickinson, ND St. Joseph Church.
Kavcak, John *m.s.c.* '73 (SB) Upland, CA St. Joseph Church.
Kaveney, Thomas J. '47 (CHI) Berwyn, IL St. Odilo Church; Retired.
Kavin, Msgr. Edward F. '56 (NEW) [N] Rutherford, NJ St. John Vianney Residence for Priests.
Kavookjian, Perry '87 (FRS) [12] Fresno, CA St. Paul Church; [H] Fresno, CA St. Paul Newman Center.
Kavunkal, Joseph '66 (CHI) [85] Chicago, IL Holy Rosary Church.
Kawa, Edward *s.d.s.* '64 (GRY) [K] Merrillville, IN Salvatorian Fathers (Society of the Divine Savior).
Kawa, Msgr. Robert J. '69 (STU) Beverly, OH St. Bernard Church; [J] Beverly, OH Marriage Encounter.
Kawamata, Louis *ss.cc.* '74 (FR) [K] Fairhaven, MA Sacred Hearts Provincial House.
Kawamura, Peter *o.s.b.* '88 (SCL) [I] Collegeville, MN St. John's Abbey, of the Order of St. Benedict.
Kawamura, Shinzo *s.j.* '92 (WDC) [M] Washington, DC The Jesuit Community at Georgetown University.
Kawanguzi, Emmanuel (AUS) [H] Austin, TX St. Joseph Hall; [H] Austin, TX St. Edward's University.
Kawczynski, Ronald '90 (FAR) Military Chaplains.
Kawecki, Andrew M. '80 (GBG) Leckrone, PA Our Lady of Perpetual Help (St. Mary) Church.
Kawiak, Matthew A. '77 (ROC) Rochester, NY Strong Memorial Hospital.
Kawka, Frederick J. '64 (SAG) Frankenmuth, MI Blessed Trinity Church.
Kawlak, Matthew '77 (ROC) [J] Rochester, NY Sisters of Mercy of the Americas Regional Community of Rochester.
Kawola, Marion '45 (PSC) [B] Sybertsville, PA Holy Dormition Monastery.
Kay, Joseph '48 (LR) Paragould, AR St. Mary's Church.
Kay, Kieran M. *o.f.m.* '55 (Y) [K] Canton, OH Sancta Clara Monastery.
Kayatta, Francis P. '80 (PRO) [A] Providence, RI Seminary of Our Lady of Providence.
Kayler, Gary W. '75 (OKL) Jones, OK St. Robert Bellarmine Church; [E] Oklahoma City, OK Mercy Health Center.
Kaylor, Lee '81 (SFR) On Duty Outside the Archdiocese.
Kaylor, Robert W. '62 (Y) [C] Canton, OH Central Catholic High.
Kayrouz, Victor '64 (OLL) Hillside, IL Our Lady of Lebanon Church; Louisville, KY Maronite Catholic Community Church.
Kayser, Leonard '59 (SFS) Mayfield, SD St. Columba Church; Sigel, SD St. Agnes Church; Yankton, SD State Hospital.
Kayser, Robert (RVC) Retired.
Kaywell, Jerome P. '91 (VEN) Cape Coral, FL St. Andrew Church.
Kaza, Msgr. Charles A. '72 (E) Brockway, PA St. Tobias Church.
Kazanchy, Cordius P. *o.f.m.* '60 (PAT) [M] Butler, NJ St. Anthony Friary.
Kazanecki, Thaddeus J. *c.o.* '77 (BRK) [13] Brooklyn, NY St. Athanasius Church.
Kazarnowicz, Anthony S. '75 (WOR) [9] Worcester, MA Our Lady of Czestochowa Church.
Kazer, Michael '80 (DET) [1] Warren, MI St. Anne's Church.
Kazista, Francis G. '66 (WDC) [6] Silver Spring, MD St. John the Baptist Church.
Kazmierczak, Carl M. '55 (MIL) [43] Milwaukee, WI St. John Kanty's Church.
Kazmierczak, Msgr. Edward L. '51 (BUF) Retired.
Kazmierczak, Eugene J. '51 (FTW) New Carlisle, IN St. Stanislaus Kostka Church.
Kaznowski, Valentine J. '41 (DET) Retired.
Kcira, Anton '67 (DET) [10] Warren, MI St. Paul Albanian Catholic Community Church.
Keahi, Christopher *ss.cc.* '65 (HON) [H] Honolulu, HI St. Patrick's Monastery.
Kealey, Edward J. '89 (RVC) Medford, NY St. Sylvester Church.
Kealy, Francis de Paul *o.f.m.* '50 (NY) [35] New York, NY St. Francis of Assisi Church.
Kealy, Hubert J. '64 (GAL) [53] Houston, TX Notre Dame Church.
Kealy, Robert L. '72 (CHI) Highland Park, IL Immaculate Conception Church; [X] Chicago, IL Court of Appeals-Province of Chicago.
Kealy, Sean *c.s.sp.* '65 (PIT) [B] Pittsburgh, PA Duquesne University of the Holy Ghost.
Kean, Cary *o.f.m.* '55 (PAT) [M] Butler, NJ St. Anthony Friary.
Kean, Msgr. John J. '40 (BRK) Retired.
Kean, Joseph H. '64 (ALN) Unassigned; [J] Bethlehem, PA Holy Family Villa.
Keane, Alfred *m.m.* '58 (BO) [W] East Walpole, MA Maryknoll Department of Development.
Keane, Aquinas *o.c.s.o.* '73 (WOR) [N] Spencer, MA St. Joseph's Abbey.
Keane, Denis J. '63 (GF) Fort Benton, MT Immaculate Conception Church.
Keane, Dennis P. '71 (NY) [85] New York, NY Our Lady of Good Counsel Church.
Keane, Edward M. '39 (BRK) [178] Queens, NY Holy Family Church.
Keane, Eugene '55 (NY) Highland, NY St. Augustine Church.
Keane, James '47 (OAK) Retired.
Keane, Msgr. James P. '45 (SFR) Retired.
Keane, James T. '55 (LFT) Muncie, IN St. Mary Church.
Keane, John *s.a.* '62 (MRY) [J] Monterey, CA Department of Campus Ministry.
Keane, John F. '57 (SAT) On Duty Outside the Archdiocese.
Keane, John F. '65 (BO) On Special or Other Diocesan Assignment.
Keane, John J. '62 (HRT) [10] New Haven, CT St. John the Baptist Church.
Keane, John J. *s.a.* '62 (MRY) Seaside, CA St. Francis Xavier Church.
Keane, John J. '62 (PIT) [6] McKeesport, PA St. Pius V Church; [Q] Pittsburgh, PA Office of Chaplaincies.
Keane, Joseph P. '49 (BRK) Retired.
Keane, M. Brendan '50 (SFD) [3] Springfield, IL Christ The King Church.
Keane, Martin T. '43 (HRT) Retired.
Keane, Michael J. '57 (SFR) [2] San Rafael, CA St. Isabella Church.
Keane, Patrick '73 (NO) Absent on Leave.
Keane, Patrick J. '51 (SFR) Retired.
Keane, Patrick J. *o.s.a.* '52 (LA) Ojai, CA St. Thomas Aquinas Church.
Keane, Philip S. *s.s.* '67 (BAL) [A] Baltimore, MD St. Mary's Seminary and University.
Keane, Philip S. *s.s.* '67 (SY) On Duty Outside the Diocese.
Keane, Robert E. '78 (STP) Retired.
Keane, Robert L. *s.j.* '78 (BO) [W] Boston, MA The Society of Jesus of New England-Provincial Offices.
Keane, Thomas F. '56 (BO) [1] Quincy, MA St. Ann Church.
Keane, Thomas S. *m.m.* '56 (SJ) [M] Los Altos, CA Maryknoll.
Keane, Msgr. Vincent A. '58 (BRK) [B] Douglaston, NY Cathedral Residence of the Immaculate Conception.
Keane, Msgr. Vincent A. '59 (BRK) [A] Douglaston, NY

Immaculate Conception Pastoral Center.
Keane, Vincent E. '83 (TR) Eatontown, NJ St. Dorothea Church.
Keane, William *s.d.b.* '74 (OAK) [N] Berkeley, CA Salesian Community.
Keaney, Denis P. '61 (SAC) Folsom, CA St. John the Baptist Church; Folsom, CA State Prison.
Keaney, Francis J. *s.s.c.* '66 (BO) [W] Quincy, MA St. Columban's Foreign Mission Society.
Keaney, James P. '54 (R) Retired.
Keaney, Joseph F. *s.j.* '48 (BO) [W] Boston, MA Loyola House.
Kearney, A. Damian *o.s.b.* '56 (PRO) [P] Portsmouth, RI Abbey of St. Gregory the Great.
Kearney, Brendan *s.j.* (LA) Redondo Beach, CA St. James Church.
Kearney, Christopher '68 (LA) [B] Santa Ynez, CA San Lorenzo Novitiate and Seminary.
Kearney, Daniel S. '87 (NY) [95] New York, NY Our Lady Queen of Martyrs Church.
Kearney, Edward J. '51 (NEW) [23] Jersey City, NJ St. Patrick's Church; Woodcliff Lake, NJ Our Lady Mother of the Church.
Kearney, George W. '53 (DEN) Retired.
Kearney, John T. '83 (NY) Lake Katrine, NY St. Catherine Laboure Church.
Kearney, Joseph A. '67 (SCR) [2] Wilkes-Barre, PA Blessed Sacrament Church; Wilkes-Barre, PA Geisinger Wyoming Valley Hospital.
Kearney, Msgr. Joseph V. '46 (LA) Carpinteria, CA St. Joseph Church; Retired.
Kearney, Lawrence '50 (BAK) Jordan Valley, OR St. Bernard's Church.
Kearney, Michael J. (BO) Absent on Sick Leave.
Kearney, Myles J. '71 (BR) [13] Baton Rouge, LA St. Jude the Apostle Church; Baton Rouge, LA Woman's Hospital.
Kearney, Msgr. Patrick J. '53 (SD) San Diego, CA Nazareth House; Retired; [G] San Diego, CA Nazareth House Retirement Home.
Kearney, Msgr. Philip J. '36 (BO) Retired.
Kearney, Thomas L. *o.p.* '50 (CHI) [N] Chicago, IL Dominicans (Provincial Office).
Kearney, Timothy '96 (BO) [4] Lynn, MA St. Mary Church.
Kearney, Msgr. Vincent L. '43 (KC) Retired.
Kearney, William '83 (SP) Retired.
Kearns, Adam '54 (TR) Marlton, NJ St. Joan of Arc Church.
Kearns, Daniel J. '86 (PH) [32] Philadelphia, PA St. Cecilia Church.
Kearns, Daniel P. *c.m.* '69 (STL) [P] St. Louis, MO Vincentian Henrietta Residence.
Kearns, David *o.carm.* '61 (NY) Middletown, NY Our Lady of Mt. Carmel Church.
Kearns, Edward A. '63 (MET) Three Bridges, NJ St. Elizabeth Ann Seton Church.
Kearns, Edward T. '77 (PH) Newtown, PA St. Andrew Church.
Kearns, Harold M. '61 (HRT) Thomaston, CT St. Thomas Church.
Kearns, John P. '88 (BO) [CC] Bridgewater, MA Bridgewater State College Catholic Center.
Kearns, Joseph J. '48 (SAG) St. Charles, MI Immaculate Conception Church.
Kearns, Owen *l.c.* '83 (HRT) [B] Cheshire, CT Novitiate of the Legion of Christ.
Kearns, Robert M. *s.s.j.* '63 (BAL) [M] Baltimore, MD St. Joseph Society of the Sacred Heart House of Central Administration.
Kearns, Thomas '60 (KCK) [4] Overland Park, KS Queen of the Holy Rosary Church.
Keary, William M. '84 (HBG) Carlisle, PA St. Patrick Church.
Keating, Msgr. Bernard A. '47 (BAK) Retired.
Keating, C. Patrick '69 (SY) [6] Binghamton, NY St. John the Evangelist Church.
Keating, Carroll *s.j.* '61 (SAC) Fair Oaks, CA St. Mel Church.
Keating, David '54 (SFS) Retired.
Keating, Douglas '61 (MRY) Retired.
Keating, Earl *c.p.* '58 (HRT) [M] West Hartford, CT Holy Family Monastery/Retreat.
Keating, Earl *c.p.* '59 (HRT) [Q] Farmington, CT Holy Family Retreat House.
Keating, Edward C. *o.f.m.* '58 (SP) [10] Tampa, FL St. Lawrence Church.
Keating, Edward J. '94 (HBG) Coal Township, PA Our Lady of Hope Church; Trevorton, PA St. Patrick Church.
Keating, George M. '54 (NEW) Kenilworth, NJ St. Theresa's Church; Union, NJ Union Hospital.
Keating, James *o.s.a.* '84 (BRK) [205] Queens, NY St. Nicholas of Tolentine Church.
Keating, James D. *o.p.* '56 (TR) New Monmouth, NJ St. Mary Church.
Keating, James P. '51 (CHI) [65] Chicago, IL St. Francis de Sales Church.
Keating, Msgr. James V. '43 (NY) [3] Kingston, NY St. Joseph Church; Retired.
Keating, James W. '34 (CHI) Lyons, IL St. Hugh Church; Retired.
Keating, John R. *s.j.* '61 (WDC) [M] Washington, DC The Jesuit Community at Georgetown University; [V] Washington, DC Theological Studies, Inc.
Keating, Joseph H. '77 (HRT) [3] Bristol, CT St. Gregory's Church.
Keating, Joseph R. '57 (LC) Retired.
Keating, Pius F. *s.a.* '46 (CHR) Military Chaplains.
Keating, Thomas *o.c.s.o.* '49 (DEN) [M] Snowmass, CO St. Benedict's Monastery.
Keating, Thomas F. '66 (SY) Maine, NY Holy Rosary Church.
Keating, Timothy F. *c.ss.r.* '66 (ROC) [K] Canandaigua, NY Notre Dame Retreat House.
Keating, Timothy G. *s.m.* '85 (WDC) [M] Washington, DC Marist Provincial House.
Keaty, Jerome R. '62 (STL) Ladue, MO Church of the Annunziata.
Keaveney, George J. *c.ss.r.* '66 (BRK) [U] Brooklyn, NY Our Lady of Good Counsel Residence.
Keaveney, John '59 (NY) Wesley Hills, NY St. Boniface Church.
Keblesh, John W. '93 (PRM) Brunswick, OH St. Emilian Church.
Keck, Barnabas J. *o.f.m.cap.* '51 (SPR) [L] Springfield, MA St. Francis of Assisi Chapel and Catholic Information Center.
Keck, Edward L. '73 (COL) Newcomerstown, OH St. Francis de Sales Church.
Keck, Robert J. *s.j.* '60 (NY) [Z] New York, NY West Side Jesuit Community.
Kedzierski, Casimir '60 (PIT) Glassport, PA Queen of the Rosary Church.
Kee, James S. '95 (MOB) [19] Mobile, AL St. Pius X Church.
Keebler, Paul J. '66 (SY) [2] Binghamton, NY St. Ann Church; Binghamton, NY Broome Developmental Center.
Keebler, William C., Jr. '91 (PEO) Alexis, IL St. Theresa's Church.
Keech, William J. *o.s.f.s.* '57 (WIL) [I] Wilmington, DE DeSales House.
Keefe, Anthony J. '63 (SY) Sabbatical.
Keefe, Bernard A. '63 (BGP) [4] Stamford, CT St. Maurice Church.
Keefe, Charles R. '76 (MIL) [N] Milwaukee, WI Milwaukee Catholic Home.
Keefe, Danel T. '54 (OG) [4] Plattsburgh, NY St. Mary of the Lake Church.
Keefe, Daniel G. '83 (HRT) [2] Meriden, CT St. Joseph Church, Cheshire, CT Connecticut Correctional Institution.
Keefe, Dennis A. (BO) Awaiting Assignment.
Keefe, Donald J. *s.j.* '62 (NY) [A] Yonkers, NY St. Joseph's Seminary.
Keefe, Francis J. '58 (PRO) North Scituate, RI St. Joseph's Church.
Keefe, Francis L. *c.s.s.* '55 (BO) [W] Waltham, MA Stigmatine House.
Keefe, Gerald E. '47 (STP) Cologne, MN St. Bernard Church; [A] St. Paul, MN The Saint Paul Seminary.
Keefe, James *ss.cc.* '42 (FR) [K] Fairhaven, MA Sacred Hearts Provincial House.
Keefe, Jeffrey *o.f.m.conv.* '52 (SY) [2] Syracuse, NY Assumption B.V.M. Church.
Keefe, John A. '49 (ALB) [5] Albany, NY St. Catherine of Siena Church; Retired.
Keefe, John J. '68 (LIN) On Duty Outside the Diocese.
Keefe, John W. '32 (ALB) Retired.
Keefe, Joseph L. '71 (WIN) [4] Winona, MN St. Mary's Church; [J] Winona, MN St. Mary's Parish of Winona Endowment Fund, Inc.
Keefe, Thomas H. *m.m.* '55 (NY) [Z] Maryknoll, NY Maryknoll Fathers and Brothers.
Keefe, William '36 (CR) Retired.
Keefer, Hugh *o.s.b.* '67 (KCK) [H] Atchison, KS St. Benedict's Abbey.
Keefer, John E. *o.p.* '56 (CHR) [3] Columbia, SC Saint Martin de Porres Church.
Keefer, John E. *o.p.* '56 (NO) [P] New Orleans, LA Dominican Fathers & Brothers, Southern Dominican Province.
Keefer, Msgr. Oliver D. '28 (PIT) Retired.
Keefner, James *o.f.m.* '54 (SFD) Madison, IL Our Lady of Czestochowa Church.
Keegan, A. Peter '62 (SFR) Absent on Leave.
Keegan, Fintan *s.s.c.* '33 (PRO) [P] Bristol, RI St. Columban's Retirement House.
Keegan, Gregory J. *m.m.* '43 (NY) [Z] Maryknoll, NY Maryknoll Fathers and Brothers.
Keegan, James M. *s.j.* '71 (BO) [W] Boston, MA The Society of Jesus of New England-Provincial Offices.
Keegan, John *m.m.* (RVC) Stony Brook, NY Stony Brook University Hospital.
Keegan, John E. *m.m.* '60 (NY) [Z] Maryknoll, NY Maryknoll Fathers and Brothers.
Keegan, John W. *s.j.* '69 (PRT) [9] Portland, ME St. Pius X Church; [C] Portland, ME Cheverus High School; [C] Portland, ME Cheverus High School.
Keegan, Terence J. *o.p.* (PRO) [B] Providence, RI Providence College.
Keegan, Terence S. *o.p.* '68 (PRO) [P] Providence, RI St. Thomas Aquinas Priory at Providence College.
Keegstra, Garrett *o.f.m.* '86 (MAD) [G] Madison, WI St. Marys Hospital Medical Center.
Keegstra, Gary *o.f.m.cap.* '86 (MAD) [M] Madison, WI San Damiano Friary.
Keehan, Msgr. Daniel J. '54 (NY) [141] Bronx, NY St. Frances de Chantal Church.
Keehan, Edward J. '57 (NY) [16] Yonkers, NY St. Peter Church.
Keehan, John J. '60 (CHI) [14] Chicago, IL St. Ann Church.
Keehan, Terence M. '86 (CHI) [180] Chicago, IL Queen of Angels Church.
Keehner, John '93 (Y) Boardman, OH St. Charles Borromeo's Church.
Keel, Edwin L. *s.m.* '70 (WDC) [B] Washington, DC Marist College, The-Scholasticate.
Keelen, Kevin J. *o.s.a.* '91 (PH) [C] Villanova, PA Villanova University.
Keeler, Christian *s.j.* '52 (RC) St. Francis, SD Rosebud Reservation Church.
Keeler, Gregory *o.p.* '82 (NY) [CC] New York, NY University Apostolate.
Keeler, Gregory *o.p.* '82 (RIC) Charlottesville, VA St. Thomas Aquinas Church.
Keeley, Alban F. '38 (HRT) Retired.
Keeley, Isaac *o.c.s.o.* '92 (WOR) [N] Spencer, MA St. Joseph's Abbey.
Keeley, James T. '56 (OAK) [17] Oakland, CA St. Mary, Immaculate Conception-St. Francis de Sales Church.
Keeley, John A. '40 (BO) Retired.
Keeley, Patrick J. *c.m.* '58 (STL) Sappington, MO St. Catherine Laboure Church.
Keeley, Patrick P. '54 (NY) Military Chaplains.
Keeley, Thomas R. '76 (CHI) Other Assignments.
Keeling, Paul M. *c.r.s.p.* '75 (BUF) [B] Youngstown, NY St. Anthony Zaccaria Seminary.
Keen, William '89 (ATL) Roswell, GA St. Andrew Church.
Keena, James *c.ss.r.* '57 (CHI) [136] Chicago, IL St. Michael Church.
Keenan, Alexander J. '76 (BO) [25] Boston, MA Gate of Heaven Church.
Keenan, Basil *o.s.b.* '67 (OKL) Shawnee, OK St. Benedict Church; [I] Shawnee, OK St. Gregory's Abbey.
Keenan, Msgr. Charles J. '42 (LIN) Retired; [E] Lincoln, NE Bonacum House.
Keenan, Christopher B. *o.f.m.* '71 (WDC) [B] Silver Spring, MD Holy Name College.
Keenan, Eugene T. (TR) Lavallette, NJ St. Bonaventure Church.
Keenan, Francis T. *s.m.* '63 (RVC) [N] Mineola, NY Provincial Residence and Novitiate.
Keenan, Francis X. *c.p.* '61 (CHI) [N] Chicago, IL Immaculate Conception Monastery.
Keenan, James *s.j.* '61 (BO) [W] Cambridge, MA Weston Jesuit Community.
Keenan, James D. *o.s.f.s.* '49 (PH) [Z] Philadelphia, PA Father Judge Faculty House.
Keenan, James F. *s.j.* '69 (NEW) [C] Jersey City, NJ St. Peter's Preparatory School.
Keenan, John *s.s.s.* (CHI) [U] Chicago, IL Trinity House.
Keenan, Msgr. John '51 (ORG) [1] Santa Ana, CA Immaculate Heart of Mary Church.
Keenan, John *s.s.s.* '69 (CLV) [P] Cleveland, OH Congregation of the Blessed Sacrament Provincial House.
Keenan, John J. '43 (SD) Retired.
Keenan, John J. *s.j.* '55 (ALN) [A] Wernersville, PA Novitiate of St. Isaac Jogues.
Keenan, Joseph A. *c.ss.r.* '47 (BRK) [107] Brooklyn, NY Our Lady of Perpetual Help Basilica.
Keenan, Joseph F. '84 (PIT) [74] Pittsburgh, PA Incarnation of the Lord Church.
Keenan, Joseph P. *s.t.* '79 (JKS) Camden, MS Immaculate Conception Church.
Keenan, Msgr. Patrick J. '69 (NY) Cortlandt Manor, NY St. Columbanus Church.
Keenan, Paul *s.t.* '50 (WDC) [M] Adelphi, MD Missionary Servants of the Most Holy Trinity.
Keenan, Paul A. '77 (NY) [93] New York, NY Our Lady of Peace Church.
Keenan, Terence F. '65 (FR) [4] Swansea, MA Our Lady of Fatima Church.
Keenan, Thomas E. '55 (MAN) Retired.
Keenan, Thomas L. '63 (PRO) Rumford, RI St. Margaret Church.
Keenan, Vincent *s.s.j.* '52 (NO) [P] New Orleans, LA Josephite Fathers and Brothers.
Keene, James H. *s.j.* '73 (LA) [C] Los Angeles, CA Loyola Marymount University.
Keene, Kenneth R. '95 (PIT) Crafton, PA St. Philip Church.
Keene, Mark A. '84 (COV) [5] Covington, KY St. Benedict Church.
Keene, Michael *o.s.b.* '37 (IND) [J] St. Meinrad, IN St. Meinrad Archabbey.

Keene, Warren '81 (STA) [8] Jacksonville, FL Immaculate Conception Church.
Keener, Michael '92 (MIA) [28] Miami, FL SS. Peter and Paul Church; [C] Miami, FL Archbishop Curley-Notre Dame High School.
Keener, Robert J. '95 (CHI) Chicago Ridge, IL Our Lady of the Ridge Church.
Keeney, Charles P. '78 (BRK) [190] Queens, NY St. Leo Church.
Keeney, Edward *ss.cc.* '61 (FR) [K] Fairhaven, MA Sacred Hearts Provincial House.
Keeney, Timothy '96 (RIC) Graduate Studies.
Keenoy, John A. '87 (STL) Crystal City, MO Sacred Heart Church.
Keese, John '74 (LA) Sepulveda, CA Our Lady of Peace Church.
Keeshan, Paul '38 (ALB) Retired.
Keesler, Robert L. '36 (WDC) Laurel, MD St. Mary Church; Retired.
Keferl, Francis J. '73 (CIN) Piqua, OH St. Mary Church.
Keffer, Joseph D. *o.s.a.* '47 (ALB) Greenwich, NY St. Joseph Church; [2] Troy, NY St. Augustine Church.
Keffer, Robert F. '68 (WDC) Special Ministries; [S] Washington, DC Archdiocesan Campus Ministry.
Keffer, Thomas '77 (SR) Middletown, CA St. Joseph Church.
Keffler, Leopold *o.f.m.conv.* '63 (IND) [B] Indianapolis, IN Marian College.
Kegel, William M. *s.j.* '42 (MIL) [P] Milwaukee, WI Jesuit Provincial Office, Wisconsin Province.
Kegel, William M. *s.j.* '42 (OAK) [22] Oakland, CA St. Theresa of the Infant Jesus (The Little Flower) Church; [N] Berkeley, CA Jesuit Community at Jesuit School of Theology at Berkeley.
Kegler, Maynard C. *o.m.i.* '51 (STP) [N] St. Paul, MN Oblate Provincial Offices; [N] St. Paul, MN Oblate Residence.
Kegley, Jeffrey J. '96 (TR) New Monmouth, NJ St. Mary Church.
Kehew, Donal R. '63 (PRO) Block Island, RI St. Andrew's Church.
Kehoe, Charles B. '73 (BRK) [189] Queens, NY St. Kevin Church.
Kehoe, Daniel J. '39 (PH) Sharon Hill, PA Holy Spirit Church; Retired.
Kehoe, James P. '70 (CHI) [142] Chicago, IL Nativity of Our Lord Church.
Kehoe, Joel *o.s.b.* '78 (B) [C] Jerome, ID Ascension Priory.
Kehoe, Joseph A. *c.s.c.* '39 (FTW) [J] South Bend, IN Congregation of Holy Cross Indiana Province Provincial House.
Kehoe, Joseph F. '66 (SY) Durhamville, NY St. Francis Church; New London, NY Holy Cross Church.
Kehoe, Richard J. '51 (BRK) [U] Jamaica, NY Vincentian Residence.
Kehoe, Richard J. *c.m.* '57 (BRK) [D] Queens and Staten Island, NY St. John's University.
Kehoe, Richard J. *c.m.* '57 (PH) [B] Philadelphia, PA St. Vincent's Seminary.
Kehoe, Thomas F. '75 (WDC) [3] Bowie, MD St. Edward Church.
Kehres, Franklin P. '68 (TOL) Sandusky, OH SS. Peter and Paul Church.
Kehres, John C. *s.j.* '50 (DET) [K] Detroit, MI Jesuit Community at the University of Detroit.
Keigher, Bernard J. '74 (TR) Maple Shade, NJ Our Lady of Perpetual Help Church.
Keilty, Msgr. John P. '41 (BO) Retired.
Keiser, Jerome F. '71 (STP) [27] St. Paul, MN St. Mark Church.
Keiser, Ray W. '70 (BIR) Gardendale, AL St. Elizabeth Ann Seton Church.
Keith, Christopher R. '89 (GI) Bridgeport, NE All Souls Church.
Keith, John C. '56 (SD) Retired.
Keitz, Bernard L. *o.p.* '54 (NEW) Harrington Park, NJ Our Lady of Victories Church.
Keitz, Bernard L. *o.p.* '54 (NY) [CC] New York, NY University Apostolate.
Kekeisen, Robert E. '44 (COS) Retired.
Kekeisen, William E. '58 (SFD) Jerseyville, IL St. Francis Xavier Church.
Kekumano, Msgr. Charles A. '49 (JUN) Retired.
Kelaher, Msgr. Felix R. '48 (CHL) Retired.
Kelash, David '94 (PHX) [9] Phoenix, AZ St. Catherine of Siena Church.
Kelbel, Joseph '80 (BAK) Hood River, OR Immaculate Conception Church.
Kelchak, Joseph M. '50 (SUP) Retired.
Keleher, J. Patrick '68 (BUF) [R] Williamsville, NY Newman Club Chaplains.
Keliher, Michael P. *c.s.v.* '76 (JOL) [2] Kankakee, IL St. Patrick Church.
Kell, Robert *o.m.i.* '79 (STP) [N] St. Paul, MN Oblate Residence.
Kelleher, Cornelius '56 (DUL) Brainerd, MN St. Andrew's Church.
Kelleher, Cyril *o.f.m.cap.* '46 (LA) Solvang, CA Old Mission Santa Ines Church.
Kelleher Denis *s.d.b.* '52 (BO) [Y] Ipswich, MA Sacred Heart Retreat Center.
Kelleher Denis *s.d.b.* '52 (NY) [72] New York, NY Mary Help of Christians Church.
Kelleher Dennis *c.ss.r.* '63 (NY) [Z] Esopus, NY Redemptorist Priests and Brothers C.Ss.R. (Province of Baltimore); [BB] Esopus, NY Mount St. Alphonsus Redemptorist Retreat Center.
Kelleher, James L. '54 (PRO) [1] Johnston, RI St. Brigid Church.
Kelleher, James P. '40 (DAV) Retired.
Kelleher, James R. *s.o.l.t.* '96 (CC) Skidmore, TX Immaculate Conception Church.
Kelleher, Jerome '83 (COS) On Administrative Leave.
Kelleher, John *o.f.m.* '89 (NEW) [N] Hohokus, NJ St. Anthony of Padua.
Kelleher, Lawrence A. '93 (GAY) Black River, MI St. Gabriel Church; Ossineke, MI St. Catherine Church.
Kelleher, M. Joseph '53 (CHL) Lexington, NC Our Lady of the Rosary Church.
Kelleher, Mark A. '96 (WIL) Fairfax, DE St. Mary Magdalen Church.
Kelleher, Michael '65 (BLX) Gautier, MS St. Mary Church.
Kelleher, Robert N. '59 (BO) [3] Brockton, MA St. Edward Church.
Kelleher, Msgr. Stephen '40 (NY) Retired.
Kelleher, Timothy J. '71 (BO) Walpole, MA Blessed Sacrament Church.
Kelleher, William A. '91 (NY) Congers, NY St. Paul Church.
Kelleher, William J. '52 (ALB) [17] Schenectady, NY St. Thomas the Apostle Church.
Kellen, Elmer W. '50 (WIN) Retired.
Keller, Bernard C. *s.v.d.* '55 (GAL) Prairie View, TX St. Martin de Porres Church.
Keller, Bernard C. *s.v.d.* '55 (LR) Pine Bluff, AR St. Peter's Church.
Keller, Brendan J. '60 (MOB) Ozark, AL St. John Church.
Keller, Brian M. '73 (BRK) [192] Queens, NY St. Margaret's Church.
Keller, Daniel E. '82 (OM) Columbus, NE St. Bonaventure Church.
Keller, Gerald J. '65 (CLV) Berea, OH St. Adalbert Church.
Keller, Harvey M. '45 (TOL) Norwalk, OH St. Paul Church; Retired.
Keller, Herbert B. *s.j.* '81 (PH) [G] Philadelphia, PA St. Joseph's Preparatory School; [Z] Philadelphia, PA St. Joseph's Preparatory School Jesuit Community, Arrupe House.
Keller, John D. *o.s.a.* '64 (SD) [B] San Diego, CA University of San Diego; [H] San Diego, CA Augustinian Community.
Keller, John F. *s.j.* '47 (NO) [C] New Orleans, LA Loyola University.
Keller, John R. '54 (ORG) [1] Huntington Beach, CA St. Bonaventure Church.
Keller, John T. '74 (GAL) [42] Houston, TX St. Justin Martyr Church.
Keller, Ken '69 (AMA) [10] Amarillo, TX St. Mary's Church.
Keller, Lawrence E. '47 (STP) Retired.
Keller, Lawrence W. '53 (COV) Bellevue, KY Sacred Heart Church; Retired.
Keller, Neil J. '55 (CIN) Retired.
Keller, Paul *c.m.f.* '96 (AUS) San Marcos, TX St. John the Evangelist Church.
Keller, Paul *c.m.f.* '96 (SAT) [B] San Antonio, TX Immaculate Heart Claretian Seminary.
Keller, Paul J. *o.p.* '93 (HRT) [14] New Haven, CT St. Mary's Priory Church.
Keller, Robb '84 (B) Twin Falls, ID St. Edward's Church.
Keller, Robert *o.p.* '83 (SFE) [M] Albuquerque, NM St. Thomas Aquinas.
Keller, Robert E. '67 (CIN) [77] Cincinnati, OH Resurrection of Our Lord Church.
Keller, Robert J. '74 (DET) Harper Woods, MI St. Peter the Apostle Church.
Keller, Robert J. *o.p.* '83 (SFE) [29] Albuquerque, NM St. Thomas Aquinas University Parish Church.
Keller, Theodore '46 (LEX) [7] Lexington, KY St. Peter Church; Retired.
Keller, Thomas F. '84 (B) Hailey, ID St. Charles Borromeo Church.
Keller, Thomas W. '58 (LR) [10] Little Rock, AR Our Lady of Good Counsel Church.
Kellerman, Raymond C. '73 (CIN) [14] Cincinnati, OH St. Bartholomew Church.
Kellermann, Leonard P. *s.m.* '46 (WDC) [M] Washington, DC Marist Provincial House.
Kellett, William *s.j.* '65 (PBL) [8] Pueblo, CO Our Lady of Mt. Carmel Church.
Kelley, Aloysius P. *s.j.* '62 (BGP) [A] Fairfield, CT Fairfield University; [D] Fairfield, CT Fairfield College Preparatory School; [O] Fairfield, CT The Fairfield Jesuit Community-Fairfield University.
Kelley, Arnold E. (BO) Awaiting Assignment.
Kelley, Bennet *c.p.* '44 (NY) [Z] Chelsea, NY Word of the Cross Passionist Community.
Kelley, Bennet *c.p.* '49 (HRT) [M] West Hartford, CT Holy Family Monastery/Retreat.
Kelley, Charles F. *s.j.* '84 (BO) [W] Boston, MA The Society of Jesus of New England-Provincial Offices.
Kelley, Charles F. *s.j.* '84 (BUF) [D] Buffalo, NY Canisius High School; [O] Buffalo, NY Canisius Jesuit Community.
Kelley, Clark T. *o.s.f.s.* '64 (STO) [A] Stockton, CA St. Mary's High School.
Kelley, Danny '95 (FWT) [11] Fort Worth, TX St. John the Apostle Church.
Kelley, David F. '88 (WIL) Salisbury, MD St. Francis De Sales Church.
Kelley, David J. *o.s.a.* '73 (ALB) Greenwich, NY St. Joseph Church.
Kelley, David J. '74 (CIN) [K] Cincinnati, OH Mercy Hospital Anderson.
Kelley, Edward J. '68 (BO) On Duty Outside the Archdiocese.
Kelley, Edward J. '68 (PRO) On Duty Outside the Diocese.
Kelley, Edward J.V. '66 (MAN) North Conway, NH Our Lady of the Mountains Church.
Kelley, Francis H. '68 (BO) [69] Boston, MA Sacred Heart Church.
Kelley, J. Ralph '34 (NOR) Retired.
Kelley, James *c.pp.s.* '43 (CIN) [B] Carthagena, OH St. Charles.
Kelley, James F. '61 (ANC) Dillingham, AK Holy Rosary Church.
Kelley, John '70 (BO) Westwood, MA St. Denis Church.
Kelley, John E. '61 (WOR) Baldwinville, MA St. Vincent De Paul Church; Otter River, MA Walter E. Fernald State School.
Kelley, John J. '45 (SCR) Olyphant, PA St. Patrick's Church.
Kelley, John J. *s.m.* '53 (CIN) [M] Dayton, OH Marianist Provincialate.
Kelley, John W. '59 (STP) [8] St. Paul, MN The Nativity of Our Lord Church.
Kelley, Joseph '46 (SPK) Retired.
Kelley, Joseph J. '87 (PH) [D] Philadelphia, PA Little Flower Catholic High School for Girls.
Kelley, Laurence E. '60 (BO) West Newbury, MA St. Ann Church.
Kelley, Michael J. '75 (WDC) [28] Washington, DC St. Martin of Tours Church.
Kelley, Micheal (IND) Universal, IN St. Joseph Church.
Kelley, Micheal '85 (IND) Clinton, IN Sacred Heart Church.
Kelley, N. F. '62 (SPK) Retired.
Kelley, Omer (GB) White Lake, WI Ss. James and Stanislaus Congregation Church; [F] Antigo, WI Langlade Memorial Hospital.
Kelley, Paul G. '49 (BO) Winchester, MA St. Mary Church; Retired.
Kelley, Richard J. '72 (MAN) Jaffrey, NH St. Patrick Church.
Kelley, Robert E. '79 (WOR) Millbury, MA St. Brigid Church.
Kelley, Thomas '67 (E) On Duty Outside Diocese.
Kelley, Thomas J. '51 (PH) [11] Philadelphia, PA St. Anne Church.
Kelley, Thomas L. '88 (MAD) [6] Madison, WI Our Lady, Queen of Peace Church; [2] Janesville, WI St. John Vianney Church.
Kelley, Msgr. Thomas P. '67 (WDC) [1] Silver Spring, MD St. Andrew Apostle Church.
Kelley, William *s.v.d.* '67 (BLX) [A] Bay St. Louis, MS St. Augustine's.
Kelley, William F. *s.j.* '44 (OM) [K] Omaha, NE Jesuit Community At Creighton University.
Kelley, William H. *c.s.c.* '70 (BUR) Bennington, VT Sacred Heart-St. Francis de Sales Church.
Kelley, William J. '54 (MAN) Peterborough, NH St. Peter Church.
Kelley, William J. *s.j.* '85 (R) [7] Raleigh, NC St. Raphael Church; [E] Durham, NC Jesuit Community.
Kellick, John W. (GAL) Retired.
Kelligar, William L. '53 (OM) [29] Omaha, NE St. Mary Magdalene Church.
Kelliher, Alexander *s.a.* (NY) [Z] Garrison, NY Franciscan Friars of the Atonement.
Kelliher, Arthur J. '56 (MAN) Hanover, NH St. Denis Church.
Kelliher, Daniel *o.c.s.o.* '48 (DEN) [M] Snowmass, CO St. Benedict's Monastery.
Kelliher, Msgr. John J. '58 (WOR) [14] Worcester, MA Our Lady of the Rosary Church.
Kelliher, Michael M. *s.j.* '67 (SEA) [A] Seattle, WA Seattle University.
Kelliher, Vincent *s.j.* '55 (FBK) [C] Fairbanks, AK Jesuit Residence.
Kellner, Winfried M. '63 (ROC) [39] Rochester, NY Our Lady of Victory-St. Joseph Church.
Kelly, William A. '59 (STA) Jacksonville Beach, FL St. Paul's Church.
Kelly, Albert P. '72 (MOB) Millbrook, AL St. Elizabeth Ann Seton Church.

Kelly, Alfred '50 (SJ) Retired.
Kelly, Andrew E. '70 (DAV) Iowa City, IA Veteran's Administration Hospital; [J] Iowa City, IA Mercy Hospital.
Kelly, Anthony *s.a.c.* '59 (NY) [91] New York, NY Our Lady of Mt. Carmel Church.
Kelly, Anthony *s.c.j.* '73 (SFS) Chamberlain, SD St. James Church.
Kelly, Augustine G. *o.s.b.* '88 (MAN) [K] Manchester, NH St. Anselm Abbey.
Kelly, Augustine M. *o.f.m.conv.* (BAL) [M] Ellicott City, MD St. Joseph Cupertino Friary, Friars Minor Conventual of St. Francis of Assisi.
Kelly, Bernard *c.sp.* '73 (NY) [Z] New York, NY Apostolic Society of the Crusade of the Holy Spirit.
Kelly, Bernard R. '61 (FR) Wellfleet, MA Our Lady of Lourdes Church.
Kelly, Bernard T. '41 (LC) Retired.
Kelly, Brian F. '77 (SCR) Military Chaplains.
Kelly, C. Richard '70 (DET) Canton, MI St. Thomas a Becket Church.
Kelly, Charles *s.c.j.* '71 (GAL) [34] Houston, TX Holy Name Church.
Kelly, Charles A. '67 (RIC) [1] Richmond, VA Cathedral of the Sacred Heart.
Kelly, Charles F. '48 (CHI) [48] Chicago, IL St. Daniel the Prophet Church; Retired; [X] Chicago, IL Apostolate of the Handicapped.
Kelly, Charles F. '64 (MET) Old Bridge, NJ St. Ambrose Church.
Kelly, Charles H. '54 (PEO) [1] Spring Valley, IL Immaculate Conception Church.
Kelly, Charles S. '69 (NY) Haverstraw, NY St. Peter Church.
Kelly, Columba *o.s.b.* '58 (IND) [B] St. Meinrad, IN St. Meinrad Seminary-College of Liberal Arts; [J] St. Meinrad, IN St. Meinrad Archabbey.
Kelly, Cornelius F. *o.f.m.* '39 (BO) [Z] Boston, MA Saint Anthony Residence.
Kelly, Daniel '56 (LC) Oxford, WI Federal Correctional Institute.
Kelly, Daniel A. '87 (PAT) [1] Passaic, NJ St. Nicholas Church.
Kelly, Daniel J. '59 (DAV) Retired.
Kelly, Daniel L. '72 (RIC) Onley, VA St. Peter's the Apostle Church.
Kelly, David A. *c.pp.s.* '83 (CHI) [20] Chicago, IL Assumption Church; [X] Chicago, IL Kolbe House.
Kelly, David F. '66 (PIT) [B] Pittsburgh, PA Duquesne University of the Holy Ghost.
Kelly, David F. '66 (WOR) On Duty Outside the Diocese.
Kelly, Donald '63 (ALB) Green Island, NY St. Joseph Church; Retired.
Kelly, E. Francis '67 (SCR) [8] Wilkes-Barre, PA Holy Saviour Church.
Kelly, Edgar M. '43 (MEM) Retired.
Kelly, Msgr. Edward '56 (DM) [3] Council Bluffs, IA St. Patrick Church.
Kelly, Edward '65 (MEM) On Duty Outside the Diocese.
Kelly, Edward '80 (SAT) [42] San Antonio, TX St. John, The Evangelist Church.
Kelly, Edward C. '90 (PH) [70] Philadelphia, PA Immaculate Heart of Mary Church.
Kelly, Edward J. *c.s.sp.* '49 (ARL) [7] Arlington, VA Our Lady, Queen of Peace Church.
Kelly, Edward J. '68 (PH) Lafayette Hill, PA St. Philip Neri Church.
Kelly, Edward M. '68 (MIA) Coral Springs, FL St. Elizabeth Ann Seton Church.
Kelly, Emmett '55 (HEL) Retired.
Kelly, Ernest *o.p.* '43 (Y) [13] Youngstown, OH St. Dominic's Church.
Kelly, Eugene A. '38 (OG) Rosiere, NY St. Vincent de Paul Church; Retired.
Kelly, Eugene D. *s.j.* '53 (PBL) [8] Pueblo, CO Our Lady of Mt. Carmel Church.
Kelly, Eugene L. *o.s.f.s.* '65 (PH) [D] Philadelphia, PA Father Judge High School for Boys; [Z] Philadelphia, PA Father Judge Faculty House.
Kelly, Evangelist *o.f.m.cap.* '49 (BAK) Bend, OR St. Francis of Assisi Church.
Kelly, Francis '57 (LA) West Los Angeles, CA Veterans Administration Wadsworth Hospital Center; Military and VA Chaplains.
Kelly, Francis *o.f.m.* '89 (PH) [D] Philadelphia, PA Archbishop Ryan High School.
Kelly, Msgr. Francis D. '63 (BO) [A] Weston, MA Pope John XXIII National Seminary.
Kelly, Msgr. Francis D. '80 (WOR) On Duty Outside the Diocese.
Kelly, Francis E. '55 (PH) Valley Forge, PA St. Teresa of Avila Church.
Kelly, Francis J. '51 (COV) Retired.
Kelly, Francis X. *o.f.m.* '88 (PH) [Z] Philadelphia, PA St. Pius X Friary.
Kelly, Frank F. '77 (GF) Retired.
Kelly, George *c.ss.r.* '59 (NEW) [2] East Orange, NJ Holy Spirit-Our Lady Help of Christians Church.
Kelly, George *c.ss.r.* '59 (ORL) [F] New Smyrna Beach, FL Redemptorist Fathers of the Vice Province of Richmond.
Kelly, Msgr. George A. '42 (NY) [58] New York, NY St. John the Evangelist Church; Retired.
Kelly, George F. *c.ss.r.* '59 (MET) Lyons, NJ U.S. Veterans Medical Center.
Kelly, Gerald E. *m.m.* '67 (BO) [W] East Walpole, MA Maryknoll Department of Development.
Kelly, Gerald G. '34 (ROC) Retired.
Kelly, Gerard D. '49 (PIT) Jefferson Boro, PA St. Thomas A Becket Church.
Kelly, Gerard P. *c.m.* '82 (STL) Perryville, MO St. Vincent De Paul Church.
Kelly, Gregory (DAL) McKinney, TX St. Gabriel the Archangel Church.
Kelly, Msgr. J. Morgan '45 (MET) East Brunswick, NJ St. Bartholomew Church; Retired.
Kelly, J Patrick *o.f.m.* '71 (NY) [Z] New York, NY Franciscan Friars, Order of Friars Manor; [Z] New York, NY Franciscan Friars, Order of Friars Manor.
Kelly, James '44 (DOD) Retired.
Kelly, James '47 (MRY) Retired.
Kelly, James *glmy.* '48 (CIN) [M] Fairfield, OH Headquarters of Glenmary Home Missioners.
Kelly, James *c.m.* '53 (BRK) [U] Jamaica, NY Vincentian Residence.
Kelly, James '57 (ALB) Special Assignment; On Duty Outside the Diocese.
Kelly, James *o.s.b.* '59 (ROC) [I] Pine City, NY Mount Saviour Monastery.
Kelly, James '60 (PHX) Camp Verde, AZ St. Frances Cabrini Church.
Kelly, James *o.f.m.* '78 (SFD) [B] Quincy, IL Quincy University.
Kelly, Msgr. James A. '82 (NY) [EE] New Rochelle, NY Opus Dei (Prelature of the Holy Cross and Opus Dei).
Kelly, James B. *o.p.* '62 (CHI) River Forest, IL St. Vincent Ferrer Priory Church.
Kelly, James E. *c.s.c.* '58 (SCR) [C] Wilkes-Barre, PA Kings College.
Kelly, Msgr. James G. '62 (BUF) [44] Buffalo, NY St. Margaret Church.
Kelly, James J. '50 (PH) Brookhaven, PA Our Lady of Charity Church; Broomall, PA St. Pius X Church; Retired.
Kelly, Msgr. James J. '60 (BRK) [24] Brooklyn, NY St. Brigid Church.
Kelly, James J. '83 (LA) [8] Long Beach, CA St. Joseph Church.
Kelly, James M. *c.m.* '53 (BRK) [D] Queens and Staten Island, NY St. John's University.
Kelly, Msgr. James P. '62 (RVC) Williston Park, NY St. Aidan's Church.
Kelly, James Patrick *o.s.f.s.* '63 (PRO) [K] Providence, RI St. Joseph Health Services of Rhode Island - St. Joseph Hospital for Specialty Care.
Kelly, James S. *c.ss.r.* '37 (STL) [P] Liguori, MO St. Clement Health Care Center.
Kelly, James T. '92 (BO) [7] Haverhill, MA Sacred Hearts Church.
Kelly, James W. *o.p.* '63 (CHI) [J] Elk Grove Village, IL Alexian Brothers Medical Center, Inc.
Kelly, Jerome *o.f.m.* '37 (BO) [Z] Boston, MA Saint Anthony Residence.
Kelly, Joel *o.s.b.* '66 (SCL) St. Cloud, MN Minnesota State Reformatory for Men; [I] Collegeville, MN St. John's Abbey, of the Order of St. Benedict.
Kelly, John *o.m.i.* '47 (OAK) [N] Oakland, CA Oblate Provincial House & Procure.
Kelly, John A. *s.j.* '53 (SAC) [C] Sacramento, CA Jesuit High School; [H] Carmichael, CA Jesuit High School Community of Sacramento.
Kelly, John D. '86 (ARL) McLean, VA St. Luke's Church.
Kelly, John E. '87 (BUF) Angelica, NY Sacred Heart Church; Belmont, NY St. Mary Church.
Kelly, John F. '84 (PT) Bonifay, FL Blessed Trinity Church; Chipley, FL St. Joseph the Worker Church.
Kelly, Msgr. John J. '28 (CAM) Retired.
Kelly, John J. *o.s.a.* '42 (MIA) [H] Miami, FL Casa San Lorenzo.
Kelly, Msgr. John J. '44 (CAM) Wildwood Crest, NJ Assumption B.V.M. Church.
Kelly, John J. '64 (BLX) Clermont Harbor, MS St. Ann Church.
Kelly, John J. *o.s.f.s.* '71 (HBG) [K] Harrisburg, PA Catholic Campus Ministry.
Kelly, John J. '87 (PH) Huntingdon Valley, PA St. Albert the Great Church.
Kelly, John L. '54 (BAL) Glen Burnie, MD Church of the Good Shepherd.
Kelly, John P. '45 (BO) [6] Somerville, MA Patronage of St. Joseph Church; Retired.
Kelly, John R. '68 (NY) Military Chaplains.
Kelly, John T. '61 (ALB) Albany, NY Memorial Hospital; Special Assignment.
Kelly, John T. *s.j.* '74 (WDC) [M] Washington, DC The Jesuit Community at Georgetown University.
Kelly, John W. '44 (LIN) Retired; [E] Lincoln, NE Bonacum House.
Kelly, John W. *c.ss.r.* '51 (HBG) [H] Ephrata, PA St. Clement's Mission House.
Kelly, Joseph '63 (NEW) [B] Jersey City, NJ Saint Peter's College.
Kelly, Joseph A. '39 (CHI) [52] Chicago, IL St. Edward Church; Retired.
Kelly, Joseph A. *o.praem.* '47 (HBG) Millersburg, PA Queen of Peace Church.
Kelly, Joseph A. *o.praem.* '47 (PH) [Z] Paoli, PA Daylesford Abbey.
Kelly, Joseph A. *s.j.* '63 (NEW) [N] Jersey City, NJ Jesuits of Saint Peter's College, Inc.
Kelly, Joseph A. *s.j.* '63 (NY) [68] New York, NY St. Malachy's Church.
Kelly, Joseph Anthony '31 (ALB) Retired.
Kelly, Joseph J. '57 (PEO) Brimfield, IL St. Joseph's Church.
Kelly, Joseph J. '78 (NY) [127] Bronx, NY St. Anthony Church.
Kelly, Msgr. Joseph P. '66 (SCR) [9] Scranton, PA Holy Rosary Church; [Q] Tunkhannock, PA Camp St. Andrew.
Kelly, Kenneth W. '79 (KCK) Burlington, KS St. Francis Xavier's Church; Emerald, KS St. Patrick's Church; Waverly, KS St. Joseph's Church; Westphalia, KS St. Teresa's Church.
Kelly, Msgr. Laurence F. '36 (PH) West Chester, PA St. Agnes Church; Retired.
Kelly, Lawrence D. *s.j.* '46 (MIL) [P] Milwaukee, WI Arrupe House Jesuit Community.
Kelly, Leonard A. *o.f.m.* '43 (PAT) [M] Butler, NJ St. Anthony Friary.
Kelly, Msgr. Martin '47 (NEW) [2] Jersey City, NJ St. Aloysius Church.
Kelly, Martin C. '48 (PHX) Retired.
Kelly, Martin T. '89 (MAN) [8] Nashua, NH St. Patrick Church.
Kelly, Msgr. Matthew H. '42 (LA) Retired.
Kelly, Maurus *o.f.m.* '56 (LA) [4] Santa Barbara, CA St. Barbara Church; [R] Santa Barbara, CA Franciscan Friary, Order of Friars Minor (Old Mission).
Kelly, Michael (MOB) [K] Montgomery, AL Huntington College Newman Center.
Kelly, Michael (OAK) [N] Oakland, CA Dominican Order, Siena House.
Kelly, Michael *ss.cc.* '65 (FR) [K] Fairhaven, MA Sacred Hearts Provincial House.
Kelly, Michael D. '71 (MOB) [7] Montgomery, AL Our Lady, Queen of Mercy Church.
Kelly, Michael D. '76 (SFS) Huron, SD St. Martin Church.
Kelly, Michael D. '95 (ARL) Falls Church, VA St. James Church.
Kelly, Msgr. Michael E. '66 (NEW) [C] West Orange, NJ Seton Hall Preparatory School.
Kelly, Michael E. '71 (SR) Graduate Studies.
Kelly, Michael E. '73 (STO) Sonora, CA St. Patrick Church.
Kelly, Michael J. '53 (OM) Retired.
Kelly, Michael J. '82 (PH) [A] Wynnewood, PA Theological Seminary of St. Charles Borromeo, Overbrook.
Kelly, Michael M. '81 (SR) Arcata, CA St. Mary's Church.
Kelly, Omer '49 (GB) Retired.
Kelly, Pat '58 (IND) [14] Indianapolis, IN St. Andrew the Apostle Church.
Kelly, Patrick J. '48 (BO) Wayland, MA St. Ann Church.
Kelly, Patrick J. '58 (IND) [33] Indianapolis, IN St. Matthew the Apostle Church; [D] Indianapolis, IN Cathedral High School (Cathedral Trustees, Inc.).
Kelly, Paul *s.c.j.* '77 (MIL) [B] Hales Corners, WI Sacred Heart School of Theology; [P] Milwaukee, WI St. Joseph House of Formation.
Kelly, Paul J. '74 (OG) Adams, NY St. Cecilia Church.
Kelly, Paul J. '83 (SC) Halbur, IA St. Augustine's Church; Roselle, IA Holy Angels Church.
Kelly, Paul M. '47 (LA) Retired.
Kelly, Philip '93 (NY) [14] New York, NY Ascension Church.
Kelly, Philip C.M. *c.s.c.* '42 (ORL) [F] Cocoa Beach, FL Holy Cross Fathers, Eastern Priests Province.
Kelly, Randy '94 (SAG) Ubly, MI St. Columbkille Church; Ubly, MI St. John the Evangelist Church.
Kelly, Raymond J. '61 (BRK) [77] Brooklyn, NY St. Malachy's Church; [L] Brooklyn, NY Catholic Charities.
Kelly, Raymond M. '49 (PRO) [26] Providence, RI St. Patrick's Church.
Kelly, Richard J. '88 (NEW) South Orange, NJ Our Lady of Sorrows Church.
Kelly, Robert '68 (WOR) Absent on Leave.
Kelly, Robert F. *o.praem.* '53 (PH) [B] Paoli, PA Daylesford Abbey; [Z] Paoli, PA Daylesford Abbey.
Kelly, Robert G. *s.j.* '57 (NY) [A] Yonkers, NY St. Joseph's Seminary; [Z] New York, NY Jesuit Community at Fordham University.
Kelly, Msgr. Robert J. '34 (NY) [200] Staten Island, NY St. Charles Church; Retired.
Kelly, Msgr. Robert J. '53 (CHR) [11] Charleston, SC Church of the Nativity.
Kelly, Robert J. '74 (ALT) [12] Altoona, PA St. Rose of Lima Church; [J] Loretto, PA Prince Gallitzin Chapel

House (Diocesan).
Kelly, Robert L. '77 (SY) [1] Utica, NY Blessed Sacrament Church.
Kelly, Robert M. '68 (SAN) Retired.
Kelly, Robert M. *o.p.* '89 (STP) [15] Minneapolis, MN St. Albert the Great Church.
Kelly, Thomas *o.f.m.* '62 (NEW) Wood-Ridge, NJ Our Lady of the Assumption Church.
Kelly, Thomas '90 (BIR) [A] Birmingham, AL John Carroll High School.
Kelly, Thomas D. (LA) Lompoc, CA Vandenberg Air Force Base.
Kelly, Thomas D. '77 (DEN) On Duty Outside the Archdiocese.
Kelly, Thomas D. '77 (LA) Military and VA Chaplains.
Kelly, Thomas E.J. *s.j.* '79 (STL) [C] St. Louis, MO Saint Louis University; [P] St. Louis, MO Leo Brown Jesuit Community.
Kelly, Thomas F. '41 (BRK) Retired.
Kelly, Thomas F. '47 (Y) Retired.
Kelly, Thomas F. '56 (PEO) Bartonville, IL St. Anthony Church.
Kelly, Msgr. Thomas J. '36 (CLV) Peninsula, OH Mother of Sorrows Church; Retired.
Kelly, Thomas J. '43 (PH) Maple Glen, PA St. Alphonsus Church; Retired.
Kelly, Thomas J. '68 (ALB) [10] Troy, NY St. Patrick Church.
Kelly, Thomas J. '86 (HRT) [I] New Haven, CT Hospital of St. Raphael.
Kelly, Thomas J. C. *s.j.* '48 (BO) [E] Boston, MA Boston College High School & Jesuit Community.
Kelly, Thomas M. '90 (BIR) [16] Birmingham, AL Our Lady of Sorrows Church.
Kelly, Thomas P. (BO) Awaiting Assignment.
Kelly, Thomas R. '61 (NY) [144] Bronx, NY St. Gabriel Church.
Kelly, Thomas W. *o.s.f.s.* '50 (CAM) [L] Pittsgrove, NJ Villa St. Joseph.
Kelly, Timothy *o.s.b.* '61 (SCL) [B] Collegeville, MN St. John's University.
Kelly, Tony *s.a.c.* '55 (NY) [Z] New York, NY Pallottine Fathers.
Kelly, Vincent J. *c.ss.r.* '39 (BO) [13] Boston, MA Basilica of Our Lady of Perpetual Help.
Kelly, Vincent J. '57 (SY) Oriskany Falls, NY St. Joseph Church.
Kelly, Vincent T. '56 (MIA) [9] Fort Lauderdale, FL St. John the Baptist Church; [C] Fort Lauderdale, FL St. Thomas Aquinas High School.
Kelly, William *s.v.d.* '49 (TR) [M] Bordentown, NJ Society of the Divine Word.
Kelly, William E. '40 (NY) Retired; [Z] New York, NY Our Lady of Consolation Residence.
Kelly, William J. '48 (CHI) Retired.
Kelly, William J. *s.j.* '54 (MIL) [P] Milwaukee, WI Jesuit Community at Marquette University.
Kelly, Msgr. William M. '47 (SY) [3] Rome, NY St. Paul Church.
Kelly, William M. *s.d.s.* '79 (BIR) [2] Huntsville, AL St. Mary of the Visitation Church.
Kelly, William T. '78 (CIN) On Duty Outside the Archdiocese.
Kelly, William T. '88 (BO) Graduate Studies.
Kelmartin, John '49 (BAL) [75] Baltimore, MD Our Lady of Victory Church.
Kelmartin, John J. '49 (BAL) Retired.
Kelpsas, Anthony '53 (JOL) Darien, IL Our Lady of Peace Church.
Kelpsas, Francis J. '50 (CHI) [141] Chicago, IL Nativity of the Blessed Virgin Mary Church; Retired.
Kelsch, Dennis J. *o.s.f.s.* '72 (TOL) [37] Toledo, OH St. Pius X Church.
Kelsch, Emmanuel *o.s.b.* '38 (SCL) [I] Collegeville, MN St. John's Abbey, of the Order of St. Benedict.
Kelso, Francis E. '61 (MAN) Rochester, NH St. Mary Church.
Keltos, Adam *o.f.m.conv.* '62 (SY) [5] Endicott, NY St. Joseph Church.
Kelty, Charles J. '40 (L) Retired.
Kelty, Edward *o.s.* '89 (PCE) On Duty Outside the Diocese.
Kelty, Msgr. Leo A. '60 (TR) Howell Township, NJ St. William the Abbot Church.
Kelty, Matthew *o.c.s.o.* '46 (L) [L] Trappist, KY Abbey of Our Lady of Gethsemani, of the Order of Cistercians of the Strict Observance.
Kemberling, Andrew J. *o.s.b.* '88 (DEN) [2] Boulder, CO Sacred Heart of Mary Church; [N] Boulder, CO Abbey of St. Walburga.
Kemberling, Andrew J. *o.s.b.* '88 (PBL) [E] Canon City, CO Holy Cross Abbey.
Kemeter, Robert '72 (PSC) Pittston, PA St. Michael Church.
Kemme, Allan (SFD) [M] Jacksonville, IL MacMurray College Newman Center.
Kemme, Allen '91 (SFD) Jacksonville, IL Our Saviour Church; [M] Jacksonville, IL Illinois College Newman Center.
Kemme, Carl A. '86 (SFD) [1] Decatur, IL Holy Family Church; Mt. Zion, IL Our Lady of the Holy Spirit Church.
Kemme, Joseph A. *s.j.* '64 (WDC) [P] Faulkner, MD Loyola on the Potomac Retreat House.
Kemmer, Victor A. '43 (MIL) St. Kilian, WI St. Kilian's Church; Retired.
Kemmery, Robert J. '54 (MAN) Retired.
Kemner, Kieran *o.f.m.* '53 (CHI) [N] Countryside, IL St. Gratian Friary, Franciscan Friars.
Kemo, Kurt H. '83 (STU) Toronto, OH St. Francis of Assisi Church; Toronto, OH St. Joseph's Church; [J] Steubenville, OH RCIA.
Kemp, Dennis '73 (SEA) [14] Seattle, WA St. Mark Church.
Kemp, Patrick W. '55 (WDC) Retired.
Kemp, Raymond B. '67 (WDC) [40] Washington, DC St. Stephen Martyr Church; Special Ministries; [V] Washington, DC Woodstock Theological Center.
Kemp, Thomas L. '52 (BUF) East Bethany, NY Immaculate Conception Church.
Kempczynski, Msgr. John '51 (BUF) Retired.
Kempczynski, Msgr. John '57 (BUF) [5] Tonawanda, NY St. Timothy Church.
Kempen, Gerald B. *o.praem.* '51 (GB) Tisch Mills, WI Nativity of the Blessed Virgin Mary Church.
Kemper, Jeffrey M. '79 (CIN) [B] Cincinnati, OH Mt. St. Mary's Seminary of the West.
Kemper, John C. *s.s.* '83 (DET) [A] Orchard Lake, MI SS. Cyril and Methodius Seminary.
Kemper, John C. *s.s.* '83 (HBG) On Duty Outside the Diocese.
Kempf, Joseph G. '80 (STL) Ballwin, MO Holy Infant Church.
Kempf, William G. '84 (STL) Richmond Heights, MO St. Luke the Evangelist Church.
Kempfer, James T. '69 (JOL) Addison, IL St. Joseph Church.
Kempfirl, Fred '65 (NY) Milton, NY St. James Church.
Kempkes, Lambert *c.m.m.* '50 (CHI) [J] Evergreen Park, IL Little Company of Mary Hospital and Health Care Centers.
Kempski, Leonard J. '66 (WIL) [4] Wilmington, DE Christ Our King Church.
Kencik, Marian M. '62 (KAL) [1] Kalamazoo, MI St. Augustine Cathedral.
Kendall, Michael *s.d.s.* '61 (FRS) [C] Fresno, CA Saint Agnes Medical Center.
Kendall, Philip *c.s.v.* '62 (KCK) [1] Kansas City, KS Cathedral of St. Peter the Apostle; [I] Kansas City, KS Convent of the Sisters, Servants of Mary.
Kendall, R. Daniel *s.j.* '70 (SFR) [N] San Francisco, CA Jesuit Community at University of San Francisco.
Kendzierski, James *o.f.m.* '81 (MIL) Sturtevant, WI St. Sebastian's Church.
Kendzierski, Norbert V. '64 (DET) Farmington, MI St. Colman Church.
Kenealy, Thomas L. *s.j.* '58 (CHI) [N] Evanston, IL Canisius House.
Kenefick, Paul F. '56 (HRT) [11] Hartford, CT St. Lawrence O'Toole Church; [3] West Hartford, CT St. John the Evangelist Church.
Keneham, David A. *o.s.f.s.* '74 (TOL) [K] Toledo, OH Oblates of St. Francis de Sales.
Kenkel, Benedict J. '53 (DM) Guthrie Center, IA St. Mary Church.
Kenkel, Leonard A. '60 (DM) Creston, IA Holy Spirit Church.
Kenlon, Joseph *o.f.m.cap.* (NY) State, NY Shawangunk Correctional Facility; State, NY Wallkill Correctional Facility.
Kenlon, Knute *o.f.m.cap.* '58 (NY) New Paltz, NY St. Joseph Church; [Z] New Paltz, NY St. Joseph Friary.
Kenna, Daniel *o.f.m.* '73 (R) [4] Raleigh, NC St. Francis of Assisi Church.
Kenna, Donald J. '64 (BRK) [4] Brooklyn, NY All Saints Church.
Kenna, John A. '39 (DET) Retired.
Kenna, John Thomas '88 (CC) On Special Assignment; [F] Corpus Christi, TX Mount Carmel Home.
Kenna, Joseph J. '67 (YAK) On Duty Outside the Diocese.
Kenna, Thomas J. '63 (NEW) On Duty Outside the Archdiocese.
Kennard, George V. *s.j.* '50 (SFR) [N] San Francisco, CA Jesuit Community at University of San Francisco.
Kennard, George V. *s.j.* '50 (STL) [P] St. Louis, MO Jesuit Community Corporation at St. Louis University - Jesuit Hall.
Kenneally, James P. '62 (DET) [8] Dearborn, MI Sacred Heart Church.
Kenneally, John A. '69 (SAV) [8] Savannah, GA St. James Church.
Kenneally, William F. '53 (BO) [2] Plymouth, MA St. Bonaventure Church.
Kenneally, William G. '61 (CHI) [71] Chicago, IL St. Gertrude Church.
Kennealy, Thomas P. *s.j.* '62 (CIN) [D] Cincinnati, OH Xavier University; [M] Cincinnati, OH Jesuit Community at Xavier Unversity.
Kennedy, Alan '52 (P) Retired.
Kennedy, Alex '90 (TLS) [2] Tulsa, OK St. Augustine's Church; [11] Tulsa, OK St. Monica's Church.
Kennedy, Andrew '63 (BIR) [15] Birmingham, AL Our Lady of Lourdes Church.
Kennedy, Arthur L. '67 (BO) On Duty Outside the Archdiocese.
Kennedy, Arthur L. '67 (STP) [C] St. Paul, MN University of St. Thomas.
Kennedy, Charles J. '66 (PH) Bridgeport, PA St. Augustine Church.
Kennedy, Charles T. '57 (BGP) [K] Trumbull, CT St. Joseph's Manor.
Kennedy, Charles T. '57 (HRT) Retired.
Kennedy, Msgr. Christopher J. '44 (LA) [3] Long Beach, CA St. Barnabas Church; Retired.
Kennedy, Daniel J. *o.p.* '60 (L) [46] Louisville, KY St. Louis Bertrand Church.
Kennedy, David G. '55 (BUR) Retired.
Kennedy, Msgr. David W. '53 (GAL) Conroe, TX Sacred Heart Church.
Kennedy, Donal P. '60 (YAK) Prosser, WA Sacred Heart Church.
Kennedy, Edward F.X. *s.j.* '52 (NY) [166] Bronx, NY St. Michael Church.
Kennedy, Msgr. Edward J. (CAM) Retired.
Kennedy, Edward J. '68 (PH) [53] Philadelphia, PA St. Hedwig Church; [W] Darby, PA St. Francis Country House.
Kennedy, Edward J. '93 (GRY) Highland, IN Our Lady of Grace Church.
Kennedy, Msgr. Edwin J. (SFR) [K] San Francisco, CA Home for the Aged of the Little Sisters of the Poor.
Kennedy, Msgr. Edwin J. '32 (SFR) Retired.
Kennedy, Ernest E. (CHR) Special Assignment.
Kennedy, Msgr. Francis B. '39 (CIN) [89] Cincinnati, OH St. William Church; Retired.
Kennedy, Francis M. '64 (SPR) [7] Chicopee, MA St. Mary's Church.
Kennedy, Francis P. '46 (RCK) Rochelle, IL St. Patrick Church.
Kennedy, Gary L. '68 (PBL) Alamosa, CO Sacred Heart Church.
Kennedy, George *o.carm.* '78 (WDC) [B] Washington, DC Whitefriars Hall.
Kennedy, Hugh A. *s.j.* '48 (BAL) [M] Baltimore, MD Jesuit Fathers and Brothers Maryland Provincial Curia.
Kennedy, Msgr. J. Nevin '58 (MET) Somerville, NJ Immaculate Conception Church.
Kennedy, James '94 (SD) Leave of Absence.
Kennedy, James M. '54 (SY) North Syracuse, NY St. Rose of Lima Church.
Kennedy, Jerrold F. '66 (OAK) [4] Alameda, CA St. Philip Neri Church.
Kennedy, Msgr. John '50 (MRY) Retired.
Kennedy, John '56 (SFD) Retired.
Kennedy, John A. '50 (LA) Retired.
Kennedy, John D. '93 (SHP) [5] Monroe, LA St. Matthew Church; [A] Monroe, LA St. Frederick High School; [G] Monroe, LA Catholic Campus Ministry at Northeast Louisiana University.
Kennedy, John F. '63 (NEW) Scotch Plains, NJ Immaculate Heart of Mary Church.
Kennedy, Msgr. John J. '49 (STL) Richmond Heights, MO St. Luke the Evangelist Church; Retired.
Kennedy, Msgr. John S. '35 (HRT) Retired.
Kennedy, John V. *c.m.* '49 (MIA) [34] Miami, FL St. Vincent De Paul Church.
Kennedy, Joseph J. '48 (PH) Media, PA Nativity of the Blessed Virgin Mary Church; Retired.
Kennedy, Joseph M. *s.j.* '55 (BAL) [C] Baltimore, MD Loyola College; [M] Baltimore, MD Jesuit Community of Loyola College, Inc.; [Q] Baltimore, MD Jesuit Seminary Guild & Jesuit Mission Bureau, Maryland Province, Inc.; [Q] Baltimore, MD Jesuit Jamshedpur Mission Society, Inc.
Kennedy, Joseph P. '56 (SY) Camden, NY St. John Church.
Kennedy, Joseph P. '73 (WDC) Landover Hills, MD St. Mary's Catholic Church.
Kennedy, Kevin C. '95 (WDC) Kensington, MD Holy Redeemer Church.
Kennedy, Laurence W. '57 (SY) [13] Syracuse, NY St. Brigid and St. Joseph Church.
Kennedy, Leo *o.f.m.conv.* (L) [6] Louisville, KY St. Anthony Church.
Kennedy, Leonard A. *c.s.b.* '47 (GAL) [Q] Sugar Land, TX Basilian Mission Center.
Kennedy, Malcolm M. '61 (WDC) [T] Washington, DC Opus Dei.
Kennedy, Michael E. *s.j.* '77 (LA) [10] Los Angeles, CA Dolores Mission Church.
Kennedy, Michael J. *c.m.* '67 (BAL) Emmitsburg, MD St. Joseph Church; [M] Emmitsburg, MD Vincentian House.
Kennedy, Michael J. '67 (STP) Cedar, MN St. Patrick Church.
Kennedy, Oliver *s.s.c.* '47 (OM) [K] St. Columbans, NE St. Columban's Foreign Mission Society.
Kennedy, Patrick '53 (DEN) [18] Denver, CO Our Lady of Grace Church.

Kennedy, Patrick A. '77 (STP) Fridley, MN St. William Church.
Kennedy, Patrick J. R. '70 (NO) Luling, LA St. Anthony of Padua Church.
Kennedy, Patrick J.R. '70 (NO) Retired.
Kennedy, Paul M. '77 (PH) Rydal, PA St. Hilary of Poitiers Church; [D] Philadelphia, PA Cardinal Dougherty High School.
Kennedy, Richard '67 (TOL) Mansfield, OH St. Peter Church.
Kennedy, Richard C. '73 (ORG) [7] Santa Ana, CA St. Barbara's Church.
Kennedy, Robert (ROC) [A] Rochester, NY St. Bernard's Institute.
Kennedy, Robert E. *s.j.* '65 (NEW) [B] Jersey City, NJ Saint Peter's College; [N] Jersey City, NJ Jesuits of Saint Peter's College, Inc.
Kennedy, Robert J. *o.f.m.* '90 (NY) [48] New York, NY Holy Name of Jesus Church.
Kennedy, Robert R. '66 (BO) [48] Boston, MA St. Mary, Star of the Sea Church.
Kennedy, Robert T. '59 (NY) On Duty Outside the Archdiocese.
Kennedy, Robert T. '59 (WDC) [C] Washington, DC Catholic University of America, The.
Kennedy, Russell F. '75 (NOR) [4] Norwich, CT St. Mary Church.
Kennedy, Russell P. '75 (NOR) New London, CT St. Mary, Star of the Sea Church; New London, CT St. Mary, Star of the Sea Church.
Kennedy, T. Frank *s.j.* '76 (BO) [W] Chestnut Hill, MA The Jesuit Community at Boston College.
Kennedy, Thaddeus J. *o.c.s.o.* '58 (DUB) [K] Peosta, IA New Melleray Abbey, Order of Cistercians of the Strict Observance.
Kennedy, Msgr. Thomas I. '41 (SFR) Marin, CA Serra Club of Marin; Retired; [K] San Rafael, CA Nazareth House.
Kennedy, Thomas R. *c.m.* '64 (PH) [Z] Philadelphia, PA Congregation of the Mission.
Kennedy, Victor P. '77 (NEW) [3] Jersey City, NJ St. Anne's Church.
Kennedy, Vincent A. '44 (RVC) East Meadow, NY Nassau County, Fire Chiefs, Council of; Retired; [N] Uniondale, NY St. Pius X Residence.
Kennedy, William H. '65 (ALB) Stottville, NY Holy Family Church; Coxsackie, NY Coxsackie Correctional Facility.
Kennedy, William J. *s.j.* '65 (BGP) [2] Greenwich, CT St. Michael the Archangel Church; [O] Fairfield, CT The Fairfield Jesuit Community-Fairfield University.
Kennedy, William J. *s.j.* '65 (BO) [W] Boston, MA The Society of Jesus of New England-Provincial Offices.
Kennedy, William J. '69 (NY) Retired; [Z] New York, NY Pope John Paul II Residence.
Kennedy, William M. '71 (BO) Military & VA Chaplains.
Kennedy, William M. '71 (CIN) [8] Cincinnati, OH St. Ann Church.
Kennedy, Msgr. William P. '33 (STO) Modesto, CA Our Lady of Fatima Church; Retired.
Kennehan, John P. '62 (OG) Potsdam, NY St. Mary Church.
Kennelley, James J. '70 (E) Du Bois, PA St. Joseph Church.
Kennelly, Daniel '77 (BGP) [2] Stratford, CT St. James Church; [I] Bridgeport, CT St. Vincent's Medical Center.
Kennelly, Michael F. *s.j.* '46 (SP) [C] Tampa, FL Jesuit High School.
Kennelly, Stephen '69 (SAN) Miles, TX St. Thomas Church; Olfen, TX St. Boniface Church; Rowena, TX St. Joseph's Church.
Kenney, Albert A. '94 (PRO) [9] Pawtucket, RI St. Mary's Church.
Kenney, Daniel J. *s.j.* '63 (MIL) [P] Milwaukee, WI Jesuit Provincial Office, Wisconsin Province.
Kenney, Francis J. *s.m.* '49 (CIN) [9] Dayton, OH Emmanuel Church; [M] Dayton, OH Marianist Provincialate.
Kenney, Francis P. '87 (WIL) Hockessin, DE St. Mary of the Assumption Church.
Kenney, Henry *s.j.* '52 (LEX) Special Assignment.
Kenney, Msgr. Jeremiah '72 (BAL) [Q] Baltimore, MD Holy Name Society.
Kenney, Msgr. Jeremiah F. '72 (BAL) [84] Baltimore, MD St. Rose of Lima Church; Special Assignment.
Kenney, John B. '57 (BUR) Stowe, VT Blessed Sacrament Church.
Kenney, Joseph A. '43 (BAL) [25] Baltimore, MD St. Clement Church; Retired; [K] Baltimore, MD Stella Maris Operating Corporation.
Kenney, Kevin T. '94 (STP) [31] Minneapolis, MN St. Olaf Church.
Kenney, Mark G. *s.m.* '79 (WDC) [M] Washington, DC Marist Provincial House.
Kenney, Martin F. *s.s.j.* '54 (BR) Donaldsonville, LA St. Catherine of Siena Church.
Kenney, Paul C. *s.j.* '72 (BO) [W] Boston, MA The Society of Jesus of New England-Provincial Offices.
Kenney, Peter J. *s.s.j.* '46 (BAL) [M] Baltimore, MD St. Joseph Society of the Sacred Heart House of Central Administration.
Kenney, Msgr. Philip J. '39 (MAN) Retired.
Kenney, Robert D. *o.s.f.s.* '52 (WIL) [B] Wilmington, DE Salesianum School.
Kenney, Sean W. '91 (MET) Woodbridge, NJ St. James Church.
Kenney, Timothy '58 (Y) Kent, OH St. Patrick's Church.
Kenney, Timothy M. *s.m.* '82 (SFR) [D] San Francisco, CA Archbishop Riordan High School (Boys); [N] San Francisco, CA Marianist Community.
Kenney, William J. *c.s.p.* '51 (NY) [Z] Scarsdale, NY Paulist Fathers Generalate.
Kenney, William J. '56 (STP) [11] Minneapolis, MN Our Lady of Mount Carmel Church.
Kenney, William T. *c.s.p.* '51 (LA) [86] Los Angeles, CA St. Paul the Apostle Church.
Kenning, Herman H. '43 (CIN) Retired; [N] Cincinnati, OH St. Clare Convent, Franciscan Sisters of the Poor; [S] Cincinnati, OH Archdiocesan Central Council of Cincinnati.
Kennington, John *c.ss.r.* '59 (NY) [Z] Esopus, NY Redemptorist Priests and Brothers C.Ss.R. (Province of Baltimore); [DD] Esopus, NY Holy Shroud Guild.
Kenny, Albert N. '54 (BRK) Absent on Sick Leave; Retired.
Kenny, Donald '66 (JOL) [5] Naperville, IL St. Thomas the Apostle Church.
Kenny, Msgr. Donald A. (ATL) [3] Marietta, GA St. Joseph Church; Special or Other (Arch)Diocesan Assignment.
Kenny, Eugene P. '53 (DOD) McCracken, KS St. Mary Church; Loretto, KS St. Mary Help of Christians.
Kenny, Msgr. Francis P. (OM) Retired.
Kenny, Gregory D. *c.m.f.* '59 (ATL) Stone Mountain, GA Corpus Christi Church; [L] Atlanta, GA Campus Ministry.
Kenny, Gregory D. *c.m.f.* '59 (CHI) [N] Oak Park, IL Claretian Fathers Headquarters of U.S.A. Eastern Province.
Kenny, James E. '49 (OM) Retired.
Kenny, Msgr. James T. (SLC) Retired.
Kenny, John F. *o.s.f.s.* '69 (HBG) Manheim, PA St. Richard Church.
Kenny, Msgr. John J. '29 (SFR) Belmont, CA Immaculate Heart of Mary Church; Retired
Kenny, John R. '51 (OAK) [3] Walnut Creek, CA St. Mary's Church.
Kenny, Johns J. *c.s.p.* '58 (CHR) Clemson, SC St. Andrew Church.
Kenny, Joseph P. *o.p.* '63 (CHI) [N] Chicago, IL Dominicans (Provincial Office).
Kenny, Kevin *o.f.m.conv.* '66 (ALB) [O] Fonda, NY Blessed Kateri Retreat House; [R] Fonda, NY The National Shrine of Blessed Kateri Tekakwitha and Friary.
Kenny, Michael '73 (SAT) [52] San Antonio, TX St. Margaret Mary Church.
Kenny, Michael J. '35 (BRK) Retired.
Kenny, Myles J. *c.s.sp.* '51 (LC) Tomah, WI Veterans Administration Medical Center.
Kenny, P. Edward, Jr. '74 (BAL) [18] Baltimore, MD Blessed Sacrament Church; [57] Baltimore, MD St. Mary of the Assumption Church.
Kenny, Patrick J. *o.s.a.* '35 (PH) [Z] Villanova, PA St. Thomas Monastery.
Kenny, Pierce *c.ss.r.* '69 (ALB) Saratoga Springs, NY St. Clement Church.
Kenny, Raymond G. '63 (SJ) [23] San Jose, CA Santa Teresa Church.
Kenny, Simon *o.carm.* '64 (TUC) [A] Tucson, AZ Salpointe Catholic High School; [F] Tucson, AZ Carmelite Priory.
Kenny, Msgr. Simon E. '38 (BAL) Retired; [K] Baltimore, MD Stella Maris Operating Corporation.
Kenny, Stephen K. '91 (MEM) Camden, TN St. Mary Church.
Kenny, Stephen Paul *c.p.* '30 (HRT) [M] West Hartford, CT Holy Family Monastery/Retreat.
Kenny, Msgr. Thomas '65 (ATL) [1] Atlanta, GA Cathedral of Christ the King.
Kenny, Thomas A. '46 (NEW) Retired.
Kenny, Thomas C. *o.s.a.* '56 (BO) Boston, MA Lawrence General Hospital; [C] North Andover, MA Merrimack College.
Kenny, Msgr. Walter F. '54 (NY) Larchmont, NY St. Augustine Church.
Kenny, William J.M. '71 (LAV) [2] Las Vegas, NV Christ the King Church.
Kenshol, Joseph W. '73 (GR) Sand Lake, MI Mary Queen of Apostles Church.
Kent, Daniel '63 (MIA) [17] Miami, FL St. Catherine of Siena Church; [B] Opa Locka, FL St. Thomas University.
Kent, James *o.f.m.conv.* '91 (L) Pleasure Ridge Park, KY St. Paul Church.
Kent, Joseph E. '48 (SY) Retired.
Kent, Thomas J. *s.j.* '47 (SY) [S] Syracuse, NY Jesuits at LeMoyne, Inc.
Keogh, James P. *s.j.* '52 (CHL) [J] Charlotte, NC Jesuit Community.
Keogh, James V. *s.j.* '52 (CHL) Mooresville, NC St. Therese Church.
Keogh, Msgr. John '37 (NY) Retired.
Keogh, Simeon '49 (GB) [I] Appleton, WI St. Fidelis Friary.
Keogh, Stephen *s.a.c.* '53 (DET) [K] Wyandotte, MI Pallottine Fathers.
Keogh, Thomas '45 (SR) Retired.
Keogh, Msgr. Thomas J. '33 (NY) [70] New York, NY St. Mary Church; Retired.
Keogh, William '78 (JC) Absent on Leave.
Keohan, Edward M. '59 (BO) [7] Salem, MA St. Mary's Italian Church; Boston, MA North Shore Medical Center.
Keohane, Daniel C. '52 (TLS) Retired.
Keohane, Daniel G. '78 (BRK) [153] Queens, NY Ascension Church.
Keohane, Daniel T. '78 (SFR) [1] San Mateo, CA St. Bartholomew Church.
Keohane, Donal '68 (SAV) On Duty Outside the Diocese.
Keohane, Msgr. Mark H. '29 (BO) Retired.
Keohane, William *o.m.i.* '36 (BO) [Z] Tewksbury, MA Immaculate Heart of Mary Novitiate-Infirmary.
Keolker, Richard F. '63 (YAK) On Duty Outside the Diocese.
Keon, James J. *c.s.b.* '52 (GAL) [Q] Houston, TX Residence of the Basilian Fathers of the University of St. Thomas.
Keonig, Paul *o.c.d.* '93 (LA) Alhambra, CA St. Therese Church.
Keough, Joseph F. '96 (HRT) Southington, CT St. Thomas Church.
Keppeler, Richard J. '54 (BUF) Bergen, NY St. Brigid Church.
Keppens, Gustaaf M. *s.j.* '61 (WDC) [K] Washington, DC Georgetown University Hospital; [M] Washington, DC The Jesuit Community at Georgetown University.
Kepple, Robert '74 (LR) Retired.
Keppler, Daniel J. '58 (DUB) Spillville, IA St. Wenceslaus Church.
Keppler, John F. '60 (BRK) [148] Queens, NY American Martyrs Church.
Keppner, Paul *s.s.c.* '42 (BUF) [5] Tonawanda, NY St. Timothy Church.
Kerbawy, Kevin '76 (SAG) Kinde, MI St. Mary-St. Edward Church.
Kerber, John V. '58 (STL) Festus, MO Our Lady Church.
Kerber, Joseph P. '88 (SFD) Alexander, IL Visitation B.V.M. Church; Franklin, IL Sacred Heart of Jesus Church; New Berlin, IL Sacred Heart of Mary Church.
Kerber, Justin *c.p.* '72 (BRK) [U] Jamaica, NY Immaculate Conception Monastery.
Kerby, Robert L. '70 (NTN) South Bend, IN St. John of Damascus Church.
Kerch, Rudolph S. '40 (GB) Retired.
Kerdiejus, John B. *s.j.* '58 (BO) [Y] Gloucester, MA Eastern Point Retreat House.
Kerestes, Michael '89 (PSC) Beltsville, MD St. Gregory of Nyssa Church.
Kerestus, Thomas J. '69 (ALN) Unassigned; [J] Bethlehem, PA Holy Family Villa.
Kereszty, Rochus *o.cist.* '60 (DAL) [M] Irving, TX Cistercian Abbey of Our Lady of Dallas.
Kerin, Msgr. Joseph A. '57 (CHL) Sabbatical.
Kerivan, William C. '48 (BO) Permanent Disability.
Kerketta, Telesphore *s.j.* '62 (BO) [W] Chestnut Hill, MA The Jesuit Community at Boston College.
Kern, Charles '77 (NEW) Kenilworth, NJ St. Theresa's Church.
Kern, Msgr. Crosby W. '65 (NO) [2] Metairie, LA St. Angela Merici Church.
Kern, Jerome C. '66 (STP) Forest Lake, MN St. Peter Church.
Kern, John R. '68 (MIL) [66] Milwaukee, WI SS. Peter and Paul Church.
Kern, Joseph R. '57 (IND) Montezuma, IN Immaculate Conception Church; Rockville, IN St. Joseph Church.
Kern, Martin F. '94 (ALN) [9] Allentown, PA Sacred Heart of Jesus Church.
Kern, Msgr. Walter O. '58 (BUF) Bowmansville, NY Sacred Heart Church; [T] Bowmansville, NY International Institute of the Heart of Jesus.
Kern, Msgr. Walter O. '58 (MIL) [Y] Milwaukee, WI International Institute of the Heart of Jesus.
Kernan, Eugene J. '49 (CAM) Stone Harbor, NJ St. Paul's Church.
Kernan, James *o.m.i.* '59 (SD) Calipatria, CA St. Patrick Church.
Kernan, Michael H. '54 (PIT) Retired.
Kernan, Timothy J. '65 (STP) [11] St. Paul, MN St. Adalbert Church.
Kernan, William A. '93 (SD) [1] El Cajon, CA Holy Trinity Church.
Kerner, Howard L. *s.j.* '43 (DET) [P] Clarkston, MI Colombiere Center.

Kerner, Terrence D. '72 (DET) [2] Monroe, MI St. John Church.
Kerner, Timothy *c.ss.r.* '81 (BR) [10] Baton Rouge, LA St. Gerard Majella Church.
Kerns, John '85 (P) [3] Portland, OR All Saints Church.
Kerns, Paul R. '71 (PRT) Augusta, ME St. Mary's Church.
Kerper, Michael '85 (MAN) Franklin, NH St. Paul Church.
Kerper, Michael '85 (PH) [T] Philadelphia, PA Nazareth Hospital.
Kerr, Charles L. *s.j.* '50 (WIN) [1] Mankato, MN SS. Peter and Paul's Church.
Kerr, Cherubin *o.s.a.* '44 (CAM) [C] Richland, NJ St. Augustine Preparatory School.
Kerr, Joseph L. *s.m.* '46 (CIN) [M] Cincinnati, OH Marianist Community.
Kerr, Robert '95 (KC) [40] Kansas City, MO St. Thomas More Church.
Kerr, Robert T. '64 (LAN) [3] Ypsilanti, MI St. Joseph Church.
Kerr, Seamus '60 (YAK) East Wenatchee, WA Holy Apostles Church.
Kerr, Msgr. William A. '66 (PIT) [B] Pittsburgh, PA La Roche College.
Kerr, Msgr. William A. '66 (PT) On Duty Outside the Diocese.
Kerrigan, Bernard '48 (WIN) Retired.
Kerrigan, James P. '70 (WOR) Rutland, MA St. Patrick's Church.
Kerrigan, Joseph '90 (MEM) [1] Memphis, TN Cathedral of the Immaculate Conception.
Kerrigan, Joseph P. '45 (PH) [2] Bensalem, PA St. Elizabeth Ann Seton Church; Retired.
Kerrigan, Michael F. '64 (DEN) Idaho Springs, CO St. Paul's Church.
Kerrigan, Michael P. *c.s.p.* '87 (NY) [Z] Scarsdale, NY Paulist Fathers Generalate.
Kerrigan, Neal *o.f.m.cap.* '52 (NY) Yonkers, NY St. John Hospital; [Z] Yonkers, NY St. Clare Friary.
Kerschen, Leo A. '62 (WCH) Coffeyville, KS Holy Name Church.
Kerschen, Leon J. '62 (WCH) Iola, KS St. John Church.
Kerschen, Matthew J. *c.ss.r.* '48 (BLX) [E] Biloxi, MS St. John Neumann Residence.
Kerscher, Charles J. '79 (ATL) Conyers, GA St. Pius X Catholic Church.
Kerscher, Francis R. '55 (GB) Seymour, WI St. John Church.
Kersey, Walter L. '81 (BR) Retired.
Kersgieter, Paul J. '45 (STL) Retired.
Kershner, Joseph J. *sch.p.* '64 (MIA) [C] Fort Lauderdale, FL Cardinal Gibbons High School.
Kerst, Pat '90 (SPK) Brewster, WA Sacred Heart Church; Twisp, WA St. Genevieve Church.
Kerstein, Thomas F. '70 (MIL) Whitefish Bay, WI Holy Family Church.
Kersten, Edward J. *o.s.a.* '56 (CHI) [185] Chicago, IL St. Rita of Cascia Church.
Kersten, John *s.v.d.* '40 (BLX) [A] Bay St. Louis, MS St. Augustine's.
Kersten, Kevin *s.j.* '72 (BO) [W] Chestnut Hill, MA The Jesuit Community at Boston College.
Kertz, Raymond N. '67 (MAD) [1] Janesville, WI Nativity of St. Mary Church.
Kerwan, Francis T. '43 (HRT) [1] Enfield, CT Holy Family Church.
Kerwick, Robert J. '48 (PH) Retired.
Kerwin, Eugene H. '52 (OM) [40] Omaha, NE St. Robert Bellarmine Church.
Kerwin, Joseph A. '62 (SC) Retired.
Kerwin, Kilian *o.s.b.* '68 (IND) [42] Indianapolis, IN St. Therese of the Infant Jesus (Little Flower) Church; [J] St. Meinrad, IN St. Meinrad Archabbey.
Kerze, William F. '69 (LA) Malibu, CA Our Lady of Malibu Church.
Kesecki, Michael T. '88 (E) On Duty Outside Diocese.
Kessel, Gerald *o.f.m.cap.* '82 (DET) [P] Washington, MI Capuchin Retreat.
Kessing, Bernadine *o.f.m.* (BUF) Vandalia, NY St. John the Baptist Church.
Kessing, Bernardine *o.f.m.* '60 (BUF) Allegany, NY St. Bonaventure Church.
Kessinger, David R. *o.s.b.* '58 (CHL) [J] Belmont, NC Belmont Abbey.
Kessler, Edward L. '48 (COL) Lancaster, OH Southeastern Correctional Institution; Retired.
Kessler, Matthew *c.ss.r.* '91 (DEN) Greeley, CO Our Lady of Peace Church.
Kessler, Thomas '74 (COL) [10] Columbus, OH Christ the King Church.
Kessler, Thomas '75 (EVN) [8] Evansville, IN Holy Spirit Church.
Kessler, Thomas J. '84 (ALN) [2] Easton, PA St. Bernard Church; [C] Easton, PA Notre Dame High School.
Kester, Kevin A. '81 (LA) Norwalk, CA St. Linus Church.
Kester, William J. '70 (STL) [6] Lemay, MO St. Matthias Church.
Kestermeier, Charles T. *s.j.* '75 (OM) [K] Omaha, NE Jesuit Community At Creighton University.
Kesterson, John C. '72 (LA) Van Nuys, CA St. Bridget of Sweden Church.
Kesting, Philip A. '41 (CIN) Retired.
Kestler, Theodore E. *s.j.* '75 (FBK) St. Marys, AK Church of the Nativity; [C] Fairbanks, AK Jesuit Residence; [E] St. Marys, AK Native Ministry Training Program; [E] St. Marys, AK Brother Joe Prince Jesuit Community.
Ketcham, Gregory K. '94 (PEO) Monmouth, IL Immaculate Conception Church; Raritan, IL Church of St. Patrick.
Ketchersid, Corbin W. (R) Retired.
Kettelberger, John *c.m.* (BUF) [C] Niagara University, NY Niagara University.
Ketteler, Aloys *s.v.d.* '40 (LSC) Deming, NM St. Ann's Church.
Ketteler, Ronald M. '61 (COV) Crescent Springs, KY St. Joseph Church.
Kettleberger, John A. *c.m.* '78 (BUF) [O] Niagara University, NY Vincentian Community at Niagara University.
Kettler, Msgr. Donald '70 (SFS) [5] Sioux Falls, SD St. Lambert Church.
Kettner, Joseph *m.s.* '50 (ORL) [3] Orlando, FL Good Shepherd Church.
Kettron, W. Michael '57 (LFT) Cicero, IN Sacred Heart Church.
Keu Sin, Peter Young (CLV) [6] Cleveland, OH St. Andrew Kim Church.
Keul, Msgr. Francis X. '48 (PH) Retired.
Keulman, Kenneth P. '69 (NO) [C] New Orleans, LA Loyola University.
Keulman, Kenneth P. '69 (SJ) On Duty Outside the Diocese.
Keutzer, Walter '56 (STL) Military Chaplains.
Kevane, Msgr. Eugene '37 (SC) Retired.
Keveney, William J. '56 (DET) Eastpointe, MI St. Barnabas Church.
Keveny, M. Valentine '73 (WDC) [40] Washington, DC St. Stephen Martyr Church.
Keville, Joseph '96 (BO) Beverly, MA St. John the Evangelist Church.
Kew, Larry J. '66 (GRY) [1] East Chicago, IN Assumption Church.
Key, Oren W. *s.j.* '53 (FWT) Crowell, TX St. Joseph Church; Quanah, TX St. Mary Church; Vernon, TX Holy Family Church.
Key, William W. '75 (MIL) [46] Milwaukee, WI St. Lawrence Church.
Keyes, Jeffrey R. *c.pp.s.* '91 (OAK) [2] Alameda, CA St. Barnabas Church.
Keyes, Paul T. '63 (BO) North Andover, MA St. Michael Church.
Keyes, Raphael '64 (JC) Missionary Assignment in Peru.
Keyes, Thomas E. '73 (BO) [1] Methuen, MA St. Lucy Church.
Keymont, Walter E. '80 (BO) [8] Boston, MA St. Ann Church.
Keyrouze, Joseph E. '50 (ALB) [14] Troy, NY St. Williams Church.
Keys, Gordon L. *s.j.* '55 (P) [D] Portland, OR Jesuit High School.
Keys, Msgr. Thomas J. '70 (SFR) [U] San Francisco, CA The Ordinary Mutual, RRG.
Keys, Msgr. Thomas J. '70 (SR) [3] Santa Rosa, CA St. Rose of Lima Church; [F] Rohnert Park, CA Society of St. Vincent de Paul, District Council of Sonoma County; [O] Santa Rosa, CA Apostolic Endowment Trust.
Kezmarsky, Kenneth '86 (PIT) Library, PA St. Joan of Arc Church.
Khachan, Bernard C. '60 (OLL) Cleveland, OH St. Maron Church.
Kharuk, Wasyl '92 (PHU) Trenton, NJ St. Josaphat's Church.
Khoury, Ghattas '90 (OLL) Wheeling, WV Our Lady of Lebanon Church.
Khoury, Msgr. James T. '75 (BO) [2] Lawrence, MA St. Anthony Church.
Khoury, Msgr. James T. '75 (SAM) Lawrence, MA St. Anthony Church.
Khue, Thomas L.T. '91 (SPK) Cusick, WA Our Lady of Sorrows Church; Ione, WA St. Bernard Church; Metaline Falls, WA St. Joseph Church; Newport, WA St. Anthony Church; Usk, WA St. Jude Church.
Kibby, Patrick J. '84 (NSH) [1] Nashville, TN Cathedral of the Incarnation.
Kichak, Joseph A. '43 (MAR) Retired.
Kicia, Chester *o.f.m.conv.* '36 (BGP) [14] Bridgeport, CT St. Michael The Archangel Church.
Kicmal Casimir C. *c.s.v.* '57 (CHI) [N] Arlington Heights, IL Viatorian Province Center-Clerics of St. Viator.
Kiczuk, Casimir *c.m.* '34 (SY) [S] Utica, NY St. Vincent's Mission House.
Kidd, Colin *o.f.m.* '48 (ORL) Merritt Island, FL Divine Mercy Church; Retired.
Kidd, Michael C. '54 (WDC) Mitchellville, MD Holy Family Church.
Kidd, Wayne R. '73 (LC) Richland Center, WI St. Mary (Assumption of B.V.M.) Church.
Kidd, William J. *s.j.* '63 (MIL) [P] Milwaukee, WI Jesuit Community at Marquette University.
Kidder, Msgr. James C. '67 (SAC) El Dorado Hills, CA Holy Trinity Church.
Kidder, Lawrence *o.f.m.* '32 (BO) [Z] Boston, MA Saint Anthony Residence.
Kiddy, Curtis '92 (MIA) [33] Miami, FL St. Timothy Church.
Kidner, M. Paul *o.s.b.* '58 (STL) [F] Creve Coeur, MO St. Louis Priory School; [P] St. Louis, MO The Abbey of St. Mary and St. Louis.
Kidney, Liam J. '68 (LA) Camarillo, CA Blessed Junipero Serra Church.
Kidney, Timothy '71 (SJ) [2] San Jose, CA St. Patrick Proto-Cathedral.
Kidwell, William *s.j.* '55 (MIA) [5] Miami, FL Gesu Church; [C] Miami, FL Our Lady of Lourdes Academy; [G] Miami, FL Mercy Hospital.
Kidykas, Jonas *s.j.* '35 (CHI) [N] Chicago, IL Lithuanian American Jesuits.
Kiedinger, Daniel J. '91 (LC) Cazenovia, WI St. Anthony de Padua Church; Keyesville, WI Nativity of the Blessed Virgin Mary Church; Lone Rock, WI Sacred Heart Church.
Kiefer, John D. '70 (LFT) Muncie, IN St. Francis of Assisi Church; [H] Muncie, IN St. Francis of Assisi University Church.
Kiefer, R. David '62 (GB) Mattoon, WI Holy Family Church; Neopit, WI St. Anthony Church; Phlox, WI St. Joseph Church.
Kiefer, Msgr. Thomas '46 (LA) [2] North Hollywood, CA St. Charles Borromeo Church.
Kiefer, Thomas P. '81 (SPC) [1] Springfield, MO Cathedral of St. Agnes.
Kiefer, William J. '58 (SB) Trona, CA St. Madeleine Sophie Barat Church; Retired.
Kieferle, Norbert '66 (AMA) On Duty Outside the Diocese.
Kieffer, Charles G. '80 (PHX) [24] Phoenix, AZ St. Theresa Church.
Kieffer, Henry '40 (SAL) [C] Concordia, KS Mount Joseph Senior Community.
Kieffer, Henry '54 (SAL) Aurora, KS St. Peter's Church.
Kieffer, John *s.j.* '68 (LEX) Monticello, KY St. Peter Church.
Kieffer, John L. *s.j.* (DET) [K] Detroit, MI Jesuit Provincial Office-Detroit Province of the Society of Jesus.
Kieffer, John L. *s.j.* '68 (LEX) [J] Livingston, KY Appalachia Science in the Public Interest.
Kieffer, Kenneth *o.f.m.* '55 (STL) [P] St. Louis, MO Franciscan Friary of St. Anthony of Padua.
Kieffer, Lawrence J. '50 (MAD) [4] Madison, WI Holy Redeemer Church; Madison, WI University Hospitals.
Kieffer, Merlin '60 (SAL) Hoxie, KS St. Frances Xavier Cabrini Church.
Kieffer, Robert J. '69 (SCL) Elk River, MN The Church of St. Andrew.
Kieffer, Thomas A. '65 (MRY) [G] Monterey, CA Oratorian Community-Congregation of the Oratory of Pontifical Right; [L] Monterey, CA Newman Institute for Historical and Religious Studies.
Kiel, William J. '93 (GBG) Kittanning, PA St. Mary, Our Lady of Guadalupe Church.
Kielb, John T. '75 (TR) Monmouth Beach, NJ Church of the Precious Blood.
Kielbasa, Richard A. '59 (SC) Lidderdale, IA Holy Family Church.
Kieliszewski, Jan M. '73 (MIL) Cudahy, WI St. Frederick's Church.
Kielkowski, Andrzej *s.d.s.* '81 (NEW) [N] Verona, NJ The Salvatorian Fathers.
Kielty, Henry *c.p.* '50 (L) [L] Louisville, KY Sacred Heart Retreat.
Kiely, Brian P. '78 (BO) Dracut, MA St. Francis Church.
Kiely, Cornelius '67 (BAK) On Duty Outside the Diocese.
Kiely, John J. '60 (HRT) [5] West Hartford, CT St. Peter Claver Church.
Kiely, Thomas P. '88 (NY) Briarcliff Manor, NY St. Theresa Church.
Kiem, Anthony '46 (PT) Retired.
Kiem, Anthony '46 (VIC) Port Lavaca, TX Our Lady of the Gulf Church.
Kiemen, Mathias *o.f.m.* '43 (FWT) [G] Crowley, TX St. Francis Village, Inc.; [H] Crowley, TX St. Maximilian Kolbe Friary.
Kiener, Hugolinus *o.f.m.* (SFD) [K] Sherman, IL Our Lady of Angels Friary.
Kienzle, Jerome C. '72 (MIL) Military Chaplains.
Kiepura, Kenneth G. '69 (CHI) Buffalo Grove, IL St. Mary Church.
Kieran, Benet *c.p.* '39 (LA) [R] Pasadena, CA Passionist Community.
Kieran, Ed '59 (AMA) Bovina, TX St. Ann's Church.
Kieran, John C. '67 (ATL) [L] Atlanta, GA Campus Ministry.
Kieran, John C. '77 (ATL) Conyers, GA St. Pius X

Catholic Church.
Kieran, Richard A. '65 (ATL) [4] Atlanta, GA Immaculate Heart of Mary Church.
Kierce, J. Joseph '43 (BO) [27] Boston, MA Holy Family Church; Retired.
Kiernan, Arthur C. *m.m.* '32 (NY) [Z] Maryknoll, NY Maryknoll Fathers and Brothers.
Kiernan, Msgr. Donald '49 (ATL) [M] Dorville, GA Korean Martyrs Pastoral Center.
Kiernan, Edward J. '54 (BRK) [30] Brooklyn, NY St. Columba Church.
Kiernan, James F. *c.m.* '70 (NY) [C] Staten Island, NY St. John's University Staten Island Campus.
Kiernan, James O. *c.m.* '70 (BRK) [D] Queens and Staten Island, NY St. John's University; [U] Jamaica, NY St. Vincent's House.
Kiernan, James W. '62 (DM) [1] Des Moines, IA St. Ambrose Cathedral.
Kiernan, John G. '55 (PBL) Retired.
Kiernan, John L. '48 (BRK) [U] Jamaica, NY Parsons Manor.
Kiernan, Joseph V. *o.f.m.* (ARL) Triangle, VA St. Francis of Assisi Church.
Kiernan, Michael F. '73 (SAC) Anderson, CA Sacred Heart Church.
Kiernan, Patrick J. '52 (P) North Bend, OR Holy Redeemer Church.
Kiernan, Msgr. R. Donald '49 (ATL) Dunwoody, GA All Saints Catholic Church.
Kiernan, Robert J. *o.s.b.* '60 (BUR) [G] Weston, VT Priory of Benedictine Monks.
Kiernan, Thomas '48 (SY) Retired.
Kies, Emil '44 (P) Retired.
Kiesel, James '95 (BAL) Annapolis, MD St. Andrew by the Bay Church.
Kiesel, Leo C. '63 (EVN) Loogootee, IN St. John Church; [J] Loogootee, IN American-Innsbruck Alumni Association.
Kieselbach, Joseph '61 (CR) Dilworth, MN St. Elizabeth Church.
Kieser, Ellwood E. *c.s.p.* '56 (LA) [86] Los Angeles, CA St. Paul the Apostle Church; [CC] Pacific Palisades, CA Paulist Productions.
Kiesling, John *s.a.* '68 (NY) [Z] Garrison, NY Generalate of the Franciscan Friars of the Atonement-St. James Friary.
Kieton, Dennis J. '85 (PRO) [11] Woonsocket, RI Sacred Heart Church.
Kiff, Herbert J., Jr. '95 (NO) Reserve, LA St. Peter Church.
Kiffmeyer, James G. '85 (CIN) [E] Cincinnati, OH Elder High School.
Kiggins, Roy J. '64 (ROC) Brockport, NY Nativity of the Blessed Virgin Mary Church.
Kigozi, Dennis S. '91 (COL) Pickerington, OH Seton Parish Church.
Kihm, Frederick C. '93 (STU) Burkhart, OH St. Joseph's Church; Woodsfield, OH St. Sylvester Church.
Kihm, Peter J. '81 (NY) Nyack, NY St. Ann Church.
Kihneman, Msgr. Louis F. '77 (CC) Rockport, TX Sacred Heart Church.
Kijauskas, Gediminas *s.j.* '60 (CLV) [59] Cleveland, OH Our Lady of Perpetual Help Church.
Kikowski, Zdzislaw *o.s.p.p.e.* '61 (PH) [Z] Doylestown, PA Pauline Fathers Monastery, Shrine of Our Lady of Czestochowa.
Kilarecki, George W. '46 (PIT) Retired; [N] Pittsburgh, PA St. John Vianney Manor.
Kilas, Joseph F. '54 (JOL) [6] Joliet, IL St. Ambrose Church; Joliet, IL Joliet Correctional Depot.
Kilbride, Eugene M. '59 (HRT) [2] West Hartford, CT St. Helena Church.
Kilbridge, Robert A. *o.p.* '47 (CHI) [131] Chicago, IL St. Mary, Star of the Sea Church; [N] River Forest, IL St. Thomas Aquinas Priory.
Kilburn, Clayton F. *c.m.* (GLP) Keams Canyon, AZ St. Joseph's Indian Mission Church.
Kilcarr, Stephen M. '56 (NEW) [C] West Orange, NJ Seton Hall Preparatory School.
Kilcline, Francis I. '81 (LFT) Kokomo, IN St. Patrick Church.
Kilcourse, George A. '76 (L) [A] Louisville, KY Bellarmine College.
Kilcoyne, John '45 (CLV) Retired.
Kilcoyne, Patrick '75 (SJ) Milpitas, CA Elmwood Rehabilitation Center.
Kilcoyne, Terence T. '76 (WOR) On Special or Other (Arch)Diocesan Assignment; [J] Worcester, MA Saint Vincent Hospital, Inc.
Kilcullen, John M. '55 (STL) Crestwood, MO St. Elizabeth of Hungary Church.
Kiley, Bonaventure *t.o.r.* '42 (ARL) [J] Winchester, VA Sacred Heart Friary.
Kiley, J. Cletus '74 (CHI) [5] Chicago, IL St. Agnes of Bohemia Church.
Kiley, John A. '66 (PRO) [7] Pawtucket, RI St. Leo's Church.
Kiley, John G. '70 (BO) Tyngsborough, MA St. Mary Magdalen Church.
Kiley, Philip *s.j.* (NOR) [A] Cromwell, CT Holy Apostles College and Seminary.
Kiley, Philip S. *s.j.* '71 (BO) [W] Boston, MA The Society of Jesus of New England-Provincial Offices; [W] Weston, MA Campion Center.
Kiley, Phillip C. '78 (CHI) [183] Chicago, IL Resurrection Church.
Kiley, Raymond P. '96 (BO) Canton, MA St. John the Evangelist Church.
Kilfoil, Msgr. Patrick '37 (EVN) Retired.
Kilgallen, John J. *s.j.* '65 (CHI) [C] Chicago, IL Jesuit Community at Loyola University of Chicago.
Kilgallon, John J. '69 (PH) Roslyn, PA St. John of the Cross Church.
Kilgarriff, John J. '36 (PH) Morton, PA Our Lady of Perpetual Help Church; Retired.
Kilian, John '68 (BUF) Attica, NY Attica Correctional Facility.
Kilian, Sabbas J. *o.f.m.* '43 (NY) [7] Mt. Vernon, NY St. Ursula Church.
Kilian, Waldemar *o.s.j.* '87 (CHI) River Grove, IL St. Cyprian Church.
Kilian, William T. '53 (SAL) Retired.
Kilianski, Edward *s.c.j.* '83 (MIL) [P] Franklin, WI Dehon House; [Y] Franklin, WI Congregation of the Priests of the Sacred Heart Support and Maintenance Trust.
Kilichumala, Varughese '87 (NEW) [12] Jersey City, NJ St. John the Baptist Church.
Kill, Robert J. '71 (TOL) Hamler, OH St. Paul Church; Holgate, OH St. Mary Church.
Killackey, Cyprian *o.c.d.* '52 (TUC) [21] Tucson, AZ Santa Cruz Church.
Killackey, Edward R. *m.m.* '57 (NY) [Z] Maryknoll, NY Maryknoll Fathers and Brothers.
Killackey, Thomas B. *m.m.* '56 (HON) Mililani Town, HI St. John Apostle and Evangelist Church; [H] Honolulu, HI Maryknoll Fathers House.
Killeen, Bernard D. '49 (HRT) Orange, CT Holy Infant Church.
Killeen, John C. '59 (CAM) [1] Cherry Hill, NJ St. Mary's Church.
Killeen, John F. *s.j.* '56 (LA) [C] Los Angeles, CA Loyola Marymount University.
Killeen, John J. '47 (HRT) Retired.
Killeen, John P. '57 (CC) George West, TX St. George Church; George West, TX St. George Church.
Killeen, Joseph P. '62 (DET) Holly, MI St. Rita Church.
Killeen, Msgr. Michael F. '59 (LA) Rowland Heights, CA St. Elizabeth Ann Seton Church.
Killeen, Thomas M. *o.m.i.* '58 (COS) Leadville, CO Catholic Community of Leadville, Annunciation & St. Joseph Church.
Killeen, Thomas M. *o.m.i.* '58 (STP) [N] St. Paul, MN Oblate Provincial Offices; [N] St. Paul, MN Oblate Residence.
Killeen, William E. '75 (CHI) Midlothian, IL St. Christopher Church.
Killeen, William J. '59 (HRT) Derby, CT St. Jude Church.
Killian, Wayne E. '84 (ALN) Pen Argyl, PA St. Elizabeth of Hungary Church; [C] Bangor, PA Pius X High School.
Killilea, Patrick *ss.cc.* '69 (FR) [K] Fairhaven, MA Sacred Hearts Provincial House.
Killingsworth, Bradley '70 (P) On Duty Outside the Archdiocese.
Killion, Dennis W. *o.s.f.s.* '80 (PH) [D] Philadelphia, PA Father Judge High School for Boys; [Z] Philadelphia, PA Father Judge Faculty House.
Killion, Robert L. '53 (WOR) Bolton, MA St. Francis Xavier Church.
Killoren, John (STL) [P] St. Louis, MO Jesuit Community Corporation at St. Louis University - Jesuit Hall.
Kilmartin, John *f.d.p.* '86 (BO) Waltham, MA Coordinator of Prison Ministry; [U] Boston, MA Don Orione Nursing Home; [BB] Boston, MA Madonna Queen Shrine.
Kilmurray, Fintan J. '77 (BLX) [1] Gulfport, MS St. Ann Church.
Kilpatrick, Andrew W. '96 (SCR) [1] Scranton, PA St. Peter's Cathedral.
Kilpatrick, Vincent J. '50 (SY) Warners, NY Our Lady of Good Counsel Church.
Kilroy, Brendan K. *s.p.s.* '62 (NEW) [C] Ramsey, NJ Don Bosco Preparatory High School for Boys; [N] Cliffside Park, NJ St. Patrick's Missionary Society.
Kilroy, C. A. *o.p.* '61 (STP) [15] Minneapolis, MN St. Albert the Great Church.
Kilroy, Paul E. '70 (BO) [7] Boston, MA St. Ann Church; [6] Newton, MA Our Lady Help of Christians Church; [CC] Boston, MA St. Ann's University Parish.
Kilroy, Robert F. *o.m.i.* '40 (BO) [Z] Tewksbury, MA Immaculate Heart of Mary Novitiate-Infirmary.
Kilsdonk, Edward P. '37 (GB) Retired.
Kilty, Cornelius F. *o.s.f.s.* '69 (PH) [Z] Philadelphia, PA Oblates of St. Francis De Sales.
Kim, Alapaki K. *c.s.p.* '82 (HON) Pahoa, HI Sacred Heart Church.
Kim, Albert K.H. *c.s.p.* '82 (NY) [Z] Scarsdale, NY Paulist Fathers Generalate.
Kim, Alex K. '91 (ORG) Irvine, CA St. Elizabeth Ann Seton Church.
Kim, Andrew '87 (LA) [14] Los Angeles, CA Holy Trinity Church.
Kim, Anthony (RVC) New Hyde Park, NY Notre Dame Church.
Kim, Barthasar '77 (WDC) [5] Washington, DC St. Anthony Church.
Kim, Benedict '64 (ORG) Special Assignment; [G] Anaheim, CA St. Thomas Korean Catholic Center.
Kim, Benedict *s.j.* '95 (NY) [Z] New York, NY West Side Jesuit Community.
Kim, Benedict Yong Tae '71 (GAL) [R] Houston, TX Handmaids of the Sacred Heart of Pohang (H.S.H.).
Kim, Carlos C. '93 (BO) Ashland, MA St. Cecilia Church.
Kim, Chrysostom *o.s.b.* '60 (SCL) [I] Collegeville, MN St. John's Abbey, of the Order of St. Benedict.
Kim, Francis *o.f.m.* '96 (NY) [35] New York, NY St. Francis of Assisi Church.
Kim, Francis K. '75 (LA) Carson, CA St. Philomena Church.
Kim, Garino '62 (BRK) [226] Queens, NY St. Paul Chong Ha-Sang Roman Catholic Chapel.
Kim, Jeong Uk '92 (IND) [29] Indianapolis, IN St. Lawrence Church.
Kim, John Sung Kyu (BIR) [11] Birmingham, AL Korean Catholic Community, St. Luke Hwang Church.
Kim, Joseph Sy '90 (LAN) [3] Jackson, MI St. Mary, Star of the Sea Church.
Kim, Joseph Y. (BAL) [16] Baltimore, MD St. Bernard Church.
Kim, Mary Joseph *o.cart* '92 (BUR) [G] Arlington, VT Carthusian Foundation, Charterhouse of the Transfiguration.
Kim, Michael '87 (CAM) Pleasantville, NJ St. Peter's Church.
Kim, Nam Van '90 (ELP) Fort Davis, TX St. Joseph Church.
Kim, Paul Chun-Ho '71 (GAL) [6] Houston, TX St. Andrew Kim Church.
Kim, Roy '94 (ORG) Cypress, CA St. Irenaeus Church.
Kim, Sae Eul '84 (LA) [38] Los Angeles, CA St. Agnes Church.
Kim, Thomas (CHI) [2] Des Plaines, IL St. Paul Chong Hasang Church.
Kim Ngo, Anthony Trang '94 (RIC) [4] Hampton, VA Our Lady of Viet Nam Chapel; [L] Richmond, VA Ethnic and Special Ministries.
Kim Thien, Joseph Tran '81 (PH) Upper Darby, PA St. Alice Church.
Kimathy, Alphonce *c.s.sp.* '80 (NO) [7] New Orleans, LA Holy Ghost Church.
Kimbrough, Conrad L. '78 (CHL) Mooresville, NC St. Therese Church; [Q] Charlotte, NC Room at the Inn, Inc.
Kimecz, Aloysius *o.cist.* '53 (DAL) [M] Irving, TX Cistercian Abbey of Our Lady of Dallas.
Kimla, James E. '69 (MIL) Awaiting Assignment.
Kimm, Gregory '87 (SJ) [8] San Jose, CA Holy Family Church.
Kimminau, Bernard V. '94 (LIN) [10] Lincoln, NE St. Peter Church.
Kimminau, Irenaeus *o.f.m.* '49 (SFD) [6] Quincy, IL St. Joseph Church.
Kimmons, Steven *s.j.* '94 (CHI) [C] Chicago, IL Jesuit Community at Loyola University of Chicago.
Kimpel, Edward J. *o.praem.* '49 (PH) [48] Philadelphia, PA St. Gabriel Church; [Z] Paoli, PA Daylesford Abbey.
Kin, Bohdan '77 (PHU) Great Meadows, NJ St. Nicholas Church; West Easton, PA Holy Ghost Church.
Kinane, Gerard P. '73 (NO) [28] New Orleans, LA St. Cecilia Church.
Kinane, James G. (MOB) On Leave from the Archdiocese.
Kinane, Joseph J. '52 (CHI) Park Ridge, IL St. Paul of the Cross Church; Retired.
Kinane, William P. '57 (SAC) Vallejo, CA St. Catherine of Siena Church.
Kinast, Robert L. '68 (ATL) On Duty Outside the Archdiocese.
Kinast, Timothy '90 (CC) Military Chaplains.
Kinch, Edwin M. *o.s.b.* '45 (CHI) [N] Chicago, IL Servite Friars - Eastern Province.
Kindall, John J. *s.j.* '57 (P) Yamhill, OR St. John Church; [A] Portland, OR Jesuit Novitiate of St. Francis Xavier.
Kinderman, Dennis J. *c.pp.s.* '67 (LFT) [A] Rensselaer, IN Saint Joseph's College.
Kindon, W. Fred '74 (PH) [137] Philadelphia, PA St. Philip Neri Church.
Kinel, Robert *s.s.j.* '67 (AUS) On Duty Outside the Diocese.
Kinel, Robert *s.s.j.* '67 (WDC) [B] Washington, DC St. Joseph's Seminary.
Kinerk, E. Edward *s.j.* '72 (STL) [P] St. Louis, MO Jesuit Community Corporation at St. Louis University - Jesuit Hall; [P] St. Louis, MO The Jesuits of the Missouri Province.
Kines, G. Jerome *o.s.a.* '62 (CHI) [N] Olympia Fields, IL

Austin Friary.
King, Andrew '96 (NY) Graduate Studies.
King, Anthony S. '59 (YAK) Grand Coulee, WA St. Henry's Church; Hartline, WA St. Patrick's Church.
King, Arthur *o.m.i.* '59 (GR) [9] Grand Rapids, MI Immaculate Heart of Mary Church.
King, Brian M. (LKC) [B] Lake Charles, LA St. Patrick Hospital of Lake Charles.
King, Msgr. Charles B. '56 (FWT) [11] Fort Worth, TX St. John the Apostle Church.
King, David G. *s.j.* '49 (P) [L] Portland, OR Jesuit Provincial Office (Oregon Prov.).
King, Donald E. '74 (Y) [1] Warren, OH Blessed Sacrament Church.
King, Donald J. '37 (PRO) Retired; [P] Providence, RI St. John Vianney Residence.
King, Edward L. '42 (BO) [2] Haverhill, MA St. James Church.
King, Francis *o.c.s.o.* '58 (P) [L] Lafayette, OR The Cistercian (Trappist) Abbey of Our Lady of Guadalupe.
King, Francis E. *s.j.* '62 (SFR) [N] San Francisco, CA Jesuit Community at University of San Francisco.
King, Frederick Bruce *i.c.* '85 (PEO) Galesburg, IL St. Patrick's Church.
King, George L. '53 (B) Kamiah, ID St. Catherine's of Siena Church; Orofino, ID St. Theresa's Church.
King, Gerard '84 (LA) On Duty Outside the Archdiocese.
King, Gregory '76 (LA) On Duty Outside the Archdiocese.
King, Howard J. '63 (E) Lewis Run, PA Our Mother of Perpetual Help Church.
King, James (ALB) [L] Saratoga Springs, NY St. John Neumann Residence.
King, James *c.s.c.* (P) [B] Portland, OR University of Portland; [L] Portland, OR Holy Cross Father & Brother, C.S.C. - University of Portland.
King, James *c.ss.r.* '58 (PH) [135] Philadelphia, PA St. Peter the Apostle Church.
King, James '90 (BRK) [36] Brooklyn, NY St. Ephrem's Church.
King, James E. (PBL) Montrose, CO St. Mary Church.
King, James E. *o.s.f.s.* (PH) Philadelphia, PA Veterans Administration Medical Center.
King, James E. '71 (NTN) Retired.
King, James E. '71 (PBL) Sabbatical.
King, James E. '92 (PEO) Creve Coeur, IL Sacre Coeur Church.
King, James J. *s.j.* '63 (CLV) [E] Cuyahoga Falls, OH Walsh Jesuit High School.
King, Msgr. James P. '46 (BRK) [200] Queens, NY St. Mel Church; Retired.
King, Jeffrey '87 (GLP) Chichiltah, NM St. Patrick Navajo Mission Church; Pinehaven, NM Good Shepherd Catholic Mission Church.
King, Jeremy *o.s.b.* '75 (IND) [A] St. Meinrad, IN St. Meinrad Seminary; [B] St. Meinrad, IN St. Meinrad Seminary-College of Liberal Arts; [J] St. Meinrad, IN St. Meinrad Archabbey.
King, John '48 (PEO) Retired.
King, John D. '88 (CLV) El Salvador, C.A., OH Parroquial de Nuestra Senora de Guadalupe.
King, John F. *c.m.* '42 (BAL) [M] Emmitsburg, MD Vincentian House.
King, John F. *c.m.* '42 (PH) [Z] Philadelphia, PA Congregation of the Mission.
King, John J. *s.j.* '53 (NY) [BB] Staten Island, NY Mount Manresa Jesuit Retreat House.
King, John J. *s.j.* '63 (NY) [Z] New York, NY Jesuit Community at Fordham University.
King, John R. *m.m.* '53 (NY) [Z] Maryknoll, NY Maryknoll Fathers and Brothers.
King, Kenneth A. '57 (TLS) Grove, OK St. Elizabeth Church.
King, Larry '89 (GR) [12] Grand Rapids, MI St. John Vianney Church.
King, Leo *ss.cc.* '45 (FR) Fairhaven, MA St. Joseph's Church.
King, Martin L. '96 (P) Corvallis, OR St. Mary Church.
King, Michael J. '77 (WDC) Largo, MD St. Joseph Church.
King, Nicholas '66 (ORL) Rockledge, FL St. Mary's Church.
King, Nicholas *s.j.* '80 (BO) [W] Cambridge, MA Faber House.
King, Norbert E. '33 (LC) Retired.
King, Norman '88 (RNO) [6] Reno, NV St. Therese Church of the Little Flower.
King, Philip J. '49 (BO) On Special or Other Diocesan Assignment; On Duty Outside the Archdiocese.
King, Stephen *o.f.m.conv.* '96 (TR) Riverside, NJ St. Casimir Church.
King, Stephen D. '50 (FAR) Retired.
King, Thomas '64 (LA) Temple City, CA St. Luke the Evangelist Church.
King, Thomas J. '60 (ALN) Miller Heights, PA Sacred Heart of Jesus Church.
King, Thomas M. *s.j.* '64 (WDC) [M] Washington, DC The Jesuit Community at Georgetown University.
King, Thomas M. '73 (CIN) [85] Cincinnati, OH St. Therese, The Little Flower Church.
King, Thomas P. *c.s.c.* '69 (FTW) [B] Notre Dame, IN University of Notre Dame Du Lac; [J] Notre Dame, IN Holy Cross Community, Corby Hall, University of Notre Dame.
King, Msgr. William '35 (NY) Retired.
King, William *s.j.* '61 (SFE) [6] Albuquerque, NM Immaculate Conception Church.
King, William F. *s.j.* '57 (CIN) [M] Cincinnati, OH Jesuit Community at Xavier Unversity.
King, William F. *s.j.* '57 (DET) [K] Detroit, MI Jesuit Provincial Office-Detroit Province of the Society of Jesus.
King, William J. '83 (HBG) Mechanicsburg, PA St. Joseph Church.
Kingery, Patrick J. '93 (ATL) Cedartown, GA St. Bernadette's Church.
Kingery, Victor *o.f.m.* '49 (SFD) [B] Quincy, IL Quincy University.
Kingsbury, John G. *c.ss.r.* '80 (NY) [Z] Esopus, NY Redemptorist Priests and Brothers C.Ss.R. (Province of Baltimore); [BB] Esopus, NY Mount St. Alphonsus Redemptorist Retreat Center.
Kingsley, Richard '83 (TUC) [19] Tucson, AZ St. Pius X Church.
Kiniry, Msgr. Joseph R. '50 (ALT) [22] Johnstown, PA St. Benedict's Church.
Kiniry, Lawrence R. '65 (GBG) [3] Greensburg, PA Our Lady of Grace Church.
Kinkead, Cormac *c.p.* '51 (HRT) [M] West Hartford, CT Holy Family Monastery/Retreat.
Kinkead, James A. '55 (BR) French Settlement, LA St. Joseph Church.
Kinkel, Robert J. '70 (DEN) Arvada, CO Spirit of Christ Parish Church.
Kinkopf, John J. '57 (CLV) Chagrin Falls, OH St. Joan of Arc Church; Kirtland, OH Divine Word Church; Retired.
Kinlough, Msgr. William C. '43 (AUS) Lampasas, TX St. Mary's Church; Lometa, TX Good Shepherd Church.
Kinlough, Msgr. William C. '43 (CC) Retired.
Kinn, James W. '57 (CHI) Mundelein, IL Santa Maria Del Popolo Church.
Kinnaman, Leroy G. '73 (LFT) Covington, IN St. Joseph Church; [H] Crawfordsville, IN Newman Center at Wabash College.
Kinnane, James F. '63 (HRT) Newington, CT Holy Spirit Church; Special and other (Arch)Diocesan Assignment.
Kinney, David *o.c.s.o.* '37 (SLC) [F] Huntsville, UT Abbey of Our Lady of the Holy Trinity of the Order of Cistercians.
Kinney, Donald *o.c.d.* '88 (SJ) [M] San Jose, CA Carmelite Monastery, Novitiate.
Kinney, Francis L. *c.pp.s.* '47 (STU) Pine Grove, OH St. Mary Church.
Kinney, George R. '63 (STP) Corcoran, MN St. Thomas the Apostle Church.
Kinney, John M. '76 (LFT) Military Chaplains.
Kinney, Leo '92 (FAR) Anamoose, ND St. Francis Xavier Church.
Kinney, M. Eugene '84 (MIL) Horicon, WI St. Malachy Church; [W] Horicon, WI Legion of Mary.
Kinney, Thomas '77 (NO) [9] Metairie, LA St. Francis Xavier Church.
Kinney, William *m.s.* '42 (ORL) [2] Orlando, FL Blessed Trinity Church.
Kinney, William Gladstone, Jr. '96 (CHR) [11] Charleston, SC Church of the Nativity.
Kinross, Knute *o.f.m.* '51 (CIN) Centerville, OH St. Francis of Assisi Church.
Kinsella, Arthur L. *o.p.* '46 (STL) [P] St. Louis, MO St. Dominic Priory.
Kinsella, Charles R. '75 (BO) Absent on Sick Leave.
Kinsella, Gerald A. *s.j.* '46 (BO) [W] Weston, MA Campion Health Center, Inc.
Kinsella, Msgr. John (BAL) Absent on Leave.
Kinsella, John J. *s.j.* '59 (CHI) [C] Chicago, IL Jesuit Community at Loyola University of Chicago.
Kinsky, Richard C. *c.s.b.* '50 (ROC) [13] Rochester, NY Christ the King Church.
Kinter, John P. '67 (WDC) [43] Washington, DC St. Thomas More Church.
Kintop, Ferdinand *o.f.m.conv.* '48 (CHI) [N] Chicago, IL Franciscan House of Studies.
Kintop, Ferdinand *o.f.m. conv.* '48 (DET) [59] Detroit, MI Our Lady Queen of Angels Church.
Kinzer, Gary '70 (ORG) Absent on Sick Leave.
Kinzer, Victor '49 (SCL) Osakis, MN Immaculate Conception Church.
Kinzig, James J. '53 (JOL) Retired.
Kinzig, James J. '53 (SD) [3] Chula Vista, CA St. Pius X Church.
Kinzler, Dale '74 (FAR) [3] Fargo, ND Nativity Church.
Kipfer, David M. '88 (PEO) [1] Peoria, IL St. Mary's Cathedral.
Kippley, Robert H. '83 (BIS) [2] Minot, ND Our Lady of Grace Church.
Kirby, Dan '94 (DM) [2] Council Bluffs, IA Our Lady, Queen of Apostles Church.
Kirby, Donald J. *s.j.* '72 (SY) [S] Syracuse, NY Jesuits at LeMoyne, Inc.
Kirby, Edward A. '61 (PT) Mary Esther, FL St. Peter Church.
Kirby, Gerald S. '84 (NOR) On Duty Outside the Diocese.
Kirby, James '96 (DM) [12] Des Moines, IA St. Theresa of the Child Jesus Church.
Kirby, Larry Joseph '81 (BAK) Absent on Leave.
Kirby, Louis M. *o.s.b.* '44 (PBL) [E] Canon City, CO Holy Cross Abbey.
Kirby, Martin F. '67 (BRK) [B] Douglaston, NY Cathedral Residence of the Immaculate Conception.
Kirby, Martin F. '67 (RVC) Oceanside, NY St. Anthony Church.
Kirby, Robert F. '59 (FR) [5] Attleboro, MA St. Theresa of the Child Jesus Church.
Kirby, Thomas M. '57 (PIT) Blawnox, PA St. Edward Church; Allegheny County, PA St. Margaret Memorial Hospital; Allegheny County, PA Harmarville Rehabilitation Center.
Kircher, August R. *m.m.* '41 (NY) [Z] Maryknoll, NY Maryknoll Fathers and Brothers.
Kircher, Edward (CC) Retired.
Kirchgessner, Christopher A. *o.s.b.* '80 (CHL) [J] Belmont, NC Belmont Abbey.
Kirchmeyer, Robert W. '52 (BO) Danvers, MA St. Alphonsus Church.
Kirchmyer, Thomas B. *m.m.* '59 (NY) [Z] Maryknoll, NY Maryknoll Fathers and Brothers.
Kirchner, James A. '63 (NEW) On Duty Outside the Archdiocese.
Kirchner, James A. '63 (SAV) Tifton, GA Our Divine Saviour Church.
Kirchner, Paul *o.carm.* '40 (NEW) [P] Mahwah, NJ Carmel Retreat House.
Kirchner, Peter K., Jr. '93 (SCL) BlueGrass, MN St. Hubert's Church; Verndale, MN St. Frederick's Church.
Kireilis, Fabian P. (CHI) Retired.
Kireilis, Fabian V. '39 (CHI) [92] Chicago, IL Immaculate Conception Church.
Kirila, Michael '87 (ROM) Detroit, MI St. John the Baptist Church.
Kirk, Albert E. '68 (MEM) [11] Memphis, TN Holy Spirit Church.
Kirk, Allan F. *s.j.* '65 (CHI) [C] Chicago, IL Jesuit Community at Loyola University of Chicago; [J] Maywood, IL Foster G. McGaw Hospital of Loyola University of Chicago.
Kirk, Daniel *o.s.b.* '49 (WDC) [M] Washington, DC St. Anselm's Abbey.
Kirk, David '64 (NTN) On Special Projects; [D] New York, NY Emmaus House/Harlem.
Kirk, David R. (TOL) Military Chaplains.
Kirk, James T., Jr. '86 (WIL) Brandywood, DE Church of the Holy Child.
Kirk, Msgr. John A. '47 (E) McKean, PA St. Francis Xavier Church.
Kirk, John L. '70 (NSH) Tullahoma, TN St. Paul the Apostle Church.
Kirk, Msgr. Raymond C. '59 (SD) Lemon Grove, CA St. John of the Cross Church.
Kirk, Thomas '69 (MEM) [C] Memphis, TN Immaculate Conception Cathedral Middle and High School.
Kirk, Thomas D. '69 (MEM) [1] Memphis, TN Cathedral of the Immaculate Conception.
Kirk, William J. *o.s.b.* '46 (PEO) [A] Peru, IL St. Bede Abbey and Academy.
Kirk, William S. '72 (PH) Secane, PA Our Lady of Fatima Church.
Kirke, Eugene K. (BO) Society of St. James the Apostle.
Kirkendoll, Thomas E., Jr. *glmy.* '87 (SAV) McRae, GA Holy Redeemer Church.
Kirkhoff, Gerald J. '69 (IND) [28] Indianapolis, IN St. Jude Church.
Kirkilas, Michael '36 (CHI) Retired.
Kirkness, Michael (LA) Lompoc, CA U.S. Penitentiary.
Kirkness, Michael D. '77 (GF) On Duty Outside of the Diocese.
Kirkpatrick, Cletus '56 (BAK) [A] Ontario, OR Holy Rosary Medical Center.
Kirkpatrick, Robert *c.ss.r.* '33 (OAK) [N] Oakland, CA Redemptorists.
Kirlin, Bernard G. '71 (MIA) North Miami, FL Holy Family Church.
Kirouac, Richard '85 (STN) [1] Chicago, IL St. Nicholas Ukrainian Catholic Cathedral.
Kirrane, James A. '46 (BRK) Retired.
Kirrane, James A. '46 (RVC) East Northport, NY St. Anthony of Padua Church.
Kirsch, Edmund D. '88 (CHL) Murphy, NC St. William Church.
Kirsch, Gerard D. *o.s.b.* '70 (SEA) [M] Lacey, WA St. Martin's Abbey.
Kirsch, Gregory A. '81 (E) [1] Erie, PA St. Peter Cathedral.
Kirsch, Gregory G. '88 (STL) [30] St. Louis, MO St. Cecilia Church; St. Louis, MO Saint Louis University Hospital; [K] St. Louis, MO Saint Louis University Hospital.

Kirsch, John B. '69 (HEL) Retired.
Kirsch, Myron M. *o.s.b.* '73 (GBG) [H] Latrobe, PA Saint Vincent Archabbey.
Kirsch, Patrick V. '81 (SB) Phelan, CA Blessed Junipero Serra Church; Wrightwood, CA Our Lady of the Snows Church.
Kirschner, Anthony *c.m.m.* '37 (DET) [K] Dearborn Heights, MI Our Lady of Grace Monastery.
Kirtland, Robert B. '55 (TOL) Perrysburg, OH St. Rose Church.
Kirtz, Raymond *o.m.i.* '58 (DUL) International Falls, MN St. Thomas Aquinas Church.
Kirwan, Christopher J., Jr. '92 (BO) Walpole, MA Blessed Sacrament Church.
Kirwan, Thomas P. '69 (DET) [1] Sterling Heights, MI St. Blase Church.
Kirwin, Arthur R. *o.p.* '84 (R) [E] Raleigh, NC Dominican Community; [E] Raleigh, NC De Porres House.
Kirwin, George *o.m.i.* '58 (BUF) [27] Buffalo, NY Holy Angels Church.
Kirwin, John '66 (ALB) [2] Albany, NY St. John-St. Ann Church; Special Assignment.
Kirwin, Michael J. '76 (SCR) [1] Old Forge, PA St. Lawrence O'Toole Church.
Kirwin, Peter *o.f.m.* '81 (P) [6] Portland, OR Ascension Church.
Kirwin, Msgr. Robert J. '45 (RVC) Williston Park, NY St. Aidan's Church; Retired.
Kirwin, William J. *o.m.i.* '38 (BO) [Z] Tewksbury, MA Immaculate Heart of Mary Novitiate-Infirmary.
Kis-Horvath, Pascal *o.cist.* '57 (DAL) [M] Irving, TX Cistercian Abbey of Our Lady of Dallas.
Kiselica, John *s.m.* '84 (DET) [E] Harper Woods, MI Notre Dame High School.
Kish, Carl '62 (Y) Cortland, OH St. Robert Bellarmine Parish Church.
Kish, Matthew J. '43 (GRY) [8] East Chicago, IN St. John Cantius Church; Retired.
Kish, Michael A. '65 (MIA) [26] Miami, FL St. Louis Church.
Kisicki, Michael (E) [B] Erie, PA Gannon University.
Kisluk, Aloysius J. '57 (NOR) [3] Middletown, CT St. Mary of Czestochowa Church.
Kiss, Barnabas G. *o.f.m.* '78 (DET) [32] Detroit, MI Holy Cross Church.
Kiss, Gabriel *s.j.* '55 (NY) [12] Yonkers, NY St. Margaret of Hungary Church.
Kiss, Matthew J. *o.f.m.* '40 (Y) [J] Youngstown, OH Mt. Alvernia Friary.
Kissam, Angelus *o.f.m.conv.* '96 (TR) [5] Trenton, NJ Immaculate Conception Church.
Kissane, James M. '92 (RVC) Hempstead, NY Our Lady of Loretto Church.
Kissane, Maurice J. '64 (CHI) Brookfield, IL St. Barbara Church.
Kissane, Michael *o.carm.* '86 (NY) [189] Bronx, NY St. Simon Stock Church; [Z] Middletown, NY St. Albert's Priory; [Z] Tappan, NY St. Eliseus Priory.
Kissane, Richard *c.s.sp.* '45 (SB) [E] Hemet, CA Holy Ghost Fathers.
Kissel, Anthony (SP) [A] St. Leo, FL Saint Leo College.
Kissel, Msgr. Anthony '73 (EVN) On Duty Outside the Diocese.
Kissel, Francis J. *s.m.* '71 (ATL) [C] Atlanta, GA Marist School.
Kissel, Ignatius M. *o.s.m.* '65 (ORG) Fullerton, CA St. Philip Benizi Church; [H] Buena Park, CA Servite Fathers And Brothers.
Kissel, Terrence T. '78 (DEN) [8] Denver, CO Church of the Good Shepherd.
Kissell, Wilbur '51 (MOB) [2] Montgomery, AL Church of St. Andrew The Apostle; [K] Montgomery, AL Faulkner University Newman Center.
Kissinger, Rodney T. *s.j.* '53 (SP) [C] Tampa, FL Jesuit High School.
Kissling, John M. '53 (DUB) Grundy Center, IA Sacred Heart Church; Reinbeck, IA Queen of Heaven Church.
Kissling, Joseph L. '44 (DUB) Retired.
Kist, Harold W. '74 (CIN) Greenville, OH St. Mary Church.
Kisting, Thomas J. '73 (DUL) Longville, MN St. Edward's Church.
Kistler, Leonard A. *c.pp.s.* '61 (TOL) Alvada, OH St. Peter Church; New Riegel, OH St. Boniface Church.
Kistner, Hilarion H. *o.f.m.* '55 (CIN) [P] Cincinnati, OH Friarhurst Retreat Center.
Kita, August *s.d.b.* '60 (NY) [BB] West Haverstraw, NY Don Bosco Retreat Center and Marian Shrine; [BB] West Haverstraw, NY Marian Shrine.
Kitchin, George '70 (BLX) Ocean Springs, MS St. Elizabeth Ann Seton Church.
Kitko, Joseph F. '55 (BAL) Laurel, MD Resurrection of Our Lord Church.
Kitt, Liam J. '43 (CLV) Elyria Township, OH St. Vincent de Paul Church.
Kitt, William J. '43 (CLV) Retired.
Kitten, Marvin C. *s.j.* '65 (NO) [C] New Orleans, LA Loyola University.
Kittock, Francis R. '55 (STP) [21] Minneapolis, MN St. Charles Borromeo Church.
Kitz, Raphael *o.c.d.* '59 (LR) [A] Little Rock, AR Marylake - Carmelite Novitiate.
Kitzke, Timothy L. '89 (MIL) Whitefish Bay, WI Holy Family Church; [Y] Shorewood, WI Association of Ladies of Charity of Milwaukee, Wisconsin.
Kivel, Joseph G. '61 (STP) [17] Minneapolis, MN St. Anthony of Padua Church.
Kiwanuka, Henry W. '81 (MIL) [3] West Allis, WI Holy Assumption Church.
Kizis, Kenneth G. '59 (SCR) Olyphant, PA St. Michael the Archangel Church.
Klaas, Gregory '67 (SR) [H] Sonoma, CA Hanna Boys Center.
Klaas, Msgr. Raymond E. '50 (MAD) Marshall, WI St. Mary's of the Nativity Church.
Klaers, Marvin J. '50 (STP) Miesville, MN St. Joseph Church; New Trier, MN St. Mary Church.
Klaia, John J. *o.p.* '52 (SFR) [13] San Francisco, CA St. Dominic Church; [N] San Francisco, CA St. Dominic Priory.
Klaiber, Jeffrey L. *s.j.* '74 (CHI) [N] Chicago, IL Chicago Province of the Society of Jesus-Provincial Office.
Klajbor, Richard J. '79 (CHI) [82] Chicago, IL Holy Innocents Church.
Klak, Jan Piotr '79 (SAT) Falls City, TX Holy Trinity Church; Panna Maria, TX Immaculate Conception of the Blessed Virgin Mary Church.
Klamet, Francis X. '78 (CLV) [30] Cleveland, OH Holy Rosary Church; Released from Diocesan Assignment.
Klapp, John S. '45 (PH) [97] Philadelphia, PA St. Mary of Czestochowa Church; Retired.
Klapperich, Giles *o.p.* (CHI) River Forest, IL St. Vincent Ferrer Priory Church.
Klapps, William J. '58 (WIL) Woodcrest, DE St. Matthew Church; Retired.
Klarer, Michael E. '79 (MAD) Military Chaplains.
Klasek, Stephen A. '83 (NSH) [7] Nashville, TN Holy Rosary Church.
Klasinski, George '51 (KCK) Retired.
Klasinski, Stanley '77 (CLV) [35] Cleveland, OH Immaculate Heart of Mary Church.
Klasinski, Stanley J. '61 (CLV) Lyndhurst, OH St. Clare Church.
Klassen, John *o.s.b.* '77 (SCL) [I] Collegeville, MN St. John's Abbey, of the Order of St. Benedict.
Klassen, Roger *o.s.b.* '66 (SCL) Freeport, MN Sacred Heart Church.
Klatka, Joseph S. '67 (MAN) Littleton, NH St. Rose of Lima Church.
Klauck, Michael (BIR) On Duty Outside the Diocese.
Klauck, Msgr. Peter N. '55 (GB) [1] Green Bay, WI St. Francis Xavier Cathedral.
Klauck, Stanley B. '46 (MIL) Retired.
Klauder, Frank '47 (NEW) [N] South Orange, NJ Don Bosco Residence.
Klauer, Gary *o.f.m.conv.* '75 (LA) [K] Torrance, CA Little Company of Mary Health Services; [R] Torrance, CA Franciscan Friars, St. Bonaventure Friary.
Klauke, Raymond '49 (LAN) Retired.
Klaus, Donald R. '42 (TOL) Retired.
Klaus, Joseph J. '54 (R) Absent on Leave.
Kleas, Msgr. Milam E. '51 (GAL) Dickinson, TX Shrine of the True Cross Church.
Kleba, Gerald J. '67 (STL) Clayton, MO St. Joseph Church.
Kleber, Cecil *o.f.m.* '50 (SFE) [1] Santa Fe, NM The Cathedral of San Francisco de Asis.
Klecha, Joseph A. *m.m.* '69 (LA) [R] Los Angeles, CA Maryknoll Fathers and Brothers.
Kleczewski, Kieran *o.s.b.* '78 (PHX) [H] Phoenix, AZ Office of Youth and Young Adult Ministries.
Klee, Robert '49 (COL) Retired.
Kleefisch, Charles A. '42 (MIL) [17] Milwaukee, WI St. Catherine Church; Retired.
Kleem, Ferris '56 (OLL) Retired.
Kleem, Ferris '56 (SAM) Retired.
Kleene, Regis *s.d.s.* '60 (CHI) [3] Waukegan, IL St. Dismas Church.
Klees, Raymond F. '73 (CHI) La Grange, IL St. Cletus Church.
Kleffman, James F. '60 (DM) Missouri Valley, IA St. Patrick Church.
Kleffman, William C. '41 (OM) [3] Omaha, NE St. Agnes Church.
Kleiber, Kenneth R. '68 (CHI) Retired.
Kleiber, Richard J. '47 (GB) Retired.
Klein, Albert J. '36 (Y) Retired.
Klein, Bernard C. '49 (STP) Retired.
Klein, Charles R. '54 (NY) [Z] New York, NY Our Lady of Consolation Residence.
Klein, Charles R. '59 (BAL) [86] Baltimore, MD Sacred Heart of Mary Church; Retired.
Klein, David *c.s.b.* '74 (SFE) Albuquerque, NM Presbyterian Hospital.
Klein, David F. *s.j.* '71 (PHX) [B] Phoenix, AZ Brophy College Preparatory.
Klein, David J. '90 (CAM) [1] Camden, NJ Immaculate Conception Cathedral.
Klein, Dennis D. '66 (BRK) [B] Douglaston, NY Cathedral Residence of the Immaculate Conception.
Klein, Donald L. '65 (DUB) [7] Cedar Rapids, IA St. Pius X Church.
Klein, Douglas Michael '96 (SC) Carroll, IA St. Lawrence Church.
Klein, Msgr. Edward '43 (WIN) Retired.
Klein, Eugene J. '45 (DM) Retired.
Klein, Msgr. Frank W. '45 (WIN) Retired.
Klein, George W. '54 (CIN) Trenton, OH Holy Name Church.
Klein, George W. '59 (CHI) Wilmette, IL St. Francis Xavier Church.
Klein, Gregory L. *o.carm.* (BUF) [C] Niagara University, NY Niagara University.
Klein, Gregory L. *o.carm.* '75 (JOL) [J] Darien, IL Carmelite Fathers Provincial Office.
Klein, J. Leo *s.j.* '64 (CIN) [D] Cincinnati, OH Xavier University; [M] Cincinnati, OH Jesuit Community at Xavier University.
Klein, James T. '78 (CLV) Westlake, OH St. Bernadette Church.
Klein, John G. '75 (CHI) [187] Chicago, IL St. Roman Church; [A] Chicago, IL Archbishop Quigley Preparatory Seminary; [A] Chicago, IL Institute of Vocation Awareness.
Klein, John J. '70 (PAT) Dover, NJ St. Mary's Church.
Klein, John P. '62 (PIT) Retired.
Klein, John P. '78 (LAN) [1] Flint, MI St. Agnes Church.
Klein, John Paul *o.m.v.* '89 (SFD) [2] Alton, IL Immaculate Conception-St. Mary's Church; [3] Alton, IL St. Patrick Church.
Klein, Karl J. '43 (DUB) Retired.
Klein, Lawrence J. '84 (BWN) Mercedes, TX Sacred Heart Church.
Klein, Louis S. (BUF) [K] Buffalo, NY Sisters of Charity Hospital of Buffalo, NY.
Klein, Martin '91 (RVC) Westbury, NY St. Brigid Church.
Klein, Pascal L. '87 (DOD) Deerfield, KS Christ the King Church; Garden City, KS St. Mary Church.
Klein, Peter J. '74 (WIN) Madelia, MN St. Mary Church.
Klein, Pius *o.s.b.* '74 (EVN) Huntingburg, IN Visitation of the Blessed Virgin Mary Church.
Klein, Pius *o.s.b.* '74 (IND) [J] St. Meinrad, IN St. Meinrad Archabbey.
Klein, Robert P. '53 (COV) Retired.
Klein, Robert W. '56 (DUL) On Leave Without Assignment.
Klein, Msgr. Stanley H. '44 (BUF) Retired.
Klein, Msgr. Sylvester '35 (LFT) Retired.
Klein, Terrance W. '84 (COL) Graduate Studies.
Klein, Theodore J. '69 (NOR) Groton, CT St. Mary Church.
Kleiner, James E. '67 (DEN) Arvada, CO St. Joan of Arc Church.
Kleiner, Robert *m.c.c.j.* '71 (CHI) Blue Island, IL St. Donatus Church; Calumet Park, IL Seven Holy Founders Church.
Kleinfehn, Walter J. '60 (DUB) Norway, IA St. Michael's Church; Watkins, IA St. Patrick's Church.
Kleinhans, Msgr. Thomas G. '67 (FRS) Visalia, CA St. Mary Church.
Kleinheinz, Joseph L. '54 (SUP) Manitowish Waters, WI Our Lady Queen of Peace Church; Mercer, WI St. Isaac Jogues and Companions Church.
Kleinhenz, John H. *s.j.* '52 (CLV) [E] Cleveland, OH St. Ignatius High School.
Kleinmann, Dennis W. '93 (ARL) Winchester, VA Sacred Heart of Jesus Church.
Kleinschmidt, Msgr. Anthony '33 (SCL) Retired.
Kleinschmidt, Msgr. Anthony A. '43 (COL) [A] Columbus, OH Pontifical College Josephinum.
Kleinschmidt, Sylvester '50 (SCL) Retired.
Kleinstuber, Joseph J. '64 (WDC) [1] Silver Spring, MD St. Andrew Apostle Church; Special Ministries.
Kleinwachter, John '77 (CR) Mahnomen, MN St. Michael's Church.
Kleinweber, Dennis J. '78 (CLV) East Cleveland, OH St. Philomena Church.
Kleinworth, Robert (ELP) Absent on Leave.
Kleiser, Msgr. William J. '50 (MEM) On Special Assignment.
Klejnowski, Arcadius '54 (TR) [15] Trenton, NJ St. Hedwig Church.
Klem, Daniel N. '83 (RIC) [9] Virginia Beach, VA St. Mark Church.
Klem, Leo J. *c.s.b.* '40 (ROC) [I] Rochester, NY Basilian Residence.
Klem, Robert J. *c.s.b.* '56 (GAL) [Q] Sugar Land, TX Basilian Mission Center.
Klemash, Dennis *o.f.m.cap.* '90 (PH) [79] Philadelphia, PA St. John the Evangelist Church.
Klementowicz, Chester '46 (ALB) Retired.
Klemme, Dennis C. '57 (MIL) [Q] Pewaukee, WI Carmel of the Mother of God.
Klemme, Robert W. '91 (LFT) Carmel, IN St. Elizabeth Ann Seton Church.
Klemmer, Marvin J. '66 (BIS) [2] Bismarck, ND Ascension Church.
Klenke, Elmer A. '65 (DOD) Retired.
Klepac, Msgr. Kenneth J. '58 (MOB) [12] Mobile, AL St. Mary Church.
Klepacki, Michael S. '78 (CHL) Military Chaplains.

Klepec, George F. '71 (JOL) [12] Joliet, IL St. Joseph Church.
Kleppner, Joseph J. '46 (PIT) Center Township, PA St. Frances Cabrini Church.
Kleszcz, Piotr *o.f.m.conv.* (BO) [55] Boston, MA Our Lady of Czestochowa Church.
Klettner, Frederick J. '65 (DET) Farmington Hills, MI St. Clare of Assisi Church.
Kletzel, Thomas P. '83 (PH) [119] Philadelphia, PA Our Lady of Hope Church; Quakertown, PA St. Isidore Church.
Kleve, A. W. '57 (DUB) [H] Waterloo, IA Covenant Medical Center.
Klevence, John P. '85 (WIL) Brandywood, DE Church of the Holy Child.
Kliche, Anthony S. *c.s.sp.* '44 (PH) [Z] Bensalem, PA Congregation of the Holy Ghost Fathers and Brothers.
Klieber, Kenneth '68 (PHX) Phoenix, AZ United States Veterans Affairs Medical Center.
Klikunas, Bruce J. *o.s.m.* '72 (OAK) [K] Hayward, CA St. Rose Hospital; [N] Berkeley, CA Servite Community, Sarpi Priory.
Klim, Vincent M. '89 (PAT) Haskell, NJ St. Francis of Assisi Church.
Klima, James A. '76 (COL) Marion, OH St. Mary Church.
Klimanskis, Adolph '53 (PRO) [10] Providence, RI St. Casimir's Church.
Klimas, George H. '51 (SAG) Retired.
Klimczyk, John '81 (FTW) [2] South Bend, IN St. Adalbert Church.
Klimczyk, Leon F. *s.j.* '79 (STP) [31] Minneapolis, MN St. Olaf Church; [N] Minneapolis, MN La Storta Jesuit Community.
Klimek, Edmund J. '53 (LC) [2] Eau Claire, WI Newman Community Church; [E] Eau Claire, WI Sacred Heart Hospital; [L] Eau Claire, WI Newman Parish.
Klimowicz, Sigmund M. *o.f.m.cap.* '45 (PAT) [M] Oak Ridge-Milton, NJ St. Stanislaus B. M. Friary.
Kline, Charles '62 (LFT) Attica, IN St. Francis Xavier Church.
Kline, Donald '95 (PHX) [2] Tempe, AZ Our Lady of Mt. Carmel Church.
Kline, John J. '47 (CLV) [8] Lorain, OH St. Mary Church; Retired.
Kline, Omer U. *o.s.b.* '49 (GBG) [H] Latrobe, PA Saint Vincent Archabbey.
Kline, Msgr. Robert R. '45 (BAL) [C] Emmitsburg, MD Mount Saint Mary's College.
Kline, Msgr. Robert R. '45 (SCR) On Duty Outside the Diocese.
Kline, Robert W. '48 (CLV) Mentor, OH St. John Vianney Church.
Kline, Msgr. Roy F. '51 (ALT) Duncansville, PA St. Catherine of Siena Church.
Klinec, Msgr. Julius G. '36 (COL) Retired.
Klingeisen, Richard H. '72 (GB) [1] Manitowoc, WI St. Boniface Church; [F] Manitowoc, WI Holy Family Memorial, Inc.
Klinger, Attilio *s.d.b* '54 (PMB) Belle Glade, FL St. Philip Benizi Church.
Klinger, Charles F. '83 (COL) Zanesville, OH St. Nicholas Church.
Klinger, John *s.c.j.* '67 (RC) [B] Eagle Butte, SD Sacred Heart Community House.
Klinger, Msgr. Nevin J. '82 (ALN) On Duty Outside the Diocese.
Klingler, Donald P. '61 (KAL) Otsego, MI St. Margaret Church.
Klingler, John *s.c.j.* '67 (RC) Eagle Butte, SD All Saints Church; Eagle Butte, SD Cheyenne River Reservation Church.
Klingler, Ronald M. '65 (Y) [7] Canton, OH St. John the Baptist Church.
Klingshirn, Charles '66 (GAY) Absent on Leave.
Klink, Anthony G. '58 (MIL) [1] Menomonee Falls, WI St. Anthony's Church.
Klink, Delbert D. '60 (MAD) [4] Janesville, WI St. William Church.
Klink, Eugene A. '63 (LC) [1] Eau Claire, WI Immaculate Conception Church.
Klink, Kenneth J. '66 (MAD) Belleville, WI St. Mary of Lourdes Church.
Klink, Peter J. *s.j.* '81 (RC) Pine Ridge, SD Holy Rosary Church; [B] Pine Ridge, SD Jesuit Community of Holy Rosary Mission.
Klinzing, Msgr. Thomas '71 (PMB) [1] Palm Beach, FL Cathedral of St. Ignatius Loyola.
Klister, Msgr. Roy M. *j.c.l.* '69 (GB) [13] Green Bay, WI SS. Peter and Paul Church.
Klister, Msgr. Roy M. *j.c.l.* '69 (MIL) [B] Hales Corners, WI Sacred Heart School of Theology.
Klitsch, Anthony L. '49 (PH) Retired.
Klizek, Duane R. '82 (BUF) [3] West Seneca, NY Fourteen Holy Helpers Church.
Kloak, David G. '78 (CHI) Military Chaplains.
Klobuchar, John Mary *m.f.v.a.* '93 (BIR) [E] Birmingham, AL Franciscan Missionaries of the Eternal Word, A Public Association of the Christian Faithful.
Klobuka, John J. *s.m.* '78 (KAL) Portage, MI St. Catherine of Siena Church; [E] Portage, MI Society of Mary.
Kloc, Thaddeus '70 (VEN) Bonita Springs, FL St. Leo Church.
Klocker, Harry R. *s.j.* '51 (STL) [P] St. Louis, MO Jesuit Community Corporation at St. Louis University - Jesuit Hall.
Klocker, Msgr. Henry J. '43 (CIN) Retired.
Klocker, John G. '58 (STL) Webster Groves, MO Annunciation Church.
Kloda, Marshall J. '89 (PH) [83] Philadelphia, PA St. Katherine of Siena Church.
Kloeckner, William '43 (SCL) Retired.
Kloepfer, John S. '53 (JOL) Retired.
Kloepfer, John S. '53 (RIC) Retired.
Klohr, Paul McC. '30 (BRK) Retired; [R] Queens Village, NY Queen of Peace Residence.
Klopke, John R. *c.pp.s.* '53 (OAK) [N] San Leandro, CA Society of the Precious Blood.
Kloppenborg, Thomas *c.m.* '91 (COS) Cheyenne Wells, CO Sacred Heart Church.
Klores, Stanley J. '82 (NO) [A] New Orleans, LA Notre Dame Seminary Graduate School of Theology.
Klos, Joseph '80 (BUF) [1] Lackawanna, NY Basilica of Our Lady of Victory.
Klos, Walter '40 (BUF) Retired.
Klose, Kenneth P. '39 (CHI) Skokie, IL St. Peter Church; Retired.
Kloskowski, Stanley E. '58 (CAM) Bridgeton, NJ St. Teresa of Avila Church.
Kloss, Anthony *o.s.b.* '91 (WOR) [N] Still River, MA Benedictine Monks, St. Benedict Abbey.
Kloster, Carl G. *s.j.* '48 (DEN) [M] Denver, CO Xavier Jesuit Center.
Kloster, Donald L. '95 (BGP) [4] Stratford, CT Our Lady of Grace Church.
Kloster, George M. '68 (CHL) Gastonia, NC St. Michael Church.
Kloster, Robert J. '65 (SY) Holland Patent, NY St. Leo Church.
Kloton, Michael J. '87 (SCR) Plains, PA SS. Peter and Paul Church; [D] Kingston, PA Bishop O'Reilly High School.
Klotter, Frederick W. (L) Graduate Studies.
Klotz, Claude *s.d.s.* '43 (MIL) [P] Milwaukee, WI Salvatorians - Jordan Hall.
Klotz, David R. *o.s.a.* '71 (CHI) [N] Olympia Fields, IL The Augustinian Provincialate Tolentine Center.
Kluba, Zbigniew (PAT) Convent Station, NJ St. Thomas More Church; Morristown, NJ Morristown Memorial Hospital.
Klubertanz, Kenneth E. '66 (MAD) Spring Green, WI St. John the Evangelist Church.
Klucinec, Benedict *m.ss.a.* '87 (NOR) [A] Cromwell, CT Holy Apostles College and Seminary; [F] Cromwell, CT Missionaries of the Holy Apostles.
Kluckman, T. Anthony *s.c.j.* '73 (SFS) [B] Chamberlain, SD St. Joseph Indian School.
Kluczynski, Campion *o.f.m.* '59 (GB) [F] Green Bay, WI St. Vincent Hospital; [I] Green Bay, WI St. Mary of the Angels Friary.
Klug, Jerome G. '49 (CHI) Bartlett, IL St. Peter Damien Church; Retired.
Klug, Richard L. '51 (CIN) [9] Cincinnati, OH Annunciation of the Blessed Virgin Mary Church.
Klunk, Timothy B. '79 (BAL) [12] Baltimore, MD St. Athanasius Church.
Kluonius, Joseph V. '47 (GAY) Retired.
Kluthe, Paul *s.s.j.* (MOB) [5] Mobile, AL St. Francis Xavier Church.
Klyber, Arthur B. *c.ss.r.* '32 (STL) [P] Liguori, MO St. Clement Health Care Center.
Kmech, John '61 (STN) [4] Chicago, IL St. Michael's Church.
Kmiec, Roman *c.m.* '86 (MAN) [2] Concord, NH St. Peter Church.
Kmiecik, Joseph M. *c.s.c.* '34 (AUS) [H] Austin, TX Congregation of Holy Cross - Southern Province.
Kmiecik, Joseph M. *c.s.c.* '34 (FTW) [J] South Bend, IN Congregation of Holy Cross Indiana Province Provincial House.
Knab, George *o.m.i.* (BO) Tewksbury, MA St. William Church.
Knapek, John A. *s.j.* '57 (CLV) [C] Cleveland, OH John Carroll Jesuit Community.
Knapik, Andrew G. (ALT) Retired.
Knapp, Charles D. '63 (TUC) [8] Tucson, AZ Our Mother of Sorrows Church.
Knapp, Gerard J. *c.ss.r.* '75 (BRK) [U] Brooklyn, NY Our Lady of Good Counsel Residence.
Knapp, James G. *s.j.* '81 (STL) [P] St. Louis, MO St. Louis University High School Jesuit Community.
Knapp, James G. *s.j.* '94 (STL) [F] St. Louis, MO St. Louis University High School, George H. Backer Memorial.
Knapp, John M. '86 (NY) [177] Bronx, NY Our Lady of Solace Church.
Knapp, Joseph G. *o.c.s.o.* '48 (DUB) [K] Peosta, IA New Melleray Abbey, Order of Cistercians of the Strict Observance.
Knapp, Msgr. Kenneth R. '63 (EVN) [3] Evansville, IN Christ the King Church; Special Assignment.
Knapp, Msgr. Richard S. '55 (SFR) [3] San Rafael, CA St. Raphael Church.
Knapp, Roger A. (DET) Gibraltar, MI St. Victor Church.
Knapp, Msgr. Stephen V. '32 (STN) Retired.
Knapp, William L. '48 (SFR) [2] San Rafael, CA St. Isabella Church; Retired.
Knappik, Richard *c.ss.r.* '58 (ALB) [L] Saratoga Springs, NY St. John Neumann Residence.
Knaresborough, Francis J. '89 (TYL) Retired.
Knauer, Msgr. Paul F. '64 (PAT) Sparta, NJ Our Lady of the Lake Church.
Knauf, Edwin L. '33 (LC) Retired.
Knauf, Randall *o.f.m.cap.* '91 (MIL) [B] Mount Calvary, WI St. Lawrence Seminary; [P] Mount Calvary, WI St. Lawrence Friary.
Knaup, Alan J. '77 (STL) Mehlville, MO St. Margaret Mary Alacoque Church.
Kneafsey, Msgr. Cornelius T. '58 (BRK) [208] Queens, NY Our Lady of the Cenacle Church.
Kneal, Msgr. Ellsworth '44 (STP) Retired; [A] St. Paul, MN The Saint Paul Seminary.
Kneifl, Rodney V. '85 (OM) [6] Omaha, NE Assumption, B.V.M. Church.
Kneip, Paschal *o.s.b.* '51 (RIC) [6] Virginia Beach, VA St. Gregory the Great Church.
Kneipp, August J. '41 (CIN) Retired.
Kneis, G. Jerome *o.s.a.* '62 (CHI) [N] Olympia Fields, IL The Augustinian Provincialate Tolentine Center.
Knelleken, James '51 (SEA) Retired.
Knepper, Daniel J. '70 (DUB) Bellevue, IA St. Joseph's Church.
Knerr, Joseph '80 (ORG) Fountain Valley, CA Holy Spirit Church.
Knestout, Barry '89 (WDC) Pastoral Center Special Ministries.
Kniepp, August J. '41 (CIN) [L] Cincinnati, OH Archbishop Leibold Home for the Aged.
Knier, Aloysius M. '42 (GB) Retired.
Kniewel, Edward J. '38 (CHI) Melrose Park, IL Sacred Heart Church; Retired.
Knight, David B. '61 (MEM) [25] Memphis, TN Sacred Heart Church.
Knight, Jeffrey '88 (STL) Manchester, MO St. Joseph Church.
Knight, Robert D. '83 (STL) Leave of Absence.
Knipe, Michael J. '88 (TLS) [15] Tulsa, OK Resurrection Church.
Knippel, Kenneth P. '76 (MIL) Fox Point, WI St. Eugene Church.
Knipper, Daniel J. '67 (DUB) Dike, IA St. Mary Church; [M] Cedar Falls, IA American Martyrs Retreat House.
Knittel, Kilian J. '60 (CHI) [43] Chicago, IL St. Columba Church.
Knoblach, Thomas '87 (SCL) Wadena, MN St. Ann's Church.
Knoebel, Thomas L. '69 (MIL) [B] Hales Corners, WI Sacred Heart School of Theology.
Knoeber, Joseph *o.m.i.* '59 (BEL) [G] Belleville, IL Missionary Oblates of Mary Immaculate - St. Henry's Oblate Residence.
Knoernschild, John *o.carm.* '70 (CHI) [D] Chicago, IL Mt. Carmel High School.
Knoernschild, William F. '47 (MIL) Retired.
Knoerschild, John *o.carm.* '70 (CHI) [N] Chicago, IL Carmelite Priory of St. Cyril.
Knoke, Kenneth F. '55 (FAR) Reynolds, ND Our Lady of Perpetual Help Church.
Knoll, Jerome E. *c.s.c.* '60 (FTW) [B] Notre Dame, IN University of Notre Dame Du Lac; [J] Notre Dame, IN Holy Cross Community, Corby Hall, University of Notre Dame.
Knoll, Lester *o.f.m.cap.* '64 (PIT) [N] Herman, PA St. Mary's Friary.
Knoll, Mark *c.ss.r.* '36 (ORL) Retired; [F] New Smyrna Beach, FL St. Alphonsus Villa-Redemptorist Fathers and Brothers; [F] New Smyrna Beach, FL Redemptorist Fathers of the Vice Province of Richmond.
Knoll, Urban H. '69 (STL) Retired.
Knop, Andrew *o.m.i.* '89 (DUL) [3] Duluth, MN Holy Family, Church.
Knopik, Andrew J. '83 (BEL) [4] Belleville, IL St. Augustine of Canterbury Church.
Knopke, Roch *o.f.m.* '31 (PAT) [M] Ringwood, NJ Holy Name Friary.
Knopp, Benjamin *o.f.m.conv.* '55 (MIL) Brandon, WI St. Brendan Church; Springvale, WI St. Mary Church; Waupun, WI St. Joseph's Church.
Knopp, John '78 (ELP) Absent on Leave.
Knotek, John T. '38 (MIL) Retired.
Knotek, Marcel '92 (PH) [32] Philadelphia, PA St. Cecilia Church.
Knotek, Michael P. '96 (CHI) Oak Forest, IL St. Damian Church.
Knotek, Wenceslaus F. *m.m.* '41 (SJ) [M] Los Altos, CA Maryknoll.
Knoth, Bernard P. *s.j.* '77 (NO) [C] New Orleans, LA Loyola University.
Knott, Edward J. '45 (MAN) Retired.

Knott, Francis X. *s.j.* '45 (BAL) [M] Baltimore, MD Jesuit Fathers and Brothers Maryland Provincial Curia.
Knott, J. Ronald '70 (L) [1] Louisville, KY Cathedral of the Assumption.
Knott, Peter *s.j.* '70 (BO) [W] Cambridge, MA Faber House.
Knott, William P. '59 (RCK) Retired; [D] Elgin, IL St. Joseph Hospital.
Knox, James '51 (PRT) Retired.
Knox, Stephen J. '89 (RCK) DeKalb, IL Christ the Teacher, University Parish of Northern Illinois University Church; [M] DeKalb, IL Newman Foundation for Catholic Students of Northern Illinois University.
Knudsen, Ronald '72 (SEA) Puyallup, WA All Saints Church.
Knueven, Gerald E. '68 (TOL) [7] Toledo, OH Good Shepherd Church; [18] Toledo, OH St. Anthony Church; [38] Toledo, OH St. Stanislaus Church.
Knueven, Harold L. '58 (IND) Greenwood, IN Our Lady of the Greenwood Church.
Knuffman, Donald E. '65 (SFD) [2] Decatur, IL Our Lady of Lourdes Church.
Knuge, Richard K. *s.m.* '56 (CIN) [M] Dayton, OH Marianist Provincialate.
Knurek, Dennis A. '77 (BGP) Retired.
Knusel, Frank '73 (P) [26] Portland, OR St. Patrick Church.
Kobak, Cantius J. *o.f.m.* '57 (MIL) [P] Milwaukee, WI Francis and Clare House.
Kobasuk, Masim *o.s.b.m.* '77 (STF) Kenmore, NY St. John the Baptist Church.
Kobayashi, Augustine *ss.cc.* '64 (FR) [K] Fairhaven, MA Sacred Hearts Provincial House.
Kobbeman, Gerald P. '66 (RCK) [2] Aurora, IL Holy Angels Church.
Kobe, Robert S. '79 (ELP) [5] El Paso, TX Christ The Savior Church.
Kobida, Vincent F. '80 (MIL) On Duty Outside the Archdiocese.
Kobler, John F. *c.p.* '54 (CHI) [N] Chicago, IL Immaculate Conception Monastery.
Kobos, Martin *o.f.m.conv.* '76 (BAL) [M] Ellicott City, MD Order of Friars Minor Conventual.
Kobti, Labib '74 (SFR) [4] San Francisco, CA St. Anne Church.
Kobti, Labib '75 (LA) Pomona, CA St. Joseph Church.
Kobularik, Robert J. '73 (HBG) New Freedom, PA St. John the Baptist Church.
Kobus, Damian M. *o.s.m.* '49 (CHI) [N] Chicago, IL Servite Friars - Eastern Province.
Kobus, Damian M. *o.s.m.* '49 (TUC) Yuma, AZ St. John Neumann Church.
Kobus, John '77 (CHI) [J] Chicago, IL St. Mary of Nazareth Hospital Center.
Kobuszewski, Thomas P. '64 (SY) [2] Liverpool, NY Immaculate Heart of Mary Church.
Kobza, John *m.i.c.* '54 (WDC) [B] Washington, DC Marian Fathers Scholasticate.
Koch, Msgr. Charles J. '63 (EVN) Special Assignment.
Koch, David J. '69 (GB) Neenah, WI St. Margaret Mary Church.
Koch, Donald J. '60 (STL) [1] Lemay, MO Mary Queen of the Universe Church.
Koch, Eugene R. '59 (DM) Granger, IA Assumption of the Blessed Virgin Mary Church.
Koch, Eugene R. '69 (NEW) [4] Linden, NJ St. Theresa of the Child Jesus Church.
Koch, Msgr. Frederick A. '43 (R) Retired.
Koch, George J. *s.j.* '59 (SJ) [M] Los Gatos, CA California Province of the Society of Jesus, Jesuit Provincial Office; [M] Los Gatos, CA Sacred Heart Jesuit Center.
Koch, Ivor '84 (FWT) Wichita Falls, TX Sacred Heart Church.
Koch, J. Robert *s.j.* '43 (DET) [P] Clarkston, MI Colombiere Center.
Koch, Kevin A. '85 (CHY) Torrington, WY St. Rose Church.
Koch, Michael R. '53 (GB) Special Assignment; [J] Oshkosh, WI SSM Franciscan Courts.
Koch, Patrick H. *s.j.* '57 (SP) [8] Tampa, FL Sacred Heart Church; [8] Tampa, FL Sacred Heart Church.
Koch, Paul M. '61 (DM) On Duty Outside the Diocese.
Koch, Terence E. *s.j.* '60 (SJ) [L] Los Altos, CA Jesuit Retreat House.
Kochaba, Myron E. *o.s.b.* '55 (PBR) Portage, PA SS. Peter and Paul Church; South Fork, PA St. Michael's Church.
Kochan, Frederick A. '55 (WIL) Garfield Park, DE Holy Spirit Church.
Kochithara, Joseph '82 (SLC) [5] Salt Lake City, UT St. Ambrose Church; Salt Lake City, UT Oxbow Correctional Facility.
Kochon, Michael A. '81 (MET) Washington, NJ St. Joseph Church.
Kochuparackal, Sebastian *c.m.i.* '75 (BRK) [56] Brooklyn, NY Holy Family Church; [U] Brooklyn, NY Carmelites of Mary Immaculate, Inc.
Kocik, Franc W. '76 (CAM) On Duty Outside the Diocese.
Kociolek, Charles J. *c.s.c.* '79 (SCR) [C] Wilkes-Barre, PA Kings College.
Kocour, Robert F. '54 (WCH) On Duty Outside the Diocese.
Kodakal, Berchmans '78 (MEM) [25] Memphis, TN Sacred Heart Church.
Kodekkanel, Mathew Jayanth *s.j.* '86 (OAK) [N] Berkeley, CA Jesuit Community at Jesuit School of Theology at Berkeley.
Koebel, Joseph A. '54 (VIC) Nada, TX Nativity of the Blessed Virgin Mary Church.
Koegel, Victor C. '43 (CIN) Retired.
Koehler, C. Frederick *s.j.* '51 (PH) [Z] Philadelphia, PA Jesuit Community at St. Joseph's University.
Koehler, John '65 (SEA) [1] Tacoma, WA St. Ann Church; [5] Tacoma, WA St. John of the Woods Church; [15] Tacoma, WA Sacred Heart Church.
Koehler, Jon C. '74 (BR) [19] Baton Rouge, LA St. Pius X Church.
Koehler, Kenneth '72 (DEN) [15] Denver, CO Most Precious Blood Church.
Koehler, Paul G. *o.s.b.* '36 (BIR) [E] Cullman, AL St. Bernard Abbey.
Koehler, Paul L. '38 (FAR) Retired; [E] Hankinson, ND St. Gerard Community Nursing Home.
Koehler, Ralph C. *c.s.b.* '40 (GRY) [B] Merrillville, IN Andrean High School; [K] Merrillville, IN Basilian Fathers Residence.
Koehler, Steven C. '82 (DET) Madison Heights, MI St. Vincent Ferrer Church.
Koehler, Theodore A. *s.m.* '41 (CIN) [D] Dayton, OH The University of Dayton; [D] Dayton, OH The University of Dayton; [M] Dayton, OH Marianist Provincialate.
Koehler, William *c.ss.r.* '83 (TUC) Tucson, AZ Tucson Medical Center.
Koehne, David '49 (GB) Retired.
Koehr, Louis A. '87 (BEL) Sesser, IL St. Mary Church.
Koelker, Harry A. '68 (DUB) [4] Cedar Rapids, IA St. Ludmila's Church; [F] Cedar Rapids, IA Holy Family Catholic Consolidated School.
Koelsch, John W. '56 (B) [6] Boise, ID Sacred Heart Church
Koelzer, Bonaventure *s.a.* '38 (NY) [Z] Garrison, NY Franciscan Friars of the Atonement.
Koen, Stephen E. (BO) [5] Newton, MA Mary Immaculate of Lourdes Church.
Koenig, Bernard J. '56 (HEL) Ronan, MT Sacred Heart Church
Koenig, Msgr. Harry C. '32 (CHI) Retired.
Koenig, Msgr. John H. '42 (NEW) Summit, NJ St. Teresa's Church; Union, NJ Holy Spirit Church; Retired
Koenig, Paul *o.f.m.cap.* '96 (MIL) [B] Mount Calvary, WI St. Felix Friary.
Koenig, Robert B. '45 (DET) Retired.
Koenig, Msgr. William A. '32 (PH) Retired; [S] Philadelphia, PA St. Vincent's Day Care Center.
Koenig, William E. '83 (RVC) [1] Rockville Centre, NY St. Agnes Cathedral.
Koenigsfeld, James F. '68 (PBL) Crested Butte, CO Queen of All Saints Church; Gunnison, CO St. Peter Church; Montrose, CO St. Mary Church.
Koenigsknecht, William J. '68 (LAN) [5] Lansing, MI Resurrection Church; Retired.
Koeninger, Francis F.. '79 (STL) Mattese, MO Assumption Church.
Koeplin, John P. *s.j.* '91 (FWT) [J] Lake Dallas, TX Montserrat Jesuit Retreat House.
Koerber, George M. '60 (TOL) Retired; [H] Oregon, OH St. Charles Hospital.
Koerner, Frederick C. '59 (NEW) [2] Irvington, NJ St. Leo's Church.
Koerner, Robert *o.m.i.* '37 (SAT) [K] San Antonio, TX Oblate Madonna Residence.
Koerner, Robert H. (GF) [G] Billings, MT Saint Vincent Hospital and Health Center.
Koers, Eugene A. '62 (FTW) Arcola, IN St. Patrick Church.
Koesel, Douglas H. '78 (CLV) [46] Cleveland, OH St. Mark Church.
Koesler, Leo '46 (LR) [A] Subiaco, AR Subiaco Monastery.
Koester, Timothy J. '83 (BUF) Military Chaplains.
Koesterer, David W. *s.j.* '64 (STL) [P] St. Louis, MO White House Retreat Jesuit Community; [T] St. Louis, MO White House Retreat.
Koestner, Alfred G. *o.s.b.* '39 (KCK) Wetmore, KS St. James Church.
Koetter, Paul D. '77 (IND) [1] Indianapolis, IN SS. Peter and Paul Cathedral; Nashville, IN St. Agnes Church.
Koeune, August '84 (CHY) Evanston, WY St. Mary Magdalen Church.
Koeune, George '95 (CHI) Niles, IL St. Isaac Jogues Church.
Koharchik, George D. '74 (ALT) [1] Portage, PA St. Joseph's Church.
Kohler, Edward '77 (HEL) Browning, MT Church of the Little Flower.
Kohler, Joseph M. '54 (STL) [W] St. Louis, MO Dismas House of St. Louis.
Kohler, Lawrence A. *m.s.* '61 (LKC) [2] Sulphur, LA Our Lady of LaSalette Church.
Kohler, Peter D. '68 (STL) Maplewood, MO Immaculate Conception Church.
Kohler, Russell E. '73 (DET) [51] Detroit, MI Most Holy Trinity Church; [Q] Detroit, MI Pope John XXIII Hospitality House; [Q] Onsted, MI St. Patrick's Retreat.
Kohler, Thomas M. '68 (PH) [1] Bensalem, PA St. Charles Borromeo Church; Absent on Sick Leave.
Kohler, William E. '67 (MIL) [6] West Allis, WI Mary, Queen of Heaven Church.
Kohler, William F. '55 (PIT) [4] Bridgeville, PA St. Barbara Church.
Kohlerman, Charles W. *c.s.c.* '63 (FTW) [L] Notre Dame, IN Holy Cross Mission House; [M] Notre Dame, IN Our Lady of Fatima Retreat Center.
Kohli, Charles F. '61 (RVC) Stony Brook, NY L.I. State Veterans' Home.
Kohls, Msgr. Eugene C. '57 (STA) [1] Jacksonville, FL Assumption Church.
Kohls, Henry H. *s.j.* '42 (P) [L] Portland, OR Jesuit Provincial Office (Oregon Prov.).
Kohmescher, Matthew F. *s.m.* '48 (CIN) [D] Dayton, OH The University of Dayton; [M] Dayton, OH Marianist Provincialate.
Kohner, David W. '90 (STP) Faribault, MN Sacred Heart - St. Lawrence of Fairbault Church.
Kohrman, Glenn '83 (FTW) [14] Fort Wayne, IN St. Paul Church.
Kohrman, Glenn '92 (FTW) [17] Fort Wayne, IN Sacred Heart Church; [C] Fort Wayne, IN Bishop Luers High School.
Kohuch, Robert Andrew '66 (PIT) Elrama, PA St. Isaac Jogues Church.
Kohut, Msgr. Joseph J. '62 (BGP) Darien, CT St. John Church.
Koilparampil, Augustine '64 (OAK) Livermore, CA St. Michael's Church; Livermore, CA Veterans Administration Hospital; Military Chaplains.
Kok, Bede *o.c.s.o.* '41 (L) [L] Trappist, KY Abbey of Our Lady of Gethsemani, of the Order of Cistercians of the Strict Observance.
Kokjohn, Joseph '54 (DAV) [B] Davenport, IA St. Ambrose University.
Kokocinski, Bernard A. '66 (TOL) [29] Toledo, OH St. Jude Church.
Kolaczek, John Baptista *o.c.d.* (GRY) [K] Munster, IN Discalced Carmelite Fathers Monastery.
Kolakowski, Marcel *o.f.m.* '49 (PH) [2] Philadelphia, PA St. Adalbert Church.
Kolanda, George A. '44 (MIL) Retired.
Kolanda, George A. '45 (MIL) [N] Wauwatosa, WI St. Camillus Health Center, Inc.
Kolanko, John R. '40 (MIL) [58] Milwaukee, WI Our Lady of Good Hope Church; Retired.
Kolar, Thomas F. '60 (STP) Retired.
Kolarec, William T. *s.j.* '69 (OM) [K] Omaha, NE Jesuit Community At Creighton University.
Kolasa, Stanley *ss.cc.* '70 (FR) [K] Fairhaven, MA Sacred Hearts Provincial House.
Kolasinski, Daniel '57 (P) Reedsport, OR St. John the Apostle Church.
Kolath, George (STP) North St. Paul, MN St. Peter Church.
Kolb, James *c.s.p.* '76 (NY) [Z] Scarsdale, NY Paulist Fathers Generalate.
Kolb, James M. *c.s.p.* '76 (FBK) [3] Fairbanks, AK St. Mark University Parish Church; [4] Fairbanks, AK St. Raphael's Church.
Kolb, Joseph C. '53 (OKL) Hennessey, OK St. Joseph's Church.
Kolb, Joseph E. *s.j.* '63 (WH) [A] Wheeling, WV Wheeling Jesuit University.
Kolb, Michael R. *s.j.* '82 (MIL) [E] Milwaukee, WI Marquette University High School; [P] Milwaukee, WI Arrupe House Jesuit Community.
Kolberg, Lawrence R. '68 (ORG) Absent on Sick Leave.
Kolbusz, Stanley F. '55 (GB) [3] Oshkosh, WI St. Josaphat Church.
Kolcun, Stephen '46 (PBR) Beaverdale, PA St. Mary's Church.
Kolczaski, Richard '55 (PEO) Peru, IL St. Mary's Church.
Kolda, Donald *s.j.* '55 (ORG) Laguna Niguel, CA St. Timothy Church; [H] Laguna Niguel, CA Jesuits.
Kole, Eugene R. *o.f.m.conv.* '75 (PH) [C] Philadelphia, PA Chestnut Hill College.
Kole, Eugene R. *o.f.m.conv.* '75 (TR) [22] Trenton, NJ St. Stanislaus Church.
Kolenkiewicz, Louis J. '93 (PH) Hatboro, PA St. John Bosco Church.
Kolenski, Robert D. '62 (LAN) Owosso, MI St. Paul Church.
Kolesar, Casimir *o.f.m.* '61 (PEO) [3] Peoria, IL Sacred Heart Church.
Kolesar, Msgr. John C. '64 (STU) Adena, OH St. Casimir's Church.
Kolf, Gerry (FTW) [I] South Bend, IN Prelature of the Holy Cross and Opus Dei.

Kolibas, Kenneth R. '94 (MET) Phillipsburg, NJ SS. Philip and James Church.
Kolinovsky, Sebastian *c.p.* '51 (NEW) [N] Union City, NJ Congregation of the Passion (Passionists)-St. Michael's Residence.
Koll, Jude *o.s.b.* '40 (SCL) [I] Collegeville, MN St. John's Abbey, of the Order of St. Benedict.
Kollar, Anton *o.carm.* '51 (JOL) [J] Darien, IL Carmelite Fathers Provincial Office.
Kollar, Edmund '46 (ARL) Retired.
Kollar, Rene M. *o.s.b.* '74 (GBG) [H] Latrobe, PA Saint Vincent Archabbey.
Kollasch, Eugene C. *s.j.* '59 (MIL) [P] Milwaukee, WI Jesuit Provincial Office, Wisconsin Province.
Kollasch, Msgr. Louis H. '58 (SC) Madrid, IA St. Malachy's Church; Woodward, IA St. John of God Church; Woodward, IA Woodward State Hospital and School.
Kollasch, Merle F. '64 (SC) Pocahontas, IA Church of the Resurrection; [G] Pocahontas, IA Opus Spiritus Sancti.
Koller, Gerold *c.pp.s.* '49 (CIN) [B] Carthagena, OH St. Charles.
Koller, Thomas '90 (SB) [G] Redlands, CA El Carmelo Retreat House.
Kolling, James L. '65 (LA) [1] Los Angeles, CA Cathedral of Our Lady of the Angels; [CC] Los Angeles, CA Rosary Hour Inc., The.
Kollithanath, Philip '84 (CHL) High Point, NC Christ the King Church.
Kollross, Dennis D. '81 (SFD) [5] Decatur, IL St. Thomas the Apostle Church; [M] Decatur, IL Millikin University Newman Catholic Community.
Kolmaga, Bogdan *o.s.p.* '92 (NY) [113] New York, NY St. Stanislaus Church.
Kolmaga, Jan *o.s.p.p.e.* '82 (PH) [Z] Doylestown, PA Pauline Fathers Monastery, Shrine of Our Lady of Czestochowa.
Kolo, Vincent F. '95 (PIT) [54] Pittsburgh, PA St. John Vianney Church.
Kolodziej, Maynard *o.f.m.* '53 (FTW) [K] Mishawaka, IN Our Lady of the Angels Convent.
Kolodziej, Maynard *o.f.m.* '53 (GRY) [K] Cedar Lake, IN Our Lady of Lourdes Friary.
Kolodziej, Michael *o.f.m.conv.* '70 (SPR) [10] Chicopee, MA St. Stanislaus Basilica.
Kolodziej, Ryszard '96 (R) Wilmington, NC St. Mark Church.
Kolodziejski, Karl *o.f.m.conv.* '78 (BUF) [21] Buffalo, NY Corpus Christi Church.
Kolota, Dominik P. '65 (ALN) Frackville, PA St. Ann Church; Frackville, PA Annunciation B.V.M. Church.
Kolp, James R. '50 (Y) [4] Massillon, OH St. Mary's Church.
Kolson, Lawrence F. '74 (BAL) Bradshaw, MD St. Stephen Church.
Kolton, Stanislaus J. '46 (CAM) Retired.
Koltuniak, Michael P. '39 (DET) Retired.
Koltzenburg, Otto '81 (SPK) Walla Walla, WA Assumption of the Blessed Virgin Mary Church.
Kolumber, Denis *m.s.* '67 (ATL) Canton, GA Our Lady of LaSalette Church.
Kolzow, Andrew K. *o.p.* '58 (DAL) [M] Irving, TX Dominican Priory of St. Albert the Great.
Koma, Joseph W. *c.s.c.* '61 (KAL) Niles, MI St. Mark Church.
Komar, John E. '64 (NEW) Ridgefield, NJ St. Matthew's Church; Englewood, NJ Englewood Hospital.
Komar, Msgr. Michael A. '36 (NEW) [2] Linden, NJ Holy Family Church; Retired.
Komaska, James R. '54 (STL) Dardenne, MO Immaculate Conception Church.
Komatz, David M. *o.praem.* '75 (GB) [B] De Pere, WI St. Norbert College; [I] De Pere, WI St. Joseph Priory.
Komechak, Michael E. *o.s.b.* '59 (JOL) [A] Lisle, IL Benedictine University; [J] Lisle, IL St. Procopius Abbey.
Kommer, Jason *o.f.m.* '43 (JOL) Kinsman, IL Sacred Heart Church.
Kommer, Venard *o.f.m.* '46 (JOL) Clarendon Hills, IL Notre Dame Church.
Kommers, Thomas M. '80 (STP) Eagan, MN St. Thomas Becket Church.
Komonchak, Joseph A. '64 (NY) On Duty Outside the Archdiocese.
Komonchak, Joseph A. '64 (WDC) [C] Washington, DC Catholic University of America, The.
Komorowski, Louis A. *o.s.f.s.* '56 (LAN) Adrian, MI St. Mary of Good Counsel Church.
Komosinski, Msgr. Martin M. '51 (TR) Burlington, NJ All Saints Church.
Konath, Jacob '95 (BIS) Glenburn, ND St. Philomena Church.
Koncewicz, Lawrence W. *c.m.* '66 (MIL) Wood, WI Veterans Administration Medical Center.
Koncik, Michael *c.ss.r.* (VEN) Wauchula, FL St. Michael Church.
Konda, Bernard A. *j.c.d.* '67 (JUN) Ketchikan, AK Holy Name Church.
Kondeja, Stanley '62 (RVC) Southampton, NY Our Lady of Poland Church.
Konderla, David '95 (AUS) [16] Austin, TX St. Louis Church.
Kondik, David M. *o.s.m.* '48 (CHI) [N] Chicago, IL Servite Friars - Eastern Province.
Kondik, David M. *o.s.m.* '48 (ORG) Fullerton, CA St. Juliana Falconieri Church.
Kondrath, James A. '50 (SFD) Retired.
Kondzielski, Thaddeus T. '67 (E) Crossingsville, PA St. Philip Church.
Kondziolka, Ronald L. '76 (CHI) [J] Chicago Heights, IL St. James Hospital and Health Centers.
Konechne, Louis D. '82 (GLP) [D] Gallup, NM Carmelite Monastery.
Konen, Lyle *c.ss.r.* '61 (SEA) [32] Seattle, WA Sacred Heart of Jesus Church.
Konerman, Edward H. *s.j.* '58 (CHI) [C] Chicago, IL Jesuit Community at Loyola University of Chicago.
Konerman, Gregory J. '93 (CIN) [58] Cincinnati, OH St. Martin of Tours Church.
Kong, Denis *s.d.b* '90 (OAK) [N] Berkeley, CA Salesian Community.
Konicek, John J. *s.j.* '93 (NO) [C] New Orleans, LA Loyola University.
Konieczka, Edward J. '63 (SAG) Harbor Beach, MI Our Lady of Lake Huron Church.
Konieczny, Anthony M. *o.f.m.conv.* '43 (BUF) [21] Buffalo, NY Corpus Christi Church.
Koninkx, Msgr. William '46 (HT) [6] Houma, LA St. Gregory Barbarigo Church; Retired.
Konisky, Edward '38 (ALB) Retired.
Konkel, Eugene J. *s.s.* '57 (MIL) On Duty Outside the Archdiocese.
Konkel, Eugene J. *s.s.* '57 (SFR) [U] Menlo Park, CA Vatican II Institute for Clergy Formation.
Konkel, Joseph D. *o.p.* '70 (GAL) [35] Houston, TX Holy Rosary Church.
Konkler, Paul Jerome *o.c.s.o.* '68 (SAC) [A] Vina, CA Abbey of New Clairvaux, Trappist Seminary; [H] Vina, CA Abbey of New Clairvaux, Trappist.
Konkol, Robert *o.f.m.* '94 (MIL) [P] Burlington, WI Queen of Peace Friary.
Konobrocki, Marian '91 (VEN) [5] Fort Myers, FL St. Francis Xavier Church.
Konold, Lon *o.m.i.* '77 (BEL) [G] Belleville, IL Missionary Oblates of Mary Immaculate - St. Henry's Oblate Residence; [K] Belleville, IL Oblate Preaching Team.
Konopa, Robert *o.f.m.* '91 (SAG) [18] Saginaw, MI St. Thomas Aquinas Church.
Konopacky, Joseph R. '82 (LC) Custer, WI Immaculate Conception Church; Rosholt, WI St. Adalbert Church.
Konopacky, Joseph R. '85 (LC) Polonia, WI Sacred Heart Church.
Konopka, Edward F. '45 (DET) [2] Troy, MI St. Alan Church; Retired.
Konopka, Edward M. '60 (NOR) Higganum, CT St. Peter Church.
Konopka, Thomas '90 (ALB) Loudonville, NY St. Pius X Church.
Konoske, Msgr. Paul M. '31 (LA) San Marino, CA Saints Felicitas and Perpetua Church; Retired.
Konowalek, Zanon '89 (CC) Three Rivers, TX Sacred Heart Church.
Konrad, Erwin R. '89 (JC) [2] Jefferson City, MO St. Peter Church; Jefferson City, MO Capital Region Medical Center, Memorial Campus; [C] Jefferson City, MO St. Marys Health Center.
Konrad, Msgr. Joseph G. '43 (BRK) [199] Queens, NY St. Matthias Church; Retired.
Konz, Gregory N. *s.j.* '90 (STL) [P] St. Louis, MO Jesuit Community Corporation at St. Louis University - Jesuit Hall.
Konzen, Joel M. *s.m.* '79 (AUS) [C] Austin, TX St. Michaels's Catholic Academy.
Koo, Il Mo (Peter) '79 (SEA) Special Assignment.
Koo, Matthew '88 (SJ) [14] San Jose, CA St. Leo the Great Church; [1] Santa Clara, CA Chinese Catholic Community Church.
Koob, Edward H. '45 (PH) Retired.
Kookoothe, Neil P. '95 (CLV) [5] Parma, OH St. Francis de Sales Church.
Koons, James W. '83 (FTW) [13] Fort Wayne, IN St. Patrick Church.
Koonz, John A. '63 (SPR) Dalton, MA St. Agnes Church.
Koop, Cecil *o.f.m.* '45 (CLV) [P] Cleveland, OH Padua Franciscan Friary.
Koopman, Bernard V. '61 (IND) Bradford, IN St. Michael Church.
Koopman, Dennis *o.f.m.* '70 (CHI) [N] Countryside, IL St. Gratian Friary, Franciscan Friars.
Koopmann, Robert *o.s.b.* '81 (SCL) [I] Collegeville, MN St. John's Abbey, of the Order of St. Benedict.
Koos, Gerald J. '66 (E) [13] Erie, PA St. Ann Church; Erie, PA Hamot Medical Center.
Kopacek, Jerry F. '88 (DUB) Marshalltown, IA St. Mary's Church.
Kopacz, Joseph R. '77 (SCR) [20] Scranton, PA Nativity of Our Lord Church.
Kopacz, Kazimierz '95 (FAR) [3] Fargo, ND Nativity Church.
Kopacz, Mark W. '92 (WIL) Easton, MD SS. Peter and Paul Church.
Kopacz, Msgr. Matthew S. '63 (BUF) [18] Buffalo, NY St. Casimir Church.
Kopacz, Stephen A. '72 (NEW) North Arlington, NJ Queen of Peace Church.
Kopaczynski, Germain *o.f.m. conv.* '74 (BO) [55] Boston, MA Our Lady of Czestochowa Church; [FF] Braintree, MA Pope John Center.
Kopchik, Martin J. *m.s.f.s.* '86 (ATL) Norcross, GA Saint Patrick's Church.
Kopczewski, Linus E. *o.f.m.* '65 (PH) [Z] Philadelphia, PA St. Pius X Friary.
Kopczewski, Linus E. *o.f.m.* '65 (TR) Trenton, NJ St. Francis Medical Center; [I] Trenton, NJ St. Francis Medical Center.
Kopczynski, Michael R. (BUF) [4] North Tonawanda, NY Our Lady of Czestochowa Church.
Kopec, Chester *o.p.* '63 (SB) Chino, CA California Institute for Men.
Kopec, Christopher A. '93 (WIL) Milford, DE St. John the Apostle Church; Salisbury, MD Salisbury State College.
Kopec, Edward S. '92 (PEO) Delavan, IL St. Mary's Church.
Kopec, Jerome E. '79 (BUF) [1] Buffalo, NY St. Joseph's Cathedral.
Kopecky, Joseph A. '45 (PIT) Retired.
Kopek, Rajmund '92 (NEW) Rochelle Park, NJ Sacred Heart Church.
Kopel, Jerry '77 (SFS) Tyndall, SD St. Leo Church.
Koper, Msgr. Francis B. '71 (DET) [A] Orchard Lake, MI SS. Cyril and Methodius Seminary; [C] Orchard Lake, MI Saint Mary's College.
Koper, Msgr. Francis B. '71 (WIL) On Duty Outside the Diocese.
Koper, Ryszard '78 (BRK) [177] Queens, NY Holy Cross Church.
Kopfensteiner, Thomas R. '81 (STL) On Duty Outside the Archdiocese.
Kopff, Herbert C. '38 (BEL) Retired.
Kopff, Marvin C. '63 (STL) Special Assignment; [I] St. Louis, MO Cardinal Ritter Institute.
Kopinski, Richard '64 (RVC) Glen Head, NY St. Hyacinth Church.
Koplik, Msgr. William J. '62 (NEW) [1] Hackensack, NJ Holy Trinity Church.
Koplinka, Quentin S. *o.s.b.* '79 (MIL) [P] Benet Lake, WI St. Benedict's Abbey.
Koplinka, Quentin S. *o.s.b.* '79 (PRM) Cleveland, OH Holy Ghost Church; Cleveland, OH St. Nicholas Church.
Kopp, Anthony Mary *o.praem.* '93 (ORG) [H] Silverado, CA Norbertine Fathers.
Kopp, Richard M. '69 (SY) Baldwinsville, NY St. Mary Church; Special Assignment.
Kopp, Thomas A. '72 (BO) [8] Brockton, MA Sacred Heart Church.
Koppert, Elias *o.f.m.* '41 (IND) [13] Indianapolis, IN Sacred Heart of Jesus Church.
Koppes, Albert *o.carm.* '59 (JOL) [J] Darien, IL Carmelite Fathers Provincial Office.
Koprowski, Mitchell J. '41 (GI) Retired.
Kopystynski, Andrzej R. *c.m.* '88 (BRK) [134] Brooklyn, NY St. Stanislaus Kostka Church.
Korabik, Joseph *c.r.* '38 (CHI) [D] Chicago, IL Weber High School.
Korba, Msgr. Frank '66 (PRM) Munster, IN Saint Nicholas Church.
Korbelak, John J. '74 (NEW) North Bergen, NJ Our Lady of Fatima Church.
Korbic, Benno *o.f.m.* '40 (CHI) [N] Lemont, IL The Slovene Franciscan Fathers, Order of Friars Minor, Commissariat of the Holy Cross.
Korcsmar, John S. *c.s.c.* '74 (AUS) [8] Austin, TX Nuestra Senora De Dolores Church.
Korda, Msgr. Edward L. '49 (CAM) Magnolia, NJ St. Gregory's Church.
Korda, J. James '79 (Y) [3] Youngstown, OH Immaculate Conception Church.
Kordas, Edward J. '68 (CLV) South Amherst, OH Nativity of Blessed Virgin Mary Church; [Y] Cleveland, OH Office of Newman Campus Ministry.
Kordek, Frank *o.f.m.* '72 (GAY) Harbor Springs, MI Holy Childhood of Jesus Church.
Kordsmeier, John W. '49 (LR) Harrison, AR Mary, Mother of God Church.
Korecki, Maximilian *o.f.m. conv.* '62 (IND) [I] Mount Saint Francis, IN Mount Saint Francis Friary and Retreat Center.
Koreger, Gerald *o.p.* '58 (CHI) [24] Chicago, IL St. Basil/Visitation Church.
Koren, Henry J. *c.s.sp.* '37 (PIT) [N] Bethel Park, PA Holy Ghost Fathers and Brothers Provincialate; [P] Bethel Park, PA Holy Ghost Animation Center.
Koren, Louis F. '32 (MIL) Retired.
Korenek, Gregory E. '93 (VIC) [2] Victoria, TX Holy Family of Joseph, Mary & Jesus Church.
Koressel, James '69 (EVN) Boonville, IN St. Clement Church.
Korf, Joseph '74 (SCL) Fergus Falls, MN Our Lady of Victory Church.

Korgie, Humbert *o.f.m.* '43 (SUP) Washburn, WI St. Louis Church.
Korinchock, Joseph '85 (PHU) Absent on Leave.
Kornacki, Matthew J. '73 (PH) [70] Philadelphia, PA Immaculate Heart of Mary Church.
Kornath, Edwin M. '84 (MIL) Campbellsport, WI St. Matthew's Church.
Kornbrust, Herman *o.s.b.* '62 (OM) [K] Schuyler, NE Benedictine Mission House.
Kornely, Benno G. *s.j.* '59 (DET) [P] Bloomfield Hills, MI Manresa Jesuit Retreat House.
Kornely, Benno G. *s.j.* '59 (MIL) [P] Milwaukee, WI Jesuit Provincial Office, Wisconsin Province.
Kornmeyer, Thomas E. '90 (OG) Malone, NY Notre Dame Church.
Kornoski, Joseph C. '88 (MET) South Plainfield, NJ Sacred Heart Church.
Korogi, Dale J. '83 (STP) [1] Minneapolis, MN The Basilica of St. Mary Co-Cathedral.
Koros, John J. '45 (OM) Retired.
Koros, John J. '50 (VEN) Lake Placid, FL St. James Church.
Korte, Ed (BIS) Crosby, ND St. Patrick Church.
Korte, Harry *c.ss.r.* '46 (STL) [P] Liguori, MO Liguori Mission House/Redemptorists.
Korte, Owen W. '81 (OM) Elgin, NE St. Boniface Church.
Korte, William L. '83 (JC) Mary's Home, MO Our Lady of the Snows Church.
Kortendick, Steven J. '85 (MAD) [1] Madison, WI St. Raphael Cathedral; [12] Madison, WI St. Paul University Parish Church.
Korth, David M. '92 (OM) Fremont, NE St. Patrick Church.
Korycki, Walter R. '49 (RVC) Retired.
Korytkowski, George J. *o.f.m.cap.* '70 (MET) [4] New Brunswick, NJ St. Joseph Church.
Korytkowski, George J. *o.f.m.cap.* '70 (PAT) [M] Oak Ridge-Milton, NJ St. Stanislaus B. M. Friary.
Korzinek, Richard *o.s.cam.* '53 (MAD) Durward's Glen, WI St. Camillus Church; [A] Durward's Glen, WI St. Camillus Monastery and Retreat Center.
Kos, Donald *o.f.m.conv.* '61 (BAL) [M] Ellicott City, MD Order of Friars Minor Conventual.
Kos, Joseph S. '66 (IND) Indianapolis, IN Indiana University Hospital; Indianapolis, IN Wishard Memorial Hospital; Indianapolis, IN Larue D. Carter Hospital.
Kosak, Msgr. Michael F. '70 (STV) [1] Barrenspot, VI Church St. Ann Church; [B] St. Thomas, VI Miscellaneous Organizations; [B] St. Thomas, VI Miscellaneous Organizations.
Kosaka, Paulo *o.f.m.cap.* '84 (AGN) [F] Agana Heights, GU St. Fidelis Friary.
Kosaka, Paulo *o.f.m.cap.* '84 (HON) Aiea, HI St. Elizabeth Church.
Kosanke, Charles '85 (DET) [A] Detroit, MI Sacred Heart Major Seminary, Inc.
Kosch, Leo D. '93 (LIN) Bellwood, NE Presentation Church.
Kosciesza, Bogumil '94 (CR) Pennington, MN St. Charles Church.
Kosciesza, Bogumil '94 (DUL) Cass Lake, MN St. Charles Church.
Kosco, Arnold J. '60 (DET) West Bloomfield, MI Prince of Peace Church.
Kose, Robert *o.f.m.cap.* '92 (MIL) [25] Milwaukee, WI St. Francis of Assisi Church.
Kosem, Frank P. '70 (CLV) [3] Elyria, OH St. Jude Church.
Koser, Albert C. '59 (PIT) Boyers, PA St. Alphonsus Church.
Koser, Rudolph J., Jr. '74 (GBG) Military Chaplains.
Koshko, Dennis M. '75 (HON) Honokaa, HI Our Lady of Lourdes Church.
Kosiba, Mark *o.s.b.* '57 (KC) [O] Conception, MO Conception Benedictine Trust.
Kosicki, Bohdan W. '50 (DET) [5] St. Clair Shores, MI St. Lucy Church; [T] St. Clair Shores, MI Catholic Kolping Society of America, Detroit Branch, Inc.
Kosicki, George *c.s.b.* '54 (ROC) [I] Rochester, NY Basilian Residence.
Kosicki, George *c.s.b.* '54 (SPR) [I] Stockbridge, MA Congregation of Marians.
Kosik, Msgr. Edward J. '65 (E) Warren, PA Holy Redeemer Church.
Kosiki, George (SPR) [I] Stockbridge, MA Congregation of Marians.
Kosinski, Stephen D. '81 (GRY) [7] Gary, IN St. Ann Church.
Kosisko, Richard J. '85 (GBG) Slickville, PA St. Sylvester Church.
Kosler, Timothy '71 (VIC) Ammannsville, TX St. John The Baptist Church; Schulenburg, TX St. Rose of Lima Church.
Kosmal, John '56 (JOL) Retired.
Kosmicki, Raymond M. '68 (GI) Wood River, NE St. Mary's Church.
Kosmoski, David B. *o.m.v.* '81 (MET) Avenel, NJ St. Andrew Church.
Kosmowski, Gary J. (MAN) Laconia, NH St. Joseph Church.
Kosnik, Anthony '55 (DET) Special Assignment.
Kosnik, Eugene A. '60 (NY) [5] Yonkers, NY St. Casimir Church.
Kosowicz, Wojciech '65 (CC) Vattman, TX Our Lady of Consolation Church.
Koss, David F. '78 (DET) Absent on Leave.
Kossak, Michael J. *s.j.* '87 (BO) [W] Boston, MA The Society of Jesus of New England-Provincial Offices.
Kossak, Michael J. *s.j.* '87 (MIA) [5] Miami, FL Gesu Church.
Kosse, Gerald C. '76 (WIN) Adrian, MN St. Adrian Church; Lismore, MN St. Anthony's Church.
Kosse, Theodore C. '71 (CIN) New Richmond, OH St. Peter Church.
Kossel, Clifford *s.j.* '48 (SPK) [C] Spokane, WA Gonzaga University.
Kost, Harold J. '45 (SCL) Belle Prairie, MN Holy Family Church.
Kostek, John '73 (ALB) [13] Schenectady, NY Our Lady of the Assumption Church.
Kostelnick, Albert T. '54 (PH) Bristol, PA St. Mark Church.
Kostelnik, Msgr. Kevin '82 (LA) [1] Los Angeles, CA Cathedral of Our Lady of the Angels.
Kostelz, Richard F. '52 (JOL) Cabery, IL St. Joseph Church.
Koster, Dale F. '54 (SC) Retired.
Koster, John *s.v.d.* '44 (CHI) [B] Techny, IL Divine Word Residence.
Koster, Kenneth '76 (SFS) Tea, SD St. Nicholas Church.
Koster, Theodore *o.c.s.o.* '59 (SPC) [E] Ava, MO Assumption Abbey (Trappist).
Kosterman, Richard A. '93 (GAY) Copemish, MI St. Raphael Church.
Kostic, Andrew (PAT) Permanent Deacons.
Kostick, Msgr. Adam J. '54 (WDC) [3] Rockville, MD St. Mary Church.
Kostiuk, Nick '80 (PHU) Nanticoke, PA Transfiguration of Our Lord Church; Plymouth, PA SS. Peter and Paul Church.
Kostka, Leonard J. *c.pp.s.* '40 (LFT) Rensselaer, IN St. Augustine Church; [A] Rensselaer, IN Saint Joseph's College.
Kostrzomb, Stanley '77 (NEW) [6] Jersey City, NJ St. Anthony of Padua Church.
Kosty, Robert J. '74 (WDC) Medley's Neck, MD Our Lady's Church.
Kostyk, Marijan '90 (STF) [4] Colchester, CT St. Mary Dormition Church.
Koszarek, Msgr. Paul P. '54 (GB) Antigo, WI St. Hyacinth Church.
Koszarek, Robert J. '74 (SUP) Eagle River, WI St. Peter the Fisherman Church.
Koszarek, Thaddeus J. '39 (GB) Retired; [H] Green Bay, WI The McCormick Memorial Home for the Aged.
Koszyk, Seweryn J. *s.a.c* '59 (BUF) [2] Niagara Falls, NY St. George Church; [O] North Tonawanda, NY Society of the Catholic Apostolate.
Kot, Luke C. *o.c.s.o.* '48 (ATL) [I] Conyers, GA The Monastery of the Holy Spirit.
Kotara, James '76 (SAT) [5] San Antonio, TX Holy Family Church.
Kotecki, Ronald E. '72 (MIL) [40] Milwaukee, WI St. Hyacinth's Church.
Koterski, Joseph W. *s.j.* '92 (NY) [Z] New York, NY Jesuit Community at Fordham University.
Koth, Arthur R. '57 (MAD) McFarland, WI Christ the King Church.
Kotheimer, Alex L. '42 (L) Retired.
Kothuis, Hans '81 (SD) Leave of Absence.
Kotkowski, Matthew *o.f.m.conv.* '45 (BAL) [88] Baltimore, MD St. Stanislaus Kostka Church.
Kotlanger, Michael J. *s.j.* '78 (SFR) [E] San Francisco, CA St. Ignatius College Preparatory (Coed); [N] San Francisco, CA Jesuit Community at St. Ignatius College Preparatory.
Kotlarz, Robert '69 (DET) [9] Detroit, MI St. Anthony Church.
Kotlinski, Bede *o.s.b.* (CLV) [E] Cleveland, OH Benedictine High School; [P] Cleveland, OH Benedictine Order of Cleveland; [Q] Cleveland, OH Sisters of the Incarnate Word and Blessed Sacrament.
Kotnis, Gregory M. '56 (PHX) Retired.
Kottar, Michael T. '94 (MET) Colonia, NJ St. John Vianney Church.
Kottaram, Mathew '63 (RVC) Elmont, NY St. Boniface Church.
Kottarczyk, Mark E. (SB) Victorville, CA Holy Innocents Church.
Kottas, Charles '70 (DM) [4] Council Bluffs, IA St. Peter Church.
Kottayil, Joseph '79 (MIA) Pembroke Pines, FL St. Maximilian Kolbe Church.
Kottenstette, William P. '73 (JC) Kirksville, MO Mary Immaculate Church; Memphis, MO St. John Church; [F] Kirksville, MO Catholic Newman Center, Truman State University.
Kottiry, Alphonsus '59 (DUL) On Duty Outside the Diocese.
Kotula, Gerard *o.f.m.* '39 (GB) [I] Pulaski, WI Assumption of B.V.M. Friary.
Kotyuk, Stephen '47 (E) Retired.
Kotz, Anthony A. '50 (LIN) Retired.
Kotzbauer, Leonard F. '65 (SY) [3] Liverpool, NY St. John Church.
Kouba, Charles J. '51 (CHI) [191] Chicago, IL St. Simon the Apostle Church; Retired.
Kouba, John *s.d.s.* '52 (SAC) West Sacramento, CA Holy Cross Church.
Koury, Msgr. Joseph A. '50 (JKS) Retired.
Koury, Joseph J. '77 (PRT) Orono, ME Our Lady of Wisdom Personal Campus Parish Church; [M] Orono, ME University of Maine.
Kovach, Blaise '55 (PBR) Braddock, PA SS. Peter and Paul Church.
Kovach, John '65 (PRM) Burton, OH Church of Weeping Madonna; [B] Burton, OH Shrine of the Weeping Madonna of Mariapoch.
Kovach, John '65 (VNN) On Special Assignment.
Kovach, Raymond J. '69 (NY) Absent on Leave.
Kovach, William J. '55 (ALT) Revloc, PA Most Holy Redeemer Church.
Kovacs, Msgr. John F. '41 (DM) Retired.
Kovacs, Louis D. '44 (PH) East Goshen, PA SS. Peter and Paul Church; Retired.
Kovacs, Matthew *o.cist.* '57 (DAL) [M] Irving, TX Cistercian Abbey of Our Lady of Dallas.
Kovacsik, Clement *s.t.* '44 (BLX) [3] Gulfport, MS St. John the Evangelist Church.
Kovalcin, John A. '81 (STL) Military Chaplains.
Kovalik, George J. '47 (STP) [2] Minneapolis, MN All Saints Church.
Kovanis, Joel M. '94 (SP) [1] St. Petersburg, FL Cathedral of St. Jude the Apostle.
Kovar, Vaclav '37 (OM) Retired.
Kovarik, James *o.s.cam.* '90 (MIL) [P] Wauwatosa, WI St. Camillus Provincialate; [P] Wauwatosa, WI St. Camillus Community House; [Y] Wauwatosa, WI St. Camillus Institute, Inc.
Kovarik, Peter '91 (RC) Piedmont-Black Hawk, SD Our Lady of the Black Hills Church.
Kovascik, Clement *s.t.* '44 (BLX) Gulfport, MS U.S. Naval Home.
Kovattiyil, Thomas *s.v.d.* '82 (CHI) [N] Chicago, IL Divine Word Theologate.
Kowal, John P. '57 (DOD) Johnson, KS St. Bernadette Church; Ulysses, KS Mary Queen of Peace Church.
Kowalchik, Demetrius *o.s.b.* '45 (JOL) [J] Lisle, IL St. Procopius Abbey.
Kowalczyk, Sigismund '56 (DET) Anchorville, MI Immaculate Conception Church.
Kowalczyk, Thomas M. '67 (SAG) Linwood, MI St. Anne Church.
Kowaleski, Edward '53 (Y) Rock Creek, OH Sacred Heart Church.
Kowalewski, Francis P. '59 (BUF) Fillmore, NY St. Patrick Church.
Kowalewski, Vincent J. *o.s.f.s.* '64 (WIL) [I] Childs, MD Oblates of St. Francis De Sales.
Kowalik, Jacek '79 (VEN) Military Chaplains.
Kowalkowski, Bruno H. *o.p.* '64 (CHI) Chicago, IL Hines V.A. Hospital; [N] Chicago, IL Dominicans (Provincial Office).
Kowalozyk, Adolph M. '88 (BUF) [2] Kenmore, NY Blessed Sacrament Church.
Kowalske, Kevin J. '95 (MIL) [9] West Allis, WI St. Rita's Church.
Kowalski, Alfred J. '51 (NEW) [5] Elizabeth, NJ Immaculate Conception Church.
Kowalski, Edmund *c.m.* '44 (SY) [S] Utica, NY St. Vincent's Mission House.
Kowalski, Eric L. '93 (NEW) [1] East Orange, NJ Holy Name of Jesus Church.
Kowalski, Eugene S. '42 (NEW) [4] Garfield, NJ St. Stanislaus Kostka Church; Retired.
Kowalski, Francis *s.v.d.* '42 (CHI) [B] Techny, IL Divine Word Residence.
Kowalski, George '56 (DET) [2] Wyandotte, MI St. Helena Church; Detroit, MI Wyandotte General Hospital.
Kowalski, Isidore *o.f.m.conv.* '43 (FR) [7] New Bedford, MA Our Lady of Perpetual Help Church.
Kowalski, James C. '43 (GR) On Special Assignment.
Kowalski, John *c.m.* '38 (SY) [S] Utica, NY St. Vincent's Mission House.
Kowalski, Kasimierz A. '91 (NY) [2] New York, NY St. Agnes Church.
Kowalski, Lawrence T. '69 (OKL) Pauls Valley, OK St. Catherine of Siena Church.
Kowalski, Leo S. '39 (MIL) Retired.
Kowalski, Matthew F. *o.s.b.* '87 (RCK) [H] Aurora, IL Marmion Abbey-St. Augustine's Abbey.
Kowalski, Ralph E. '42 (DET) Retired.
Kowalski, Ronald C. '81 (MIL) Twin Lakes, WI St. John's Church.
Kowalski, Wladyslaw J. '51 (LC) Peplin, WI St. John the Baptist Church.
Kowalski, Wladyslaw J. '51 (SUP) Retired.

Kowalsky, Myron *o.f.m.cap* '58 (MIL) [P] Milwaukee, WI St. Conrad House.
Kowatch, Thomas P. '85 (CLV) [4] Lakewood, OH St. James Church; Cleveland, OH Lakewood Hospital.
Kownacki, Francis J. *s.j.* '60 (SCR) [C] Scranton, PA University of Scranton.
Kownacki, Raymond F. '60 (BEL) Leave of Absence.
Kownacki, Robert '63 (CHI) [J] Chicago, IL Resurrection Medical Center.
Kownacki, Robert '63 (SAT) On Duty Outside the Archdiocese.
Kowrach, Edward '38 (SPK) Retired.
Koychick, George J. '49 (HBG) Palmyra, PA Holy Spirit Church.
Koys, Thomas R. '85 (CHI) [25] Chicago, IL St. Bede the Venerable Church.
Koza, John J., III '77 (PBR) Warren, OH SS. Peter and Paul's Church.
Kozacheson, Roman M. *o.f.m.cap.* '61 (PH) [79] Philadelphia, PA St. John the Evangelist Church.
Kozak, David J. '83 (ALN) Frackville, PA Annunciation B.V.M. Church; [C] Ashland, PA Cardinal Brennan Jr./Sr. High School.
Kozak, Eligius *o.f.m.conv.* '42 (BUF) [O] Athol Springs, NY Father Justin Rosary Hour Radio Apostolate.
Kozak, Remiquius A. '54 (BLX) Leakesville, MS South Mississippi Correctional Institution.
Kozak, Richard J. '67 (CHI) Melrose Park, IL Sacred Heart Church.
Kozanecki, Charles *o.f.m.conv.* '53 (MRY) Pismo Beach, CA St. Paul the Apostle Church.
Kozar, Joseph F. *s.m.* '77 (CIN) [D] Dayton, OH The University of Dayton; [M] Dayton, OH Marianist Provincialate.
Kozel, Msgr. Robert F. '61 (ALN) [1] Bethlehem, PA St. Anne Church.
Kozen, Bert S. '82 (SCR) Canton, PA St. Michael Church.
Koziczuk, Andrew '79 (SAC) [15] Sacramento, CA St. Joseph's Church.
Kozien, Casimir J. '50 (CHI) [23] Chicago, IL St. Bartholomew Church; Retired.
Kozikowski, Thad '75 (GF) Glasgow, MT St. Raphael's Church.
Kozina, Mark *o.f.m.* (CHI) [101] Chicago, IL St. Jerome Church; [N] Chicago, IL Croatian Franciscan Custody of the Holy Family.
Kozina, Vladimir '45 (OAK) Retired.
Koziol, John A. *o.f.m.conv.* '88 (ATL) Jonesboro, GA St. Philip Benizi Church.
Koziol, Stanley N. '58 (BGP) [3] Stratford, CT St. Mark's Church.
Kozlak, Stanley F. '74 (STP) Lonsdale, MN Immaculate Conception Church; Special Assignment.
Kozlowski, Daniel E. '72 (LC) Tomah, WI St. Mary (Immaculate Conception) Church; Warrens, WI St. Andrew Church.
Kozlowski, Edward A. '38 (NY) Bronx, NY Veterans Administration Hospital.
Kozlowski, Joseph F. '73 (BUF) Holley, NY St. Mary Church; Kendall, NY St. Mark Church.
Kozlowski, Joseph P. '49 (RVC) Glen Head, NY St. Hyacinth Church; Retired.
Kozlowski, Louis '38 (E) Retired.
Kozlowski, Msgr. Raymond J. '61 (BUF) [34] Buffalo, NY Immaculate Heart of Mary Church.
Kozlowski, Theodore '58 (GR) [18] Grand Rapids, MI Our Lady of Sorrows Church.
Kozma, Raymond M. '70 (BRK) Absent on Leave.
Kozminski, Msgr. Max M. '60 (BUF) [10] Cheektowaga, NY Queen of Martyrs Church.
Kozoil, Micah E. '76 (GBG) Clymer, PA Church of the Resurrection.
Kozon, John A. '32 (NOR) Retired.
Kozub, Tomasz *s.ch.* '92 (BAL) [36] Baltimore, MD Holy Rosary Church.
Kozuch, John L. *s.d.s.* '58 (NEW) [N] Verona, NJ The Salvatorian Fathers.
Kozyra, Oscar *o.de.m.* '73 (SP) [O] St. Petersburg, FL St. Peter Nolasco Residence.
Krach, Joseph W. '57 (BAL) Retired.
Kraeger, David *t.o.r.* '68 (FWT) Scotland, TX St. Boniface Church; Windthorst, TX St. Mary Church.
Kraemer, Bartholomew *o.s.b.* '64 (DET) [K] Detroit, MI St. Sylvester Monastery.
Kraemer, Edwin J. '55 (SCL) [7] St. Cloud, MN St. Michael Church.
Kraemer, John A. '57 (RCK) Sandwich, IL St. Paul Church.
Kraeszig, Charles J. '52 (IND) Retired.
Krafchak, John S. '56 (SCR) [5] Nanticoke, PA St. Mary of Czestochowa Church.
Krafcik, Andrew W.P. '59 (ARL) Dale City, VA Holy Family Church; Manassas, VA Sacred Heart Church; Retired.
Krafinski, Thomas S. *c.m.* '68 (BRK) [66] Brooklyn, NY St. John the Baptist Church; [U] Brooklyn, NY St. John the Baptist Rectory.
Kraft, Niles E. *o.f.m.* '55 (GLP) Navajo, NM St. Berard Church.
Kraft, Thomas D. *o.p.* '86 (OAK) [N] Oakland, CA Western Dominican Province.
Kraft, Msgr. William A. '51 (SD) Retired.
Kraft, William L. '86 (STO) San Andreas, CA St. Andrew Church.
Krah, James B. '71 (PIT) Darlington, PA St. Rose of Lima Church.
Krah, Joseph '63 (SB) Ontario, CA St. George Church.
Krahel, David H. '86 (BGP) [6] Stamford, CT Our Lady Star of the Sea Church.
Krahenbuhl, Gary L. '84 (MAD) [1] Beloit, WI Our Lady of the Assumption Church.
Krahman, Philip G. '72 (STL) Richmond Heights, MO Little Flower, St. Teresa of the Infant Jesus Church; St. Louis, MO St. John's Mercy Medical Ctr.; [K] Creve Coeur, MO St. John's Mercy Medical Center.
Kraig, Robert J. '72 (CLV) Strongsville, OH St. John Neumann Church.
Krajci, Anthony *s.v.d.* '45 (CHI) [B] Techny, IL Divine Word Residence.
Krajcovic, Bernard '56 (STU) Yorkville, OH St. Lucy's Church.
Krajewski, Henry T. *o.f.m.cap.* '58 (PAT) [M] Oak Ridge-Milton, NJ St. Stanislaus B. M. Friary.
Krajewski, Henry T. *o.f.m.cap.* '58 (TR) [4] Trenton, NJ Holy Cross Church.
Krajewski, Joseph A. '73 (MET) South Amboy, NJ Sacred Heart Church.
Krajewski, Paul A. (PAT) Retired.
Krajewski, Msgr. Walter M. (BUF) Retired.
Krajicek, Robert P. (OM) Retired.
Krajnik, Paul '50 (CLV) [2] Lorain, OH SS. Cyril and Methodius Church.
Kraker, James J. '65 (SUP) Erin, WI St. Patrick Church; Hammond, WI Immaculate Conception Church.
Kraker, John J. '59 (CLV) [2] Euclid, OH St. Felicitas Church.
Kraker, Joseph H. '64 (CLV) [18] Akron, OH St. Vincent Church.
Krakovsky, Reginald *t.o.r.* '52 (ALT) [F] Newry, PA St. Bernardine Monastery.
Kraljic, John R. '69 (NY) [E] New York, NY Cardinal Spellman High School.
Krall, Jack '63 (P) [22] Portland, OR Church of St. Joseph the Worker.
Krall, Kenneth R. *s.j.* '71 (SPK) [C] Spokane, WA Gonzaga University.
Kralovich, Louis W. '60 (TR) [3] Toms River, NJ St. Luke Church; [R] Princeton, NJ Campus Ministry for the Diocese of Trenton.
Kram, Charles '75 (VIC) Yoakum, TX St. Joseph Church.
Kram, Thomas '49 (PIT) [O] Pittsburgh, PA Sisters of St. Francis of the Providence of God; [R] Pittsburgh, PA Priests' Benefit Plan of the Diocese of Pittsburgh.
Kramarz, Anthony '50 (MET) Retired.
Kramberg, Donald F. '74 (OG) Au Sable Forks, NY Holy Name Church; Black Brook, NY St. Matthew Church.
Kramer, Anthony '95 (RC) [B] Bethlehem, SD Holy Nativity Monastery.
Kramer, Bernard *c.ss.r.* '36 (KC) [32] Kansas City, MO Our Lady of Perpetual Help Church; [J] Kansas City, MO Redemptorists of Kansas City.
Kramer, Carl '52 (SAL) Hays, KS Immaculate Heart of Mary Church.
Kramer, Daniel J. *c.m.* '47 (PH) [Z] Philadelphia, PA Congregation of the Mission.
Kramer, Frank (WDC) [44] Washington, DC St. Vincent De Paul Church.
Kramer, George C. '53 (BO) On Duty Outside the Archdiocese.
Kramer, George J. '62 (JC) Special Assignments.
Kramer, Herbert *s.m.* '34 (SAT) [K] San Antonio, TX St. Joseph's Community.
Kramer, James F. '68 (CLV) Westlake, OH St. Bernadette Church.
Kramer, James G. '48 (MAD) Westport, WI St. Mary of the Lake Church.
Kramer, James K. (PEO) [1] Rock Island, IL St. Mary Church.
Kramer, Lawrence A. '60 (FTW) [12] Fort Wayne, IN Our Lady of Good Hope Church.
Kramer, Noel *o.f.m. conv.* (LSC) Carlsbad, NM St. Edward Church.
Kramer, Peter L. '79 (BIS) [5] Dickinson, ND St. Wenceslaus Church.
Kramer, Richard R. '66 (RCK) Harvard, IL St. Joseph Church.
Kramer, Robert L. *c.s.c.* '64 (PHX) [F] Phoenix, AZ Holy Cross Congregation of Casa Santa Cruz.
Kramer, Scott T. *c.pp.s.* '90 (CIN) [U] Dayton, OH Community Support Charitable Trust.
Kramer, Scott T. *c.pp.s.* '90 (COL) [23] Columbus, OH St. James the Less Church.
Kramer, Thomas '78 (DET) Absent on Leave.
Kramer, Thomas E. '58 (BIS) [1] Bismarck, ND Cathedral of the Holy Spirit.
Kramer, Urban J. *s.j.* '49 (STL) [P] St. Louis, MO The Jesuits of the Missouri Province.
Kramer, Urban J. *s.j.* '49 (TLS) [E] Tulsa, OK Saint Francis Hospital, Inc.
Kramer, William J. *c.pp.s.* '44 (LFT) [A] Rensselaer, IN Saint Joseph's College.
Kramer, William J. '73 (CIN) Beavercreek, OH St. Luke Church.
Kramis, Joseph '57 (SEA) Retired.
Kramlich, Lloyd P. *s.d.s.* '58 (PHX) [4] Mesa, AZ Queen of Peace Church.
Kramper, James P. *s.j.* '44 (OM) [K] Omaha, NE Jesuit Community At Creighton University.
Kramper, James V. '73 (OM) Emerson, NE Sacred Heart Church; Pender, NE St. John Church.
Kranch, Peter V. '51 (ALB) West Taghkanic, NY Holy Cross Church.
Krank, Michael T. '52 (BIS) Regent, ND St. Henry Church.
Krantz, Ernest *c.pp.s.* '76 (GRY) [A] Whiting, IN Calumet College of St. Joseph.
Krantz, Robert V. '78 (SFS) Parkston, SD Sacred Heart Church.
Kranyc, Andrew G. '87 (WH) [3] Huntington, WV Sacred Heart Church; [4] Huntington, WV St. Peter Claver Church.
Kranz, Stephen *o.s.b.* '55 (BIS) Mandaree, ND St. Anthony Church; Fort Berthold Reservation, ND Sacred Heart Indian Mission Church; [A] Richardton, ND Assumption Abbey.
Krapfl, Daniel A. '58 (DUB) [5] Dubuque, IA St. Patrick's Church; [9] Dubuque, IA Holy Trinity Church.
Krapfl, Gary '72 (DUB) Decorah, IA St. Benedict's Church.
Krasauskas, Rapolas (NOR) [G] Putnam, CT Matulaitis Nursing Home Inc.
Krasen, John W. '60 (CLV) Westlake, OH St. Bernadette Church.
Krasevac, Edward *o.p.* '77 (OAK) [A] Berkeley, CA Dominican School of Philosophy and Theology; [A] Berkeley, CA Dominican School of Philosophy and Theology; [N] Berkeley, CA St. Thomas Aquinas House.
Krasic, Ljubo *o.f.m.* (CHI) [N] Chicago, IL Croatian Franciscan Custody of the Holy Family.
Krasman, James *o.f.m.* '83 (DET) [T] Detroit, MI St. John Health System.
Krasman, James *o.f.m.* '86 (SAG) Hemlock, MI St. Mary Church.
Krason, Edward J. '58 (FTW) Goshen, IN St. John the Evangelist Church.
Krastel, Francis W. '54 (WDC) St. Mary's City, MD St. Cecilia Church; [S] Washington, DC Archdiocesan Campus Ministry.
Kratz, Conrad J. *o. praem.* '73 (GB) [5] De Pere, WI Our Lady of Lourdes Church; [I] De Pere, WI St. Joseph Priory.
Kratz, Lawrence *o.s.b.* '52 (SFS) [F] Marvin, SD Blue Cloud Abbey.
Kraus, Bill *o.f.m.cap.* '73 (SAL) [H] Hays, KS Comeau Catholic Campus Center at Fort Hays State University; [H] Hays, KS Comeau Catholic Campus Center at Fort Hays State University.
Kraus, Charles A. '58 (BRK) [29] Brooklyn, NY St. Charles Borromeo Church.
Kraus, Conrad L. '67 (E) Girard, PA St. John the Evangelist Church.
Kraus, David *o.m.i.* '57 (BEL) [I] Belleville, IL Retreat and Renewal Center.
Kraus, David H. '67 (DOD) Elkhart, KS St. Joan of Arc Church.
Kraus, Msgr. Donald W. '54 (PIT) [73] Pittsburgh, PA Holy Wisdom Church.
Kraus, Leonard E. *s.j.* '72 (STL) [35] St. Louis, MO St. Francis Xavier Church; [P] St. Louis, MO Jesuit Community Corporation at St. Louis University - Jesuit Hall.
Kraus, Philip D. *s.j.* '75 (STL) [P] St. Louis, MO White House Retreat Jesuit Community; [T] St. Louis, MO White House Retreat.
Kraus, Robert J. '42 (STL) Retired.
Kraus, Stephen (ROC) Dansville, NY St. Mary Church.
Kraus, Msgr. Theodore W. '63 (BUF) On Duty Outside the Diocese.
Kraus, William *o.f.m.cap.* '73 (SAL) [D] Hays, KS St. Bonaventure's Friary.
Krause, Bruce J. *c.m.* '82 (PH) [Z] Philadelphia, PA Congregation of the Mission.
Krause, Edward *c.s.c.* '70 (E) [6] Erie, PA Immaculate Conception Church.
Krause, Edward C. *c.s.c.* '66 (E) [B] Erie, PA Gannon University.
Krause, Edward C. *c.s.c.* '66 (FTW) [J] South Bend, IN Congregation of Holy Cross Indiana Province Provincial House.
Krause, Frederick *o.f.m.cap.* '67 (PH) [79] Philadelphia, PA St. John the Evangelist Church.
Krause, Joseph A. '68 (TUC) Payson, AZ Saint Philip the Apostle Church.
Krause, Karl H. '92 (HON) [9] Honolulu, HI St. John the Baptist Church.
Krause, Kenneth J. '65 (ORG) Costa Mesa, CA St. Joachim Church.
Krauth, Lothar '73 (GF) [4] Great Falls, MT Our Lady

of Lourdes Church.
Krautkremer, Leo D. '66 (STP) Golden Valley, MN North Memorial Hospital.
Krautsack, Blaise P. *o.praem.* '74 (WIL) [B] Claymont, DE Archmere Academy; [I] Claymont, DE Immaculate Conception Priory of the Canons Regular of Premontre.
Krawczyk, Henry R. '78 (PIT) [2] Munhall, PA St. Maximilian Kolbe Church.
Krawinkel, Msgr. Robert M. '58 (STL) Ladue, MO Church of the Annunziata.
Krawontka, Stefan '77 (SCR) Dickson City, PA Visitation of the Blessed Virgin Mary Church.
Kraynak, Nicholas '59 (PSC) Old Forge, PA St. Nicholas Church.
Kraynak, William B. '81 (Y) Louisville, OH Sacred Heart of Mary Church.
Kraynyak, Basil William '66 (PSC) New Port Richey, FL St. Anne's Church.
Krebs, Bruce '78 (BIS) Hettinger, ND Holy Trinity Church.
Krebs, Msgr. Donald H. '55 (CR) Moorhead, MN St. Joseph's Church.
Krebs, Gerard H. '63 (E) [20] Erie, PA St. Joseph Church.
Krebs, Msgr. Henry L. '60 (E) Du Bois, PA St. Michael Church.
Krebs, John F. '57 (CHI) Ingleside, IL St. Bede Church.
Krebs, Paul F. '57 (COV) Retired.
Krebs, Peter *s.t.* '69 (PAT) [M] Stirling, NJ Holy Spirit Missionary Cenacle; [M] Stirling, NJ Shrine of St. Joseph.
Kreckel, Robert G. '54 (ROC) Ontario, NY St. Mary of the Lake Church.
Kredel, Thomas E. '72 (PIT) [31] Pittsburgh, PA St. Louise de Marillac Church.
Kreder, Michael J. '85 (NEW) Garwood, NJ Church of St. Anne.
Kreft, Henry S. '45 (DET) Retired.
Kreher, Albert E. '64 (BEL) Prairie du Rocher, IL St. Joseph Church.
Kreidler, Thomas W. (CIN) Twenty Mile Stand, OH St. Margaret of York Church.
Kreig, Robert A. *c.s.c.* '73 (FTW) [A] Notre Dame, IN Moreau Seminary.
Kreikemeier, Leo A. '43 (OM) Retired.
Kreilein, Philip J. '74 (EVN) Ferdinand, IN St. Ferdinand Church.
Kreimer, Richard *glmy.* '79 (CIN) [M] Fairfield, OH Headquarters of Glenmary Home Missioners.
Kreimes, Paul '72 (DET) [A] Detroit, MI Sacred Heart Major Seminary, Inc.
Kreiser, Thomas L. '94 (NY) Monroe, NY Sacred Heart Church.
Krejci, Msgr. Albert L. '41 (OM) [8] Sarpy Co., NE St. Bernadette Church; Retired.
Krekelberg, Richard G. '73 (LA) Santa Monica, CA St. Clement Church.
Krekelberg, William '70 (ORG) Laguna Beach, CA St. Catherine of Siena Church.
Krelovich, Michael '95 (SB) Indio, CA Our Lady of Perpetual Help Church.
Kremeier, James '55 (GI) Retired.
Kremen, Timothy M. *o.s.m.* '61 (CHI) [N] Chicago, IL Servite Friars - Eastern Province.
Kremen, Timothy M. *o.s.m.* '61 (STL) Affton, MO Seven Holy Founders Church.
Kremer, Barry *o.carm.* '46 (JOL) [J] Darien, IL Carmelite Fathers Provincial Office.
Kremer, John R. '59 (DUB) Mason City, IA Holy Family Church; [G] Mason City, IA Newman Catholic.
Kremer, Leroy M. '68 (SCL) Little Falls, MN Our Lady of Lourdes Church.
Kremer, Philip *o.s.b.* '57 (RCK) [H] Aurora, IL Marmion Abbey-St. Augustine's Abbey.
Kremmell, William T. '66 (BO) [1] Plymouth, MA Blessed Kateri Tekakwitha Church.
Kremp, Bruno *o.f.m.* '65 (CIN) [M] Cincinnati, OH St. Francis Seraph Friary; [M] Cincinnati, OH St. Francis Center.
Krempa, Adam J. '90 (BUR) Chittenden, VT St. Robert Church; Rutland, VT Immaculate Heart of Mary Church; Sherburne, VT Our Lady of the Mountains Church.
Krempa, Stanley J. '70 (ARL) [7] Alexandria, VA St. Mary's Church.
Krenek, Fred '92 (VIC) [5] Victoria, TX St. Mary's Church.
Krenik, Michael J. '84 (STP) White Bear Lake, MN St. Pius X Church.
Krenik, Robert L. '84 (RIC) Abingdon, VA Christ the King Church; Marion, VA St. John the Evangelist Church.
Krenik, Thomas '77 (STP) [A] St. Paul, MN The Saint Paul Seminary; [C] St. Paul, MN University of St. Thomas.
Krepp, Theodore '82 (PSC) Kingston, PA St. Mary's Church.
Kreps, Anthony L. '38 (CLV) Amherst, OH St. Joseph Church; Retired.
Kresinski, Daniel J. '70 (E) [1] Sharon, PA Sacred Heart Church.
Kresmer, Donald J. '56 (DET) Detroit, MI Bon Secours; Retired.
Kress, Joseph J. '37 (DET) Retired.
Kress, Msgr. Justin A. '39 (DUB) Retired.
Kress, Robert '58 (EVN) On Duty Outside the Diocese.
Kret, John A. '61 (CHI) [N] Chicago, IL St. Rita Monastery.
Krettek, Daniel '78 (DM) Cumberland, IA St. Timothy Church; Griswold, IA Our Lady Of Grace Church.
Krettek, G. Thomas *s.j.* '82 (OM) [K] Omaha, NE Campion House.
Kretz, Edward J. '56 (GBG) [G] Greensburg, PA St. Anne Home.
Kretz, James C. '91 (PEO) Rutland, IL Sacred Heart Church, Toluca, IL St. Ann's Church.
Kreuzer, Eugene T. '52 (MIL) Retired.
Kreuzer, Msgr. Gerald J. '38 (BUF) Retired.
Kreuzer, Msgr. Gerald J. '56 (BUF) Angola, NY Most Precious Blood Church.
Krewer, Edward M. '43 (PEO) Retired.
Kribs, Charles R. '51 (BEL) Retired.
Kribs, Don R. (LA) Monrovia, CA Immaculate Conception Church.
Kricek, Henry C. '80 (CHI) Skokie, IL St. Peter Church.
Krick, Howard K. '58 (PH) Retired.
Krieg, Charles F. *c.m.* '63 (MET) [J] Plainsboro, NJ Vincentian Renewal Center.
Krieg, Msgr. Gerald C. '53 (ROC) [M] Rochester, NY Diocesan Office of Campus Ministry.
Krieg, Msgr. Gerard C. '53 (ROC) Geneva, NY St. Stephen Church.
Krieg, Jerome L. '38 (DET) Retired; [I] Waterford, MI Lourdes Nursing Home.
Krieg, Michael '82 (SPK) [N] Pullman, WA Washington State University - St. Thomas More Chapel, Newman Center.
Krieg, Peter *o.f.m.* '40 (OAK) [9] Oakland, CA St. Elizabeth's Church.
Krieg, Peter *o.f.m.* '43 (OAK) [N] Oakland, CA Franciscan Friars.
Krieg, Robert A. *c.s.c.* '73 (FTW) [B] Notre Dame, IN University of Notre Dame Du Lac.
Krieg, Thomas J. '92 (LC) [2] Eau Claire, WI Newman Community Church; [J] Eau Claire, WI St. Bede Priory; [L] Eau Claire, WI Newman Parish.
Kriege, Roger L. '64 (COV) Williamstown, KY St. William Church.
Kriegel, Msgr. Henry A. '70 (E) [21] Erie, PA St. Jude the Apostle Church.
Krieger, Msgr. Wilfred L. '46 (STL) Retired.
Kriegshauser, J. Laurence *o.s.b.* '69 (STL) [F] Creve Coeur, MO St. Louis Priory School; [P] St. Louis, MO The Abbey of St. Mary and St. Louis.
Kriegsmann, William A. '44 (RCK) Retired.
Krier, John P. '69 (GF) On Duty Outside of the Diocese.
Krier, John P. '69 (SPK) Davenport, WA Immaculate Conception Church; Harrington, WA St. Francis of Assisi Church; Reardan, WA St. Michael Church.
Krigler, Bela *sch.p.* '50 (MIL) [22] Milwaukee, WI St. Emeric's Church.
Krijnen, Joseph G. '46 (PHX) [3] Tempe, AZ Resurrection Church; Retired.
Krile, George F. '41 (FAR) Retired.
Krile, Stephen '83 (COL) Wellston, OH SS. Peter and Paul Church.
Kriley, Victor *o.f.m.cap.* '64 (HBG) [2] York, PA St. Joseph Church.
Krill, Jude Michael *o.s.f.conv.* '83 (PH) [C] Aston, PA Neumann College.
Krill, Jude Michael *o.f.m.conv.* '83 (TR) Riverside, NJ St. Casimir Church.
Kringe, Charles J. '64 (SCR) Unassigned or Leave of Absence.
Krings, James A. '71 (STL) [31] St. Louis, MO St. Cronan Church; St. Louis, MO St. Mary's Health Ctr.; [K] St. Louis, MO St. Mary's Health Center.
Krinzner, William R. '79 (CLV) [D] Cleveland, OH Holy Name High School.
Krisak, Anthony F. (WDC) [V] Washington, DC Missionary Vehicle Association, Inc.
Krisak, Anthony F. *s.s.* '75 (TR) On Duty Outside the Diocese.
Krisanda, Stephen J. *m.s.* '60 (ORL) [3] Orlando, FL Good Shepherd Church.
Krische, Francis '57 (KCK) [4] Topeka, KS Most Pure Heart of Mary Church.
Krische, James J. '91 (BRK) [244] Queens, NY St. Teresa of Avila Church.
Krische, Otto *o.f.m.* '37 (CIN) [M] Cincinnati, OH St. Clement Friary.
Krische, Vincent E. '64 (KCK) [J] Lawrence, KS St. Lawrence Catholic Campus Center at the University of Kansas and Residence.
Krisciunevicius, Victor '49 (DET) Retired.
Krisman, Ronald F. '73 (LUB) Levelland, TX St. Michael's Church.
Krispinsky, Msgr. Joseph A. '23 (Y) Retired.
Kriss, Aaron J. '91 (PIT) Natrona Heights, PA Our Lady of the Most Blessed Sacrament Church.
Kriss, David J. '79 (PIT) Clairton, PA St. Clare of Assisi Church.
Kriss, Zigford J. '58 (HRT) [2] West Hartford, CT St. Helena Church; Special and other (Arch)Diocesan Assignment.
Kristancic, Dennis J. '83 (CLV) [26] Cleveland, OH St. Henry Church; [11] Lorain, OH St. Stanislaus Church.
Kristofak, Terence *c.p.* (HRT) [C] West Hartford, CT Saint Joseph College; [M] West Hartford, CT Holy Family Monastery/Retreat; [Q] Farmington, CT Holy Family Retreat House.
Kristofak, Terence *c.p.* '69 (MET) [H] South River, NJ Passionist Provincial Office.
Kristy, Mark *o.c.d.* '85 (SR) [M] Oakville, CA Carmelite House of Prayer.
Krivak, John A. '82 (ALN) [C] Allentown, PA Allentown Central Catholic High School; [O] Kutztown, PA Christopher House; [O] Kutztown, PA Christopher House.
Krivanek, George E. *s.j.* '59 (LA) [R] Los Angeles, CA Columbiere House.
Kriz, Mark G. *s.j.* '95 (BUF) [O] Buffalo, NY Canisius Jesuit Community; [R] Williamsville, NY Newman Club Chaplains.
Krizmanich, Germain *o.f.m.* (CIN) [M] Cincinnati, OH St. Francis Center.
Krizner, William R. '79 (CLV) [2] Parma, OH St. Bridget Church.
Krlis, William F. '68 (BRK) [176] Queens, NY Holy Child Jesus Church.
Krock, George E. *c.m.* '50 (ALN) Roseto, PA Our Lady of Mt. Carmel Church.
Kroeger, Gerald C. *o.p.* '58 (CHI) Summit, IL St. Joseph Church; [N] Chicago, IL Dominicans (Provincial Office).
Kroeger, James H. *m.m.* '75 (NY) [Z] Maryknoll, NY Maryknoll Fathers and Brothers.
Kroeger, John '72 (CIN) Monroe, OH Our Lady of Sorrows Church.
Kroeger, Robert S. '94 (MIL) [48] Milwaukee, WI St. Margaret Mary Church.
Kroeger, Timothy D. '90 (LFT) Kokomo, IN St. Joan of Arc Church.
Kroger, Daniel *o.f.m.* '73 (CIN) [M] Cincinnati, OH St. Francis Seraph Friary.
Kroger, John H. '55 (COV) Bellevue, KY St. Anthony Church.
Krogman, David L. '81 (SFS) Military Chaplains.
Krogman, Philip J. '60 (MAD) Kieler, WI Immaculate Conception Church.
Krogmann, David J. (FAR) Grand Forks, ND Grand Forks Air Force Base; [I] Grand Forks, ND Air Force Base.
Krogol, Jude *o.s.b.* '65 (SP) [O] St. Leo, FL St. Leo Abbey.
Krol, Boleslaus '61 (DET) [13] Detroit, MI St. Bartholomew Church; [44] Detroit, MI St. Louis the King Church.
Krolczyk, David B. '72 (CHI) Posen, IL St. Stanislaus Bishop and Martyr Church.
Krolikowski, Lucian *o.f.m.conv.* '46 (BUF) [O] Athol Springs, NY Father Justin Rosary Hour Radio Apostolate.
Krolikowski, Walter P. *s.j.* '57 (CHI) [C] Chicago, IL Jesuit Community at Loyola University of Chicago.
Kroll, Anthony '61 (SCL) Flensburg, MN Sacred Heart Church.
Kroll, Lawrence W. '86 (KAL) [3] Kalamazoo, MI St. Mary Church.
Kromenaker, Joseph (CHI) [58] Chicago, IL St. Ferdinand Church.
Kromer, Stanley S. *o.carm.* '50 (VEN) Englewood, FL St. Raphael Church.
Kron, Kenneth M. '87 (YAK) Quincy, WA St. Pius X Church.
Kronewitter, Frank '62 (FTW) [H] Fort Wayne, IN Saint Anne Home & Retirement Community.
Kronkowski, Leonard J. '55 (GRY) Rolling Prairie, IN St. John Kanty Church.
Kropac, Robert J. '82 (CLV) [26] Cleveland, OH St. Henry Church.
Kropf, Richard '58 (GAY) [H] Johannesburg, MI Stella Maris Hermitage.
Kropf, Richard '58 (LAN) On Duty Outside the Diocese.
Kropiwnicki, Henry K. '58 (FR) [11] New Bedford, MA St. Casimir Church.
Kros, Donald M. '59 (OM) Lynch, NE Assumption B.V.M. Church; [O] Lynch, NE Niobrara Valley House of Renewal.
Krosfield, George '70 (ALX) Simmesport, LA Christ the King Church.
Krosnicki, Thomas A. *s.v.d.* '66 (CHI) [B] Techny, IL Divine Word Residence; [N] Techny, IL Society of the Divine Word, Provincial Headquarter-Chicago Prov.; [U] Techny, IL S.V.D., Catholic Universities, Inc.; [U] Techny, IL Divine Word Missionaries, Inc., Divine Word Funds, Inc.
Krotec, Ivan '70 (STN) [3] Chicago, IL SS. Volodymyr and Olha Church.
Krough, Jack L. '76 (WIN) Austin, MN St. Edward's Church.

Krouse, Dennis W. '68 (SD) [B] San Diego, CA University of San Diego.
Krozser, John J. *c.m.* '56 (MOB) [8] Montgomery, AL Resurrection Catholic Church.
Krozser, John J. *c.m.* '56 (NEW) On Duty Outside the Archdiocese.
Krudwig, William C. '61 (SPC) El Dorado Springs, MO St. Elizabeth Church.
Krueger, Robert W. '56 (P) [4] Portland, OR St. Andrew Church.
Kruel, Ronald G. *o.p.* '78 (DEN) [28] Denver, CO St. Dominic's Church.
Krugel, Stephen A. '88 (HRT) [4] New Haven, CT St. Bernadette's Church.
Krukowski, Francis V. '58 (HRT) South Windsor, CT St. Margaret Mary Church.
Krul, Valentine C. '77 (SY) New York Mills, NY St. Mary Church.
Krulak, Michael '95 (PSC) Jacksonville, FL Protection of the Mother of God Church; Ormond Beach, FL Holy Dormition Church.
Krull, Michael G. '86 (MET) Port Reading, NJ St. Anthony of Padua Church.
Krumm, Gustave R. *o.f.m.* '82 (ORG) [3] Huntington Beach, CA SS. Simon and Jude Church.
Krumm, John E. '76 (CIN) [6] Dayton, OH Assumption Church; [20] Dayton, OH Our Lady of Mercy Church.
Krumpe, William F. '66 (CIN) [14] Cincinnati, OH St. Bartholomew Church.
Krupa, Alexander *o.f.m.* '31 (TR) Roebling, NJ Holy Assumption Church.
Krupa, Msgr. Francis A. (BUF) Retired.
Krupa, Msgr. Francis A. '40 (BUF) [K] Buffalo, NY Mercy Hospital.
Krupa, James M. *s.j.* '88 (BO) [W] Boston, MA The Society of Jesus of New England-Provincial Offices.
Krupa, Stephen T. *s.j.* '86 (DET) [K] Detroit, MI Jesuit Provincial Office-Detroit Province of the Society of Jesus.
Krupa, Stephen T. *s.j.* '86 (OAK) [N] Berkeley, CA Jesuit Community at Jesuit School of Theology at Berkeley.
Krupa, Thomas J. '71 (ALB) Castleton-on-Hudson, NY Sacred Heart Church.
Krupa, William J. *o.s.a.* '44 (PH) [18] Philadelphia, PA St. Augustine Church.
Krupich, Thomas J. '88 (FAR) Tappen, ND St. Paul's Church.
Krupka, Michael '77 (SJP) [4] Akron, OH Holy Ghost Church.
Krupnick, Marion I. '54 (HRT) [2] New Britain, CT Holy Cross Church.
Krupp, Albert '65 (CLV) El Salvador, C.A., OH Parroquial Immaculada Concepcion.
Kruse, Clarence '57 (DUB) Retired.
Kruse, Msgr. Clement '41 (SAL) Retired.
Kruse, David '94 (BAL) [70] Baltimore, MD Our Lady of Mount Carmel Church.
Kruse, James '96 (PEO) Pekin, IL St. Joseph's Church.
Kruse, Jay L. '91 (OM) [38] Omaha, NE St. Pius X Church; [B] Omaha, NE V.J. & Angela Skutt Catholic High School of Omaha.
Kruse, Phillip '81 (DM) [2] Council Bluffs, IA Our Lady, Queen of Apostles Church.
Kruse, Robert J. *c.s.c.* '58 (FR) [B] North Easton, MA Stonehill College.
Krusinski, Andrew J. '45 (SCR) [4] Williamsport, PA Holy Rosary Church.
Krusling, Msgr. James L. '32 (CIN) Retired.
Krusling, Lawrence R. '51 (CIN) [79] Cincinnati, OH St. Rose of Lima Church.
Krutcik, Stanley F. '80 (WOR) Manchaug, MA St. Anne's Church.
Krutzik, Norman '57 (GB) Special Assignment.
Kruzel, Leonard M. '83 (CHI) [60] Chicago, IL Five Holy Martyrs Church.
Krylowicz, Mark J. '91 (CHI) [73] Chicago, IL St. Gregory Church.
Krymski, Christopher L. *o.s.m.* '83 (CHI) [15] Chicago, IL Annunciata Church.
Krymski, Christopher M. *o.s.m.* '83 (CHI) [N] Chicago, IL Servite Friars - Eastern Province.
Krynski, Leo '52 (SUP) Retired.
Krysa, Czeslaw M. '80 (BUF) On Duty Outside the Diocese.
Krysa, Czeslaw M. '80 (DET) [A] Orchard Lake, MI SS. Cyril and Methodius Seminary.
Kryston, Edward '74 (PIT) Baldwin Boro, PA St. Albert the Great Church.
Krystosek, Robert H. '56 (GI) Retired.
Krystosek, Robert H. '56 (NU) Retired.
Kryszak, Marian '56 (SAG) Retired.
Kryszkiewicz, Pawel '93 (CAM) Merchantville, NJ St. Peter's Church.
Krysztofik, Msgr. Joseph M. '50 (MET) Retired.
Kryzston, Stanley W. '88 (TR) [3] Trenton, NJ Holy Angels Church.
Kryzyanski, John *o.f.m.conv.* '82 (BRK) [146] Queens, NY St. Adalbert Church.
Krzysiak, Casimir J. '50 (SY) [15] Utica, NY St. Stanislaus Church.
Krzywda, Leonard *c.r.* '65 (CHI) [D] Chicago, IL Weber High School.
Krzywda, Leonard *c.r.* '65 (SB) [1] Fontana, CA Church of the Resurrection.
Krzywicki, Lance P. '83 (PT) Military Chaplains.
Krzyzaniak, Timothy D. '91 (LAN) Hamburg, MI Holy Spirit Church.
Krzyzanowski, Casimir *m.i.c.* '56 (SPR) [I] Stockbridge, MA Congregation of Marians.
Krzyzopolski, Al '50 (SFS) Retired.
Kselman, John J. *s.s.* '67 (BAL) [M] Baltimore, MD Sulpician Provincial House.
Kselman, John J. *s.s.* '67 (BO) [W] Cambridge, MA Weston Jesuit Community.
Kselman, John J. *s.s.* '67 (TR) On Duty Outside the Diocese.
Kub, Francis Q. '65 (CHI) [191] Chicago, IL St. Simon the Apostle Church.
Kuba, William M. '62 (E) Kane, PA St. Callistus Church.
Kubacki, Anthony '80 (SJP) Johnstown, PA St. John the Baptist Church.
Kubacki, William J. '78 (TOL) [14] Toledo, OH Sacred Heart of Jesus Church.
Kubajak, James '77 (PRM) Northwood, OH St. Michael the Archangel Church.
Kubala, Daniel I. '76 (MIA) [32] Miami, FL St. Thomas the Apostle Church.
Kubart, Francis E. '49 (OM) Leigh, NE St. Mary Church.
Kubat, Alphonse M. '42 (STP) Retired.
Kubeck, John C. '65 (MIL) [O] Brookfield, WI Opus Dei-Prelature of the Holy Cross and Opus Dei.
Kuberski, Leonard '67 (PSC) Dunellen, NJ St. Nicholas Church.
Kubiak, Edward J. '34 (GR) Retired.
Kubiak, Joseph M. *o.f.m.cap.* '74 (MET) [4] New Brunswick, NJ St. Joseph Church; New Brunswick, NJ Robert Wood Johnson University Hospital.
Kubiak, Joseph M. *o.f.m.cap.* '74 (PAT) [M] Oak Ridge-Milton, NJ St. Stanislaus B. M. Friary.
Kubicki, James M. *s.j.* '83 (MIL) [P] Milwaukee, WI Jesuit Provincial Office, Wisconsin Province; [P] Milwaukee, WI Jesuit Community at Marquette University.
Kubik, John M. '49 (DET) [63] Detroit, MI SS. Peter and Paul Church; Retired.
Kubik, Thomas *c.r.* '72 (CHI) [D] Chicago, IL Gordon Technical High School.
Kubina, Eugene *t.o.r.* '53 (ALT) [F] Newry, PA St. Bernardine Monastery.
Kubinski, Scott M. '84 (ROC) Horseheads, NY St. Mary Our Mother Church.
Kubinyi, Julius '51 (PBR) Erie, PA SS. Peter and Paul Church.
Kubis, Alcuin *o.s.b.* '32 (LR) Morrison Bluff, AR SS. Peter and Paul Church.
Kubisiak, Robert P. '72 (OAK) Pleasant Hill, CA Christ the King Church.
Kucan, Jerome *o.f.m.* (CHI) [N] Chicago, IL Croatian Franciscan Custody of the Holy Family.
Kucera, Edward *o.s.b.* '53 (DEN) Aurora, CO Fitzsimons Army Medical Center.
Kucera, Edward *o.s.b.* '53 (JOL) [J] Lisle, IL St. Procopius Abbey.
Kucera, Edward C., Jr. *m.th.* '73 (GAL) Hempstead, TX St. Mary Church.
Kucera, Robert M. *o.s.m.* '53 (CHI) [N] Chicago, IL Servite Friars - Eastern Province.
Kuchar, Bryan '93 (STL) Affton, MO St. Timothy Church.
Kuchar, Michael W. '80 (LAN) [7] Lansing, MI St. Therese Church.
Kucharczyk, Dennis '80 (SAG) Caseville, MI St. Roch Church; Pinnebog, MI St. Felix Church.
Kucharski, Steven M. '77 (MAN) Rollinsford, NH St. Mary Church; Somersworth, NH Holy Trinity Church.
Kuchera, Michael J. *s.j.* '87 (BAL) [D] Baltimore, MD Loyola High School.
Kuchta, Waldemar J. '89 (PRM) Dayton, OH St. Barbara Church.
Kucingis, Msgr. John A. '37 (LA) [54] Los Angeles, CA St. Casimir Church; Retired.
Kucyk, Msgr. Herman W. '57 (DET) [5] Dearborn, MI Divine Child Church.
Kuczaik, Stanislaw *s.ch.* '57 (DET) [K] Sterling Heights, MI Society of Christ Provincial Home.
Kuczborski, Bernard *o.f.m.conv.* '47 (BAL) [20] Baltimore, MD St. Casimir Church.
Kuczborski, Joseph M. '82 (PEO) On Duty Outside the Diocese.
Kuczborski, Joseph M. '82 (PMB) [2] Boca Raton, FL Our Lady of Lourdes Church.
Kuczmanski, Gregory M. '75 (BWN) Edcouch, TX St. Theresa of the Infant Jesus Church.
Kuczynski, Edward P. '77 (PH) Pottstown, PA St. Peter Church.
Kuczynski, Edwin R. *o.s.a.* '47 (CHI) [N] Olympia Fields, IL Tolentine Monastery at Tolentine Center.
Kuczynski, Francis I. '43 (PIT) Retired.
Kuczynski, James H. *m.s.* '73 (HRT) [M] Hartford, CT Missionaries of LaSalette Provincial Secretary.
Kuczynski, John *c.m.* '44 (HRT) Derby, CT St. Michael Church.
Kuczynski, Kazimierz '76 (NEW) [6] Bayonne, NJ Mt. Carmel Church.
Kuder, Donald E. *c.s.b.* '63 (GAL) [K] Houston, TX The Catholic Chaplain Corps.
Kuder, Stephen R. *s.j.* '73 (SPK) [C] Spokane, WA Gonzaga University.
Kudilil, Jim '63 (FRS) Los Banos, CA St. Joseph Church.
Kudlo, Frank '88 (MIA) Absent on Leave.
Kudrick, John '75 (PBR) McKees Rocks, PA Holy Ghost Church.
Kuebler, A.M. Seamus *o.a.s.* (PRT) [L] Peaks Island, ME Mother of the Good Shepherd Monastery by the Sea.
Kuebler, A.M. Seamus '75 (WDC) On Duty Outside the Archdiocese.
Kuechmann, Theodore M. *m.m.* '53 (NY) [Z] Maryknoll, NY Maryknoll Fathers and Brothers.
Kuefer, Edward A. *o.s.f.s.* '55 (TOL) [K] Toledo, OH Oblates of St. Francis de Sales.
Kuehler, Msgr. Norbert '55 (AMA) Borger, TX St. John the Evangelist Church.
Kuehmeier, Carl L. '64 (BUF) West Valley, NY St. John the Baptist Church.
Kuehnemund, H. Thomas '93 (DET) [6] Westland, MI St. Theodore of Canterbury Church.
Kuehner, Joe '91 (SFE) Clayton, NM St. Francis Xavier Church; Roy, NM Holy Family-St. Joseph Church.
Kuehner, Msgr. Ralph J. '50 (WDC) Retired.
Kuenzig, Aloysius A. '43 (PIT) Retired.
Kuenzig, Peter A. '46 (PIT) Retired.
Kuffel, Thomas P. *o.s.* '89 (LIN) Davey, NE St. Mary's Church.
Kuffel, Thomas P. *o.s.* '89 (PCE) On Duty Outside the Diocese.
Kugler, Michael '89 (GLP) Absent on Leave.
Kuhl, Charles E. '54 (CAM) Waterford, NJ St. Anthony Church.
Kuhl, Morgan J. '93 (NY) [204] Staten Island, NY Holy Child Church.
Kuhl, Msgr. Urban B. '45 (BEL) Retired; [K] Belleville, IL Catholic War Veterans.
Kuhlmann, John L. '68 (BUF) Jamestown, NY St. James Church; Jamestown, NY Jamestown Women's Christian Association Hospital.
Kuhlmann, Steven F. *o.p.* '92 (CHI) River Forest, IL St. Vincent Ferrer Priory Church; [N] Chicago, IL Dominicans (Provincial Office).
Kuhn, Christopher A. *c.s.c.* '77 (CHI) [D] Niles, IL Notre Dame High School.
Kuhn, Dennis R. '82 (CHL) [5] Charlotte, NC St. Gabriel Church.
Kuhn, George J. '64 (NY) Rhinebeck, NY The Good Shepherd Church; City, NY Bronx House of Detention; [O] Rhinebeck, NY Astor Home for Children, The.
Kuhn, Herbert C. '57 (SAL) Retired.
Kuhn, James G. '71 (MAD) Roxbury, WI St. Norbert Church.
Kuhn, John C. *ss.cc.* '76 (HON) [11] Honolulu, HI St. Patrick Church.
Kuhn, John G. '58 (WDC) Special Ministries.
Kuhn, John H. '43 (BIS) Retired; [G] Bismarck, ND Emmaus Place.
Kuhn, Richard V. *s.m.* '58 (CAM) [O] Cape May Point, NJ Marianist Family Retreat Center.
Kuhn, Richard W. '53 (DUB) Ossian, IA St. Francis de Sales Church; [E] Calmar, IA Christian Family School.
Kuhn, Thomas A. '67 (CIN) Centerville, OH Incarnation Church.
Kuhn, Thomas W. '57 (TOL) New Washington, OH St. Bernard Church; North Auburn, OH Mother of Sorrows Church.
Kuhns, Howard *c.s.c.* '46 (PHX) Gila Bend, AZ St. Michael Church.
Kuhns, James '61 (SPK) [4] Spokane, WA Our Lady of Fatima Church.
Kuhr, William M. '67 (GB) [6] Appleton, WI Sacred Heart Church.
Kujawa, Patrick R. '95 (HT) [1] Houma, LA Cathedral of St. Francis De Sales.
Kujovsky, Msgr. Thomas (HBG) Retired.
Kujovsky, Thomas J. '57 (HBG) Elizabethtown, PA St. Peter Church.
Kujundzija, Zravko (BO) [3] Cambridge, MA St. Francis of Assisi Church.
Kukla, Gerald F. '67 (SAG) [4] Bay City, MI St. Hyacinth Church.
Kukucka, Joseph G. '65 (PBL) Retired.
Kukulka, Janusz '85 (DET) [A] Orchard Lake, MI SS. Cyril and Methodius Seminary.
Kukulski, Stanislaus C. '55 (DET) Detroit, MI Northville State Hospital; [O] Northville, MI Our Lady of Providence Center.
Kukura, Joseph W. '67 (NEW) On Duty Outside the Archdiocese.
Kula, Frances *m.s.* '54 (MIL) [P] Milwaukee, WI La

Salette Fathers.
Kula, Frank *m.s.* '54 (MIL) [65] Milwaukee, WI St. Paul Church.
Kula, Joseph '55 (BIR) Retired.
Kulak, Joseph F. '66 (RCK) [2] Elgin, IL St. Laurence Church.
Kulandai, Peter '69 (NY) Red Hook, NY St. Christopher Church.
Kulandairajan, S. (NY) Shrub Oak, NY Saint Elizabeth Ann Seton Church.
Kulapurath, Mathew (BRK) [208] Queens, NY Our Lady of the Cenacle Church.
Kulas, John *o.s.b.* '57 (SCL) [I] Collegeville, MN St. John's Abbey, of the Order of St. Benedict.
Kulas, Robert A. '54 (WIN) Retired.
Kulas, William J. '74 (WIN) Rushford, MN St. Joseph's Church.
Kulathinal, Joseph *o.s.b.* (PAT) [M] Clifton, NJ Holy Face of Jesus Monastery.
Kulavich, John J. '83 (SCR) Great Bend, PA St. Lawrence's Church.
Kulbicki, Timothy *o.f.m.conv.* '86 (BAL) [26] Baltimore, MD St. Clement Mary Hofbauer Church.
Kulbis, Augustine M. *o.s.m.* '58 (CHI) [18] Chicago, IL Assumption of the Blessed Virgin Mary Church; [N] Chicago, IL Servite Friars - Eastern Province.
Kulczycki, Roman *c.m.* '83 (HRT) [18] New Haven, CT St. Stanislaus Church.
Kulczynski, Jason V. '89 (PH) Pottstown, PA St. Aloysius Church.
Kulesa, Daniel J. '62 (Y) McDonald, OH Our Lady of Perpetual Help Church.
Kulhawik, Frank '40 (CR) Retired.
Kulick, Larry J. '92 (GBG) Irwin, PA Immaculate Conception Church.
Kulig, Anthony J. '61 (NEW) [6] Bayonne, NJ Mt. Carmel Church.
Kulig, Francis G. '74 (SCR) [L] Dallas, PA Mercy Center Nursing Unit, Inc.; [O] Dallas, PA Mercy Center Convent.
Kulik, Msgr. Alexander T. '54 (SCR) [15] Wilkes-Barre, PA Maternity of the Blessed Virgin Mary Church.
Kulik, Francis J. '69 (SCR) Unassigned or Leave of Absence.
Kulinski, Kenneth E. '72 (OKL) [9] Oklahoma City, OK St. Paul, Apostle Church.
Kull, Jack *o.f.m.* '66 (NEW) Fair Lawn, NJ St. Anne's Church.
Kull, Martin '76 (BRK) [115] Brooklyn, NY St. Patrick Church.
Kulleck, Msgr. Donald R. '52 (SD) [3] Chula Vista, CA St. Pius X Church.
Kulleck, Thomas '74 (BWN) McCook, TX Immaculate Conception Church; [4] Mission, TX St. Paul Church.
Kuller, Thomas *s.j.* '90 (ALN) [G] Reading, PA Saint Joseph Medical Center.
Kuller, Thomas J. *s.j.* '79 (ALN) [A] Wernersville, PA Novitiate of St. Isaac Jogues.
Kullmann, Charles *c.s.p.* '78 (NY) [104] New York, NY St. Paul the Apostle Church.
Kulovits, Fred A. '59 (LC) Retired.
Kulwicki, Raymond J. *c.s.sp.* '56 (VEN) [G] Sarasota, FL Congregation of the Holy Ghost.
Kulwiec, Richard *o.m.i.* '81 (NY) [BB] Newburgh, NY Our Lady of Hope Center.
Kumbalaparambil, Xavier '66 (SAV) [2] Savannah, GA St. Anthony's Church.
Kumle, Peter *c.p.* '52 (LA) [R] Pasadena, CA Passionist Community.
Kummer, John R. '72 (CIN) Fairborn, OH Mary Help of Christians Church.
Kummer, William '75 (FTW) [7] Fort Wayne, IN St. John Baptist Church.
Kummerer, Timothy '83 (TOL) On Duty Outside the Diocese; [O] Toledo, OH Office of Global Concerns.
Kumontis, Msgr. Francis M. '73 (HBG) Hershey, PA St. Joan of Arc Church.
Kumplamthanam, Chacko '80 (HRT) [I] New Haven, CT Hospital of St. Raphael.
Kumse, John M. '79 (CLV) [47] Cleveland, OH St. Mary Church.
Kuna, Lech '74 (HRT) [5] Bristol, CT St. Stanislaus Church.
Kunco, Edward '69 (PIT) Pleasant Hills, PA St. Elizabeth Church.
Kunda, Brendan J. '65 (SUP) Boulder Junction, WI St. Anne Church; Presque Isle, WI St. Rita Church; Sayner, WI St. Mary Church.
Kundert, Rudolph '82 (PHX) On Leave.
Kundrat, Michael J. '41 (DET) Retired.
Kunert, Kenneth M. *s.j.* (DET) [K] Detroit, MI Jesuit Provincial Office-Detroit Province of the Society of Jesus.
Kunes, James F. *s.m.* '60 (CIN) [M] Dayton, OH Marianist Provincialate.
Kunisch, Robert *c.pp.s.* '56 (TOL) Marywood, OH St. Michael's Church; [M] Bellevue, OH Sorrowful Mother Shrine; [O] Bellevue, OH Mary Lay Center.
Kunkel, A. Henry, III '70 (BAL) Pylesville, MD St. Mary Church.
Kunkel, Albert A. '57 (CLV) [5] Barberton, OH Sacred Heart Church.
Kunkel, Charles *o.s.c.* '67 (PHX) [F] Phoenix, AZ Crosier Community of Phoenix (Canons Regular of the Order of the Holy Cross).
Kunkel, George C. '77 (CIN) [58] Cincinnati, OH St. Martin of Tours Church.
Kunkel, James E. '73 (PIT) [1] McKeesport, PA St. Martin de Porres Church.
Kunkel, Raymond W. '60 (SPC) Joplin, MO St. Mary Church.
Kunnakkattuthara, Zacharias '75 (TYL) Palestine, TX Sacred Heart Church.
Kunnath, Matthew (NEW) Nutley, NJ St. Mary's Church
Kunnath, Msgr. Sebastian '73 (NEW) [2] Linden, NJ Holy Family Church; Jersey City, NJ B.S. Pollak Hospital.
Kunnath, Thomas '85 (NEW) [1] Jersey City, NJ St. Aedan's Church; Jersey City, NJ St. Francis Health Center; [G] Hoboken, NJ St. Mary Hospital; [G] Jersey City, NJ St. Francis Hospital.
Kunnel, Lawrence '60 (TR) Neptune, NJ Holy Innocents Church.
Kunnumpuram, Paul *m.s.f.s.* '76 (ALX) Ferriday, LA St. Patrick Church; Vidalia, LA Our Lady of Lourdes Church.
Kunsch, William C. '42 (DUB) Retired.
Kuntz, Aloysius G. '47 (BUF) Retired.
Kuntz, Aloysius G. '49 (BUF) [O] Buffalo, NY Sheehan Residence for Priests.
Kuntz, Donald B. '41 (DET) Retired.
Kuntz, Ildephonse *ss.cc.* '46 (HON) [H] Honolulu, HI St. Patrick's Monastery.
Kuntz, Kenneth E. '77 (DAV) [1] Iowa City, IA St. Mary of the Assumption Church.
Kunz, Alfred J. '56 (MAD) Dane, WI St. Michael Church.
Kunz, David C. '80 (WIN) [A] Winona, MN Immaculate Heart of Mary Seminary, Saint Mary's University of MN #43.
Kunz, Francis P. '49 (WIN) Retired.
Kunz, James '73 (WIN) [G] Rochester, MN General Motherhouse of the Sisters of the Third Order Regular of St. Francis of the Congregation of Our.
Kunz, John M. '76 (WIN) Waseca, MN Sacred Heart Church.
Kunze, Robert W. '74 (NEW) On Duty Outside the Archdiocese.
Kunze, Robert W. '74 (WIL) Newark, DE St. John the Baptist-Holy Angels Church.
Kunzman, Richard T. '63 (CAM) On Duty Outside the Diocese.
Kuolt, Benedict J. '47 (NY) [3] White Plains, NY St. Bernard Church; White Plains, NY White Plains Hospital.
Kupczak, Jaroslaw *o.p.* '90 (WDC) [B] Washington, DC Dominican House of Studies.
Kuper, Raymond L. '64 (EVN) [12] Evansville, IN St. Agnes Church.
Kupferman, Lawrence '88 (RVC) Farmingdale, NY St. Kilian Church.
Kupinski, Raymond P. '45 (CHI) Retired.
Kupisz, Julian F. '74 (FAR) Sykeston, ND St. Elizabeth's Church.
Kupke, Raymond J. '73 (PAT) Florham Park, NJ Holy Family Church.
Kuppe, Paul M. *o.f.m.cap.* '70 (PIT) [29] Pittsburgh, PA Our Lady of the Angels Church.
Kuppens, Sjef *m.afr.* '67 (LA) [4] North Hollywood, CA St. Patrick Church.
Kuragama, Cyril '64 (NY) Pleasant Valley, NY St. Stanislaus Kostka Church.
Kuras, Alexander A. '69 (DET) [3] Westland, MI Church of the Divine Savior.
Kuras, Felix '38 (DUL) Retired.
Kuras, Hippolite *o.f.m.conv.* '35 (RCK) [11] Rockford, IL St. Stanislaus Kostka Church.
Kurash, Stanley J. '71 (SCR) [2] Old Forge, PA St. Mary's Church.
Kurber, Robert '60 (ORL) [4] Orlando, FL Holy Cross Church.
Kurdziel, Dennis M. '75 (ALT) Williamsburg, PA St. Joseph Church; Smithfield, PA State Correctional Institution.
Kurech, Gerard '51 (BAL) [85] Baltimore, MD Sacred Heart of Jesus Church.
Kurera, Pius (STO) Stockton, CA O.H. Close School.
Kurgan, Charles *o.carm.* '65 (JOL) [J] Darien, IL Carmelite Fathers Provincial Office.
Kurilec, Robert '68 (SB) On Duty Outside the Diocese.
Kurimay, Michael D. *s.j.* '73 (MIL) [P] Milwaukee, WI Jesuit Community at Marquette University.
Kurimsky, Frank '86 (PIT) Washington County, PA Washington County Jail.
Kurimsky, Frank M. '86 (PIT) Washington, PA Immaculate Conception Church.
Kurkiewicz, Raymond J. '42 (MIL) Retired.
Kurkowski, Innocent *o.f.m.conv.* '56 (BGP) [1] Fairfield, CT St. Anthony of Padua Church.
Kurnath, Joseph G. '91 (HRT) Newington, CT St. Mary Church.
Kurovsky, Andrew '85 (SCR) [3] Williamsport, PA St. Boniface's Church; [D] Williamsport, PA Bishop Neumann Junior/Senior High School.
Kurowski, Andrzej *s.a.c.* '76 (BRK) [177] Queens, NY Holy Cross Church.
Kurowski, Andrzej *s.a.c.* '76 (BUF) [O] North Tonawanda, NY Society of the Catholic Apostolate.
Kurowski, Clement *o.f.m.* '53 (PH) [106] Philadelphia, PA St. Monica Church.
Kurps, Jack *s.c.j.* '77 (MIL) [P] Hales Corners, WI Priests of the Sacred Heart; [P] Milwaukee, WI St. Joseph House of Formation.
Kurt, Allan J. '55 (DUB) Retired.
Kurt, David L. '77 (PEO) Bushnell, IL St. Bernard Church.
Kurt, Msgr. Edgar J. '41 (DUB) Retired.
Kurtenbach, Harold R. '60 (GI) Pleasanton, NE St. Mary's Church.
Kurth, Earl J. *s.j.* '49 (RC) Pine Ridge, SD Holy Rosary Church; [B] Pine Ridge, SD Jesuit Community of Holy Rosary Mission.
Kurty, Msgr. John (PRM) Allen Park, MI St. Stephen Church; Retired.
Kurtyka, Edward J. '71 (PAT) Prospect Park, NJ St. Paul's Church.
Kurtz, Msgr. George J. '40 (STL) Retired.
Kurtz, James *o.f.m.cap.* '87 (PIT) Herman, PA St. Mary of the Assumption Church; [N] Herman, PA St. Mary's Friary.
Kurtz, Jeffrey A. '90 (MAR) Leave of Absence.
Kurtz, Msgr. Joseph E. '72 (ALN) [7] Bethlehem, PA Notre Dame of Bethlehem Church; [F] Allentown, PA Catholic Social Agency-Catholic Charities Administrative Office.
Kurtz, R. James *s.j.* '77 (DET) [E] Detroit, MI University of Detroit Jesuit High School and Academy.
Kurtzke, John *c.s.c.* '85 (P) [B] Portland, OR University of Portland; [L] Portland, OR Holy Cross Father & Brother, C.S.C. - University of Portland.
Kurutz, Gregory *o.f.m.* '54 (GAY) Lewiston, MI St. Francis of Assisi Church.
Kurutz, Joseph V. '59 (PIT) [35] Pittsburgh, PA St. Raphael Church.
Kuruvila, Jose P. *o.i.c.* '86 (SB) Lake Elsinore, CA St. Frances of Rome Church.
Kurwicki, Robert A. '85 (JC) Marceline, MO St. Bonaventure Church.
Kurylo, Michael '34 (STN) San Diego, CA Our Lady of Perpetual Help Church; Retired.
Kurylowicz, Martin S. '79 (GR) Sparta, MI Holy Family Church.
Kurz, Michael A. '75 (CHI) Calumet City, IL St. Victor Church.
Kurz, Michael A. '75 (PBL) On Duty Outside the Diocese.
Kurz, William S. *s.j.* '70 (MIL) [P] Milwaukee, WI Jesuit Community at Marquette University.
Kurzaj, Franciszek '76 (SAT) [6] San Antonio, TX Holy Name Church.
Kurzak, John '75 (SC) On Duty Outside the Diocese.
Kurzawa, Ronald W. '64 (DET) [6] St. Clair Shores, MI St. Margaret Church.
Kurzawski, Casimir J. '58 (WOR) Retired.
Kurzendoerfer, Mark A. '81 (EVN) [4] Vincennes, IN St. Thomas Church; Special Assignment; [A] Evansville, IN Mater Dei High School.
Kurzyna, Andrew E. '74 (NY) Verplanck, NY St. Patrick Church.
Kus, Sebastian *o.f.m.* (NEW) [O] Lodi, NJ Immaculate Conception Convent.
Kuse, Michael '67 (SFD) [7] Quincy, IL St. Mary Church.
Kusevich, Nicholas '69 (PSC) Fort Pierce, FL SS. Cyril and Methodius Church; Lake Worth, FL Holy Apostles Church.
Kusevich, Nicholas '69 (ROM) Special Assignment.
Kusibab, Justin *o.f.m.conv.* '87 (CHI) [N] Chicago, IL Conventual Franciscans of St. Bonaventure Province.
Kuska, George *o.s.b.* '39 (JOL) [J] Lisle, IL St. Procopius Abbey.
Kusmirek, Mark '77 (TYL) Kilgore, TX Christ the King Church.
Kuss, Allen R. '84 (BIS) On Duty Outside the Diocese.
Kustanto, Johannes B. Hari *s.j.* '91 (BGP) [O] Fairfield, CT The Fairfield Jesuit Community-Fairfield University.
Kustanto, Johannes B. Hari *s.j.* '91 (HRT) [5] New Haven, CT St. Boniface's Church.
Kusunoki, Peter *ss.cc.* '79 (FR) [K] Fairhaven, MA Sacred Hearts Provincial House.
Kuta, Frank J. '53 (CLV) Rittman, OH St. Anne Church; Retired.
Kutch, Joseph J. '88 (SCR) [2] Nanticoke, PA Holy Trinity Church.
Kutch, Peter P. *o.f.m.cap.* '66 (MIL) Mount Calvary, WI Holy Cross Church; St. Cloud, WI St. Cloud Church; St. Joe, WI St. Joseph's Church.
Kutil, Dale '73 (RC) Fort Pierre, SD St. John Church; [D] Rapid City, SD Priest Retirement and Aid Association.

Kutipurath, Joseph *o.de.m.* '79 (SP) [10] Tampa, FL St. Lawrence Church.
Kutiuk, Casimir R. '57 (GB) Retired.
Kutlesa, Zvonimir *o.f.m.* '66 (CHI) [101] Chicago, IL St. Jerome Church.
Kutner, Raymond W. '64 (BRK) [157] Queens, NY Blessed Sacrament Church.
Kutsch, Eugene C. '51 (DUB) [2] Dubuque, IA St. Anthony's Church.
Kutsche, Javier F. '81 (OAK) [8] Oakland, CA St. Cyril Church.
Kuttikattukunnel, Francis *s.v.d.* '88 (DUB) [B] Epworth, IA Divine Word College.
Kutys, Daniel J. '80 (PH) [2] Drexel Hill, PA St. Bernadette Church.
Kutz, Lawrence A. '65 (WDC) [T] Washington, DC Opus Dei.
Kutz, Msgr. Ralph G. '37 (JC) Argyle, MO St. Aloysius Church.
Kuveikis, Rufin *o.f.m.cap.* '42 (BGP) Norwalk, CT Norwalk Hospital.
Kuveikis, Rufin *o.f.m.cap.* '48 (BGP) [O] Stamford, CT Lourdes Capuchin Chaplains Community.
Kuykendall, Andy '78 (WCH) Haysville, KS St. Cecilia Church.
Kuykendall, Henry '86 (EVN) [9] Evansville, IN Nativity Church.
Kuykendall, Thomas S. '94 (YAK) Richland, WA Christ the King Church.
Kuzara, George *c.pp.s.* '78 (CIN) Fort Recovery, OH St. Peter Church; St. Joseph, OH St. Joseph Church.
Kuzdal, Anthony P. '56 (NOR) Retired.
Kuzhippallil, George '67 (PAT) Budd Lake, NJ St. Jude Church.
Kuzia, Anthony F. *c.m.* '76 (PRT) Lisbon Falls, ME Holy Trinity Church.
Kuziemski, Ignatius H. '60 (MET) Great Meadows, NJ SS. Peter and Paul Church.
Kuzilla, John A. '55 (E) Kersey, PA St. Boniface Church.
Kuzinskas, John A. '52 (CHI) [141] Chicago, IL Nativity of the Blessed Virgin Mary Church.
Kuzma, Mykhailo '81 (STN) [6] Palatine, IL Immaculate Conception Church.
Kuzmann, Robert J. '85 (ALN) [2] Mahanoy City, PA St. Canicus Church; [4] Mahanoy City, PA St. Fidelis Church; [C] Tamaqua, PA Marian Catholic High School.
Kuzmeski, Charles H. '75 (SPR) Ware, MA St. Mary's Church.
Kuzmich, John M. '65 (FTW) [19] Fort Wayne, IN St. Vincent de Paul Church.
Kuzniewski, Anthony J. *s.j.* '79 (WOR) [N] Worcester, MA Jesuits of Holy Cross College, Inc.
Kuzy, Paul S. *c.pp.s.* '62 (SLC) St. George, UT St. George's Church; [H] St. George, UT Dixie College, Newman Center.
Kvedas, Leonard J. '61 (HRT) Beacon Falls, CT St. Michael's Church.
Kvedrovicz, Richard J. '72 (SCR) Duryea, PA Sacred Heart of Jesus Church.
Kwak, John A. '51 (PEO) Hennepin, IL St. Patrick's Church.
Kwak, Thaddeus '59 (FTW) [15] South Bend, IN Our Lady of Hungary Church.
Kwapisz, Gregory *o.f.m.conv.* (BUF) [21] Buffalo, NY Corpus Christi Church.
Kwatera, Michael *o.s.b.* '77 (SCL) Jacob's Prairie, MN St. James Church; [I] Collegeville, MN St. John's Abbey, of the Order of St. Benedict.
Kweder, Joseph K. '85 (ALN) Fountain Hill, PA St. Ursula Church.
Kwiatkowski, Constantine '47 (BUF) Salamanca, NY Holy Cross Church.
Kwiatkowski, Michael '78 (SPK) Colbert, WA St. Joseph Church.
Kwiatkowski, Paul M. '64 (TOL) [9] Toledo, OH Immaculate Conception Church; [25] Toledo, OH St. James Church.
Kwiatkowski, Richard P. '72 (NEW) Bloomfield, NJ Sacred Heart Church.
Kwiatkowski, Robert M. '83 (HRT) [6] Hamden, CT St. Rita's Church.
Kwiecen, Wojiech (CHI) [63] Chicago, IL St. Francis of Assisi/Our Lady of the Angels Church.
Kwiecien, Jan '80 (NEW) [4] Linden, NJ St. Theresa of the Child Jesus Church.
Kwiecien, John S. '76 (BUF) Perrysburg, NY St. Joan of Arc Church; South Dayton, NY St. John Fisher Church.
Kwiecien, Michael *o.carm.* '80 (PHX) [6] Phoenix, AZ St. Agnes Church; [I] Phoenix, AZ Kino Institute.
Kwoka, Edward '78 (SY) [14] Utica, NY St. Peter Church.
Kwolek, Joseph '45 (BUF) Retired; [P] Buffalo, NY Immaculate Heart of Mary Provincial House and Convent.
Ky, Joseph Cao *s.s.* '59 (HON) [2] Honolulu, HI Co-Cathedral of St. Theresa of the Child Jesus; [H] Honolulu, HI Society of the Priests of St. Sulpice (Sulpicians) S.S.
Kyfes, Robert J. '77 (CHI) [31] Chicago, IL St. Bride Church.
Kyle, Eric *o.f.m.* '52 (NY) [V] Staten Island, NY Carmel Richmond Nursing Home, Inc.
Kyle, John M. '36 (CHI) Streamwood, IL St. John the Evangelist Church; Retired.
Kylius, Ferdinand W. '37 (CIN) Retired.
Kyne, John J. '50 (SAC) Dixon, CA St. Peter Church; Retired and in Senior Ministry.
Kyrie, James *o.f.m.* '57 (SJ) [18] San Jose, CA Our Lady of Guadalupe Church.
Kyrpczak, James A. '96 (MET) Alpha, NJ St. Mary Church.
Kyte, Michael G. *o.p.* '87 (DEN) [28] Denver, CO St. Dominic's Church; [A] Denver, CO St. Dominic Priory.

L

L'Arche, Jeffrey M. *m.s.* '75 (ORL) [3] Orlando, FL Good Shepherd Church.
L'Heureux, Ernest L. '62 (PRT) Gorham, ME St. Anne Church; [M] Portland, ME University of Southern Maine.
L'Heureux, William D. (OM) Hooper, NE St. Rose of Lima Church.
La Belle, Ralph '78 (NY) Manhattan, NY Columbia Presbyterian Medical Center.
La Brake, John R. *s.s.e.* '57 (MOB) Belle Fontaine, AL St. Philip Neri Church.
La Casa, Vicente Paz en '66 (PBL) [17] Pueblo, CO Shrine of St. Therese Church.
La France, Val *o.p.* '58 (NEW) [27] Jersey City, NJ Sacred Heart Church.
La Fratta, William E. '63 (RIC) Charlottesville, VA Church of the Incarnation.
La Mazza, Carmen G. *m.m.* '55 (NY) [Z] Maryknoll, NY Maryknoll Fathers and Brothers.
La Mere, Cletus E. *s.d.s.* '48 (GB) Kiel, WI SS. Peter and Paul Church.
La Monte, Richard A. '66 (NY) [4] Poughkeepsie, NY St. John the Baptist Church.
La Pan, Kenneth *t.o.r.* '52 (ALT) [F] Newry, PA St. Bernardine Monastery.
La Plante, Philip *s.m.* '48 (BO) [BB] Boston, MA Our Lady of Good Voyage Chapel.
La Porta, Gerald '57 (BAL) Retired.
La Puebla, Enrique *m.s.* '80 (SB) Moreno Valley, CA St. Christopher Church.
La Rocca, Jack '88 (SJ) [5] San Jose, CA Five Wounds Portuguese National Church.
La Rocca, Vincent '49 (BRK) [131] Brooklyn, NY Sacred Hearts of Jesus and Mary and St. Stephen Church.
La Rosa, Stephen J. *o.s.a.* '65 (CAM) [C] Richland, NJ St. Augustine Preparatory School.
Lab, Robert J. *s.j.* '60 (CHI) [T] Barrington, IL Bellarmine Hall.
Lab, Robert J. *s.j.* '60 (DET) [K] Detroit, MI Jesuit Provincial Office-Detroit Province of the Society of Jesus.
Laba, Gerald *c.p.* '73 (PIT) [N] Pittsburgh, PA St. Paul of the Cross Monastery.
LaBaff, Arthur J. '66 (OG) Chasm Falls, NY St. Helen Church; Malone, NY Notre Dame Church.
LaBaire, Steven M. '87 (WOR) Westborough, MA St. Luke the Evangelist Church.
Labaj, Stephen V. '36 (MIL) Retired.
Labak, Joseph L. '77 (CLV) Brunswick, OH St. Ambrose Church.
Labaka, Jose Francisco *o.f.m.* '68 (SJN) [3] Carolina, PR Santa Clara de Asis Church.
Labarda, Nathaniel C. '93 (HRT) Wallingford, CT Holy Trinity Church.
LaBarge, Charles F. '46 (DUB) Retired.
LaBarge, Christopher '85 (WIL) Marydel, MD Immaculate Conception Church.
Labat, Dennis C. '74 (NU) Special or Diocesan Assignment.
LaBau, Anthony F. *s.j.* '46 (NY) [Z] New York, NY St. Ignatius Loyola Residence; [Z] New York, NY Jesuit Seminary and Mission Bureau, Inc. (Jesuit Deferred Funds); [DD] New York, NY Jesuit Seminary and Mission Bureau, Inc.
Labauve, J. Joel '70 (BR) Angola, LA Louisiana State Penitentiary.
LaBauve, John *s.v.d.* '51 (BLX) [A] Bay St. Louis, MS St. Augustine's.
Labbe, Clifton *s.v.d.* '96 (BLX) [E] Bay St. Louis, MS Southern Province of St. Augustine - Provincial Residence.
Labbe, Emil J. *c.pp.s.* '68 (CIN) Maria Stein, OH St. John the Baptist Church.
Labbe, Joseph P. '75 (CLV) Bainbridge Township, OH Holy Angels Church.
Labedis, Anthony *o.f.m.conv.* '60 (CHI) [N] Chicago, IL Conventual Franciscans of St. Bonaventure Province.
Labella, Robert '54 (CLV) [2] Akron, OH St. Anthony of Padua Church.
LaBelle, Jeffrey *s.j.* '88 (SJ) [17] San Jose, CA Most Holy Trinity Church.
LaBelle, Patrick *o.p.* '65 (SJ) [O] Palo Alto, CA Newman Center, Catholic Community at Stanford.
Labieniec, Alphonse S. '61 (HRT) [7] West Hartford, CT St. Timothy's Church; Cheshire, CT Manson Youth Institution.
Labinski, Jacek '83 (TR) Hightstown, NJ St. Anthony of Padua Church.
Labinsky, Paul '81 (PHU) Manville, NJ St. Michael's Church; New Brunswick, NJ Nativity of B.V.M. Church.
Labita, Francis J. '49 (BRK) [211] Queens, NY Our Lady of Grace Church; Retired.
Labonte, L. Roger '66 (MET) Edison, NJ St. Helena Church.
Labonte, Richard H. '70 (WOR) Blackstone, MA St. Theresa Church.
Labonte, Roger '94 (LA) [1] Oxnard, CA St. Anthony Church.
Laboon, Joseph D. '57 (NO) New Orleans, LA Veterans Affairs Medical Center.
Laboon, Joseph D. '57 (PIT) Military Chaplains.
Labosky, James M. '79 (R) Wilson, NC Church of St. Therese.
Labove, M. Keith (LAF) [6] Lafayette, LA Our Lady of Wisdom, University of Southwestern Louisiana Church; On Special Assignment.
LaBran, Joseph J. *s.j.* '47 (WOR) [N] Worcester, MA Jesuits of Holy Cross College, Inc.; [Q] Worcester, MA Campus Ministry.
Labranche, Raymond '94 (NEW) New Milford, NJ Ascension Church.
LaBrecque, Frederick '67 (CHR) Conway, SC St. James Church.
Labrie, Jean Paul '82 (PRT) Daigle, ME Holy Family Church; Fort Kent, ME St. Louis Church.
Labrie, Robert G. '64 (BO) Newburyport, MA St. Louis de Gonzague Church.
Labrosse, Paul E. *m.s.c.* '42 (OG) [2] Watertown, NY Our Lady of the Sacred Heart, Missionaries of the Sacred Heart Church.
LaBurt, Brian '86 (SAV) Waynesboro, GA Sacred Heart Church.
LaCanne, Stephen J. '76 (STP) Wayzata, MN St. Bartholomew Church.
Lacasse, Aime F. *m.afr.* '38 (SP) [O] St. Petersburg, FL Missionaries of Africa.
Lacasse, Andre-Joseph *o.p.* '92 (Y) [13] Youngstown, OH St. Dominic's Church.
Lacasse, Eugene *o.c.s.o.* '54 (WOR) [N] Spencer, MA St. Joseph's Abbey.
LaCasse, John P. '74 (DET) Ida, MI St. Joseph Church.
LaCasse, Raymond *o.m.i.* '58 (NOR) [F] Willimantic, CT Oblates of Mary Immaculate; [I] Willimantic, CT Immaculata Retreat House.
Lacasse, Roger '53 (PRO) Retired.
Lacasse, Roland *s.m.* (BO) [3] Methuen, MA Our Lady of Mount Carmel Church.
LaCaze, Msgr. J. Carson '57 (SHP) [4] Shreveport, LA Our Lady of the Holy Rosary Church.
Lacchin, Mario *i.m.c.* '63 (MET) [N] Somerset, NJ Mission International, Inc.
Lacerna, Rodolfo '68 (ELP) [16] El Paso, TX Our Lady of the Light Church.
LaCerra, Msgr. Gerard T. '69 (MIA) [33] Miami, FL St. Timothy Church; [B] Opa Locka, FL St. Thomas University.
LaCerte, Henri *o.s.b.* (P) [P] Portland, OR University of Portland.
Lacerte, Henry W. *o.s.b.* '59 (PBL) [E] Canon City, CO Holy Cross Abbey.
Lacey, Msgr. Francis A. '51 (SFR) Tiburon, CA St. Hilary Church.
Lacey, George F. '45 (STO) [7] Stockton, CA St. Luke Church; Retired.
Lacey, James (ALB) [L] Saratoga Springs, NY St. John Neumann Residence.
Lacey, Joseph P. *s.j.* '71 (WDC) [20] Washington, DC Holy Trinity Church.
Lacey, Mark W. '95 (ATL) [L] Atlanta, GA Campus Ministry.
Lacey, Michael *m.s.c.* '78 (OAK) [4] Alameda, CA St. Philip Neri Church.
Lacey, Thomas E. '43 (SFR) Redwood City, CA St. Matthias Church; Retired.
LaChance, Charles P. '74 (CHI) Other Assignments.
Lachance, Paul (CHI) [N] Chicago, IL St. Peter's Friary.
Lachance, Pierre E. *o.p.* '42 (FR) [12] Fall River, MA St. Anne's Church; [K] Fall River, MA Dominican House.
LaChance, Roger '67 (B) Coeur D'Alene, ID St. Pius X Church; [F] Coeur D'Alene, ID North Idaho College.
Lachapelle, Alphonsus *s.o.cist.* '82 (ALN) [K] New Ringgold, PA Cistercian Conventual Priory, St. Mary's Priory.
LaChapelle, Hector O. *m.s.* '68 (BO) [Y] Ipswich, MA LaSalette Retreat House at Newman Hall.
LaChapelle, Hector O. *m.s.* '68 (NY) Phoenicia, NY St. Francis de Sales Church.
LaCharite, Roger J. *s.s.e.* '55 (MOB) [H] Selma, AL Edmundite Fathers.
LaCharite, Roger J. *s.s.e.* '55 (NOR) [A] Mystic, CT Edmundite Seminary Guild.

Lache, Rodolfo '81 (LA) Sun Valley, CA Our Lady of the Holy Rosary Church.
Lachendro, Vincent *o.f.m.conv.* '63 (BAL) [M] Ellicott City, MD Order of Friars Minor Conventual.
Lachowicz, Francis B. '60 (PIT) [4] McKeesport, PA St. Mary Czestochowa Church.
Lachowitzer, Charles V. '90 (STP) Maplewood, MN Presentation of the Blessed Virgin Mary Church.
Lachowski, Joseph *c.m.* '54 (BRK) [134] Brooklyn, NY St. Stanislaus Kostka Church.
Lachowsky, Clement *c.s.sp.* '47 (SB) Hemet, CA Our Lady of the Valley Church.
Lacienski, Michael *o.f.m.* '43 (PIT) [N] Ben Avon, PA St. Anthony Friary and Mission House.
Lack, Christopher '90 (CIN) [68] Cincinnati, OH Our Lady of Lourdes Church.
Lackamp, Franklin J. '58 (KC) Lexington, MO Immaculate Conception Church.
Lackenmier, James R. *c.s.c.* '64 (SCR) [C] Wilkes-Barre, PA Kings College.
Lackie, Daniel *o.f.m.* '96 (SFR) [5] San Francisco, CA St. Anthony Church.
Lackner, Bede *o.cist.* '52 (DAL) [M] Irving, TX Cistercian Abbey of Our Lady of Dallas.
Lackner, Francis J.X. '44 (PIT) Retired.
Lackner, Joseph H. *s.m.* '72 (CIN) [D] Dayton, OH The University of Dayton; [M] Dayton, OH Marianist Provincialate.
Lackner, Joseph H. *s.m.* '72 (SFR) [N] San Francisco, CA Marianist Community.
Lackner, Msgr. Paul M. '42 (PIT) Retired.
Lackovic, Msgr. Stephen F. '39 (BUF) [7] Lackawanna, NY Our Lady of Bistrica Church; Retired.
Lacombe, Robert E. '91 (PRO) Greenville, RI St. Philip's Church.
LaCorte, Richard P. '87 (FAR) On Duty Outside the Diocese.
LaCosse, Norbert R. '52 (MAR) Retired.
LaCount, Daniel E. (SFD) Auburn, IL St. Benedict Church; Divernon, IL Sacred Heart Church.
LaCount, Daniel E. '89 (SFD) Waverly, IL St. Sebastian Church.
Lacovic, Lawrence L. '69 (ALT) [5] Johnstown, PA St. Stephen, First King of Hungary Church.
Lacroix, Daniel W. '88 (FR) Mansfield, MA St. Mary's Church.
Lacroix, Maurice R. '53 (MAN) [2] Berlin, NH St. Joseph Church.
LaCroix, Wilfred L. *s.j.* '69 (KC) [B] Kansas City, MO Rockhurst College; [J] Kansas City, MO Rockhurst College - Jesuit Community.
LaCrosse, James *s.m.* '67 (WH) [11] Wheeling, WV St. Vincent de Paul's Church.
Lacruz, Alfredo Alvarez '86 (PCE) [A] Ponce, PR Diocesan Seminary; [B] Ponce, PR The Pontifical Catholic University of Puerto Rico.
Lacruz, Cecilio *sch.p.* (SJN) [58] San Juan, PR Santisimo Salvador Church.
Lacson, Tony '86 (RVC) Levittown, NY St. Bernard Church.
Lacy, Aidan '93 (PMB) [4] Delray Beach, FL St. Vincent Ferrer Church.
Laczko, T. Ansgar '60 (WDC) [6] Washington, DC Assumption Church.
Ladd, John O. '79 (GAY) Prudenville, MI Our Lady of the Lake Church.
Ladden, Timothy M. '53 (OG) Cape Vincent, NY St. Vincent of Paul Church; Rosiere, NY St. Vincent de Paul Church.
Ladewski, Roman S. *c.s.c.* '45 (FTW) [J] South Bend, IN Congregation of Holy Cross Indiana Province Provincial House.
Ladish, Robert W. '53 (HRT) [1] Torrington, CT St. Francis of Assisi Church.
Ladkau, William D. '84 (CHR) [6] Columbia, SC Good Shepherd Church.
Ladra, Jose '82 (NO) Terrytown, LA Christ the King Church.
Ladzinski, Msgr. Casimir H. *v.g.* '62 (TR) Jackson, NJ St. Aloysius Gonzaga Church.
Laenen, Hendrik *o.m.i.* '52 (SAN) Sweetwater, TX Immaculate Heart of Mary Church.
Laenen, Joseph C. *o.praem.* '51 (PH) [T] Darby, PA Mercy Catholic Medical Center; [Z] Paoli, PA Daylesford Abbey.
Laesch, Dennis C. '96 (DET) Rochester, MI St. Andrew Church.
LaFache, Anthony '68 (SY) [6] Utica, NY St. Anthony of Padua Church.
LaFavia, Louis M. *c.pp.s.* '47 (WDC) [C] Washington, DC Catholic University of America, The.
LaFay, Michael *o.carm.* '60 (JOL) [J] Darien, IL Carmelite Fathers Provincial Office.
LaFemina, Msgr. Anthony A. '61 (VEN) Absent on Sick Leave.
Laferrera, John J. '73 (NEW) Caldwell, NJ St. Aloysius Church.
Laferrera, Robert G. '88 (NEW) [11] Jersey City, NJ Holy Rosary Church.
Laferriere, Raymond '60 (MAN) [3] Manchester, NH St. Anthony of Padua Church.
Laferty, Charles P. *o.s.a.* '53 (PH) [C] Villanova, PA Villanova University; [Z] Villanova, PA St. Thomas Monastery.
Lafey, Kevin *o.carm.* '72 (JOL) [J] Darien, IL Carmelite Fathers Provincial Office.
Lafferty, Charles L. '55 (BAL) [39] Baltimore, MD Immaculate Conception Church.
Lafferty, David '85 (OKL) Graduate Studies.
Lafferty, Msgr. James K. '54 (SC) Arcadia, IA St. John the Baptist Church.
Lafferty, Msgr. John J. (ALT) Retired.
Lafferty, Owen J. '66 (NY) [1] Mt. Vernon, NY Sacred Heart Church.
LaFlamme, Julien J. '58 (BUR) Manchester Center, VT Conversion of St. Paul Church.
LaFleur, Alfred *o.s.a.* '44 (FWT) Hillsboro, TX Our Lady of Mercy Church.
LaFleur, Angelus *o.f.m.conv.* '35 (STL) [P] St. Louis, MO St. Bonaventure Friary (Province of Our Lady of Consolation).
LaFleur, Gerard A. '53 (SPR) [1] Chicopee, MA Assumption Church.
LaFleur, Paul J. '85 (LAF) Carencro, LA Our Lady of the Assumption Church.
Lafond, Donald E. '62 (MAN) Merrimack, NH Our Lady of Mercy Church.
LaFontaine, James F. *s.j.* '87 (BO) [W] Boston, MA The Society of Jesus of New England-Provincial Offices; [W] Boston, MA The Society of Jesus of New England-Provincial Offices.
LaFontaine, Paul A. '72 (STP) [19] St. Paul, MN St. Columba Church.
LaForest, Conrad V. '72 (MAN) Absent on Sick Leave.
Laforge, Joseph M. (TR) On Duty Outside the Diocese.
LaForge, Joseph M. '65 (R) Rocky Mount, NC Our Lady of Perpetual Help Church.
LaFosse, William D. *m.s.* '68 (SPR) [4] Holyoke, MA Immaculate Conception Church.
Lafrenz, James '54 (ELP) Retired.
Lafrenz, James '54 (LSC) Retired.
Lagan, Hugh F. '54 (SP) Plant City, FL St. Clement Church.
Lagana, Msgr. Frank A. '39 (GAL) Retired; [U] Houston, TX St. Mary's Orphanage Board
Lagasse, C. Brian '93 (PRO) [1] North Providence, RI St. Anthony's Church.
Lagasse, Ronald J. (OAK) Military Chaplains.
Lager, John *o.f.m.cap.* '79 (DEN) [M] Denver, CO St. Francis of Assisi Friary.
Lages de Silva, Fernando Eurico (BGP) [15] Bridgeport, CT Our Lady of Fatima Church.
Lagges, Patrick R. '77 (CHI) [153] Chicago, IL Our Lady of Mercy Church.
Lagiouane, John M. '92 (NY) Pearl River, NY St. Aedan Church.
Lagiovane, John M. '92 (NY) [4] Newburgh, NY Sacred Heart Church.
Lago, Danilo *s.x.* '77 (PAT) [M] Wayne, NJ Xaverian Missionary Fathers.
Lagoa, Raul M. '79 (FR) Somerset, MA St. John of God Church.
Lagodinski, Dale '72 (FAR) Wahpeton, ND St. John's Church; Wahpeton, ND Newman Student Parish Church; [H] Wahpeton, ND State College of Science Newman Student Parish.
LaGoe, John P. '61 (GR) On Special Assignment; [L] Muskegon Heights, MI Christian Community Center.
Lagomarsino, John *s.s.c.* '70 (SAC) Carmichael, CA St. John the Evangelist Church.
Lagomarsino, Vincent J. *s.j.* '56 (WH) [A] Wheeling, WV Wheeling Jesuit University.
Lagonegro, Msgr. Dominick J. '69 (NY) Hopewell Junction, NY St. Columba Church.
Lagor, Joseph J. '54 (BUR) Retired.
Lagos, Benito M. *i.v.e.* '93 (FR) [17] New Bedford, MA St. Kilian Church; [Q] New Bedford, MA The Institute of the Incarnate Word, Inc.
Laguna-Vargas, Enrique *o.carm.* '90 (JOL) [J] Darien, IL Carmelite Fathers Provincial Office.
Lahart, Daniel K. *s.j.* '94 (WDC) [E] Washington, DC Gonzaga College High School.
LaHart, Msgr. Richard T. '52 (PH) Lafayette Hill, PA St. Philip Neri Church.
Lahens, Alberto '95 (MIA) [1] Hialeah, FL Immaculate Conception Church.
Laheta, Andrew P. '43 (CLV) [55] Cleveland, OH Our Lady of Mercy Church; Retired.
Lahey, John '67 (SAL) Solomon, KS Immaculate Conception Church.
Lahey, John F. *c.s.c.* '70 (FTW) [A] Notre Dame, IN Moreau Seminary; [B] Notre Dame, IN University of Notre Dame Du Lac; [J] Notre Dame, IN Holy Cross Community, Corby Hall, University of Notre Dame.
Lahey, Msgr. Joseph T. '48 (BRK) [115] Brooklyn, NY St. Patrick Church; Retired.
Lahey, Msgr. Maurice '50 (FRS) Retired.
Lahey, Piers M. '82 (SFR) [23] San Francisco, CA Holy Name of Jesus Church; Novato, CA Serra Club of Marin.
Lahoud, Joseph F. '59 (BO) [54] Boston, MA Our Lady of The Cedars of Lebanon Church.
Lahoud, Msgr. Joseph F. '59 (SAM) Jamaica Plain, MA Our Lady of the Cedars of Lebanon Church.
Lahout, Francis M. '53 (HBG) [F] Camp Hill, PA Holy Spirit Hospital and Community Mental Health Center.
Lahrs, Carey *s.d.s.* '72 (SAV) [A] Columbus, GA Pacelli High School.
Lai, Doan Van '73 (SD) [7] San Diego, CA Holy Spirit Church.
Laible, Jeffrey G. '88 (PEO) Colfax, IL St. Joseph's Church; [B] Bloomington, IL Central Catholic High School.
Laicha, Michael M. '89 (HBG) [7] (Penbrook), PA St. Margaret Mary Alacoque Church.
Laini, Valerian '69 (CHI) Evanston, IL St. Mary Church.
Lair, Gerald P. *o.s.b.* '60 (PAT) [M] Morristown, NJ St. Mary's Abbey.
Laird, Kenneth W. '75 (BR) Zachary, LA St. John the Baptist Church.
Laird, Martin S. *o.s.a.* '91 (CHI) [N] Olympia Fields, IL The Augustinian Provincialate Tolentine Center.
Laird, William F. '75 (ROC) Churchville, NY St. Vincent De Paul Church.
Lajack, Edward F. '68 (CLV) [2] Barberton, OH SS. Cyril and Methodius Church.
Lajack, Jerome M. '66 (CLV) [77] Cleveland, OH St. Wendelin Church.
Lajiness, Todd J. '95 (DET) Northville, MI Our Lady of Victory Church.
Lajo, Saturnino *o.m.i.* '63 (SAT) [T] San Antonio, TX Oblate Missions.
Lajoie, David *s.m.* '48 (PRT) Van Buren, ME St. Bruno - St. Remi Church.
Lajoie, Marcel *s.m.* '56 (PRT) Van Buren, ME St. Bruno - St. Remi Church.
Lajoie, Roland L. '88 (WOR) Warren, MA St. Paul's Church; West Warren, MA St. Thomas Aquinas Church.
Lajoie, Ronald A. *s.m.* (BO) [10] Cambridge, MA Our Lady of Pity Church.
Lakers, John J. *o.f.m.* '58 (SFD) [B] Quincy, IL Quincy University.
Lal, Tej *i.m.s.* '68 (TYL) Crockett, TX St. Francis of the Tejas Church.
Laliberte, George G. '56 (HRT) Woodbury, CT St. Teresa's Church.
Laliberte, Robert L. '73 (FAR) Special Assignment; [A] Fargo, ND Cardinal Muench Seminary.
Laliberte, Stephen *o.f.m.cap.* '80 (PAT) [M] Oak Ridge-Milton, NJ St. Stanislaus B. M. Friary.
Laliberte, Stephen P. '81 (GAL) Baytown, TX St. John the Evangelist Church.
Laliberte, William F. '43 (BUR) Retired.
Lalic, Paul B. '58 (BGP) [3] Stamford, CT St. Mary's Church; [J] Stamford, CT St. Camillus Health Center.
Lalli, Tony *s.x.* '66 (BO) [W] Holliston, MA Xaverian Missionaries; [BB] Holliston, MA Our Lady of Fatima Shrine.
Lally, Brendan G. *s.j.* '77 (SCR) [C] Scranton, PA University of Scranton.
Lally, Msgr. Dennis '65 (GB) Lebanon Township, WI St. Patrick Church.
Lally, Edward J. (PAT) Permanent Deacons.
Lally, Joachim *c.s.p.* '65 (NY) [Z] Scarsdale, NY Paulist Fathers Generalate.
Lally, M. Terrance (P) [L] Portland, OR Holy Cross Father & Brother, C.S.C. - University of Portland.
Lally, M. Terrance *c.s.c.* '67 (FTW) [J] South Bend, IN Congregation of Holy Cross Indiana Province Provincial House.
Lally, Martin '78 (DEN) Northglenn, CO Immaculate Heart of Mary Church.
Lally, Owen *c.p.* '34 (NY) [Z] Chelsea, NY Word of the Cross Passionist Community.
Lally, Owen *c.p.* '59 (BRK) [U] Jamaica, NY Immaculate Conception Monastery.
Lally, Owen *c.p.* '59 (NY) [DD] Chelsea, NY The Fellowship of the Beloved Disciple.
LaLonde, Emile G. '41 (OG) Retired.
Lalonde, Venant *o.f.m.* '54 (NY) [Z] New York, NY Franciscan Friars, Order of Friars Manor; [Z] New York, NY Franciscan Friars, Order of Friars Manor.
Lalor, Thomas '66 (JKS) [4] Jackson, MS St. Therese Church.
Lam, John *s.d.b.* '71 (SFR) [45] San Francisco, CA SS. Peter and Paul Church.
Lama, Michael '84 (SB) Banning, CA Precious Blood Church.
Lamadrid, Arthur Gilde (SUP) [1] Superior, WI Cathedral of Christ the King.
Lamanna, Alfred '49 (ALB) Retired.
Lamantia, A. Robert '48 (TOL) Retired.
LaMar, Joseph P. *m.m.* '83 (NY) [Z] Maryknoll, NY Maryknoll Fathers and Brothers.
LaMarre, Theodore E. '45 (SAG) Retired.
LaMartina, Liborio J. *s.j.* '67 (BAL) [M] Baltimore, MD Jesuit Fathers and Brothers Maryland Provincial Curia.
Lamas, Rodolfo '80 (SJN) [7] Guaynabo, PR Divino

Nino Jesus Church.
Lamb, Bruce '89 (SR) [1] Santa Rosa, CA Cathedral of St. Eugene.
Lamb, Gary E. '83 (MEM) Military Chaplains.
Lamb, Louis J. '61 (OKL) [13] Oklahoma City, OK St. Joseph's Church.
Lamb, Matthew L. '62 (MIL) On Duty Outside the Archdiocese.
Lamb, Patrick H. *o.f.m.* '83 (ALN) [C] Reading, PA Reading Central Catholic High School (Monsignor Bornemann Memorial); [L] Reading, PA Sacred Heart Convent.
Lamb, Paul T. '96 (FR) West Harwich, MA Holy Trinity Church.
Lamb, Thomas J. '71 (NEW) [M] South Orange, NJ Opus Dei.
Lamb, Wes *o.s.s.t.* (IND) Terre Haute, IN U.S. Penitentiary.
Lamb, Weston J. *o.ss.t.* '81 (BAL) [M] Baltimore, MD Holy Trinity Monastery.
Lambe, Jeremiah F. *c.s.sp.* '52 (STA) [1] St. Augustine, FL Cathedral of St. Augustine.
Lambe, William (VIC) Yoakum, TX St. Joseph Church.
Lambeck, Robert W. *s.j.* '49 (MIL) [P] Milwaukee, WI Jesuit Community at Marquette University.
Lambert, Christopher *o.f.m.* (STL) [P] St. Louis, MO Franciscan Friary of St. Anthony of Padua.
Lambert, Cornelius F. '83 (CAM) Blackwood, NJ St. Agnes Church.
Lambert, Curtis '74 (CHI) [151] Chicago, IL Our Lady of Lourdes Church.
Lambert, James J. '80 (PT) Panama City, FL St. Dominic Church.
Lambert, James L. *s.j.* '68 (SAT) [17] San Antonio, TX Our Lady of Guadalupe Church.
Lambert, John C. '69 (BWN) Retired.
Lambert, John C. '84 (SCR) Jersey Shore, PA St. Luke's Church.
Lambert, Joseph J. '43 (PRO) Retired; [P] Providence, RI St. John Vianney Residence.
Lambert, Leo M. '45 (MIL) Retired.
Lambert, Louis J. *s.j.* '66 (ELP) [21] El Paso, TX Sacred Heart Church.
Lambert, Peter '72 (MIA) [5] Fort Lauderdale, FL St. Clement Church.
Lambert, Peter '79 (DUL) Military Chaplains.
Lambert, Raymond P. (BO) Retired.
Lambert, Richard '75 (PBR) [4] Pittsburgh, PA St. John Chrysostom Church.
Lambert, Richard D. '80 (CR) Fosston, MN St. Mary's Church.
Lambert, Robert E. '65 (SAT) [C] San Antonio, TX Oblate School of Theology.
Lambert, Rollins E. '49 (CHI) Retired.
Lambert, Theodore '76 (STO) Manteca, CA St. Anthony Church; Stockton, CA Karl Holton School.
Lambert, Timothy J. '92 (MET) On Duty Outside the Diocese.
Lambert, William '55 (RC) Retired.
Lamberty, Darrell V. '79 (SFS) Pierre, SD SS. Peter and Paul Church.
Lamberty, Philip J. *o.p.* '59 (STL) [P] St. Louis, MO St. Dominic Priory.
Lambertz, Wilfrid *o.s.b.* '58 (SFS) [F] Marvin, SD Blue Cloud Abbey.
Lambeth, K. Michael '94 (TR) Spring Lake, NJ St. Catharine Church.
Lambing, Gregory *o.c.s.o.* '59 (L) [L] Trappist, KY Abbey of Our Lady of Gethsemani, of the Order of Cistercians of the Strict Observance.
Lambino, Miguel *s.j.* '93 (NY) [Z] New York, NY Jesuit Community at Fordham University.
Lambour, C. Stephen *c.s.c.* '55 (ORL) Indialantic, FL Holy Name of Jesus Church.
Lambro, Edward '74 (PAT) Unassigned.
Lamby, Robert *s.s.c.* '75 (OM) [K] St. Columbans, NE St. Columban's Foreign Mission Society.
Lamela, Juan *c.m.* '62 (MGZ) [8] Mayaquez, PR San Vicente Church.
Lamela, Juan *c.m.* '62 (PCE) [B] Ponce, PR The Pontifical Catholic University of Puerto Rico.
Lamendola, Francis S. '36 (NO) Retired.
Lamendola, Salvatore '90 (GBG) [3] Greensburg, PA Our Lady of Grace Church.
Lamica, Alan J. '78 (OG) Keene, NY St. Brendan Church; Moriah, NY Moriah Shock Incarceration Correctional Facility.
Lamitie, James F. '53 (OG) Malone, NY Franklin Correctional Facility.
Lamitie, Robert O. '57 (OG) Malone, NY Barehill Correctional Facility.
Lamm, Timothy *o.s.b.* '56 (SD) [C] San Diego, CA St. Augustine High School.
Lamm, Timothy J. *o.s.b.* '54 (SEA) [M] Lacey, WA St. Martin's Abbey.
Lamm, William F. *s.j.* '57 (BAL) [M] Baltimore, MD Jesuit Fathers and Brothers Maryland Provincial Curia.
Lammeier, Francis G. '55 (CIN) [13] Cincinnati, OH Assumption Church.
Lammers, Donald W. '72 (JC) [2] Jefferson City, MO St. Peter Church.
Lammers, Ralph A. '63 (OM) Schuyler, NE St. Mary Church.
Lammers, William F. (TOL) Retired.
Lammert, Edward H. *o.f.m.* '58 (LEX) Cumberland, KY St. Stephen Church; Harlan, KY Holy Trinity Church; Lynch, KY Church of the Resurrection.
LaMoine, Gary W. '81 (CR) Red Lake Falls, MN St. Joseph's Church.
Lamonde, Joseph R. '74 (PIT) Military Chaplains.
LaMontagne, Bernard L. '63 (PRO) On Duty Outside the Diocese.
Lamore, Victor E. '80 (OG) Indian Lake, NY St. Mary's Church.
LaMorte, Joseph P. '81 (NY) [3] Poughkeepsie, NY Holy Trinity Church.
LaMorte, Richard A. '66 (NY) [7] Poughkeepsie, NY Our Lady of Mt. Carmel Church.
Lamothe, C. Romero '48 (WOR) Retired.
Lamothe, Daniel O. '62 (MAN) Dover, NH St. Joseph Church.
Lamothe, Donat R. *a.a.* '62 (WOR) [N] Worcester, MA Assumptionists of Assumption College.
Lamothe, Philip R. '55 (BUR) Bradford, VT Our Lady of Perpetual Help Church.
LaMotte, Victor S. *o.p.* '56 (CHI) [N] River Forest, IL St. Thomas Aquinas Priory.
LaMountain, Michael V. '76 (PRO) Absent on Leave.
Lamoureaux, Richard L. *a.a.* '71 (WOR) [N] Worcester, MA Assumptionists of Assumption College.
Lamoureux, Roger '62 (SR) [2] Santa Rosa, CA Holy Spirit Church.
Lamoureux, Roger E. *o.m.i.* '83 (BO) [4] Lowell, MA Sainte Jeanne d'Arc Church.
Lamoureux, Roger J. *o.m.i.* '59 (NOR) Willimantic, CT St. Mary Church.
Lamp, Edward '82 (SP) Ruskin, FL St. Anne Church.
Lampe, Msgr. Irvin F. '43 (WCH) Retired.
Lampe, Stephen J. '82 (MIL) [80] Milwaukee, WI St. Vincent de Paul's Church; [A] Milwaukee, WI Saint Francis Seminary.
Lampert, Robert E. '65 (STL) On Duty Outside the Archdiocese.
Lampert, Vincent P. '91 (IND) Danville, IN Mary Queen of Peace Church.
Lamping, Thomas E. '84 (CHI) [180] Chicago, IL Queen of Angels Church.
Lamprich, Mark *m.i.c.* '90 (CHL) [1] Greensboro, NC Our Lady of Grace Church.
Lampron, Alfred J. '75 (PAT) Pequannock, NJ Holy Spirit Church.
Lampron, Maurice W. '63 (MAN) Retired.
Lamy, Raymond J. '81 (MAN) Military Chaplains.
Lamy, Robert E. *c.m.* '51 (NO) [P] New Orleans, LA Vincentian Fathers.
Lan Tran, Anthony '70 (SEA) Federal Way, WA St. Vincent De Paul Church.
Lanagan, Vincent F. '60 (SCR) Athens, PA St. Joseph Church.
Lanahan, Daniel *o.f.m.* '62 (NEW) [N] Hohokus, NJ St. Anthony of Padua.
Lanahan, William F. '55 (BRK) Released from Diocesan Assignment.
Lancaster, Leo '54 (WOR) Shrewsbury, MA St. Mary's Church.
Lancellotti, Vincent A. '68 (NY) Elmsford, NY Our Lady of Mt. Carmel Church.
Land, Jerome *o.s.b.* '80 (NO) [P] St. Benedict, LA St. Joseph Abbey.
Land, Philip S. *s.j.* (WDC) [V] Washington, DC Center of Concern.
Landa, Salvador '94 (ORG) [6] Santa Ana, CA St. Anne's Church.
Landauer, Joseph '78 (PIT) [M] Pittsburgh, PA Opus Dei.
Landewe, Robert A. '59 (SPC) Salem, MO Sacred Heart Church.
Landeza, Jayson J. '87 (OAK) [4] Fremont, CA St. Joseph Mission Church.
Landgraff, Thomas *o.s.f.s.* (TOL) Sandusky, OH St. Mary Church.
Landherr, Clayton R. '91 (DUB) [6] Dubuque, IA Church of the Resurrection.
Landi, Msgr. Andrew P. '34 (BRK) Retired.
Landi, Msgr. Andrew P. '34 (NY) [97] New York, NY Our Lady of the Scapular/St. Stephen Church.
Landi, L. Joseph (SFR) [U] San Francisco, CA Charismatic Movement.
Landi, Lodovico Joseph '90 (SFR) [10] San Francisco, CA St. Cecilia Church.
Lando Camillo *c.s.* (BO) [1] Everett, MA St. Anthony Church.
Landoll, Msgr. Gilbert J. '50 (SAL) Retired.
Landrau, Jose Antonio '90 (SJN) [34] San Juan, PR San Luis Gonzaga Church.
Landreau, Edward J. '57 (LA) Azusa, CA St. Frances of Rome Church.
Landreville, Norbert B. '58 (MAR) Ironwood, MI Our Lady of Peace Church.
Landry, Alduce '80 (HT) Permanent Deacons.
Landry, Alfred R. '32 (NOR) Retired.
Landry, Charles R. *c.ss.r.* '83 (NO) [23] New Orleans, LA St. Alphonsus Church; [4] New Orleans, LA St. Mary's Assumption Church.
Landry, Clyde B. '73 (BR) On Duty Outside the Diocese.
Landry, David J. '87 (FR) [2] Taunton, MA Our Lady of the Immaculate Conception Church.
Landry, Francis *c.p.* '76 (WOR) [N] Shrewsbury, MA Passionist Fathers of Shrewsbury, Inc., Calvary Retreat Center; [P] Shrewsbury, MA Calvary Retreat Center, Passionist Community.
Landry, Gary *c.m.* '73 (LA) [A] Camarillo, CA St. John's Seminary College of the Archdiocese of Los Angeles.
Landry, George *s.m.a.* '54 (NEW) [N] Tenafly, NJ Society of African Missions, Provincialate, S.M.A. Fathers.
Landry, George A. '43 (HT) Retired.
Landry, Ken Ramon (BLX) Waynesboro, MS St. Bernadette Church.
Landry, Laval L. *m.s.* '25 (STL) [P] St. Louis, MO La Salette Missionaries.
Landry, Maurice A. *s.m.m.* '41 (RVC) [N] Bay Shore, NY Montfort Missionaries.
Landry, Msgr. Michael '48 (NO) Retired.
Landry, Oneil A. '47 (LAF) Centerville, LA St. Joseph Church.
Landry, Phillip G. '88 (NO) Chalmette, LA St. Mark Church.
Landry, Ralph J. '62 (LAF) Washington, LA Immaculate Conception Church.
Landry, Richard *m.s.* '69 (FR) [K] Attleboro, MA La Salette Shrine; [M] Attleboro, MA La Salette Center for Christian Living.
Landry, Thomas G. '83 (WOR) Auburn, MA St. Joseph's Church.
Landsberger, Nicholas '61 (SCL) Little Falls, MN St. Mary Church.
Landsberger, Robert '57 (SCL) Motley, MN St. Michael's Church.
Landwerlen, Paul '54 (IND) St. Vincent de Paul, IN St. Vincent de Paul Church.
Landwermeyer, Bart J. '56 (FWT) Megargel, TX St. Mary Church; Seymour, TX Sacred Heart Church.
Landwermeyer, Francis M. *s.j.* '66 (SAT) [31] San Antonio, TX St. Brigid Church.
Landy, Joseph V. *s.j.* '54 (NY) [Z] New York, NY Murray-Weigel Hall.
Lane, Andrew *c.p.* '47 (CHI) [N] Chicago, IL Immaculate Conception Monastery; [N] Chicago, IL Daneo Hall.
Lane, Brian '89 (RC) Winner, SD Immaculate Conception Church.
Lane, C. Vincent '61 (SY) Vestal, NY St. Vincent de Paul Church.
Lane, Edmund C. *s.s.p.* '64 (NY) [B] New York, NY Society of St. Paul.
Lane, Msgr. Frank '67 (COL) [5] Columbus, OH St. Andrew Church.
Lane, George A. *s.j.* '67 (CHI) [N] Chicago, IL Chicago Province of the Society of Jesus-Provincial Office; [X] Chicago, IL Loyola Press.
Lane, James H. '62 (BO) [15] Boston, MA St. Brendan Church.
Lane, John H. *s.j.* '38 (CHI) [D] Chicago, IL St. Ignatius Jesuit Community.
Lane, John Thomas *s.s.s.* '92 (CLV) [B] Cleveland, OH Blessed Sacrament Seminary, Congregation of the Blessed Sacrament; [P] Cleveland, OH Blessed Sacrament Community.
Lane, Mark '74 (RIC) Special Assignment.
Lane, Mark *c.o.* '83 (BRK) [22] Brooklyn, NY St. Boniface Church.
Lane, Mark J. *c.o.* '83 (BRK) [U] Brooklyn, NY Oratory of Saint Philip Neri, Congregation Pontifical Right.
Lane, Michael '74 (JOL) Elmhurst, IL Visitation Church.
Lane, Robert C. '69 (STL) St. Peters, MO All Saints Church.
Lane, Thomas '29 (SEA) Retired.
Lane, Thomas V. '64 (YAK) Goldendale, WA Holy Trinity Church.
Lane, Timothy P. *c.j.* '95 (LA) [3] Santa Barbara, CA Our Lady of Guadalupe Church.
Lane, Msgr. William '46 (MRY) Retired.
Lane, William '50 (SEA) Retired.
Laner, Leander *o.f.m.* '39 (LA) [R] Santa Barbara, CA Franciscan Friary, Order of Friars Minor (Old Mission).
Lanergan, James F. (BO) [3] Plymouth, MA St. Mary Church; Waltham, MA Coordinator of Prison Ministry.
Lanese, John R. '73 (ALB) Clifton Park, NY St. Edward the Confessor Church.
Lanese, Pasquale *o.m.i.* '53 (BWN) [1] Brownsville, TX Immaculate Conception Cathedral.
Lang, Arnold *s.v.d.* '53 (WH) Marlinton, WV St. John Neumann Church.
Lang, B. Benedict *o.s.b.* '53 (PRO) [P] Portsmouth, RI Abbey of St. Gregory the Great.
Lang, Charles E. '65 (DUB) Anamosa, IA St. Patrick's Church; Belle Plaine, IA St. Michael Church; [2]

Cedar Rapids, IA All Saints Church; Chelsea, IA St. Joseph's Church.
Lang, Charles F. '75 (CIN) Fryburg, OH St. John Church; Glynwood, OH St. Patrick Church.
Lang, Msgr. Cordell J. '79 (MOB) [12] Mobile, AL St. Mary Church.
Lang, Henry A. '46 (BRK) Retired.
Lang, Hugh J. '56 (PIT) [5] Munhall, PA St. Theresa of Lisieux Church.
Lang, James Paul '75 (SY) Special Assignment; [V] Syracuse, NY Syracuse University, St. Thomas More Foundation, Inc.
Lang, James Paul '75 (Y) Windham, OH St. Michael's Church.
Lang, Joseph J. '65 (CLV) Released from Diocesan Assignment.
Lang, Joseph R. *m.m.* '52 (NY) [Z] Maryknoll, NY Maryknoll Fathers and Brothers.
Lang, Jovian *o.f.m.* '46 (FWT) Carrollton, TX St. Catherine of Siena Church; [H] Crowley, TX St. Maximilian Kolbe Friary.
Lang, Julius '42 (FAR) Retired.
Lang, Julius '42 (VEN) [1] Naples, FL St. Ann Church.
Lang, Leonard P. '75 (TR) Asbury Park, NJ Holy Spirit Church.
Lang, Michael P. '92 (TR) [14] Trenton, NJ St. Gregory the Great Church.
Lang, Raymond '43 (SCL) Retired.
Langan, James J. '57 (SCR) Retired.
Langan, John P. *s.j.* (DET) [K] Detroit, MI Jesuit Provincial Office-Detroit Province of the Society of Jesus.
Langan, John P. *s.j.* '72 (CHI) [C] Chicago, IL Jesuit Community at Loyola University of Chicago.
Langan, John P. *s.j.* '72 (WDC) [V] Washington, DC Woodstock Theological Center.
Langan, Patrick *l.c.* '91 (HRT) [V] Orange, CT Legion of Christ, Inc.
Langan, Thomas F. '59 (HBG) Abbottstown, PA Immaculate Heart of Mary Church.
Langan, Vincent F. '60 (SCR) South Waverly, PA St. John the Evangelist Church.
Langan, William J.P. '77 (SCR) Friendsville, PA St. Francis Xavier's Church.
Langdon, Robert H. '56 (NEW) Rutherford, NJ St. Mary's Church.
Lange, Donald F. '70 (MAD) Sinsinawa, WI St. Joseph Church.
Lange, George O. '57 (WOR) Westborough, MA St. Luke the Evangelist Church.
Lange, John W. *s.j.* '61 (SCR) [C] Scranton, PA University of Scranton.
Lange, Joseph '59 (PRT) Mexico, ME St. Theresa Church.
Lange, Lawrence P. '63 (TLS) Retired.
Lange, Matthew '38 (FTW) Retired.
Lange, Maurice *o.m.i.* '90 (GAL) [S] Dickinson, TX Christian Renewal Center.
Lange, Michael *o.f.m.* '46 (SUP) Odanah, WI St. Mary Church.
Lange, Raymond L. '50 (WOR) Retired.
Lange, Robert A. '86 (ARL) [6] Arlington, VA Our Lady of Lourdes Church.
Lange, Timothy J. '61 (OM) Stanton, NE St. Peter Church.
Lange, William S. '92 (PH) [12] Philadelphia, PA Annunciation B.V.M. Church; Highland Park, PA St. Laurence Church.
Langelier, Msgr. Gerald J. '61 (BRK) [214] Queens, NY Our Lady of Mercy Church.
Langell, Michael (SAV) Swainsboro, GA Holy Trinity Church.
Langenbrunner, Norman '70 (CIN) Fairfield, OH Sacred Heart of Jesus Church.
Langenderfer, Carl *o.f.m.* '71 (CIN) [M] Cincinnati, OH St. Ann Friary.
Langenderfer, Max *o.f.m.* '73 (CIN) [M] Cincinnati, OH St. Francis Seraph Friary.
Langenfeld, Thomas *c.s.v.* '60 (LAV) [15] Las Vegas, NV St. Viator Church.
Langenkamp, August *s.v.d.* '57 (JKS) Greenville, MS Sacred Heart Church.
Langer, Thomas E. '56 (LC) Bloomer, WI St. Paul Church; New Auburn, WI St. Jude Church.
Langerholz, Callistus F. *o.f.m.* '35 (CHI) [194] Chicago, IL St. Stephen Church.
Langevin, Fernand *m.s.* '48 (FR) [K] Attleboro, MA La Salette Provincial House.
Langford, Terry Lee '96 (L) Bardstown, KY St. Joseph Church.
Langguth, Laurence C. *s.j.* '40 (BO) [W] Weston, MA Campion Health Center, Inc.
Langhals, Henry *c.pp.s.* '37 (CIN) [B] Carthagena, OH St. Charles.
Langhans, Victor '84 (HEL) Frenchtown, MT St. John the Baptist Church.
Langheim, Albert *o.f.m.* '55 (GAY) Cross Village, MI Holy Cross Church; Good Hart, MI St. Ignatius Church; Larks Lake, MI St. Nicholas Church.
Langhirt, Carl J. *c.s.s.r.* '35 (ALB) [L] Saratoga Springs, NY St. John Neumann Residence.
Langhorst, Randall L. '92 (LIN) Weston, NE St. John Nepomucene Church.
Langille, Justin '80 (SD) Unassigned.
Langley, Barry *o.f.m.* '94 (WIL) [10] Wilmington, DE St. Paul's Church.
Langley, Barry J. *o.f.m.* '94 (WIL) [7] Wilmington, DE St. Joseph's R.C. Church of Wilmington, Inc.; [N] Wilmington, DE The Franciscan Center.
Langley, Joseph W. '42 (BO) Retired.
Langley, Terence *s.c.j.* '79 (BO) Carlisle, MA St. Irene Church.
Langley, Terence *s.c.j.* '79 (MIL) [P] Hales Corners, WI Priests of the Sacred Heart.
Langley, Wendell E. *s.j.* '53 (MIL) [P] Milwaukee, WI Jesuit Community at Marquette University.
Langlinais, J. Willis *s.m.* '52 (SAT) [C] San Antonio, TX St. Mary's University of San Antonio, Texas; [M] San Antonio, TX Casa Maria Marianist Community.
Langlois, Charles '96 (LAF) [3] New Iberia, LA Our Lady of Perpetual Help Church.
Langlois, Frederick M. '91 (HRT) [4] Milford, CT St. Mary's Church.
Langlois, John A. *o.p.* '91 (PRO) [P] Providence, RI St. Thomas Aquinas Priory at Providence College.
Langlois, Robert *s.m.* '61 (BO) [W] Cambridge, MA Our Lady of Mercy Marist Novitiate.
Langlois, William A. '74 (GR) Grand Haven, MI St. Patrick's Church.
Langone, Robert E. *s.a.* '89 (ARL) Sterling, VA Christ the Redeemer Church.
Langsch, Gerold M. '72 (MIL) [T] Waukesha, WI Secular Institute of Schoenstatt Fathers.
Langsdorf, Karl '72 (CHI) [N] Chicago, IL St. Patrick's Missionary Society.
Langsdorf, Michael (CHL) Clemmons, NC Holy Family Church
Langsfeld, Msgr. Paul J. '77 (BAL) [A] Emmitsburg, MD Mount St. Mary's Seminary.
Langsfeld, Msgr. Paul J. '77 (WDC) On Duty Outside the Archdiocese.
Langston, Micheas *o.s.b.* '65 (EVN) New Boston, IN St. John Chrysostom Church.
Langston, Micheas *o.s.b.* '65 (IND) [B] St. Meinrad, IN St. Meinrad Seminary-College of Liberal Arts; [J] St. Meinrad, IN St. Meinrad Archabbey.
Langton, Bernard F. *o.p.* '69 (PRO) [F] Providence, RI St. Thomas Aquinas Priory at Providence College.
Langton, Edmund T. *c.ss.r.* '44 (STL) [P] Liguori, MO St. Clement Health Care Center.
Langweld John *o.f.m.cap.* '46 (NY) [Z] Wassaic, NY Guardian Angel Chapel.
LaNier, Michael L. '83 (LA) Sick Leave.
Lanigan, Leo *c.ss.r.* '44 (ORL) [F] New Smyrna Beach, FL St. Alphonsus Villa-Redemptorist Fathers and Brothers.
Lanigan, Patrick J. '51 (SAC) Retired and in Senior Ministry.
Lankford, Michael G. '91 (TR) Red Bank, NJ St. James Church.
Lannan, Patrick D. '68 (STP) [8] St. Paul, MN The Nativity of Our Lord Church; [W] St. Paul, MN Nativity of Our Lord Endowment Fund.
Lannan, Paul A. '66 (LA) [86] Los Angeles, CA St. Paul the Apostle Church.
Lanning, Michael *o.f.m.* '78 (NY) [50] New York, NY Holy Trinity Church.
Lanning, Michael *o.f.m.* '78 (STL) [P] St. Louis, MO Franciscan Friary of St. Anthony of Padua.
Lannon, Timothy R. *s.j.* '86 (MIL) [P] Milwaukee, WI Jesuit Provincial Office, Wisconsin Province.
LaNoue, Bertrand *o.s.b.* '52 (KCK) [A] Atchison, KS Benedictine College; [H] Atchison, KS St. Benedict's Abbey.
Lanser, Jerome E. '58 (MIL) On Leave.
Lantry, Jerome *o.c.d.* '46 (LA) Alhambra, CA St. Therese Church.
Lantsberger, James *o.m.i.* '57 (SR) Imola, CA Napa State Hospital.
Lantsberger, John R. '76 (SFS) Aberdeen, SD Sacred Heart Church.
Lantz, David S. '78 (SFD) [3] Springfield, IL Christ The King Church; [C] Springfield, IL Springfield College in Illinois.
Lantz, Gary *s.c.j.* '80 (SFS) Lake Andes, SD St. Mark Church; Pierre, SD SS. Peter and Paul Church.
Lanuevo, Victor '75 (HON) Military Chaplains.
Lanuza, Antonio G. '62 (TR) Eatontown, NJ St. Dorothea Church.
Lanwermeyer, Francis M. *s.j.* '66 (SAT) [D] San Antonio, TX Antonian College Preparatory High School.
Lanz, Mathias F. '94 (FAR) Leeds, ND St. Vincent de Paul Church.
Lanz, Placido *o.a.r.* '32 (NEW) [N] West Orange, NJ Augustinian Recollects.
Lanza, Daniel A. *m.m.* '59 (NY) [Z] Maryknoll, NY Maryknoll Fathers and Brothers.
Lanza, Steven M. '81 (CHI) [144] Chicago, IL Notre Dame Church.
Lanzaderas, Francisco H. '82 (NY) [211] Staten Island, NY St. Joseph, St. Thomas Church.
Lanzalaco, Joseph M. *c.s.b.* '87 (GRY) Michigan City, IN Indiana State Prison; [B] Merrillville, IN Andrean High School; [K] Merrillville, IN Basilian Fathers Residence.
Lanzon, Paul *s.d.s.* '71 (LC) [D] Marshfield, WI Holy Family Middle School.
Lanzrath, Curt *o.f.m.* '54 (HT) [4] Houma, LA Our Lady of the Most Holy Rosary Church.
Lanzrath, John *o.f.m.* '53 (LSC) Roswell, NM St. Peter Church.
Lanzrath, John P. '88 (WCH) Mulvane, KS St. Michael the Archangel Church.
LaPan, Kenneth C. *t.o.r.* '52 (ALT) [F] Hollidaysburg, PA St. Joseph Friary.
Lapan, Robert '60 (BUR) St. Johnsbury, VT St. John the Evangelist Church.
LaPata, Richard C. *o.p.* '59 (CHI) [J] Elk Grove Village, IL Alexian Brothers Medical Center, Inc.; [N] River Forest, IL St. Thomas Aquinas Priory.
Lapauw, Joseph *c.i.c.m.* '73 (ARL) [J] Arlington, VA Missionhurst, C.I.C.M.-Central House and Provincialate.
LaPaz, Gabriel '78 (NY) [53] New York, NY Incarnation Church.
Lape, Lydell T '90 (OM) Butte, NE SS. Peter and Paul Church.
Lapean, Gerald J. '57 (SPR) [11] Springfield, MA Our Lady of the Sacred Heart Church.
Lapensky, John G. '77 (STP) Veseli, MN Most Holy Trinity Church.
LaPenta, Charles A. *o.s.f.s.* '54 (OKL) Duncan, OK Assumption Church.
LaPenta, Charles A. *o.s.f.s.* '54 (TOL) [K] Toledo, OH Oblates of St. Francis de Sales.
Lapera, John M. '84 (SCR) [15] Scranton, PA St. Joseph's Church.
Laperle, Theodore R. '54 (WOR) [2] Fitchburg, MA St. Bernard's Church; Retired.
LaPierre, David *o.f.m.cap.* '69 (FRS) Fresno, CA Community Hospital, Veterans' Hospital.
Lapinski, Daniel A. '79 (BUF) Westfield, NY St. James Church.
LaPlante, David W. '78 (OM) Bancroft, NE Holy Cross Church; Lyons, NE St. Joseph Church.
Laplante, Jean-Paul '50 (BUR) Retired.
LaPlante, Joseph A. '54 (WIN) Retired; [A] Winona, MN Immaculate Heart of Mary Seminary, Saint Mary's University of MN #43.
Laplante, Laurant R. '57 (PRT) Kennebunk, ME St. Martha's Church.
Laplante, Louis A. '87 (MET) Retired.
Laplante, Philip *s.m.* '48 (BO) [59] Boston, MA Our Lady of Victories Church; [W] Boston, MA Marist Fathers of Our Lady of Victories (Boston Prov.).
LaPlante, Robert J. '95 (CR) Thief River Falls, MN St. Bernards Church.
LaPlante, Roland M. '62 (HRT) South Meriden, CT Holy Angels Church.
Lapointe, J. Donald R. '67 (SPR) [3] Northampton, MA Sacred Heart Church; [4] Northampton, MA St. John Cantius Church.
Lapointe, Jean Marie *o.p.* '39 (PRT) [I] Lewiston, ME SS. Peter and Paul Priory.
LaPointe, John G. '72 (PRO) [3] Johnston, RI St. Robert Bellarmine Church.
LaPointe, Laurence A.M. '70 (NOR) [K] Willimantic, CT Campus Ministry; [K] Willimantic, CT Campus Ministry.
Lapolla, Daniel *c.s.* '74 (CHI) [137] Chicago, IL St. Michael Archangel Church.
Lapomarda, Vincent A. *s.j.* '64 (WOR) [N] Worcester, MA Jesuits of Holy Cross College, Inc.
LaPore, Arthur '76 (JOL) [8] Joliet, IL St. Anthony Church.
LaPorta, Ross A. '51 (BAL) [55] Baltimore, MD St. Mark Church.
LaPorte, Gerard B. *c.ss.r.* '65 (NO) [23] New Orleans, LA St. Alphonsus Church.
Laporte, Paul J. '65 (PRO) Coventry, RI St. Vincent de Paul's Church.
Lappin, Peter *s.d.b.* '43 (NY) [BB] West Haverstraw, NY Don Bosco Retreat Center and Marian Shrine; [BB] West Haverstraw, NY Marian Shrine.
LaPrad, Steve '95 (KNX) Johnson City, TN St. Mary Church.
Laptuta, Demetrius *c.ss.r.* '45 (STF) Niagara Falls, NY Protection of B.V.M. Church.
Laqueux, Maurice R. '61 (MAN) Absent on Sick Leave.
Lara, Delfino *ss.cc.* '63 (SB) Cathedral City, CA St. Louis Church.
Lara, Gustavo (LA) [53] Los Angeles, CA St. Camillus De Lellis Church.
Lara, Gustavo '57 (LA) [24] Los Angeles, CA Our Lady of Guadalupe Church.
Lara, James '57 (SP) Brandon, FL Church of the Nativity.
LaRaia, Joseph P. '46 (BO) Westford, MA St. Catherine Church.
Larche, James M. '91 (OG) Massena, NY Sacred Heart Church.
Lardner, Gerald V. '67 (BAL) [M] Baltimore, MD

Sulpician Provincial House.
Laredo, Leopoldo *sch.p.* '40 (SJN) [58] San Juan, PR Santisimo Salvador Church.
Larena, Ismael '47 (PCE) Santa Isabel, PR St. James Church.
Large, John J. '75 (PH) Norwood, PA St. Gabriel Church.
Largent, Jeffery '84 (FTW) Culver, IN St. Mary of the Lake Church.
Largente, Laurent '59 (SJ) Retired.
Larger, Raymond E. '77 (CIN) [40] Cincinnati, OH St. James the Greater Church.
Larguier, Everett H. *s.j.* '41 (MOB) [B] Mobile, AL Spring Hill College.
Lariviere, Robert D. '78 (PRT) Kittery, ME St. Raphael's Church.
Larkin, Alexander C. '67 (SJ) Saratoga, CA Sacred Heart Church.
Larkin, Bartholomew *o.carm.* '58 (VEN) Grove City, FL St. Francis of Assisi Church.
Larkin, Edward A. *s.j.* '54 (OM) [C] Omaha, NE Creighton Preparatory School.
Larkin, Ernest *o.carm.* '46 (PHX) [6] Phoenix, AZ St. Agnes Church; [I] Phoenix, AZ Kino Institute.
Larkin, James (NY) White Plains, NY St. Agnes Hospital.
Larkin, John *o.carm.* '51 (PHX) [6] Phoenix, AZ St. Agnes Church.
Larkin, John P. '44 (NY) Retired; [Z] New York, NY Pope John Paul II Residence.
Larkin, Joseph M. '57 (SY) Minetto, NY Our Lady of Perpetual Help Church.
Larkin, Kevin J. '59 (LA) Sherman Oaks, CA St. Francis de Sales Church.
Larkin, Michael J. '59 (STA) [12] Jacksonville, FL Prince of Peace Church.
Larkin, Michael T. '68 (SC) Humboldt, IA St. Mary's Church; Livermore, IA Sacred Heart Church.
Larkin, Patrick '57 (WCH) Caldwell, KS St. Martin of Tours Church.
Larkin, Richard '47 (STP) Retired.
Larkin, Msgr. Robert W. '73 (NY) [193] Bronx, NY Visitation Church.
Larkin, Ron *m.s.c.* '61 (SB) Upland, CA St. Joseph Church.
Larkin, William D. *c.s.p.* '81 (BO) [W] Boston, MA Paulist Fathers Residence.
Larkin, William J. *s.j.* '52 (BO) [W] Boston, MA Loyola House; [W] Chestnut Hill, MA The Jesuit Community at Boston College.
Larko, Ronald *v.f.* '82 (PBR) Irving, TX St. Basil the Great Church.
Larmann, Marian E. *o.s.b.* '47 (NO) St. Benedict, LA St. Benedict Church; [A] St. Benedict, LA St. Joseph's Seminary College; [P] St. Benedict, LA St. Joseph Abbey.
Larmore, Donald E. '63 (GI) [2] Grand Island, NE Blessed Sacrament Church.
Larner, James M. '57 (BO) [26] Boston, MA St. Gregory Church.
LaRocca, Christopher *o.c.d.* (TUC) [21] Tucson, AZ Santa Cruz Church.
LaRocca, Jack '88 (SJ) San Jose, CA Detention Ministry for Juveniles.
LaRocca, John J. *s.j.* '75 (CIN) [M] Cincinnati, OH Jesuit Community at Xavier Unversity.
LaRocca, Msgr. Vincent R. '49 (BRK) Released from Diocesan Assignment.
LaRoche, Christopher J. '95 (PRT) Caribou, ME Holy Rosary Church.
Laroche, Leonidas B. '61 (BUR) St. Albans, VT Immaculate Conception Church.
Larochelle, Alphonse *m.s.* '59 (HON) Waipahu, HI St. Joseph Church.
Larochelle, Maurice R. '87 (MAN) Lancaster, NH All Saints Church.
LaRocque, Benedict J. *o.s.b.* '42 (KCK) [H] Atchison, KS St. Benedict's Abbey.
LaRocque, Benedict J. *o.s.b.* '42 (OM) Retired.
LaRocque, Leonard *a.a.* '56 (WOR) [N] Worcester, MA Assumptionists (Augustinians of the Assumption).
LaRocque, Msgr. Richard P. '63 (NOR) Old Lyme, CT Christ the King Church.
LaRoque, Paul M. '45 (TUC) Retired.
LaRosa, John J. '81 (PH) [147] Philadelphia, PA Stella Maris Church; [152] Philadelphia, PA St. Timothy Church.
LaRose, Edward M. '66 (HRT) [7] New Britain, CT St. Jerome's Church.
Larrea, Luis Eduardo '77 (LA) [68] Los Angeles, CA Santa Isabel Church.
Larreategui, Jose Luis *sch.p.* '53 (PCE) Jayuya, PR Our Lady of Monserrate Church; [B] Ponce, PR The Pontifical Catholic University of Puerto Rico.
Larrivee, Leo J. *s.s.* '77 (BAL) [65] Baltimore, MD Our Lady of the Angels Catholic Community Church.
Larrivee, Leo J. *s.s.* '77 (SEA) On Duty Outside the Archdiocese.
Larriviere, Marshall (LAF) Retired.
Larroque, Msgr. H. Alexandre '55 (LAF) On Special Assignment; [I] Lafayette, LA Discalced Carmelites.
Larry, Anthony J. *o.s.f.s.* '67 (HBG) New Bloomfield, PA St. Bernard Church.
Larsen, Kevin '93 (ARL) Springfield, VA St. Bernadette's Church.
Larson, F. James '62 (RCK) Special Assignment.
Larson, Jan '56 (SEA) Snoqualmie, WA Our Lady of Sorrows Church.
Larson, Jan '68 (SEA) Snoqualmie, WA Echo Glen School
Larson, Lawrence A. '77 (BGP) Newtown, CT St. Rose of Lima Church.
Larson, Paul J. '79 (DUL) Coleraine, MN Mary Immaculate Church; Marble, MN St. Mary's Church.
Larue, Charles '93 (SAN) Retired.
LaRue, Joseph *o.f.m.* '32 (LA) [R] Santa Barbara, CA Franciscan Friary, Order of Friars Minor (Old Mission).
LaRusch, Msgr. Alton J. '41 (BUF) Retired.
Larussa, Raymond '74 (COL) [9] Columbus, OH St. Cecilia Church.
Larve, Charles '93 (SAT) [K] San Antonio, TX Padua Place.
Las, Stefan '88 (PAT) [4] Passaic, NJ Holy Rosary Church.
Las, Wlodzimierz R. *s.d.s.* '86 (BRK) [93] Brooklyn, NY Our Lady of Consolation Church.
Las, Wlodzimierz R. *s.d.s.* '86 (NEW) [N] Verona, NJ The Salvatorian Fathers.
Lasalle, Donald *s.m.m.* '83 (HRT) [M] Litchfield, CT Montfort Missionaries.
LaSalle, Donald G. *s.m.m.* '83 (WDC) [M] Washington, DC Missionaries of the Company of Mary-Montfort Missionaries.
Lascelle, Roger L. '77 (DEN) Meeker, CO Holy Family Church; Rangely, CO St. Ignatius Church; [P] Rangely, CO Colorado Northwestern Community College (Rangely).
Lascelle, Roger L. '77 (WOR) On Duty Outside the Diocese.
Lasch, Msgr. Kenneth E. '62 (PAT) Mendham, NJ St. Joseph's Church.
Lasecki, Daniel J. '64 (MIL) Elkhart Lake, WI St. George's Church; Glenbeulah, WI St. Fridolin Church.
Lash, Joseph J. '57 (CHL) Retired.
Lasheras, Antonio *o.a.r.* '62 (NY) [157] Bronx, NY St. John Vianney, Cure of Ars Church.
Lasic, Dionizije *o.f.m.* '37 (CHI) [N] Chicago, IL Croatian Franciscan Custody of the Holy Family.
Lasic, Miron '40 (CHI) [N] Chicago, IL Croatian Franciscan Custody of the Holy Family.
Laska, William M. '88 (E) [4] Erie, PA Holy Rosary Church.
Laske, Kenneth S. '58 (CHI) Berwyn, IL St. Leonard Church.
Lasko, Stephen J. *c.s.sp.* '47 (VEN) [G] Sarasota, FL Congregation of the Holy Ghost.
Laskowski, Norbert '71 (NEW) Kearny, NJ St. Cecilia's Church.
Lasky, Joseph J. '55 (SCR) Kingston, PA St. Mary's Annunciation Church.
Laslavich, Luke *o.praem.* '94 (ORG) [H] Silverado, CA Norbertine Fathers.
Lasley, Jerry D. '92 (DAV) Iowa City, IA State University of Iowa Hospital.
Lasrado, Maxim *o.c.d.* (CHI) [58] Chicago, IL St. Ferdinand Church.
Lassuy, Raymond J. '39 (PEO) Retired.
Last, Carl A. '69 (MIL) [53] Milwaukee, WI St. Matthias Church.
Lastiri, Jean-Michael '85 (FRS) Merced, CA Our Lady of Mercy/St. Patricks Church.
Latcovich, Mark '81 (CLV) [A] Wickliffe, OH St. Mary Seminary.
Latella, Joseph A. *s.j.* '58 (NY) [Z] New York, NY St. Ignatius Loyola Residence.
Later, Msgr. Morse A. (B) Retired.
Later, Morse A. '55 (B) Idaho City, ID St. Joseph's Church; [B] Boise, ID St. Alphonsus Regional Medical Center, Inc.
Lathem, Msgr. E. Christopher '65 (CHR) Summerville, SC St. John the Beloved Church.
Latimer, Msgr. Edward H. '39 (E) [1] Erie, PA St. Peter Cathedral; Retired.
Latino, Msgr. Joseph N. '63 (HT) [1] Houma, LA Cathedral of St. Francis De Sales.
Latka, John '56 (CHI) [60] Chicago, IL Five Holy Martyrs Church.
Latona, Marcello J. '70 (BRK) [179] Queens, NY Holy Trinity Church.
LaTorre, Abraham '51 (SAT) [20] San Antonio, TX Our Lady of Sorrows Church.
Latosynski, Roger '84 (PT) Apalachicola, FL St. Patrick Church.
Latre, Msgr. Angel '54 (MGZ) [1] Mayaquez, PR Cathedral of Our Lady of Purification.
Latronico, P. '86 (NEW) [S] Rutherford, NJ The Community of God's Love.
Latsko, Andrew J. '92 (CHL) Swannanoa, NC St. Margaret Mary Church.
Latterell, Glenn '81 (SFS) Retired.
Lattis, Herbert L. '64 (L) Goshen, KY Transfiguration of Our Lord Church.
Latus, Charles J. '68 (ROC) Mendon, NY St. Catherine of Siena Church.
Latzko, Frank '84 (CHI) [199] Chicago, IL St. Teresa Church; [A] Chicago, IL Archbishop Quigley Preparatory Seminary.
Lau, Ignatius '58 (ORG) [1] Santa Ana, CA Immaculate Heart of Mary Church.
Lau, John Raymond *o.m.i.* '91 (MIA) [19] Miami, FL St. Francis Xavier Church.
Lau, Michael '61 (P) Seaside, OR Our Lady of Victory Church.
Lau, Vincent '52 (FRS) [9] Fresno, CA St. Genevieve Church.
Laubach, Barnabas *o.s.b.* '52 (SB) San Bernardino, CA San Bernardino Medical Center; [D] San Bernardino, CA St. Bernardine Medical Center.
Laubach, Barnabas *o.s.b.* '52 (SCL) [I] Collegeville, MN St. John's Abbey, of the Order of St. Benedict.
Laubacker, Jerome *o.de.m.* '74 (BUF) [O] LeRoy, NY Order of the BVM of Mercy/Mercedarian Friars; [Q] LeRoy, NY St. Peter Nolasco Spiritual Center.
Lauck, Anthony J. *c.s.c.* '46 (FTW) [A] Notre Dame, IN Moreau Seminary.
Laudati, Joseph J. '56 (NEW) Retired.
Lauder, Robert E. '60 (BRK) Released from Diocesan Assignment; [B] Douglaston, NY Cathedral Residence of the Immaculate Conception.
Laudick, John R. '64 (TOL) [H] Sandusky, OH Providence Hospital Inc.
Lauducci, V. James '57 (SY) Special Assignment; [V] Utica, NY SUNY Institute of Technology at Utica/Rome Newman Center; [V] Utica, NY Utica College of Syracuse University Newman Center.
Laudwein, James R. *s.j.* '62 (P) [L] Portland, OR Jesuit Provincial Office (Oregon Prov.).
Laudwein, Joseph *s.j.* '62 (FBK) Tanana, AK St. Aloysius Church; [C] Fairbanks, AK Jesuit Residence.
Lauenstein, Gary *c.ss.r.* '71 (STL) [B] St. Louis, MO St. John Neumann House.
Lauer, Albert E. '74 (CIN) On Special and Diocesan Assignment.
Lauer, Douglas J. '94 (COV) Crescent Springs, KY St. Joseph Church; [C] Covington, KY Villa Madonna High School.
Lauer, Eugene A. *o.s.b.* '43 (PEO) [A] Peru, IL St. Bede Abbey and Academy.
Lauer, Eugene F. '61 (FTW) [B] Notre Dame, IN University of Notre Dame Du Lac.
Lauer, Eugene F. '61 (PIT) On Duty Outside the Diocese.
Lauer, J. Quentin *s.j.* '48 (NY) [Z] New York, NY Murray-Weigel Hall.
Lauerman, James P. '70 (FAR) Napoleon, ND St. Philip Neri Church.
Laughery, Kevin M. '83 (SFD) Farmersville, IL St. Mary Church; Girard, IL St. Patrick Church.
Laughlin, James L. (BO) Winchester, MA St. Eulalia Church.
Laughlin, Joseph R. *s.j.* '57 (BO) [E] Boston, MA Boston College High School & Jesuit Community.
Laughlin, Martin T. '52 (DUB) Retired.
Laughlin, Martin T. . '67 (CHR) Hilton Head Island, SC St. Francis By the Sea Church.
Launderville, Dale *o.s.b.* '79 (SCL) [A] Collegeville, MN St. John's Seminary; [B] Collegeville, MN St. John's University; [I] Collegeville, MN St. John's Abbey, of the Order of St. Benedict.
Launtrie, Francis J. *c.s.b.* '56 (GAL) [Q] Sugar Land, TX Basilian Mission Center.
Laurance, John D. *s.j.* '70 (MIL) [P] Milwaukee, WI Jesuit Community at Marquette University.
Laurano, Anthony J. (BO) Retired.
Laurello, Msgr. Bartholomew J. '46 (BGP) Retired.
Laurent, Edward *o.f.m.cap.* '64 (PIT) [N] Pittsburgh, PA St. Patrick Friary.
Laurenzano, Roch M. '49 (NY) Retired.
Laurenzo, James M. (DM) [A] West Des Moines, IA St. Joseph Educational Center.
Lauretti, George F. '56 (HRT) Southington, CT St. Thomas Church.
Lauri, John F. '73 (NY) [E] New York, NY Cardinal Spellman High School.
Laurick, Richard A. *c.s.c.* '54 (FTW) [16] South Bend, IN St. Patrick Church.
Laurinaitis, Saulius P. '48 (COL) Retired.
Lauriola, Guglielmo *o.f.m.* '53 (SFR) [5] San Francisco, CA St. Anthony Church.
Lause, Richard *c.m.* '77 (SPC) Charleston, MO St. Henry Church.
Laushway, Aaron *o.p.* '80 (RIC) Charlottesville, VA St. Thomas Aquinas Church.
Lautenschlager, Bruno *s.j.* '64 (BO) [W] Cambridge, MA Faber House.
Lautermilch, David J. '62 (TOL) Awaiting Assignment.
Lautner, Msgr. William A. '38 (EVN) Retired.
Lautz, Boniface *o.s.b.* '60 (B) [C] Jerome, ID Ascension Priory.
Laux, Donald J. '48 (GB) Retired.
Lauze, Michael *o.m.i.* '75 (PRT) [I] Augusta, ME St.

Paul Retreat House and Cursillo Center; [L] Augusta, ME St. Paul Retreat House and Cursillo Center.
Lauzon, Kris C. '91 (OG) [1] Ogdensburg, NY St. Mary's Cathedral.
Lauzon, Paul *s.d.s.* '71 (LC) [C] Marshfield, WI Columbus High School.
Lauzon, Raymond J. '55 (PRT) Retired.
Lavagetto, Xavier M. *o.p.* '96 (SFR) [13] San Francisco, CA St. Dominic Church; [N] San Francisco, CA St. Dominic Priory.
Lavallee, Pierre A. '61 (BUR) [4] Burlington, VT St. Joseph's Church.
LaValley, Richard G. '64 (BUR) Winooski, VT St. Francis Xavier Church; [J] Burlington, VT University of Vermont-The Catholic Center at UVM.
LaVan, Kenneth G. '58 (STP) Lino Lakes, MN St. Joseph Church.
Lavaroni, Rino '67 (NEW) Oradell, NJ St. Joseph's Church.
Lavastida, Jose I. '87 (NO) [A] New Orleans, LA Notre Dame Seminary Graduate School of Theology.
Lavelle, Donald *c.m.f.* '46 (CHI) [N] Oak Park, IL Claretian Fathers Headquarters of U.S.A. Eastern Province.
Lavelle, Edward R. '63 (HBG) [8] Harrisburg, PA Our Lady of the Blessed Sacrament Church.
Lavelle, Francis '70 (SPR) [M] Northampton, MA Spanish Apostolate.
Lavelle, Francis P. '70 (SPR) [2] Northampton, MA Blessed Sacrament Church; [P] Amherst, MA University of Massachusetts and Amherst College, Newman Center.
Lavelle, Raymond E. '57 (COL) Powell, OH St. Joan of Arc Church.
Lavely, Charles J. *c.s.c.* '65 (FTW) [16] South Bend, IN St. Patrick Church.
LaVerde, Calogero N. '68 (CAM) Egg Harbor City, NJ St. Nicholas Church.
LaVerde, Charles *c.s.* '65 (CHI) [17] Chicago, IL St. Anthony Church.
LaVerdiere, Eugene *s.s.s.* '64 (CLV) [B] Cleveland, OH Blessed Sacrament Seminary, Congregation of the Blessed Sacrament.
LaVerdiere, Eugene *s.s.s.* '64 (NY) [55] New York, NY St. Jean Baptiste Church.
LaVerdiere, Eugene A. *s.s.s.* '56 (CHI) [B] Chicago, IL The Catholic Theological Union at Chicago.
Lavere, Philip *o.f.m.* '47 (BO) [BB] Boston, MA St. Anthony Shrine.
LaVerghetta, Richard D. '86 (TR) [14] Trenton, NJ St. Gregory the Great Church.
Lavergne, Carlos J. *s.j.* '65 (SJN) [22] San Juan, PR San Ignacio de Loyola Church.
Laverone, Kenneth J. '79 (MRY) Aptos, CA Resurrection Church.
Laverty, Joseph F. *o.s.a.* '48 (PH) [Z] Villanova, PA St. Thomas Monastery.
Laverty, Seamus '68 (SEA) [9] Tacoma, WA St. Patrick's Church.
Laverty, Tod *o.f.m.* '72 (CHI) [N] Chicago, IL St. Joseph Friary; [N] Chicago, IL St. Mary Magdalene Friary.
Lavery, Bruce '67 (ORG) Laguna Niguel, CA St. Timothy Church.
Lavery, Phillip M. '88 (PIT) Absent on Sick Leave.
Laviano, Vincent A. *o.f.m.* '74 (NY) [35] New York, NY St. Francis of Assisi Church.
Lavich, David *o.c.s.o.* '73 (WOR) [A] Spencer, MA St. Joseph's Abbey School of Theology and Institute of Monastic Studies.
Lavigne, Lionel *s.s.s.* '41 (NY) [8] New York, NY St. Andrew Church.
Lavigne, Maurice D. '68 (MAN) [13] Manchester, NH Our Lady of Perpetual Help Church.
Lavigne, Richard R. '66 (SPR) Absent on Leave.
Lavin, Bernard C. '79 (PRO) [5] Pawtucket, RI St. John the Baptist Church.
Lavin, Msgr. James M. '45 (STP) Retired; [C] St. Paul, MN University of St. Thomas.
Lavin, Msgr. John B. '64 (BRK) [235] Queens, NY St. Robert Bellarmine Church.
Lavin, John J. '64 (PRO) [3] Newport, RI St. Joseph's Church.
Lavin, John P. *c.ss.r.* '66 (BAL) [60] Baltimore, MD St. Michael Church; [76] Baltimore, MD St. Patrick Church.
Lavin, Martin '67 (RIC) Martinsville, VA St. Joseph Church.
Lavin, Paul E. '69 (WDC) [24] Washington, DC St. Joseph on Capitol Hill Church.
Lavin, Msgr. Robert F. '56 (SY) East Syracuse, NY St. Matthew Church; Retired.
Lavin, Thomas '41 (MIL) [P] East Troy, WI Divine Word Seminary.
Lavin, Thomas *o.f.m.conv.* '87 (HRT) Kensington, CT St. Paul's Church.
Lavin, Wayne Patrick '71 (CAM) [3] Camden, NJ St. Bartholomew's Church.
LaViolette, Msgr. Matt H. '34 (MAR) Retired.
Laviste, Manuel J. '91 (HON) Kekaha, HI St. Theresa Church.
Lavitch, David *o.c.s.o.* '73 (WOR) [N] Spencer, MA St. Joseph's Abbey.
Lavoie, Merle L. '68 (SPR) [13] Springfield, MA St. Aloysius Church; [17] Springfield, MA St. Matthew's Church.
Lavoie, Rene G. '51 (PRT) [3] Lewiston, ME Holy Family Church; Retired.
Lavoie, Richard *m.s.* '64 (FR) Brewster, MA Our Lady of the Cape Church.
Lavoie, Msgr. Robert G. '53 (PRT) Westbrook, ME St. Hyacinth Church.
Lavoie, Robert R. '40 (PRT) Retired; [I] Waterville, ME Mt. St. Joseph Priest Retirement Home.
LaVoie, Victor (BO) Boston, MA Lahey Clinic.
Lavoie, Victor '71 (BO) Winchester, MA St. Eulalia Church.
Lavorin, Anthony F. *o.f.m.* (MRY) Jolon, CA San Antonio Mission Church.
Lavoy, Elwood '53 (LAV) Retired.
Lavrih, John '39 (DOD) Retired.
Law, Msgr. Joseph A. '49 (SCR) Retired.
Lawie, Richard J. '69 (GR) On Special Assignment.
Lawler, Bruce A. '80 (SC) Salix, IA St. Joseph's Church.
Lawler, Daniel F. *s.j.* '48 (HBG) Chambersburg, PA Corpus Christi Church.
Lawler, David '62 (IND) Indianapolis, IN Methodist Hospital.
Lawler, Msgr. John F. (BO) Retired.
Lawler, John T. '43 (BO) Retired.
Lawler, Joseph A. '61 (BEL) Piopolis, IL St. John the Baptist Church.
Lawler, Msgr. Richard C. '59 (IND) [31] Indianapolis, IN St. Mark the Evangelist Church.
Lawler, Msgr. Robert L. '56 (OG) Waddington, NY St. Mary Church.
Lawler, Ronald '51 (PIT) [N] Pittsburgh, PA St. Francis Friary
Lawler, Terrance M. '74 (MET) Sayreville, NJ Our Lady of Victories Church.
Lawler, William J. '72 (WIL) Centreville, MD Mother of Sorrows Church.
Lawless, Brendan '64 (JC) Richland, MO St. Jude Church; Waynesville, MO St. Robert Bellarmine Church.
Lawless, Joseph *m.s.f.* '71 (CC) [15] Corpus Christi, TX St. Joseph Church.
Lawless, Timothy J. *s.j.* '61 (DEN) [M] Denver, CO Xavier Jesuit Center.
Lawlor, Brendan '55 (SP) Temple Terrace, FL Corpus Christi Church.
Lawlor, Brendan W. '44 (BUR) Retired.
Lawlor, David T. *o.praem.* '71 (BAL) Grantsville, MD St. Ann Church; Mount Savage, MD St. Patrick Church.
Lawlor, David T. *o.praem.* '71 (PH) [Z] Paoli, PA Daylesford Abbey.
Lawlor, Edward J. *s.s.j.* '40 (NO) [N] New Orleans, LA Chateau de Notre Dame.
Lawlor, Francis *o.s.a.* '45 (STL) [6] St. Louis, MO Immaculate Conception-St. Henry Church.
Lawlor, Francis '69 (SAC) [21] Sacramento, CA St. Rose Church.
Lawlor, J. Michael '73 (BO) Lynnfield, MA St. Maria Goretti Church.
Lawlor, James '63 (ROC) [45] Rochester, NY St. Mary Church.
Lawlor, Msgr. John F. (BO) Needham, MA St. Bartholomew Church.
Lawlor, John J. *c.m.* '44 (BAL) [M] Emmitsburg, MD Vincentian House.
Lawlor, John J. *c.m.* '44 (PH) [Z] Philadelphia, PA Congregation of the Mission.
Lawlor, John L. *c.m.* '44 (CHR) Gloverville, SC Our Lady of the Valley Church.
Lawlor, Joseph '62 (JC) Missionary Assignment in Peru.
Lawlor, Msgr. Joseph F. '35 (RVC) Baldwin, NY St. Christopher Church; Retired.
Lawlor, Mark '95 (CHL) Winston-Salem, NC St. Leo's Church.
Lawlor, Msgr. Timothy '43 (SB) Ontario, CA St. George Church; Retired.
Lawlor, William G. *s.j.* '49 (NY) [Z] New York, NY Murray-Weigel Hall.
Lawrence, David L. *s.j.* '74 (OAK) [N] Berkeley, CA Jesuit Community at Jesuit School of Theology at Berkeley.
Lawrence, Emeric *o.s.b.* '35 (SCL) [I] Collegeville, MN St. John's Abbey, of the Order of St. Benedict.
Lawrence, Francis '45 (JOL) [J] Lisle, IL St. Procopius Abbey.
Lawrence, James A. '70 (BUR) Ludlow, VT Annunciation Church.
Lawrence, James T. '61 (DAV) [M] Davenport, IA St. Vincent Center.
Lawrence, Jeffrey '96 (PEO) Rantoul, IL St. Malachy's Church.
Lawrence, John (SAC) Fort Jones, CA Sacred Heart Church.
Lawrence, Joseph '77 (FTW) [1] Fort Wayne, IN Cathedral of the Immaculate Conception.
Lawrence, Kenneth F. '60 (HBG) Columbia, PA Holy Trinity Church.
Lawrence, Kevin C. '87 (PH) [144] Philadelphia, PA Sacred Heart of Jesus Church.
Lawrence, Michael S. '73 (ALN) [7] Allentown, PA St. Paul Church; [L] Coopersburg, PA Carmelite Monastery.
Lawrence, Neal Henry *o.s.b.* '60 (SCL) [I] Collegeville, MN St. John's Abbey, of the Order of St. Benedict.
Lawrence, Ralph J. '53 (CIN) Eaton, OH Visitation of the Blessed Virgin Mary Church; New Paris, OH St. John Church.
Lawrence, Richard T. '68 (BAL) [93] Baltimore, MD St. Vincent de Paul Church.
Lawrence, Walter L. '73 (WDC) Kensington, MD Holy Redeemer Church.
Lawryniuk, Lawrence *o.s.b.m.* '64 (STF) New York, NY St. George Church.
Lawsine, Robert S. '81 (BRK) [84] Brooklyn, NY St. Mary, Star of the Sea Church.
Lawson, Harold F. '59 (BO) Absent on Sick Leave.
Lawson, Meinrad J. *o.s.b.* '67 (SAV) [F] Savannah, GA The Benedictine Priory.
Lawson, Robert T. '62 (R) Pinehurst, NC Sacred Heart Church.
Lawson, Ronald (BO) [1] Arlington, MA St. Agnes Church; Boston, MA V.A. Medical Centers.
Lawson, Theodore *c.ss.r.* '89 (DAV) [4] Davenport, IA St. Alphonsus Church.
Lawson, Willaim T. '86 (SD) National City, CA St. Anthony of Padua Church.
Lawton, Robert B. *s.j.* '81 (WDC) [C] Washington, DC Georgetown University; [M] Washington, DC The Jesuit Community at Georgetown University.
Lawton, Thomas E. *c.s.c.* '36 (FR) [M] North Easton, MA Holy Cross Fathers Retreat House.
Lawyer, Jerome R. *c.s.c.* '39 (BRK) [95] Brooklyn, NY Our Lady of Good Counsel Church.
Lay, Thomas N. *s.j.* '66 (KC) [B] Kansas City, MO Rockhurst College; [J] Kansas City, MO Rockhurst College - Jesuit Community.
Layton, Richard *o.c.s.o.* '82 (P) [L] Lafayette, OR The Cistercian (Trappist) Abbey of Our Lady of Guadalupe.
Laz, Medard P. '69 (CHI) [5] Cicero, IL Our Lady of Charity Church.
Lazar, Francis M. '60 (GRY) Highland, IN St. James the Less Church.
Lazar, John '42 (STN) Dearborn Heights, MI Our Lady of Perpetual Help Church; Flint, MI St. Vladimir's Church.
Lazar, John E. '80 (BRK) Absent on Leave.
Lazaro, Angel Millan *sch.p.* '55 (SJN) [58] San Juan, PR Santisimo Salvador Church.
Lazaro, Felix *sch.p.* '61 (PCE) Jayuya, PR Our Lady of Monserrate Church; [B] Ponce, PR The Pontifical Catholic University of Puerto Rico.
Lazaro, Lesmes Bernabe *o.s.a.* '49 (MGZ) Aguada, PR St. Francis of Assisi Church.
Lazarski, Marvin I. '62 (MIL) [28] Milwaukee, WI St. Gerard's Church.
Lazek, Aleck '60 (AUS) Retired; [J] Waco, TX The Regis Retirement Home and St. Elizabeth Nursing Home.
Lazor, Bernard A. *o.s.a.* '51 (PH) [C] Villanova, PA Villanova University; [Z] Villanova, PA St. Thomas Monastery.
Lazor, Joseph '90 (STF) Manchester, NH Protection of B.V.M. Church.
Lazzaro, Nicholas A. '41 (PH) Conshohocken, PA SS. Cosmas and Damian Church; Retired.
Le, Hoang Viet '61 (TLS) [8] Tulsa, OK St. Joseph Church.
Le, James Vinh '87 (KAL) Dorr, MI St. Stanislaus Church.
Le, Joseph Ahn *s.d.b.* '95 (LA) [F] Bellflower, CA St. John Bosco High School.
Le, Paul Vung *s.v.d.* '85 (SB) [7] San Bernardino, CA St. Anthony Church.
Le, Peter Quang '88 (STP) [11] St. Paul, MN St. Adalbert Church.
Le, Tan Van '73 (CHL) [4] Charlotte, NC St. Ann Church.
Le, Thang T. '93 (CHI) Berwyn, IL St. Mary of Celle Church.
Le Beau, Philip '93 (PAT) [8] Paterson, NJ St. Gerard Majella Church.
Le Fevre, Francis J. '71 (BAL) Absent on Leave; [K] Baltimore, MD Stella Maris Operating Corporation.
Le Frois, Christian G. *o.s.b.* '46 (GBG) [H] Latrobe, PA Saint Vincent Archabbey.
Le Jacq, Peter M. *m.m.* '87 (NY) [Z] Maryknoll, NY Maryknoll Fathers and Brothers.
Leach, Gregory '93 (DM) Ankeny, IA Our Lady's Immaculate Heart Church.
Leach, Jerome '76 (SFR) Absent on Leave.
Leach, Phillip M. '85 (R) Chapel Hill, NC Newman Catholic Student Center, University of North Carolina Church; [H] Chapel Hill, NC Newman Catholic Student Center.
Leach, Thomas F. '73 (BRK) [103] Brooklyn, NY Our Lady of Miracles Church.

Leach, William J. '58 (STL) Gildehaus, MO St. John the Baptist Church.
Leack, Lawrence J. '50 (MIL) Retired; [V] Milwaukee, WI Our Blessed Lady of Victory Mission, Inc.
Leahey, Patrick R. '77 (ALT) Dudley, PA Immaculate Conception Church.
Leahy, Anthony '55 (SB) Retired.
Leahy, Clement '50 (CHI) [N] Chicago, IL St. Peter's Friary.
Leahy, Edward W. *o.p.* '94 (STP) [8] Minneapolis, MN Holy Rosary Church; [15] Minneapolis, MN St. Albert the Great Church.
Leahy, Edwin D. *o.s.b.* '72 (NEW) [C] Newark, NJ St. Benedict's Preparatory School; [N] Newark, NJ Newark Abbey.
Leahy, John A. '57 (CLV) Middleburg Heights, OH St. Bartholomew Church.
Leahy, Liam '72 (TUC) [14] Tucson, AZ St. John the Evangelist Church.
Leahy, Msgr. Patrick J. '38 (DOD) Retired.
Leahy, Robert T. '60 (NEW) On Duty Outside the Archdiocese.
Leahy, Robert T. '60 (TR) Forked River, NJ St. Pius X Church.
Leahy, Thomas W. *s.j.* '51 (SJ) [M] Los Gatos, CA California Province of the Society of Jesus, Jesuit Provincial Office; [M] Los Gatos, CA Sacred Heart Jesuit Center.
Leahy, William *s.j.* '78 (BO) [W] Chestnut Hill, MA The Jesuit Community at Boston College.
Leahy, William J. '66 (SAV) St. Marys, GA Our Lady Star of the Sea Church.
Leahy, William P. *s.j.* '78 (BO) [C] Chestnut Hill, MA Boston College.
Leake, Jerome L. '68 (RCK) [1] Elgin, IL St. Joseph Church.
Lealofi, Msgr. Etuale '69 (SPP) [4] (Lauli'i), AS Church of St. Peter and Paul.
Leannah, Scott R. '93 (MIL) Lake Geneva, WI St. Francis de Sales Church.
Leary, Albert R. '54 (BIS) Huff, ND St. Martin Church; Mandan, ND Christ the King Church; Mandan, ND Christ the King Church.
Leary, Donald G. '51 (WIN) Retired.
Leary, Edward *s.s.e.* '53 (VEN) [G] Englewood, FL Society of St. Edmund Residence.
Leary, James *o.f.m.cap.* '70 (DET) [K] Detroit, MI St. Bonaventure Friary; [T] St. Clair Shores, MI Catholic Kolping Society of America, Detroit Branch, Inc.
Leary, James *o.f.m.cap.* '80 (DET) [Q] Detroit, MI Capuchin Soup Kitchen.
Leary, James F. '68 (HRT) [4] Bristol, CT St. Joseph Church; [C] West Hartford, CT Saint Joseph College.
Leary, James V. '56 (PH) Retired.
Leary, Msgr. Joseph W. '53 (CAM) Retired.
Leary, Patrick *o.f.m.* '62 (BO) [BB] Boston, MA St. Anthony Shrine.
Leary, Patrick R. *v.g.* '76 (LAV) [16] Las Vegas, NV Shrine of the Most Holy Redeemer Church.
Leason, Antoine G. *s.v.d.* '96 (LAF) [4] Lafayette, LA Immaculate Heart of Mary Church.
Leatham, Gerald '65 (LUB) Ralls, TX St. Michael Church.
Leavey, Msgr. Thomas G. '51 (RVC) Seaford, NY St. William, the Abbot Church.
Leavins, Brice A. *o.f.m.* '69 (BO) [BB] Boston, MA St. Anthony Shrine.
Leavitt, Robert F. *s.s.* '68 (BAL) [A] Baltimore, MD St. Mary's Seminary and University; [A] Baltimore, MD St. Mary's Seminary and University.
Leavitt, Robert F. *s.s.* '68 (HRT) On Duty Outside the Archdiocese.
Lebanowski, Gerald '59 (STL) [P] St. Louis, MO La Salette Missionaries.
Lebar, Ivan M. *t.o.r.* '58 (WH) Keyser, WV Assumption Church.
LeBar, James J. '62 (NY) Hyde Park, NY Regina Coeli Church; Poughkeepsie, NY Hudson River Psychiatric Center.
LeBarre, Renald D. '60 (PRT) Biddeford, ME St. Joseph's Church.
LeBauve, J. Joel '70 (BR) New Roads, LA St. Mary of False River Church.
Lebdowicz, Jan Krzysztof '80 (NEW) Wallington, NJ Most Sacred Heart of Jesus Church.
LeBeau, Cyril A. '48 (WOR) [16] Worcester, MA Sacred Heart Church; [M] Worcester, MA Vianney House.
LeBeau, Joseph *s.v.d.* '49 (CHI) [B] Techny, IL Divine Word Residence.
Lebel, Guy *s.m.* '39 (BO) [Y] Framingham Centre, MA The Marist House.
Lebel, Maurice T. '67 (PRT) Auburn, ME Sacred Heart Church.
Lebiedz, Bernard *o.s.b.* '59 (SFE) [L] Pecos, NM Our Lady of Guadalupe Benedictine Abbey.
LeBlanc, Alvin J. '82 (HRT) [8] Waterbury, CT St. Anne Church; Special and other (Arch)Diocesan Assignment; [A] Bloomfield, CT St. Thomas Seminary.
LeBlanc, Charles R. '79 (NOR) Plainfield, CT St. John the Apostle Church.
LeBlanc, David E. '61 (GR) [8] Grand Rapids, MI Holy Spirit Church.
LeBlanc, Etienne '71 (HT) Morgan City, LA Holy Cross Church.
LeBlanc, Gregory S. '94 (DOD) [1] Dodge City, KS Cathedral of the Sacred Heart.
LeBlanc, Harold E. '61 (BO) [4] Woburn, MA St. Joseph Church.
LeBlanc, J. Whitney '63 (LAF) Retired.
LeBlanc, James Leo '96 (CHR) [17] Charleston, SC Christ Our King Church.
LeBlanc, Keith '96 (BO) [2] Everett, MA Immaculate Conception Church.
LeBlanc, Kenneth A. '76 (BO) [5] Waltham, MA Our Lady, Comforter of the Afflicted Church.
LeBlanc, Leo *o.m.i.* '67 (MIA) Opa Locka, FL St. Monica Church.
LeBlanc, Leo A. '74 (MAN) [11] Manchester, NH St. John the Baptist Church.
LeBlanc, Omer *c.j.m.* '61 (SD) [2] El Cajon, CA Our Lady of Grace Church.
LeBlanc, Paul '69 (NY) Absent on Leave.
LeBlanc, Paul J. '69 (NY) [184] Bronx, NY St. Pius V Church.
LeBlanc, Steven C. '77 (LAF) [5] New Iberia, LA Sacred Heart of Jesus Church.
LeBleu, Vernon W. '95 (LKC) [6] Lake Charles, LA St. Theodore's Church.
LeBoeuf, Gerald J. '93 (DET) Allen Park, MI St. Frances Cabrini Church.
LeBouef, Raymond (HT) [4] Houma, LA Our Lady of the Most Holy Rosary Church.
LeBourgeois, Msgr. Louis P. '61 (NO) Jefferson, LA St. Agnes Church.
Lebrun, Maurice '34 (PRT) [I] Lewiston, ME SS. Peter and Paul Priory.
LeBrun, Paul *c.s.c.* '83 (FTW) [20] South Bend, IN St. Therese, Little Flower Church.
Lebrun, Raymond *o.m.i.* '68 (PRT) [I] Augusta, ME St. Paul Retreat House and Cursillo Center; [L] Augusta, ME St. Paul Retreat House and Cursillo Center.
LeCaptain, Douglas '93 (GB) [15] Green Bay, WI Resurrection Church.
Lecchin, Mario *i.m.c.* '63 (MET) [H] Somerset, NJ Consolata Society for Foreign Missions.
Lech, Ferdinand F. '48 (PIT) Meadowlands, PA Our Lady of the Miraculous Medal Church.
Lech, Waclaw L. *o.c.d.* '74 (GRY) [K] Munster, IN Discalced Carmelite Fathers Monastery.
Lecheler, Anton L. '46 (LC) Rock Falls, WI St. Joseph Church.
Lechiara, Francis J. '59 (PMB) Palm Beach, FL St. Edward Church; [J] Palm Beach Gardens, FL Diocesan Health Plan Trust; [J] Palm Beach Gardens, FL Diocesan Pension Plan Trust.
Lechner, Robert *c.pp.s.* '46 (CIN) [B] Carthagena, OH St. Charles.
Lechner, Robert *c.pp.s.* '46 (WOR) [P] Spencer, MA Ecumenical Institute of Spirituality.
Lechner, Msgr. Roger A. '66 (SD) [7] San Diego, CA Holy Spirit Church.
Lechtenberg, Msgr. Edward W. '51 (DUB) Lycurgus, IA St. Mary's Church; Waukon, IA St. Patrick's Church.
Leckie, Michael J. '76 (PRO) Hope Valley, RI St. Joseph's Church.
LeClair, Lawrence J. '53 (HRT) [6] Waterbury, CT Our Lady of Mt. Carmel Church; Waterbury, CT Waterbury Hospital; Retired.
LeClaire, Fred *c.m.f.* '87 (PHX) Prescott, AZ Sacred Heart Church.
LeClaire, Karl '86 (PHX) [4] Mesa, AZ Queen of Peace Church.
Leclerc, Leo A. '61 (SPR) [9] Chicopee, MA St. Rose de Lima Church.
Leclercq, M. Duane '64 (PEO) [4] La Salle, IL St. Patrick's Church.
Leclere, Gerard P. '60 (BUR) Enosburg Falls, VT St. John the Baptist Church.
LeCompte, Glenn D. '86 (HT) Raceland, LA St. Hilary of Poitiers Church.
LeCompte, Glenn D. '86 (NO) [A] New Orleans, LA Notre Dame Seminary Graduate School of Theology.
LeCours, Sylva P. '47 (NOR) Ballouville, CT St. Anne Church.
Lecuivre, Joel A. '72 (PRO) [5] Cranston, RI St. Mary Church.
Lecumberri, Rufino '54 (NY) [158] Bronx, NY St. Joseph Church.
Leddy, Aidan J. '56 (CC) Violet, TX St. Anthony Church.
Leddy, John J. *o.m.i.* '51 (WDC) [B] Washington, DC Oblate College/Oblate Center for Mission Studies; [Q] Washington, DC Basilica of the National Shrine of the Immaculate Conception.
Leddy, Leonard '59 (AUS) Cyclone, TX St. Joseph's Church; Marak, TX SS. Cyril and Methodius Church.
Leddy, Seamus *s.s.c.* '42 (LA) [R] Los Angeles, CA Columban Fathers, Procure House.
Leder, Dennis M. *s.j.* '76 (NY) [Z] New York, NY Jesuit Provincial's Office.
Lederman, Paul '50 (DET) Retired.
Ledermann, Paul F. '63 (OG) On Duty Outside the Diocese.
Ledermann, Paul F. '63 (SR) Yountville, CA Veterans Administration Home.
Ledet, Msgr. Donald L. '63 (HT) Raceland, LA St. Mary's Nativity Church.
Ledford, John S. '75 (WH) Berkeley Springs, WV St. Vincent de Paul Church.
Ledoux, Albert H. '87 (WDC) Beltsville, MD St. Joseph Church.
LeDoux, Jerome *s.v.d.* '57 (NO) [26] New Orleans, LA St. Augustine Church.
Ledoux, John C. '50 (BUR) Retired.
Ledoux, Louis V. '52 (LAF) Military Chaplains.
Ledoux, Michael Dominic *o.f.m.* '86 (PIT) [C] McKeesport, PA Serra Catholic High School.
Ledoux, Michael Dominic W. *o.f.m.* (PIT) [N] McKeesport, PA Franciscan Friars.
Ledoux, William J. '93 (PRO) Coventry, RI SS. John and Paul Church.
LeDuc, Roger D. '60 (FR) [2] Swansea, MA St. Louis de France Church.
Ledwidge, Brendan K. '55 (LAN) Retired.
Ledwith, Harry '74 (TUC) [19] Tucson, AZ St. Pius X Church.
Ledwon, Jacob C. '72 (BUF) [40] Buffalo, NY St. Joseph Church; [R] Williamsville, NY Newman Club Chaplains.
Ledwon, Josaphat *o.f.m.* '56 (GB) [I] Pulaski, WI Assumption of B.V.M. Friary.
Lee, Andrew '83 (RIC) [1] Newport News, VA Catholic Community of the Korean Martyrs Church; [L] Richmond, VA Ethnic and Special Ministries.
Lee, Bernard J. *s.m.* '67 (NO) [C] New Orleans, LA Loyola University.
Lee, Blose '76 (DET) [6] Detroit, MI St. Andrew Kim Korean Catholic Church.
Lee, Msgr. David M. '68 (BUF) [R] Williamsville, NY Newman Club Chaplains.
Lee, Dominic Savio '94 (SFR) [4] San Francisco, CA St. Anne Church.
Lee, Francis D. '42 (SFD) [9] Quincy, IL St. Rose of Lima Church.
Lee, Gerard *o.f.m.* '50 (NY) [Z] New York, NY Franciscan Friars, Order of Friars Manor.
Lee, Gerard *o.f.m.* '71 (ALB) [J] Albany, NY Teresian House.
Lee, Henry H. '54 (LC) Retired.
Lee, Msgr. Howard T. '54 (FRS) Retired.
Lee, James '75 (SEA) Bellingham, WA Assumption B.V.M. Church.
Lee, Jeffrey E. '92 (TR) Cinnaminson, NJ St. Charles Borromeo Church.
Lee, John (SC) [D] Sioux City, IA Marian Health Center.
Lee, John M. *c.p.* '72 (MET) [H] South River, NJ Passionist Provincial Office; [H] South River, NJ Passionist Provincial Office.
Lee, John R. *c.s.b.* '56 (ROC) [I] Rochester, NY Basilian Residence.
Lee, John B. Yong-woo '92 (WDC) [M] Washington, DC Carroll House.
Lee, Joseph '55 (CHI) [98] Chicago, IL St. James Church.
Lee, Joseph Chun Yuan '58 (SFR) Retired.
Lee, Joseph P. '57 (LA) Sick Leave.
Lee, Joshua '87 (LA) [40] Los Angeles, CA St. Alphonsus Church.
Lee, Keun-Soo '95 (BR) [12] Baton Rouge, LA St. Jean Vianney Church.
Lee, Kevin '89 (LR) Mena, AR St. Agnes Church.
Lee, Lawrence '49 (GAL) Retired.
Lee, Matthew (J.T.) '93 (WDC) Military Chaplains.
Lee, Michael (TR) Eatontown, NJ Immaculate Conception Church.
Lee, Michael G. '64 (WH) Absent on Sick Leave.
Lee, Michael G. *s.j.* '96 (MIL) [29] Milwaukee, WI Gesu Parish Church.
Lee, Michael J. *o.praem.* '70 (PH) [D] Philadelphia, PA St. John Neumann High School; [Z] Philadelphia, PA St. Norbert Priory.
Lee, Patrick J. '76 (CHI) [90] Chicago, IL Immaculate Conception of the Blessed Virgin Mary Church.
Lee, Patrick J. *s.j.* '78 (P) [A] Portland, OR Jesuit Novitiate of St. Francis Xavier.
Lee, Paul '90 (SD) [H] San Luis Rey, CA San Luis Rey.
Lee, Paul D. '83 (WDC) Pastoral Center Special Ministries.
Lee, Peter '51 (LA) Retired.
Lee, R. Anthony '93 (PEO) Danville, IL St. Paul's Church; [B] Danville, IL Schlarman High School.
Lee, Robert E. *m.m.* '43 (NY) [Z] Maryknoll, NY Maryknoll Fathers and Brothers.
Lee, Robert E. *o.carm.* '55 (JOL) [J] Darien, IL Carmelite Community; [M] Darien, IL Provincial Office of Lay Carmelites and Scapular Confraternity.
Lee, Robert E. *o.carm.* '55 (PRT) [1] Portland, ME Cathedral of the Immaculate Conception; Portland, ME St. Joseph's Manor; Retired.
Lee, Robert E. '59 (PEO) Moline, IL Sacred Heart Church.

Lee, Roy A. '68 (MIL) Military Chaplains.
Lee, San Yil '92 (AUS) Leander, TX St. Yoo Peter Catholic Church.
Lee, Terence J. *m.h.m.* '57 (NY) [Z] Hartsdale, NY Mill Hill Fathers Residence.
Lee, Msgr. Thaddeus (PAT) Retired.
Lee, Thomas M. '53 (PRT) Lyman, ME St. Philip Church.
Lee, William '62 (HON) On Duty Outside the Diocese.
Lee, William J. *s.s.* '46 (BAL) [K] Baltimore, MD St. Charles Villa; [M] Baltimore, MD St. Charles Villa.
Leeber, Victor F. *s.j.* '53 (BGP) [A] Fairfield, CT Fairfield University; [O] Fairfield, CT The Fairfield Jesuit Community-Fairfield University.
Leech, George T. '56 (PIT) [O] Elizabeth, PA Divine Redeemer Motherhouse.
Leedale, Walter F. *s.j.* '59 (SPK) [C] Spokane, WA Gonzaga University.
Leehan, Patrick *c.ss.r.* '48 (OAK) [N] Oakland, CA Redemptorists.
Leehy, Stephen G. '73 (OG) On Duty Outside the Diocese.
Leek, Michael *o.s.b.* '93 (SFE) [L] Pecos, NM Our Lady of Guadalupe Benedictine Abbey.
Leeuw, Daniel '57 (FTW) Fort Wayne, IN Veterans Administration Hospital; [H] Avilla, IN Sacred Heart Home; [H] Avilla, IN LaVerna Terrace Apartments.
Lefebure, Leo D. '78 (CHI) [A] Mundelein, IL University of St. Mary of the Lake-Mundelein Seminary; [A] Mundelein, IL University of St. Mary of the Lake-Mundelein Seminary.
Lefebvre, Bruce A. '73 (SC) West Bend, IA SS. Peter and Paul Church.
Lefebvre, Msgr. Gerald M. '56 (BR) Maurepas, LA St. Stephen Martyr Church.
Lefebvre, James '59 (ALB) [11] Albany, NY St. Mary Church.
Lefebvre, Leo P. '55 (MAN) Penacook, NH Immaculate Conception Church.
Lefebvre, Simon *c.s.v.* '56 (SD) Borrego Springs, CA St. Richard Church.
LeFevre, Msgr. Michael C. '82 (DET) [1] Sterling Heights, MI St. Blase Church.
LeFevre, Robert J. '66 (ALB) Saratoga Springs, NY St. Peter Church.
Leffler, Richard J. '78 (MAD) Tennyson-Potosi, WI SS. Andrew-Thomas Church.
Lefko, John *c.pp.s.* '38 (CIN) [B] Carthagena, OH St. Charles.
Lefler, John '57 (EVN) Retired.
LeFleur, R.K. '61 (SAG) Bannister, MI St. Cyril Church.
LeFrois, Christian *o.s.b* '46 (SAV) Lakeland, GA Queen of Peace Church.
LeFrois, Msgr. Marvin J. '49 (SAV) Retired.
Legarra, Francisco J. *o.a.r.* '74 (LA) [R] Oxnard, CA St. Augustine Priory O.A.R.
Legarski, Anthony J. '83 (ALT) Military Chaplains.
Legaspi, Alex '76 (SFR) [16] San Francisco, CA St. Emydius Church.
Legendre, Msgr. Francis J. '61 (HT) Cut-Off, LA Sacred Heart Church.
Leger, Donald Nicholas '68 (LAF) Evangeline, LA St. Joseph Church.
Leger, G. Robert '71 (SJ) [6] San Jose, CA St. Frances Cabrini Church.
Leger, Laurie *m.s.* '54 (WOR) [3] Gardner, MA Our Lady of the Holy Rosary Church.
Leger, P. Austin '62 (LAF) Lawtell, LA St. Bridget Church.
Leger, Paul P. '33 (PIT) Monongahela, PA Transfiguration Church.
Leger, Steven '86 (BEA) Absent On Leave.
Legere, Germain *c.p.* '42 (L) [K] Louisville, KY Nazareth Home; [L] Louisville, KY Sacred Heart Retreat.
LeGere, Vincent '60 (VEN) Bokeelia, FL Our Lady of the Miraculous Medal Church.
Legerski, John '81 (B) Absent on Sick Leave.
Lego, William E. *o.s.a.* '83 (CHI) [185] Chicago, IL St. Rita of Cascia Church.
Lehane, Joseph E. '77 (CLV) Macedonia, OH Our Lady of Guadalupe Church.
Leheny, Msgr. Bernard M. '66 (LA) Norwalk, CA St. John of God Church.
Lehman, Darold R. '58 (NU) Springfield, MN St. Raphael Church.
Lehman, Joseph *t.o.r.* '96 (FWT) [4] Arlington, TX St. Maria Goretti Church.
Lehman, Joseph P. '80 (RIC) [2] Norfolk, VA Christ the King Church.
Lehman, Mark A. '88 (PHX) Unassigned.
Lehman, Paul J. '54 (NEW) [5] Newark, NJ St. Antoninus Church.
Lehmann, Anthony *s.j.* '56 (SPK) [C] Spokane, WA Gonzaga University.
Lehmkuhl, Gerhardt B. *s.j.* '74 (STL) [P] St. Louis, MO Jesuit Community Corporation at St. Louis University - Jesuit Hall.
Lehmkuhl, John '45 (TOL) Retired.
Lehner, John *o.s.f.s.* '70 (DET) Inkster, MI Holy Family Parish Church; Inkster, MI St. Kevin and St. Norbert Church.
Lehnerd, Frank M. '58 (Y) [14] Youngstown, OH St. Edward's Church.
Lehning, Thomas J. '70 (ARL) Manassas, VA Sacred Heart Church.
Lehocky, Msgr. Leigh A. '68 (CHR) [1] Columbia, SC St. Peter's Church.
Lehr, Theodore F. *o.f.m.* '56 (NEW) Elmwood Park, NJ St. Leo's Church.
Lehrberger, James *o.cist.* '76 (DAL) [B] Irving, TX University of Dallas; [M] Irving, TX Cistercian Abbey of Our Lady of Dallas.
Leibenguth, Gerald T. *o.s.b.* '72 (BO) [W] Hingham, MA Glastonbury Abbey.
Leibham, David M. '87 (AUS) Giddings, TX St. Margaret Church.
Leibinger, Arthur B. '38 (STL) Retired.
Leiblinger, Frank J. '38 (LIN) Retired.
Leibold, Alcuin *o.s.b.* '56 (IND) [J] St. Meinrad, IN St. Meinrad Archabbey.
Leibold, James C. '80 (BRK) Military Chaplains.
Leibrecht, Robert G. '58 (STL) [3] St. Louis, MO Holy Family Church.
Leicht, Gerard *ss.cc.* '40 (HON) [11] Honolulu, HI St. Patrick Church.
Leicht, Gerard *ss.cc.* '45 (HON) [H] Honolulu, HI St. Patrick's Monastery.
Leidich, Kevin A. *s.j.* '82 (LA) [F] Los Angeles, CA Loyola High School.
Leies, John A. *s.m.* '56 (SAT) [C] San Antonio, TX St. Mary's University of San Antonio, Texas; [M] San Antonio, TX Marianist Residence.
Leies, John G. *s.m.* '38 (SAT) [M] San Antonio, TX Marianist Residence.
Leif, Gregory P. '78 (WIN) Adams, MN Sacred Heart Church.
Leifeld, Msgr. Antony J. '38 (NU) [1] New Ulm, MN Cathedral of The Holy Trinity; Retired.
Leigh, David J. *s.j.* '68 (SEA) [A] Seattle, WA Seattle University.
Leighton, Donald E. '62 (PH) Collingdale, PA St. Joseph Church.
Leiker, Francis R. *s.j.* '54 (STL) [O] St. Louis, MO Fusz Pavilion.
Leiker, Perry D. '76 (LA) [17] Los Angeles, CA Mother of Sorrows Church.
Leikhim, Joel J. *o.s.b.* '61 (PAT) [M] Morristown, NJ St. Mary's Abbey.
Leinen, Ronald *m.s.c.* '57 (RCK) [H] Aurora, IL Missionaries of the Sacred Heart Community.
Leinfelder, Philip '39 (LC) Retired; [I] La Crosse, WI Holy Cross (Seminary) Diocesan Center.
Leininger, Charles A. *s.j.* '53 (DAL) [D] Dallas, TX Jesuit College Preparatory School.
Leininger, Donald F. '58 (SP) Palm Harbor, FL St. Luke the Evangelist Church; [F] Palm Harbor, FL St. Luke Early Childhood Center.
Leininger, Joseph B. *s.j.* '53 (GAL) [F] Houston, TX Strake, Jesuit College Preparatory Inc.
Leininger, William C. '56 (SJ) [24] San Jose, CA Church of the Transfiguration.
Leipert, Jack J. '75 (SAG) Bad Axe, MI Sacred Heart Church.
Leiphon, Donald A. '68 (FAR) Fairmount, ND St. Anthony's Church; [F] Wahpeton, ND Carmel of Mary.
Leis, Edward C. *o.f.m.conv.* '58 (IND) [J] Mount Saint Francis, IN Provincial Headquarters for the Conventual Franciscan Province.
Leise, Gerald A., Jr. '74 (OM) Ewing, NE St. Peter de Alcantara Church; St. John, NE St. John Church.
Leise, Leo V. *s.j.* '94 (NO) [P] New Orleans, LA Jesuit Provincial Office.
Leisen, Leo '54 (SCL) Lake Henry, MN St. Margaret's Church; Roscoe, MN St. Agnes Church; Spring Hill, MN St. Michael's Church.
Leisen, Richard '56 (SCL) Paynesville, MN St. Louis Church.
Leising, Msgr. Frederick D. '71 (BUF) Lancaster, NY St. Mary of the Assumption Church.
Leising, John J. '69 (BUF) Newfane, NY St. Bridget Church; Wilson, NY Our Lady of the Rosary Church.
Leising, Robert *o.m.i.* '90 (HBG) Dallastown, PA St. Joseph Church.
Leisle, Charles E. '58 (LC) Retired.
Leissa, Eric B. '95 (CLV) Chesterland, OH St. Anselm Church.
Leissler, Joseph L. '32 (SB) Retired.
Leisy, Christian *o.s.b.* '88 (SFE) [J] Abiquiu, NM Monastery of Christ in the Desert.
Leitem, Leon *o.f.m.cap.* '57 (PIT) Freedom, PA St. Felix Church; [N] Rochester, PA St. Cecilia Friary.
Leith, James A. '81 (FAR) West Fargo, ND Holy Cross Church.
Leitheiser, Douglas '49 (FRS) Retired.
Leiting, Robert L. '67 (SC) Carroll, IA St. Anthony Regional Hospital; [D] Carroll, IA St. Anthony Regional Hospital; [D] Carroll, IA St. Anthony Regional Hospital; [E] Carroll, IA St. Anthony Nursing Home.
Leitner, John E. (KC) [2] Independence, MO St. Joseph the Worker Church.
Leiva, Emilio (ARE) On Duty Outside the Diocese.
Leiweke, Robert W. *s.j.* '58 (MIL) [P] Milwaukee, WI Jesuit Community at Marquette University.
Leja, Casimir '85 (CHI) Other Assignments.
LeJeune, Ronald J. '71 (TOL) [4] Fremont, OH St. Joseph Church.
Leketas, Peter J. '43 (LC) Retired.
Lekwot, Peter (NY) [F] New York, NY All Hallows Institute.
Leliaert, Richard M. *o.s.c.* '67 (DET) Riverview, MI St. Cyprian Church; [K] Riverview, MI Crosier Community of Riverview.
Lelii, Raymond M. *s.j.* '61 (WDC) [E] North Bethesda, MD Georgetown Preparatory School.
Lelo-Luemba, Albert *c.i.c.m.* '96 (BWN) [4] McAllen, TX St. Joseph the Worker Church.
Leloczky, Julius *o.cist.* '61 (DAL) [M] Irving, TX Cistercian Abbey of Our Lady of Dallas.
LeLonde, Venant *o.f.m.* '54 (NY) [2] New York, NY St. Agnes Church.
Lelonis, Richard M. '71 (PIT) [62] Pittsburgh, PA St. Pius X Church.
Lemanski, William E. *s.a.c.* '74 (MIL) [P] Milwaukee, WI Pallotti House.
Lemarie, Marie Tarcisius *f.j.* '90 (CC) [G] Laredo, TX Holy Spirit Retreat and Conference Center; [H] Laredo, TX St. John's Priory, (F.J.).
Lemaster, Scott G. '85 (DAV) Richmond, IA Holy Trinity Church; Wellman, IA St. Joseph Church.
LeMay, Donald *o.s.b.* '57 (SCL) [I] Collegeville, MN St. John's Abbey, of the Order of St. Benedict.
Lemay, Donald H. '89 (RIC) Blacksburg, VA St. Mary & Newman Community Church.
Lemay, Jean M. (SJ) Gilroy, CA St. Mary Church.
LeMay, John M. *o.s.m.* '84 (CHI) [N] Chicago, IL Servite Friars - Eastern Province.
Lembo, Richard A. '75 (PRT) Lubec, ME Sacred Heart Church.
Lemen, William F. '36 (CR) Bemidji, MN St. Philip's Church; Retired.
LeMieux, Thomas A. '59 (MIL) [11] Kenosha, WI St. Thomas Aquinas Church.
Lemire, Paul W. '89 (WOR) [4] Southbridge, MA St. Mary's Church.
Lemke, Norbert J. *s.j.* '44 (OM) [K] Omaha, NE Jesuit Community At Creighton University.
Lemkuhl, David A. '79 (CIN) On Duty Outside the Archdiocese.
Lemlin, Timothy J. '78 (PRO) Mapleville, RI Our Lady of Good Help Church.
Lemm, Eugene '57 (SCL) Brandon, MN Church of St. Ann; Millerville, MN Seven Dolors Church.
Lemmens, Henry C. *c.s.sp.* '34 (VEN) [G] Sarasota, FL Congregation of the Holy Ghost.
Lemmert, Ronald J. '51 (NY) State, NY Sing Sing Correctional Facility; [DD] Peekskill, NY My Father's House, Inc.
Lemming, Patrick W. '81 (MOB) On Leave from the Archdiocese.
Lemoi, Paul R. '75 (PRO) [2] West Warwick, RI Our Lady of Good Counsel Church.
Lemoine, Msgr. J. Guy '56 (LAF) [1] New Iberia, LA St. Peter Church.
Lemoine, Russell J. '70 (ALX) Mansura, LA St. Paul the Apostle Church.
Lemoine, Msgr. Vincent P. '51 (SAL) Retired.
Lemon, Msgr. Clement P. '64 (WIL) Hockessin, DE St. Mary of the Assumption Church.
Lemoncelli, Henry L. *o.m.i.* '79 (WDC) [B] Washington, DC Oblate College/Oblate Center for Mission Studies; [B] Washington, DC Oblates of Mary Immaculate, De Mazenod Residence.
Lemos, Thomas F. *c.s.c.* '74 (FTW) [5] South Bend, IN St. Casimir Church; [19] South Bend, IN St. Stephen Church; [J] South Bend, IN Congregation of Holy Cross Indiana Province Provincial House.
Lemoyne, William '49 (ALB) Retired.
Lemp, Joseph R. *s.t.l.* '56 (PIT) Koppel, PA Queen of Heaven Church.
Lempart, Ignatius *o.s.c.* '43 (LIN) [A] Hastings, NE Crosier Monastery.
Lemrise, Arthur *c.s.v.* '44 (JOL) [E] Momence, IL Good Shepherd Manor.
Lemrise, John-Marie *c.m.f.* '52 (CHI) [149] Chicago, IL Our Lady of Guadalupe Church.
Lemus, Francisco Arrivillaga *o.s.b.* '95 (SFS) [F] Marvin, SD Blue Cloud Abbey.
Lemus, Francisco J. *s.j.* '62 (MIA) [22] Miami, FL St. John Bosco Church; [D] Miami, FL Belen Jesuit Preparatory School.
Lemus, Ovidio Ortega '83 (SJN) [41] San Juan, PR Ntra. Sra. de la Medalla Milagrosa Church.
Lenaghan, Charles G. *s.j.* '58 (CHI) [172] Chicago, IL St. Philomena Church.
Lenaghan, Jordan *o.p.* '96 (RIC) Charlottesville, VA St. Thomas Aquinas Church.
Lenahan, John B. '49 (L) Retired; [K] Louisville, KY St. Joseph Home for the Aged.
Lenane, William '50 (SJ) [3] Palo Alto, CA St. Ann

Chapel; Retired.
Lenarz, Richard J. '56 (MAD) Benton, WI St. Patrick Church.
Lencewicz, Leonard E. '63 (SP) [O] St. Petersburg, FL St. Anthony Friary.
Lenchak, Timothy A. *s.v.d.* '75 (CHI) [B] Chicago, IL The Catholic Theological Union at Chicago; [B] Techny, IL Divine Word Residence; [N] Chicago, IL Divine Word Theologate; [N] Techny, IL Society of the Divine Word, Provincial Headquarter-Chicago Prov.
Lenczycki, Frederick '72 (STL) [K] Bridgeton, MO De Paul Health Center.
Lendacky, Francis G. '61 (PH) [4] Philadelphia, PA St. Agnes-St. John Nepomucene Church.
Lendvai, John B. '94 (PIT) [63] Pittsburgh, PA Prince of Peace Church.
Lenehan, Claude *o.f.m.* (PAT) [M] Paterson, NJ St. Benedict the Moor Friary.
Lenehan, Vincent '54 (SAC) Retired and in Senior Ministry.
Lengen, Msgr. James G. '29 (BGP) Retired; [O] Stamford, CT Our Lady Queen of the Clergy Home.
Lengerich, Ambrose R. *c.pp.s.* '42 (CIN) [B] Carthagena, OH St. Charles; [M] Dayton, OH Provincial House of the Cincinnati Province of the Society of the Precious Blood.
Lengerich, Msgr. Vincent L. '48 (GRY) Retired.
Lengwin, Ronald P. '66 (PIT) [26] Pittsburgh, PA St. Mary of Mercy Church.
Lenihan, Daniel F. *o.c.s.o.* '55 (DUB) [K] Peosta, IA New Melleray Abbey, Order of Cistercians of the Strict Observance.
Lenihan, Msgr. John J. '53 (STA) [20] Jacksonville, FL San Jose Church.
Lenihan, John P. '69 (ORG) Dana Point, CA St. Edward Church.
Lenihan, Msgr. Michael '52 (LA) Redondo Beach, CA St. Lawrence Martyr Church.
Lenihan, Michael '71 (CC) [1] Kingsville, TX Our Lady of Good Counsel Church.
Lenk, Charles E. '52 (WOR) Retired.
Lenning, Terry A. '96 (RIC) [9] Richmond, VA St. Edward The Confessor Church.
Lennon, Charles (RVC) Absent on Leave.
Lennon, Francis P. '40 (PH) Collegeville, PA St. Eleanor Church; Retired.
Lennon, James M. '58 (JOL) [17] Joliet, IL St. Patrick Church.
Lennon, John W. '55 (NY) [11] Yonkers, NY St. John the Baptist Church.
Lennon, Joseph L. '44 (BRK) Retired.
Lennon, Joseph L. *o.p.* '47 (PRO) [P] Providence, RI St. Thomas Aquinas Priory at Providence College.
Lennon, Peter F. '55 (NEW) [B] South Orange, NJ Seton Hall University.
Lennon, Raymond T. *s.v.d.* '64 (WDC) [M] Washington, DC Divine Word College.
Lennon, Richard G. '73 (BO) [4] Brookline, MA St. Mary of the Assumption Church.
Lennon, Msgr. Robert T. '50 (NEW) Livingston, NJ St. Philomena Church.
Lenoch, Francis J. (DAV) Retired.
Lenoci, Dominick '95 (NEW) Kenilworth, NJ St. Theresa's Church.
Lenoir, Jean (SB) Retired.
Lenti, Arthur *s.d.b.* '50 (OAK) [A] Berkeley, CA Dominican School of Philosophy and Theology; [N] Berkeley, CA Salesian Community.
Lentine, Peter S. '50 (DET) [64] Detroit, MI St. Philomena Church.
Lentocha, Msgr. George V. '55 (HBG) Middletown, PA Seven Sorrows of the Blessed Virgin Mary Church.
Lentz, Gerald J. *s.j.* '60 (SJ) [D] San Jose, CA Bellarmine College Preparatory.
Lentz, Lawrence D. *c.s.v.* '81 (JOL) Bourbonnais, IL Maternity of the Blessed Virgin Mary Church.
Lentz, Robert F. '64 (BAL) [71] Baltimore, MD Our Lady of Perpetual Help Church.
Lenz, Daniel *o.s.b.* '85 (OM) [C] Elkhorn, NE Mount Michael High School; [K] Elkhorn, NE Mount Michael Abbey.
Lenz, David *o.f.m.conv.* '86 (STL) [P] St. Louis, MO St. Bonaventure Friary (Province of Our Lady of Consolation).
Lenz, David *o.f.m.conv.* '87 (IND) [J] Mount Saint Francis, IN Provincial Headquarters for the Conventual Franciscan Province.
Lenz, Frank B. '94 (VIC) Yorktown, TX Holy Cross Church.
Lenz, Frank M. '69 (MAR) Marquette, MI Marquette General Hospital.
Lenz, Henry J. *m.s.* '41 (TYL) Union Grove-Gladewater, TX St. Theresa of the Infant Jesus Church.
Lenz, Michael *o.f.m.* '76 (ALN) [K] Easton, PA St. Francis Friary.
Lenz, Msgr. Paul A. '49 (ALT) On Duty Outside the Diocese.
Lenzini, Donald J. '51 (BEL) Benton, IL St. Joseph Church.
Lenzner, George G. '57 (GB) Oneida, WI St. Joseph Church.
Leo, Arthur R. '85 (NY) Peekskill, NY Assumption Church.
Leo, Frederick '79 (NY) Nyack, NY St. Ann Church.
Leon, Antonio '57 (STA) [8] Jacksonville, FL Immaculate Conception Church.
Leon, Bartholomew *o.s.b.* '85 (CC) [G] Sandia, TX Benedictine Retreat Center; [H] Sandia, TX Corpus Christi Abbey.
Leon, J Francisco *o.s.a.* '78 (GAL) Pasadena, TX Blessed Juan Diego Church.
Leon, Jose M. '81 (OAK) Union City, CA Our Lady of the Rosary Church.
Leon, Juan *o.f.m.* '57 (FRS) [G] Three Rivers, CA St. Anthony's Retreat House.
Leonard, Clyde A. (BO) Retired.
Leonard, Edmond J. *c.s.sp.* '37 (SB) [E] Hemet, CA Holy Ghost Fathers.
Leonard, Edward '53 (COS) Retired.
Leonard, Edwin M. '84 (CLV) [6] Parma, OH Holy Family Church.
Leonard, Eugene A. '66 (CHR) Spartanburg, SC Jesus Our Risen Savior Church.
Leonard, Msgr. Francis '45 (NY) Retired.
Leonard, Francis B. '50 (BO) [3] Revere, MA St. John Vianney Church.
Leonard, John *o.f.m.* (PAT) Little Falls, NJ Our Lady of the Holy Angels Church.
Leonard, John '48 (JKS) Retired.
Leonard, John E. '65 (RIC) Glen Allen, VA St. Michael Church.
Leonard, John F. '55 (BO) [3] Salem, MA St. James Church.
Leonard, John J. *s.j.* '50 (NY) [F] New York, NY Fordham Preparatory School; [Z] New York, NY Jesuit Community at Fordham University.
Leonard, Joseph '45 (MRY) Retired.
Leonard, Lawrence J. *c.m.* (GAL) Retired.
Leonard, Patrick J. '63 (NEW) Mountainside, NJ Our Lady of Lourdes Church.
Leonard, Paul F. '89 (SCR) [21] Scranton, PA St. Patrick's Church.
Leonard, Peter (WDC) [B] Washington, DC Oblates of St. Francis de Sales House of Studies.
Leonard, Peter *o.s.f.s.* '85 (ALN) [B] Center Valley, PA Allentown College of St. Francis de Sales.
Leonard, Peter J. *o.s.f.s.* '86 (ALN) [K] Center Valley, PA Oblates of St. Francis de Sales.
Leonard, Raymond J. '90 (MET) Middlesex, NJ Our Lady of Mount Virgin Church; [A] Edison, NJ Bishop Ahr High School.
Leonard, Robert *s.j.* '49 (LA) [R] Los Angeles, CA Columbiere House.
Leonard, Sebastian *o.s.b.* '57 (HRT) [E] New Milford, CT Canterbury School.
Leonard, Sebastian *o.s.b.* '57 (IND) [J] St. Meinrad, IN St. Meinrad Archabbey.
Leonard, Msgr. Thomas P. '56 (NY) [50] New York, NY Holy Trinity Church.
Leonard, William F. '70 (MET) South Amboy, NJ St. Mary Church.
Leonard, William J. *s.j.* '37 (BO) [W] Chestnut Hill, MA The Jesuit Community at Boston College.
Leonard, Msgr. William P. '43 (DUB) Retired.
Leonard, William T. (BO) Boston, MA Walter E. Fernald School.
Leonardis, Charles F. '54 (ALT) [5] Windber, PA Holy Child Jesus Church.
Leonards, Martin C. '66 (LAF) Maurice, LA St. Alphonsus Church.
Leone, Arthur '56 (NY) [85] New York, NY Our Lady of Good Counsel Church.
Leone, James M. '60 (BRK) Military Chaplains.
Leone, Kenneth '67 (DEN) Littleton, CO St. Frances Cabrini Parish Church.
Leone, Mark *o.f.m.* '40 (NY) [Z] New York, NY Franciscan Province of the Immaculate Conception.
Leone, Richard D. *o.s.f.s.* '59 (WIL) [I] Wilmington, DE DeSales House.
Leone, William B. '74 (ROC) Cato, NY St. Patrick Church; Weedsport, NY St. John Church; Weedsport, NY St. Joseph Church.
Leong, Francis J. *m.m.* '87 (NY) [Z] Maryknoll, NY Maryknoll Fathers and Brothers.
Leong, Herman M. '91 (OAK) San Ramon, CA St. Joan of Arc Church.
Leonhardt, Douglas J. *s.j.* '69 (MIL) [E] Milwaukee, WI Marquette University High School; [P] Milwaukee, WI Pere Marquette House Jesuit Community.
Leonhardt, Louis J. '56 (DAV) Hills, IA St. Joseph's Church; Iowa City, IA Veteran's Administration Hospital.
Leonhardt, Robert *o.f.m.* '59 (SHP) West Monroe, LA St. Paschal Church.
Leopold, David C. '82 (BGP) Westport, CT Assumption Church.
Leotilc, Rocco *c.s.s.* '53 (BO) [Z] Waltham, MA Stigmatine Fathers and Brothers.
Leoz, Maximo '56 (BRK) [77] Brooklyn, NY St. Malachy's Church.
Lepak, Roy C. '62 (STP) Special Assignment.
LePine, Clement J. '46 (MAR) Retired.
Lepire, Roland M. '75 (PRO) Absent on Leave.
Lepleiter, Robert P. '63 (PH) Retired.
Lepping, George M. *s.m.* '38 (WDC) [M] Washington, DC Marist Provincial House.
Lequin, Thomas '77 (PRT) Mars Hill, ME St. Joseph Church; Presque Isle, ME Nativity of B.V.M. Church.
Lerch, Joseph R. *s.j.* '56 (BAL) Woodstock, MD St. Alphonsus Rodriguez Church.
Leroux, Edward N. '56 (ALB) Fort Edward, NY St. Joseph Church.
Leroux, Roger M. *m.s.* '52 (MAN) [L] Littleton, NH Provincial House of Daughters of the Charity of the Sacred Heart of Jesus.
LeRoux, William F. *s.j.* '53 (SEA) [A] Seattle, WA Seattle University.
Lerox, Edward '56 (ALB) Retired.
Lery, Bruce *s.m.* '87 (HON) Kapaa, HI St. Catherine Church.
Lesak, William P. '75 (NEW) Military Chaplains.
Lesch, Howard J. *c.pp.s.* '44 (CIN) [M] Dayton, OH Provincial House of the Cincinnati Province of the Society of the Precious Blood.
Lescoe, Francis J. '42 (HRT) Retired.
Lesczynski, James J. '64 (LC) Necedah, WI St. Francis of Assisi Church.
Leser, Msgr. William J. *c.b.* '63 (LA) Westlake Village, CA St. Jude Church.
Leshney, Michael F. '73 (CIN) [E] Cincinnati, OH Moeller High School.
LeSieur, David '76 (LR) [11] Little Rock, AR Our Lady of the Holy Souls Church.
Leskiw, Msgr. Peter '45 (LA) [19] Los Angeles, CA Nativity of Blessed Virgin Mary Church.
Leskiw, Msgr. Peter '45 (STN) Retired.
Leskovar, Richard J. '68 (ALB) Special Assignment.
Leslie, Larry B. '80 (COV) Military Chaplains.
Leslie, Patrick J. '69 (SAC) On Duty Outside the Diocese.
Leslie, Patrick J. '69 (SR) [5] Santa Rosa, CA Star of the Valley Church; Eldridge, CA Sonoma Developmental Center.
Lesniak, David '91 (DET) Lapeer, MI Immaculate Conception of the Blessed Virgin Mary Church.
Lesniak, John E. '48 (CLV) [6] Euclid, OH St. William Church; Retired.
Lesniak, Marian J. '50 (LAN) [2] Jackson, MI St. Joseph Church.
Lesniak, Richard D. '66 (MAD) Berlin, WI St. Joseph Church; Berlin, WI St. Michael Church.
Lesnick, John F. '78 (BAL) [61] Baltimore, MD St. Michael Church.
Lesnick, Richard '67 (SEA) Unassigned.
Lesniewski, Stephen F. (CHI) [172] Chicago, IL St. Philomena Church.
Lesniowski, Francis A. '63 (GBG) [4] Connellsville, PA St. Rita Church.
Lesniowski, Stanley '70 (PAT) [4] Passaic, NJ Holy Rosary Church.
Lesousky, John *c.r.* '56 (L) [17] Louisville, KY St. Cecilia Church.
Lessard, Anatole *o.m.i.* '44 (BO) [4] Lowell, MA Sainte Jeanne d'Arc Church.
Lessard, Eugene R. '59 (PRO) [3] Central Falls, RI St. Matthew's Church.
Lessard, Gerard Arthur *o.p.* '84 (L) [4] Springfield, KY St. Rose Church.
Lessard, Joseph '80 (PHX) On Duty Outside the Diocese.
Lessard, Joseph M. '80 (RCK) [4] Aurora, IL St. Mary Church; [D] Aurora, IL Mercy Health Corporation.
Lessard, Joseph P. '52 (STL) Retired.
Lessard, Leo R. '60 (GB) Aurora, WI Sacred Heart Church; Florence, WI Immaculate Conception Church.
Lessard-Thibodeau, John G. '92 (SPR) [14] Springfield, MA St. Catherine of Siena Church.
Lesseps, Roland J. *s.j.* '65 (NO) [P] New Orleans, LA Jesuit Provincial Office.
Lester, Msgr. J. William '45 (FTW) [1] Fort Wayne, IN Cathedral of the Immaculate Conception.
Lester, John E. '59 (TOL) Retired.
Lester, John J. '62 (NEW) Scotch Plains, NJ St. Bartholomew Church.
Lester, Thomas '57 (OAK) [4] San Leandro, CA St. Leander Church.
Lester, William F. *s.j.* '54 (SJ) [M] Los Gatos, CA California Province of the Society of Jesus, Jesuit Provincial Office; [M] Los Gatos, CA Sacred Heart Jesuit Center.
LeStrange, Gregory C. '82 (SY) Fayetteville, NY Immaculate Conception Church.
Leszczynski, Steven '89 (NO) Des Allemands, LA St. Gertrude Church.
Lethiez, Alphonse O. '55 (PRO) [6] West Warwick, RI St. John's Church.
Letko, Anthony '37 (FTW) Retired.
Leto, Nelo A. '54 (DM) Carlisle, IA St. Elizabeth Seton Church.
Letoile, Kenneth R. *o.p.* '74 (PRO) [27] Providence, RI St. Pius V Church; [P] Providence, RI St. Pius Priory.
Letourneau, F. E. (ORL) Retired.
Letourneau, Francis E. '36 (PRT) Retired.

Letourneau, Msgr. Paul R. '54 (BUF) [7] Cheektowaga, NY Our Lady Help of Christians Church; [T] Buffalo, NY Kolping Catholic Young Men's Association of Buffalo, NY dba Kolping Society of Buffalo.
Lettau, David '53 (Y) Retired.
Letteer, Michael C. (HBG) [1] York, PA Immaculate Conception of the Blessed Virgin Mary Church.
Lettic, Edward P. '73 (WOR) Lancaster, MA Immaculate Conception Church.
Lettre, Msgr. Achille W. '33 (MAN) Retired.
Lettre, Raymond '88 (SP) Spring Hill, FL St. Frances Xavier Cabrini Church.
LeTure, Theodore J. '49 (RVC) Valley Stream, NY Holy Name of Mary Church; Retired; Retired.
Leu, James E. '71 (DAV) Absent on Leave.
Leuer, Msgr. Anthony '61 (LA) [13] Los Angeles, CA Holy Spirit Church.
Leurck, Raymond J. '67 (CIN) Military Chaplains.
Leute, Charles J. *o.p.* '69 (FAR) Fort Totten, ND Seven Dolors Church; Fort Totten Reservation, ND (Sioux Indians) Church; Fort Totten Reservation, ND (Sioux Indians) Church.
Leva, Stephen F. '88 (ARL) [3] Arlington, VA St. Ann Church.
Levan, Donald E. '96 (BUF) [P] Buffalo, NY Immaculate Heart of Mary Provincial House and Convent.
Levandusky, Edward '65 (PHU) Palmerton, PA St. Vladimir's Church.
Levantino, Noel J. '93 (NEW) Cranford, NJ St. Michael's Church.
Levario, Gilbert *o.c.d.* '83 (TUC) [16] Tucson, AZ St. Margaret's Church; [F] Tucson, AZ Discalced Carmelite Fathers of St. Margaret's.
Levasque, Denis Antoine *c.f.r.* (NY) [W] New York, NY Padre Pio Shelter for Homeless Men.
LeVasseur, Angelo '83 (PRT) Frenchville, ME St. Luce's Church; [L] Upper Frenchville, ME Christian Life Center.
LeVasseur, Giles *o.s.b.* '84 (WDC) [M] Washington, DC St. Anselm's Abbey.
LeVasseur, Lawrence A. *c.s.c.* '51 (SAT) [B] San Antonio, TX Congregation of Holy Cross - Formation Community; [M] San Antonio, TX Holy Cross Community.
LeVay, R. Joseph '50 (SPR) Hinsdale, MA St. Patrick's Church.
LeVecke, John R. *s.j.* '84 (SJ) [B] Santa Clara, CA Santa Clara University.
Leveille, Andre E. *c.s.c.* '78 (FTW) [A] Notre Dame, IN Moreau Seminary.
Leveille, Roger L. '79 (SPC) Portageville, MO St. Eustachius Church.
Leveille, Rudolph J. '57 (PRT) Brewer, ME St. Teresa's Church.
Leveling, Carlos F. '59 (DAV) Retired.
Leven, Marvin F. '59 (OKL) Lawton, OK Holy Family Church; [K] Norman, OK Campus Ministry for the Archdiocese of Oklahoma City.
Levenhagen, Robert J. '57 (DUB) Cherry Mound, IA St. Pius Church; McGregor, IA St. Mary's Church.
Levens, Robert J. *s.j.* '81 (BO) [W] Boston, MA The Society of Jesus of New England-Provincial Offices; [W] Boston, MA The Society of Jesus of New England-Provincial Offices.
Levernier, Donald *glmy.* '61 (CIN) [M] Fairfield, OH Headquarters of Glenmary Home Missioners.
Levesque, Edmond R. '55 (FR) [10] New Bedford, MA St. Anthony of Padua's Church.
Levesque, Gerald A. '64 (PRT) Farmington, ME St. Joseph's Church; [M] Farmington, ME University of Maine at Farmington.
Levesque, Joseph L. *c.m.* '67 (PH) [B] Philadelphia, PA St. Vincent's Seminary; [B] Philadelphia, PA DePaul Novitiate; [Z] Philadelphia, PA Congregation of the Mission; [Z] Philadelphia, PA Congregation of the Mission.
Levesque, Louis *c.j.m.* '50 (BUF) [1] West Seneca, NY St. Bonaventure Church; [O] West Seneca, NY St. Bonaventure.
Levesque, Paul '89 (ORG) [1] Anaheim, CA St. Anthony Claret Church.
Levesque, Rene R. '55 (FR) Retired.
Levesque, Robert G. *o.m.i.* '60 (BO) [11] Lowell, MA Notre Dame de Lourdes Church.
Levesque, Robert G. *o.m.i.* '60 (NOR) [F] Willimantic, CT Oblates of Mary Immaculate.
Levesque, Roger J. '59 (FR) [16] New Bedford, MA St. Joseph's Church.
Levesque, Sylvio E. '46 (SPR) Three Rivers, MA St. Anne's Church.
Levesque, Sylvio J. '55 (PRT) Winthrop, ME St. Francis Xavier Church.
Levi, Anthony J. '93 (LFT) West Lafayette, IN St. Thomas Aquinas Church.
Levi, Tony '93 (LFT) [H] West Lafayette, IN St. Thomas Aquinas Parish and Foundation for Catholic Students attending Purdue Univ.
Levis, Robert J. '48 (E) Retired; [B] Erie, PA Gannon University.
Levitre, J. Albert, Jr. '80 (FBK) North Pole, AK St. Nicholas Church.
Levitt, Donald L. '79 (PEO) East Moline, IL St. Mary's Church.
Levko, John J. *s.j.* '78 (SCR) [C] Scranton, PA University of Scranton; [C] Scranton, PA University of Scranton.
Levkulic, Msgr. William '55 (PBR) Duquesne, PA SS. Peter and Paul Church.
LeVoir, John M. '81 (STP) South St. Paul, MN Holy Trinity Church.
LeVoy, Joseph T. '54 (CHI) [6] Cicero, IL Our Lady of the Mount Church.
Levri, Fidelis *glmy.* '67 (TYL) Daingerfield, TX Our Lady of Fatima Church.
Levy, Cyril '53 (GLP) McNary, AZ St. Anthony Church.
Levy, Michael *o.m.i.* '57 (SAT) [55] San Antonio, TX St. Mary Church.
Levytsky, Bohdan '32 (PHU) Retired.
Lewandowski, Andrew *o.f.m.* '76 (STL) [P] St. Louis, MO Franciscan Friary of St. Anthony of Padua.
Lewandowski, Andrzej *c.r.* (CHI) [88] Chicago, IL St. Hyacinth Church.
Lewandowski, Bruce *c.ss.r.* '93 (NY) [23] New York, NY St. Cecilia Church.
Lewandowski, David J. '55 (HRT) Southington, CT Immaculate Conception Church.
Lewandowski, Dennis '85 (JOL) [3] Naperville, IL St. Raphael Church.
Lewandowski, Donald R. *o.s.a.* '69 (JOL) [B] Kankakee, IL Bishop McNamara High School.
Lewandowski, John '96 (FAR) Jamestown, ND The Basilica of St. James.
Lewandowski, Michael *o.f.m.conv.* '75 (SPR) [5] Chicopee, MA St. Anthony's Church.
Lewandowski, Raymond H. '85 (DET) [5] Wyandotte, MI St. Patrick Church.
Lewandowski, Richard P. '74 (WOR) [3] Fitchburg, MA St. Camillus de Lellis Church; [Q] Worcester, MA Campus Ministry.
Lewandowski, Robert M. *s.m.* '64 (FWT) Denton, TX Immaculate Conception Church; [M] Arlington, TX University of Texas at Arlington; [M] Denton, TX University of North Texas and Texas Woman's University.
Lewandowski, Ronald C. '95 (CHI) Arlington Heights, IL Our Lady of the Wayside Church.
Lewanski, Gary J. '82 (CHI) [161] Chicago, IL Our Lady of Victory Church.
Lewczak, Thomas J. '65 (NEW) [7] Elizabeth, NJ St. Hedwig's Church.
Lewers, William M. *c.s.c.* '65 (FTW) [B] Notre Dame, IN University of Notre Dame Du Lac; [J] Notre Dame, IN Holy Cross Community, Corby Hall, University of Notre Dame.
Lewinski, Cassian *o.p.* '69 (SLC) [7] Salt Lake City, UT St. Catherine of Siena Church; [H] Salt Lake City, UT University of Utah, Newman Center.
Lewinski, Ronald J. '72 (CHI) Mundelein, IL St. Mary Church.
Lewinski, Stanislaus '86 (BRK) [140] Brooklyn, NY St. Thomas Aquinas Church.
Lewis, Alexander J. *o.f.m.conv.* '85 (LA) [R] Torrance, CA Franciscan Friars, St. Bonaventure Friary.
Lewis, Clyde A. '64 (OG) [1] Watertown, NY Holy Family Church.
Lewis, Daniel C. *s.j.* '62 (BO) [E] Boston, MA Boston College High School & Jesuit Community.
Lewis, David '90 (CI) Moen, FM Holy Family Church; [C] Tunnuk, Chuuk, FM Vicariate Residence.
Lewis, Dennis J. '75 (MIL) [54] Milwaukee, WI St. Michael's Church; [71] Milwaukee, WI St. Rose Church.
Lewis, Edward J. '84 (SAC) Vallejo, CA St. Vincent Ferrer Church; [L] Sacramento, CA Catholic Charities of Sacramento, Inc.
Lewis, Edward J. '92 (GBG) Harrison City, PA St. Barbara Church.
Lewis, Eric A. '69 (LA) Monterey Park, CA St. Stephen Church; West Covina, CA St. Christopher Church.
Lewis, Francis C. '68 (PH) [1] Coatesville, PA St. Cecilia Church.
Lewis, Francis W. *s.j.* '60 (BGP) [A] Fairfield, CT Fairfield University; [O] Fairfield, CT The Fairfield Jesuit Community-Fairfield University.
Lewis, Gerald *s.v.d.* '52 (GAL) [1] Galveston, TX St. Mary's Cathedral Basilica; [K] Houston, TX The Catholic Chaplain Corps.
Lewis, Gerald *s.v.d.* '52 (LAF) [4] New Iberia, LA St. Edward Church.
Lewis, Gerald F. '88 (PAT) Sparta, NJ Our Lady of the Lake Church.
Lewis, Gerard *o.f.m.* '85 (PAT) [M] Ringwood, NJ Holy Name Friary.
Lewis, Harry J. '50 (SCR) Retired; [N] Dunmore, PA Villa St. Joseph.
Lewis, James *o.carm.* '83 (JOL) [J] Darien, IL Carmelite Fathers Provincial Office.
Lewis, James V. *s.j.* '69 (CLV) [E] Cleveland, OH St. Ignatius High School.
Lewis, Kenneth W. '91 (TLS) Fairfax, OK Sacred Heart Church; Pawnee, OK St. John Church.
Lewis, Lawrence J. *m.m.* '75 (NY) [Z] Maryknoll, NY Maryknoll Fathers and Brothers.
Lewis, Leo T. '60 (STL) Sunset Hills, MO St. Justin Martyr Church.
Lewis, Mark *s.j.* '91 (NO) [P] New Orleans, LA Jesuit Provincial Office.
Lewis, Mark E. '93 (SFD) Effingham, IL St. Anthony of Padua Church.
Lewis, Sebastian C. *o.s.b.* '51 (CHI) [110] Chicago, IL St. Joseph Church.
Lewis, Sebastian C. *o.s.b.* '51 (PEO) [A] Peru, IL St. Bede Abbey and Academy.
Lewis, Walter G. '79 (RIC) [12] Richmond, VA St. Mary Church.
Lewkiewicz, Richard M. '68 (BRK) [50] Brooklyn, NY Good Shepherd Church.
Lex, Henry V. '51 (BUF) Retired.
Lex, Henry V. '57 (BUF) [O] Buffalo, NY Sheehan Residence for Priests.
Lex, James '50 (EVN) [13] Evansville, IN St. Anthony Church; Retired.
Lexa, Robert '70 (GB) Neenah, WI St. Gabriel the Archangel Church.
Ley, Richard J. '71 (ARL) [6] Alexandria, VA St. Louis Church.
Leydon, William M. '86 (NY) [76] New York, NY St. Monica Church.
Leykam, John J. '72 (STL) St. Ann, MO St. Kevin Church.
Leykam, Lambert *o.f.m.* '56 (SFD) Teutopolis, IL St. Francis of Assisi Church; [K] Teutopolis, IL St. Francis Assisi Friary.
Leykem, Lambert *o.f.m.* '40 (SFD) Montrose, IL St. Rose of Lima Church.
Leyland, Thomas '65 (TOL) Bowling Green, OH St. Aloysius Church.
Leyrita, Norbert L. '63 (GR) Saranac, MI St. Anthony Church.
Lezochowski, Walter '59 (DET) Detroit, MI Crittendon Hospital.
Li-Chung-Lun, Francis *o.f.m.* '46 (STL) [P] St. Louis, MO Franciscan Friary of St. Anthony of Padua.
Liable, Adrian *o.s.b.* '58 (OM) [K] Elkhorn, NE Mount Michael Abbey.
Liagas, Carlos *s.j.* (CHI) [151] Chicago, IL Our Lady of Lourdes Church.
Libaire, Nathan *o.s.b.* '78 (SFE) [5] Santa Fe, NM St. John Baptist Church.
Libaire, Nathan *o.s.b.* '81 (SCL) [I] Collegeville, MN St. John's Abbey, of the Order of St. Benedict.
Libanati, Ciro '93 (SB) Rialto, CA St. Catherine of Siena Church.
Libasci, Peter A. '78 (RVC) Inwood, NY Our Lady of Good Counsel Church.
Libbey, Louis E. *s.j.* '91 (LA) [C] Los Angeles, CA Loyola Marymount University.
Libens, John F. *s.j.* '70 (DET) [E] Detroit, MI University of Detroit Jesuit High School and Academy; [K] Detroit, MI Jesuit Provincial Office-Detroit Province of the Society of Jesus.
Libera, Angelo '57 (SY) Retired.
Libera, Thomas '69 (CHI) Orland Park, IL Our Lady of the Woods Church.
Liberatore, Albert M. '89 (SCR) [A] Dalton, PA Saint Pius X Seminary.
Liberatore, David D. '60 (CLV) Parma Heights, OH St. John Bosco Church.
Liberty, Donald *c.ss.r.* '61 (LA) Whittier, CA St. Mary of the Assumption Church; [R] Whittier, CA Redemptorist Fathers Mission House.
Libone, John '80 (DAL) Plano, TX St. Elizabeth Ann Seton Church.
Librandi, Michael A. '78 (RCK) Hanover, IL St. John the Evangelist Church.
Licari, Jonathan *o.s.b.* '76 (SCL) Collegeville, MN St. John the Baptist Church; [A] Collegeville, MN St. John's Seminary; [B] Collegeville, MN St. John's University; [I] Collegeville, MN St. John's Abbey, of the Order of St. Benedict.
LiCastro, Antonio (HRT) [3] New Haven, CT St. Anthony's Church.
Licata, Donald B. '59 (NY) Beacon, NY St. Joachim Church; State, NY Downstate Correction Facility; State, NY Fishkill Correctional Facility; Castle Point, NY Veterans Administration Medical Center.
Licciardi, Frederick T. *c.pp.s.* '82 (CIN) [M] Dayton, OH Provincial House of the Cincinnati Province of the Society of the Precious Blood.
Lichtefeld, James J. '59 (L) [70] Louisville, KY St. Stephen, Martyr Church.
Lichtenthal, Msgr. James J. '63 (BUF) Snyder, NY Christ the King Church.
Lichter, Mark '92 (SFS) Aberdeen, SD St. Mary Church.
Lichtle, Thomas A. '61 (LA) Retired.
Lickman, Peter '68 (PSC) Miami, FL St. Basil's Church.
Lickteig, Anthony J. '54 (KCK) Wea, KS Holy Rosary Church.
Lickteig, Fergus *o.carm.* '55 (WDC) [B] Washington, DC Whitefriars Hall.
Lickteig, Norbert '61 (KCK) [2] Topeka, KS Christ the King Church.

Liddy, Msgr. Richard M. '63 (NEW) [B] South Orange, NJ Seton Hall University.
Liddy, Msgr. Richard M. '63 (WDC) [M] Washington, DC Woodstock Jesuit Community; [V] Washington, DC Woodstock Theological Center.
Liderbach, Daniel P. *s.j.* '73 (BUF) [O] Buffalo, NY Canisius Jesuit Community.
Liderbach, Daniel P. *s.j.* '73 (DET) [K] Detroit, MI Jesuit Provincial Office-Detroit Province of the Society of Jesus.
Lieb, Germain L. *o.s.b.* '45 (ALT) Hastings, PA St. Bernard Church.
Lieb, Joel R. *o.s.b.* '46 (GBG) Trauger, PA Forty Martyrs Church; [H] Latrobe, PA Saint Vincent Archabbey.
Lieb, Marianus D. *t.o.r.* '44 (ALT) [F] Loretto, PA Mount Assisi Monastery.
Lieberth, Joseph J. '68 (CLV) Stow, OH Holy Family Church.
Liebhardt, Kevin M. '74 (CLV) Eastlake, OH St. Justin Martyr Church.
Liebl, Harold J. *s.a.c.* '48 (MIL) [P] Milwaukee, WI St. Vincent Community; [Y] Milwaukee, WI Pallottine Fathers and Brothers, Inc., Disability Trust; [Y] Milwaukee, WI Pallottine Fathers and Brothers, Inc., Educational and Apostolic Ministry Trust.
Liebl, Michael *o.s.b.* '77 (OM) [C] Elkhorn, NE Mount Michael High School; [K] Elkhorn, NE Mount Michael Abbey.
Liebler, Thomas '81 (SFD) Granite City, IL St. Elizabeth Church.
Liebner, David C. '80 (ALN) [1] Allentown, PA Cathedral of St. Catharine of Siena.
Liebner, David M. '60 (ALN) Girardville, PA St. Vincent de Paul Church.
Liebscher, Arthur F. *s.j.* '84 (SJ) [B] Santa Clara, CA Santa Clara University.
Liem, Joseph Than Van *c.m.c.* (SPC) Seneca, MO St. Mary Church.
Lienert, Charles J. '68 (P) Gresham, OR St. Henry Church.
Lienhard, Joseph T. *s.j.* '71 (NY) [Z] New York, NY Jesuit Community at Fordham University.
Liepold, Donald F. '47 (SFS) Retired.
Liermann, Raymond B. '53 (STL) Josephville, MO St. Joseph Church.
Lies, Eric *o.s.b.* '45 (IND) [J] St. Meinrad, IN St. Meinrad Archabbey.
Lies, Jim *c.s.c.* (FTW) [B] Notre Dame, IN University of Notre Dame Du Lac.
Lies, William M. *c.s.c.* '94 (FTW) [J] South Bend, IN Congregation of Holy Cross Indiana Province Provincial House.
Lieser, Gregory '63 (SCL) [9] St. Cloud, MN St. Peter Church.
Lieser, Vincent '67 (SCL) Special Assignment; [A] Collegeville, MN St. John's Seminary.
Liew, Richard (NY) White Plains, NY New York Hospital - Cornell Medical Center.
Liewer, David F. '74 (OM) South Sioux City, NE St. Michael Church.
Lifrak, Richard *ss.cc.* '95 (FR) [3] New Bedford, MA Our Lady of the Assumption Church.
Ligato, Anthony '95 (ALB) [3] Albany, NY Blessed Sacrament Church.
Ligeti, Angelus *o.f.m.* '79 (DET) [32] Detroit, MI Holy Cross Church.
Liggio, John R. *o.s.a.* '75 (PH) [G] Malvern, PA Malvern Preparatory School for Boys.
Ligonde, Jean-Marie Fritz '89 (NEW) [7] Jersey City, NJ Assumption/All Saints Church; [23] Jersey City, NJ St. Patrick's Church.
Ligos, George A. '53 (NEW) [24] Jersey City, NJ St. Paul of the Cross Church.
Liguori, Henry A. '66 (TR) Military Chaplains.
Lihvar, Francis P. *s.j.* '61 (CLV) [C] Cleveland, OH John Carroll Jesuit Community.
Liistro, Frank J. '74 (WOR) [7] Fitchburg, MA Madonna of the Holy Rosary Church.
Lijewski, Thomas F. '70 (MIL) [2] Racine, WI St. John Nepomuk Church.
Lijewski, Timothy M. '93 (CHR) Union, SC St. Augustine's Church.
Like, Wayne '63 (BEL) [I] Belleville, IL Retreat and Renewal Center.
Lileart, Richard (DET) Detroit, MI Oakwood Hospital.
Lill, Kenneth J. '91 (TOL) Sylvania, OH St. Joseph Church.
Lilly, Msgr. E. C. '29 (SC) Retired.
Lilly, Robert A. *m.m.* '62 (STL) [P] St. Louis, MO Maryknoll House.
Lim, Andrew '85 (STP) [15] St. Paul, MN St. Andrew Kim Church.
Lim, Candido O. *s.j.* '69 (SJ) [25] San Jose, CA St. Victor Church.
Lim, Michael '87 (NEW) [6] Orange, NJ St. Andrew Kim Church.
Lima, Fernando Henrique *o.s.b.* '78 (GBG) [H] Latrobe, PA Saint Vincent Archabbey.
Lima, John Bosco '92 (NEW) [25] Newark, NJ St. Michael's Church.
Lima, John H. '63 (LAV) Tonopah, NV St. Patrick Church.
Lima, Joseph *c.pp.s.* '44 (CIN) [B] Carthagena, OH St. Charles.
Lima, Vivian Ben '85 (LA) San Pedro, CA Mary, Star of the Sea Church.
Limanni, Joseph A. '87 (GAL) [70] Houston, TX Queen of Peace Church.
Limanowski, Stanley C. '42 (CHI) Glenwood, IL St. John Church; Retired.
Limbani, George '94 (SEA) [2] Seattle, WA St. Alphonsus Church.
Limbert, William G. '51 (KAL) Retired.
Limmer George A. '64 (BAL) Hagerstown, MD St. Mary Church.
Limon, Lidio '92 (MRY) [G] Monterey, CA Oratorian Community-Congregation of the Oratory of Pontifical Right.
Linakis, William *s.a.* '77 (NY) [Z] Garrison, NY Generalate of the Franciscan Friars of the Atonement-St. James Friary.
Linakis, William *s.a.* '77 (STO) Stockton, CA DeWitt Nelson Training Center.
Linares, Jose R. '86 (MGZ) Cabo Rojo, PR St. Michael Church.
Linbeck, Augustine *o.s.b.* '32 (CC) [H] Sandia, TX Corpus Christi Abbey.
Linck, Joseph C. *c.o.* '94 (PIT) [N] Pittsburgh, PA Congregation of the Oratory of St. Philip Neri; [Q] Slippery Rock, PA Office for Campus Ministry; [Q] Slippery Rock, PA Office for Campus Ministry; [Q] Slippery Rock, PA Office for Campus Ministry.
Lincoln, Daniel L. '84 (L) Jamestown, KY Holy Spirit Church.
Lincoln, Howard A. '93 (SB) Rialto, CA St. Catherine of Siena Church.
Lincon, J. Bruce '89 (BGP) Darien, CT St. John Church.
Lind, Joseph G. '65 (BO) Wellesley, MA St. Paul Church.
Lind, Thomas *s.c.j.* '58 (JKS) [E] Nesbit, MS St. Michael Community House.
Lindauer, Msgr. Clarence '37 (EVN) Retired.
Lindauer, Msgr. Clarence '38 (EVN) [F] Evansville, IN St. John's Home for the Aged.
Lindauer, Prosper *o.s.b.* '50 (IND) [J] St. Meinrad, IN St. Meinrad Archabbey.
Lindblad, Karl-Albert '87 (NY) Military Chaplains; [DD] New York, NY St. Ansgar Scandinavian Catholic League.
Lindbloom, Eric *o.f.m.* '67 (DEN) [M] Denver, CO St. Francis of Assisi Friary.
Lindemann, Gene E. '83 (BIS) Garrison, ND St. Nicholas Church.
Linden, Emmet *c.p.* '51 (L) [68] Louisville, KY St. Rita Church; [L] Louisville, KY Sacred Heart Retreat.
Lindenfelser, Timothy M. '94 (STA) [1] St. Augustine, FL Cathedral of St. Augustine.
Lindenmeyer, Msgr. James '48 (GLP) Farmington, NM St. Mary's Church.
Linder, Michael J. '85 (KNX) Dayton, TN St. Bridget Church.
Linder, Msgr. William J. '63 (NEW) [33] Newark, NJ St. Rose of Lima Church.
Lindle, Lawrence H. '59 (L) Culvertown, KY Immaculate Conception Church; [Q] Louisville, KY Perpetual Eucharistic Adoration; [Q] New Haven, KY World Apostolate of Fatima (Blue Army); [Q] New Haven, KY World Apostolate of Fatima (Blue Army).
Lindley, Phillip '83 (AMA) [3] Amarillo, TX Blessed Sacrament Church.
Lindner, Jerold W. *s.j.* '76 (LA) [F] Los Angeles, CA Loyola High School.
Lindner, Thomas F. '95 (LC) [1] La Crosse, WI St. Joseph the Workman Cathedral.
Lindquist, Ted (MAD) [G] Madison, WI St. Marys Hospital Medical Center.
Lindsay, John A. *o.s.f.s.* '70 (STO) [A] Stockton, CA St. Mary's High School.
Lindsay, Michael P. '87 (LSC) Santa Clara, NM Santa Clara Church.
Lindsay, Stewart M. *o.s.f.s.* '74 (BUF) [11] Niagara Falls, NY Prince of Peace Church.
Lindsay, Stewart M. *o.s.f.s.* '74 (TOL) [K] Toledo, OH Oblates of St. Francis de Sales.
Linebach, Martin A. '87 (L) [1] Louisville, KY Cathedral of the Assumption.
Linehan, Brian *o.f.m.* '67 (NEW) East Rutherford, NJ St. Joseph's Church.
Linehan, Cornelius '43 (P) Retired.
Linehan, David '56 (SEA) Retired.
Linehan, Dennis *s.j.* '72 (NY) [Z] New York, NY "America;" Residence and publication office of the America Press.
Linehan, Eugene J. *s.j.* '53 (WDC) Bethesda, MD National Institutes of Health, Clinical Center; [E] North Bethesda, MD Georgetown Preparatory School.
Linehan, Jeremiah '48 (P) Retired.
Linehan, Maurice F. *m.s.* '52 (TYL) Lufkin, TX St. Patrick Church.
Linehan, Patrick M. *o.m.i.* '34 (BO) [Z] Tewksbury, MA Immaculate Heart of Mary Novitiate-Infirmary.
Linehan, Stephen J. (BO) Military & VA Chaplains.
Linehan, William J. '36 (BO) Retired.
Liners, David *c.m.f.* '85 (CHI) [N] Oak Park, IL Claretian Fathers Headquarters of U.S.A. Eastern Province.
Ling, Peter '60 (LA) Montebello, CA Our Lady of the Miraculous Medal Church.
LIngan, Joseph E. *s.j.* '90 (SPK) [B] Spokane, WA St. Michael's Institute.
Liniger, Paul *o.f.m.conv.* (WDC) [B] Washington, DC St. Bonaventure Friary.
Liningstone, Benedict *s.p.* (SFE) [N] Jemez Springs, NM Fitzgerald Charitable Trust.
Link, David '91 (OAK) San Lorenzo, CA St. John the Baptist Church.
Link, Fred *o.f.m.* '70 (HT) [4] Houma, LA Our Lady of the Most Holy Rosary Church.
Link, Frederick G. '69 (CAM) Westville, NJ St. Anne's Church.
Link, Linus F. '45 (KC) Retired.
Link, Mark J. *s.j.* '60 (CHI) [C] Chicago, IL Jesuit Community at Loyola University of Chicago.
Link, Paul *c.pp.s.* (STL) O'Fallon, MO Assumption Church.
Linkchorst, William J. '73 (ALN) Tamaqua, PA SS. Peter and Paul Church.
Linn, Msgr. Francis J. '40 (BAL) Retired; [K] Baltimore, MD Stella Maris Operating Corporation.
Linn, Matthew L. *s.j.* '73 (STP) [N] Minneapolis, MN La Storta Jesuit Community; [Q] Wayzata, MN Cenacle Retreat House.
Linnan, John E. *c.s.v.* '61 (CHI) [B] Chicago, IL The Catholic Theological Union at Chicago; [N] Chicago, IL Viatorian Residence.
Linnan, Roger J. '62 (SC) Rockwell City, IA St. Francis of Assisi Church; Rockwell City, IA Calhoun County State Reformatory, Minimum Security for Men.
Linnane, Brian F. *s.j.* '86 (WOR) [N] Worcester, MA Jesuits of Holy Cross College, Inc.
Linnebur, David W. (WCH) [4] Wichita, KS Christ the King Church.
Linnebur, Leroy '61 (WCH) Clonmel, KS St. John Church.
Linnebur, Vincent '60 (JC) Absent on Leave.
Linnemann, Eugene C. '80 (BEL) Leave of Absence.
Linnenbrink, Harry H. '57 (DAV) [4] Iowa City, IA St. Wenceslaus Church.
Linowski, Eugene R. '57 (PRM) Columbus, OH St. John Chrysostom Church; Dayton, OH St. Barbara Church.
Lins, James R. '64 (MAD) Seymour, WI Our Lady of Hope Church; Shullsburg, WI St. Matthew Church.
Linsay, Robert E. *s.j.* '60 (BO) [W] Boston, MA Jesuit Urban Center & Immaculate Conception Community.
Linse, Henry *c.s.s.* '48 (BO) [Z] Waltham, MA Stigmatine Fathers and Brothers.
Linsky, Gary S. '95 (CHR) [2] Columbia, SC St. Joseph Church.
Linsky, Thomas J. *s.j.* '52 (ALN) [A] Wernersville, PA Novitiate of St. Isaac Jogues.
Linsler, Christopher E. '77 (ROC) [5] Elmira, NY St. Casimir Church.
Linsler, Christopher E. '78 (ROC) Elmira Heights, NY St. Charles Borromeo Church.
Linster, Joseph B. '69 (RCK) St. Charles, IL St. Patrick Church.
Linton, Edward *o.s.b.* '91 (IND) [J] St. Meinrad, IN St. Meinrad Archabbey.
Linton, Terence H. *c.s.c.* '73 (FTW) [J] Notre Dame, IN Holy Cross Community, Corby Hall, University of Notre Dame.
Linton, Terence H. *c.s.c.* '80 (OAK) [N] Berkeley, CA Holy Cross Fathers-Holy Cross Center.
Lintz, Christoph '94 (NEW) Ridgefield Park, NJ St. Francis of Assisi Church.
Lintzenich, Stephen P. '74 (EVN) [19] Evansville, IN St. Mary Church.
Linz, Lester A. *s.j.* (CIN) [M] Cincinnati, OH Jesuit Community at St. Xavier High School.
Lioi, Frank E. '67 (ROC) [4] Rochester, NY St. Anne Church.
Lion, William J. '58 (CHI) [1] Oak Lawn, IL St. Catherine of Alexandria Church.
Liona, Kenneth J. '78 (BRK) Absent on Leave.
Lionelli, Anthony J. '72 (NEW) [21] Newark, NJ Immaculate Conception Church.
Lipareli, Michael '80 (NY) [125] Bronx, NY St. Ann Church.
Lipari, Anthony '89 (NEW) Bergenfield, NJ St. John the Evangelist Church.
Lipczewski, Boleslaus '58 (DET) [11] Detroit, MI Assumption Grotto Church; Absent on Sick Leave.
Lipiec, Bart '83 (BUF) Warsaw, NY St. Michael Church.
Lipinski, Alberic *s.o.cist.* '83 (CHI) [N] Willow Springs, IL Cistercian Fathers.
Lipinski, Edward J. '71 (CAM) Audubon, NJ Church of the Holy Maternity.
Lipinski, Paul M. '73 (RCK) [B] Woodstock, IL Marian Central Catholic High School.
Lipnicki, Thomas Paul '78 (NEW) [2] East Orange, NJ Holy Spirit-Our Lady Help of Christians Church.

Lipp, John F. *o.s.a.* '54 (PH) [T] Norristown, PA Sacred Heart Hospital and Rehabilitation Center; [Z] Villanova, PA St. Thomas Monastery.
Lippert, Donald *o.f.m.cap.* '85 (CLV) [A] Wickliffe, OH Borromeo Seminary.
Lippert, Paul R. '61 (MIL) Retired.
Lippold, John L. '57 (BAL) Linthicum Heights, MD St. Philip Neri Church.
Lipps, Frank J. '68 (NO) Violet, LA Our Lady of Lourdes Church.
Lipps, Louis *s.j.* '52 (LEX) [1] Lexington, KY Cathedral of Christ the King; Special Assignment.
Lippstock, Paul E. '78 (DUB) [6] Waterloo, IA Blessed Sacrament Church; [D] Waterloo, IA Columbus High School.
Liprie, James *o.s.b.* '83 (LAF) [H] Opelousas, LA Mother of the Redeemer Monastery.
Lipscomb, N. Alan '94 (RIC) Lexington, VA St. Patrick Church.
Liptak, David Q. '53 (HRT) Broad Brook, CT St. Catherine's Church; Special and other (Arch)Diocesan Assignment.
Liptak, David Q. '53 (NOR) [A] Cromwell, CT Holy Apostles College and Seminary.
Liptock, Edward R. *v.f.* '55 (SCR) [1] Dunmore, PA All Saints Church.
LiPuma, David G. '87 (BUF) [60] Buffalo, NY St. Rose of Lima Church.
Lira, Juan R. '85 (DAL) Sherman, TX St. Mary Church.
Lirette, Msgr. Arthur J. '49 (LA) Glendale, CA Holy Family Church; Retired.
Lis, Albert *o.f.m.* '86 (GB) Pulaski, WI Assumption of the Blessed Virgin Mary Church.
Lis, John S. '73 (SPR) [1] Northampton, MA Annunciation Church.
Lisante, Msgr. James P. '81 (RVC) West Hempstead, NY St. Thomas, the Apostle Church.
Lisbeth, Michael L. *s.m.* '80 (CIN) [M] Cincinnati, OH Marianist Community.
Lischaa, Msgr. Sharbel '61 (SAM) Philadelphia, PA St. Maron Church.
Lischwe, Bruno V. *c.ss.r.* '52 (STL) [P] Liguori, MO St. Clement Health Care Center.
Lisik, Paul A. '81 (GBG) Monessen, PA The Epiphany of Our Lord Church.
Liska, Richard A. '70 (MIL) Butler, WI St. Agnes Church.
Lism, Joseph Tran Van *c.m.c.* (SPC) Neosho, MO St. Canera Church.
Lisowski, Brian A. (CHI) Evergreen Park, IL Most Holy Redeemer Church.
Lisowski, Edward E. '64 (CHI) [3] Waukegan, IL St. Dismas Church.
Lisowski, Edward E. '64 (MIL) On Duty Outside the Archdiocese.
Lisowski, Jan '39 (SC) Retired.
Lisowski, Lawrence M. '84 (CHI) La Grange, IL St. Francis Xavier Church.
Lisowski, William J. '50 (CHI) [115] Chicago, IL St. Ladislaus Church; Retired.
Liss, Robert C. '62 (STL) Richwoods, MO St. Stephen's Church.
Liss, Valentine '40 (PEO) [4] Spring Valley, IL SS. Peter and Paul's Church; Retired.
Lisson, Edwin L. *s.j.* '69 (STL) [C] St. Louis, MO Saint Louis University; [P] St. Louis, MO Jesuit Community Corporation at St. Louis University - Jesuit Hall.
List, John E. '85 (LEX) Georgetown, KY St. John's Church.
Listecki, Jerome E. '75 (CHI) [A] Mundelein, IL University of St. Mary of the Lake-Mundelein Seminary.
Lister, Alfred Q. *o.p.* '59 (NO) [P] New Orleans, LA Dominican Fathers & Brothers, Southern Dominican Province.
Liston, Daniel P. '85 (SPR) West Springfield, MA St. Louis de France Church.
Liston, Paul F. '58 (WDC) [36] Washington, DC St. Patrick Church.
Liszewski, Francis A. '69 (NOR) Absent on Leave; Retired.
Liszewski, Peter B. '76 (NOR) Lebanon, CT St. Francis of Assisi Church.
Litavec, Edward S. '60 (PIT) Fredericktown, PA St. Oliver Plunkett Church.
Litcheck, Michael P. '71 (SCR) Carbondale, PA Our Lady of Mt. Carmel Church.
Literal, Peter (MEM) Memphis, TN Federal Correctional Institute at Memphis.
Literski, Msgr. Roy E. '53 (WIN) Retired.
Litot, Msgr. Edward F. '47 (GRY) Retired.
Littelmann, Edward J. '69 (TOL) Huron, OH St. Peter Church.
Little, Msgr. Anthony B. '82 (ALT) [13] Altoona, PA St. Therese of the Child Jesus Church.
Little, Gregory (NY) Bronx, NY U.S.V.A. Medical Center.
Little, John '87 (OWN) [I] Bowling Green, KY Western Kentucky University Newman Center.
Little, Msgr. John J. '77 (ALT) Nanty-Glo, PA St. Mary's Church.
Little, John J. L. '88 (ALN) Northampton, PA Our Lady of Hungary Church.
Little, Richard P. '62 (BO) [2] Methuen, MA St. Monica Church.
Littlefield, Philaret '87 (NTN) Milwaukee, WI St. George Church.
Litwin, Paul A. '79 (BUF) [O] Buffalo, NY Bishop's Residence.
Litzau, John B. '51 (MIL) Retired.
Liu, Peter '60 (RVC) Hicksville, NY Our Lady of Mercy Church.
Liu, Vincent '54 (RVC) Smithtown, NY St. Patrick Church.
Liuima, Francis *s.j.* '45 (BO) [W] Chestnut Hill, MA The Jesuit Community at Boston College.
Liuzzi, Kenneth J. '75 (DEN) Arvada, CO Shrine of St. Anne Church.
Liuzzi, Peter J. *o.carm.* '65 (LA) [B] North Hills, CA Carmel West Community.
Liuzzo, Vincent *o.f.m.cap.* '49 (PAT) Passaic, NJ St. Mary Hospital; [J] Passaic, NJ St. Mary's Hospital.
Lively, Joseph A. '57 (BUR) Gilman, VT St. Theresa Church; St. Johnsbury, VT St. John the Evangelist Church.
Livigni, Salvatore J. '61 (BAL) [39] Baltimore, MD Immaculate Conception Church; Baltimore, MD Greater Baltimore Medical Center.
Livingston, Benedict *s.p.* '72 (SFE) [J] Jemez Springs, NM The Jemez Program, Our Lady of Lourdes Novitiate.
Livingston, James G. '91 (DET) Plymouth, MI Our Lady of Good Counsel Church.
Livingston, James T. '90 (STP) Delano, MN St. Mary of Czestochowa Church; St. Bonifacius, MN St. Boniface Church.
Livingston, Morson Ravi *s.a.c.* '85 (ALX) Brouillette, LA St. Genevieve Church.
Livingston, Msgr. Robert C. '45 (PEO) Kickapoo, IL St. Mary's of Kickapoo Church; Retired.
Livojevich, Ronald '70 (KCK) Shawnee, KS St. Joseph's Church
Livolsi, Silvester J. '48 (PAT) [I] Branchville, NJ Sanctuary of Mary-Our Lady of the Holy Spirit.
Livolsi, Sylvester J. '48 (NEW) On Duty Outside the Archdiocese.
Liwanag, Paul '67 (CHI) [J] Chicago, IL St. Mary of Nazareth Hospital Center.
Lizarraga, Joaquin (ARE) Retired.
Lizarralde, Luis *o.f.m.* '51 (SJN) [4] Toa Baja, PR Jose Obrero Church.
Lizio, John R. '57 (BO) [4] Marlboro, MA St. Matthias Church.
Lizor, Joseph S., Jr. '58 (BAL) [54] Baltimore, MD St. Luke Church.
Llamas, Rodolfo DLC *v.d.c.* '93 (SFR) [N] San Francisco, CA Verbum Dei Community.
Llambias, Martin (SJN) [F] Guaynabo, PR Opus Dei.
Llano, Isidoro '51 (GLP) On Duty Outside of Diocese.
Llanos, Philip S. '78 (LA) Military and VA Chaplains.
Llaria, Vincent '59 (VEN) Lake Placid, FL St. James Church.
Lleo, Pedro '76 (MIA) Miami Shores, FL St. Rose of Lima Church.
Llorente, Amando *s.j.* '48 (MIA) [J] Miami, FL John Paul II Retreat House.
Llorente, Ricardo San '51 (ARE) [1] Arecibo, PR Cathedral of San Felipe Apostol.
Lloyd, James B. *c.s.p.* '48 (NY) [104] New York, NY St. Paul the Apostle Church; [A] Yonkers, NY St. Joseph's Seminary; [Z] Scarsdale, NY Paulist Fathers Generalate.
Lloyd, Patrick J. *s.c.j.* '69 (GB) New Holstein, WI Holy Rosary Church; St. Anna, WI St. Ann Church.
Lloyd, Patrick J. *s.c.j.* '69 (MIL) [P] Hales Corners, WI Sacred Heart Monastery.
Lloyd, Msgr. Paul A. '37 (PRO) Retired [M] Pawtucket, RI Jeanne Jugan Residence.
Lloyd, Robert J. *m.m.* '62 (NY) [Z] Maryknoll, NY Maryknoll Fathers and Brothers.
Lloyd, Ronald L. *s.m.m.* '43 (RVC) [N] Bay Shore, NY Montfort Missionaries.
Lloyd, Vincent A. '42 (TR) Retired.
Lloyd, Vincent A. '45 (ORL) Retired.
Lluch, Santiago *c.m.* '42 (NY) [Z] New York, NY Vincentian Fathers.
Lluch, Santiago *c.m.* '62 (NY) [44] New York, NY Holy Agony Church.
Lluria, Carmel *o.f.m.* '55 (PAT) [M] Ringwood, NJ Holy Name Friary.
Lo Bianco, Msgr. Francis R. '54 (NEW) Paramus, NJ Our Lady of the Visitation Church.
Lo Pinto, Alfred '70 (SB) [1] San Bernardino, CA Our Lady of the Rosary Cathedral; San Bernardino, CA San Bernardino Juvenile Hall & Verdemont Boys Ranch.
Lobacz, James E. '79 (MIL) [C] Milwaukee, WI Cardinal Stritch College.
Lobato, Nicanor '61 (VEN) Palmetto, FL Holy Cross Church.
Lobaton, Jose *o.f.m.* '73 (WDC) [1] Washington, DC St. Matthew Cathedral.
Lobby, Basil F. *o.f.m.* '46 (PAT) [M] Butler, NJ St. Anthony Friary.
Lobert, Richard C. '75 (BAL) Special Assignment.
Lobert, Richard C. '75 (LAN) [3] Ann Arbor, MI St. Thomas the Apostle Church.
LoBianco, Paschal *s.v.d.* '50 (CHI) [B] Techny, IL Divine Word Residence.
LoBianco, Paschal *s.v.d.* '50 (SFD) [1] Springfield, IL Cathedral of the Immaculate Conception.
LoBianco, Richard J. '79 (CHI) [2] Oak Lawn, IL St. Gerald Church.
LoBiondo, Gasper F. *s.j.* '68 (WDC) [M] Washington, DC Woodstock Jesuit Community; [V] Washington, DC Woodstock Theological Center.
Lobo, Anthony *s.s.* '70 (LA) [A] Camarillo, CA St. John's Seminary College of the Archdiocese of Los Angeles.
Lobo, Benjamin '63 (GF) Glendive, MT Sacred Heart Church.
Lobo, Raphael *s.d.b.* '82 (OAK) [N] Berkeley, CA Salesian Community.
Lobo, Stanley '65 (NEW) Rutherford, NJ St. Mary's Church.
Lobo, Theodore '57 (TUC) Parker, AZ Sacred Heart Church.
Loc, Timothy Mai Vinh *c.m.c.* '77 (SPC) Carthage, MO St. Ann Church.
LoCascio, Thomas M. *o.s.m.* '38 (CHI) [N] Chicago, IL Servite Friars - Eastern Province.
Locatelli, Paul L. *s.j.* '74 (SJ) [B] Santa Clara, CA Santa Clara University; [B] Santa Clara, CA Santa Clara University.
Loch, Richard J. '79 (SCR) [17] Scranton, PA St. Mary of the Assumption Church.
Lochner, Robert J. *c.s.c.* '46 (FTW) [J] South Bend, IN Congregation of Holy Cross Indiana Province Provincial House.
Lochner, Robert J. *c.s.c.* '46 (ORL) Retired; [F] Cocoa Beach, FL Holy Cross Fathers, Eastern Priests Province.
Lochs, Matthew *ss.cc.* '36 (HON) [11] Honolulu, HI St. Patrick Church.
Lock, Bertram *ss.cc.* '89 (HON) Kaneohe, HI St. Ann Church.
Lockard, Msgr. David A. '75 (ALT) Huntingdon, PA Most Holy Trinity Church.
Locke, James E. '61 (PH) Chadds Ford, PA St. Cornelius Church.
Lockey, Paul E. (BO) Awaiting Assignment.
Lockman, V. James '67 (WDC) Laurel, MD St. Mary Church.
Lockwood, Charles P. '54 (ALB) Altamont, NY St. Lucy Church.
Lockwood, Gregory J. '88 (STL) Hazelwood, MO Our Lady of Mercy Church; [A] St. Louis, MO Kenrick-Glennon Seminary.
Lodge, John G. '73 (CHI) [A] Mundelein, IL University of St. Mary of the Lake-Mundelein Seminary.
Lodge, Richard J. '69 (CAM) West Collingswood, NJ Transfiguration Church.
Lodi, George C. '74 (NY) [4] Newburgh, NY Sacred Heart Church.
Lody, John R. '62 (Y) Canal Fulton, OH SS. Philip and James Church.
Loeb, Karl E. '95 (BUF) Amherst, NY St. Leo Church.
Loeber, Germain *o.s.b* '55 (SCL) [I] Collegeville, MN St. John's Abbey, of the Order of St. Benedict.
Loebl, Jeffrey R. *s.j.* '82 (MIL) [P] Milwaukee, WI Jesuit Community at Marquette University.
Loecke, Douglas J. '89 (DUB) Blessing, IA Immaculate Conception Church; Cedar Falls, IA St. Patrick Church.
Loecker, Craig J. '92 (OM) [46] Omaha, NE St. Thomas More Church.
Loeffer, Earl '51 (TOL) [5] Toledo, OH Corpus Christi, University of Toledo Church.
Loeffler, Richard A. *c.m.* '32 (PH) [Z] Philadelphia, PA Congregation of the Mission.
Loegering, Leonard '73 (FAR) [1] Grand Forks, ND Holy Family Church.
Loehr, Alfred M. '37 (GB) Retired.
Loehr, Charles D. '47 (MIL) Retired.
Loehr, James P. '67 (MIL) Okauchee, WI St. Joan of Arc Church.
Loehrlein, Richard A. *s.m.* '61 (CIN) [M] Dayton, OH Marianist Provincialate.
Loehrlein, Sylvester '56 (EVN) Red Brush, IN St. Rupert Church.
Loeper, David J. '83 (ALN) [10] Bethlehem, PA SS. Simon and Jude Church.
Loeper, Msgr. Richard J. '50 (ALN) [3] Bethlehem, PA Holy Ghost Church.
Loffredo, Peter J. '70 (TR) On Duty Outside the Diocese.
Lofgren, Eric D. (SAC) Burney, CA St. Francis of Assisi Church.
LoFranco, Sofronio '60 (BRK) [B] Elmhurst, NY Cathedral Preparatory Seminary of the Immaculate Conception; [N] Jamaica, NY Catholic Medical Center of Brooklyn & Queens.

Loftin, Don '94 (AUS) Round Rock, TX St. William's Church.
Lofton, Msgr. Edward D. '82 (CHR) [14] Charleston, SC St. Thomas The Apostle Church.
Lofton, James J. '61 (ALN) New Philadelphia, PA Sacred Heart Church.
Loftus, Msgr. Anthony '43 (NY) [V] New York, NY Kateri Residence.
Loftus, Conrad W. *o.f.m.* '54 (NY) [Z] New York, NY Franciscan Friars, Order of Friars Manor.
Loftus, David '94 (LA) La Mirada, CA Beatitudes of Our Lord Church.
Loftus, J. Allan *s.j.* '74 (BAL) [M] Baltimore, MD Jesuit Fathers and Brothers Maryland Provincial Curia.
Loftus, Joseph J. (ARL) Falls Church, VA St. Philip Church.
Loftus, Joseph V. *s.j.* '40 (DET) [P] Clarkston, MI Colombiere Center.
Loftus, Kenneth G. *s.j.* '91 (BO) [W] Boston, MA The Society of Jesus of New England-Provincial Offices.
Loftus, Kenneth G. *s.j.* '91 (SCR) [C] Scranton, PA University of Scranton.
Loftus, Msgr. Padraic '62 (LA) Woodland Hills, CA St. Mel Church.
Loftus, Msgr. Robert '43 (NY) Retired.
Loftus, Robert A. '91 (BGP) Riverside, CT St. Catherine of Siena Church.
Loftus, Thomas B. *c.ss.r.* '57 (BAL) [85] Baltimore, MD Sacred Heart of Jesus Church.
Lofy, Guy *o.c.d.* '48 (MIL) [P] Milwaukee, WI Provincial Offices - Discalced Carmelites.
Lofy, Joseph M. *c.s.v.* '73 (CHI) [N] Arlington Heights, IL Viatorian Province Center-Clerics of St. Viator.
Logan, Aidan *o.c.s.o.* '85 (WOR) [N] Spencer, MA St. Joseph's Abbey; [P] Spencer, MA St. Joseph Abbey.
Logan, Msgr. Daniel B. '63 (STA) [5] Jacksonville, FL Holy Family Church.
Logan, David '79 (VNN) Spokane, WA SS. Cyril & Methodius Church.
Logan, Francis A. *s.j.* '33 (SEA) [A] Seattle, WA Seattle University.
Logan, Gary '93 (SR) Graduate Studies.
Logan, J. M. '79 (PEO) [3] Rock Island, IL St. Joseph's Church.
Logan, James J. '59 (LC) Marshfield, WI Our Lady of Peace Church.
Logan, James P. '86 (BAK) [1] Baker, OR Cathedral of St. Francis De Sales.
Logan, Msgr. James T. '54 (FRS) [2] Fresno, CA Holy Spirit Church; [J] Fresno, CA Apostolate of Christian Action.
Logan, John *o.carm.* '64 (NY) [97] New York, NY Our Lady of the Scapular/St. Stephen Church; Manhattan, NY Bellevue Hospital.
Logan, John D. *o.p.* '56 (TYL) [D] Nacogdoches, TX Stephen F. Austin University Catholic Student Center.
Logan, Joseph P. *s.j.* '54 (SJ) [L] Los Altos, CA Jesuit Retreat House.
Logan, Michael *c.ss.r.* '57 (B) Coeur D'Alene, ID St. Thomas Church.
Logan, William R. '69 (RVC) Brentwood, NY St. Luke Church.
Logan, Wm. John Dominic *o.p.* '57 (TYL) Nacogdoches, TX Sacred Heart Church.
LoGatto, Joseph J. '57 (PAT) Retired.
LoGatto, Rosario J. '42 (BRK) Retired.
LoGrasso, Pasquale '57 (DET) [2] Clinton Twp., MI St. Louis Church.
Logrip, Joseph L. '72 (PH) [100] Philadelphia, PA Mater Dolorosa Church.
Logsdon, Wilfrid *o.f.m.conv.* '59 (SAV) Brunswick, GA St. Francis Xavier Church.
Logue, Charles D. '48 (BO) Halifax, MA Our Lady of the Lake Church.
Logue, Dennis *s.v.d.* '83 (WH) Camden, WV St. Boniface Church.
Logue, Louis R. '53 (BUR) Waterbury, VT State Hospital.
Logue, Mark '73 (BAL) Owensville, MD Our Lady of Sorrows Church.
Lohan, James '73 (NO) [5] Metairie, LA St. Catherine of Siena Church.
Lohan, Louis '71 (BLX) Long Beach, MS St. Thomas the Apostle Church; [G] Long Beach, MS University of Southern Mississippi, Gulf Park.
Lohkamp, Nicholas *o.f.m.* '52 (CIN) [M] Cincinnati, OH St. Ann Friary.
Lohr, Charles H. *s.j.* '61 (NY) [Z] New York, NY Jesuit Provincial's Office.
Lohrmeyer, Kenneth P. '70 (SAL) Mankato, KS St. Theresa of Infant Jesus Church.
Lohse, Edward M. '89 (E) [A] Erie, PA St. Mark's Seminary.
Lohse, Walter H. '40 (E) Retired.
Loi, Nguyen '66 (OM) [4] Omaha, NE St. Ann Church.
Loiacono, James *o.m.i.* '71 (BO) [12] Lowell, MA Nuestra Senora del Carmen 1990 Church.
Loiselle, Joseph G. '57 (WOR) East Brookfield, MA St. John the Baptist Church.
Loiselle, Lucien H. '49 (BO) Dracut, MA St. Mary of the Assumption Church.
Lojewicz, John '72 (PAT) Absent on Leave.
Lolio, John W. '70 (PRO) East Greenwich, RI Our Lady of Mercy Church.
Lomasiewicz, Donald E. '62 (GR) [10] Grand Rapids, MI St. Isidore's Church.
Lomax, Mark '80 (NO) [2] Slidell, LA St. Genevieve Church.
Lombard, Richard J. '53 (SHP) [8] Shreveport, LA St. Joseph Church.
Lombard, Roy A. '47 (WH) Retired.
Lombard, Samuel J. '46 (BO) Middleton, MA St. Agnes Church.
Lombardi, Albert U. '47 (DET) Retired.
Lombardi, Gary '69 (SR) Petaluma, CA St. Vincent de Paul Church.
Lombardi, John '79 (BAL) [10] Baltimore, MD St. Anthony of Padua Church; Special Assignment.
Lombardi, Joseph L. *s.j.* '75 (PH) [C] Philadelphia, PA St. Joseph's University; [Z] Philadelphia, PA Jesuit Community at St. Joseph's University.
Lombardi, Nicholas D. *s.j.* '72 (NY) [Z] New York, NY Jesuit Community at Fordham University.
Lombardi, Thomas '75 (FTW) Besancon, IN St. Louis Church.
Lombardo, Msgr. Angelo J. '55 (BEL) Okawville, IL St. Barbara Church.
Lombardo, Francis J. *o.f.m.conv.* '71 (NOR) Stafford Springs, CT St. Edward Church.
Lombardo, Gerard '86 (NEW) Livingston, NJ St. Barnabas Medical Center.
Lombardo, Gregory J. *c.s.c.* '45 (FTW) [J] South Bend, IN Congregation of Holy Cross Indiana Province Provincial House.
Lombardo, Joseph A. '85 (TUC) Green Valley, AZ Our Lady of the Valley Church.
Lombardo, Michael J. '78 (PAT) Pompton Plains, NJ Our Lady of Good Counsel Church; Pompton Plains, NJ Chilton Memorial Hospital; Wayne, NJ Wayne General Hospital.
Lombardo, Robert *c.f.r.* '90 (NY) [Z] New York, NY St. Crispin Friary.
Lombardo, Msgr. Samuel L. '39 (BUF) Retired.
Lombo, German *o.s.a.* '53 (MGZ) Aguada, PR St. Francis of Assisi Church.
Lommel, George D. '46 (FAR) Retired.
Lonardo, Alfred C. '63 (PRO) [5] Cranston, RI St. Mary Church.
Loncar, Sebastian '37 (VEN) Retired.
Loncar, Stephen *o.f.m.conv.* '88 (GRY) [12] Gary, IN St. Joseph The Worker Church.
Loncarcic, Stanley J. '36 (KCK) Louisburg, KS Immaculate Conception Church.
Lonchyna, Taras R. '77 (PHU) Silver Spring, MD Holy Trinity Church; Manassas, VA Annunciation of the Blessed Virgin Mary Church; Richmond, VA St. John the Baptist Church.
London, Lawrence '53 (RCK) Retired.
Londono, Diego '96 (ORL) Daytona Beach, FL St. Paul's Church.
Londono, Heriberto '84 (SJN) [2] Toa Baja, PR Ntra. Sra. de la Candelaria Church.
Londono, Hugo '74 (ORL) [1] Ocala, FL Blessed Trinity Church.
Londono, Orlando '77 (SJN) [3] Canovanas, PR Sagrado Corazon de Jesus Church.
Lonek, Stephen C. '76 (NY) On Duty Outside the Archdiocese.
Lonek, Stephen C. '76 (WIL) Newark, DE St. John the Baptist-Holy Angels Church.
Lonergan, David W. '61 (HRT) Wethersfield, CT Corpus Christi Church; Wethersfield, CT Sacred Heart Church.
Lonergan, James Barry '66 (ALB) Berlin, NY Sacred Heart Church; Military Chaplains.
Lonergan, Michael J. '93 (PH) Collingdale, PA St. Joseph Church.
Long, Daniel *l.c.* (WDC) [M] Potomac, MD Legionaries of Christ.
Long, Francis C. '51 (PHX) Retired.
Long, Galen J. '91 (SAL) Ellis, KS St. Mary's Church.
Long, Garrett J. *s.m.* '76 (RVC) [D] Mineola, NY Chaminade High School (Boys); [N] Mineola, NY Provincial Residence and Novitiate.
Long, J. William '89 (R) Henderson, NC St. James the Greater Church.
Long, James T. '63 (BEL) Fairview Heights, IL St. Albert the Great Church.
Long, John '61 (JC) Lake Ozark, MO Our Lady of the Lake Church.
Long, John F. *s.j.* '56 (NY) [Z] New York, NY Jesuit Provincial's Office.
Long, John G. *o.carm.* '86 (PHX) Special Assignment; [F] Phoenix, AZ Carmelite Community; [I] Phoenix, AZ Kino Institute.
Long, John J. *s.j.* '56 (BAL) [A] Baltimore, MD St. Mary's Seminary and University.
Long, John M. '78 (STP) Hopkins, MN St. Joseph's Church.
Long, John R. '89 (SUP) Bruce, WI St. Mary Church; Strickland, WI Assumption of the Blessed Virgin Mary Church; Weyerhauser, WI SS. Peter and Paul Church.
Long, Joseph J. *c.s.c.* '59 (SCR) [C] Wilkes-Barre, PA Kings College.
Long, Melvin T. '66 (SAL) Manhattan, KS St. Thomas More Parish Church.
Long, Msgr. Michael J. '54 (PH) Sellersville, PA St. Agnes Church.
Long, Richard E. '89 (BRK) [23] Brooklyn, NY St. Brendan's Church.
Long, Thomas *c.s.v.* '69 (MRY) Hollister, CA Sacred Heart Church.
Long, Tran Phuc '48 (ORG) Costa Mesa, CA St. John the Baptist Church.
Long, Valentine *o.f.m.* '27 (PAT) [M] Ringwood, NJ Holy Name Friary.
Long, Vincent P. '69 (SY) [2] Rome, NY St. Mary of the Assumption Church.
Long, W. Thomas '91 (GB) [2] Green Bay, WI Nativity of Our Lord Church.
Longanback, Carl *c.pp.s.* '34 (CIN) [B] Carthagena, OH St. Charles.
Longbucco, John L. '90 (MAR) Ontonagon, MI Holy Family Church; Rockland, MI St. Mary Church.
Longchamps, Adrien R. '75 (MAN) [4] Manchester, NH St. Augustin Church.
Longen, Louis *o.m.i.* '79 (BUF) [27] Buffalo, NY Holy Angels Church.
Longo, Robert M. *o.f.m.cap.* '85 (BRK) Released from Diocesan Assignment.
Longo, Robert M. *o.f.m.cap.* '85 (WIL) [F] Wilmington, DE Ministry of Caring, Inc.
Longo, Roque *m.ss.cc.* '33 (CAM) [L] Linwood, NJ Villa Pieta.
Longres, Joaquin S. '62 (BRK) [191] Queens, NY St. Luke Church.
Longtin, Lucien F. *s.j.* '65 (WDC) [E] Washington, DC Gonzaga College High School.
Longua, Msgr. Paul '61 (PAT) Sabbatical.
Longweld, John *o.f.m.cap.* (NY) Wassaic, NY Wassaic Development Center.
Longwill, Cathal '54 (DEN) Craig, CO St. Michael Church.
Longworth, Kevin J. *s.p.s.* '53 (SFR) [2] San Mateo, CA St. Gregory Church.
Lonney, Thomas P. *c.s.c.* '87 (SCR) [M] Wilkes-Barre, PA Moreau House.
Lonsdale, Richard G. '66 (PRT) Hallowell, ME Sacred Heart Church.
Lonteen, Daniel A. '94 (CLV) Eastlake, OH St. Justin Martyr Church.
Looby, John J. '66 (OG) Dannemora, NY St. Joseph Church.
Loomie, Albert J. *s.j.* '52 (NY) [Z] New York, NY Jesuit Community at Fordham University.
Loomis, Dennis J. *m.s.* '77 (MAN) [K] Enfield, NH Shrine of Our Lady of La Salette; [M] Enfield, NH La Salette Shrine and Center of Enfield.
Loomis, Msgr. Richard '76 (LA) [2] North Hollywood, CA St. Charles Borromeo Church.
Loomis, Richard P. '52 (WIN) Fairmont, MN St. John Vianney Church.
Loomis, Thomas A. '92 (WIN) [2] Rochester, MN Pax Christi Church.
Looney, Daniel A. '71 (SAC) Davis, CA St. James Church.
Looney, Joseph E. '67 (HRT) [7] Waterbury, CT Sacred Heart Church.
Looney, Matthew D. '58 (NEW) Westfield, NJ Holy Trinity Church.
Looney, Thomas P. *c.s.c.* '87 (SCR) [C] Wilkes-Barre, PA Kings College.
Loos, Francis *c.i.c.m.* '41 (ARL) [J] Arlington, VA Missionhurst, C.I.C.M.-Central House and Provincialate.
Loos, Frederick C. '63 (SAG) On Duty Outside the Diocese.
Loosbrock, Donald L. '51 (WIN) Retired.
Lopardo, Vito R. '55 (BEL) Retired.
Lopatesky, Raymond M. '75 (PAT) [P] Chester, NJ Nazareth Village.
Lopera, Rafael I. *c.s.b.* '94 (GAL) [Q] Sugar Land, TX Basilian Mission Center.
Lopes, Richard *o.f.m.cap.* '82 (SFR) [N] Burlingame, CA Capuchin Provincial House.
Lopes, Thomas C. '65 (FR) Nantucket, MA St. Mary's, Our Lady of the Isle Church.
Lopez, Abel '56 (SJ) [1] San Jose, CA St. Joseph Cathedral.
Lopez, Adolfo '87 (GLP) Absent on Leave.
Lopez, Agustin *sch.p.* '57 (PCE) [4] Ponce, PR Our Lady of Mt. Carmel Church.
Lopez, Alberto '87 (SJN) [3] Guaynabo, PR Maria Madre de Mi Senor Church.
Lopez, Alvaro '95 (STO) Modesto, CA St. Stanislaus Church.
Lopez, Amador *o.m.i.* '58 (SD) Calipatria, CA St. Patrick Church.
Lopez, Antonio '95 (FR) [17] Fall River, MA St. Louis Church; [Q] Fall River, MA Priestly Fraternity of the Missionaries of St. Charles Borromeo, Inc.

Lopez, Armando *o.f.m.* '88 (SD) San Luis Rey, CA Mission San Luis Rey de Francia Church; [H] San Luis Rey, CA San Luis Rey.
Lopez, Benigno *o.de. m.* '62 (PCE) [13] Ponce, PR Santuario San Judas Tadeo Church.
Lopez, Bruce D. '88 (PEO) Galva, IL St. John's Church; Woodhull, IL St. John's Church.
Lopez, Calixto *c.m.* '80 (LA) [A] Camarillo, CA St. John's Seminary College of the Archdiocese of Los Angeles.
Lopez, Camilo L. '93 (NEW) Fort Lee, NJ Madonna Church.
Lopez, Msgr. Daniel M. '63 (FRS) Chowchilla, CA St. Columba Church.
Lopez, Edgardo '83 (MGZ) Rosario, PR Rosary Church.
Lopez, Efrain (CGS) [B] Aibonito, PR Casa Manresa.
Lopez, Enrique '94 (LSC) [2] Las Cruces, NM Holy Cross Church.
Lopez, Enrique A. *c.ss.r.* '64 (LA) Whittier, CA St. Mary of the Assumption Church; [R] Whittier, CA Redemptorist Fathers Mission House.
Lopez, Eugenio '84 (SAC) Vacaville, CA St. Mary Church.
Lopez, Fausto (SJ) [1] San Jose, CA St. Joseph Cathedral.
Lopez, Felipe '59 (NEW) [2] Union City, NJ St. Augustine's Church.
Lopez, Felix M. *c.r.* '64 (PBL) Conejos, CO Our Lady of Guadalupe Church.
Lopez, Fernando *s.j.* '54 (MIA) [5] Miami, FL Gesu Church.
Lopez, Msgr. Francis R. '57 (MGZ) San German, PR San German de Auxerre Church.
Lopez, Francisco Javier *sch.p.* '78 (SJN) [58] San Juan, PR Santisimo Salvador Church.
Lopez, Frank '93 (ELP) [22] El Paso, TX St. Frances Xavier Cabrini Parish Church.
Lopez, G. *m.s.w.* (LA) [Y] Los Angeles, CA Catholic Charities of Los Angeles, Inc.
Lopez, Guillermo Velez '88 (NY) [137] Bronx, NY Christ the King Church.
Lopez, Humberto '86 (MGZ) San German, PR San German de Auxerre Church.
Lopez, Jairo '94 (AUS) Round Rock, TX St. William's Church.
Lopez, Jairo '94 (ELP) On Duty Outside of Diocese.
Lopez, Jesus Francisco (CC) [4] Corpus Christi, TX Holy Family Church.
Lopez, Jose '91 (JKS) On Duty Outside the Diocese.
Lopez, Jose A. '71 (SAT) [A] San Antonio, TX The Assumption-St. John's Seminary; [C] San Antonio, TX Oblate School of Theology.
Lopez, Jose D. '91 (MIA) [24] Miami, FL St. Kevin Church.
Lopez, Jose M. '78 (ARE) [4] Arecibo, PR Santa Ana Church; [8] Arecibo, PR Inmaculado Corazon de Maria Church; Special Assignment.
Lopez, Joseph '59 (KCK) [1] Overland Park, KS Church of the Ascension.
Lopez, Juan '87 (SAV) Special Assignment.
Lopez, Juan M. '62 (MIA) [28] Miami, FL SS. Peter and Paul Church.
Lopez, Kharlosg '77 (CGS) Fajardo, PR Santisimo Redentor Church.
Lopez, Leonidas '85 (SLC) [4] Salt Lake City, UT Sacred Heart Church.
Lopez, Lionel '96 (BWN) [10] Brownsville, TX Saint Mary, Mother of the Church.
Lopez, Luis E. *c.s.v.* '95 (CHI) [N] Arlington Heights, IL Viatorian Province Center-Clerics of St. Viator.
Lopez, Mauricio A. '92 (SAT) Asherton, TX Immaculate Conception Church.
Lopez, Pedro J. '81 (LA) El Monte, CA Nativity Church.
Lopez, Ramon *o.f.m.cap.* '76 (SJN) [4] San Juan, PR San Antonio Church.
Lopez, Richard '73 (ATL) [H] Atlanta, GA Our Lady of Perpetual Help Home.
Lopez, Richard A. '82 (SFR) San Francisco, CA St. Mary's Medical Center.
Lopez, Serapio '82 (STV) [4] Mt. Pleasant, VI Church of St. Joseph.
Lopez, Severino *c.m.f.* '44 (ATL) Stone Mountain, GA Corpus Christi Church.
Lopez, Victor '64 (ELP) [30] El Paso, TX St. Pius X Church.
Lopez, Victor *o.carm.* '68 (NEW) Englewood, NJ St. Cecilia's Church.
Lopez, Vincent *o.p.* '56 (P) [6] Eugene, OR St. Thomas More Church; [D] Eugene, OR Marist High School.
Lopez Aponte, Nelson '90 (CGS) [6] Caguas, PR Nuestra Senora del Perpetuo Socorro Church.
Lopez-Tovar, Ireneo '50 (CAM) Landisville, NJ Our Lady of Victories Church.
Lopez-Velez, Mauricio '92 (LKC) On Duty Outside the Diocese.
Lopilato, Art *s.j.* '80 (ANC) [6] Anchorage, AK Our Lady of Guadalupe Church; [G] Anchorage, AK Jesuit House.
LoPinto, Alfred P. '70 (BRK) Released from Diocesan Assignment.
Lorance, Douglas '84 (SJP) Jeannette, PA St. Demetrius Church.
Lord, David *m.i.c.* '91 (CHL) [1] Greensboro, NC Our Lady of Grace Church.
Lord, Gary (MAN) Salem, NH St. Joseph Church.
Lord, John *o. carm.* '81 (NEW) Bogota, NJ St. Joseph's Church.
Lord, Laurence J. '64 (SY) [3] Binghamton, NY St. Catherine of Siena Church.
Lord, Norman *c.s.sp.* '48 (SB) [E] Hemet, CA Holy Ghost Fathers.
Lord, Robert J. '60 (HRT) Woodbridge, CT Church of the Assumption.
Lord, Ronald A. '64 (BUF) [53] Buffalo, NY Our Lady of Loretto Church.
Lordemann, Francis W. '72 (OM) Fremont, NE St. Patrick Church.
Lorden, Demetrio L. '70 (SP) Temple Terrace, FL Corpus Christi Church.
Loredo, Miguel A. *o.f.m.* '64 (NY) [35] New York, NY St. Francis of Assisi Church.
Lorento, Anthony *s.a.c.* '72 (BRK) [110] Brooklyn, NY Our Lady of the Rosary of Pompeii Church.
Lorentsen, Michael *o.f.m.conv.* '94 (R) Burlington, NC Blessed Sacrament Church; [H] Elon College, NC Elon College.
Lorenz, Bernard A. '85 (LIN) Harvard, NE St. Joseph's Church.
Lorenz, John F. '54 (DM) [7] Des Moines, IA St. Augustin's Church; [F] Des Moines, IA Institute of the Heart of Jesus.
Lorenz, Matthais E. '69 (CHI) On Duty Outside the Archdiocese.
Lorenz, Richard J. *s.a.c.* '60 (MIL) Wauwatosa, WI Milwaukee Regional Medical Center; Wauwatosa, WI Froedtert Memorial Lutheran Hospital; [P] Milwaukee, WI Pallotti House.
Lorenz, Msgr. Victor O. '31 (DET) Retired.
Lorenz, Vincent E. '53 (SD) Retired.
Lorenzana, Elias *o.de.m.* '82 (CGS) Cayey, PR Nuestra Senora de la Merced Church.
Lorenzetti, Msgr. Dino J. '53 (BUF) [5] Depew, NY Our Lady of the Blessed Sacrament Church; Retired.
Lorenzo, Avelino *s.d.b.* (SFE) [18] Albuquerque, NM San Jose Church.
Lorenzo, Eduardo '66 (LAN) [6] Flint, MI Our Lady of Guadalupe Church.
Lorenzo, Elias R. *o.s.b.* '89 (PAT) [M] Morristown, NJ St. Mary's Abbey.
Lorenzo, Joseph F. *o.f.m.* '76 (MAN) Derry, NH St. Thomas Aquinas Church.
Lorenzoni, Larry *s.d.b.* (SFR) [N] San Francisco, CA Salesian Provincial Residence.
Loreti, Msgr. Joseph F. '59 (NEW) Roselle Park, NJ The Assumption Church.
Lorfanfant, Ernest P. *s.m.* '68 (RVC) [N] Mineola, NY Provincial Residence and Novitiate.
Lorge, Felix P. '50 (SPK) Colfax, WA St. Patrick Church; Lacrosse, WA St. Joseph Church.
Lorig, Douglas E. '84 (PHX) Gilbert, AZ St. Anne Church.
Lorigan, Thomas '39 (PT) Milton, FL St. Rose of Lima Church; Retired.
Lorilla, Wilfredo '68 (AGN) Piti, GU Assumption of Our Lady Church.
Lorio, Msgr. Joseph O. '54 (NO) [11] Metairie, LA St. Louis King of France Church.
Lorkowski, Robert A. '77 (CLV) Solon, OH St. Rita Church.
Lorrain, Matthew P. '86 (BR) Lakeland, LA Immaculate Conception Church.
Losarcos, Javier '51 (NEW) [4] Newark, NJ St. Aloysius Church.
LoSchiavo, John J. *s.j.* '55 (SFR) [C] San Francisco, CA University of San Francisco; [N] San Francisco, CA Jesuit Community at University of San Francisco.
Loscocco, Angelo P. '53 (BO) [1] Methuen, MA St. Lucy Church.
Losemann, Heinrich J., Jr. (BAL) Absent on Leave.
Losh, Joseph '64 (COL) La Rue, OH St. Joseph's Church.
Loshe, Norbert *c.pp.s.* '40 (CIN) Fort Recovery, OH Mary Help of Christians Church.
Losiewicz, George H. '74 (TOL) Clyde, OH St. Mary Church.
Losito, Msgr. Felix A. '58 (ALN) [6] Reading, PA Holy Rosary Church.
Loskarn, George '65 (BAL) [28] Baltimore, MD St. Dominic Church.
Loskot, Donald *s.d.s.* '76 (MIL) [P] Milwaukee, WI Salvatorian Formation Community.
Losoya, Jose Encarnacion *c.o.* '91 (BWN) Pharr, TX St. Jude Thaddeus Church; [E] Pharr, TX Oratory of St. Philip Neri, of Pontifical Right.
Lossing, Larry '84 (ORL) [10] Orlando, FL St. Joseph Church; Special Assignment.
Lostrittu, Paul *o.f.m.* '96 (NY) [48] New York, NY Holy Name of Jesus Church.
Loth, Alan J. '68 (OKL) Bison, OK St. Joseph's Church.
Lothamer, James W. *s.s.* '71 (LAN) Adrian, MI St. Joseph Church.
Lotief, Cecil '64 (SAN) Absent on Leave.
Lotito, Floyd A. *o.f.m.* '60 (SFR) [5] San Francisco, CA St. Anthony Church; [U] San Francisco, CA Franciscan Friars of California, Office of Communications.
Lott, Franklin '69 (SEA) Battle Ground, WA Sacred Heart Church.
Lott, Lawrence (MOB) On Leave from the Archdiocese.
Lott, Michael D. '92 (L) LaGrange, KY Immaculate Conception Church.
Lott, Robert V. '65 (NY) [36] New York, NY St. Francis de Sales Church.
Lott, Roger R.S. *o.s.b.* '54 (BIR) [E] Cullman, AL St. Bernard Abbey.
Lotz, Joseph *o.f.m.conv.* '92 (PAT) [6] Clifton, NJ St. John Kanty Church.
Lotz, Robert J. '73 (MIL) [C] Milwaukee, WI Mount Mary College; [X] Milwaukee, WI Milwaukee Archdiocesan Campus Ministry.
Lotze, James F. *s.j.* '69 (DET) [28] Detroit, MI Gesu Church.
Lou, Aloysius '65 (HON) Pearl City, HI Our Lady of Good Counsel Church.
Louapre, Albert C. *s.j.* '60 (LAF) [A] Grand Coteau, LA St. Charles College.
Loucks, Thomas J. '77 (B) Twin Falls, ID Our Lady of Guadalupe Church; [F] Twin Falls, ID College of Southern Idaho.
Loughery, Robert J. *c.s.c.* '89 (OAK) [3] Hayward, CA St. Clement Church; [Q] Hayward, CA California State University/Campus Ministry Center.
Loughlin, James F. '52 (NEW) Retired.
Loughlin, William J. '69 (BGP) [7] Fairfield, CT St. Thomas Aquinas Church.
Loughman, Kenneth M. '58 (NY) Walden, NY Most Precious Blood Church.
Loughnane, Msgr. James J. '61 (LA) Diamond Bar, CA St. Denis Church.
Loughnane, John B., Jr. '88 (BUR) Canaan, VT Assumption of the Blessed Virgin Mary Church.
Loughnane, John B., Jr. '88 (MAN) West Stewartstown, NH St. Albert Church.
Loughran, Francis J. '56 (PH) Upper Gwynedd, PA Corpus Christi Church; Retired.
Loughran, James N. *s.j.* '70 (NEW) [B] Jersey City, NJ Saint Peter's College; [B] Jersey City, NJ Saint Peter's College; [N] Jersey City, NJ Jesuits of Saint Peter's College, Inc.
Loughran, John J. *o.s.f.s.* '80 (TOL) [K] Toledo, OH Oblates of St. Francis de Sales.
Loughran, Peter G. '48 (SPR) [1] Holyoke, MA Blessed Sacrament Church.
Loughren, James P. '91 (OG) Morrisonville, NY St. Alexander Church; [3] Plattsburgh, NY St. Joseph Church.
Loughrey, Thomas F. '45 (PH) [19] Philadelphia, PA St. Barbara Church; Retired.
Louis, A. J. *s.d.b.* '44 (PAT) [D] Paterson, NJ Don Bosco Technical High School.
Louis, Anthony M. '36 (STP) Retired.
Louis, Conrad *o.s.b.* '40 (IND) [J] St. Meinrad, IN St. Meinrad Archabbey.
Louis, Jean Woady (VEN) Immokalee, FL Our Lady of Guadalupe Church.
Louis, John F. *o.m.i.* '43 (STP) [N] St. Paul, MN Oblate Provincial Offices; [N] St. Paul, MN Oblate Residence.
Louis, Msgr. John H. '62 (SCR) Clarks Green, PA St. Gregory Church.
Louis, Kevin C. '89 (LC) Cashton, WI Sacred Heart of Jesus Church; Norwalk, WI St. Augustine of Hippo Church; Saint Mary's Ridge, WI Nativity of the Blessed Virgin Mary Church; Summit, WI St. John the Baptist Church.
Lourdusamy, M.A. '87 (MIL) [17] Milwaukee, WI St. Catherine Church.
Louzon, Bede G. *o.f.m.cap.* '86 (MAR) Chassell, MI St. Anne Church.
Lovas, Donald J. '63 (WIN) [5] Rochester, MN St. Francis of Assisi Church.
Lovat, Rene *s.x.* '57 (PAT) [M] Wayne, NJ Xaverian Missionary Fathers.
Lovato, Charles *s.f.* (NY) Manhattan, NY U.S.V.A. Medical Center.
Lovato, Charles *s.f.* (PAT) [J] Denville, NJ Sisters of the Sorrowful Mother Health Care Ministry Corp.
Love, John '90 (LA) Moorpark, CA Holy Cross Church.
Love, Lester E. *s.j.* '91 (OAK) [N] Berkeley, CA Jesuit Community at Jesuit School of Theology at Berkeley.
Loveless, William J. '75 (Y) [7] Warren, OH St. Pius X Church.
Loveley, Arthur E. *s.j.* '44 (DET) [62] Detroit, MI SS. Peter and Paul Jesuit Church.
Loveley, Edward M. *s.j.* '47 (DET) [P] Clarkston, MI Colombiere Center.
Lover, Lawrence E. *c.ss.r.* '51 (BAL) [66] Baltimore, MD Our Lady of Fatima Church.
Lovett, Gerald F. '59 (SEA) Redmond, WA St. Jude Church.
Lovett, Msgr. John (RVC) Riverhead, NY St. John the Evangelist Church.
Lovisa, Eugene L. '49 (TOL) Retired.
Lovrencic, Athanasius *o.f.m.* '48 (CHI) [N] Lemont, IL

The Slovene Franciscan Fathers, Order of Friars Minor, Commissariat of the Holy Cross.
Low, Msgr. Albert W. '47 (BO) Retired.
Lowe, Frank '85 (SB) On Duty Outside the Diocese.
Lowe, Philip J. '82 (PH) Collegeville, PA St. Eleanor Church; [D] Pottstown, PA St. Pius X High School.
Lowe, Russell P. '92 (CLV) [3] Parma, OH St. Charles Borromeo Church.
Lowell, Ben (TOL) [H] Lima, OH St. Rita's Medical Center.
Lower, Richard T. '71 (MAN) New London, NH Our Lady of Fatima Church; [N] Durham, NH Campus Ministries; [N] New London, NH Colby-Sawyer College Newman Center.
Lowery, Daniel L. *c.ss.r.* '55 (GR) [3] Grand Rapids, MI St. Alphonsus Church.
Lowery, James T. *m.s.* '55 (HRT) [M] Hartford, CT Missionaries of LaSalette Provincial Secretary.
Lowery, Martin J. *m.m.* '68 (NY) [Z] Maryknoll, NY Maryknoll Fathers and Brothers.
Lowery, Philip A. '76 (TR) Red Bank, NJ St. James Church.
Lowery, Wilfred *c.ss.r.* '49 (CHI) [N] Glenview, IL The Redemptorists of Glenview, Illinois.
Lowery, Wilfrid *c.ss.r.* '49 (STL) [P] Liguori, MO Liguori Mission House/Redemptorists.
Lowery, William R. '53 (SFR) [1] San Mateo, CA St. Bartholomew Church; Retired.
Lowicz, Myron *o.f.m.* '60 (GRY) [I] Crown Point, IN St. Anthony Home, Inc.
Lowney, Edward *o.m.i.* '40 (BO) Tewksbury, MA St. William Church; Boston, MA Tewksbury Hospital.
Lowney, Jeremiah '88 (HEL) [B] Helena, MT Carroll College.
Lowrey, Robert *o.m.v.* '78 (BO) [BB] Boston, MA St. Francis Chapel.
Lowry, Msgr. James M. '42 (SCR) Retired; [N] Dunmore, PA Villa St. Joseph.
Lowry, Joseph K., Jr. '66 (BUF) Little Valley, NY St. Mary Church; Retired.
Loy, Vincent P. '49 (RVC) Retired.
Loya, Alfredo (LUB) [2] Lubbock, TX Our Lady of Grace Church.
Loya, Daniel '66 (PBR) Windber, PA St. Mary (Dormition) Church.
Loya, John F. '74 (CLV) [A] Wickliffe, OH Borromeo Seminary; [A] Wickliffe, OH St. Mary Seminary.
Loya, Joseph *o.s.a.* '79 (PH) Havertown, PA St. Denis Church; [C] Villanova, PA Villanova University.
Loya, Thomas '82 (PRM) Chicago, IL St. Mary Church; Joliet, IL St. Mary Assumption Church.
Loyacono, Charles '57 (JKS) Woodville, MS St. Joseph Church.
Loyd, Frederick A. '70 (COL) Powell, OH St. Joan of Arc Church.
Loyens, William J. *s.j.* '58 (P) [L] Portland, OR Jesuit Provincial Office (Oregon Prov.).
Loyson, Michael '92 (DET) Absent on Leave.
Lozano, Jose '65 (PCE) [2] Ponce, PR Church San Patricio Church; Jayuya, PR Our Lady of Monserrate Church.
Lozano, Roland *c.m.f.* '75 (LA) [R] Los Angeles, CA Missionary Sons of the Immaculate Heart of Mary; [R] Los Angeles, CA Claretian Retreat Center Community.
Lozier, Donald *o.m.i.* '60 (BO) [4] Lowell, MA Sainte Jeanne d'Arc Church.
Lozier, Timothy R. '88 (STA) [4] Gainesville, FL St. Augustine Church; [L] Gainesville, FL University of Florida-St. Augustine Parish and Student Center.
Lozinski, Eugene L. '72 (NU) Glencoe, MN St. Pius X Church.
Lozinski, Robert W. *c.s.c.* '73 (PSC) Scranton, PA St. John the Baptist Church.
Lu, Matthias '42 (OAK) Retired.
Luat Nguyen, John *o.f.m.* '94 (SFR) [7] San Francisco, CA St. Boniface Church.
Lubanski, Armand *o.f.m.* '47 (FWT) [G] Crowley, TX St. Francis Village, Inc.; [H] Crowley, TX St. Maximilian Kolbe Friary.
Lubas, Feliks '57 (FAR) Minto, ND Sacred Heart Church.
Lubbers, John W. *c.s.c.* '57 (FTW) [J] South Bend, IN Congregation of Holy Cross Indiana Province Provincial House.
Lubbers, John W. *c.s.c.* '57 (SAT) [C] San Antonio, TX Our Lady of the Lake University; [M] San Antonio, TX Holy Cross Community.
Lubbers, Leland E. *s.j.* '59 (OM) [K] Omaha, NE Jesuit Community At Creighton University.
Lubeley, Msgr. Richard J. '49 (STL) Webster Groves, MO Mary, Queen of Peace Church.
Lubey, John A. '43 (WDC) Retired; [L] Washington, DC Cardinal O'Boyle Residence for Priests.
Lubic, Robert T. '96 (GBG) New Kensington, PA Mt. St. Peter Church.
Lubicky, Msgr. John R. '48 (CAM) Blackwood, NJ St. Agnes Church; Retired.
Lubinsky, Michael C. '78 (SAV) Warner Robins, GA Sacred Heart Church.
Lubrano, Joseph *s.d.s.* '74 (MIL) [P] Milwaukee, WI Salvatorian Provincial Residence.
Luca, Edward J. '54 (CLV) Sheffield, OH St. Teresa Church.
Luca, Msgr. Joseph L. '70 (BAL) Clarksville, MD St. Louis Church.
Lucal, John A. *s.j.* (DET) [K] Detroit, MI Jesuit Provincial Office-Detroit Province of the Society of Jesus.
Lucarelli, Gabriel M. *c.r.m.* '36 (NEW) Lodi, NJ St. Joseph's Church.
Lucas, Christopher *o.f.m.conv.* '85 (MRY) [G] Arroyo Grande, CA St. Joseph's Cupertino Novitiate.
Lucas, Donald *o.f.m.* (JKS) Greenwood, MS St. Francis of Assisi Church.
Lucas, Edward '61 (PBR) Duquesne, PA St. Mary's Church.
Lucas, Msgr. George J. '75 (STL) Special Assignment; [A] St. Louis, MO Kenrick-Glennon Seminary.
Lucas, Jeffery J. '81 (E) [20] Erie, PA St. Joseph Church.
Lucas, John (STN) San Francisco, CA Immaculate Conception Church.
Lucas, Msgr. John J. '65 (E) Conneaut Lake, PA Our Lady Queen of the Americas Church.
Lucas, John P. '69 (CHI) [3] Oak Park, IL St. Edmund Church; [X] Chicago, IL Court of Appeals-Province of Chicago.
Lucas, Lawrence E. '59 (NY) [89] New York, NY Our Lady of Lourdes Church; City, NY North Infirmary Command; City, NY Otis Bantum Correctional Center; Manhattan, NY North General Hospital.
Lucas, Neil '67 (TOL) [3] Toledo, OH Christ the King Church.
Lucas, Robert '59 (PSC) Doylestown, PA Christ the Savior Byzantine Catholic Church at Our Lady of Czestochawa Shrine Church.
Lucas, Robert *c.m.* '74 (CHI) [J] Chicago, IL St. Joseph Hospital; [N] Chicago, IL Vincentian Community, Congregation of the Mission, Midwest Province.
Lucas, Theodore '84 (CLV) Solon, OH Resurrection of Our Lord Church.
Lucas, Thomas M. *s.j.* '85 (SFR) [N] San Francisco, CA Jesuit Community at University of San Francisco.
Lucas, William '90 (BIR) Jacksonville, AL St. Charles Church; [H] Jacksonville, AL Jacksonville State University.
Lucasinsky, Raymond *c.m.m.* '62 (DET) [K] Dearborn Heights, MI Our Lady of Grace Monastery.
Lucatero, Heliodoro '86 (SPK) Othello, WA Sacred Heart Church.
Lucavei, Tarcisio *o.s.b.m.* (STN) Hamtramck, MI Immaculate Conception of B.V.M. Church.
Lucca, Augustine *s.d.s.* '51 (NSH) Smyrna, TN St. Luke Church.
Lucchesi, Joseph *o.carm.* '84 (JOL) [J] Darien, IL Carmelite Fathers Provincial Office.
Lucci, Fred *o.p.* '93 (TUC) [I] Tucson, AZ University of Arizona.
Lucero, Leo E. '60 (SFE) [3] Santa Fe, NM Cristo Rey Church.
Lucero, Lorenzo '56 (ELP) San Elizario, TX San Elceario Church.
Lucev, John '65 (SD) Retired.
Lucey, Beatus T. *o.s.b.* '59 (PAT) [I] Morristown, NJ St. Mary's Abbey Retreat Center; [M] Morristown, NJ St. Mary's Abbey.
Lucey, Gregory F. *s.j.* '64 (MIL) [P] Milwaukee, WI Jesuit Provincial Office, Wisconsin Province.
Lucey, Gregory F. *s.j.* '64 (WDC) [M] Washington, DC Leonard Neale House; [V] Washington, DC Jesuit Conference, Inc.
Lucey, J. Roger *s.j.* '58 (MIL) [P] Milwaukee, WI Jesuit Provincial Office, Wisconsin Province.
Lucey, J. Roger *s.j.* '58 (OAK) Orinda, CA Santa Maria Church; [N] Berkeley, CA Jesuit Community at Jesuit School of Theology at Berkeley.
Lucey, John P. '32 (SPR) Retired.
Lucey, John P. *c.s.c.* '45 (FTW) [J] South Bend, IN Congregation of Holy Cross Indiana Province Provincial House.
Lucey, Paul T. *s.j.* '48 (BO) [W] Boston, MA Loyola House.
Lucey, William F. (BO) Retired.
Luchi, Robert J. *s.j.* '93 (BEL) [3] East St. Louis, IL St. Joseph Church.
Luchi, Robert J. *s.j.* '93 (STL) [52] St. Louis, MO St. Matthew, Apostle Church.
Lucia, Douglas J. '89 (OG) [1] Ogdensburg, NY St. Mary's Cathedral.
Luciana, Msgr. Lawrence J. '63 (STU) Retired.
Luciana, Msgr. Lawrence J. '63 (WH) Ona, WV St. Stephen Church.
Luciani, Pompeo *s.a.c.* '36 (NEW) Fairview, NJ Our Lady of Grace Church.
Luciano, William J. '83 (NY) [166] Bronx, NY St. Michael Church.
Lucid, Msgr. Michael '54 (OAK) [1] San Leandro, CA Assumption of the Blessed Virgin Mary Church.
Lucid, Philip J. *s.j.* '55 (SEA) [A] Seattle, WA Seattle University.
Lucid, Vincent F. '43 (BO) Retired.
Lucido, John '73 (ELP) Monahans, TX St. John the Apostle and Evangelist Church.
Lucier, Charles V. *o.p.* '41 (WDC) [11] Washington, DC St. Dominic Church & Priory Church.
Lucier, Jude *o. praem* '74 (ORG) [3] Orange, CA St. Norbert Church.
Lucio, Justin '72 (DAL) Special Assignment.
Luck, Robert O. '62 (LA) Retired.
Lucking, Aloysius '50 (MIA) Retired.
Lucko, Aidan *o.f.m.cap.* '40 (PIT) [N] Pittsburgh, PA St. Augustine Friary.
Lucree, Lawrence A. '60 (SAV) Americus, GA St. Mary Church.
Luczak, Andrew E. '70 (CHI) Skokie, IL St. Lambert Church.
Luczak, Jay R. '92 (TUC) [20] Tucson, AZ Saints Peter and Paul Church.
Luczak, Thomas W. *o.f.m.* '70 (GB) [I] Pulaski, WI Assumption of B.V.M. Friary.
Luczak, Thomas W. *o.f.m.* '70 (GRY) [K] Cedar Lake, IN San Damiano Friary.
Luczycki, Msgr. Matthew C. '45 (SY) Oneida, NY St. Joseph Church; Retired.
Ludeman, Edward '95 (SFR) [4] South San Francisco, CA St. Veronica Church.
Ludescher, Kenneth F. '61 (STP) Maplewood, MN St. Jerome Church.
Ludlum, William '46 (NEW) Retired.
Ludvik, John J. *s.j.* '71 (P) [N] Portland, OR Loyola Renewal Center.
Ludwig, Alexander P. '58 (SCL) Alexandria, MN St. Mary's Church.
Ludwig, Augustine W. *o.s.b.* '86 (RIC) [7] Richmond, VA St. Benedict Church; [M] Richmond, VA Mary Mother of the Church Abbey.
Ludwig, Eugene M. *o.f.m.cap.* '71 (NTN) Oakland, CA St. John The Theologian Church.
Ludwig, Eugene M. *o.f.m.cap.* '71 (OAK) [A] Berkeley, CA Dominican School of Philosophy and Theology.
Ludwig, John '74 (DM) [4] Des Moines, IA Drake Newman Parish Church; [H] Des Moines, IA Drake Newman Center.
Ludwig, Raphael A. '57 (DUB) St. Lucas, IA St. Luke's Church; Waucoma, IA St. Mary's Church; [F] St. Lucas, IA Fort Atkinson-St. Lucas Catholic School.
Ludwig, Roman E. '43 (FAR) Larimore, ND St. Stephen's Church.
Ludwig, Thomas K. '87 (KC) Savannah, MO St. Rose of Lima Church; [C] St. Joseph, MO Bishop LeBlond High School.
Ludwikoski, James E. '73 (KCK) Military Chaplains.
Luebke, Martial *o.f.m.* '39 (LA) [72] Los Angeles, CA St. Joseph Church.
Luebking, Msgr. Thomas A. '71 (TR) Spring Lake, NJ St. Catharine Church.
Lueckenotte, Daniel I. '90 (JC) Ewing, MO Queen of Peace Church; Palmyra, MO St. Joseph Church.
Lueckenotto, Arthur A. *m.s.* '63 (STL) [P] St. Louis, MO La Salette Missionaries.
Luehrmann, Stanley E. '53 (CIN) Hillsboro, OH St. Mary's Church.
Luera, Ruben '86 (LUB) On Duty Outside the Diocese.
Lueras, Charles R. *c.r.i.c.* '81 (LA) [64] Los Angeles, CA St. Francis of Assisi Church; [B] Los Angeles, CA Canons Regular of the Immaculate Conception-Novitiate; [R] Los Angeles, CA Canons Regular of the Immaculate Conception.
Luerman, John H. '56 (IND) Cambridge City, IN St. Elizabeth of Hungary Church.
Luetkemeyer, Alexander *o.s.b.* '53 (KC) Bethany, MO Blessed Sacrament Church.
Luettgen, Lawrence J. *s.j.* '60 (NO) [P] New Orleans, LA Ignatius Residence.
Luevano, Rafael '81 (ORG) Los Alamitos, CA St. Hedwig Church.
Luft, Raymond P. '68 (PRO) [24] Providence, RI Our Lady of Mt. Carmel Church.
Luger, Paul P. *s.j.* '42 (SPK) [K] Spokane, WA Regis Community.
Lugger, William Robert '89 (LAN) [12] Flint, MI St. Michael Church.
Lugo, Camilo '69 (RVC) Brentwood, NY St. Luke Church.
Lugo, Joseph W. '62 (PAT) Retired.
Lugo, Martin *o.s.b.* '62 (OKL) [I] Shawnee, OK St. Gregory's Abbey.
Lugue, Peter '63 (SB) [2] Corona, CA St. Edward Church.
Lui, Gabriel '79 (LA) Monterey Park, CA St. Thomas Aquinas Church.
Luisi, Joseph G. '83 (PIT) [66] Pittsburgh, PA St. Wendelin Church.
Luisini, Msgr. Anthony J. '56 (MET) Alpha, NJ St. Mary Church.
Luistro, Abelardo '50 (LA) [47] Los Angeles, CA St. Basil's Church.
Luiten, Gary '92 (FAR) Ellendale, ND St. Helena's Church.
Luiz, Gary M. *c.pp.s.* '77 (OAK) [N] Berkeley, CA Society of the Precious Blood.
Luka, Ronald *c.m.f.* '63 (CHI) [N] Oak Park, IL

Claretian Fathers Headquarters of U.S.A. Eastern Province.
Lukac, Thomas M. '63 (GBG) [3] Latrobe, PA St. John the Evangelist Church.
Lukachinsky, Jerome A. '88 (CLV) [2] Parma, OH St. Bridget Church.
Lukaczyk, George '54 (STF) [9] Terryville, CT St. Michael Church.
Lukas, Andrew F. '58 (WH) Retired.
Lukas, Joseph S. '46 (BO) Ipswich, MA Sacred Heart Church.
Lukas, Martin C. *o.s.f.s.* '80 (TOL) [C] Toledo, OH St. Francis de Sales High School; [K] Toledo, OH Oblates of St. Francis de Sales.
Lukas, Michael '36 (SEA) Retired.
Lukasik, Alexius *o.f.m.* '49 (GB) Stangelville, WI St. Lawrence Church; West Kewaunee, WI St. Hedwig Church.
Lukasik, Alexius *o.f.m.* '49 (MIL) [P] Burlington, WI Queen of Peace Friary.
Lukaszczyk, Josef '80 (STL) [P] Eureka, MO Our Lady of the Angels Monastery.
Lukaszewicz, John C. '55 (MIL) [1] Waukesha, WI St. Joseph's Church.
Lukaszewski, Jerome *o.f.m.conv.* '48 (BAL) [M] Ellicott City, MD Order of Friars Minor Conventual.
Lukaszewski, Joseph C. '79 (RVC) West Islip, NY Our Lady of Lourdes Church.
Lukaszewski, Leonard '54 (GRY) Retired.
Lukaszewski, Stanley P. '79 (TR) Willingboro, NJ Corpus Christi Church.
Luke, Eugene *o.s.b.* '61 (FWT) Lindsay, TX St. Peter Church.
Lukefahr, Oscar *c.m.* '66 (STL) [P] Perryville, MO Congregation of The Mission; [W] Perryville, MO Catholic Home Study Service.
Lukehart, Frederick '63 (Y) [16] Youngstown, OH St. Joseph Church.
Lukenda, Raymond T. '56 (NEW) Secaucus, NJ Immaculate Conception Church.
Lukes, Duane '57 (OM) [G] Norfolk, NE Our Lady of Lourdes Hospital.
Lukianiuk, Andriej '86 (BRK) [43] Brooklyn, NY St. Frances de Chantal Church.
Lukoskie, Raymond M. '58 (PEO) Warsaw, IL Sacred Heart Church.
Luljak, Louis P. '61 (MIL) [4] Racine, WI Holy Trinity Church; [11] Racine, WI St. Stanislaus Church.
Lulko, Leo T. '65 (DET) Highland, MI Church of the Holy Spirit.
Lulloff, William '48 (GB) [I] Appleton, WI St. Fidelis Friary.
Lum, William '69 (ROC) Absent on Leave.
Luminais, Msgr. J. Anthony '54 (NO) Bridge City, LA Holy Guardian Angels Church.
Lumpkin, Thomas '64 (DET) Detroit, MI Southwest Detroit Hospital.
Lumsden, Patrick '96 (DAV) [3] Davenport, IA Holy Family Church.
Luna, Ezequiel Bas *o.s.b.* '84 (SFE) [J] Abiquiu, NM Monastery of Christ in the Desert.
Luna, Henry *c.m.f.* '55 (AUS) San Marcos, TX St. John the Evangelist Church.
Luna, Ignacio '65 (BWN) Ranchito, TX St. Ignatius Church.
Luna, Lambert Joseph '78 (SFE) [16] Albuquerque, NM San Felipe de Neri Church.
Luna, Miguel '89 (ELP) [28] El Paso, TX St. Matthew Church.
Luna, Roger *s.d.b.* (SFR) [N] San Francisco, CA Salesian Provincial Residence.
Lund, Donald F. *c.s.v.* '46 (JOL) Bourbonnais, IL Maternity of the Blessed Virgin Mary Church.
Lund, Donald J. '69 (CHI) [72] Chicago, IL Good Shepherd Church.
Lundberg, Jan *o.c.d.* '93 (SJ) [M] San Jose, CA Carmelite Monastery, Novitiate.
Lundberg, John W. '60 (TLS) On Duty Outside the Diocese.
Lundergan, Barnabas *o.s.b.* '45 (RCK) [H] Aurora, IL Marmion Abbey-St. Augustine's Abbey.
Lundgren, Richard '96 (JOL) [5] Naperville, IL St. Thomas the Apostle Church.
Lundgren, Russell J. (SUP) Montreal, WI Sacred Heart of Jesus Church.
Lundgren, Stephen A. '79 (DUB) [H] Dubuque, IA Mercy Health Center-St. Joseph's Unit.
Lundy, George F. *s.j.* '78 (DET) [K] Detroit, MI Jesuit Community at the University of Detroit.
Lungay, Jose Roel G. '84 (NO) [3] Metairie, LA St. Ann Church and Shrine Church.
Luniw, Paul '82 (STF) [8] New Haven, CT St. Michael Church.
Lunney, Msgr. John A. '56 (ANC) [6] Anchorage, AK Our Lady of Guadalupe Church; Retired.
Lunney, William H. '94 (SPR) [9] Holyoke, MA Sacred Heart Church; [M] Holyoke, MA Casa Maria.
Lunnon, William '82 (DET) [M] Detroit, MI St. Mary's Residence.
Lunsford, Keith '92 (KCK) Leawood, KS Church of the Nativity.
Lunsford, Robert D. '60 (LAN) Ovid, MI Holy Family Church; St. Johns, MI St. Joseph Church.
Luo, Matteo *o.f.m.conv.* '59 (BAL) [M] Ellicott City, MD Order of Friars Minor Conventual.
Luong, Dominic *s.s.s.* '67 (SAT) [74] San Antonio, TX Vietnamese Martyers Catholic Center Church.
Luong, Msgr. Dominic Mai Thanh '66 (NO) [14] New Orleans, LA Mary, Queen of Vietnam Church; [5] New Orleans, LA Chapel of the Vietnamese Martyrs Church.
Luong, Tri M. '94 (HBG) [3] York, PA St. Patrick Church.
Luong Kim Dinh, Dominic (SPC) [E] Carthage, MO Congregation of the Mother Co-Redemptrix, United States Assumption Province.
Luong Mihn Tuat, Francis M. *c.m.c.* (SPC) [E] Springfield, MO Congregation of Mother Co-Redemptrix, Our Lady of the Rosary House.
Luongo, Anthony (NEW) [C] Ramsey, NJ Don Bosco Preparatory High School for Boys.
Luongo, John '78 (ORG) Absent on Sick Leave.
Lupa, Gerard (OG) Malone, NY Notre Dame Church.
Lupa, Gerard (SY) Absent on Leave.
Lupico, Samuel J. '70 (BAL) Special Assignment.
Lupo, Joseph F. *o.ss.t.* (NY) [218] Staten Island, NY Our Lady of Mt. Carmel-St. Benedicta Church.
Lupo, William L. '65 (CHI) Bartlett, IL St. Peter Damian Church.
Lusch, Daniel J. *s.j.* '62 (BO) [W] Boston, MA The Society of Jesus of New England-Provincial Offices; [W] Chestnut Hill, MA The Jesuit Community at Boston College.
Lusch, Daniel J. *s.j.* '62 (BUF) [O] Buffalo, NY Canisius Jesuit Community.
Luschen, Timothy D. '89 (OKL) Altus, OK Prince of Peace Church.
Lusoski, Thomas J. '57 (CLV) South Euclid, OH St. Margaret Mary Church.
Lussier, Andre '55 (FR) [K] Attleboro, MA La Salette Provincial House.
Lussier, Bonaventure *o.c.d.* (CHI) [N] Chicago, IL Edith Stein House of Studies.
Lussier, Bonaventure *o.c.d.* (WH) [N] Hinton, WV Monastery of Christ on the Mountain.
Lussier, Louis *o.s.cam.* '90 (MIL) [P] Wauwatosa, WI St. Camillus Provincialate; [P] St. Francis, WI St. Camillus Formation Community; [Y] Wauwatosa, WI St. Camillus Institute, Inc.
Lussier, Robert *o.s.b.* (SFE) [L] Pecos, NM Our Lady of Guadalupe Benedictine Abbey.
Lussier, Robert *s.s.s.* '56 (GB) Menasha, WI St. Mary Church.
Lussier, Ronald P. '52 (SPR) [6] Chicopee, MA St. George's Church.
Lusson, David R. '80 (SUP) On Leave.
Lustig, Victor Joseph '42 (B) Retired.
Luszczak, Francis J. '39 (ALN) Retired.
Luteri, Evaristo '30 (PIT) Retired; [N] Pittsburgh, PA St. John Vianney Manor.
Lutgen, Richard E. '62 (SAL) Chapman, KS St. Michael's Church.
Luther, Benjamin F. '64 (OWN) [3] Paducah, KY St. John the Evangelist Church.
Luther, Philip L '87 (LIN) Trenton, NE St. James Church.
Lutjen, George J. '68 (BRK) [149] Queens, NY St. Anastasia Church.
Lutkenhoff, Bernard '71 (LFT) Unassigned.
Lutmer, Joseph H. '46 (CIN) Retired.
Lutostanski, Anthony '58 (BUF) [39] Buffalo, NY St. John Kanty Church.
Luttenberger, Gerard H. *c.m.* '65 (RVC) [A] Huntington, NY Diocesan Seminary of the Immaculate Conception; [N] Oyster Bay, NY Vincentian Community.
Lutz, Bernard A. '63 (EVN) Fort Branch, IN Holy Cross Church.
Lutz, Donald J. '70 (BUF) [13] Buffalo, NY St. Bernard Church.
Lutz, Frederick J. '73 (SPC) Advance, MO St. Joseph Church; Oran, MO Guardian Angel Church.
Lutz, George (NEW) [17] Newark, NJ St. James Church.
Lutz, Gerald '56 (PIT) McKeesport, PA St. Patrick Church.
Lutz, Herman G. (IND) [37] Indianapolis, IN St. Philip Neri Church.
Lutz, Joseph L. '87 (RCK) [3] Freeport, IL St. Mary Church; Shannon, IL St. Wendelin Church.
Lutz, Kevin '78 (COL) Plain City, OH St. Joseph Church.
Lutz, Robert J. '50 (CHI) Northbrook, IL St. Norbert Church; Retired.
Lutz, Thomas '93 (NY) Highland, NY St. Augustine Church.
Luu, Joseph '66 (HT) Amelia, LA Thanh Gia Church.
Lux, Joachim N. *o.f.m.* '61 (CIN) [M] Cincinnati, OH St. Clement Friary.
Lux, Joseph W. *s.j.* '71 (NEW) [B] Jersey City, NJ Saint Peter's College; [N] Jersey City, NJ Jesuits of Saint Peter's College, Inc.
Lux, Robert *c.pp.s.* '42 (CIN) [B] Carthagena, OH St. Charles.
Lux, Thomas J. '85 (LIN) Bruno, NE St. Anthony Church; [C] David City, NE Aquinas/St. Mary's Schools.
Luyet, Gregory '95 (LR) Fort Smith, AR Immaculate Conception Church.
Luzbetak, Louis *s.v.d.* '45 (CHI) [B] Techny, IL Divine Word Residence.
Luzetsky, Stephen '50 (PSC) Retired.
Luznicky, George M. *o.s.m.* '55 (DEN) Westminster, CO Holy Trinity Church.
Luzzi, Anthony *s.d.b.* '49 (NY) West Haverstraw, NY Helen Hayes Hospital; [BB] West Haverstraw, NY Don Bosco Retreat Center and Marian Shrine; [BB] West Haverstraw, NY Marian Shrine.
Lybarger, Curtis F. '77 (STP) Osseo, MN St. Vincent de Paul Church.
Lyddy, Daniel F. '34 (OG) Retired.
Lyddy, Vincent E. '45 (HRT) North Haven, CT St. Therese's Church; Retired.
Lyden, Dennis P. '63 (STU) Retired.
Lydon, Leo B. '50 (WH) Retired.
Lydon, Michael '74 (SP) [2] Largo, FL St. Justin Martyr Church.
Lydon, Michael J. '84 (STL) [57] St. Louis, MO St. Pius the Fifth Church.
Lyle, Dennis J. '91 (CHI) [A] Chicago, IL St. Joseph Seminary; [C] Chicago, IL Loyola University-Chicago.
Lyle, John W. *o.s.f.s.* (ARL) [D] Fairfax, VA Paul VI High School; [J] Fairfax, VA Oblates of St. Francis de Sales Residence.
Lyman, Edward P. '67 (SCR) Archbald, PA St. Thomas Aquinas Church.
Lynam, Gerald J. '50 (HEL) Retired; [B] Helena, MT Carroll College.
Lynam, Robert G. '84 (MET) Kendall Park, NJ St. Augustine of Canterbury Church.
Lynaugh, Msgr. Joseph E. '36 (PH) Ardsley, PA Queen of Peace Church; Retired.
Lynch, Antone J. '81 (BLX) [4] Gulfport, MS St. Joseph Catholic Church.
Lynch, Charles E. *c.s.b.* '58 (GAL) Rosenberg, TX Our Lady of Guadalupe Church.
Lynch, Charles M. '78 (NEW) Retired.
Lynch, Cletus J. '30 (CHI) La Grange Park, IL St. Louise de Marillac Church; Retired.
Lynch, Conall P. *o.f.m.* '51 (GLP) Houck, AZ St. John Church; [F] Gallup, NM Southwest Indian Foundation.
Lynch, Cornelius B. '54 (PRO) On Duty Outside the Diocese.
Lynch, Cyprian J. *o.f.m.* '48 (BUF) [O] St. Bonaventure, NY St. Bonaventure Friary.
Lynch, Damion J. '91 (CHL) [3] Charlotte, NC Our Lady of Consolation Church.
Lynch, Daniel C. '48 (SC) Retired.
Lynch, Daniel F. *o.carm.* '54 (NY) Montrose, NY Franklin D. Roosevelt Hospital; Montrose, NY FDR DVA Hospital; [Z] Middletown, NY St. Albert's Priory.
Lynch, Daniel G. '51 (BO) Retired.
Lynch, Daniel J. *s.m.a.* '67 (WDC) [M] Takoma Park, MD Society of African Missions (S.M.A.).
Lynch, Denis '57 (GAL) Retired.
Lynch, Dennis J. '68 (LC) Mill Creek, WI St. Bartholomew Church; [6] Stevens Point, WI St. Stephen Church.
Lynch, Donald D. *s.j.* '59 (BGP) [A] Fairfield, CT Fairfield University; [O] Fairfield, CT The Fairfield Jesuit Community-Fairfield University.
Lynch, Edward C. *s.j.* '64 (NY) [Z] New York, NY Murray-Weigel Hall.
Lynch, Msgr. Edward J. '57 (BAL) [39] Baltimore, MD Immaculate Conception Church.
Lynch, Eugene *s.m.m.* '54 (HRT) [M] Litchfield, CT Montfort Missionaries.
Lynch, Francis A. *c.m.* '50 (MOB) Tallassee, AL St. Vincent De Paul Church.
Lynch, Frank '57 (BRK) [216] Queens, NY Our Lady of Mount Carmel Church.
Lynch, Gerald P. '73 (SLC) [8] Salt Lake City, UT St. Patrick's Church.
Lynch, Gerard F. *o.ss.t.* '74 (TR) Asbury Park, NJ Our Lady of Mt. Carmel Church.
Lynch, Ibar '52 (SEA) Retired.
Lynch, James M. '74 (CLV) Released from Diocesan Assignment.
Lynch, John A. '60 (ROC) [28] Rochester, NY St. James Church.
Lynch, John E. *c.s.p.* '51 (WDC) [B] Washington, DC St. Paul's College; [C] Washington, DC Catholic University of America, The; [C] Washington, DC Catholic University of America, The.
Lynch, John J. *s.j.* '66 (OM) [23] Omaha, NE St. John Church; [K] Omaha, NE Jesuit Community At Creighton University.
Lynch, John J. '96 (NY) Woodbourne, NY Immaculate Conception Church.
Lynch, John K. '56 (HRT) Cheshire, CT St. Bridget's Church.

Lynch, John R. '67 (CHI) [2] Oak Park, IL St. Catherine of Siena-St. Lucy Church.
Lynch, John S. '63 (E) Sharpsville, PA St. Bartholomew Church.
Lynch, Joseph *s.m.* '64 (RVC) [N] Hewlett, NY Marianist Community.
Lynch, Joseph P. '53 (CHI) Burbank, IL St. Albert the Great Church; Retired.
Lynch, Kenny '42 (L) [L] Louisville, KY Sacred Heart Retreat.
Lynch, Kevin A. *c.s.p.* '53 (NEW) [S] Mahwah, NJ Paulist Press.
Lynch, Kevin A. *c.s.p.* '53 (NY) [104] New York, NY St. Paul the Apostle Church.
Lynch, Leo A. '93 (ALT) [4] Altoona, PA Sacred Heart Church; [D] Altoona, PA Mercy Regional Health System.
Lynch, Leo X. '56 (BO) [1] Woburn, MA St. Anthony Church.
Lynch, M. Kevin '74 (PRO) [4] Cranston, RI St. Mark Church.
Lynch, Maurice J. '65 (DUB) [4] Dubuque, IA St. Mary's Church; [D] Dubuque, IA Wahlert High School.
Lynch, Michael '89 (MIA) Margate, FL St. Vincent Church.
Lynch, Michael J. '71 (LC) Wausau, WI Wausau Hospital Center.
Lynch, Michael J. '82 (TR) Marlboro, NJ St. Gabriel Church.
Lynch, Michael J. '88 (BRK) [215] Queens, NY Our Lady of the Miraculous Medal Church.
Lynch, Myles *o.s.m.* '58 (ORG) [H] Buena Park, CA Servite Fathers And Brothers.
Lynch, Noel '62 (SAC) Susanville, CA Sacred Heart Church.
Lynch, Patrick J. '46 (ALB) Retired.
Lynch, Msgr. Patrick J. '50 (MEM) Retired.
Lynch, Patrick J. *s.j.* '72 (BUF) [O] Buffalo, NY Canisius Jesuit Community.
Lynch, Ralph *o.s.b.* '46 (IND) [J] St. Meinrad, IN St. Meinrad Archabbey.
Lynch, Raymond J. *o.f.m.* '51 (SCR) [12] Wilkes-Barre, PA St. Joseph Church; [M] Wilkes-Barre, PA St. Joseph's Friary.
Lynch, Msgr. Richard '46 (LSC) Retired.
Lynch, Richard D. '63 (E) [4] Erie, PA Holy Rosary Church.
Lynch, Robert *o.f.m.* '43 (BO) [Z] Boston, MA Saint Anthony Residence.
Lynch, Robert B. '60 (NOR) [4] Norwich, CT St. Mary Church.
Lynch, Robert G. *s.j.* '56 (CHY) Pinedale, WY Our Lady of Peace Church.
Lynch, Robert N. '78 (MIA) [B] Opa Locka, FL St. Thomas University.
Lynch, Stephen *o.f.m.* '55 (PRO) [P] Providence, RI St. Francis Friary.
Lynch, Stephen '77 (BRK) [229] Queens, NY Presentation of the Blessed Virgin Mary Church.
Lynch, T. Patrick '61 (NEW) [B] Jersey City, NJ Saint Peter's College; [N] Jersey City, NJ Jesuits of Saint Peter's College, Inc.
Lynch, Thomas '92 (NY) Graduate Studies.
Lynch, Thomas F. '48 (NEW) [2] Hackensack, NJ Immaculate Conception Church.
Lynch, Thomas F. '71 (BGP) [2] Stratford, CT St. James Church.
Lynch, Thomas J. '56 (HRT) Newington, CT St. Mary Church.
Lynch, Thomas P. *o.p.* '86 (CHI) [N] Chicago, IL Dominicans (Provincial Office).
Lynch, Timothy J. '71 (PMB) [2] West Palm Beach, FL Mary Immaculate Church.
Lynch, Victor K. '92 (NEW) Ramsey, NJ St. Paul Church.
Lynch, William B. (CHI) Palos Heights, IL Incarnation Church.
Lynch, William B. '35 (CHI) Retired.
Lynch, William F. '57 (HRT) [4] Manchester, CT St. James Church.
Lynch, William J. *s.j.* '48 (CHL) Mooresville, NC St. Therese Church; [J] Charlotte, NC Jesuit Community.
Lynes, James F. '79 (GAL) Clute, TX St. Jerome Church.
Lynes, James F. '79 (SAN) On Duty Outside the Diocese.
Lynes, John '87 (MOB) Chickasaw, AL St. Thomas the Apostle Church.
Lynes, Thomas E. '43 (SPR) Retired.
Lynette, C. Franklyn *s.j.* '47 (NO) [C] New Orleans, LA Loyola University.
Lyng, Msgr. Eamonn F. '58 (SD) La Jolla, CA Mary, Star of the Sea Church.
Lyng, Matthew '57 (CC) Robstown, TX St. Thomas the Apostle Church.
Lynn, Joseph F. *o.s.f.s.* '42 (WIL) [I] Childs, MD Oblates of St. Francis De Sales.
Lynn, William D. *s.j.* '54 (COL) [A] Columbus, OH Pontifical College Josephinum.
Lynn, William J. '76 (PH) Ardsley, PA Queen of Peace Church.
Lyon, Msgr. E. Carl '46 (WDC) [6] Silver Spring, MD St. John the Baptist Church; Retired.
Lyon, George *o.s.b.* '50 (SFS) [F] Marvin, SD Blue Cloud Abbey.
Lyon, Msgr. Gerald F. '49 (SC) Le Mars, IA St. Joseph's Church; Retired.
Lyon, Joseph A. '50 (L) Retired.
Lyons, Denis '58 (ORG) Dana Point, CA St. Edward Church.
Lyons, Edward D. '62 (CAM) Ocean City, NJ St. Augustine's Church; [A] Absecon, NJ Holy Spirit High School.
Lyons, Edward J. *c.s.p.* '53 (NY) [Z] Scarsdale, NY Paulist Fathers Generalate.
Lyons, Edward J. *c.s.p.* '53 (PMB) [G] Vero Beach, FL Paulist Fathers Retirement Home.
Lyons, Msgr. Eugene F. '42 (CHI) Winnetka, IL SS. Faith, Hope and Charity Church; Retired.
Lyons, Francis A. '59 (MIA) North Lauderdale, FL Our Lady Queen of Heaven Church.
Lyons, Msgr. Frederick J. '52 (ALX) Retired.
Lyons, James A. '94 (PH) [13] Philadelphia, PA St. Anselm Church.
Lyons, James D. (BO) Rowley, MA St. Mary Church.
Lyons, James F. '43 (FR) Retired.
Lyons, James H.C. '96 (CR) Bemidji, MN St. Philip's Church; [F] Bemidji, MN Holy Spirit Newman Center.
Lyons, James M. *v.g.* '88 (HBG) [2] Harrisburg, PA St. Catherine Laboure Church.
Lyons, James P. '45 (KC) Retired.
Lyons, James W. (CHI) Retired.
Lyons, John '80 (SAV) [6] Savannah, GA Sacred Heart of Jesus Church.
Lyons, John *o.m.v.* '84 (MET) [H] Asbury, NJ Lanteri House.
Lyons, John F. '46 (Y) Retired.
Lyons, John J. *o.m.i.* '42 (BO) [3] Lowell, MA Immaculate Conception Church.
Lyons, John P. '55 (BO) Rochester, MA St. Rose of Lima Church.
Lyons, John P. '88 (TUC) [F] Tucson, AZ Regina Cleri Center.
Lyons, John T. '74 (PH) [19] Philadelphia, PA St. Barbara Church.
Lyons, Joseph *o.m.i.* '29 (SAT) [K] San Antonio, TX Oblate Madonna Residence.
Lyons, Lawrence '54 (MIA) Retired.
Lyons, Leo J. (CHI) Retired.
Lyons, Mark J. '38 (MIL) Retired.
Lyons, Michael '96 (VIC) El Campo, TX St. Philip's Church.
Lyons, Michael J. '70 (DUL) Pine City, MN Immaculate Conception Church.
Lyons, Michael Patrick (BGP) [2] Stratford, CT St. James Church.
Lyons, Patrick J. '45 (LIN) Hebron, NE Sacred Heart Church.
Lyons, Patrick M. '70 (CHI) Evergreen Park, IL Queen of Martyrs Church.
Lyons, Peter *t.o.r.* '66 (WDC) [M] Washington, DC St. Louis Friary.
Lyons, Peter A. *t.o.r.* '66 (BAL) [A] Baltimore, MD St. Mary's Seminary and University.
Lyons, Richard J. '74 (MET) Dunellen, NJ St. John the Evangelist Church.
Lyons, Robert *s.j.* '77 (SPK) [C] Spokane, WA Gonzaga University.
Lyons, Thomas J. '52 (BRK) [141] Brooklyn, NY St. Thomas Aquinas Church.
Lyons, Timothy *o.f.m.conv.* '42 (TR) Seaside Park, NJ St. Catharine of Siena Church.
Lyons, Timothy J. *c.m.* '86 (RVC) [N] Oyster Bay, NY Vincentian Community.
Lyons, Vincent '48 (SAC) Retired and in Senior Ministry.
Lyons, William J. '56 (CHI) Alsip, IL St. Terrence Church.
Lyons, Msgr. William J. '56 (STL) [A] St. Louis, MO Kenrick-Glennon Seminary; [A] St. Louis, MO Kenrick-Glennon Seminary; [V] St. Louis, MO Washington University Newman Centers.
Lyons, William P. '51 (CLV) [12] Akron, OH St. Matthew Church; Retired.
Lysaght, John *o.c.d.* '48 (SR) [M] Oakville, CA Carmelite House of Prayer.
Lysogorski, John '75 (ALB) [3] Troy, NY St. Francis de Sales Church; Albany, NY Albany Medical Center Hospital; Special Assignment.
Lysz, Robert J. '75 (HRT) Forestville, CT St. Matthew Church.
Lytle, Gerald A. '60 (HBG) [1] Lancaster, PA St. Anne Church.
Lyttle, Eugene '93 (DUL) Duluth, MN Indian Missions Church; Duluth, MN Indian Missions Church.
Lyttle, Eugene Francis '93 (DUL) Cloquet, MN Holy Family Church.
Lyttle, Gregory '75 (NY) [131] Bronx, NY St. Augustine Church.

M

Ma, Didacus '52 (SFR) Burlingame, CA St. Catherine of Siena Church.
Ma, Peter (NY) Manhattan, NY Beekman Downtown - New York Infirmary.
Ma, Peter '55 (NY) [70] New York, NY St. Mary Church.
Maag, Ronald E. '78 (BAK) The Dalles, OR St. Peter's Church.
Maag, Timothy J. '92 (TOL) Absent on Leave.
Maas, Francis *m.s.f.* '35 (SAT) [K] San Antonio, TX Padua Place.
Maat, William A. *o.s.b.* '33 (P) Rockaway, OR St. Mary by the Sea Church.
Maat, William A. *o.s.b.* '33 (SEA) [M] Lacey, WA St. Martin's Abbey.
Mabango, Ashiono Anthony '95 (PAT) Parsippany, NJ St. Peter the Apostle Church.
Mabarak, John R. *o.s.a.* '60 (CHI) [N] Olympia Fields, IL The Augustinian Provincialate Tolentine Center; [N] Olympia Fields, IL Tolentine Monastery at Tolentine Center.
Mabon, Msgr. Thomas K. '57 (ALT) [13] Johnstown, PA Our Mother of Sorrows Church.
MacAdam, Austin *m.afr.* '58 (CHI) [124] Chicago, IL St. Martin De Porres Church; [N] Chicago, IL Missionaries of Africa.
Macalintal, Dionisio '63 (SD) National City, CA St. Mary Church.
Macaluso, Msgr. Christie A. '71 (HRT) [1] Hartford, CT Cathedral of St. Joseph.
MacArthur, Bruce '53 (SFS) Retired.
Macartney, Ross J. '64 (PH) [101] Philadelphia, PA Maternity B.V.M. Church; Oreland, PA Holy Martyrs Church.
MacAulay, A. Gerard '59 (OKL) [11] Oklahoma City, OK Immaculate Conception Church.
MacAulay, Stephen A. '51 (TLS) Coweta, OK St. Vincent de Paul Church; Wagoner, OK Holy Cross Church.
Macaya, Miguel '65 (LSC) Dona Ana, NM Our Lady of the Purification Church.
MacCandless, William J. *o.s.b.* '58 (NO) Abita Springs, LA St. Jane de Chantal Church; [A] St. Benedict, LA St. Joseph's Seminary College; [P] St. Benedict, LA St. Joseph Abbey.
Maccarone, Patrick C. '91 (MET) Flemington, NJ St. Magdalen de Pazzi Church.
MacCarthy, John P. *o.praem.* '69 (GB) [I] De Pere, WI St. Norbert Abbey.
MacCarthy, Justin H. '64 (ORG) La Habra, CA Our Lady of Guadalupe Church.
MacCarthy, Liam '68 (SAC) Sutter Creek, CA Immaculate Conception Church; [K] Chico, CA Director of Campus Ministry.
MacCarthy, Peter T. '50 (BIR) Leeds, AL St. Theresa's Church.
MacCarthy, Timothy '60 (ORG) Tustin, CA St. Cecilia Church.
Macchi, William V. '64 (OAK) [3] Concord, CA St. Francis of Assisi Church.
Macchietto, Robert G. '71 (NY) [E] New York, NY Monsignor Farrell High School.
Macchler, Robert '62 (LA) Glendale, CA Church of the Incarnation.
MacDonald, Msgr. Arthur F. '52 (GLP) Alpine, AZ St. Helena Church.
MacDonald, Charles J. '67 (HRT) Wallingford, CT Holy Trinity Church.
MacDonald, Colin (SAC) Antelope, CA St. Clare Church.
MacDonald, Msgr. Colin A. '45 (MAN) [8] Manchester, NH St. Francis of Assisi Church; Retired.
MacDonald, David W. *s.j.* '61 (LA) [F] Los Angeles, CA Loyola High School.
MacDonald, Edward J. '42 (MAN) Retired.
MacDonald, Fabian '77 (SEA) [5] Seattle, WA St. Bernadette Church.
MacDonald, Hugh J. '64 (HRT) North Haven, CT St. Barnabas Church.
MacDonald, James *c.ss.r.* (STV) [2] Christiansted, VI Church of the Holy Cross.
MacDonald, James *s.a.c.* '35 (NEW) [S] South Orange, NJ The Pallottines of South Orange, Inc.
MacDonald, James H. '67 (SFR) Belmont, CA Immaculate Heart of Mary Church.
MacDonald, Kevin *c.ss.r.* (RVC) Bethpage, NY St. Martin of Tours Church.
MacDonald, Paul V. '59 (BO) [5] Weymouth, MA Sacred Heart Church.
MacDonald, Richard J. *s.c.j.* '65 (BWN) Lyford, TX Prince of Peace Church; Raymondville, TX Our Lady of Guadalupe Church.
MacDonald, Rupert A. *s.s.j.* '40 (BAL) [M] Baltimore, MD St. Joseph's Manor.
MacDonald, Stirling B. '88 (BO) Scituate, MA St. Mary of the Nativity Church.
MacDonald, Timothy *s.a.* '67 (NY) [Z] Garrison, NY Generalate of the Franciscan Friars of the Atonement-St. James Friary.
MacDonnell, John J. *s.j.* '58 (WOR) [N] Worcester, MA Jesuits of Holy Cross College, Inc.

MacDonnell, Joseph F. *s.j.* (BGP) [A] Fairfield, CT Fairfield University; [O] Fairfield, CT The Fairfield Jesuit Community-Fairfield University.
MacDonnell, Martin *s.j.* '66 (NOR) Storrs, CT St. Thomas Aquinas Church; [K] Willimantic, CT Campus Ministry.
MacDonnell, Martin P. *s.j.* '66 (BO) [W] Boston, MA The Society of Jesus of New England-Provincial Offices.
MacDonough, Richard *s.s.* '60 (LA) [A] Camarillo, CA St. John's Seminary College of the Archdiocese of Los Angeles.
MacDougall, James L. *o.s.a.* '59 (MIA) [B] Opa Locka, FL St. Thomas University; [H] Miami, FL Casa San Lorenzo.
MacEachen, Bede *s.a.* '42 (NY) [Z] Garrison, NY Generalate of the Franciscan Friars of the Atonement-St. James Friary.
Maceda, Thomas *c.ss.r.* '63 (NY) [23] New York, NY St. Cecilia Church.
Macedo, Charles '48 (SJ) Retired.
Macedo, Charles B. '67 (SJ) [2] Palo Alto, CA St. Albert the Great Church.
Macedo, Stephen A. '93 (HON) Naalehu, HI Sacred Heart Church; Pahala, HI Holy Rosary Church.
Maceli, Anthony J. '48 (BRK) Retired.
MacEntee, Francis J. *s.j.* '54 (SCR) [C] Scranton, PA University of Scranton.
MacEwen, Michael W. '85 (BO) On Special or Other Diocesan Assignment.
Macey, Richard '75 (DET) [4] Taylor, MI St. Paschal Church.
MacFarland, Francis L. *c.s.c.* (BO) Boston, MA Brockton Hospital.
MacFarlane, John F. '66 (WDC) [1] Rockville, MD St. Elizabeth Church.
MacGabhann, Kevin '63 (PMB) Lantana, FL Holy Spirit Church.
MacGee, James B. *o.m.i.* '57 (PT) Medart, FL St. Elizabeth Ann Seton Church.
MacGillivray, Arthur A. *s.j.* '44 (BO) [W] Chestnut Hill, MA The Jesuit Community at Boston College.
Macgregor, Donald '64 (HON) [2] Honolulu, HI Co-Cathedral of St. Theresa of the Child Jesus.
Machado, Domingos *o.a.r.* '95 (NY) [154] Bronx, NY St. John's Church; [BB] Bronx, NY St. Joseph's Center.
Machado, Jose '93 (WCH) On Duty Outside the Diocese.
Machado, Manuel '64 (NY) [109] New York, NY St. Rose of Lima Church.
Machain, David '52 (PH) [23] Philadelphia, PA St. Bernard Church.
Machak, James A. '49 (DET) Retired.
Machalski, Thomas C. '85 (BRK) [207] Queens, NY Our Lady of the Blessed Sacrament Church.
Machar, Jerome J. *o.c.s.o.* '75 (ROC) [I] Piffard, NY Abbey of the Genesee.
Machcinski, Anthony J. '50 (GAY) Retired.
Machesky, Peter I. *o.f.m.* '50 (JKS) Charleston, MS St. John Church.
Machlik, Jerome J. '71 (DET) Shelby Twp., MI St. John Vianney Church.
Machnik, Theodore '91 (COL) Westerville, OH St. Paul the Apostle Church.
Macho, George S. '53 (NEW) Retired.
Macho, Tomas *s.j.* '46 (MIA) [H] Miami, FL Jesuit Fathers of the Province of the Antilles, Inc.
Machovec, Frank J. '59 (LIN) Superior, NE St. Joseph's Church.
Machovec, Martin F. *o.m.i.* '61 (CR) Ogema, MN Most Holy Redeemer Church; White Earth, MN St. Benedict Church.
Macias, Francisco A. '94 (SAT) Gonzales, TX St. James Church.
Macias, Salvadore (OAK) Graduate Studies.
Maciej, David '80 (SCL) [4] St. Cloud, MN St. Anthony of Padua Church.
Maciejewski, Gerard *o.f.m.conv.* '59 (BRK) [146] Queens, NY St. Adalbert Church.
Maciejewski, Norbert '69 (DET) [2] Warren, MI Ascension Church.
Maciejewski, Richard J. '56 (STU) Retired.
Maciejewski, Tadeusz *c.m.* '88 (BRK) [32] Brooklyn, NY SS. Cyril and Methodius Church.
MacInnis, John E. '69 (BO) [A] Boston, MA St. John's Seminary School of Theology.
Macior, Lazarus *o.f.m.* '56 (CLV) [P] Cleveland, OH St. Stanislaus Friary.
Macior, Lazarus *o.f.m.* '56 (GB) [I] Pulaski, WI Assumption of B.V.M. Friary.
MacIssac, Charles S. *o.s.* '83 (PCE) On Duty Outside the Diocese.
Maciukiewicz, David J. '81 (E) [5] Erie, PA Holy Trinity Church.
Mack, Msgr. Ferdinand A. '31 (MAD) Retired.
Mack, Henry J. '49 (SFD) Retired.
Mack, John P. '85 (BUF) Lancaster, NY Our Lady of Pompeii Church; [D] Lancaster, NY St. Mary's High School.
Mack, Joseph W. '89 (CHL) Asheboro, NC St. Joseph Church.
Mack, Msgr. Robert A. '57 (BUF) [42] Buffalo, NY St. Louis Church.
Mack, Thomas E. '78 (PEO) Monmouth, IL Immaculate Conception Church; Raritan, IL Church of St. Patrick.
Macke, Paul B. *s.j.* '73 (ANC) [G] Anchorage, AK Jesuit House.
Macke, Richard J. '54 (SC) Pomeroy, IA St. Mary's Church.
Macken, Forrest *c.p.* '47 (L) [L] Louisville, KY Sacred Heart Retreat.
MacKenzie, William M. '66 (BO) Medway, MA St. Joseph Church.
Mackert, Albert J. '61 (CLV) [34] Cleveland, OH Immaculate Conception Church; Retired.
Mackesy, Robert L. *m.m.* '47 (NY) [Z] Maryknoll, NY Maryknoll Fathers and Brothers.
Mackey, James M. '61 (ALB) [8] Troy, NY St. Michael the Archangel Church.
Mackey, John J. '49 (BAL) Mount Savage, MD St. Patrick Church.
Mackiewicz, Richard E. '69 (GBG) Fayette City, PA Holy Spirit Church.
Mackin, Eamon *c.h.s.* '70 (ORG) [2] Huntington Beach, CA St. Mary's by the Sea Church.
Mackin, Francis C. *s.j.* '54 (BO) [W] Chestnut Hill, MA The Jesuit Community at Boston College.
Mackin, Gerard *m.s.f.* '66 (SAT) Seguin, TX Our Lady of Guadalupe Church.
Mackin, John J. '38 (CHI) Arlington Heights, IL Our Lady of the Wayside Church; Hometown, IL Our Lady of Loretto Church; Retired.
Mackin, Kevin E. '64 (ALB) [B] Loudonville, NY Siena College. [B] Loudonville, NY Siena College.
Mackin, William H. '38 (MIL) Retired.
Mackinnon, Donald *c.ss.r.* '59 (OAK) [N] Oakland, CA Redemptorists.
Mackle, Daniel E. '80 (PH) [1] Philadelphia, PA Cathedral Basilica of SS. Peter and Paul.
Mackle, Liam *o.s.m.* '58 (ORG) [H] Buena Park, CA Servite Fathers And Brothers.
Macklin, Eckley *s.o.l.t.* '94 (CC) [H] Robstown, TX Society of Our Lady of the Most Holy Trinity.
Macklin, Eckley *s.o.l.t.* '94 (KC) [O] Kansas City, MO Society of Our Lady of the Most Holy Trinity.
Macko, Msgr. John '41 (PBR) Retired.
Mackowiak, Edward M. '55 (CHI) Burbank, IL St. Albert the Great Church.
Mackowski, Richard M. *s.j.* '61 (DET) [K] Detroit, MI Jesuit Provincial Office-Detroit Province of the Society of Jesus.
Macl, Joel P. *o.s.b.* '78 (PAT) [M] Newton, NJ St. Paul's Abbey.
MacLeay, Richard Paul *o.p.* '57 (NO) [P] New Orleans, LA Dominican Fathers & Brothers, Southern Dominican Province.
MacLellan, Iain G. *o.s.b.* '87 (MAN) [K] Manchester, NH St. Anselm Abbey.
MacLellan, Richard H. '51 (CHY) Newcastle, WY Corpus Christi Church.
MacLennan, Donald '67 (DET) Absent on Sick Leave.
MacLeod, Thomas P. '56 (BO) Wakefield, MA Most Blessed Sacrament Church.
MacLoughlin, James '63 (ORL) Belleview, FL St. Theresa Church.
MacMahon, Craig *o.m.v.* '90 (SFD) [2] Alton, IL Immaculate Conception-St. Mary's Church; [3] Alton, IL St. Patrick Church; [H] Alton, IL Saint Anthony's Health Center; [N] Alton, IL Saint Anthony's Health System, Inc.; [N] Alton, IL Saint Clare's Hospital.
MacMahon, Msgr. Eamon '47 (MRY) Retired.
MacMahon, Michael '66 (BIR) [17] Birmingham, AL Our Lady of the Valley Church.
MacMahon, Patrick '69 (SPK) Colton, WA St. Gall Church; Uniontown, WA St. Boniface Church.
MacMaster, Thomas A. *o.c.s.o.* '57 (DUB) [K] Peosta, IA New Melleray Abbey, Order of Cistercians of the Strict Observance.
MacMillan, Len '91 (B) McCall, ID Our Lady of the Lake Church.
MacMillan, Leonard '91 (B) Council, ID St. Jude Church.
MacNamara, Patrick *o.c.d.* '80 (WDC) [B] Washington, DC Monastery of Our Lady of Mount Carmel.
MacNamara, Robert C. '51 (ROC) Horseheads, NY St. Mary Our Mother Church; Retired.
MacNevin, Stanley F. *c.s.p.* '60 (BO) [P] Boston, MA Paulist Center; [W] Boston, MA Paulist Fathers Residence.
MacNevin, Stanley F. *c.s.p.* '60 (NY) [Z] Scarsdale, NY Paulist Fathers Generalate.
MacNew, James J. *o.s.f.s.* '80 (WIL) [I] Wilmington, DE Oblates of St. Francis De Sales.
Maco, Stephen L. '76 (ALN) [5] Allentown, PA Our Lady Help of Christians Church; [1] Bethlehem, PA St. Anne Church; [C] Bethlehem, PA Bethlehem Catholic High School.
Macoskie, Melvin H. '55 (MIL) Retired.
MacPeck, Francis *s.j.* '67 (SFR) [44] San Francisco, CA St. Peter Church.
MacPhaidin, Bartley J. *c.s.c.* '63 (FR) [B] North Easton, MA Stonehill College.
MacPherson, Albert P. *o.s.a.* '74 (BO) [C] North Andover, MA Merrimack College.
MacPherson, Damian *s.a.* '78 (NY) [Z] Garrison, NY Generalate of the Franciscan Friars of the Atonement-St. James Friary.
MacPherson, Stephen '86 (SR) McKinleyville, CA Christ the King Church.
MacPherson, Walter E. '55 (BEL) Retired.
MacPherson, Walter J. '86 (CIN) [15] Dayton, OH Holy Trinity Church.
MacQuarrie, John '78 (CIN) New Carlisle, OH Sacred Heart Church.
MacRory, Camillus *o.f.m.cap.* '51 (SFR) [N] Burlingame, CA Capuchin Provincial House.
Macul, Joel P. *o.s.b.* '78 (PAT) [M] Newton, NJ St. Paul's Abbey.
Macunas, Theodore S. '64 (ALN) [10] Reading, PA St. Paul Church.
MacVeigh, Donal T. *s.j.* '72 (NEW) [B] Jersey City, NJ Saint Peter's College; [N] Jersey City, NJ Jesuits of Saint Peter's College, Inc.
MacVeigh, Michael C. '56 (PIT) Overbrook, PA St. Norbert Church.
Madaj, John A. '39 (SCR) Retired.
Madariaga, Jesus M. *o.p.* '54 (CC) [13] Laredo, TX St. Joseph Church.
Maday, Norbert J. '64 (CHI) Other Assignments.
Maddalena, Joseph P. '86 (GBG) [B] Greensburg, PA Seton Hill College.
Madden, Benjamin *o.f.m.cap.* '58 (WDC) [B] Washington, DC St. Francis Friary-Capuchin College.
Madden, Msgr. Brendan P. '51 (PAT) [4] Clifton, NJ St. Clare's Church.
Madden, Daniel P. *o.p.* '60 (MIA) [B] Miami, FL Barry University; [H] Bal Harbour, FL Dominican Friars Residence.
Madden, Declan A. *o.f.m.conv.* (DEN) [I] Denver, CO Francis Heights, Inc.; [K] Denver, CO Francis Heights.
Madden, Denis J. '67 (BAL) Special Assignment.
Madden, Edward T. '52 (DEN) [1] Boulder, CO Sacred Heart of Jesus Church.
Madden, Henry L. *o.f.m.* '46 (ALB) [B] Loudonville, NY Siena College.
Madden, J. Thomas '53 (SFR) [M] Menlo Park, CA Vallombrosa Center.
Madden, James *c.s.c.* (BGP) [P] Wilton, CT School Sisters of Notre Dame Motherhouse (Northeastern Province); [P] Wilton, CT Lourdes Health Care Center.
Madden, James J. (OG) Watertown, NY U.S. Army Headquarters Fort Drum.
Madden, Msgr. James J. '55 (GAL) Retired.
Madden, James J. *m.m.* '60 (CHI) [N] Chicago, IL Maryknoll Fathers & Brothers.
Madden, John '62 (NEW) [N] Rutherford, NJ St. John Vianney Residence for Priests.
Madden, John '86 (Y) Struthers, OH St. Nicholas Church.
Madden, John F. *c.s.b.* '47 (GAL) Retired; [Q] Houston, TX Dillon House.
Madden, John F. '84 (WOR) [27] Worcester, MA St. Peter Church; [C] Worcester, MA Holy Name Central Catholic High School.
Madden, John J. '62 (NEW) Retired.
Madden, Msgr. John R. '59 (SY) Hamilton, NY St. Mary Church.
Madden, Lawrence J. *s.j.* '64 (WDC) [20] Washington, DC Holy Trinity Church.
Madden, Michael G. '62 (TOL) [4] Toledo, OH Community of the Risen Christ Church.
Madden, Michael J. '95 (BGP) Ridgefield, CT St. Mary's Church.
Madden, Michael T. '75 (EVN) St. James, IN St. James Church.
Madden, Patrick '74 (SHP) On Duty Outside the Diocese.
Madden, Patrick '83 (MOB) Bayou LaBatre, AL St. Margaret Church.
Madden, Msgr. Patrick J. '45 (CAM) Retired.
Madden, Patrick J. '74 (BAL) [A] Baltimore, MD St. Mary's Seminary and University.
Madden, Msgr. Patrick M. '53 (STA) [14] Jacksonville, FL Sacred Heart Church.
Madden, Paul '70 (JKS) On Duty Outside the Diocese.
Madden, Ronald '70 (SAV) Military Chaplains.
Madden, Stephen J. '88 (BO) Foxboro, MA St. Mary Church.
Madden, Thomas '53 (SFR) Special Assignment.
Madden, Thomas '81 (SP) Dunedin, FL Our Lady of Lourdes Church.
Madden, Msgr. Thomas E. '32 (ALT) [1] Altoona, PA Cathedral of the Blessed Sacrament; Retired.
Madden, Thomas F. '76 (NY) [Z] New York, NY St. John Neumann Residence; [DD] New York, NY The Center for Spirituality and Justice.
Madden, Msgr. Thomas G. '55 (NEW) North Arlington, NJ Queen of Peace Church.
Madden, Thomas J. *s.j.* '57 (MIA) [5] Miami, FL Gesu Church.
Madden, William O. *s.j.* '57 (CHI) Chicago, IL Cook County Hospital; [D] Chicago, IL St. Ignatius Jesuit Community.

Madden, William T. *m.m.* '58 (NY) [Z] Maryknoll, NY Maryknoll Fathers and Brothers; [DD] Maryknoll, NY Friends of St. Maria Goretti, U.S.A., Inc.
Maddock, Andrew L. *s.j.* '85 (FBK) [2] Fairbanks, AK Immaculate Conception Church; [C] Fairbanks, AK Jesuit Residence.
Maddock, George *o.f.m.cap.* '64 (AGN) [F] Agana Heights, GU St. Fidelis Friary.
Maddock, Jay T. '75 (FR) [22] Fall River, MA St. William's Church; [O] Fall River, MA Diocesean Catholic Youth Organization.
Maddock, Laurence F. '56 (CHI) [96] Chicago, IL Saint Ita Church.
Maddox, Msgr. Edward C. '50 (LA) Inglewood, CA St. John Chrysostom Church.
Maddox, Edward Milton '96 (AUS) [14] Austin, TX St. John Neumann Church.
Madeiros, Antonio (BO) [1] Lowell, MA St. Anthony Church.
Madej, Paul D. '90 (SY) Military Chaplains.
Madejczyk, Louis S. '36 (GRY) Retired.
Mader, George '59 (NEW) Oakland, NJ Our Lady of Perpetual Help Church; [Q] Mahwah, NJ Ramapo College.
Mader, Joseph '67 (IND) On Disability Leave.
Mader, Stan '92 (STP) [27] St. Paul, MN St. Mark Church.
Madey, Louis '68 (LAN) On Duty Outside the Diocese.
Madigan, Arthur R. *s.j.* '77 (BO) [W] Chestnut Hill, MA The Jesuit Community at Boston College.
Madigan, Daniel '64 (SAC) Clarksburg, CA St. Joseph Church.
Madigan, Daniel *s.j.* '72 (NY) [Z] New York, NY West Side Jesuit Community.
Madigan, Henry F. *o.f.m.conv.* '56 (SY) Minoa, NY St. Mary Church.
Madigan, Msgr. James '32 (MOB) Retired; [F] Mobile, AL Little Sisters of the Poor, Home For the Aged, Inc.
Madigan, John *o.m.i.* '77 (MIA) Opa Locka, FL St. Philip Church.
Madigan, John A. *o.p.* '66 (RVC) [B] Rockville Centre, NY Molloy College.
Madigan, John Alphonsus *o.p.* (NY) [Z] New York, NY St. Catherine of Siena Priory.
Madigan, John C. '74 (SEA) Renton, WA St. Stephen the Martyr Church.
Madigan, Msgr. John J. '54 (WDC) [9] Silver Spring, MD Our Lady of Grace Church.
Madigan, Kevin '92 (CHI) [B] Chicago, IL The Catholic Theological Union at Chicago.
Madigan, Kevin V. '71 (NY) [18] New York, NY Blessed Sacrament Church.
Madigan, Patrick S. *s.j.* '83 (NO) [P] New Orleans, LA Jesuit Provincial Office.
Madison, Martan *s.a.* '62 (BRK) [113] Brooklyn, NY Our Lady of Victory Church.
Madley, Jeffrey J. '76 (RVC) Commack, NY Christ the King Church.
Madlon, Daniel *o.s.b.* '33 (SFS) [F] Marvin, SD Blue Cloud Abbey.
Madori, Peter J. '69 (NY) Warwick, NY St. Stephen Church.
Madrazo, Higinio *c.m.* '44 (SJN) [47] San Juan, PR Nuestra Senora del Pilar Church; [E] Rio Piedras, PR Asylum For Orphan Girls.
Madrid, J. Saul '85 (PHX) [7] Phoenix, AZ SS. Anthony and Pius X Church.
Madrid, Jaime '68 (ELP) Absent on Leave.
Madrid, Ramon '53 (NY) Rhinebeck, NY The Good Shepherd Church; State, NY Eastern Correctional Facility.
Madrigal, Hector '87 (AMA) Absent on Leave.
Madrigal, Idelfonso '57 (LA) Paramount, CA Our Lady of the Rosary Church.
Madrilejos, J. Rico '93 (NEW) Rahway, NJ St. Mary's Church.
Madsen, Msgr. Cletus P. (DAV) Retired; [B] Davenport, IA St. Ambrose University; [M] Davenport, IA St. Vincent Center.
Madsen, Msgr. John W. '66 (BUF) [2] Depew, NY St. Barnabas Church.
Madu, Emmanuel '78 (NO) [5] New Orleans, LA Corpus Christi Church.
Maduike, Basil '66 (SFS) [D] Sioux Falls, SD McKennan Hospital.
Madumere, Ignatius *o.p.* '87 (HBG) [2] Harrisburg, PA St. Catherine Laboure Church.
Maduri, John '87 (BRK) [126] Brooklyn, NY St. Rosalia-Regina Pacis Church.
Maduro, Gabriel '59 (ARE) [12] Arecibo, PR Church of Santa Teresita.
Madus, Msgr. Peter P. '68 (SCR) [14] Scranton, PA St. Joseph's Church.
Maduzia, Norbert J., Jr. '82 (GAL) Navasota, TX Christ Our Light Church.
Maechler, Edmund F. '49 (LA) Retired.
Maechler, Gerald T. '55 (LA) Retired.
Maes, Allen *o.m.i.* '68 (STL) [W] St. Louis, MO Oblate House of Studies.
Maes, Clarence '87 (SFE) Chama, NM St. Patrick Church.
Maes, Clark B. '95 (STL) Brentwood, MO St. Mary Magdalen Church.
Maes, David *c.r.* '85 (ORG) [H] Orange, CA Theatine Fathers.
Maes, John J. '67 (DOD) Dubuque, KS St. Catherine Church; Hoisington, KS St. John the Evangelist Church; Odin, KS Holy Family Church.
Maestri, William F. '77 (NO) [A] St. Benedict, LA St. Joseph's Seminary College.
Maestrini, Nicholas *p.i.m.e.* '30 (PMB) [G] Tequesta, FL P.I.M.E. Missionaries.
Mafezzini, Angel '54 (LA) [26] Los Angeles, CA Our Lady of Lourdes Church.
Maffei, Joseph *s.d.b.* '58 (NY) [Z] New Rochelle, NY Salesian Provincial House.
Maffei, Vincent R. '64 (BO) Plainville, MA St. Martha Church.
Maffeo, Michael '91 (RVC) Rocky Point, NY St. Anthony of Padua Church.
Magadia, Jose *s.j.* '91 (NY) [Z] New York, NY West Side Jesuit Community.
Magaldi, Phillip '60 (FWT) [11] Fort Worth, TX St. John the Apostle Church.
Magallanes, Alejandro *o.f.m.cap.* '69 (FRS) Fresno, CA Community Hospital, Veterans' Hospital.
Magallanes, Manuel *o.s.b.* '76 (LA) Montebello, CA St. Benedict Church.
Magary, Thomas A. '66 (STU) Martins Ferry, OH St. Mary Church.
Magdaleno, Richard D. '89 (FRS) Corcoran, CA Our Lady of Lourdes Church.
Magdaraog, Vicente '66 (TR) Medford, NJ St. Mary of the Lakes Church.
Magee, Andrew T. '45 (NY) Maybrook, NY Assumption Church; Retired; [Z] New York, NY Pope John Paul II Residence.
Magee, Ernest *s.m.a.* '46 (NEW) [N] Tenafly, NJ Society of African Missions, Provincialate, S.M.A. Fathers.
Magee, George P. *o.s.a.* '68 (PH) [D] Drexel Hill, PA Monsignor Bonner High School.
Magee, Michael K. '91 (PH) Graduate Studies.
Magee, Patrick F. '70 (TR) Point Pleasant, NJ St. Martha Church.
Magee, Paul L. '94 (STP) Chanhassen, MN St. Hubert Church.
Magee, Robert L. '70 (PMB) Jensen Beach, FL St. Martin de Porres Church.
Magel, John E. '60 (L) Retired.
Mager, Martin J. *o.s.b.* '63 (SFR) [N] Portola Valley, CA Woodside Priory.
Mages, Mark C. *o.s.b.* '39 (BIR) [E] Cullman, AL St. Bernard Abbey.
Maggio, J. Mark '90 (BR) On Leave.
Maggioni, Luigi *p.i.m.e.* '57 (DET) [K] Detroit, MI P.I.M.E. Missionaries of SS. Peter and Paul.
Maggs, William C. *c.ss.r.* '66 (PH) [135] Philadelphia, PA St. Peter the Apostle Church.
Maginnis, Andrew F. *s.j.* '52 (SFR) [N] San Francisco, CA Jesuit Community at University of San Francisco.
Maginnis, Edward L. *s.j.* '53 (COS) [10] Colorado Springs, CO St. Francis of Assisi Church.
Maginnis, Edward L. *s.j.* '53 (DEN) [M] Denver, CO Regis Jesuit Community (The Jesuits at Regis University).
Maginnis, Robert P. '61 (PH) Ardmore, PA St. Colman Church.
Maginot, Michael (GRY) [G] Dyer, IN St. Margaret Mercy Healthcare Centers, South Campus; [G] Hobart, IN St. Mary Medical Center.
Maginot, Richard J. '50 (CHI) Prospect Heights, IL St. Alphonsus Liguori Church; Retired.
Maglione, Joseph J. '42 (BGP) Retired.
Magnan, Oscar '63 (NEW) [B] Jersey City, NJ Saint Peter's College; [N] Jersey City, NJ Jesuits of Saint Peter's College, Inc.
Magnano, Paul A. '67 (SEA) Burlington, WA St. Charles Church; LaConner, WA Sacred Heart Church; LaConner, WA St. Paul Church; Mount Vernon, WA Immaculate Conception Church; Sedro Woolley, WA Immaculate Heart of Mary Church; [Q] LaConner, WA Skagit Valley Regional Ministry.
Magni, Daniel M. '83 (BO) [15] Lowell, MA Shrine of St. Rita Church.
Magnier, Patrick *c.ss.r.* '35 (BAL) [94] Baltimore, MD St. Wenceslaus Church; [Q] Baltimore, MD Legion of Mary.
Magoon, R. Dale '60 (GAY) Afton, MI St. Monica Church; Onaway, MI St. Paul Church.
Magraw, Msgr. Daniel E. '75 (E) [7] Erie, PA Mount Calvary Church.
Magri, Thomas '79 (RIC) Williamsburg, VA St. Bede's Church.
Magro, Emanuel '79 (WDC) [35] Washington, DC Our Lady of Victory Church.
Maguire, Alban *o.f.m.* '41 (WDC) [3] Silver Spring, MD St. Camillus Church; [3] Silver Spring, MD St. Camillus Church.
Maguire, Connell J. '45 (PH) Retired.
Maguire, Daniel J. '69 (SFR) Half Moon Bay, CA Our Lady of the Pillar Church.
Maguire, Enda J. '59 (STO) Lockeford, CA St. Joachim Church.
Maguire, Eugene (PHX) Retired; [G] Phoenix, AZ Mt. Claret Retreat Center.
Maguire, Felix H. '50 (HRT) Retired.
Maguire, Francis *o.p.* '57 (DET) [21] Detroit, MI St. Dominic Church.
Maguire, Francis X. *c.m.* '78 (PH) [Z] Philadelphia, PA Congregation of the Mission.
Maguire, Hugh '57 (MOB) Enterprise, AL St. John Church.
Maguire, James F. *s.j.* '35 (CHI) [C] Chicago, IL Jesuit Community at Loyola University of Chicago.
Maguire, John J. '40 (BO) Retired.
Maguire, Msgr. John R. '50 (STL) [1] St. Louis, MO St. Louis Cathedral.
Maguire, Joseph D. (FR) [7] Taunton, MA St. Joseph's Church.
Maguire, Joseph T. (MAN) Retired.
Maguire, Paul J. '48 (CAM) Wildwood, NJ St. Ann's Church; Retired.
Maguire, Robert *o.cist.* '76 (DAL) [B] Irving, TX University of Dallas; [M] Irving, TX Cistercian Abbey of Our Lady of Dallas.
Maguire, Robert E. *s.j.* '63 (BO) [69] Boston, MA Sacred Heart Church; [W] Weston, MA Campion Center.
Maguire, Seamus J. '53 (WH) Retired.
Maguire, Thomas '71 (SAC) Sacramento, CA Mule Creek State Prison.
Maguire, Thomas H. '76 (BO) Bridgewater, MA St. Thomas Aquinas Church; Canton, MA St. John the Evangelist Church.
Maguire, Vincent E. '55 (LR) [E] Fort Smith, AR St. Edward Mercy Medical Center.
Maguire, Msgr. William E. '50 (TR) Retired.
Maguire, William J. *c.s.sp.* '49 (PH) [EE] Philadelphia, PA Shrine of Our Lady of Victories at St. Peter Claver.
Magulick, Daniel A. '78 (PBR) Weirton, WV St. Mary's Church.
Magyar, Ladislaus *sch.p.* '38 (PH) [G] Devon, PA Devon Preparatory School; [Z] Devon, PA Piarist Fathers (Order of the Pious Schools).
Mahalic, Philip A. '83 (LFT) Wheatfield, IN Sorrowful Mother Church.
Mahan, Daniel J. '88 (IND) [30] Indianapolis, IN St. Luke Church.
Mahan, George S. *s.j.* '40 (BO) [W] Boston, MA Loyola House.
Mahan, Paul J. '68 (BO) Absent on Sick Leave.
Mahan, Terrance L. *s.j.* '54 (LA) [C] Los Angeles, CA Loyola Marymount University; [C] Los Angeles, CA Loyola Marymount University.
Mahaney, Hilary F. '69 (CHI) [127] Chicago, IL St. Mary of the Angels Church.
Mahar, Raymond '58 (BUF) [K] Lackawanna, NY Our Lady of Victory Hospital.
Mahedy, Brian *c.p.* '33 (CHI) [N] Chicago, IL Immaculate Conception Monastery.
Mahedy, Oliver '59 (WDC) [7] Silver Spring, MD St. John the Evangelist Church.
Maher, Arthur '54 (JOL) In Residence.
Maher, Byron G. '50 (CHI) Wauconda, IL Transfiguration Church; Retired.
Maher, Charles E. '60 (PRO) [9] Providence, RI Blessed Sacrament Church.
Maher, Daniel J. '62 (ALB) [7] Albany, NY Church of the Holy Cross.
Maher, Daniel J. '91 (ARL) On Duty Outside the Diocese.
Maher, Daniel J. '91 (WDC) [Q] Washington, DC Basilica of the National Shrine of the Immaculate Conception.
Maher, Edward A. *c.s.p.* '49 (NY) [Z] Scarsdale, NY Paulist Fathers Generalate.
Maher, Edward A. *c.s.p.* '49 (SFR) [31] San Francisco, CA Old St. Mary's Cathedral.
Maher, Edward J. '81 (CAM) Mays Landing, NJ St. Vincent de Paul Church.
Maher, Francis '54 (JOL) Wilmington, IL St. Rose Church.
Maher, Gerald John '94 (MRY) [1] Monterey, CA Cathedral of San Carlos Borromeo.
Maher, J. David '71 (JC) Kirksville, MO Mary Immaculate Church.
Maher, Msgr. James '43 (SJ) Retired.
Maher, James J. *c.m.* (BRK) [D] Queens and Staten Island, NY St. John's University; [L] Brooklyn, NY Catholic Charities; [U] Jamaica, NY St. Vincent's House.
Maher, James J. '92 (LA) [Z] Los Angeles, CA Scouting and Camp Fire Ministry/Catholic Youth Camps.
Maher, James M. (LA) Sherman Oaks, CA St. Francis de Sales Church.
Maher, John *c.m.* '81 (PH) [155] Philadelphia, PA St. Vincent de Paul Church.
Maher, John J. '39 (NY) Retired.
Maher, Joseph G. '55 (CHR) [11] Charleston, SC Church of the Nativity.
Maher, Michael L. '48 (SAG) Retired.
Maher, Michael N. *ss.cc.* '63 (SB) Chino Hills, CA St.

Paul the Apostle Church.
Maher, Michael W. *s.j.* '86 (MIL) [P] Milwaukee, WI Jesuit Provincial Office, Wisconsin Province; [P] Milwaukee, WI Jesuit Community at Marquette University.
Maher, Patrick '53 (MOB) [3] Montgomery, AL St. Bede Church.
Maher, Msgr. Patrick K. '47 (STU) Retired.
Maher, Patrick S. '71 (LUB) Snyder, TX Our Lady of Guadalupe Church.
Maher, Paul P. *o.m.i.* '58 (P) Lebanon, OR St. Edward Church.
Maher, Raymond '44 (SJ) Retired.
Maher, Robert E. '71 (BWN) Edinburg, TX St. Joseph Church.
Maher, Robert G. '57 (WIN) On Duty Outside the Diocese.
Maher, Robert L. *o.f.m.cap.* '74 (AGN) Talofofo, GU San Miguel Church.
Maher, Thomas *l.c.* '94 (LA) [R] Pasadena, CA Legionaries of Christ.
Maher, Thomas F. '47 (CHI) [69] Chicago, IL St. Genevieve Church; [132] Chicago, IL St. Mary of the Woods Church; Retired.
Maher, Thomas J. *c.ss.r.* '40 (BRK) [107] Brooklyn, NY Our Lady of Perpetual Help Basilica.
Maher, Thomas J. '62 (ALT) Loretto, PA St. Michael's Church.
Maher, William F.X. *s.j.* '57 (NEW) [B] Jersey City, NJ Saint Peter's College; [N] Jersey City, NJ Jesuits of Saint Peter's College, Inc.
Mahfoud, Peter '55 (SAM) Retired.
Mahler, Joachim A. *o.f.m.* '49 (NY) [146] Bronx, NY Holy Cross Church.
Mahler, Michael '73 (ROC) [M] Rochester, NY Diocesan Office of Campus Ministry.
Mahlmann, Raymond (GLP) Farmington, NM St. Mary's Church.
Mahnke, Ronald *o.s.b.* '62 (CLV) Broadview Heights, OH Assumption Church; [P] Cleveland, OH Benedictine Order of Cleveland.
Mahon, Ambrose J. '58 (STP) Edina, MN St. Patrick Church.
Mahon, Msgr. David L. '65 (PAT) Mountain Lakes, NJ St. Catherine of Siena Church.
Mahon, Msgr. Dennis (WDC) [C] Washington, DC Catholic University of America, The.
Mahon, Msgr. Dennis '70 (WDC) [C] Washington, DC Catholic University of America, The.
Mahon, Francis *s.v.d.* '40 (TR) [M] Bordentown, NJ Society of the Divine Word.
Mahon, Gerald A. '71 (WIN) [6] Rochester, MN St. John's Church.
Mahon, Joseph F. *c.s.p.* '56 (NY) [104] New York, NY St. Paul the Apostle Church.
Mahon, Leo '51 (CHI) [132] Chicago, IL St. Mary of the Woods Church.
Mahon, M. Shawn '88 (BAL) [41] Baltimore, MD St. Isaac Jogues Church.
Mahon, William (NEW) Scotch Plains, NJ Immaculate Heart of Mary Church.
Mahone, Casey B. '89 (WH) [2] Fairmont, WV Immaculate Conception Church.
Mahone, Michael Q. '80 (RNO) Incline Village, NV St. Francis of Assisi Church.
Mahoney, Arthur J. *c.ss.r.* '51 (HBG) [H] Ephrata, PA St. Clement's Mission House.
Mahoney, Bernard '53 (AUS) On Duty Outside the Diocese.
Mahoney, Bryan '95 (BO) Wellesley, MA St. John the Evangelist Church.
Mahoney, Charles J. *c.s.c.* '40 (FTW) [J] South Bend, IN Congregation of Holy Cross Indiana Province Provincial House.
Mahoney, Cornelius H. (BRK) Released from Diocesan Assignment.
Mahoney, Cornelius H. (RVC) [A] Huntington, NY Diocesan Seminary of the Immaculate Conception.
Mahoney, Daniel C. '70 (GBG) Murrysville, PA Mother of Sorrows Church.
Mahoney, Daniel F. '46 (NEW) Retired.
Mahoney, Daniel J. '52 (HBG) [5] (Lower Paxton Twp.), PA Holy Name of Jesus Church.
Mahoney, Daniel J. '56 (BO) [23] Boston, MA St. Francis de Sales Church.
Mahoney, Edward P. '86 (R) Chapel Hill, NC Newman Catholic Student Center, University of North Carolina Church; Special Assignment; [H] Chapel Hill, NC Newman Catholic Student Center.
Mahoney, Msgr. Francis '30 (NY) Retired.
Mahoney, Francis L. '60 (FR) [5] Fall River, MA Holy Name Church.
Mahoney, Gerard J. *o.s.f.s.* '71 (PH) [D] Philadelphia, PA Father Judge High School for Boys; [Z] Philadelphia, PA Father Judge Faculty House.
Mahoney, Gordon '56 (JOL) [2] Naperville, IL Sts. Peter and Paul Church.
Mahoney, Msgr. James '73 (PAT) Chatham Township, NJ Corpus Christi Church.
Mahoney, James F. '45 (BO) Pembroke, MA St. Thecla Church.
Mahoney, James M. '92 (BO) Watertown, MA St. Patrick Church.
Mahoney, Jeremia W. '46 (KC) Retired.
Mahoney, John A. '56 (PEO) Geneseo, IL St. Malachy's Church; Retired.
Mahoney, John E. *s.j.* '36 (DET) [P] Clarkston, MI Colombiere Center.
Mahoney, John E. *o.f.m.cap.* '64 (NY) [Z] Garrison, NY St. Francis Friary.
Mahoney, John E. '72 (BRK) [21] Brooklyn, NY Blessed Sacrament Church.
Mahoney, John F. '60 (RVC) Priests Released from Diocesan Assignment.
Mahoney, John J., Jr. '85 (MAN) [7] Manchester, NH St. Edmond Church.
Mahoney, John L. *s.j.* '51 (BO) [E] Boston, MA Boston College High School & Jesuit Community.
Mahoney, John P. '48 (BO) Hanover, MA St. Mary of the Sacred Heart Church; Retired.
Mahoney, Joseph E. '85 (MAN) Newport, NH St. Patrick Church.
Mahoney, Joseph P. '57 (WOR) [1] Worcester, MA St. Paul's Cathedral; [25] Worcester, MA St. John's Church.
Mahoney, Kevin J. '81 (STL) [3] St. Charles, MO St. Elizabeth Ann Seton Church.
Mahoney, Leo R. '53 (BO) Hudson, MA Christ the King Church.
Mahoney, Mark A. '86 (BO) Holliston, MA St. Mary Church.
Mahoney, Martin J. '94 (NY) Hopewell Junction, NY St. Columba Church.
Mahoney, Michael *o.f.m.cap.* '74 (SFR) Burlingame, CA Our Lady of Angels Church.
Mahoney, Michael T. '75 (CIN) [22] Dayton, OH St. Peter Church.
Mahoney, Neil J. '70 (NEW) [2] Newark, NJ St. Patrick's Pro-Cathedral.
Mahoney, Peter A. '61 (BRK) [15] Brooklyn, NY St. Barbara Church.
Mahoney, Richard J. '58 (STP) Retired.
Mahoney, Robert '59 (AUS) Manor, TX St. Joseph's Church.
Mahoney, Robert J. '55 (KC) Special Assignment; [B] Kansas City, MO Rockhurst College.
Mahoney, Shaun L. '91 (PH) Graduate Studies.
Mahoney, Thomas E. '68 (WOR) Mendon, MA St. Michael's Church.
Mahony, John '58 (SP) On Duty Outside the Diocese.
Mahony, Thomas J. *o.s.a.* '54 (PH) [C] Villanova, PA Villanova University; [Z] Villanova, PA St. Thomas Monastery.
Mahowald, Paul A. *s.j.* '68 (OM) [C] Omaha, NE Creighton Preparatory School.
Mahowald, Msgr. Richard '55 (SFS) [2] Sioux Falls, SD Christ the King Church.
Mahrer, James *o.s.b.* '30 (PBL) Westcliffe, CO Our Lady of the Assumption Church.
Mahrer, James A. *o.s.b.* '37 (PBL) [E] Canon City, CO Holy Cross Abbey.
Mai, Dai Viet *i.c.* '90 (SP) Seffner, FL St. Francis of Assisi Church.
Mai, Emmanuel K. '86 (MRY) Absent on Sick Leave.
Mai, Michael '93 (SY) [7] Syracuse, NY Our Lady of Pompei Church.
Mai Chi Thanh, Joseph M. '58 (PEO) Pesotum, IL St. Mary Church; Pesotum, IL St. Joseph Church.
Maibusch, Henry B. *o.s.a.* '54 (MIL) [8] Kenosha, WI Our Lady of the Holy Rosary Church.
Maichen, Richard F. '54 (DUB) Retired.
Maida, Thaddeus S. '58 (PIT) Perrysville, PA St. Teresa of Avila Church.
Maier, John C. '90 (DM) Audubon, IA St. Patrick Church.
Maier, Paul '70 (RIC) St. Paul, VA St. Therese Church.
Maierle, John P. '55 (DET) [5] Livonia, MI St. Maurice Church.
Maiers, Brennan *o.s.b.* '63 (SCL) [I] Collegeville, MN St. John's Abbey, of the Order of St. Benedict.
Maikowski, Thomas '76 (GLP) [2] Gallup, NM St. Francis of Assisi Church; Special Assignment.
Mailloux, Normand F. *m.s.* '55 (SPR) Bondsville, MA St. Adalbert's Church.
Mailloux, Orville C. *c.ss.r.* '42 (STL) [P] Liguori, MO St. Clement Health Care Center.
Mailloux, Thomas B. *c.s.b.* (GAL) [7] Houston, TX St. Anne Church.
Mainardi, Donald G. '63 (ORL) [7] Orlando, FL St. Charles Borromeo Church.
Mainelli, Vincent P. *c.o.* '63 (HON) [8] Honolulu, HI Holy Trinity Church.
Mainelli, Vincent P. *c.o.* '63 (OM) Absent on Leave.
Mainzer, James S. '87 (WCH) Augusta, KS St. James Church.
Maio, Anthony V. '49 (SAC) Retired and in Senior Ministry.
Maione, Anthony '85 (ALB) Special Assignment.
Maione, Francis T. '65 (NEW) East Newark, NJ St. Anthony's Church; [K] Kearny, NJ New Jersey Boystown.
Mair, Henry *s.a.* '62 (MRY) Seaside, CA St. Francis Xavier Church.
Mair, Robert G. '65 (CHI) [128] Chicago, IL St. Mary of the Lake Church.
Mairal, Jose Ma. Lopez '54 (SJN) [10] San Juan, PR Santa Cecilia Church.
Mairal, Jose Ma. Lopez '54 (SJN) Resident Chaplains.
Maisano, Richard J. '69 (PH) New Garden Township, PA St. Gabriel of the Sorrowful Mother Church.
Maiser, Raymond *c.s.sp.* '64 (SEA) [O] Federal Way, WA Palisades Retreat House.
Maison, Gabriel '78 (VIC) Moulton, TX St. Joseph's Church.
Maisonet, Msgr. Tomas (SJN) [16] Carolina, PR Ntra. Sra. Reina de los Angeles Church.
Maisonneuve, Joseph *o.carm.* '86 (JOL) [J] Joliet, IL St. Elias Carmelites.
Maivelett, Bruce A. *s.j.* '88 (SY) [A] Syracuse, NY Saint Andrew Hall.
Maiza, Felix *s.j.* '52 (LA) [K] Duarte, CA Santa Teresita Hospital.
Maiza, Felix A. *s.j.* '52 (LA) [R] Los Angeles, CA Columbiere House.
Maiza, Jesus Maria *s.s.s.* '67 (CGS) [5] Caguas, PR Santisimo Sacramento Church.
Maj, Msgr. George C. *s.a.c.* '58 (BUF) [O] North Tonawanda, NY Society of the Catholic Apostolate.
Maj, Msgr. George E. *s.a.c.* '58 (BUF) [11] Cheektowaga, NY Resurrection Church.
Maj, George J. *o.s.p.p.e.* '89 (PH) [Z] Doylestown, PA Pauline Fathers Monastery, Shrine of Our Lady of Czestochowa.
Majan, Ricardo '54 (ARE) [3] Vega-Baja, PR The Blessed Trinity Church.
Majarucon, Jon '84 (LA) Santa Monica, CA St. Monica Church.
Majcher, Tadeusz *s.d.s.* '87 (BRK) [93] Brooklyn, NY Our Lady of Consolation Church.
Majchrowski, Anthony P. '44 (LAN) [2] Flint, MI All Saints Church.
Majchrzak, Colman *o.f.m.* '51 (CHI) [N] Chicago, IL Holy Name Friary-Franciscan House of Formation.
Majda, Francis A. '39 (PIT) Retired.
Majdanik, Albin J. '42 (SY) Retired.
Majerus, Daniel '57 (SCL) On Duty Outside the Diocese.
Majewicz, Frank *c.r.* '74 (CHI) [D] Chicago, IL Weber High School.
Majewski, Edmund W. *s.j.* '83 (NEW) [B] Jersey City, NJ Saint Peter's College; [N] Jersey City, NJ Jesuits of Saint Peter's College, Inc.
Majewski, Eugene *c.r.* '74 (RCK) Woodstock, IL Resurrection Church.
Majewski, Francis *o.f.m.cap.* '64 (PAT) [M] Oak Ridge-Milton, NJ St. Stanislaus B. M. Friary.
Majewski, John E. '53 (STL) Clover Bottom, MO St. Ann's Church.
Majewski, Joseph B. '66 (RIC) [3] Newport News, VA St. Jerome Church.
Majewski, Joseph J. *c.ss.r.* '67 (RIC) [2] Hampton, VA St. Joseph Church.
Majewski, Stephen *o.f.m.conv.* '34 (BO) [55] Boston, MA Our Lady of Czestochowa Church.
Majic, Timothy *o.f.m.* '39 (CHI) [N] Chicago, IL Croatian Franciscan Custody of the Holy Family.
Majka, Frank A. *s.j.* '74 (MIL) [P] Milwaukee, WI Jesuit Community at Marquette University.
Majka, George '72 (MAN) Pittsfield, NH Our Lady of Lourdes Church.
Majka, Philip S. '65 (ARL) Chancellorsville, VA St. Patrick's Church.
Majkut, Thaddeus '84 (TYL) Longview, TX St. Anthony Church.
Major, Charles M. '59 (SY) [4] Liverpool, NY St. Joseph the Worker Church.
Major, Stephen P. '87 (LIN) Nebraska City, NE St. Mary's Church.
Major, Thomas J. '91 (SCR) Clarks Summit, PA Our Lady of the Snows Church.
Majoros, Stephen '57 (TOL) [28] Toledo, OH St. Joseph Church.
Makacinas, Stanley *o.carm.* '70 (JOL) [J] Darien, IL Carmelite Fathers Provincial Office.
Makalla, Peter *a.l.c.p.* '86 (P) Tigard, OR St. Anthony Church.
Makaras, Joseph V. '40 (CHI) Retired.
Makarewicz, Sylvester E. *o.f.m.* '48 (GB) [I] Pulaski, WI Assumption of B.V.M. Friary.
Makarewicz, Sylvester E. *o.f.m.* '48 (PIT) [N] Ben Avon, PA St. Anthony Friary and Mission House.
Makerewicz, Marion J. '87 (JC) [A] Hannibal, MO St. Thomas Aquinas Seminary.
Maki, George S. '88 (MAR) Newberry, MI St. Gregory Church.
Makothakat, John M. '62 (SAT) [66] San Antonio, TX St. Thomas More Church; [C] San Antonio, TX Oblate School of Theology.
Makowski, Douglas '66 (CLV) Strongsville, OH St. Joseph Church.
Makowski, Edward J. '32 (SCR) Retired.
Makowski, Lee J. *o.s.a.* '80 (PH) [2] Norristown, PA St. Francis of Assisi Church; [C] Villanova, PA Villanova

University; [Z] Villanova, PA St. Thomas Monastery.
Makowski, Mariusz '87 (MAR) [5] Marquette, MI St. Michael Church.
Makowski, Tomasz '93 (PMB) Sebastian, FL St. Sebastian Church.
Makranyi, Steven F. '69 (LAN) Flushing, MI St. Robert Church.
Maksimovich, Victor *o.f.m.* '54 (E) [4] Sharon, PA St. Stanislaus Kostka Church.
Maksvytis, Jerome J. '74 (MAD) Berlin, WI St. Stanislaus Church.
Maksymowicz, Msgr. John H. '70 (BRK) Released from Diocesan Assignment.
Makuch, Thaddeus J. '53 (CHI) [3] Cicero, IL St. Mary of Czestochowa Church.
Malabad, Antonio R. '53 (RIC) Williamsburg, VA St. Bede's Church.
Malacaman, Pericles P. '72 (WH) Mullens, WV St. John the Evangelist Church.
Malacari, Carmelo V. *o.f.m.conv.* '93 (CHL) [6] Charlotte, NC St. John Neumann Church.
Malachowski, Christopher *o.s.* '58 (PCE) On Duty Outside the Diocese.
Malagreca, Joseph P. '76 (BRK) [183] Queens, NY SS. Joachim and Anne Church.
Malain, Dan '66 (BEA) Nederland, TX St. Charles Borromeo Church; [G] Beaumont, TX Rev. Herman Vincent Scholarship Fund.
Malanga, Salvatore T. '57 (NEW) Belleville, NJ St. Anthony's Church.
Malanowski, Msgr. Thaddeus F. '47 (NOR) Retired.
Malanyaon, Joven '72 (TOL) [J] Oregon, OH Sacred Heart Home.
Malaric, Stephen L. '51 (DET) Retired.
Malarz, Andrew '92 (GRY) Hobart, IN St. Bridget Church; [G] Hobart, IN St. Mary Medical Center.
Malatesta, Charles R. *o.p.* '44 (STL) [P] St. Louis, MO St. Dominic Priory.
Malatesta, Christopher A. '93 (SPR) Easthampton, MA Immaculate Conception Church.
Malatesta, Edward J. *s.j.* '61 (SFR) [N] San Francisco, CA Jesuit Community at University of San Francisco; [U] San Francisco, CA The Ricci Institute for Chinese-Western Cultural History at the Center for the Pacific Rim.
Malatesta, Vincent R. *s.j.* '61 (ATL) [K] Atlanta, GA Ignatius House.
Malave, Gervasio *c.ss.r.* '87 (STV) [1] St. Thomas, VI Cathedral of Sts. Peter and Paul.
Malave, Will Roger '86 (WH) Cameron, WV St. Martin Church; St. Joseph Settlement, WV St. Joseph's Church.
Malave, Will-Roger '86 (HRT) On Duty Outside the Archdiocese.
Malawy, Michael D. '81 (DET) Romulus, MI St. Aloysius Church.
Malboeuf, Gerald L. '54 (SPR) [4] Ludlow, MA St. Mary Church; Retired.
Malcolm, Dennis E. '73 (NY) On Duty Outside the Archdiocese.
Malcolm, Lawrence J. '70 (CHI) [48] Chicago, IL St. Daniel the Prophet Church.
Malcom-Hollis, Raphael *o.ss.t.* '47 (TR) [16] Trenton, NJ St. James Church.
Malczyk, Joseph *c.r.* '69 (CHI) [D] Chicago, IL Gordon Technical High School.
Maldari, Donald C. *s.j.* '85 (NY) [Z] New York, NY Jesuit Provincial's Office.
Maldonado, Angel M. *o.s.m.* '79 (ELP) [24] El Paso, TX St. Ignatius of Loyola Church.
Maldonado, Edward *o.f.m.cap.* '83 (PCE) [5] Ponce, PR Santa Teresita Church; [E] Ponce, PR Residencia Asis.
Maldonado, Francisco '90 (TUC) [10] Tucson, AZ St. Ambrose Church.
Maldonado, Hector *s.v.d.* '91 (CHI) [16] Chicago, IL St. Anselm Church.
Maldonado, Jorge Rivera *o.carm.* '96 (MGZ) Anasco, PR St. Anthony Abbot Church.
Maldonado, P. Jose A. Rivera '84 (CGS) Naguabo, PR Nuestra Senora del Rosario Church.
Maldonado, Santos Rene (WDC) [4] Silver Spring, MD St. Catherine Laboure Church.
Malec, Raymond S. '54 (BEL) Retired.
Malecki, John '48 (ALB) Special Assignment.
Malek, Eugene F. *o.f.m.* '51 (PRO) [P] Providence, RI St. Francis Friary.
Malene, Robert '72 (E) On Duty Outside Diocese.
Males, Jake A. '76 (TLS) Sapulpa, OK Sacred Heart Church.
Malesic, Edward C. '87 (HBG) [7] (Penbrook), PA St. Margaret Mary Alacoque Church.
Maletta, Sammie L. '80 (GRY) [3] Merrillville, IN St. Joan of Arc Church.
Maletz, Leo J. '73 (ALN) [4] Minersville, PA St. Stanislaus Kostka Church.
Malewitz, Joseph M. '55 (GR) Retired.
Malgeri, Albert '94 (NEW) Nutley, NJ Holy Family Church.
Malia, Thomas R. '84 (BAL) Bel Air, MD St. Margaret Church.
Maliakal, Varghese '85 (NY) [7] Yonkers, NY St. Denis Church.
Malicki, Jan '73 (MIA) Davie, FL St. David Church.
Maliekal, Cyriac '71 (HRT) [2] New Haven, CT St. Aedan's Church.
Malik, John E. '53 (LC) Colby, WI St. Mary Help of Christians Church.
Malik, Joseph '52 (Y) Retired.
Malin, Delbert J. '58 (LC) Holmen, WI St. Elizabeth Ann Seton Church.
Malin, Gary J. '86 (CLV) [4] Elyria, OH St. Mary Church.
Malin, George '46 (SP) Retired.
Malin, Peter '37 (ALB) Retired.
Malinak, Joseph G. '33 (PIT) Retired.
Malinowski, Francis *c.s.sp.* '50 (PIT) [B] Pittsburgh, PA Duquesne University of the Holy Ghost.
Malinowski, Hilary L. '56 (SCR) Simpson, PA St. Michael's Church.
Malinowski, Msgr. John C. '63 (AUS) College Station, TX St. Thomas Aquinas Church; [F] Bryan, TX St. Joseph Hospital and Health Center of Bryan, Inc.
Malinowski, Stanley J. '54 (PEO) Rantoul, IL St. Malachy's Church.
Malinsky, Gregory J. '74 (PIT) Military Chaplains.
Maliszewski, Edward C. '45 (PIT) Retired.
Maliszewski, Francis '46 (PAT) [15] Paterson, NJ St. Stephen's Church; Retired.
Maliszewski, Francis S. '41 (DET) Retired.
Maliyekal, John '60 (SFS) Scotland, SD St. George Church.
Malkiewicz, Edward S. '71 (NEW) [12] Jersey City, NJ St. John the Baptist Church; Retired.
Malkiewicz, Stephen *o.f.m.* '69 (MIL) [P] Milwaukee, WI Francis and Clare House.
Malkov, Leonid *c.ss.r.* '90 (PHU) Newark, NJ St. John the Baptist Church.
Mallaghan, Thomas P. *c.m.* '60 (BUF) [O] Niagara University, NY Vincentian Community at Niagara University.
Mallahan, James '52 (SEA) Retired.
Mallak, Mark S. '88 (NU) Comfrey, MN St. Paul Church; Leavenworth, MN Japanese Martyrs Church.
Malleck, Joseph L. '56 (BRK) Absent on Sick Leave.
Mallen, Charles *c.ss.r.* '44 (VEN) [G] Venice, FL St. Alphonsus Residence; [I] Venice, FL Our Lady of Perpetual Help Retreat and Spirituality Center.
Mallen, Santiago *c.ss.r.* '47 (CGS) San Lorenzo, PR Nuestra Senora de la Mercedes Church.
Mallet, W. Curtis '92 (LAF) [11] Lafayette, LA St. Genevieve Church.
Mallett, James K. '66 (NSH) [4] Nashville, TN Church of Christ the King.
Mallette, Daniel J. '57 (CHI) [120] Chicago, IL St. Margaret of Scotland Church.
Malley, James '56 (NY) [209] Staten Island, NY St. John Neumann Church.
Malley, James B. *s.j.* '64 (BO) [W] Chestnut Hill, MA The Jesuit Community at Boston College.
Malley, John *o.carm.* (JOL) [M] Darien, IL Carmelite Mission Office.
Malley, John *o.carm.* '56 (JOL) [J] Darien, IL Carmelite Community.
Malley, Michael A. '34 (HRT) Canaan, CT St. Joseph's Church; Retired.
Malley, Raymond E. *s.m.* '68 (HON) Wailuku, HI St. Anthony Church; [H] Wailuku, Maui, HI Wailuku Marianist Community.
Malley, Vernon '59 (TUC) [F] Tucson, AZ Carmelite Priory.
Mallia, Joseph '92 (DET) [9] Warren, MI St. Martin de Porres Church.
Mallick, Andrew '84 (ORL) [1] Lakeland, FL Church of the Resurrection.
Mallin, Maximilian *o.f.m.conv.* '90 (LA) Hermosa Beach, CA Our Lady of Guadalupe Church.
Mallinson, Arthur D. '81 (DAL) Forney, TX St. Martin Church; Kaufman, TX St. Ann Church.
Mallo, Walter '90 (SJ) [2] San Jose, CA St. Patrick Proto-Cathedral.
Mallon, Elias D. *s.a.* '71 (NY) [Z] New York, NY Atonement Friars; [Z] Garrison, NY Generalate of the Franciscan Friars of the Atonement-St. James Friary; [Z] Garrison, NY Franciscan Friars of the Atonement.
Mallon, John F. '40 (ALB) Cairo, NY Sacred Heart Church; Retired.
Mallon, John J. '50 (OAK) [3] Walnut Creek, CA St. Mary's Church.
Mallonee, Robert *s.v.d.* '67 (BO) [W] Duxbury, MA Society of the Divine Word.
Malloy, Brendan *o.f.m.cap.* '54 (PIT) [N] Pittsburgh, PA St. Augustine Friary.
Malloy, Msgr. David J. '83 (MIL) On Duty Outside the Archdiocese.
Malloy, Edward A. *c.s.c.* '70 (FTW) [B] Notre Dame, IN University of Notre Dame Du Lac; [J] Notre Dame, IN Holy Cross Community, Corby Hall, University of Notre Dame.
Malloy, Msgr. Faber J. '50 (ALT) Ebensburg, PA Holy Name Church; Retired.
Malloy, Francis X. '85 (MIL) Military Chaplains.
Malloy, Joseph J. '70 (BGP) [4] Bridgeport, CT St. Ann's Church.
Malloy, Michael B. '76 (OM) Bow Valley, NE SS. Peter and Paul Church; St. Helena, NE Immaculate Conception Church.
Malloy, Peter V. *s.d.b.* '74 (BIR) [8] Birmingham, AL Holy Rosary Church; [A] Birmingham, AL John Carroll High School.
Malloy, Richard G. *s.j.* '88 (CAM) [4] Camden, NJ Holy Name Church.
Malloy, Robert *o.f.m.cap.* '70 (SAG) [G] Saginaw, MI Queen of Angels Friary and Retreat House.
Malloy, Robert P. '60 (SFE) [13] Albuquerque, NM Queen of Heaven Church.
Malloy, Stephen J. (BO) [1] Newton, MA St. Bernard Church.
Malloy, Thomas F. *o.s.f.s.* '67 (WIL) [I] Childs, MD Oblates of St. Francis De Sales.
Malloy, William E. '73 (CHI) [3] Oak Lawn, IL St. Germaine Church.
Mally, Edward J. *s.j.* '61 (NY) [Z] New York, NY Jesuit Provincial's Office.
Mallya, Gregory '83 (PIT) Glade Mills, PA Holy Sepulcher Church.
Malm, Raymond B. '76 (PRO) [21] Providence, RI St. Michael's Church.
Malnar, Matthew '66 (AMA) On Duty Outside the Diocese.
Malnar, Stan '72 (HEL) Special Assignments.
Malo, John B. *c.s.b.* '78 (OAK) [C] Oakland, CA Bishop O'Dowd High School.
Malo, Richard C. '87 (PRT) Jackman, ME St. Anthony Church.
Malonda, Anselme *c.i.c.m.* '92 (BWN) Alton, TX San Martin de Porres Church.
Malone, Alan '59 (PHX) [2] Scottsdale, AZ Our Lady of Perpetual Help Church; Special Assignment.
Malone, Bernard G. '50 (LR) [8] Little Rock, AR Immaculate Heart of Mary Church.
Malone, Donald '60 (NY) Absent on Leave.
Malone, Edward T. '72 (BO) [7] Lynn, MA St. Pius the Fifth Church.
Malone, Francis I. '77 (LR) [7] Little Rock, AR Immaculate Conception Church; [L] Little Rock, AR The "Arkansas Catholic".
Malone, H. Patrick '69 (WCH) [7] Wichita, KS Holy Savior Church.
Malone, James P. *s.j.* '45 (ROC) [B] Rochester, NY McQuaid Jesuit High School.
Malone, John (RVC) Seaford, NY Maria Regina Church.
Malone, John M. '67 (STP) [2] St. Paul, MN Assumption Church; [C] St. Paul, MN University of St. Thomas.
Malone, Michael T. *c.ss.sp.* '65 (PRO) [B] Newport, RI Salve Regina University.
Malone, Msgr. Quintin J. '38 (WCH) Retired.
Malone, Msgr. Richard '62 (PH) [A] Wynnewood, PA Theological Seminary of St. Charles Borromeo, Overbrook.
Malone, Richard J. '72 (BO) [28] Boston, MA Holy Name Church; [4] Somerville, MA St. Catherine of Genoa Church.
Malone, Robert J. *c.s.c.* '61 (WIL) Newark, DE St. Thomas More Oratory Church; Dover, DE Wesley College; Newark, DE University of Delaware; [O] Newark, DE Wesley College Newman Center; [O] Newark, DE Univ. of Delaware Newman Center; [O] Newark, DE Univ. of Delaware Newman Center.
Malone, William P. '92 (CHI) [160] Chicago, IL Our Lady of Tepeyac Church.
Maloney, Andrew P. '34 (SCR) Retired.
Maloney, Bernard M. *o.f.m.cap.* '69 (NY) [17] Yonkers, NY Sacred Heart Church.
Maloney, Charles F. '57 (TUC) Apache Junction, AZ St. George Church.
Maloney, Msgr. Christopher '66 (NY) [82] New York, NY Notre Dame Church; [CC] New York, NY University Apostolate.
Maloney, Daniel *o.s.b.* '68 (BIS) [A] Richardton, ND Assumption Abbey; [B] Bismarck, ND University of Mary; [H] Bismarck, ND Annunciation Priory.
Maloney, Edward F. '55 (NY) [Z] New York, NY Jesuit Community at Fordham University.
Maloney, Edward J. '55 (CHI) Mundelein, IL Santa Maria Del Popolo Church.
Maloney, Francis E. '59 (PMB) Port St. Lucie, FL St. Elizabeth Ann Seton Church.
Maloney, Francis G. '56 (R) Fuquay-Varina, NC St. Bernadette Church; Garner, NC St. Mary, Mother of the Church.
Maloney, George A. *s.j.* '57 (MIL) [P] Milwaukee, WI Jesuit Provincial Office, Wisconsin Province.
Maloney, James *c.m.f.* '60 (CHI) [N] Oak Park, IL Claretian Fathers Headquarters of U.S.A. Eastern Province.
Maloney, James C. '37 (L) Retired; [J] Louisville, KY Boys' Haven.
Maloney, James G. '71 (CLV) Norton, OH St. Andrew the Apostle Church.
Maloney, John '75 (BRK) [196] Queens, NY St. Mary

Magdalene Church.
Maloney, John '87 (MAR) Retired.
Maloney, John P. '64 (PIT) Glade Mills, PA Holy Sepulcher Church.
Maloney, John P. '66 (BRK) [189] Queens, NY St. Kevin Church.
Maloney, John W. '75 (BRK) [223] Queens, NY St. Pascal Baylon Church; [G] Brooklyn, NY Catherine McAuley.
Maloney, Joseph *o.f.m.cap.* '58 (DET) [K] Detroit, MI St. Bonaventure Friary.
Maloney, Joseph '91 (PH) [D] Springfield, PA Cardinal O'Hara High School.
Maloney, Joseph L. '91 (PH) Swarthmore, PA Notre Dame de Lourdes Church.
Maloney, Malcolm *o.f.m.cap.* '55 (DET) Hazel Park, MI St. Mary Magdalen Church.
Maloney, Patrick H. *c.s.c.* '54 (FTW) [B] Notre Dame, IN University of Notre Dame Du Lac; [J] Notre Dame, IN Holy Cross Community, Corby Hall, University of Notre Dame.
Maloney, Raymond G. '59 (BUR) Fair Haven, VT Our Lady of Seven Dolors Church.
Maloney, Richard *s.d.s.* '69 (WDC) [B] Silver Spring, MD Salvatorian Community.
Maloney, Richard E. '50 (DET) Retired.
Maloney, Robert L. *s.j.* '61 (SFR) [N] San Francisco, CA Jesuit Community at University of San Francisco.
Maloney, Robert S. *s.x.* '57 (BO) [W] Holliston, MA Xaverian Missionaries.
Maloney, Rufino *o.f.m.conv.* '59 (ALB) [12] Albany, NY Our Lady of Angels Church; Albany, NY Albany County Nursing Home.
Maloney, Msgr. Thomas F. '68 (BUF) [1] Tonawanda, NY St. Amelia Church.
Maloney, Thomas J. '65 (SCR) Pocono Pines, PA Our Lady of the Lake Church.
Maloney, Thomas J. *s.j.* '69 (LA) [C] Los Angeles, CA Loyola Marymount University.
Maloney, Thomas P. '70 (RVC) Babylon, NY St. Joseph's Church.
Maloney, Timothy P. *o.s.b.* '50 (LA) Montebello, CA St. Benedict Church.
Maloney, Tom '67 (PEO) Normal, IL Epiphany Church.
Maloney, Walter '47 (JKS) Retired.
Maloney, Wilfred F. '55 (PH) Maple Glen, PA St. Alphonsus Church.
Maloney, William '76 (CHI) [34] Chicago, IL St. Cajetan Church.
Maloney, William J. '48 (E) Retired.
Malooly, Msgr. Francis '70 (BAL) [90] Baltimore, MD St. Thomas More Church.
Malooly, Msgr. Francis W. '70 (BAL) Special Assignment.
Malorzo, Luigi *c.p.* '52 (MET) [H] South River, NJ Passionist Provincial Office.
Malovetz, Gregory E. S. '83 (MET) Skillman, NJ St. Charles Borromeo Church.
Maloy, Dale R. '54 (PEO) [1] La Salle, IL Queen of the Holy Rosary Church.
Malpide, Jeff *c.m.* '80 (SAT) [T] San Antonio, TX Intercongregational Justice & Peace Office.
Malpiede, Jeff *c.m.* '80 (SAT) [M] San Antonio, TX Vincentian Residence.
Maltese, Msgr. Anthony '54 (NY) Tuckahoe, NY Immaculate Conception Church; Tuckahoe, NY Assumption Church.
Maltese, James L. '65 (RVC) Valley Stream, NY Holy Name of Mary Church.
Malthaner, John P. '93 (E) [16] Erie, PA St. George Church.
Maluafiti, Soke *o.f.m.cap.* (AGN) [F] Agana Heights, GU St. Fidelis Friary.
Malvey, Killian *o.s.b.* '73 (SEA) [M] Lacey, WA St. Martin's Abbey.
Malvey, Sean R. *o.s.b.* '89 (SEA) [M] Lacey, WA St. Martin's Abbey.
Mamede, Carlos C. '69 (NEW) [26] Newark, NJ Our Lady of Fatima Church.
Mammarella, Dominick A. '53 (HBG) Berwick, PA St. Joseph's Church.
Mamo, Nathan '78 (HON) [1] Honolulu, HI Cathedral of Our Lady of Peace.
Mampaey, Lawrence *ss.cc.* '29 (HON) [H] Honolulu, HI St. Patrick's Monastery.
Mampara, Mathew '60 (PHX) On Leave.
Mampilly, Joy *c.m.i.* '84 (NY) [206] Staten Island, NY Holy Rosary Church.
Mampuzhakal, Kuriakose '52 (PH) [44] Philadelphia, PA Epiphany of Our Lord Church.
Man, Matthias Tinh An Tran '63 (FWT) [19] Fort Worth, TX Christ the King Church.
Man Tran, Joseph '95 (NO) Chalmette, LA St. Mark Church.
Manahan, John J. *s.m.* '68 (SAT) [8] San Antonio, TX Holy Rosary Church; [M] San Antonio, TX Holy Rosary Marianist Community.
Manahan, Martin J. '52 (WOR) Retired.
Manahan, Thomas *s.j.* '95 (OM) [K] Omaha, NE Jesuit Community At Creighton University.
Manalel, Matthew '72 (BRK) [58] Brooklyn, NY Holy Name Church.
Manalili, Feliciano '62 (CHR) [E] Moncks Corner, SC Mepkin Abbey.
Manalis, Edward W. '77 (BAL) Hagerstown, MD St. Ann Church.
Manalo, Pantaleon O. '63 (RIC) [E] Portsmouth, VA Maryview Medical Center; [L] Richmond, VA Ethnic and Special Ministries.
Manarchuck, Josepha J.. '78 (SCR) Friendsville, PA St. Joseph's Church.
Mancha, George '88 (SJ) [1] Palo Alto, CA St. Thomas Aquinas Church; [2] Palo Alto, CA St. Albert the Great Church.
Manchapilly, George *c.m.i.* '71 (BRK) [3] Brooklyn, NY St. Agnes Church.
Manchas, Lawrence L. '79 (GBG) Herminie, PA St. Edward Church.
Manchino, John '65 (LR) Retired.
Mancilla, Pedro M. '58 (FRS) Riverdale, CA St. Ann Church.
Mancini, Anthony '78 (PRO) [14] Providence, RI Holy Cross Church.
Mancini, Domenic '76 (PIT) [35] Pittsburgh, PA St. Raphael Church; Imperial, PA St. Columbkille Church.
Mancini, James E. '66 (LR) [2] Little Rock, AR St. Anne Church; [9] Little Rock, AR St. Mary Church; [12] Little Rock, AR St. Patrick's Church.
Mancini, John S. *o.s.f.s.* '80 (SAG) [4] Saginaw, MI SS. Simon and Jude Church.
Mancini, Marc '92 (PAT) Succasunna, NJ St. Therese Church.
Mancini, Nicholas J. '75 (ALT) Beaverdale, PA St. Joseph's Church; Beaverdale, PA St. Agnes Church; Dunlo, PA Corpus Christi Church.
Mancuso, Anthony '83 (SJ) [8] San Jose, CA Holy Family Church; [10] San Jose, CA St. Anthony Church.
Mancuso, Dennis J. '96 (BUF) [5] Buffalo, NY All Saints Church.
Mancuso, Henry '75 (LKC) [5] Lake Charles, LA St. Margaret Church.
Mancuso, Joseph A. '64 (KC) [4] Kansas City, MO St. Anthony Church; [O] Kansas City, MO Diocesan Council of Catholic Women.
Mancuso, Joseph A. '70 (ALB) [15] Schenectady, NY Our Lady of Mt. Carmel Church.
Mancuso, Luke *o.s.b.* '83 (SCL) [I] Collegeville, MN St. John's Abbey, of the Order of St. Benedict.
Mandala, Michael J. *s.j.* '77 (LA) [R] Los Angeles, CA Columbiere House.
Mandarino, Constantino *o.m.* '65 (LA) [3] Los Angeles, CA All Saints Church; [R] Los Angeles, CA Minim Fathers.
Mandato, Kieran '87 (NY) Military Chaplains.
Mandel, Brian L. '94 (NU) Marshall, MN Holy Redeemer Church.
Manderfield, Paul G. '60 (MAR) Baraga, MI St. Ann Church.
Manders, Norbert R. *o.praem.* '54 (SFE) [J] Albuquerque, NM Santa Maria de la Vid Priory.
Mandile, John J. *s.j.* '57 (BO) [W] Weston, MA Campion Center.
Manding, Benito O. '64 (SJ) [4] Sunnyvale, CA St. Martin Church.
Mandl, Maximus J. *o.f.m.* '41 (TR) Roebling, NJ Holy Assumption Church.
Mandock, Patrick H. '72 (GBG) Military Chaplains.
Mandoli, Richard *o.c.d.* '92 (SB) [G] Redlands, CA El Carmelo Retreat House.
Mandry, Stephen A. *s.t.d.* '66 (GAL) Baytown, TX St. Joseph Church.
Mandziuk, Paul *m.s.* (GAL) Friendswood, TX Mary, Queen Church.
Mandziuk, Paul *m.s.* '80 (STL) [K] St. Louis, MO Saint Louis University Hospital.
Manente, Vladimiro *o.m.i.* '46 (CC) [6] Laredo, TX San Augustine Church.
Manero, Ismael '37 (GLP) Retired.
Manerowski, Joseph '95 (ALB) Delhi, NY St. Peter Church; [S] Delhi, NY State University of New York College of Agricultural & Technology at Delhi.
Maney, Robert L. '51 (MIL) Retired.
Maney, Thomas J. *m.m.* '56 (NY) [Z] Maryknoll, NY Maryknoll Fathers and Brothers.
Manfred, Donald J. '67 (OG) Tupper Lake, NY St. Alphonsus Church.
Mangampo, Gil '91 (GLP) On Duty Outside of Diocese.
Mangampo, Gil '91 (ORG) [F] Fullerton, CA St. Jude Medical Center.
Mangan, Charles '89 (SFS) Kranzburg, SD Holy Rosary Church.
Mangan, Eugene V. '58 (NY) [229] Staten Island, NY St. Sylvester Church.
Mangan, James '69 (SPK) Otis Orchards, WA St. Joseph Church.
Mangan, John J. '40 (PH) Retired.
Mangan, Joseph T. *s.j.* '42 (DET) [P] Clarkston, MI Colombiere Center.
Mangan, Martin '57 (SFD) [4] Decatur, IL St. James Church.
Mangan, Timothy *s.s.s.* '59 (ALB) Broadalbin, NY St. Joseph Church.
Manganello, Salvatore '82 (BUF) [14] Buffalo, NY Blessed Sacrament Church.
Mangano, Charles N. '90 (RVC) Bohemia, NY St. John Nepomucene Church.
Mangen, Daniel J. *c.pp.s.* '80 (CIN) [M] Dayton, OH Provincial House of the Cincinnati Province of the Society of the Precious Blood.
Manger, William '62 (BEA) [2] Beaumont, TX St. Anne Church.
Mangiafico, Paul '70 (HRT) [13] Waterbury, CT St. Lucy's Church.
Mangiaracina, Cayet *o.p.* '64 (SAT) [26] San Antonio, TX St. Ann Church; [B] San Antonio, TX Dominican Priory of Juan Macias.
Mangiaracina, George *o.c.d* '93 (MIL) [P] Milwaukee, WI Provincial Offices - Discalced Carmelites.
Mangini, Charles M. '56 (BRK) Absent on Sick Leave.
Mangini, Richard A. '67 (OAK) [2] Concord, CA St. Bonaventure Church.
Mangum, Peter '90 (SHP) Minden, LA St. Paul Church.
Manhard, Edward P. *s.j.* '32 (STL) [O] St. Louis, MO Fusz Pavilion.
Manhart, Paul *s.j.* '58 (RC) Pine Ridge, SD Holy Rosary Church; [B] Pine Ridge, SD Jesuit Community of Holy Rosary Mission.
Maniamkerry, Matthew *o.ss.t.* '84 (VIC) [4] Victoria, TX Our Lady of Sorrows Church.
Maniangat, Joseph '64 (STA) Macclenny, FL St. Mary's Church.
Maniangatt, Joseph '72 (RVC) Roslyn, NY St. Francis Hospital.
Manickam, Selvaraj '73 (NY) [227] Staten Island, NY Sacred Heart Church.
Manieri, Msgr. Francis '60 (STU) Bridgeport, OH St. Anthony of Padua Church; [J] Bridgeport, OH Cursillo Moderator.
Manikowski, Stanislaus J. (HT) Raceland, LA St. Mary's Nativity Church; Retired.
Maniola, Francis N. '38 (CHI) [197] Chicago, IL St. Symphorosa and Seven Sons Church; Retired.
Manion, Dominic *o.f.m.conv.* '68 (LSC) Loving, NM Our Lady of Grace Church.
Manion, Kevin *c.m.f.* '89 (SAT) [32] San Antonio, TX St. Cecilia Church.
Manion, Lawrence G. '93 (GF) Culbertson, MT St. Anthony's Church.
Manion, Thomas F. '57 (PIT) [11] Pittsburgh, PA Epiphany Church; On Duty Outside the Diocese.
Maniscalco, Msgr. Francis '71 (RVC) West Hempstead, NY St. Thomas, the Apostle Church; Priests Released from Diocesan Assignment.
Manista, Clemens D. '74 (WIL) Bear, DE St. Elizabeth Ann Seton Church.
Maniyangat, Jose '75 (STA) [1] Jacksonville, FL Assumption Church.
Mank, Virgil '65 (SFD) Godfrey, IL St. Ambrose Church.
Mankel, Xavier '61 (KNX) [1] Knoxville, TN Cathedral of the Sacred Heart of Jesus; [K] Knoxville, TN Diocesan Council of Catholic Women.
Manko, Rodney A. '78 (NO) Absent on Leave.
Mankowski, Edmund A. '46 (BRK) Retired.
Mankowski, Paul V. *s.j.* '65 (CHI) [N] Chicago, IL Chicago Province of the Society of Jesus-Provincial Office.
Manley, Bernard A. '87 (CHL) Retired.
Manly, Msgr. Alex F. '57 (RVC) Kings Park, NY St. Joseph's Church.
Mann, Francis J. '79 (BRK) [149] Queens, NY St. Anastasia Church.
Mann, Gordon '92 (EVN) Chrisney, IN St. Martin Church; Santa Claus, IN St. Nicholas Church.
Mann, Lawrence *s.m.* '45 (LA) [F] Chatsworth, CA Chaminade College Preparatory.
Mann, Peter '67 (RVC) Absent on Leave.
Mann, Raymond *o.f.m.* '59 (BO) [BB] Boston, MA St. Anthony Shrine.
Mann, Robert G. '59 (PEO) [J] Danville, IL United Samaritans Medical Center.
Manna, Louis *o.f.m.conv.* '73 (IND) Dover, IN St. John the Baptist Church; St. Leon, IN St. Joseph Church.
Mannara, Frederick R. '63 (SY) New Hartford, NY St. John the Evangelist Church; Sabbatical.
Mannelli, David F. '80 (CHI) Niles, IL St. John Brebeuf Church.
Mannetta, Andrew *o.f.m.cap.* '83 (AGN) [F] Agana Heights, GU St. Fidelis Friary.
Mannetta, Andrew *o.f.m.cap.* '83 (HON) Aiea, HI St. Elizabeth Church.
Mannhardt, Daniel C. '57 (DAV) [2] Davenport, IA Our Lady of Victory Church.
Manning, Aedan *s.t.* '63 (JKS) [3] Jackson, MS St. Richard Church.
Manning, Brian F. '74 (BO) [4] Somerville, MA St. Catherine of Genoa Church.
Manning, Charles T. '75 (ROC) Cohocton, NY St. Pius V Church.
Manning, Daniel J. '91 (SFS) Britton, SD St. John de Britto Church.
Manning, Edward J. *m.m.* '47 (NY) [Z] Maryknoll, NY

Maryknoll Fathers and Brothers.
Manning, Francis J. '51 (SPR) [4] Ludlow, MA St. Mary Church.
Manning, Msgr. J. Leroy '40 (SAT) Retired; [K] San Antonio, TX Casa De Padres.
Manning, James *s.m.m.* '58 (RVC) [N] Bay Shore, NY Montfort Missionaries.
Manning, James J. '75 (CIN) [3] Dayton, OH St. Albert the Great Church.
Manning, John '55 (OAK) Retired.
Manning, John E. '72 (CLV) [75] Cleveland, OH St. Vincent de Paul Church.
Manning, Joseph H. '61 (BO) [5] Brockton, MA Our Lady of Lourdes Church.
Manning, Justinian *c.p.* '54 (BO) [24] Boston, MA St. Gabriel's Church; [W] Brighton, MA St. Gabriel's Passionist Community.
Manning, Martin B. '43 (DAV) Retired; [M] Davenport, IA St. Vincent Center.
Manning, Michael '69 (SB) [A] Riverside, CA Divine Word Seminary; [I] Riverside, CA Wordnet, Inc.
Manning, Paul F. (BO) Awaiting Assignment.
Manning, Paul S. '85 (PAT) Rockaway, NJ St. Cecilia's Church; [C] Denville, NJ Morris Catholic High School.
Manning, Robert '54 (COL) Retired.
Manning, Robert E. *s.j.* '67 (BO) [B] Cambridge, MA Weston Jesuit School of Theology; [W] Cambridge, MA Weston Jesuit Community.
Manning, Robert T. '54 (COL) New Philadelphia, OH Sacred Heart Church.
Manning, Thomas D. *o.m.i.* '35 (BO) [Z] Tewksbury, MA Immaculate Heart of Mary Novitiate-Infirmary.
Manning, Thomas J. '65 (SY) Retired.
Manning, Thomas V. '84 (PIT) Mt. Lebanon, PA St. Bernard Church.
Manning, William F. *c.s.p.* '44 (NY) [Z] Scarsdale, NY Paulist Fathers Generalate.
Mannion, Bernard J. '50 (STO) Oakdale, CA St. Mary of the Annunciation Church.
Mannion, Edward C. *c.m.* '39 (PH) [Z] Philadelphia, PA Congregation of the Mission.
Mannion, Frank *s.s.c.* '52 (LA) Whittier, CA St. Bruno Church.
Mannion, James '81 (RVC) Wantagh, NY St. Frances de Chantal Church.
Mannion, John H. '68 (IND) [F] Beech Grove, IN St. Francis Hospital and Health Centers.
Mannion, John H. '68 (LFT) On Duty Outside the Diocese.
Mannion, John Patrick '55 (WCH) St. Mark's, KS St. Mark Church.
Mannion, Msgr. M. Francis '73 (SLC) [1] Salt Lake City, UT Cathedral of the Madeleine.
Mannion, Martin '66 (STL) [N] Normandy, MO St. Vincent Home for Children.
Mannion, Msgr. Martin J. '62 (CAM) Collingswood, NJ St. John's Church.
Mannion, Martin K. '66 (STL) Special Assignment.
Mannion, Michael '71 (CAM) On Duty Outside the Diocese.
Mannion, Michael '71 (WDC) [C] Washington, DC Catholic University of America, The; [C] Washington, DC Catholic University of America, The.
Mannion, P. John *m.s.c.* '66 (SAT) [4] San Antonio, TX Divine Providence Church.
Mannion, Thomas F. '46 (BRK) Retired.
Mannion, Thomas F. '46 (P) Brookings, OR Star of the Sea Church.
Mannion, Thomas Ignatius '65 (HBG) Roaring Creek, PA Our Lady of Mercy Church; Danville, PA State Hospital.
Mannion, Thomas J. '52 (LC) Prescott, WI St. Joseph Church.
Mannion, William D. '63 (CHI) Evanston, IL St. Athanasius Church.
Mannion, William M. '89 (BAL) [3] Baltimore, MD St. Agnes Church.
Mannis, James B. *c.s.c.* '55 (SCR) [4] Wilkes-Barre, PA St. Casimir's Church.
Manno, John K. '68 (SCR) Conyngham, PA St. John Bosco Church.
Manny, Msgr. Howard F. '44 (ALB) [11] Schenectady, NY St. Luke Church; Retired.
Manos, James A. '96 (NEW) [26] Newark, NJ Our Lady of Fatima Church.
Manrique, Wilfredo S. '88 (SJ) Milpitas, CA St. John the Baptist Church.
Mansell, C. Kirk *s.j.* '84 (LAF) [J] Grand Coteau, LA Our Lady of the Oaks Retreat House.
Mansfield, John L. '53 (BO) On Special or Other Diocesan Assignment.
Manship, D. Joseph '76 (PRT) Augusta, ME St. Mary's Church.
Manship, Paul E. '88 (SPR) [5] Springfield, MA Holy Family Church.
Mansilla, Joaquin '56 (SJN) [6] San Juan, PR Nuestra Senora de Belen Church.
Mansini, Guy *o.s.b.* '77 (IND) [A] St. Meinrad, IN St. Meinrad Seminary; [B] St. Meinrad, IN St. Meinrad Seminary-College of Liberal Arts; [J] St. Meinrad, IN St. Meinrad Archabbey.
Manske, James J. '62 (JUN) Retired.
Mansour, Gregory J. '82 (OLL) Los Angeles, CA Our Lady of Mt. Lebanon-St. Peter Cathedral.
Manternach, Msgr. Albert V. '52 (DUB) Retired.
Manternach, Carl J. '55 (DUB) New Melleray, IA Holy Family Church; Peosta, IA St. John the Baptist Church.
Manternach, Neil J. '85 (DUB) Fillmore, IA Sacred Heart Church.
Mantia, Armand '85 (NEW) Clark, NJ St. Agnes Church.
Mantica, A. Donald '60 (STU) Piney Fork, OH St. Therese Church; Smithfield, OH Our Lady, Queen of Peace Church.
Mantilla, Jorge I. *o.ss.t.* '89 (ARE) Isabela, PR St. Anthony Church.
Manton, Joseph E. *c.ss.r.* '29 (BO) [13] Boston, MA Basilica of Our Lady of Perpetual Help.
Mantovani, Firmo *c.s.* '73 (SD) Imperial, CA St. Anthony of Padua Church.
Manuel, Albert William '87 (MIL) [P] Milwaukee, WI Jesuit Community at Marquette University.
Manuel, Armand *s.s.j.* (MOB) Chastang, AL St. Peter the Apostle Church.
Manuel, Gerdenio M. *s.j.* '79 (SJ) [M] Los Gatos, CA California Province of the Society of Jesus, Jesuit Provincial Office.
Manuel, Vincent *s.a.c.* '81 (ALX) Bordelonville, LA St. Peter Church; Kleinwood, LA St. Michael Church.
Manuppella, Anthony J. '76 (CAM) Millville, NJ St. Mary Magdalen's Church.
Manville, Alexander *o.f.m.* '53 (PHX) [G] Scottsdale, AZ Franciscan Renewal Center, Inc. (Casa de Paz Y Bien)
Manwelo, Paul *s.j.* '93 (BO) [W] Chestnut Hill, MA The Jesuit Community at Boston College.
Manz, John R. '71 (CHI) [144] Chicago, IL Notre Dame Church.
Manz, Msgr. Joseph C. '40 (NEW) [18] Jersey City, NJ St. Nicholas Church; Woodcliff Lake, NJ Our Lady Mother of the Church; Retired.
Manz, Michael J. '79 (PRO) [O] Providence, RI Opus Dei, Mathewson House.
Manzaro, Paul L. '60 (FRS) Wasco, CA Prison Facility.
Manzelli, Michael '57 (RVC) Freeport, NY Our Holy Redeemer Church.
Manzi, Arcangelo *o.de.m.* '64 (SP) [1] St. Petersburg, FL Cathedral of St. Jude the Apostle; [O] St. Petersburg, FL St. Peter Nolasco Residence.
Manzo, Fernando L. '83 (TUC) Somerton, AZ Immaculate Heart of Mary Church.
Manzo, Msgr. Francis J. '62 (BRK) Absent on Leave.
Manzo, Louis A. *c.s.c.* '65 (FR) [B] North Easton, MA Stonehill College.
Maples, Frederic A. *s.j.* '72 (BO) [W] Boston, MA The Society of Jesus of New England-Provincial Offices.
Maquire, Thomas J. '69 (SAC) Ione, CA Sacred Heart Church.
Mara, John J. '48 (SPR) [6] Pittsfield, MA St. Francis Church.
Marable, Gerald C. '88 (CAM) Gibbsboro, NJ St. Andrew the Apostle Church.
Maraczewski, Edward S. '45 (CHI) [1] Waukegan, IL St. Anastasia Church; Retired.
Maraist, Martin C. '80 (LAF) Morrow, LA St. Peter Church.
Maraldo, Angelo F. *o.s.f.s.* '86 (ARL) Vienna, VA Our Lady of Good Counsel Church.
Maraldo, Angelo F. *o.s.f.s.* '86 (VEN) [6] Fort Myers, FL Our Lady of Light Church.
Maramot, Faustino (GAL) Galena Park, TX Our Lady of Fatima Church.
Marancu, Bede (SJ) [5] Sunnyvale, CA Church of The Resurrection.
Marancu, Nicolaus '52 (P) [20] Portland, OR Immaculate Heart of Mary Church.
Marangone, Mark *s.x.* '84 (PAT) [M] Wayne, NJ Xaverian Missionary Fathers; [M] Wayne, NJ Xaverian Missionary Fathers.
Marani, Philip *o.carm.* (NY) Manhattan, NY Bellevue Hospital.
Marani, Philip *o.carm.* '65 (NY) [97] New York, NY Our Lady of the Scapular/St. Stephen Church.
Marano, Fred '91 (BRK) [B] Elmhurst, NY Cathedral Preparatory Seminary of the Immaculate Conception.
Maranowski, Michael '87 (PIT) Scott Township, PA Our Lady of Grace Church.
Maranto, Charles L. *c.s.v.* '50 (CHI) [N] Arlington Heights, IL Viatorian Province Center-Clerics of St. Viator.
Maranto, Samuel C. *c.ss.r.* '72 (BR) [H] Baton Rouge, LA Redemptorist Fathers Vice Provincialate.
Marasciulo, Msgr. John '45 (YAK) Cle Elum, WA St. John the Baptist Church.
Maravilla, Primitivo (MOB) Fairhope, AL St. Lawrence Church.
Maravilla-Vigil, Juan *f.m.m.* (BEA) Livingston, (1970) St. Joseph Church.
Maraye, Felipe '62 (ELP) Absent on Leave.
Marbach, Msgr. Joseph '43 (NY) Retired.
Marbach, Lawrence J. '52 (SFS) Retired.
Marbaugh, Meinrad '39 (LR) [A] Subiaco, AR Subiaco Monastery.
Marbury, Cabell '64 (ALB) Special Assignment.
Marbury, Cabell B. '64 (ALB) [C] Albany, NY Bishop Maginn High School.
Marcaccio, Anthony J. '91 (CHL) Special Assignment.
Marcantonio, Clement '59 (PBL) Retired.
Marceau, Emmett L. '67 (SAG) [12] Bay City, MI Our Lady of the Visitation Church.
Marceau, Timothy R. *o.s.b.* '52 (ALX) Belledeau, LA St. Martin of Tours Church.
Marceau, Timothy R. *o.s.b.* '52 (JOL) [J] Lisle, IL St. Procopius Abbey.
Marceau, William C. *c.s.b.* '57 (ROC) [I] Rochester, NY Basilian Residence.
Marceaux, Msgr. Sidney J. '70 (BEA) Military Chaplains.
Marceaux, Timothy *o.s.b.* '52 (ALX) Pineville, LA Central Louisiana State Hospital.
Marcell, Robert G. '56 (BR) St. Gabriel, LA St. Gabriel Church.
March, Ralph *o.cist.* '45 (DAL) [M] Irving, TX Cistercian Abbey of Our Lady of Dallas.
March, Thomas *o.f.m.cap.* '78 (RVC) East Patchogue, NY St. Joseph the Worker Church.
Marchand, Gerald A. '54 (NEW) West Orange, NJ Our Lady of Lourdes Church.
Marchand, Robert A. '52 (MAN) [18] Manchester, NH St. Theresa Church.
Marchesani, Gino *f.d.p.* (BO) [Y] Bradford, MA Don Orione Center.
Marchesani, Gino *f.d.p.* '56 (BO) [B] Haverhill, MA Sons of Divine Providence School for Exceptional Boys; [U] Boston, MA Don Orione Nursing Home.
Marchese, Dominic A. *s.s.j.* '40 (BAL) [M] Baltimore, MD St. Joseph Society of the Sacred Heart House of Central Administration.
Marchese, Dominic A. *s.s.j.* '40 (TR) Bay Head, NJ Sacred Heart Church.
Marchese, Henry *s.a.* '64 (NY) [Z] Garrison, NY Generalate of the Franciscan Friars of the Atonement-St. James Friary; [Z] Garrison, NY Franciscan Friars of the Atonement.
Marchese, Joseph P. '69 (SPR) On Duty Outside the Diocese.
Marchese, Richard E. '70 (BRK) [B] Elmhurst, NY Cathedral Preparatory Seminary of the Immaculate Conception.
Marchesin, Ivan J. *s.x.* '66 (CHI) [N] Chicago, IL Xaverian Missionaries (S.X.).
Marchetti, Carlo M. *o.s.m.* '59 (ORG) [H] Buena Park, CA Servite Fathers And Brothers.
Marchetti, Michael H. '82 (SCR) White Mills, PA St. Joseph's Church.
Marchino, Louis H. '39 (IND) Retired.
Marchionda, James V. *o.p.* '73 (CHI) [N] Chicago, IL Dominicans (Provincial Office); [N] Chicago, IL Dominicans (Provincial Office).
Marchitelli, Anthony D. '76 (NY) [E] Somers, NY John F. Kennedy High School; [L] New York, NY Catholic Youth Organization of the Archdiocese of New York Inc.
Marchlewski, Michael A. *s.j.* '67 (STL) [P] St. Louis, MO De Smet Jesuit High School Community.
Marchukonis, Frank V. '97 (PIT) Holiday Park, PA Our Lady of Joy Church.
Marchulones, Kenneth L. '65 (PEO) East Peoria, IL St. Monica's Church.
Marciano, Charles A. '72 (ALN) [11] Reading, PA St. Peter Church.
Marciano, Robert L. '83 (PRO) [9] Warwick, RI St. Rose of Lima Church.
Marcil, Leo L. '47 (ALB) Hudson Falls, NY Church of St. Mary's/St. Paul's; Retired.
Marciniak, Felix R. '79 (NEW) [10] Newark, NJ St. Casimir's Church.
Marciniak, Henry P. '61 (NEW) Harrison, NJ Our Lady of Czestochowa Church.
Marciniak, John '56 (NOR) Retired.
Marciniak, Piotr *o.s.p.p.e.* (PH) [Z] Doylestown, PA Pauline Fathers Monastery, Shrine of Our Lady of Czestochowa.
Marciniak, Thomas R. *s.j.* '76 (SY) [S] Syracuse, NY Jesuits at LeMoyne, Inc.
Marcinkiewicz, Msgr. Eugene V. '36 (BUF) [18] Buffalo, NY St. Casimir Church; Retired.
Marciulonis, Benedict J. '43 (GAY) Retired.
Marck, Marianus *o.cart.* '50 (BUR) [G] Arlington, VT Carthusian Foundation, Charterhouse of the Transfiguration.
Marck, Ray John *o.m.i.* (NO) [17] New Orleans, LA Our Lady of Guadalupe /International Shrine of St. Jude Church.
Marco, Alfredo '60 (LKC) [3] Lake Charles, LA Sacred Heart of Jesus Church.
Marco, Michael J. *s.j.* '96 (OM) [C] Omaha, NE Creighton Preparatory School.
Marcone, Eugene F. '64 (NEW) Clark, NJ St. Agnes Church.

Marconi, John '87 (LR) Benton, AR Our Lady of Fatima Church.
Marconi, Paul *c.r.s.p.* '58 (SD) Pala, CA Mission San Antonio de Pala Church.
Marconi, Theodore B. '84 (E) Smethport, PA St. Elizabeth Church.
Marconyak, Albert J. '43 (PIT) Retired.
Marcotte, David P. '92 (NY) [Z] New York, NY Jesuit Provincial's Office; [Z] New York, NY Xavier Jesuit Community.
Marcotte, Joseph A. '69 (WOR) Webster, MA St. Louis Church.
Marcotte, Wayne E. '66 (MAR) Hancock, MI Resurrection Church.
Marcotte, William '60 (SB) Fontana, CA Kaiser Permanente Hospital.
Marcouiller, Douglas *s.j.* '86 (BO) [W] Chestnut Hill, MA The Jesuit Community at Boston College.
Marcoux, John *m.ss.a.* '87 (NOR) [A] Cromwell, CT Holy Apostles College and Seminary; [F] Cromwell, CT Missionaries of the Holy Apostles.
Marcoux, Stephen '93 (MAN) Hampton, NH Our Lady of the Miraculous Medal Church.
Marcucci, John A. '68 (PIT) [3] Charleroi, PA Mary Mother of the Church.
Marcynski, Christopher '91 (BRK) [192] Queens, NY St. Margaret's Church.
Marczewski, Robert '95 (PH) [35] Philadelphia, PA St. Christopher Church.
Marczewski, Ronald J. '74 (NEW) [2] Elizabeth, NJ St. Adalbert's Church.
Marczuk, Scott L. *j.c.l.* '81 (LR) [1] Little Rock, AR Cathedral of St. Andrew.
Mardelli, Maximos '38 (NTN) Retired.
Mardian, Joseph P. '45 (SFS) Retired.
Mardian, Pius '44 (SFS) Retired.
Mardones, Gustavo *l.d.* '93 (PCE) [18] Ponce, PR Church Santisimo Sacramento Church.
Marecki, Ronald A. '83 (CHL) On Duty Outside the Diocese.
Marek, Dean V. '65 (MIL) On Duty Outside the Archdiocese.
Marek, Ray J. *o.m.i.* '89 (NO) [1] New Orleans, LA St. Louis Cathedral.
Marek, Walter '46 (GAY) Retired.
Maresca, Ralph J. '78 (BRK) Special Assignment.
Maresh, Mark A. '94 (GI) [1] Grand Island, NE Cathedral of the Nativity of the Blessed Virgin Mary.
Marflak, Albert *o.s.b.* '75 (CLV) [E] Cleveland, OH Benedictine High School; [P] Cleveland, OH Benedictine Order of Cleveland.
Marfori, Antonio '78 (SCL) Zimmerman, MN St. Pius X Church.
Margalef, Jose *sch.p.* '67 (LA) [R] Los Angeles, CA Piarist Fathers.
Margason, James E. '71 (BEL) [6] Belleville, IL St. Luke Church; [9] Belleville, IL Chapel of St. John Children's Home Church; Lebanon, IL St. Joseph Church; [D] Belleville, IL St. John Children's Home.
Marggraf, Brian *ss.cc.* '55 (FR) [K] Fairhaven, MA Sacred Hearts Provincial House.
Margherio, Ronald L. *o.s.b.* '78 (PEO) [A] Peru, IL St. Bede Abbey and Academy; [C] Peru, IL St. Bede Academy.
Margiotta, Msgr. Vincent S. '29 (RVC) Retired.
Margola, Joseph F. '84 (PCE) On Duty Outside the Diocese.
Maria Alabanza de la Trin, David A. *s.e.m.v.* '95 (ARE) Hatillo, PR Our Lady of Guadalupe Church.
Marian, Anthony S. '58 (NY) [2] Poughkeepsie, NY St. Mary Church; Poughkeepsie, NY Vassar Brothers Hospital.
Mariani, Charles J. '43 (BRK) [131] Brooklyn, NY Sacred Hearts of Jesus and Mary and St. Stephen Church; Retired.
Mariano, Angel *s.j.* '92 (SJ) [17] San Jose, CA Most Holy Trinity Church.
Mariano, John M. '58 (BRK) Released from Diocesan Assignment.
Mariano, Remigio Tupaz, Jr. '94 (TUC) [22] Tucson, AZ St. Elizabeth Ann Seton Church.
Marickovic, Thomas C. (HBG) Lewistown, PA Sacred Heart of Jesus Church; Mifflintown, PA St. Jude Church.
Marie, Adrien Ste. *c.s.c.* (P) [B] Portland, OR University of Portland.
Marie, Louis '70 (RC) [B] Bethlehem, SD Holy Nativity Monastery.
Marien, Roy C. '85 (PT) Destin, FL Church of the Resurrection.
Marier, Edward '88 (SPK) Odessa, WA St. Joseph Church; Wilbur, WA Sacred Heart Church.
Marier, Euclid A. '72 (OG) [1] Ogdensburg, NY St. Mary's Cathedral; Ogdensburg, NY Ogdensburg Correctional Facility; Retired.
Marigliano, Michael *o.f.m.cap.* '84 (MIL) [B] Mount Calvary, WI St. Felix Friary.
Marin, James (SJN) [44] San Juan, PR Santos Pedro y Pablo los Apostoles Church.
Marin, John L. '83 (MET) On Duty Outside the Diocese.
Marin, Jose N. '81 (MGZ) Rincon, PR St. Rose of Lima Church.
Marin, Moises M. '95 (CHI) [8] Chicago, IL St. Aloysius Church.
Marin, Rafael *m.afr.* '78 (LA) [4] North Hollywood, CA St. Patrick Church.
Marin, Tomas M. '89 (MIA) [B] Opa Locka, FL St. Thomas University.
Marinacci, Msgr. Nicholas '38 (NY) [102] New York, NY St. Patrick Old Cathedral; Retired.
Marinak, Andrew P. '56 (HBG) Cornwall, PA Sacred Heart of Jesus Church.
Marinak, Msgr. Thomas A. '54 (NY) [205] Staten Island, NY Holy Family Church.
Marincel, Frank '58 (DUL) Retired.
Marinciori, Raniero C. *s.j.s.* '85 (TR) Keyport, NJ Jesus the Lord Church.
Marinciori, Raniero C. '90 (MET) Bernardsville, NJ Our Lady of Perpetual Help Church.
Marine, John C. '76 (PH) [A] Wynnewood, PA Theological Seminary of St. Charles Borromeo, Overbrook.
Marine, Robert A. '73 (CIN) [44] Cincinnati, OH St. John the Baptist Church.
Maring, William J. *s.j.* '45 (SJ) [M] Los Gatos, CA California Province of the Society of Jesus, Jesuit Provincial Office; [M] Los Gatos, CA Sacred Heart Jesuit Center.
Marini, Francis J. '95 (SAM) [D] Staten Island, NY Pastoral Center.
Marini, John L. *c.s.sp.* '92 (PIT) [3] Millvale, PA Holy Spirit Church.
Marini, Joseph J. '52 (SFR) San Bruno, CA St. Robert Church; Retired.
Marini, Michael A. '72 (MRY) Santa Cruz, CA Holy Cross Church.
Marinko, John S. '55 (SCR) Olyphant, PA Holy Ghost Church.
Marino, Chris '93 (MIA) [15] Miami, FL St. Agatha Church; [D] Miami, FL Christopher Columbus High School.
Marino, Edward J. *c.s.* '57 (PRO) [M] North Kingstown, RI Scalabrini Villa.
Marino, Francis J. *s.m.* '57 (MET) [L] Phillipsburg, NJ The Anawim Community.
Marino, John J. *o.f.m.* '88 (PRO) [P] Providence, RI St. Francis Friary.
Marino, Msgr. Joseph '79 (BIR) On Duty Outside the Diocese.
Marino, Joseph *o.s.b.* '94 (STL) [F] Creve Coeur, MO St. Louis Priory School; [P] St. Louis, MO The Abbey of St. Mary and St. Louis.
Marino, Joseph T. '75 (PH) Gladwyne, PA St. John Baptist Vianney Church; [A] Wynnewood, PA Theological Seminary of St. Charles Borromeo, Overbrook.
Marino, Ronald T. '73 (BRK) [126] Brooklyn, NY St. Rosalia-Regina Pacis Church; [T] Brooklyn, NY Catholic Migration & Refugee Office, Catholic Migration Services, Inc.; [T] Brooklyn, NY Catholic Migration & Refugee Office, Catholic Migration Services, Inc.; [T] Brooklyn, NY Catholic Migration & Refugee Office, Catholic Migration Services, Inc.
Marino, Umberto J. '54 (NY) On Duty Outside the Archdiocese.
Marinucci, Stephen J. '74 (PH) [A] Wynnewood, PA Theological Seminary of St. Charles Borromeo, Overbrook.
Maristany, Edward '80 (NY) [EE] New Rochelle, NY Opus Dei (Prelature of the Holy Cross and Opus Dei).
Maristela, Victor '86 (SD) Escondido, CA St. Mary Church.
Marjanczyk, Msgr. Joseph A. '45 (NEW) [6] Bayonne, NJ Mt. Carmel Church; Retired.
Markaitis, Bruno *s.j.* '48 (CHI) [N] Chicago, IL Lithuanian American Jesuits.
Markell, John W. '84 (PIT) Turtle Creek, PA St. Colman Church.
Markelz, Carl *o.carm.* '91 (CHI) [N] Chicago, IL Carmelite Priory of St. Cyril.
Markelz, Carl J. *o.carm.* '91 (CHI) [D] Chicago, IL Mt. Carmel High School.
Markert, Leo F. '62 (ALB) Rotterdam, NY St. Gabriel the Archangel Church.
Market, John C. *o.f.m.* '45 (DET) [5] Southfield, MI St. Michael Church.
Markewuch, Uriy '65 (PHU) Whippany, NJ St. John the Baptist Church.
Markey, Earle L. *s.j.* '63 (WOR) [N] Worcester, MA Jesuits of Holy Cross College, Inc.
Markey, Francis '61 (MRY) Retired.
Markey, Gerard *s.s.c.* '71 (OM) [K] St. Columbans, NE St. Columban's Foreign Mission Society.
Markey, John *o.p.* '93 (OAK) [N] Oakland, CA Order of Preachers (Southern Province).
Markey, John J. *o.p.* '93 (DEN) [28] Denver, CO St. Dominic's Church; Longmont, CO Spirit of Peace Parish Church.
Markey, Thomas J. '51 (WOR) Millbury, MA St. Brigid Church.
Markham, Msgr. James '51 (MAN) [11] Manchester, NH St. John the Baptist Church.
Markham, Msgr. James J. '51 (MAN) Retired.
Markham, John W. '54 (DET) [22] Detroit, MI St. Elizabeth Church.
Markiewicz, Stanley T. *o.s.b.* '61 (GBG) [2] Latrobe, PA St. Vincent Basilica; [H] Latrobe, PA Saint Vincent Archabbey.
Markley, Edward P. *o.s.b.* '66 (BIR) [E] Cullman, AL St. Bernard Abbey.
Markowicz, Joseph A. *m.s.* '43 (HRT) [M] Hartford, CT Missionaries of LaSalette Provincial Secretary.
Markowski, Clement A. '53 (SCR) Retired; [N] Dunmore, PA Villa St. Joseph.
Marks, Kenneth L. '77 (NY) [133] Bronx, NY St. Benedict Church.
Marks, Thomas C. '79 (LR) Wynne, AR St. Peter's Church.
Marks, William G. '92 (IND) [23] Indianapolis, IN St. Gabriel the Archangel Church.
Markunas, Robert *s.c.j.* '76 (MIL) [P] Hales Corners, WI Priests of the Sacred Heart.
Markunas, Robert *s.c.j.* '76 (ORL) Special Assignment.
Markus, Anthony L. '80 (CHI) Evergreen Park, IL Most Holy Redeemer Church.
Markwell, Ben *o.f.m.cap.* '66 (DET) [16] Detroit, MI St. Charles Borromeo Church.
Markwell, George J. *m.afr.* '65 (LA) [4] North Hollywood, CA St. Patrick Church.
Marley, Edward G. *c.s.sp.* '44 (LR) Center Ridge, AR St. Joseph's Church.
Marley, Edward G. *c.s.sp.* '45 (LR) Atkins, AR Assumption B.V.M. Church.
Marley, Msgr. Michael F. '40 (PH) [94] Philadelphia, PA St. Martin of Tours Church; Retired.
Marley, Thomas J. *c.s.p.* '49 (NY) [Z] Scarsdale, NY Paulist Fathers Generalate.
Marley, Thomas J. *c.s.p.* '49 (PMB) [G] Vero Beach, FL Paulist Fathers Retirement Home.
Marlow, Ransom *s.j.* '66 (NO) [C] New Orleans, LA Loyola University.
Marmentini, Alvadi *o.f.m.cap.* '73 (WDC) [B] Washington, DC St. Francis Friary-Capuchin College.
Marmion, Joseph '62 (GF) Chester, MT St. Mary's Church.
Marmolejo, Joan '92 (BGP) [2] Bridgeport, CT St. Ambrose Church.
Marneni, M. Julian '67 (WH) [1] Huntington, WV St. Joseph's Church.
Marohn, Donald '62 (SFS) Grenville, SD St. Joseph Church; Waubay, SD Immaculate Conception Church.
Maroney, Frank '92 (DEN) Basalt, CO St. Vincent Church.
Maroney, Maurice J. '67 (HRT) [3] Milford, CT St. Gabriel Church.
Maroon, Donald '67 (COL) London, OH St. Patrick's Church.
Maroon, Msgr. William J. '67 (COL) Hilliard, OH St. Brendan Church.
Maroor, Joseph '63 (MIA) [3] Pompano Beach, FL St. Coleman Church.
Marot, Roger L. '50 (PRO) Retired; [N] Woonsocket, RI Fr. Marot CYO Center.
Marotta, Robert (NEW) Lyndhurst, NJ Our Lady of Mount Carmel Church.
Maroun, George F. '74 (OG) [A] Ogdensburg, NY Wadhams Hall.
Maroun, Sharbel G. '89 (OLL) Minneapolis, MN St. Maron Church.
Marpes, Thomas M. '50 (PIT) [62] Pittsburgh, PA St. Pius X Church; [L] Pittsburgh, PA St. Pius X Residence, Inc.
Marquard, Elmer E. '66 (CLV) North Olmsted, OH St. Richard Church.
Marquardt, Donald F. '51 (GB) [2] Two Rivers, WI Sacred Heart Church; Retired.
Marquardt, John J. (TLS) Antlers, OK St. Agnes Church.
Marquart, Ernest J. '70 (SPC) Mountain View, MO St. John Vianney Church.
Marquart, Joseph M. '57 (SEA) Everett, WA St. Mary Magdalen Church.
Marquez, Esteban '95 (LA) Bell Gardens, CA St. Gertrude Church.
Marquina, Luis '64 (MIA) [G] Miami, FL Mercy Hospital.
Marquis, J. Alphee '39 (PRT) Retired.
Marquis, John Clifton *s.t.* '69 (LA) Compton, CA Our Lady of Victory Church.
Marquis, John E. *s.m.* '78 (PRT) [M] Waterville, ME Colby College; [M] Waterville, ME Thomas College.
Marquis, John J. '62 (COL) Portsmouth, OH St. Mary Church.
Marquis, Paul '42 (BO) [W] Lowell, MA Missionary Oblates of Mary Immaculate.
Marquis, Paul R. '86 (PRT) [1] Portland, ME Cathedral of the Immaculate Conception; Portland, ME Maine Medical Center.
Marquis, William Paul *o.p.* '83 (PRO) [P] Providence, RI St. Thomas Aquinas Priory at Providence College.
Marr, James G. '60 (NEW) [10] Elizabeth, NJ St. Patrick's Church.
Marr, James G. '60 (STU) Retired.

Marr, Thomas P. '70 (MAD) Watertown, WI St. Bernard Church.
Marra, Msgr. Anthony C. '51 (SCR) [3] Dunmore, PA St. Anthony of Padua Church.
Marrapese, Casto *p.i.m.e.* '44 (COL) [H] Newark, OH P.I.M.E. Mission & Prayer Center.
Marredan, Francisco J. *c.m.* (ARE) [3] Manati, PR Sagrada Familia Church.
Marrell, Dennis P. '78 (LA) Military and VA Chaplains.
Marren, Hugh '76 (ATL) [9] Atlanta, GA St. Anthony of Padua Church.
Marren, Martin T. '84 (CHI) [22] Chicago, IL St. Barnabas Church.
Marrero, Francisco *s.j.* '70 (SJN) [22] San Juan, PR San Ignacio de Loyola Church.
Marrion, Malachy *o.c.s.o.* '54 (ARL) [J] Berryville, VA Cistercian Abbey of Our Lady of the Holy Cross.
Marro, Nicholas A. *c.s.* '63 (CHI) [118] Chicago, IL Santa Lucia-Santa Maria Incoronata Church.
Marro, Simeon D. *o.carm.* '55 (GBG) [H] New Florence, PA Mount Carmel Hermitage.
Marrodon, Javier *c.m.* '63 (SJN) [24] San Juan, PR Jesus Maestro Church.
Marrokal, Donald '58 (Y) Retired.
Marron, Msgr. James '43 (MRY) Retired.
Marron, James F. '62 (BRK) [228] Queens, NY St. Pius X Church.
Marron, Joseph *c.ss.r.* '48 (BRK) [107] Brooklyn, NY Our Lady of Perpetual Help Basilica.
Marron, Patrick L. '67 (SAT) Leon Springs, TX St. Elizabeth Ann Seton Church.
Marron, Peter J. *o.s.a.* '36 (SD) [H] San Diego, CA Augustinian Community.
Marrone, Robert J. '73 (CLV) [63] Cleveland, OH St. Peter Church.
Marroquin, Luis Antonio (WDC) [5] Silver Spring, MD Christ the King Church.
Marrow, Stanley B. *s.j.* '61 (BO) [W] Cambridge, MA Weston Jesuit Community.
Marrufo, Manuel *c.m.f.* (LA) [20] Los Angeles, CA Our Lady of Solitude Church.
Marrufo, Ramon R. '76 (SD) Vista, CA St. Francis Church.
Marsar, Msgr. Joseph '44 (HEL) Retired.
Marsch, Dwaine J. *c.ss.r.* '49 (STL) [P] Liguori, MO St. Clement Health Care Center.
Marschner, Msgr. Aloysius J. '36 (STL) Retired.
Marse, John J. '81 (NO) Norco, LA Sacred Heart of Jesus Church.
Marsh, Ivan Cormac *o.carm.* '80 (NEW) [P] Mahwah, NJ Carmel Retreat House.
Marshall, Alan '66 (SEA) Puyallup, WA All Saints Church.
Marshall, Albert *s.d.b.* '69 (SFR) [N] San Francisco, CA Salesian Provincial Residence.
Marshall, David C. *c.s.sp.* '46 (VEN) [G] Sarasota, FL Congregation of the Holy Ghost.
Marshall, Eugene C. *o.s.b.* '50 (OKL) McLoud, OK St. Vincent de Paul Church; [I] Shawnee, OK St. Gregory's Abbey.
Marshall, Hugh *s.t.* '56 (SAV) [E] Columbus, GA St. Francis Hospital.
Marshall, James A. *s.j.* (DAL) [D] Dallas, TX Jesuit College Preparatory School.
Marshall, Msgr. James C. '57 (STU) [3] Steubenville, OH Holy Rosary Church.
Marshall, James C. '59 (STL) Glasgow Village, MO St. Pius X Church.
Marshall, John J. '59 (ALT) [7] Johnstown, PA St. Casimir's Church; [9] Johnstown, PA St. Emerich's Church.
Marshall, Joseph *s.m.* '93 (BO) [CC] Waltham, MA Brandeis University Campus Ministry.
Marshall, Oswald J. *s.j.* '46 (DET) [P] Clarkston, MI Colombiere Center.
Marshall, Patrick M. '79 (CHI) [V] Chicago, IL Ministry in Higher Education; [V] Chicago, IL Ministry in Higher Education.
Marshall, Paul M. *s.m.* '76 (CLV) [4] Cleveland, OH St. Aloysius - St. Agatha Church.
Marshall, Raymond '43 (DET) Retired.
Marshall, Robert A. '61 (STL) Sullivan, MO Church of the Holy Martyrs of Japan.
Marshall, Thomas R. *c.s.p.* '59 (NY) [Z] Scarsdale, NY Paulist Fathers Generalate.
Marshall, W. Hodgson *c.s.b.* '51 (GAL) [Q] Sugar Land, TX Basilian Mission Center.
Marshall, William '63 (OAK) Retired.
Marsicek, Robert R. *s.d.s.* '68 (SAC) Orangevale, CA Divine Savior Church; [M] Orangevale, CA Catholic Committee on Scouting.
Marsick, James J. '72 (CLV) Cuyahoga Falls, OH St. Joseph Church.
Marszal, Theodore '68 (CLV) [1] Cleveland, OH Cathedral of St. John the Evangelist.
Marszalek, Francis G. '67 (PH) Pottstown, PA St. Aloysius Church.
Marszalek, Paul B. '52 (CHI) [99] Chicago, IL St. Jane de Chantal Church.
Marta, Raul '72 (FRS) Tulare, CA St. Aloysius Church.
Marteja, Vincent '67 (RVC) East Islip, NY St. Mary's Church.
Marteka, Anthony T. '61 (WOR) Grafton, MA St. Philip's Church.
Martel, C. James '70 (PRT) Pittsfield, ME St. Agnes Church.
Martel, Leo E. '63 (BO) Bellingham, MA Assumption Church.
Martel, Luc *a.a.* '73 (BO) [W] Brighton, MA Assumptionist Center.
Martel, Marcel I. '79 (MAN) [1] Berlin, NH St. Anne Church.
Martel, Robert T. '49 (PRT) Retired; [I] Waterville, ME Mt. St. Joseph Priest Retirement Home.
Martell, James Joseph '88 (MEM) Savannah, TN St. Mary's Church; [M] Savannah, TN Charismatic Prayer Groups.
Martell, John J. *s.m.* '48 (WDC) [M] Washington, DC Marist Provincial House.
Martelli, Jose M. *c.s.c.* '73 (FTW) Notre Dame, IN Sacred Heart Church; [B] Notre Dame, IN University of Notre Dame Du Lac; [J] Notre Dame, IN Holy Cross Community, Corby Hall, University of Notre Dame.
Martello, Lawrence N. '74 (CLV) Amherst, OH St. Joseph Church.
Martens, Francis E. *c.i.c.m.* '43 (HRT) Plainville, CT Our Lady of Mercy Church.
Martens, L. Gene *s.j.* '63 (STL) [P] St. Louis, MO Hallahan House; [P] St. Louis, MO The Jesuits of the Missouri Province; [W] St. Louis, MO The Jesuits of the Missouri Province.
Martensen, Carsten P. *s.j.* '77 (NEW) [B] Jersey City, NJ Saint Peter's College; [N] Jersey City, NJ Jesuits of Saint Peter's College, Inc.
Marth, Msgr. Loydell J. '56 (FRS) Buttonwillow, CA St. Mary Church; Taft, CA St. Mary Church.
Marthaler, Andrew '90 (SCL) Elbow Lake, MN St. Olaf Church; Tintah, MN St. Gall's Church.
Marthaler, Berard L. *o.f.m.conv.* '52 (WDC) [5] Washington, DC St. Anthony Church; [B] Washington, DC St. Bonaventure Friary; [C] Washington, DC Catholic University of America, The.
Marti, Thomas J. *m.m.* '65 (SEA) [M] Seattle, WA Maryknoll Fathers.
Marti, Tony *o.f.m.cap.* '96 (LA) [74] Los Angeles, CA St. Lawrence of Brindisi Church.
Martignon, John E. '84 (MAR) Cooks, MI St. Mary Magdalene Church; Garden, MI St. John the Baptist Church; Nahma, MI St. Andrew Church.
Martin, Andrew '67 (CAM) [7] Camden, NJ St. Joseph's Pro-Cathedral.
Martin, Andrew E. '67 (CAM) [A] Cherry Hill, NJ Camden Catholic High School.
Martin, Anselm *o.f.m.cap.* '45 (PH) [79] Philadelphia, PA St. John the Evangelist Church.
Martin, Bernard E. '60 (WDC) [2] Silver Spring, MD St. Bernadette Church.
Martin, C. Lou '76 (BAL) [10] Baltimore, MD St. Anthony of Padua Church; [64] Baltimore, MD Most Precious Blood, Community of Church.
Martin, Charles A. *c.s.p.* '65 (BO) [W] Boston, MA Paulist Fathers Residence.
Martin, Charles A. *c.s.p.* '65 (STP) [29] Minneapolis, MN St. Lawrence Church; [V] Minneapolis, MN University of Minnesota Newman Center and Chapel.
Martin, Clarence A. *s.j.* '46 (ALN) [A] Wernersville, PA Novitiate of St. Isaac Jogues.
Martin, Clifford A. '76 (SFR) Belmont, CA Immaculate Heart of Mary Church.
Martin, Msgr. Daniel J. '43 (E) Retired.
Martin, David A. '76 (EVN) Washington, IN St. Simon Church.
Martin, David L. '73 (ARL) Gordonsville, VA St. Mark's Church; Orange, VA St. John's Church.
Martin, Dean J. '88 (BR) Independence, LA Mater Dolorosa Church.
Martin, Dennis A. '75 (E) Erie, PA St. Vincent's Health Center; [G] Erie, PA Saint Vincent Health Center.
Martin, Dennis C. '67 (DAV) Washington, IA St. James Church.
Martin, Diosdado '66 (LA) [5] Los Angeles, CA Assumption Church; On Duty Outside the Archdiocese.
Martin, Donald J. *s.j.* '62 (NO) [P] New Orleans, LA Jesuit Provincial Office.
Martin, Edward C. *ss.cc.* '77 (HON) Waialua, HI St. Michael Church.
Martin, Edward L. *o.p.* '59 (NY) [DD] New York, NY Dominican Friars' Guild.
Martin, Emilio '52 (MIA) [5] Hialeah, FL St. John the Apostle Church.
Martin, Msgr. F. Gerald '54 (DET) Grosse Pointe Farms, MI St. Paul Catholic Church; [Q] Detroit, MI St. Vincent de Paul Society.
Martin, Francis '43 (LAN) [F] Lansing, MI St. Lawrence Hospital and Healthcare Services.
Martin, Francis *o.s.m.* '48 (STL) Affton, MO Seven Holy Founders Church.
Martin, Francis M. *o.s.m.* '48 (CHI) [N] Chicago, IL Servite Friars - Eastern Province.
Martin, Francis T. '39 (LAN) Retired.
Martin, Francisco '53 (MIA) Miami Lakes, FL Our Lady of the Lakes Church.
Martin, George W. *o.s.f.s.* '71 (PH) [75] Philadelphia, PA St. Joachim Church.
Martin, Gerard R. '73 (BR) [21] Baton Rouge, LA St. Thomas More Church.
Martin, Gilmer J. '74 (NO) [8] Metairie, LA St. Edward the Confessor Church.
Martin, Msgr. Harrison A. '37 (NO) Retired.
Martin, Harry '66 (SAT) San Antonio, TX Audie Murphy VA Hospital.
Martin, Msgr. Ignatius (LAF) Retired.
Martin, J. Dennis *c.m.* '61 (STL) [A] St. Louis, MO Kenrick-Glennon Seminary; [P] St. Louis, MO Vincentian-St. Lazare Residence.
Martin, James A. *s.j.* '34 (WDC) [M] Washington, DC The Jesuit Community at Georgetown University.
Martin, James J. '63 (PH) [59] Philadelphia, PA Holy Family Church.
Martin, James J. '68 (CHI) [27] Chicago, IL St. Benedict the African (West) Church.
Martin, James R. *c.s.c.* '93 (AUS) [24] Austin, TX San Francisco Church.
Martin, Joel W. *o.s.b.* '91 (BIR) [B] Cullman, AL St. Bernard Preparatory School, Inc.; [E] Cullman, AL St. Bernard Abbey.
Martin, John *c.ss.r.* (NY) [42] New York, NY Guardian Angel Church.
Martin, John *o.s.m.* '53 (ORL) Palm Bay, FL Our Lady of Grace Church.
Martin, John *a.a.* '57 (BO) [W] Brighton, MA Assumptionist Center; [W] Brighton, MA Assumptionist Center.
Martin, John B. '65 (NEW) [15] Jersey City, NJ St. Mary's Church.
Martin, John F. *s.j.* '74 (BAL) [M] Baltimore, MD Jesuit Fathers and Brothers Maryland Provincial Curia.
Martin, John H. *s.j.* '41 (SFR) [N] San Francisco, CA Jesuit Community at University of San Francisco.
Martin, John Hilary *o.p.* '55 (OAK) [A] Berkeley, CA Dominican School of Philosophy and Theology; [N] Berkeley, CA St. Thomas Aquinas House.
Martin, John J. *o.s.m.* '53 (CHI) [N] Chicago, IL Servite Friars - Eastern Province.
Martin, John J. '65 (SR) Mendocino, CA St. Anthony Church.
Martin, Msgr. John J. '72 (ALN) Colesville, PA Assumption B.V.M. Church.
Martin, John L. *m.m.* '65 (NY) [Z] Maryknoll, NY Maryknoll Fathers and Brothers.
Martin, John M. *s.j.* '84 (SJ) [2] Santa Clara, CA St. Clare Church.
Martin, Msgr. John P. '48 (WOR) Retired.
Martin, John P. *m.m.* '66 (NY) [Z] Maryknoll, NY Maryknoll Fathers and Brothers.
Martin, Jon C. '65 (BO) [2] Lowell, MA Holy Trinity Church; Essex County, MA Essex County Correctional Facility, Middleton.
Martin, Msgr. Joseph A. '67 (NY) Fishkill, NY Church of St. Mary, Mother of the Church.
Martin, Joseph C. *s.s.* '48 (BAL) Special Assignment; [M] Baltimore, MD Sulpician Provincial House.
Martin, Joseph I. (BO) Society of St. James the Apostle.
Martin, Joseph L. *s.j.* '45 (SJ) [M] Los Gatos, CA California Province of the Society of Jesus, Jesuit Provincial Office; [M] Los Gatos, CA Sacred Heart Jesuit Center.
Martin, Joseph P. '64 (Y) [11] Canton, OH St. Paul's Church.
Martin, Kenneth *s.s.* '89 (WDC) [35] Washington, DC Our Lady of Victory Church.
Martin, Kenneth J. *s.s.* '89 (BAL) [M] Baltimore, MD Sulpician Provincial House.
Martin, Kenneth J. '89 (WIL) On Duty Outside the Diocese.
Martin, Msgr. Kieran J. '50 (BRK) [141] Brooklyn, NY St. Thomas Aquinas Church; Retired.
Martin, Larok Obwano '80 (OKL) [5] Oklahoma City, OK Corpus Christi Church.
Martin, Leon J. *s.a.c.* '75 (MIL) [P] Milwaukee, WI Pallotti House.
Martin, Leonard A. *s.j.* '73 (SCR) [C] Scranton, PA University of Scranton; [E] Scranton, PA Scranton Preparatory School.
Martin, Luis '55 (ELP) [35] El Paso, TX San Antonio Church.
Martin, Malcolm *s.a.* '62 (BO) [P] Brockton, MA Chapel of Our Savior-Catholic Pastoral and Information Center; [W] Brockton, MA Chapel of Our Saviour; [BB] Brockton, MA Chapel of Our Saviour.
Martin, Malcolm *s.a.* '62 (NY) [Z] Garrison, NY Generalate of the Franciscan Friars of the Atonement-St. James Friary.
Martin, Manuel '45 (MIA) [1] Miami Beach, FL St. Francis de Sales Church.
Martin, Marciano G. *c.pp.s.* '64 (SP) [1] Tampa, FL Blessed Sacrament Church.
Martin, Michael *c.s.p.* '79 (GR) Grand Rapids, MI Chapel of St. Paul-Catholic Information Center.
Martin, Michael *o.f.m.conv.* '89 (BAL) [D] Baltimore, MD Archbishop Curley High School; [M] Baltimore,

MD Immaculate Heart of Mary Friary.
Martin, Michael '94 (CHK) San Antonio Village, District 6, MP San Antonio De Padua Parish Church; Saipan, MP San Jude Parish Church.
Martin, Michael '94 (SFR) [1] San Francisco, CA Cathedral of St. Mary (Assumption).
Martin, Msgr. Myron F. '35 (SFS) Retired.
Martin, Norman F. *s.j.* '47 (SJ) [B] Santa Clara, CA Santa Clara University.
Martin, Normand *s.m.* (DET) [E] Harper Woods, MI Notre Dame High School.
Martin, Patrick '78 (NOR) [I] Wauregan, CT Ministry of His Able People.
Martin, Msgr. Paul M. '58 (ORG) San Juan Capistrano, CA (Old Mission) Church.
Martin, Ralph L. '65 (WIL) Smyrna, DE St. Polycarp Church; Smyrna, MD Delaware Home & Hospital for the Chronically Ill.
Martin, Raymond '94 (BAL) Glen Burnie, MD Holy Trinity Church.
Martin, Reginald *o.p.* (SFR) [13] San Francisco, CA St. Dominic Church.
Martin, Reginald E. *o.p.* '74 (OAK) [N] Oakland, CA Western Dominican Province; [N] Oakland, CA Western Dominican Province.
Martin, Reginald E. *o.p.* '74 (SFR) [N] San Francisco, CA St. Dominic Priory.
Martin, Richard B. '66 (ARL) Burke, VA Church of the Nativity.
Martin, Richard J. '63 (CHI) Palos Heights, IL Incarnation Church.
Martin, Robert A. '83 (BUF) [2] Batavia, NY St. Joseph Church; [D] Batavia, NY Notre Dame High School of Batavia.
Martin, Roger (OG) Retired.
Martin, Roosevelt '88 (GAL) [45] Fort Bend Co., TX St. Mark the Evangelist Church.
Martin, Sean C. '81 (DAL) On Duty Outside the Diocese.
Martin, Sean C. '81 (GAL) [A] Houston, TX St. Mary's Seminary.
Martin, Shane P. *s.j.* '92 (LA) [C] Los Angeles, CA Loyola Marymount University.
Martin, Susan (RVC) Seaford, NY St. William, the Abbot Church.
Martin, Thomas *o.c.d.* '61 (MIL) [P] Milwaukee, WI Provincial Offices - Discalced Carmelites.
Martin, Thomas *o.s.a.* '69 (PH) [C] Villanova, PA Villanova University.
Martin, Thomas '70 (OAK) [3] Berkeley, CA St. Joseph The Worker Church.
Martin, Thomas '79 (COL) On Duty Outside the Diocese.
Martin, Thomas A. '79 (KAL) Mendon, MI St. Edward Church.
Martin, Thomas F. '56 (CLV) [24] Cleveland, OH St. Francis Church; [X] Cleveland, OH Diocesan Hispanic Office.
Martin, Thomas F. *o.s.a.* '69 (CHI) [N] Olympia Fields, IL The Augustinian Provincialate Tolentine Center.
Martin, Thomas P. *s.j.* '66 (BAL) [M] Baltimore, MD Jesuit Fathers and Brothers Maryland Provincial Curia.
Martin, Vicente Moreno '75 (CAM) Somers Point, NJ St. Joseph's Church.
Martin, Victor T. '80 (BGP) [7] Fairfield, CT St. Thomas Aquinas Church.
Martin, Vincent *o.s.b.* '36 (LA) [R] Valyermo, CA St. Andrew's Abbey.
Martin, Warren S. *s.j.* '32 (NO) [P] New Orleans, LA Ignatius Residence.
Martin, William *o.m.i.* '61 (PMB) [4] West Palm Beach, FL St. John Fisher Church; [C] West Palm Beach, FL Rosarian Academy.
Martin, Msgr. William C. '47 (SAT) [63] San Antonio, TX St. Pius X Church.
Martin, William F. '78 (STP) Waverly, MN St. Mary Church.
Martin, William J. '50 (TOL) Marysdale, OH Immaculate Conception Church; The Bend, OH St. Stephen Church.
Martin, William J. '55 (CHI) Western Springs, IL St. John of the Cross Church.
Martin, William J. '71 (L) [68] Louisville, KY St. Rita Church.
Martin, Msgr. William L. '56 (GRY) Cedar Lake, IN Holy Name Church.
Martin, Zenaido '91 (ARE) [2] Camuy, PR Our Lady of the Miraculous Medal Church.
Martina, Joseph A., Jr. '89 (SHP) Bastrop, LA St. Joseph Church; Oak Grove, LA Sacred Heart Church.
Martineau, Laurier J. (BO) [3] Marlboro, MA St. Mary Church.
Martineau, Maurice '63 (LKC) Big Lake, LA St. Mary of the Lake Church.
Martinek, John B. '73 (CHI) On Duty Outside the Archdiocese.
Martinek, John B. '73 (FBK) Kotzebue, AK St. Francis Xavier Church.
Martinelli, Januarius *s.a.* '30 (NY) [Z] Garrison, NY Franciscan Friars of the Atonement.
Martinex, Gilbert S. *c.s.p.* '95 (BO) [W] Boston, MA Paulist Fathers Residence.
Martinez, Adam '85 (AUS) Lockhart, TX St. Mary's Church.
Martinez, Alberto '62 (CGS) [13] Barrio Rio Canas, PR Maria Madre de la Iglesia Church.
Martinez, Alfonso '85 (P) Cornelius, OR St. Alexander Church.
Martinez, Alfredo (CGS) Retired.
Martinez, Anthony L. '89 (SFE) Portales, NM St. Helen Church; [M] Portales, NM University Catholic Center - St. Thomas More Chapel.
Martinez, Antonio *o.a.r.* '48 (LSC) [3] Las Cruces, NM Our Lady of Health Church.
Martinez, Antonio Felipe '96 (TUC) Nogales, AZ Sacred Heart Church.
Martinez, Balduino *c.m.* (BRK) [116] Brooklyn, NY St. Peter-St. Paul-Our Lady of Pilar Church; [W] Brooklyn, NY Centro Evangelizacion San Vicente de Paul; [Y] Brooklyn, NY Jornada Movement.
Martinez, Benjamin (CC) On Duty Outside the Diocese.
Martinez, Benjamin *c.m.f.* '58 (MET) [4] Perth Amboy, NJ Our Lady of Fatima Church.
Martinez, Bulmaro Alvarado '88 (YAK) Prosser, WA Sacred Heart Church.
Martinez, Carlos '89 (ORG) [1] Anaheim, CA St. Anthony Claret Church.
Martinez, Celso '52 (SJN) [5] Carolina, PR Santo Cristo de los Milagros Church.
Martinez, Charles (DEN) [1] Denver, CO Cathedral of the Immaculate Conception.
Martinez, Chas. *o.f.m.* '80 (DEN) [M] Denver, CO Holy Trinity Friary.
Martinez, Dario '87 (SJN) [21] Bayamon, PR Nuestra Sra. del Rosario Church.
Martinez, Felipe J. *c.m.* '55 (STL) Brewer, MO Christ the Savior Church.
Martinez, Francisco (ARE) Retired.
Martinez, Francisco *ss.cc.* '58 (SJN) [6] Guaynabo, PR Nuestra Senora de la Paz Church.
Martinez, Francisco X. '90 (CC) Alice, TX St. Joseph Church.
Martinez, Frank R. '82 (DAV) Special Assignment; [M] Davenport, IA St. Vincent Center.
Martinez, Msgr. George W. '46 (SHP) [5] Monroe, LA St. Matthew Church; Retired.
Martinez, German *o.s.b.* '67 (BGP) [1] Greenwich, CT St. Mary's Church.
Martinez, Gilbert *c.s.p.* '95 (MEM) [20] Memphis, TN St. Patrick's Church; [J] Memphis, TN Paulist Fathers (New York).
Martinez, Ignacio *o.f.m.cap.* '60 (FWT) [6] Fort Worth, TX Our Lady of Guadalupe Church.
Martinez, Ignacio '93 (MRY) Watsonville, CA St. Patrick Church.
Martinez, James E. *o.s.a.* '57 (PH) Bryn Mawr, PA Our Mother of Good Counsel Church.
Martinez, Joachim *s.j.* '55 (BO) [3] Somerville, MA St. Benedict Church.
Martinez, John J. *s.j.* '62 (RIC) Dinwiddie County, VA St. John Church.
Martinez, Jose Luis *o.a.r.* '64 (LA) [R] Oxnard, CA St. Augustine Priory O.A.R.
Martinez, Juan *s.d.b.* '73 (SJN) [28] San Juan, PR San Juan Bosco Church.
Martinez, Julian *c.m.* (SJN) [24] San Juan, PR Jesus Maestro Church.
Martinez, Msgr. Leo '63 (SAT) [11] San Antonio, TX Immaculate Conception Church.
Martinez, Leonel *o.s.a.* '46 (GAL) Pasadena, TX Blessed Juan Diego Church.
Martinez, Lorenzo (NSH) Smyrna, TN St. Luke Church.
Martinez, Luis '75 (LA) Van Nuys, CA St. Elisabeth Church.
Martinez, Luis '96 (SR) Napa, CA St. John the Baptist Church.
Martinez, Manuel '66 (SAT) On Duty Outside the Archdiocese.
Martinez, Manuel C. *o.r.c.* '94 (PCE) Adjuntas, PR St. Joachim Church.
Martinez, Marco A. '74 (LA) [R] Los Angeles, CA Guadalupe Missioners Procure.
Martinez, Marcos '52 (CC) [9] Corpus Christi, TX Our Lady of the Pillar Church.
Martinez, Mariano '52 (CC) [10] Laredo, TX Santa Rita De Casia Independent Mission Church.
Martinez, Mark A. '96 (LA) Venice, CA St. Mark Church.
Martinez, Martin S. '93 (TUC) Yuma, AZ Immaculate Conception Church.
Martinez, Michael '89 (TUC) [17] Tucson, AZ St. Monica Church.
Martinez, Otto *s.j.* '63 (MIA) [H] Miami, FL Villa Arrieta.
Martinez, Ramon *o.s.a.* (GAL) Baytown, TX Our Lady of Guadalupe Church.
Martinez, Raymond *c.m.f.* '41 (LA) [R] Rancho Dominguez, CA Dominguez Seminary Inc.
Martinez, Raymond P. '89 (NO) [24] New Orleans, LA St. Andrew the Apostle Church.
Martinez, Roberto *o.f.m.cap.* '96 (PCE) [5] Ponce, PR Santa Teresita Church; [E] Ponce, PR Residencia Asis.
Martinez, Rogelio '67 (SAT) Retired; [K] San Antonio, TX Casa De Padres.
Martinez, Roy *o.f.m.cap.* '84 (ARE) [1] Utuado, PR San Miquel Church.
Martinez, Ruben *o.m.i.* '68 (OAK) [N] Oakland, CA Oblate Provincial House & Procure.
Martinez, Timothy A. '90 (SFE) Mora, NM St. Gertrude Church.
Martinez, Vidal *o.s.m.* '75 (CHI) [N] Chicago, IL Servite Friars - Eastern Province.
Martinez, Vidal *o.s.m.* '75 (ORL) Kissimmee, FL Holy Redeemer Church.
Martinez, Virgilio '65 (SJN) [35] San Juan, PR San Luis Rey Church.
Martinez y Alire, Jerome J. '76 (SFE) [7] Santa Fe, NM Santa Maria de La Paz Catholic Community Church; [N] Albuquerque, NM Fraternidad de Nuestro Padre Jesus Nazareno.
Martinez-Mari, Joaquin *s.j.* '55 (BO) [E] Boston, MA Boston College High School & Jesuit Community.
Martinez-Mata, Jose '89 (ELP) [7] El Paso, TX Cristo Rey Church.
Martini, Alexis *o.f.m.conv.* '41 (L) [6] Louisville, KY St. Anthony Church.
Martini, Ivo '84 (SFS) Highmore, SD St. Mary Church.
Martini, Richard M. '80 (LA) Pacific Palisades, CA Corpus Christi Church.
Martinka, Stanley V. '61 (NU) On Duty Outside the Diocese.
Martinkovic, Joseph '54 (ALN) [2] McAdoo, PA St. Mary Church.
Martino, Msgr. Joseph F. '70 (PH) [A] Wynnewood, PA Theological Seminary of St. Charles Borromeo, Overbrook.
Martino, Nicholas J. '82 (PH) [140] Philadelphia, PA Resurrection of Our Lord Church.
Martino, Steven '87 (SR) On Leave.
Martinosky, Joseph A. '57 (STU) Retired.
Martins, John C. '55 (FR) [13] Fall River, MA St. Anthony of Padua Church.
Martis, Albin A. '43 (WH) Retired.
Martis, Douglas A. '89 (JOL) [1] Joliet, IL The Cathedral of St. Raymond; Hinsdale, IL St. Isaac Jogues Church.
Martis, John *s.j.* '91 (WDC) [M] Washington, DC The Jesuit Community at Georgetown University.
Martlock, Loville N. '63 (BUF) Retired.
Marto, Lawrence T. '88 (GB) [1] Marinette, WI Holy Family Church.
Martocchio, Peter T. '57 (BO) [3] Weymouth, MA Immaculate Conception Church.
Marton, Bernard *o.cist.* '67 (DAL) [M] Irving, TX Cistercian Abbey of Our Lady of Dallas.
Marton, Henry *o.cist.* '49 (DAL) [M] Irving, TX Cistercian Abbey of Our Lady of Dallas.
Martone, James '79 (BR) Darrow, LA St. Anthony of Padua Church; Sorrento, LA St. Anne Church.
Martorano, Nicholas *o.s.a.* '77 (PH) [111] Philadelphia, PA St. Nicholas of Tolentine Church.
Martorell, Jose A. *t.o.r.* '64 (AUS) Satin, TX Santa Rita Shrine Church; [2] Waco, TX St. Francis on the Brazos Church.
Martus, Joseph A. *s.j.* '40 (BO) [W] Weston, MA Campion Health Center, Inc.
Martusciello, Msgr. Joseph A. '54 (BRK) [245] Queens, NY St. Thomas Apostle Church.
Martusevich, Msgr. Vito J. '31 (PH) [49] Philadelphia, PA St. George Church; Retired.
Martyn, George W. *o.s.f.s.* '71 (WIL) [I] Childs, MD Oblates of St. Francis De Sales.
Martyniuk, Joseph '58 (PHU) Cherry Hill, NJ St. Michael's Church.
Martyniuk, Pawlo '92 (STF) [10] Willimantic, CT Protection of B.V.M. Church.
Maruca, Dominic W. *s.j.* '58 (BAL) [M] Baltimore, MD Jesuit Fathers and Brothers Maryland Provincial Curia.
Maruca, Michael J. *s.j.* '90 (BAL) [M] Baltimore, MD Jesuit Fathers and Brothers Maryland Provincial Curia.
Marucci, Msgr. Carl J. '83 (CAM) On Duty Outside the Diocese.
Marucci, Msgr. Carl J. '83 (NY) [2] New York, NY St. Agnes Church.
Marucci, Louis A. '87 (CAM) [N] Blackwood, NJ St. Pius X Spiritual Life Center.
Marullo, Lawrence *v.f.* '75 (OG) Inlet, NY St. Anthony of Padua Church; Old Forge, NY St. Bartholomew Church; Raquette Lake, NY St. William Church.
Marus, Msgr. Andrew G. '71 (BGP) [17] Bridgeport, CT St. Patrick Church.
Marusa, Henry *s.v.d.* '33 (ORG) [H] Santa Ana, CA Divine Word.
Maruscak, Roland *o.f.m.* '41 (ALN) [K] Easton, PA St. Francis Friary.
Marusceac, Vladimir '88 (STF) Cohoes, NY SS. Peter and Paul Church; Troy, NY Protection of B.V.M. Church.
Marut, Paul *o.f.m.conv.* '72 (BAL) [M] Ellicott City, MD

Order of Friars Minor Conventual.
Marut, Thomas '74 (STU) Malvern, OH St. Francis Xavier Church.
Marvin, James J. '48 (ROC) Retired.
Marx, John '60 (ANC) Retired.
Marx, Lambert M. '44 (MAD) Retired.
Marx, Louis '66 (SB) [7] Riverside, CA St. Francis de Sales Church.
Marx, Paul *o.s.b.* '47 (SCL) [I] Collegeville, MN St. John's Abbey, of the Order of St. Benedict.
Marx, Paul B. *o.s.b.* '41 (WDC) [V] Front Royal, VA Human Life International.
Maryanski, Fabian J. '71 (BUF) Absent on Leave.
Maryland, Joseph A. '40 (E) Retired.
Marzen, Msgr. Francis A. '51 (HON) Retired.
Marzheuser, Richard A. '77 (CIN) [B] Cincinnati, OH Mt. St. Mary's Seminary of the West; [B] Cincinnati, OH Mt. St. Mary's Seminary of the West.
Marzilli, Raphael '42 (GBG) On Duty Outside the Diocese.
Marzluf, George J. '46 (COL) Retired.
Marzocchi, Mario *s.s.s.* '84 (CLV) Highland Heights, OH St. Paschal Baylon Church.
Marzocchi, Mario T. '84 (CLV) [P] Cleveland, OH Blessed Sacrament Community.
Marzolf, John G. *s.j.* '66 (ALB) [O] Auriesville, NY Jesuit Retreat House for Priests, Religious and Lay People; [O] Auriesville, NY Shrine of Our Lady of Martyrs.
Marzolf, John G. *s.j.* '66 (NY) [Z] New York, NY Jesuit Seminary and Mission Bureau, Inc. (Jesuit Deferred Funds).
Marzullo, Robert *o.p.* '78 (PHX) [F] Tempe, AZ Dominicans (Dominican Community-Jordan House); [H] Phoenix, AZ Office of Youth and Young Adult Ministries.
Masabakhwa, Raphael '95 (DM) [3] Council Bluffs, IA St. Patrick Church.
Masad, Frederick F. '60 (CHR) [5] Columbia, SC St. John Neumann Church.
Masakowski, Edward M. '57 (SCR) Glen Lyon, PA St. Adalbert's Church.
Masakowski, Msgr. John C. '49 (SCR) [2] Plymouth, PA St. John the Baptist Church.
Masar, Joseph G. '89 (SD) Brawley, CA Sacred Heart Church.
Mascardo, Editho '83 (STO) [4] Stockton, CA St. George Church.
Mascarella, Patrick J. '66 (BR) [6] Baton Rouge, LA Christ the King Church; [K] Baton Rouge, LA Christ the King Parish and Catholic Student Center.
Mascarenhas, Oswald A. *s.j.* '66 (DET) [K] Detroit, MI Jesuit Community at the University of Detroit.
Mascareno, Jose Ramon *o.s.b.* '81 (BIR) [E] Cullman, AL St. Bernard Abbey.
Mascari, Michael A. *o.p.* '87 (STL) [P] St. Louis, MO St. Dominic Priory.
Mascari, Peter '52 (SFD) Retired.
Mascherino, Alphonse '76 (ALT) Absent on Leave.
Maschmann, Elvan *o.f.m.* '46 (STL) [R] St. Louis, MO Villa Gesu.
Masciarelli, Rudolph '49 (BO) Society of St. James the Apostle; Retired.
Masciocchi, Robert *c.s.s.* '54 (BO) [Y] Waltham, MA Espousal Retreat House and Conference Center; [Z] Waltham, MA Stigmatine Fathers and Brothers.
Mascioli, Joseph M. *v.f.* '57 (WH) Grafton, WV St. Augustine Church.
Mascolino, Charles E. '54 (STU) Barnesville, OH Assumption Church; Temperanceville, OH St. Mary's Church.
Mascolino, Robert A. '45 (STU) Retired.
Masek, James J. '74 (CLV) [54] Cleveland, OH Our Lady of Lourdes Church.
Masello, David W. '78 (PRO) [1] Warren, RI St. Alexander Church.
Mash, Wesley M. '90 (PBR) Charleroi, PA Holy Ghost Church.
Masiar, Paul E. '69 (ALN) [3] Saint Clair, PA Immaculate Conception Church; Coaldale, PA Coaldale State Hospital.
Masich, Emil G. '45 (PRM) Retired.
Masiello, Johon *s.d.b.* '58 (NEW) [3] Elizabeth, NJ St. Anthony's Church.
Masiello, Joseph P. '69 (NEW) Westfield, NJ Holy Trinity Church.
Masin, Richard H. '85 (CC) On Duty Outside the Diocese.
Maskell, A. Joseph (BAL) Absent on Leave.
Maskell, Stephen J. *m.m.* '48 (SJ) [M] Los Altos, CA Maryknoll.
Maslach, Paul *o.f.m.* '62 (CHI) [189] Chicago, IL Sacred Heart Church.
Maslak, Gregory '72 (PHU) Pottstown, PA St. Michael's Church; Reading, PA Nativity of Blessed Virgin Mary Church.
Maslar, George *o.f.m.conv.* '63 (BAL) [M] Ellicott City, MD Order of Friars Minor Conventual.
Maslar, William J. '56 (ALN) [1] Mahanoy City, PA Assumption B.V.M. Church; [6] Mahanoy City, PA Sacred Heart Church.
Maslejak, Andrzej *s.ch.* '79 (DET) [K] Sterling Heights, MI Society of Christ Provincial Home.
Maslinski, Reginald *o.f.m.* '44 (MIL) [P] Burlington, WI Queen of Peace Friary.
Maslowski, Krzysztof '88 (NEW) Cranford, NJ St. Michael's Church.
Maslowski, Stanley '63 (STP) North St. Paul, MN St. Peter Church.
Maslowsky, Michael '86 (P) [5] Portland, OR St. Anthony Church.
Masluk, Alexander (PH) [132] Philadelphia, PA Our Mother of Sorrows Church.
Masnicki, Marek '92 (NOR) Old Saybrook, CT St. John Church.
Maso, Dario *s.x.* '82 (PAT) [M] Wayne, NJ Xaverian Missionary Fathers.
Mason, Albert M. (BO) Awaiting Assignment.
Mason, Brian G. '93 (MIL) [53] Milwaukee, WI St. Matthias Church.
Mason, Charlon O. '79 (GR) Pewamo, MI St. Joseph's Church.
Mason, Dennis *o.f.m.conv.* '78 (TR) Riverside, NJ St. Casimir Church.
Mason, Edward J. '87 (BRK) Absent on Leave.
Mason, James E. '67 (LC) On Duty Outside the Diocese.
Mason, James H. '80 (SD) Leave of Absence.
Mason, Mark (OKL) [5] Oklahoma City, OK Corpus Christi Church; Special Assignment.
Mason, Robert '56 (NY) Massapequa Park, NY Our Lady of Lourdes Church.
Mason, Robert E. '56 (RVC) Massapequa Park, NY Our Lady of Lourdes Church.
Mason, William *o.m.i.* '71 (CHI) [174] Chicago, IL Precious Blood Church.
Mass, Ronald J. '70 (CHI) Hometown, IL Our Lady of Loretto Church.
Massa, James (BO) [A] Weston, MA Pope John XXIII National Seminary.
Massa, Mark S. *s.j.* '80 (DET) [K] Detroit, MI Jesuit Provincial Office-Detroit Province of the Society of Jesus.
Massa, Mark S. *s.j.* '80 (NY) [Z] New York, NY Jesuit Community at Fordham University.
Massacavalo, Bruno '77 (JOL) Absent on Sick Leave.
Massanet, Louis '93 (VEN) [1] Naples, FL St. Ann Church.
Massar, Richard A. '69 (BUF) [2] Cheektowaga, NY Infant of Prague Church.
Massarella, Francis A. '46 (CIN) Retired; [L] Dayton, OH Mercy Siena Woods.
Massaro, Gabriel *o.f.m.cap.* '66 (NY) [Z] Garrison, NY St. Francis Friary.
Massaro, Joseph *c.s.s.* '48 (SPR) [9] Springfield, MA Our Lady of Mt. Carmel Church.
Massaro, Michael A. *c.s.c.* '81 (NOR) [C] Baltic, CT Academy and Boarding-School of the Holy Family.
Massaro, Thomas J. *s.j.* '93 (BO) [W] Boston, MA The Society of Jesus of New England-Provincial Offices.
Massaro, Thomas J. *s.j.* '93 (WDC) [M] Washington, DC Leonard Neale House.
Massart, James '66 (GB) Special Assignment.
Massett, Msgr. Robert D. '66 (NO) [12] Metairie, LA St. Mary Magdalen Church.
Massetti, Philip '76 (SAC) [16] Sacramento, CA St. Mary Church.
Massey, Robert E. '73 (MIL) [1] Wauwatosa, WI St. Bernard's Church; Special Assignment.
Massi, Anthony '84 (MIA) [13] Miami, FL Our Lady of Lourdes Church.
Massicotte, Bernard *o.s.b.cam.* '57 (MRY) [G] Big Sur, CA New Camaldoli Hermitage.
Massie, Daniel J. '80 (MIL) [1] West Allis, WI St. Aloysius Church.
Massie, Guy '83 (BRK) [98] Brooklyn, NY Our Lady Help of Christians Church; [E] Brooklyn, NY Office of the Superintendent of Schools.
Massie, Guy A. '83 (BRK) Special Assignment.
Massimino, Jerome *o.f.m.* '77 (HRT) [14] Hartford, CT St. Patrick-St. Anthony Church.
Massingale, Bryan N. '83 (MIL) [A] Milwaukee, WI Saint Francis Seminary.
Massion, John C. '56 (CHI) Wheeling, IL St. Joseph the Worker Church.
Massmann, Albert *o.s.b.* '54 (OM) [K] Elkhorn, NE Mount Michael Abbey.
Masson, Paul R. *m.m.* '72 (GAL) [Q] Houston, TX Maryknoll Fathers and Brothers.
Massoth, Charles *o.s.b.* '51 (OKL) Shawnee, OK St. Benedict Church.
Massucci, Joseph D. '70 (CIN) [D] Dayton, OH The University of Dayton.
Massucci, Joseph D. '70 (STU) On Duty Outside the Diocese.
Massung, Francis G. '40 (PIT) Retired; [N] Pittsburgh, PA St. John Vianney Manor.
Mast, Paul '72 (WIL) Hockessin, DE St. Mary of the Assumption Church.
Mastalir, Peter W. '92 (GB) Shawano, WI Sacred Heart Church.
Masters, Andrew *s.v.d.* '34 (CHI) [B] Techny, IL Divine Word Residence.
Masters, Gerard G. '66 (HRT) [4] Torrington, CT St. Peter's Church.
Masterson, Clyde (CC) On Duty Outside the Diocese.
Masterson, Clyde G. '85 (MAN) Absent on Sick Leave.
Masterson, Frank D. *s.j.* '53 (P) [D] Portland, OR Jesuit High School.
Masterson, Harold J. *c.s.p.* '37 (NY) [Z] Scarsdale, NY Paulist Fathers Generalate.
Masterson, John J. '57 (WIL) Bethany Beach, DE St. Ann Church.
Masterson, Thomas D. *s.j.* '64 (SCR) [C] Scranton, PA University of Scranton.
Mastey, Gregory J. '95 (SCL) Alexandria, MN St. Mary's Church.
Mastey, Walter S. '40 (GRY) Retired.
Mastrangelo, Joseph A. '40 (PIT) Retired.
Mastrangelo, Mario *o.f.m.cap.* '58 (SJN) [B] Rio Piedras, PR Fraternidad Santa Maria de Los Angeles.
Mastrangelo, Nicholas M. '64 (PIT) Monaca, PA St. John the Baptist Church.
Mastria, Angelo *o.carm.* '58 (TUC) [D] Tucson, AZ Social Service Agencies: Pima County; [F] Tucson, AZ Carmelite Priory.
Mastrian, Mark J. '87 (E) [3] Oil City, PA St. Joseph Church; Polk, PA Polk Center.
Mastrobuono, Peter *s.c.j.* '66 (GAL) Sweeny, TX Our Lady of Perpetual Help Church.
Mastroeni, Anthony '72 (PAT) On Duty Outside the Diocese.
Mastroeni, Anthony '72 (STU) [A] Steubenville, OH Franciscan University of Steubenville.
Mastrolia, Arthur '87 (NY) [A] New York, NY Cathedral Preparatory Seminary; [A] New York, NY Cathedral Preparatory Seminary.
Mastrovito, Francis *t.o.r.* '51 (OWN) Central City, KY St. Joseph Church.
Maszkiewicz, Msgr. Mark '36 (TLS) Retired.
Mata, Antonio *o.c.d.* '46 (CGS) [2] Caguas, PR San Jose Church.
Matanic, George M. *o.p.* '70 (OAK) [4] Berkeley, CA St. Mary Magdalen Church; [N] Oakland, CA Western Dominican Province.
Matano, Msgr. Salvatore R. '71 (PRO) [7] Providence, RI St. Augustine's Church.
Matarazzo, Francis '67 (PAT) [3] Clifton, NJ St. Brendan Church; Passaic, NJ Passiac General Hospital.
Matarazzo, Salvatore *o.p.* '60 (NY) Valhalla, NY Holy Name of Jesus Church.
Matas, Msgr. Juan '65 (LA) Montebello, CA Our Lady of the Miraculous Medal Church.
Matash, Msgr. Edward M. '56 (NEW) [4] Bayonne, NJ St. Joseph's Church.
Matei, Andrei '84 (ROM) Chesterland, OH Most Holy Trinity Church; Cleveland, OH St. Helena Church; Lorain, OH St. Basil Church.
Matejek, Wladyslav *o.f.m. conv.* (BO) [55] Boston, MA Our Lady of Czestochowa Church; [3] Chelsea, MA St. Stanislaus Church.
Matejune, Gerald *c.p.* '38 (HRT) [M] West Hartford, CT Holy Family Monastery/Retreat.
Mateljan, Roy A. '67 (MIL) [C] Fond du Lac, WI Marian College of Fond du Lac.
Mateo, Arturo *m.s.c.* '76 (SJ) San Jose, CA Alexian Brothers Hospital; [H] San Jose, CA Alexian Brothers Hospital.
Mateo, Jose *sch.p.* '49 (PCE) [4] Ponce, PR Our Lady of Mt. Carmel Church.
Mateo, Mateo *ss.cc.* (SJN) [9] Guaynabo, PR Sagrados Corazones Church.
Mateo, Miguel *s.f.* '81 (SFE) Chimayo, NM Holy Family Church.
Mateos, Francisco *c.m.* '58 (LA) [29] Los Angeles, CA Our Lady of the Rosary of Talpa Church.
Mateos, Tomas '45 (BWN) Retired; [I] McAllen, TX Secular Franciscan Order, Fraternity of Our Lady of Guadalupe.
Matera, Frank J. '68 (HRT) On Duty Outside the Archdiocese.
Matera, Frank J. '68 (WDC) [C] Washington, DC Catholic University of America, The.
Matera, Philip T. '51 (TR) Retired.
Maternoski, Robert '62 (JOL) [2] Lockport, IL St. Dennis Church.
Mateus, Norberto '81 (ATL) [12] Atlanta, GA Shrine of the Immaculate Conception Church.
Matheis, Joseph *m.m.* '56 (HON) [H] Honolulu, HI Maryknoll Fathers House.
Matheny, William K., Jr. '96 (WH) Beckley, WV St. Francis De Sales Church.
Mathes, Thomas '84 (B) Leave of Absence.
Mathesius, William P. '76 (WIL) Secretary, MD Our Lady of Good Counsel Church.
Matheson, Paul V. '47 (DET) Retired.
Mathew, Armand *o.m.i.* '49 (WDC) [B] Washington, DC Oblates of Mary Immaculate, De Mazenod Residence.
Mathews, Abraham '79 (TYL) Atlanta, TX St. Catherine of Siena Church.
Mathews, James D. '62 (SY) [19] Syracuse, NY St. Lucy Church.

Mathews, Kenneth M. '78 (ALX) [1] Alexandria, LA St. Francis Xavier Cathedral.
Mathews, Paul *s.m.* '60 (B) Nampa, ID St. Paul's Church.
Mathews, Robert A. '64 (OAK) [10] Oakland, CA St. Jarlath's Church.
Mathewson, Dean '73 (COL) Newark, OH St. Francis de Sales Church.
Mathewson, Robert B. *s.j.* '62 (SFR) [N] San Francisco, CA Jesuit Community at University of San Francisco.
Mathias, Edwin J. '67 (TR) Browns Mills, NJ St. Ann Church.
Mathias, Gregory A. '91 (FR) Norton, MA St. Mary's Church.
Mathias, Victor '71 (AUS) Lexington, TX Holy Family Church; Rockdale, TX St. Joseph's Church.
Mathie, D. Edward *s.j.* '68 (MIL) [P] Milwaukee, WI Jesuit Provincial Office, Wisconsin Province; [P] Milwaukee, WI Jesuit Community at Marquette University.
Mathieu, Rene T. '77 (PRT) [2] Lewiston, ME Holy Cross Church.
Mathieu, Robert '76 (GLP) Springerville, AZ St. Peter Church.
Mathis, George *glmy.* '55 (CIN) [M] Fairfield, OH Headquarters of Glenmary Home Missioners.
Mathis, R. Paul '72 (SY) Lee Center, NY St. Joseph Church.
Matienzo, Msgr. Rafael '68 (SJN) [16] Carolina, PR Ntra. Sra. Reina de los Angeles Church.
Matlak, Marion A. '43 (CHI) [46] Chicago, IL St. Cornelius Church; Retired.
Matlenga, Joseph '40 (DET) Retired.
Matocha, Msgr. Edward C. '45 (AUS) [1] Austin, TX St. Mary's Cathedral; Special Assignments.
Matocha, Msgr. John L. '47 (SAT) Retired.
Matonti, Charles '60 (BRK) Released from Diocesan Assignment.
Matos, David Diaz '79 (CGS) Humacao, PR Dulce Nombre de Jesus Church.
Matrishion, Joseph (PSC) Leave of Absence.
Matro, Justin M. *o.s.b.* '89 (GBG) [A] Latrobe, PA St. Vincent Seminary; [H] Latrobe, PA Saint Vincent Archabbey.
Matsko, John M. '39 (PH) Bridgeport, PA Our Mother of Sorrows Church; Retired.
Matson, Mark *c.r.* (DEN) [A] Denver, CO Provincial House at St. Andrew, Seminary (C.R.).
Matt, Erwin H. '56 (MIL) Retired.
Matt, Joseph H. '74 (KC) Belton, MO St. Sabina's Church.
Matt, Thomas S. '86 (OM) Absent on Leave.
Matta, Pablo (ELP) Horizon City, TX Holy Spirit Church.
Mattaliano, James *s.j.* '90 (BO) [3] Newton, MA St. Ignatius Church; [W] Chestnut Hill, MA The Jesuit Community at Boston College.
Mattas, Louis S. '60 (SAL) Abilene, KS St. Andrew's Church.
Mattath, Joseph *c.m.i.* '64 (SY) [2] Endicott, NY St. Ambrose Church.
Matte, Richard O. '64 (BO) Absent on Sick Leave.
Mattei, Msgr. Saverio C. '55 (RVC) Dix Hills, NY St. Matthew Church.
Matteo, James P. '72 (PH) [76] Philadelphia, PA St. Joan of Arc Church.
Mattern, Joseph A. '59 (GB) Omro, WI St. Mary Church.
Matteucig, Joseph *s.x.* '84 (PAT) [M] Wayne, NJ Xaverian Missionary Fathers.
Mattey, Joseph J. '65 (SCR) Taylor, PA St. John the Baptist Church.
Matthew, Augustine *c.m.i.* '81 (NY) [6] Mt. Vernon, NY SS. Peter and Paul Church.
Matthews, Donald C. *s.j.* '63 (NY) [Z] New York, NY Jesuit Community at Fordham University.
Matthews, Edward *o.m.i.* (JUN) Wrangell, AK St. Rose of Lima Church.
Matthews, Francis *o.f.m.* '88 (NY) [35] New York, NY St. Francis of Assisi Church.
Matthews, James '74 (OAK) [5] Oakland, CA St. Benedict Church.
Matthews, Ron '75 (ALX) On Duty Outside the Diocese.
Matthews, Ron '75 (SHP) Bossier City, LA Christ the King Church.
Matthiesen, Msgr. Monroe J. '43 (AMA) [D] Panhandle, TX St. Ann's Nursing Home; [D] Panhandle, TX St. Joseph's Home for Retired Priests.
Matthys, Donald R. *s.j.* '68 (MIL) [P] Milwaukee, WI Jesuit Community at Marquette University.
Mattice, George F. (SY) Special Assignment.
Mattie, Msgr. John G. '36 (SEA) Retired.
Mattiello, Lucian C. '45 (ALT) Retired.
Mattimoe, Edward J. *s.j.* '65 (DET) [K] Detroit, MI Jesuit Provincial Office-Detroit Province of the Society of Jesus.
Mattimoe, Edward J. *s.j.* '65 (NY) [Z] New York, NY "America;" Residence and publication office of the America Press.
Mattimore, John J. *s.j.* '88 (NY) [74] New York, NY St. Michael Church; [F] New York, NY Fordham Preparatory School; [Z] New York, NY Jesuit Community at Fordham University.
Mattimore, William F. '51 (HON) Kahuku, HI St. Roch Church.
Mattimore, William F. '51 (WOR) On Duty Outside the Diocese.
Mattina, Louis A. '95 (MET) Bound Brook, NJ St. Joseph Church.
Mattingly, Allen J. *o.s.b.* '57 (PEO) [A] Peru, IL St. Bede Abbey and Academy.
Mattingly, Basil *o.s.b.* '46 (SD) [H] Oceanside, CA Prince of Peace Abbey, Benet Hill.
Mattingly, Jerry Alan '95 (JKS) Natchez, MS St. Mary Church.
Mattingly, John F. *s.s.* '48 (SFR) [A] Menlo Park, CA St. Patrick Seminary; [A] Menlo Park, CA St. Patrick Seminary.
Mattingly, John S. '72 (WDC) Newtowne, MD St. Francis Xavier Church.
Mattingly, Lawrence *o.f.m.conv.* '64 (AUS) [3] Austin, TX Cristo Rey Church.
Mattingly, Martin '50 (OWN) Dawson Springs, KY Resurrection Church; Earlington, KY Immaculate Conception Church.
Mattingly, Robert '68 (VEN) Murdock, FL St. Maximilian Kolbe Church.
Mattioni, George *o.a.r.* '53 (NY) Suffern, NY Good Samaritan Hospital; [B] Suffern, NY Tagaste Monastery; [S] Suffern, NY Good Samaritan Hospital of Suffern
Mattison, James H. '78 (BUR) Barton, VT Conversion of St. Paul Church.
Mattison, Thomas V. '82 (BUR) Fairfield, VT St. Patrick Church.
Mattler, Albert A. '56 (STL) Flint Hill, MO St. Theodore Church
Mattosha, Mansour '73 (OLD) Jacksonville, FL St. Ephrem Church.
Mattosha, Mansour '73 (STA) [21] Jacksonville, FL Syriac Antiochian-Rite Mission St. Ephrem Church.
Mattscheck, John J. '53 (CIN) [38] Cincinnati, OH St. Ignatius Loyola Church; [V] Cincinnati, OH Priests Eucharistic League.
Mattucci, James J. (MAD) Retired; [H] Janesville, WI St. Elizabeth Home.
Mattulke, Arthur (BUF) Blossom, NY St. Gabriel Church.
Matula, Lawrence *v.f.* '62 (VIC) El Campo, TX St. Robert Bellarmine Church.
Matula, Stanley '59 (SY) [9] Syracuse, NY Sacred Heart Church.
Matulenas, Raymond A. *o.s.b.* '40 (PEO) [A] Peru, IL St. Bede Abbey and Academy.
Matulewicz, Ronald '59 (ALB) Hagaman, NY St. Stephen Church.
Matulik, Martin '52 (Y) Retired.
Matulis, Albert J. '58 (NEW) [8] Bayonne, NJ St. Michael's Church.
Maturi, John Alexander Gregory *o.p.* (NY) Manhattan, NY Hospital for Special Surgery; [Z] New York, NY St. Catherine of Siena Priory.
Maturi, John Alexander Gregory *o.p.* '94 (NY) [22] New York, NY St. Catherine of Siena Church.
Matus, Walter J. '70 (AUS) Killeen, TX St. Joseph's Church.
Matusak, Michael W. '75 (GBG) Kent, PA Church of the Good Shepherd.
Matusz, Michael A. '89 (CLV) [4] Garfield Heights, OH St. Timothy Church; Cleveland, OH Meridia South Pointe Hospital.
Matuszak, Walter L. '58 (BUF) [11] Cheektowaga, NY Resurrection Church.
Matuszewski, Ramon '57 (SAG) Pinconning, MI St. Michael Church.
Matutis, Joseph J. '41 (HRT) Retired.
Matveenko, Michael J. '82 (CAM) Woodbury Heights, NJ St. Margaret's Church.
Maty, Robert J. '57 (BGP) [4] Trumbull, CT St. Theresa's Church.
Matya, Robert A. '95 (LIN) Hastings, NE St. Cecilia's Church.
Matyas, Francis B. '42 (STL) Retired.
Matyas, William T. *o.s.b.* '53 (CLV) Broadview Heights, OH Assumption Church; [P] Cleveland, OH Benedictine Order of Cleveland.
Matysik, Robert T. '84 (CAM) Somers Point, NJ St. Joseph's Church.
Matz, David *c.pp.s.* '95 (SAN) [3] Abilene, TX St. Francis of Assisi Church; [4] Abilene, TX St. Vincent Pallotti Church.
Matz, George A. '66 (KCK) Garnett, KS Holy Angels Church.
Matz, Joseph A. '64 (SCR) Jessup, PA St. Michael's Church.
Matz, Leo '61 (MRY) Retired.
Matz, Michael J. '84 (PH) Bryn Mawr, PA St. John Neumann Church.
Matzek, William J. '63 (LC) Onalaska, WI St. Patrick Church.
Matzinger, Robert J. *c.s.b.* '57 (GAL) Sugar Land, TX St. Theresa Church.
Matzko, David G. *s.j.* '79 (OM) [K] Omaha, NE Jesuit Community At Creighton University.
Mau, Joseph '39 (LAF) Retired.
Mau, Nguyen Duc *c.ss.r.* '70 (LA) [R] Baldwin Park, CA Vietnamese Redemptorist Mission.
Mauck, George A. '77 (BEL) Carlyle, IL St. Mary Church.
Maudlin, Stanislaus *o.s.b.* '42 (SFS) [F] Marvin, SD Blue Cloud Abbey.
Mauel, James E. *s.j.* '57 (MIL) [P] Milwaukee, WI Jesuit Community at Marquette University; [Q] Milwaukee, WI St. Joseph Convent, General Motherhouse of the School Sisters of St. Francis; [S] Milwaukee, WI Cardoner Retreat Center.
Mauel, John N. '50 (LC) Retired.
Mauer, Elmar *o.m.i.* '64 (BEL) Centreville, IL Immaculate Conception Church.
Maufort, Msgr. Richard A. '54 (GB) Special Assignment.
Maughan, Michael *s.m.a.* '43 (BEL) Enfield, IL St. Patrick Church.
Maughan, Richard N. '72 (NO) [10] Metairie, LA St. Lawrence the Martyr Church.
Maul, William '55 (SFD) Raymond, IL St Raymond Church.
Maullon, Alberto A., Jr. '82 (GAL) Katy, TX St. Bartholomew Church.
Maung, Chrysostom Ah (WCH) Columbus, KS St. Rose Church; Scammon, KS St. Bridget's Church.
Maung, John S. '63 (IND) Shelbyville, IN St. Joseph Church.
Mauntel, Robert J. '49 (CIN) Retired.
Maurer, Edward L. '69 (BRK) [242] Queens, NY St. Stanislaus Kostka Church.
Maurer, Paul F. '43 (PH) [44] Philadelphia, PA Epiphany of Our Lord Church; Retired.
Maurer, Russell J. '60 (PIT) Blawnox, PA St. Edward Church.
Maurer, Thomas *s.d.s.* '64 (NSH) Dover, TN St. Francis of Assisi Church.
Mauricci, Bruno *o.p.* '90 (PHX) [5] Phoenix, AZ Most Holy Trinity Church.
Mauriello, Matthew R. '88 (BGP) Monroe, CT St. Jude Church.
Mauritzen, Joseph '96 (FR) Orleans, MA St. Joan of Arc Church.
Maurizio, Joseph D. '86 (ALT) [19] Johnstown, PA St. Andrew's Church.
Maus, Christopher '93 (DET) [42] Detroit, MI St. Jude Church.
Maus, LeRoy '66 (P) Sheridan, OR Federal Correctional Institution.
Maus, LeRoy '66 (SCL) On Duty Outside the Diocese.
Maus, Marc T. '91 (STP) Little Canada, MN St. John the Evangelist Church; Monticello, MN St. Henry Church.
Maus, Omer *o.s.b.* '45 (SCL) [I] Collegeville, MN St. John's Abbey, of the Order of St. Benedict.
Maus, Msgr. Rudolph E. '39 (LR) Retired.
Mausolf, James H. '50 (GAY) Retired.
Mauthe, Richard '58 (GB) Dyckesville, WI St. Louis Church.
Mavs, Jasper *o.f.m.* '39 (SAT) [T] San Antonio, TX Pilgrim Center of Hope - Evangelization Center.
Mawicke, Joseph '63 (SB) Thousand Palms, CA St. Philip the Apostle Church.
Mawn, Benedict *c.p.* '45 (MET) [H] South River, NJ Passionist Provincial Office.
Mawn, Francis X. '82 (BO) [2] Chelsea, MA St. Rose Church.
Maxa, Edward J. '59 (CHI) [92] Chicago, IL Immaculate Conception Church.
Maxfield, Leo *m.s.* '55 (FR) [K] Attleboro, MA La Salette Shrine.
Maxwell, Bruce C. *o.s.c.* '75 (DET) [K] Riverview, MI Crosier Community of Riverview.
Maxwell, John '59 (OAK) El Cerrito, CA St. John the Baptist Church.
Maxwell, Palmer *o.c.d.* '88 (SAT) [H] San Antonio, TX Santa Rosa Health Care System.
May, Anthony C. '75 (SD) Lakeside, CA Blessed Kateri Tekakwitha Church.
May, Douglas *m.m.* '86 (BUF) [O] Buffalo, NY Maryknoll House.
May, Herbert '75 (LKC) Welsh, LA Our Lady of the Seven Dolors Church.
May, James *c.ss.r.* '41 (ALB) [L] Saratoga Springs, NY St. John Neumann Residence.
May, James *c.ss.r.* '41 (NY) [92] New York, NY Our Lady of Perpetual Help Church.
May, Michael K. *s.j.* '93 (STL) [C] St. Louis, MO Saint Louis University; [P] St. Louis, MO Jesuit Community Corporation at St. Louis University - Jesuit Hall.
May, Raymond '93 (KCK) [J] Lawrence, KS St. Lawrence Catholic Campus Center at the University of Kansas and Residence.
May, Ronald P. '86 (HRT) Collinsville, CT St. Patrick's Church.
May, Thomas P. '83 (CHI) [108] Chicago, IL St. John Fisher Church.

Maya, Manuel *o.s.m.* '58 (ORG) Fullerton, CA St. Philip Benizi Church.
Maya, Tulio *s.d.s.* '56 (PHX) [17] Phoenix, AZ St. Mark Church; Phoenix, AZ Maricopa Medical Center.
Mayall, Daniel G. '77 (CHI) [64] Chicago, IL St. Francis Borgia Church.
Maybrier, Michael J. '86 (WCH) Chanute, KS St. Patrick Church; Humboldt, KS St. Joseph Church.
Mayefske, Thomas '62 (GB) On Duty Outside the Diocese.
Mayer, Arthur *o.s.b.* '46 (PAT) [M] Morristown, NJ St. Mary's Abbey.
Mayer, Charles P. '96 (LA) Northridge, CA Our Lady of Lourdes Church.
Mayer, Douglas J. '86 (GRY) Valparaiso, IN Our Lady of Sorrows Church; [O] Valparaiso, IN Newman Apostolate-Valparaiso University.
Mayer, James *o.de.m.* '93 (BUF) [O] LeRoy, NY Order of the BVM of Mercy/Mercedarian Friars; [O] LeRoy, NY St. Raymond Nonnatus Novitiate.
Mayer, John L. '64 (STL) Millwood, MO St. Alphonsus Church.
Mayer, Jules A. '64 (LA) [77] Los Angeles, CA St. Marcellinus Church.
Mayer, Kenneth H. *o.s.b.* '42 (PAT) [M] Morristown, NJ St. Mary's Abbey.
Mayer, Laurence A. *o.praem.* '65 (GB) [I] De Pere, WI St. Norbert Abbey.
Mayer, Msgr. Richard G. '61 (E) West Middlesex, PA Good Shepherd Church.
Mayer, Walter W. '59 (OAK) Livermore, CA St. Michael's Church.
Mayer, William J. *s.j.* '74 (PMB) [3] West Palm Beach, FL St. Ann Church.
Mayers, Gregory *c.ss.r.* '70 (AMA) [H] Amarillo, TX Bishop DeFalco Retreat Center.
Mayfield, Olin W. '96 (LA) Diamond Bar, CA St. Denis Church.
Mayhew, John A. *c.j.* '65 (LA) Santa Maria, CA St. Louis de Montfort Church; [B] Santa Maria, CA St. Joseph Seminary (Josephite Fathers' Novitiate).
Maynard, George C. *s.j.* '61 (DET) [K] Detroit, MI Jesuit Provincial Office-Detroit Province of the Society of Jesus.
Maynard, George C. *s.j.* '61 (LEX) Lexington, KY Veterans Administration Hospital.
Maynard, Jack *s.f.o.* '78 (COL) Lancaster, OH St. Mary Church.
Maynard, Leo E. '47 (HRT) Retired.
Maynard, Leon C. '54 (PRO) Retired; [P] Providence, RI St. John Vianney Residence.
Maynard, Lewis H. '69 (BRK) [2] Brooklyn, NY St. Agatha's Church.
Maynard, Richard C. '56 (PRO) [11] Pawtucket, RI Sacred Heart Church.
Maynard, Robert J. '48 (PRO) [7] Cranston, RI St. Paul Church; Retired.
Mayne, Kenneth '94 (LAF) Abbeville, LA St. Mary Magdalen Church.
Mayo, Aiden J. '76 (P) Sandy, OR St. Michael Church.
Mayo, James M. '79 (SAV) [3] Savannah, GA St. Benedict the Moor Church.
Mayo, Joseph M. '73 (SLC) [2] Kearns, UT St. Francis Xavier Church; [C] Kearns, UT St. Francis Xavier Regional School.
Mayo, Reid C. '63 (BUR) Rutland, VT Christ the King Church.
Mayoros, George A. '79 (PH) [33] Philadelphia, PA St. Charles Borromeo Church.
Mayotte, Allan J. '60 (MAR) Wakefield, MI Immaculate Conception of the Blessed Virgin Mary Church.
Mayovsky, Frederick P. *s.j.* '75 (SEA) [C] Tacoma, WA Bellarmine Preparatory School.
Mayovsky, Gerald L. '59 (SEA) [30] Seattle, WA Our Lady of Lourdes Church; Tukwila, WA St. Thomas Church.
Mayworm, James A. '64 (DET) Centerline, MI St. Clement Church.
Mayzik, James J. *s.j.* '85 (BGP) [A] Fairfield, CT Fairfield University; [O] Fairfield, CT The Fairfield Jesuit Community-Fairfield University.
Mazaika, Joseph J. '53 (TLS) Retired.
Mazanec, James F. '81 (CLV) Chagrin Falls, OH St. Joan of Arc Church.
Maziarz, Edward A. *c.pp.s.* '40 (CIN) [M] Dayton, OH Provincial House of the Cincinnati Province of the Society of the Precious Blood.
Mazon, Diego *o.f.m.* '60 (GLP) [2] Gallup, NM St. Francis of Assisi Church.
Mazouch, Charles J. '73 (DOD) Great Bend, KS St. Rose of Lima Church.
Mazuchowski, Hyacinth '63 (BEL) Flora, IL St. Stephen Church.
Mazuelas, Paulino *o.s.b.* '54 (MGZ) [6] Mayaquez, PR Sacred Heart Church; [6] Mayaquez, PR Sacred Heart Church.
Mazur, Clarence *o.f.m.* '42 (GRY) [K] Cedar Lake, IN Our Lady of Lourdes Friary.
Mazur, Francis X. '76 (BUF) Grand Island, NY St. Stephen Church.
Mazur, Robert C. '76 (ALT) [1] Altoona, PA Cathedral of the Blessed Sacrament.
Mazur, Timothy P. '95 (DET) [3] Sterling Heights, MI St. Ephrem Church.
Mazurek, James K. (DET) [A] Orchard Lake, MI SS. Cyril and Methodius Seminary; [C] Orchard Lake, MI Saint Mary's College.
Mazurek, James K. (PIT) On Duty Outside the Diocese.
Mazurkiewicz, Msgr. Benedict J. '55 (AUS) Fayetteville, TX St. John's Church.
Mazurkiewicz, Msgr. Harry C. '51 (AUS) La Grange, TX Sacred Heart of Jesus Church.
Mazurkiewicz, Joseph '84 (ALT) Somerset, PA St. Peter's Church; Somerset, PA State Correctional Institution.
Mazuryk, Ivan '95 (STF) Syracuse, NY St. John the Baptist Church.
Mazza, Louis J. '53 (NY) North Tarrytown, NY Immaculate Conception Church.
Mazza, Mark G. '80 (GRY) North Judson, IN Ss. Cyril and Methodius Church.
Mazza, Victor J. '70 (PAT) [7] Clifton, NJ St. Paul Church.
Mazzarella, Cadmus D. '85 (CAM) Clayton, NJ St. Catherine's Church; [Q] Glassboro, NJ Rowan College of New Jersey.
Mazzarella, Frederick *o.f.m.* '61 (NY) [Z] New York, NY Franciscan Province of the Immaculate Conception.
Mazziotta, Msgr. Robert R. '41 (NY) [220] Staten Island, NY Our Lady of Pity Church; Retired.
Mazzitello, John A. *s.j.* '69 (STP) [N] Minneapolis, MN La Storta Jesuit Community.
Mazzocchia, George *o.f.m.* '40 (NY) [Z] New York, NY Padua Friary.
Mazzola, Robert E. *s.t.b.* '63 (IND) Greenfield, IN St. Michael Church.
Mazzotta, George J. '66 (PH) [109] Philadelphia, PA Mother of Divine Grace Church.
Mazzuchelli, Matthew C. *o.s.b.* '58 (PEO) [A] Peru, IL St. Bede Abbey and Academy.
Mbemba, Jean Claude *c.s.s.p.* '86 (PIT) [40] Pittsburgh, PA St. Patrick-St. Stanislaus Kostka Church.
Mbogu, Christopher '83 (PIT) [3] McKees Rocks, PA St. John of God Church.
Mc Cauley, James R. *c.s.p.* '74 (PAT) [A] Oak Ridge, NJ Paulist Novitiate.
Mc Cullough, Michael '74 (LA) Burbank, CA St. Finbar Church.
Mc Menemie, Msgr. James '53 (NEW) Lyndhurst, NJ St. Michael's Church.
McAfee, Franklyn M. '71 (ARL) [5] Alexandria, VA St. Lawrence Church.
McAlear, Richard *o.m.i.* '70 (WDC) [B] Washington, DC Oblate College/Oblate Center for Mission Studies.
McAleer, Robert T. '71 (DAV) [3] Fort Madison, IA SS. Mary & Joseph Church.
McAlinden, Terence O. '67 (TR) Tuckerton, NJ St. Teresa Church.
McAlister, Msgr. Lawrence J. '44 (BRK) [150] Queens, NY St. Andrew Avellino Church.
McAlister, Msgr. Lawrence J. '59 (BRK) Retired.
McAlister, Richard A. *o.p.* '61 (PRO) [P] Providence, RI St. Thomas Aquinas Priory at Providence College.
McAllister, Alex '86 (SR) On Leave.
McAllister, Donald '71 (PRT) Portland, ME Mercy Hospital; Portland, ME Maine Medical Center; [H] Portland, ME Mercy Hospital.
McAllister, Forest *o.f.m.* '67 (SFE) [K] Rio Rancho, NM Felician Sisters.
McAllister, Leo '54 (SAC) Carmichael, CA Our Lady of the Assumption Church.
McAllister, Robert J. *s.j.* '51 (ALN) [A] Wernersville, PA Novitiate of St. Isaac Jogues.
McAloon, Francis X. *s.j.* '92 (OAK) [N] Berkeley, CA Jesuit Community at Jesuit School of Theology at Berkeley.
McAlpin, James C. '64 (SC) Sheldon, IA St. Patrick's Church.
McAlpin, Leonard J. '69 (GBG) Donegal, PA St. Raymond Church.
McAlpine, Harry D. '87 (SC) Fort Dodge, IA Sacred Heart Church.
McAndrew, David T. '63 (HBG) [1] Lebanon, PA Assumption of the Blessed Virgin Mary Church; [G] Lebanon, PA Villa Vianney.
McAndrew, John '86 (ORG) Brea, CA St. Angela Merici Church.
McAndrew, John P. *c.s.sp.* '67 (PIT) [P] Bethel Park, PA Holy Ghost Animation Center.
McAndrew, Joseph P. '85 (NY) [147] Bronx, NY Holy Family Church.
McAndrew, Michael *c.ss.r.* '73 (DEN) [32] Denver, CO St. Joseph's Church.
McAndrew, Stephen *o.m.v.* '91 (BO) [B] Boston, MA Oblate Provincialate.
McAndrew, Thomas F. '61 (DUB) Manly, IA Sacred Heart Church; Plymouth, IA St. Michael Church.
McAndrews, Msgr. Donald A. '54 (SCR) [1] Wilkes-Barre, PA St. Aloysius Church.
McAndrews, James F. *s.j.* '62 (BAL) [D] Baltimore, MD Loyola High School.
McAndrews, Richard J. '67 (PH) [110] Philadelphia, PA Nativity of the Blessed Virgin Mary Church.
McAndrews, Walter J. '43 (BO) Retired.
McAnerney, Brendan *o.p.* '88 (P) Ashland, OR Our Lady of the Mountain Church.
McAnulty, John D. *s.j.* '57 (LA) [R] Los Angeles, CA Columbiere House.
McArdle, John F. '51 (MAR) Retired.
McArdle, Msgr. Joseph G. '38 (MOB) Retired; [F] Mobile, AL Little Sisters of the Poor, Home For the Aged, Inc.
McArdle, Kevin *o.c.d.* '43 (TUC) [16] Tucson, AZ St. Margaret's Church; [F] Tucson, AZ Discalced Carmelite Fathers of St. Margaret's.
McArdle, Sean '67 (CAM) Cedarville, NJ St. Michael's Church; Leesburg, NJ New Jersey State Medium Security Prison.
McAree, Msgr. Francis J. '75 (NY) [A] Yonkers, NY St. Joseph's Seminary.
McArthur, John B. '74 (MEM) [21] Memphis, TN St. Paul The Apostle Church.
McArthur, Luke *s.d.s.* '57 (MIL) [P] Milwaukee, WI Salvatorian Provincial Residence.
McArtney, Robert J. '60 (BUF) [K] Lackawanna, NY Our Lady of Victory Hospital.
McAskill, Kenneth F. (BO) Retired.
McAskill, Kenneth F. '50 (BO) [3] Arlington, MA St. James the Apostle Church.
McAtavey, John J. '54 (PMB) Tequesta, FL St. Jude Church; Retired.
McAtee, John F. *o.s.a.* (PH) [B] Villanova, PA St. Augustine Friary.
McAteer, James P. *i.c.* '64 (PEO) Galesburg, IL Corpus Christi Church.
McAteer, Kenneth P. '73 (PH) [119] Philadelphia, PA Our Lady of Hope Church.
McAteer, Patrick J. *s.j.* '73 (CHI) [C] Chicago, IL Jesuit Community at Loyola University of Chicago.
McAuley, John J. *m.m.* '81 (NY) [46] New York, NY Holy Family Church; [Z] Maryknoll, NY Maryknoll Fathers and Brothers.
McAuliff, R. Richard *s.j.* '92 (MI) Majuro, MH Cathedral of the Assumption.
McAuliffe, Dennis '73 (BRK) [13] Brooklyn, NY St. Athanasius Church; [E] Brooklyn, NY Office of Religious Education: Evangelization and Catholic Formation.
McAuliffe, Kevin '90 (LAV) Laughlin, NV St. John the Baptist Catholic Mission Church.
McAuliffe, Robert F. (BO) [3] Arlington, MA St. James the Apostle Church.
McAuliffe, Robert J. (BO) Awaiting Assignment.
McAuliffe, Roger B. *s.j.* '49 (SJ) [M] Los Gatos, CA California Province of the Society of Jesus, Jesuit Provincial Office.
McAuliffe, Roger D. *s.j.* '49 (SJ) [M] Los Gatos, CA Sacred Heart Jesuit Center.
McAvey, James R. *o.p.* '39 (PRO) [P] Providence, RI St. Thomas Aquinas Priory at Providence College.
McAvoy, Msgr. Ambrose A. '39 (DUB) Retired.
McAvoy, Msgr. C. J. '63 (OG) [2] Plattsburgh, NY St. John the Baptist Church.
McBrearity, Gerald *s.s.* '73 (SAT) [A] San Antonio, TX The Assumption-St. John's Seminary.
McBrearity, Gerald D. '84 (ATL) On Duty Outside the Archdiocese.
McBrearty, John J. *s.s.j.* '68 (BEA) Raywood, TX Sacred Heart Church.
McBrearty, William J. *s.j.* '47 (SY) [S] Syracuse, NY Jesuits at LeMoyne, Inc.
McBriar, David J. *o.f.m.* (R) [3] Durham, NC Immaculate Conception Church.
McBride, Alfred *o.praem.* (BO) [A] Weston, MA Pope John XXIII National Seminary.
McBride, Alfred A. '53 (GB) [I] De Pere, WI St. Norbert Abbey.
McBride, Brendan (SFR) [46] San Francisco, CA St. Philip the Apostle Church.
McBride, Daniel '95 (PHX) [1] Glendale, AZ Our Lady of Perpetual Help Church.
McBride, Eugene J. *o.s.f.s.* '89 (PH) [75] Philadelphia, PA St. Joachim Church.
McBride, Gerald E. '91 (TR) New Monmouth, NJ St. Mary Church.
McBride, Harold E. *s.m.m.* '47 (RVC) Bay Shore, NY Southside Hospital; [N] Bay Shore, NY Montfort Missionaries.
McBride, Henry J. '61 (CAM) Berlin, NJ Our Lady of Mt. Carmel Church.
McBride, Msgr. James P. '56 (PH) [83] Philadelphia, PA St. Katherine of Siena Church.
McBride, John *s.j.* '61 (P) [L] Portland, OR Jesuit Provincial Office (Oregon Prov.).
McBride, John F. '62 (PH) Hilltown, PA Our Lady of the Sacred Heart Church.
McBride, Larry '87 (OWN) [6] Owensboro, KY St. Pius Tenth Church.
McBride, Malachy R. *o.f.m. cap.* '62 (DEN) [1] Aurora, CO Queen of Peace Church; [M] Denver, CO St. Francis of Assisi Friary.
McBride, Msgr. Peter A. '60 (PAT) [2] Clifton, NJ St. Andrew the Apostle Church.

McBride, Robert G. '72 (NEW) Saddle Brook, NJ St. Philip the Apostle Church.
McBride, William F. '82 (MAD) Leave of Absence.
McBride, William T. '42 (PH) Richboro, PA St. Vincent de Paul Church; Retired.
McBrien, Kevin *o.carm.* '70 (SAC) Fairfield, CA Our Lady of Mount Carmel, Church.
McBrien, Kevin F. '86 (BRK) [174] Queens, NY St. Gregory the Great Church.
McBrien, Richard P. '62 (FTW) [B] Notre Dame, IN University of Notre Dame Du Lac.
McBrien, Richard P. '62 (HRT) On Duty Outside the Archdiocese.
McBurney, James D. *o.s.a.* '84 (MIL) [P] Racine, WI Augustinian Novitiate.
McCaa, Msgr. Francis B. '48 (ALT) Retired.
McCabe, Brendan (NY) [16] Yonkers, NY St. Peter Church; County, NY Westchester County Jail; Bronx, NY Montefiore Medical Center.
McCabe, Charles J. '92 (MOB) [19] Mobile, AL St. Pius X Church.
McCabe, Edward D. (BO) Awaiting Assignment.
McCabe, Edwin J. *o.c.s.o.* '39 (SAC) [A] Vina, CA Abbey of New Clairvaux, Trappist Seminary.
McCabe, George V. *s.j.* '45 (BO) [W] Weston, MA Campion Health Center, Inc.
McCabe, George V. *s.j.* '45 (SPK) Spokane, Wa U.S. Veterans Hospital; Retired.
McCabe, James F. *c.s.p.* '57 (AUS) [11] Austin, TX St. Austin's Church; Austin, TX State School.
McCabe, James F. *c.pp.s.* '58 (CIN) [M] Dayton, OH Provincial House of the Cincinnati Province of the Society of the Precious Blood; [M] Dayton, OH Provincial House of the Cincinnati Province of the Society of the Precious Blood.
McCabe, James T. '71 (PH) Broomall, PA St. Pius X Church.
McCabe, John H. '55 (RVC) Uniondale, NY Holly Patterson Home for Nassau Community Aged and Infirm; [C] Hicksville, NY Holy Trinity.
McCabe, John J. *m.m.* '42 (SJ) [M] Los Altos, CA Maryknoll.
McCabe, John J. '59 (LIN) Hastings, NE St. Cecilia's Church.
McCabe, Kenneth O. *ss.cc.* '65 (LA) [K] Burbank, CA Providence Health System; [R] Mission Hills, CA Congregation of the Sacred Hearts.
McCabe, Louis J. *s.j.* '71 (STL) [P] St. Louis, MO Bellarmine House of Studies; [P] St. Louis, MO The Jesuits of the Missouri Province.
McCabe, Michael G. '89 (LIN) Dawson, NE St. Mary's Church; [C] Falls City, NE Sacred Heart High School/Elementary Schools.
McCabe, Patrick A. '61 (CAM) Lindenwold, NJ St. Lawrence's Church.
McCabe, Paul J. '59 (ROC) [8] Elmira, NY Our Lady of Lourdes Church.
McCabe, Peter '70 (AUS) Giddings, TX State School.
McCabe, Raymond M. *o.p.* (CAM) [L] Camden, NJ Dominican Sisters of the Perpetual Rosary Chaplain's Residence.
McCabe, Raymond M. *o.p.* '57 (CAM) [M] Camden, NJ Monastery of the Dominican Nuns of the Perpetual Rosary.
McCabe, Msgr. Richard '58 (AUS) [7] Austin, TX Emmaus Catholic Church.
McCabe, Robert '89 (DET) [2] Livonia, MI St. Colette Church.
McCabe, Msgr. Robert J. '64 (NY) Forestburgh, NY St. Thomas Aquinas Church.
McCabe, Thomas E. '92 (STP) Crystal, MN St. Raphael Church.
McCabe, Msgr. Vincent '46 (LA) Retired.
McCabe, William J. '41 (SY) Retired.
McCafferty, David L. '64 (CLV) Wickliffe, OH Our Lady of Mount Carmel Church.
McCafferty, James B. *s.m.* '70 (WH) Buckhannon, WV Holy Rosary Church; [Q] Buckhannon, WV West Virginia Wesleyan College Newman Center.
McCafferty, Joseph F. '61 (PH) [X] Lansdale, PA St. Mary Manor.
McCafferty, Michael F. '87 (CHR) [2] Columbia, SC St. Joseph Church; [H] Columbia, SC University of South Carolina, Columbia College, Thomas More Center.
McCafferty, Richard *s.j.* '62 (OAK) Livermore, CA St. Charles Borromeo Church.
McCafferty, Richard B. *s.j.* '62 (BO) [W] Boston, MA The Society of Jesus of New England-Provincial Offices.
McCaffrey, Daniel '58 (SAN) On Duty Outside the Diocese.
McCaffrey, Edmund *o.carm.* '53 (NY) [97] New York, NY Our Lady of the Scapular/St. Stephen Church; New York, NY New York City Veterans Administration Hospital; Manhattan, NY U.S.V.A. Medical Center.
McCaffrey, Edmund M. '59 (CHR) Hilton Head Island, SC Holy Family Church.
McCaffrey, Gerald T. *o.f.m.* '58 (BO) [BB] Boston, MA St. Anthony Shrine.
McCaffrey, Gerard D. '45 (PH) Retired.
McCaffrey, Howard A. *s.j.* '47 (NY) [Z] New York, NY Murray-Weigel Hall.
McCaffrey, James L. (SFR) Retired.
McCaffrey, James Leo '58 (STO) Retired.
McCaffrey, James P. *s.j.* '52 (BO) [W] Weston, MA Campion Center.
McCaffrey, Msgr. John '44 (CAM) Retired.
McCaffrey, John '76 (AUS) Bryan, TX St. Joseph's Church.
McCaffrey, John J. '48 (CLV) Sheffield Lake, OH St. Thomas the Apostle Church.
McCaffrey, Joseph (PIT) Lawrence County, PA Youth Development Center.
McCaffrey, Joseph J. '77 (ROC) [7] Elmira, NY St. Anthony Church.
McCaffrey, Joseph P. *c.m.* '54 (PH) [Z] Philadelphia, PA Congregation of the Mission.
McCaffrey, Joseph P. '77 (ROC) [2] Elmira, NY St. Patrick Church.
McCaffrey, Joseph R. '87 (PIT) New Bedford, PA St. James Church.
McCaffrey, Lawrence X. *s.j.* '51 (NY) Harriman, NY St. Anastasia Church; [AA] Harriman, NY St. Patrick's Villa.
McCaffrey, Michael *o.f.m.conv.* '94 (CHL) Winston-Salem, NC Our Lady of Mercy Church; [L] Charlotte, NC Diocesan Office of Campus Ministry.
McCaffrey, Patrick J. '59 (WDC) [15] Washington, DC St. Gabriel Church.
McCaffrey, Richard L. *s.j.* '73 (FBK) Bethel, AK Immaculate Conception Church.
McCaffrey, Thomas J. '47 (NY) Scarsdale, NY Our Lady of Fatima Church.
McCaffrey, Msgr. William J. '72 (PRO) [18] Providence, RI St. Joseph's Church.
McCahill, Msgr. Patrick P. '68 (NY) [32] New York, NY St. Elizabeth of Hungary Church; [I] New York, NY The Catholic Charities of the Archdiocese of New York.
McCahon, Joseph F.S. '75 (SP) Military Chaplains.
McCaig, John J. '58 (CHI) [5] Lemont, IL St. Patrick Church; Retired.
McCain, William '86 (SFR) Special Assignment.
McCall, James T. '60 (CAM) Delair, NJ St. Veronica's Church.
McCall, Msgr. John H. '49 (BAL) Fallston, MD St. Mark Church.
McCall, Msgr. John M. '58 (SP) [4] Largo, FL St. Patrick Church.
McCall, Peter *o.f.m.cap.* '62 (NY) [17] Yonkers, NY Sacred Heart Church; [DD] New York, NY House of Peace, Inc.
McCall, Robert E. *s.s.j.* '46 (BAL) [M] Baltimore, MD St. Joseph Society of the Sacred Heart House of Central Administration; [M] Baltimore, MD St. Joseph's Manor.
McCall, Msgr. Stephen '79 (SD) Carlsbad, CA St. Patrick Church.
McCall, Thomas D. *s.j.* '52 (NY) [51] New York, NY St. Ignatius Loyola Church; [Z] New York, NY Jesuit Provincial's Office; [Z] New York, NY St. Ignatius Loyola Residence.
McCallin, Frederick D. '42 (DEN) Retired.
McCallister, Charles E. '71 (WH) Absent on Sick Leave; [N] Wheeling, WV Webb Farm Residence.
McCallister, Richard '91 (SEA) Lynden, WA St. Joseph's Church.
McCallum, Msgr. John V. '43 (DAL) Retired.
McCallum, Paul F. '62 (AUS) [18] Austin, TX St. Paul's Church; [N] Austin, TX Society of St. Vincent de Paul.
McCamley, Martin Dugan '62 (ALT) State College, PA Our Lady of Victory Church.
McCandless, William T. *o.s.f.s.* '94 (PH) [D] Philadelphia, PA Northeast Catholic High School for Boys; [Z] Philadelphia, PA Oblates of St. Francis De Sales.
McCann, Arthur '62 (DM) Des Moines, IA City Chaplaincy Program; [I] Des Moines, IA City Hospital Chaplaincy Service.
McCann, Bill '94 (LSC) Hatch, NM Our Lord of Mercy Church.
McCann, Charles '69 (WDC) Camp Springs, MD St. Philip the Apostle Church.
McCann, James M. *s.j.* '79 (CHI) [C] Chicago, IL Jesuit Community at Loyola University of Chicago.
McCann, Joachim *o.s.b.* '91 (P) [L] St. Benedict, OR Mt. Angel Abbey.
McCann, Msgr. John B. '85 (ALN) [3] Allentown, PA Immaculate Conception Church; [F] Allentown, PA Catholic Social Agency-Catholic Charities Administrative Office.
McCann, John H. *s.m.m.* '55 (HRT) Bantam, CT Our Lady of Grace Church.
McCann, Msgr. John J. '65 (RVC) Glen Cove, NY St. Patrick's Church.
McCann, Joseph H. '57 (HRT) [2] New Haven, CT St. Aedan's Church.
McCann, Luke (NY) [CC] New York, NY University Apostolate.
McCann, Robert J. '81 (OAK) [1] Hayward, CA All Saints Church.
McCann, Thomas *c.p.* '66 (R) Greenville, NC St. Gabriel Church.
McCann, Thomas A. '76 (PH) Levittown, PA Queen of the Universe Church.
McCann, Thomas E. '59 (SCR) Harding, PA Church of the Holy Redeemer.
McCann, Thomas W. '68 (CLV) Cuyahoga Falls, OH Immaculate Heart of Mary Church.
McCann, Vincent *o.f.m.* '41 (NY) [35] New York, NY St. Francis of Assisi Church.
McCarragher, Timothy '91 (Y) Absent on Leave.
McCarren, Charles K. '45 (RCK) Retired.
McCarren, Msgr. Edgar (SJ) Retired.
McCarren, Msgr. Edgar P. '43 (OAK) [B] Moraga, CA Saint Mary's College.
McCarren, Msgr. Edgar P. '43 (RVC) Retired.
McCarren, Msgr. Edgar P. '43 (SJ) [5] Santa Clara, CA Our Lady of Peace Church.
McCarren, Gerald H. '91 (NEW) [B] South Orange, NJ Seton Hall University.
McCarren, Msgr. John C. '46 (PIT) Aleppo Township, PA St. Mary Church.
McCarren, Paul J. *s.j.* '74 (WDC) [20] Washington, DC Holy Trinity Church.
McCarren, Msgr. Stephen A. '55 (GBG) On Duty Outside the Diocese.
McCarren, William J. '47 (BRK) Retired.
McCarron, Francis X. *o.m.i.* '45 (BO) [Z] Tewksbury, MA Immaculate Heart of Mary Novitiate-Infirmary.
McCarron, Gerard J. '70 (TR) Freehold, NJ St. Rose of Lima Church.
McCarron, Michael D. '77 (RIC) [2] Newport News, VA Our Lady of Mount Carmel Church; [4] Newport News, VA St. Vincent de Paul Church.
McCarthy, Anthony T. '71 (MIL) North Lake, WI St. Clare's Church.
McCarthy, Bernard '47 (HEL) Retired.
McCarthy, Brian P. '75 (NY) [132] Bronx, NY St. Barnabas Church.
McCarthy, Brien R. '81 (WDC) [4] Washington, DC Annunciation Church; Special Ministries; [S] Washington, DC Archdiocesan Campus Ministry.
McCarthy, Carl '95 (OWN) [2] Owensboro, KY Blessed Mother Church.
McCarthy, Charles '81 (NTN) On Special Projects.
McCarthy, Charles A. *c.s.sp.* '51 (PEO) Eagle Township, IL Annunciation of Blessed Virgin Mary Church; Leonore, IL SS. Peter and Paul's Church.
McCarthy, Charles L. '50 (ROC) Retired.
McCarthy, Msgr. Charles W. '48 (BO) Retired; [Q] Brighton, MA St. Elizabeth's Hospital of Boston.
McCarthy, Cornelius '74 (MRY) Carmel Valley, CA Our Lady of Mt. Carmel Church.
McCarthy, D. Joseph '78 (SAC) [K] Chico, CA Director of Campus Ministry.
McCarthy, Daniel *c.s.sp.* '66 (NY) [69] New York, NY St. Mark the Evangelist Church.
McCarthy, Daniel *o.s.b.* '91 (KCK) Wathena, KS St. Joseph's Church.
McCarthy, Daniel A. '37 (SCR) Retired; [N] Dunmore, PA Villa St. Joseph.
McCarthy, Daniel J. *ss.cc.* '42 (BO) [31] Boston, MA St. James the Greater in Chinatown Church; Boston, MA New England Medical Center.
McCarthy, Daniel P. '43 (SR) [2] Santa Rosa, CA Holy Spirit Church; Retired.
McCarthy, Daniel P. '67 (CHI) [161] Chicago, IL Our Lady of Victory Church.
McCarthy, Daniel P. *o.s.b.* '91 (KCK) Bendena, KS St. Benedict's Church; Troy, KS St. Charles Church.
McCarthy, David F. *s.j.* '52 (DET) [P] Clarkston, MI Colombiere Center.
McCarthy, David J. '60 (CLV) Doylestown, OH SS. Peter and Paul Church.
McCarthy, Donal *ss.cc.* '65 (LA) [D] La Verne, CA Damien Boys High School; [R] La Verne, CA Congregation of the Sacred Hearts.
McCarthy, Donald (SAL) Ellis, KS St. Mary's Church.
McCarthy, Donald E. *c.s.b.* '58 (ROC) Webster, NY St. Rita Church; [I] Rochester, NY Basilian Residence.
McCarthy, Donald G. '54 (CIN) [11] Cincinnati, OH St. Antoninus Church.
McCarthy, Donald P. '59 (SAL) Hill City, KS Immaculate Heart of Mary Church.
McCarthy, Edward '71 (ORL) Merritt Island, FL Divine Mercy Church.
McCarthy, Edward A. '43 (MIA) Retired.
McCarthy, Edward J. *s.j.* '49 (MIL) [P] Milwaukee, WI Jesuit Provincial Office, Wisconsin Province.
McCarthy, Edward P. *c.pp.s.* '40 (LFT) [A] Rensselaer, IN Saint Joseph's College.
McCarthy, Msgr. Emmett '43 (ORG) Brea, CA St. Angela Merici Church; Retired.
McCarthy, Eugene J. '60 (VEN) Marco Island, FL San Marco Church.
McCarthy, Francis *o.carm.* '51 (JOL) [J] Darien, IL Carmelite Fathers Provincial Office.
McCarthy, Francis *o.carm.* '51 (TUC) [B] Nogales, AZ Our Lady of Lourdes High School.
McCarthy, Francis J. *s.s.j.* '51 (BEA) [6] Port Arthur,

TX St. John Church.
McCarthy, Francis W. *c.pp.s.* '42 (CIN) [M] Dayton, OH Provincial House of the Cincinnati Province of the Society of the Precious Blood.
McCarthy, Francis X. '54 (MIA) [8] Fort Lauderdale, FL St. Jerome Church.
McCarthy, George B. '56 (PRO) [4] Newport, RI St. Mary's Church.
McCarthy, Gerald '57 (FAR) St. John, ND St. John the Baptist Church.
McCarthy, J. Joseph (BO) Society of St. James the Apostle.
McCarthy, James '45 (FR) Retired.
McCarthy, Msgr. James '68 (NY) [1] New York, NY Cathedral of St. Patrick.
McCarthy, James C. '62 (HEL) [E] Butte, MT St. James Community Hospital, Inc.
McCarthy, James H. '55 (CHI) Other Assignments.
McCarthy, James J. '64 (BO) On Special or Other Diocesan Assignment.
McCarthy, Jeremiah (LA) [A] Camarillo, CA St. John's Seminary.
McCarthy, Jeremiah *m.s.c.* '50 (SAN) Eldorado, TX Our Lady of Guadalupe Church.
McCarthy, Jeremiah J. '72 (LA) [A] Camarillo, CA St. John's Seminary.
McCarthy, Jeremiah J. '72 (TUC) On Duty Outside the Diocese.
McCarthy, Jeremiah J. '78 (SAV) [4] Savannah, GA Most Blessed Sacrament Church.
McCarthy, Jerry '45 (TLS) Retired.
McCarthy, John E. *c.s.c.* '58 (FR) [B] North Easton, MA Stonehill College.
McCarthy, Msgr. John F. '55 (HEL) On Duty Outside the Diocese.
McCarthy, John J. *s.j.* '52 (NY) [Z] New York, NY Jesuit Community at Fordham University.
McCarthy, John J. *m.s.* '69 (HRT) [M] Hartford, CT Missionaries of LaSalette Provincial Secretary.
McCarthy, John J. '84 (HRT) [1] Hartford, CT Cathedral of St. Joseph; Special and other (Arch)Diocesan Assignment.
McCarthy, John L. *s.j.* '62 (MIL) [P] Milwaukee, WI Jesuit Provincial Office, Wisconsin Province.
McCarthy, John L. *s.j.* '62 (STL) [P] St. Louis, MO Jesuit Community Corporation at St. Louis University - Jesuit Hall.
McCarthy, Msgr. John M. '54 (NY) [222] Staten Island, NY St. Patrick Church.
McCarthy, John M. *m.s.* '69 (STL) [P] St. Louis, MO La Salette Missionaries.
McCarthy, John P. '51 (BUF) Retired.
McCarthy, John R. '55 (CLV) East Cleveland, OH St. Philomena Church.
McCarthy, John R. '55 (STU) On Duty Outside the Diocese.
McCarthy, Jose *o.f.m.cap.* '60 (ARE) [1] Utuado, PR San Miquel Church.
McCarthy, Jose *o.f.m.cap.* '60 (NY) [Z] White Plains, NY St. Conrad Friary.
McCarthy, Joseph '48 (BUR) Retired.
McCarthy, Joseph F. '48 (SFD) Retired.
McCarthy, Joseph J. *o.carm.* '66 (GAL) [14] Houston, TX St. Bernadette Soubirous Church.
McCarthy, Joseph L. '69 (CHL) Retired.
McCarthy, Joseph S. '96 (BO) [16] Boston, MA St. Brigid Church.
McCarthy, Kevin P. '89 (GRY) Portage, IN Nativity of Our Savior Church.
McCarthy, Leo *o.carm.* '62 (JOL) [J] Darien, IL Carmelite Community; [J] Darien, IL Carmelite Fathers Provincial Office.
McCarthy, Msgr. Leo F. (BUF) [2] Batavia, NY St. Joseph Church.
McCarthy, Leo F. *m.m.* '47 (BO) [W] East Walpole, MA Maryknoll Department of Development.
McCarthy, Leo F. *m.m.* '47 (NY) [Z] Maryknoll, NY Maryknoll Fathers and Brothers.
McCarthy, Msgr. Leo F. '59 (BUF) [2] Batavia, NY St. Joseph Church.
McCarthy, Martin F. *s.j.* '54 (BO) [W] Boston, MA The Society of Jesus of New England-Provincial Offices.
McCarthy, Martin F. *s.j.* '54 (TUC) [F] Tucson, AZ Jesuit Community of the Vatican Observatory.
McCarthy, Michael J. *c.s.sp.* '48 (BRK) [U] Long Island City, NY Holy Ghost Fathers of Ireland.
McCarthy, Michael J. '58 (BGP) [P] Ridgefield, CT Provincial House, Congregation de Notre Dame.
McCarthy, Michael J. '65 (PH) Absent on Sick Leave.
McCarthy, Mick *s.j.* (SFR) [2] San Francisco, CA St. Agnes Church.
McCarthy, Patrick *m.s.* '78 (LKC) De Ridder, LA St. Joseph's Church.
McCarthy, Patrick P. '44 (SFR) [4] South San Francisco, CA St. Veronica Church; Retired.
McCarthy, Paul '84 (FTW) [14] South Bend, IN St. Mary of the Assumption Church.
McCarthy, Paul J. *s.j.* '57 (BUF) [O] Buffalo, NY Canisius Jesuit Community.
McCarthy, Paul R. (BO) Absent on Leave.
McCarthy, Raymond *c.ss.r.* '47 (NY) [92] New York, NY Our Lady of Perpetual Help Church.
McCarthy, Richard C. '69 (PRT) Retired.
McCarthy, Richard J. *c.m.* '58 (SAT) Losoya, TX El Carmen Catholic Church.
McCarthy, Msgr. Robert J. '46 (OG) Retired.
McCarthy, Msgr. Robert L. '58 (STL) [2] Jennings, MO St. Frances Xavier Cabrini Church.
McCarthy, Robert P. *c.ss.r.* '47 (DET) [34] Detroit, MI Holy Redeemer Church.
McCarthy, Sean M. (BO) [4] Norwood, MA St. Timothy Church.
McCarthy, Terrence A. '74 (CHI) [1] Waukegan, IL St. Anastasia Church.
McCarthy, Thomas '61 (Y) [L] Kent, OH Family and Community Services of Catholic Charities.
McCarthy, Thomas *s.j.* '64 (P) Sherwood, OR St. Francis Church.
McCarthy, Thomas *o.s.a.* '94 (CHI) [N] Chicago, IL St. Rita Monastery.
McCarthy, Thomas A. '59 (NEW) Washington Township, NJ Our Lady of Good Counsel Church.
McCarthy, Thomas E. '49 (HRT) Avon, CT St. Ann's Church.
McCarthy, Thomas H. '43 (KC) Retired.
McCarthy, Thomas J. '51 (SPR) Retired.
McCarthy, Thomas J. '53 (RVC) Glen Cove, NY St. Patrick's Church.
McCarthy, Thomas J. '61 (Y) Mantua, OH St. Joseph's Church.
McCarthy, Thomas J. '80 (BUF) [3] Kenmore, NY St. John the Baptist Church.
McCarthy, Thomas M. *s.j.* '62 (P) [L] Portland, OR Jesuit Provincial Office (Oregon Prov.).
McCarthy, Thomas P. *c.s.v.* '52 (CHI) [N] Arlington Heights, IL Viatorian Province Center-Clerics of St. Viator.
McCarthy, Warren J. '52 (CHI) Schaumburg, IL St. Marcelline Church.
McCarthy, William *m.ss.a.* '59 (NOR) [I] Moodus, CT My Father's House.
McCarthy, Msgr. William '63 (PAT) East Hanover, NJ St. Rose of Lima Church.
McCarthy, William D. *m.m.* '56 (NY) [B] Maryknoll, NY Center for Mission Research and Study at Maryknoll; [Z] Maryknoll, NY Maryknoll Fathers and Brothers.
McCarthy, William E. *m.m.* '58 (NY) [Z] Maryknoll, NY Maryknoll Fathers and Brothers.
McCarthy, William E. '58 (RVC) Shoreham, NY St. Mark Church.
McCarthy, William R. (BO) Retired.
McCarthy, William R. *m.m.* '40 (NY) [Z] Maryknoll, NY Maryknoll Fathers and Brothers.
McCarthy, William R. '52 (BO) [3] Quincy, MA St. John the Baptist Church.
McCartin, Francis P. *o.m.i.* '38 (BO) [Z] Tewksbury, MA Immaculate Heart of Mary Novitiate-Infirmary.
McCartney, James J. *o.s.a.* '70 (PH) Havertown, PA St. Denis Church; [C] Villanova, PA Villanova University; [Z] Havertown, PA Augustinians (O.S.A.).
McCartney, Jim '84 (LUB) Slaton, TX St. Joseph's Church.
McCartney, Louis R. *o.s.f.s.* '52 (WIL) [I] Childs, MD Oblates of St. Francis De Sales.
McCartney, Marcellus A. *o.f.m.* '44 (NY) [35] New York, NY St. Francis of Assisi Church.
McCarty, Bruce '89 (OWN) Absent on Leave.
McCarty, Kieran *o.f.m.* '49 (TUC) [4] Tucson, AZ Mission San Xavier del Bac Church.
McCarty, Lawrence L. '63 (SC) [8] Sioux City, IA St. Michael Church.
McCarty, Paul T. *s.j.* '67 (BO) [W] Weston, MA Campion Center.
McCarty, Robert E. *s.j.* '67 (NEW) [B] Jersey City, NJ Saint Peter's College; [N] Jersey City, NJ Jesuits of Saint Peter's College, Inc.
McCarty, Shaun *s.t.* '56 (WDC) [M] Adelphi, MD Missionary Servants of the Most Holy Trinity.
McCarty, Thomas J. *o.c.s.o.* '56 (DUB) [K] Peosta, IA New Melleray Abbey, Order of Cistercians of the Strict Observance.
McCarver, Jim '91 (MEM) Union City, TN Immaculate Conception Church.
McCarville, John J. '65 (CHI) Bellwood, IL St. Simeon Church.
McCasland, Howard (OG) Retired.
McCasland, Howard '44 (OG) Churubusco, NY Immaculate Heart of Mary Church.
McCaslin, John O. '55 (OM) [20] Omaha, NE Immaculate Conception, B.V.M. Church; [25] Omaha, NE St. Joseph Church.
McCaslin, John T. *s.j.* '66 (ALN) [A] Wernersville, PA Novitiate of St. Isaac Jogues.
McCaslin, R. Patrick '61 (OM) [26] Omaha, NE St. Leo Church.
McCaslin, Richard F. *s.j.* '65 (GB) [M] Oshkosh, WI Jesuit Retreat House.
McCauley, Daniel *o.c.d.* '55 (MIL) [P] Milwaukee, WI Provincial Offices - Discalced Carmelites.
McCauley, David '63 (FAR) On Duty Outside the Diocese.
McCauley, David F. '63 (STP) [S] St. Paul, MN Minnesota Catholic Conference.
McCauley, George C. *s.j.* '61 (NY) [Z] New York, NY Jesuit Community at Fordham University.
McCauley, James P. *s.j.* '56 (NY) [222] Staten Island, NY St. Patrick Church.
McCauley, James S. '56 (WIN) Lake City, MN St. Mary's Church.
McCauley, Walter C. *s.j.* '56 (FWT) [J] Lake Dallas, TX Montserrat Jesuit Retreat House.
McCaulley, Cornelius W. '66 (PIT) [41] Pittsburgh, PA St. Stephen Church.
McCausland, Joseph E. '50 (CLV) Military Chaplains.
McCawley, Scott '93 (JOL) Downers Grove, IL St. Mary Church.
McCawley, William J. '60 (SCR) Brodheadsville, PA Our Lady Queen of Peace Church.
McChesney, Robert W. *s.j.* '81 (WDC) [M] Washington, DC Leonard Neale House; [V] Washington, DC Jesuit Missions, Inc.
McClain, J. Thomas *s.j.* (DET) [K] Detroit, MI Jesuit Provincial Office-Detroit Province of the Society of Jesus.
McClain, J. Thomas *s.j.* '77 (NY) [F] New York, NY Regis High School; [Z] New York, NY St. Ignatius Loyola Residence.
McClain, Joseph P. *c.m.* (ALN) [A] Northampton, PA Mary Immaculate Seminary; [K] Northhampton, PA Vincentian Community.
McClanahan, Robert P. '84 (PT) Military Chaplains.
McClean, Msgr. John R. '57 (DUB) Marion, IA St. Joseph's Church; Springville, IA St. Isidore's Church.
McCleane, Michael J. '81 (PH) [1] Philadelphia, PA Cathedral Basilica of SS. Peter and Paul.
McClear, J. Edmund *m.m.* '42 (NY) [Z] Maryknoll, NY Maryknoll Fathers and Brothers.
McCleary, Michael L. '78 (PBL) Durango, CO St. Columba Church; [D] Durango, CO Mercy Medical Center.
McClellan, Keith *o.s.b.* '79 (IND) [A] St. Meinrad, IN St. Meinrad Seminary; [J] St. Meinrad, IN St. Meinrad Archabbey.
McClellan, Robert J. '81 (RCK) [3] Aurora, IL St. Joseph Church.
McClintock, Jim '86 (BEA) Special Assignment.
McClory, Bernard J. '53 (COL) [27] Columbus, OH St. Leo Church.
McCloskey, Daniel J. '83 (WIL) Absent on Sick Leave.
McCloskey, Francis '63 (ALB) Special Assignment.
McCloskey, Gary N. *o.s.a.* '77 (MIA) [B] Opa Locka, FL St. Thomas University; [H] Miami, FL Casa San Lorenzo.
McCloskey, J. Terrence *c.ss.r.* '66 (WCH) [G] Wichita, KS Redemptorist Community; [I] Wichita, KS Spiritual Life Center.
McCloskey, Msgr. James A. (SY) Retired.
McCloskey, James F. '43 (NEW) Retired.
McCloskey, James P. *c.s.sp.* '80 (PH) [G] Bensalem, PA Holy Ghost Preparatory School; [Z] Bensalem, PA Congregation of the Holy Ghost Fathers and Brothers.
McCloskey, Joseph A. '39 (PH) [39] Philadelphia, PA St. Dominic Church; Retired.
McCloskey, Joseph M. *s.j.* '63 (WDC) [2] Washington, DC St. Aloysius Church; [E] Washington, DC Gonzaga College High School.
McCloskey, Joseph W. '61 (PH) [36] Philadelphia, PA St. Clement Church.
McCloskey, Kevin *c.p.* '48 (SCR) [M] Scranton, PA Saint Ann's Passionist Monastery.
McCloskey, Lester J. '64 (SEA) [17] Seattle, WA St. Patrick Church; [18] Seattle, WA St. Paul Church; [20] Seattle, WA St. Therese Church; [31] Seattle, WA Our Lady of Mount Virgin Church; Vashon, WA St. John Vianney Church.
McCloskey, Patrick *o.f.m.* '75 (CIN) [E] Cincinnati, OH Roger Bacon High School; [M] Cincinnati, OH St. Clare Friary.
McClosky, Adam S. '67 (GAL) [48] Houston, TX St. Maximilian Kolbe Catholic Community Church.
McClure, Jack '95 (KC) [J] Liberty, MO Precious Blood Center.
McClure, John A. '62 (TOL) [L] Sylvania, OH Sisters of St. Francis of the Congregation of Our Lady of Lourdes.
McCluskey, James F. '68 (OM) Duncan, NE St. Stanislaus Church.
McCluskey, John D. *s.j.* '45 (SEA) Bellevue, WA Sacred Heart Church.
McCluskey, Raymond E. *s.j.* '45 (BO) [W] Weston, MA Campion Health Center, Inc.
McCluskey, Vincent S. '59 (PAT) Flanders, NJ St. Elizabeth Ann Seton Church; [N] Hewitt, NJ St. Joseph's Convent.
McCoart, Charles C., Jr. '90 (ARL) [2] Alexandria, VA Good Shepherd Church.
McCole, John F. '58 (PH) Pottstown, PA St. Aloysius Church.
McColl, Scott J. '80 (SD) [26] San Diego, CA St. Didacus Church.
McColligan, Raymond A. '43 (PIT) Retired.

McComiskey, Joseph C. '70 (RVC) Syosset, NY St. Edward Confessor Church.
McConaghy, R. Thomas '81 (NOR) Pawcatuck, CT St. Michael Church.
McConaghy, Robert J. '75 (ALN) Lehighton, PA SS. Peter and Paul Church.
McConnell, Bernard J. '36 (PH) [Z] Philadelphia, PA Jesuit Community at St. Joseph's University.
McConnell, James *s.m.a.* '72 (NEW) [N] Tenafly, NJ Society of African Missions, Provincialate, S.M.A. Fathers.
McConnell, James J. '54 (TR) Pennington, NJ St. James Church.
McConnell, James J. *s.m.a.* '72 (NEW) [14] Newark, NJ Queen of Angels Church.
McConnell, John *s.j.* '55 (NY) [Z] New York, NY Murray-Weigel Hall.
McConnell, William J. '53 (BO) [4] Brockton, MA St. Margaret Church.
McConnin, Robert J. '73 (BRK) [83] Brooklyn, NY Mary Queen of Heaven Church.
McConvey, Michael '79 (GLP) Absent on Leave.
McConville, James P. '90 (STP) Special Assignment.
McConville, Philip G.J. '43 (BO) Retired.
McConville, William E. *o.f.m.* '73 (ALB) [B] Loudonville, NY Siena College.
McConway, Sean J. *o.p.* '87 (NY) Pleasantville, NY Holy Innocents Church.
McCoog, Thomas M. *s.j.* '71 (BAL) [M] Baltimore, MD Jesuit Fathers and Brothers Maryland Provincial Curia.
McCool, Gerald A. *s.j.* '52 (NY) [Z] New York, NY Jesuit Community at Fordham University.
McCool, Malachy '71 (HT) On Leave.
McCool, Patrick *o.s.b.* '63 (OKL) [I] Shawnee, OK St. Gregory's Abbey.
McCord, Kent G. '81 (MET) On Duty Outside the Diocese.
McCorkle, Louis W. '53 (JC) [A] Hannibal, MO St. Thomas Aquinas Seminary.
McCormack, Andrew *s.m.* '57 (ATL) [6] Atlanta, GA Our Lady of the Assumption Church; [L] Atlanta, GA Campus Ministry.
McCormack, Brendan '60 (WDC) Retired.
McCormack, Daniel J. '94 (CHI) [6] Chicago, IL St. Ailbe Church.
McCormack, Douglas '69 (LFT) Zionsville, IN St. Alphonsus Church.
McCormack, John '61 (KC) [39] (Kansas City North), MO St. Therese Parish Church.
McCormack, John K. '42 (PH) [Z] Philadelphia, PA Jesuit Community at St. Joseph's University.
McCormack, Keith J. '76 (TOL) Columbus Grove, OH St. Anthony of Padua Church.
McCormack, Martin L. *o.f.m.* '48 (BO) [Z] Boston, MA Saint Anthony Residence.
McCormack, Michael (RVC) [B] Rockville Centre, NY Molloy College.
McCormack, Michael *s.a.c.* '62 (FWT) Weatherford, TX St. Stephen Church.
McCormack, Michael Joseph *o.p.* (NY) [Z] New York, NY St. Catherine of Siena Priory.
McCormack, Richard J. '61 (BRK) [143] Brooklyn, NY St. Vincent de Paul Church.
McCormack, Msgr. Robert '47 (NY) Retired.
McCormack, Thomas A. *s.s.c.* '35 (PRO) [P] Bristol, RI St. Columban's Retirement House.
McCormick, Andrew D. '82 (PH) [78] Philadelphia, PA St. John Cantius Church.
McCormick, Brian '66 (TR) [S] Trenton, NJ Martin House.
McCormick, Daniel J. '57 (ATL) Dunwoody, GA All Saints Catholic Church.
McCormick, Frank '68 (HEL) [3] Missoula, MT Pope John XXIII Church.
McCormick, George '84 (CAM) Retired.
McCormick, George '84 (PRT) Stonington, ME St. Mary Star of the Sea Church.
McCormick, Gerard *o.m.i.* '47 (NY) [BB] Newburgh, NY Our Lady of Hope Center.
McCormick, Gregory *s.p.* '49 (SB) [G] Cherry Valley, CA Servants of the Paraclete Guadalupe Retreat Center.
McCormick, Harold W. '63 (WCH) [1] Wichita, KS Cathedral of the Immaculate Conception.
McCormick, Howard W. '57 (SPR) Agawam, MA St. John the Evangelist Church.
McCormick, James '63 (SFS) On Leave of Absence.
McCormick, James '82 (E) [18] Erie, PA St. James Church; [C] Erie, PA Cathedral Preparatory School.
McCormick, James D. '62 (SC) Carroll, IA Holy Spirit Church.
McCormick, Msgr. James R. '39 (BEL) Retired.
McCormick, Jeffrey '96 (MIA) [26] Miami, FL St. Louis Church.
McCormick, Jerry '73 (MRY) Pacific Grove, CA St. Angela Church.
McCormick, John '75 (ORL) Kissimmee, FL Holy Redeemer Church.
McCormick, John D. '75 (DEN) Arvada, CO Shrine of St. Anne Church.
McCormick, John J. '56 (BO) Billerica, MA St. Theresa Church.
McCormick, Joseph E. *o.s.a.* '77 (DET) Grosse Pointe Park, MI St. Clare of Montefalco Church.
McCormick, Justin J. *c.s.p.* '61 (NY) [Z] Scarsdale, NY Paulist Fathers Generalate.
McCormick, Kieran J. '64 (SFR) [4] San Mateo, CA St. Timothy Church.
McCormick, Louis *o.f.m.* '65 (BUF) [Q] West Clarksville, NY Mount Irenaeus, Franciscan Mountain Retreat & Holy Peace Friary.
McCormick, Mark '91 (RC) Hot Springs, SD St. Anthony's Church.
McCormick, Martin F. *o.p.* '61 (CHI) River Forest, IL St. Vincent Ferrer Priory Church.
McCormick, Maurice M. '58 (SFR) Pacifica, CA Good Shepherd Church; [U] Pacifica, CA Cursillo.
McCormick, Michael '85 (WH) Absent on Sick Leave.
McCormick, Myron *o.f.m.* '52 (BO) [BB] Boston, MA St. Anthony Shrine.
McCormick, Patrick '75 (FRS) On Special Assignment.
McCormick, Patrick G. '96 (PH) [1] Norristown, PA Epiphany of Our Lord Church.
McCormick, Patrick J. '57 (ATL) Military Chaplains.
McCormick, Patrick Joseph '75 (FRS) [11] Fresno, CA St. Mary Church.
McCormick, Peter *s.p.* '70 (SB) Palm Desert, CA Sacred Heart Church.
McCormick, Richard A. *s.j.* (DET) [K] Detroit, MI Jesuit Provincial Office-Detroit Province of the Society of Jesus.
McCormick, Richard A. *s.j.* '53 (FTW) [B] Notre Dame, IN University of Notre Dame Du Lac.
McCormick, Richard J. *s.d.b.* '70 (BO) [E] Boston, MA Don Bosco Preparatory School of Technology.
McCormick, Msgr. Robert F. '47 (NY) Ossining, NY St. Augustine Church.
McCormick, Robert J. '42 (MIL) Retired.
McCormick, Thomas '59 (DEN) Commerce City, CO Our Lady Mother of the Church.
McCormick, Thomas F. *s.j.* '67 (LA) [F] Los Angeles, CA Loyola High School.
McCormick, Thomas G. '81 (RVC) Babylon, NY St. Joseph's Church.
McCormley, Hugh J. '62 (PIT) Harmarville, PA St. Francis of Assisi Church.
McCorry, Msgr. Edward J. '56 (NY) Hastings-on-Hudson, NY St. Matthew Church; Hastings-on-Hudson, NY St. Stanislaus Kostka Church.
McCotter, Daniel E. *c.s.p.* (SFR) [22] San Francisco, CA Holy Family Chinese Mission Church; [31] San Francisco, CA Old St. Mary's Cathedral.
McCouch, Richard S. *s.j.* '93 (SCR) [C] Scranton, PA University of Scranton; [E] Scranton, PA Scranton Preparatory School.
McCourt, Gerald P. *s.j.* '72 (SJ) [L] Los Altos, CA Jesuit Retreat House.
McCourt, Msgr. Robert R. '61 (BRK) [223] Queens, NY St. Pascal Baylon Church.
McCown, Robert M. *s.j.* '54 (MOB) Daphne, AL Shrine of the Holy Cross Church.
McCoy, Alan *o.f.m.* '38 (LA) [72] Los Angeles, CA St. Joseph Church.
McCoy, Alfred E. '54 (SC) Onawa, IA St. John's Church.
McCoy, Bernard *o.cist.* '95 (LC) [I] Sparta, WI Our Lady of Spring Bank, Cistercian Abbey.
McCoy, Charles J. '61 (BO) [7] Newton, MA St. Philip Neri Church; On Special or Other Diocesan Assignment.
McCoy, Msgr. James P. '63 (PH) Chalfont, PA St. Jude Church.
McCoy, John '93 (STU) [3] Steubenville, OH Holy Rosary Church; [E] Steubenville, OH Trinity Health System; [E] Steubenville, OH Trinity Health System.
McCoy, Kevin C. '81 (SC) [H] Sioux City, IA Diocese of Sioux City Priests' Welfare Foundation.
McCoy, Msgr. Patrick (SR) [G] Santa Rosa, CA Santa Rosa Memorial Hospital.
McCoy, Perry *o.s.m.* '93 (TUC) Yuma, AZ St. Francis of Assisi Church; Yuma, AZ St. John Neumann Church.
McCracken, John E. '79 (GAY) Roscommon, MI St. Michael Church.
McCracken, Msgr. John T. '44 (OAK) [1] Walnut Creek, CA St. Anne Church.
McCracken, Kevin *c.m.* (LA) [A] Camarillo, CA St. John's Seminary.
McCrann, Peter J. *s.m.m.* '58 (RVC) Bay Shore, NY Southside Hospital; [N] Bay Shore, NY Montfort Missionaries.
McCrate, D. Stephen '89 (BEA) [7] Port Arthur, TX St. Joseph Church.
McCready, Daniel A. '47 (PHX) Retired.
McCready, James *s.j.* '63 (SPK) [K] Spokane, WA Regis Community.
McCreanor, David '75 (PT) [4] Tallahassee, FL St. Louis Church.
McCreanor, James '78 (MIA) [23] Miami, FL St. John Neumann Church.
McCreary, Glenn E. '95 (SCR) Kingston, PA St. Ignatius Church; Sayre, PA Church of the Epiphany.
McCreary, Robert E. *o.f.m.cap.* '64 (BAL) Cresaptown, MD St. Ambrose Church.
McCreary, Robert L. *o.f.m.cap.* '59 (PIT) [N] Pittsburgh, PA St. Conrad Friary.
McCreary, Roberto *o.f.m.cap.* '64 (BAL) [M] Cumberland, MD SS. Peter and Paul Friary.
McCreedy, Harry E. '72 (PH) [5] Norristown, PA St. Paul Church.
McCreedy, Justin D. *o.s.b.* '70 (SEA) [M] Lacey, WA St. Martin's Abbey.
McCreedy, Justin D. *o.s.b.* '70 (YAK) [B] Yakima, WA Providence Yakima Medical Center.
McCreesh, Eugene P. *s.j.* '54 (CHL) [9] Charlotte, NC St. Peter Church; [J] Charlotte, NC Jesuit Community.
McCreesh, Thomas P. *o.p.* '72 (WDC) [B] Washington, DC Cluster of Independent Theological School, The; [B] Washington, DC Dominican House of Studies.
McCreight, James H. '68 (CLV) [20] Cleveland, OH Cristo Rey, Capilla De Church; [50] Cleveland, OH St. Michael Church.
McCreight, Jim (CLV) [X] Cleveland, OH Diocesan Hispanic Office.
McCrillis, Philip '61 (SJ) Special Assignment.
McCrone, John '82 (NEW) Paramus, NJ Bergen Pines County Hospital.
McCrone, John M. '82 (NEW) Paramus, NJ Annunciation Church.
McCue, Michael J. *o.s.f.s.* '90 (ARL) [D] Alexandria, VA Bishop Ireton High School; [J] Alexandria, VA Oblates of St. Francis de Sales Residence.
McCue, Richard T. '58 (CHL) Franklin, NC St. Francis of Assisi Church.
McCue, Will *s.c.* '74 (BR) Special Assignment.
McCulken, Michael T. '76 (PH) Brookline, PA Annunciation B.V.M. Church.
McCullagh, Francis '37 (BUF) [M] Silver Creek, NY St. Columbans on the Lake, Home for the Aged.
McCullagh, Msgr. John P. '55 (BRK) [143] Brooklyn, NY St. Vincent de Paul Church.
McCullen, John L. '44 (MIA) Deerfield Beach, FL St. Ambrose Church.
McCullen, John L. '44 (TOL) On Duty Outside the Diocese.
McCullough, Hugh J. *s.j.b.* '79 (FR) South Yarmouth, MA St. Pius Tenth Church.
McCullough, J. Edward '67 (GBG) Dunbar, PA St. Aloysius Church.
McCullough, James '57 (E) [B] Erie, PA Gannon University.
McCullough, Michael P. '73 (LA) Los Angeles, CA L.A. Police Department.
McCumber, William '83 (STL) [2] St. Charles, MO St. Cletus Church.
McCune, James L. '58 (BO) Canton, MA St. John the Evangelist Church.
McCurdy, Richard L. *s.j.* (SAC) [C] Sacramento, CA Jesuit High School; [H] Carmichael, CA Jesuit High School Community of Sacramento.
McCurdy, William J. *s.j.* '61 (ROC) [B] Rochester, NY McQuaid Jesuit High School.
McCurry, James E. *o.f.m.conv.* '77 (SPR) [A] Granby, MA St. Hyacinth College and Seminary; [Q] Granby, MA Knights of the Immaculata Movement (Militia Immaculatae, M.I.).
McCusker, William C. *s.j.* '51 (ROC) [B] Rochester, NY McQuaid Jesuit High School.
McDade, Msgr. Thomas J. '74 (NEW) On Duty Outside the Archdiocese.
McDaid, Msgr. Edward J. (CAM) Retired.
McDaid, Henry A. '63 (BIR) Sylacauga, AL St. Jude Church; Talladega, AL St. Francis of Assisi Church; [H] Talladega, AL Talladega College Catholic Campus Ministry.
McDaid, J. Anthony '75 (DEN) On Duty Outside the Archdiocese.
McDaniel, George '70 (DAV) [B] Davenport, IA St. Ambrose University.
McDaniel, Isaac *o.s.b.* '82 (IND) St. Croix, IN Holy Cross Church; St. Croix, IN St. Isidore the Farmer Church; [J] St. Meinrad, IN St. Meinrad Archabbey.
McDaniel, John W. *s.j.* '71 (PH) [Z] Philadelphia, PA Jesuit Community at St. Joseph's University.
McDaniel, Rodney '58 (CIN) [L] Cincinnati, OH St. Margaret Hall.
McDarby, J. Patrick *o.s.b.* '53 (SCL) [I] Collegeville, MN St. John's Abbey, of the Order of St. Benedict.
McDermott, Brian O. *s.j.* '68 (BO) [B] Cambridge, MA Weston Jesuit School of Theology; [W] Cambridge, MA Weston Jesuit Community.
McDermott, Charles B. '63 (PRO) [6] Pawtucket, RI St. Joseph's Church.
McDermott, Charles B. '73 (NEW) Union, NJ St. Michael's Church.
McDermott, Charles S. '60 (SAC) [21] Sacramento, CA St. Rose Church.
McDermott, Christopher H. *c.s.sp.* '81 (PH) [Z] Bensalem, PA Congregation of the Holy Ghost Fathers and Brothers.
McDermott, Edwin J. *s.j.* '49 (SFR) [N] San Francisco, CA Jesuit Community at University of San Francisco.

McDermott, Eric *s.j.* '43 (PH) [Z] Philadelphia, PA Jesuit Community at St. Joseph's University.
McDermott, Francis A. '38 (PH) [133] Philadelphia, PA St. Patrick Church; Retired.
McDermott, Msgr. Ignatius D. '36 (CHI) Retired.
McDermott, Msgr. James M. '48 (NY) [2] White Plains, NY St. John the Evangelist Church.
McDermott, James P. '42 (BRK) Retired.
McDermott, John '89 (BUR) [J] Burlington, VT University of Vermont-The Catholic Center at UVM.
McDermott, Msgr. John F. '57 (NEW) Upper Saddle River, NJ Church of the Presentation.
McDermott, John J. '86 (DUB) [C] Dubuque, IA Loras College.
McDermott, John J. '89 (BUR) Middlebury, VT Assumption of the Blessed Virgin Mary Church.
McDermott, John M. *s.j.* '71 (NY) [Z] New York, NY Jesuit Provincial's Office.
McDermott, Joseph *s.v.d.* '52 (DUB) [B] Epworth, IA Divine Word College.
McDermott, Joseph J. '42 (BRK) Retired.
McDermott, Joseph M. '95 (PH) Warrington, PA St. Robert Bellarmine Church.
McDermott, Joseph P. '62 (BO) Stoughton, MA Immaculate Conception Church.
McDermott, Michael '65 (SEA) [14] Tacoma, WA Our Lady, Queen of Heaven Church.
McDermott, Michael '66 (PIT) Allegheny County, PA Eye and Ear Hospital; Allegheny County, PA Montefiore Hospital; Allegheny County, PA Presbyterian-University Hospital; Allegheny County, PA Western Psychiatric Hospital.
McDermott, Michael F. '79 (GI) St. Paul, NE SS. Peter and Paul Church.
McDermott, Michael J. '75 (WIL) Wilmington Manor, DE Our Lady of Fatima Church.
McDermott, Neal *o.p.* '61 (NO) [30] New Orleans, LA St. Dominic Church.
McDermott, Patrick '67 (SEA) Aberdeen, WA St. Mary's Church; Aberdeen, WA SS. Peter and Paul Church; Hoquiam, WA Our Lady of Good Help Church; Ocean Shores, WA St. Jerome Church.
McDermott, Patrick M. '64 (BLX) [4] Biloxi, MS Sacred Heart Church.
McDermott, Paul B. '59 (CHI) Wadsworth, IL St. Patrick Church.
McDermott, Paul B. '59 (PEO) Absent on Leave.
McDermott, Robert B. '90 (PH) West Chester, PA St. Agnes Church.
McDermott, Msgr. Robert T. '69 (CAM) [7] Camden, NJ St. Joseph's Pro-Cathedral.
McDermott, Robert T. '81 (MIL) [2] Kenosha, WI St. Casimir's Church.
McDermott, Robert T. '81 (STA) [17] Jacksonville, FL St. Patrick Church.
McDermott, Thomas F. *s.j.* '38 (BO) [W] Weston, MA Campion Health Center, Inc.
McDermott, Thomas F. *m.m.* '44 (NY) [Z] Maryknoll, NY Maryknoll Fathers and Brothers.
McDermott, Msgr. Thomas J. '55 (SD) Retired.
McDermott, Thomas J. '56 (SCR) Wyalusing, PA St. Mary's Assumption Church.
McDermott, Thomas K. *o.p.* '83 (CHI) [N] Chicago, IL Dominicans (Provincial Office).
McDevitt, Msgr. Anthony '49 (MOB) [17] Mobile, AL Our Savior Church.
McDevitt, Edward P. *c.o.* '71 (CHR) York, SC Divine Saviour Church; [E] Rock Hill, SC Oratory of St. Philip Neri, Congregation of the Oratory of Pontifical Rite.
McDevitt, Edwin R. *m.m.* '49 (NY) [Z] Maryknoll, NY Maryknoll Fathers and Brothers.
McDevitt, Francis N. '41 (PH) Malvern, PA St. Patrick Church; Retired.
McDevitt, James A. '90 (BGP) [3] Stamford, CT St. Mary's Church; Danbury, CT Federal Correctional Institution.
McDevitt, James J. '35 (PBL) Retired.
McDevitt, John M. *o.s.f.s.* '66 (CAM) [L] Pittsgrove, NJ Villa St. Joseph.
McDevitt, Michael V. '71 (SPC) Poplar Bluff, MO Sacred Heart Church.
McDevitt, Patrick J. *c.m.* '86 (STL) [P] St. Louis, MO Vincentian Residence.
McDevitt, Robert L. *s.j.* '60 (SFR) [N] San Francisco, CA Jesuit Community at University of San Francisco.
McDevitt, Thomas D. '58 (LAN) East Lansing, MI St. John the Evangelist, Student Parish Church.
McDonagh, Andrew J. '42 (CHI) [132] Chicago, IL St. Mary of the Woods Church; Retired.
McDonagh, Msgr. Charles (NY) [3] Kingston, NY St. Joseph Church.
McDonagh, Donald *s.p.s.* '55 (NEW) [N] Cliffside Park, NJ St. Patrick's Missionary Society.
McDonagh, Edward C. '62 (BO) West Bridgewater, MA St. Ann Church.
McDonagh, John J. '81 (NY) North Tarrytown, NY St. Teresa of Avila Church.
McDonagh, John P. '82 (SPR) [1] Springfield, MA St. Michael's Cathedral.
McDonagh, Michael *m.s.h.s.* '74 (DAL) [L] Dallas, TX Marian Servants of the Holy Spirit.
McDonald, A. John '56 (BR) Retired.
McDonald, Allan J. '80 (SAV) [1] Augusta, GA Church of the Most Holy Trinity; [I] Augusta, GA Catholic Cemetery.
McDonald, Bernard (NY) Port Jervis, NY Mercy Community Hospital.
McDonald, C. Alexander '91 (CHR) North Augusta, SC Our Lady of Peace Church.
McDonald, Charles *c.ss.r.* '71 (HBG) [2] Lancaster, PA St. Anthony of Padua Church.
McDonald, Charles J. '65 (LEX) Lawrenceburg, KY St. Lawrence Church.
McDonald, Daniel C. *s.j.* '81 (MIL) [P] Milwaukee, WI Jesuit Provincial Office, Wisconsin Province.
McDonald, Daniel C. *s.j.* '81 (WDC) [M] Washington, DC Leonard Neale House; [V] Washington, DC Jesuit Conference, Inc.
McDonald, David M. '55 (HRT) [2] Hamden, CT Blessed Sacrament Church.
McDonald, Edward J. *c.s.p.* '41 (BO) [P] Boston, MA Paulist Center; [W] Boston, MA Paulist Fathers Residence.
McDonald, Edward J. *c.s.p.* '41 (NY) [Z] Scarsdale, NY Paulist Fathers Generalate.
McDonald, Elmer J. '49 (ROC) Retired.
McDonald, Eustace *c.p.* '45 (BAL) [M] Baltimore, MD St. Joseph's Passionist Community.
McDonald, Finian *o.s.b.* '62 (SCL) [I] Collegeville, MN St. John's Abbey, of the Order of St. Benedict.
McDonald, Francis B. '60 (JOL) Roselle, IL St. Walter Church.
McDonald, Gerald R. *o.f.m.* '45 (PAT) [M] Butler, NJ St. Anthony Friary.
McDonald, J. Robert '37 (DUB) Retired.
McDonald, James E. *c.s.c.* '84 (FTW) [J] South Bend, IN Congregation of Holy Cross Indiana Province Provincial House.
McDonald, Msgr. James M. '67 (RVC) Center Moriches, NY St. John the Evangelist Church.
McDonald, James T. (BO) Retired.
McDonald, John F. '47 (HRT) South Glastonbury, CT St. Augustine Church.
McDonald, John J. *o.p.* '36 (CHI) [N] Chicago, IL Dominicans (Provincial Office).
McDonald, John J. *s.j.* '57 (PAT) [I] Morristown, NJ Loyola House of Retreats.
McDonald, Joseph F., III '87 (B) Pocatello, ID St. Anthony's Church; Pocatello, ID St. John's Community Church; [F] Pocatello, ID Idaho State University, St. John's Community.
McDonald, Joseph S. *s.m.* '61 (CIN) [M] Dayton, OH Marianist Provincialate.
McDonald, Kenneth '57 (LAN) Mason, MI St. James Church.
McDonald, Kevin *c.s.s.r.* (RVC) Bethpage, NY Mid-Island Hospital.
McDonald, Malcolm '85 (PIT) East McKeesport, PA St. Robert Bellarmine Church.
McDonald, Mark *m.s.c.* '68 (RCK) [H] Aurora, IL Missionaries of the Sacred Heart Community.
McDonald, Martin '62 (MRY) Boulder Creek, CA St. Michael Church; Boulder Creek, CA Ben Lomond Youth Authority Camp.
McDonald, Matthew D. '40 (CHI) Skokie, IL St. Joan of Arc Church; Retired.
McDonald, Maurice *c.s.s.r.* '25 (ALB) [L] Saratoga Springs, NY St. John Neumann Residence.
McDonald, Michael D. '85 (GI) Burwell, NE Sacred Heart Church.
McDonald, Michael J. '50 (PRT) [1] Portland, ME Cathedral of the Immaculate Conception; Retired.
McDonald, Paul *o.s.b.* '70 (PRO) [P] Portsmouth, RI Abbey of St. Gregory the Great.
McDonald, Paul F. '51 (DUB) Retired.
McDonald, Perry *o.f.m.cap.* '67 (DET) [K] Detroit, MI St. Bonaventure Friary; [K] Detroit, MI St. Bonaventure Friary.
McDonald, Peter '59 (SFR) San Anselmo, CA St. Anselm Church.
McDonald, Raphael *o.f.m.* '44 (PAT) [M] Ringwood, NJ Holy Name Friary.
McDonald, Raphael *o.f.m.* '44 (SP) [O] St. Petersburg, FL St. Anthony Friary.
McDonald, Robert *s.m.* '50 (PRT) Brunswick, ME St. John the Baptist Church.
McDonald, Sebastian *c.p.* '58 (DET) [K] Detroit, MI St. Paul of the Cross Community, Congregation of the Passion.
McDonald, Thomas A. '52 (NY) Poughkeepsie, NY St. Francis Hospital; [S] Poughkeepsie, NY St. Francis Hospital.
McDonald, Thomas M. '56 (NY) On Duty Outside the Archdiocese.
McDonald, Vincent *o.carm.* (ALB) [5] Troy, NY St. Joseph Church.
McDonald, Vincent *s.c.j.* '58 (GAL) [34] Houston, TX Holy Name Church.
McDonald, William '89 (LAV) [3] Las Vegas, NV Holy Family Church.
McDonnell, Anthony '70 (LA) Sick Leave.
McDonnell, Charles J. '54 (NEW) South Orange, NJ Our Lady of Sorrows Church.
McDonnell, Cyril '43 (CAM) Retired.
McDonnell, David '72 (PAT) Randolph, NJ St. Matthew the Apostle Church.
McDonnell, Donald C. '47 (SFR) Retired.
McDonnell, Francis E. '51 (RCK) Sterling, IL Sacred Heart Church.
McDonnell, Francis P. '58 (HRT) Windsor Locks, CT St. Mary Church.
McDonnell, Francis R. *o.s.a.* '42 (DET) Grosse Pointe Park, MI St. Clare of Montefalco Church.
McDonnell, Francis W. '60 (SD) San Diego, CA Mercy Hospital; Retired; [F] San Diego, CA Mercy Hospital and Medical Center dba Mercy Healthcare San Diego.
McDonnell, Msgr. James T. '35 (NY) Retired.
McDonnell, John (CHI) [38] Chicago, IL Christ the Redeemer Byzantine Bielarusian Church.
McDonnell, John *c.m.* '43 (BRK) [U] Jamaica, NY Vincentian Residence.
McDonnell, John H. '56 (WH) [3] Charleston, WV St. Agnes Church.
McDonnell, John J. *c.m.* '43 (BRK) [D] Queens and Staten Island, NY St. John's University.
McDonnell, Msgr. John J. '44 (YAK) [2] Yakima, WA Holy Family Church.
McDonnell, John J. '73 (CHI) [1] Chicago, IL Cathedral of the Holy Name; [A] Mundelein, IL University of St. Mary of the Lake-Mundelein Seminary.
McDonnell, Joseph F. '55 (CHI) Western Springs, IL St. John of the Cross Church; Retired.
McDonnell, Msgr. Joseph J. '67 (DM) West Des Moines, IA Sacred Heart Church.
McDonnell, Joseph M. '30 (ROC) Newark, NY St. Michael Church; Retired.
McDonnell, Joseph T. '50 (SD) Retired.
McDonnell, Kilian *o.s.b.* '51 (SCL) [I] Collegeville, MN St. John's Abbey, of the Order of St. Benedict.
McDonnell, Lawrence V. *c.s.p.* '53 (NY) [104] New York, NY St. Paul the Apostle Church.
McDonnell, Martin '68 (PAT) Parsippany, NJ St. Ann Church.
McDonnell, Michael *o.f.m.* '65 (NY) [35] New York, NY St. Francis of Assisi Church.
McDonnell, P. William '64 (RCK) [4] Freeport, IL St. Thomas Aquinas Church.
McDonnell, Msgr. Patrick '57 (MIA) [13] Fort Lauderdale, FL St. Sebastian Church.
McDonnell, Patrick '73 (BWN) Alamo, TX Resurrection Church.
McDonnell, Paul A. *o.s.j.* '91 (SCR) [1] Pittston, PA Our Lady of Mt. Carmel Church.
McDonnell, Robert *c.s.c.* '57 (ORL) [F] Cocoa Beach, FL Holy Cross Fathers, Eastern Priests Province.
McDonnell, Sean (PAT) Parsippany, NJ St. Christopher Church.
McDonnell, Stephen '89 (RVC) Absent on Leave.
McDonnell, Thomas *s.j.* '68 (RIC) [4] Richmond, VA Our Lady of Lourdes Church.
McDonnell, Thomas J. '60 (BO) [12] Boston, MA St. Augustine Church.
McDonnell, Thomas P. *m.m.* '65 (NY) [Z] Maryknoll, NY Maryknoll Fathers and Brothers.
McDonnell, Msgr. Timothy A. '63 (NY) Chappaqua, NY St. John and St. Mary Church.
McDonnell, Vincent (MOB) Retired.
McDonnell, Msgr. William J. '54 (BUF) Amherst, NY St. Leo Church.
McDonough, Donat Michael '74 (SP) On Duty Outside the Diocese.
McDonough, Edward *c.ss.r.* '48 (BO) [13] Boston, MA Basilica of Our Lady of Perpetual Help.
McDonough, James '42 (AGN) Dededo, GU Santa Barbara Church.
McDonough, James '84 (PIT) [2] Munhall, PA St. Maximilian Kolbe Church.
McDonough, James A. *o.p.* '62 (AUS) [H] Austin, TX Dominican Fathers.
McDonough, James A. *o.p.* '62 (NO) [P] New Orleans, LA Dominican Fathers & Brothers, Southern Dominican Province; [S] Metairie, LA Southern Dominican Foundation.
McDonough, James E. *ss.cc.* '68 (FR) [K] Fairhaven, MA Sacred Hearts Provincial House.
McDonough, James M. *s.j.* '61 (P) [L] Portland, OR Jesuit Provincial Office (Oregon Prov.).
McDonough, Msgr. James T. '57 (PH) Strafford, PA Our Lady of the Assumption Church; [EE] Philadelphia, PA Ladies of Charity.
McDonough, John *o.p.* (OAK) [N] Moraga, CA Dominican Community.
McDonough, John *s.d.b.* '89 (OAK) [A] Berkeley, CA Dominican School of Philosophy and Theology; [B] Moraga, CA Saint Mary's College; [Q] Moraga, CA St. Mary's College Campus Ministry.
McDonough, Msgr. John P. '52 (BO) [3] Peabody, MA St. John the Baptist Church.
McDonough, John P. '95 (WH) [1] Charleston, WV Sacred Heart Co-Cathedral.

McDonough, John T. '50 (CLV) [17] Akron, OH St. Sebastian Church; Hinckley, OH Our Lady of Grace Church; Retired.
McDonough, Joseph *s.t.* '68 (WDC) [B] Silver Spring, MD Holy Trinity Mission Seminary (1926).
McDonough, Joseph F. *c.s.sp.* '53 (PRO) Tiverton, RI St. Madeleine Church.
McDonough, Kevin M. '80 (STP) [32] St. Paul, MN St. Peter Claver Church.
McDonough, Msgr. Martin J. '40 (PH) Doylestown, PA Our Lady of Mount Carmel Church; Retired.
McDonough, Patrick M. '68 (WH) St. Albans, WV St. Francis of Assisi Church.
McDonough, Raymond *c.p.* '47 (SAC) [H] Citrus Heights, CA Christ the King Retreat; [J] Citrus Heights, CA Christ the King Retreat Center.
McDonough, Roger F. '76 (BGP) [3] Greenwich, CT St. Paul's Church.
McDonough, Msgr. T. Joseph '46 (MAN) [8] Nashua, NH St. Patrick Church.
McDonough, Thomas R. '89 (STP) [3] St. Paul, MN Blessed Sacrament Church.
McDonough, Timothy T. *c.s.sp.* '56 (WDC) [B] Wheaton, MD Holy Ghost Fathers Development Office.
McDonough, Vincent *s.j.* '62 (ROC) [B] Elmira, NY Notre Dame High School.
McDonough, William C. '82 (STP) [A] St. Paul, MN The Saint Paul Seminary; [C] St. Paul, MN University of St. Thomas.
McDougal, Jon '79 (LR) Camden, AR St. Louis Church.
McDougall, James '75 (LAN) Saline, MI St. Andrew Church.
McDougall, Russell K. *c.s.c.* '91 (FTW) [J] South Bend, IN Congregation of Holy Cross Indiana Province Provincial House.
McDowell, John W. *o.f.m.* '77 (NY) [35] New York, NY St. Francis of Assisi Church.
McDowell, Leo George '94 (GF) [1] Billings, MT St. Patrick's Co-Cathedral; [2] Billings, MT Holy Rosary Church.
McDowell, Patrick '54 (DUL) [4] Duluth, MN Our Lady of Mercy Church; [13] Duluth, MN St. Mary Star of the Sea Church; [15] Duluth, MN St. Peter's Church.
McDowell, Patrick D. '68 (SCR) Meshoppen, PA St. Joachim's Church.
McDuffie, Paul A. '95 (CHR) Myrtle Beach, SC St. Andrew's Church.
McDyre, Cajetan *s.t.* '45 (PAT) [M] Stirling, NJ Holy Spirit Missionary Cenacle.
McEachin, Cornelius '48 (SAG) Retired.
McEachin, Donald *c.s.sp.* (PIT) [B] Pittsburgh, PA Duquesne University of the Holy Ghost; [Q] Slippery Rock, PA Office for Campus Ministry.
McElaney, Robert *o.s.b.* '82 (IND) [J] Indianapolis, IN St. Maur Priory.
McElaney, Robert *o.s.b.* '82 (NEW) [N] Newark, NJ Newark Abbey.
McElaney, Robert D. '82 (PRM) Indianapolis, IN St. Athanasius Church.
McElduff, Edward W. '53 (ALN) Berlinsville, PA St. Nicholas Church.
McEleney, Neil J. *c.s.p.* '53 (NY) [Z] Scarsdale, NY Paulist Fathers Generalate.
McEleney, Neil J. *c.s.p.* '53 (WDC) [B] Washington, DC St. Paul's College.
McEleney, Robert J. '58 (RIC) Hurt, VA St. Victoria Church.
McElhinney, Thomas *glmy.* '62 (NSH) Fayetteville, TN St. Anthony Church; Pulaski, TN Immaculate Conception Church.
McElhinny, Michael *s.m.* '80 (BO) [W] Boston, MA Marist Fathers and Brothers Provincial House; [W] Cambridge, MA Our Lady of Mercy Marist Novitiate.
McElligott, Msgr. Francis J. '38 (CHI) [108] Chicago, IL St. John Fisher Church; Retired.
McElligott, Thomas J. '69 (OAK) [3] Berkeley, CA St. Joseph The Worker Church.
McElligott, Thomas J. '69 (SFR) On Duty Outside the Archdiocese.
McElnee, Michael A. *s.j.* '95 (PH) [C] Philadelphia, PA St. Joseph's University.
McElroy, Charles J. '64 (PH) Delphi, PA St. Mary Church.
McElroy, Francis P. *c.ss.r.* '48 (BRK) [107] Brooklyn, NY Our Lady of Perpetual Help Basilica; Brooklyn, NY Lutheran Medical Center.
McElroy, Herbert '34 (BRK) Retired.
McElroy, James E. '56 (LA) [14] Los Angeles, CA Holy Trinity Church.
McElroy, John J. '45 (PRO) [6] Pawtucket, RI St. Joseph's Church; Retired.
McElroy, John W. (BO) Avon, MA St. Michael Church.
McElroy, Msgr. Robert W. '80 (SFR) [2] San Mateo, CA St. Gregory Church; Special Assignment.
McElroy, Thomas *ss.cc.* (FR) [A] Wareham, MA Sacred Hearts Retreat Center.
McElroy, William J. *c.s.sp.* '45 (ALX) [F] Natchitoches, LA Holy Ghost Fathers Home, Maison Brothier.
McElwee, Michael A. *s.j.* '95 (PH) [Z] Philadelphia, PA Jesuit Community at St. Joseph's University.
McElwee, Robert W. '83 (WCH) Pittsburg, KS Our Lady of Lourdes Church.
McElynn, John D. *c.m.* '81 (BRK) [U] Queens Village, NY DePaul Residence.
McEnaney, Msgr. Owen J. '43 (NY) Retired; [V] New York, NY Kateri Residence.
McEneaney, Msgr. John P.A. '43 (SFS) Retired.
McEneany, Joseph *ss.cc.* '57 (ORG) Costa Mesa, CA Fairview Developmental Center; [H] Costa Mesa, CA Sacred Heart Fathers.
McEnery, Dennis '50 (DUL) Retired.
McEnery, James J. '53 (MAD) Milton, WI St. Mary Church.
McEnhill, Gerald A. '72 (DET) Farmington, MI St. Gerald Church.
McEnhill, John *s.m.* '56 (SFR) [B] San Francisco, CA Marianist Seminary; [N] San Francisco, CA Marianist Community.
McEniry, Robert F. *s.j.* '51 (OM) [K] Omaha, NE Jesuit Community At Creighton University.
McEnnis, Thomas '45 (SEA) Retired.
McEntee, John B. '61 (STL) Luebbering, MO St. Francis of Assisi Church.
McEntee, Paul H. '57 (BO) Watertown, MA Sacred Heart Church.
McEvilly, John W. '64 (BEL) [3] Belleville, IL Our Lady Queen of Peace Church.
McEvoy, David *o.carm.* '88 (NY) [Z] Middletown, NY Brandsma Priory.
McEvoy, John '52 (MRY) Retired.
McEvoy, William '87 (KCK) [2] Kansas City, KS Blessed Sacrament Church.
McFadden, Brian '88 (NEW) [3] Linden, NJ St. John the Apostle Church.
McFadden, Edward J. *s.j.* '54 (SJ) [D] San Jose, CA Bellarmine College Preparatory.
McFadden, Frank C. '83 (BAL) Bel Air, MD St. Margaret Church.
McFadden, George B. '52 (SC) Retired.
McFadden, J. Michael '74 (HBG) [3] Lebanon, PA St. Cecilia Church.
McFadden, James J. *m.m.* '61 (HON) [9] Honolulu, HI St. John the Baptist Church; [H] Honolulu, HI Maryknoll Fathers House.
McFadden, John R. '62 (PH) Cheltenham, PA Presentation of Blessed Virgin Mary Church.
McFadden, Msgr. Joseph P. '81 (PH) Morton, PA Our Lady of Perpetual Help Church; [D] Springfield, PA Cardinal O'Hara High School.
McFadden, Msgr. Leo E. '53 (RNO) Retired.
McFadden, Michael '61 (SAC) [11] Sacramento, CA St. Charles Borromeo Church.
McFadden, Michael J. *o.s.a.* '67 (LA) [31] Los Angeles, CA Mother of Good Counsel Church.
McFadden, William C. *s.j.* '59 (WDC) [M] Washington, DC The Jesuit Community at Georgetown University.
McFadin, Marcus '92 (ELP) [30] El Paso, TX St. Pius X Church.
McFalls, Dean '95 (STO) [7] Stockton, CA St. Luke Church.
McFarland, Msgr. Edward J. '55 (COL) Gahanna, OH St. Matthew Church.
McFarland, Eugene H. '43 (ROC) Geneseo, NY St. Mary Church; Retired.
McFarland, Francis T. '57 (BO) [3] Medford, MA St. Joseph Church.
McFarland, H. James *s.j.* '69 (SAC) Sacramento, CA Sutter General Hospital; Sacramento, CA Sutter Memorial Hospital.
McFarland, H. James *s.j.* '69 (STL) [P] St. Louis, MO The Jesuits of the Missouri Province.
McFarland, James W. '47 (NEW) Retired.
McFarland, Michael C. *s.j.* '84 (BO) [W] Boston, MA The Society of Jesus of New England-Provincial Offices.
McFarland, Michael C. *s.j.* '84 (SPK) [C] Spokane, WA Gonzaga University.
McFarland, Timothy D. *c.pp.s.* '83 (LFT) [A] Rensselaer, IN Saint Joseph's College.
McFarlane, Dale F. '66 (GF) Retired.
McGaffin, Joseph '96 (PHX) Chandler, AZ St. Mary's Church.
McGagh, Martin '54 (FRS) Retired.
McGahagan, James E. '68 (SCR) Buttonwood, PA Exaltation of the Holy Cross Church.
McGahee, Thomas *s.d.b.* '77 (PAT) [D] Paterson, NJ Don Bosco Technical High School.
McGahren, Joseph J. *m.m.* '51 (PH) [Z] Philadelphia, PA Maryknoll House.
McGanhey, Charles (BO) [1] Arlington, MA St. Agnes Church.
McGann, Diarmuid F. '64 (RVC) Blue Point, NY Our Lady of the Snow Church.
McGann, Francis J. (BO) Needham, MA St. Joseph Church; Retired.
McGann, Gerard J. '48 (BO) Retired.
McGann, Joseph F. '44 (NY) Retired.
McGann, L. Philip '71 (WIL) Retired.
McGann, Richard P. '70 (HRT) Plainville, CT Our Lady of Mercy Church.
McGann, Thomas F. *s.j.* '45 (NY) [Z] New York, NY Murray-Weigel Hall.
McGannon, J. Barry *s.j.* '55 (STL) [C] St. Louis, MO Saint Louis University; [P] St. Louis, MO Jesuit Community Corporation at St. Louis University - Jesuit Hall.
McGarr, Joseph '86 (ALN) [2] Allentown, PA St. Francis of Assisi Church.
McGarrigle, Michael '49 (PRT) Retired.
McGarrill, Colman *t.o.r.* '54 (SP) [13] Tampa, FL St. Patrick Church.
McGarrity, Patrick J. *c.ss.r.* '61 (HBG) New Holland, PA Our Lady of Lourdes Church; [H] Ephrata, PA St. Clement's Mission House.
McGarrity, Richard A. *s.j.* '70 (MIL) [P] Milwaukee, WI Jesuit Community at Marquette University.
McGarry, Gerard J. '34 (NEW) Mountainside, NJ Our Lady of Lourdes Church.
McGarry, James J. '70 (SCR) Clarks Summit, PA Our Lady of the Snows Church; Clarks Summit, PA Clarks Summit State Hospital.
McGarry, John P. *s.j.* '93 (LA) [F] Los Angeles, CA Loyola High School.
McGarry, Joseph P. '55 (HRT) [5] West Hartford, CT St. Peter Claver Church.
McGarry, Michael B. *c.s.p.* '75 (OAK) [2] Berkeley, CA Holy Spirit Parish Church; [Q] Berkeley, CA Holy Spirit Parish, University of California, Newman Hall.
McGarry, Peter *o.carm.* '69 (CHI) [68] Chicago, IL St. Gelasius Church.
McGarry, Thomas (NY) Bronx, NY St. Barnabas Hospital.
McGarry, William C. '59 (BUF) [11] Niagara Falls, NY Prince of Peace Church.
McGarry, William J. '58 (CI) [C] Kolonia, Pohnpei, FM Jesuit House.
McGarty, Bernard O. '49 (LC) [2] La Crosse, WI Blessed Sacrament Church.
McGarvey, Joseph F. '50 (CAM) Retired.
McGaugh, Philip E. (BO) [35] Boston, MA St. Joseph Church; Boston, MA Massachusetts General Hospital; Boston, MA South Shore Hospital.
McGauley, Francis H. *s.j.* '55 (PH) [Z] Philadelphia, PA Jesuit Community at St. Joseph's University.
McGee, Dominic *o.f.m.conv.* '67 (TR) [5] Trenton, NJ Immaculate Conception Church.
McGee, Francis J. '45 (BRK) [236] Queens, NY St. Rose of Lima Church; Retired.
McGee, H. Desmond, Jr. '71 (E) [C] Bradford, PA Bradford Central Christian High School.
McGee, James J. *s.s.* '85 (SCR) On Duty Outside the Diocese.
McGee, Jim *s.s.* '85 (OAK) Pleasant Hill, CA Christ the King Church.
McGee, John E. *o.s.f.s.* '82 (R) [2] Durham, NC Holy Infant Church.
McGee, Leo J. '57 (PH) [117] Philadelphia, PA Our Lady Help of Christians Church.
McGee, Michael J. '77 (BRK) [188] Queens, NY St. Joseph Church.
McGee, Peter '53 (LA) Gardena, CA St. Anthony of Padua Church.
McGee, Richard F. *c.r.* '74 (SB) [3] Fontana, CA St. Joseph Church.
McGee, Thomas J. *o.s.f.s.* '71 (WIL) [B] Wilmington, DE Salesianum School.
McGee, Timothy H. '87 (CR) East Grand Forks, MN Sacred Heart Church.
McGee, W. Desmond '71 (E) Bradford, PA St. Francis of Assisi Church.
McGeean, John T. '86 (JOL) Oswego, IL St. Anne Church.
McGeory, Peter '76 (NY) Military Chaplains.
McGeough, Jude P. '58 (PRO) [2] East Providence, RI St. Martha Church.
McGeough, Martin *c.m.* '76 (BIR) Lanett, AL Holy Family Church.
McGeown, Joseph P. '65 (PH) Wallingford, PA St. John Chrysostom Church.
McGeown, William F. '70 (PH) [126] Philadelphia, PA Our Lady of Ransom Church.
McGerity, Francis X. '84 (CC) On Duty Outside the Diocese.
McGettigan, Msgr. D. James '67 (PH) [U] Darby, PA Villa Saint Joseph; [U] Ventnor, PA Villa St. Joseph by the Sea.
McGettigan, Neil J. *o.s.a.* '53 (PH) [C] Villanova, PA Villanova University; [Z] Villanova, PA St. Thomas Monastery.
McGettrick, Msgr. Thomas P. '56 (CC) [20] Corpus Christi, TX St. Philip The Apostle Church.
McGhee, James '95 (AMA) Canadian, TX Sacred Heart Church.
McGhee, William P. '82 (BEL) Mound City, IL Church of the Immaculate Conception-St. Mary.
McGill, Joseph F. '56 (NY) Absent on Leave.
McGill, Joseph P. *s.j.* '60 (FWT) [J] Lake Dallas, TX Montserrat Jesuit Retreat House.
McGill, Malachy *c.p.* '46 (ALT) [J] Bedford, PA St. Mary's House of Greater Solitude.
McGilley, Michael J. '65 (CAM) Audubon, NJ Church of

the Holy Maternity.
McGillicuddy, Sean J. *c.ss.r.* '86 (PH) [25] Philadelphia, PA St. Boniface Church.
McGilvary, A. Robert *o.s.f.s.* '62 (ALN) [B] Center Valley, PA Allentown College of St. Francis de Sales.
McGilvray, A. Robert *o.s.f.s.* '62 (ALN) [K] Center Valley, PA Oblates of St. Francis de Sales.
McGing, Thomas '71 (JKS) Vicksburg, MS St. Paul Church.
McGinley, Anthony J. '45 (HBG) Retired.
McGinley, Bernard P. *m.a.* '61 (HBG) [4] Harrisburg, PA Holy Family Church.
McGinley, James J. *s.j.* '40 (ALB) [O] Auriesville, NY Jesuit Retreat House for Priests, Religious and Lay People.
McGinley, Jeremiah V. *o.f.m.* '55 (NEW) Fair Lawn, NJ St. Anne's Church.
McGinley, John F. *o.s.f.s.* '68 (ALN) [B] Center Valley, PA Allentown College of St. Francis de Sales; [K] Center Valley, PA Oblates of St. Francis de Sales.
McGinley, Kevin P. *s.j.* '91 (SPK) [B] Spokane, WA St. Michael's Institute; [C] Spokane, WA Gonzaga University; [E] Spokane, WA Gonzaga Preparatory School.
McGinn, Anthony F. *s.j.* '79 (NO) [F] New Orleans, LA Jesuit High School; [H] New Orleans, LA Jesuit High School.
McGinn, Charles T. '69 (KCK) Olathe, KS St. Paul's Church.
McGinn, Daniel A. *s.s.c.* '53 (LA) Granada Hills, CA St. Euphrasia Church.
McGinn, Finian *o.f.m.* (OAK) [R] Berkley, CA Multicultural Institute.
McGinn, Finian *o.f.m.* '60 (OAK) [N] Oakland, CA Franciscan Friars Provincial Office, Province of St. Barbara.
McGinn, Finian *o.f.m.* '60 (SFR) [5] San Francisco, CA St. Anthony Church.
McGinn, John J. '52 (DEN) [4] Englewood, CO St. Thomas More Church.
McGinn, Msgr. Malachy M. '61 (SB) Palm Springs, CA St. Theresa Church.
McGinn, Sylvester P. '56 (NY) [195] Staten Island, NY St. Ann Church.
McGinness, Matthew C. '89 (WCH) [18] Wichita, KS St. Paul Parish Church; [K] Wichita, KS Wichita State University.
McGinnis, Albin C. '77 (PIT) Waynesburg, PA St. Ann Church; Greene County, PA Greene County Memorial; Greene County, PA Curry Memorial Home; Greene County, PA Franklin Care Center; Greene County, PA Waynesburg County Jail; [Q] Slippery Rock, PA Office for Campus Ministry.
McGinnis, Gary *s.d.s.* '62 (MIL) [P] Milwaukee, WI Salvatorians - Jordan Hall.
McGinnis, James '78 (PH) [93] Philadelphia, PA St. Martin De Porres Church.
McGinnis, Jay W. '76 (BUF) Lancaster, NY Our Lady of Pompeii Church.
McGinnis, Joseph '46 (WIN) [F] Wabasha, MN St. Elizabeth's Health Care Center.
McGinnis, Msgr. Joseph R. '46 (WIN) Retired; [D] Wabasha, MN St. Elizabeth's Hospital; [F] Wabasha, MN St. Elizabeth's Health Care Center.
McGinnis, N. Charles '41 (LR) Retired.
McGinnity, Ambrose T. '45 (GRY) Retired.
McGinnity, John C. '75 (WH) Ronceverte, WV St. Catherine of Siena Church.
McGinnity, Joseph P. '56 (CHI) [4] Des Plaines, IL St. Zachary Church.
McGinnity, P. J. '91 (KNX) [4] Chattanooga, TN St. Stephen Church.
McGinnity, Robert F. '55 (CHI) Palos Hills, IL Sacred Heart Church.
McGinty, John P. (BO) [71] Boston, MA St. Theresa Church; [A] Boston, MA St. John's Seminary School of Theology.
McGinty, John P. *s.j.* '58 (BAL) [M] Baltimore, MD Jesuit Fathers and Brothers Maryland Provincial Curia.
McGinty, Msgr. Michael J. '31 (OAK) Retired.
McGinty, Vincent T. *s.j.* '51 (SJ) [M] Los Gatos, CA California Province of the Society of Jesus, Jesuit Provincial Office; [M] Los Gatos, CA Sacred Heart Jesuit Center.
McGivern, Carroll A. '35 (DAV) [B] Davenport, IA St. Ambrose University.
McGivern, John W. '91 (CHI) [41] Chicago, IL St. Clement Church.
McGivney, Thomas '91 (JOL) Addison, IL St. Joseph Church.
McGlade, Desmond *c.s.sp.* '41 (SJ) Mountain View, CA St. Athanasius Church.
McGlade, Thomas F. '43 (RVC) Setauket, NY St. James Church; Retired.
McGlauchlin, Michael '86 (STP) Hassan Township, MN St. Walburga Church; Rogers, MN St. Martin Church.
McGlinchey, James J. '56 (TLS) Retired.
McGlinchy, Edward H. *s.j.* '49 (NY) [Z] Cornwall, NY Jogues Retreat.
McGlinn, Charles '67 (KCK) Leawood, KS Cure of Ars Church.
McGlinn, Msgr. Joseph J. '42 (PH) [126] Philadelphia, PA Our Lady of Ransom Church; Retired.
McGlinn, Robert J. '55 (CHI) Other Assignments.
McGlinn, Robert J. '55 (MIL) [2] Racine, WI Cristo Rey Church.
McGloin, Peter M. '56 (TUC) [6] Tucson, AZ Our Lady of Fatima Church.
McGloin, Richard D. *s.j.* '45 (OM) [K] Omaha, NE Jesuit Community At Creighton University.
McGlone, Gerald J. *s.j.* '87 (BAL) [M] Baltimore, MD Jesuit Fathers and Brothers Maryland Provincial Curia.
McGlone, Gerard M. '84 (SCR) Elkland, PA St. Thomas the Apostle Church.
McGlone, Joseph F. '52 (BO) [2] Newton, MA Corpus Christi Church.
McGlothlin, Eugene J. *o.s.b.* '60 (STP) Hastings, MN St. Elizabeth Ann Seton Church.
McGlynn, Daniel J. '82 (WIL) Elkton, MD Immaculate Conception Church.
McGlynn, Francis '54 (KC) Retired.
McGlynn, Francis '54 (PRM) Sugar Creek, MO St. Luke Byzantine Catholic Parish Church.
McGlynn, Philip M. *o.s.m.* '65 (CHI) [N] Chicago, IL Servite Friars - Eastern Province.
McGlynn, Thomas E. '84 (FR) South Dartmouth, MA St. Mary's Church.
McGoldrick, James F. *s.m.* '67 (WDC) [B] Washington, DC Marist College, The-Scholasticate.
McGoldrick, John T. '38 (B) Retired.
McGoldrick, William J. '43 (DET) Retired.
McGonagle, James E. *c.ss.r.* '44 (ATL) Griffin, GA Sacred Heart Church.
McGonegal, James R. '71 (CLV) [33] Cleveland, OH St. Ignatius Church.
McGonigle, Thomas D. *o.p.* '68 (PRO) [P] Providence, RI St. Thomas Aquinas Priory at Providence College.
McGough, Frank C. *s.j.* '58 (DET) [K] Detroit, MI Jesuit Community at the University of Detroit.
McGough, Msgr. James P. '57 (BLX) [2] Gulfport, MS St. James Church.
McGough, Stephen D. '68 (SCR) Montoursville, PA Our Lady of Lourdes Church.
McGough, Msgr. Thomas J. '32 (HBG) Retired.
McGough, Timothy *o.c.d.* '49 (MIL) [24] Milwaukee, WI St. Florian's Church.
McGough, William J. '47 (NO) Covington, LA St. Peter Church.
McGourty, Thomas P. *c.m.* '53 (BUF) [C] Niagara University, NY Niagara University; [O] Niagara University, NY Vincentian Community at Niagara University.
McGovern, Arthur F. *s.j.* '62 (DET) [K] Detroit, MI Jesuit Community at the University of Detroit.
McGovern, Bonfilius M. *o.s.m.* (ORG) [D] Anaheim, CA Servite High School; Servite High School Development Fund.
McGovern, Bonifilius M. *o.s.m.* (CHI) [N] Chicago, IL Servite Friars - Eastern Province.
McGovern, Brian '69 (SEA) [I] Seattle, WA Providence Mount St. Vincent.
McGovern, Msgr. Damian E. '48 (HBG) [6] Lancaster, PA Sacred Heart of Jesus Church.
McGovern, Donan *o.f.m* '55 (BO) [BB] Boston, MA St. Anthony Shrine.
McGovern, Edward J. '51 (PRO) [3] North Providence, RI Mary, Mother of Mankind Church; [P] Providence, RI St. John Vianney Residence.
McGovern, Eugene F. '56 (BRK) [147] Queens, NY St. Aloysius Church.
McGovern, Msgr. James J. '58 (TR) Moorestown, NJ Our Lady of Good Counsel Church.
McGovern, James O. '67 (BAL) Ellicott City, MD Resurrection Church.
McGovern, John P. *o.p.* '58 (WDC) [B] Washington, DC Dominican House of Studies.
McGovern, John P. '65 (NEW) Berkeley Heights, NJ Church of the Little Flower.
McGovern, Joseph A. '79 (WIL) Absent on Sick Leave.
McGovern, Joseph J. *s.j.* '48 (CHL) Mars Hill, NC St. Andrew the Apostle Church; [J] Charlotte, NC Jesuit Community; [M] Hot Springs, NC Jesuit House of Prayer.
McGovern, Lawrence J. '67 (STO) Manteca, CA St. Anthony Church.
McGovern, Mark J. '67 (DUB) Fairbank, IA Immaculate Conception Church; Independence, IA Mental Health Institute.
McGovern, Martin D. '46 (LA) Retired.
McGovern, Michael A. '45 (PHX) Retired.
McGovern, Michael G. '94 (CHI) [181] Chicago, IL Queen of the Universe Church.
McGovern, Msgr. Thomas '46 (LA) Retired.
McGovern, Thomas A. '58 (CLV) [12] Akron, OH St. Matthew Church.
McGovern, Walter J. '64 (BAL) Randallstown, MD Holy Family Church.
McGovern, William W. '55 (WOR) Retired; [M] Worcester, MA Vianney House.
McGowan, Msgr. Anthony '41 (ORG) San Clemente, CA Our Lady of Fatima Church; Retired.
McGowan, Dennis M.. *o.s.a.* (BO) [6] Lawrence, MA Holy Rosary Church.
McGowan, Frederick R. '49 (BO) [2] Haverhill, MA St. James Church.
McGowan, James J. '62 (BO) Belmont, MA Our Lady of Mercy Church.
McGowan, Jeffrey A. '89 (STA) [3] Gainesville, FL Queen of Peace Church.
McGowan, John *c.ss.r.* '62 (PH) [135] Philadelphia, PA St. Peter the Apostle Church.
McGowan, John *c.ss.r.* '62 (TR) [Q] Long Branch, NJ San Alfonso Retreat House.
McGowan, John J. '52 (RCK) Retired.
McGowan, Msgr. Joseph '53 (PEO) [J] Bloomington, IL St. Joseph Medical Center.
McGowan, Joseph F. *o.carm.* '62 (TUC) [9] Tucson, AZ Sacred Heart Church.
McGowan, Joseph O. *s.j.* '74 (SEA) [20] Seattle, WA St. Therese Church; [A] Seattle, WA Seattle University.
McGowan, Kenan *o.f.m.conv.* '52 (SY) [5] Binghamton, NY SS. Cyril and Method Church.
McGowan, Kilian *c.p.* '46 (NEW) [N] Union City, NJ Congregation of the Passion (Passionists)-St. Michael's Residence.
McGowan, Msgr. Myles '37 (BAL) [91] Baltimore, MD St. Ursula Church; Retired.
McGowan, Myles P. '45 (NU) Retired.
McGowan, Richard A. *s.j.* '83 (BO) [W] Chestnut Hill, MA The Jesuit Community at Boston College.
McGowan, Richard W. *s.j.* '60 (SP) [8] Tampa, FL Sacred Heart Church.
McGowan, Seamus J. '57 (CC) Sinton, TX Sacred Heart Church.
McGowan, Thomas A. *o.s.a.* '45 (CHI) [N] Olympia Fields, IL Tolentine Monastery at Tolentine Center.
McGowan, Thomas C. *o.p.* '29 (BO) [W] Dover, MA St. Stephen Priory.
McGowan, Wallace A. '62 (MIA) [26] Miami, FL St. Louis Church.
McGowan, William J. *s.j.* '62 (NY) [F] New York, NY Xavier High School.
McGrade, Kevin M. '85 (BO) Permanent Disability.
McGrade, William H. '49 (STP) Retired.
McGrail, Charles A. '80 (NOR) Mystic, CT St. Patrick Church.
McGrail, John A. *s.j.* '57 (DET) [P] Bloomfield Hills, MI Manresa Jesuit Retreat House.
McGrann, John '67 (SPK) On Duty Outside the Diocese.
McGrath, Andre *o.f.m.* '67 (NO) [44] New Orleans, LA St. Mary Of The Angels Church.
McGrath, Msgr. Andrew '38 (LA) Lompoc, CA La Purisima Concepcion Church; Retired.
McGrath, Brian F. '92 (SPR) Lee, MA St. Mary's Church.
McGrath, Conor '74 (SAT) Selma, TX Our Lady of Perpetual Help Church.
McGrath, Daniel F. (NOR) Retired.
McGrath, Msgr. Edmond G. '37 (YAK) Moxee City, WA Holy Rosary Church.
McGrath, Edward F. '80 (WIN) Rollingstone, MN Holy Trinity Church.
McGrath, Felix P. *o.f.m.* '61 (NY) [35] New York, NY St. Francis of Assisi Church.
McGrath, Francis '78 (TR) Leave of Absence.
McGrath, Frank C. '70 (BGP) Westport, CT Assumption Church.
McGrath, Gerald F. '58 (MIA) Key West, FL St. Mary, Star of the Sea Church.
McGrath, Msgr. James '43 (PH) Manoa, PA Sacred Heart Church; Retired.
McGrath, James J. *c.s.c.* '59 (FTW) [B] Notre Dame, IN University of Notre Dame Du Lac; [J] Notre Dame, IN Holy Cross Community, Corby Hall, University of Notre Dame.
McGrath, James R. '54 (BUF) Retired.
McGrath, Jeremiah '80 (BEA) [1] Beaumont, TX St. Anthony Cathedral.
McGrath, John *o.m.i.* '53 (SAT) Eagle Pass, TX St. Joseph's Church.
McGrath, John A. *s.m.* '66 (CIN) [D] Dayton, OH The University of Dayton; [M] Dayton, OH Marianist Provincialate.
McGrath, John D. '59 (MIA) Tavernier, FL San Pedro Church.
McGrath, John F. (CHI) Retired.
McGrath, John J. *s.j.* '51 (BO) [W] Weston, MA Campion Center.
McGrath, John R. '82 (BLX) Pass Christian, MS St. Paul Church.
McGrath, Jordan *o.p.* '59 (MAD) [3] Madison, WI Blessed Sacrament Church.
McGrath, Joseph '85 (LKC) Oberlin, LA St. Joan of Arc Church.
McGrath, Kevin *o.p.* '96 (WDC) [B] Washington, DC Dominican House of Studies.
McGrath, Kevin D. *o.s.b.* '74 (BIR) Cullman, AL Sacred Heart Church; [E] Cullman, AL St. Bernard Abbey.
McGrath, Laurence W. '57 (BO) [A] Boston, MA St. John's Seminary School of Theology.
McGrath, Leonard T. '53 (BO) [6] Lowell, MA St.

Joseph Church.
McGrath, Patrick M. (SAC) Rio Vista, CA St. Joseph Church.
McGrath, Peter *s.j.* '88 (OAK) [17] Oakland, CA St. Mary, Immaculate Conception-St. Francis de Sales Church.
McGrath, Peter R. *s.j.* '88 (BO) [W] Boston, MA The Society of Jesus of New England-Provincial Offices.
McGrath, Peter R. *s.j.* '88 (OAK) [N] Berkeley, CA Jesuit Community at Jesuit School of Theology at Berkeley.
McGrath, Philip J. '54 (LA) Bellflower, CA St. Bernard Church.
McGrath, Richard H. '50 (COV) Wilder, KY St. John Church; [M] Fort Thomas, KY Sisters of the Good Shepherd.
McGrath, Richard J. *o.s.a.* '73 (JOL) [C] New Lenox, IL Providence Catholic High School; [J] New Lenox, IL Augustinian Friary.
McGrath, Robert *o.m.i.* '55 (CC) [I] Corpus Christi, TX Incarnate Word Convent.
McGrath, Robert B. '71 (DET) Highland Park, MI St. Benedict Church.
McGrath, Robert D. '43 (HRT) Retired.
McGrath, Roger E. *s.s.* '71 (BAL) [A] Baltimore, MD St. Mary's Seminary and University; [A] Baltimore, MD St. Mary's Seminary and University.
McGrath, Roger E. *s.s.* '71 (CAM) On Duty Outside the Diocese.
McGrath, Sean *s.s.c.* '54 (OM) [K] St. Columbans, NE St. Columban's Foreign Mission Society.
McGrath, Sean J. '91 (DEN) [23] Denver, CO Church of the Risen Christ.
McGrath, Thomas E. '77 (JC) Jefferson City, MO Missouri Intermediate Reformatory; Jefferson City, MO Capital Region Medical Center, Still Campus; [D] Jefferson City, MO St. Joseph's Home.
McGrath, Thomas J. '59 (SY) Skaneateles, NY St. Mary of the Lake Church.
McGrath, Thomas M. (PAT) Special Assignment.
McGrath, W. Aedan *s.s.c.* '29 (OM) [K] St. Columbans, NE St. Columban's Foreign Mission Society.
McGrath, William E. '47 (HRT) [3] East Hartford, CT St. Christopher Church; Retired.
McGrath, William J. *s.j.* '59 (SCR) [C] Scranton, PA University of Scranton; [E] Scranton, PA Scranton Preparatory School.
McGratty, John J. (RVC) Manorville, NY St. Peter & Paul Church.
McGraw, John '81 (VEN) Absent on Leave.
McGraw, John T. '56 (SY) [S] Syracuse, NY St. Pius X Home, Inc.
McGraw, Rene *o.s.b.* '62 (SCL) [I] Collegeville, MN St. John's Abbey, of the Order of St. Benedict.
McGraw, Robert H. '76 (LAN) Grand Ledge, MI St. Michael Church.
McGraw, W. Howard *o.s.a.* '62 (ALB) Waterford, NY St. Mary of the Assumption Church.
McGray, James W. '67 (SD) [B] San Diego, CA University of San Diego.
McGread, Thomas '53 (WCH) [13] Wichita, KS St. Francis of Assisi Church; [M] Wichita, KS Serra Club of Wichita - Metro.
McGready, Oliver '62 (WDC) [2] Rockville, MD Shrine of St. Jude Church.
McGreal, James '48 (SEA) Retired.
McGreal, Msgr. James R. '34 (MAN) Retired.
McGreevy, James V. '64 (SPK) Lind, WA St. Ambrose Church; Ritzville, WA St. Agnes Church; Sprague, WA Mary Queen of Heaven Church; Washtunca, WA Holy Trinity Church.
McGreevy, John G. *o.p.* '64 (CHI) River Forest, IL St. Vincent Ferrer Priory Church.
McGreevy, Thomas J. *o.p.* '64 (P) [18] Portland, OR Holy Rosary Parish & Dominican Priory Church.
McGregor, John F. *s.m.* '63 (SFR) [B] San Francisco, CA St. Peter Chanel Seminary; [N] San Francisco, CA Provincial Residence.
McGregor, Mark *s.j.* '96 (P) [N] Portland, OR Loyola Renewal Center.
McGrenehan, Msgr. Bernard J. '45 (PMB) Palm Beach, FL St. Edward Church; Retired.
McGrenra, Cornelius D. '51 (TUC) Retired.
McGroarty, Msgr. Charles E. '62 (PH) [102] Philadelphia, PA St. Matthew Church.
McGroarty, Hugh H. '45 (SCR) [4] Pittston, PA St. John the Evangelist Church.
McGroarty, Joseph *o.p.* '46 (TR) Holmdel, NJ St. Catharine Church.
McGroarty, William K. *s.j.* '55 (BAL) [C] Baltimore, MD Loyola College; [M] Baltimore, MD Jesuit Community of Loyola College, Inc.
McGrogan, James P. '64 (GRY) [1] Michigan City, IN St. Mary of the Immaculate Conception Church.
McGuffey, James W.. '95 (MET) Old Bridge, NJ St. Ambrose Church.
McGuigan, Francis W. *s.j.* '52 (FBK) [E] Fairbanks, AK Monroe Foundation, Inc.
McGuigan, John J. '68 (PAT) Hopatcong, NJ St. Jude's Church.
McGuigan, Patrick *o.carm.* '79 (NY) Middletown, NY Our Lady of Mt. Carmel Church; [Z] Middletown, NY St. Albert's Priory.
McGuigan, Robert '78 (WDC) Retired.
McGuigan, Steven '90 (SPR) [2] Springfield, MA All Souls Church; Springfield, MA Baystate Medical Center, Springfield Hospital Unit.
McGuill, Martin '64 (ARL) McLean, VA St. Luke's Church.
McGuine, Peter '90 (SD) Carlsbad, CA St. Thomas More Church.
McGuiness, Edward '61 (SB) Desert Hot Springs, CA St. Elizabeth of Hungary Church.
McGuinn, James T. '88 (PH) [4] Norristown, PA St. Patrick Church.
McGuinness, Msgr. Brendan '47 (MRY) Retired.
McGuinness, David I. '73 (MOB) Dauphin Island, AL St. Edmund-by-the-Sea Church.
McGuinness, Fergal '86 (SR) Napa, CA St. Apollinaris Church.
McGuinness, Fergus *c.p.* '47 (LA) [R] Pasadena, CA Passionist Community.
McGuinness, Gerard J. '60 (SB) Sun City, CA St. Vincent Ferrer Church.
McGuinness, J. Roger '65 (OG) [6] Plattsburgh, NY Newman Parish, John XXIII College Community Church.
McGuinness, Joseph P. '52 (PBL) Cortez, CO St. Margaret Mary Church; Mancos, CO St. Rita Church.
McGuinness, Lester A. '49 (NEW) Caldwell, NJ St. Aloysius Church; Retired.
McGuinness, Msgr. Michael (MOB) Retired.
McGuinness, Msgr. Richard M. '51 (NEW) [3] Linden, NJ St. John the Apostle Church.
McGuire, Anthony *o.f.m.* '52 (PAT) [M] Butler, NJ St. Anthony Friary.
McGuire, Anthony '65 (SFR) [4] San Francisco, CA St. Anne Church.
McGuire, Msgr. Anthony W. '57 (PH) [101] Philadelphia, PA Maternity B.V.M. Church.
McGuire, Augustus *c.s.p.* '59 (AUS) [11] Austin, TX St. Austin's Church.
McGuire, Daniel J. *s.j.* '50 (BAL) [C] Baltimore, MD Loyola College; [M] Baltimore, MD Jesuit Community of Loyola College, Inc.
McGuire, David V. '88 (RIC) Danville, VA Sacred Heart Church.
McGuire, Donald J. *s.j.* '66 (CHI) [N] Evanston, IL Canisius House.
McGuire, Edward A. *o.f.m.* '40 (PAT) [M] Butler, NJ St. Anthony Friary.
McGuire, Francis X. *o.s.a.* '35 (PH) [Z] Villanova, PA St. Thomas Monastery.
McGuire, J. Frederick '81 (CIN) [2] Springfield, OH St. Joseph Church.
McGuire, James *o.a.r.* '54 (LA) [82] Los Angeles, CA San Miguel Church.
McGuire, James E. '70 (PH) [3] Bensalem, PA Saint Ephrem Church.
McGuire, James J. *o.s.f.s.* '50 (WIL) [I] Childs, MD Oblates of St. Francis De Sales.
McGuire, John *c.ss.r.* '44 (BRK) [107] Brooklyn, NY Our Lady of Perpetual Help Basilica.
McGuire, John *o.p.* '79 (NY) [CC] New York, NY University Apostolate.
McGuire, Msgr. John A. '50 (RVC) Sound Beach, NY St. Louis de Montfort Church.
McGuire, John C. '79 (NY) East Kingston, NY St. Colman Church.
McGuire, John F. '76 (P) Coquille, OR Holy Name Church.
McGuire, John J. '60 (COV) Erlanger, KY Mary, Queen of Heaven Church; [S] Fort Thomas, KY Mission Share.
McGuire, John P. *o.p.* '73 (HRT) [V] New Haven, CT Angelicum Fund.
McGuire, John V. *c.ss.r.* '41 (NY) [DD] Esopus, NY Holy Shroud Guild.
McGuire, Joseph E. '65 (DUB) Dysart, IA St. Joseph Church; Vinton, IA St. Mary's Church.
McGuire, Kenneth H. *c.s.p.* '68 (NY) [Z] Scarsdale, NY Paulist Fathers Generalate.
McGuire, Michael A. '58 (MET) South Plainfield, NJ Sacred Heart Church.
McGuire, Paul J. *s.c.j.* '68 (MIL) [P] Franklin, WI Dehon House.
McGuire, Richard '67 (SCL) Isanti, MN St. Elizabeth Ann Seton Church.
McGuire, Richard *o.s.c.* '73 (STP) Shoreview, MN St. Odilia Church; [N] Shoreview, MN Crosier Community of Shoreview.
McGuire, Richard G. *o.c.s.o.* '57 (CHR) [E] Moncks Corner, SC Mepkin Abbey.
McGuire, Msgr. Richard J. '60 (E) [22] Erie, PA St. Julia Church.
McGuire, Robert A. *s.j.* '58 (NY) [Z] New York, NY Jesuit Provincial's Office.
McGuire, Robert A. *s.j.* '58 (RVC) Plainview, NY St. Pius X Church.
McGuire, Thomas D. '81 (LIN) Wallace, NE St. Mary's Church.
McGuire, Timothy P. '84 (STU) Neffs, OH Sacred Heart Church; Powhatan Point, OH St. John Vianney Church.
McGuire, William A. *o.s.a.* '65 (PH) [C] Villanova, PA Villanova University; [Z] Villanova, PA St. Thomas Monastery.
McGuirk, Alan *m.s.* '56 (TYL) Lufkin, TX St. Patrick Church.
McGuirk, John J. '70 (SC) Remsen, IA St. Mary's Church.
McGuirk, Raymond A. '47 (BRK) Retired; [U] Douglaston, NY Bishop Mugavero Residence.
McGuirk, William C. '82 (GBG) Delmont, PA St. John Baptist de La Salle Church.
McGuirl, John A. '72 (BRK) [184] Queens, NY St. Joan of Arc Church.
McGurk, Patrick '58 (HEL) Deer Lodge, MT Immaculate Conception Church.
McGurn, Richard H. *s.j.* '75 (CHI) [N] Chicago, IL Chicago Province of the Society of Jesus-Provincial Office.
McHale, Anthony I. *s.j.* '53 (WDC) [E] Washington, DC Gonzaga College High School.
McHale, Damian *c.p.* '61 (LA) [R] Pasadena, CA Passionist Community.
McHale, Msgr. James J. '60 (ALN) Bath, PA Sacred Heart Church.
McHall, Charles P. '50 (NY) Retired.
McHarness, Paul *o.s.b.* '60 (SFS) [F] Marvin, SD Blue Cloud Abbey.
McHatton, James S. *o.p.* '43 (NO) [25] New Orleans, LA St. Anthony Of Padua Church.
McHenry, Joel T. '94 (OG) Absent on Leave.
McHenry, John *s.v.d.* '55 (SB) [A] Riverside, CA Divine Word Seminary.
McHenry, Stephen P. '73 (PH) Ambler, PA St. Anthony of Padua Church; [A] Wynnewood, PA Theological Seminary of St. Charles Borromeo, Overbrook.
McHenry, Vincent Ferrer *o.p.* (NY) Manhattan, NY New York Hospital.
McHenry, Vincent Ferrer *o.p.* '49 (NY) [22] New York, NY St. Catherine of Siena Church; [Z] New York, NY St. Catherine of Siena Priory.
McHugh, Alphonsus *ss.cc.* (FR) Fairhaven, MA St. Mary's Church.
McHugh, Brian J. '88 (BO) [5] Weymouth, MA Sacred Heart Church.
McHugh, Conall *o.f.m.conv.* '56 (CHL) Winston-Salem, NC Our Lady of Mercy Church.
McHugh, Connell A. '72 (SCR) West Hazleton, PA St. Francis of Assisi Church.
McHugh, Dennis (PAT) Retired.
McHugh, Donald '57 (P) Absent on Leave.
McHugh, Edward T. *o.m.i.* '37 (SEA) [4] Seattle, WA St. Benedict Church.
McHugh, Francis B. *o.praem.* '40 (GB) [I] De Pere, WI St. Norbert Abbey.
McHugh, Frank *o.f.m.* '75 (PAT) Butler, NJ St. Anthony Church.
McHugh, James *c.p.* '61 (MET) [H] South River, NJ Passionist Provincial Office.
McHugh, James L. '60 (COV) Brooksville, KY St. James Church.
McHugh, James P. (HRT) Newington, CT St. Mary Church.
McHugh, James P. *o.s.f.s.* '77 (SLC) [B] Salt Lake City, UT Judge Memorial Catholic High School; [F] Salt Lake City, UT Oblate House.
McHugh, Jerome *o.f.m.cap.* '60 (NY) [Z] White Plains, NY St. Conrad Friary.
McHugh, John (NOR) [A] Cromwell, CT Holy Apostles College and Seminary.
McHugh, John *s.o.l.t.* '52 (CC) [H] Robstown, TX Society of Our Lady of the Most Holy Trinity.
McHugh, John '54 (LA) Santa Fe Springs, CA St. Pius X Church.
McHugh, John *o.f.m.cap.* '69 (MAN) [N] Durham, NH Campus Ministries.
McHugh, John F. *o.m.i.* (BO) [3] Lowell, MA Immaculate Conception Church.
McHugh, Msgr. John L. '31 (BUF) [1] Tonawanda, NY St. Amelia Church; Retired.
McHugh, John P. *o.f.m.cap.* '69 (MAN) [N] Hanover, NH The Catholic Student Center at Dartmouth, Aquinas House, Aquinas at Dartmouth, Inc.
McHugh, John T. '93 (LC) Special Assignment; [A] La Crosse, WI Holy Cross Seminary House of Formation; [C] La Crosse, WI Aquinas High School; [D] La Crosse, WI Aquinas Middle School; [I] La Crosse, WI Holy Cross (Seminary) Diocesan Center.
McHugh, John W. '76 (HRT) Guilford, CT St. George Church; [C] West Hartford, CT Saint Joseph College.
McHugh, Joseph B. *s.j.* '58 (BO) [Y] Gloucester, MA Eastern Point Retreat House.
McHugh, Joseph F. (TR) Leave of Absence.
McHugh, Joseph F. *s.j.* '83 (BO) [Y] Weston, MA Campion Renewal Center.
McHugh, Kieran A. '70 (PAT) [C] Sparta, NJ Pope John XXIII High School.
McHugh, Msgr. Martin '32 (FRS) Retired.
McHugh, Michael *s.j.* '51 (HEL) Browning, MT Church of the Little Flower.

McHugh, Michael J. '80 (BRK) [203] Queens, NY Most Precious Blood Church.
McHugh, Owen J. '50 (COS) [10] Colorado Springs, CO St. Francis of Assisi Church.
McHugh, Patrick J. '50 (LA) Torrance, CA Nativity Church.
McHugh, Paul F. '53 (MAN) Retired.
McHugh, Msgr. Peter J. (PAT) [2] Clifton, NJ St. Andrew the Apostle Church.
McHugh, Richard P. *s.j.* '60 (WDC) [20] Washington, DC Holy Trinity Church.
McHugh, Thomas J. '49 (CHI) [134] Chicago, IL St. Matthias Church; Retired.
McHugh, William *o.m.i.* '52 (P) Shady Cove, OR Our Lady of Fatima Church.
McIlhenny, Bernard R. *s.j.* '56 (SCR) [C] Scranton, PA University of Scranton.
McIlhon, Msgr. John J. '48 (DM) Retired.
McIlhone, James P. '74 (CHI) [A] Mundelein, IL University of St. Mary of the Lake-Mundelein Seminary.
McIlvane, Donald W. (PIT) Retired.
McIlwain, Michael A. *o.s.b.* '94 (GBG) Latrobe, PA Latrobe Area Hospital; [H] Latrobe, PA Saint Vincent Archabbey.
McInerney, Blaise *o.carm.* '54 (JOL) [J] Darien, IL Carmelite Fathers Provincial Office.
McInerney, Henry '77 (BLX) Kiln, MS Annunciation Church.
McInerney, Maurice '59 (DEN) Absent on Leave.
McInerney, Walter L. *c.s.c.* '36 (FTW) [J] South Bend, IN Congregation of Holy Cross Indiana Province Provincial House.
McInerny, Msgr. Lawrence B. '79 (CHR) [10] Charleston, SC Stella Maris Church; [A] Charleston, SC Bishop England High School.
McInerny, Paul B. '72 (BO) On Special or Other Diocesan Assignment.
McInnes, Val A. *o.p.* '61 (NO) [30] New Orleans, LA St. Dominic Church; [P] New Orleans, LA Dominican Fathers & Brothers, Southern Dominican Province; [S] New Orleans, LA The Patrons of the Vatican Museums in the South, Inc.; [S] Metairie, LA Southern Dominican Foundation.
McInnes, William *s.j.* '57 (BO) [W] Chestnut Hill, MA The Jesuit Community at Boston College.
McInnis, Francis L. '56 (GF) Retired.
McInnis, Kevin *s.c.j.* '57 (MIL) [P] Hales Corners, WI Sacred Heart Monastery.
McInnis, Richard W. '69 (PRT) Retired.
McInnis, Thomas J. '57 (LC) Ettrick, WI St. Bridget Church; Melrose, WI St. Kevin Church.
McIntosh, Alan R. *o.s.b.* '61 (IND) St. Meinrad, IN St. Meinrad Church; [J] St. Meinrad, IN St. Meinrad Archabbey.
McIntrye, Allen J. '56 (STP) Hamel, MN St. Anne Church.
McIntyre, Frederick H. '92 (WDC) Newport, MD St. Mary Church.
McIntyre, James *o.f.m.cap.* '53 (BGP) Greenwich, CT Greenwich Hospital; [O] Stamford, CT Lourdes Capuchin Chaplains Community.
McIntyre, Msgr. James P. '38 (CLV) [33] Cleveland, OH St. Ignatius Church; Rocky River, OH St. Christopher Church; Retired.
McIntyre, Msgr. James P. '71 (CAM) Runnemede, NJ St. Maria Goretti Church.
McIntyre, John J. '92 (PH) Bristol, PA St. Mark Church.
McIntyre, John P. *s.j.* '63 (BO) [W] Boston, MA The Society of Jesus of New England-Provincial Offices.
McIntyre, Justin '81 (SR) Retired.
McIntyre, Louis *t.o.r.* '53 (VEN) [2] Sarasota, FL Our Lady Queen of Martyrs Church.
McIntyre, Raymond T. '52 (RIC) Retired.
McIntyre, Thomas J. '50 (LA) [R] Los Angeles, CA Amat House; [W] Montebello, CA DePaul Center.
McIntyre, Msgr. Thomas J. '66 (CAM) Blackwood, NJ St. Jude's Church; [F] Camden, NJ The Tuition Assistance Fund, Inc.
McIntyre, William *o.f.m.* '95 (WIL) [10] Wilmington, DE St. Paul's Church.
McIsaac, Edward F. '48 (FR) Retired.
McKamy, Eldon J. '63 (OM) [37] Omaha, NE St. Philip Neri Church.
McKane, Paul *o.s.b.* '88 (WDC) [M] Washington, DC St. Anselm's Abbey.
McKarns, James E. '62 (Y) North Canton, OH St. Paul's Church.
McKay, Anthony *c.s.sp.* '60 (LR) Conway, AR St. Joseph's Church.
McKay, Douglas M. '82 (PH) [X] Philadelphia, PA Holy Family Home.
McKay, Frank '54 (NY) Absent on Sick leave.
McKay, Henry *m.s.* '48 (BEA) Orange, TX St. Therese Church.
McKay, Msgr. James '56 (SFR) [3] San Mateo, CA St. Matthew Church; San Mateo, CA Serra Club of San Mateo.
McKay, James R. *s.m.* '50 (PIT) [N] Pittsburgh, PA Marianist Community.
McKay, Joseph A. '84 (ALB) [16] Schenectady, NY St. Paul the Apostle Church.
McKay, Michael *o.s.b.* '86 (GBG) [H] Latrobe, PA Saint Vincent Archabbey.
McKay, Robert J. '51 (SY) Retired; [S] Syracuse, NY St. Pius X Home, Inc.
McKay, William E. '49 (PHX) Retired.
McKean, Benedict B. *o.s.b.* '59 (PEO) [A] Peru, IL St. Bede Abbey and Academy.
McKean, Dan '87 (LAN) Williamston, MI St. Mary Church.
McKean, Louis '47 (P) Retired.
McKeaney, James J. (PH) West Conshohocken, PA St. Gertrude Church.
McKee, Msgr. Francis J. '39 (LR) Retired; [H] Little Rock, AR St. John Manor.
McKee, Francis X. '66 (PH) [59] Philadelphia, PA Holy Family Church.
McKee, Henry J. '72 (PH) [129] Philadelphia, PA Our Lady of Victory Church.
McKee, James C. *s.j.* '69 (E) Curwensville, PA St. Timothy Church; Curwensville, PA St. Timothy Church; Grampian, PA St. Bonaventure Church.
McKee, John '46 (FRS) Retired.
McKee, Keith '54 (SP) [2] Clearwater, FL Light of Christ Church.
McKee, Roderick D. '66 (WDC) Beltsville, MD St. Joseph Church.
McKee, William *c.ss.r.* '48 (STL) [P] Liguori, MO Liguori Mission House/Redemptorists; [W] Liguori, MO Liguori Mission House, The Redemptorists.
McKee, William A. '83 (SEA) [10] Seattle, WA St. John Church.
Mckeefry, Brendan '67 (SAC) Paradise, CA St. Thomas More Church.
McKeever, Frederick *o.f.m.* '54 (PAT) [M] Butler, NJ St. Anthony Friary.
McKeever, Henry *c.ss.r.* '48 (STL) [P] Liguori, MO Liguori Mission House/Redemptorists.
McKeever, William '45 (MIA) Retired.
McKeever, Msgr. William F. '45 (MIA) [22] Miami, FL St. John Bosco Church.
McKelvey, James P. '93 (PH) Collegeville, PA St. Eleanor Church.
McKelvey, Thomas P. '62 (PH) Linwood, PA Holy Saviour Church.
McKendrick, Norman G. *s.j.* '61 (DET) [K] Detroit, MI Jesuit Community at the University of Detroit.
McKenna, Brian *o.f.m.cap.* '65 (BAK) Bend, OR St. Francis of Assisi Church.
McKenna, Daniel *o.m.i.* '58 (GAL) Alvin, TX St. John the Baptist Church.
McKenna, Denis R. '47 (NEW) Retired.
McKenna, Dennis '47 (NEW) [2] Irvington, NJ St. Leo's Church.
McKenna, Edward J. (CHI) [93] Chicago, IL Immaculate Conception of the Blessed Virgin Mary Church.
McKenna, Msgr. Edward J. '36 (NOR) Retired.
McKenna, Enda '64 (SAT) [49] San Antonio, TX St. Leo Church.
McKenna, Eugene F. *m.s.* '53 (LKC) Hackberry, LA St. Peter Apostle Church.
McKenna, Eugene J. *s.s.j.* '47 (BAL) [M] Baltimore, MD St. Joseph's Manor.
McKenna, Eugene J. '63 (PRO) Middletown, RI St. Lucy's Church.
McKenna, F. Charles '60 (ALN) Retired; [J] Bethlehem, PA Holy Family Villa.
McKenna, Frank W. '94 (NOR) Colchester, CT St. Andrew Church.
McKenna, George P. '44 (CHI) [1] Oak Lawn, IL St. Catherine of Alexandria Church; Retired.
McKenna, Hugh J. *o.s.f.s.* '44 (WIL) [I] Childs, MD Oblates of St. Francis De Sales.
McKenna, James '50 (SPR) Retired.
McKenna, James *s.d.s.* '52 (MOB) Phenix City, AL Mother Mary Parish Church.
McKenna, James A. *s.d.b.* '80 (NY) [2] Port Chester, NY Corpus Christi Church.
McKenna, James D. '50 (SPR) [1] Holyoke, MA Blessed Sacrament Church.
McKenna, James George (DAL) [5] Dallas, TX Holy Cross Church; On Duty Outside the Diocese.
McKenna, Msgr. James J. '42 (BRK) [198] Queens, NY St. Mary Star of the Sea Church; Retired.
McKenna, James T. '64 (NEW) Closter, NJ St. Mary's Church.
McKenna, Jerome *c.p.* '58 (WH) Kingwood, WV St. Sebastian's Church; Masontown, WV St. Zita's Church.
McKenna, John *c.m.* '64 (BRK) [U] Jamaica, NY St. Vincent's House.
McKenna, John *c.ss.r.* '84 (MGZ) [2] Mayaquez, PR Our Lady of Mt. Carmel Church.
McKenna, John '88 (PIT) Glenshaw, PA St. Mary Church.
McKenna, John H. *c.m.* '64 (BRK) [D] Queens and Staten Island, NY St. John's University.
McKenna, John J. '45 (WOR) Retired.
McKenna, John J. '47 (NY) Sloatsburg, NY St. Joan of Arc Church.
McKenna, Joseph C. *s.j.* '49 (NY) [Z] New York, NY Murray-Weigel Hall.
McKenna, Joseph J. *o.s.f.s.* '57 (WIL) Newark, DE Medical Center of Delaware; [B] Wilmington, DE Salesianum School.
Mckenna, Joseph R. '57 (PRT) Bath, ME Immaculate Conception Church.
McKenna, Kenneth N. *o.s.f.s.* '85 (DET) [Q] Warren, MI St. John's Deaf Center.
McKenna, Kevin (ROC) Scottsville, NY St. Mary of the Assumption Church.
McKenna, Michael G. '73 (GR) Big Rapids, MI St. Mary's Church.
McKenna, Peter '57 (SAT) La Vernia, TX St. Ann Church.
McKenna, Philip A. '62 (MOB) On Duty Outside the Archdiocese.
McKenna, Thomas F. *c.m.* '70 (BRK) [D] Queens and Staten Island, NY St. John's University.
McKenna, Thomas F. *c.m.* '70 (PH) [B] Philadelphia, PA St. Vincent's Seminary; [B] Philadelphia, PA DePaul Novitiate; [Z] Philadelphia, PA Congregation of the Mission; [Z] Philadelphia, PA Congregation of the Mission.
McKenna, Thomas J. '72 (PIT) Hopewell Township, PA Our Lady of Fatima Church.
McKenna, Timothy J. '79 (SEA) Military Chaplains.
McKenna, William *s.s.j.* '64 (MOB) [15] Mobile, AL Most Pure Heart of Mary Church.
McKenna, William A. *s.j.* '68 (NEW) [B] Jersey City, NJ Saint Peter's College; [N] Jersey City, NJ Jesuits of Saint Peter's College, Inc.
McKenney, Charles R. *s.j.* '44 (WOR) [N] Worcester, MA Jesuits of Holy Cross College, Inc.
McKenney, William G. *s.j.* '94 (RC) Pine Ridge, SD Holy Rosary Church; [B] Pine Ridge, SD Jesuit Community of Holy Rosary Mission.
McKenzie, John Harold *o.s.b.* '85 (CC) [H] Sandia, TX Corpus Christi Abbey.
McKenzie, John J. *o.s.a.* '65 (PH) [C] Villanova, PA Villanova University; [Z] Villanova, PA St. Thomas Monastery.
McKenzie, Mark D. *s.j.* '69 (PBL) Trinidad, CO Most Holy Trinity, Trinidad Area Catholic Community (Trinidad Cluster) Church; Trinidad, CO Our Lady of Mt. Carmel, Trinidad Area Catholic Community (Trinidad Cluster) Church; Trinidad, CO St. Joseph, Trinidad Area Catholic Community (Trinidad Cluster) Church; [E] Trinidad, CO Trinidad Area Catholic Community.
McKeon, Brian A. '77 (RVC) Garden City, NY St. Anne Church.
McKeon, Gerard R. *s.j.* '86 (BO) [Y] Gloucester, MA Eastern Point Retreat House.
McKeon, John Aedan *o.p.* '56 (NY) [Z] New York, NY St. Vincent Ferrer Priory.
McKeon, Michael '65 (SAC) [1] Sacramento, CA Cathedral of the Blessed Sacrament.
McKeon, Raymond T. '63 (NEW) Retired.
McKeon, Robert '90 (NY) [A] Yonkers, NY St. Joseph's Seminary; [Z] New York, NY St. John Neumann Residence.
McKeon, Robert F. '59 (LAN) Mount Morris, MI St. Mary Church.
McKeon, Thomas *s.s.s.* '50 (NY) [8] New York, NY St. Andrew Church; Manhattan, NY Beekman Downtown - New York Infirmary.
McKeon, William '57 (GAY) East Jordan, MI St. Joseph Church; Praga, MI St. John Nepomucene Church.
McKeon, William E. *c.m.* (BUF) [8] Niagara Falls, NY Our Lady of Lebanon Church.
McKeon, William J. '57 (LAN) Retired.
McKeone, William '72 (TR) On Duty Outside the Diocese.
McKeough, Brendan J. '53 (GB) [I] De Pere, WI St. Joseph Priory.
McKeown, Peter *m.s.* '59 (ORL) [2] Orlando, FL Blessed Trinity Church.
McKeown, Peter '67 (NY) [11] Yonkers, NY St. John the Baptist Church.
McKernan, Kenneth B. *c.s.b.* '66 (DET) [E] Redford, MI Catholic Central High School.
McKernan, Leo J. (SCR) Avoca, PA St. Mary's Church.
McKernan, Louis F. *c.s.p.* '54 (NY) [Z] Scarsdale, NY Paulist Fathers Generalate.
McKevitt, Gerald L. *s.j.* '75 (SJ) [B] Santa Clara, CA Santa Clara University.
McKevitt, Msgr. Nolan B. '35 (MAR) Retired.
McKiernan, J. Michael '91 (ORG) Garden Grove, CA St. Columban Church.
McKiernan, Joseph W. '51 (WOR) Sutton, MA St. Mark Church.
McKiernan, Raymond '56 (BRK) [58] Brooklyn, NY Holy Name Church.
McKiernan, Thomas M. '51 (CHI) Palos Heights, IL St. Alexander Church.
McKiernan, Vincent *c.s.p.* '57 (COL) [J] Columbus, OH Campus Ministry.
McKillin, David '76 (LR) [A] Subiaco, AR Subiaco Monastery.
McKillop, Michael J. *m.m.* '35 (NY) [Z] Maryknoll, NY

Maryknoll Fathers and Brothers.
McKinley, Joseph J. *s.s.j.* '85 (NO) [6] New Orleans, LA Epiphany Church.
McKinley, Michael J. '85 (LFT) Lake Village, IN St. Augusta Church.
McKinley, Steve *o.f.m.conv.* '94 (PEO) [2] Peoria, IL Holy Family Church.
McKinney, Floyd '80 (WCH) [9] Wichita, KS Our Lady of Perpetual Help Church.
McKinney, Francis *t.o.r.* '34 (ARL) [J] Winchester, VA Sacred Heart Friary.
McKinney, James F. '96 (FAR) [3] Grand Forks, ND St. Michael's Church.
McKinney, Michael A. '93 (LFT) Fishers, IN Holy Spirit Church.
McKinney, Ronald H. *s.j.* '83 (SCR) [C] Scranton, PA University of Scranton.
McKinney, Thomas A. '61 (GR) Greenville, MI St. Charles Church.
McKinnon, Eymard *o.f.m.cap.* '54 (AGN) [F] Agana Heights, GU St. Fidelis Friary.
McKinstra, William M. '62 (RCK) Dundee, IL St. Catherine of Siena Church.
McKitrick, James V. '58 (RCK) McHenry, IL St. Patrick Church.
McKloskey, Msgr. James A. '46 (SY) Fayetteville, NY Immaculate Conception Church.
McKnight, James '59 (SAC) Nevada City, CA St. Canice Church.
McKnight, Kevin F. '94 (PIT) Washington, PA Immaculate Conception Church; [Q] Slippery Rock, PA Office for Campus Ministry.
McKnight, Robert J. '73 (BUR) Orwell, VT St. Paul Church.
McKnight, W. Shawn '94 (WCH) [3] Wichita, KS Blessed Sacrament Church.
McKnight, William F. '48 (GR) Custer, MI St. Mary's Church.
McLachlan, Frederick E. *s.s.e.* '64 (BUR) Putney, VT Our Lady of Mercy Church.
McLain, J. Clyde '57 (STL) Retired.
McLaughlin, Adrian T. *o.s.b.* '41 (PAT) [M] Morristown, NJ St. Mary's Abbey.
McLaughlin, Andrew '87 (DET) Absent on Leave.
McLaughlin, Bernard P. '59 (BO) Canton, MA St. Gerard Majella Church.
McLaughlin, Charles '62 (BRK) [10] Brooklyn, NY St. Anselm's Church.
McLaughlin, Charles J. (CHI) Retired.
McLaughlin, Daniel *o.s.a.* '83 (PH) [D] Drexel Hill, PA Monsignor Bonner High School.
McLaughlin, Daniel P. *s.t.* '63 (TUC) [2] Tucson, AZ Blessed Kateri Tekakwitha Church; [J] Tucson, AZ St. Nicholas Indian Center.
McLaughlin, David S. '96 (NEW) Rahway, NJ St. Mary's Church.
McLaughlin, Don E. '81 (JOL) Bensenville, IL St. Charles Borromeo Church.
McLaughlin, Donald '67 (NEW) Dumont, NJ St. Mary's Church.
McLaughlin, Edward J. '52 (BO) Bridgewater, MA St. Thomas Aquinas Church.
McLaughlin, Edward J. '59 (CHI) Orland Park, IL St. Michael Church.
McLaughlin, Eugene '85 (STU) Absent on Leave.
McLaughlin, Farrell E. '71 (PRO) [2] North Providence, RI St. Lawrence's Church.
McLaughlin, Francis J. '62 (CAM) Barrington, NJ St. Francis de Sales Church.
McLaughlin, Gregory '85 (AUS) Calvert, TX St. Mary Church; Hearne, TX St. Mary's Church.
McLaughlin, Hugh J. '63 (HBG) Spring Grove, PA Sacred Heart Church.
McLaughlin, James '73 (SB) [9] Riverside, CA St. Patrick Church.
McLaughlin, James C., II '78 (GAY) Absent on Leave.
McLaughlin, James E. *m.m.* '40 (NY) [Z] Maryknoll, NY Maryknoll Fathers and Brothers.
McLaughlin, James J. '70 (PH) [20] Philadelphia, PA St. Barnabas Church.
McLaughlin, James W. '96 (MET) Old Bridge, NJ St. Ambrose Church.
McLaughlin, John '61 (SEA) Elma, WA St. Joseph's Church.
McLaughlin, John *c.ss.r.* '92 (BAL) [94] Baltimore, MD St. Wenceslaus Church.
McLaughlin, John E. (BO) [5] Somerville, MA St. Clement Church.
McLaughlin, John E. '62 (BO) [3] Somerville, MA St. Benedict Church.
McLaughlin, John F. '56 (GB) Amberg, WI St. Agnes Church; Wausaukee, WI St. Augustine Church.
McLaughlin, John P. '66 (MIA) [1] Fort Lauderdale, FL Blessed Sacrament Church.
McLaughlin, Joseph '55 (OKL) Retired.
McLaughlin, Joseph A. *o.praem.* '70 (WIL) [I] Claymont, DE Immaculate Conception Priory of the Canons Regular of Premontre.
McLaughlin, Joseph J. '66 (PH) Richboro, PA St. Vincent de Paul Church.
McLaughlin, Joseph J. *s.m.* '72 (BR) Paulina, LA St. Joseph Church.
McLaughlin, Joseph M. *s.s.e.* '70 (BUR) [G] Colchester, VT Society of St. Edmund.
McLaughlin, Joseph P. *o.praem.* '70 (WIL) [B] Claymont, DE Archmere Academy.
McLaughlin, Michael P. '77 (TOL) Absent on Leave.
McLaughlin, Mike '82 (DM) [5] Des Moines, IA Holy Trinity Church.
McLaughlin, Neil P. *s.j.* '59 (SCR) [C] Scranton, PA University of Scranton.
McLaughlin, Owen F. '41 (MIL) Retired.
McLaughlin, Patrick J. '61 (BO) [3] Medford, MA St. Joseph Church; [3] Medford, MA St. Joseph Church.
McLaughlin, Patrick J. '74 (SCR) Dushore, PA St. Basil's Church.
McLaughlin, Paul E. '71 (VEN) Military Chaplains.
McLaughlin, Paul J. '55 (BO) [2] Marlboro, MA Immaculate Conception Church.
McLaughlin, Peter A. '78 (CAM) Military Chaplains.
McLaughlin, Richard '74 (PRT) [1] Lewiston, ME St. Joseph's Church.
McLaughlin, Richard P. '68 (BO) [37] Boston, MA St. Joseph-St. Lazarus Church.
McLaughlin, Robert A. '73 (PH) [91] Philadelphia, PA St. Malachy Church; [DD] Philadelphia, PA Newman Apostolate; [DD] Philadelphia, PA Newman Apostolate.
McLaughlin, Robert E. '66 (CHI) [1] Chicago, IL Cathedral of the Holy Name.
McLaughlin, Thomas *o.s.b.* '83 (RCK) [H] Aurora, IL Marmion Abbey-St. Augustine's Abbey.
McLaughlin, Thomas D. '76 (SCR) Stroudsburg, PA St. Luke's Church.
McLaughlin, Thomas J. *o.s.a.* '53 (SD) [34] San Diego, CA St. Patrick Church.
McLaughlin, Thomas R. '81 (NEW) Hillside, NJ St. Catherine of Siena Church; Newark, NJ Beth Israel Hospital.
McLaughlin, Thomas W. '49 (LA) [91] Los Angeles, CA St. Teresa of Avila Church; Retired.
McLaughlin, Msgr. William '58 (ORG) Newport Beach, CA Our Lady Queen of Angels Church.
McLaughlin, William H. '68 (BO) [38] Boston, MA St. Joseph Church.
McLaughlin, William J. '70 (TR) [S] Trenton, NJ Martin House.
McLean, Barry L. '90 (SAN) McCamey, TX Sacred Heart Church.
McLean, Edward J. '48 (ARL) Retired.
McLean, Edward J. '52 (HRT) [1] West Hartford, CT St. Brigid's Church; Special and other (Arch)Diocesan Assignment.
McLean, George F. *o.m.i.* '55 (WDC) [B] Washington, DC Oblate College/Oblate Center for Mission Studies; [V] Washington, DC Council for Research in Values and Philosophy.
McLean, Jack (SFR) [S] San Francisco, CA Newman Center, San Francisco State University.
McLean, James F. *c.s.p.* '41 (NY) [Z] Scarsdale, NY Paulist Fathers Generalate.
McLean, William A. '69 (LA) [37] Los Angeles, CA St. Agatha Church.
McLearen, Daniel J. '92 (HRT) [6] Waterbury, CT Our Lady of Mt. Carmel Church.
McLellan, Daniel *o.f.m.* '76 (WDC) [B] Silver Spring, MD Holy Name College.
McLellan, James '70 (FR) North Dighton, MA St. Joseph's Church.
McLellan, Michael F. '76 (BO) [14] Boston, MA Blessed Sacrament Church; [56] Boston, MA Our Lady of Lourdes Church.
McLellan, Thomas J. *c.ss.r.* '56 (BRK) [107] Brooklyn, NY Our Lady of Perpetual Help Basilica.
McLeod, Daniel '42 (OAK) Retired.
McLeod, David (PAT) On Duty Outside the Diocese.
McLeod, Donald *c.s.b.* '78 (DET) Special Assignment.
McLeod, Frederick G. *s.j.* '62 (BO) [W] Boston, MA The Society of Jesus of New England-Provincial Offices.
McLeod, Frederick G. *s.j.* '62 (STL) [C] St. Louis, MO Saint Louis University; [P] St. Louis, MO Jesuit Community Corporation at St. Louis University - Jesuit Hall.
McLeod, Malcolm C. *m.ss.cc.* '87 (CAM) Linwood, NJ Our Lady of Sorrows Church.
McLeod, Paul *ss.cc.* (HON) Lihue, HI Immaculate Conception Church.
McLeon, Robert (NY) [D] New York, NY Department of Education.
McLernan, Richard L. *o.s.f.s.* '57 (LAN) [B] Jackson, MI Lumen Christi High School.
McLernon, Thomas M. '57 (BGP) [A] Fairfield, CT Sacred Heart University; [V] Bridgeport, CT Newman Centers.
McLernon, Thomas M. '57 (HBG) On Duty Outside the Diocese.
McLinden, James E. *s.s.j.* '71 (WDC) [B] Washington, DC St. Joseph's Seminary.
McLoone, Joseph C. '88 (PH) [94] Philadelphia, PA St. Martin of Tours Church.
McLoraine, John A. '35 (CHI) [2] Mt. Prospect, IL St. Emily Church; Retired.
McLoud, Steven J. '94 (SC) Carroll, IA Holy Spirit Church.
McLoughlin, Brendan '70 (PAT) Randolph, NJ Resurrection Church.
McLoughlin, Edward '78 (VEN) Absent on Leave.
McLoughlin, James W. '65 (RCK) Geneva, IL St. Peter Church.
McLoughlin, John *c.ss.r.* (BAL) [94] Baltimore, MD St. Wenceslaus Church.
McLoughlin, John Francis *c.p.* '54 (HRT) [M] West Hartford, CT Holy Family Monastery/Retreat.
McLoughlin, John T. '73 (NY) West Point, NY Catholic Chapel of the Most Holy Trinity Church; [CC] New York, NY University Apostolate.
McLoughlin, Luke '66 (STA) [16] Jacksonville, FL St. Matthew's Church.
McLoughlin, Michael P. '81 (NY) Highland Falls, NY Sacred Heart of Jesus Church.
McLoughlin, Nicholas '66 (VEN) Port Charlotte, FL St. Charles Borromeo Church.
McLoughlin, Patrick '86 (COS) [11] Colorado Springs, CO St. Joseph's Church.
McLoughlin, Paul J. '71 (SPC) Ozark, MO St. Joseph the Worker Church.
McLoughlin, Richard J. '69 (PH) Absent on Leave.
McLoughlin, William J. *s.j.* '43 (PAT) [I] Morristown, NJ Loyola House of Retreats.
McLoughlin, William J. '57 (BRK) [78] Brooklyn, NY St. Margaret Mary Church.
McLoy, Alfred E. '54 (SC) [B] Sioux City, IA Bishop Heelan Catholic High School.
McLucas, James '79 (NY) Absent on Leave.
McMackin, Thomas P. '63 (ORL) Ormond Beach, FL Prince of Peace Church.
McMahan, Frederick J. '40 (DAV) Retired; [B] Davenport, IA St. Ambrose University.
McMahon, Albert F. *o.f.m.* (BO) Boston, MA Metro West Medical Center; [W] Brighton, MA St. Bonaventure Friary, Franciscan Friars.
McMahon, Bernard '48 (NY) [C] New Rochelle, NY College of New Rochelle.
McMahon, Brian '66 (BO) [1] Medford, MA St. Francis of Assisi Church.
McMahon, Brian F. '80 (BO) [Q] Brighton, MA St. Elizabeth's Hospital of Boston.
McMahon, Desmond '60 (SEA) Medical Leave.
McMahon, Edward J. *s.j.* '60 (NY) [Z] New York, NY Jesuit Provincial's Office; [Z] New York, NY Xavier Jesuit Community.
McMahon, Edward M. '70 (BO) Billerica, MA St. Mary Church.
McMahon, Francis *c.ss.r.* '58 (OAK) [N] Oakland, CA Redemptorists.
McMahon, Francis X. *s.s.e.* '54 (NOR) Groton, CT Sacred Heart Church.
McMahon, George J. *s.j.* '53 (NY) [C] Bronx, NY Fordham University; [Z] New York, NY Jesuit Community at Fordham University.
McMahon, Gerald F. *c.s.c.* '41 (SY) [9] Binghamton, NY St. Patrick Church.
McMahon, Gerald J. *s.j.* '62 (NY) [Z] New York, NY Murray-Weigel Hall.
McMahon, Gerard J. '59 (ROC) On Duty Outside the Diocese.
McMahon, Gerard J. '59 (SCR) [4] Scranton, PA St. David's Church.
McMahon, Gerard T. '61 (BO) On Duty Outside the Archdiocese.
McMahon, Msgr. James B. '53 (BRK) [23] Brooklyn, NY St. Brendan's Church.
McMahon, Msgr. John '66 (PMB) [3] Boca Raton, FL St. Joan of Arc Church.
McMahon, John A. *o.p.* '68 (WDC) [11] Washington, DC St. Dominic Church & Priory Church.
McMahon, John B. '60 (WDC) Retired.
McMahon, John F. '76 (CLV) [64] Cleveland, OH SS. Philip and James Church; Cleveland, OH Cuyahoga County Nursing Home; Retired.
McMahon, Msgr. John J. (PHX) [J] Phoenix, AZ St. Vincent De Paul Society.
McMahon, John J. '38 (CHI) Skokie, IL St. Joan of Arc Church; Retired.
McMahon, Msgr. John J. '48 (PHX) Special Assignment; [G] Phoenix, AZ Mt. Claret Retreat Center.
McMahon, Joseph M. '43 (P) Retired.
McMahon, Joseph R. '71 (WIL) [2] Wilmington, DE St. Ann Church.
McMahon, Joseph S. '68 (P) Gresham, OR St. Henry Church.
McMahon, Joseph V. '84 (NSH) [6] Nashville, TN St. Henry Church; [B] Nashville, TN Father Ryan High School.
McMahon, Kevin T. '75 (PH) [A] Wynnewood, PA Theological Seminary of St. Charles Borromeo, Overbrook.
McMahon, Kevin T. '75 (WIL) On Duty Outside the Diocese.
McMahon, Kieran F. *o.f.m.* '47 (PAT) [M] Ringwood, NJ Holy Name Friary.
McMahon, Kieran M. '65 (SAC) [20] Sacramento, CA St. Robert Church.

McMahon, Msgr. Lawrence J. '55 (BGP) [3] Stratford, CT St. Mark's Church.
McMahon, Martin J. *o.m.i.* '56 (BUF) [27] Buffalo, NY Holy Angels Church.
McMahon, Marvin J. '51 (SFS) Retired.
McMahon, Michael F. '88 (CHI) Lake Forest, IL St. Mary Church.
McMahon, Patrick *o.carm.* '76 (WDC) [B] Washington, DC Whitefriars Hall.
McMahon, Sean '62 (ALB) Cairo, NY Sacred Heart Church.
McMahon, Msgr. Thomas '34 (NY) Rye, NY Resurrection Church; Retired.
McMahon, Thomas D. *s.j.* '51 (BUF) [50] Buffalo, NY St. Michael Church.
McMahon, Thomas F. *c.s.v.* '54 (CHI) [N] Chicago, IL Viatorian Residence.
McMahon, Msgr. Thomas V. '34 (NY) [E] White Plains, NY Archbishop Stepinac High School.
McMahon, Timothy M. *s.j.* '87 (KC) [12] Kansas City, MO St. Francis Xavier Church; [J] Kansas City, MO St. Francis Xavier - Jesuit Community.
McMahon, Walter M. '73 (SJ) [19] San Jose, CA St. Thomas of Canterbury Church.
McMahon, Msgr. William J. '45 (NY) Cortlandt Manor, NY Holy Spirit Church; Retired; [DD] New York, NY St. Anthony Welfare Center.
McMain, Msgr. Robert O. '49 (WDC) Special Ministries; [V] Washington, DC Catholic Historical Society of Washington.
McManamin, Francis G. *s.j.* '61 (BAL) [C] Baltimore, MD Loyola College; [M] Baltimore, MD Jesuit Community of Loyola College, Inc.
McManamon, James *o.f.m.* '49 (CLV) [6] Parma, OH Holy Family Church.
McManamon, John M. *s.j.* (DET) [K] Detroit, MI Jesuit Provincial Office-Detroit Province of the Society of Jesus.
McManamon, John M. *s.j.* '80 (CHI) [C] Chicago, IL Jesuit Community at Loyola University of Chicago.
McManimon, James P. '59 (TR) [3] Trenton, NJ Holy Angels Church; Leave of Absence.
McManus, Msgr. Charles '42 (NY) [144] Bronx, NY St. Gabriel Church.
McManus, Msgr. Charles J. '42 (NY) [4] Yonkers, NY St. Bartholomew Church; Retired.
McManus, Dennis *c.s.sp.* '58 (SFR) San Anselmo, CA St. Anselm Church; San Quentin, CA California State Prison.
McManus, Eamon '54 (WDC) Lanham, MD St. Matthias Church.
McManus, Edward '34 (ALB) Retired.
McManus, Eugene J. '57 (RVC) Hewlett, NY St. Joseph's Church; Retired.
McManus, Eugene P. *s.s.j.* '49 (BAL) [M] Baltimore, MD St. Joseph Society of the Sacred Heart House of Central Administration.
McManus, Fidelis *o.f.m.cap.* '45 (SAL) [D] Hays, KS St. Joseph's Friary.
McManus, Francis J. *s.j.* '73 (BGP) [O] Fairfield, CT The Fairfield Jesuit Community-Fairfield University.
McManus, Francis J. *s.j.* '73 (BO) [W] Boston, MA The Society of Jesus of New England-Provincial Offices.
McManus, Francis J. *s.j.* '73 (FR) [14] New Bedford, MA St. James Church.
McManus, Msgr. Frederick R. '47 (BO) On Duty Outside the Archdiocese.
McManus, Msgr. Frederick R. '47 (WDC) [C] Washington, DC Catholic University of America, The.
McManus, Gerald D. '79 (PH) Military Chaplains.
McManus, Msgr. Hugh F. '61 (NY) Scarsdale, NY Our Lady of Fatima Church.
McManus, Msgr. J. Fleming '47 (CHR) Retired.
McManus, John E. *c.s.b.* '55 (GAL) [Q] Houston, TX Residence of the Basilian Fathers of the University of St. Thomas.
McManus, John H. *o.m.i.* '56 (SCL) [M] St. Cloud, MN St. Therese Center for Special Ministry.
McManus, John H. *o.m.i.* '56 (STP) [Q] Buffalo, MN Christ the King Retreat Center.
McManus, Joseph '56 (BAL) [40] Baltimore, MD Immaculate Heart of Mary Church.
McManus, Martin '59 (SD) Retired.
McManus, Msgr. Michael G. '48 (SAT) Bandera, TX St. Stanislaus Church.
McManus, Michael K. '85 (FR) Somerset, MA St. Thomas More Church.
McManus, Paul C. '65 (DUB) Urbana, IA St. Mary Church; Walker, IA Sacred Heart Church; [H] Waterloo, IA Covenant Medical Center.
McManus, Paul G. (BO) Society of St. James the Apostle.
McManus, Msgr. Paul J. '42 (BO) Retired.
McManus, Richard *o.f.m.* '83 (MRY) [I] San Juan Bautista, CA St. Francis Retreat Center.
McManus, Robert J. '78 (PRO) Barrington, RI St. Luke's Church.
McManus, Msgr. Robert T. '52 (PH) Downingtown, PA St. Joseph Church.
McManus, Thomas F. *s.j.* '63 (ROC) [B] Rochester, NY McQuaid Jesuit High School.
McManus, Thomas J. *s.t.l.* '68 (PH) [157] Philadelphia, PA St. William Church.
McMenamin, John (OKL) Prison Ministry.
McMillan, Cliff J. '90 (DEN) Glenwood Springs, CO St. Stephen Church.
McMillan, John F. *c.p.* '56 (PIT) [N] Pittsburgh, PA St. Paul of the Cross Monastery.
McMillan, Robert G. *s.j.* '62 (BO) [22] Boston, MA St. Francis de Sales-St. Philip Church; [W] Boston, MA Loyola House; [W] Boston, MA The Society of Jesus of New England-Provincial Offices.
McMillen, Michael *s.c.j.* '67 (CHI) [N] Chicago, IL Priests of the Sacred Heart.
McMonagle, Edward J. *s.m.* '47 (HON) Kapaa, HI St. Catherine Church.
McMorrow, Kevin *s.a.* '58 (NY) [A] Yonkers, NY St. Joseph's Seminary; [Z] Garrison, NY Franciscan Friars of the Atonement.
McMullan, John E. '61 (SEA) [16] Seattle, WA St. Matthew Church; [29] Seattle, WA Our Lady of the Lake Church.
McMullan, John E. '75 (SEA) [21] Seattle, WA Assumption Church.
McMullan, Msgr. Seamus O. '46 (FRS) Tehachapi, CA St. Malachy Church; Retired.
McMullen, Aidan C. '47 (NEW) [B] Jersey City, NJ Saint Peter's College; [N] Jersey City, NJ Jesuits of Saint Peter's College, Inc.
McMullen, Brendan J. *o.p.* '43 (STP) [15] Minneapolis, MN St. Albert the Great Church; Bloomington, MN Nativity of the Blessed Virgin Mary Church.
McMullen, Charles P. '34 (PH) Eddystone, PA St. Rose of Lima Church; Retired.
McMullen, Francis R. '51 (RVC) Priests Released from Diocesan Assignment.
McMullen, John *o.s.b.* '66 (SFS) Wilmot, SD St. Mary Church; [F] Marvin, SD Blue Cloud Abbey; [I] Marvin, SD Blue Cloud Abbey Retirement Trust.
McMullen, Roger '67 (SHP) Retired.
McMullin, Daniel '81 (ROC) [6] Rochester, NY St. Anthony of Padua Church; [15] Rochester, NY St. Francis Assisi Church; [20] Rochester, NY Holy Apostles Church; [51] Rochester, NY SS. Peter and Paul Church.
McMullin, Ernan '49 (FTW) [B] Notre Dame, IN University of Notre Dame Du Lac.
McMullin, Finian *o.f.m.* '46 (SFD) [H] Granite City, IL St. Elizabeth Medical Center.
McMurry, John E. *s.s.* '56 (BAL) [L] Baltimore, MD St. Mary's Spiritual Center.
McMurry, John E. *s.s.* '56 (NSH) On Duty Outside the Diocese.
McMurry, Vincent deP. *s.s.* '49 (NSH) On Duty Outside the Diocese.
McMurtrie, Msgr. James W. '62 (ARL) Ashburn, VA St. Theresa Church.
McNalis, John P. '75 (CHI) [94] Chicago, IL Immaculate Heart of Mary Church.
McNally, Dennis E. *s.j.* '74 (PH) [C] Philadelphia, PA St. Joseph's University; [Z] Philadelphia, PA Jesuit Community at St. Joseph's University.
McNally, Donald *o.m.i.* (GAL) Richmond, TX Jester IV Unit.
McNally, Donald *o.m.i.* '60 (SAT) [M] San Antonio, TX Provincial Administration Office, Oblates of Mary Immaculate (Southern Prov.).
McNally, Edward F. '95 (SY) Mattydale, NY St. Margaret Church.
McNally, James P. '80 (JC) Absent on Leave.
McNally, Joseph '58 (IND) [17] Indianapolis, IN St. Barnabas Church.
McNally, Lawrence R. '77 (CHI) [181] Chicago, IL Queen of the Universe Church.
McNally, Michael '73 (PMB) On Duty Outside the Diocese.
McNally, Michael J. '73 (PH) [A] Wynnewood, PA Theological Seminary of St. Charles Borromeo, Overbrook.
McNally, Michael R. '59 (SB) Colton, CA Immaculate Conception Church.
McNally, Nathan *o.f.m.* '57 (STL) [T] Dittmer, MO Il Ritiro-The Little Retreat.
McNally, Richard *ss.cc.* '75 (FR) [K] Fairhaven, MA Sacred Hearts Provincial House.
McNally, Stephen '86 (RIC) On Duty Outside the Diocese.
McNally, Theodore A. *o.f.m.* '55 (PAT) [M] Butler, NJ St. Anthony Friary.
McNally, Thomas *c.s.c.* '61 (OAK) [3] Hayward, CA St. Clement Church.
McNally, Thomas C. '46 (Y) Retired.
McNally, Vincent '84 (MIL) [B] Hales Corners, WI Sacred Heart School of Theology.
McNally, Vincent M. *s.j.* '48 (ALB) [O] Auriesville, NY Jesuit Retreat House for Priests, Religious and Lay People.
McNamara, Brian J. '84 (RVC) Plainview, NY St. Pius X Church.
McNamara, Dennis L. *s.j.* '76 (WDC) [M] Washington, DC The Jesuit Community at Georgetown University.
McNamara, Donald P. '61 (PH) On Duty Outside the Archdiocese.
McNamara, Elmer A. '33 (BUF) Kendall, NY St. Mark Church.
McNamara, Elmer A. '33 (ROC) Retired.
McNamara, Msgr. Eugene P. '53 (BO) Scituate, MA St. Mary of the Nativity Church.
McNamara, Francis J. *s.j.* '54 (ROC) [B] Rochester, NY McQuaid Jesuit High School.
McNamara, Msgr. James '71 (RVC) West Babylon, NY Our Lady of Grace Church.
McNamara, John '32 (ALB) Retired.
McNamara, John J. '53 (ALN) Port Carbon, PA St. Stephen Church.
McNamara, John P. '56 (CHI) Palatine, IL St. Theresa Church.
McNamara, Joseph *s.p.* '56 (STL) [P] St. Louis, MO Servants of the Paraclete.
McNamara, Joseph C. *o.s.f.s.* '56 (PAT) Denville, NJ St. Clare Hospital; [J] Denville, NJ Sisters of the Sorrowful Mother Health Care Ministry Corp.
McNamara, Joseph F. *c.s.sp.* '42 (PRO) Tiverton, RI St. Madeleine Church.
McNamara, Joseph M. '39 (ROC) Groton, NY St. Anthony Church; Retired.
McNamara, Michael J. '79 (BO) Awaiting Assignment.
McNamara, Patrick M. *o.s.m.* '49 (P) [L] Portland, OR The Grotto, The National Sanctuary of Our Sorrowful Mother.
McNamara, Patrick V. '60 (NY) [2] New Rochelle, NY St. Gabriel Church.
McNamara, Peter J. '64 (CC) Zapata, TX Our Lady of Lourdes Church.
McNamara, Philip *s.a.c.* '58 (FWT) Comanche, TX Sacred Heart Church; De Leon, TX Our Lady of Guadalupe Church; Dublin, TX St. Mary Church; Stephenville, TX St. Brendan Church.
McNamara, Philip D. '56 (WOR) Retired.
McNamara, Robert F. '36 (ROC) [59] Rochester, NY St. Thomas the Apostle Church; Retired; [L] Rochester, NY Archivist.
McNamara, Robert J. '69 (LA) Chatsworth, CA St. John Eudes Church.
McNamara, Stephen E. '67 (VEN) [2] Fort Myers, FL Church Of The Resurrection Of Our Lord.
McNamara, Thomas E. '67 (NY) [182] Bronx, NY SS. Philip and James Church.
McNamara, Thomas F. *m.s.* '47 (GAL) [J] Nassau Bay, TX St. John Hospital.
McNamara, Thomas J. '82 (SAG) Mount Pleasant, MI Sacred Heart Church; Rosebush, MI St. Henry Church.
McNamara, Thomas L. *o.s.f.s.* '52 (TOL) [C] Toledo, OH St. Francis de Sales High School; [K] Toledo, OH Oblates of St. Francis de Sales.
McNamara, Vincent P. '60 (NY) City, NY Bronx House of Detention.
McNamara, William *o.c.d.* '51 (MIL) [P] Milwaukee, WI Provincial Offices - Discalced Carmelites.
McNamara, William *o.c.d.* '51 (PBL) [I] Crestone, CO Spiritual Life Institute of America, Inc.
McNamara, William '65 (SAT) Elmendorf, TX St. Anthony Church.
McNamee, Msgr. Charles W. '50 (RCK) Special Assignment.
McNamee, Francis G. '95 (ATL) Peachtree City, GA Holy Trinity Catholic Church.
McNamee, James P. '73 (LC) Kendall, WI St. Joseph Church; Wilton, WI St. John the Baptist Church.
McNamee, John P. '59 (PH) [91] Philadelphia, PA St. Malachy Church.
McNamee, Maurice B. *s.j.* '40 (STL) [P] St. Louis, MO Jesuit Community Corporation at St. Louis University - Jesuit Hall.
McNamee, Patrick '70 (P) Salem, OR St. Vincent de Paul Church.
McNamee, Msgr. William J. '26 (FAR) Retired.
McNanna, Neal *o.carm.* '59 (SAC) Fairfield, CA Our Lady of Mount Carmel, Church.
McNea, Mark C. '89 (WIN) [A] Winona, MN Immaculate Heart of Mary Seminary, Saint Mary's University of MN #43; [C] Winona, MN Cotter High School.
McNearney, John *glmy.* '62 (CIN) [M] Fairfield, OH Headquarters of Glenmary Home Missioners.
McNeely, Maurice '58 (HON) [6] Honolulu, HI Holy Family Church.
McNeff, Thomas C. '77 (CHI) Schiller Park, IL St. Maria Goretti Church.
McNeice, Charles *s.s.e.* '62 (BIR) Marion, AL Marion Military Institute Church.
McNeice, Charles *s.s.e.* '62 (MOB) Plateau, AL Our Mother of Mercy Church; Prichard, AL Our Lady of Fatima Church.
McNeil, Aubrey *o.f.m.* '85 (NY) [146] Bronx, NY Holy Cross Church.
McNeil, Dennis M. '75 (CLV) Brook Park, OH Assumption of Mary Church.
McNeil, Frank J. '71 (SFS) On Leave of Absence.
McNeil, Joel (OM) Absent on Leave.
McNeil, Joel D. '87 (AUS) [25] Austin, TX San Jose Church; Somerville, TX St. Ann's Church.

McNeil, John R. (BO) On Duty Outside the Archdiocese.
McNeil, Lawrence J. '73 (HBG) [K] Harrisburg, PA Catholic Campus Ministry.
McNeil, Nicholas J. *s.j.* '46 (BO) [W] Weston, MA Campion Health Center, Inc.
McNeill, Donald P. *c.s.c.* '65 (FTW) [B] Notre Dame, IN University of Notre Dame Du Lac; [J] Notre Dame, IN Holy Cross Community, Corby Hall, University of Notre Dame.
McNeill, Douglas '70 (GLP) Absent on Leave.
McNeill, John A. '46 (BRK) [213] Queens, NY Our Lady of Lourdes Church; Retired.
McNeill, Malachy '44 (B) Retired.
McNeill, Msgr. Robert W. '47 (BO) Kingston, MA St. Joseph Church.
McNeilly, Dennis P. *s.j.* '85 (OM) [K] Omaha, NE Jesuit Community At Creighton University.
McNelis, Dennis M. *c.s.c.* '62 (FR) [I] Fall River, MA Rose Hawthorne Lathrop Home.
McNelis, Francis J. '65 (ALN) Sinking Spring, PA St. Ignatius Loyola Church.
McNelis, Patrick J. '62 (BRK) [64] Brooklyn, NY Immaculate Heart of Mary Church.
McNelis, Paul D. *s.j.* '77 (WDC) [M] Washington, DC The Jesuit Community at Georgetown University.
McNellis, Paul W. *s.j.* '87 (NY) [Z] New York, NY Jesuit Provincial's Office.
McNerney, James '81 (ALB) [11] Troy, NY St. Paul the Apostle Church.
McNerney, Malachy *o.s.b.* '67 (LR) Booneville, AR Church of Our Lady of the Assumption; [A] Subiaco, AR Subiaco Monastery.
McNew, Dwayne A. '95 (COL) Zanesville, OH St. Nicholas Church; [C] Zanesville, OH Bishop Rosecrans High School.
McNichol, Daniel J. '67 (HON) [2] Honolulu, HI Co-Cathedral of St. Theresa of the Child Jesus.
McNichol, Fabian *t.o.r.* '55 (ALT) [F] Loretto, PA St. Francis Friary, Third Order Regular of St. Francis of Penance.
McNicholas, Edward J. '54 (BRK) Released from Diocesan Assignment.
McNicholas, Raymond *s.s.c.* '49 (BUF) [2] Orchard Park, NY St. Bernadette Church.
McNicholas, Stephen '53 (ORL) Retired.
McNicholas, Timothy J. '43 (CIN) Retired.
McNicholas, Walter *o.s.a.* (CHI) [J] Chicago, IL Holy Cross Hospital.
McNicholl, Michael P. '66 (BUF) Strykersville, NY St. Mary, Queen of the Rosary Church.
McNichols, William *s.j.* '79 (BO) [W] Chestnut Hill, MA The Jesuit Community at Boston College.
McNichols, Msgr. William J. '38 (CHI) [2] Oak Lawn, IL St. Gerald Church; Retired.
McNiff, Msgr. James '36 (SFE) Retired.
McNiff, William T. *o.s.c.* '43 (SCL) Onamia, MN The Church of the Holy Cross of Onamia; [I] Onamia, MN Crosier Monastery.
McNulty, Charles L. '37 (ALN) Retired; [J] Bethlehem, PA Holy Family Villa.
McNulty, Edward '93 (SD) [8] San Diego, CA Immaculata Church.
McNulty, Edwin J. '44 (COL) Retired; [G] Columbus, OH St. Rita Home.
McNulty, Frank J. '52 (NEW) Roseland, NJ Our Lady of the Blessed Sacrament Church.
McNulty, Gerard J. '67 (LA) Military and VA Chaplains.
McNulty, J. Brendan '74 (CLV) [64] Cleveland, OH SS. Philip and James Church.
McNulty, James '53 (LA) [86] Los Angeles, CA St. Paul the Apostle Church.
McNulty, James D. *c.s.p.* '53 (NY) [Z] Scarsdale, NY Paulist Fathers Generalate.
McNulty, Jerry (LAV) Military Chaplains.
McNulty, John '74 (PRO) Bristol, RI St. Mary's Church.
McNulty, John P. '73 (CLV) [3] Euclid, OH Holy Cross Church.
McNulty, Joseph D. '69 (CLV) [9] Cleveland, OH St. Augustine Church.
McNulty, Joseph P. '43 (BO) Retired.
McNulty, Michael A. '50 (MET) Blairstown, NJ St. Jude Church.
McNulty, Msgr. Patrick (LA) [49] Los Angeles, CA St. Bernard Church.
McNulty, Msgr. Patrick '53 (LA) Retired.
McNulty, Patrick J. '60 (FTW) On Special Assignment.
McNulty, Robert E. '56 (NOR) Retired.
McNulty, T. Michael *s.j.* '73 (MIL) [P] Milwaukee, WI Jesuit Community at Marquette University.
McNulty, Theodore '66 (CHI) [206] Chicago, IL St. Thomas More Church.
McNulty, Theodore '66 (SAN) Absent on Leave.
McNulty, William C. '46 (STP) Retired.
McNulty, William J. '61 (CHI) Lake Forest, IL St. Patrick Church.
McNulty, William J. '64 (NOR) Dayville, CT St. Joseph Church; Rogers, CT St. Ignatius Church.
McOwen, James F. '41 (LA) [R] Los Angeles, CA Amat House; [W] Santa Barbara, CA St. Mary's Seminary Center.
McPadden, Charles J. *m.m.* '69 (CHR) Greenville, SC St. Mary's Church.
McPadden, Malachy M. *o.s.b.* '57 (NEW) [N] Newark, NJ Newark Abbey.
McPartland, Aloysius M. *m.s.* '47 (NY) Phoenicia, NY St. Francis de Sales Church.
McPartland, Guy *o.carm.* '55 (JOL) [J] Darien, IL Carmelite Fathers Provincial Office.
McPartland, Guy I. *o.carm.* '55 (MET) [F] New Brunswick, NJ St. Peter's Medical Center.
McPartland, Paul G. '57 (BO) Halifax, MA Our Lady of the Lake Church.
McPartland, Thomas *c.ss.r.* '32 (NY) [92] New York, NY Our Lady of Perpetual Help Church.
McPeak, George *m.m.* '59 (NY) [Z] Maryknoll, NY Maryknoll Fathers and Brothers.
McPeak, William J. '45 (NY) Retired; [Z] New York, NY Our Lady of Consolation Residence.
McPhail, J. Stuart *o.p.* '69 (PRO) [B] Providence, RI Providence College; [P] Providence, RI St. Thomas Aquinas Priory at Providence College.
McPhee, John *c.ss.r.* '46 (CHI) [N] Bangkok, Thailand.
McPhee, John *c.ss.r.* '46 (DEN) [M] Denver, CO The Redemptorists/Denver Province.
McPhee, Marvin E. '65 (SFS) Groton, SD St. John Baptist Church.
McPhillips, James G. '83 (CLV) Newbury, OH St. Helen Church.
McPhillips, Thomas J. '44 (SFS) Retired; [E] Mitchell, SD Brady Memorial Home.
McPolin, Patrick *c.m.f.* '43 (LA) [R] Rancho Dominguez, CA Dominguez Seminary Inc.
McQuade, Brian D. '94 (RVC) St. James, NY SS. Philip and James Church.
McQuade, James F. *c.s.p.* '56 (NY) [104] New York, NY St. Paul the Apostle Church; Manhattan, NY St. Luke's-Roosevelt Hospital Center.
McQuade, Richard E. '57 (BO) On Special or Other Diocesan Assignment; Awaiting Assignment.
McQuaid, Msgr. Eugene (PAT) Retired.
McQuaid, Thomas W. (CHI) [4] Waukegan, IL Holy Family Church.
McQueeney, Robert *m.ss.a.* '82 (NOR) [A] Cromwell, CT Holy Apostles College and Seminary; [F] Cromwell, CT Missionaries of the Holy Apostles.
McQueeny Thomas F. *s.j.* '56 (STL) [P] St. Louis, MO De Smet Jesuit High School Community.
McQuester, Mark A. '87 (MAR) Norway, MI St. Mary Church; Vulcan, MI St. Barbara Church.
McQuillan, Cornelius T. *c.s.sp.* (SJN) [B] Bayamon, PR Seminario Misionero del Espiritu Santo.
McQuillan, Edward *c.m.* '44 (STA) [E] Jacksonville, FL St. Vincent's Medical Center, Inc.
McQuillan, Edward F. *c.m.* '44 (PH) [Z] Philadelphia, PA Congregation of the Mission.
McQuillen, Paul G. *s.s.e.* '77 (NO) [4] Marrero, LA St. Joseph the Worker Church.
McQuillen, Thomas '96 (TOL) Norwalk, OH St. Paul Church.
McQuinn, James '88 (PH) [D] Norristown, PA Kennedy-Kenrick Catholic High School.
McQuinn, Maurice '39 (KC) Retired.
McQuinn, Peter B. '91 (CHI) [123] Chicago, IL St. Mark Church.
McRae, Cornelius (BO) On Duty Outside the Archdiocese.
McRae, Roderick *b.s.o.* '92 (NTN) Waterford, CT St. Ann Church.
McReavy, Thomas J. *c.s.b.* '59 (GAL) [7] Houston, TX St. Anne Church.
McReynolds, Eugene *o.s.b.* '70 (OM) Boys Town, NE Immaculate Conception B.V.M. Church; [I] Boys Town, NE Father Flanagan's Boys' Home; [K] Elkhorn, NE Mount Michael Abbey.
McShane, James J. '66 (BUR) Bellows Falls, VT St. Charles Church.
McShane, John '74 (LAV) [3] Las Vegas, NV Holy Family Church.
McShane, John A. '57 (BRK) [55] Brooklyn, NY Holy Family Church.
McShane, Joseph M. *s.j.* '77 (NY) [C] Bronx, NY Fordham University; [Z] New York, NY Jesuit Community at Fordham University.
McShane, Patrick (BO) Boston, MA V.A. Medical Centers.
McShane, Patrick E. '79 (CLV) Released from Diocesan Assignment.
McShane, Thomas S. *s.j.* '60 (OM) [K] Omaha, NE Jesuit Community At Creighton University.
McShane, Vincent J. '39 (NY) Retired; [E] White Plains, NY Archbishop Stepinac High School.
McSheffery, Daniel F. '56 (HRT) North Branford, CT St. Augustine Church.
McSherry, John G. *s.j.* '72 (NY) [Z] New York, NY West Side Jesuit Community.
McSherry, Patrick *o.f.m.cap.* (DET) [K] Detroit, MI St. Mary's Friary.
McSherry, Patrick *o.f.m.cap.* '78 (DET) [K] Detroit, MI St. Bonaventure Friary.
McSherry, Thomas '71 (OKL) Special Assignment.
McSherry, Tom '53 (TLS) On Duty Outside the Diocese.
McSorley, Aidan *o.s.b.* '69 (KC) [J] Conception, MO Conception Abbey.
McSorley, Gerald '64 (LA) [49] Los Angeles, CA St. Bernard Church.
McSorley, James P. *o.m.i.* '46 (OAK) [N] Oakland, CA Oblate Provincial House & Procure.
McSorley, Matthew T. *o.s.b.* '49 (CHL) [J] Belmont, NC Belmont Abbey.
McSorley, Richard T. *s.j.* '46 (WDC) [M] Washington, DC The Jesuit Community at Georgetown University.
McSpiritt, John *s.t.* '59 (ARL) [J] Arlington, VA Missionary Servants of the Most Holy Trinity, S.T.
McSweeney, Brian '86 (NY) [E] Somers, NY John F. Kennedy High School.
McSweeney, Edward F. '52 (PIT) West View, PA St. Athanasius Church; [L] Allison Park, PA Regency Hall Nursing Home, Inc.
McSweeney, Godfrey D. *o.f.m.* '42 (MRY) [I] San Juan Bautista, CA St. Francis Retreat Center; [I] Soquel, CA St. Clare's Retreat House.
McSweeney, James '47 (GI) Retired.
McSweeney, James '74 (SR) Sonoma, CA St. Francis Solano Church.
McSweeney, Msgr. James E. '50 (R) Retired.
McSweeney, Jeremiah F. '72 (WH) Cheat Lake, WV St. Luke Church.
McSweeney, John '48 (MRY) Retired.
McSweeney, Msgr. John J. '74 (CHL) Asheville, NC Basilica of St. Lawrence.
McSweeney, Msgr. John R. '61 (BUR) [5] Burlington, VT St. Mark's Church.
McSweeney, Joseph *s.s.c.* '58 (PRO) [P] Bristol, RI St. Columban's Retirement House.
McSweeney, Noel *s.a.* '48 (NY) [Z] Garrison, NY Generalate of the Franciscan Friars of the Atonement-St. James Friary.
McSweeney, Placid *o.s.c.o.* (WOR) [N] Spencer, MA St. Joseph's Abbey; [P] Spencer, MA St. Joseph Abbey.
McSweeney, Reginald *o.c.d.* '52 (SB) [G] Redlands, CA El Carmelo Retreat House.
McSweeney, Thomas J. (NY) [DD] New York, NY The Christophers.
McSweeney, William M. *o.m.i.* '52 (PMB) Riviera Beach, FL St. Francis of Assisi Church.
McSweeney, William P. '69 (SAC) [2] Sacramento, CA All Hallows Church; Sacramento, CA California Youth Authority.
McSwiggan, Thomas '67 (SAT) [59] San Antonio, TX St. Patrick Church.
McTaggart, Msgr. Edward P. '55 (SFR) [8] San Francisco, CA St. Brendan Church; San Francisco, CA Young Ladies' Institute; San Francisco, CA Serra Club of San Francisco (Golden Gate).
McTague, Charles H. '47 (NEW) [17] Newark, NJ St. James Church; Retired.
McTague, Thomas '57 (GF) Retired.
McTarsney, John F. '88 (DUB) Decorah, IA St. Benedict's Church; On Leave of Absence.
McTavey, Lawrence G. '55 (ALB) [2] Cohoes, NY St. Bernard Church.
McTighe, Edward P. *s.j.* '61 (P) [D] Portland, OR Jesuit High School; [J] Portland, OR Providence St. Vincent Medical Center.
McTighe, John *c.ss.r.* '94 (NY) [150] Bronx, NY Immaculate Conception Church.
McTighe, Simon *o.s.b.* '53 (IND) [J] St. Meinrad, IN St. Meinrad Archabbey.
McTigue, Norman P. (BUF) [4] Niagara Falls, NY St. John de La Salle Church.
McVean, John J. *o.f.m.* '67 (NY) [35] New York, NY St. Francis of Assisi Church.
McVeigh, James E. '73 (PH) [1] Drexel Hill, PA St. Andrew Church.
McVeigh, John J. '58 (LAV) Retired.
McVernon, John J. '58 (BRK) [191] Queens, NY St. Luke Church; Released from Diocesan Assignment.
McVinney, Paul *s.v.d.* '50 (TR) [M] Bordentown, NJ Society of the Divine Word.
McWeeney, Brian E. '73 (NY) [6] Poughkeepsie, NY St. Martin de Porres Church.
McWeeney, John W. *m.s.* '55 (NOR) Brooklyn, CT Our Lady of La Salette Church.
McWhorter, Michael L. (ATL) Milledgeville, GA Sacred Heart of Jesus Church.
McWilliam, James J. '49 (CIN) Retired; [B] Cincinnati, OH Mt. St. Mary's Seminary of the West.
Mead, Brian E. '69 (BUR) Colchester, VT Our Lady of Grace Church.
Mead, Leland C. '68 (NU) On Duty Outside the Diocese.
Meade, Denis *o.s.b.* '55 (KCK) [A] Atchison, KS Benedictine College.
Meade, Emilian *o.f.m.cap.* '46 (SFR) Burlingame, CA Our Lady of Angels Church.
Meade, Garvey G. '65 (BRK) [50] Brooklyn, NY Good Shepherd Church.
Meade, Henry J. '57 (BO) Needham, MA St. Bartholomew Church; Retired.
Meade, James '52 (BRK) [R] Queens Village, NY Queen

of Peace Residence.
Meade, James C. '52 (RVC) Retired.
Meade, James W. '81 (CIN) West Chester, OH St. John Church.
Meade, James W. '86 (GRY) Griffith, IN St. Mary Church.
Meade, John *s.m.* '53 (BO) [3] Methuen, MA Our Lady of Mount Carmel Church.
Meade, John F. (RVC) Malverne, NY Our Lady of Lourdes Church.
Meade, John F. '43 (NY) Retired.
Meade, Maurice P. '48 (BO) Boston, MA Cambridge Hospital; Boston, MA Mount Auburn Hospital; Retired.
Meade, William *l.c.* '91 (HRT) [B] Cheshire, CT Novitiate of the Legion of Christ.
Meaden, Paul *o.s.b.* '84 (SFE) [L] Pecos, NM Our Lady of Guadalupe Benedictine Abbey.
Meagher, Msgr. Frank J. '60 (COL) Buckeye Lake, OH Our Lady of Mt. Carmel Church.
Meagher, Jerome *o.m.i.* '49 (SAT) [K] San Antonio, TX Oblate Madonna Residence.
Meagher, John J. *s.s.e.* '66 (NOR) Groton, CT Sacred Heart Church.
Meagher, Joseph A. '92 (NEW) [3] Linden, NJ St. John the Apostle Church.
Meagher, Michael T. '65 (SY) [16] Syracuse, NY St. James Church.
Meagher, Patrick *o.s.b.* '35 (P) [L] St. Benedict, OR Mt. Angel Abbey.
Meagher, Msgr. Thomas '40 (SB) Guasti, CA San Secondo d'Asti Church; Retired.
Meagher, Thomas L. '64 (DET) White Lake, MI St. Patrick Church.
Mealey, John H. '60 (ALB) [16] Albany, NY St. Teresa of Avila Church.
Mealey, Mark *o.s.f.s.* '78 (ARL) Vienna, VA Our Lady of Good Counsel Church.
Meaney, Brendan J. '65 (CAM) Sicklerville, NJ St. John Neumann Church.
Meaney, John '59 (HRT) [D] Waterbury, CT Sacred Heart High School.
Meaney, John J. *m.m.* '59 (NY) [Z] Maryknoll, NY Maryknoll Fathers and Brothers.
Meaney, Joseph P. *m.m.* '26 (NY) [Z] Maryknoll, NY Maryknoll Fathers and Brothers.
Meaney, M. Brendan *f.j.* '87 (CC) [H] Hebbronville, TX Catholic Solitudes.
Meaney, Peter J. *o.s.b.* '51 (PAT) [M] Morristown, NJ St. Mary's Abbey.
Means, David '81 (ANC) On Duty Outside Archdiocese.
Means, David A. '81 (STL) On Duty Outside the Archdiocese.
Meany, John J. *o.p.* '87 (CHI) [N] Chicago, IL Dominicans (Provincial Office).
Meany, Michael G. '80 (CHI) [42] Chicago, IL St. Clotilde Church.
Meany, Neill R. *s.j.* '54 (YAK) [4] Yakima, WA St. Joseph's Church.
Meany, Stephen J. *s.j.* '67 (NY) [Z] New York, NY Murray-Weigel Hall.
Meany, Msgr. Thomas '55 (CC) On Special Assignment; [I] Corpus Christi, TX Pax Christi Residence.
Mears, Charles T. '51 (GF) Retired.
Measer, Donald L. '63 (BUF) [2] Depew, NY St. Barnabas Church; Retired.
Meaux, Glenn *s.o.l.t.* '80 (CC) [H] Robstown, TX Society of Our Lady of the Most Holy Trinity.
Meaux, Glenn '80 (LAF) On Duty Outside the Diocese.
Mecca, Gregg Daniel '96 (BGP) [5] Danbury, CT St. Peter's Church.
Mecca, Msgr. Mark A. '36 (SCR) Retired.
Meccia, Francis S. *m.m.* '66 (NY) [Z] Maryknoll, NY Maryknoll Fathers and Brothers.
Mech, John J. '95 (DET) Grosse Pointe, MI Our Lady Star of the Sea Church.
Mecir, Joseph S. '80 (CLV) Painesville, OH St. Mary Church.
Mecker, Lawrence A. (NO) Terrytown, LA Christ the King Church.
Mecwel, Pawel J. '90 (MAR) Grand Marais, MI Holy Rosary Church.
Medairos, Anthony J. '70 (BO) [25] Boston, MA Gate of Heaven Church.
Medas, Michael (BO) [4] Newton, MA St. John the Evangelist Church.
Medeiros, Antonio S. (BO) Retired.
Medeiros, Arnold R. '75 (FR) Norton, MA St. Mary's Church.
Medeiros, Benjamin *t.o.r.* '77 (FWT) [8] Fort Worth, TX St. Andrew Church.
Medeiros, James S. '92 (FR) North Dartmouth, MA St. Julie Billiart Church; [C] North Dartmouth, MA Bishop Stang High School.
Meder, James R. '39 (L) Rhodelia, KY St. Theresa Church; Retired.
Meder, Stephen A. *s.j.* '43 (DET) [P] Clarkston, MI Colombiere Center.
Medina, Antonio *m.g.* '82 (SJ) Los Gatos, CA Presentation Center.
Medina, Fabio (SFR) Half Moon Bay, CA Our Lady of the Pillar Church.
Medina, Francisco '89 (SJN) [8] San Juan, PR Nuestra Senora del Carmen Church.
Medina, George '87 (PCE) On Duty Outside the Diocese.
Medina, George A. '87 (TR) [1] Trenton, NJ St. Mary Cathedral.
Medina, Hector '84 (FWT) Wichita Falls, TX Our Lady of Guadalupe Church.
Medina, Ignazio C. '77 (JC) Fulton, MO St. Peter Church.
Medina, Jose A. *c.m.* '88 (PH) [Z] Philadelphia, PA Congregation of the Mission.
Medina, Julian '73 (SAC) Gridley, CA Sacred Heart Church.
Medina, Mauricio '64 (B) Blackfoot, ID St. Bernard's Church.
Medina, Miguel Arango (SAT) Uvalde, TX Sacred Heart Church.
Medina, Tito *m.s.c.* '92 (RCK) [H] Aurora, IL Missionaries of the Sacred Heart Community.
Medinski, Francis J. '48 (BGP) Retired.
Medley, Robert C. '90 (MET) [1] Metuchen, NJ Cathedral of St. Francis.
Medley, William F. '82 (L) Bardstown, KY St. Joseph Church.
Medlock, Scott '96 (ANC) [4] Anchorage, AK St. Elizabeth Ann Seton Church.
Medrano, Marcus '86 (DEN) [24] Denver, CO Sacred Heart Church.
Medwid, John '90 (ALB) Catskill, NY St. Patrick Church.
Meegan, William H. '50 (BUF) Retired.
Meehan, Andrew M. '93 (MAN) Salem, NH Mary, Queen of Peace Church.
Meehan, Barry C. *s.j.* '86 (NOR) [5] Norwich, CT SS. Peter and Paul Church.
Meehan, Barry M. '78 (PRO) [6] West Warwick, RI St. John's Church.
Meehan, Francis X. '61 (PH) West Chester, PA SS. Simon and Jude Church.
Meehan, Gabriel '59 (CHL) Forest City, NC Immaculate Conception Church.
Meehan, Gery G. *o.praem.* '60 (GB) [6] De Pere, WI St. Norbert College Parish Church; [B] De Pere, WI St. Norbert College; [I] De Pere, WI St. Joseph Priory.
Meehan, James *s.j.* '59 (SEA) Vashon, WA St. John Vianney Church; [C] Tacoma, WA Bellarmine Preparatory School.
Meehan, Msgr. James H. '50 (PH) Bryn Mawr, PA St. John Neumann Church.
Meehan, James L. '41 (OG) Redwood, NY St. Francis Xavier Church.
Meehan, James L. '51 (OG) Retired.
Meehan, John T. '64 (NY) [4] Mt. Vernon, NY St. Mary Church.
Meehan, Joseph '66 (STA) Atlantic Beach, FL St. John the Baptist Church.
Meehan, Joseph F. *s.j.* '49 (SJ) [M] Los Gatos, CA California Province of the Society of Jesus, Jesuit Provincial Office; [M] Los Gatos, CA Sacred Heart Jesuit Center.
Meehan, Joseph J. '61 (PH) Primos, PA St. Eugene Church.
Meehan, Msgr. Joseph P. '54 (NY) Suffern, NY Sacred Heart Church.
Meehan, Kenneth E. *s.j.* '71 (WDC) [E] Washington, DC Gonzaga College High School.
Meehan, Kevin *l.c.* '91 (HRT) [B] Cheshire, CT Novitiate of the Legion of Christ.
Meehan, Patrick *s.s.c.* '49 (BRK) [U] Kew Gardens, NY St. Columbans Foreign Mission Society.
Meehan, Peter K. '68 (NY) [33] New York, NY St. Emeric Church.
Meehan, Richard '69 (SPR) Absent on Leave.
Meehan, T.J. '72 (ATL) [12] Atlanta, GA Shrine of the Immaculate Conception Church.
Meehan, Terence A. '67 (CIN) [7] Cincinnati, OH St. Andrew Church; [34] Cincinnati, OH Holy Cross-Immaculata Church; [36] Cincinnati, OH Holy Name Church.
Meehan, Thomas '72 (CIN) [M] Fairfield, OH Headquarters of Glenmary Home Missioners.
Meehan, Thomas J. *o.s.a.* '80 (ALB) [2] Troy, NY St. Augustine Church.
Meehan, Timothy A. '59 (HRT) North Haven, CT St. Therese's Church.
Meehling, Donald '58 (SFD) [6] Springfield, IL St. Aloysius Church.
Meeks, Delphyn '83 (BEA) [1] Beaumont, TX St. Anthony Cathedral.
Meemken, Eugene A. '59 (SCL) Clarissa, MN St. Joseph Church; Moran, MN St. Isidore Church.
Meenan, Francis P. *c.s.sp.* '44 (PIT) Emsworth, PA Sacred Heart Church.
Meenan, Msgr. Joseph S. '37 (PIT) Retired.
Meenihan, Regis J. (E) North East, PA St. Gregory Thaumaturgus Church; [C] Erie, PA Cathedral Preparatory School.
Meersman, Jerome *c.i.c.m.* '49 (ARL) [J] Arlington, VA Missionhurst, C.I.C.M.-Central House and Provincialate.
Meffan, Robert V. (BO) Retired.
Meger, Msgr. Thomas *v.g.* '62 (RNO) [2] Reno, NV Our Lady of the Snows Church.
Mehan, Joseph '96 (DAL) [21] Dallas, TX St. Monica Church.
Mehm, Richard J. '77 (BO) [5] Boston, MA St. Andrew Church.
Mehm, Msgr. Walter '46 (LAN) Retired.
Mehok, Charles J. *s.j.* '48 (MIL) [P] Milwaukee, WI Jesuit Community at Marquette University; [Y] Milwaukee, WI Catholic Information Center.
Mehok, William J. *s.j.* '43 (FAR) Retired; [E] Fargo, ND Riverview Place, Inc.
Mehok, William J. *s.j.* '43 (MIL) [P] Milwaukee, WI Jesuit Provincial Office, Wisconsin Province.
Mehrkens, Msgr. William '50 (CR) Red Lake, MN St. Mary's Mission Church; [A] Red Lake, MN St. Mary's Mission School.
Meidl, Gerald S. '74 (NU) Marshall, MN Holy Redeemer Church.
Meier, Msgr. Allen J. '51 (COV) Retired; [C] Covington, KY Academy of Notre Dame.
Meier, Alphonse H. *o.s.b.* '48 (GBG) [H] Latrobe, PA Saint Vincent Archabbey.
Meier, Cyprian T. '69 (BIS) Mandan, ND Spirit of Life Church.
Meier, David E. *s.j.* '53 (DET) [P] Clarkston, MI Colombiere Center.
Meier, Denis '63 (SFS) Beresford, SD St. Teresa of Avila Church.
Meier, Emeric *o.f.m.* '68 (BO) [BB] Boston, MA St. Anthony Shrine.
Meier, Gerald A. '66 (STL) [62] St. Louis, MO St. Stephen, Protomartyr Church.
Meier, Msgr. John P. '67 (NY) On Duty Outside the Archdiocese.
Meier, John P. '67 (WDC) [C] Washington, DC Catholic University of America, The.
Meier, Msgr. Joseph F. '39 (SCR) Retired.
Meier, Laverne G. '58 (MAD) Montfort, WI St. Thomas Church; Madison, WI Madison-Meriter General Hospital.
Meier, Msgr. Raymond O. '36 (E) [3] Sharon, PA St. Joseph Church; Retired.
Meier, Timothy J. *s.j.* (DET) [K] Detroit, MI Jesuit Provincial Office-Detroit Province of the Society of Jesus.
Meier, Timothy J. *s.j.* '91 (SJ) [L] Los Altos, CA Jesuit Retreat House.
Meiergerd, Godfrey A. '42 (OM) Retired.
Meighan, Joseph F. '68 (SCR) [L] Scranton, PA Home for Aged of the Little Sisters of the Poor, Holy Family Residence; [N] Dunmore, PA Villa St. Joseph.
Meighan, Thomas A. '63 (WDC) [7] Silver Spring, MD St. John the Evangelist Church.
Meik, Thomas J. *c.m.* '48 (CHI) [C] Chicago, IL Vincentian Community at DePaul University.
Meiklejohn, Norman '54 (BO) [W] Brighton, MA Assumptionist Center.
Meilak, John '47 (LA) Retired.
Meiluta, George J. *s.m.* '40 (WDC) [M] Washington, DC Marist Provincial House.
Meiman, Louis J. '87 (L) [37] Louisville, KY Immaculate Heart of Mary Church.
Meinen, Dennis W. '87 (SC) Churdan, IA St. Columbkille's Church; Scranton, IA St. Paul's Church.
Meiners, Andrew *c.ss.r.* '70 (KC) [32] Kansas City, MO Our Lady of Perpetual Help Church; [J] Kansas City, MO Redemptorists of Kansas City.
Meinhart, C. Joseph '91 (OKL) Norman, OK St. Thomas More University Parish Church; [K] Norman, OK Campus Ministry for the Archdiocese of Oklahoma City; [K] Norman, OK Campus Ministry for the Archdiocese of Oklahoma City.
Meinhart, Joseph C. '91 (OKL) Special Assignment.
Meinholz, David J. '94 (MIL) Awaiting Assignment.
Meinholz, John M. '77 (MAD) [5] Madison, WI Immaculate Heart of Mary Church.
Meiring, Arnold *c.pp.s.* '40 (CIN) [B] Carthagena, OH St. Charles.
Meiring, Bernard *c.pp.s.* '55 (CIN) St. Anthony, OH St. Anthony Church.
Meirose, Harold R. *s.j.* '62 (DET) [P] Clarkston, MI Colombiere Center.
Meisburger, Joseph '66 (KC) [4] Independence, MO St. Mary's Church.
Meisburger, Joseph C. '66 (KC) Retired.
Meisel, Msgr. Charles F. (BAL) Retired.
Meisel, Msgr. Charles F. '50 (BAL) Timonium, MD Church of the Nativity.
Meisel, Gerald '61 (LA) [11] Long Beach, CA St. Matthew Church.
Meismer, Paul J. '69 (PEO) Sheffield, IL St. Patrick's Church.
Meissner, Robert J. '69 (SAG) [12] Saginaw, MI St. Helen Church.
Meissner, William W. *s.j.* '61 (BO) [W] Chestnut Hill, MA The Jesuit Community at Boston College.
Meister, Andrew H. '44 (OM) Retired.

Meitl, Roger K. '59 (SAL) Grinnell, KS Immaculate Conception Church; Oakley, KS St. Joseph's Church.
Mejak, Msgr. Heliodore '35 (KCK) [4] Kansas City, KS Holy Family Church.
Mejia, Jose '91 (LA) [1] Oxnard, CA St. Anthony Church.
Mejia, Leoncio *m.ss.cc.* (SJN) [1] Trujillo Alto, PR San Bartolome Church.
Mejia, Manuel J. *m.m.* '63 (SFR) [N] San Francisco, CA Maryknoll Fathers and Brothers, Catholic Foreign Mission Society of America, Inc.
Mejia, Ricardo '76 (SD) San Ysidro, CA Our Lady of Mt. Carmel Church.
Melancon, Bill John '93 (LAF) Baldwin, LA Sacred Heart Church.
Melancon, Leo J. *m.m.* '32 (LA) [R] Los Angeles, CA Maryknoll Fathers and Brothers.
Melancon, Msgr. Louis J. '63 (LKC) [6] Lake Charles, LA St. Theodore's Church.
Melancon, Robert '62 (HT) On Leave.
Melancon, Thomas J. *s.j.* '74 (STL) [P] St. Louis, MO Leo Brown Jesuit Community.
Melaniuk, Joseph M. '86 (MET) South River, NJ St. Mary of Ostrabrama Church.
Melbourne, David '39 (JUN) Retired.
Melcher, Francis L. *o.s.a.* '53 (PH) [Z] Villanova, PA St. Thomas Monastery.
Melcher, Michael '92 (LUB) Stamford, TX St. Ann Church.
Melchior, Frank D. '59 (GB) Suring, WI St. Michael Church.
Melchior, Gerald P. '90 (OM) [9] Omaha, NE St. Bernard Church.
Melchior, Thomas '65 (KCK) [4] Topeka, KS Most Pure Heart of Mary Church.
Melchoir, Frank '59 (GB) Retired.
Melchor, Filiberto *f.m.m.* '93 (MIA) [2] Pompano Beach, FL San Isidro Church.
Meldrum, James *o.c.d.* '42 (MIL) [P] Milwaukee, WI Provincial Offices - Discalced Carmelites.
Meldrum, James *o.c.d.* '42 (MOB) [F] Mobile, AL Little Sisters of the Poor, Home For the Aged, Inc.
Mele, Carmen *o.p.* '80 (NO) [P] New Orleans, LA Dominican Fathers & Brothers, Southern Dominican Province.
Mele, Joseph M. '73 (PIT) Unity, PA St. John the Baptist Church.
Mele, Rudolph '77 (NO) Retired.
Mele, Tom '77 (SPK) Medical Lake, WA St. Anne Church.
Mele, Vincent *o.f.m.* '40 (NY) [V] New York, NY Kateri Residence; [Z] New York, NY Franciscan Province of the Immaculate Conception.
Meledom, Joseph '68 (GAL) [76] Houston, TX St. Thomas More Church.
Melel, Andrew *o.i.c.* '51 (TYL) Gun Barrel City, TX St. Jude Church.
Melendez, Hector '80 (PAT) [8] Passaic, NJ Our Lady of Fatima Church.
Melendez, Michael S. '89 (BRK) [166] Queens, NY St. Elizabeth's Church.
Melepuram, John '78 (DET) Melvindale, MI St. Mary Magdalen Church.
Melevage, Msgr. F. J. '42 (GRY) Retired.
Melican, Msgr. Francis J. '50 (NY) Scarsdale, NY St. Pius X Church; Yonkers, NY Yonkers Fire Department.
Melican, Thomas J. '39 (NY) Port Jervis, NY Immaculate Conception Church.
Melillo, William J. '66 (NEW) [C] West Orange, NJ Seton Hall Preparatory School.
Melito, August A. '64 (DAL) [14] Dallas, TX St. Bernard of Clairvaux Church.
Melito, Ignatius M. *c.m.* '51 (STL) [P] Earth City, MO Congregation of the Mission Midwest Province (Vincentians); [P] St. Louis, MO Vincentian Residence.
Melito, Joseph '75 (ORG) Inactive Leave.
Melka, John *o.c.d.* '64 (OAK) [N] Berkeley, CA Carmelite (Discalced) House of Studies.
Melki, Pierre '65 (OLD) Laval, Eglise St. Ephrem Church.
Mell, Darrell J. (NEW) [N] Union City, NJ Congregation of the Passion (Passionists)-St. Michael's Residence.
Melle, James J. '72 (PH) West Chester, PA SS. Simon and Jude Church; [D] West Chester, PA Bishop Shanahan High School.
Melleck, Joseph L. '56 (BRK) Retired.
Melley, James '77 (MIA) Military Chaplains.
Mellitt, John *o.f.m.cap* '75 (NY) [98] New York, NY Our Lady of Sorrows Church.
Mello, Edward '46 (SAC) Nevada City, CA St. Canice Church; Walnut Grove, CA St. Anthony Church; Retired and in Senior Ministry.
Mello, Matthew '87 (ORL) Melbourne, FL Our Lady of Lourdes Church; [A] Melbourne, FL Central Catholic High School.
Melloh, John A. *s.m.* '73 (FTW) [B] Notre Dame, IN University of Notre Dame Du Lac.
Mellone, Michael J. '76 (WDC) Gaithersburg, MD St. Martin Church.
Mellone, Vincent P. '65 (BO) [2] Woburn, MA St. Barbara Church.
Mellott, Bob (PIT) [J] Pittsburgh, PA Mercy Providence Hospital.
Mellott, David '92 (STU) On Duty Outside the Diocese.
Mellott, David M. '92 (BAL) [A] Baltimore, MD St. Mary's Seminary and University.
Melner, John H. '91 (ARL) Vienna, VA St. Mark's Church.
Melnic, Msgr. James '78 (PHU) [4] Philadelphia, PA Annunciation of the B.V.M. Church; [6] Philadelphia, PA St. Josaphat's Church; [D] Philadelphia, PA Ascension Manor, Inc.
Melnick, John '86 (SCR) [M] Elmhurst, PA Priestly Fraternity of St. Peter (F.S.S.P.).
Melnick, William D. '75 (WIL) [2] Wilmington, DE St. Ann Church.
Melo, Ficel '96 (CHL) Clemmons, NC Holy Family Church.
Melo, Nicholas P. '83 (HRT) [2] Bristol, CT St. Anthony's Church.
Meloch, Msgr. Chester A. '43 (BUF) Retired.
Melody, William P. *c.s.c.* '59 (FTW) [L] Notre Dame, IN Holy Cross Mission House.
Melone, Mark E. '78 (NTN) Sacramento, CA St. George Church.
Melovasich, Frank '50 (DUL) [14] Duluth, MN St. Michael's Church.
Meloy, Bernard F. '54 (MAD) Retired.
Melton, John H. *o.s.a.* '55 (PH) [G] Malvern, PA Malvern Preparatory School for Boys.
Melton, Thomas K. '59 (TLS) Bixby, OK St. Clement's Church.
Meluskey, Andre J. '59 (HBG) McSherrystown, PA Annunciation of the Blessed Virgin Mary Church.
Melville, Raymond P. '85 (PRT) Machias, ME Holy Name of Jesus Church; [M] Machias, ME University of Maine at Machias.
Melvin, James M. '54 (CAM) Retired.
Melycher, Stephen D. '36 (BAL) Retired.
Melzer, Howard *s.c.j.* '58 (MIL) [P] Franklin, WI St. Francis Residence; [P] Hales Corners, WI Priests of the Sacred Heart.
Memenas, Vytas '57 (JOL) Frankfort, IL St. Anthony Church.
Memolo, Rocco C. '76 (MAN) Absent on Leave.
Men, Vincent Mao '84 (LA) [CC] Granada Hills, CA Chinese Catholic Bishops Conference Vocations Center.
Mena, Antonio '81 (ELP) Pecos, TX Santa Rosa Church.
Mena, Jose '61 (ORL) Retired.
Menapace, James L. '63 (MAR) Retired.
Menard, Clarence C. *o.m.i.* '58 (NO) [A] New Orleans, LA Notre Dame Seminary Graduate School of Theology.
Menard, Francis A. '54 (OG) Retired.
Menard, Gilbert B. '55 (OG) Ellenburg, NY St. Edmund Church.
Menard, J. Godden *c.m.* '55 (GLP) Tuba City, AZ St. Jude Church.
Menard, James R. *s.j.* '54 (PHX) [3] Phoenix, AZ Brophy College Preparatory.
Menard, Msgr. Raymond '39 (SAL) [1] Salina, KS Cathedral of the Sacred Heart.
Menard, Robert *o.f.m.* '72 (ARL) Triangle, VA St. Francis of Assisi Church.
Menard, Roland V. '64 (OG) Malone, NY St. John Bosco Church.
Menard, Wilfrid A. *c.s.c.* '55 (KAL) Three Oaks, MI St. Mary of the Assumption Church.
Menasco, Edward '90 (OKL) Woodward, OK St. Peter's Church.
Menchaca, Gerardo '95 (SJ) [15] San Jose, CA St. Maria Goretti Church.
Mende, Dennis W. '83 (BUF) [29] Buffalo, NY Holy Cross Church.
Mender, Lawrence *o.s.b.* (SEA) Longview, WA St. Rose de Viterbo Church.
Mendes, Joseph *m.s.f.s.* '63 (ATL) Norcross, GA Saint Patrick's Church.
Mendez, Angel '90 (MGZ) [9] Mayaquez, PR Church of the Resurrection.
Mendez, David Perez '87 (MGZ) Moca, PR Our Lady of Monserrate Church.
Mendez, Edwin '95 (ATL) Jonesboro, GA St. Philip Benizi Church.
Mendez, Enrique *s.d.b.* '52 (SJN) [28] San Juan, PR San Juan Bosco Church.
Mendez, Jose *o.a.r.* '83 (NEW) [N] West Orange, NJ Augustinian Recollects.
Mendez, Juan '73 (SFE) [5] Santa Fe, NM St. John Baptist Church.
Mendez, Oscar *s.j.* '64 (MIA) [33] Miami, FL St. Timothy Church.
Mendez, Rafael '93 (MGZ) San German, PR San German de Auxerre Church.
Mendez, Rafael '94 (PH) [156] Philadelphia, PA Visitation B.V.M. Church.
Mendis, Nimal '82 (NY) Beacon, NY St. John Evangelist Church; [Z] New York, NY Apostolic Society of the Crusade of the Holy Spirit.
Mendis, Nimal B. '82 (NY) Haverstraw, NY St. Peter Church.
Mendl, Michael *s.d.b.* '79 (NY) [Z] New Rochelle, NY Salesian Provincial House.
Mendonca, John '79 (BRK) [201] Queens, NY St. Michael Church.
Mendonca, Jose '53 (BGP) [7] Stamford, CT Sacred Heart Church.
Mendonca, Lucas *s.d.b.* '80 (OAK) [N] Berkeley, CA Salesian Community.
Mendonca, Msgr. Luiz G. '44 (FR) Retired.
Mendonsa, August F. '42 (PRO) Retired.
Mendoza, Andres '95 (LUB) Denver City, TX St. William Church.
Mendoza, Armando Guerrero *m.n.m.* '90 (SAT) Del Rio, TX Our Lady of Guadalupe Church; Del Rio, TX Our Lady of Guadalupe Church.
Mendoza, Eduardo '84 (SFR) [1] Menlo Park, CA St. Anthony Church.
Mendoza, Fernando *o.f.m.* '74 (ELP) [B] El Paso, TX St. Anthony's School of Theology.
Mendoza, Gerardo '88 (SB) Victorville, CA St. Joan of Arc Church.
Mendoza, Msgr. Miguel A. '70 (CGS) Barranquitas, PR Church of St. Anthony of Padua.
Mendoza, Pablo Mora *s.j.* '91 (CHI) [N] Chicago, IL Chicago Province of the Society of Jesus-Provincial Office.
Mendoza, Santos '54 (DAL) [15] Dallas, TX St. Cecilia Church.
Mendrick, Paul P. '47 (PBL) Retired.
Menegatto, Gaetano *c.s.j.* '42 (CLV) [P] Avon, OH Congregation of St. Joseph.
Menegay, David C. '88 (PIT) [C] Baden, PA Quigley Catholic High School.
Menegay, David C. '93 (PIT) [O] Baden, PA St. Joseph Convent.
Meneghello, Serafino '49 (GRY) Retired.
Menei, Francis T. '67 (PH) On Duty Outside the Archdiocese.
Menendez, Adolph *s.x.* '68 (PAT) [M] Wayne, NJ Xaverian Missionary Fathers.
Menendez, Jose L. '77 (MIA) [3] Miami, FL Corpus Christi Church.
Meneses, Miguel '61 (ELP) [19] El Paso, TX Our Lady of the Valley Church.
Menezes, Glenn A. *s.j.* '90 (MIL) [P] Milwaukee, WI Jesuit Community at Marquette University.
Menezes, Mark '59 (JOL) Monee, IL St. Boniface Church.
Meng, David P. '89 (ARL) Ashburn, VA St. Theresa Church.
Meng, Robert A. '45 (ROC) Retired.
Menge, James Paul '62 (SPR) [8] Chicopee, MA St. Patrick's Church.
Menge, Msgr. Kenneth M. '54 (BUF) [3] Kenmore, NY St. John the Baptist Church.
Mengel, Mark *s.s.c.* (CHI) [N] Chicago, IL Columban Fathers Theologate.
Menghini, Peter D. '80 (SCR) [7] Wilkes-Barre, PA Holy Rosary Church.
Menihane, Daniel J. *o.s.a.* '57 (ALB) Hoosick Falls, NY Immaculate Conception Church; Pittstown, NY St. George Church.
Meninger, William *o.c.s.o.* '58 (DEN) [M] Snowmass, CO St. Benedict's Monastery.
Menke, George R. *s.j.* '75 (CHI) [D] Chicago, IL St. Ignatius College Prep; [D] Chicago, IL St. Ignatius Jesuit Community.
Menke, Paul F. '66 (LA) [60] Los Angeles, CA St. Eugene Church.
Menke, Msgr. S. G. '38 (DAV) Retired.
Menke, Msgr. Sebastian J. '38 (DAV) [M] Davenport, IA St. Vincent Center.
Menker, Joseph *o.m.i.* '53 (STP) [28] St. Paul, MN St. Mary Church; St. Paul, MN St. Paul-Ramsey Hospital; St. Paul, MN Gillette Children's Hospital.
Menna, F. Dominic '58 (BO) [1] Revere, MA St. Anthony of Padua Church.
Mennella, Luke *o.ss.t.* '56 (BAL) [M] Baltimore, MD Holy Trinity Monastery.
Menner, John H. *c.s.b.* '58 (DET) [E] Redford, MI Catholic Central High School.
Menner, Michael '93 (PEO) [K] Lacon, IL St. Joseph's Nursing Home.
Menner, Robert J. '68 (STL) On Duty Outside the Archdiocese.
Mennis, James F. '62 (SAC) Military Chaplains.
Menniti, Daniel J. '53 (HBG) Carlisle, PA St. Patrick Church.
Mens, Theodore J. '67 (GRY) Griffith, IN St. Mary Church.
Mensah, Gabriel '83 (VIC) On Duty Outside the Diocese.
Menster, William J. '38 (DUB) Retired.
Mentel, Joseph C. '40 (FAR) Retired.
Mentrup, Charles '88 (CIN) [8] Cincinnati, OH St. Ann Church; [E] Cincinnati, OH McAuley High School.
Menty, Ronald A. '69 (ALB) Scotia, NY St. Joseph Church.
Meny, Hilary G. '40 (IND) Retired.

Menz, Anthony (SB) Military Chaplains.
Menz, Anthony *o.c.s.o.* '68 (SPC) [E] Ava, MO Assumption Abbey (Trappist).
Menzel, William G. '67 (LC) [3] Wisconsin Rapids, WI St. Vincent de Paul Church.
Menzies, Scott '85 (VEN) Graduate Studies.
Meograssi, Romuald *o.f.m.conv.* (BAL) [B] Ellicott City, MD Friary of St. Joseph Cupertino; [M] Ellicott City, MD St. Joseph Cupertino Friary, Friars Minor Conventual of St. Francis of Assisi.
Mercado, Edwin '86 (ARE) Special Assignment.
Mercado, Edwin '87 (ARE) [6] Arecibo, PR Our Lady of Hope Church.
Mercado, Miguel '83 (ARE) Special Assignment; [A] Arecibo, PR Seminario de Jesus Maestro.
Mercer, David '87 (SJ) [O] San Jose, CA The Newman Center/Catholic Campus Ministry.
Mercer, John E. '70 (NY) [220] Staten Island, NY Our Lady of Pity Church.
Mercer, Robert *s.a.* '82 (NY) [Z] Garrison, NY Generalate of the Franciscan Friars of the Atonement-St. James Friary.
Mercer, Timmothy '90 (CC) On Duty Outside the Diocese.
Merchant, David M. *o.s.f.s.* '73 (PH) [D] Philadelphia, PA Father Judge High School for Boys; [Z] Philadelphia, PA Father Judge Faculty House.
Mercieca, Anthony '62 (MIA) Miami Springs, FL Blessed Trinity Church.
Mercier, J. Patrick '93 (IND) [17] Indianapolis, IN St. Barnabas Church.
Mercier, Msgr. Joseph (BLX) Retired.
Mercier, Ronald A. *s.j.* '87 (BO) [W] Boston, MA The Society of Jesus of New England-Provincial Offices.
Mercure, Gary '74 (ALB) Clinton Heights, NY St. Mary Church; [S] Glens Falls, NY Adirondack Community College.
Mercurio, Gregory J. *o.f.m.* '80 (BO) [1] Lynn, MA Holy Family Church; Winthrop, MA St. John the Evangelist Church.
Mercurio, Roger *c.p.* '44 (CHI) [N] Chicago, IL Immaculate Conception Monastery.
Mercy, Richard R. *s.j.* '71 (SPK) [E] Spokane, WA Gonzaga Preparatory School; [O] Spokane, WA Kateri Northwest Ministry Institute.
Merdian, Mark J. '93 (PEO) [4] Champaign, IL St. Matthew Church.
Merdinger, Philip E. '64 (NEW) On Duty Outside the Archdiocese.
Meredith, John '80 (OWN) [4] Owensboro, KY Our Lady of Lourdes Church.
Meredith, Philip S. '74 (DEN) [1] Fort Collins, CO St. Joseph Church.
Meredith, Richard '78 (OWN) Bowling Green, KY St. Joseph's Church.
Merfeld, Vincent (LA) Retired.
Merfeld, Vincent C. '44 (DUB) Retired.
Mergenhagen, John J. '54 (BUF) [Q] Stella Niagara, NY Stella Niagara Center of Renewal.
Mericantante, John J. '75 (PMB) Pahokee, FL St. Mary Church.
Meridier, Wilfred F. '69 (NO) [36] New Orleans, LA St. Henry Church; Jefferson, LA Ochsner Foundation Hospital.
Merino, Msgr. Baudilio '48 (SJN) [49] San Juan, PR Nuestra Senora de la Providencia Church.
Merino, Santiago '46 (LA) Retired.
Merino, Sean Paris '94 (BIR) [4] Huntsville, AL Holy Spirit Church.
Merino, Zenon R. '32 (BR) Retired.
Merity, John A. '49 (NEW) Glen Rock, NJ St. Catharine Church; Retired.
Meriwether, Stephen A. '83 (SFR) [2] South San Francisco, CA Mater Dolorosa Church; Special Assignment.
Merkatoris, Ralph C. '58 (GB) Pine Grove, WI Holy Trinity Church.
Merkel, Francis J. '30 (SCR) Retired.
Merkel, James '73 (SP) Crystal River, FL St. Benedict Church.
Merkel, Mark K. '92 (OM) O'Neill, NE St. Patrick Church.
Merkelis, John *o.s.a.* '85 (JOL) [C] New Lenox, IL Providence Catholic High School.
Merkelis, John D. *o.s.a.* '85 (JOL) [J] New Lenox, IL Augustinian Friary.
Merkle, Charles W., III '88 (ARL) [1] Alexandria, VA Blessed Sacrament Church.
Merkovsky, Paul W. '90 (PIT) Bellevue, PA Assumption of the Blessed Virgin Mary on the Beautiful River Church.
Merkt, Joseph T. '66 (L) [26] Louisville, KY St. Francis of Assisi Church; [K] Louisville, KY Marian Home.
Merkt, Michael F. '81 (MIL) [6] West Allis, WI Mary, Queen of Heaven Church.
Merlandk, J. Gordon *s.j.* '64 (P) [L] Portland, OR Jesuit Provincial Office (Oregon Prov.).
Merlino, James T. *o.f.m.* '87 (PIT) [60] Pittsburgh, PA St. Pamphilus Church.
Merlucci, Michael A. '75 (NEW) [17] Jersey City, NJ Mt. Carmel Church.
Merman, Msgr. Raymond F. '60 (ALN) Hellertown, PA St. Theresa of the Child Jesus Church.
Merold, James E. '71 (CHI) North Chicago, IL Queen of Peace Church.
Merolla, George R. '87 (BRK) Absent on Leave.
Meronek, Andrew '43 (GRY) [K] Cedar Lake, IN Our Lady of Lourdes Friary.
Merrell, Arthur R. '70 (PIT) [22] Pittsburgh, PA St. Lawrence O'Toole Church; Allegheny County, PA Allegheny County Jail; Allegheny County, PA Shuman Center.
Merrifield, Donald P. *s.j.* '65 (LA) [C] Los Angeles, CA Loyola Marymount University; [C] Los Angeles, CA Loyola Marymount University.
Merrigan, Daniel M. *s.j.* '85 (BO) [W] Boston, MA The Society of Jesus of New England-Provincial Offices.
Merrill, Paul *c.s.s.* '61 (BO) [Z] Waltham, MA Stigmatine Fathers and Brothers.
Merrill, Thomas J. *o.f.m. conv.* '79 (LSC) Carlsbad, NM San Jose Church.
Merris, Christopher '82 (SD) [14] San Diego, CA Our Lady of Refuge Church; Unassigned.
Merry, Christopher C. '92 (E) Bradford, PA St. Bernard Church; [P] Erie, PA Newman Centers and Campus Ministry.
Merry, Paul F. '71 (BGP) [6] Bridgeport, CT Blessed Sacrament Church.
Mersberger, Jerome '42 (MAD) Retired.
Mersinger, Arthur '42 (JC) Retired.
Mersinger, Arthur J. '42 (STL) Retired.
Mersinger, Norbert A. '55 (STL) Bel-Ridge, MO St. Thomas More Church.
Merson, Thomas S. '83 (SFR) [4] San Francisco, CA St. Anne Church; Special Assignment.
Mertens, Msgr. Arthur '49 (SPK) Retired.
Mertens, Michael G. '45 (LC) Retired; [I] La Crosse, WI Holy Cross (Seminary) Diocesan Center.
Mertensotto, Leon J. *c.s.c.* '56 (FTW) [B] Notre Dame, IN University of Notre Dame Du Lac; [J] Notre Dame, IN Holy Cross Community, Corby Hall, University of Notre Dame.
Mertes, Mark '87 (KCK) Hartford, KS St. Mary's Church; Olpe, KS St. Joseph's Church.
Mertes, Robert *s.v.d.* '78 (WDC) [L] Hyattsville, MD Sacred Heart Home Inc.; [M] Washington, DC Divine Word College.
Mertes, William H. '59 (COV) Retired.
Merth, John P. '32 (CR) Retired.
Merth, Robert J. '44 (NU) Retired.
Mertz, Frederick A. '49 (STP) Retired.
Mertz, William H. '47 (STP) Retired.
Merwald, Melvin '71 (OM) [27] Omaha, NE St. Margaret Mary Church.
Merz, Albert *o.f.m.* '66 (CHI) [N] Countryside, IL St. Gratian Friary, Franciscan Friars.
Merz, Eugene F. *s.j.* '61 (MIL) [P] Milwaukee, WI Jesuit Community at Marquette University.
Merz, Fabiano *o.f.m.* (SFD) [K] Sherman, IL Our Lady of Angels Friary.
Merzena, Carl J. '41 (NEW) Retired; [N] Rutherford, NJ St. John Vianney Residence for Priests.
Merzweiler, David W. '77 (Y) Lake Milton, OH St. Catherine Church; North Jackson, OH St. James Parish Family Church.
Mesa, Jose A. *s.j.* '92 (BO) [W] Boston, MA Loyola House.
Mesa, Manuel *o.m.i.* '72 (SD) Westmorland, CA St. Joseph Church.
Mesa, Mario *o.f.m.cap.* '64 (SJN) [29] San Juan, PR San Juan de La Cruz Church.
Mescall, Msgr. John '52 (NY) [4] New Rochelle, NY Holy Family Church.
Mescall, John R. *c.p.* '59 (BRK) [U] Jamaica, NY Immaculate Conception Monastery.
Mescher, Michael '83 (DUB) [3] Waterloo, IA Sacred Heart Church.
Mesi, Vincent *o.f.m.* '72 (LA) [4] Santa Barbara, CA St. Barbara Church; [R] Santa Barbara, CA Franciscan Friary, Order of Friars Minor (Old Mission).
Mesiona, Erwin C. (SAC) [11] Sacramento, CA St. Charles Borromeo Church.
Meskell, David B. '55 (BO) Absent on Sick Leave.
Meskenas, Vincent A. '49 (BEL) Retired.
Meskenas, Vincent A. '49 (SAC) Yuba City, CA St. Isidore Church.
Meskill, M. Francis '58 (LA) [47] Los Angeles, CA St. Basil's Church.
Meskill, Patrick A. '53 (LA) Retired.
Meskill, Thomas A. '60 (LA) Sick Leave.
Mesko, Louis G. *sch.p.* '36 (PH) [G] Devon, PA Devon Preparatory School; [Z] Devon, PA Piarist Fathers (Order of the Pious Schools).
Mesley, Jerry T. '73 (GLP) Cuba, NM Immaculate Conception Church.
Mesmer, William A. '68 (SY) Oneida, NY St. Patrick Church.
Messaro, Michael A. *m.ss.cc.* '68 (HBG) Blue Ridge Summit, PA St. Rita Church; Fairfield, PA Immaculate Conception of the Blessed Virgin Mary Church.
Messaros, Msgr. Michael F. '36 (ALN) Retired.
Messenger, William '77 (LA) [32] Los Angeles, CA Our Saviour Catholic Center Church; [BB] Los Angeles, CA Archdiocesan Office for Campus Ministry.
Messer, Joseph V. '61 (BAL) Glen Burnie, MD Church of the Good Shepherd; Retired.
Messer, Paul A. *s.j.* '67 (BO) [W] Chestnut Hill, MA The Jesuit Community at Boston College.
Messer, Terry *c.f.r.* '94 (NY) [Z] New York, NY St. Crispin Friary.
Messerich, Valerius U. *o.f.m.* '46 (STP) Hampton, MN St. Mathias Church.
Messick, Severin *o.s.b.* '82 (IND) Cannelton, IN St. Michael Church; Tell City, IN St. Paul Church; Troy, IN St. Pius Church; [J] St. Meinrad, IN St. Meinrad Archabbey.
Messier, Bernard H. '56 (BUR) Barre, VT St. Monica Church.
Messier, Raymond P. '68 (WOR) Athol, MA St. Francis Church; Petersham, MA St. Peter Church.
Messina, Angelo '68 (ALX) Leesville, LA St. Michael Church.
Messina, John A. '96 (BAL) Bradshaw, MD St. Stephen Church.
Messina, Joseph M. '72 (CAM) [N] Blackwood, NJ St. Pius X Spiritual Life Center.
Messina, Richard C. '65 (BO) Winchester, MA St. Mary Church.
Messina, Samuel '65 (JKS) Belzoni, MS All Saints Church.
Messina, Victor G. '74 (BR) [16] Baton Rouge, LA Our Lady of Mercy Church.
Messing, Arnold A. '56 (GAY) Absent on Leave.
Messing, Francis '59 (MOB) Grove Hill, AL Sacred Heart Church.
Messman, Gerald C. '31 (LIN) Retired.
Messner, Thomas *o.f.m.* (MRY) [G] San Miguel, CA Franciscan Friars, O.F.M.; [G] San Miguel, CA Novitiate House for the Franciscan Friars, O.F.M.
Messner, Thomas *o.f.m.* '67 (MRY) [I] San Miguel, CA San Miguel Retreat House.
Mestas, Leonard '81 (SB) Loma Linda, CA Loma Linda Community Hospital; Loma Linda, CA Loma Linda University Medical Center.
Mestas, Leonard J. '81 (BWN) On Assignment Outside the Diocese.
Mestriparampil, Thomas D. '89 (NY) [1] Port Chester, NY Our Lady of Mercy Church.
Mesure, Gerard C. '84 (PH) Graduate Studies.
Meszaros, James J. '69 (BRK) [241] Queens, NY St. Stanislaus Bishop and Martyr Church.
Metcalf, Andrew '86 (SR) Sonoma, CA St. Francis Solano Church.
Metcko, Leo E. '43 (WCH) Retired.
Meter, Msgr. Charles N. '36 (CHI) Wilmette, IL St. Joseph Church; Retired.
Methe, Msgr. Normand A. '58 (BGP) Stamford Co., CT Holy Spirit Church.
Method, Fredrick '66 (DUL) Hibbing, MN St. Leo's Church.
Metrejean, Msgr. Paul '63 (LAF) Mermentau, LA St. John the Evangelist Church.
Metro, LeRoy '63 (SAL) [2] Salina, KS St. Elizabeth Ann Seton Church.
Metro, Michael A. '96 (ALN) [1] Bethlehem, PA St. Anne Church.
Metsy, Msgr. Norman G. '47 (PRO) Retired.
Metts, Ralph E. *s.j.* '73 (WDC) [M] Washington, DC The Jesuit Community at Georgetown University; [V] Washington, DC Jesuit Secondary Education Association.
Metz, Earl O. '58 (CIN) Georgetown, OH St. George Church; Mount Orab, OH St. Michael Church.
Metz, Kenneth J. '65 (MIL) [5] Kenosha, WI St. Mark's Church.
Metzbower, Francis X. *s.j.* '63 (BAL) [M] Baltimore, MD Jesuit Fathers and Brothers Maryland Provincial Curia.
Metzdorf, William C. '73 (WDC) Potomac, MD Our Lady of Mercy Church.
Metzger, Alvin P. *o.s.a.* '54 (MIL) [P] Racine, WI Augustinian Novitiate.
Metzger, Andrew *o.s.b.* '56 (SP) [O] St. Leo, FL St. Leo Abbey.
Metzger, Clement *s.j.* '65 (TOL) [6] Toledo, OH Gesu Church.
Metzger, Dennis M. '74 (TOL) [35] Toledo, OH St. Patrick of Heatherdowns Church.
Metzger, Edward C. *o.f.m.* '59 (BUF) [3] Kenmore, NY St. John the Baptist Church.
Metzger, Edward C. *o.f.m.* '59 (NY) [Z] New York, NY Franciscan Friars, Order of Friars Manor.
Metzger, Edwin B. '55 (ROC) On Duty Outside the Diocese.
Metzger, John L. '67 (COL) Corning, OH St. Bernard Church.
Metzger, Joseph H., III '91 (RIC) Farmville, VA St. Theresa Church.
Metzger, Msgr. Paul E. '43 (STU) Retired.
Metzger, Richard L. '67 (COL) Johnstown, OH Church of the Ascension.
Metzger, Msgr. Robert E. '60 (COL) Jackson, OH Holy Trinity Church.

Metzger, Msgr. Samuel S. '59 (TYL) Athens, TX St. Edward Church.
Metzger, Stephen A. '70 (COL) Utica, OH Church of the Nativity.
Metzger, Thomas H. '82 (LFT) Lebanon, IN St. Joseph Church.
Metzger, William A. '78 (COL) [3] Columbus, OH St. Agnes Church.
Metzger, William J. '62 (COL) Waverly, OH St. Mary, Queen of the Missions Church.
Metzger, William J. *o.s.f.s.* '71 (ARL) [D] Alexandria, VA Bishop Ireton High School; [J] Alexandria, VA Oblates of St. Francis de Sales Residence.
Metzinger, John '82 (OKL) Norman, OK Church of St. Mark the Evangelist.
Metzinger, John R. (OKL) Special Assignment.
Metzler, Warren W. '64 (PIT) Wilkinsburg, PA St. James Church; Allegheny County, PA Forbes Health Metropolitan Health Center.
Metzler, William R. '72 (HRT) Kent, CT Sacred Heart Church.
Meulemans, Carl *m.m.* '60 (GB) [1] Manitowoc, WI St. Boniface Church.
Meulemans, Dennis T. '61 (SUP) Medford, WI Our Lady of the Holy Rosary Church.
Meulemans, Edward G. '60 (SUP) [1] Superior, WI Cathedral of Christ the King.
Meulemans, Thomas O. *o.praem.* '59 (GB) [A] De Pere, WI St. Norbert Abbey; [I] De Pere, WI St. Norbert Abbey; [I] De Pere, WI St. Joseph Priory.
Meulemans, Thomas O. *o.praem.* '59 (PH) [Z] Paoli, PA Daylesford Abbey.
Meuree, James *c.i.c.m.* '47 (SAT) [M] San Antonio, TX Missionhurst Community Residence.
Meurer, David C. '51 (SAT) Harper, TX St. Anthony's Church.
Meuret, Donald L., Jr. '84 (WH) War, WV Christ the King Church; Welch, WV St. Peter Church.
Mevissen, Richard *c.ss.r.* '66 (DET) [34] Detroit, MI Holy Redeemer Church.
Meyer, Albert *o.s.b.* '56 (MRY) [G] San Luis Obispo, CA Monastery of the Risen Christ.
Meyer, Alfred *o.s.b.* '35 (KC) [J] Conception, MO Conception Abbey.
Meyer, Arthur D. '61 (PEO) Canton, IL St. Mary's Church.
Meyer, Ben *o.p.* '54 (GAL) [J] Houston, TX St. Joseph Hospital.
Meyer, Benedict *o.s.b.* '54 (IND) [J] St. Meinrad, IN St. Meinrad Archabbey.
Meyer, Benedict *o.s.b.* '54 (LR) Brinkley, AR St. John the Baptist Church.
Meyer, Bernard *s.m.* '51 (SAT) [8] San Antonio, TX Holy Rosary Church; [M] San Antonio, TX Marianist Residence.
Meyer, Bernard A. '59 (SFD) On Duty Outside the Diocese.
Meyer, Charles *c.pp.s.* '31 (CIN) [B] Carthagena, OH St. Charles.
Meyer, Charles R. '45 (CHI) Retired; [A] Mundelein, IL University of St. Mary of the Lake-Mundelein Seminary.
Meyer, Clayton '66 (SEA) [19] Seattle, WA St. Peter Church; Special Assignment.
Meyer, Cosmas A. *s.v.d.* '47 (SB) [A] Riverside, CA Divine Word Seminary.
Meyer, Daniel J. '82 (CIN) Centerville, OH Incarnation Church; [V] Centerville, OH Catholic Alumni Club (Dayton Chapter).
Meyer, Dennis J. *m.s.* '70 (STL) [P] St. Louis, MO La Salette Missionaries; [P] St. Louis, MO La Salette Missionaries.
Meyer, Earl R. *o.f.m.cap.* '60 (STL) Arnold, MO Immaculate Conception Church; [P] Arnold, MO Immaculate Conception Friary.
Meyer, Emmett F. '64 (OM) [22] Omaha, NE St. Joan of Arc Church.
Meyer, Eric *c.p.* '66 (CHI) [91] Chicago, IL Immaculate Conception Church; [N] Chicago, IL Immaculate Conception Monastery.
Meyer, Fred A. '65 (STL) [6] St. Charles, MO St. Robert Bellarmine Church.
Meyer, Frederick C. '56 (STP) St. Henry, MN Church of St. Henry.
Meyer, George R. '46 (SFR) [1] San Mateo, CA St. Bartholomew Church; Retired.
Meyer, Gerald J. '96 (PEO) [1] Ottawa, IL St. Columba Church.
Meyer, Msgr. Gilbert '42 (FRS) Retired.
Meyer, Harold K. *o.c.s.o.* '62 (SAC) [A] Vina, CA Abbey of New Clairvaux, Trappist Seminary; [H] Vina, CA Abbey of New Clairvaux, Trappist.
Meyer, Harry J. '64 (CIN) Mason, OH St. Susanna Church.
Meyer, Henry H. '35 (SC) Retired.
Meyer, James A. '94 (FAR) Wyndmere, ND St. John the Baptist Church.
Meyer, James L. '60 (DET) Detroit, MI Hutzel Hospital.
Meyer, Jerome P. '85 (MIL) [14] Milwaukee, WI Congregation of the Blessed Trinity Church.
Meyer, John A. '82 (IND) Madison, IN Prince of Peace Church; Vevay, IN Most Sorrowful Mother of God Church; [N] Madison, IN Hanover College Newman Center.
Meyer, John D. (RVC) Absent on Leave.
Meyer, John R. '89 (CHI) [W] Chicago, IL Opus Dei.
Meyer, Msgr. Joseph J. '45 (PAT) Retired.
Meyer, Leo A. '65 (NO) [37] New Orleans, LA St. James Major Church.
Meyer, Msgr. Louis F. '44 (STL) Retired; [W] St. Louis, MO Missionaries of the Kingship of Christ.
Meyer, Michael W. '93 (LA) [69] Los Angeles, CA St. Jerome Church.
Meyer, Nicholas W. *o.f.m.* '52 (STP) [10] St. Paul, MN Sacred Heart Church.
Meyer, Msgr. Omer F. '49 (EVN) [11] Evansville, IN Sacred Heart Church; Special Assignment.
Meyer, Pacian *o.f.m.* '46 (GLP) Tohatchi, NM St. Mary Church.
Meyer, Paul Wayne '49 (COL) Retired.
Meyer, Robert G. '74 (WIN) [5] Winona, MN St. Stanislaus Church.
Meyer, Robert J. '64 (PIT) [43] Pittsburgh, PA St. Basil Church.
Meyer, Robert L. '57 (SFD) Charleston, IL St. Charles Borromeo Church; [M] Charleston, IL Eastern Illinois University Newman Center.
Meyer, Robert S. '88 (NEW) [B] South Orange, NJ Seton Hall University; [B] South Orange, NJ Seton Hall University.
Meyer, Ronald J. *o.m.i.* '71 (CR) Waubun, MN St. Ann Church.
Meyer, Sebastian *o.carm.* '62 (GAL) [14] Houston, TX St. Bernadette Soubirous Church.
Meyer, Stephen *c.ss.r.* '76 (DEN) [M] Denver, CO The Redemptorists/Denver Province.
Meyer, Stephen *c.ss.r.* '76 (OAK) [N] Oakland, CA Redemptorists.
Meyer, Stephen L. '79 (DUB) Dougherty, IA St. Patrick's Church; Rockwell, IA Sacred Heart Church.
Meyer, Steven '90 (FAR) Hope, ND St. Agatha's Church.
Meyer, Theo (DET) Detroit, MI Bi-County Osteopathic.
Meyer, Thomas C. '55 (SCL) Swanville, MN St. John the Baptist Church.
Meyer, Thomas E. '70 (CIN) [12] Dayton, OH Holy Angels Church.
Meyer, Thomas G. *o.m.i.* '70 (SFD) [1] Alton, IL SS. Peter and Paul Church.
Meyer, Vernon J. '79 (PHX) [I] Phoenix, AZ Kino Institute.
Meyer, Wayne '49 (COL) Mount Vernon, OH Mount Vernon State Institute.
Meyer, William C. *c.s.v.* '56 (CHI) [N] Arlington Heights, IL Viatorian Province Center-Clerics of St. Viator.
Meyer, William O. '49 (DAV) Mechanicsville, IA St. Mary's Church.
Meyers, Frederick *ss.cc.* '71 (FR) Fairhaven, MA St. Joseph's Church.
Meyers, James E. *s.s.* '80 (SFR) [27] San Francisco, CA St. John the Evangelist Church.
Meyers, James P. '70 (WDC) Leonardtown, MD St. Aloysius Church.
Meyers, John F. '56 (DAL) [21] Dallas, TX St. Monica Church.
Meyers, John F. '83 (PH) Lansdowne, PA St. Philomena Church.
Meyers, Joseph L. *c.s.b.* '43 (GAL) [Q] Houston, TX Residence of the Basilian Fathers of the University of St. Thomas.
Meyers, Louis E. *s.j.* '62 (NO) New Orleans, LA Delgado Community College, School of Nursing; New Orleans, LA Louisiana State University Medical Center.
Meyers, Msgr. Michael W. '77 (LA) [13] Los Angeles, CA Holy Spirit Church.
Meyers, Robert V. '87 (MET) Kendall Park, NJ St. Augustine of Canterbury Church.
Meyett, Irving C. '53 (SUP) Retired.
Meyr, Herbert J. '60 (CHI) Maywood, IL St. James Church.
Meysenburg, James J. '89 (LIN) Rulo, NE Immaculate Conception Church; [C] Falls City, NE Sacred Heart High School/Elementary Schools.
Meystrik, Gregory C. '90 (JC) Baring, MO St. Aloysius Church; Edina, MO St. Joseph Church.
Meza, Arturo '88 (AMA) On Duty Outside the Diocese.
Meza, Arturo '88 (SFE) [A] Santa Fe, NM Immaculate Heart of Mary Seminary.
Meznar, Joseph A. '58 (DEN) [13] Denver, CO Holy Rosary Church.
Meznar, Robert P. '60 (DEN) [27] Denver, CO St. Catherine of Siena Church.
Mezquida, Ramon '58 (PCE) On Duty Outside the Diocese.
Mezydlo, James A. '77 (CHI) [158] Chicago, IL Our Lady of the Snows Church.
Mezydlo, Leonard T. '50 (CHI) [3] Des Plaines, IL St. Stephen Protomartyr Church; Retired.
Mezyk, Walter *o.f.m.conv.* '95 (BUF) [O] Athol Springs, NY Father Justin Rosary Hour Radio Apostolate.
Mezzanote, Joseph *o.f.m.cap.* '39 (NEW) [5] Hoboken, NJ St. Ann's Church.
Mezzomo, Charles '71 (STF) Hempstead, NY St. Vladimir Church.
Mghanga, Anthony (PIT) [31] Pittsburgh, PA St. Louise de Marillac Church.
Miah, Gabriel '77 (RVC) Roslyn, NY St. Francis Hospital.
Miani, Titian A. '55 (STO) [7] Stockton, CA St. Luke Church; Retired.
Mibach, Everett J. *s.j.* '51 (SFR) [N] San Francisco, CA Jesuit Community at University of San Francisco.
Micali, Cuthbert *s.a.* '48 (NY) [Z] Garrison, NY Franciscan Friars of the Atonement.
Micarelli, Edmond C. '59 (PRO) Retired.
Micca, Louis *s.a.c.* '66 (BAL) [49] Baltimore, MD St. Jude Shrine Church.
Micek, Joseph S. '42 (OM) Retired.
Micek, Sylvester *o.f.m.* '51 (GAY) Burt Lake, MI Assumption of St. Mary Church; Pellston, MI St. Clement Church.
Miceli, James A. '75 (ATL) Rome, GA St. Mary's Church; [L] Atlanta, GA Campus Ministry.
Miceli, John P. '94 (CLV) [7] Akron, OH St. Hilary Church.
Miceli, Matthew M. *c.s.c.* '52 (FTW) [B] Notre Dame, IN University of Notre Dame Du Lac; [J] Notre Dame, IN Holy Cross Community, Corby Hall, University of Notre Dame.
Miceli, Paul W. '72 (BO) [14] Cambridge, MA Sacred Heart of Jesus Church; On Special or Other Diocesan Assignment.
Miceli, Vincent F. '91 (BRK) [203] Queens, NY Most Precious Blood Church.
Mich, Kenneth A. '70 (MIL) West Bend, WI St. Frances Cabrini Church.
Mich, Mario *s.d.b.* '48 (SFR) [N] San Francisco, CA Salesian Provincial Residence.
Michael, Msgr. Chester P. '42 (RIC) Retired.
Michael, David C. '86 (BO) Swampscott, MA St. John the Evangelist Church.
Michael, David F. '96 (SAM) [A] Washington, DC Our Lady of Lebanon Maronite Seminary.
Michael, Msgr. Kenneth A. '65 (OLL) Detroit, MI St. Maron/St. Sharbel Church.
Michael, Lawrence P. '75 (SAM) Torrington, CT St. Maron Church.
Michael, Matthew '73 (PH) Upper Darby, PA St. Alice Church.
Michael, Susainathan '88 (SFS) Elkton, SD Our Lady of Good Counsel Church.
Michaelraj, Anthony S. '75 (STA) [4] Gainesville, FL St. Augustine Church; [L] Gainesville, FL University of Florida-St. Augustine Parish and Student Center.
Michaels, Msgr. Anthony B. (OM) Retired.
Michaels, Dana '82 (OAK) Pittsburg, CA St. Peter Martyr of Verona Church.
Michaels, Emmett T. '38 (ALT) Retired.
Michaels, John L. '39 (PIT) Retired; [N] Pittsburgh, PA St. John Vianney Manor.
Michaels, Patrick T. '82 (SFR) [4] Menlo Park, CA St. Raymond Church.
Michalak, Jaromir '91 (CAM) North Cape May, NJ St. John of God Church.
Michalak, John *o.s.p.p.e.* '81 (PH) [Z] Doylestown, PA Pauline Fathers Monastery, Shrine of Our Lady of Czestochowa.
Michalak, John S. '51 (OM) [15] Omaha, NE St. Francis Assisi Church.
Michalek, George C. '78 (LAN) [1] Lansing, MI St. Mary Cathedral.
Michalek, Henry J. '43 (CHI) [214] Chicago, IL St. William Church; Retired.
Michalek, Stanislaw *s.ch.* '88 (DAL) [23] Dallas, TX St. Peter Church.
Michalenko, Alexei '68 (VNN) On Special Assignment.
Michalenko, Seraphim *m.i.c.* '56 (SPR) [I] Stockbridge, MA Congregation of Marians; [I] Stockbridge, MA Congregation of Marians; [I] Stockbridge, MA Congregation of Marians.
Michalicka, John J. '59 (OKL) Ponca City, OK Church of St. Mary; [H] Ponca City, OK St. Mary's Housing Foundation.
Michalik, Bernard *o.f.m.conv.* '47 (RNO) Virginia City, NV St. Mary in the Mountains Church.
Michalik, Gary M. '80 (DET) Hamtramck, MI Our Lady Queen of Apostles Church.
Michalik, Walter G. *c.s.c.* '56 (SP) Tarpon Springs, FL St. Ignatius Church.
Michalisin, Geoffrey '92 (PBR) North Huntingdon, PA St. Stephen's Church.
Michalka, Msgr. Arthur '51 (AUS) Jarrell, TX Holy Trinity Church.
Michalowski, John W. *s.j.* '81 (PRT) [C] Portland, ME Cheverus High School; [I] Portland, ME St. Ignatius Residence.
Michalski, James L. *s.j.* '72 (OM) [F] Omaha, NE The Jesuit Middle School of Omaha; [K] Omaha, NE Jesuit Community At Creighton University.
Michalski, Melvin E. '70 (MIL) [A] Milwaukee, WI

Saint Francis Seminary.
Michalski, Michael F. '76 (MIL) [39] Milwaukee, WI Holy Trinity-Our Lady of Guadalupe Church.
Michalski, Thaddeus C. '43 (CLV) Retired; [J] Cleveland, OH Marymount Hospital, Inc.
Michand, Leo James '77 (PRT) Ellsworth, ME St. Joseph's Church.
Michatek, William C. '66 (ROC) Spencerport, NY St. John the Evangelist Church.
Michel, Delix '81 (SFD) East Alton, IL St. Kevin Church.
Michel, Delix '88 (SFD) Venice, IL St. Mark Church.
Michel, Engelbert G. '66 (PH) Secane, PA Our Lady of Fatima Church; [K] Philadelphia, PA St. Vincent's Orphanage Tacony; [EE] Philadelphia, PA Catholic Kolping Society.
Michel, Eugene *o.f.m.* '64 (SAT) [46] San Antonio, TX St. Joseph Church.
Michel, Richard *o.s.b.* '86 (GBG) [A] Latrobe, PA St. Vincent Seminary.
Michel, Richard B. *o.s.b.* '86 (GBG) [H] Latrobe, PA Saint Vincent Archabbey.
Michele, Robert *c.s.p.* '55 (AUS) [11] Austin, TX St. Austin's Church; Austin, TX St. David's Hospital.
Michele, Robert P. *c.s.p.* '55 (NY) [Z] Scarsdale, NY Paulist Fathers Generalate.
Michelini, Michael S. '71 (CHI) [8] Chicago, IL St. Aloysius Church.
Michell, George J. '64 (RVC) Southold, NY St. Patrick's Church.
Michell, Timothy *o.c.s.o.* '65 (P) [L] Lafayette, OR The Cistercian (Trappist) Abbey of Our Lady of Guadalupe.
Michels, Aloysius *o.s.b.* '39 (SCL) [I] Collegeville, MN St. John's Abbey, of the Order of St. Benedict.
Michels, Andrew J. '85 (NU) Nassau, MN St. James Church; Ortonville, MN St. John Church; Rosen, MN St. Joseph Church.
Michelson, Chris '80 (KNX) [2] Knoxville, TN All Saints Catholic Church.
Michet, John M. '78 (CHI) [66] Chicago, IL St. Gabriel Church.
Michiels, Kenneth J. '91 (ALX) Mansura, LA Our Lady of Prompt Succor Church; Marksville, LA Holy Ghost Church.
Michiels, Philip F. '69 (SHP) [9] Shreveport, LA St. Mary of the Pines Church; Shreveport, LA Overton Brooks Veteran's Administration Medical Center.
Michini, F. Joseph *s.j.* '80 (PH) [G] Philadelphia, PA St. Joseph's Preparatory School; [Z] Philadelphia, PA St. Joseph's Preparatory School Jesuit Community, Arrupe House.
Michler, James '87 (STL) On Duty Outside the Archdiocese.
Michlik, Michael '63 (PHU) Baltimore, MD St. Michael's Church.
Michniewicz, Martin E. '86 (CHI) Calumet City, IL St. Andrew the Apostle Church.
Michota, Piotr '85 (NEW) Harrison, NJ Our Lady of Czestochowa Church.
Miciunas, Anthony *m.i.c.* '40 (CHI) [N] Chicago, IL Congregation of Marian Fathers of the Immaculate Conception.
Mick, Lawrence E. '72 (CIN) On Special and Diocesan Assignment.
Mick, Lawrence J. '49 (CIN) [45] Cincinnati, OH St. John the Evangelist Church.
Mick, Robert J. '49 (CIN) [16] Cincinnati, OH St. Bernard Church.
Micka, Alphonse *m.i.c.* '49 (JOL) Darien, IL Our Lady of Peace Church.
Micka, Ermin *o.f.m.* '38 (STL) Oakville, MO St. Francis of Assisi Church; [P] Oakville, MO St. Francis Friary.
Mickelson, Michael T. '76 (NEW) Fort Lee, NJ Holy Trinity Church.
Micketti, Gerald F. '83 (GAY) Traverse City, MI St. Patrick Church.
Mickey, Richard L. '88 (MEM) [4] Memphis, TN Church of the Ascension.
Mickiewicz, David '62 (ALB) Special Assignment.
Mickiewicz, David '84 (ALB) Albany, NY Albany Medical Center Hospital.
Mickiewicz, J. William '62 (MET) Califon, NJ St. John Neumann Church.
Mickler, Jeffrey *s.s.p.* '74 (BUF) [O] Derby, NY Society of St. Paul Provincial Residence.
Mickus, James J. '72 (OKL) Enid, OK St. Francis Xavier Church.
Miclot, Brian *ph.d.* '74 (DAV) [B] Davenport, IA St. Ambrose University.
Middendorf, Cyril *s.m.* '53 (CIN) [M] Dayton, OH Marianist Provincialate.
Middendorf, Eugene *o.f.m.* '45 (SFD) [4] Quincy, IL St. Francis Solanus Church; [K] Quincy, IL St. Francis Solanus Friary.
Middendorf, Frederic G. *s.j.* '42 (CIN) [28] Cincinnati, OH St. Francis Xavier Church.
Middendorf, Raymar *o.f.m.* '50 (IND) Oldenburg, IN Holy Family Church; [K] Oldenburg, IN Motherhouse of the Congregation of the Sisters of the Third Order of St. Francis.
Middendorf, Raymond D. *s.m.* '57 (PCE) Villalba, PR Our Lady Mother of Divine Providence Church.
Middleeamp, Eric *s.d.s.* '52 (MIL) [P] Milwaukee, WI Salvatorians - Jordan Hall.
Middleton, Charles '51 (WCH) Baxter Springs, KS St. Joseph Church; Galena, KS St. Patrick Church.
Midgley, James J. '90 (BGP) [10] Bridgeport, CT Holy Rosary Church; [C] Bridgeport, CT Kolbe-Cathedral High School.
Midile, Theodore *t.o.r.* '60 (WH) [F] Kearneysville, WV Priest Field Pastoral Center.
Midor, Adam *s.v.d.* '91 (TR) Neptune, NJ Our Lady of Providence Church.
Midowski, Leonard '51 (NEW) [N] Rutherford, NJ St. John Vianney Residence for Priests.
Midura, Msgr. Francis S. '70 (RVC) Carle Place, NY Church of Our Lady of Hope.
Midzak, Ihor '90 (STF) [6] Hartford, CT St. Michael Church.
Miechielsen, Albert *ss.cc.* '46 (HON) [H] Honolulu, HI St. Patrick's Monastery.
Mieczkowski, Msgr. Chester J. '45 (BAL) [13] Baltimore, MD St. Augustine Church.
Mieczkowski, Msgr. Chester J. '45 (BAL) Retired.
Miekina, Stanislaw *c.m.* '59 (BRK) [134] Brooklyn, NY St. Stanislaus Kostka Church.
Miele, Joseph J. '56 (TR) Red Bank, NJ St. Anthony Church.
Mier, Cristian '95 (ELP) [A] El Paso, TX St. Charles Seminary College Program.
Mierenfeld, Lawrence E. '73 (CIN) [11] Dayton, OH St. Henry Church.
Mierzwa, Ronald B. '76 (BUF) Ellicottville, NY Holy Name of Mary Church.
Mietelski, Joseph *c.m.* '59 (BRK) [32] Brooklyn, NY SS. Cyril and Methodius Church.
Mifkovic, Francis S. '32 (KC) Retired.
Mifsud, Carmelo '59 (OAK) Retired.
Mifsud, James J. *s.m.* '65 (SJ) [20] San Jose, CA Queen of Apostles Church.
Miglarese, Msgr. Sam R. (CHR) [H] Charleston, SC The College of Charleston Newman Center, Medical University of South Carolina.
Miglarese, Msgr. Sam R. '69 (CHR) [1] Charleston, SC Cathedral of St. John the Baptist.
Migliazzo, Felix '49 (MRY) Retired; [F] Monterey, CA Ave Maria Convalescent Hospital.
Migliazzo, Filex '49 (MRY) [H] Monterey, CA Ave Maria Convent.
Migliore, Angelus *t.o.r.* '64 (SP) [13] Tampa, FL St. Patrick Church.
Mignogna, Joe (GAL) [2] Spring, TX St. Edward Church.
Mignot, Msgr. John W. '54 (E) Reynoldsville, PA St. Mary Church.
Miguel, Eutiquiano *o.f.m.cap.* '51 (NO) [61] New Orleans, LA St. Theresa Of Avila Church; New Orleans, LA Charity Hospital.
Miguelez, Valeriano '66 (SJN) [15] San Juan, PR Espiritu Santo Church.
Migueli, Peter A. '91 (NY) [11] Yonkers, NY St. John the Baptist Church.
Miguerza, Octavio '92 (GAL) Humble, TX St. Mary Magdalene Church.
Mihai, Eugen '88 (ROM) Astoria, NY St. Mary Romanian Catholic Mission Church.
Mihalak, James J. '76 (ALN) [3] Pottsville, PA Mary Queen of Peace Church.
Mihalco, John J. '83 (PBR) Houston, TX St. John Chrysostom Church; San Antonio, TX Byzantine Catholic Mission Church.
Mihalec, Peter M. '76 (CLV) Fairport Harbor, OH St. Anthony of Padua Church.
Mihalic, Peter M. '76 (CLV) [A] Wickliffe, OH St. Mary Seminary.
Mihalik, Msgr. Alexis E. '64 (PBR) Boardman, OH Infant Jesus of Prague Church.
Mihalyi, Gilbert E. *o.praem.* '43 (GB) [I] De Pere, WI St. Norbert Abbey.
Mihan, Msgr. John A. '59 (LA) Pacific Palisades, CA Corpus Christi Church.
Mihayi, Gilbert *o.praem.* '43 (GB) [I] De Pere, WI St. Joseph Priory.
Mihelich, Leopold '32 (DEN) Retired.
Mihelko, John J. *m.m.* '38 (NY) [Z] Maryknoll, NY Maryknoll Fathers and Brothers.
Mihm, Richard L. '90 (DUB) On Leave of Absence.
Mihm, Xavier R. *o.s.b.* '43 (GBG) [H] Latrobe, PA Saint Vincent Archabbey.
Mihovilovich, John B. '52 (SFR) Retired.
Mijas, Paul (RVC) Glen Head, NY St. Hyacinth Church.
Mika, John M. '72 (LIN) Sick Leave.
Mika, Joseph *o.f.m.* (CHI) [M] Justice, IL Rosary Hill Home.
Mika, Joseph *o.f.m.* '51 (CHI) [N] Chicago, IL Holy Name Friary-Franciscan House of Formation.
Mikalajunas, John '69 (SY) Binghamton, NY Binghamton General Hospital.
Mikalajunas, John E. '69 (SY) [7] Binghamton, NY St. Joseph Church.
Mikalofsky, Hilarion '75 (BEL) [K] Belleville, IL Scott Air Force Base.
Mikalofsky, Hilarion A. '75 (MIL) Military Chaplains.
Mikasauskas, Ronald *m.ss.a.* '77 (NOR) [F] Cromwell, CT Missionaries of the Holy Apostles.
Mikasauskas, Ronald H. *m.ss.a.* '77 (NOR) [A] Cromwell, CT Holy Apostles College and Seminary.
Mikes, Pavel '90 (VIC) East Bernard, TX Holy Cross Church.
Mikesch, Gregory R. '75 (STL) Ferguson, MO Good Shepherd Church.
Miketinac, Hilary '45 (SY) [5] Binghamton, NY SS. Cyril and Method Church.
Mikkelson, Scott '82 (AUS) Mexia, TX St. Mary's Church; Mexia, TX State School.
Miklas, Sebastian F. *o.f.m.cap.* '39 (WDC) [B] Washington, DC St. Francis Friary-Capuchin College.
Miklaszewski, Albin *o.f.m.* '46 (MIL) [P] Burlington, WI Queen of Peace Friary.
Mikolaitis, Vito E. '43 (CHI) [141] Chicago, IL Nativity of the Blessed Virgin Mary Church; Retired.
Mikolajczyk, Bruno '88 (CC) [18] Corpus Christi, TX St. Paul the Apostle Church.
Mikolajczyk, Edward M. '73 (CHI) [161] Chicago, IL Our Lady of Victory Church; [A] Chicago, IL Archbishop Quigley Preparatory Seminary.
Mikolajczyk, George *m.m.* '55 (NY) [201] Staten Island, NY St. Christopher Church.
Mikolajczyk, George M. *m.m.* '55 (NY) [Z] Maryknoll, NY Maryknoll Fathers and Brothers.
Mikonis, Gerald S. '74 (PIT) Port Vue, PA St. Mark Church.
Miksch, Joseph A. '66 (OM) Columbus, NE St. Anthony Church.
Mikschl, Luke *s.t.* '53 (STP) [4] Minneapolis, MN Ascension Church.
Mikstay, Michael '59 (Y) Military Chaplains.
Mikula, Gregory '87 (PEO) [2] Streator, IL St. Anthony of Padua Church; [3] Streator, IL St. Casimir Church.
Mikula, John J. *o.f.m.conv.* '56 (RCK) [11] Rockford, IL St. Stanislaus Kostka Church.
Mikulanis, Alcuin L. *o.f.m.* '55 (CLV) [71] Cleveland, OH St. Stanislaus Church; [P] Cleveland, OH St. Stanislaus Friary.
Mikulanis, Dennis '77 (SD) [23] San Diego, CA St. Charles Church.
Mikulich, Joseph *o.f.m.* '22 (SJ) [26] San Jose, CA St. Mary of the Assumption Church.
Mikulik, Kenneth E. '52 (GAL) Wallis, TX Guardian Angel Church.
Mikulski, Isadore J. '50 (GAY) Retired.
Mikulski, Michael '95 (LA) Norwalk, CA St. Linus Church.
Mikus, Elemir Joseph '57 (DET) [2] Sterling Heights, MI SS. Cyril and Methodius Church.
Mikus, Frank P. '41 (SCR) Retired; [N] Dunmore, PA Villa St. Joseph.
Milanese, John M. '74 (BUR) Randolph, VT SS. Donatian and Rogatian Church; [J] Burlington, VT University of Vermont-The Catholic Center at UVM.
Milani, Joseph J. '50 (SJ) Cupertino, CA St. Joseph of Cupertino Church; Retired.
Milani, Vasco J. *s.x.* '67 (MIL) [B] Franklin, WI Xaverian Missionary Fathers College Seminary.
Milano, Cleo J. '83 (BR) Denham Springs, LA Immaculate Conception Church.
Milano, Msgr. James '40 (LSC) Retired.
Milanowski, Paul A. '65 (GR) Newaygo, MI St. Bartholomew's Church.
Milazzo, Nicholas F. '52 (NY) [128] Bronx, NY St. Anthony Church.
Milbauer, Robert '66 (LA) Van Nuys, CA St. Bridget of Sweden Church; [D] Mission Hills, CA Alemany High School.
Milby, Lawrence M. '65 (BUF) Gowanda, NY St. Joseph Church.
Milcetich, Paul P. *o.s.f.s.* '65 (R) Roxboro, NC SS. Mary and Edward Church.
Milde, Robert F. '48 (BRK) Brooklyn, NY Veterans Administration Medical Center; Absent on Sick Leave; Retired.
Milek, Richard '83 (CHI) [82] Chicago, IL Holy Innocents Church.
Miles, Cassian *o.f.m.* '61 (NY) [35] New York, NY St. Francis of Assisi Church.
Miles, Cassian A. *o.f.m.* '61 (PAT) [P] Paterson, NJ St. Anthony's Guild.
Miles, Francis J. *s.j.* '60 (WDC) [P] Faulkner, MD Loyola on the Potomac Retreat House.
Miles, James '78 (BAL) [36] Baltimore, MD Holy Rosary Church.
Miles, James '78 (LKC) On Duty Outside the Diocese.
Miles, Michael '70 (BAK) Merrill, OR St. Augustine Church.
Miles, Richard M. '83 (NO) [2] Kenner, LA Our Lady of Perpetual Help Church.
Milewski, Casimir '69 (TR) Burlington, NJ All Saints Church.
Milewski, Douglas J. '89 (NEW) [B] South Orange, NJ Seton Hall University.

Milewski, John '93 (KNX) Oak Ridge, TN St. Mary Church.
Milewski, Richard '83 (TR) Tabernacle, NJ Holy Eucharist Church; New Lisbon, NJ New Jersey State Colony.
Milewski, Robert '80 (E) On Duty Outside Diocese.
Milewski, Msgr. Stanley E. '55 (DET) [A] Orchard Lake, MI SS. Cyril and Methodius Seminary; [C] Orchard Lake, MI Saint Mary's College; [E] Orchard Lake, MI St. Mary's Preparatory.
Milewski, Stanley J. '44 (GRY) [3] Gary, IN Holy Family Church.
Miley, Eamon '73 (MOB) Butler, AL St. John Church.
Miley, Edward *p.i.m.e.* '67 (DET) [K] Detroit, MI P.I.M.E. Missionaries of SS. Peter and Paul.
Milford, Joseph *o.m.i.* '46 (PMB) [4] West Palm Beach, FL St. John Fisher Church.
Milford, Kenneth F. *c.s.sp.* '33 (SB) [E] Hemet, CA Holy Ghost Fathers.
Mili, Jude J. *o.f.m.* '59 (WH) [G] Morgantown, WV Our Lady of Good Counsel Franciscan Friary.
Milia, Msgr. Anthony A. '50 (OG) [3] Watertown, NY St. Anthony Church.
Milienewicz, Frank J. '76 (NTN) Birmingham, AL St. George Church; [E] Birmingham, AL National Shrine of St. George.
Militello, Benedict P. '57 (NEW) [2] Garfield, NJ Holy Name Church.
Militello, Cosmo F. '60 (CHI) Melrose Park, IL Sacred Heart Church.
Millane, Thomas J. '63 (TUC) [22] Tucson, AZ St. Elizabeth Ann Seton Church.
Millar, Andrew L. '58 (RVC) Seaford, NY Maria Regina Church.
Millea, Thomas V. (CHI) Retired.
Millea, Msgr. William V. '80 (BGP) On Duty Outside the Diocese.
Millen, Edwin F. '56 (RCK) [7] Aurora, IL St. Peter Church.
Miller, A. Andrew '45 (MAN) Retired.
Miller, Abraham (STN) Chicago, IL St. Mary of Nazareth Hospital Center.
Miller, Abraham '79 (CHI) [J] Chicago, IL St. Mary of Nazareth Hospital Center.
Miller, Alfred J. '64 (DET) Temperance, MI Our Lady of Mt. Carmel Church.
Miller, Bernard *m.s.c.* '59 (RCK) [H] Aurora, IL Missionaries of the Sacred Heart Community.
Miller, Bert '91 (FAR) Grafton, ND St. John the Evangelist's Church.
Miller, Bertin *o.f.m.* '64 (STL) [T] Dittmer, MO Il Ritiro-The Little Retreat.
Miller, Brendan '83 (LR) [A] Subiaco, AR Subiaco Monastery.
Miller, Brendan '83 (NSH) On Duty Outside the Diocese.
Miller, Brian J. *t.o.r.* '53 (SP) [6] St. Petersburg, FL St. Mary Our Lady of Grace Church.
Miller, Bruce '77 (ALX) [6] Alexandria, LA St. Rita Church.
Miller, Burt '91 (FAR) Grafton, ND Grafton State School.
Miller, Byron *c.ss.r.* '90 (SAT) [B] San Antonio, TX Redemptorist Seminary, Liguori House.
Miller, C. Anthony '80 (HBG) [3] York, PA St. Patrick Church.
Miller, Charles *o.f.m.* '66 (NY) [48] New York, NY Holy Name of Jesus Church.
Miller, Charles B. *o.f.m.* '38 (PEO) Metamora, IL St. Mary's Church.
Miller, Charles E. *c.m.* '56 (LA) [A] Camarillo, CA St. John's Seminary.
Miller, Charles E. '91 (SB) Yucaipa, CA St. Frances Xavier Cabrini Church.
Miller, Charles H. *s.m.* '64 (SAT) [C] San Antonio, TX St. Mary's University of San Antonio, Texas; [C] San Antonio, TX St. Mary's University of San Antonio, Texas; [M] San Antonio, TX Chaminade Community House.
Miller, Charles J. *o.f.m.* '66 (NY) [Z] New York, NY Franciscan Friars, Order of Friars Manor.
Miller, Charles J. '72 (NEW) Lyndhurst, NJ Sacred Heart Church.
Miller, Christopher T. '93 (LFT) [4] Lafayette, IN St. Lawrence Church.
Miller, Cletus *o.s.b.* '44 (SFS) [F] Marvin, SD Blue Cloud Abbey.
Miller, Conrad *o.f.m.conv.* '38 (BAL) [D] Baltimore, MD Archbishop Curley High School; [M] Baltimore, MD Immaculate Heart of Mary Friary.
Miller, David L. '81 (SPC) Pulaskifield, MO SS. Peter and Paul Church.
Miller, Donald A. *o.f.m.* '72 (Y) [B] North Canton, OH Walsh University.
Miller, Donald S. '42 (KC) Maryville, MO St. Gregory Barbarigo Church; Retired.
Miller, Edward M. '71 (BAL) [17] Baltimore, MD St. Bernardine Church.
Miller, Elden J. '54 (FTW) [4] Mishawaka, IN Queen of Peace Church.
Miller, Ferdinand B. '46 (NEW) Retired.
Miller, Francis *o.c.d.* '49 (WDC) [B] Washington, DC Monastery of Our Lady of Mount Carmel.
Miller, Francis J. '50 (CIN) Retired.
Miller, Francis N. '37 (BUF) Retired; [K] Lackawanna, NY Our Lady of Victory Hospital.
Miller, Francis X. *s.j.* '59 (WOR) [N] Worcester, MA Jesuits of Holy Cross College, Inc.
Miller, Msgr. Frank '54 (AUS) Absent on Sick Leave.
Miller, Frank P. '54 (COL) Dresden, OH St. Ann's Church.
Miller, Franklin '89 (FAR) Zeeland, ND St. Andrew's Church.
Miller, Frederick J. '41 (NY) Retired.
Miller, Frederick L. '72 (NEW) On Duty Outside the Archdiocese.
Miller, Frederick L. '72 (NY) [A] Yonkers, NY St. Joseph's Seminary.
Miller, Frederick L. '72 (PH) [A] Wynnewood, PA Theological Seminary of St. Charles Borromeo, Overbrook.
Miller, Gary A. '70 (COV) [K] Fort Thomas, KY Carmel Manor; [K] Fort Thomas, KY Regina Cleri Home for Retired Priests.
Miller, Gary M. '72 (CHI) [164] Chicago, IL St. Pascal Church.
Miller, Gary R. '83 (TOL) [21] Toledo, OH St. Clement Church.
Miller, George '78 (DET) Special Assignment.
Miller, George '79 (DET) [4] Dearborn Heights, MI St. Linus Church.
Miller, Henry A. *o.s.c.* '43 (DUL) St. Mathias, MN St. Mathias Church.
Miller, Henry A. *o.s.c.* '43 (SCL) [I] Onamia, MN Crosier Monastery.
Miller, James '54 (CIN) [B] Carthagena, OH St. Charles.
Miller, James *o.m.i.* '57 (GAL) [36] Houston, TX Immaculate Conception Church.
Miller, James '68 (FWT) [3] Arlington, TX St. Joseph's Church.
Miller, James C. (RVC) Graduate Studies.
Miller, James C. '83 (RVC) Garden City, NY St. Anne Church; Port Jefferson, NY St. Charles Hospital, Port Jefferson, New York; [I] Port Jefferson, NY St. Charles Hospital, Port Jefferson, New York.
Miller, Msgr. James F. '61 (JUN) Haines, AK Sacred Heart Church; Retired.
Miller, James H. '68 (LC) Viroqua, WI Annunciation of the Blessed Virgin Mary Church.
Miller, James L. '76 (DUB) Waverly, IA St. Mary's Church.
Miller, James Norman '59 (NSH) [9] Nashville, TN St. Mary's of the Seven Sorrows Church.
Miller, James W. '67 (CHI) [160] Chicago, IL Our Lady of Tepeyac Church.
Miller, Joe *s.v.d.* (LA) [R] Los Angeles, CA Casa Guadalupe.
Miller, John '58 (SCL) St. Stephen, MN St. Stephen's Church.
Miller, John '82 (WCH) Cunningham, KS Sacred Heart Church; St. Leo, KS St. Leo the Great Church.
Miller, John C. '95 (BRK) [97] Brooklyn, NY Our Lady of Guadalupe Church.
Miller, John H. *c.s.c.* '51 (STL) [W] St. Louis, MO Central Bureau of the CCUA.
Miller, Msgr. John J. '64 (PH) Fairless Hills, PA St. Frances Cabrini Church.
Miller, John P. '78 (HEL) [4] Missoula, MT St. Anthony Church.
Miller, John P. '82 (WCH) Willowdale, KS St. Peter's Church; Zenda, KS St. John Church.
Miller, Joseph '36 (SFD) Retired.
Miller, Joseph *c.pp.s.* '77 (DAV) Centerville, IA St. Mary's Church.
Miller, Joseph A. '89 (BRK) Absent on Leave.
Miller, Joseph B. '36 (TR) Retired.
Miller, Joseph C. '49 (OWN) Retired.
Miller, Joseph K. '57 (SAG) Nine Mile, MI St. Mary Church; Pinconning, MI St. Agnes Church.
Miller, Joseph N. '48 (SUP) Minocqua, WI St. Patrick Church.
Miller, Joseph W. '59 (PIT) Retired.
Miller, Kenneth '77 (Y) Boardman, OH St. Luke Church.
Miller, Lawrence J. '69 (NEW) [1] Bayonne, NJ St. Mary Star of the Sea Church.
Miller, Leo M. *o.m.i.* '52 (LA) Long Beach, CA Veterans Affairs Medical Center; Military and VA Chaplains.
Miller, Leo M. *o.m.i.* '52 (STP) [N] St. Paul, MN Oblate Residence.
Miller, Loran *o.f.m.cap.* '64 (DET) [K] Detroit, MI St. Bonaventure Friary.
Miller, Loran *o.f.m. cap.* '64 (LC) [I] Marathon City, WI St. Anthony Retreat Center.
Miller, Louis '56 (L) [N] Louisville, KY Sacred Heart Home, Inc.
Miller, Mark *c.pp.s.* '71 (KC) [A] Kansas City, MO Precious Blood Mission House; [A] Liberty, MO Society of the Precious Blood Provincial Offices; [J] Liberty, MO Precious Blood Society Provincial Office.
Miller, Mark A. '69 (ROC) Stanley, NY St. Theresa Church.
Miller, Martin E. '94 (PH) [6] Norristown, PA St. Titus Church.
Miller, Martin J. '94 (NY) [EE] New Rochelle, NY Opus Dei (Prelature of the Holy Cross and Opus Dei).
Miller, Maurice R. '49 (LFT) [2] Lafayette, IN St. Ann Church.
Miller, Meinrad *o.s.b.* '94 (KCK) [A] Atchison, KS Benedictine College; [H] Atchison, KS St. Benedict's Abbey.
Miller, Michael '72 (MRY) [4] Salinas, CA Madonna Del Sasso Church; Special Assignment.
Miller, Michael *m.s.c.* '85 (RCK) [H] Aurora, IL Missionaries of the Sacred Heart Community.
Miller, Michael '86 (ALB) Colonie, NY St. Clare Church.
Miller, Michael J. '96 (STP) West St. Paul, MN St. Joseph Church.
Miller, Milton Peter '82 (LKC) [8] Lake Charles, LA Our Lady Queen of Heaven Church.
Miller, Neil '61 (ROC) [37] Rochester, NY Our Lady of Perpetual Help Church.
Miller, Oscar J. *c.m.* '39 (SAT) Losoya, TX El Carmen Catholic Church.
Miller, Paul '44 (FTW) [10] South Bend, IN Holy Family Church.
Miller, Paul A. *c.ss.r.* '33 (NY) Port Ewen, NY Presentation of the Virgin Mary Church.
Miller, Paul A. *c.ss.r.* '62 (NY) [Z] Esopus, NY Redemptorist Priests and Brothers C.Ss.R. (Province of Baltimore).
Miller, Paul A. '67 (SCR) [1] Wilkes-Barre, PA St. Aloysius Church.
Miller, Paul N. '56 (HBG) Bonneauville, PA St. Joseph Church.
Miller, Paul W. '44 (KCK) Eudora, KS Holy Family Church.
Miller, Peter *s.c.j.* '45 (MIL) [P] Franklin, WI St. Francis Residence; [P] Hales Corners, WI Priests of the Sacred Heart.
Miller, Philip '77 (Y) Ashtabula, OH St. Joseph's Church.
Miller, Randall J. '89 (LAN) Blissfield, MI St. Peter the Apostle Church.
Miller, Richard E. '76 (LFT) Reynolds, IN St. Joseph Church; Grissom, IN Grissom Air Force Base, St. Michael's Chapel; Special Assignment.
Miller, Richard G. '50 (TOL) [16] Toledo, OH St. Agnes Church.
Miller, Robert G. *c.s.b.* '43 (ROC) [I] Rochester, NY Basilian Residence.
Miller, Robert J. *o.p.* '56 (CHI) [J] Blue Island, IL St. Francis Hospital and Health Center; [N] Chicago, IL Dominicans (Provincial Office); [N] River Forest, IL St. Thomas Aquinas Priory.
Miller, Robert J. '61 (MET) Edison, NJ Guardian Angels Church.
Miller, Robert J. '80 (PIT) [43] Pittsburgh, PA St. Basil Church.
Miller, Robert M. '92 (PIT) [1] New Castle, PA Mary, Mother of Hope Church.
Miller, Roger F. '54 (KC) Lee's Summit, MO Holy Spirit Church.
Miller, Theodore '75 (TOL) [22] Toledo, OH St. Francis de Sales Church; [32] Toledo, OH St. Mary of the Assumption Church.
Miller, Thomas C. '93 (STL) [7] Florissant, MO Sacred Heart Church.
Miller, Thomas G. '71 (RIC) [8] Richmond, VA St. Bridget Church.
Miller, Thomas J. *c.s.sp* '58 (NO) Pointe a la Hache, LA St. Thomas Church.
Miller, Thomas M. *c.s.b.* '45 (ROC) [I] Rochester, NY Residence of Basilian Fathers-The Aquinas Institute.
Miller, Thomas R. '77 (PIT) Clarksville, PA St. Thomas Church.
Miller, Thomas R. '79 (PEO) [15] Peoria, IL St. Vincent De Paul Church.
Miller, Thomas W. '77 (BEL) Anna, IL St. Mary Church; Anna, IL Anna State Hospital; Vienna, IL Vienna Correctional Center; Vienna, IL Shawnee Correctional Center.
Miller, Walt *s.v.d.* (SB) [A] Riverside, CA Divine Word Seminary; [G] Riverside, CA Divine Word Retreat Center.
Miller, Walter D. *j.c.d.* '61 (BUR) Hinesburg, VT St. Jude the Apostle Church.
Miller, Wayne '61 (COL) [35] Columbus, OH Our Lady of Victory Church.
Miller, Whitney '80 (LKC) [7] Lake Charles, LA Our Lady of Good Counsel Church; [F] Lake Charles, LA Catholic Student Center.
Miller, William '61 (L) [58] Louisville, KY Our Lady of Lourdes Church.
Miller, William *c.pp.s.* '63 (JC) Sedalia, MO Sacred Heart Church.
Miller, William *s.j.* '72 (P) [A] St. Benedict, OR Mount Angel Seminary.
Miller, William C. '83 (E) [3] Oil City, PA St. Joseph Church.

Miller, William M. '56 (PIT) [26] Pittsburgh, PA St. Mary of Mercy Church.
Miller, William M. '91 (LKC) [5] Lake Charles, LA St. Margaret Church.
Miller, William T. *s.j.* '55 (DEN) [M] Denver, CO Xavier Jesuit Center.
Miller, William T. *i.c.* '84 (PEO) [A] Peoria, IL Rosminian Novitiate.
Millerd, William H. *s.j.* '68 (WDC) [M] Washington, DC The Jesuit Community at Georgetown University.
Millet, John H. *s.j.* (LAF) Retired.
Millican, Ron '81 (P) Vernonia, OR St. Mary Church; [C] Portland, OR Central Catholic High School.
Milligan, Richard A. '60 (PHX) [16] Phoenix, AZ St. Luke Church.
Milligan, Ronald '72 (DET) [3] Sterling Heights, MI St. Ephrem Church.
Milliken, Damian J. *o.s.b.* '58 (PAT) [M] Newton, NJ St. Paul's Abbey.
Milliken, David '77 (NEW) Berkeley Heights, NJ Church of the Little Flower.
Millisor, Daniel J. '86 (COL) Ada, OH Our Lady of Lourdes Church.
Millot, Andre '69 (WDC) [26] Washington, DC Church of St. Louis.
Millott, Thirburse F. '75 (WOR) Southborough, MA St. Anne Church.
Mills, Alexander '80 (TUC) Tucson, AZ Villa Maria.
Mills, Alexander *o.s.b.* '90 (TUC) [F] St. David, AZ Holy Trinity Monastery.
Mills, Brindley '64 (DAL) [21] Dallas, TX St. Monica Church.
Mills, Henry '88 (NY) [63] New York, NY St. Joseph of the Holy Family Church.
Mills, James Leo '62 (NEW) Retired.
Mills, Joseph M. '53 (OWN) Rome, KY St. Martin Church.
Mills, Robert N. '55 (L) Retired.
Milon, Augustin *o.f.m.* (CHI) [I] Chicago, IL The Port.
Milosz, Bogdan '81 (DET) Capac, MI St. Nicholas Church.
Milota, Thomas A. '92 (JOL) [2] Naperville, IL Sts. Peter and Paul Church.
Milsted, Gordon '63 (MOB) Fairhope, AL St. Lawrence Church.
Milton, Hilary *o.carm.* '63 (NEW) Teaneck, NJ St. Anastasia's Church.
Mimms, Wolfgang *o.ss.t.* '70 (VIC) [4] Victoria, TX Our Lady of Sorrows Church.
Mimnagh, Msgr. Peter F. '48 (SD) Retired.
Mina, John Louis '89 (PBR) Leisenring, PA St. Stephen Church; Perryopolis, PA St. Nicholas Church.
Minamicki, George *s.j.* '54 (FTW) [B] Notre Dame, IN University of Notre Dame Du Lac.
Minassian, Raphael '73 (ARM) Los Angeles, CA Our Lady Queen of Martyrs Church.
Minassian, Raphael *p.i.a.* '73 (LA) [30] Los Angeles, CA Our Lady Queen of Martyrs Church.
Minch, Richard '69 (SAV) Military Chaplains.
Minchak, Paul *o.f.m.cap.* '69 (AGN) [F] Agana Heights, GU St. Fidelis Friary.
Minchak, Paul *o.f.m. cap.* '69 (HON) Kailua, HI St. Anthony Church.
Minchiatti, Francis *c.s.* '45 (HRT) [15] New Haven, CT St. Michael's Church.
Minder, Kevin W. '89 (YAK) Wapato, WA St. Peter Claver Church.
Minder, Lawrence *o.s.b.* '89 (P) [L] St. Benedict, OR Mt. Angel Abbey.
Mindling, J. Daniel *o.f.m.cap.* '80 (BAL) [A] Emmitsburg, MD Mount St. Mary's Seminary; [A] Emmitsburg, MD Mount St. Mary's Seminary.
Mindling, J. Daniel *o.f.m.cap.* '80 (WDC) [B] Washington, DC St. Francis Friary-Capuchin College.
Mindling, Joseph *o.f.m.cap.* '67 (WDC) [39] Washington, DC Shrine of the Sacred Heart Church.
Mindrup, Mark F. *o.f.m.conv.* '39 (STP) [Q] Prior Lake, MN Franciscan Retreat House.
Minehan, Michael P. (SY) Special Assignment; [W] Syracuse, NY David W. Barry Foundation.
Minehan, Michael P. '80 (SY) Lafayette, NY St. Joseph Church.
Minelli, Peter A. '63 (MAR) [1] Escanaba, MI St. Anne Church.
Minette, James '41 (SCL) Retired.
Minh, Joseph Duc (LA) [A] Camarillo, CA St. John's Seminary.
Minh, Matthew T. '53 (COS) [1] Colorado Springs, CO St. Mary's Cathedral.
Minh, Vincent *c.ss.r.* '68 (P) [17] Portland, OR Holy Redeemer Church; [1] Portland, OR Southeast Asian Vicariate Church.
Minh, Vu Duc '80 (TLS) On Duty Outside the Diocese.
Minh Thanh Tran, Matthew T. '53 (COS) [14] Colorado Springs, CO The Vietnamese Holy Martyrs Quasi-Parish Church.
Minh Thu, Anthony Hoang '68 (ARL) [5] Arlington, VA Holy Martyrs of Vietnam Church.
Minhoto, Msgr. Walter '64 (FRS) [1] Fresno, CA St. John Cathedral.
Minhoto, Msgr. Walter F. (FRS) Retired.
Minic, John F. '71 (CIN) Retired.
Minichello, Arthur '73 (BRK) [33] Brooklyn, NY St. Dominic Church.
Minielli, Anthony '45 (NY) Retired.
Minigan, Frederick J. '39 (BO) Retired.
Minigan, William J. '86 (BO) [8] Cambridge, MA St. John the Evangelist Church.
Miniscalco, Donald C. *c.ss.r.* '68 (PH) [135] Philadelphia, PA St. Peter the Apostle Church.
Mink, John J. '85 (WIL) Wilmington Manor, DE Our Lady of Fatima Church; Wilmington, DE Delaware Army National Guard.
Minkiel, Stephen J. *c.m.* '57 (BRK) [32] Brooklyn, NY SS. Cyril and Methodius Church.
Minkler, John '72 (ALB) Albany, NY Veterans' Administration Hospital; Special Assignment; Military Chaplains.
Minnich, John F. (GRY) Retired.
Minnihan, Paul D. '93 (OAK) Pleasanton, CA St. Augustine Church.
Minniti, Anthony L. '70 (CAM) Elmer, NJ St. Ann's Church.
Minniti, David V. '72 (CAM) Millville, NJ St. Mary Magdalen's Church.
Minnoggio, Ferrando '47 (CLV) Retired.
Minogue, Austin F. *c.m.* '41 (CHI) [C] Chicago, IL Vincentian Community at DePaul University.
Minogue, John P. *c.m.* '72 (CHI) [C] Chicago, IL De Paul University; [C] Chicago, IL Vincentian Community at DePaul University.
Minogue, Liam A. '68 (MET) Hillsborough, NJ Mary, Mother of God Church.
Minogue, Michael '81 (PHX) Sun City West, AZ Our Lady of Lourdes Church.
Minsterman, Joseph '61 (GBG) East Vandergrift, PA Our Lady, Queen of Peace Church.
Minta, John J. '50 (IND) Milan, IN St. Charles Borromeo Church; Retired.
Mintegui, Marc '68 (AGN) On Duty Outside the Archdiocese.
Mintegui, Marc A. '68 (CHR) Military Chaplains.
Mintjal, Frank D. '59 (Y) Alliance, OH Regina Coeli Church.
Minturn, Joseph '57 (RVC) Manorhaven, NY Our Lady of Fatima Church.
Minvielle, John Q. *s.j.* '43 (NO) [P] New Orleans, LA Ignatius Residence.
Miodowski, Chester A. '46 (NEW) Retired.
Miodowski, Leonard A. '51 (NEW) Retired.
Miola, Luigi C. '77 (CLV) Madison, OH Immaculate Conception Church.
Miorin, Albert C. '64 (TOL) Cloverdale, OH St. Barbara Church; Continental, OH St. John the Baptist Church.
Miotke, Carmel *o.f.m.* '60 (BO) [BB] Boston, MA St. Anthony Shrine.
Mirabelli, Daniel J. *c.s.v.* '60 (PEO) [B] Rock Island, IL Alleman High School.
Miracky, James J. *s.j.* '88 (WOR) [N] Worcester, MA Jesuits of Holy Cross College, Inc.
Miraglia, Salvatore J. '75 (RVC) Priests Released from Diocesan Assignment.
Miralbes-Drago, Julio E. '72 (MIL) [81] Milwaukee, WI St. Wenceslaus Church.
Miranda, Juan '51 (SJN) [21] San Juan, PR Nuestra Sra. de Guadalupe Church.
Miranda, Lorenzo '91 (LA) Lynwood, CA St. Emydius Church.
Miranda, Luis *o.carm.* '84 (ARE) Ciales, PR Holy Rosary Church.
Miranda, Luke '55 (FWT) Absent on Leave.
Miranda, R. Dario '92 (LA) Canoga Park, CA St. Joseph the Worker Church.
Miranda, Msgr. Rafael '56 (ELP) [38] El Paso, TX San Judas Tadeo Church.
Miranda, Victor '86 (CHI) Calumet City, IL St. Victor Church.
Miranne, Paul *o.s.b.* '47 (NO) [P] St. Benedict, LA St. Joseph Abbey.
Mire, Msgr. Jerome T. '51 (NO) [15] New Orleans, LA Mater Dolorosa Church.
Mirecki, Msgr. John '55 (RVC) Riverhead, NY St. Isidore's Church.
Mireles, Richard '74 (BWN) Absent.
Miriani, Gerald C. '62 (BEL) Shiloh, IL Corpus Christi Church.
Miroslaw, '77 (PIT) Wildwood, PA St. Catherine of Sweden Church.
Mirro, Joseph A. '76 (RVC) Mastic Beach, NY St. Jude Church.
Mirsberger, Richard E. '66 (MIL) [9] West Allis, WI St. Rita's Church.
Mirto, Gregorio '65 (DEN) Littleton, CO Light of the World Parish Church.
Misbrener, David M. '95 (PBR) North Hills-Gibsonia, PA St. Andrew the Apostle Church.
Miscamble, Wilson D. *c.s.c.* '88 (FTW) [B] Notre Dame, IN University of Notre Dame Du Lac; [J] Notre Dame, IN Holy Cross Community, Corby Hall, University of Notre Dame.
Mischke, Bernard C. *o.s.c.* '51 (SCL) St. Nicholas, MN St. Nicholas Church; [I] Onamia, MN Crosier Monastery.
Mischke, Fridolin P. *o.s.c.* '42 (PHX) [F] Phoenix, AZ Crosier Community of Phoenix (Canons Regular of the Order of the Holy Cross).
Mischke, Gerald '64 (SCL) Holdingford, MN St. Hedwig's Church; Holdingford, MN St. Mary's Church; Opole, MN Our Lady of Mt. Carmel Church; St. Anna, MN Immaculate Conception Church; St. Wendel, MN St. Columbkille's Church.
Mischke, Walter *c.m.f.* (CHI) [N] Oak Park, IL Claretian Fathers Headquarters of U.S.A. Eastern Province.
Mischke, Walter *c.m.f.* '43 (LA) [R] Rancho Dominguez, CA Dominguez Seminary Inc.
Mischkowiuski, Henry B. '65 (LR) Lake Village, AR Our Lady of the Lake Church.
Mischler, Thomas E. '81 (GRY) Lowell, IN St. Edward Church; Shelby, IN St. Theresa Church.
Misenko, John A. '78 (CLV) [4] Parma, OH St. Columbkille Church.
Misercola, Chester A. '64 (SY) [1] Oswego, NY St. John the Evangelist Church.
Misey, Leonard S. '63 (JC) Brunswick, MO St. Boniface Church; Indian Grove, MO St. Raphael Church.
Mish, Roy L. '60 (LC) Awaiting Assignment.
Misho, Lloyd P. '58 (BEL) Retired.
Misiewicz, Chester J. '73 (WOR) Gilbertville, MA St. Aloysius Church.
Misiolek, Frederick '65 (DET) Flat Rock, MI St. Roch Church.
Miskella, Richard '64 (LA) Palmdale, CA St. Mary Church.
Miskiewicz, Paul *o.f.m.conv.* '82 (BRK) [146] Queens, NY St. Adalbert Church.
Miskolczy, Kalman *sch.p.* '45 (BUF) [3] Lackawanna, NY Assumption Church; [O] Derby, NY Piarist Fathers.
Missa, Msgr. John B. '32 (BO) [6] Brockton, MA Our Lady of Ostrobrama Church.
Missett, Luke *c.p.* '40 (HRT) [M] West Hartford, CT Holy Family Monastery/Retreat.
Missimi, Anthony N. '62 (COL) [22] Columbus, OH Immaculate Conception Church.
Missler, John C. '78 (TOL) Shelby, OH Most Pure Heart of Mary Church.
Missler, Othmar *c.pp.s.* '37 (CIN) [B] Carthagena, OH St. Charles.
Mistretta, Msgr. Vito F. '42 (SAC) Citrus Heights, CA Holy Family Church; Retired and in Senior Ministry.
Misulich, Msgr. Raymond M. *j.c.l.* '56 (PSC) New York, NY St. Mary's Church.
Misurda, Matthew E. (ALT) [B] Johnstown, PA Bishop McCort High School.
Misurda, Matthew E. '77 (ALT) Twin Rocks, PA St. Charles Church.
Miszkel, Ivot *o.f.m.cap.* '80 (PAT) [M] Oak Ridge-Milton, NJ St. Stanislaus B. M. Friary.
Mitas, Matthew M. '79 (STL) Kirkwood, MO St. Gerard Majella Church.
Mitchell, Charles I. '84 (ORL) Altamonte Springs, FL St. Mary Magdalen Church.
Mitchell, Conan *o.f.m.* '43 (SUP) Ashland, WI Our Lady of the Lake Catholic Community Church.
Mitchell, Edward J. '54 (DET) Rochester, MI St. Irenaeus Church.
Mitchell, Eugene *b.s.o.* '92 (NTN) Manchester, NH Our Lady of the Cedars Church; [B] Methuen, MA Basilian Salvatorian Order.
Mitchell, John C. '55 (BGP) On Duty Outside the Diocese.
Mitchell, John D. *c.s.p.* '38 (NY) [104] New York, NY St. Paul the Apostle Church.
Mitchell, John Dennis *c.s.p.* '38 (NY) [Z] Scarsdale, NY Paulist Fathers Generalate.
Mitchell, John E. '54 (STP) [22] St. Paul, MN St. James Church.
Mitchell, Msgr. John J. '63 (RCK) Loves Park, IL St. Bridget Church.
Mitchell, John J. '96 (STP) Eagan, MN St. John Neumann Church.
Mitchell, John T. *s.j.* '72 (SJ) [M] Los Gatos, CA California Province of the Society of Jesus, Jesuit Provincial Office.
Mitchell, Joseph '56 (DAL) McKinney, TX St. Michael Church.
Mitchell, Joseph O. *c.p.* '81 (SAC) [H] Citrus Heights, CA Christ the King Retreat; [J] Citrus Heights, CA Christ the King Retreat Center.
Mitchell, Joseph P. '79 (SEA) Bremerton, WA Our Lady, Star of the Sea Church.
Mitchell, Kenneth *s.c.j.* (SP) [O] Pinellas Park, FL Priests of the Sacred Heart.
Mitchell, Lester *o.f.m.* '55 (PHX) [19] Phoenix, AZ St. Mary's Basilica.
Mitchell, Mark E. '76 (GR) On Special Assignment.
Mitchell, Michael J. '65 (SJ) Cupertino, CA St. Joseph of Cupertino Church; Special Assignment; [P] Santa Clara, CA St. Joseph Seminary Corporation; [P] Santa Clara, CA The Roman Catholic Welfare Corporation of San Jose.

Mitchell, Peter '78 (ORL) Port Orange, FL Epiphany Church.
Mitchell, Peter G. '51 (HRT) [I] Hartford, CT Saint Francis Hospital and Medical Center.
Mitchell, Robert A. *s.j.* '56 (SY) [B] Syracuse, NY Le Moyne College; [S] Syracuse, NY Jesuits at LeMoyne, Inc.
Mitchell, Robert J. '85 (PAT) [3] Clifton, NJ St. Brendan Church.
Mitchell, Royce '74 (NO) Retired.
Mitchell, Msgr. Salvatore P. '42 (E) Retired.
Mitchell, Thomas R. '79 (HRT) On Duty Outside the Archdiocese.
Mitchell, Thomas R. '79 (MGZ) [4] Mayaquez, PR Church De El Buen Pastor Church.
Mitchell, Walter '61 (BRK) Brooklyn, NY Brooklyn House of Detention; Brooklyn, NY Brooklyn Correctional Facility.
Mitchell, Walter '91 (MIA) Pembroke Pines, FL St. Maximilian Kolbe Church.
Mitchell, Walter A. '61 (BRK) [118] Brooklyn, NY SS. Peter and Paul's Church.
Mitchell, William *ss.cc.* (FR) [A] Wareham, MA Sacred Hearts Retreat Center.
Mitchell, William J. '49 (PHX) Retired.
Mitchko, James A. '77 (PSC) Swoyersville, PA St. Nicholas Church.
Mitek, Jozef '84 (DET) [63] Detroit, MI SS. Peter and Paul Church.
Mitera, Stanislaus C. '41 (OM) Retired.
Mitka, John J. '66 (BUF) Jamestown, NY St. Peter and Paul Church.
Mitko, Joseph K. *o.ss.t.* '80 (TR) Asbury Park, NJ Our Lady of Mt. Carmel Church.
Mitolo, Frank A. '68 (PIT) Allegheny County, PA Allegheny General Hospital.
Mitolo, Msgr. Nicholas A. '54 (GBG) Jeannette, PA Ascension Church.
Mitrano, Joseph *c.s.b.* '41 (AUS) Kingsland, TX St. Charles Borromeo Church.
Mitros, Joseph *s.j.* '47 (NY) [Z] New York, NY Jesuit Community at Fordham University.
Mittelstadt, John *o.f.m.* '62 (GLP) Tohatchi, NM St. Mary Church.
Mitten, Stephen F. *s.j.* '95 (RC) [B] Howes, SD Kino Jesuit Community; [B] Howes, SD Kino Jesuit Community; [D] Howes, SD The Diocese of Rapid City Mahpiya na Maka Okoigna.
Mitty, Msgr. Edward J. '50 (NY) [99] New York, NY Our Lady of Victory Church.
Mitzel, Daniel C. '81 (HBG) [3] Harrisburg, PA St. Francis of Assisi Church.
Mitzi, John J. '57 (ORL) Retired.
Miyares, Carlos '81 (MIA) Absent on Leave.
Miyares, Gustavo J. '73 (MIA) [1] Hialeah, FL Immaculate Conception Church; [B] Opa Locka, FL St. Thomas University; [C] Miami, FL Msgr. Edward Pace High School.
Mizener, Paul *o.f.m.conv.* '64 (SP) Pinellas Park, FL Sacred Heart Church.
Mizeur, Thomas '73 (PEO) [J] Peoria, IL St. Francis' Medical Center.
Mizicko, Carroll *o.f.m.* '68 (SHP) [2] Monroe, LA Little Flower of Jesus Church.
Mlapah, Bernard *o.ss.t.* '80 (CC) [2] Corpus Christi, TX Christ the King Church.
Mmassi, Gabriel '93 (WDC) [M] Washington, DC Carroll House.
Moan, Francis X. *s.j.* (WDC) [E] Washington, DC Gonzaga College High School.
Mobley, William A. '73 (SLC) Retired.
Mocco, Charles W. '57 (GB) Special Assignment; [N] Green Bay, WI University of Wisconsin Ecumenical Center.
Mocio, Stephen J. '76 (DAL) Lancaster, TX St. Francis of Assisi Church.
Mociun, Casimir T. '42 (SFS) Retired.
Mock, Robert M. '84 (BUF) Canaseraga, NY St. Mary Church; Portageville, NY Assumption B.V.M. Church.
Mock, Timothy *c.m.m.* '52 (DET) [K] Dearborn Heights, MI Our Lady of Grace Monastery.
Mockaitis, Timothy '78 (P) [4] Eugene, OR St. Paul Church.
Mockel, George E. '75 (OAK) [1] Concord, CA St. Agnes Church.
Mockevicius, Charles *o.f.m.* (ROC) [I] Rochester, NY St. George's Rectory.
Mockevicius, Charles L. '47 (ROC) [17] Rochester, NY St. George Church; Retired.
Mockevicius, Charles L. '47 (RVC) Northport, NY Veteran's Hospital; Retired.
Mockevicius, Dominic '48 (ROC) Retired.
Mockler, Patrick J. '79 (BLX) Wiggins, MS St. Francis Xavier Church; [G] Perkinston, MS Perkinston Junior College.
Mockler, Peter F. '73 (BLX) Bay St. Louis, MS Our Lady of the Gulf Church.
Mockos, William J. '74 (PAT) Absent on Leave.
Moczarny, Chester B. '47 (LC) Retired; [I] La Crosse, WI Holy Cross (Seminary) Diocesan Center.
Moczydlowski, Chester M. '73 (CHR) Taylors, SC Prince of Peace Church.
Mode, Daniel L. '92 (ARL) McLean, VA St. John's Church; [D] Arlington, VA Bishop Denis J. O'Connell High School.
Modeen, James '81 (TUC) [E] Tucson, AZ Carondelet Health Care Corporation of Arizona, Inc.; [F] Tucson, AZ Regina Cleri Center.
Moder, John *s.m.* '79 (SAT) [B] San Antonio, TX Marianist Formation Community; [C] San Antonio, TX The United Colleges of San Antonio; [C] San Antonio, TX St. Mary's University of San Antonio, Texas; [M] San Antonio, TX Marianist Formation Community.
Moder, John *s.m.* '79 (STL) [P] St. Louis, MO Provincialate of the Society of Mary, Province of St. Louis.
Moder, John J. *s.m.* '79 (SAT) [C] San Antonio, TX St. Mary's University of San Antonio, Texas.
Modica, John '45 (COV) [M] Melbourne, KY Holy Family Home.
Modino, Roman A. '86 (TR) [1] Trenton, NJ St. Mary Cathedral.
Modlin, William F. '96 (PRT) [1] Portland, ME Cathedral of the Immaculate Conception; South Portland, ME Maine Youth Center; South Portland, ME Men's Correctional Center; Thomaston, ME Maine State Prison; Warren, ME Super Maximum Facility & Minimum Facility; Awaiting Assignment.
Modrys, Walter F. *s.j.* '78 (NY) [51] New York, NY St. Ignatius Loyola Church; [Z] New York, NY St. Ignatius Loyola Residence.
Modugno, Msgr. Thomas A. '66 (NY) [76] New York, NY St. Monica Church.
Moeder, August L. '53 (SAL) Retired.
Moeder, John A. '57 (SAL) Belleville, KS St. Edward's Church
Moeggenberg, Raymond '56 (SAG) [E] Saginaw, MI St. Mary's Medical Center of Saginaw, Inc.
Moeglein, James G. *o.s.c.* '70 (LIN) [A] Hastings, NE Crosier Monastery.
Moell, Carl J. *s.j.* '53 (CIN) [28] Cincinnati, OH St. Francis Xavier Church.
Moellenberndt, Duane R. '76 (MAD) Fort Atkinson, WI St. Joseph Church.
Moeller, Msgr. George B. '62 (BAL) [47] Baltimore, MD St. Joseph Church.
Moeller, Louis '51 (SAN) Ballinger, TX St. Mary Star of the Sea Church.
Moelter, Joel *o.carm.* '51 (JOL) [J] Darien, IL Carmelite Fathers Provincial Office.
Moen, Larry *c.m.f.* (LA) [R] Los Angeles, CA Claretian Retreat Center Community.
Moenkedrick, Leo '86 (SCL) Breckenridge, MN St. Mary of the Presentation Church.
Moerman, Stephen A. '94 (PH) Lansdale, PA St. Stanislaus Church.
Moert, Jerome S. '44 (L) Retired; [L] Louisville, KY Bishop David Apartments.
Moeschler, William H. *m.m.* '44 (NY) [Z] Maryknoll, NY Maryknoll Fathers and Brothers.
Moeslein, Francis R. '58 (R) Morehead City, NC St. Egbert Church.
Mofan, Feliciano '79 (SFR) San Carlos, CA St. Charles Church.
Moffat, Gerald '56 (SEA) Langley, WA St. Hubert Church.
Moffat, Joseph *c.s.b.* '61 (CHI) [30] Chicago, IL St. Bonaventure Church.
Moffatt, Charles P. *s.s.j.* '57 (MOB) [15] Mobile, AL Most Pure Heart of Mary Church.
Moffatt, Timothy *t.o.r.* '66 (SP) [2] Tampa, FL Christ the King Church.
Moffitt, Joseph M. *s.j.* '44 (WDC) [M] Washington, DC The Jesuit Community at Georgetown University.
Moffitt, Venard *t.o.r.* '55 (SP) [13] Tampa, FL St. Patrick Church.
Moffo, James '77 (SD) Absent on Sick Leave.
Moffo, Joseph G. *c.s.* '59 (HRT) [3] New Haven, CT St. Anthony's Church.
Moga, Michael D. *s.j.* '64 (NY) [Z] New York, NY Jesuit Community at Fordham University.
Mogilka, Erwin E. '49 (MIL) Retired.
Mohan, Oliver *o.m.i.* '48 (PHX) [6] Scottsdale, AZ St. Maria Goretti Church.
Mohan, Msgr. Robert Paul '46 (WDC) Retired; [C] Washington, DC Catholic University of America, The.
Mohan, Msgr. Thomas J. '35 (CHI) [69] Chicago, IL St. Genevieve Church; Retired.
Mohen, Bernard N. '61 (NEW) [3] East Orange, NJ St. Joseph's Church.
Mohl, Andrew '84 (BAL) Hagerstown, MD St. Ann Church.
Mohnickey, Ronald *t.o.r.* '71 (STU) [A] Steubenville, OH Franciscan University of Steubenville; [F] Steubenville, OH Holy Spirit Monastery.
Mohnickey, Ronald H. '71 (STU) [I] Steubenville, OH Jefferson County Technical Institute
Moholy, Noel *o.f.m.* '41 (LA) [R] Santa Barbara, CA Franciscan Friary, Order of Friars Minor (Old Mission).
Moholy, Ralph J. *s.j.* '44 (SJ) [M] Los Gatos, CA California Province of the Society of Jesus, Jesuit Provincial Office.
Mohr, J. Patrick *s.j.* '75 (SCR) [C] Scranton, PA University of Scranton.
Mohr, Richard G. '67 (BEL) Marion, IL St. Joseph Church.
Mohr, Simon *o.f.m.conv.* '57 (ALB) [A] Rensselaer, NY Conventual Franciscan Friars.
Mohr, Thomas H. '58 (DAV) Absent on Leave.
Mohrman, J. Gregory *o.s.b.* '86 (STL) [F] Creve Coeur, MO St. Louis Priory School; [G] Creve Coeur, MO St. Louis Priory School; [P] St. Louis, MO The Abbey of St. Mary and St. Louis.
Moineau, John A. '87 (GBG) Murrysville, PA Mother of Sorrows Church.
Moise, Burnet '94 (NEW) [3] Irvington, NJ Sacred Heart of Jesus Church; On Duty Outside the Archdiocese.
Moisin, Michael '88 (ROM) Special Assignment.
Mokarzel, Galeb *o.m.i.* '57 (SAT) [72] San Antonio, TX San Juan De Los Lagos Church.
Mokluk, John M. *o.s.f.s.* '70 (WIL) [B] Wilmington, DE Salesianum School.
Mokris, Michael '61 (PBR) Retired.
Mokris, Michael '61 (PSC) Lopez, PA SS. Peter and Paul Church.
Mokrzycki, M. Joseph '65 (TR) [1] Long Branch, NJ Our Lady Star of the Sea Church.
Mol, Joseph C. '77 (CHI) Hickory Hills, IL St. Patricia Church.
Molan, Msgr. John E. '53 (MAN) Auburn, NH St. Peter Church.
Molano, Ernesto '56 (MIA) Miami Shores, FL St. Rose of Lima Church.
Moleski, Martin X. *s.j.* '81 (BUF) [O] Buffalo, NY Canisius Jesuit Community.
Molewski, Andrew '82 (WIL) [5] Wilmington, DE St. Elizabeth Church.
Moley, Kevin *c.ss.r.* '68 (BRK) [107] Brooklyn, NY Our Lady of Perpetual Help Basilica.
Moley, Kevin *c.ss.r.* '70 (SJN) [2] San Juan, PR San Agustin Church.
Molina, Angel '88 (DEN) [A] Denver, CO Redemptoris Mater House of Formation.
Molina, Arturo '83 (LEX) Manchester, KY St. Ann Church; Manchester, KY Federal Correctional Institution.
Molina, Jose F. '95 (ELP) [4] El Paso, TX Blessed Sacrament Church.
Molinari, Todd '95 (P) Grants Pass, OR St. Anne Church.
Molinaro, Kenneth *c.s.c.* '76 (CHI) [D] Niles, IL Notre Dame High School.
Molinaro, Kenneth M. *c.s.c.* '76 (FTW) [J] South Bend, IN Congregation of Holy Cross Indiana Province Provincial House.
Molinaro, Matthew J. '49 (LC) Arkansaw, WI St. Joseph Church.
Molinelli, Louis *s.d.b.* '86 (NEW) [C] Ramsey, NJ Don Bosco Preparatory High School for Boys.
Molini, Thomas M. '85 (STL) [A] St. Louis, MO Kenrick-Glennon Seminary.
Moliski, Wendel *o.f.m.cap.* '50 (PIT) [5] Butler, PA St. Wendelin Church; [N] Herman, PA St. Mary's Friary.
Molitor, Donald '63 (STL) [1] University City, MO All Saints Church; [A] St. Louis, MO Kenrick-Glennon Seminary.
Molka, Victor J., Jr. '78 (PIT) [1] New Castle, PA Mary, Mother of Hope Church.
Moll, Walter J. '85 (ALT) Ebensburg, PA Holy Name Church.
Mollan, Paul F. '54 (OKL) [6] Oklahoma City, OK Church of the Epiphany of the Lord; Special Assignment.
Mollan, Ralph R. '43 (CHI) [4] Mt. Prospect, IL St. Thomas a Becket Church; Retired.
Molling, Mark L. '80 (MIL) Wales, WI Ethan Allen School for Boys.
Mollison, Roger W. '64 (DEN) [3] Englewood, CO St. Louis Church.
Mollohan, James L. '51 (CHI) [79] Chicago, IL Holy Angels Church; Retired.
Molloy, Msgr. Cronan T. '44 (STU) Minerva, OH St. Gabriel the Archangel Church; Retired.
Molloy, Francis P. *s.j.* '50 (BO) [W] Chestnut Hill, MA The Jesuit Community at Boston College.
Molloy, Msgr. James E. '72 (PH) [A] Wynnewood, PA Theological Seminary of St. Charles Borromeo, Overbrook.
Molloy, John *c.p.m.* '46 (OWN) [F] South Union, KY Fathers of Mercy.
Molloy, Joseph '83 (SFD) Newton, IL St. Thomas Church.
Molloy, Msgr. Patrick J. '40 (STL) Retired.
Molloy, Msgr. Thomas E. *j.c.d.* '70 (RVC) Roosevelt, NY Queen of the Most Holy Rosary Church.
Molloy, William T. '88 (MET) Retired.
Molnar, Anthony '34 (FTW) [15] South Bend, IN Our Lady of Hungary Church; Retired.
Molnar, John J. *o.s.a.* '66 (MIL) [8] Kenosha, WI Our Lady of the Holy Rosary Church.

Molnar, Jude *t.o.r.* '65 (WH) [Q] Fairmont, WV Fairmont State College Newman Center.
Molnar, Michael A. '76 (DET) [6] Westland, MI St. Theodore of Canterbury Church.
Molnar, Richard L. '39 (PIT) Retired.
Molodowitz, Augustine '59 (PHU) Perth Amboy, NJ Assumption of B.V.M. Church.
Molokie, Jerome M. *o.praem.* '95 (ORG) [D] Siverado, CA St. Michael's College Preparatory High School; [H] Silverado, CA Norbertine Fathers.
Molon, Erlindo N. '59 (STA) [2] Gainesville, FL Holy Faith Church.
Moloney, Msgr. Alphonsus '63 (SD) [9] San Diego, CA Immaculate Conception Church.
Moloney, Bean '58 (SAC) Retired and in Senior Ministry.
Moloney, Msgr. James A. '56 (DET) [2] Dearborn Heights, MI St. Anselm Church.
Moloney, John '72 (LA) Downey, CA Our Lady of Perpetual Help Church.
Moloney, John C. '91 (PH) Ardsley, PA Queen of Peace Church.
Moloney, Patrick W. '77 (NTN) Leave of Absence.
Moloney, Msgr. Stephan J. '82 (COL) [39] Columbus, OH Saint Stephen the Martyr Church; Gahanna, OH St. Matthew Church.
Moloney, Thomas J. *s.a.c.* '73 (DET) [6] Sterling Heights, MI St. Matthias Church.
Molony, Francis J. '42 (NY) Retired; [Z] New York, NY Our Lady of Consolation Residence.
Molter, Richard J. '64 (MIL) [1] Racine, WI St. Edward's Church.
Moltesz, Joseph E. *s.j.* '57 (NY) [BB] Staten Island, NY Mount Manresa Jesuit Retreat House.
Molumby, Donald J. '56 (SFS) Miller, SD St. Ann Church.
Molumby, John '77 (SAC) Auburn, CA St. Joseph Church.
Molyn, John A. '81 (ALB) Special Assignment; [G] Watervliet, NY St. Colman's Home; [M] Watervliet, NY St. Colman's Convent.
Monacell, Cornelius J. *s.j.* '59 (SFR) [N] San Francisco, CA Jesuit Community at University of San Francisco.
Monaco, James M. '85 (BUF) [8] Buffalo, NY Annunciation Church.
Monaco, Samuel '88 (NEW) North Arlington, NJ Queen of Peace Church.
Monaco, Vincent *c.s.* '57 (BO) [2] Somerville, MA St. Anthony Church.
Monaghan, Msgr. Charles J. '41 (PH) Retired.
Monaghan, Fergus '72 (SPC) [5] Springfield, MO St. Elizabeth Ann Seton Church.
Monaghan, Msgr. George (SFR) [K] San Rafael, CA Nazareth House.
Monaghan, Msgr. George D. '41 (SR) Retired.
Monaghan, George P. '80 (DAL) Denison, TX St. Patrick Church.
Monaghan, James *s.j.* '46 (SJ) [M] Los Gatos, CA California Province of the Society of Jesus, Jesuit Provincial Office; [M] Los Gatos, CA Sacred Heart Jesuit Center.
Monaghan, John T. '63 (NY) [E] New York, NY Cardinal Spellman High School.
Monaghan, Justin '66 (SPC) West Plains, MO St. Mary Church.
Monaghan, Robert '62 (STP) [9] Minneapolis, MN Incarnation Church.
Monaghan, Thomas E. *c.ss.r.* '44 (STL) [P] Liguori, MO St. Clement Health Care Center.
Monaghan, Thomas J. '70 (MAD) Mount Horeb, WI St. Ignatius Church.
Monagle, Robert J. '70 (BO) [4] Quincy, MA St. Joseph Church.
Monahan, David '53 (OKL) Mangum, OK Sacred Heart Church.
Monahan, Gregory *t.o.r.* '90 (WH) [H] Wheeling, WV Wheeling Hospital.
Monahan, Msgr. Jeremiah P. '60 (NY) [E] New York, NY Cardinal Spellman High School.
Monahan, Joseph E. '77 (DEN) Littleton, CO St. Mary Church.
Monahan, Joseph R. '62 (STL) Ballwin, MO Holy Infant Church.
Monahan, Kieran *o.f.m.* '65 (PRT) [6] Portland, ME St. Peter's Church.
Monahan, Paul '60 (DM) Glenwood, IA Our Lady of the Holy Rosary Church.
Monahan, Richard J. '59 (BGP) Retired.
Monan, J. Donald *s.j.* '55 (BO) [W] Chestnut Hill, MA The Jesuit Community at Boston College.
Monan, J. Donald *s.j.* '55 (WDC) [M] Washington, DC Leonard Neale House.
Moncher, Raymond F. '58 (MAR) Munising, MI Sacred Heart of Jesus Church.
Mondello, Donald J. '60 (GBG) [1] Latrobe, PA Holy Family Church.
Mondik, Michael '73 (PSC) Minersville, PA SS. Peter and Paul Church.
Mondor, Christian *o.f.m.* '51 (ORG) [3] Huntington Beach, CA SS. Simon and Jude Church.
Mondragon, Anselmo *t.o.r.* '91 (AUS) [2] Waco, TX St. Francis on the Brazos Church.
Mondragon, Antonio '63 (SFE) [3] Albuquerque, NM Community of the Risen Saviour Church.
Mondragon, Ezequiel '62 (DET) Imlay City, MI Sacred Heart Church.
Mondzelewski, Dominic '69 (CLV) [E] Cleveland, OH Benedictine High School; [P] Cleveland, OH Benedictine Order of Cleveland.
Moneck, George J. '89 (PIT) Roscoe, PA St. Joseph Church; Greene County, PA State Correctional Institution at Waynesburg.
Mones, Benjamin S. '58 (ELP) Canutillo, TX St. Patrick Church.
Monestero, John '75 (ORG) [3] Anaheim, CA St. Justin Martyr Church; Absent on Sick Leave.
Monestime, Perard C. *s.j.* '85 (BO) [W] Boston, MA The Society of Jesus of New England-Provincial Offices.
Monestine, Perard C. *s.j.* '85 (STL) [P] St. Louis, MO Bellarmine House of Studies.
Monet, Zachary *o.carm.* '60 (NEW) Paramus, NJ Carmelite Chapel of St. Therese Church.
Moneta, Msgr. Robert G. '51 (PSC) Newark, NJ St. George Church.
Monforton, Jeffrey '94 (DET) Graduate Studies.
Mongelluzzo, Msgr. James A. '74 (WOR) [5] Leominster, MA Our Lady of the Lake Church.
Mongeon, Peter M. '83 (NO) On Duty Outside the Archdiocese.
Mongiello, Anthony P. '80 (ALN) Girardville, PA St. Joseph Church; [C] Ashland, PA Cardinal Brennan Jr./Sr. High School.
Mongiello, Robert '87 (VEN) Punta Gorda, FL Sacred Heart Church.
Mongrain, Dennis '77 (LA) Simi Valley, CA St. Peter Claver Church.
Monica, Ted J. '86 (OG) Absent on Leave.
Moniz, Hyacinth '40 (PRO) Retired.
Moniz, Joseph '64 (LA) Hawthorne, CA St. Joseph Church.
Monks, James L. *s.j.* '34 (BO) [W] Weston, MA Campion Health Center, Inc.
Monmonier, Hugh *o.s.b.* '45 (WDC) [M] Washington, DC St. Anselm's Abbey.
Monnens, Merle W. '56 (NU) De Graff, MN St. Bridget Church; Lucan, MN Our Lady of Victory Church; Milroy, MN St. Michael Church.
Monnerat, Brian W. '88 (HRT) [3] Enfield, CT St. Bernard's Church.
Monnig, Francis R. '60 (CIN) Camden, OH St. Mary's Church.
Monnin, Robert J. '55 (CIN) Vandalia, OH St. Christopher Church.
Monogue, Michael G. '85 (STP) [16] Minneapolis, MN St. Anne Church.
Monohan, Duncan W. '77 (SD) Winterhaven, CA St. Thomas Church.
Monohan, Thomas J. '58 (RCK) Durand, IL St. Mary Church.
Monostori, Benedict *o.cist.* '44 (DAL) [M] Irving, TX Cistercian Abbey of Our Lady of Dallas.
Monreal, Jesus *o.carm.* '69 (ARE) Morovis, PR Nuestra Senora del Carmen Church.
Monroe, Charles F. '75 (WOR) [8] Worcester, MA Our Lady of the Angels Church.
Monroe, Clement *c.ss.r.* '53 (NO) New Orleans, LA Memorial Medical Center.
Monroe, Edward *c.ss.r.* '61 (STP) Brooklyn Center, MN St. Alphonsus Church.
Monroe, Msgr. Henry T. *p.a., v.e.* '53 (FR) Centerville, MA Our Lady of Victory Church.
Monroe, Lee '69 (CLV) [A] Wickliffe, OH Borromeo Seminary.
Monsalue, Alfred (BO) [9] Cambridge, MA St. Mary of the Annunciation Church.
Monshau, Michael *o.p.* '88 (DET) [2] St. Clair Shores, MI St. Gertrude Church; [A] Orchard Lake, MI SS. Cyril and Methodius Seminary.
Monsour, Raymond G. '63 (STP) Le Center, MN St. Mary Church.
Montag, Bernard J. '32 (SC) Retired.
Montag, John F. *s.j.* '93 (MIL) [P] Milwaukee, WI Jesuit Provincial Office, Wisconsin Province.
Montague, George *s.m.* '58 (SAT) [C] San Antonio, TX St. Mary's University of San Antonio, Texas.
Montague, George T. *s.m.* '58 (SAT) [M] San Antonio, TX Casa Maria Marianist Community.
Montague, Hugh *s.o.cist.* '82 (ALN) [K] New Ringgold, PA Cistercian Conventual Priory, St. Mary's Priory.
Montague, James G. '84 (BO) Absent on Leave.
Montalbano, Daniel F. '72 (CHI) [183] Chicago, IL Resurrection Church.
Montalbano, Frank *o.m.i.* '47 (NO) [1] New Orleans, LA St. Louis Cathedral; [A] New Orleans, LA Notre Dame Seminary Graduate School of Theology.
Montalbano, Joseph E. '55 (ALX) Moreauville, LA Our Lady of Sorrows Church; Moreauville, LA Sacred Heart Church.
Montanaro, Guido G. '69 (BGP) [10] Bridgeport, CT Holy Rosary Church.
Montanaro, James *o.m.v.* '83 (BO) [B] Boston, MA Oblate Provincialate.
Montano, Angel *m.j.* '92 (GAL) [74] Houston, TX St. Stephen Church.
Montano, Msgr. Edward J. '45 (NY) Retired.
Montavon, Thomas G. '61 (CLV) Brunswick, OH St. Colette Church.
Montcalm, Msgr. Rosario L.U. '36 (SPR) Retired.
Monte, Dominic V. *o.f.m.* (WDC) [M] Silver Spring, MD Gemelli House.
Montealegre, Ruy '93 (MIA) [20] Miami, FL St. James Church.
Montecalvo, Carlo F. '73 (PRO) On Duty Outside the Diocese.
Montecino, Henry R. *s.j.* '47 (LAF) [A] Grand Coteau, LA St. Charles College.
Monteiro, Alfredo '73 (NY) [116] New York, NY St. Teresa Church.
Monteiro, Galdino *s.f.x.* '65 (P) Sublimity, OR St. Boniface Church.
Monteiro, Ralph *o.s.a.* '66 (SR) Hoopa, CA Mission of Blessed Kateri Tekakwitha Church.
Montejano, John '94 (LA) Baldwin Park, CA St. John the Baptist Church.
Montelaro, Thomas (LAF) Leroy, LA Our Lady of Perpetual Help Church; Absent on Sick Leave.
Monteleone, Jacob A. '75 (SP) Zephyrhills, FL St. Joseph Church.
Monteleone, Pascal A. '72 (PH) Wayne, PA St. Katharine of Siena Church; [D] Springfield, PA Cardinal O'Hara High School.
Monteleone, Raphael D. '30 (RVC) Retired.
Montella, Alban V. *o.f.m.* '55 (NY) [Z] New York, NY Franciscan Province of the Immaculate Conception; [Z] Mount Vernon, NY St. Bernardine of Siena Friary.
Montemayor, Teodoro *s.d.b.* '83 (LA) [W] Rosemead, CA St. Joseph's Salesian Youth Renewal Center.
Montenegro, Blas *o.a.r.* '49 (NY) [126] Bronx, NY St. Anselm Church; [157] Bronx, NY St. John Vianney, Cure of Ars Church.
Montero, Eduardo G. '73 (PH) [K] Philadelphia, PA St. Vincent's Orphanage Tacony; [EE] Philadelphia, PA St. Vincent's Orphan Asylum-St. Vincent's Comprehensive Emergency Shelter Program.
Montero, Hugo L. '91 (STP) [9] St. Paul, MN Our Lady of Guadalupe Church.
Montes, Jesse *s.d.b.* '79 (MRY) [D] Watsonville, CA St. Francis Youth Center.
Montes De Oca, Jose '96 (NEW) [10] Elizabeth, NJ St. Patrick's Church.
Montesino, Efrain '85 (ARE) [5] Vega-Baja, PR Parroquia de San Martin de Porres Church.
Montgomery, Msgr. James F. '56 (WDC) [4] Washington, DC Annunciation Church.
Montgomery, Matthias *o.c.d.* '62 (MIL) [P] Holy Hill, WI Discalced Carmelite Monastery.
Montgomery, William L. '79 (WDC) Special Ministries; [D] Washington, DC Archbishop Carroll High School.
Monti, Dominic V. *o.f.m.* '71 (WDC) [U] West Bethesda, MD Missionaries of the Kingship of Christ.
Monti, Robert M. '61 (LC) On Duty Outside the Diocese.
Monticello, Msgr. Robert V. '51 (DET) [J] Livonia, MI Ryan Senior Residences of the Archdiocese of Detroit, Inc.
Montiel, Jose M. '57 (FRS) Merced, CA Sacred Heart Church.
Montilla, Felix Abreu *c.s.sp.* (SJN) [B] Bayamon, PR Teologado Padre Liberman.
Montminy, Marc R. '77 (MAN) [12] Manchester, NH St. Marie Church; [17] Manchester, NH Sacred Heart of Jesus Church.
Montminy, Paul D. '78 (MAN) Gonic, NH St. Leo Church; Rochester, NH Holy Rosary Church.
Montondon, Walter '57 (BEA) Retired.
Montoro, Joseph J. '92 (GRY) Absent on Leave.
Montoya, Ernest '89 (LA) [12] Long Beach, CA Our Lady of Refuge Church.
Montoya, Ernest '89 (SFE) Retired.
Montoya, Jose J. '57 (PBL) Retired.
Montoya, Juan '89 (MIA) [3] Pompano Beach, FL St. Coleman Church.
Montoya, Leobardo D. (SFR) [41] San Francisco, CA St. Patrick Church.
Montoya, Luis F. '87 (PCE) [G] Alhambra, Ponce, PR Prelature of the Holy Cross and Opus Dei.
Montoya, Michael *c.i.c.m.* '94 (BWN) La Joya, TX Our Lady, Queen of Angels Church.
Montoya, Msgr. Paul '73 (LA) Inglewood, CA St. John Chrysostom Church.
Montplaisir, Roland A. '40 (MAN) Retired.
Montville, Edmund J. *s.j.* '45 (DET) [P] Clarkston, MI Colombiere Center.
Monzillo, Oneil '53 (NO) Retired.
Moodie, Michael R. *s.j.* '79 (LA) [C] Los Angeles, CA Loyola Marymount University.
Moody, Michael *s.v.d.* '64 (LAF) Plaisance, LA St. Joseph Church.
Moody, Quentin '85 (NO) [62] New Orleans, LA St. Theresa Of The Child Jesus Church.
Moody, Thomas A. '67 (OG) Louisville, NY St. Lawrence

Church; Madrid, NY St. John the Baptist Church.
Moody, William (BAL) Retired.
Mooney, Charles A. *s.j.* '42 (DET) [P] Clarkston, MI Colombiere Center.
Mooney, Dennis M. '77 (PH) [66] Philadelphia, PA St. Hugh of Cluny Church.
Mooney, Msgr. George A. '48 (BRK) Retired.
Mooney, Harold T. '55 (PEO) Retired.
Mooney, J. Terence *c.m.* '48 (MIA) [34] Miami, FL St. Vincent De Paul Church.
Mooney, Michael P. '63 (PT) [4] Pensacola, FL Nativity of Our Lord Church.
Mooney, Richard T. '79 (RIC) [4] Virginia Beach, VA Holy Family Church.
Mooney, Robert J. '68 (CIN) [A] Cincinnati, OH The Athenaeum of Ohio; [B] Cincinnati, OH Mt. St. Mary's Seminary of the West; [B] Cincinnati, OH Mt. St. Mary's Seminary of the West.
Mooney, Thomas J. '47 (BO) Lakeville, MA Saints Martha and Mary Church; Retired.
Mooney, William '55 (SD) Poway, CA St. Michael Church.
Mooney, William C. '68 (STA) St. Augustine Shores, FL Corpus Christi Church.
Mooney, William J. '68 (PAT) Florham Park, NJ Holy Family Church.
Moons, Joseph *c.p.* '77 (CHI) [N] Chicago, IL Passionist Provincial Office.
Mooradd, Paul '84 (SAM) Newtown Square, PA St. Sharbel Mission Church.
Moorby, William A. '82 (ROC) Newark Valley, NY St. John the Evangelist Church; [L] Rochester, NY Catholic Charismatic Renewal.
Moore, Anthony F. *o.f.m.* '51 (HRT) Winsted, CT St. Joseph's Church.
Moore, Augustine '60 (SFE) Espanola, NM Sacred Heart Church.
Moore, Brian R. '83 (COL) [A] Columbus, OH Pontifical College Josephinum.
Moore, Brian R. '83 (DOD) On Duty Outside the Diocese.
Moore, Charles E. '36 (CIN) [S] Cincinnati, OH Archdiocesan Central Council of Cincinnati.
Moore, Charles F. '88 (TR) Neptune, NJ Holy Innocents Church.
Moore, Charles L. '36 (CIN) Retired.
Moore, Charles L. '38 (CIN) Middletown, OH Holy Family Church.
Moore, Christian *o.f.m.conv.* '65 (CLV) [1] Lorain, OH St. Anthony of Padua Church.
Moore, Christopher P. '77 (BAL) [30] Baltimore, MD St. Elizabeth of Hungary Church.
Moore, Clarke W. '64 (TUC) Tubac, AZ St. Ann Church.
Moore, Daniel F. '84 (MEM) [24] Memphis, TN Church of the Resurrection.
Moore, Donald C. '65 (OKL) [15] Oklahoma City, OK St. Patrick's Church; Special Assignment; [H] Oklahoma City, OK St. Ann's Home, Inc.
Moore, Donald J. *s.j.* '60 (NY) [Z] New York, NY West Side Jesuit Community.
Moore, Msgr. Edmund J. '59 (SHP) [1] Monroe, LA Jesus the Good Shepherd Church.
Moore, Edmund R. *o.f.m.* '45 (L) [15] Louisville, KY St. Boniface Church; [L] Louisville, KY St. Boniface Friary.
Moore, Edward F. *m.m.* '58 (SJ) [M] Los Altos, CA Maryknoll.
Moore, Edward F. '59 (BUR) Essex Center, VT St. Pius X Church.
Moore, Elmer R. '54 (LEX) Retired.
Moore, Francis A. *s.j.* '47 (PHX) [B] Phoenix, AZ Brophy College Preparatory.
Moore, Francis M. *s.j.* '50 (DET) [P] Clarkston, MI Colombiere Center.
Moore, Frederick B. (DET) [H] Pontiac, MI St. Joseph Mercy - Oakland.
Moore, George B. '66 (PH) [22] Philadelphia, PA St. Benedict Church.
Moore, Gerald T. '39 (SEA) Retired.
Moore, Gregory *o.f.m.conv.* '82 (SPR) [A] Granby, MA St. Hyacinth College and Seminary.
Moore, Gregory J. *o.p.* (MAD) [3] Madison, WI Blessed Sacrament Church.
Moore, Harold W. '50 (WH) Oak Hill, WV SS. Peter and Paul Church.
Moore, J. Patrick '89 (P) Hillsboro, OR St. Matthew Church.
Moore, Msgr. J. Raymond '56 (SD) Retired.
Moore, James (SB) [6] San Bernardino, CA St. Anne Church.
Moore, James P. '88 (SFE) [22] Albuquerque, NM St. Bernadette Church.
Moore, Msgr. James R. '67 (NY) Crestwood, NY Church of the Annunciation.
Moore, James T. '84 (GAL) [60] Houston, TX Our Lady of Walsingham Church.
Moore, James W. *s.j.* '59 (PH) [C] Philadelphia, PA St. Joseph's University; [Z] Philadelphia, PA Jesuit Community at St. Joseph's University.
Moore, John '45 (FAR) [E] Fargo, ND Riverview Place, Inc.
Moore, John Charles '78 (BAL) Middletown, MD Holy Family Catholic Community Church.
Moore, John E. '45 (FAR) Retired.
Moore, John F. '60 (FR) North Falmouth, MA St. Elizabeth Seton Church.
Moore, John J. *s.m.* '43 (WDC) [M] Washington, DC Marist Provincial House.
Moore, John J. '57 (FRS) Corcoran, CA Calif. State Prison.
Moore, John J. '57 (GF) On Duty Outside of the Diocese.
Moore, John P. *c.p.* '47 (BRK) [U] Jamaica, NY Immaculate Conception Monastery.
Moore, John P. '55 (NY) [52] New York, NY Immaculate Conception Church.
Moore, John Patrick *c.p.* '47 (BRK) [W] Jamaica, NY Bishop Molloy Retreat House for Laymen.
Moore, John R. '64 (RVC) Babylon, NY St. Joseph's Church
Moore, Jon H. '81 (WIN) Absent on Leave.
Moore, Joseph P. '71 (BGP) On Duty Outside the Diocese.
Moore, Joseph P. '71 (PRO) [A] Coventry, RI The Society of St. John Vianney.
Moore, Lawrence *s.j.* '77 (NO) [C] New Orleans, LA Loyola University.
Moore, Manning C. *o.s.f.s.* '67 (ARL) [D] Alexandria, VA Bishop Ireton High School; [J] Alexandria, VA Oblates of St. Francis de Sales Residence.
Moore, Matthias *c.s.sp.* '52 (NO) [39] New Orleans, LA St. John The Baptist Church.
Moore, Michael '77 (YAK) On Duty Outside the Diocese
Moore, Michael *s.p.s.* '84 (NEW) [N] Cliffside Park, NJ St. Patrick's Missionary Society.
Moore, Neil J. '60 (P) [29] Portland, OR St. Pius X Church.
Moore, Raymond H. '81 (WDC) [4] Bowie, MD St. Pius X Church.
Moore, Msgr. Robert (NY) North Tarrytown, NY Phelps Memorial Hospital.
Moore, Robert A. '46 (BRK) [36] Brooklyn, NY St. Ephrem's Church; Retired.
Moore, Msgr. Robert E. '55 (NY) Gardiner, NY St. Charles Borromeo Church; North Tarrytown, NY St. Teresa of Avila Church; Retired.
Moore, Robert J. *o.c.s.o.* '49 (ROC) [I] Piffard, NY Abbey of the Genesee.
Moore, Robert J. '83 (NY) [165] Bronx, NY St. Mary Star of the Sea Church.
Moore, Steven C. '76 (ANC) [8] Anchorage, AK St. Patrick Church.
Moore, Terence M. '67 (SLC) [9] Salt Lake City, UT St. Thomas More Church.
Moore, Thomas G. '88 (MET) Middlesex, NJ Our Lady of Mount Virgin Church.
Moore, Thomas M. *o.s.f.s.* '66 (SAG) [4] Saginaw, MI SS. Simon and Jude Church.
Moore, Timothy *o.carm.* '35 (JOL) [J] Darien, IL Carmelite Fathers Provincial Office.
Moore, Timothy *o.carm.* '35 (NEW) Englewood, NJ St. Cecilia's Church.
Moore, Ward P. '72 (NEW) Westwood, NJ St. Andrew's Church.
Moore, Wilbur E. '57 (OKL) Nicoma Park, OK Our Lady of Fatima Church.
Moore, William *ss.cc.* '75 (LA) San Dimas, CA Holy Name of Mary Church.
Moore, William C. '68 (STO) [2] Stockton, CA St. Bernadette Church.
Moore, William F. '69 (CAM) Pennsville, NJ Queen of the Apostles Church.
Moorman, John V. *s.j.* '68 (CHI) [D] Wilmette, IL Loyola Academy.
Moorman, Marcellus *o.f.m.* '45 (BR) [G] Baton Rouge, LA Ollie Steele Burden Manor; [H] Baton Rouge, LA Franciscan Residence; [I] Baton Rouge, LA Maryville Novitiate and Provincial House.
Moorman, Raymond J. '46 (STP) Retired.
Moorman, William J. *o.ss.t.* '79 (BAL) [M] Baltimore, MD Holy Trinity Monastery.
Moorman, William J. *o.ss.t.* '79 (WDC) [A] Washington, DC Theological College of the Catholic University of America
Moors, Clifton W. *s.m.* (BO) [12] Lawrence, MA Sacred Heart Church.
Moorse, Dustan *o.s.b.* '78 (SCL) [I] Collegeville, MN St. John's Abbey, of the Order of St. Benedict.
Moosbrugger, Robert F. *o.m.i.* '70 (STP) [N] St. Paul, MN Oblate Provincial Offices; [N] St. Paul, MN Oblate Residence.
Moquin, Raymond *m.s.* '54 (FR) [J] North Attleboro, MA Madonna Manor Inc.; [K] Attleboro, MA La Salette Shrine.
Mora, Juan R. '92 (ARE) [2] Arecibo, PR Church of Sagrado Corazon de Jesus.
Mora, Sergio '94 (OAK) [4] Hayward, CA St. Joachim Church.
Morabito, James *s.d.b.* '78 (PMB) Belle Glade, FL St. Philip Benizi Church.
Morabito, Vincent R. '87 (PH) Royersford, PA Sacred Heart Church.
Moraczewski, Albert S. *o.p.* '54 (BO) [FF] Braintree, MA Pope John Center.
Moraczewski, Albert S. *o.p.* '54 (STL) [P] St. Louis, MO St. Dominic Priory.
Moraes, Claudio *o.s.b.* '84 (GBG) [H] Latrobe, PA Saint Vincent Archabbey.
Moraga, Cecilio T. '84 (SD) Holtville, CA St. Joseph Church.
Moraghan, Vincent J. '65 (CLV) [28] Cleveland, OH Holy Name Church.
Moragne, Msgr. James C. '75 (NO) Paradis, LA St. John the Baptist Church.
Morahan, Gerald B. *o.p.* '52 (DET) [2] St. Clair Shores, MI St. Gertrude Church.
Morais, Jeremy J. *m.s.* '81 (STL) [P] St. Louis, MO La Salette Missionaries.
Moral, Alejandro *o.c.d.* '60 (CGS) [2] Caguas, PR San Jose Church.
Morales, Anibal '93 (MIA) [8] Miami, FL Mother of Christ Church.
Morales, Dan *o.m.i.* '90 (VIC) Port Lavaca, TX Our Lady of the Gulf Church.
Morales, Eduardo D. '96 (SAT) Fredericksburg, TX St. Mary's Church.
Morales, Elias '91 (PCE) Ensenada, PR Sacred Heart Church; Guanica, PR St. Anthony Abbot Church.
Morales, Eusebio Ramos '83 (CGS) Humacao, PR Dulce Nombre de Jesus Church.
Morales, Gonzalo '85 (FWT) Bridgeport, TX St. John the Baptizer Church; Decatur, TX Assumption of the Blessed Virgin Mary Church; Jacksboro, TX St. Mary Church.
Morales, Guillermo '88 (AMA) Dimmitt, TX Immaculate Conception Church.
Morales, J. Trinidad *s.m.* '61 (ELP) [39] El Paso, TX Santa Lucia Church.
Morales, Msgr. John F. '60 (GRY) Retired.
Morales, Jose '47 (ORG) Brea, CA St. Angela Merici Church; Retired.
Morales, Juan Bautista '83 (MGZ) Moca, PR Our Lady of Monserrate Church.
Morales, Luis Angel '83 (ARE) On Duty Outside the Diocese.
Morales, Raul '75 (PHX) Retired.
Morales, Raymond '81 (LA) Van Nuys, CA St. Bridget of Sweden Church.
Morales, Robert P. '66 (BRK) [63] Brooklyn, NY Immaculate Conception of the Blessed Virgin Mary Church.
Morales, Romain G. *c.m.* '73 (STL) [P] St. Louis, MO Vincentian Henrietta Residence.
Morales, Salomon (ARE) On Duty Outside the Diocese.
Morales, Salomon '63 (SJN) [21] Carolina, PR San Francisco de Asis Church.
Morales Berrios-Parroco, Raul '88 (CGS) Comerio, PR Santo Cristo de la Salud Church.
Moran, Msgr. Bernard J. '53 (OAK) [22] Oakland, CA St. Theresa of the Infant Jesus (The Little Flower) Church.
Moran, Chalres '67 (STU) Absent on Leave.
Moran, Charles *o.m.i.* '54 (BWN) [1] Brownsville, TX Immaculate Conception Cathedral.
Moran, Daniel F. '47 (BO) Lakeville, MA Saints Martha and Mary Church.
Moran, Donald V. '61 (MAD) Ridgeway, WI St. Bridget Church.
Moran, Edward C. '89 (RIC) Military Chaplains.
Moran, Edward F. '34 (HEL) Retired.
Moran, Edward J. '62 (WOR) Shrewsbury, MA St. Anne's Church.
Moran, Edward M. '76 (HRT) [6] West Hartford, CT St. Thomas the Apostle Church.
Moran, Edwin *c.p.* '61 (PIT) [N] Pittsburgh, PA St. Paul of the Cross Monastery; [N] Pittsburgh, PA St. Paul of the Cross Monastery.
Moran, Frank '59 (ORG) San Clemente, CA Our Lady of Fatima Church.
Moran, Gerard K. '71 (OAK) [2] Fremont, CA Holy Spirit Church.
Moran, Howard L. *s.j.* '51 (SPK) [K] Spokane, WA Regis Community.
Moran, Msgr. J. Thomas '57 (BUF) Youngstown, NY St. Bernard's Church.
Moran, James *c.o.* '89 (ALX) Mansura, LA Our Lady of Prompt Succor Church; Marksville, LA Holy Ghost Church.
Moran, James *c.o.* '89 (CHR) [E] Rock Hill, SC Oratory of St. Philip Neri, Congregation of the Oratory of Pontifical Rite.
Moran, James E. '59 (NU) Lafayette, MN St. Gregory the Great Church; West Newton Township, MN St. George Church.
Moran, James F. '71 (BO) Military & VA Chaplains.
Moran, James M. '74 (HRT) [5] West Hartford, CT St. Peter Claver Church.
Moran, Msgr. James P. '45 (GR) Retired.
Moran, Msgr. James P. '72 (MET) Iselin, NJ St. Cecelia Church.
Moran, James W. *c.s.p.* '64 (SD) [M] San Diego, CA

University of California at San Diego (Campus Ministry).
Moran, John V. '53 (MAN) Rye Beach, NH St. Theresa Church.
Moran, John W. '51 (DUB) Monona, IA St. Patrick's Church.
Moran, Joseph P. '56 (VEN) Retired.
Moran, Joseph P. '71 (HEL) Shelby, MT St. William Church.
Moran, Kevin '65 (SEA) Federal Way, WA St. Theresa Church.
Moran, Lawrence '52 (IND) Seelyville, IN Holy Rosary Church.
Moran, Lawrence J. '52 (IND) [6] Terre Haute, IN St. Patrick Church.
Moran, Leonard J. *s.m.* '45 (WDC) [M] Washington, DC Marist Provincial House.
Moran, Martin O., III '88 (HBG) [1] Lebanon, PA Assumption of the Blessed Virgin Mary Church.
Moran, Michael '63 (VNN) Van Nuys, CA Cathedral of St. Mary.
Moran, Michael F. '82 (MIL) Sheboygan Falls, WI St. Mary's Church.
Moran, Michael J. '58 (NEW) Hillsdale, NJ St. John the Baptist Church.
Moran, Owen '91 (PAT) Chatham, NJ St. Patrick's Church.
Moran, Patrick '43 (JOL) [I] Naperville, IL St. John Vianney Villa.
Moran, Patrick A. '43 (GF) Retired.
Moran, Patrick J. '58 (DUL) [7] Gary-New Duluth, MN St. Elizabeth's Church.
Moran, Msgr. Peter C. '65 (LA) Northridge, CA Our Lady of Lourdes Church.
Moran, Richard S. *c.ss.r.* '61 (BO) [13] Boston, MA Basilica of Our Lady of Perpetual Help; [3] Quincy, MA St. John the Baptist Church.
Moran, Robert B. '64 (SJ) Mountain View, CA St. Joseph the Worker Church.
Moran, Robert E. *c.s.p.* '64 (NY) [Z] Scarsdale, NY Paulist Fathers Generalate.
Moran, Robert E. '69 (LFT) Hartford City, IN St. John the Evangelist Church.
Moran, Stephen P. '92 (CLV) North Olmsted, OH St. Brendan Church.
Moran, Terence J. (BO) [60] Boston, MA St. Patrick Church.
Moran, Terrance *c.ss.r.* '82 (NY) [78] New York, NY Most Holy Redeemer Church.
Moran, Thomas *c.m.f.* '55 (CHI) [N] Oak Park, IL Claretian Fathers Headquarters of U.S.A. Eastern Province.
Moran, Thomas '88 (SFR) [20] San Francisco, CA St. Gabriel Church.
Moran, Thomas A. '71 (CHI) Lyons, IL St. Hugh Church.
Moran, Thomas A. '77 (CLV) [58] Cleveland, OH Our Lady of Peace Church.
Moran, Thomas J. '48 (NY) Retired.
Moran, Msgr. Timothy J. '76 (BO) [A] Boston, MA St. John's Seminary School of Theology.
Moran, W. Lawrence *c.s.b.* '46 (GAL) [Q] Sugar Land, TX Basilian Mission Center.
Moran, William H. *s.j.* '55 (LR) Siloam Springs, AR St. Mary's Church.
Morand, Robert '57 (DET) [57] Detroit, MI Our Lady of the Rosary Church.
Moras, Edward '81 (OKL) [12] Oklahoma City, OK St. James Church.
Moratelli, Ronald J. '69 (HBG) Bloomsburg, PA St. Columba Church.
Moratiel, Felix *o.s.a.* '62 (SJN) [18] Bayamon, PR Santa Rita de Casia Church.
Moraus, Govie '82 (SHP) [F] Shreveport, LA Motherhouse of the Daughters of the Cross in America.
Morawski, Stefan *o.f.m.conv.* '68 (BGP) [14] Bridgeport, CT St. Michael The Archangel Church.
Morbeck, George '52 (SPK) Curlew, WA St. Patrick Church.
Morbeck, George H. '52 (SPK) Republic, WA Immaculate Conception Church.
Morbito, Angelo L. '56 (SY) Solvay, NY St. Cecilia Church.
Morciniec, Peter J. '70 (SPC) Aurora, MO Holy Trinity Church; Verona, MO Sacred Heart Church.
Mordino, Robert F. '63 (WDC) Special Ministries; [P] Upper Marlboro, MD Our Lady of Mattaponi Youth Retreat and Conference Center.
Moreau, Charles *o.m.i.* '44 (MAN) [K] Colebrook, NH Shrine of Our Lady of Grace.
Moreau, Ernest P. '51 (SPR) Retired.
Moreau, George '51 (ORL) Retired.
Moreau, Randall P. '87 (LAF) Grand Prairie, LA St. Peter Church.
Moreau, Raymond J. '85 (OG) North Bangor, NY St. Augustine Church.
Moreci, Francis A. '33 (OM) Retired.
Moredo, Wilfredo Pena '74 (SJN) [2] Carolina, PR Santa Bernardita Soubirous Church.
Moreeuw, Leroy *c.pp.s.* (CLV) [53] Cleveland, OH Our Lady of Good Counsel Church.
Moreira, Nelson A. *s.s.j.* '72 (NO) [P] New Orleans, LA Josephite Fathers and Brothers.
Morel, Albert J. *s.c.* (PRO) [P] Harrisville, RI Provincial House.
Morel, John F. *c.i.c.m.* '39 (ARL) Madison, VA Our Lady of the Blue Ridge Church.
Morel, Paul A. '78 (WDC) Norbeck, MD St. Patrick Church.
Moreland, J. Gordon *s.j.* '64 (ORG) Special Assignment; [H] Orange, CA Jesuits; [K] Orange, CA House of Prayer for Priests.
Morell, Fernando '87 (ARE) Hatillo, PR Our Lady of Mt. Carmel Church.
Morell, J. William *o.m.i.* (SAT) [C] San Antonio, TX The United Colleges of San Antonio.
Morell, J. William *o.m.i.* '70 (SAT) [C] San Antonio, TX Oblate School of Theology.
Morelle, Edmund J. '53 (SY) Verona, NY Our Lady of Good Counsel Church.
Morelli, Gary '81 (DET) [3] Taylor, MI St. Cyril of Jerusalem Church.
Morelli, Gary J. '74 (SEA) Bellingham, WA Sacred Heart Church.
Morello, Msgr. Amedeo L. (TR) Retired.
Morello, Carl '83 (CHI) Park Ridge, IL St. Paul of the Cross Church.
Morello, Peter '78 (GLP) On Duty Outside of Diocese.
Morello, Peter '78 (PHX) Phoenix, AZ United States Veterans Affairs Medical Center.
Morello, Sam Anthony *o.c.d.* '62 (DAL) [K] Dallas, TX Mount Carmel Center.
Morelock, George L. '65 (SFD) Hillsboro, IL St. Agnes Church; Hillsboro, IL Graham Correctional Center.
Morency, Raymond P. '87 (PRT) Military Chaplains.
Moreno, Antonio *o.f.m.conv.* '80 (IND) [J] Mount Saint Francis, IN Provincial Headquarters for the Conventual Franciscan Province.
Moreno, David *s.d.b.* '79 (NY) [Z] New Rochelle, NY Salesian Provincial House.
Moreno, Joaquin *o.f.m.* (SFR) [7] San Francisco, CA St. Boniface Church.
Moreno, Jorge '63 (SD) Brawley, CA Our Lady of Perpetual Help Church.
Moreno, Jose (DAL) [1] Garland, TX Good Shepherd Church.
Moreno, Joseph '86 (BUF) [L] Buffalo, NY St. Francis Geriatric & Healthcare Services, Inc.
Moreno, Joseph F. '86 (BUF) [44] Buffalo, NY St. Margaret Church.
Moreno, Juan '60 (LSC) [5] Las Cruces, NM St. Genevieve Church.
Moreno, Kolbe *o.praem.* '93 (ORG) [H] Silverado, CA Norbertine Fathers.
Moreno, Robert '93 (STF) Lancaster, NY St. Basil Church.
Mores, Bernard J. *c.pp.s.* '40 (CIN) [M] Dayton, OH Provincial House of the Cincinnati Province of the Society of the Precious Blood.
Moreschi, Alex *i.m.c.* '73 (PIT) [N] Pittsburgh, PA Consolata Fathers.
Moreshead, Harold D. '55 (PRT) Mechanic Falls, ME Our Lady of Ransom Church.
Moretta, Msgr. John T. '68 (LA) [35] Los Angeles, CA Resurrection Church.
Moretti, Msgr. August '54 (LA) Pasadena, CA Assumption of the Blessed Virgin Mary Church.
Moretti, Edward D. '60 (VEN) Bradenton, FL SS. Peter and Paul the Apostles Church.
Moretti, Mark E. '95 (ARL) Vienna, VA St. Mark's Church.
Morey, Charles W. '80 (SPC) Sabbatical.
Morey, Daniel *o.f.m.* (NY) [13] New York, NY St. Anthony of Padua Church.
Morey, Robert E. '96 (BAL) Westminster, MD St. John Church.
Morfeld, Msgr. Frank G. '51 (DEN) [29] Denver, CO St. Francis de Sales Church.
Morfin, Francois J. *c.s.b.* '77 (GAL) [Q] Sugar Land, TX Basilian Mission Center.
Morfin, John N. '67 (GAL) [40] Houston, TX St. John Vianney Church.
Morgan, Arthur (BEA) Orangefield, TX St. Helen Church.
Morgan, Arthur '59 (LSC) Special Assignment.
Morgan, Brendan '64 (NO) River Ridge, LA St. Matthew the Apostle Church.
Morgan, Charles J. '79 (ALX) Winnsboro, LA St. Mary Church.
Morgan, Colum '51 (DET) Absent on Sick Leave.
Morgan, D. Terrence '76 (STA) Atlantic Beach, FL St. John the Baptist Church; On Duty Outside the Diocese.
Morgan, Dave J. *s.j.* '53 (SJ) [L] Los Altos, CA Jesuit Retreat House.
Morgan, Drew P. *c.o.* (PIT) [N] Pittsburgh, PA Congregation of the Oratory of St. Philip Neri; [Q] Slippery Rock, PA Office for Campus Ministry.
Morgan, Drew P. *c.o.* '94 (PIT) [Q] Slippery Rock, PA Office for Campus Ministry.
Morgan, Edward *c.ss.r.* '64 (WCH) [14] Wichita, KS St. Joseph Church; [G] Wichita, KS Redemptorist Mission House.
Morgan, Edward J. '37 (CHI) Retired.
Morgan, Francis C. *ss.cc.* (NY) Manhattan, NY U.S.V.A. Medical Center.
Morgan, George *c.m.f.* '88 (CHI) [149] Chicago, IL Our Lady of Guadalupe Church.
Morgan, George R. *o.s.a.* (BO) Andover, MA St. Augustine Church; Boston, MA Lawrence General Hospital.
Morgan, Greg *v.d.c.* '95 (SFR) [N] San Francisco, CA Verbum Dei Community.
Morgan, Guy *o.f.m.* '54 (NY) [Z] New York, NY Franciscan Friars, Order of Friars Manor.
Morgan, J.P. '91 (ORL) [1] Orlando, FL St. James Cathedral.
Morgan, James '60 (ALN) [G] Pottsville, PA Good Samaritan Regional Medical Center.
Morgan, James F. *s.j.* '54 (BO) [3] Newton, MA St. Ignatius Church.
Morgan, Jerome '62 (SAL) Dorrance, KS St. Joseph's Church; Wilson, KS St. Wenceslaus Church.
Morgan, John '58 (OAK) Retired.
Morgan, John A. '40 (ROC) Retired.
Morgan, John H. '51 (L) Retired.
Morgan, John W. '58 (B) Hailey, ID St. Charles Borromeo Church; Sun Valley, ID Our Lady of the Snows Church.
Morgan, John W. '58 (OAK) [3] Fremont, CA St. James The Apostle Church.
Morgan, Joseph '81 (OG) Champlain, NY St. Mary Church.
Morgan, Jude *ss.cc.* '50 (FR) [K] Fairhaven, MA Sacred Hearts Provincial House.
Morgan, Julian *c.p.* '53 (HRT) [M] West Hartford, CT Holy Family Monastery/Retreat.
Morgan, Kirk '74 (GF) Miles City, MT Sacred Heart Church.
Morgan, Maron '95 (RC) [B] Bethlehem, SD Holy Nativity Monastery.
Morgan, Martin '70 (TLS) [5] Tulsa, OK Christ the King Church.
Morgan, Matthew A. '51 (PMB) [1] Boca Raton, FL Ascension Church.
Morgan, Michael T. *o.s.b.* '40 (BIR) [E] Cullman, AL St. Bernard Abbey.
Morgan, Oliver J. *s.j.* '79 (SCR) [C] Scranton, PA University of Scranton.
Morgan, Raymond J. '42 (BRK) Retired; [U] Douglaston, NY Bishop Mugavero Residence.
Morgan, Msgr. Thomas '39 (MRY) Retired.
Morgan, Thomas '84 (SP) Lecanto, FL St. Scholastica Church.
Morgan, Thomas B. '55 (BO) Salisbury, MA Star of the Sea Church.
Morgan, Msgr. Thomas J. '65 (CAM) Haddonfield, NJ Christ the King Regional School Church.
Morgan, Walter N. '44 (MIL) Retired.
Morgan, William H. '50 (BO) Retired.
Morgan, William P. '57 (BUR) Washington, VT St. Cecilia Church.
Morgen, Paul '62 (SFS) Retired.
Morgenroth, Anton *c.s.sp.* (GAL) [B] Houston, TX Holy Ghost Fathers.
Morgenthaler, John N. *o.p.* '41 (NO) [25] New Orleans, LA St. Anthony Of Padua Church.
Morgera, Michael A. '85 (MEM) [21] Memphis, TN St. Paul The Apostle Church.
Morgia, Robustiano D. '76 (NO) Jefferson, LA St. Agnes Church.
Morhous, Robert *o.c.s.o.* '59 (WOR) [N] Spencer, MA St. Joseph's Abbey.
Moriarity, Daniel J. '64 (PH) [110] Philadelphia, PA Nativity of the Blessed Virgin Mary Church.
Moriarity, William J. '66 (CHI) [1] Chicago, IL Cathedral of the Holy Name.
Moriarty, Francis *s.s.e.* '45 (VEN) [G] Englewood, FL Society of St. Edmund Residence.
Moriarty, Frederick L. *s.j.* '44 (BO) [W] Chestnut Hill, MA The Jesuit Community at Boston College.
Moriarty, James F. '51 (CHI) Skokie, IL St. Joan of Arc Church; Stickney, IL St. Pius X Church; Retired.
Moriarty, James J. '48 (NY) Pawling, NY St. John the Evangelist Church; Retired.
Moriarty, John '62 (JOL) On Duty Outside the Diocese.
Moriarty, John P. '91 (LEX) Prestonsburg, KY St. Martha Church.
Moriarty, Joseph B. '93 (IND) [35] Indianapolis, IN St. Monica Church.
Moriarty, Msgr. Joseph T. '34 (CLV) Retired; [F] Cleveland, OH Incarnate Word Academy; [Q] Cleveland, OH Sisters of the Incarnate Word and Blessed Sacrament.
Moriarty, Philip M. '80 (JC) Wien, MO St. Mary of the Angels Church.
Moriarty, Quentin E. *o.p.* '59 (CHI) [N] River Forest, IL St. Thomas Aquinas Priory.
Moriarty, Thomas M., Jr. '92 (RVC) Valley Stream, NY Holy Name of Mary Church.
Moriarty, Thomas W. '42 (BO) Retired.
Morillo, Jose '49 (VEN) Absent on Sick Leave.
Morin, Frank P. '73 (PRT) [2] Portland, ME St.

Dominic's Church; [7] Portland, ME Sacred Heart Church.
Morin, George E. (BO) Saugus, MA St. Margaret Church.
Morin, Henri D. '44 (PRO) [10] Woonsocket, RI Precious Blood Church; Retired.
Morin, John *o.m.i.* '51 (BO) [6] Boston, MA St. Angela Church.
Morin, Joseph *c.ss.r.* '64 (CHI) [9] Chicago, IL St. Alphonsus Church.
Morin, Michael J. '88 (LIN) Cortland, NE St. James Church; [C] Lincoln, NE Pius X Central High School; [K] Lincoln, NE Pius X Foundation and Pius X Endowment Fund.
Morin, Robert *o.m.i.* '69 (BEL) [G] Belleville, IL Missionary Oblates of Mary Immaculate - St. Henry's Oblate Residence; [K] Belleville, IL Oblate Preaching Team.
Morin, Msgr. Roger P. '71 (NO) [13] New Orleans, LA Incarnate Word Church.
Morin, Timothy '77 (STP) Lino Lakes, MN St. Joseph Church.
Moriones, Francis *o.a.r.* '34 (NY) [B] Suffern, NY Tagaste Monastery.
Morisco, Cyril *o.f.m.* '45 (NY) [Z] New York, NY Franciscan Province of the Immaculate Conception.
Morisette, Alfred *s.j.* '61 (SPK) [C] Spokane, WA Gonzaga University.
Morisette, Richard P. '61 (SY) Onondaga Hill, NY St. Michael Church.
Moritz, Paul L. '41 (BO) [7] Brockton, MA St. Patrick Church; Retired.
Morkunas, Msgr. Simon '33 (SC) Retired.
Morlan, Lawrence A. '95 (PEO) [4] Bloomington, IL St. Patrick Church of Merna.
Morley, Edward *o.c.s.o.* '83 (PMB) Fort Pierce, FL St. Mark Church.
Morley, Edward T. *o.c.s.o.* '83 (ATL) [I] Conyers, GA The Monastery of the Holy Spirit.
Morley, John F. '62 (NEW) [B] South Orange, NJ Seton Hall University.
Morley, John J. '32 (PH) [141] Philadelphia, PA St. Richard Church; Retired.
Morlino, Paschal A. *o.s.b.* '66 (BAL) [15] Baltimore, MD St. Benedict Church.
Morlino, Robert C. '74 (KAL) [1] Kalamazoo, MI St. Augustine Cathedral.
Morman, David '54 (BIS) [F] Sentinel Butte, ND Home on the Range.
Morman, David G. '89 (BIS) Beach, ND St. John the Baptist Church.
Morman, James *t.o.r.* '92 (ALT) [A] Loretto, PA St. Francis College; [F] Loretto, PA St. Francis Friary, Third Order Regular of St. Francis of Penance.
Morman, Kenneth G. '73 (TOL) [1] Toledo, OH Queen of the Most Holy Rosary Cathedral; [8] Toledo, OH Holy Rosary Church; [30] Toledo, OH St. Louis Church; Special Assignment.
Morman, Wilbert *s.v.d.* '46 (CHI) [B] Techny, IL Divine Word Residence.
Mormando, Franco *s.j.* '93 (BO) [W] Chestnut Hill, MA The Jesuit Community at Boston College.
Moroney, Joseph E. '54 (CHY) [1] Cheyenne, WY St. Mary's Cathedral; Retired.
Moroney, Martin J. '67 (SAC) Rancho Cordova, CA St. John Vianney Church.
Moroney, Michael J. '71 (BR) [16] Baton Rouge, LA Our Lady of Mercy Church.
Moroney, William F. *m.afr.* '61 (WDC) [M] Washington, DC Missionaries of Africa.
Morozowich, Mark '91 (SJP) Graduate Studies.
Morras, Ignacio '49 (MIA) [5] Hialeah, FL St. John the Apostle Church; Retired.
Morras, Xavier '50 (MIA) Coral Gables, FL Little Flower Church.
Morrell, Joseph J. '57 (ALN) [2] Allentown, PA St. Francis of Assisi Church.
Morrell, William *o.m.i.* '70 (SAT) [M] San Antonio, TX De Mazenod House.
Morrelly, Leonard (RVC) Absent on Leave.
Morrill, Bruce *s.j.* '92 (BO) [W] Chestnut Hill, MA The Jesuit Community at Boston College.
Morrill, Giles '50 (ALB) Retired.
Morris, Alan E. '92 (PIT) Whitehall, PA St. Gabriel of the Sorrowful Virgin Church.
Morris, Alexis P. '56 (SP) [O] St. Petersburg, FL St. Anthony Friary.
Morris, Anthony *c.ss.r.* '94 (ORL) New Smyrna Beach, FL Sacred Heart Church.
Morris, C. Eugene '96 (STL) [36] St. Louis, MO St. Gabriel the Archangel Church.
Morris, Charles M. '83 (DET) [1] Wyandotte, MI St. Elizabeth Church; [T] Roseville, MI Cursillos in Christianity Movement of the Archdiocese of Detroit.
Morris, George O. *s.j.* '68 (SPK) [C] Spokane, WA Gonzaga University.
Morris, Gerald R. '70 (MIA) Marathon, FL San Pablo Church.
Morris, James '63 (BO) [5] Salem, MA St. John the Baptist Ukrainian Catholic Church.
Morris, James '93 (STF) Salem, MA St. John the Baptist Church.
Morris, James A. '80 (BRK) [U] Jamaica, NY Vincentian Residence.
Morris, James A. '94 (KAL) St. Joseph, MI St. Joseph Church.
Morris, James H. '66 (SFR) San Bruno, CA St. Robert Church.
Morris, James J. '89 (BRK) Absent on Leave.
Morris, John *o.p.* '66 (OAK) [B] Moraga, CA Saint Mary's College.
Morris, John *o.p.* '66 (SAC) Benicia, CA St. Dominic Church.
Morris, Msgr. John E. '47 (PAT) [5] Passaic, NJ Holy Trinity Church.
Morris, John J. '44 (CHI) Retired.
Morris, John J. '60 (NEW) Military Chaplains.
Morris, John J. *s.j.* '62 (P) [14] Portland, OR St. Francis of Assisi Church; [L] Portland, OR Jesuit Provincial Office (Oregon Prov.).
Morris, John S. '62 (BO) Absent on Sick Leave.
Morris, Joseph A. *c.m.* '80 (BRK) [D] Queens and Staten Island, NY St. John's University.
Morris, Joseph E. '96 (ATL) [4] Marietta, GA Church of the Transfiguration.
Morris, Joseph W. *s.j.* '59 (SLC) East Carbon, UT Good Shepherd Church.
Morris, Ken *c.s.v.* (LAV) Henderson, NV St. Thomas More Church.
Morris, Kenan *o.f.m.* '50 (BO) [Z] Boston, MA Saint Anthony Residence.
Morris, Lester G. '91 (NOR) Middlefield, CT St. Colman Church.
Morris, Loyd '95 (DAL) Allen, TX St. Jude Church.
Morris, Michael *o.p.* '77 (OAK) [B] Moraga, CA Saint Mary's College.
Morris, Michael P. '89 (NY) [132] Bronx, NY St. Barnabas Church.
Morris, Michael T. *o.p.* '77 (OAK) [A] Berkeley, CA Dominican School of Philosophy and Theology; [N] Moraga, CA Dominican Community
Morris, Msgr. Philip D. '63 (NEW) Hillsdale, NJ St. John the Baptist Church.
Morris, Robert (SP) [12] Tampa, FL St. Mary Church.
Morris, Robert '49 (SFD) Collinsville, IL SS. Peter and Paul Church.
Morris, Robert '91 (SP) [4] Largo, FL St. Patrick Church
Morris, Robert Alan *o.p.* '50 (NY) [Z] New York, NY St. Vincent Ferrer Priory.
Morris, Robert F. '66 (PT) Destin, FL Corpus Christi Church
Morris, Robert J. '53 (PAT) Retired; [P] Chester, NJ Nazareth Village.
Morris, Stephen P. '79 (RVC) Absent on Leave.
Morris, Thomas A. *o.ss.t.* '81 (WDC) [M] Hyattsville, MD St. John de Matha Monastery, Order of Most Holy Trinity.
Morris, William J. *s.m.* '38 (STL) [P] St. Louis, MO Provincialate of the Society of Mary, Province of St. Louis.
Morris, William S. *s.s.* '31 (BAL) [K] Baltimore, MD St. Charles Villa; [M] Baltimore, MD St. Charles Villa.
Morris, William T. '69 (MET) [B] Watchung, NJ Mount St. Mary Academy.
Morris, William T. '69 (NEW) Westfield, NJ St. Helen Church.
Morrisette, Robert H. '75 (BO) Absent on Sick Leave.
Morrison, Anselm *a.a.* '48 (BO) [W] Brighton, MA Assumptionist Center.
Morrison, Anselm Harry *a.a.* '48 (SP) Dade City, FL St. Rita Church.
Morrison, Carl T. '69 (MIA) Miami Shores, FL St. Martha Church; [G] Miami, FL Mercy Hospital.
Morrison, Craig *o.carm.* '87 (JOL) [J] Darien, IL Carmelite Fathers Provincial Office.
Morrison, Craig *o.carm.* '87 (WDC) [B] Washington, DC Whitefriars Hall.
Morrison, Msgr. David J. '54 (ALN) [8] Bethlehem, PA Our Lady of Perpetual Help Church.
Morrison, Douglas A. '59 (HRT) On Duty Outside the Archdiocese.
Morrison, Francis X. '55 (PH) [152] Philadelphia, PA St. Timothy Church.
Morrison, Harry B. '76 (OAK) Lafayette, CA St. Perpetua Church; [4] Walnut Creek, CA St. Stephen Church.
Morrison, Howard L. *s.j.* '58 (P) [L] Portland, OR Jesuit Provincial Office (Oregon Prov.).
Morrison, James J. '74 (PRT) York Harbor, ME St. Christopher-by-the-Sea Church.
Morrison, James R. '87 (HT) [2] Houma, LA Annunziata Church.
Morrison, John A. *s.j.* '36 (NY) [Z] New York, NY Murray-Weigel Hall.
Morrison, John A. '92 (SAM) Troy, NY St. Ann Church.
Morrison, Larry '79 (RNO) Sun Valley, NV St. Peter Canisius Church.
Morrison, Michael G. *s.j.* '68 (OM) [A] Omaha, NE Creighton University; [K] Omaha, NE Jesuit Community At Creighton University.
Morrison, Raymond J. '39 (CHI) Northlake, IL St. John Baptist Vianney, Cure of Ars Church; Retired.
Morrison, Thomas A. *o.p.* '55 (CHI) [J] Chicago, IL Holy Cross Hospital; [N] Chicago, IL Dominicans (Provincial Office).
Morrison, Thomas F. '76 (CHR) Chester, SC St. Joseph's Church; Lancaster, SC St. Catherine's Church.
Morrissette, Dominic '45 (JOL) Retired.
Morrissette, Dominic '45 (LAV) [16] Las Vegas, NV Shrine of the Most Holy Redeemer Church.
Morrissette, Joseph H. '56 (NOR) Retired.
Morrissey, Daniel W. *o.p.* '62 (CHI) [N] Chicago, IL Dominicans (Provincial Office).
Morrissey, Dunstan R. *o.s.b.* '53 (PEO) [A] Peru, IL St. Bede Abbey and Academy.
Morrissey, J. Michael '78 (P) Gresham, OR St. Anne Church.
Morrissey, James E. '38 (CHI) Mundelein, IL St. Mary Church; Retired.
Morrissey, Msgr. James L. '55 (PEO) [1] Streator, IL Immaculate Conception Church.
Morrissey, Jerome V. '47 (PEO) Retired; [L] Peoria, IL St. Augustine Manor.
Morrissey, John '63 (PMB) Stuart, FL St. Joseph Church.
Morrissey, John J. '37 (DAV) Retired; [M] Davenport, IA St. Vincent Center.
Morrissey, Joseph G. *o.s.f.s.* '77 (WIL) [I] Wilmington, DE Oblates of St. Francis De Sales.
Morrissey, Lawrence M. '54 (PEO) Retired; [L] Peoria, IL St. Augustine Manor.
Morrissey, Lawrence P. '57 (PEO) El Paso, IL St. Mary's Church.
Morrissey, Michael *s.s.c.* '51 (LAV) [13] Las Vegas, NV St. Mary the Virgin Church; [14] Las Vegas, NV St. Paul Jung-Ha-Sang Church.
Morrissey, Michael E. '86 (RCK) [9] Rockford, IL SS. Peter and Paul Church.
Morrissey, Msgr. Michael J. '65 (DAV) [M] Davenport, IA St. Vincent Center; [P] Davenport, IA Kingdom Co.
Morrissey, Paul F. *s.m.* '75 (STP) [25] St. Paul, MN St. Louis King of France Church.
Morrissey, Philip T. '46 (BGP) Retired.
Morrissey, Robert '80 (RVC) Ocean Beach, NY Our Lady of the Magnificat Church.
Morrissey, Robert O. '83 (RVC) New Hyde Park, NY Holy Spirit Church.
Morrissey, Robert P. '76 (BGP) Ridgefield, CT St. Mary's Church.
Morrissey, Thomas E. '61 (FR) [6] Taunton, MA St. James Church.
Morrissey, William F. '52 (RCK) [4] Aurora, IL St. Mary Church.
Morrone, Louis S. *o.p.* '92 (DEN) [28] Denver, CO St. Dominic's Church; [P] Denver, CO Regis University (Denver).
Morrow, Brian S. '80 (DEN) [31] Denver, CO St. James Church.
Morrow, Dennis '75 (GR) [20] Grand Rapids, MI SS. Peter and Paul's Church.
Morrow, Lambert W. *o.s.b.* '42 (PBL) [E] Canon City, CO Holy Cross Abbey.
Morrow, Michael J. '86 (NY) [135] Bronx, NY St. Brendan Church.
Morrow, Richard B. '55 (ATL) [1] Atlanta, GA Cathedral of Christ the King.
Morrow, Thomas G. '82 (WDC) [42] Washington, DC St. Thomas Apostle Church.
Morrow, Thomas O. '71 (BRK) Absent on Leave.
Morry, Matthew F. *o.p.* '50 (PRO) [P] Providence, RI St. Thomas Aquinas Priory at Providence College.
Morsch, Msgr. Peter '31 (AMA) Retired.
Morse, Frederick H. '95 (PRT) South Portland, ME Church of the Holy Cross; South Portland, ME St. John the Evangelist Church.
Morse, Guy E. '81 (CHL) Retired.
Morse, James E. *s.j.* '50 (SJ) [D] San Jose, CA Bellarmine College Preparatory.
Morse, James H. '67 (FR) Special Assignment.
Morse, John *s.j.* '61 (YAK) Moses Lake, WA Our Lady of Fatima Church; Warden, WA Queen of All Saints Church.
Morse, John A. '52 (STL) Retired.
Morse, Jonathan '88 (STF) Special Assignment; [F] Stamford, CT Missionary Sisters of Mother of God.
Morse, Michael E. '84 (STA) Live Oak, FL St. Francis Xavier Church.
Morse, Richard *o.s.f.s.* (TOL) [C] Toledo, OH St. Francis de Sales High School.
Morse, Richard E. *o.s.f.s.* '69 (TOL) [K] Toledo, OH Oblates of St. Francis de Sales.
Morslander, Edward '52 (SCL) Retired.
Mort, Ernest C. *c.s.p.* '59 (NY) [Z] Scarsdale, NY Paulist Fathers Generalate.
Mort, Ernest C. *c.s.p.* '59 (SD) Special Assignment.
Mortell, Anthony *s.s.c.* '60 (LA) [R] Los Angeles, CA Columban Fathers, Procure House.
Mortimer, Msgr. James E. '52 (PH) [157] Philadelphia, PA St. William Church.
Morton, Jake *s.j.* '75 (SPK) Ford, WA St. Philip Benizi

Church; Inchelium, WA St. Michael's Mission Church; Wellpinit, WA Sacred Heart Church; Westend, WA Our Lady of Lourdes Church.
Morton, John *c.ss.r.* '53 (DAV) [4] Davenport, IA St. Alphonsus Church.
Morton, Vincent '86 (SP) [4] Largo, FL St. Patrick Church; [O] St. Leo, FL St. Leo Abbey.
Morvant, Kenneth '61 (OLL) Lafayette, LA Maronite Catholic Community Church.
Morvant, Kenneth R. (LAF) On Special Assignment.
Morvay, Andrew '60 (RC) Buffalo, SD St. Anthony Church; Retired.
Mosbrucker, Jacob '66 (P) [10] Portland, OR St. Charles Church.
Moscaritolo, Mario P. '64 (KC) [1] Kansas City, MO Cathedral of Immaculate Conception.
Moscato, Angelo *c.s.* '62 (CHI) [N] Chicago, IL Scalabrini House of Theology.
Moschini, Christopher H. *o.p.* '52 (P) [18] Portland, OR Holy Rosary Parish & Dominican Priory Church.
Mosele, Victor *s.x.* '60 (PAT) [M] Wayne, NJ Xaverian Missionary Fathers.
Moseley, Stan *o.s.b.* '53 (NO) [P] St. Benedict, LA St. Joseph Abbey.
Moseley, Stanley '53 (NY) [118] New York, NY St. Thomas More Church.
Moser, Albert *c.s.p.* '60 (OAK) [2] Berkeley, CA Holy Spirit Parish Church; [Q] Berkeley, CA Holy Spirit Parish, University of California, Newman Hall.
Moser, Charles J. *s.m.a.* '32 (ORL) Retired.
Moser, Claudio *o.f.m.* '63 (NY) [Z] New York, NY Franciscan Province of the Immaculate Conception.
Moser, John A. '86 (DUB) New Haven, IA St. Peter's Church; Riceville, IA Immaculate Conception Church.
Moser, Thomas W. '94 (KNX) Alcoa, TN Our Lady of Fatima Church.
Moser, Msgr. Victor G. '46 (KC) [5] St. Joseph, MO St. Mary's Church.
Mosey, Douglas L. *c.s.b.* '74 (NOR) [A] Cromwell, CT Holy Apostles College and Seminary.
Mosher, Mark L. '88 (SAC) [4] Sacramento, CA Immaculate Conception Church.
Mosher, Thomas '81 (BUR) Lyndonville, VT St. Elizabeth Church; [J] Burlington, VT University of Vermont-The Catholic Center at UVM.
Moskal, Joseph E. '65 (SY) Hinckley, NY St. Ann Church; [10] Utica, NY St. Joseph and St. Patrick Church; Absent on Sick Leave.
Mosko, Msgr. Leon A. '56 (STF) Special Assignment.
Moskus, John T. '63 (HRT) [1] Milford, CT Christ the Redeemer Church.
Moskva, Emil '47 (PSC) Retired.
Moslener, Robert E. '76 (GBG) Sagamore, PA Sacred Heart Church; Yatesboro, PA St. Mary Church.
Mosley, Charles A. '85 (GRY) [5] Gary, IN Holy Trinity Church.
Mosley, Daniel E. '77 (STL) Berger, MO St. Paul Church; New Haven, MO Assumption Church.
Mosley, Francis J. '39 (BO) Retired.
Mosley, Godfrey '79 (WDC) Oxon Hill, MD St. Columba Church.
Moslosky, Robert *c.s.b.* '74 (OAK) [C] Oakland, CA Bishop O'Dowd High School.
Mosovsky, James J. '42 (CLV) Avon Lake, OH Holy Spirit Church; Retired.
Moss, Msgr. Charles T. '58 (ALN) West Bangor, PA St. Roch Church.
Moss, Donald G. '86 (AUS) Military Chaplains.
Moss, Donald G. '86 (LA) Military and VA Chaplains.
Moss, Donald Roy (LA) Point Mugu, CA Naval Air Station.
Moss, James T. '82 (PAT) Sparta, NJ Our Lady of the Lake Church.
Moss, James T. '82 (STA) Williston, FL Holy Family Church.
Moss, Ray '86 (CHY) Laramie, WY St. Laurence O'Toole Church.
Moss, Robert D. '69 (BUF) Sloan, NY St. Andrew Church.
Moss, Robert H. *c.s.c.* '74 (FTW) [A] Notre Dame, IN Old College; [A] Notre Dame, IN Moreau Seminary; [B] Notre Dame, IN University of Notre Dame Du Lac; [J] Notre Dame, IN Holy Cross Community, Corby Hall, University of Notre Dame.
Mossett, Robert *o.s.f.s.* (LAN) Adrian, MI St. Mary of Good Counsel Church.
Mossi, John P. *s.j.* '73 (SPK) [C] Spokane, WA Gonzaga University.
Mossing, Msgr. Lawrence A. '40 (TOL) Retired.
Most, William G. '40 (DUB) Retired.
Mostardi, Joseph S. *o.s.a.* '75 (NY) [216] Staten Island, NY Our Lady of Good Counsel Church.
Moster, Humbert *o.f.m.* (IND) Oldenburg, IN Holy Family Church; St. Mary-of-the-Rock, IN St. Mary-of-the-Rock Church; St. Peter, IN St. Peter Church.
Moster, James *o.f.m.cap.* '72 (KCK) [H] Lawrence, KS St. Conrad's Friary.
Moszur, Edward J. '71 (GRY) Highland, IN Our Lady of Grace Church.
Motherway, Thomas F. '69 (BO) Absent on Sick Leave.
Motl, James R. *o.p.* '62 (STP) [15] Minneapolis, MN St. Albert the Great Church; [A] St. Paul, MN The Saint Paul Seminary; [C] St. Paul, MN University of St. Thomas.
Motolinia, Arturo *o.s.a.* '82 (NY) [40] New York, NY St. Gregory Church.
Motsay, Joseph '78 (RC) Ellsworth, SD Ellsworth AFB.
Motsay, Joseph R. '78 (SCR) Military Chaplains.
Motsett, Msgr. C. Bourke '34 (PEO) Retired.
Mott, James A. *o.s.a.* '65 (SD) [B] San Diego, CA Austin House - House of Formation; [H] San Diego, CA Augustinian Community.
Mott, Msgr. John D. '56 (RVC) Hicksville, NY Our Lady of Mercy Church.
Motta, Anthony '63 (ALB) Haines Falls, NY Immaculate Conception Church.
Motta, Michael (NOR) [A] Cromwell, CT Holy Apostles College and Seminary.
Motta, Michael J. '60 (HRT) Special and other (Arch-)Diocesan Assignment.
Mottau, Robert S. (BO) Retired.
Mottet, Marvin A. '56 (DAV) [1] Davenport, IA Sacred Heart Cathedral; [K] Davenport, IA Thomas Merton House, Inc.; [P] Davenport, IA Interfaith Housing, Ltd.
Mottin, Msgr. Charles A. '49 (STL) [S] St. Louis, MO Father Jim's Home; [S] St. Louis, MO Father Dempsey's Hotel, Inc.
Motycka, Robert R. '79 (CHI) Other Assignments.
Mouannes, Nabil '84 (OLL) San Diego, CA Saint Ephrem Mission Church; Phoenix, AZ Maronite Catholic Community Church.
Mouawad, Paul '69 (SAM) Pawtucket, RI Holy Trinity-St. George Church.
Mouch, Msgr. Frank M. '58 (VEN) On Duty Outside the Diocese.
Moudry, Paul G. '87 (STP) Columbia Heights, MN Immaculate Conception Church.
Moudry, Richard P. '50 (STP) Retired.
Mould, Christopher J. '88 (ARL) Burke, VA Church of the Nativity.
Moulder, John '90 (CHI) [1] Oak Park, IL Ascension Church.
Mountain, Edward C. '47 (WIN) Retired.
Mountain, Harold B. '42 (WIN) Retired.
Mountain, Joseph W. '52 (WIN) Mapleton, MN St. Teresa's Church; Retired.
Mounteer, Louis A. *s.j.* '56 (ALB) [O] Auriesville, NY Jesuit Retreat House for Priests, Religious and Lay People.
Mousbrugger, Edwin A. *s.j.* '36 (DET) [P] Clarkston, MI Colombiere Center.
Mouser, J. Irvin '65 (L) St. Thomas, KY St. Thomas Church; [M] Nerinx, KY Motherhouse and Novitiate of the Sisters of Loretto at the Foot of the Cross.
Moussier, Howard R. *o.s.b.* '65 (BIR) [E] Cullman, AL St. Bernard Abbey.
Moussier, Howard R. *o.s.b.* '65 (MOB) Elberta, AL St. Bartholomew Church.
Moutenot, Charles L. *s.j.* '84 (NY) [Z] New York, NY Jesuit Provincial's Office.
Moutenot, Charles L. *s.j.* '84 (OAK) [N] Berkeley, CA Jesuit Community at Jesuit School of Theology at Berkeley.
Mouton, Msgr. C. Burton '49 (LAF) On Duty Outside the Diocese.
Mouton, Thomas Jason '92 (LAF) [7] Lafayette, LA Our Lady Queen of Peace Church.
Mowatt, John J. (BO) Awaiting Assignment.
Mowry, Raymond G. '44 (SFS) Ipswich, SD Holy Cross Church; Retired.
Moy, Francis J. *s.j.* '69 (BGP) [1] Greenwich, CT St. Mary's Church; [O] Fairfield, CT The Fairfield Jesuit Community-Fairfield University.
Moy, Francis J. *s.j.* '69 (BO) [W] Boston, MA The Society of Jesus Of New England-Provincial Offices.
Moy, Gregory *c.ss.r.* '88 (DET) [34] Detroit, MI Holy Redeemer Church.
Moya, Peter O. '85 (MET) On Duty Outside the Diocese.
Moyano, Felipe (CAM) [1] Atlantic City, NJ Holy Spirit Church.
Moyer, Joseph M. *c.s.c.* '94 (AUS) [H] Austin, TX Congregation of Holy Cross - Southern Province.
Moyer, Joseph M. *c.s.c.* '94 (NO) [22] New Orleans, LA Sacred Heart Of Jesus Church.
Moyer, Msgr. Richard '64 (PHX) Carefree, AZ Our Lady of Joy Church.
Moylan, Thomas *l.c.* '69 (MAD) [I] Edgerton, WI Legion of Christ, Inc.
Moyna, James Moneta *o.p.* '70 (NY) [Z] New York, NY St. Vincent Ferrer Priory.
Moyna, James P. '70 (RVC) East Rockaway, NY St. Raymond's Church.
Moyna, John L. '73 (ALB) Coxsackie, NY St. Mary Church; Coxsackie, NY Coxsackie Correctional Facility.
Moynahan, Joseph A. '34 (WOR) Retired.
Moynahan, Kevin '54 (LSC) Retired.
Moynahan, Michael E. *s.j.* '73 (SPK) [C] Spokane, WA Gonzaga University.
Moynihan, Cornelius A. '47 (PHX) Retired.
Moynihan, Eugene J. *s.m.m.* '33 (RVC) [N] Bay Shore, NY Montfort Missionaries.
Moynihan, Eugene R. *s.s.j.* '57 (GAL) [61] Houston, TX Our Mother of Mercy Church.
Moynihan, George F. '74 (CHR) North Myrtle Beach, SC Our Lady Star of the Sea Church.
Moynihan, James M. (SY) Special Assignment; [W] Syracuse, NY David W. Barry Foundation.
Moynihan, Jeremiah P. '74 (ROC) Hornell, NY St. Ignatius Loyola Church; Hornell, NY St. James Mercy Hospital.
Moynihan, Michael (NY) [CC] New York, NY University Apostolate.
Moynihan, Michael Robert '79 (BGP) [2] Greenwich, CT St. Michael the Archangel Church.
Moynihan, Noel '77 (BRK) [237] Queens, NY Sacred Heart of Jesus Church.
Moynihan, Paul V. (BO) Retired.
Moynihan, T. Joseph '57 (BO) Westwood, MA St. Margaret Mary Church.
Moynihan, Timothy '32 (SEA) [2] Seattle, WA St. Alphonsus Church; Retired.
Moys, Gregory '64 (P) Stayton, OR Immaculate Conception Church; [Q] Portland, OR Oregon Catholic Conference.
Mozeris, Msgr. Damasus A. '39 (CHI) [92] Chicago, IL Immaculate Conception Church; Retired.
Mozos, Sebastian *o.m.i.* '33 (SAT) [K] San Antonio, TX Oblate Madonna Residence.
Mrakuzic, Stephen A. '48 (CLV) [62] Cleveland, OH St. Paul Church; Retired.
Mraz, John S. '75 (ALN) [11] Allentown, PA St. Thomas More Church; Catasauqua, PA Annunciation B.V.M. - St. Mary's Church.
Mraz, Louis R. *o.s.c.* '59 (PHX) [2] Glendale, AZ St. Helen Church; [F] Phoenix, AZ Crosier Community of Phoenix (Canons Regular of the Order of the Holy Cross).
Mraz, Method J. *o.s.b.* '34 (GBG) [H] Latrobe, PA Saint Vincent Archabbey.
Mraz, Robert J. '74 (NU) Silver Lake, MN Church of the Holy Family.
Mrnarevic, Daniel Miho '84 (FAR) Rugby, ND St. Therese, Little Flower Church.
Mroczkowski, Msgr. Joseph '42 (CHI) [209] Chicago, IL St. Turibius Church.
Mroczkowski, Joseph A. '45 (LIN) Retired.
Mroczkowski, Msgr. Joseph J. '42 (CHI) Retired.
Mroczkowski, Leonard A. '46 (CAM) Retired.
Mroczynski, Edward *s.chr.* '57 (LA) [22] Los Angeles, CA Our Lady of the Bright Mount Church.
Mrowinski, Charles *c.r.* '55 (CHI) [D] Chicago, IL Weber High School; [M] Chicago, IL St. Joseph Home of Chicago, Inc.
Mrowka, Chester R. *c.m.* '59 (HRT) [M] Manchester, CT DePaul Provincial Residence.
Mroz, Richard J. '92 (NEW) Saddle Brook, NJ St. Philip the Apostle Church.
Mroziewski, Witold '91 (BRK) [94] Brooklyn, NY Our Lady of Czestochowa-St. Casimir Church.
Mruk, Walter *o.f.m.conv.* '49 (FR) [4] Fall River, MA Holy Cross Church.
Mubiru, Peter (DET) [1] Roseville, MI St. Angela Church.
Muc, John *s.o.cist.* '90 (CHI) [N] Willow Springs, IL Cistercian Fathers.
Muccilli, Sebastian L. '57 (MET) On Duty Outside the Diocese.
Muccitelli, Mario *s.d.v.* '48 (PAT) [M] Florham Park, NJ Father Justin Vocationary.
Mucha, Jan '54 (DEN) [33] Denver, CO St. Joseph's Church.
Mucha, John '53 (STU) [I] Nelsonville, OH Hocking Technical College.
Mucha, John '81 (STU) Glouster, OH Holy Cross Church; Nelsonville, OH St. Mary of the Hills Church.
Mucharski, Francis *o.f.m.cap.* '33 (PAT) [M] Oak Ridge-Milton, NJ St. Stanislaus B. M. Friary.
Muckenhaupt, Gregory F. *s.j.* '88 (CI) [C] Kolonia, Pohnpei, FM Jesuit House.
Muckerman, Norman J. *c.ss.r.* '42 (STL) [P] Liguori, MO Liguori Mission House/Redemptorists.
Mucowski, Richard J. *o.f.m.* '71 (Y) [B] North Canton, OH Walsh University.
Mudd, David A. '80 (WDC) Military Chaplains.
Mudd, Earl '60 (BEA) [2] Beaumont, TX St. Anne Church.
Mudd, James T. '64 (L) Hodgenville, KY Our Lady of Mercy Church; Howardstown, KY St. Ann Church.
Mudd, John '69 (WDC) Special Ministries; [D] Washington, DC Archbishop Carroll High School.
Mudrak, Lloyd '62 (DUL) Virginia, MN Holy Spirit Church.
Mudry, Lubomyr '51 (STF) Staten Island, NY Holy Trinity Church.
Mueggenborg, Daniel H. '89 (TLS) [9] Tulsa, OK The Madalene Church.
Muehlberger, Howard J. *s.s.e.* '71 (BUR) [G] Colchester, VT Society of St. Edmund.
Mueller, Anthony E. '36 (BRK) Retired.
Mueller, Charles L. '57 (NO) [6] Metairie, LA St.

Christopher the Martyr Church; Metairie, LA East Jefferson General Hospital.
Mueller, Donald R. '61 (TOL) [1] Fremont, OH Sacred Heart Church; [I] Green Springs, OH St. Francis Health Care Center, Rehab Hospital Section; [J] Green Springs, OH St. Francis Health Care Centre (ICF & Skilled).
Mueller, Eugene J. (CIN) Retired.
Mueller, Francis E. *s.j.* '53 (FBK) Barrow, AK St. Patrick Church; [C] Fairbanks, AK Jesuit Residence.
Mueller, Gary A. *c.m.* '95 (DEN) [12] Denver, CO Holy Ghost Church; [P] Denver, CO Auraria Campus.
Mueller, George E. '59 (DOD) Fowler, KS St. Anthony Church; Meade, KS St. John the Baptist Church; Plains, KS St. Patrick Church.
Mueller, Glenn R. *s.j.* '73 (STL) [35] St. Louis, MO St. Francis Xavier Church; [P] St. Louis, MO Jesuit Community Corporation at St. Louis University - Jesuit Hall.
Mueller, James *o.carm.* '69 (PHX) [5] Glendale, AZ St. Raphael Church.
Mueller, James J. '66 (BRK) [152] Queens, NY St. Anthony of Padua Church.
Mueller, John F. *s.m.* '41 (CIN) [M] Huntsville, OH St. George Chapel of Marianist Community.
Mueller, John J. '59 (CLV) Wooster, OH St. Mary of the Immaculate Conception Church.
Mueller, John J. *s.j.* '75 (STL) [C] St. Louis, MO Saint Louis University.
Mueller, Joseph G. *s.j.* (DET) [K] Detroit, MI Jesuit Provincial Office-Detroit Province of the Society of Jesus.
Mueller, Joseph J. '44 (MIL) Retired.
Mueller, Joseph P. '39 (BEL) Retired.
Mueller, Kevin A. '92 (BAL) Cockeysville, MD St. Joseph Church.
Mueller, Matthias R. *o.p.* '49 (CHI) [173] Chicago, IL St. Pius V Church; [N] Chicago, IL Dominican Community.
Mueller, Maurice M. '48 (FAR) Retired; [E] Fargo, ND Riverview Place, Inc.; [F] Fargo, ND Presentation Center-Sacred Heart Convent.
Mueller, Michael '85 (ORL) On Duty Outside the Diocese.
Mueller, Noel *o.s.b.* '68 (IND) [B] St. Meinrad, IN St. Meinrad Seminary-College of Liberal Arts; [J] St. Meinrad, IN St. Meinrad Archabbey.
Mueller, Paul '49 (TOL) Bowling Green, OH St. Thomas More University Parish Church; Retired.
Mueller, Paul R. *s.j.* '93 (CHI) [N] Chicago, IL Chicago Province of the Society of Jesus-Provincial Office.
Mueller, Peter F. *c.s.c.* '42 (FTW) [J] South Bend, IN Congregation of Holy Cross Indiana Province Provincial House.
Mueller, Richard J. '44 (IND) Retired.
Mueller, Richard J. '63 (CHI) Northbrook, IL St. Norbert Church.
Mueller, Richard J. '66 (PIT) Penn Hills, PA St. Bartholomew Church.
Mueller, Richard J. '66 (VEN) [1] Venice, FL Epiphany Cathedral.
Mueller, Robert F. '46 (MIL) [7] Milwaukee, WI St. Anthony's Church; Retired.
Mueller, Roman C. *s.d.s.* '74 (PHX) [4] Mesa, AZ Queen of Peace Church.
Mueller, W. W. (STL) [P] St. Louis, MO Jesuit Community Corporation at St. Louis University - Jesuit Hall.
Muellerleile, Ernest H. '44 (ANC) [5] Anchorage, AK Holy Cross Church.
Muench, Joseph '81 (LEX) Harrodsburg, KY St. Andrew Church.
Muench, R. Francis '81 (RIC) [3] Hampton, VA St. Rose of Lima Church.
Muench, William G. '59 (OG) Crown Point, NY Sacred Heart Church; Ticonderoga, NY St. Mary Church.
Muerder, Edward E. '58 (BUF) Bliss, NY St. Joseph Church; Java Center, NY St. Patrick Church; North Java, NY St. Nicholas Church.
Mueserfechter, Msgr. Robert J. '51 (STL) Fenton, MO St. Paul Church.
Mugan, William L. *s.j.* '55 (MIL) [P] Milwaukee, WI Jesuit Community at Marquette University.
Mugavero, Anthony P. '81 (ROC) [10] Rochester, NY St. Bridget Church; [37] Rochester, NY Our Lady of Perpetual Help Church.
Muggli, Boniface *o.s.b.* '90 (BIS) [A] Richardton, ND Assumption Abbey.
Muggli, Florian *o.s.b.* '51 (SCL) St. Joseph, MN St. Joseph's Church.
Muggli, Odo *o.s.b.* '66 (BIS) [A] Richardton, ND Assumption Abbey.
Muha, Edward J. '45 (HRT) Retired.
Muha, Joseph '60 (B) Cottonwood, ID St. Mary's Church.
Muha, Peter J. '88 (GRY) [5] Hammond, IN St. John Bosco Church.
Muheim, Martin *o.s.b.* '88 (PBL) [D] Canon City, CO St. Thomas More Hospital and Progressive Care Center.
Muheim, Martin de Porres J. *o.s.b.* '88 (PBL) [E] Canon City, CO Holy Cross Abbey.
Muhich, Peter '89 (DUL) Proctor, MN St. Rose Catholic Church.
Muhiirwa, Robert *c.s.c.* '95 (FTW) [13] South Bend, IN St. Jude Church.
Muhlbaier, Howard E. '65 (CAM) Atco, NJ Assumption Church.
Muhlen, Micah *o.f.m.* '91 (JOL) [10] Joliet, IL SS. Cyril and Methodius Church.
Muhr, Michael '83 (SP) [2] Tampa, FL Christ the King Church.
Muhs, Edward J. '51 (RVC) Bellmore, NY St. Barnabas the Apostle Church; Retired.
Muir, Edmund D. '49 (DET) Retired.
Muir, Gavin W. (PH) [72] Philadelphia, PA Saint Irenaeus Church; Ridley Park, PA St. Madeline Church.
Muka, John R. *c.s.sp.* '39 (PH) [Z] Bensalem, PA Congregation of the Holy Ghost Fathers and Brothers.
Mukald, Joseph (NEW) Roselle Park, NJ The Assumption Church.
Mukasa, Michael '96 (PIT) [62] Pittsburgh, PA St. Pius X Church.
Mula, Zarco *o.f.m.conv.* '85 (BUF) [7] Lackawanna, NY Our Lady of Bistrica Church.
Mulanjanany, Augustine '69 (LKC) Fenton, LA St. Charles Borromeo Church.
Mulcahy, Brian Martin *o.p.* (NY) [Z] New York, NY St. Catherine of Siena Priory.
Mulcahy, Daniel R., Jr. '79 (WOR) Linwood, MA Good Shepherd Church.
Mulcahy, Msgr. Donal '51 (LA) Ventura, CA Our Lady of the Assumption Church.
Mulcahy, Gerald F. '62 (CHI) Hickory Hills, IL St. Patricia Church.
Mulcahy, Howard J. '44 (ALB) Retired.
Mulcahy, Msgr. James R. '37 (LA) La Puente, CA St. Louis of France Church; Retired.
Mulcahy, John M. *c.s.c.* '65 (FTW) [J] South Bend, IN Congregation of Holy Cross Indiana Province Provincial House.
Mulcahy, Louis *o.s.b.* '89 (IND) [J] St. Meinrad, IN St. Meinrad Archabbey.
Mulcahy, Patrick J. '95 (SD) Encinitas, CA St. John the Evangelist Church.
Mulcahy, Msgr. Philip '51 (NY) [145] Bronx, NY St. Helena Church.
Mulcahy, Richard E. *s.j.* '46 (SFR) [N] San Francisco, CA Jesuit Community at University of San Francisco.
Mulcahy, Sean C. '62 (MIA) [11] Fort Lauderdale, FL St. Maurice Church.
Mulcair, William W. *m.s.* '65 (HRT) [M] Hartford, CT Missionaries of LaSalette Provincial Secretary.
Mulcrone, Charles '53 (SFD) Retired.
Mulcrone, Joseph '71 (CHI) [X] Chicago, IL Catholic Office of the Deaf.
Mulcrone, Joseph A. '71 (CHI) [64] Chicago, IL St. Francis Borgia Church.
Mulcrone, Thomas *s.j.* '46 (NO) New Orleans, LA Orleans Parish House of Detention; [C] New Orleans, LA Loyola University.
Mulcrone, Thomas '77 (CHI) [144] Chicago, IL Notre Dame Church.
Mulderry, Anthony J. '67 (MIA) Sunrise, FL All Saints Church.
Muldoon, Brendan '64 (SP) Indian Rocks Beach, FL St. Jerome Church; [F] Largo, FL St. Jerome Early Childhood Center.
Muldoon, P. Christopher '71 (PAT) Lake Hopatcong, NJ Our Lady Star of the Sea Church.
Muldowney, James D. '52 (ARL) Middleburg, VA St. Stephen the Martyr Church.
Mulert, Donovan *m.s.c.* '54 (Y) [A] Youngstown, OH Sacred Heart Retreat House & Renewal Center.
Mulewski, Patrick M. '79 (NEW) Ridgewood, NJ Our Lady of Mount Carmel Church.
Mulgrew, John E. '56 (PH) [63] Philadelphia, PA Holy Spirit Church.
Mulhall Emmanuel F. *o.praem.* '41 (GB) [I] De Pere, WI St. Norbert Abbey.
Mulhall Msgr. Francis X. '47 (BRK) Retired; [U] Douglaston, NY Bishop Mugavero Residence.
Mulhall J. Gregory '37 (ALB) Retired.
Mulhall John W. *c.s.p.* '56 (LA) [86] Los Angeles, CA St. Paul the Apostle Church.
Mulhall John W. *c.s.p.* '56 (NY) [Z] Scarsdale, NY Paulist Fathers Generalate.
Mulhauser, Daniel J. *s.j.* '60 (CI) Koror, FM Sacred Heart Church; [C] Koror, Palau, PW Manresa Jesuit House.
Mulhearn, Michael *c.m.* '68 (KC) [J] Kansas City, MO Vincentian Parish Mission Center.
Mulhern, Bernard J. *s.j.* '51 (CHI) [T] Barrington, IL Bellarmine Hall.
Mulhern, James P. *o.f.m.* '44 (SP) [O] St. Petersburg, FL St. Anthony Friary.
Mulhern, Joseph Hugh *o.p.* (NY) [Z] New York, NY St. Vincent Ferrer Priory.
Mulhern, Kevin P. '76 (SCR) Honesdale, PA St. John the Evangelist Church.
Mulhern, Patrick F. '64 (ATL) Decatur, GA St. Thomas More Church.
Mulhern, Raymond F. '52 (COV) Retired.
Mulholland, Charles H. (R) Retired.
Mulholland, John '65 (PH) Levittown, PA Immaculate Conception B.V.M. Church.
Mulica, James '67 (CLV) Retired.
Mulka, Arthur C. '51 (GAY) Retired.
Mulka, Raymond C. '49 (GAY) Retired.
Mulkerin, Terrence J. '61 (BRK) Military Chaplains.
Mulkern, John F. '43 (BO) Retired.
Mulkern, Stephen M. '49 (PRT) Retired.
Mull, Thomas P. '76 (ROC) [1] Rochester, NY Sacred Heart Cathedral; [L] Rochester, NY Apostleship of Prayer.
Mullady, Brian T. *o.p.* '72 (NOR) [A] Cromwell, CT Holy Apostles College and Seminary.
Mullady, Brian T. *o.p.* '72 (SFR) [13] San Francisco, CA St. Dominic Church; [N] San Francisco, CA St. Dominic Priory.
Mullakkara, Joseph *m.s.f.s.* '75 (ATL) Norcross, GA Saint Patrick's Church.
Mullally, Gerald F. '76 (SCR) Milford, PA St. Patrick's Church.
Mullally, Thomas A. *s.v.d.* (LAF) St. Martinville, LA Notre Dame de Perpetuel Secours Church.
Mullan, Glen '94 (CC) [17] Corpus Christi, TX St. Patrick Church.
Mullan, Patrick '67 (PAT) Retired; [P] Chester, NJ Nazareth Village.
Mullan, Raymund A. '62 (FWT) Graham, TX St. Mary Church; Olney, TX St. Theresa of the Infant Jesus Church.
Mullan, William F. *m.m.* '62 (NY) [Z] Maryknoll, NY Maryknoll Fathers and Brothers.
Mullane, Bernard J. '56 (RCK) Belvidere, IL St. James Church.
Mullane, Thomas '68 (MIA) Big Pine Key, FL St. Peter Church.
Mullaney, Aidan *t.o.r.* '52 (STU) [A] Steubenville, OH Franciscan University of Steubenville.
Mullaney, Aidan *t.o.r.* '54 (STU) [F] Steubenville, OH Holy Spirit Monastery.
Mullaney, Msgr. Bernard C. '58 (SAT) Retired; [K] San Antonio, TX Casa De Padres.
Mullaney, Cornelius J. '71 (BO) Braintree, MA St. Thomas More Church.
Mullaney, Edward John *o.c.s.o.* '73 (WOR) [N] Spencer, MA St. Joseph's Abbey.
Mullaney, Gregory C. '90 (PBR) Tarentum, PA Sts. Peter and Paul Church.
Mullaney, Lawrence '88 (RIC) Clifton Forge, VA St. Joseph Church.
Mullaney, Leonard '62 (FR) East Falmouth, MA St. Anthony's Church.
Mullarkey, John T. '64 (GB) Kaukauna, WI Holy Cross Church.
Mullarkey, Msgr. Patrick J. '64 (SD) [25] San Diego, CA St. Columba Church.
Mullelly, Thomas J. '80 (TR) [R] Princeton, NJ Campus Ministry for the Diocese of Trenton.
Mullen, Anthony P. *c.ss.p.* '90 (BRK) [144] Brooklyn, NY St. Vincent Ferrer Church.
Mullen, Austin M. (SP) [11] Tampa, FL St. Mark the Evangelist Church.
Mullen, Bernard *c.pp.s.* (KCK) Blue Rapids, KS St. Elizabeth Church; Frankfort, KS Annunciation Church; Waterville, KS St. Monica's Church.
Mullen, Bernard J. '61 (DET) Lake Orion, MI St. Joseph Church.
Mullen, Charles F. *s.j.* '43 (OM) [C] Omaha, NE Creighton Preparatory School.
Mullen, Charles F. *c.pp.s.* '64 (FTW) Rome City, IN St. Gaspar del Bufalo Church.
Mullen, David J. '46 (BO) Bellingham, MA St. Brendan Church.
Mullen, Dennis M. '70 (SUP) Cumberland, WI St. Anthony The Abbot Church.
Mullen, Msgr. Edward F. '54 (CAM) Ocean City, NJ St. Augustine's Church.
Mullen, Edward F. '58 (CHR) Retired.
Mullen, Francis '36 (ALB) Retired.
Mullen, Godfrey *o.s.b.* '94 (IND) [A] St. Meinrad, IN St. Meinrad Seminary; [J] St. Meinrad, IN St. Meinrad Archabbey.
Mullen, John '52 (WCH) Retired.
Mullen, John J. *s.j.* (BO) Suffolk County, MA Boston-Nashua Street Jail.
Mullen, John J. '49 (RVC) Selden, NY St. Margaret of Scotland Church; Retired.
Mullen, John J. *s.j.* '62 (BO) [23] Boston, MA St. Francis de Sales Church; [W] Weston, MA Campion Center.
Mullen, Joseph *o.f.m.cap.* '47 (NY) [57] New York, NY St. John the Baptist Church.
Mullen, Joseph *s.j.* '50 (SD) Carlsbad, CA St. Patrick Church.
Mullen, Joseph A. '48 (BRK) Retired.
Mullen, Joseph E. *s.j.* '50 (BO) [W] Boston, MA The Society of Jesus of New England-Provincial Offices.
Mullen, Kevin J. *o.f.m.* '80 (BO) [BB] Boston, MA St.

Anthony Shrine.
Mullen, L. James '53 (PH) [W] Philadelphia, PA St. John Neumann Nursing Home.
Mullen, Michael '62 (KCK) [14] Kansas City, KS St. Patrick's Church.
Mullen, Michael *i.c.* '75 (VEN) Bradenton, FL Sacred Heart Church.
Mullen, Michael F. *c.m.* '41 (BRK) [U] Jamaica, NY Vincentian Residence.
Mullen, Owen J. '64 (NY) West Point, NY Catholic Chapel of the Most Holy Trinity Church.
Mullen, Owen J. '64 (WIL) Military Chaplains.
Mullen, Paul M. '73 (SCR) Mountaintop, PA St. Jude's Church.
Mullen, Peter P. *m.m.* '62 (NY) [Z] Maryknoll, NY Maryknoll Fathers and Brothers.
Mullen, Peter P. *m.m.* '62 (OG) Ray Brook, NY Federal Correctional Institution.
Mullen, Richard L. '55 (PEO) [1] Champaign, IL Holy Cross Church.
Mullen, Thomas '56 (LKC) On Duty Outside the Diocese.
Mullen, Thomas J. *ss.cc.* '75 (LA) San Dimas, CA Holy Name of Mary Church.
Mullen, Timothy F. *o.praem.* '73 (WIL) [B] Claymont, DE Archmere Academy; [I] Claymont, DE Immaculate Conception Priory of the Canons Regular of Premontre.
Mullen, William E. '76 (ALT) Cresson, PA St. Aloysius Church.
Mullen, William G. *o.m.v.* '92 (BO) [BB] Boston, MA St. Francis Chapel.
Mullen, Msgr. William J. '47 (OAK) Orinda, CA Santa Maria Church; Retired.
Mullen, Msgr. William J. '51 (HRT) [4] West Hartford, CT St. Mark the Evangelist Church.
Muller, Anthony '68 (CIN) [73] Cincinnati, OH Our Lord, Christ the King Church.
Muller, Earl C. *s.j.* '77 (NO) [P] New Orleans, LA Jesuit Provincial Office.
Muller, Francis J. *o.f.m.* '42 (NY) [35] New York, NY St. Francis of Assisi Church.
Muller, Herman J. *s.j.* '41 (DET) [K] Detroit, MI Jesuit Community at the University of Detroit.
Muller, James B. *o.p.* '59 (NY) Hawthorne, NY Holy Rosary Church.
Muller, Joseph T. *m.s.c.* '58 (RCK) [10] Aurora, IL St. Therese of Jesus Church.
Muller, Kennard '66 (BAL) Retired.
Muller, Lutz *s.j.* '93 (CHI) [C] Chicago, IL Jesuit Community at Loyola University of Chicago.
Muller, Martin M. '57 (BIR) [16] Birmingham, AL Our Lady of Sorrows Church.
Muller, Michael '94 (NEW) Higher Studies.
Muller, Myles '48 (BAL) Retired; [K] Baltimore, MD Stella Maris Operating Corporation.
Muller, Peter D. *o.praem.* '93 (ORG) [H] Silverado, CA Norbertine Fathers.
Muller, William H. *s.j.* '73 (SJ) [D] San Jose, CA Bellarmine College Preparatory.
Mullet, John '91 (SAG) Coleman, MI St. Philip Neri Church.
Mullett, Msgr. Gene W. '76 (STU) Bellaire, OH St. John Church; Bellaire, OH St. Michael's Church.
Mulligan, Bede J.K. *o.carm.* '58 (GBG) [H] New Florence, PA Mount Carmel Hermitage.
Mulligan, Bernard *c.ss.r.* '42 (SEA) [32] Seattle, WA Sacred Heart of Jesus Church.
Mulligan, Bertrand *o.f.m.cap.* '49 (SFR) [N] Burlingame, CA Capuchin Provincial House.
Mulligan, Charles (ROC) Penn Yan, NY St. Michael Church; [M] Rochester, NY Diocesan Office of Campus Ministry.
Mulligan, Charles '64 (ROC) [M] Penn Yan, NY St. Michael's Church.
Mulligan, Colm *m.s.c.* '58 (SAT) [M] San Antonio, TX Missionaries of the Sacred Heart.
Mulligan, Edward J. '56 (SP) [3] Clearwater, FL St. Brendan Church.
Mulligan, Emmett *o.f.m.* '52 (PMB) [D] West Palm Beach, FL St. Mary's Hospital, Inc.
Mulligan, George B. *c.s.c.* '82 (PRT) Saco, ME Most Holy Trinity Church.
Mulligan, Msgr. James J. '61 (ALN) Northampton, PA Our Lady of Hungary Church.
Mulligan, James J. '66 (PH) Glenside, PA St. Luke the Evangelist Church; [D] Wyncote, PA Bishop McDevitt High School.
Mulligan, John D. *s.m.* '57 (CIN) [M] Dayton, OH Marianist Provincialate; [M] Dayton, OH Marianist Provincialate.
Mulligan, John M. *v.g.* '64 (ROC) Henrietta, NY Church of the Good Shepherd; Rush, NY St. Joseph Church.
Mulligan, John T. '64 (NY) [E] New York, NY Cardinal Hayes High School.
Mulligan, Joseph '37 (SPR) [H] Holyoke, MA Sisters of Providence Care Centers, Inc.
Mulligan, Joseph E. *s.j.* (DET) [K] Detroit, MI Jesuit Provincial Office-Detroit Province of the Society of Jesus.
Mulligan, Joseph V. '75 (CHL) [7] Charlotte, NC St Luke Church.
Mulligan, Louis J. '61 (DAV) Special Assignment.
Mulligan, Paul F. '57 (BO) Ashland, MA St. Cecilia Church.
Mulligan, Robert G. *o.s.f.s.* '85 (PH) [Z] Philadelphia, PA Father Judge Faculty House.
Mulligan, Robert H. (PH) South Coventry, PA St. Thomas More Church.
Mulligan, Robert W. *s.j.* '49 (CHI) [C] Chicago, IL Jesuit Community at Loyola University of Chicago.
Mulligan, Timothy *o.f.m.conv.* '96 (SY) Minoa, NY St. Mary Church.
Mulligan, William L. *s.j.* '65 (BO) [R] Cambridge, MA Youville Hospital & Rehabilitation Center, Inc.; [U] Cambridge, MA Youville Healthcare Center, Inc.; [W] Boston, MA Loyola House; [FF] Cambridge, MA The Youville House, Inc.
Mulligan, William R. '45 (BUR) Retired.
Mullin, Edward J. *c.m.* '54 (STL) [P] St. Louis, MO Vincentian Residence.
Mullin, Francis R. *o.p.* '71 (HBG) [I] Lancaster, PA Monastery of the Dominican Nuns of the Perpetual Rosary.
Mullin, Henry *c.s.sp.* '59 (MIA) [5] Fort Lauderdale, FL St. Clement Church.
Mullin, Hugh J. '46 (KC) Retired.
Mullin, Jay M. '69 (BO) Absent on Sick Leave.
Mullin, John A. *s.j.* '75 (NY) [Z] New York, NY Jesuit Community at Fordham University; [CC] New York, NY University Apostolate.
Mullin, John F. *s.j.* '65 (BO) [W] Boston, MA The Society of Jesus of New England-Provincial Offices; [W] Chestnut Hill, MA The Jesuit Community at Boston College.
Mullin, John F. *s.j.* '65 (MAN) Lebanon, NH Sacred Heart Church; Hanover, NH Mary Hitchcock Hospital.
Mullin, Patrick J. '75 (LA) [R] Los Angeles, CA Amat House; [W] Montebello, CA DePaul Center.
Mullin, Thomas M. (ALN) [A] Northampton, PA Mary Immaculate Seminary.
Mullin, Thomas M. '75 (PH) [A] Wynnewood, PA Theological Seminary of St. Charles Borromeo, Overbrook.
Mullin, William H. '64 (BO) Braintree, MA St. Francis of Assisi Church.
Mullink, Michael D. '88 (SFD) Arcola, IL St. John the Baptist Church; Tuscola, IL Forty Martyrs Church.
Mullins, Carlos A. '55 (NY) [102] New York, NY St. Patrick Old Cathedral; [124] Bronx, NY St. Angela Merici Church.
Mullins, Charles R. '50 (HRT) [3] Bristol, CT St. Gregory's Church.
Mullins, Kevin C. *o.s.a.* '90 (LA) [31] Los Angeles, CA Mother of Good Counsel Church.
Mullins, Kevin C. *o.s.a.* '90 (ORL) Casselberry, FL St. Augustine Church.
Mullins, Patrick *c.m.* '39 (CHI) [C] Chicago, IL Vincentian Community at DePaul University.
Mullins, Msgr. Raymond '52 (PT) Fort Walton Beach, FL St. Mary Church.
Mullins, Richard A. '95 (ARL) Annandale, VA St. Michael's Church.
Mullins, Robert J. '45 (FAR) Retired.
Mullonkal, George *m.c.b.s.* '71 (SFR) [26] San Francisco, CA St. James Church; San Francisco, CA San Francisco General Hospital.
Mullowney, Edward J. *s.s.j.* '55 (BAL) [M] Baltimore, MD St. Joseph Society of the Sacred Heart House of Central Administration.
Mullowney, Thomas E. '55 (GI) Retired.
Mulloy, Francis *c.s.sp.* '52 (SFR) Millbrae, CA St. Dunstan Church.
Mulloy, James *s.d.b.* '85 (BO) [E] Boston, MA Don Bosco Preparatory School of Technology.
Mulloy, John F. (BO) Saugus, MA Blessed Sacrament Church.
Mulloy, Matthew F. '53 (NY) Absent on Sick leave.
Mulloy, Michael '79 (RC) [2] Rapid City, SD Blessed Sacrament Church.
Mulloy, Sylvester '38 (JOL) Retired.
Mulloy, William '54 (NY) Absent on Leave.
Mulnix, John Gabriel R. *c.p.* '68 (CHI) [N] Chicago, IL Passionist Provincial Office.
MulQueen, John D. '34 (Y) East Liverpool, OH St. Aloysius Church.
Mulqueen, Joseph C. '57 (BRK) Released from Diocesan Assignment.
Mulqueen, Martin B. '74 (PMB) [2] Boca Raton, FL Our Lady of Lourdes Church.
Mulranen, Francis J. '82 (PH) Trooper, PA Visitation B.V.M. Church.
Mulranen, John J. '50 (SY) [2] Binghamton, NY St. Ann Church; Retired.
Mulrenan, Alexus J. *o.f.m.* '60 (PAT) [M] Butler, NJ St. Anthony Friary.
Mulrenan, Donald P. *s.v.d.* '60 (BO) [W] Boston, MA Divine Word Missionaries.
Mulroney, Joseph G. *j.c.l.* '93 (R) Smithfield, NC St. Ann Church.
Mulrooney, Charles F. '42 (SCR) Retired; [N] Dunmore, PA Villa St. Joseph.
Mulrooney, Conan P. *o.praem.* '67 (GB) [F] Green Bay, WI St. Vincent Hospital; [I] De Pere, WI St. Norbert Abbey.
Mulrooney, F. Harold '37 (SCR) Retired.
Mulroy, Richard D. *o.praem.* '40 (GB) [I] De Pere, WI St. Norbert Abbey.
Mulsoff, Donald J. '69 (CHI) [130] Chicago, IL St. Mary of Perpetual Help Church.
Mulvanerty, Thomas '65 (NY) Absent on Leave.
Mulvanerty, Thomas F. '79 (RVC) Farmingville, NY Church of the Resurrection.
Mulvanerty, Thomas M. (OAK) Moraga, CA St. Monica Church.
Mulvaney, Andrew R. '68 (OG) Military Chaplains.
Mulvaney, James J. '53 (BIR) Retired.
Mulvanity, Francis C. '59 (CLV) [4] Euclid, OH St. Paul Church.
Mulvany, Michael '88 (KCK) Lapeer, KS St. Francis Church; Osage City, KS St. Patrick's Church; Scranton, KS St. Patrick's Church.
Mulvehill, John R. '57 (BO) Cohasset, MA St. Anthony Church.
Mulvehill, Louis J. '53 (ALT) South Fork, PA Most Holy Trinity Church; South Fork, PA St. James Church.
Mulvey, Gerard *o.f.m.cap.* '91 (NY) [57] New York, NY St. John the Baptist Church; [T] New York, NY St. Rose's Home.
Mulvey, John J. '62 (NEW) On Duty Outside the Archdiocese.
Mulvey, John J. '62 (VEN) Port Charlotte, FL St. Charles Borromeo Church.
Mulvey, Michael '75 (AUS) On Duty Outside the Diocese.
Mulvihill, Daniel R. '53 (WCH) Retired.
Mulvihill, David J. '72 (CHI) Berwyn, IL St. Odilo Church.
Mulvihill, John Edward '65 (CHI) [106] Chicago, IL St. John Bosco Church.
Mulvihill, Martin J. '83 (STL) Shrewsbury, MO St. Michael Church.
Mumper, Ed (JOL) Beaverville, IL St. Mary Church; Martinton, IL St. Martin Church.
Mun, Byung Hak, Joseph '83 (STL) Ellisville, MO St. Andrew Kim Korean Catholic Community Church.
Munari, Mario '36 (SR) Retired.
Mundakal, Joseph A. *c.m.i.* '83 (JOL) Wheaton, IL St. Michael Church.
Mundell, Msgr. J. Joshua '47 (WDC) [22] Washington, DC Immaculate Conception Church.
Mundy, Joseph T. '81 (RVC) Wading River, NY St. John Baptist Church.
Mundy, Patrick W. '66 (OG) On Duty Outside the Diocese.
Mungari, Joseph *s.a.c.* '45 (CAM) Hammonton, NJ St. Joseph's Church.
Munguia, Jorge *s.j.* '67 (MIA) [D] Miami, FL Belen Jesuit Preparatory School; [H] Miami, FL Villa Arrieta.
Muniz, Alberto '77 (PCE) Patillas, PR Inmaculado Corazon de Maria Church.
Muniz, William '94 (MIA) [2] Fort Lauderdale, FL Our Lady Queen of Martyrs Church.
Munley, Jay '93 (LAN) East Lansing, MI St. John the Evangelist, Student Parish Church.
Munn, Daniel '80 (NTN) Augusta, GA St. Ignatios of Antioch Church.
Munn, Daniel '82 (SAV) [1] Augusta, GA Church of the Most Holy Trinity.
Munn, Daniel M. '82 (SAV) [E] Augusta, GA St. Joseph Hospital, Augusta, GA, Inc.
Munn, Thomas J. '51 (SC) Dayton, IA Christ the King Church; Ogden, IA St. John's Church.
Munoz, Antonio '60 (CGS) [10] Barrio Rio Canas, PR San Pedro Apostol Church.
Munoz, Arcadio '76 (NEW) [1] Hoboken, NJ Our Lady of Grace Church.
Munoz, Msgr. Ernesto '55 (ARE) Quebradillas, PR San Raphael Church.
Munoz, Eusiquio '64 (WOR) Milford, MA St. Mary of the Assumption Church.
Munoz, Fernando Gil '53 (PCE) Jayuya, PR Our Lady of Monserrate Church.
Munoz, J. Francisco *s.d.b.* '73 (LA) [79] Los Angeles, CA St. Mary Church.
Munoz, Jose *c.m.* '90 (SJN) [27] San Juan, PR San Jose Obrero Church.
Munoz, Jose F. '96 (ORL) Altamonte Springs, FL St. Mary Magdalen Church.
Munoz, Rafael '60 (PCE) On Duty Outside the Diocese.
Munoz, Rafael '69 (ARE) [3] Camuy, PR Our Lady of Asumption Church.
Munoz, Raul Saez '82 (SJN) [1] San Juan, PR Catedral De San Juan Bautista Church.
Munoz, Tomas G. '85 (TUC) Yuma, AZ Immaculate Conception Church.
Munro, Donald R. '87 (PMB) [1] Boca Raton, FL Ascension Church.
Munro, Hugh J. '57 (FR) [J] Taunton, MA Marian Manor Inc.
Munsch, Nathan *o.s.b.* (BO) [3] Brookline, MA St.

Lawrence Church.
Munsch, Nathan *o.s.b.* '91 (GBG) [H] Latrobe, PA Saint Vincent Archabbey.
Munsell, Richard F. '79 (GF) Military Chaplains.
Munshower, William G. '58 (IND) [43] Indianapolis, IN St. Thomas Aquinas Church.
Munson, Thomas N. (PBL) Montrose, CO St. Mary Church.
Munster, Thomas P. *c.m.* '48 (CHI) [C] Chicago, IL De Paul University; [C] Chicago, IL Vincentian Community at DePaul University.
Muntone, Msgr. Anthony D. '64 (ALN) Whitehall, PA St. Elizabeth Church.
Munzing, Joel *o.f.m.* '47 (CAM) [L] Margate, NJ Franciscan Friars' Vacation Home.
Muodiaju, Samuel *c.s.sp.* '85 (MIA) [15] Miami, FL St. Agatha Church.
Muoneke, Romanus O. '74 (GAL) Kingwood, TX St. Martha Church.
Murasso, Jeremiah N. '79 (HRT) Naugatuck, CT St. Vincent Ferrer Church; Special and other (Arch)Diocesan Assignment; [G] New Haven, CT St. Francis Home for Children, Inc.
Murawski, Apolinary '34 (GBG) Retired; [G] Greensburg, PA Neumann House.
Murawski, Edward J. *s.j.* '66 (BO) [W] Boston, MA Loyola House.
Murcko, Charles S. '52 (E) [4] Farrell, PA St. Ann Church.
Murd, Francis A. '76 (TOL) Tiffin, OH St. Mary Church.
Murd, Frank A. '60 (TOL) Sycamore, OH St. Pius X Church.
Murdick, Msgr. Olin J. '45 (SAG) Essexville, MI St. John the Evangelist Church; Retired.
Murdock, Paul J. '75 (NOR) Windham, CT Sagrado Corazon de Jesus Church.
Murhammer, Francis J. '88 (PIT) [38] Pittsburgh, PA Sacred Heart Church.
Murnan, Sean *o.f.m.* '73 (SFE) Los Ojos, NM San Jose Church; Tierra Amarilla, NM Santo Nino Church.
Murnane, Patrick J. '60 (MIA) Hollywood, FL Nativity Church.
Murnion, Msgr. Philip J. '63 (NY) [88] New York, NY Our Lady of Loreto Church; On Duty Outside the Archdiocese.
Muro, Msgr. Victor S. '66 (CAM) [3] Vineland, NJ St. Francis of Assisi Church; [O] Vineland, NJ Spanish Catholic Center.
Muroski, Leon T. '60 (E) [15] Erie, PA St. Casimir Church.
Murphy, Alfred E. *o.s.a.* '56 (BO) [C] North Andover, MA Merrimack College.
Murphy, Alfred E. *o.s.a.* '56 (PH) [Z] Villanova, PA Provincial Offices of the Order of St. Augustine, Province of St. Thomas of Villanova.
Murphy, Arthur J. '55 (HRT) [6] West Hartford, CT St. Thomas the Apostle Church.
Murphy, B. James '78 (CHI) [A] Mundelein, IL University of St. Mary of the Lake-Mundelein Seminary.
Murphy, Bartholomew J. *s.j.* '72 (P) [L] Portland, OR Jesuit Provincial Office (Oregon Prov.).
Murphy, Brendan *s.v.d.* (LAF) Broussard, LA St. Joseph Church.
Murphy, Brian *o.carm.* '58 (ROC) [B] Rochester, NY McQuaid Jesuit High School; [I] Rochester, NY Whitefriars Priory.
Murphy, Campion *s.t.* '56 (PAT) [M] Stirling, NJ Holy Spirit Missionary Cenacle.
Murphy, Charles *s.a.* '61 (NY) [Z] Garrison, NY Franciscan Friars of the Atonement.
Murphy, Charles C. *s.j.* '62 (MIL) [P] Milwaukee, WI Jesuit Provincial Office, Wisconsin Province.
Murphy, Charles J. (BO) [2] Weymouth, MA St. Francis Xavier Church.
Murphy, Charles J. '76 (SUP) On Leave.
Murphy, Msgr. Charles M. '61 (PRT) Falmouth, ME Holy Martyrs Church.
Murphy, Charles R. '91 (OKL) Guymon, OK St. Peter's Church; [K] Norman, OK Campus Ministry for the Archdiocese of Oklahoma City.
Murphy, Christopher '96 (ARL) [7] Alexandria, VA St. Mary's Church.
Murphy, Clarence '20 (FR) Retired.
Murphy, Columba *o.f.m.* '41 (SP) [O] St. Petersburg, FL St. Anthony Friary.
Murphy, Msgr. D. Declan '49 (MRY) Carmel, CA San Carlos Borromeo Basilica.
Murphy, Daniel A. '39 (NEW) Retired; [B] South Orange, NJ Seton Hall University.
Murphy, Daniel C. '51 (SB) [E] Hemet, CA Holy Ghost Fathers.
Murphy, Daniel G. '56 (SY) Windsor, NY Our Lady of Lourdes Church.
Murphy, Daniel J. '56 (DET) [4] Birmingham, MI St. Regis Church.
Murphy, Daniel S. '70 (BRK) [7] Brooklyn, NY St. Andrew the Apostle Church.
Murphy, Daniel T. '62 (MIL) [N] Greenfield, WI Clement Manor Health Center.
Murphy, Daniel W. '73 (PAT) Sparta, NJ Blessed Kateri Tekakwitha Church.
Murphy, David *o.carm.* '42 (JOL) [J] Darien, IL Carmelite Fathers Provincial Office.
Murphy, David C. '63 (BO) [5] Brockton, MA Our Lady of Lourdes Church.
Murphy, David F. '87 (WIL) Claymont, DE Holy Rosary Church; Wilmington, DE Delaware Army National Guard.
Murphy, David M. (ROC) On Duty Outside the Diocese.
Murphy, Denis J. '53 (LA) Retired.
Murphy, Dennis *s.a.* '39 (NY) [Z] Garrison, NY Generalate of the Franciscan Friars of the Atonement-St. James Friary.
Murphy, Dennis '74 (RIC) On Duty Outside the Diocese.
Murphy, Dennis *s.a.* '89 (WDC) [B] Washington, DC Atonement Seminary-Francisan Friars of the Atonement.
Murphy, Dennis P. '75 (ALB) [1] Albany, NY Cathedral of the Immaculate Conception; On Duty Outside the Diocese; Unassigned.
Murphy, Desmond P. '57 (WDC) Mitchellville, MD Holy Family Church; Retired.
Murphy, Edward (ALB) [H] Troy, NY Seton Health System, Inc.
Murphy, Edward '93 (STA) Palm Coast, FL St. Elizabeth Ann Seton Church.
Murphy, Edward J. *s.j.* '68 (NY) [Z] New York, NY West Side Jesuit Community.
Murphy, Emmet *o.f.m.* '86 (NEW) [N] Hohokus, NJ St. Anthony of Padua.
Murphy, Eoin '64 (LAN) Clio, MI SS. Charles and Helena Church.
Murphy, Msgr. Eugene '34 (MAN) Retired.
Murphy, Msgr. Eugene F. '52 (RVC) Mineola, NY Corpus Christi Church; Mineola, NY Winthrop Hospital.
Murphy, F. Kevin '81 (NEW) [D] Summit, NJ The Oratory Catholic Preparatory School.
Murphy, Francis (BO) Boston, MA Holy Family Hospital Medical Center.
Murphy, Msgr. Francis (MOB) Retired.
Murphy, Msgr. Francis '43 (R) Retired.
Murphy, Francis '58 (RNO) Dayton, NV St. Ann Church.
Murphy, Msgr. Francis A. '57 (ANC) Retired.
Murphy, Msgr. Francis C. (MOB) [4] Mobile, AL St. Dominic Church.
Murphy, Msgr. Francis H. '41 (PAT) Retired.
Murphy, Francis J. '35 (BO) On Special or Other Diocesan Assignment.
Murphy, Francis J. '51 (LIN) Ashland, NE St. Mary's Church.
Murphy, Francis J. *s.j.* '56 (KC) [B] Kansas City, MO Rockhurst College.
Murphy, Francis J. '66 (GAY) [1] Gaylord, MI St. Mary Cathedral.
Murphy, Francis J. *c.s.c.* '86 (FTW) [J] South Bend, IN Congregation of Holy Cross Indiana Province Provincial House.
Murphy, Francis W. '49 (NOR) Essex, CT Our Lady of Sorrows Church.
Murphy, Francis X. *c.ss.r.* '40 (BAL) Annapolis, MD St. Mary Church; [M] Annapolis, MD Saint Mary Rectory.
Murphy, Frank J. *s.j.* '56 (KC) [J] Kansas City, MO Rockhurst College - Jesuit Community.
Murphy, Frederick J. '57 (BO) [1] Boston, MA Cathedral of the Holy Cross.
Murphy, G. Ronald *s.j.* '69 (WDC) [M] Washington, DC The Jesuit Community at Georgetown University.
Murphy, George '66 (BLX) Hattiesburg, MS Sacred Heart Church.
Murphy, George R. *s.j.* '71 (BO) [W] Boston, MA The Society of Jesus of New England-Provincial Offices.
Murphy, George R. *s.j.* '71 (OAK) [A] Berkeley, CA The Jesuit School of Theology at Berkeley; [N] Berkeley, CA Jesuit Community at Jesuit School of Theology at Berkeley.
Murphy, Gerard '79 (SP) New Port Richey, FL Our Lady Queen of Peace Church.
Murphy, Gerasimos *b.s.o.* '67 (NTN) [A] Methuen, MA Seminary of St. Basil the Great.
Murphy, Gordon A. *o.f.m.* '55 (BO) [Z] Boston, MA Saint Anthony Residence.
Murphy, H. Joseph '61 (BO) Wakefield, MA St. Florence Church.
Murphy, Harold B. '68 (CHI) [207] Chicago, IL St. Timothy Church.
Murphy, Harry J. '40 (GBG) Retired.
Murphy, Harry J. '40 (SB) [E] Morongo Valley, CA St. Michael's of Morongo Valley, Inc.
Murphy, Henry *m.m.* '58 (STA) [H] Jacksonville, FL Maryknoll Fathers & Brothers.
Murphy, Henry J. *s.j.* '57 (BGP) [A] Fairfield, CT Fairfield University; [O] Fairfield, CT The Fairfield Jesuit Community-Fairfield University.
Murphy, Hugh J. '59 (NOR) Retired.
Murphy, Hugh P. '71 (PAT) [P] Morristown, NJ Priests Residence.
Murphy, J. E. '60 (SFS) Huron, SD Church of the Resurrection.
Murphy, Msgr. J. Emmett '38 (ROC) Retired.
Murphy, J. Patrick *c.m.* '76 (CHI) [N] Chicago, IL Vincentian Community, Congregation of the Mission, Midwest Province.
Murphy, James (ORL) Retired.
Murphy, James *o.s.b.* '46 (OKL) Harrah, OK St. Teresa of Avila Church.
Murphy, James *c.s.c.* '58 (PRT) [J] Biddeford, ME Marie Joseph Spiritual Center.
Murphy, James '65 (L) [E] Louisville, KY Thomas Merton Academy.
Murphy, James '70 (MIA) Miami Lakes, FL Our Lady of the Lakes Church.
Murphy, James '78 (JOL) On Duty Outside the Diocese.
Murphy, James A. '39 (PH) Stowe, PA St. Gabriel Church; Retired.
Murphy, James D. *o.s.b.* '46 (OKL) [I] Shawnee, OK St. Gregory's Abbey.
Murphy, James E. '52 (STL) Bridgeton, MO St. Lawrence the Martyr Church.
Murphy, James E. '55 (GI) Retired.
Murphy, James F. '47 (PH) Retired.
Murphy, James F. *c.s.c.* '58 (PRT) Saco, ME Most Holy Trinity Church; [L] Biddeford, ME Marie Joseph Spiritual Center.
Murphy, James F. '70 (PIT) [1] Butler, PA St. Fidelis of Sigmaringen Church.
Murphy, James H. '81 (MAD) Platteville, WI St. Augustine University Parish Church.
Murphy, James J. (RCK) [4] Rockford, IL St. Edward Church.
Murphy, James J. '45 (PH) Retired.
Murphy, James J. '54 (WH) Weston, WV St. Patrick's Church.
Murphy, James P. '65 (CHI) Glenview, IL St. Catherine Laboure Church.
Murphy, James T. '68 (SAC) [11] Sacramento, CA St. Charles Borromeo Church.
Murphy, James W. '48 (MEM) Retired.
Murphy, James W. '65 (L) [29] Louisville, KY Guardian Angels Church.
Murphy, Jeremiah *m.s.c.* '46 (SAT) Rocksprings, TX Sacred Heart of Mary Church.
Murphy, Msgr. Jeremiah T. '63 (LA) [50] Los Angeles, CA St. Brendan Church.
Murphy, Jerome A. *c.ss.r.* '51 (SP) [9] Tampa, FL St. Joseph Church.
Murphy, Jerome J. '43 (NY) New York, NY New York Postal Service; Retired.
Murphy, John *c.s.b.* (GRY) [K] Merrillville, IN Basilian Fathers Residence.
Murphy, John '50 (LA) On Duty Outside the Archdiocese.
Murphy, John *o.f.m.* '54 (HRT) [14] Hartford, CT St. Patrick-St. Anthony Church.
Murphy, John *f.m.s.i.* '72 (BO) [B] Framingham, MA Sylva Maria.
Murphy, John '79 (MRY) Retired.
Murphy, John B. *o.s.f.s.* '57 (CHL) Thomasville, NC Our Lady of the Highways Church; [I] High Point, NC Maryfield Nursing Home.
Murphy, John C. '65 (SP) St. Pete Beach, FL St. John Church.
Murphy, John D. *s.j.* '77 (SJ) [D] San Jose, CA Bellarmine College Preparatory.
Murphy, John D. '79 (MET) Colonia, NJ St. John Vianney Church.
Murphy, Msgr. John E. '38 (LR) Retired; [H] Little Rock, AR St. John Manor.
Murphy, Msgr. John F. '47 (COV) Retired.
Murphy, Msgr. John F. '47 (MIL) Retired.
Murphy, John F. '59 (CLV) [1] Cleveland, OH Cathedral of St. John the Evangelist.
Murphy, John G. '79 (MRY) [1] Monterey, CA Cathedral of San Carlos Borromeo.
Murphy, John J. *c.s.c.* (BO) Boston, MA Good Samaritan Medical Center.
Murphy, John J. '39 (FR) Somerset, MA St. Thomas More Church; Retired.
Murphy, John J. *c.s.c.* '49 (FR) [B] North Easton, MA Holy Cross Fathers Religious.
Murphy, Msgr. John J. '51 (SFR) Burlingame, CA St. Catherine of Siena Church; Retired.
Murphy, Msgr. John J. '54 (WDC) Retired.
Murphy, John J. '57 (ALB) Catskill, NY St. Patrick Church.
Murphy, John J. '68 (DEN) Evergreen, CO Christ the King Church.
Murphy, John M. (ATL) LaGrange, GA St. Peter's Church.
Murphy, John M. '45 (MIL) Retired.
Murphy, John M. '51 (NU) Retired.
Murphy, John M. '65 (CHI) [52] Chicago, IL St. Edward Church.
Murphy, John P. *s.d.b.* '45 (NEW) [3] Elizabeth, NJ St. Anthony's Church.
Murphy, John P. *o.s.a.* '57 (JOL) New Lenox, IL St. Jude Church.
Murphy, Msgr. John P. '64 (ALN) [11] Allentown, PA St. Thomas More Church.

Murphy, John P. *s.j.* '69 (CHI) [N] Chicago, IL Chicago Province of the Society of Jesus-Provincial Office.
Murphy, John T. *o.p.* (NY) Manhattan, NY Rockefeller University.
Murphy, John T. '31 (LC) Retired; [I] La Crosse, WI Holy Cross (Seminary) Diocesan Center.
Murphy, John Thaddeus *o.p.* '54 (NY) [22] New York, NY St. Catherine of Siena Church; [Z] New York, NY St. Catherine of Siena Priory.
Murphy, John V. *s.j.* '52 (P) [L] Portland, OR Jesuit Provincial Office (Oregon Prov.); [Q] Portland, OR Jesuit Development & Communications Office.
Murphy, Joseph (BO) Boston, MA McLean Hospital.
Murphy, Joseph *o.m.i.* '27 (BO) [Z] Tewksbury, MA Immaculate Heart of Mary Novitiate-Infirmary.
Murphy, Joseph '61 (PAT) Totowa Borough, NJ St. James of the Marches Church.
Murphy, Joseph B. *c.s.sp.* '33 (SB) [E] Hemet, CA Holy Ghost Fathers.
Murphy, Joseph F. (PRO) Chepachet, RI St. Eugene's Church.
Murphy, Joseph F. '49 (PRO) Retired.
Murphy, Joseph G. '44 (HRT) Retired.
Murphy, Joseph H. '61 (NEW) Old Tappan, NJ St. Pius X Church.
Murphy, Joseph J. '43 (CHR) Retired.
Murphy, Msgr. Joseph P. '54 (NY) [202] Staten Island, NY St. Clare Church.
Murphy, Joseph P. '88 (NOR) Warrenville, CT St. Philip Church.
Murphy, Joseph R. *s.s.j.* (GAL) Retired.
Murphy, Joseph R. *s.s.j.* '43 (BAL) [M] Baltimore, MD St. Joseph Society of the Sacred Heart House of Central Administration.
Murphy, Joseph T. '47 (PH) Glenside, PA St. Luke the Evangelist Church; Retired.
Murphy, Jude R. *o.f.m.* '61 (PRO) [P] Providence, RI St. Francis Friary.
Murphy, Kenneth *o.carm.* '81 (NY) [97] New York, NY Our Lady of the Scapular/St. Stephen Church.
Murphy, Kenneth B. (BO) Retired.
Murphy, Kenneth G. '55 (RVC) Great Neck, NY St. Aloysius Church.
Murphy, Kenneth J. '65 (IND) Military Chaplains.
Murphy, Kenneth R. '86 (MET) Spotswood, NJ Immaculate Conception Church.
Murphy, Kevin *o.s.b.* (LR) [2] Little Rock, AR St. Anne Church; [12] Little Rock, AR St. Patrick's Church.
Murphy, Kevin J. *o.s.b.* '62 (MIL) [P] Benet Lake, WI St. Benedict's Abbey.
Murphy, Kevin P. (ROC) Penfield, NY St. Joseph Church.
Murphy, Laurence T. *m.m.* '54 (NY) [Z] Maryknoll, NY Maryknoll Fathers and Brothers.
Murphy, Lawrence B. *s.j.* '64 (LA) [F] Los Angeles, CA Loyola High School.
Murphy, Lawrence C. '50 (MIL) Retired.
Murphy, Lawrence F. '56 (BO) Retired.
Murphy, Lawrence J. '43 (PH) Retired.
Murphy, Lawrence V. '58 (ROC) [26] Rochester, NY Holy Rosary Church.
Murphy, Michael A. '92 (BAL) Columbia, MD St. John the Evangelist Church.
Murphy, Michael D. '66 (LAN) East Lansing, MI St. Thomas Aquinas Church.
Murphy, Michael D. '77 (PH) [4] Drexel Hill, PA St. Dorothy Church.
Murphy, Michael F. '83 (SD) Coronado, CA Sacred Heart Church.
Murphy, Michael G. '87 (STL) [6] Florissant, MO St. Ferdinand Church.
Murphy, Michael J. *c.s.c.* '49 (FTW) [B] Notre Dame, IN University of Notre Dame Du Lac; [J] Notre Dame, IN Holy Cross Community, Corby Hall, University of Notre Dame.
Murphy, Michael P. '89 (JC) Kahoka, MO St. Michael the Archangel Church; St. Patrick, MO The Shrine of St. Patrick Church.
Murphy, Myles P. '90 (NY) [144] Bronx, NY St. Gabriel Church.
Murphy, Owen *s.a.* '52 (NY) [Z] Garrison, NY Franciscan Friars of the Atonement.
Murphy, Pat *c.s.* '80 (LA) Sun Valley, CA Our Lady of the Holy Rosary Church.
Murphy, Patrick (LIN) [D] Lincoln, NE St. Elizabeth Community Health Center.
Murphy, Patrick '53 (BIR) Madison, AL St. John the Baptist Church.
Murphy, Patrick E. '85 (MAR) Iron Mountain, MI Veterans Administration Hospital; [E] Iron Mountain, MI Monastery of the Holy Cross.
Murphy, Msgr. Patrick J. '50 (ALX) Tallulah, LA St. Edward Church.
Murphy, Patrick J. '53 (BIR) [I] Madison, AL St. John's Educational Foundation.
Murphy, Paul G. '94 (BGP) Shelton, CT St. Joseph's Church.
Murphy, Paul M. *c.m.* '60 (PH) [Z] Philadelphia, PA Congregation of the Mission.
Murphy, Peter *s.c.* '84 (MET) [B] Metuchen, NJ St. Joseph High School.
Murphy, Peter J. (BO) [1] Malden, MA Immaculate Conception Church.
Murphy, Peter P. '68 (PIT) Clairton, PA St. Clare of Assisi Church.
Murphy, Philip *ss.cc.* '70 (FR) [K] Fairhaven, MA Sacred Hearts Provincial House.
Murphy, Ralph J. *s.d.b.* '56 (OAK) [N] Berkeley, CA Salesian Community.
Murphy, Richard *o.p.* '35 (NO) [30] New Orleans, LA St. Dominic Church.
Murphy, Richard '57 (PMB) Fort Pierce, FL St. Mark Church.
Murphy, Richard '65 (PMB) Stuart, FL St. Joseph Church; [J] Palm Beach Gardens, FL Diocesan Property & Liability Insurance Committee.
Murphy, Richard '65 (ROC) [M] Rochester, NY Diocesan Office of Campus Ministry.
Murphy, Richard '80 (Y) Mineral Ridge, OH St. Mary's Church; [C] Youngstown, OH Ursuline High School.
Murphy, Richard Daniel '96 (BGP) [7] Norwalk, CT St. Thomas the Apostle Church.
Murphy, Richard J. *s.j.* '64 (CHI) [89] Chicago, IL St. Ignatius Church.
Murphy, Richard J. '73 (BAL) Walkersville, MD St. Timothy Church.
Murphy, Robert '74 (KC) [2] St. Joseph, MO Our Lady of Guadalupe Church.
Murphy, Robert *m.ss.a.* '93 (NOR) [A] Cromwell, CT Holy Apostles College and Seminary; [F] Cromwell, CT Missionaries of the Holy Apostles.
Murphy, Msgr. Robert E. '42 (BUF) [1] Lackawanna, NY Basilica of Our Lady of Victory; Retired.
Murphy, Robert J. *s.j.* '54 (LEX) [1] Lexington, KY Cathedral of Christ the King.
Murphy, Robert L. *s.j.* '59 (STL) [T] St. Louis, MO White House Retreat.
Murphy, Robert M. '93 (VEN) [3] Naples, FL St. Peter Church.
Murphy, Roland *o.carm.* '42 (WDC) [B] Washington, DC Whitefriars Hall.
Murphy, Romeo J. *o.m.i.* (BO) Boston, MA Saints Memorial Medical Center.
Murphy, Rory '88 (SFR) [2] San Rafael, CA St. Isabella Church.
Murphy, Msgr. Terrance J. '46 (STP) Retired.
Murphy, Msgr. Terrence J. '46 (STP) [C] St. Paul, MN University of St. Thomas.
Murphy, Theodore *s.m.m.* '58 (RVC) [N] Bay Shore, NY Montfort Missionaries.
Murphy, Thomas *o.f.m.cap.* (NY) Yonkers, NY St. Joseph Hospital.
Murphy, Thomas '36 (PIT) [K] Pittsburgh, PA Villa De Marillac Nursing Home.
Murphy, Thomas '51 (VEN) Port Charlotte, FL St. Charles Borromeo Church.
Murphy, Thomas *s.j.* '57 (NY) [161] Bronx, NY St. Margaret of Cortona Church.
Murphy, Thomas *m.s.c.* '65 (RCK) [H] Aurora, IL Missionaries of the Sacred Heart Community.
Murphy, Msgr. Thomas '66 (SAT) [61] San Antonio, TX St. Peter Prince of the Apostles Church.
Murphy, Thomas *o.f.m.cap.* '71 (NY) [17] Yonkers, NY Sacred Heart Church; [S] Yonkers, NY St. Joseph's Medical Center.
Murphy, Thomas '85 (IND) [26] Indianapolis, IN St. John the Evangelist Church.
Murphy, Thomas A. *s.j.* '39 (BGP) [O] Fairfield, CT The Fairfield Jesuit Community-Fairfield University.
Murphy, Thomas E. '73 (WDC) [B] Washington, DC Diocesan Laborer Priests, House of Studies.
Murphy, Thomas E. *o.s.f.s.* '76 (VEN) [3] Fort Myers, FL St. Cecilia Church.
Murphy, Thomas F. '51 (Y) Vienna, OH St. Vincent de Paul Church.
Murphy, Thomas F. '70 (RVC) Mineola, NY Corpus Christi Church.
Murphy, Thomas K. *o.f.m.* '58 (SP) [O] St. Petersburg, FL St. Anthony Friary.
Murphy, Thomas M. '79 (PRT) [A] Standish, ME Saint Joseph's College; [M] Standish, ME Saint Joseph's College.
Murphy, Thomas P. *c.s.p.* '62 (NY) [Z] Scarsdale, NY Paulist Fathers Generalate; [Z] Scarsdale, NY Paulist Fathers Generalate.
Murphy, Thomas R. '36 (PIT) Retired.
Murphy, Thomas W. '44 (NOR) Somersville, CT All Saints Church.
Murphy, Timothy '60 (VEN) Cape Coral, FL St. Andrew Church.
Murphy, Timothy *o.ss.t.* '67 (BAL) [L] Baltimore, MD Holy Trinity Spiritual Center; [M] Baltimore, MD Holy Trinity Monastery.
Murphy, Timothy '67 (P) [C] Portland, OR Central Catholic High School.
Murphy, Timothy *glmy.* '93 (JKS) Aberdeen, MS St. Francis of Assisi Church.
Murphy, Timothy J. (BO) [2] Salem, MA Immaculate Conception Church.
Murphy, Msgr. Timothy J. (SAN) [1] Midland, TX St. Ann's Church.
Murphy, Timothy J. '74 (SPR) Hampden, MA St. Mary's Church.
Murphy, Ultan P. '53 (DOD) Olmitz, KS St. Ann Church; Timken, KS Holy Trinity Church.
Murphy, Venard *o.f.m.* '61 (SP) [O] St. Petersburg, FL St. Anthony Friary.
Murphy, W. Maximus *c.s.b.* '44 (GAL) [Q] Sugar Land, TX Basilian Mission Center.
Murphy, Msgr. Walter C. '58 (BRK) [128] Brooklyn, NY Sacred Heart Church.
Murphy, Warren *t.o.r.* '60 (FWT) [8] Fort Worth, TX St. Andrew Church.
Murphy, William *s.a.* '40 (NY) [Z] Garrison, NY Franciscan Friars of the Atonement.
Murphy, William *c.p.* '73 (R) Tarboro, NC St. Catherine Church.
Murphy, William F. (BO) [28] Boston, MA Holy Name Church.
Murphy, William F. '56 (PRO) Retired; [P] Providence, RI St. John Vianney Residence.
Murphy, Msgr. William F. '65 (BO) Wellesley, MA St. John the Evangelist Church; [DD] Boston, MA Chancery Office.
Murphy, William F. '88 (BO) [3] Weymouth, MA Immaculate Conception Church.
Murphy, William J. '57 (DET) Orchard Lake, MI Our Lady of Refuge Church.
Murphy, William J. '96 (SUP) Hudson, WI St. Patrick Church.
Murphy, William P. '43 (CHI) Evergreen Park, IL Queen of Martyrs Church; Retired.
Murphy, William P. '65 (DEN) [2] Englewood, CO Holy Name Church.
Murphy, William P. '86 (SPR) Hadley, MA Holy Rosary Church; Longmeadow, MA St. Mary's Church.
Murphy, William S. '90 (PH) [1] Philadelphia, PA Cathedral Basilica of SS. Peter and Paul; [123] Philadelphia, PA Chapel of Our Lady of the Miraculous Medal.
Murphy, William T. '50 (RVC) Retired.
Murr, Charles T. '77 (NY) [62] New York, NY St. Joseph Church.
Murray, Adrian '51 (OAK) Retired.
Murray, Adrian L. '43 (OAK) [M] Oakland, CA Bishop Begin Villa.
Murray, Msgr. Andrew '73 (BLX) [4] Biloxi, MS Sacred Heart Church.
Murray, Arthur *o.f.m.* '49 (SP) [O] St. Petersburg, FL St. Anthony Friary.
Murray, Bernard *o.c.s.o.* '50 (L) [L] Trappist, KY Abbey of Our Lady of Gethsemani, of the Order of Cistercians of the Strict Observance.
Murray, Brendan J. '68 (PAT) Rockaway, NJ St. Cecilia's Church.
Murray, Celestine '55 (CC) Woodsboro, TX St. Therese, The Little Flower Church.
Murray, Cornelius J. '63 (CLV) North Olmsted, OH St. Brendan Church.
Murray, Cyprian *o.f.m.cap.* '64 (NOR) [4] Middletown, CT St. Pius X Church.
Murray, Msgr. Daniel A. '64 (PH) [3] Drexel Hill, PA St. Charles Borromeo Church.
Murray, Msgr. Daniel J. '73 (ORG) Garden Grove, CA St. Callistus Church.
Murray, Daniel L. '86 (WIN) Litomysl, MN Holy Trinity Church.
Murray, Donald J. '61 (MAD) [14] Madison, WI St. Thomas Aquinas Church.
Murray, Edmund J. *c.s.c.* '38 (FTW) [J] South Bend, IN Congregation of Holy Cross Indiana Province Provincial House.
Murray, Edward (SFR) Special Assignment; [J] San Francisco, CA St. Mary's Medical Center.
Murray, Edward *o.m.i.* '37 (SAT) San Antonio, TX Baptist Memorial Hospital; [M] San Antonio, TX Oblate Benson Residence (Southern Prov.); [M] San Antonio, TX Provincial Administration Office, Oblates of Mary Immaculate (Southern Prov.).
Murray, Edward G. '69 (SC) Whittemore, IA St. Michael's Church.
Murray, Edward K. '62 (SFR) [50] San Francisco, CA St. Teresa Church; San Francisco, CA St. Mary's Medical Center.
Murray, Edward L. *c.s.sp.* '45 (PIT) [B] Pittsburgh, PA Duquesne University of the Holy Ghost.
Murray, Eugene L. '65 (SC) Emmetsburg, IA Holy Family Church.
Murray, Msgr. Francis '49 (SAG) Retired.
Murray, Francis '53 (SFR) San Carlos, CA St. Charles Church; San Francisco, CA Kaiser Hospital Redwood City; San Francisco, CA Sequoia Hospital; Special Assignment.
Murray, Francis J. '51 (LAN) Manchester, MI St. Mary Church.
Murray, Frank J. '81 (PRT) Bangor, ME St. Mary's Church.
Murray, Frederick J. '53 (BO) Westwood, MA St. Denis Church.
Murray, George B. *s.j.* (DET) [K] Detroit, MI Jesuit Provincial Office-Detroit Province of the Society of Jesus.
Murray, George B. *s.j.* '65 (BO) [W] Weston, MA

Campion Center.
Murray, Gerald '84 (NY) Graduate Studies.
Murray, Msgr. Harold A. '49 (NEW) Retired.
Murray, Ignatius L. '57 (PH) Brookline, PA Annunciation B.V.M. Church.
Murray, J. Glenn *s.j.* '79 (CLV) [26] Cleveland, OH St. Henry Church.
Murray, James *o.p.* '50 (DET) [21] Detroit, MI St. Dominic Church.
Murray, James A. '58 (LAN) [1] Lansing, MI St. Mary Cathedral.
Murray, James B. '57 (NSH) Retired.
Murray, Msgr. James H. '56 (PAT) Denville, NJ St. Mary's Church.
Murray, Msgr. James J. '56 (NY) [I] New York, NY The Catholic Charities of the Archdiocese of New York; [I] New York, NY The Catholic Charities of the Archdiocese of New York; [V] New York, NY Mary Manning Walsh Home; [DD] New York, NY The Housing Fund of the Archdiocese of New York.
Murray, James M. *o.s.b.* '93 (PEO) [A] Peru, IL St. Bede Abbey and Academy.
Murray, Msgr. Jerome E. '49 (LIN) Curtis, NE St. James Church.
Murray, John '54 (Y) Retired.
Murray, John *c.s.b.* '67 (ROC) [L] Rochester, NY Marriage Encounter Apostolate.
Murray, John '67 (RVC) New Hyde Park, NY Notre Dame Church.
Murray, John A. *c.m.* '49 (PH) [Z] Philadelphia, PA Congregation of the Mission.
Murray, John A. '54 (Y) Hubbard, OH St. Patrick's Church.
Murray, John A. '62 (BO) Concord, MA St. Bernard Church.
Murray, John B. *c.m.* '42 (BRK) [D] Queens and Staten Island, NY St. John's University; [U] Jamaica, NY Vincentian Residence.
Murray, John C. *c.s.b.* '57 (ROC) [I] Rochester, NY Basilian Residence.
Murray, John D. '62 (LA) Canoga Park, CA Our Lady of the Valley Church.
Murray, John E. '60 (CHY) Douglas, WY St. James Church.
Murray, John E. '63 (HEL) [4] Anaconda, MT Anaconda Catholic Community Church.
Murray, John E. '67 (RVC) Retired.
Murray, John F. *c.ss.r.* '73 (TR) [Q] Long Branch, NJ San Alfonso Retreat House.
Murray, John Francis *s.m.a.* '57 (NEW) [N] Tenafly, NJ Society of African Missions, Provincialate, S.M.A. Fathers.
Murray, John I. '55 (SFS) Retired.
Murray, John J. '47 (PH) Retired.
Murray, John J. '61 (NY) Port Jervis, NY Immaculate Conception Church.
Murray, John J. '65 (BRK) [148] Queens, NY American Martyrs Church.
Murray, John J. '78 (CHL) Morganton, NC St. Charles Borromeo Church.
Murray, John L. '47 (E) Retired.
Murray, John P. *c.m.* '48 (PH) [A] Wynnewood, PA Theological Seminary of St. Charles Borromeo, Overbrook; [Z] Philadelphia, PA Congregation of the Mission.
Murray, John P. '54 (RVC) Merrick, NY Cure of Ars Church; East Meadow, NY Nassau County Medical Center.
Murray, John P. *s.j.* '87 (BO) [W] Boston, MA Loyola House.
Murray, John S. '69 (ORL) Titusville, FL St. Teresa Church.
Murray, John W. '68 (CHI) Military Chaplains.
Murray, Joseph '55 (NEW) [5] Bayonne, NJ St. Vincent de Paul Church.
Murray, Msgr. Joseph M. '56 (RVC) Westhampton Beach, NY Immaculate Conception Church.
Murray, Joseph P. *s.j.* '49 (BO) [W] Boston, MA Loyola House.
Murray, Msgr. Joseph W. '61 (PH) Lansdale, PA St. Stanislaus Church.
Murray, Kevin P. '77 (PH) Morton, PA Our Lady of Perpetual Help Church.
Murray, Kevin R. *c.ss.r.* '86 (PH) [25] Philadelphia, PA St. Boniface Church.
Murray, Leo A. *s.j.* '62 (PH) [82] Philadelphia, PA Old St. Joseph's Church.
Murray, Leonard M. *s.j.* '40 (STL) [O] St. Louis, MO Fusz Pavilion; [T] St. Louis, MO White House Retreat.
Murray, Maximillian '46 (SEA) Retired.
Murray, Michael *o.s.b.* '81 (PBL) Florence, CO St. Benedict Church.
Murray, Michael D. *o.s.b.* '56 (PBL) [E] Canon City, CO Holy Cross Abbey.
Murray, Michael J. '76 (WDC) Forestville, MD Church of the Holy Spirit.
Murray, Michael S. *o.s.f.s.* '86 (PH) [D] Philadelphia, PA Northeast Catholic High School for Boys; [Z] Philadelphia, PA Oblates of St. Francis De Sales.
Murray, Patrick '37 (MIA) Retired.
Murray, Patrick F. *s.j.* '45 (PH) [Z] Philadelphia, PA Jesuit Community at St. Joseph's University.
Murray, Msgr. Patrick J. '48 (SAT) [K] San Antonio, TX Casa De Padres; [S] San Antonio, TX Casa de Padres Endowment Fund; [S] San Antonio, TX St. Peter and Joseph Childrens' Home Endowment Fund; [S] San Antonio, TX Archdiocesan Endowment Fund; [S] San Antonio, TX Assumption Seminary Endowment Fund; [S] San Antonio, TX Seton Home Endowment Fund.
Murray, Paul E. '75 (WDC) [40] Washington, DC St. Stephen Martyr Church.
Murray, Peter *s.j.* '72 (NY) [Z] New York, NY West Side Jesuit Community.
Murray, Peter J. *s.j.* '72 (MET) [F] New Brunswick, NJ St. Peter's Medical Center.
Murray, Pius C.W. *c.s.s.* (BO) [6] Waltham, MA Sacred Heart Church.
Murray, Msgr. Richard H. '43 (LA) Woodland Hills, CA St. Bernardine of Siena Church; Retired.
Murray, Robert J. *o.s.a.* '83 (PH) [C] Villanova, PA Villanova University; [D] Drexel Hill, PA Monsignor Bonner High School.
Murray, Robert P. '46 (TR) Retired; [L] Lawrenceville, NJ Morris Hall-Saint Lawrence, Inc.
Murray, Robert W. '88 (BO) [3] Framingham, MA St. Jeremiah Church; [D] Framingham, MA Marian High School.
Murray, Msgr. Sean '52 (SD) [21] San Diego, CA St. Brigid Church; Retired.
Murray, Sean *c.ss.r.* '57 (SR) [L] Sebastopol, CA Diocesan House of Prayer.
Murray, Senan *c.s.sp.* '55 (MIA) [1] Pompano Beach, FL Assumption Church.
Murray, Steven (OG) [C] Watertown, NY Immaculate Heart Central High School.
Murray, Steven M. '88 (OG) [3] Watertown, NY St. Anthony Church.
Murray, Thomas '44 (SJ) Los Altos, CA St. Simon Church; Retired.
Murray, Thomas A. '68 (PH) [94] Philadelphia, PA St. Martin of Tours Church.
Murray, Thomas F. '57 (BO) Natick, MA Sacred Heart Church.
Murray, Timothy J. '77 (DET) [9] Warren, MI St. Martin de Porres Church.
Murray, Msgr. William F. '45 (PRO) Retired.
Murray, William F. '54 (MIL) Retired.
Murray, William J. *o.s.a.* '47 (PH) [Z] Villanova, PA St. Thomas Monastery.
Murray, Yhomas P. '81 (RVC) Sound Beach, NY St. Louis de Montfort Church.
Murrin, Donald *s.v.d.* '60 (JKS) Vicksburg, MS St. Mary Church.
Murrin, Joseph *s.s.c.* '44 (PRO) [P] Bristol, RI St. Columban's Retirement House.
Murrin, Raymond J. '61 (BIR) [19] Birmingham, AL St. Patrick's Church.
Murrman, Jonathan J. *o.s.b.* '65 (GBG) [H] Latrobe, PA Saint Vincent Archabbey.
Murrman, Warren D. *o.s.b.* '65 (GBG) [H] Latrobe, PA Saint Vincent Archabbey.
Murtagh, George O. '50 (BUR) Retired.
Murtagh, James '66 (PMB) [1] West Palm Beach, FL Holy Name of Jesus Church.
Murtagh, John J. '69 (YAK) [2] Yakima, WA Holy Family Church.
Murtagh, Lawrence '53 (WIN) On Duty Outside the Diocese.
Murtagh, Thomas P. '81 (BRK) [218] Queens, NY Our Lady, Queen of Martyrs Church.
Murtaugh, Daniel J. '54 (CHI) [114] Chicago, IL St. Kilian Church; Retired.
Murtaugh, James J. '48 (CHI) Skokie, IL St. Lambert Church; Retired.
Murtaugh, Lewis C. *s.j.* '69 (CHI) [N] Chicago, IL Chicago Province of the Society of Jesus-Provincial Office.
Murtaugh, William '72 (STP) New Brighton, MN St. John the Baptist Church.
Murtha, Chester '93 (SFS) [7] Sioux Falls, SD St. Michael Church.
Murtha, John *o.s.b.* (SAV) [B] Savannah, GA Benedictine Military School; [F] Savannah, GA The Benedictine Priory.
Murtha, Michael G. '93 (PH) [1] Phoenixville, PA St. Ann Church.
Murugarren, Jesus *o.s.a.* '55 (SAT) [58] San Antonio, TX St. Michael Church.
Murzyn, John A. '59 (GRY) Absent on Leave.
Muscalino, Daniel C. '78 (SY) [18] Syracuse, NY St. John the Evangelist Church; Special Assignment.
Muscat, John '51 (NY) [2] New Rochelle, NY St. Gabriel Church; New Rochelle, NY New Rochelle Hospital Medical Center.
Muscat, John '84 (CAM) Williamstown, NJ St. Mary's Church.
Muschette, Emilian *o.s.b.* '58 (NEW) [N] Newark, NJ Newark Abbey.
Muscolino, Frank J. '68 (BIR) [24] Birmingham, AL St. Stephen University Parish Church; [H] Birmingham, AL St. Stephen University Parish.
Mushi, Peter *a.j.* '87 (PIT) [5] Pittsburgh, PA St. Bede Church.
Mushinsky, John E. (PAT) Retired.
Musholt, Silas *o.f.m.* '55 (STL) Oakville, MO St. Francis of Assisi Church.
Musial, Msgr. Edward S. '46 (PH) [3] Bensalem, PA Saint Ephrem Church; Retired.
Musial, George '67 (CHI) [N] Chicago, IL St. Peter's Friary.
Musinski, Donald T. '62 (MIL) Johnsburg, WI St. John the Baptist Church.
Musiol, Jozef '72 (AUS) Bremond, TX St. Mary's Church.
Musko, Andrew (PSC) Retired.
Musngi, Efren *m.s.* '61 (SB) Moreno Valley, CA St. Christopher Church.
Musselman, Joseph G. *s.j.* '52 (NY) [Z] New York, NY Jesuit Provincial's Office; [Z] New York, NY Xavier Jesuit Community.
Mustaciuolo, Gregory '90 (NY) [1] New York, NY Cathedral of St. Patrick; Graduate Studies.
Musteikis, Leonard '38 (OM) Retired.
Mustos, Stephen N. *sch.p.* '58 (PAT) [9] Passaic, NJ St. Stephen's Church.
Musumbu, Gilberto Malu *m.s.p.* '88 (TUC) Yuma, AZ St. Francis of Assisi Church.
Musumeci, James S. '76 (BRK) [233] Queens, NY Resurrection-Ascension Church; [L] Brooklyn, NY Catholic Charities.
Mutefunya, Deo Gratias R. '63 (PEO) Moline, IL St. Mary's Church.
Muteru, Gabriel '87 (NY) Mamaroneck, NY Holy Trinity Church.
Muth, Joseph R. '74 (BAL) [59] Baltimore, MD St. Matthew Church.
Muthukattil, Thomas '66 (BRK) [152] Queens, NY St. Anthony of Padua Church.
Muthuplakel, James '67 (HBG) [5] Lancaster, PA St. Joseph Church; Lancaster, PA Lancaster General Hospital and Lancaster Community Hospital.
Mutlow, Robert *o.p.* '58 (CHI) [24] Chicago, IL St. Basil/Visitation Church.
Muyombo, Gaston '83 (DEN) [3] Englewood, CO St. Louis Church; [N] Littleton, CO Carmel of Holy Spirit.
Muzdakis, John J. *o.s.f.s.* '65 (ARL) [D] Alexandria, VA Bishop Ireton High School; [J] Alexandria, VA Oblates of St. Francis de Sales Residence.
Muzic, Anthony J. '63 (CLV) [46] Cleveland, OH St. Mark Church.
Muzquiz, Lino *c.p.* '47 (MGZ) San Sebastian, PR San Sebastian Martir Church.
Muzzey, Charles H. '65 (WDC) Derwood, MD St. Francis of Assisi Church.
Muzzin, Victor *f.d.p.* '72 (NY) [11] New York, NY St. Ann Church.
Mwangi, Paul (PIT) [64] Pittsburgh, PA Resurrection Church.
Mwariri, Alphonsus *i.m.c.* '86 (PIT) [N] Pittsburgh, PA Consolata Fathers.
Mwau, Julius '82 (NY) [153] Bronx, NY St. Joan of Arc Church.
Mychajlenko, Jaroslaw '78 (SJP) [10] Solon, OH Protection B.V.M. Church.
Mycue, Gordon E. '49 (STP) Retired.
Myer, Blase '68 (PHX) [6] Scottsdale, AZ St. Maria Goretti Church.
Myers, Albert J. '51 (CLV) North Olmsted, OH St. Brendan Church; Retired.
Myers, Chris *o.f.m.* (BO) [W] Andover, MA St. Francis Friary.
Myers, Christopher *s.o.l.t.* '90 (CC) [H] Robstown, TX Society of Our Lady of the Most Holy Trinity.
Myers, David A. *s.j.* '70 (P) [L] Portland, OR Jesuit Provincial Office (Oregon Prov.).
Myers, Edward F. '45 (CHI) [37] Chicago, IL Christ the King Church; Retired.
Myers, Edward J. '55 (NEW) Rahway, NJ St. Mary's Church.
Myers, Edward T. *o.p.* '65 (NY) [Z] New York, NY St. Vincent Ferrer Priory.
Myers, Gerald '94 (FAR) Walhalla, ND St. Boniface's Church.
Myers, James E. '80 (PEO) On Duty Outside the Diocese.
Myers, James R. '57 (FTW) Elkhart, IN St. Vincent de Paul Church.
Myers, Jeremy '84 (DAL) Sherman, TX St. Mary Church.
Myers, John *o.f.m.cap.* '54 (DET) [K] Detroit, MI St. Bonaventure Friary.
Myers, Kenneth C. '68 (CLV) Released from Diocesan Assignment; [AA] Cleveland, OH COAR Peace Mission, Inc.; [AA] San Antonio, TX.
Myers, Kenneth C. '68 (SAT) [T] San Antonio, TX Missionaries of Pastoral Charity Society.
Myers, Rawley '49 (COS) Retired.
Myers, Regis F. '54 (ALT) Retired.
Myers, Robert *s.v.d.* '49 (CHI) [B] Techny, IL Divine Word Residence.

Myers, William F. '56 (RCK) Active Outside the Diocese.
Myers, Msgr. William R. '69 (STU) Gallipolis, OH St. Louis Church; [I] Rio Grande, OH Rio Grande University.
Myers, William S. '88 (STO) Absent on Leave.
Myett, Robert D. *o.p.* '60 (PRO) [P] Providence, RI St. Thomas Aquinas Priory at Providence College.
Myhalyk, Richard M. *s.s.e.* (MOB) [A] Selma, AL Edmundite House of Formation.
Mykyta, Andrew (SD) San Diego, CA Our Lady of Perpetual Help Church.
Mykyta, Andrew (STN) [1] Chicago, IL St. Nicholas Ukrainian Catholic Cathedral; Retired.
Myladil, Thomas *o.c.d.* '78 (NY) [165] Bronx, NY St. Mary Star of the Sea Church.
Mylchreest, William F. '80 (MIA) [13] Fort Lauderdale, FL St. Sebastian Church.
Myler, John T. '82 (BEL) Cahokia, IL Holy Family Church.
Myles, A. James '62 (WH) [3] Wheeling, WV Corpus Christi Church.
Myles, John '64 (SAC) Maxwell, CA Sacred Heart Church.
Mynaugh, Msgr. Charles B. '42 (PH) Retired.
Myrand, Pierre *c.p.* '63 (WOR) [N] Shrewsbury, MA Passionist Fathers of Shrewsbury, Inc., Calvary Retreat Center; [P] Shrewsbury, MA Calvary Retreat Center, Passionist Community.
Myshchuk, Mikhail '94 (STF) Watervliet, NY St. Nicholas Church.
Myslinski, John F. '80 (WDC) Great Mills, MD Holy Face Church.
Mysliwiec, Haldane R. '70 (CHI) Other Assignments.
Mysliwiec, Jan J. *s.d.s.* '62 (NEW) [N] Verona, NJ The Salvatorian Fathers.
Mysliwiec, Jordan *s.d.s.* '62 (NEW) [3] Irvington, NJ Sacred Heart of Jesus Church.
Myszel, George G. '53 (MIL) Retired.
Myszka, Msgr. Daniel J. '58 (BUF) [10] Buffalo, NY Assumption Church.
Mytych, Joseph '39 (CHI) Argo, IL St. Blase Church.
Mytych, Joseph F. '39 (CHI) [170] Chicago, IL SS. Peter and Paul Church; Retired.
Myvett, Manuel *s.v.d.* '62 (TR) Lakewood, NJ St. Anthony Claret Church.

N

Naas, Stephen E. '78 (KAL) Niles, MI St. Mary Church.
Naber, Herman J. '59 (L) [23] Louisville, KY St. Elizabeth of Hungary Church; [71] Louisville, KY St. Therese Church; [F] Louisville, KY St. Joseph Child Development Center; [G] Louisville, KY St. Joseph Children's Home; [G] Louisville, KY St. Joseph Catholic Orphan Society.
Naber, John T. '45 (BUF) Retired.
Nabozny, Peter J. '55 (ALB) Herkimer, NY St. Francis de Sales Church.
Nacarino, Raymond L. '85 (MET) [3] New Brunswick, NJ Our Lady of Mt. Carmel Church.
Nacauili, John '61 (FRS) Absent on Sick Leave.
Nacca, John J. (ORL) Retired.
Nacca, John J. '41 (ROC) Retired.
Naccarato, Francis A. '79 (NY) [199] Staten Island, NY Blessed Sacrament Church.
Naccarato, Frank '79 (NY) State, NY Arthur Kill Correctional Facility.
Nace, Msgr. Arthur J. '57 (PH) Absent on Sick Leave.
Nachajski, Richard E. '71 (ALN) [2] Reading, PA St. Anthony of Padua Church.
Nachef, Anthony *b.s.o.* '91 (NTN) Akron, OH St. Joseph Church.
Nachtigal, Fred '58 (Y) Retired.
Nacional, Perfecto '62 (SR) [3] Santa Rosa, CA St. Rose of Lima Church.
Nacius, Michael A. '89 (CHI) Orland Park, IL St. Michael Church.
Nacke, Xavier *o.s.b.* '63 (KC) Maryville, MO St. Gregory Barbarigo Church; [A] Conception, MO Conception Seminary College; [N] Maryville, MO Northwest Missouri State University Newman House.
Nacu, Joseph *m.s.* '57 (SB) Barstow, CA St. Philip Neri Church.
Nadackal, Zacharias *c.m.i.* '64 (NY) Rye, NY Resurrection Church.
Nadal, Bart *c.r.* '47 (DEN) [A] Denver, CO Provincial House at St. Andrew, Seminary (C.R.).
Naddeo, Henry M. '56 (NEW) Lyndhurst, NJ Our Lady of Mount Carmel Church.
Nadeau, Armand J. *m.s.* '39 (HRT) [M] Hartford, CT Missionaries of LaSalette Provincial Secretary.
Nadeau, J.H. Normand '68 (BUR) Brattleboro, VT St. Michael Church.
Nadeau, James A. '88 (PRT) [1] Portland, ME Cathedral of the Immaculate Conception.
Nadeau, Leon C. '39 (SPR) Retired.
Nadeau, Real J. '62 (PRT) [5] Lewiston, ME St. Patrick's Church; [6] Lewiston, ME SS. Peter and Paul Church.
Nadeau, Richard A. '80 (PRT) Bradley, ME St. Ann Church.
Nadeau, Roland A. *m.s.* '42 (HRT) [M] Hartford, CT Missionaries of LaSalette Provincial Secretary.
Nadeau, Roland S. *m.s.* '69 (MAN) Hanover, NH Mary Hitchcock Hospital; [K] Enfield, NH Shrine of Our Lady of La Salette; [M] Enfield, NH La Salette Shrine and Center of Enfield.
Nadeau, Timothy J. '91 (PRT) [4] Old Town, ME St. Ann Church, Indian Island Church; Orono, ME St. Mary's Church.
Nadeau, William E. *o.m.i.* '68 (STP) [N] St. Paul, MN Oblate Provincial Offices; [N] St. Paul, MN Oblate Residence.
Nadicksbernd, Elmer *s.v.d.* '64 (WH) Gassaway, WV St. Thomas Church; Maysel, WV Church of The Risen Lord.
Nadine, Jerome E. '58 (BRK) Released from Diocesan Assignment.
Nadine, Jerry '58 (LAV) [8] Las Vegas, NV St. Elizabeth Ann Seton Church.
Nadolny, Edmund S. '59 (HRT) [6] Meriden, CT St. Stanislaus Church.
Nadolny, Stanley '68 (TUC) Bisbee, AZ St. Patrick Church.
Nadrach, Adolph W. '42 (KAL) Retired.
Nadura, John '58 (NEW) [22] Jersey City, NJ Our Lady of Victories Church.
Naduvilekoot, Augustine '71 (NOR) Durham, CT Notre Dame Church.
Nadzam, John B. '50 (STU) Retired.
Naegele, Gary P. '79 (WH) [3] Fairmont, WV St. Anthony Church.
Naessens, Philip *o.f.m.cap.* '86 (DET) [K] Detroit, MI St. Bonaventure Friary.
Naffah, Msgr. John '39 (OLL) Hillside, IL Our Lady of Lebanon Church; Retired.
Naffah, Msgr. John '39 (SAM) Retired.
Nagai, Msgr. Alan '58 (HON) Kailua, HI St. John Vianney Church.
Nagaroor, Joseph '66 (MAR) Perkins, MI St. Joseph Church.
Nagele, John *c.pp.s.* (TOL) [M] Bellevue, OH Sorrowful Mother Shrine.
Nagengast, Maynard G. *o.s.b.* '62 (NEW) [N] Newark, NJ Newark Abbey.
Nagle, Austin *ss.cc.* '54 (BO) Boston, MA V.A. Medical Centers; [U] Brockton, MA St. Joseph Manor Nursing & Extended Care Facility.
Nagle, Austin *ss.cc.* '54 (FR) [K] Fairhaven, MA Sacred Hearts Provincial House.
Nagle, Edmund W. *s.j.* '63 (PAT) [I] Morristown, NJ Loyola House of Retreats.
Nagle, Gerald J. *m.m.* '57 (SFR) [N] San Francisco, CA Maryknoll Fathers and Brothers, Catholic Foreign Mission Society of America, Inc.
Nagle, James B. *m.m.* '52 (NY) [Z] Maryknoll, NY Maryknoll Fathers and Brothers.
Nagle, John *s.a.c.* '47 (FWT) Mineral Wells, TX Our Lady of Lourdes Church.
Nagle, Msgr. Joseph P. '71 (BRK) [132] Brooklyn, NY St. Saviour Church; [U] Douglaston, NY Institutional Services Residence.
Nagle, Michael R. '72 (FR) Edgartown, MA St. Elizabeth Church; Oak Bluffs, MA Sacred Heart Church; Vineyard Haven, MA St. Augustine Church.
Nagle, Richard *o.carm.* '37 (NY) [Z] Middletown, NY St. Albert's Priory.
Nagle, Vincent '92 (FR) [17] Fall River, MA St. Louis Church; [P] Buzzards Bay, MA Massachusetts Maritime Academy Newman Center; [Q] Fall River, MA Priestly Fraternity of the Missionaries of St. Charles Borromeo, Inc.
Nagle, William A. '49 (BGP) [1] Stamford, CT St. John's Church.
Nagler, Robert '56 (SB) Retired.
Nagler, Robert J. '56 (SD) [31] San Diego, CA St. Mary Magdalene Church.
Naglich, Robert *s.c.j.* '91 (GAL) [20] Houston, TX Christ the Redeemer Church.
Naguszewski, Edward B. '30 (BO) Retired.
Nagy, Joseph '40 (LA) Retired.
Nagy, Moses *o.cist.* '53 (DAL) [B] Irving, TX University of Dallas.
Nahman, Richard M. *o.s.a.* '58 (BRK) [205] Queens, NY St. Nicholas of Tolentine Church.
Nahn, William J. '76 (ALN) [2] Easton, PA St. Bernard Church.
Nahoe, Francisco *o.f.m.conv.* '94 (LA) [R] Torrance, CA Franciscan Friars, St. Bonaventure Friary.
Nairn, Thomas *o.f.m.* (CHI) [D] Chicago, IL Hales Franciscan High School, Inc.
Nairn, Thomas *o.f.m.* '75 (CHI) [B] Chicago, IL The Catholic Theological Union at Chicago.
Najdowski, Msgr. John A. '51 (GR) Grandville, MI St. Pius X Church.
Najjar, Samuel A. '84 (SAM) Waterville, ME St. Joseph Church.
Nakagawa, Francis *s.m.* '57 (SJ) [M] Cupertino, CA Marianist Provincial Residence.
Nakowicz, Stanley T. '67 (PRO) [3] East Providence, RI Our Lady of Loreto Church.
Nalepa, Damien '70 (BAL) [34] Baltimore, MD St. Gregory the Great Church; Baltimore, MD Baltimore City Jail.
Nalepa, Richard *c.p.* '70 (SCR) [M] Scranton, PA Saint Ann's Passionist Monastery.
Nall, Brent '93 (SAC) Chico, CA St. John the Baptist Church.
Nall, James M. '87 (BEL) Special Assignment.
Nallen, James F. '66 (CHI) [55] Chicago, IL St. Ethelreda Church.
Nalley, Robert W. '75 (GAY) Grayling, MI St. Mary Church; Special Assignment.
Nally, J. Brendan '56 (WOR) Clinton, MA Our Lady of the Rosary Church; Lancaster, MA Massachusetts Correctional Institution.
Nally, John J. *m.s.* '54 (WOR) [6] Fitchburg, MA St. Joseph's Church.
Nally, Joseph M. '72 (WOR) [24] Worcester, MA St. Joan of Arc Church.
Nalysnyk, Bohoan (STN) [1] Chicago, IL St. Nicholas Ukrainian Catholic Cathedral.
Nalysnyk, Jaroslav (BO) [20] Boston, MA Christ The King Church.
Nalysnyk, Jaroslaw '91 (STF) Boston, MA Christ the King Church.
Nam, Joseph Phan *c.m.c.* (SB) [6] San Bernardino, CA St. Anne Church.
Nam, Kim Van '90 (ELP) Alpine, TX Our Lady of Peace Church.
Nam, Simon '52 (NY) [156] Bronx, NY St John Nam Church.
Nami, Peter *o.m.i.* '76 (BUF) [35] Buffalo, NY St. James Church.
Namie, James B. '54 (SAM) [D] Brooklyn, NY Archbishop's Residence.
Namie, Msgr. James B. '54 (STP) On Duty Outside the Archdiocese.
Namiotka, Edward F. '87 (CAM) [5] Vineland, NJ St. Mary's Church; [A] Hammonton, NJ St. Joseph.
Namocatcat, Felix S. '62 (SFR) [3] South San Francisco, CA St. Augustine Church.
Nan, Dale '78 (DUL) [F] Duluth, MN University of MN-Duluth.
Nangle, C. Richard '45 (ROC) [7] Auburn, NY St. Francis of Assisi Church; Retired.
Nangle, Joseph *o.f.m.* '58 (WDC) [B] Washington, DC Franciscan Mission Service of North America.
Nangle, Thomas R. '70 (CHI) Other Assignments.
Nanley, William (ORL) Melbourne, FL Our Lady of Lourdes Church.
Nanthiyattu, Zacharias *o.i.c.* (CHI) [73] Chicago, IL St. Gregory Church; Chicago, IL Syro-Malankara Catholic Mission of the Archdiocese of Chicago Church.
Nanz, Jack '71 (PIT) [4] Butler, PA St. Peter Church.
Napier, Robert L. '90 (STA) Jacksonville Beach, FL St. Paul's Church.
Napierkowski, Joseph J. *s.m.* '55 (HON) Wailuku, HI St. Anthony Church; [H] Wailuku, Maui, HI Wailuku Marianist Community.
Napoli, Carlo *t.o.r.* (PIT) Allegheny County, PA Eye and Ear Hospital; Allegheny County, PA Montefiore Hospital; Allegheny County, PA Presbyterian-University Hospital; [N] Pittsburgh, PA Franciscan Friars, T.O.R.
Napoli, Felician *o.f.m.* (SP) [5] Tampa, FL Incarnation Church.
Napoli, Felician *o.f.m.* '51 (NY) [Z] New York, NY Franciscan Province of the Immaculate Conception.
Napoli, Peter *o.f.m.cap.* '73 (PAT) [12] Paterson, NJ Our Lady of Lourdes Church.
Napolitano, Anthony M. '66 (NY) [3] Yonkers, NY St. Ann Church.
Napolitano, Joseph V. '76 (HRT) [11] New Britain, CT St. Maurice Church; [E] New Britain, CT St. Thomas Aquinas High School.
Nappo, Michael *o.f.m.* (BO) [42] Boston, MA St. Leonard of Port Maurice Church.
Naquin, Roch R. '62 (HT) Grand Caillou, LA Holy Family Church.
Naranjo, Francisco '95 (STO) Manteca, CA St. Anthony Church.
Narbekovas, Andrius '93 (WDC) [B] Washington, DC Marian Fathers Scholasticate.
Nardo, Anthony J. '87 (NEW) Springfield, NJ St. James Church.
Nardoianni, Antonio *o.f.m.* ' 7 (NY) [Z] New York, NY Franciscan Province of the Immaculate Conception.
Nardone, Amadeo *o.f.m.* '68 (NY) [Z] New York, NY Franciscan Province of the Immaculate Conception.
Nardone, Richard M. '54 (NEW) [B] South Orange, NJ Seton Hall University.
Nardoni, Enrique *s.s.d.* '48 (DAL) [B] Irving, TX University of Dallas.
Narewski, Peter J. (PRO) [P] Providence, RI St. John Vianney Residence.
Narewski, Peter J. '47 (PRO) Retired.
Narez, Juan '93 (ELP) [30] El Paso, TX St. Pius X Church.
Nargaj, Andrew *o.f.m.* (NY) [171] Bronx, NY Our Lady of Good Counsel Church; [Z] New York, NY Franciscan Friars, Order of Friars Manor.
Narimattam, Joseph '64 (WIL) Claymont, DE Holy

Rosary Church; Wilmington, DE St. Francis Hospital; [H] Wilmington, DE St. Francis Hospital, Inc.
Narita, Michael *ss.cc.* '68 (FR) [K] Fairhaven, MA Sacred Hearts Provincial House.
Narkun, Msgr. Peter P. '45 (NY) Retired; [E] New York, NY Cardinal Hayes High School.
Narlaly, Jose T. *o.ss.t.* '81 (BAL) [M] Baltimore, MD Holy Trinity Monastery.
Naro, Carl J. '52 (RIC) Retired.
Narowich, Edward '53 (FTW) Geneva, IN St. Mary of the Presentation Church.
Naseman, Alfred *c.pp.s.* '67 (CIN) [B] Carthagena, OH St. Charles.
Nash, Denis P. '54 (GR) Jenison, MI Holy Redeemer Church.
Nash, Francis J. *s.j.* '69 (BAL) [C] Baltimore, MD Loyola College; [M] Baltimore, MD Jesuit Community of Loyola College, Inc.
Nash, Howard J. '61 (HRT) [4] New Haven, CT St. Bernadette's Church.
Nash, James '94 (WIL) Ogletown, DE Holy Family Church.
Nash, Msgr. James F. '34 (ORG) [1] Anaheim, CA St. Anthony Claret Church; Retired.
Nash, James R. '89 (SCR) Montrose, PA Holy Name of Mary Church.
Nash, John C. '75 (NOR) North Stonington, CT St. Thomas More Church.
Nash, Michael '80 (JUN) Hoonah, AK Sacred Heart Church; Skagway, AK St. Therese of the Child Jesus Church; Yakutat, AK St. Ann Church.
Nash, Paul A. *s.j.* '52 (BO) [W] Chestnut Hill, MA The Jesuit Community at Boston College.
Nash, Robert C. '48 (WH) [1] Wheeling, WV St. Joseph's Cathedral; [J] Wheeling, WV Welty Home for the Aged, Inc.
Nash, Thomas C. (SC) Armstrong, IA St. Mary's Church; Estherville, IA St. Patrick's Church.
Nasini, Gino *s.x.* '65 (PAT) [M] Wayne, NJ Xaverian Missionary Fathers.
Naslund, Sebastian C. '67 (PT) Chattahoochee, FL Holy Cross Parish Church; Chattahoochee, FL Florida State Hospital.
Nason, Dennis T. '66 (BO) [4] Medford, MA St. Raphael Church.
Nasr, Toufic '97 (OLL) Awaiting Assignment.
Nasri, Youssef Bochra '85 (BRK) [86] Brooklyn, NY St. Michael's Church; [123] Brooklyn, NY Resurrection Catholic Coptic Chapel.
Nassal, Joseph F. *c.pp.s.* '82 (KCK) [K] Easton, KS Shantivanam Archdiocesan House of Prayer.
Nassaney, Daniel *o.m.i.* '74 (NOR) [F] Willimantic, CT Oblates of Mary Immaculate; [I] Willimantic, CT Immaculata Retreat House.
Nasser, Joseph M. *s.j.* '75 (GAL) [3] Spring, TX St. Ignatius of Loyola Church.
Nassetta, Peter W. '89 (ARL) Falls Church, VA St. James Church.
Nassr, Martin '67 (TOL) Findlay, OH St. Michael Church.
Nasta, Thomas A. '82 (PH) Abington, PA Our Lady Help of Christians Church.
Nastold, Donald O. *s.j.* '58 (CIN) [28] Cincinnati, OH St. Francis Xavier Church.
Natale, Samuel '79 (RIC) On Duty Outside the Diocese.
Natali, Alfred M. *o.s.a.* '43 (PH) [99] Philadelphia, PA St. Mary Magdalen de Pazzi Church.
Natalizia, Louis T. '80 (PRO) [4] North Providence, RI Presentation of the Blessed Virgin Mary Church.
Nathe, Joel '93 (SCL) Grey Eagle, MN St. Joseph's Church; Ward Springs, MN St. Bernard's Church.
Natho, Clifton J. '60 (GAL) [1] Spring, TX Christ the Good Shepherd Church; Retired.
Nativo, Joseph S. '56 (NEW) [22] Newark, NJ St. Lucy's Church.
Natsuhara, Bruce K. '78 (OKL) Okeene, OK St. Anthony's Church.
Nau, Dale '78 (DUL) [G] Duluth, MN The Human Life and Development Fund of the Diocese of Duluth; [G] Duluth, MN Calvary Cemetery.
Nau, Thomas R. '78 (STU) Ironton, OH St. Joseph Church; Ironton, OH St. Lawrence Church.
Naucke, Alfred E. *s.j.* '65 (SAC) [C] Sacramento, CA Jesuit High School; [H] Carmichael, CA Jesuit High School Community of Sacramento.
Naughton, James *s.d.b.* '67 (BIR) [8] Birmingham, AL Holy Rosary Church; [9] Birmingham, AL St. John Bosco Church.
Naughton, Msgr. John T. '49 (LA) Woodland Hills, CA St. Mel Church; Retired.
Naughton, Msgr. Louis '71 (ATL) [1] Atlanta, GA Cathedral of Christ the King.
Naughton, Michael *o.s.b.* '66 (SCL) [I] Collegeville, MN St. John's Abbey, of the Order of St. Benedict.
Naughton, Patrick J. '91 (COL) [2] Columbus, OH St. Agatha Church.
Naughton, Thomas J. '61 (BO) Winchester, MA Immaculate Conception Church.
Naughton, William M. '72 (PAT) Randolph, NJ Resurrection Church.
Naumann, Msgr. Joseph F. '75 (STL) [41] St. Louis, MO St. John the Baptist Church.
Naumann, Paul S. *s.j.* '63 (SY) [S] Syracuse, NY Jesuits at LeMoyne, Inc.
Naumes, Matthew '63 (SEA) Medical Leave.
Naus, John E. *s.j.* '55 (MIL) [P] Milwaukee, WI Jesuit Community at Marquette University.
Navarra, Peter '81 (SD) Escondido, CA St. Mary Church.
Navarre, Robert G. '45 (SAG) Retired.
Navarria, Antony '59 (TUC) [I] Thatcher, AZ Eastern Arizona Junior College.
Navarro, Jose Luis Duenas *o.a.r.* '59 (NY) [Z] New York, NY Augustinian Recollects Provincial Residence, Province of St. Nicholas of Tolentine.
Navarro, Martin *s.s.s.* '68 (CGS) [5] Caguas, PR Santisimo Sacramento Church.
Navarro, Modesto Martinez *t.c.* (BAL) Odenton, MD St. Joseph Church.
Navarro, Nicolas Parroco (SJN) [37] San Juan, PR Maria Auxiliadora Church.
Navarro, Olga (BWN) [D] San Juan, TX San Juan Home Health and Hospice.
Navarro, Msgr. Pablo A. '78 (MIA) On Duty Outside the Archdiocese.
Navarro, Msgr. Pablo A. '78 (PMB) [A] Boynton Beach, FL St. Vincent de Paul Regional Seminary.
Navarro, Pedro '63 (NEW) [2] Union City, NJ St. Augustine's Church.
Navarroli, Frederick '43 (RVC) Retired.
Navascues, Moises *sch.p.* '54 (PCE) Santa Isabel, PR St. James Church; [B] Ponce, PR The Pontifical Catholic University of Puerto Rico
Nave, Francis A. '92 (ALN) Bath, PA Sacred Heart Church.
Nave, Francis R. '60 (ALN) Retired; [J] Bethlehem, PA Holy Family Villa.
Navien, Thomas A. '42 (BO) Retired.
Navin, Msgr. Cyril '45 (LA) Encino, CA St. Cyril Church; Retired.
Navin, Timothy M. '79 (VEN) [3] Naples, FL St. Peter Church.
Navins, Robert J. '50 (NY) [212] Staten Island, NY St. Margaret Mary Church.
Navit, Zachary W. '94 (PH) Trooper, PA Visitation B.V.M. Church.
Navone, John J. *s.j.* '62 (P) [L] Portland, OR Jesuit Provincial Office (Oregon Prov.).
Navoy, Ronald E. '71 (CHI) River Grove, IL St. Cyprian Church.
Nawarskas, Msgr. Frederick '67 (SAN) [2] Abilene, TX Holy Family Church.
Nawrocki, Norman '82 (DET) [4] Redford, MI St. Valentine Church; Special Assignment.
Nawrocki, Robert W. '61 (MIL) [5] Milwaukee, WI St. Alexander's Church.
Nawrocki, Xavier *o.f.m.conv.* '57 (BGP) [6] Danbury, CT Sacred Heart Church.
Nawrocki, Zozislaw *s.ch.* '75 (PAT) Boonton, NJ SS. Cyril and Methodius Church.
Nay, Msgr. Thomas '78 (STU) [I] St. Clairsville, OH Ohio University - Eastern.
Nayak, Christudas '68 (ALX) [C] Alexandria, LA St. Frances Cabrini Hospital.
Naylor, Ronald J. '60 (RIC) Retired.
Nazabal, Isidro '63 (CGS) Cidra, PR Nuestra Senora de Fatima Church.
Nazareth, Longinus '62 (NY) [203] Staten Island, NY St. Clement Church; [215] Staten Island, NY St. Michael Church.
Nazario, Herber *o.s.a.* '65 (SJN) [42] San Juan, PR Ntra. Sra. de la Monserrate Church.
Nazimek, David J. '93 (GBG) North Huntingdon, PA St. Agnes Church.
Nazimek, Francis A. '48 (PIT) Carmichaels, PA St. Hugh Church.
Nazzaro, John *s.d.b.* '83 (SP) [E] Tampa, FL Mary Help of Christians School.
Nazzaro, Stanley J. '48 (HRT) Retired.
Ndagizimana, Isidore '85 (AUS) [4] Austin, TX Holy Cross Church.
Ndeukoya, Msgr. Augustine (SP) Ruskin, FL St. Anne Church.
Ndiokwere, Nathaiel '75 (SFS) [1] Sioux Falls, SD St. Joseph Cathedral.
Ndrevashay, Primus P. '61 (DET) Beverly Hills, MI Our Lady of Albanians Church.
Ndulaka, Matthias '78 (NY) [224] Staten Island, NY St. Peter Church.
Nealen, Giles L. *o.s.b.* '51 (GBG) [H] Latrobe, PA Saint Vincent Archabbey; [I] Latrobe, PA Discalced Carmelite Nuns.
Nealon, Msgr. Joseph A. '61 (STU) Retired.
Nealon, Joseph W. '40 (NEW) Haworth, NJ Sacred Heart Church; Retired.
Nealy, Francis D. *o.p.* '39 (PRO) [P] Providence, RI St. Thomas Aquinas Priory at Providence College.
Neary, Anthony *c.p.* '54 (PIT) [N] Pittsburgh, PA St. Paul of the Cross Monastery.
Neary, Mark J. '83 (SJ) [3] Sunnyvale, CA St. Cyprian Church.
Neary, Patrick *c.s.c.* '91 (FTW) [A] Notre Dame, IN Moreau Seminary; [A] Notre Dame, IN Moreau Seminary; [B] Notre Dame, IN University of Notre Dame Du Lac.
Neary, Patrick M. *c.s.c.* '91 (FTW) [J] Notre Dame, IN Holy Cross Community, Corby Hall, University of Notre Dame.
Neary, Thomas E. '54 (SY) [5] Syracuse, NY Most Holy Rosary Church; Retired.
Neault, Armand R. '52 (PRT) Springvale, ME Notre Dame Church.
NeBel, Msgr. Charles A. '38 (BEL) Equality, IL St. Joseph Church; Ridgway, IL St. Joseph Church; Retired.
Nebiolo, Emilio '52 (KCK) Retired.
Nedder, Edward T. '87 (SAM) Springfield, MA St. Anthony Church.
Nee, Eugene O. '64 (SAT) Military Chaplains.
Nee, Kenneth T. '53 (RVC) Manorhaven, NY Our Lady of Fatima Church.
Nee, Robert *o.f.m.* '62 (NY) [35] New York, NY St. Francis of Assisi Church.
Nee, Robert E. '71 (BO) [10] Lowell, MA St. Michael Church.
Nee, Thomas B. '66 (RIC) Smithfield, VA Good Shepherd Church; Suffolk, VA St. Mary of the Presentation Church.
Nee, Thomas M. '39 (PIT) Retired; [N] Pittsburgh, PA St. John Vianney Manor.
Needham, Msgr. Thomas J. '61 (WOR) [6] Worcester, MA Immaculate Conception Church.
Neeley, Peter *s.j.* '81 (LA) [6] Los Angeles, CA Blessed Sacrament Church.
Neely, Harry M. *o.s.a.* '53 (SD) [C] San Diego, CA St. Augustine High School; [H] San Diego, CA Augustinian Community.
Neenan, Aidan *o.f.m.cap.* '44 (RVC) Nesconset, NY Nesconset Nursing Home; St. James, NY St. James Nursing Home; [N] Smithtown, NY St. Ann's Friary.
Neenan, Benedict *o.s.b.* '88 (KC) [A] Conception, MO Conception Seminary College; [J] Conception, MO Conception Abbey.
Neenan, Robert P. *s.j.* '51 (STP) [N] Minneapolis, MN La Storta Jesuit Community.
Neenan, William B. *s.j.* '61 (BO) [C] Chestnut Hill, MA Boston College; [W] Chestnut Hill, MA The Jesuit Community at Boston College.
Nees, John '51 (PH) [D] Philadelphia, PA Father Judge High School for Boys.
Neff, Alfred F. *c.s.c.* '40 (FTW) [J] South Bend, IN Congregation of Holy Cross Indiana Province Provincial House.
Neff, Eugene J. '71 (BEL) Lebanon, IL St. Joseph Church.
Neff, Msgr. John F. '60 (SP) [14] Tampa, FL St. Paul Church; [F] Tampa, FL St. Paul Preschool.
Neff, John R. '86 (E) Brandy Camp, PA Holy Cross Church; Du Bois, PA Du Bois Regional Hospital.
Neffy, Arthur '47 (DET) Retired.
Negele, R. Philip *o.c.s.o.* '66 (DEN) [H] Denver, CO St. Joseph Hospital.
Negherbon, Vincent R. '46 (ALT) [F] Loretto, PA Mount Assisi Monastery.
Negley, Phil M. *m.s.* (GAL) Friendswood, TX Mary, Queen Church.
Negley, Phil M. *m.s.* '73 (BO) [Y] Ipswich, MA LaSalette Retreat House at Newman Hall.
Negrete, Wayne *s.j.* '91 (SD) [4] San Diego, CA Christ the King Church.
Negrillos, Ferdinand *sch.p.* '41 (PH) [G] Devon, PA Devon Preparatory School; [Z] Devon, PA Piarist Fathers (Order of the Pious Schools).
Negro, Carmelo *c.s.* '52 (WDC) [L] Mitchellville, MD Villa Rosa Nursing Home, Inc.
Negro, Sergio P. '53 (FRS) On Special Assignment; [C] Fresno, CA Saint Agnes' Medical Center.
Negron, Hermin *d.d.* (SJN) [17] Bayamon, PR La Resurreccion del Senor Church.
Neidhart, William J. *c.s.c.* (FTW) Granger, IN St. Pius X Church.
Neiheisel, Stanley H. '61 (CIN) [34] Cincinnati, OH Holy Cross-Immaculata Church.
Neilson, Joseph *o.c.d.* '62 (DAL) [K] Dallas, TX Mount Carmel Center.
Neilson, Kieran A. *o.s.b.* '60 (CHL) [J] Belmont, NC Belmont Abbey.
Neilson, Richard J. '83 (NY) [101] New York, NY Our Saviour Church.
Neiman, John W. '86 (LA) Redondo Beach, CA St. Lawrence Martyr Church.
Neis, Thomas A. '52 (GAY) Charlevoix, MI St. Mary Church.
Neis, William P. '67 (LC) Menomonie, WI St. Joseph Church; [L] Menomonie, WI The Ministry to the University of Wisconsin-Stout.
Nejasmich, Stephen C. *s.j.* '78 (SFR) [E] San Francisco, CA St. Ignatius College Preparatory (Coed); [N] San Francisco, CA Jesuit Community at St. Ignatius College Preparatory.
Nekic, Simon J. '43 (CLV) [12] Lorain, OH St. Vitus Church.

Nekoliczak, Ted A. '59 (GI) Sidney, NE St. Patrick's Church.
Nelan, Francis *m.s.c.* '53 (SAT) [K] San Antonio, TX Padua Place.
Nelan, Kevin J. '77 (NY) [16] New York, NY St. Benedict the Moor Church; [110] New York, NY Sacred Heart of Jesus Church.
Nelipowitz, Charles *o.f.m.conv.* '54 (SY) [2] Syracuse, NY Assumption B.V.M. Church.
Nelke, Richard '51 (STL) Chesterfield, MO Ascension Church.
Nelligan, Paul J. *s.j.* '54 (WOR) [N] Worcester, MA Jesuits of Holy Cross College, Inc.
Nellis, Thomas F. '66 (ROC) Webster, NY Holy Trinity Church.
Nelson, Andrew L. '57 (MIL) [A] Milwaukee, WI Saint Francis Seminary.
Nelson, Caye A. '88 (BR) [15] Baton Rouge, LA Most Blessed Sacrament Church.
Nelson, Charles T. '87 (SFD) Bluffs, IL St. Patrick Church; Murrayville, IL St. Bartholomew Church; Winchester, IL St. Mark Church.
Nelson, Daniel C. *o.f.m.* '77 (ALB) [B] Loudonville, NY Siena College.
Nelson, Francis J. '66 (SAV) [7] Savannah, GA St. Frances Xavier Cabrini Church.
Nelson, Francis P. *c.ss.r.* '64 (BRK) [U] Brooklyn, NY Our Lady of Good Counsel Residence.
Nelson, Frank M. (RVC) Valley Stream, NY Blessed Sacrament Church.
Nelson, Glenn L. '93 (RCK) Special Assignment.
Nelson, James D. *s.j.* '57 (SPK) [K] Spokane, WA Regis Community.
Nelson, Linden '81 (LC) [E] Marshfield, WI St. Joseph's Hospital.
Nelson, Paul E. '61 (WIN) Austin, MN St. Augustine's Church.
Nelson, Robert W. '77 (LC) Boyd, WI Sacred Heart of Jesus-St. Joseph Church; Stanley, WI Holy Family Church; [E] Stanley, WI Victory Medical Center, Inc.
Nelson, Thomas *o.praem.* '81 (ORG) [H] Silverado, CA Norbertine Fathers.
Nelson, Thomas J. *c.m.* '75 (DEN) [M] Denver, CO Congregation of the Mission Midwest Province: De Paul House.
Nelson, Thomas J. '93 (WDC) [1] Bethesda, MD St. Bartholomew Church.
Nelson, Thomas W. *o.praem.* '81 (ORG) [A] Silverado, CA St. Michael's Norbertine Postulancy, Novitiate and Juniorate.
Nelson, William R. '82 (PBL) Center, CO St. Francis Jerome Church; Del Norte, CO Holy Name of Mary Church; Monte Vista, CO St. Joseph Church.
Nemec, Joseph J. '84 (LIN) [11] Lincoln, NE St. Teresa's Church; [G] Lincoln, NE Adoration Convent and Church of Christ the King.
Nemecek, M. Cyril '60 (CHI) North Riverside, IL Mater Christi Church.
Nemeck, Francis Kelly *o.m.i.* '61 (CC) [G] Sarita, TX Lebh Shomea House of Prayer.
Nemeck, Francis Kelly *o.m.i.* '61 (SAT) [C] San Antonio, TX Oblate School of Theology.
Nemergut, Robert '77 (EVN) [2] Vincennes, IN Basilica of St. Francis Xavier; [3] Vincennes, IN St. John the Baptist Church.
Nemeth, Edward M. *s.j.* '65 (CLV) University Heights, OH Gesu Church.
Nemeth, Maurus B. *o.s.b.* '72 (SFR) [N] Portola Valley, CA Woodside Priory.
Nemeth, Robert *o.f.m.* '67 (BGP) [3] Fairfield, CT St. Emery's Church.
Nemmers, Francis J. '57 (SC) Larchwood, IA St. Mary Church.
Nemmers, Mark R. '66 (DUB) St. Theresa, IA St. Theresa's Church; Sylvia, IA Assumption Church.
Nemmers, Reinhard E. '35 (SC) Retired.
Nenneau, Thomas D. '81 (LAN) Charlotte, MI St. Mary Church.
Nentwick, John '65 (Y) [2] Canton, OH Our Lady of Peace Church.
Nero, James *o.f.m.* (NEW) Fair Lawn, NJ St. Anne's Church.
Neroda, Edward J. '57 (Y) [21] Youngstown, OH St. Stanislaus Kostka's Church.
Nesbit, Walter G. *s.j.* '59 (KC) [B] Kansas City, MO Rockhurst College; [J] Kansas City, MO Rockhurst College - Jesuit Community.
Nesbitt, James B. '53 (SUP) Retired.
Nesbitt, John B. '62 (SD) Retired.
Nesevitch, Joseph '51 (SJP) Retired.
Neske, Mark I. '83 (MOB) [11] Mobile, AL Little Flower Church.
Nespolo, Umberto (FRS) On Special Assignment.
Nespolo, Umberto *o.m.i.* '59 (FRS) [1] Fresno, CA St. John Cathedral.
Nesrsta, Steven '95 (AUS) Temple, TX St. Mary's Church.
Ness, Bernardine *o.s.b.* '64 (SFS) [F] Marvin, SD Blue Cloud Abbey.
Ness, Scott C. *o.s.a.* '90 (BO) [CC] North Andover, MA Merrimack College Campus Ministry Center.
Nessel, William J. *o.s.f.s.* '56 (HBG) Lewisburg, PA Sacred Heart of Jesus Church.
Nessinger, Philip *o.carm.* '50 (CHI) Gurnee, IL St. Paul the Apostle Church.
Nession, Mark R. '84 (FR) [1] Fall River, MA Cathedral of St. Mary of the Assumption.
Nester, Edward J. '46 (MET) Retired; [H] Somerset, NJ Maria Regina Residence.
Nesti, Donald S. *c.s.sp.* (GAL) [Q] Houston, TX Western Province of the Congregation of the Holy Ghost.
Nestler, W. David *o.f.m.cap.* '89 (PIT) [N] Pittsburgh, PA St. Conrad Friary.
Nestor, Msgr. Michael '65 (SJP) Retired.
Nestor, Robert P. '70 (NEW) [B] South Orange, NJ Seton Hall University.
Nestor, Thomas E. '81 (BO) [A] Boston, MA St. John's Seminary School of Theology.
Nestor, Thomas F. '80 (BO) [A] Boston, MA St. John's Seminary.
Nesvadba, Msgr. Reginald '66 (GAL) [A] Houston, TX St. Mary's Seminary.
Netta, John G. '57 (NEW) [6] Elizabeth, NJ St. Genevieve's Church; Elizabeth, NJ Union County Jail.
Nettekoven, Joseph '75 (ORG) [3] Anaheim, CA St. Justin Martyr Church.
Netter, Msgr. Edmund '51 (NY) Nyack, NY St. Ann Church.
Netter, Msgr. Edmund W. '51 (NY) Retired.
Netzer, Angelus *o.f.m.conv.* '51 (ALB) [A] Rensselaer, NY Conventual Franciscan Friars.
Neu, Msgr. Hubert '51 (FWT) [1] Fort Worth, TX St. Patrick Cathedral.
Neu, Msgr. Leon M. '76 (BUF) Randolph, NY St. Patrick Church.
Neubeck, Robert H. *s.j.* '55 (NY) [Z] New York, NY Murray-Weigel Hall.
Neuberger, Michael T. '62 (MIL) On Leave.
Neubert, Germar '65 (OM) [K] Schuyler, NE Benedictine Mission House.
Neudecker, Urban C. '45 (WIN) Retired.
Neufelder, Jerome '55 (IND) [A] St. Meinrad, IN St. Meinrad Seminary.
Neufelder, Msgr. Jerome M. '55 (EVN) On Duty Outside the Diocese.
Neugebauer, John J. '55 (ALT) [11] Altoona, PA Our Lady of Lourdes Church.
Neugebauer, Robert G. '73 (ALT) [2] Altoona, PA Immaculate Conception Church.
Neuhaus, Richard J. '91 (NY) [52] New York, NY Immaculate Conception Church; [A] Yonkers, NY St. Joseph's Seminary.
Neuhaus, William B. '83 (COV) Carrollton, KY St. John the Evangelist Church.
Neuman, Eugene C. '70 (MIL) [5] Fond du Lac, WI Sacred Heart Church; [W] Milwaukee, WI Cursillos in Christianity.
Neuman, James L. '71 (SFD) Wood River, IL St. Bernard Church.
Neuman, Matthias *o.s.b.* '67 (EVN) [H] Ferdinand, IN Sisters of St. Benedict of Ferdinand, IN, Inc., Monastery Immaculate Conception.
Neuman, Matthias *o.s.b.* '67 (IND) [B] St. Meinrad, IN St. Meinrad Seminary-College of Liberal Arts; [J] St. Meinrad, IN St. Meinrad Archabbey.
Neuman, Peter *i.c.* '80 (NO) [14] New Orleans, LA Mary, Queen of Vietnam Church.
Neumann, Aloysius J. '60 (RCK) Stockton, IL Holy Cross Church.
Neumann, August '52 (MET) Retired.
Neumann, Charles *s.m.* '52 (SAT) [C] San Antonio, TX St. Mary's University of San Antonio, Texas; [M] San Antonio, TX Marianist Residence.
Neumann, Don A. '72 (GAL) [K] Houston, TX The Catholic Chaplain Corps.
Neumann, Paul *s.m.* '59 (FWT) [12] Fort Worth, TX St. Mary of the Assumption Church.
Neumann, Richard J. '65 (HRT) Windsor, CT St. Gabriel's Church.
Neumann, William J. '75 (ORL) [2] Ocala, FL Our Lady of the Springs Church.
Neumeier, Larry '95 (LA) Paramount, CA Our Lady of the Rosary Church.
Neuner, Donald L. '56 (STL) [3] St. Charles, MO St. Elizabeth Ann Seton Church.
Neurohr, Gilbert N. '54 (MAR) Retired; [D] Escanaba, MI Bishop Noa Home for Senior Citizens.
Neuroth, William C. '65 (COV) [R] Covington, KY Interfaith Commission of Northern Kentucky.
Neuser, John '62 (GB) Mishicot, WI Holy Cross Church.
Neuville, Joseph '46 (P) Retired.
Neuville, Joseph J. '47 (P) Milwaukie, OR St. John the Baptist Church.
Neuzil, Greg '67 (KNX) LaFollette, TN Our Lady of Perpetual Help Church.
Neva, Roman G. '35 (FAR) Retired.
Nevans, Robert V. '49 (DEN) Retired.
Nevares, Eduardo *m.s.* '81 (TYL) Lufkin, TX St. Patrick Church.
Neveu, Armand A. '45 (HRT) Retired.
Neville, Gary J. *o.praem.* '78 (GB) [I] De Pere, WI St. Norbert Abbey.
Neville, James J. *s.j.* '56 (WH) Monongah, WV Holy Spirit Church.
Neville, John J. *o.s.c.* '61 (STP) [N] Shoreview, MN Crosier Provincial House Province of St. Odilia.
Neville, Joseph B. *s.j.* '60 (SY) [S] Syracuse, NY Jesuits at LeMoyne, Inc.
Neville, Thomas W. '52 (RCK) Virgil, IL SS. Peter and Paul Church.
Nevin, Emmet R. '77 (NY) [E] New York, NY Monsignor Farrell High School.
Nevins, Albert J. *m.m.* '42 (NY) [Z] Maryknoll, NY Maryknoll Fathers and Brothers.
Nevins, Donald J. '75 (CHI) [62] Chicago, IL St. Francis of Assisi Church; [81] Chicago, IL Holy Family Church.
Nevins, Eugene J. *s.j.* '80 (CIN) [K] Cincinnati, OH Good Samaritan Hospital; [M] Cincinnati, OH Jesuit Community at St. Xavier High School.
Nevins, John J. '57 (PH) Essington, PA St. Margaret Mary Alacoque Church.
Nevins, Troy '96 (GR) Portland, MI St. Patrick's Church.
Nevlud, Gregory '82 (SAT) [C] San Antonio, TX University of the Incarnate Word.
New, Gary *s.d.s.* '91 (GB) Charlesburg, WI St. Charles Borromeo Church; Charlestown, WI St. Martin Church; Chilton, WI St. Augustine Church; Chilton, WI St. Mary Church; Jericho, WI Holy Trinity Church; Kloten, WI St. Elizabeth Church.
Newberry, Austin *o.s.b.* '87 (IND) [B] St. Meinrad, IN St. Meinrad Seminary-College of Liberal Arts; [J] St. Meinrad, IN St. Meinrad Archabbey.
Newbold, Robert C. '45 (PRO) [23] Providence, RI Our Lady of Lourdes Church.
Newbold, Thomas M. *c.p.* '42 (CHI) [N] Chicago, IL Passionist Provincial Office.
Newbold, Thomas More *c.p.* '42 (SAC) [H] Citrus Heights, CA Christ the King Retreat.
Newburn, Charles *sch.p.* '79 (MIA) [C] Fort Lauderdale, FL Cardinal Gibbons High School.
Newcomer, Joseph '71 (B) [B] Nampa, ID Mercy Medical Center.
Newell, John J. '58 (BRK) Absent on Sick Leave.
Newell, Joseph A. *s.j.* '66 (CAM) Washington Township, NJ SS. Peter and Paul Church.
Newell, Joseph P. '45 (PIT) Cranberry Township, PA St. Ferdinand Church.
Newell, Matthias '87 (RIC) Brookneal, VA St. Elizabeth of Hungary Church; South Boston, VA St. Paschal Baylon Church.
Newfield, John L. '48 (HT) Retired.
Newhouse, Paul M. *c.i.c.m.* '54 (SAT) Somerset, TX St. Mary's Church.
Newland, Ronald A. '67 (NEW) Military Chaplains.
Newman, Aloysius T. '54 (WDC) Retired.
Newman, Charles *o.f.m.* '85 (PH) [D] Philadelphia, PA Archbishop Ryan High School; [Z] Philadelphia, PA St. Pius X Friary.
Newman, Earle A. *s.s.j.* '53 (BAL) [M] Baltimore, MD St. Joseph Society of the Sacred Heart House of Central Administration.
Newman, Francis M. '47 (NY) Verplanck, NY St. Patrick Church; Retired.
Newman, J. Scott '93 (CHR) [9] Charleston, SC Divine Redeemer Church.
Newman, Louis '58 (SD) [25] San Diego, CA St. Columba Church.
Newman, Louis I. '58 (RVC) Priests Released from Diocesan Assignment.
Newman, Mark L. *c.j.* '60 (LA) Santa Maria, CA St. Louis de Montfort Church.
Newman, Michael J. *s.d.s.* '67 (SAC) [K] Chico, CA Director of Campus Ministry; [K] Chico, CA Director of Campus Ministry.
Newman, Michael T. '69 (MIL) [2] Waukesha, WI St. Mary Church.
Newman, Nelson A. '54 (OM) Central City, NE St. Michael Church.
Newman, Robert V. *s.c.* '81 (HRT) [1] New Haven, CT Sacred Heart Church; [16] New Haven, CT St. Peter Church.
Newman, William '54 (BAL) [Q] Baltimore, MD Catholic Daughters of the Americas.
Newman, William A. *o.p.* '57 (WDC) [11] Washington, DC St. Dominic Church & Priory Church.
Newmeyer, George C. '68 (PIT) Glenshaw, PA St. Bonaventure Church.
Newns, John J. '74 (PH) [1] Phoenixville, PA St. Ann Church.
Newton, David J. '88 (LFT) Carmel, IN Our Lady of Mount Carmel Church.
Newton, John G. '53 (CAM) Military Chaplains.
Newton, John G. '53 (HON) Retired.
Newton, Stephen *c.s.c.* '89 (FTW) [J] Notre Dame, IN Holy Cross Community, Corby Hall, University of Notre Dame.
Newton, Stephen P. *c.s.c.* '89 (FTW) [B] Notre Dame, IN University of Notre Dame Du Lac.
Newton, Thomas A. '88 (CAM) Mantua, NJ Incarnation

Church; [Q] Camden, NJ Rutgers College of South Jersey.
Ney, Charles N. '74 (NSH) Absent on Leave.
Neyland, Malcolm '73 (LUB) Shallowater, TX St. Phillip Benizi Church.
Neyland, Quintin A. *o.f.m.* '46 (NY) [35] New York, NY St. Francis of Assisi Church.
Neylon, Bruce M. '75 (FR) Seekonk, MA St. Mary's Church.
Neyra, Hugo '84 (LA) Pico Rivera, CA St. Hilary Church; Los Angeles, CA L.A. County/University of Southern California Hospitals.
Neyrey, Jerome H. *s.j.* '70 (FTW) [B] Notre Dame, IN University of Notre Dame Du Lac; [O] Granger, IN Jesuit Community.
Ng, Thomas '61 (OAK) [12] Oakland, CA St. Leo's Church.
Ng'iela, Pius '88 (PIT) [J] Pittsburgh, PA St. Francis Medical Center.
Ngbatana, Tongele (SAC) Carmichael, CA St. John the Evangelist Church.
Nghi, John T. '71 (LA) Burbank, CA St. Finbar Church.
Nghiem, Peter Hoan-Xuan '72 (GR) On Special Assignment.
Nghiem, Vu Minh *c.ss.r.* '51 (LA) [R] Baldwin Park, CA Vietnamese Redemptorist Mission; [CC] Baldwin Park, CA The Redemptorist Vietnamese Mission Corporation.
Ngo, Anthony Trang Kim '94 (RIC) [6] Norfolk, VA Our Lady of Lavang Church.
Ngo, Francis Huan Ton '89 (GAL) [39] Houston, TX St. John Neumann Church.
Ngo, Joseph Linh Duy '52 (NO) Retired.
Ngo, Peter T.C. '93 (LA) [1] Los Angeles, CA Cathedral of Our Lady of the Angels.
Ngo Chau Minh, Peter M. *c.m.c.* (SPC) [E] Carthage, MO Congregation of the Mother Co-Redemptrix, United States Assumption Province.
Ngo hoang Khoi, Joachim '91 (SB) [E] Corona, CA Congregation of the Mother Coredemptrix.
Ngoc Diep, Joseph M. Tran *c.m.c.* '82 (SPC) [A] Carthage, MO Congregation of the Mother Co-Redemptrix.
Ngugi Kaihu, Dominic (ROC) [I] Rochester, NY Basilian Residence.
Nguyen, Alfonso T. '89 (MET) Woodbridge, NJ St. James Church.
Nguyen, Am *s.d.b.* '94 (OAK) [N] Berkeley, CA Salesian Community.
Nguyen, Andrew *c.m.c.* (BO) [62] Boston, MA St. Peter Church.
Nguyen, Andrew Cuu (NY) Manhattan, NY Manhattan Psychiatric Center.
Nguyen, Anthony Giang '66 (BO) [2] Chelsea, MA St. Rose Church; [13] Lowell, MA St. Patrick Church.
Nguyen, Anthony Phuc *c.s.s.r.* '92 (P) [17] Portland, OR Holy Redeemer Church.
Nguyen, Augustine '70 (DAL) [2] Garland, TX Mother of Perpetual Help Church.
Nguyen, Binh *c.m.* '82 (LA) San Gabriel, CA San Gabriel Church.
Nguyen, Chanh '96 (LA) Canoga Park, CA St. Joseph the Worker Church.
Nguyen, Chau '86 (ORL) Palm Bay, FL St. Joseph Church.
Nguyen, Chinh '94 (SR) Petaluma, CA St. Vincent de Paul Church.
Nguyen, Dam '93 (PIT) Castle Shannon, PA St. Anne Church.
Nguyen, Dau '84 (NO) [A] New Orleans, LA Notre Dame Seminary Graduate School of Theology.
Nguyen, Doakim '93 (GAL) [40] Houston, TX St. John Vianney Church.
Nguyen, Doanh (PHX) [B] Phoenix, AZ Brophy College Preparatory.
Nguyen, Dominic Hoa '95 (ORG) Garden Grove, CA St. Columban Church.
Nguyen, Dominic Hung *s.j.* '92 (P) [L] Portland, OR Jesuit Provincial Office (Oregon Prov.).
Nguyen, Dominic Huyen Duc '64 (NO) [14] New Orleans, LA Mary, Queen of Vietnam Church.
Nguyen, Dominic Khoai *i.c.m.* (BR) [H] Baton Rouge, LA Incarnational Consecration Mission.
Nguyen, Dovan '93 (TLS) Poteau, OK Immaculate Conception Church.
Nguyen, Francis X. Khoi '90 (DOD) Dighton, KS St. Theresa Church; Scott City, KS St. Joseph Church.
Nguyen, Hien Minh '85 (SJ) Milpitas, CA St. Elizabeth Church.
Nguyen, Hieu '69 (SC) [1] Sioux City, IA Cathedral of the Epiphany.
Nguyen, Hoa '95 (OKL) [1] Oklahoma City, OK Cathedral of Our Lady of Perpetual Help.
Nguyen, Huan Tien '66 (CIN) On Special and Diocesan Assignment; [V] Cincinnati, OH Vietnamese-Catholic Community.
Nguyen, Hung '94 (SEA) Poulsbo, WA St. Olaf Church.
Nguyen, Hung Joseph (STO) [10] Stockton, CA Presentation of B.V.M. Church.
Nguyen, Hung Viet *i.c.m.* '69 (BR) [4] Baton Rouge, LA St. Anthony of Padua Church; [H] Baton Rouge, LA Incarnational Consecration Mission; [L] Baton Rouge, LA St. Michael's Home.
Nguyen, Huy '95 (LA) Claremont, CA Our Lady of the Assumption Church.
Nguyen, Joe Van Anh '88 (AUS) [5] Austin, TX Holy Vietnamese Martyrs Church.
Nguyen, John '72 (LA) Torrance, CA St. Catherine Laboure Church.
Nguyen, Joseph '80 (NOR) [B] Uncasville, CT St. Bernard High School.
Nguyen, Joseph An '92 (CAM) [7] Camden, NJ St. Joseph's Pro-Cathedral; [5] Atlantic City, NJ Our Lady Star of the Sea Church.
Nguyen, Joseph Chinh (BO) [74] Boston, MA St. William Church.
Nguyen, Joseph Chuan '78 (ORG) Inactive Leave.
Nguyen, Joseph Dau Van '84 (NO) [4] Metairie, LA St. Benilde Church.
Nguyen, Joseph Kahn V. '63 (DAV) [M] Davenport, IA St. Vincent Center.
Nguyen, Joseph Luan '90 (ORG) [1] Huntington Beach, CA St. Bonaventure Church.
Nguyen, Joseph Ngoc Tu *o.p.* '64 (GAL) [Q] Houston, TX Dominican Fathers and Brothers, St. Mark Priory, Inc.
Nguyen, Joseph Phiet The '73 (GAL) Madisonville, TX St. Elizabeth Ann Seton Church.
Nguyen, Joseph Son '89 (ORG) Laguna Hills, CA St. Nicholas Church.
Nguyen, Joseph Son Van '82 (DAL) [7] Dallas, TX Mary Immaculate Church.
Nguyen, Joseph Tan Doan *o.f.m.* '86 (SFD) [B] Quincy, IL Quincy University.
Nguyen, Joseph Thai-Doan '88 (BR) Gonzales, LA St. Theresa of Avila Church.
Nguyen, Joseph Thinh '94 (MEM) [22] Memphis, TN Our Lady Of Perpetual Help Church.
Nguyen, Jude Ban '73 (SAC) [22] Sacramento, CA Vietnamese Catholic Martyrs Church.
Nguyen, Khiet '96 (TLS) [1] Tulsa, OK Holy Family Cathedral.
Nguyen, Khoa *o.f.m.* '95 (BO) [BB] Boston, MA St. Anthony Shrine.
Nguyen, Lich Van '84 (NO) Arabi, LA St. Robert Bellarmine Church.
Nguyen, Liem *o.s.b.* '94 (P) [A] St. Benedict, OR Mount Angel Seminary; [L] St. Benedict, OR Mt. Angel Abbey.
Nguyen, Liep Van Joseph '63 (CC) On Special Assignment.
Nguyen, Manh H. *c.m.* '95 (CHL) [3] Greensboro, NC St. Mary Church.
Nguyen, Martin Lam *c.s.c.* '89 (FTW) [B] Notre Dame, IN University of Notre Dame Du Lac; [J] Notre Dame, IN Holy Cross Community, Corby Hall, University of Notre Dame.
Nguyen, Michael Joseph Vinh Ngoc '90 (NO) On Duty Outside the Archdiocese.
Nguyen, Michael N. '93 (NO) La Place, LA St. Joan of Arc Church.
Nguyen, Minh Hai '92 (NEW) West New York, NJ St. Joseph of the Palisades Church.
Nguyen, Nghiem Vinh '89 (NO) [12] Metairie, LA St. Mary Magdalen Church.
Nguyen, Pascal *o.praem.* '94 (ORG) [H] Silverado, CA Norbertine Fathers.
Nguyen, Paul Chuong *s.d.b.* '88 (NEW) [C] Ramsey, NJ Don Bosco Preparatory High School for Boys.
Nguyen, Peter '61 (SD) Oceanside, CA Tri City Hospital.
Nguyen, Peter '90 (OKL) [2] Oklahoma City, OK St. Andrew Dung-Lac Church.
Nguyen, Peter Phong '46 (DAL) Grand Prairie, TX St. Joseph Vietnamese Catholic Community Church.
Nguyen, Peter Quang '90 (DEN) [17] Denver, CO Notre Dame Church.
Nguyen, Peter Vinh Q. '86 (NEW) South Orange, NJ Our Lady of Sorrows Church.
Nguyen, Fhien '92 (CHI) [26] Chicago, IL St. Benedict Church.
Nguyen, Phillip D. '87 (GR) On Duty Outside the Diocese.
Nguyen, Quang '91 (NO) Gretna, LA St. Cletus Church.
Nguyen, Quang Dang '44 (CC) Rockport, TX St. Peter Indo-Chinese Parish Church; Retired.
Nguyen, Raphael Ho Xuan '96 (ORG) Garden Grove, CA St. Columban Church.
Nguyen, Stephen Tan *o.f.m.* '59 (SFR) [7] San Francisco, CA St. Boniface Church.
Nguyen, Sy Uy '91 (ORG) [4] Huntington Beach, CA St. Vincent de Paul Church.
Nguyen, Tam N. '82 (TLS) [13] Tulsa, OK SS. Peter and Paul Church.
Nguyen, Te Van '86 (SFR) [3] San Mateo, CA St. Matthew Church.
Nguyen, Thai Van '95 (CHI) [11] Chicago, IL St. Andrew Church.
Nguyen, Thanh N. '95 (R) [3] Raleigh, NC Our Lady of Lourdes Church.
Nguyen, Thanh T. '91 (STA) [3] Jacksonville, FL Christ the King Church.
Nguyen, Thien Chi *s.o.l.t.* '91 (CC) [H] Robstown, TX Society of Our Lady of the Most Holy Trinity.
Nguyen, Thien Van '89 (WIN) New Richland, MN All Saints Church.
Nguyen, Thomas Thanh '69 (LAF) Louisa, LA St. Helen Church.
Nguyen, Thong *c.ss.r.* '56 (DAL) [2] Garland, TX Mother of Perpetual Help Church.
Nguyen, Thu Ngoc '93 (GAL) [44] Houston, TX St. Luke the Evangelist Church.
Nguyen, Thu Van '92 (VIC) El Campo, TX St. Philip's Church.
Nguyen, Thuong Hoai '91 (OAK) [3] Oakland, CA St. Anthony's Church.
Nguyen, Tien Tri '96 (SFE) Rio Rancho, NM St. Thomas Aquinas Church.
Nguyen, Toan *s.j.* '96 (SFR) Novato, CA St. Anthony of Padua Church.
Nguyen, Tran V. '86 (JOL) Villa Park, IL St. Alexander Church.
Nguyen, Trong Duc '69 (SFR) [23] San Francisco, CA Holy Name of Jesus Church; Special Assignment.
Nguyen, Trung '94 (GAL) Pearland, TX St. Helen Church.
Nguyen, Trung John '95 (MOB) Bayou LaBatre, AL St. Margaret Church.
Nguyen, Tuan *s.d.b.* '88 (STO) [7] Stockton, CA St. Luke Church.
Nguyen, Tuan '92 (SEA) Centralia, WA St. Mary's Church; Chehalis, WA St. Joseph's Church; Chehalis, WA State Training School for Boys.
Nguyen, Tuan '95 (ORG) Westminster, CA Blessed Sacrament Church.
Nguyen, Tuyen Van '87 (ORG) [7] Santa Ana, CA St. Barbara's Church.
Nguyen, Vandennis (PEO) Pekin, IL St. Joseph's Church.
Nguyen, Vien The '89 (NO) [8] Metairie, LA St. Edward the Confessor Church; [A] New Orleans, LA Notre Dame Seminary Graduate School of Theology.
Nguyen, Vincent The' Quang '75 (CHR) Greenville, SC St. Mary's Church.
Nguyen Chau Dien, Raymond M. *c.m.c.* (SPC) [E] Carthage, MO Congregation of the Mother Co-Redemptrix, United States Assumption Province.
Nguyen Du Tuan, Camillus M. *c.m.c.* '84 (SB) [E] Corona, CA Congregation of the Mother Coredemptrix.
Nguyen Duc Kien, Barnabas M. *c.m.c.* (SPC) [E] Carthage, MO Congregation of the Mother Co-Redemptrix, United States Assumption Province.
Nguyen Duc Thuan, Polycarp M. *c.m.c.* (SPC) [E] Carthage, MO Congregation of the Mother Co-Redemptrix, United States Assumption Province.
Nguyen Hai Duong, Ignatius Antioch M. *c.m.c.* (SPC) [E] Carthage, MO Congregation of the Mother Co-Redemptrix, United States Assumption Province.
Nguyen Linh Uy, Athanasius M. *c.m.c.* (SPC) [E] Carthage, MO Congregation of the Mother Co-Redemptrix, United States Assumption Province.
Nguyen Mang Cach, Paul M. *c.m.c.* (SPC) [E] Carthage, MO Congregation of the Mother Co-Redemptrix, United States Assumption Province.
Nguyen Minh Tu, Andrew '69 (PT) Panama City, FL SS. Peter & Paul Mission Church.
Nguyen Ngoc Tu, Joseph *o.p.* '64 (GAL) [35] Houston, TX Holy Rosary Church.
Nguyen Phuoc, Joseph *s.d.b.* '95 (OAK) [N] Berkeley, CA Salesian Community.
Nguyen Quang Dan, Pius M. *c.m.c.* (SPC) [E] Carthage, MO Congregation of the Mother Co-Redemptrix, United States Assumption Province.
Nguyen Thanh Hue, Augustine '64 (PT) [5] Pensacola, FL Our Lady Queen of Martyrs, Mission Church.
Nguyen-Thanh-Long, Peter '65 (WDC) [5] Bethesda, MD Our Lady of Vietnam Church.
Nhan, Tran Tu *c.ss.r.* '47 (LA) [R] Baldwin Park, CA Vietnamese Redemptorist Mission.
Nhan Van Tran, John '92 (NO) [5] Marrero, LA The Visitation of Our Lady Church.
Nhi, Tran Dinh '71 (ARL) [3] Alexandria, VA Queen of Apostles Church.
Nhien, Louis '95 (ROC) [6] Rochester, NY St. Anthony of Padua Church.
Nho, Do Duy '66 (LR) [12] Little Rock, AR St. Patrick's Church.
Nibberich, Msgr. Lawrence C. '50 (STL) Retired.
Nibler, James *o.m.v.* '87 (BO) [BB] Boston, MA St. Francis Chapel.
Niblick, Charles W. '74 (GRY) [5] Whiting, IN Sts. Peter and Paul Church.
Nicastro, Thomas D., Jr. '90 (BGP) Ridgefield, CT St. Mary's Church.
Nicastro, Thomas More *o.f.m.* '42 (NY) [BB] Wappingers Falls, NY Mt. Alvernia Retreat House.
Niccoli, Andrew '42 (BRK) [203] Queens, NY Most Precious Blood Church.
Niccolls, Edward D. '74 (WOR) Lunenburg, MA St. Boniface Church.
Nicewicz, Edward '62 (WOR) Absent on Leave.
Nicgorski, David J. *o.m.v.* '91 (MET) Avenel, NJ St.

Andrew Church.
Nicholas, Gerald A. *o.s.a.* '66 (JOL) [C] New Lenox, IL Providence Catholic High School; [J] New Lenox, IL Augustinian Friary.
Nicholas, John *c.m.* '54 (BIR) Ashland, AL Catholic Community of Ashland Church.
Nicholas, John J. *c.m.* '54 (BIR) Alexander City, AL St. John the Apostle Church.
Nicholl, Rex F. '67 (AMA) Perryton, TX Immaculate Conception Church.
Nicholls, Trevor '90 (NY) [E] Goshen, NY John S. Burke Catholic High School.
Nichols, Aquinas *o.s.b.* '80 (SD) [H] Oceanside, CA Prince of Peace Abbey, Benet Hill.
Nichols, Charles '48 (BRK) [131] Brooklyn, NY Sacred Hearts of Jesus and Mary and St. Stephen Church.
Nichols, Charles P. '48 (BRK) Retired.
Nichols, Earl W. '46 (OG) Retired.
Nichols, Edward P., Jr. '75 (SP) Brandon, FL Church of the Nativity.
Nichols, Harry E. '73 (PIT) Green Tree, PA St. Margaret Church.
Nichols, Henry P. '70 (BO) Boston, MA V.A. Medical Centers; Military & VA Chaplains.
Nichols, Herbert T. '75 (FR) [K] Fall River, MA Priests' Hostel.
Nichols, John J. '62 (BO) Watertown, MA St. Theresa of the Child Jesus Church.
Nichols, Joseph E. (NOR) Retired.
Nichols, Louis J. '60 (SR) Willits, CA St. Anthony Church.
Nichols, Louis J. '60 (SY) On Duty Outside the Diocese.
Nichols, Rodrick '89 (LSC) Silver City, NM St. Vincent de Paul Church.
Nichols, Stephen J. '86 (BUR) Troy, VT Sacred Heart of Jesus Church.
Nichols, Timothy '73 (LA) Redondo Beach, CA St. James Church.
Nichols, William H. *s.j.* '60 (CLV) [C] Cleveland, OH John Carroll Jesuit Community.
Nicholson, David *o.s.b.* '49 (P) [L] St. Benedict, OR Mt. Angel Abbey.
Nicholson, Francis J. *s.j.* '53 (BO) [W] Chestnut Hill, MA The Jesuit Community at Boston College.
Nicholson, George M. '74 (BRK) [185] Queens, NY St. John Vianney Church.
Nicholson, John A. *s.j.* '46 (NY) [Z] New York, NY Murray-Weigel Hall.
Nicholson, Patrick '69 (MOB) On Leave from the Archdiocese.
Nickas, John P. '66 (NEW) [32] Newark, NJ St. Rocco's Church; Montclair, NJ St. Peter Claver Church.
Nickel, James *ss.cc.* '70 (FR) [K] Fairhaven, MA Sacred Hearts Provincial House.
Nickel, Leander F. '47 (GB) Stockbridge, WI St. Mary Church.
Nickels, Larry *o.f.m.* '86 (STL) [R] St. Louis, MO Franciscan Sisters of Our Lady of Perpetual Help.
Nickels, Peter '60 (LAN) [1] Lansing, MI St. Mary Cathedral.
Nickerson, Russell *o.m.i.* '47 (MIA) Miramar, FL St. Stephen Church.
Nickle, Frederick *o.f.m.cap.* '65 (NOR) [4] Middletown, CT St. Pius X Church.
Nickless, R. Walker '73 (DEN) [3] Lakewood, CO Our Lady of Fatima Church.
Nicknair, Bernand L. '54 (PRT) Caribou, ME Sacred Heart Church; Stockholm, ME St. Therese Church.
Nicknair, Harold '61 (PRT) [1] Portland, ME Cathedral of the Immaculate Conception; Retired.
Nicknair, Leopold G. '58 (PRT) Caribou, ME Holy Rosary Church.
Nickol, G. Eugene '73 (BAL) Glen Burnie, MD Holy Trinity Church.
Nickolai, Arthur A. '43 (MIL) Retired.
Nickse, Jose P. '73 (MIA) [16] Miami, FL St. Brendan Church; [B] Opa Locka, FL St. Thomas University; [M] Key Largo, FL 1-800-Mass-Times Trust.
Nicola, John J. '55 (CHI) Other Assignments.
Nicolas, Jeffrey S. '93 (L) Elizabethtown, KY St. James Church; White Mills, KY St. Ignatius Church.
Nicolas, Marcos '36 (LA) Retired.
Nicolau, Bernardo *t.o.r.* '65 (FWT) [2] Fort Worth, TX All Saints Church.
Nicolau, Juan '60 (BWN) [9] Brownsville, TX St. Luke Church.
Nicoletti, Maurizio *o.cist* '65 (TR) Mount Laurel, NJ St. John Neumann Church; [M] Mount Laurel, NJ Cistercian Monastery of Our Lady of Fatima.
Nicoletti, Robert *m.j.* '92 (PCE) On Duty Outside the Diocese.
Nicolicchia, James A. *o.p.* '65 (NY) Hawthorne, NY Holy Rosary Church.
Nicoll, Leo A. *s.j.* '61 (NO) [C] New Orleans, LA Loyola University.
Nicolo, Joseph J. '74 (PH) [127] Philadelphia, PA Our Lady of the Rosary Church.
Nicolodi, Lodovico *c.s.s.* '39 (NY) [4] White Plains, NY Our Lady of Mt. Carmel Church.
Nicolosi, Mark Ronald *o.s.b.* '67 (BUR) [G] Weston, VT Priory of Benedictine Monks.
Nicosia, Peter *o.f.m.cap.* '59 (NEW) [4] Hackensack, NJ St. Francis Church.
Nicosia, Vincent A. *s.o.l.t.* '92 (CC) [H] Robstown, TX Society of Our Lady of the Most Holy Trinity.
Nicosia, Vincent A. *s.o.l.t.* '92 (SFE) La Joya, NM Our Lady of Sorrows Church.
Nieberding, Richard *c.pp.s.* '80 (CIN) [P] Maria Stein, OH Maria Stein Center.
Nieberding, Robert H. '56 (LEX) [3] Lexington, KY Mary, Queen of the Holy Rosary Church.
Nieblas, James *s.d.b.* '86 (LA) [79] Los Angeles, CA St. Mary Church; [D] Los Angeles, CA Bishop Mora Salesian High School.
Niebrugge, Herman J. '56 (SFD) Mattoon, IL Immaculate Conception Church.
Niebrzydowski, Msgr. Walter J. '59 (NY) [34] New York, NY Epiphany Church.
Nieckarz, James P. *m.m.* '66 (NY) [Z] Maryknoll, NY Maryknoll Fathers and Brothers.
Niederauer, George H. '62 (SLC) [1] Salt Lake City, UT Cathedral of the Madeleine.
Niederberger, Vincent J. *c.s.sp.* '50 (PH) [Z] Bensalem, PA Congregation of the Holy Ghost Fathers and Brothers.
Niedergeses, W. Bernard '50 (NSH) [3] Nashville, TN Assumption Church; [12] Nashville, TN St. Pius X Church.
Niedermier, Jerome G. '52 (TOL) Retired.
Niedhammer, Cosmas *o.f.m.cap.* '27 (NY) [B] Beacon, NY St. Lawrence of Brindisi Friary.
Niedzwicki, Thomas C. '53 (GR) Irons, MI St. Bernard's Church.
Niedzwiecki, Harold *o.f.m.* (NEW) [O] Lodi, NJ Immaculate Conception Convent.
Niehaus Charles W. *s.p.* '74 (CHI) [177] Chicago, IL St. Procopius Church.
Niehaus Francis H. '55 (CIN) Retired.
Niehaus Jonathan J. '94 (MIL) [T] Waukesha, WI Secular Institute of Schoenstatt Fathers.
Niehoff, Edmund A. '64 (SHP) Mansfield, LA St. Joseph Church.
Niehoff, Kevin *o.p.* '93 (CHI) [24] Chicago, IL St. Basil/Visitation Church; [D] Oak Park, IL Fenwick High School.
Niehoff, Robert L. *s.j.* '82 (SFR) [N] San Francisco, CA Jesuit Community at University of San Francisco.
Nieli, Bruce *c.s.p.* '73 (WDC) [B] Washington, DC St. Paul's College.
Nielsen, Eric '95 (MAD) [5] Madison, WI Immaculate Heart of Mary Church.
Nielsen, James P. *o.praem.* '93 (GB) [I] De Pere, WI St. Norbert Abbey.
Nielsen, Kenneth M. '80 (BUF) On Duty Outside the Diocese.
Nielsen, Philip W. *o.f.m.* '48 (PAT) [N] Parsippany, NJ St. Francis of Assisi Novitiate-Franciscan Sisters of St. Elizabeth.
Nielson, Kenneth (BO) Danvers, MA St. Mary of the Annunciation Church.
Nielson, Thomas A. '59 (NY) [1] New York, NY Cathedral of St. Patrick; [DD] New York, NY St. Ansgar Scandinavian Catholic League.
Nieman, Frank B. (OAK) [R] Oakland, CA Institute of Lay Theology.
Nieman, Raymond L. '54 (COV) Retired.
Niemann, Mark E. *s.j.* '50 (OM) [C] Omaha, NE Creighton Preparatory School.
Niemann, Paul '80 (PRM) St. Louis, MO St. Louis Mission Church.
Niemczyk, Joseph W. '68 (BRK) Absent on Sick Leave.
Niemczyk, Stefan J. '87 (SPR) [7] Springfield, MA Immaculate Conception Church.
Niemeier, Dennis '73 (CIN) Military Chaplains.
Niemeyer, Elmer L. '41 (SFE) Retired.
Niemeyer, James '74 (JC) Missionary Assignment in Peru.
Niemeyer, John '41 (JKS) Retired.
Niemeyer, John '55 (PEO) Retired.
Niemeyer, Roger *o.f.m.* (SFD) [K] Sherman, IL Our Lady of Angels Friary.
Niemier, Roch *o.f.m.* '65 (MIL) [P] Milwaukee, WI Francis and Clare House; [Y] Milwaukee, WI Franciscan Pilgrimage Programs, Inc.
Niemira, Thomas '65 (JKS) On Duty Outside the Diocese.
Niemira, Thomas J. '53 (AUS) Waco, TX V.A. Hospital.
Nienaber, Msgr. Leonard B. '34 (LEX) Retired.
Nienaber, Robert H. '63 (OM) Genoa, NE St. Rose of Lima Church; Krakow, NE SS. Peter and Paul Church.
Nienhaus, Bernard '65 (STL) Hawk Point, MO St. Mary Church.
Nienhaus, Gerald T. '62 (STL) Spanish Lake, MO St. Aloysius Church.
Nienhaus, Ivan R. '89 (DUB) Masonville, IA Immaculate Conception Church; Winthrop, IA St. Patrick's Church.
Niese, Larry P. '95 (ATL) [2] Atlanta, GA Holy Cross Church.
Nieset, Frank '56 (TOL) Absent on Sick Leave.
Nieset, Frank E. '56 (TOL) Retired.
Niessen, John '51 (SB) Perris, CA St. James Church.
Nietfeld, Fred J. '46 (TOL) Retired.
Nietlong, Joseph '86 (NY) [S] New York, NY Saint Vincent's Medical Center of Richmond.
Nieto, Jose *c.m.f.* '66 (SJN) [9] Bayamon, PR San Jose Church.
Nieto-Ruiz, Jose de Jesus '94 (OAK) [2] Hayward, CA St. Bede Church.
Nieva, Constantino '55 (RVC) Bellport, NY Mary Immaculate Church.
Nieves, Carlos '86 (PCE) Arroyo, PR Our Lady of Mt. Carmel Church.
Nieves, Encarnacion (CGS) Aguas Buenas, PR Espiritu Santo Church.
Nieves, Jose Javier '95 (PAT) [7] Paterson, NJ St. George Church.
Niewczas, Msgr. Tadeus '52 (RVC) Cutchogue, NY Our Lady of Ostrabrama Church.
Niewiadomski, Arthur '94 (TOL) [1] Lima, OH St. Charles Borromeo Church.
Niezgoda, Joseph R. (GRY) [8] East Chicago, IN St. John Cantius Church.
Niggemann, Bernard '31 (SUP) Retired.
Nightengale, Msgr. Francis '42 (SB) Retired.
Niglis, Joseph C. '37 (MAD) Retired.
Nigro, Armond *s.j.* (SPK) [B] Spokane, WA Mater Dei Institute.
Nigro, Dominick '88 (TOL) Absent on Sick Leave.
Nijem, Fred J. '68 (SAV) Warner Robins, GA Sacred Heart Church.
Nijenhuis, John *o.carm.* '54 (GAL) Baytown, TX St. John the Evangelist Church.
Niklas, Gerald R. '59 (CIN) [K] Cincinnati, OH Good Samaritan Hospital.
Nikliborc, Francis U. '47 (CHI) Retired.
Nikliborc, Robert D. '55 (SD) [20] San Diego, CA St. Anne Church.
Nikodem, Martin J. '67 (BGP) [16] Bridgeport, CT Our Lady of Good Counsel Church.
Nikodem, Ronald J. *s.m.* '94 (ATL) [C] Atlanta, GA Marist School.
Nikolai, William V. '48 (LC) Retired; [I] La Crosse, WI Holy Cross (Seminary) Diocesan Center.
Niland, Jack *o.f.m.cap.* '76 (AGN) Santa Rita, GU Our Lady of Guadalupe Church.
Nilema, Nicholas E. *a.l.c.p.* '88 (P) [36] Portland, OR St. Therese of the Child Jesus Church.
Nilges, Harold L. '53 (RCK) Genoa, IL St. Catherine of Genoa Church.
Nilles, Msgr. Allan F. '49 (FAR) Park River, ND St. Mary's Church.
Nilles, Roger G. '59 (MAD) [13] Madison, WI St. Peter Church.
Nilsson, Richard A. '71 (RVC) Long Beach, NY St. Ignatius Martyr Church.
Nimal, George '76 (STO) Modesto, CA St. Stanislaus Church.
Nimerichter, Dean '92 (DM) Greenfield, IA St. John Church; Orient, IA St. Mark Church.
Nimocks, Michael F. '96 (COL) [32] Columbus, OH St. Michael Church; Bolivar, OH Holy Trinity Church.
Ninedorf, Robert W. '89 (CHR) Edgefield, SC St. Mary's Church; Ward, SC St. William's Church.
Ninemire, Kerry '75 (SAL) Phillipsburg, KS SS. Philip and James Church.
Nino, Andres G. *o.s.a.* '62 (BO) [9] Cambridge, MA St. Mary of the Annunciation Church.
Nintemann, George B. *o.p.* '59 (WIN) [4] Rochester, MN St. Bridget's Church.
Nir, Roman '64 (DET) [A] Orchard Lake, MI SS. Cyril and Methodius Seminary.
Nirappel, Antony '63 (MOB) [2] Mobile, AL St. Catherine of Siena Church.
Nirrengarten, Andrew (RVC) Absent on Leave.
Nirschl, Nicholas E. *o.praem.* '56 (SFE) Isleta, NM St. Augustine Church; [J] Albuquerque, NM Santa Maria de la Vid Priory.
Nisbet, Jim '69 (MRY) Spreckels, CA St. Joseph Church.
Nischan, James R. '83 (PCE) On Duty Outside the Diocese.
Nishigaya, Msgr. Raymond J. '64 (HON) [14] Honolulu, HI St. Stephen Church.
Niskanen, Stephen *c.m.f.* '90 (LA) San Gabriel, CA San Gabriel Church; [R] San Gabriel, CA Claretian Missionaries (Missionary Sons of the Immaculate Heart of Mary).
Niskanen, Steven *c.m.f.* '90 (SAT) [B] San Antonio, TX St. Anthony Mary Claret Seminary.
Nist, Arthur '40 (Y) Retired.
Nistal, Alejandro *o.ss.t.* '66 (PCE) [10] Ponce, PR La Santisima Trinidad Church.
Nistler, Edward '54 (CR) Akeley, MN St. John's Church.
Nitural, Leo (BRK) [54] Brooklyn, NY Holy Family Church.
Nitz, Eliot *s.d.s.* '68 (WDC) [B] Silver Spring, MD Salvatorian Community; [K] Silver Spring, MD Holy Cross Hospital of Silver Spring, Inc.
Nitzki, John *s.c.j.* '56 (MIL) Franklin, WI Sacred Hearts of Jesus and Mary Church.

Nix, Albert (PAT) Stirling, NJ St. Vincent de Paul Church.
Nix, Julian *o.s.b.* '87 (BIS) [A] Richardton, ND Assumption Abbey.
Nixon, Edmond J. *c.ss.r.* '71 (NY) [34] New York, NY Epiphany Church.
Nixon, Joseph J. '85 (RVC) [C] Hicksville, NY Holy Trinity.
Niziolek, Terrence *m.s.* '66 (MIL) [P] Twin Lakes, WI La Salette Missionaries Shrine.
Njoku, Gregory *c.s.sp.* '82 (MIA) Opa Locka, FL Our Lady of Perpetual Help Church.
Njoku, Hyacinth '86 (NY) [162] Bronx, NY St. Margaret Mary Church.
Njoku, Peter C. '74 (STP) [32] Minneapolis, MN St. Philip Church.
Nleedife, Peter '76 (LKC) Jennings, LA Our Lady of Perpetual Help Church.
Nmana, Pedro *o.f.m.* '89 (OAK) [N] Oakland, CA Franciscan Friars.
Noah, Daniel '50 (CR) Retired.
Noah, Timothy T. '47 (CR) Hallock, MN St. Patrick's Church.
Nobile, Angelo '53 (MEM) On Duty Outside the Diocese.
Nobiletti, Raymond J. *m.m.* '69 (NY) [119] New York, NY Transfiguration Church; [Z] Maryknoll, NY Maryknoll Fathers and Brothers.
Noble, Bruce H. '87 (GAL) [K] Houston, TX The Catholic Chaplain Corps.
Noble, Charles F. '55 (NEW) Weehawken, NJ St. Lawrence's Church.
Noble, David H. '87 (GAL) [K] Houston, TX The Catholic Chaplain Corps.
Noble, Jeffrey J. '86 (E) [4] Oil City, PA St. Stephen Church; [P] Erie, PA Newman Centers and Campus Ministry.
Noble, Paul A. '81 (COL) [1] Columbus, OH St. Joseph Cathedral.
Nobleza, Dennis A., Jr. '70 (LA) Monrovia, CA Immaculate Conception Church.
Noboa, Origenes (VEN) LaBelle, FL Our Lady Queen of Heaven Church.
Nocero, Pascal F. '48 (LA) Retired.
Nochelski, Paul W. *s.j.* '71 (BUF) [O] Buffalo, NY Canisius Jesuit Community.
Nock, James J. '64 (HRT) [2] East Hartford, CT Our Lady of Peace Church.
Nockunas, Anthony N. *m.i.c.* '57 (WOR) [19] Worcester, MA St. Casimir's Church.
Noda, Jorge '84 (MIA) [1] Hialeah, FL Immaculate Conception Church.
Noe, John P. '74 (LEX) Ashland, KY Federal Correctional Institution; [D] Ashland, KY Our Lady of Bellefonte Hospital, Inc.
Noecker, Ronald J. '85 (OM) Beemer, NE Holy Cross Church.
Noel, Damian L. *t.o.r.* '53 (ALT) [F] Loretto, PA Mount Assisi Monastery.
Noel, Donald C. *o.praem.* '59 (GB) [I] De Pere, WI St. Norbert Abbey.
Noesen, Gerald L. '55 (CR) Fertile, MN St. Joseph Church; Mentor, MN St. Lawrence Church.
Noesen, Robert '93 (JOL) Mokena, IL St. Mary Church.
Noeson, Thomas *o.p.* '76 (DEN) [34] Denver, CO St. Mary Magdalene's Church.
Noetzel, Kenneth J. *s.j.* (DET) [28] Detroit, MI Gesu Church.
Nofaley, Thomas Simon '92 (EST) Southfield, MI Our Lady of Chaldeans Cathedral, Mother of God Chaldean Parish Church.
Nofi, Michael A. *m.ss.a.* (WH) Moorefield, WV Epiphany of the Lord Church.
Noga, Edward P. '76 (Y) [18] Youngstown, OH St. Patrick's Church.
Noga, Gregory J. '79 (PSC) Coatesville, PA St. Mary's Church; Mont Clare, PA St. Michael Church.
Nogaro, Paul M. '71 (BUF) [4] Kenmore, NY St. Paul Church.
Nogosek, Bob '56 (SB) Thermal, CA San Felipe de Jesus Church.
Nogosek, Robert J. *c.s.c.* '56 (SB) Coachella, CA Our Lady of Soledad Church.
Noguera, Dagoberto '85 (BRK) [63] Brooklyn, NY Immaculate Conception of the Blessed Virgin Mary Church.
Noguera, Ronald '81 (MIA) Homestead, FL Sacred Heart Church.
Nohava, Douglas J. '70 (PHX) [9] Phoenix, AZ St. Catherine of Siena Church.
Nohilly, Thomas B. '81 (BRK) [127] Brooklyn, NY St. Rose of Lima Church.
Nohs, Joseph E. '93 (RVC) East Meadow, NY St. Raphael Church.
Noia, Leonel C. '73 (SJ) [5] San Jose, CA Five Wounds Portuguese National Church.
Noiseux, Donald A. '84 (SPR) Huntington, MA St. Thomas Church.
Nojek, Mark *o.c.d.* (GRY) [K] Munster, IN Discalced Carmelite Fathers Monastery.
Nolan, Brian J. '91 (MET) Sayreville, NJ Our Lady of Victories Church.
Nolan, Colman J. *s.t.* '56 (TUC) Sierra Vista, AZ St. Andrew Church.
Nolan, Dan *c.s.v.* (LAV) Henderson, NV St. Thomas More Church.
Nolan, David F. '95 (NY) [135] Bronx, NY St. Brendan Church.
Nolan, Msgr. Edward J. '48 (BRK) [182] Queens, NY The Incarnation Church; Retired.
Nolan, Eugene A. *s.j.* '71 (SCR) [C] Scranton, PA University of Scranton; [E] Scranton, PA Scranton Preparatory School.
Nolan, George W. *s.j.* '54 (BO) [W] Boston, MA Loyola House.
Nolan, James L. *o.s.a.* '46 (PH) [Z] Villanova, PA St. Thomas Monastery.
Nolan, Jerome M. '74 (TR) Fair Haven, NJ Nativity Church.
Nolan, John '77 (SFD) Military Chaplains.
Nolan, Joseph *m.s.* (ATL) [2] Marietta, GA Church of St. Ann.
Nolan, Joseph A. '60 (ORL) Melbourne Beach, FL Immaculate Conception Church.
Nolan, Joseph M. '47 (BRK) [238] Queens, NY Sacred Heart Church.
Nolan, Joseph T '53 (WCH) On Duty Outside the Diocese.
Nolan, Justin *o.s.b.* '55 (GBG) [H] Latrobe, PA Saint Vincent Archabbey.
Nolan, Kevin '90 (LA) Van Nuys, CA St. Elisabeth Church.
Nolan, Kieran *o.s.b.* '59 (SCL) [I] Collegeville, MN St. John's Abbey, of the Order of St. Benedict.
Nolan, Larry '58 (COL) [G] Columbus, OH St. Raphael Home for the Aged, Inc.
Nolan, Msgr. Michael '48 (SB) Retired.
Nolan, Michael '87 (KNX) Cleveland, TN St. Therese of Lisieux Church.
Nolan, Michael E. '84 (WCH) Oxford, KS St. Mary Church; Winfield, KS Holy Name Church.
Nolan, Niall '66 (GAL) [23] Houston, TX St. Cyril of Alexandria Church.
Nolan, Norbert L. '51 (ROC) Retired.
Nolan, Msgr. Patrick '50 (SAC) Retired and in Senior Ministry.
Nolan, Msgr. Patrick M. (SAC) [19] Sacramento, CA St. Philomene Church.
Nolan, Paul '75 (NEW) Maywood, NJ Our Lady Queen of Peace Church.
Nolan, Raymond A. *s.j.* '43 (NY) [Z] New York, NY Murray-Weigel Hall.
Nolan, Robert J. *s.a.c.* '70 (CAM) [C] Pennsauken, NJ Bishop Eustace Prep School.
Nolan, Shawn *o.f.m.conv.* '55 (NY) [B] New York, NY St. Francis Novitiate.
Nolan, Msgr. Terence '66 (SAT) [16] San Antonio, TX Our Lady of Grace Church.
Nolan, Timothy '92 (PEO) [13] Peoria, IL St. Philomena's Church.
Nolan, Timothy F. '67 (STP) Ham Lake, MN Saint Paul Church.
Nolan, Msgr. Walter E. '69 (TR) Washington Crossing, NJ St. George Church.
Nolan, William A. '85 (MAD) Cambridge, WI St. Pius X Church.
Nolan, William J. '69 (TR) [2] Toms River, NJ St. Justin Church.
Nolan, Msgr. William L. '43 (MAN) Retired.
Nolan, William N (NSH) Retired.
Nold, Joseph K. '45 (SY) Retired.
Nolen, Joseph *c.ss.r.* '76 (STL) [B] St. Louis, MO St. John Neumann House.
Nolette, Mark P. '87 (PRT) Ashland, ME St. Mark's Church.
Nolin, Joseph A. '49 (ORL) Retired.
Nolker, Thomas C. '72 (CIN) [32] Cincinnati, OH Guardian Angels Church.
Noll, Claire *o.f.m.cap.* '37 (SJN) [4] San Juan, PR San Antonio Church.
Noll, Daniel J. '76 (LEX) [2] Lexington, KY The Newman Center, Holy Spirit Church; [L] Lexington, KY The Newman Center Holy Spirit Parish University of Kentucky.
Noll, Donald T. '61 (CIN) Fayetteville, OH St. Patrick's Church.
Noll, Joseph *c.ss.r.* '33 (ALB) [L] Saratoga Springs, NY St. John Neumann Residence.
Noll, Joseph *c.ss.r.* '33 (NY) [92] New York, NY Our Lady of Perpetual Help Church.
Nollette, Louis A. '75 (GI) Mullen, NE St. Mary's Church.
Nollette, Neal P. '80 (GI) Elm Creek, NE Immaculate Conception Church.
Nolte, William J., Jr. '67 (WH) Retired.
Nombrado, Benjamin '79 (SFR) [15] San Francisco, CA St. Elizabeth Church.
Nomellini, Paul J. '77 (MAR) Kingsford, MI St. Mary Queen of Peace Church.
Nondorf, Aloysius J. '57 (GRY) Military Chaplains.
Noon, Msgr. Robert L. '51 (COL) Retired.
Noonan, John '83 (MIA) [A] Miami, FL St. John Vianney College Seminary; [C] Miami, FL St. Brendan High School.
Noonan, Joseph T. '95 (CHI) [64] Chicago, IL St. Francis Borgia Church.
Noonan, Mark L. '59 (BO) [A] Boston, MA St. John's Seminary.
Noonan, Michael A. '80 (CIN) [49] Cincinnati, OH St. Joseph Church; [76] Cincinnati, OH St. Pius Church.
Noonan, Patrick '63 (JKS) Canton, MS Sacred Heart Church; Canton, MS Holy Child Jesus Church; Carthage, MS St. Anne Church.
Noonan, Robert C. '64 (HEL) Choteau, MT St. Joseph Church; Fairfield, MT St. John Church; Kalispell, MT St. Matthew Church.
Noonan, Msgr. Thomas F. '55 (BRK) [34] Brooklyn, NY St. Edmund's Church.
Noonan, William J. '39 (BO) Retired.
Noone, Charles J. '67 (PH) Absent on Leave.
Noone, David E. '66 (ALB) Loudonville, NY St. Francis de Sales Church.
Noone, John '67 (BLX) Picayune, MS St. Charles Borromeo Church.
Noone, Msgr. Kevin B. '70 (BRK) [97] Brooklyn, NY Our Lady of Guadalupe Church.
Noone, Sean '52 (CC) Retired.
Nooney, P. Joseph '52 (SC) Fort Dodge, IA Trinity Regional Hospital.
Nooney, Patrick J. '52 (SC) Retired.
Norbeck, Ernest '84 (JOL) [1] Naperville, IL St. Elizabeth Seton Church.
Norcavage, Albert R. '50 (ALT) Absent on Leave.
Nord, Clarence C. '43 (L) Retired.
Norden, Emmett M. '62 (MAR) Bark River, MI St. Elizabeth Ann Seton Church; Perronville, MI St. Elizabeth Ann Seton Church; Schaffer, MI St. Elizabeth Ann Seton Church.
Nordenbrock, William A. *c.pp.s.* '83 (CIN) [M] Dayton, OH Provincial House of the Cincinnati Province of the Society of the Precious Blood.
Norder, John '66 (MAD) Cassville, WI St. Charles Borromeo Church.
Nordhaus, Jeffrey J. '72 (TOL) Military Chaplains.
Nordick, Benedict *o.s.b.* '78 (SCL) [I] Collegeville, MN St. John's Abbey, of the Order of St. Benedict.
Nordick, Jerome G. '83 (SCL) Chokio, MN St. Mary's Church; Herman, MN St. Charles Church.
Nordick, John A. '90 (NU) Beardsley, MN St. Mary Church; Graceville, MN Holy Rosary Church.
Nordmeyer, Emeric *o.f.m.* '56 (GLP) Grants, NM St. Teresa Church.
Nordquist, Theodore A. '80 (GRY) La Porte, IN St. Joseph Church; [N] Gary, IN Catholic Charities.
Noreika, Michael *s.s.s.* '70 (GB) Menasha, WI St. Mary Church.
Noriega, Arnoldo '75 (TUC) Absent on Leave.
Norkett, Edward J. '36 (CHI) Retired.
Norkett, Michael '68 (OAK) [1] San Leandro, CA Assumption of the Blessed Virgin Mary Church.
Norkiewicz, Chester *c.r.* '44 (CHI) [D] Chicago, IL Gordon Technical High School.
Norkunas, Msgr. Anthony J. '44 (SCR) Retired.
Norman, Charles J. *o.s.f.s.* '65 (PH) [75] Philadelphia, PA St. Joachim Church.
Norman, Clifford A. '60 (PBL) On Duty Outside the Diocese.
Norman, Gary R. *o.m.i.* '80 (JUN) Petersburg, AK St. Catherine of Siena Church.
Norman, Gary R. '94 (YAK) On Duty Outside the Diocese.
Norman, Gregory *o.cist.* '53 (LC) [I] Sparta, WI Our Lady of Spring Bank, Cistercian Abbey.
Norman, John E. '79 (SLC) [2] Ogden, UT St. James Church; [B] Ogden, UT St. Joseph Catholic High School.
Norman, Richard W. *s.j.* '58 (ALN) [A] Wernersville, PA Novitiate of St. Isaac Jogues.
Normanly, Thomas *s.s.c.* '52 (OM) [K] St. Columbans, NE St. Columban's Foreign Mission Society.
Noronha, Valerian *o.c.d.* '91 (WDC) [B] Washington, DC Monastery of Our Lady of Mount Carmel.
Norrell, Msgr. Albert V. '88 (PH) [29] Philadelphia, PA St. Carthage Church.
Norris, David J. '74 (FRS) Hilmar, CA Holy Rosary Church.
Norris, Frank B. *s.s.* '50 (SFR) [A] Menlo Park, CA St. Patrick Seminary.
Norris, John P. '46 (ROC) Mendon, NY St. Catherine of Siena Church; Retired.
Norris, Mark *o.s.b.* '95 (SFE) [L] Pecos, NM Our Lady of Guadalupe Benedictine Abbey.
Norris, Patrick F. *o.p.* '89 (STL) [P] St. Louis, MO St. Dominic Priory.
Norris, Thomas P. *o.s.f.s.* '73 (CHL) High Point, NC Immaculate Heart of Mary Church.
Norris, Timothy L. '94 (STP) [1] St. Paul, MN Cathedral of St. Paul.
Norris, Walter J. '41 (WDC) Damascus, MD St. Paul Church; Retired.
Norsworthy, Richard '85 (SHP) Bossier City, LA St. Jude Church.
North, Robert G. *s.j.* '44 (MIL) [P] Milwaukee, WI

Jesuit Provincial Office, Wisconsin Province.
Northridge, Keith C. (PAT) Absent on Leave.
Norton, Arthur E. '59 (BGP) Danbury, CT Danbury Area Mental Health Authority.
Norton, Claude B. '43 (DUB) Retired.
Norton, Daniel J. '65 (CAM) On Duty Outside the Diocese.
Norton, Edward *s.v.d.* '45 (CHI) [B] Techny, IL Divine Word Residence.
Norton, Emmet J. *s.j.* '48 (PAT) [I] Morristown, NJ Loyola House of Retreats.
Norton, George '83 (ROC) [8] Rochester, NY Blessed Sacrament Church; Rochester, NY Genesee Hospital; [L] Rochester, NY Family Rosary For Peace, Inc.
Norton, John *o.p.* '56 (CHY) Sheridan, WY U.S. Veterans Administration Hospital.
Norton, Michael *c.pp.s.* '70 (SAT) [H] San Antonio, TX Santa Rosa Health Care System.
Norton, Robert A. '72 (PIT) West View, PA St. Athanasius Church.
Norton, Robert J. *o.f.m.* '74 (NEW) Elmwood Park, NJ St. Leo's Church.
Norton, Thomas '63 (NEW) Northvale, NJ St. Anthony's Church; Westwood, NJ Pascack Valley Hospital.
Norton, Thomas *s.t.* '76 (SJN) [4] Canovanas, PR Santa Maria Madre de Dios Church.
Norton, William W. '67 (FR) Woods Hole, MA St. Joseph's Church.
Nortz, Alfred E. '55 (SY) [24] Syracuse, NY St. Vincent de Paul Church.
Norusis, Nicholas M. *o.s.m.* '44 (DEN) Westminster, CO Holy Trinity Church.
Norvel, William L. *s.s.j.* (BAL) [33] Baltimore, MD St. Francis Xavier Church.
Nosbush, Peter C. '70 (NU) Litchfield, MN St. Philip Church.
Noser, J. Homer '43 (STL) Retired.
Nosser, Msgr. Charles J. '53 (RVC) Floral Park, NY Our Lady of Victory Church.
Nosser, Msgr. John C. '64 (RVC) Cutchogue, NY Our Lady of Ostrabrama Church.
Notabartolo, Charles '77 (PMB) Jupiter, FL St. Peter Church.
Notaro, Carlo *o.s.cam.* '88 (MIL) [N] Wauwatosa, WI St. Camillus Health Center, Inc.; [N] Wauwatosa, WI San Camillo, Inc.; [P] Wauwatosa, WI St. Camillus Community House.
Notarpole, Joseph '49 (STA) [11] Jacksonville, FL Our Lady of the Angels Church.
Notebaart, James C. '71 (STP) Special Assignment.
Noto, James M. '63 (RIC) [11] Virginia Beach, VA St. Nicholas Church.
Nott, David L. '93 (RIC) Covington, VA Church of the Sacred Heart; Hot Springs, VA The Shrine of the Sacred Heart Church.
Notter, Richard E. (TOL) [O] Toledo, OH The Catholic Migrant Farmworker Network.
Notter, Richard E. '63 (TOL) [36] Toledo, OH SS. Peter and Paul Church.
Nouws, Jacques J. '46 (LA) [R] Los Angeles, CA Amat House.
Nouws, James J. *c.m.* '46 (LA) [W] Montebello, CA DePaul Center.
Nouza, Frank M. *o.p.* '58 (CHI) [N] Chicago, IL Dominicans (Provincial Office).
Novack, Kevin F. *c.s.p.* '81 (NY) [Z] Scarsdale, NY Paulist Fathers Generalate.
Novack, Kevin F. *c.s.p.* '81 (PBL) Telluride, CO St. Patrick Church.
Novacki, Michael Leo *o.p.* '35 (PH) [61] Philadelphia, PA Holy Name of Jesus Church; [Z] Philadelphia, PA Holy Name Priory, Dominican Friars.
Novak, Alfred *c.ss.r.* '56 (DEN) [M] Denver, CO The Redemptorists/Denver Province.
Novak, David A. '79 (CLV) [34] Cleveland, OH Immaculate Conception Church; [39] Cleveland, OH St. Josaphat Church.
Novak, David M. '77 (STL) Hazelwood, MO St. Bartholomew Church.
Novak, Francis *c.ss.r.* '49 (CHI) [136] Chicago, IL St. Michael Church.
Novak, Henry *c.ss.r.* (CHI) [N] Glenview, IL The Redemptorists of Glenview, Illinois.
Novak, James M. '57 (LAN) Westphalia, MI St. Mary Church.
Novak, John '42 (JOL) Retired.
Novak, Joseph A. *s.j.* '57 (NY) [Z] New York, NY Jesuit Community at Fordham University; [Z] New York, NY Jesuit Community at Fordham University.
Novak, Msgr. Leonard J. '56 (SCR) [24] Scranton, PA Sacred Hearts of Jesus and Mary Church.
Novak, Norbert *o.s.b.* '64 (P) [J] Portland, OR Providence Portland Medical Center; [L] St. Benedict, OR Mt. Angel Abbey.
Novak, Paul M. *o.s.m.* '90 (CHI) [N] Chicago, IL Servite Friars - Eastern Province; [N] Chicago, IL Servite Friars - Eastern Province.
Novak, Robert J. '42 (CHI) Retired.
Novak, Thomas *s.d.s.* '59 (MIL) [P] Milwaukee, WI Salvatorian Provincial Residence.
Novak, Vincent M. *s.j.* '55 (NY) [C] Bronx, NY Fordham University; [Z] New York, NY Jesuit Community at Fordham University.
Novakowski, James E. '95 (GI) Stapleton, NE St. John the Evangelist Church.
Novello, Lawrence E. '84 (BO) [4] Waltham, MA St. Mary Church.
Novello, Msgr. Russell R. '53 (BO) Retired.
Novelly, Duane R. '79 (DET) [50] Detroit, MI St. Matthew Church.
Novicky, Msgr. William N. '46 (CLV) South Euclid, OH St. Gregory the Great Church.
Novielli, John J. *o.praem.* '74 (PH) [48] Philadelphia, PA St. Gabriel Church.
Noviello, Anthony A. '43 (SCR) Retired.
Novoa, Dominic '83 (PMB) [D] West Palm Beach, FL St. Mary's Hospital, Inc.
Novoa, Dominic E. '83 (HRT) On Duty Outside the Archdiocese.
Novotney, Andrew J. *s.j.* '71 (BAL) [M] Baltimore, MD Jesuit Fathers and Brothers Maryland Provincial Curia.
Novotny, Allen P. *s.j.* '82 (BAL) [Q] Baltimore, MD Jesuit Educational Association of Maryland, Inc.
Novotny, Allen P. *s.j.* '82 (WDC) [E] Washington, DC Gonzaga College High School.
Novotny, James F. '64 (OM) Lindsay, NE Holy Family Church.
Novotny, Richard '81 (RC) On Duty Outside the Diocese.
Novotny, Richard P. '81 (B) Mountain Home Air Force Base, ID St. Mary's Church.
Novotny, Robert J. '50 (MIL) Retired.
Nowacki, Jerome A. '93 (MAR) Rudyard, MI St. Joseph Church.
Nowacki, Peter *o.p.* (CHI) [3] Lemont, IL SS. Cyril and Methodius Church.
Nowak, Bernard '52 (ROC) Retired.
Nowak, Bernard J. '52 (LC) Retired.
Nowak, Bernard U. (BUF) Military Chaplains.
Nowak, Daniel *o.f.m.* '59 (SAG) Bridgeport, MI Assumption of the Blessed Virgin Mary Church.
Nowak, David G. (GRY) [5] Merrillville, IN St. Stephen, Martyr Church.
Nowak, Edward C. *c.s.p.* '89 (LA) Goleta, CA St. Mark University Parish Church; [BB] Los Angeles, CA Archdiocesan Office for Campus Ministry.
Nowak, Eugene J. '70 (CHI) Hoffman Estates, IL St. Hubert Church.
Nowak, Francis T. '58 (BUF) Alden, NY Erie County Correctional Facility.
Nowak, Jacek *s.ch.* '92 (DET) [8] Sterling Heights, MI Our Lady of Czestochowa Church.
Nowak, James A. '67 (JOL) Westmont, IL Holy Trinity Church.
Nowak, John H. *c.r.* '71 (CHI) [D] Chicago, IL Weber High School; [N] Chicago, IL Provincial Office of the Congregation of the Resurrection.
Nowak, Joseph G. '42 (CHI) [138] Chicago, IL St. Michael Church; Retired.
Nowak, Mark A. '75 (E) Cambridge Springs, PA St. Anthony Church; [P] Erie, PA Newman Centers and Campus Ministry.
Nowak, Randolph *o.f.m.cap.* '52 (AGN) [F] Agana Heights, GU St. Fidelis Friary.
Nowak, Stanley F. '58 (BUF) [4] Depew, NY SS. Peter and Paul Church.
Nowak, Vincent A. '36 (ALB) Retired.
Nowakowski, Edward S. '48 (GB) Armstrong Creek, WI St. Stanislaus Kostka Church; Goodman, WI St. Joan of Arc Church.
Nowakowski, Francis M. '39 (ALB) Retired.
Nowakowski, Jerome '63 (TOL) [7] Toledo, OH Good Shepherd Church.
Nowakowski, Stanislaus A. '37 (KAL) Battle Creek, MI St. Joseph Church; Retired.
Nowel, Mark D. *o.p.* '86 (PRO) [P] Providence, RI St. Thomas Aquinas Priory at Providence College.
Nowery, C. Richard *c.s.c.* '68 (NO) [22] New Orleans, LA Sacred Heart Of Jesus Church.
Nowicki, Chester *s.v.d.* '46 (CHI) [B] Techny, IL Divine Word Residence; [N] Techny, IL Society of the Divine Word, Provincial Headquarter-Chicago Prov.; [N] Techny, IL Society of the Divine Word, Provincial Headquarter-Chicago Prov.
Nowicki, Gary D. '96 (MIL) [79] Milwaukee, WI St. Veronica's Church.
Nowinski, Dennis '73 (DET) Memphis, MI All Saints Church.
Nowlan, Edward H. *s.j.* '41 (BO) [W] Chestnut Hill, MA The Jesuit Community at Boston College.
Nowlan, John T. '77 (DET) Redford Township, MI St. Hilary Church.
Nuanez, Anthony '79 (LA) Sick Leave.
Nuelle, John *m.s.* '64 (STL) [P] St. Louis, MO La Salette Missionaries.
Nuelle, John R. *m.s.* '64 (HRT) [M] Hartford, CT Missionaries of LaSalette Provincial Secretary; [M] Hartford, CT Missionaries of LaSalette Provincial Secretary.
Nugent, Anthony A. '72 (JOL) Plainfield, IL St. Mary Immaculate Church.
Nugent, Msgr. Arthur W. '47 (PH) Retired.
Nugent, C. Robert *s.d.s.* '65 (MIL) [P] Milwaukee, WI Salvatorian Provincial Residence.
Nugent, Frank '56 (NEW) [N] South Orange, NJ Salesian Residence.
Nugent, Frank McG. *s.j.* '50 (SCR) [C] Scranton, PA University of Scranton.
Nugent, Msgr. Irvine '54 (PMB) Vero Beach, FL St. Helen Church; [J] Palm Beach Gardens, FL Diocesan Council of Catholic Women.
Nugent, Msgr. James (COL) [40] Columbus, OH St. Timothy Church.
Nugent, James *c.ss.r.* '50 (STL) [P] Liguori, MO Liguori Mission House/Redemptorists.
Nugent, James *i.c.* '69 (PEO) [A] Peoria, IL Rosminian Novitiate.
Nugent, Msgr. James B. '56 (STU) Retired.
Nugent, John G. *c.m.* (ALN) [A] Northampton, PA Mary Immaculate Seminary; [K] Northhampton, PA Vincentian Community.
Nugent, Msgr. Joseph A. '71 (BRK) [234] Queens, NY St. Rita Church.
Nugent, Msgr. Michael A. '43 (COL) [40] Columbus, OH St. Timothy Church; Retired.
Nugent, Msgr. Peter D. '62 (LA) [2] Oxnard, CA Santa Clara Church.
Nugent, Raymond H. '58 (RVC) Montauk, NY St. Therese of Lisieux Church.
Nugent, Msgr. Richard T. '49 (BUF) [2] Orchard Park, NY St. Bernadette Church.
Nugent, Robert '65 (ALB) South Glens Falls, NY St. Michael the Archangel Church.
Nugent, Vincent J. *c.m.* '42 (PH) [Z] Philadelphia, PA Congregation of the Mission.
Nunan, Jeremiah '63 (ALB) Cairo, NY Sacred Heart Church.
Nunes, James (RVC) Freeport, NY Our Holy Redeemer Church.
Nunes, James *m.s.* '91 (MAN) [K] Enfield, NH Shrine of Our Lady of La Salette; [M] Enfield, NH La Salette Shrine and Center of Enfield.
Nunes, Jose '68 (PH) [71] Philadelphia, PA Incarnation of Our Lord Church.
Nunez, Albert G. '64 (LAF) Lyons Point, LA St. John the Baptist Church.
Nunez, Edgardo '96 (ARE) [1] Vega-Baja, PR Holy Rosary Church.
Nunez, Edward H. '76 (PBL) [6] Pueblo, CO Our Lady of Guadalupe Church; [13] Pueblo, CO St. Leander Church.
Nunez, Felipe '88 (ARE) Vega-Alta, PR Perpetuo Socorro Church.
Nunez, Mario '79 (SAC) Fairfield, CA Holy Spirit Church.
Nunez, Pedro F. '77 (NO) [35] New Orleans, LA St. Gerard Church; [65] New Orleans, LA St. Vincent De Paul Church; [1] New Orleans, LA Holy Trinity Church.
Nunning, David H. '69 (EVN) St. Wendel, IN St. Wendel Church.
Nuno, Rafael '69 (ARE) [2] Utuado, PR San Pedro y San Pablo Church.
Nurre, Henry V. *o.s.b.* '56 (MIL) [P] Benet Lake, WI St. Benedict's Abbey.
Nusbaum, Daniel C. '61 (ALB) On Duty Outside the Diocese.
Nusbaum, Daniel C. '61 (BAL) [C] Emmitsburg, MD Mount Saint Mary's College.
Nusbaum, Michael L. (CLV) [C] Cleveland, OH John Carroll Jesuit Community.
Nuss, David W. '93 (TOL) Sandusky, OH St. Mary Church.
Nuss, Francis B. '61 (RVC) Sayville, NY Good Samaritan Nursing Home.; [C] West Islip, NY St. John the Baptist; [K] Sayville, NY Good Samaritan Nursing Home.
Nutt, Maurice *c.ss.r.* '89 (STL) [22] St. Louis, MO St. Alphonsus Liguori Church; [P] St. Louis, MO St. Alphonsus Rectory of the Redemptorist.
Nuttall, William I. *s.j.* '41 (PH) [82] Philadelphia, PA Old St. Joseph's Church.
Nutter, N. John '89 (BR) Amite, LA St. Helena Church.
Nuttman, Joseph *c.ss.r.* '52 (RNO) Carlin, NV Sacred Heart Church; Eureka, NV St. Brendan's Church.
Nuttman, Joseph K. *c.s.s.r.* '52 (P) [17] Portland, OR Holy Redeemer Church.
Nuttmann, Joseph *c.ss.r.* '52 (CHI) [N] Bangkok, Thailand; [N] Parana, Brazil Rua Consulheiro Sinimbu.
Nuttmann, Joseph *c.ss.r.* '52 (DEN) [M] Denver, CO The Redemptorists/Denver Province.
Nuwer, Herold M. '61 (BUF) Ransomville, NY Immaculate Conception Church.
Nuytten, Ralph *c.i.c.m.* '49 (SAT) [M] San Antonio, TX Missionhurst Community Residence.
Nuzzi, Ronald '84 (CIN) [5] Dayton, OH Ascension Church.
Nuzzi, Ronald '84 (Y) Absent on Leave.
Nuzzo, Peter Damian *o.f.m.* '69 (NY) [175] Bronx, NY Our Lady of Pity Church.

Nwachukwu, Oliver (CHI) [121] Chicago, IL St. Margaret Mary Church.
Nwachukwu, Paschal '89 (GAL) [65] Houston, TX St. Peter the Apostle Church.
Nwachukwu, Raphael '74 (NY) Rosendale, NY St. Peter Church.
Nwachukwu, Thomas Kizito '82 (SHP) [3] Monroe, LA Our Lady of Fatima Church.
Nwachukwu-Udaku, Anthony Okey *s.s.j.* '93 (WDC) [32] Washington, DC Our Lady of Perpetual Help Church.
Nwamadi, Chima Eva (LA) [67] Los Angeles, CA St. Ignatius of Loyola Church.
Nwanze, John *o.p.* (SEA) [26] Seattle, WA Immaculate Conception Church.
Nwaogu, Anthony '77 (DAL) [12] Dallas, TX St. Anthony Church.
Nwaorgu, Anselm I. '92 (NEW) Union, NJ St. Michael's Church.
Nwaru, Romanus '95 (MIL) Elm Grove, WI St. Mary's Church.
Nwoga, Laserian I. '95 (CAM) Pleasantville, NJ St. Peter's Church.
Nwogwugwu, Emmanuel '86 (NY) [204] Staten Island, NY Holy Child Church.
Nwosuh, Cosmas *m.s.p.* '89 (WDC) [B] Washington, DC St. Joseph's Seminary.
Nyambo, Callist N. '69 (SP) [15] Tampa, FL St. Peter Claver Church.
Nyardy, Jeffrey S. *o.s.b.* '90 (SAV) [B] Savannah, GA Benedictine Military School; [F] Savannah, GA The Benedictine Priory.
Nycz, Mieczyslaw F. '94 (BUF) [3] Orchard Park, NY Our Lady of the Sacred Heart Church.
Nydegger, Thomas P. '92 (NEW) [1] Newark, NJ Cathedral of the Sacred Heart Basilica.
Nyein, Isidore Usit *s.o.l.t.* '73 (CC) Robstown, TX St. Anthony Church.
Nygaard, Robert C. '64 (STP) Roseville, MN Corpus Christi Church; [A] St. Paul, MN The Saint Paul Seminary.
Nygren, David *c.m.* '77 (CHI) [N] Chicago, IL Vincentian Community, Congregation of the Mission, Midwest Province.
Nygren, David J. *c.m.* '77 (STL) [P] Earth City, MO Congregation of the Mission Midwest Province (Vincentians).
Nyhan, W. James (BO) [7] Cambridge, MA Immaculate Conception Church.
Nyquist, Raymond J. '54 (GF) Black Eagle, MT Most Blessed Sacrament Church.
Nys, Loren G. *s.d.s.* '67 (GB) Kiel, WI SS. Peter and Paul Church.
Nyssen, Jacques *s.v.d.* '59 (TR) [M] Bordentown, NJ Society of the Divine Word.
Nytes, Raymond *o.f.m.* '45 (FWT) [G] Crowley, TX St. Francis Village, Inc.; [H] Crowley, TX St. Maximilian Kolbe Friary.

O

O Shea, David T. '61 (PT) Panama City Beach, FL St. Bernadette Church.
O'Bell, John C. '91 (SCR) [1] Hazleton, PA St. Gabriel's Church.
O'Bierne, William M. *o.p.* '38 (WDC) [11] Washington, DC St. Dominic Church & Priory Church.
O'Blaney, James *c.ss.r.* (ALB) Saratoga Springs, NY St. Clement Church.
O'Boyle, Andrew F. '54 (CLV) Brooklyn, OH St. Thomas More Church; Newbury, OH St. Helen Church; Retired.
O'Boyle, Leo *c.p.* '96 (CHI) [N] Chicago, IL Passionist Community-CTU.
O'Brien, Allan *o.f.m.cap.* '34 (NY) [Z] White Plains, NY St. Conrad Friary.
O'Brien, Anthony *ss.cc.* '34 (HON) [H] Honolulu, HI St. Patrick's Monastery.
O'Brien, Anthony '88 (MIA) Coral Gables, FL Little Flower Church.
O'Brien, Arthur '83 (HON) Retired.
O'Brien, Bartholomew J. '40 (ROC) Retired.
O'Brien, Bartholomew J. '65 (PH) [70] Philadelphia, PA Immaculate Heart of Mary Church.
O'Brien, Bernard P. '49 (PIT) Retired.
O'Brien, Charles H. *o.p.* '54 (L) [46] Louisville, KY St. Louis Bertrand Church.
O'Brien, Christian T. *o.praem.* '62 (SFE) Albuquerque, NM St. Joseph Medical Center; [J] Albuquerque, NM Santa Maria de la Vid Priory.
O'Brien, Christopher '54 (EVN) On Duty Outside the Diocese.
O'Brien, Msgr. Cornelius '36 (NY) [E] White Plains, NY Archbishop Stepinac High School.
O'Brien, Cornelius '55 (ARL) Chantilly, VA St. Timothy Church.
O'Brien, Msgr. Cornelius M. '36 (NY) [1] Port Chester, NY Our Lady of Mercy Church; Retired.
O'Brien, Daniel '75 (VIC) Shiner, TX SS. Cyril and Methodius Church; Retired.
O'Brien, Msgr. Daniel B. '39 (SY) Dewitt, NY Holy Cross Church; Retired.
O'Brien, Daniel J. *s.j.* '59 (NY) [Z] New York, NY Jesuit Community at Fordham University.
O'Brien, Daniel P. '85 (HBG) Camp Hill, PA Good Shepherd Church.
O'Brien, David *c.s.p.* '56 (COL) [J] Columbus, OH Campus Ministry.
O'Brien, David G. '62 (BRK) Absent on Sick Leave.
O'Brien, Denis *m.m.* '53 (DAL) [25] Dallas, TX St. Pius X Church.
O'Brien, Denis J. '44 (RVC) Retired.
O'Brien, Dennis '81 (PT) [1] Tallahassee, FL Co-Cathedral of St. Thomas More; On Duty Outside the Diocese.
O'Brien, Dennis J. '77 (WOR) [N] Leicester, MA Father James Fitton House of Priestly Formation.
O'Brien, Donald *o.m.i.* '65 (BO) [3] Lowell, MA Immaculate Conception Church.
O'Brien, Donald J. '61 (GI) Cozad, NE Christ the King Church.
O'Brien, Donald J. '93 (TR) Howell Township, NJ St. Veronica Church.
O'Brien, Donald V. *s.j.* '55 (NY) [2] White Plains, NY St. John the Evangelist Church.
O'Brien, Edmund M. '57 (HRT) Lakeville, CT St. Mary's Church.
O'Brien, Edward C. *s.j.* '61 (STL) [P] St. Louis, MO Jesuit Community Corporation at St. Louis University - Jesuit Hall.
O'Brien, Edward J. '37 (PRT) [1] Portland, ME Cathedral of the Immaculate Conception; Retired.
O'Brien, Msgr. Edward M. '62 (NY) [27] New York, NY St. Columba Church; [42] New York, NY Guardian Angel Church.
O'Brien, Edward P. '52 (CHI) [142] Chicago, IL Nativity of Our Lord Church; [2] Oak Lawn, IL St. Gerald Church; Retired.
O'Brien, Edwin F. '65 (NY) [A] Yonkers, NY St. Joseph's Seminary; [D] New York, NY Department of Education.
O'Brien, Eugene C. '57 (MIL) Retired.
O'Brien, Eugene J. *s.j.* '56 (NY) [Z] New York, NY "America;" Residence and publication office of the America Press; [DD] New York, NY Gregorian University Foundation, The.
O'Brien, Forrest '55 (TLS) [6] Tulsa, OK St. Francis Xavier-Our Lady of Guadalupe Church.
O'Brien, Francis C. '87 (BO) [49] Boston, MA St. Matthew Church.
O'Brien, Francis E. '66 (BO) [2] Framingham, MA St. George Church.
O'Brien, Francis P. '85 (BO) [6] Newton, MA Our Lady Help of Christians Church.
O'Brien, Frederick J. *s.j.* '62 (BO) [W] Boston, MA The Society of Jesus of New England-Provincial Offices.
O'Brien, Frederick J. *s.j.* '62 (NY) [Z] New York, NY "America;" Residence and publication office of the America Press; [Z] New York, NY Jesuit Provincial's Office.
O'Brien, Frederick W. (BO) Retired.
O'Brien, George '57 (LA) Beverly Hills, CA Good Shepherd Church.
O'Brien, George L. '58 (WOR) East Templeton, MA Holy Cross Church.
O'Brien, Gerard '95 (LA) La Crescenta, CA St. James the Less Church.
O'Brien, Gerard C. *s.j.* '59 (BO) [W] Chestnut Hill, MA The Jesuit Community at Boston College.
O'Brien, Gilbert *o.praem.* '90 (ORG) [H] Silverado, CA Norbertine Fathers.
O'Brien, Hugh V. '38 (CHI) [114] Chicago, IL St. Kilian Church; Arlington Heights, IL St. James Church; Retired.
O'Brien, J. Paul *s.j.* '68 (CIN) [F] Cincinnati, OH St. Xavier High School; [M] Cincinnati, OH Jesuit Community at St. Xavier High School.
O'Brien, James (BO) [W] Quincy, MA St. Columban's Foreign Mission Society.
O'Brien, James (SAC) Paradise, CA St. Thomas More Church.
O'Brien, James A. *s.j.* '60 (WH) [A] Wheeling, WV Wheeling Jesuit University.
O'Brien, James C. *s.j.* '61 (BO) [W] Chestnut Hill, MA The Jesuit Community at Boston College.
O'Brien, James E. '60 (Y) Canfield, OH St. Michael's Church.
O'Brien, James F. '49 (NEW) [21] Jersey City, NJ Church of Our Lady of Sorrows.
O'Brien, James F. *s.j.* '67 (NY) [Z] New York, NY St. Ignatius Loyola Residence; [Z] New York, NY Jesuit Seminary and Mission Bureau, Inc. (Jesuit Deferred Funds); [DD] New York, NY Jesuit Seminary and Mission Bureau, Inc.
O'Brien, Msgr. James J. '40 (NOR) Retired.
O'Brien, James J. '60 (CHI) [56] Chicago, IL St. Eugene Church.
O'Brien, James R. '66 (HBG) Mechanicsburg, PA Blessed Katharine Drexel Church.
O'Brien, James T. '63 (BRK) [122] Brooklyn, NY Resurrection Church.
O'Brien, James T. '70 (SY) [3] Syracuse, NY Blessed Sacrament Church.
O'Brien, John *c.p.* (BO) Burlington, MA St. Malachy Church.
O'Brien, John *o.s.b.* (IND) Liberty, IN St. Bridget Church.
O'Brien, John *s.j.* (MIL) [N] Wauwatosa, WI St. Camillus Health Center, Inc.
O'Brien, John (PAT) Absent on Leave.
O'Brien, Msgr. John (TR) [L] Lawrenceville, NJ Morris Hall-Saint Lawrence, Inc.
O'Brien, John '45 (BLX) Retired.
O'Brien, John *c.p.m.* '52 (OWN) [F] South Union, KY Fathers of Mercy.
O'Brien, John *s.d.b.* '62 (SFR) [45] San Francisco, CA SS. Peter and Paul Church.
O'Brien, John '69 (SAV) Valdosta, GA St. John the Evangelist Church.
O'Brien, John '75 (PIT) Retired.
O'Brien, John A. '64 (MIL) North Fond du Lac, WI Presentation of the Blessed Virgin Church.
O'Brien, John E. '46 (NEW) Livingston, NJ St. Raphael Church; Retired.
O'Brien, John E. '50 (CHI) Highland Park, IL Immaculate Conception Church; Retired.
O'Brien, John E. '87 (BAL) [L] Sparks, MD Msgr. Clare J. O'Dwyer Retreat House.
O'Brien, Msgr. John F. '42 (NEW) Retired.
O'Brien, John F. '55 (GB) [12] Green Bay, WI St. Patrick Church.
O'Brien, John F. '61 (PH) [139] Philadelphia, PA St. Raymond of Penafort Church.
O'Brien, John F. '62 (WIL) [5] Wilmington, DE St. Elizabeth Church.
O'Brien, John G. '53 (R) Retired.
O'Brien, Msgr. John H. '62 (BRK) [155] Queens, NY St. Benedict Joseph Labre Church.
O'Brien, Msgr. John J. '38 (WOR) Retired.
O'Brien, John J. '40 (NEW) [B] Jersey City, NJ Saint Peter's College; [N] Jersey City, NJ Jesuits of Saint Peter's College, Inc.
O'Brien, Msgr. John J. '42 (SCR) Retired; [N] Dunmore, PA Villa St. Joseph.
O'Brien, John J. *s.j.* '49 (NEW) Saddle River Borough, NJ St. Gabriel the Archangel Church.
O'Brien, John J. *m.m.* '52 (NY) [Z] Maryknoll, NY Maryknoll Fathers and Brothers.
O'Brien, John J. *s.a.c.* '62 (RNO) Sparks, NV Immaculate Conception Church.
O'Brien, John M. *o.c.s.o.* '81 (ATL) [I] Conyers, GA The Monastery of the Holy Spirit.
O'Brien, John P. '49 (SPK) Retired.
O'Brien, John P. '90 (NY) [Z] New York, NY St. John Neumann Residence.
O'Brien, John T. '45 (BLX) Bay St. Louis, MS Our Lady of the Gulf Church.
O'Brien, John T. *s.j.* '58 (MIL) [P] Wauwatosa, WI Jesuit Community at St. Camillus.
O'Brien, John W. (BO) [8] Quincy, MA Sacred Heart Church.
O'Brien, John W. '82 (PRO) [4] North Providence, RI Presentation of the Blessed Virgin Mary Church; Providence, RI Rhode Island Hospital.
O'Brien, Jon J. *s.j.* '63 (BAL) [M] Baltimore, MD Jesuit Fathers and Brothers Maryland Provincial Curia.
O'Brien, Msgr. Joseph (STL) [O] Kirkwood, MO St. Agnes Home for the Elderly.
O'Brien, Joseph '49 (ALB) North Creek, NY St. James Church.
O'Brien, Joseph *o.carm.* '63 (NEW) Englewood, NJ St. Cecilia's Church.
O'Brien, Joseph *o.p.* '78 (PHX) [J] Phoenix, AZ The Malta Center.
O'Brien, Joseph '91 (ALB) Chestertown, NY St. John the Baptist Church; Hague, NY Blessed Sacrament Church.
O'Brien, Joseph A. '44 (STL) Retired.
O'Brien, Joseph A. '56 (WDC) Special Ministries; [L] Washington, DC Cardinal O'Boyle Residence for Priests.
O'Brien, Joseph E. '51 (PH) [87] Philadelphia, PA St. Leo Church.
O'Brien, Joseph J. *o.m.i.* '54 (BWN) Port Isabel, TX Our Lady Star of the Sea Church.
O'Brien, Joseph J. '56 (CHI) Other Assignments.
O'Brien, Joseph L. '55 (TOL) Retired.
O'Brien, Msgr. Joseph M. '57 (STL) Special Assignment.
O'Brien, Msgr. Joseph T. '46 (STL) Retired.
O'Brien, Joseph V. '57 (DUB) [1] Dubuque, IA St. Raphael's Cathedral.
O'Brien, Msgr. Kenneth R. '40 (LA) Retired.
O'Brien, Kevin '79 (RIC) Lynchburg, VA St. Thomas More Church.
O'Brien, Kevin J. '81 (OG) Massena, NY Sacred Heart Church; [A] Ogdensburg, NY Wadhams Hall.
O'Brien, Kevin P. '54 (DET) [7] Livonia, MI St. Priscilla Church.
O'Brien, Msgr. Kevin P. '73 (NY) [10] New York, NY St. Ann's Roman Catholic Church; [52] New York, NY Immaculate Conception Church.
O'Brien, Msgr. Laurence '43 (LA) Glendale, CA Church of the Incarnation.

O'Brien, Leo P. '56 (ALB) [17] Albany, NY St. Vincent de Paul Church; Special Assignment.
O'Brien, Mark J. '84 (PH) Absent on Leave.
O'Brien, Martin F. '52 (NEW) [A] South Orange, NJ Immaculate Conception Seminary; [B] South Orange, NJ Seton Hall University.
O'Brien, Maurice '68 (SAC) Dixon, CA St. Peter Church.
O'Brien, Michael '43 (NY) Retired.
O'Brien, Michael '72 (JKS) Starkville, MS St. Joseph Church; [G] Starkville, MS Mississippi State University Catholic Student Association.
O'Brien, Michael '79 (SP) [3] St. Petersburg, FL Holy Cross Church.
O'Brien, Michael G. *c.s.c.* '42 (FTW) [J] South Bend, IN Congregation of Holy Cross Indiana Province Provincial House.
O'Brien, Michael J. '43 (NY) Mamaroneck, NY Holy Trinity Church.
O'Brien, Michael J. *c.s.v.* '48 (CHI) [N] Arlington Heights, IL Viatorian Province Center-Clerics of St. Viator.
O'Brien, Michael J. '63 (NEW) Kearny, NJ Our Lady of Sorrows Church.
O'Brien, Nicholas J. '83 (ORL) Leesburg, FL St. Paul's Church.
O'Brien, Patrick *o.m.i.* '37 (SAT) [K] San Antonio, TX Oblate Madonna Residence.
O'Brien, Patrick '64 (PIT) [B] Pittsburgh, PA La Roche College.
O'Brien, Patrick *c.ss.r.* '64 (TUC) [H] Tucson, AZ Redemptorist Picture Rocks Retreat.
O'Brien, Patrick '69 (SAV) [9] Savannah, GA St. Peter the Apostle Church.
O'Brien, Patrick '74 (HT) [3] Thibodaux, LA Christ The Redeemer Church; [5] Thibodaux, LA St. John The Evangelist Church.
O'Brien, Msgr. Patrick J. '56 (LA) Ventura, CA San Buenaventura Mission Church.
O'Brien, Patrick K. '46 (SEA) [8] Tacoma, WA St. Martin of Tours Church.
O'Brien, Paul B. '91 (BO) Graduate Studies.
O'Brien, Paul B. '95 (BO) [3] Brookline, MA St. Lawrence Church.
O'Brien, Peter F. *s.j.* '71 (RVC) [P] Manhasset, NY St. Ignatius Retreat House, Inisfada.
O'Brien, Peter K. '83 (NEW) Westfield, NJ St. Helen Church.
O'Brien, Raymond C. '75 (WDC) Special Ministries; [C] Washington, DC Catholic University of America, The.
O'Brien, Richard *c.m.* '61 (KC) [J] Kansas City, MO Vincentian Parish Mission Center.
O'Brien, Richard J. *s.j.* '54 (WDC) [M] Washington, DC The Jesuit Community at Georgetown University.
O'Brien, Richard M. '92 (BO) Hudson, MA St. Michael Church.
O'Brien, Robert E. *s.j.* '54 (NY) [46] New York, NY Holy Family Church.
O'Brien, Robert E. '59 (BO) [5] Boston, MA St. Andrew Church; Retired.
O'Brien, Roger '61 (SEA) [12] Seattle, WA St. Luke Church.
O'Brien, Msgr. Roger E. '42 (DUB) Retired.
O'Brien, Scott I. *o.p.* '92 (NO) [P] New Orleans, LA Dominican Fathers & Brothers, Southern Dominican Province.
O'Brien, Scott T. *o.p.* '92 (NO) [25] New Orleans, LA St. Anthony Of Padua Church.
O'Brien, Sean P. '93 (SY) [3] Utica, NY Our Lady of Lourdes Church.
O'Brien, Steven G. '86 (DUB) Belle Plaine, IA St. Michael Church; [1] Cedar Rapids, IA Immaculate Conception Church; Chelsea, IA St. Joseph's Church; [D] Cedar Rapids, IA LaSalle High School; [D] Cedar Rapids, IA Regis High School.
O'Brien, Terrance P. '81 (PEO) [4] Champaign, IL St. Matthew Church.
O'Brien, Msgr. Terrence '43 (ORG) Retired.
O'Brien, Thomas '47 (SAC) Retired and in Senior Ministry.
O'Brien, Thomas *o.s.c.* '74 (STP) [N] Shoreview, MN Crosier Community of Shoreview.
O'Brien, Thomas F. '55 (OM) [47] Omaha, NE St. Vincent de Paul Church.
O'Brien, Thomas F. '56 (WOR) Retired.
O'Brien, Thomas G. *c.s.v.* '47 (CHI) [N] Arlington Heights, IL Viatorian Province Center-Clerics of St. Viator.
O'Brien, Msgr. Thomas J. '50 (KC) Retired.
O'Brien, Thomas J. '55 (SAT) Martinez, TX St. Jerome Church.
O'Brien, Msgr. Thomas L. '43 (LA) Retired.
O'Brien, Msgr. Thomas M. '52 (BRK) [229] Queens, NY Presentation of the Blessed Virgin Mary Church.
O'Brien, Msgr. Timothy '54 (SJ) Retired.
O'Brien, Timothy A. '94 (HRT) New Milford, CT St. Francis Xavier's Church.
O'Brien, Timothy J. '69 (MIL) Special Assignment.
O'Brien, Vincent M. *s.j.* '55 (WDC) [E] North Bethesda, MD Georgetown Preparatory School.
O'Brien, Walter *o.f.m.cap.* '37 (SPR) [L] Springfield, MA St. Francis of Assisi Chapel and Catholic Information Center.
O'Brien, William (DUB) Haverhill, IA Immaculate Conception Church.
O'Brien, William *m.s.* '49 (LKC) [3] Sulphur, LA Our Lady of Prompt Succor Church.
O'Brien, William '78 (BAL) Special Assignment.
O'Brien, William '80 (E) [C] Oil City, PA Venango Christian High School.
O'Brien, William '88 (VNN) Sacramento, CA St. Philip the Apostle Church; San Jose-Palo Alto, CA St. Basil the Great Church.
O'Brien, Msgr. William B. '51 (NY) [135] Bronx, NY St. Brendan Church; On Duty Outside the Archdiocese.
O'Brien, William D. '50 (DUB) Haverhill, IA Immaculate Conception Church.
O'Brien, William G. (WOR) Otter River, MA St. Martin's Church.
O'Brien, William G. '90 (GB) Brillion, WI St. Mary Church.
O'Brien, William H. '77 (BAL) Baltimore, MD University of Maryland Hospital.
O'Brien, William J. *c.m.* '67 (BUF) [T] Niagara University, NY Our Lady of Angels Association.
O'Brien, William J. *c.m.* '67 (PH) [69] Philadelphia, PA Immaculate Conception Church; [B] Philadelphia, PA St. Vincent's Seminary; [EE] Philadelphia, PA The Central Association of the Miraculous Medal.
O'Brien, William J. '80 (E) [2] Oil City, PA Our Lady Help of Christians Church.
O'Brien, William P. *s.j.* (IND) [D] Indianapolis, IN Brebeuf Jesuit Preparatory School, Inc.
O'Brien, William P. *m.s.* '49 (LKC) Sulphur, LA West Clacasieu Cameron Hospital.
O'Brien, William S. '61 (NEW) Ridgewood, NJ Our Lady of Mount Carmel Church.
O'Brien, William S. '69 (RIC) Waynesboro, VA St. John the Evangelist Church.
O'Bryan, Henry '41 (OWN) Retired.
O'Bryan, Msgr. J. A. '35 (L) Retired.
O'Bryan, James *s.t.* '56 (BLX) Pineville, MS Our Lady of Lourdes Church.
O'Byrne, John '61 (LA) Torrance, CA St. Catherine Laboure Church.
O'Byrne, Patrick J. '60 (LIN) Colon, NE St. Joseph's Church.
O'Byrne, Msgr. Sylvester '51 (LA) Montecito, CA Our Lady of Mount Carmel Church.
O'Callaghan, Dominic *o.c.d.* '44 (SB) [G] Redlands, CA El Carmelo Retreat House.
O'Callaghan, Msgr. Eugene '55 (SAT) New Braunfels, TX SS. Peter and Paul Church.
O'Callaghan, Msgr. James A. '43 (LA) Hacienda Heights, CA St. John Vianney Church; Retired.
O'Callaghan, John '65 (ORG) Inactive Leave.
O'Callaghan, John F. '45 (DET) Retired.
O'Callaghan, John J. *s.j.* '62 (CHI) [C] Chicago, IL Jesuit Community at Loyola University of Chicago.
O'Callaghan, Matthias J. '62 (SAC) Willows, CA St. Monica Church; Special Assignment.
O'Callaghan, Patrick '55 (SAT) Retired.
O'Callaghan, Msgr. Peter '52 (SAT) [24] San Antonio, TX St. Agnes Church.
O'Callaghan, Thomas '54 (SEA) Retired.
O'Callaghan, Tiernan *o.carm.* '56 (PHX) [6] Phoenix, AZ St. Agnes Church.
O'Carroll, Msgr. Donal '56 (STU) Lafferty, OH St. Mary Church.
O'Carroll, Eugene '62 (PHX) [21] Phoenix, AZ St. Paul Church.
O'Carroll, Philip A. '58 (SB) [2] Fontana, CA St. George Church.
O'Ceochain, Donie '68 (LA) [78] Los Angeles, CA St. Martin of Tours Church.
O'Cinnsealaigh, Benedict (CIN) [3] Dayton, OH St. Albert the Great Church.
O'Connell, Anthony M. *o.s.m.* '67 (CHI) [18] Chicago, IL Assumption of the Blessed Virgin Mary Church; [A] Mundelein, IL University of St. Mary of the Lake-Mundelein Seminary; [N] Chicago, IL Servite Friars - Eastern Province.
O'Connell, Brian J. *c.m.* '68 (PH) [Z] Philadelphia, PA Congregation of the Mission.
O'Connell, Brian J. *c.m.* '68 (WDC) [K] Washington, DC Providence Hospital; [V] Washington, DC Carroll Manor Nursing & Rehabilitation Center.
O'Connell, Cuthbert '86 (BLX) Bassfield, MS St. Peter Church.
O'Connell, Damian A. *s.j.* '75 (NY) [51] New York, NY St. Ignatius Loyola Church; [Z] New York, NY St. Ignatius Loyola Residence.
O'Connell, Daniel '71 (SAV) Douglas, GA St. Paul's Church.
O'Connell, Daniel C. *s.j.* '58 (WDC) [M] Washington, DC The Jesuit Community at Georgetown University.
O'Connell, Daniel P. '71 (SAV) [I] Willacoochee, GA Catholic Cemetery.
O'Connell, David '79 (LA) [61] Los Angeles, CA St. Frances Xavier Cabrini Church.
O'Connell, David M. *c.m.* '82 (BRK) [D] Queens and Staten Island, NY St. John's University; [D] Queens and Staten Island, NY St. John's University; [D] Jamaica, NY St. John's University; [U] Jamaica, NY Vincentian Residence.
O'Connell, George *o.m.i.* '41 (SAT) [K] San Antonio, TX Oblate Madonna Residence.
O'Connell, George M. *o.s.m.* '37 (CHI) [N] Chicago, IL Servite Friars - Eastern Province.
O'Connell, Msgr. James E. '33 (LR) [L] Little Rock, AR St. John's Home Missions Seminary, Inc.
O'Connell, James F. '36 (ROC) Retired.
O'Connell, Msgr. James P. '53 (STL) Retired.
O'Connell, James R. *o.f.m.* '83 (NY) [35] New York, NY St. Francis of Assisi Church.
O'Connell, John '59 (SFD) Taylorville, IL St. Mary Church.
O'Connell, John B. '40 (HRT) [4] Enfield, CT St. Martha's Church.
O'Connell, John G. *o.p.* '44 (STP) [15] Minneapolis, MN St. Albert the Great Church.
O'Connell, John Q. *c.m.* '53 (DEN) [M] Denver, CO Congregation of the Mission Midwest Province: De Paul House; [Q] Denver, CO Kateri Catholic Indian Community of Colorado.
O'Connell, John R. '73 (NEW) Midland Park, NJ Nativity Church.
O'Connell, Joseph '51 (SFR) Mill Valley, CA Our Lady of Mt. Carmel Church.
O'Connell, Joseph *s.o.l.t.* '91 (CC) Robstown, TX St. John Nepomucene Church; [H] Robstown, TX Society of Our Lady of the Most Holy Trinity.
O'Connell, Msgr. Joseph F. '64 (CAM) Washington Township, NJ St. Charles Borromeo Church.
O'Connell, Joseph F. *s.j.* '73 (WDC) [M] Washington, DC The Jesuit Community at Georgetown University; [V] Washington, DC Jesuit Secondary Education Association.
O'Connell, Luke A. *o.f.m.* '55 (ALB) [B] Loudonville, NY Siena College.
O'Connell, Mark '90 (BO) Danvers, MA St. Mary of the Annunciation Church; [CC] Salem, MA Salem State College, Catholic Campus Ministry.
O'Connell, Mark A. '79 (NEW) Belleville, NJ St. Peter's Church.
O'Connell, Marvin '56 (FTW) [B] Notre Dame, IN University of Notre Dame Du Lac.
O'Connell, Marvin R. '56 (STP) On Duty Outside the Archdiocese.
O'Connell, Maurice J. '85 (TLS) Broken Arrow, OK St. Anne Church.
O'Connell, Maurice J. '86 (TLS) [G] Broken Arrow, OK St. Anne Church.
O'Connell, Maurice V. '72 (WDC) Riverdale, MD St. Bernard Church.
O'Connell, Michael '67 (STP) [1] Minneapolis, MN The Basilica of St. Mary Co-Cathedral.
O'Connell, Michael W. '83 (CHI) Graduate Studies.
O'Connell, Neil J. *o.f.m.* '64 (NY) [115] New York, NY St. Stephen of Hungary Church; [DD] New York, NY Shrine of St. Jude, Inc.
O'Connell, Msgr. Patrick '55 (BEA) Retired.
O'Connell, Paul T. '60 (WOR) Shrewsbury, MA St. Mary's Church.
O'Connell, Richard C. '51 (ROC) [48] Rochester, NY St. Monica Church; Retired.
O'Connell, Robert '71 (SUP) Saxon, WI St. Ann's Church.
O'Connell, Robert E. '71 (SUP) Hurley, WI St. Mary of the Seven Dolors Church; Montreal, WI Sacred Heart of Jesus Church; Pence, WI Holy Redeemer Church.
O'Connell, Robert J. *s.s.j.* '41 (BAL) [M] Baltimore, MD St. Joseph's Manor.
O'Connell, Robert J. '70 (RVC) Patchogue, NY Our Lady of Mt. Carmel Church.
O'Connell, Robert Jerome *s.j.* '46 (NY) [Z] New York, NY Murray-Weigel Hall.
O'Connell, Robert John *s.j.* '57 (NY) [Z] New York, NY Murray-Weigel Hall.
O'Connell, Msgr. Robert M. '51 (NY) [105] New York, NY St. Peter Church.
O'Connell, Terrence E. *o.m.i.* (BO) [12] Lowell, MA Nuestra Senora del Carmen 1990 Church.
O'Connell, Terry J. '92 (P) Coos Bay, OR St. Monica Church.
O'Connell, Thomas (CHL) Winston-Salem, NC St. Leo's Church.
O'Connell, Msgr. Thomas '45 (LA) Westlake Village, CA St. Jude Church; Retired.
O'Connell, Thomas *c.ss.r.* '49 (NY) [92] New York, NY Our Lady of Perpetual Help Church.
O'Connell, Thomas C. '46 (PIT) Retired; [N] Pittsburgh, PA St. John Vianney Manor.
O'Connell, Msgr. Timothy '63 (LA) Lancaster, CA Sacred Heart Church.
O'Connell, Vincent *c.s.sp.* '59 (BRK) [U] Long Island City, NY Holy Ghost Fathers of Ireland.
O'Connell, Walter *o.p.* '58 (DUL) Grand Marais, MN St. John's Church.
O'Connell, Walter T. *o.p.* '58 (CHI) [N] River Forest, IL St. Thomas Aquinas Priory.
O'Connell, William '54 (CHI) [4] Waukegan, IL Holy

Family Church.
O'Connell, Msgr. William '57 (RC) McIntosh, SD St. Bonaventure's Church; McLaughlin, SD St. Bernard Church.
O'Connell, William '66 (VEN) Priests Released from Diocesan Assignment.
O'Connell, William A. '55 (SFR) Pacifica, CA St. Peter Church; Special Assignment.
O'Connell, Msgr. William J. '57 (RC) Gregory, SD St. Joseph Church.
O'Connell, William M. (CHI) Retired.
O'Conner, Kevin *o.m.i.* '58 (P) Scio, OR St. Bernard Church.
O'Conner, William *o.m.i.* '43 (SAT) [M] San Antonio, TX Oblate Benson Residence (Southern Prov.).
O'Connor, Msgr. Albert G. '67 (SAC) Elk Grove, CA St. Joseph Church.
O'Connor, Msgr. Aloysius E. '40 (WDC) Avenue, MD Holy Angels Church; Retired.
O'Connor, Andrew '96 (NY) [70] New York, NY St. Mary Church.
O'Connor, Andrew J. '87 (STL) St. Ann, MO St. Kevin Church.
O'Connor, Bernard *c.m.f.* '50 (LA) Santa Monica, CA St. Monica Church.
O'Connor, Bernard F. *o.s.f.s.* '73 (ALN) [B] Center Valley, PA Allentown College of St. Francis de Sales; [K] Center Valley, PA Oblates of St. Francis de Sales.
O'Connor, Charles '58 (WCH) On Duty Outside the Diocese.
O'Connor, Charles *o.f.m., s.t.d.* '73 (BUF) [A] East Aurora, NY Christ the King Seminary.
O'Connor, Charles J. *c.m.* '34 (PH) [Z] Philadelphia, PA Congregation of the Mission.
O'Connor, Charles P. '50 (NEW) Fairfield, NJ St. Thomas More Church.
O'Connor, Charles T. '83 (MET) Bound Brook, NJ St. Joseph Church.
O'Connor, Msgr. Daniel J. '61 (ATL) [10] Atlanta, GA St. Jude Church.
O'Connor, Daniel P. (ALX) Fifth Ward, LA Our Lady of Lourdes Church.
O'Connor, David *s.t.* (WDC) [M] University Park, MD Holy Trinity Missionary Cenacle.
O'Connor, David '64 (JKS) On Duty Outside the Diocese.
O'Connor, David F. *s.t.* '55 (WDC) [B] Silver Spring, MD Holy Trinity Mission Seminary (1926).
O'Connor, David H. '86 (DUB) [C] Dubuque, IA Loras College.
O'Connor, Desmond *s.p.s.* '50 (PAT) Mount Arlington, NJ Our Lady of the Lake Church.
O'Connor, Desmond '80 (NY) [A] New York, NY Cathedral Preparatory Seminary; [A] New York, NY Cathedral Preparatory Seminary.
O'Connor, Donal P. '55 (LA) Lynwood, CA St. Emydius Church.
O'Connor, Donald '64 (JOL) [9] Joliet, IL St. Bernard Church.
O'Connor, Edward '60 (ATL) Thomson, GA Queen of Angels Church.
O'Connor, Edward D. *c.s.c.* '48 (FTW) [B] Notre Dame, IN University of Notre Dame Du Lac; [J] Notre Dame, IN Holy Cross Community, Corby Hall, University of Notre Dame.
O'Connor, Msgr. Edward J. '39 (CAM) Retired.
O'Connor, Edward J. '81 (ALN) Branchdale, PA St. Mary Star of the Sea Church; Newtown, PA Sacred Heart Church.
O'Connor, Edward T. '44 (BRK) [64] Brooklyn, NY Immaculate Heart of Mary Church; Retired.
O'Connor, Eugene '54 (BIR) [3] Birmingham, AL St. Barnabas Church.
O'Connor, Msgr. Francis '46 (MOB) Retired.
O'Connor, Francis A. '28 (SPR) Retired.
O'Connor, Francis A. '62 (ALB) [4] Albany, NY St. Casimir Church; [14] Albany, NY St. Patrick Church.
O'Connor, Francis J. '53 (MAN) Retired.
O'Connor, Francis M. '58 (WDC) [2] Washington, DC St. Aloysius Church; [E] Washington, DC Gonzaga College High School.
O'Connor, Msgr. Fred P. '52 (GAL) Crosby, TX Sacred Heart Church.
O'Connor, Frederic M. *s.j.* '40 (NY) [Z] New York, NY West Side Jesuit Community.
O'Connor, Gerald T. '66 (ROC) Addison, NY St. Catherine of Siena Church; Bradford, NY St. Stanislaus Church.
O'Connor, Gerald V. *s.j.* '76 (WDC) [E] Washington, DC Gonzaga College High School.
O'Connor, Glenn L. '80 (IND) [27] Indianapolis, IN St. Joseph Church; Indianapolis, IN Indianapolis International Airport.
O'Connor, Msgr. Hugh '39 (ORG) [3] Anaheim, CA St. Justin Martyr Church; Retired.
O'Connor, J. Kieran '45 (MAN) Retired; [J] Manchester, NH St. Teresas Manor & Bishop Primeau Apartments.
O'Connor, J. Paul *s.j.* '53 (STL) [O] St. Louis, MO Fusz Pavilion.
O'Connor, James (NOR) [A] Cromwell, CT Holy Apostles College and Seminary.
O'Connor, Msgr. James '40 (NY) Retired.
O'Connor, James '69 (AUS) [5] Waco, TX St. Joseph Church.
O'Connor, James '70 (LUB) [3] Lubbock, TX Our Lady of Guadalupe Church.
O'Connor, James C. '71 (BUF) Fredonia, NY St. Joseph Church.
O'Connor, James E. *o.c.s.o.* '57 (DUB) [K] Peosta, IA New Melleray Abbey, Order of Cistercians of the Strict Observance.
O'Connor, James E. '82 (WH) Madison, WV St. Mary, Queen of Heaven Church.
O'Connor, James J. '43 (FTW) Retired.
O'Connor, James J. '54 (CIN) Botkins, OH Immaculate Conception Church; Rhine, OH St. Lawrence Church.
O'Connor, James M. '52 (LIN) Minden, NE St. John's Church.
O'Connor, James T. '54 (CHI) [6] Cicero, IL Our Lady of the Mount Church; Retired.
O'Connor, James T. '66 (NY) Millbrook, NY St. Joseph Church.
O'Connor, Jay '74 (BAL) Annapolis, MD St. Andrew by the Bay Church.
O'Connor, John C. '61 (LA) Lynwood, CA St. Emydius Church; Sick Leave.
O'Connor, John F. *s.t.b.* (NEW) [21] Newark, NJ Immaculate Conception Church.
O'Connor, John F. '44 (PEO) Retired.
O'Connor, John F. *o.f.m.* '73 (ARL) Triangle, VA St. Francis of Assisi Church.
O'Connor, John F. '73 (R) [1] Raleigh, NC Cathedral of the Sacred Heart.
O'Connor, John H. (PAT) Absent on Leave.
O'Connor, John J. '42 (BUF) Buffalo, NY Buffalo Psychiatric Center.
O'Connor, John J. '58 (DUB) New Vienna, IA St. Boniface's Church; Petersburg, IA SS. Peter and Paul Church.
O'Connor, Msgr. John J. '60 (SFR) [33] San Francisco, CA Mission Dolores Basilica.
O'Connor, John J. '68 (DUB) [F] New Vienna, IA Archbishop Hennessy Catholic School.
O'Connor, John J. *s.l.l.* '93 (BRK) [13] Brooklyn, NY St. Athanasius Church.
O'Connor, John L. '60 (CAM) [2] Atlantic City, NJ St. Michael's Church.
O'Connor, John L. '63 (ROC) [34] Rochester, NY Our Lady of Lourdes Church.
O'Connor, John P. '45 (PH) [83] Philadelphia, PA St. Katherine of Siena Church.
O'Connor, Msgr. John Philip '61 (NEW) Garwood, NJ Church of St. Anne.
O'Connor, John R. '33 (BGP) [K] Trumbull, CT St. Joseph's Manor.
O'Connor, John R. '33 (HRT) Retired.
O'Connor, John T. '46 (HRT) Newington, CT Holy Spirit Church.
O'Connor, John T. '52 (MIL) [B] Hales Corners, WI Sacred Heart School of Theology; [P] Hales Corners, WI Sacred Heart Monastery.
O'Connor, Msgr. Joseph A. (TR) [M] Trenton, NJ Villa Neumann.
O'Connor, Msgr. Joseph A. '47 (TR) Retired.
O'Connor, Joseph E. *s.j.* '59 (BO) [3] Newton, MA St. Ignatius Church.
O'Connor, Joseph X. *o.s.a.* '53 (CAM) [4] Atlantic City, NJ St. Nicholas of Tolentine Church.
O'Connor, Kyron *c.p.* '40 (CHI) [N] Chicago, IL Daneo Hall.
O'Connor, Mark *s.a.* '84 (NY) [Z] Garrison, NY Franciscan Friars of the Atonement.
O'Connor, Matthew '71 (MOB) Tillman's Corner, AL St. Vincent de Paul Church.
O'Connor, Matthew J. '56 (SPR) [8] Springfield, MA Our Lady of Hope Church; [C] Springfield, MA Cathedral High School; [O] Goshen, MA Holy Cross Camp Grounds.
O'Connor, Maurice '52 (NY) Absent on Sick leave.
O'Connor, Maurice J. '53 (BO) Stoughton, MA Our Lady of the Rosary Church.
O'Connor, Msgr. Michael '47 (FRS) Lamont, CA St. Augustine Church; Retired.
O'Connor, Michael F. '44 (NU) Retired.
O'Connor, Michael F. '44 (STP) Miesville, MN St. Joseph Church.
O'Connor, Msgr. Michael J. '34 (LA) Woodland Hills, CA St. Mel Church; Retired.
O'Connor, Michael J. '65 (SJ) [5] Sunnyvale, CA Church of The Resurrection.
O'Connor, Michael J. *o.s.a.* '71 (CHI) [D] Chicago, IL St. Rita High School; [N] Chicago, IL St. Rita Monastery.
O'Connor, Michael J. *o.s.a.* '71 (MIL) [F] Oconomowoc, WI Austin Hall.
O'Connor, Michael J. '72 (TR) Delran, NJ Holy Name Church.
O'Connor, Neil D. '69 (CLV) [4] Parma, OH St. Columbkille Church.
O'Connor, Norman J. *c.s.p.* '48 (NY) [Z] Scarsdale, NY Paulist Fathers Generalate.
O'Connor, Oliver J. *o.f.m.cap.* '42 (ROC) [I] Interlaken, NY St. Fidelis Friary.
O'Connor, Patrick (BRK) [N] Jamaica, NY Catholic Medical Center of Brooklyn & Queens.
O'Connor, Patrick *m.s.c.* '52 (CC) Bishop, TX St. James Church.
O'Connor, Patrick '55 (KC) Retired.
O'Connor, Msgr. Patrick C. '54 (MOB) Gulf Shores, AL Our Lady of the Gulf Church.
O'Connor, Patrick C. '78 (SAG) [1] Bay City, MI Holy Trinity Church.
O'Connor, Patrick J. '58 (SAC) Tahoe City, CA Corpus Christi Church.
O'Connor, Patrick J. '64 (GBG) New Alexandria, PA St. James Church.
O'Connor, Patrick J. '85 (CLV) [3] Elyria, OH St. Jude Church.
O'Connor, Msgr. Paul '45 (CAM) Retired.
O'Connor, Paul *c.s.b.* '60 (PHX) Phoenix, AZ Arizona State Hospital.
O'Connor, Pio *o.f.m.* '94 (GLP) Chinle, AZ Our Lady of Fatima, Indian Mission Church; [A] Chinle, AZ Native American Lay Ministry and Diaconate Program.
O'Connor, Raymond *c.m.f.* '64 (CHI) [N] Oak Park, IL Claretian Fathers Headquarters of U.S.A. Eastern Province.
O'Connor, Richard C. '37 (STP) [8] St. Paul, MN The Nativity of Our Lord Church.
O'Connor, Richard T. '37 (NU) Retired.
O'Connor, Robert B. '56 (NY) [18] New York, NY Blessed Sacrament Church.
O'Connor, Robert C. *s.j.* '64 (CHI) [C] Chicago, IL Jesuit Community at Loyola University of Chicago.
O'Connor, Robert D. '55 (PEO) East Moline, IL St. Anne Church.
O'Connor, Robert F. *s.j.* '79 (STP) [6] St. Paul, MN The Immaculate Heart of Mary Church.
O'Connor, Robert W. '48 (PEO) Lewistown, IL St. Mary's Church.
O'Connor, Samuel *o.f.m.* '56 (BO) [BB] Boston, MA St. Anthony Shrine.
O'Connor, Shaun *m.i.c.* '82 (WDC) [B] Washington, DC Marian Fathers Scholasticate.
O'Connor, Stephen '48 (ALB) Retired.
O'Connor, Steven J. '77 (PT) Tiger Point, FL St. Sylvester Church; [H] Navarre, FL Casa Stella Maris.
O'Connor, Thomas *c.ss.r.* '50 (GR) [3] Grand Rapids, MI St. Alphonsus Church.
O'Connor, Thomas A. *s.j.* '62 (BUF) [O] Buffalo, NY Canisius Jesuit Community; [R] Williamsville, NY Newman Club Chaplains.
O'Connor, Thomas J. '55 (TR) Freehold, NJ St. Robert Bellarmine Church.
O'Connor, Thomas J. *o.s.b.* '56 (BIR) [E] Cullman, AL St. Bernard Abbey.
O'Connor, Thomas J. '93 (BO) [W] Hingham, MA Glastonbury Abbey.
O'Connor, Thomas P. '56 (FTW) [10] Fort Wayne, IN St. Mary Church.
O'Connor, Thomas V. *s.j.* '63 (NEW) [C] Jersey City, NJ St. Peter's Preparatory School.
O'Connor, Timothy J. '75 (CLV) Avon Lake, OH St. Joseph's Church.
O'Connor, Vincent M. '48 (SPR) Leeds, MA St. Catherine's Church.
O'Connor, William '49 (SJ) Retired.
O'Connor, William B. '47 (BO) Braintree, MA St. Clare Church.
O'Connor, William C. *c.s.c.* (LA) Burbank, CA St. Francis Xavier Church.
O'Connor, William F. *s.j.* '48 (BO) [W] Weston, MA Campion Health Center, Inc.
O'Connor, William J. '58 (BO) [3] Framingham, MA St. Jeremiah Church.
O'Connor, William T. '68 (CHI) Chicago Heights, IL St. Paul Church.
O'Curneen, Hugh '57 (SD) Retired.
O'Day, Msgr. Martin J. '47 (CHI) Oak Forest, IL St. Damian Church; Retired.
O'Day, Michael '38 (SB) Sun City, CA St. Vincent Ferrer Church; Retired.
O'Dea, George F. *s.s.j.* '43 (BAL) [M] Baltimore, MD St. Joseph's Manor.
O'Dea, James F. '38 (HRT) Beacon Falls, CT St. Michael's Church; Retired.
O'Dea, John W. '52 (SPK) Retired.
O'Dea, Msgr. Joseph J. '42 (PEO) Retired.
O'Dea, Loren F. '93 (DET) Farmington, MI Our Lady of Sorrows Church.
O'Dea, Sean '54 (MIA) Hollywood, FL St. Bernadette Church.
O'Dea, Thomas '58 (PHX) Fountain Hills, AZ Ascension Church.
O'Dea, Thomas E. '60 (FR) [18] New Bedford, MA St. Lawrence Martyr Church.
O'Dea, Vincent P. '36 (CLV) Hudson, OH St. Mary Church; Retired.
O'Dea, William L. '56 (PMB) Lantana, FL Holy Spirit Church.
O'Dell, W. Paul '93 (SFR) Kentfield-Greenbrae, CA St.

Sebastian Church.
O'Doherty, Dermot '52 (DUL) Retired.
O'Doherty, Edward '28 (CHL) Retired.
O'Doherty, Gerard *s.v.d.* (LA) [25] Los Angeles, CA Our Lady of Loretto Church.
O'Doherty, John *s.s.c.* '39 (PRO) [P] Bristol, RI St. Columban's Retirement House.
O'Doherty, Msgr. Jude '65 (MIA) [4] Miami, FL Epiphany Church.
O'Doherty, Liam '65 (OG) Antwerp, NY St. Michael Church.
O'Doherty, Patrick J. '70 (ORL) [3] Ocala, FL Queen of Peace Church.
O'Donnell, Brian P. *s.j.* '86 (DET) [K] Detroit, MI Jesuit Community at the University of Detroit.
O'Donnell, Cornelius '55 (SAC) Dunsmuir, CA St. John the Evangelist Church; McCloud, CA St. Joseph Church.
O'Donnell, David P. '95 (BO) Lexington, MA St. Brigid Church.
O'Donnell, Dennis '83 (GR) Ludington, MI St. Stanislaus Church.
O'Donnell, Dennis J.W. '74 (PH) [BB] Malvern, PA St. Joseph's in the Hills.
O'Donnell, Edmond G. '64 (SB) Upland, CA St. Anthony Church.
O'Donnell, Msgr. Edward C. '41 (OM) [16] Omaha, NE Holy Cross Church; Retired.
O'Donnell, Msgr. Edward D. '54 (NY) [110] New York, NY Sacred Heart of Jesus Church.
O'Donnell, Edward T. *s.j.* '74 (CIN) [M] Cincinnati, OH Jesuit Community at Xavier Unversity.
O'Donnell, Eugene P. '73 (SJ) Morgan Hill, CA St. Catherine of Alexandria Church; [P] Mountain View, CA St. Joseph the Worker Center.
O'Donnell, Francis P. *s.j.* '69 (CHI) [N] Chicago, IL Chicago Province of the Society of Jesus-Provincial Office.
O'Donnell, Gabriel *o.p.* '70 (HRT) [14] New Haven, CT St. Mary's Priory Church.
O'Donnell, Gabriel B. *o.p.* '70 (PH) [A] Wynnewood, PA Theological Seminary of St. Charles Borromeo, Overbrook.
O'Donnell, Gregory A. *o.f.m.* '41 (PAT) [M] Ringwood, NJ Holy Name Friary.
O'Donnell, Harold F. *s.j.* '64 (NY) [Z] New York, NY Jesuit Provincial's Office; [Z] New York, NY Xavier Jesuit Community.
O'Donnell, Harold F.X. *s.j.* (NY) Manhattan, NY Bird S. Coler Memorial Hospital and Home.
O'Donnell, Hugh '58 (SFR) [2] South San Francisco, CA Mater Dolorosa Church.
O'Donnell, Msgr. Hugh A. '54 (NEW) [6] Elizabeth, NJ St. Genevieve's Church.
O'Donnell, James *o.s.b.* '42 (PAT) [M] Morristown, NJ St. Mary's Abbey.
O'Donnell, James '56 (CLV) Cleveland, OH Northeast Pre Release Center.
O'Donnell, James P. '56 (CLV) Cleveland, OH Cuyahoga County Detention Home.
O'Donnell, John '72 (DUL) Hibbing, MN Blessed Sacrament Church; Hibbing, MN Immaculate Conception Church; [F] Duluth, MN University of MN-Duluth.
O'Donnell, Msgr. John F. '54 (LR) Fort Smith, AR Immaculate Conception Church; Hartford, AR St. Leo's Church.
O'Donnell, John F. '63 (BO) [26] Boston, MA St. Gregory Church.
O'Donnell, John J. *s.j.* '74 (BO) [W] Cambridge, MA Weston Jesuit Community.
O'Donnell, Joseph *glmy.* '48 (OWN) Fordsville, KY St. John the Baptist Church.
O'Donnell, Joseph '76 (CLV) [J] Cleveland, OH Marymount Hospital, Inc.
O'Donnell, Joseph A. *glmy.* '48 (OWN) Beaver Dam, KY Holy Redeemer Church; Morgantown, KY Holy Trinity Church.
O'Donnell, Joseph F. *c.s.c.* '60 (FTW) [J] South Bend, IN Congregation of Holy Cross Indiana Province Provincial House.
O'Donnell, Joseph M. *c.m.* '43 (BRK) [D] Queens and Staten Island, NY St. John's University; [U] Jamaica, NY Vincentian Residence.
O'Donnell, Luke *o.s.b.* '41 (P) Beaverton, OR St. Cecilia Church.
O'Donnell, Luke N. *o.s.b.* '41 (SEA) [M] Lacey, WA St. Martin's Abbey.
O'Donnell, Mark D. '85 (NOR) Montville, CT St. John Church.
O'Donnell, Matthew '95 (STO) Tracy, CA St. Bernard's Church.
O'Donnell, Msgr. Michael F. '33 (NY) [170] Bronx, NY Our Lady of the Assumption Church; [V] Staten Island, NY Carmel Richmond Nursing Home, Inc.
O'Donnell, Patrick *glmy.* '49 (CIN) [M] Fairfield, OH Headquarters of Glenmary Home Missioners.
O'Donnell, Msgr. Peter C. '58 (NY) [84] New York, NY Our Lady of Esperanza Church.
O'Donnell, Philip '58 (LAV) [11] Las Vegas, NV St. Joan of Arc Church.
O'Donnell, Raymond G. '72 (SD) [5] El Cajon, CA St. Luke Church.
O'Donnell, Richard '59 (PMB) Retired.
O'Donnell, Richard A. '55 (PRT) Yarmouth, ME Sacred Heart Church.
O'Donnell, Richard J. '35 (CHI) [147] Chicago, IL Our Lady of Good Counsel Church; Retired.
O'Donnell, Robert A. *c.s.p.* '51 (NY) [104] New York, NY St. Paul the Apostle Church; [Z] Scarsdale, NY Paulist Fathers Generalate.
O'Donnell, Robert J. *c.s.p.* '74 (NY) [Z] Scarsdale, NY Paulist Fathers Generalate.
O'Donnell, Simon *o.s.b.* '68 (LA) [R] Valyermo, CA St. Andrew's Abbey.
O'Donnell, Simon J. *o.s.b.* '68 (MAN) [K] Manchester, NH St. Anselm Abbey.
O'Donnell, Terence *s.d.b.* '70 (BO) [N] Boston, MA Salesian Boys & Girls Club.
O'Donnell, Terence M. *c.m.* '55 (LA) [R] Los Angeles, CA Amat House; [W] Montebello, CA DePaul Center.
O'Donnell, Thomas D. *s.m.* '44 (ATL) [C] Atlanta, GA Marist School.
O'Donnell, Thomas M. '60 (PIT) [66] Pittsburgh, PA St. Wendelin Church.
O'Donnell, Thomas M. '61 (HEL) East Helena, MT SS. Cyril and Methodius Church.
O'Donnell, Thomas P. '55 (RVC) Long Beach, NY St. Ignatius Martyr Church.
O'Donnell, Thomas V. '67 (CLV) [50] Cleveland, OH St. Michael Church; Cleveland, OH Metro Health Medical Center.
O'Donnell, Timothy R. '86 (MAN) Center Ossipee, NH St. Joseph Church.
O'Donnell, Walter *s.t.* '55 (BLX) DeLisle, MS The Catholic Church in DeLisle Church.
O'Donnell, William A. *c.pp.s.* '77 (CIN) Wapakoneta, OH St. Joseph Church; [M] Dayton, OH Provincial House of the Cincinnati Province of the Society of the Precious Blood.
O'Donnell, Msgr. William F '62 (WDC) [V] Washington, DC The Catholic Cemeteries of the Archdiocese of Washington, Inc.
O'Donnell, Msgr. William F. '62 (WDC) [42] Washington, DC St. Thomas Apostle Church; Special Ministries; [V] Capital Plaza, MD Archdiocese of Washington Division, The Blue Army, World Apostolate of Fatima.
O'Donnell, William J. (NO) Unassigned.
O'Donnell, William J. (NY) Montrose, NY FDR DVA Hospital.
O'Donnell, William J. '52 (ALN) New Philadelphia, PA Holy Family Church.
O'Donnell, William J. '52 (PH) Warminster, PA Nativity of Our Lord Church.
O'Donnell, William J. '56 (OAK) [3] Berkeley, CA St. Joseph The Worker Church.
O'Donnell, William J. '58 (NY) Montrose, NY Franklin D. Roosevelt Hospital; On Duty Outside the Archdiocese.
O'Donnell, William M. *o.m.i.* '70 (WDC) [B] Washington, DC Oblate College/Oblate Center for Mission Studies; [M] Washington, DC Missionary Oblates of Mary Immaculate.
O'Donoghue, Brendon W. '50 (WOR) Retired.
O'Donoghue, Msgr. James P. '43 (SD) Retired.
O'Donoghue, John '64 (SAT) [2] San Antonio, TX Blessed Sacrament Church; [A] San Antonio, TX Permanent Diaconate.
O'Donoghue, Kevin J. '58 (BRK) [28] Brooklyn, NY St. Cecilia Church.
O'Donoghue, Patrick '61 (BIR) Trussville, AL Holy Infant of Prague Church.
O'Donohoe, James '70 (BO) [X] Lexington, MA Grey Nuns Provincial House.
O'Donohoe, James A. '47 (BO) On Special or Other Diocesan Assignment.
O'Donohue, James A. (BO) On Duty Outside the Archdiocese.
O'Donovan, Daniel *s.d.b.* '40 (NY) [BB] West Haverstraw, NY Don Bosco Retreat Center and Marian Shrine; [BB] West Haverstraw, NY Marian Shrine.
O'Donovan, Daniel '51 (SB) Retired.
O'Donovan, Dennis J. '69 (P) Beaverton, OR St. Cecilia Church.
O'Donovan, Donal '50 (WH) Retired.
O'Donovan, John '55 (SP) [1] Largo, FL St. Catherine of Siena Church.
O'Donovan, L. Aidan *m.s.c.* '80 (DAL) [I] Dallas, TX Parkland Hospital.
O'Donovan, L. Aidan *m.s.c.* '80 (SAT) [M] San Antonio, TX Missionaries of the Sacred Heart.
O'Donovan, Leo J. *s.j.* '66 (WDC) [C] Washington, DC Georgetown University; [M] Washington, DC The Jesuit Community at Georgetown University.
O'Donovan, Martin E. '78 (CHI) [39] Chicago, IL St. Christina Church.
O'Donovan, Patrick G. '72 (PAT) New Vernon, NJ Christ the King Church.
O'Donovan, Rickard J. '49 (BO) Wilmington, MA St. Dorothy Church.
O'Donovan, Thomas P. '70 (CC) On Special Assignment; [E] Laredo, TX Mercy Regional Medical Center.
O'Donovan, Timothy John '49 (B) Retired.
O'Dougherty, Msgr. Loyola A. '40 (TUC) San Manuel, AZ St. Bartholomew Church; Retired.
O'Dowd, Bernard J. *o.s.a.* '58 (CAM) [4] Atlantic City, NJ St. Nicholas of Tolentine Church.
O'Dowd, Brendan '49 (SAC) Retired and in Senior Ministry.
O'Dowd, Msgr. John '42 (VEN) Retired.
O'Down, M. Brendan '49 (P) Brookings, OR Star of the Sea Church.
O'Driscoll, James J. '79 (BO) [1] Gloucester, MA St. Ann Church.
O'Driscoll, John C. '87 (PH) Graduate Studies.
O'Dwyer, Dominick '66 (MIA) Tamarac, FL St. Malachy Church.
O'Dwyer, James F. '65 (STO) Escalon, CA St. Patrick Church.
O'Dwyer, Patrick '72 (LA) Whittier, CA St. Bruno Church.
O'Dwyer, Thomas '70 (MIA) Hollywood, FL Little Flower Church.
O'Farrell, Donal *s.s.c.* '53 (OM) [K] St. Columbans, NE St. Columban's Foreign Mission Society.
O'Farrell, Michael J. '43 (RVC) Northport, NY St. Philip Neri Church; Northport, NY St. Philip Neri Church; Retired.
O'Farrell, William J. '39 (ORL) Retired.
O'Flaherty, Edward M. *s.j.* '65 (BO) [W] Chestnut Hill, MA The Jesuit Community at Boston College.
O'Flaherty, John '61 (STA) Flagler Beach, FL Santa Maria Del Mar Church; Korona, FL St. Mary's Church.
O'Flaherty, John P. '43 (WOR) Retired.
O'Flaherty, Michael '75 (PMB) [5] West Palm Beach, FL St. Juliana Church.
O'Flanagan, Thomas P. '95 (PMB) North Palm Beach, FL St. Clare Church.
O'Flannigan, Thomas L. '55 (TUC) Retired.
O'Flynn, John (PBL) Florence, CO Federal Correctional Institute at Florence.
O'Flynn, Seamus '59 (STA) [3] St. Augustine, FL St. Anastasia Church.
O'Friel, Demetrius *o.f.m.* '50 (NY) [Z] New York, NY Franciscan Friars, Order of Friars Manor.
O'Friel, Msgr. John '45 (FRS) Lemoore, CA St. Peter Church.
O'Friel, LaSalle *o.f.m.* '54 (PAT) [M] Butler, NJ St. Anthony Friary.
O'Friel, Zachary *o.f.m.* '47 (BO) [BB] Boston, MA St. Anthony Shrine.
O'Gara, James *c.s.p.* '61 (CHI) [125] Chicago, IL Old St. Mary Church.
O'Gara, Stephen R. '71 (STP) [34] Minneapolis, MN St. Thomas the Apostle Church.
O'Gorman, Msgr. Charles F. '49 (LA) [2] Oxnard, CA Santa Clara Church.
O'Gorman, Eamon '67 (ORG) La Habra, CA Our Lady of Guadalupe Church.
O'Gorman, Msgr. George '37 (NEW) North Bergen, NJ Our Lady of Fatima Church; [N] Rutherford, NJ St. John Vianney Residence for Priests.
O'Gorman, Msgr. George A. '37 (NEW) Retired.
O'Gorman, Michael B. '64 (SAT) [38] San Antonio, TX St. Gregory's Church.
O'Gorman, Richard '57 (NY) Bangall, NY Immaculate Conception Church.
O'Grady, Dennis R. '61 (CLV) [50] Cleveland, OH St. Michael Church; [X] Cleveland, OH Diocesan Hispanic Office.
O'Grady, Edward F. '46 (LAN) Retired; [E] Jackson, MI St. Joseph Home for Children, Inc.
O'Grady, Frank (PAT) Military Chaplains.
O'Grady, James '50 (KCK) Retired.
O'Grady, James F. '54 (LA) El Segundo, CA St. Anthony Church.
O'Grady, James F. '58 (LA) [98] Los Angeles, CA Visitation Church.
O'Grady, James W. '42 (TOL) Retired.
O'Grady, John F. '66 (ALB) On Duty Outside the Diocese.
O'Grady, John F. '66 (MIA) [B] Miami, FL Barry University.
O'Grady, John G. '35 (ALB) Windham, NY St. Theresa of Child Jesus Church.
O'Grady, John G. '66 (ALB) Retired.
O'Grady, Michael '58 (PHX) [1] Phoenix, AZ SS. Simon and Jude Cathedral.
O'Grady, Michael J. '56 (NEW) [5] Bayonne, NJ St. Vincent de Paul Church.
O'Grady, Peter '63 (NO) Jefferson, LA St. Agnes Church.
O'Grady, Robert A. '72 (HRT) Windsor Locks, CT St. Mary Church.
O'Grady, Robert M. '78 (BO) Watertown, MA Sacred Heart Church; [P] Boston, MA Archdiocesan Information Center.
O'Guinn, Jon '93 (BEL) Salem, IL St. Theresa of Avila Church.
O'Hagan, James P. '47 (DET) Waterford, MI St. Benedict Church.

O'Hagan, Patrick *ss.cc.* (LA) Sepulveda, CA Veterans Administration Medical Center.
O'Haire, John A. '56 (SCR) Retired; [N] Dunmore, PA Villa St. Joseph.
O'Hala, Stephen '88 (MIA) On Duty Outside the Archdiocese.
O'Hala, Steven '88 (PMB) [A] Boynton Beach, FL St. Vincent de Paul Regional Seminary.
O'Hallaran, John E. *s.s.j.* '85 (NO) [5] New Orleans, LA Corpus Christi Church.
O'Halloran, Edward '78 (NY) [7] Yonkers, NY St. Denis Church.
O'Halloran, Martin J. '47 (PH) Gladwyne, PA St. John Baptist Vianney Church; Retired.
O'Halloran, Michael *o.p.* '56 (SAC) Ione, CA Sacred Heart Church; Preston, CA School of Industry; Special Assignment.
O'Halloran, Richard '51 (MRY) Retired.
O'Halloran, Richard '59 (MRY) [H] Salinas, CA Congregation of the Sisters of the Holy Cross; [K] Salinas, CA Madonna Manor Retirement Home.
O'Halloran, William *s.s.s.* '50 (GB) Menasha, WI St. Mary Church.
O'Halloran, William *s.s.s.* '50 (NY) [55] New York, NY St. Jean Baptiste Church.
O'Halloran, William J. *s.j.* '58 (WOR) [B] Worcester, MA College of the Holy Cross, Inc; [N] Worcester, MA Jesuits of Holy Cross College, Inc.
O'Hanlon, James J. '57 (SY) [2] Endicott, NY St. Ambrose Church; Retired.
O'Hanlon, Michael A. '57 (GF) Retired.
O'Hanlon, Richard Thomas *o.f.m.conv.* (BAL) [M] Ellicott City, MD St. Joseph Cupertino Friary, Friars Minor Conventual of St. Francis of Assisi.
O'Hanlon, Thomas '83 (LA) Thousand Oaks, CA St. Paschal Baylon Church.
O'Hanlon, Msgr. William '49 (SHP) [2] Shreveport, LA Holy Trinity Church.
O'Hara, Arthyr T. '78 (TLS) Pryor, OK St. Mark's Church.
O'Hara, Charles R. '70 (PH) [U] Downingtown, PA St. John Vianney Hospital.
O'Hara, Daniel J. '87 (SY) [16] Syracuse, NY St. James Church.
O'Hara, Edward '60 (SAC) West Sacramento, CA Our Lady of Grace Church.
O'Hara, Eugene *o.f.m. cap.* '61 (ROC) Trumansburg, NY St. James the Apostle Church; [I] Interlaken, NY St. Fidelis Friary.
O'Hara, Eugene P. '45 (NY) [Z] New York, NY Our Lady of Consolation Residence.
O'Hara, Eugene R. (NY) Retired.
O'Hara, Francis A. '56 (BO) [3] Plymouth, MA St. Mary Church.
O'Hara, Francis W. '59 (PRO) Lincoln, RI St. Jude Church; [6] Warwick, RI St. Kevin Church.
O'Hara, Frank J. '41 (SFD) [10] Springfield, IL SS. Peter and Paul Church.
O'Hara, Harold T. '30 (CHI) Arlington Heights, IL Our Lady of the Wayside Church; Retired.
O'Hara, James T. '66 (E) [3] Erie, PA Holy Family/St. Ann/St. Casimir Church; [13] Erie, PA St. Ann Church; [15] Erie, PA St. Casimir Church.
O'Hara, John F. '71 (PRT) Bucksport, ME St. Vincent de Paul Church; Stonington, ME St. Mary Star of the Sea Church; [M] Castine, ME Maine Maritime Academy.
O'Hara, John T. '80 (ARL) [6] Arlington, VA Our Lady of Lourdes Church.
O'Hara, Kieran *o.carm.* '37 (JOL) [J] Darien, IL Carmelite Fathers Provincial Office.
O'Hara, Kieran '37 (NO) Lacombe, LA St. John of the Cross Church.
O'Hara, Martin '41 (SFD) Stonington, IL Holy Trinity Church.
O'Hara, Martin F. '41 (PH) [74] Philadelphia, PA St. Jerome Church; Retired.
O'Hara, Maurice *o.f.m.* '55 (SP) [O] St. Petersburg, FL St. Anthony Friary.
O'Hara, Michael *o.m.i.* (NY) Federal, NY Federal Correctional Institution.
O'Hara, Michael '59 (NY) State, NY Beacon Correctional Facility.
O'Hara, Michael '67 (SAC) [8] Sacramento, CA Sacred Heart of Jesus Church.
O'Hara, Michael D. '60 (BUF) Franklinville, NY St. Philomena Church.
O'Hara, Michael J. '47 (DET) Retired.
O'Hara, Michael J. '67 (NOR) Killingworth, CT St. Lawrence Church.
O'Hara, Peter J. '59 (BO) Townsend, MA St. John Church.
O'Hara, Robert E. *m.s.f.* '65 (SAT) [M] San Antonio, TX MSF Center & Provincialate.
O'Hara, Msgr. Robert J. '46 (MAD) Retired.
O'Hara, Thomas J. *c.s.c.* '78 (SCR) [C] Wilkes-Barre, PA Kings College.
O'Hare, Daniel G. *s.j.* '79 (NY) [Z] New York, NY St. Ignatius Loyola Residence.
O'Hare, Dennis *c.s.c.* '73 (P) [B] Portland, OR University of Portland.
O'Hare, Dennis P. *c.s.c.* '73 (P) [L] Portland, OR Holy Cross Father & Brother, C.S.C. - University of Portland.
O'Hare, Donal J. '54 (PMB) Vero Beach, FL Holy Cross Church.
O'Hare, Donal J. '54 (WCH) Retired.
O'Hare, Francis C. '51 (BO) Reading, MA St. Athanasius Church.
O'Hare, John B. '53 (PMB) Vero Beach, FL Holy Cross Church.
O'Hare, Msgr. John J. '55 (SR) Boyes Hot Springs, CA St. Leo Church.
O'Hare, Joseph A. *s.j.* '61 (NY) [C] Bronx, NY Fordham University; [Z] New York, NY Jesuit Community at Fordham University.
O'Hare, Joseph P. '65 (STO) Modesto, CA St. Joseph Church.
O'Hare, Robert V. *s.j.* '95 (NY) [F] New York, NY Xavier High School.
O'Hear, Daniel J. '62 (SPR) [4] North Adams, MA St. Anthony of Padua Church.
O'Hearn, James E. *s.j.* '59 (MIL) [F] Milwaukee, WI Jesuit Provincial Office, Wisconsin Province.
O'Hearn, Michael '95 (FR) Edgartown, MA St. Elizabeth Church; Oak Bluffs, MA Sacred Heart Church; Vineyard Haven, MA St. Augustine Church.
O'Hearn, Paul V. (BO) Permanent Disability.
O'Hern, Charles A. '46 (PHX) Retired.
O'Hern, Edward P. *c.s.p.* '32 (NY) [Z] Scarsdale, NY Paulist Fathers Generalate.
O'Hern, Edward Philip *c.s.p.* '32 (AUS) [11] Austin, TX St. Austin's Church.
O'Heron, Edward J. '57 (SY) Special Assignment; [V] Cortland, NY Newman Foundation of Cortland, Inc. at the State University College of New York.
O'Holohan, John *s.j.* '55 (ORL) [5] Orlando, FL Holy Family Church.
O'Hotto, Kenneth L. '80 (STP) Le Sueur, MN St. Anne Church.
O'Kane, James D. '65 (GI) Scottsbluff, NE St. Agnes Church.
O'Kane, Patrick J. '77 (SC) [F] Sioux City, IA Monastery of the Discalced Carmelite Nuns.
O'Keefe, Daniel Paul *o.s.b.* '93 (GBG) [H] Latrobe, PA Saint Vincent Archabbey.
O'Keefe, Edward *o.f.m.cap.* '65 (LA) [74] Los Angeles, CA St. Lawrence of Brindisi Church.
O'Keefe, Francis J. '60 (NOR) Putnam, CT St. Mary Church.
O'Keefe, George L. *o.carm.* '48 (CHI) [D] Chicago, IL Mt. Carmel High School; [N] Chicago, IL Carmelite Priory of St. Cyril.
O'Keefe, Msgr. John J. '72 (NY) [E] White Plains, NY Archbishop Stepinac High School.
O'Keefe, Joseph *s.j.* '86 (BO) [W] Chestnut Hill, MA The Jesuit Community at Boston College.
O'Keefe, Kevin '95 (ARL) [3] Alexandria, VA Queen of Apostles Church.
O'Keefe, Lawrence '70 (GLP) Holbrook, AZ Our Lady of Guadalupe Church; [A] Gallup, NM Diocesan Diaconate Formation Program.
O'Keefe, Mark *o.s.b.* '83 (IND) [A] St. Meinrad, IN St. Meinrad Seminary; [B] St. Meinrad, IN St. Meinrad Seminary-College of Liberal Arts; [J] St. Meinrad, IN St. Meinrad Archabbey.
O'Keefe, Martin D. *s.j.* '66 (STL) [C] St. Louis, MO Saint Louis University; [P] St. Louis, MO Jesuit Community Corporation at St. Louis University - Jesuit Hall.
O'Keefe, Maurice L. '57 (NEW) Retired; [N] Rutherford, NJ St. John Vianney Residence for Priests.
O'Keefe, Michael *o.carm.* '75 (JOL) Darien, IL Our Lady of Mount Carmel Church.
O'Keefe, Michael A. '56 (JOL) Glen Ellyn, IL St. Petronille Church.
O'Keefe, Millard '65 (CHI) Other Assignments.
O'Keefe, Patrick T. (BUF) Swormville, NY St. Mary Church.
O'Keefe, Thomas E. '48 (NY) Retired; [E] White Plains, NY Archbishop Stepinac High School.
O'Keefe, Vincent T. *s.j.* '50 (NY) [Z] New York, NY "America;" Residence and publication office of the America Press; [DD] New York, NY John LaFarge Institute, The.
O'Keefe, William F. '60 (HRT) [3] Enfield, CT St. Bernard's Church; On Duty Outside the Archdiocese.
O'Keeffe, Dennis J. '84 (LFT) Muncie, IN St. Lawrence Church.
O'Keeffe, Jeremiah '66 (LA) Temple City, CA St. Luke the Evangelist Church.
O'Keeffe, L. Joseph *s.j.* '75 (NY) [Z] New York, NY Jesuit Provincial's Office.
O'Keeffe, Michael J. '68 (SAV) Perry, GA St. Patrick Church.
O'Keeffe, Patrick '59 (SB) Retired.
O'Keeffe, Msgr. Richard W. '59 (TUC) Yuma, AZ Immaculate Conception Church; Yuma, AZ Immaculate Conception Church.
O'Keeffe, William J. '59 (LA) [12] Long Beach, CA Our Lady of Refuge Church.
O'Keeffe, William T. *s.s.* '45 (BAL) [K] Baltimore, MD St. Charles Villa; [M] Baltimore, MD St. Charles Villa.
O'Kelly, Colm (SAC) Woodland, CA Holy Rosary Church.
O'Kennedy, Philip N. '71 (BIR) [1] Huntsville, AL Good Shepherd Church.
O'Kere, Michael '90 (NY) [124] Bronx, NY St. Angela Merici Church.
O'Kielty, James '54 (PAT) Madison, NJ St. Vincent Martyr Church.
O'Konsky, Stanley J. *s.j.* '72 (NY) [F] New York, NY Fordham Preparatory School; [Z] New York, NY Jesuit Community at Fordham University.
O'Kruta, Francis A. '94 (WH) Weirton, WV St. Paul's Church.
O'Laughlin, Patrick J. '67 (STL) [2] Creve Coeur, MO St. John Bosco Church.
O'Leary, Adrian P. '47 (BO) Retired.
O'Leary, Arthur P. (BO) Retired.
O'Leary, Bartholomew J. '70 (HON) Retired.
O'Leary, Bernard C. *s.j.* '48 (WDC) La Plata, MD Sacred Heart Church.
O'Leary, Msgr. Cornelius '48 (CAM) On Duty Outside the Diocese.
O'Leary, Msgr. Cornelius '48 (SB) Retired.
O'Leary, Cornelius F. '56 (WOR) Otter River, MA St. Martin's Church.
O'Leary, Daniel F. *o.m.i.* '50 (BUF) [27] Buffalo, NY Holy Angels Church; [C] Niagara University, NY Niagara University; [O] Niagara University, NY Vincentian Community at Niagara University.
O'Leary, David '74 (BAL) [A] Baltimore, MD St. Mary's Seminary and University.
O'Leary, David A. '45 (WCH) Retired.
O'Leary, David M. (BO) On Duty Outside the Archdiocese.
O'Leary, Donald J. '37 (HRT) Plantsville, CT St. Aloysius Church; Retired.
O'Leary, Harold V. *c.s.b.* '49 (GAL) [Q] Houston, TX Residence of the Basilian Fathers of the University of St. Thomas.
O'Leary, Hilary *o.s.b.* '68 (PAT) Cedar Knolls, NJ Notre Dame of Mt. Carmel Church; [M] Morristown, NJ St. Mary's Abbey.
O'Leary, James E. '68 (BO) [2] Arlington, MA St. Camillus Church.
O'Leary, James J. '56 (DET) Harrison Twp., MI St. Hubert Church.
O'Leary, James J. *s.j.* '65 (MIL) [P] Milwaukee, WI Jesuit Provincial Office, Wisconsin Province.
O'Leary, James J. '65 (SD) Special Assignment.
O'Leary, James M. *s.j.* '91 (CHI) [N] Chicago, IL Chicago Province of the Society of Jesus-Provincial Office.
O'Leary, James S. '61 (KAL) Battle Creek, MI St. Joseph Church.
O'Leary, Jerome A. *o.p.* '57 (CHI) [N] River Forest, IL St. Thomas Aquinas Priory.
O'Leary, John '67 (MIA) On Duty Outside the Archdiocese.
O'Leary, John '78 (CAM) Washington Township, NJ St. Charles Borromeo Church.
O'Leary, John P. '54 (BIS) New Town, ND St. Anthony Church.
O'Leary, Kevin J. '95 (BO) Lynnfield, MA Our Lady of the Assumption Church.
O'Leary, Msgr. Lawrence '53 (LA) [78] Los Angeles, CA St. Martin of Tours Church.
O'Leary, Lawrence J. '56 (RVC) East Northport, NY St. Anthony of Padua Church; West Brentwood, NY Pilgrim Psychiatric Center.
O'Leary, Malcolm *s.v.d.* '61 (LAF) [4] Opelousas, LA Holy Ghost Church.
O'Leary, Mark G. *o.p.* '84 (SR) [G] Santa Rosa, CA Santa Rosa Memorial Hospital.
O'Leary, Mark G. *o.p.* '85 (OAK) [N] Oakland, CA Dominican Order, Siena House.
O'Leary, Michael G. '43 (DET) Grosse Pointe Farms, MI St. Paul Catholic Church; Retired.
O'Leary, Niall F. '60 (LA) West Covina, CA St. Christopher Church.
O'Leary, Patrick B. *s.j.* '61 (SEA) [A] Seattle, WA Seattle University.
O'Leary, Patrick C. '76 (SY) [1] Liverpool, NY Christ the King Church.
O'Leary, Patrick D. '51 (Y) Retired.
O'Leary, Raymond J. '62 (ORL) Port Orange, FL Our Lady of Hope Church.
O'Leary, Robert A. '53 (NEW) Livingston, NJ St. Philomena Church.
O'Leary, Sean *o.carm.* '55 (GAL) [Q] Houston, TX Carmelite Priory.
O'Leary, Sean '61 (SAC) Red Bluff, CA Sacred Heart Church.
O'Leary, Msgr. Thomas M. '57 (NEW) Wyckoff, NJ St. Elizabeth Church.
O'Leary, Todd '58 (TUC) [23] Tucson, AZ St. Thomas the Apostle Church.
O'Leary, William A. '40 (BRK) Retired.
O'Leary, William F. *s.j.* '62 (OM) [C] Omaha, NE Creighton Preparatory School.
O'Leary, William R. *s.j.* '73 (PAT) [I] Morristown, NJ

Loyola House of Retreats.
O'Lenny, Patrick J. '56 (LC) On Duty Outside the Diocese.
O'Liddy, Patrick H. *s.j.* '90 (DEN) [M] Denver, CO Regis Jesuit Community (The Jesuits at Regis University).
O'Loghlen, Martin P. *ss.cc.* '61 (LA) [R] La Verne, CA Congregation of the Sacred Hearts.
O'Looney, Martin J. *c.s.p.* '46 (NY) [Z] Scarsdale, NY Paulist Fathers Generalate.
O'Loughlin, Msgr. Eugene E. '44 (BUF) [64] Buffalo, NY St. Thomas Aquinas Church; Retired.
O'Loughlin, Eugene P. '43 (WH) Retired.
O'Loughlin, Francis A. '80 (PRO) [3] Newport, RI St. Joseph's Church; Newport, RI Newport Hospital.
O'Loughlin, Frank '65 (PMB) Boynton Beach, FL St. Thomas More Church.
O'Loughlin, S. Raphael *c.s.b.* '42 (GAL) Retired; [Q] Houston, TX Dillon House.
O'Mahoney, Finbar P. *o.s.b.* '43 (MAN) [K] Manchester, NH St. Anselm Abbey.
O'Mahony, Donal *o.f.m.cap.* '66 (SFR) Burlingame, CA Our Lady of Angels Church.
O'Mahony, Jerome *m.s.c.* '50 (LA) Sherman Oaks, CA St. Francis de Sales Church.
O'Mahony, Maurice '67 (LA) Pomona, CA St. Joseph Church.
O'Mahony, Tom *s.s.s.* '95 (SLC) [7] Taylorsville, UT St. Martin de Porres Church.
O'Malley, Bartholomew J. *c.m.* '40 (PH) [Z] Philadelphia, PA Congregation of the Mission.
O'Malley, Dennis O. '90 (WOR) [24] Worcester, MA St. Joan of Arc Church.
O'Malley, Edward J. '60 (JOL) Manhattan, IL St. Joseph Church.
O'Malley, Francis P. '73 (NY) [193] Bronx, NY Visitation Church; On Special or Other (Arch)Diocesan Assignment.
O'Malley, James *c.ss.r.* '55 (ORL) [F] New Smyrna Beach, FL St. Alphonsus Villa-Redemptorist Fathers and Brothers.
O'Malley, James '56 (CHI) Highwood, IL St. James Church.
O'Malley, James E. '46 (SFR) Novato, CA St. Anthony of Padua Church; Retired.
O'Malley, James J. '46 (SPK) Retired.
O'Malley, John A. '55 (BWN) Weslaco, TX San Martin de Porres Church.
O'Malley, John J. *o.p.* '59 (CHI) River Forest, IL St. Vincent Ferrer Priory Church.
O'Malley, John J. '65 (PIT) Wilmerding, PA St. Jude the Apostle Church.
O'Malley, John W. *s.j.* (DET) [K] Detroit, MI Jesuit Provincial Office-Detroit Province of the Society of Jesus.
O'Malley, John W. *s.j.* '59 (BO) [W] Cambridge, MA Weston Jesuit Community.
O'Malley, Joseph M. '50 (DEN) Retired.
O'Malley, Joseph T. '54 (GAL) [76] Houston, TX St. Thomas More Church; [K] Houston, TX The Catholic Chaplain Corps.
O'Malley, Kenneth *c.p.* '64 (CHI) [B] Chicago, IL The Catholic Theological Union at Chicago; [N] Chicago, IL Passionist Community-CTU.
O'Malley, Kevin *c.p.* '59 (CHI) [N] Chicago, IL Passionist Community-CTU.
O'Malley, Leonard F. '74 (BO) Burlington, MA St. Malachy Church.
O'Malley, Mark Francis '95 (NEW) Caldwell, NJ St. Aloysius Church.
O'Malley, Michael P. '92 (PH) Media, PA St. Mary Magdalen Church.
O'Malley, Michael W. '52 (WCH) Retired.
O'Malley, Patrick J. '57 (CHI) [128] Chicago, IL St. Mary of the Lake Church.
O'Malley, Paul '57 (LA) [56] Los Angeles, CA St. Columban Church.
O'Malley, Thomas J. '66 (SCR) Ashley, PA St. Leo's Church.
O'Malley, Thomas P. *s.j.* '61 (BO) [W] Boston, MA The Society of Jesus of New England-Provincial Offices.
O'Malley, Thomas P. *s.j.* '61 (LA) [C] Los Angeles, CA Loyola Marymount University; [C] Los Angeles, CA Loyola Marymount University.
O'Malley, Vincent J. *c.m.* '73 (BUF) [C] Niagara University, NY Niagara University; [O] Niagara University, NY Vincentian Community at Niagara University.
O'Malley, William *o.carm.* '65 (NEW) Demarest, NJ St. Joseph's Church.
O'Malley, William J. *s.j.* '51 (NY) [Z] New York, NY Jesuit Community at Fordham University.
O'Malley, William J. *s.j.* '63 (NY) [F] New York, NY Fordham Preparatory School.
O'Malley, William M. *s.j.* '62 (P) Sublimity, OR St. Boniface Church; [L] Portland, OR Jesuit Provincial Office (Oregon Prov.).
O'Malley, William P. '70 (PIT) Beaver Falls, PA Divine Mercy Church.
O'Mara, Dennis *s.s.c.* '61 (DAL) Grand Prairie, TX Immaculate Conception Church.
O'Mara, Michael '88 (IND) Bloomington, IN St. Paul Catholic Center Church; [N] Bloomington, IN Indiana University, Bloomington Newman Center.
O'Mara, William T. '58 (CHI) Orland Hills, IL St. Elizabeth Seton Church.
O'Meara, Donagh (BRK) [158] Queens, NY Blessed Virgin Mary, Help of Christians Church.
O'Meara, Gerard J. (BO) Society of St. James the Apostle.
O'Meara, Gregory J. *s.j.* (NY) [Z] New York, NY Xavier Jesuit Community.
O'Meara, Henry *c.ss.r.* '43 (BAL) Annapolis, MD St. Mary Church; [M] Annapolis, MD Saint Mary Rectory.
O'Meara, James J. '49 (KAL) Retired.
O'Meara, Joseph M. '67 (BAL) [84] Baltimore, MD St. Rose of Lima Church.
O'Meara, Joseph P. '53 (NY) [155] Bronx, NY St. John Chrysostom's Church.
O'Meara, Marcian T. '59 (DEN) [8] Denver, CO Church of the Good Shepherd.
O'Meara, Thomas *o.p.* '62 (FTW) [B] Notre Dame, IN University of Notre Dame Du Lac.
O'Meara, Thomas Aquinas F. *o.p.* '62 (CHI) [N] River Forest, IL St. Thomas Aquinas Priory.
O'Mearain, Msgr. Ciaran P. '60 (CAM) Bridgeton, NJ Immaculate Conception Church.
O'Melia, Edward A. '77 (DAV) West Branch, IA St. Bernadette Church; West Liberty, IA St. Joseph's Church.
O'Neal, James '80 (STA) [1] Jacksonville, FL Assumption Church.
O'Neal, Norman B. *s.j.* '59 (NO) [F] New Orleans, LA Jesuit High School.
O'Neal, Patrick K. '90 (PEO) Granville, IL Sacred Heart Of Jesus Church.
O'Neil, Charles H. '56 (SAG) Auburn, MI St. Joseph Church.
O'Neil, Dennis '66 (LA) [93] Los Angeles, CA St. Thomas the Apostle Church.
O'Neil, Flann *o.f.m.* '52 (GLP) Ganado, AZ All Saints Church.
O'Neil, Francis J. *s.j.* '50 (BO) Boston, MA Bethany Hospital; [FF] Framingham, MA Bethany Health Care Center, Inc.
O'Neil, James '85 (GF) Malta, MT St. Mary's Church; [K] Malta, MT St. Mary's Catholic Education Trust.
O'Neil, James W. *s.j.* '57 (BO) [E] Boston, MA Boston College High School & Jesuit Community.
O'Neil, Joseph M. *m.s.* '93 (HRT) [5] Hartford, CT Our Lady of Sorrows Church; [M] Hartford, CT Missionaries of LaSalette Provincial Secretary.
O'Neil, Kevin *c.ss.r.* '81 (WDC) [M] Washington, DC Holy Redeemer College.
O'Neil, Lee '56 (MOB) Gulf Shores, AL Our Lady of the Gulf Church.
O'Neil, Lee E. '56 (TLS) On Duty Outside the Diocese.
O'Neil, Leo J. '56 (WOR) [4] Leominster, MA St. Leo's Church; Boylston, MA Worcester County Sanitarium; Boylston, MA Worcester County Jail and House of Correction.
O'Neil, Lewis B. *s.j.* '63 (SFR) [53] San Francisco, CA St. Vincent de Paul Church.
O'Neil, Maurice *s.s.* '50 (TUC) Willcox, AZ Sacred Heart Church; Willcox, AZ Federal Prison Camp; Fort Grant Rural Station, AZ Fort Grant Training Center.
O'Neil, Maurice L. '57 (OG) On Duty Outside the Diocese.
O'Neil, Michael '59 (SEA) Retired.
O'Neil, Patrick J. '83 (WIL) Ocean City, MD St. Luke and St. Andrew Church.
O'Neil, Msgr. Philip E. '54 (RCK) Marengo, IL Sacred Heart Church.
O'Neil, Thomas D. '69 (PIT) Washington, PA St. Hilary Church.
O'Neil, W. Laurence *s.j.* '61 (BGP) [A] Fairfield, CT Fairfield University; [O] Fairfield, CT The Fairfield Jesuit Community-Fairfield University.
O'Neil, William J. '37 (Y) Retired.
O'Neill, Blane *o.f.m.* '51 (STL) Oakville, MO St. Francis of Assisi Church; [P] Oakville, MO St. Francis Friary.
O'Neill, Brian E. '68 (CAM) Gloucester, NJ St. Mary's Church.
O'Neill, Charles '46 (DET) [6] Dearborn Heights, MI Our Lady of Grace Church.
O'Neill, Charles E. *s.j.* '57 (NO) [C] New Orleans, LA Loyola University.
O'Neill, Charles F. '46 (DET) Retired.
O'Neill, Cornelius J. '50 (FR) Retired.
O'Neill, Daniel *o.carm.* (CHI) [N] Chicago, IL Carmelite Fathers Residence.
O'Neill, Daniel *o.carm.* '69 (JOL) [J] Darien, IL Carmelite Fathers Provincial Office.
O'Neill, Msgr. Daniel J. '76 (ALT) [20] Johnstown, PA St. Gregory's Church; [21] Johnstown, PA St. Barnabas Church; [H] Huntingdon, PA Juniata College.
O'Neill, Dennis B. '73 (CHI) [26] Chicago, IL St. Benedict Church.
O'Neill, Desmond '59 (ROC) [9] Rochester, NY St. Boniface Church.
O'Neill, Edward M. '71 (MET) Colonia, NJ St. John Vianney Church.
O'Neill, Msgr. Felix M. '55 (CAM) Woodbury Heights, NJ St. Margaret's Church.
O'Neill, Francis J. *s.j.* '50 (BO) [E] Boston, MA Boston College High School & Jesuit Community; [W] Boston, MA The Society of Jesus of New England-Provincial Offices.
O'Neill, Francis S. '37 (HRT) Retired.
O'Neill, George T. '41 (HRT) Retired.
O'Neill, Msgr. James '54 (CHY) Casper, WY St. Anthony of Padua Church; [B] Casper, WY St. Anthony Manor.
O'Neill, James '57 (ALB) Stillwater, NY St. Peter the Apostle Church.
O'Neill, James A. '41 (CLV) Westlake, OH St. Bernadette Church; Retired.
O'Neill, James R. '40 (NEW) Ramsey, NJ St. Paul Church; Retired.
O'Neill, James V. *o.s.f.s.* '41 (WIL) [I] Childs, MD Oblates of St. Francis De Sales.
O'Neill, James W. *o.s.f.s.* '67 (CHL) [4] Greensboro, NC St. Paul the Apostle Church.
O'Neill, Jeremiah '59 (LA) Alhambra, CA St. Thomas More Church.
O'Neill, Jeremiah P. '57 (NY) [217] Staten Island, NY Our Lady Help of Christians Church.
O'Neill, John D. *s.j.* '60 (DET) [K] Detroit, MI Jesuit Community at the University of Detroit.
O'Neill, John J. *m.s.* '62 (NOR) Danielson, CT St. James Church.
O'Neill, John J. '67 (SFR) Novato, CA Our Lady of Loretto Church.
O'Neill, John M. *o.s.f.s.* '73 (ARL) Vienna, VA Our Lady of Good Counsel Church.
O'Neill, Joseph J. *m.m.* '49 (SJ) [M] Los Altos, CA Maryknoll.
O'Neill, Joseph P. *s.j.* '54 (BO) [E] Boston, MA Boston College High School & Jesuit Community.
O'Neill, Keith *o.f.m.conv.* '66 (SAV) Jesup, GA St. Joseph Church.
O'Neill, Msgr. Kevin P. '77 (SCR) Bushkill, PA St. John Church.
O'Neill, Kevin S. '77 (HEL) [1] Butte, MT Butte Catholic Community North Church; [4] Butte, MT Immaculate Conception Church; [11] Butte, MT St. Patrick Church.
O'Neill, Msgr. Kevin T. '61 (BUF) East Aurora, NY Immaculate Conception Church.
O'Neill, Laurence M. *s.j.* '35 (NO) [P] New Orleans, LA Ignatius Residence.
O'Neill, Michael *i.c.* '70 (VEN) Bradenton, FL Sacred Heart Church.
O'Neill, Michael '76 (LA) San Pedro, CA Fort MacArthur Annex.
O'Neill, Michael '78 (HEL) Special Assignments.
O'Neill, Michael '81 (SP) Palm Harbor, FL St. Luke the Evangelist Church.
O'Neill, Michael F. (LA) Military and VA Chaplains.
O'Neill, Michael F. '76 (NO) Military Chaplains.
O'Neill, Msgr. Patrick '45 (SD) La Mesa, CA St. Martin of Tours Church.
O'Neill, Patrick '53 (SEA) [1] Tacoma, WA St. Ann Church; [15] Tacoma, WA Sacred Heart Church; Retired.
O'Neill, Patrick G. '53 (SEA) [5] Tacoma, WA St. John of the Woods Church.
O'Neill, Patrick H. '67 (MIA) Special Assignment.
O'Neill, Msgr. Patrick J. '45 (SD) Retired.
O'Neill, Msgr. Patrick J. '47 (SAC) Retired and in Senior Ministry.
O'Neill, Patrick J. '90 (CHI) Alsip, IL St. Terrence Church.
O'Neill, Raymond '66 (SP) Gulfport, FL Most Holy Name of Jesus Church.
O'Neill, Richard (SY) Marcy, NY Central New York Psychiatric Center.
O'Neill, Richard V. '54 (SY) [12] Utica, NY St. Mary Church.
O'Neill, Robert '96 (STO) Lodi, CA St. Anne Church.
O'Neill, Robert F. '62 (ROC) [5] Rochester, NY Church of the Annunciation.
O'Neill, Rory '55 (DOD) Retired.
O'Neill, Thomas '62 (FRS) Shafter, CA St. Therese Church.
O'Neill, Thomas D. '68 (PRO) On Duty Outside the Diocese.
O'Neill, Thomas H. *s.j.* '90 (LA) [F] Los Angeles, CA Loyola High School.
O'Neill, Thomas M. '78 (LC) [B] La Crosse, WI Viterbo College.
O'Neill, Thomas P. *o.s.f.s.* '57 (TOL) [C] Toledo, OH St. Francis de Sales High School; [K] Toledo, OH Oblates of St. Francis de Sales.
O'Neill, Timothy '67 (Y) Hubbard, OH St. Patrick's Church.
O'Neill, Vincent '71 (SR) Windsor, CA Our Lady of Guadalupe Church.
O'Neill, Virgil *o.s.b.* '46 (SCL) [I] Collegeville, MN St. John's Abbey, of the Order of St. Benedict.
O'Neill, William (SJ) Retired.
O'Neill, William *c.s.sp.* '42 (SJ) Mountain View, CA St. Athanasius Church.

O'Neill, William J. '65 (PRO) Jamestown, RI St. Mark Church.

O'Neill, William O. '67 (SAV) [1] Savannah, GA Cathedral of St. John the Baptist.

O'Neill, William P. '61 (CLV) Hinckley, OH Our Lady of Grace Church.

O'Neill, William R. *s.j.* '81 (OAK) [A] Berkeley, CA The Jesuit School of Theology at Berkeley; [N] Berkeley, CA Jesuit Community at Jesuit School of Theology at Berkeley.

O'Pira, Simon Peter '93 (STV) [1] Barrenspot, VI Church St. Ann Church.

O'Rafferty, Patrick (SAC) Carmichael, CA St. John the Evangelist Church.

O'Rafferty, Patrick '51 (SAC) Retired and in Senior Ministry.

O'Regan, Denis '61 (STA) [2] Jacksonville, FL Blessed Trinity Church.

O'Regan, Hugh H. '57 (BO) [29] Boston, MA Holy Trinity Church; [31] Boston, MA St. James the Greater in Chinatown Church.

O'Reilly, Aidan '60 (SAC) Mount Shasta, CA St. Anthony Church.

O'Reilly, Msgr. Alvin J. '51 (NO) [3] New Orleans, LA St. Mary Church; New Orleans, LA Shrine of St. Lazarus of Jerusalem Church; Retired.

O'Reilly, Andrew *c.pp.s.* '74 (ORL) Winter Garden, FL Resurrection Church.

O'Reilly, Msgr. Bernard '45 (LA) Paramount, CA Our Lady of the Rosary Church; Retired.

O'Reilly, Bernard M. '69 (PRO) Harrisville, RI St. Patrick's Church.

O'Reilly, Edward M. '68 (NY) Military Chaplains.

O'Reilly, Francis J. '45 (PHX) Retired.

O'Reilly, Gabriel '67 (MIA) Davie, FL St. David Church.

O'Reilly, Gerald K. '85 (CHI) [116] Chicago, IL St. Laurence Church.

O'Reilly, James E. *s.j.* '57 (DET) [24] Detroit, MI St. Francis de Sales Church.

O'Reilly, James P. *m.s.* '37 (STL) [P] St. Louis, MO La Salette Missionaries.

O'Reilly, James P. *c.s.sp.* '42 (SB) [E] Hemet, CA Holy Ghost Fathers.

O'Reilly, Msgr. John L. '40 (WH) Retired.

O'Reilly, Joseph '49 (SFD) Retired.

O'Reilly, Joseph F. '56 (WH) White Sulphur Springs, WV St. Charles Borromeo Church.

O'Reilly, Joseph P. '39 (SFR) [49] San Francisco, CA St. Stephen Church; Retired.

O'Reilly, Kevin '96 (NY) [169] Bronx, NY Our Lady of Angels Church.

O'Reilly, Kevin P. '84 (WDC) Laurel, MD St. Mary Church.

O'Reilly, Michael '96 (SAC) South Lake Tahoe, CA St. Theresa Church.

O'Reilly, Michael P. '61 (WH) Parkersburg, WV St. Francis Xavier's Church.

O'Reilly, P. J. '53 (ORL) Retired.

O'Reilly, Patrick J. '44 (GF) Retired.

O'Reilly, Msgr. Peter A. '61 (LA) Oak Park, CA St. Maximilian Kolbe Church.

O'Reilly, Vincent '62 (SAC) Vacaville, CA St. Joseph Church.

O'Riley, Dennis H. '59 (PEO) Tolono, IL St. Patrick's Church.

O'Riley, James K. '67 (IND) Retired.

O'Riley, Robert F. *o.p.* '58 (CHI) [N] River Forest, IL St. Thomas Aquinas Priory.

O'Riordan, James '64 (JKS) Vicksburg, MS St. Michael Church.

O'Riordan, Msgr. Jeremiah '68 (PAT) Sabbatical.

O'Riordan, William '85 (NO) [3] Harvey, LA St. Martha Church.

O'Roake, Patrick J. *o.s.b.* '60 (MIL) [P] Benet Lake, WI St. Benedict's Abbey.

O'Rorke, Msgr. James H. '61 (PAT) [5] Wayne, NJ Our Lady of the Valley Church.

O'Rourke, Arthur G. *o.s.a.* (BO) [9] Lawrence, MA St. Mary Immaculate Conception Church.

O'Rourke, Bryan A. '66 (STP) Plymouth, MN St. Mary of the Lake Church.

O'Rourke, Carl '88 (JOL) [I] Naperville, IL St. John Vianney Villa.

O'Rourke, Charles M. '58 (PH) Milmont Park, PA Our Lady of Peace Church.

O'Rourke, Colin *o.f.m.* '61 (BO) [BB] Boston, MA St. Anthony Shrine.

O'Rourke, Daniel J. '88 (GF) Scobey, MT St. Philip Bonitus Church.

O'Rourke, David *o.p.* '62 (OAK) [4] Berkeley, CA St. Mary Magdalen Church.

O'Rourke, Dennis J. '80 (PHX) [5] Scottsdale, AZ St. Daniel the Prophet Church; [H] Phoenix, AZ Office of Youth and Young Adult Ministries.

O'Rourke, Edmund F. *o.s.f.s.* '56 (CAM) [L] Pittsgrove, NJ Villa St. Joseph.

O'Rourke, Francis J. '52 (MIL) Fox Point, WI St. Eugene Church; Retired.

O'Rourke, Francis J. *c.ss.r.* '62 (BRK) [U] Brooklyn, NY Our Lady of Good Counsel Residence.

O'Rourke, Francis J. '75 (CHL) Clemmons, NC Holy Family Church.

O'Rourke, Gabriel A. '45 (SC) Retired.

O'Rourke, Hugh *s.s.c.* '52 (PRO) [12] Pawtucket, RI St. Teresa Church.

O'Rourke, James J. '58 (BO) [21] Boston, MA St. Columbkille Church.

O'Rourke, John F. *o.s.a.* '61 (PH) [142] Philadelphia, PA St. Rita of Cascia Church.

O'Rourke, Msgr. John G. '48 (DAL) Retired.

O'Rourke, John J. *s.s.j.* '66 (BIR) [14] Birmingham, AL Our Lady of Fatima Church.

O'Rourke, Kevin David *o.p.* '54 (STL) [P] St. Louis, MO Dominican Community of St. Louis.

O'Rourke, Michael *o.p.* '96 (NO) [25] New Orleans, LA St. Anthony Of Padua Church; [25] New Orleans, LA St. Anthony Of Padua Church.

O'Rourke, Michael J. *o.p.* '96 (SAT) On Duty Outside the Archdiocese.

O'Rourke, Michael K. '69 (GB) [4] Appleton, WI St. Mary Church.

O'Rourke, P. Gerard '50 (SFR) [46] San Francisco, CA St. Philip the Apostle Church; Special Assignment.

O'Rourke, Paul J. *s.s.c.* '61 (BRK) [U] Kew Gardens, NY St. Columbans Foreign Mission Society.

O'Rourke, Richard *m.s.c.* (AUS) Harker Heights, TX St. Paul Chong Hasang Church.

O'Rourke, Robert *s.s.c.* '58 (DAL) Grand Prairie, TX Immaculate Conception Church.

O'Rourke, Terence J. *o.s.a.* '64 (CAM) [4] Atlantic City, NJ St. Nicholas of Tolentine Church.

O'Rourke, Thomas J. '63 (BRK) [84] Brooklyn, NY St. Mary, Star of the Sea Church.

O'Rourke, Thomas J. '64 (HRT) [1] Hamden, CT Ascension Church.

O'Rourke, Thomas P. *m.m.* '41 (NY) [Z] Maryknoll, NY Maryknoll Fathers and Brothers.

O'Rourke, William '58 (RVC) Port Washington, NY St. Peter of Alcantara Church.

O'Rourke, William J. '56 (NOR) Quinebaug, CT St. Stephen Church.

O'Ryan, Colm '55 (LA) Beverly Hills, CA Good Shepherd Church.

O'Shaughnessy, Donald J. *s.j.* '55 (DET) [P] Clarkston, MI Colombiere Center.

O'Shaughnessy, James J. '68 (NY) [E] New York, NY Cardinal Spellman High School.

O'Shaughnessy, Michael A. '50 (VIC) Edna, TX St. Agnes Church.

O'Shaughnessy, Patrick '68 (BLX) [8] Biloxi, MS St. Michael Church.

O'Shaughnessy, Seamus '70 (MIA) [6] Fort Lauderdale, FL St. George Church.

O'Shaughnessy, William J. *o.p.* '49 (PRO) [P] Providence, RI St. Thomas Aquinas Priory at Providence College

O'Shea, Daniel *o.s.b.* '35 (KCK) [I] Leavenworth, KS Motherhouse of the Sisters of Charity of Leavenworth.

O'Shea, Daniel *s.a.* '64 (NY) [14] Yonkers, NY Our Lady of the Rosary Church.

O'Shea, Howard '58 (NY) [Z] New York, NY Franciscan Friars, Order of Friars Manor.

O'Shea, James '89 (NEW) [3] Union City, NJ SS. Joseph and Michael Church.

O'Shea, James B. '65 (WOR) [12] Worcester, MA Our Lady of Lourdes Church.

O'Shea, James D. '64 (SFD) [1] Decatur, IL Holy Family Church Mt. Zion, IL Our Lady of the Holy Spirit Church

O'Shea, James R. '56 (WCH) Halstead, KS Sacred Heart of Jesus Church.

O'Shea, Jeremiah T. '64 (PIT) Mt. Lebanon, PA St. Winifred Church.

O'Shea, John F. *s.j.* '52 (STL) [P] St. Louis, MO The Jesuits of the Missouri Province.

O'Shea, John G. '60 (YAK) Kennewick, WA Holy Spirit Church.

O'Shea, John J. '36 (CHI) [121] Chicago, IL St. Margaret Mary Church; Retired.

O'Shea, John J. '41 (ATL) Retired.

O'Shea, John J. '50 (WCH) [19] Wichita, KS St. Thomas Aquinas Church.

O'Shea, John L. '81 (PIT) [4] Donora, PA Our Lady of the Valley Church.

O'Shea, John T. '54 (BUF) Retired.

O'Shea, Joseph '61 (SEA) Woodland, WA St. Philip's Church.

O'Shea, Msgr. Joseph H. '47 (PMB) [2] Boca Raton, FL Our Lady of Lourdes Church; Retired.

O'Shea, Joseph J. '42 (NY) [145] Bronx, NY St. Helena Church; Retired.

O'Shea, Lawrence '56 (DUL) [17] Duluth, MN St. Raphael's Church.

O'Shea, Michael (NY) County, NY Westchester County Jail.

O'Shea, Michael '52 (LA) Bellflower, CA St. Bernard Church.

O'Shea, Michael *o.f.m.cap.* '54 (FRS) [D] Fresno, CA Nazareth House.

O'Shea, Patrick '61 (LA) On Duty Outside the Archdiocese.

O'Shea, Patrick '61 (MIA) [3] Fort Lauderdale, FL St. Anthony Church.

O'Shea, Patrick *m.s.c.* '73 (SAT) [M] San Antonio, TX Missionaries of the Sacred Heart.

O'Shea, Msgr. Patrick J. '58 (SFR) Absent on Leave.

O'Shea, Paul *o.p.* '89 (WDC) [B] Washington, DC Dominican House of Studies.

O'Shea, Philip *o.f.m.* '75 (BO) [W] Boston, MA Ministry of the Word.

O'Shea, Philip A. '54 (WDC) [10] Washington, DC Blessed Sacrament, Shrine of the Most Church; Retired.

O'Shea, Robert J. '63 (BEL) [E] Breese, IL St. Joseph Hospital.

O'Shea, Vincent M. *o.s.m.* '38 (CHI) [N] Chicago, IL Servite Friars - Eastern Province.

O'Shea, William D. '62 (PMB) North Palm Beach, FL St. Clare Church.

O'Shea, William J. '63 (JOL) [4] Naperville, IL St. Margaret Mary Church.

O'Sullivan, Andrew C. *o.s.b.* '43 (PAT) [M] Newton, NJ St. Paul's Abbey.

O'Sullivan, Brendan '54 (SB) Retired.

O'Sullivan, Brendan *s.s.c.* '70 (OM) [K] St. Columbans, NE St. Columban's Foreign Mission Society.

O'Sullivan, Carrol '51 (LA) Montecito, CA Our Lady of Mount Carmel Church.

O'Sullivan, Carroll M. *s.j.* '38 (SJ) [M] Los Gatos, CA Sacred Heart Jesuit Center.

O'Sullivan, Cyril '80 (SFR) [18] San Francisco, CA St. Finn Barr Church.

O'Sullivan, Daniel '60 (DET) New Haven, MI St. Francis of Assisi Church; Detroit, MI Detroit Psychiatric Institute.

O'Sullivan, Daniel '63 (LA) Ventura, CA Sacred Heart Church.

O'Sullivan, Daniel A. *s.j.* '55 (SFR) [N] San Francisco, CA Jesuit Community at University of San Francisco.

O'Sullivan, Daniel J. '62 (CHI) Park Forest, IL St. Irenaeus Church.

O'Sullivan, Denis A. '72 (SR) [3] Santa Rosa, CA St. Rose of Lima Church.

O'Sullivan, Eugene (BO) Awaiting Assignment.

O'Sullivan, Msgr. Francis G. (BO) [3] Peabody, MA St. John the Baptist Church; Retired.

O'Sullivan, James '49 (CAM) On Sick Leave; [L] Cherry Hill, NJ Vianney Villa.

O'Sullivan, James *s.m.a.* '54 (NEW) [N] Tenafly, NJ Society of African Missions, Provincialate, S.M.A. Fathers.

O'Sullivan, James J. '60 (JC) Eldon, MO Sacred Heart Church.

O'Sullivan, Msgr. Jeremiah '58 (SD) Coronado, CA Sacred Heart Church; Retired.

O'Sullivan, John '50 (B) Retired.

O'Sullivan, John C. '45 (PBL) Retired.

O'Sullivan, John J. '50 (BRK) Absent on Sick Leave.

O'Sullivan, John V. '68 (PT) [2] Tallahassee, FL Blessed Sacrament Church.

O'Sullivan, Laurence '48 (MRY) Retired.

O'Sullivan, Leo *o.s.a.* '49 (ORG) Buena Park, CA St. Pius V Church.

O'Sullivan, Martin J. '53 (BRK) [R] Bayside, NY Ozanam Hall of Queens Nursing Home, Inc.

O'Sullivan, Michael '48 (MRY) Retired.

O'Sullivan, Michael '55 (SAT) On Leave.

O'Sullivan, Michael J. '55 (WDC) [37] Washington, DC St. Peter Church.

O'Sullivan, Msgr. Peter '34 (LA) Granada Hills, CA St. John Baptist de la Salle Church; Retired.

O'Sullivan, Peter '83 (KCK) Emporia, KS Sacred Heart Church.

O'Sullivan, Raymond (BO) Society of St. James the Apostle.

O'Sullivan, Robert '43 (BIR) Retired.

O'Sullivan, Sarsfield '51 (HEL) Retired.

O'Sullivan, Sean *i.c.* '47 (SP) Indian Rocks Beach, FL St. Jerome Church.

O'Sullivan, Sean '64 (MIA) Coral Gables, FL Little Flower Church; Retired.

O'Sullivan, T. Brendan '56 (SAC) [10] Sacramento, CA St. Anthony Church.

O'Sullivan, Thomas C. '51 (LA) Retired.

O'Sullivan, Msgr. Thomas Joseph '28 (LA) [98] Los Angeles, CA Visitation Church; Retired.

O'Sullivan, Thomas P. '71 (SR) Point Arena, CA St. Aloysius Church.

O'Sullivan, Timothy *o.f.m.cap.* '36 (LA) Solvang, CA Old Mission Santa Ines Church.

O'Sullivan, Timothy F. '94 (PH) [60] Philadelphia, PA Holy Innocents Church.

O'Sullivan, Timothy J. '52 (BO) [44] Boston, MA St. Mark Church.

O'Sullivan, Timothy J. '71 (SR) Napa, CA St. John the Baptist Church.

O'Sullivan, Tracy *o.carm.* '62 (LA) [88] Los Angeles, CA St. Raphael Church.

O'Toole, Msgr. Anthony J. '44 (ALT) Retired.

O'Toole, Brian '86 (WOR) Shrewsbury, MA St. Mary's Church.

O'Toole, Charles '72 (SP) Retired.
O'Toole, Coleman P. '61 (PRT) [5] Portland, ME St. Patrick's Church.
O'Toole, Msgr. Fursey '60 (BRK) [115] Brooklyn, NY St. Patrick Church.
O'Toole, Henry *c.ss.r.* '44 (ORL) [F] New Smyrna Beach, FL St. Alphonsus Villa-Redemptorist Fathers and Brothers.
O'Toole, James '64 (FWT) Bedford, TX St. Michael Church.
O'Toole, John J. '52 (PEO) Retired.
O'Toole, John M. '67 (PIT) [26] Pittsburgh, PA St. Mary of Mercy Church.
O'Toole, Msgr. Joseph M. '39 (ALT) Retired.
O'Toole, Kenneth '44 (NY) Chappaqua, NY St. John and St. Mary Church.
O'Toole, Kenneth E. '44 (NY) Retired.
O'Toole, Lawrence J. *s.j.* '58 (BO) Billerica, MA St. Mary Church; [W] Weston, MA Campion Center.
O'Toole, Lawrence J. *s.j.* '88 (BO) [W] Boston, MA The Society of Jesus of New England-Provincial Offices.
O'Toole, Matthew L. '95 (STL) [58] St. Louis, MO St. Raphael The Archangel Church.
O'Toole, Terrence *o.f.m.cap.* '55 (NOR) [4] Middletown, CT St. Pius X Church.
O'Toole, Thomas F. *c.ss.r.* '51 (ALB) [L] Saratoga Springs, NY St. John Neumann Residence.
O'Toole, Thomas L. '69 (OKL) Sterling, OK Our Lady of Perpetual Help Church.
O'Toole, Timothy L. '89 (B) Idaho Falls, ID Christ the King Church.
O'Toole, William F. '96 (GRY) [3] Michigan City, IN Queen of All Saints Church.
O'Toole, Msgr. William P. '61 (LA) Alhambra, CA All Souls Church.
O.Connell, James R. *o.f.m.* (BO) Boston, MA Massachusetts General Hospital.
Oakes, Edward T. *s.j.* '79 (DEN) [M] Denver, CO Regis Jesuit Community (The Jesuits at Regis University).
Oakham, Ronald *o. carm.* '77 (TUC) [F] Tucson, AZ Carmelite Priory.
Oates, Eugene *c.ss.r.* '44 (DEN) Greeley, CO Our Lady of Peace Church.
Oates, Thomas F. (BO) Society of St. James the Apostle.
Obaza, Theodore L. '61 (SCR) [9] Wilkes-Barre, PA Holy Trinity Church.
Obee, Gregory *o.s.b.* '56 (RCK) [H] Aurora, IL Marmion Abbey-St. Augustine's Abbey.
Obeng-Kyeremeh, Simon '89 (BAL) [47] Baltimore, MD St. Joseph Church.
Obenrader, Paul F. '39 (E) Retired.
Ober, Anselm *o.s.b.* '42 (RIC) [6] Virginia Beach, VA St. Gregory the Great Church.
Ober, Lawrence M. *s.j.* '77 (CLV) [E] Cleveland, OH St. Ignatius High School.
Oberch, Msgr. Rick J. '85 (PEO) [N] East Peoria, IL Mt. Alverno Novitiate.
Oberg, Paul *s.s.j.* '85 (MOB) [5] Mobile, AL St. Francis Xavier Church.
Oberg, Paul J. *s.s.j.* '85 (MOB) [18] Mobile, AL Prince of Peace Church.
Obergefell, Sylvan W. '58 (TOL) Ottoville, OH Immaculate Conception Church.
Oberhausen, James *o.f.m.conv.* '82 (IND) Clarksville, IN St. Anthony of Padua Church.
Oberkirch, Msgr. James W. '62 (MOB) [1] Mobile, AL Cathedral of the Immaculate Conception.
Oberle, James '87 (WDC) On Duty Outside the Archdiocese.
Oberle, James P. *s.s.* '87 (SFR) [A] Menlo Park, CA St. Patrick Seminary.
Oberle, Joseph *c.s.s.r.* '37 (ALB) [L] Saratoga Springs, NY St. John Neumann Residence; [L] Saratoga Springs, NY St. John Neumann Residence.
Obermiller, Edwin *c.s.c.* '96 (P) [B] Portland, OR University of Portland; [L] Portland, OR Holy Cross Father & Brother, C.S.C. - University of Portland; [P] Portland, OR University of Portland.
Obersinner, Joseph *s.j.* '57 (P) Tillamook, OR Sacred Heart Church.
Oberstar, Richard *m.s.f.* '65 (SAT) New Braunfels, TX Our Lady of Perpetual Help Church.
Obersteiner, Ernest '77 (GLP) Absent on Leave.
Obert, Martin '56 (SP) Retired.
Oberto, Peter '78 (MAR) Ishpeming, MI St. John the Evangelist Church.
Oberts, David P. '69 (SUP) Hawkins, WI St. Mary Czestowchowa Church; Ladysmith, WI Our Lady of Sorrows Church; Tony, WI St. Anthony de Padua Church.
Oberwinder, Robert J. '35 (LC) Retired.
Obiajunwa, Chukwuol '82 (PAT) Sparta, NJ Our Lady of the Lake Church.
Obijiski, Herbert '65 (HRT) Kensington, CT St. Paul's Church.
Obin, Arthur *o.m.i.* '64 (MAN) Claremont, NH St. Mary Church.
Obin, Gilbert *c.i.c.m.* '67 (SAT) [54] San Antonio, TX St. Martin de Porres Church.
Obiulewu, Innocent '91 (LKC) [1] Sulphur, LA Immaculate Conception of the B.V.M. Church.
Oblinger, Joseph B. '46 (HEL) West Yellowstone, MT Our Lady of the Pines Church; Retired.
Obloj, Stanislaw J. '93 (DET) [11] Warren, MI St. Sylvester Church.
Obloy, Leonard G. (BAL) [A] Emmitsburg, MD Mount St. Mary's Seminary.
Obloy, Leonard G. '77 (CLV) Released from Diocesan Assignment.
Obloy, Leonard J. (BAL) [A] Emmitsburg, MD Mount St. Mary's Seminary.
Obmann, Msgr. Russell J. '51 (STL) Retired.
Oborny, Paul J. '63 (WCH) Council Grove, KS St. Rose Church; Strong City, KS St. Anthony of Padua Church.
Oborny, Rudolf F. '71 (LIN) [6] Lincoln, NE St. John the Apostle Church.
Obregon, Miguel *o.f.m.* '81 (OAK) [N] Oakland, CA Franciscan Friars Provincial Office, Province of St. Barbara.
OBrien, Michael C. '65 (SEA) [3] Vancouver, WA St. John Church.
Obrimski, Paul G. '70 (BAL) On Duty Outside the Archdiocese.
Ocampo, Ramon Conde *o.de.m.* '59 (PCE) [13] Ponce, PR Santuario San Judas Tadeo Church.
Occhiuto, Joseph L. '79 (MRY) [1] Monterey, CA Cathedral of San Carlos Borromeo.
Ochiltree, Richard *c.ss.r.* '53 (SEA) [O] Federal Way, WA Palisades Retreat House.
Ochoa, David '72 (LA) Lynwood, CA St. Emydius Church.
Ochoa, Einer (SB) Barstow, CA St. Joseph Church.
Ochoa, Einer M.De J. '85 (SAT) Special Assignment.
Ochoa, Javier *m.s.c.* '79 (LA) Cudahy, CA Cudahy Mission Church.
Ochoa, Jose Luis '66 (LA) La Puente, CA St. Louis of France Church; [R] Los Angeles, CA Guadalupe Missioners Procure.
Ochoa, Rafael '78 (LA) [15] Los Angeles, CA Immaculate Conception Church.
Ochoa, Xavier '69 (SR) Windsor, CA Our Lady of Guadalupe Church.
Ochs, Daniel L. '76 (COL) Reynoldsburg, OH St. Pius X Church.
Ochs, Robert J. *s.j.* '61 (OAK) [N] Berkeley, CA Jesuit Community at Jesuit School of Theology at Berkeley.
Ochylski, Ronald S. *s.s.* '87 (BAL) [M] Baltimore, MD Sulpician Provincial House.
Ochylski, Ronald S. '87 (SFR) On Duty Outside the Archdiocese.
Ocilka, John A. '94 (CLV) [43] Cleveland, OH St. Leo the Great Church.
Ockay, Msgr. Clement A. '41 (NEW) Retired.
Odama, Joseph '93 (CHI) [51] Chicago, IL St. Dorothy Church.
Odbert, Jerome (STL) [P] St. Louis, MO Jesuit Community Corporation at St. Louis University - Jesuit Hall.
Odbert, Jerome K. *s.j.* '69 (DET) [K] Detroit, MI Jesuit Provincial Office-Detroit Province of the Society of Jesus.
Oddo, Peter A. '61 (NEW) Military Chaplains.
Odenbrett, Stephen *o.s.b.* '46 (MRY) [G] San Luis Obispo, CA Monastery of the Risen Christ.
Odermann, John *o.s.b.* '55 (BIS) [A] Richardton, ND Assumption Abbey.
Odermann, John *o.s.b.* '55 (FAR) [F] Valley City, ND Sisters of Mary of the Presentation.
Odermann, Valerian *o.s.b.* '73 (BIS) [A] Richardton, ND Assumption Abbey; [B] Bismarck, ND University of Mary.
Odie, John P. '61 (BGP) Retired; [O] Stamford, CT Our Lady Queen of the Clergy Home.
Odien, Terry M. '73 (CAM) Westmont, NJ Holy Saviour Church.
Odoemela, Richard (NEW) Nutley, NJ Our Lady of Mount Carmel Church.
Odom-Green, William '91 (OWN) Absent on Leave.
Odor, Luke '80 (FAR) Cooperstown, ND St. George's Church.
Odorizzi, Thomas A. '92 (MET) Monmouth Junction, NJ St. Cecilia Church.
Odufuye, Francis '79 (RVC) Elmont, NY St. Boniface Church; Valley Stream, NY Franklin Medical Center Hospital.
Oedy, Thomas E. '71 (TOL) Edgerton, OH St. Mary Church; Hicksville, OH St. Michael Church.
Oehmler, Gary W. '83 (PIT) [37] Pittsburgh, PA St. Rosalia Church.
Oehrlein, Felix G. '65 (MAD) Pine Bluff, WI St. Mary of Pine Bluff Church.
Oelerich, Robert *c.ss.r.* '49 (OM) [19] Omaha, NE Holy Name Church.
Oelrich, Anthony '92 (SCL) Holdingford, MN St. Hedwig's Church; Holdingford, MN St. Mary's Church; Opole, MN Our Lady of Mt. Carmel Church; St. Anna, MN Immaculate Conception Church; St. Wendel, MN St. Columbkille's Church.
Oen, Edward J. *c.pp.s.* '64 (SAL) Greenleaf, KS Sacred Heart Church; Hanover, KS St. John the Baptist Church.
Oesterle, John G. '67 (PIT) East McKeesport, PA St. Robert Bellarmine Church.
Oestreich, Brian W. '93 (NU) [1] New Ulm, MN Cathedral of The Holy Trinity.
Oestreich, Emil C. '45 (PH) [96] Philadelphia, PA St. Mary of the Assumption Church; [139] Philadelphia, PA St. Raymond of Penafort Church; Retired.
Oetgen, John A. *o.s.b.* '51 (CHL) [J] Belmont, NC Belmont Abbey.
Offer, Henry *s.s.j.* '44 (BEA) [7] Beaumont, TX Our Mother of Mercy Church.
Offerman, Paul '57 (SFS) Bridgewater, SD St. Stephen Church.
Offutt, Bradley S. '86 (KC) Harrisonville, MO Our Lady of Lourdes Church.
Ofoha, Paul N. *m.s.p.* (GAL) [Q] Barrett Station, TX Missionary Society of St. Paul, Inc. - U.S. Region.
Ofoha, Paul Ngozichukwu *m.s.p.* '88 (BEA) Ames, TX Our Mother of Mercy Church.
Oftutt, J. James '62 (JC) [3] Jefferson City, MO Immaculate Conception Church.
Ogbemure, Raymond '74 (OAK) El Cerrito, CA St. John the Baptist Church.
Ogbonna, Edmund '78 (MIA) Miramar, FL St. Bartholomew Church.
Ogbonna, Stanislaus (NY) State, NY Sullivan Correctional Facility.
Ogden, Louis P. '85 (HBG) Middletown, PA Seven Sorrows of the Blessed Virgin Mary Church.
Oge, Raymond J. '67 (STL) Bloomsdale, MO St. Agnes Church; Lawrenceton, MO St. Lawrence's Church.
Ogg, Thomas '68 (CHY) Gillette, WY St. Matthew's Church.
Oggero, Roy J. *c.s.b.* '61 (GAL) Sugar Land, TX St. Theresa Church.
Ogle, Sean '77 (BRK) [198] Queens, NY St. Mary Star of the Sea Church.
Oglesby, J. Leonard '48 (MEM) Retired.
Ognibene, Joseph F. '52 (CHI) [154] Chicago, IL Our Lady, Mother of the Church; Rolling Meadows, IL St. Colette Church; Retired.
Ognibene, Salvatore J. '47 (CHI) [106] Chicago, IL St. John Bosco Church; Retired; [L] Chicago, IL St. Mary of Providence.
Ogolla, Julius '91 (CHI) [110] Chicago, IL St. Joseph Church.
Ogorzaly, Adam '85 (TYL) [1] Tyler, TX Cathedral of the Immaculate Conception.
Ogrodowski, William M. '75 (PIT) On Duty Outside the Diocese.
Ogu, Cletus (RVC) Glen Cove, NY St. Rocco Church.
Ogunnaike, Emmanuel *m.s.p.* '90 (STL) [33] St. Louis, MO St. Elizabeth, Mother of John the Baptist Church.
Ohirko, Peter '55 (STF) Ozone Park, (1954) St. Mary Protectress Church.
Ohlemacher, Richard N. *o.s.c.* '55 (PHX) [F] Phoenix, AZ Crosier Community of Phoenix (Canons Regular of the Order of the Holy Cross).
Ohlig, John '95 (LUB) [1] Lubbock, TX Cathedral Christ the King Church; Floydada, TX St. Mary Magdalen Church.
Ohno, Ignatius F. *s.j.* '92 (P) [L] Portland, OR Jesuit Provincial Office (Oregon Prov.).
Oho, Ray *o.s.b.* '82 (SFS) Revillo, SD Annunciation Church; [E] Milbank, SD St. William Home for the Aged.
Ojeda, Filemon G. '46 (SFR) Retired.
Ojeda, Rodrigo (SAC) Woodland, CA Holy Rosary Church.
Ojibway, Paul *s.a.* '78 (WDC) [B] Washington, DC Atonement Seminary-Franciscan Friars of the Atonement.
Okere, Remigius '94 (DM) [9] Des Moines, IA St. Joseph's Church.
Okoli, Peter '67 (NY) [63] New York, NY St. Joseph of the Holy Family Church.
Okon, Jack '44 (IND) [33] Indianapolis, IN St. Matthew the Apostle Church.
Okonski, Joseph F. '90 (PH) [13] Philadelphia, PA St. Anselm Church.
Okopinski, Louis S. '51 (MIL) Retired.
Okorie, Joseph '81 (SJ) Milpitas, CA Elmwood Rehabilitation Center.
Okorie, Joseph B.C. '81 (SJ) Milpitas, CA St. Elizabeth Church.
Okorn, Dusan A. '47 (HEL) Swan Valley, MT Swan Valley Catholic Community Church; Retired; [G] Swan Lake, MT The Sycamore Tree Contemplative Prayer Center.
Okoro, Joseph E. *c.m.f.* '90 (NO) [4] New Orleans, LA Blessed Sacrament Church.
Okorochukwu, Wilfred C. '75 (LR) Fordyce, AR Good Shepherd Church; Sheridan, AR Holy Cross Church.
Okoye, James C. *c.ss.sp.* '70 (CHI) [B] Chicago, IL The Catholic Theological Union at Chicago.
Okroy, Francis *s.ch.* '48 (BAL) [36] Baltimore, MD Holy Rosary Church.
Okumu, Richard U.O. '81 (DAV) Victor, IA St. Bridget's Church.
Okuroski, Michael *o.c.d.* '44 (SAT) [18] San Antonio, TX

Our Lady of Mt. Carmel and St. Therese, Discalced Carmelite Fathers Church; [M] San Antonio, TX Discalced Carmelites (Prov. of St. Therese).
Ola'aiga, Vitaliano '91 (P) [A] St. Benedict, OR Mount Angel Seminary.
Olczak, Joseph '65 (NOR) [A] Cromwell, CT Holy Apostles College and Seminary.
Olczak, Joseph M. '65 (NOR) Rockville, CT St. Joseph Church.
Oldani, Louis J. *s.j.* '64 (KC) [J] Kansas City, MO Rockhurst College - Jesuit Community.
Oldenski, Kenneth E. (PIT) Richland Township, PA Saint Richard Church.
Oldershaw, Robert H. '62 (CHI) Evanston, IL St. Nicholas Church.
Oldfield, Albert E. '59 (SCR) [18] Scranton, PA St. Mary's Church.
Oldfield, John J. '63 (NY) [B] Suffern, NY Tagaste Monastery.
Olds, Daryld *c.m.f.* '92 (SAT) [B] San Antonio, TX St. Anthony Mary Claret Seminary.
Olds, Steve '88 (ORL) Sabbatical.
Olejniczak, Henry A. '51 (CHI) [43] Chicago, IL St. Columba Church; Retired.
Olek, Ralph F. *s.m.* '74 (ATL) [C] Atlanta, GA Marist School.
Oleksiak, Donald P. '89 (CLV) [1] Garfield Heights, OH St. Monica Church.
Oleksy, Stanislaus '82 (LR) [E] Rogers, AR St. Mary-Rogers Memorial Hospital.
Olendzki, Joaquim J. '58 (NY) Pine Island, NY St. Stanislaus Church.
Olenowski, Msgr. Mark '85 (PAT) Randolph, NJ Resurrection Church; Sabbatical.
Olesh, Msgr. Bohdan '42 (PHU) Alden Station, PA St. Vladimir Church; Glen Lyon, PA St. Nicholas Church.
Oleshko, Myroslaw '40 (STN) Retired.
Olesik, William J. '72 (NOR) Bolton, CT St. Maurice Church.
Olges, H. Anthony '70 (L) [23] Louisville, KY St. Elizabeth of Hungary Church; [71] Louisville, KY St. Therese Church.
Olguin, Jacinto '74 (VIC) Bloomington, TX St. Patrick Church.
Olguin, Luis '92 (SY) [13] Utica, NY St. Mary of Mt. Carmel Church; Rome, NY Walsh Facility; Special Assignment.
Oliana, Guido *m.c.c.j.* '78 (CHI) [N] Chicago, IL Comboni Missionaries Theologate (M.C.C.J.), Verona Fathers.
Oligschlaeger, P. Gregory '93 (JC) [A] Hannibal, MO St. Thomas Aquinas Seminary.
Oliva, George M. *s.j.* '72 (SD) Special Assignment.
Oliva, Max *s.j.* '72 (SD) [12] San Diego, CA Our Lady of Guadalupe Church.
Olivares, Romero "Butch" *c.i.c.m.* '74 (BWN) La Joya, TX Our Lady, Queen of Angels Church.
Olivas, J. Alfredo '81 (ELP) [40] El Paso, TX Santo Nino De Atocha Church.
Olive, Louis A. *c.ss.r.* '64 (TOL) [2] Lima, OH St. Gerard Church.
Oliveira, Albano '55 (OAK) Piedmont, CA Corpus Christi Church; [R] Oakland, CA The Roman Catholic Cemeteries of the Diocese of Oakland.
Oliveira, Aventino *i.m.c.* '57 (MET) [H] Somerset, NJ Consolata Society for Foreign Missions.
Oliveira, Gastao A. '72 (FR) [23] Fall River, MA Santo Christo Church.
Oliveira, Humbert M. '77 (MAN) [1] Manchester, NH St. Joseph Cathedral.
Oliveira, Joel D. '54 (BO) On Duty Outside the Archdiocese.
Oliveira, Joel D. '54 (PRO) [5] Warren, RI St. Thomas the Apostle Church.
Oliveira, Msgr. John J. *p.a., v.e.* '67 (FR) [19] New Bedford, MA St. Mary's Church.
Oliveira, John J. '77 (FR) [15] New Bedford, MA St. John the Baptist Church.
Oliveira, Joseph '49 (FR) Retired.
Oliveira, Robert A. '77 (FR) North Attleboro, MA St. Mary's Church.
Oliveira, Vitor '73 (SPR) [2] Ludlow, MA Our Lady of Fatima Church.
Oliver, Harry T. *s.j.* '57 (PHX) [B] Phoenix, AZ Brophy College Preparatory.
Oliver, Homer G. '43 (Y) Louisville, OH St. Louis Church; Retired.
Oliver, James M. '88 (PH) Graduate Studies.
Oliver, Msgr. John A. '52 (TUC) Sunsites, AZ St. Jude Thaddius Church.
Oliver, Jorge *t.o.r.* '52 (NEW) [14] Elizabeth, NJ Immaculate Heart of Mary Church.
Oliver, Marc '89 (NY) [CC] New York, NY University Apostolate.
Oliver, R.B. Michael '91 (BUF) [6] Buffalo, NY St. Ambrose Church.
Oliver, William A. '77 (GAL) Danbury, TX St. Anthony de Padua Church.
Oliver, William R. *s.v.d.* '58 (LAF) Maurice, LA St. Joseph Church.
Olivera, Fernando *o.a.r.* '94 (NY) [154] Bronx, NY St. John's Church.
Oliveras, Evaristo *c.m.* '88 (SJN) [62] San Juan, PR San Vicente de Paul Church.
Oliveras, Jose *o.carm.* '95 (ARE) Morovis, PR Nuestra Senora del Carmen Church.
Olivere, Michael S. '94 (PH) [15] Philadelphia, PA Ascension of Our Lord Church.
Oliveri, Armand *s.d.b.* '50 (SFR) [12] San Francisco, CA Corpus Christi Church.
Oliveri, Richard H. '66 (PAT) Dover, NJ St. Mary's Church.
Olivero, Michael A. '74 (CHI) [3] Des Plaines, IL St. Stephen Protomartyr Church.
Olivier, David S. *s.j.* '62 (P) [D] Portland, OR Jesuit High School.
Olivier, John H. *s.s.* '47 (MAR) Retired.
Olivier, Robert '57 (JKS) [C] Jackson, MS St. Dominic-Jackson Memorial Hospital.
Olivo, Stephen *s.j.* '69 (SFR) [N] San Francisco, CA Jesuit Community at University of San Francisco.
Olkovikas, Msgr. Albert W. '53 (MAN) [L] Manchester, NH Monastery of the Precious Blood.
Ollivier, John '50 (TOL) Retired.
Olmer, Vernon J. *o.f.m.* '62 (SUP) Ashland, WI Our Lady of the Lake Catholic Community Church.
Olmos, Pedro '78 (FRS) Faculties Only.
Olmstead, Daryl '75 (SAL) Goodland, KS Our Lady of Perpetual Help Church.
Olmsted, Msgr. Thomas J. '73 (COL) [A] Columbus, OH Pontifical College Josephinum.
Olmsted, Msgr. Thomas J. '73 (LIN) On Duty Outside the Diocese.
Olowin, Msgr. Jan C. '68 (E) [16] Erie, PA St. George Church.
Ols, James R. '75 (CLV) Elyria Township, OH St. Vincent de Paul Church.
Olsaukas, Msgr. Algirdas '52 (LA) [54] Los Angeles, CA St. Casimir Church.
Olsavsky, John R. '62 (CLV) Chagrin Falls, OH St. Joan of Arc Church.
Olsem, Andrew D. '67 (WIN) Worthington, MN St. Mary's Church.
Olsen, Charles R. *s.j.* '68 (SAC) [C] Sacramento, CA Jesuit High School; [H] Carmichael, CA Jesuit High School Community of Sacramento.
Olsen, Joseph J. '82 (E) Shinglehouse, PA St. Theresa Church.
Olsen, Kenneth '73 (P) On Duty Outside the Archdiocese.
Olsen, Thomas F. '53 (NEW) Cliffside Park, NJ Epiphany Church
Olson, Benedict *c.p.* '61 (LA) [R] Pasadena, CA Passionist Community; [W] Sierra Madre, CA Mater Dolorosa Retreat Center.
Olson, Dennis '74 (LC) [E] Marshfield, WI St. Joseph's Hospital.
Olson, Eric E. '84 (MAR) Hubbell, MI St. Cecilia Church; Lake Linden, MI St. Joseph Church.
Olson, Hans '83 (SEA) [4] Vancouver, WA St. Joseph Church.
Olson, James P. '88 (PH) [5] Philadelphia, PA All Saints Church; [D] Philadelphia, PA St. Hubert's Catholic High School for Girls.
Olson, Michael '94 (FWT) Bedford, TX St. Michael Church.
Olson, Randy E. '90 (LC) Athens, WI St. Anthony de Padua Church; Poniatowski, WI Holy Family Church.
Olson, Richard F. *s.j.* '59 (BO) [W] Weston, MA Campion Health Center, Inc.
Olson, Robert J. *o.m.i.* '65 (SPC) Mansfield, MO Immaculate Heart of Mary Church.
Olson, Ronald *o.f.m.conv.* '58 (SUP) Danbury, WI Our Lady of Perpetual Help Church; Webster, WI St. John the Baptist Church.
Olson, Ronald *o.f.m.conv.* '75 (SUP) Crescent Lake, WI Sacred Hearts of Jesus and Mary Church.
Olson, Theodore '72 (ORG) Brea, CA St. Angela Merici Church.
Olson, Theodore E. '79 (WIL) Elsmere, DE Corpus Christi Church.
Olson, Thomas F. '73 (SCL) Brennyville, MN St. Elizabeth Church; Morrill, MN St. Joseph's Church.
Olsovsky, George J. '56 (GAL) Huffman, TX St. Philip the Apostle Church.
Olszak, Len (JOL) Steger, IL St. Liborius Church.
Olszamowski, Leon M. *s.m.* '76 (DET) [D] Pontiac, MI Notre Dame Preparatory High School and Marist Academy.
Olszewski, Bernard *o.f.m.conv.* '79 (BUF) [C] Hamburg, NY Hilbert College; [D] Athol Springs, NY St. Francis High School; [O] Athol Springs, NY St. Francis of Assisi Friary; [R] Williamsville, NY Newman Club Chaplains.
Olszewski, Clarence A. '57 (HBG) York Haven, PA Holy Infant Church.
Olszewski, Daniel D. '51 (SCR) Dupont, PA Sacred Heart of Jesus Church.
Olszewski, Darryl (MIL) [17] Milwaukee, WI St. Catherine Church.
Olszewski, Edward '60 (MIA) Key Largo, FL St. Justin Martyr Church.
Olszewski, John S. '47 (NEW) Retired.
Olszewski, Laurence M. *c.s.c.* '64 (BUR) Bennington, VT Sacred Heart-St. Francis de Sales Church.
Olszewski, Paul A. '93 (CAM) Lindenwold, NJ St. Lawrence's Church.
Olszewski, Richard *o.f.m.* '62 (PH) [92] Philadelphia, PA Saint Martha Church.
Olszewski, Ronald W. *o.s.f.s.* '74 (TOL) [C] Toledo, OH St. Francis de Sales High School; [K] Toledo, OH Oblates of St. Francis de Sales; [K] Toledo, OH Oblates of St. Francis de Sales.
Olszyk, Thomas P. '71 (MIL) Military Chaplains.
Olvida, Victor '82 (SEA) Sedro Woolley, WA Immaculate Heart of Mary Church.
Olzacki, Tadeusz *o.s.p.p.e.* (PH) [Z] Doylestown, PA Pauline Fathers Monastery, Shrine of Our Lady of Czestochowa.
Oman, Francis M. *i.c.* '57 (PEO) Abingdon, IL Sacred Heart Church; St. Augustine, IL St. Augustine Church.
Ombao, Manuel '70 (AGN) Tamuning, GU St. Anthony and St. Victor Church.
Omernick, Kenneth E. '74 (MIL) [A] Milwaukee, WI Saint Francis Seminary.
Onaindia, Bernardo *c.p.* '46 (MGZ) San Sebastian, PR San Sebastian Martir Church.
Ondecko, Roman *o.f.m.conv.* '43 (ALB) [A] Rensselaer, NY Conventual Franciscan Friars.
Onderko, John M. '62 (PEO) [3] La Salle, IL Resurrection Church.
Ondic, John L. '65 (ALN) Tresckow, PA St. Bartholomew Church; Tresckow, PA St. Michael Church.
Ondik, Michael J. '37 (CLV) Avon, OH Holy Trinity Church; Retired.
Ondo, Michael A. '54 (LFT) Carmel, IN Our Lady of Mount Carmel Church.
Ondrako, Edward J. (ROC) [M] Rochester, NY Diocesan Office of Campus Ministry.
Ondreyka, Richard J. *m.s.* '54 (CLV) [2] Lakewood, OH SS. Cyril and Methodius Church.
Onesko, John '46 (PSC) Edison, NJ St. Nicholas Church.
Ong, Walter J. *s.j.* '46 (STL) [P] St. Louis, MO Jesuit Community Corporation at St. Louis University - Jesuit Hall.
Ongaro, Mario *m.c.c.j.* '51 (CIN) [M] Cincinnati, OH Comboni Missionaries (Verona Fathers)-Comboni Mission Center.
Onger, John '84 (JOL) Frankfort, IL St. Anthony Church.
Oniskiewicz, Mieczyslaw T. '92 (MAR) Engadine, MI Our Lady of Lourdes Church.
Ontiveros, Roy *o.carm.* '78 (GAL) [57] Houston, TX Our Lady of Mt. Carmel Church.
Onufer, Paul P. '59 (CAM) [5] Vineland, NJ St. Mary's Church.
Onuh, William I. '79 (ROC) [60] Rochester, NY St. Thomas More Church; Rochester, NY Monroe Community Hospital; Sonyea, NY Groveland Correctional Facility.
Onuoha, Anselm E. '83 (BRK) [21] Brooklyn, NY Blessed Sacrament Church.
Onuora, Felix *c.s.sp.* '79 (DM) [1] Des Moines, IA St. Ambrose Cathedral.
Onushco, William J. '76 (ALN) Weatherly, PA St. Nicholas Church.
Onwana, Jude '86 (CLV) [3] Akron, OH St. Bernard Church.
Onyango, Paul G. '80 (ARL) [2] Arlington, VA St. Agnes Church.
Onyebuchi, Martin (NY) [183] Bronx, NY St. Philip Neri Church.
Onyeihe, Cyprian I. '82 (NY) [132] Bronx, NY St. Barnabas Church.
Onyekwere, Michael '95 (STV) [4] Mt. Pleasant, VI Church of St. Joseph.
Onze, Robert E. '64 (BGP) [1] Stamford, CT St. John's Church.
Oommen, Joseph Valakuzhy *o.i.c.* '80 (SCR) [17] Scranton, PA St. Mary of the Assumption Church.
Oosbree, Christian Van '92 (SC) [4] Sioux City, IA St. Casimir Church; [5] Sioux City, IA St. Francis of Assisi Church; [6] Sioux City, IA Immaculate Conception Church.
Oosdyke, Raymond *o.f.m.conv.* '37 (GR) [4] Grand Rapids, MI St. Anthony of Padua Church.
Opalenick, Msgr. John '61 (PSC) Hazleton, PA St. John the Baptist Church.
Opalewski, Walter '85 (GLP) [4] Gallup, NM St. John Vianney Church.
Opara, Ben M. '85 (ARL) Falls Church, VA St. Anthony's Church.
Opat, Kenneth *o.s.c.* '69 (STP) Anoka, MN St. Stephen Church; [N] Anoka, MN Crosier Community of Anoka.
Opeil, Cyril *s.j.* '94 (BO) [W] Chestnut Hill, MA The Jesuit Community at Boston College.
Opem, Anthony '68 (SFS) Madison, SD St. Thomas Aquinas Church.
Ophals, Donald J. '61 (ALB) [3] Troy, NY St. Francis de Sales Church.

Opoka, Lloyd E. '68 (KC) Blue Springs, MO St. Robert Bellarmine Church.
Oppenheim, Frank M. *s.j.* '55 (CIN) [P] Milford, OH Milford Spiritual Center.
Oppenheimer, Daniel W. '91 (SCR) [M] Scranton, PA St. Gregory's Priory (Priestly Fraternity of St. Peter); [M] Elmhurst, PA Priestly Fraternity of St. Peter (F.S.S.P.).
Oppido, Harold J. *s.j.* '55 (NEW) [C] Jersey City, NJ St. Peter's Preparatory School.
Oppitz, Joseph '53 (PH) [135] Philadelphia, PA St. Peter the Apostle Church.
Opps, Francis J. '58 (ALN) Tower City, PA SS. Peter and Paul Church.
Oranczak, Ronald J. '78 (ALN) [3] Shenandoah, PA St. George Church; [5] Shenandoah, PA Our Lady of Mt. Carmel Church.
Orapankal, Abraham '83 (NY) Blauvelt, NY St. Catharine Church.
Oravec, Christian R. *t.o.r.* '64 (ALT) [A] Loretto, PA St. Francis College; [F] Loretto, PA St. Francis Friary, Third Order Regular of St. Francis of Penance.
Oravec, Gregory *o.s.b.* '44 (CLV) [P] Cleveland, OH Benedictine Order of Cleveland.
Oravecz, John '35 (RVC) Woodbury, NY Holy Name of Jesus Church.
Oravecz, John F. '35 (BRK) Retired; [U] Douglaston, NY Bishop Mugavero Residence.
Orbanek, Gerald L. '66 (E) [B] Erie, PA Gannon University; [M] Erie, PA Villa Maria.
Orchik, Michael J. '73 (BAL) [53] Baltimore, MD Little Flower, Shrine of Church.
Ordax, Emiliano '48 (MIA) [4] Hialeah, FL St. Cecilia Church.
Ordonez, Juan Alonso '58 (CGS) [3] Caguas, PR Sagrado Corazon de Jesus Church.
Orel, Paul '84 (PHX) [4] Glendale, AZ St. Louis The King Church; Special Assignment.
Orellana, Samuel '68 (LA) Gardena, CA St. Anthony of Padua Church.
Orengo, Juan Rodriguez '79 (PCE) [2] Ponce, PR Christ the King Church.
Oreshoski, Gary '88 (RC) Sturgis, SD St. Francis of Assisi Church.
Orf, Msgr. Raymond V. '55 (SPC) Lebanon, MO St. Francis De Sales Church.
Organ, Patrick C. '71 (VEN) North Port, FL San Pedro Church.
Oria, Enrique *o.c.* '58 (SJN) [61] San Juan, PR Santa Teresita Del Nino Jesus Church.
Oria, Manuel '57 (PCE) Retired.
Orians, David '85 (RC) Belle Fourche, SD St. Paul Church.
Orians, Thomas *s.a.* '92 (NY) [Z] Garrison, NY Franciscan Friars of the Atonement.
Orimaco, Domingo B. '72 (SFR) [3] South San Francisco, CA St. Augustine Church.
Oriole, Philip M. '70 (E) [19] Erie, PA St. John the Baptist Church.
Oris, Fabian G. '42 (GBG) Retired.
Orlandi, Joseph J. '73 (PAT) [11] Paterson, NJ St. Michael the Archangel Church.
Orlandi, Nazareno '61 (NEW) [5] Union City, NJ St. Rocco's Church.
Orlando, Gerard *c.p.* '46 (NY) [V] Bronx, NY St. Patrick's Home for the Aged and Infirm.
Orlando, Gerard A. *c.p.* '46 (MET) [H] South River, NJ Passionist Provincial Office.
Orlando, John V. (ALT) Retired.
Orlando, Richard J. '47 (ROC) [60] Rochester, NY St. Thomas More Church; Retired.
Orlando, Samuel W. '91 (CHL) Salisbury, NC Sacred Heart Church.
Orlando, Vincent A. *s.j.* '74 (GAL) [F] Houston, TX Strake, Jesuit College Preparatory Inc.
Orlett, Raymond *glmy.* '53 (CIN) [M] Fairfield, OH Headquarters of Glenmary Home Missioners.
Orlik, Dale A. '67 (SAG) [13] Saginaw, MI St. John Vianney Church.
Orlikiewicz, Stanley '53 (JOL) [1] Joliet, IL The Cathedral of St. Raymond.
Orlinski, Richard A. '73 (GRY) [4] Hammond, IN St. Catherine of Siena Church.
Orloski, Joseph F. '94 (SCR) [10] Scranton, PA Immaculate Conception Church.
Orloski, Raymond J. '62 (HBG) Kulpmont, PA Holy Angels Church.
Orlosky, Anselm *o.s.b.* '53 (PBR) Wall, PA Holy Trinity Church; [D] Butler, PA Holy Trinity Monastery.
Orlowski, Walter C. '79 (BGP) [5] Norwalk, CT St. Matthew Church.
Orlowsky, Michael T. '93 (ARL) Fredericksburg, VA St. Mary Church.
Ormaza, Antonio Liberman *s.c.s.* (DAL) [28] Dallas, TX Santa Clara Church.
Ormechea, John Baptist *c.p.* '65 (L) [2] Louisville, KY St. Agnes Church; [L] Louisville, KY Sacred Heart Retreat.
Ormond, Henry *o.carm.* (OAK) [B] Oakland, CA Holy Names College.
Ormond, Henry *o.carm.* '77 (JOL) [J] Darien, IL Carmelite Fathers Provincial Office.
Ormsby, Msgr. Basil A. '42 (BUF) Retired.
Ormsby, Owen J. *o.f.m.* '50 (PAT) [M] Ringwood, NJ Holy Name Friary.
Ornelas, Angel, Jr. '65 (CHY) Laramie, WY St. Laurence O'Toole Church.
Ornowski, Gerald *m.i.c.* (WDC) [B] Brookeville, MD Marian Novitiate; [B] Brookeville, MD Marian Spiritual Center.
Orobiourritia, Juan J. *o.a.r.* '43 (LA) [8] Los Angeles, CA Cristo Rey Church.
Oroquieta, Jose Maria *o.f.m.* '53 (FWT) [5] Fort Worth, TX Immaculate Heart of Mary Church.
Orosco, James S. '81 (DAL) [22] Dallas, TX St. Patrick Church.
Orozco, Argemiro '92 (YAK) Moses Lake, WA Our Lady of Fatima Church; Warden, WA Queen of All Saints Church.
Orozco, Raphael '50 (CHI) Palatine, IL Santa Teresita Vicariate Church.
Orozco, Raphael R. (CHI) Retired.
Orozco, Rodolfo '48 (FRS) Parlier, CA Our Lady of Sorrows Church.
Orr, Garrett D. *s.j.* '83 (WDC) [E] North Bethesda, MD Georgetown Preparatory School.
Orr, Jim '79 (PIT) Etna, PA All Saints Church.
Orr, Joseph T. '82 (ALT) McConnellsburg, PA St. Stephen's Church.
Orr, Sherman A. '91 (WCH) [4] Wichita, KS Christ the King Church; [B] Wichita, KS Bishop Mark K. Carroll High School.
Orr, Msgr. Stephen '74 (DM) West Des Moines, IA St. Francis of Assisi Church.
Orrico, Msgr. Caesar G. '43 (NEW) Emerson, NJ Church of the Assumption.
Orrico, Msgr. Caeser G. '43 (NEW) Retired.
Orru, Bruno *s.x.* '63 (PAT) [M] Wayne, NJ Xaverian Missionary Fathers.
Orsborn, Bruce '81 (SD) [6] San Diego, CA Holy Family Church.
Orsi, Cyril *o.p.* (HBG) Mechanicsburg, PA St. Joseph Church.
Orsi, Michael P. '76 (CAM) Westmont, NJ Holy Saviour Church.
Orsini, James '74 (HON) Kaunakakai, HI Molokai Catholic Community Church.
Orsini, Joseph E. '64 (CAM) Retired.
Orsino, Gordon *o.m.i.* '84 (NY) [BB] Newburgh, NY Our Lady of Hope Center.
Orsino, Jerry *o.m.i.* '66 (WDC) [B] Washington, DC Oblate College/Oblate Center for Mission Studies.
Orso, Claire Antonio *c.s.* '91 (CHI) Melrose Park, IL St. Charles Borromeo Church.
Orsolin, Vilmar *c.s.* '80 (VEN) Immokalee, FL Our Lady of Guadalupe Church.
Orsolits, Norbert F. '65 (BUF) [41] Buffalo, NY St. Lawrence Church; Buffalo, NY Buffalo General Hospital.
Orsulak, Thomas J. '90 (ALN) [11] Reading, PA St. Peter Church; [C] Reading, PA Holy Name High School.
Orsy, Ladislas *s.j.* '51 (NY) [Z] New York, NY Jesuit Community at Fordham University.
Orsy, Ladislas *s.j.* '51 (WDC) [M] Washington, DC The Jesuit Community at Georgetown University.
Orszulak, Henry A. '67 (BUF) [5] Lackawanna, NY St. Hyacinth Church.
Ortega, Eduardo '77 (SFE) Absent on Leave.
Ortega, Eduardo '95 (BWN) [4] Brownsville, TX Holy Family Church.
Ortega, Efren '72 (DAL) [18] Dallas, TX St. James Church.
Ortega, Manuel '76 (MIA) [3] Miami Beach, FL St. Mary Magdalen Church.
Ortega, Ovidio (SJN) Resident Chaplains; [E] Puerta De Tierra, PR Asylum For The Aged and Infirm.
Ortega, Russell A. *o.s.a.* '86 (BO) [9] Lawrence, MA St. Mary Immaculate Conception Church.
Ortega, Santos Leonel '96 (SB) Ontario, CA St. George Church.
Ortega, Vidal *o.s.a.* '65 (SJN) [42] San Juan, PR Ntra. Sra. de la Monserrate Church.
Ortega y Ortiz, Adam Lee '92 (SFE) Penasco, NM San Antonio de Padua Church.
Ortega-Ruiz, Augustin '93 (JOL) Glen Ellyn, IL St. Petronille Church.
Orteneau, Eugene F. *s.j.* '82 (BO) [W] Boston, MA The Society of Jesus of New England-Provincial Offices.
Ortez, Sofonias '96 (VEN) Bonita Springs, FL St. Leo Church.
Orth, Anthony F. '75 (PH) [147] Philadelphia, PA Stella Maris Church; [3] Bensalem, PA Saint Ephrem Church.
Orthel, Joseph A. '89 (SPC) [3] Springfield, MO Immaculate Conception Church.
Orthmann, James *o.c.s.o.* '94 (ARL) [J] Berryville, VA Cistercian Abbey of Our Lady of the Holy Cross.
Ortiz, Alex *c.ss.r.* '69 (BO) [13] Boston, MA Basilica of Our Lady of Perpetual Help.
Ortiz, Alexander F. *c.s.s.r.* '76 (PH) [25] Philadelphia, PA St. Boniface Church.
Ortiz, Alfredo (ORL) Mount Dora, FL St. Patrick's Church.
Ortiz, Angel '87 (MGZ) Cabo Rojo, PR St. Michael Church.
Ortiz, Arnold *o.s.j.* '72 (FRS) Madera, CA St. Joachim Church.
Ortiz, Benedicto '57 (BWN) Retired.
Ortiz, Edwin Rafael Hernandez '83 (CGS) Cidra, PR Nuestra Senora del Carmen Church.
Ortiz, Emerito '96 (WOR) [24] Worcester, MA St. Joan of Arc Church.
Ortiz, Msgr. Hector '33 (MGZ) Moca, PR Our Lady of Monserrate Church.
Ortiz, J.C. '91 (PHX) Sedona, AZ St. John Vianney Church.
Ortiz, Jose Antonio '85 (CGS) Aibonito, PR Church of St. Joseph.
Ortiz, Michael *s.c.j.* '56 (GAL) [34] Houston, TX Holy Name Church.
Ortiz, Miguel *o.f.m.cap* '86 (LA) Solvang, CA Old Mission Santa Ines Church.
Ortiz, Rodrigo *o.f.m.* '75 (FRS) [1] Fresno, CA St. John Cathedral.
Ortiz, Msgr. Romualdo M. '39 (MGZ) San German, PR San German de Auxerre Church; [A] San German, PR Hospital of the Immaculate Conception.
Ortiz, Victor Raul '86 (CGS) Barranquitas, PR San Andres Apostol Church.
Ortmann, William '57 (SD) [1] San Diego, CA St. Joseph Cathedral.
Ortmeier, Paul '72 (OM) Bloomfield, NE St. Andrew Church.
Ortmeier, Richard J. '56 (SFS) Retired.
Ortner, John W. *s.j.* '44 (NY) [Z] New York, NY Jesuit Community at Fordham University.
Ortner, Paul *s.s.j.* '45 (VEN) [D] Port Charlotte, FL Bon Secours-St. Joseph Hospital.
Ortner, Paul A. *s.s.j.* '45 (BAL) [M] Baltimore, MD St. Joseph Society of the Sacred Heart House of Central Administration.
Ortyl, Stanley E. '80 (NEW) Union, NJ Holy Spirit Church.
Oruche, Michael (BO) [5] Somerville, MA St. Clement Church.
Orumpakkat, James S. *c.m.i.* '64 (BEL) [5] Belleville, IL St. Henry Church; [H] Belleville, IL Poor Clare Monastery of Our Lady of Mercy.
Oryshkewych, Ostap '80 (PHU) [3] Philadelphia, PA St. Andrew Church; Retired.
Orzech, Eric S. '93 (CLV) Concord Twp., OH St. Gabriel Church.
Orzechowski, Aloysius M. *c.r.* '46 (CHI) [D] Chicago, IL Gordon Technical High School.
Orzechowski, Walter B. '49 (MIL) Retired.
Orzel, David J. '79 (SY) Boonville, NY St. Joseph Church.
Osbahr, Theodore '67 (NEW) Bloomfield, NJ Sacred Heart Church.
Osborn, Douglas '68 (LAN) [7] Flint, MI St. John Vianney Church.
Osborn, Michael A. '92 (KAL) Hartford, MI Immaculate Conception Church.
Osborn, William A. '66 (SFS) Hoven, SD St. Anthony of Padua Church.
Osborne, Francis J. *s.j.* '37 (BO) [W] Weston, MA Campion Health Center, Inc.
Osborne, Msgr. Francis M. '38 (LA) Encino, CA Our Lady of Grace Church; Retired.
Osborne, Herb (LEX) [D] Lexington, KY St. Joseph Hospital.
Osborne, Kenan B. *o.f.m.* '55 (OAK) [A] Berkeley, CA Franciscan School of Theology; [R] Berkley, CA Multicultural Institute.
Osborne, Martin J. '50 (RVC) Southold, NY St. Patrick's Church; Retired.
Osborne, Paul *o.f.m.* '64 (BUF) [59] Buffalo, NY SS. Rita & Patrick Church.
Osborne, Robert E. '54 (L) [58] Louisville, KY Our Lady of Lourdes Church; Louisville, KY Baptist Hospital East.
Osborne, Robert R. *s.m.* '66 (STL) [F] Kirkwood, MO Vianney High School.
Osborne, Ronald J. '83 (HRT) [6] East Hartford, CT St. Rose's Church.
Osborne, Stanley L. '59 (L) Cecilia, KY St. Ambrose Church; St. John, KY St. John the Baptist Church.
Osborne, Thomas *o.s.a.* '66 (JOL) New Lenox, IL St. Jude Church.
Osborne, Msgr. William J. '24 (BRK) [167] Queens, NY St. Fidelis Church; Retired.
Osburg, Frank C. '60 (LEX) [6] Lexington, KY St. Paul Church.
Osburg, Gregory E. (COV) Kenton, KY St. Matthew Church.
Osebold, Richard A. '60 (DET) [2] Redford, MI St. John Bosco Church.
Osendorf, Cassian *o.s.b.* '39 (SCL) [I] Collegeville, MN St. John's Abbey, of the Order of St. Benedict.
Oser, Donald '53 (Y) Retired.
Oser, Richard *s.j.* '92 (ORL) Eustis, FL St. Mary of the Lakes Church.

Oses, Jesus M. *c.m.* '65 (NY) [44] New York, NY Holy Agony Church; [Z] New York, NY Vincentian Fathers.
Osiander, Alfons M. '73 (BUF) Williamsville, NY SS. Peter and Paul Church; [A] East Aurora, NY Christ the King Seminary.
Osinski, Peter J. '69 (CAM) Pennsville, NJ Queen of the Apostles Church; [A] Carneys Point, NJ St. James High School.
Osinski, Ronald V. '72 (ALT) [2] Portage, PA Sacred Heart Church; [3] Portage, PA Assumption B.V.M. Church.
Oska, Krzysztof *s.ch.* '78 (WDC) [10] Silver Spring, MD Our Lady Queen of Poland and Saint Maximilian Kolbe Church.
Oslance, Michael E. '83 (STL) Washington, MO St. Francis Borgia Church.
Osle, Enrique *s.j.* '45 (MIA) [H] Miami, FL Jesuit Fathers of the Province of the Antilles, Inc.
Oslovich, Paul *c.ss.r.* (PH) [135] Philadelphia, PA St. Peter the Apostle Church.
Osorio, Celimo '87 (ELP) [34] El Paso, TX Sts. Peter and Paul Church; San Elizario, TX San Felipe de Jesus Church.
Osorio, Edison *c.s.* '95 (CHI) [N] Chicago, IL Scalabrini House of Theology.
Osorio, RudolfoEdward B. '55 (NEW) Retired.
Osowski, Chester J. '49 (LC) Arpin, WI St. Francis Church; Sigel, WI Holy Rosary Church; Vesper, WI St. James Church.
Ossa, Pedro Nel '63 (BRK) [90] Brooklyn, NY St. Nicholas Church.
Ossino, Angelo '57 (DEN) [3] Aurora, CO St. Pius X Church.
Ossola, John R. '64 (SFD) [1] Springfield, IL Cathedral of the Immaculate Conception.
Ossowski, Msgr. Casimir B. '37 (ALT) [7] Johnstown, PA St. Casimir's Church; Retired.
Ostaszewski, George '58 (PH) [85] Philadelphia, PA St. Ladislaus Church.
Ostatek, Albert P. *o.s.p.p.e.* '45 (PH) [Z] Doylestown, PA Pauline Fathers Monastery, Shrine of Our Lady of Czestochowa.
Ostdick, Rupert *o.s.b.* '48 (IND) [J] St. Meinrad, IN St. Meinrad Archabbey.
Ostdiek, Dan *o.p.* '60 (CHI) [4] Oak Park, IL St. Giles Church.
Ostdiek, Gil *o.f.m.* '60 (CHI) [N] Chicago, IL St. Joseph Friary.
Ostdiek, John *o.f.m.* '49 (FWT) [G] Crowley, TX St. Francis Village, Inc.; [H] Crowley, TX St. Maximilian Kolbe Friary.
Ostendorf, Mark G. '81 (SCL) Becker, MN Immaculate Conception Church.
Osterhage, Louis *c.pp.s.* (CIN) [17] Dayton, OH St. Joseph Church.
Osterhaus, Mark '85 (DUB) Worthington, IA St. Paul's Church.
Osterhout, Conrad *c.f.r.* '83 (NY) [Z] Yonkers, NY Saint Felix Friary; [Z] New York, NY St. Joseph's Friary.
Osterle, Paul V. *s.j.* '59 (SFE) [6] Albuquerque, NM Immaculate Conception Church.
Osterman, Gerald J. '67 (BO) [32] Boston, MA St. John-St. Hugh Church.
Osterman, Richard D. '69 (GF) Red Lodge, MT St. Agnes Church.
Ostertag, Robert C. *s.j.* '49 (MIL) [P] Wauwatosa, WI Jesuit Community at St. Camillus.
Ostini, Anthony *s.j.* '72 (BR) [J] Convent, LA Manresa, House of Retreats.
Ostrander, Gary L. '71 (OM) West Point, NE Assumption B.V.M. Church; [G] West Point, NE Franciscan Care Services, Inc., (d.b.a. St. Francis Memorial Hospital.
Ostrowski, David T. *o.s.b.* '89 (STP) [6] Minneapolis, MN Holy Cross Church.
Ostrowski, Eugene S. '77 (WH) [1] Wheeling, WV St. Joseph's Cathedral.
Ostrowski, Joseph C. '52 (SCR) [L] Elmhurst, PA St. Mary's Villa Nursing Home.
Ostrowski, Max J. '39 (GR) Retired.
Ostrowski, Theodore L. (CHI) [3] Chicago, IL St. Adrian Church.
Ostrowski, Walter *s.v.d.* '65 (PIT) [N] Pittsburgh, PA Society of The Divine Word.
Osuagwu, Denis A. *c.m.f.* (GAL) [21] Houston, TX St. Christopher Church.
Osuangwa, Peter Chidi '89 (BRK) [153] Queens, NY Ascension Church.
Osuch, Joseph C. *s.j.* '49 (DET) [P] Clarkston, MI Colombiere Center.
Osuch, Michael *c.r.* (CHI) [88] Chicago, IL St. Hyacinth Church.
Osuji, Boniface A.A. '66 (PH) Wayne, PA St. Isaac Jogues Church.
Osuji, Canice '79 (NY) [10] Yonkers, NY St. Joseph Church.
Osuji, Emmanuel '77 (LA) [65] Los Angeles, CA St. Gerard Majella Church.
Osuji, Ngozi '81 (NY) [82] New York, NY Notre Dame Church.
Osuji, Samuel '87 (LKC) [B] Lake Charles, LA St. Patrick Hospital of Lake Charles.
Osuji, Urban *c.m.* (CHI) [151] Chicago, IL Our Lady of Lourdes Church.
Osuna, E. Donald '63 (OAK) El Cerrito, CA St. Jerome's Church.
Oswald, Leo P. '78 (PH) Fairless Hills, PA St. Frances Cabrini Church.
Oswald, Norman R. '72 (MIL) Wood, WI Veterans Administration Medical Center.
Oswald, Richard S. '65 (LR) Rogers, AR St. Vincent de Paul Church.
Oswald, Ted '84 (SR) Lakeport, CA St. Mary Church.
Oswalt, Matthew Price '96 (OKL) Norman, OK St. Joseph's Church.
Otazua-Fena, Francisco *s.j.* '53 (SJ) [M] Los Gatos, CA Sacred Heart Jesuit Center.
Otellini, Msgr. Steven '78 (SFR) [10] San Francisco, CA St. Cecilia Church.
Oterino, Francis L. '87 (MET) On Duty Outside the Diocese.
Otero, Msgr. Henry '62 (WDC) [42] Washington, DC St. Thomas Apostle Church.
Otero, Jose (NY) [103] New York, NY St. Paul Church.
Otero, Manuel '62 (SJN) [48] San Juan, PR San Pio X Church.
Otero, Neil '49 (HRT) Retired.
Otillio, Peter *o.p.* '57 (CHI) [N] Chicago, IL Dominicans (Provincial Office).
Ott, Msgr. Alfred R. '60 (ALN) [1] Allentown, PA Cathedral of St. Catharine of Siena.
Ott, Francis M. '42 (GBG) Retired; [G] Greensburg, PA Neumann House.
Ott, Vincent *o.m.i.* (DUL) Garrison, MN Our Lady of Fatima Church; Hillman, MN Holy Family Church.
Ottelini, Msgr. Steven D. (SFR) [U] San Francisco, CA Catholics for Truth & Justice.
Otten, Lammert B. *s.j.* '65 (SEA) [A] Seattle, WA Seattle University.
Ottensmeyer, Hilary *o.s.b.* '50 (IND) [J] St. Meinrad, IN St. Meinrad Archabbey; [K] Beech Grove, IN Our Lady of Grace Monastery for Sisters of St. Benedict of Beech Grove, IN, Inc.
Ottenweller, Albert '43 (TOL) [1] Toledo, OH Queen of the Most Holy Rosary Cathedral.
Otterbacher, John *glmy.* '56 (CIN) [M] Fairfield, OH Headquarters of Glenmary Home Missioners.
Otterbein, Adam *c.s.s.r.* '51 (ALB) [L] Saratoga Springs, NY St. John Neumann Residence.
Otterbein, Adam J. *c.ss.r.* '40 (NY) [DD] Esopus, NY Holy Shroud Guild.
Otting, Loras C. '62 (DUB) Retired.
Ottman, Timothy *o.s.b.* '78 (HON) [H] Waialua, Oahu, HI Benedictine Monastery of Hawaii.
Otto, David C. '77 (KAL) Edwardsburg, MI Our Lady of the Lake Church.
Otto, John A. '39 (DAV) On Duty Outside the Diocese.
Otto, Leo '56 (SCL) Dent, MN Sacred Heart Church; Rush Lake, MN St. Lawrence Church; Retired.
Otto, Peter B. '77 (AMA) Military Chaplains.
Otto, Raymond *o.s.b.* '82 (SFS) Big Stone City, SD St. Charles Church; [F] Marvin, SD Blue Cloud Abbey.
Otto, Richard *o.f.m.conv.* '68 (MRY) [G] Arroyo Grande, CA St. Joseph's Cupertino Novitiate.
Ottoline, Robert A. '53 (STL) Retired.
Oubre, Carroll L. '91 (ARL) [7] Alexandria, VA St. Mary's Church.
Oubre, Louis T. '86 (BR) Morganza, LA St. Ann Church.
Ouderkirk, Lloyd Paul '59 (DUB) Garwin, IA St. Boniface Church; Marshalltown, IA St. Mary's Church.
Ouellet, Maurice F. *s.s.e.* '52 (VEN) [G] Englewood, FL Society of St. Edmund Residence.
Ouellette, Donald C. (WOR) Lunenburg, MA St. Boniface Church.
Ouellette, Donald C. '89 (WOR) [C] Fitchburg, MA St. Bernard's Central Catholic High School.
Ouellette, John C. '95 (CC) [1] Corpus Christi, TX Corpus Christi Cathedral.
Ouellette, Lionel P. '57 (BO) [3] Marlboro, MA St. Mary Church.
Ouellette, Raymond *s.m.* '52 (DET) [E] Harper Woods, MI Notre Dame High School.
Ouellette, Richard R. '75 (PRT) Grand Isle, ME St. Gerard-Mt. Carmel Church; Madawaska, ME St. David's Church.
Ouellette, Richard T. '63 (SEA) [M] Seattle, WA Maryknoll Fathers.
Ouellette, Roger J. '42 (PRT) Retired; [I] Waterville, ME Mt. St. Joseph Priest Retirement Home.
Ouellette, Vincent L. '63 (MAR) Ishpeming, MI St. Joseph Church.
Ouillette, Arthur A. '55 (WOR) Jefferson, MA St. Mary's Church.
Ouimet, J. Lawrence '74 (NOR) [2] Norwich, CT Sacred Heart Church.
Oulds, John V. '68 (PH) [4] Coatesville, PA St. Stanislaus Kostka Church.
Ouletta, James F. '60 (CHI) Lake Villa, IL Prince of Peace Church.
Oulvey, William T. *s.j.* '85 (STL) [P] St. Louis, MO Bellarmine House of Studies; [P] St. Louis, MO The Jesuits of the Missouri Province.
Ours, Donald *c.m.* '94 (CHI) [211] Chicago, IL St. Vincent de Paul Church; [C] Chicago, IL Vincentian Community at DePaul University.
Ours, Robert A. '80 (SY) [1] Endicott, NY Our Lady of Good Counsel Church; Special Assignment; [C] Binghamton, NY Seton Catholic Central High School of Broome County.
Oury, Dom Guy-Marie *o.s.b.* '54 (BUR) [H] Westfield, VT Monastery of the Immaculate Heart of Mary.
Ousepparampil, Sebastian '76 (NY) [99] New York, NY Our Lady of Victory Church.
Outlaw, S. Keith '89 (NY) [131] Bronx, NY St. Augustine Church.
Ovalle, Thomas *o.m.i.* '77 (SAT) [C] San Antonio, TX Oblate School of Theology; [M] San Antonio, TX De Mazenod House; [O] San Antonio, TX Oblate Renewal Center.
Overbaugh, Msgr. Hugh A. '61 (HBG) [2] Harrisburg, PA St. Catherine Laboure Church.
Overbaugh, Msgr. Lawrence R. '55 (HBG) [5] Mount Carmel, PA Our Lady of Mount Carmel Church.
Overbeck, Jerome T. *s.j.* '74 (CHI) [C] Chicago, IL Jesuit Community at Loyola University of Chicago.
Overberg, Kenneth *s.j.* '73 (CIN) [P] Milford, OH Milford Spiritual Center.
Overend, James *c.m.f.* '77 (LA) [R] Rancho Dominguez, CA Dominguez Seminary Inc.
Overman, Conleth *c.p.* (ORL) [F] Orlando, FL Bethany House of Beutel.
Overman, Msgr. Robert F. '45 (STL) Retired.
Overmann, William J. '62 (SFD) North Arm, IL St. Aloysius Church; Paris, IL St. Mary Church.
Oviedo, Francisco *o.a.r.* '25 (NY) [179] Bronx, NY Our Saviour Church; [187] Bronx, NY St. Roch Church.
Owambo, Cyril (NY) Ossining, NY St. Ann Church.
Owen, David (FWT) Absent on Leave.
Owen, John J. '48 (BIR) Retired.
Owens, Benjamin *c.ss.r.* '75 (OAK) [C] Oakland, CA Bishop O'Dowd High School.
Owens, Bernard J. *s.j.* '72 (DET) [P] Bloomfield Hills, MI Manresa Jesuit Retreat House.
Owens, Edward *o.ss.t.* (LA) [A] Camarillo, CA St. John's Seminary.
Owens, Edward M. '36 (JC) Retired.
Owens, Jesse *c.s.b.* '67 (GAL) [Q] Sugar Land, TX Basilian Mission Center.
Owens, John '48 (BIR) Trussville, AL Holy Infant of Prague Church.
Owens, John J. '60 (BIS) Menoken, ND St. Hildegard Church.
Owens, Joseph P. *s.j.* '48 (CLV) Cleveland, OH Cleveland Clinic Hospital; [C] Cleveland, OH John Carroll Jesuit Community.
Owens, Leroy E. '64 (BO) [1] Framingham, MA St. Bridget Church.
Owens, Michael J. '84 (HON) Pearl City, HI Our Lady of Good Counsel Church.
Owens, Msgr. Peter J. '58 (SY) [9] Binghamton, NY St. Patrick Church.
Owens, S. Brian '95 (WH) [7] Wheeling, WV St. Alphonsus Church; [4] Fairmont, WV St. Joseph's Church.
Owens, Thomas J. '74 (PH) [A] Wynnewood, PA Theological Seminary of St. Charles Borromeo, Overbrook.
Owens-Howard, Robert J. '74 (CHR) Retired.
Owlrich, Robert E. '89 (DEN) On Duty Outside the Archdiocese.
Owusu-Boateng, Johnson '85 (VIC) Cuero, TX St. Michael Church.
Oya, Msgr. Eufrasio (SJN) Retired.
Oyabu, Charles *s.m.* '70 (HON) Kahului, HI Christ the King Church.
Oyama, Michel *s.s.* (WDC) [A] Washington, DC Theological College of the Catholic University of America.
Oyanguren, Angel *c.m.* '53 (LA) [29] Los Angeles, CA Our Lady of the Rosary of Talpa Church.
Oyarbide, Pedro '62 (CGS) Humacao Playa, PR Nuestra Senora del Carmen Church.
Oyeyipo, Anthony (BO) [32] Boston, MA St. John-St. Hugh Church.
Oyler, George F. '57 (L) Retired.
Ozalas, Msgr. Michael C. '39 (SCR) Retired.
Ozanne, Thomas *c.pp.s.* '74 (KC) Liberty, MO St. James Church; [J] Liberty, MO Precious Blood Center.
Ozbun, John W. '84 (WIN) Slayton, MN St. Ann's Church.
Ozimek, Adam Z. '94 (ATL) [3] Atlanta, GA Holy Spirit Church.
Ozimek, Anthony *o.s.b.* '68 (CLV) [P] Cleveland, OH Benedictine Order of Cleveland.
Ozimek, Anthony *osm* '68 (GF) [K] Billings, MT St. Vincent de Paul Society of Yellowstone County.
Ozimek, Anthony J. *osb* '68 (GF) [G] Billings, MT Saint Vincent Hospital and Health Center.
Ozimek, Eugene F. '45 (SPR) Retired.
Ozimek, Joseph J. '47 (CLV) [5] Barberton, OH Sacred Heart Church.
Ozminkowsi, Clyde R. *o.carm.* '54 (KCK) Richmond, KS St. Therese Church; Scipio, KS St. Boniface Church.

Ozug, John C. '77 (FR) [11] Fall River, MA Sacred Heart Church.

P

Paa, Donald R. '47 (KC) Retired.
Paa, Joseph F. '41 (BUF) Retired.
Paa, Msgr. Raymond F. '55 (BUF) Harris Hill, NY Nativity of the Blessed Virgin Mary Church.
Paala, Jonathan '75 (SFR) [34] San Francisco, CA St. Monica Church.
Pabin, Chester '92 (STU) Marietta, OH St. Mary's Church; Miltonsburg, OH St. John the Baptist Church.
Pable, Martin *o.f.m.cap.* '58 (MIL) [Y] Milwaukee, WI House of Peace.
Pabon, Jose R. Oquendo '80 (CGS) Ceiba, PR San Antonio de Padua Church.
Pabst, Peter J. *s.j.* '86 (PHX) [B] Phoenix, AZ Brophy College Preparatory.
Pacacha, Joseph E. '45 (NY) Retired.
Pace, David F. '78 (OAK) [K] Hayward, CA St. Rose Hospital; [O] Hayward, CA Sisters of St. Joseph of Wichita, KS.
Pace, Paul J. '66 (HRT) [10] Waterbury, CT St. Francis Xavier's Church.
Pace, William J. '51 (SCR) Retired; [N] Dunmore, PA Villa St. Joseph.
Pace, Woodrow H. '95 (LC) [2] Wausau, WI St. Anne Church; [C] Wausau, WI Newman High School; [D] Wausau, WI Wausau Area Catholic Schools.
Pacheco, Agostinho S. '60 (BWN) [2] McAllen, TX Our Lady of Sorrows Church.
Pacheco, Alexandre '68 (STO) Turlock, CA Sacred Heart Church.
Pacheco, Andres *c.ss.r.* '84 (MGZ) [2] Mayaquez, PR Our Lady of Mt. Carmel Church.
Pacheco, Mario '76 (LA) Covina, CA Sacred Heart Church.
Pacheco-Sanchez, Luis '79 (MIL) [N] West Allis, WI Villa Clement Health Center.
Pachence, Ronald A. '74 (SAV) On Duty Outside the Diocese.
Pachence, Ronald A. '74 (SD) [B] San Diego, CA University of San Diego.
Pachla, Stanley L., Jr. '83 (DET) Eastpointe, MI St. Veronica Church.
Pacho, Jesus '51 (PCE) [1] Ponce, PR Cathedral of Our Lady of Guadalupe.
Pacholec, Daniel S. '96 (SPR) [4] Springfield, MA Holy Cross Church.
Pachorek, Joseph J. (CHI) [61] Chicago, IL St. Florian Church; Retired.
Pacini, Mario *s.a.c.* '66 (ALB) [T] Cohoes, NY Apostolate for the Suffering.
Paciorek, Joseph C. *c.m.* '35 (HRT) [6] Meriden, CT St. Stanislaus Church; [M] Manchester, CT DePaul Provincial Residence.
Pacitti, Gary (PH) Holland, PA St. Bede the Venerable Church.
Packard, Nathan '87 (SCL) Hillman, MN St. Rita's Church; Wahkon, MN Sacred Heart Church.
Packard, Walter E. '71 (E) Warren, PA St. Joseph Church.
Pacocha, Edwin D. '62 (CHI) [46] Chicago, IL St. Cornelius Church.
Pacudan, Roland '83 (HON) Makakilo, HI St. Jude Church.
Pacwa, Mitchell *s.j.* '76 (DAL) [D] Dallas, TX Jesuit College Preparatory School.
Paczek, Valerian '34 (FAR) Retired.
Paczesny, John R. '61 (MIL) Whitefish Bay, WI St. Monica's Church; [K] Milwaukee, WI St. Mary's Hospital of Milwaukee; [K] Mequon, WI St. Mary's Hospital Ozaukee, Inc.
Paczkowski, Vincent *s.d.b.* (NY) [117] New York, NY St. Thomas the Apostle Church.
Padavick, William B. '63 (CLV) Oberlin, OH Sacred Heart Church.
Padazinski, C. Michael '88 (SFR) Special Assignment.
Padberg, John R. *s.j.* '41 (STL) [O] St. Louis, MO Fusz Pavilion.
Padberg, John W. *s.j.* '57 (STL) [P] St. Louis, MO Jesuit Community Corporation at St. Louis University - Jesuit Hall; [W] St. Louis, MO Institute of Jesuit Sources; [W] St. Louis, MO Seminar on Jesuit Spirituality.
Paddack, John N. '84 (NY) [53] New York, NY Incarnation Church; [E] New York, NY Cardinal Hayes High School.
Padden, Neil *o.f.m.* '55 (SP) [O] St. Petersburg, FL St. Anthony Friary.
Paddock, Richard W. '59 (RCK) Elburn, IL St. Gall Church.
Padelli, Emilio P. '62 (HRT) [4] East Hartford, CT St. Isaac Jogues Church.
Padilla, Aquino '60 (SFR) [3] San Mateo, CA St. Matthew Church.
Padilla, Gilbert '55 (TUC) Mammoth, AZ Blessed Sacrament Church.
Padilla, Norberto *c.m.f.* '90 (SJN) [9] Bayamon, PR San Jose Church.
Padilla, Rafael '89 (VEN) Cape Coral, FL St. Andrew Church.
Padilla, Steven V. '79 (DEN) [27] Denver, CO St. Catherine of Siena Church.
Padilla Ruiz, Juan Pablo '96 (P) Woodburn, OR St. Luke Church.
Padinjarepeedika, Jose L.F. *c.m.i.* '72 (LAF) Melville, LA St. John the Evangelist Church.
Pado, Thomas '75 (ORG) Irvine, CA St. Elizabeth Ann Seton Church.
Padovani, Martin *s.v.d.* '60 (TR) [M] Bordentown, NJ Society of the Divine Word.
Padovano, Louis A. *s.j.* '69 (NY) [Z] New York, NY Jesuit Provincial's Office.
Padrez, Mark C. *o.p.* (OAK) Antioch, CA Holy Rosary Church.
Padron, Julio Victor Garcia '89 (SJN) Catano, PR Santa Rosa de Lima Church.
Paduch, Frank '89 (BEA) Sour Lake, TX Our Lady of Victory Church.
Padula, Armand *o.f.m.* '56 (NY) [BB] Wappingers Falls, NY Mt. Alvernia Retreat House.
Pafchik, Lawrence F. *o.f.m.* '42 (PAT) [M] Ringwood, NJ Holy Name Friary.
Pagan, Alberto *o.p.* '93 (SJN) Catano, PR Nuestra Senora del Carmen Church.
Pagan, Angel '80 (ARE) [2] Manati, PR Our Savior Church.
Pagan, Tomas '83 (ARE) Morovis, PR St. Paul Apostle Church.
Pagano, Bernard T. '58 (WIL) On Duty Outside the Diocese.
Pagano, Peter E. '52 (SPR) Retired.
Page, Anthony '69 (LA) [50] Los Angeles, CA St. Brendan Church; [D] Los Angeles, CA Bishop Conaty-Our Lady of Loretto High School.
Page, Charles T. '91 (KAL) Mattawan, MI St. John Bosco Church.
Page, David '58 (ORL) Indialantic, FL Holy Name of Jesus Church.
Page, Hugh H. '80 (FTW) [B] Notre Dame, IN University of Notre Dame Du Lac.
Page, Leon J. '56 (DET) [4] Sterling Heights, MI St. Jane Frances de Chantal Church.
Page, Msgr. Raymond J. '46 (WOR) Retired.
Page, Stephen C. '87 (DAV) Fairfield, IA St. Mary's Church.
Page, Thomas P. '79 (GR) Big Rapids, MI St. Paul's Campus Parish Church; On Special Assignment.
Pagel, John M. '80 (CHL) On Duty Outside the Diocese.
Pagel, John M. '80 (SAT) [62] San Antonio, TX St. Philip of Jesus Church.
Pageot, Roger *s.s.s.* '53 (NY) [8] New York, NY St. Andrew Church.
Pagliara, Alfonso *o.f.m.cap.* '81 (CHL) Hendersonville, NC Immaculate Conception Church.
Pagliari, Robert *c.ss.r.* '75 (STL) [P] Liguori, MO Liguori Mission House/Redemptorists.
Pagliari, Robert M. *c.ss.r.* '75 (ORL) [F] New Smyrna Beach, FL Redemptorist Fathers of the Vice Province of Richmond.
Pagliuca, Joseph P. '43 (BUR) Retired.
Pagnotta, James V. '69 (NEW) [13] Jersey City, NJ St. Joseph's Church.
Pagone, Joseph '55 (WDC) Retired.
Pagones, Peter N. '68 (ALB) Averill Park, NY St. Henry Church.
Pahamtang, Leonardo '77 (SAC) Vallejo, CA St. Vincent Ferrer Church.
Pahl, Norman *o.m.i.* '58 (DUL) Willow River, MN St. Mary's Church; Willow River, MN Youth Conservation Camp.
Pahler, Robert E. '57 (CLV) Green, OH Queen of Heaven Church.
Pai, Simon (RVC) Retired.
Paiano, Angelo *s.j.* '90 (NY) [Z] New York, NY West Side Jesuit Community.
Paider, Paul '92 (GB) Kaukauna, WI Holy Cross Church.
Paik, Francis M. '54 (CLV) [1] Euclid, OH St. Christine Church; Retired.
Paillacho, Jose Joffre '87 (MOB) Dothan, AL St. Columba Church.
Painter, Emmett B. *s.j.* '75 (P) Rainier, OR Nativity B.V.M. Church; [L] Portland, OR Jesuit Provincial Office (Oregon Prov.).
Painter, George F. *m.m.* '44 (NY) [Z] Maryknoll, NY Maryknoll Fathers and Brothers.
Paisley, James J. '85 (SCR) Laflin, PA St. Maria Goretti Church.
Paiva, Antonio M. '49 (PRO) [25] Providence, RI Our Lady of the Rosary Church.
Paiz, William *c.m.f.* '79 (ORG) [2] Orange, CA La Purisima Church.
Pajk, Thomas J. '87 (CLV) Gates Mills, OH St. Francis of Assisi Church.
Pajkos, James *o.f.m.* '58 (JOL) [10] Joliet, IL SS. Cyril and Methodius Church.
Pakalniskis, John L. '39 (BRK) Retired; [U] Douglaston, NY Bishop Mugavero Residence.
Pakenham, Daniel J. '65 (MIL) Elm Grove, WI St. Mary's Church.
Pakianather, Aloysius P. '78 (RVC) Valley Stream, NY Blessed Sacrament Church.
Pakiz, Rudolph '46 (DUL) Tower, MN St. Martin's Church.
Pakosta, Francis '52 (SUP) Retired.
Pakula, Michael G. '73 (PEO) Geneseo, IL St. Malachy's Church.
Pakulniewicz, Msgr. Raphael F. '50 (NY) [196] Staten Island, NY St. Anthony Church.
Pakutka, Msgr. William J. '43 (SCR) Retired; [N] Dunmore, PA Villa St. Joseph.
Pala, Francis *sch.p.* '55 (MIA) [C] Fort Lauderdale, FL Cardinal Gibbons High School.
Pala, Manuel Soler *m.ss.cc.* '70 (SJN) [10] Bayamon, PR San Juan Bautista de la Salle Church.
Palacino, Joseph '82 (BGP) [1] Norwalk, CT St. Jerome Church.
Palacio, Fernando '79 (MGZ) [7] Mayaquez, PR Santa Teresita Church.
Palacios, Joseph M. *s.j.* '87 (OAK) [N] Berkeley, CA Jesuit Community at Jesuit School of Theology at Berkeley.
Palacios, Joseph W. '87 (LA) On Duty Outside the Archdiocese.
Palacioz, Robert '87 (WCH) Newton, KS Our Lady of Guadalupe Church.
Palackal, Joseph *c.m.i.* (BRK) [242] Queens, NY St. Stanislaus Kostka Church.
Palad, Pio C. '47 (KNX) [3] Chattanooga, TN St. Jude Church.
Paladino, John J.F. '91 (NEW) [4] Hoboken, NJ SS. Peter and Paul's Church; [Q] Hoboken, NJ Stevens Institute of Technology; [Q] Jersey City, NJ Jersey City State College.
Palafox, Lorenzo J. *s.j.* '67 (SAC) [C] Sacramento, CA Jesuit High School; [H] Carmichael, CA Jesuit High School Community of Sacramento.
Palamattathil, George '86 (OAK) [3] Walnut Creek, CA St. Mary's Church.
Palaming, Ernest *o.f.m.cap.* '78 (SAT) [73] San Antonio, TX Senyor Santo Nino de Cebu Church.
Palang, Mansueto P. '77 (BR) Belle Rose, LA St. Jules Church.
Palardy, William B. '85 (BO) [A] Boston, MA St. John's Seminary School of Theology.
Palaroan, Moises (STA) Keystone Heights, FL St. William Church.
Palasits, John A. '58 (NEW) South Orange, NJ Our Lady of Sorrows Church.
Palazzolo, Anthony P. '93 (STA) [20] Jacksonville, FL San Jose Church.
Palcheck, Gerald F. '67 (SD) Descanso, CA Our Lady of Light Church.
Palcisko, Raymond '58 (CR) Roseau, MN Sacred Heart Church.
Paleari, Giorgio *p.i.m.e.* '75 (DET) [K] Detroit, MI P.I.M.E. College Community; [K] Detroit, MI P.I.M.E. Missionaries of SS. Peter and Paul.
Palen, Robert L. '41 (DUB) Retired.
Palepale, Marisi *ss.cc.* '86 (HON) Lahaina, HI Maria Lanakila Church.
Palermo, Albert A. '63 (AUS) [2] Austin, TX St. Albert The Great Church.
Palermo, Albert A. '63 (MIL) On Duty Outside the Archdiocese.
Palermo, Angelo *s.a.c.* '34 (NEW) [S] South Orange, NJ The Pallottines of South Orange, Inc.
Palermo, Angelo *s.a.c.* '60 (NY) [221] Staten Island, NY Our Lady Star of the Sea Church.
Palermo, Frank C. '55 (SPC) [2] Springfield, MO Holy Trinity Church; Springfield, MO Diocesan Hospital Ministry.
Palermo, Joseph S. '94 (NO) Harahan, LA St. Rita Church.
Paliathayil, Rubin R. '79 (BR) [9] Baton Rouge, LA St. George Church.
Palick, George '58 (PIT) [1] Butler, PA St. Fidelis of Sigmaringen Church.
Paliokas, Algirdas *s.j.* '73 (CHI) [2] Lemont, IL Blessed Jurgis Matulaitis Church; [N] Chicago, IL Lithuanian American Jesuits.
Palis, Theo '45 (OAK) Pittsburg, CA Our Lady Queen of the World Church.
Paliwoda, Steven '94 (SJP) [8] Lorain, OH St. John the Baptist Church.
Palka, Bernard *s.a.* (NY) [Z] Garrison, NY Generalate of the Franciscan Friars of the Atonement-St. James Friary.
Palka, Bernard *s.a.* '72 (NY) [W] Garrison, NY St. Christopher's Inn; [Z] Garrison, NY Franciscan Friars of the Atonement.
Palka, Bogdan *s.d.s.* '92 (NEW) [4] Garfield, NJ St. Stanislaus Kostka Church.
Palka, Edwin '96 (SP) [2] Tampa, FL Christ the King Church.
Palko, John A. '54 (PIT) Retired.
Palko, John J. '67 (ALT) Hollidaysburg, PA St. Mary's Church.
Palko, Thomas J. *o.s.f.s.* '59 (VEN) [6] Fort Myers, FL Our Lady of Light Church.

Palkowski, Jan '76 (PH) Clifton Heights, PA Sacred Heart Church.
Palladino, Msgr. Alfonso G. '43 (BO) Melrose, MA St. Mary of the Annunciation Church; Retired.
Palladino, Robert J. '58 (P) Gresham, OR St. Henry Church; Sandy, OR St. Michael Church.
Pallard, John *o.m.i.* '72 (WDC) [B] Washington, DC Oblate College/Oblate Center for Mission Studies.
Pallardy, James G. '87 (PEO) Andalusia, IL St. Patrick's Church.
Pallas, Raymond A. *s.j.* '46 (SJ) [M] Los Gatos, CA Sacred Heart Jesuit Center.
Palliparambil, Jose Simon '62 (RVC) Plainview, NY Central General Hospital.
Pallivathuckal, Joseph '73 (MIA) Hollywood, FL Nativity Church.
Pallivathukkall, Jacob M. '65 (PT) Fort Walton Beach, FL St. Mary Church.
Pallo, Joseph L. '61 (LR) Blytheville, AR Immaculate Conception Church; Osceola, AR St. Matthew's Church; [L] Blytheville, AR Immaculate Conception Trust Fund.
Palluck, M. Charles '66 (SEA) Black Diamond, WA St. Barbara Church.
Palma, Gregory *o.f.m.* '40 (ALB) [A] Catskill, NY St. Anthony Friary.
Palma, Raul *sch.p.* '58 (LA) [21] Los Angeles, CA Our Lady Help of Christians (Maria Auxiliadora) Church; [R] Los Angeles, CA Piarist Fathers.
Palmatier, David *o.s.b.* '57 (RCK) [H] Aurora, IL Marmion Abbey-St. Augustine's Abbey.
Palmeno, Alberto *o.s.a.* '68 (CC) [17] Laredo, TX St. Vincent de Paul Church.
Palmer, Edwin G. '56 (KAL) Battle Creek, MI St. Jerome Church.
Palmer, Frank '62 (DM) Indianola, IA St. Thomas Aquinas Church.
Palmer, Herbert *o.s.b.* '39 (SD) [H] Oceanside, CA Prince of Peace Abbey, Benet Hill.
Palmer, John *c.s.v.* '71 (JOL) [A] Lisle, IL Benedictine University.
Palmer, Martin E. *s.j.* '64 (STL) [P] St. Louis, MO Jesuit Community Corporation at St. Louis University - Jesuit Hall.
Palmer, Michael C. '63 (BGP) Wilton, CT Our Lady of Fatima Church.
Palmer, Michael J. '70 (STL) [23] St. Louis, MO St. Ambrose Church.
Palmer, Patrick J. '48 (SAT) Canyon Lake, TX St. Thomas the Apostle Church.
Palmer, Richard D. *o.s.a.* '87 (CHI) [N] Olympia Fields, IL The Augustinian Provincialate Tolentine Center.
Palmer, Ronald L. '80 (PEO) [O] Normal, IL St. Robert Bellarmine Newman Center, Illinois State University.
Palmer, Samuel '57 (DM) Urbandale, IA St. Pius X Church.
Palmer, Msgr. Thomas M. '58 (SAT) LaCoste, TX Our Lady of Grace Church.
Palmese, Anthony '76 (ORL) [4] Ocala, FL St. Jude's Church.
Palmieri, Alexander J. '76 (PH) Conshohocken, PA SS. Cosmas and Damian Church; [A] Wynnewood, PA Theological Seminary of St. Charles Borromeo, Overbrook.
Palmieri, Frank *c.r.m.* '62 (CHR) Goose Creek, SC Immaculate Conception Church.
Palmieri, John A. '41 (BO) Retired.
Palmieri, Louis R. '93 (BO) Abington, MA St. Bridget Church.
Palmieri, Luigi '67 (ALN) [7] Allentown, PA St. Paul Church.
Palmieri, Luigi '67 (JC) On Duty Outside the Diocese.
Palmieri, Thaddeus *o.f.m.* '48 (NY) [Z] New York, NY Franciscan Province of the Immaculate Conception.
Palmigiano, James *o.c.s.o.* '88 (WOR) [N] Spencer, MA St. Joseph's Abbey.
Palmigiano, James M. *s.j.* '88 (BO) [W] Boston, MA The Society of Jesus of New England-Provincial Offices.
Palmiotto, Paul (BRK) [159] Queens, NY St. Bonaventure's Church.
Palmiotto, Paul C. (BRK) [156] Queens, NY St. Benedict, the Moor Church.
Palmisano, Peter J. '93 (NEW) Oradell, NJ St. Joseph's Church.
Palmitessa, Paul '56 (SD) [13] San Diego, CA Our Lady of Mt. Carmel Church.
Palo, Anthony *o.carm.* '64 (NEW) Englewood, NJ St. Cecilia's Church.
Paloma, Victor '70 (NEW) [5] Bayonne, NJ St. Vincent de Paul Church.
Palombo, Albert B. '42 (PH) [100] Philadelphia, PA Mater Dolorosa Church; Retired.
Palomino, Esviardo '49 (NY) [67] New York, NY St. Lucy Church.
Palomino, Ignacio '85 (HBG) [3] Lancaster, PA Assumption of the Blessed Virgin Mary Church; [J] Lancaster, PA Iglesia de San Juan Bautista.
Palos, Anthony *o.a.r.* '60 (ORG) [3] Santa Ana, CA Our Lady of Guadalupe Church.
Palsa, Steven '79 (PIT) Wexford, PA St. Alexis Church.
Palubinskas, Vytautas A. '54 (BRK) [9] Brooklyn, NY Annunciation of the Blessed Virgin Mary Church.
Paluck, Casimir A. *o.s.b.* '61 (BIS) Fort Yates, ND St. Peter - Catholic Indian Mission Church; Selfridge, ND St. Philomena Church.
Palumbo, Jospeh '93 (LA) [2] North Hollywood, CA St. Charles Borromeo Church.
Palumbo, Richard W. '93 (MET) Somerville, NJ Immaculate Conception Church; [L] Phillipsburg, NJ The Anawim Community.
Palumbos, Edward L. '72 (ROC) [12] Rochester, NY St. Charles Borromeo Church.
Paluse, Richard V. '42 (PIT) Retired.
Palys, Daniel J. '69 (BUF) Blossom, NY St. Gabriel Church.
Pambello, Louis '81 (NEW) Montclair, NJ Immaculate Conception Church; Montclair, NJ Mountainside Hospital.
Pamment, Duaine H. '64 (LAN) Laingsburg, MI St. Isidore Church.
Pamment, Gary W. '63 (KAL) Wayland, MI St. Therese Church.
Pamplaniyil, Matthew (FAR) [1] Fargo, ND St. Mary's Cathedral.
Pan, Philip *o.p.* '84 (WDC) [B] Washington, DC Dominican House of Studies.
Panagia, Sal J. '73 (PAT) [13] Paterson, NJ Our Lady of Pompei Church.
Panagoplos, Christopher *t.o.r.* '76 (ALT) [12] Johnstown, PA SS. Peter and Paul's Church; Johnstown, PA Memorial Hospital; Johnstown, PA Lee Hospital.
Panahal, John Bosco '70 (JOL) West Chicago, IL St. Mary Church.
Panakal, Thomson '60 (JOL) [2] Lockport, IL St. Dennis Church.
Panares, Auxentius '62 (WDC) Mount Rainier, MD St. James Church; Washington, DC Washington Hospital Center; Hospital & Nursing Home Ministries.
Panchuk, Myron '82 (STN) [3] Chicago, IL SS. Volodymyr and Olha Church.
Pancorbo, Msgr. Marcos A. '58 (PCE) [1] Ponce, PR Cathedral of Our Lady of Guadalupe; [1] Ponce, PR Church Our Lady of Miraculous Medal; [H] Penuelas, PR Training School for the Lay Apostolate (Hermanos Cheos).
Panczuk, Bernard '63 (STF) New York, NY St. George Church.
Pandarathikudiyil, Sebastian *v.c.* '88 (NY) Highland Mills, NY St. Patrick Church.
Pandola, Oreste '69 (BAL) [52] Baltimore, MD St. Leo Church; [M] Baltimore, MD Pallottine Center for Apostolic Causes.
Pandolfo, Anthony '60 (STU) Retired.
Pandolfo, Lawrence *o.p.* '39 (NO) Jefferson, LA Elmwood Medical Center.
Pane, Andrew '87 (NY) Absent on Leave.
Panek, Edward B. '91 (CHI) [140] Chicago, IL St. Monica Church.
Panek, Robert M. '70 (NY) Military Chaplains.
Panepinto, Vincent '67 (ROC) Willard, NY Drug Treatment Center.
Paner, Robert (TR) Colts Neck, NJ Naval Weapons Station Earle.
Pangelinan, Ferdinand *o.f.m.cap.* '81 (AGN) [F] Agana Heights, GU St. Fidelis Friary.
Pangratz, Clement H. *o.s.b.* '47 (SEA) [M] Lacey, WA St. Martin's Abbey.
Paniagua, Jose L. '62 (MIA) [3] Hialeah, FL St. Benedict Church.
Paniagua, Pablo '59 (SAT) [62] San Antonio, TX St. Philip of Jesus Church.
Paninski, John (PEO) [M] Georgetown, IL LaSalette Missionaries.
Paninski, John *m.s.* '61 (PEO) Georgetown, IL St. Isaac Jogues Church.
Pank, Julian F. '40 (L) Retired.
Pank, William H. '40 (L) Retired.
Panke, Robert '96 (WDC) Olney, MD St. Peter Church.
Pankiw, Roman '86 (PHU) [6] Philadelphia, PA St. Josaphat's Church.
Panos, Msgr. Patrick G. '68 (PAT) Ringwood, NJ St. Catherine of Bologna Church.
Pansini, Francis David *c.m.* '42 (LA) [R] Los Angeles, CA Vincentian Fathers and Brothers.
Pansza, Ralph C. *c.m.* '68 (CHI) [C] Chicago, IL Vincentian Community at DePaul University.
Pantaleo, Daniel C. (PH) [C] Philadelphia, PA LaSalle University.
Pantano, Salvatore *o.f.m.conv.* '51 (ALB) [12] Albany, NY Our Lady of Angels Church.
Panthalani, Thomas '64 (LKC) De Ridder, LA St. Joseph's Church.
Pantle, G. Donald *s.j.* '60 (SCR) [C] Scranton, PA University of Scranton.
Pantyra, Anthony F. *m.s.* '78 (KAL) Bangor, MI Sacred Heart of Jesus Church.
Panula, Arne A. '73 (SFR) [T] San Francisco, CA Opus Dei.
Panuska, Joseph A. *s.j.* '60 (SCR) [C] Scranton, PA University of Scranton.
Panyadimai, Simon '82 (NY) Wappingers Falls, NY St. Mary Church.
Panza, Msgr. Paul D. (ALT) Retired.
Panza, Robert S. '83 (HBG) Camp Hill, PA Good Shepherd Church.
Panzer, Joel S. '94 (LIN) [4] Lincoln, NE North American Martyrs Church.
Paoli, Livius *o.s.b.* '37 (DET) [71] Detroit, MI St. Scholastica Church; [K] Detroit, MI St. Sylvester Monastery.
Paolicelli, Lawrence M. '84 (NY) [E] New York, NY Cardinal Spellman High School; [DD] New York, NY Legion of Mary, Office.
Paolo, Francis de Sales *o.f.m.* (BO) [57] Boston, MA Our Lady of Mt. Carmel Church.
Paolo, Francis DeSales *o.f.m.* '58 (BO) [W] Boston, MA St. Christopher Friary.
Paolozzi, Joseph L. '61 (MEM) Martin, TN St. Jude's Church; [L] Martin, TN Cooperative Ministries Interfaith Center.
Paone, Ernest C. '57 (PIT) On Duty Outside the Diocese.
Paonessa, Ralph *o.f.m.* '63 (NY) [Z] New York, NY Franciscan Province of the Immaculate Conception.
Papa, Charles E. '67 (RVC) Medford, NY St. Sylvester Church.
Papa, Christopher J. '89 (PH) [106] Philadelphia, PA St. Monica Church.
Papa, Dominic *c.p.* '60 (BRK) [U] Jamaica, NY Immaculate Conception Monastery.
Papa, Frank *s.o.l.t.* '89 (CC) [H] Robstown, TX Society of Our Lady of the Most Holy Trinity.
Papa, Frank E. *s.o.l.t.* '89 (HRT) [5] East Hartford, CT St. Mary's Church.
Papaj, Joseph J. *s.j.* '70 (NY) [F] New York, NY Loyola School; [Z] New York, NY St. Ignatius Loyola Residence.
Papalia, Pasquale '74 (PSC) Somerset, NJ SS. Peter and Paul Church.
Papalia, Pasquale A. '74 (NEW) On Duty Outside the Archdiocese.
Pape, William '70 (ALB) [1] Albany, NY Cathedral of the Immaculate Conception.
Papen, Gerald T. *c.s.c.* '63 (FTW) [J] South Bend, IN Congregation of Holy Cross Indiana Province Provincial House.
Papera, Lewis V. '67 (NEW) Rochelle Park, NJ Sacred Heart Church.
Paperini, Richard '77 (P) [A] St. Benedict, OR Mount Angel Seminary; [A] St. Benedict, OR Mount Angel Seminary.
Papes, Joseph T. '59 (GF) On Duty Outside of the Diocese.
Papes, Louis M. '88 (CLV) East Cleveland, OH Christ the King Church.
Papes, Rudy *c.ss.r.* '65 (GR) [3] Grand Rapids, MI St. Alphonsus Church.
Papesh, Michael L. '83 (STP) [5] St. Paul, MN Holy Spirit Church.
Papiernik, Roman J. '40 (LC) Retired.
Papineau, Andre *s.d.s.* '65 (MIL) [B] Hales Corners, WI Sacred Heart School of Theology.
Papp, Christopher '86 (WIL) Military Chaplains.
Papp, Edward E. '60 (OG) Brushton, NY St. Mary Church.
Paprocki, John L. '59 (NEW) Fort Lee, NJ Madonna Church.
Paprocki, Thomas J. '78 (CHI) [1] Chicago, IL Cathedral of the Holy Name.
Paquet, Hubert J. '55 (PRT) Limerick, ME St. Matthew Church.
Paquet, Joseph A. *s.j.* '59 (BO) [W] Weston, MA Campion Health Center, Inc.
Paquet, Michael *o.s.c.* '78 (STP) Anoka, MN St. Stephen Church; [N] Anoka, MN Crosier Community of Anoka.
Paquet, Robert J. *s.j.* '45 (CHL) [9] Charlotte, NC St. Peter Church; [J] Charlotte, NC Jesuit Community.
Paquette, Francis '57 (DUL) Silver Bay, MN St. Mary's Church.
Paquette, Joseph R. '78 (PRO) [31] Providence, RI St. Thomas Church.
Paquette, Neil *o.c.s.o.* '94 (DUB) [K] Peosta, IA New Melleray Abbey, Order of Cistercians of the Strict Observance.
Paquin, Ronald H. '73 (BO) Absent on Sick Leave.
Paradis, Donald L. *m.s.* '58 (PRO) [B] Newport, RI Salve Regina University.
Paradis, Robert M. *o.m.i.* '37 (MAN) [K] Colebrook, NH Shrine of Our Lady of Grace.
Paradis, Msgr. Wilfrid '49 (MAN) [11] Manchester, NH St. John the Baptist Church.
Paradis, Msgr. Wilfrid H. '49 (MAN) Retired.
Parambi, Thomas Seraphin *c.s.t.* (NY) [177] Bronx, NY Our Lady of Solace Church.
Paramo, Raymond *c.s.b.* '66 (DET) [E] Redford, MI Catholic Central High School.
Paramo, Thomas *c.m.f.* '56 (CHI) [N] Oak Park, IL Claretian Fathers Headquarters of U.S.A. Eastern Province.
Parampath, Joseph K. '53 (BGP) Easton, CT Notre Dame of Easton Church; Weston, CT St. Francis of

Assisi Church.
Paraniuk, Michael '81 (CIN) [15] Cincinnati, OH St. Bernard Church; [K] Cincinnati, OH Franciscan Hospital, Western Hills Campus; [K] Cincinnati, OH Franciscan Hospital, Mt. Airy Campus.
Parappally, James '59 (MIA) [5] Pompano Beach, FL St. Gabriel Church.
Parappully, Jose *s.d.b.* '78 (SFR) [8] San Francisco, CA St. Brendan Church.
Parchem, Peter *o.f.m.conv.* '51 (MRY) Pismo Beach, CA St. Paul the Apostle Church.
Pardee, Charles D. '84 (JC) Boonville, MO SS. Peter and Paul Church.
Pardue, John D. '88 (SHP) [10] Shreveport, LA St. Pius X Church.
Pare, Arthur H. *s.j.* (PRT) [9] Portland, ME St. Pius X Church.
Pare, Arthur H. *s.j.* '60 (BO) [W] Boston, MA The Society of Jesus of New England-Provincial Offices.
Pare, Jean Dominique *o.p.* '41 (FR) [12] Fall River, MA St. Anne's Church.
Pare, Paul M. '53 (PRT) Richmond, ME St. Ambrose Church.
Pare, Paul U. '52 (PRT) Retired.
Paredes, Edmundo '85 (DAL) [15] Dallas, TX St. Cecilia Church.
Parekkat, Winson *c.m.i.* '72 (PH) [39] Philadelphia, PA St. Dominic Church.
Parel, Joseph '57 (HRT) Northford, CT St. Monica's Church.
Parella, Francis J. *s.s.p.* '47 (BUF) [O] Derby, NY Society of St. Paul Provincial Residence.
Parello, Joseph J. '74 (SJN) On Duty Outside the Archdiocese.
Parent, Basil R. '86 (NTN) Danbury, CT St. Ann Church.
Parent, J. Wilfrid '91 (WDC) Waldorf, MD St. Peter Church.
Parent, Norman *o.m.i.* '64 (MIA) Opa Locka, FL St. Monica Church.
Parent, Philip *s.m.* '81 (BO) [W] Cambridge, MA Our Lady of Mercy Marist Novitiate.
Parent, Philip *s.m.* '81 (RC) Standing Rock, SD Standing Rock Reservation Church.
Parent, Rene L. *m.s.* '76 (NOR) Jewett City, CT St. Mary Church.
Parent, Royal J. '56 (PRT) Boothbay Harbor, ME Our Lady, Queen of Peace Church.
Parente, Lino S. *o.cist.* '65 (TR) Mount Laurel, NJ St. John Neumann Church; [M] Mount Laurel, NJ Cistercian Monastery of Our Lady of Fatima.
Parente, Michael *s.a.c.* '47 (CAM) Hammonton, NJ St. Joseph's Church.
Parenteau, William J. '70 (TUC) Tombstone, AZ Sacred Heart Church.
Parenti, Robert J. '72 (TR) Manasquan, NJ St. Denis Church.
Parenti, Thomas '74 (SFR) Kentfield-Greenbrae, CA St. Sebastian Church.
Parenza, John Anthony '50 (DET) [H] Livonia, MI St. Mary Hospital; [K] Detroit, MI St. Paul of the Cross Community, Congregation of the Passion.
Paret, Joaquin '82 (MIA) Miami Springs, FL Blessed Trinity Church.
Paret, John J. *s.j.* '51 (ALB) [O] Auriesville, NY Shrine of Our Lady of Martyrs.
Parham, William J. '76 (MEM) Brownsville, TN St. John Church; Jackson, TN St. Mary's Church.
Pariante, Mario *s.m.* '90 (HON) [B] Honolulu, HI Chaminade University of Honolulu; [D] Honolulu, HI St. Louis School; [H] Honolulu, HI Center Marianist Community.
Parillo, Emery *o.f.m.* '55 (ALB) [3] Watervliet, NY Our Lady of Mt. Carmel Church.
Parina, Jesus '63 (SFR) [2] San Rafael, CA St. Isabella Church.
Paris, Benedetto J. '95 (MAR) Norway, MI St. Mary Church; Vulcan, MI St. Barbara Church.
Paris, Charles W. '55 (WIL) Retired.
Paris, John *s.j.* '69 (BO) [W] Chestnut Hill, MA The Jesuit Community at Boston College.
Paris, John U. '50 (BO) [4] Malden, MA St. Peter Church; [E] Needham, MA St. Sebastian's Country Day School, Inc.
Paris, Joseph *o.m.i.* '53 (SFD) [A] Godfrey, IL Immaculate Heart of Mary Novitiate.
Paris, Thomas *m.s.* '46 (FR) [K] Attleboro, MA La Salette Shrine.
Parise, Michael '79 (BO) [1] Malden, MA Immaculate Conception Church.
Parish, John G. '84 (LA) On Duty Outside the Archdiocese.
Parisi, Enrique *o.f.m.* '60 (LA) [72] Los Angeles, CA St. Joseph Church.
Parisi, Frank J. '85 (RVC) Smithtown, NY St. Patrick Church.
Parisi, Joseph L. '74 (STL) West Overland, MO St. Jude Church.
Parisi, Michael (PAT) Military Chaplains.
Parisi, Michael R. '55 (BRK) Special Assignment.
Parisi, Salvador *o.f.m.* '54 (MRY) Jolon, CA San Antonio Mission Church; San Miguel, CA San Miguel Church; [G] San Miguel, CA Franciscan Friars, O.F.M.; [I] San Miguel, CA San Miguel Retreat House.
Parizek, Msgr. James F. '72 (DAV) [M] Davenport, IA St. Vincent Center; [P] Davenport, IA Quad Cities Catholic Deaf Ministry.
Park, Augustin C. '61 (NEW) [6] Orange, NJ St. Andrew Kim Church.
Park, Augustine '92 (MIL) [Y] Milwaukee, WI Korean Catholic Community.
Park, Austin *s.j.* '55 (LKC) Kinder, LA St. Philip Neri Church.
Park, John '82 (ORL) [1] Orlando, FL St. James Cathedral.
Park, John '93 (BRK) [226] Queens, NY St. Paul Chong Ha-Sang Roman Catholic Chapel.
Park, John Jong-Man '82 (SJ) [2] Sunnyvale, CA Sts. Andrew and Paul Korean Catholic Mission of San Jose Church.
Park, Jung-Woo '91 (NY) [Z] New York, NY Jesuit Community at Fordham University.
Park, Morton '52 (P) [35] Portland, OR St. Stephen Church.
Park, Robert G. '57 (WH) [1] Wheeling, WV St. Joseph's Cathedral.
Park, Thomas *o.s.b.* '65 (SEA) Seattle, WA Veterans Administration Medical Center.
Park, Thomas R. *o.s.b.* '65 (SEA) [M] Lacey, WA St. Martin's Abbey.
Parke, Frederick '75 (STA) Bunnell, FL St. Stephen Church; Palm Coast, FL St. Elizabeth Ann Seton Church.
Parke, James E. '65 (RIC) [1] Virginia Beach, VA Church of the Ascension.
Parker, Charles '71 (PHX) [C] Phoenix, AZ St. Joseph's Hospital and Medical Center.
Parker, Edmond L '56 (BO) Acton, MA St. Elizabeth of Hungary Church.
Parker, Frank J. *s.j.* '73 (BO) [W] Chestnut Hill, MA The Jesuit Community at Boston College.
Parker, George '83 (NOR) North Grosvenordale, CT St. Joseph Church.
Parker, Glenn D. *c.ss.r.* (STA) [6] Jacksonville, FL Holy Rosary Church.
Parker, James '82 (CHR) [15] Charleston, SC Church of the Holy Spirit.
Parker, John W. '70 (CHI) [11] Chicago, IL St. Andrew Church.
Parker, Kenneth '65 (R) Retired.
Parker, Larry '84 (WCH) [E] Pittsburg, KS Mount Carmel Medical Center; Mount Carmel Foundation.
Parker, Michael J. (BUF) [1] Tonawanda, NY St. Amelia Church.
Parker, Paul M. '82 (BO) [A] Weston, MA Pope John XXIII National Seminary.
Parker, Richard (SB) [B] Riverside, CA Notre Dame High School.
Parker, Rick '77 (OKL) On Duty Outside the Archdiocese.
Parker, Theodore K. *o.s.c.* '72 (NY) [4] New York, NY All Saints Church; [Z] New Rochelle, NY Crosier (Canons Regular of the Order of the Holy Cross).
Parker, Thomas '85 (SR) On Leave.
Parker, Thomas P. *s.s.c.* '47 (LA) [R] Los Angeles, CA Columban Fathers, Procure House.
Parker, William C. '64 (TOL) Walbridge, OH St. Jerome Church.
Parker, William J. *c.ss.r.* '73 (WCH) [G] Wichita, KS Redemptorist Community; [I] Wichita, KS Spiritual Life Center.
Parkes, Joseph P. *s.j.* '76 (NY) [F] New York, NY Fordham Preparatory School; [Z] New York, NY Jesuit Community at Fordham University.
Parkinson, Forrest T. '94 (RVC) Deer Park, NY SS. Cyril and Methodius Church.
Parkos, John F. '64 (STP) Maple Grove, MN St. Joseph the Worker Church.
Parks, Jonathan *s.d.b.* '78 (NO) [4] Harvey, LA St. Rosalie Church.
Parks, Msgr. Joseph K. '39 (BRK) [115] Brooklyn, NY St. Patrick Church; Retired; [V] Brooklyn, NY Monastery of the Sisters Adorers of the Precious Blood.
Parks, Richard E. '59 (BAL) [86] Baltimore, MD Sacred Heart of Mary Church.
Parks, Richard L. *c.p.* '70 (L) [L] Louisville, KY Sacred Heart Retreat.
Parlanti, Gregory J. '82 (PH) [A] Wynnewood, PA Theological Seminary of St. Charles Borromeo, Overbrook.
Parle, Richard '56 (SEA) Lacey, WA Sacred Heart of Jesus Church.
Parlette, Thomas L. '89 (DAV) Knoxville, IA St. Anthony's Church; Melcher, IA Sacred Heart Church; Pella, IA St. Mary's Church.
Parlsi, Michael '73 (BRK) [189] Queens, NY St. Kevin Church.
Parmar, Francis *s.j.* '79 (WDC) [M] Washington, DC The Jesuit Community at Georgetown University.
Parme, George J. '48 (PIT) Retired; [N] Pittsburgh, PA St. John Vianney Manor.
Parmisano, Fabian *o.p.* '53 (OAK) [N] Oakland, CA Dominican Order (Western Province), St. Albert's Priory.
Parnassus, Msgr. George J. '53 (LA) West Hollywood, CA St. Victor Church.
Parnell, Dennis R. *s.j.* '93 (SJ) [B] Santa Clara, CA Santa Clara University.
Paroh, Paul *o.f.m.conv.* '85 (FTW) LaGrange, IN St. Joseph Church.
Paron, William J. '69 (STP) New Prague, MN St. Wenceslaus Church.
Parr, John L. '78 (LC) Special Assignment; [I] La Crosse, WI Holy Cross (Seminary) Diocesan Center.
Parr, Norman B. '50 (OM) [36] Omaha, NE SS. Peter and Paul Church.
Parr, Raymond A. '39 (MIL) Retired.
Parra, Jesus A. '93 (LA) Lomita, CA St. Margaret Mary Alacoque Church.
Parrales, Napoleon J. '57 (SD) On Duty Outside the Diocese.
Parrini, Warren (RVC) Retired.
Parrish, Bryan K. '88 (BO) Wellesley, MA St. Paul Church.
Parrish, Francis J. *s.j.* '42 (LA) [R] Los Angeles, CA Columbiere House.
Parrotta, Arthur J. '50 (MAR) Retired.
Parry, Charles '81 (WDC) Hyattsville, MD St. Mark Church; Pastoral Center Special Ministries.
Parsch, David '80 (SAG) Alma, MI St. Mary Church.
Parsienïczyk, Stanley '68 (BO) [4] Salem, MA St. John the Baptist Church.
Parson, Donald J. (BAL) Ellicott City, MD Resurrection Church.
Parsons, Harold J. '29 (NY) Retired.
Parsons, Harry E. '56 (PIT) New Brighton, PA Holy Family Church.
Parsons, Myles *o.f.m.cap.* '43 (NY) [98] New York, NY Our Lady of Sorrows Church.
Parsons, Neil J. *c.p.* '37 (SAC) [H] Citrus Heights, CA Christ the King Retreat.
Parsons, Samuel *o.p.* '57 (OAK) [A] Berkeley, CA Dominican School of Philosophy and Theology.
Parsons, Samuel R. *o.p.* '57 (SFR) [N] San Francisco, CA St. Dominic Priory.
Partee, Chrysostom *o.f.m.* '50 (SFE) Jemez Pueblo, NM San Diego Indian Missions Church.
Partensky, Leonard J. (DET) Retired.
Parthie, Ralph R. *o.f.m.* '75 (NO) [P] New Orleans, LA Franciscan Fraternity.
Partida, Rafael A. '86 (SB) Indio, CA Our Lady of Perpetual Help Church.
Partika, Richard '51 (DUL) [12] Duluth, MN St. Margaret Mary Church.
Partridge, Bede *o.s.b.* '58 (P) [L] St. Benedict, OR Mt. Angel Abbey.
Partridge, Donald F. '90 (NY) [165] Bronx, NY St. Mary Star of the Sea Church.
Partridge, Francis C. '60 (GAY) Boyne City, MI St. Matthew Church; Boyne Falls, MI St. Augustine Church.
Partusch, Frank A. '72 (OM) [2] Omaha, NE St. Adalbert Church; [33] Omaha, NE Our Lady of Lourdes Church.
Parvensky, Msgr. Andrew D. '50 (PBR) Monessen, PA Assumption of the Blessed Virgin Church.
Parzymies, Joseph K. '77 (HRT) [6] Meriden, CT St. Stanislaus Church.
Pasadilla, Nicholas '72 (GAL) [13] Houston, TX St. Benedict the Abbot Church.
Pascale, Anthony '58 (HON) Retired.
Pascazi, Louis F. '80 (PIT) Sewickley, PA St. James Church.
Paschak, Patrick *o.s.b.m.* '47 (STF) New York, NY St. George Church.
Pasche, Fred *o.f.m.conv.* '64 (L) Pleasure Ridge Park, KY St. Paul Church.
Pasciak, Marcel J. '74 (CHI) [197] Chicago, IL St. Symphorosa and Seven Sons Church.
Pasciuto, Joseph D. '91 (BRK) [98] Brooklyn, NY Our Lady Help of Christians Church.
Pasciutto, Joseph (NY) City, NY Spofford Juvenile Center.
Pascoe, Louis B. *s.j.* '64 (NY) [Z] New York, NY Jesuit Community at Fordham University.
Pascual, Antonio S. '60 (RVC) East Rockaway, NY St. Raymond's Church.
Pascual, Elias *o.carm.* '51 (ARE) Morovis, PR Nuestra Senora del Carmen Church.
Pascual, Lope '82 (MET) [B] New Brunswick, NJ Shoreless Lake School; [H] New Village, NJ Society of Jesus Christ the Priest; [H] Raritan, NJ Clairvaux House.
Pascual, Manuel '46 (FRS) Retired.
Pascucci, Philip *s.d.b.* '51 (NY) [Z] New Rochelle, NY Salesian Provincial House.
Pasek, Timothy *o.f.m.conv.* '75 (BRK) [146] Queens, NY St. Adalbert Church.
Pash, Joseph '48 (SPK) Retired.
Pashak, Lawrence M. '63 (SAG) Freeland, MI St. Agnes Church.
Pashby, John J. (BO) Society of St. James the Apostle.

Pashley, Msgr. Wilfred J. '63 (PH) [143] Philadelphia, PA St. Rose of Lima Church.
Pasiecznik, Marcel M. *o.f.m.* '37 (PIT) [N] Ben Avon, PA St. Anthony Friary and Mission House.
Pasieczny, Roman '80 (DET) [4] St. Clair Shores, MI St. Joan of Arc Church.
Pasiewala, Jan *s.a.c.* '76 (BUF) [23] Buffalo, NY St. Florian Church.
Pasik, Mark A. '76 (SY) [4] Endicott, NY St. Casimir Church.
Paska, Walter '47 (PHU) Millville, NJ St. Nicholas Church.
Paskert, Leonard '36 (STL) [T] Dittmer, MO Il Ritiro-The Little Retreat.
Paskey, Robert V. *s.j.* (PRT) Bingham, ME St. Peter's Church.
Paskowicz, Marian '54 (ALN) Retired.
Pasley, Robert C. '82 (CAM) Collingswood, NJ St. John's Church; [A] Cherry Hill, NJ Camden Catholic High School.
Pasqualetto, Vicente *s.t.* '70 (SJN) [4] Canovanas, PR Santa Maria Madre de Dios Church.
Pasquinelli, Msgr. Frederick A. '52 (STU) [8] Steubenville, OH St. Pius X Church; Retired.
Passalacqua, Robert '84 (SJ) Campbell, CA St. Lucy Church.
Passamonte, Philip B. '67 (RVC) Absent on Leave.
Passarella, Msgr. Anthony F. '42 (BRK) [11] Brooklyn, NY St. Anthony of Padua-St. Alphonsus Church; Retired.
Passarelli, Msgr. Robert S. '52 (BAL) Hagerstown, MD St. Mary Church; Retired.
Passauer, Gregory '86 (E) Franklin, PA St. Patrick Church.
Passenant, Francis J. '79 (BRK) [210] Queens, NY Our Lady of Fatima Church; Released from Diocesan Assignment.
Passenant, Frank (NY) City, NY Correctional Institution for Men; City, NY West Facility.
Passeri, Richard *o.f.m.* (BO) [42] Boston, MA St. Leonard of Port Maurice Church.
Passero, Ernest *s.j.* '70 (BUR) Derby Line, VT St. Edward Church.
Passero, Ernest F. *s.j.* '70 (BO) [W] Boston, MA The Society of Jesus of New England-Provincial Offices.
Pastick, Joseph A. (CHI) Retired.
Pastirik, Joachim *o.s.b.* '69 (CLV) [E] Cleveland, OH Benedictine High School; [P] Cleveland, OH Benedictine Order of Cleveland.
Pastizzo, Michael H. *s.j.* '70 (BUF) [O] Buffalo, NY Canisius Jesuit Community.
Pastor, Eduardo '50 (MIA) [27] Miami, FL St. Michael the Archangel Church.
Pastorius, Vance *o.f.m.cap.* '60 (BAL) Cumberland, MD SS. Peter and Paul Church; [M] Cumberland, MD SS. Peter and Paul Friary.
Pastro, Vincent '78 (SEA) [1] Tacoma, WA St. Ann Church; [5] Tacoma, WA St. John of the Woods Church; [15] Tacoma, WA Sacred Heart Church.
Pastucci, Anthony '80 (VEN) Bradenton, FL SS. Peter and Paul the Apostles Church.
Paszko, John M. '74 (MIA) [3] Hialeah, FL St. Benedict Church.
Patacconi, Noel *o.s.b.* '32 (DET) [33] Detroit, MI Holy Family Church; [K] Detroit, MI St. Sylvester Monastery.
Patala, William S. '56 (STU) Retired.
Patalano, Anthony *o.p.* '86 (P) [18] Portland, OR Holy Rosary Parish & Dominican Priory Church.
Patat, St. John E. '42 (CHR) Retired.
Patella, Michael *o.s.b.* '90 (SCL) [I] Collegeville, MN St. John's Abbey, of the Order of St. Benedict.
Patenaude, Andre *m.s.* '69 (FR) [K] Attleboro, MA La Salette Provincial House.
Patenaude, Gilbert A. '46 (PRT) Retired.
Patenaude, Laurent '43 (PRT) [I] Waterville, ME Mt. St. Joseph Priest Retirement Home.
Patenaude, Laurent O. '43 (PRT) Retired.
Pater, Aurel '90 (ROM) Chicago, IL Ss. Peter and Paul Mission Church; East Chicago, IN St. Nicholas Church.
Pater, Daniel R. '79 (CIN) On Duty Outside the Archdiocese.
Pater, Giles H. '58 (CIN) [46] Cincinnati, OH St. John Fisher Church.
Pater, Thomas '42 (WDC) [C] Washington, DC Catholic University of America, The.
Pater, Thomas G. '42 (CIN) Retired.
Paterno, Salvatore D. '64 (BRK) Released from Diocesan Assignment.
Paternoster, Alejandro '94 (LFT) Muncie, IN St. Mary Church.
Pates, Msgr. Richard E. '68 (STP) [12] Minneapolis, MN Our Lady of Peace Church.
Patete, Michael A. '62 (NEW) [5] Bayonne, NJ St. Vincent de Paul Church.
Pathe, Eugene W. '56 (PT) [11] Pensacola, FL St. Mary Church.
Pathiyamoola, Paul '70 (SFS) Watertown, SD Immaculate Conception Church.
Patil, Gabriel M. *c.r.s.p.* '72 (ALN) [K] Bethlehem, PA The Barnabite Fathers Barnabite Spiritual Center.
Patillo, Bennie J. '67 (BEA) Port Neches, TX St. Elizabeth Church.
Patin, Paul B. *s.j.* '73 (GAL) [3] Spring, TX St. Ignatius of Loyola Church.
Patino, Ruben M. *c.s.p.* '79 (LA) Goleta, CA St. Mark University Parish Church; [BB] Los Angeles, CA Archdiocesan Office for Campus Ministry.
Patnode, Msgr. Michael '72 (CR) Bemidji, MN St. Philip's Church; [F] Bemidji, MN Holy Spirit Newman Center.
Patnode, Ronald J. '61 (YAK) Wenatchee, WA St. Joseph's Church.
Patout, Rivers A. '67 (GAL) [4] Houston, TX St. Alphonsus Church.
Patragnoni, Ettore '42 (CLV) Retired.
Patras, Adam *o.s.b.* '94 (OM) [K] Schuyler, NE Benedictine Mission House.
Patricius, J. M. (NEW) [8] Bayonne, NJ St. Michael's Church; Bayonne, NJ Bayonne Hospital.
Patrick, Ernest '46 (PT) [2] Pensacola, FL Little Flower Church.
Patrick, Ernest E. '46 (PT) Retired.
Patrick, John E. '67 (MAR) [5] Marquette, MI St. Michael Church.
Patrick, Mary *s.c.m.c.* (NOR) [B] Uncasville, CT St. Bernard High School.
Patrick, Maurice '33 (SFS) Retired.
Patrick, Richard Martin *o.p.* '65 (GAL) [J] Houston, TX St. Joseph Hospital; [Q] Houston, TX Dominican Fathers and Brothers, St. Mark Priory, Inc.
Patrick, William '57 (ORG) [F] Fullerton, CA St. Jude Medical Center.
Patrick, William J. '58 (CLV) Released from Diocesan Assignment.
Patriquin, Garry '84 (PIT) [J] Pittsburgh, PA St. Francis Central Hospital.
Patriquin, Garry G. '84 (PIT) [11] Pittsburgh, PA Epiphany Church; Allegheny County, PA St. Francis Central.
Patrizi, Vincent M. '52 (CC) [10] Corpus Christi, TX Our Lady Star of the Sea Church.
Patrizio, Anthony *m.ss.cc.* '66 (CAM) [L] Linwood, NJ Villa Pieta.
Patron, Charles '62 (SB) Temecula, CA St. Catherine Church
Patron, Juan (SJN) [5] Toa Baja, PR San Pedro Apostol Church
Patrylak, T. Frank '62 (PHU) [2] Philadelphia, PA Protection of Blessed Virgin Mary Church; Clifton Heights, PA SS. Peter and Paul Church.
Patte, Steven W. '69 (CHI) [76] Chicago, IL St. Helena Church.
Pattee, Daniel *t.o.r* '87 (STU) [A] Steubenville, OH Franciscan University of Steubenville; [F] Steubenville, OH Holy Spirit Monastery.
Patterson Alfred *o.s.b.* '90 (E) St. Marys, PA St. Mary Church.
Patterson Bernard J. *o.s.b.* '44 (BIR) [E] Cullman, AL St. Bernard Abbey.
Patterson Bernardin *o.s.b.* '53 (IND) [J] Indianapolis, IN St. Maur Priory.
Patterson, Bernardin J. *o.s.b.* '53 (NEW) [N] Newark, NJ Newark Abbey.
Patterson, Bruce A. '86 (ORG) Costa Mesa, CA St. John the Baptist Church.
Patterson, Msgr. Charles H. '51 (JC) Westphalia, MO St. Joseph Church.
Patterson, David L. '68 (ATL) On Duty Outside the Archdiocese.
Patterson, Frank '67 (SAV) [1] Columbus, GA Holy Family Church.
Patterson, Herbert *o.f.m.* '34 (LA) [P] Los Angeles, CA St. Anne's.
Patterson, James *c.ss.r.* '54 (STL) [P] Liguori, MO Liguori Mission House/Redemptorists.
Patterson, Patrick E. *c.pp.s.* '65 (CIN) [M] Dayton, OH Provincial House of the Cincinnati Province of the Society of the Precious Blood.
Patterson, Randall P. '70 (ALB) [9] Troy, NY Our Lady of Victory Church.
Patterson, Richard '89 (LA) Arcadia, CA Holy Angels Church.
Patterson, Robert A. '71 (STP) Osseo, MN St. Vincent de Paul Church; Minneapolis, MN Abbott-Northwestern Hospital; Minneapolis, MN Minneapolis Children's Medical Center.
Patterson, Robert J. '58 (NEW) [1] Orange, NJ St. John's Church.
Patterson, Ronald '64 (LIN) [K] Lincoln, NE Calvary Cemetery and Mausoleum Association.
Patterson, Ronald E. '64 (LIN) [5] Lincoln, NE Sacred Heart Church.
Patterson, Terrence R. '66 (OG) Retired.
Patterson, William C. '51 (COL) New Boston, OH St. Monica Church; Portsmouth, OH Holy Redeemer Church; Wheelersburg, OH St. Peter Church.
Patti, Angelo J. '82 (ALT) Everett, PA St. John the Evangelist Church.
Pattison, Msgr. Francis '58 (SD) [35] San Diego, CA St. Rita Church.
Pattok, Raymond J. '48 (GR) Retired.
Patton, James J. '65 (CLV) Perry, OH St. Cyprian Church.
Patton, Mel *o.s.b.* '56 (IND) [J] St. Meinrad, IN St. Meinrad Archabbey.
Patton, Mel *o.s.b.* '56 (SFS) [G] Yankton, SD Sacred Heart Monastery.
Patton, Patrick G. '78 (HEL) Military Chaplains.
Pattussi, Roque R. *c.s.* (BO) [5] Framingham, MA St. Tarcisius Church.
Paturzo, Louis S. '73 (HRT) [2] Bristol, CT St. Anthony's Church; [4] Bristol, CT St. Joseph Church.
Paul, Alexis *c.p.* '63 (PH) [Z] Philadelphia, PA St. Michael's Passionist Residence.
Paul, Bededict (NY) [182] Bronx, NY SS. Philip and James Church.
Paul, David *s.m.* '70 (STL) [P] St. Louis, MO Provincialate of the Society of Mary, Province of St. Louis.
Paul, Dennis '93 (JOL) [18] Joliet, IL St. Paul the Apostle Church.
Paul, Gerald *m.s.c.* '60 (RCK) [H] Aurora, IL Missionaries of the Sacred Heart Community.
Paul, Gregory *c.p.* '58 (BAL) [48] Baltimore, MD St. Joseph Passionist Monastery Parish Church; [M] Baltimore, MD St. Joseph's Passionist Community.
Paul, John '72 (PH) Bridgeport, PA Our Mother of Sorrows Church.
Paul, John *s.j.* '92 (ELP) [21] El Paso, TX Sacred Heart Church.
Paul, John J. *m.s.c.* '58 (ALN) [K] Reading, PA Missionaries of the Sacred Heart.
Paul, John M. *s.j.* '80 (STP) [B] St. Paul, MN Jesuit Novitiate.
Paul, John P. '72 (PH) [D] Norristown, PA Kennedy-Kenrick Catholic High School.
Paul, Raphael '87 (SFD) Medora, IL St. John the Evangelist Church.
Paul, Raymond F. '55 (HRT) [2] Ansonia, CT Holy Rosary Church.
Paul, Raymond L. '62 (Y) [3] Massillon, OH St. Joseph's Church.
Paul, Stanislaus '67 (LA) Temple City, CA St. Luke the Evangelist Church.
Paul, Thomas '77 (JOL) Downers Grove, IL St. Mary Church.
Paul, Msgr. William J. '63 (PH) Lower Makefield, PA St. John the Evangelist Church.
Paulantonio, Joseph '45 (MAR) Retired.
Paulicek, Louis (AUS) Temple, TX St. Luke's Church.
Paulin, George A. '70 (BUR) North Troy, VT St. Vincent de Paul Church.
Paulish, Jeffrey '88 (PHU) Nanticoke, PA St. Nicholas Church.
Paulissen, Richard E. *m.m.* '63 (GAL) [Q] Houston, TX Maryknoll Fathers and Brothers; [U] Houston, TX Catholic Charismatic Center.
Paulissen, Richard E. *m.m.* '63 (NY) [Z] Maryknoll, NY Maryknoll Fathers and Brothers.
Paulits, Walter J. '72 (BAL) Retired.
Paulli, Kenneh *o.f.m.* '90 (PAT) Little Falls, NJ Our Lady of the Holy Angels Church.
Paulo, Maselino '80 (SPP) [7] Pago Pago, AS Church of Christ the King.
Paulraj, Jude '68 (NY) [2] New Rochelle, NY St. Gabriel Church.
Paulsen, Harold P. '78 (TYL) Palestine, TX Sacred Heart Church.
Paulshock, Emil '65 (PSC) Lansford, PA St. John the Baptist Church.
Paulson, Brian G. *s.j.* (CHI) [C] Chicago, IL Jesuit Community at Loyola University of Chicago; [N] Chicago, IL Chicago Province of the Society of Jesus-Provincial Office.
Paulson, Jerome E. '76 (NU) Montevideo, MN St. Joseph Church.
Paulson, Warren (LAN) Chelsea, MI Cassidy Lake Tech. School.
Paulus, Donard *o.f.m.* '48 (GAY) Indian River, MI Cross in the Woods Catholic Shrine Church.
Pauly, William *s.j.* '79 (RC) Pine Ridge, SD Holy Rosary Church; [B] Pine Ridge, SD Jesuit Community of Holy Rosary Mission.
Paur, Roman *o.s.b.* '66 (SCL) [B] Collegeville, MN St. John's University; [I] Collegeville, MN St. John's Abbey, of the Order of St. Benedict.
Paurazas, Peter P. '55 (CHI) [182] Chicago, IL St. Rene Goupil Church.
Pausche, Frederick F. '57 (CLV) Concord Twp., OH St. Gabriel Church.
Pauselli, Francis L. '75 (SCR) South Williamsport, PA St. Lawrence's Church.
Pautler, Mark '74 (SPK) [14] Spokane, WA St. Joseph Church.
Pavalkis, Victor '32 (SJ) Milpitas, CA St. John the Baptist Church; Retired.
Pavela, Wayne S. '77 (OM) Columbus, NE St. Anthony Church; [B] Columbus, NE Scotus Central Catholic High School.
Pavelis, Harold '51 (SCL) Retired.
Pavese, Paul J. *o.s.j.* '42 (SCR) [1] Pittston, PA Our Lady of Mt. Carmel Church; [M] Pittston, PA Eastern

Province of the Oblates of St. Joseph.
Pavignano, Steven J. *o.f.m.* '78 (ATL) [L] Atlanta, GA Campus Ministry.
Pavis, Raymond A. '45 (CHI) [1] Mt. Prospect, IL St. Cecilia Church; Retired.
Pavis, Msgr. Victor C. '42 (NY) Retired; [E] New York, NY Cardinal Hayes High School.
Pavlak, Robert P. *s.s.j.* '55 (NO) [P] New Orleans, LA Josephite Fathers and Brothers.
Pavlakovich, Michael G. '87 (DEN) Brush, CO St. Mary Church.
Pavlicek, Edward A., Jr. '83 (SAT) [29] San Antonio, TX St. Benedict Church.
Pavlick, Clement *c.p.* '42 (PIT) [N] Pittsburgh, PA St. Paul of the Cross Monastery.
Pavlick, Michael *s.m.* '53 (BO) [W] Boston, MA Marist Fathers Lourdes Residence; [BB] Boston, MA Chapel of Our Lady of Lourdes.
Pavlick, Raymond (NY) Castle Point, NY Veterans Administration Medical Center.
Pavlick, Raymond A. '71 (PAT) On Duty Outside the Diocese.
Pavlik, Albert *o.carm.* '61 (ALB) [5] Troy, NY St. Joseph Church.
Pavlik, James J. '63 (STL) Ozora, MO Sacred Heart Church.
Pavlik, John A. *o.f.m.cap.* '78 (WDC) [B] Washington, DC St. Francis Friary-Capuchin College.
Pavlina, Mark S. '75 (GRY) Dyer, IN St. Joseph Church.
Pavlish, W. Jeffrey '88 (SCR) [L] Wilkes-Barre, PA Little Flower Manor of the Diocese of Scranton.
Pavlock, Martin L. '66 (BUF) [7] Cheektowaga, NY Our Lady Help of Christians Church.
Pavlosky, John J. '71 (ALN) Northampton, PA St. Michael Church.
Pavlovsky, Wencil C. *c.s.b.* '91 (GAL) Richmond, TX St. John Fisher Church; [Q] Sugar Land, TX Basilian Mission Center.
Pavone, Frank A. '88 (NY) On Duty Outside the Archdiocese.
Pavur, Claude N. *s.j.* '84 (STL) [C] St. Louis, MO Saint Louis University; [P] St. Louis, MO Jesuit Community Corporation at St. Louis University - Jesuit Hall.
Pawelk, Steven P. *glmy.* '89 (JKS) New Albany, MS St. Francis of Assisi Church.
Pawelko, Mitchell *c.r.* '43 (CHI) [D] Chicago, IL Weber High School.
Pawelski, John '50 (GB) Absent on Leave.
Pawlak, Ed '68 (AMA) Retired.
Pawlak, Edwin F. '68 (ORL) Retired.
Pawlicki, James *s.v.d.* '73 (BLX) [A] Bay St. Louis, MS St. Augustine's; [E] Bay St. Louis, MS Media Production Center "In A Word".
Pawlicki, Joseph *c.s.c.* '50 (SB) Coachella, CA Our Lady of Soledad Church.
Pawlik, Wladyslaw *s.d.s.* '58 (GRY) [K] Merrillville, IN Salvatorian Fathers (Society of the Divine Savior).
Pawlikowski, John M. *o.s.m.* '67 (CHI) [18] Chicago, IL Assumption of the Blessed Virgin Mary Church; [B] Chicago, IL The Catholic Theological Union at Chicago; [N] Chicago, IL Servite Friars - Eastern Province.
Pawlos, John D. *s.m.* '59 (BAL) [M] Baltimore, MD Marianists Community (New York Province).
Pawloski, Gregory P. '74 (LIN) Imperial, NE St. Patrick's Church.
Pawlowski, Darius '87 (TYL) Nacogdoches, TX Sacred Heart Church.
Pawlowski, Joseph M. '73 (GRY) [15] Gary, IN St. Mary of the Lake Church.
Pawson, Msgr. Robert J. '66 (BRK) [197] Queens, NY Mary's Nativity Church.
Pax, Bart *o.f.m.* '68 (CIN) [U] Cincinnati, OH Community Support Charitable Trust.
Pax, Bart *o.f.m.* '68 (NO) [44] New Orleans, LA St. Mary Of The Angels Church.
Pax, Joseph *c.pp.s.* '47 (CIN) [N] Dayton, OH Sisters of the Precious Blood, Salem Heights Convent.
Pax, Maurus *o.f.m.* '50 (GLP) Grants, NM St. Teresa Church.
Pax, Ulric *o.f.m.* '59 (GLP) [2] Gallup, NM St. Francis of Assisi Church.
Paxton, Philip *c.p.* '95 (LA) [R] Pasadena, CA Passionist Community; [W] Sierra Madre, CA Mater Dolorosa Retreat Center.
Payant, Remi J. '38 (STP) Retired.
Payant, Romain *o.c.s.o.* '53 (P) [L] Lafayette, OR The Cistercian (Trappist) Abbey of Our Lady of Guadalupe.
Payea, Gerald *o.carm.* '69 (JOL) [J] Darien, IL Carmelite Fathers Provincial Office.
Payer, Emil S. '71 (GBG) Scottdale, PA St. John the Baptist Church.
Payikat, Zacharias *c.m.i.* '70 (NSH) Lewisburg, TN St. John the Evangelist Church; Shelbyville, TN St. William Church.
Payne, Charles E. *o.f.m.* (CHI) [D] Chicago, IL Hales Franciscan High School, Inc.
Payne, Gary '85 (OWN) Absent on Leave.
Payne, John *o.s.a.* '89 (WDC) [7] Washington, DC St. Augustine Church.
Payne, John Michael *o.c.d.* '70 (DAL) [K] Dallas, TX Mount Carmel Center.
Payne, John R. *s.j.* '70 (MOB) [B] Mobile, AL Spring Hill College.
Payne, John T. *c.s.c.* '46 (AUS) [13] Austin, TX St. Ignatius Martyr Church.
Payne, Joseph *o.p.* '63 (NY) Pleasantville, NY Holy Innocents Church.
Payne, Mark '94 (GB) [I] De Pere, WI St. Joseph Priory.
Payne, Mark M. *o.s.b.* '81 (NEW) [N] Newark, NJ Newark Abbey.
Payne, Stephen J. '91 (GAL) Huntsville, TX St. Thomas the Apostle Church.
Payne, Steven *o.c.d.* '82 (WDC) [B] Washington, DC Monastery of Our Lady of Mount Carmel; [V] Washington, DC Institute of Carmelite Studies and ICS Publications.
Payne, Thomas H. '50 (SAV) Retired.
Payo, Reuben (DEN) Conifer, CO Our Lady of The Pines Church.
Paysse, Wayne C. '87 (NO) [31] New Orleans, LA St. Frances Xavier Cabrini Church.
Paz, Jose M. '52 (MIA) [27] Miami, FL St. Michael the Archangel Church.
Pazera, Casimir A. *o.s.a.* '51 (JOL) [C] New Lenox, IL Providence Catholic High School; [J] New Lenox, IL Augustinian Friary.
Pazmany, Geza *sch.p.* '61 (PH) [G] Devon, PA Devon Preparatory School; [Z] Devon, PA Piarist Fathers (Order of the Pious Schools).
Pazo, John T. '55 (RVC) Retired.
Peace, John '36 (SJ) Retired.
Peacha, Thomas J. '59 (LA) [55] Los Angeles, CA St. Cecilia Church.
Peacock, Francis A. '53 (PHX) [7] Phoenix, AZ SS. Anthony and Pius X Church; [25] Phoenix, AZ St. Thomas the Apostle Church.
Peacock, Joseph '78 (ATL) Decatur, GA St. Thomas More Church; Retired.
Peacock, Thomas E. *s.j.* '63 (BAL) [M] Baltimore, MD Jesuit Fathers and Brothers Maryland Provincial Curia.
Peake, Msgr. Daniel A. '49 (NY) Rye, NY Resurrection Church.
Peaker, James N. '48 (CIN) Retired; [S] Cincinnati, OH Archdiocesan Central Council of Cincinnati.
Pearce, J. Donald *s.j.* '59 (NO) [8] New Orleans, LA Holy Name of Jesus Church.
Pearce, Jeff *a.a.* (BO) [W] Brighton, MA Assumptionist Center.
Pearce, John S. *c.m.* '57 (PH) [Z] Philadelphia, PA Congregation of the Mission.
Pearsall, Ernest P. '37 (BO) Retired.
Pearsall, William T. (BO) Society of St. James the Apostle.
Pearson, Everett '91 (WDC) Forestville, MD Mt. Calvary Church.
Pearson, John A. '66 (NU) Cottonwood, MN St. Mary Church; Green Valley, MN St. Clotilde Church.
Pearson, John H. *c.s.c.* '73 (FTW) [B] Notre Dame, IN University of Notre Dame Du Lac; [J] Notre Dame, IN Holy Cross Community, Corby Hall, University of Notre Dame.
Pearson, Robert A. '65 (SPK) [9] Spokane, WA St. Augustine Church.
Pearson, Robert L. *o.c.s.o.* '60 (ATL) [I] Conyers, GA The Monastery of the Holy Spirit.
Pease, Anthony F. '61 (OG) On Duty Outside the Diocese.
Pease, Joseph M. '61 (HBG) [1] Mount Carmel, PA Divine Redeemer Church.
Peatee, Greg '92 (TOL) [3] Toledo, OH Christ the King Church.
Pecaric, Alfred F. '82 (BGP) [7] Fairfield, CT St. Thomas Aquinas Church.
Pecchie, Paul '95 (SP) [4] St. Petersburg, FL Holy Family Church.
Pecci, Ronald *o.f.m.* '83 (BUF) [59] Buffalo, NY SS. Rita & Patrick Church.
Pecevich, Conrad S. '77 (WOR) [Q] Worcester, MA Campus Ministry.
Pecharich, Michael '73 (ORG) Rancho Santa Margarita, CA San Francisco Solano Church.
Pecharroman, Ovidio '87 (ARL) Falls Church, VA St. Philip Church.
Pecht, Gerard J. *c.ss.r.* '50 (WCH) [G] Wichita, KS Redemptorist Community; [I] Wichita, KS Spiritual Life Center.
Pechulis, John Baptist *c.p.* '47 (DET) [K] Detroit, MI St. Paul of the Cross Community, Congregation of the Passion.
Pecinovsky, Albert '65 (KCK) Absent on Sick Leave.
Peck, David A. '94 (RCK) [3] Elgin, IL St. Mary Church; [B] Elgin, IL St. Edward Central Catholic High School.
Peck, John '89 (RIC) [6] Virginia Beach, VA St. Gregory the Great Church.
Peck, Msgr. Leon J. '42 (PH) Warrington, PA St. Joseph Church; Retired.
Pecklers, Keith F. *s.j.* '91 (NY) [Z] New York, NY Jesuit Provincial's Office.
Pecoraro, James A. '53 (KC) Retired.
Pecovnik, Karel '44 (SCL) Retired.
Pedata, Msgr. Armand A. '58 (TR) Marlton, NJ St. Joan of Arc Church.
Peddicord, Richard A. *o.p.* '86 (STL) [B] St. Louis, MO Aquinas Institute of Theology; [P] St. Louis, MO St. Dominic Priory.
Pedelesky, Nestor '67 (STN) Absent on Sick Leave.
Pedi, Mario *o.s.b.* '57 (RCK) [1] Aurora, IL Annunciation of the Blessed Virgin Mary Church; [H] Aurora, IL Marmion Abbey-St. Augustine's Abbey.
Pedigo, John '91 (SJ) [12] San Jose, CA St. John Vianney Church.
Pednekar, Joseph C. *m.s.f.s.* '62 (CLV) [61] Cleveland, OH St. Patrick Church.
Pedone, F. Stephen '78 (WOR) [23] Worcester, MA St. George Church.
Pedrano, Stephanos *o.s.b.* '91 (SD) [H] Oceanside, CA Prince of Peace Abbey, Benet Hill.
Pedraz, Juan Lopez *s.j.* (SJN) [C] Rio Piedras, PR Centro Universitario Catolico.
Pedraz, Juan Lopez *s.j.* '46 (SJN) [22] San Juan, PR San Ignacio de Loyola Church.
Pedretti, Raymond J. '56 (LC) Arcadia, WI Our Lady of Perpetual Help Church; Arcadia, WI St. Stanislaus Church.
Pedretti, Robert F. '64 (LC) Amherst, WI St. James Church; Fancher, WI St. Mary of Mount Carmel Church.
Pedrizetti, Raymond *o.s.b.* '58 (SCL) [I] Collegeville, MN St. John's Abbey, of the Order of St. Benedict.
Pedrosa, Agustin *s.m.* '59 (NEW) West New York, NJ St. Joseph of the Palisades Church.
Pedroso, Rafael '64 (MIA) Hialeah Gardens, FL Santa Barbara Church.
Pedrotti, Francis L. *s.j.* '70 (KC) [B] Kansas City, MO Rockhurst College; [J] Kansas City, MO Rockhurst College - Jesuit Community.
Pedroza, Salvador '81 (SAT) Dilley, TX St. Joseph's Church.
Pedulla, John G. '93 (NY) [222] Staten Island, NY St. Patrick Church.
Peduti, Douglas F. *s.j.* '96 (WDC) [20] Washington, DC Holy Trinity Church.
Pedzich, Henry J. '72 (SY) Cazenovia, NY St. James Church.
Pedzik, Vitalis '61 (RVC) Lindenhurst, NY Our Lady of Perpetual Help Church.
Peet, Msgr. Arthur V. '41 (STL) Retired.
Peeters, Ambrose J. *o.praem.* '53 (GB) [A] De Pere, WI St. Norbert Abbey; [I] De Pere, WI St. Norbert Abbey.
Peeters, John N. *c.s.v.* '83 (JOL) Bourbonnais, IL Maternity of the Blessed Virgin Mary Church.
Peeters, R. Thomas '42 (GB) Retired.
Peffley, Francis J. '90 (ARL) Woodbridge, VA Our Lady of Angels Church.
Pegnan, William *o.f.m.cap.* '67 (SJ) [16] San Jose, CA St. Martin of Tours Church.
Pegoraro, Germano *s.c.* (LAN) [L] Grass Lake, MI The Pious Union of St. Joseph.
Peguero, Msgr. Lawrence '47 (GAL) Retired.
Pehl, Jeffery '95 (SAT) [49] San Antonio, TX St. Leo Church.
Pehler, Gerald *o.f.m.cap.* '88 (DET) [P] Washington, MI Capuchin Retreat.
Pehrsson, Alfred *c.m.* '58 (GR) [J] Spring Lake, MI St. Lazare Retreat House.
Pehrsson, Alfred R. *c.m.* '58 (PH) [Z] Philadelphia, PA Congregation of the Mission.
Pei, Maurus *o.c.s.o.* '82 (SAC) [A] Vina, CA Abbey of New Clairvaux, Trappist Seminary; [H] Vina, CA Abbey of New Clairvaux, Trappist.
Peifer, Claude *o.s.b.* (HRT) [N] Bethlehem, CT Abbey of Regina Laudis.
Peifer, Claude J. *o.s.b.* '52 (PEO) [A] Peru, IL St. Bede Abbey and Academy.
Peiffer, James E. (TOL) Oak Harbor, OH St. Boniface Church.
Peil, William '49 (FTW) Retired.
Peil, William L. '49 (GRY) Retired.
Peinado, Louis A. *s.j.* '60 (LA) [F] Los Angeles, CA Loyola High School.
Peiris, Richard (OAK) Fremont, CA Washington Hospital.
Peiris, Richard '68 (NY) [V] New York, NY Mary Manning Walsh Home.
Pejza, John P. *o.s.a.* '61 (LA) [F] Ojai, CA Villanova Preparatory School.
Pekar, Atanasius B. *o.s.b.m.* '46 (RVC) [N] Glen Cove, NY St. Josaphatis Monastery, Novitiate and Retreat House.
Pekar, Athanasius B. *o.s.b.m.* '46 (STF) [B] Glen Cove, NY Basilian Fathers Novitiate of the Order of St. Basil the Great.
Pekar, Florian *c.p.* '40 (HRT) [M] West Hartford, CT Holy Family Monastery/Retreat.
Pekar, Msgr. Gilbert F. (GAL) Retired.
Pekar, Joseph W. '57 (BGP) [8] Bridgeport, CT SS. Cyril and Methodius Church.

Pekarske, Daniel T. *s.d.s.* '90 (MIL) [55] Milwaukee, WI Mother of Good Counsel Church.
Peklo, Edward *s.v.d.* '69 (CHI) [B] Techny, IL Divine Word Residence; [N] Techny, IL Society of the Divine Word, Provincial Headquarter-Chicago Prov.
Pekola, David J. '86 (MET) Iselin, NJ St. Cecelia Church.
Pelaez, Oscar A. '94 (STO) Turlock, CA Sacred Heart Church.
Pelant, William G. '94 (STP) Burnsville, MN Mary, Mother of the Church.
Pelc, Timothy R. '74 (DET) Grosse Pointe Park, MI St. Ambrose Church.
Pelcyn, Robert F. *o.f.m.* '68 (LC) [E] Arcadia, WI Franciscan Skemp Healthcare, Mayo Health System, Arcadia Campus Hospital.
Pelczar, Edward A. '62 (PH) Absent on Leave.
Pelczynski, Walter *m.i.c.* '42 (SPR) [I] Stockbridge, MA Congregation of Marians.
Pelensky, Thor (STF) Retired.
Pelep, Etwel '95 (CI) Sokens, FM St. Peter's Church.
Peles, David S. '84 (ALT) [22] Johnstown, PA St. Benedict's Church.
Pelkey, Richard '84 (SY) On Duty Outside the Diocese.
Pelkington, Leo *o.p.* '68 (NY) Valhalla, NY Holy Name of Jesus Church.
Pelky, Theron E. '85 (GAY) Lake City, MI St. Stephen Church; Manton, MI St. Theresa Church.
Pellegrini, Frederick J. *s.j.* '84 (RVC) Oceanside, NY St. Anthony Church.
Pellegrino, Francis B. '51 (SLC) [9] West Valley City, UT SS. Peter and Paul Church; Salt Lake City, UT Decker Lake Youth Center.
Pellegrino, Gerard *s.d.b.* '74 (BO) [Y] Ipswich, MA Sacred Heart Retreat Center.
Pellegrino, Joseph A. *v.f.* '77 (SP) Tarpon Springs, FL St. Ignatius Church; [F] Tarpon Springs, FL St. Ignatius Early Childhood Center.
Pelleteri, Manuel J. *c.m.* '53 (CHI) [C] Chicago, IL Vincentian Community at DePaul University.
Pelletier, Adrien O. *s.m.* (BUR) White River Junction, VT St. Anthony Church; White River Junction, VT Veterans Administration Hospital.
Pelletier, Clement L. *s.j.* '62 (BO) [E] Boston, MA Boston College High School & Jesuit Community.
Pelletier, Donald *m.s.* '56 (STL) [P] St. Louis, MO La Salette Missionaries.
Pelletier, Edgar A. '47 (WOR) Retired.
Pelletier, Emile '94 (PHX) [12] Phoenix, AZ St. Gregory Church.
Pelletier, Eugene J. '53 (MAN) Retired.
Pelletier, George C. '79 (PRT) Jay, ME St. Rose of Lima Church.
Pelletier, Gerard *s.m.* '60 (HRT) [I] New Haven, CT Hospital of St. Raphael.
Pelletier, Gerard G. *s.m.* '51 (BRK) [45] Brooklyn, NY St. Francis of Assisi-St. Blaise Church.
Pelletier, Leonard E. '69 (BO) [7] Lowell, MA St. Louis de France Church.
Pelletier, Norman *s.s.s.* (CLV) [P] Cleveland, OH Congregation of the Blessed Sacrament Provincial House.
Pelletier, Rosaire *o.p.* '50 (PRT) [I] Lewiston, ME SS. Peter and Paul Priory.
Pelletier, Walter R. *s.j.* '60 (BGP) [D] Fairfield, CT Fairfield College Preparatory School; [O] Fairfield, CT The Fairfield Jesuit Community-Fairfield University.
Pellett, Marcian *o.f.m.cap.* '38 (AGN) [F] Agana Heights, GU St. Fidelis Friary.
Pellettieri, Joseph F. *c.ss.r.* '65 (ALX) Deville, LA St. John the Baptist Church.
Pellicane, Albert *c.p.* '56 (BRK) [U] Jamaica, NY Immaculate Conception Monastery.
Pellicane, Albert *c.p.* '56 (NY) [V] Bronx, NY Franciscan Health System of New York, Inc.; [Z] New York, NY Pope Paul VI Residence.
Pellicore, Msgr. Edward M. (CHI) [12] Chicago, IL St. Angela Church.
Pellicore, Msgr. Edward M. '36 (CHI) Retired.
Pelligrin, Joseph '81 (BRK) [55] Brooklyn, NY Holy Family Church.
Pellissier, Francois '81 (JKS) Starkville, MS St. Joseph Church.
Peloso, Alex *c.s.* (CHI) [122] Chicago, IL Santa Maria Addolorata Church.
Peloso, John '96 (MIA) Coral Springs, FL St. Andrew Church.
Pelous, Donald P. '77 (LAF) Breaux Bridge, LA St. Bernard Church.
Pelton, Robert S. *c.s.c.* '49 (FTW) [B] Notre Dame, IN University of Notre Dame Du Lac; [J] Notre Dame, IN Holy Cross Community, Corby Hall, University of Notre Dame.
Pelton, Thomas (CHI) [133] Chicago, IL Maternity of the Blessed Virgin Mary Church.
Peltz, Carl '77 (STU) On Duty Outside the Diocese.
Peltzer, H. Michael '80 (WCH) Eureka, KS Sacred Heart Church; Hamilton, KS St. John Church; Madison, KS St. Teresa of Avila Church.
Peluse, Dominic A. *s.c.j.* '74 (GAL) [20] Houston, TX Christ the Redeemer Church.
Peluso, Francis E. *o.a.r.* '61 (NEW) [N] West Orange, NJ Augustinian Recollects.
Peluso, Francis E. *o.a.r.* '61 (NY) [154] Bronx, NY St. John's Church; [BB] Bronx, NY St. Joseph's Center; [DD] Bronx, NY St. Joseph's Center.
Peluso, Michael J. '58 (NY) Absent on Leave.
Pemberton, Joseph '77 (FWT) [3] Fort Worth, TX Holy Family Church.
Pena, Francisco *s.j.* '53 (SJ) [M] Los Gatos, CA California Province of the Society of Jesus, Jesuit Provincial Office.
Pena, Gustaro Aldolfo Tenorio '81 (SCR) [20] Scranton, PA Nativity of Our Lord Church.
Pena, Joseph '67 (SAT) [34] San Antonio, TX St. Dominic Church.
Pena, Luis '82 (SFE) [2] Santa Fe, NM Our Lady of Guadalupe Church.
Pena, Raymundo J. '57 (BWN) [C] Brownsville, TX Catholic Charities; [D] San Juan, TX San Juan Nursing Home.
Pena, Richard '92 (SAT) [3] San Antonio, TX Christ the King Church; [T] San Antonio, TX Archdiocesan Union of Holy Name Societies.
Pena, Roberto *o.m.i.* '55 (SAT) Del Rio, TX St. Joseph's Church.
Pena, Vicente M. *o.p.* '36 (SAT) [B] San Antonio, TX Dominican Priory of Juan Macias.
Pena-Martinez, Gilberto '68 (SAC) Chico, CA St. John the Baptist Church.
Penafiel, Fausto '83 (PHX) [8] Phoenix, AZ St. Augustine Church.
Penalba, Vincente *c.m.* '69 (CGS) [8] Barrio Rio Canas, PR Immaculado Corozon de Maria Church.
Penaloza, Jorge '60 (LA) Pico Rivera, CA St. Francis Xavier Church.
Penchi, Edward J. '56 (LC) Foreign Missions.
Penczynski, Richard M. '75 (GRY) [3] Hammond, IN St. Casimir Church.
Pendergast, Msgr. John F. '54 (OG) Massena, NY Sacred Heart Church.
Pendergast, Richard J. *s.j.* '63 (NY) [Z] New York, NY Murray-Weigel Hall.
Penderghest, William T. *ss.cc.* '67 (FR) [K] Fairhaven, MA Sacred Hearts Provincial House.
Pendergraft, Michael '81 (STA) Chiefland, FL St. John the Evangelist Church.
Pendleton, Arthur J. *o.s.b.* '64 (CHL) [J] Belmont, NC Belmont Abbey.
Pendolphi, Richard J. '76 (COL) Logan, OH St. John Church.
Penebsky, John P. '65 (SFR) Redwood City, CA St. Pius Church.
Peng, John B. (CHI) Retired.
Penkala, Msgr. Edmund S. '45 (SCR) Retired; [N] Dunmore, PA Villa St. Joseph.
Penko, Francis G. '60 (SD) [3] El Cajon, CA St. Kieran Church.
Penn, Michael A. '54 (SCR) [3] Scranton, PA St. Anthony of Padua Church.
Penna, Anthony *c.s.s.* '75 (BO) [W] Waltham, MA Stigmatine House.
Penna, Msgr. Joseph P. '67 (NY) Pearl River, NY St. Aedan Church.
Penna, Marshall Della *o.f.m.* '60 (PAT) [M] Ringwood, NJ Holy Name Friary.
Pennett, Frederick J. '71 (MAN) [J] Dover, NH St. Ann; [N] Durham, NH Campus Ministries; [N] Durham, NH Campus Ministries; [N] Durham, NH St. Thomas More Catholic Student Center at the University of New Hampshire.
Pennington, John F. *s.j.* '70 (CHI) [N] Chicago, IL Chicago Province of the Society of Jesus-Provincial Office.
Pennington, John R., III '79 (WDC) Burtonsville, MD Resurrection Parish Church.
Pennington, M. Basil *o.c.s.o.* '57 (WOR) [N] Spencer, MA St. Joseph's Abbey; [R] Spencer, MA Cistercian Publications, Inc.
Pennington, Matthew '88 (MRY) Scotts Valley, CA San Agustin Church.
Pennisi, Celestine *o.f.m.* '52 (NY) [Z] New York, NY Franciscan Province of the Immaculate Conception.
Pennisi, Ignatius F. *s.j.* '43 (BO) [E] Boston, MA Boston College High School & Jesuit Community.
Pennock, Michael (JOL) Bolingbrook, IL St. Francis of Assisi Church.
Penonzek, Edward M. *o.s.m.* '58 (ORG) [D] Anaheim, CA Servite High School; Servite High School Development Fund; [H] Anaheim, CA Servite Fathers and Brothers.
Pensia, William *c.s.c.* (NY) [188] Bronx, NY Sacred Heart Church.
Penta, Leo J. '78 (BRK) Released from Diocesan Assignment.
Pentecost, Denver B. '69 (NO) [1] Marrero, LA Immaculate Conception Church; Marrero, LA West Jefferson General Hospital; Marrero, LA Wynhoven Health Care Center.
Pentello, Richard J. '79 (Y) Garrettsville, OH St. Ambrose Church.
Pentis, William F. *c.o.* '66 (CHR) Rock Hill, SC St. Anne's Church; [E] Rock Hill, SC Oratory of St. Philip Neri, Congregation of the Oratory of Pontifical Rite.
Pentony, Liam '55 (JKS) Brookhaven, MS St. Francis Church; [G] Brookhaven, MS Lincoln Junior College Newman Center.
Penzes, Lawrence M. '78 (RVC) Lynbrook, NY Our Lady of Peace Church.
Penzimas, Joseph A. '40 (NU) Retired.
Peoples, J. Eugene '66 (HEL) [B] Helena, MT Carroll College.
Pepe, Msgr. Joseph A. '70 (PH) On Duty Outside the Archdiocese.
Pepe, Msgr. Joseph A. *j.c.d.* '70 (SFE) [1] Albuquerque, NM Annunciation Church.
Pepe, Mario P. '56 (HRT) Marlborough, CT St. John Fisher Church.
Pepe, Robert F. '50 (WCH) Retired.
Pepel, Anthony '75 (SY) [7] Oswego, NY St. Stephen the King Church.
Pepel, Clement '82 (MET) On Duty Outside the Diocese.
Pepel, Klemens '44 (PHX) Special Assignment.
Pepeu, Luis *o.f.m.cap.* '82 (WDC) [B] Washington, DC St. Francis Friary-Capuchin College.
Pepin, Darryl J. '78 (MAR) Iron Mountain, MI Immaculate Conception of the Blessed Virgin Mary Church.
Pepin, Normand A. *s.j.* '63 (FBK) [A] Fairbanks, AK Monroe Catholic Junior-Senior High School; [C] Fairbanks, AK Jesuit Residence; [E] Fairbanks, AK House of Prayer.
Pepin, Paul H. *s.m.* '39 (BO) [W] Boston, MA Marist Fathers Lourdes Residence; [BB] Boston, MA Chapel of Our Lady of Lourdes.
Pepka, Edward *a.a.* '77 (BO) [W] Brighton, MA Assumptionist Center.
Pepka, Edward '77 (SAC) Colusa, CA Our Lady of Lourdes Church.
Peplansky, Joseph *c.m.f.* '60 (SPC) [4] Springfield, MO Sacred Heart Church; [E] Springfield, MO Claretians Missionaries' Residence-Villa Claret.
Peplinski, Msgr. Raymond J. '42 (B) Retired.
Pepowski, Bert '61 (GRY) [K] Cedar Lake, IN Our Lady of Lourdes Friary.
Peppard, Patrick F. *s.j.* '73 (DET) [E] Detroit, MI University of Detroit Jesuit High School and Academy.
Pepper, David J. '58 (DUB) Retired.
Pera, Sylvano *o.f.m.* (SFD) Belleview, IL St. Agnes Church; Hardin, IL St. Norbert Church; Kampsville, IL St. Anselm Church; Michael, IL St. Michael Church.
Perales, Jorge '78 (MIA) Hialeah Gardens, FL Santa Barbara Church.
Perata, Stephen F. '58 (SJ) [25] San Jose, CA St. Victor Church.
Perdue, John *m.ss.cc.* '90 (CAM) Linwood, NJ Our Lady of Sorrows Church.
Pere, Adrian C. '93 (BR) Prairieville, LA St. John the Evangelist Church.
Perea, Michael U. *o.praem.* '90 (ORG) [H] Silverado, CA Norbertine Fathers.
Pereda, James F. (RVC) Seaford, NY St. William, the Abbot Church; Graduate Studies.
Pereira, Albert F. '40 (RIC) Retired.
Pereira, Anthony '82 (SJ) Los Gatos, CA St. Mary of the Immaculate Conception Church.
Pereira, Cyril F. '54 (ALB) [10] Troy, NY St. Patrick Church; Special Assignment.
Pereira, Luciano J. '54 (FR) Retired.
Pereira, Manuel *m.s.* '95 (FR) [K] Attleboro, MA La Salette Shrine.
Perelli, Robert J. *c.j.m.* '76 (BUF) [1] West Seneca, NY St. Bonaventure Church; [O] West Seneca, NY St. Bonaventure.
Perera, *o.s.b.* '71 (FRS) Avenal, CA California State Prison, Kings Co.
Perera, Denzil M. '58 (NO) [19] New Orleans, LA Our Lady Of The Rosary Church; Retired.
Perera, Paul (ELP) Retired.
Peres, Mark R. *c.pp.s.* '85 (LFT) Rensselaer, IN St. Augustine Church.
Peretta, Andrew J. (PAT) Unassigned.
Peretti, Peter L. '73 (GBG) Leisenring, PA St. Vincent de Paul Church.
Perez, Anthony *s.s.* '77 (BAL) [M] Baltimore, MD Sulpician Provincial House.
Perez, Antonio '77 (AGN) On Duty Outside the Archdiocese.
Perez, Armando '62 (MIA) [2] Fort Lauderdale, FL Our Lady Queen of Martyrs Church.
Perez, Arturo J. (CHI) [187] Chicago, IL St. Roman Church.
Perez, Arturo J. '72 (CHI) [62] Chicago, IL St. Francis of Assisi Church.
Perez, Aurelio '86 (MIL) Greendale, WI St. Alphonsus Church.
Perez, Carlos (NY) [31] New York, NY St. Elizabeth Church.

Perez, Carlos '60 (MIA) [2] Hialeah, FL San Lazaro Church.
Perez, Carlos '92 (B) Nampa, ID Our Lady of Guadalupe Parish Church.
Perez, Edwardo '86 (SB) Ontario, CA Our Lady of Guadalupe Church.
Perez, Francisco Javier '73 (LA) South Gate, CA St. Helen Church.
Perez, Gabino *o.a.r.* '51 (ORG) [5] Santa Ana, CA Our Lady of the Pillar Church.
Perez, Greg '86 (AUS) On Duty Outside the Diocese.
Perez, Gregory G. '86 (AUS) [1] Austin, TX St. Mary's Cathedral.
Perez, Gustavo '64 (SFR) [44] San Francisco, CA St. Peter Church.
Perez, Hector R.G. '81 (PT) [14] Pensacola, FL St. Stephen Church.
Perez, Henry '73 (ORG) Inactive Leave.
Perez, Isidro '81 (MIA) [4] Hialeah, FL St. Cecilia Church.
Perez, Javier '93 (TUC) [14] Tucson, AZ St. John the Evangelist Church.
Perez, Jesse L. '74 (PBL) [3] Pueblo, CO Holy Family Church.
Perez, Jesu "Jay" *o.f.m. cap.* (CHL) [8] Charlotte, NC St. Matthew Church.
Perez, Jose '65 (LA) [93] Los Angeles, CA St. Thomas the Apostle Church.
Perez, Jose Caracoza *m.n.m.* '82 (SAT) Del Rio, TX Our Lady of Guadalupe Church.
Perez, Joseph '69 (GAL) On Duty Outside the Diocese.
Perez, Juan Antonio *o.ss.t.* '88 (VIC) [4] Victoria, TX Our Lady of Sorrows Church.
Perez, Leo *o.m.i.* '84 (SAT) [M] San Antonio, TX St. Anthony Catholic High School House.
Perez, Leon '60 (ARE) Barceloneta, PR Our Lady of Victory Church.
Perez, Leopoldo *o.m.i.* '84 (SAT) [C] San Antonio, TX Oblate School of Theology.
Perez, Luis A. '95 (MIA) North Miami, FL Holy Family Church.
Perez, Maximiliano '49 (MIA) Retired.
Perez, Modesto '88 (LA) [1] Los Angeles, CA Cathedral of Our Lady of the Angels.
Perez, Nelson J. '89 (PH) [66] Philadelphia, PA St. Hugh of Cluny Church.
Perez, Pedro Luis '52 (MIA) [2] Hialeah, FL San Lazaro Church.
Perez, Rafael '74 (GLP) On Duty Outside of Diocese.
Perez, Rafael '74 (LSC) Hurley, NM Infant Jesus Church.
Perez, Rafael *o.s.b.* '79 (CGS) Humacao, PR Maria Reina de la Paz Church.
Perez, Ramon '75 (CHI) Franklin Park, IL St. Gertrude Church.
Perez, Raul '86 (SAV) Cordele, GA St. Theresa Church.
Perez, Raymond *o.praem.* (LA) San Pedro, CA Mary, Star of the Sea Church.
Perez, Raymond L. *o.praem.* '88 (ORG) [H] Silverado, CA Norbertine Fathers.
Perez, Restituto *o.p.* '60 (MIA) [18] Miami, FL St. Dominic Church.
Perez, Robert R. '86 (CHI) [178] Chicago, IL Providence of God Church.
Perez, Sacramento *o.m.* (SB) Ontario, CA Our Lady of Guadalupe Church.
Perez, Salvador *o.s.a.* '61 (FWT) Clifton, TX Holy Angels Church; Morgan, TX Our Lady of Guadalupe Church.
Perez, Santos *o.f.m.* '85 (ELP) [15] El Paso, TX Our Lady of Guadalupe Church.
Perez, Tomas *o.a.r.* '67 (LSC) La Mesa, NM San Jose Church; [B] Mesilla, NM Augustinian Recollects Fathers.
Perez, Vicente '58 (MGZ) [1] Mayaquez, PR Cathedral of Our Lady of Purification.
Perez, Victor *o.p.* '67 (SJN) [16] Bayamon, PR Nuestra Senora del Perpetuo Socorro Church.
Perez, Victor '75 (P) [P] Portland, OR University of Portland.
Perez, Victoriano '75 (P) Independence, OR St. Patrick Church.
Perez, Viktor *o.f.m.conv.* '89 (RNO) [1] Reno, NV St. Thomas Aquinas Cathedral.
Perez, William A. *o.s.a.* '62 (TLS) [B] Tulsa, OK Cascia Hall Preparatory School.
Perez-Castaneda, Daniel G. '96 (LA) Hawthorne, CA St. Joseph Church.
Perez-Lerena, Francisco *s.j.* '58 (MIA) [D] Miami, FL Belen Jesuit Preparatory School; [H] Miami, FL Jesuit Fathers of the Province of the Antilles, Inc.
Perez-Santiago, Enrique A. '71 (ARE) [7] Arecibo, PR Nuestra Senora de Fatima Church.
Perfetto, Anthony *s.m.* '66 (CIN) [L] Centerville, OH The Franciscan at St. Leonard.
Perfetto, Richard A. '66 (DET) Canton, MI Resurrection Church.
Pergl, James F. *c.s.sp.* '44 (PIT) [P] Bethel Park, PA Holy Ghost Animation Center.
Perham, Arnold E. *c.s.v.* '56 (CHI) [D] Arlington Heights, IL St. Viator High School.
Peri, Paul '71 (P) Wilsonville, OR St. Cyril Church.
Pericone, Nicholas '96 (NO) [1] Marrero, LA Immaculate Conception Church.
Peries, Angelito *c.ss.r.* '74 (SR) [L] Sebastopol, CA Diocesan House of Prayer.
Peries, Ignatius *c.sp.* '79 (NY) [Z] New York, NY Apostolic Society of the Crusade of the Holy Spirit.
Perin, Glen W. '53 (CIN) Sidney, OH Holy Angels Church.
Perin, Isidro *m.s.* '67 (STL) [P] St. Louis, MO La Salette Missionaries.
Perini, Msgr. Armando J. '56 (MET) Edison, NJ St. Helena Church.
Perino, John M. '79 (NO) Ama, LA St. Mark Church.
Perjak, Edmond J. '67 (BEL) Retired.
Perkin, David R. '78 (NSH) Old Hickory, TN St. Stephen Church.
Perkins, Bernard '43 (TUC) [16] Tucson, AZ St. Margaret's Church.
Perkins, Bernard *o.c.d.* '82 (TUC) [F] Tucson, AZ Discalced Carmelite Fathers of St. Margaret's.
Perkins, Charles J. '78 (HT) Amelia, LA St. Andrew Church.
Perkins, Dennis M. '95 (NOR) New London, CT St. Mary, Star of the Sea Church.
Perkins, Joseph F. '68 (WDC) [7] Silver Spring, MD St. John the Evangelist Church.
Perkins, Robert '71 (RIC) [1] Richmond, VA Cathedral of the Sacred Heart.
Perkins, Robert S. '72 (CHI) Other Assignments.
Perkins, Russell H. '58 (WIL) Retired.
Perkinton, John J. '85 (LIN) [2] Lincoln, NE Blessed Sacrament Church; [H] Lincoln, NE Villa Marie School and Home for the Educable Mentally Handicapped.
Perkl, James M. '84 (STP) Jordan, MN St. John the Baptist Church.
Perko, F. Michael *s.j.* '75 (CHI) [C] Chicago, IL Jesuit Community at Loyola University of Chicago.
Perkovic, Anton '46 (NO) Retired.
Perkovich, Frank '54 (DUL) Biwabik, MN St. John's Church; Gilbert, MN St. Joseph's Church.
Perkowski, Joseph '46 (DET) Retired.
Perlite, John J. *s.j.* '49 (PHX) [B] Phoenix, AZ Brophy College Preparatory.
Perlite, Paul A. '46 (SFR) Fairfax, CA St. Rita Church; Retired.
Perluzzi, James *o.f.m.* '65 (STL) [P] St. Louis, MO Franciscan Friary of St. Anthony of Padua.
Pernia, Msgr. John R. '58 (SFR) Daly City, CA Our Lady of Perpetual Help Church.
Peron, Bartholomew (NY) [122] New York, NY St. Vincent de Paul Church.
Perozich, Richard L. '92 (SD) [16] San Diego, CA Our Lady of the Sacred Heart Church.
Perozzi, Julian *s.x.* '82 (PAT) [M] Wayne, NJ Xaverian Missionary Fathers.
Perpete, Louis M. *m.s.* '45 (HRT) [M] Hartford, CT Missionaries of LaSalette Provincial Secretary.
Perreault, Aurele R. '53 (HRT) Retired.
Perreault, Joseph A. '75 (CAM) Brigantine, NJ St. Thomas Church; [A] Absecon, NJ Holy Spirit High School.
Perreault, Leonard '54 (SPR) Stockbridge, MA St. Joseph's Church; West Stockbridge, MA St. Patrick's Church.
Perreault, Louis G. *c.s.sp.* '62 (SB) Hemet, CA Our Lady of the Valley Church.
Perrello, Blaise '77 (RIC) Richmond, VA MCV Hospital.
Perretta, Andrew T. (PAT) [1] Clifton, NJ Sacred Heart Church.
Perri, Joseph E. *s.j.* '51 (P) Oakridge, OR St. Michael Church.
Perricone, Charles A. '74 (PAT) Sussex, NJ St. Monica Church.
Perricone, John A. '75 (NY) [2] New York, NY St. Agnes Church.
Perricone, John A. '76 (NEW) On Duty Outside the Archdiocese.
Perriello, Robert A. '76 (WH) Clarksburg, WV St. James Church.
Perrier, Martin '88 (RNO) Fernley, NV St. Robert Bellarmine Church.
Perrier, Monroe G. *c.ss.r.* '58 (BR) [H] Baton Rouge, LA Redemptorist Fathers Vice Provincialate.
Perrier, Thomas *o.s.b.* '80 (NO) [R] St. Benedict, LA Abbey Christian Life Center.
Perrier, Thomas E. *o.s.b.* '80 (NO) [A] St. Benedict, LA St. Joseph's Seminary College; [P] St. Benedict, LA St. Joseph Abbey.
Perrins, Samuel T. '86 (SCR) [1] Plymouth, PA Nativity of the Blessed Virgin Mary Church.
Perron, Gary *a.a.* '66 (BO) [W] Brighton, MA Assumptionist Center.
Perron, Richard J. '46 (BO) Retired.
Perron, Robert P. '81 (PRO) [4] Central Falls, RI Notre Dame Church.
Perrone, Eduard '78 (DET) [11] Detroit, MI Assumption Grotto Church.
Perry, Ashley J. *s.s.j.* '75 (NO) [6] New Orleans, LA Epiphany Church.
Perry, Carmen J. '77 (SCR) Stroudsburg, PA St. Luke's Church.
Perry, Daniel *ss.cc.* '49 (FR) [K] Fairhaven, MA Sacred Hearts Provincial House.
Perry, David T. '72 (PRO) Valley Falls, RI St. Patrick Church.
Perry, Francis J. '50 (DUB) Ionia, IA St. Boniface's Church; North Washington, IA Immaculate Conception Church.
Perry, Frederick J. '53 (LFT) Montpelier, IN St. Margaret of Scotland Church.
Perry, John A. '63 (FR) East Freetown, MA St. John Neumann Church.
Perry, John J. '83 (FR) [16] Fall River, MA St. Joseph's Church.
Perry, Joseph N. '75 (MIL) [63] Milwaukee, WI All Saints Church; [B] Hales Corners, WI Sacred Heart School of Theology; [Y] Milwaukee, WI St. Thomas More Lawyers Society.
Perry, Killian J. *t.o.r.* '74 (STP) [20] Minneapolis, MN St. Bridget Church.
Perry, Michael '71 (BRK) [47] Brooklyn, NY St. Francis Xavier Church.
Perry, Michael *o.f.m.* '84 (CHI) [47] Chicago, IL Corpus Christi Church.
Perry, Michael *o.de.m.* '85 (SP) [O] St. Petersburg, FL St. Peter Nolasco Residence.
Perry, Michael A. '82 (BRK) [E] Brooklyn, NY Office of the Superintendent of Schools.
Perry, Michael V. *o.f.m.* '45 (PAT) [M] Butler, NJ St. Anthony Friary.
Perry, Paul '67 (SFR) Mill Valley, CA Our Lady of Mt. Carmel Church.
Perry, Paul E. '78 (TOL) Plymouth, OH St. Joseph Church; Willard, OH St. Francis Xavier Church.
Perry, Robert U. *o.p.* '59 (BR) Hammond, LA Holy Ghost Church.
Perry, Ronald V. *s.j.* '76 (BGP) [D] Fairfield, CT Fairfield College Preparatory School; [O] Fairfield, CT The Fairfield Jesuit Community-Fairfield University.
Perryman, John E. '45 (CIN) Retired.
Persac, Louis A. '47 (NO) Gretna, LA St. Anthony Church; Retired.
Persha, Gerald *m.m.* '78 (CHI) [B] Chicago, IL The Catholic Theological Union at Chicago; [B] Chicago, IL The Catholic Theological Union at Chicago.
Pershe, Joseph N. *s.j.* '66 (NY) Manhattan, NY Bird S. Coler Memorial Hospital and Home; [Z] New York, NY West Side Jesuit Community.
Persich, Nicholas E. *c.m.* '46 (STL) [P] Perryville, MO Congregation of The Mission.
Persich, Roy A. *c.m.* '60 (LA) [R] Los Angeles, CA Amat House; [W] Santa Barbara, CA St. Mary's Seminary Center.
Persico, Lawrence T. '77 (GBG) [I] Greensburg, PA Benedictine Sisters (Eichstatt, Bavaria).
Persico, Pasquale *p.i.m.e.* '44 (PMB) [G] Tequesta, FL P.I.M.E. Missionaries.
Persons, Jeffrey L. *o.s.f.s.* (LAN) Adrian, MI St. Mary of Good Counsel Church.
Perunilam, Thomas V. '64 (MET) Milltown, NJ Our Lady of Lourdes Church.
Peruti, John J. '55 (HRT) [12] Hartford, CT St. Luke Church.
Perzan, Stephan B. '73 (GLP) Lumberton, NM St. Francis of Assisi Church.
Perzan, Stephen B. '73 (PH) On Duty Outside the Archdiocese.
Pesanka, Nicholas A. '75 (PIT) Bethel Park, PA St. Germaine Church.
Pesarchick, Robert A. '91 (PH) Graduate Studies.
Pesaresi, Constantine V. '35 (BRK) [221] Queens, NY Our Lady of Sorrows Church; Retired.
Pescatello, Joseph A. '89 (PRO) [5] Cranston, RI St. Mary Church.
Pescatore, Terence *o.f.m.conv.* (NEW) [2] Hoboken, NJ St. Joseph's Church.
Pesce, John Baptist *c.p.* '51 (HRT) [M] West Hartford, CT Holy Family Monastery/Retreat.
Pesch, Elroy *o.f.m.cap.* '63 (MIL) [B] Mount Calvary, WI St. Lawrence Seminary; [P] Mount Calvary, WI St. Lawrence Friary.
Peschel, Msgr. Anthony R. '35 (FAR) Retired.
Peschel, Joseph E. *s.j.* '76 (CIN) [P] Milford, OH Milford Spiritual Center.
Peschel, Roland '60 (OM) [9] Omaha, NE St. Bernard Church.
Pesci, Thomas A. *s.j.* '79 (KC) [D] Kansas City, MO Rockhurst High School; [J] Kansas City, MO Rockhurst High School - Jesuit Community.
Pesek, Anthony '65 (SAT) [9] San Antonio, TX Holy Spirit Church.
Pesek, Fred C. '89 (CHI) Streamwood, IL St. John the Evangelist Church.
Pesenti, Paul *o.m.i.* '66 (NEW) [7] Bayonne, NJ Our Lady of the Assumption Church.
Pestun, Aloysius *s.d.b.* '59 (SFR) [12] San Francisco, CA Corpus Christi Church.
Pesut, Louis J. '55 (RCK) Lee, IL St. James Church.
Peszkowski, Msgr. Zdzislaw '54 (DET) [A] Orchard

Lake, MI SS. Cyril and Methodius Seminary.
Petcavage, Leonard *c.s.j.* '81 (CLV) Released from Diocesan Assignment.
Petcavage, Leonard *c.s.j.* '81 (LA) [D] Lancaster, CA Paraclete High School.
Petche, Daniel *o.s.b.* '67 (KC) Stanberry, MO St. Peter's Church.
Pete, Joseph P. '76 (WIN) Lake Crystal, MN Holy Family Church; [4] Mankato, MN St. Joseph the Worker Church.
Petekiewicz, Robert '91 (RVC) Bellmore, NY St. Barnabas the Apostle Church.
Peter, David J. '66 (BUF) Eden, NY Immaculate Conception Church.
Peter, Martin A. '67 (IND) [38] Indianapolis, IN St. Pius X Church.
Peter, Patrick N. '75 (BEL) Breese, IL St. Dominic Church.
Peter, Paul F. '52 (OM) Retired.
Peter, Valentine J. '59 (OM) Boys Town, NE Immaculate Conception B.V.M. Church; [C] Boys Town, NE Father Flanagan's Boys' Home; [E] Boys Town, NE Father Flanagan's Boys' Home; [I] Boys Town, NE Father Flanagan's Boys' Home.
Peterka, Dale '68 (CIN) [22] Cincinnati, OH St. Clare Church.
Peterka, Sylvester *c.m.* (BAL) [21] Baltimore, MD St. Cecilia Church; [38] Baltimore, MD Immaculate Conception Church.
Peterka, Theodore '47 (SCL) Retired.
Peterlini, Luciano *s.x.* '63 (PAT) [M] Wayne, NJ Xaverian Missionary Fathers.
Peterman, Charles '58 (MIA) [16] Miami, FL St. Brendan Church.
Peterman, Thomas J. '57 (WIL) Galena, MD St. Dennis Church.
Peternel, Warren *o.f.m.* (SFD) [K] Sherman, IL Our Lady of Angels Friary.
Peters, Aaron *o.s.b.* '77 (KCK) [H] Atchison, KS St. Benedict's Abbey; [I] Paola, KS Our Lady of Lourdes Convent.
Peters, Daniel E. '89 (RCK) Prophetstown, IL St. Catherine Church; [B] Sterling, IL Newman Central Catholic High School; Newman Middle School.
Peters, David L. '58 (SFD) Highland, IL St. Paul Church.
Peters, Donald R. '50 (MIL) Retired.
Peters, Eric '80 (SP) [16] Tampa, FL St. Timothy Church.
Peters, Fred *s.d.s.* '56 (GB) Charlesburg, WI St. Charles Borromeo Church; Charlestown, WI St. Martin Church; Chilton, WI St. Augustine Church; Chilton, WI St. Mary Church; Jericho, WI Holy Trinity Church; Kloten, WI St. Elizabeth Church.
Peters, Herman B. '41 (CLV) [16] Cleveland, OH St. Cecilia Church; Shaker Heights, OH St. Dominic Church; Retired.
Peters, Msgr. John '60 (ELP) [26] El Paso, TX St. Luke Church.
Peters, John C. *v.f.* '74 (VIC) Hallettsville, TX Sacred Heart Church; Hallettsville, TX St. Mary Church.
Peters, John M. '44 (DUB) Retired.
Peters, Joseph J. *s.j.* '40 (DET) [P] Clarkston, MI Colombiere Center.
Peters, Jude *o.c.d.* '89 (MIL) [P] Holy Hill, WI Discalced Carmelite Monastery.
Peters, Julian *o.s.b.* '88 (IND) [A] St. Meinrad, IN St. Meinrad Seminary; [B] St. Meinrad, IN St. Meinrad Seminary-College of Liberal Arts; [J] St. Meinrad, IN St. Meinrad Archabbey.
Peters, Kenan *c.p.* '60 (BRK) [U] Jamaica, NY Immaculate Conception Monastery.
Peters, Kevin '90 (Y) [6] Canton, OH St. Joan of Arc Church.
Peters, Lyle '96 (DM) [B] West Des Moines, IA Dowling High School.
Peters, Mark M. *o.s.b.* '80 (GBG) Whitney, PA St. Cecilia Church.
Peters, Michael G. '88 (DM) Panama, IA St. Mary of the Assumption Church.
Peters, Noel *o.m.i.* '63 (FRS) Faculties Only.
Peters, Paul R. '62 (DUB) Guttenberg, IA St. Mary's Church; North Buena Vista, IA Immaculate Conception Church; [F] Guttenberg, IA Guttenberg-North Buena Vista Consolidated School.
Peters, Raymond W. '47 (LC) Suspended.
Peters, Msgr. Roy V. '48 (HON) [17] Honolulu, HI Saints Peter and Paul Church.
Peters, Msgr. Roy V. '48 (SAC) Retired and in Senior Ministry.
Peters, Stephen '67 (ELP) [4] El Paso, TX Blessed Sacrament Church.
Petersen, Msgr. E. James (FRS) On Duty Outside the Diocese.
Petersen, Msgr. E. James (SAC) [3] Sacramento, CA Holy Spirit Church.
Petersen, Michael C. '92 (MIL) Burlington, WI Immaculate Conception Church.
Petersen, Vincent *o.f.m.conv.* '85 (WDC) [B] Washington, DC St. Bonaventure Friary.
Peterson, Bradley *o.carm.* '92 (TUC) [A] Tucson, AZ Salpointe Catholic High School; [F] Tucson, AZ Carmelite Priory.
Peterson, Bruce '57 (STP) Belle Creek, MN St. Columbkill Church.
Peterson, C. Vincent '74 (SEA) [24] Seattle, WA Holy Family Church.
Peterson, Casimir M. '47 (BAL) Retired; [Q] Baltimore, MD Reparation Society of the Immaculate Heart of Mary.
Peterson, Charles J. *s.j.* '69 (FBK) Marshall, AK Immaculate Heart of Mary Church; St. Marys, AK Church of the Nativity; [E] St. Marys, AK Native Ministry Training Program; [E] St. Marys, AK Brother Joe Prince Jesuit Community.
Peterson, Cyril P. '41 (DM) Retired.
Peterson, Cyril P. '41 (WIN) Retired.
Peterson, Dennis L. '73 (GAL) [27] Houston, TX St. Frances Cabrini Church.
Peterson, Francis A. '46 (B) Retired.
Peterson, Frederick *o.s.b.* '95 (RCK) [H] Aurora, IL Marmion Abbey-St. Augustine's Abbey.
Peterson, Frederick *o.s.b.* '95 (ROM) Aurora, IL St. George Church.
Peterson, G. Paul *s.j.* '61 (BGP) [O] Fairfield, CT The Fairfield Jesuit Community-Fairfield University.
Peterson, G. Paul *s.j.* '86 (BGP) [A] Fairfield, CT Fairfield University.
Peterson, Gerald *glmy.* '56 (BIR) Winfield, AL Holy Spirit Church.
Peterson, Msgr. James W. '47 (E) [M] Erie, PA Holy Family Monastery; [O] Erie, PA Office of the Marginalized.
Peterson, Jay H. '78 (GF) Lewistown, MT St. Leo's Church; [K] Lewistown, MT St. Leo's Catholic Education Trust.
Peterson, John P. '89 (ARL) Chancellorsville, VA St. Patrick's Church.
Peterson, John S. *o.p.* '62 (PRO) [P] Providence, RI St. Thomas Aquinas Priory at Providence College.
Peterson, Joseph L. '75 (WH) [2] Huntington, WV Our Lady of Fatima Church.
Peterson, Leonard N. '67 (PH) Newtown Square, PA St. Anastasia Church; [DD] Philadelphia, PA Newman Apostolate.
Peterson, Louis P. '74 (BEL) Leave of Absence.
Peterson, Martin *c.m.* '47 (BRK) [U] Jamaica, NY Vincentian Residence.
Peterson, Maurice F. '87 (YAK) Cashmere, WA St. Francis Xavier Church; Leavenworth, WA Our Lady of the Snows Church.
Peterson, Paul *s.s.c.* '55 (LA) [Q] Los Angeles, CA Nazareth House; [S] Los Angeles, CA Congregation of the Poor Sisters of Nazareth Motherhouse, U.S.A. and Novitiate.
Peterson, Steven J. '73 (RVC) East Islip, NY St. Mary's Church.
Peterson, Steven J. '94 (WIN) Heron Lake, MN Sacred Heart Church.
Peterson, Thomas R. *o.p.* '56 (NEW) [A] South Orange, NJ Immaculate Conception Seminary; [A] South Orange, NJ Seton Hall University College Seminary; [B] South Orange, NJ Seton Hall University; [B] South Orange, NJ Seton Hall University.
Peterson, Vincent *o.f.m.conv.* (WDC) [1] Washington, DC St. Matthew Cathedral.
Peterson, William *c.ss.r.* '67 (CHI) [N] Bangkok, Thailand; [N] Parana, Brazil Rua Consulheiro Sinimbu.
Peterson, William *c.ss.r.* '67 (DEN) [M] Denver, CO The Redemptorists/Denver Province.
Peterson, William F. '59 (RCK) Retired.
Petilla, Antonio '61 (SFR) Daly City, CA Our Lady of Perpetual Help Church.
Petinge, Roland *o.f.m.* '61 (BO) [P] Andover, MA Franciscan Center; [W] Andover, MA St. Francis Friary; [Y] Andover, MA Franciscan Center - Retreat House.
Petit, Clement P. '40 (RCK) Retired.
Petit, Edmund P. '46 (RCK) Retired.
Petit, Eliades '80 (MIA) [17] Miami, FL St. Catherine of Siena Church.
Petit, Leo *m.s.c.* '51 (RCK) [H] Aurora, IL Missionaries of the Sacred Heart Community.
Petit, Roland '38 (ALB) Retired.
Petit-Monsieur, Lamartine (BO) [4] Lynn, MA St. Mary Church.
Petkash, Donald J. *s.j.* '71 (CLV) [E] Cuyahoga Falls, OH Walsh Jesuit High School.
Petko, Paul S. *f.ss.p.* '95 (OM) [34] Omaha, NE St. Patrick Church.
Petko, Paul S. *f.s.s.p.* '95 (SCR) [M] Elmhurst, PA Priestly Fraternity of St. Peter (F.S.S.P.).
Petosa, Joseph '55 (SEA) Retired.
Petracca, Anthony '85 (ALT) State College, PA Our Lady of Victory Church.
Petraitis, David *o.s.a.* '79 (FWT) Gainesville, TX St. Mary Church.
Petraitus, Donald *m.i.c.* '64 (CHI) [N] Chicago, IL Congregation of Marian Fathers of the Immaculate Conception.
Petrarca, Anthony *o.p.* '89 (SAC) Benicia, CA St. Dominic Church.
Petrarulo, John D. '53 (PIT) [4] New Castle, PA St. Vitus Church.
Petras, David M. '67 (PBR) [A] Pittsburgh, PA Byzantine Catholic Seminary of SS. Cyril and Methodius.
Petras, David M. '67 (PRM) On Duty Outside the Diocese.
Petrash, Reginald F. '84 (GAL) Freeport, TX St. Mary: Star of the Sea Church.
Petrasic, Martin J. '43 (OM) Retired.
Petrella, Robert '64 (WDC) Retired.
Petri, Gregg D. '61 (LSC) Alamogordo, NM Immaculate Conception Church.
Petri, John C. '45 (TR) Retired.
Petriano, Thomas '79 (RVC) Absent on Leave; [B] Patchogue, NY St. Joseph's College.
Petrich, John C. '83 (DUL) [4] Duluth, MN Our Lady of Mercy Church; Duluth, MN St. Luke's Hospital; Duluth, MN Miller Dwan Hospital; Saginaw, MN Northeast Regional Correctional Institution.
Petrie, Harry F. '45 (PIT) Wexford, PA St. Alexis Church; Retired.
Petrie, Michael J. '87 (MIL) Hartford, WI St. Kilian Church.
Petrie, Roderic *o.f.m.* '59 (SP) [O] Belleair Bluffs, FL St. James Friary.
Petrie, William *ss.cc.* '69 (FR) [K] Fairhaven, MA Sacred Hearts Provincial House.
Petrikovic, John *o.f.m.cap.* '81 (PIT) [N] Pittsburgh, PA St. Conrad Friary.
Petrillo, Joseph A. '77 (NEW) [2] Jersey City, NJ St. Aloysius Church.
Petrillo, Thomas J. '59 (NEW) Montclair, NJ Our Lady of Mt. Carmel Church.
Petrimoulx, Leo *o.f.m.cap.* '66 (MAD) [M] Madison, WI San Damiano Friary.
Petringa, Gerard '88 (BO) [3] Quincy, MA St. John the Baptist Church.
Petro, John G. '68 (PBR) Beaver, PA Saint Nicholas Chapel; [A] Pittsburgh, PA Byzantine Catholic Seminary of SS. Cyril and Methodius.
Petro, William J. '68 (WH) [Q] Huntington, WV Marshall Newman Center.
Petrocelli, John '71 (PRO) [K] North Providence, RI St. Joseph Health Services of Rhode Island - Our Lady of Fatima Hospital.
Petron, William G. '57 (DET) [5] Dearborn Heights, MI St. Mel Church.
Petronek, Msgr. Thomas '65 (STU) On Duty Outside the Diocese.
Petroske, Peter '84 (DET) Southgate, MI St. Pius X Church.
Petrosky, Arnold *t.o.r.* '57 (SFS) White Lake, SD St. Peter Church.
Petrosky, Christopher *t.o.r.* (ARL) [J] Winchester, VA Sacred Heart Friary.
Petrovsky, Felix *o.f.m.cap.* '55 (SAL) [D] Victoria, KS St. Fidelis Friary.
Petrovsky, James F. '68 (GBG) Ligonier, PA Holy Trinity Church.
Petroy, Dominic J. *o.s.b.* '86 (GBG) Jeannette, PA Sacred Heart Church; Jeannette, PA Jeannette District Memorial Hospital; Jeannette, PA Monsour Medical Center; [F] Jeannette, PA Jeannette District Memorial Hospital.
Petru, Msgr. Julius A. '37 (VIC) New Taiton, TX St. John Nepomucene Church.
Petru, Msgr. Stanley J. '48 (VIC) Cistern, TX SS. Cyril and Methodius Church; Hostyn, TX Holy Rosary Church.
Petruaskas, John C. *m.i.c.* '43 (WOR) [17] Worcester, MA St. Andrew the Apostle Church; [19] Worcester, MA St. Casimir's Church.
Petrucci, Dominic '82 (SFS) Retired.
Petrucci, Raymond '73 (BGP) [C] Trumbull, CT St. Joseph High School; [P] Monroe, CT Provincial House, Immaculate Heart of Mary Province, Sisters of the Holy Family of Nazareth, C.S.F.N.
Petruha, Louis J. *o.f.m.cap.* '65 (PIT) Cabot, PA St. Joseph Church; [N] Herman, PA St. Mary's Friary.
Petrunak, William (Y) [C] Warren, OH John F. Kennedy High School.
Petrusic, Anthony A. '57 (OM) Retired.
Petruska, Christopher '59 (PSC) St. Clair, PA St. Mary's Church.
Petruska, William M. '73 (SCR) Military Chaplains.
Petry, Thomas G. '78 (COL) [14] Columbus, OH St. Dominic Church.
Petsch, Joseph P. '50 (SAT) Comfort, TX Sacred Heart Church.
Petsche, Daniel *o.s.b.* '67 (KC) [A] Conception, MO Conception Seminary College; [J] Conception, MO Conception Abbey.
Petta, Gerard A. *m.ss.a.* (WH) Moorefield, WV Epiphany of the Lord Church.
Petta, LeRoy A. '60 (MIL) [74] Milwaukee, WI St. Stanislaus Church.
Pettei, Thomas G. '86 (BRK) [G] Fresh Meadows, NY St. Francis Preparatory School.
Petter, Henry V. '76 (DAL) Richardson, TX St. Paul the Apostle Church.
Pettingill, David M. '62 (SFR) Special Assignment.

Pettit, Edward G. '51 (PBL) [5] Pueblo, CO Our Lady of the Assumption Church; [14] Pueblo, CO St. Mary Church; [15] Pueblo, CO St. Patrick Church.
Pettit, Joseph H. '56 (HRT) Forestville, CT St. Matthew Church.
Pettit, Joseph J. '55 (GR) [20] Grand Rapids, MI SS. Peter and Paul's Church; Retired.
Pettit, William J. '54 (DET) Plymouth, MI St. Kenneth Church.
Pettke, Lawrence A. '81 (DET) [2] Southfield, MI St. Bede Church.
Petty, Edward C. '77 (DUB) Dyersville, IA Basilica of St. Francis Xavier.
Petuskey, John A. '66 (OKL) Edmond, OK St. John the Baptist Church.
Peverada, Augustine J. *c.s.c.* '45 (FR) [B] North Easton, MA Holy Cross Fathers Religious.
Peyton, John T. '61 (BRK) [124] Brooklyn, NY St. Rita's Church.
Peyton, Mark J. '77 (CLV) [66] Cleveland, OH St. Procop Church.
Peyton, Thomas '86 (BRK) Absent on Leave.
Pezzotti, Mario *s.x.* '59 (PAT) [M] Wayne, NJ Xaverian Missionary Fathers.
Pezzullo, Angelo B. '62 (BRK) [204] Queens, NY Nativity of the Blessed Virgin Mary Church.
Pfab, Charles *s.m.* '53 (ATL) [C] Atlanta, GA Marist School.
Pfaff, Aaron J. '96 (MAN) Keene, NH St. Bernard Church.
Pfaff, Joseph A. '75 (BRK) [179] Queens, NY Holy Trinity Church.
Pfalzer, Juvenal *o.f.m.* '42 (CIN) [L] Centerville, OH The Franciscan at St. Leonard.
Pfalzer, Miles *o.f.m.* '47 (MAR) Calumet, MI St. Paul the Apostle Church; Mohawk, MI Keweenaw Catholic Missions Church.
Pfannenstial, Celestine E. *s.t.* '41 (JKS) Camden, MS Immaculate Conception Church.
Pfannenstiel, Donald F. '75 (SAL) Herington, KS St. John the Evangelist Church.
Pfannenstiel, John *o.f.m.cap.* '82 (BAL) [6] Baltimore, MD St. Ambrose Church.
Pfau, Bernard A. '65 (FAR) Jamestown, ND The Basilica of St. James; [I] Jamestown, ND Jamestown College.
Pfeffer, Charles J. '77 (PH) [3] Philadelphia, PA St. Agatha-St. James Church; [DD] Philadelphia, PA Newman Apostolate.
Pfeffer, Msgr. Edward B. '56 (DM) Winterset, IA St. Joseph Church.
Pfeffer, Thomas '60 (DM) [13] Des Moines, IA Visitation Church.
Pfeifer, Frederick A. '93 (NEW) [15] Newark, NJ St. Francis Xavier Church.
Pfeifer, James *o.m.i.* '51 (BWN) [3] McAllen, TX Sacred Heart Church.
Pfeifer, John M. '65 (BIS) Watford City, ND Epiphany Church.
Pfeifer, William A. '36 (TOL) Retired.
Pfeiffer, Carl A. *o.ss.t.* '87 (NY) [218] Staten Island, NY Our Lady of Mt. Carmel-St. Benedicta Church.
Pfeiffer, Charles A. '54 (JC) Indian Creek, MO St. Stephen Church.
Pfeiffer, James S. '70 (NY) [Z] New York, NY Pope John Paul II Residence.
Pfeiffer, Msgr. Joseph C. '58 (BRK) [175] Queens, NY St. Helen Church.
Pfeiffer, Mark S. '82 (LIN) Benkelman, NE St. Joseph's Church.
Pfeiffer, Robert F. '61 (CLV) Medina, OH Holy Martyrs Church.
Pfender, Terrence *o.carm.* '77 (LA) [B] North Hills, CA Carmel West Community; [BB] Los Angeles, CA Archdiocesan Office for Campus Ministry.
Pfiester, Emeric J. *o.s.b.* '48 (GBG) [H] Latrobe, PA Saint Vincent Archabbey.
Pfister, J. Emile *s.j.* '58 (NO) [A] New Orleans, LA Notre Dame Seminary Graduate School of Theology.
Pfister, John F. '66 (FTW) [16] Fort Wayne, IN Queen of Angels Church.
Pfister, Neal A. '90 (DEN) Holyoke, CO St. Patrick Church.
Pfisterer, Robert *o.f.m.* '51 (SFR) [5] San Francisco, CA St. Anthony Church.
Pfleger, Michael L. '75 (CHI) [188] Chicago, IL St. Sabina Church.
Pfleger, Phillip C. '79 (TR) Evesham Township, NJ St. Isaac Jogues Church.
Pflomm, Peter '70 (RVC) New Hyde Park, NY Notre Dame Church.
Pflumm, Robert '60 (KCK) [2] Overland Park, KS Holy Cross Church.
Pfnausch, Edward G. '68 (HRT) On Duty Outside the Archdiocese.
Pfnausch, Edward G. '68 (WDC) [C] Washington, DC Catholic University of America, The; [C] Washington, DC Catholic University of America, The.
Pfotenhauer, Frederick W. '57 (FTW) [B] Notre Dame, IN University of Notre Dame Du Lac.
Pfundstein, George A. '63 (BRK) [151] Queens, NY St. Ann's Church.
Phalen, John J. *c.s.c.* '74 (FR) [B] North Easton, MA Holy Cross Fathers Religious.
Phalen, John L. '59 (DET) Lake Orion, MI St. Joseph Church.
Phalen, John P. *c.s.c.* '74 (LA) [CC] Hollywood, CA Family Theater Productions.
Pham, Chau *s.v.d.* '95 (STL) [57] St. Louis, MO St. Pius the Fifth Church.
Pham, Dominic Chinh *i.c.m.* '95 (BR) [4] Baton Rouge, LA St. Anthony of Padua Church; [H] Baton Rouge, LA Incarnational Consecration Mission.
Pham, Francis *c.ss.r.* (GAL) [42] Houston, TX St. Justin Martyr Church.
Pham, Hanh Van '93 (CC) [23] Corpus Christi, TX Collegiate Parish of St. Thomas More Church.
Pham, Hung Q. '89 (WCH) [11] Wichita, KS St. Anthony Church.
Pham, John '56 (SPR) [20] Springfield, MA St. Thomas Aquinas Church; [1] Holyoke, MA Blessed Sacrament Church.
Pham, Joseph '70 (BRK) [216] Queens, NY Our Lady of Mount Carmel Church.
Pham, Joseph Than Xuan '85 (RIC) [16] Richmond, VA Church of the Vietnamese Martyrs; [L] Richmond, VA Ethnic and Special Ministries.
Pham, Joseph Tuan '88 (ORG) Garden Grove, CA St. Callistus Church.
Pham, Khoi '94 (STO) Modesto, CA Our Lady of Fatima Church.
Pham, Le-Mihn '93 (AUS) Temple, TX St. Mary's Church.
Pham, Minh J. *c.m.* '91 (STO) Patterson, CA Sacred Heart Church.
Pham, Peter Chinh '71 (SJ) [21] San Jose, CA Our Lady Queen of Martyrs, Vietnamese Mission Church.
Pham, Phong Q. '91 (GR) Howard City, MI Christ the King Church; Lakeview, MI St. Francis de Sales Church.
Pham, Pierre '71 (SPR) On Duty Outside the Diocese.
Pham, Tan *s.o.l.t.* '91 (CC) [H] Robstown, TX Society of Our Lady of the Most Holy Trinity.
Pham, Tin Cosmas Kim '95 (GAL) [13] Houston, TX St. Benedict the Abbot Church.
Pham, Tuan '94 (ORG) Fountain Valley, CA Holy Spirit Church.
Pham, Vincent The Tung '85 (PH) [60] Philadelphia, PA Holy Innocents Church.
Pham An Su, Bartholomew M. *c.m.c.* (SPC) [E] Carthage, MO Congregation of the Mother Co-Redemptrix, United States Assumption Province.
Pham duc Trin, Joseph '70 (VIC) Palacios, TX St. Anthony's Church.
Pham Minh Van, Bartholomew *c.m.c.* (SPC) [E] Carthage, MO Congregation of the Mother Co-Redemptrix, United States Assumption Province.
Pham Tien Duc, John Bosco M. *c.m.c.* (SPC) [E] Carthage, MO Congregation of the Mother Co-Redemptrix, United States Assumption Province.
Pham Trung Thuc, John Bosco M. *c.m.c.* (SPC) [E] Carthage, MO Congregation of the Mother Co-Redemptrix, United States Assumption Province.
Pham Van Lan, Augustine '63 (CLV) [13] Cleveland, OH St. Boniface Church.
Pham Van Tue, Joseph '73 (NO) [2] Marrero, LA St. Agnes Le Thi Thanh Church.
Pham-Van-Ninh, James '67 (P) [1] Portland, OR Southeast Asian Vicariate Church.
Phan, Cho Dink Peter '72 (DAL) On Duty Outside the Diocese.
Phan, Dominic '70 (BLX) [8] Biloxi, MS St. Michael Church.
Phan, John-Peter '95 (PEO) [4] Champaign, IL St. Matthew Church.
Phan, Joseph Duong '93 (OAK) Dublin, CA St. Raymond Church; [1] San Leandro, CA Assumption of the Blessed Virgin Mary Church.
Phan, Nguyen Van *c.ss.r.* '93 (LA) [R] Baldwin Park, CA Vietnamese Redemptorist Mission.
Phan, Peter C. '72 (WDC) [C] Washington, DC Catholic University of America, The.
Phan, Peter Luc '90 (SJ) Cupertino, CA St. Joseph of Cupertino Church.
Phan, Philip '65 (NY) [42] New York, NY Guardian Angel Church.
Phan, Phu T. '92 (AMA) [11] Amarillo, TX St. Thomas the Apostle Church; Canyon, TX St. Ann's Church.
Phan, Vincent '95 (MOB) [11] Mobile, AL Little Flower Church.
Phan Cong Binh, John M. (SPC) [E] Carthage, MO Congregation of the Mother Co-Redemptrix, United States Assumption Province.
Phan Lam, Anthony '62 (OAK) [8] Oakland, CA St. Cyril Church.
Phan Sa Dominic '88 (PT) Niceville, FL Holy Name of Jesus Church.
Pharr, Msgr. William N. '60 (CHL) [11] Charlotte, NC St. Vincent de Paul Church.
Phelan, Cornelius '59 (LA) Newbury Park, CA St. Julie Billiart Church.
Phelan, Edward '63 (SFR) [15] San Francisco, CA St. Elizabeth Church.
Phelan, Gerald J. *s.j.* '62 (SJ) [2] Santa Clara, CA St. Clare Church.
Phelan, John E. '74 (SY) Forestport, NY St. Patrick Church.
Phelan, Msgr. John F. '41 (BAK) Retired.
Phelan, John P. *c.s.c.* '74 (ALB) [T] Albany, NY The Family Rosary Worldwide Office; [T] Albany, NY The Family Rosary Worldwide Office.
Phelan, John R. '46 (STL) Retired.
Phelan, Julian *o.f.m.cap.* '46 (ROC) [I] Interlaken, NY St. Fidelis Friary.
Phelan, Murray *o.carm.* '47 (JOL) [J] Darien, IL Carmelite Fathers Provincial Office.
Phelan, Nicholas '52 (SAC) Grass Valley, CA St. Patrick Church.
Phelan, Reginald L. '51 (TUC) Retired.
Phelan, Thomas '51 (ALB) [S] Troy, NY Rensselaer Polytechnic Institute.
Phelan, Thomas '53 (SEA) Retired.
Phelan, Thomas '76 (BEA) Absent On Leave.
Phelan, Walter M. '49 (GI) Grand Island, NE U.S. Veterans' Hospital; Retired.
Phelps, John *c.ss.r.* '66 (CHI) [29] Chicago, IL Blessed Sacrament Church.
Phelps, Lawrence J. *o.s.b.* '63 (NO) [A] St. Benedict, LA St. Joseph's Seminary College; [P] St. Benedict, LA St. Joseph Abbey.
Phelps, Robert *o.f.m.cap.* '66 (AGN) [F] Agana Heights, GU St. Fidelis Friary.
Phelps, Robert *o.f.m.cap.* '66 (HON) Ewa Beach, HI Our Lady of Perpetual Help Church.
Phen Van Pham, Joseph '78 (SD) [16] San Diego, CA Our Lady of the Sacred Heart Church.
Philbin, John J. '44 (BO) Middleboro, MA Sacred Heart Church; Retired.
Philbin, Patrick *s.m.* '24 (ORG) [H] Orange, CA Marianists.
Philbin, Patrick *s.m.* '72 (ORG) [L] Irvine, CA Campus Ministry-Diocese of Orange; [L] Irvine, CA Campus Ministry-Diocese of Orange.
Philbin, Patrick B. *s.m.* '72 (ORG) [K] Orange, CA House of Prayer for Priests.
Philbin, William '37 (RC) Retired.
Philibert, Paul *o.p.* '63 (FTW) [B] Notre Dame, IN University of Notre Dame Du Lac.
Philion, Richard *o.m.i.* '61 (CC) [3] Kingsville, TX St. Joseph Church.
Philiposki, Richard G. *s.ch.* '79 (P) [34] Portland, OR St. Stanislaus Church.
Philipps, John J. '55 (ROC) East Bloomfield, NY St. Bridget Church.
Philips, Joseph H. (SY) Special Assignment.
Philips, Salvator J. *o.f.m.* '46 (PAT) [M] Ringwood, NJ Holy Name Friary.
Philipsen, Martin *o.praem.* '42 (JKS) [2] Jackson, MS St. Mary Church; [E] Jackson, MS Priory of St. Moses the Black.
Philipsen, Todd K. '89 (GI) Crawford, NE St. John the Baptist Church.
Phillip, Alan *c.p.* '67 (CHI) [91] Chicago, IL Immaculate Conception Church; [N] Chicago, IL Immaculate Conception Monastery.
Phillipino, Lucio B. '60 (FR) North Easton, MA Immaculate Conception Church.
Phillippino, Michael L. '90 (NOR) [2] Norwich, CT Sacred Heart Church.
Phillips, A. Patrick *s.j.* '62 (BR) [J] Convent, LA Manresa, House of Retreats.
Phillips, Ambrose K. *t.o.r.* '71 (WDC) [B] Wheaton, MD St. Thomas More Friary, Third Order Regular of St. Francis.
Phillips, Benet C. *o.s.b.* '92 (MAN) [K] Manchester, NH St. Anselm Abbey; [N] Durham, NH Campus Ministries.
Phillips, C. Frank *c.r.* '77 (CHI) [107] Chicago, IL St. John Cantius Church.
Phillips, Christopher G. '83 (SAT) [14] San Antonio, TX Our Lady of the Atonement Catholic Church.
Phillips, Gene D. *s.j.* '65 (CHI) [C] Chicago, IL Jesuit Community at Loyola University of Chicago.
Phillips, George *c.ss.r.* (SP) [9] Tampa, FL St. Joseph Church.
Phillips, George '45 (ALB) Latham, NY St. Ambrose Church; Retired.
Phillips, Msgr. George M. '40 (OG) Retired.
Phillips, Glenn *o.f.m.* '66 (SUP) Bayfield, WI Holy Family Church; Cornucopia, WI St. Ann Church; LaPointe, WI St. Joseph Church; Red Cliff, WI St. Francis Church.
Phillips, Msgr. Hugh J. '35 (BAL) Retired; [C] Emmitsburg, MD Mount Saint Mary's College.
Phillips, John M. '87 (STA) [4] Gainesville, FL St. Augustine Church; [L] Gainesville, FL University of Florida-St. Augustine Parish and Student Center.
Phillips, Joseph H. '68 (SY) [11] Syracuse, NY St. Ann Church; [N] Syracuse, NY Family Life Education.
Phillips, Joseph J. *s.p.* '66 (Y) [I] Canton, OH House of Loreto; [N] Canton, OH Servants of the Paraclete.
Phillips, Kenneth G. '91 (BIS) Carson, ND St. Theresa the Child Jesus Church; Flasher, ND St. Lawrence

Church; Raleigh, ND St. Gertrude Church.
Phillips, Louis *f.a.c.* (NY) [CC] New York, NY University Apostolate.
Phillips, Louis J. *s.a.c.* '81 (BAL) [49] Baltimore, MD St. Jude Shrine Church.
Phillips, Msgr. Michael J. '60 (BRK) [10] Brooklyn, NY St. Anselm's Church.
Phillips, Michael T. '69 (DAV) [3] Davenport, IA Holy Family Church.
Phillips, Paschal *o.c.s.o.* '57 (L) [L] Trappist, KY Abbey of Our Lady of Gethsemani, of the Order of Cistercians of the Strict Observance.
Phillips, Randall R. '83 (DET) [4] Dearborn Heights, MI St. Linus Church.
Phillips, Rene F. *o.f.m.* '56 (NY) [Z] New York, NY Franciscan Friars, Order of Friars Manor.
Phillips, Robert L. *s.j.* '72 (STL) [P] St. Louis, MO Jesuit Community Corporation at St. Louis University - Jesuit Hall.
Phillips, Robert W. '49 (SC) Retired.
Phillips, Steven '87 (ORL) [1] Ocala, FL Blessed Trinity Church.
Phillips, Thomas '42 (NY) Retired.
Phillips, Thomas L. '71 (BAL) Abingdon, MD St. Francis de Sales Church.
Phillips, Walter W. '55 (GI) Retired.
Philominathan, Sagayaraj *s.d.b.* '88 (OAK) [N] Berkeley, CA Salesian Community.
Philominsamy, Michaelraj *c.pp.s.* '91 (SR) Philo, CA St. Elizabeth Seton Church.
Phinn, Gilbert S. '53 (BO) [2] Milton, MA St. Elizabeth Church.
Phinn, Paul A. '57 (BO) [34] Boston, MA St. John Chrysostom Church.
Phipps, Charles T. *s.j.* '59 (SJ) [B] Santa Clara, CA Santa Clara University.
Phuc, Anthony *c.ss.r.* '56 (MRY) Pacific Grove, CA St. Angela Church.
Phuc, Hong *c.ss.r.* '48 (LA) [R] Baldwin Park, CA Vietnamese Redemptorist Mission.
Phuc, John '83 (NO) Destrehan, LA St. Charles Borromeo Church.
Phuc, Tran Dinh *c.ss.r.* '56 (LA) [R] Baldwin Park, CA Vietnamese Redemptorist Mission.
Phung, Chi Peter '90 (TLS) Krebs, OK St. Joseph's Church.
Phung, Le Quang *c.ss.r.* '69 (LA) [R] Baldwin Park, CA Vietnamese Redemptorist Mission.
Phung, Vincent '96 (DEN) Littleton, CO St. Mary Church.
Physician, Thomas R. '58 (DET) [2] Clinton Twp., MI St. Louis Church; Clinton Township, MI State Prisons; [T] Detroit, MI St. Mary Magdalen Catholic Community.
Piacentini, David A. '71 (PRO) Barrington, RI Holy Angels Church.
Piacitelli, Henry J. *c.m.* (SLC) Huntsville, UT St. Florence Catholic Community Church.
Piano, Timothy '77 (MIA) Absent on Leave.
Piansay, Victor Villegas '64 (FRS) Earlimart, CA St. Jude Church.
Piasecki, Timothy R. '73 (RCK) [9] Aurora, IL Sacred Heart Church.
Piatek, Ignatius M. *o.f.m.conv.* '61 (BAL) [D] Baltimore, MD Archbishop Curley High School; [M] Baltimore, MD Immaculate Heart of Mary Friary.
Piatek, Joseph '69 (ORL) [10] Orlando, FL St. Joseph Church.
Piatkowski, Adalbert *o.f.m.conv.* '84 (SPR) [10] Chicopee, MA St. Stanislaus Basilica.
Piatkowski, Robert J. '53 (NEW) Springfield, NJ St. James Church.
Piazza, Msgr. Benjamin A. '49 (NEW) Retired.
Piazza, Salvatore J. '48 (BUF) Ransomville, NY Immaculate Conception Church; Retired.
Picado, Rodrigo '71 (NO) On Duty Outside the Archdiocese.
Picard, Daniel '79 (LAF) [3] New Iberia, LA Our Lady of Perpetual Help Church.
Picard, Howard *c.i.c.m.* '56 (ARL) [J] Arlington, VA Missionhurst, C.I.C.M.-Central House and Provincialate.
Picard, Michael C. '66 (PH) Newtown, PA St. Andrew Church.
Picard, Raymond '65 (PRT) Newcastle, ME St. Patrick Church.
Picardi, Aubert Marie *o.f.m.* '62 (BO) [57] Boston, MA Our Lady of Mt. Carmel Church.
Picardi, John J. (BO) Awaiting Assignment.
Picarella, Dale M. '84 (BAL) [24] Baltimore, MD St. Clare Church.
Picariello, Anthony R. *s.j.* '80 (BO) [W] Weston, MA Campion Center.
Picazo, Luis *s.f.* '72 (WDC) [B] Silver Spring, MD Holy Family Seminary.
Picciano, Daniel A. '71 (RVC) Seaford, NY St. James Church.
Piccinini, Claudio *c.p.* '72 (BRK) [U] Jamaica, NY Immaculate Conception Monastery.
Piccinino, Corey V. '86 (BGP) [5] Danbury, CT St. Peter's Church; [C] Danbury, CT Immaculate High School.
Piccioli, Giovanna (BRK) [103] Brooklyn, NY Our Lady of Miracles Church.
Piccione, John T. *o.f.m.* '95 (PAT) [5] Paterson, NJ St. Bonaventure Church.
Piccola, Michael J. *v.f.* '78 (SCR) Drums, PA Church of the Good Shepherd.
Piccoli, Gino *o.f.m.* '65 (PHX) [G] Scottsdale, AZ Franciscan Renewal Center, Inc. (Casa de Paz Y Bien).
Piccolo, Bruno *p.i.m.e.* '65 (DET) [K] Detroit, MI P.I.M.E. College Community; [K] Detroit, MI P.I.M.E. Missionaries of SS. Peter and Paul; [T] Detroit, MI Foster Parents Mission Club.
Piccolomini, Rocco '85 (WOR) [13] Worcester, MA Our Lady of Mt. Carmel and St. Ann Church.
Pichard, Msgr. Lawrence '73 (DAL) [1] Dallas, TX Cathedral-Santuario de Guadalupe Church.
Piche, Donald J. '77 (STP) New Hope, MN St. Joseph Church.
Piche, Lee '84 (STP) [C] St. Paul, MN University of St. Thomas.
Piche, Marc A. '68 (BO) [7] Haverhill, MA Sacred Hearts Church.
Picher, Leo J. '34 (HRT) Retired.
Pichette, David '67 (SY) Absent on Leave.
Pichette, Msgr. Fernand L. '58 (MAN) Meredith, NH St. Charles Church.
Pick, Anthony P. '67 (SC) Royal, IA St. Louis Church.
Pick, Edward '60 (VEN) Longboat Key, FL St. Mary Star of the Sea Church.
Pick, Philip E. *s.j.* '50 (MIL) [P] Milwaukee, WI Jesuit Provincial Office, Wisconsin Province.
Pickard, William B. '76 (SCR) [22] Scranton, PA St. Paul's Church; [J] Scranton, PA St. Joseph's Center.
Pickard, Msgr. William M. '54 (GAL) [28] Houston, TX St. Francis de Sales Church.
Pickarts, Bernard J. '55 (MAD) Footville, WI St. Augustine Church.
Pickert, Cecil *o.carm.* '58 (BEL) [J] Carbondale, IL The Newman Center.
Pickett, James '61 (COL) On Duty Outside the Diocese.
Pickett, James '61 (OAK) Pleasanton, CA St. Augustine Church.
Pickett, Robert T. '55 (TLS) Retired.
Pico, Fernando *s.j.* (SJN) [E] Hato Rey, PR Jesuit Community - Casa Claver.
Pico, Jaime *c.m.* '42 (BRK) [104] Brooklyn, NY Our Lady of Monserrate-St. Ambrose Church.
Picornell, Antonio *m.ss.cc.* '42 (SJN) [25] Bayamon, PR Santiago Apostol Church.
Picton, James (SEA) Hoquiam, WA Our Lady of Good Help Church; Ocean Shores, WA St. Jerome Church.
Picton, James '75 (SEA) Aberdeen, WA St. Mary's Church; Aberdeen, WA SS. Peter and Paul Church; Special Assignment.
Picton, Thomas *c.ss.r.* '71 (SAT) [M] San Antonio, TX Redemptorists of Texas-Redemptorist Community at St. Gerard.
Piderit, John J. *s.j.* (CHI) [C] Chicago, IL Loyola University-Chicago; [C] Chicago, IL Jesuit Community at Loyola University of Chicago.
Pidgeon, John J. '87 (PH) Newtown, PA St. Andrew Church; [D] Warminster, PA Archbishop Wood Catholic High School.
Pidlypczak, Orest *o.s.b.m.* '75 (PHU) Carteret, NJ St. Mary's Church.
Pieber, Carl L. *c.m.* '80 (PH) [Z] Philadelphia, PA Congregation of the Mission.
Pieber, Carl L. *c.m.* '80 (WDC) [C] Washington, DC Catholic University of America, The.
Pieber, Carl L. *c.m.* '80 (WH) [A] Wheeling, WV Wheeling Jesuit University.
Piechocinski, Thomas A. '61 (MET) Monmouth Junction, NJ St. Cecilia Church.
Piechocki, Bruce (FTW) [16] Fort Wayne, IN Queen of Angels Church; Pierceton, IN St. Francis Xavier Church; On Special Assignment.
Piechocki, Raymond S. '47 (ALB) Special Assignment; [J] Amsterdam, NY Mt. Loretto Nursing Home.
Piechowski, Leonard E. '51 (MIL) [5] West Allis, WI St. Joseph's Church.
Pieczka, Walenty *c.m.* '43 (HRT) Derby, CT St. Michael Church.
Pied, Wilfred L. '51 (BO) Retired.
Pied, Wilfrid L. '51 (BO) Canton, MA St. John the Evangelist Church.
Piedahita, Msgr. Hernan '77 (SJN) Luquillo, PR Madre del Redentor Church.
Piedra, Ruskin S. *c.ss.r.* '60 (BRK) [U] Brooklyn, NY Our Lady of Good Counsel Residence.
Piegl, Fred '70 (CHI) [W] Chicago, IL Northview University Center.
Piekarczyk, Marian *s.d.s.* '80 (SAT) [20] San Antonio, TX Our Lady of Sorrows Church; San Antonio, TX Methodist Hospital.
Piekarski, Joseph J. '86 (WIL) [6] Wilmington, DE St. Hedwig Church.
Pieklo, Chris *o.carm.* '77 (LA) [3] North Hollywood, CA St. Jane Frances de Chantal Church.
Pienciak, Daniel B. '87 (TR) Leave of Absence.
Pientek, Placid *o.s.b.* '44 (CLV) [P] Cleveland, OH Benedictine Order of Cleveland.
Pieper, George M. *s.j.* '48 (STL) [O] St. Louis, MO Fusz Pavilion.
Pieper, Herbert W. *s.m.* '38 (STL) [4] Creve Coeur, MO Our Lady of the Pillar Church.
Pieper, Msgr. James E. '57 (STL) Des Peres, MO St. Clement Church.
Pieper, Robert F. *o.p.* '54 (CHI) [M] Palatine, IL St. Joseph's Home for the Elderly; [N] Chicago, IL Dominicans (Provincial Office).
Pieper, Theodore X. '62 (STL) Old Mines, MO St. Joachim's Church; Tiff, MO St. Joseph's Church.
Pier, Andrew *o.s.b.* '37 (CLV) [P] Cleveland, OH Benedictine Order of Cleveland.
Pier, Msgr. Joseph '38 (ALT) Retired.
Pierce, Blaine F. '46 (Y) Retired.
Pierce, Bradley *m.ss.a.* (NOR) Essex, CT Our Lady of Sorrows Church; [A] Cromwell, CT Holy Apostles College and Seminary; [F] Cromwell, CT Missionaries of the Holy Apostles.
Pierce, Brian J. *o.p.* '88 (NO) [P] New Orleans, LA Dominican Fathers & Brothers, Southern Dominican Province.
Pierce, Edward J. '72 (SFS) Mitchell, SD Holy Family Church.
Pierce, George R. '59 (GBG) Maxwell, PA St. James Church.
Pierce, James L. *s.j.* '77 (NY) [Z] New York, NY Jesuit Provincial's Office; [Z] New York, NY Xavier Jesuit Community; [CC] New York, NY University Apostolate.
Pierce, John J. *o.f.m.* '63 (PAT) [M] Butler, NJ St. Anthony Friary.
Pierce, Joseph B. '92 (WDC) [3] Washington, DC St. Ann Church.
Pierce, Justin A. *s.d.s.* '48 (GB) [B] Manitowoc, WI Silver Lake College of the Holy Family.
Pierce, Larry E. '58 (SAL) Retired.
Pierce, Mark R. '81 (LC) [1] Stevens Point, WI Newman University Parish Church; [5] Stevens Point, WI St. Stanislaus Church; [L] Stevens Point, WI Newman University Parish.
Pierce, Michael G. *s.j.* '40 (BO) [W] Weston, MA Campion Health Center, Inc.
Pierce, Msgr. Robert T. '54 (LA) Covina, CA St. Louise de Marillac Church.
Pierce, William C. '71 (CAM) National Park, NJ St. Matthew's Church.
Pierce, William J. '52 (SHP) Retired.
Pierceall, Patrick L. '69 (JC) Clarence, MO St. Patrick Church; Shelbina, MO St. Mary Church.
Pierick, Bernard E. '47 (MAD) Retired.
Pierini, Pascal *o.c.d.* '48 (SJ) [M] San Jose, CA Carmelite Monastery, Novitiate.
Pierini, Raymond G. *m.m.* '87 (NY) Manhattan, NY Cabrini Medical Center; [Z] Maryknoll, NY Maryknoll Fathers and Brothers.
Pieris, Timothy '46 (NO) Retired.
Pierjok, Harry A. '88 (PEO) Kickapoo, IL St. Mary's of Kickapoo Church.
Piermarini, Msgr. Louis R. '69 (WOR) Oxford, MA St. Roch's Church.
Pierog, Stanislaus '76 (VEN) [5] Fort Myers, FL St. Francis Xavier Church.
Pieroni, Edward L. '85 (PRO) [3] Woonsocket, RI St. Ann's Church; [8] Woonsocket, RI Our Lady of Victories Church.
Pierre, Jean '88 (MIA) [1] Miami, FL St. Mary's Cathedral.
Pierre, Kenneth J. '63 (STP) [3] Minneapolis, MN Annunciation Church.
Pierre, Roger A. '79 (BRK) [57] Brooklyn, NY Holy Innocents Church.
Pierre, Roger P. '63 (STP) White Bear Lake, MN St. Mary of the Lake Church.
Pierre-Louis, Jean Marx '87 (BO) [8] Brockton, MA Sacred Heart Church.
Pierro, Sebastian C. '82 (BUF) [2] Dunkirk, NY Holy Trinity Church.
Pierse, Msgr. James J. '44 (ORG) Seal Beach, CA Holy Family Church; Retired.
Pierson, Robert *o.s.b.* '84 (SCL) [I] Collegeville, MN St. John's Abbey, of the Order of St. Benedict.
Piesiur, Joseph '75 (PH) [81] Philadelphia, PA St. Josaphat Church.
Pietramale, John L. '92 (OM) [12] Omaha, NE Christ the King Church.
Pietrantonio, Thomas *o.f.m.cap.* '49 (WIL) [I] Wilmington, DE Capuchin Franciscan Friars, St. Francis Renewal Center; [L] Wilmington, DE St. Francis Renewal Center.
Pietras, Robert E. '62 (JOL) Downers Grove, IL Divine Savior Church.
Pietropaoli, David '84 (BAL) Educational Sabbatical.
Pietropinto, Joseph P. '70 (NEW) Maywood, NJ Our Lady Queen of Peace Church.
Pietrowski, Stephen '92 (RVC) Williston Park, NY St. Aidan's Church.
Pietrucha, Edward S. *c.s.p.* '57 (TUC) [11] Tucson, AZ

St. Cyril of Alexandria Church.
Pietrus, Henryk '70 (FAR) Absent on Leave.
Pietrzak, Bernard J. '81 (CHI) [3] Mt. Prospect, IL St. Raymond de Penafort Church.
Pietrzak, Daniel *o.f.m.conv.* (BAL) [M] Ellicott City, MD Order of Friars Minor Conventual.
Pietrzyk, John Michael *o.p.* '73 (NEW) [27] Jersey City, NJ Sacred Heart Church.
Pietrzynski, Boleslaus J. '42 (PIT) Retired.
Piette, Gilbert M. '79 (BWN) [4] Harlingen, TX St. Anthony Church.
Pifher, Cletus *o.f.m.conv.* '64 (SAV) Brunswick, GA St. Francis Xavier Church.
Pifher, William A. *c.s.c.* '94 (FTW) [5] South Bend, IN St. Casimir Church; [19] South Bend, IN St. Stephen Church.
Pighini, Richard *c.s.v.* '85 (JOL) [2] Kankakee, IL St. Patrick Church.
Pignato, Salvatore A. '68 (PSC) Orlando, FL St. Nicholas of Myra Church.
Pigott, Edward L. *s.j.* '68 (CIN) [F] Cincinnati, OH St. Xavier High School; [M] Cincinnati, OH Jesuit Community at St. Xavier High School.
Piguet, Leo A. '51 (LFT) Carmel, IN St. Elizabeth Ann Seton Church.
Pihale, Robert I. *s.j.* '48 (OM) [K] Omaha, NE Jesuit Community At Creighton University.
Pijoan, L. Adrian M. Figuerola '71 (NO) Retired.
Pijunowski, Joseph J. '85 (WOR) [1] Southbridge, MA St. Hedwig's Church.
Pikturna, Vytautas '45 (BRK) Retired.
Pikula, Roman *s.d.s.* '94 (MIL) [P] Milwaukee, WI Salvatorian Provincial Residence.
Pikulski, John F. '60 (BGP) [6] Stamford, CT Holy Name of Jesus Church; Danbury, CT Danbury Hospital.
Pikus, Karl A. *s.j.* (SCR) [M] Elmhurst, PA Priestly Fraternity of St. Peter (F.S.S.P.).
Pikus, Karl A. *f.s.s.p.* '92 (RC) [1] Rapid City, SD Cathedral of Our Lady of Perpetual Help.
Pilaczynski, John E. *o.m.i.* '68 (STP) [E] St. Paul, MN The Saint Thomas Academy.
Pilarski, Bernard '56 (DET) Detroit, MI Annapolis; Detroit, MI Garden City Osteopathic Hospital.
Pilarski, Chester J. '50 (SAG) Kawkawlin, MI Sacred Heart Church.
Pilarski, Raymond J. '55 (GAY) Atlanta, MI Jesus the Good Shepherd Church; Hillman, MI St. Augustine Church.
Pilarz, Scott R. *s.j.* (WDC) [M] Washington, DC The Jesuit Community at Georgetown University.
Pilarz, Scott R. *s.j.* '92 (PH) [C] Philadelphia, PA St. Joseph's University.
Pilat, Edmund S. '56 (SY) Fulton, NY St. Michael Church.
Pilato, Sabato '92 (LA) Torrance, CA St. Catherine Laboure Church; [D] Gardena, CA Junipero Serra High School.
Pilatowski, Augustine *o.f.m.conv.* '48 (HRT) [K] New Britain, CT St. Lucian's Home for the Aged.
Pilatowski, Augustine *o.f.m.conv.* '59 (HRT) [M] New Britain, CT Conventual Franciscans.
Pilatowski, Eugene '60 (NOR) [3] Norwich, CT St. Joseph Church.
Pilcher, Gregory A. *o.s.b.* '78 (LR) El Dorado, AR Holy Redeemer Church.
Pilecki, Walter J. '43 (KC) Sugar Creek, MO St. Cyril Church.
Pileggi, Francis J. *o.s.f.s.* '61 (PH) [Z] Philadelphia, PA Oblates of St. Francis De Sales.
Piletic, William R. *c.m.* '45 (CHI) [C] Chicago, IL Vincentian Community at DePaul University.
Pilger, G. Richard *i.c.* '79 (SP) Seminole, FL Blessed Sacrament Church.
Pilger, Joseph J. '55 (LEX) Retired.
Pilgram, Paul C. *s.j.* '70 (STL) [O] St. Louis, MO Fusz Pavilion.
Pilipie, John P. '82 (PAT) Whippany, NJ Our Lady of Mercy Church.
Pilla, P. Carl '54 (SY) Retired; [S] Syracuse, NY St. Pius X Home, Inc.
Pillar, Conrad *o.s.b.* '47 (KCK) Fidelity, KS St. Augustine's Church; Sabetha, KS Sacred Heart Church.
Pillar, James J. *o.m.i.* '54 (STP) [N] St. Paul, MN Oblate Provincial Offices; [N] St. Paul, MN Oblate Residence.
Pilliod, Francis B. '39 (CIN) [22] Dayton, OH St. Peter Church; Retired.
Pillon, Gordon '79 (CHL) [11] Charlotte, NC St. Vincent de Paul Church.
Pillon, Gordon '79 (PEO) On Duty Outside the Diocese.
Pilola, Joseph S. '87 (HT) [4] Thibodaux, LA St. Genevieve Church.
Pilon, Daniel J. '76 (FAR) Wild Rice, ND St. Benedict's Church.
Pilon, James F. (HRT) Cornwall Bridge, CT St. Bridget Church; Sharon, CT St. Bernard's Church.
Pilon, Jerome R. '89 (PEO) Hoopeston, IL St. Anthony's Church.
Pilon, Mark A. '75 (ARL) Annandale, VA St. Ambrose Church.
Pilones, Loji *r.c.j.* '86 (FRS) Sanger, CA St. Mary Church.
Pilsner, Peter R. '89 (NY) [211] Staten Island, NY St. Joseph, St. Thomas Church.
Pilson, Paul '53 (ALB) On Duty Outside the Diocese.
Pimental, Francis Mary of the Angels *f.f.i.* '83 (FR) [K] New Bedford, MA Marian Friary of Our Lady, Queen of the Seraphic Order.
Pimentel, Jose *o.p.* '90 (P) [6] Eugene, OR St. Thomas More Church; [P] Portland, OR University of Portland.
Pina, Joseph D. '72 (LA) Ventura, CA San Buenaventura Mission Church.
Pina, Martin '93 (LUB) Hale Center, TX St. Theresa's Church.
Pina, Paolino *o.f.m.cap.* '73 (BO) [60] Boston, MA St. Patrick Church.
Pinard, Paul *s.s.e.* '59 (NOR) [A] Enders Island, CT St. Edmund's Novitiate; [F] Mystic, CT Society of St. Edmund.
Pincelli, Thomas '70 (BWN) La Feria, TX St. Francis Xavier Church.
Pinchock, Joseph '72 (ORL) Winter Haven, FL St. Joseph's Church.
Pinci, August *o.ss.t.* '36 (BAL) [M] Baltimore, MD Holy Trinity Monastery.
Pinciaro, Albert G., III '84 (BGP) [6] Norwalk, CT St. Philip Church.
Pincince, Gerald P. '65 (PRO) On Duty Outside the Diocese.
Pincince, Marcel E. '83 (PRO) [A] Providence, RI Seminary of Our Lady of Providence.
Pinczewski, Philip A. '87 (E) Meadville, PA St. Agatha Church.
Pineau, Gerard J. '81 (BO) [4] Weymouth, MA St. Jerome Church.
Pineda, Juan *m.s.c.* '77 (LA) Cudahy, CA Cudahy Mission Church.
Pineda, Serafin *o.a.r.* '18 (NY) [179] Bronx, NY Our Saviour Church.
Pinero, Geraldo J. '91 (PH) [71] Philadelphia, PA Incarnation of Our Lord Church.
Pinette, Stuart H. '95 (HRT) [2] Hamden, CT Blessed Sacrament Church.
Pingatore, Thomas J. '44 (STP) [13] St. Paul, MN St. Ambrose Church.
Pinho, Antonio M. '66 (NEW) Military Chaplains.
Pinizotto, Anthony J. *o.s.f.s.* '78 (ARL) Stafford, VA St. William of York Church.
Pinizzotto, Anthony J. *o.s.f.s.* '78 (WIL) [I] Wilmington, DE Oblates of St. Francis De Sales.
Pinkerton, Samuel J. '95 (WCH) Pittsburg, KS Our Lady of Lourdes Church; [E] Pittsburg, KS Mount Carmel Medical Center; Mount Carmel Foundation.
Pinkston, Robert L. *c.s.p.* '69 (GR) Grand Rapids, MI Chapel of St. Paul-Catholic Information Center.
Pinne, Christopher P. *s.j.* '87 (KC) [D] Kansas City, MO Rockhurst High School; [J] Kansas City, MO Rockhurst High School - Jesuit Community.
Pins, Herbert '71 (SEA) Unassigned.
Pins, Msgr. Joseph '70 (STL) Chesterfield, MO Ascension Church.
Pintacura, Michael '76 (STO) [9] Stockton, CA St. Michael Church.
Pinterbone, John A. '79 (NY) [197] Staten Island, NY Assumption Church; [228] Staten Island, NY St. Stanislaus Kostka Church.
Pinti, Domenico C. '85 (TUC) Safford, AZ St. Rose of Lima Church.
Pinto, Alex '69 (NEW) [D] Clark, NJ Mother Seton (Girls) Regional High School.
Pinto, Danny '63 (FTW) Churubusco, IN St. John Bosco Church; Ege, IN Immaculate Conception Church.
Pinto, Edgar '80 (SJN) [2] Trujillo Alto, PR Santa Cruz Church.
Pinto, Peter J. '56 (HRT) [4] West Haven, CT St. Louis Church.
Pinto, Santan *s.o.l.t.* '77 (CC) [H] Robstown, TX Society of Our Lady of the Most Holy Trinity.
Pintye, Louis M. *o.f.m.* '90 (ALB) [1] Troy, NY St. Anthony of Padua Church.
Pinyan, Charles '92 (NEW) Paramus, NJ Annunciation Church.
Pinzon, Eduardo *s.j.* '60 (CHI) [128] Chicago, IL St. Mary of the Lake Church.
Piontkowski, Richard L. '82 (GI) St. Libory, NE St. Libory's Church.
Piorkowski, Robert '76 (STN) [5] Madison, IL St. Mary's Church; St. Louis, MO Assumption B.V.M. Church.
Piorkowski, Msgr. Stanley W. '51 (SCR) Dickson City, PA Visitation of the Blessed Virgin Mary Church.
Piotrowicz, Maciej '95 (PMB) Wellington, FL St. Rita Church.
Piotrowski, Adrian C. *o.s.c.* '64 (NY) Katonah, NY St. Mary of the Assumption Church; [Z] New Rochelle, NY Crosier (Canons Regular of the Order of the Holy Cross).
Piotrowski, Leonard '93 (SP) Indian Rocks Beach, FL St. Jerome Church.
Piovan, Benjamin '64 (NO) La Place, LA Ascension of Our Lord Church.
Pipala, Edward A. '66 (NY) Absent on Leave.
Piper, Norbert G. *o.carm.* '32 (JOL) Glendale Heights, IL St. Matthew Church.
Pipp, Thomas J. *s.j.* '92 (TOL) [C] Toledo, OH St. John's Jesuit High School.
Pipta, Robert M. '94 (VNN) Phoenix, AZ St. Stephen Church.
Piquado, Thomas G. *s.j.* '72 (SFR) [24] San Francisco, CA St. Ignatius Church; [N] San Francisco, CA Jesuit Community at University of San Francisco.
Piraro, Don '67 (LKC) [C] Moss Bluff, LA St. Charles Center.
Pires, Francisco '84 (SLC) Brigham City, UT St. Henry Church.
Piro, Francis '54 (PH) [103] Philadelphia, PA St. Michael Church.
Piro, Frank R. '62 (SFR) Daly City, CA St. Andrew Church.
Piro, Gerald J. '79 (BRK) Absent on Leave.
Pirrera, Aaron *o.s.b.* '85 (LR) [A] Subiaco, AR Subiaco Monastery.
Pirrone, Roberto '88 (LA) Maywood, CA St. Rose of Lima Church.
Pirrung, George F. '54 (PHX) Cottonwood, AZ Immaculate Conception Church.
Pirulli, Francis D. '45 (GBG) Retired; [G] Greensburg, PA Neumann House.
Pisanelli, Humbert D. '37 (NY) Retired; [Z] New York, NY Our Lady of Consolation Residence.
Pisanello, George M. '86 (MET) [7] Perth Amboy, NJ Holy Spirit Church.
Pisano, Andrew '42 (LA) Retired.
Pisarcik, John G. (PAT) Absent on Leave.
Piscilli, Constanzo J. '69 (PRT) Belfast, ME St. Francis of Assisi Church.
Pisciotta, Justin M. *o.s.m.* '64 (DEN) [21] Denver, CO Our Lady of Mt. Carmel Church.
Piscitelli, Vincent J. '37 (BO) Retired.
Piscitello, Primo P. *o.f.m.* '60 (BO) [W] Boston, MA St. Christopher Friary.
Pisclotta, Justin M. *o.s.m.* '64 (ORG) [H] Buena Park, CA Servite Fathers And Brothers.
Pisegna, Cedric *c.p.* '91 (SAC) [H] Citrus Heights, CA Christ the King Retreat.
Pisik, Timothy E. '74 (CAM) On Sick Leave.
Piskula, Louis '75 (OWN) Non-Parochial Assignments; [G] Whitesville, KY St. Joseph's Monastery.
Piskura, Joseph H. '54 (CLV) Released from Diocesan Assignment.
Pisoni, Otto B. '41 (E) Retired.
Pisors, John A. *c.s.v.* '66 (CHI) [N] Arlington Heights, IL Viatorian Province Center-Clerics of St. Viator.
Pispeky, Steve '88 (GLP) Tinaja, NM San Lorenzo Church.
Pistacchio, Gene B. (WDC) [M] Silver Spring, MD Gemelli House.
Pistone, Bernardo '73 (HBG) [3] Lancaster, PA Assumption of the Blessed Virgin Mary Church; [J] Lancaster, PA Iglesia de San Juan Bautista.
Pistone, Dominic J., Jr. '78 (GAL) [64] Houston, TX St. Paul Church.
Pistorius, Francis X. *s.j.* (GAL) [3] Spring, TX St. Ignatius of Loyola Church.
Pistulka, Celestine C. '56 (NU) Marshall, MN Holy Redeemer Church.
Piszczatowski, Maurice *o.f.m.conv.* '53 (BAL) [88] Baltimore, MD St. Stanislaus Kostka Church.
Piszker, James E. '91 (E) Meadville, PA St. Brigid Church.
Pitkiewicz, Vincent '45 (BRK) Retired.
Pitlok, Andrew J. *s.d.s.* '52 (NEW) [N] Verona, NJ The Salvatorian Fathers.
Pitre, Eric J. '81 (GAL) Richmond, TX Sacred Heart Church.
Pitruzzello, Raymond '53 (HRT) [2] Waterbury, CT Immaculate Conception Church.
Pitstick, Rory '94 (SPK) Pasco, WA St. Patrick Church.
Pitt, William L. '61 (RIC) [A] Virginia Beach, VA Catholic High School.
Pittappilly, Thomas '61 (BIS) Williston, ND St. Joseph Church.
Pittard, Wayne '83 (GF) Roundup, MT St. Benedict's Church.
Pittman, Robert S. *s.s.s.* '58 (CLV) [P] Cleveland, OH Congregation of the Blessed Sacrament Provincial House.
Pittman, Robert S. *s.s.s.* '58 (WDC) [V] Washington, DC Black Leadership and Christ's Kingdom Society; [V] Waldorf, MD Body of Christ Farm Community, Inc.
Pitts, Joseph A. *o.m.i.* '59 (CHI) [174] Chicago, IL Precious Blood Church; [V] Chicago, IL Ministry in Higher Education.
Pitts, William L. '70 (R) Wrightsville Beach, NC St. Therese Church; [H] Wilmington, NC Catholic Student Center.
Pitula, Zygmunt J. '39 (TOL) Retired.
Pitzen, John J. '45 (DUB) Retired.
Pius, Jung Bio (ALB) Special Assignment.
Pivonka, David *t.o.r.* '96 (STU) [A] Steubenville, OH

Franciscan University of Steubenville; [F] Steubenville, OH Holy Spirit Monastery.
Pivonka, Msgr. Leonard *j.c.d.* '77 (CC) [1] Corpus Christi, TX Corpus Christi Cathedral.
Piwowar, Stanley J. '51 (MAN) Claremont, NH St. Joseph Church.
Piwowarczyk, Darius *s.v.d.* '90 (WDC) [M] Washington, DC Divine Word College.
Pizmoht, Louis A. '66 (CLV) Lyndhurst, OH St. Clare Church.
Pizzamiglio, Ernest E. '66 (PEO) Galesburg, IL Immaculate Heart of Mary Church.
Pizzarelli, Frank *s.m.m.* '80 (RVC) [B] Patchogue, NY St. Joseph's College.
Pizzo, Anthony B. *o.s.a.* '84 (CHI) [40] Chicago, IL St. Clare of Montefalco Church.
Pizzo, Philip '77 (BRK) [138] Brooklyn, NY St. Teresa of Avila Church.
Pizzuto, Alfred R. '55 (NY) Marlboro, NY St. Mary Church.
Placa, Msgr. Alan J. '70 (RVC) Deer Park, NY SS. Cyril and Methodius Church.
Placa, Stephen '95 (BRK) [47] Brooklyn, NY St. Francis Xavier Church.
Place, Michael D. '70 (CHI) Wilmette, IL St. Francis Xavier Church.
Place, Terry E. '72 (FTW) [11] South Bend, IN St. John the Baptist Church.
Placek, Paul *c.p.* '45 (CHI) [N] Chicago, IL Passionist Provincial Office.
Plafcan, Paul '47 (CLV) Retired.
Plagens, James '65 (SAN) Absent on Leave.
Plagge, Robert J. '43 (CIN) Retired; [V] Cincinnati, OH Marian Center of Cincinnati.
Plaisted, Eugene D. *o.s.c.* '61 (STP) Anoka, MN St. Stephen Church; [N] Anoka, MN Crosier Community of Anoka.
Plakut, Peter *o.c.s.o.* '58 (P) [L] Lafayette, OR The Cistercian (Trappist) Abbey of Our Lady of Guadalupe.
Plamondon, Donald J. '72 (DUB) Holy Cross, IA Holy Cross Church; Luxemburg, IA Holy Trinity Church; [F] Holy Cross, IA Rickardsville-Holy Cross-Luxemburg (RHCL) Catholic School.
Planas, Salvador '54 (MIA) Retired.
Planea, John '82 (NO) On Duty Outside the Archdiocese.
Planinsek, Henry J. *c.s.sp.* '57 (ALX) [F] Natchitoches, LA Holy Ghost Fathers Home, Maison Brothier.
Plank, Stephen J. *o.s.b.* '94 (OM) [C] Elkhorn, NE Mount Michael High School; [K] Elkhorn, NE Mount Michael Abbey.
Plans, John *s.f.* (SFE) [28] Albuquerque, NM St. Therese of the Infant Jesus Shrine of the Little Flower Church.
Plante, Albert R. '48 (OG) [1] Watertown, NY Holy Family Church.
Plante, Georges J. '53 (PRT) Madison, ME St. Sebastian Church.
Plante, Msgr. Jacques L. '82 (PRO) [1] Providence, RI Cathedral of SS. Peter and Paul; [19] Providence, RI St. Maron Church; [T] Providence, RI Miscellaneous Listings for the Diocese of Providence.
Plante, Paul A. '71 (PRT) Winslow, ME St. John the Baptist Church.
Plante, Pierre J. '78 (PRO) Albion, RI St. Ambrose's Church; [S] Smithfield, RI Bryant College.
Plante, Richard A. '53 (RC) Retired.
Plante, Roger J. *m.s.* '61 (MAN) [K] Enfield, NH Shrine of Our Lady of La Salette; [M] Enfield, NH La Salette Shrine and Center of Enfield.
Plantes, Francis P. '45 (PIT) Retired; [N] Pittsburgh, PA St. John Vianney Manor.
Plascencia, Miguel '53 (LA) [9] Los Angeles, CA Divine Saviour Church.
Plasker, Alexander *o.s.b.* '62 (P) [L] St. Benedict, OR Mt. Angel Abbey.
Plasker, Robert L. *c.s.c.* '57 (FTW) [J] South Bend, IN Congregation of Holy Cross Indiana Province Provincial House.
Plasse, Eugene J. '72 (SPR) Bondsville, MA St. Bartholomew's Church; Palmer, MA St. Thomas the Apostle Church.
Plasserry, George C. *c.m.i.* '74 (PH) [157] Philadelphia, PA St. William Church.
Plaster, George '80 (LFT) On Duty Outside the Diocese.
Plaster, George F. '80 (IND) [F] Indianapolis, IN St. Vincent Hospital and Health Care Center, Inc.
Plastino, James L. '94 (MRY) Carmel, CA San Carlos Borromeo Basilica.
Plate, Brian G. '96 (NEW) Franklin Lakes, NJ Most Blessed Sacrament Church.
Plathe, Anthony H. '63 (NU) On Duty Outside the Diocese.
Plathottam, Matthew '67 (PHX) [1] Scottsdale, AZ Blessed Sacrament Church.
Plathottam, Thomas '74 (NOR) Putnam, CT St. Mary Church.
Platt, Stewart '51 (Y) Retired.
Platt, W. Wallace *c.s.b.* '43 (GAL) [Q] Sugar Land, TX Basilian Mission Center.
Platt, William F. '88 (BGP) Riverside, CT St. Catherine of Siena Church.
Plaushin, Mark F. *o.s.f.s.* '89 (PH) [Z] Philadelphia, PA Oblates of St. Francis De Sales.
Plavac, Timothy '86 (CLV) [A] Wickliffe, OH Borromeo Seminary.
Plavcan, Jon J. '94 (GRY) Griffith, IN St. Mary Church.
Plawecki, Joseph '83 (DET) Erie, MI St. Joseph Church.
Plawny, Thaddeus *m.s.* (PEO) [M] Georgetown, IL LaSalette Missionaries.
Playoust, Alfred G. *s.j.* '46 (SJ) Santa Clara, CA Santa Clara Valley Medical Center; [D] San Jose, CA Bellarmine College Preparatory; [M] Los Gatos, CA California Province of the Society of Jesus, Jesuit Provincial Office.
Plazewski, Leonard J.M. '91 (SP) Temple Terrace, FL Corpus Christi Church.
Pleban, Alexander L. '57 (GBG) [2] Uniontown, PA St. Joseph Church.
Pleban, Leo J. '60 (Y) Campbell, OH St. Joseph the Provider Church.
Plechta, Sabin *o.f.m.* '43 (WDC) [M] Washington, DC Commissariat of the Holy Land, Franciscan Monastery - Mount St. Sepulchre.
Pledl, Mariangela (MIL) Eagle, WI St. Theresa's Church
Pleho, Anthony J. '79 (NY) [18] Yonkers, NY Most Holy Trinity Church.
Plei, Stephen *c.ss.r.* '56 (LAF) Crowley, LA Immaculate Heart of Mary Church.
Pleier, David J. '75 (GB) Glenmore, WI Immaculate Conception Church; Stark, WI St. Mary Church.
Pleiman, Kenneth F. *c.pp.s.* '70 (CIN) [M] Dayton, OH Provincial House of the Cincinnati Province of the Society of the Precious Blood.
Pleiness, Gregg '81 (LAN) Absent on Leave.
Plesa, Andrew J. '56 (RCK) Spring Grove, IL St. Peter Church
Pleskac, Msgr. Myron J. '60 (LIN) [7] Lincoln, NE St. Joseph Church.
Pleva, Gerald *s.m.* '77 (SAT) Helotes, TX Our Lady of Guadalupe Church.
Plevyak, Valentine R. '44 (SCR) Retired; [N] Dunmore, PA Villa St. Joseph.
Plewka, Edwin J. '40 (GR) Retired.
Plewka, Mark A. '76 (PBL) [4] Pueblo, CO Holy Rosary Church
Pliauplis, Christopher '87 (BRK) [133] Brooklyn, NY SS. Simon and Jude Church.
Pliauplis, Christopher '87 (STU) On Duty Outside the Diocese.
Plichta, Felician *o.f.m.conv.* '41 (BAL) [M] Ellicott City, MD Order of Friars Minor Conventual.
Plichta, Felician *o.f.m.conv.* '41 (FR) Sandwich, MA Corpus Christi Church.
Plo, John '61 (NY) Absent on Leave.
Ploch, Timothy C. *s.d.b.* '76 (NY) [Z] New Rochelle, NY Salesian Provincial House.
Plocharczyk, Msgr. Daniel J. '74 (HRT) Special and other (Arch)Diocesan Assignment.
Plock, Charles T. *c.m.* '73 (PH) [69] Philadelphia, PA Immaculate Conception Church.
Plocke, Donald J. *s.j.* '84 (BO) [W] Chestnut Hill, MA The Jesuit Community at Boston College.
Plocki, Msgr. Robert '45 (SFD) Retired.
Plocki, Msgr. Robert '45 (SFR) Retired.
Plocki, Msgr. Robert J. '54 (SFR) Tiburon, CA St. Hilary Church
Ploeckl, Joseph M. '40 (SY) Retired.
Plokhooy, Christopher H. '59 (WIL) Sherwood Park, DE St. John the Beloved Church; Retired.
Plominski, Walter J. '68 (ROC) Caledonia, NY St. Columba Church.
Plominski, Walter J. '68 (SCR) On Duty Outside the Diocese.
Ploof, Gerald '75 (LAN) [I] De Witt, MI St. Francis Retreat Center.
Ploof, Msgr. Thomas M. '45 (WIN) Retired.
Ploplis, Theodore '77 (CHI) [J] Chicago, IL St. Anthony Hospital; [J] Chicago, IL Columbus Hospital; [J] Chicago, IL St. Joseph Hospital.
Plotka, Frank W. '68 (CHI) [6] Waukegan, IL Immaculate Conception B.V.M. Church.
Plotkowski, Jerome '65 (SFE) On Duty Outside the Archdiocese.
Plotkowski, Jerome '65 (WDC) Hyattsville, MD St. Jerome Church.
Plotkowski, John S. '74 (CHI) Buffalo Grove, IL St. Mary Church.
Ploude, Thomas E. '64 (CAM) Brooklawn, NJ St. Maurice's Church.
Plough, James H. '58 (PBL) Grand Junction, CO Immaculate Heart of Mary Church.
Plourde, Carroll W. *s.s.e.* '87 (MOB) Selma, AL Our Lady Queen of Peace Church; [H] Selma, AL Edmundite Fathers; [K] Selma, AL Marion Institute Newman Center.
Plourde, James S. '82 (PRT) Waterville, ME Holy Spirit Church
Plourde, John '84 (SP) Military Chaplains.
Plourde, Peter '83 (PMB) [A] Boynton Beach, FL St. Vincent de Paul Regional Seminary.
Plourde, Peter '83 (SP) On Duty Outside the Diocese.
Plourde, Raymond C. '58 (BO) On Special or Other Diocesan Assignment.
Plummer, J. Bruce '40 (HEL) Retired.
Plummer, James R. '58 (CAM) Wildwood Crest, NJ Assumption B.V.M. Church.
Plunkett, Gregory J. '88 (PEO) Aledo, IL St. Catherine's Church.
Plunkett, Msgr. Joseph P. '60 (NEW) New Providence, NJ Our Lady of Peace Church.
Plushkell, Robert B. *s.j.* '48 (SFR) [N] San Francisco, CA Jesuit Community at University of San Francisco.
Pluth, Paul *o.s.b.* (LA) [R] Valyermo, CA St. Andrew's Abbey.
Poage, Godfrey *c.p.* '46 (LA) [R] Pasadena, CA Passionist Community.
Poandl, Robert *glmy.* '68 (TYL) Pittsburg, TX Holy Cross Church.
Poblocki, Richard M. '83 (BUF) Bolivar, NY St. Mary Church; Portville, NY Sacred Heart Church.
Pocernich, Eugene S. '74 (MIL) On Duty Outside the Archdiocese.
Pocetto, Alexander T. *o.s.f.s.* '55 (ALN) [B] Center Valley, PA Allentown College of St. Francis de Sales; [K] Center Valley, PA Oblates of St. Francis de Sales.
Poche, Daniel M. '78 (HT) Gheens, LA Community of St. Anthony Church; Raceland, LA St. Hilary of Poitiers Church.
Poche, Msgr. Gerard W. '48 (NO) Gretna, LA St. Anthony Church.
Pock, Donald P. '58 (JOL) Itasca, IL St. Peter the Apostle Church.
Pocovi, Juan *m.ss.cc.* '64 (SJN) Rio Grande, PR Nuestra Senora del Carmen Church.
Pocus, Msgr. Dominick A. '45 (NEW) Kearny, NJ Our Lady of Sorrows Church.
Poczworowski, Luke *o.f.m.conv.* '64 (RCK) [2] Rockford, IL St. Anthony of Padua Church.
Podesta, Msgr. John F. '35 (JOL) Retired.
Podgorny, Msgr. John '55 (PAT) [4] Passaic, NJ Holy Rosary Church.
Podgorski, Clarence '77 (PMB) Port St. Lucie, FL St. Elizabeth Ann Seton Church.
Podlesny, James *o.s.b.* '80 (GBG) [H] Latrobe, PA Saint Vincent Archabbey.
Podolak, William S. '50 (MIL) Retired.
Podrasky, Michael P. '43 (BEL) Retired.
Podrosky, Alfred '52 (SCL) Retired.
Podsiadlo, John J. *s.j.* '72 (NY) [80] New York, NY Nativity Church; [DD] New York, NY Nativity Mission Center, Inc.
Podskoch, Clement J. *c.s.c.* '56 (SCR) [C] Wilkes-Barre, PA Kings College.
Podson, Theodore E. *sch.p.* '76 (AMA) [6] Amarillo, TX St. Francis Church; Clarendon, TX St. Mary's Church.
Podson, Theodore E. *sch.p.* '76 (WDC) [B] Washington, DC Queen of Pious Schools House of Studies-Piarist Fathers.
Podvin, Albert J. '62 (SFE) [20] Albuquerque, NM Sangre de Cristo Church.
Poecking, David G. '96 (PIT) Perrysville, PA St. Teresa of Avila Church.
Poehlmann, Edward J. '67 (DEN) Edwards, CO St. Clare of Assisi Church.
Poelker, Msgr. Gerard L. '42 (JC) Retired.
Poerio, John A. '59 (LKC) Bell City, LA St. John Vianney Church.
Poettgen, Edward '80 (ORG) Stanton, CA St. Polycarp Church.
Poetz, Lawrence *s.v.d.* '44 (CHI) [B] Techny, IL Divine Word Residence.
Poetzel, Richard K. *c.ss.r.* '63 (BAL) [66] Baltimore, MD Our Lady of Fatima Church.
Poff, Edward '57 (JOL) [G] Kankakee, IL St. Mary's Hospital.
Poff, Pius *o.f.m.conv.* '61 (TOL) Carey, OH Our Lady of Consolation, Basilica-National Shrine Church; Salem Twp., OH St. Joseph Church.
Poggi, Giulio *c.s.* (NY) [DD] New York, NY American Committee on Italian Immigration, Inc.
Pogorelc, Anthony (LFT) [4] Lafayette, IN St. Lawrence Church.
Pogorelc, Anthony *s.m.* '88 (STL) [P] St. Louis, MO Provincialate of the Society of Mary, Province of St. Louis.
Pogorzelski, Eugeniusz '35 (GRY) Retired.
Pohl, Msgr. Daniel J. '53 (LIN) Indianola, NE St. Catherine's Church.
Pohl, Jerome H. '67 (PH) [2] Philadelphia, PA St. Adalbert Church.
Pohl, Leon H. '56 (KAL) Sturgis, MI Holy Angels Church.
Pohl, Stephen A. (L) Bardstown, KY St. Monica Church; St. Thomas, KY St. Thomas Church.
Pohley, Robert G. '75 (BGP) [7] Stamford, CT Sacred Heart Church; [W] Shelton, CT Fr. McKenna St. Vincent de Paul Shoppe; [W] Stamford, CT Stamford Catholic Library.

Pohlman, Stephen J. '84 (SFD) Glen Carbon, IL St. Cecilia Church.
Pohlmeier, Loren G. '82 (GI) Greeley, NE Sacred Heart Church.
Pohorlak, John G. '54 (PBR) Newton Falls, OH St. Michael Church.
Pohorlak, Joseph '61 (PRM) Whiting, IN Assumption of the Blessed Virgin Church.
Pohto, Tom *o.s.a.* (VEN) Cape Coral, FL Blessed Katharine Drexel Church.
Pointek, Msgr. Francis J. '40 (FRS) Tehachapi, CA St. Malachy Church; Retired.
Poirier, David *s.a.* '77 (NY) [Z] Garrison, NY Generalate of the Franciscan Friars of the Atonement-St. James Friary.
Poirier, J. Eugene *s.j.* (ARL) Annandale, VA St. Michael's Church.
Poirier, J. Eugene *s.j.* (WDC) [M] Washington, DC The Jesuit Community at Georgetown University.
Poirier, John '71 (MAN) Dover, NH St. Joseph Church.
Poirier, Joseph *s.c.j.* '73 (SP) [O] Pinellas Park, FL Priests of the Sacred Heart.
Poirier, Ralph J. *c.s.sp.* '63 (PIT) Emsworth, PA Sacred Heart Church.
Poirier, Raoul J. '42 (OG) Retired.
Poirier, Robert (STL) [P] St. Louis, MO Jesuit Community Corporation at St. Louis University - Jesuit Hall.
Poirier, Robert *s.m.* '54 (BO) [W] Boston, MA Marist Fathers and Brothers Provincial House.
Poirier, Ronald '88 (SP) [2] Clearwater, FL Light of Christ Church.
Poirier, Vincent H. '85 (BO) [2] Newton, MA Corpus Christi Church; [CC] Framingham, MA Framingham State College Campus Ministry; [CC] Wellesley, MA Wellesley College Campus Ministry.
Poissant, Msgr. Leeward J. '63 (OG) [1] Ogdensburg, NY St. Mary's Cathedral; [A] Ogdensburg, NY Wadhams Hall.
Poisson, Joseph *f.s.s.p.* '96 (SCR) [M] Elmhurst, PA Priestly Fraternity of St. Peter (F.S.S.P.).
Poisson, Thomas L. '78 (MAR) L'Anse, MI Sacred Heart Church.
Poitras, Steven (BO) [1] Somerville, MA St. Ann Church.
Pokladowski, Gregory F. (OAK) Military Chaplains.
Pokladowski, Gregory S. '73 (CHI) Other Assignments.
Pokladowski, Gregory S. '73 (LA) Port Hueneme, CA Naval Construction Battalion Center; Military and VA Chaplains; Retired.
Pokornowski, Daniel A. '54 (BUF) [3] Cheektowaga, NY St. John Gualbert Church.
Pokorsky, Jerry '90 (ARL) Annandale, VA Holy Spirit Church.
Pokrzewinski, Justus M. *o.p.* '60 (CHI) [N] Chicago, IL Dominicans (Provincial Office).
Pokusa, Msgr. Joseph W. '70 (CAM) Runnemede, NJ St. Teresa of the Infant Jesus Church.
Pol, Dom Te '70 (HT) Retired.
Polak, Michael J. '58 (PIT) [1] West Mifflin, PA St. Agnes Church.
Polakowski, Joseph '59 (MAR) Retired.
Polanco, Dennis *s.a.* '74 (NY) [Z] Garrison, NY Generalate of the Franciscan Friars of the Atonement-St. James Friary.
Poland, Sean '94 (KNX) [1] Knoxville, TN Cathedral of the Sacred Heart of Jesus.
Polando, Peter M. *j.c.l.* '80 (Y) [17] Youngstown, OH St. Matthias Church.
Polasek, Jeffrey S. '91 (TLS) Sallisaw, OK St. Francis Xavier Church.
Polc, Msgr. Jaroslav '55 (GB) On Duty Outside the Diocese.
Polcyn, Robert F. *o.f.m.cap.* '68 (LC) Pine Creek, WI Most Sacred Heart Church; [G] Arcadia, WI Franciscan Skemp Healthcare, Mayo Health System, Arcadia Campus Nursing Home.
Polczyk, Stanislaus T. '82 (TR) Union Beach, NJ Holy Family Church.
Polednak, John V. '76 (SCR) Nicholson, PA St. Patrick's Church.
Polek, David *c.ss.r.* '62 (STL) [B] St. Louis, MO St. John Neumann House.
Polenz, Gordon '82 (ALB) Sidney, NY Sacred Heart Church.
Poletunow, Mark *o.f.m.cap.* '86 (WDC) [B] Washington, DC St. Francis Friary-Capuchin College.
Polewczak, Michael J. '73 (ALB) On Duty Outside the Diocese.
Polewczak, Michael J. '73 (CHR) Orangeburg, SC Holy Trinity Church.
Polgar, Capistran *o.f.m.* '67 (MET) [6] New Brunswick, NJ St. Ladislaus Church.
Poliafico, David A. '95 (COL) Pickerington, OH Seton Parish Church.
Policetta, Sleeva R. '87 (CHI) [198] Chicago, IL St. Tarcissus Church.
Polich, David J. '76 (DM) [3] Des Moines, IA Christ the King Church.
Polich, James (DM) On Duty Outside the Diocese.
Polich, James (KC) [A] Conception, MO Conception Seminary College.
Polichnowski, Nicholas *t.o.r.* (BRK) [131] Brooklyn, NY Sacred Hearts of Jesus and Mary and St. Stephen Church.
Policicchio, Luke *o.s.b.* '88 (RIC) [6] Virginia Beach, VA St. Gregory the Great Church.
Polidano, Carmel F. '81 (CAM) Blackwood, NJ St. Jude's Church.
Polifka, Charles *o.f.m.cap.* '71 (KCK) Lawrence, KS St. John the Evangelist Church; [H] Lawrence, KS St. Conrad's Friary.
Polimine, Alan *t.o.r.* '59 (ALT) [7] Altoona, PA Our Lady of Mt. Carmel Church.
Polinski, Casimir V. *c.r.* '44 (CHI) [74] Chicago, IL St. Hedwig Church.
Polinsky, John R. '60 (BGP) Retired.
Polito, Martin F. '76 (CLV) [29] Cleveland, OH Holy Redeemer Church.
Polito, Victor J. '54 (MAN) Retired.
Polizzi, Daniel '69 (SD) La Jolla, CA All Hallows Church; San Diego, CA Scripps Hospital.
Polizzi, Msgr. Salvatore E. '56 (STL) [59] St. Louis, MO St. Roch Church.
Poljicak, Vlatko '65 (LA) Panorama City, CA St. Genevieve Church.
Polk, Page E. *o.f.m.* '86 (GAL) [4] Galveston, TX St. Patrick Church.
Polk, Thomas '67 (BAL) Urbana, MD St. Ignatius Loyola Church.
Pollack, Andrew *c.pp.s.* '35 (CIN) [B] Carthagena, OH St. Charles.
Pollack, Anthony J. '55 (ALT) [6] Altoona, PA Our Lady of Fatima Church.
Pollack, Msgr. Joseph '49 (STU) Retired.
Pollak, Claude W. *o.s.b.* '57 (ALT) Nicktown, PA St. Nicholas Church.
Pollard, Daniel E. '53 (PRT) [1] Portland, ME Cathedral of the Immaculate Conception; Retired.
Pollard, John E. '74 (CHI) On Duty Outside the Archdiocese.
Pollard, John L. (STA) Absent on Sick Leave.
Pollard, Leo E. *s.j.* '47 (BO) [E] Boston, MA Boston College High School & Jesuit Community.
Pollard, Marcus A. '90 (ARL) [6] Alexandria, VA St. Louis Church.
Pollard, Martin *o.s.b.* '32 (P) [L] St. Benedict, OR Mt. Angel Abbey.
Pollard, Patrick J. '72 (CHI) [50] Chicago, IL St. Denis Church; [Y] Chicago, IL Central Office.
Pollard, Msgr. Raymond J. '50 (NEW) Retired.
Pollard, Roy F. '66 (WIL) Hockessin, DE St. Mary of the Assumption Church.
Pollard, Thomas W. '66 (WDC) Clinton, MD Church of St. John the Evangelist.
Pollauf, Robert A. *s.j.* '46 (DET) [P] Clarkston, MI Colombiere Center.
Pollie, A. Frank '67 (DET) Ortonville, MI St. Anne Church.
Pollis, Roberg '57 (BO) [31] Boston, MA St. James the Greater in Chinatown Church.
Pollis, Robert G. '57 (BO) Absent on Sick Leave.
Pollitt, Michael J. '83 (MAN) Absent on Leave.
Pollock, Martin *l.c.* (DAL) [M] Irving, TX Legionaries of Christ.
Pollock, Msgr. Robert C. '48 (SLC) Retired.
Pollone, Ralph A. '83 (SPR) [9] Pittsfield, MA St. Mary the Morning Star Church.
Polmounter, Richard J. '78 (SCR) [6] Pittston, PA St. Mary, Help of Christians Church.
Polo, Antonio *s.d.b.* (SJN) [28] San Juan, PR San Juan Bosco Church; [37] San Juan, PR Maria Auxiliadora Church.
Polo, Peter P. *c.s.* '68 (BRK) [U] Jamaica, NY Saint Charles House of Studies.
Pologruto, C.S.P., Donald C. '82 (OAK) [Q] Oakland, CA Mills College Newman Center.
Polosky, Michael '91 (SJP) Ambridge, PA Ss. Peter and Paul Church.
Poloway, Msgr. Michael '54 (SJP) Pittsburgh, PA St. John the Baptist Church.
Polselli, Leo *c.s.c.* '70 (ALB) [T] Albany, NY The Family Rosary Worldwide Office; [T] Albany, NY The Family Rosary Worldwide Office.
Polt, Albert *o.a.r.* '54 (LA) [R] Oxnard, CA St. Augustine Priory O.A.R.
Poltorak, George *s.a.c.* '90 (BUF) [O] North Tonawanda, NY Society of the Catholic Apostolate.
Poltorak, Stanley '82 (SAC) Truckee, CA Assumption of the Blessed Virgin Mary Church.
Poluikis, John A. *c.s.b.* '51 (ROC) [I] Rochester, NY Basilian Residence.
Polyak, John V. '69 (MET) North Brunswick, NJ Our Lady of Peace Church.
Polzer, Charles W. *s.j.* '64 (TUC) [F] Tucson, AZ Kino House.
Polzer, Daniel *l.c.* '94 (LIN) [F] Waverly, NE Our Lady of Good Counsel Retreat House.
Pomaville, Raymond *o.m.i.* '55 (SAT) [K] San Antonio, TX Oblate Madonna Residence.
Pomerlau, Claude *c.s.c.* '65 (P) [L] Portland, OR Holy Cross Father & Brother, C.S.C. - University of Portland.
Pomerleau, Claude *c.s.c.* '65 (P) [B] Portland, OR University of Portland.
Pomerleau, William A. '79 (SPR) [20] Springfield, MA St. Thomas Aquinas Church.
Pomeroy, Joseph B. *s.j.* '62 (WOR) [N] Worcester, MA Jesuits of Holy Cross College, Inc.
Pomeroy, Thomas K. '93 (GB) [3] Green Bay, WI St. Agnes Church.
Pomilio, Matthew J. '62 (BRK) Released from Diocesan Assignment.
Pompei, Francis *o.f.m.* '74 (PH) [Z] Philadelphia, PA Order of Friars Minor, Holy Name Province.
Pompei, Frederick A. '66 (SY) [7] Syracuse, NY Our Lady of Pompei Church; Special Assignment.
Ponce, Demetrio '88 (ELP) Marfa, TX St. Mary's Church.
Ponce, Francisco R. '67 (NEW) Plainfield, NJ St. Mary Church.
Ponce, Gonzalo *s.s.p.* '76 (LA) [R] Los Angeles, CA Society of St. Paul.
Poncelet, Frank '87 (SCL) Sedan, MN Immaculate Conception Church.
Ponciroli, Robert '69 (OAK) [8] Oakland, CA St. Cyril Church.
Pondant, Anthony W. '73 (DAL) Wylie, TX St. Anthony Church.
Ponessa, Joseph '74 (GF) Glendive, MT Sacred Heart Church; [K] Glendive, MT Sacred Heart Educational Endowment Trust.
Ponisciak, Cyril S. '53 (PH) [3] Coatesville, PA St. Joseph Church.
Ponnapati, Shoury '89 (OKL) Edmond, OK St. John the Baptist Church.
Ponnet, Christopher D. '83 (LA) [53] Los Angeles, CA St. Camillus De Lellis Church.
Pons, Antonio '60 (ORL) Haines City, FL St. Ann Church.
Pons, Miguel '53 (SJN) [5] Trujillo Alto, PR San Judas Tadeo Church.
Pons, Ramon de Jesus *o.a.r.* '88 (ORG) Fullerton, CA St. Mary's Church.
Ponso, Andres *o.s.m.* '50 (ELP) [18] El Paso, TX Our Lady of Sorrows Church.
Pontarelli, Michael M. *o.s.m.* '88 (ORG) [H] Anaheim, CA Servite Fathers and Brothers.
Pontarelli, Michael P. *o.s.m.* '82 (ORG) [D] Anaheim, CA Servite High School; Servite High School Development Fund; [H] Buena Park, CA Servite Fathers And Brothers.
Ponticello, Robert D. '81 (MEM) [19] Memphis, TN Church Of The Nativity.
Pontolillo, Dominic T. *o.f.m.cap.* '49 (FRS) Chowchilla, CA Department of Corrections, Central California Women's Facility.
Pontones, Manuel '58 (LA) Pico Rivera, CA St. Marianne de Paredes Church.
Ponzini, Thomas V. '96 (GAL) [69] Houston, TX Prince of Peace Church.
Pool, Robert '55 (KCK) Retired.
Poole, Msgr. James D. '43 (SAC) Retired and in Senior Ministry.
Poole, James E. *s.j.* '53 (SEA) [C] Tacoma, WA Bellarmine Preparatory School; [G] Tacoma, WA St. Joseph Medical Center.
Poole, Richard '94 (SPK) Connell, WA St. Vincent Church; Eltopia, WA St. Paul Church.
Poole, Stafford *c.m.* '56 (LA) [R] Los Angeles, CA Vincentian Fathers and Brothers.
Poole, Steven F. '96 (BEL) [1] Belleville, IL Cathedral of St. Peter.
Poole, William G. '63 (LEX) Ravenna, KY St. Elizabeth Church.
Pooler, Alfred *c.p.* '60 (CHI) [N] Chicago, IL Passionist Community-CTU.
Poore, Charles T. '89 (Y) [10] Canton, OH St. Michael the Archangel Church.
Poorman, James E. '71 (SJP) Ramey, PA Annunciation B.V.M. Church.
Poorman, Mark L. *c.s.c.* '82 (FTW) [B] Notre Dame, IN University of Notre Dame Du Lac; [J] Notre Dame, IN Holy Cross Community, Corby Hall, University of Notre Dame; [J] South Bend, IN Congregation of Holy Cross Indiana Province Provincial House.
Poorten, William P. *s.j.* '63 (ALB) [O] Auriesville, NY Jesuit Retreat House for Priests, Religious and Lay People.
Poovakulam, Antony P. '63 (TR) Whiting, NJ St. Elizabeth Ann Seton Church.
Poovakulath, Jose *s.a.c.* '81 (VEN) [3] Sarasota, FL St. Martha Church.
Poovannal, Thomas '76 (WDC) Landover Hills, MD Syro-Malankara Mission Church; Washington, DC General Hospital.
Popadick, Msgr. Peter J. '70 (BUF) [O] Buffalo, NY Bishop's Residence.
Popadiuk, Mauricio *o.s.b.m.* '84 (RVC) [N] Glen Cove, NY St. Josaphatis Monastery, Novitiate and Retreat House.
Popadiuk, Mauricio *o.s.b.m.* '84 (STF) Bronx, NY St.

Mary Protectress Church; [B] Glen Cove, NY Basilian Fathers Novitiate of the Order of St. Basil the Great.
Pope, Charles '89 (WDC) [16] Washington, DC Holy Comforter—St. Cyprian Church.
Pope, L. Michael *s.j.* '81 (P) [19] Portland, OR St. Ignatius Church.
Pope, Nicholas F. *s.j.* '72 (MIL) [P] Milwaukee, WI Jesuit Provincial Office, Wisconsin Province.
Pope, Nicholas F. *s.j.* '72 (STL) [P] St. Louis, MO Jesuit Community Corporation at St. Louis University - Jesuit Hall.
Popeleski, Frank '79 (BLX) Biloxi, MS V.A. Center; Gulfport, MS V.A. Hospital.
Popelka, Joseph '92 (SAL) Hays, KS Immaculate Heart of Mary Church.
Popesh, Msgr. Bernard '49 (DUL) Retired.
Popish, Edward *ss.cc.* '90 (HON) [F] Honolulu, HI St. Francis Healthcare System of Hawaii; [H] Honolulu, HI St. Patrick's Monastery.
Popivchak, Msgr. Ronald P. '67 (PHU) Bridgeport, PA SS. Peter and Paul Church; Phoenixville, PA SS. Peter and Paul Church.
Popochock, James L. '68 (GBG) Footedale, PA St. Thomas Church; New Salem, PA St. Procopius Church.
Popovich, George '51 (Y) [5] Warren, OH St. Joseph Church; [G] Warren, OH St. Joseph Health Center.
Popovich, Josaphat '51 (PBR) Retired.
Popovich, Peter '85 (NY) [171] Bronx, NY Our Lady of Good Counsel Church; Greenburgh, NY Church of Our Lady of Shkodra.
Popovich, Stephen '81 (Y) [4] Youngstown, OH Immaculate Heart of Mary Church.
Popowski, Stanley '83 (HEL) Cut Bank, MT St. Margaret Church; Valier, MT St. Francis Church.
Popp, Kenneth J. '83 (SCL) Greenwald, MN St. Andrew's Church; Meire Grove, MN St. John's Church.
Poppa, Chester *o.f.m.cap.* '53 (GF) Broadus, MT St. David's Church.
Popravak, Christopher *o.f.m.cap.* '74 (STL) [P] St. Louis, MO St. Crispin's Friary.
Popson, Michael George '87 (PSC) Danbury, CT St. Nicholas Church.
Porada, Casey *o.s.* '89 (LIN) David City, NE St. Mary's Church.
Porada, Casey *o.s.* '89 (PCE) On Duty Outside the Diocese.
Porada, Charles *o.f.m.conv.* '43 (FR) [4] Fall River, MA Holy Cross Church.
Porazzo, Francis J. '44 (TR) Retired.
Porcari, Ernest M. '59 (DET) Northville, MI Our Lady of Victory Church.
Pore, Victor G. (OG) [2] Plattsburgh, NY St. John the Baptist Church.
Porpigilia, Joseph D. '85 (BUF) [1] Orchard Park, NY Nativity Church.
Porpora, Robert '90 (NY) [221] Staten Island, NY Our Lady Star of the Sea Church.
Porras-Landeo, Juan '46 (KAL) Battle Creek, MI Veteran's Administration Hospital.
Porrello, Joseph J. '51 (WOR) Retired.
Porsch, Ernest '49 (CIN) [M] Cincinnati, OH St. Francis Center.
Port, Dennis R. '74 (STL) Overland, MO Our Lady of the Presentation Church.
Portalatin, Antonio '91 (ARE) [14] Arecibo, PR Santisimo Sacramento Church.
Porten, Henry F. *c.ss.r.* '41 (BR) [10] Baton Rouge, LA St. Gerard Majella Church.
Porten, Henry F. *c.ss.r.* '41 (STL) [P] Liguori, MO St. Clement Health Care Center.
Porter, John '56 (CIN) Princeton, OH St. Maximilian Kolbe Church.
Porter, John Baptist *o.c.s.o.* '90 (SAC) [A] Vina, CA Abbey of New Clairvaux, Trappist Seminary; [H] Vina, CA Abbey of New Clairvaux, Trappist.
Porter, John E. '56 (CIN) [V] Cincinnati, OH St. Andrew Kim Korean Catholic Society.
Porter, John F. '57 (GR) Conklin, MI St. Francis Xavier Church; Ravenna, MI St. Catherine Church.
Porter, Lawrence B. '74 (NEW) [A] South Orange, NJ Immaculate Conception Seminary; [B] South Orange, NJ Seton Hall University.
Porter, Richard L. *s.j.* '47 (MIL) [P] Wauwatosa, WI Jesuit Community at St. Camillus.
Porter, Robert A. '81 (SFD) Pana, IL St. Patrick Church.
Porter, Robert N. '64 (SFD) Bunker Hill, IL St. Mary Church; Shipman, IL St. Denis Church; Wilsonville, IL Holy Cross Church.
Porter, Stephen C. '80 (SB) [4] Fontana, CA St. Mary Church.
Porter, Thomas *o.c.s.o.* '42 (SLC) [F] Huntsville, UT Abbey of Our Lady of the Holy Trinity of the Order of Cistercians.
Porter, William B. '80 (KCK) [J] Emporia, KS Didde Catholic Campus Center, Emporia State University.
Porter, William J. '75 (WIL) Ocean City, MD St. Luke and St. Andrew Church.
Porterfield, David J. *c.s.c.* '79 (FTW) [18] South Bend, IN St. Stanislaus Church.
Porterfield, Mark A. '94 (JC) Hannibal, MO Holy Family Church; [A] Hannibal, MO St. Thomas Aquinas Seminary.
Portland, Paul *s.d.s.* '76 (PHX) [4] Mesa, AZ Queen of Peace Church.
Portman, Msgr. John R. '56 (SD) Coronado, CA Sacred Heart Church; Retired.
Portmann, Frederick '79 (PHX) Retired.
Portrey, Msgr. Lawrence A. '39 (GI) Retired.
Portucheck, Joseph J. '49 (STL) [42] St. Louis, MO St. John Nepomuk Church.
Portz, Bernard J. *s.j.* '52 (OM) [K] Omaha, NE Jesuit Community At Creighton University.
Porunnolil, Abraham Z. '66 (RVC) Port Jefferson, NY Infant Jesus Church.
Posadas, Jose Antonio *o.f.m.* '95 (CLV) [P] Cleveland, OH Padua Franciscan Friary.
Posadas, Tony *o.f.m.* '95 (CLV) [E] Cleveland, OH Padua Franciscan High School.
Posanski, James B. '65 (MIL) [8] West Allis, WI Our Lady of Mt. Carmel Church.
Posch, Christopher *o.f.m.* '95 (CAM) [2] Camden, NJ St. Anthony of Padua Church.
Poschen, Msgr. Edward '53 (FRS) [13] Fresno, CA St. Therese Church.
Posco, Raphael A. '38 (SPR) Retired.
Posey, Patrick L. '91 (ARL) Dominican Republic, VA San Jose, Pedro Santana Church; On Duty Outside the Diocese.
Posey, Thadeus J. *o.f.m.cap.* (STP) [C] St. Paul, MN University of St. Thomas.
Posiewala, Jan B. *s.a.c.* '76 (BUF) [O] North Tonawanda, NY Society of the Catholic Apostolate.
Poslusney, Venard *o.carm.* '42 (JOL) [J] Darien, IL Carmelite Fathers Provincial Office.
Posluszny, Francis '62 (BGP) On Duty Outside the Diocese.
Posluszny, Sylvester '34 (GAL) Retired.
Pospichal, Leo C. '56 (SFS) Epiphany, SD Church of the Epiphany.
Pospishil, Msgr. Victor J. '40 (PHU) Retired.
Post, Robert J. '82 (BGP) [7] Stamford, CT Sacred Heart Church.
Postell, Philip S. *s.j.* '70 (DAL) [D] Dallas, TX Jesuit College Preparatory School.
Poster, Richard J. '92 (DAV) Bettendorf, IA St. John Vianney Church; [B] Davenport, IA St. Ambrose University.
Postlethwaite, Basil (SFR) [C] Belmont, CA College of Notre Dame.
Poterucha, Michael '85 (SFD) Absent on Leave.
Poth, Thomas *s.m.m.* '83 (HRT) [M] Litchfield, CT Montfort Missionaries.
Pothier, Glen K. '95 (PMB) [1] Palm Beach, FL Cathedral of St. Ignatius Loyola.
Potocek, Msgr. Cyril J. '36 (NY) North Tarrytown, NY Holy Cross Church; Retired.
Potter, Gerald L. '54 (FAR) Special Assignment.
Potter, Msgr. Joseph D. '54 (BGP) [7] Bridgeport, CT St. Charles Church; [U] Bridgeport, CT The Urban Center of St. Charles Parish.
Potter, Stephen K. '78 (RCK) Crystal Lake, IL St. Elizabeth Ann Seton Church.
Potterton, Msgr. Daniel J. '37 (RVC) Bellmore, NY St. Barnabas the Apostle Church; Retired.
Potthoff, Donald W. '49 (LA) Diamond Bar, CA St. Denis Church; Retired.
Potthoff, Msgr. Frederick E. '44 (LFT) Retired.
Pottorff, Lisle J. '49 (DOD) Retired.
Potts, Donald G. '60 (KAL) Cassopolis, MI St. Ann Church.
Potts, Kenneth M. '68 (OM) Osmond, NE St. Mary of the Seven Dolors Church.
Potts, Richard *c.ss.r.* '91 (STL) [22] St. Louis, MO St. Alphonsus Liguori Church; [P] St. Louis, MO St. Alphonsus Rectory of the Redemptorist.
Potts, Robert J. '64 (ALN) [3] Shenandoah, PA St. George Church; [5] Shenandoah, PA Our Lady of Mt. Carmel Church.
Potts, Ronald A. '89 (WDC) [2] Bethesda, MD St. Jane Frances de Chantal Church.
Potvin, Leo F. '64 (ALB) Dolgeville, NY St. Joseph Church; Newport, NY St. John the Baptist Church.
Potvin, Raymond H. '48 (SPR) On Duty Outside the Diocese.
Potvin, Raymond H. '58 (WDC) [C] Washington, DC Catholic University of America, The.
Potvin, Raymond J. '80 (MAN) Hinsdale, NH St. Joseph Church.
Potvin, Thomas R. *o.p.* '62 (PRT) [I] Lewiston, ME SS. Peter and Paul Priory.
Poulin, Donald J. '66 (NY) Beacon, NY St. Joachim Church.
Poulin, Edward C. '54 (NOR) Retired.
Poulin, Hector *s.d.b.* '68 (NY) [F] New Rochelle, NY Salesian High School.
Poulin, Neil C. *s.j.* '66 (CI) Gagil, FM St. Joseph Church; Tomil, FM St. Peter Chanel Church.
Poulin, Robert P. '48 (WOR) Retired.
Pouliot, Eugene A. '70 (STP) Farmington, MN St. Michael Church.
Pouliot, Francis A. '58 (STP) [35] Minneapolis, MN Visitation Church.
Poulsen, James N. '68 (SD) [27] San Diego, CA St. Gregory The Great Church.
Poulsen, Thomas *o.p.* '63 (DET) [L] Farmington Hills, MI Monastery of the Blessed Sacrament.
Poulson, David L. '79 (E) [B] Erie, PA Gannon University.
Poupore, J. Gareth *c.s.b.* '53 (ROC) [I] Rochester, NY Basilian Residence.
Poupore, Norman E. '50 (OG) Retired.
Poussard, Bertrand R. '67 (PRT) Lewiston, ME St. Mary's Regional Medical Center; [H] Lewiston, ME St. Mary's Regional Medical Center.
Pousson, Donald '66 (LAF) Morse, LA Immaculate Conception Church.
Poux, Francis A. *c.ss.r.* '62 (BAL) Odenton, MD St. Joseph Church.
Poveromo, Robert J. '72 (NY) [54] New York, NY St. James Church.
Povish, Robert W. '90 (PH) Jamison, PA St. Cyril of Jerusalem Church; [D] Warminster, PA Archbishop Wood Catholic High School.
Powderly, James J. '58 (WDC) [3] Rockville, MD St. Mary Church; Special Ministries.
Powell, Bernard F. '58 (PMB) Palm City, FL Holy Redeemer Church.
Powell, Daniel F. X. '92 (HBG) Mechanicsburg, PA St. Joseph Church.
Powell, Edward F. '54 (SUP) Retired.
Powell, Eric S. '90 (PEO) On Duty Outside the Diocese.
Powell, Harold W. '77 (KC) Retired.
Powell, John *o.s.b.cam.* '76 (MRY) [G] Big Sur, CA New Camaldoli Hermitage.
Powell, John J. *s.j.* '56 (CHI) [C] Chicago, IL Jesuit Community at Loyola University of Chicago.
Powell, Leon A. '71 (LC) Special Assignment; [I] La Crosse, WI Holy Cross (Seminary) Diocesan Center.
Powell, Matthew D. *o.p.* '75 (CHI) [N] Chicago, IL Dominicans (Provincial Office).
Powell, Matthew D. *o.p.* '75 (PRO) [P] Providence, RI St. Thomas Aquinas Priory at Providence College.
Powell, Michael '89 (JOL) [16] Joliet, IL St. Mary Nativity Church.
Powell, Paul P. '48 (OWN) Stanley, KY St. Peter of Alcantara Church.
Powell, Ralph A. *o.p.* '51 (STL) [P] St. Louis, MO Dominican Community of St. Louis.
Powell, Robert '66 (CHI) [N] Chicago, IL The Holy Evangelists Friary.
Powell, Robert J. *d.m.a., m.a., m.div.* '74 (PH) Jamison, PA St. Cyril of Jerusalem Church.
Power, Bernard J. *c.ss.r.* '43 (RIC) [O] Hampton, VA Holy Family Retreat House.
Power, David N. *o.m.i.* '56 (WDC) [B] Washington, DC Oblate College/Oblate Center for Mission Studies; [C] Washington, DC Catholic University of America, The.
Power, Eugene J. *s.j.* '51 (ALN) [A] Wernersville, PA Novitiate of St. Isaac Jogues.
Power, J. Timothy '66 (STP) Eden Prairie, MN Pax Christi Church.
Power, James E. *c.m.* '57 (PH) [Z] Philadelphia, PA Congregation of the Mission.
Power, James E. *c.m.* '57 (WDC) [K] Washington, DC Providence Hospital.
Power, James F. (BO) Awaiting Assignment.
Power, Joseph *o.s.f.s.* '62 (BUF) [P] Stella Niagara, NY Stella Niagara Education Park; [Q] Stella Niagara, NY Stella Niagara Center of Renewal.
Power, Patrick A. '55 (LA) Santa Clarita, CA Our Lady of Perpetual Help Church.
Power, Robert E. *c.s.b.* '66 (LSC) Hatch, NM Our Lord of Mercy Church; [B] Las Cruces, NM Basilian Fathers.
Power, Thomas E. '44 (ANC) Retired.
Power, Virgil '39 (ORL) Retired.
Power, Virgil '39 (RVC) Retired.
Power, Walter D. '52 (WIL) Perryville, MD Church of the Good Shepherd; Retired.
Power, William J. *s.j.* '41 (BO) [W] Weston, MA Campion Health Center, Inc.
Powers, Alfred J. '43 (CIN) Retired.
Powers, Aloysius '48 (OWN) Calvert City, KY St. Pius Tenth Church.
Powers, Anthony F. '42 (BRK) Retired.
Powers, Msgr. Bernard '52 (OWN) Reed, KY St. Augustine Church; [H] Maple Mount, KY Mt. St. Joseph Retreat Center.
Powers, Bruce J. '73 (RVC) Melville, NY St. Elizabeth Church.
Powers, Msgr. Charles F. '48 (PAT) Dover, NJ Sacred Heart Church.
Powers, Daniel *s.j.* '68 (HEL) Heart Butte, MT St. Anne Church.
Powers, Donald E. '58 (JC) Camdenton, MO St. Anthony Church.
Powers, Donald E. '58 (KC) Retired.
Powers, Edward R. *s.j.* '45 (SCR) [C] Scranton, PA

University of Scranton.
Powers, Gerard E. '69 (SP) New Port Richey, FL Our Lady Queen of Peace Church.
Powers, Glenn E. '87 (MIL) [5] Sheboygan, WI Immaculate Conception Church.
Powers, Harold J. *c.s.p.* '48 (LA) [86] Los Angeles, CA St. Paul the Apostle Church.
Powers, Harold J. *c.s.p.* '48 (NY) [Z] Scarsdale, NY Paulist Fathers Generalate.
Powers, Isaias *c.p.* '61 (PMB) [G] North Palm Beach, FL Our Lady of Florida Spiritual Center.
Powers, James E. *s.j.* '45 (BO) [W] Weston, MA Campion Health Center, Inc.
Powers, James G. *s.j.* '62 (SPK) [C] Spokane, WA Gonzaga University.
Powers, James P. '90 (SUP) Graduate Studies.
Powers, Jerome C. '47 (CHR) Retired.
Powers, Msgr. John '38 (SJ) Retired.
Powers, John *c.p.* '77 (NY) [Z] New York, NY Passionist Spiritual Center.
Powers, John A. *o.p.* '52 (NO) [25] New Orleans, LA St. Anthony Of Padua Church; [N] Metairie, LA Metairie Manor, Metairie II, and Metairie III.
Powers, John E. '36 (JC) Hermitage, MO St. Bernadette Church.
Powers, John J. (CHI) Retired.
Powers, John J. '38 (ALB) Retired.
Powers, John J. '51 (CHI) South Holland, IL St. Jude the Apostle Church.
Powers, Joseph '50 (ORG) Retired.
Powers, Joseph B. '79 (KC) [15] Kansas City, MO Holy Cross Church.
Powers, Joseph L. '46 (FR) Retired.
Powers, Joseph M. *s.j.* '58 (OAK) [N] Berkeley, CA Jesuit Community at Jesuit School of Theology at Berkeley.
Powers, Msgr. Raymond T. *s.t.d.* '51 (NY) Mahopac, NY St. John the Evangelist Church.
Powers, Richard '47 (BO) [13] Cambridge, MA St. Peter Church.
Powers, Richard E. *s.j.* (E) [26] Erie, PA St. Matthew in the Woods Church; Waterford, PA St. Cyprian Church.
Powers, Richard E. *s.j.* (STA) [8] Jacksonville, FL Immaculate Conception Church.
Powers, Richard J. (BO) Retired.
Powers, Richard M. '59 (OWN) Whitesville, KY St. Mary of the Woods Church.
Powers, Msgr. Richard T. '63 (PH) [71] Philadelphia, PA Incarnation of Our Lord Church; Levittown, PA St. Michael the Archangel Church.
Powers, Msgr. Robert J. '45 (BO) [1] Weymouth, MA St. Albert the Great Church.
Powers, Msgr. Robert J. '45 (BUR) Retired.
Powers, Robert M. '92 (BRK) [26] Brooklyn, NY St. Catharine of Alexandria Church.
Powers, Thomas '62 (ALB) Special Assignment.
Powers, Thomas F. '40 (GF) Retired.
Powers, Thomas F. '66 (BO) Wellesley, MA St. John the Evangelist Church.
Powers, Thomas J. *s.j.* '72 (TOL) [K] Toledo, OH St. Mary's Jesuit Community.
Powers, Thomas J. *s.j.* '95 (BO) Reading, MA St. Agnes Church.
Powers, Thomas J. *s.j.* '95 (SFR) [N] San Francisco, CA Jesuit Community at University of San Francisco.
Powers, Thomas M. '49 (CHI) River Grove, IL St. Cyprian Church; Retired.
Powers, Thomas M. '62 (ALB) Valatie, NY St. John the Baptist Church.
Powers, Troy David '87 (SAC) Oroville, CA St. Thomas the Apostle Church.
Powers, Vincent J. '45 (RVC) Retired.
Powers, Msgr. William E. '36 (GR) Retired.
Powers, Msgr. William E. '36 (MIA) [7] Fort Lauderdale, FL St. Helen Church.
Powers, William V. '58 (PBL) Retired.
Powhida, Robert W. '78 (ALB) Glens Falls, NY St. Alphonsus Church; [C] Glens Falls, NY St. Mary-St. Alphonsus Regional Catholic School.
Powis, Msgr. John J. '59 (BRK) [15] Brooklyn, NY St. Barbara Church.
Poyatt, Msgr. William F. '49 (CAM) Barrington, NJ St. Francis de Sales Church.
Poynter, Gail A. '51 (CIN) Retired.
Pozdol, Henry '50 (CHI) Summit, IL St. Joseph Church; Retired.
Poznakowski, Gilbert '75 (PIT) Allegheny County, PA Shadyside Hospital.
Pozzuoli, Dominic G. '55 (GBG) Leechburg, PA St. Catherine of Alexandria Church.
Prabell, Paul '72 (LEX) Danville, KY SS. Peter & Paul Church.
Prabhu, Alphonse (NY) Millbrook, NY St. Joseph Church.
Prachar, Andrew (NEW) Livingston, NJ St. Raphael Church.
Pracz, Ted '66 (PEO) Danville, IL Holy Family Church.
Prado, Alfred *o.m.i.* '57 (SAT) [K] San Antonio, TX Oblate Madonna Residence.
Prado, Cletus '58 (CHY) Retired.
Prado, Manuel *c.m.* (SJN) Loiza, PR Santiago Apostol, El Mayor Church.
Prado, Teodoro Tim Y. '77 (GAL) [K] Houston, TX The Catholic Chaplain Corps.
Prakasam, John '88 (BRK) [52] Brooklyn, NY Guardian Angel Church.
Prakuzhy, Zacharias *c.m.i.* '68 (SHP) [B] Monroe, LA St. Francis Medical Center.
Pralzer, Roman *o.f.m.* '47 (CIN) [L] Centerville, OH The Franciscan at St. Leonard.
Pramuk, Chris (DEN) [D] Aurora, CO Regis Jesuit High School.
Pranaitis, Mark *c.m.* '93 (DEN) [12] Denver, CO Holy Ghost Church.
Pranaitis, Mark S. *c.m.* (STL) [P] St. Louis, MO Vincentian-St. Lazare Residence.
Pranckus, Msgr. Francis J. '45 (BGP) Retired.
Pranzo, Joseph F. *c.s.* '71 (PRO) [8] Providence, RI St. Bartholomew's Church.
Praski, Jacek '91 (CHI) [193] Chicago, IL St. Stanislaus Kostka Church.
Prasser, Jeffery A. '89 (MIL) [18] Milwaukee, WI St. Catherine Church.
Prat, Camille *s.j.* '62 (PHX) Chandler, AZ St. Andrew the Apostle Church.
Prather, Edward W. '71 (OKL) Absent on Sick Leave.
Pratico, Patrick J. '79 (SCR) Eynon, PA St. Mary's Czestochowa Church.
Prats, Charles V. '84 (MET) [H] Raritan, NJ Clairvaux House; [K] Raritan, NJ Shrine Chapel of the Blessed Sacrament.
Pratt, Burton W. *s.j.* '50 (LC) Prairie du Chien, WI St. Gabriel Church; Prairie du Chien, WI St. John Nepomucene Church.
Pratt, Edward C. '72 (ALB) Hudson Falls, NY Church of St. Mary's/St. Paul's.
Pratt, James F.X. *s.j.* '86 (BO) [W] Boston, MA The Society of Jesus of New England-Provincial Offices.
Pratt, James F.X. *s.j.* '96 (NSH) [1] Nashville, TN Cathedral of the Incarnation.
Pratt, James L. *s.m.* '46 (SFR) [B] San Francisco, CA St. Peter Chanel Seminary; [N] San Francisco, CA Provincial Residence.
Pratt, Lawrence E. '62 (BO) Melrose, MA Incarnation Church.
Pratt, Oscar J. '96 (BO) [8] Lynn, MA Sacred Heart Church.
Pravetz, Matthew A. *o.f.m.* (NY) [146] Bronx, NY Holy Cross Church.
Pray, Joseph N '50 (BUR) Retired.
Prazan, Ceslaus R. *o.p.* '63 (BR) Tickfaw, LA Our Lady of Pompeii Church.
Prazan, Ceslaus R. *o.p.* '63 (CHI) [N] Chicago, IL Dominicans (Provincial Office).
Prebula, David W. *o.s.b.* '44 (SEA) Tacoma, WA Veterans Admin. Medical Center; [M] Lacey, WA St. Martin's Abbey.
Prechasniuk, *o.s.b.m.* '91 (STN) Detroit, MI St. John the Baptist Church.
Prechtl, Ronald G. '80 (WH) [7] Wheeling, WV St. Alphonsus Church.
Preciado, Rudolph J. '69 (ORG) Garden Grove, CA St. Callistus Church.
Precourt, Peter R. *a.a.* '76 (NY) [87] New York, NY Our Lady of Guadalupe Church.
Prefontaine, Roger C. *s.s.s.* '53 (GAL) [24] Houston, TX Corpus Christi Church.
Pregana, Craig A. '89 (FR) [11] Fall River, MA Sacred Heart Church.
Pregana, David A. '96 (FR) [1] Attleboro, MA St. John the Evangelist Church.
Preisinger, Robert F. '63 (OM) [8] Sarpy Co., NE St. Bernadette Church.
Preisner, Msgr. A. F. '40 (DOD) Retired.
Premoshis, Gregory F. '68 (GBG) Mount Pleasant, PA Visitation of the Blessed Virgin Mary Church; [C] Connellsville, PA Geibel Catholic High School.
Prempeh, John Duah *s.v.d.* '95 (GAL) [46] Houston, TX St. Mary of the Purification Church.
Prenatt, David E. '95 (E) [23] Erie, PA St. Luke Church.
Prendergast, Edmond '73 (MIA) [4] Fort Lauderdale, FL St. Bonaventure Church.
Prendergast, Edward F. '51 (CLV) Rocky River, OH St. Christopher Church.
Prendergast, Fergus '94 (MOB) [3] Montgomery, AL St. Bede Church.
Prendergast, Francis '54 (STO) Turlock, CA Sacred Heart Church; [G] Turlock, CA The McElligott Sacred Heart School Foundation.
Prendergast, John J. '76 (PEO) On Duty Outside the Diocese.
Prendergast, Joseph '54 (SJ) [3] Santa Clara, CA St. Justin Church.
Prendergast, Noel '58 (JKS) Clinton, MS Holy Savior Church; [G] Clinton, MS Mississippi College Newman Center; [G] Raymond, MS Hinds Community College Catholic Student Organization.
Prendergast, Richard J. '79 (CHI) Berwyn, IL St. Mary of Celle Church.
Prendergast, Robert E. '22 (PEO) Retired.
Prendergast, Msgr. Thomas '56 (SD) [10] San Diego, CA Mission Basilica San Diego De Alcala Church.
Prendeville, Eugene *o.m.i.* (PEO) Lincoln, IL Lincoln State School.
Prendiville, Edmond P. '63 (PRO) On Duty Outside the Diocese.
Prendiville, Joseph A. '47 (L) Retired.
Prendiville, Kerry '84 (RC) Spearfish, SD St. Joseph Church.
Prendiville, Thomas *s.d.b.* '56 (OAK) [N] Berkeley, CA Salesian Community.
Preneta, Henry S. '67 (GBG) On Duty Outside the Diocese.
Preneta, Henry S. '67 (PIT) [3] Butler, PA St. Paul Church.
Prengaman, Leo Peter *s.j.* '93 (NY) [Z] New York, NY Jesuit Provincial's Office; [Z] New York, NY Xavier Jesuit Community.
Prengaman, Leo Peter *s.j.* '93 (RVC) Farmingdale, NY St. Kilian Church.
Prescott, Herbert W. '55 (KNX) Retired.
Prescott, Leslie T.H. '54 (LAF) Pine Prairie, LA St. Peter Church.
Presenti, Richard R. *s.d.b.* '68 (LA) [F] Bellflower, CA St. John Bosco High School.
Presinell, Joseph C. '44 (SFS) Retired.
Preske, Venantius '52 (LR) Retired.
Preskenis, James T. *c.s.c.* '75 (FR) [B] North Easton, MA Holy Cross Fathers Religious.
Presley, William F. '56 (E) Sykesville, PA Assumption of Blessed Virgin Mary Church.
Presmanes, Jorge *o.p.* '91 (MIA) [18] Miami, FL St. Dominic Church.
Presta, James (CHI) [A] Chicago, IL St. Joseph Seminary; [A] Chicago, IL St. Joseph Seminary.
Prestera, Vincent J. '47 (HON) Retired.
Prestera, Vincent J. '47 (NEW) Retired.
Preston, Richard '74 (LAN) [F] Lansing, MI St. Lawrence Hospital and Healthcare Services.
Pretto, Franklin D. '72 (SFE) [6] Santa Fe, NM San Isidro Church.
Preuss, David *o.f.m.cap.* '79 (DET) [16] Detroit, MI St. Charles Borromeo Church; [58] Detroit, MI Our Lady of Sorrows Church.
Prevost, Frederick J. '48 (SY) Whitesboro, NY St. Anne Church.
Prevost, Normand *s.a.* '47 (NY) [Z] Garrison, NY Franciscan Friars of the Atonement.
Prevost, Robert F. *o.s.a.* '82 (CHI) [N] Olympia Fields, IL The Augustinian Provincialate Tolentine Center.
Prevosto, Paul J. '96 (NEW) Mountainside, NJ Our Lady of Lourdes Church.
Prez, Daniel J. '74 (E) Union City, PA St. Teresa of Avila Church.
Pribonic, Phillip '67 (PIT) Library, PA St. Joan of Arc Church.
Pribula, Duane J. '70 (CR) Oklee, MN St. Francis Xavier's Church.
Pribyl, Francis T. '39 (CHI) [5] Chicago, IL St. Agnes of Bohemia Church; Retired.
Pricco, Richard A. '62 (PEO) Macomb, IL St. Paul's Church.
Price, Bede *o.s.b.* '96 (STL) [F] Creve Coeur, MO St. Louis Priory School; [P] St. Louis, MO The Abbey of St. Mary and St. Louis.
Price, Msgr. Edward G. '44 (NEW) [6] Elizabeth, NJ St. Genevieve's Church; Roselle Park, NJ The Assumption Church; Retired.
Price, Francis R. '44 (OM) Retired.
Price, James *c.p.* '94 (BRK) [180] Queens, NY Immaculate Conception Church; [U] Jamaica, NY Immaculate Conception Monastery.
Price, John R. '66 (CHI) [4] Cicero, IL Mary, Queen of Heaven Church.
Price, Msgr. Leo J. '41 (GAL) Retired.
Price, Rothell '88 (SHP) [1] Shreveport, LA St. John Berchmans Cathedral.
Price, Wayne (STA) Jacksonville Beach, FL St. Paul's Church.
Prichard, James F. '39 (ALB) Retired.
Prickel, Nicholas *s.c.j.* '77 (GB) Institute, WI SS. Peter and Paul Church.
Priebe, Msgr. Norman F. '67 (LA) Arcadia, CA Holy Angels Church.
Priest, Msgr. Gerald '68 (TYL) Texarkana, TX Sacred Heart Church.
Priester, Robert E. '59 (BUF) Retired; [M] Niagara Falls, NY St. Mary's Manor.
Prieto, Frank '64 (SFE) [15] Albuquerque, NM Saint Joseph on the Rio Grande Church.
Prieto, Luis '36 (PCE) [9] Ponce, PR La Merced Church.
Prietto, Mario J. *s.j.* '73 (SJ) [B] Santa Clara, CA Santa Clara University; [B] Santa Clara, CA Santa Clara University.
Prill, John '55 (GAL) [39] Houston, TX St. John Neumann Church.
Primavera, Msgr. Santi J. (BRK) [18] Brooklyn, NY St. Bernadette Church.
Primeaux, Patrick D. *s.m.* '77 (WDC) [M] Washington, DC Marist Provincial House.
Primich, John F. '95 (MET) Basking Ridge, NJ St. James Church.
Primozic, Robert *o.carm.* '64 (JOL) [J] Darien, IL

Carmelite Fathers Provincial Office.
Prince, Joseph A. '71 (BGP) Ridgefield, CT St. Elizabeth Seton Church.
Prince, Leo R. '86 (NY) [1] Poughkeepsie, NY St. Peter Church.
Principe, Francis J. '53 (NY) [E] New York, NY Cardinal Spellman High School.
Prindiville, Gerard T. '96 (NEW) [1] Bayonne, NJ St. Mary Star of the Sea Church.
Prindle, Richard G. '78 (LA) Altadena, CA St. Elizabeth of Hungary Church.
Prinelli, John A. '78 (RIC) Chincoteague, VA St. Andrew Church.
Pringle, Denis *s.a.* '89 (SEA) [4] Seattle, WA St. Benedict Church.
Pringle, John R. '72 (MET) Bridgewater, NJ Holy Trinity Church.
Printy, Michael G. '57 (OM) Jackson, NE St. Patrick Church.
Prinz, Gerald '68 (HT) On Leave.
Prior, Eugene J. *s.j.* '55 (NY) [F] New York, NY Loyola School; [Z] New York, NY St. Ignatius Loyola Residence.
Prior, Felix *o.carm.* '58 (JOL) [J] Darien, IL Carmelite Fathers Provincial Office.
Prior, Francis X. *c.m.* '51 (BUF) [C] Niagara University, NY Niagara University.
Prior, James G. *c.m.* '53 (ALN) Roseto, PA Our Lady of Mt. Carmel Church.
Prior, Joseph G. '90 (PH) Graduate Studies.
Prior, Robert J. *c.m.* '94 (CHL) [3] Greensboro, NC St. Mary Church.
Prior, Thomas *c.m.* '59 (BRK) [U] Jamaica, NY Vincentian Residence.
Priscaro, Jerry S. '93 (E) [3] Sharon, PA St. Joseph Church.
Prist, Wayne F. '67 (CHI) [179] Chicago, IL Queen of All Saints Basilica.
Pritchard, Edward '74 (WDC) Retired.
Pritt, Phillip P. '62 (CLV) Rittman, OH St. Anne Church.
Pritzl, Kurt *o.p.* '91 (WDC) [B] Washington, DC Dominican House of Studies; [C] Washington, DC Catholic University of America, The.
Prive, Francis R. '69 (BUR) Underhill Center, VT St. Thomas Church.
Privett, John A. *s.j.* '72 (OAK) [R] Oakland, CA Institute of Lay Theology.
Privett, John A. *s.j.* '72 (SJ) [M] Los Gatos, CA California Province of the Society of Jesus, Jesuit Provincial Office; [M] Los Gatos, CA Sacred Heart Jesuit Center.
Privett, Stephen A. *s.j.* '72 (SJ) [B] Santa Clara, CA Santa Clara University; [B] Santa Clara, CA Santa Clara University.
Privitera, Msgr. Santi J. '27 (BRK) Retired.
Proback, Adrian *o.c.s.o.* '54 (WOR) [N] Spencer, MA St. Joseph's Abbey.
Probst, R. Dean (SFD) Carlinville, IL SS. Mary & Joseph Church.
Probst, Msgr. Robert L. '45 (STP) Retired; [C] St. Paul, MN University of St. Thomas.
Probstfield, Edgar *o.s.b.* '52 (KC) Trenton, MO St. Joseph's Church.
Probstfield, Regis *o.s.b.* '57 (KC) [J] Conception, MO Conception Abbey.
Procaccini, David C. '93 (PRO) Barrington, RI St. Luke's Church.
Procaccini, Joseph J. '58 (TR) Allentown, NJ St. John Church.
Procella, Paul '87 (GAL) Humble, TX St. Mary Magdalene Church.
Prochaska, John '93 (OAK) [4] San Leandro, CA St. Leander Church.
Prochaski, Adam F. '68 (BRK) Absent on Sick Leave.
Procopio, Charles '56 (HBG) [5] Mount Carmel, PA Our Lady of Mount Carmel Church.
Procopio, Clement *o.f.m.* '44 (NY) [Z] New York, NY Franciscan Province of the Immaculate Conception.
Procopio, Clement *o.f.m.* '44 (PHX) Carefree, AZ Our Lady of Joy Church.
Procter, John W. '85 (ORG) Dana Point, CA St. Edward Church.
Proctor, Burton *s.j.* '62 (ALN) [A] Wernersville, PA Novitiate of St. Isaac Jogues.
Proctor, John G., Jr. '72 (SD) Bonita, CA Corpus Christi Church.
Procyk, Marijan '80 (STF) Buffalo, NY St. Nicholas Church.
Prodehl, Richard B. '66 (JOL) [1] Lockport, IL St. Bernard Church.
Prodywus, Alexander (STN) Absent on Sick Leave.
Proehl, Douglas M. '74 (CLV) Fairview Park, OH St. Angela Merici Church.
Proeller, Ullric (FAR) Retired.
Proeller, Ullric J. (SAT) [K] San Antonio, TX Padua Place.
Profeta, Salvatore '50 (PMB) Retired.
Profitt, James D.. (BAL) [39] Baltimore, MD Immaculate Conception Church.
Profota, James H. '75 (DET) Eastpointe, MI St. Basil Church.
Prohens, James *c.r.* '36 (DEN) [26] Denver, CO St. Cajetan's Church.
Prokes, Francis A. *s.j.* '57 (OM) [K] Omaha, NE Jesuit Community At Creighton University.
Prokop, Msgr. Andrew A. '35 (Y) Retired; [I] North Lima, OH The Assumption Village.
Prokop, Roger '87 (LAN) [3] Ann Arbor, MI St. Thomas the Apostle Church.
Prokopiw, Taras *o.s.b.m.* '58 (STF) New York, NY St. George Church.
Prokopiw, Wasyl (STN) Denver, CO Transfiguration of Our Lord Church.
Promesso, William J. '87 (DET) [9] Sterling Heights, MI St. Rene Goupil Church.
Promis, Christopher P. *c.s.sp.* '72 (PIT) [N] Bethel Park, PA Holy Ghost Fathers and Brothers Provincialate.
Pronesti, Salvatore J. '67 (PH) Bridgeport, PA Our Lady of Mt. Carmel Church; Springfield, PA St. Kevin Church.
Proodian, Paul C. *c.o.* '51 (CHR) [E] Rock Hill, SC Oratory of St. Philip Neri, Congregation of the Oratory of Pontifical Rite.
Proppe, John *o.f.m.cap.* '47 (NY) Hawthorne, NY Rosary Hill Home; [T] Hawthorne, NY Rosary Hill Home; [AA] Hawthorne, NY Motherhouse & Novitiate of the Sisters of St. Dominic, Congregation of St. Rose of Li.
Propst, Sergius R. *o.p.* '73 (OAK) [N] Oakland, CA Dominican Order (Western Province), St. Albert's Priory; [N] Oakland, CA Western Dominican Province.
Prosen, Anthony J. (LFT) Muncie, IN St. Mary Church; Pendleton, IN Indiana State Reformatory, St. Christopher Chapel; Pendleton, IN Correctional Industrial Complex Ecumenical Chapel; Special Assignment.
Prost, Charles E. *c.m.* '78 (DEN) [12] Denver, CO Holy Ghost Church.
Protack, Thomas J. '96 (WIL) Wilmington Manor, DE Our Lady of Fatima Church.
Protano, Joseph, Jr. '63 (PRO) [5] Providence, RI St. Anthony's Church.
Proterra, Michael *s.j.* '71 (OM) [A] Omaha, NE Creighton University; [K] Omaha, NE Jesuit Community At Creighton University.
Protomastro, Camillus *o.f.m.cap.* '59 (NY) [151] Bronx, NY Immaculate Conception Church.
Protopapas, George *o.m.i.* '43 (BO) [12] Lowell, MA Nuestra Senora del Carmen 1990 Church.
Proud, Albert J. '68 (SY) Jordan, NY St. Patrick Church.
Proulx, Arthur '80 (SP) [5] St. Petersburg, FL St. Joseph Church; [F] St. Petersburg, FL Immaculate Conception Pre-School.
Proulx, Donald R. '60 (PRT) Windham, ME Our Lady of Perpetual Help Church.
Proulx, Raymond G. '60 (HRT) Goshen, CT St. Thomas of Villanova Church.
Proulx, Roger F. '47 (PRT) Retired; [I] Waterville, ME Mt. St. Joseph Priest Retirement Home.
Prout, Thomas S. *s.j.* '92 (NY) [F] New York, NY Loyola School; [Z] New York, NY St. Ignatius Loyola Residence.
Provensano, Francis A. *c.s.c.* '44 (FTW) [J] South Bend, IN Congregation of Holy Cross Indiana Province Provincial House.
Provenza, Msgr. Earl V. '64 (SHP) Bossier City, LA Christ the King Church.
Provenza, John '90 (LA) [81] Los Angeles, CA St. Michael Church; [D] Playa Del Rey, CA St. Bernard High School.
Provinsal, Thomas G. *s.j.* '75 (FBK) Alakanuk, AK St. Ignatius Church; Emmonak, AK Sacred Heart Church.
Provinzano, Rocco F. '66 (NEW) Westwood, NJ St. Andrew's Church.
Provost, Armand J. '38 (MAN) Dover, NH St. Charles Church; Retired.
Provost, Msgr. Glen John '75 (LAF) [1] Lafayette, LA St. John the Evangelist Cathedral.
Provost, James H. '63 (HEL) On Duty Outside the Diocese.
Provost, James H. '63 (WDC) [C] Washington, DC Catholic University of America, The
Provost, John T. '73 (ALB) [6] Schenectady, NY Holy Cross Church; [9] Schenectady, NY St. John the Evangelist Church; [12] Schenectady, NY St. Mary Church.
Provost, Raymond C. '36 (BUR) Retired.
Provosty, William B. '59 (ALX) Cottonport, LA St. Mary Assumption Church.
Proxell, Leo G. '77 (HEL) [A] Helena, MT Carroll College; [B] Helena, MT Carroll College.
Prozny, Leopold V. '42 (SY) Retired.
Prucha, Francis Paul *s.j.* '57 (MIL) [P] Milwaukee, WI Jesuit Community at Marquette University.
Prudell, Msgr. Harold O. '39 (MIL) Retired.
Prudencio, Rodriguez *c.m.* '65 (PHX) Special Assignment.
Pruemer, Alexis *o.f.m.* '47 (SFD) Shumway, IL Church of the Annunciation; [K] Teutopolis, IL St. Francis Assisi Friary.
Pruett, Bill '79 (OKL) [7] Oklahoma City, OK St. Eugene's Church.
Pruett, John M. '55 (STO) Modesto, CA Our Lady of Fatima Church.
Prunier, Arthur J. '48 (WOR) Retired.
Prunty, Brian *o.praem.* '65 (CHI) [N] Chicago, IL Premonstratensian Fathers and Brothers (Norbertines).
Prus, Edward '61 (DET) Garden City, MI St. Raphael the Archangel Church.
Prus, Msgr. Eugene '64 (MET) Martinsville, NJ Blessed Sacrament Church.
Prusaitis, John P. '78 (BO) [1] Brockton, MA St. Casimir Church.
Prusakowski, Gerald *o.f.m.* '65 (GB) Abrams, WI St. Louis Church; Chase, WI St. Joseph Church; Sobieski, WI St. John Cantius Church.
Pruschowitz, Walter M. '61 (PAT) [5] Passaic, NJ Holy Trinity Church.
Prushinski, Carl T. '64 (SCR) Mocanaqua, PA St. Mary, Our Lady of Perpetual Help Church.
Pruss, Rodney Lee A. '69 (GI) Ravenna, NE Our Lady of Lourdes Church.
Prussing, Charles *s.j.* '55 (LA) [R] Los Angeles, CA Columbiere House.
Prusynski, Chester *c.s.c.* '62 (P) [B] Portland, OR University of Portland; [L] Portland, OR Holy Cross Father & Brother, C.S.C. - University of Portland.
Pruys, George L. '75 (STN) Milwaukee, WI St. Michaels Church.
Prybis, Raymond *o.m.i.* '67 (WDC) [B] Washington, DC Oblate College/Oblate Center for Mission Studies.
Pryor, Msgr. Donald J. (NY) Pocantico Hills, NY The Magdalene Church.
Pryor, G. Robert '55 (CR) Retired.
Pryor, Patrick W. '92 (NU) Absent on Leave.
Pryor, Msgr. Thomas P. '37 (PH) Retired.
Przechacki, Casimir J. '44 (MET) Retired.
Przepierski, Frank J. '62 (E) Clarion, PA Immaculate Conception Church.
Przewozny, Bernard *o.f.m.conv.* '69 (BAL) [M] Ellicott City, MD Order of Friars Minor Conventual.
Przyblski, Kevin *o.f.m.conv.* '89 (IND) [I] Mount Saint Francis, IN Mount Saint Francis Friary and Retreat Center.
Przybocki, Bernard A. '58 (ALT) Gallitzin, PA St. Patrick's Church; Gallitzin, PA Our Lady of Czestochowa Church.
Przybyla, Kenneth '77 (COS) Salida, CO St. Joseph Church.
Przybyla, Kenneth '77 (PEO) On Duty Outside the Diocese.
Przybyla, Philip J. '70 (PIT) Canonsburg, PA St. Patrick Church.
Przybyla, Raymond C. '40 (TOL) Retired.
Przybylo, William P. '68 (HRT) [9] Hartford, CT SS. Cyril and Methodius Church; [N] Hartford, CT SS. Cyril & Methodius Convent.
Przybylski, Donald L. '74 (LC) [5] Stevens Point, WI St. Stanislaus Church.
Przybysz, Joseph J. '75 (TOL) [23] Toledo, OH St. Hedwig Church.
Przybysz, Mark C. '90 (GR) [8] Grand Rapids, MI Holy Spirit Church; [22] Grand Rapids, MI St. Stephen's Church.
Przydacz, John '33 (TYL) Retired.
Przydzial, Frederick '56 (ALN) [11] Bethlehem, PA St. Stanislaus Church.
Przysucha, Joseph *c.r.* '53 (CHI) [D] Chicago, IL Weber High School.
Przywara, Gerald A. '67 (RIC) Columbia, VA St. Joseph Church; Palmyra, VA Ss. Peter & Paul Church.
Ptacek, Benedict *o.de.m.* '59 (SP) [O] St. Petersburg, FL St. Peter Nolasco Residence.
Ptacek, John P. '55 (DUB) Farley, IA St. Joseph's Church; [F] Epworth, IA Seton Catholic Elementary School.
Ptak, Walter J. '87 (DET) [4] Wyandotte, MI Our Lady of Mt. Carmel Church.
Ptaszynski, Stephen F. '45 (HRT) Retired.
Ptaszynski, Thomas E. '73 (HRT) New Milford, CT Our Lady of the Lakes Church.
Pu, Matthew C. '53 (B) On Duty Outside the Diocese.
Pu, Matthew C. '53 (BAK) Burns, OR Holy Family Church.
Publicover, James L. '56 (BO) [4] Arlington, MA St. Jerome Church.
Pucar, August '63 (BEA) Liberty, TX Immaculate Conception Church.
Pucci, Alfred J. '54 (NY) [226] Staten Island, NY St. Roch Church.
Pucci, Anthony A. (NY) [18] Yonkers, NY Most Holy Trinity Church; Yonkers, NY Yonkers General Hospital.
Pucci, Francis L. '57 (PIT) Retired.
Pucci, Joseph *o.m.i.* '41 (PMB) [4] West Palm Beach, FL St. John Fisher Church.
Pucciarelli, George W. '74 (BO) Military & VA Chaplains.

Puccinelli, Alfred H. *s.m.* '66 (B) Nampa, ID St. Paul's Church.
Puccini, Alfred V. '53 (BO) [4] Malden, MA St. Peter Church.
Puchenski, Anthony C. '71 (CHI) [92] Chicago, IL Immaculate Conception Church.
Pucke, Michael U. '73 (CIN) [64] Cincinnati, OH St. Michael Church.
Pudenz, Anthony '48 (JKS) Port Gibson, MS St. Joseph Church; Retired.
Pudichery, Joseph '62 (PIT) [B] Pittsburgh, PA Duquesne University of the Holy Ghost.
Pudichery, Joseph P. '62 (PIT) Overbrook, PA St. Norbert Church.
Puerner, John W. '55 (LC) Thorp, WI St. Bernard-St. Hedwig Parish Church.
Puerta, Jorge '89 (MIA) Absent on Sick Leave.
Puetz, Richard W. '45 (LFT) [D] Delphi, IN St. Elizabeth Healthcare Center.
Pugevicius, Casimir A. '53 (BAL) [5] Baltimore, MD St. Alphonsus Church; [10] Baltimore, MD St. Anthony of Padua Church.
Pugevicues, Casimir A. '53 (BAL) Retired.
Pugh, Msgr. Charles '60 (SAT) Von Ormy, TX St. Peter the Fisherman Church.
Pugh, James L. '67 (MEM) [3] Memphis, TN St. Anne's Church.
Pugliese, Francis A. '68 (NY) Military Chaplains.
Pugliese, Steven *s.j.* '93 (BRK) [62] Brooklyn, NY St. Ignatius Church.
Puglisi, Msgr. Guy J. '71 (BRK) [3] Brooklyn, NY St. Agnes Church; [E] Brooklyn, NY Office of the Superintendent of Schools.
Puglisi, James *s.a.* '73 (NY) [Z] Garrison, NY Generalate of the Franciscan Friars of the Atonement-St. James Friary.
Puhak, Msgr. Nicholas I. '57 (PSC) Trenton, NJ St. Mary of the Assumption Church.
Puhl, Albert E. '44 (DEN) Retired.
Puhlman, Robert W.P. '84 (ORG) Newport Beach, CA Our Lady Queen of Angels Church.
Puisis, John C. *c.s.v.* '45 (CHI) [N] Arlington Heights, IL Viatorian Province Center-Clerics of St. Viator.
Puisis, Leonard '52 (MIA) Hallandale, FL St. Matthew Church.
Pujdak, Steve *s.c.j.* '69 (BWN) Raymondville, TX Our Lady of Guadalupe Church.
Pulaski, Joseph S. *m.m.* '47 (NY) [Z] Maryknoll, NY Maryknoll Fathers and Brothers.
Puleo, Edward C. '88 (MET) [1] Carteret, NJ St. Joseph Church.
Pulicare, Michael J. '71 (SCR) Susquehanna, PA St. John the Evangelist Church.
Pulice, John J. '66 (MIL) [69] Milwaukee, WI St. Robert's Church.
Pulikoottil, Abraham '56 (BUF) Clarence, NY Our Lady of Peace Church.
Pulikoottil, Abroham '65 (BUF) Retired.
Pulikoottil, Berard '62 (BUF) Lancaster, NY St. Mary of the Assumption Church.
Puljic, Marko *o.f.m.* '81 (NY) [29] New York, NY SS. Cyril and Methodius - St. Raphael Church.
Pullo, Francis S. '42 (BRK) Retired; [U] Douglaston, NY Bishop Mugavero Residence.
Pulskamp, Msgr. James E. '67 (SR) [2] Santa Rosa, CA Holy Spirit Church.
Pulvermacher, Claude *o.f.m.cap.* '60 (MIL) [N] Wauwatosa, WI St. Camillus Health Center, Inc.; [P] Milwaukee, WI St. Conrad House.
Pulvermacher, Pius '48 (GB) [I] Appleton, WI St. Fidelis Friary.
Puma, Msgr. Vincent E. '51 (PAT) Special Assignment.
Punch, David '68 (MIA) Retired.
Punch, Nicholas W. *o.p.* '66 (SUP) [I] Webster, WI Thomas More Center for Preaching and Prayer, Inc.
Punderson, Msgr. Joseph R. '76 (TR) On Duty Outside the Diocese.
Punke, Msgr. Robert H. '54 (STU) St. Clairsville, OH St. Mary's Church; [I] St. Clairsville, OH Ohio University - Eastern.
Puntal, Pedro C. '82 (ORL) Goldenrod, FL Saints Peter and Paul Church.
Punti, George '55 (RVC) Elmont, NY St. Boniface Church.
Puntino, John '78 (NEW) [N] South Orange, NJ Don Bosco Residence.
Puodziunas, John *o.f.m.* '87 (GB) [3] Manitowoc, WI St. Mary Church; [I] Pulaski, WI Assumption of B.V.M. Friary.
Pupin, Vito A. '41 (BRK) Retired.
Pupius, George J. '63 (OKL) Moore, OK St. Andrew's Church.
Pupsys, Adam '52 (NOR) Retired.
Purcell, Arthur D. '79 (BRK) [43] Brooklyn, NY St. Frances de Chantal Church.
Purcell, James E. '53 (PEO) Eureka, IL St. Luke's Church.
Purcell, Msgr. Lawrence M. '65 (SD) Solana Beach, CA St. James Church.
Purcell, Owen *o.s.b.* '57 (KCK) Kelly, KS St. Bede's Church.
Purcell, Msgr. Paul J. '54 (SCR) [22] Scranton, PA St. Paul's Church.
Purcell, Robert F. *s.j.* '67 (MIL) [P] Milwaukee, WI Jesuit Community at Marquette University.
Purcell, Robert H. '74 (ALB) Margaretville, NY Sacred Heart Church.
Purcell, William F. '47 (SCR) Peckville, PA Sacred Heart of Jesus Church.
Purdy, David T. *s.d.b.* '70 (SFR) [45] San Francisco, CA SS. Peter and Paul Church.
Purdy, George *s.j.* '53 (YAK) Naches, WA St. John's Church.
Purdy, Robert M. (BO) Absent on Leave.
Purfield, James R. '54 (DEN) [2] Denver, CO All Saints Church.
Puricell, Stephen G. '91 (STL) Maryland Heights, MO St. Blaise Church.
Puricelli, Stephen G. '91 (STL) Webster Groves, MO Holy Redeemer Church.
Purnam, Richard *s.d.b.* '89 (MIA) [25] Miami, FL St. Kieran Church.
Purnell, Mark E. '85 (GBG) Republic, PA Holy Rosary Church.
Purta, Jerome J. '61 (SCR) Unassigned or Leave of Absence.
Purtell, John *s.o.l.t.* '95 (CC) [H] Robstown, TX Society of Our Lady of the Most Holy Trinity.
Purtell, John J. '68 (DUB) Hawkeye, IA St. Francis Xavier Church; Sumner, IA Immaculate Conception Church.
Purtell, Thomas J. '61 (CHI) [108] Chicago, IL St. John Fisher Church.
Purtell, Thomas W. '53 (DUB) Unassigned.
Purvey, J. James '84 (BAL) [61] Baltimore, MD St. Michael Church.
Puryear, Stan '95 (OWN) Bowling Green, KY Holy Spirit Church.
Pusak, Ronald '61 (MIA) [30] Miami, FL St. Richard Church.
Pusateri, Christian *o.s.b.* '55 (RCK) [H] Aurora, IL Marmion Abbey-St. Augustine's Abbey.
Pusateri, Joseph E. '54 (GRY) Otis, IN St. Mary Church.
Pusateri, Philip A. *s.j.* '72 (BO) [E] Boston, MA Boston College High School & Jesuit Community.
Pusateri, Samuel D. *o.s.b.* '79 (PEO) [A] Peru, IL St. Bede Abbey and Academy.
Puscas, Louis *d.d.* '42 (ROM) Aurora, IL St. Michael Church.
Pusch, Richard K. '71 (SHP) [3] Shreveport, LA Our Lady of the Blessed Sacrament Church.
Pustaver, John '87 (LA) Redondo Beach, CA St. James Church.
Puthenparambil, Joseph '78 (NEW) Newark, NJ Beth Israel Hospital.
Puthiyadom, Thomas '94 (HRT) [I] Hartford, CT Saint Francis Hospital and Medical Center.
Puthoff, Chad *s.d.s.* '71 (MIL) [P] Milwaukee, WI Salvatorian Provincial Residence.
Puthota, Charles Isaac *s.j.* '89 (MIL) [P] Milwaukee, WI Jesuit Community at Marquette University.
Puthotta, Patrick '75 (NY) [1] New Rochelle, NY Blessed Sacrament Church.
Puthuppally, Joseph '66 (SHP) [5] Monroe, LA St. Matthew Church; [B] Monroe, LA St. Francis Medical Center.
Puthusseril, George '79 (MIA) [4] Miami Beach, FL St. Patrick Church.
Putich, Michael J. *o.f.m.* '68 (Y) [B] North Canton, OH Walsh University.
Putka, John S. *s.m.* '69 (CIN) [D] Dayton, OH The University of Dayton; [M] Cincinnati, OH Marianist Community.
Putnam, J.T. (WDC) [B] Washington, DC St. Joseph's Seminary.
Putnam, John T., Jr. '92 (CHL) Graduate Studies.
Putnam, Richard *s.d.b.* '89 (MIA) [C] Miami, FL La Salle High School.
Putnick, Robert J. '45 (CIN) Retired.
Putz, Kenneth G. '73 (PH) Warminster, PA Nativity of Our Lord Church.
Putz, Louis *c.s.c.* (FTW) [B] Notre Dame, IN University of Notre Dame Du Lac.
Puza, Paul G. '75 (ALN) Barnesville, PA St. Richard Church; [C] Tamaqua, PA Marian Catholic High School.
Puzio, Thomas '70 (DET) [4] Warren, MI St. Dorothy Church.
Pyka, Francis *c.m.f.* '46 (PHX) Prescott, AZ Sacred Heart Church.
Pyka, Frank *c.m.f.* '46 (LA) [R] San Gabriel, CA Claretian Missionaries (Missionary Sons of the Immaculate Heart of Mary).
Pyne, Donald E. '56 (SFR) Retired.
Pyne, William F. (PRO) [M] North Smithfield, RI St. Antoine Residence.
Pyne, William F. '41 (PRO) Retired.
Pyo, Edward '85 (PBR) Ernest, PA St. Jude Thaddeus Church.
Pysz, Bruno *o.f.m.conv.* '48 (BUF) [21] Buffalo, NY Corpus Christi Church.
Pytel, Ronald '73 (BAL) [36] Baltimore, MD Holy Rosary Church.
Pytlik, Conrad E. '66 (LSC) Mesilla, NM St. Albino Church.

Q

Quach, Binh The *c.s.sp.* (GAL) [B] Houston, TX Holy Ghost Fathers.
Quach, Binh The '91 (WCH) On Duty Outside the Diocese.
Quackenbush, Daniel M. *o.f.m.conv.* '88 (R) Burlington, NC Blessed Sacrament Church; Siler City, NC St. Julia Church.
Quade, Alvin '54 (SCL) Randall, MN St. James Church.
Quadrini, Angelo '85 (EVN) [F] Jasper, IN Providence Home, Nursing Home for the Needy.
Quaine, Michael W. '85 (DET) [1] Dearborn, MI St. Alphonsus Church.
Quainoo, Clement '82 (VIC) Hillje, TX St. Andrew Church.
Qualizza, Frank *s.x.* '71 (PAT) [M] Wayne, NJ Xaverian Missionary Fathers.
Quane, Joseph F. *s.j.* '38 (BO) [W] Chestnut Hill, MA The Jesuit Community at Boston College; [W] Weston, MA Campion Health Center, Inc.
Quane, Ralph L. '78 (DET) Royal Oak, MI Shrine of the Little Flower Church.
Quang, John '70 (SAV) Military Chaplains.
Quang Huy, John Vu *c.m.c.* '85 (FWT) Wichita Falls, TX Sacred Heart Church.
Quangle, Peter '88 (STP) [11] St. Paul, MN St. Adalbert Church.
Quant, Roberto '91 (OKL) [10] Oklahoma City, OK Holy Angels Church.
Quante, Paul *o.s.a.* '84 (OAK) Castro Valley, CA Our Lady of Grace Church.
Quanz, Paul E. *c.s.b.* '84 (GRY) [B] Merrillville, IN Andrean High School; [K] Merrillville, IN Basilian Fathers Residence.
Quarato, Robert A. '92 (NY) [161] Bronx, NY St. Margaret of Cortona Church.
Quartana, Donald F. '53 (MIL) [1] Wauwatosa, WI St. Bernard's Church; Retired.
Quartier, Neal E. (SY) Special Assignment.
Quartier, Neal E. '76 (SY) [1] Syracuse, NY The Cathedral of the Immaculate Conception.
Quattropane, Joseph '72 (LA) Canyon Country, CA St. Clare Church.
Quaye-Foli, Anumu *s.v.d.* '85 (WDC) [M] Washington, DC Divine Word College.
Que, Dinh Ngoc *c.ss.r.* '56 (LA) [R] Baldwin Park, CA Vietnamese Redemptorist Mission.
Quealy, Philip J. '83 (NY) [E] White Plains, NY Archbishop Stepinac High School.
Queen, James T. '65 (SY) [C] Rome, NY Rome Catholic Junior-Senior High School.
Queen, James T. '66 (SY) Florence, NY St. Mary Church; [3] Rome, NY St. Paul Church.
Queenan, John M. (NY) [Q] Ossining, NY The Cardinal McCloskey Emergency Residential School.
Queenan, William J. *s.s.* '60 (SFR) [3] Menlo Park, CA The Church of the Nativity.
Quenum, Andre '93 (PIT) [78] Pittsburgh, PA Most Holy Name of Jesus Church.
Quesada, Manuel '53 (RVC) Sag Harbor, NY St. Andrew's Church.
Quesada, Raul A. '80 (SJN) [1] Carolina, PR San Andres Church.
Quetchenbach, Raymond *s.v.d.* '57 (CHI) [B] Techny, IL Divine Word Residence; [N] Techny, IL Society of the Divine Word, Provincial Headquarter-Chicago Prov.
Quevedo, Alfredo S. *s.j.* '56 (BRK) [62] Brooklyn, NY St. Ignatius Church.
Quezada, Francisco (GAL) [1] Spring, TX Christ the Good Shepherd Church.
Quezada, Sixto '81 (NY) [14] New York, NY Ascension Church.
Qui, Vincent '68 (NO) Retired.
Quiambo, Hermogenes '66 (AGN) Tamuning, GU St. Anthony and St. Victor Church.
Quibuyen, Rogelio S. '86 (HON) Waihee, HI St. Ann Church.
Quic, Cristobal Coche '92 (RCK) [H] Aurora, IL Marmion Abbey-St. Augustine's Abbey.
Quiceno, Jose Francisco '72 (SJN) [57] San Juan, PR Santismo Sacramento Church.
Quick, Emmanuel '84 (SEA) [G] Tacoma, WA St. Joseph Medical Center.
Quigg, Harold '60 (SEA) [6] Seattle, WA St. Bridget Church.
Quigley, Eugene J. *s.j.* '55 (NY) [Z] New York, NY Murray-Weigel Hall.
Quigley, J. Joseph '56 (SPR) Retired; [P] Amherst, MA University of Massachusetts and Amherst College, Newman Center.
Quigley, James Ferrer *o.p.* '65 (PRO) [P] Providence, RI St. Thomas Aquinas Priory at Providence College.
Quigley, John *o.f.m.* '72 (CIN) [M] Cincinnati, OH St. Francis Seraph Friary.
Quigley, Joseph (SPR) Hadley, MA St. John's Church.

Quigley, Joseph P. '60 (BRK) [79] Brooklyn, NY St. Mark's Church; Brooklyn, NY Coney Island Hospital.
Quigley, Martin J. '46 (BAK) Retired.
Quigley, Patrick '81 (NY) Absent on Leave.
Quigley, Robert L. '58 (NEW) [I] Jersey City, NJ St. Joseph's Home for the Blind.
Quigley, William *c.i.c.m.* '74 (SAT) [B] San Antonio, TX Missionhurst Formation Community.
Quihuis, Luis H. *s.j.* '92 (SFR) [N] San Francisco, CA Jesuit Community at University of San Francisco.
Quijano, Antonio *m.s.* '92 (HON) Waipahu, HI St. Joseph Church.
Quijano, Juan '73 (PMB) [A] Boynton Beach, FL St. Vincent de Paul Regional Seminary.
Quilici, Lawrence '68 (RNO) On Duty Outside the Diocese.
Quilici, Lawrence '68 (TUC) Florence, AZ Arizona State Prison.
Quill, J. Michael '82 (WDC) Pomfret, MD St. Joseph Church.
Quill, James E. '53 (COV) [2] Covington, KY St. Agnes Church; Retired.
Quill, John '74 (NEW) Summit, NJ Overlook Hospital.
Quillen, Andrew M. '91 (BO) [W] Hingham, MA Glastonbury Abbey.
Quilligan, Maurice '57 (SFD) Maryville, IL Mother of Perpetual Help Church.
Quilligan, Michael '71 (MIA) West Hollywood, FL Annunciation Church.
Quilty, James B. '65 (HRT) Rocky Hill, CT Veterans' Home and Hospital; [M] Hartford, CT Missionaries of LaSalette Provincial Secretary.
Quinkert, Denis *o.s.b.* '76 (SFS) Yankton, SD State Hospital; [A] Yankton, SD Mount Marty College; [G] Yankton, SD Sacred Heart Monastery.
Quinlan, Edward J. '78 (HBG) Danville, PA St. Joseph Church.
Quinlan, Eugene '62 (MIA) Retired.
Quinlan, James V. '76 (CHI) Maywood, IL St. Eulalia Church.
Quinlan, John J. '70 (PAT) Swartswood, NJ Our Lady of Mt. Carmel Church; Newton, NJ Newton Memorial Hospital.
Quinlan, Joseph M. '52 (NEW) Retired.
Quinlan, Thomas J. '58 (RIC) Tabb, VA Blessed Kateri Tekawitha Church.
Quinlan, William J. '38 (CHI) Forest Park, IL St. Bernardine Church; Retired.
Quinlivan, Anthony *c.ss.r.* '71 (ORL) Melbourne, FL Ascension Church.
Quinlivan, Thomas J. '72 (BUF) Olean, NY St. Mary of the Angels Church.
Quinlivan, William J. '75 (BUF) [4] Kenmore, NY St. Paul Church.
Quinn, Msgr. Andrew F. '35 (NY) [227] Staten Island, NY Sacred Heart Church; Retired.
Quinn, Bernard '53 (HBG) Hanover, PA St. Vincent Church.
Quinn, Bernard J. '72 (LA) [R] Los Angeles, CA Amat House.
Quinn, Brendan H. '74 (NEW) Kearny, NJ St. Cecilia's Church.
Quinn, Bruce *o.f.m.cap* '57 (BGP) [O] Stamford, CT Lourdes Capuchin Chaplains Community.
Quinn, Charles H. '43 (BAL) Retired.
Quinn, Charles J. '61 (WIN) Windom, MN St. Francis Xavier's Church.
Quinn, Charles P. '59 (NY) Pleasant Valley, NY St. Stanislaus Kostka Church.
Quinn, Charles P. '66 (PRO) North Tiverton, RI Holy Ghost Church.
Quinn, Charles T. *o.p.* '55 (NEW) [27] Jersey City, NJ Sacred Heart Church.
Quinn, Don '83 (IND) [N] Indianapolis, IN Butler University Newman Center; [N] Indianapolis, IN Indiana University-Purdue University, Indianapolis Newman Center; [N] Indianapolis, IN University of Indianapolis Newman Center.
Quinn, Frank C. *o.p.* '59 (STL) [B] St. Louis, MO Aquinas Institute of Theology; [P] St. Louis, MO St. Dominic Priory.
Quinn, Gavin *o.carm.* '65 (JOL) Darien, IL Our Lady of Mount Carmel Church.
Quinn, J. Gregory *s.j.* '85 (BAL) [D] Baltimore, MD Loyola High School.
Quinn, J. Patrick '65 (JC) St. Clement, MO St. Clement Church.
Quinn, J. Patrick *t.o.r.* '84 (STP) [20] Minneapolis, MN St. Bridget Church.
Quinn, James '60 (NY) Absent on Leave.
Quinn, James A. '67 (SY) Absent on Leave.
Quinn, James E. '54 (MIA) Retired.
Quinn, James F. (SY) Special Assignment.
Quinn, James F. '58 (SY) [5] Syracuse, NY Most Holy Rosary Church.
Quinn, James J. *s.j.* '50 (OM) [K] Omaha, NE Jesuit Community At Creighton University.
Quinn, James P. '92 (TR) Browns Mills, NJ St. Ann Church.
Quinn, James Q. '67 (SY) [10] Utica, NY St. Joseph and St. Patrick Church.
Quinn, Jarlath '96 (NY) [170] Bronx, NY Our Lady of the Assumption Church.
Quinn, John (NY) White Plains, NY Burke Rehabilitation Center.
Quinn, John F. '71 (NY) Armonk, NY St. Patrick Church.
Quinn, Msgr. John J. '43 (NY) Retired; [A] Yonkers, NY St. Joseph's Seminary.
Quinn, John J. '50 (HRT) Retired.
Quinn, John J. *s.j.* '54 (SCR) [C] Scranton, PA University of Scranton.
Quinn, John J. '63 (ROC) [43] Rochester, NY St. Margaret Mary Church.
Quinn, John J. '86 (TR) Moorestown, NJ Our Lady of Good Counsel Church.
Quinn, John L. (NY) Gardiner, NY St. Charles Borromeo Church.
Quinn, John M. *o.s.a.* '49 (PH) [Z] Villanova, PA St. Thomas Monastery.
Quinn, John M. '57 (SY) New Hartford, NY St. Thomas Church.
Quinn, Msgr. John M. '72 (DET) [45] Detroit, MI St. Luke Church; Special Assignment.
Quinn, Msgr. John P. '68 (MAN) [1] Manchester, NH St. Joseph Cathedral; [G] Manchester, NH Catholic Charities Administration.
Quinn, Msgr. John S. '40 (CHI) [11] Chicago, IL St. Andrew Church.
Quinn, Msgr. John S. '44 (CHI) Retired.
Quinn, John T. '67 (SD) Retired.
Quinn, John T. *s.j.* '92 (SAC) [C] Sacramento, CA Jesuit High School; [H] Carmichael, CA Jesuit High School Community of Sacramento.
Quinn, Joseph G. '85 (SCR) [1] Scranton, PA St. Peter's Cathedral.
Quinn, Msgr. Joseph J. '45 (NY) Retired; [Z] New York, NY Pope John Paul II Residence.
Quinn, Joseph L. *s.j.* '66 (SCR) [C] Scranton, PA University of Scranton.
Quinn, Joseph M. *c.s.c.* '50 (BUR) Wallingford, VT St. Patrick Church.
Quinn, Kenneth '71 (BO) Maynard, MA St. Bridget Church.
Quinn, Kevin P. *s.j.* '85 (WDC) [M] Washington, DC The Jesuit Community at Georgetown University.
Quinn, Kieran *o.f.m.cap.* '44 (WH) [2] Charleston, WV St. Anthony's Church; [N] Charleston, WV Capuchins-St. Anthony Friary.
Quinn, Lawrence J. '71 (NY) [173] Bronx, NY Our Lady of Mercy Church; [L] New York, NY Catholic Youth Organization of the Archdiocese of New York Inc.
Quinn, Lawrence T. '67 (NY) [195] Staten Island, NY St. Ann Church.
Quinn, Liam '83 (MIA) [A] Miami, FL St. John Vianney College Seminary; [D] Miami, FL Christopher Columbus High School.
Quinn, Matthew *s.s.c.* '43 (LA) Montrose, CA Holy Redeemer Church.
Quinn, Michael *c.ss.r.* '72 (OM) [19] Omaha, NE Holy Name Church.
Quinn, Michael F. '70 (JC) Columbia, MO Columbia Newman Center, University of Missouri Church; [F] Columbia, MO University of Missouri-Columbia, Campus Ministry.
Quinn, Patrick '54 (JKS) On Duty Outside the Diocese; [H] Jackson, MS Nuestra Senora Del Perpetuo Socorro.
Quinn, Patrick T. *s.j.* '88 (WH) [A] Wheeling, WV Wheeling Jesuit University.
Quinn, Peter '50 (ORL) Retired.
Quinn, Peter '62 (JKS) On Duty Outside the Diocese.
Quinn, Peter F. '72 (BO) [3] Quincy, MA St. John the Baptist Church.
Quinn, Peter N. '75 (PH) [51] Philadelphia, PA Good Shepherd Church.
Quinn, Peter O. (BLX) [3] Biloxi, MS Our Mother of Sorrows Church.
Quinn, Msgr. Richard M. '40 (ROC) Retired.
Quinn, Richard M. *c.ss.r.* '62 (KC) [32] Kansas City, MO Our Lady of Perpetual Help Church; [J] Kansas City, MO Redemptorists of Kansas City.
Quinn, Robert C. '61 (ALN) Boyertown, PA St. Columbkill Church.
Quinn, Robert F. *c.s.p.* '53 (NY) [Z] Scarsdale, NY Paulist Fathers Generalate.
Quinn, Msgr. Robert J. '34 (SC) Retired.
Quinn, Seamus M. *c.ss.r.* '58 (PH) [135] Philadelphia, PA St. Peter the Apostle Church.
Quinn, Stephen *s.t.* '44 (PAT) [M] Stirling, NJ Holy Spirit Missionary Cenacle.
Quinn, Thomas '62 (SEA) [27] Seattle, WA Our Lady of Fatima Church.
Quinn, Thomas J. *s.j.* '68 (NY) [BB] Staten Island, NY Mount Manresa Jesuit Retreat House.
Quinn, Thomas J. '69 (PBL) Sabbatical.
Quinn, Thomas P. '48 (HRT) Farmington, CT St. Patrick's Church.
Quinn, Thomas S. '85 (TOL) Genoa, OH Our Lady of Lourdes Church.
Quinn, Vincent J. '54 (NEW) Palisades Park, NJ St. Michael's Church.
Quinn, Msgr. W. Louis '45 (WDC) [4] Bethesda, MD Our Lady of Lourdes Church; Retired.
Quinn, Walter J. *o.s.a.* '61 (PH) [18] Philadelphia, PA St. Augustine Church.
Quinn, Msgr. William '62 (CAM) Wildwood, NJ St. Ann's Church.
Quinn, Msgr. William J. '41 (CHI) Maywood, IL St. Eulalia Church; Retired.
Quinn, William J. '59 (CHI) [5] Oak Lawn, IL St. Louis De Montfort Church.
Quinn, William P. '55 (SFR) [23] San Francisco, CA Holy Name of Jesus Church.
Quinnan, Edward J. *s.j.* '87 (CHI) [C] Chicago, IL Jesuit Community at Loyola University of Chicago.
Quinnan, Michael F. '86 (SCR) [20] Scranton, PA Nativity of Our Lord Church; [A] Dalton, PA Saint Pius X Seminary.
Quinones, Benjamin *c.r.l.* '85 (ARE) Corozal-Palos Blancos, PR Christ the King Church.
Quinones, Francisco (SJN) [A] Santurce, PR Academia Sagrado Corazon.
Quinones, Leoncio '46 (PCE) On Duty Outside the Diocese.
Quinones, Miguel P. '52 (WDC) Retired; [L] Washington, DC Cardinal O'Boyle Residence for Priests.
Quint, Dennis J. '96 (DUB) [3] Cedar Rapids, IA St. Jude Church.
Quintal, Gerald '65 (P) Dallas, OR St. Philip Church.
Quintana, Carlos *o.s.b.* '49 (RCK) [H] Aurora, IL Marmion Abbey-St. Augustine's Abbey.
Quintana, Edward '50 (GLP) Retired.
Quintana, Jose Luis '95 (GR) Holland, MI St. Francis de Sales Church.
Quinter, Paul S. '82 (PH) [A] Wynnewood, PA Theological Seminary of St. Charles Borromeo, Overbrook; [A] Wynnewood, PA Theological Seminary of St. Charles Borromeo, Overbrook.
Quintero, Francisco (SJN) [5] Canovanas, PR San Jose Church.
Quintero, Gustavo '96 (STO) Lodi, CA St. Anne Church.
Quintero, Manuel (LAV) North Las Vegas, NV St. Christopher Church.
Quinters, Msgr. Elmer T. '50 (GAL) Deer Park, TX St. Hyacinth Church.
Quinto, Armand *s.d.b.* '75 (NY) [2] Port Chester, NY Corpus Christi Church.
Quirk, Msgr. Edward J. '45 (NY) Pearl River, NY St. Aedan Church; Retired.
Quirk, Kevin M. (WH) On Duty Outside the Diocese.
Quirk, Richard J. '78 (STL) [46] St. Louis, MO Basilica of St. Louis, the King; [W] St. Louis, MO Catholic Commission on Housing.
Quirk, William L. '54 (MAN) Bristol, NH St. Timothy Church.
Quiroz, Guido M. '44 (VIC) Retired.
Quitugua, David C. '83 (AGN) [1] Agana, GU Dulce Nombre de Maria Cathedral - Basilica.
Quitugua, David I.A. '64 (AGN) Ordot, GU San Juan Bautista Church.
Qunidlen, Joseph J. '73 (PH) Cheltenham, PA St. Joseph Church.
Quyet, Anthony '83 (JKS) Indianola, MS Immaculate Conception Church; Indianola, MS St. Benedict the Moor Church.

R

Raab, Alexander '36 (STU) Retired.
Raab, Ronald P. *c.s.c.* '83 (LA) Burbank, CA St. Francis Xavier Church.
Raaser, Eric P. '85 (NY) [E] White Plains, NY Archbishop Stepinac High School.
Raaz, Paul A. '70 (SAT) [22] San Antonio, TX Resurrection of the Lord Church.
Rabatsky, Raymond J. '74 (SB) Yucca Valley, CA St. Mary of the Valley Church.
Rabaut, Francis D. *s.j.* '44 (DET) [P] Clarkston, MI Colombiere Center.
Rabay, Christopher *o.cist.* '44 (DAL) [M] Irving, TX Cistercian Abbey of Our Lady of Dallas.
Rabbat, Robert '94 (NTN) Hammond, IN St. Michael the Archangel Church.
Rabbitte, Martin *m.s.c.* '60 (AUS) [6] Waco, TX St. Louis Church.
Rabe, David L. '83 (NO) [A] New Orleans, LA Notre Dame Seminary Graduate School of Theology.
Rabelo, William *o. de m.* '95 (PCE) [13] Ponce, PR Santuario San Judas Tadeo Church.
Rabenecker, David *o.s.b.* '91 (IND) [B] St. Meinrad, IN St. Meinrad Seminary-College of Liberal Arts; [J] St. Meinrad, IN St. Meinrad Archabbey.
Rabideau, Richard L. '46 (ORL) Retired.
Rabideau, Richard L. '46 (SAG) Retired.
Rabideau, Thomas R. *o.s.b.* '43 (OKL) Seminole, OK Immaculate Conception Church; [I] Shawnee, OK St. Gregory's Abbey.
Rable, Cyril J. '56 (SCR) [4] Old Forge, PA St. Stanislaus Church.
Rabroker, Msgr. Edward '48 (AUS) Granger, TX SS. Cyril and Methodius Church.
Rabroker, Msgr. George F. '41 (BEA) [6] Beaumont, TX Our Lady of the Assumption Church; Retired.

Rabusa, Romeo '95 (HON) Waikane, HI Our Lady of Mt. Carmel Church.
Racco, Philip G. '77 (CLV) [30] Cleveland, OH Holy Rosary Church.
Racette, Norman *o.m.i.* '39 (BWN) [1] Mission, TX Our Lady of Guadalupe Church.
Rachford, Nicholas '71 (PRM) Parma, OH Saint John the Baptist, Cathedral.
Rachunek, Henry C. '62 (GAL) Beasley, TX St. Wenceslaus Mission Church.
Rachunek, Henry C. '62 (VIC) Hungerford, TX St. John the Baptist Church.
Racine, Michael S. '95 (FR) [6] Fall River, MA Notre Dame de Lourdes Church.
Racivitch, Herve P. *s.j.* '62 (NO) [P] New Orleans, LA Ignatius Residence.
Rackensperger, Norbert *o.f.m.conv.* '54 (LA) New Cuyama, CA Immaculate Conception Church.
Rackensperger, Norbert *o.f.m.conv.* '54 (MRY) [G] Arroyo Grande, CA St. Joseph's Cupertino Novitiate.
Racki, Leonard E. '62 (PBL) Retired.
Rackliffe, Donald O. (HRT) Bristol, CT Bristol Hospital.
Raczek, Kenneth T. '56 (LFT) Elwood, IN St. Joseph Church.
Raczka, Philip G. '80 (NTN) Cliffside Park, NJ St. Demetrius Church; [A] Newton, MA Seminary of St. Gregory the Theologian.
Raczynski, Paul L. '72 (MIL) [21] Milwaukee, WI SS. Cyril and Methodius Church; [26] Milwaukee, WI St. Gabriel Church.
Raczynski, Theodore T. '56 (HRT) Suffield, CT Sacred Heart Church.
Radaich, Thomas '70 (DUL) Grand Rapids, MN St. Joseph's Church.
Radano, Msgr. John A. '65 (NEW) On Duty Outside the Archdiocese.
Radasky, Robert M. (ALT) On Special Assignment.
Radchuk, Anthony '62 (PHU) [D] Philadelphia, PA Home of Divine Providence.
Radde, James M. *s.j.* '72 (OM) [C] Omaha, NE Creighton Preparatory School.
Radecki, Albin A. '49 (TOL) Retired.
Radecki, Dane *o.praem.* '77 (CHI) [N] Chicago, IL Premonstratensian Fathers and Brothers (Norbertines).
Radecky, Stephen F. '45 (CLV) [54] Cleveland, OH Our Lady of Lourdes Church; [4] Parma, OH St. Columbkille Church; Retired.
Radek, James '89 (JOL) Woodridge, IL St. Scholastica Church.
Rademacher, Germain P. '58 (NU) Morton, MN St. John Church; Redwood Falls, MN St. Catherine Church.
Rademacher, Msgr. Glen A. '44 (LA) Santa Fe Springs, CA St. Pius X Church; Retired.
Rademacher, John R. '70 (GI) [4] Grand Island, NE St. Leo Church.
Rademacher, Raymond M. '62 (LAN) [2] Lansing, MI St. Casimir Church.
Rademacher, Robert B. *glmy.* '55 (RIC) Clintwood, VA St. Joseph Church.
Rademacher, William '54 (LAN) Retired.
Rademaker, Jan *o.m.i.* '69 (BWN) [8] Brownsville, TX St. Joseph Church.
Rademaker, Martan *o.f.m.* '55 (GLP) Fort Defiance, AZ Our Lady of Blessed Sacrament Church.
Rademaker, Martin *o.f.m.* '55 (SFE) [J] Albuquerque, NM San Antonio Provincial Friary Franciscan Friars.
Rader, John S. (SFS) [4] Sioux Falls, SD Our Lady of Guadalupe Church.
Radetic, Branimir '52 (Y) [19] Youngstown, OH SS. Peter and Paul's Church.
Radetski, John J. '77 (MIL) Beaver Dam, WI St. Michael's Church.
Radetski, Paul J. '82 (GB) Peshtigo, WI St. Mary Church.
Radloff, James A. '93 (BAK) La Pine, OR Holy Redeemer Church.
Radloff, Thomas H. *s.j.* '61 (DET) [K] Detroit, MI Jesuit Provincial Office-Detroit Province of the Society of Jesus.
Radocha, Stephen J. '77 (ALN) Catasauqua, PA St. Andrew Church; Northampton, PA Assumption of the Blessed Virgin Mary Church.
Radomski, Joseph A. '62 (TR) Avon, NJ St. Elizabeth Church.
Radon, Msgr. Eugene M. '47 (BUF) [20] Buffalo, NY Coronation of the Blessed Virgin Mary Church.
Radosevich, Eugene A. '90 (PEO) Havana, IL St. Patrick's Church.
Radosevich, George '68 (SFD) Livingston, IL Sacred Heart Church; Staunton, IL St. Michael Church.
Radtke, Fred '67 (CHI) [N] Chicago, IL St. Peter's Friary.
Radvansky, Joseph R. '65 (PRM) Marblehead, OH St. Marys Church.
Radvansky, Robert J. '55 (PSC) Perth Amboy, NJ St. Nicholas Church.
Rae Cho, Andrew Myeong '85 (DEN) [5] Aurora, CO St. Lawrence Korean Catholic Community Church.
Raef, Scott '94 (AMA) Gruver, TX Cristo Redentor Church; Spearman, TX Sacred Heart Church.
Raeke, Joseph K. '80 (BO) Duxbury, MA Holy Family Church.
Rafacz, Joseph J. *v.g.* '56 (LC) [8] La Crosse, WI St. Pius X Church; Special Assignment; [I] La Crosse, WI Holy Cross (Seminary) Diocesan Center.
Rafalowski, Leonard '42 (SEA) Retired.
Raffel, Godfrey '53 (FRS) Tehachapi, CA St. Malachy Church; Retired.
Rafferty, Brian '94 (RIC) Wytheville, VA St. Mary's Church.
Rafferty, Brian M. '62 (BAL) Pasadena, MD Our Lady of the Chesapeake Church.
Rafferty, Gerard F. '79 (NY) Scarsdale, NY Our Lady of Fatima Church; [A] Yonkers, NY St. Joseph's Seminary.
Rafferty, James A. '94 (SCR) Carbondale, PA St. Rose of Lima Church; [A] Dalton, PA Saint Pius X Seminary; [D] Carbondale, PA Sacred Heart Junior/Senior High School.
Rafferty, James E. '72 (SD) Escondido, CA Church of St. Timothy.
Rafferty, James F. '63 (BO) Hingham, MA St. Paul Church.
Rafferty, Joseph P. '83 (SCR) Mansfield, PA Holy Child Church.
Rafferty, Lawrence B. '67 (RVC) Seaford, NY Maria Regina Church.
Rafferty, Michael J. '57 (SCR) West Wyoming, PA Our Lady of Sorrows Church.
Rafferty, Raymond J. '54 (PRO) Retired.
Rafferty, Raymond M. '66 (NY) [40] New York, NY St. Gregory Church; On Duty Outside the Archdiocese.
Rafferty, Thomas A. '38 (WH) Retired.
Rafferty, Thomas F. '83 (GAL) La Porte, TX St. Mary of the Immaculate Conception Church.
Raffo-Rivasplata, Cesar '85 (LA) Carson, CA St. Philomena Church.
Raftery, Paul *o.p.* '55 (SFR) [13] San Francisco, CA St. Dominic Church.
Raftery, Paul *o.p.* '84 (P) [18] Portland, OR Holy Rosary Parish & Dominican Priory Church.
Raftery, Thomas J. '44 (CHI) [37] Chicago, IL Christ the King Church; Winnetka, IL Sacred Heart Church; Retired.
Raftery, William J. '45 (WOR) Retired.
Raftery, William J. *s.j.* '57 (BO) [W] Boston, MA The Society of Jesus of New England-Provincial Offices; [W] Weston, MA Campion Health Center, Inc.
Raftis, J. Duane '47 (DUB) Retired.
Ragan, Gerald '79 (SAV) Dublin, GA Immaculate Conception Church.
Ragan, Gerald P. '79 (PH) On Duty Outside the Archdiocese.
Rager, Msgr. Charles D. '67 (ALT) Beans Cove, PA Seven Dolors B.V.M. Church; Retired.
Rager, Patrick F. '85 (PIT) Absent on Sick Leave.
Ragis, Gerald *o.s.b.* '63 (BUR) Charlotte, VT Our Lady of Mount Carmel Church.
Ragis, Gerald *o.s.b.* '63 (ROC) [I] Pine City, NY Mount Saviour Monastery.
Ragni, Richard R. '64 (PIT) Renton, PA St. Januarius Church.
Ragnoni, James V. '60 (CLV) [2] Akron, OH St. Anthony of Padua Church.
Ragsdale, Patrick J. '72 (SAT) [51] San Antonio, TX St. Luke Church.
Ragusa, Salvatore *s.d.s.* '88 (OAK) [B] Moraga, CA Saint Mary's College; [Q] Moraga, CA St. Mary's College Campus Ministry.
Rahilly, James T. *c.s.c.* '64 (FTW) [A] Notre Dame, IN Moreau Seminary.
Rahilly, Paul '81 (RVC) Cedarhurst, NY St. Joachim Church.
Rahn, David C. '94 (ARL) Fairfax, VA St. Leo's Church.
Rahoy, Nicholas '77 (CI) Ulithi & Neighboring Islands, FM Queen of Heaven Church; Woleai & Neighboring Islands, FM St. Ignatius Church.
Rahrig, Gilbert O. '49 (LAN) Howell, MI St. Joseph Church.
Rai, Kevin '87 (AUS) Pflugerville, TX St. Elizabeth Church.
Raible, Daniel *c.pp.s.* '43 (CIN) [B] Carthagena, OH St. Charles.
Raible, Roland *o.f.m.cap.* '35 (PIT) [N] Pittsburgh, PA St. Augustine Friary.
Raica, Stephen '78 (LAN) [2] Lansing, MI St. Casimir Church; Bellevue, MI St. Ann Church.
Raich, Stephen *o.f.m.* '43 (NY) [29] New York, NY SS. Cyril and Methodius - St. Raphael Church.
Raiche, Brian '95 (ALB) Oneonta, NY St. Mary Church; [S] Oneonta, NY New York State University at Oneonta and Hartwick College.
Raila, Donald *o.s.b.* '83 (GBG) [H] Latrobe, PA Saint Vincent Archabbey.
Raila, Stanislaus '33 (BRK) Retired; [U] Douglaston, NY Bishop Mugavero Residence.
Railey, Clayton A. *s.j.* '87 (BAL) [M] Baltimore, MD Jesuit Fathers and Brothers Maryland Provincial Curia.
Raimer, Chester J. '74 (GBG) Blairsville, PA SS. Simon and Jude Church; Torrance, PA Torrance State Hospital.
Raimondi, Michele '50 (SFR) Retired.
Raimondo, Msgr. Joseph J. '40 (NY) Harrison, NY St. Gregory the Great Church; Retired.
Rainaldo, John H. *s.j.* '64 (MIL) [P] Milwaukee, WI Jesuit Provincial Office, Wisconsin Province.
Rainaldo, John H. *s.j.* '64 (NY) [Z] New York, NY Jesuit Provincial's Office.
Rainaldo, John H. *s.j.* '64 (RVC) [R] New Hyde Park, NY Apostleship of Prayer, National Office for the U.S.
Rainey, R. Randall *s.j.* '87 (WDC) [V] Washington, DC Woodstock Theological Center.
Rainforth, Thomas G. '73 (PAT) Hainesville, NJ St. Thomas the Apostle Church; Montague, NJ St. James the Greater Church.
Rainone, John J. '70 (PRO) [18] Providence, RI St. Joseph's Church; Providence, RI Rhode Island Hospital.
Rainville, Laurence P. *o.f.m.* '47 (ALB) [B] Loudonville, NY Siena College.
Rainville, Marcel *s.s.e.* '71 (BUR) [G] Colchester, VT Society of St. Edmund.
Rainville, Paul *m.s.* '65 (MAN) Enfield, NH St. Helena Church.
Raiser, Jerome K. '58 (COL) Washington Court House, OH St. Colman Church.
Raj, M. Arul '82 (CHI) [207] Chicago, IL St. Timothy Church.
Raj, Simon '72 (NY) [206] Staten Island, NY Holy Rosary Church.
Rajanayagam, Thomas M. '66 (STO) Riverbank, CA St. Frances of Rome Church.
Rajendram, Christlin *s.j.* '73 (COL) [35] Columbus, OH Our Lady of Victory Church.
Rajter, Valentine *o.f.m.conv.* '48 (BUF) [21] Buffalo, NY Corpus Christi Church.
Raju, Anthony Prem (LA) Covina, CA St. Louise de Marillac Church.
Raju, Martin '85 (NY) [S] New York, NY St. Vincent's Hospital and Medical Center of New York.
Rakaczki, Andor '73 (PSC) Bridgeport, CT Holy Trinity Church.
Rakaczky, Basil M. *o.s.b.m.* '60 (PSC) Perth Amboy, NJ St. Michael Church; [B] Matawan, NJ Basilian Fathers of Mariapoch.
Rakatonocliarimanana, Raphael *m.s.* '65 (STL) [P] St. Louis, MO La Salette Missionaries.
Raker, Msgr. Clarence J. '39 (DUB) Retired.
Rakiej, Stanislaw *s.ch.* '74 (STP) [6] Minneapolis, MN Holy Cross Church.
Rakoczy, Richard S. '59 (DET) Waterford, MI St. Perpetua Church.
Rakoczy, Walter J. '78 (GRY) [3] Whiting, IN St. Adalbert Church.
Ralenkotter, Howard *c.p.* '38 (L) [L] Louisville, KY Sacred Heart Retreat.
Ralko, Martin J. '84 (COL) Dennison, OH Immaculate Conception Church.
Rallis, Stephen (DM) [4] Council Bluffs, IA St. Peter Church.
Ralph, John (WH) Retired.
Ralph, Msgr. Thomas J. '56 (DUB) Otter Creek, IA St. Lawrence Church.
Ramacciotti, Gabriel M. *o.s.m.* '51 (DEN) [4] Denver, CO Assumption Church.
Ramacciotti, James J. '85 (STL) [23] St. Louis, MO St. Ambrose Church; [A] St. Louis, MO Kenrick-Glennon Seminary.
Ramacher, Edward '45 (SCL) Retired.
Ramaeker, Victor F. '61 (SC) Vail, IA St. Ann's Church.
Ramaekers, Timothy L. '82 (ORG) [1] Orange, CA Cathedral of the Holy Family.
Ramellini, Msgr. P. Lino '47 (GBG) Retired.
Ramen, Paul F. '60 (NOR) Retired.
Ramenaden, Ronald *o.m.i.* '70 (FTW) [3] Fort Wayne, IN St. Charles Borromeo Church.
Ramer, Leo '54 (LAN) Retired.
Ramirez, Adalberto *o.f.m.* '64 (CC) Hebbronville, TX Our Lady of Guadalupe Church; [H] Hebbronville, TX Franciscan Friars - O.F.M.
Ramirez, Allen A. *o.f.m.conv.* '72 (MRY) [G] Arroyo Grande, CA St. Joseph Cupertino Province, Provincial Center.
Ramirez, Cesar '96 (ARE) [1] Arecibo, PR Cathedral of San Felipe Apostol.
Ramirez, Charles '87 (LA) [34] Los Angeles, CA Presentation of the B.V.M. Church; Claremont, CA Our Lady of the Assumption Church.
Ramirez, Cornelio C. *s.a.c.* '67 (LUB) [6] Lubbock, TX St. Joseph's Church.
Ramirez, Enrique Espinosa *m.sp.s.* '79 (LA) [3] Oxnard, CA Our Lady of Guadalupe Parish Church.
Ramirez, Fernando '78 (SD) [5] San Diego, CA Good Shepherd Church.
Ramirez, Francisco X. '78 (LA) South El Monte, CA Epiphany Church.
Ramirez, Francisco X. '79 (LA) [84] Los Angeles, CA St.

Patrick Church.
Ramirez, Gerardo '91 (PCE) Ensenada, PR Sacred Heart Church; Guanica, PR St. Anthony Abbot Church.
Ramirez, Hernando *s.j.* '75 (CC) On Special Assignment; [E] Laredo, TX Mercy Regional Medical Center.
Ramirez, J. Jesus '86 (YAK) Granger, WA Our Lady of Guadalupe Church.
Ramirez, Jairo H. '88 (STO) [8] Stockton, CA St. Mary of the Assumption Church.
Ramirez, Jose *s.m.* '69 (STL) [P] St. Louis, MO Marianist Community; [T] Eureka, MO Marianist Retreat & Conference Center.
Ramirez, Jose Nieves '79 (ELP) Absent on Leave.
Ramirez, Millan *ss.cc.* '57 (SJN) [9] Guaynabo, PR Sagrados Corazones Church.
Ramirez, Renelmo '84 (CGS) Culebra, PR Nuestra Senora del Carmen Church.
Ramirez-Alejos, Pedro '74 (SPK) Pasco, WA St. Patrick Church.
Ramler, Michael '74 (LEX) Frankfort, KY Good Shepherd Church.
Ramon, Robert (GAL) New Caney, TX St. John of the Cross Church.
Ramon, Valentin *c.m.f.* '64 (ORG) [2] Orange, CA La Purisima Church.
Ramon, Valentin L. *c.m.f.* '64 (LA) San Gabriel, CA San Gabriel Church; [R] San Gabriel, CA Claretian Missionaries (Missionary Sons of the Immaculate Heart of Mary).
Ramon-Landry, Kenneth '87 (BLX) Laurel, MS Immaculate Conception Church; [G] Ellisville, MS Jones Junior College.
Ramos, Andre '88 (SD) [33] San Diego, CA St. Michael Church.
Ramos, Angel Roman '90 (MGZ) Hormigueros, PR Shrine of Our Lady of Monserrate Church.
Ramos, Antonio W. '94 (SFS) Mellette, SD All Saints Church.
Ramos, Cipriano '52 (SAC) Retired and in Senior Ministry.
Ramos, Danielo '79 (DAL) [17] Dallas, TX St. Elizabeth Church.
Ramos, Eleuterio '66 (ORG) Inactive Leave.
Ramos, Fausto '35 (PCE) Retired.
Ramos, Fausto '46 (PCE) Villalba, PR Our Lady of Mt. Carmel Church.
Ramos, Gilbert '61 (LA) Graduate Studies.
Ramos, Justin S. *o.praem.* '95 (ORG) [D] Siverado, CA St. Michael's College Preparatory High School; [H] Silverado, CA Norbertine Fathers.
Ramos, Victoriano '54 (SJN) [33] San Juan, PR Santa Luisa de Marillac Church.
Ramoso, Irenio (SFR) Foster City, CA St. Luke Church.
Ramsey, Boniface *o.p.* '73 (NEW) [A] South Orange, NJ Immaculate Conception Seminary.
Ramsey, James '84 (GAL) Damon, TX SS. Cyril and Methodius Church; Needville, TX St. Michael Church.
Ramsey, James Boniface *o.p.* '73 (NY) [121] New York, NY St. Vincent Ferrer Church; [Z] New York, NY St. Vincent Ferrer Priory.
Ramson, Ronald W. *c.m.* '59 (CHI) [C] Chicago, IL Vincentian Community at DePaul University.
Ranahan, Michael J. *c.s.v.* '41 (CHI) [N] Arlington Heights, IL Viatorian Province Center-Clerics of St. Viator.
Ranaivsoon, Marc *m.s.* '67 (STL) [P] St. Louis, MO La Salette Missionaries.
Ranalletti, Richard A. *c.s.b.* '73 (OAK) [C] Oakland, CA Bishop O'Dowd High School.
Ranalli, John '83 (R) Special Assignment.
Ranalli, John A. '83 (R) [I] Raleigh, NC Vocations Office.
Ranallo, John *o.s.a.* (OAK) Castro Valley, CA Eden Hospital.
Ranallo, John E. '75 (OAK) Castro Valley, CA Transfiguration Church.
Rancourt, Henry *s.m.* '57 (BO) [Y] Framingham Centre, MA The Marist House.
Randall, Msgr. Edward '64 (GAL) [23] Houston, TX St. Cyril of Alexandria Church.
Randall, Edward L. *o.m.i.* '50 (LEX) Jenkins, KY St. George Church.
Randall, John F. '53 (PRO) [11] Providence, RI St. Charles Borromeo Church.
Randall, Jude *o.s.b.* '60 (JOL) [J] Lisle, IL St. Procopius Abbey.
Randall, Jude D. '60 (JOL) [C] Lisle, IL Benet Academy.
Randall, Kevin S. '92 (NOR) Gales Ferry, CT Our Lady of Lourdes Church.
Randall, Robert J. '51 (PRO) Retired.
Randazzo, Anthony J. '86 (NEW) North Caldwell, NJ Notre Dame Church.
Randone, Michael C '95 (BO) North Andover, MA St. Michael Church.
Ranek, Jerome M. '91 (SFS) Mobridge, SD St. Joseph Church.
Raneri, Carmine B. '55 (HRT) [6] Waterbury, CT Our Lady of Mt. Carmel Church.
Raney, Isaac *m.ss.a.* '67 (DEN) Greeley, CO St. Peter Church.
Raney, Richard E. '38 (PEO) Retired.
Ranft, Paul J. '40 (TUC) San Manuel, AZ St. Bartholomew Church; Retired.
Ranges, Charles H. *s.s.e.* '72 (BUR) Highgate Center, VT St. Louis Church; Swanton, VT Nativity of the Blessed Virgin Mary Church.
Ranieri, John J. '82 (NEW) [B] South Orange, NJ Seton Hall University.
Ranieri, Msgr. Joseph A. '57 (WDC) Hyattsville, MD St. Jerome Church.
Rank, Robert *s.o.l.t.* '67 (CC) Robstown, TX St. Anthony Church; [B] Robstown, TX St. Anthony School; [H] Robstown, TX Society of Our Lady of the Most Holy Trinity.
Rank, Robert F. '68 (GB) On Duty Outside the Diocese.
Rank, Ronald G. '58 (MAD) Waterloo, WI St. Joseph Church.
Rankin, James '65 (SD) [37] San Diego, CA St. Vincent de Paul Church.
Rankin, Joseph M. '79 (L) [26] Louisville, KY St. Francis of Assisi Church.
Rankin, Paul B. *c.s.c.* '48 (AUS) [H] Austin, TX Congregation of Holy Cross - Southern Province.
Rankin, Paul B. *c.s.c.* '48 (FTW) [J] South Bend, IN Congregation of Holy Cross Indiana Province Provincial House.
Rankin, Robert '80 (LA) Montrose, CA Holy Redeemer Church
Ranly, Ernest W. *c.pp.s.* '56 (CIN) [M] Dayton, OH Provincial House of the Cincinnati Province of the Society of the Precious Blood.
Rans, Norbert J. *m.m.* '64 (NY) [Z] Maryknoll, NY Maryknoll Fathers and Brothers.
Ransing, Bernard E. *c.s.c.* '35 (FTW) [J] South Bend, IN Congregation of Holy Cross Indiana Province Provincial House.
Ransom, Donald B. '64 (NEW) Kearny, NJ St. Stephen's Church.
Ransom, Ralph R. *s.s.j.* '61 (BAL) [M] Baltimore, MD St. Joseph Society of the Sacred Heart House of Central Administration.
Ranzino, Thomas C. '78 (BR) [9] Baton Rouge, LA St. George Church.
Rapczynski, Joseph B. '34 (ALN) Retired; [J] Bethlehem, PA Holy Family Villa.
Raphael, John *s.s.j.* '95 (BEA) [7] Beaumont, TX Our Mother of Mercy Church.
Rapin, Cyril W. '46 (OG) Mooers, NY St. Joseph Church; Retired.
Raposo, John A. '77 (FR) Provincetown, MA St. Peter the Apostle Church.
Rapp, Bernard A. '77 (SD) Calexico, CA Our Lady of Guadalupe Church.
Rapp, Bertrand J. (L) Retired.
Rapp, Bertrand J. '50 (L) [3] Louisville, KY St. Albert the Great Church; [11] Louisville, KY St. Bartholomew Church.
Rapp, James F. *o.s.f.s.* '67 (OKL) Duncan, OK Assumption Church.
Rappl, Joseph P. '78 (BUF) Military Chaplains.
Rareshide, Msgr. Lanaux J. '61 (NO) [47] New Orleans, LA St. Monica Church.
Raretsky, Albert *o.p.* '81 (WDC) [B] Washington, DC Dominican House of Studies.
Rarus, Boleslaus J. '40 (BGP) Retired.
Rasby, Msgr. James W. '52 (DEN) Retired.
Rasch, Richard *o.de.m.* '84 (CLV) [57] Cleveland, OH Our Lady of Mount Carmel Church; [P] Cleveland, OH Mercedarians.
Rascher, Joseph C. '81 (BEL) Evansville, IL St. Boniface Church; Menard, IL Menard Psychiatric Center.
Raschke, Bernard L. '58 (LC) Edgar, WI St. John the Baptist Church.
Raschko, Michael '75 (SEA) Special Assignment.
Rashford, John T. *s.j.* '71 (YAK) [4] Yakima, WA St. Joseph's Church; [B] Yakima, WA Providence Yakima Medical Center.
Rashford, Nicholas J. *s.j.* '71 (PH) [C] Philadelphia, PA St. Joseph's University; [Z] Philadelphia, PA Jesuit Community at St. Joseph's University.
Rasing, Linus E. '53 (DUB) Bankston, IA St. Clement's Church.
Rask, Phillip J. '72 (STP) [A] St. Paul, MN The Saint Paul Seminary; [C] St. Paul, MN University of St. Thomas.
Rasky, Joseph G. *s.m.* '65 (SAT) [F] San Antonio, TX Central Catholic High School; [M] San Antonio, TX Central Catholic Marianist Community.
Rasmussen, Harry *s.d.b.* '62 (LA) [W] Rosemead, CA St. Joseph's Salesian Youth Renewal Center.
Rasmussen, John C. '69 (SFS) Elk Point, SD St. Joseph Church.
Rasmussen, Terrence *o.f.m.conv.* '79 (DUB) Ames, IA St. Cecilia Church; Gilbert, IA SS. Peter and Paul Church.
Rasner, David L. '72 (LFT) Special Assignment.
Rasner, David L. '82 (LFT) Otterbein, IN St. Charles Church.
Raso, Anthony '75 (BRK) [216] Queens, NY Our Lady of Mount Carmel Church.
Raspallo, Domenic (PRO) Retired.
Raspudic, Bruno *o.f.m.* '43 (PIT) [N] Beaver Falls, PA Our Lady of Peace Monastery.
Rasquinha, Dionysius *s.j.* '86 (BO) [W] Cambridge, MA Faber House.
Rasquiuha, Ignatius '96 (SB) Running Springs, CA St. Anne in the Mountains Church.
Rassas, George J. '68 (CHI) Lake Forest, IL St. Mary Church.
Rassley, George *c.ss.r.* '53 (B) Coeur D'Alene, ID St. Thomas Church.
Rasura, James I. *s.j.* '56 (SD) [12] San Diego, CA Our Lady of Guadalupe Church; San Diego, CA Central Detention Facility and San Diego City Jail.
Raszeja, Norbert W. *c.r.* '72 (CHI) [N] Chicago, IL Provincial Office of the Congregation of the Resurrection.
Raszkowski, Robert P. *s.j.* '46 (MIL) [P] Milwaukee, WI Jesuit Provincial Office, Wisconsin Province.
Rataj, Stanley G. '79 (CHI) [143] Chicago, IL St. Nicholas of Tolentine Church.
Ratajczak, Justin *o.f.m.conv.* '77 (E) [4] Sharon, PA St. Stanislaus Kostka Church.
Ratajczak, Michael '75 (SD) Spring Valley, CA Santa Sophia Church.
Ratajczak, Richard C. '58 (SAG) Beaver, MI St. Valentine Church.
Ratazak, Bernard A. '76 (RCK) Retired.
Ratchford, Robert J. *s.j.* '61 (NO) Gretna, LA Jefferson Parish Correctional Center; [C] New Orleans, LA Loyola University; [P] New Orleans, LA Jesuit Provincial Office.
Raterman, Herbert J *s.j.* '55 (CIN) [M] Cincinnati, OH Faber Jesuit Community.
Raterman, Herbert J. *s.j.* '55 (CIN) [V] Cincinnati, OH Living Monuments of Reparation.
Ratermann, Msgr. David A. '51 (STL) On Duty Outside the Archdiocese.
Ratermann, George H. *m.m.* '47 (CLV) [P] Cleveland, OH Maryknoll Fathers.
Ratermann, Jerome B. '57 (BEL) Retired.
Rath, John G. '36 (Y) Retired.
Rath, Martin *o.s.b.* (NU) Winsted, MN St. Mary's Care Center.
Rath, Thomas V. '49 (CLV) [5] Lorain, OH St. John Church; Retired.
Rathapilly, Emanuel '71 (SJP) Altoona, PA Immaculate Conception Church; Barnesboro, PA Immaculate Conception Church.
Rathfon, John R. (CLV) Cuyahoga Falls, OH Immaculate Heart of Mary Church; Retired.
Rathgeb, William R. '67 (GBG) [E] Greensburg, PA Clelian Heights School for Exceptional Children; [I] Greensburg, PA Apostles of the Sacred Heart of Jesus.
Rathschmidt, John *o.f.m.cap.* '69 (NY) [C] New Rochelle, NY College of New Rochelle; [Z] White Plains, NY St. Conrad Friary.
Ratigan, James '65 (JOL) Woodridge, IL Christ The Servant Parish Church.
Ratigan, Patrick A. '83 (OG) Military Chaplains.
Ratterman, Kevin J. '94 (OKL) Edmond, OK St. John the Baptist Church; [K] Norman, OK Campus Ministry for the Archdiocese of Oklahoma City.
Ratzenberger, Raymond '85 (TUC) Benson, AZ Our Lady of Lourdes Church.
Ratzmann, George '87 (VEN) [1] Venice, FL Epiphany Cathedral.
Rau, Msgr. Donald E. '56 (STL) [51] St. Louis, MO St. Mary of Victories Church.
Rau, Peter J. '85 (ATL) Cumming, GA Good Shepherd Church.
Rau, Msgr. Raymond '49 (BRK) [21] Brooklyn, NY Blessed Sacrament Church.
Rau, Raymond F. '49 (BRK) Retired.
Rau, Msgr. Raymond F. '49 (CC) [22] Corpus Christi, TX St. Theresa Church.
Raub, Jacob *o.c.s.o.* '62 (L) [L] Trappist, KY Abbey of Our Lady of Gethsemani, of the Order of Cistercians of the Strict Observance.
Rauch, David E. '70 (STL) [38] St. Louis, MO St. James the Greater Church.
Rauch, Edward L. *o.s.f.s.* '64 (PH) [D] Philadelphia, PA Father Judge High School for Boys; [Z] Philadelphia, PA Father Judge Faculty House.
Rauch, Laszlo F. '49 (TR) Normandy Beach, NJ Our Lady of Peace Church.
Raudabaugh, Joseph R. '62 (CIN) Fairborn, OH Mary Help of Christians Church.
Raudeliunas, Kazimieras *s.j.* '43 (CHI) [N] Chicago, IL Lithuanian American Jesuits.
Raught, Msgr. Horton '44 (NEW) [2] Newark, NJ St. Patrick's Pro-Cathedral.
Raulli, Enrico *s.j.* '65 (NEW) [C] Jersey City, NJ St. Peter's Preparatory School.
Raulli, Enrico *s.j.* '65 (NY) [Z] New York, NY West Side Jesuit Community.
Raum, Blair '71 (BAL) [89] Baltimore, MD St. Thomas Aquinas Church; Special Assignment.

Raun, Msgr. Douglas A. '82 (SFE) Rio Rancho, NM St. Thomas Aquinas Church.
Rausch, Dale J. '68 (DUB) Fayette, IA St. Francis of Assisi Church; West Union, IA Holy Name Church; [N] West Union, IA Upper Iowa University.
Rausch, Dennis *s.v.d.* '80 (MIA) [5] Fort Lauderdale, FL St. Clement Church.
Rausch, John *o.f.m.* (STL) [R] St. Louis, MO Franciscan Sisters of Mary Administrative Offices.
Rausch, John '72 (CIN) [M] Fairfield, OH Headquarters of Glenmary Home Missioners.
Rausch, John *o.f.m.* '76 (STL) [P] St. Louis, MO Franciscan Friary of St. Anthony of Padua.
Rausch, John W. '47 (MIL) Retired.
Rausch, Leon S. *s.j.* '59 (LC) Gays Mills, WI St. Mary Church; Rolling Ground, WI St. Philip Church.
Rausch, Leon S. *s.j.* '59 (MIL) [P] Milwaukee, WI Jesuit Provincial Office, Wisconsin Province.
Rausch, Nicholas *o.s.b.* '56 (SEA) [M] Lacey, WA St. Martin's Abbey.
Rausch, Thomas P. *s.j.* '72 (LA) [C] Los Angeles, CA Loyola Marymount University.
Rauscher, Donald F. *s.j.* '68 (MIL) [P] Milwaukee, WI Jesuit Provincial Office, Wisconsin Province.
Rauscher, Msgr. Joseph G. '67 (SCR) [16] Wilkes-Barre, PA St. Nicholas Church.
Rauscher, Msgr. Martin F. '60 (PAT) Morristown, NJ Assumption of the Blessed Virgin Mary Church.
Rauscher, Russell G. '75 (CLV) [5] Parma, OH St. Francis de Sales Church.
Rauseo, Francis J. (PH) [88] Philadelphia, PA St. Lucy Church.
Rautenberg, Joseph F. '73 (IND) Beech Grove, IN Holy Name Church; Knightstown, IN St. Rose Church; New Castle, IN St. Anne Church; [F] Indianapolis, IN St. Vincent Hospital and Health Care Center, Inc.
Rauth, Philip J. '59 (LIN) Auburn, NE St. Joseph's Church.
Raux, Redmond (BO) Military & VA Chaplains.
Raux, Redmond '82 (PHX) Luke Air Force Base, AZ Luke Air Force Base.
Rauzi, Daniel *s.d.b.* '85 (BIR) [8] Birmingham, AL Holy Rosary Church.
Rauzi, Mario *c.s.* '45 (CIN) [80] Cincinnati, OH Sacred Heart Church.
Raveneau, Ricardo '90 (BRK) [86] Brooklyn, NY St. Michael's Church.
Ravey, Donald J. '61 (BUR) Williston, VT Immaculate Heart of Mary Church.
Ravlic, Msgr. Cornelius C. '37 (LA) Retired.
Rawa, Jerome D. *s.m.* '55 (WH) Richwood, WV Holy Family Church; Summersville, WV St. John The Evangelist Church.
Rawlins, John J. *s.s.j.* '45 (BAL) [M] Baltimore, MD St. Joseph's Manor.
Ray, James M. '75 (CHI) Other Assignments; [G] Chicago, IL Catholic Charities of the Archdiocese of Chicago-Archdiocesan Offices.
Ray, Robert E. '69 (L) Fairdale, KY St. Jerome Church.
Raya, Gregorio (BGP) [5] Stamford, CT Our Lady of Montserrat Church.
Rayalipunna, Mark *c.i.c.m.* '94 (SAT) [23] San Antonio, TX Sacred Heart Church.
Rayas, Tomas Martinez *s.s.p.* (LA) [R] Los Angeles, CA Society of St. Paul.
Rayer, Thomas '93 (STP) Crystal, MN St. Raphael Church.
Rayes, Emanuel '54 (EST) Troy, MI St. Joseph Chaldean Parish Church.
Rayes, Joseph *o.f.m.* '57 (CIN) [M] Cincinnati, OH St. Ann Friary.
Raymaker, John *c.i.c.m.* (BO) [4] Boston, MA St. Ambrose Church.
Raymond, David R. '89 (SPR) South Hadley, MA St. Patrick's Church; [C] Springfield, MA Cathedral High School; [C] Holyoke, MA Holyoke Catholic High School.
Raymond, Maurice L. '62 (SCR) [2] Hazleton, PA Church of the Most Precious Blood.
Raymond, Wilfred J. '71 (BGP) [O] Bridgeport, CT Provincial Offices of the Priests and Brothers of Holy Cross, Eastern Province.
Raymundo, Gregorio G. '46 (LA) Retired.
Raynor, John P. *s.j.* '54 (MIL) [C] Milwaukee, WI Marquette University.
Re, Angelo (SJ) Retired.
Rea, John W. '45 (ARL) Chantilly, VA St. Timothy Church; Retired.
Read, Denis *o.c.d.* '52 (MIL) [P] Holy Hill, WI Discalced Carmelite Monastery; [W] Milwaukee, WI Cursillos in Christianity.
Read, Ignacio *o.c.d.* '56 (MIL) [P] Milwaukee, WI Provincial Offices - Discalced Carmelites.
Reading, Edward '72 (PAT) On Duty Outside the Diocese.
Ready, Francis P. '50 (BO) [8] Cambridge, MA St. John the Evangelist Church; Retired.
Ready, Frank J. '59 (ARL) Annandale, VA Holy Spirit Church.
Reagan, Msgr. Donald '47 (Y) Retired.
Real, Fernando *m.id.* '81 (NY) [180] Bronx, NY Santa Maria Church; [Z] Bronx, NY Idente Missionaries of Santa Maria Residence.
Real, Gabriel D. *c.m.* '48 (BRK) [116] Brooklyn, NY St. Peter-St. Paul-Our Lady of Pilar Church.
Real, Jorge del (SFR) [4] San Mateo, CA St. Timothy Church.
Reale, Frank E. *s.j.* '81 (STL) [F] St. Louis, MO St. Louis University High School, George H. Backer Memorial; [P] St. Louis, MO St. Louis University High School Jesuit Community; [P] St. Louis, MO The Jesuits of the Missouri Province.
Reale, Sante *c.pp.s.* '60 (ORL) Kissimmee, FL Holy Redeemer Church.
Realmuto, George '87 (NOR) [F] Cromwell, CT Missionaries of the Holy Apostles.
Ream, Gerard J. (ALT) Retired.
Reamer, Mark *o.f.m.* '91 (R) [4] Raleigh, NC St. Francis of Assisi Church.
Reamer, William G. '87 (OG) Crown Point, NY Sacred Heart Church; Ticonderoga, NY St. Mary Church.
Reardon, Arthur L. '52 (BO) Permanent Disability.
Reardon, Daniel *c.s.v.* '61 (LAV) [1] Las Vegas, NV Guardian Angel Cathedral.
Reardon, Dennis A. '72 (PRO) [21] Providence, RI St. Michael's Church.
Reardon, Francis H. '78 (PMB) Fort Pierce, FL St. Anastasia Church.
Reardon, James E. '65 (BIS) Beulah, ND St. Joseph Church; Hazen, ND St. Martin Church.
Reardon, John D. '73 (PH) Wyndmoor, PA Seven Dolors Church.
Reardon, John F. '50 (NY) [225] Staten Island, NY St. Rita Church.
Reardon, John I. *o.p.* '49 (NSH) [F] Nashville, TN St. Thomas Hospital; [H] Nashville, TN Dominican Friars.
Reardon, John J. '39 (STU) Retired.
Reardon, Michael '74 (LA) [5] Long Beach, CA St. Cornelius Church.
Reardon, Robert J. '59 (PIT) Upper St. Clair, PA St. John Capistran Church.
Reardon, Thomas J. '51 (LC) Mauston, WI St. Patrick Church.
Reasbeck, Msgr. David E. '56 (STU) Colerain, OH St. Frances Cabrini Church.
Reaume, Michael R. *s.m.* '69 (CIN) [M] Dayton, OH Marianist Provincialate.
Reaves, Phillip A. '94 (LR) Springdale, AR St. Raphael's Church; Tontitown, AR St. Joseph's Church.
Rebain, Daniel '67 (DET) Auburn Hills, MI Sacred Heart Church.
Rebaldo, Ronald '91 (RVC) Sayville, NY St. Lawrence the Martyr Church.
Rebamontan, Marito F. '70 (ORG) [1] Anaheim, CA St. Anthony Claret Church.
Rebanal, Jeremias R. '95 (NEW) [1] Jersey City, NJ St. Aedan's Church.
Rebaque, Jose *s.a.c.* '70 (BGP) [9] Bridgeport, CT St. George's Church; [18] Bridgeport, CT St. Peter's Church.
Rebatzki, George M. '64 (MIL) [49] Milwaukee, WI Old St. Mary's Church.
Rebebes, Florencio B. '78 (HON) Lanai City, HI Sacred Hearts Church.
Rebeck, Eugene M. '65 (TR) Holmdel, NJ St. Catharine Church.
Rebeiro, Anthony J. '56 (BO) [1] Revere, MA St. Anthony of Padua Church.
Rebel, John W. '65 (PIT) Mars, PA St. Kilian Church.
Rebel, Patrick '85 (SP) New Port Richey, FL St. Thomas Aquinas Church.
Rebeyro, Lloyd (ALB) [11] Albany, NY St. Mary Church.
Rebman, Msgr. Joseph F. '60 (WIL) [1] Wilmington, DE Cathedral of St. Peter.
Rebol, Anthony '56 (CLV) [42] Cleveland, OH St. Lawrence Church.
Reboli, John P. *s.j.* '70 (WOR) [N] Worcester, MA Jesuits of Holy Cross College, Inc.
Rebong, Nestor '86 (LA) Glendora, CA St. Dorothy Church.
Rebosura, II, Sabino B. '87 (HT) Cut-Off, LA Sacred Heart Church.
Rebovich, John '67 (PRM) Absent on Leave.
Rebuldella, Alfred '72 (HON) Pearl City, HI Our Lady of Good Counsel Church.
Recchuti, William A. *o.s.a.* '44 (PH) [Z] Flourtown, PA Augustinians (O.S.A.).
Recchuti, William A. *o.s.a.* '61 (PH) Flourtown, PA St. Genevieve Church.
Receconi, Edward R. *o.s.b.* '79 (SEA) [13] Tacoma, WA Holy Rosary Church; [M] Lacey, WA St. Martin's Abbey.
Recera, Ricardo '89 (CHI) [J] Des Plaines, IL Holy Family Medical Center.
Rechenburg, Basil *o.s.b.* '68 (WOR) [N] Still River, MA Benedictine Monks, St. Benedict Abbey.
Rechtein, John *s.m.* '70 (SAT) [C] San Antonio, TX St. Mary's University of San Antonio, Texas.
Rechtien, John *s.m.* '70 (SAT) [M] San Antonio, TX Marianist Residence.
Recio, Jesus Perez *o.a.r.* '68 (NY) [186] Bronx, NY St. Rita of Cascia Shrine Church.
Reck, Donald W. *s.j.* '65 (BEL) [A] Cahokia, IL Parks College of Saint Louis University.
Reck, Donald W. *s.j.* '65 (STL) [C] St. Louis, MO Saint Louis University; [P] St. Louis, MO Leo Brown Jesuit Community.
Recker, Odo *o.s.b.* '78 (P) [A] St. Benedict, OR Mount Angel Seminary; [L] St. Benedict, OR Mt. Angel Abbey.
Recker, Philip F. '59 (DUB) Jewell, IA Good Shepherd Church; Williams, IA St. Mary's Church.
Reckinger, Robert A. '51 (DET) Retired.
Reckker, Stephen C. '63 (DET) Romeo, MI St. Clement of Rome Church.
Rector, Warren *o.f.m.* '68 (CAM) [G] Camden, NJ Our Lady of Lourdes Medical Center, Inc.
Rector, Warren *o.f.m.* '68 (PH) [Z] Philadelphia, PA St. Pius X Friary.
Reczek, Felix J. *o.f.m.* '44 (BUR) Bellows Falls, VT Sacred Heart Church.
Reczek, Paul *o.f.m.* '72 (GB) [I] Pulaski, WI Assumption of B.V.M. Friary.
Redahan, Msgr. Patrick J. '33 (LA) Hawthorne, CA St. Joseph Church; Retired.
Redcay, T. Christopher '89 (PH) Penn Valley, PA St. Justin Martyr Church; [D] Radnor, PA Archbishop John Carroll High School.
Redden, Don '59 (PMB) Fellsmere, FL Our Lady of Guadalupe Mission Church.
Redden, Michael J. '72 (ATL) Covington, GA St. Augustine Church.
Reddick, E. Peter '72 (SY) [20] Syracuse, NY St. Patrick Church.
Reddick, James (BRK) [N] Jamaica, NY Catholic Medical Center of Brooklyn & Queens.
Reddington, Benjamin J. '43 (MAD) Retired.
Reddington, John A. '37 (ROC) Pittsford, NY St. Louis Church; Retired.
Reddy, Albert F. *s.j.* '51 (BGP) [A] Fairfield, CT Fairfield University.
Reddy, Albert F. *s.j.* '58 (BGP) [O] Fairfield, CT The Fairfield Jesuit Community-Fairfield University.
Reddy, Reginald J. *o.f.m.* '61 (ALB) [B] Loudonville, NY Siena College.
Reddy, Thomas J. *o.m.i.* '52 (BO) [W] Tewksbury, MA Oblate Fathers-Oblate World/Missionary Association of Mary Immaculate; [Z] Tewksbury, MA Immaculate Heart of Mary Novitiate-Infirmary.
Redinbo, Joseph *o.f.m.* '59 (SFE) Pena Blanca, NM Nuestra Senora De Guadalupe Church.
Reding, Aquinas *o.f.m.* '53 (BUF) Allegany, NY St. Bonaventure Church.
Redlon, Reginald A. *o.f.m.* '49 (NY) [115] New York, NY St. Stephen of Hungary Church.
Redmerski, Stanley '58 (LIN) [E] Lincoln, NE Madonna Rehabilitation Hospital.
Redmond, Arthur S. '55 (LC) Edson, WI Sacred Heart of Jesus Church; Rozellville, WI St. Andrew Church; Retired.
Redmond, Daniel P. '96 (CLV) [75] Cleveland, OH St. Vincent de Paul Church.
Redmond, Donald *o.s.b.* '57 (KCK) Atchison, KS St. Benedict's Church; Atchison, KS Sacred Heart Church.
Redmond, Lawrence '64 (ORL) Retired.
Redmond, Paul '54 (ALB) On Duty Outside the Diocese.
Redmond, Paul V. '54 (BAL) [C] Emmitsburg, MD Mount Saint Mary's College.
Redmond, Sean P. '90 (LIN) Paul, NE St. Joseph's Church.
Redstone, James '90 (NEW) [15] Newark, NJ St. Francis Xavier Church.
Redwanski, Dale H. *o.s.c.* '71 (DET) Riverview, MI St. Cyprian Church; [K] Riverview, MI Crosier Community of Riverview.
Redwick, Adolph '59 (DET) [6] Dearborn, MI St. Joseph Church.
Redwick, Stanislaus J. '54 (DET) Retired.
Reeb, Edward J. '45 (BEL) Retired.
Reece, Frederick W. '44 (DM) Retired.
Reece, Richard T. '65 (PH) [Z] Philadelphia, PA Father Judge Faculty House.
Reece, Robert *o.s.f.s.* '65 (ALN) [L] Reading, PA St. Joseph Villa.
Reed, Alan *o.s.b.* (SCL) [I] Collegeville, MN St. John's Abbey, of the Order of St. Benedict.
Reed, Albert A. *c.pp.s.* '54 (CIN) Burkettsville, OH St. Bernard Church; [U] Dayton, OH Community Support Charitable Trust.
Reed, Bruce '93 (RVC) Elmont, NY St. Vincent de Paul Church.
Reed, Dennis L. '69 (DOD) Garden City, KS St. Dominic Church; Ingalls, KS St. Stanislaus Church.
Reed, Douglas *o.f.m.conv.* '71 (R) Castle Hayne, NC St. Stanislaus Kostka Church; [E] Wilmington, NC Conventual Franciscans O.F.M.Conv.
Reed, H. William '62 (NO) [58] New Orleans, LA St. Rose Of Lima Church.
Reed, John C. *s.j.* '50 (TOL) [K] Toledo, OH St. Mary's Jesuit Community.
Reed, Michael '84 (PT) [1] Pensacola, FL Cathedral of

the Sacred Heart.
Reed, Robert '85 (BO) [49] Boston, MA St. Matthew Church.
Reed, Robert A. '42 (BAL) [15] Baltimore, MD St. Benedict Church; [78] Baltimore, MD St. Peter the Apostle Church; Retired.
Reed, Robert J. '61 (ALN) [10] Bethlehem, PA SS. Simon and Jude Church.
Reed, Thomas A. *s.j.* '47 (SFR) [N] San Francisco, CA Jesuit Community at University of San Francisco.
Reed, William C. '71 (NEW) [9] Elizabeth, NJ Our Lady of Most Holy Rosary/St. Michael Church; Elizabeth, NJ Elizabeth General Medical Center.
Reedy, Francis C. *o.s.b.* '58 (MIL) [P] Benet Lake, WI St. Benedict's Abbey.
Reedy, Gerard *s.j.* '70 (WOR) [B] Worcester, MA College of the Holy Cross, Inc.
Reedy, Gerard C. *s.j.* '70 (NY) [C] Bronx, NY Fordham University.
Reedy, Gerard C. *s.j.* '70 (WOR) [N] Worcester, MA Jesuits of Holy Cross College, Inc.
Reedy, John J. '35 (P) Retired.
Reehil, Philip J. '46 (RVC) Setauket, NY St. James Church; Retired.
Reemmer, A. Leonard '56 (LFT) Gas City, IN Holy Family Church; Marion, IN U.S. Veteran's Hospital.
Reen, Jeremiah *s.d.b.* '71 (PMB) Belle Glade, FL St. Philip Benizi Church.
Reese, Benjamin '91 (RC) [3] Rapid City, SD St. Therese the Little Flower Church.
Reese, Charles T. '49 (CHL) Retired.
Reese, Donald B. '63 (CAM) On Duty Outside the Diocese.
Reese, Edward *s.j.* '73 (PHX) [B] Phoenix, AZ Brophy College Preparatory.
Reese, Harry A. *s.j.* '69 (BUF) [O] Buffalo, NY Canisius Jesuit Community.
Reese, Harry A. *s.j.* '69 (NY) [Z] New York, NY Jesuit Provincial's Office.
Reese, Robert P. '89 (ALT) [2] Altoona, PA Immaculate Conception Church.
Reese, Thomas J. *s.j.* '74 (WDC) [M] Washington, DC Woodstock Jesuit Community; [V] Washington, DC Woodstock Theological Center.
Reeson, David G. '80 (OM) Military Chaplains.
Reeves, Joseph '76 (BAK) On Duty Outside the Diocese.
Reeves, Joseph '76 (P) [J] Portland, OR Providence St. Vincent Medical Center.
Reeves, Nathaniel *o.s.b.* '78 (IND) [A] St. Meinrad, IN St. Meinrad Seminary; [J] St. Meinrad, IN St. Meinrad Archabbey.
Refalo, Anthony E. '89 (RVC) Manhasset, NY St. Mary's Church.
Refermat, Thomas '94 (CHI) Grayslake, IL St. Gilbert Church.
Regalado, Gonzalo E. '66 (NOR) Canterbury, CT St. Augustine Church.
Regalado, Luis *o.s.b.* '84 (SFE) [J] Abiquiu, NM Monastery of Christ in the Desert.
Regan, Charles W. '58 (WCH) [4] Wichita, KS Christ the King Church.
Regan, Columkille *c.p.* '49 (PH) [Z] Philadelphia, PA St. Michael's Passionist Residence.
Regan, Msgr. Dennis M. '64 (RVC) Port Jefferson, NY Infant Jesus Church.
Regan, Desmond '46 (BIR) [1] Birmingham, AL St. Paul's Cathedral; Retired.
Regan, Francis A. '53 (BO) Marshfield, MA St. Christine Church.
Regan, Gerald T. *s.j.* '64 (MIL) [P] Milwaukee, WI Jesuit Provincial Office, Wisconsin Province.
Regan, Gerald T. *s.j.* '64 (MOB) [B] Mobile, AL Spring Hill College.
Regan, James *o.p.* '36 (CHI) [N] River Forest, IL St. Thomas Aquinas Priory.
Regan, John '89 (JOL) Frankfort, IL St. Anthony Church.
Regan, John D. '53 (HRT) Middlebury, CT St. John of the Cross Church.
Regan, John J. '48 (BO) On Duty Outside the Archdiocese.
Regan, Msgr. John J. '53 (FR) Falmouth, MA St. Patrick's Church.
Regan, Matthew R.D. '70 (OAK) [4] San Leandro, CA St. Leander Church.
Regan, Msgr. Michael F. '38 (STL) Bridgeton, MO St. Lawrence the Martyr Church; Retired.
Regan, Msgr. Michael J. '46 (ATL) Carrollton, GA Church of Our Lady of Perpetual Help; Retired; [L] Atlanta, GA Campus Ministry.
Regan, Michael J. '62 (BO) Bridgewater, MA St. Thomas Aquinas Church.
Regan, Richard '85 (SAN) Military Chaplains.
Regan, Richard J. (SJ) Military Chaplains.
Regan, Richard J. *s.j.* '63 (NY) [Z] New York, NY Jesuit Community at Fordham University.
Regan, Robert F. *s.j.* (PRT) [9] Portland, ME St. Pius X Church.
Regan, Terrence P. '68 (GF) Stanford, MT St. Rose of Lima Church.
Regan, Thomas J. *s.j.* '87 (BGP) [A] Fairfield, CT Fairfield University; [O] Fairfield, CT The Fairfield Jesuit Community-Fairfield University.
Regan, Timothy J. '91 (DAV) Keota, IA Holy Trinity Church.
Regan, William D. '44 (STL) Retired.
Regan, William P. '56 (SY) Retired; [S] East Syracuse, NY Bishop Grimes Priests Residence.
Regensburger, Edmund *c.ss.r.* (VEN) Wauchula, FL St. Michael Church.
Reger, George L. '69 (BUF) [15] Buffalo, NY Blessed Trinity Church.
Regh, John '53 (SUP) Retired.
Reginato, Julian '65 (GR) Portland, MI St. Patrick's Church.
Regnier, William H. '48 (RCK) Retired.
Rego, Richard J. (TUC) Ajo, AZ Immaculate Conception Church.
Regoli, John A. '61 (GBG) [4] Uniontown, PA St. Therese, the Little Flower of Jesus Church.
Regula, Ronald R. '67 (NEW) Cedar Grove, NJ Essex County Hospital Center.
Regynski, Lawrence '95 (SFS) Yankton, SD Sacred Heart Church.
Rehage, Joseph W. *c.s.c.* '46 (AUS) [H] Austin, TX St. Joseph Hall; [H] Austin, TX Congregation of Holy Cross - Southern Province.
Rehauer, Stephen *c.ss.r.* (CHI) [9] Chicago, IL St. Alphonsus Church.
Rehkemper, Msgr. Robert C. '49 (DAL) [2] Dallas, TX All Saints Church.
Rehling, Paul '56 (CIN) [4] Cincinnati, OH St. Aloysius Gonzaga Church.
Rehme, Albert A. '56 (STL) Retired.
Rehrauer, Matthew J. '92 (SPC) Piedmont, MO St. Catherine of Siena Church.
Reich, John C. '84 (WH) Elkview, WV Our Lady of the Hills Church.
Reich, Paul A. *s.m.* '57 (BAL) Sykesville, MD St. Joseph Church; [M] Baltimore, MD Marianist Community.
Reichart, Charles V. *o.p.* '38 (PRO) [P] Providence, RI St. Thomas Aquinas Priory at Providence College.
Reichel, William *o.f.m.* '61 (CIN) [M] Cincinnati, OH St. Clement Friary.
Reicher, A Paul '62 (CHI) River Forest, IL St. Luke Church.
Reichert, Eldon *s.m.* '52 (CLV) [4] Cleveland, OH St. Aloysius - St. Agatha Church.
Reichert, Henry J. '63 (JC) Tipton, MO St. Andrew Church; Tipton, MO State Correctional Pre-Release Center.
Reichert, J. Lawrence '71 (COL) Groveport, OH St. Mary's Church.
Reichert, James *o.s.b.* '59 (SCL) Avon, MN St. Benedict's Church.
Reichert, James J. '71 (ALN) West Reading, PA Sacred Heart Church.
Reichert, Kenneth *o.s.b.* '59 (KC) [A] Conception, MO Conception Seminary College; [J] Conception, MO Conception Abbey; [O] Conception, MO Conception Benedictine Trust.
Reichert, Ralph '49 (TOL) Retired.
Reichlin, Urban A. '39 (CLV) [75] Cleveland, OH St. Vincent de Paul Church; Retired.
Reichling, David *o.f.m.cap.* '67 (GF) [4] Billings, MT St. Bernard's Church.
Reichling, Paul *o.f.m.cap.* '65 (GF) [3] Billings, MT Little Flower Church; [5] Billings, MT Our Lady of Guadalupe Church.
Reichmann, James B. *s.j.* '53 (SEA) [A] Seattle, WA Seattle University.
Reicks, Allen '76 (SC) Ruthven, IA Sacred Heart Church.
Reicks, Msgr. Leander H. '44 (DUB) Retired.
Reid, Damian *c.p.* '29 (HRT) [M] West Hartford, CT Holy Family Monastery/Retreat.
Reid, David P. *ss.cc.* '66 (FR) [3] New Bedford, MA Our Lady of the Assumption Church.
Reid, Francis R. '64 (CR) Retired.
Reid, Frank '64 (CR) Mahnomen, MN St. Michael's Church.
Reid, George B. '53 (WDC) Barnesville, MD St. Mary Church and Shrine of Our Lady of Fatima Church.
Reid, James H. *s.j.* '46 (NY) [Z] New York, NY Jesuit Community at Fordham University.
Reid, John J. *o.p.* '73 (PRO) [P] Providence, RI St. Thomas Aquinas Priory at Providence College.
Reid, Malcolm '57 (CHY) Rawlins, WY St. Joseph's Church; Rawlins, WY Wyoming State Penitentiary.
Reid, Msgr. Marion M. '40 (NO) Retired.
Reid, Michael '69 (RVC) Uniondale, NY Holly Patterson Home for Nassau Community Aged and Infirm; [C] Hicksville, NY Holy Trinity.
Reid, Michael R. '55 (BRK) Special Assignment.
Reid, Nicholas R. *o.p.* '59 (PH) [61] Philadelphia, PA Holy Name of Jesus Church; [Z] Philadelphia, PA Holy Name Priory, Dominican Friars.
Reid, Paul *s.c.j.* '72 (MIL) [P] Hales Corners, WI Sacred Heart Monastery.
Reid, Sean *o.carm.* '33 (NY) [Z] Middletown, NY St. Albert's Priory.
Reidmann, Gary P. (SC) [H] Carroll, IA St. Anthony Foundation.
Reidy, Edward J. *c.s.c.* '62 (FTW) [J] South Bend, IN Congregation of Holy Cross Indiana Province Provincial House.
Reidy, James '56 (STP) [C] St. Paul, MN University of St. Thomas.
Reidy, Martin F. '41 (RVC) Retired.
Reidy, Ned *c.s.c.* '62 (SB) Palm Desert, CA Christ of the Desert Church; [H] Palm Desert, CA Christ of the Desert Newman Center.
Reidy, Richard F. '94 (WOR) [1] Worcester, MA St. Paul's Cathedral.
Reidy, Robert '62 (Y) Military Chaplains.
Reidy, Robert J. '75 (CLV) [4] Lorain, OH Sacred Heart Chapel; [6] Lorain, OH St. Joseph Church; [X] Cleveland, OH Diocesan Hispanic Office.
Reidy, Msgr. Thomas E. '67 (SPC) [2] Springfield, MO Holy Trinity Church.
Reif, John T. '65 (ROC) Webster, NY St. Rita Church.
Reif, Marvin W. '89 (DOD) Ness City, KS Sacred Heart Church.
Reif, Marvin. W. '89 (DOD) Ransom, KS St. Aloysius Church.
Reifel, Mark *t.o.r.* '55 (ALT) [3] Windber, PA St. Anthony of Padua Church.
Reifenberg, Philip D. '79 (MIL) [62] Milwaukee, WI St. Martin de Porres Church.
Reiff, Dale E. '67 (SC) Barnum, IA St. Joseph's Church; Clare, IA St. Matthew's Church.
Reiff, Dennis E. '81 (NEW) [2] Orange, NJ Our Lady of the Valley Church.
Reifsnyder, John A. (COV) Retired.
Reifsnyder, John A. (PIT) [38] Pittsburgh, PA Sacred Heart Church.
Reigel, Joseph P. (E) [1] Erie, PA St. Peter Cathedral.
Reiker, H. John '78 (STL) [7] St. Louis, MO Immaculate Heart of Mary Church.
Reiker, Robert J. '73 (STL) Dardenne, MO Immaculate Conception Church.
Reikowski, Miroslaw '96 (RCK) Cary, IL SS. Peter & Paul Church.
Reile, Louis *s.m.* '60 (SAT) [M] San Antonio, TX Marianist Residence.
Reiley, Robert J. *m.m.* '59 (NY) [Z] Maryknoll, NY Maryknoll Fathers and Brothers.
Reilley, Thomas J. *s.j.* '95 (LA) [F] Los Angeles, CA Loyola High School.
Reilly, Bernard L. '73 (LAN) De Witt, MI St. Jude Church.
Reilly, Cristobal *s.t.* '55 (PCE) Coamo, PR St. Blase Church.
Reilly, David '75 (CIN) [17] Cincinnati, OH St. Bonaventure Church.
Reilly, Denis Daniel *o.p.* '70 (OAK) [N] Oakland, CA Dominican Order (Western Province), St. Albert's Priory.
Reilly, Donald F. *o.s.a.* '74 (PH) [C] Villanova, PA Villanova University; [Z] Villanova, PA Order of St. Augustine.
Reilly, Msgr. Edward '54 (STL) Mattese, MO Mary, Mother of the Church.
Reilly, F. Joseph '58 (STL) Coffman, MO St. Catherine of Alexandria Church; River Aux Vases, MO SS. Phillip and James Church.
Reilly, Francis E. '80 (SPR) [9] Holyoke, MA Sacred Heart Church; [M] Holyoke, MA Casa Maria.
Reilly, Gavin *o.f.m.cap.* '54 (NY) [98] New York, NY Our Lady of Sorrows Church.
Reilly, George M. '60 (NEW) Oradell, NJ St. Joseph's Church.
Reilly, James F. '68 (NEW) Teaneck, NJ Holy Name Hospital; [G] Teaneck, NJ Holy Name Hospital.
Reilly, James J. (NEW) [Q] Bloomfield, NJ Bloomfield College.
Reilly, Msgr. James J. '45 (FWT) Retired.
Reilly, Msgr. James J. '45 (PH) Chalfont, PA St. Jude Church.
Reilly, James J. '68 (NEW) Harrison, NJ Holy Cross Church; [Q] Cranford, NJ Union County College.
Reilly, John '78 (SD) On Duty Outside the Diocese.
Reilly, John C. '39 (BRK) [231] Queens, NY Queen of Peace Church; Retired.
Reilly, John E. *s.j.* '59 (CHI) [C] Chicago, IL Jesuit Community at Loyola University of Chicago.
Reilly, John H. '63 (BRK) [11] Brooklyn, NY St. Anthony of Padua-St. Alphonsus Church.
Reilly, Msgr. John J. '48 (LA) [8] Long Beach, CA St. Joseph Church; Retired.
Reilly, Msgr. John J. '48 (SFR) [3] Menlo Park, CA The Church of the Nativity; Special Assignment.
Reilly, Joseph L. '36 (BO) Retired.
Reilly, Joseph M. '84 (CAM) Marmora, NJ The Church of the Resurrection.
Reilly, Joseph R. '91 (NEW) [C] West Orange, NJ Seton Hall Preparatory School.
Reilly, Lawrence T. '64 (YAK) Cowiche, WA St. Peter's Church; [F] Cowiche, WA St. Peter the Apostle Retreat Center.
Reilly, Mathew V. *o.p.* '54 (NEW) [O] Summit, NJ Monastery of Our Lady of the Rosary.

Reilly, Michael P. '92 (NY) [205] Staten Island, NY Holy Family Church; [F] New York, NY St. Joseph by the Sea, High School.
Reilly, Msgr. Patrick '58 (LA) Burbank, CA St. Robert Bellarmine Church.
Reilly, Peter J. '58 (NEW) Rutherford, NJ St. Mary's Church.
Reilly, Msgr. Philip J. '60 (BRK) Special Assignment; [V] Brooklyn, NY Monastery of the Sisters Adorers of the Precious Blood.
Reilly, Rembert F. *o.s.b.* '59 (PAT) [M] Morristown, NJ St. Mary's Abbey.
Reilly, Robert '55 (COL) Circleville, OH St. Joseph's Church.
Reilly, Robert E. '58 (L) [57] Louisville, KY Our Lady Church.
Reilly, Msgr. Robert J. (E) [25] Erie, PA St. Mary Church.
Reilly, Steven *l.c.* (DAL) [D] Irving, TX Highland School; [G] Irving, TX Highland School; [M] Irving, TX Legionaries of Christ.
Reilly, Terrence J. *o.p.* '59 (SFR) [13] San Francisco, CA St. Dominic Church; [N] San Francisco, CA St. Dominic Priory.
Reilly, Thomas A. *m.s.* '72 (HRT) [M] Hartford, CT Missionaries of LaSalette Provincial Secretary.
Reilly, Thomas J. '67 (BO) [50] Boston, MA St. Monica Church.
Reilly, Msgr. William J. '65 (NEW) [1] Union City, NJ Holy Family Church.
Reilman, Thomas J. '61 (DAV) [L] Burlington, IA St. Francis Continuation Care and Nursing Home.
Reim, Daniel T. *s.j.* '95 (CLV) [C] Cleveland, OH John Carroll Jesuit Community.
Reiman, Frederick *o.s.m.* '45 (CHI) [N] Chicago, IL Servite Friars - Eastern Province.
Reimann, Oswald S. '53 (JOL) Bensenville, IL St. Alexis Church.
Reimer, Edward J. '67 (SY) [23] Syracuse, NY St. Therese the Little Flower of Jesus Church; Jamesville, NY Jamesville Penitentiary.
Reimer, Elroy '57 (GB) Wrightstown, WI St. Paul Church.
Reimer, Ronald P. '62 (GB) [6] Manitowoc, WI St. Paul Church.
Reina, Nicholas J. *s.d.b.* '78 (LA) [C] Rosemead, CA Don Bosco Technical Institute; [D] Rosemead, CA Don Bosco Technical Institute.
Reina, Richard A. '70 (BUF) [41] Buffalo, NY St. Lawrence Church.
Reinbold, Charles (NEW) On Duty Outside the Archdiocese.
Reinbold, Msgr. Francis A. '40 (NEW) Scotch Plains, NJ St. Bartholomew Church; Retired.
Reiner, Charles J. *o.s.b.* '42 (BIR) [E] Cullman, AL St. Bernard Abbey.
Reiner, Charles J. *o.s.b.* '42 (MOB) Foley, AL St. Margaret Church.
Reinersman, Gerald L. '79 (COV) [M] Covington, KY St. Walburg Monastery.
Reinert, Duane F. *o.f.m.cap.* '76 (KC) [A] Conception, MO Conception Seminary College.
Reinert, Duane F. *o.f.m.cap.* '76 (KCK) Lawrence, KS Haskell Institute; [H] Lawrence, KS St. Conrad's Friary; [J] Lawrence, KS Haskell Catholic Campus Center.
Reinert, Ellis *o.carm.* '49 (NEW) Englewood, NJ St. Cecilia's Church.
Reinert, James M. '83 (LIN) On Duty Outside the Diocese.
Reinert, James M. '83 (NY) [2] New York, NY St. Agnes Church.
Reinert, Paul C. *s.j.* '40 (STL) [C] St. Louis, MO Saint Louis University; [P] St. Louis, MO Jesuit Community Corporation at St. Louis University - Jesuit Hall.
Reinhardt, Leo J. '78 (ROC) Clyde, NY St. John the Evangelist Church.
Reinhardt, Leo S. '55 (BEL) Albers, IL St. Bernard Church; Damiansville, IL St. Damian Church.
Reinhardt, Mark S. '96 (PRT) [2] Lewiston, ME Holy Cross Church.
Reinhart, Blaise R. *o.f.m.* '55 (ALB) [B] Loudonville, NY Siena College.
Reinhart, Kenneth W. *o.f.m.cap.* '68 (LC) [H] Marathon City, WI St. Anthony Retreat Center; [I] Marathon City, WI St. Anthony Retreat Center.
Reinhart, Ralph W. '52 (SC) Manning, IA Sacred Heart Church.
Reinhart, Robert '61 (TOL) [2] Toledo, OH Blessed Sacrament Church.
Reinhart, Robert C. *c.pp.s.* '53 (LFT) Bryant, IN Holy Trinity Church.
Reinke, Francis '57 (GB) Poy Sippi, WI Sacred Heart of Jesus Church; Redgranite, WI St. Mark Church.
Reinke, John H. *s.j.* '45 (CHI) [C] Chicago, IL Jesuit Community at Loyola University of Chicago.
Reinke, Robert J. '57 (COV) [4] Newport, KY St. Vincent de Paul Church.
Reinkemeyer, John C. '51 (WCH) Kingman, KS St. Patrick Church.
Reino, Joseph C. '93 (PH) [115] Philadelphia, PA Our Lady of Consolation Church.
Reinsfelder, Msgr. John L. '49 (BAL) [35] Baltimore, MD Holy Cross Church; Retired.
Reiran, Eric A. *o.p.* '91 (STL) [P] St. Louis, MO Dominican Community of St. Louis.
Reis, Antonio (OAK) [4] San Leandro, CA St. Leander Church.
Reis, Daniel O. '75 (FR) [5] New Bedford, MA Our Lady of the Immaculate Conception Church.
Reis, John *o.f.m.* '25 (Y) [J] Youngstown, OH Mt. Alvernia Friary.
Reis, Justin J. '69 (COL) Lancaster, OH St. Bernadette Church.
Reis, Lancelot '67 (PAT) Chester, NJ St. Lawrence the Martyr Church.
Reis, Michael J. '67 (COL) [11] Columbus, OH St. Christopher Church.
Reis, Raymond H. *s.j.* '37 (STL) [P] St. Louis, MO Jesuit Community Corporation at St. Louis University - Jesuit Hall.
Reis, Richard M. '61 (Y) Girard, OH St. Rose Church.
Reis, Timothy P. '86 (FR) Seekonk, MA Our Lady of Mt. Carmel Church.
Reisch, Milton L. '60 (NO) [1] Metairie, LA Our Lady of Divine Providence Church.
Reischl, Fred P. '55 (DM) Avoca, IA St. Mary, Mediatrix of All Graces Church; Walnut, IA St. Patrick Church.
Reischman, Placidus G. *o.s.b.* '54 (SEA) [M] Lacey, WA St. Martin's Abbey.
Reischman, Virgil '69 (STU) Amsterdam, OH St. Joseph Church.
Reisdorff, Clarence P. '46 (LIN) Retired; [E] Lincoln, NE Bonacum House.
Reiser, Bernard A. '49 (STP) Coon Rapids, MN Church of the Epiphany.
Reiser, John '56 (MIA) Absent on Sick Leave.
Reiser, Richard J. '80 (OM) O'Neill, NE St. Patrick Church.
Reiser, William E. *s.j.* '72 (WOR) [N] Worcester, MA Jesuits of Holy Cross College, Inc.; [N] Worcester, MA Jesuits of Holy Cross College, Inc.; [R] Worcester, MA Casa Santa Maria del Camino, Inc.
Reisert, Frederick J. *s.j.* '54 (BUF) [O] Buffalo, NY Canisius Jesuit Community.
Reisert, Gregory *o.f.m.cap.* '64 (NY) [Z] White Plains, NY St. Conrad Friary.
Reisig, Msgr. William E. '45 (NY) Retired.
Reising, Joseph H. '71 (NO) [F] New Orleans, LA Jesuit High School; [P] New Orleans, LA Jesuit Provincial Office.
Reising, Raymond '45 (EVN) Retired.
Reisinger, Walter J. *c.m.* '55 (JC) Crocker, MO St. Cornelius Church; Dixon, MO St. Theresa Church.
Reiske, Steven '90 (FAR) [6] Fargo, ND St. Paul Newman Center, N.D.S.U. Church; Special Assignment.
Reiss, Francis R. '66 (DET) [63] Detroit, MI SS. Peter and Paul Church.
Reiss, John E. *o.f.m.* '69 (Y) [5] Youngstown, OH Our Lady of Hungary Church.
Reiss, Robert J. '55 (DUB) Retired.
Reissmann, Richard A. '63 (WIL) Newark, DE St. John the Baptist-Holy Angels Church.
Reist, Thomas *o.f.m.conv.* '79 (BAL) [M] Ellicott City, MD Order of Friars Minor Conventual.
Reist, Thomas *o.f.m.conv.* '79 (WDC) [B] Washington, DC St. Bonaventure Friary.
Reisteter, William *o.f.m.* '71 (ALN) [K] Easton, PA St. Francis Friary; [M] Easton, PA St. Francis Retreat House.
Reisz, Adam '41 (DM) Retired.
Reisz, Leonard '50 (OWN) Non-Parochial Assignments.
Reiter, James E. '90 (ROM) McKeesport, PA St. Mary Church.
Reites, James W. *s.j.* '71 (SJ) [B] Santa Clara, CA Santa Clara University.
Reith, David H. '76 (MIL) Burlington, WI Immaculate Conception Church.
Reith, Herman R. *c.s.c.* '42 (FTW) [B] Notre Dame, IN University of Notre Dame Du Lac; [J] Notre Dame, IN Holy Cross Community, Corby Hall, University of Notre Dame.
Reitl, Andrew J. '71 (TR) Brant Beach, NJ St. Francis of Assisi Church.
Reitter, Frank *s.m.* '84 (BO) [W] Boston, MA Marist Fathers and Brothers Provincial House.
Reitter, Frank *s.m.* '84 (RC) Standing Rock, SD Standing Rock Reservation Church.
Reitz, Joseph A. '53 (GAY) Retired.
Reitz, Louis M. *s.s.* '55 (BAL) [82] Baltimore, MD St. Pius X Church; [M] Baltimore, MD Sulpician Provincial House.
Reitz, William J. '47 (GR) Carson City, MI St. Mary's Church; Hubbardston, MI St. John the Baptist Church.
Rejent, Michael *o.s.f.s.* '68 (LAN) [6] Lansing, MI St. Gerard Church; [B] Lansing, MI Lansing Catholic Central High School.
Rejsek, J. Brian '86 (PEO) Princeville, IL St. Mary of the Woods Church.
Rekasi, Joseph '46 (GB) [I] De Pere, WI St. Joseph Priory.
Rekasi, Joseph S. *o.praem.* '46 (GB) [O] De Pere, WI Canons Regular of Magnovarad, Ltd.
Reker, Timothy T. (WIN) On Duty Outside the Diocese.
Rekofke, Robert *s.j.* '59 (SEA) [12] Tacoma, WA Holy Cross Church.
Relihan, Thomas '47 (SAC) Ione, CA Sacred Heart Church.
Reller, Gary W. '71 (HEL) Polson, MT Immaculate Conception Church.
Remaklus, Charles W. '47 (LFT) Retired.
Rementeria, Alfonso *o.ss.t.* '76 (PCE) [10] Ponce, PR La Santisima Trinidad Church.
Remes, James A. '55 (STP) Retired.
Remillard, Andre N. '70 (WOR) Sterling, MA St. Richard of Chichester Church.
Remillard, Bernard M. *o.p.* '37 (PRT) [I] Lewiston, ME SS. Peter and Paul Priory.
Remirez, Pascual '92 (OAK) Richmond, CA St. Cornelius Church.
Remke, Raymond J. '88 (BIR) Montevallo, AL St. Thomas the Apostle Church; [H] Montevallo, AL University of Montevallo.
Remm, George F. '60 (PEO) Urbana, IL St. Patrick's Church.
Remmel, William J. *s.d.s.* '67 (BAL) [83] Baltimore, MD St. Rita Church.
Remmes, Richard R. '62 (SC) Marcus, IA Holy Name Church.
Rempe, Melvin L. '65 (LIN) Cambridge, NE St. John's Church.
Remy, Adrien T. '34 (SPR) Retired; [J] Holyoke, MA Mont Marie.
Remy, David P. '67 (DUB) Military Chaplains.
Renaldo, Daniel *c.m.* '48 (ALN) Roseto, PA Our Lady of Mt. Carmel Church.
Renard, Eugene C. *s.j.* '60 (PBL) Trinidad, CO Most Holy Trinity, Trinidad Area Catholic Community (Trinidad Cluster) Church; Trinidad, CO Our Lady of Mt. Carmel, Trinidad Area Catholic Community (Trinidad Cluster) Church; Trinidad, CO St. Joseph, Trinidad Area Catholic Community (Trinidad Cluster) Church; [E] Trinidad, CO Trinidad Area Catholic Community.
Renard, John F. '65 (NEW) Guttenberg, NJ St. John Nepomucene Church.
Renard, Peter J. *o.praem.* '68 (GB) [F] Green Bay, WI St. Vincent Hospital; [I] De Pere, WI St. Norbert Abbey.
Renaud, Oliver *o.m.i.* '50 (NOR) [F] Willimantic, CT Oblates of Mary Immaculate; [I] Willimantic, CT Immaculata Retreat House.
Renaud, Roland A. '60 (SPR) [6] Holyoke, MA Our Lady of Perpetual Help Church.
Render, Msgr. Bernard A. '40 (PEO) Retired; [L] Peoria, IL St. Augustine Manor.
Render, John T. *c.p.* '52 (CHI) [N] Chicago, IL Immaculate Conception Monastery.
Render, Patrick W. *c.s.v.* '68 (SFD) [8] Springfield, IL St. Joseph Church.
Rendon, Luis A. '73 (PAT) [1] Paterson, NJ Cathedral of St. John the Baptist.
Rendon, Raul P. *o.ss.t.* '87 (VIC) [4] Victoria, TX Our Lady of Sorrows Church.
Rendon, Samuel '92 (LA) [40] Los Angeles, CA St. Alphonsus Church.
Renehan, Edmond M. '58 (LA) Canyon Country, CA St. Clare Church.
Renfroe, Francis E. *s.j.* '68 (SFE) [6] Albuquerque, NM Immaculate Conception Church.
Rengers, Christopher *o.f.m.cap.* '42 (RCK) [N] St. Charles, IL Queen of Americas Guild.
Rengers, Christopher *o.f.m.cap.* '42 (WDC) [B] Washington, DC St. Francis Friary-Capuchin College.
Rengers, Joseph F. *c.s.sp.* '41 (PIT) [3] Millvale, PA Holy Spirit Church.
Renggli, John J. '68 (SEA) Lynnwood, WA St. Thomas More Church.
Rengifo, J. Orlando '85 (NEW) [1] Hackensack, NJ Holy Trinity Church.
Renken, John A. '79 (SFD) Riverton, IL St. James Church.
Renkiewicz, Adolphe T. '56 (HRT) [N] Enfield, CT Felician Sisters - Our Lady of the Angels.
Renna, Anton J. *s.j.* '65 (PHX) [B] Phoenix, AZ Brophy College Preparatory.
Rennell, Albert F. '59 (RCK) Retired.
Renner, Christopher A. '91 (DEN) Julesburg, CO St. Anthony Church.
Renner, Frank G. '81 (EVN) Cannelburg, IN All Saints Church.
Renner, Louis L. *s.j.* '57 (FBK) [C] Fairbanks, AK Jesuit Residence.
Renner, Ralph C. *s.j.* '70 (STL) [C] St. Louis, MO Saint Louis University; [P] St. Louis, MO Jesuit Community Corporation at St. Louis University - Jesuit Hall.
Renninger, Michael '93 (RIC) [2] Newport News, VA Our Lady of Mount Carmel Church.
Rensing, William F. '55 (BEL) Sparta, IL Our Lady of

Lourdes Church.
Renteria, Rudy '79 (DAL) [I] Dallas, TX St. Paul Medical Center.
Renteria, Rudy '79 (FWT) On Duty Outside the Diocese.
Rentino, Pablo (NY) [173] Bronx, NY Our Lady of Mercy Church.
Rentner, Randall *c.s.c.* '90 (CHI) [D] Niles, IL Notre Dame High School.
Rento, Richard G. '58 (PAT) [3] Clifton, NJ St. Brendan Church.
Repchick, George *m.s.* '56 (LKC) [3] Sulphur, LA Our Lady of Prompt Succor Church.
Repela, Vasyl '86 (PHU) [A] Washington, DC St. Josaphat Seminary.
Repenshek, Jerome V. '63 (MIL) West Bend, WI Holy Angels Church.
Repko, Joseph '95 (PRM) Bedford, OH St. Eugene Church.
Repole, Celsus '43 (NY) [Z] Yonkers, NY St. Clare Friary.
Repole, Charles '43 (NY) [Z] Yonkers, NY St. Clare Friary.
Reppen, Robert B. *o.praem.* '46 (GB) [I] De Pere, WI St. Norbert Abbey.
Repschinski, Liborius *s.j.* '90 (CHI) [C] Chicago, IL Jesuit Community at Loyola University of Chicago.
Resch, Gerard F. *c.ss.r.* '44 (STL) [P] Liguori, MO St. Clement Health Care Center.
Resch, Julian C. *o.praem.* '38 (GB) [I] De Pere, WI St. Norbert Abbey.
Reschick, Joseph W. '77 (PIT) [37] Pittsburgh, PA St. Rosalia Church.
Resconich, Emil C. *t.o.r.* '54 (ALT) [A] Loretto, PA St. Francis College; [F] Loretto, PA St. Francis Friary, Third Order Regular of St. Francis of Penance.
Resheske, Florian '55 (GB) Champion, WI St. Joseph Church; New Franken, WI St. Kilian Church; Absent on Leave.
Reskey, George (MOB) On Leave from the Archdiocese.
Resko, Blane *o.s.b.* '57 (ALT) Carrolltown, PA St. Benedict's Church.
Resma, Louis (DET) Farmington, MI Botsford General Hospital; Detroit, MI Saratoga General Hospital.
Resop, Michael A. '79 (MAD) Plain, WI St. Luke Church.
Ressler, Mark A. '76 (DUB) [A] Dubuque, IA Seminary of St. Pius X; [C] Dubuque, IA Loras College; [C] Dubuque, IA Clarke College.
Ressler, Wayne A. '64 (DUB) [10] Dubuque, IA Nativity Church.
Resta, Vincent A. '55 (NY) [181] Bronx, NY St. Peter and St. Paul Church.
Restrepo, George *s.j.* '65 (BAL) [89] Baltimore, MD St. Thomas Aquinas Church.
Restrepo, Jairo '92 (B) [2] Boise, ID St. Mark's Church.
Restrick, Jacob *o.p.* '89 (BUF) [P] Buffalo, NY Monastery of Our Lady of the Rosary.
Restrick, Jacob *o.p.* '89 (Y) [13] Youngstown, OH St. Dominic's Church.
Resultay, Angel V. '67 (RVC) Farmingdale, NY St. Kilian Church.
Reszel, Marc W. '88 (CHI) Glenview, IL Our Lady of Perpetual Help Church.
Reszkowski, Msgr. Joseph V. '54 (E) [9] Erie, PA Our Lady of Mt. Carmel Church.
Reteneller, Charles E. '60 (L) Elizabethtown, KY St. James Church; White Mills, KY St. Ignatius Church; [M] St. Catharine, KY St. Catharine of Siena Convent.
Rethamel, Roger R. '60 (DUB) Alta Vista, IA St. Bernard Church; Elma, IA Immaculate Conception Church.
Rethinger, Omer '53 (TOL) Kansas, OH St. James Church; Millersville, OH St. Mary Church.
Retortillo, Benito *o.p.* '62 (CC) San Diego, TX St. Francis de Paula Church; [H] San Diego, TX Vicariate of Holy Rosary.
Rettger, Emmeran A. *o.s.b.* '38 (GBG) [H] Latrobe, PA Saint Vincent Archabbey.
Rettger, Thaddeus E. *o.s.b.* '74 (GBG) Vandergrift, PA St. Gertrude Church.
Rettig, Donald R. '71 (CIN) [5] Cincinnati, OH St. Aloysius-on-the-Ohio Church; [E] Cincinnati, OH Elder High School.
Rettig, Hermann-Joseph K. *o.praem.* '84 (LA) [90] Los Angeles, CA St. Stephen Church.
Rettig, Hermann-Joseph K. *o.praem.* '84 (ORG) [H] Silverado, CA Norbertine Fathers.
Retzel, Joseph R. *s.j.* '60 (GF) Hays, MT St. Paul's Indian Mission Church.
Retzner, James P. *o.s.a.* '95 (LA) Ojai, CA St. Thomas Aquinas Church.
Reuse, Patrick J. *s.j.* '73 (PHX) [11] Phoenix, AZ St. Francis Xavier Church.
Reusing, James '94 (BAL) Pasadena, MD St. Jane Frances de Chantal Church.
Reuss, Louis L. '38 (RVC) Bohemia, NY St. John Nepomucene Church; Retired.
Reuss, Norbert C. *c.s.b.* '38 (GAL) [F] Houston, TX St. Thomas High School.
Reuten, Lloyd '57 (DUB) Blessing, IA Immaculate Conception Church.
Reuter, Arnold F. '52 (LC) Retired; [I] La Crosse, WI Holy Cross (Seminary) Diocesan Center.
Reuter, Charles *o.f.m.* '49 (STL) Oakville, MO St. Francis of Assisi Church; [P] Oakville, MO St. Francis Friary.
Reuter, Christian *o.f.m.* '66 (CHI) [47] Chicago, IL Corpus Christi Church.
Reuter, John F. '67 (GB) On Duty Outside the Diocese.
Reuter, Lars *s.j.* '86 (STL) [C] St. Louis, MO Saint Louis University; [P] St. Louis, MO Jesuit Community Corporation at St. Louis University - Jesuit Hall.
Reuter, Lawrence *s.j.* '71 (CHI) [C] Chicago, IL Loyola University-Chicago; [C] Chicago, IL Jesuit Community at Loyola University of Chicago; [V] Chicago, IL Ministry in Higher Education.
Reuter, Leon *o.f.m.* '62 (STL) [P] St. Louis, MO Franciscan Friary of St. Anthony of Padua.
Reuter, Lloyd E. '57 (DUB) Eagle Center, IA St. Mary of Mt. Carmel Church; La Porte City, IA Sacred Heart Church.
Revak, Msgr. Francis C. '40 (ALN) Catasauqua, PA St. Lawrence Church; [C] Allentown, PA Allentown Central Catholic High School.
Revak, Msgr. Raymond '59 (PHU) Scranton, PA St. Vladimir's Church.
Revel, Peter '82 (TYL) Jacksonville, TX Our Lady of Sorrows Church.
Revello, James K.I. '73 (DEN) On Duty Outside the Archdiocese.
Revilla, Francisco '54 (STA) Special Assignment.
Revilla, Isaias *o.s.a.* '60 (MGZ) Aguada, PR St. Francis of Assisi Church.
Revuelto, Manuel '59 (NEW) [1] Orange, NJ St. John's Church.
Rewak, William J. *s.j.* '64 (MOB) [B] Mobile, AL Spring Hill College.
Rewtiuk, Msgr. Michael '69 (SJP) [1] Parma, OH St. Josaphat Cathedral.
Reycraft, Robert J. '75 (DEN) [9] Denver, CO Guardian Angels Church.
Reyes, Andres (NEW) Belleville, NJ St. Peter's Church.
Reyes, Francisco *o.f.m.* '42 (SFR) [5] San Francisco, CA St. Anthony Church.
Reyes, Jorge A. *o.s.a.* (BO) [9] Lawrence, MA St. Mary Immaculate Conception Church.
Reyes, Jose *o.f.m.conv.* '84 (LSC) Hobbs, NM St. Helena Church.
Reyes, Jose Luis '93 (MIA) [28] Miami, FL SS. Peter and Paul Church.
Reyes, Jose Maria *o.de.m.* (SJN) [40] San Juan, PR Nuestra Senora de la Merced Church.
Reyes, Msgr. Lonnie C. '69 (AUS) [15] Austin, TX St. Julia Church.
Reyes, Marco '85 (LA) San Gabriel, CA St. Anthony Church.
Reyes, Pedro Luis '90 (SJN) Graduate Studies.
Reyes, Ralph *o.c.d.* '69 (SAT) [18] San Antonio, TX Our Lady of Mt. Carmel and St. Therese, Discalced Carmelite Fathers Church; [M] San Antonio, TX Discalced Carmelites (Prov. of St. Therese).
Reyes, Reynaldo '93 (LUB) [4] Lubbock, TX St. Elizabeth University Parish Church; Snyder, TX St. Elizabeth's Church.
Reyes, Victor J. '94 (ATL) [10] Atlanta, GA St. Jude Church.
Reyes, Wilberto *l.d.* '83 (PCE) [18] Ponce, PR Church Santisimo Sacramento Church.
Reymann, Albert I. *m.m.* '47 (CLV) [3] Akron, OH St. Bernard Church.
Reymann, Albert I. *m.m.* '47 (NY) [Z] Maryknoll, NY Maryknoll Fathers and Brothers.
Reymann, James J. '58 (CLV) Wellington, OH St. Patrick Church.
Reyna, Cecilio '91 (LAN) [1] Jackson, MI St. John the Evangelist Church.
Reyna, Joseph A. '71 (SAT) Pearsall, TX Immaculate Heart of Mary Church.
Reyna, Marcos O. *o.f.m.conv.* '86 (LSC) [D] Mesilla Park, NM Holy Cross Retreat and Friary.
Reynebeau, Thomas '87 (GB) Absent on Leave.
Reynierse, Peter J. '95 (WDC) Pastoral Center Special Ministries.
Reynolds, Brad R. *s.j.* '77 (P) [L] Portland, OR Jesuit Provincial Office (Oregon Prov.).
Reynolds, Daniel '53 (P) [2] Eugene, OR St. Mark Church.
Reynolds, Msgr. Edward J. '45 (NY) Retired; [Z] New York, NY Pope John Paul II Residence.
Reynolds, Fred G. *s.j.* '78 (LAF) [A] Grand Coteau, LA St. Charles College.
Reynolds, Ignatius C. '35 (PH) Gladwyne, PA St. John Baptist Vianney Church; Retired.
Reynolds, J. Patrick '80 (OWN) Sorgho, KY St. Mary Magdalene Church.
Reynolds, James B. '50 (MIA) [6] Pompano Beach, FL St. Henry Church.
Reynolds, James J.M. '84 (BRK) [199] Queens, NY St. Matthias Church.
Reynolds, James L. '71 (SPC) Billings, MO St. Joseph Church.
Reynolds, Jeffrie S. '90 (BIR) On Duty Outside the Diocese.
Reynolds, Jeffrie S. '90 (NO) New Orleans, LA Memorial Medical Center.
Reynolds, Jeffrie S. '90 (PAT) Dover, NJ Dover General Hospital.
Reynolds, John C. *c.s.p.* '47 (NY) [104] New York, NY St. Paul the Apostle Church; [Z] Scarsdale, NY Paulist Fathers Generalate.
Reynolds, John C. '90 (KCK) Alma, KS Holy Family Church; Eskridge, KS St. John Vianney's Church; Paxico, KS Sacred Heart Church.
Reynolds, Msgr. John P. '49 (NO) [49] New Orleans, LA St. Patrick Church; [S] New Orleans, LA Stella Roman Foundation, Inc.
Reynolds, John R. '83 (STA) [16] Jacksonville, FL St. Matthew's Church.
Reynolds, Joseph F. '59 (NY) Harriman, NY St. Anastasia Church.
Reynolds, Kirk R. *s.j.* '79 (RVC) Oceanside, NY St. Anthony Church.
Reynolds, Paul *c.s.p.* '94 (WH) Morgantown, WV St. John's University Parish, Newman Hall Church.
Reynolds, Paul F. '65 (PRO) [8] West Warwick, RI St. Mary Church.
Reynolds, Paul H. '63 (ATL) Roswell, GA St. Andrew Church.
Reynolds, Robert E. '52 (PEO) Rushville, IL St. Rose Church; Retired.
Reynolds, Msgr. Roger A. '43 (NEW) Harrington Park, NJ Our Lady of Victories Church; Retired.
Reynolds, Stephen B. '89 (GAL) [19] Houston, TX Christ the King Church.
Reynolds, Thomas D. '58 (BO) [4] Brockton, MA St. Margaret Church.
Reynolds, Thomas J. '54 (NY) Massapequa Park, NY Our Lady of Lourdes Church.
Reynolds, Thomas J. '54 (RVC) Massapequa Park, NY Our Lady of Lourdes Church.
Reynolds, Thomas P. *s.s.c.* '61 (CHI) [N] Chicago, IL Columban Fathers Mission Center.
Reynolds, William E. '81 (DAV) Lost Nation, IA Sacred Heart Church; Toronto, IA St. James Church.
Reynolds, William E. '81 (DUB) Oxford Junction, IA Sacred Heart Church.
Reynolds, William V. '55 (NY) Nanuet, NY St. Anthony Church.
Rezabek, Msgr. William J. '31 (LIN) Retired; [E] Lincoln, NE Bonacum House.
Rezac, Keith D. '87 (OM) Coleridge, NE St. Michael Church; [B] Hartington, NE Cedar Catholic High School.
Rezula, Leon J. '69 (CHI) [201] Chicago, IL St. Thecla Church.
Rezza, Boniface *o.f.m.* '44 (NY) [Z] New York, NY Franciscan Province of the Immaculate Conception.
Rhatigan, Msgr. John '49 (SD) Retired.
Rheault, Francois *o.cart.* '93 (BUR) [G] Arlington, VT Carthusian Foundation, Charterhouse of the Transfiguration.
Rhein, Msgr. George V. '39 (GAL) Retired.
Rhinehart, R. William *c.m.* '79 (COS) Limon, CO Our Lady of Victory Church.
Rhoades, C. Michael '70 (MAR) St. Ignace, MI St. Ignatius Loyola Church.
Rhoades, Kevin C. '83 (BAL) [A] Emmitsburg, MD Mount St. Mary's Seminary; [A] Emmitsburg, MD Mount St. Mary's Seminary.
Rhoden, Raymond R. '76 (PIT) [4] Donora, PA Our Lady of the Valley Church.
Rhodes, C. Michael '70 (MAR) Moran, MI Immaculate Conception Church.
Rhodes, David W. '65 (Y) [11] Youngstown, OH St. Christine's Church.
Rhodes, Edmund L. *s.m.* '41 (CIN) [M] Dayton, OH Marianist Provincialate.
Rhodes, George V. '53 (WIL) Retired.
Rhodes, Joseph '41 (OWN) Retired; [E] Owensboro, KY Carmel Home.
Rhodes, Ronald E. '81 (R) Graduate Studies.
Rhodes, Terence *o.f.m.* '43 (GLP) Zuni, NM St. Anthony Indian Mission, Our Lady of Guadalupe Church.
Rhomberg, Thomas W. '53 (DUB) Elkader, IA St. Joseph's Church; Volga, IA Sacred Heart Church.
Rhyner, Robert E. '59 (GB) [9] Green Bay, WI Holy Martyrs of Gorcum Church.
Riani, Peter R. '55 (OG) Peru, NY St. Augustine Church.
Riano, Camilo '47 (SJN) [2] Bayamon, PR San Antonio Maria Claret Church.
Ribando, William R. *c.s.c.* '64 (SCR) [C] Wilkes-Barre, PA Kings College.
Ribaudo, Msgr. Charles A. '67 (RVC) Oyster Bay, NY St. Dominic's Church.
Ribble, James M. *ph.d.* '57 (SPK) [1] Spokane, WA Cathedral of Our Lady of Lourdes.
Ribeiro, Alvaro *s.j.* '87 (WDC) [M] Washington, DC The Jesuit Community at Georgetown University.
Ribeiro, George *s.a.* '67 (NY) [14] Yonkers, NY Our

Lady of the Rosary Church; [Z] Garrison, NY Franciscan Friars of the Atonement.
Ribeiro, Nelson *c.m.* '54 (HRT) [3] Waterbury, CT Our Lady of Fatima Church.
Ribero, Arthur '50 (OAK) Retired.
Ribezzi, Rinaldo A. *c.s.s.* '39 (SPR) [3] Pittsfield, MA Our Lady of Mt. Carmel Church.
Ribits, Thomas A. *o.s.f.s.* '82 (TOL) [K] Toledo, OH Oblates of St. Francis de Sales.
Ribotta, Frank *s.d.b.* '47 (LA) [F] Bellflower, CA St. John Bosco High School.
Ribotta, Michael *s.d.b.* '49 (OAK) [A] Berkeley, CA Dominican School of Philosophy and Theology; [N] Berkeley, CA Salesian Community.
Ricafort, Juvencio D. '82 (SD) [35] San Diego, CA St. Rita Church.
Ricard, David F. '69 (PRO) [1] West Warwick, RI Christ the King Church; Warwick, RI Kent County Memorial Hospital.
Ricard, Joseph M. '64 (NOR) Retired.
Ricard, Rodney Anthony '95 (NO) [57] New Orleans, LA St. Rita Church.
Riccardi, Salvatore *c.p.* '62 (MET) [H] South River, NJ Passionist Provincial Office.
Riccardi, Salvatore *c.p.* '62 (NY) Crestwood, NY Church of the Annunciation.
Riccardo, John C. '96 (DET) [5] Dearborn, MI Divine Child Church.
Riccardo, Joseph J. '75 (E) Punxsutawney, PA SS. Cosmas and Damian Church.
Ricchini, Joseph *o.f.m.* '64 (CIN) [M] Cincinnati, OH St. Ann Friary.
Ricci, Alfred V. '80 (PRO) [18] Providence, RI St. Joseph's Church; [S] Providence, RI Brown University.
Ricci, Daniel A. *c.m.* '74 (STL) [P] St. Louis, MO Vincentian Residence.
Ricci, Philip C. '65 (PH) North Wales, PA Mary, Mother of the Redeemer Church.
Ricci, Roberto J. *s.j.* '37 (NY) [28] New York, NY Corpus Christi Church.
Ricciardelli, Albert '84 (TR) [2] Long Branch, NJ Holy Trinity Church.
Ricciardi, August A. '83 (SCR) Throop, PA St. Anthony's Church; Throop, PA St. Bridget's Church; Throop, PA St. John the Baptist Church.
Ricciardi, Robert P. '79 (HRT) [6] East Hartford, CT St. Rose's Church.
Riccio, Alexis D. '34 (HRT) Retired.
Riccio, Fred A. '77 (OAK) San Ramon, CA St. Joan of Arc Church.
Riccio, Salvatore M. '66 (PH) Springfield, PA St. Francis of Assisi Church.
Riccitelli, Dennis '85 (PHX) [3] Mesa, AZ Holy Cross Church.
Riccomini, Msgr. Dino F. '57 (FRS) Wasco, CA St. John the Evangelist Church.
Rice, Charles F. *c.m.* '43 (STL) [P] Perryville, MO Congregation of The Mission.
Rice, Msgr. Charles O. '34 (PIT) Castle Shannon, PA St. Anne Church; Retired.
Rice, Edward M. '87 (STL) [A] St. Louis, MO Kenrick-Glennon Seminary.
Rice, George N. '67 (L) On Special Assignment.
Rice, John A. '57 (SEA) Retired.
Rice, Joseph P. '77 (NEW) Paramus, NJ Bergen Pines County Hospital.
Rice, Lawrence *c.s.p.* (WDC) [B] Washington, DC St. Paul's College; [V] Washington, DC ITP Paulist Communications.
Rice, Michael D. '64 (KC) Lee's Summit, MO Our Lady of the Presentation Church.
Rice, Owen (ALB) [L] Saratoga Springs, NY St. John Neumann Residence.
Rice, Patrick J. *o.s.a.* '48 (PH) [C] Villanova, PA Villanova University; [Z] Villanova, PA St. Thomas Monastery.
Rice, Patrick J. *s.j.* '54 (DET) [E] Detroit, MI University of Detroit Jesuit High School and Academy.
Rice, Patrick J. '74 (PAT) McAfee, NJ St. Francis de Sales Church.
Rice, Richard M. *s.j.* '72 (STP) [6] St. Paul, MN The Immaculate Heart of Mary Church; [Q] St. Paul, MN Loyola.
Rice, Richard P. '60 (PRT) Sanford, ME Holy Family Church.
Rice, Thomas G. '77 (DET) [7] Warren, MI St. Louise Church.
Rice, William A. '63 (E) [1] Farrell, PA Holy Trinity Church; [3] Farrell, PA St. Adalbert Church.
Rich, John A. *m.m.* '58 (NY) [Z] Maryknoll, NY Maryknoll Fathers and Brothers.
Rich, Joseph '74 (SJ) Los Altos, CA St. Simon Church.
Rich, Orlando S. '43 (Y) Girard, OH St. Rose Church; Retired.
Rich, William W. '80 (BAL) [A] Baltimore, MD St. Mary's Seminary and University.
Richard, Alain *o.f.m.* (LAV) Special Assignment.
Richard, Antonio J. '38 (FAR) Retired.
Richard, Charles J. (OG) Retired.
Richard, Claude *o.p.* (PRT) [I] Lewiston, ME SS. Peter and Paul Priory.
Richard, Edward '41 (TLS) Retired.
Richard, Edward D. '68 (MAN) Pelham, NH St. Patrick Church.
Richard, Msgr. Eugene F. '45 (NY) [1] New Rochelle, NY Blessed Sacrament Church; Retired.
Richard, Hudson R. '73 (HRT) Hartford, CT Hartford Hospital.
Richard, James S. *s.j.* '70 (DEN) [M] Denver, CO Regis Jesuit Community (The Jesuits at Regis University).
Richard, Joseph *a.a.* '46 (BO) [W] Brighton, MA Assumptionist Center.
Richard, Joseph E. '58 (RNO) Winnemucca, NV St. Paul Church.
Richard, Joseph E. '58 (SFR) On Duty Outside the Archdiocese.
Richard, Louis J. '81 (LAF) Crowley, LA St. Michael Archangel Church; Milton, LA St. Joseph Church.
Richard, Lucien *o.m.i.* '59 (BO) [W] Lowell, MA Missionary Oblates of Mary Immaculate.
Richard, Mark '96 (LAF) Rayne, LA St. Joseph Church.
Richard, Normand P. '72 (PRT) Millinocket, ME St. Martin of Tours Church.
Richard, Theodule *m.s.* '51 (FR) [K] Attleboro, MA La Salette Provincial House.
Richard, Timothy '92 (LAF) Mamou, LA St. Ann Church.
Richard, Msgr. Wayne R. '40 (LAF) Retired.
Richard, William '81 (DAL) Rockwall, TX Our Lady of the Lake Church.
Richards, Damian '92 (SAL) Atwood, KS Sacred Heart Church; Herndon, KS Assumption Church.
Richards, Edward W. '59 (BRK) [217] Queens, NY Our Lady of Perpetual Help Church.
Richards, Fabian '80 (ORG) Brea, CA St. Angela Merici Church.
Richards, George J. '95 (NOR) [1] Norwich, CT St. Patrick Cathedral.
Richards, Harry G. '91 (PH) North Wales, PA Mary, Mother of the Redeemer Church.
Richards, John M. '85 (CLV) Absent on Leave.
Richards, Joseph D. '90 (CR) Leave of Absence.
Richards, Lawrence '89 (E) [23] Erie, PA St. Luke Church; [C] Erie, PA Cathedral Preparatory School; [P] Erie, PA Newman Centers and Campus Ministry.
Richards, Richard E. *a.a.* '50 (BO) [W] Brighton, MA Assumptionist Center.
Richardson, Albert '83 (HT) Retired.
Richardson, Donald '57 (GLP) On Duty Outside of Diocese.
Richardson, Francis X. '93 (ATL) Lookout Mountain, GA Our Lady of the Mount Church.
Richardson, James *s.c.* '92 (HRT) [1] New Haven, CT Sacred Heart Church; [16] New Haven, CT St. Peter Church.
Richardson, James E. '65 (WIL) Special Assignment.
Richardson, John L. '54 (R) Retired.
Richardson, John T. *c.m.* '49 (CHI) [C] Chicago, IL De Paul University; [C] Chicago, IL Vincentian Community at DePaul University.
Richardson, M. Paul '91 (ARL) Falls Church, VA St. Philip Church.
Richardson, Peter *glmy.* (CIN) [M] Fairfield, OH Headquarters of Glenmary Home Missioners.
Richardson, Peter *glmy.* (LEX) West Liberty, KY Prince of Peace Church.
Richardson, Robert C. '71 (WDC) Chillum, MD St. John Baptist de la Salle Church.
Richardson, Robert C. '87 (BUR) Cambridge, VT St. Mary Church; [J] Burlington, VT University of Vermont-The Catholic Center at UVM.
Richardson, Msgr. Ronald A. '61 (RVC) Babylon, NY St. Joseph's Church.
Richardson, William *s.s.j.* (BEA) Beaumont, TX Baptist Hospital; Beaumont, TX Columbia Beaumont Hospital.
Richardson, William J. *s.j.* '53 (BO) [W] Chestnut Hill, MA The Jesuit Community at Boston College.
Richardson, Msgr. William M. '72 (HBG) [1] Harrisburg, PA Cathedral Parish of St. Patrick Church.
Richardson, William O. *s.j.* '52 (SFR) [N] San Francisco, CA Jesuit Community at University of San Francisco.
Richardt, J. Lawrence '62 (IND) [A] St. Meinrad, IN St. Meinrad Seminary.
Richart, Paul F. '61 (IND) Sellersburg, IN St. Paul Church.
Richel, Michael C. '87 (MAD) Lodi, WI St. Patrick Church.
Richers, David *s.s.c.* '52 (OM) [K] St. Columbans, NE St. Columban's Foreign Mission Society.
Richert, Antoine *s.m.m.* '62 (PMB) Fort Pierce, FL Notre Dame Mission Church.
Richetta, John J. '55 (MIL) [7] Kenosha, WI Our Lady of Mount Carmel Church.
Richey, Msgr. Dennis A. '66 (ALN) [I] Pottsville, PA Queen of Peace Apartments.
Richey, Herbert '78 (TOL) Absent on Sick Leave.
Richey, Msgr. Terrence '64 (LA) [53] Los Angeles, CA St. Camillus De Lellis Church; Los Angeles, CA St. Camillus Center for Pastoral Care.
Richling, Theodore L. '71 (OM) [39] Omaha, NE St. Richard Church.
Richman, Bertrand N. '62 (PRO) Tiverton, RI St. Theresa's Church.
Richman, Randy (DM) Ankeny, IA Our Lady's Immaculate Heart Church; Elkhart, IA St. Mary/Holy Cross Church.
Richmeier, Garry *c.pp.s.* '83 (KC) [8] Kansas City, MO St. Charles Borromeo Church.
Richmond, John A. *s.m.* '39 (WDC) [M] Washington, DC Marist Provincial House.
Richmond, Thomas C. '93 (OM) [C] Omaha, NE Creighton Preparatory School.
Richstatter, Thomas *o.f.m.* '66 (IND) [A] St. Meinrad, IN St. Meinrad Seminary.
Richter, David T. '86 (SHP) Zwolle, LA St. Joseph Church.
Richter, Helmut '94 (OAK) [2] Fremont, CA Holy Spirit Church.
Richter, Msgr. James B. '51 (RVC) Huntington, NY St. Patrick's Church.
Richter, John '78 (DM) On Duty Outside the Diocese.
Richter, John A. '64 (NU) Sleepy Eye, MN St. Mary Church.
Richter, Msgr. Kevin M. '88 (SC) Hawarden, IA St. Mary's Church.
Richter, Norbert M. '41 (RCK) Retired.
Richter, Raynor E. '47 (JOL) Lombard, IL Sacred Heart Church; Retired.
Richter, Robert J. '67 (MIL) Military Chaplains.
Richter, Thomas J. '96 (BIS) [1] Bismarck, ND Cathedral of the Holy Spirit.
Richter, William '58 (TOL) Retired.
Richtsteig, Erik J. '94 (SLC) Helper, UT St. Anthony's Church.
Ricken, David L. *j.c.l.* '80 (PBL) On Duty Outside the Diocese.
Rickert, William J. '45 (GB) Hollandtown, WI St. Francis Church; Retired.
Rickey, James E. '69 (PEO) Campus, IL Sacred Heart Church; Dwight, IL St. Patrick's Church; Dwight, IL Dwight Correctional Center.
Rickle, William C. *s.j.* '79 (PH) [82] Philadelphia, PA Old St. Joseph's Church.
Ricks, Paul C. '78 (SAC) Jackson, CA St. Patrick's Church.
Rickson, Stephen E. '90 (TUC) Absent on Leave.
Rico, Herminio *s.j.* '93 (BO) [W] Chestnut Hill, MA The Jesuit Community at Boston College.
Ridella, Joseph '52 (VNN) Retired.
Ridge, Thomas P. '38 (TR) Retired.
Ridgell, John E. '67 (RIC) Gloucester, VA St. Therese, the Little Flower Church.
Ridgeway, Kenneth *s.m.* '69 (PRT) Brunswick, ME St. John the Baptist Church.
Ridgway, John K. *s.j.* '82 (DEN) [M] Denver, CO Regis Jesuit Community (The Jesuits at Regis University).
Ridi, Pio '47 (P) Retired.
Ridick, George J. '73 (WOR) [20] Worcester, MA St. Catherine of Sweden Church.
Riding, Ratmond *s.t.* (SJN) [2] Canovanas, PR Resurreccion del Senior Church.
Ridley, Harold E. *s.j.* '69 (BAL) [C] Baltimore, MD Loyola College; [C] Baltimore, MD Loyola College; [M] Baltimore, MD Jesuit Community of Loyola College, Inc.
Ridore, Danis '67 (PMB) [2] Delray Beach, FL Our Lady of Perpetual Help Mission Church.
Ridyard, John J. *m.m.* '56 (SJ) [M] Los Altos, CA Maryknoll.
Riebe, Bruce '85 (PRM) Brecksville, OH St. Joseph Church.
Riebe, Gary *s.v.d.* '71 (LA) Graduate Studies.
Riebe, Loren '70 (PHX) [6] Scottsdale, AZ St. Maria Goretti Church.
Riebe, Todd M. *m.c.c.j.* '80 (IND) Richmond, IN Holy Family Church; Richmond, IN St. Andrew Church; Richmond, IN St. Mary Church; Richmond, IN Richmond State Hospital; [N] Richmond, IN Earlham College Newman Center.
Riebe-Estrella, Gary '71 (CHI) [B] Chicago, IL The Catholic Theological Union at Chicago; [B] Chicago, IL The Catholic Theological Union at Chicago; [B] Techny, IL Divine Word Residence; [N] Techny, IL Society of the Divine Word, Provincial Headquarter-Chicago Prov.
Riebe-Estrella, Gary L. *s.v.d.* '71 (CHI) [N] Chicago, IL Divine Word Theologate.
Rieboldt, Richard '75 (LAF) On Duty Outside the Diocese.
Rieck, Raymond '56 (SFD) Retired.
Riede, Clifford A. '52 (L) Retired.
Riedel, Richard R. *c.pp.s.* '52 (CIN) Celina, OH Immaculate Conception of the Blessed Virgin Mary Church.
Riedel, Robert B. '92 (WDC) Valley Lee, MD St. George Church.
Riedemann, Kenneth '64 (SCL) Kensington, MN Our Lady of the Runestone Church; Lake Reno, MN St. John Nepomuk Church.
Rieden, Thomas W. *o.s.f.s.* '68 (LAN) [B] Jackson, MI Lumen Christi High School.

Rieder, David J. '56 (SCL) Perham, MN St. Henry's Church; Perham, MN St. Stanislaus Church.
Rieder, Donald '55 (SCL) Retired.
Rieder, Michael J. '94 (RVC) Port Jefferson, NY Infant Jesus Church.
Rieder, Ronald *o.f.m.cap.* '63 (FTW) Huntington, IN SS. Peter and Paul Church.
Riedl, Paul D. '35 (SPR) Retired; [H] Holyoke, MA Sisters of Providence Care Centers, Inc.
Riedman, John '62 (SFS) Garretson, SD St. Rose of Lima Church.
Riedman, Joseph G. '56 (IND) [8] Indianapolis, IN Holy Spirit Church.
Riedmann, Boniface *s.a.* '45 (BO) [P] Brockton, MA Chapel of Our Savior-Catholic Pastoral and Information Center; [W] Brockton, MA Chapel of Our Saviour; [BB] Brockton, MA Chapel of Our Saviour.
Riedmann, Boniface *s.a.* '45 (LUB) Anson, TX St. Michael's Church.
Riedmueller, Leo A. '48 (LR) Hot Springs National Park, AR St. Mary's of the Springs Church.
Riedy, Robert I. (PH) Spring City, PA St. Joseph Church.
Riedy, Robert I. '39 (PH) Retired.
Rieger, Alan J. *o.c.d.* '61 (MIL) [P] Milwaukee, WI Provincial Offices - Discalced Carmelites.
Riegler, Frederick J. '67 (PH) [77] Philadelphia, PA St. John the Baptist Church.
Riehle, James L. *c.s.c.* '64 (FTW) [B] Notre Dame, IN University of Notre Dame Du Lac; [J] Notre Dame, IN Holy Cross Community, Corby Hall, University of Notre Dame.
Riel, James A. '83 (MAN) Derry, NH Holy Cross Church.
Riel, Robert H. '80 (SPR) [3] Chicopee, MA Nativity of the Blessed Virgin Mary Church.
Rielly, John *s.m.* '53 (SJ) [M] Cupertino, CA Marianist Provincial Residence.
Rieman, Richard W. '58 (BO) [V] Chestnut Hill, MA Opus Dei.
Riemer, Matthew *m.s.h.s.* '95 (DAL) [L] Dallas, TX Marian Servants of the Holy Spirit.
Rien, Robert K. '74 (OAK) [19] Oakland, CA St. Paschal Baylon Church.
Riendeau, Richard '57 (SPR) South Hadley, MA St. Theresa of the Infant Jesus Church.
Riendeau, Walter A. *s.s.s.* '50 (SLC) Eureka, UT St. Patrick's Church; Payson, UT San Andres Church.
Riepe, Charles K. '60 (BAL) Special Assignment; [O] Baltimore, MD Archdiocesan Office-Newman Center.
Riera, John *t.o.r.* '48 (NEW) [20] Newark, NJ Immaculate Heart of Mary Church.
Ries, Carl A. '70 (DUB) Mason City, IA St. Joseph's Church.
Ries, Donald C. '59 (SC) Fort Dodge, IA Corpus Christi Church.
Ries, James C. '93 (ORG) Placentia, CA St. Joseph Church.
Ries, Richard S. '63 (SC) Le Mars, IA St. James Church.
Ries, Victor F. (CIN) Retired.
Riesberg, Leo L. '57 (SC) Wall Lake, IA St. Joseph's Church.
Riesenberg, John J. '60 (COV) Fort Thomas, KY St. Thomas Church.
Riesthuis, Henk *m.h.m.* '59 (LA) [R] Los Angeles, CA Mill Hill Missionaries Procure.
Rietti, John '57 (JKS) Lexington, MS St. Thomas Church; [G] Lexington, MS Holmes Community College Newman Center.
Riffle, David '67 (B) Emmett, ID Sacred Heart Church.
Riffle, Donald J. '62 (B) [1] Boise, ID Cathedral of St. John the Evangelist.
Riffle, Douglas H. '57 (B) Retired.
Riffle, Henry J. *o.s.b.* '70 (SP) Beverly Hills, FL Our Lady of Grace Church; [O] St. Leo, FL St. Leo Abbey.
Riffle, Raymond E. '79 (GBG) [4] Greensburg, PA St. Paul Church.
Rigali, Norbert J. *s.j.* '59 (SD) [B] San Diego, CA University of San Diego.
Rigatuso, Leo '94 (OM) [48] Douglas Co., NE St. Wenceslaus Church.
Rigdon, Vincent J. '77 (WDC) [1] Silver Spring, MD St. Andrew Apostle Church; Special Ministries.
Rigert, James A. *c.s.c.* '66 (FTW) [A] Notre Dame, IN Moreau Seminary; [B] Notre Dame, IN University of Notre Dame Du Lac; [J] Notre Dame, IN Holy Cross Community, Corby Hall, University of Notre Dame.
Riggie, Kloman F. '60 (BAL) Hagerstown, MD St. Joseph, Half Way Church.
Rigney, Msgr. Dennis A. '66 (ALN) [2] Allentown, PA St. Francis of Assisi Church; [H] Bethlehem, PA Holy Family Manor; [I] Bethlehem, PA Holy Family Apartments; [I] Bethlehem, PA Trexler Pavilion, Personal Care Residence of Holy Family Manor; [I] Easton, PA Antonian Towers; [I] New Philadelphia, PA Holy Family Apartments; [I] Orwigsburg, PA Holy Family Residence; [I] Orwigsburg, PA Holy Family Adult Day Care at St. Francis Center; [I] Reading, PA Queen of Angels Apartment; [I] Bethlehem, PA Grace Mansion Personal Care Residence of Holy Manor; [J] Bethlehem, PA Holy Family Villa.
Rigney, Msgr. James '47 (NY) Retired.
Rigney, Msgr. Philip '49 (CAM) Retired.
Rigney, Msgr. Raymond P. '42 (NY) Retired; [E] White Plains, NY Archbishop Stepinac High School.
Rigoli, Anthony *o.m.i.* '72 (BUF) [27] Buffalo, NY Holy Angels Church; [R] Williamsville, NY Newman Club Chaplains.
Rigonan, Antonio R. '77 (SPC) Springfield, MO U.S. Medical Center.
Rihn, Msgr. Roy '42 (SAT) Retired; [K] San Antonio, TX Casa De Padres.
Rikteraitis, John E. '56 (HRT) [4] New Britain, CT St. Andrew's Church.
Riler, Robert '94 (SEA) Olympia, WA St. Michael's Church.
Riley, Andrew *p.i.m.e.* '80 (PMB) Lake Worth, FL Sacred Heart Church.
Riley, Daniel *o.f.m.* '71 (BUF) [Q] West Clarksville, NY Mount Irenaeus, Franciscan Mountain Retreat & Holy Peace Friary.
Riley, Daniel J. '84 (BO) [74] Boston, MA St. William Church; [4] Quincy, MA St. Joseph Church.
Riley, David J. '64 (BGP) Sherman, CT Holy Trinity Church; [E] Danbury, CT Catholic Elementary Schools-Region IX.
Riley, Dennis S. (CHI) [12] Chicago, IL St. Angela Church.
Riley, Edward H. *o.p.* '60 (CHI) [N] Chicago, IL Dominicans (Provincial Office).
Riley, George F. *o.s.a.* '62 (PH) [C] Villanova, PA Villanova University; [Z] Villanova, PA St. Thomas Monastery.
Riley, J. Norman '57 (CLV) Copley, OH Guardian Angels Church.
Riley, James *s.j.* (CLV) [U] Cleveland, OH Jesuit Retreat House.
Riley, James H. (BO) Retired.
Riley, James L. '70 (SY) New Hartford, NY Our Lady of the Rosary Church.
Riley, John '56 (ALB) Waterford, NY St. Anne Church.
Riley, John F. '55 (STP) Retired.
Riley, John J. '91 (ARL) Manassas, VA All Saints Church.
Riley, John P. *c.s.c.* '94 (FTW) [6] South Bend, IN Christ the King Church.
Riley, Kenneth A. '92 (KC) Lee's Summit, MO Our Lady of the Presentation Church.
Riley, Leo P. '82 (DUB) Clermont, IA St. Peter's Church; Postville, IA St. Bridget's Church.
Riley, Mark J. (BO) Stoneham, MA St. Patrick Church.
Riley, Mark R. '95 (CLV) [4] Lakewood, OH St. James Church.
Riley, Miles O'Brien '63 (SFR) Belmont, CA St. Mark Church; Special Assignment.
Riley, Patric '84 (KCK) [8] Topeka, KS St. Matthew Church.
Riley, Patrick '48 (SCL) Retired.
Riley, Placidus H. *o.s.b.* '46 (MAN) [K] Manchester, NH St. Anselm Abbey.
Riley, Robert D. *o.p.* '60 (WDC) [11] Washington, DC St. Dominic Church & Priory Church.
Rilley, John F. '53 (PH) Retired.
Rimassa, Paul S. '83 (TR) [10] Trenton, NJ Our Lady of Sorrows Church; Trenton, NJ Donnelly Memorial Hospital of City of Trenton.
Rimelspach, Jeffrey J. '85 (COL) Bremen, OH St. Mary Church.
Rimes, Robert B. *s.j.* '55 (MOB) [B] Mobile, AL Spring Hill College.
Rimmele, Leo *o.s.b.* '55 (P) [L] St. Benedict, OR Mt. Angel Abbey.
Rimselis, Victor *m.i.c.* '43 (CHI) [N] Chicago, IL Congregation of Marian Fathers of the Immaculate Conception.
Rimshaw, Joseph J. *s.s.j.* '48 (ORL) Retired.
Rinaldi, Francis J. *o.s.f.s.* '69 (WIL) [C] Ridgely, MD The Benedictine School for Exceptional Children; [J] Ridgely, MD St. Gertrude's Monastery, Motherhouse and Novitiate of the Sisters of St. Benedict.
Rinaldi, Nicholas *s.a.c.* '39 (CAM) Hammonton, NJ St. Joseph's Church.
Rinaldi, Vincent *o.f.m.conv.* '55 (TR) [5] Trenton, NJ Immaculate Conception Church.
Rinaldo, Alexander '39 (SP) Retired.
Rinaldo, Joseph *s.c.* '67 (LAN) [E] Chelsea, MI St. Louis Center for Exceptional Children & Adults; [L] Grass Lake, MI The Pious Union of St. Joseph.
Rindos, Paul T. '59 (HBG) Mount Joy, PA Mary, Mother of the Church.
Riney, C. Phil '48 (OWN) [2] Owensboro, KY Blessed Mother Church.
Riney, Maury '77 (OWN) Whitesville, KY St. Mary of the Woods Church.
Riney, William Jerry '75 (OWN) LaCenter, KY St. Mary Church; [4] Paducah, KY St. Thomas More Church.
Rinfret, T. Donald *s.j.* '56 (BAL) [M] Baltimore, MD Jesuit Fathers and Brothers Maryland Provincial Curia; [Q] Baltimore, MD Jesuit Seminary Guild & Jesuit Mission Bureau, Maryland Province, Inc.
Ring, Msgr. Arthur R. '37 (DM) Retired.
Ring, Daniel J. '68 (TOL) Fostoria, OH St. Wendelin Church.
Ring, Francis J. *s.j.* '47 (MIL) [P] Milwaukee, WI Jesuit Provincial Office, Wisconsin Province.
Ring, James W. *s.j.* '41 (BO) [W] Chestnut Hill, MA The Jesuit Community at Boston College.
Ring, John K. '61 (SFR) [53] San Francisco, CA St. Vincent de Paul Church.
Ring, Joseph G. '88 (SFD) Charleston, IL St. Charles Borromeo Church.
Ring, Michael '70 (SAV) [2] Augusta, GA St. Joseph's Church.
Ring, Paul L. '95 (BO) North Reading, MA St. Theresa Church.
Ring, Vincent D. '64 (SFR) San Bruno, CA St. Robert Church.
Ringenback, Gerard A. '72 (RVC) Islip Terrace, NY St. Peter the Apostle Church.
Ringenberger, Harry '69 (MIA) [12] Fort Lauderdale, FL St. Pius X Church.
Ringholz, Benedict E. '45 (TOL) Retired.
Ringwood, Joseph D. *s.j.* '59 (SPK) [K] Spokane, WA Regis Community.
Rini, John '67 (ELP) [19] El Paso, TX Our Lady of the Valley Church.
Rink, George O. '57 (SEA) Bellevue, WA St. Madeleine Sophie Church.
Rinkowski, George M. '41 (TOL) Retired.
Rinn, Richard A. *c.s.v.* '48 (CHI) [N] Arlington Heights, IL Viatorian Mission House.
Rinn, Richard A. *c.s.v.* '78 (CHI) [N] Arlington Heights, IL Clerics of St. Viator-Provincial Residence.
Rinn, Richard A. *c.s.v.* '81 (CHI) [N] Arlington Heights, IL Viatorian Province Center-Clerics of St. Viator.
Rinschler, Msgr. William J. '38 (NY) [111] New York, NY Sacred Hearts of Jesus and Mary Church; Retired.
Rinzel, Jerome A. '64 (MIL) Muskego, WI St. Leonard Congregation Church.
Riordan, Msgr. Brendan P. '70 (RVC) Deer Park, NY SS. Cyril and Methodius Church.
Riordan, Brice E. *o.carm.* '44 (NEW) Paramus, NJ Carmelite Chapel of St. Therese Church.
Riordan, Daniel F. '28 (BO) Retired.
Riordan, Eugene *s.m.a.* '53 (WDC) [M] Takoma Park, MD Society of African Missions (S.M.A.).
Riordan, Jerome F. '43 (CHI) Hanover Park, IL St. Ansgar Church; Retired.
Riordan, John B. *o.f.m.cap.* '71 (NY) [17] Yonkers, NY Sacred Heart Church.
Riordan, Patrick M. '90 (PEO) Silvis, IL Our Lady of Guadalupe Church.
Riordan, Richard J. '60 (WIN) Retired.
Rios, Angel L. *m.c.* (MGZ) Maricao, PR St. John the Baptist Church.
Rios, Francisco '91 (SJ) [14] San Jose, CA St. Leo the Great Church; San Jose, CA Santa Clara County Jail; Milpitas, CA Elmwood Rehabilitation Center.
Rios, Juan Carlos '93 (MIA) Higher Studies.
Rios, Manuel D. '86 (NEW) [1] Elizabeth, NJ St. Mary of the Assumption Church.
Rios Cappiello, Luis B. '81 (SP) New Port Richey, FL Our Lady Queen of Peace Church.
Rioux, J. Robert *c.s.c.* '56 (FR) [K] North Dartmouth, MA St. Joseph's Hall.
Rioux, Raymond '94 (LAV) [8] Las Vegas, NV St. Elizabeth Ann Seton Church.
Rioux, Raymond '94 (SR) [3] Santa Rosa, CA St. Rose of Lima Church; On Duty Outside the Diocese.
Ripko, DePaul *o.f.m.cap.* '53 (PIT) [N] Herman, PA St. Mary's Friary.
Riplog, Duane T. '84 (CHR) Summerville, SC St. John the Beloved Church.
Ripoli, Roland *o.s.b.* (PIT) Bairdford, PA St. Victor Church.
Ripoli, Roland R. *o.s.b.* '64 (GBG) [H] Latrobe, PA Saint Vincent Archabbey.
Ripp, Anthony *m.s.c.* '67 (ALN) [A] Center Valley, PA Missionaries of the Sacred Heart.
Ripp, Joseph '64 (SFS) Salem, SD St. Mary Church.
Ripper, Thomas J. *m.s.* '68 (STL) Maplewood, MO Immaculate Conception Church.
Ripperger, Edward J. '61 (IND) Mooresville, IN St. Thomas More Church.
Ripperger, Harold A. '58 (IND) Lanesville, IN St. Mary Church.
Ripperger, Mark *o.cist.* '93 (DAL) [M] Irving, TX Cistercian Abbey of Our Lady of Dallas.
Ripperger, William G. '41 (IND) Napoleon, IN St. Maurice Church.
Ripperger, William G. '55 (IND) Millhousen, IN Immaculate Conception Church.
Rippinger, Joel *o.s.b.* '74 (RCK) [H] Aurora, IL Marmion Abbey-St. Augustine's Abbey.
Ripple, Michael E. '92 (GBG) Lower Burrell, PA St. Margaret Mary Church.
Rippy, Robert J. '84 (ARL) [6] Arlington, VA Our Lady of Lourdes Church.
Risacher, James E. '52 (TOL) Retired.
Rischmann, Edward '48 (NEW) Retired.
Rischmann, Robert J. '61 (NEW) [1] East Orange, NJ

Holy Name of Jesus Church.
Risden, George '84 (SR) Clearlake, CA Our Lady, Queen of Peace Church.
Rishel, Robert F. '55 (PIT) Creighton, PA Holy Family Church.
Risley, John C. *o.p.* '65 (DEN) [28] Denver, CO St. Dominic's Church.
Risley, L. Thomas '64 (RCK) Carpentersville, IL St. Monica Church.
Riss, Dennis '84 (RC) Faith, SD St. Joseph Church.
Risse, Claire *s.v.d.* '47 (CHI) [B] Techny, IL Divine Word Residence.
Rissling, Ron *o.m.i.* (STO) Tracy, CA Deuel Vocational Institution.
Ristori, Michael *o.f.m.cap.* '53 (NY) [151] Bronx, NY Immaculate Conception Church.
Ristori, Michael *o.f.m.cap.* '60 (NEW) [4] Hackensack, NJ St. Francis Church.
Ristuccia, Leon *o.f.m.* '45 (HRT) Winsted, CT St. Joseph's Church.
Rita, Carmine J. '94 (NY) Bronxville, NY St. Joseph Church.
Rita, Thomas L. '70 (FR) Osterville, MA Our Lady of the Assumption Church.
Ritacco, Richard '76 (WOR) Absent on Leave.
Ritari, Raymond '83 (PHX) [18] Phoenix, AZ St. Martin de Porres Church; [20] Phoenix, AZ St. Matthew Church.
Ritchey, Samuel E. '73 (COL) [12] Columbus, OH Corpus Christi Church; Columbus, OH Regency Manor.
Ritchey, Scott '94 (PHX) [22] Phoenix, AZ Our Lady of the Valley Church.
Ritchey, Timothy M. '85 (B) Meridian, ID Holy Spirit Church.
Ritchie, Donald E. '59 (BUR) Waitsfield, VT Our Lady of the Snows Church; Waterbury, VT St. Andrew Church.
Ritchie, Francis J. (BO) [3] Salem, MA St. James Church.
Ritchie, Msgr. G. Carlton '32 (E) Retired.
Ritchie, Gerald T. '68 (E) [8] Erie, PA Our Lady of Mercy Church.
Ritchie, Robert T. '71 (NY) [21] New York, NY St. Catherine of Genoa Church; [M] New York, NY Society of St. Vincent De Paul, Archdiocesan Central Council of New York.
Ritchie, Vincent J. *s.j.* '74 (RVC) [P] Manhasset, NY St. Ignatius Retreat House, Inisfada.
Riter, Dennis G. '71 (BUF) [55] Buffalo, NY Our Lady of Perpetual Help Church; [66] Buffalo, NY St. Valentine Church.
Ritt, Paul E. '81 (BO) [A] Boston, MA St. John's Seminary School of Theology.
Rittenhouse, Thomas R. '76 (TR) Leave of Absence; Retired.
Ritter, Charles F. '67 (TOL) Bryan, OH St. Patrick Church.
Ritter, David '77 (JC) Missionary Assignment in Peru.
Ritter, Edward W. '51 (DET) St. Clair, MI St. Mary Church.
Ritter, J. Patrick *s.d.s.* '76 (SAC) Orangevale, CA Divine Savior Church.
Ritter, Patrick J. '74 (SEA) [2] Tacoma, WA St. Charles Borromeo Church.
Rittmeyer, Robert '80 (SP) Zephyrhills, FL St. Joseph Church; Retired.
Ritz, Robert G. *c.s.b.* '51 (GAL) Sugar Land, TX St. Theresa Church.
Ritzert, William J. '64 (PIT) Evans City, PA St. Matthias Church; Butler County, PA Deshon Veterans Hospital.
Riva, Gerald '68 (JOL) Elmhurst, IL Immaculate Conception Church.
Riva, Hugo *m.c.c.j.* '50 (CHI) Blue Island, IL St. Donatus Church; Calumet Park, IL Seven Holy Founders Church.
Riva, Paolo *c.r.s.* (MAN) [H] Allenstown, NH Pine Haven Boys Center.
Rivard, George '36 (BO) [W] Lowell, MA Missionary Oblates of Mary Immaculate.
Rivard, Robert *f.m.s.i.* '77 (BO) Waltham, MA Coordinator of Prison Ministry; [B] Framingham, MA Sylva Maria.
Rivard, Robert J. *c.m.* '44 (BRK) [D] Queens and Staten Island, NY St. John's University; [U] Jamaica, NY Vincentian Residence.
Rivard, Roland J. '56 (BUR) [2] Burlington, VT St. Anthony's Church; [F] Burlington, VT St. Joseph's Home for Aged; [F] Derby Line, VT Michaud Memorial Manor; [F] Rutland, VT Loretto Home for Aged.
Rivas, David '85 (ARE) [1] Camuy, PR St. Joseph Church.
Rivas, Jorge *o.f.m.* '48 (ELP) [B] El Paso, TX St. Anthony's School of Theology.
Rivas, Jose '70 (SJN) [23] San Juan, PR Inmaculado Corazon de Maria Church.
Rivas, Juan *l.c.* '82 (LA) [R] Pasadena, CA Legionaries of Christ; [CC] El Monte, CA Hombre Nuevo.
Rivas, Romeo '59 (MIA) [K] Miami, FL Shrine of Our Lady of Charity.
Rively, William E. *s.j.* '46 (CI) [C] Tunnuk, Chuuk, FM Vicariate Residence.
Rivera, Adalin '77 (PCE) Juana Diaz, PR Santa Teresita Church; [B] Ponce, PR The Pontifical Catholic University of Puerto Rico.
Rivera, Anastacio *s.j.* '74 (LA) [6] Los Angeles, CA Blessed Sacrament Church.
Rivera, Andres *s.d.b.* (SJN) [37] San Juan, PR Maria Auxiliadora Church.
Rivera, Antonio *m.j.* '59 (GAL) [74] Houston, TX St. Stephen Church.
Rivera, Eddie '90 (SJN) [50] San Juan, PR Nuestra Senora de la Providencia Church.
Rivera, Felix *o.carm.* (LA) [88] Los Angeles, CA St. Raphael Church.
Rivera, Guadalupe '49 (SFE) Retired.
Rivera, Hector E. '82 (MGZ) Sabana Grande, PR Church of San Isidro.
Rivera, Hilario '74 (CGS) [4] Caguas, PR Nuestra Senora de la Providencia Church.
Rivera, Jaime Velasco *o.s.b.* '93 (MIL) [P] Benet Lake, WI St. Benedict's Abbey.
Rivera, Javier *c.m.f.* '94 (SJN) [9] Bayamon, PR San Jose Church.
Rivera, Jesus *s.t.* '81 (ARL) [J] Arlington, VA Missionary Servants of the Most Holy Trinity, S.T.
Rivera, Joaquin '79 (SJN) [8] Carolina, PR San Fernando Church.
Rivera, Jose Luis *o.s.a.* '95 (GAL) Baytown, TX Our Lady of Guadalupe Church.
Rivera, Luis '84 (MIA) [11] Miami, FL Our Lady of Divine Providence Church.
Rivera, Luis Antonio '83 (CGS) San Lorenzo, PR Sagrado Corazon de Jesus y 12 Apostoles Church.
Rivera, Msgr. Manuel '79 (SJN) [39] San Juan, PR San Mateo Church.
Rivera, Miguel '83 (ARE) Corozal-Padilla, PR Our Lady of the Seven Sorrows Church.
Rivera, Narciso *o.a.r.* '77 (LSC) [3] Las Cruces, NM Our Lady of Health Church.
Rivera, Orlando '90 (PCE) Guayanilla, PR Immaculate Conception Church.
Rivera, Oscar *o.s.b.* (CGS) [6] Caguas, PR Nuestra Senora del Perpetuo Socorro Church; [C] Humacao, PR San Antonio Abad Abbey of the Order of St. Benedict.
Rivera, Ramon J. Casellas *o.f.m.cap.* '85 (SJN) [C] Rio Piedras, PR Centro Capuchino.
Rivera, Raymond L. '86 (PCE) Guayanilla, PR Immaculate Conception Church.
Rivera-Lopez, Ramon '82 (HBG) Trevorton, PA St. Patrick Church.
Rivera-Martinez, Pius *o.s.c.o.* '53 (WOR) [N] Spencer, MA St. Joseph's Abbey.
Rivero, Jordi '88 (MIA) [27] Miami, FL St. Michael the Archangel Church.
Rivero, Jordi S. '82 (MIA) [K] Miami, FL Respect Life Office.
Rivero, Juan '72 (FWT) Denton, TX Immaculate Conception Church; Denton, TX State School.
Rivero, Julio B. *t.o.r.* '69 (SP) St. Pete Beach, FL St. John Church.
Rivero, Leonides '78 (ELP) [27] El Paso, TX St. Mark Church.
Rivers, Clarence J. '56 (CIN) On Special and Diocesan Assignment.
Rivers, Clarence R.J. *ph.d.* '56 (CIN) [V] Cincinnati, OH Stimuli, Inc.
Rivers, Robert S. *c.s.p.* '68 (WDC) [B] Washington, DC St. Paul's College; [V] Washington, DC Paulist National Catholic Evangelization Assoc.
Rivet, Hilton L. *s.j.* '54 (BR) [11] Baton Rouge, LA Immaculate Conception Church.
Rivi, Geno G. '57 (GBG) Retired.
Rivituso, Mark S. '88 (STL) Bissell Hills, MO St. Jerome Church.
Rivoire, S. Joseph *s.j.* '49 (NO) [P] New Orleans, LA Ignatius Residence.
Rizo, Sergio '89 (FWT) Cleburne, TX St. Joseph Church.
Rizzi, Salvatore '41 (BRK) Retired.
Rizzo, John C. '56 (OM) [4] Omaha, NE St. Ann Church; [35] Omaha, NE St. Peter Church.
Rizzo, John V. *f.s.s.p.* '85 (SCR) [M] Elmhurst, PA Priestly Fraternity of St. Peter (F.S.S.P.).
Rizzo, Mateo J. '73 (BRK) [72] Brooklyn, NY Shrine Church of St. Jude.
Rizzo, Robert C. '74 (CHI) [214] Chicago, IL St. William Church.
Rizzotto, Msgr. Vincent M. '56 (GAL) [17] Houston, TX St. Cecilia Church.
Rizzuto, Mariano J. *s.m.* '59 (BR) Convent, LA St. Michael the Archangel Church.
Roach, Charles B. '45 (PIT) Retired.
Roach, Francis J. '56 (STP) Rosemount, MN St. Joseph Church.
Roach, Francis J. '73 (WOR) Worcester, MA Worcester State Hospital; [J] Worcester, MA Saint Vincent Hospital, Inc.
Roach, John A. (SPR) Shelburne Falls, MA St. Joseph's Church.
Roach, John E. '43 (ROC) Retired.
Roach, Joseph W. *s.a.g.* '48 (SAG) Retired.
Roach, Joseph W. *s.a.g.* '48 (SB) Retired; [E] Morongo Valley, CA St. Michael's of Morongo Valley, Inc.
Roach, Michael G. '81 (KC) [34] Kansas City, MO St. Patrick Church.
Roach, Michael J. '71 (BAL) Manchester, MD St. Bartholomew Church; [A] Emmitsburg, MD Mount St. Mary's Seminary.
Roach, Richard *s.j.* '69 (NY) [82] New York, NY Notre Dame Church.
Roach, Richard R. *s.j.* '69 (MIL) [P] Milwaukee, WI Jesuit Community at Marquette University.
Roach, Richard R. *s.j.* '69 (P) [L] Portland, OR Jesuit Provincial Office (Oregon Prov.).
Roach, Robert N. *c.s.sp.* '48 (PH) [Z] Bensalem, PA Congregation of the Holy Ghost Fathers and Brothers.
Roach, Thomas E. *s.j.* '70 (WDC) [E] North Bethesda, MD Georgetown Preparatory School.
Roach, Virgil J. *s.j.* '43 (OM) [K] Omaha, NE Jesuit Community At Creighton University.
Roache, James P. '60 (CHI) [1] Chicago, IL Cathedral of the Holy Name.
Roark, John L. '56 (SY) [11] Syracuse, NY St. Ann Church.
Roark, Michael B. '70 (KNX) Crossville, TN St. Alphonsus Church.
Robak, Anthony G. '74 (NEW) North Bergen, NJ Sacred Heart Church.
Robards, Charles P. (PEO) Thomasboro, IL St. Elizabeth's Church.
Robb, Dennis E. '74 (SEA) Everett, WA Immaculate Conception Church; Everett, WA Our Lady of Perpetual Help Church.
Robb, Kevin D. *o.p.* '77 (PRO) [P] Providence, RI St. Thomas Aquinas Priory at Providence College.
Robb, Paul V. *s.j.* '60 (CHI) [N] Chicago, IL Chicago Province of the Society of Jesus-Provincial Office.
Robbins, Charles J. *c.pp.s.* '39 (LFT) [A] Rensselaer, IN Saint Joseph's College.
Robbins, Robert J. '74 (NY) [46] New York, NY Holy Family Church.
Robbins, Roger P. '63 (SAT) Schertz, TX Church of the Good Shepherd.
Robbins, Thomas P. '74 (COV) Taylor Mill, KY St. Anthony Church; [B] Covington, KY Holy Cross High School.
Robello, Louis J. '65 (SFR) Retired.
Roberge, Francis A. '78 (WOR) Westminster, MA St. Edward the Confessor Church; [P] Worcester, MA Community of Teresian Carmelites.
Roberge, Frederick *s.s.s.* '35 (CLV) [P] Cleveland, OH Blessed Sacrament Community.
Roberge, Richard A. '85 (MAN) [3] Berlin, NH St. Kieran Church.
Roberson, Henry '71 (OKL) Special Assignment; [E] Enid, OK St. Mary Mercy Hospital.
Roberson, Michael '74 (NO) [52] New Orleans, LA SS. Peter and Paul Church.
Roberson, Ronald G. *c.s.p.* '77 (WDC) [B] Washington, DC St. Paul's College.
Robert, Darin '71 (LAN) Ann Arbor, MI University of Michigan Hospitals.
Robert, Emile A. '50 (PRO) [3] Warren, RI St. Jean Baptiste Church.
Robert, Rene '89 (STA) [1] St. Augustine, FL Cathedral of St. Augustine; [D] St. Augustine, FL Religious Education for Catholic Deaf and Blind.
Roberts, Allan '80 (LA) [10] Long Beach, CA St. Maria Goretti Church.
Roberts, Art *c.s.b.* '55 (LSC) Truth or Consequences, NM Our Lady of Perpetual Help Church.
Roberts, Don J. '78 (SFD) Oconee, IL Sacred Heart of Jesus Church; Ramsey, IL St. Joseph Church.
Roberts, Edward '41 (KCK) Retired.
Roberts, Edward *s.s.s.* '60 (CLV) [P] Cleveland, OH Congregation of the Blessed Sacrament Provincial House.
Roberts, Edward A. *s.s.c.* '60 (BO) [W] Quincy, MA St. Columban's Foreign Mission Society.
Roberts, Edward J. '96 (PEO) Pontiac, IL St. Mary's Church.
Roberts, Eugene J. '75 (TR) Marlboro, NJ St. Gabriel Church.
Roberts, G. Richard '91 (LC) Elroy, WI St. Patrick Church; Wonewoc, WI St. Jerome Church.
Roberts, Kenneth J. '66 (DAL) On Duty Outside the Diocese.
Roberts, Mark (LAV) Henderson, NV St. Peter the Apostle Church.
Roberts, Randall *o.f.m.* '84 (GB) [I] Pulaski, WI Assumption of B.V.M. Friary.
Roberts, Thomas C. '84 (NEW) Plainfield, NJ St. Bernard's Church.
Roberts, Victor W. *o.s.b.* '69 (OKL) [I] Shawnee, OK St. Gregory's Abbey.
Robertson, Douglas C. '96 (LC) Marshfield, WI St. John the Baptist Church; [C] Marshfield, WI Columbus High School; [D] Marshfield, WI Holy Family Middle School.

Robertson, Eugene '78 (STL) Fenton, MO St. Paul Church; Farmington, MO St. Joseph Church.
Robertson, Msgr. Glendon E. '57 (CAM) Gibbsboro, NJ St. Andrew the Apostle Church.
Robertson, Msgr. Harold J. '49 (NY) [1] Yonkers, NY St. Anthony Church.
Robertson, J. Felton *o.f.m.* '47 (PAT) [M] Butler, NJ St. Anthony Friary.
Robertson, James E. '77 (BO) Pembroke, MA St. Thecla Church.
Robertson, John W. '71 (HEL) Special Assignments.
Robertson, Theophane *o.f.m.* '54 (LA) [R] Santa Barbara, CA Franciscan Friary, Order of Friars Minor (Old Mission).
Robertson, Thomas J. '41 (STP) Retired.
Robertson, Thomas M. '65 (STL) Hazelwood, MO St. Bartholomew Church; Riverview Gardens, MO St. Catherine of Alexandria Church.
Robertson, Vernon W. '67 (L) [9] Louisville, KY St. Augustine Church; Retired.
Robertson, Msgr. William P. '60 (GAL) [1] Spring, TX Christ the Good Shepherd Church.
Robeson, Steve '84 (STL) Mattese, MO Mary, Mother of the Church.
Robichand, Paul G. *c.s.p.* '75 (NY) [Z] Scarsdale, NY Paulist Fathers Generalate.
Robichaud, George H. '75 (MAN) Ashland, NH St. Agnes Church.
Robichaud, J. Armand *s.m.* '50 (BO) [W] Boston, MA Marist Fathers Lourdes Residence; [BB] Boston, MA Chapel of Our Lady of Lourdes.
Robichaud, James P. *o.m.i.* '79 (BO) [11] Lowell, MA Notre Dame de Lourdes Church.
Robichaud, Paul G. *c.s.p.* '75 (WDC) [C] Washington, DC Catholic University of America, The.
Robichaux, Robie E. '76 (LAF) [15] Lafayette, LA St. Patrick Church; On Special Assignment.
Robida, Raymond A. '48 (FR) Retired.
Robillard, George M. *o.p.* '43 (PRO) [P] Providence, RI St. Thomas Aquinas Priory at Providence College.
Robillard, Joseph '84 (ORG) [6] Santa Ana, CA St. Anne's Church.
Robillard, Raymond A. '66 (FR) Absent on Leave; [K] Fall River, MA Priests' Hostel.
Robillard, Msgr. Thomas J. '44 (OG) Norfolk, NY Visitation of the B.V.M. Church; Retired.
Robin, Richard A. *s.j.* '67 (LA) [C] Los Angeles, CA Loyola Marymount University; [C] Los Angeles, CA Loyola Marymount University.
Robine, Paul M. '59 (ALT) Mundys Corner, PA St. John Vianney's Church.
Robins, Dean '85 (NO) Mandeville, LA Our Lady of the Lake Church.
Robinson, Charles *o.f.m.cap.* '70 (GF) Crow Agency, MT St. Dennis Church.
Robinson, Christopher S. *c.m.* '89 (STL) [P] Earth City, MO Congregation of the Mission Midwest Province (Vincentians).
Robinson, David C. *s.j.* '92 (SFR) [N] San Francisco, CA Jesuit Community at University of San Francisco.
Robinson, David J. *s.j.* '90 (SFR) [E] San Francisco, CA St. Ignatius College Preparatory (Coed); [N] San Francisco, CA Jesuit Community at St. Ignatius College Preparatory.
Robinson, Denis P. *c.s.sp.* '79 (PH) [Z] Bensalem, PA Congregation of the Holy Ghost Fathers and Brothers.
Robinson, Donald '80 (OG) [A] Ogdensburg, NY Wadhams Hall.
Robinson, Edmund J. *s.j.* '55 (SPK) [K] Spokane, WA Regis Community.
Robinson, Edward M. *o.p.* '41 (DAL) [M] Irving, TX Dominican Priory of St. Albert the Great.
Robinson, Edwin *o.f.m.* '68 (NEW) Wood-Ridge, NJ Our Lady of the Assumption Church.
Robinson, Ernest E. '79 (RVC) Huntington, NY St. Patrick's Church.
Robinson, Fisher *s.v.d.* '56 (LA) [71] Los Angeles, CA St. John, The Evangelist Church.
Robinson, Gerald H. *s.j.* '77 (SAC) [14] Sacramento, CA St. Ignatius Church.
Robinson, Gerald J. '64 (TOL) [29] Toledo, OH St. Jude Church; [42] Toledo, OH St. Vincent de Paul Church.
Robinson, Jack Clark *o.f.m.* '86 (SFE) [4] Albuquerque, NM Holy Family Church.
Robinson, Msgr. James P. *s.s.e.* '57 (DET) [1] Detroit, MI Cathedral, Church of the Most Blessed Sacrament.
Robinson, Jerome (MOB) On Leave from the Archdiocese.
Robinson, John *o.s.b.* '61 (CHY) On Leave of Absence.
Robinson, John *o.s.b.* '61 (PBL) [E] Canon City, CO Holy Cross Abbey.
Robinson, John A. '71 (CHI) Elk Grove Village, IL Queen of the Rosary Church.
Robinson, John C. '54 (MOB) [6] Mobile, AL Holy Family Church.
Robinson, Joseph A. '64 (CIN) [18] Cincinnati, OH St. Boniface Church.
Robinson, Joseph P. '68 (BO) Bedford, MA St. Michael Church; Boston, MA V.A. Medical Centers; Military & VA Chaplains.
Robinson, Ken '92 (FWT) [10] Fort Worth, TX St. George Church.
Robinson, Lawrence F. *s.j.* '65 (P) [D] Portland, OR Jesuit High School.
Robinson, Lynn *o.s.b.* '93 (IND) [J] St. Meinrad, IN St. Meinrad Archabbey.
Robinson, Michael Dean '96 (SD) [23] San Diego, CA St. Charles Church.
Robinson, Monte E. '75 (MAD) Belmont, WI St. Philomena Church.
Robinson, Patrick '91 (PHX) Chandler, AZ St. Benedict Church
Robinson, Paul *o.carm.* '67 (JOL) [J] Darien, IL Carmelite Fathers Provincial Office.
Robinson, Perry L. *s.j.* '72 (OM) [K] Omaha, NE Jesuit Community At Creighton University.
Robinson, Richard J. '71 (MIL) Armstrong, WI Our Lady of Angels Church; Dotyville, WI St. Michael Church
Robinson, Robert M. '69 (BRK) [224] Queens, NY St. Patrick Church.
Robinson, Tyrone '79 (DET) [47] Detroit, MI Martyrs of Uganda Church.
Robisch, David C. '62 (CIN) [61] Cincinnati, OH St. Mary Church.
Robitaille, Henry J. '39 (PRO) Retired.
Robitaille, Jean C. *m.afr.* '73 (SP) [O] St. Petersburg, FL Missionaries of Africa.
Robitaille, Joseph S. '57 (ALB) [3] Cohoes, NY St. Joseph Church.
Robitaille, Marcel '64 (PRT) [I] Waterville, ME Mt. St. Joseph Priest Retirement Home.
Robitaille, Raymond '45 (LAF) [G] New Iberia, LA Consolata Home.
Robitaille, Raymond '47 (LAF) Retired.
Robitaille, Yves '53 (ALX) Retired.
Robl, Eugene J. '50 (JC) Columbia, MO Veterans' Administration Medical Center.
Robles, Antonio '61 (CGS) [C] Aibonito, PR Casa Salesiana de Retiros.
Robles, Victor G. '86 (AUS) Bryan, TX Santa Teresa's Church.
Robles-Sanchez, Jose' A. '95 (ALX) Marksville, LA St. Joseph's Church.
Robling, Landelin *o.s.b.* '52 (SCL) New Munich, MN Immaculate Conception Church; St. Martin, MN St. Martin's Church.
Robotnik, Lawrence R. '57 (COV) Bellevue, KY Sacred Heart Church.
Robouam, Thierry-Jean *s.j.* '92 (OAK) [N] Berkeley, CA Jesuit Community at Jesuit School of Theology at Berkeley.
Roby, Brian '96 (OWN) LaCenter, KY St. Mary Church; [4] Paducah, KY St. Thomas More Church.
Roca, Albert L. '77 (MET) Port Murray, NJ St. Theodore Church.
Roca, Casimiro *s.f.* '43 (SFE) Chimayo, NM Holy Family Church.
Roca, W. Wayne *s.j.* '70 (NO) [C] New Orleans, LA Loyola University.
Rocca, Gregory *o.p.* '77 (OAK) [A] Berkeley, CA Dominican School of Philosophy and Theology; [A] Berkeley, CA Dominican School of Philosophy and Theology; [N] Oakland, CA Dominican Order, Siena House.
Rocca, Peter D. *c.s.c.* '74 (FTW) [A] Notre Dame, IN Moreau Seminary; [B] Notre Dame, IN University of Notre Dame Du Lac; [B] Notre Dame, IN University of Notre Dame Du Lac.
Rocchi, Frank J. '82 (NEW) Maplewood, NJ Immaculate Heart of Mary Church.
Rocco, Daniel '90 (CAM) Haddonfield, NJ Christ the King Regional School Church.
Rocco, Msgr. Remigio G. '66 (PAT) Haskell, NJ St. Francis of Assisi Church.
Rocha, Ivo D. '66 (STO) Tracy, CA St. Bernard's Church.
Rocha, Manuel '30 (SPR) Retired; [H] Springfield, MA St. Michael's Residence.
Rocha, Michael '88 (LA) Santa Monica, CA St. Monica Church.
Rocha, Victor J. '53 (PIT) [64] Pittsburgh, PA Resurrection Church.
Rocha-Sosa, Carlos '96 (ATL) [8] Atlanta, GA Sacred Heart of Jesus Church.
Rochacewicz, Thomas *c.ss.r.* (BRK) [U] Brooklyn, NY Our Lady of Good Counsel Residence.
Roche, Allan E. '46 (BO) Retired.
Roche, Christopher J. '31 (BUF) Retired; [O] Buffalo, NY Sheehan Residence for Priests.
Roche, David '58 (PEO) [J] Pontiac, IL Saint James Hospital.
Roche, David V. '42 (BUF) Retired.
Roche, Evan *o.f.m.* '43 (ALB) [12] Albany, NY Our Lady of Angels Church.
Roche, John S. *s.s.c.* '59 (BO) [W] Quincy, MA St. Columban's Foreign Mission Society.
Roche, Msgr. M. Edward '36 (CHI) Chicago Ridge, IL Our Lady of the Ridge Church; Retired.
Roche, Matthew F. *s.j.* '81 (RVC) Oceanside, NY St. Anthony Church.
Roche, Randall H. *s.j.* '68 (HON) [7] Honolulu, HI Newman Center at the University of Hawaii, Holy Spirit Parish Church; [H] Honolulu, HI Jesuit Fathers House.
Roche, Robert *o.s.b.* '62 (ALT) Patton, PA Our Lady of Perpetual Help Church; Patton, PA Queen of Peace Church.
Roche, Ronald '61 (PBL) [11] Pueblo, CO St. Francis Xavier Church.
Roche, Msgr. William H. '50 (BO) [1] Boston, MA Cathedral of the Holy Cross; Retired.
Roche, William J. '59 (BUF) [M] Lancaster, NY St. Elizabeth's Home.
Roche, Msgr. William M. '55 (ROC) Retired.
Roche, Msgr. William M. '55 (SFR) Redwood City, CA Our Lady of Mount Carmel Church.
Rocheford, Dennis J. '77 (WOR) Military Chaplains.
Rochefort, Maurice J. '66 (MAN) Exeter, NH St. Michael Church.
Rochel, Anthony J. *s.j.* '51 (STL) [P] St. Louis, MO Jesuit Community Corporation at St. Louis University - Jesuit Hall.
Rocheleau, Raymond '52 (BR) Retired.
Rochford, E. Michael '62 (CHI) Missionary Work.
Rochford, John J. '47 (CHI) Country Club Hills, IL St. Emeric Church; Retired.
Rochford, Michael '62 (CHI) [148] Chicago, IL Our Lady of Grace Church.
Rochon, Bernard M. *s.m.* '58 (SAT) [67] San Antonio, TX St. Timothy's Church.
Rochon, Bernard M. *s.m.* '58 (STL) [P] St. Louis, MO Provincialate of the Society of Mary, Province of St. Louis.
Rochon, Robert A. '74 (FR) [H] Fall River, MA Saint Anne's Hospital.
Rochon, Robert A. '74 (PRO) [4] Central Falls, RI Notre Dame Church; On Duty Outside the Diocese.
Rock, John J. '54 (NEW) Retired.
Rock, John J. *s.j.* '87 (WH) [A] Wheeling, WV Wheeling Jesuit University.
Rock, Joseph A. '72 (ALN) [H] Bethlehem, PA Holy Family Manor; [J] Bethlehem, PA Holy Family Villa.
Rock, Leo P. *s.j.* '58 (SJ) [B] Santa Clara, CA Santa Clara University.
Rock, Martin *s.j.* '59 (SLC) [4] Ogden, UT St. Mary's Church.
Rock, Michael *o.de.m.* '86 (BUF) [O] LeRoy, NY Order of the BVM of Mercy/Mercedarian Friars.
Rock, Richard J. *c.m.* '73 (PH) [69] Philadelphia, PA Immaculate Conception Church.
Rock, Russell L. '62 (CAM) Haddon Township, NJ St. Vincent Pallotti Church; [A] Haddonfield, NJ Paul VI High School.
Rock, Stephen B. '74 (BO) Military & VA Chaplains.
Rock, William J. *o.p.* '58 (Y) [13] Youngstown, OH St. Dominic's Church.
Rockenstein, James *o.f.m.* '57 (SAC) Lincoln, CA St. Joseph Church.
Rocker, Stephen R. '79 (OG) [A] Ogdensburg, NY Wadhams Hall.
Rockers, Alfred '62 (KCK) Leawood, KS Church of the Nativity.
Rockford, Thomas M. *s.j.* '76 (WDC) [M] Washington, DC Leonard Neale House.
Rocky, Ronald *o.f.m.conv.* '84 (SB) [3] Riverside, CA Queen of Angels Church.
Rodak, Joseph V. *c.pp.s.* '62 (LFT) [A] Rensselaer, IN Saint Joseph's College.
Rodakowski, Louis '42 (P) Retired.
Rodas, Mauro G. '65 (IND) [32] Indianapolis, IN St. Mary/Immaculate Conception Church.
Rodda, Regis *o.f.m.conv.* '59 (SY) [2] Syracuse, NY Assumption B.V.M. Church.
Roddy, James *s.s.c.* '41 (PRO) [P] Bristol, RI St. Columban's Retirement House.
Rodeghero, Jeffery A.G. '84 (STF) Pittsfield, MA St. John the Baptist Church; Hudson, NY St. Nicholas Church.
Rodell, Jeremiah J. '47 (CHI) Retired.
Roden, Raymond P. '81 (BRK) [216] Queens, NY Our Lady of Mount Carmel Church; [G] Astoria, NY St. John Preparatory School.
Roden-Lucero, Edward G. '82 (ELP) [3] El Paso, TX Blessed Juan Diego Parish Church.
Rodenfels, Jerome P. '74 (COL) New Albany, OH Church of the Resurrection.
Rodenspiel, James E. '64 (B) Chubbuck, ID St. Paul's Church.
Roder, Terry A. '88 (SC) Dedham, IA St. Joseph's Church; [B] Carroll, IA Kuemper Catholic High School.
Rodgers, Arthur E. '65 (PH) Bala-Cynwyd, PA St. Matthias Church.
Rodgers, Dermot *o.f.m.cap.* '91 (HBG) [2] York, PA St. Joseph Church.
Rodgers, Francis M. '41 (PIT) Retired; [N] Pittsburgh, PA St. John Vianney Manor.
Rodgers, Kenneth W. '43 (GB) Retired.
Rodgers, Kieran *o.s.b.* '46 (ALT) Carrolltown, PA St. Benedict's Church.

Rodgers, Philip F. '81 (ALN) Boyertown, PA St. Columbkill Church.
Rodgers, Thomas M. '44 (PIT) Retired; [R] Pittsburgh, PA Society of Saint Vincent de Paul.
Rodgers, Msgr. William J. '49 (BRK) Retired; [R] Queens Village, NY Queen of Peace Residence.
Rodi, Msgr. Thomas J. '78 (NO) Unassigned.
Rodia, James C. *o.praem.* '72 (PH) [D] Philadelphia, PA St. John Neumann High School; [Z] Philadelphia, PA St. Norbert Priory.
Rodighiero, Dominic *c.s.* '61 (NY) [Z] Staten Island, NY Scalabrinian Missionaries.
Rodini, Rick '83 (SJ) [C] San Jose, CA Archbishop Mitty High School.
Rodino, Salvatore A. '80 (ALB) Speigletown, NY St. Bonaventure Church.
Rodis, James '60 (STL) [19] St. Louis, MO St. Agatha Church.
Rodis, Rodney '86 (RIC) Buckner, VA Immaculate Conception Church; Mineral, VA St. Jude Church.
Rodman, Hugh B. *s.j.* '42 (CHI) [C] Chicago, IL Jesuit Community at Loyola University of Chicago.
Rodney, John *s.v.d.* '60 (WDC) [5] Washington, DC St. Anthony Church; [M] Washington, DC Divine Word College.
Rodney, Joseph C. *s.s.j.* '68 (BR) Napoleonville, LA St. Benedict the Moor Church.
Rodo, Anthony C. '55 (PH) Ridley Park, PA St. Madeline Church.
Rodoni, Rick '91 (SJ) [1] San Jose, CA St. Joseph Cathedral.
Rodrigo, Marcelo Blazquez (NY) State, NY Woodbourne Correctional Facility.
Rodrigo, Salvador *o.carm.* '62 (ARE) Ciales, PR Holy Rosary Church.
Rodrigues, Alberto *o.s.s.t.* '87 (PMB) [1] West Palm Beach, FL Holy Name of Jesus Church.
Rodrigues, Alberto Edgardo *o.ss.t.* '87 (BAL) [M] Baltimore, MD Holy Trinity Monastery.
Rodrigues, Amancio '66 (P) [30] Portland, OR Queen of Peace Church.
Rodrigues, Anthony '54 (RIC) Big Stone Gap, VA Sacred Heart Church; Pennington Gap, VA Church of the Holy Spirit.
Rodrigues, Antonio '33 (MRY) Retired.
Rodrigues, Carlos '95 (BGP) [3] Bridgeport, CT St. Andrew Church.
Rodrigues, Ignatius '66 (SB) [2] Riverside, CA Our Lady of Perpetual Help Church.
Rodrigues, Januarius E. '59 (SAC) [9] Sacramento, CA St. Anne Church.
Rodrigues, Joseph *s.d.s.* '93 (MIL) [P] Milwaukee, WI Salvatorian Provincial Residence.
Rodrigues, Sabbas '61 (RVC) Commack, NY Christ the King Church.
Rodrigues, Santos '70 (SFR) [33] San Francisco, CA Mission Dolores Basilica.
Rodriguez, Alberto *o.p.* '71 (NO) [25] New Orleans, LA St. Anthony Of Padua Church; [P] New Orleans, LA Dominican Fathers & Brothers, Southern Dominican Province; [P] New Orleans, LA Dominican Fathers & Brothers, Southern Dominican Province; [S] Metairie, LA Southern Dominican Foundation.
Rodriguez, Aloysius M. '66 (BR) Military Chaplains.
Rodriguez, Anthony *l.c.* '83 (HRT) [B] Cheshire, CT Novitiate of the Legion of Christ.
Rodriguez, Antonio *i.s.s.s.* (CC) On Special Assignment.
Rodriguez, Antonio *o.carm.* '79 (ARE) Morovis, PR Nuestra Senora del Carmen Church.
Rodriguez, Antonio '93 (MAD) Sun Prairie, WI Sacred Hearts of Jesus and Mary Church.
Rodriguez, Antonio *c.c.* '93 (MIL) [T] Waukesha, WI Secular Institute of Schoenstatt Fathers.
Rodriguez, Antonio L. '49 (BUF) [33] Buffalo, NY Immaculate Conception Church.
Rodriguez, Armando J. '55 (GAL) [58] Houston, TX Our Lady of St. John Church.
Rodriguez, Arturo '84 (YAK) Bridgeport, WA St. Anne's Church.
Rodriguez, Astor L. *c.m.* '93 (BRK) [116] Brooklyn, NY St. Peter-St. Paul-Our Lady of Pilar Church; [116] Brooklyn, NY St. Peter-St. Paul-Our Lady of Pilar Church.
Rodriguez, Ben M. '91 (PEO) [11] Peoria, IL St. Martin de Porres Church.
Rodriguez, Benigno Antonio '66 (LA) Baldwin Park, CA St. John the Baptist Church.
Rodriguez, Bernardo '80 (BGP) [5] Stamford, CT Our Lady of Montserrat Church.
Rodriguez, Carlos *o.c.s.o.* '70 (L) [L] Trappist, KY Abbey of Our Lady of Gethsemani, of the Order of Cistercians of the Strict Observance.
Rodriguez, Carlos M. '87 (NY) [134] Bronx, NY Blessed Sacrament Church.
Rodriguez, D. Andres G. '36 (RIC) Retired.
Rodriguez, David *o.f.m.* (CHI) [D] Chicago, IL Hales Franciscan High School, Inc.
Rodriguez, Delfin '86 (ARE) [3] Arecibo, PR Nuestra Senora del Carmen Church.
Rodriguez, Domingo *s.t.* '67 (ARL) [J] Arlington, VA Missionary Servants of the Most Holy Trinity, S.T.
Rodriguez, Edmundo *s.j.* '66 (LAF) [A] Grand Coteau, LA St. Charles College.
Rodriguez, Eduardo *m.id.* (NY) [180] Bronx, NY Santa Maria Church; [Z] Bronx, NY Idente Missionaries of Santa Maria Residence; [CC] New York, NY University Apostolate.
Rodriguez, Eduardo *o.c.s.o.* '69 (ATL) [I] Conyers, GA The Monastery of the Holy Spirit.
Rodriguez, Msgr. Efranin '74 (SJN) [31] San Juan, PR Nuestra Senora de Lourdes Church.
Rodriguez, Epifanio *o.p.* '54 (CC) Benavides, TX St. Rose of Lima Church; [H] San Diego, TX Vicariate of Holy Rosary.
Rodriguez, Fabian *s.j.* '66 (SJN) [22] San Juan, PR San Ignacio de Loyola Church.
Rodriguez, Francis *o.c.s.o.* '55 (WOR) [N] Spencer, MA St. Joseph's Abbey.
Rodriguez, Gilbert '74 (SAN) [2] Midland, TX Our Lady of Guadalupe Church; [3] Midland, TX Our Lady of San Juan de Los Lagos Church.
Rodriguez, Guillermo '56 (SFR) Retired.
Rodriguez, Guillermo '69 (LA) [11] Long Beach, CA St. Matthew Church.
Rodriguez, Guillermo '75 (SAC) Marysville, CA St. Joseph Church.
Rodriguez, Henry '86 (SD) [30] San Diego, CA St. Jude Church.
Rodriguez, J. Rigoberto '89 (LA) [93] Los Angeles, CA St. Thomas the Apostle Church.
Rodriguez, Jesse *s.j.* '95 (BO) [W] Chestnut Hill, MA The Jesuit Community at Boston College.
Rodriguez, Jesus A. '93 (ARE) [4] Manati, PR Nuestra Senora del Mar Church.
Rodriguez, Joaquin '72 (MIA) Coconut Grove, FL St. Hugh Church.
Rodriguez, Msgr. John F. '59 (SFR) [2] Menlo Park, CA St. Denis Church.
Rodriguez, Jorge *o.f.m.conv.* (PAT) [10] Paterson, NJ St. Mary's Church.
Rodriguez, Jose *o.s.b.* '63 (CGS) [C] Humacao, PR San Antonio Abad Abbey of the Order of St. Benedict.
Rodriguez, Jose '75 (GLP) Overgaard, AZ Our Lady of Assumption Church; Snowflake, AZ Our Lady of the Snows Church.
Rodriguez, Jose A. (SFR) [11] San Francisco, CA St. Charles Borromeo Church.
Rodriguez, Jose A. '80 (ARE) [1] Vega-Baja, PR Holy Rosary Church.
Rodriguez, Jose Andres '95 (WOR) [27] Worcester, MA St. Peter Church.
Rodriguez, Jose Diego '81 (PCE) Villalba, PR Our Lady of Mt. Carmel Church.
Rodriguez, Jose Trinidad '92 (LA) [15] Los Angeles, CA Immaculate Conception Church.
Rodriguez, Juan '79 (PCE) [B] Ponce, PR The Pontifical Catholic University of Puerto Rico.
Rodriguez, Lawrence '52 (LA) Retired.
Rodriguez, Luis *s.j.* '65 (MIL) [P] Wauwatosa, WI Jesuit Community at St. Camillus.
Rodriguez, Luis R. '93 (HBG) New Cumberland, PA St. Theresa of the Infant Jesus Church.
Rodriguez, Manuel '62 (ATL) [I] Conyers, GA The Monastery of the Holy Spirit.
Rodriguez, Manuel J. *o.s.a.* '59 (BRK) [U] Forest Hills, NY Augustinian Fathers-Province of Castile, Spain.
Rodriguez, Martin S. *o.r.c.* '82 (SB) [5] San Bernardino, CA Our Lady of Guadalupe Church.
Rodriguez, Martin S. '92 (SB) [1] Riverside, CA Our Lady of Guadalupe Shrine Church; Riverside, CA Riverside Community Hospital.
Rodriguez, Michael '90 (SAN) Eden, TX St. Charles Church.
Rodriguez, Msgr. Pablo M. '61 (RVC) Hempstead, NY Our Lady of Loretto Church.
Rodriguez, Peter *c.m.f.* '57 (CHI) [80] Chicago, IL Holy Cross/Immaculate Heart of Mary Church.
Rodriguez, Plinio '70 (PCE) On Duty Outside the Diocese.
Rodriguez, Rafael A. '75 (CGS) Cayey, PR San Esteban Protomartir Church.
Rodriguez, Reyes G. (SLC) Salt Lake City, UT Salt Lake County Jail.
Rodriguez, Reyes G. '67 (SLC) [6] Salt Lake City, UT St. Ann Church.
Rodriguez, Ricardo *o.f.m.* '82 (ELP) [15] El Paso, TX Our Lady of Guadalupe Church.
Rodriguez, Richard *s.j.* '74 (SFE) [6] Albuquerque, NM Immaculate Conception Church.
Rodriguez, Robert '53 (MIL) Retired.
Rodriguez, Robin E. *c.m.* '73 (BRK) [104] Brooklyn, NY Our Lady of Monserrate-St. Ambrose Church.
Rodriguez, Roy '94 (CHY) [1] Cheyenne, WY St. Mary's Cathedral.
Rodriguez, Ruben *o.carm.* (NY) [189] Bronx, NY St. Simon Stock Church.
Rodriguez, Salvador (ARE) On Duty Outside the Diocese.
Rodriguez, Salvador '62 (SJN) [20] Carolina, PR San Valentin Church.
Rodriguez, Silvestre *o.f.m.* '48 (CC) [6] Laredo, TX San Augustine Church.
Rodriguez Gamboa, John E. '77 (NEW) [27] Newark, NJ Our Lady of Good Counsel Church.
Rodriguez-Hernandez, Edwin '95 (ALX) [2] Alexandria, LA Our Lady of Prompt Succor Church; [J] Alexandria, LA Louisiana State University at Alexandria.
Rodriguez-Ochoa, Leonardo '91 (SJN) [10] Carolina, PR Inmaculata Concepcion Church.
Rodriguez-Utia, Mhilivetr F. '80 (ORG) [7] Santa Ana, CA St. Barbara's Church.
Rodriquez, Arturo '84 (YAK) Chelan, WA St. Francis de Sales Church.
Rodriquez, Gus, Sr. (ELP) [32] El Paso, TX St. Stephen, Deacon and Martyr Church.
Rodriquez, Nestor L. '93 (PMB) [1] Palm Beach, FL Cathedral of St. Ignatius Loyola.
Rodriquez, Reyes (SLC) Park City, UT St. Mary of the Assumption Church.
Rodulfa, Julius '85 (NY) [209] Staten Island, NY St. John Neumann Church.
Roebert, Michael '66 (LA) [9] Long Beach, CA St. Lucy Church.
Roebuck, John H. '76 (PH) [2] Drexel Hill, PA St. Bernadette Church.
Roedel, Richard P. '59 (STP) Heidelberg, MN St. Scholastica Church; Lexington, MN St. Joseph Church.
Roedel, Robert H. '56 (PH) Feasterville, PA Assumption B.V.M. Church; Absent on Sick Leave.
Roedig, Louis '53 (STL) Richmond Heights, MO Immacolata Church.
Roehrich, Andrew '50 (FAR) Windsor, ND St. Mathias Church.
Roehrich, David '84 (SFS) Colman, SD St. Peter Church; Flandreau, SD SS. Simon and Jude Church.
Roehrig, Matthew *s.s.p.* '84 (Y) [A] Canfield, OH Society of St. Paul.
Roelke, Joseph Paul *m.s.f.* '81 (STL) [66] St. Louis, MO St. Wenceslaus Church.
Roeltgen, Msgr. Kenneth W. '79 (BAL) [A] Emmitsburg, MD Mount St. Mary's Seminary; [C] Emmitsburg, MD Mount Saint Mary's College.
Roeltgen, Msgr. Kenneth W. '79 (WDC) On Duty Outside the Archdiocese.
Roensch, Frederick J. '55 (MIL) Retired.
Roensch, Msgr. Roger C. '57 (WDC) Special Ministries.
Roerig, Peter A. '64 (P) [1] Eugene, OR St. Jude Church.
Roesch, David H. '66 (ALT) Bellwood, PA St. Joseph's Church.
Roesch, Joseph *m.i.c.* '92 (SPR) [I] Stockbridge, MA Congregation of Marians; [I] Stockbridge, MA Congregation of Marians.
Roesch, Karl J. *o.s.b.* '60 (NEW) [1] Linden, NJ St. Elizabeth's Church.
Roesch, Karl J. *o.s.b.* '60 (PAT) [M] Morristown, NJ St. Mary's Abbey.
Roesslein, Charles *s.v.d.* '36 (CHI) [B] Techny, IL Divine Word Residence.
Roeten, Msgr. Winus '48 (NO) Retired.
Roets, Perry J. *s.j.* '52 (MIL) [P] Wauwatosa, WI Jesuit Community at St. Camillus.
Roetzel, Robert E. *c.s.c.* '87 (FTW) [J] South Bend, IN Congregation of Holy Cross Indiana Province Provincial House.
Roetzer, Russell G. (MIL) [1] Racine, WI St. Casimir's Church; [9] Racine, WI St. Rose Church.
Roetzer, Russell G. '63 (MIL) [E] Racine, WI St. Catherine's High School.
Rofrano, Peter J. *s.a.c.* '39 (NY) [91] New York, NY Our Lady of Mt. Carmel Church; [Z] New York, NY Pallottine Fathers.
Rog, Francis *c.r.* '55 (CHI) [88] Chicago, IL St. Hyacinth Church; [D] Chicago, IL Weber High School.
Rog, Theodore C. '64 (BUF) [4] Orchard Park, NY St. John Vianney Church.
Rogala, Gerard E. '66 (CHI) [201] Chicago, IL St. Thecla Church.
Rogalla, William '96 (LAF) [1] New Iberia, LA St. Peter Church.
Rogalski, Christopher '80 (STF) [3] Bridgeport, CT Protection of B.V.M. Church.
Rogawski, Ralph *o.p.* '59 (AUS) [H] Austin, TX Dominican Fathers.
Rogenski, Joseph (SUP) Ashland, WI Our Lady of the Lake Catholic Community Church.
Roger, Richard G. '64 (WOR) [7] Worcester, MA Notre Dame des Canadiens - St. Joseph Church; Otter River, MA Walter E. Fernald State School.
Rogers, Daniel J. (DUB) Retired.
Rogers, Foster P. '66 (ROC) [4] Auburn, NY St. Alphonsus Church.
Rogers, Francis J. '81 (WIL) Elsmere, DE Corpus Christi Church; Wilmington, DE Pennsylvania Air National Guard.
Rogers, Francis P. '46 (PH) [152] Philadelphia, PA St. Timothy Church; Retired.
Rogers, Furman '78 (MOB) Retired.
Rogers, Gary P. '72 (BRK) [51] Brooklyn, NY St. Gregory the Great Church.
Rogers, Herbert W. *s.j.* '44 (NY) [Z] New York, NY Jesuit Community at Fordham University.

Rogers, James '39 (EVN) Retired.
Rogers, James M. '51 (BO) Retired.
Rogers, Jerry '76 (CR) Detroit Lakes, MN Holy Rosary Church.
Rogers, Joseph '54 (DAV) Brooklyn, IA St. Patrick Church; [P] Brooklyn, IA St. Patrick Parish Foundation.
Rogers, Nicholas P. '55 (MAN) [14] Manchester, NH St. Patrick Church.
Rogers, Patrick W. '82 (COL) [38] Columbus, OH St. Philip The Apostle Church.
Rogers, Paul J. '77 (RVC) Holbrook, NY Good Shepherd Church.
Rogers, Peter S. *s.j.* '74 (CHL) [J] Charlotte, NC Jesuit Community.
Rogers, Peter S. *s.j.* '74 (NO) [C] New Orleans, LA Loyola University.
Rogers, Philip E. '80 (Y) Struthers, OH St. Nicholas Church.
Rogers, Robert '92 (HT) Raceland, LA St. Mary's Nativity Church.
Rogers, Stephen G. '95 (TOL) Mansfield, OH St. Peter Church.
Rogers, Thomas W. '52 (GBG) Rostraver, PA St. Anne Church.
Rogers, Vincent (KC) [4] St. Joseph, MO St. James Church.
Rogerson, Daniel '77 (SEA) On Duty Outside the Archdiocese.
Rogerson, Dave *o.s.b.* '82 (P) [A] St. Benedict, OR Mount Angel Seminary.
Rogge, Louis *o.carm.* '54 (JOL) [J] Joliet, IL St. Elias Carmelites.
Rogge, Norman J. *s.j.* '56 (LAF) [A] Grand Coteau, LA St. Charles College.
Rogina, Walter, Jr. '85 (SR) [1] Santa Rosa, CA Cathedral of St. Eugene.
Rogliano, Joseph S. '85 (BUF) Williamsville, NY St. Gregory the Great Church.
Rogusz, Joseph A. *c.s.c.* '46 (FTW) [J] South Bend, IN Congregation of Holy Cross Indiana Province Provincial House.
Roh, Raymond V. *o.s.b.* '59 (MRY) [G] San Luis Obispo, CA Monastery of the Risen Christ.
Roh, Robert A. '65 (LIN) Falls City, NE SS. Peter and Paul Church; [C] Falls City, NE Sacred Heart High School/Elementary Schools; [K] Falls City, NE Sacred Heart High School Endowment Fund.
Rohan, John P. '72 (HRT) South Windsor, CT St. Francis of Assisi Church.
Rohen, Patrick J. '96 (TOL) [2] Toledo, OH Blessed Sacrament Church.
Rohleder, Earl '63 (EVN) [13] Evansville, IN St. Anthony Church; New Harmony, IN Holy Angels Church.
Rohlfs, Msgr. Steven P. '76 (PEO) [13] Peoria, IL St. Philomena's Church.
Rohling, Msgr. George W. '39 (NSH) [8] Nashville, TN St. Mary Villa Parish Community Church; [E] Nashville, TN St. Mary Orphanage, Inc. dba St. Mary Villa; [L] Nashville, TN Ladies of Charity Welfare Agency, Inc.
Rohling, Paul '75 (BIR) [6] Birmingham, AL St. Francis Xavier Church; [I] Birmingham, AL Agape Institute of St. Teresa of Jesus.
Rohlinger, Joseph A. *o.praem* '43 (GB) [I] De Pere, WI St. Norbert Abbey.
Rohmiller, Christian A. '79 (CIN) [4] Dayton, OH St. Anthony of Padua Church; [Q] Fairborn, OH Wright State Campus Ministry Center.
Rohr, Jerome M. '94 (DEN) [1] Boulder, CO Sacred Heart of Jesus Church.
Rohr, John J. *s.j.* '60 (NEW) [C] Jersey City, NJ St. Peter's Preparatory School.
Rohr, Richard *o.f.m.* '70 (SFE) [N] Albuquerque, NM Center for Action and Contemplation.
Rohrer, Jerome E. *s.j.* '54 (MIL) [P] Wauwatosa, WI Jesuit Community at St. Camillus.
Rohrer, Richard '94 (PSC) Cary, NC SS. Cyril & Methodius Byzantine Catholic Church.
Rohrkemper, Charles B. '43 (CIN) Troy, OH St. Patrick Church; Retired.
Roia, Martino *s.x.* '82 (PAT) [M] Wayne, NJ Xaverian Missionary Fathers.
Roide, Russell J. *s.j.* '70 (SFR) [2] San Francisco, CA St. Agnes Church.
Rojas, Jaime Vazquez '83 (SJN) [20] Bayamon, PR Nuestra Senora del Rosario Church.
Rojas, Manuel I. '64 (NY) [203] Staten Island, NY St. Clement Church; [215] Staten Island, NY St. Michael Church.
Rojas, Melquiades '91 (ARE) [10] Arecibo, PR San Juan Bosco Church.
Rojas, Tito '68 (ORL) [6] Orlando, FL St. Andrew Church; Apopka, FL St. Francis of Assisi Church.
Rojas, Victor '85 (ARE) On Duty Outside the Diocese.
Rokicinski, Stanley J. '39 (CHI) [148] Chicago, IL Our Lady of Grace Church; [209] Chicago, IL St. Turibius Church; Retired.
Rokos, Richard V. '56 (PRT) Bangor, ME St. Joseph's Hospital; [H] Bangor, ME St. Joseph Hospital.
Rokosz, Charles W. '70 (SCR) Duryea, PA Holy Rosary Church.
Rolak, Patrick *o.f.m.conv.* '56 (BAL) [M] Ellicott City, MD Order of Friars Minor Conventual.
Rolak, Patrick *o.f.m.conv.* '56 (BUF) [M] Clarence, NY Brothers of Mercy Sacred Heart Home, Inc.
Roland, Charles '67 (PT) On Duty Outside the Diocese.
Roland, Charles W. '67 (SAV) Waycross, GA St. Joseph's Church.
Roldan, Basilio '59 (SJN) [55] San Juan, PR Sagrado Corazon de Jesus Church.
Roldan, Juan '56 (SJN) On Duty Outside the Archdiocese.
Rolek, John A. '61 (CHI) [5] Cicero, IL Our Lady of Charity Church.
Roleke, H. James *s.j.* '62 (BUF) [50] Buffalo, NY St. Michael Church.
Rolf, Msgr. John '57 (LEX) Mt. Sterling, KY St. Patrick Church.
Rolfes, Robert E. '77 (SCL) Rockville, MN Mary of the Immaculate Conception Church; Special Assignment.
Rolfs, Richard W. *s.j.* '61 (LA) [C] Los Angeles, CA Loyola Marymount University.
Rolfson, Gunther *o.s.b.* '46 (SCL) Farming, MN St. Catherine's Church.
Roll, Bertin *o.f.m.cap.* '42 (PIT) [N] Pittsburgh, PA St. Augustine Friary.
Roll, David H. '70 (SD) Retired.
Roll, Robert J. '77 (CHI) [170] Chicago, IL SS. Peter and Paul Church.
Roll, Ron *o.f.m.conv.* '80 (BAL) [M] Ellicott City, MD Order of Friars Minor Conventual.
Rolland, Daniel *o.p.* '93 (PHX) [F] Tempe, AZ Dominicans (Dominican Community-Jordan House); [H] Phoenix, AZ Office of Youth and Young Adult Ministries.
Rolland, Michael *o.p.* '88 (OAK) [N] Oakland, CA Western Dominican Province.
Roller, John W. '60 (CHI) [4] Mt. Prospect, IL St. Thomas a Becket Church.
Rolwing, Msgr. Richard C. '53 (SPC) [1] Cape Girardeau, MO Cathedral of St. Mary.
Rom, Gregory A. '75 (CHI) Blue Island, IL St. Isidore Church.
Roma, Paul E. '88 (MAN) Military Chaplains.
Romage, George J. '95 (WH) Clarksburg, WV Immaculate Conception Church.
Romagno, Michael '37 (ALN) Retired.
Romagosa Edward J. *s.j.* '54 (BR) [J] Convent, LA Manresa, House of Retreats.
Romagosa Msgr. Elmo L. '47 (NO) [1] Harvey, LA Infant Jesus of Prague Church.
Roman, Bede *o.s.b.* '66 (SFS) [F] Marvin, SD Blue Cloud Abbey.
Roman, Carlos '89 (PCE) [1] Ponce, PR Cathedral of Our Lady of Guadalupe.
Roman, Carlos '89 (WDC) [4] Bethesda, MD Our Lady of Lourdes Church.
Roman, Charles '70 (HEL) Whitefish, MT St. Charles Church.
Roman, Darrell *s.ch.* (DET) Hamtramck, MI St. Florian Church.
Roman, Manuel R. '56 (BAL) [11] Baltimore, MD Ascension Church.
Roman, Paul A. '71 (ALB) Oneonta, NY St. Mary Church.
Roman, Stephen '57 (SEA) Aberdeen, WA St. Mary's Church; Aberdeen, WA St. Mary's Church; Aberdeen, WA SS. Peter and Paul Church; Hoquiam, WA Our Lady of Good Help Church; Ocean Shores, WA St. Jerome Church.
Roman, Victor '84 (DET) [14] Detroit, MI St. Brendan Church.
Roman Toro, Carlos R. '89 (PCE) [B] Ponce, PR The Pontifical Catholic University of Puerto Rico.
Romanenko, Oleh '93 (STN) Los Angeles, CA Nativity of B.V.M Church.
Romani, Joseph '34 (PRT) Retired.
Romano, Blase *t.o.r.* '89 (ORL) Mount Dora, FL St. Patrick's Church.
Romano, Charles P. '79 (RVC) Farmingdale, NY St. Kilian Church.
Romano, Chuck (RVC) New Hyde Park, NY Holy Spirit Church.
Romano, Eugene L. '57 (PAT) [I] Chester, NJ Hermits of Bethlehem of the Heart of Jesus.
Romano, Harry A. '57 (PH) [2] Coatesville, PA Our Lady of the Rosary Church.
Romano, Joseph '66 (ALB) [5] Albany, NY St. Catherine of Siena Church; Coxsackie, NY Greene County Correctional Institution; Special Assignment.
Romano, Joseph E. '63 (BUR) Pittsford, VT St. Alphonsus Liguori Church.
Romano, Joseph L. '63 (DET) [7] Dearborn Heights, MI St. Sabina Church.
Romano, Philip *o.f.m.cap.* '94 (NY) [57] New York, NY St. John the Baptist Church.
Romano, Robert J. *m.div.* '77 (BRK) [18] Brooklyn, NY St. Bernadette Church.
Romanoski, Joseph V. '86 (MET) South Amboy, NJ Sacred Heart Church.
Romanowski, Francis C. '39 (BRK) [241] Queens, NY St. Stanislaus Bishop and Martyr Church; Retired.
Romanski, Aloysius *o.f.m.conv.* '57 (CHI) [L] Lake Zurich, IL Mt. St. Joseph Home.
Romanski, Edward '75 (CHI) Harvey, IL St. John the Baptist Church.
Romanski, Greg *c.s.p.* (AUS) [20] Austin, TX St. Theresa Church.
Romanski, Gregory A. *c.s.p.* '77 (NY) [Z] Scarsdale, NY Paulist Fathers Generalate.
Romansky, Joseph A. '75 (CLV) [N] Cleveland, OH St. Augustine Manor.
Romeo, Peter A. '72 (LAV) [3] Las Vegas, NV Holy Family Church.
Romeo, Peter A. '72 (MET) On Duty Outside the Diocese.
Romeo, Robert A. '87 (RVC) Merrick, NY Cure of Ars Church.
Romero, Anthony E. *o.p.* '70 (CHI) [N] Chicago, IL Dominicans (Provincial Office).
Romero, Antonio *o.p.* (CHI) [173] Chicago, IL St. Pius V Church.
Romero, Antonio *m.ss.cc.* (SJN) Rio Grande, PR Nuestra Senora del Carmen Church.
Romero, David H. *s.j.* '91 (NO) [P] New Orleans, LA Jesuit Provincial Office.
Romero, Donald G. '91 (DEN) [1] Aurora, CO Queen of Peace Church.
Romero, Gilbert '61 (LA) [BB] Los Angeles, CA Archdiocesan Office for Campus Ministry.
Romero, J. Robert '75 (LAF) Ville Platte, LA Sacred Heart of Jesus Church.
Romero, Jose *o.s.a.* '77 (CC) [4] Laredo, TX Holy Redeemer Church.
Romero, Joseph *c.r.* '81 (DEN) [2] Fort Collins, CO Holy Family Church.
Romero, Joseph J. '69 (BEA) [4] Port Arthur, TX St. Catherine of Siena Church.
Romero, Juan '64 (LA) [62] Los Angeles, CA San Francisco Church.
Romero, Mario '90 (LAF) Leroy, LA Our Lady of Perpetual Help Church.
Romero, Oswald E. '50 (PIT) Retired.
Romero, Tobias *c.m.f.* '75 (LA) San Gabriel, CA San Gabriel Church; [R] San Gabriel, CA Claretian Missionaries (Missionary Sons of the Immaculate Heart of Mary).
Romero, William '67 (VEN) Retired.
Romero-Rios, Adolfo '88 (NY) [184] Bronx, NY St. Pius V Church.
Romfh, Paul *o.s.b.* '63 (SP) [O] St. Leo, FL St. Leo Abbey.
Romito, Donald '74 (ORG) Garden Grove, CA St. Columban Church.
Romo, Eugenio *m.g.* (LA) [85] Los Angeles, CA St. Paul Church.
Romo, Sergio '93 (CHI) [69] Chicago, IL St. Genevieve Church.
Rompa, John '51 (SPK) Retired.
Romza, Msgr. Victor G. '54 (PBR) Campbell, OH St. Michael Church.
Ronaghan, John J. '80 (BO) Melrose, MA St. Mary of the Annunciation Church; Boston, MA Carney Hospital.
Ronald, Roy K. '60 (BUF) Absent on Leave.
Ronan, Charles E. *s.j.* '45 (CHI) [C] Chicago, IL Jesuit Community at Loyola University of Chicago.
Ronan, Eugene T. *m.s.f.* (CC) [3] Beeville, TX St. James Church.
Ronan, Henry T. '55 (BO) [1] Malden, MA Immaculate Conception Church; Retired.
Ronan, Msgr. Hugh F. '61 (TR) [6] Trenton, NJ Incarnation Church.
Ronan, James J. '82 (BO) On Duty Outside the Archdiocese.
Roncase, Robert A. '82 (PH) Penndel, PA Our Lady of Grace Church.
Ronconi, Ferdinando *c.s.s.* '69 (BO) [W] Waltham, MA Stigmatine Fathers & Brothers Provincial House.
Rondeau, John S. *c.s.sp.* '38 (PIT) [P] Bethel Park, PA Holy Ghost Animation Center.
Rondeau, Julian *s.m.* '71 (BO) [4] Haverhill, MA St. Joseph's Church.
Rondeau, Lawrence J. '58 (BO) [6] Salem, MA St. Joseph Church.
Rondon, Pedro Arturo *m.ss.cc.* '94 (SJN) [25] Bayamon, PR Santiago Apostol Church.
Roney, David A. '45 (NU) Retired.
Roney, George '78 (LUB) Woodrow, TX San Ramon Church.
Ronik, Michael E. '57 (Y) [2] Youngstown, OH Holy Name Church.
Ronquest, Msgr. John T. '45 (STL) Concord Village, MO St. Simon the Apostle Church; Retired.
Roock, John D. '59 (SY) Endwell, NY Our Lady of Angels Church.
Roodbeen, Henry W. '75 (DET) [2] Livonia, MI St. Colette Church.
Roof, Francis M. '72 (OWN) Livermore, KY St. Charles Church.

Roof, Frank '72 (OWN) Calhoun, KY St. Sebastian Church.
Rook, Paul '47 (TUC) Retired.
Rookey, Peter M. *o.s.m.* '41 (CHI) [N] Chicago, IL Servite Friars - Eastern Province.
Rooks, Charles W. '52 (COV) Retired; [M] Covington, KY St. Joseph Heights Provincialate and Novitiate of the Sisters of Notre Dame.
Rooney, Aidan R. *c.m.* '84 (PH) [155] Philadelphia, PA St. Vincent de Paul Church.
Rooney, Bernard *c.ss.r.* '59 (GR) [3] Grand Rapids, MI St. Alphonsus Church.
Rooney, Bill *o.f.m.* '81 (CHI) [167] Chicago, IL St. Peter's Church; [N] Chicago, IL St. Peter's Friary.
Rooney, Donald A. '79 (CLV) Mentor, OH St. John Vianney Church; [4] Parma, OH St. Columbkille Church.
Rooney, Donald J. '94 (ARL) Dominican Republic, VA San Francisco de Asis, Banica Church; On Duty Outside the Diocese.
Rooney, Edward '62 (STA) Middleburg, FL St. Luke's Church.
Rooney, Msgr. Francis J. '41 (PIT) Retired; [N] Pittsburgh, PA St. John Vianney Manor.
Rooney, Francis V. *s.j.* '60 (NY) [Z] New York, NY Murray-Weigel Hall.
Rooney, Msgr. Hugh J. '45 (NY) Retired; [Z] New York, NY Our Lady of Consolation Residence.
Rooney, James T. '64 (BRK) [247] Queens, NY Transfiguration Church.
Rooney, John C. '89 (LIN) Hastings, NE St. Michael's Church; [C] Hastings, NE St. Cecilia's Middle School/High School; [K] Hastings, NE St. Cecilia High School Endowment Fund.
Rooney, John E. '37 (NY) Port Jervis, NY Immaculate Conception Church.
Rooney, John J. '62 (ALB) [5] Watervliet, NY Sacred Heart of Mary Church.
Rooney, Jordon *o.carm.* '54 (JOL) [J] Darien, IL Carmelite Fathers Provincial Office.
Rooney, Joseph S. *s.j.* '66 (NY) [F] New York, NY Fordham Preparatory School; [Z] New York, NY Jesuit Community at Fordham University.
Rooney, Kevin E. '62 (BUR) Northfield, VT St. John the Evangelist Church.
Rooney, Leo J. '73 (SJ) Cupertino, CA St. Joseph of Cupertino Church.
Rooney, Martin D. *m.ss.a.* (NOR) [A] Cromwell, CT Holy Apostles College and Seminary; [F] Cromwell, CT Missionaries of the Holy Apostles.
Rooney, Michael J. *s.m.a.* '41 (BO) [W] Dedham, MA African Mission House and African Cultural Center.
Rooney, Michael R. '89 (TLS) Miami, OK Sacred Heart Church; [I] Miami, OK Northeastern Oklahoma A & M College Newman Center.
Rooney, Robert '63 (GI) Broken Bow, NE St. Joseph's Church.
Rooney, Sean *s.d.b.* '66 (BIR) [9] Birmingham, AL St. John Bosco Church.
Rooney, Stephen '85 (DET) [5] Monroe, MI St. Michael Church.
Rooney, Msgr. Thaddeus '47 (RVC) Retired.
Rooney, Thomas J. '91 (PH) [39] Philadelphia, PA St. Dominic Church.
Rooney, William A. '51 (NY) Mamaroneck, NY Holy Trinity Church.
Rooney, William J. (CHI) Retired.
Rooney, William J. '40 (WDC) [C] Washington, DC Catholic University of America, The.
Roos, Edward M. '66 (NY) [3] White Plains, NY St. Bernard Church.
Roos, H. Jules '56 (PIT) On Duty Outside the Diocese.
Roos, John R. '55 (ALB) Cooperstown, NY St. Mary Church.
Roos, Leo R. '90 (ARL) McLean, VA St. Luke's Church.
Roos, Paul '61 (EVN) Mariah Hill, IN Mary, Help of Christians Church.
Roos, William A. '59 (MET) Retired.
Roost, Joseph F. '89 (DAV) Marengo, IA St. Patrick's Church; Williamsburg, IA St. Mary's Church.
Root, James A. '84 (SAM) Pittsburgh, PA Our Lady of Victory Church.
Root, Richard '90 (SPK) [A] Spokane, WA Bishop White Seminary.
Ropelski, Msgr. Stanley A. (BUF) Hamburg, NY SS. Peter and Paul Church.
Ropke, John '78 (SJP) New Kensington, PA St. Vladimir Church.
Roppolo, Msgr. Ignatius M. '54 (NO) [A] New Orleans, LA Notre Dame Seminary Graduate School of Theology.
Ropret, Rafko *s.s.s.* (CLV) [P] Cleveland, OH Congregation of the Blessed Sacrament Provincial House.
Roque, Alejandro '88 (MIA) Opa Locka, FL St. Monica Church.
Rori, Benedict M. *o.s.m.* '37 (DEN) [21] Denver, CO Our Lady of Mt. Carmel Church.
Ros, Joseph *s.d.b.* '61 (NY) [Z] New Rochelle, NY Salesian Provincial House.
Ros, Manuel '60 (BRK) [221] Queens, NY Our Lady of Sorrows Church.
Rosa, Joseph '76 (BRK) [119] Brooklyn, NY Most Precious Blood Church.
Rosa, Salvatore J. '68 (HRT) [10] New Britain, CT St. Mary's Church.
Rosack, Msgr. Edward V. '54 (PBR) Ambridge, PA St. Mary's Church.
Rosaforte, Msgr. Anthony S. '70 (NOR) [1] Norwich, CT St. Patrick Cathedral.
Rosage, Msgr. David E. '43 (SPK) Retired.
Rosales, Angelito *s.d.v.* '96 (NEW) [25] Newark, NJ St. Michael's Church.
Rosales, Cris *s.d.b.* '88 (LA) [D] Los Angeles, CA Bishop Mora Salesian High School.
Rosales, Fredi A. '92 (BRK) [99] Brooklyn, NY Our Lady of Loreto Church; [108] Brooklyn, NY Our Lady of the Presentation Church.
Rosales, Fruto '70 (RVC) Hempstead, NY Our Lady of Loretto Church.
Rosales, Ramon '81 (SB) [5] San Bernardino, CA Our Lady of Guadalupe Church.
Rosales, Raul H. '93 (TUC) Morenci, AZ Holy Cross Church.
Rosales, Samuel *s.j.* '73 (SAT) [17] San Antonio, TX Our Lady of Guadalupe Church.
Rosario, Jose Francisco *o.c.d.* '86 (MIA) [M] Miami, FL Discalced Carmelite Friars of Miami, Inc.
Rosario, Juan *c.ss.r.* (SJN) [2] San Juan, PR San Agustin Church.
Rosario, Juan Edgardo *c.ss.r.* '79 (MGZ) Aguadilla, PR St. Charles Borromeo Church.
Rosario, Socorro D. '87 (BEA) [5] Port Arthur, TX St. James Church.
Rosato, Philip J. *s.j.* '71 (BAL) [M] Baltimore, MD Jesuit Fathers and Brothers Maryland Provincial Curia.
Rosca, Paschal *o.de.m.* '63 (CLV) [67] Cleveland, OH St. Rocco Church.
Rosch, James '72 (ALB) Queensbury, NY Our Lady of the Annunciation Church.
Roscioli, Dominic J. '74 (MIL) Retired.
Rosczewski, Steven M. *o.de.m.* '89 (PH) [Z] Philadelphia, PA Monastery of Our Lady of Mercy.
Rose, Alphonse G. '56 (BAL) Baltimore, MD Johns Hopkins Medical Institutions; Special Assignment; [Q] Baltimore, MD Johns Hopkins Hospital Apostolate.
Rose, Msgr. Donald '53 (GB) Retired.
Rose, Frank '90 (NEW) West New York, NJ St. Joseph of the Palisades Church.
Rose, James '57 (FTW) Retired.
Rose, James '57 (LFT) Marion, IN U.S. Veteran's Hospital.
Rose, John '72 (SY) Baldwinsville, NY St. Augustine Church.
Rose, Michael F. '81 (WOR) South Grafton, MA St. James Church.
Rose, William J. '56 (TOL) Sycamore, OH St. Pius X Church.
Rose, William J. '96 (TOL) Tiffin, OH St. Mary Church.
Rosebaugh, Laurence E. '63 (STP) [N] St. Paul, MN Oblate Residence.
Rosebrough, Robert T. '69 (STL) Valley Park, MO Sacred Heart Church.
Roselada, Eulogio '93 (CHI) [N] Chicago, IL The Holy Evangelists Friary.
Roselli, Marc J. *s.j.* '85 (NY) [F] New York, NY Xavier High School.
Rosemeyer, John C. '58 (CHI) Westchester, IL Divine Providence Church.
Rosemeyer, Paul F. '52 (CHI) [1] Des Plaines, IL St. Mary Church; Retired.
Rosen, Cyprian *o.f.m.cap.* '62 (NEW) [N] Union City, NJ Capuchin Friars - Prov. Stigmata of St. Francis.
Rosen, Cyprian *o.f.m.cap.* '62 (WIL) [I] Wilmington, DE Capuchin Franciscan Friars, St. Francis Renewal Center; [L] Wilmington, DE St. Francis Renewal Center.
Rosenau, Alan '88 (LR) [E] Hot Springs National Park, AR St. Joseph's Regional Health Center.
Rosenbaum, William E. '76 (ALT) [18] Johnstown, PA St. Clement's Church.
Rosenfelder, Richard M. *s.j.* '51 (CLV) [E] Cuyahoga Falls, OH Walsh Jesuit High School.
Rosenfelder, Robert D. *s.j.* '46 (DET) [P] Clarkston, MI Colombiere Center.
Rosenkranz, George J. '62 (BO) Absent on Sick Leave.
Rosensteel, William A. '69 (ALT) Newry, PA St. Patrick's Church.
Rosensweig, Walter F. '53 (TUC) Absent on Leave; [F] Tucson, AZ Regina Cleri Center.
Rosero, Leo V. '90 (BRK) [181] Queens, NY Immaculate Conception Church.
Rosette, Fabian Maria *h.o.carm.* '80 (SAN) [A] Christoval, TX Mount Carmel Hermitage.
Rosetti, Gabriel A. *o.f.m.* '59 (PH) [D] Philadelphia, PA Archbishop Ryan High School; [Z] Philadelphia, PA St. Pius X Friary.
Rosettie, Msgr. Frederick D. '45 (TUC) Retired.
Rosevear, Anthony *o.p.* '78 (P) Ashland, OR Our Lady of the Mountain Church.
Rosie, Joseph '90 (TR) Freehold, NJ St. Rose of Lima Church.
Rosielski, Eugene '54 (SY) [5] Rome, NY Transfiguration Church.
Rosin, Richard *s.d.b.* '95 (NY) [F] New Rochelle, NY Salesian High School.
Rosing, Paul J. '73 (CLV) [1] Akron, OH Annunciation Church.
Rosing, Robert '53 (COV) [H] Covington, KY St. Elizabeth Medical Center, North.
Rosinski, Edward B. '63 (CAM) Sicklerville, NJ St. John Neumann Church.
Rosinski, Richard A. '91 (RCK) DeKalb, IL St. Mary Church.
Rosko, Ladislaus '52 (CLV) Orange Village, OH St. Margaret of Hungary Church.
Rosloniec, Leo S. '54 (GR) Wright Township, MI St. Joseph's Church.
Roslovich, Peter J. *s.j.* '63 (NY) [Z] New York, NY Murray-Weigel Hall.
Roslowski, Romulus *o.f.m. conv.* '74 (ALT) Hooversville, PA Holy Family Church.
Rosner, William F. *c.ss.r.* '51 (HBG) Ephrata, PA Mother of Perpetual Help Church; [H] Ephrata, PA St. Clement's Mission House.
Rosoh, James '72 (ALB) Fort Edward, NY St. Joseph Church.
Rosolen, Emil '86 (AMA) Absent on Leave.
Rosonke, Steven J. '82 (DUB) [6] Cedar Rapids, IA St. Patrick's Church.
Rosonke, Vince G. '75 (DM) Altoona, IA SS. John and Paul Church.
Rospond, Paul S. *c.s.p.* '81 (STP) [29] Minneapolis, MN St. Lawrence Church; [V] Minneapolis, MN University of Minnesota Newman Center and Chapel.
Ross, Brendan A. '87 (NY) [213] Staten Island, NY St. Mary Church.
Ross, Msgr. Charles E. '37 (IND) Retired.
Ross, Christopher *o.s.m.* '54 (ORG) [H] Buena Park, CA Servite Fathers And Brothers.
Ross, David M. '75 (TOL) [1] Lima, OH St. Charles Borromeo Church.
Ross, James H. '46 (OKL) Kingfisher, OK SS. Peter and Paul Church.
Ross, Joseph *c.s.c.* (GRY) Michigan City, IN Indiana State Prison.
Ross, Joseph *m.s.* '55 (FR) [K] Attleboro, MA La Salette Shrine.
Ross, Joseph D. '69 (STL) [31] St. Louis, MO St. Cronan Church.
Ross, Joseph D. *c.s.c.* '89 (FTW) [B] Notre Dame, IN University of Notre Dame Du Lac; [J] Notre Dame, IN Holy Cross Community, Corby Hall, University of Notre Dame.
Ross, Joseph R. '69 (OKL) [4] Oklahoma City, OK Christ the King Church.
Ross, Kenneth '92 (ORL) Retired.
Ross, Laurence *s.m.* (BO) [12] Lawrence, MA Sacred Heart Church.
Ross, Mark J. '88 (SAV) Vidalia, GA Sacred Heart Church.
Ross, Raymond *c.m.* '48 (STL) Sappington, MO St. Catherine Laboure Church.
Ross, Richard G. '67 (JOL) [15] Joliet, IL St. Mary Magdalene Church.
Ross, Robert *s.d.s.* '58 (WDC) [B] Silver Spring, MD Salvatorian Community.
Ross, Robert J. *s.j.* '72 (CIN) [M] Cincinnati, OH Faber Jesuit Community.
Ross, Robert J. *s.j.* '72 (COV) [H] Covington, KY St. Elizabeth Medical Center, North; [H] Edgewood, KY St. Elizabeth Medical Center, South; [H] Williamstown, KY St. Elizabeth Medical Center, Grant County.
Ross, Stephen-Joseph *o.c.d.* '84 (BO) [W] Brighton, MA Carmelite Monastery.
Ross, Theodore C. *s.j.* '67 (CHI) [C] Chicago, IL Jesuit Community at Loyola University of Chicago.
Ross, William B. '54 (OKL) Purcell, OK Our Lady of Victory Church.
Rossbach, Msgr. George '44 (HON) Retired.
Rossbach, Msgr. George F. '36 (NY) Retired.
Rossbach, Robert *c.ss.r.* '47 (STL) [P] Liguori, MO Liguori Mission House/Redemptorists.
Rosse, John V. '54 (ROC) [24] Rochester, NY Holy Name of Jesus Church.
Rossell, Richard *o.f.m.conv.* '61 (TR) Point Pleasant Beach, NJ St. Peter Church.
Rosselli, Msgr. Charles '36 (NY) Retired.
Rossello, Nicholas A. '60 (BUF) [3] Lockport, NY St. Joseph Church.
Rosser, Aelred *o.s.b.* '67 (KC) [J] Conception, MO Conception Abbey.
Rossetti, Mark T. '85 (SCR) Unassigned or Leave of Absence.
Rossetti, Salvatore J. *o.p.* '42 (MET) Edison, NJ St. Helena Church.
Rossetti, Stephen '84 (SY) On Duty Outside the Diocese.
Rossetti, Stephen J. (WDC) [V] Silver Spring, MD Saint Luke Institute, Inc.

Rossey, Stephen J. *o.praem.* '59 (GB) [I] De Pere, WI St. Norbert Abbey.
Rossi, Anthony M. '49 (PH) Retired.
Rossi, Desmond '92 (ALB) Guilderland, NY St. Madeleine Sophie Church.
Rossi, Domenic *o.praem.* '74 (SFE) [11] Albuquerque, NM Our Lady of Most Holy Rosary Church; [J] Albuquerque, NM Santa Maria de la Vid Priory.
Rossi, Domenic A. *o.praem.* '74 (PH) [Z] Paoli, PA Daylesford Abbey.
Rossi, Frank H. '83 (GAL) On Special Assignment.
Rossi, John B. '92 (NEW) Military Chaplains.
Rossi, Joseph M. '84 (BO) Braintree, MA St. Thomas More Church.
Rossi, Joseph S. *s.j.* '80 (BAL) [C] Baltimore, MD Loyola College; [M] Baltimore, MD Jesuit Community of Loyola College, Inc.
Rossi, Joseph S. '80 (NY) [Z] New York, NY Jesuit Provincial's Office; [Z] New York, NY Xavier Jesuit Community.
Rossi, Pat '82 (NY) [Z] New York, NY St. John Neumann Residence.
Rossi, Paul J. '74 (SFR) Sausalito, CA St. Mary Star of the Sea Church.
Rossi, Philip J. *s.j.* '71 (MIL) [P] Milwaukee, WI Arrupe House Jesuit Community.
Rossi, Raymond R. '58 (LR) Hot Springs Village, AR Sacred Heart of Jesus Church.
Rossi, Ronald J. *o.praem.* '70 (PH) [D] Philadelphia, PA St. John Neumann High School; [Z] Philadelphia, PA St. Norbert Priory.
Rossi, Thomas J. *o.praem.* '73 (PH) [134] Philadelphia, PA St. Paul Church; [Z] Paoli, PA Daylesford Abbey.
Rossi, Thomas P. '56 (BO) Absent on Sick Leave.
Rossi, Thomas P. '83 (BO) Stoneham, MA St. Patrick Church.
Rossi, Walter R. '87 (SCR) Sabbatical or Graduate Studies.
Rossi, Msgr. Walter R. '87 (WDC) [Q] Washington, DC Basilica of the National Shrine of the Immaculate Conception.
Rossie, Arthur *c.s.s.r.* '57 (STP) Brooklyn Center, MN St. Alphonsus Church.
Rossiter, Msgr. Francis '42 (BO) Middlesex County, MA East Cambridge and Billerica; Retired.
Rossiter, John F. '58 (KCK) [1] Topeka, KS Assumption Church.
Rossitto, Joseph V. '69 (BGP) [4] Danbury, CT St. Joseph's Church; Retired.
Rossman, George M. '66 (SFR) [T] San Francisco, CA Opus Dei.
Rossman, Richard '71 (P) Tualatin, OR Church of the Resurrection.
Rosso, Norbert *c.s.sp.* '54 (SAT) [7] San Antonio, TX Holy Redeemer Church.
Rosson, John Peter '75 (ALB) [8] Schenectady, NY St. John the Baptist Church; Special Assignment.
Rosswog, Bernard L. *o.s.b.* '37 (CHL) [J] Belmont, NC Belmont Abbey.
Rosswog, Kenneth *o.f.m.* '57 (STL) [25] St. Louis, MO St. Anthony of Padua Church; [P] St. Louis, MO Franciscan Friary of St. Anthony of Padua.
Rosswurm, Michael J. '73 (FTW) [18] Fort Wayne, IN St. Therese Church.
Rost, Msgr. George W. '51 (HBG) Conewago Township, PA Basilica of the Sacred Heart of Jesus.
Rost, Robert A. (KC) [5] Independence, MO Nativity of the Blessed Virgin Church.
Roszko, Edward J. *o.s.f.s.* '70 (PH) [D] Philadelphia, PA Father Judge High School for Boys; [Z] Philadelphia, PA Father Judge Faculty House.
Rotelle, John E. *o.s.a.* '65 (PH) [Z] Villanova, PA Provincial Offices of the Order of St. Augustine, Province of St. Thomas of Villanova; [Z] Villanova, PA St. John Stone Friary.
Roten, Johann B.G. *s.m.* '69 (CIN) [D] Dayton, OH The University of Dayton; [D] Dayton, OH The University of Dayton; [M] Dayton, OH Marianist Provincialate.
Rotert, J. Matthew '94 (KC) [9] Kansas City, MO Christ the King Church.
Rotert, Norman '57 (KC) [41] Kansas City, MO Visitation of the Blessed Virgin Church.
Rotert, Msgr. Norman '57 (OAK) [R] Oakland, CA Pacific Institute for Community Organization.
Roth, Jacob P. '53 (DUB) Festina, IA Our Lady of Seven Dolors Church; Fort Atkinson, IA St. John Nepomucene's Church.
Roth, Jake '53 (JKS) Clarksdale, MS Immaculate Conception Church.
Roth, James H. *o.s.f.s.* '95 (TOL) [C] Toledo, OH St. Francis de Sales High School; [K] Toledo, OH Oblates of St. Francis de Sales.
Roth, James J. '46 (WCH) Bushton, KS Holy Name of Jesus Church.
Roth, Msgr. Joseph (CHI) [U] Chicago, IL National Association of Diaconate Directors (NADD).
Roth, Msgr. Joseph R. '79 (CHR) Myrtle Beach, SC St. Andrew's Church.
Roth, Robert J. *s.j.* '51 (NY) [Z] New York, NY Jesuit Community at Fordham University.
Roth, Timothy *m.i.c.* '74 (CHI) [N] Chicago, IL Congregation of Marian Fathers of the Immaculate Conception.
Roth, Timothy *m.i.c.* '74 (NOR) [C] Thompson, CT Marianapolis Preparatory School; [F] Thompson, CT Marian Fathers.
Roth, Wallace F. '47 (CLV) South Amherst, OH Nativity of Blessed Virgin Mary Church; Retired.
Rothbauer, Francis J. '66 (STU) Retired.
Rothe, James A. '56 (LA) Santa Paula, CA St. Sebastian Church.
Rothermel, Paul L. (ALN) [7] Bethlehem, PA Notre Dame of Bethlehem Church; [3] Reading, PA St. Catharine of Siena Church; [C] Reading, PA Reading Central Catholic High School (Monsignor Bornemann Memorial).
Rothfuchs, Gregory '95 (JOL) [2] Naperville, IL Sts. Peter and Paul Church.
Rothrauff, Leo P. *o.s.b.* '56 (GBG) [H] Latrobe, PA Saint Vincent Archabbey.
Rothrauff, Noel H. *o.s.b.* '54 (GBG) [H] Latrobe, PA Saint Vincent Archabbey.
Rothrock, Theodore D. '83 (LFT) Oxford, IN St. Patrick Church; Special Assignment.
Rothschild, Paul J. (STL) [39] St. Louis, MO St. Joan of Arc Church.
Rothwell, Joseph T. '52 (BO) Permanent Disability.
Rotola, Albert C. *s.j.* '68 (STL) [C] St. Louis, MO Saint Louis University; [P] St. Louis, MO Jesuit Community Corporation at St. Louis University - Jesuit Hall.
Rotolo, Michael '51 (STU) Barton, OH Our Lady of Angels Church; Blaine, OH All Saints Church.
Rotondi, Paul A. *o.f.m.* '56 (MET) [6] New Brunswick, NJ St. Ladislaus Church.
Rotrige, Msgr. Henry J. '38 (STL) Retired.
Rott, Bernard E. '79 (MAD) Watertown, WI St. Henry Church.
Rottloff, Linus *c.p.* '51 (HRT) [M] West Hartford, CT Holy Family Monastery/Retreat.
Rotunno, Anthony '61 (PRT) Greenville, ME Holy Family Church.
Rotunno, Floyd '70 (NEW) [2] Orange, NJ Our Lady of the Valley Church.
Rotunno, Philip J. '66 (NEW) West New York, NJ Our Lady of Libera Church.
Rouch, Nicholas J. '89 (E) [A] Erie, PA St. Mark's Seminary; [B] Erie, PA Gannon University; [P] Erie, PA Newman Centers and Campus Ministry.
Rouech, Chris '96 (GR) [12] Grand Rapids, MI St. John Vianney Church.
Roueche, Msgr. John F. '33 (CHL) Retired.
Rouelle, Forrest '56 (STU) [J] Steubenville, OH The Fraternity of Priests, Inc.
Rouelle, Forrest W. '56 (BUR) Newport, VT St. Mary Star of the Sea Church.
Rougeau, Marc *s.d.b.* '77 (LA) [C] Rosemead, CA Don Bosco Technical Institute; [D] Rosemead, CA Don Bosco Technical Institute.
Roughan, Richard F. '63 (NOR) Waterford, CT St. Paul Church.
Rourke, John C. '63 (VEN) Sabbatical.
Rouse, John-Vincent '74 (GAL) Channelview, TX St. Andrew Church.
Rouse, Paul (BO) [28] Boston, MA Holy Name Church.
Rouse, Silvan *c.p.* '49 (ALT) [J] Bedford, PA St. Mary's House of Greater Solitude.
Rouse, Warren J. *o.f.m.* '57 (SD) [H] San Luis Rey, CA San Luis Rey.
Rousseau, Julian *s.s.s.* '50 (SFE) [23] Albuquerque, NM St. Charles Borromeo Church; Albuquerque, NM Veterans Administration Medical Center.
Rousseau, Peter A. '49 (BUR) Retired.
Rousseau, Richard W. *s.j.* '54 (BO) [W] Boston, MA The Society of Jesus of New England-Provincial Offices.
Rousseau, Richard W. *s.j.* '54 (SCR) [C] Scranton, PA University of Scranton.
Rousseau, Robert J. '67 (HRT) [1] Bristol, CT St. Ann Church.
Rousseau, Robert P. *s.s.s.* '76 (GAL) [24] Houston, TX Corpus Christi Church.
Rousseau, Sean K. '95 (ARL) Fairfax, VA St. Leo's Church.
Rousseau, Msgr. Stanley B. '56 (BGP) [1] Bridgeport, CT St. Augustine Cathedral.
Rousseau, William C. '95 (SPR) [8] Chicopee, MA St. Patrick's Church.
Roussel, Joseph P. *c.s.b.* '52 (GAL) Retired; [Q] Houston, TX Residence of the Basilian Fathers of the University of St. Thomas.
Roussel, Matthew '96 (LAF) Ville Platte, LA Sacred Heart of Jesus Church.
Routhier, Peter A. '78 (BUR) Winooski, VT St. Stephen Church.
Roux, Gerard *o.m.i.* '64 (MAN) [M] Hudson, NH Oblates of Mary Immaculate Retreat House.
Roux, Philippe D. '73 (SPR) [5] North Adams, MA St. Francis Church.
Roux, Randy P. '76 (NO) Madisonville, LA St. Anselm Church.
Rovira, Ivan M. '71 (BWN) [4] Brownsville, TX Holy Family Church.
Rovira, Luis Iscla *s.j.* '49 (DET) [P] Clarkston, MI Colombiere Center.
Rowan, Gerald F. '57 (WCH) Castleton, KS St. Agnes Church; Hutchinson, KS St. Teresa Church.
Rowan, Gerard J. '47 (STP) Carver, MN St. Nicholas Church.
Rowan, Msgr. John '61 (RVC) Sayville, NY St. Lawrence the Martyr Church.
Rowan, John M. '89 (BO) [5] Quincy, MA St. Mary Church.
Rowan, Joseph C. *c.ss.r.* '45 (ORL) [F] New Smyrna Beach, FL St. Alphonsus Villa-Redemptorist Fathers and Brothers; [F] New Smyrna Beach, FL Redemptorist Fathers of the Vice Province of Richmond.
Rowan, Mark P. '91 (RVC) Lynbrook, NY Our Lady of Peace Church.
Rowan, Stephen '70 (SEA) Special Assignment.
Rowe, Donald F. *s.j.* '72 (CHI) [C] Chicago, IL Jesuit Community at Loyola University of Chicago; [D] Chicago, IL St. Ignatius College Prep.
Rowe, Douglas L. '67 (OM) Absent on Leave.
Rowe, William J. '64 (BEL) Mount Carmel, IL St. Mary Church.
Rowgh, T. Matthew '75 (WH) Shepherdstown, WV St. Agnes Church.
Rowland, Msgr. Charles H. '70 (CHR) [2] Columbia, SC St. Joseph Church.
Rowland, Edward P. '53 (JOL) [19] Joliet, IL St. Thaddeus Church.
Rowland, Thomas '49 (ELP) On Duty Outside of Diocese.
Rowland, William F. *c.j.m.* '70 (SD) [3] San Diego, CA Blessed Sacrament Church.
Rowland, William F. *s.m.* '79 (WDC) [M] Washington, DC Marist Provincial House.
Rowley, Charles *o.f.m.* '55 (BO) [BB] Boston, MA St. Anthony Shrine.
Rowley, James J. '37 (CHI) Palatine, IL St. Thomas of Villanova Church; Retired.
Rowntree, Stephen C. *s.j.* '75 (NO) [P] New Orleans, LA Jesuit Provincial Office.
Rowsome, Morgan '70 (CC) [19] Corpus Christi, TX St. Peter Prince of Apostles Church.
Roxas, Rodolfo P. '69 (SAV) [E] Savannah, GA St. Joseph's Hospital.
Roy, Msgr. Allen J. '54 (NO) [10] New Orleans, LA Holy Spirit Church.
Roy, Donald J. '70 (BUR) Milton, VT St. Ann Church.
Roy, F. Gilles '57 (WOR) On Duty Outside the Diocese.
Roy, Gregory *s.j.* '46 (ALB) [L] Valatie, NY St. Joseph.
Roy, Gregory R. *s.j.* '46 (BO) [W] Boston, MA The Society of Jesus of New England-Provincial Offices.
Roy, J. Jean '56 (WDC) Retired.
Roy, James '61 (ALX) Hessmer, LA St. Alphonsus Church.
Roy, John J. '90 (WOR) West Boylston, MA Our Lady of Good Counsel Church; [C] Worcester, MA St. Peter-Marian Central Catholic Junior-Senior High School.
Roy, Joseph *s.s.s.* '56 (SFE) [23] Albuquerque, NM St. Charles Borromeo Church.
Roy, Kenneth J. '78 (ALX) Natchitoches, LA Immaculate Conception Church; Powhatan, LA St. Francis Church.
Roy, Maurice J. '73 (BUR) St. Albans, VT Holy Angels Church.
Roy, Michael J. '75 (WOR) Webster, MA Sacred Heart of Jesus Church.
Roy, Oscar *c.j.m.* '64 (SD) [3] San Diego, CA Blessed Sacrament Church.
Roy, Paul M. *m.s.* '58 (FR) [K] Attleboro, MA La Salette Provincial House.
Roy, Richard M. '75 (FR) Orleans, MA St. Joan of Arc Church.
Roy, Robert P. '94 (HRT) [2] Meriden, CT St. Joseph Church; [4] Meriden, CT St. Mary Church.
Roy, Sheldon L. '86 (ALX) Natchitoches, LA Holy Cross Church; [J] Natchitoches, LA Northwestern State University.
Royal, E. Peter (AUS) Marlin, TX V.A. Hospital.
Royal, E. Peter '53 (AUS) Lott, TX Sacred Heart Church; Marlin, TX St. Joseph's Church.
Royal, Kevin T. '85 (BGP) New Canaan, CT St. Aloysius Church; [O] Stamford, CT St. John Fisher Seminary Residence.
Royce, Thomas R. *s.j.* '56 (YAK) [4] Yakima, WA St. Joseph's Church.
Royer, Msgr. George C. '27 (MOB) Retired; [F] Mobile, AL Little Sisters of the Poor, Home For the Aged, Inc.
Royer, Msgr. Ronald E. '58 (LA) Lakewood, CA St. Pancratius Church.
Royer, Thomas J. '60 (PEO) [3] Champaign, IL St. Mary's Church; Ivesdale, IL St. Joseph's Church.
Royer, Yvon J. '90 (BUR) [4] Burlington, VT St. Joseph's Church.
Rozanski, Mitchell T. '84 (BAL) [35] Baltimore, MD Holy Cross Church; [58] Baltimore, MD St. Mary, Star of the Sea Church.
Rozansky, Joseph G. *o.f.m.* '76 (NY) [146] Bronx, NY Holy Cross Church.
Rozansky, Joseph G. *o.f.m.* '76 (WDC) [B] Silver Spring,

MD Holy Name College.
Rozario, Bimal *c.s.c.* '68 (FTW) [A] Notre Dame, IN Moreau Seminary.
Rozewicz, Michael *o.f.m.conv.* '51 (DET) [59] Detroit, MI Our Lady Queen of Angels Church.
Rozman, Thomas J. '86 (HBG) [1] Harrisburg, PA Cathedral Parish of St. Patrick Church.
Rozniak, Msgr. Ronald J. '71 (NEW) [1] Newark, NJ Cathedral of the Sacred Heart Basilica; [S] Newark, NJ New Jersey Caritas Corporation, Inc.; [S] Newark, NJ CatholiCare, Inc.
Roznowski, Thomas *o.s.b.* '76 (SFS) Milbank, SD St. Lawrence Church; [F] Marvin, SD Blue Cloud Abbey.
Rozum, George A. *c.s.c.* '68 (FTW) [B] Notre Dame, IN University of Notre Dame Du Lac; [J] Notre Dame, IN Holy Cross Community, Corby Hall, University of Notre Dame.
Rozycki, George '70 (HON) On Duty Outside the Diocese.
Rozycki, George '70 (SP) Brandon, FL Church of the Nativity.
Rozycki, Isidore '68 (AUS) Tours, TX St. Martin Church.
Ruane, Dennis *s.s.s.* '59 (SFE) [23] Albuquerque, NM St. Charles Borromeo Church.
Ruane, Edward M. *o.p.* '69 (CHI) [N] Chicago, IL Dominicans (Provincial Office); [N] Chicago, IL Dominicans (Provincial Office); [X] Chicago, IL St. Thomas Aquinas Foundation.
Ruane, George (NEW) Fairfield, NJ St. Thomas More Church.
Ruane, John P. *s.j.* '49 (NEW) [B] Jersey City, NJ Saint Peter's College; [N] Jersey City, NJ Jesuits of Saint Peter's College, Inc.
Ruane, Martin '63 (JKS) Pearl, MS St. Jude Church; Pearl, MS Rankin County Prison; Whitfield, MS Mississippi State Hospital.
Ruane, Michael '69 (BAL) Poplar Springs, MD St. Michael Church.
Ruba, Msgr. Nicholas J. '51 (SC) Retired.
Rubadue, Paul E. *o.s.b.* '86 (GBG) [1] Latrobe, PA Holy Family Church.
Rubaj, Leon (SAT) On Duty Outside the Archdiocese.
Rubalcaba, Francisco '57 (SJN) [13] Carolina, PR Nuestra Senora de Lourdes Church.
Rubba, John C. *o.p.* '32 (PRO) [P] Providence, RI St. Thomas Aquinas Priory at Providence College.
Rubbelke, Ronald J. '64 (STL) O'Fallon, MO Assumption Church.
Rubey, Charles T. '66 (CHI) [G] Chicago, IL Catholic Charities of the Archdiocese of Chicago-Archdiocesan Offices; [L] Chicago, IL St. Joseph's Carondelet Child Center.
Rubino, Msgr. David A. '73 (E) [B] Erie, PA Gannon University.
Rubio, Gerardo '78 (SAC) Vallejo, CA St. Vincent Ferrer Church.
Rubio, Jo '80 (SJ) On Duty Outside the Diocese.
Rubio-Boitel, Fernando '75 (SFE) [A] Santa Fe, NM Immaculate Heart of Mary Seminary.
Rubsys, Anthony L. *f.s.c.a.* '38 (NY) [Z] New York, NY Brothers of the Christian Schools of Manhattan College, Inc.
Ruby, David C. '91 (GB) Little Chute, WI St. John Nepomucene Church.
Rucando, Anthony M. '70 (BRK) [98] Brooklyn, NY Our Lady Help of Christians Church.
Ruchgy, Wayne J. '66 (STN) Dearborn, MI St. Michael's Church.
Rucinski, Joseph S. '42 (TR) Retired.
Rucinski, Willard *o.s.f.s.* '65 (R) Fayetteville, NC St. Elizabeth Ann Seton Church.
Ruck, Michael J. *m.m.* '46 (SJ) [M] Los Altos, CA Maryknoll.
Rucker, G. Neville '46 (LA) Pacific Palisades, CA Corpus Christi Church.
Rucker, Lawrence *s.c.j.* '66 (JKS) Holly Springs, MS St. Joseph Church; [G] Holly Springs, MS Rust College Newman Center.
Rucker, Neville '46 (LA) Retired.
Rudcki, Stanley R. '53 (CHI) Palos Heights, IL St. Alexander Church.
Rudd, C. Richard '54 (FAR) Hillsboro, ND St. Rose of Lima Church.
Rudd, Thad B. '91 (ATL) Atlanta, GA Atlanta Veterans Administration Hospital.
Rudden, Matthew T. '59 (RCK) [3] Rockford, IL St. Bernadette Church.
Ruddick, James J. *s.j.* '55 (BUF) [O] Buffalo, NY Canisius Jesuit Community; [T] Amherst, NY St. Andrew Kim Roman Catholic Church Society of Amherst, NY, Diocese of Buffalo.
Ruddy, Msgr. Donald J. '55 (LA) Whittier, CA St. Gregory the Great Church.
Ruddy, Edward J. '40 (PAT) Retired.
Ruddy, H. Paul *o.s.f.s.* '64 (LAN) Hudson, MI Sacred Heart Church.
Rude, James A. *s.j.* '64 (LA) [6] Los Angeles, CA Blessed Sacrament Church.
Rudemiller, Edward L. '58 (CIN) [68] Cincinnati, OH Our Lady of Lourdes Church.
Rudisill, James A. '51 (NSH) Retired.
Rudnay, Clement A. *o.praem.* '38 (ORG) [H] Silverado, CA Norbertine Fathers.
Rudnick, Kenneth J. *s.j.* '91 (SPK) [C] Spokane, WA Gonzaga University.
Rudnicki, Msgr. Walter '56 (RVC) Syosset, NY St. Edward Confessor Church.
Rudnik, John J. '61 (CHI) [208] Chicago, IL Transfiguration of Our Lord Church.
Rudnik, Tadeusz '55 (SY) [22] Syracuse, NY St. Stephen Church.
Rudolf, Roger G. '92 (IND) Rushville, IN Immaculate Conception/St. Mary Church.
Rudolph, Frederick *s.v.d.* '54 (CHI) [B] Techny, IL Divine Word Residence.
Rudolph, Patrick N. '88 (ORG) [1] Orange, CA Cathedral of the Holy Family.
Rudolph, Thomas J. '61 (LC) Rozellville, WI St. Andrew Church; Stratford, WI St. Joseph Church.
Rudolphi, Stephen A. '79 (BEL) Carmi, IL St. Polycarp Church.
Rudolphi, Timothy '89 (STP) Chaska, MN Guardian Angels Church.
Rudy, John W. *o.f.m.* '77 (HRT) Winsted, CT St. Joseph's Church.
Rudy, Noel T. '53 (SAG) AuGres, MI St. Mark Church.
Rudy, Richard E. '76 (PH) [102] Philadelphia, PA St. Matthew Church.
Rudy, Theodore '54 (PSC) Dunmore, PA St. Michael Church.
Rudzewicz, Jan *s.ch.* '83 (DET) [8] Sterling Heights, MI Our Lady of Czestochowa Church.
Rueda, John (NY) [173] Bronx, NY Our Lady of Mercy Church.
Rueda, Silverio '81 (SJN) [12] Carolina, PR San Juan de Dios Church.
Ruede, Ernest '66 (R) Fayetteville, NC St. Ann Church.
Ruedel, Richard P. '59 (STP) St. Thomas, MN St. Thomas Church.
Ruedisueli, Robert A. '69 (DET) [8] Warren, MI St. Mark Church.
Ruef, Msgr. James L.T. '78 (COL) [20] Columbus, OH Holy Name Church.
Ruef, John *c.ss.r.* '50 (TR) [Q] Long Branch, NJ San Alfonso Retreat House.
Rueger, William J. '75 (BRK) [207] Queens, NY Our Lady of the Blessed Sacrament Church.
Ruehl, William F. '58 (ARL) Front Royal, VA St. John the Baptist Church.
Ruekert, Thomas E. *s.d.b.* '73 (NO) [4] Harvey, LA St. Rosalie Church.
Ruelle, Gerald *o.s.b.* '50 (BIS) Halliday, ND St. Paul Church; Killdeer, ND St. Joseph Church.
Ruelle, Gerald *o.s.b.* '52 (BIS) [A] Richardton, ND Assumption Abbey.
Ruess, Charles W. '31 (TOL) Retired.
Rueter, Joseph J. '46 (COV) Cold Spring, KY St. Joseph Church; Retired.
Rueve, Charles R. *c.pp.s.* '43 (LFT) [A] Rensselaer, IN Saint Joseph's College.
Ruff, Anthony *o.s.b.* '93 (SCL) [I] Collegeville, MN St. John's Abbey, of the Order of St. Benedict.
Ruff, Charles R. '46 (STL) Retired.
Ruff, Daniel M. *s.j.* '86 (BAL) [A] Baltimore, MD St. Mary's Seminary and University.
Ruff, Frank '63 (NSH) [L] Nashville, TN Glenmary Department of Pastoral Services.
Ruff, Frank *glmy.* '72 (OWN) Franklin, KY St. Mary of the Woods Church; Scottsville, KY Christ the King Church.
Ruffalo, Richard M. '59 (JOL) [2] Joliet, IL Holy Cross Church.
Ruffing, Norman '63 (OAK) Retired.
Ruffo, John *o.f.m. conv.* '74 (R) Jacksonville, NC Shrine of the Infant of Prague, Church of the Holy Spirit.
Ruffolo, George *c.m.f.* '56 (CHI) [166] Chicago, IL St. Paul Church.
Ruge, Kenneth C. '63 (CHI) Other Assignments.
Rugel, Msgr. James J. (PAT) Paterson, NJ St. Joseph Hospital; Retired.
Rugen, Patrick J. '76 (CHI) On Duty Outside the Archdiocese.
Rugen, Patrick J. '76 (WIN) [4] Winona, MN St. Mary's Church.
Ruggere, Peter *m.m.* '68 (WDC) [B] Washington, DC Maryknoll Fathers and Brothers.
Ruggeri, Joseph A. '65 (BO) [8] Lowell, MA St. Margaret Church.
Ruggieri, James T. '95 (PRO) [6] Cranston, RI St. Matthew Church.
Ruggieri, Joseph '95 (Y) Kent, OH St. Patrick's Church.
Ruggieri, Pasquale *f.d.p.* '52 (NY) [11] New York, NY St. Ann Church.
Ruggiero, James S. '70 (PIT) Penn Hills, PA St. Bartholomew Church.
Ruggles, John J. '60 (BEL) Retired.
Ruglovsky, Robert '61 (PRM) Absent on Leave.
Ruhl, George J. '38 (PH) Milmont Park, PA Our Lady of Peace Church; Retired.
Ruhl, John '64 (ORG) Inactive Leave.
Ruhl, Matthew D. *s.j.* '92 (STL) [52] St. Louis, MO St. Matthew, Apostle Church; [P] St. Louis, MO St. Matthew Jesuit Community.
Ruhl, William J. *o.s.f.s.* '62 (WDC) [B] Washington, DC Deshairs Community-Oblates of St. Francis de Sales Residence.
Ruhland, Carl J. '45 (DUB) Retired.
Ruhling, James '60 (E) [10] Erie, PA Our Lady of Peace Church; Erie, PA Soldiers and Sailors Home.
Ruhnke, Robert *c.ss.r.* '66 (SAT) [M] San Antonio, TX Redemptorists of Texas-Redemptorist Community at St. Gerard.
Ruhnke, Robert A. *c.ss.r.* (BR) [H] Baton Rouge, LA The Redemptorist Education and Formation.
Ruisanchez, Jose P. '86 (LA) [X] Los Angeles, CA Opus Dei. Prelature of the Holy Cross and Opus Dei.
Ruiz, Adan Martinez *s.s.p.* '77 (LA) [R] Los Angeles, CA Society of St. Paul.
Ruiz, Adolfo '29 (BR) Retired.
Ruiz, Msgr. Agustin '56 (BRK) [118] Brooklyn, NY SS. Peter and Paul's Church.
Ruiz, Albert '73 (AUS) Killeen, TX St. Joseph's Church.
Ruiz, Alberto M. *c.m.f.* '84 (LA) [R] Rancho Dominguez, CA Dominguez Seminary Inc.
Ruiz, Antonio A. '71 (TUC) Nogales, AZ San Felipe de Jesus Church.
Ruiz, Dominic *o.s.b.* '83 (SCL) Richmond, MN SS. Peter and Paul's Church; [I] Collegeville, MN St. John's Abbey, of the Order of St. Benedict.
Ruiz, Enrique '56 (SAT) On Leave.
Ruiz, Faustino C. '91 (MET) On Duty Outside the Diocese.
Ruiz, Gabriel *c.m.f.* '89 (LA) [R] Los Angeles, CA Claretian Retreat Center Community.
Ruiz, J. Antonio *c.m.* '65 (PHX) [26] Phoenix, AZ St. Vincent de Paul Church.
Ruiz, Jean-Pierre *s.t.d.* '82 (BRK) [224] Queens, NY St. Patrick Church; Released from Diocesan Assignment.
Ruiz, John '55 (HT) Pointe-Aux-Chenes, LA St. Charles Borromeo Church.
Ruiz, Jose Domingo (STO) [6] Stockton, CA St. Linus Church.
Ruiz, Jose H. '58 (VEN) Sebring, FL St. Catherine Church.
Ruiz, Joseph B. '66 (CHI) [3] Oak Park, IL St. Edmund Church.
Ruiz, Juan Carlos '95 (PAT) [2] Paterson, NJ St. Agnes Church.
Ruiz, Lorenzo '63 (SJN) [28] San Juan, PR San Juan Bosco Church.
Ruiz, Lorenzo *o.f.m.* '66 (GLP) St. Michaels, AZ St. Michael Church.
Ruiz, Luis E. '68 (SAT) Special Assignment.
Ruiz, Luis Manuel '84 (CGS) Barranquitas, PR San Andres Apostol Church.
Ruiz, Pedro *o.de.m.* '88 (PCE) [13] Ponce, PR Santuario San Judas Tadeo Church.
Ruiz, Ricardo '93 (ELP) Alpine, TX Our Lady of Peace Church.
Ruiz, Rudy '79 (MRY) Castroville, CA Our Lady of Refuge Church.
Rukavina, Steven '87 (B) Pocatello, ID St. Joseph's Church.
Ruland, Vernon J. *s.j.* '63 (SFR) [N] San Francisco, CA Jesuit Community at University of San Francisco.
Rule, Philip C. *s.j.* (DET) [K] Detroit, MI Jesuit Provincial Office-Detroit Province of the Society of Jesus.
Rule, Philip C. *s.j.* '62 (WOR) [N] Worcester, MA Jesuits of Holy Cross College, Inc.
Rule, Steven R. '75 (RIC) Roanoke, VA St. Andrew Church.
Rulli, Joseph A. '92 (FTW) Elkhart, IN St. Vincent de Paul Church.
Rumble, Clarence F. '86 (SY) [3] Endicott, NY St. Anthony of Padua Church.
Runde, David H. '57 (MAD) Cottage Grove, WI St. Patrick Church.
Runde, Raymond E. '56 (MAD) Absent on Sick Leave.
Rundzio, Mark A. '81 (MAN) Winchester, NH St. Stanislaus Church.
Runge, Msgr. Fenton J. '53 (STL) [50] St. Louis, MO SS. Mary and Joseph Church.
Runte, Richard M. '73 (SPR) Easthampton, MA Immaculate Conception Church.
Ruoff, John C. *s.j.* '61 (STL) [P] St. Louis, MO Jesuit Community Corporation at St. Louis University - Jesuit Hall.
Ruoff, Lou '84 (RIC) [3] Norfolk, VA Holy Trinity Church.
Rupert, Msgr. Dale R. '77 (SCR) [A] Dalton, PA Saint Pius X Seminary.
Rupiper, Darrell *o.m.i.* '63 (SFD) [A] Godfrey, IL Immaculate Heart of Mary Novitiate.
Rupp, Daniel N. '66 (MAR) Leave of Absence.
Ruppe, Thomas G. '45 (MAR) Retired.
Ruppenthal, William J. *s.j.* '48 (PH) [Z] Philadelphia, PA Jesuit Community at St. Joseph's University.
Ruppert, Donald R. '78 (VIC) On Sick Leave.
Ruppert, E. Alan '78 (BEL) Dahlgren, IL St. John

Nepomucene Church; McLeansboro, IL St. Clement Church.
Ruppert, Nelson J. *o.f.m.cap.* '66 (ROC) Interlaken, NY St. Francis Solanus Church; Ovid, NY Holy Cross Church; [I] Interlaken, NY St. Fidelis Friary.
Rupprecht, Norbert A. *o.s.b.* '34 (GBG) [H] Latrobe, PA Saint Vincent Archabbey.
Rusay, Leonard F.A. '85 (MET) Phillipsburg, NJ SS. Philip and James Church.
Rusch, Donald P. '61 (LAN) Clinton, MI St. Dominic's Church.
Ruschau, Ambrose *c.pp.s.* '50 (CIN) [B] Carthagena, OH St. Charles.
Ruschman, Albert E. '53 (COV) Fort Mitchell, KY Blessed Sacrament Church.
Rusconi, Richard A. '71 (PAT) [4] Paterson, NJ Blessed Sacrament Church.
Ruse, Fred R. '76 (ORL) Winter Haven, FL St. Matthew Church.
Rush, Alfred C. *c.ss.r.* '36 (ALB) [L] Saratoga Springs, NY St. John Neumann Residence.
Rush, Gerald V. '89 (OM) Absent on Leave.
Rush, J. Kenneth '71 (RIC) Lynchburg, VA Holy Cross Church.
Rush, James C. '68 (HRT) Windsor, CT St. Gabriel's Church.
Rush, James P. '72 (CAM) [5] Camden, NJ St. Joan of Arc Church.
Rush, Joseph P. '62 (CAM) Pomona, NJ Assumption Church.
Rush, Michael P. '73 (CAM) Mullica Hill, NJ Holy Name of Jesus Church.
Rush, Patrick J. '69 (KC) [35] Kansas City, MO St. Peter's Church; Special Assignment.
Rush, Thomas *o.m.i.* '73 (LA) Pacoima, CA Mary Immaculate Church.
Rush, Thomas *o.m.i.* '73 (OAK) [N] Oakland, CA Oblate Provincial House & Procure.
Rush, Msgr. Vincent '72 (RVC) Huntington Station, NY St. Hugh of Lincoln Church.
Rushford, William A. '55 (BIS) Retired; [G] Bismarck, ND Emmaus Place.
Rushman, John '55 (GAY) Retired.
Rushofsky, John R. '79 (PIT) [1] McKeesport, PA St. Martin de Porres Church.
Rusin, Joseph C. '46 (SCR) Mayfield, PA Sacred Heart of Jesus Church.
Rusk, John '68 (SB) Blythe, CA Chuckawalla Valley State Prison.
Rusk, Richard (ROC) [K] Corning, NY Anawim Community Center.
Rusk, Richard M. '90 (MET) Martinsville, NJ Blessed Sacrament Church; [L] Phillipsburg, NJ The Anawim Community.
Ruskamp, Robert L. (ARL) Woodstock, VA St. John Bosco Church.
Ruskoski, William '74 (LAF) Arnaudville, LA St. Francis Regis Church; Arnaudville, LA St. Catherine Church.
Ruskowski, Clifford '62 (DET) [3] Clinton Twp., MI St. Paul of Tarsus Church; [A] Detroit, MI Sacred Heart Major Seminary, Inc.
Rusnak, Mark E. '87 (E) Emlenton, PA St. Michael Church.
Rusnak, Melvin E. '70 (Y) [22] Youngstown, OH St. Stephen of Hungary Church.
Russ, Francis J. '51 (KC) Retired.
Russel, James *s.m.* '64 (MIA) Hollywood, FL Nativity Church.
Russel, William *s.j.* '65 (BO) [W] Cambridge, MA Faber House.
Russell, Alfred *o.s.f.s.* '66 (LAN) Brooklyn, MI St. Joseph's Shrine Church.
Russell, David '64 (MIA) [23] Miami, FL St. John Neumann Church.
Russell, David P. '81 (WDC) [17] Washington, DC Holy Name Church.
Russell, J. Christopher '79 (STP) Annandale, MN St. Ignatius Church.
Russell, James A. *s.m.* '64 (CIN) [M] Dayton, OH Marianist Provincialate.
Russell, James D. '60 (WIN) Madison Lake, MN All Saints Church.
Russell, Msgr. James M. '70 (BLX) [1] Biloxi, MS Cathedral of the Nativity of the Blessed Virgin Mary.
Russell, John F. *o.carm.* '60 (NEW) [A] South Orange, NJ Immaculate Conception Seminary; [B] South Orange, NJ Seton Hall University.
Russell, Kenneth '58 (OAK) Retired.
Russell, Patrick '86 (B) Boise, ID Chateau de Boise Retirement Center.
Russell, Paul F. '87 (BO) Graduate Studies.
Russell, Paul M. '32 (L) Retired; [K] Louisville, KY Nazareth Home.
Russell, Raymond R. '56 (BUF) [64] Buffalo, NY St. Thomas Aquinas Church.
Russell, Richard '60 (LA) [V] Los Angeles, CA Catholic Kolping House.
Russell, Richard J. '60 (SD) Retired.
Russell, Richard R. '61 (HRT) West Simsbury, CT St. Catherine of Siena Church.
Russell, Samuel *o.s.b.* '94 (KC) [A] Conception, MO Conception Seminary College; [J] Conception, MO Conception Abbey.
Russell, Stanley J. '61 (WIL) Bellefonte, DE St. Helena Church.
Russell, Msgr. W. Joyce '30 (WDC) [4] Silver Spring, MD St. Catherine Laboure Church; Retired.
Russell, William C. *s.j.* '65 (BO) [W] Boston, MA The Society of Jesus of New England-Provincial Offices; [W] Cambridge, MA Weston Jesuit Community.
Russi, Fred F. '66 (LKC) Raymond, LA St. Lawrence Church.
Russi, John *s.m.* '67 (HON) [D] Honolulu, HI St. Louis School; [H] Honolulu, HI Center Marianist Community.
Russman, Thomas *o.f.m.cap.* '72 (WDC) [B] Washington, DC St. Francis Friary-Capuchin College.
Russman, Thomas A. *o.f.m.cap.* '70 (GAL) [C] Houston, TX University of St. Thomas.
Russo, Alfred E. '62 (BGP) [K] Trumbull, CT St. Joseph's Manor.
Russo, Anthony P. *s.c.j.* '66 (MIL) Franklin, WI Sacred Hearts of Jesus and Mary Church; St. Martins, WI Holy Assumption Church; [P] Franklin, WI St. Francis Residence; [P] Hales Corners, WI Priests of the Sacred Heart.
Russo, Anthony T. *c.ss.r.* '65 (PH) [25] Philadelphia, PA St. Boniface Church; [R] Philadelphia, PA Catholic Center for the Deaf and Hard of Hearing.
Russo, Armando C. '44 (SPR) Russell, MA Our Lady of the Rosary Church.
Russo, Caesar '74 (STA) On Duty Outside the Diocese.
Russo, Caesar '75 (NY) [Z] New York, NY Brothers of the Christian Schools of Manhattan College, Inc.
Russo, Carmen *c.s.s.* '45 (BO) [W] Waltham, MA Stigmatine Fathers & Brothers Provincial House.
Russo, Cesar (NY) [CC] New York, NY University Apostolate.
Russo, Msgr. Charles J. '65 (PAT) [16] Paterson, NJ St. Therese Church.
Russo, Francis X. *o.f.m.cap.* '59 (WDC) [39] Washington, DC Shrine of the Sacred Heart Church.
Russo, Frank '81 (LA) Pico Rivera, CA St. Hilary Church.
Russo, James E. '70 (SP) [5] Clearwater, FL St. Michael The Archangel Church.
Russo, John W. (TR) Leave of Absence.
Russo, Lawrence J. '80 (BO) Military & VA Chaplains.
Russo, Michael '88 (LAF) Franklin, LA Assumption B.V.M. Church.
Russo, Michael A. '71 (NEW) On Duty Outside the Archdiocese.
Russo, Michael A. '71 (OAK) [B] Moraga, CA Saint Mary's College.
Russo, Nicodemus A. '48 (PEO) Retired.
Russo, Peter '76 (ALB) Copake Falls, NY St. Bridget Church.
Russo, Reginald *o.f.m.cap.* '67 (HBG) [2] York, PA St. Joseph Church.
Russo, Ricardo *o.f.m.* '74 (SFE) Santa Fe, NM New Mexico State Penitentiary.
Russo, Richard M. '82 (RCK) [4] Elgin, IL St. Thomas More Church.
Russo, Robert T. '61 (HRT) East Windsor, CT St. Philip's Church.
Russo, Romanos V. '77 (NTN) West Paterson, NJ St. Ann's Church.
Russo, Thomas *o.s.j.* '56 (MRY) [G] Santa Cruz, CA Oblates of St. Joseph Provincial House and Shrine.
Rusteika, John B. '45 (WCH) Retired.
Ruston, Robert L. '76 (ALT) Cassandra, PA St. Agnes Church; Wilmore, PA St. Bartholomew's Church.
Ruszel, Henry *c.r.* '54 (SB) [3] Fontana, CA St. Joseph Church
Ruszel, Humphrey *c.r.* '46 (SB) [1] Fontana, CA Church of the Resurrection.
Rutan, Albert E. '57 (GF) Absent on Leave.
Ruth, A. John *c.s.b.* '42 (GAL) [Q] Sugar Land, TX Basilian Mission Center.
Ruth, John C. '85 (SCR) [20] Scranton, PA Nativity of Our Lord Church; [I] Scranton, PA Mercy Hospital.
Ruth, Robert F. '60 (RIC) Retired.
Ruth, Ronald A. '70 (RIC) [9] Richmond, VA St. Edward The Confessor Church.
Ruthenberg, Gari *o.m.i.* '95 (SFS) Sisseton, SD St. Catherine Church; Sisseton, SD St. Peter Church.
Ruthenberg, Michael B. *o.p.* '88 (DET) [2] St. Clair Shores, MI St. Gertrude Church.
Ruther, William E. '90 (LA) La Puente, CA St. Joseph Church.
Rutherford, Donald L. '81 (ALB) Military Chaplains.
Rutherford, Richard *c.s.c.* '64 (P) [B] Portland, OR University of Portland; [L] Portland, OR Holy Cross Father & Brother, C.S.C. - University of Portland.
Rutkowski, George A. '60 (DET) [55] Detroit, MI Our Lady Help of Christians Church.
Rutkowski, James N. '77 (STL) St. Louis, MO St. Mary's Health Ctr.
Rutkowski, Ronald J. '69 (GBG) Cardale, PA Madonna of Czestochowa Church; Palmer, PA St. Albert Church.
Rutkowski, Stephen C. '58 (NEW) Retired.
Rutkowski, Theodore A. '63 (PIT) Scott Township, PA Our Lady of Grace Church.
Rutkowski, William J. '87 (SAG) Shepherd, MI St. Vincent De Paul Church.
Rutledge, Arthur F. *s.j.* '51 (SJ) [M] Los Gatos, CA California Province of the Society of Jesus, Jesuit Provincial Office; [M] Los Gatos, CA Sacred Heart Jesuit Center.
Rutledge, Robert M. *o.s.f.s.* '89 (ALN) [B] Center Valley, PA Allentown College of St. Francis de Sales; [K] Center Valley, PA Oblates of St. Francis de Sales.
Rutledge, William G. '53 (PIT) Reserve Township, PA St. Aloysius Church.
Rutler, George W. (NY) [DD] New York, NY Guild of Catholic Lawyers, The.
Rutler, George W. '81 (NY) [2] New York, NY St. Agnes Church; On Duty Outside the Archdiocese.
Ruttle, Paul *c.p.* '80 (MET) [H] South River, NJ Passionist Provincial Office.
Rutz, Gilbert '66 (PHX) [I] Phoenix, AZ Kino Institute.
Rutz, Gilbert J. '66 (COV) On Duty Outside the Diocese.
Ruvalcaba, Victor J. '96 (LA) Pasadena, CA St. Andrew Church.
Ruvo, Msgr. John A. '54 (NY) [174] Bronx, NY Our Lady of Mt. Carmel Church.
Ruyechan, Matthew *o.f.m.* (E) [2] Sharon, PA St. Anthony Church.
Ruygt, Hans '85 (SR) Ukiah, CA St. Mary of the Angels Church.
Ruzich, Boniface *o.ss.t.* '59 (TR) [16] Trenton, NJ St. James Church.
Ruzicka, Gary J. '76 (CHY) Casper, WY Saint Patrick's Church.
Ruzzo, Paul F. '83 (MAN) [8] Manchester, NH St. Francis of Assisi Church.
Rweyemamu, Justinian B. '93 (NOR) Gales Ferry, CT Our Lady of Lourdes Church.
Rweza, Anthony Zachary (FTW) [A] Notre Dame, IN Moreau Seminary.
Ryalt, Lawrence *c.p.* '92 (BRK) [W] Jamaica, NY Bishop Molloy Retreat House for Laymen.
Ryan, Adam *o.s.b.* '90 (KC) [J] Conception, MO Conception Abbey.
Ryan, Alan J. *m.m.* '60 (NY) [Z] Maryknoll, NY Maryknoll Fathers and Brothers.
Ryan, Albert J. '58 (FR) [12] New Bedford, MA St. Francis of Assisi Church.
Ryan, Alphonsus '64 (SD) Absent on Sick Leave.
Ryan, Barry '76 (BRK) Absent on Leave.
Ryan, Msgr. Bernard J. '55 (RVC) Bellport, NY Mary Immaculate Church.
Ryan, Brian G. '64 (PT) Crestview, FL Our Lady of Victory Church.
Ryan, C. Duane '54 (KC) Retired.
Ryan, Clarence R. '56 (KC) Retired.
Ryan, Daniel J. '89 (TR) Keyport, NJ St. Joseph Church; [B] Holmdel, NJ St. John Vianney High School.
Ryan, David '79 (CHI) [X] Chicago, IL Catholic Youth, Archdiocese of Chicago.
Ryan, Dennis K. '66 (DEN) Broomfield, CO Nativity of Our Lord Church.
Ryan, Dennis M. '74 (GB) Freedom, WI St. Nicholas Church.
Ryan, Donald L. '63 (L) Fairfield, KY St. Michael Church; Fairfield, KY St. Michael Church.
Ryan, Edmund G. *s.j.* '59 (SY) [B] Syracuse, NY Le Moyne College; [S] Syracuse, NY Jesuits at LeMoyne, Inc.
Ryan, Edmund K. *o.p.* '65 (P) Brookings, OR Star of the Sea Church.
Ryan, Edward '47 (ALB) Retired.
Ryan, Edward A. '71 (BRK) [166] Queens, NY St. Elizabeth's Church.
Ryan, Msgr. Edward J. '33 (SY) Fayetteville, NY Immaculate Conception Church; Retired.
Ryan, Edward M. '74 (WOR) [10] Worcester, MA Our Lady of Fatima Church; Worcester, MA University of Mass Medical Center.
Ryan, Eugene D. '69 (VEN) [6] Sarasota, FL St. Thomas More Church.
Ryan, F. Lee '68 (JOL) Watseka, IL St. Edmund Church.
Ryan, Francis J. *c.ss.r.* '44 (STL) [P] Liguori, MO St. Clement Health Care Center.
Ryan, Francis J. '58 (PEO) Odell, IL St. Paul's Church.
Ryan, Frank *o.m.i.* '54 (STP) Albertville, MN St. Albert Church.
Ryan, Frederick J. '64 (BO) On Special or Other Diocesan Assignment; Priestly Renewal.
Ryan, G. Philip '88 (ATL) Washington, GA St. Joseph's Church.
Ryan, George J. '62 (BRK) [188] Queens, NY St. Joseph Church.
Ryan, Gerald E. '55 (DM) [10] Des Moines, IA St. Mary of Nazareth Church.
Ryan, Msgr. Gerald J. '45 (NY) [160] Bronx, NY St. Luke Church; Retired.
Ryan, Greg (SP) Absent on Leave.
Ryan, Herbert J. *s.j.* '62 (LA) [C] Los Angeles, CA

Loyola Marymount University.
Ryan, J. Patrick (PAT) Rockaway, NJ St. Cecilia's Church.
Ryan, Jack '76 (HON) Holualoa, HI St. Michael The Archangel Church; Holualoa, HI St. Michael The Archangel Church.
Ryan, James '60 (JUN) Retired.
Ryan, James F. *s.s.e.* '56 (MOB) [H] Selma, AL Edmundite Fathers.
Ryan, James G. *o.s.a.* '49 (FWT) Abbott, TX Immaculate Heart of Mary Church.
Ryan, James H. *s.j.* '69 (RC) Rosebud, SD St. Bridget Church.
Ryan, James M. '75 (COV) Melbourne, KY St. Philip Church.
Ryan, James R. '66 (CAM) Pennsauken, NJ St. Cecilia's Church.
Ryan, James S. *s.j.* '69 (RC) St. Francis, SD Rosebud Reservation Church.
Ryan, James W. '48 (BRK) [39] Brooklyn, NY St. Fortunata Church.
Ryan, James W. '70 (BIS) Underwood, ND St. Bonaventure Church.
Ryan, John '45 (MAR) Retired.
Ryan, John '50 (SB) Highland, CA St. Adelaide Church; Highland, CA St. Adelaide Church.
Ryan, John *c.ss.r.* '53 (BO) [13] Boston, MA Basilica of Our Lady of Perpetual Help.
Ryan, John '53 (Y) Absent on Leave.
Ryan, John '54 (ALX) Retired.
Ryan, John '64 (JOL) Park Forest, IL St. Mary Church.
Ryan, John '74 (NO) Lafitte, LA St. Anthony Church.
Ryan, John A. '70 (SFR) San Carlos, CA St. Charles Church.
Ryan, John Chrysostom *c.p.* '48 (BRK) [U] Jamaica, NY Immaculate Conception Monastery.
Ryan, Msgr. John F.C. '50 (FRS) Retired.
Ryan, John J. *c.ss.r.* (BO) Boston, MA New England Baptist Hospital.
Ryan, John J. *o.p.* '42 (WDC) [11] Washington, DC St. Dominic Church & Priory Church.
Ryan, John J. '51 (PEO) Absent on Leave.
Ryan, John J. '71 (ORL) Ormond Beach, FL St. Brendan Church.
Ryan, John J. *c.s.c.* '90 (SCR) [C] Wilkes-Barre, PA Kings College.
Ryan, Msgr. John M. '55 (BUF) Eggertsville, NY St. Benedict Church.
Ryan, John M. '64 (CHI) [3] Waukegan, IL St. Dismas Church.
Ryan, John P. '63 (NEW) Fort Lee, NJ Madonna Church.
Ryan, Msgr. John R. '46 (PAT) Retired.
Ryan, Msgr. John R. '47 (PAT) [P] Chester, NJ Nazareth Village.
Ryan, John R. '50 (DM) Retired.
Ryan, John T. '56 (IND) [16] Indianapolis, IN St. Anthony Church.
Ryan, John T. *s.j.* '76 (NY) [BB] Staten Island, NY Mount Manresa Jesuit Retreat House.
Ryan, Joseph (PAT) Mount Arlington, NJ Our Lady of the Lake Church.
Ryan, Joseph '58 (SAG) Clare, MI St. Cecilia Church.
Ryan, Joseph A. *o.m.i.* '42 (BO) [Z] Tewksbury, MA Immaculate Heart of Mary Novitiate-Infirmary.
Ryan, Joseph D. '43 (CHI) [212] Chicago, IL St. Walter Church; Flossmoor, IL Infant Jesus of Prague Church; Retired.
Ryan, Joseph D. *s.j.* '43 (NY) [Z] New York, NY Murray-Weigel Hall.
Ryan, Joseph E. '47 (BO) Retired.
Ryan, Joseph F. '46 (SCR) Retired.
Ryan, Joseph G. *o.s.a.* '87 (WDC) [B] Silver Spring, MD Austin Friars Hall, Order of St. Augustine.
Ryan, Joseph J. '51 (STL) Retired.
Ryan, Joseph L. *s.j.* '51 (BGP) [O] Fairfield, CT The Fairfield Jesuit Community-Fairfield University.
Ryan, Msgr. Joseph P. '38 (DM) Retired.
Ryan, Kenan *s.t.* (JKS) Philadelphia, MS Holy Cross Church.
Ryan, Kenan *s.t.* '59 (PAT) [M] Stirling, NJ Holy Spirit Missionary Cenacle.
Ryan, Kevin *o.s.b.* '42 (IND) [H] Beech Grove, IN St. Paul Hermitage; [J] St. Meinrad, IN St. Meinrad Archabbey.
Ryan, Kevin E. '70 (SAT) [53] San Antonio, TX St. Mark the Evangelist Church.
Ryan, Laurence D. *s.j.* '77 (BGP) [O] Fairfield, CT The Fairfield Jesuit Community-Fairfield University.
Ryan, Lawrence A. '42 (SAC) Vacaville, CA St. Mary Church; Retired and in Senior Ministry.
Ryan, Lawrence D. *s.j.* '77 (BGP) [D] Fairfield, CT Fairfield College Preparatory School.
Ryan, Msgr. Leo P. '54 (PAT) Retired; [P] Chester, NJ Nazareth Village.
Ryan, LeRoy F. *s.j.* '56 (DET) [P] Clarkston, MI Colombiere Center.
Ryan, Martin E. *s.j.* '48 (BO) [W] Weston, MA Campion Health Center, Inc.
Ryan, Msgr. Martin P. '76 (BGP) New Fairfield, CT St. Edward the Confessor Church.
Ryan, Michael G. '66 (SEA) [1] Seattle, WA St. James Cathedral.
Ryan, Michael J. '68 (SEA) Olympia, WA St. Michael's Church.
Ryan, Michael J. '72 (PH) [140] Philadelphia, PA Resurrection of Our Lord Church.
Ryan, Milton Fleming *c.m.* (SPC) [2] Cape Girardeau, MO St. Vincent de Paul Church.
Ryan, Noel S. *s.s.c.* '63 (SD) [25] San Diego, CA St. Columba Church.
Ryan, Patrick '53 (ALB) On Duty Outside the Diocese.
Ryan, Patrick '85 (PMB) On Duty Outside the Diocese.
Ryan, Patrick D. '70 (STL) [2] Lemay, MO Most Precious Blood Church.
Ryan, Patrick J. '58 (STP) On Duty Outside the Archdiocese.
Ryan, Patrick J. *s.j.* '59 (BO) [W] Chestnut Hill, MA The Jesuit Community at Boston College.
Ryan, Patrick J. *s.j.* '68 (NY) [Z] New York, NY Jesuit Community at Fordham University.
Ryan, Patrick J. *m.m.* '77 (NY) [Z] Maryknoll, NY Maryknoll Fathers and Brothers.
Ryan, Paul *s.m.* '45 (SAT) [M] San Antonio, TX Marianist Residence.
Ryan, Paul J. '73 (ROC) Aurora, NY St. Patrick Church; Cayuga, NY St. Joseph Church; King Ferry, NY Our Lady of the Lake, King Ferry Church; Union Springs, NY St. Michael's Church; [M] Rochester, NY Diocesan Office of Campus Ministry.
Ryan, Paul T. '58 (BO) [26] Boston, MA St. Gregory Church.
Ryan, Peter F. *s.j.* '87 (BAL) [C] Baltimore, MD Loyola College; [M] Baltimore, MD Jesuit Community of Loyola College, Inc.
Ryan, Philip J. '57 (SR) Guerneville, CA St. Elizabeth Church.
Ryan, Philip R. '57 (DAV) Keswick, IA Our Lady of Lourdes Church.
Ryan, Philip V. '57 (DAV) Sigourney, IA St. Mary's Church.
Ryan, Raymond R. *o.s.a.* '57 (JOL) New Lenox, IL St. Jude Church.
Ryan, Regis J. '66 (PIT) [3] McKees Rocks, PA St. John of God Church; Allegheny County, PA Ohio Valley General Hospital.
Ryan, Msgr. Richard '73 (STO) [9] Stockton, CA St. Michael Church.
Ryan, Richard '77 (PHX) Sun City, AZ Church of St. Joachim & St. Anne.
Ryan, Richard R. *c.m.* '69 (DEN) [M] Denver, CO Congregation of the Mission Midwest Province: De Paul House.
Ryan, Robert F. '47 (PH) Retired.
Ryan, Robin *c.p.* '84 (BRK) [U] Jamaica, NY Immaculate Conception Monastery; [W] Jamaica, NY Bishop Molloy Retreat House for Laymen.
Ryan, Robin C. *c.p.* '84 (BO) [A] Boston, MA St. John's Seminary School of Theology.
Ryan, Stephen *s.d.b.* '92 (PAT) [D] Paterson, NJ Don Bosco Technical High School.
Ryan, Stephen '95 (NY) [183] Bronx, NY St. Philip Neri Church.
Ryan, Stephen D. *o.p.* '93 (BO) [W] Dover, MA St. Stephen Priory.
Ryan, Steve *o.s.m.* '55 (LA) [K] Los Angeles, CA Queen of Angels-Hollywood Presbyterian Medical Center.
Ryan, Steven P. *s.j.* '82 (AUS) [21] Austin, TX St. Thomas More Church; [H] Austin, TX Jesuit Fathers and Brothers.
Ryan, T. Kenneth '30 (STP) Retired.
Ryan, Msgr. T. Peter '62 (RVC) Centerport, NY Our Lady Queen of Martyrs Church.
Ryan, Terrence P. *c.s.p.* '77 (KNX) [4] Knoxville, TN John XXIII Catholic Center Church; [J] Knoxville, TN UT-Knoxville, Newman Foundation, Inc.
Ryan, Thomas '59 (SAC) Folsom, CA St. John the Baptist Church.
Ryan, Thomas '68 (FTW) Elkhart, IN St. Thomas the Apostle Church.
Ryan, Thomas '73 (BAL) [1] Baltimore, MD Cathedral of Mary Our Queen.
Ryan, Thomas A. '64 (GI) [1] Grand Island, NE Cathedral of the Nativity of the Blessed Virgin Mary.
Ryan, Thomas F. '93 (MET) [8] Perth Amboy, NJ La Asuncion Church.
Ryan, Thomas J. '54 (SFS) Retired.
Ryan, Thomas J. '69 (OAK) [1] Berkeley, CA St. Ambrose Church.
Ryan, Thomas J. '79 (SY) Johnson City, NY St. James Church.
Ryan, Thomas M. *s.j.* '71 (CLV) [E] Cuyahoga Falls, OH Walsh Jesuit High School.
Ryan, Msgr. Timothy A. '57 (CAM) Cape May, NJ Our Lady Star of the Sea Church.
Ryan, Timothy K. '62 (SAV) Special Assignment.
Ryan, Vincent B. *s.j.* '45 (SY) [S] Syracuse, NY Jesuits at LeMoyne, Inc.
Ryan, William *o.p.* '47 (NY) Valhalla, NY Holy Name of Jesus Church.
Ryan, William '55 (JOL) Retired; [I] Naperville, IL St. John Vianney Villa.
Ryan, William A. *c.m.* '41 (CHI) [C] Chicago, IL Vincentian Community at DePaul University.
Ryan, William A. *s.j.* '45 (PH) [Z] Philadelphia, PA Jesuit Community at St. Joseph's University.
Ryan, William A. *o.s.a.* '66 (P) Myrtle Creek, OR All Souls Church.
Ryan, William A. '80 (WDC) Gaithersburg, MD St. Martin Church.
Ryan, William Arthur '59 (PEO) Ransom, IL St. Patrick's Church.
Ryan, William F. '62 (CAM) Bellmawr, NJ Annunciation Church.
Ryan, William F. *s.j.* '62 (SPK) [C] Spokane, WA Gonzaga University.
Ryan, Msgr. William H. '48 (ELP) [10] El Paso, TX Immaculate Conception Church.
Ryan, William J. '68 (STO) [1] Stockton, CA Cathedral of the Annunciation.
Ryan, William P. *s.j.* '94 (BAL) [C] Baltimore, MD Loyola College; [M] Baltimore, MD Jesuit Community of Loyola College, Inc.
Ryba, Charles J. '69 (CLV) Columbia Station, OH St. Elizabeth Ann Seton Church.
Rybacki, Czeslew *s.ch.* '92 (SFR) [36] San Francisco, CA Nativity Church.
Rybarczyk, Melvin *c.r.* '69 (VNN) San Diego, CA Holy Angels Church.
Ryberg, James C. '57 (OM) Platte Center, NE St. Joseph Church.
Rybicki, Daryl '79 (FTW) [2] South Bend, IN St. Adalbert Church; [4] South Bend, IN St. Augustine Church.
Rybicky, Walter *o.s.b.m.* '83 (STN) [7] Palos Park, IL Nativity of B. V. M. Church.
Rybinski, Marvin '59 (DET) Retired.
Rybka, Damien *o.f.m.* '52 (GB) [I] Pulaski, WI Assumption of B.V.M. Friary.
Rybolt, John E. *c.m.* '67 (STL) [P] St. Louis, MO Vincentian Residence.
Rydelek, Theodore '89 (TYL) Fairfield, TX St. Bernard of Clarivaux Church.
Ryder, Frederick *c.pp.s.* '63 (CIN) Cassella, OH Nativity of the Blessed Virgin Mary Church; St. Rose, OH St. Rose Church.
Ryder, Joseph F. '46 (DET) Retired.
Ryder, Matthais '62 (ORG) Inactive Leave.
Rydz, Zygmund S. '48 (LIN) Retired.
Rydzon, Walter C. '76 (PIT) [55] Pittsburgh, PA St. Justin Church.
Ryfinski, Gerald J. '90 (CHR) Hartsville, SC St. Mary the Virgin Mother Church; [H] Hartsville, SC Coker College Newman Center.
Rykowski, Jerome A. '55 (PBL) Retired.
Rykowski, Valerian J. '43 (GAY) [D] Traverse City, MI Infant Jesus of Prague Monastery.
Rykowski, Valerian J. '43 (MIL) Retired.
Rykwalder, David L. '85 (GI) Farwell, NE St. Anthony of Padua Church.
Ryland, Raymond '83 (SD) Unassigned.
Ryle, Edward J. '56 (PHX) Special Assignment.
Ryle, Edward J. '56 (TUC) On Duty Outside the Diocese.
Ryle, Gerald '68 (SAC) North Highlands, CA St. Lawrence Church.
Rymdeika, Joseph F. '82 (PH) Delphi, PA St. Mary Church.
Rynes, Theodore J. *s.j.* '62 (SJ) [B] Santa Clara, CA Santa Clara University.
Rynish, Msgr. John F. '43 (SPC) Retired.
Rynne, Msgr. James J. '59 (CAM) Deptford, NJ St. John Vianney Church.
Rynne, Paul P. (BO) Retired.
Rynne, Thomas J. '56 (PMB) Jensen Beach, FL St. Martin de Porres Church.
Rys, Paschal *o.f.m.conv.* '51 (OG) Constableville, NY St. Mary Church.
Ryscavage, Richard J. *s.j.* '77 (WDC) [M] Washington, DC Leonard Neale House; [V] Washington, DC Jesuit Missions, Inc.; [V] Washington, DC Jesuit Refugee Service.
Ryu, Hae-Wuk *s.j.* '91 (BO) [W] Cambridge, MA Faber House.
Rywalt, Lawrence *c.p.* '92 (BRK) [U] Jamaica, NY Immaculate Conception Monastery.
Rzeczkowski, Matthew *o.p.* '69 (WDC) [B] Washington, DC Dominican House of Studies.
Rzepiela, Thomas R. '72 (CHI) [45] Chicago, IL St. Constance Church.
Rzeszutek, Martin *m.i.c.* '51 (SPR) [I] Stockbridge, MA Congregation of Marians.
Rzonca, Michael W. '73 (PH) Spring City, PA St. Joseph Church; Graterford, PA Graterford State Correctional Institution.

S

Saad, Antoun '47 (OLL) Retired.
Saad, Antoun '47 (SAM) Retired.
Saad, Msgr. Richard D. '72 (OLL) Birmingham, AL St. Elias Church.
Saade, Bassam '92 (SAM) Utica, NY St. Louis Gonzaga Church.

Saale, Richard T. '50 (KC) Retired.
Saalfeld, Lawrence '44 (P) Retired.
Saathoff, Alexis *o.s.b.* '59 (KC) [A] Conception, MO Conception Seminary College; [J] Conception, MO Conception Abbey.
Saato, Fred '67 (NTN) Yonkers, NY Christ the Savior Church.
Saavedra, Juan de Dios '89 (CC) [H] Laredo, TX St. John's Priory, (F.J.).
Saba, Joseph '74 (JUN) On Duty Outside the Diocese.
Saba, Joseph '74 (TUC) [E] Tucson, AZ Carondelet Health Care Corporation of Arizona, Inc.
Saba, Joseph J. '70 (BGP) [18] Bridgeport, CT St. Peter's Church.
Sabadell, Juan *l.c.* (PRO) [T] South Kingston, RI Hombre Nueva (RI), Inc.; [T] Wakefield, RI Mater Ecclesiae, Inc.; [T] Wakefield, RI Overbrook, Incorporated; [T] Wakefield, RI The Legion of Christ (RI) Incorporated.
Sabadish, Joseph F. '45 (PH) Lansdale, PA St. Stanislaus Church; [T] Norristown, PA Sacred Heart Hospital and Rehabilitation Center.
Saban, Michael J. '89 (PH) [157] Philadelphia, PA St. William Church.
Sabatini, Francis J. '63 (PH) [88] Philadelphia, PA St. Lucy Church.
Sabatino, Robert A. '56 (Y) Ravenna, OH Immaculate Conception Church.
Sabatos, Daniel C. '62 (BRK) Absent on Sick Leave.
Sabatte, Frank *c.s.p.* '80 (OAK) [2] Berkeley, CA Holy Spirit Parish Church; [Q] Berkeley, CA Holy Spirit Parish, University of California, Newman Hall.
Sabbagh, Stephen F. *o.f.m.* '59 (WDC) [M] Washington, DC Commissariat of the Holy Land, Franciscan Monastery - Mount St. Sepulchre.
Sabella, Charles A. '94 (MET) Kendall Park, NJ St. Augustine of Canterbury Church; [L] Phillipsburg, NJ The Anawim Community.
Sabia, Msgr. John B. '64 (BGP) Monroe, CT St. Jude Church.
Sable, Msgr. Robert M. '74 (DET) Special Assignment.
Sable, Thomas F. *s.j.* '75 (SCR) [C] Scranton, PA University of Scranton; [C] Scranton, PA University of Scranton.
Sablica, Michael J. '56 (MIL) Retired.
Sabo, Edward *t.o.r.* '68 (WH) Stonewood, WV Our Lady of Perpetual Help Church.
Sabo, Gerald J. *s.j.* '80 (CLV) [C] Cleveland, OH John Carroll Jesuit Community.
Sabo, Paul P. '69 (BUF) [68] Buffalo, NY The Visitation of the B.V.M. Church.
Sabog, Henry '60 (HON) Waimanalo, HI St. George Church.
Sabol, Casimir *o.f.m.conv.* '49 (R) Hampstead, NC St. Jude the Apostle Church; [E] Wilmington, NC Conventual Franciscans O.F.M.Conv.
Sabol, Sebastian *o.s.b.m.* '34 (STN) Warren, MI St. Josaphat Church.
Sabourin, Gerard O. '60 (PRO) Wickford, RI St. Bernard's Church.
Sabourin, Leo F. '58 (DET) [75] Detroit, MI St. Thomas Aquinas Church.
Sabulis, Paul P. '43 (HRT) [11] Waterbury, CT St. Joseph Church; Retired.
Saburo, Rusk R. '93 (CI) Babeldaob, FM Catholic Churches Church.
Saccacio, Msgr. Robert J. '61 (RVC) Amityville, NY St. Martin's Church.
Sacco, Carmine J. *s.j.* '57 (SEA) [11] Tacoma, WA St. Rita Church.
Saccoman, Robert '57 (NY) Nanuet, NY St. Anthony Church.
Sachs, John R. *s.j.* '76 (BO) [W] Cambridge, MA Weston Jesuit Community.
Sackett, Frederick *o.m.i.* '41 (SAT) [C] San Antonio, TX Oblate School of Theology; [M] San Antonio, TX De Mazenod House.
Sackevich, Paul E. '84 (BUR) Middletown Springs, VT St. Anne Church.
Sacks, Msgr. Edward R. '64 (ALN) [8] Bethlehem, PA Our Lady of Perpetual Help Church.
Sacks, Francis W. *c.m.* '67 (BIR) Roanoke, AL The Vincentian Mission of East Central Alabama Church.
Sacks, Francis W. *c.m.* '67 (BRK) [D] Queens and Staten Island, NY St. John's University.
Sacks, Francis W. *c.m.* '67 (PH) [Z] Philadelphia, PA Congregation of the Mission.
Sacus, Samuel S. '66 (WH) Beckley, WV St. Francis De Sales Church.
Sadaba, Eugenio *c.m.* '62 (SJN) [62] San Juan, PR San Vicente de Paul Church.
Sadek, Ignace '56 (SAM) Wilkes-Barre, PA St. Anthony Church.
Sadie, P. Edward '57 (WH) [1] Charleston, WV Sacred Heart Co-Cathedral.
Sadler, Alfred H. '34 (DET) Retired.
Sadlier, Richard T. *s.s.j.* '63 (BR) New Roads, LA St. Augustine Church.
Sadlowski, Ronald F. '72 (SPR) Easthampton, MA Sacred Heart Church.
Sadowski, Robert J. *c.s.p.* (BO) [P] Boston, MA Paulist Center; [W] Boston, MA Paulist Fathers Residence.
Sadowsky, James A. *s.j.* '57 (NY) [Z] New York, NY Jesuit Community at Fordham University.
Sadusky, Msgr. Joseph F. '70 (WDC) [37] Washington, DC St. Peter Church; Pastoral Center Special Ministries.
Saelzler, Richard J. '76 (TOL) [34] Toledo, OH St. Patrick Historic Church; [B] Toledo, OH Central Catholic High School.
Saenz, Roberto B. *s.j.* '59 (YAK) [3] Yakima, WA Holy Redeemer Church.
Saenz, Urbano *o.s.a.* '70 (SJN) [42] San Juan, PR Ntra. Sra. de la Monserrate Church.
Saez, Jose '49 (ELP) Retired.
Saez, Raul (SJN) [C] San Juan, PR Santa Ana Chapel.
Safiejko, Edward M. '48 (MIL) [19] Milwaukee, WI St. Charles Borromeo Church.
Safko, Gerard F. '90 (SCR) [1] Freeland, PA St. Ann's Church.
Safko, Stephen '73 (PSC) Phillipsburg, NJ SS. Peter and Paul Church.
Safranek, William '96 (OM) [13] Omaha, NE St. Elizabeth Ann Church.
Safraniec, Joseph '76 (STU) On Duty Outside the Diocese.
Sagala, James F. (NEW) East Orange, NJ Veterans Administration Hospital.
Sagala, James F. '61 (PIT) Military Chaplains.
Sagardia, Reinaldo '79 (SJN) [32] San Juan, PR San Lucas Church.
Sagardoy, Angel (LA) [65] Los Angeles, CA St. Gerard Majella Church.
Sagayaraj, Sekar '88 (LIN) Plattsmouth, NE Church of the Holy Spirit.
Saglimbeni, Bernardine (NY) Bronx, NY U.S.V.A. Medical Center.
Saglio, Charles A. '74 (RIC) [E] Newport News, VA Mary Immaculate Hospital.
Sagorski, Peter A. '95 (ORL) Daytona Beach, FL St. Paul's Church.
Sah, Sushil '87 (DET) [K] Detroit, MI Jesuit Community at the University of Detroit.
Saharic, Michael C. '88 (MET) Edison, NJ St. Matthew Church.
Sahlfeld, Francis J. '48 (CIN) Retired.
Saidi, Joseph '33 (SAM) Worcester, MA Our Lady of Mercy Church.
Sailstad, Kenton '88 (DUL) Cloquet, MN Queen of Peace Church.
Saja, Thaddeus A. '46 (BO) [2] Boston, MA St. Adalbert Church; Retired.
Sajda, Michael *o.f.m.conv.* '79 (PMB) [B] Fort Pierce, FL John Carroll High School.
Sajdak, Ronald P. '96 (BUF) [38] Buffalo, NY St. John the Evangelist Church.
Sakalys, Raphael J. *o.f.m.* '53 (PRT) [I] Kennebunkport, ME St. Anthony's Friary.
Sakano, Msgr. Donald '71 (NY) [47] New York, NY Holy Innocents Church; [DD] New York, NY The Housing Fund of the Archdiocese of New York.
Sakkal, Georges '96 (OLD) Laval, Eglise St. Ephrem Church.
Saksons, Richard *o.praem.* '92 (BAK) Milton Freewater, OR St. Francis of Assisi Church.
Sakwoicz, Gregory '79 (CHI) [132] Chicago, IL St. Mary of the Woods Church.
Sala, Charles *p.i.m.e.* '38 (COL) [H] Newark, OH P.I.M.E. Mission & Prayer Center.
Sala, Michael J. *s.j.* (NY) Manhattan, NY Metropolitan Hospital.
Sala, Michael J. *s.j.* '77 (NY) [80] New York, NY Nativity Church.
Salach, Conrad M. *o.f.m.conv.* '71 (ALT) Davidsville, PA St. Anne Church.
Salada, Urbano '59 (SD) Retired.
Saladna, George E. '58 (PIT) Springdale, PA St. Alphonsus Church.
Salah, Michael A. '91 (WDC) [14] Washington, DC St. Francis Xavier Church.
Salamon, John *c.ss.r.* '45 (ORL) [F] New Smyrna Beach, FL St. Alphonsus Villa-Redemptorist Fathers and Brothers.
Salamone, Charles E. '75 (BO) Braintree, MA St. Clare Church.
Salamone, Gregory R. *o.p.* '72 (PH) [A] Wynnewood, PA Theological Seminary of St. Charles Borromeo, Overbrook.
Salamone, Michael J. '75 (BRK) Absent on Sick Leave.
Salanitro, Alfred J. '89 (OM) Laurel, NE St. Mary Church.
Salanitro, Carl A. '70 (OM) [30] Omaha, NE Mary Our Queen Church.
Salas, Raul *o.m.i.* '80 (SAT) [F] San Antonio, TX St. Anthony Catholic High School; [M] San Antonio, TX St. Anthony Catholic High School House.
Salas, Sipio '50 (SFE) Retired.
Salas, Vicente *o.m.* '66 (PCE) [B] Ponce, PR The Pontifical Catholic University of Puerto Rico.
Salata, Gregory '94 (MEM) [16] Memphis, TN St. Louis Church.
Salatino, John C. '94 (SPR) [4] Westfield, MA St. Mary's Church.
Salazar, Alejandro '91 (CC) Encinal, TX Immaculate Heart of Mary Church; [3] Laredo, TX Holy Family Church.
Salazar, Alexander '84 (LA) [91] Los Angeles, CA St. Teresa of Avila Church.
Salazar, Cesar '93 (ORG) La Habra, CA Our Lady of Guadalupe Church.
Salazar, Claudio Manuel '90 (P) Salem, OR St. Joseph Church.
Salazar, Felipe '86 (SEA) Unassigned.
Salazar, Franklin '75 (RVC) Mastic Beach, NY St. Jude Church.
Salazar, George V. '67 (SFE) Las Vegas, NM Immaculate Conception Church; [M] Las Vegas, NM St. Paul, Highlands University Newman Center.
Salazar, Jairo '91 (SJN) [3] Toa Alta, PR San Jose Church.
Salazar, Jose Angel '85 (CC) Mathis, TX Sacred Heart Church.
Salazar, Joseph A. *m.ss.a.* '77 (WH) Romney, WV Our Lady of Grace Church.
Salazar, Mario A. '61 (YAK) Grandview, WA Blessed Sacrament Church.
Salazar, Mario P. '90 (YAK) Quincy, WA St. Pius X Church.
Salazar, Oscar '96 (ORL) Deltona, FL Our Lady of the Lakes Church.
Salazar-Jimenez, John '84 (AMA) Tulia, TX Church of the Holy Spirit.
Salberg, James G. '69 (PIT) Allegheny County, PA Dismas House; Allegheny County, PA State Correctional Institution of Pittsburgh.
Salca, Louis A. '65 (SD) [4] El Cajon, CA St. Louise de Marillac Church.
Salcedo, Cresenciano *s.d.b.* '59 (LA) [79] Los Angeles, CA St. Mary Church.
Salcedo, Luis G. '89 (WDC) [1] Bethesda, MD St. Bartholomew Church; Retired.
Salciccia, Ralph '49 (STU) Bellaire, OH St. John Church.
Salcido, Romeo *m.j.* '86 (PCE) [7] Ponce, PR Santa Maria Church; [B] Ponce, PR The Pontifical Catholic University of Puerto Rico.
Saldana, Jesus '82 (MIA) [21] Miami, FL St. Joachim Church.
Saldana, Jose '61 (DAL) Bonham, TX St. Elizabeth Church; Bonham, TX Veterans Administration Hospital.
Salditos, Ricardito P. '80 (LUB) Morton, TX St. Ann Church.
Salem, George J. *o.s.b.* '40 (BIR) [E] Cullman, AL St. Bernard Abbey.
Salemi, Msgr. Cajetan P. '61 (NEW) Allendale, NJ Guardian Angel Church.
Salemi, Vincenzo *i.m.c.* '68 (MET) [H] Somerset, NJ Consolata Society for Foreign Missions.
Salera, Alfredo J. (CHI) Evergreen Park, IL St. Bernadette Church.
Salerno, Emilio J. '59 (BRK) [41] Brooklyn, NY St. Frances Cabrini Church.
Salerno, Joseph '80 (SY) [13] Utica, NY St. Mary of Mt. Carmel Church.
Salerno, Joseph A. '65 (CAM) Rosenhayn, NJ St. Mary's Church.
Salerno, Michael *s.a.c.* '93 (BRK) [110] Brooklyn, NY Our Lady of the Rosary of Pompeii Church.
Saletrik, E. George '96 (GBG) Belle Vernon, PA St. Sebastian Church.
Salgado, Jose '93 (SCR) [M] Elmhurst, PA Priestly Fraternity of St. Peter (F.S.S.P.).
Salgueiro da Costa, Jose *i.m.c.* '73 (MET) [H] Somerset, NJ Consolata Society for Foreign Missions.
Saliba, John A. *s.j.* '65 (DET) [K] Detroit, MI Jesuit Community at the University of Detroit.
Salicone, Aniello *s.x.* '66 (BO) [W] Holliston, MA Xaverian Missionaries.
Salim, Anthony J. '74 (OLL) Youngstown, OH St. Maron Church.
Salinas, Marcel H. *c.m.f.* '54 (PHX) [6] Mesa, AZ St. Timothy Church; Special Assignment.
Salinas, Octavio Jose *o.f.m.* '83 (NY) [5] Mt. Vernon, NY Our Lady of Mount Carmel Church.
Salisbury, Paschal Donald *o.p.* '67 (P) White City, OR U.S. Veteran's Affiars Domiciliary.
Salisbury, W. Dayton *s.s.j.* '59 (BAL) [M] Baltimore, MD St. Joseph Society of the Sacred Heart House of Central Administration.
Saliva, Juan J. '90 (PCE) Yauco, PR St. Martin de Porres Church.
Salko, John H. '60 (PBR) Scottdale, PA St. John the Baptist Church.
Salkovski, Basil *o.s.b.m.* (STN) Warren, MI St. Josaphat Church.
Saller, Neil *t.o.r.* '56 (PH) [Z] Fairless Hills, PA St. Anthony Friary.
Sallese, Albert J. '66 (BO) [33] Boston, MA St. John Baptist Church; [68] Boston, MA Sacred Heart Church.

Sallis, Steven '80 (SEA) Bothell, WA St. Brendan Church.
Sallot, Steven '80 (ORG) [8] Santa Ana, CA St. Joseph's Church; [C] Santa Ana, CA Mater Dei High School.
Salmani, Frank S. '82 (PRO) [4] Providence, RI St. Ann's Church.
Salmi, Richard P. *s.j.* '82 (CLV) [C] Cleveland, OH John Carroll University; [C] Cleveland, OH John Carroll Jesuit Community.
Salmon, Albert G. '54 (OG) Brushton, NY St. Mary Church.
Salmon, Charles P. '44 (DEN) Retired; [I] Denver, CO Gardens at St. Elizabeth.
Salmon, Edward M. '59 (CHI) [4] Oak Park, IL St. Giles Church.
Salmon, James F. *s.j.* '64 (BAL) [C] Baltimore, MD Loyola College; [M] Baltimore, MD Jesuit Community of Loyola College, Inc.; [M] Baltimore, MD Jesuit Fathers and Brothers Maryland Provincial Curia.
Salmon, William F. '65 (BO) [58] Boston, MA Our Lady of the Presentation Church.
Salocks, Stephen E. '80 (BO) [A] Boston, MA St. John's Seminary School of Theology.
Salois, Phillip (BO) Boston, MA V.A. Medical Centers.
Salomon, Jean F. '80 (NEW) [9] Elizabeth, NJ Our Lady of Most Holy Rosary/St. Michael Church.
Salomone, Gregory *o.p.* '72 (RIC) Charlottesville, VA St. Thomas Aquinas Church.
Saloy, Lee John '72 (NO) [13] Metairie, LA St. Philip Neri Church.
Saloy, Thomas '88 (RVC) West Babylon, NY Our Lady of Grace Church.
Salt, Donald L. '47 (STP) Retired.
Saltarin, Jose '67 (NEW) [18] Jersey City, NJ St. Nicholas Church.
Salter, Bartholomew C. *c.s.c.* '71 (BGP) [4] Greenwich, CT St. Roch Church; [I] Bridgeport, CT St. Vincent's Medical Center.
Saltry, Joseph A. '44 (SCR) Retired.
Saltysiak, Paul M. '92 (WDC) Military Chaplains.
Salus, Jude S. *o.s.b.* '75 (PAT) [M] Morristown, NJ St. Mary's Abbey.
Salvador, John '54 (PHX) Prescott, AZ Sacred Heart Church.
Salvador, Stephen B. '74 (FR) [4] Attleboro, MA Holy Ghost Church.
Salvagna, Michael *c.p.* '69 (PIT) [N] Pittsburgh, PA St. Paul of the Cross Monastery; [N] Pittsburgh, PA St. Paul of the Cross Monastery; [P] Pittsburgh, PA St. Paul of the Cross Retreat Center.
Salvana, Bonifacio '56 (YAK) Waterville, WA St. Joseph's Church.
Salvas, John V. *o.f.m.cap.* '88 (SP) [6] Tampa, FL Most Holy Redeemer Church.
Salvaturian, Stanley Oleksy '82 (LR) Huntsville, AR St. John's Church.
Salvi, Americo *c.r.m.* '55 (NEW) Lodi, NJ St. Joseph's Church.
Salwach, Jeffery '84 (JOL) [11] Joliet, IL St. John the Baptist Church; [J] Joliet, IL St. John the Baptist Friary.
Salwowski, Francis J. *o.f.m.cap.* '45 (PAT) [M] Oak Ridge-Milton, NJ St. Stanislaus B. M. Friary.
Salwowski, John F. *o.f.m.cap.* '45 (MET) [4] New Brunswick, NJ St. Joseph Church.
Saly, Msgr. Robert J. '85 (ALT) [3] Altoona, PA St. Mark's Church; [E] Hollidaysburg, PA Dmitri Manor Priests' Residence.
Salz, Marvin C. '64 (DUB) Lawler, IA Our Lady of Mt. Carmel Church; New Hampton, IA St. Mary's Church; [E] New Hampton, IA St. John's School.
Salzbrunn, Tony '52 (SCL) Dumont, MN St. Peter's Church; Wheaton, MN Ave Maria Church.
Salzmann, George S. *o.s.f.s.* '77 (BO) [CC] Cambridge, MA Harvard-Radcliffe Catholic Student Center.
Salzmann, George S. *o.s.f.s.* '77 (WIL) [I] Wilmington, DE Oblates of St. Francis De Sales.
Salzmann, George S. *o.s.f.s.* '78 (BO) [12] Cambridge, MA St. Paul Church.
Sam, James '75 (DET) Absent on Leave.
Samaha, Jeffrey F. '78 (WDC) Hospital & Nursing Home Ministries.
Samaniego, Eduardo A. *s.j.* '90 (SD) [4] San Diego, CA Christ the King Church.
Samaniego, Tarciscio *l.c.* (HRT) [B] Cheshire, CT Novitiate of the Legion of Christ.
Samay, Sebastian A. *o.s.b.* '59 (GBG) [H] Latrobe, PA Saint Vincent Archabbey.
Samayoa, Emmanuel G. '89 (ROM) Special Assignment.
Sambor, David R. '78 (SY) Special Assignment; [S] East Syracuse, NY Bishop Grimes Priests Residence.
Samiano, Marvin J. '92 (HON) Mountain View, HI St. Theresa Church.
Sammon, Msgr. John F. '42 (ORG) Special Assignment.
Sammon, Peter J. '47 (SFR) [50] San Francisco, CA St. Teresa Church.
Sammons, Msgr. Francis L. '47 (SY) Retired.
Sammons, Msgr. Frank L. '47 (SY) [S] East Syracuse, NY Bishop Grimes Priests Residence.
Sammons, Joseph F. '49 (SCR) Retired.
Sammut, Tito '52 (GB) New London, WI Most Precious Blood Church.
Samonie, Jacob '56 (DET) Retired.
Sampana, Narcisco '84 (CHK) Tanapag Village, District 8, MP Santa Remedios Church; San Roque Village, District 9, MP San Roque Parish Church.
Samperi, Charles J. '96 (GAL) [53] Houston, TX Notre Dame Church.
Sampietro, Vincent *c.s.p.* '45 (P) [28] Portland, OR St. Philip Neri Church.
Sampietro, Vincent J. *c.s.p.* '45 (NY) [Z] Scarsdale, NY Paulist Fathers Generalate.
Sample, Alexander K. '90 (MAR) [2] Marquette, MI St. Christopher Church; Special Assignment.
Sampon, Robert G. '53 (MIL) Newburg, WI Holy Trinity Church.
Sampon, Robert G. '54 (MIL) [W] Milwaukee, WI People's Eucharistic League.
Sampson, Elric '85 (CHI) [N] Chicago, IL St. Peter's Friary.
Sampson, J. Gregory *c.j.m.* '54 (BUF) [1] West Seneca, NY St. Bonaventure Church; [O] West Seneca, NY St. Bonaventure.
Sampson, James *s.p.* '65 (SFE) [J] Jemez Springs, NM The Jemez Program, Our Lady of Lourdes Novitiate.
Sampson, James G. *s.j.* '87 (DEN) [M] Denver, CO Regis Jesuit Community (The Jesuits at Regis University).
Sampson, Patrick '55 (GF) Retired.
Sampson, William P. *s.j.* '59 (WDC) [E] Washington, DC Gonzaga College High School.
Samra, Basil '86 (NTN) Phoenix, AZ St. John of the Desert Church.
Sams, Ronald W. *s.j.* '59 (BUF) [D] Buffalo, NY Canisius High School; [O] Buffalo, NY Canisius Jesuit Community.
Samsa, Bertin L. *o.f.m.cap.* (GB) Weyauwega, WI SS. Peter and Paul Church.
Samson, John F. '61 (SCR) Ashley, PA Holy Rosary Church.
Samson, Robert J. '79 (STL) [28] St. Louis, MO St. Boniface Church.
Samter, James '87 (GB) Special Assignment.
Samuel, Abraham '75 (DAL) [1] Garland, TX Good Shepherd Church.
Samuel, Francis '72 (RVC) Seaford, NY St. James Church.
Samway, Patrick H. *s.j.* '69 (NY) [Z] New York, NY "America;" Residence and publication office of the America Press.
Samy, Edward (SJ) Milpitas, CA St. Elizabeth Church.
Samy, S. Anthony '85 (NY) [138] Bronx, NY St. Dominic Church.
Samyn, Rick *o.f.m.cap.* (DET) [K] Detroit, MI St. Mary's Friary.
San Andres, Vito B. '79 (AGN) Yigo, GU Our Lady of Lourdes Church.
San Filipo, David (PHX) [18] Phoenix, AZ St. Martin de Porres Church.
San Fratello, Sennen C. *o.f.m.* '58 (ALB) [B] Loudonville, NY Siena College.
San Llorente, Faustino '41 (ARE) Retired.
San Marco, Salvator J. *s.j.* '53 (MIA) [5] Miami, FL Gesu Church.
San Martin, Miguel Angel *c.p.* '63 (MGZ) San Sebastian, PR San Sebastian Martir Church.
San Nicasio, Julian *s.d.b.* '76 (ARE) Orocovis, PR San Juan Bautista Church.
San Nicasio, Julian '77 (CGS) [C] Aibonito, PR Casa Salesiana de Retiros.
Sana, Yoshia '84 (EST) San Jose, CA St. Mary Assyrian-Caldean Parish Church.
Sanahuja, Manuel *sch.p.* '67 (LA) [92] Los Angeles, CA Santa Teresita Church.
Sanches, Joseph A. '70 (ATL) On Duty Outside the Archdiocese.
Sanches, Joseph A. '70 (NSH) [10] Nashville, TN Church of the Most Holy Name; [11] Nashville, TN St. Patrick's Church.
Sanchez, Alejandro '93 (STV) [1] St. Thomas, VI Cathedral of Sts. Peter and Paul.
Sanchez, Angel '75 (MGZ) Lajas, PR Our Lady of the Purification Church.
Sanchez, Angel '90 (PCE) Salinas, PR Our Lady of Monserrat Church.
Sanchez, Angelo G. *c.ss.r.* '41 (MGZ) Aguadilla, PR St. Charles Borromeo Church.
Sanchez, Antonio '90 (MRY) Watsonville, CA Assumption Church; Special Assignment.
Sanchez, Msgr. Carlos '50 (BR) Retired.
Sanchez, Castor G. '61 (TR) [13] Trenton, NJ St. Francis of Assisium Church.
Sanchez, D. Ignacio '40 (LA) Pomona, CA Sacred Heart Church.
Sanchez, Eliseo '57 (LA) Retired.
Sanchez, Enrique '55 (SAC) Isleton, CA St. Therese's Church.
Sanchez, Esequiel '95 (CHI) [148] Chicago, IL Our Lady of Grace Church.
Sanchez, Felix '65 (SP) Dade City, FL St. Rita Church.
Sanchez, Frank *o.carm.* '54 (JOL) [J] Darien, IL Carmelite Fathers Provincial Office.
Sanchez, Guadalupe *o.s.j.* '60 (FRS) Madera, CA St. Joachim Church.
Sanchez, Jose '61 (BRK) [225] Queens, NY St. Paul the Apostle Church; Queens, NY Elmhurst General Hospital.
Sanchez, Jose C. *c.m.* '62 (MIA) [34] Miami, FL St. Vincent De Paul Church.
Sanchez, Jose L. *c.m.f.* '95 (AUS) Martindale, TX Immaculate Heart of Mary Church.
Sanchez, Jose M. '58 (GAL) Freeport, TX St. Henry Church.
Sanchez, Joseph '60 (SFR) Special Assignment; [K] San Francisco, CA Home for the Aged of the Little Sisters of the Poor.
Sanchez, Joseph G. '83 (LA) Lynwood, CA St. Philip Neri Church.
Sanchez, Juan '93 (CHI) [100] Chicago, IL St. Jerome Church.
Sanchez, Juan Luis '84 (MIA) [13] Miami, FL Our Lady of Lourdes Church.
Sanchez, Julio (SLC) [C] Ogden, UT St. Joseph Regional School.
Sanchez, Julio E. '92 (SLC) [3] Ogden, UT St. Joseph's Church.
Sanchez, Msgr. Manuel O. '54 (LA) Pomona, CA Sacred Heart Church.
Sanchez, Paul R. '71 (BRK) [2] Brooklyn, NY St. Agatha's Church.
Sanchez, Prudencio '59 (WDC) Waldorf, MD St. Peter Church.
Sanchez, Raul '74 (GLP) On Duty Outside of Diocese.
Sanchez, Raul '93 (FRS) Fowler, CA St. Lucy Church; Selma, CA St. Joseph Church.
Sanchez, Stephen *o.c.d.* '92 (LR) [A] Little Rock, AR Marylake - Carmelite Novitiate.
Sanchez, Steve '82 (SFE) Albuquerque, NM Lovelace Hospital.
Sanchez, Victor '90 (ARE) Quebradillas, PR San Raphael Church.
Sanchez, Vincente '88 (BRK) [24] Brooklyn, NY St. Brigid Church.
Sanchez, William E. '83 (SFE) Bernalillo, NM Our Lady of Sorrows Church.
Sancho, Jesus *o.c.d.* (DAL) [20] Dallas, TX St. Mary of Carmel Church.
Sancho Piquer, Enrique '50 (PCE) On Duty Outside the Diocese.
Sancho-Boyles, Anthony (FRS) Retired.
Sand, John P. '55 (SPK) Dayton, WA St. Joseph Church; Pomeroy, WA Holy Rosary Church; Waitsburg, WA St. Mark Church.
Sandberg, Stuart '68 (NY) [DD] White Plains, NY Company of St. Paul.
Sander, Bernard *o.s.b.* '44 (P) [L] St. Benedict, OR Mt. Angel Abbey.
Sander, Francis *o.s.b.* '49 (NO) [P] St. Benedict, LA St. Joseph Abbey.
Sander, Reginald *o.s.b.* '63 (KC) Chillicothe, MO St. Columban's Church.
Sander, Timothy *o.s.b.* '41 (P) [L] St. Benedict, OR Mt. Angel Abbey.
Sanders, Daniel J. '78 (MIL) [4] Sheboygan, WI Holy Name Church.
Sanders, Edwin J. *s.j.* '59 (ALN) [A] Wernersville, PA Novitiate of St. Isaac Jogues.
Sanders, Gary E. *o.s.a.* '75 (SD) [34] San Diego, CA St. Patrick Church.
Sanders, Msgr. John C. '73 (BGP) [4] Norwalk, CT St. Mary's Church.
Sanders, John R. *o.s.a.* '74 (SD) [C] San Diego, CA St. Augustine High School; [H] San Diego, CA Augustinian Community.
Sanders, Joseph P. *s.j.* '61 (WH) [A] Wheeling, WV Wheeling Jesuit University.
Sanders, Larry *c.ss.r.* '93 (DET) [34] Detroit, MI Holy Redeemer Church.
Sanders, Patrick B. '90 (NO) [2] Metairie, LA St. Angela Merici Church.
Sanders, Peter C. '84 (MRY) [G] Monterey, CA Oratorian Community-Congregation of the Oratory of Pontifical Right.
Sanders, Raymond *s.v.d.* '45 (WDC) [M] Washington, DC Divine Word College.
Sanders, Robert E. '40 (HRT) Retired.
Sanders, William F. '75 (WOR) [28] Worcester, MA St. Stephen's Church.
Sandersfeld, John '66 (SJ) [3] San Jose, CA St. Francis of Assisi/Edendale Church.
Sanderson, William E. '83 (OM) Hartington, NE Holy Trinity Church.
Sandford, Mark *o.f.m.* '43 (L) [K] Louisville, KY Franciscan Health Care Center/Retirement Center.
Sandhage, Martin J. '86 (LFT) Noblesville, IN Our Lady of Grace Church.
Sandheinrich, Msgr. Bernard H. '60 (STL) [46] St. Louis, MO Basilica of St. Louis, the King.
Sandi, Thomas P. '73 (NY) Military Chaplains.
Sandman, Gregory '80 (MRY) Watsonville, CA St. Patrick Church.
Sandmann, Augustus C. *o.s.a.* '47 (NY) [216] Staten

Island, NY Our Lady of Good Counsel Church.
Sandor, Albert *o.f.m.cap.* '82 (DET) [K] Detroit, MI St. Bonaventure Friary.
Sandor, George *o.f.m.conv.* '72 (SY) [5] Binghamton, NY SS. Cyril and Method Church.
Sandoval, Clarence J. '87 (SLC) Logan, UT St. Thomas Aquinas Church; [H] Logan, UT St. Thomas Aquinas, Newman Center.
Sandoval, Jose Luis '74 (SAT) [25] San Antonio, TX St. Alphonsus Church.
Sandoval, Victoriano F. *o.s.a.* '59 (TR) Mount Holly, NJ Christ the Redeemer Church.
Sandoz, Robert J. *o.f.m.* '86 (PRO) [P] Providence, RI St. Francis Friary.
Sandrick, Philip *o.s.b.m.* '84 (STF) Long Island City, NY Holy Cross Church.
Sands, Francis *c.ss.r.* '47 (CHL) Concord, NC St. James Church.
Sands, Joseph C. *s.j.* '92 (BAL) [M] Baltimore, MD Jesuit Fathers and Brothers Maryland Provincial Curia.
Sandstrom, Philip J. '62 (NY) Absent on Sick leave; [DD] New York, NY St. Ansgar Scandinavian Catholic League.
Sandweg, Michael J. '79 (STL) Portage Des Sioux, MO St. Francis Church.
Saner, Daniel J. '69 (COV) Augusta, KY St. Augustine Church.
Sanfelippo, Frank J. '58 (MIL) Retired.
Sanfilippo, David '94 (PHX) [20] Phoenix, AZ St. Matthew Church.
Sanfilippo, Ronald J. *s.j.* '76 (SJ) [2] Santa Clara, CA St. Clare Church.
Sanford, Harry L. *s.j.* (PBL) [8] Pueblo, CO Our Lady of Mt. Carmel Church.
Sanford, James R. *o.s.f.s.* '86 (TOL) [37] Toledo, OH St. Pius X Church; [C] Toledo, OH St. Francis de Sales High School.
Sanford, Stephen J. *s.j.* '93 (BO) [W] Chestnut Hill, MA The Jesuit Community at Boston College.
Sang, Francis '73 (RVC) Amityville, NY St. Martin's Church.
Sanger, Charles P. '37 (DEN) Retired.
Sangermano, Charles L. '78 (PH) [106] Philadelphia, PA St. Monica Church.
Sangiovanni, William F. '77 (BGP) [4] Trumbull, CT St. Theresa's Church; [C] Fairfield, CT Notre Dame Catholic High School.
Sangl, Harry R. '54 (PIT) Chippewa Township, PA Christ the Divine Teacher Church.
Sanguinetti, Joseph P. *o.p.* '44 (SFR) [N] San Francisco, CA St. Dominic Priory.
Sanguinetti, Peter J. *o.p.* '44 (SFR) [13] San Francisco, CA St. Dominic Church.
Sankoorikal, George '71 (BGP) [6] Fairfield, CT St. Pius X Church.
Sankoorikal, Paul L. '59 (LC) Bangor, WI St. Mary Church; [E] La Crosse, WI Franciscan Skemp Healthcare, Mayo Health System, La Crosse Campus Medical Center.
Sankovitz, Msgr. John P. '47 (STP) Retired; [C] St. Paul, MN University of St. Thomas.
Sanks, T. Howland *s.j.* '65 (OAK) [A] Berkeley, CA The Jesuit School of Theology at Berkeley; [A] Berkeley, CA The Jesuit School of Theology at Berkeley; [N] Berkeley, CA Jesuit Community at Jesuit School of Theology at Berkeley.
Sanllorente, Santiago *c.m.* '46 (PCE) [14] Ponce, PR San Vicente-Cantera Church.
Sanner, Msgr. James E. '59 (E) On Duty Outside Diocese.
Sans, Pablo '53 (BRK) [208] Queens, NY Our Lady of the Cenacle Church.
Sans, Theodore R. '59 (L) [3] Louisville, KY St. Albert the Great Church.
Sansaricq, Carl '51 (NY) Spring Valley, NY St. Joseph Church.
Sansaricq, Guy '60 (BRK) [65] Brooklyn, NY St. Jerome's Church; [T] Brooklyn, NY Catholic Migration & Refugee Office, Catholic Migration Services, Inc.; [Y] Cambria Heights, NY National Center of the Haitian Apostolate.
Sansom, Lawrence W. '41 (ROC) Retired.
Sanson, Robert J. '67 (CLV) Strongsville, OH St. Joseph Church.
Sansone, Anthony J. '80 (BRK) [188] Queens, NY St. Joseph Church.
Sansone, Paul D. *o.f.m.* '83 (PAT) Little Falls, NJ Our Lady of the Holy Angels Church.
Sansone, Simon *o.c.s.o.* '89 (WOR) [N] Spencer, MA St. Joseph's Abbey.
Santa, Michael *o.s.b.* '56 (KCK) [H] Atchison, KS St. Benedict's Abbey.
Santa Barbara, Robert L. '90 (MET) [1] Metuchen, NJ Cathedral of St. Francis.
Santa-Bibiana, Joseph *s.d.b.* '66 (PAT) [3] Paterson, NJ St. Anthony's Church.
Santa-Olaya, Aureliano '63 (VEN) Palmetto, FL Holy Cross Church.
Santaella, Esteban '58 (PCE) [3] Ponce, PR Church of the Resurrection; Jayuya, PR Our Lady of Monserrate Church; [B] Ponce, PR The Pontifical Catholic University of Puerto Rico.
Santamaria, Max '56 (MRY) Retired.
Santana, Edward '86 (CGS) [B] San Lorenzo, PR Casa Charlie Rodriguez; [D] San Lorenzo, PR Diocesan Shrine Our Lady of Mount Carmel; [E] Caguas, PR Diocesan Tribunal of Caguas.
Santana, Francisco '68 (MIA) [K] Miami, FL Shrine of Our Lady of Charity.
Santana, Franklin *m.c.* (MGZ) Aguadilla, PR San Jose Obrero Church.
Santana, Ramon '89 (CGS) Yabucoa, PR Santos Angeles Cutodios Church.
Santangelo, Michael A. '95 (TR) Marlton, NJ St. Joan of Arc Church.
Santen, Thomas J. '70 (STL) [23] St. Louis, MO St. Ambrose Church.
Santerre, Richard R. '82 (BO) Belmont, MA St. Joseph Church; Absent on Sick Leave.
Santiago, Angelo (ARE) On Duty Outside the Diocese.
Santiago, Felipe *c.ss.r.* '81 (MGZ) Aguadilla, PR St. Charles Borromeo Church.
Santiago, Florentino '78 (HT) [4] Thibodaux, LA St. Genevieve Church.
Santiago, Francisco *s.j.* '64 (SJN) [22] San Juan, PR San Ignacio de Loyola Church.
Santiago, Hiram *s.d.b.* (SJN) [37] San Juan, PR Maria Auxiliadora Church.
Santiago, Hiran (MGZ) Aguadilla, PR San Jose Obrero Church.
Santiago, Jorge *s.d.b.* '94 (ARE) Orocovis, PR San Juan Bautista Church.
Santiago, Jose M. *o.p.* '93 (DEN) [28] Denver, CO St. Dominic's Church.
Santiago, Juan J. *s.j.* '66 (SJN) [22] San Juan, PR San Ignacio de Loyola Church; [22] San Juan, PR San Ignacio de Loyola Church.
Santiago, Leonicia S. (CHI) [153] Chicago, IL Our Lady of Mercy Church.
Santiago, Manuel '85 (PCE) [17] Ponce, PR Our Lady of Mt. Carmel Church.
Santiago, Marciano, II '78 (OAK) [2] Hayward, CA St. Bede Church.
Santiago, Msgr. Rafael '69 (PCE) [16] Ponce, PR Church of the Good Shepherd.
Santiago, Samuel *c.ss.r.* (CGS) San Lorenzo, PR Nuestra Senora de la Mercedes Church.
Santich, Jan *o.s.b.* '90 (SCL) [I] Collegeville, MN St. John's Abbey, of the Order of St. Benedict.
Santich, Jan J. *o.s.b.* '90 (CHY) Riverton, WY St. Margaret's Church.
Santilian, John *sch.p.* '69 (LA) [R] Los Angeles, CA Piarist Fathers.
Santillan, Juan *sch.p.* '69 (LA) [21] Los Angeles, CA Our Lady Help of Christians (Maria Auxiliadora) Church.
Santillanes, Jose Flavio (SFE) Pojoaque, NM N.S. de Guadalupe del Valle de Pojoaque Church.
Santilli, Francis C. '80 (PRO) [2] Pawtucket, RI St. Cecilia's Church; [C] Pawtucket, RI St. Raphael Academy.
Santillo, Michael P. '75 (MET) On Duty Outside the Diocese.
Santitoro, Francis E. '66 (TR) [4] Toms River, NJ St. Maximilian Kolbe Church.
Santo, Mark (LA) Los Angeles, CA Metropolitan Detention Center.
Santo, Vincent '45 (SCL) Retired.
Santoalla, Jesus '57 (SJN) [25] San Juan, PR San Jorge Church.
Santor, John E. '65 (E) [12] Erie, PA St. Andrew Church; [M] Erie, PA Congregation of the Divine Spirit.
Santora, Alexander M. '82 (NEW) [19] Jersey City, NJ Our Lady of Czestochowa Church; [Q] Union, NJ Kean College.
Santora, Gerard M. '38 (NEW) [11] Jersey City, NJ Holy Rosary Church; Retired; [N] Rutherford, NJ St. John Vianney Residence for Priests.
Santoro, Charles M. *o.p.* '71 (STP) [8] Minneapolis, MN Holy Rosary Church; [15] Minneapolis, MN St. Albert the Great Church.
Santoro, David *o.p.* '77 (DM) [10] Des Moines, IA St. Mary of Nazareth Church.
Santoro, David J. *o.p.* '77 (CHI) [N] River Forest, IL St. Thomas Aquinas Priory.
Santoro, Michael C. '79 (NEW) Bloomfield, NJ St. Valentine Church.
Santorsola, Albert J. (PH) Abington, PA Our Lady Help of Christians Church.
Santos, Angel M. '77 (ARE) [9] Arecibo, PR La Milagrosa Church.
Santos, Cesar '93 (ARE) Vega-Alta, PR Immaculate Conception of Blessed Virgin Mary Church.
Santos, Frankie L. G. *c.s.sp.* '84 (GAL) [B] Houston, TX Holy Ghost Fathers.
Santos, Gregory *o.c.s.o.* (SLC) [F] Huntsville, UT Abbey of Our Lady of the Holy Trinity of the Order of Cistercians.
Santos, Lito B. (OG) Watertown, NY U.S. Army Headquarters Fort Drum.
Santos, Raul '63 (CGS) Barranquitas, PR San Andres Apostol Church.
Santos, Sergio *o.f.m.* '85 (SFR) [5] San Francisco, CA St. Anthony Church.
Santos, Tomas '95 (ARE) Quebradillas, PR San Raphael Church.
Santos, Ubaldo *c.m.f.* '87 (SAT) Gonzales, TX St. James Church.
Santos, Victor '49 (SJN) [62] San Juan, PR San Vicente de Paul Church.
Santre, William *t.o.r.* '61 (ALT) [3] Windber, PA St. Anthony of Padua Church.
Santry, Robert '86 (HON) Military Chaplains.
Santucci, Hugo *s.d.b.* '55 (SFR) [12] San Francisco, CA Corpus Christi Church.
Santucci, Louis '74 (Y) Absent on Leave.
Santulin, Msgr. Joseph M. '39 (NY) Retired; [Z] New York, NY Pope John Paul II Residence.
Santurri, Joseph '42 (PRO) Retired.
Sanz, Eleutherio '59 (MRY) Soledad, CA Our Lady of Solitude Church.
Sanz, Florentino '65 (SJN) [4] Guaynabo, PR San Juan M. Vianney Church.
Sanz, Jose (WDC) On Duty Outside the Archdiocese.
Sanz, Jose '73 (SB) [A] Riverside, CA Blessed Junipero Serra House of Formation.
Sanz, Julian '77 (TUC) Somerton, AZ Immaculate Heart of Mary Church.
Saoncella, Valentino *m.c.c.j.* '44 (CHI) [N] La Grange Park, IL Comboni Mission Center.
Sapeta, Joseph S. '47 (NEW) Retired.
Sapio, Thadeus M. *o.f.m.* (NY) [146] Bronx, NY Holy Cross Church.
Saplak, Sergio *o.s.b.m.* '92 (STN) Hamtramck, MI Immaculate Conception of B.V.M. Church.
Saplis, Raymond A. '58 (LA) Granada Hills, CA St. Euphrasia Church.
Saporito, Msgr. Cosmo G. '54 (BRK) [18] Brooklyn, NY St. Bernadette Church.
Saporito, Louis R. *s.s.j.* '60 (GAL) [62] Houston, TX Our Lady Star of the Sea Church.
Saporito, Michael A. '92 (NEW) River Edge, NJ St. Peter the Apostle Church.
Saporito, Peter '77 (CAM) Villas, NJ St. Raymond Church.
Sapp, James '86 (FTW) [7] Fort Wayne, IN St. John Baptist Church.
Sapporito, Msgr. Cosmo G. '54 (BRK) Retired.
Saprano, Samuel '71 (STU) Carlisle, OH St. Michael Church; Fulda, OH Immaculate Conception Church.
Sapuay, Orlando '73 (STL) [P] St. Louis, MO La Salette Missionaries.
Sara, Solomon I. *s.j.* '63 (BO) [W] Boston, MA The Society of Jesus of New England-Provincial Offices.
Sara, Solomon I. *s.j.* '63 (WDC) [M] Washington, DC The Jesuit Community at Georgetown University.
Sarachaga, Felix *c.m.* '52 (LA) [29] Los Angeles, CA Our Lady of the Rosary of Talpa Church.
Sarachit, Niphon *s.d.b.* '85 (OAK) [N] Berkeley, CA Salesian Community.
Sarah-Buckman, Michael *s.s.j.* '93 (BR) [8] Baton Rouge, LA St. Francis Xavier Church.
Sarauskas, Msgr. R. George '73 (CHI) On Duty Outside the Archdiocese.
Sardina, John J. '60 (BUF) [10] Cheektowaga, NY Queen of Martyrs Church; [M] Clarence, NY Brothers of Mercy Nursing & Rehabilitation Center; [M] Clarence, NY Brothers of Mercy Sacred Heart Home, Inc.; [O] Clarence, NY Provincial Motherhouse of Brothers of Mercy.
Sardina, Jorge *s.j.* '59 (MIA) [D] Miami, FL Belen Jesuit Preparatory School; [H] Miami, FL Jesuit Fathers of the Province of the Antilles, Inc.
Sardinas, Jorge A. '77 (MIA) [30] Miami, FL St. Richard Church.
Sarge, John S. '73 (SAG) [10] Saginaw, MI St. Casimir Church; [11] Saginaw, MI St. George Church.
Sargent, Benjamin F. *s.j.* '51 (SJ) [M] Los Gatos, CA Sacred Heart Jesuit Center.
Sargent, John '53 (Y) Retired.
Sargus, Edward T. '39 (BAL) Retired.
Sariego, Francis *o.f.m.cap.* '69 (NEW) [N] Union City, NJ Capuchin Friars - Prov. Stigmata of St. Francis.
Sariego, Francis '69 (NY) [151] Bronx, NY Immaculate Conception Church.
Sarjeant, Francis X. *s.j.* '61 (BO) [W] Boston, MA The Society of Jesus of New England-Provincial Offices.
Sarjeant, Francis X. *s.j.* '61 (SP) [4] Clearwater, FL St. Cecelia Church.
Sarjumanarsa, Thomas *s.j.* '75 (CHI) [C] Chicago, IL Jesuit Community at Loyola University of Chicago.
Sarkies, Jeffery L. '65 (SEA) [25] Seattle, WA Holy Rosary Church.
Sarmiento, Oscar '78 (MIA) [2] Miami Beach, FL St. Joseph Church.
Sarmiento, Oscar '82 (PT) On Duty Outside the Diocese.
Sarno, Msgr. Robert J. '73 (BRK) Released from Diocesan Assignment.
Sarosiek, John H. '93 (GAY) Retired.
Sarrazin, Victor J. *c.m.* '85 (LA) [W] Montebello, CA

DePaul Center.
Sarrazin, Victor J. '90 (LA) [R] Los Angeles, CA Amat House.
Sarrazine, Kenneth '62 (FTW) [5] Fort Wayne, IN St. Henry Church.
Sarro, John A. '79 (WIL) Bellefonte, DE St. Helena Church.
Sartain, J. Peter '78 (MEM) [16] Memphis, TN St. Louis Church.
Sartor, Alfred J. *o.f.m.conv.* '58 (TOL) Carey, OH Our Lady of Consolation, Basilica-National Shrine Church; Frenchtown, OH St. Nicholas Church.
Sartorelli, Otto J. '50 (MAR) Caspian, MI St. Cecilia Church.
Sartori, Hector *c.s.* '54 (PRO) [4] Johnston, RI St. Rocco Church.
Sartori, Peter V. '40 (STU) Retired.
Sarzynski, Edward W. '79 (ALN) [2] Shenandoah, PA St. Casimir Church; [6] Shenandoah, PA St. Stanislaus Church.
Sas, Thomas J. '76 (HRT) [4] West Hartford, CT St. Mark the Evangelist Church.
Sash, Theodore *o.f.m.conv.* '58 (SY) [10] Utica, NY St. Joseph and St. Patrick Church.
Sasin, Jan '77 (NEW) [9] Elizabeth, NJ Our Lady of Most Holy Rosary/St. Michael Church.
Sass, Donald E. '60 (MIL) Milwaukee, WI St. Luke's Medical Center.
Sassani, John E. '80 (BO) [4] Newton, MA St. John the Evangelist Church.
Sassano, Rock '63 (P) Lake Oswego, OR Our Lady of the Lake Church.
Sasso, Frank M. '73 (CHI) [102] Chicago, IL St. Joachim Church.
Sasso, Joseph M. '58 (ROC) [4] Rochester, NY St. Anne Church; Retired.
Sassone, James '57 (SD) [2] San Diego, CA Ascension Church.
Sastre, Raphael '51 (MGZ) Hormigueros, PR El Salvador Church.
Sasway, Msgr. John R. '62 (ALT) Lilly, PA St. Brigid's Church; Lilly, PA Our Lady of Mt. Carmel Church; Lilly, PA Our Lady of the Alleghenies Church.
Satchell, Martin J. '93 (PH) Absent on Sick Leave.
Sato, Damian *s.a.* '45 (NY) [Z] Garrison, NY Generalate of the Franciscan Friars of the Atonement-St. James Friary.
Satterfield, Msgr. Carroll E. '54 (BAL) Retired.
Sattler, Frederick F. '70 (ALN) [4] Pottsville, PA St. Patrick Church.
Sattler, Henry E. *c.ss.r.* '76 (BAL) [66] Baltimore, MD Our Lady of Fatima Church.
Sattler, Henry V. '43 (BAL) [85] Baltimore, MD Sacred Heart of Jesus Church.
Sattler, John C. *o.f.m.conv.* '42 (SAV) St. Simons Island, GA St. Williams Church.
Sattler, Paul E. *c.pp.s.* '58 (KC) [8] Kansas City, MO St. Charles Borromeo Church.
Sauber, A. Michael '69 (STP) Shakopee, MN St. Mary Church.
Sauchelli, James J. (TR) Leave of Absence.
Saucier, Thomas *o.p.* (CHI) River Forest, IL St. Vincent Ferrer Priory Church.
Saudis, Richard B. '55 (CHI) Berwyn, IL St. Odilo Church.
SauelKoul, Leonard *o.s.b.* '95 (BIS) Fort Yates, ND St. Peter - Catholic Indian Mission Church.
Sauer, Alban '59 (SCL) Absent on Leave.
Sauer, Anthony P. *s.j.* '71 (SFR) [E] San Francisco, CA St. Ignatius College Preparatory (Coed); [N] San Francisco, CA Jesuit Community at St. Ignatius College Preparatory.
Sauer, Bonaventure *o.c.d.* '92 (NO) [A] New Orleans, LA Notre Dame Seminary Graduate School of Theology.
Sauer, David J. (NY) [DD] New York, NY International Catholic Child Bureau/North America, Inc.
Sauer, James '77 (EVN) [7] Evansville, IN Holy Rosary Church.
Sauer, John M. '85 (WIN) [1] Winona, MN Cathedral of the Sacred Heart.
Sauer, Simon *o.f.m.conv.* '57 (L) [6] Louisville, KY St. Anthony Church; Louisville, KY Vencor Veterans Hospital.
Sauer, Timothy J. '76 (SEA) Ferndale, WA St. Joseph Church.
Sauerbier, Paul W. *c.m.* '68 (DAL) [6] Dallas, TX Holy Trinity Church.
Sauerwein, Msgr. Anthony L. (BAL) Retired.
Saul, James *o.s.b.* '52 (JOL) [J] Lisle, IL St. Procopius Abbey; [J] Lisle, IL St. Procopius Abbey.
Saulaitis, Antanas V. *s.j.* '69 (CHI) [N] Chicago, IL Lithuanian American Jesuits.
Saulenas, Simeon W. '44 (BO) [6] Cambridge, MA Immaculate Conception Church.
Saulino, Joseph A. '67 (LEX) Winchester, KY St. Joseph Church.
Saulnier, Joseph *f.m.s.i.* '72 (BO) [B] Framingham, MA Sylva Maria.
Saumell, Amaro '92 (SB) Barstow, CA St. Joseph Church; Ontario, CA St. George Church.
Saunders, Allan L. '86 (SPC) Chaffee, MO St. Ambrose Church.
Saunders, Charles D. *c.m.* '43 (STL) [P] Perryville, MO Congregation of The Mission.
Saunders, Donald W. *s.j.* '84 (SP) [C] Tampa, FL Jesuit High School.
Saunders, John A. '40 (BO) Retired.
Saunders, Msgr. Kenneth W. '38 (CLV) [43] Cleveland, OH St. Leo the Great Church; Middleburg Heights, OH St. Bartholomew Church.
Saunders, Robert E. '68 (HRT) Retired; [D] Bristol, CT St. Paul Catholic High School.
Saunders, Robert J. '41 (DUB) Retired.
Saunders, Ronald *s.m.* '59 (BUR) White River Junction, VT St. Anthony Church.
Saunders, William P. '84 (ARL) [3] Alexandria, VA Queen of Apostles Church; [B] Arlington, VA Notre Dame Institute for Catechetics.
Sauppe, Timothy '92 (PEO) [4] Rock Island, IL St. Pius X Church; [B] Rock Island, IL Alleman High School.
Saurimakel, Joseph '75 (BRK) [T] Brooklyn, NY Catholic Migration & Refugee Office, Catholic Migration Services, Inc.
Sauter, David A. *s.j.* '72 (PH) [G] Philadelphia, PA St. Joseph's Preparatory School; [Z] Philadelphia, PA St. Joseph's Preparatory School Jesuit Community, Arrupe House.
Sauter, John '85 (GLP) Shiprock, NM Christ the King Church.
Sauter, John D. (SB) [E] Morongo Valley, CA St. Michael's of Morongo Valley, Inc.
Sauter, Thomas M. '47 (DET) Rockwood, MI St. Mary Church.
Savage, Charles H. '81 (WH) Retired.
Savage, James W. (BO) [12] Cambridge, MA St. Paul Church.
Savage, John J. *o.m.i.* '39 (BO) [3] Lowell, MA Immaculate Conception Church.
Savage, Paul J. '57 (PIT) Beaver Falls, PA Divine Mercy Church; Beaver County, PA Beaver Valley Geriatric Center.
Savage, Robert *s.d.b.* '46 (NY) [Z] New Rochelle, NY Salesian Provincial House.
Savage, Roger A. '77 (MIL) Eldorado, WI St. Mary Church; Woodhull, WI St. John the Baptist Church.
Savage, Thomas J. '47 (MAN) Retired.
Savage, Thomas J. *s.j.* '79 (BO) [W] Boston, MA The Society of Jesus of New England-Provincial Offices.
Savage, Warren J. '79 (SPR) [1] North Adams, MA Holy Family Church; [2] North Adams, MA Notre Dame Church; [3] North Adams, MA Our Lady of The Incarnation Church.
Savard, John *s.j.* '91 (BO) [W] Chestnut Hill, MA The Jesuit Community at Boston College.
Savard, Wilfred '48 (SFE) Retired.
Savarimuthu, Simon (NY) Staten Island, NY Staten Island University Hospital North.
Savary, James '60 (LR) Retired.
Savastano, Msgr. Anthony J. '56 (RVC) Woodbury, NY Holy Name of Jesus Church.
Savelesky, Michael '73 (SPK) Walla Walla, WA St. Francis of Assisi Church; Walla Walla, WA St. Patrick Church.
Savial, Clarence '70 (LAV) [5] Las Vegas, NV Prince of Peace Church.
Saviane, Frederick L. '68 (BGP) [3] Danbury, CT Our Lady of Guadalupe Church.
Savickas, Michael G. '74 (DET) Walled Lake, MI St. William Church.
Savidge, Peter '89 (KC) Leave of Absence.
Savilla, Edmund '77 (SFE) Taos, NM Nuestra Senora De Guadalupe Church.
Savino, Dominic *o.carm.* '65 (LA) [B] North Hills, CA Carmel West Community.
Savino, Michael A. '82 (CIN) Blanchester, OH Holy Name Church; Saint Martin, OH Saint Martin Church; [B] Cincinnati, OH Mt. St. Mary's Seminary of the West; [B] Cincinnati, OH Mt. St. Mary's Seminary of the West.
Savinski, John M. *m.div.* (ALN) [A] Northampton, PA Mary Immaculate Seminary.
Savinski, John M. '71 (PH) [A] Wynnewood, PA Theological Seminary of St. Charles Borromeo, Overbrook.
Savio, John '67 (CHY) Lander, WY Holy Rosary Church.
Savio, Michael G. '92 (MIL) [59] Milwaukee, WI Our Lady of Lourdes Church.
Savio, Samuel '83 (NY) [1] New Rochelle, NY Blessed Sacrament Church.
Savitt, Alan F. '73 (PAT) [3] Clifton, NJ St. Brendan Church.
Savoca, Americo '93 (NY) Carmel, NY St. James the Apostle Church.
Savoie, Johnny S. '95 (MOB) [4] Mobile, AL St. Dominic Church.
Savores, John M. '63 (SFD) Pawnee, IL St. Mary Church.
Savukynas, John *m.i.c.* '44 (JOL) Plano, IL St. Mary Church.
Saw, Paul Fatt Lean *f.m.s.* '81 (CHI) [N] Chicago, IL Passionist Community-CTU.
Sawdy, Wallace E. '51 (HBG) Retired.
Sawher, Msgr. Clifford F. '52 (DET) Retired.
Sawick, John *c.s.s.p.* (BO) [1] Somerville, MA St. Ann Church.
Sawicki, Eugene A. '86 (NY) [100] New York, NY Our Lady of Vilna Church.
Sawicki, Gregory *s.d.s.* (SAT) Cestohowa, TX Nativity of the Blessed Virgin Mary Church; Hobson, TX St. Boniface Church.
Sawicki, Henry *c.m.* '36 (HRT) [18] New Haven, CT St. Stanislaus Church.
Sawicki, John A. *c.s.sp.* '86 (PH) [Z] Bensalem, PA Congregation of the Holy Ghost Fathers and Brothers.
Sawyer, Donald '74 (OLL) Austin, TX Our Lady's Maronite Parish Church; El Paso, TX Maronite Catholic Community Church.
Sawyer, Lucien A. *o.m.i.* '49 (BO) On Special or Other Diocesan Assignment; [Q] Boston, MA Carney Hospital.
Sawyer, Michael *o.s.b.* '74 (HON) [H] Waialua, Oahu, HI Benedictine Monastery of Hawaii.
Sax, John C. *o.m.i.* '73 (NO) [1] New Orleans, LA St. Louis Cathedral.
Saxe, Joseph '90 (BRK) [176] Queens, NY Holy Child Jesus Church.
Saxon, JaVan J. '83 (R) [5] Raleigh, NC St. Joseph Church.
Say, Celestino '58 (VIC) [3] Victoria, TX Our Lady of Lourdes Church.
Say, James K. '60 (TOL) Tiffin, OH St. Joseph Church.
Sayasaya, Fernando '95 (FAR) [1] Fargo, ND St. Mary's Cathedral.
Sayers, James M. '58 (CHI) Homewood, IL St. Joseph Church.
Sayers, Monty '86 (E) Frenchtown, PA St. Hippolyte Church.
Sayers, Raymond J. '64 (DET) [42] Detroit, MI St. Jude Church.
Sayes, Ronald '57 (DET) [1] Westland, MI St. Bernardine Church.
Sayles, Bartholomew *o.s.b.* '48 (SCL) [I] Collegeville, MN St. John's Abbey, of the Order of St. Benedict.
Saylor, Msgr. Philip P. '55 (ALT) Philipsburg, PA SS. Peter and Paul Church.
Sazama, Warren J. *s.j.* '77 (MIL) [P] Milwaukee, WI Jesuit Provincial Office, Wisconsin Province; [P] Milwaukee, WI Pere Marquette House Jesuit Community; [Y] Milwaukee, WI The Jesuit Partnership.
Sbordone, Gaetano J. '83 (BRK) [212] Queens, NY Our Lady of Hope Church.
Scadron, Christopher '83 (RC) Retired.
Scafidi, William *m.ss.a.* '83 (NY) [1] New York, NY Cathedral of St. Patrick.
Scaglione, Paul A. '73 (TR) Manalapan, NJ St. Thomas More Church.
Scagnelli, Louis *o.c.d.* '42 (SAT) [18] San Antonio, TX Our Lady of Mt. Carmel and St. Therese, Discalced Carmelite Fathers Church; [M] San Antonio, TX Discalced Carmelites (Prov. of St. Therese).
Scagnelli, Peter J. '76 (PRO) Absent on Leave.
Scahill, James J. '74 (SPR) [16] Springfield, MA St. Mary's Church.
Scahill, John J. '46 (PRT) [1] Portland, ME Cathedral of the Immaculate Conception; Retired.
Scala, Thomas A. '73 (HBG) Milton, PA St. Joseph Church.
Scalco, Joseph *c.s.j.* '78 (LA) [D] Lancaster, CA Paraclete High School.
Scalco, Joseph *c.s.j.* '79 (LA) Lancaster, CA Blessed Junipero Serra Church.
Scales, Donald *o.s.b.* '55 (RIC) [7] Richmond, VA St. Benedict Church.
Scales, Donald F. *o.s.b.* '55 (RIC) [M] Richmond, VA Mary Mother of the Church Abbey.
Scales, George B. '88 (FR) Falmouth, MA St. Patrick's Church.
Scaletty, Thomas F. '63 (WCH) [15] Wichita, KS St. Jude Church.
Scalia, Paul D. '96 (ARL) Springfield, VA St. Bernadette's Church.
Scallon, Joseph D. *s.j.* '59 (DET) [P] Clarkston, MI Colombiere Center.
Scallon, Joseph D. *s.j.* '59 (MIL) [P] Milwaukee, WI Jesuit Provincial Office, Wisconsin Province.
Scallon, Kevin *c.m.* (SP) [T] Palm Harbor, FL St. Vincent Ministry to Priests, Inc.
Scalone, Jonathan '87 (FWT) Lewisville, TX St. Philip the Apostle Church.
Scanagatta, Joseph *s.d.b.* '47 (SFR) [N] San Francisco, CA Salesian Provincial Residence.
Scanlan, Charles V. '54 (NEW) Retired; [N] Rutherford, NJ St. John Vianney Residence for Priests.
Scanlan, Cornelius J. *o.m.i.* '59 (SAN) Big Spring, TX Sacred Heart Church; Big Spring, TX St. Thomas Church.
Scanlan, Msgr. Edward J. '53 (BUF) [9] Niagara Falls, NY Our Lady of Mount Carmel Church.
Scanlan, Francis G. '61 (CHI) [25] Chicago, IL St. Bede the Venerable Church.

Scanlan, John '75 (SHP) Lake Providence, LA St. Patrick Church.
Scanlan, Msgr. John J. '59 (WDC) Lanham, MD St. Matthias Church.
Scanlan, Kevin *s.m.a.* '55 (NEW) [N] Tenafly, NJ Society of African Missions, Provincialate, S.M.A. Fathers.
Scanlan, Lambert D. '33 (GB) Retired.
Scanlan, Michael *t.o.r.* '64 (STU) [A] Steubenville, OH Franciscan University of Steubenville; [F] Steubenville, OH Holy Spirit Monastery.
Scanlan, Michael J. *o.s.a.* '64 (PH) [Z] Villanova, PA St. John Stone Friary.
Scanlan, Patrick J. '28 (SB) Retired.
Scanlin, Joseph T. '89 (HBG) Carlisle, PA St. Patrick Church; [K] Harrisburg, PA Catholic Campus Ministry.
Scanlon, Msgr. Bernard S. '45 (BGP) Retired; [O] Stamford, CT Our Lady Queen of the Clergy Home.
Scanlon, Frank '83 (NY) [27] New York, NY St. Columba Church.
Scanlon, James M. *m.m.* '52 (NY) [Z] Maryknoll, NY Maryknoll Fathers and Brothers.
Scanlon, Msgr. John J. (NY) Scarsdale, NY Immaculate Heart of Mary Church.
Scanlon, John J. '42 (PIT) Retired.
Scanlon, Michael J. *o.s.a.* '64 (PH) [C] Villanova, PA Villanova University.
Scanlon, Michael M. *o.s.m.* '30 (CHI) [N] Chicago, IL Servite Friars - Eastern Province.
Scanlon, Noel '51 (NY) [Z] Yonkers, NY St. Clare Friary.
Scanlon, Paul *o.p.* '59 (LA) [59] Los Angeles, CA St. Dominic Church.
Scanlon, Paul J.D. *o.p.* '49 (COL) Zanesville, OH St. Thomas Aquinas Church.
Scanlon, Peter J. '57 (WOR) [16] Worcester, MA Sacred Heart Church; [Q] Worcester, MA Campus Ministry; [Q] Worcester, MA Campus Ministry; [Q] Worcester, MA Campus Ministry; [Q] Worcester, MA Campus Ministry.
Scanlon, Regis *o.f.m.cap.* '72 (DEN) [M] Denver, CO St. Francis of Assisi Friary.
Scanlon, Richard M. '28 (RVC) Blue Point, NY Our Lady of the Snow Church; Retired.
Scanlon, Msgr. Thomas F. '49 (NY) [3] Mt. Vernon, NY Our Lady of Victory Church.
Scanlon, Msgr. Thomas J. '59 (PH) [140] Philadelphia, PA Resurrection of Our Lord Church.
Scanlon, Thomas M. *t.o.r.* '53 (SP) [6] St. Petersburg, FL St. Mary Our Lady of Grace Church.
Scanlon, Thomas R. (BAK) Retired.
Scanlon, Wilfred *c.p.* '45 (MET) [H] South River, NJ Passionist Provincial Office.
Scanlon, William '72 (BO) Stoughton, MA St. James Church.
Scanlon, William J. *s.j.* '70 (NY) [Z] New York, NY St. Ignatius Loyola Residence; [Z] New York, NY Jesuit Seminary and Mission Bureau, Inc. (Jesuit Deferred Funds); [DD] New York, NY Jesuit Seminary and Mission Bureau, Inc.
Scannel, Anthony *o.f.m.cap.* '55 (LA) [F] La Canada Flintridge, CA St. Francis High School.
Scannell, Anthony *o.f.m.cap.* (DET) [K] Detroit, MI St. Mary's Friary.
Scannell, Anthony *o.f.m.cap.* '55 (MIL) [Y] Milwaukee, WI Santa Fe Communications, Inc.
Scannell, John W. '34 (DEN) Retired.
Scannell, Joseph S. *s.j.* '50 (WOR) [N] Worcester, MA Jesuits of Holy Cross College, Inc.
Scannell, Msgr. Peter '46 (ORG) Retired.
Scannell, Msgr. Thomas P. '37 (ARL) [2] Arlington, VA St. Agnes Church; Retired.
Scannell, Timothy J. '69 (NY) Irvington-on-the-Hudson, NY Immaculate Conception Church.
Scantlebury, Neil '95 (STV) [3] Estate Tutu, VI Holy Family Parish Church.
Scantlin, Joseph S. '59 (FWT) [2] Arlington, TX Most Blessed Sacrament Church.
Scaramella, Renzo L. '95 (NEW) Plainfield, NJ St. Mary Church.
Scaramuzzo, Peter C. '66 (NY) [1] White Plains, NY St. Anthony Church.
Scarangella, Joseph A. '92 (NEW) Cliffside Park, NJ Epiphany Church.
Scarangello, John R. *o.f.m.* '81 (NY) [Z] Mount Vernon, NY St. Bernardine of Siena Friary.
Scarborough, Henry *o.c.s.o.* '63 (WOR) [N] Spencer, MA St. Joseph's Abbey.
Scarcella, Philip J. '77 (MET) On Duty Outside the Diocese.
Scarcello, Michael S. '56 (B) Rathdrum, ID St. Stanislaus Church.
Scarcia, John J. '74 (PH) East Greenville, PA St. Philip Neri Church.
Scardella, Joseph E. '81 (SY) [7] Syracuse, NY Our Lady of Pompei Church.
Scarff, Msgr. Stanley J. '31 (BAL) Retired.
Scarff, Msgr. Stanley J. '93 (BAL) [K] Baltimore, MD Stella Maris Operating Corporation.
Scarfia, Gabriel *o.f.m., s.t.d.* '64 (BUF) [A] East Aurora, NY Christ the King Seminary.
Scarlata, Ronald E. '66 (CHI) Highwood, IL St. James Church.
Scepaniak, Russell G. '93 (WIN) St. Clair, MN Immaculate Conception Church; [I] Mankato, MN Newman Center.
Scerbo, Joseph *s.a.* '70 (NY) [Z] Garrison, NY Generalate of the Franciscan Friars of the Atonement-St. James Friary.
Sceski, Alfred '91 (HBG) [5] (Lower Paxton Twp.), PA Holy Name of Jesus Church.
Scesney, Everard S. *o.f.m.* '68 (GB) Aniwa, WI St. Boniface Church; Birnamwood, WI St. Philomena Church.
Scezney, Leonard J. '85 (DEN) Absent on Leave.
Schaab, Dennis *c.pp.s.* '68 (JC) Warsaw, MO St. Ann Church.
Schaab, Denny M. '76 (STL) Webster Groves, MO Annunciation Church.
Schaab, R. Michael '71 (PEO) Orion, IL Mary, Our Lady of Peace Church.
Schaab, Thomas J. '74 (STL) [2] Florissant, MO Our Lady of Fatima Church.
Schaad, Jerome *s.c.j.* '66 (MIL) [P] Hales Corners, WI Priests of the Sacred Heart; [P] Hales Corners, WI Sacred Heart Monastery.
Schaaf, Paul F. *c.pp.s.* '60 (CIN) [M] Dayton, OH Provincial House of the Cincinnati Province of the Society of the Precious Blood.
Schaal, John K. '90 (SCR) Clarks Summit, PA Our Lady of the Snows Church.
Schabel, Joseph A. '56 (SAG) Retired.
Schabowski, Henry F. '60 (TR) [15] Trenton, NJ St. Hedwig Church.
Schackmuth, William A. '47 (CHI) Norridge, IL Divine Savior Church; Retired.
Schad, Edward J. '48 (OM) Columbus, NE St. Bonaventure Church; Retired.
Schad, Joseph J. *s.j.* '91 (BGP) [A] Fairfield, CT Fairfield University; [O] Fairfield, CT The Fairfield Jesuit Community-Fairfield University.
Schad, Sylvester *o.s.b.* '38 (CC) [H] Sandia, TX Corpus Christi Abbey.
Schaden, J. Robert '62 (DET) [S] Livonia, MI Schoolcraft College, Newman House.
Schaedel, Joseph F. '82 (IND) [16] Indianapolis, IN St. Anthony Church; Brownsburg, IN St. Malachy Church.
Schaefer, Bernard *o.s.b.* '56 (RCK) [H] Aurora, IL Marmion Abbey-St. Augustine's Abbey.
Schaefer, Dennis R. '75 (BEL) Chester, IL St. Mary Help of Christians Church.
Schaefer, Edgar J. '54 (WIN) Spring Valley, MN St. Ignatius Church.
Schaefer, Edward F. '75 (BEL) St. Rose, IL St. Rose Church.
Schaefer, Ferdinand T. *o.carm.* '48 (BO) [P] Peabody, MA Catholic Information Center; [BB] Peabody, MA St. Theresa Carmelite Chapel.
Schaefer, Francis R. '55 (COL) Retired.
Schaefer, James F. '61 (LC) Dorchester, WI St. Louis Church
Schaefer, James W. '56 (STL) [8] Florissant, MO St. Norbert Church.
Schaefer, Joseph P. *o.s.f.s.* '56 (CAM) [L] Pittsgrove, NJ Villa St. Joseph.
Schaefer, Kenneth J. '74 (BEL) Herrin, IL Our Lady of Mount Carmel Church.
Schaefer, Les F. *c.s.b.* '61 (OAK) [C] Oakland, CA Bishop O'Dowd High School.
Schaefer, Martin T. '92 (WIN) Adrian, MN St. Adrian Church
Schaefer, Philip *c.p.* '58 (DET) [K] Detroit, MI St. Paul of the Cross Community, Congregation of the Passion.
Schaefer, Richard L. '68 (DUB) [C] Dubuque, IA Loras College.
Schaefer, Roman J. '42 (MIA) [2] Fort Lauderdale, FL Our Lady Queen of Martyrs Church.
Schaefer, Roman J. '42 (NU) Retired.
Schaefer, Thomas '53 (WDC) Retired.
Schaefer, Thomas *c.s.sp.* '82 (PIT) [B] Pittsburgh, PA Duquesne University of the Holy Ghost.
Schaefer, Thomas G. *c.s.sp.* '82 (PIT) [40] Pittsburgh, PA St. Patrick-St. Stanislaus Kostka Church.
Schaefer, Verne B. '55 (MIL) Retired.
Schaefer, Vernon J. '45 (WIN) Eyota, MN Holy Redeemer Church.
Schaefers, Francis J. '33 (P) Retired.
Schaeffer, Bradley M. *s.j.* '77 (CHI) [D] Chicago, IL St. Ignatius Jesuit Community; [N] Chicago, IL Chicago Province of the Society of Jesus-Provincial Office.
Schaeffer, Richard C. '83 (MAR) Wells, MI St. Anthony Church.
Schaeffer, Richard L. (DUB) [5] Dubuque, IA St. Patrick's Church.
Schaeflein, Msgr. Charles J. '49 (PH) Retired; [U] Philadelphia, PA Mount Nazareth.
Schaeper, Jerome A. '60 (CIN) [E] Cincinnati, OH Elder High School; [L] Cincinnati, OH St. Margaret Hall.
Schaeufele, Robert L. '75 (SP) [3] St. Petersburg, FL Holy Cross Church.
Schafer, Dennis *o.f.m.* '80 (SFD) [B] Quincy, IL Quincy University.
Schafer, Dennis R. '89 (BIS) Mott, ND St. Vincent de Paul Church.
Schafer, Raymond E. '89 (IND) Aurora, IN St. Mary of the Immaculate Conception Church.
Schafer, William *s.d.b.* '61 (SFR) [N] San Francisco, CA Salesian Provincial Residence.
Schaff, Tyrone J. '73 (SPK) [13] Spokane, WA St. John Vianney Church.
Schaffer, Gregory J. '94 (STP) Maplewood, MN Presentation of the Blessed Virgin Mary Church.
Schaffer, Msgr. Gregory T. '60 (NU) On Duty Outside the Diocese.
Schaffer, J. Darrell '90 (DEN) [6] Denver, CO Christ the King Church.
Schaffner, Mark J. *o.carm.* '89 (GAL) [3] Houston, TX St. Albert of Trapani Church.
Schaffner, William E. '48 (ALN) [A] Wernersville, PA Novitiate of St. Isaac Jogues.
Schaftlein, Stephen '78 (IND) Greensburg, IN St. Mary Church.
Schaible, Donald J. '89 (ALN) Nesquehoning, PA Our Lady of Mount Carmel Church; Tamaqua, PA St. Jerome Church; [C] Tamaqua, PA Marian Catholic High School.
Schak, John R. *s.j.* '61 (MIL) [P] Milwaukee, WI Jesuit Provincial Office, Wisconsin Province.
Schalk, Sebastian R. *o.praem.* '60 (GB) [I] De Pere, WI St. Norbert Abbey.
Schall, James V. *s.j.* '63 (WDC) [M] Washington, DC The Jesuit Community at Georgetown University.
Schallberger, Meinrad *o.s.b.* '64 (B) [C] Jerome, ID Ascension Priory.
Schaller, Harvey B. *o.p.* '37 (CIN) [30] Cincinnati, OH St. Gertrude Church; [M] Cincinnati, OH St. Gertrude Priory.
Schaller, Pascal *o.f.m.cap.* '51 (PIT) [N] Pittsburgh, PA St. Augustine Friary.
Schaller, Robert A. '87 (LC) Bakerville, WI Corpus Christi Church; Marshfield, WI Sacred Heart of Jesus Church.
Schanz, John P. '50 (E) [B] Erie, PA Gannon University; [B] Erie, PA Gannon University.
Schapper, Norbert *o.s.b.* '52 (KC) [J] Conception, MO Conception Abbey.
Schappert, James P. *s.s.j.* '49 (BAL) [M] Baltimore, MD St. Joseph Society of the Sacred Heart House of Central Administration.
Schardt, William B. '75 (ARL) [3] Arlington, VA St. Ann Church.
Scharf, David E. '85 (PIT) Hopewell Township, PA Our Lady of Fatima Church.
Scharf, Joseph *s.j.* '51 (CLV) [U] Cleveland, OH Jesuit Retreat House.
Scharf, Lawrence C. '65 (TOL) Monroeville, OH St. Joseph Church.
Scharf, T. Patrick '68 (TOL) [10] Toledo, OH Little Flower of Jesus Church.
Scharfenberger, Msgr. Edward B. '77 (BRK) [214] Queens, NY Our Lady of Mercy Church.
Scharinger, James G. '69 (STN) Belfield, ND St. John the Baptist Church; Fairfield, ND St. Demetrius Church.
Schario, D. Clayton *s.j.* '56 (DET) [K] Detroit, MI Jesuit Community at the University of Detroit.
Schartz, Kenneth E. '85 (CIN) Centerville, OH Incarnation Church.
Schatteman, Rene J. '60 (LA) [X] Los Angeles, CA Opus Dei. Prelature of the Holy Cross and Opus Dei.
Schatzel, John E. '61 (BO) [2] Brockton, MA St. Colman of Cloyne Church.
Schatzle, Michael J. *c.s.s.r.* '74 (BR) New Roads, LA St. Mary of False River Church.
Schaub, Martin R. '91 (GAY) Absent on Leave.
Schauer, David V. '80 (SFD) [7] Springfield, IL St. Frances Cabrini Church.
Schauerman, Msgr. Henry J. '51 (E) Meadville, PA St. Agatha Church.
Schaukowitch, James V. *s.j.* '79 (LA) [F] Los Angeles, CA Loyola High School.
Schaut, Gregory F. '85 (CLV) Brooklyn, OH St. Thomas More Church.
Schavitz, Peter *c.ss.r.* (CHI) [9] Chicago, IL St. Alphonsus Church.
Scheaffer, Msgr. Walter T. '66 (ALN) Kutztown, PA St. Mary Church.
Scheble, Carl J. '83 (STL) [33] St. Louis, MO St. Elizabeth, Mother of John the Baptist Church.
Scheck, Frances M. '36 (LFT) Retired.
Scheckel, Roger J. '84 (LC) [5] La Crosse, WI St. James the Less Church.
Scheckenback, Robert C. '89 (RVC) Holbrook, NY Good Shepherd Church.
Schecker, Robert J.W. '71 (TR) Mount Holly, NJ Sacred Heart Church; Burlington, NJ Burlington County Hospital & Extended Care Center; Burlington, NJ Burlington County Jail.
Scheel, Msgr. Daniel '69 (GAL) [38] Houston, TX St. Jerome Church.
Scheeler, Jeffrey *o.f.m.* '80 (CIN) [65] Cincinnati, OH

St. Monica-St. George Parish Newman Center Church; [Q] Cincinnati, OH University of Cincinnati Newman Center.
Scheeler, Jeffrey *o.f.m.* '80 (GAL) [Q] Houston, TX Franciscan Friars.
Scheer, Allen '95 (SAL) [3] Salina, KS St. Mary's Church.
Scheer, Joseph O. '42 (STL) Retired.
Scheerer, Dominic T. *o.c.d.* '47 (MIL) [24] Milwaukee, WI St. Florian's Church.
Scheets, Francis Kelly *o.s.c.* '51 (NY) [4] New York, NY All Saints Church.
Scheetz, Daniel L. '65 (SAL) Ellsworth, KS St. Bernard's Church; Gorham, KS St. Mary's Church; Holyrood, KS St. Mary's Church; Kanopolis, KS St. Ignatius Loyola Church.
Scheetz, Joseph H. '54 (SAL) WaKeeney, KS Christ the King Church.
Schefers, Eberhard '64 (SCL) Sartell, MN St. Francis Xavier Church.
Scheffler, Mark *c.ss.r.* '70 (SAT) San Antonio, TX Santa Rosa Hospital System; [H] San Antonio, TX Santa Rosa Health Care System.
Schehr, Timothy P. '73 (CIN) [B] Cincinnati, OH Mt. St. Mary's Seminary of the West.
Scheib, Joseph C. '76 (PIT) [43] Pittsburgh, PA St. Basil Church.
Scheible, Alan D. *o.praem.* '69 (CHI) [N] Chicago, IL Premonstratensian Fathers and Brothers (Norbertines).
Scheible, Allan '69 (GB) [I] De Pere, WI St. Joseph Priory.
Scheich, Gene '66 (L) [54] Louisville, KY St. Matthias Church.
Scheick, James C. '63 (DET) [3] Livonia, MI St. Edith Church.
Scheid, W. Bernard (CHI) [113] Chicago, IL St. Kevin Church.
Scheid, W. Bernard '36 (CHI) Retired.
Scheider, David J. '53 (BUF) East Pembroke, NY Holy Name of Mary Church.
Scheiding, Philip '81 (MIA) On Duty Outside the Archdiocese.
Scheidler, Alfred J. *o.s.b.* '52 (PEO) [A] Peru, IL St. Bede Abbey and Academy.
Scheidler, David J. *c.s.c.* '94 (FTW) [B] Notre Dame, IN University of Notre Dame Du Lac; [J] Notre Dame, IN Holy Cross Community, Corby Hall, University of Notre Dame.
Scheidler, Robert E. '70 (IND) Leave of Absence.
Scheierl, LeRoy '91 (SCL) Belgrade, MN St. Francis De Sales Church; Elrosa, MN SS. Peter and Paul Church.
Scheiner, Richard *c.p.* '60 (NY) [Z] New York, NY Passionist Spiritual Center.
Scheinost, Douglas P. '92 (OM) Humphrey, NE St. Francis Church.
Scheip, Michael A. '93 (NEW) Newark, NJ St. Michael Medical Center; [G] Newark, NJ Saint Michael's Medical Center.
Schelble, T. Michael '61 (LC) Auburndale, WI Nativity of the Blessed Virgin Mary Church.
Schelble, T. Michael '71 (LC) Hewitt, WI St. Michael Church.
Schelble, Thomas M. *s.m.* '46 (SAT) [K] San Antonio, TX St. Joseph's Community.
Schelich, Anthony T. *o.s.f.s.* '65 (WIL) [G] Newark, DE Jeanne Jugan Residence; [I] Childs, MD Oblates of St. Francis De Sales.
Schelich, Theodosius *o.f.m.* '59 (STL) [P] St. Louis, MO Franciscan Friary of St. Anthony of Padua.
Schelich, Theodosius A. *o.f.m.* '59 (SFD) [H] Litchfield, IL St. Francis Hospital.
Schell, Joseph O. *s.j.* '44 (CLV) [C] Cleveland, OH John Carroll Jesuit Community.
Schellberg, L. Eugene '60 (MET) Parlin, NJ St. Bernadette Church.
Schellemans, Francis *ss.cc.* '49 (HON) [H] Honolulu, HI St. Patrick's Monastery.
Schellenberg, James '77 (SAT) San Antonio, TX Brooke Army Medical Center.
Schellenberg, Milton A. '46 (WDC) Retired.
Scheller, Albert J. '61 (EVN) [5] Vincennes, IN St. Vincent de Paul Church.
Scheller, John '58 (OKL) Retired.
Scheller, Raymund B. '47 (FAR) Retired.
Schelling, Michael '74 (TOL) Fort Jennings, OH St. Joseph Church.
Schemel, Francis *s.j.* '58 (WDC) [M] Washington, DC The Jesuit Community at Georgetown University.
Schemel, George J. *s.j.* '64 (SCR) [C] Scranton, PA University of Scranton; [R] Scranton, PA ISECP, Inc.
Schemm, Michael J. '93 (WCH) Parsons, KS St. Patrick Church.
Schenck, Stephen *s.d.b.* '81 (NY) [BB] West Haverstraw, NY Don Bosco Retreat Center and Marian Shrine; [BB] West Haverstraw, NY Marian Shrine.
Schendt, Richard L. '63 (CHI) [W] Oak Park, IL Oak Park Study Center.
Schenick, Joseph D. '51 (PRO) [9] Woonsocket, RI Our Lady, Queen of Martyrs Church.
Schenk, Arthur J. *s.j.* '45 (SJ) [M] Los Gatos, CA California Province of the Society of Jesus, Jesuit Provincial Office; [M] Los Gatos, CA Sacred Heart Jesuit Center.
Schenk, Francisco *glmy.* '55 (CIN) [M] Fairfield, OH Headquarters of Glenmary Home Missioners.
Schenk, Mark *o.f.m.cap.* (STL) [P] St. Louis, MO St. Crispin's Friary.
Schenk, Richard *o.p.* '78 (OAK) [A] Berkeley, CA Dominican School of Philosophy and Theology; [N] Oakland, CA Dominican Order (Western Province), St. Albert's Priory.
Schenkelberg, Edwin J. '51 (CLV) [49] Cleveland, OH St. Mel Church.
Schenning, Kevin T. '81 (BAL) Aberdeen, MD St. Joan of Arc Church.
Scheper, Msgr. John B. '30 (LR) Retired.
Schepers, Frank '55 (KCK) Greeley, KS St. John the Baptist's Church.
Scherba, Raymond M. '82 (BGP) [1] Danbury, CT St. Gregory's Church.
Scherer, Albert *o.f.m.conv.* '85 (SPR) [10] Chicopee, MA St. Stanislaus Basilica.
Scherer, Donald R. '67 (NEW) Retired.
Scherer, Gary M. *c.pp.s.* '67 (CIN) [K] Dayton, OH St. Elizabeth Medical Center, Inc.
Scherer, Gerald N. '54 (RC) Retired.
Scherer, James F. '64 (ATL) On Duty Outside the Archdiocese.
Scherer, Philip M. *o.s.m.* '55 (CHI) [N] Chicago, IL Servite Friars - Eastern Province.
Scherer, Richard '49 (MIA) Retired.
Scherer, Steven J. '79 (GB) Absent on Leave.
Scherf, Gerard H. '47 (PH) [92] Philadelphia, PA Saint Martha Church; Retired.
Scherger, Herman F. '58 (TOL) Antwerp, OH St. Mary Church; Cecil, OH Immaculate Conception Church.
Scherman, Charles J. *s.j.* '57 (LC) Chippewa Falls, WI Holy Ghost Church; Springfield, WI St. Bridget Church.
Scherman, Charles J. *s.j.* '57 (MIL) [P] Milwaukee, WI Jesuit Provincial Office, Wisconsin Province.
Schermer, Paul '82 (LAN) [5] Flint, MI Holy Rosary Church.
Scherpenberg, Sergius H. *o.f.m.* '51 (L) [15] Louisville, KY St. Boniface Church; [L] Louisville, KY St. Boniface Friary.
Scherrer, Carl E. '73 (BEL) Carbondale, IL St. Francis Xavier Church.
Scherrer, George H. *s.m.* '45 (SAT) [K] San Antonio, TX St. Joseph's Community.
Scherrer, Ralph *o.f.m.* (SFD) [K] Sherman, IL Our Lady of Angels Friary.
Scherrer, Steven *m.m.* '72 (NY) [Z] Maryknoll, NY Maryknoll Fathers and Brothers.
Scherzer, Edwin J. '50 (L) Retired; [L] Louisville, KY Bishop David Apartments; [Q] Louisville, KY Our Lady's Rosary Makers.
Scheteliek, Paul D. '76 (NEW) [3] Newark, NJ Blessed Sacrament Church.
Schetter, Albert E. '55 (CIN) Retired.
Schettler, Charles H. '54 (OKL) [8] Oklahoma City, OK St. Francis of Assisi Church.
Scheuer James W. '59 (DUL) Beroun, MN St. Joseph's Church; Hinckley, MN St. Patrick's Church.
Scheuerell, Charles A. '57 (MIL) Beaver Dam, WI St. Patrick's Church.
Scheuerman, Edward L. '50 (DET) Retired.
Schevers, Joel *o.carm.* '42 (VEN) [1] Venice, FL Epiphany Cathedral; [G] Venice, FL Carmel in Venice.
Schexnayder, Daniel '63 (LAF) Leonville, LA St. Leo the Great Church.
Schexnayder, Gary '69 (LAF) [9] Lafayette, LA St. Edmond Church.
Schexnayder, James (OAK) [H] Oakland, CA Catholic Charities of the Diocese of Oakland, Inc.
Scheyd, Msgr. William J. '65 (BGP) [7] Norwalk, CT St. Thomas the Apostle Church.
Schiavi, Giulio *p.i.m.e.* (DET) [7] Clinton Twp., MI San Francesco Community Church.
Schiavone, Alphonse A. *m.m.* '46 (RVC) [N] West Hempstead, NY Maryknoll Residence.
Schiavone, Christopher F. '84 (BO) Absent on Leave.
Schiavone, Jeldo '52 (LFT) Retired.
Schiavone, John S. '73 (LA) Culver City, CA St. Augustine Church.
Schiavone, Robert '69 (MIL) [B] Hales Corners, WI Sacred Heart School of Theology.
Schiavone, Robert W. '69 (GB) On Duty Outside the Diocese.
Schiblin, Richard *c.s.s.r.* '61 (P) [17] Portland, OR Holy Redeemer Church.
Schichtel, Kenneth H. '62 (GR) Ludington, MI St. Simon's Church.
Schidel, George E. *c.s.c.* '41 (FTW) [J] South Bend, IN Congregation of Holy Cross Indiana Province Provincial House.
Schieber, Joachim *o.s.b.* (KC) [H] Blue Springs, MO St. Mary's Manor.
Schieber, Lawrence J. '49 (STL) Moselle, MO St. Mary's Church.
Schiefen, Richard J. *c.s.b.* '61 (GAL) [Q] Houston, TX Residence of the Basilian Fathers of the University of St. Thomas.
Schiefen, Msgr. Robert W. '46 (VEN) Sanibel, FL St. Isabel Church.
Schieffer, Stanley F. '56 (LIN) Red Cloud, NE Sacred Heart Church.
Schiel, Nicholas E. *s.j.* '55 (MIL) [P] Milwaukee, WI Jesuit Provincial Office, Wisconsin Province.
Schiele, John D. '93 (PH) Brookhaven, PA Our Lady of Charity Church.
Schierse, Msgr. Paul J. '55 (WIL) Ocean City, MD St. Mary, Star of the Sea Church.
Schifalacqua, Ildebrando E. '43 (PH) [21] Philadelphia, PA St. Bartholomew Church; Retired.
Schifano, James R. *s.c.j.* '75 (GAL) [47] Houston, TX St. Matthew the Evangelist Church.
Schiff, John S. '74 (OKL) Absent on Sick Leave.
Schiffbauer, Rory '91 (CHY) [1] Cheyenne, WY St. Mary's Cathedral.
Schiffer, James A. '71 (MET) [H] South River, NJ Passionist Provincial Office.
Schiffer, Thomas E. '63 (WH) Weirton, WV St. Paul's Church.
Schifferli, Jerome F. '45 (ROC) Retired.
Schik, Jerome *o.s.c.* '75 (STP) Shoreview, MN St. Odilia Church; [N] Shoreview, MN Crosier Community of Shoreview.
Schilder, David M. '68 (COL) [26] Columbus, OH St. Ladislas Church; Orient, OH Orient Correctional Institution.
Schilken, Karl '80 (FWT) Mansfield, TX St. Jude Church.
Schill, Damien '87 (FAR) [2] Fargo, ND Holy Spirit Church.
Schill, Frederick J. '57 (TOL) Gibsonburg, OH St. Michael Church.
Schill, Paul '80 (E) Anita, PA St. Joseph Church.
Schill, Paul A. '63 (E) Walston, PA St. Anthony Church.
Schill, Paul A., Jr. '63 (E) Delancey, PA St. Adrian Church.
Schill, Victor J. '50 (FAR) Retired.
Schiller, Daniel (AUS) [M] Brenham, TX Blinn College Catholic Student Union.
Schiller, David J. '55 (CHR) Summerville, SC St. Theresa the Little Flower Church.
Schiller, Francis E. '65 (NEW) [23] Jersey City, NJ St. Patrick's Church.
Schiller, Thomas A. '55 (GR) Montague, MI St. James Church.
Schilli, Richard J. '77 (STL) Mattese, MO Assumption Church.
Schilling, Francis X. '57 (KNX) Gatlinburg, TN St. Mary Church.
Schillinger, James '84 (ATL) [L] Atlanta, GA Campus Ministry.
Schilly, Msgr. Adolph M. '44 (STL) Retired.
Schilly, Joseph '48 (SB) Retired; [B] San Bernardino, CA Aquinas High School.
Schiltz, Roger J. '68 (WIN) Retired.
Schimelpfening, James *s.m.* '80 (STL) [P] St. Louis, MO Provincialate of the Society of Mary, Province of St. Louis.
Schiml, Ronald J. *c.pp.s.* '55 (LFT) Star City, IN St. Joseph Church.
Schimmer, Robert J. '68 (SC) [7] Sioux City, IA St. Joseph Church.
Schimscheiner, Francis *o.s.f.s.* '65 (BUF) [5] Lockport, NY St. Patrick Church.
Schindler, Carl A. *c.ss.r.* '63 (BR) [H] Baton Rouge, LA Redemptorist Fathers Vice Provincialate.
Schindler, Frederick *o.s.b.* '45 (OM) [K] Elkhorn, NE Mount Michael Abbey.
Schindler, John H. '49 (YAK) Retired.
Schindler, John L. '85 (L) [61] Louisville, KY St. Patrick Church.
Schindler, Paul E. '67 (CLV) [3] Akron, OH St. Bernard Church; [X] Cleveland, OH Diocesan Hispanic Office.
Schindler, Robert '54 (FRS) Faculties Only.
Schindler-McGraw, Kevin *o.f.m.conv.* '54 (RNO) [1] Reno, NV St. Thomas Aquinas Cathedral.
Schinelli, Giles A. *t.o.r.* '70 (ALT) [7] Altoona, PA Our Lady of Mt. Carmel Church.
Schinn, Dom Bernard *o.s.b.* (DET) [K] Detroit, MI St. Sylvester Monastery.
Schinski, Msgr. Stanislaus E. '51 (PAT) [1] Wayne, NJ Annunciation Church.
Schipp, John H. '64 (EVN) [2] Vincennes, IN Basilica of St. Francis Xavier; [J] Vincennes, IN Old Cathedral Library & Museum, Inc.
Schipp, Ralph (EVN) Special Assignment; [E] Evansville, IN St. Mary's Medical Center of Evansville, Inc.
Schipper, Carl A. '68 (SFR) Special Assignment; [A] Menlo Park, CA St. Patrick Seminary.
Schipper, William *o.s.b.* '94 (IND) [J] St. Meinrad, IN St. Meinrad Archabbey.
Schiro, Nicholas T. *s.j.* '57 (NO) [F] New Orleans, LA Jesuit High School.
Schirra, Peter M. '37 (PIT) Retired.

Schiska, Paul A. '57 (MAR) Retired.
Schissel, Gregory A. *s.j.* '79 (MIL) [P] Milwaukee, WI Jesuit Community at Marquette University.
Schissel, John G. '40 (SC) Retired.
Schlachter, Msgr. Clarence A. '46 (EVN) Special Assignment.
Schlachter, Eric A. '81 (JC) Chamois, MO Most Pure Heart of Mary Church; Morrison, MO Assumption Church.
Schlade, Joseph F. '58 (RCK) Retired.
Schladen, Donald R. '56 (PEO) Marseilles, IL St. Joseph's Church.
Schladen, Robert G. '59 (PEO) [10] Peoria, IL St. Mark's Church.
Schlaefer, Joseph H. '58 (MAD) Neshkoro, WI St. James Church.
Schlaf, John E. '64 (GI) Ogallala, NE St. Luke's Church.
Schlafer, Joseph M. '75 (RVC) Nesconset, NY Church of the Holy Cross.
Schlaffer, James J. '45 (MIL) Retired.
Schlageter, Robert *o.f.m.conv.* '83 (BGP) [6] Danbury, CT Sacred Heart Church; [V] Bridgeport, CT Newman Centers.
Schlagheck, Regis T. *o.f.m.conv.* '66 (STP) Bloomington, MN St. Bonaventure Church.
Schlatter, Fredric *s.j.* '56 (SPK) [C] Spokane, WA Gonzaga University.
Schlatter, Glen '55 (P) Retired.
Schlattmann, Edward B. '34 (STL) Retired.
Schlautman, Wayne W. '65 (OM) Randolph, NE St. Frances de Chantal Church.
Schlax, Charles M. '66 (CHI) Palatine, IL St. Theresa Church.
Schlegel, Daniel F. '88 (CLV) [3] Euclid, OH Holy Cross Church.
Schlegel, Msgr. George J. '66 (COL) New Philadelphia, OH Sacred Heart Church.
Schlegel, John P. *s.j.* '73 (SFR) [C] San Francisco, CA University of San Francisco; [N] San Francisco, CA Jesuit Community at University of San Francisco.
Schlegel, Lawrence *o.s.b.* '54 (MAN) [K] Manchester, NH St. Anselm Abbey.
Schleicher, Edward R. '83 (PIT) Muse, PA Holy Rosary Church.
Schleicher, James R. '54 (CLV) [5] Akron, OH St. Francis de Sales Church; [V] Cleveland, OH Society of St. Vincent de Paul, Diocesan Central Council.
Schlenker, Richard '56 (MIL) [B] Hales Corners, WI Sacred Heart School of Theology.
Schlert, Alfred A. '87 (ALN) [C] Easton, PA Notre Dame High School; [O] Kutztown, PA Christopher House.
Schlesselmann, Gregory '93 (FAR) Oriska, ND St. Bernard's Church.
Schleter, Edward J. '67 (TOL) Defiance, OH St. Mary Church.
Schlett, Francis J. '70 (PH) [1] Coatesville, PA St. Cecilia Church.
Schleupner, Msgr. G. Michael '72 (BAL) [87] Baltimore, MD Shrine of the Sacred Heart Church; Special Assignment.
Schlich, James J. (L) Retired.
Schlick, Regis *o.f.m.cap.* '65 (SJN) [4] San Juan, PR San Antonio Church.
Schliessmann, Thomas '89 (IND) Scottsburg, IN American Martyrs Church.
Schliessmann, Thomas L. '89 (IND) Salem, IN St. Patrick Church.
Schlim, Robert J. *s.j.* '62 (SPK) [K] Spokane, WA Regis Community.
Schlimm, Chrysostom V. *o.s.b.* '61 (GBG) [H] Latrobe, PA Saint Vincent Archabbey.
Schlinkmann, John W. '31 (MIA) Retired.
Schlitt, Dale M. *o.m.i.* '69 (STP) [N] St. Paul, MN Oblate Provincial Offices; [N] St. Paul, MN Oblate Residence.
Schlitt, Harry G. '64 (SFR) [20] San Francisco, CA St. Gabriel Church; Special Assignment.
Schlitt, Robert T. '56 (TLS) Stillwater, OK St. Francis Xavier Church.
Schloeder, Paul '87 (SAC) Vacaville, CA California Medical Facility, South.
Schloemer, Bernard J. '60 (STL) Sunset Hills, MO St. Justin Martyr Church.
Schloemer, Leo *glmy.* '56 (TYL) New Boston, TX St. Mary of the Cenacle Church.
Schloemer, Thomas N. *s.j.* '68 (MIL) [P] Milwaukee, WI Jesuit Community at Marquette University.
Schloesser, Stephen R. *s.j.* '92 (MIL) [P] Milwaukee, WI Jesuit Provincial Office, Wisconsin Province.
Schloesser, Stephen R. *s.j.* '92 (SJ) [B] Santa Clara, CA Santa Clara University.
Schlosser, Leo *o.s.b.* '59 (PBR) [3] Youngstown, OH St. George Church; [4] Youngstown, OH St. John the Baptist Church.
Schlosser, Richard '74 (GF) [2] Great Falls, MT Eastside Catholic Communities Church.
Schloth, Brian D. *m.s.* '89 (NOR) Danielson, CT St. James Church.
Schludecker, Andre *o.f.m.* '64 (GAY) Bay Shore, MI St. Francis Solanus Church; Petoskey, MI St. Francis Xavier Church.
Schlueter, Clemens M. '58 (TUC) Retired.
Schlut, Michael '86 (DEN) Absent on Leave.
Schluter O. Charles '78 (MAD) Mazomanie, WI St. Barnabas Church.
Schmainda, Robert D. '64 (SCL) St. Augusta, MN St. Mary Help of Christians Church.
Schmalhofer, John '74 (HBG) [1] Harrisburg, PA Cathedral Parish of St. Patrick Church.
Schmaltz, Albert F. '43 (STL) Retired.
Schmaltz, Bernard W. '73 (NO) [34] New Orleans, LA St. Gabriel the Archangel Church; Absent on Leave.
Schmalzried, Bernard R. '69 (Y) [6] Warren, OH St. Mary's Church.
Schmaus, James E. '92 (CHI) Libertyville, IL St. Joseph Church.
Schmeer, John P. '64 (PH) New Hope, PA St. Martin of Tours Church.
Schmelz, Damian *o.s.b.* '58 (IND) [B] St. Meinrad, IN St. Meinrad Seminary-College of Liberal Arts; [J] St. Meinrad, IN St. Meinrad Archabbey.
Schmelzer, Delbert L. '56 (MAD) Verona, WI St. Andrew Church.
Schmelzer, Joseph M. '77 (TOL) Payne, OH St. John the Baptist Church; Van Wert, OH St. Mary Church.
Schmelzer, Linus L. '45 (MIL) Retired.
Schmelzer, Paul '43 (SCL) Retired.
Schmenk, Cleo '53 (TOL) Paulding, OH St. Joseph Church.
Schmid, Wayne L. '68 (WCH) Military Chaplains.
Schmidberger, Richard M. '57 (DET) North Branch, MI St. Mary's Burnside Church.
Schmidlin, Donald L. '57 (IND) [33] Indianapolis, IN St. Matthew the Apostle Church.
Schmidlkofer, Bruce J. *s.j.* '91 (P) [D] Portland, OR Jesuit High School.
Schmidt, Anthony '50 (SFD) Retired.
Schmidt, Bosco *s.a.* '49 (NY) [Z] Garrison, NY Franciscan Friars of the Atonement.
Schmidt, Carl '50 (SFD) Coffeen, IL St. John the Baptist Church; Panama, IL Sacred Heart Church.
Schmidt, Charles W. *m.m.* '48 (HON) [H] Honolulu, HI Maryknoll Fathers House.
Schmidt, David L. '77 (SFD) Litchfield, IL Holy Family Church.
Schmidt, David R. '81 (GB) [5] Appleton, WI St. Pius X Church.
Schmidt, Dennis '80 (JC) Columbia, MO Columbia Newman Center, University of Missouri Church; [F] Columbia, MO University of Missouri-Columbia, Campus Ministry.
Schmidt, Dennis C. '80 (STL) On Duty Outside the Archdiocese.
Schmidt, Donald A. '73 (MIL) Belgium, WI St. Mary's Church.
Schmidt, Donald P. (WIN) Chatfield, MN St. Mary's Church.
Schmidt, Edward W. *s.j.* '73 (CHI) [N] Chicago, IL Chicago Province of the Society of Jesus-Provincial Office.
Schmidt, Edwin A. '63 (JC) St. Martins, MO St. Martin Church.
Schmidt, Elmer J. '56 (ROC) Hornell, NY St. Ann Church; Retired.
Schmidt, Eugene '56 (GB) Retired.
Schmidt, Florian J. '61 (DUB) [4] Dubuque, IA St. Mary's Church.
Schmidt, Francis J. '58 (MAD) Edgerton, WI St. Joseph Church.
Schmidt, Msgr. Francis X. '57 (PH) Bridgeport, PA St. Augustine Church.
Schmidt, Frederick N. '42 (MIL) Retired.
Schmidt, George, Jr. '70 (KNX) [K] Chattanooga, TN Mount Olivet.
Schmidt, George E., Jr. '70 (KNX) [1] Chattanooga, TN SS. Peter and Paul Church.
Schmidt, Msgr. George N. '41 (WCH) Retired.
Schmidt, Gerald *o.f.m.cap.* '66 (GB) Lakewood, WI St. Mary of the Lake Church; Wabeno, WI St. Ambrose Church.
Schmidt, Gregory L. '61 (STL) Old Monroe, MO Immaculate Conception Church.
Schmidt, Gustav H. *s.j.* '66 (HEL) St. Ignatius, MT St. Ignatius Church.
Schmidt, Henry C. '57 (SFD) [4] Springfield, IL Little Flower Church.
Schmidt, Jan Kevin '90 (CIN) [39] Cincinnati, OH Immaculate Heart of Mary Church.
Schmidt, Jerome J. '49 (BRK) [122] Brooklyn, NY Resurrection Church; Retired.
Schmidt, John *c.ss.r.* '89 (CHI) [9] Chicago, IL St. Alphonsus Church; [136] Chicago, IL St. Michael Church.
Schmidt, John Berchmans *o.f.m.cap.* '34 (PIT) [N] Pittsburgh, PA St. Conrad Friary.
Schmidt, John W. '56 (Y) Retired.
Schmidt, Joseph F. '66 (B) Moscow, ID St. Mary's Church.
Schmidt, Kenneth W. '81 (KAL) [5] Kalamazoo, MI St. Thomas More Student Parish Church; [H] Kalamazoo, MI Western Michigan University, Kalamazoo College-Kalamazoo Valley Community College.
Schmidt, Leo C. '56 (COV) [4] Covington, KY St. Augustine Church.
Schmidt, Leslie *glmy.* '61 (RIC) Big Stone Gap, VA Sacred Heart Church.
Schmidt, Louis R. '54 (LEX) [3] Lexington, KY Mary, Queen of the Holy Rosary Church; Retired.
Schmidt, Lukas *o.carm.* '65 (WDC) [B] Washington, DC Whitefriars Hall.
Schmidt, Nicholas '67 (ORG) Inactive Leave.
Schmidt, Paul *s.v.d.* '81 (SB) [A] Riverside, CA Divine Word Seminary.
Schmidt, Paul J. '64 (OAK) [14] Oakland, CA St. Margaret Mary Church.
Schmidt, Ralph G., Jr. '73 (GAL) Texas City, TX St. Mary Church.
Schmidt, Raymond F. '60 (BRK) [194] Queens, NY St. Mary Church.
Schmidt, Raymond F. '84 (WDC) [10] Washington, DC Blessed Sacrament, Shrine of the Most Church.
Schmidt, Richard C. *s.j.* '61 (WDC) [E] North Bethesda, MD Georgetown Preparatory School.
Schmidt, Msgr. Robert R. '43 (COL) Retired.
Schmidt, Robert W. *s.j.* '42 (CIN) [M] Cincinnati, OH Jesuit Community at Xavier University.
Schmidt, Sebastian *o.s.b.* '60 (BIS) [A] Richardton, ND Assumption Abbey.
Schmidt, Stanley A. '41 (L) Retired.
Schmidt, Thomas *c.ss.r.* (RVC) Bethpage, NY St. Martin of Tours Church.
Schmidt, Thomas '76 (STL) Arnold, MO St. David Church.
Schmidt, Vincent F. '49 (COV) Retired.
Schmidt, Msgr. W. Robert '57 (DAV) [M] Davenport, IA St. Vincent Center.
Schmidt, Wilfred W. '50 (DUB) [4] Dubuque, IA St. Mary's Church; Retired.
Schmidt, William *o.f.m.* (STP) [10] St. Paul, MN Sacred Heart Church.
Schmidt, William F. *s.a.* '59 (R) Apex, NC St. Andrew the Apostle Church.
Schmidt, William T. '76 (BO) Stoneham, MA St. Patrick Church.
Schmidtzinsky, Msgr. Victor '41 (SAT) [K] San Antonio, TX Padua Place.
Schmidtzinsky, Msgr. Victor '41 (VIC) Retired.
Schmied, Michael S. '71 (RIC) [6] Richmond, VA St. Augustine Church.
Schmied, Thomas *o.f.m.cap.* '69 (MAR) Special Assignment.
Schmieder, Mark '66 (CIN) [3] Cincinnati, OH All Saints Church.
Schmieg, Brennan *o.f.m.* '58 (SUP) Sanborn, WI St. Anne Church; Washburn, WI St. Louis Church.
Schmiesing, Julian *o.s.b.* '58 (SCL) Cold Spring, MN St. Boniface Church.
Schmit, Arthur G. *o.s.b.* '57 (PEO) [A] Peru, IL St. Bede Abbey and Academy.
Schmit, Fred *s.d.s.* '46 (MIL) [55] Milwaukee, WI Mother of Good Counsel Church.
Schmit, George V., Jr. '68 (NU) [1] New Ulm, MN Cathedral of The Holy Trinity; Searles, MN St. John the Baptist Church.
Schmit, Msgr. Jerome '41 (TOL) Retired.
Schmit, Jerome L. '57 (LA) Altadena, CA Sacred Heart Church.
Schmit, Kenneth A. '79 (ORG) El Toro, CA Santiago de Compostela Church.
Schmit, Louis L. *c.pp.s.* '63 (CIN) [M] Dayton, OH Provincial House of the Cincinnati Province of the Society of the Precious Blood.
Schmit, Meyrl E. '65 (JKS) Tupelo, MS St. James Church.
Schmit, Msgr. Ralph R. '46 (MIL) Retired.
Schmit, Roger W. *o.s.b.* '62 (CHY) Laramie, WY St. Paul's Newman Center Church; [E] Laramie, WY University of Wyoming.
Schmit, Ronald G. (OAK) Byron, CA St. Anne Church.
Schmit, Ronald N. '75 (PRT) Brewer, ME St. Joseph's Church.
Schmit, Stanley T. '94 (OM) [33] Omaha, NE Our Lady of Lourdes Church.
Schmitmeyer, James M. '81 (CIN) North Star, OH St. Louis Church; Osgood, OH St. Nicholas Church.
Schmitt, Adam '57 (FTW) [8] Fort Wayne, IN St. Joseph Church.
Schmitt, Allen M. '71 (DUB) Little Turkey, IA Assumption of the B. V. M. Church; Protivin, IA Holy Trinity Church.
Schmitt, Bernard *c.pp.s.* '40 (CIN) [B] Carthagena, OH St. Charles.
Schmitt, Carl L. '61 (DUB) New Hampton, IA St. Joseph's Church.
Schmitt, Charles R. '59 (E) Port Allegany, PA St. Gabriel the Archangel Church.
Schmitt, Christopher '60 (PMB) [F] Delray Beach, FL Opus Dei.
Schmitt, Conrad *s.t.* '55 (SAV) Blakely, GA Holy Family Church.
Schmitt, David J. '67 (WH) Logan, WV St. Francis of Assisi Church; Man, WV St. Edmund Church.

Schmitt, Donald P. '62 (DUB) Barclay, IA St. Francis Church; Jesup, IA St. Athanasius Church.
Schmitt, Ervin J. '58 (PBL) [5] Pueblo, CO Our Lady of the Assumption Church; [14] Pueblo, CO St. Mary Church; [15] Pueblo, CO St. Patrick Church.
Schmitt, Eugene A. '45 (WH) Retired.
Schmitt, Gregory *c.ss.r.* '69 (KC) [32] Kansas City, MO Our Lady of Perpetual Help Church; [J] Kansas City, MO Redemptorists of Kansas City; [O] Kansas City, MO Our Lady of Perpetual Help Charitable Trust.
Schmitt, Harold F. '59 (PEO) [3] Ottawa, IL St. Mary's Church.
Schmitt, Msgr. J. Harley '40 (DEN) Retired; [I] Denver, CO Mullen Home.
Schmitt, James, J. '51 (LAN) Retired.
Schmitt, James C. '66 (GI) [3] Grand Island, NE Resurrection Church; Grand Island, NE Nebraska Veterans Home.
Schmitt, James J. '74 (PIT) Crafton, PA St. Philip Church.
Schmitt, John P. '44 (GB) Retired.
Schmitt, Msgr. Joseph J. '55 (AUS) Lago Vista, TX St. Mary, Our Lady of the Lake Church.
Schmitt, Kent A. '73 (MAD) [7] Madison, WI St. Dennis Church.
Schmitt, Leo J. '43 (GB) Retired.
Schmitt, Michael T. '71 (ALB) Colonie, NY St. Clare Church.
Schmitt, Myles *o.f.m.cap.* '43 (PIT) [N] Pittsburgh, PA St. Conrad Friary.
Schmitt, Phillip E. '56 (DUB) Iowa Falls, IA St. Mark's Church.
Schmitt, Reinhold *c.m.m.* '52 (AUS) Westphalia, TX Visitation Church.
Schmitt, Reinhold *c.m.m.* '52 (DET) [K] Dearborn Heights, MI Our Lady of Grace Monastery.
Schmitt, Silverius J. '58 (SCL) Bowlus, MN St. Stanislaus Kostka Church; North Prairie, MN Holy Cross Church.
Schmitt, Thomas '91 (SPR) Graduate Studies.
Schmitt, Thomas G. '45 (DET) Retired.
Schmitt, Urban J. *o.s.c.* '49 (LIN) [A] Hastings, NE Crosier Monastery.
Schmitt, Warren J. '42 (MIL) Retired.
Schmitter, Phillip '71 (LAN) Special Assignment.
Schmittgens, Kevin V. '83 (STL) Gildehaus, MO St. John the Baptist Church.
Schmitz, Allan *o.f.m.* (CIN) [V] Cincinnati, OH Catholic Cursillo of Cincinnati.
Schmitz, Aloysius F. *s.j.* '59 (STP) [N] Minneapolis, MN La Storta Jesuit Community.
Schmitz, Bernard A. '74 (DEN) On Duty Outside the Archdiocese.
Schmitz, Msgr. Bernard R. '57 (IND) Milan, IN St. Charles Borromeo Church; Morris, IN St. Anthony of Padua Church; St. Nicholas, IN St. Nicholas Church.
Schmitz, Charles E. *s.j.* '72 (P) [L] Portland, OR Jesuit Provincial Office (Oregon Prov.); [Q] Portland, OR Jesuit Development & Communications Office.
Schmitz, Dennis E. '89 (KCK) [8] Kansas City, KS St. Mary-St. Anthony Church.
Schmitz, Donald J. '80 (WIN) Caledonia, MN St. Mary Church.
Schmitz, Donald P. '64 (WIN) [3] Rochester, MN Resurrection Church.
Schmitz, George '69 (CIN) [7] Dayton, OH St. Charles Borromeo Church.
Schmitz, Gerald P. '62 (MIL) [3] Kenosha, WI St. George Church.
Schmitz, Gerald T. '48 (MIL) Retired.
Schmitz, Gerard G. '68 (HRT) Madison, CT St. Margaret Church.
Schmitz, James P. '86 (CLV) Amherst, OH St. Joseph Church.
Schmitz, John A. '52 (MIL) Ripon, WI St. Patrick Church.
Schmitz, John J. '91 (JC) Vienna, MO Visitation Church.
Schmitz, Michael D '96 (OM) Columbus, NE St. Isidore Church.
Schmitz, Robert A. '55 (OM) Tilden, NE Our Lady of Mt. Carmel Church.
Schmitz, Robert E. '75 (CIN) [19] Cincinnati, OH St. Catharine Church.
Schmitzer, Richard C. '46 (STP) Retired.
Schmock, Hilarion *o.c.s.o.* '43 (L) [L] Trappist, KY Abbey of Our Lady of Gethsemani, of the Order of Cistercians of the Strict Observance.
Schmoldt, William F. *s.j.* '54 (DET) [P] Clarkston, MI Colombiere Center.
Schmoll, John '85 (FRS) Lamont, CA St. Augustine Church.
Schmuhl, Lawrence *s.m.* '47 (ATL) [6] Atlanta, GA Our Lady of the Assumption Church.
Schnacky, Paul R. '53 (ROC) Wayland, NY St. Joseph's Church.
Schnaubelt, Joseph C. *o.s.a.* '57 (PH) [Z] Villanova, PA St. Thomas Monastery.
Schnaus, Urban *o.s.b.* '40 (WDC) [M] Washington, DC St. Anselm's Abbey.
Schneebeck, Paul O. *c.m.* '69 (STL) [P] St. Louis, MO Vincentian-St. Lazare Residence.
Schneibel, Jeffrey *c.s.c.* (P) [L] Portland, OR Holy Cross Father & Brother, C.S.C. - University of Portland.
Schneibel, Jeffrey *c.s.c.* '85 (P) [B] Portland, OR University of Portland.
Schneible, Peter *o.f.m.* '89 (BUF) [O] St. Bonaventure, NY St. Bonaventure Friary.
Schneid, Michael '58 (CLV) Retired.
Schneider, Adrian *o.f.m.* '41 (CIN) [M] Cincinnati, OH St. Francis Center.
Schneider, Msgr. Alfred A. '38 (GB) Retired.
Schneider, Anthony *o.f.m.* (NY) [146] Bronx, NY Holy Cross Church.
Schneider, Msgr. Arnold J. (BUF) Bowmansville, NY Sacred Heart Church.
Schneider, Barry *o.f.m.* '56 (SUP) Dauby, WI St. Peter Church; Iron River, WI St. Michael Church.
Schneider, Bernard R. '67 (FAR) Mayville, ND Our Lady of Peace Church; [H] Mayville, ND Mayville State University Newman Center.
Schneider, Charles J. '63 (WH) New Martinsville, WV St. Vincent de Paul Church.
Schneider, Christopher *o.f.m.* '49 (CIN) [M] Cincinnati, OH St. Clement Friary.
Schneider, Conrad *o.f.m.* '51 (CHI) [N] Oak Forest, IL St. Roch Friary-Franciscan Fathers.
Schneider, Craig '89 (CIN) [K] Dayton, OH St. Elizabeth Medical Center, Inc.
Schneider, Donald A. '50 (GB) Retired.
Schneider, Edward '64 (EVN) Petersburg, IN SS. Peter and Paul Church.
Schneider, Msgr. Ernest P. '77 (GR) Ada, MI St. Robert Church.
Schneider, Francis J. '83 (RVC) Elmont, NY St. Vincent de Paul Church.
Schneider, Fredrick *o.f.m.* (LR) Horseshoe Bend, AR St. Mary of the Mount Church.
Schneider, George D. '56 (FAR) Rolla, ND St. Joachim's Church.
Schneider, George E. '58 (COV) Florence, KY St. Paul Church.
Schneider, George P. '45 (PH) Parkesburg, PA Our Lady of Consolation Church; Retired.
Schneider, Gilbert *o.f.m.* '64 (SFE) [J] Albuquerque, NM San Antonio Provincial Friary Franciscan Friars.
Schneider, Harold '74 (KCK) [3] Topeka, KS Holy Name Church.
Schneider, Harold E. '62 (COL) Heath, OH St. Leonard Church.
Schneider, Henry W. '53 (BIS) [3] Minot, ND St. John the Apostle Church.
Schneider, J. Daniel *m.m.* '77 (NY) [Z] Maryknoll, NY Maryknoll Fathers and Brothers.
Schneider, Jerzy *s.d.b.* '53 (NEW) [C] Ramsey, NJ Don Bosco Preparatory High School for Boys.
Schneider, John G. '48 (STL) Retired.
Schneider, John H. '68 (STL) Bonne Terre, MO St. Joseph's Church.
Schneider, John W. '83 (CHL) Arden, NC St. Barnabas Church.
Schneider, Joseph M. '74 (DUB) Meyer, IA Sacred Heart Church; St. Ansgar, IA St. Ansgar Church; Stacyville, IA Church of the Visitation.
Schneider, Juniper *o.f.m.conv.* '72 (OAK) San Pablo, CA St. Paul Church.
Schneider, Karl J. '59 (MIL) [4] West Allis, WI Immaculate Heart of Mary Church.
Schneider, Kevin C. *s.j.* '94 (RC) Pine Ridge, SD Holy Rosary Church; [B] Pine Ridge, SD Jesuit Community of Holy Rosary Mission.
Schneider, Leo J. '83 (LC) [9] La Crosse, WI Roncalli Newman Parish Church; [L] La Crosse, WI Roncalli Newman Parish.
Schneider, Leon J. '53 (MIL) [5] Racine, WI St. Mary's by the Lake Church.
Schneider, Mark *o.s.b.* '41 (SCL) [H] Cold Spring, MN Assumption Home; [H] Cold Spring, MN John Paul Apartments; [H] Cold Spring, MN Assumption Court.
Schneider, Michael '94 (GF) Poplar, MT Our Lady of Lourdes Church.
Schneider, Michael R. '81 (SFS) Gettysburg, SD Sacred Heart Church; Onida, SD St. Pius X Church.
Schneider, Msgr. Nicholas A. '56 (STL) [3] Creve Coeur, MO St. Monica Church.
Schneider, Paul *o.f.m.* '43 (SFE) [K] Rio Rancho, NM Felician Sisters.
Schneider, Philip *o.f.m.conv.* '61 (FTW) Angola, IN St. Anthony Church; Clear Lake, IN St. Paul Chapel.
Schneider, Ralph *c.pp.s.* '64 (TOL) Ottawa, OH SS. Peter and Paul Church.
Schneider, Ric *o.f.m.* '59 (PEO) [2] Bloomington, IL St. Mary's Church.
Schneider, Richard J. *s.m.* '83 (SAT) [K] San Antonio, TX St. Joseph's Community.
Schneider, Msgr. Robert E. '57 (COL) Coshocton, OH Sacred Heart Church.
Schneider, Robert J. '78 (WIN) Albert Lea, MN St. Theodore's Church; [J] Albert Lea, MN St. Theodore Catholic School Endowment.
Schneider, Robert J. '81 (SP) [4] St. Petersburg, FL Holy Family Church.
Schneider, Robert W. '55 (MIL) Retired.
Schneider, Ronald '75 (GB) Absent on Leave.
Schneider, Ronald F. '67 (GR) Hart, MI St. Gregory's Church.
Schneider, Stephen *o.f.m.* '38 (L) [L] Louisville, KY St. Boniface Friary.
Schneider, Stephen A. '72 (SPC) [3] Springfield, MO Immaculate Conception Church.
Schneider, Stephen V. *o.f.m.* '38 (L) [15] Louisville, KY St. Boniface Church.
Schneider, Terrance L. '79 (CIN) Oxford, OH St. Mary Church and Catholic Campus Ministry Church; [Q] Oxford, OH Miami University Catholic Campus Ministry.
Schneider, Todd '85 (SCL) Elmdale, MN St. Edward's Church; Upsala, MN St. Mary Church.
Schneider, Vincent N. '38 (MIL) Retired.
Schneider, William F. '68 (NOR) Gales Ferry, CT Our Lady of Lourdes Church.
Schneider, William T. '63 (TR) Freehold, NJ St. Rose of Lima Church; Marlboro, NJ New Jersey State Hospital.
Schneller, Michael J. '72 (NO) Belle Chasse, LA Our Lady of Perpetual Help Church.
Schneweis, Emil F. *o.f.m.cap.* '39 (MIL) [P] Mount Calvary, WI St. Lawrence Friary.
Schnipke, Eugene '80 (SB) Military Chaplains.
Schnipke, Eugene H. *c.pp.s.* '80 (CIN) [M] Dayton, OH Provincial House of the Cincinnati Province of the Society of the Precious Blood.
Schnipke, Kenneth R. *c.pp.s.* '90 (ORL) Longwood, FL Church of the Nativity.
Schnitzius, Donald J. '48 (STP) Retired.
Schnoebelen, Kenneth F. '46 (LIN) Retired.
Schnorr, Charles A. *s.j.* '50 (PH) [Z] Philadelphia, PA Jesuit Community at St. Joseph's University.
Schnupp, Luzerne A. '57 (NSH) Franklin, TN St. Matthew Church.
Schnur, Edward C. '91 (EVN) Rockport, IN St. Bernard Church.
Schnurr, Msgr. Dennis M. '74 (SC) On Duty Outside the Diocese.
Schnurr, Herman J. '39 (FTW) Avilla, IN St. Mary of the Assumption Church; Retired.
Schnurr, Thomas J. *o.s.b.* '32 (BIR) [E] Cullman, AL St. Bernard Abbey.
Schober, Robert J. '77 (BUF) [2] Depew, NY St. Barnabas Church; Williamsville, NY SS. Peter and Paul Church; Buffalo, NY Millard Fillmore Hospital.
Schock, Ronald A. '96 (TOL) Findlay, OH St. Michael Church.
Schoderbek, Charles *s.v.d.* '47 (CHI) [B] Techny, IL Divine Word Residence.
Schoech, Frowin *o.s.b.* '66 (FWT) Muenster, TX Sacred Heart Church.
Schoellmann, Edward E. *m.m.* '65 (GAL) [Q] Houston, TX Maryknoll Fathers and Brothers.
Schoellmann, Edward R. *m.m.* '65 (NY) [Z] Maryknoll, NY Maryknoll Fathers and Brothers.
Schoemann, Robert L. '66 (DM) Waukee, IA St. Boniface Church.
Schoen, Thomas A. *s.m.* '87 (CIN) [D] Dayton, OH The University of Dayton; [M] Dayton, OH Marianist Provincialate.
Schoen, Timothy *o.s.b.* '64 (KC) [A] Conception, MO Conception Seminary College; [J] Conception, MO Conception Abbey.
Schoenauer, Francis P. '73 (ALN) [1] Saint Clair, PA St. Boniface Church; [4] Saint Clair, PA St. Mary Church; [5] Saint Clair, PA SS. Peter and Paul Church.
Schoenbachler, Charles *c.r.* '42 (L) [17] Louisville, KY St. Cecilia Church.
Schoenbachler, Timothy M. '78 (L) Leave of Absence.
Schoenberg, Oscar C. *o.s.c.* '48 (LIN) [A] Hastings, NE Crosier Monastery.
Schoenberg, Wilfred *s.j.* '51 (P) [L] Portland, OR Jesuit Provincial Office (Oregon Prov.).
Schoenberger, James T. '57 (STP) North Branch, MN St. Gregory Church; Shakopee, MN Women's State Reformatory.
Schoenfeldt, Arthur *c.s.c.* '59 (P) [B] Portland, OR University of Portland; [L] Portland, OR Holy Cross Father & Brother, C.S.C. - University of Portland.
Schoenhofen, Darr '82 (SY) On Duty Outside the Diocese.
Schoenhofen, Roger *o.m.i.* '66 (BEL) [I] Belleville, IL Retreat and Renewal Center.
Schoening, Sylvester H. '58 (PBL) Retired.
Schoenstene, Robert L. '75 (CHI) [A] Mundelein, IL University of St. Mary of the Lake-Mundelein Seminary.
Schoenstene, Robert L. '75 (JOL) On Duty Outside the Diocese.
Schoeppe, F. Warren *s.j.* '58 (SLC) Brigham City, UT St. Henry Church.
Schoettelkotte, Msgr. Charles T. '34 (EVN) Retired.
Schoettelkotte, John B. '60 (IND) North Vernon, IN St. Mary/Nativity of the Blessed Virgin Mary Church; St. Joseph, IN St. Joseph Church.

Schoettelkotte, Lawrence A. *s.m.* '70 (KAL) Portage, MI St. Catherine of Siena Church; [E] Portage, MI Society of Mary.
Schoettmer, Kenneth J. (CIN) Millville, OH Queen of Peace Church.
Schoffelmeer, Arnold L. '56 (SPK) Retired.
Scholl, William G. *o.s.f.s.* '61 (PH) [Z] Philadelphia, PA Oblates of St. Francis De Sales.
Scholla, Robert *s.j.* (BO) [W] Cambridge, MA Weston Jesuit Community.
Scholsky, Martin J. '56 (HRT) [5] East Hartford, CT St. Mary's Church.
Scholz, James P. '71 (OM) [42] Omaha, NE Sacred Heart Church; [F] Omaha, NE Christian Urban Education Service Foundation; [O] Omaha, NE Christian Urban Education Service.
Scholz, LeRoy '66 (SCL) Clear Lake, MN St. Marcus Church.
Scholz, William J. '52 (PIT) Robinson Township, PA Holy Trinity Church.
Schoming, Henry C. *c.s.sp.* '43 (VEN) [G] Sarasota, FL Congregation of the Holy Ghost.
Schommer, George '94 (CIN) [30] Cincinnati, OH St. Gertrude Church; [M] Cincinnati, OH St. Gertrude Priory.
Schommer, Msgr. Mark J. '63 (GB) Bear Creek, WI St. Mary Church; Clintonville, WI St. Rose Church.
Schommer, Michael '93 (FAR) Langdon, ND St. Alphonsus Church.
Schon, Randy L. '88 (SC) Oyens, IA St. Catherine's Church.
Schons, Msgr. Gerard '47 (SAC) Retired and in Senior Ministry.
Schook, James R. '75 (L) Payneville, KY St. Mary Magdalen of Pazzi Church; Rhodelia, KY St. Theresa Church.
Schooler, William C. '74 (FTW) [9] Fort Wayne, IN St. Jude Church.
Schoone, Raymond L. (SUP) Retired.
Schopfer, John C. '69 (SY) [1] Syracuse, NY The Cathedral of the Immaculate Conception; Special Assignment.
Schopman, Joop *s.j.* '66 (BO) [W] Chestnut Hill, MA The Jesuit Community at Boston College.
Schopp, George L. '74 (CHI) Blue Island, IL St. Benedict Church.
Schoppe, Msgr. Charles K. '49 (GAL) Retired.
Schopps, William J. '85 (ARL) Colonial Beach, VA St. Elizabeth Church; Colonial Beach, VA St. Elizabeth Church.
Schork, John *c.p.* '76 (GAL) [S] Houston, TX Holy Name Retreat Center.
Schorp, W. Franz *s.m.* '64 (SAT) [C] San Antonio, TX St. Mary's University of San Antonio, Texas; [M] San Antonio, TX Marianist Residence.
Schorr, James D. '68 (CLV) [2] Elyria, OH Holy Cross Church.
Schorr, W. David '73 (PIT) [78] Pittsburgh, PA Most Holy Name of Jesus Church.
Schott, Brett T. '91 (STL) [57] St. Louis, MO St. Pius the Fifth Church.
Schott, Edward *s.j.* '63 (ELP) [21] El Paso, TX Sacred Heart Church.
Schott, Fred '88 (COV) Leave of Absence.
Schott, James '61 (NO) [45] New Orleans, LA St. Matthias Church.
Schott, Kevin J. '90 (NEW) Cedar Grove, NJ St. Catherine of Siena Church.
Schott, Paul W. *s.j.* '53 (NO) [11] New Orleans, LA Immaculate Conception Church.
Schott, Timothy R. '70 (SC) Spencer, IA Sacred Heart Church.
Schott, Valerian *o.f.m.* '32 (STL) Oakville, MO St. Francis of Assisi Church; [P] Oakville, MO St. Francis Friary.
Schott, Victor '56 (LFT) [C] Lafayette, IN St. Elizabeth Hospital Medical Center.
Schotzko, Philip M. '73 (NU) Hector, MN Church of St. John.
Schotzko, Philip M. '77 (NU) Bird Island, MN St. Mary Church.
Schouten, Frank L. '58 (CHI) [56] Chicago, IL St. Eugene Church.
Schoutteten, Francis *o.m.i.* '41 (BWN) San Juan, TX Virgen de San Juan del Valle Shrine Church; [I] San Juan, TX Virgen de San Juan del Valle Shrine.
Schrad, Merlin J. '77 (SC) Auburn, IA St. Mary's Church; [B] Carroll, IA Kuemper Catholic High School.
Schrader, James C., Jr. '76 (LIN) Campbell, NE St. Ann's Church.
Schrader, James H. *c.pp.s.* '56 (KC) Nevada, MO St. Mary's Church.
Schrader, Robert J. '78 (ROC) [3] Auburn, NY St. Mary Church.
Schrage, Frank P. '68 (GB) [F] Green Bay, WI St. Mary's Hospital-Medical Center.
Schramel, Michael J. (ROC) [2] Rochester, NY St. Ambrose Church.
Schramel, Sebastian *o.s.b.* '45 (SCL) [I] Collegeville, MN St. John's Abbey, of the Order of St. Benedict.
Schramko, Stewart *c.s.v.* '64 (LAV) [9] Las Vegas, NV St. Francis de Sales Church.
Schramm, Charles H. '71 (MIL) [73] Milwaukee, WI St. Sebastian's Church.
Schramm, Donald C. '67 (STL) Troy, MO Sacred Heart Church.
Schramm, Edward J. '69 (STL) Kinloch, MO Holy Angels Church.
Schramm, Robert *o.s.f.s.* '69 (SAG) [4] Saginaw, MI SS. Simon and Jude Church.
Schramm, Robert F. *o.s.f.s.* (LAN) Adrian, MI St. Mary of Good Counsel Church.
Schratz, Martin A. *o.f.m.cap.* '83 (ARL) Purcellville, VA St. Francis de Sales Church.
Schray, Karl G. '65 (P) Grants Pass, OR St. Anne Church.
Schreck, Christopher J. '77 (PH) [A] Wynnewood, PA Theological Seminary of St. Charles Borromeo, Overbrook.
Schreck, Christopher J. '77 (SAV) On Duty Outside the Diocese.
Schreck, J. Gerard (SAV) [A] Columbus, GA Pacelli High School.
Schreck, Joseph *o.f.m.cap.* '55 (ARE) [1] Utuado, PR San Miquel Church.
Schreck, Joseph Gerard '83 (SAV) [3] Columbus, GA St. Anne Church.
Schreck, Paul C. '45 (BUF) [K] Lewiston, NY Mount St. Mary's Hospital of Niagara Falls.
Schreiber, Bernard G. '47 (LC) Retired.
Schreiber, Edmund J. '44 (CHI) Franklin Park, IL St. Gertrude Church; Retired.
Schreiber, William A. '79 (SC) Le Mars, IA St. Joseph's Church; [B] Le Mars, IA Gehlen Catholic School.
Schreiner, Bernard P. '42 (NU) Retired.
Schreiner, Robert C. '89 (CR) Middle River, MN St. Joseph, Husband of Mary Church; Stephen, MN St. Stephen's Church.
Schreiner, William M. *c.s.c.* '42 (FTW) [L] Notre Dame, IN Holy Cross Mission House.
Schreiter, Daniel A. '50 (GB) Retired.
Schreiter, John P. '69 (MIL) Dousman, WI St. Bruno's Church.
Schreiter, Robert *c.pp.s.* '75 (CHI) [B] Chicago, IL The Catholic Theological Union at Chicago.
Schreitmueller, Henry J. '56 (NEW) [B] South Orange, NJ Seton Hall University.
Schremmer, Robert A. '76 (DOD) Belpre, KS St. Bernard Church; Larned, KS Sacred Heart Church.
Schrenger, Arthur C. '75 (MOB) [4] Montgomery, AL Church of the Holy Spirit.
Schriber, Robert T. '96 (R) Cary, NC St. Michael the Archangel Church.
Schrieber, Gerard H. *c.ss.r.* '54 (RIC) [O] Hampton, VA Holy Family Retreat House.
Schriefer, Msgr. Robert F. '44 (E) Retired.
Schrimpf, Raymond *s.d.s.* '56 (MIL) [P] Milwaukee, WI Salvatorian Provincial Residence.
Schrimpf, Reginald '50 (MIL) [P] Milwaukee, WI Salvatorians - Jordan Hall.
Schriver, Ragan '95 (KNX) Kingsport, TN St. Dominic Church.
Schroder, John F. *s.j.* '53 (NO) [P] New Orleans, LA Jesuit Provincial Office.
Schroeder, Dennis A. '61 (TOL) Bucyrus, OH Holy Trinity Church.
Schroeder, Edward H. '58 (BUF) Clarence Center, NY St. Augustine Church.
Schroeder, Eugene '79 (EVN) [20] Evansville, IN St. Theresa Church.
Schroeder, Francis J. *s.s.j.* '45 (BR) [8] Baton Rouge, LA St. Francis Xavier Church.
Schroeder, Fred A. '42 (LFT) Carmel, IN St. Elizabeth Ann Seton Church.
Schroeder, George *o.f.m.conv.* '43 (TOL) Carey, OH Our Lady of Consolation, Basilica-National Shrine Church; Salem Twp., OH St. Joseph Church.
Schroeder, George J. '42 (PEO) [1] Rock Island, IL St. Mary Church; Retired.
Schroeder, George M. '62 (DEN) Steamboat Springs, CO Holy Name Church; [P] Steamboat Springs, CO Colorado Mountain College.
Schroeder, James *s.c.j.* '70 (MIL) [P] Franklin, WI Dehon House.
Schroeder, Jerome *o.f.m.cap.* '70 (MIL) [S] Milwaukee, WI The Dwelling Place.
Schroeder, Karl G. '34 (DUB) Retired; [C] Dubuque, IA Loras College.
Schroeder, Kenneth J. *c.pp.s.* '65 (CIN) [M] Dayton, OH Provincial House of the Cincinnati Province of the Society of the Precious Blood.
Schroeder, Richard F. '45 (CHI) Retired.
Schroeder, Roger P. *s.v.d.* '79 (CHI) [B] Chicago, IL The Catholic Theological Union at Chicago; [B] Techny, IL Divine Word Residence; [N] Chicago, IL Divine Word Theologate; [N] Techny, IL Society of the Divine Word, Provincial Headquarter-Chicago Prov.
Schroeder, Thomas H. '64 (MAD) Martinsville, WI St. Martin Church.
Schroeder, Timothy C. '88 (FAR) Forman, ND St. Mary's Church.
Schroeder, Msgr. Walter L. '41 (NY) Armonk, NY St. Patrick Church; Retired.
Schroeder, William H. '55 (PIT) Wexford, PA St. Alphonsus Church.
Schroeder, William L. '45 (CIN) [32] Cincinnati, OH Guardian Angels Church; Retired.
Schroeppel, Stephen L. *m.m.* '58 (STL) [P] St. Louis, MO Maryknoll House.
Schroer, Joseph *o.c.s.o.* '52 (SLC) [F] Huntsville, UT Abbey of Our Lady of the Holy Trinity of the Order of Cistercians.
Schroer, Thomas A. *s.m.* '72 (CIN) [D] Dayton, OH The University of Dayton; [M] Dayton, OH Marianist Provincialate.
Schroering, Francis A. '59 (EVN) Haubstadt, IN SS. Peter and Paul Church.
Schroering, Raymond A. '49 (EVN) Retired.
Schroll, Bernard A. '69 (DET) Clawson, MI Guardian Angels Church; Retired.
Schroth, Raymond A. *s.j.* '67 (NO) [C] New Orleans, LA Loyola University.
Schubeck, Thomas L. *s.j.* '68 (CLV) [C] Cleveland, OH John Carroll Jesuit Community.
Schubert, Gerard H. *o.s.f.s.* '59 (ALN) [B] Center Valley, PA Allentown College of St. Francis de Sales; [K] Center Valley, PA Oblates of St. Francis de Sales.
Schubert, Gerold *o.f.m.* '54 (JOL) [J] Joliet, IL St. John the Baptist Friary.
Schubert, Herbert B. '56 (MIL) [1] South Milwaukee, WI St. Adalbert's Church.
Schubiger, Albert B. '49 (MAD) Retired.
Schuck, Hugh *o.s.b.* '34 (RCK) [H] Aurora, IL Marmion Abbey-St. Augustine's Abbey.
Schuck, Joseph J. '53 (ALB) Sidney, NY Sacred Heart Church.
Schuck, Joseph J. '53 (BRK) Released from Diocesan Assignment.
Schuckenbrock, Harry *o.m.i.* '59 (BWN) [7] Brownsville, TX St. Eugene De Mazenod Church.
Schuckman, Kenneth J. '92 (WCH) Newton, KS St. Mary Church; [M] Wichita, KS Serra Club of Wichita - Downtown.
Schue, Dennis L. '57 (FAR) Retired; [D] Devils Lake, ND Mercy Hospital.
Schuele, Francis J. (KC) [I] Kansas City, MO Jeanne Jugan Center.
Schuele, John C. '76 (KC) [7] Kansas City, MO St. Catherine of Siena Church.
Schueller, Anthony L. *s.s.s.* '77 (CLV) [B] Cleveland, OH Blessed Sacrament Seminary, Congregation of the Blessed Sacrament; [P] Cleveland, OH Congregation of the Blessed Sacrament Provincial House; [P] Cleveland, OH Blessed Sacrament Community.
Schueller, La Verne L. '66 (DUB) Military Chaplains.
Schuer, Robert J. '48 (COL) [2] Columbus, OH St. Agatha Church; Retired.
Schuerger, Anthony J. '77 (CLV) [44] Cleveland, OH Community of St. Malachi Church; [45] Cleveland, OH St. Malachi Church.
Schuerman, James T. '86 (MIL) Graduate Studies.
Schuessler, Peter *s.d.s.* '80 (MIL) [B] Hales Corners, WI Sacred Heart School of Theology; [P] Milwaukee, WI Salvatorian Provincial Residence.
Schuessler, William R. '67 (RCK) Special Assignment.
Schuett, John T. *s.j.* '58 (DET) [P] Bloomfield Hills, MI Manresa Jesuit Retreat House.
Schug, John *o.f.m.cap.* '54 (SPR) [L] Springfield, MA St. Francis of Assisi Chapel and Catholic Information Center.
Schuh, Earl J. '43 (GB) [13] Green Bay, WI SS. Peter and Paul Church; Retired.
Schuh, Msgr. John H. '65 (GB) Special Assignment.
Schuhmacher, George J. '57 (COV) Warsaw, KY St. Joseph Church.
Schuler, A. John '74 (STL) Ferguson, MO Our Lady of Guadalupe Church.
Schuler, Emett '69 (PIT) [N] Pittsburgh, PA St. Francis Friary.
Schuler, Emitt *o.f.m.cap.* '69 (PIT) Allegheny County, PA Veterans Administration - Aspinwall; Allegheny County, PA Veterans Administration - Oakland.
Schuler, Gregory '77 (LEX) [1] Lexington, KY Cathedral of Christ the King.
Schuler, Norbert *s.v.d.* '26 (TR) [M] Bordentown, NJ Society of the Divine Word.
Schuler, Msgr. Richard J. '45 (STP) [12] St. Paul, MN St. Agnes Church.
Schuler, Robert J. '89 (JOL) Clarendon Hills, IL Notre Dame Church.
Schuler, Stephen *s.v.d.* '79 (BLX) [A] Bay St. Louis, MS St. Augustine's.
Schuller, Frederick E. *s.j.* '52 (STL) [P] St. Louis, MO The Jesuits of the Missouri Province.
Schulmeister, Lawrence *o.f.m.* (BAL) Baltimore, MD University of Maryland Hospital.
Schulmeister, Lawrence *o.f.m.* '67 (NY) [Z] New York, NY Franciscan Friars, Order of Friars Manor.
Schulte, Bernard C. *s.j.* '47 (STL) [O] St. Louis, MO Fusz Pavilion; [P] St. Louis, MO Jesuit Community Corporation at St. Louis University - Jesuit Hall.
Schulte, Carl G. *c.m.* '48 (KC) [J] Kansas City, MO

Vincentian Parish Mission Center.
Schulte, Daniel R. *c.m.* '87 (STL) [P] St. Louis, MO Vincentian Residence.
Schulte, Francisco *o.s.b.* '79 (SCL) [I] Collegeville, MN St. John's Abbey, of the Order of St. Benedict.
Schulte, Gary '72 (DET) [11] Warren, MI St. Sylvester Church.
Schulte, John R. '77 (COV) [M] Erlanger, KY Monastery of the Sacred Passion.
Schulte, Msgr. Joseph M. '37 (DM) Retired.
Schulte, Lyle L. '60 (LC) Boyceville, WI St. Luke Church; Menomonie, WI St. Joseph Church.
Schulte, Oswald W. '45 (LC) Retired; [I] La Crosse, WI Holy Cross (Seminary) Diocesan Center.
Schulte, Robert '75 (FTW) [4] Fort Wayne, IN St. Elizabeth Ann Seton Church.
Schulte, William P. '52 (NEW) Retired.
Schultenover, David G. *s.j.* '69 (OM) [K] Omaha, NE Campion House.
Schultheis, Michael J. *s.j.* '65 (P) [L] Portland, OR Jesuit Provincial Office (Oregon Prov.).
Schultheis, Raymond *c.pp.s.* '56 (CLV) Cleveland, OH Deaconess Hospital.
Schultz, Blaine *o.s.b.* '60 (KCK) [A] Atchison, KS Benedictine College; [H] Atchison, KS St. Benedict's Abbey.
Schultz, Brian '82 (DUL) Virginia, MN Sacred Heart Church; [F] Duluth, MN University of MN-Duluth.
Schultz, Bruce B. *o.p.* '88 (NO) [P] New Orleans, LA Dominican Fathers & Brothers, Southern Dominican Province.
Schultz, C. Ray '91 (BEL) Lawrenceville, IL St. Lawrence Church.
Schultz, Charles F. '80 (SB) Murrietta, CA St. Martha's Church.
Schultz, Henry A. *c.ss.r.* '49 (STL) [P] Liguori, MO St. Clement Health Care Center.
Schultz, John (PEO) Danville, IL Veterans' Administration Hospital.
Schultz, John A. '65 (LC) [4] Eau Claire, WI St. James the Greater Church.
Schultz, John C. '57 (LFT) On Duty Outside the Diocese.
Schultz, John M. '82 (E) [3] Oil City, PA St. Joseph Church; [C] Oil City, PA Venango Christian High School.
Schultz, Msgr. Raymond T. '47 (PIT) Beaver, PA SS. Peter and Paul Church; Beaver County, PA Beaver County Jail.
Schultz, Ronald *o.f.m.conv.* '39 (ALB) Fonda, NY St. Cecilia Church.
Schultz, Russell '66 (SAN) Retired.
Schultz, Russell '66 (SAT) [K] San Antonio, TX Padua Place.
Schultz, Msgr. William E. (ALT) Roaring Spring, PA St. Thomas More Church.
Schultz, Msgr. William F. '64 (BGP) [4] Stratford, CT Our Lady of Grace Church.
Schultze, George E. *s.j.* '94 (LA) [R] Culver City, CA Ignatius House, The Novitiate of the California Province, Society of Jesus.
Schulz, Albert H. *s.j.* '44 (STL) [P] St. Louis, MO Jesuit Community Corporation at St. Louis University - Jesuit Hall.
Schulz, Msgr. Donald C. '53 (COL) [4] Columbus, OH St. Aloysius Church; Retired.
Schulz, James W. *s.j.* '77 (GRY) [K] East Chicago, IN Roque Gonzalez Residence-Jesuit Fathers; [P] Hammond, IN Heartland Center.
Schulz, Raymond B. '37 (LC) Retired.
Schulz, Ronald '68 (PMB) [4] Boca Raton, FL St. John the Evangelist Church.
Schulz, Wilfred *o.s.b.* '53 (NEW) [1] Linden, NJ St. Elizabeth's Church.
Schulz, Wilfred G. *o.s.b.* '53 (PAT) [M] Morristown, NJ St. Mary's Abbey.
Schulze, Paul *s.d.s.* (GB) [H] Kaukauna, WI St. Paul Home, Inc.
Schulzetenberg, Raymond A. '46 (SCL) Gilman, MN SS. Peter and Paul Church.
Schumacher, Andrew J. '59 (B) [3] Boise, ID St. Mary's Church.
Schumacher, Anthony J. '60 (MAD) Oregon, WI Holy Mother of Consolation Church.
Schumacher, Bernard '54 (LR) [A] Subiaco, AR Subiaco Monastery.
Schumacher, Charles P. '48 (LC) Bakerville, WI Corpus Christi Church; Retired.
Schumacher, Ernest *c.r.* (L) Raywick, KY St. Francis Xavier Church; St. Mary, KY St. Charles Church.
Schumacher, Eugene T. '56 (SC) Rock Rapids, IA Holy Name Church.
Schumacher, Gerard (CHL) Clemmons, NC Holy Family Church.
Schumacher, Jacob '52 (BIS) South Heart, ND St. Mary Church.
Schumacher, James A. '95 (CHY) Sheridan, WY Holy Name Church.
Schumacher, Msgr. Joseph A. '57 (FWT) [5] Arlington, TX St. Matthew Church.
Schumacher, Leo C. '32 (SC) Retired.
Schumacher, Louis E. '47 (IND) Brookville, IN St. Michael Church; Cedar Grove, IN Holy Guardian Angels Church.
Schumacher, Mark R. '84 (B) Moscow, ID St. Augustine's Church; Potlatch, ID St. Mary's Church; [F] Moscow, ID University of Idaho, St. Augustine Catholic Center.
Schumacher, Patrick A. (BIS) New England, ND St. Mary Church.
Schumacher, Paul A. '48 (GB) [4] Two Rivers, WI Most Holy Redeemer Church.
Schumacher, Paul A. '62 (NU) Faxon Township, MN St. John-Assumption Church; Green Isle, MN St. Brendan Church.
Schumacher, Robert A. '49 (SPC) Sikeston, MO St. Francis Xavier's Church.
Schuster, Anthony J. '70 (GF) [5] Great Falls, MT St. Luke the Evangelist Church; [K] Great Falls, MT St. Joseph's Education Trust.
Schuster, Francis J. *k.h.s.* '63 (ALN) Whitehall, PA St. John the Baptist Church.
Schuster, Msgr. George J. '38 (LIN) Retired.
Schuster, Msgr. George M. '57 (BRK) [215] Queens, NY Our Lady of the Miraculous Medal Church.
Schuster, Paul '93 (FAR) [4] Grand Forks, ND St. Thomas Aquinas Parish, UND Church; Manvel, ND St. Timothy's Church; [H] Grand Forks, ND Univ. of North Dakota Newman Center.
Schuster, Peter L. '95 (WIN) [6] Rochester, MN St. John's Church.
Schuster, Philip *o.s.b.* '48 (KC) Parnell, MO St. Joseph's Church.
Schuster, Philip *o.s.b.* '58 (KC) [G] Maryville, MO St. Francis Hospital & Health Services.
Schuster, Raymond '93 (SAT) [30] San Antonio, TX St. Bonaventure Church.
Schuster, Robert C. '95 (DET) Utica, MI St. Lawrence Church.
Schuster, Roy *o.f.m.cap.* '59 (PIT) Conway, PA Our Lady of Peace Church; [N] Rochester, PA St. Cecilia Friary.
Schuster, Valery P. '41 (MIL) Retired.
Schuster, Vincent *c.pp.s.* '44 (CIN) [B] Carthagena, OH St. Charles.
Schuster, Vincent *c.pp.s.* '44 (TOL) [M] Bellevue, OH Sorrowful Mother Shrine.
Schuster, Wilfred J. '46 (MAD) [10] Madison, WI St. Maria Goretti Church; Retired.
Schute, Arthur B. '67 (NEW) [4] Newark, NJ St. Aloysius Church.
Schute, Bruce J. *s.a.c.* '60 (MIL) Wauwatosa, WI Froedtert Memorial Lutheran Hospital; [P] Milwaukee, WI Pallotti House.
Schutte, James R. '79 (CIN) [2] Dayton, OH St. Agnes Church; [8] Dayton, OH Corpus Christi Church.
Schutte, Robert W. '43 (CIN) Retired.
Schutten, Msgr. Marion '45 (NO) Mandeville, LA Southeast Louisiana Hospital.
Schutter, Thomas '68 (JOL) Carol Stream, IL St. Luke Church.
Schutty, John J. '83 (JC) Brinktown, MO Guardian Angels Church; Meta, MO St. Cecilia Church.
Schutzman, John S. '52 (COV) Retired.
Schuwey, Emil A. *c.pp.s.* '49 (CIN) [M] Dayton, OH Provincial House of the Cincinnati Province of the Society of the Precious Blood.
Schuyler, David *s.m.* '60 (SJ) Special Assignment.
Schuyler, Henry C. '45 (PH) Trooper, PA Visitation B.V.M Church; Retired.
Schuyler, Joseph B. *s.j.* '51 (NY) [Z] New York, NY Murray-Weigel Hall.
Schwaab, Paul J. '54 (OM) [24] Omaha, NE St. John Vianney Church.
Schwab, Donald F. '73 (ROC) Absent on Leave.
Schwab, Elwin C. '60 (P) St. Helens, OR St. Frederic Church.
Schwab, James A. '81 (JOL) [13] Joliet, IL St. Jude Church.
Schwab, Jerome F. '92 (CHR) Lexington, SC Corpus Christi Church.
Schwab, Joseph '48 (OAK) Retired.
Schwab, Joseph C. *o.m.i.* '53 (PT) Madison, FL St. Vincent de Paul Church; Monticello, FL St. Margaret Church.
Schwab, Msgr. Robert C. '41 (BUF) Retired.
Schwab, Steven '90 (IND) [11] Indianapolis, IN Nativity of Our Lord Jesus Christ Church.
Schwab, Thomas E. '56 (CHI) Rosemont-Des Plaines, IL Our Lady of Hope Church.
Schwaegel, Msgr. Joseph R. '65 (BEL) Leave of Absence.
Schwaig, R. John '90 (STL) Chesterfield, MO Ascension Church.
Schwalenberg, Msgr. Martin '45 (BAL) Retired.
Schwalm, Donald '52 (KCK) On Duty Outside the Archdiocese.
Schwan, Paul Mark *o.c.s.o.* '88 (SAC) [A] Vina, CA Abbey of New Clairvaux, Trappist Seminary; [H] Vina, CA Abbey of New Clairvaux, Trappist.
Schwane, Robert A. *c.m.* '53 (DEN) [12] Denver, CO Holy Ghost Church.
Schwanger, Kenneth '90 (MIA) [2] Hialeah, FL San Lazaro Church.
Schwantes, John A. *s.j.* '69 (MIL) [E] Milwaukee, WI Marquette University High School; [P] Milwaukee, WI Pere Marquette House Jesuit Community.
Schwantner, James *o.f.m.* '55 (SP) [O] St. Petersburg, FL St. Anthony Friary.
Schware, Richard A. '75 (ALN) Pen Argyl, PA St. Elizabeth of Hungary Church.
Schwarte, Michael '95 (JUN) Ketchikan, AK Holy Name Church; Metlakatla, AK Holy Family Church.
Schwarte, Msgr. Michael W. '38 (DM) Retired.
Schwarting, J. Donald '66 (GAL) Military Chaplains.
Schwartz, Anthony '49 (PHX) Retired.
Schwartz, Christopher *o.s.b.* '74 (CLV) Broadview Heights, OH Assumption Church; [P] Cleveland, OH Benedictine Order of Cleveland.
Schwartz, Clarence J. (L) Retired.
Schwartz, David C. *s.j.* '85 (HON) [7] Honolulu, HI Newman Center at the University of Hawaii, Holy Spirit Parish Church; [F] Honolulu, HI St. Francis Healthcare System of Hawaii; [H] Honolulu, HI Jesuit Fathers House.
Schwartz, Edwin V. '60 (ALN) Northampton, PA Our Lady of Hungary Church.
Schwartz, Hugh F. '56 (OM) Blair, NE St. Francis Borgia Church.
Schwartz, James A. '68 (ROC) Pittsford, NY St. Louis Church.
Schwartz, John *s.j.* '64 (SEA) Mount Vernon, WA Immaculate Conception Church.
Schwartz, Kevin '93 (SCL) Bluffton, MN St. John the Baptist Church; Butler, MN Holy Cross Church; Menahga, MN The Church of the Assumption of Our Lady of Menahga.
Schwartz, Norman R. '69 (MIL) [K] Milwaukee, WI St. Joseph's Hospital of Franciscan Sisters, Milwaukee, Inc.
Schwartz, Paul E. '53 (CHI) Glenwood, IL St. John Church.
Schwartz, Peter *o.s.b.* '62 (SFS) [F] Marvin, SD Blue Cloud Abbey.
Schwartz, Robert M. '67 (STP) Eagan, MN St. John Neumann Church.
Schwartz, Rodney A. '92 (SFD) [4] Springfield, IL Little Flower Church.
Schwartz, William H. '53 (CIN) [4] Hamilton, OH St. Peter in Chains Church.
Schwartz, William J. '68 (PIT) Oakdale, PA St. Patrick Church.
Schwartz, William T. '58 (DUB) Retired.
Schwartzkopf, Gary W. *s.j.* '69 (NY) [Z] New York, NY Murray-Weigel Hall.
Schwarz, Msgr. Aloysius B. '37 (SFD) Divernon, IL Sacred Heart Church.
Schwarz, Bernard F. '66 (OKL) Retired.
Schwarz, Carl *c.ss.r.* '42 (STL) [P] Liguori, MO Liguori Mission House/Redemptorists.
Schwarz, Elmer C. '53 (OKL) Chickasha, OK Holy Name Church; [K] Norman, OK Campus Ministry for the Archdiocese of Oklahoma City.
Schwarz, Paul E. *c.ss.r.* '39 (STL) [P] Liguori, MO St. Clement Health Care Center.
Schwarz, Robert '65 (MRY) Retired.
Schwarzhaupt, Robert '86 (HON) Nanakuli, HI St. Rita Church.
Schwatrz, Msgr. William H. '68 (RCK) [1] Rockford, IL St. Peter Cathedral.
Schwebs, Daniel L. *o.s.j.* '86 (NOR) [5] Middletown, CT St. Sebastian Church.
Schweda, Phillip '79 (LAN) [3] Jackson, MI St. Mary, Star of the Sea Church.
Schweder, Msgr. John F. '60 (DET) [41] Detroit, MI St. Joseph Church.
Schweers, Gregory *o.cist.* '81 (DAL) [M] Irving, TX Cistercian Abbey of Our Lady of Dallas.
Schwehr, Charles '76 (LA) West Covina, CA St. Christopher Church.
Schweibold, Conrad L. *o.f.m.conv.* '47 (FTW) Angola, IN St. Anthony Church; Big Long Lake, IN St. Mary of the Angels Church.
Schweifler, Michael *o.s.a.* '84 (TLS) [B] Tulsa, OK Cascia Hall Preparatory School.
Schweigardt, Erwin H. '67 (ALB) [4] Watervliet, NY St. Patrick Church.
Schweiger, Troy J. '95 (LIN) [6] Lincoln, NE St. John the Apostle Church.
Schweihofer, Frederick J. '68 (DET) [9] Sterling Heights, MI St. Rene Goupil Church.
Schweihofer, Walter J. '38 (DET) Retired.
Schweikert, John *m.s.c.* '96 (ALN) Nazareth, PA Holy Family Church.
Schweitzer, Msgr. Francis X. '45 (COL) [19] Columbus, OH Holy Family Church.
Schweitzer, Gerald H. '71 (GRY) Wanatah, IN Sacred Heart Church.
Schweitzer, Joachim B. *o.s.b.* '58 (PAT) [M] Morristown, NJ St. Mary's Abbey.
Schweitzer, Peter '93 (SP) [4] Clearwater, FL St. Cecilia Church; [L] Clearwater, FL The Tepeyac Corporation dba Clinica Guadalupana.

Schweitzer, Robert '67 (PIT) [83] Pittsburgh, PA Risen Lord Church.
Schweitzer, Tom '82 (LA) Vernon, CA Holy Angels Parish of the Deaf Church.
Schweizer, Paul *o.carm.* '62 (NEW) Bogota, NJ St. Joseph's Church.
Schweizer, Vincent J. '58 (L) Pewee Valley, KY St. Aloysius Church.
Schwellenbach, Aloysius '48 (SFD) Absent on Leave.
Schwemin, Ralph H. '41 (SPK) Retired.
Schwendeman, Msgr. Francis J. '31 (COL) Retired.
Schwenk, William M. '60 (EVN) [15] Evansville, IN St. Boniface Church.
Schwenzer, Ronald G. *c.s.b.* '68 (SFE) [D] Albuquerque, NM St. Pius X High School; [N] Albuquerque, NM St. Pius X High School Foundation, Inc.
Schwertley, James F. '61 (OM) Fort Calhoun, NE St. John the Baptist Church.
Schwet, Edward N. '82 (CLV) [18] Akron, OH St. Vincent Church.
Schwetner, Msgr. Timothy '65 (LUB) Plainview, TX St. Alice Church.
Schwieters, Severin '50 (SCL) Special Assignment.
Schwietz, Paul *o.s.b.* '82 (SCL) [I] Collegeville, MN St. John's Abbey, of the Order of St. Benedict.
Schwind, Donald F. '46 (BRK) Retired.
Schwinger, Msgr. William A. '58 (BUF) [1] Buffalo, NY St. Joseph's Cathedral; Retired.
Schwinghammer, Claude '35 (SCL) Retired.
Schwinn, Alexander L. '35 (NU) Retired.
Schwinn, Joseph F. '43 (MIL) Retired.
Schwinn, Thomas J. '58 (DUB) Fairfax, IA St. Patrick's Church; Walford, IA Holy Trinity Church.
Scianna, Bernard C. *o.s.a.* '93 (JOL) [C] New Lenox, IL Providence Catholic High School; [J] New Lenox, IL Augustinian Friary.
Sciarra, John N. '45 (IND) [17] Indianapolis, IN St. Barnabas Church; Retired.
Sciarrotta, Lee *s.m.* '67 (CIN) [9] Dayton, OH Emmanuel Church; [M] Dayton, OH Marianist Provincialate.
Sciarrotta, Paul J. '62 (CLV) [Q] Chardon, OH Provincial House of the Sisters of Notre Dame, Juniorate, Novitiate.
Sciberras, Michael J. '67 (GBG) [1] Connellsville, PA Immaculate Conception Church.
Sciera, Msgr. Ronald P. '61 (BUF) [56] Buffalo, NY Precious Blood Church.
Scillieri, Charles P. '73 (MET) Jamesburg, NJ St. James the Less Church.
Scioli, Richard A. *c.s.s.* '79 (SPR) [9] Springfield, MA Our Lady of Mt. Carmel Church.
Sciumbato, Michael R. '94 (SLC) Richfield/Monroe, UT St. Elizabeth's Church; [H] Ephraim, UT St. Jude Mission.
Sciurba, Salvatore *o.c.d.* '71 (BO) [W] Brighton, MA Carmelite Monastery.
Scocco, Victor *o.ss.t.* '81 (VIC) [4] Victoria, TX Our Lady of Sorrows Church; [F] Victoria, TX Trinity House.
Scolamiero, Dominic A. '69 (PAT) Unassigned.
Scollen, Francis J. '71 (WOR) [27] Worcester, MA St. Peter Church.
Scopa, Joseph A. *c.s.* '48 (BO) [5] Framingham, MA St. Tarcisius Church.
Scopp, Andrew *s.j.* (HRT) [K] Enfield, CT The Home for the Aged of the Little Sisters of the Poor.
Scopp, Andrew J. *s.j.* '63 (BO) [W] Boston, MA The Society of Jesus of New England-Provincial Offices.
Scornaienchi, Frank *t.o.r.* '79 (ALT) [F] Newry, PA St. Bernardine Monastery.
Scorzello, Joseph F. '65 (BO) [4] Brookline, MA St. Mary of the Assumption Church.
Scotchie, David '93 (ORL) Indialantic, FL Holy Name of Jesus Church.
Scott, Alfonso '59 (LA) [12] Long Beach, CA Our Lady of Refuge Church; [D] Lakewood, CA Saint Joseph High School.
Scott, Brendan T. *s.j.* '78 (BUF) [O] Buffalo, NY Canisius Jesuit Community.
Scott, Charles '61 (DM) [C] Council Bluffs, IA Bergan Mercy Health System: Mercy Hospital.
Scott, Daniel *m.s.* '73 (HRT) West Haven, CT Veterans' Medical Center.
Scott, Daniel J. *m.s.* '73 (HRT) [10] New Haven, CT St. John the Baptist Church; [M] Hartford, CT Missionaries of LaSalette Provincial Secretary.
Scott, Delroy Thomas '86 (MGZ) Las Marias, PR Immaculate Heart of Mary Church.
Scott, Edward R. '56 (SCR) Lake Ariel, PA St. Thomas More Church.
Scott, Frank '79 (BLX) Vancleave, MS Catholic Church of the Holy Spirit.
Scott, Hilary *o.f.m.* '49 (PAT) [M] Ringwood, NJ Holy Name Friary.
Scott, James A. '66 (WDC) Absent On Leave.
Scott, John *o.s.b.* '72 (SEA) [M] Lacey, WA St. Martin's Abbey.
Scott, John M. *s.j.* '44 (OM) [K] Omaha, NE Jesuit Community At Creighton University.
Scott, John V. '69 (GRY) Portage, IN Nativity of Our Savior Church.
Scott, Joseph *s.v.d.* '75 (OAK) [6] Oakland, CA St. Bernard's Church.
Scott, Joseph J. *c.s.p.* '73 (P) [28] Portland, OR St. Philip Neri Church; [Q] Portland, OR Paulist Fathers Catholic Center for Evangelization.
Scott, Kenny *o.f.m.* '57 (OAK) [N] Oakland, CA Franciscan Friars.
Scott, Msgr. Leonard G. '64 (CAM) [2] Cherry Hill, NJ Holy Rosary Church.
Scott, Mark A. *o.c.s.o.* '87 (SAC) [A] Vina, CA Abbey of New Clairvaux, Trappist Seminary; [H] Vina, CA Abbey of New Clairvaux, Trappist.
Scott, Michael Craig '96 (ALX) [2] Alexandria, LA Our Lady of Prompt Succor Church.
Scott, Michael P. '87 (MET) [1] Perth Amboy, NJ St. Mary Church.
Scott, Patrick J. '60 (PAT) Pompton Plains, NJ Our Lady of Good Counsel Church.
Scott, Philip '89 (SP) Sun City Center, FL Prince of Peace Church.
Scott, Philip P. '79 (PSC) Roswell, GA Epiphany Byzantine Church.
Scott, Raymond J. '48 (DAL) Terrell, TX St. John Church; Terrell, TX State Hospital.
Scott, Richard '88 (WDC) [15] Washington, DC St. Gabriel Church.
Scott, Robert T. '49 (ALB) [L] Lake George, NY St. Mary of the Lake.
Scott, Robert T. *c.s.p.* '49 (AUS) Horseshoe Bay, TX St. Paul the Apostle Church.
Scott, Samuel V. '95 (BGP) Westport, CT St. Luke Church.
Scott, Vincent J. '75 (OAK) [2] Walnut Creek, CA St. John Vianney Church.
Scotti, P. Paschal *o.s.b.* '89 (PRO) [P] Portsmouth, RI Abbey of St. Gregory the Great.
Scrima, Claude *o.f.m.* '61 (NY) [Z] New York, NY Franciscan Province of the Immaculate Conception.
Scuderi, Carmen *o.f.m.* '83 (GRY) [G] Crown Point, IN St. Anthony Medical Center, Inc.; [I] Crown Point, IN St. Anthony Home, Inc.; [K] Cedar Lake, IN Our Lady of Lourdes Friary.
Scuderi, Salvatore A. *m.ss.cc.* '88 (CAM) [8] Camden, NJ Our Lady of Fatima and Mount Carmel Church.
Scull, Edward J. '51 (BGP) [6] Fairfield, CT St. Pius X Church.
Scull, James P. *s.j.* '58 (BGP) [O] Fairfield, CT The Fairfield Jesuit Community-Fairfield University.
Scull, James P. *s.j.* '58 (MIL) [P] Milwaukee, WI Jesuit Provincial Office, Wisconsin Province.
Scullin, Robert J. *s.j.* '76 (COL) [25] Columbus, OH Community of Holy Rosary and St. John Church.
Scullion, James P. *o.f.m.* '80 (WDC) [B] Silver Spring, MD Holy Name College.
Scully, Msgr. Donald J. '51 (E) [1] Sharon, PA Sacred Heart Church.
Scully, G. Michael *c.s.c.* '58 (FR) [B] North Easton, MA Holy Cross Fathers Religious.
Scully, Msgr. John '48 (SP) Spring Hill, FL St. Theresa Church.
Scully, John J. (TR) Matawan, NJ St. Clement Church.
Scully, John J. *s.j.* '57 (NY) [Z] New York, NY Jesuit Community at Fordham University.
Scully, John T. *s.s.e.* '55 (BUR) Putney, VT Our Lady of Mercy Church.
Scully, Michael *o.f.m.cap.* '65 (SAL) Hays, KS St. Joseph's Church; [B] Hays, KS Thomas More Prep-Marian; [D] Hays, KS St. Joseph's Friary.
Scully, Michael G. *s.j.* '86 (SJ) [D] San Jose, CA Bellarmine College Preparatory.
Scully, Patrick A. '56 (SHP) Shreveport, LA Louisiana State University Medical Center.
Scully, Philip A. '42 (PH) Springfield, PA St. Kevin Church; Retired.
Scully, Richard D. '78 (AMA) Dumas, TX SS. Peter and Paul Church.
Scully, Robert E. *s.j.* '96 (SY) [S] Syracuse, NY Jesuits at LeMoyne, Inc.
Scully, Timothy R. *c.s.c.* '81 (FTW) [B] Notre Dame, IN University of Notre Dame Du Lac; [B] Notre Dame, IN University of Notre Dame Du Lac; [J] Notre Dame, IN Holy Cross Community, Corby Hall, University of Notre Dame.
Scully, William *o.f.m.* '67 (PAT) Hewitt, NJ Our Lady Queen of Peace Church.
Scurti, Louis J. '73 (PAT) Totowa, NJ North Jersey Developmental Center; [O] Haledon, NJ William Paterson College Catholic Campus Ministry Center.
Sdyrcz, Michael '73 (CLV) Painesville, OH St. Mary Church.
Seabold, John P. '88 (CLV) [1] Garfield Heights, OH St. Monica Church.
Seabridge, Thomas L. '88 (SAC) Corning, CA Immaculate Conception Church; Orland, CA St. Dominic Church; Special Assignment.
Seagrave, Thomas L. '68 (SFR) [54] San Francisco, CA Visitacion, Church of the.
Seagraves, Richard '91 (NY) Hartsdale, NY Sacred Heart Church.
Seagriff, Edward M. '81 (RVC) Lindenhurst, NY Our Lady of Perpetual Help Church.
Sealy, Robert J. *s.j.* '51 (NY) [Z] New York, NY Jesuit Community at Fordham University.
Seaman, Cyril *o.f.m.* '56 (BO) [BB] Boston, MA St. Anthony Shrine.
Seaman, Paul G. '85 (CHI) Country Club Hills, IL St. Emeric Church.
Searles, Lawrence P. *s.j.* '87 (NY) [Z] New York, NY Jesuit Provincial's Office.
Searles, Thaddeus *s.t.* '56 (MOB) Holy Trinity, AL St. Joseph Church.
Searles, Wendell H. '55 (BUR) [H] Burlington, VT Mount St. Mary Convent.
Sears, Eugene A. '58 (KAL) St. Joseph, MI St. Joseph Church.
Sears, G. David '63 (NY) [226] Staten Island, NY St. Roch Church.
Sears, G. David '63 (SY) On Duty Outside the Diocese.
Sears, Gerald *o.c.s.o.* '73 (WOR) [N] Spencer, MA St. Joseph's Abbey; [P] Spencer, MA St. Joseph Abbey.
Sears, Michael J. '94 (LA) Encino, CA Our Lady of Grace Church.
Sears, Robert T. *s.j.* '66 (CHI) [C] Chicago, IL Jesuit Community at Loyola University of Chicago.
Sears, William F. '84 (PRO) Point Judith, RI St. Mary, Star of the Sea Church.
Sears, William J. '62 (BRK) Released from Diocesan Assignment.
Seasoltz, Kevin *o.s.b.* '56 (SCL) [I] Collegeville, MN St. John's Abbey, of the Order of St. Benedict.
Seaver, Paul E. *o.p.* '59 (PRO) [P] Providence, RI St. Thomas Aquinas Priory at Providence College.
Seavey, Michael J. '86 (PRT) Biddeford, ME St. Joseph's Church; [M] Biddeford, ME University of New England.
Seay, Robert *o.f.m.* (HT) [4] Houma, LA Our Lady of the Most Holy Rosary Church.
Sebaali, George M. '83 (SAM) Richmond, VA St. Anthony Church.
Sebahar, John M. '58 (JOL) Glen Ellyn, IL St. James the Apostle Church.
Sebastian, Benjamin '66 (BRK) [84] Brooklyn, NY St. Mary, Star of the Sea Church.
Sebastian, Gregory *o.s.b.* '83 (SCL) [I] Collegeville, MN St. John's Abbey, of the Order of St. Benedict.
Sebescak, Gary '94 (BEL) Leave of Absence.
Sebesta, James A. *s.j.* '70 (STL) [C] St. Louis, MO Saint Louis University; [P] St. Louis, MO Jesuit Community Corporation at St. Louis University - Jesuit Hall.
Sebra, Anthony G. '72 (STA) Lake City, FL Epiphany Church.
Secondo, Louis J. *t.o.r.* '46 (ALT) [7] Altoona, PA Our Lady of Mt. Carmel Church.
Secor, Gary '77 (HON) Mililani Town, HI St. John Apostle and Evangelist Church.
Secora, James L. '75 (DUB) Gilbertville, IA Immaculate Conception Church; [D] Gilbertville, IA Don Bosco High School.
Seculoff, James F. '62 (FTW) Bristol, IN St. Mary of the Annunciation Church.
Seda, Jon M. '88 (DUB) Ames, IA St. Thomas Aquinas Church (and Catholic Student Center) Church; [N] Ames, IA St. Thomas Aquinas Church and Catholic Student Center (Iowa State University).
Sederwall, Donald F. '85 (SFD) Barry, IL Holy Redeemer Church; Pittsfield, IL Immaculate Conception Church.
Sedita, Msgr. Vincent A. '72 (LKC) Jennings, LA Our Lady Help of Christians Church.
Sedlacek, Richard D. '79 (YAK) Benton City, WA St. Frances Xavier Cabrini Church; Kennewick, WA St. Joseph's Church.
Sedlacko, Louis S. *o.s.b.* '44 (GBG) [H] Latrobe, PA Saint Vincent Archabbey.
Sedlak, John A. '82 (GBG) Grindstone, PA St. Cecilia Church; [K] Smock, PA Ladies of Charity.
Sedlak, Kenneth *c.ss.r.* '72 (CHI) [136] Chicago, IL St. Michael Church.
Sedlak, Valentine G. '44 (PIT) Retired.
Sedley, Joseph *c.p.* '69 (WOR) [N] Shrewsbury, MA Passionist Fathers of Shrewsbury, Inc., Calvary Retreat Center; [P] Shrewsbury, MA Calvary Retreat Center, Passionist Community.
Sedlmayer, Lauro C. '85 (MET) [9] Perth Amboy, NJ Our Lady of the Rosary of Fatima Church.
Sedlock, David W. '91 (MAR) [4] Escanaba, MI St. Thomas the Apostle Church.
Sedlock, Stephen *c.s.c.* '66 (P) [L] Portland, OR Holy Cross Father & Brother, C.S.C. - University of Portland.
Sedlock, Stephen J. *c.s.c.* '66 (P) [38] Portland, OR St. Vincent de Paul Church; [B] Portland, OR University of Portland.
Seeberger, Claude *o.s.b.* '49 (BIS) Glen Ullin, ND Sacred Heart of Jesus Church; [A] Richardton, ND Assumption Abbey.
Seed, Michael *s.a.* '86 (NY) [Z] Garrison, NY Generalate of the Franciscan Friars of the Atonement-St. James Friary.
Seedorf, Warren H. *c.s.p.* '49 (NY) [Z] Scarsdale, NY Paulist Fathers Generalate.
Seefeldt, Wilbert T. '39 (STP) Retired.

Seegar, Kenneth M. '87 (SCR) Shavertown, PA St. Therese Church.
Seeger, Francis J. '41 (BRK) Retired.
Seeger, James E. '85 (PIT) Canonsburg, PA St. Patrick Church.
Seeger, Peter J. '35 (BRK) [167] Queens, NY St. Fidelis Church; Retired.
Seekamp, Walter J. '79 (BGP) [4] Trumbull, CT St. Theresa's Church.
Seelaus, William O. *o.s.f.s.* '51 (PH) [D] Philadelphia, PA Father Judge High School for Boys; [Z] Philadelphia, PA Father Judge Faculty House.
Seelman, Patrick *t.o.r.* '63 (ALT) [10] Johnstown, PA St. Anthony's Church.
Seeman, Robert L. '79 (PIT) [Q] Slippery Rock, PA Office for Campus Ministry; [Q] Slippery Rock, PA Office for Campus Ministry.
Seery, William O. '95 (HRT) Naugatuck, CT St. Francis of Assisi Church; Oakville, CT St. Mary Magdalen Church.
Seetch, William D. *c.s.c.* '79 (FTW) [B] Notre Dame, IN University of Notre Dame Du Lac; [J] Notre Dame, IN Holy Cross Community, Corby Hall, University of Notre Dame.
Seethaler, Scott *o.f.m.cap.* '69 (PIT) [N] Pittsburgh, PA St. Augustine Friary.
Seeton, Philip '91 (OKL) Special Assignment.
Seeton, Philip '95 (OKL) [B] Oklahoma City, OK Bishop McGuinness High School.
Seewald, Carl H. *s.v.d.* '68 (OAK) Martinez, CA St. Catherine of Siena Church.
Sefcik, Dennis L. '65 (SC) Lohrville, IA St. Joseph's Church.
Segadelli, Joseph D. '42 (BO) Retired.
Segaric, John '48 (LA) [45] Los Angeles, CA St. Anthony Church.
Segatta, Bruno '74 (B) On Duty Outside the Diocese.
Seger, Michael '88 (CIN) [B] Cincinnati, OH Mt. St. Mary's Seminary of the West.
Seger, Oscar H. '70 (CIN) Egypt, OH St. Joseph Church; On Special and Diocesan Assignment.
Segerson, Thomas M. '69 (MAD) Mineral Point, WI Congregation of St. Mary-St. Paul Church.
Seginak, Theodore J. *o.s.b.* '49 (PBR) Punxsutawney, PA SS. Peter and Paul Church.
Sego, Msgr. Arthur A. '46 (LFT) Retired.
Segotta, Vincent *c.p.* '77 (PIT) [N] Pittsburgh, PA St. Paul of the Cross Monastery; [N] Pittsburgh, PA St. Paul of the Cross Monastery.
Segovia, Norman '67 (SJ) [4] San Jose, CA Edenvale Catholic Mission Church.
Segreve., Richard J. *c.s.c.* '61 (FR) [B] North Easton, MA Holy Cross Fathers Religious.
Segrue, Joseph D. '53 (SY) Retired.
Seguin, Robert J. *c.s.b.* '69 (GAL) [Q] Sugar Land, TX Basilian Mission Center.
Segura, Leonicio '63 (ORG) [6] Santa Ana, CA St. Anne's Church.
Seher, Philip O. '65 (CIN) [89] Cincinnati, OH St. William Church.
Sehler, Michael E. *s.j.* '73 (NY) [F] New York, NY Loyola School; [Z] New York, NY Jesuit Community at Fordham University.
Seib, Herbert *o.c.s.o.* '37 (L) [L] Trappist, KY Abbey of Our Lady of Gethsemani, of the Order of Cistercians of the Strict Observance.
Seibert, Gary G. *s.j.* '73 (NY) [62] New York, NY St. Joseph Church; [Z] New York, NY West Side Jesuit Community.
Seibert, Herman *o.f.m.conv.* '45 (SY) [2] Syracuse, NY Assumption B.V.M. Church.
Seibert, James C. *c.pp.s.* '77 (CIN) Celina, OH Immaculate Conception of the Blessed Virgin Mary Church; [M] Dayton, OH Provincial House of the Cincinnati Province of the Society of the Precious Blood.
Seibert, Thomas E. *i.c.* '75 (PEO) Elmwood, IL St. Patrick's Church; Farmington, IL St. Matthew's Church; [B] Peoria, IL Notre Dame High School.
Seichepine, Albert M. *c.s.sp.* '51 (PH) [Z] Bensalem, PA Congregation of the Holy Ghost Fathers and Brothers.
Seidel, George J. *o.s.b.* '58 (SEA) [M] Lacey, WA St. Martin's Abbey.
Seidel, Michael L. '87 (STL) [46] St. Louis, MO Basilica of St. Louis, the King.
Seidel, Ricardo '65 (RIC) [6] Richmond, VA St. Augustine Church; [L] Richmond, VA Ethnic and Special Ministries.
Seidel, Victor *s.t.* '61 (SAV) Thomasville, GA St. Augustine's Church.
Seidenburg, Msgr. Augustine J. (CAM) Retired.
Seidl, Larry J. '75 (GB) [1] Two Rivers, WI St. Luke Church; [3] Two Rivers, WI St. Mark Church.
Seidl, Neil W. *s.d.s.* '54 (SAC) Orangevale, CA Divine Savior Church.
Seifert, Michael *s.m.* '85 (BWN) [11] Brownsville, TX San Felipe de Jesus Church.
Seifert, Michael D. '84 (Y) Waynesburg, OH St. James Church.
Seifert, Raymond *c.pp.s.* '44 (CIN) [B] Carthagena, OH St. Charles.
Seifert, William N. '81 (ALN) [10] Bethlehem, PA SS. Simon and Jude Church; [C] Bethlehem, PA Bethlehem Catholic High School.
Seifferly, Richard R. '63 (GAY) West Branch, MI St. Joseph Church.
Seifner, Thomas J. '92 (JC) Mokane, MO St. Jude Thaddeus Church; Rhineland, MO Church of the Risen Savior.
Seifried, Gerardo A. *c.s.sp.* '38 (SJN) [E] Dorado, PR Santuario del Espiritu Santo.
Seifried, Kenneth A. (ATL) Atlanta, GA Fort McPherson.
Seifried, Kenneth A. '63 (SC) On Duty Outside the Diocese.
Seigel, Timothy '91 (RCK) Crystal Lake, IL St. Thomas the Apostle Church.
Seiker, Daniel J. '87 (LIN) Syracuse, NE St. Paulinus Church.
Seiker, Leo V. '91 (LIN) Bellwood, NE St. Peter's Church.
Seiker, Mark E. '84 (LIN) Beatrice, NE St. Joseph's Church.
Seil, Paul D. '89 (BUF) [32] Buffalo, NY Holy Spirit Church.
Seiler, Andrew J. '88 (WCH) Wellington, KS St. Anthony Church; Wellington, KS St. Rose of Lima Church.
Seiler, Gerald L., Jr. '90 (NO) Gretna, LA St. Anthony Church; [A] New Orleans, LA Notre Dame Seminary Graduate School of Theology.
Seiler, John A. '59 (COV) Fort Thomas, KY St. Luke Hospital East.
Seipp, William J. '63 (MAD) Sauk City, WI St. Aloysius Church.
Seis, Michael '93 (GB) [5] Green Bay, WI St. Bernard Church; On Duty Outside the Diocese.
Seiter, Joseph A. *c.s.sp.* '62 (LR) Morrilton, AR Sacred Heart Church.
Seitz, Cyprian *o.s.b.* '37 (SCL) [I] Collegeville, MN St. John's Abbey, of the Order of St. Benedict.
Seitz, Gilbert '82 (BAL) Abingdon, MD St. Francis de Sales Church.
Seitz, James J. '94 (WIN) [4] Mankato, MN St. Joseph the Worker Church; [C] Mankato, MN Mankato Area Catholic Schools.
Seitz, Joseph W. '58 (CHI) [37] Chicago, IL Christ the King Church.
Seitz, Mark Joseph '80 (DAL) Waxahachie, TX St. Joseph Church.
Seitz, Patrick K. '92 (BWN) San Benito, TX St. Theresa Church.
Seitz, Paul F.X. '58 (CHR) Walterboro, SC St. Anthony's Church.
Seitz, Thomas R. '52 (CHI) [204] Chicago, IL St. Thomas Apostle Church; Retired.
Seitzinger, Msgr. John P. '60 (ALN) [10] Reading, PA St. Paul Church.
Sekellick, Msgr. John T. '69 (PSC) Wilkes-Barre, PA St. Mary's Church.
Seleccion, Romeo *m.s.* '92 (SB) Moreno Valley, CA St. Christopher Church.
Selemobri, Matthias *m.s.p.* (GAL) Barrett Station, TX St. Martin de Porres Church.
Seli, Msgr. John J. '46 (PIT) Verona, PA St. Joseph Church; Retired.
Seli, William F. *s.m.* (WH) Richwood, WV Holy Family Church; Summersville, WV St. John The Evangelist Church.
Sell, Robert L., III '78 (LFT) Special Assignment.
Sella, Donald '83 (PAT) [N] West Paterson, NJ Missionary Sisters of the Immaculate Conception, Convent of the Immaculate Conception.
Sella, Peter *s.d.b.* '68 (NEW) [C] Ramsey, NJ Don Bosco Preparatory High School for Boys.
Selle, Paulinus J. *o.s.b.* '39 (GBG) [H] Latrobe, PA Saint Vincent Archabbey.
Selleck, John P. '57 (CAM) On Duty Outside the Diocese.
Selleck, John P. '57 (PT) Blountstown, FL St. Francis of Assisi Church.
Sellentin, Thomas J. '65 (OM) Howells, NE SS. Peter and Paul Church; Howells, NE St. John Nepomucene Church.
Sellers, Benedict *o.s.b.* '75 (CLV) [E] Cleveland, OH Benedictine High School; [P] Cleveland, OH Benedictine Order of Cleveland.
Sellers, Charles *o.m.i.* (BEA) Silsbee, TX St. Mark the Evangelist Church.
Selvam, Xavier Panneer '81 (P) Lake Oswego, OR Our Lady of the Lake Church; [P] Portland, OR University of Portland.
Selvaraj, Balappa '86 (ATL) Decatur, GA St. Thomas More Church.
Selzer, Eugene '61 (PRM) St. Louis, MO St. Louis Mission Church.
Selzer, Eugene P. '61 (STL) Woodson Terrace, MO St. William Church.
Selzler, Norbert E. '38 (BUF) Retired.
Semaan, Charbel T. '89 (SAM) New Bedford, MA Our Lady of Purgatory Church; [E] New Bedford, MA Cedar Holdings, Inc.
Semancik, Msgr. Joseph F. '53 (GRY) [6] East Chicago, IN Sacred Heart Church; [N] Gary, IN Catholic Charities.
Semeniuk, Gregory *c.m.* '89 (RVC) Freeport, NY Our Holy Redeemer Church; Uniondale, NY St. Martha Church.
Semenych, Petro '91 (PHU) Washington, DC Ukrainian Catholic National Shrine of the Holy Family Church.
Seminack, Msgr. Richard '67 (SJP) Carnegie, PA Holy Trinity Church.
Seminara, Ronald S. *s.j.* '74 (RC) Manderson, SD St. Agnes Church; Porcupine, SD Church of Christ the King; Pine Ridge, SD Holy Rosary Church; [B] Pine Ridge, SD Jesuit Community of Holy Rosary Mission.
Seminatore, Joseph J. '69 (CLV) [M] Parma, OH Parmadale.
Semko, Edward '69 (PSC) Carteret, NJ St. Elias Church.
Semler, Albert J. '67 (PIT) [A] Pittsburgh, PA Saint Paul Seminary.
Semner, Dean F. '79 (CHI) Westchester, IL Divine Infant Church.
Semonin, James R. '71 (CLV) Cleveland, OH Parma Community Hospital; [M] Parma, OH Parmadale.
Sempa, John J. '80 (SCR) Swoyersville, PA St. Mary of Czestochowa Church.
Sempko, Walter A. '50 (HBG) [G] Harrisburg, PA Villa Teresa Nursing Home.
Semple, James '61 (SLC) [3] Salt Lake City, UT Our Lady of Lourdes Church.
Sena, Charles A. '92 (PBL) Delta, CO St. Michael Church.
Sena, Sotero A. '81 (SFE) Fort Sumner, NM St. Anthony Church; Santa Rosa, NM St. Rose of Lima Church.
Senchur, Becket G. *o.s.b.* '73 (GBG) [H] Latrobe, PA Saint Vincent Archabbey.
Senderak, Msgr. Casimir E. '44 (GRY) Retired.
Sendlein, Thomas A. *c.m.* '72 (PH) [Z] Philadelphia, PA Congregation of the Mission.
Sendra, Jesus (ARE) On Duty Outside the Diocese.
Senecal, Gerard *o.s.b.* '54 (KCK) Atchison, KS St. Joseph's Church; St. Patrick, KS St. Patrick's Church.
Seneschal, Theodore T. *o.s.b.* '70 (OKL) [I] Shawnee, OK St. Gregory's Abbey.
Senetsky, Msgr. Robert *j.c.d.* '60 (PSC) Peekskill, NY SS. Peter and Paul Church.
Senger, Daniel *o.f.m.* '93 (CLV) [E] Cleveland, OH Padua Franciscan High School; [P] Cleveland, OH Padua Franciscan Friary.
Senger, Joseph P. '54 (FAR) Velva, ND St. Cecilia's Church.
Senior, Donald *c.p.* '67 (CHI) [B] Chicago, IL The Catholic Theological Union at Chicago; [N] Chicago, IL Passionist Community-CTU.
Senior, Timothy C. '85 (PH) [J] Philadelphia, PA The Catholic Social Services of the Archdiocese of Philadelphia.
Seniw, John '82 (PHU) Frackville, PA St. Michael's Church.
Senk, Christopher L. '20 (NEW) [B] Caldwell, NJ Caldwell College.
Senk, Christopher L. *o.s.b.* '76 (MAN) [K] Manchester, NH St. Anselm Abbey.
Senkewicz, Robert M. *s.j.* '76 (SJ) [B] Santa Clara, CA Santa Clara University.
Senko, Martin R. '56 (P) Cornelius, OR St. Alexander Church.
Senn, Edward R. '58 (SUP) Sarona, WI St. Catherine Church; Shell Lake, WI St. Joseph Church.
Sennik, Thomas W. '76 (NOR) West Willington, CT St. Jude Church.
Sennott, Msgr. Robert J. '40 (BO) Retired.
Senske, Joseph A. '48 (PH) Retired.
Sepe, Kevin M. '86 (BO) Randolph, MA St. Mary Church.
Seper, John M. '83 (STL) Ste. Genevieve, MO Ste. Genevieve's Church.
Sepich, Lawrence '74 (MIL) Brighton, WI St. Francis Xavier Church.
Sepich, Lawrence '74 (PEO) On Duty Outside the Diocese.
Sepulveda, Juan J. *c.m.f.* (SJN) [23] Bayamon, PR Santa Maria Church.
Sepulveda, Miguel A. *o.f.m.* '85 (NY) [35] New York, NY St. Francis of Assisi Church.
Sepulveda, Miguel A. '89 (FRS) Porterville, CA St. Anne Church.
Sepulveda, Thomas W. *c.s.b.* '74 (GAL) [Q] Sugar Land, TX Basilian Mission Center.
Sequeira, Glenn N. '91 (LA) Glendale, CA Holy Family Church.
Sequeira, Lazarus '56 (NY) [76] New York, NY St. Monica Church.
Sequeira, Michael '66 (NOR) Clinton, CT St. Mary of the Visitation Church.
Sera, Enrique '78 (ORG) [1] Santa Ana, CA Immaculate Heart of Mary Church.
Serado, Msgr. William '40 (SR) Retired.
Serafin, Thomas J. '93 (MET) Edison, NJ St. Matthew Church.

Serafini, Augustine '62 (GB) [I] Oshkosh, WI Community of Our Lady.
Seramur, Leo J. '45 (MIL) Retired.
Serano, Joseph '69 (SFE) [J] Albuquerque, NM Santa Maria de la Vid Priory.
Serban, Ron '93 (SR) Military Chaplains.
Seremet, Hyacinth '51 (SY) [4] Utica, NY Sacred Heart Church; Special Assignment.
Serena, Edward T. '68 (BO) Marshfield, MA St. Ann's by the Sea Church.
Sergi, Michael *c.ss.r.* '79 (BAL) [94] Baltimore, MD St. Wenceslaus Church.
Sergot, Stanley *o.m.i.* '35 (STP) [N] St. Paul, MN Oblate Residence.
Serio, Anthony M. '67 (NO) Westwego, LA Our Lady of Prompt Succor Church.
Serio, John J. *s.d.b.* '82 (NY) [F] New Rochelle, NY Salesian High School.
Sermak, Jerzy *s.j.* '79 (CHI) [N] Chicago, IL Sacred Heart Mission House.
Sermak, Ronald *o.f.m.conv.* '60 (BAL) [M] Ellicott City, MD Order of Friars Minor Conventual.
Sermak, Ronald *o.f.m.conv.* '60 (BUF) [P] Hamburg, NY Immaculate Conception Convent.
Serna, F. Marc *o.s.b.* (PRO) [E] Portsmouth, RI Portsmouth Abbey School.
Serna, Luis '96 (DAL) [16] Dallas, TX St. Edward Church.
Sernett, Msgr. Michael D. '70 (SC) [9] Sioux City, IA Nativity of Our Lord Jesus Christ Church.
Serour, George A. '59 (SAG) Gagetown, MI St. Agatha Church.
Serour, George J. '59 (SAG) Sebewaing, MI Holy Family Church.
Serowik, James P. '87 (SY) Whitney Point, NY St. Patrick Church.
Serpa, Vincent A. *o.p.* '68 (OAK) [N] Oakland, CA Dominican Order (Western Province), St. Albert's Priory; [N] Oakland, CA Western Dominican Province.
Serra, Dominic '72 (NY) On Duty Outside the Archdiocese.
Serra, Dominic '72 (STP) [A] St. Paul, MN The Saint Paul Seminary; [C] St. Paul, MN University of St. Thomas.
Serraglio, Mario '58 (COL) [24] Columbus, OH St. John the Baptist Church.
Serraino, Fred *c.s.c.* '68 (LA) [CC] Hollywood, CA Family Theater Productions.
Serraino, Frederick *c.s.c.* (ORL) Retired.
Serrano, Edgar '87 (HON) [3] Honolulu, HI St. Anthony Church.
Serrano, Heriberto '67 (SAC) Colusa, CA Our Lady of Lourdes Church.
Serrano, Heriberto '70 (SAC) Maxwell, CA Sacred Heart Church.
Serrano, John J. '42 (RVC) Retired; [N] Uniondale, NY St. Pius X Residence.
Serrano, Jose '95 (NY) [31] New York, NY St. Elizabeth Church.
Serrano, Jose Orlando '96 (CGS) [1] Caguas, PR Cathedral Dulce Nombre de Jesus Church.
Serrano, Salvador V. '85 (SFR) [T] San Francisco, CA Opus Dei.
Serratelli, Arthur J. '68 (NEW) [A] South Orange, NJ Immaculate Conception Seminary; [B] South Orange, NJ Seton Hall University.
Serrick, James K. *s.j.* '62 (DET) [P] Bloomfield Hills, MI Manresa Jesuit Retreat House.
Serter, George C. '83 (CAM) [L] Blackwood, NJ Bishop's Residence.
Serva, Donald M. *s.j.* (DET) [K] Detroit, MI Jesuit Provincial Office-Detroit Province of the Society of Jesus.
Serva, Donald M. *s.j.* (WH) [A] Wheeling, WV Wheeling Jesuit University.
Servatius, Msgr. Robert R. '64 (SLC) [6] Sandy, UT Blessed Sacrament Church.
Service, Msgr. Gerald H. (OG) Canton, NY St. Mary Church.
Servinsky, Msgr. Michael E. '70 (ALT) Coupon, PA St. Joseph's Church.
Servodidio, Msgr. John T. '54 (NY) [210] Staten Island, NY St. Joseph Church.
Serwa, Gregory P. *s.a.c.* '70 (MIL) [S] Elkhorn, WI St. Vincent Pallotti Center.
Sescon, Esteban '77 (ELP) [23] El Paso, TX St. Francis Xavier Church.
Sesek, Raphael A. *o.f.m.* '41 (CHI) [70] Chicago, IL St. George Church.
Sestito, Joseph N. '59 (OG) On Duty Outside the Diocese.
Sesto, Gennaro *s.d.b.* '50 (NY) [BB] West Haverstraw, NY Don Bosco Retreat Center and Marian Shrine; [BB] West Haverstraw, NY Marian Shrine.
Setelik, James J., Jr. '84 (RNO) Elko, NV St. Joseph's Church.
Setlock, Msgr. William A. '68 (BUF) Retired.
Setter, H. Jay '88 (WCH) Derby, KS St. Mary's Church.
Settle, Anthony P. '90 (NY) [185] Bronx, NY St. Raymond Church.
Settles, Dennis F. '65 (JOL) [1] Kankakee, IL St. Martin of Tours Church.
Setzer, Frank *s.m.m.* '37 (BRK) [U] Ozone Park, NY Montfort Missionaries Provincialate.
Seubert, Xavier *o.f.m.* '71 (NY) [Z] New York, NY Franciscan Friars, Order of Friars Manor.
Seuferling, George '56 (KCK) Shawnee, KS Good Shepherd Church.
Seung Chi Baek, John '81 (RVC) Great Neck, NY St. Aloysius Church.
Seuntjens, LeRoy L. (SC) Special Assignment.
Seuntjens, LeRoy L. '60 (SC) [E] Sioux City, IA Holy Spirit Retirement Home.
Sevastian, M.R.P. (NOR) [G] Baltic, CT Holy Family Motherhouse.
Sevcik, Lawrence *o.s.b.* '53 (CLV) [P] Cleveland, OH Benedictine Order of Cleveland.
Severson, Richard '82 (ALB) Wilton, NY Mount McGregor Correctional Facility; Special Assignment.
Severt, William H. '74 (CLV) Absent on Leave.
Sevick, John M. '73 (CHI) [212] Chicago, IL St. Walter Church.
Sevigny, Michael E. *o.f.m.cap.* '78 (MAN) [5] Manchester, NH Blessed Sacrament Church.
Sevigny, Robert '53 (HT) Chauvin, LA St. Joseph Church.
Sevilla, Dennis C. '69 (SEA) Port Orchard, WA St. Gabriel's Church; Retsil, WA Washington Veterans Home Hospital.
Sewall, Msgr. Charles H. '60 (SY) [14] Utica, NY St. Peter Church; On Duty Outside the Diocese.
Sewar, Dennis R. '83 (ROC) [41] Rochester, NY St. Lawrence Church.
Sewell, Jack '78 (ORG) Westminster, CA Blessed Sacrament Church.
Sewertz, Thaddeus (Ted) *c.s.c.* '40 (NOR) [D] Deep River, CT Mount St. John.
Sewvello, Robert '94 (YAK) Wenatchee, WA St. Joseph's Church.
Sexstone, James H. '69 (ATL) [4] Atlanta, GA Immaculate Heart of Mary Church.
Sexton, Charles E. '38 (IND) Retired.
Sexton, Cornelius *s.s.j.* '43 (MOB) [10] Mobile, AL St. Joseph Church.
Sexton, John J. '36 (SPR) Retired; [H] Springfield, MA St. Michael's Residence.
Sexton, Joseph G. (NY) Peekskill, NY The Community Hospital.
Sexton, Msgr. Michael '61 (BIR) Florence, AL St. Joseph's Church; [H] Florence, AL University of North Alabama.
Sexton, Patrick D. '77 (BRK) Absent on Leave.
Sexton, Thomas J. *s.j.* '49 (P) [L] Portland, OR Jesuit Provincial Office (Oregon Prov.).
Seyer, Francis L. '52 (BEL) Waterloo, IL SS. Peter and Paul Church.
Seyer, James A. '50 (SPC) Retired.
Seymour, Msgr. Francis R. '63 (NEW) Kearny, NJ St. Cecilia's Church.
Seymour, James W. '87 (OG) On Duty Outside the Diocese.
Seymour, John *s.t.* '71 (LA) [4] Los Angeles, CA Ascension Church.
Seynaeve, Jaak *m.afr.* '44 (BR) Special Assignment.
Sezzi, Michael J. '96 (LA) South Pasadena, CA Holy Family Church.
Sgarbossa, Lino *s.x.* '64 (CHI) [N] Chicago, IL Xaverian Missionaries (S.X.).
Sgarioto, Michael *o.carm.* '85 (JOL) [J] Darien, IL Carmelite Fathers Provincial Office.
Sgueglia, Charles J.M. '52 (SPR) Retired.
Shackelford, Christopher '91 (TYL) Sulphur Springs, TX St. James Church; Sulphur Springs, TX St. James Church.
Shad, Joseph J. *s.j.* '91 (BGP) [V] Bridgeport, CT Newman Centers.
Shadwell, Damian '90 (WDC) Olney, MD St. Peter Church.
Shadwell, Steven G. '89 (PAT) Prospect Park, NJ St. Paul's Church.
Shafer, Drake R. '73 (DAV) [B] Davenport, IA St. Ambrose University; [B] Davenport, IA St. Ambrose University.
Shafer, James A. '75 (FTW) [1] Mishawaka, IN St. Bavo Church.
Shafer, Richard '46 (GB) Retired.
Shaffer, Scott '89 (TR) Lawrenceville, NJ St. Ann Church; [B] Trenton, NJ Notre Dame High School.
Shafran, Steven *s.d.b.* '85 (COL) [H] Columbus, OH Salesian Center.
Shaheen, Joseph '59 (SAM) Unassigned.
Shakalis, Peter A. (BO) Retired.
Shaleta, Emanuel Isho '84 (LA) [5] North Hollywood, CA St. Paul Assyrian-Chaldean Church.
Shallbetter, Martin B. '69 (STP) Bloomington, MN St. Edward Church.
Shallow, Edmund J. '81 (MET) [2] Carteret, NJ Holy Family Church.
Shamleffer, John B. '83 (STL) Warson Woods, MO Ste. Genevieve Du Bois Church.
Shamon, Albert J. '40 (ROC) Fleming, NY St. Isaac Jogues Church; Retired.
Shamsher, Paul '67 (HRT) Branford, CT St. Therese Church; Retired.
Shanahan, Daniel A. *o.p.* '62 (DAL) [M] Irving, TX Dominican Priory of St. Albert the Great.
Shanahan, Edward J. '52 (RVC) Retired; [N] Uniondale, NY St. Pius X Residence.
Shanahan, John '48 (TOL) Retired.
Shanahan, John D. '50 (SFR) Larkspur, CA St. Patrick Church.
Shanahan, Michael *ss.cc.* '62 (FR) [K] Fairhaven, MA Sacred Hearts Provincial House.
Shanahan, Michael J. '92 (CHI) La Grange, IL St. Francis Xavier Church.
Shanahan, Robert J. *s.j.* '55 (OM) [K] Omaha, NE Jesuit Community At Creighton University.
Shanahan, Thomas J. *s.j.* '67 (OM) [K] Omaha, NE Jesuit Community At Creighton University; [K] Omaha, NE Jesuit Community At Creighton University.
Shane, Donald R. '54 (RVC) Ronkonkoma, NY St. Joseph's Church.
Shane, Donald W. '69 (OM) [36] Omaha, NE SS. Peter and Paul Church.
Shaner, Edward G. '96 (MET) Old Bridge, NJ St. Thomas the Apostle Church.
Shanfelt, Thomas G. '78 (ALN) [7] Reading, PA St. Joseph Church.
Shangrow, Philip A. '79 (GR) On Special Assignment.
Shank, Bernard F. '42 (GRY) Retired.
Shanks, Thomas E. *s.j.* '77 (SJ) [B] Santa Clara, CA Santa Clara University.
Shanley, Albert J. *m.s.* '38 (STP) Taylors Falls, MN St. Joseph's Church.
Shanley, Brian J. *o.p.* '87 (WDC) [B] Washington, DC Dominican House of Studies; [C] Washington, DC Catholic University of America, The.
Shanley, Charles M. *c.m.* '55 (PH) [B] Philadelphia, PA DePaul Novitiate; [Z] Philadelphia, PA Congregation of the Mission.
Shanley, Gerry *ss.cc.* '61 (BWN) Pharr, TX St. Anne, Mother of Mary Church.
Shanley, James A. '80 (HRT) Rocky Hill, CT St. Elizabeth Seton Church.
Shanley, Joseph D. '43 (PRO) Retired; [M] Woonsocket, RI Saint Francis House.
Shanley, Kevin *o.carm.* '56 (JOL) [J] Darien, IL Carmelite Community; [L] Darien, IL Carmelite Spiritual Center.
Shanley, Matthew R. '55 (HRT) East Haven, CT Our Lady of Pompeii Church.
Shanley, Matthias *ss.cc.* '65 (BWN) [3] Harlingen, TX Queen of Peace Church.
Shanley, Owen F. '53 (ALB) Corinth, NY Immaculate Conception Church.
Shanley, Paul R. (BO) Retired.
Shanley, Thomas Q. *o.p.* '40 (HRT) [14] New Haven, CT St. Mary's Priory Church.
Shannon, Albert C. *o.s.a.* '44 (PH) [Z] Villanova, PA St. Thomas Monastery.
Shannon, Bernard E. *s.j.* '80 (RVC) [P] Manhasset, NY St. Ignatius Retreat House, Inisfada.
Shannon, Brendan '62 (MIA) [5] Hialeah, FL St. John the Apostle Church.
Shannon, Charles T. *o.p.* '77 (HRT) [14] New Haven, CT St. Mary's Priory Church.
Shannon, David *c.ss.r.* '48 (STP) Brooklyn Center, MN St. Alphonsus Church.
Shannon, Francis '87 (BRK) [15] Brooklyn, NY St. Barbara Church.
Shannon, Joseph E. '64 (CAM) On Sick Leave.
Shannon, Joseph L. *o.s.a.* '37 (PH) [Z] Villanova, PA St. Thomas Monastery.
Shannon, Joseph P. *c.s.b.* '48 (GAL) [Q] Sugar Land, TX Basilian Mission Center.
Shannon, Michael T. *s.j.* '44 (SPK) [K] Spokane, WA Regis Community.
Shannon, Patrick J. '72 (HBG) Lewisburg, PA Sacred Heart of Jesus Church.
Shannon, Richard J. '59 (CHI) [5] Lemont, IL St. Patrick Church.
Shannon, Robert J. (CHI) Retired.
Shannon, Timothy '75 (STU) [1] Steubenville, OH Holy Name Cathedral; [6] Steubenville, OH St. Anthony of Padua Church.
Shannon, Timothy T. *s.j.* '88 (DET) [E] Detroit, MI University of Detroit Jesuit High School and Academy.
Shannon, William *o.f.m.cap.* '71 (AGN) [F] Agana Heights, GU St. Fidelis Friary.
Shannon, Msgr. William H. '43 (ROC) Retired; [J] Rochester, NY Sisters St. Joseph Motherhouse; [L] Rochester, NY Censores Librorum.
Shappard, Christopher *o.s.b.* '62 (IND) [B] St. Meinrad, IN St. Meinrad Seminary-College of Liberal Arts; [J] St. Meinrad, IN St. Meinrad Archabbey.
Shappelle, James '48 (CIN) [15] Cincinnati, OH St. Bernard Church; [66] Cincinnati, OH Mother of Christ Church.
Sharanevych, Emile '32 (STF) Retired.
Sharkey, Msgr. John A. '56 (PH) [95] Philadelphia, PA

Old St. Mary's Church.
Sharkey, Owen *c.p.* '45 (HRT) [M] West Hartford, CT Holy Family Monastery/Retreat.
Sharkey, Robert Urban *o.p.* (NY) [Z] New York, NY St. Vincent Ferrer Priory.
Sharkey, Thomas *c.s.sp.* '51 (ARE) Barceloneta, PR Church of Our Lady of Mt. Carmel.
Sharkey, Msgr. Thomas H. '48 (CAM) Ocean City, NJ Our Lady of Good Counsel Church; [F] Ocean City, NJ The Sharkey Family Charitable Trust.
Sharkey, William *s.o.l.t.* '89 (CC) [H] Robstown, TX Society of Our Lady of the Most Holy Trinity.
Sharman, Robert F. '84 (HBG) Mechanicsburg, PA St. Elizabeth Ann Seton Church.
Sharon, Charles *s.a.* '72 (NY) [Z] New York, NY Atonement Friars.
Sharon, Norbert *s.t.* '48 (LA) [27] Los Angeles, CA Our Lady of Victory Church.
Sharp, David L. *c.s.b.* '70 (PHX) Special Assignment; [H] Phoenix, AZ Office of Youth and Young Adult Ministries.
Sharp, Donald B. *s.j.* '71 (SFR) [N] San Francisco, CA Jesuit Community at University of San Francisco.
Sharp, Edward A. *s.j.* '53 (OM) [K] Omaha, NE Jesuit Community At Creighton University.
Sharp, George (NEW) Maplewood, NJ St. Joseph's Church.
Sharp, James R. '84 (DAL) [27] Dallas, TX St. Thomas Aquinas Church.
Sharp, Kenneth W. '81 (PH) Lansdale, PA St. Stanislaus Church.
Sharpe, John O'M. *c.m.* '38 (PHX) [26] Phoenix, AZ St. Vincent de Paul Church.
Sharpe, Msgr. Joseph F. '43 (LA) Retired.
Sharpe, Msgr. Joseph F. '43 (ORG) Newport Beach, CA Our Lady Queen of Angels Church.
Sharpe, Patrick F. '42 (E) Retired.
Sharrett, Victor F. '65 (PH) Kennett Square, PA St. Patrick Church.
Sharrock, David J. *c.ss.r.* '55 (CHR) Sumter, SC St. Anne's Church.
Sharum, Peter *o.s.b.* '52 (LR) Charleston, AR Sacred Heart Church.
Shashy, Daniel '91 (STA) [13] Jacksonville, FL Resurrection Church.
Shatzel, Richard J. '69 (ROC) [40] Rochester, NY Our Mother of Sorrows Church.
Shaughnessey, Angelus *o.f.m.cap.* '56 (GBG) Export, PA St. Mary Church.
Shaughnessy, James D. '40 (PEO) Retired.
Shaughnessy, James E. '73 (KCK) Lawrence, KS Corpus Christi Church.
Shaughnessy, James M. *s.j.* '79 (BO) [30] Boston, MA Immaculate Conception Church; Boston, MA New England Medical Center; [W] Boston, MA Jesuit Urban Center & Immaculate Conception Community.
Shaughnessy, John *c.ss.r.* '49 (OAK) [N] Oakland, CA Redemptorists.
Shaughnessy, John A. *c.m.* '49 (STL) [P] St. Louis, MO Vincentian Henrietta Residence.
Shaughnessy, Martin G. *s.j.* '63 (BGP) [D] Fairfield, CT Fairfield College Preparatory School; [O] Fairfield, CT The Fairfield Jesuit Community-Fairfield University.
Shaughnessy, Paul J. *s.j.* '87 (BAL) [M] Baltimore, MD Jesuit Fathers and Brothers Maryland Provincial Curia.
Shaughnessy, Thomas *o.f.m.* '60 (STL) [P] St. Louis, MO Franciscan Friary of St. Anthony of Padua.
Shaughnessy, William *o.f.m.* '73 (SD) [H] San Luis Rey, CA San Luis Rey.
Shaughnessy, William G. '92 (WDC) [T] Washington, DC Opus Dei.
Shaughnessy, William Rusty *o.f.m.* '73 (SD) [K] San Luis Rey, CA Mission San Luis Rey Retreat.
Shaules, Patrick R. *s.j.* '48 (PH) [Z] Philadelphia, PA Jesuit Community at St. Joseph's University.
Shaum, David (BAL) Retired.
Shaum, David W. '46 (BAL) [C] Emmitsburg, MD Mount Saint Mary's College.
Shaunessy, Francis W. '45 (CHI) [56] Chicago, IL St. Eugene Church; Retired.
Shaver, James R. '89 (LAN) [1] Jackson, MI St. John the Evangelist Church.
Shaw, Brian A. '66 (HRT) [5] Bristol, CT St. Stanislaus Church.
Shaw, Charles E. '51 (HRT) Retired.
Shaw, David '68 (SR) [4] Santa Rosa, CA Resurrection Church.
Shaw, Dennis '74 (ROC) [25] Rochester, NY Holy Redeemer-St. Francis Xavier Church; [36] Rochester, NY Our Lady of Mount Carmel Church.
Shaw, Dennis J. '74 (ROC) [47] Rochester, NY St. Michael Church.
Shaw, Eugene F. *s.j.* '60 (MIL) [P] Milwaukee, WI Jesuit Provincial Office, Wisconsin Province.
Shaw, Eugene F. *s.j.* '60 (PH) [Z] Philadelphia, PA Jesuit Community at St. Joseph's University.
Shaw, John M. '57 (YAK) Toppenish, WA St. Aloysius Church.
Shaw, Kenneth *s.d.b.* (PAT) [3] Paterson, NJ St. Anthony's Church; [D] North Haledon, NJ Mary Help of Christians Academy.
Shaw, Mario '56 (PEO) [P] Peoria, IL St. Augustine Community.
Shaw, Mario W. '56 (PEO) [L] Peoria, IL St. Augustine Manor.
Shaw, Michael B. '96 (PT) [1] Pensacola, FL Cathedral of the Sacred Heart.
Shaw, Richard '68 (ALB) Albany, NY Albany County Jail; Special Assignment.
Shaw, William (CHL) [4] Greensboro, NC St. Paul the Apostle Church.
Shaw, William E. '57 (YAK) Zillah, WA Resurrection Church.
Shay, Michael *s.d.s.* '73 (MIL) [P] Milwaukee, WI Salvatorian Provincial Residence.
Shay, Robert *s.t.* '59 (WDC) [M] Adelphi, MD Missionary Servants of the Most Holy Trinity.
Shea, Baldwin *o.c.s.o.* '53 (SLC) [F] Huntsville, UT Abbey of Our Lady of the Holy Trinity of the Order of Cistercians.
Shea, Daniel B. '69 (HEL) [B] Helena, MT Carroll College.
Shea, Donald *c.pp.s.* '53 (TOL) [M] Bellevue, OH Sorrowful Mother Shrine.
Shea, Msgr. Donald W. '62 (HEL) Military Chaplains.
Shea, Edward *o.f.m.* (CHI) [47] Chicago, IL Corpus Christi Church.
Shea, Evan P. '86 (CHY) Lusk, WY St. Leo's Church.
Shea, James *c.ss.r.* (DEN) Fort Lupton, CO St. William Church.
Shea, James J. *sch.p.* '92 (PH) [Z] Devon, PA Piarist Fathers (Order of the Pious Schools).
Shea, James M. '65 (BUR) Springfield, VT Maternity of the Blessed Virgin Mary Church.
Shea, James M. *s.j.* '75 (BO) [W] Boston, MA The Society of Jesus of New England-Provincial Offices.
Shea, James M. *s.j.* '75 (WDC) [K] Washington, DC Georgetown University Hospital; [M] Washington, DC The Jesuit Community at Georgetown University.
Shea, James M. '85 (WOR) [14] Worcester, MA Our Lady of the Rosary Church.
Shea, James P. *sch.p.* '66 (PH) [G] Devon, PA Devon Preparatory School.
Shea, John J. (BO) [4] Plymouth, MA St. Peter Church.
Shea, John J. '45 (SPR) Granby, MA Immaculate Heart of Mary Church.
Shea, John J. '67 (CHI) Other Assignments.
Shea, John J. *s.j.* '75 (CLV) [C] Cleveland, OH John Carroll University; [C] Cleveland, OH John Carroll Jesuit Community.
Shea, John J. *s.j.* '75 (NY) [C] Bronx, NY Fordham University.
Shea, Joseph *o.f.m.cap.* '67 (RVC) East Patchogue, NY St. Joseph the Worker Church.
Shea, Joseph '78 (LA) Glendale, CA Holy Family Church.
Shea, Joseph C. *m.s.* '57 (STL) Maplewood, MO Immaculate Conception Church; [P] St. Louis, MO La Salette Missionaries.
Shea, Leo A. '64 (MAN) Absent on Leave.
Shea, Leo B. *m.m.* '66 (NY) [Z] Maryknoll, NY Maryknoll Fathers and Brothers.
Shea, Lewis M. *o.p.* '66 (CHI) [N] Chicago, IL Dominicans (Provincial Office).
Shea, Maurice F. '56 (SJ) [14] San Jose, CA St. Leo the Great Church; Special Assignment.
Shea, Michael J. *c.m.* '70 (GR) [J] Spring Lake, MI St. Lazare Retreat House.
Shea, Michael J. *c.m.* '70 (PH) [Z] Philadelphia, PA Congregation of the Mission.
Shea, Michael J. '76 (SFE) Alameda, NM Nativity of the Blessed Virgin Mary Church.
Shea, Peter D. '75 (WOR) West Brookfield, MA Sacred Heart of Jesus Church.
Shea, Peter G. *c.s.p.* '56 (SFR) [31] San Francisco, CA Old St. Mary's Cathedral.
Shea, Msgr. Richard J. '61 (BGP) [2] Trumbull, CT St. Catherine of Siena Church.
Shea, Robert F. '55 (R) Roanoke Rapids, NC St. John the Baptist Church.
Shea, Thomas '73 (PEO) Absent on Leave.
Shea, Thomas F. '64 (PH) Retired.
Shea, Thomas J. *o.s.a.* '52 (PH) [Z] Villanova, PA St. Thomas Monastery.
Shea, Thomas M. '66 (SPR) [4] Springfield, MA Holy Cross Church.
Shea, Timothy J. '61 (BO) Wellesley, MA St. James the Great Church.
Shea, Vincent *o.f.m.* '51 (PAT) [M] Ringwood, NJ Holy Name Friary.
Shea, Vincent M. *o.s.m.* (SP) St. Pete Beach, FL St. John Church.
Shea, William *s.v.d.* '64 (DUB) [B] Epworth, IA Divine Word College.
Shea, Msgr. William B. (BO) Retired.
Sheaffer, John K. '93 (SPR) Agawam, MA St. John the Evangelist Church.
Sheahan, Msgr. Donal C. '60 (SD) [17] San Diego, CA Our Mother of Confidence Church.
Sheahan, Gerald R. *s.j.* '51 (STL) [P] St. Louis, MO St. Louis University High School Jesuit Community.
Sheahan, Gerald R. *s.j.* '89 (STL) [F] St. Louis, MO St. Louis University High School, George H. Backer Memorial.
Sheahan, John A. '60 (ORG) Retired.
Sheahan, John F. '46 (SFD) Retired.
Sheahan, Kevin J. '88 (CHI) [186] Chicago, IL St. Robert Bellarmine Church.
Sheahan, Richard D. '69 (PRO) [2] Cranston, RI Holy Apostles Church.
Shear, Michael P. '64 (PSC) Harrisburg, PA St. Ann Church.
Shearer, Thomas M. '78 (CIN) [4] Dayton, OH St. Anthony of Padua Church.
Shebuski, Charles '65 (GB) Absent on Leave.
Shecterle, Ross A. '86 (MIL) Graduate Studies.
Shedlock, John '94 (SFE) Ribera, NM San Miguel Del Vado Church; Villanueva, NM Our Lady of Guadalupe Church.
Sheedlo, Walter J. '71 (MAR) [2] Escanaba, MI St. Joseph Church.
Sheeds, Gerald E. '68 (KCK) Gardner, KS Sacred Heart Church.
Sheedy, Edward J. (BUF) On Duty Outside the Diocese.
Sheedy, Edward J. '72 (BUF) Silver Springs, NY St. Mary Church.
Sheedy, Edward J. '72 (OG) [A] Ogdensburg, NY Wadhams Hall.
Sheedy, Mateo E. '77 (SJ) [22] San Jose, CA Sacred Heart of Jesus Church.
Sheedy, Patrick J. '65 (ORL) [1] Ocala, FL Blessed Trinity Church.
Sheedy, Timothy J. '76 (DAV) [4] Fort Madison, IA Sacred Heart Church.
Sheedy, Val J. '55 (ORL) [1] Lakeland, FL Church of the Resurrection.
Sheehan, Augustine J. '55 (RVC) Central Islip, NY St. John of God Church; Northport, NY Veteran's Hospital.
Sheehan, Bernard *o.s.b.* '68 (OM) [K] Elkhorn, NE Mount Michael Abbey.
Sheehan, Daniel J. '53 (BO) [8] Salem, MA St. Thomas the Apostle Church.
Sheehan, Daniel J. '79 (BRK) [R] Bayside, NY Ozanam Hall of Queens Nursing Home, Inc.; [U] Jamaica, NY Parsons Manor.
Sheehan, Msgr. Dennis F. (BO) [12] Cambridge, MA St. Paul Church.
Sheehan, Donald P. '68 (NEW) Dumont, NJ St. Mary's Church.
Sheehan, Edward *s.m.* '61 (PRT) Brunswick, ME St. John the Baptist Church.
Sheehan, George F. (SY) [C] East Syracuse, NY Bishop Grimes Jr./Sr. High School; [S] East Syracuse, NY Bishop Grimes Priests Residence.
Sheehan, Gerald *s.o.l.t.* '85 (CC) [H] Robstown, TX Society of Our Lady of the Most Holy Trinity.
Sheehan, Gerald P. '64 (BUF) Forestville, NY St. Rose of Lima Church; Sheridan, NY St. John Bosco Church.
Sheehan, J. Peter '56 (BIR) Retired.
Sheehan, J. William *o.m.i.* '65 (WDC) [B] Washington, DC Oblate College/Oblate Center for Mission Studies; [M] Washington, DC Missionary Oblates of Mary Immaculate.
Sheehan, James '75 (PMB) Retired.
Sheehan, James C. *o.p.* '37 (HRT) [14] New Haven, CT St. Mary's Priory Church.
Sheehan, James T. *s.j.* '59 (BO) [W] Boston, MA Loyola House.
Sheehan, John F.X. *s.j.* '64 (BO) [W] Boston, MA The Society of Jesus of New England-Provincial Offices.
Sheehan, John F.X. *s.j.* '64 (STL) [C] St. Louis, MO Saint Louis University; [P] St. Louis, MO Jesuit Community Corporation at St. Louis University - Jesuit Hall.
Sheehan, Msgr. John J. '37 (BO) Retired.
Sheehan, John J. '54 (NY) [219] Staten Island, NY Our Lady, Queen of Peace Church.
Sheehan, John P. '89 (NY) [155] Bronx, NY St. John Chrysostom's Church.
Sheehan, Joseph *o.carm.* '63 (SFS) [A] Aberdeen, SD Presentation College.
Sheehan, Joseph A. (ALN) [4] Easton, PA St. Joseph Church.
Sheehan, Joseph D. *s.j.* '49 (MIL) [P] Milwaukee, WI Jesuit Provincial Office, Wisconsin Province.
Sheehan, Joseph G. '48 (NEW) Retired.
Sheehan, Justin R. *o.c.s.o.* '91 (ROC) [I] Piffard, NY Abbey of the Genesee.
Sheehan, Lawrence A. *s.j.* '47 (RVC) Massapequa, NY St. Rose of Lima Church; Retired.
Sheehan, Lourdes *r.s.m.* (FTW) [B] Notre Dame, IN University of Notre Dame Du Lac.
Sheehan, Mark S. '63 (BO) Bedford, MA St. Michael Church.
Sheehan, Maurice *o.f.m.cap.* (NOR) [A] Cromwell, CT Holy Apostles College and Seminary.

Sheehan, Maurice '55 (PIT) [N] Pittsburgh, PA St. Francis Friary.
Sheehan, Michael J. (NEW) Paramus, NJ Annunciation Church.
Sheehan, Michael J. '64 (PH) [144] Philadelphia, PA Sacred Heart of Jesus Church.
Sheehan, Myles N. *s.j.* '94 (BO) [W] Boston, MA The Society of Jesus of New England-Provincial Offices.
Sheehan, Myles N. *s.j.* '94 (CHI) [C] Chicago, IL Jesuit Community at Loyola University of Chicago.
Sheehan, Richard J. *o.m.i.* '61 (BWN) San Juan, TX St. John the Baptist Church.
Sheehan, Thomas *o.f.m.* '60 (BUF) [A] East Aurora, NY Christ the King Seminary.
Sheehan, Thomas '70 (CLV) [6] Parma, OH Holy Family Church.
Sheehan, Thomas D. *o.p.* '45 (GAL) [Q] Houston, TX Dominican Fathers and Brothers, St. Mark Priory, Inc.
Sheehan, Thomas J. '53 (WDC) [40] Washington, DC St. Stephen Martyr Church.
Sheehan, William *o.m.i.* '58 (BO) [DD] Tewksbury, MA The Society of Oblate Fathers for Missions Among the Poor Formation Charitable Trust; [DD] Tewksbury, MA The Society of Oblate Fathers Continuing Support Fund.
Sheehan, William J. *s.j.* '65 (BO) [W] Weston, MA Campion Center; [Y] Weston, MA Campion Renewal Center.
Sheehan, William J. *c.s.b.* '66 (ROC) [I] Rochester, NY Basilian Residence.
Sheehey, Robert J. *s.s.e.* '47 (BUR) [G] Colchester, VT Society of St. Edmund.
Sheehy, Charles I. '44 (BO) Braintree, MA St. Francis of Assisi Church.
Sheehy, Charles I. '64 (BO) Retired.
Sheehy, Dennis E. '68 (GBG) Yukon, PA Seven Dolors Church.
Sheehy, Joseph T. '53 (BO) Swampscott, MA St. John the Evangelist Church.
Sheehy, Paul E. '54 (LIN) Ulysses, NE Immaculate Conception Church.
Sheehy, Sean O. '70 (BR) [K] Hammond, LA St. Albert the Great Catholic Center.
Sheehy, Vincent J. '61 (VEN) [2] Venice, FL Our Lady of Lourdes Church.
Sheehy, Wilfred '60 (SR) Retired.
Sheehy, Yvon *s.c.j.* '78 (RC) Lower Brule, SD St. Mary's Church; Lower Brule, SD Lower Brule Reservation Church; [B] Lower Brule, SD SCJ Community House.
Sheehy, Yvon *s.c.j.* '78 (SFS) Fort Thompson, SD St. Joseph Church; Stephan, SD Immaculate Conception Church.
Sheekey, Philip P. '64 (WIL) Rehoboth, DE St. Edmond Church.
Sheeran, Kevin J. *o.s.b.* '65 (JOL) [A] Lisle, IL Benedictine University; [J] Lisle, IL St. Procopius Abbey.
Sheeran, Michael J. *s.j.* '70 (DEN) [M] Denver, CO Regis Jesuit Community (The Jesuits at Regis University).
Sheeran, Michael J. *s.j.* '93 (DEN) [B] Denver, CO Regis University.
Sheeran, Msgr. Robert T. '70 (NEW) [A] South Orange, NJ Immaculate Conception Seminary; [A] South Orange, NJ Seton Hall University College Seminary; [B] South Orange, NJ Seton Hall University; [B] South Orange, NJ Seton Hall University.
Sheerin, James O. '56 (NEW) Little Ferry, NJ St. Margaret of Cortona Church.
Sheerin, Philip F. *m.m.* '55 (SJ) [M] Los Altos, CA Maryknoll.
Sheets, Francis K. *o.s.c.* '51 (NY) [Z] New Rochelle, NY Crosier (Canons Regular of the Order of the Holy Cross).
Sheets, Joseph B. '57 (IND) Brownstown, IN Our Lady of Providence Church; Seymour, IN St. Ambrose Church.
Sheetz, Stephen A. '57 (HBG) Millersville, PA St. Philip the Apostle Church.
Sheffield, Walter N. '82 (GAL) [64] Houston, TX St. Paul Church.
Sheffler, Mark *c.ss.r.* '70 (SAT) [M] San Antonio, TX Redemptorists of Texas-Redemptorist Community at St. Gerard.
Sheherd, Eugene '78 (AUS) Chappell Hill, TX St. Stanislaus Church.
Sheil, James '66 (CLV) Military Chaplains.
Shelander, Donald E. '70 (CIN) Newport, OH SS. Peter and Paul Church.
Shelby, Charles F. *c.m.* '68 (STL) [P] Perryville, MO Congregation of The Mission; [W] Perryville, MO The Association of the Miraculous Medal.
Sheldon, Denis (FBK) Alakanuk, AK St. Ignatius Church.
Sheldon, William W. *c.m.* (ALN) [A] Northampton, PA Mary Immaculate Seminary; [K] Northhampton, PA Vincentian Community.
Sheley, John '73 (SPC) Dexter, MO Sacred Heart Church.
Shellem, John J. '52 (PH) Newtown Square, PA St. Anastasia Church.
Shelley, John J. '61 (PH) Cheltenham, PA Presentation of Blessed Virgin Mary Church.
Shelley, Jonathan P. '95 (STP) Bayport, MN St. Charles Church; Stillwater, MN St. Michael Church.
Shelley, Owen *o.f.m.cap.* '45 (RVC) Huntington, NY St. Patrick's Church; Huntington, NY Huntington Hospital.
Shelley, Thomas (NY) [118] New York, NY St. Thomas More Church.
Shelley, William M. '50 (NY) [2] New York, NY St. Agnes Church.
Shellman, Richard L. '86 (HRT) Bethlehem, CT Church of the Nativity.
Shelly, Roy J. *s.d.b.* '78 (NY) [BB] West Haverstraw, NY Don Bosco Retreat Center and Marian Shrine; [BB] West Haverstraw, NY Marian Shrine.
Shelly, Thomas J. '62 (NY) [A] Yonkers, NY St. Joseph's Seminary.
Shelton, Charles *o.f.m.conv.* '81 (MRY) [G] Arroyo Grande, CA St. Joseph's Cupertino Novitiate.
Shelton, Charles *o.f.m.conv.* '81 (RNO) [1] Reno, NV St. Thomas Aquinas Cathedral.
Shelton, Charles M. *s.j.* '82 (DEN) [M] Denver, CO Regis Jesuit Community (The Jesuits at Regis University).
Shelton, Henry '69 (JKS) Shaw, MS St. Francis of Assisi Church.
Shelton, Lawrence '66 (LA) [44] Los Angeles, CA St. Anselm Church.
Sheltz, Anton R. '76 (GAL) [25] Houston, TX St. Dominic Church.
Sheltz, George A. '71 (GAL) [69] Houston, TX Prince of Peace Church.
Shema, George T. '67 (PAT) [3] Wayne, NJ Immaculate Heart of Mary Church.
Shemuga, Kevin C. '83 (CLV) [43] Cleveland, OH St. Leo the Great Church.
Shen, Louis *s.j.* '83 (OAK) Union City, CA St. Anne Church.
Shen, Raphael *s.j.* '70 (DET) [K] Detroit, MI Jesuit Community at the University of Detroit.
Shenk, Bertrand J. '37 (TOL) Sandusky, OH Soldiers and Sailors Home; Retired.
Shenk, Joseph D. '34 (TOL) Retired; [J] Oregon, OH Sacred Heart Home.
Shenoy, Leslie F. '76 (FRS) Mojave, CA St. Francis Church.
Shenrock, Msgr. Joseph C. '53 (TR) Whiting, NJ St. Elizabeth Ann Seton Church.
Shepanski, Don C. '62 (SAT) [57] San Antonio, TX St. Matthew's Church.
Shepard, Thomas B. '77 (HRT) Rocky Hill, CT St. James Church.
Shepard, Timothy J. *s.j.* '82 (DET) [B] Berkley, MI Loyola House; [K] Detroit, MI Jesuit Provincial Office-Detroit Province of the Society of Jesus.
Shepardson, Eleanor '90 (OAK) [R] Oakland, CA St. Mary's Center.
Sheperd, Raymond C. '57 (TOL) [13] Toledo, OH Regina Coeli Church; Special Assignment.
Shepherd, Maurice *s.o.l.t.* '88 (CC) [H] Robstown, TX Society of Our Lady of the Most Holy Trinity.
Shepherd, Thomas N. '45 (BUF) [46] Buffalo, NY St. Martin Church; Retired.
Shepler, Charles C. '43 (DAV) Retired; [B] Davenport, IA St. Ambrose University.
Shepley, Brian J. '92 (DAV) [1] Iowa City, IA St. Mary of the Assumption Church.
Sheputa, Albin *m.i.c.* '43 (NOR) [F] Thompson, CT Marian Fathers.
Sherba, Girard M. '79 (R) Kinston, NC Holy Trinity-Our Lady of the Atonement Church.
Sherbno, John '49 (TOL) Retired.
Sherbo, Albert '87 (DM) Anita, IA St. Mary Church; Casey, IA St. Joseph Church.
Sherbo, Albert G. '87 (DM) Adair, IA St. John Church.
Sherburne, Richard F. *s.j.* '56 (MIL) [P] Milwaukee, WI Jesuit Community at Marquette University.
Sherdel, Lawrence '81 (HBG) [K] Harrisburg, PA Catholic Campus Ministry.
Sherdel, Lawrence W. '81 (HBG) Shippensburg, PA Our Lady of the Visitation Church.
Sherer, Richard B. '58 (HRT) [1] West Hartford, CT St. Brigid's Church.
Sheridan, Brian R. *m.s.* '83 (HRT) [M] Hartford, CT Missionaries of LaSalette Provincial Secretary.
Sheridan, Daniel P. (RVC) St. James, NY SS. Philip and James Church.
Sheridan, Denis J. '81 (RVC) Hempstead, NY St. Ladislaus Church; Rockville Centre, NY Mercy Medical Center; [I] Rockville Centre, NY Mercy Medical Center.
Sheridan, Edward J. '63 (CHL) [5] Charlotte, NC St. Gabriel Church.
Sheridan, Eugene '45 (NY) Retired.
Sheridan, Eugene *c.m.* '60 (MOB) Phenix City, AL St. Patrick Church.
Sheridan, James B. *o.p.* '35 (NY) Pleasantville, NY Holy Innocents Church.
Sheridan, James B. '50 (PH) Retired.
Sheridan, James J. *o.s.a.* '61 (TLS) [B] Tulsa, OK Cascia Hall Preparatory School.
Sheridan, John E. '91 (BO) [8] Boston, MA St. Ann Church.
Sheridan, John F. '87 (ALN) [3] Easton, PA St. Jane Frances de Chantal Church.
Sheridan, John J. *o.s.a.* '85 (ALB) Hoosick Falls, NY Immaculate Conception Church; Pittstown, NY St. George Church.
Sheridan, Msgr. John V. '43 (LA) Malibu, CA Our Lady of Malibu Church; Retired.
Sheridan, Mark *o.s.b.* '65 (WDC) [M] Washington, DC St. Anselm's Abbey.
Sheridan, Matthew W. '54 (BRK) [230] Queens, NY Queen of Angels Church.
Sheridan, Michael (PRT) Woodland, ME St. James the Greater Church.
Sheridan, Michael '75 (PRT) Indian Township, ME St. Ann Church.
Sheridan, Michael J. '71 (STL) Richmond Heights, MO Immacolata Church.
Sheridan, Paul G. *s.j.* '75 (STL) [W] St. Louis, MO Boys Hope.
Sheridan, Msgr. Paul W. '56 (SFD) Pierron, IL Immaculate Conception Church; Pocahontas, IL St. Nicholas Church.
Sheridan, Peter C. *o.f.m.* '41 (WDC) [B] Silver Spring, MD Holy Name College.
Sheridan, Philip A. '51 (HRT) Union City, CT St. Mary's Church.
Sheridan, Robert A. '43 (CHI) [120] Chicago, IL St. Margaret of Scotland Church; Retired.
Sheridan, Thomas L. *s.j.* '57 (NEW) [B] Jersey City, NJ Saint Peter's College; [N] Jersey City, NJ Jesuits of Saint Peter's College, Inc.
Sheridan, William H. '54 (CHI) [171] Chicago, IL St. Philip Neri Church.
Sheridan, William J. '72 (CHI) [1] Chicago, IL Cathedral of the Holy Name.
Sheridan, William P. '89 (NEW) Lyndhurst, NJ Sacred Heart Church; [A] South Orange, NJ Seton Hall University College Seminary; [B] South Orange, NJ Seton Hall University.
Sherlock, J. Alex '66 (MOB) [19] Mobile, AL St. Pius X Church.
Sherlock, James C. '64 (PH) [121] Philadelphia, PA Our Lady of Lourdes Church.
Sherlock, John '69 (WCH) [19] Wichita, KS St. Thomas Aquinas Church; [B] Wichita, KS Kapaun Mt. Carmel High School.
Sherlock, R. Marc '79 (CIN) Wilmington, OH St. Columbkille Church; [Q] Wilmington, OH Wilmington College Campus Ministry.
Sherman, Msgr. Anthony F. '70 (BRK) [199] Queens, NY St. Matthias Church.
Sherman, Charles E. '51 (RCK) Retired.
Sherman, Daniel J. *m.m.* '47 (NY) [Z] Maryknoll, NY Maryknoll Fathers and Brothers.
Sherman, Daniel M. '77 (CAM) Pomona, NJ Assumption Church.
Sherman, Edward '56 (FAR) St. Michael, ND St. Michael's Church; St. Michael, ND St. Michael's Indian Mission Church.
Sherman, Gary '85 (TLS) [1] Tulsa, OK Holy Family Cathedral.
Sherman, Kenneth '80 (NTN) Rochester, NY St. Nicholas Church.
Sherman, Thomas P. *s.j.* '87 (MIL) [P] Milwaukee, WI Jesuit Provincial Office, Wisconsin Province.
Sherman, William C. '55 (FAR) [3] Grand Forks, ND St. Michael's Church; Grand Forks, ND School for the Blind.
Sherpenski, Donald A.J. *s.j.* '69 (BO) [E] Boston, MA Boston College High School & Jesuit Community; [W] Boston, MA The Society of Jesus of New England-Provincial Offices.
Sherpenski, Donald A.J. *s.j.* '88 (BO) [2] Plymouth, MA St. Bonaventure Church.
Sherrer, Charles D. *c.s.c.* '61 (P) [B] Portland, OR University of Portland; [L] Portland, OR Holy Cross Father & Brother, C.S.C. - University of Portland.
Sherry, Brendan '52 (AMA) Absent on Leave.
Sherry, Bryan W. '62 (TUC) Florence, AZ Assumption of the Blessed Virgin Mary Church; Special Assignment.
Sherry, Edward F. '68 (BO) Wilmington, MA St. Thomas of Villanova Church.
Sherry, Peter Thomas *o.carm.* '38 (BO) [P] Peabody, MA Catholic Information Center; [BB] Peabody, MA St. Theresa Carmelite Chapel.
Sherry, Robert N. '66 (RCK) McHenry, IL Church of Holy Apostles.
Shershanovich, Michael '74 (SPR) [7] Pittsfield, MA St. Joseph's Church.
Sherwin, Michael *o.p.* '91 (FTW) [A] Notre Dame, IN Moreau Seminary.
Sherwood, Lan S. '75 (PHX) Unassigned.
Sherwood, Stephen K. *c.m.f.* '71 (SAT) [B] San Antonio, TX St. Anthony Mary Claret Seminary; [C] San Antonio, TX Oblate School of Theology.

Sherwood, Timothy J. '93 (SP) [7] St. Petersburg, FL St. Paul Church.
Sherzer, Msgr. William J. '46 (DET) Bloomfield Hills, MI St. Owen Church; Retired.
Sheslo, Charles W. '61 (SD) Ramona, CA Immaculate Heart of Mary Church.
Shetler, Msgr. Carl '47 (EVN) St. Martin, IN St. Martin's Church.
Shetler, John '92 (PHX) [13] Phoenix, AZ St. Jerome Church.
Shetler, John E. '57 (ORG) Irvine, CA St. John Neumann Church.
Shevlin, John *s.v.d.* '60 (SB) [A] Riverside, CA Divine Word Seminary.
Shevlin, Msgr. John G. '48 (NY) Bangall, NY Immaculate Conception Church; Retired.
Shevlin, Msgr. Raymond R. '44 (BRK) [122] Brooklyn, NY Resurrection Church; Retired.
Shibley, Amel A. (SPC) Retired.
Shidler, Anthony *o.s.b.* '64 (SPC) [6] Springfield, MO St. Joseph's Church; [C] Springfield, MO St. John's Regional Health Center.
Shields, David M. '73 (MIL) [64] Milwaukee, WI St. Patrick's Church; [P] Milwaukee, WI Jesuit Community at Marquette University.
Shields, Hugh J. '72 (PH) On Duty Outside the Archdiocese.
Shields, James E. '75 (NY) [Z] New York, NY Jesuit Provincial's Office.
Shields, James J. '63 (PH) [13] Philadelphia, PA St. Anselm Church.
Shields, James P. '52 (CHI) Other Assignments.
Shields, Joseph '72 (BO) [W] Boston, MA The Society of St. James the Apostle, Inc.
Shields, Msgr. Joseph A. '49 (PH) Kimberton, PA St. Basil the Great Church.
Shields, Joseph E. '36 (MAN) Newmarket, NH St. Mary Church; Retired.
Shields, Msgr. Maurice L. '57 (MOB) [11] Mobile, AL Little Flower Church.
Shields, Michael '79 (ANC) On Duty Outside Archdiocese.
Shields, Patrick J. '64 (CLV) [7] Lorain, OH St. Ladislaus Church.
Shields, Robert J. '64 (YAK) Grand Coulee, WA St. Henry's Church.
Shields, Stephen L. '74 (CLV) Parma Heights, OH St. John Bosco Church.
Shields, W. Bry '84 (MOB) [7] Mobile, AL St. Ignatius Church; [C] Mobile, AL McGill-Toolen High School.
Shields, William J. '52 (CHI) Mundelein, IL Santa Maria Del Popolo Church.
Shields, William J. '58 (ALN) [J] Bethlehem, PA Holy Family Villa.
Shiffer, Jim *s.s.c.* '65 (LA) [R] Los Angeles, CA Columban Fathers, Procure House.
Shigo, Francis (LA) [K] Torrance, CA Little Company of Mary Health Services.
Shigo, Francis L. *s.v.d.* '60 (LA) [R] Los Angeles, CA Society of the Divine Word Western Province.
Shih, John M. '49 (NEW) Retired.
Shikany, Paul M. '79 (IND) Edinburgh, IN Holy Trinity Church; Franklin, IN St. Rose of Lima Church; [N] Franklin, IN Franklin College Newman Center.
Shilala, Robert N. '58 (SCR) Dorrance, PA Our Lady Help of Christians Church.
Shillcox, Timothy '87 (GB) [I] De Pere, WI St. Joseph Priory.
Shillcox, Timothy D. *o.praem.* '87 (GB) Bay Settlement, WI Holy Cross Church.
Shiller, Francis E. (NEW) [7] Jersey City, NJ Assumption/All Saints Church.
Shillito, Edward D. '55 (RVC) [N] Uniondale, NY St. Pius X Residence.
Shimanek, Joseph '54 (JOL) Retired.
Shimkus, Bernard A. '43 (PH) Retired.
Shimmaly, Edward E. '61 (B) Retired.
Shimmaly, Edward E. '61 (LA) Sick Leave.
Shimotsu, John '94 (ORG) Stanton, CA St. Polycarp Church.
Shin, Jung Soon (Benedict) (WDC) College Park, MD St. Andrew Kim Church.
Shindelar, Vincent J. '56 (RCK) Tampico, IL St. Mary Church.
Shine, Con '60 (ORL) Silver Springs Shores, FL Immaculate Heart of Mary Church.
Shine, Cornelius '60 (LA) On Duty Outside the Archdiocese.
Shine, Daniel J. *s.j.* '51 (BO) [W] Weston, MA Campion Health Center, Inc.
Shine, Edward J. '57 (CIN) [44] Cincinnati, OH St. John the Baptist Church.
Shine, Francis J. *c.m.* '55 (STL) St. Louis, MO Regional Hospital; [P] St. Louis, MO Vincentian Henrietta Residence.
Shine, John V. *c.m.* '63 (PHX) [26] Phoenix, AZ St. Vincent de Paul Church.
Shine, Robert W. '55 (SAG) Port Austin, MI St. Michael Church.
Shine, Sean '52 (ORL) Silver Springs Shores, FL Immaculate Heart of Mary Church.
Shiner, Kenneth H. '71 (HRT) Branford, CT St. Elizabeth Church.
Shinners, Charles T. *s.j.* '50 (MIL) [P] Wauwatosa, WI Jesuit Community at St. Camillus.
Shinney, Robert J. *s.j.* '68 (SJ) [D] San Jose, CA Bellarmine College Preparatory.
Shinnick, Edward P. '56 (GF) Retired.
Shinnick, James F. '39 (B) Retired.
Shinnick, Patrick J. '69 (SAV) Macon, GA Holy Spirit Church.
Shinos, Robert '63 (ALB) Herkimer, NY St. Anthony-St. Joseph Church.
Shinsky, John C. *c.j.m.* '93 (SD) [M] San Diego, CA San Diego State University Newman Center.
Shipe, William '61 (Y) [3] Canton, OH Sacred Heart Church.
Shipley, Msgr. William L. '54 (SD) [B] San Diego, CA University of San Diego.
Shipp, Edmund M. '61 (SFR) [44] San Francisco, CA St. Peter Church; San Francisco, CA San Francisco General Hospital.
Shipps, Frank B. *o.p.* '85 (L) [46] Louisville, KY St. Louis Bertrand Church.
Shiraki, Gabriel *s.a.* '89 (NY) [Z] Garrison, NY Generalate of the Franciscan Friars of the Atonement-St. James Friary.
Shirey, John W. '43 (CHI) [114] Chicago, IL St. Kilian Church; Retired.
Shirey, Joseph E. *s.j.* '56 (P) White City, OR U.S. Veteran's Affiars Domiciliary; [J] Medford, OR Providence Medford Medical Center; [L] Portland, OR Jesuit Provincial Office (Oregon Prov.).
Shirilla, Gerald '68 (DET) Absent on Leave.
Shirima, Amadeus *s.j.* '92 (CHI) [C] Chicago, IL Jesuit Community at Loyola University of Chicago.
Shirley, John T. *o.s.a.* '65 (MIL) [8] Racine, WI St. Rita's Church.
Shirley, Msgr. Richard '67 (CC) [21] Corpus Christi, TX St. Pius X Church.
Shirley, Ronald R. '73 (MRY) [4] Salinas, CA Madonna Del Sasso Church.
Shiroda, Donald L. '59 (MAR) Sault Sainte Marie, MI St. Joseph Church.
Shiverski, John J. '68 (MAR) Negaunee, MI St. Paul Church.
Shlesinger, Bernard E., III '96 (R) Wilmington, NC St. Mary Church.
Shmaruk, Richard J. '65 (BO) [21] Boston, MA St. Columbkille Church.
Shmauz, Donald '60 (MAD) Madison, WI Mendota State Hospital.
Shmauz, Donald A. '60 (MIL) On Duty Outside the Archdiocese.
Shnob, Alan D. '78 (OG) Massena, NY St. Mary Church.
Shoback, Edward J. '67 (SCR) [23] Scranton, PA SS. Peter and Paul Church.
Shoback, Thomas P. '77 (SCR) Blossburg, PA St. Mary's Church.
Shockey, David P. '56 (COV) Retired; [M] Walton, KY St. William Convent.
Shocklee, Msgr. John A. '42 (STL) Retired.
Shoda, D. Brian '87 (WH) Inwood, WV St. Leo Church.
Shoda, Richard W. '78 (WH) [Q] Bethany, WV St. John Fisher Catholic Chapel; [Q] West Liberty, WV West Liberty State College, St. Thomas Aquinas Campus Ministry.
Shoemaker, Msgr. Samuel E. '66 (PH) Yardley, PA St. Ignatius of Antioch Church.
Shoemaker, Thomas R. '90 (FTW) [1] South Bend, IN St. Matthew Cathedral.
Sholander, Anthony E. *s.j.* '84 (SJ) [B] Santa Clara, CA Santa Clara University.
Shoneberger, Thomas (COL) [40] Columbus, OH St. Timothy Church.
Shonis, Anthony J. '71 (OWN) Non-Parochial Assignments; [A] Owensboro, KY Brescia College; [G] Maple Mount, KY Mount St. Joseph.
Shoppe Eric *o.f.m.* '45 (PAT) [M] Ringwood, NJ Holy Name Friary.
Shore, Ray '93 (BR) On Leave.
Shore, Zachary J. '81 (SFR) [35] San Francisco, CA Most Holy Redeemer Church.
Shori, Nicholas R. '74 (Y) New Middletown, OH St. Paul the Apostle Church.
Short, Anthony J. *s.j.* '71 (DEN) [M] Denver, CO Xavier Jesuit Center.
Short, Gregory J. *o.m.v.* '79 (MET) [H] Asbury, NJ Lanteri House.
Short, Joseph '90 (SFS) Clear Lake, SD St. Mary Church.
Short, Redemptus *o.c.d.* '47 (MIL) [P] Holy Hill, WI Discalced Carmelite Monastery.
Shortall, Robert '74 (DAL) Plano, TX St. Elizabeth Ann Seton Church.
Shortall, Robert '74 (DAV) On Duty Outside the Diocese.
Shorter, Melvin *c.p.* '86 (ATL) [11] Atlanta, GA St. Paul of the Cross Church.
Shortt, David J. '89 (PBR) Donora, PA St. Michael Church.
Shortt, Patrick J. (JC) Moberly, MO St. Pius X Church; Moberly, MO Missouri Training Center For Men.
Shott, Stephen E. *o.s.f.s.* '95 (WIL) [B] Wilmington, DE Salesianum School.
Shoup, Steven L. '84 (CIN) [11] Dayton, OH St. Henry Church.
Shovelton, Gerald T. *v.f.* '56 (FR) West Harwich, MA Holy Trinity Church.
Shovelton, William J. '46 (FR) Retired.
Showalter, Joseph L. *s.j.* '57 (P) [L] Portland, OR Jesuit Provincial Office (Oregon Prov.).
Showalter, Msgr. Paul E. '66 (PEO) [4] Rock Island, IL St. Pius X Church.
Showfety, Msgr. Joseph S. '55 (CHL) [2] Greensboro, NC St. Benedict Church.
Shrader, Dwight E. '82 (RIC) [7] Virginia Beach, VA St. John the Apostle Church.
Shreenan, Timothy J. *o.f.m.* '84 (NY) [35] New York, NY St. Francis of Assisi Church.
Shreve, Thomas F. '61 (RIC) [2] Richmond, VA Church of the Epiphany.
Shubiak, Stephen '88 (STF) Special Assignment; [F] Sloatsburg, NY Immaculate Conception Provincialate.
Shuda, Paul R. '60 (HBG) [8] Harrisburg, PA Our Lady of the Blessed Sacrament Church.
Shuda, Msgr. Robert J. '59 (GBG) [1] Greensburg, PA Blessed Sacrament Cathedral.
Shugrue, Michael P. '66 (R) [H] Durham, NC Catholic Student Center for Students at Duke University.
Shugrue, Msgr. Timothy J. '73 (NEW) Montclair, NJ Immaculate Conception Church.
Shuhler, Ralph V. *o.s.a.* '39 (PH) [Z] Villanova, PA St. Thomas Monastery.
Shuley, Keith '92 (CC) Military Chaplains.
Shulik, Bernard P. '74 (PIT) Monongahela, PA St. Anthony Church.
Shuman, Killian E. *t.o.r.* '59 (E) Ramey, PA Holy Trinity Church.
Shuppert, William T. '71 (TUC) [1] Tucson, AZ St. Augustine's Cathedral; Special Assignment.
Shurer, Ralph C. *o.s.a.* '54 (PH) [C] Villanova, PA Villanova University; [Z] Villanova, PA St. Thomas Monastery.
Shurtleff, F. James '66 (OG) Malone, NY St. Joseph's Church.
Shurtleff, Robert M. '70 (OG) Tupper Lake, NY Holy Name of Jesus Church.
Shust, Yaroslav '30 (STF) Retired.
Shuster, Anthony J. '70 (GF) [3] Great Falls, MT St. Joseph's Church.
Shuttleworth, Edward J. '90 (LC) Durand, WI St. Mary's Assumption Church; Lima, WI Holy Rosary Church.
Shwe, Jerome Aung (CHL) Morganton, NC St. Charles Borromeo Church.
Sibenik, Simeon B. '81 (PBR) Du Bois, PA Nativity of the Mother of God Church; Sykesville, PA Holy Trinity Church.
Sibilano, Joseph *o.s.j.* '65 (SCR) [M] Pittston, PA Eastern Province of the Oblates of St. Joseph.
Sibilano, Joseph D. *o.s.j.* '65 (NOR) [5] Middletown, CT St. Sebastian Church.
Sica, Joseph F. '82 (SCR) Tunkhannock, PA Nativity of Blessed Virgin Mary Church.
Sicard, Kenneth *o.p.* '90 (COL) [36] Columbus, OH St. Patrick Church.
Sicari, Joseph J. '82 (BUF) [H] Buffalo, NY The Catholic Charities of the Diocese of Buffalo.
Sicilia, Msgr. Pablo A. '60 (SAT) Carrizo Springs, TX Our Lady of Guadalupe Church.
Siciliano, Donald E. '93 (JC) Vandalia, MO Sacred Heart Church.
Siciliano, John M. '82 (WOR) [1] Fitchburg, MA St. Anthony of Padua Church.
Siciliano, Jude *o.p.* (R) [E] Raleigh, NC De Porres House.
Siciliano, Jude *o.p.* '69 (OAK) [N] Oakland, CA Order of Preachers (Southern Province).
Siciliano, Jude *o.p.* '69 (R) [E] Raleigh, NC Dominican Community.
Sickler, Robert *m.ss.a.* '87 (NOR) [A] Cromwell, CT Holy Apostles College and Seminary.
Sickler, Thomas G. *m.s.* '73 (WOR) [6] Fitchburg, MA St. Joseph's Church.
Sicoli, David C. '75 (PH) [14] Philadelphia, PA St. Anthony of Padua Church.
Siconolfi, Msgr. Constantine V. '59 (SCR) [7] Scranton, PA Holy Family Church; [R] Scranton, PA St. Francis of Assisi Kitchen.
Siconolfi, Michael *s.j.* '72 (SPK) [C] Spokane, WA Gonzaga University.
Siconolfi, Thomas *c.ss.r.* '70 (BAL) Annapolis, MD St. Mary Church; [M] Annapolis, MD Saint Mary Rectory.
Sidera, Joseph A. *c.s.c.* '68 (SCR) [C] Wilkes-Barre, PA Kings College.
Sides, Gary '73 (AMA) Panhandle, TX St. Theresa Church.
Sidler, Fred '92 (DAL) Ennis, TX St. John Nepomucene Church.

Sidler, Peter *o.s.b.* '46 (PRO) [P] Portsmouth, RI Abbey of St. Gregory the Great.
Sidney, Walter T. *s.j.* '78 (DEN) [D] Aurora, CO Regis Jesuit High School; [M] Aurora, CO Regis Jesuit High School - Jesuit Community.
Sidoti, Anthony '40 (ALB) [8] Albany, NY St. James Church; Retired.
Sidoti, James *o.carm.* '92 (BRK) [140] Brooklyn, NY St. Thomas Aquinas Church.
Siebenaler, John M. '61 (STP) Dayton, MN St. John the Baptist Church.
Siebenaler, Leonard '59 (STP) St. Michael, MN St. Michael Church.
Siebenaler, Martin J. '59 (STP) Waconia, MN St. Joseph Church.
Siebenand, Ambrose F. '41 (NU) Retired.
Siebenand, John N. '38 (NU) Retired.
Siebenand, Paul Alcuin '60 (LA) Avalon, CA St. Catherine of Alexandria Church.
Siebenand, Richard '67 (LA) [26] Los Angeles, CA Our Lady of Lourdes Church.
Siebeneck, Robert *c.pp.s.* '44 (CIN) [B] Carthagena, OH St. Charles.
Siebers, Glen F. *o.praem* '50 (GB) [I] De Pere, WI St. Norbert Abbey.
Siebert, Anthony G. '59 (STL) On Duty Outside the Archdiocese.
Siebert, Paul S. '86 (E) Ridgway, PA St. Leo the Great Church.
Siebert, William P. '79 (DET) [5] Sterling Heights, MI St. Malachy Church.
Siebold, Gerard F. *c.ss.r.* '58 (SAT) [37] San Antonio, TX St. Gerard Majella Church; [B] San Antonio, TX Redemptorist Seminary, Liguori House.
Siebor, John '58 (RVC) Hempstead, NY St. Ladislaus Church.
Siebs, Robert L. '49 (OKL) Absent on Leave.
Siecienski, A. Edward '95 (TR) Medford, NJ St. Mary of the Lakes Church.
Siedlecki, Aloysius M. '48 (BRK) Absent on Sick Leave.
Siedlicki, Edmund J. '52 (CHI) [T] Mundelein, IL Cardinal Stritch Retreat House.
Siefer, Richard R. '75 (E) Du Bois, PA St. Catherine Church; [P] Erie, PA Newman Centers and Campus Ministry.
Siefert, John S. '89 (STL) Leave of Absence.
Siefert, Ralph A. *s.m.* '73 (STL) [F] Creve Coeur, MO Chaminade College Preparatory School Inc.; [G] Creve Coeur, MO Chaminade College Preparatory.
Sieg, Leslie M. *c.s.p.* '76 (NY) [Z] Scarsdale, NY Paulist Fathers Generalate.
Sieg, Leslie M. *o.f.m.* '76 (P) Tigard, OR St. Anthony Church.
Sieg, Robert *o.f.m.* '75 (IND) [13] Indianapolis, IN Sacred Heart of Jesus Church.
Sieg, Thomas H. '71 (STP) Burnsville, MN Church of the Risen Savior.
Siegel, Joseph '88 (JOL) Plainfield, IL St. Mary Immaculate Church.
Siegel, Kenan *o.f.m.cap.* '56 (MIL) [B] Mount Calvary, WI St. Lawrence Seminary; [P] Mount Calvary, WI St. Lawrence Friary.
Siegfried, Gerard *c.s.sp.* '37 (ARE) Barceloneta, PR Church of Our Lady of Mt. Carmel.
Siekaniec, Ladislas *o.f.m.* '40 (STL) [P] St. Louis, MO Franciscan Friary of St. Anthony of Padua.
Siekierski, Msgr. John J. '67 (GRY) [13] East Chicago, IN St. Stanislaus Church.
Siekierski, Matthew J. '77 (WDC) La Plata, MD Sacred Heart Church.
Sielski, Joseph *m.i.c.* '41 (BAL) [K] Baltimore, MD St. Joseph's Nursing Home; [N] Baltimore, MD Sisters Servants of Mary Immaculate, Inc.
Sielski, Joseph *m.i.c.* '41 (WDC) [B] Washington, DC Marian Fathers Scholasticate.
Siemanowski, John S. '89 (CHI) Chicago Heights, IL St. Agnes Church.
Siener, Albert '46 (NSH) Retired.
Siener, Msgr. Leo C. '48 (KNX) Retired.
Sienkiewicz, Msgr. Alfred J. '43 (BGP) Retired.
Siepka, Richard W. '82 (BUF) [A] East Aurora, NY Christ the King Seminary.
Siepker, Dan '93 (DM) [C] Corning, IA Mercy Midlands: Mercy Hospital.
Siepker, Daniel E. '93 (DM) Corning, IA St. Patrick's Church.
Sieracki, Aloysius *o.carm.* '59 (JOL) [J] Darien, IL Carmelite Community.
Sieradski, Alfred A. *c.ss.r.* (STA) [6] Jacksonville, FL Holy Rosary Church.
Sierminski, Vernon '56 (SAG) Retired.
Sierocki, Paul E. '44 (DET) Retired.
Sierra, Daniel M. *o.s.m.* '92 (ELP) [18] El Paso, TX Our Lady of Sorrows Church.
Sierra, Francis A. '46 (SD) Retired.
Sierra, John A. *s.f.* '40 (WDC) [B] Silver Spring, MD Holy Family Seminary.
Sierra, Luis Alberto '73 (SJN) [4] Toa Alta, PR Nuestra Senora de la Medalla Milagrosa Church.
Sierra-Posada, Pedro J. '76 (ALX) [1] Alexandria, LA St. Francis Xavier Cathedral; Glenmora, LA St. Louis Church; [D] Forest Hill, LA Our Lady of Guadalupe Mission.
Siesle, John W. '75 (STL) [1] Lemay, MO Mary Queen of the Universe Church.
Sievel, Thomas A. '78 (HRT) [3] West Haven, CT St. Lawrence's Church.
Sieverding, Dale '89 (SFS) Graduate Studies.
Siffert, Etienne *s.m.* '58 (SFR) [37] San Francisco, CA Notre Dame des Victoires Church.
Siffrin, Robert '79 (Y) [9] Youngstown, OH St. Brendan's Church.
Sigaran, Mamerto (SFR) [42] San Francisco, CA St. Paul Church.
Sigler, Gary L. '79 (FTW) Huntington, IN St. Mary Church; Lagro, IN St. Patrick Church.
Sigler, John W. '94 (LA) Simi Valley, CA St. Rose of Lima Church.
Sigman, Louis A. '67 (PHX) [2] Phoenix, AZ Corpus Christi Church.
Sigmund, Andrew J. '64 (STL) Kimmswick, MO St. Joseph's Church.
Signey, Lawrence '37 (LA) La Canada Flintridge, CA St. Bede the Venerable Church.
Signiski, Michael M. '66 (CAM) [2] Cherry Hill, NJ Holy Rosary Church.
Signorelli Francis *s.x.* '59 (PAT) [M] Wayne, NJ Xaverian Missionary Fathers.
Siguan, Francis *o.s.j.* '81 (SCR) Exeter, PA St. Anthony of Padua Church.
Siguenza, Francisco *o.a.r.* '56 (ELP) [12] El Paso, TX Saint Therese of the Little Flower Parish Church.
Sigur, Msgr. Alexander O. '46 (LAF) Retired.
Sigwarth, Reynold J. '41 (DUB) Retired.
Sihuay, Francis X. *o.f.m.* '51 (WDC) [M] Washington, DC Commissariat of the Holy Land, Franciscan Monastery - Mount St. Sepulchre.
Sikiric, Grgo *t.o.r.* (PIT) [5] Millvale, PA St. Nicholas Church; [N] Pittsburgh, PA Croatian Commissariate, T.O.R.
Siklodi, Sandor '71 (CLV) [22] Cleveland, OH St. Emeric Church.
Sikon, Michael P. '96 (GBG) [1] Greensburg, PA Blessed Sacrament Cathedral.
Sikora, James M. '67 (NEW) On Duty Outside the Archdiocese.
Sikora, James R. '67 (GF) Special Assignment; [A] Great Falls, MT University of Great Falls.
Sikora, Msgr. Joseph G. '49 (PH) [39] Philadelphia, PA St. Dominic Church; Retired.
Sikorski, Andrew '29 (GR) Retired.
Sikorski, Harold R. '56 (SAG) On Duty Outside the Diocese.
Sikorski, Jeffery P. '73 (TOL) Maumee, OH St. Joseph Church.
Sikorski, Louis S. '64 (GAL) Anderson, TX St. Stanislaus Church.
Silcox, John D., Jr. '95 (PH) Exton, PA SS. Philip and James Church.
Sileo, Joseph R. '71 (WDC) [30] Washington, DC Nativity Church.
Siler, Francis A. '63 (PIT) [26] Pittsburgh, PA St. Mary of Mercy Church.
Siler, Paschal *o.f.m.cap.* '60 (GF) Ashland, MT St. Labre's Church.
Siliako, Petelo '86 (SPP) [8] Pago Pago, AS Church of Sacred Heart.
Silio, Antonio R. '88 (MIA) Pembroke Pines, FL St. Boniface Church.
Silipigni, Stephan A. '81 (PRO) Coventry, RI SS. John and Paul Church.
Silk, John D. '59 (BO) Amesbury, MA St. Joseph Church; Retired.
Silk, William J. '60 (WDC) [4] Bethesda, MD Our Lady of Lourdes Church.
Silko, Herbert *o.f.m.* '55 (MIL) [P] Burlington, WI Queen of Peace Friary.
Sill, Theodore '89 (COL) [30] Columbus, OH St. Mary Magdalene Church.
Silva, Alfredo (TUC) [8] Tucson, AZ Our Mother of Sorrows Church.
Silva, Alvaro '74 (BO) [V] Chestnut Hill, MA Opus Dei.
Silva, Alvaro '87 (SJN) [22] Bayamon, PR Sagrada Familia Church.
Silva, Caesar '74 (HT) [3] Houma, LA Maria Immacolata Church.
Silva, David E. '54 (CLV) Retired.
Silva, Edwin Lugo '89 (MGZ) [5] Mayaquez, PR Nuestra Senora De Fatima Church.
Silva, Francis J. *s.j.* '42 (SJ) [D] San Jose, CA Bellarmine College Preparatory.
Silva, Frank J. '76 (BO) [1] Malden, MA Immaculate Conception Church.
Silva, Ismael '79 (ORG) [1] Santa Ana, CA Immaculate Heart of Mary Church.
Silva, James M. '67 (PRO) Retired.
Silva, John F. '34 (BO) Retired.
Silva, Jose D. '51 (HRT) [4] Hartford, CT Our Lady of Fatima Church.
Silva, Juan '92 (LA) [93] Los Angeles, CA St. Thomas the Apostle Church.
Silva, Langes '95 (SLC) [1] Salt Lake City, UT Cathedral of the Madeleine; [2] Salt Lake City, UT Our Lady of Guadalupe Church.
Silva, Larry '75 (OAK) [2] Oakland, CA St. Andrew-St. Joseph Church.
Silva, Miguel '84 (SAC) Corning, CA Immaculate Conception Church; Orland, CA St. Dominic Church.
Silva, Robert J. '65 (STO) [10] Stockton, CA Presentation of B.V.M. Church.
Silveira, Eduino '87 (SAC) [12] Sacramento, CA St. Elizabeth Church; Special Assignment.
Silver, Jeffrey P. '84 (CIN) [3] Hamilton, OH St. Julie Billiart Church.
Silver, John '92 (OG) Peru, NY St. Augustine Church.
Silver, Martin J. '54 (NEW) [3] Hackensack, NJ St. Joseph's Church.
Silveri, Donato P. '64 (PH) [99] Philadelphia, PA St. Mary Magdalen de Pazzi Church.
Silverio, Gilbert J. *o.f.m.* (FR) [K] Onset, MA St. Joseph Novitiate-Franciscan Friars.
Silverman, Robert '67 (SAT) [44] San Antonio, TX St. John Neumann Church; [T] San Antonio, TX The Blue Army.
Silvers, Rudolph M. '75 (PIT) Bulger, PA St. Ann Church.
Silvester, George E. *c.s.b.* '46 (GAL) Sugar Land, TX St. Theresa Church.
Silvester, Peter *s.v.d.* '78 (TR) [M] Bordentown, NJ Society of the Divine Word.
Silvestri, Luke '52 (PHX) Camp Verde, AZ St. Frances Cabrini Church.
Silvestri, Luke A. '52 (SCR) On Duty Outside the Diocese.
Silvestri, Vincent A. '64 (MIL) Retired.
Silvestrini, Dino F. '85 (MAR) Menominee, MI Resurrection Church.
Silvestro, Dominic '60 (SPR) [L] Springfield, MA St. Francis of Assisi Chapel and Catholic Information Center.
Silvia, Kenneth *c.s.c.* (SJ) Saratoga, CA Sacred Heart Church.
Sima, John R. *s.j.* '71 (CHI) [N] Chicago, IL Chicago Province of the Society of Jesus-Provincial Office.
Simard, Robert E. '56 (BAK) Prineville, OR St. Joseph's Church.
Simas, Msgr. Manuel C. '61 (OAK) [4] Fremont, CA St. Joseph Mission Church.
Simboli, Ronald L. '75 (GBG) Apollo, PA St. James the Greater Church.
Simburger, R. Joseph '79 (SFD) Military Chaplains.
Simcox, Thomas *s.c.j.* '40 (SP) [O] Pinellas Park, FL Priests of the Sacred Heart.
Simeone, Francis P. *o.s.f.s.* (R) Shallotte, NC St. Brendan the Navigator Church.
Simeone, Gary F. '75 (HRT) East Haven, CT St. Vincent de Paul's Church.
Simeone, Ronald P. '82 (PRO) [2] Johnston, RI Our Lady of Grace Church.
Simington, Ralph P. '62 (DUB) Manchester, IA St. Mary's Church; [E] Manchester, IA St. Paul's School of Religion.
Simko, James G. '91 (DEN) Estes Park, CO Our Lady of the Mountains Church.
Simko, Michael S. '44 (NEW) Retired.
Simlik, Frank P. '54 (PHX) Sun City, AZ Church of St. Joachim & St. Anne.
Simmions, James S. '68 (E) [11] Erie, PA Sacred Heart Church.
Simmons, Msgr. Donald W. '43 (B) Retired.
Simmons, Franklin '79 (GAL) [72] Houston, TX St. Rose of Lima Church; [K] Houston, TX The Catholic Chaplain Corps.
Simmons, Hilary F. '43 (LC) Retired.
Simmons, Jerome '68 (E) [O] Erie, PA Ecclesia Center.
Simmons, Joseph C. '61 (BAL) Joppa, MD Church of the Holy Spirit.
Simmons, Norman *c.ss.r.* '73 (PH) [25] Philadelphia, PA St. Boniface Church.
Simmons, Msgr. Walter E. '55 (RVC) Port Washington, NY St. Peter of Alcantara Church.
Simmons, William B. *c.s.c.* '52 (FTW) [L] Notre Dame, IN Holy Cross Mission House.
Simms, William '62 (BAL) [89] Baltimore, MD St. Thomas Aquinas Church; Special Assignment.
Simodejka, Msgr. Michael A. '40 (PBR) Aliquippa, PA St. George Church.
Simoes, Gilbert '61 (FR) Absent on Leave.
Simon, Ambrose '50 (GB) [I] Appleton, WI St. Fidelis Friary.
Simon, Bernard '42 (SP) Retired.
Simon, Brian '96 (SFS) [2] Sioux Falls, SD Christ the King Church.
Simon, Carl A. '71 (LAN) Deerfield, MI St. Augustine Church.
Simon, David P. '67 (ROC) Apalachin, NY St. Margaret Mary Church.
Simon, Eugene P. *s.j.* '57 (DET) [P] Bloomfield Hills, MI Manresa Jesuit Retreat House; [T] Detroit, MI Jesuit Seminary Association.
Simon, George H. '57 (LAF) Scott, LA Saint Martin de Porres Church.

Simon, John A. '76 (MET) On Duty Outside the Diocese.
Simon, John L. '73 (MIL) Beaver Dam, WI St. Peter's Church.
Simon, Joseph *s.v.d.* '61 (BLX) [A] Bay St. Louis, MS St. Augustine's.
Simon, Joseph M. '71 (STL) Webster Groves, MO Holy Redeemer Church.
Simon, Julian *o.s.b.* '45 (CGS) [C] Humacao, PR San Antonio Abad Abbey of the Order of St. Benedict.
Simon, Martin M. '55 (MIL) Retired.
Simon, Raphael *o.c.s.o.* '47 (WOR) [N] Spencer, MA St. Joseph's Abbey.
Simon, Richard T. '75 (CHI) [205] Chicago, IL St. Thomas of Canterbury Church.
Simon, Robert *c.ss.r.* '48 (B) Coeur D'Alene, ID St. Thomas Church.
Simon, Robert G. *c.s.c.* '61 (FTW) [J] South Bend, IN Congregation of Holy Cross Indiana Province Provincial House.
Simon, Robert J. '90 (SCR) Clarks Summit, PA Our Lady of the Snows Church.
Simon, Vincent J. '46 (DUB) Retired.
Simonds, Donald D. *m.s.* '63 (HRT) [M] Hartford, CT Missionaries of LaSalette Provincial Secretary.
Simone, Earl Francis '77 (CIN) [22] Dayton, OH St. Peter Church.
Simone, Michael A. *m.m.* '56 (NY) [Z] Maryknoll, NY Maryknoll Fathers and Brothers.
Simoneau, Norman J. '67 (MAN) On Duty Outside the Diocese.
Simoneau, Norman J. '67 (SR) Fortuna, CA St. Joseph Church.
Simoneau, Ronald L. '78 (PRO) Greenville, RI St. Philip's Church.
Simoneaux, Jody '82 (LAF) [11] Lafayette, LA St. Genevieve Church.
Simonelli, Gerald '90 (JOL) Bolingbrook, IL St. Dominic Church.
Simonetti, Gennaro M. '38 (BRK) [103] Brooklyn, NY Our Lady of Miracles Church; Retired.
Simoni, Salvador '80 (CHI) Northlake, IL St. John Baptist Vianney, Cure of Ars Church.
Simonin, Msgr. John A. '47 (CHR) [2] Charleston, SC St. Mary's Church.
Simonini, Michael F. '75 (RCK) Active Outside the Diocese.
Simonnet, Philippe *s.s.e.* '52 (BUR) [G] Colchester, VT Society of St. Edmund.
Simons, Derek *s.v.d.* '70 (CHI) [B] Techny, IL Divine Word Residence; [N] Chicago, IL Divine Word Theologate; [N] Techny, IL Society of the Divine Word, Provincial Headquarter-Chicago Prov.
Simons, Edward J. *o.s.f.s.* '43 (PH) [Z] Philadelphia, PA Oblates of St. Francis De Sales.
Simons, Lawrence D. '48 (HEL) Retired.
Simons, Msgr. Richard J. '38 (PH) Newtown Square, PA St. Anastasia Church; Retired.
Simons, Thomas G. '77 (GR) [2] Muskegon, MI St. Francis de Sales Church.
Simonson, Earl C. '69 (STP) [22] Minneapolis, MN St. Clement Church.
Simpson, Brian C. '72 (CHI) Military Chaplains.
Simpson, David *o.carm.* '70 (NEW) [P] Mahwah, NJ Carmel Retreat House.
Simpson, Gerald T. '57 (STL) Neier, MO St. Joseph's Church.
Simpson, Kenneth C. '78 (CHI) [V] Chicago, IL Ministry in Higher Education.
Simpson, Mark '79 (CHI) Winnetka, IL Sacred Heart Church.
Simpson, Mauro *o.s.b.* '52 (CGS) Humacao, PR Maria Reina de la Paz Church.
Simpson, Robert A. '65 (RNO) [4] Reno, NV St. Albert the Great Church.
Simpson, Roger '52 (SFD) Retired.
Sims, Henry F.H. '51 (PRT) Retired.
Sims, Paul *c.r.* '86 (CHI) [D] Chicago, IL Gordon Technical High School.
Sims, Robert W. '71 (IND) Leave of Absence.
Sinasac, Alvin A. *c.s.b.* '78 (GAL) [B] Houston, TX Casa San Basilio.
Sinatra, Leonard '67 (PHU) Northampton, PA St. John the Baptist Church.
Sinatra, William D. '64 (DET) [4] Southfield, MI St. Ives Church.
Sinclair, Alexander B. '57 (KC) [36] Kansas City, MO St. Raphael the Archangel Church.
Sinclair, Calvin F. *s.s.j.* '79 (BAL) [M] Baltimore, MD St. Joseph's Manor.
Sinclair, Roger A. (BO) Boston, MA V.A. Medical Centers.
Sinclair, Roger A. '74 (GBG) Military Chaplains.
Sindik, Msgr. George E. '59 (PT) [13] Pensacola, FL St. Paul Church.
Sindik, Matthew A. '62 (MOB) [6] Montgomery, AL St. Jude Church; [F] Montgomery, AL City of St. Jude, Inc., The; [L] Montgomery, AL The City of St. Jude, Inc.
Sindler, Jeffrey R. (BAL) [F] Baltimore, MD St. Ignatius Loyola Academy.
Singarayar, Philip *o.m.i.* '64 (WDC) [B] Washington, DC Oblates of Mary Immaculate, De Mazenod Residence.
Singelyn, Robert K. '60 (DET) On Duty Outside the Archdiocese.
Singer, Jerome C. '63 (DET) [52] Detroit, MI Nativity of Our Lord Church.
Singer, Thomas J. *o.m.i.* '57 (STP) [N] St. Paul, MN Oblate Provincial Offices; [N] St. Paul, MN Oblate Residence.
Singler, Charles E. '84 (TOL) Perrysburg, OH St. Rose Church.
Singler, James E. '82 (CLV) Cleveland Heights, OH St. Ann Church.
Singler, John P. '82 (CLV) Willowick, OH St. Mary Magdalene Church.
Singleton, William (RVC) Retired.
Singleton, William V. '50 (RVC) East Rockaway, NY St. Raymond's Church.
Sinibaldi, Daniel I. '96 (MAN) Merrimack, NH Our Lady of Mercy Church.
Sinisi, Daniel *t.o.r.* '66 (STU) [A] Steubenville, OH Franciscan University of Steubenville; [F] Steubenville, OH Holy Spirit Monastery.
Siniskey, Joseph M. '48 (ALB) East Greenbush, NY Holy Spirit Church.
Sinisky, Joseph '48 (ALB) Retired.
Sinkler, Michael D. '81 (LR) Bentonville, AR St. Stephen Church; Rogers, AR St. Vincent de Paul Church.
Sinnema, Paul *o.f.m.* '63 (NEW) East Rutherford, NJ St. Joseph's Church; Wood-Ridge, NJ Our Lady of the Assumption Church.
Sinner, Msgr. Emil E. '42 (SAL) Retired.
Sinner, Richard W. '52 (FAR) Retired.
Sinnerud, James A. *s.j.* '72 (OM) [C] Omaha, NE Creighton Preparatory School.
Sinnige, J. C. '36 (LAF) Retired.
Sinor, Michael J. '88 (SD) Calexico, CA Our Lady of Guadalupe Church.
Sinski, Norbert J. *c.s.c.* '77 (FTW) [J] South Bend, IN Congregation of Holy Cross Indiana Province Provincial House.
Sinz, Eugene R. '60 (STL) High Ridge, MO St. Anthony of Padua Church.
Siok, Slavomir *s.a.c.* '90 (BUF) Lewiston, NY St. Peter Church; [O] North Tonawanda, NY Society of the Catholic Apostolate.
Siola, Roman *o.f.m.conv.* '56 (BUF) [21] Buffalo, NY Corpus Christi Church.
Sioleti, Andrew *o.f.m.* (NY) Manhattan, NY Cabrini Medical Center.
Sioleti, Andrew *o.f.m.conv.* '84 (NEW) [2] Hoboken, NJ St. Joseph's Church.
Sipaco, Cecilio E. '67 (MET) [F] New Brunswick, NJ St. Peter's Medical Center.
Sipe, Robert J. '59 (STP) Forest Lake, MN St. Peter Church.
Siple, Donald M. *o.s.m.* '92 (CHI) [N] Chicago, IL Servite Friars - Eastern Province; [N] Chicago, IL Servite Friars - Eastern Province.
Siple, Donald M. *o.s.m.* '92 (ORG) [H] Buena Park, CA Servite Fathers And Brothers.
Siple, William R. '92 (PIT) [16] Pittsburgh, PA Immaculate Conception Church; [20] Pittsburgh, PA St. Joseph Church.
Sippel, Bernard S. '65 (MIL) Germantown, WI St. Boniface Church.
Sippel, David E. *s.j.* '61 (NY) [Z] New York, NY Murray-Weigel Hall.
Sippel, Edward F. '47 (MIL) Retired.
Sipperly, Edward '53 (ALB) [8] Amsterdam, NY St. Stanislaus Church.
Sipulski, Vianney *o.f.m.* '60 (GB) Hofa Park, WI St. Stanislaus Church.
Siracuse, Guy F. '67 (BUF) [4] Buffalo, NY St. Agnes Church.
Sirba, Joseph '87 (DUL) Aurora, MN Holy Rosary Church; Hoyt Lakes, MN Queen of Peace Church.
Sirba, Paul D. '86 (STP) [A] St. Paul, MN St. John Vianney Seminary; [C] St. Paul, MN University of St. Thomas.
Siriani, Klaus-Werner J. '78 (WDC) Military Chaplains.
Sirianni, Anthony '89 (MET) [2] New Brunswick, NJ St. John the Baptist Church; New Brunswick, NJ Robert Wood Johnson University Hospital.
Sirianni, Jasper F. '46 (DET) Emmett, MI Our Lady of Mount Carmel Church; Retired.
Sirianni, Louis A. '74 (ROC) [22] Rochester, NY Holy Family Church.
Sirianni, Richard D. '78 (P) [23] Portland, OR St. Mary Magdalene Church.
Sirianni, Sam A. '84 (TR) [3] Trenton, NJ Holy Angels Church.
Sirico, Robert *c.s.p.* '89 (GR) Grand Rapids, MI Chapel of St. Paul-Catholic Information Center.
Sirico, Robert A. *c.s.p.* '89 (NY) [Z] Scarsdale, NY Paulist Fathers Generalate.
Sirois, George *o.m.i.* '53 (PRT) Lincoln, ME St. Mary Church.
Sirois, Gerald *s.d.s.* '61 (GB) St. Nazianz, WI St. Gregory Church.
Sirois, Msgr. Joseph V. '51 (WOR) [5] Worcester, MA Holy Name of Jesus Church.
Sirois, Lionel *c.ss.r.* '38 (LA) Whittier, CA St. Mary of the Assumption Church; [R] Whittier, CA Redemptorist Fathers Mission House.
Siroki, David (PSC) Leave of Absence.
Sirolli, Francis A. *o.s.a.* '65 (PH) [130] Philadelphia, PA Our Mother of Consolation Church.
Siroskey, P. Larry '80 (DET) Allen Park, MI St. Frances Cabrini Church.
Sirvent-Dominguez, Francisco '87 (PCE) Penuelas, PR St. Joseph Church; [B] Ponce, PR The Pontifical Catholic University of Puerto Rico.
Siry, Philip L. '62 (WIL) Delaware City, DE St. Paul Church; Delaware City, DE Governor Bacon Health Center.
Sis, Michael J. '86 (AUS) College Station, TX St. Mary's Church; [M] College Station, TX St. Mary's Catholic Center.
Sise, John '45 (ALB) Retired.
Sisk, Richard J. *s.j.* '51 (SPK) [K] Spokane, WA Regis Community.
Sisk, William *o.f.m.* '48 (SPK) [11] Spokane, WA St. Francis of Assisi, Friars Church.
Siska, Ernest J. '60 (TR) [21] Trenton, NJ St. Raphael Church.
Sison, Alden '87 (LA) Woodland Hills, CA St. Bernardine of Siena Church.
Sison, Bernabe '65 (NY) [94] New York, NY Our Lady of Pompeii Church.
Sisul, Paul A. '72 (CHI) [N] Chicago, IL Vincentian Community, Congregation of the Mission, Midwest Province.
Sitar, Richard T. '79 (GAY) Retired.
Sitko, Joseph S. '68 (SCR) Forest City, PA Sacred Heart of Jesus Church.
Sito, Joseph '62 (DET) Retired.
Sitter, Leonard F. *s.j.* '61 (SPK) [C] Spokane, WA Gonzaga University.
Sittinger, Edward J. *s.t.* '77 (LA) [27] Los Angeles, CA Our Lady of Victory Church.
Sitzmann, Eugene E. '62 (SC) Cherokee, IA St. Dymphna Church; Maryhill, IA Visitation of the B.V.M. Church; Cherokee, IA State Mental Health Institute.
Sitzmann, Richard A. '62 (SC) [3] Sioux City, IA St. Boniface Church; Sioux City, IA Marian Health Center; [D] Sioux City, IA Marian Health Center.
Siu, Robert K.C. '54 (CHY) Lander, WY Holy Rosary Church; In Residence.
Siu, Robert K.C. '54 (HON) Retired.
Sivillo, Msgr. Nicholas W. '64 (BRK) [212] Queens, NY Our Lady of Hope Church.
Sivinsky, Wasyl '92 (PHU) [5] Philadelphia, PA St. Nicholas Church.
Sivore, Victor J. '64 (CHI) [3] Lemont, IL SS. Cyril and Methodius Church.
Sivric, Ivo *o.f.m.* '41 (STL) [44] St. Louis, MO St. Joseph Church.
Siwek, Daniel S. '73 (CHI) [A] Mundelein, IL University of St. Mary of the Lake-Mundelein Seminary.
Siwek, Jerome S. '56 (CHI) [184] Chicago, IL St. Richard Church.
Sizelove, Dennis M. '90 (NO) Military Chaplains.
Sizemore, David W. '96 (COL) Dublin, OH St. Brigid of Kildare Church.
Sizing, Theodore '55 (SY) Retired.
Skach, Charles J. (CHI) Retired.
Skaff, Elias B. '36 (NTN) Retired.
Skagen, Robert '70 (PHX) [2] Glendale, AZ St. Helen Church.
Skaj, John P. *c.s.sp.* '63 (PIT) Emsworth, PA Sacred Heart Church.
Skalb, Antoni '81 (STL) [P] St. Louis, MO La Salette Missionaries.
Skalko, J. Dominic *o.p.* '39 (PRO) [P] Providence, RI St. Thomas Aquinas Priory at Providence College.
Skalski, Francis S. '56 (DET) [35] Detroit, MI St. Hyacinth Church.
Skalsky, Ted A. '72 (DOD) Pratt, KS Sacred Heart Church.
Skarbek, Richard *m.ss.a.* '86 (NOR) [A] Cromwell, CT Holy Apostles College and Seminary; [F] Cromwell, CT Missionaries of the Holy Apostles.
Skarohlid, Robert F. '88 (FAR) Lakota, ND St. Mary's Church.
Skaskiw, Bohdan '80 (STN) Retired.
Skeabeck, Andrew *c.ss.r.* '47 (TR) [Q] Long Branch, NJ San Alfonso Retreat House.
Skechus, Francis E. *s.j.* '75 (PH) [G] Philadelphia, PA St. Joseph's Preparatory School; [Z] Philadelphia, PA Jesuit Community at St. Joseph's University.
Skeehan, William K. '60 (TLS) Bartlesville, OK St. James Church.
Skehan, James W. *s.j.* '54 (BO) [W] Chestnut Hill, MA The Jesuit Community at Boston College.
Skehan, John A. '52 (PMB) [4] Delray Beach, FL St. Vincent Ferrer Church.
Skehan, John R. '86 (PRT) Special or Other Diocesan Assignment.

Skehan, Msgr. Martin O. '44 (YAK) Moses Lake, WA Our Lady of Fatima Church; Retired.
Skelly, Francis *c.ss.r.* '72 (NY) [150] Bronx, NY Immaculate Conception Church.
Skelly, Msgr. John J. '53 (RVC) Manhasset, NY St. Mary's Church.
Skelly, Laurence J. *s.j.* '56 (BO) [W] Weston, MA Campion Health Center, Inc.
Skelly, Msgr. Richard J. '54 (PH) Morton, PA Our Lady of Perpetual Help Church.
Skelton, Paul H. '64 (SFD) Hume, IL St. Michael Church; Villa Grove, IL Sacred Heart Church.
Skenderovic, Ivan '76 (BUF) Alden, NY St. John the Baptist Church.
Skeris, Robert A. '61 (ARL) [A] Front Royal, VA Christendom College.
Skeris, Robert A. '61 (MIL) On Duty Outside the Archdiocese.
Skerl, Alphonse '55 (GRY) [3] East Chicago, IN Holy Trinity Church.
Skerry, Donald *s.v.d.* '62 (BO) [W] Boston, MA Divine Word Missionaries.
Skertich, Mark J. '77 (PIT) Ellsworth, PA Ave Maria Church.
Skiba, Andrew *o.f.m.conv.* '47 (SPR) [5] Holyoke, MA Mater Dolorosa Church.
Skiba, Walter F. '56 (SCR) Wyoming, PA St. Joseph's Church.
Skillin, Harmon D. *j.c.d.* '60 (STO) [7] Stockton, CA St. Luke Church.
Skillingst, M. Delmar '60 (SPK) [C] Spokane, WA Gonzaga University.
Skindeleski, Thomas J. '71 (PH) On Duty Outside the Archdiocese.
Skindeleski, Thomas J. '71 (PMB) [3] Boca Raton, FL St. Joan of Arc Church.
Skinner, Charles D. '53 (E) Retired.
Skinner, Mary (ROC) [M] Rochester, NY Diocesan Office of Campus Ministry.
Skinta, Stephen J. *o.s.b.m.* '59 (PSC) [B] Matawan, NJ Basilian Fathers of Mariapoch.
Skirkus, Joseph K. '28 (PEO) Retired.
Skirtich, John '90 (PIT) [6] Ambridge, PA Good Samaritan Church.
Skitzki, Francis P. '70 (SCR) Duryea, PA Holy Rosary Church.
Skluzacek, Michael C. '80 (STP) Stillwater, MN St. Michael Church; [H] Stillwater, MN St. Croix Catholic Educational Programs.
Skoczylas, Walter '75 (CR) On Duty Outside the Diocese.
Skok, Charles D. '52 (SPK) [13] Spokane, WA St. John Vianney Church.
Skoneki, William J. (MOB) [4] Mobile, AL St. Dominic Church.
Skonezny, Ray '61 (ORG) Irvine, CA St. John Neumann Church.
Skonny, Thomas F. *o.c.s.o.* '51 (ATL) [I] Conyers, GA The Monastery of the Holy Spirit.
Skonseng, Dennis A. '82 (FAR) Special Assignment; [A] Fargo, ND Cardinal Muench Seminary.
Skornia, Bernard L. '57 (SAG) Retired.
Skorup, Ildephonse *o.f.m.* '59 (CHI) [65] Chicago, IL St. Francis de Sales Church; [N] Countryside, IL St. Gratian Friary, Franciscan Friars.
Skotek, Thomas D. '63 (SCR) [1] Wilkes-Barre, PA St. Aloysius Church.
Skotnicki, Andrew *o.carm.* '77 (WDC) [B] Washington, DC Whitefriars Hall.
Skowronski, John P. '36 (SPR) [10] Springfield, MA Our Lady of the Rosary Church.
Skrapits, John '51 (BUF) [22] Buffalo, NY St. Elizabeth of Hungary Church.
Skriba, Raymond F. '57 (CHI) Round Lake, IL St. Joseph Church.
Skriba, Richard L. '49 (CHI) [181] Chicago, IL Queen of the Universe Church; Retired.
Skrincosky, Msgr. Peter '47 (STF) [A] Stamford, CT St. Basil College.
Skrypek, Gregory A. '70 (STP) Stillwater, MN Minnesota State Prison.
Skrzypiec, Andrzej '82 (SLC) [3] Magna, UT Our Lady of Lourdes Church.
Skudlarek, William *o.s.b.* '64 (SCL) [I] Collegeville, MN St. John's Abbey, of the Order of St. Benedict.
Skufca, Ronald J. '79 (MAR) [3] Escanaba, MI St. Patrick Church.
Skupien, Edward D. '37 (CHI) [21] Chicago, IL St. Barbara Church; Retired.
Skupien, Msgr. Francis M. '51 (BUF) Retired.
Skupien, Msgr. Joseph F. (BUF) Retired.
Skura, Mark David *ofm conv.* '82 (BUF) [D] Athol Springs, NY St. Francis High School; [O] Athol Springs, NY St. Francis of Assisi Friary.
Skurla, Anthony *o.f.m.* (PSC) [B] Sybertsville, PA Holy Dormition Monastery.
Skurla, Anthony *o.f.m.* '54 (PHU) [E] Sybertsville, PA Holy Dormition Monastery.
Skurla, Robert J. '56 (PSC) Jersey City, NJ St. Mary's Church.
Skurla, William '87 (VNN) Tucson, AZ St. Melany Church.
Skwara, John M. '59 (MET) South Plainfield, NJ Our Lady of Czestochowa Church.
Skwor, Donald *s.d.s.* '53 (MIL) [P] Milwaukee, WI Salvatorian Provincial Residence.
Skyva, Joseph '72 (BO) Randolph, MA St. Bernadette Church.
Slacke, Varian *o.f.m.* '44 (CIN) [C] Cincinnati, OH St. Anthony Shrine, Francisan Candidacy.
Sladek, Robert F. '47 (GB) Black Creek, WI St. Mary Church; Retired.
Sladicka, Phillip J. '76 (SCR) Muncy, PA Resurrection Church; Muncy, PA Muncy Prison.
Slafkosky, Andrew L. '38 (ORL) Retired.
Slafkosky, Andrew L. '38 (PH) Pottstown, PA Holy Trinity Church; Retired.
Slampak, John A. '66 (RCK) Byron, IL St. Mary Church.
Slane, Anthony *c.ss.r.* '42 (SEA) [32] Seattle, WA Sacred Heart of Jesus Church.
Slate, William '55 (SEA) Retired.
Slater, Dennis W. (SY) Special Assignment.
Slater, Ed '82 (CIN) [M] Cincinnati, OH St. Francis Center.
Slater, Msgr. John J. '52 (E) Retired.
Slater, William T. '77 (RVC) New Hyde Park, NY Notre Dame Church.
Slatterie, Leo '51 (LAV) Caliente, NV Holy Child Church.
Slatterie, Leo '51 (P) [Q] Beaverton, OR Our Lady of Peace Institute in Catholic Teaching.
Slattery, Dennis J. *m.m.* '37 (NY) [Z] Maryknoll, NY Maryknoll Fathers and Brothers.
Slattery, Edmund *s.s.s.* '40 (NY) [55] New York, NY St. Jean Baptiste Church; Manhattan, NY Lenox Hill Hospital.
Slattery, James F. '41 (ROC) Pittsford, NY St. Louis Church; Retired.
Slattery, John F. '57 (COS) [1] Colorado Springs, CO St. Mary's Cathedral.
Slattery, Msgr. John T. '54 (SB) Lucerne Valley, CA St. Paul Church; Retired.
Slattery, Joseph A. '66 (RIC) On Duty Outside the Diocese.
Slattery, Ken '94 (SP) Dunedin, FL Our Lady of Lourdes Church.
Slattery, Kenneth F. *c.m.* '48 (BRK) [D] Queens and Staten Island, NY St. John's University; [U] Jamaica, NY Vincentian Residence.
Slattery, Kevin '86 (JKS) Oxford, MS St. John Church; [G] Oxford, MS University of Mississippi Newman Center.
Slattery, Maurice C. '55 (NY) Absent on Sick leave; [Z] New York, NY Our Lady of Consolation Residence.
Slattery, Michael *o.m.i.* '41 (SAT) [K] San Antonio, TX Oblate Madonna Residence.
Slattery, Michael *o.s.a.* '77 (CHI) [N] Chicago, IL St. John Stone Friary.
Slattery, Michael J. '62 (LA) Granada Hills, CA St. John Baptist de la Salle Church.
Slattery, William *l.c.* '91 (NY) [Z] Rye, NY Legionaries of Christ.
Slaughter, Martin '85 (LA) Pico Rivera, CA St. Marianne de Paredes Church.
Slaven, Donald J. '64 (SC) Graduate Studies.
Slaven, Frederick '59 (Y) Louisville, OH St. Louis Church.
Slavish, Richard '59 (PEO) Matherville, IL St. Anthony's Church.
Sleasman, Martin J. *c.m.* '42 (BUF) [O] Niagara University, NY Vincentian Community at Niagara University.
Sledesky, Stephen '93 (HRT) Suffield, CT Sacred Heart Church.
Sledz, Stanley V. '69 (STP) [16] St. Paul, MN St. Bernard Church.
Sledzaus, Alexander L. '50 (RVC) Patchogue, NY Our Lady of Mt. Carmel Church; Retired.
Sledziona, John S. *c.m.* '70 (HRT) [M] Manchester, CT DePaul Provincial Residence.
Slejzer, Ferdinand E. '53 (BO) Retired.
Slemba, Dominic *o.f.m.conv.* '51 (BAL) [M] Ellicott City, MD Order of Friars Minor Conventual.
Slepicka, Msgr. Joseph J. '55 (DUB) Clear Lake, IA St. Patrick's Church.
Slesinski, Robert '76 (PSC) Bethlehem, PA SS. Peter and Paul Church.
Slesinski, Sebastian *o.f.m.conv.* '51 (FR) [7] New Bedford, MA Our Lady of Perpetual Help Church.
Sleszynski, Darius '66 (BO) Ashland, MA St. Cecilia Church.
Slevin, Henry '62 (WDC) [13] Washington, DC St. Francis de Sales Church; On Duty Outside the Archdiocese.
Slevin, Patrick C. '57 (MIA) [12] Fort Lauderdale, FL St. Pius X Church.
Slezak, Raymond P. '74 (ALN) Shepptor, PA St. Joseph Church.
Slight, William *m.s.* '65 (FR) [K] Attleboro, MA La Salette Provincial House.
Slikas, William L. '86 (JOL) Piper City, IL St. Peter Church.
Slimak, Bernard *o.s.b.* '40 (CLV) [P] Cleveland, OH Benedictine Order of Cleveland.
Slinger, Msgr. Joseph T. '70 (NEW) Belleville, NJ St. Peter's Church.
Slipe, Robert H. '73 (NEW) River Edge, NJ St. Peter the Apostle Church.
Slipski, William P. '46 (Y) Retired.
Slisz, Charles E. '71 (BUF) [4] Cheektowaga, NY St. Josaphat Church.
Slivonik, Stanley '69 (ARL) Retired.
Sliwiak, Stanley A. '66 (CC) Alice, TX St. Elizabeth Church.
Sloan, Daniel *i.c.* '41 (VEN) Bradenton, FL Sacred Heart Church.
Sloan, Daniel '82 (MET) Manville, NJ Christ the King Church.
Sloan, James *c.pp.s.* '62 (OAK) [N] Berkeley, CA Society of the Precious Blood.
Slobig, Charles *o.carm.* '34 (L) [B] Louisville, KY St. Francis DeSales High School.
Slobig, John '90 (PHX) [4] Glendale, AZ St. Louis The King Church.
Slobogin, Roland D. (PH) [107] Philadelphia, PA Most Blessed Sacrament Church.
Slocum, Samuel B. '80 (E) Eldred, PA St. Raphael Church.
Slodowski, Bronislaw '68 (MIL) [40] Milwaukee, WI St. Hyacinth's Church.
Slodowski, Bruno '68 (MIL) Awaiting Assignment.
Slomba, Eugene S. '64 (BUF) [4] Batavia, NY Sacred Heart Church; [3] Cheektowaga, NY St. John Gualbert Church.
Slominski, Fabian B. '48 (DET) Pontiac, MI St. Joseph Church; Retired.
Slominski, George A. '38 (CHI) Retired; [D] Chicago, IL Maria High School.
Slominski, Leon '58 (SCL) Luxemburg, MN St. Wendelin's Church.
Slomski, Joseph P. '53 (WCH) Chase, KS St. Mary Church.
Slon, Thomas R. *s.j.* '90 (SCR) [C] Scranton, PA University of Scranton.
Slonecki, Michael *o.f.m.conv.* '41 (SPR) [5] Chicopee, MA St. Anthony's Church.
Slosarcik, Edward A. (CHI) Retired.
Slota, Frederick V. '53 (PRO) [2] Providence, RI St. Adalbert's Church.
Slough, Charles R. '56 (HBG) Elysburg, PA Queen of the Most Holy Rosary Church.
Sloun, Russell J. *s.j.* '73 (NY) [F] New York, NY Xavier High School.
Sloup, Ernest O. '53 (LIN) Retired; [E] Lincoln, NE Bonacum House.
Slovikovski, John J. '96 (ALT) [1] Altoona, PA Cathedral of the Blessed Sacrament.
Slowey, John P. '57 (SUP) Retired.
Slowiak, Allan L. '73 (LC) Rothschild, WI St. Mark Church.
Slowik, Joseph S. '72 (RIC) Portsmouth, VA St. Paul Church.
Slowinski, Jerome '90 (DET) [1] Warren, MI St. Anne's Church; Special Assignment.
Slowinski, Thomas F. '81 (DET) [1] Redford, MI St. Agatha Church.
Sloyan, Gerard S. '44 (TR) On Duty Outside the Diocese.
Slubecky, Msgr. David S. '73 (BUF) [3] West Seneca, NY Fourteen Holy Helpers Church.
Slusser, Michael '66 (PIT) [B] Pittsburgh, PA Duquesne University of the Holy Ghost.
Slusser, Michael S. '66 (STP) On Duty Outside the Archdiocese.
Smaistrla, Benjamin '72 (GAL) [75] Houston, TX St. Theresa Church.
Smalarz, Msgr. Jerome S. '37 (DET) [A] Orchard Lake, MI SS. Cyril and Methodius Seminary.
Small, Edward J. *s.j.* '70 (BGP) [1] Trumbull, CT Christ the King Church; [O] Fairfield, CT The Fairfield Jesuit Community-Fairfield University.
Small, Edward J. *s.j.* '70 (BO) [W] Boston, MA The Society of Jesus of New England-Provincial Offices.
Small, James *c.ss.r.* '54 (HBG) [2] Lancaster, PA St. Anthony of Padua Church.
Small, Jeffery '93 (PEO) [4] Streator, IL St. Stephen's Church.
Small, Joseph F. *s.j.* '48 (CHI) [C] Chicago, IL Jesuit Community at Loyola University of Chicago; [N] Chicago, IL Chicago Province of the Society of Jesus-Provincial Office.
Small, Joseph H. *s.j.* '60 (P) [L] Portland, OR Jesuit Provincial Office (Oregon Prov.).
Small, William T. '77 (PH) Broomall, PA St. Pius X Church.
Smalley, William R. '55 (NEW) [4] Irvington, NJ St. Paul the Apostle Church.
Smar, Michael J. '69 (Y) Champion, OH St. William Church.
Smarsh, Charles F. '64 (NY) On Duty Outside the Archdiocese.

Smart, Raymond W. '70 (PH) Absent on Sick Leave.
Smegal, John T. '77 (SPR) Lanesboro, MA North American Martyrs Church; [P] Amherst, MA University of Massachusetts and Amherst College, Newman Center.
Smegelsky, John J. '66 (SY) Central Square, NY St. Michael Church.
Smeltzer, Stuart M. '96 (WCH) [12] Wichita, KS St. Elizabeth Ann Seton Church.
Smet, Joachim *o.carm.* '42 (JOL) [J] Darien, IL Carmelite Fathers Provincial Office.
Smet, Leroy R. '59 (GB) Winneconne, WI St. Mary Church.
Smetana, Brendan L. *o.s.b.* '40 (GBG) [H] Latrobe, PA Saint Vincent Archabbey.
Smetanka, Gary T. '82 (DET) [5] Clinton Twp., MI St. Thecla Church.
Smialowski, Raymond S. '82 (HRT) Newington, CT Holy Spirit Church; [R] Hartford, CT University of Hartford Newman Center; [R] Hartford, CT University of Hartford Newman Center.
Smiciklas, Msgr. Nicholas X. *v.f.* '56 (PBR) [6] Pittsburgh, PA St. Pius X Church.
Smidt-Jernstrom, Kurt '85 (P) [K] Mt. Angel, OR Benedictine Nursing Center.
Smiech, Charles *o.f.m.* '81 (DET) [3] Detroit, MI St. Aloysius Church.
Smiga, George '75 (CLV) Willoughby Hills, OH St. Noel Church.
Smigiel, Edgar *o.f.m.* '47 (RCK) [6] Rockford, IL St. James Church.
Smigiel, Walter J. '50 (PBL) Retired.
Smilanic, Daniel A. (CHI) Park Ridge, IL St. Paul of the Cross Church.
Smilga, Zenon A. '50 (NOR) Fishers Island, NY Our Lady of Grace Church.
Smiroldo, Msgr. Onofrio R. '53 (BUF) [3] Tonawanda, NY St. Edmund Church.
Smit, Gerard C. '50 (LKC) Retired.
Smith, A. Philip *o.p.* '68 (PRO) [P] Providence, RI St. Thomas Aquinas Priory at Providence College.
Smith, Al '65 (PH) [D] Philadelphia, PA Father Judge High School for Boys.
Smith, Alberic *o.f.m.* '58 (LA) [R] Santa Barbara, CA St. Anthony's Seminary.
Smith, Albert J. *o.s.f.s.* '65 (PH) [C] Philadelphia, PA Holy Family College; [Z] Philadelphia, PA Father Judge Faculty House.
Smith, Alexei '87 (LA) El Segundo, CA St. Andrew Church.
Smith, Alexei R. '87 (NTN) El Segundo, CA St. Paul Church.
Smith, Msgr. Alfred D. '53 (TR) Belmar, NJ St. Rose Church.
Smith, Alfred E. *m.m.* '45 (SJ) [M] Los Altos, CA Maryknoll.
Smith, Alfred E. '56 (BAL) Williamsport, MD St. Augustine Church.
Smith, Alphonsus M. '56 (WDC) Retired.
Smith, Andrew T. *o.s.b.* '64 (PAT) [M] Morristown, NJ St. Mary's Abbey.
Smith, Anthony *c.ss.r.* '84 (CHI) [N] Bangkok, Thailand; [N] Parana, Brazil Rua Consulheiro Sinimbu.
Smith, Anthony *c.ss.r.* '84 (DEN) [M] Denver, CO The Redemptorists/Denver Province.
Smith, Aquinas '59 (SD) Retired.
Smith, Arnold R. '51 (SCR) Retired; [N] Dunmore, PA Villa St. Joseph.
Smith, Arthur F. *o.s.a.* '54 (PH) [Z] Villanova, PA St. Thomas Monastery.
Smith, Arthur J. '71 (BUF) [64] Buffalo, NY St. Thomas Aquinas Church.
Smith, Bernard *o.f.m.cap.* '64 (NY) [Z] White Plains, NY St. Conrad Friary.
Smith, Msgr. Bernard E. '33 (TOL) Retired; [L] Toledo, OH Notre Dame Provincialate.
Smith, Bernardine J. *t.o.r.* '59 (SP) [6] St. Petersburg, FL St. Mary Our Lady of Grace Church.
Smith, Brendan *s.t.* '54 (ORG) Orange, CA Juvenile Hall; Orange, CA Theo Lacy Minimum Security Facility; [A] Santa Ana, CA Trinity Missions House of Studies; [H] Santa Ana, CA Trinitarian Missionaries/ Missionary Servants of the Most Holy Trinity.
Smith, Brian P. '86 (STL) [8] Florissant, MO St. Norbert Church.
Smith, Charles *s.v.d.* '95 (IND) [39] Indianapolis, IN St. Rita Church.
Smith, Msgr. Charles A. '45 (WCH) Retired.
Smith, Charles C. *c.s.b.* '60 (DET) [E] Redford, MI Catholic Central High School.
Smith, Charles Clyde (FBK) Alakanuk, AK St. Ignatius Church.
Smith, Charles D. '65 (PH) [94] Philadelphia, PA St. Martin of Tours Church.
Smith, Charles F. '76 (FRS) [5] Fresno, CA Sacred Heart Church.
Smith, Chester *s.v.d.* '95 (IND) [39] Indianapolis, IN St. Rita Church.
Smith, Christopher H. '78 (ORG) [8] Santa Ana, CA St. Joseph's Church.
Smith, Clifford G. '96 (DAL) Richardson, TX St. Joseph Church.
Smith, Cyril J. *o.s.a.* '55 (MIA) [C] Miami, FL Msgr. Edward Pace High School; [H] Miami, FL Casa San Lorenzo.
Smith, D. Gregory '91 (HEL) [3] Helena, MT Our Lady of the Valley Church.
Smith, D. Stephen '73 (MAD) Cross Plains, WI St. Francis Xavier Church.
Smith, Daniel *o.carm.* '46 (NEW) Paramus, NJ Carmelite Chapel of St. Therese Church.
Smith, David '82 (MIA) Special Assignment.
Smith, David G. '73 (BAL) [67] Baltimore, MD Our Lady of Good Counsel Church; [Q] Baltimore, MD Apostleship of the Sea.
Smith, David L. *c.s.sp.* '58 (PIT) [B] Pittsburgh, PA Duquesne University of the Holy Ghost.
Smith, David L. *s.j.* '85 (RC) Pine Ridge, SD Holy Rosary Church; [B] Pine Ridge, SD Jesuit Community of Holy Rosary Mission.
Smith, David W. '64 (STP) [C] St. Paul, MN University of St. Thomas.
Smith, Dennis '75 (FWT) [1] Fort Worth, TX St. Patrick Cathedral.
Smith, Donald C. '61 (NEW) [B] South Orange, NJ Seton Hall University.
Smith, Donald R. '57 (SC) Retired.
Smith, Douglas *o.f.m.cap.* '57 (GAL) [38] Houston, TX St. Jerome Church.
Smith, Earl L. *s.j.* '87 (CHI) [C] Chicago, IL Jesuit Community at Loyola University of Chicago.
Smith, Edmund *o.s.b.* '65 (P) Mt. Angel, OR St. Mary Church; [L] St. Benedict, OR Mt. Angel Abbey.
Smith, Edward E. '82 (MOB) On Leave from the Archdiocese.
Smith, Edward J. *o.praem.* (GB) [O] Green Bay, WI Green Bay Area Catholic High School Foundation, L.T.D.
Smith, Edward J. '65 (BRK) [85] Brooklyn, NY St. Matthew's Church; [92] Brooklyn, NY Our Lady of Charity Church.
Smith, Edward J. *o.praem.* '73 (PH) [B] Paoli, PA Daylesford Abbey; [Z] Paoli, PA Daylesford Abbey.
Smith, Edward P. '82 (CIN) On Duty Outside the Archdiocese.
Smith, Elmer W. '50 (CIN) [20] Cincinnati, OH St. Cecilia Church; [V] Cincinnati, OH Legion of Mary.
Smith, Ermin R. *o.s.b.* '45 (GBG) Latrobe, PA Latrobe Area Hospital; [H] Latrobe, PA Saint Vincent Archabbey.
Smith, Eugene D. '50 (LC) Retired.
Smith, Eugene M. *o.s.m.* '88 (ORG) [D] Anaheim, CA Servite High School; Servite High School Development Fund; [H] Anaheim, CA Servite Fathers and Brothers; [H] Buena Park, CA Servite Fathers And Brothers.
Smith, Eugene P. '50 (LC) Boyd, WI Sacred Heart of Jesus-St. Joseph Church.
Smith, F. Harold '50 (L) Retired.
Smith, Francis J. *s.j.* '52 (CLV) [C] Cleveland, OH John Carroll Jesuit Community.
Smith, Msgr. Francis J. '67 (ELP) [31] El Paso, TX St. Raphael Church.
Smith, Francis N. *o.f.m.* '86 (NEW) [N] Hohokus, NJ St. Anthony of Padua.
Smith, Francis R. *s.j.* '70 (SJ) [B] Santa Clara, CA Santa Clara University.
Smith, Francis X.J. '64 (ORL) Melbourne, FL Ascension Church; [G] Melbourne, FL Ascension Housing, Inc.
Smith, Fred A. '47 (MIL) Retired.
Smith, Gabriel J. '82 (CHR) [12] Charleston, SC St. Joseph Church.
Smith, Gary N. *s.j.* '71 (P) [38] Portland, OR St. Vincent de Paul Church; [L] Portland, OR Jesuit Provincial Office (Oregon Prov.).
Smith, Gene F. '84 (CHI) [165] Chicago, IL St. Patrick Church.
Smith, Geoffrey '74 (HRT) [7] New Haven, CT St. Casimir's Church.
Smith, Gerald S. '64 (PH) North Wales, PA St. Rose of Lima Church.
Smith, Gerard *c.ss.r.* '45 (WIL) Seaford, DE Our Lady of Lourdes Church.
Smith, Gregory J. '74 (GB) Howard, WI St. John the Baptist Church.
Smith, Msgr. Gregory M. '67 (BGP) [16] Bridgeport, CT Our Lady of Good Counsel Church; [A] Fairfield, CT Sacred Heart University; [W] Fairfield, CT The Institute for Religious Education and Pastoral Studies (REAPS).
Smith, Herbert F. *s.j.* '62 (PH) [Z] Philadelphia, PA Jesuit Community at St. Joseph's University; [EE] Philadelphia, PA Apostleship of Prayer.
Smith, Howard C. *s.m.* '72 (WDC) [M] Washington, DC Marist Provincial House.
Smith, Ignatius *o.s.b.* '54 (PBL) [D] Canon City, CO St. Thomas More Hospital and Progressive Care Center.
Smith, Ignatius E. *o.f.m.* '56 (NY) Callicoon, NY Holy Cross Church.
Smith, Ignatius J. *o.s.b.* '46 (PBL) [E] Canon City, CO Holy Cross Abbey.
Smith, Ivan E. '91 (GB) Special Assignment.
Smith, James *o.praem.* '77 (ORG) [H] Silverado, CA Norbertine Fathers.
Smith, James A. '52 (CLV) Retired.
Smith, James A.D. '56 (PAT) Succasunna, NJ St. Therese Church.
Smith, James B. '85 (WIL) Salisbury, MD St. Francis De Sales Church.
Smith, James D. '87 (STP) Oakdale, MN Transfiguration Church.
Smith, James E. *c.m.* '61 (ALB) [L] Albany, NY Vincentian Fathers Residence; [M] Menands, NY De Paul Provincial House.
Smith, James F. *m.m.* '35 (NY) [Z] Maryknoll, NY Maryknoll Fathers and Brothers.
Smith, James F. *s.j.* '62 (SY) [A] Syracuse, NY Saint Andrew Hall.
Smith, James H. '63 (HRT) Derby, CT St. Mary's Church.
Smith, James R. '67 (SC) Cherokee, IA Immaculate Conception Church.
Smith, James T. '56 (BRK) [189] Queens, NY St. Kevin Church.
Smith, James T. '65 (COL) [31] Columbus, OH St. Matthias Church.
Smith, Jerry A. (AUS) [1] Austin, TX St. Mary's Cathedral.
Smith, John *s.s.c.* (CHI) [N] Chicago, IL Korean Catholic Center.
Smith, John B. '59 (STP) Military Chaplains.
Smith, John F. '62 (HBG) Columbia, PA St. Peter Church.
Smith, John F.X. '61 (NY) Cornwall-on-Hudson, NY St. Thomas of Canterbury Church; Tuxedo, NY Our Lady of Mt. Carmel Church.
Smith, Msgr. John J. '59 (FR) South Yarmouth, MA St. Pius Tenth Church.
Smith, John P. '42 (DUB) Retired.
Smith, Joseph A. '96 (SAV) [3] Columbus, GA St. Anne Church.
Smith, Joseph F. '35 (PH) [35] Philadelphia, PA St. Christopher Church; Trooper, PA Visitation B.V.M. Church; Retired.
Smith, Joseph F.X. *c.s.p.* '74 (NY) [Z] Scarsdale, NY Paulist Fathers Generalate.
Smith, Msgr. Joseph P.T. '60 (ALN) [3] Reading, PA St. Catharine of Siena Church.
Smith, Joseph S. *m.m.* '51 (NY) [Z] Maryknoll, NY Maryknoll Fathers and Brothers.
Smith, Jude *o.f.m.* '53 (MET) Bound Brook, NJ St. Mary of Czestochowa Church.
Smith, Jude *o.f.m.* '53 (PAT) [M] Butler, NJ St. Anthony Friary.
Smith, Kenneth A. '63 (BR) [20] Baton Rouge, LA Sacred Heart of Jesus Church.
Smith, Kenneth G. '84 (HBG) Rohrerstown, PA St. Leo the Great Church.
Smith, Kenneth J. '64 (NY) [17] New York, NY St. Bernard Church; [120] New York, NY St. Veronica Church.
Smith, Kevin M. '88 (RVC) Manhasset, NY St. Mary's Church.
Smith, Laurence H. '68 (MET) High Bridge, NJ St. Joseph Church.
Smith, Lawrence C. *s.j.* '82 (BO) [W] Boston, MA The Society of Jesus of New England-Provincial Offices.
Smith, Lawrence R. '76 (PIT) [3] McKees Rocks, PA St. John of God Church.
Smith, Leland J. '53 (WIN) Retired.
Smith, Leonard A. '91 (WH) Williamson, WV Sacred Heart Church.
Smith, Leroy (SPR) Pittsfield, MA Berkshire Medical Center.
Smith, LeRoy J. '78 (BRK) Released from Diocesan Assignment.
Smith, Lester E. '75 (SY) Marathon, NY St. Stephen Church.
Smith, Malachy *o.carm.* '43 (JOL) [J] Darien, IL Carmelite Fathers Provincial Office.
Smith, Malcolm *m.afr.* '69 (ORG) [1] Orange, CA Cathedral of the Holy Family.
Smith, Mark *o.f.m.* '61 (BO) [BB] Boston, MA St. Anthony Shrine.
Smith, Mark S. '96 (JC) [3] Jefferson City, MO Immaculate Conception Church; [B] Jefferson City, MO Helias High School.
Smith, Martin '73 (CIN) [76] Cincinnati, OH St. Pius Church.
Smith, Martin D. '79 (STU) On Duty Outside the Diocese.
Smith, Martin G. '36 (PH) Retired.
Smith, Martin L. *o.s.a.* '77 (WDC) [B] Washington, DC Augustinian College, Order of St. Augustine.
Smith, Matthew '95 (BAL) [28] Baltimore, MD St. Dominic Church.
Smith, Maury *o.f.m.* '66 (MEM) [17] Memphis, TN St. Mary's Church; [J] Memphis, TN Franciscan Friars (Sacred Heart Prov.) of Memphis.
Smith, Michael '73 (SD) Retired.
Smith, Michael '77 (HEL) Bonner, MT St. Ann Church.
Smith, Michael B. '74 (CLV) Cuyahoga Falls, OH

Immaculate Heart of Mary Church.
Smith, Michael H. '66 (SAV) Statesboro, GA St. Matthew's Church.
Smith, Michael N. *s.j.* '67 (PBL) Paonia, CO Sacred Heart Church.
Smith, Michael S. '92 (NOR) [B] Middletown, CT Mercy High School; [B] Middletown, CT Xavier High School.
Smith, Myles H. '70 (IND) Leave of Absence.
Smith, Neil B. '48 (MAR) Retired.
Smith, Nicholas '94 (STL) [5] Lemay, MO St. Martin of Tours Church.
Smith, Nicholas P. '65 (PRO) North Kingstown, RI St. Francis De Sales Church.
Smith, Norman (GLP) Retired.
Smith, Norman N. '70 (CLV) Kirtland, OH Divine Word Church.
Smith, Paschal *c.p.* '51 (NY) [Z] Pelham Manor, NY St. Vincent's Residence; [DD] Pelham, NY Passionist Communications, Inc.
Smith, Patrick '67 (PHX) [5] Scottsdale, AZ St. Daniel the Prophet Church; Scottsdale, AZ Scottsdale Memorial Hospital.
Smith, Patrick A. '90 (WDC) St. Inigoes, MD St. Peter Claver Church.
Smith, Paul '59 (ALB) Special Assignment; [D] Albany, NY Academy of the Holy Names Upper, Middle and Lower Schools.
Smith, Paul '62 (ALX) On Duty Outside the Diocese.
Smith, Paul '62 (HON) Retired.
Smith, Paul B. (CHI) [79] Chicago, IL Holy Angels Church.
Smith, Paul F. '73 (CLV) Thompson, OH St. Patrick Church.
Smith, Paul H. '62 (NEW) On Duty Outside the Archdiocese.
Smith, Paul P. '46 (PHX) Retired.
Smith, Paul R. '59 (ALB) [B] Albany, NY Maria College.
Smith, Peter '51 (NY) [V] Rhinebeck, NY Ferncliff Nursing Home.
Smith, Peter H. '26 (ALB) Retired.
Smith, Peter J. '51 (BWN) Retired.
Smith, Philip *o.praem.* '84 (ORG) [H] Silverado, CA Norbertine Fathers.
Smith, Philip A. *o.p.* (PRO) [B] Providence, RI Providence College.
Smith, R. Douglas *o.s.f.s.* '62 (WIL) [B] Wilmington, DE Salesianum School.
Smith, R. Leroy '54 (COV) Retired.
Smith, Ramon *o.f.m.* '53 (LSC) Roswell, NM St. Peter Church.
Smith, Raymond J. '50 (CLV) [11] Akron, OH St. Mary Church.
Smith, Raymond K. '56 (SFR) Special Assignment; On Duty Outside the Archdiocese; [M] Petaluma, CA Silver Penny Farm Retreat Center.
Smith, Richard '76 (JOL) Channahon, IL St. Ann Parish Church.
Smith, Richard '84 (JKS) Forest, MS St. Michael Church; Paulding, MS St. Michael Church; [G] Forest, MS East Central Community College Newman Center.
Smith, Richard A. '56 (MAN) Whitefield, NH St. Matthew Church.
Smith, Richard E. (BAL) Ellicott City, MD Our Lady of Perpetual Help Church.
Smith, Richard F. *s.j.* '50 (STL) [P] St. Louis, MO Jesuit Community Corporation at St. Louis University - Jesuit Hall.
Smith, Richard J. '49 (FTW) Lakeville, IN Sacred Heart Church.
Smith, Richard J. '60 (BO) Norwell, MA St. Helen Church.
Smith, Robert '89 (ATL) Roswell, GA St. Andrew Church.
Smith, Robert D. '56 (BO) [2] Haverhill, MA St. James Church.
Smith, Robert G. '53 (ROC) Red Creek, NY Butler Correctional Facility.
Smith, Robert H. '56 (LIN) Retired.
Smith, Robert J. '55 (OM) Valley, NE St. John Church.
Smith, Msgr. Robert J. '70 (E) [J] Erie, PA Bishop Michael J. Murphy Residence for Retired Priests.
Smith, Robert J. '83 (RVC) [A] Huntington, NY Diocesan Seminary of the Immaculate Conception.
Smith, Robert S. '58 (RVC) Stony Brook, NY Stony Brook University Hospital; [Q] Rockville Centre, NY The Campus Parish of Long Island.
Smith, Robert V. '61 (CAM) Glassboro, NJ St. Bridget's Church.
Smith, Roger '76 (CC) [2] Kingsville, TX St. Gertrude Church; [5] Kingsville, TX Collegiate Parish of St. Thomas Aquinas Church.
Smith, Roger J. '73 (SEA) Morton, WA Sacred Heart Church; Pe Ell, WA St. Joseph's Church; Raymond, WA St. Lawrence Church.
Smith, Ronald T. '73 (HRT) [4] New Britain, CT St. Andrew's Church; New Britain, CT New Britain General Hospital.
Smith, Russell E. '74 (RIC) On Duty Outside the Diocese.
Smith, Russell E. '80 (BAL) [A] Emmitsburg, MD Mount St. Mary's Seminary; [A] Emmitsburg, MD Mount St. Mary's Seminary.
Smith, S. Douglas *c.s.c.* '76 (FTW) [J] South Bend, IN Congregation of Holy Cross Indiana Province Provincial House.
Smith, Sherrill '55 (SAT) [65] San Antonio, TX St. Stephen Church.
Smith, Simon E. *s.j.* '61 (BO) [W] Boston, MA Jesuit Urban Center & Immaculate Conception Community.
Smith, Stanley C. *o.s.a.* '60 (BO) [C] North Andover, MA Merrimack College.
Smith, Stephen K. *o.p.* '58 (KNX) Elizabethton, TN St. Elizabeth Church.
Smith, Terrance W. '73 (CIN) Loveland, OH St. Columban Church.
Smith, Terrence T. *t.o.r.* '73 (ALT) [7] Altoona, PA Our Lady of Mt. Carmel Church.
Smith, Terry *c.s.sp.* '80 (STA) [1] St. Augustine, FL Cathedral of St. Augustine.
Smith, Theodore *o.praem.* '91 (ORG) [H] Silverado, CA Norbertine Fathers.
Smith, Thomas '51 (ORL) Altamonte Springs, FL St. Mary Magdalen Church.
Smith, Thomas A. *o.f.m.conv.* '79 (IND) [I] Mount Saint Francis, IN Mount Saint Francis Friary and Retreat Center.
Smith, Thomas A. '83 (L) Flaherty, KY St. Martin of Tours Church; Vine Grove, KY St. Brigid Church.
Smith, Thomas E. '51 (PIT) Retired.
Smith, Thomas E. '67 (E) [27] Erie, PA St. Patrick/St. Hedwig Church.
Smith, Thomas E. *s.j.* '74 (NY) [Z] New York, NY Jesuit Provincial's Office; [Z] New York, NY St. Ignatius Loyola Residence.
Smith, Thomas F. *o.c.s.o.* '58 (ATL) [I] Conyers, GA The Monastery of the Holy Spirit.
Smith, Msgr. Thomas H. '57 (HBG) [5] Lancaster, PA St. Joseph Church.
Smith, Thomas J. *o.s.f.s.* '58 (LAN) Michigan Center, MI Our Lady of Fatima Church.
Smith, Thomas J. '60 (LC) [G] La Crosse, WI St. Joseph's Nursing Home; [G] La Crosse, WI Bethany-St. Joseph Care Center; [I] La Crosse, WI Holy Cross (Seminary) Diocesan Center.
Smith, Thomas J. '73 (PH) [51] Philadelphia, PA Good Shepherd Church.
Smith, Thomas J. '82 (NOR) New London, CT St. Mary, Star of the Sea Church.
Smith, Thomas R. '81 (CLV) [5] Lorain, OH St. John Church
Smith, Vernon '90 (FAR) Harvey, ND St. Cecilia's Church
Smith, Msgr. Vincent J. '55 (HBG) Camp Hill, PA Good Shepherd Church.
Smith, Vincent Leo '66 (DEN) Breckenridge, CO St. Mary Church.
Smith, W. Andrew '80 (LR) Pine Bluff, AR St. Joseph's Church.
Smith, Walter J. *s.j.* '72 (BO) [W] Boston, MA The Society of Jesus of New England-Provincial Offices.
Smith, Walter J. *s.j.* '72 (NY) [Z] New York, NY "America;" Residence and publication office of the America Press.
Smith, Walter N. '68 (CAM) Gloucester, NJ St. Mary's Church.
Smith, Wilfred T. '56 (CLV) Mentor, OH St. Mary of the Assumption Church.
Smith, William (BRK) [59] Brooklyn, NY Holy Rosary Church.
Smith, William *glmy.* '47 (CIN) [M] Fairfield, OH Headquarters of Glenmary Home Missioners.
Smith, William *o.carm.* '54 (JOL) [J] Darien, IL Carmelite Fathers Provincial Office.
Smith, William *c.s.sp.* '74 (PIT) [B] Pittsburgh, PA Duquesne University of the Holy Ghost.
Smith, William A. '74 (BRK) [47] Brooklyn, NY St. Francis Xavier Church; [76] Brooklyn, NY St. Lucy-St. Patrick Church.
Smith, Msgr. William B. '66 (NY) [A] Yonkers, NY St. Joseph's Seminary.
Smith, William C. '45 (HRT) Retired.
Smith, William F. '52 (JOL) Gibson City, IL Our Lady of Lourdes Church.
Smith, William J. '47 (PH) Downingtown, PA St. Joseph Church; Retired.
Smith, Msgr. William J. '60 (NY) [130] Bronx, NY St. Athanasius Church.
Smith, William J. '81 (MET) [5] Perth Amboy, NJ Our Lady of Hungary Church.
Smith, William P. '67 (BO) Bedford, MA St. Michael Church.
Smith, Wilton S. '58 (SFR) [4] South San Francisco, CA St. Veronica Church.
Smithers, Stephen T. *o.p.* '53 (GAL) [Q] Houston, TX Dominican Fathers and Brothers, St. Mark Priory, Inc.
Smithes, Donald F. '79 (RCK) Polo, IL St. Mary's Church.
Smits, Joseph *c.i.c.m.* '56 (ARL) [J] Arlington, VA Missionhurst, C.I.C.M.-Central House and Provincialate.
Smits, Joseph B. *c.i.c.m.* '56 (PH) [C] Gwynedd Valley, PA Gwynedd-Mercy College.
Smits, Kenneth *o.f.m.* (MAD) [4] Madison, WI Holy Redeemer Church.
Smits, Lambert *c.i.c.m.* '48 (DET) [1] Roseville, MI St. Angela Church.
Smits, Pete *s.v.d.* '41 (BLX) [A] Bay St. Louis, MS St. Augustine's.
Smochko, Msgr. Basil '46 (PRM) Lakewood, OH St. Gregory the Theologian Church.
Smolar, Joseph *c.pp.s.* '42 (CIN) [B] Carthagena, OH St. Charles.
Smolarski, Dennis C. *s.j.* '79 (SJ) [B] Santa Clara, CA Santa Clara University.
Smolenski, Stanley '68 (HRT) [4] Enfield, CT St. Martha's Church.
Smoley, Rudolph F. '69 (PIT) [1] Carnegie, PA St. Elizabeth Ann Seton Church.
Smolich, Thomas L. *s.j.* (SFR) [2] San Francisco, CA St. Agnes Church.
Smolinski, Arcadius *o.f.m.* '47 (GB) [I] Pulaski, WI Assumption of B.V.M. Friary.
Smolinski, Clarence D. '53 (GAY) Retired.
Smolinski, Joseph J. (NY) Thiells, NY Letchworth Village.
Smolira, David *s.j.* (CHI) [89] Chicago, IL St. Ignatius Church.
Smolko, John F. '57 (BGP) On Duty Outside the Diocese.
Smolko, John F. '57 (WDC) [C] Washington, DC Catholic University of America, The.
Smolley, Robert '82 (STF) [A] Stamford, CT St. Basil College.
Smolley, Robert J. '82 (BR) On Duty Outside the Diocese.
Smoot, K. Robert '95 (STL) Dardenne, MO Immaculate Conception Church.
Smulders, Raphael M. *ss.cc.* '34 (HON) Lahaina, HI Maria Lanakila Church.
Smullen, Martin J. '82 (NO) [59] New Orleans, LA St. Simon Peter Church.
Smutelovic, Peter '95 (NEW) North Arlington, NJ Queen of Peace Church.
Smutny, Jan '42 (GI) Retired.
Smutny, Wenceslaus J. *c.ss.r.* '53 (PH) [25] Philadelphia, PA St. Boniface Church.
Smyda, August *s.j.* '64 (CHI) [N] Chicago, IL Sacred Heart Mission House.
Smyer, Msgr. Francis A. '46 (AMA) [10] Amarillo, TX St. Mary's Church.
Smyka, James *o.f.m.conv.* '73 (BGP) [14] Bridgeport, CT St. Michael The Archangel Church.
Smylie, Benjamin '85 (TYL) Carthage, TX St. William of Vercelli Church.
Smyth, Msgr. Claude '53 (DAL) Plano, TX St. Mark the Evangelist Church.
Smyth, Edmond J. *s.j.* '50 (SJ) [M] Los Gatos, CA Sacred Heart Jesuit Center.
Smyth, Henry J. '50 (PH) Horsham, PA St. Catherine of Siena Church.
Smyth, James '56 (NY) Hastings-on-Hudson, NY St. Matthew Church.
Smyth, John L. *c.ss.r.* '64 (ATL) Griffin, GA Sacred Heart Church.
Smyth, John P. '62 (CHI) [H] Des Plaines, IL Maryville Academy; [X] Chicago, IL Catholic Youth, Archdiocese of Chicago.
Smyth, Joseph P. '59 (BO) Chelmsford, MA St. Mary Church.
Sneck, William J. *s.j.* '71 (BAL) [C] Baltimore, MD Loyola College; [M] Baltimore, MD Jesuit Community of Loyola College, Inc.
Snedeker, Arthur A. '74 (CLV) [8] Akron, OH Immaculate Conception Church.
Snee, Msgr. Joseph T.V. '42 (NY) [17] New York, NY St. Bernard Church; Retired.
Snell, Roger K. '72 (FAR) Retired.
Snella, Adolph A. '51 (ARL) Retired.
Sneyd, Derrick '70 (FTW) New Haven, IN St. John the Baptist Church.
Snider, Harold *o.f.m.cap.* (SFR) Burlingame, CA Our Lady of Angels Church.
Snieg, Marion J. '55 (CHI) [M] Wheeling, IL Addolorata Villa, Inc.
Snieg, Peter '93 (CHI) [155] Chicago, IL Our Lady of Mount Carmel Church; [A] Chicago, IL Archbishop Quigley Preparatory Seminary.
Sniegowski, Msgr. Thaddeus R. '43 (GR) Retired.
Sniezyk, Richard S. '62 (SPR) [16] Springfield, MA St. Mary's Church.
Snincak, Stephen A. '35 (WH) Retired.
Snipes, Roy Lee *o.m.i.* '80 (BWN) [1] Mission, TX Our Lady of Guadalupe Church.
Snock, Bernard C. '62 (GAL) Frydek, TX St. Mary's Church.
Snock, Francis '50 (Y) Retired.
Snodgrass, Thomas A. '76 (CIN) [6] Cincinnati, OH St. Aloysius Church; [21] Cincinnati, OH St. Charles Borromeo Church.

Snoeren, Cornelius M. *m.h.m.* '52 (NY) [Z] Hartsdale, NY Mill Hill Fathers Residence.
Snoha, Joseph J. *c.m.* '90 (STL) [P] St. Louis, MO Vincentian-St. Lazare Residence.
Snoich, Stephen *o.s.b.* '72 (IND) [J] St. Meinrad, IN St. Meinrad Archabbey.
Snoj, Joseph '37 (SB) Retired.
Snoke, F. Richard '65 (COL) Danville, OH St. Luke Church.
Snopek, Charles J. '86 (CHR) Pawleys Island, SC Precious Blood of Christ Church.
Snouffer, Philip T. '62 (BAL) Special Assignment.
Snow, Glen *o.carm.* '89 (CHI) [D] Chicago, IL Mt. Carmel High School; [N] Chicago, IL Carmelite Priory of St. Cyril.
Snow, Harry K. '77 (OG) Morristown, NY St. John the Evangelist Church.
Snow, J. Lee '55 (OG) Retired.
Snyder, Alexander N. '59 (OAK) [5] San Leandro, CA Our Lady of Good Counsel Church.
Snyder, Brian '79 (SEA) [Q] Seattle, WA Catholic Hospital Ministries.
Snyder, Chester P. '77 (HBG) Mechanicsburg, PA St. Joseph Church.
Snyder, Clatus E. '34 (BUF) Retired.
Snyder, Daniel L. '84 (KAL) Absent on Leave.
Snyder, Donald '93 (CLV) [U] Cleveland, OH St. Joseph Christian Life Center.
Snyder, Edward J. *s.j.* '52 (NEW) [C] Jersey City, NJ St. Peter's Preparatory School.
Snyder, Frederick N. '52 (GI) Ashton, NE St. Francis Church.
Snyder, Gary B. '74 (SC) Templeton, IA Sacred Heart Church.
Snyder, Joachim J. *o.carm.* '48 (NY) [Z] Scarborough, NY Carmelite Fathers, NY Prov. of St. Elias.
Snyder, John F. *s.j.* '55 (STL) [P] St. Louis, MO Jesuit Community Corporation at St. Louis University - Jesuit Hall; [W] St. Louis, MO Gregorian University Foundation.
Snyder, Larry J. '88 (STP) Special Assignment.
Snyder, Michael J. *m.m.* '79 (NY) [Z] Maryknoll, NY Maryknoll Fathers and Brothers.
Snyders, William J. *s.j.* '66 (STL) [P] St. Louis, MO De Smet Jesuit High School Community.
Snyderwine, L. Thomas '68 (E) [28] Erie, PA St. Paul Church; Erie, PA Erie County Geriatric Center Annex.
Snyers, Peter '53 (SCL) [6] St. Cloud, MN St. John Cantius Church.
Soares, Bernardo '54 (MRY) Watsonville, CA Our Lady Help of Christians Church.
Soares, John P. '93 (PRO) [S] Kingston, RI University of Rhode Island Catholic Center.
Soares, Msgr. Nicholas J. '64 (NY) [203] Staten Island, NY St. Clement Church; [215] Staten Island, NY St. Michael Church.
Soares, Patrick *c.s.sp.* '73 (STA) [15] Jacksonville, FL St. Joseph's Church.
Soave, Msgr. Alfred '48 (RVC) Retired; [N] Uniondale, NY St. Pius X Residence.
Sobalvarro, Alfredo '71 (RVC) Patchogue, NY Our Lady of Mt. Carmel Church.
Sobczak, Marek W. '81 (HRT) [4] Ansonia, CT St. Joseph's Church.
Sobejano, Jesus *o.a.r.* '51 (NY) [157] Bronx, NY St. John Vianney, Cure of Ars Church.
Soberal, Jose '60 (ARE) Special Assignment.
Soberick, George J. '62 (MAN) Lakeport, NH Our Lady of the Lakes Church.
Sobiech, Stanley *o.f.m.conv.* '62 (SPR) [5] Holyoke, MA Mater Dolorosa Church.
Sobieck, Elmer '46 (SCL) Retired.
Sobiecki, Peter S. '66 (HRT) [2] New Britain, CT Holy Cross Church.
Sobierajski, Msgr. Edward J. '61 (BUF) Retired; [O] Tonawanda, NY O'Hara Residence.
Sobierajski, Joseph A. *s.j.* '74 (BAL) [C] Baltimore, MD Loyola College; [M] Baltimore, MD Jesuit Community of Loyola College, Inc.
Sobiesiak, Msgr. Joseph R. '76 (ALN) [6] Allentown, PA Our Lady of Mt. Carmel Church; [9] Allentown, PA Sacred Heart of Jesus Church; [C] Allentown, PA Allentown Central Catholic High School.
Sobieszczyk, David '64 (DEN) [31] Denver, CO St. James Church.
Sobolewski, Edward F. '69 (CAM) National Park, NJ St. Matthew's Church.
Sobon, Walter A. '67 (PIT) Ingram, PA Ascension Church.
Sobosan, Jeffrey *c.s.c.* '73 (P) [B] Portland, OR University of Portland; [L] Portland, OR Holy Cross Father & Brother, C.S.C. - University of Portland.
Sobotka, De Paul *o.f.m.* '63 (GB) [I] Pulaski, WI Assumption of B.V.M. Friary.
Sobr, Clement *o.s.b.* '51 (JOL) [J] Lisle, IL St. Procopius Abbey.
Sobr, Clement *o.s.b.* '51 (SUP) [C] Fifield, WI King of Martyrs Priory.
Sobus, James M. '86 (WH) [10] Wheeling, WV St. Michael's Church.
Soce, Jago *o.f.m.* '94 (CHI) [189] Chicago, IL Sacred Heart Church.
Socha, Bronislaw F. *o.c.d.* '89 (GRY) [K] Munster, IN Discalced Carmelite Fathers Monastery.
Sochacki Walter L. '68 (STP) Roseville, MN St. Rose of Lima Church.
Socias, James '78 (CHI) [W] Chicago, IL Midtown Center
Sockol, Timothy '77 (PMB) Sebastian, FL St. Sebastian Church.
Sodano, Ralph (TUC) Yuma, AZ MCAS Chapel.
Sodano, Ralph H. '67 (PAT) Military Chaplains.
Sodano, Thomas M. '91 (PH) [101] Philadelphia, PA Maternity B.V.M. Church.
Soderlund, David '65 (ALN) Unassigned.
Sodini, Pierre G. '68 (PIT) Avella, PA St. Michael Church.
Sodja, Richard H. '65 (HEL) Bigfork, MT St. Catherine Church.
Sodomora, John *c.ss.r.* '78 (BAL) Annapolis, MD St. Mary Church; [M] Annapolis, MD Saint Mary Rectory.
Sodoro, Carl F. '77 (OM) [5] Omaha, NE St. Anthony Church; [L] Omaha, NE Sisters of the Annunciation of the Archdiocese of Omaha.
Soehner, Mark *o.f.m.* '87 (DET) [3] Detroit, MI St. Aloysius Church.
Soerries, Denis *o.s.b.* '56 (LR) Subiaco, AR St. Benedict Church.
Sofie, J. Frank, Jr. '94 (MOB) [7] Mobile, AL St. Ignatius Church.
Sogliuzzo, Gerard (NEW) Nutley, NJ St. Mary's Church.
Sogliuzzo, Louis P. *s.j.* '80 (NY) [Z] New York, NY Xavier Jesuit Community.
Sogliuzzo, Louis S. *s.j.* '87 (NY) [37] New York, NY St. Francis Xavier Church.
Soha, Roderick *t.o.r.* '95 (ORL) [2] Lakeland, FL St. Anthony's Church.
Sohm, John E. '58 (SFD) Sullivan, IL St. Columcille Church.
Sohn, Frederick H. *c.s.b.* '55 (GAL) [Q] Houston, TX Residence of the Basilian Fathers of the University of St. Thomas.
Soileau, Charles L. '57 (LKC) Vinton, LA St. Joseph Church.
Soisson, Clifford F. '37 (PIT) Retired.
Soisson, F. Clifford '37 (PIT) [N] Pittsburgh, PA St. John Vianney Manor.
Sojka, Msgr. Ferdinand M. '44 (PIT) Retired; [N] Pittsburgh, PA St. John Vianney Manor.
Sojka, Louis *o.s.b.* '90 (OM) [C] Elkhorn, NE Mount Michael High School.
Sojka, Louis L. *o.s.b.* '90 (OM) [K] Elkhorn, NE Mount Michael Abbey.
Sojka, Remi '95 (RIC) [8] Richmond, VA St. Bridget Church.
Sokalski, Marcel *o.f.m.conv.* '50 (BGP) [C] Bridgeport, CT Kolbe-Cathedral High School.
Sokalski, Marcel '59 (BGP) [14] Bridgeport, CT St. Michael The Archangel Church.
Sokol, Alfred J. *s.d.b.* '47 (NEW) Mahwah, NJ Immaculate Heart of Mary Church.
Sokol, Stanley (SPR) Sheffield, MA Our Lady of the Valley Church.
Sokolowski, Bernard T. '45 (BUF) [4] Cheektowaga, NY St. Josaphat Church; Retired.
Sokolowski, Edward V. '44 (SCR) Retired.
Sokolowski, Robert S. '61 (WDC) [C] Washington, DC Catholic University of America, The.
Sokolowski, Msgr. Robert S. '65 (HRT) On Duty Outside the Archdiocese.
Sokolowski, Thomas J. '79 (SCR) East Stroudsburg, PA St. Matthew's Church.
Sokolowski, Waclaw *o.f.m.conv.* '84 (PAT) [6] Clifton, NJ St. John Kanty Church.
Sokolowski, William R. '65 (HRT) Wolcott, CT St. Maria Goretti Church.
Sokolski, John *o.m.i.* (NO) [17] New Orleans, LA Our Lady of Guadalupe /International Shrine of St. Jude Church.
Sokolski, John *o.m.i.* '55 (NO) [1] New Orleans, LA St. Louis Cathedral.
Sola, Jeronimo *c.m.* '35 (MGZ) [8] Mayaquez, PR San Vicente Church.
Solan, Lawrence T. '80 (DEN) Aspen, CO St. Mary Church.
Solano, Julio '93 (MIA) [4] Miami Beach, FL St. Patrick Church.
Solari, James K. '55 (CHL) Winston-Salem, NC St. Leo's Church.
Solari, Placid D. *o.s.b.* '80 (CHL) [A] Belmont, NC Belmont Abbey College; [J] Belmont, NC Belmont Abbey.
Solarski, Jack '76 (DAL) [L] Irving, TX Opus Dei.
Solazzo, Michael J. '76 (CHI) Other Assignments.
Solcia, Louis M. *c.r.s.p.* '57 (SD) [15] San Diego, CA Our Lady of the Rosary Church.
Soldo, Slavko '72 (CHI) [N] Chicago, IL Croatian Franciscan Custody of the Holy Family.
Soler, Lawrence *t.o.r.* '51 (AUS) [1] Waco, TX Sacred Heart Church.
Soler, Luis Augusto '67 (CHR) North Augusta, SC Our Lady of Peace Church.
Soler, Roberto '62 (MGZ) Aguada, PR Santuario Protomartires de la Concepcion Church.
Soles, John (BRK) [T] Brooklyn, NY Catholic Migration & Refugee Office, Catholic Migration Services, Inc.
Soles, John '64 (NY) [75] New York, NY St. Michael Chapel.
Soles, Juan (NY) Federal, NY Metropolitan Correctional Center.
Soleta, Chester A. *c.s.c.* '42 (FTW) [J] South Bend, IN Congregation of Holy Cross Indiana Province Provincial House.
Soley, Roger A. '78 (WDC) Huntingtown, MD Jesus the Divine Word Parish Church.
Solier, Jess Eric '57 (NY) [3] New Rochelle, NY St. Joseph Church.
Solis, Oscar A. '79 (HT) Golden Meadow, LA Our Lady of Prompt Succor Church.
Solis, Ralph, Jr. '93 (ELP) Van Horn, TX Our Lady of Fatima Church.
Solla, Santiago '53 (PCE) Juana Diaz, PR St. Raymond Nonato Church.
Solma, Martin A. *s.m.* '78 (CIN) [M] Dayton, OH Marianist Provincialate.
Soloman, Louis E. *s.j.* '64 (NY) [Z] New York, NY Murray-Weigel Hall.
Solomia, Paul '59 (DM) [C] Des Moines, IA Mercy Hospital Medical Center.
Solors, Stephen '91 (DUL) Bigfork, MN Our Lady of the Snows Church.
Solorzano, Marcelo *o.p.* '95 (NO) [25] New Orleans, LA St. Anthony Of Padua Church; [64] New Orleans, LA St. Thomas More Church; New Orleans, LA Tulane-Newcomb.
Solorzano, Miguel A. '93 (GAL) [5] Houston, TX St. Ambrose Church.
Soltis, Anthony '35 (SCR) Retired.
Soltys, Daniel F. '68 (OM) Gretna, NE St. Patrick Church.
Soltys, Raymond A. '79 (SPR) [1] Ludlow, MA Christ the King Church.
Somers, Eldon K. '51 (E) Retired.
Somers, Michael '82 (GB) Absent on Leave.
Somers, Richard '66 (JKS) [3] Jackson, MS St. Richard Church; Jackson, MS Institute for the Blind, Institute for the Deaf and Speech Impaired.
Somerville, Alvin *o.f.m.* '57 (ALB) [4] Albany, NY St. Casimir Church; [L] Rensselaer, NY Provincialate, Immaculate Conception Friary - Order of Friars Minor Conventual.
Somerville, Alvin *o.f.m.conv.* '58 (ALB) [12] Albany, NY Our Lady of Angels Church.
Somerville, Conrad *o.f.m.conv.* '54 (ALB) Tribes Hill, NY Sacred Heart Church.
Somerville, Joseph W. '86 (WDC) [34] Washington, DC Our Lady Queen of Peace Church.
Somerville, Walter F. (CHI) Retired.
Somerville, William P. '93 (GAL) [4] Spring, TX St. James the Apostle Church.
Somma, James E. '59 (PIT) Pitcairn, PA St. Michael Church; Allegheny County, PA Forbes Regional Health Center.
Sommer, Allan J. '66 (MIL) Port Washington, WI St. Mary's Church.
Sommer, Gerald R.J. *m.s.c.* '47 (Y) [9] Canton, OH St. Mary Church; [A] Youngstown, OH Sacred Heart Retreat House & Renewal Center.
Sommer, Harold *s.j.* '65 (CIN) [M] Cincinnati, OH Faber Jesuit Community.
Sommer, Msgr. Jerome '40 (JC) Retired.
Sommer, Jerome '40 (STL) Retired; Retired.
Sommer, Kenneth J. *s.m.* '59 (CIN) [M] Dayton, OH Marianist Provincialate.
Sommer, Leo J. *m.m.* '48 (NY) [Z] Maryknoll, NY Maryknoll Fathers and Brothers.
Sommer, Paul J. *m.m.* '44 (NY) [Z] Maryknoll, NY Maryknoll Fathers and Brothers.
Sommer, Ralph '83 (RVC) Hauppauge, NY St. Thomas More Church.
Sommermeyer, Gary '91 (BRK) [197] Queens, NY Mary's Nativity Church.
Sommers, Edward P. '73 (CAM) [4] Vineland, NJ St. Isidore Church; [H] Vineland, NJ Bishop McCarthy Residence.
Somos, Joseph '59 (CHI) [195] Chicago, IL St. Stephen, King of Hungary Church.
Somos, Joseph '59 (STL) On Duty Outside the Archdiocese.
Somoza, Jose I. *o.f.m.* '65 (WDC) [33] Washington, DC Our Lady Queen of the Americas Church.
Son, Kyungsu *m.m.* '79 (LA) [R] Los Angeles, CA Maryknoll Fathers and Brothers.
Son, Nguyen Thanh *c.ss.r.* '85 (LA) [R] Baldwin Park, CA Vietnamese Redemptorist Mission.
Son Le, Peter Ha '74 (LA) Santa Fe Springs, CA St. Pius X Church.
Sondej, Cyprian *o.f.m.conv.* '48 (SPR) [A] Granby, MA St. Hyacinth College and Seminary.
Sondergeld, Theodore '59 (SEA) Medical Leave.
Sonderman, Msgr. James W. '45 (AMA) Retired; [D]

Panhandle, TX St. Joseph's Home for Retired Priests.
Sondgeroth, Louis *o.m.i.* '57 (DUL) International Falls, MN St. Thomas Aquinas Church; Littlefork, MN St. Columban Church.
Sonefeld, Raymond G. '48 (KAL) Retired.
Song, James '82 (OAK) [8] Oakland, CA St. Cyril Church.
Song, S. Jin-yeul *s.j.* '96 (BO) [W] Boston, MA Loyola House.
Songeroth, Louis *o.m.i.* (DUL) International Falls, MN St. Thomas Aquinas Church.
Songster, John *s.j.* '44 (WDC) [M] Washington, DC The Jesuit Community at Georgetown University.
Songy, Msgr. Donald J. '53 (BR) [20] Baton Rouge, LA Sacred Heart of Jesus Church; Retired.
Songy, Msgr. James B. (HT) Special and other Diocesan Assignment.
Sonnberger, Albert W. '56 (LC) Chippewa Falls, WI Notre Dame Church.
Sonnier, Charles '64 (VIC) Koerth, TX St. John the Baptist Church; Sweet Home, TX Queen of Peace Church.
Sonnier, T. Alcide '56 (LAF) Chataignier, LA Our Lady of Mount Carmel Church.
Sonntag, Luis *o.f.m.cap.* '42 (MIL) [P] Mount Calvary, WI St. Lawrence Friary.
Sontheimer, W. Wendell '47 (NO) [1] Metairie, LA Our Lady of Divine Providence Church; Retired.
Soosaipillai, Manuelpillai (WH) Parkersburg, WV St. Francis Xavier's Church.
Soper, Paul R. (BO) [15] Lowell, MA Shrine of St. Rita Church; [CC] Lowell, MA The Catholic Center U Mass, Lowell.
Sopiak, Donald A. '78 (DET) [60] Detroit, MI Our Lady Queen of Heaven Church.
Sopke, Philip *c.s.c.* (P) [L] Portland, OR Holy Cross Father & Brother, C.S.C. - University of Portland.
Sopke, Philip *c.s.c.* '69 (P) [B] Portland, OR University of Portland.
Sopke, Philip *c.s.c.* '88 (P) [P] Portland, OR University of Portland.
Sopp, Michael '75 (SJP) Ford City, PA St. Mary Church.
Soprano, Ernest R. '79 (CAM) Landisville, NJ Our Lady of Victories Church.
Soprych, Marion A. '75 (CHI) [5] Oak Lawn, IL St. Louis De Montfort Church.
Soraci, John (NY) White Plains, NY St. Agnes Hospital.
Soranno, Joseph M. '74 (SPR) Wilbraham, MA St. Cecilia's Church.
Sorce, John J. '61 (CHR) Absent On Leave.
Sorci, Msgr. Francis P. '42 (BUF) Retired.
Sordi, Peter *c.s.* '45 (CHI) Melrose Park, IL Our Lady of Mount Carmel Church.
Sordillo, Ronald '75 (PAT) Morris Plains, NJ St. Virgilius Church.
Sorensen, Bartley A. '76 (PIT) Chicora, PA Mater Dolorosa Church; North Oakland, PA St. Joseph Church.
Sorensen, Bryan '88 (RC) Custer, SD St. John the Baptist Church; Hill City, SD St. Rose of Lima Church.
Sorenson, Phil (PBL) [D] Pueblo, CO St. Mary-Corwin Hospital.
Sorento, Armand *o.f.m.conv.* '42 (TR) Seaside Park, NJ St. Catharine of Siena Church.
Soreth, James F. '41 (PH) Retired.
Sorgie, Anthony D. '82 (NY) [A] Yonkers, NY St. Joseph's Seminary.
Soria, George '86 (SD) [4] Chula Vista, CA St. Rose of Lima Church.
Soria, Manuel '81 (ELP) On Duty Outside of Diocese.
Soria, Manuel B. '81 (SAC) Lincoln, CA St. Joseph Church.
Soria, Santiago *o.c.d.* '59 (PCE) [12] Ponce, PR San Jose Church.
Soriano, Danilo C. '78 (CHI) Matteson, IL St. Lawrence O'Toole Church.
Soriano, Eugene '52 (BRK) [154] Queens, NY St. Bartholomew's Church; [T] Brooklyn, NY Catholic Migration & Refugee Office, Catholic Migration Services, Inc.
Soriano, Jesus '70 (SAC) Vallejo, CA St. Catherine of Siena Church.
Sork, David A. '70 (LA) La Puente, CA St. Louis of France Church.
Sorohan, Msgr. David V. '59 (COL) [8] Columbus, OH St. Catharine Church.
Sors, Vladimir '28 (PEO) Retired.
Sorvillo, Mark B. '78 (CHI) [121] Chicago, IL St. Margaret Mary Church.
Sosa, Carlos '89 (MIL) On Leave.
Sosa, Juan J. '72 (MIA) [17] Miami, FL St. Catherine of Siena Church.
Sosa, Philip *m.s.f.* '68 (BWN) Donna, TX St. Joseph Church.
Soseman, Richard '92 (PEO) [L] Peoria, IL St. Joseph's Home of Peoria; [P] Moline, IL The Order of the Legion of Little Souls of the Merciful Heart of Jesus.
Sosinski, Thomas P. '58 (MAD) Absent on Sick Leave.
Sosnowski, Msgr. Stanley T. '77 (ALN) Whitehall, PA Holy Trinity Church.
Sostrich, John L. '62 (SD) Retired.
Sota, Pascual *c.m.* '56 (SJN) [62] San Juan, PR San Vicente de Paul Church.
Sotak, Donald J. '62 (PIT) Natrona, PA St. Joseph Church.
Sotak, John *o.s.a.* '92 (JOL) [B] Kankakee, IL Bishop McNamara High School.
Sotelo, Andrew *s.j.* (SB) [B] San Bernardino, CA Aquinas High School.
Sotelo, Angel L. '91 (FRS) Orange Cove, CA St. Isidore the Farmer Church.
Sotelo, Antonio '58 (PHX) [4] Phoenix, AZ Immaculate Heart of Mary Church.
Sotiroff, Stephen T. '81 (SFD) Vandalia, IL Mother of Dolors Church.
Soto, Angel Leonides '89 (MGZ) [1] Mayaquez, PR Cathedral of Our Lady of Purification.
Soto, Calixto '85 (SJN) Palmer, PR Cristo Rey Church.
Soto, Carmelo '89 (SJN) [1] Canovanas, PR Nuestra Senora del Pilar Church.
Soto, Charles *o.f.m.* '70 (NY) [Z] New York, NY Franciscan Province of the Immaculate Conception.
Soto, Edward '58 (LA) Maywood, CA St. Rose of Lima Church.
Soto, Msgr. Jaime '82 (ORG) [2] Santa Ana, CA Our Lady of Guadalupe Church.
Soto, Roberto Angel '95 (CGS) Comerio, PR Santo Cristo de la Salud Church.
Soto, Ruben Albano *f.m.m.* '96 (WIL) [I] Seaford, DE Missionary Fraternity of Mary, USA, Ltd.
Sottek, James J. *o.s.f.s.* '57 (TOL) [K] Toledo, OH Oblates of St. Francis de Sales.
Soucey, Louis A. '74 (MAN) North Conway, NH Our Lady of the Mountains Church; Retired.
Soucie, Edward A. *s.j.* '62 (CI) [B] Pohnpei, FM PATS (Pohnpei Agriculture and Trade School).
Souckar, Michael '88 (MIA) Higher Studies.
Soucy, A. Francis *o.f.m.* '67 (PAT) [M] Ringwood, NJ Holy Name Friary.
Soucy, D. Wilfrid '30 (PRT) Retired.
Soucy, Maurice P. '49 (HRT) [3] Meriden, CT St. Laurent Church.
Soucy, Robert P. '62 (BO) Stow, MA St. Isidore Church.
Soucy, Timothy J. '73 (OG) Saranac Lake, NY St. Bernard Church.
Souffrant, Claude *s.j.* '65 (CHI) [120] Chicago, IL St. Margaret of Scotland Church.
Soukup, Gervase *o.s.b.* '45 (SCL) [I] Collegeville, MN St. John's Abbey, of the Order of St. Benedict.
Soukup, Gregory *o.s.b.* '41 (SCL) [I] Collegeville, MN St. John's Abbey, of the Order of St. Benedict.
Soukup, Paul *s.j.* '79 (SJ) San Jose, CA Catholic Scouting.
Soukup, Paul A. *s.j.* '79 (SJ) [B] Santa Clara, CA Santa Clara University.
Soule, W. Becket *o.p.* '93 (WDC) [11] Washington, DC St. Dominic Church & Priory Church.
Soulliere, John Richard '76 (MIA) Lighthouse Point, FL St. Paul the Apostle Church.
Sousa, Douglas H. '91 (FR) [5] Taunton, MA St. Anthony's Church.
Sousa, Eugene *o.p.* '58 (PHX) [5] Phoenix, AZ Most Holy Trinity Church.
Sousa, Jose M. '85 (FR) [6] New Bedford, MA Our Lady of Mt. Carmel Church.
Sousa, Kevin '82 (SPR) Absent on Leave.
Sousa, Manuel F. '80 (STO) Turlock, CA Our Lady of the Assumption of the Portuguese Church.
Sousa, Peter E. *c.ss.r.* '78 (BRK) [C] Whitestone, NY St. Alphonsus Formation Residence.
Sousa, Peter E. *c.ss.r.* '78 (RIC) [O] Hampton, VA Holy Family Retreat House.
Souse, Stephen J. *o.s.b.* '40 (PEO) [C] Peru, IL St. Bede Academy.
Souse, Stephen J. *o.s.b.* '43 (PEO) [A] Peru, IL St. Bede Abbey and Academy.
Southerton, Gary '88 (SEA) Puyallup, WA All Saints Church; Puyallup, WA Holy Disciples Church.
Soutiere, Ronald '74 (BUR) Military Chaplains.
Soutus, Hugo '94 (STN) Phoenix, AZ Assumption of B.V.M. Church.
Soutuyo, Raul '93 (MIA) [16] Miami, FL St. Brendan Church.
Souva, Eileen *o.p.* (LAN) [1] Jackson, MI St. John the Evangelist Church.
Sowada, Arlie '73 (SCL) Brown's Valley, MN St. Anthony's Church.
Sowada, Terrance '92 (SP) [14] Tampa, FL St. Paul Church.
Sowinski, Albin F. '51 (MIL) Retired.
Sowinski, Richard E. '74 (BUF) [4] Kenmore, NY St. Paul Church.
Soy, Esteban G. '52 (VEN) [1] Venice, FL Epiphany Cathedral.
Soyka, Giles '50 (GB) [I] Appleton, WI St. Fidelis Friary.
Spacek, William F. (BAL) [10] Baltimore, MD St. Anthony of Padua Church.
Spacht, Andres *c.ss.r.* '61 (CGS) Aguas Buenas, PR Church of Tres Santos Reyes.
Spada, Rino CS (LA) Retired.
Spadaro, Thomas L. '64 (RVC) Holbrook, NY Good Shepherd Church.
Spadini, Marian '62 (JKS) On Duty Outside the Diocese.
Spadini, Marian '62 (MEM) [22] Memphis, TN Our Lady of Perpetual Help Church.
Spagnolia, D. George '64 (BO) Franklin, MA St. Mary Church.
Spagnolo, Nicholas *c.s.s.* '52 (BO) [W] Waltham, MA Stigmatine House.
Spahn, James A. *o.p.* '81 (CHI) [N] Chicago, IL Dominicans (Provincial Office).
Spahr, Matthew D. '92 (SD) Alpine, CA Queen of Angels Church; [B] San Diego, CA University of San Diego.
Spaight, Msgr. Robert L. '56 (DUB) Nashua, IA St. Michael's Church.
Spain, John H. *m.m.* '70 (NY) [Z] Maryknoll, NY Maryknoll Fathers and Brothers.
Spain, P. Arnold '47 (BIS) Retired.
Spaits, George S. '43 (PH) Retired.
Spalding, J. Mark '91 (L) Lebanon, KY St. Augustine Church.
Spalding, Leon C. '59 (L) [1] Springfield, KY St. Dominic Church.
Spalding, William '45 (GB) Retired.
Spalding, William '48 (LEX) Retired.
Spanel, Hubert J. '59 (GI) Hemingford, NE St. Bridget Church.
Spangenberg, Robert *c.s.sp.* '74 (CHL) Hamlet, NC St. James Church.
Spanier, Marian '81 (NEW) [4] Garfield, NJ St. Stanislaus Kostka Church.
Spanjers, John J. '59 (SUP) Almena, WI Sacred Heart of Jesus Church of Almena; Turtle Lake, WI St. Ann Church.
Spanley, Anthony L. '68 (GRY) Hamlet, IN Holy Cross Church.
Spano, Anthony *s.d.b.* '43 (NY) [Z] New Rochelle, NY Salesian Provincial House.
Spano, Philip F. '82 (BR) Gonzales, LA St. Theresa of Avila Church.
Sparklin, Paul '91 (BAL) [47] Baltimore, MD St. Joseph Church.
Sparks, Joseph R. '66 (DAV) Solon, IA St. Mary's Church.
Sparks, Kenneth A. '95 (PIT) Ross Township, PA St. Sebastian Church.
Sparks, Richard C. *c.s.p.* '78 (CHI) [125] Chicago, IL Old St. Mary Church.
Sparks, Thomas J. (MAN) [B] Warner, NH Magdalen College.
Sparks, Thomas J. '56 (LAN) Retired.
Sparks, Timothy H. *o.p.* '30 (CHI) [N] River Forest, IL St. Thomas Aquinas Priory.
Sparough, J. Michael *s.j.* '78 (CHI) [T] Barrington, IL Bellarmine Hall.
Spatorico, Joseph S. '66 (BUF) Military Chaplains.
Spatt, John *c.pp.s.* '43 (CIN) [B] Carthagena, OH St. Charles.
Spaulding, Donald E. '57 (EVN) Dubois, IN St. Raphael Church.
Spaulding, John '71 (PHX) [25] Phoenix, AZ St. Thomas the Apostle Church.
Spear, Arthur J. *c.s.p.* '38 (NY) [Z] Scarsdale, NY Paulist Fathers Generalate.
Specht, Terry W. '96 (ARL) Fairfax, VA St. Mary of Sorrows Church.
Speck, Gregory M. *s.c.j.* '76 (BWN) Raymondville, TX Our Lady of Guadalupe Church.
Speck, James A. '50 (WIN) Retired.
Speckman, Harry *o.f.m.* '61 (SFD) [B] Quincy, IL Quincy University.
Speer, Patrick '41 (BGP) [K] Trumbull, CT St. Joseph's Manor.
Speer, Patrick J. '41 (HRT) Retired.
Speers, David B. '90 (TUC) Absent on Leave.
Speerstra, William F. '59 (SUP) Land-O'-Lakes, WI St. Albert Church; Phelps, WI Holy Redeemer Church.
Spegele, Michael A. '41 (B) Retired.
Speice, Msgr. Lawrence T. '61 (E) [A] Erie, PA St. Mark's Seminary.
Speicher, Charles W. '75 (PIT) Baldwin Boro, PA St. Albert the Great Church.
Speicher, David '86 (LAN) Hartland, MI St. John The Baptist Church.
Speichinger, Lawrence '55 (KC) Retired.
Speier, Francis J. '75 (TOL) [12] Toledo, OH Our Lady of Perpetual Help Church.
Speier, Thomas *o.f.m.* (CIN) [24] Cincinnati, OH Corpus Christi Church.
Speiler, Joe *s.j.* '75 (SD) [4] San Diego, CA Christ the King Church.
Speiser, Allan '48 (SCL) Retired.
Speiser, Thomas '77 (DAL) Forney, TX St. Martin Church; Kaufman, TX St. Ann Church.
Speiss, Kevin J. '86 (CHI) [1] Lemont, IL St. Alphonsus Church.
Speitel, Edmond J. '55 (PH) Brookhaven, PA Our Lady of Charity Church; East Greenville, PA St. Philip Neri Church.
Spekschate, John '42 (LAF) Retired.

Spelgatti, Msgr. David P. '41 (MAR) Retired.
Spell, August '54 (SFD) Palmyra, IL Holy Rosary Church.
Spellen, Lawrence M. '46 (SLC) Retired.
Spellerberg, Joseph R. *s.j.* '53 (BUF) [50] Buffalo, NY St. Michael Church.
Spellman, Francis J. '40 (CHI) [4] Cicero, IL Mary, Queen of Heaven Church; Retired; [M] Niles, IL St. Benedict Home for the Aged.
Spellman, John P. *o.s.f.s.* '66 (WIL) [B] Wilmington, DE Salesianum School.
Spellman, Robert (WOR) Shrewsbury, MA St. Anne's Church.
Speltz, Msgr. Richard '33 (WIN) Retired.
Spenard, James T. *o.s.a.* '72 (OG) Carthage, NY St. James Minor Church; Deferiet, NY St. Rita Church.
Spencer, F. Richard '88 (BAL) Oakland, MD St. Peter the Apostle Church.
Spencer, Francis M. *m.s.* '50 (MAN) [2] Nashua, NH St. Casimir Church.
Spencer, Gregory '89 (EVN) St. Joseph, IN St. Joseph's Church.
Spencer, Jeremiah L. '65 (KCK) [5] Kansas City, KS Holy Name Church; Kansas City, KS K.U. Medical Center and Chapel.
Spencer, John *s.j.* '79 (BO) [W] Chestnut Hill, MA The Jesuit Community at Boston College.
Spencer, John P. *s.j.* '79 (BO) [30] Boston, MA Immaculate Conception Church.
Spencer, Robert (NY) City, NY Manhattan Detention Center.
Spencer, Robert '85 (WCH) On Duty Outside the Diocese.
Spencer, William *o.f.m.* '74 (SHP) [6] Shreveport, LA St. Catherine of Siena Church.
Spendov, Vendelin *o.f.m.* '47 (CHI) [N] Lemont, IL The Slovene Franciscan Fathers, Order of Friars Minor, Commissariat of the Holy Cross.
Spener, Robert M. '82 (RIC) Petersburg, VA St. Joseph Church.
Spengler, Msgr. James F. '68 (BRK) [172] Queens, NY St. Gerard Majella Church.
Spenner, Jerome I. '64 (OM) Creighton, NE St. Ludger Church.
Spenner, Wilfred J. '73 (OM) Albion, NE St. Michael Church.
Speno, Eugene '60 (SB) Palm Springs, CA Our Lady of Guadalupe Church.
Spera, James F. '77 (NEW) [B] South Orange, NJ Seton Hall University; [B] South Orange, NJ Seton Hall University.
Sperber, Timothy '78 (HBG) On Duty Outside the Diocese.
Sperber, Timothy '78 (MIA) Pembroke Pines, FL St. Boniface Church.
Sperger, Herbert J. '79 (PH) [9] Philadelphia, PA St. Ambrose Church.
Sperl, August J. '54 (SFD) Virden, IL Sacred Heart Church.
Sperlak, Charles S. '64 (ALN) [4] Reading, PA SS. Cyril and Methodius Church.
Sperry, Msgr. James E. '41 (E) Retired.
Spexarth, Daniel J. '84 (WCH) Schulte, KS St. Peter's Church; Wichita, KS Sedgwick County Adult Local Detention Facility.
Spexarth, James '55 (WCH) Retired.
Spexarth, Joachim *o.s.b.* '65 (OKL) [I] Shawnee, OK St. Gregory's Abbey.
Speyrer, Jules (LAF) Retired.
Spezia, Leo J. '76 (STL) Wentzville, MO St. Patrick Church.
Spezia, Robert '95 (DET) Graduate Studies.
Spicer, Kevin P. *c.s.c.* '92 (FR) [B] North Easton, MA Holy Cross Fathers Religious.
Spicer, Leo M. *o.s.m.* '76 (ORG) [H] Buena Park, CA Servite Fathers And Brothers.
Spicer, Richard J. '86 (SEA) Arlington, WA Immaculate Conception Church.
Spicijaric, Anthony '33 (PH) Retired.
Spicuzza, Anthony P. '46 (IND) Brazil, IN Annunciation of the Blessed Virgin Mary Church.
Spiece, Lawrence '61 (E) [C] Erie, PA Cathedral Preparatory School.
Spiegel, John D. '76 (DAV) Houghton, IA St. John's Church; St. Paul, IA St. James Church.
Spiegel, Robert H. '66 (DAV) Military Chaplains.
Spiegel, Thomas J. '67 (DAV) Bettendorf, IA Our Lady of Lourdes Church.
Spiekermeier, Michael J. '69 (DAV) Keokuk, IA All Saints Church.
Spielman, Paul J. '61 (STL) [3] Lemay, MO St. Andrew Church.
Spielmann, Henry V. *o.s.a.* '39 (TLS) [B] Tulsa, OK Cascia Hall Preparatory School.
Spier, Mathias *o.s.b.* '58 (STP) [19] Minneapolis, MN St. Boniface Church.
Spiers, Msgr. Edward F. '39 (COL) On Duty Outside the Diocese.
Spika, Anthony (SFR) [K] San Rafael, CA Nazareth House.
Spika, Anthony L. '35 (SJ) Retired.
Spilka, Anthony Francis *o.f.m.conv.* '69 (SPR) [10] Chicopee, MA St. Stanislaus Basilica.
Spillane, Emmanuel *o.c.s.o.* '44 (SLC) [F] Huntsville, UT Abbey of Our Lady of the Holy Trinity of the Order of Cistercians.
Spillane, Jeremiah '86 (VEN) [1] Sarasota, FL Incarnation Church.
Spillane, Michael '68 (BAL) Special Assignment.
Spillane, Thomas J. *s.j.* '53 (BO) [W] Weston, MA Campion Center.
Spillane, Walter J. '60 (KAL) Retired.
Spillane, William *c.ss.r.* '58 (PCE) Guayama, PR St. Anthony of Padua Church.
Spillett, Thomas '64 (SP) [3] Largo, FL St. Matthew Church.
Spilly, Alphonse P. *c.pp.s.* '53 (CIN) [M] Dayton, OH Provincial House of the Cincinnati Province of the Society of the Precious Blood.
Spilly, William V. '74 (ROC) [29] Rochester, NY St. John Evangelist Church.
Spilman, Robert D. '96 (PEO) [1] Champaign, IL Holy Cross Church.
Spina, Douglas J. '76 (PRO) [4] Woonsocket, RI St. Anthony's Church.
Spine, William J. *s.j.* '73 (CHI) [C] Chicago, IL Jesuit Community at Loyola University of Chicago.
Spinelli, Joseph A. *o.s.a.* '55 (VEN) Golden Gate, FL St. Elizabeth Seton Church.
Spinks, W. Robert (CHL) [A] Belmont, NC Belmont Abbey College.
Spinler, Ruben C. '94 (WIN) Rose Creek, MN St. Peter's Church.
Spinner, Hubert '50 (RVC) Retired; [N] Uniondale, NY St. Pius X Residence.
Spino, John J. '90 (NEW) [13] Jersey City, NJ St. Joseph's Church.
Spinos, Vincent J. *t.o.r.* '50 (STP) [20] Minneapolis, MN St. Bridget Church.
Spinosa, Anthony S. '83 (OLL) Flint, MI Our Lady of Lebanon Church.
Spirko, Nicholas A. '72 (PIT) Ellwood City, PA Purification of the Blessed Virgin Mary Church.
Spisak, Paul G. '73 (PIT) Center Township, PA St. Andrew Church.
Spisak, Stephen '82 (CLV) [1] Barberton, OH St. Augustine Church.
Spisak, Thomas M. '77 (Y) [2] Warren, OH Christ Our King Church; [3] Warren, OH SS. Cyril and Methodius Church.
Spishak, Carl A. '59 (ALT) [5] Altoona, PA Holy Rosary Church.
Spitale, John '26 (Y) Retired.
Spiteri, George '70 (NY) [3] White Plains, NY St. Bernard Church.
Spiteri, Laurence '78 (LA) [98] Los Angeles, CA Visitation Church.
Spittler, Ernest G. *s.j.* '62 (CLV) [C] Cleveland, OH John Carroll Jesuit Community.
Spitz, Gregory M. '67 (MIL) Mequon, WI St. James Church.
Spitzer, Robert J. *s.j.* '83 (SEA) [A] Seattle, WA Seattle University.
Spitzig, Msgr. Joseph '42 (CLV) Retired.
Spitzley, Denis R. '75 (LAN) Burton, MI Blessed Sacrament Church.
Splawski, Bernard J. *o.f.m.* '63 (PAT) West Milford Township, NJ St. Joseph Church.
Spleet, Julius A. '62 (SAG) Gladwin, MI Sacred Heart Church.
Splonskowski, Wilfrid J. *o.s.b.* '52 (BIS) New Hradec, ND SS. Peter and Paul Church; [A] Richardton, ND Assumption Abbey.
Spodnik, A. Leo '48 (HRT) [2] Torrington, CT Sacred Heart Church.
Spoletini, Pasquale M. *s.j.* '54 (SEA) [31] Seattle, WA Our Lady of Mount Virgin Church.
Spolny, Joseph R. '78 (CLV) [38] Cleveland, OH St. John Nepomucene Church.
Sponder, John '93 (JOL) Steger, IL St. Liborius Church.
Spong, William '79 (FWT) On Duty Outside the Diocese.
Spontak, James '75 (PBR) Morgantown, WV St. Mary's Holy Protection Church; [E] Mount St. Macrina, PA Motherhouse and Novitiate of the Sisters of St. Basil the Great.
Spors, Roman '58 (DUL) Emily, MN St. Emily's Church.
Sprague, George Raymond '34 (PEO) Retired; [L] Peoria, IL St. Augustine Manor.
Spraker, Msgr. Gerard W. '34 (BAL) [11] Baltimore, MD Ascension Church; Retired.
Spranger, William J. '56 (GRY) San Pierre, IN All Saints Church; [I] San Pierre, IN Holy Cross Care Services dba Little Company of Mary Health Facility, Inc.
Sprauer, Michael '72 (P) Salem, OR Oregon State Correctional Institution; Salem, OR Oregon Women's Correction Center.
Sprecace, Msgr. Francis A. '55 (CAM) [2] Atlantic City, NJ St. Michael's Church.
Spreen, John W. '53 (SFD) Ashland, IL St. Augustine Church.
Spreitsma, Leo *o.f.m.conv.* '53 (TUC) Apache Junction, AZ St. George Church.
Sprenger, Alan M. '60 (COL) Special Assignment.
Spriggs, Robert W. '65 (SFD) Highland, IL St. Paul Church.
Sprigler, William A. '75 (NU) Clara City, MN St. Clara Church; Granite Falls, MN St. Andrew Church.
Spring, Mark P. '80 (DAV) Military Chaplains.
Springer, Francis *s.m.* '55 (HON) Kapaa, HI St. Catherine Church.
Springer, Francis *s.m.* '55 (SFR) [B] San Francisco, CA St. Peter Chanel Seminary; [N] San Francisco, CA Provincial Residence.
Springer, James *c.ss.r.* '49 (KC) [32] Kansas City, MO Our Lady of Perpetual Help Church; [J] Kansas City, MO Redemptorists of Kansas City.
Springer, Lawrence F. '59 (CHI) [4] Des Plaines, IL St. Zachary Church.
Springer, Robert *s.j.* '48 (NY) [Z] New York, NY West Side Jesuit Community.
Springer, William A. '72 (SD) [10] San Diego, CA Mission Basilica San Diego De Alcala Church.
Springman, Donald W. '67 (L) [3] Valley Station, KY Our Lady of Consolation Church.
Sprouffske, Matthew *o.carm.* '54 (JOL) [J] Darien, IL Carmelite Fathers Provincial Office.
Sproul, John M. '63 (SD) La Mesa, CA St. Martin of Tours Church.
Sproule, Robert N. *s.j.* '61 (BGP) [O] Fairfield, CT The Fairfield Jesuit Community-Fairfield University.
Sprute, Mel '69 (B) Kellogg, ID St. Rita's Church; Wallace, ID St. Alphonsus Church.
Spychala, Daniel S. '84 (ARL) Winchester, VA Sacred Heart of Jesus Church.
Spyrka, Edward C. *o.c.d.* '62 (GRY) [K] Munster, IN Discalced Carmelite Fathers Monastery.
Squeo, Eugene P. '71 (NEW) [7] Jersey City, NJ Assumption/All Saints Church; [23] Jersey City, NJ St. Patrick's Church.
Squiller, Msgr. John '56 (STF) Hamptonburgh, NY St. Andrew's Chapel.
Squire, Aelred *o.s.b.cam.* '52 (MRY) [G] Big Sur, CA New Camaldoli Hermitage.
Srebernak, Francis '37 (LAN) Retired.
Sreboth, Michael (MOB) Atmore, AL St. Robert Bellarmine Church.
Sredzinski, Joseph L. '70 (GBG) Everson, PA St. Joseph Church.
Srenn, Thomas E. '77 (CHI) [155] Chicago, IL Our Lady of Mount Carmel Church.
Srion, Charles N. '78 (RVC) Floral Park, NY Our Lady of Victory Church.
Sroba, Andrew '93 (ALN) [4] Allentown, PA St. John the Baptist Church.
Srode, John S. *c.pp.s.* '72 (CIN) [M] Dayton, OH Provincial House of the Cincinnati Province of the Society of the Precious Blood.
Sroka, Gerald A. '60 (GRY) Valparaiso, IN St. Elizabeth Seton Church.
Srumpf, David *o.f.m.* '90 (CHI) [N] Lemont, IL The Slovene Franciscan Fathers, Order of Friars Minor, Commissariat of the Holy Cross.
Ssebadduka, George '78 (MIL) Mequon, WI St. James Church.
Sserunjogi, Expedit '86 (LA) Culver City, CA St. Augustine Church.
St-Pierre, Michel J. '57 (BUR) [2] Burlington, VT St. Anthony's Church.
St. Charles, Paul W. '66 (MEM) Retired.
St. Clair, Joseph A. '40 (PH) Ardmore, PA St. Colman Church; Retired.
St. Clair, Robert L. *s.j.* (OAK) [R] Oakland, CA Institute of Lay Theology.
St. Clair, Robert L. *s.j.* '58 (SJ) [M] Los Gatos, CA California Province of the Society of Jesus, Jesuit Provincial Office.
St. Cyr, Richard E. '66 (PRT) Saco, ME Notre Dame de Lourdes Church.
St. George, John P. *s.j.* '66 (NEW) [B] Jersey City, NJ Saint Peter's College; [N] Jersey City, NJ Jesuits of Saint Peter's College, Inc.
St. George, Peter Thomas '95 (CIN) [71] Cincinnati, OH Our Lady of Victory Church.
St. Germain, Antoine F. '76 (CAM) Pennsauken, NJ St. Stephen Church.
St. Germain, Brian '88 (PRM) Absent on Leave.
St. Godard, Edward G. '64 (PRO) [6] Woonsocket, RI Holy Family Church.
St. Jacques, Clement *s.a.* '45 (WDC) [B] Washington, DC Atonement Seminary-Francisan Friars of the Atonement.
St. James, Paul F. '68 (BUR) Essex Junction, VT St. Lawrence, Martyr Church.
St. Jean, Marcel '96 (BGP) [7] Bridgeport, CT St. Charles Church.
St. Jean, Mary Kidney '92 (MIA) [10] Miami, FL Notre Dame d'Haiti Church.
St. John, George G. '52 (ALB) East Greenbush, NY Holy Spirit Church.

St. John, Norman R. *s.v.d.* '62 (MET) Belle Mead, NJ Carrier Clinic.
St. John, Norman R. *s.v.d.* '62 (TR) [M] Bordentown, NJ Society of the Divine Word.
St. Jules, Stephen '79 (RCK) Batavia, IL Holy Cross Church.
St. Laurent, Daniel A. '71 (MAN) [4] Nashua, NH St. Francis Xavier Church.
St. Marie, Denis L. '59 (CLV) Independence, OH St. Michael Church; El Salvador, C.A., OH The Catholic Center.
St. Marie, Michael '93 (B) Gooding, ID St. Elizabeth's Church; Shoshone, ID St. Peter's Church.
St. Martin, Robert *o.f.m.conv.* '77 (FTW) Angola, IN St. Anthony Church.
St. Martin, Robert J. '56 (HRT) Unionville, CT St. Mary's Church.
St. Onge, Omer *s.m.* '46 (BRK) [45] Brooklyn, NY St. Francis of Assisi-St. Blaise Church.
St. Onge, Msgr. Paul J. '41 (NOR) New London, CT St. Joseph Church; Retired.
St. Peter, Lawrence '59 (DEN) Absent on Leave.
St. Pierre, Anthony *o.s.b.* '78 (GBG) [H] Latrobe, PA Saint Vincent Archabbey.
St. Pierre, Leo L. '39 (MAN) Wolfeboro, NH St. Cecilia Church.
St. Pierre, Roland *o.m.i.* '52 (MAN) [K] Colebrook, NH Shrine of Our Lady of Grace.
St. Pierre, Romeo A. '54 (PRT) Retired.
St. Pierre, Ronald L. '83 (BO) Tyngsborough, MA St. Mary Magdalen Church.
St. Pierre, Thomas J. '80 (RVC) Brentwood, NY St. Anne's Church.
St. Sure, Donald F. *s.j.* '39 (SJ) [M] Los Gatos, CA California Province of the Society of Jesus, Jesuit Provincial Office; [M] Los Gatos, CA Sacred Heart Jesuit Center.
St.John, Norman *s.v.d.* (TR) Howell Township, NJ St. Veronica Church.
Sta. Maria, Nicanor *s.d.b.* (SJN) [37] San Juan, PR Maria Auxiliadora Church.
Staab, Gregory *o.m.v.* '84 (BO) [B] Boston, MA Our Lady of Grace Seminary.
Staal, David E. '90 (OAK) Livermore, CA St. Michael's Church; [R] Oakland, CA Adventus; [R] Oakland, CA The Roman Catholic Cemeteries of the Diocese of Oakland.
Staar, Robert J. '77 (NY) Stony Point, NY Immaculate Conception Church.
Stab, Herbert J. '59 (MET) Piscataway, NJ Our Lady of Fatima Church.
Stabene, Edmondo '45 (STU) Hopedale, OH Sacred Heart Church.
Staber, Francis H. '43 (SC) Retired.
Stacer, John R. *s.j.* '63 (NO) [P] New Orleans, LA Jesuit Provincial Office.
Stacherczak, Idzi '75 (CHI) [33] Chicago, IL St. Bruno Church.
Stachewicz, Msgr. Henry J. '47 (BUF) [1] Depew, NY St. Augustine Church.
Stachnik, Kenneth R. '86 (GAY) [3] Alpena, MI St. John the Baptist Church.
Stachowiak, Conrad P. '74 (BUF) [7] Cheektowaga, NY Our Lady Help of Christians Church.
Stachura, Thaddeus X. '64 (WOR) [9] Worcester, MA Our Lady of Czestochowa Church.
Stachurski, David *o.f.m.conv.* '80 (ATL) Lithia Springs, GA St. John Vianney Church.
Stack, Aquinas E. *o.carm.* '85 (PMB) [5] Boca Raton, FL St. Jude Church.
Stack, Christopher '66 (PMB) Retired.
Stack, Daniel '82 (ATL) Dalton, GA St. Joseph's Church; [L] Atlanta, GA Campus Ministry.
Stack, Gabriel D. *o.praem.* '82 (ORG) [D] Siverado, CA St. Michael's College Preparatory High School; [H] Silverado, CA Norbertine Fathers; [M] El Toro, CA Aid to the Church In Need, Inc.
Stack, George J. '59 (BRK) [220] Queens, NY Our Lady of the Snows Church.
Stack, Gilbert *o.s.b.* '39 (KC) [J] Conception, MO Conception Abbey.
Stack, James M. '86 (WDC) [4] Washington, DC Annunciation Church; Special Ministries.
Stack, Jerome *c.pp.s.* '72 (LA) Norwalk, CA Metropolitan State Hospital.
Stack, John '88 (DAV) [L] Clinton, IA The Alverno Health Care Facility; [N] Clinton, IA Mount St. Clare Convent.
Stack, John G. *s.j.* '71 (DAL) [D] Dallas, TX Jesuit College Preparatory School.
Stack, John J. '53 (HRT) [6] West Hartford, CT St. Thomas the Apostle Church; [C] West Hartford, CT Saint Joseph College.
Stack, John J. '88 (DAV) Camanche, IA Church of the Visitation; [J] Clinton, IA Samaritan Health System, Inc.
Stack, John P. '55 (WDC) Chaptico, MD Our Lady of the Wayside Church.
Stack, John P. *o.s.a.* '74 (PH) [C] Villanova, PA Villanova University; [Z] Villanova, PA St. Thomas Monastery.
Stack, Joseph O. *o.m.i.* '34 (BO) [Z] Tewksbury, MA Immaculate Heart of Mary Novitiate-Infirmary.
Stack, Lambert *s.t.* '44 (WDC) [M] Adelphi, MD Missionary Servants of the Most Holy Trinity.
Stack, Philip Dan '48 (SUP) Sugar Camp, WI St. Kunegunda Church.
Stack, Msgr. Richard J. '56 (E) [23] Erie, PA St. Luke Church.
Stack, T. Mannix '73 (MIA) Miami Lakes, FL Our Lady of the Lakes Church.
Stack, William E. '48 (MAD) Retired.
Stackpoole, Edward V. *s.j.* '56 (SFR) [N] San Francisco, CA Jesuit Community at University of San Francisco.
Stacy, Bernard *c.m.f.* '47 (LA) [R] Rancho Dominguez, CA Dominguez Seminary Inc.
Stacy, Ronald W. '72 (ROC) Absent on Leave.
Stadalnikas, Casimir J. '40 (MIA) Retired.
Stadler, Joseph '32 (SB) Retired.
Stadler, Robert G. '48 (SFR) Foster City, CA St. Luke Church.
Stadtmueller, Msgr. Fred '40 (SFE) Retired.
Stadtmueller, Roman *s.d.s.* '54 (WDC) [B] Silver Spring, MD Salvatorian Community.
Staebell, Msgr. Francis J. *s.j.* (BUF) [K] Buffalo, NY Mercy Hospital.
Staebell, James E. '57 (BUF) Farnham, NY St. Anthony's Church.
Staehler, Adrian *o.f.m.cap.* '67 (MIL) [P] Milwaukee, WI St. Conrad House.
Staes, Robert *o.p.* '71 (DEN) [34] Denver, CO St. Mary Magdalene's Church.
Staff, Stephen M. *c.m.* '90 (MOB) Auburn, AL St. Michael Church.
Stafford, Dennis J. '91 (CHI) Barrington, IL St. Anne Church; Vernon Hills, IL St. Mary of Vernon Church.
Stafford, James D.M. '61 (OKL) Lawton, OK Blessed Sacrament Church.
Stafford, Joseph E. *o.s.f.s.* '52 (WIL) [I] Childs, MD Oblates of St. Francis De Sales.
Stafford, Msgr. Joseph L. '57 (BRK) [178] Queens, NY Holy Family Church.
Stafford, Michael *o.s.b.* '58 (KAL) Battle Creek, MI Veteran's Administration Hospital.
Stafford, Michael *o.s.b.* '58 (PRO) [P] Portsmouth, RI Abbey of St. Gregory the Great.
Stafford, Raymond W. '59 (BRK) [203] Queens, NY Most Precious Blood Church.
Stagaman, David J. *s.j.* '66 (OAK) [A] Berkeley, CA The Jesuit School of Theology at Berkeley; [N] Berkeley, CA Jesuit Community at Jesuit School of Theology at Berkeley.
Stagg, Robert B. '75 (NEW) Springfield, NJ St. James Church.
Stagnaro, John J. '76 (BO) Holbrook, MA St. Joseph Church; Lynnfield, MA St. Maria Goretti Church; On Special or Other Diocesan Assignment.
Stahel, Thomas H. *s.j.* '71 (NO) [P] New Orleans, LA Jesuit Provincial Office.
Stahl, Allen '75 (ORL) On Duty Outside the Diocese.
Stahl, David A. '91 (DEN) [22] Denver, CO Presentation of Our Lady Church.
Stahl, George '56 (IND) On Disability Leave.
Stahura, Joseph L. '81 (HBG) Greencastle, PA St. Mark the Evangelist Church.
Staiger, Charles '56 (RVC) Sick Leave.
Staigers, P. Del '87 (CIN) [B] Cincinnati, OH Mt. St. Mary's Seminary of the West.
Stajkowski, Leo S. '66 (ALN) [9] Reading, PA St. Mary Church.
Stake, Ronald P. '85 (CHI) Military Chaplains.
Stakem, Gary *o.f.m.cap.* '51 (CLV) [65] Cleveland, OH St. Philip Neri Church; [P] Cleveland, OH St. Paul Friary.
Stakem, Ward *o.f.m.cap.* '78 (PIT) Rochester, PA St. Cecilia Church; [N] Rochester, PA St. Cecilia Friary.
Stalavicz, George P. '51 (SCR) Retired.
Staley, Robert '95 (R) Fayetteville, NC St. Patrick Church.
Stallings, John E. '50 (BEL) Harrisburg, IL St. Mary Church.
Stalter, Cal '94 (AMA) Wellington, TX Our Mother of Mercy Church.
Stalzer, David '74 (JOL) [16] Joliet, IL St. Mary Nativity Church.
Stalzer, Joseph '59 (JOL) Itasca, IL St. Peter the Apostle Church.
Stamborski, James J. '55 (GB) [5] Manitowoc, WI St. Andrew Church.
Stampiglia, Fausto *s.a.c.* '60 (VEN) [3] Sarasota, FL St. Martha Church; [F] Sarasota, FL St. Martha's Housing, Inc.; [F] Sarasota, FL St. Martha's Housing II, Inc.
Stamschror, Robert P. '61 (WIN) [J] Winona, MN Saint Mary's Press, Christian Brothers Publications.
Stanal, Frank J. (JC) Retired.
Stanbery, Stephen '80 (TOL) New Bavaria, OH Sacred Heart of Jesus Church; North Creek, OH St. Joseph Church.
Stanchik, Dennis P. '59 (LC) Adams, WI St. Joseph Church; Brooks, WI St. Ann Church.
Stander, Charles J. *s.m.* '81 (CIN) [M] Dayton, OH Marianist Provincialate.
Stander, Edwin L. '63 (LIN) [5] Lincoln, NE Sacred Heart Church; Lincoln, NE Nebraska Penal Complex.
Stanek, Msgr. Wenceslaus '30 (CHI) Retired.
Stanfield, Francis E. '80 (GLP) Retired; [F] Gallup, NM Southwest Indian Foundation.
Stanfield, William L. '76 (MIL) On Duty Outside the Archdiocese.
Stang, Charles L. *s.j.* '67 (MIL) [E] Milwaukee, WI Marquette University High School; [P] Milwaukee, WI Arrupe House Jesuit Community.
Stang, Mark '90 (SCL) Long Prairie, MN St. Mary of Mt. Carmel Church.
Stang, William J. *c.pp.s.* '77 (LFT) [A] Rensselaer, IN Saint Joseph's College.
Stanganelli, Anthony M. '79 (RVC) Franklin Square, NY St. Catherine of Sienna Church.
Stange, Frank (R) Rocky Mount, NC Our Lady of Perpetual Help Church.
Stange, Henry '90 (ALT) [3] Altoona, PA St. Mark's Church.
Stange, James '95 (P) [3] Eugene, OR St. Mary Church.
Stangel, Mark J. '65 (MIL) [1] West Allis, WI St. Aloysius Church.
Stanger, Edward J. '91 (STL) [58] St. Louis, MO St. Raphael The Archangel Church.
Stanger, Harold B. '77 (CHI) [1] Oak Park, IL Ascension Church; [A] Chicago, IL Institute of Vocation Awareness.
Stangl, Alfred '63 (SCL) St. Cloud, MN U.S. Veteran's Hospital.
Stangl, Alfred '67 (SCL) Special Assignment.
Stanibula, Christopher '95 (FR) [15] New Bedford, MA St. John the Baptist Church.
Stanichar, Joseph '68 (VNN) Portland, OR Byzantine Catholic Community of Portland, OR Church; Lacy, WA Byzantine Catholic Community Attended from St. John Chrysostom, Seattle, WA Church; Seattle, WA St. John Chrysostom Church.
Stanievich, J. Walter '46 (DET) Retired.
Stanion, Robert *c.f.r.* '92 (NY) [Z] Yonkers, NY Saint Felix Friary.
Staniskis, Daniel '84 (PSC) Flanders, NJ Holy Wisdom Church.
Staniszewski, Ignatius *s.s.p.* '64 (NY) [B] New York, NY Society of St. Paul.
Staniszewski, Jerome B. *o.f.m.* '48 (PIT) [N] Ben Avon, PA St. Anthony Friary and Mission House.
Staniszewski, Stanley *c.m.* '63 (HRT) [M] Manchester, CT DePaul Provincial Residence.
Staniszewski, Stanley T. '74 (KAL) [1] Kalamazoo, MI St. Augustine Cathedral.
Stankard, Albert H. '59 (BO) [4] Framingham, MA St. Stephen Church.
Stankavage, Joseph G. '90 (WDC) Laurel, MD St. Mary Church.
Stankevicius, John P. '37 (CHI) Retired.
Stankiewicz, John A. *s.s.e.* '41 (BUR) [G] Colchester, VT Society of St. Edmund.
Stanko, Andrew C. '71 (ALT) [3] Johnstown, PA Immaculate Conception Church; [11] Johnstown, PA St. Michael's Church; [D] Johnstown, PA Good Samaritan Medical Center.
Stanko, Edward '56 (PSC) Forest City, PA St. John the Baptist Church.
Stankus, Gregory A. '78 (BRK) [81] Brooklyn, NY St. Mary Mother of Jesus Church.
Stanley, Brian L. '96 (KAL) [4] Kalamazoo, MI St. Monica Church.
Stanley, Charles R. (BO) Society of St. James the Apostle.
Stanley, Colm *s.s.c.* '69 (OM) [K] St. Columbans, NE St. Columban's Foreign Mission Society.
Stanley, Matthew '91 (SJ) [1] Palo Alto, CA St. Thomas Aquinas Church.
Stanley, Matthew D. '91 (SJ) [2] Palo Alto, CA St. Albert the Great Church.
Stanley, Richard J. *s.j.* '74 (BGP) [A] Fairfield, CT Fairfield University; [O] Fairfield, CT The Fairfield Jesuit Community-Fairfield University; [V] Bridgeport, CT Newman Centers.
Stanley, Ronald A. *o.p.* '67 (MET) [H] New Brunswick, NJ De Porres House; [M] New Brunswick, NJ Catholic Center at Rutgers University.
Stanley, Thomas J. *s.m.* '50 (CIN) [M] Dayton, OH Marianist Provincialate.
Stano, Luke *o.s.m.* '61 (DET) [38] Detroit, MI St. John Berchmans-St. Juliana Church.
Stano, Luke M. *o.s.m.* '61 (CHI) [N] Chicago, IL Servite Friars - Eastern Province.
Stanonik, Anthony '82 (SD) Fallbrook, CA St. Peter Church.
Stanosz, Paul A. '84 (MIL) [58] Milwaukee, WI Our Lady of Good Hope Church.
Stansberry, Richard, Jr. '92 (OKL) [3] Oklahoma City, OK St. Charles Borromeo Church.
Stansley, Ralph W. '73 (TR) Hopewell, NJ St. Alphonsus Church.

Stanton, Finbarr P. '67 (SAV) Albany, GA St. Teresa Church.
Stanton, Francis M. '59 (COL) [34] Columbus, OH Our Lady of Peace Church.
Stanton, Joseph '51 (COL) Retired.
Stanton, Joseph F. *o.c.s.o.* '84 (ROC) [I] Piffard, NY Abbey of the Genesee.
Stanton, Leonard F. '43 (SFS) Retired.
Stanton, Terence *o.s.b.* '43 (RCK) [H] Aurora, IL Marmion Abbey-St. Augustine's Abbey.
Stanton, Thomas J. '92 (BO) [68] Boston, MA Sacred Heart Church.
Stanton, Msgr. William G. '49 (BUF) [6] Buffalo, NY St. Ambrose Church.
Stanton, William J. '52 (PH) Wyndmoor, PA Seven Dolors Church.
Stanton, Msgr. William J. '56 (SPC) Sikeston, MO St. Francis Xavier's Church.
Stapenhorst, Verne P. '61 (SC) [1] Sioux City, IA Cathedral of the Epiphany; [B] Sioux City, IA Bishop Heelan Catholic High School.
Staples, Terrence R. '95 (ARL) Fairfax, VA St. Mary of Sorrows Church.
Stapleton, Edward J. *s.s.s.* '60 (CLV) [P] Cleveland, OH Congregation of the Blessed Sacrament Provincial House; [P] Cleveland, OH Blessed Sacrament Community.
Stapleton, Gerard '85 (NO) [11] Metairie, LA St. Louis King of France Church.
Stapleton, James *c.s.p.* '74 (BRK) [239] Queens, NY Sacred Heart Church.
Starbuck, James (OAK) Military Chaplains.
Starc, Martin '30 (STO) San Andreas, CA St. Andrew Church.
Staricek, Andrew '40 (RC) Retired.
Stark, John W. '57 (DUB) Retired.
Stark, Paul V. *s.j.* '85 (STL) [C] St. Louis, MO Saint Louis University; [P] St. Louis, MO Jesuit Community Corporation at St. Louis University - Jesuit Hall.
Stark, Robert *s.s.s.* '77 (SFE) [23] Albuquerque, NM St. Charles Borromeo Church.
Stark, Ronald P. *o.f.m.* '66 (NY) [35] New York, NY St. Francis of Assisi Church.
Starks, R. Mansfield '42 (ALB) Glenville, NY Immaculate Conception Church; Retired.
Starmann, Joseph W. '63 (JC) On Duty Outside the Diocese; Absent on Leave.
Staron, Stanley R. '74 (HRT) [I] Waterbury, CT St. Mary Hospital.
Starostka, John C. '61 (OM) Cedar Rapids, NE St. Anthony Church.
Starus, Ralph E. '60 (CHI) [119] Chicago, IL St. Malachy Church.
Starzynski, Stefan P. '96 (ARL) Annandale, VA St. Michael's Church.
Stasell, Dean *l.c.* (ATL) [I] Dunwoody, GA Legionaries of Christ.
Stash, Robert '82 (PRM) Bay City, MI Saint George Church; Omer Co., MI St. John Mission Church.
Stashek, Leonard C. '56 (LC) Milan, WI St. Thomas Church; Wuerzburg, WI St. John the Baptist Church.
Stasiak, Kurt *o.s.b.* '80 (IND) [A] St. Meinrad, IN St. Meinrad Seminary; [J] St. Meinrad, IN St. Meinrad Archabbey.
Stasik, Thaddeus '60 (NEW) [5] Jersey City, NJ St. Ann's Church.
Stasiowski, John S. '65 (FWT) Bowie, TX St. Jerome Church; Henrietta, TX St. Mary Church; Montague, TX St. William Church; Nocona, TX St. Joseph Church.
Stasker, R. Louis '65 (GR) [19] Grand Rapids, MI St. Paul the Apostle Church.
Stasyszen, Lawrence R. *o.s.b.* '94 (OKL) [I] Shawnee, OK St. Gregory's Abbey.
Staszak, Bernard C. '65 (BUF) French Creek, NY St. Matthias Church.
Staszak, David J. *o.p.* '55 (CHI) [N] Chicago, IL Dominicans (Provincial Office).
Staszewski, Joseph P. '64 (E) Lucinda, PA St. Joseph Church.
Staszewski, Robert M. '72 (PIT) [1] Carnegie, PA St. Elizabeth Ann Seton Church.
Statkus, Edward '38 (GR) Retired.
Statkus, Msgr. Francis J. '46 (PH) Ardmore, PA St. Colman Church; Retired.
Statnick, Roger A. '73 (GBG) Derry, PA St. Joseph Church.
Statt, Thomas R. '58 (ROC) [40] Rochester, NY Our Mother of Sorrows Church.
Stattmiller, John E. '66 (COL) Otway, OH Our Lady of Lourdes Church; West Portsmouth, OH Our Lady of Sorrows Church.
Statz, James '84 (SCL) Brooten, MN St. Donatus Church; Padua, MN Church of St. Anthony of Padua.
Staub, Msgr. Edward F. '61 (BAL) Severna Park, MD St. John the Evangelist Church.
Staub, Eugene J. *c.ss.r.* '52 (BR) [H] Baton Rouge, LA Redemptorist Fathers Vice Provincialate.
Stauber, James '59 (SB) On Leave.
Staublin, Daniel J. '82 (IND) Brownsburg, IN St. Malachy Church.
Staud, Paul R. '70 (PIT) Kennedy Township, PA St. Malachy Church.
Staud, Msgr. Sylvester W. '42 (WH) Retired.
Staudenmaier, John M. *s.j.* '70 (DET) [K] Detroit, MI Jesuit Community at the University of Detroit.
Staudenmaier, Wilbert N. '43 (GB) Retired.
Stauder, Paul W. '48 (BEL) Retired.
Stauder, William V. *s.j.* '52 (STL) [C] St. Louis, MO Saint Louis University; [P] St. Louis, MO Jesuit Community Corporation at St. Louis University - Jesuit Hall.
Staudinger, Greg '81 (GF) Sidney, MT St. Matthew Church.
Staudt, Joseph W. '78 (RVC) Bay Shore, NY St. Patrick's Church.
Staunton, Patrick J. '60 (LA) La Puente, CA St. Joseph Church.
Stauter, Andrew (MOB) On Leave from the Archdiocese.
Stauter, Msgr. Patrick C. '40 (PBL) Retired.
Stavinoha, Donald *o.m.i.* '70 (SAT) [K] San Antonio, TX Oblate Madonna Residence.
Stavoy, Stephen J. '79 (SCR) Military Chaplains.
Stawasz, John B. '53 (HON) Kihei, HI St. Theresa Church.
Stawowy, Norbert *s.d.s.* '58 (GRY) [K] Merrillville, IN Salvatorian Fathers (Society of the Divine Savior).
Staysniak, Dale W. '75 (CLV) [1] Parma, OH St. Anthony of Padua Church.
Ste. Marie, Adrien *c.s.c.* (P) [L] Portland, OR Holy Cross Father & Brother, C.S.C. - University of Portland.
Ste. Marie, Adrien J. *c.s.c.* '50 (FTW) [L] Notre Dame, IN Holy Cross Mission House.
Stead, Julian *o.s.b.* '52 (PRO) [P] Portsmouth, RI Abbey of St. Gregory the Great.
Stead, Mell '56 (P) Lincoln City, OR St. Augustine Church.
Steakem, John J. '60 (FR) Somerset, MA St. Thomas More Church.
Stearns, John '53 (FAR) [E] Fargo, ND Riverview Place, Inc.
Stearns, Msgr. John D. '53 (CR) Retired.
Stearns, Joseph E. '63 (VEN) [4] Naples, FL St. William Church.
Steber, Michael '86 (MAR) Channing, MI St. Rose Church.
Stebler, Lawrence F. '63 (PIT) Perrysville, PA St. Teresa of Avila Church.
Stec, Emil *c.r.* '48 (CHI) [193] Chicago, IL St. Stanislaus Kostka Church.
Stec, John P. '94 (MET) [2] Perth Amboy, NJ St. Stephen Church.
Stec, Joseph C. '57 (PH) [2] Philadelphia, PA St. Adalbert Church; [53] Philadelphia, PA St. Hedwig Church; [A] Wynnewood, PA Theological Seminary of St. Charles Borromeo, Overbrook.
Stec, Mark D. '88 (BEL) Special Assignment.
Stec, Michael S. '94 (LIN) Wahoo, NE St. Wenceslaus Church.
Stec, Robert '88 (CLV) [A] Wickliffe, OH Borromeo Seminary.
Stecher John E. '72 (DAV) [H] Iowa City, IA Newman Catholic Student Center; [M] Iowa City, IA O'Keefe Hall.
Stecher, Kenneth C. '68 (DUB) Parkersburg, IA St. Patrick's Church.
Steck, Christopher W. *s.j.* '94 (BGP) [O] Fairfield, CT The Fairfield Jesuit Community-Fairfield University.
Steck, Christopher W. *s.j.* '94 (HRT) [12] New Haven, CT St. Joseph's Church.
Steckbauer, Linus J. '42 (GB) Retired.
Steckel, Gregory A. '81 (DAV) On Duty Outside the Diocese.
Stecklein, Warren L. '90 (DOD) Wright, KS St. Andrew Church.
Steckler, Gerard *s.j.* (P) Waldport, OR St. Anthony Church.
Steckler, Gerard *s.j.* '57 (AUS) [H] Austin, TX Jesuit Fathers and Brothers.
Steckler, Gerard G. *s.j.* '57 (P) [L] Portland, OR Jesuit Provincial Office (Oregon Prov.).
Steckler, Kenneth '96 (EVN) Jasper, IN St. Joseph Church.
Steed, Donald R. *m.m.* '54 (NY) [Z] Maryknoll, NY Maryknoll Fathers and Brothers.
Steele, Michael J. '77 (BO) Wakefield, MA St. Joseph Church.
Steele, Peter *s.j.* '70 (WDC) [M] Washington, DC The Jesuit Community at Georgetown University.
Steele, Philip G. *s.j.* '80 (DEN) [D] Aurora, CO Regis Jesuit High School; [M] Aurora, CO Regis Jesuit High School - Jesuit Community.
Steele, Steven G. '90 (MAD) [1] Madison, WI St. Raphael Cathedral; [12] Madison, WI St. Paul University Parish Church.
Steele, Thomas J. *s.j.* '64 (DEN) [M] Denver, CO Regis Jesuit Community (The Jesuits at Regis University).
Steenken, George W. *s.j.* '54 (CHI) [T] Barrington, IL Bellarmine Hall.
Stefan, Bonaventure *o.f.m.cap.* '56 (PIT) [N] Pittsburgh, PA St. Patrick Friary.
Stefanelli, Joseph *s.m.* '51 (SJ) [M] San Jose, CA Marianist Community.
Stefaniuk, Msgr. Dmytro '58 (PHU) Retired.
Stefanko, Paul F. '76 (PRT) Special or Other Diocesan Assignment.
Stefanotti, Robert A. *o.carm.* (TR) Delran, NJ Holy Name Church.
Stefanski, Gery W. '79 (CHI) River Forest, IL St. Luke Church.
Stefanski, Jacek (CAM) [6] Camden, NJ St. Joseph's Church.
Stefanski, Walter '40 (CHI) [163] Chicago, IL St. Pancratius Church; Retired.
Steffan, Paul *o.f.m.cap.* '57 (NY) New Paltz, NY St. Joseph Church; [Z] New Paltz, NY St. Joseph Friary.
Steffen, Carl J. '58 (HBG) Buchanan Valley, PA St. Ignatius Loyola Church.
Steffen, Francis J. '57 (MAD) [1] Madison, WI St. Raphael Cathedral; [K] Madison, WI Society of St. Vincent de Paul.
Steffen, Kenneth C. '84 (SFD) Riverton, IL St. James Church.
Steffens, Terrence J. '82 (GRY) Crown Point, IN St. Matthias Church.
Steffensmeier, Ralph J. '59 (OM) [18] Omaha, NE Holy Ghost Church.
Steffes, James D. *s.c.j.* '63 (GAL) [55] Houston, TX Our Lady of Guadalupe Church.
Steffes, James P. '93 (WIN) [1] Winona, MN Cathedral of the Sacred Heart.
Steffes, Joseph X. *c.ss.r.* '40 (LAF) Crowley, LA Immaculate Heart of Mary Church.
Steffes, LuVerne W. '95 (OM) [37] Omaha, NE St. Philip Neri Church.
Steffes, Marvin J. *c.pp.s.* '58 (MRY) Los Gatos, CA Christ Child Church.
Steffes, Raymond *o.s.c.* '58 (SCL) Vineland, MN St. Therese, Little Flower Indian Mission Church.
Steffes, Raymond A. *o.s.c.* '58 (SCL) [I] Onamia, MN Crosier Monastery.
Steffey, John M. '53 (KAL) Parchment, MI St. Ambrose Church.
Stefula, Salvator *t.o.r.* '74 (FWT) [16] Fort Worth, TX St. Thomas Church.
Stefun, Bonaventure *o.f.m.cap.* '56 (PIT) Allegheny County, PA St. Francis Medical Center; [J] Pittsburgh, PA St. Francis Medical Center.
Steger, Francis R. *o.c.s.o.* '56 (ROC) [I] Piffard, NY Abbey of the Genesee.
Steger, John J. '51 (ROC) [32] Rochester, NY St. Jude the Apostle Church.
Steggert, Bruce A. *s.j.* '93 (WDC) [E] Washington, DC Gonzaga College High School.
Stegman, Leonard F. '40 (ELP) Retired.
Stegman, Thomas D. *s.j.* (MIL) [P] Milwaukee, WI Jesuit Provincial Office, Wisconsin Province.
Stegmann, Msgr. Raymond V. '50 (RVC) Retired.
Stegmann, Robert '95 (GB) [5] Appleton, WI St. Pius X Church.
Stehly, Dennis '77 (STL) Mehlville, MO St. Margaret Mary Alacoque Church.
Stehly, James '85 (LA) [A] Camarillo, CA St. John's Seminary College of the Archdiocese of Los Angeles.
Stehly, Mark '66 (SEA) [Q] Seattle, WA Catholic Hospital Ministries.
Stehly, Thomas '61 (LA) Whittier, CA St. Gregory the Great Church.
Steibel, Gary R. '63 (MIA) Hallandale, FL St. Charles Borromeo Church.
Steichen, John A. '54 (OKL) Union City, OK St. Joseph's Church.
Steidle, Mark '93 (COV) [3] Covington, KY St. Ann Church; [B] Covington, KY Covington Latin School.
Steier, Charles '73 (SAL) Russell, KS St. Mary's Church.
Steiger, Richard A. '67 (PAT) Andover, NJ Good Shepherd Church.
Steigmeyer, Robert C. *c.s.c.* '47 (GR) [E] Grand Rapids, MI St. Mary's Health Services.
Steik, Dennis *s.m.* '69 (MRY) [G] Santa Cruz, CA Society of Mary, Marists; [J] Monterey, CA Department of Campus Ministry; [J] Monterey, CA Department of Campus Ministry.
Steimel, Craig E. '89 (DUB) Buffalo Center, IA St. Patrick's Church; Forest City, IA St. James Church; Lake Mills, IA St. Patrick Church.
Steimel, Msgr. Paul T. '52 (DUB) Cedar Falls, IA St. Patrick Church.
Stein, Benjamin *o.s.b.* '36 (SCL) [I] Collegeville, MN St. John's Abbey, of the Order of St. Benedict.
Stein, E. John *o.f.m.* '85 (CIN) [26] Cincinnati, OH St. Francis Seraph Church.
Stein, James *o.praem.* '86 (CHI) [N] Chicago, IL Premonstratensian Fathers and Brothers (Norbertines).
Stein, Jerry '66 (AMA) Happy, TX Holy Name of Jesus Church; Nazareth, TX Holy Family Church.
Stein, John *o.f.m.* '85 (CIN) [M] Cincinnati, OH St. Francis Seraph Friary.

Stein, Norbert W. *s.s.j.* (LAF) Cecilia, LA St. Rose of Lima Church.
Stein, Robert E. '81 (CLV) [5] Akron, OH St. Francis de Sales Church.
Stein, Timothy P. '84 (ALT) Chest Springs, PA St. Monica's Church.
Steinauer, Carl J. '76 (SAC) Absent on Leave.
Steinbacher, Will *glmy.* '62 (CIN) [M] Fairfield, OH Headquarters of Glenmary Home Missioners.
Steinbauer, Joseph '79 (TOL) Rossford, OH All Saints Church.
Steinbeissen, Joseph A. '86 (NU) Willmar, MN St. Mary Church.
Steinberger, Edward J. '45 (WCH) Caney, KS Sacred Heart Church; Moline, KS St. Mary's Church; Sedan, KS St. Robert Bellarmine Church.
Steinbicker, Carl R. '34 (CIN) Retired.
Steinbock, Leo '54 (LA) [73] Los Angeles, CA St. Kevin Church.
Steinbrunner, Jerome *c.pp.s.* '74 (CLV) [2] Cleveland, OH St. Adalbert Church.
Steiner, Bernard J. '61 (NU) Lamberton, MN St. Joseph Church; Sanborn, MN St. Thomas Church; Wanda, MN St. Mathias Church.
Steiner, Msgr. Carl E. '55 (GB) Oconto Falls, WI St. Anthony Church; Stiles, WI St. Patrick Church.
Steiner, Msgr. Clarence J. '44 (STP) [8] St. Paul, MN The Nativity of Our Lord Church; Retired.
Steiner, Daniel R. '79 (CHI) Evergreen Park, IL Queen of Martyrs Church.
Steiner, Edward F., III '82 (NSH) Madison, TN St. Joseph's Church.
Steiner, John M. '69 (SPK) [19] Spokane, WA St. Thomas More Church.
Steiner, John W. '74 (LC) [3] Eau Claire, WI Sacred Heart of Jesus Church; [6] Eau Claire, WI St. Patrick Church.
Steiner, Luke *o.s.b.* '56 (SCL) [I] Collegeville, MN St. John's Abbey, of the Order of St. Benedict.
Steiner, William H. *s.j.* '52 (KC) [J] Kansas City, MO Arrupe Jesuit Community.
Steinert, Thomas J. *o.s.cam.* '85 (LC) Camp Douglas, WI St. James Church; Indian Creek, WI St. Michael Church; Mauston, WI St. Patrick Church.
Steingraeber, John *c.ss.r.* '74 (DEN) [M] Denver, CO The Redemptorists/Denver Province.
Steingreaber, Paul *o.s.b.* '65 (KCK) [H] Atchison, KS St. Benedict's Abbey.
Steinhauser, Kenneth B. '70 (BRK) Released from Diocesan Assignment.
Steinhauser, Michael G. '67 (BRK) Released from Diocesan Assignment.
Steinhauser, Raymond W. '54 (COV) Retired.
Steinhilber, Richard *s.s.c.* '51 (OM) [K] St. Columbans, NE St. Columban's Foreign Mission Society.
Steinhoff, Henry '67 (B) Retired.
Steinhoff, Henry '67 (HEL) Eureka, MT Our Lady of Mercy Church.
Steinkirchner, Edward E. '49 (ROC) Penfield, NY St. Joseph Church; Retired.
Steinle, David G. '79 (DAV) Charlotte, IA Assumption and St. Patrick's Church.
Steinle, James '53 (TOL) Retired.
Steinman, Robert E. *o.s.a.* '50 (PH) [Z] Villanova, PA St. Thomas Monastery.
Steinmetz, Paul B. *s.j.* '59 (MIL) [P] Milwaukee, WI Jesuit Provincial Office, Wisconsin Province.
Steinmetz, Paul B. *s.j.* '59 (OAK) Orinda, CA Santa Maria Church.
Steinmiller, G. Alexander *c.p.* '70 (SAT) [M] San Antonio, TX Casa Pasionista Guadalupe.
Stella, Livio *c.s.* '75 (CHI) [N] Oak Park, IL Missionaries of Saint Charles.
Stella, Thomas A. *c.s.c.* '72 (COS) [B] Colorado Springs, CO Penrose-St. Francis Health Services; [E] Cascade, CO Holy Cross Novitiate.
Steller, Paul W. *episcopal* '65 (BUF) [R] Williamsville, NY Newman Club Chaplains; [R] Williamsville, NY Newman Club Chaplains.
Stelling, William F. '64 (MEM) [15] Memphis, TN St. Joseph's Church.
Stelmach, Jerome J. '80 (BUF) Limestone, NY St. Patrick Church; Olean, NY Transfiguration Church.
Stelmach, Michael '70 (STN) Minneapolis, MN St. Constantine Church.
Stelten, Leo F. '50 (FAR) Retired.
Steltenkamp, Michael F. *s.j.* (DET) [K] Detroit, MI Jesuit Provincial Office-Detroit Province of the Society of Jesus.
Steltenkamp, Michael F. *s.j.* '76 (WH) [A] Wheeling, WV Wheeling Jesuit University.
Stelter, Richard T. (RVC) Amityville, NY St. Martin's Church.
Stelzer, Mark S. '83 (SPR) [12] Springfield, MA Sacred Heart Church; Graduate Studies.
Stelzner, Barnabas W. *o.s.b.* '88 (PBL) [E] Canon City, CO Holy Cross Abbey.
Stemac, Msgr. Louis V. '42 (LR) Retired; [H] Little Rock, AR St. John Manor.
Stembler, James G. '89 (CC) On Special Assignment; [A] Corpus Christi, TX Corpus Christi Academy; [B] Corpus Christi, TX Bishop Garriga Middle School.
Stemmann, Joseph H. '63 (LAF) Henry, LA St. John Church.
Stempora, Daniel F. '60 (JOL) Oswego, IL St. Anne Church.
Stempsey, William E. *s.j.* '92 (WOR) [N] Worcester, MA Jesuits of Holy Cross College, Inc.
Stencil, Rallen H. '63 (GB) Hilbert, WI St. Mary Church.
Stencil, Steven G. '81 (TUC) Casa Grande, AZ St. Anthony Church; [I] Casa Grande, AZ Central Arizona College, Holy Family Newman Center.
Stengel, Msgr. Charles G. '56 (NEW) [12] Jersey City, NJ St. John the Baptist Church.
Stengel, Mark '72 (LR) [A] Subiaco, AR Subiaco Monastery.
Stengel, Michael Joseph *c.p.* '57 (CHI) [N] Chicago, IL Passionist Provincial Office.
Stengel, Msgr. Paul F. '59 (BUF) Boston, NY St. John the Baptist Church.
Stengel, William '55 (GB) Wausaukee, WI St. Augustine Church.
Stengel, William J. '57 (GB) [F] Green Bay, WI St. Vincent Hospital.
Stenger, Msgr. Frederick R. '28 (JOL) Retired.
Stenger, William J., Sr. '94 (WH) Glen Dale, WV St. Jude Church.
Stenson, James F. '51 (Y) Streetsboro, OH St. Joan of Arc Church; Retired.
Stenson, Patrick *m.s.c.* '63 (SAT) [M] San Antonio, TX Missionaries of the Sacred Heart.
Stenzel, Duane R. *o.f.m.* '54 (HT) [C] Schriever, LA Lumen Christi Retreat Center.
Stenzel, Eugene F. '67 (WIN) Wells, MN St. Casimir's Church
Stenzel, William J. '75 (CHI) La Grange, IL St. Francis Xavier Church.
Stepanich, Martin *o.f.m.* '41 (CHI) [N] Lemont, IL The Slovene Franciscan Fathers, Order of Friars Minor, Commissariat of the Holy Cross.
Stepanski, Thomas *s.t.* (IND) [29] Indianapolis, IN St. Lawrence Church.
Stepanski, Thomas *s.t.* '62 (WDC) [E] Silver Spring, MD Holy Trinity Mission Seminary (1926).
Stepek, Robert A. '81 (CHI) Homewood, IL St. Joseph Church.
Stephan, George *s.v.d.* '35 (LA) [71] Los Angeles, CA St. John, The Evangelist Church.
Stephan, George J. '62 (BUF) [25] Buffalo, NY St. Francis Xavier Church; [37] Buffalo, NY St. John the Baptist Church.
Stephan, Matthew J. '83 (CC) Falfurrias, TX Sacred Heart Church.
Stephen, John *c.r.* '38 (CHI) [D] Chicago, IL Gordon Technical High School.
Stephens, Gerald '63 (FWT) Retired.
Stephens, Rod '74 (ORG) Placentia, CA St. Joseph Church.
Stephenson, Alphonse J. '75 (PAT) On Duty Outside the Diocese.
Stephenson, Lloyd F. '80 (RIC) Hampton, VA VA Medical Center.
Stephenson, Patrick '68 (SR) American Canyon, CA Holy Family Church.
Stephenson, Robert B. '78 (SY) [18] Syracuse, NY St. John the Evangelist Church; [H] Syracuse, NY Catholic Charities of the Roman Catholic Diocese of Syracuse.
Stepien, Allen F. '65 (PAT) Long Valley, NJ St. Mark the Evangelist Church.
Steriti, Edward *o.c.s.o.* '57 (WOR) [N] Spencer, MA St. Joseph's Abbey.
Sterk, Francis R. '65 (CLV) [1] Euclid, OH St. Christine Church.
Sterker, Msgr. Louis F. '46 (CHR) Retired.
Sterling, Donald A. '74 (BAL) [4] Baltimore, MD The New All Saints Church.
Sterling, John J. '96 (COV) [2] Covington, KY St. Agnes Church; [B] Covington, KY Covington Catholic High School.
Sterling, John K. '94 (DAV) Burlington, IA St. Patrick's Church; Dodgeville, IA St. Mary's Church; West Burlington, IA St. Mary's Church.
Stern, Jean *m.s.* '64 (STL) [P] St. Louis, MO La Salette Missionaries.
Stern, Jerome F. '63 (LEX) London, KY St. William/St. Sylvester Church.
Stern, Msgr. Robert L. (NY) [DD] New York, NY Catholic Near East Welfare Association.
Sternemann, Reinhard J. *o.s.a.* '66 (FWT) Abbott, TX Immaculate Heart of Mary Church; Penelope, TX Nativity of the Blessed Virgin Mary Church.
Sterner, James M. '70 (HBG) Littlestown, PA St. Aloysius Church.
Sterowski, Scott P. '91 (SCR) Moscow, PA St. Catherine of Siena Church; [D] Dunmore, PA Bishop O'Hara High School.
Sterrett, Brad '85 (SAL) Manhattan, KS St. Isidore Church; [H] Manhattan, KS St. Isidore's Catholic Student Center.
Stessman, Msgr. Gerald J. '59 (DM) [5] Des Moines, IA Holy Trinity Church.
Stessman, John (DM) Harlan, IA St. Michael Church.
Stets, Ihor '85 (STF) Johnson City, NY Sacred Heart Ukrainian Catholic Church.
Stetson, William H. '62 (CHI) [W] Chicago, IL Opus Dei.
Stetz, Allan '66 (DM) Chariton, IA Sacred Heart Church.
Stetz, Mark '90 (MRY) Los Osos, CA St. Elizabeth Ann Seton Church.
Steuer, James '63 (ALB) Mohawk, NY Blessed Sacrament Church.
Steuterman, James M. '75 (WOR) North Oxford, MA St. Ann's Church.
Stevens, Clifford J. '56 (OM) Absent on Leave.
Stevens, George E. *c.m.* '83 (LA) [95] Los Angeles, CA St. Vincent De Paul Church.
Stevens, Michael J. '80 (STP) [11] St. Paul, MN St. Adalbert Church; Special Assignment.
Stevensky, Msgr. John '63 (SJP) Miami, FL Assumption of B.V.M. Church.
Stevenson, Alden J. *s.j.* '46 (SFR) [N] San Francisco, CA Jesuit Community at University of San Francisco.
Stevenson, Anthony '81 (OWN) Bardwell, KY St. Charles Church; Fancy Farm, KY St. Denis Church.
Stevenson, Dennis E. *j.c.l.* '88 (COL) [4] Columbus, OH St. Aloysius Church.
Stevenson, Msgr. Frederick J. '42 (PH) Wallingford, PA St. John Chrysostom Church; Retired.
Stevenson, R. Francis (SAC) [9] Sacramento, CA St. Anne Church.
Stevenson, William J. '82 (LAN) [4] Ann Arbor, MI St. Mary Student Parish Church; [J] Ann Arbor, MI St. Mary Student Parish.
Stevenson, William P. '86 (SD) Santa Ysabel, CA Santa Ysabel Indian Mission Church.
Stevernol, Slider '96 (P) Gresham, OR St. Henry Church.
Stewart, August '94 (COS) [13] Colorado Springs, CO Saint Paul Church.
Stewart, Columba *o.s.b.* '90 (SCL) [I] Collegeville, MN St. John's Abbey, of the Order of St. Benedict.
Stewart, Msgr. Dell F. '49 (KAL) Retired.
Stewart, Edward R. '89 (BRK) [19] Brooklyn, NY St. Bernard's Church.
Stewart, George (NY) Pearl River, NY St. Margaret Church.
Stewart, Msgr. George N. '35 (DOD) Retired.
Stewart, J. Keith '93 (MEM) Jackson, TN St. Mary's Church.
Stewart, J. Patrick *s.j.* '61 (SPK) [C] Spokane, WA Gonzaga University.
Stewart, James *o.f.m.cap.* (NY) Valhalla, NY Westchester County Medical Center.
Stewart, James *o.f.m.cap.* '85 (NY) [Z] White Plains, NY St. Conrad Friary.
Stewart, Jonathan '91 (IND) Enochsburg, IN St. John the Evangelist Church; Hamburg, IN St. Anne Church; St. Maurice, IN St. Maurice Church.
Stewart, Kenneth C. *o.f.m.cap.* '67 (DET) [66] Detroit, MI Presentation-Our Lady of Victory Church.
Stewart, Kenneth K.J. '78 (PH) Absent on Leave.
Stewart, Michael L. '75 (MEM) [6] Memphis, TN St. Brigid Church.
Stewart, Patrick F. '78 (LEX) Somerset, KY St. Mildred Church.
Stewart, Paul '73 (PT) Military Chaplains.
Stewart, Robert *o.f.m.* '80 (BUF) [O] St. Bonaventure, NY St. Bonaventure Friary.
Stewart, Robert H. '82 (KC) [16] Kansas City, MO Holy Family Church.
Stewart, Msgr. Terrence L. '70 (GR) Marne, MI St. Mary's Church; On Special Assignment.
Sthokal, Edward S. *s.j.* '54 (STP) [Q] Lake Elmo, MN Jesuit Retreat House.
Sticco, Peter T. *s.a.c.* (BRK) [Y] Brooklyn, NY Bay Webster Corporation, Inc.
Sticco, Peter T. *s.a.c.* '69 (BAL) [M] Baltimore, MD Pallottine Center for Apostolic Causes.
Sticco, Peter T. *s.a.c.* '69 (CAM) [L] Camden, NJ Dominican Sisters of the Perpetual Rosary Chaplain's Residence.
Stickle, William '50 (RIC) Retired.
Stieferman, Lowell L. '63 (OKL) [6] Oklahoma City, OK Church of the Epiphany of the Lord.
Stiefvater, Robert X. '77 (MIL) Special Assignment.
Stiegeler, A. Francis *s.j.* '78 (SAC) [C] Sacramento, CA Jesuit High School; [H] Carmichael, CA Jesuit High School Community of Sacramento.
Stieger, Msgr. Joseph '50 (MRY) Retired.
Stier, Joseph S. '38 (MIL) Retired.
Stier, Timothy '79 (OAK) [1] Fremont, CA Corpus Christi Church.
Stika, Msgr. Richard F. '85 (STL) Special Assignment.
Stikel, Roman S. '88 (MIL) [67] Milwaukee, WI St. Philip Neri Church; [69] Milwaukee, WI St. Robert's Church.
Stiles, J. Roy '63 (L) [41] Louisville, KY St. John Vianney Church; Fairdale, KY St. Jerome Church.
Stiles, Wallis '61 (SAT) D'Hanis, TX Holy Cross Church.

Stillmank, John G. '93 (MAD) [I] Madison, WI Holy Name Catholic Center, Inc.
Stillmock, Martin *c.ss.r.* '58 (STP) Brooklyn Center, MN St. Alphonsus Church.
Stillmunks, Steven J. '77 (OM) Papillion, NE St. Columbkille Church.
Stillwell, Msgr. William J. '67 (BUF) [7] Niagara Falls, NY St. Mary of the Cataract Church.
Stilwell, Dennis R. '71 (GAY) Traverse City, MI Immaculate Conception Church.
Stine, Jerome E. '48 (DET) Retired.
Stine, Robert F. '73 (BR) St. Amant, LA Holy Rosary Church.
Stinebrickner, Msgr. David W. '63 (OG) [1] Ogdensburg, NY St. Mary's Cathedral; Retired.
Stineman, William F. '49 (IND) Retired.
Stingel, Louis F. '60 (MET) Jamesburg, NJ St. James the Less Church.
Stingle, Lawrence A. '41 (GB) Retired.
Stinner, Francis J. '67 (NY) Bronxville, NY St. Joseph Church.
Stinson, James G. *s.j.* '94 (BGP) [O] Fairfield, CT The Fairfield Jesuit Community-Fairfield University.
Stipe, Jack H. '61 (P) Retired.
Stirniman, Jeffrey D. '95 (PEO) [13] Peoria, IL St. Philomena's Church.
Stislow, Louis *o.f.m.* '61 (PH) [D] Philadelphia, PA Archbishop Ryan High School.
Stislow, Louis *o.f.m.* '64 (PH) [Z] Philadelphia, PA St. Pius X Friary.
Stiteler, Francis Michael *o.c.s.o.* '83 (ATL) [I] Conyers, GA The Monastery of the Holy Spirit.
Stites, John '76 (TOL) Lima, OH St. Rita Hospital and Medical Center; [H] Lima, OH St. Rita's Medical Center.
Stitz, John '53 (KCK) Retired.
Stivason, Paul R. '89 (GBG) Indiana, PA St. Bernard Church.
Stluka, Jerome '69 (COL) [11] Columbus, OH St. Christopher Church.
Stobba, Joseph G. *o.s.a.* '59 (MIL) [8] Racine, WI St. Rita's Church.
Stober, William P. '73 (PAT) Branchville, NJ Our Lady Queen of Peace Church.
Stobie, Stephen (P) [K] Portland, OR Mt. St. Joseph Residence and Extended Care Center.
Stochmal, Marek '95 (DET) Lincoln Park, MI Christ the Good Shepherd Church.
Stock, Augustine *o.s.b.* '48 (KC) [J] Conception, MO Conception Abbey.
Stock, Michael E. *o.p.* '52 (BO) [W] Dover, MA St. Stephen Priory.
Stockelman, William R. '78 (CIN) Batavia, OH Holy Trinity Church; Williamsburg, OH St. Ann Church.
Stocker, Bede *o.s.b.* '42 (RCK) [H] Aurora, IL Marmion Abbey-St. Augustine's Abbey.
Stocker, Thomas '63 (GB) Absent on Leave.
Stockert, Donfred H. '58 (RIC) Retired.
Stockert, Harold '63 (PSC) Granville, NY SS. Peter and Paul Church.
Stockhausen, Gerald L. *s.j.* '79 (OM) [K] Omaha, NE Jesuit Community At Creighton University.
Stockhausen, Paul G. *s.j.* '40 (MIL) [P] Wauwatosa, WI Jesuit Community at St. Camillus.
Stocking, Joseph R. *s.j.* '67 (SEA) [23] Seattle, WA Christ the King Church; [A] Seattle, WA Seattle University.
Stockinger, Tony '63 (JOL) Winfield, IL Central DuPage Hospital.
Stockinger, Tony A. '63 (JOL) Winfield, IL St. John the Baptist Church; [C] Wheaton, IL St. Francis High School.
Stocklosa, J. Walter '40 (BO) Retired.
Stockman, Gerald '64 (JC) On Duty Outside the Diocese.
Stockmeyer, Basil *c.p.* '40 (BAL) [11] Baltimore, MD Ascension Church.
Stockmeyer, Basil *c.p.* '42 (BAL) [M] Baltimore, MD St. Joseph's Passionist Community.
Stockus, Edward S. '91 (CHI) [3] Oak Lawn, IL St. Germaine Church.
Stockwell, C. Robert '53 (LAN) Retired.
Stodola, Francis (CC) [8] Laredo, TX Santa Margarita De Escocia Independent Mission Church.
Stoeber, Charles L. *s.f.* '56 (SFE) [28] Albuquerque, NM St. Therese of the Infant Jesus Shrine of the Little Flower Church.
Stoeckig, Robert '94 (LAV) [2] Las Vegas, NV Christ the King Church.
Stoegbauer, Carlton C. '82 (CAM) [6] Cherry Hill, NJ Queen of Heaven Church.
Stoeger, James A. *s.j.* '74 (CHI) [C] Chicago, IL Jesuit Community at Loyola University of Chicago.
Stoeger, James A. *s.j.* '75 (CHI) [N] Chicago, IL Chicago Province of the Society of Jesus-Provincial Office.
Stoeger, John '72 (LA) [A] Camarillo, CA St. John's Seminary.
Stoeger, John D. '72 (LA) [A] Camarillo, CA St. John's Seminary.
Stoeger, William *s.j.* '72 (TUC) [F] Tucson, AZ Jesuit Community of the Vatican Observatory.
Stoerlein, Msgr. Joseph G. '49 (CAM) [2] Vineland, NJ Sacred Heart Church.
Stoetzel Charles D. '80 (LC) Marshfield, WI St. John the Baptist Church; Spencer, WI Christ the King Church.
Stofcik, John A. '40 (GBG) Retired.
Stoffel, Msgr. Jerome C. '36 (SLC) Retired.
Stoffel, Richard J. '79 (MIL) [3] Racine, WI St. Joseph's Church.
Stofft, Kenneth G. '75 (RIC) Roanoke, VA Our Lady of Nazareth Church.
Stoga, Stanley C. '30 (CHI) Retired.
Stohrer, Walter J. *s.j.* '60 (MIL) [P] Milwaukee, WI Jesuit Community at Marquette University.
Stokes, David *s.j.* '63 (RIC) [5] Richmond, VA Sacred Heart Church.
Stokes, Edward J. *s.j.* '51 (BEL) [1] Belleville, IL Cathedral of St. Peter.
Stokes, Thomas A. *s.m.* '63 (SP) [7] Tampa, FL Our Lady of Perpetual Help Church.
Stoklie, Eugene J. '60 (BRK) [83] Brooklyn, NY Mary Queen of Heaven Church.
Stokowski, Lucjan '77 (CLV) [2] Garfield Heights, OH SS. Peter and Paul Church.
Stolcis, Ronald A. '68 (CHY) Worland, WY St. Mary Magdalen Church.
Stoley, Lawrence J. '91 (LIN) Morse Bluff, NE St. George Church.
Stolinksi, Dennis R. '69 (OM) Bellevue, NE St. Matthew The Evangelist Church of Bellevue.
Stolinski, Robert A. (BUF) [62] Buffalo, NY St. Stephen Church.
Stolinski, Robert A. '70 (BUF) Buffalo, NY Erie County Medical Center.
Stoll, Eugene '30 (CHI) [B] Techny, IL Divine Word Residence.
Stoll, Jerome L. '59 (MIL) Special Assignment.
Stoll, Kenneth *s.c.j.* '45 (JKS) [E] Nesbit, MS St. Michael Community House.
Stoll, Mark J. '92 (SC) Graduate Studies.
Stollenwerk, Charles J. '73 (CLV) North Olmsted, OH St. Richard Church.
Stolowski, Stephen '79 (NSH) Absent on Leave.
Stoltz, John J. '90 (L) Edmonton, KY Christ the Healer Church.
Stoltz, Joseph H. '73 (L) Louisville, KY Caritas Medical Center; [H] Louisville, KY Caritas Medical Center.
Stoltz, Richard L. '74 (STL) Richmond Heights, MO St. Luke the Evangelist Church.
Stolz, Paul L. '61 (CIN) [75] Cincinnati, OH Sts. Peter and Paul Church.
Stolz, William K. *s.j.* '62 (SAC) [C] Sacramento, CA Jesuit High School; [H] Carmichael, CA Jesuit High School Community of Sacramento.
Stolze, Edward B. '72 (CIN) [54] Cincinnati, OH St. Louis Church.
Stolzman, William F. '71 (STP) Shakopee, MN St. Mark Church.
Stommel, Russell J. '67 (MIL) [31] Milwaukee, WI St. Gregory The Great Church.
Stone, Carl '42 (ALB) Retired.
Stone, Colm *o.c.d.* '62 (SEA) Stanwood, WA St. Cecilia's Church.
Stone, Michael J. '68 (ALN) Schuylkill Haven, PA St. Ambrose Church.
Stone, Robert *s.t.l.* '77 (PMB) [A] Boynton Beach, FL St. Vincent de Paul Regional Seminary.
Stone, Robert '90 (KC) Montrose, MO Immaculate Conception Church.
Stone, Robert J. *c.m.* (PH) [Z] Philadelphia, PA Congregation of the Mission.
Stone, Stanley R. '60 (SC) Special Assignment.
Stone, Theodore '52 (CHI) Park Ridge, IL Mary, Seat of Wisdom Church.
Stone, Msgr. William S. '43 (BAK) Retired.
Stoneberg, Jeff *o.f.m.* '90 (JOL) Glen Ellyn, IL St. James the Apostle Church.
Stonebridge, John (BRK) [R] Queens Village, NY Queen of Peace Residence.
Stonebridge, John H. '38 (BRK) Retired.
Stoner John Bosco *o.s.b.* '76 (LA) [R] Valyermo, CA St. Andrew's Abbey.
Stoner Timothy L. '96 (GI) Alliance, NE Holy Rosary Church.
Stonich, Raymond '56 (JOL) Addison, IL St. Philip The Apostle Church.
Stookey, Gerald L. *o.p.* '78 (CHI) [N] Chicago, IL Dominicans (Provincial Office); [N] Chicago, IL Dominicans (Provincial Office).
Stopponi, John *o.s.b.* '38 (DET) [K] Detroit, MI St. Sylvester Monastery.
Stopyra, David M. *o.f.m.conv.* '60 (BUF) Athol Springs, NY St. Francis of Assisi Church.
Storan, William P. '61 (SAC) Vallejo, CA St. Basil Church.
Storch, Richard F. *s.a.c.* '45 (MIL) [P] Milwaukee, WI Pallotti House.
Storck, Edward J. '52 (WIL) Nursing Homes.
Storey, Finan *c.p.* '39 (CHI) [N] Chicago, IL Immaculate Conception Monastery; [N] Chicago, IL Daneo Hall.
Storey, John R. '47 (CLV) Retired.
Stormes, James R. *s.j.* '79 (BAL) [M] Baltimore, MD Jesuit Fathers and Brothers Maryland Provincial Curia; [M] Baltimore, MD Ferdinand Wheeler House.
Storms, Francis *o.f.m.* '75 (BUF) [C] St. Bonaventure, NY St. Bonaventure University; [O] St. Bonaventure, NY St. Bonaventure Friary.
Storms, Louis B. *c.m.* '45 (BAL) [M] Emmitsburg, MD Vincentian House.
Stortz, Donald '64 (OM) [1] Omaha, NE St. Cecilia's Cathedral.
Stortz, Mario '49 (AMA) Retired.
Stotenbur, David M. '68 (LAN) [4] Lansing, MI Immaculate Heart of Mary Church.
Stott, Thomas D. '83 (CHL) Mt. Airy, NC Holy Angels Church.
Stoud, Frank *s.j.* (NY) [CC] New York, NY University Apostolate.
Stout, O. Hugh '61 (CAM) On Duty Outside the Diocese.
Stout, O. Hugh '61 (NO) [7] New Orleans, LA Holy Ghost Church.
Stout, Thomas '77 (BEL) Red Bud, IL St. John the Baptist Church.
Stout, William J. *s.j.* '64 (SJ) [D] San Jose, CA Bellarmine College Preparatory.
Stouvenel, Gerald E. '72 (DAV) Burlington, IA St. Patrick's Church; Dodgeville, IA St. Mary's Church; West Burlington, IA St. Mary's Church.
Stoviak, Leonard W. '73 (GBG) [4] Greensburg, PA St. Paul Church.
Stovik, Raphael *o.s.b.* '56 (BIS) [A] Richardton, ND Assumption Abbey.
Stowe, John *o.f.m.conv.* '95 (ELP) [17] El Paso, TX Our Lady of Mt. Carmel Church.
Stowell, Jerome G. *c.p.* '40 (CHI) [N] Chicago, IL Passionist Provincial Office.
Stowell, Jerome G. *c.p.* '40 (STL) [K] Lake St. Louis, MO St. Joseph Hospital West.
Stoyle, James '91 (FTW) [13] South Bend, IN St. Jude Church.
Strachota, Dennis '67 (BAK) Pendleton, OR St. Mary's Church.
Strachota, Michael D. '79 (MIL) [20] Milwaukee, WI Corpus Christi Church.
Strader, Kenneth L. '84 (Y) Newton Falls, OH St. Joseph Church; Newton Falls, OH St. Mary Church.
Strader, Mark '91 (LA) Rancho Palos Verdes, CA St. John Fisher Church.
Stradinger, Stephen J. '74 (MIL) Fontana, WI St. Benedict Church.
Strafalace, Francis *s.c.j.* '65 (GAL) [55] Houston, TX Our Lady of Guadalupe Church.
Stragisher, Raphael *o.f.m.* '39 (ALT) [17] Johnstown, PA St. Therese of the Child Jesus Church.
Strahan, Francis V. '59 (BO) [1] Framingham, MA St. Bridget Church.
Strahl, Ernest '45 (IND) Retired.
Strain, Eugene '53 (DET) Rochester Hills, MI St. Mary's of the Hills Church.
Straka, Francis P. '90 (ALN) Hellertown, PA St. Theresa of the Child Jesus Church.
Straley, Michael '83 (PHX) [12] Phoenix, AZ St. Gregory Church; Special Assignment.
Stram, Msgr. Gideon '38 (AUS) Retired.
Strancar, Ignatius '32 (SB) Retired.
Strand, Ralph S. '64 (CHI) Other Assignments.
Strange, J. Michael *s.s.* '65 (BAL) [M] Baltimore, MD Sulpician Provincial House.
Strano, Antonio *o.m.i.* '51 (SAT) [K] San Antonio, TX Oblate Madonna Residence.
Stransky, Thomas F. *c.s.p.* '57 (NY) [Z] Scarsdale, NY Paulist Fathers Generalate.
Strass, Richard *c.ss.r.* '60 (ANC) Seward, AK Sacred Heart Church.
Strass, Richard *c.ss.r.* '60 (CHI) [N] Bangkok, Thailand.
Strass, Richard *c.ss.r.* '60 (DEN) [M] Denver, CO The Redemptorists/Denver Province.
Strassberger, H. Richard '42 (BUF) Retired.
Strassberger, Richard '50 (BUF) [12] Niagara Falls, NY Sacred Heart Church.
Strasser, John R. '76 (DOD) [1] Dodge City, KS Cathedral of the Sacred Heart.
Strassle, Paul '58 (LR) Retired.
Strassner, Henry E. '47 (ALN) Tamaqua, PA St. Jerome Church.
Strasz, James G. *s.m.* '82 (DET) [D] Pontiac, MI Notre Dame Preparatory High School and Marist Academy.
Stratman, Ambrose F. '48 (STL) Park Hills, MO Immaculate Conception Church.
Stratman, Joseph '77 (BEA) China, TX Our Lady of Sorrows Church.
Stratman, Raymond R. '58 (LEX) Versailles, KY St. Leo Church.
Stratman, Thomas F. '50 (DAV) [1] Davenport, IA Sacred Heart Cathedral; Retired.
Stratman, William J. (DAV) Retired.
Straub, Carrol C. '58 (MIL) [1] Milwaukee, WI St. John Cathedral; Special Assignment.
Straub, David R. '94 (CHI) [44] Chicago, IL St. Columbanus Church.

Straub, Edward F. '65 (NY) Liberty, NY St. Peter Church.
Strausser, George '77 (PH) [3] Philadelphia, PA St. Agatha-St. James Church.
Stravinskas, Peter '77 (B) On Duty Outside the Diocese.
Stravinskas, Peter M.J. (SCR) [M] Mount Pocono, PA Diocesan Oratory of Saint Philip Neri - Newman House.
Strebel, Milton C. *o.praem.* '54 (GB) [I] De Pere, WI St. Norbert Abbey.
Strebel, Roger '66 (GB) Wagner, WI St. Edward Church; Walsh, WI St. Joseph Church.
Strebig, John J. '52 (GRY) La Porte, IN Sacred Heart Church.
Strebler, Charles F. '94 (CLV) Strongsville, OH St. Joseph Church.
Stredny, Anthony G. (GAL) Retired.
Streeter, Gerald A. *s.j.* '68 (DET) [P] Clarkston, MI Colombiere Center.
Streff, Joseph N. '42 (STP) Retired.
Streichardt, Wolfgang '82 (SAG) Croswell, MI St. Patrick Church.
Streicher, Bernard J. *s.j.* '60 (CLV) [E] Cleveland, OH St. Ignatius High School.
Streit, Joseph C. '60 (SCR) [I] Wilkes-Barre, PA Mercy Hospital.
Streit, Thomas G. *c.s.c.* '86 (FTW) [B] Notre Dame, IN University of Notre Dame Du Lac; [J] Notre Dame, IN Holy Cross Community, Corby Hall, University of Notre Dame; [J] South Bend, IN Congregation of Holy Cross Indiana Province Provincial House.
Strelick, Charles J. '56 (MAR) Retired.
Strelinski, Ernest (PIT) Allison Park, PA St. Ursula Church.
Stremel, Adolph '36 (WCH) Retired.
Strempeck, Martin R. '55 (BAL) Hydes, MD St. John the Evangelist Church.
Stremski, John P. '60 (SUP) Lac du Flambeau, WI St. Anthony Catholic Church.
Streng, Msgr. James E. '51 (BUF) Gasport, NY St. Mary Church; Middleport, NY St. Stephen Church.
Strenski, David F. *o.praem.* '68 (GB) [I] De Pere, WI St. Norbert Abbey.
Strenski, Joseph A. '45 (MIL) Retired.
Stretch, Daniel P. '53 (STL) On Duty Outside the Archdiocese.
Stretton, Noel '59 (DUL) [10] Duluth, MN St. Joseph's Church; Duluth, MN Duluth Federal Prison.
Streveler, Robert A. '69 (LC) Rothschild, WI St. Therese of the Child Jesus Church.
Streza, Charles V. '43 (ROM) Retired.
Stricker, Robert A. '48 (CIN) [85] Cincinnati, OH St. Therese, The Little Flower Church; Retired.
Strickland, Msgr. Joseph E. '85 (TYL) [1] Tyler, TX Cathedral of the Immaculate Conception.
Strieder, Leon '76 (AUS) On Duty Outside the Diocese.
Strieder, Leon '76 (GAL) [A] Houston, TX St. Mary's Seminary.
Striedl, Max J., Jr. '96 (RCK) [5] Rockford, IL Holy Family Church.
Striegel, Robert M. '73 (DAV) Ottumwa, IA St. Mary of the Visitation Church.
Stringini, John L. '79 (RCK) Dixon, IL St. Patrick Church.
Stripe, Keith A. '96 (TOL) [35] Toledo, OH St. Patrick of Heatherdowns Church.
Strish, Andrew F. '67 (SCR) [3] Pittston, PA St. John the Baptist Church.
Stritch, Morris G. '42 (MEM) Retired; [C] Memphis, TN Christian Brothers High School.
Strittmatter, Andre *t.o.r.* '61 (ALT) [F] Loretto, PA St. Francis Friary, Third Order Regular of St. Francis of Penance.
Strittmatter, Andre C. *t.o.r.* '61 (PH) [Z] Fairless Hills, PA St. Anthony Friary.
Strittmatter, J. Joseph '56 (ALT) Retired.
Strittmatter, Lawrence R. '57 (CIN) [3] Dayton, OH St. Albert the Great Church.
Strittmatter, Paul *s.j.* '77 (RC) Mission, SD St. Thomas the Apostle Church; St. Francis, SD Rosebud Reservation Church; St. Francis, SD Rosebud Reservation Church.
Strittmatter, Robert '66 (FWT) [1] Fort Worth, TX St. Patrick Cathedral.
Strmiska, John A. *c.s.sp.* '29 (SB) [E] Hemet, CA Holy Ghost Fathers.
Stroba, Mark *o.m.i.* '85 (CHI) [174] Chicago, IL Precious Blood Church.
Strobel, Charles '70 (NSH) Absent on Leave.
Strock, Richard M. '65 (LR) Slovak, AR SS. Cyril and Methodius Church.
Strohmeyer, George E. '64 (E) [F] Erie, PA L'Arche Community.
Strom, Charles W. '72 (HEL) Retired.
Stromberg, Floyd G. '59 (TUC) [7] Tucson, AZ Our Lady, Queen of All Saints Church.
Stromberg, James S. '57 (STP) Retired; [C] St. Paul, MN University of St. Thomas.
Strome, Robert '55 (HBG) [5] Mount Carmel, PA Our Lady of Mount Carmel Church.
Strommer, James G. *c.p.* '70 (SAC) [H] Citrus Heights, CA Christ the King Retreat.
Stromski, Adam F.X. '46 (STU) Retired.
Stronkowski, John '85 (BGP) [1] Danbury, CT St. Gregory's Church.
Stroot, Ralph E. '60 (STL) [21] St. Louis, MO St. Aloysius Gonzaga Church.
Stroot, Thomas J. '70 (WCH) Pittsburg, KS Our Lady of Lourdes Church; [B] Pittsburg, KS St. Mary-Colgan High School.
Stroud, J. Francis *s.j.* '61 (NY) [Z] New York, NY Jesuit Community at Fordham University.
Stroup, Edmund F. '49 (BAL) Retired.
Stroupe, Scott T. '91 (E) [12] Erie, PA St. Andrew Church.
Strub, Herman A. '34 (DAV) Retired; [L] Davenport, IA Kahl Home for the Aged and Infirm.
Struc, Marian '69 (PHU) Jersey City, NJ SS. Peter and Paul Church.
Struck, Msgr. John W. '40 (PRO) Retired.
Struckman, Timothy W. '83 (GF) Absent on Leave.
Struik, Felix *o.p.* '58 (SJN) Catano, PR Nuestra Senora del Carmen Church.
Struminski, Robert *s.m.* '71 (HRT) [12] New Haven, CT St. Joseph's Church; [I] New Haven, CT Hospital of St. Raphael.
Strumski, Matthew J. '48 (PRO) [2] Warren, RI St. Casimir Church.
Strupp, James A. '67 (MIL) Retired.
Strupp, Joachim *o.f.m.cap.* '63 (PIT) [N] Herman, PA St. Mary's Friary.
Strus, Walter A. '94 (CHI) Bridgeview, IL St. Fabian Church.
Struzik, Edward J. '85 (MET) Plainsboro, NJ Queenship of Mary Church.
Struzynski, Robert *o.f.m.* '63 (BUF) [59] Buffalo, NY SS. Rita & Patrick Church.
Struzzieri, Andrew L. '75 (BRK) [109] Brooklyn, NY Our Lady of Refuge Church.
Struzzo, John A. *c.s.c.* '65 (FTW) [J] South Bend, IN Congregation of Holy Cross Indiana Province Provincial House.
Stryjewski, John J. '66 (MOB) Grand Bay, AL St. John Baptist Church.
Stryk, Jerome J. '44 (VIC) Plum, TX SS. Peter and Paul Church.
Strynkowski, Msgr. John J. *s.t.d.* '63 (BRK) [177] Queens, NY Holy Cross Church.
Strzadala, Wieslaw P. *s.d.s.* '90 (BRK) [93] Brooklyn, NY Our Lady of Consolation Church.
Strzelec, Thaddeus B. '42 (HBG) Lewistown, PA Sacred Heart of Jesus Church.
Strzelinski, Ernest '65 (PIT) Allegheny County, PA Kane Regional Center - Ross.
Strzok, James A. *s.j.* '70 (RC) St. Francis, SD Rosebud Reservation Church.
Stua, Ronald *c.m.f.* '81 (ATL) Stone Mountain, GA Corpus Christi Church.
Stua, Ronald '81 (CHI) [N] Oak Park, IL Claretian Fathers Headquarters of U.S.A. Eastern Province.
Stuardi, Msgr. J. Edwin '41 (MOB) Retired; [F] Daphne, AL Mercy Medical; [L] Daphne, AL Apostleship of Prayer.
Stuart, Francis *o.s.b.* '61 (SAL) Sharon Springs, KS Holy Ghost Church.
Stuart, George '89 (WDC) [3] Bethesda, MD Little Flower Church.
Stubbs, Msgr. Charles W. '63 (BGP) [1] Greenwich, CT St. Mary's Church.
Stubbs, Michael C. '78 (KCK) Lansing, KS St. Francis de Sales Church.
Stubeda, Anthony J. '85 (NU) Special or Diocesan Assignment.
Stubna, Kris D. '85 (PIT) Scott Township, PA SS. Simon and Jude Church.
Stuchlak, John *c.ss.r.* '58 (PHU) Newark, NJ St. John the Baptist Church.
Stuchlik, Richard '68 (WCH) Hutchinson, KS St. Teresa Church; [B] Hutchinson, KS Trinity High School.
Stucky-Abbott, Leona (SFE) [C] Santa Fe, NM College of Santa Fe.
Stuczko, Richard J. '54 (SY) Oriskany, NY Oneida County Jail; Retired.
Studel, Louis B. *o.m.i.* '76 (BEL) [K] Belleville, IL Missionary Association of Mary Immaculate-Mission Oblates of Mary Immaculate.
Studeny, Robert *s.v.d.* '34 (CHI) [B] Techny, IL Divine Word Residence.
Studer, James *o.s.b.* '54 (SCL) [I] Collegeville, MN St. John's Abbey, of the Order of St. Benedict.
Studerus, Gregory '80 (NEW) [9] Jersey City, NJ St. Bridget's Church.
Studney, J. Edward '87 (WDC) Retired; [L] Washington, DC Cardinal O'Boyle Residence for Priests.
Studniewski, Gary R. '95 (WDC) Hollywood, MD St. John Church.
Studwell, Joachim *o.f.m.* '87 (MIL) [P] Burlington, WI Queen of Peace Friary.
Studzinski, Lambert '40 (FAR) [E] Fargo, ND Riverview Place, Inc.
Studzinski, Lambert V. '40 (FAR) Retired.
Studzinski, Raymond *o.s.b.* '69 (IND) [J] St. Meinrad, IN St. Meinrad Archabbey.
Studzinski, Raymond *o.s.b.* '69 (WDC) [C] Washington, DC Catholic University of America, The.
Stuebben, Anthony A. *c.ss.r.* '48 (STL) [P] Liguori, MO St. Clement Health Care Center.
Stuebben, Msgr. George '54 (SAT) Retired.
Stuebben, Lawrence '55 (SAT) [24] San Antonio, TX St. Agnes Church.
Stueber, Edwin *o.s.b.* '46 (SCL) [I] Collegeville, MN St. John's Abbey, of the Order of St. Benedict.
Stuecker, Henry C. '38 (L) [60] Louisville, KY Our Mother of Sorrows Church; Retired.
Stuempel, Robert L. '75 (L) [43] Louisville, KY St. Lawrence Church.
Stueve, Bernard C. *s.m.* '38 (CIN) [M] Dayton, OH Marianist Provincialate.
Stulb, Joseph A. '61 (NEW) Ridgewood, NJ Our Lady of Mount Carmel Church; Ridgewood, NJ Valley Hospital.
Stulting, Robert J. *c.s.p.* '61 (NY) [Z] Scarsdale, NY Paulist Fathers Generalate.
Stulting, Robert J. *c.s.p.* '61 (TUC) [11] Tucson, AZ St. Cyril of Alexandria Church.
Stump, David X. *s.j.* '71 (NEW) [B] Jersey City, NJ Saint Peter's College; [N] Jersey City, NJ Jesuits of Saint Peter's College, Inc.
Stump, James *o.f.m.cap.* '88 (FRS) Fresno, CA Community Hospital, Veterans' Hospital.
Stump, Reinhard *c.ss.r.* '40 (BLX) [E] Biloxi, MS St. John Neumann Residence.
Stumpf, Thomas W. *o.s.b.* '52 (RIC) [H] Richmond, VA St. Joseph's Home for the Aged; [M] Richmond, VA Mary Mother of the Church Abbey.
Stumpf, William F. '85 (IND) On Duty Outside the Archdiocese.
Stunek, Howard *o.f.m.* '57 (LAN) Milan, MI Federal Correctional Institution.
Stunek, Leonard *o.f.m.* '60 (SAG) [18] Saginaw, MI St. Thomas Aquinas Church.
Stuparitz, George P. '46 (PIT) Retired; [N] Pittsburgh, PA St. John Vianney Manor.
Stupca, Edward L. '61 (HEL) Madison, MT Madison County Catholic Community Church.
Sturm, Donald E. '58 (KC) Hamilton, MO Sacred Heart Church.
Sturm, George *c.m.f.* '37 (SAT) [12] San Antonio, TX Immaculate Heart of Mary Church.
Sturm, John G. *s.j.* '50 (BUF) [50] Buffalo, NY St. Michael Church.
Sturm, Michael O. '69 (MIL) [4] Fond du Lac, WI St. Patrick's Church.
Sturmer, Jeffrey M. '94 (BUF) [1] Kenmore, NY St. Andrew Church; [D] Buffalo, NY Nardin Academy High School.
Sturn, Michael L. '77 (SB) [3] San Bernardino, CA Our Lady of the Assumption Church.
Sturtz, Richard S. '56 (OG) Olmstedville, NY St. Joseph Church; Schroon Lake, NY Our Lady of Lourdes Church.
Stutz, Edward J. '46 (E) Retired.
Styczen, Emil '55 (SP) Holiday, FL St. Vincent De Paul Church.
Styles, Kenneth A. *s.j.* '72 (DET) [E] Detroit, MI University of Detroit Jesuit High School and Academy.
Su, Stanislaus *c.s.j.b.* '69 (LA) [CC] Monterey Park, CA Congregation of St. John the Baptist.
Su, Msgr. Tomas '50 (SJN) [54] San Juan, PR Sagrada Familia Church.
Suan, Charito '85 (SFR) Redwood City, CA Our Lady of Mount Carmel Church.
Suarez, Carlos *o.s.b.* '86 (BIS) [A] Richardton, ND Assumption Abbey.
Suarez, Jesus '86 (TYL) Fairfield, TX St. Bernard of Clarivaux Church.
Suarez, Joaquin *s.m.* (SJN) [5] Bayamon, PR Nuestra Sra. de los Dolores Church.
Suarez, Msgr. Jose V. '54 (SJ) [13] San Jose, CA St. Julie Church.
Suarez, Juan *o.p.* '56 (CC) San Diego, TX St. Francis de Paula Church; [H] San Diego, TX Vicariate of Holy Rosary.
Suarez, Leonardo '88 (STO) [4] Stockton, CA St. George Church.
Suarez, Michael F. *s.j.* '94 (NY) [Z] New York, NY Jesuit Provincial's Office.
Suarez, Octavio *c.m.f.* '64 (TYL) Henderson, TX St. Jude Church.
Suarez, Pedro A. *s.j.* '72 (MIA) [B] Miami, FL Barry University; [H] Miami, FL Villa Arrieta.
Suaybagio, Evangelio R. '75 (NY) [211] Staten Island, NY St. Joseph, St. Thomas Church.
Suazo, Rafael '64 (SJN) [7] Carolina, PR San Felipe Apostol Church.
Subb, Victor *glmy.* '87 (LR) Crossett, AR Holy Cross Church.
Suberlak, Donald *c.r.* '67 (PT) Panama City, FL St. John the Evangelist Church.
Subocz, Adam '86 (HRT) [2] Enfield, CT St. Adalbert's Church.

Suchan, William T. *s.j.* '58 (CI) [C] Tunnuk, Chuuk, FM Vicariate Residence.
Sucharski, Michael *s.v.d.* '83 (BLX) [A] Bay St. Louis, MS St. Augustine's.
Sucher, Frederick *c.p.* '44 (CHI) [N] Chicago, IL Immaculate Conception Monastery.
Suchnicki, Michael *o.f.m.cap.* '88 (DEN) [M] Denver, CO St. Francis of Assisi Friary.
Suchocki, James A. '62 (GAY) Special Assignment.
Suchocki, Marek '86 (NY) [228] Staten Island, NY St. Stanislaus Kostka Church.
Sucholet, James J. '91 (NOR) [3] Middletown, CT St. Mary of Czestochowa Church.
Suchy, Theodore D. *o.s.b.* '67 (JOL) [A] Lisle, IL Benedictine University; [J] Lisle, IL St. Procopius Abbey.
Suda, Conrad P. '40 (MAR) Retired.
Sudario, Msgr. Antonio '69 (ORG) Cypress, CA St. Irenaeus Church.
Suddes, Msgr. James A. '38 (SFD) Retired; [J] Alton, IL Marian Heights Apartments.
Sudekum, Msgr. Edward J. '61 (STL) [3] University City, MO Our Lady of Lourdes Church.
Sudhoff, Leonard *c.pp.s.* '39 (CIN) [B] Carthagena, OH St. Charles.
Sudlik, Richard *o.m.i.* '72 (MIA) [7] Miami, FL Holy Redeemer Church.
Sudol, Gerard J. '80 (NEW) [3] Jersey City, NJ St. Anne's Church; Jersey City, NJ St. Francis Health Center; [G] Jersey City, NJ St. Francis Hospital.
Suellentrop, Anthony J. '73 (DOD) Kiowa, KS St. John the Apostle Church; Medicine Lodge, KS Holy Rosary Church; Sharon, KS St. Boniface Church.
Suellentrop, Bernard '45 (STL) Shrewsbury, MO St. Michael Church.
Suellentrop, Daniel M. *o.s.b.* '51 (OKL) [I] Shawnee, OK St. Gregory's Abbey.
Suelzer, Msgr. John N. '65 (FTW) [3] Fort Wayne, IN St. Charles Borromeo Church.
Suen, Benito *o.a.r* '54 (LSC) [B] Mesilla, NM Augustinian Recollects Fathers.
Suenram, John Magdalene *o.c.d.* '87 (SAT) [18] San Antonio, TX Our Lady of Mt. Carmel and St. Therese, Discalced Carmelite Fathers Church; [M] San Antonio, TX Discalced Carmelites (Prov. of St. Therese).
Sueper, Alban *s.s.c.* '53 (OM) [K] St. Columbans, NE St. Columban's Foreign Mission Society.
Suess, Milton M. '63 (GB) Luxemburg, WI Immaculate Conception Church.
Suffredini, Louis M. '57 (MOB) [F] Mobile, AL Little Sisters of the Poor, Home For the Aged, Inc.
Suggs, Fred H. '46 (CHR) Retired.
Sughrue, Denis B. *c.s.c.* '39 (FR) [B] North Easton, MA Holy Cross Fathers Religious.
Sughrue, Paul S. '70 (BO) [3] Woburn, MA St. Charles Church.
Sugrue, John F. '62 (CAM) Mays Landing, NJ St. Vincent de Paul Church.
Sugrue, Patrick *o.c.d.* '64 (SB) [G] Redlands, CA El Carmelo Retreat House.
Sugrue, Timothy F. *s.m.* '63 (WDC) [M] Washington, DC Marist Provincial House.
Suhaka, Peter G. '86 (MET) Manville, NJ Sacred Heart of Jesus Church.
Suhoza, J. Edward '68 (PIT) Bethel Park, PA St. Thomas More Church.
Suibielski, Kenneth J. '77 (PRO) [8] Pawtucket, RI St. Maria Goretti Church.
Suing, Benedict *o.s.b.* '54 (P) [33] Portland, OR Sacred Heart Church.
Suit, Robert J. '74 (STL) De Soto, MO St. Rose of Lima Church.
Suitan, Martin '79 (NY) Pine Bush, NY The Infant Saviour Church.
Sujka, Andrew *o.f.m.conv.* '75 (BO) [55] Boston, MA Our Lady of Czestochowa Church.
Suknaic, John J. (HBG) [G] Lebanon, PA Villa Vianney.
Sukup, Joseph G. '56 (MIL) Oak Creek, WI St. Matthew's Church.
Sulahian, Mesrop (ARM) [C] Glendale, CA Mekhitarian Educational Foundation.
Sularz, Thomas '71 (JOL) Woodridge, IL St. Scholastica Church.
Sulavik, Athanasius *o.p.* (NY) [Z] New York, NY St. Catherine of Siena Priory.
Sulavik, Athanasius *o.p.* '95 (NY) [22] New York, NY St. Catherine of Siena Church.
Sulicki, Casimir F. '55 (SCR) Forest City, PA St. Joseph's Church.
Sulka, Stanley E. '59 (KAL) Absent on Sick Leave.
Sulkowski, Anthony F. '86 (DET) [4] Monroe, MI St. Mary's Church.
Sullivan, Alan *o.f.m.* '56 (NY) [Z] New York, NY Franciscan Friars, Order of Friars Manor.
Sullivan, Andrew '94 (BIR) [6] Birmingham, AL St. Francis Xavier Church; [A] Birmingham, AL John Carroll High School.
Sullivan, Andrew J. '47 (WOR) Retired.
Sullivan, Msgr. Arthur A. '37 (PRO) Retired.
Sullivan, Athanasius *o.p.* (NY) Manhattan, NY New York Hospital.
Sullivan, Msgr. Bernard O. (BEL) Retired.
Sullivan, Brendan J. '78 (BO) On Duty Outside the Archdiocese.
Sullivan, Brendan V. '60 (CAM) Ventnor, NJ St. James Church.
Sullivan, C. Otis (CHI) Retired.
Sullivan, Charles D. *s.j.* '72 (NY) [F] New York, NY Fordham Preparatory School; [Z] New York, NY Jesuit Community at Fordham University.
Sullivan, Charles J. '50 (SFR) [51] San Francisco, CA St. Thomas, The Apostle Church.
Sullivan, Charles J. '65 (SPR) Absent on Leave.
Sullivan, Charles J. '65 (WIN) Jackson, MN Good Shepherd Church.
Sullivan, Charles J. '66 (PH) [23] Philadelphia, PA St. Bernard Church.
Sullivan, Charles K. '64 (VEN) [4] Fort Myers, FL St. Columbkille Church.
Sullivan, Cletus *o.carm.* '45 (CHI) [N] Mundelein, IL Carmelite Monastery.
Sullivan, Cyprian M. *o.f.m.conv.* '37 (MET) [G] North Plainfield, NJ Villa Maria Sanitarium; [I] North Plainfield, NJ Villa Maria Regional House.
Sullivan, D. Edward '42 (CHL) Retired.
Sullivan, Dan *c.p.* '68 (PIT) [N] Pittsburgh, PA St. Paul of the Cross Monastery.
Sullivan, Daniel '75 (TR) Hainesport, NJ Our Lady Queen of Peace Church.
Sullivan, Msgr. Daniel F. '38 (LA) Beverly Hills, CA Good Shepherd Church; Retired.
Sullivan, Daniel F. '57 (CHI) Arlington Heights, IL St. Edna Church.
Sullivan, Daniel J. *c.m.* '53 (BRK) [D] Queens and Staten Island, NY St. John's University; [U] Jamaica, NY Vincentian Residence.
Sullivan, Daniel J. '53 (CHI) Retired.
Sullivan, Daniel J. *s.j.* '61 (NY) [Z] New York, NY Jesuit Community at Fordham University.
Sullivan, Daniel J. *s.j.* '72 (HON) [7] Honolulu, HI Newman Center at the University of Hawaii, Holy Spirit Parish Church; [H] Honolulu, HI Jesuit Fathers House.
Sullivan, Daniel J. *s.j.* '72 (SJ) [M] Los Gatos, CA California Province of the Society of Jesus, Jesuit Provincial Office.
Sullivan, Daniel J. '77 (PH) [93] Philadelphia, PA St. Martin De Porres Church.
Sullivan, Daniel James '63 (HRT) [3] Hamden, CT Our Lady of Mt. Carmel Church.
Sullivan, Daniel Jeremiah '63 (HRT) South Windsor, CT St. Margaret Mary Church.
Sullivan, Msgr. Daniel L. '40 (NY) Retired.
Sullivan, Msgr. Daniel L. '48 (NY) [199] Staten Island, NY Blessed Sacrament Church; [229] Staten Island, NY St. Sylvester Church.
Sullivan, David D. '58 (STL) [K] Creve Coeur, MO St. John's Mercy Medical Center.
Sullivan, Dennis J. '71 (NY) [116] New York, NY St. Teresa Church; Manhattan, NY Gouverneur Hospital.
Sullivan, Dennis L. *t.o.r.* '54 (PH) Newtown Square, PA St. Anastasia Church.
Sullivan, Donal '64 (STA) Green Cove Springs, FL Sacred Heart Church.
Sullivan, Msgr. Donald E. '52 (STL) Retired.
Sullivan, E. Hartrick *c.m.* '46 (DEN) [M] Denver, CO Congregation of the Mission Midwest Province: De Paul House.
Sullivan, Edward *o.f.m.* (NY) Warwick, NY St. Anthony Community Hospital; [S] Warwick, NY St. Anthony Community Hospital, Inc.; [V] Warwick, NY Villa Frances at the Knolls; [AA] Warwick, NY Franciscan Sisters of Poor Mt Alverno Center, Inc. Franciscan Health Systems of Warwick, Inc.; [BB] Warwick, NY Mount Alverno Center and Convent.
Sullivan Edward '55 (RVC) Copiague, NY Our Lady of the Assumption Church.
Sullivan Edward P. *s.j.* '46 (BUF) [O] Buffalo, NY Canisius Jesuit Community.
Sullivan Msgr. Edward T. '42 (SCR) Retired; [N] Dunmore, PA Villa St. Joseph.
Sullivan, Msgr. Edwin V. '46 (NEW) Retired; [B] South Orange, NJ Seton Hall University.
Sullivan, Emmanuel *o.c.d.* '52 (BO) [W] Brighton, MA Carmelite Monastery.
Sullivan, Emmanuel *o.c.d.* '52 (PRT) [A] Standish, ME Saint Joseph's College.
Sullivan, Emmanuel *s.a.* '55 (NY) [Z] Garrison, NY Generalate of the Franciscan Friars of the Atonement-St. James Friary.
Sullivan, Ernest L. '61 (LA) [R] Los Angeles, CA Columban Fathers, Procure House.
Sullivan, Eugene J. *c.s.v.* '45 (JOL) [2] Kankakee, IL St. Patrick Church.
Sullivan, Eugene P. (BO) [2] Weymouth, MA St. Francis Xavier Church.
Sullivan, Eugene P. '59 (CHY) Sheridan, WY Holy Name Church.
Sullivan, F. Norman '62 (BUF) [5] Cheektowaga, NY Most Holy Redeemer Church.
Sullivan, Francis A. *s.j.* '51 (BO) [W] Chestnut Hill, MA The Jesuit Community at Boston College.
Sullivan, Francis B. *c.pp.s.* '46 (HBG) [I] Columbia, PA Adorers of the Blood of Christ.
Sullivan, Francis D. *o.f.m.* '43 (BUF) [5] Cheektowaga, NY Most Holy Redeemer Church.
Sullivan, Francis J. '30 (SPR) Retired.
Sullivan, Francis P. '37 (BO) Retired.
Sullivan, Francis X. '48 (SPR) [2] Westfield, MA Our Lady of the Blessed Sacrament Church.
Sullivan, Frederick '53 (NY) Cold Spring-on-Hudson, NY Our Lady of Loretto Church.
Sullivan, Gael '76 (SFR) [N] San Francisco, CA Salesian Provincial Residence.
Sullivan, George *o.f.m.conv.* '74 (CHL) Winston-Salem, NC Our Lady of Mercy Church.
Sullivan, George '76 (LA) [1] Oxnard, CA St. Anthony Church.
Sullivan, George D. '80 (OAK) [14] Oakland, CA St. Margaret Mary Church.
Sullivan, George D. '80 (STO) On Duty Outside the Diocese.
Sullivan, George R. *s.j.* '75 (LA) [R] Los Angeles, CA Columbiere House.
Sullivan, George R. *s.j.* '75 (MIL) [P] Milwaukee, WI Jesuit Provincial Office, Wisconsin Province.
Sullivan, Gerald A. '59 (CHY) [2] Cheyenne, WY Holy Trinity Church.
Sullivan, Gerald P. *s.j.* '62 (SJ) [B] Santa Clara, CA Santa Clara University.
Sullivan, J. Bernard '44 (HEL) Retired.
Sullivan, J. Richard '77 (L) On Duty Outside the Archdiocese.
Sullivan, J. Richard '77 (LEX) Danville, KY SS. Peter & Paul Church.
Sullivan, James *s.m.a.* (PAT) [J] Denville, NJ Sisters of the Sorrowful Mother Health Care Ministry Corp.
Sullivan, James *c.ss.r.* '39 (DET) [34] Detroit, MI Holy Redeemer Church.
Sullivan, James '47 (SFD) Retired.
Sullivan, James B. '58 (NEW) Fort Lee, NJ Holy Trinity Church.
Sullivan, James E. '46 (BRK) [179] Queens, NY Holy Trinity Church; Retired.
Sullivan, James E. *o.m.i.* '53 (WDC) [B] Washington, DC Oblate College/Oblate Center for Mission Studies.
Sullivan, James F. '87 (PH) Military Chaplains.
Sullivan, James J. '40 (HRT) Retired.
Sullivan, James K. '65 (SAT) [C] San Antonio, TX Oblate School of Theology.
Sullivan, James L. '43 (BO) Permanent Disability.
Sullivan, James M. '60 (HEL) On Duty Outside the Diocese.
Sullivan, James M. '60 (OM) [24] Omaha, NE St. John Vianney Church.
Sullivan, James M. '66 (STL) Port Hudson, MO Holy Family Church.
Sullivan, James M. *o.p.* '95 (CIN) [M] Cincinnati, OH St. Gertrude Priory.
Sullivan, James M. *o.p.* '96 (CIN) [30] Cincinnati, OH St. Gertrude Church.
Sullivan, James T. *o.p.* '45 (PRO) [P] Providence, RI St. Thomas Aquinas Priory at Providence College.
Sullivan, Jan C.P. '91 (COL) [19] Columbus, OH Holy Family Church; Columbus, OH Children's Hospital.
Sullivan, Jeremiah *c.s.p.* '59 (LA) [86] Los Angeles, CA St. Paul the Apostle Church.
Sullivan, Jeremiah T. '62 (HEL) [B] Helena, MT Carroll College.
Sullivan, John *o.p.* (NY) Orangeburg, NY Rockland Psychiatric Center.
Sullivan, John '54 (JOL) Glen Ellyn, IL St. Petronille Church.
Sullivan, John *o.f.m.* '59 (SFD) Batchtown, IL St. Barbara Church; Brussels, IL St. Mary Church; Meppen, IL St. Joseph Church.
Sullivan, John *o.f.m.* '59 (STL) [P] Oakville, MO St. Francis Friary.
Sullivan, John *s.m.* '65 (HON) [15] Honolulu, HI Star of the Sea Church.
Sullivan, John *o.c.d.* '68 (MIL) [P] Milwaukee, WI Provincial Offices - Discalced Carmelites.
Sullivan, John '72 (SAC) Placerville, CA St. Patrick's Church.
Sullivan, John A. '55 (PAT) On Duty Outside the Diocese.
Sullivan, John A. '55 (TR) Brick Town, NJ Visitation Church.
Sullivan, John A. '78 (RNO) Stead, NV St. Michael's Church.
Sullivan, John B. '61 (NY) [164] Bronx, NY St. Mary Church.
Sullivan, John E. (TR) [M] Trenton, NJ Villa Neumann.
Sullivan, John E. '49 (TR) Retired.
Sullivan, John J. '41 (NOR) [3] Middletown, CT St. Mary of Czestochowa Church; Retired.
Sullivan, Msgr. John J. '51 (SLC) [6] Salt Lake City, UT St. Ann Church.
Sullivan, John J. '66 (DET) Plymouth, MI Our Lady of Good Counsel Church.

Sullivan, John J. '67 (CLV) Mentor, OH St. Bede the Venerable Church.
Sullivan, John J. '77 (CHI) [206] Chicago, IL St. Thomas More Church.
Sullivan, John J. *o.s.f.s.* '81 (PH) [Z] Philadelphia, PA Oblates of St. Francis De Sales.
Sullivan, John James *o.p.* '39 (NY) [Z] New York, NY St. Vincent Ferrer Priory.
Sullivan, John L. (BO) Society of St. James the Apostle.
Sullivan, John L. (SPR) Agawam, MA St. Theresa of the Child Jesus Church.
Sullivan, John L. '41 (HRT) Retired.
Sullivan, John L. '45 (PRT) Retired; [I] Waterville, ME Mt. St. Joseph Priest Retirement Home.
Sullivan, John L. *o.p.* '49 (NY) [AA] Blauvelt, NY Congregation of St. Dominic General Motherhouse of the Sisters of St. Dominic of Blauvelt.
Sullivan, John L. '71 (SPR) [J] Holyoke, MA Providence Motherhouse - Sisters of Providence.
Sullivan, John L. '74 (BO) [A] Boston, MA St. John's Seminary School of Theology.
Sullivan, John M. (BO) [1] Malden, MA Immaculate Conception Church.
Sullivan, John M. '90 (FR) North Attleboro, MA St. Mary's Church.
Sullivan, John P. *o.p.* '41 (NY) Pleasantville, NY Holy Innocents Church.
Sullivan, John P. '65 (HRT) [12] New Haven, CT St. Joseph's Church; [R] New Haven, CT Southern Connecticut State University Newman Center.
Sullivan, Msgr. John P. '65 (RVC) Greenport, NY St. Agnes Church.
Sullivan, John P. *m.s.* '70 (HRT) [M] Hartford, CT Missionaries of LaSalette Provincial Secretary.
Sullivan, John R. '94 (LIN) [9] Lincoln, NE St. Patrick's Church.
Sullivan, John T. '42 (PHX) Retired.
Sullivan, John W. *s.j.* '47 (BO) [W] Weston, MA Campion Health Center, Inc.
Sullivan, Msgr. Joseph A. '45 (DUB) Retired.
Sullivan, Joseph A. '58 (BGP) [3] Greenwich, CT St. Paul's Church.
Sullivan, Joseph C. '53 (DEN) [25] Denver, CO St. Anthony of Padua Church.
Sullivan, Joseph D. '56 (NY) Montgomery, NY Holy Name of Mary Church.
Sullivan, Msgr. Joseph J. '38 (ROC) Retired.
Sullivan, Msgr. Joseph P. '53 (SFR) [30] San Francisco, CA St. Kevin Church.
Sullivan, Joseph P. '58 (HEL) Columbia Falls, MT St. Richard Church.
Sullivan, Kevin L. '76 (NY) [40] New York, NY St. Gregory Church; [I] New York, NY The Catholic Charities of the Archdiocese of New York; [DD] New York, NY Carmel Housing Development Fund Co., Inc.; [DD] New York, NY The Housing Fund of the Archdiocese of New York.
Sullivan, Kilian *o.s.b.* '89 (KC) [J] Conception, MO Conception Abbey.
Sullivan, Lawrence F. *o.c.d.* '60 (BO) Boston, MA Lawrence F. Quigley Memorial Hospital; [W] Brighton, MA Carmelite Monastery.
Sullivan, Lawrence J. '92 (CHI) Elmwood Park, IL St. Celestine Church.
Sullivan, Liam '72 (BIR) Bessemer, AL St. Aloysius Church.
Sullivan, Martin J. '53 (BRK) [186] Queens, NY St. Josaphat Church.
Sullivan, Matthew *ss.cc.* '55 (FR) New Bedford, MA Bristol Co. House of Correction & Eastern Massachusetts Correctional Alcohol Center; [K] Fairhaven, MA Sacred Hearts Provincial House.
Sullivan, Michael '66 (MIA) Deerfield Beach, FL Our Lady of Mercy Church.
Sullivan, Michael '81 (CR) Warren, MN SS. Peter and Paul Church.
Sullivan, Michael *o.f.m.cap.* '84 (MIL) [11] Milwaukee, WI St. Benedict the Moor Church; [25] Milwaukee, WI St. Francis of Assisi Church.
Sullivan, Michael B. '75 (FTW) [J] Notre Dame, IN Holy Cross Community, Corby Hall, University of Notre Dame.
Sullivan, Michael Bruce *c.s.c.* '75 (FTW) [B] Notre Dame, IN University of Notre Dame Du Lac.
Sullivan, Michael D. '45 (BO) Retired.
Sullivan, Michael D. '91 (TR) Bayville, NJ St. Barnabas Church.
Sullivan, Michael J. '79 (SCR) Wellsboro, PA St. Peter's Church.
Sullivan, Michael P. *o.s.a.* '67 (PH) [Z] Villanova, PA St. Thomas Monastery.
Sullivan, Patrick '62 (DEN) Retired.
Sullivan, Patrick '82 (CR) Warroad, MN St. Mary's Church.
Sullivan, Patrick A. *s.j.* '45 (BO) [W] Weston, MA Campion Center.
Sullivan, Patrick H. '55 (LA) [80] Los Angeles, CA St. Mary Magdalen Church.
Sullivan, Patrick J. *s.j.* '50 (NY) [Z] New York, NY Jesuit Community at Fordham University.
Sullivan, Patrick J. *c.s.c.* '56 (FTW) [J] South Bend, IN Congregation of Holy Cross Indiana Province Provincial House.
Sullivan, Patrick J. '63 (BIR) [20] Birmingham, AL St. Peter the Apostle Church.
Sullivan, Patrick J. *s.j.* '71 (CI) [B] Chuuk, FM Xavier High School.
Sullivan, Patrick M. *o.s.b.* '87 (MAN) [K] Manchester, NH St. Anselm Abbey.
Sullivan, Patrick T. *s.j.* '64 (BUF) [50] Buffalo, NY St. Michael Church.
Sullivan, Paul '63 (BO) Winthrop, MA St. John the Evangelist Church.
Sullivan, Paul M. *s.j.* '83 (BO) [W] Boston, MA The Society of Jesus of New England-Provincial Offices.
Sullivan, Paul M. *s.j.* '83 (PRT) Eastport, ME St. Joseph Church.
Sullivan, Paul V. '50 (NY) [10] Yonkers, NY St. Joseph Church; Retired.
Sullivan, Peter '70 (ALB) [7] Albany, NY Church of the Holy Cross.
Sullivan, Peter J., III '70 (ALB) [1] Albany, NY Cathedral of the Immaculate Conception; Special Assignment.
Sullivan, R. William *o.s.a.* '67 (CHI) [N] Chicago, IL St. John Stone Friary.
Sullivan, Raymond F. *m.m.* '54 (NY) [Z] Maryknoll, NY Maryknoll Fathers and Brothers.
Sullivan, Richard H. *c.s.c.* '50 (FR) [M] North Easton, MA Holy Cross Fathers Retreat House.
Sullivan, Richard J. '58 (E) [12] Erie, PA St. Andrew Church.
Sullivan, Robert E. '80 (BO) [A] Boston, MA St. John's Seminary School of Theology.
Sullivan, Robert J. *s.j.* '40 (BO) [W] Boston, MA The Society of Jesus of New England-Provincial Offices.
Sullivan, Robert J. *s.j.* '45 (PRT) Bangor, ME St. John's Church; Bangor, ME Eastern Maine Medical Center.
Sullivan, Robert J. '63 (SY) [V] Vestal, NY Binghamton University Newman Center.
Sullivan, Robert J. '78 (BO) [71] Boston, MA St. Theresa Church.
Sullivan, Robert J. '93 (BIR) [20] Birmingham, AL St. Peter the Apostle Church; [A] Birmingham, AL John Carroll High School.
Sullivan, Robert L. *s.j.* '67 (BEL) [3] East St. Louis, IL St. Joseph Church.
Sullivan, Robert L. *s.j.* '67 (STL) [52] St. Louis, MO St. Matthew, Apostle Church; [P] St. Louis, MO The Jesuits of the Missouri Province.
Sullivan, Robert W. *s.s.j.* '72 (BLX) [5] Gulfport, MS St. Therese Church.
Sullivan, Terence *o.s.b.* '56 (KCK) Hiawatha, KS St. Ann's Church.
Sullivan, Terrence J. '64 (SJ) Campbell, CA St. Lucy Church.
Sullivan, Thomas D. *s.s.e.* '38 (VEN) [G] Englewood, FL Society of St. Edmund Residence.
Sullivan, Thomas F. '41 (CLV) Retired; [N] Akron, OH Francesca Residence; [Q] Akron, OH Provincial Motherhouse and Novitiate of the Daughters of Divine Charity.
Sullivan, Thomas G. *c.ss.r.* '72 (HRT) [5] Enfield, CT St. Patrick's Church.
Sullivan, Thomas K. '52 (STA) [18] Jacksonville, FL St. Paul's Church.
Sullivan, Thomas L. *c.s.v.* '32 (CHI) [N] Arlington Heights, IL Viatorian Province Center-Clerics of St. Viator.
Sullivan, Thomas P. '53 (BIS) Parshall, ND St. Bridget Church.
Sullivan, Timothy *s.a.* '90 (OG) [E] Saranac Lake, NY St. Joseph's Rehabilitation Center, Inc.; [F] Saranac Lake, NY Atonement Friars.
Sullivan, Msgr. Timothy E. '37 (BO) Retired.
Sullivan, Timothy F. *c.s.p.* '85 (NY) [Z] Scarsdale, NY Paulist Fathers Generalate.
Sullivan, Timothy J. (PRO) [M] Newport, RI St. Clare Home.
Sullivan, Timothy J. '38 (PRO) Retired.
Sullivan, Vincent B. *s.j.* '76 (NEW) [26] Jersey City, NJ St. Peter's Church.
Sullivan, Msgr. W. Jerome '61 (BUF) Hamburg, NY St. Mary of the Lake Church.
Sullivan, Walter A. '54 (FR) South Dartmouth, MA St. Mary's Church.
Sullivan, Walter J. *c.s.p.* '35 (BO) [P] Boston, MA Paulist Center; [W] Boston, MA Paulist Fathers Residence.
Sullivan, Walter J. *c.s.p.* '35 (NY) [Z] Scarsdale, NY Paulist Fathers Generalate.
Sullivan, Wilfred '40 (WIN) Retired.
Sullivan, William *s.j.* (MI) Kwajalein, MH Blessed Sacrament Church.
Sullivan, William '72 (FTW) [3] Mishawaka, IN St. Monica Church.
Sullivan, William *o.ss.t.* '81 (BAL) [M] Baltimore, MD Holy Trinity Monastery.
Sullivan, William F. *s.s.c.* '56 (PRO) [P] Bristol, RI St. Columban's Retirement House.
Sullivan, William H. *o.s.a.* '52 (SD) [H] San Diego, CA Augustinian Community.
Sullivan, William J. '59 (HBG) Rohrerstown, PA St. Leo the Great Church.
Sullivan, William J. *s.j.* '61 (SEA) [A] Seattle, WA Seattle University.
Sullivan, William J. *o.s.b.* '71 (SFR) [N] Portola Valley, CA Woodside Priory.
Sullivan, William J. *o.ss.t.* '81 (WDC) [E] Hyattsville, MD De Matha Catholic High School; [M] Hyattsville, MD St. John de Matha Monastery, Order of Most Holy Trinity.
Sullivan, William M. (BO) Westford, MA St. Catherine Church.
Sullivan, William P. '39 (BO) Retired.
Sullivan, William V. '66 (RIC) Ashland, VA St. Ann Church.
Sumler, Kevin '82 (BEA) Absent On Leave.
Sumler, Paul E. '80 (BEA) Kountze, TX Holy Spirit Mission Church; Lumberton, TX Infant Jesus Church.
Summerfield, Michael L. '86 (NU) [2] New Ulm, MN St. Mary Church.
Summers, Bryan F. *c.o.* '72 (PIT) [N] Pittsburgh, PA Congregation of the Oratory of St. Philip Neri; [Q] Slippery Rock, PA Office for Campus Ministry; [Q] Slippery Rock, PA Office for Campus Ministry; [Q] Slippery Rock, PA Office for Campus Ministry.
Summers, John '54 (Y) Retired.
Summers, Msgr. R. Emmett '52 (KC) Retired.
Summitt, James A. '81 (BIR) Absent on Leave.
Sumpter, Gary '79 (SR) Napa, CA St. Thomas Aquinas Church.
Sun, Paul *s.j.* '95 (BAL) [C] Baltimore, MD Loyola College; [M] Baltimore, MD Jesuit Community of Loyola College, Inc.
Sundararaj, Lazar (NY) [3] Yonkers, NY St. Ann Church.
Sunderland, James C. *s.j.* '58 (DEN) [M] Denver, CO Loyola Parish - Jesuit Community; [M] Denver, CO Xavier Jesuit Center.
Sundholm, Conrad J. '55 (ROC) [1] Auburn, NY Holy Family Church.
Sunds, Elvin '72 (JKS) Meridian, MS East Mississippi State Hospital.
Sunds, Elvin '73 (JKS) Meridian, MS St. Patrick Church; Meridian, MS St. Joseph Church.
Sung, John *s.j.* (SFR) [2] San Francisco, CA St. Agnes Church.
Sung, Thomas (BRK) [T] Brooklyn, NY Catholic Migration & Refugee Office, Catholic Migration Services, Inc.
Sung, Thomas *c.s.j.b.* '51 (BRK) [U] Elmhurst, NY Congregation of St. John the Baptist of China.
Sung, Thomas *c.s.j.b.* '69 (BRK) [209] Queens, NY Our Lady of China Chapel.
Sunoborg, Stephen V. *s.j.* '74 (P) [L] Portland, OR Jesuit Provincial Office (Oregon Prov.).
Suntum, James *s.f.* '84 (WDC) Takoma Park, MD Our Lady of Sorrows Church.
Sunturn, Jim *s.f.* '84 (WDC) [B] Silver Spring, MD Holy Family Seminary.
Supancheck, Norman A. '68 (LA) Fillmore, CA St. Francis of Assisi Church.
Super, David J. '80 (CR) Moorhead, MN St. Francis de Sales Church.
Super, Msgr. Joseph J. '44 (SCR) [3] Pittston, PA St. John the Baptist Church; Retired.
Superiaso, Jose '85 (SFR) Daly City, CA St. Andrew Church.
Suppa, F. Thomas '78 (E) [1] Oil City, PA Assumption of the Blessed Virgin Mary Church; Rouseville, PA St. Venantius Church; [O] Du Bois, PA Nazareth In The Woods, Inc.
Suppe, Bernard A. *s.j.* '56 (BAL) [I] Baltimore, MD Mercy Medical Center, Inc.
Suppe, Joseph V. '74 (HRT) Retired.
Supple, Edmund R. *c.s.sp.* '38 (PIT) [B] Pittsburgh, PA Duquesne University of the Holy Ghost.
Supple, Msgr. James '36 (DUB) Ames, IA St. Thomas Aquinas Church (and Catholic Student Center) Church.
Supple, Msgr. James A. '36 (DUB) Retired; [N] Ames, IA St. Thomas Aquinas Church and Catholic Student Center (Iowa State University).
Suquilvide, Abel '55 (LA) Guadalupe, CA Our Lady of Guadalupe Church.
Surace, Robert J. '79 (NY) Absent on Leave.
Suran, Joaquin '49 (BRK) [225] Queens, NY St. Paul the Apostle Church.
Surban, Edmundo A. '61 (NEW) Jersey City, NJ Jersey City Medical Center.
Suren, John '58 (STL) Weingarten, MO Our Lady Help of Christians Church.
Suren, Richard H. '53 (STL) High Ridge, MO St. Anthony of Padua Church.
Surette, John E. *s.j.* '67 (BO) [W] Boston, MA The Society of Jesus of New England-Provincial Offices.
Surges, Robert F. '64 (MIL) Big Bend, WI St. Joseph's Church.
Suriani, Raymond N. '85 (PRO) Westerly, RI St. Pius X Church.
Suriano, Thomas M. '64 (MIL) [59] Milwaukee, WI Our Lady of Lourdes Church.

Surman, Stanislaus '56 (SAG) Sandusky, MI St. Joseph Church.
Surmeier, William J. '65 (SAL) Hays, KS St. Nicholas of Myra Church; Munjor, KS St. Francis of Assisi Church.
Surowiec, Jude *o.f.m.conv.* '75 (SPR) [A] Granby, MA St. Hyacinth College and Seminary.
Surprenant, John L. '78 (NOR) Absent on Leave.
Surprenant, Paul W. '73 (WIN) [7] Rochester, MN St. Pius X Church.
Surufka, Michael *o.f.m.* '91 (PH) [D] Philadelphia, PA Archbishop Ryan High School; [Z] Philadelphia, PA St. Pius X Friary.
Survil, Bernard '67 (GBG) On Duty Outside the Diocese.
Surwilo, Msgr. Edward R. '63 (BGP) [6] Stamford, CT Our Lady Star of the Sea Church.
Susa, Robert P. '61 (E) [B] Erie, PA Gannon University.
Susann, Robert *m.s.* '74 (ATL) [2] Marietta, GA Church of St. Ann.
Susany, L. James '67 (PIT) Duquesne, PA St. Joseph Church.
Susi, Msgr. Joseph M. '50 (ALX) Special Assignment; Retired.
Susin, Angelo J. *c.s.* '38 (PRO) [15] Providence, RI Holy Ghost Church.
Suskey, Robert G. '90 (PH) Warrington, PA St. Joseph Church.
Susko, Martin S. '61 (Y) Girard, OH St. Rose Church.
Suslenko, Mark S. '86 (HRT) [1] West Haven, CT Our Lady of Victory Church.
Suslowicz, Michael S. '80 (PIT) Nemacolin, PA Our Lady of Consolation Church.
Susnik, Bernardin *o.f.m.* '59 (CHI) [N] Lemont, IL The Slovene Franciscan Fathers, Order of Friars Minor, Commissariat of the Holy Cross.
Suss, Thomas '73 (SEA) McNeil Island, WA McNeil Island Correction Center.
Sustarsic, John '52 (DUL) Babbitt, MN St. Pius X Church.
Sustatya, Paul A. '91 (LA) Pasadena, CA St. Andrew Church.
Sustrick, Stephen J. *o.s.b.* '42 (PBL) [E] Canon City, CO Holy Cross Abbey.
Suszek, Eugene '87 (SPR) Graduate Studies.
Suszynski, Michael *o.f.m.conv.* '86 (CHI) [O] Chicago, IL Mother of Good Counsel Convent.
Sutherland, Thomas J. '60 (DET) Shelby Twp., MI St. Therese of Lisieux Church.
Sutherland, William E. '83 (E) [27] Erie, PA St. Patrick/St. Hedwig Church.
Sutherland, Msgr. William J. '33 (BUF) Retired.
Sutil, Florencio (SJN) On Duty Outside the Archdiocese.
Sutphin, Carl '58 (LA) [1] Los Angeles, CA Cathedral of Our Lady of the Angels.
Sutschek, Francis C. '40 (MIL) Retired.
Sutter, Conrad *o.f.m.conv.* '93 (CLV) [1] Lorain, OH St. Anthony of Padua Church.
Sutter, Raymond A. '73 (CLV) [7] Parma, OH St. Matthias Church.
Suttmann, Donnul *o.f.m.* '53 (CIN) [23] Cincinnati, OH St. Clement Church; [M] Cincinnati, OH St. Clement Friary.
Sutton, Donald '82 (COS) Parker, CO Ave Maria Church.
Sutton, John (BO) [4] Peabody, MA St. Joseph Church.
Sutton, John '56 (FAR) Cando, ND Sacred Heart Church.
Sutton, John '70 (PMB) [3] Boca Raton, FL St. Joan of Arc Church.
Sutton, John H. '56 (PBL) Retired.
Sutton, John V. '83 (BO) [D] Peabody, MA Bishop Fenwick High School.
Sutton, ST Antoun '96 (OLD) [1] Newark, NJ Our Lady of Deliverance Church.
Sutton, Stephen R. '84 (BAL) [47] Baltimore, MD St. Joseph Church.
Sutton, Thomas E. '73 (SAG) [17] Saginaw, MI St. Stephen Church.
Sutula, Leo S. '49 (NOR) Quaker Hill, CT Our Lady of Perpetual Help Church.
Suver, Robert J. '40 (CIN) Retired.
Suwalsky, David J. *s.j.* '95 (KC) [D] Kansas City, MO Rockhurst High School; [J] Kansas City, MO Rockhurst High School - Jesuit Community.
Suwinski, Leo S. '43 (BGP) Retired.
Svarczkopf, Mark A. '74 (IND) [14] Indianapolis, IN St. Andrew the Apostle Church; [29] Indianapolis, IN St. Lawrence Church.
Svea, Timothy E. '92 (LC) [I] St. Mary's Ridge, WI Immaculate Conception Priory; [O] Cashton, WI Institute of Christ the King-Sovereign Priest.
Sverchek, Michael P. '34 (ALN) Retired.
Sviokla, Edmond J. '51 (BO) [2] Everett, MA Immaculate Conception Church.
Svirskas, Joseph J. '51 (BO) Retired.
Svitan, Martin '79 (NY) Kingston, NY Benedictine Hospital; [S] Kingston, NY Benedictine Hospital.
Svobodny, Aloysius *o.m.i.* '49 (STP) [Q] Buffalo, MN Christ the King Retreat Center.
Swacha, Stanley J. '79 (E) Falls Creek, PA St. Bernard Church.
Swade, Thomas J. '61 (CHI) Other Assignments.
Swain, Kenneth J. '72 (ALB) Fort Plain, NY St. James Church.
Swain, Paul J. '88 (MAD) [I] Madison, WI Holy Name Catholic Center, Inc.
Swain, Robert J. '59 (BRK) [U] Jamaica, NY Vincentian Residence.
Swalina, Msgr. Michael F. '70 (SPC) New Madrid, MO Immaculate Conception Church.
Swaner, James J. '61 (PEO) Washington, IL St. Patrick's Church.
Swanson, Charles F. '66 (OM) [16] Omaha, NE Holy Cross Church.
Swanson, Mark W. '81 (DAV) Georgetown, IA St. Patrick's Church; Melrose, IA St. Patrick's Church; Knoxville, IA Veteran's Administration Hospital.
Swarick, Joachim *o.f.m.* '52 (GB) [10] Green Bay, WI St. Mary Church; [A] Green Bay, WI St. Mary of the Angels Friary; [I] Green Bay, WI St. Mary of the Angels Friary.
Swarthout, James E. '86 (RCK) Woodstock, IL St. Mary Church.
Swartvargher, Mark '96 (BRK) Graduate Studies.
Swartz, Joseph '75 (EVN) Mount Vernon, IN St. Matthew Church.
Swartz, Lawrence *o.c.s.o.* '34 (ATL) [I] Conyers, GA The Monastery of the Holy Spirit.
Swartz, Michael R. '87 (BUF) Absent on Leave.
Swast, George W. '80 (GBG) New Kensington, PA St. Joseph Church.
Sweany, Thomas M. '80 (CLV) Chesterland, OH St. Anselm Church.
Swearingen, Eric '87 (FRS) [10] Fresno, CA St. Helen Church.
Sweeney, Charles J. *s.j.* '62 (TOL) [C] Toledo, OH St. John's Jesuit High School.
Sweeney, Cornelius '50 (MRY) Cayucos, CA St. Joseph Church; Morro Bay, CA St. Timothy Church.
Sweeney, D. Gilbert *s.j.* '54 (ALN) [A] Wernersville, PA Novitiate of St. Isaac Jogues.
Sweeney, Daniel R. *s.j.* '94 (BAL) [M] Baltimore, MD Jesuit Fathers and Brothers Maryland Provincial Curia.
Sweeney, Denis J. *c.ss.r.* '81 (TOL) [2] Lima, OH St. Gerard Church.
Sweeney, Denis R. '58 (GBG) Freeport, PA St. Mary Church.
Sweeney, Msgr. Donald F. '41 (DUB) Retired.
Sweeney, E. Daniel '82 (PIT) Absent on Sick Leave.
Sweeney, Edward '88 (AMA) Friona, TX St. Teresa of Jesus Church.
Sweeney, Edward J. *s.j.* '46 (NY) [Z] New York, NY Jesuit Community at Fordham University.
Sweeney, Ernest S. *s.j.* '63 (LA) [C] Los Angeles, CA Loyola Marymount University.
Sweeney, Eugene *s.m.* '78 (FWT) Denton, TX St. Mark Church.
Sweeney, Eugene J. '65 (PBL) Retired.
Sweeney, Eugene P. '60 (ROC) Ithaca, NY Immaculate Conception Church.
Sweeney, Francis M. *c.s.p.* '61 (BO) [P] Boston, MA Paulist Center; [W] Boston, MA Paulist Fathers Residence.
Sweeney, Francis W. *s.j.* '44 (BO) [W] Chestnut Hill, MA The Jesuit Community at Boston College.
Sweeney, Frederick E. '52 (BO) [3] Haverhill, MA St. John the Baptist Church.
Sweeney, James *m.h.m.* (CHI) [182] Chicago, IL St. Rene Goupil Church.
Sweeney, James '45 (MRY) Retired.
Sweeney, James '80 (BRK) [67] Brooklyn, NY St. John Cantius Church.
Sweeney, James E. '59 (ALN) Miller Heights, PA Sacred Heart of Jesus Church; Retired.
Sweeney, James H. '81 (BRK) [101] Brooklyn, NY Our Lady of Mercy Church.
Sweeney, James P. '63 (BRK) [N] Jamaica, NY Catholic Medical Center of Brooklyn & Queens; [U] Jamaica, NY Parsons Manor.
Sweeney, Msgr. John A. '41 (STP) Retired; [A] St. Paul, MN The Saint Paul Seminary.
Sweeney, John D. '56 (NEW) West Orange, NJ St. Joseph's Church.
Sweeney, John P. *s.m.a.* '34 (BO) [W] Dedham, MA African Mission House and African Cultural Center.
Sweeney, John P. '73 (PIT) Aliquippa, PA St. Titus Church.
Sweeney, John T. '70 (GBG) Lower Burrell, PA St. Margaret Mary Church.
Sweeney, Joseph *c.s.sp.* '40 (SB) [E] Hemet, CA Holy Ghost Fathers.
Sweeney, Joseph F. *s.j.* '57 (WDC) [M] Washington, DC The Jesuit Community at Georgetown University.
Sweeney, Joseph J. '61 (PH) [39] Philadelphia, PA St. Dominic Church; Absent on Sick Leave.
Sweeney, Msgr. Kenny C. '53 (IND) Retired.
Sweeney, Kevin '94 (ORG) Rancho Santa Margarita, CA San Francisco Solano Church.
Sweeney, Lawrence '88 (SD) Leave of Absence.
Sweeney, Lawrence P. '54 (SLC) [1] Ogden, UT Holy Family Church.
Sweeney, Leo C. *s.j.* '49 (CHI) [C] Chicago, IL Jesuit Community at Loyola University of Chicago.
Sweeney, Michael '79 (KNX) Jefferson City, TN Holy Trinity Church; Morristown, TN St. Patrick Church.
Sweeney, Michael B. *o.p.* '79 (SEA) [22] Seattle, WA Blessed Sacrament Church.
Sweeney, Patrick E. '72 (PH) [121] Philadelphia, PA Our Lady of Lourdes Church.
Sweeney, Peter J. '61 (WDC) Damascus, MD St. Paul Church.
Sweeney, Reginald *o.f.m.conv.* '44 (TR) Seaside Park, NJ St. Catharine of Siena Church.
Sweeney, Robert J. '69 (RCK) Pecatonica, IL St. Mary Church.
Sweeney, Robert J. '82 (NY) Greenwood Lake, NY Holy Rosary Church.
Sweeney, Robert L. '48 (BWN) Retired.
Sweeney, Robert S. '48 (BUF) Retired.
Sweeney, Timothy *o.s.b.* '61 (IND) [J] St. Meinrad, IN St. Meinrad Archabbey.
Sweeney, Timothy *o.s.b.* '81 (OWN) [3] Owensboro, KY The Immaculate Church.
Sweeney, William *s.s.c.* '75 (OM) [K] St. Columbans, NE St. Columban's Foreign Mission Society.
Sweeney, William *s.a.c.* '77 (LUB) Seminole, TX St. James Church.
Sweeney, William F. '81 (BRK) [160] Queens, NY St. Camillus Church.
Sweeney, William J. '59 (NY) [96] New York, NY Our Lady of the Rosary Church.
Sweeny, Msgr. Edward (RVC) Graduate Studies.
Sweeny, Msgr. Edward A. '57 (RVC) Long Beach, NY St. Ignatius Martyr Church.
Sweeny, John J. '48 (SJ) [5] Santa Clara, CA Our Lady of Peace Church; [A] Santa Clara, CA Shrine of Our Lady of Peace.
Sweeny, Louis L. '48 (STO) Newman, CA St. Joachim Church.
Sweeny, Richard R. '86 (TR) Fair Haven, NJ Nativity Church.
Sweet, Douglas S. '95 (PRO) Westerly, RI Immaculate Conception Church.
Sweetser, Thomas P. *s.j.* '70 (MIL) [P] Milwaukee, WI Jesuit Provincial Office, Wisconsin Province.
Sweitzer, Raymond M. *s.j.* '75 (NY) [F] New York, NY Fordham Preparatory School; [Z] New York, NY Jesuit Provincial's Office.
Swendrowski, Patrick R. '63 (MAD) Clinton, WI St. Stephen Church.
Swenson, Frederick O. '67 (LAF) Scott, LA SS. Peter and Paul Church.
Swenson, James L. '74 (LAV) [7] Las Vegas, NV St. Bridget Church.
Swenson, Roger A. '70 (NO) [42] New Orleans, LA St. Leo the Great Church; [A] New Orleans, LA Notre Dame Seminary Graduate School of Theology.
Swenson, Walter J. '50 (NEW) [22] Jersey City, NJ Our Lady of Victories Church.
Swertz, Thaddeus S. *c.s.c* '54 (BGP) [O] Bridgeport, CT Provincial Offices of the Priests and Brothers of Holy Cross, Eastern Province.
Swetland, Stuart '91 (WDC) [37] Washington, DC St. Peter Church.
Swetland, Stuart W. (PEO) Graduate Studies.
Swetnam, R. William '73 (STL) Military Chaplains.
Swett, Charles J. '57 (TLS) Tahlequah, OK St. Brigid Church; [I] Tahlequah, OK Northeastern State University Catholic Student Organization.
Swett, Msgr. Ronald J. '67 (FRS) [6] Bakersfield, CA St. Philip the Apostle Church.
Swiader, Msgr. James P. '75 (RVC) Merrick, NY Cure of Ars Church.
Swiat, James R. '67 (LAN) Grand Blanc, MI Holy Family Church.
Swiatecki, Emilian '56 (VEN) Moore Haven, FL St. Joseph the Worker Church.
Swiatek, Emil P. '65 (BUF) Elma, NY Annunciation of the Blessed Virgin Mary Church.
Swiatek, Nicholas *o.f.m. conv.* '68 (BAL) [M] Ellicott City, MD Order of Friars Minor Conventual.
Swiatkowski, Msgr. Francis M. '44 (BUF) Retired; [O] Tonawanda, NY O'Hara Residence.
Swiatocha, Bruno (RVC) Retired.
Swichtenberg, William '83 (GB) Howard, WI St. John the Baptist Church.
Swickard, John L. '74 (COL) [6] Columbus, OH Saint Anthony Church.
Swiderski, Gregory C. '72 (PIT) Harwick, PA Our Lady of Victory Church; Allegheny County, PA Allegheny Valley Hosptial.
Swiderski, Stan *s.d.s* '63 (LR) Mountain Home, AR St. Peter the Fisherman Church.
Swiercz, Pawel A. '94 (FR) Raynham, MA St. Ann Church; [D] Taunton, MA Taunton Catholic Middle School.
Swierczynski, Joseph E. '64 (PIT) [17] Pittsburgh, PA Immaculate Heart of Mary Church.
Swierz, Michael '85 (Y) Poland, OH Holy Family Church.

Swierzbinski, Edward '51 (NEW) Retired.
Swierzbiolek, Waclav *s.d.b.* '62 (NY) [Z] New Rochelle, NY Salesian Provincial House.
Swierzowski, Stanislaus J. '56 (ALB) [2] Amsterdam, NY St. John the Baptist Church.
Swierzy, Michael W. '75 (PH) Lower Makefield, PA St. John the Evangelist Church.
Swietek, Walter '62 (VEN) Lehigh Acres, FL St. Raphael Church.
Swietochowski, Andrew K. '78 (SFS) Jefferson, SD St. Peter Church.
Swift, Bruce *o.s.b.* '60 (SPC) Buffalo, MO St. William Church; Conway, MO Sacred Heart Church.
Swift, Bruce *o.s.b.* '90 (SPC) Fordland, MO Ozark Correctional Center.
Swift, Daniel F. '89 (TR) [1] Toms River, NJ St. Joseph Church.
Swift, Gerald *s.t.* '46 (WDC) [M] Adelphi, MD Missionary Servants of the Most Holy Trinity.
Swift, James E. *c.m.* '78 (STL) [A] St. Louis, MO Kenrick-Glennon Seminary; [P] St. Louis, MO Vincentian Residence.
Swift, John *s.v.d.* '75 (CHI) [B] Techny, IL Divine Word Residence.
Swift, Walter A. '69 (SPR) Brimfield, MA St. Christopher's Church.
Swift, William J. '44 (TLS) [10] Tulsa, OK St. Mary Church.
Swiger, Msgr. Charles W. '63 (RVC) Farmingdale, NY St. Kilian Church.
Swing, R. John '70 (LC) Babcock, WI All Saints Church; Nekoosa, WI Sacred Heart of Jesus Church; Port Edwards, WI St. Alexander Church.
Swirski, Thaddeus M. '54 (CLV) [6] Akron, OH St. Hedwig Church.
Swisshelm, Germain *o.s.b.* '60 (IND) [J] St. Meinrad, IN St. Meinrad Archabbey.
Switalksi, Casimir S. '40 (SPR) Retired.
Switalski, Bruno (CHI) [198] Chicago, IL St. Tarcissus Church.
Switalski, Casimir S. '40 (SPR) [H] Holyoke, MA Sisters of Providence Care Centers, Inc.
Switanowski, Robert Joseph *o.f.m.conv.* '90 (MIL) [45] Milwaukee, WI Basilica of St. Josaphat.
Swizdor, Matthew *o.f.m.conv.* '43 (ROC) [6] Auburn, NY St. Hyacinth Church.
Swoger, John W. '63 (E) Youngsville, PA St. Luke Church.
Swoger, Mark S. '85 (E) Du Bois, PA St. Michael Church; [C] Du Bois, PA Du Bois Area Catholic Schools; [K] Du Bois, PA Christ the King Manor, Inc.
Swolek, Richard L. '63 (OM) [43] Omaha, NE St. Stanislaus Church.
Swope, Mark G. '90 (PH) Springfield, PA Holy Cross Church.
Swope, Msgr. Timothy J. '66 (ALT) Meyersdale, PA SS. Philip and James Church.
Sykes, Gregory '77 (KCK) Fort Leavenworth, KS St. Ignatius Chapel.
Sykes, Gregory '77 (OG) Military Chaplains.
Sylva, Eugene R. '93 (PAT) Hawthorne, NJ St. Anthony's Church.
Sylvester, J. Wilfred '52 (LAF) Retired.
Sylvestre, Ernest *o.m.i.* '61 (SD) [1] Chula Vista, CA Most Precious Blood Church.
Sylvia, Albert A. '66 (BO) [11] Lawrence, MA SS. Peter and Paul Church.
Sylvia, Edmund J. '77 (STU) [A] Steubenville, OH Franciscan University of Steubenville.
Symes, David L. *c.m.* '47 (PH) [Z] Philadelphia, PA Congregation of the Mission.
Symes, Joseph J. *c.m.* '50 (PH) [Z] Philadelphia, PA Congregation of the Mission.
Symionow, Bernardine *s.s.m.i.* (STF) [G] Sloatsburg, NY St. Mary's Villa Spiritual, Cultural & Educational Center.
Symolon, Lawrence '75 (HRT) [5] West Haven, CT St. Paul's Church.
Synan, Msgr. Edward A. '42 (NEW) On Duty Outside the Archdiocese.
Synowiak, Msgr. Edward F. '51 (BUF) [23] Buffalo, NY St. Florian Church.
Sypek, Msgr. Stanislaus T. '43 (BO) [2] Boston, MA St. Adalbert Church.
Sypko, Tadeusz Marek '92 (NEW) On Duty Outside the Archdiocese.
Sypko, Tadeusz Marek '92 (TUC) Safford, AZ St. Rose of Lima Church.
Syracuse, Ross *o.f.m.conv.* '78 (BRK) [61] Brooklyn, NY Most Holy Trinity Church.
Syrianey, Robert '45 (DEN) [2] Aurora, CO St. Michael the Archangel Church; Retired.
Sys, Joseph *m.afr.* '41 (SP) [O] St. Petersburg, FL Missionaries of Africa.
Syslo, Alan M. *c.s.v.* '66 (CHI) [N] Arlington Heights, IL Viatorian Province Center-Clerics of St. Viator.
Sysol, Steven M. *o.f.m.* '79 (NY) [Z] New York, NY Franciscan Province of the Immaculate Conception.
Syverstad, Daniel *o.p.* '82 (OAK) [N] Oakland, CA Western Dominican Province.
Syvinski, Henry B. *o.s.a.* '47 (PH) [Z] Villanova, PA St. Thomas Monastery.
Szabelski, Joseph R. '70 (CHI) [98] Chicago, IL St. James Church.
Szabo, Edward J. '57 (CLV) Stow, OH Holy Family Church.
Szabo, Msgr. Julius J. '36 (BUF) Retired; [O] Tonawanda, NY O'Hara Residence.
Szabo, Marcel '71 (PSC) Passaic, NJ St. Michael Cathedral; Mahwah, NJ Holy Spirit Church.
Szada, John A., Jr. '78 (HBG) Harrisburg, PA Harrisburg Hospital; Harrisburg, PA Polyclinic Medical Clinic.
Szadiak, Frank *c.ss.r.* '73 (PHU) Newark, NJ St. John the Baptist Church.
Szafranski, Richard T. '75 (SAG) Vassar, MI St. Frances Xavier Cabrini Church.
Szakaly, Anthony V. *c.s.c.* '92 (FTW) [12] South Bend, IN St. Joseph Church; [J] South Bend, IN Congregation of Holy Cross Indiana Province Provincial House.
Szal, George *s.m.* '75 (BO) [Y] Framingham Centre, MA The Marist House.
Szal, Ignatius J. '44 (PH) Oreland, PA Holy Martyrs Church; Retired.
Szamocki, Piotr '91 (CAM) Westville Grove, NJ Most Holy Redeemer Church.
Szanto, Hubert S. *o.praem.* '48 (ORG) [D] Siverado, CA St. Michael's College Preparatory High School; [H] Silverado, CA Norbertine Fathers; [M] El Toro, CA Aid to the Church In Need, Inc.
Szantyr, Eugene R. '78 (BGP) [17] Bridgeport, CT St. Patrick Church; Bridgeport, CT Bridgeport Hospital.
Szantyr, John '57 (WOR) Absent on Leave.
Szanyi, Mark A. *o.f.m.conv.* '78 (PMB) [B] Fort Pierce, FL John Carroll High School.
Szapka, Msgr. Edward J. '38 (TYL) Retired.
Szarama, Roman J. '41 (NY) Retired.
Szarek, Eugene *c.r.* '67 (CHI) [74] Chicago, IL St. Hedwig Church.
Szarek, Joseph '39 (ALB) Retired.
Szarek, Mitchell '57 (DET) [20] Detroit, MI St. Cunegunda Church.
Szarka, B. S. *o.cist.* '49 (FWT) Grapevine, TX St. Francis of Assisi Church.
Szarka, Balthasar *o.cist.* '49 (DAL) [M] Irving, TX Cistercian Abbey of Our Lady of Dallas.
Szarnicki, Henry '56 (PIT) Allegheny County, PA Marian Manor; [L] Pittsburgh, PA Marian Manor Corp.
Szarnicki, Zygmunt V. '45 (PIT) Retired; [N] Pittsburgh, PA St. John Vianney Manor.
Szaroleta, Andrew L. '77 (MET) Clinton, NJ Immaculate Conception Church; Clinton, NJ Hunterdon State School.
Szatkowski, Casimir M. (CHI) [61] Chicago, IL St. Florian Church; Retired.
Szczapa, Stanley J. '71 (NOR) Vernon, CT Sacred Heart Church.
Szczepanik, John J. '88 (MET) Lambertville, NJ St. John the Evangelist Church.
Szczepankiewicz, Gary '75 (BUF) [1] North Tonawanda, NY Ascension Church.
Szczerbicki, Thaddeus P. '40 (LC) Retired.
Szczesniak, Harry F. '72 (BUF) [8] Cheektowaga, NY Our Lady of Czestochowa Church.
Szczesny, John S. '75 (GBG) Brownsville, PA St. Mary Church.
Szczesny, Michael S. '36 (GI) Retired.
Szczesny, Walter J. '90 (BUF) Hamburg, NY SS. Peter and Paul Church.
Szczygiel, Edwin A. '47 (DET) [39] Detroit, MI St. John Cantius Church.
Szczykowski, Jan '88 (MAR) [1] Marquette, MI St. Peter Cathedral.
Szczykutowicz, Francis S. '58 (PT) Sunny Hills, FL St. Theresa Church.
Szebenyi, Andrew L. *s.j.* '61 (SY) [S] Syracuse, NY Jesuits at LeMoyne, Inc.
Szekula, Augustin '44 (ARM) [A] La Crescenta, CA Mekhitarist School.
Szelest, Theodore A. '47 (NEW) Dumont, NJ St. Mary's Church; Retired.
Szeman, Stephen '53 (SEA) Retired.
Szemborski, Chester *s.d.b.* '50 (NY) [EB] West Haverstraw, NY Don Bosco Retreat Center and Marian Shrine; [BB] West Haverstraw, NY Marian Shrine.
Szemla, Patrick *o.f.m.* '43 (GRY) [K] Cedar Lake, IN Our Lady of Lourdes Friary.
Szepe, Ladislaus *s.f.o.* '35 (GB) [I] Pulaski, WI Assumption of B.V.M. Friary.
Szewczyk, Grzegorz *s.d.s.* '91 (NEW) [N] Verona, NJ The Salvatorian Fathers.
Szewczyk, Joseph '55 (DET) New Boston, MI St. Stephen Church; [A] Orchard Lake, MI SS. Cyril and Methodius Seminary; [H] Pontiac, MI St. Joseph Mercy - Oakland.
Szewczyk, Stanley M. '69 (SY) [25] Syracuse, NY Transfiguration Church; Oneida, NY St. Joseph Church.
Szews, George R. '78 (LC) [2] Eau Claire, WI Newman Community Church; [L] Eau Claire, WI Newman Parish.
Szklarski, Joseph '62 (NEW) Lyndhurst, NJ St. Michael's Church.
Szlanga, Edmund S. '48 (CHI) [33] Chicago, IL St. Bruno Church; [99] Chicago, IL St. Jane de Chantal Church; Retired.
Szleszinski, Peter F. '56 (SUP) Hudson, WI St. Patrick Church.
Szlezak, Emeric *o.f.m.* '44 (BGP) [3] Fairfield, CT St. Emery's Church.
Szmutko, Stephen *s.v.d.* '44 (TR) [14] Trenton, NJ St. Gregory the Great Church; [M] Bordentown, NJ Society of the Divine Word.
Szmyd, John '96 (CHI) Wilmette, IL St. Joseph Church.
Szodenyi, Damian *o.cist.* '38 (DAL) [M] Irving, TX Cistercian Abbey of Our Lady of Dallas.
Szoke, Joseph V. (MET) Permanent Deacons.
Szolack, Joseph T. '88 (CAM) Merchantville, NJ St. Peter's Church.
Szopa, Daniel F. '76 (MAN) [10] Nashua, NH St. Stanislaus Church.
Szostak, Msgr. Daniel J. '54 (BUF) North Collins, NY Holy Spirit Church.
Szott, Timothy J. '70 (DET) Utica, MI St. Lawrence Church.
Szpiech, Edward P. '67 (NEW) [4] Garfield, NJ St. Stanislaus Kostka Church.
Szpieg, Edmund L. '94 (PMB) Royal Palm Beach, FL Our Lady Queen of the Apostles Church.
Szpilski, Joseph *c.m.* '56 (HRT) [4] Ansonia, CT St. Joseph's Church.
Sztorc, Richard E. '69 (CHI) Northbrook, IL Our Lady of the Brook Church.
Sztuczko, Thaddeus J. *f.d.p.* '53 (EVN) [F] Jasper, IN Providence Home, Nursing Home for the Needy.
Szudarek, Ronald J. '81 (CLV) [19] Cleveland, OH Corpus Christi Church.
Szudera, Theodore F. '77 (GF) Belt, MT St. Mark the Evangelist Church.
Szufel, Adam E. *o.f.m.* '64 (GB) [I] Pulaski, WI Assumption of B.V.M. Friary.
Szulecki, Raymond L. '46 (MET) Retired.
Szulwach, Joseph B. '87 (MET) [2] New Brunswick, NJ St. John the Baptist Church.
Szumilo, Julian *c.m.* '50 (PRT) Lisbon Falls, ME Holy Trinity Church.
Szupa, Joseph '92 (PHU) Passaic, NJ St. Nicholas Church.
Szupper, Michael F. '57 (WIL) Newark, DE St. Thomas More Oratory Church; Newark, DE University of Delaware; [O] Newark, DE Univ. of Delaware Newman Center.
Szura, Carl A. *t.o.r.* '71 (ALT) [A] Loretto, PA St. Francis College; [A] Loretto, PA St. Francis College; [F] Loretto, PA St. Francis Friary, Third Order Regular of St. Francis of Penance; [H] Huntingdon, PA Juniata College.
Szura, John Paul *o.s.a.* '66 (JOL) New Lenox, IL St. Jude Church.
Szura, Thomas *c.m.m.* '78 (DET) [K] Dearborn Heights, MI Our Lady of Grace Monastery.
Szwach, Joseph F. '55 (WOR) Dudley, MA St. Andrew Bobola Church.
Szybka, Joseph P. '83 (TOL) Attica, OH SS. Peter and Paul Church; Republic, OH St. Aloysius Church; St. Stephen, OH St. Stephen Church.
Szybka, Stanley S. '80 (TOL) Lexington, OH Resurrection Church.
Szych, Mark *o.f.m.* '53 (MIL) [P] Burlington, WI Queen of Peace Friary.
Szydlowski, Gregory *s.o.cist.* '63 (CHI) [N] Willow Springs, IL Cistercian Fathers.
Szydlowski, Joel *o.f.m.* '67 (PH) [Z] Philadelphia, PA St. Pius X Friary.
Szydlowski, Joel F. *o.f.m.* '67 (TR) Trenton, NJ St. Francis Medical Center; [I] Trenton, NJ St. Francis Medical Center.
Szydlowski, Robert L. '62 (STL) [50] St. Louis, MO SS. Mary and Joseph Church.
Szymanski, Bronislaus '34 (PRO) Retired.
Szymanski, Edgar S. *c.s.c.* '43 (FTW) [J] South Bend, IN Congregation of Holy Cross Indiana Province Provincial House.
Szymanski, Msgr. John B. '57 (MET) Old Bridge, NJ St. Thomas the Apostle Church.
Szymanski, Pawel Z. '93 (MET) [2] Perth Amboy, NJ St. Stephen Church.
Szymborski, Alexander *c.r.l.* '54 (SPR) [1] Pittsfield, MA Holy Family Church.
Szymcik, Mark M. '75 (WOR) South Barre, MA St. Thomas-A-Becket Church.
Szymkowiak, Gerard J. *c.ss.r.* '68 (HBG) Lititz, PA St. James Church; [H] Ephrata, PA St. Clement's Mission House.
Szymusiak, Bruno '58 (SP) Ridge Manor, FL St. Anne Church.
Szymusiak, Bruno '59 (SP) Brooksville, FL St. Anthony Church.
Szyszko, Brian J. '83 (MIL) [6] Sheboygan, WI St. Peter Claver Church.

T

Ta, Binh Thanh *c.ss.r.* '93 (NO) [23] New Orleans, LA St. Alphonsus Church.
Taaffe, Charles P. '55 (P) Shaw, OR St. Mary Church.
Tabak, Thaddeus *s.d.s.* '77 (AUS) Rosebud, TX St. Ann's Church.
Tabbert, Robert D. '79 (VEN) [1] Naples, FL St. Ann Church.
Taberski, Richard M. '64 (HRT) [16] Waterbury, CT St. Patrick Church.
Tabet, Fadi E. *m.l.m.* '90 (OLL) Houston, TX Our Lady of the Cedars Mission Church; [A] San Antonio, TX The Congregation of Maronite Lebanese Missionaries.
Tabet, Marwan *m.l.m.* '86 (OLL) [A] San Antonio, TX The Congregation of Maronite Lebanese Missionaries.
Tabit, Michael J. '39 (COL) Retired.
Tabit, Michael J. '39 (MIA) [12] Miami, FL Our Lady of the Holy Rosary Church.
Tabon, Raymond *o.s.j.* '60 (SCR) [8] Pittston, PA St. Rocco Church.
Tabone, Marcel '85 (CAM) Washington Township, NJ Holy Family Church.
Tabor, Charlotte (ALB) [S] Loudonville, NY Siena College.
Tabor, Kenneth F. '75 (CHI) Northbrook, IL Our Lady of the Brook Church.
Tabor, Paul J. *s.j.* '88 (BO) [W] Boston, MA The Society of Jesus of New England-Provincial Offices.
Tabor, Paul J. *s.j.* '88 (NY) [Z] New York, NY St. Ignatius Loyola Residence.
Tabujara, Oscar D. '75 (SJ) Mountain View, CA St. Joseph the Worker Church.
Tacderas, Joseph '66 (LA) On Duty Outside the Archdiocese.
Tacelli, Ronald K. *s.j.* '82 (BO) [W] Chestnut Hill, MA The Jesuit Community at Boston College.
Tachias, Alfred A. '59 (GLP) [A] Gallup, NM Diocesan Diaconate Formation Program; [E] Gallup, NM Villa Guadalupe Home for the Aged.
Tachuah, James (E) [28] Erie, PA St. Paul Church.
Tacito, Nicholas M. *o.praem* '96 (ORG) [D] Siverado, CA St. Michael's College Preparatory High School; [H] Silverado, CA Norbertine Fathers.
Tack, Theodore E. *o.s.a.* '53 (TLS) [B] Tulsa, OK Cascia Hall Preparatory School.
Tackaberry, John P. *c.m.* '41 (STL) [P] Perryville, MO Congregation of The Mission.
Tackney, John P. '74 (BO) [14] Cambridge, MA Sacred Heart of Jesus Church.
Taddy, Jerome '60 (GB) Green Bay, WI Green Bay Correctional Institution.
Tadeusz, Majcher *s.d.s.* '87 (NEW) [N] Verona, NJ The Salvatorian Fathers.
Tadla, Casimir *c.r.* '48 (CHI) [N] Chicago, IL Provincial Office of the Congregation of the Resurrection.
Tadyszak, Leonard *s.c.j.* '51 (SP) [O] Pinellas Park, FL Priests of the Sacred Heart.
Taft, Robert F. *s.j.* '63 (BO) [W] Boston, MA The Society of Jesus of New England-Provincial Offices.
Taft, William '94 (TUC) Hayden, AZ St. Joseph's Church.
Taggart, Frederick H. *o.s.a.* '65 (LAN) [11] Flint, MI St. Matthew Church.
Taggart, J. Vincent *s.j.* '67 (PH) [G] Philadelphia, PA St. Joseph's Preparatory School; [Z] Philadelphia, PA St. Joseph's Preparatory School Jesuit Community, Arrupe House.
Taggart, James E. *o.m.i.* '85 (MIA) Miramar, FL St. Stephen Church.
Taggart, John *c.r.i.c.* '42 (LA) [B] Los Angeles, CA Canons Regular of the Immaculate Conception-Novitiate.
Taggart, John L. '70 (WIL) [13] Wilmington, DE St. Thomas Church.
Taggart, Msgr. Paul J. '51 (WIL) [1] Wilmington, DE Cathedral of St. Peter; Retired.
Tague, Charles *s.t.* '44 (WDC) [M] Adelphi, MD Missionary Servants of the Most Holy Trinity.
Tagura, Pablito *s.v.d.* '88 (MIL) [P] East Troy, WI Divine Word Seminary.
Tahaney, James L. '63 (BRK) [64] Brooklyn, NY Immaculate Heart of Mary Church.
Taheny, Mark V. '95 (SFR) [17] San Francisco, CA Church of the Epiphany.
Taheny, Robert R. *s.j.* '59 (SJ) [25] San Jose, CA St. Victor Church.
Taheny, Theodore T. *s.j.* '56 (SFR) [N] San Francisco, CA Jesuit Community at University of San Francisco.
Taillez, Daniel *o.m.i.* '63 (STP) [28] St. Paul, MN St. Mary Church.
Taillon, Marcel L. '94 (PRO) Riverside, RI St. Brendan Church.
Tait, Alexander A. *s.j.* '46 (SJ) [M] Los Gatos, CA Sacred Heart Jesuit Center.
Tajak, Ralph M. *o.s.b.* '94 (GBG) [H] Latrobe, PA Saint Vincent Archabbey.
Tajc, Edward C. '69 (GBG) Masontown, PA All Saints Church.
Takach, Brinstan G. *o.s.b.* '48 (GBG) Bovard, PA St. Bede Church; [H] Latrobe, PA Saint Vincent Archabbey.
Takeuchi, Osamu *s.j.* '96 (OAK) [N] Berkeley, CA Jesuit Community at Jesuit School of Theology at Berkeley.
Takuski, Walter '95 (CHI) [115] Chicago, IL St. Ladislaus Church.
Takyi, John K. '90 (PIT) Mt. Lebanon, PA St. Winifred Church.
Talafous, Don *o.s.b.* '52 (SCL) [I] Collegeville, MN St. John's Abbey, of the Order of St. Benedict.
Talar, Charles J.T. '79 (BGP) On Duty Outside the Diocese.
Talarico, Anthony M. '70 (CHI) [85] Chicago, IL Holy Rosary Church.
Talaska, Richard J. '68 (MIL) Greenfield, WI St. John the Evangelist Church.
Talbot, Felix F. *s.j.* '44 (BO) [W] Chestnut Hill, MA The Jesuit Community at Boston College.
Talbot, Francis A. '63 (MAN) Manchester, NH V.A. Hospital.
Talbot, James F. *s.j.* '68 (PRT) [C] Portland, ME Cheverus High School; [I] Portland, ME St. Ignatius Residence.
Talbot, John *s.j.* (SJN) [B] Rio Piedras, PR Jesuit Novitiate.
Talbott, Ron *o.f.m.cap* '81 (LA) Solvang, CA Old Mission Santa Ines Church.
Talcott, Peter '75 (SR) On Duty Outside the Diocese.
Talentino, William *o.f.m.cap.* (PIT) [R] Pittsburgh, PA The Capuchin Franciscan Volunteer Corps, Inc.
Talesfore, John '89 (SFR) [52] San Francisco, CA St. Thomas More Church; Special Assignment.
Taliercio, Pasquale *m.ss.a.* '92 (NOR) [A] Cromwell, CT Holy Apostles College and Seminary; [F] Cromwell, CT Missionaries of the Holy Apostles.
Talkin, Ralph H. *s.j.* '57 (CHI) [C] Chicago, IL Jesuit Community at Loyola University of Chicago.
Tallarida, Thomas *c.s.c.* '51 (FTW) [B] Notre Dame, IN University of Notre Dame Du Lac; [J] Notre Dame, IN Holy Cross Community, Corby Hall, University of Notre Dame.
Talley, David P. '89 (ATL) On Duty Outside the Archdiocese.
Tallman, Gilmary *o.f.m.cap.* '60 (STL) Arnold, MO Immaculate Conception Church; [P] Arnold, MO Immaculate Conception Friary.
Tallman, Stephen '59 (HEL) Stevensville, MT St. Mary Church.
Talloen, Jerome G. '45 (OKL) Retired.
Talocci, Peter J. '86 (PH) [40] Philadelphia, PA St. Donato Church.
Tam, Thomas '50 (STP) [19] St. Paul, MN St. Columba Church.
Tamalis John J. '71 (SCR) [3] Williamsport, PA St. Boniface's Church.
Tamayo, Elias '72 (PAT) [16] Paterson, NJ St. Therese Church.
Tamborino, James *s.o.l.t.* '91 (CC) [H] Robstown, TX Society of Our Lady of the Most Holy Trinity.
Tamburello, Dennis *o.f.m.* '80 (ALB) [B] Loudonville, NY Siena College.
Tamburello, Dominic J. *o.p.* '49 (NO) [30] New Orleans, LA St Dominic Church.
Tamburrini, Joseph '64 (Y) Absent on Leave.
Tamburro, Francis '74 (HBG) [G] Danville, PA Maria Joseph Manor.
Tamm, Thaddeus *c.p.* '39 (BIR) [7] Birmingham, AL Holy Family Church.
Tamminga, Robert G. '71 (TUC) [13] Tucson, AZ St. Francis de Sales Church.
Tampe, Eric *s.a.* '49 (NY) [Z] Garrison, NY Generalate of the Franciscan Friars of the Atonement-St. James Friary.
Tamulis, Anthony J. '48 (SFD) Retired.
Tamulis, John J. '40 (GAY) Retired.
Tan, John '86 (BRK) [T] Brooklyn, NY Catholic Migration & Refugee Office, Catholic Migration Services, Inc.
Tanahal, Albert '91 (CHI) [176] Chicago, IL St. Priscilla Church.
Tancrede, Msgr. Roland '47 (MAN) [11] Manchester, NH St. John the Baptist Church; Retired.
Tancredi, Carl T. '67 (HBG) [4] York, PA St. Rose of Lima Church; [K] Harrisburg, PA Catholic Campus Ministry; [K] Harrisburg, PA Catholic Campus Ministry.
Tancrell, Luke *o.p.* '59 (WDC) [B] Washington, DC Dominican House of Studies.
Taney, Francis J. *m.m.* '58 (HON) [H] Honolulu, HI Maryknoll Fathers House.
Tang, Emery *o.f.m.* '52 (ORG) [3] Huntington Beach, CA SS. Simon and Jude Church.
Tang, Michael R. *s.j.* '90 (LA) [C] Los Angeles, CA Loyola Marymount University.
Tanguay, William H. '69 (CHL) Hickory, NC St. Aloysius Church; Hickory, NC St. Aloysius Church.
Tanguay, William H. '69 (PRO) [11] Pawtucket, RI Sacred Heart Church.
Tanilong, Gerardo J. '62 (ORG) Garden Grove, CA St. Callistus Church.
Tank, Thomas '67 (KCK) [1] Kansas City, KS Cathedral of St. Peter the Apostle.
Taormina, Andrew C. '62 (NO) [9] Metairie, LA St. Francis Xavier Church.
Taosan, John *c.i.c.m.* '96 (BWN) [5] McAllen, TX Holy Spirit Church.
Tapella, Joseph J. '78 (JOL) [1] Joliet, IL The Cathedral of St. Raymond.
Tapp, John G. '84 (SP) [16] Tampa, FL St. Timothy Church; [F] Tampa, FL St. Timothy Preschool.
Tappe, Msgr. Walter (SFR) [K] San Rafael, CA Nazareth House.
Tappe, Msgr. Walter J. '39 (SR) Retired.
Tappe, Walter J. '85 (WDC) Greenbelt, MD St. Hugh Church; Pastoral Center Special Ministries.
Tapper, John W. '61 (CHI) Hanover Park, IL St. Ansgar Church.
Taraborelli, Arthur I. '64 (PH) [151] Philadelphia, PA St. Thomas Aquinas Church.
Taraborelli, Carmen F. '70 (PH) [28] Philadelphia, PA St. Callistus Church.
Tarallo, Philip *s.s.j.* '36 (BR) New Roads, LA St. Augustine Church.
Taran, Peter *s.a.* '60 (NY) [Z] Garrison, NY Franciscan Friars of the Atonement.
Tarantino, James A. '72 (NO) [19] New Orleans, LA Our Lady Of The Rosary Church.
Tarantino, James T. '81 (SFR) Special Assignment; [D] Kentfield, CA Marin Catholic College Preparatory (Coed).
Tarantino, John A. '78 (PAT) Montville, NJ St. Pius X Church.
Taranto, James '81 (KC) [25] Kansas City, MO St. Matthew The Apostle Church.
Tarasi, Carlo D. '72 (CHL) On Duty Outside the Diocese.
Tarasiw, Ihor '90 (STF) Riverhead, NY St. John the Baptist Church.
Tardiff, Charles *m.afr.* '47 (SP) [O] St. Petersburg, FL Missionaries of Africa.
Tardiff, Edward *c.s.s.r.* '42 (ALB) [L] Saratoga Springs, NY St. John Neumann Residence.
Tardivo, Mario *c.s.* '38 (BO) [67] Boston, MA Sacred Heart Church.
Targonski, Conrad *o.f.m.* '75 (GB) [I] Pulaski, WI Assumption of B.V.M. Friary.
Tarimo, Aquilene *s.j.* '95 (OAK) [N] Berkeley, CA Jesuit Community at Jesuit School of Theology at Berkeley.
Tarlizzo, David *o.m.i.* '68 (BEL) [F] Belleville, IL Our Lady of the Snows Apartment Community Retirement Home.
Tarlton, Allen *o.s.b.* '55 (SCL) [I] Collegeville, MN St. John's Abbey, of the Order of St. Benedict.
Tarnawski, Wiktor '80 (ARE) Ciales, PR N.S. Madre del Redentor Church.
Tarrant, Edward L. '50 (RVC) Hicksville, NY St. Ignatius Loyola Church.
Tarrant, Patrick (BO) Lexington, MA Sacred Heart Church.
Tarrant, Patrick J. '53 (GF) Retired.
Tarrier, William B. *o.p.* '47 (WDC) [11] Washington, DC St. Dominic Church & Priory Church.
Tarrillion, Joseph A. *s.m.* '66 (SAT) [F] San Antonio, TX Central Catholic High School; [M] San Antonio, TX Chaminade Community House.
Tartaglia, Paul '58 (ALB) Special Assignment; Retired.
Tartaglia, Richard V. '72 (PAT) Denville, NJ St. Mary's Church.
Tasch, Hugh *o.s.b.* '48 (KC) [J] Conception, MO Conception Abbey.
Tasch, Hugh *o.s.b.* '57 (KC) [A] Conception, MO Conception Seminary College.
Taschetta, Anthony '71 (JOL) [5] Kankakee, IL St. Teresa Church.
Tascon, Wilson *m.s.c.* '90 (RCK) [H] Aurora, IL Missionaries of the Sacred Heart Community.
Tash, Msgr. Joseph T. '62 (AMA) [11] Amarillo, TX St. Thomas the Apostle Church.
Tasker, Franklin R. *o.carm.* '56 (JOL) Glendale Heights, IL St. Matthew Church.
Tasler, Mak A. '90 (LIN) Nebraska City, NE St. Benedict's Church.
Tassone, Salvatore A. *s.j.* '63 (SJ) [B] Santa Clara, CA Santa Clara University.
Tasto, Harold J. '68 (STP) Blaine, MN St. Timothy's Church.
Tasto, John P. *o.s.a.* '67 (CHI) [N] Olympia Fields, IL The Augustinian Provincialate Tolentine Center.
Tasy, Msgr. Francis G. *v.s.* '52 (FRS) Reedley, CA St. Anthony Church.
Tatarczuk, Msgr. Vincent A. '49 (PRT) Retired.
Tate, Joseph H. *c.s.c.* '81 (BUR) Wilmington, VT Our Lady of Fatima Church.
Tatel, Orlando '65 (STP) [3] St. Paul, MN Blessed Sacrament Church.
Taton, Thomas P. (BUF) [8] Lackawanna, NY Queen of All Saints Church.
Tatro, Kenneth J. '76 (SPR) Feeding Hills, MA Sacred Heart Church.
Taube, Sylvester '64 (DET) Special Assignment.
Tauber, Gregory J. '77 (ALN) [1] Pottsville, PA St. John

the Baptist Church.
Taubitz, Leo A. '56 (KAL) Dowagiac, MI Holy Maternity of Mary Church.
Taufen, Daniel '56 (SCL) Special Assignment.
Taugher, Timothy J. (SY) Johnson City, NY Wilson Memorial Hospital; Special Assignment.
Tauke, Michael L. '74 (DUB) Anamosa, IA St. Patrick's Church; Andrew, IA St. John Church; La Motte, IA Holy Rosary Church.
Taurasi, David '88 (CC) Sinton, TX Our Lady of Guadalupe Church.
Tauscher, Donald *o.s.b.* '65 (SCL) [I] Collegeville, MN St. John's Abbey, of the Order of St. Benedict.
Tavai, Van Camp '89 (SPP) [3] Pago Pago, AS Church of St. Paul.
Tavard, George *a.a.* '47 (BO) [W] Brighton, MA Assumptionist Center.
Tavares, Antonino C. '43 (FR) [6] New Bedford, MA Our Lady of Mt. Carmel Church; Retired.
Tavares, Evaristo '60 (FR) [7] Fall River, MA Our Lady of the Angels Church.
Tavares, Msgr. John E. '55 (PRO) [1] East Providence, RI St. Francis Xavier Church.
Tavarro, Elly S. '81 (ORG) [F] Orange, CA St. Joseph Hospital of Orange.
Tavella, Thomas *c.s.p.* '62 (KNX) [K] Knoxville, TN Calvary.
Tavella, Thomas A. *c.s.p.* '81 (KNX) [3] Knoxville, TN Immaculate Conception Church.
Tavera, Joseph *s.x.* '71 (PAT) [M] Wayne, NJ Xaverian Missionary Fathers.
Tavis, Gordon *o.s.b.* '58 (SCL) [I] Collegeville, MN St. John's Abbey, of the Order of St. Benedict.
Tay, Msgr. Peter '54 (PBR) [2] Pittsburgh, PA Holy Ghost Church.
Taylor, Anthony B. '80 (OKL) Edmond, OK St. Monica Church; Special Assignment.
Taylor, Augustus R., Jr. '66 (PIT) On Duty Outside the Diocese.
Taylor, Benedict M. *o.f.m.* '60 (NY) [Z] New York, NY Franciscan Friars, Order of Friars Manor.
Taylor, Charles F. '53 (CHY) Kemmerer, WY St. Patrick's Church.
Taylor, Conan *o.f.m.* '45 (CIN) [M] Cincinnati, OH St. Ann Friary.
Taylor, Daniel '75 (TUC) Yuma, AZ St. Francis of Assisi Church.
Taylor, David H. '74 (PIT) [8] Pittsburgh, PA St. Charles Lwanga Church.
Taylor, Donn J. '53 (KAL) Battle Creek, MI St. Joseph Church; Retired.
Taylor, Msgr. E. Melville '41 (BAL) [87] Baltimore, MD Shrine of the Sacred Heart Church; Retired.
Taylor, Eamon G. *s.j.* '51 (NY) [Z] New York, NY Jesuit Community at Fordham University.
Taylor, Msgr. Francis J. '54 (HBG) New Cumberland, PA St. Theresa of the Infant Jesus Church.
Taylor, Gordon '85 (B) Bonners Ferry, ID St. Ann's Church.
Taylor, James B. '54 (BLX) Pascagoula, MS Sacred Heart Church; Retired.
Taylor, James E. *o.m.i.* '56 (BEL) [G] Belleville, IL Missionary Oblates of Mary Immaculate - St. Henry's Oblate Residence; [K] Belleville, IL Missionary Association of Mary Immaculate-Mission Oblates of Mary Immaculate.
Taylor, Jon '64 (GF) Special Assignment; [A] Great Falls, MT University of Great Falls.
Taylor, Jon '64 (LAN) On Duty Outside the Diocese.
Taylor, Joseph C. '53 (CHI) [52] Chicago, IL St. Edward Church.
Taylor, Kenneth E. '78 (IND) [9] Indianapolis, IN Holy Trinity Church.
Taylor, Mel *o.s.b.* '67 (SCL) [I] Collegeville, MN St. John's Abbey, of the Order of St. Benedict.
Taylor, Msgr. Melville '41 (BAL) [K] Baltimore, MD Stella Maris Operating Corporation.
Taylor, Michael '86 (ALB) [A] Rensselaer, NY Conventual Franciscan Friars.
Taylor, Michael *o.f.m.conv.* '86 (SY) [2] Syracuse, NY Assumption B.V.M. Church.
Taylor, Michael G. '93 (ARL) Warrenton, VA St. John the Evangelist Church.
Taylor, Michael J. *s.j.* '54 (SEA) [A] Seattle, WA Seattle University.
Taylor, Paul R. *o.s.b.* '92 (GBG) [H] Latrobe, PA Saint Vincent Archabbey.
Taylor, Peter '74 (GB) On Duty Outside the Diocese.
Taylor, Peter '74 (PHX) Special Assignment.
Taylor, Robert H. *s.j.* '52 (LA) [C] Los Angeles, CA Loyola Marymount University.
Taylor, Robert H. *s.j.* '52 (SAC) Placerville, CA St. Patrick's Church.
Taylor, Robert H. '56 (WIN) Absent on Leave.
Taylor, Roger H. '64 (MAD) Muscoda, WI St. John the Baptist Church.
Taylor, Senan *o.f.m.cap.* '70 (NY) [Z] Yonkers, NY St. Clare Friary.
Taylor, Thomas E. '83 (PEO) Bradford, IL St. John the Baptist Church.
Taylor, Vincent A. *s.j.* '45 (NY) [F] New York, NY Xavier High School.
Taylor, William '64 (B) Saint Maries, ID St. Mary's Church.
Taylor, William R. '67 (SAG) [2] Saginaw, MI Holy Family Church.
Teague, Bruce N. '80 (SPR) Amherst, MA St. Brigid's Church.
Teague, James B. '87 (NY) [4] New Rochelle, NY Holy Family Church.
Teahan, Timothy J. '70 (BRK) Military Chaplains.
Teall, Richard *c.s.c.* '50 (AUS) Buda, TX Santa Cruz Church.
Tearney, Thomas A. '73 (MIL) Oconomowoc, WI St. Jerome's Church.
Tebangura, Francis '68 (SFD) Granite City, IL St. Elizabeth Church.
Tebbe, Francis *o.f.m.* '75 (DET) [C] Livonia, MI Madonna University.
Tebbe, Francis S. *o.f.m.* (CHI) [U] Chicago, IL National Organization for Continuing Education of Roman Catholic Clergy, Inc.
Tebbe, Francis S. *o.f.m.* (CIN) [M] Cincinnati, OH St. Francis Seraph Friary.
Tebes, Stephen J. '68 (CHI) Norridge, IL Divine Savior Church.
Tecca, Felix '61 (Y) Absent on Sick Leave.
Teczar, Thomas '80 (WOR) Absent on Leave.
Tederous, Elias J. *m.m.* '55 (HON) Waianae, HI Sacred Heart Church; [H] Honolulu, HI Maryknoll Fathers House.
Tedesco, Joseph A. '79 (TR) Medford, NJ St. Mary of the Lakes Church.
Tedone, Michael G. '91 (BRK) [234] Queens, NY St. Rita Church; Special Assignment.
Teeling, John P. *s.j.* '55 (DEN) [M] Denver, CO Xavier Jesuit Center.
Tegeder, Michael V. '78 (STP) Mound, MN Our Lady of the Lake Church.
Tegeder, Vincent *o.s.b.* '37 (SCL) [I] Collegeville, MN St. John's Abbey, of the Order of St. Benedict.
Tegeler, Herbert L. '53 (DUB) Lansing, IA Immaculate Conception Church; [E] Lansing, IA Lansing School of Religion.
Tegels, Aelred '48 (SCL) [I] Collegeville, MN St. John's Abbey, of the Order of St. Benedict.
Tegmeyer Mark *o.f.m.conv.* '95 (ELP) [17] El Paso, TX Our Lady of Mt. Carmel Church.
Teichert, Isaiah *o.s.b.cam.* '90 (MRY) [G] Big Sur, CA New Camaldoli Hermitage.
Tejada, Denis '72 (LSC) [5] Las Cruces, NM St. Genevieve Church.
Tekippe, Terry T. '65 (NO) [A] New Orleans, LA Notre Dame Seminary Graduate School of Theology.
Teknipp, Robert J. '46 (CLV) Green, OH Queen of Heaven Church; Retired.
Teles, Dennis J. '65 (GRY) [4] Merrillville, IN Ss. Peter and Paul Church.
Telesz, Msgr. Leo '39 (CLV) [14] Cleveland, OH St. Casimir Church.
Teletchea, Msgr. Joseph L. '44 (WDC) Hyattsville, MD St. Jerome Church; Retired.
Telken, Paul E. '73 (STL) St. Clair, MO St. Clare Church.
Teller, Msgr. Raymond J. '55 (PH) Doylestown, PA Our Lady of Mount Carmel Church.
Tellers, Marven *o.s.c.* '50 (STP) Shoreview, MN St. Odilia Church; [N] Shoreview, MN Crosier Community of Shoreview.
Telles, John '75 (ELP) Kermit, TX St. Thomas & St. Joseph Church.
Tellez, Eric '86 (PHX) [7] Scottsdale, AZ St. Patrick Church.
Tellez, Jairo '62 (SAT) Military Chaplains.
Telnack, Methodius *o.c.s.o.* '57 (ATL) [I] Conyers, GA The Monastery of the Holy Spirit.
Telthorst, Msgr. James T. '68 (STL) [1] St. Louis, MO St. Louis Cathedral.
Teluma, Lukas Bao *s.v.d.* (LA) [R] Los Angeles, CA Casa Guadalupe.
Temme, Roger *o.m.i.* '76 (SAT) [K] San Antonio, TX Oblate Madonna Residence.
Tempel, Theodore G. '64 (EVN) [5] Evansville, IN Good Shepherd Church.
Temple, Matthew *o.carm.* '82 (ROC) [I] Rochester, NY Whitefriars Priory.
Templeton, Edward *s.m.* '53 (WDC) [M] Washington, DC Marist Provincial House.
Templeton, Robert E. '88 (NEW) [1] Newark, NJ Cathedral of the Sacred Heart Basilica.
Templin, Kenneth A. *s.m.* '79 (KAL) [5] Kalamazoo, MI St. Thomas More Student Parish Church; [E] Portage, MI Society of Mary; [H] Kalamazoo, MI Western Michigan University, Kalamazoo College-Kalamazoo Valley Community College.
Tenbarge, Timothy A. '73 (EVN) Bicknell, IN St. Philip Neri Church.
Tengler, Msgr. Alvin '49 (CC) Retired.
Tenhundfeld, Carl '55 (GAL) [2] Houston, TX All Saints Church.
Tenhundfeld, Paul F. '54 (COV) Camp Springs, KY St. Joseph Church.
Tenoever, Donald A. '50 (CIN) Retired.
Tenorio, Roger P.T. '93 (CHK) San Vicente Village, District 10, MP San Vicente Ferrer Parish Church; San Vicente Village, District 10, MP San Vicente Ferrer Parish Church.
Tensae, Ande *o.f.m.cap.* '81 (RVC) Manhasset, NY North Shore Univ. Hospital.
Tensi, Lawrence R. '77 (CIN) On Special and Diocesan Assignment.
Terdine, Richard '65 (PIT) Allegheny County, PA Eye and Ear Hospital; Allegheny County, PA Montefiore Hospital; Allegheny County, PA Presbyterian-University Hospital.
Terentieff, Robert '62 (BAL) [C] Emmitsburg, MD Mount Saint Mary's College.
Terentieff, Robert J. '62 (BGP) On Duty Outside the Diocese.
Terga, Richard '73 (NY) [85] New York, NY Our Lady of Good Counsel Church.
Terico, Nicholas R. *o.praem.* '89 (PH) [Z] Paoli, PA Daylesford Abbey.
Terlecky, John '76 (STF) [1] Stamford, CT St. Vladimir Cathedral; [A] Stamford, CT St. Basil College.
Termini, Mario '79 (BR) Retired.
Termyna, James J. '70 (PAT) Boonton, NJ SS. Cyril and Methodius Church.
Ternes, Gary '79 (SFS) [8] Sioux Falls, SD St. Therese Church.
Ternullo, Joseph P. '73 (SAC) Winters, CA St. Anthony Church.
Tero, Richard D. '74 (ANC) Soldotna, AK Our Lady of Perpetual Help Church.
Terra, Joseph P. *f.s.s.p.* '89 (PAT) Pequannock, NJ Our Lady of Fatima Chapel (Tridentine) Church.
Terra, Joseph P. *f.s.s.p.* '89 (SCR) [M] Elmhurst, PA Priestly Fraternity of St. Peter (F.S.S.P.).
Terra, Msgr. Russell G. '62 (SAC) Redding, CA St. Joseph Church.
Terrant, Patrick (BO) Boston, MA Youville Hospital.
Terrassa, Antonio *t.o.r.* '47 (NEW) [20] Newark, NJ Immaculate Heart of Mary Church.
Terrebonne, Burnick J. '77 (NO) [3] Marrero, LA St. Joachim Church.
Terrero, Reynaldo '85 (MIA) [11] Miami, FL Our Lady of Divine Providence Church.
Terrien, Douglas J. '79 (DET) Lapeer, MI Immaculate Conception of the Blessed Virgin Mary Church.
Terrien, Lawrence B. *s.s.* '72 (BAL) [A] Baltimore, MD St. Mary's Seminary and University.
Terrill, Richard F. '54 (IND) Retired.
Terrillion, Albert *o.s.b.* '96 (NO) [A] St. Benedict, LA St. Joseph's Seminary College; [P] St. Benedict, LA St. Joseph Abbey.
Terriquez, Enrique '63 (B) Caldwell, ID St. Mary Church; [F] Caldwell, ID Albertson's College of Idaho.
Terry, Christopher *o.p.* '91 (P) [D] Eugene, OR Marist High School.
Terry, Christopher *o.p.* '92 (P) [6] Eugene, OR St. Thomas More Church.
Terry, John S. '75 (SCR) Sugar Notch, PA Holy Family Church; [Q] Wilkes-Barre, PA Catholic Youth Center.
Tertzakian, Hovhannes *o.m.ven.* '48 (ARM) New York, NY St. Ann's Cathedral.
Terwilliger, Msgr. John G. '42 (SAC) Retired and in Senior Ministry.
Terza, William R. '69 (PIT) [3] McKees Rocks, PA St. John of God Church.
Terzano, John D. '74 (CLV) Peninsula, OH Mother of Sorrows Church.
Tesek, Albert J. '51 (CLV) North Royalton, OH St. Albert the Great Church.
Tesfamarian, Menghesteab *m.c.c.j.* '79 (CHI) [N] Chicago, IL Comboni Missionaries Theologate (M.C.C.J.), Verona Fathers.
Teske, Roland J. *s.j.* '65 (MIL) [P] Milwaukee, WI Jesuit Community at Marquette University.
Teslovic, Eugene J. '77 (RIC) [8] Virginia Beach, VA St. Luke Church.
Tessarolo, Giulivo *c.s.* '39 (NY) [94] New York, NY Our Lady of Pompeii Church.
Tessmer, Richard A. (CHI) Retired.
Testa, David '67 (ALB) On Duty Outside the Diocese.
Testa, David '67 (STU) [A] Steubenville, OH Franciscan University of Steubenville; [F] Steubenville, OH Holy Spirit Monastery.
Testa, Genaro J. '47 (HRT) Retired.
Testa, Jess '88 (JOL) Clarendon Hills, IL Notre Dame Church.
Testa, Richard '67 (ALB) Special Assignment.
Testa, Msgr. Steve J. *v.f.* '64 (ALX) Bunkie, LA St. Anthony of Padua Church.
Testagrossa, Joseph *o.f.m.cap.* '57 (SP) [O] Seminole, FL Capuchin Franciscan Residence.
Teta, Michael J. '74 (TUC) Absent on Leave.
Teter, Patrick A. '93 (SPC) [5] Springfield, MO St. Elizabeth Ann Seton Church.
Tetlow, John H. '84 (STA) [1] St. Augustine, FL Cathedral of St. Augustine; [3] Jacksonville, FL Christ the King Church.

Tetlow, Joseph A. *s.j.* '60 (NO) [P] New Orleans, LA Jesuit Provincial Office.
Tetrault, Ralph D. '65 (FR) Wareham, MA St. Patrick's Church.
Tetrault, Raymond L. '60 (PRO) [30] Providence, RI St. Teresa of Avila Church.
Tetreault, Msgr. Jean C. '49 (BGP) Newtown, CT St. Rose of Lima Church; Retired.
Tetreault, Maynard *o.f.m.* '60 (DET) [B] Detroit, MI Duns Scotus.
Tetreault, Maynard *o.f.m.* '60 (LEX) Cumberland, KY St. Stephen Church.
Tetreault, Raymond A. '71 (PRO) Slatersville, RI St. John the Evangelist Church.
Tetzlaff, Joseph W. '39 (LC) Retired.
Teufel, Charles B. '62 (WH) Wellsburg, WV St. John The Evangelist Church; [S] Wheeling, WV Mount Calvary.
Tevaga, Emani '86 (SPP) [6] (Lepua), AS Church of the Immaculate Conception; [C] Malaeloa, AS Marist High School.
Teverzczuk, William J. '73 (PH) Penndel, PA Our Lady of Grace Church.
Tevington, Thomas *o.s.a.* '34 (ORG) Buena Park, CA St. Pius V Church.
Tewes, John Edwin Thayer '96 (ARL) Fredericksburg, VA St. Mary Church.
Tewes, Msgr. Thomas J. '63 (BAL) [68] Baltimore, MD Our Lady of Hope Church.
Texada, David Ker '80 (NO) Retired.
Tey, Jose R. *s.j.* '59 (MIA) [D] Miami, FL Belen Jesuit Preparatory School; [H] Miami, FL Jesuit Fathers of the Province of the Antilles, Inc.
Tezie, John M. '59 (CLV) Grafton, OH Assumption Church.
Tezie, William F. '56 (CLV) [38] Cleveland, OH St. John Nepomucene Church.
Thaar, Gerald *o.s.c.* '65 (DET) Royal Oak, MI St. Dennis Church; [K] Riverview, MI Crosier Community of Riverview.
Thachet, Joseph '60 (KAL) Retired.
Thaden, William A. '88 (CLV) El Salvador, C.A., OH Parroquial Immaculada Concepcion.
Thadeu, Joseph S. '47 (PRO) Retired.
Thai, Thomas Vu-Minh '54 (LEX) [7] Lexington, KY St. Peter Church.
Thai Minh Tran, Joseph *s.s.s.* '94 (SFE) [23] Albuquerque, NM St. Charles Borromeo Church.
Thalanamy, Joseph '67 (SFS) Emery, SD St. Martin Church.
Thaler, Joseph L. *m.m.* '70 (NY) [Z] Maryknoll, NY Maryknoll Fathers and Brothers.
Thall, Apollinaris I. *s.j.* '83 (CI) Nemar, FM St. Mary Church.
Thalman, Eugene A. *m.m.* '60 (NY) [Z] Maryknoll, NY Maryknoll Fathers and Brothers.
Thamert, Mark *o.s.b.* '69 (SCL) [D] Collegeville, MN St. John's Preparatory School.
Thamert, Mark *o.s.b.* '79 (SCL) [I] Collegeville, MN St. John's Abbey, of the Order of St. Benedict.
Thames, Robert '64 (FWT) On Duty Outside the Diocese.
Than Nhu Huu, Joseph M. *c.m.c.* (SPC) [E] Carthage, MO Congregation of the Mother Co-Redemptrix, United States Assumption Province.
Thanh, Joachim '67 (PRT) Dover-Foxcroft, ME St. Thomas Church.
Thanh, Mark Tran-Xuan '59 (IND) [27] Indianapolis, IN St. Joseph Church.
Thanh, Nguyen Duc *c.ss.r.* '96 (LA) [R] Baldwin Park, CA Vietnamese Redemptorist Mission.
Thanh Hung, John B. '54 (MIL) [7] Milwaukee, WI St. Anthony's Church.
Thanh Huynh, Mark Nguyen *c.m.c.* '77 (BEA) [2] Port Arthur, TX Queen of Vietnam Church.
Tharappel, Augustine '70 (TYL) [1] Tyler, TX Cathedral of the Immaculate Conception.
Tharayil, John *c.m.i.* (PH) Croydon, PA St. Thomas Aquinas Church.
Tharp, Larry R. '77 (CIN) [84] Cincinnati, OH St. Teresa Church.
That Son, Nguyen Ngoc '90 (WH) Gary, WV Our Lady of Victory Church; Powhatan, WV Sacred Heart Church.
Thatcher, John R. *s.j.* '47 (SPK) [K] Spokane, WA Regis Community.
Thayer, David D. *s.s.* '75 (BAL) [A] Baltimore, MD St. Mary's Seminary and University.
Thayer, David D. *s.s.* '75 (HRT) On Duty Outside the Archdiocese.
Thein, Edward '79 (ATL) [1] Marietta, GA Holy Family Church.
Theis, Gerald J. *o.s.a.* '53 (JOL) [C] New Lenox, IL Providence Catholic High School; [J] New Lenox, IL Augustinian Friary.
Theis, Jeffrey '83 (ORG) Inactive Leave.
Theisen, Donald J. '42 (LC) Retired.
Theisen, John J. '59 (MIL) Retired.
Theisen, Kenneth *o.s.b.* '84 (RCK) [A] Aurora, IL Marmion Abbey; [H] Aurora, IL Marmion Abbey-St. Augustine's Abbey; [H] Aurora, IL Marmion Abbey-St. Augustine's Abbey.
Theisen, Wilfred *o.s.b.* '56 (SCL) [I] Collegeville, MN St. John's Abbey, of the Order of St. Benedict.
Theiss, Daniel *c.m.* '90 (CHI) [N] Chicago, IL Vincentian Community, Congregation of the Mission, Midwest Province.
Thekkedam, George '60 (LUB) Special Assignment; [B] Lubbock, TX St. Mary of the Plains Hospital.
Thelakkart, Xavier '80 (STP) [C] St. Paul, MN University of St. Thomas.
Thelakkatt, Xavier '80 (STP) [A] St. Paul, MN St. John Vianney Seminary.
Thelan, Albert R. *s.j.* '68 (RC) [B] Pine Ridge, SD Jesuit Community of Holy Rosary Mission.
Thelappilly, Walter *c.m.i.* '84 (PH) [63] Philadelphia, PA Holy Spirit Church.
Thelen, Albert *s.j.* '68 (RC) Pine Ridge, SD Sacred Heart Church.
Thelen, Frederick L. '80 (LAN) [8] Lansing, MI Cristo Rey Church.
Thelen, Jerome *o.f.m.* '66 (SHP) Ruston, LA St. Thomas Aquinas Church; [G] Ruston, LA E. Donn Piatt Catholic Student Center at Louisiana Tech University.
Thelen, Msgr. Robert J. '70 (BRK) [204] Queens, NY Nativity of the Blessed Virgin Mary Church.
Thell, Richard *o.s.b.* '74 (OM) [C] Elkhorn, NE Mount Michael High School; [K] Elkhorn, NE Mount Michael Abbey.
Thelly, Matthew '71 (SY) Utica, NY St. Elizabeth Hospital; [O] Utica, NY St. Elizabeth Hospital.
Thelly, Matthew '71 (TR) On Duty Outside the Diocese.
Thelon, Albert *s.j.* '68 (RC) Pine Ridge, SD Holy Rosary Church.
Thenen, John T. '58 (NY) [224] Staten Island, NY St. Peter Church.
Thennattil, George *t.o.r.* '76 (FWT) [16] Fort Worth, TX St. Thomas Church.
Thennes, Clarence J. '38 (RCK) Retired; [E] Freeport, IL St. Vincent Home for Children; [G] Freeport, IL St. Joseph Home for the Aged; [G] Freeport, IL St. Joseph Adult Day Care Center.
Theobald, Charles F. '58 (NEW) Lodi, NJ St. Francis de Sales Church.
Theobald, Vincent *s.v.d.* '49 (NO) [N] New Orleans, LA St. John Berchmans Manor.
Thepe, Theodore C. *s.j.* '55 (CIN) [M] Cincinnati, OH Jesuit Community at Xavier Unversity.
Theriault, A. Francis *s.v.d.* '55 (BLX) Bay St. Louis, MS St. Rose De Lima Church.
Theriault, Frank *c.s.c.* '53 (SD) [1] San Diego, CA St. Joseph Cathedral.
Theriault, H. *m.div.* '60 (NY) Tivoli, NY St. Sylvia Church.
Theriot, Donald C. '57 (LAF) Abbeville, LA St. Mary Magdalen Church.
Therly, Paul *o.praem.* '90 (CHI) [N] Chicago, IL Premonstratensian Fathers and Brothers (Norbertines).
Theroux, Bertrand L. '67 (PRO) [4] Warren, RI St. Mary of the Bay Church.
Theroux, David *s.s.e.* '74 (NO) [I] New Orleans, LA Bishop Perry Middle School.
Theroux, J. Raymond '65 (PRO) Cumberland, RI St. John Baptist Mary Vianney Church.
Theroux, Normand *m.s.* '54 (FR) [K] Attleboro, MA La Salette Shrine; [M] Attleboro, MA La Salette Center for Christian Living.
Theroux, Msgr. Paul D. '77 (PRO) On Duty Outside the Diocese.
Therrien, Shawn M. '87 (MAN) Charlestown, NH St. Catherine Church.
Thesing, Kenneth F. *m.m.* '69 (NY) [Z] Maryknoll, NY Maryknoll Fathers and Brothers.
Thesing, Mark B. *c.s.c.* '86 (FTW) [J] South Bend, IN Congregation of Holy Cross Indiana Province Provincial House.
Thesing, Mark B. *c.s.c.* '86 (R) [E] Chapel Hill, NC Jesuit Residence, Robert Southwell House.
Thesing, Robert J. *s.j.* '76 (CIN) [28] Cincinnati, OH St. Francis Xavier Church.
Thessing, Charles J. '88 (LR) Carlisle, AR St. Rose of Lima Church; Jacksonville, AR St. Jude the Apostle Church.
Thevarkunnel, Anselm '57 (DUL) Deer River, MN St. Mary's Church.
Thevis, Charles '92 (LAF) Loreauville, LA St. Joseph Church.
Thi, Andrew '85 (NY) [102] New York, NY St. Patrick Old Cathedral.
Thibault, Armand *s.m.* '85 (BO) [59] Boston, MA Our Lady of Victories Church; [W] Boston, MA Marist Fathers and Brothers Provincial House; [W] Boston, MA Marist Fathers of Our Lady of Victories (Boston Prov.).
Thibault, Camillus *a.a.* '56 (BO) [W] Brighton, MA Assumptionist Center.
Thibault, Donald P. *o.p.* '68 (WDC) [11] Washington, DC St. Dominic Church & Priory Church.
Thibeault, Raoul *o.s.cam.* '55 (MIL) [P] Wauwatosa, WI St. Camillus Community House.
Thibeault, W. Timothy '72 (MAN) Londonderry, NH St. Jude Church.
Thibedeau, Vianney '88 (GB) [I] Appleton, WI St. Fidelis Friary.
Thibodeau, Andre M. '71 (MAN) Henniker, NH St. Theresa Church; [N] Durham, NH Campus Ministries; [N] Henniker, NH New England College Newman Center.
Thibodeau, Clement D. '58 (PRT) Gardiner, ME St. Joseph's Church.
Thibodeau, Kenneth *s.m.* '68 (PRT) Brunswick, ME St. John the Baptist Church.
Thibodeau, Raynold J. '85 (MAN) [N] Durham, NH Campus Ministries.
Thibodeau, Raynold P. *o.f.m.cap.* '85 (MAN) [N] Hanover, NH The Catholic Student Center at Dartmouth, Aquinas House, Aquinas at Dartmouth, Inc.
Thibodeau, Richard *c.ss.r.* '76 (DEN) [M] Denver, CO The Redemptorists/Denver Province.
Thibodeaux, Charles B. *s.j.* '59 (NO) [P] New Orleans, LA Jesuit Provincial Office.
Thibodeaux, Mark *s.j.* (DAL) [D] Dallas, TX Jesuit College Preparatory School.
Thibodeaux, Paul A. '48 (LAF) Coteau, LA Our Lady of Prompt Succor Church.
Thibodeaux, Roger '79 (BEA) Corrigan, TX St. Martin de Porres Mission Church; Livingston, (1970) St. Joseph Church; Woodville, TX Our Lady of the Pines Church.
Thiel, Chris *o.f.m.cap.* '90 (LA) [F] La Canada Flintridge, CA St. Francis High School.
Thiel, Harold *c.ss.r.* '56 (CHI) [N] Bangkok, Thailand; [N] Parana, Brazil Rua Consulheiro Sinimbu.
Thiel, Harold *c.ss.r.* '56 (DEN) [M] Denver, CO The Redemptorists/Denver Province.
Thiel, Lloyd *o.f.m. cap.* '56 (DET) Detroit, MI Beaumont Hospital; [K] Detroit, MI St. Bonaventure Friary.
Thiele, Robert A. '55 (SC) Lake City, IA St. Mary's Church.
Thielemann, William A. *s.s.* '42 (BAL) [K] Baltimore, MD St. Charles Villa; [M] Baltimore, MD St. Charles Villa.
Thielen, Jeffrey M. '74 (MIL) [4] Racine, WI St. Lucy's Church.
Thielen, Martin '35 (P) Retired.
Thielman, Kenneth '55 (SCL) Browerville, MN Christ the King Church; Sauk Centre, MN State Home School for Girls.
Thieman, Anthony J. '89 (SFD) Camp Point, IL St. Thomas Church; Liberty, IL St. Brigid Church.
Thieman, Donald J. *c.pp.s.* '53 (CIN) [M] Dayton, OH Provincial House of the Cincinnati Province of the Society of the Precious Blood.
Thiers, George G. '70 (PH) [47] Philadelphia, PA St. Francis Xavier Church; [Z] Philadelphia, PA Archdiocesan Oratory of St. Philip Neri (C.O.).
Thieryoung, John (PEO) Galesburg, IL Immaculate Heart of Mary Church.
Thiessen, Dennis D. *s.d.s.* '78 (MIL) [P] Milwaukee, WI Salvatorian Provincial Residence.
Thill, Richard '81 (PBL) Absent on Leave.
Thillo, Marcel Van *c.i.c.m.* '56 (ARL) [J] Arlington, VA Missionhurst, C.I.C.M.-Central House and Provincialate.
Thimm, Donald H. '76 (MIL) Special Assignment.
Thimmesh, Hilary *o.s.b.* '54 (SCL) [I] Collegeville, MN St. John's Abbey, of the Order of St. Benedict.
Thinnes, John M. '64 (CHI) Deerfield, IL Holy Cross Church.
Thirukudumbam, Xavier *s.v.d.* '87 (WDC) [M] Washington, DC Divine Word College.
Thissen, Donald R. '70 (WCH) Arma, KS St. Joseph Church; Girard, KS St. Michael Church.
Thissen, Kevin C. *o.p.* '63 (GAL) Sugar Land, TX St. Thomas Aquinas Church.
Thivierge, Benoit *o.s.b.* '90 (KC) [A] Conception, MO Conception Seminary College; [J] Conception, MO Conception Abbey.
Thoa, Ngo Dinh *c.ss.r.* '62 (LA) [R] Baldwin Park, CA Vietnamese Redemptorist Mission.
Thoennes, James '64 (SCL) Special Assignment.
Thoennes, Roger '90 (SCL) Harding, MN Holy Cross Church; Lastrup, MN St. John Nepomuk Church.
Thole, Simeon *o.s.b.* '62 (SCL) [I] Collegeville, MN St. John's Abbey, of the Order of St. Benedict.
Thole, Simeon J. *o.s.b.* '62 (SP) [O] St. Leo, FL St. Leo Abbey.
Thole, Thomas *o.s.b.* '58 (SCL) [I] Collegeville, MN St. John's Abbey, of the Order of St. Benedict.
Tholen, John L. '62 (YAK) [3] Yakima, WA Holy Redeemer Church.
Thom, Elmer D. '43 (SC) Retired.
Thom, William V. *s.j.* '58 (SJ) [D] San Jose, CA Bellarmine College Preparatory.
Thoma, Anthony '37 (GB) [I] Appleton, WI St. Fidelis Friary.
Thoma, Steven R. *c.r.* '91 (STL) Spanish Lake, MO Our Lady of Loretto Church.
Thoman, Dwayne J. '76 (DUB) [1] Cedar Rapids, IA Immaculate Conception Church; [L] Cedar Rapids,

IA Sacred Heart Convent.
Thoman, James *c.p.* '75 (CHI) [N] Chicago, IL Passionist Provincial Office; [N] Chicago, IL Immaculate Conception Monastery.
Thoman, Robert A. '28 (PH) [Z] Philadelphia, PA Jesuit Community at St. Joseph's University.
Thomas, Alan E. '92 (ALT) [1] Johnstown, PA St. John Gualbert Cathedral; [B] Ebensburg, PA Bishop Carroll High School.
Thomas, Antoine '92 (PEO) [O] Peoria, IL Newman Foundation at Bradley University & Illinois Central College.
Thomas, Aquinas *s.a.* '48 (NY) [K] Barryville, NY New Hope Manor; [Z] Garrison, NY Generalate of the Franciscan Friars of the Atonement-St. James Friary; [DD] Barryville, NY New Hope Manor.
Thomas, Msgr. Arthur S. '65 (NU) Military Chaplains.
Thomas, Charles Theodore '73 (COL) Mt. Vernon, OH St. Vincent de Paul Church; [J] Columbus, OH Campus Ministry.
Thomas, Curtis R. '87 (NO) [18] New Orleans, LA Our Lady Of Lourdes Church.
Thomas, Msgr. Daniel E. '85 (PH) On Duty Outside the Archdiocese.
Thomas, David T. '52 (STL) [2] Creve Coeur, MO St. John Bosco Church.
Thomas, Donald *m.s.* '57 (LKC) [3] Sulphur, LA Our Lady of Prompt Succor Church.
Thomas, Donald '85 (HON) Retired.
Thomas, Donald N. '68 (SAM) Olean, NY St. Joseph Church.
Thomas, Fred (ORL) Mount Dora, FL St. Patrick's Church.
Thomas, Fred J. '58 (GAY) Retired.
Thomas, Fred J. '58 (ORL) Retired.
Thomas, Gary R. '83 (SJ) Los Altos, CA St. Nicholas Church.
Thomas, George '76 (SEA) Snoqualmie, WA Our Lady of Sorrows Church; Special Assignment.
Thomas, George L. '48 (SFR) [2] Menlo Park, CA St. Denis Church; Retired.
Thomas, Jacob *s.a.c.* '76 (ALX) Campti, LA Nativity of The Blessed Virgin Mary Church.
Thomas, James J. '76 (ALN) Military Chaplains.
Thomas, Jerald F. '56 (SR) [1] Santa Rosa, CA Cathedral of St. Eugene.
Thomas, John A. '62 (TOL) Perrysburg, OH St. Rose Church.
Thomas, John D. '54 (WOR) Paxton, MA St. Columba's Church.
Thomas, John E. '50 (BO) [72] Boston, MA St. Thomas Aquinas Church.
Thomas, John M. '66 (SC) Bancroft, IA St. John the Baptist's Church; Ledyard, IA Sacred Heart Church.
Thomas, John M. '93 (OWN) Henderson, KY Holy Name of Jesus Church.
Thomas, Joseph *b.s.o.* (BO) [8] Lawrence, MA St. Joseph Church.
Thomas, Joseph *b.s.o.* '71 (NTN) Lawrence, MA St. Joseph Church; [E] Lawrence, MA St. Joseph's Plains Community Center.
Thomas, Joseph '71 (SAM) On Duty Outside the Diocese.
Thomas, Joseph S. '52 (CHI) Northlake, IL St. John Baptist Vianney, Cure of Ars Church.
Thomas, Joseph W. '55 (PH) Retired.
Thomas, Juniper Jones '70 (RVC) [I] Port Jefferson, NY St. Charles Hospital, Port Jefferson, New York; [I] Port Jefferson, NY The St. Charles Corporation.
Thomas, Kevin *m.m.* '88 (DET) Macomb, MI St. Isidore Church.
Thomas, Kevin T. *m.m.* '88 (NY) [Z] Maryknoll, NY Maryknoll Fathers and Brothers.
Thomas, LaVerne, III '86 (SHP) [7] Shreveport, LA St. Elizabeth Ann Seton Church.
Thomas, Leo *o.p.* '54 (SEA) [22] Seattle, WA Blessed Sacrament Church.
Thomas, Mark '93 (PIT) [6] Ambridge, PA Good Samaritan Church.
Thomas, Mark A. '96 (PIT) [47] Pittsburgh, PA Guardian Angels Church.
Thomas, Merwyn J. *c.s.c.* '67 (FTW) [B] Notre Dame, IN University of Notre Dame Du Lac; [J] Notre Dame, IN Holy Cross Community, Corby Hall, University of Notre Dame.
Thomas, Michael G. '83 (SAM) Miami, FL Our Lady of Lebanon Church.
Thomas, Milton A. *o.s.c.* '64 (LIN) [A] Hastings, NE Crosier Monastery.
Thomas, Norman P. '55 (DET) [70] Detroit, MI Sacred Heart of Jesus Church.
Thomas, Paschal *o.s.b.* '57 (KC) [J] Conception, MO Conception Abbey.
Thomas, Paul '42 (ALT) Retired.
Thomas, Paul '63 (BAL) Special Assignment.
Thomas, Paul *o.s.b.* '82 (P) [L] St. Benedict, OR Mt. Angel Abbey.
Thomas, Philip *o.c.d.* '79 (MIL) [24] Milwaukee, WI St. Florian's Church; [P] Milwaukee, WI Provincial Offices - Discalced Carmelites.
Thomas, Ralph W. (CLV) Olmsted Falls, OH St. Mary of the Falls Church.
Thomas, Raymond '71 (COL) Absent on Sick Leave.
Thomas, Raymond J. '72 (Y) Orwell, OH St. Mary's Church.
Thomas, Richard L. '66 (GB) Oneida Township, WI Immaculate Conception Church.
Thomas, Richard M. *s.j.* '58 (ELP) [N] El Paso, TX Our Lady's Youth Center.
Thomas, Robert '60 (TUC) Sabbatical Leave.
Thomas, Robert R. '60 (TOL) On Duty Outside the Diocese.
Thomas, Robert W. (BO) Society of St. James the Apostle.
Thomas, Msgr. Royce R. '69 (LR) Fort Smith, AR Christ the King Church; [B] Fort Smith, AR Trinity Junior High.
Thomas, Sylvester J. '55 (LA) Retired; [CC] San Pedro, CA Apostleship of the Sea, Catholic Maritime Ministry.
Thomas, Wilbur N. '73 (CHL) Hickory, NC St. Aloysius Church.
Thomas, William '78 (LAN) On Duty Outside the Diocese.
Thomas, William F. '93 (LR) Hope, AR Our Lady of Good Hope Church.
Thomas, William V. '62 (CIN) Jamestown, OH St. Augustine Church; South Charleston, OH St. Charles Borromeo Church.
Thome, Edwin A. '54 (GAY) Acme, MI Christ the King Church.
Thome, Edwin J. '51 (LC) Onalaska, WI St. Patrick Church; Retired.
Thome, Francis E. '89 (MRY) San Luis Obispo, CA San Luis Obispo Church.
Thome, John J. '46 (SAG) Merrill, MI Sacred Heart Church; Ryan, MI St. Patrick Church.
Thompson, August L. '57 (ALX) [4] Alexandria, LA St. James Memorial Church; [5] Alexandria, LA St. Juliana Church.
Thompson, Augustine *o.p.* '85 (P) [6] Eugene, OR St. Thomas More Church.
Thompson, Charles C.E. '87 (L) Lebanon, KY St. Augustine Church.
Thompson, D. Timothy '82 (FWT) [14] Fort Worth, TX St. Peter The Apostle Church.
Thompson, Damien *o.c.s.o.* '61 (L) [L] Trappist, KY Abbey of Our Lady of Gethsemani, of the Order of Cistercians of the Strict Observance.
Thompson, David A. '92 (WDC) Leonardtown, MD St. Aloysius Church.
Thompson, Dennis *o.f.m.conv.* '89 (STP) St. Louis Park, MN Most Holy Trinity Church.
Thompson, Edward C, '59 (NEW) Dumont, NJ St. Mary's Church.
Thompson, Edward J. '51 (ORL) Altamonte Springs, FL St. Mary Magdalen Church.
Thompson, George M. '52 (PEO) Retired.
Thompson, Msgr. George P. '65 (NY) [60] New York, NY St. John the Martyr Church.
Thompson, J. Garret '81 (BO) [2] Marlboro, MA Immaculate Conception Church.
Thompson, J. Noel '54 (SD) Retired.
Thompson, J. Vincent *c.s.b.* '49 (GAL) [Q] Sugar Land, TX Basilian Mission Center.
Thompson, James *o.s.a.* '71 (CHI) [N] Chicago, IL St. John Stone Friary.
Thompson, James A. '44 (TR) Retired.
Thompson, James W. '44 (L) Retired; [L] Louisville, KY Bishop David Apartments.
Thompson, Jerald W. '94 (LA) Simi Valley, CA St. Rose of Lima Church.
Thompson, Jerome F. '66 (MIL) On Duty Outside the Archdiocese.
Thompson, Jerome H. '60 (LA) Sick Leave.
Thompson, John A. '79 (BRK) [88] Brooklyn, NY St. Michael Archangel and St. Edward Church.
Thompson, Kizito *o.c.s.o.* '70 (WOR) [N] Spencer, MA St. Joseph's Abbey.
Thompson, Mary Bernard *o.cart.* '91 (BUR) [G] Arlington, VT Carthusian Foundation, Charterhouse of the Transfiguration.
Thompson, Matthew E. '79 (WDC) Hilltop, MD St. Ignatius Loyola Church; McConchie, MD St. Catherine of Alexandria Church.
Thompson, Melvin F. '67 (DEN) [3] Lakewood, CO Our Lady of Fatima Church.
Thompson, Michael '96 (STA) [1] Gainesville, FL St. Patrick's Church.
Thompson, Nils Francis *o.f.m.* '63 (SFE) [4] Albuquerque, NM Holy Family Church; Albuquerque, NM U.S.P.H. Indian Hospital.
Thompson, Msgr. Patrick '60 (LA) Lomita, CA St. Margaret Mary Alacoque Church; San Fernando, CA Santa Rosa Church.
Thompson, Philip E. '78 (DUB) Cascade, IA St. Matthias Church; [E] Cascade, IA Aquin Religious Education Center; [F] Cascade, IA Aquin Elementary School.
Thompson, Richard *o.s.c.* '78 (DET) [K] Riverview, MI Crosier Community of Riverview.
Thompson, Richard '95 (P) Beaverton, OR St. Cecilia Church.
Thompson, Richard B. '69 (MAN) Plaistow, NH Holy Angels Church.
Thompson, Richard J. '96 (PIT) Wexford, PA St. Alphonsus Church.
Thompson, Richard R. '59 (SY) Fulton, NY Holy Family Church.
Thompson, Robert '65 (GB) Absent on Leave.
Thompson, Thomas A. *s.m.* '68 (CIN) [D] Dayton, OH The University of Dayton; [D] Dayton, OH The University of Dayton; [M] Dayton, OH Marianist Provincialate.
Thompson, Thomas E. '92 (SUP) Chelsea, WI Assumption of the Blessed Virgin Mary Church; Rib Lake, WI St. John the Baptist Church; Westboro, WI St. Theresa Church; Whittlesey, WI Our Lady of Perpetual Help Church.
Thompson, Thomas W. '64 (LAN) Brighton, MI St. Patrick Church.
Thompson, Thomas W. '82 (SD) Carlsbad, CA St. Patrick Church.
Thompson, Msgr. William '54 (CC) [5] Corpus Christi, TX Most Precious Blood Church.
Thompson, William D. '69 (BGP) Military Chaplains.
Thompson, William J. '71 (WDC) Bryantown, MD St. Mary Church.
Thompson, William L. *o.s.b.* '44 (PBL) [E] Canon City, CO Holy Cross Abbey.
Thomson, Edward A. '80 (PRT) Augusta, ME St. Andrew's Church.
Thomson, Paul van K. '83 (PRO) Retired.
Thomson, Richard G. *o.s.c.* '78 (WIN) Stewartville, MN St. Bernard's Church.
Thon, Andrew J. *s.j.* '74 (MIL) [P] Milwaukee, WI Jesuit Community at Marquette University.
Thong, John the Baptist '68 (BAL) [Q] Baltimore, MD Vietnamese Catholic Community at Baltimore (VCCAB).
Thong, Nguyen Duc *c.ss.r.* '56 (LA) [R] Baldwin Park, CA Vietnamese Redemptorist Mission; [CC] Baldwin Park, CA The Redemptorist Vietnamese Mission Corporation.
Thongamphai, Peter B. '56 (JOL) [3] Lockport, IL St. John Vianney Church.
Thongamphi, Peter '48 (JOL) Joliet, IL Silver Cross Hospital.
Thoni, Philip F. '49 (KNX) Fairfield Glade, TN St. Francis of Assisi Church.
Thonikuzhiyil, Mathai J. *c.m.i.* '77 (NSH) Madison, TN St. Joseph's Church.
Thoon Kuzhy, Joseph '58 (BEL) Retired.
Thorburn, Msgr. Timothy J. '83 (LIN) [F] Waverly, NE Our Lady of Good Counsel Retreat House.
Thoren, Guy S. '71 (MAR) [4] (Harvey), MI St. Louis Church.
Thorne, Carrol *c.p.* '60 (MET) [H] South River, NJ Passionist Provincial Office.
Thorne, Vance *s.v.d.* '53 (TR) [M] Bordentown, NJ Society of the Divine Word.
Thornsberry, John J. '91 (BAL) [L] Sparks, MD Msgr. Clare J. O'Dwyer Retreat House.
Thornsberry, Michael T. '91 (L) On Duty Outside the Archdiocese.
Thornton, James W. *c.s.c.* '64 (COS) [9] Colorado Springs, CO Sacred Heart Church.
Thornton, Lawrence *s.v.d.* '54 (CHI) [B] Techny, IL Divine Word Residence.
Thornton, Msgr. Michael J. '69 (BLX) Pascagoula, MS Sacred Heart Church.
Thorsen, Henry '53 (BIR) Retired.
Thorsen, Robert J. '56 (CIN) Retired.
Thorton, James W. *c.s.c.* '64 (FTW) Notre Dame, IN Sacred Heart Church.
Thottakara, Daniel *c.m.i.* '62 (DET) Lake Orion, MI St. Joseph Church; Detroit, MI Clinton Valley Center.
Thottapally, James '71 (SR) Fortuna, CA St. Joseph Church; [G] Eureka, CA St. Joseph Hospital of Eureka.
Thottungal, Thomas '70 (NEW) [2] Jersey City, NJ St. Aloysius Church.
Thozhuthumparambil, Sebastian *c.m.* '62 (NY) [229] Staten Island, NY St. Sylvester Church.
Thrasher, Robert W. '62 (SPR) [3] Holyoke, MA Holy Family Church.
Thro, Edward A. *s.j.* '42 (DEN) [M] Denver, CO Xavier Jesuit Center.
Thro, Linus J. *s.j.* '44 (STL) [P] St. Louis, MO Jesuit Community Corporation at St. Louis University - Jesuit Hall.
Thro, Thomas *s.j.* '51 (SPC) Shell Knob, MO Holy Family Church.
Thro, William *s.j.* '52 (COS) [12] Colorado Springs, CO St. Patrick's Church.
Thuer, William J. '46 (HRT) Retired.
Thuerauf, Jeffrey P. '89 (TUC) Coolidge, AZ St. James Church.
Thul, Joseph T. '55 (MET) Retired.
Thul, Robert C. *s.j.* '61 (CHI) [D] Chicago, IL St. Ignatius College Prep; [D] Chicago, IL St. Ignatius Jesuit Community.

Thuma, Clifton M (BO) [3] Peabody, MA St. John the Baptist Church.
Thuong, Msgr. Philippe Xuan Le '70 (GAL) [1] Houston, TX Sacred Heart Co-Cathedral.
Thurmer, William H. '48 (STL) Des Peres, MO St. Clement Church; Retired.
Thurmond, Benton A. '46 (VIC) Inez, TX St. Joseph's Church.
Thurner, Robert M. '51 (STP) Retired.
Thurston, Anthony (WH) Follansbee, WV St. Anthony's Church.
Thury, Gerald '67 (SFS) Woonsocket, SD St. Wilfrid Church.
Thuy, Pham Quang '73 (RIC) On Duty Outside the Diocese.
Thychery, George '60 (LAF) Franklin, LA St. Jules Church.
Thylstrup, Edward J. *s.j.* '67 (SJ) [M] Los Gatos, CA California Province of the Society of Jesus, Jesuit Provincial Office.
Thyppadth, Xavier *o.s.j.* (FRS) Madera, CA St. Joachim Church.
Tiano, Christopher M. '89 (HRT) [2] Hartford, CT Holy Trinity Church; Special and other (Arch)Diocesan Assignment.
Tibay, Ernesto '76 (NEW) Bergenfield, NJ St. John the Evangelist Church.
Tibbs, Thomas T. '74 (GRY) Kouts, IN St. Mary Church.
Tibesar, Leo J. '68 (STP) [24] Minneapolis, MN St. Frances Cabrini Church; Minneapolis, MN Riverside Medical Center.
Tiblier, Edgar J. *s.j.* '56 (BR) [16] Baton Rouge, LA Our Lady of Mercy Church.
Tiboni, Vito '69 (BRK) Brooklyn, NY Veterans Administration Medical Center.
Tiboni, Vito '69 (NEW) On Duty Outside the Archdiocese.
Tibudan, Tomasito '73 (AGN) Dededo, GU Santa Barbara Church.
Tice, Cecil W. '81 (CHL) [3] Charlotte, NC Our Lady of Consolation Church.
Tichacek, Charles P. '94 (STL) [3] Florissant, MO St. Angela Merici Church.
Tickerhoof, Bernard *t.o.r.* '77 (PIT) [N] Pittsburgh, PA Franciscan Friars, T.O.R.
Tickerhoof, Bernard F. *t.o.r.* '78 (ALT) [F] Loretto, PA St. Bonaventure Friary.
Tickerhoof, David *t.o.r.* '67 (SFS) Wagner, SD St. John the Baptist Church.
Tiedeman, Edmund '66 (SC) Mapleton, IA St. Mary's Church.
Tiedemann, Neil *c.p.* '75 (NEW) [3] Union City, NJ SS. Joseph and Michael Church.
Tiegs, James R. '74 (OM) [H] Omaha, NE New Cassel Retirement Center.
Tiell, Florian *o.f.m.conv.* '68 (SAV) Jesup, GA St. Joseph Church.
Tiell, Maurice J. '50 (OWN) Eddyville, KY St. Mark Church.
Tiemann, Stephen E. '89 (GAL) [70] Houston, TX Queen of Peace Church.
Tien, Msgr. Peter Nguyen Duc '60 (ORG) [G] Santa Ana, CA Vietnamese Catholic Center.
Tiep, John V. '89 (MAN) [2] Manchester, NH St. Anne Church.
Tiercelin, Harry '47 (NY) [122] New York, NY St. Vincent de Paul Church; [Z] New York, NY Pope John Paul II Residence.
Tiernan, John A. (ALT) Hollidaysburg, PA St. Mary's Church.
Tierney, Berard *c.p.* '48 (SCR) [M] Scranton, PA Saint Ann's Passionist Monastery.
Tierney, Francis J. *s.j.* '42 (NY) [Z] New York, NY Murray-Weigel Hall; [Z] New York, NY Jesuit Provincial's Office.
Tierney, Gary M. '67 (DET) Clawson, MI Guardian Angels Church.
Tierney, Msgr. James E. '50 (BO) [Z] Boston, MA Regina Cleri, Inc.
Tierney, Joachim *o.c.s.o.* '40 (ATL) [I] Conyers, GA The Monastery of the Holy Spirit.
Tierney, John J. '37 (BAL) Retired; [K] Baltimore, MD Stella Maris Operating Corporation; [K] Baltimore, MD Stella Maris Operating Corporation.
Tierney, Joseph P. '86 (NY) [A] Yonkers, NY St. Joseph's Seminary.
Tierney, Michael '69 (KC) Grandview, MO Coronation of Our Lady Church.
Tierney, Michael J. '67 (RCK) Algonquin, IL St. Margaret Mary Church.
Tierney, Patrick '89 (DEN) Littleton, CO Light of the World Parish Church.
Tierney, Patrick J. '69 (BIR) Tuscumbia, AL Our Lady of the Shoals Church.
Tierney, Msgr. Patrick M. '57 (CAM) Avalon, NJ Maris Stella Church.
Tierney, Robert G. '67 (SY) [2] Endicott, NY St. Ambrose Church.
Tierney, Thomas J. *s.j.* '62 (RC) [B] Howes, SD Kino Jesuit Community.
Tierney, Thomas M. '70 (WOR) [2] Fitchburg, MA St. Bernard's Church; Gardner, MA Massachusetts Correctional Institution.
Tiesi, Samuel *t.o.r.* '63 (ARL) [J] Winchester, VA Sacred Heart Friary.
Tietjen, Kenneth F. *o.c.s.o.* '56 (DUB) [K] Peosta, IA New Melleray Abbey, Order of Cistercians of the Strict Observance.
Tiffany, Eugene W. '72 (STP) Lakeville, MN All Saints Church.
Tifft, Thomas W. '69 (CLV) [A] Wickliffe, OH St. Mary Seminary.
Tigges, James '71 (SC) Alton, IA St. Mary's Church; Hospers, IA St. Anthony's Church.
Tighe, Msgr. Benedict F. '59 (BGP) [2] Stamford, CT St. Leo's Church.
Tighe, Dermot F. '54 (DOD) Great Bend, KS St. Patrick Church.
Tighe, Msgr. Emmett F. '51 (WIN) Blue Earth, MN SS. Peter and Paul's Church.
Tighe, James L. '70 (BRK) [96] Brooklyn, NY Our Lady of Grace Church.
Tighe, Leonard J. (BO) Boston, MA Lemuel Shattuck Hospital.
Tighe, Timothy '69 (NEW) Kearny, NJ Hudson County Correctional Center.
Tigreros, Ernesto '66 (DET) [K] Detroit, MI Society of St. Paul.
Tigyer, Paul (PSC) Retired.
Tijerina, Richard '85 (AUS) [1] Austin, TX St. Mary's Cathedral; Austin, TX Brackenridge Hospital.
Tikalsky, Russell F. '56 (MIL) [K] Milwaukee, WI St. Mary's Hospital of Milwaukee.
Tilford, John E. '66 (CHI) [139] Chicago, IL St. Michael the Archangel Church.
Till, Joseph E. '46 (GRY) Retired.
Tilley, Charles J. *s.j.* (MRY) [C] San Luis Obispo, CA Mission College Preparatory Catholic High School.
Tilley, Charles J. *s.j.* '85 (SJ) [D] San Jose, CA Bellarmine College Preparatory.
Tillia, Marc '59 (KCK) On Duty Outside the Archdiocese.
Tillman, Msgr. Clyde (SFR) [K] San Rafael, CA Nazareth House.
Tillman, Msgr. Clyde F. '37 (SR) Retired.
Tillman, Richard H. '65 (BAL) Columbia, MD St. John the Evangelist Church.
Tillman, Richard J. '65 (STL) [1] St. Charles, MO St. Charles Borromeo Church.
Tillman, Robert J. *s.j.* '77 (OM) [C] Omaha, NE Creighton Preparatory School.
Tillman, Stanley *s.j.* '45 (LEX) Barbourville, KY St. Gregory Church; [L] Barbourville, KY St. Gregory Church-Union College.
Tillotson, Frederick *o.carm.* '69 (LA) [F] Encino, CA Crespi Carmelite High School.
Tillrock, Raymond J. '69 (CHI) [22] Chicago, IL St. Barnabas Church.
Tillyer, Msgr. Herbert K. '68 (PAT) Parsippany, NJ St. Peter the Apostle Church; [P] Paterson, NJ Martin de Porres Village Corporation.
Tilp, John R. '69 (DUB) Clutier, IA Immaculate Conception Church; Traer, IA St. Paul's Church; Vining, IA St. Mary's Church.
Timar, Frank J. *m.s.c.* '58 (RCK) Sycamore, IL St. Mary Church.
Timbre, Roland '61 (HT) Chackbay, LA Our Lady of Prompt Succor Church.
Timby, Bryan P. '83 (MEM) [10] Memphis, TN Holy Rosary Church.
Timchak, Robert M. '92 (SCR) [8] Wilkes-Barre, PA Holy Saviour Church; [D] Wilkes-Barre, PA Bishop Hoban High School.
Timko, Philip S. *o.s.b.* '69 (JOL) [A] Lisle, IL Benedictine University; [J] Lisle, IL St. Procopius Abbey; [K] Lisle, IL Benedictine Sisters of the Sacred Heart, Sacred Heart Monastery.
Timlin, Anthony J. '56 (SB) Palm Desert, CA Sacred Heart Church.
Timlin, John P. *c.m.* '79 (BRK) [66] Brooklyn, NY St. John the Baptist Church; [U] Brooklyn, NY St. John the Baptist Rectory.
Timlin, Thomas D. '55 (CHR) Anderson, SC St. Joseph's Church; [H] Anderson, SC Anderson College Newman Center.
Timmerman, David W. '87 (MAD) Bloomington, WI St. Mary Church.
Timmerman, Gerard *s.m.* '75 (HON) [15] Honolulu, HI Star of the Sea Church.
Timmerman, Randy J. '93 (MAD) [7] Madison, WI St. Dennis Church.
Timmermans, Msgr. John '52 (ALX) Retired; [E] Moreauville, LA St. John's Village.
Timmings, Thomas '70 (FRS) Atwater, CA St. Anthony Church.
Timock, Ronald K. '83 (MAR) On Duty Outside the Diocese.
Timock, Ronald K. '83 (PRM) Cleveland, OH St. Mary Church.
Timone, Donald '60 (NY) [4] Newburgh, NY Sacred Heart Church.
Timone, Richard F. *s.j.* '64 (NY) [Z] New York, NY Murray-Weigel Hall.
Timoney, Brian '56 (OAK) [4] Walnut Creek, CA St. Stephen Church.
Timoney, Christopher *o.c.d.* '62 (SAT) [18] San Antonio, TX Our Lady of Mt. Carmel and St. Therese, Discalced Carmelite Fathers Church; [M] San Antonio, TX Discalced Carmelites (Prov. of St. Therese).
Timoney, Conan H. *c.p.* '68 (BAL) [11] Baltimore, MD Ascension Church; Baltimore, MD Veterans Hospital, Fort Howard; Baltimore, MD Veterans Hospital, Baltimore; [Q] Baltimore, MD Catholic War Veterans, Inc.
Timoney, Conan H. *c.p.* '68 (PSC) Baltimore, MD Patronage of the Mother of God Church.
Timoney, Francis '69 (LAV) [5] Las Vegas, NV Prince of Peace Church.
Timperman, Robert *c.i.c.m.* '49 (ARL) [J] Falls Church, VA Missionhurst-C.I.C.M.
Tinajero, Francisco M. *s.v.d.* '88 (LA) [71] Los Angeles, CA St. John, The Evangelist Church.
Tinajero, Frank *s.v.d.* (LA) Terminal Island, CA Federal Correction Institute.
Tinajero, Frank *s.b.d.* '89 (LA) Terminal Island, CA Federal Correction Institution.
Tindall, Harold '78 (SD) Retired.
Tindall, William H. '89 (DET) Newport, MI St. Charles Borromeo Church.
Tinder, F. Dennis '68 (BAL) Pasadena, MD St. Jane Frances de Chantal Church.
Tingerthal, James *o.s.b.* '61 (SCL) [I] Collegeville, MN St. John's Abbey, of the Order of St. Benedict.
Tinh, Joseph Nguyen '57 (SJ) On Duty Outside the Diocese.
Tinney, Edward J. *s.j.* '44 (ALN) [A] Wernersville, PA Novitiate of St. Isaac Jogues.
Tinney, Richard W. '65 (BUR) Rutland, VT Immaculate Heart of Mary Church.
Tino, Robert '71 (SEA) Steilacoom, WA Western State Hospital.
Tino, Robert F. '71 (MIL) On Duty Outside the Archdiocese.
Tinsley, Msgr. Edmond T. '51 (WOR) [I] Leicester, MA McAuley Nazareth Home for Boys; [R] Worcester, MA Monsignor Thomas Griffin Foundation.
Tintle, Ray *o.f.m.* '69 (LA) [R] Santa Barbara, CA Franciscan Friary, Order of Friars Minor (Old Mission).
Tippmann, Laurence '69 (FTW) [8] Fort Wayne, IN St. Joseph Church.
Tippmann, Lawrence '69 (FTW) [C] Fort Wayne, IN Bishop Luers High School.
Tipton, Grover B. '96 (STA) Special Assignment.
Tirabassi, Camillo '59 (FTW) [7] South Bend, IN Corpus Christi Church.
Tirado, James '56 (SJN) [26] San Juan, PR San Jose Church.
Tirado, Ramon Orlando *c.m.* (SJN) [47] San Juan, PR Nuestra Senora del Pilar Church.
Tirone, Seraphin *o.f.m.cap.* '40 (NY) [B] Beacon, NY St. Lawrence of Brindisi Friary.
Tirpak, Adrian *t.o.r.* '60 (ALT) [3] Windber, PA St. Anthony of Padua Church.
Titko, Stephen J. '79 (GRY) Saint John, IN St. John Evangelist Church.
Titmas, William D. '63 (CAM) [H] Cherry Hill, NJ St. Mary's Nursing Home; [L] Cherry Hill, NJ Vianney Villa.
Tito, Joseph (NOR) Baltic, CT St. Mary of the Immaculate Conception Church.
Tito, Joseph '96 (CHI) [196] Chicago, IL St. Sylvester Church.
Tito, Rocco A. '55 (E) Titusville, PA St. Walburga Church.
Titone, Robert '71 (BRK) [170] Queens, NY St. Gabriel Church.
Titore, Robert A. '71 (BRK) Absent on Sick Leave.
Titta, Santino '60 (ALB) Cherry Valley, NY St. Thomas the Apostle Church.
Tittler, Leo R. '63 (BAL) Emmitsburg, MD St. Anthony Shrine Church; Thurmont, MD Our Lady of Mount Carmel Church.
Titus, Austin E. '92 (NY) [142] Bronx, NY St. Frances of Rome Church.
Titus, John '89 (SFD) [6] Springfield, IL St. Aloysius Church.
Titus, Rodney Q. '95 (PMB) Port St. Lucie, FL St. Lucie Church.
Tivenan, John J. '72 (B) [B] Nampa, ID Mercy Medical Center.
Tivenan, John J. '72 (BRK) Released from Diocesan Assignment.
Tivnan, Paul J. (BO) Awaiting Assignment.
Tivnan, Paul J. '63 (BO) Braintree, MA St. Francis of Assisi Church; Boston, MA Deaconess Hospital.
Tivy, Gerald '64 (JOL) Aurora, IL Our Lady of Mercy Church.
Tivy, Thomas A. '62 (CHI) [148] Chicago, IL Our Lady of Grace Church.
Tix, Michael '92 (STP) Richfield, MN Assumption of the B.V.M. Church.
Tizio, John G. *c.ss.r.* '85 (BAL) Annapolis, MD St. Mary

Church; [M] Annapolis, MD Saint Mary Rectory.
Tizio, Joseph *c.ss.r.* '75 (NY) [78] New York, NY Most Holy Redeemer Church.
Tkach, Norman A. '56 (SLC) On Duty Outside the Diocese.
Tkachuk, William '81 (CHI) Schaumburg, IL Church of the Holy Spirit.
Tlapa, Richard J. (CHI) Retired.
Tlucek, Edward *o.f.m.* '78 (GB) Pulaski, WI Assumption of the Blessed Virgin Mary Church; [I] Pulaski, WI Assumption of B.V.M. Friary.
To, Joseph Lien *i.c.m.* (BR) [H] Baton Rouge, LA Incarnational Consecration Mission.
Toal, Bernard *s.s.c.* '43 (DAL) Grand Prairie, TX Immaculate Conception Church.
Toal, James '58 (LA) [K] Burbank, CA Providence Saint Joseph Medical Center.
Toal, James F. *o.f.m.* '75 (SFD) [B] Quincy, IL Quincy University.
Toale, Thomas E. '81 (DUB) Temple Hill, IA St. Peter's Church.
Toan, Francis '34 (MRY) Retired.
Toan, John Hoang Minh '68 (GAL) [53] Houston, TX Notre Dame Church.
Tobias, Humphrey '48 (MIL) [P] Burlington, WI Queen of Peace Friary.
Tobias, Joseph *m.s.c.* '66 (PH) Ottsville, PA St. John the Baptist Church.
Tobias, Mary Michael *o.cart.* '93 (BUR) [G] Arlington, VT Carthusian Foundation, Charterhouse of the Transfiguration.
Tobin, Chuck '68 (KC) Maryville, MO St. Gregory Barbarigo Church.
Tobin, Douglas R. '81 (CAM) Oaklyn, NJ St. Aloysius Church.
Tobin, Eamon '72 (ORL) Cocoa Beach, FL Church of Our Saviour.
Tobin, Flavian *o.f.m.* '45 (BO) [BB] Boston, MA St. Anthony Shrine.
Tobin, George W. '50 (OG) Cadyville, NY St. James Minor Church.
Tobin, James *s.m.* '69 (STL) [P] St. Louis, MO Provincialate of the Society of Mary, Province of St. Louis.
Tobin, James B. '52 (NY) Retired; [E] White Plains, NY Archbishop Stepinac High School.
Tobin, Jeremy *o.praem.* '69 (CHI) [N] Chicago, IL Premonstratensian Fathers and Brothers (Norbertines).
Tobin, Joseph *c.ss.r.* '62 (LA) Whittier, CA St. Mary of the Assumption Church; [R] Whittier, CA Redemptorist Fathers Mission House.
Tobin, Joseph W. *c.ss.r.* '78 (CHI) [N] Bangkok, Thailand; [N] Parana, Brazil Rua Consulheiro Sinimbu.
Tobin, Joseph W. *c.ss.r.* '78 (DEN) [M] Denver, CO The Redemptorists/Denver Province.
Tobin, Msgr. Neil W. '57 (DUB) Castle Grove, IA Immaculate Conception Church; Monticello, IA Sacred Heart Church.
Tobin, Paul R. '64 (Y) Geneva, OH Assumption B.V.M. Church.
Tobin, T. Michael '93 (L) [48] Louisville, KY St. Margaret Mary Church.
Tobin, Thomas '59 (GF) Baker, MT St. John the Evangelist Church.
Tobin, Thomas H. *s.j.* '73 (CHI) [C] Chicago, IL Jesuit Community at Loyola University of Chicago.
Tobin, Thomas J. '55 (FR) [K] North Dartmouth, MA Holy Cross Mission House.
Tobin, Vincent *o.s.b.* '59 (IND) [J] St. Meinrad, IN St. Meinrad Archabbey.
Tobin, William D. '34 (ROC) Elmira Heights, NY St. Charles Borromeo Church.
Tobolski, James F. '84 (SUP) [5] Superior, WI St. Francis Xavier Church.
Tobolski, Robert *m.s.c.* '55 (ALN) [K] Reading, PA Missionaries of the Sacred Heart.
Tocco, Msgr. Anthony M. '65 (DET) Bloomfield Hills, MI St. Hugo of the Hills Church.
Toczek, Melchior *o.f.m.* '49 (CHI) Oak Forest, IL Oak Forest Hospital; [N] Oak Forest, IL St. Roch Friary-Franciscan Fathers.
Todd, Richard J. *c.m.f.* '55 (CHI) [N] Oak Park, IL Claretian Fathers Headquarters of U.S.A. Eastern Province.
Todd, Wilmer '63 (HT) [5] Houma, LA St. Bernadette Church.
Toelle, William L. '56 (MIL) Ripon, WI St. Wenceslaus Church.
Toepfer, John R. *o.f.m.cap.* '86 (SAL) [D] Hays, KS St. Bonaventure's Friary; [H] Hays, KS Comeau Catholic Campus Center at Fort Hays State University; [H] Hays, KS Comeau Catholic Campus Center at Fort Hays State University.
Tofani, Richard L. '79 (TR) [2] Trenton, NJ Blessed Sacrament Church.
Togni, Peter J. *s.j.* '85 (SFR) [N] San Francisco, CA Jesuit Community at University of San Francisco.
Tokarski, Stanislaw '93 (DET) [7] Sterling Heights, MI St. Michael Church.
Tokarski, Stephen L. '69 (GF) [6] Billings, MT St. Pius X Church.
Tokarz, David J. '91 (MOB) Troy, AL St. Martin Church; [K] Troy, AL Troy State University Newman Center.
Tokarz, John '39 (SPR) Retired; [H] Springfield, MA St. Michael's Residence.
Tokarz, Robert J. '96 (GRY) [2] Gary, IN Blessed Sacrament Church.
Tokarz, Thomas M. '77 (WOR) [2] Gardner, MA St. Joseph's Church.
Tokaz, John *o.f.m.cap.* '78 (NOR) [4] Middletown, CT St. Pius X Church.
Tokus, William J. *m.m.* '60 (NY) [Z] Maryknoll, NY Maryknoll Fathers and Brothers.
Tolaas, Gregory '83 (STP) [C] St. Paul, MN University of St. Thomas.
Toland, Paul L. (BO) Retired.
Toland, Terrence *s.j.* '52 (WDC) [M] Washington, DC The Jesuit Community at Georgetown University.
Tolang, Jaime '58 (SEA) [26] Seattle, WA Immaculate Conception Church; Retired.
Tolbert, George T. *s.j.* '45 (DET) [P] Clarkston, MI Colombiere Center.
Tolczyk, Marion M. *o.f.m.conv.* '54 (BUF) [O] Athol Springs, NY Father Justin Rosary Hour Radio Apostolate.
Tolentino, Eddie '84 (WDC) [16] Washington, DC Holy Comforter—St. Cyprian Church.
Tolentino, Thomas J. '56 (NY) Scarsdale, NY Immaculate Heart of Mary Church.
Tolentino de la Rosa, Lorenzo Maria, Jr. *o.cart.* '92 (BUR) [G] Arlington, VT Carthusian Foundation, Charterhouse of the Transfiguration.
Toliusis, Msgr. Casimir '36 (SFD) Retired.
Tolland, Cyril E. '44 (BO) Permanent Disability.
Tollini, Frederick P. *s.j.* '65 (SJ) [B] Santa Clara, CA Santa Clara University.
Tollner, Gary B. '61 (OAK) [R] Oakland, CA Catholic Ladies' Aid Society, Grand Chaplain.
Toloczko, Bernard A. '58 (SCR) [2] Nanticoke, PA Holy Trinity Church; [J] Nanticoke, PA Mercy Health Care Center.
Tolosa, Braulio '64 (DM) [C] Des Moines, IA Mercy Hospital Medical Center.
Tolve, Paul *o.f.m.cap.* '84 (NY) Valhalla, NY Westchester County Medical Center; [Z] White Plains, NY St. Conrad Friary.
Tomaino, Peter *s.a.* '47 (NY) [Z] Garrison, NY Generalate of the Franciscan Friars of the Atonement-St. James Friary.
Tomalonis, John '51 (PBL) Retired.
Toman, Edward A. *s.d.s.* '83 (NEW) [N] Verona, NJ The Salvatorian Fathers.
Tomasek, Richard A. *s.j.* '73 (MIL) [P] Milwaukee, WI Jesuit Provincial Office, Wisconsin Province.
Tomasek, Richard J. *s.j.* '73 (COL) [A] Columbus, OH Pontifical College Josephinum.
Tomaselli, Msgr. Samuel J. '59 (ALT) Somerset, PA St. Peter's Church.
Tomasi, Lydio *c.s.* '63 (NY) [Z] Staten Island, NY Scalabrinian Missionaries.
Tomasi, Noel *s.x.* '60 (PAT) [M] Wayne, NJ Xaverian Missionary Fathers.
Tomasiewicz, Edward J. *c.m.* '74 (CHI) [C] Chicago, IL Vincentian Community at DePaul University.
Tomasiewicz, Frank S. '65 (SCL) Kimball, MN Church of Saint Anne.
Tomasiewicz, Mark A. '91 (OM) Papillion, NE St. Columbkille Church.
Tomasko, Andrew J. '91 (DET) [6] Warren, MI St. Leonard of Port Maurice Church; [T] Detroit, MI Guest House Alumni Association.
Tomaskovic, Emil F. *s.a.* '71 (NY) [Z] Garrison, NY Generalate of the Franciscan Friars of the Atonement-St. James Friary.
Tomasone, Richard C. '80 (E) Mercer, PA Immaculate Heart Church; [C] Hermitage, PA Kennedy Christian High School.
Tomasovich, Msgr. John A. '48 (NO) [24] New Orleans, LA St. Andrew the Apostle Church.
Tomassetti, Berard *o.f.m.cap.* '53 (SAL) [D] Victoria, KS St. Fidelis Friary.
Tomasso, Paul J. (ROC) [51] Rochester, NY SS. Peter and Paul Church.
Tomasso, Paul J. '81 (ROC) [1] Rochester, NY Sacred Heart Cathedral; [6] Rochester, NY St. Anthony of Padua Church; [15] Rochester, NY St. Francis Assisi Church; [20] Rochester, NY Holy Apostles Church.
Tomasulo, Anthony J. *o.s.a.* '61 (ALB) Mechanicville, NY Assumption-St. Paul Church; Schaghticoke, NY St. John the Baptist Church.
Tomaszewski, Mariano '91 (LA) Pasadena, CA St. Philip the Apostle Church.
Tomaszewski, Msgr. Michael J. '58 (GRY) [4] Michigan City, IN St. Stanislaus Kostka Church.
Tomatis, Christopher F. *o.f.m.* '65 (OAK) [N] Oakland, CA Franciscan Friars Provincial Office, Province of St. Barbara.
Tombasco, Anthony R. '51 (SCR) [6] Dunmore, PA St. Rocco's Church.
Tomc, Victor N. '43 (CLV) [47] Cleveland, OH St. Mary Church; Retired.
Tomiak, Walter L. '40 (BUF) Retired.
Tomich, Daniel M. '76 (CHI) Riverdale, IL Queen of Apostles Church.
Tomichek, Msgr. George (PH) [135] Philadelphia, PA St. Peter the Apostle Church.
Tomicky, Ronald '75 (CLV) Retired.
Tomiczek, Damien *s.d.s.* '82 (SAT) Cestohowa, TX Nativity of the Blessed Virgin Mary Church; Hobson, TX St. Boniface Church.
Tomkins, Robert J. '88 (SB) Joshua Tree, CA St. Christopher of the Desert Church.
Tomlian, Robert J. '53 (NY) [59] New York, NY St. John Nepomucene Church.
Tomlinson, Brian *o.f.m.cap.* '65 (PAT) [M] Lafayette, NJ St. Francis Center.
Tompkins, John-Mary *o.s.b.* '93 (PIT) [81] Pittsburgh, PA St. Peter Church.
Tompkins, Regis C. *o.c.s.o.* '54 (ROC) [I] Piffard, NY Abbey of the Genesee.
Tompkins, Terry '82 (OAK) Danville, CA St. Isidore's Church.
Tompson, Harry W. *s.j.* '67 (NO) [11] New Orleans, LA Immaculate Conception Church.
Tomsmeire, Sidney A. *s.j.* '43 (MOB) [B] Mobile, AL Spring Hill College.
Tomzik, Fred W. '84 (CHI) [56] Chicago, IL St. Eugene Church.
Ton, Anthony '66 (SEA) [2] Vancouver, WA St. James Church.
Tonary, David *m.s.f.* '81 (CC) [15] Corpus Christi, TX St. Joseph Church; [B] Corpus Christi, TX Corpus Christi Academy Middle School.
Tonelli, Robert F. '72 (CHI) Streamwood, IL St. John the Evangelist Church.
Tonelotto, Walter *c.s.* (NY) [DD] New York, NY Italian Seamen's Club, The; [DD] New York, NY Friends of RADIO MARIA, Inc.
Toner, Donald *c.s.s.* '62 (BO) [W] Waltham, MA Stigmatine Fathers & Brothers Provincial House.
Toner, Edward R. '52 (COV) Retired.
Toner, Msgr. Francis X. '55 (NY) [132] Bronx, NY St. Barnabas Church.
Toner, John G. *m.s.* '44 (HRT) [M] Hartford, CT Missionaries of LaSalette Provincial Secretary.
Toner, Jules J. *s.j.* '45 (DET) [P] Bloomfield Hills, MI Manresa Jesuit Retreat House.
Toner, Oliver *o.carm.* '71 (VEN) [2] Fort Myers, FL Church Of The Resurrection Of Our Lord.
Toner, Patrick '75 (COL) Newark, OH St. Francis de Sales Church.
Toner, Raphael F. *s.t.* '41 (TUC) [2] Tucson, AZ Blessed Kateri Tekakwitha Church.
Tong, Joseph Lien Thien '69 (DAL) [25] Dallas, TX St. Pius X Church.
Tongotani, Celestin *c.i.c.m.* '96 (SAT) [15] San Antonio, TX Our Lady of Good Counsel Church.
Tonne, Msgr. Arthur '32 (WCH) Retired.
Tonos, Habeeb Joseph, II '94 (JKS) [3] Jackson, MS St. Richard Church.
Tonry, Patrick J. *s.m.* '65 (BAL) Sykesville, MD St. Joseph Church.
Toof, Daniel '94 (ATL) Alpharetta, GA St. Thomas Aquinas Church.
Toohey, Jerome (BAL) Unassigned.
Toohey, Mark F. *s.j.* '90 (SFR) [E] San Francisco, CA St. Ignatius College Preparatory (Coed); [N] San Francisco, CA Jesuit Community at St. Ignatius College Preparatory.
Toohey, Thomas F. '42 (HRT) Retired.
Toohey, Timothy J. '65 (STL) Washington, MO St. John's Hospital; [K] Washington, MO St. John's Mercy Hospital.
Toohig, Timothy E. *s.j.* '65 (BGP) [A] Fairfield, CT Fairfield University; [O] Fairfield, CT The Fairfield Jesuit Community-Fairfield University.
Toohy, Msgr. William J. '61 (NY) [18] New York, NY Blessed Sacrament Church; [I] New York, NY The Catholic Charities of the Archdiocese of New York; [I] New York, NY The Catholic Charities of the Archdiocese of New York; [I] New York, NY The Catholic Charities of the Archdiocese of New York; [I] New York, NY The Catholic Charities of the Archdiocese of New York.
Toolan, David S. *s.j.* '67 (NY) [Z] New York, NY West Side Jesuit Community.
Toolan, John A. *c.s.v.* '43 (CHI) [N] Arlington Heights, IL Viatorian Province Center-Clerics of St. Viator.
Toole, Arthur A. '58 (ALB) Voorheesville, NY St. Matthew Church.
Toole, Lawrence E. '67 (PRO) Westerly, RI St. Pius X Church.
Toolis, Martin '70 (GR) Retired.
Tooman, Robert '77 (NEW) [27] Newark, NJ Our Lady of Good Counsel Church.
Toomey, Charles B. *s.j.* '41 (BO) [W] Chestnut Hill, MA The Jesuit Community at Boston College.
Toomey, Gregory *o.f.m.* '48 (PAT) [M] Ringwood, NJ Holy Name Friary.
Toomey, John M. '61 (BO) [38] Boston, MA St. Joseph Church.
Toomey, Kevin G. '78 (BO) [4] Somerville, MA St. Catherine of Genoa Church.

Toomey, Msgr. Leonard R. '48 (TR) Allentown, NJ St. John Church; Retired.
Toomey, Thomas *o.s.b.* '50 (PAT) [M] Clifton, NJ Holy Face of Jesus Monastery.
Toonen, Harvey H. *o.praem.* '41 (GB) [17] Green Bay, WI St. Willebrord Church; [I] De Pere, WI St. Joseph Priory.
Topel, L. John *s.j.* '65 (SEA) [A] Seattle, WA Seattle University.
Topf, Thomas J. '63 (SC) Fort Dodge, IA Holy Rosary Church.
Topmoeller, William G. *s.j.* '52 (CIN) [M] Cincinnati, OH Faber Jesuit Community.
Topper, Charles J. '68 (HBG) On Duty Outside the Diocese.
Topper, Charles J. '68 (HRT) [C] West Hartford, CT Saint Joseph College.
Topper, John M. *o.s.m.* '87 (CHI) [N] Chicago, IL Servite Friars - Eastern Province.
Topper, John M. *o.s.m.* '87 (P) [L] Portland, OR The Grotto, The National Sanctuary of Our Sorrowful Mother.
Topper, Msgr. Vincent J. '36 (HBG) Retired; [G] Lebanon, PA Villa Vianney.
Topping, Msgr. Joseph '47 (SD) Retired.
Torborg, Elmer J. '55 (SCL) Duelm, MN St. Lawrence's Church; Sauk Rapids, MN St. Patrick Church.
Torgerson, Msgr. Lloyd A. '65 (LA) Santa Monica, CA St. Monica Church.
Torina, Ronald F. *s.j.* '76 (TOL) [C] Toledo, OH St. John's Jesuit High School.
Torm, Agustin '93 (CHR) Military Chaplains.
Torma, Andrew *m.s.c.* '76 (Y) [A] Youngstown, OH Sacred Heart Retreat House & Renewal Center; [N] Youngstown, OH Sacred Heart Retreat and Renewal Center.
Tormey, Daniel '55 (ROC) Retired.
Tormey, James D. '78 (SY) [12] Binghamton, NY St. Thomas Aquinas Church.
Tornes, Dale F. '70 (STU) Belle Valley, OH Corpus Christi Church; Caldwell, OH St. Stephen Church.
Torney, Msgr. John R. '39 (MET) Retired; [H] Somerset, NJ Maria Regina Residence.
Toro, Emilio '60 (SJN) Luquillo, PR San Jose Church.
Torok, Bela E. '43 (SAG) Retired.
Torok, Delso '48 (Y) East Palestine, OH Our Lady of Lourdes Church.
Torok, Dezso '48 (Y) Retired.
Torok, George J. '58 (NY) [DD] Sparkill, NY Hallel Institute.
Torpey, Charles L. '69 (GI) Kearney, NE St. James Church.
Torpey, James M. '83 (ALN) Whitehall, PA St. Elizabeth Church.
Torpey, Matt G. *o.c.s.o.* '56 (ATL) [I] Conyers, GA The Monastery of the Holy Spirit.
Torpey, Michael J. '68 (RVC) Sea Cliff, NY St. Boniface Martyr Church.
Torquato, James R. (PIT) Glenshaw, PA St. Bonaventure Church.
Torralba, Antolin B. '48 (LA) Santa Fe Springs, CA St. Pius X Church.
Torralba, Julio *sch.p.* '58 (PCE) [C] Coto Laurel, PR Colegio Ponceno.
Torre, Emilio Diaz *l.c.* '93 (HRT) [V] Orange, CT Legion of Christ, Inc.
Torre, Jesse *o.f.m.cap.* '61 (DAL) [8] Dallas, TX Our Lady of Lourdes Church.
Torrelas, Eduardo '85 (CGS) [C] Humacao, PR San Antonio Abad Abbey of the Order of St. Benedict.
Torrente, Lorenzo T. '75 (RNO) Battle Mountain, NV St. John Bosco Church.
Torres, Adrian '75 (PMB) [5] West Palm Beach, FL St. Juliana Church.
Torres, Daniel A. '96 (LKC) [8] Lake Charles, LA Our Lady Queen of Heaven Church.
Torres, E. Fernando (R) Lumberton, NC St. Francis De Sales Church.
Torres, Ernesto '72 (DAL) [13] Dallas, TX St. Augustine Church.
Torres, Fernado *sch.p.* '93 (PCE) [C] Coto Laurel, PR Colegio Ponceno.
Torres, Frank D. '94 (GRY) [11] East Chicago, IN St. Mary Church.
Torres, Gabriel M. '95 (ARE) Ciales, PR Holy Rosary Church.
Torres, Hipolito '85 (CGS) Naranjito, PR San Miguel Arcangel Church.
Torres, Ivan '88 (BUF) [29] Buffalo, NY Holy Cross Church.
Torres, Ivan '89 (SJN) On Duty Outside the Archdiocese.
Torres, Luis Angel '85 (SJN) [17] Carolina, PR Santisima Trinidad Church.
Torres, Mario A. '96 (LA) Huntington Park, CA St. Matthias Church.
Torres, Martin Betances '87 (NY) [96] New York, NY Our Lady of the Rosary Church.
Torres, Orlando *s.j.* '73 (SJN) [B] Rio Piedras, PR Jesuit Novitiate.
Torres, Pablo *c.m.* '88 (SJN) [55] San Juan, PR Sagrado Corazon de Jesus Church.
Torres, Robert A. '66 (LR) Retired.
Torres, Ruben M. *o.s.m.* '89 (ELP) [18] El Paso, TX Our Lady of Sorrows Church.
Torres, William '90 (SJN) [11] Bayamon, PR San Miguel Arcangel Church.
Torretto, Joseph '75 (RIC) Charlottesville, VA Church of the Holy Comforter.
Torrez, Basil '56 (SAL) Collyer, KS St. Michael's Church; St. Peter, KS St. Anthony's Church.
Torsiello, Ralph C. '58 (WDC) Gaithersburg, MD St. John Neumann Church.
Torson, Daniel *c.pp.s.* '90 (KC) [B] Kansas City, MO Avila College; [N] Kansas City, MO Avila College Campus Ministry.
Tortora, James F. '72 (NEW) [8] Bayonne, NJ St. Michael's Church.
Tortora, Raymond (RVC) Retired.
Tortorelli, Kevin *o.f.m.* '73 (NY) [35] New York, NY St. Francis of Assisi Church.
Tortorici, James D. '95 (PH) Yardley, PA St. Ignatius of Antioch Church.
Tortorici, Joseph *o.p.* '72 (WDC) [B] Washington, DC Dominican House of Studies.
Tos, Aldo J. '53 (NY) [61] New York, NY St. Joseph Church.
Tosatto, Lawrence *f.d.p.* '65 (BO) [U] Boston, MA Don Orione Nursing Home.
Toscani, Peter J. *o.s.a.* '47 (PH) [111] Philadelphia, PA St. Nicholas of Tolentine Church; [Z] Philadelphia, PA Augustinian Community (O.S.A.).
Toscano, Eduardo '73 (SJN) [18] Carolina, PR Cristo Rey Church.
Toscano, Pasquale A. '44 (HRT) Retired.
Toschi, Larry *o.s.j.* '76 (MRY) Santa Cruz, CA Shrine of St. Joseph Guardian of the Redeemer Church; [G] Santa Cruz, CA Oblates of St. Joseph Provincial House and Shrine.
Tosco, Lawrence *c.s.j.* '70 (CLV) [P] Avon, OH Congregation of St. Joseph.
Tosco, Lorenzo *c.s.j.* '70 (CLV) [A] Wickliffe, OH St. Mary Seminary.
Tosello, Matthew '62 (PIT) Prospect, PA St. Christopher Church.
Tosi, John C. '73 (BRK) [1] Brooklyn, NY The Cathedral-Basilica of St. James; [Y] Brooklyn, NY St. James Cathedral Foundation, Inc.
Tosti, Anthony F. '65 (SY) Canastota, NY St. Agatha Church.
Tosti, Ronald A. '62 (FR) Mashpee, MA Christ The King Church.
Totah, Sami '71 (NY) [9] Yonkers, NY Immaculate Conception Church; [9] Yonkers, NY Immaculate Conception Church.
Toth, Joseph A. '83 (PH) Downingtown, PA St. Joseph Church.
Toth, Julius *o.f.m.conv.* '53 (TR) Riverside, NJ St. Peter Church.
Toth, Michael A. '74 (OG) Mineville, NY The Church of All Saints; Westport, NY St. Philip Neri Church.
Toth, Simon J. *o.s.b.* '59 (GBG) [5] Latrobe, PA St. Boniface Church; [H] Latrobe, PA Saint Vincent Archabbey.
Toth, Victor '48 (HT) Retired.
Totten, Raymond F. '48 (COL) Retired.
Tottle, Gregg '91 (SP) Safety Harbor, FL Espiritu Santo Church.
Tou, John '57 (NY) On Duty Outside the Archdiocese.
Tou, Louis A. '56 (WDC) Hospital & Nursing Home Ministries; [K] Silver Spring, MD Holy Cross Hospital of Silver Spring, Inc.
Touchette, Marc L. '57 (ALB) [2] Cohoes, NY St. Bernard Church.
Tougas, Paul J. '64 (WOR) Boylston, MA St. Mary of the Hills Church.
Tougas, Roger *a.a.* '60 (BO) [W] Brighton, MA Assumptionist Center.
Toulas, James J. *c.ss.r.* '54 (BRK) [C] Whitestone, NY St. Alphonsus Formation Residence.
Toups, Earl *c.ss.r.* '48 (BLX) [E] Biloxi, MS St. John Neumann Residence.
Tourangeau, John M. '86 (SFE) Ranchos De Taos, NM San Francisco de Asis Church.
Tourigney, Ernest E. '61 (BO) Absent on Sick Leave.
Tourigny, William A. '80 (SPR) [15] Springfield, MA St. Joseph's Church.
Tourneir, Msgr. Andre (SFR) [K] San Rafael, CA Nazareth House.
Tournier, Msgr. Andre '48 (SR) Retired.
Tovar, Emilio *c.m.* '50 (ARE) [1] Manati, PR La Candelaria Church.
Toven, Ronald D. '74 (E) On Leave of Absence.
Towell, Stephen A. '33 (CLV) South Euclid, OH St. Gregory the Great Church; Retired.
Towey, Cyprian *c.p.* '42 (LA) [R] Pasadena, CA Passionist Community.
Towey, Damian *c.p.* '58 (PMB) [G] North Palm Beach, FL Our Lady of Florida Spiritual Center.
Towle, Joseph C. *s.j.* '66 (NY) [Z] New York, NY Jesuit Provincial's Office.
Towle, Joseph W. *m.m.* '65 (NY) [Z] Maryknoll, NY Maryknoll Fathers and Brothers.
Townsend, C. Frederick '83 (KC) Leave of Absence.
Townsend, Charles P. '91 (LIN) Mead, NE St. James Church.
Townsend, Joe C. '88 (TLS) Stillwater, OK St. John University Parish and Catholic Student Center Church; [I] Stillwater, OK St. John's University Parish and Catholic Student Center.
Townsend, Ralph V. *o.p.* '50 (PH) [61] Philadelphia, PA Holy Name of Jesus Church; [Z] Philadelphia, PA Holy Name Priory, Dominican Friars.
Towsley, Peter J. '91 (BGP) [5] Fairfield, CT Holy Family Church.
Toye, D. Richard *s.j.* '65 (GAL) [F] Houston, TX Strake, Jesuit College Preparatory Inc.
Tra, John *s.v.d.* '44 (DUB) [B] Epworth, IA Divine Word College.
Trabold, Alphonsus A. *o.f.m.* '51 (BUF) [O] St. Bonaventure, NY St. Bonaventure Friary.
Trabold, Msgr. George R. '73 (NEW) Bergenfield, NJ St. John the Evangelist Church.
Trac, Peter Vu Dinh '54 (ORG) [2] Orange, CA La Purisima Church.
Tracey, Bernard M. *c.m.* '74 (BRK) [D] Queens and Staten Island, NY St. John's University; [U] Jamaica, NY St. Vincent's House.
Tracey, Joseph A. (PH) Cheltenham, PA Presentation of Blessed Virgin Mary Church.
Tracey, Michael J. '72 (BLX) Hattiesburg, MS St. Thomas Aquinas Church; Hattiesburg, MS University of Southern Mississippi; [G] Hattiesburg, MS University of Southern Mississippi.
Tracey, Terence '52 (SFD) Retired; [L] Springfield, IL St. Francis Convent.
Tracey, Thomas S. '63 (CAM) Blue Anchor, NJ St. Lucy's Church.
Tracy, Charles '63 (SR) Retired.
Tracy, David W. '63 (BGP) On Duty Outside the Diocese.
Tracy, Eugene '91 (SPK) [18] Spokane, WA St. Peter Church.
Tracy, George E. '84 (PRT) Retired.
Tracy, Msgr. James R. '60 (CAM) [3] Cherry Hill, NJ St. Peter Celestine Church.
Tracy, John *o.m.i.* '33 (BO) [Z] Tewksbury, MA Immaculate Heart of Mary Novitiate-Infirmary.
Tracy, John A. '52 (NEW) Retired.
Tracy, John P. '48 (HRT) [11] Hartford, CT St. Lawrence O'Toole Church; [3] West Hartford, CT St. John the Evangelist Church.
Tracy, Joseph A. '92 (PH) Graduate Studies.
Tracy, Laurence '63 (ROC) [36] Rochester, NY Our Lady of Mount Carmel Church.
Tracy, Laurence '66 (ROC) [25] Rochester, NY Holy Redeemer-St. Francis Xavier Church; [47] Rochester, NY St. Michael Church.
Tracy, Melvin *s.d.s.* '58 (GB) St. Nazianz, WI St. Gregory Church.
Tracy, Philip A. '88 (PRT) St. Francis, ME St. Charles Church; St. John, ME St. John Church.
Tracy, Philip Michael '60 (PRT) South Berwick, ME St. Michael Church.
Tracy, Robert P. *o.carm.* '63 (NY) Tarrytown, NY Transfiguration Church.
Tracy, T. Shawn *o.s.a.* '66 (PH) [C] Villanova, PA Villanova University; [Z] Villanova, PA St. John Stone Friary.
Tracy, Theodore J. *s.j.* '50 (CHI) [C] Chicago, IL Jesuit Community at Loyola University of Chicago.
Trad, John (OLL) Retired.
Trader, William A. (PH) Westtown, PA St. Maximilian Kolbe Church.
Traeger, Gregory *o.s.b.* '42 (SP) [O] St. Leo, FL St. Leo Abbey.
Traenkle, Mark *s.a.* '56 (OG) [E] Saranac Lake, NY St. Joseph's Rehabilitation Center, Inc.; [F] Saranac Lake, NY St. Joseph's Friary.
Trahan, Charles Nicholas '81 (LAF) [1] Opelousas, LA St. Landry Church.
Trahan, Harold '69 (LAF) [10] Lafayette, LA St. Elizabeth Seton Church.
Trahan, Romeo A. *s.s.e.* '45 (BUR) [G] Colchester, VT Society of St. Edmund.
Trahon, Basil *c.p.* '62 (HRT) [M] West Hartford, CT Holy Family Monastery/Retreat.
Trainer, Eugene '58 (STO) Modesto, CA Our Lady of Fatima Church.
Trainor, Daniel M. '61 (PRO) [6] Providence, RI Assumption of the Blessed Virgin Mary Church.
Trainor, Henry J. '73 (SFR) [41] San Francisco, CA St. Patrick Church; Special Assignment.
Trainor, James F. '64 (WIL) [8] Wilmington, DE St. Mary of the Immaculate Conception Church; [9] Wilmington, DE St. Patrick Church; [G] Wilmington, DE St. Patrick's House, Inc.
Trainor, James T. '44 (PRO) Retired; [P] Providence, RI St. John Vianney Residence.
Trainor, John J. *c.m.* '43 (BUF) [O] Niagara University, NY Vincentian Community at Niagara University.
Trainor, Joseph P. *m.m.* '50 (BO) [4] Brookline, MA St. Mary of the Assumption Church.

Trainor, Michael P. *o.p.* '75 (PRO) [27] Providence, RI St. Pius V Church; [P] Providence, RI St. Pius Priory.
Trainor, Msgr. Patrick '44 (SP) Retired.
Trainor, Msgr. Patrick '45 (SP) St. Pete Beach, FL St. John Church.
Trainor, Richard F. '75 (WOR) Auburn, MA St. Joseph's Church.
Trainor, Msgr. Robert M. '57 (NY) [125] Bronx, NY St. Ann Church.
Tram, Luc *s.v.d.* '96 (LA) [25] Los Angeles, CA Our Lady of Loretto Church.
Trame, Richard H. *s.j.* '52 (LA) [C] Los Angeles, CA Loyola Marymount University.
Tran, Anh Q. '90 (FWT) Breckenridge, TX Sacred Heart Church; Dodson Prairie, TX St. Boniface Church; Graford, TX St. Francis of Assisi Church; Throckmorton, TX San Patricio Church.
Tran, Anthony Doan '88 (BLX) Ocean Springs, MS St. Alphonsus Church.
Tran, Anthony Hung Ngoc *o.p.* (GAL) [56] Houston, TX Our Lady of Lavang Church.
Tran, Binh K. '92 (PEO) Ohio, IL Immaculate Conception Church.
Tran, Dac *o.f.m.* '89 (BO) [BB] Boston, MA St. Anthony Shrine.
Tran, J.B. Nuynh Ngoc '90 (GAL) [12] Houston, TX St. Augustine Church.
Tran, John '95 (NY) [127] Bronx, NY St. Anthony Church.
Tran, John Chinh Chan (GAL) Retired.
Tran, John Kha '89 (GAL) [A] Houston, TX St. Mary's Seminary.
Tran, John-Hue *s.v.d.* '95 (DUB) [B] Epworth, IA Divine Word College.
Tran, Joseph '74 (LAN) [1] Lansing, MI St. Mary Cathedral.
Tran, Joseph '95 (NY) [168] Bronx, NY St. Nicholas of Tolentine Church.
Tran, Joseph Thang Dinh '96 (NO) [31] New Orleans, LA St. Frances Xavier Cabrini Church.
Tran, Kiem Van '91 (ORG) [7] Santa Ana, CA St. Barbara's Church.
Tran, Liem *o.p.* '93 (WDC) [B] Washington, DC Dominican House of Studies.
Tran, Luan '94 (P) [1] Portland, OR Cathedral of the Immaculate Conception.
Tran, Luong Quang '89 (BEA) Nederland, TX St. Charles Borromeo Church; [G] Beaumont, TX St. Thomas More Society of Southeast Texas.
Tran, Martin Duc '90 (BAL) [M] Baltimore, MD Sulpician Provincial House.
Tran, Michael Mai *c.m.c.* '94 (ALB) [15] Albany, NY Sacred Heart of Jesus Church.
Tran, Michael X. '93 (SD) [4] Chula Vista, CA St. Rose of Lima Church.
Tran, Paul (SFE) [18] Albuquerque, NM San Jose Church.
Tran, Paul *o.p.* '86 (PHX) [5] Phoenix, AZ Most Holy Trinity Church; [5] Phoenix, AZ Most Holy Trinity Church.
Tran, Peter '73 (RIC) [2] Newport News, VA Our Lady of Mount Carmel Church.
Tran, Peter Nam Van '84 (NO) [14] New Orleans, LA Mary, Queen of Vietnam Church.
Tran, Philip '92 (NY) [6] Poughkeepsie, NY St. Martin de Porres Church.
Tran, Phuong Duc '65 (SEA) [Q] Seattle, WA Seattle, Vietnamese Catholic Center.
Tran, Quan '96 (PH) Exton, PA SS. Philip and James Church.
Tran, Quynh Dinh '93 (WOR) [21] Worcester, MA St. Charles Borromeo Church.
Tran, Sang V. '92 (LA) Sepulveda, CA Our Lady of Peace Church.
Tran, Tan Van '92 (DM) Bayard, IA St. Patrick Church.
Tran, Tan Van '96 (DM) [12] Des Moines, IA St. Theresa of the Child Jesus Church.
Tran Cao Tuong, Andrew '75 (NO) [2] Marrero, LA St. Agnes Le Thi Thanh Church.
Tran Dien, Peter (SPC) [E] Carthage, MO Congregation of the Mother Co-Redemptrix, United States Assumption Province.
Tran Ngoc Diep, Joseph M. *c.m.c.* '83 (SPC) [E] Carthage, MO Congregation of the Mother Co-Redemptrix, United States Assumption Province.
Tran Ngoc Thoai, Aloysius *c.m.c.* '92 (AMA) [5] Amarillo, TX Our Lady of Vietnam Church.
Tran Van Dong, Alphonsus '63 (BGP) [1] Bridgeport, CT St. Augustine Cathedral.
Tran Van Phat, Peter '67 (NY) Mamaroneck, NY St. Vito Church; Nanuet, NY St. Anthony Church.
Tran-cong-Ly, Hilary M. *c.m.c.* '77 (FWT) [5] Arlington, TX St. Matthew Church.
Tran-Khac-Hy, Hilarius '57 (WDC) Retired.
Trance, F. Raymond '94 (PIT) Bethel Park, PA St. Valentine Church.
Tranchida, Blaise *o.f.m.* '50 (NY) [Z] New York, NY Franciscan Province of the Immaculate Conception.
Tranchina, Joseph '68 (NO) Retired.
Trancone, Gerard A. '69 (WDC) Special Ministries; [S] Washington, DC Archdiocesan Campus Ministry; [V] Landover Hills, MD Catholic Deaf Center.
Tranel, Daniel D. '56 (RCK) Galena, IL St. Mary Church; Galena, IL St. Michael Church.
Tranel, Don *glmy.* '88 (WH) Spencer, WV Holy Redeemer Church.
Tranel, Dorrance E. '49 (RCK) Wonder Lake, IL Christ the King Church.
Trant, John P. '44 (LC) Retired.
Trapani, Anthony (RVC) Priests Released from Diocesan Assignment.
Trapasso, Msgr. Thomas J. '49 (PAT) Netcong, NJ St. Michael's Church.
Trapini, Anthony '73 (RVC) Military Chaplains.
Trapold, John T. '60 (WDC) Retired.
Trapp, Arthur L. *c.m.* '56 (STL) [P] Perryville, MO Congregation of The Mission.
Trapp, Daniel J. '84 (DET) [12] Detroit, MI St. Augustine and St. Monica Church; [A] Detroit, MI Sacred Heart Major Seminary, Inc.
Trapp, Joseph John, II '96 (COL) [8] Columbus, OH St. Catharine Church.
Trapp, Joseph L. '59 (BEL) Elizabethtown, IL St. Joseph Church; Metropolis, IL St. Rose of Lima Church.
Trapp, Raymond A. '37 (CLV) Retired.
Traser, Anthony *c.pp.s.* '40 (CIN) [B] Carthagena, OH St. Charles.
Trask, David R. (CLV) North Ridgeville, OH St. Peter Church.
Traub, George W. *s.j.* '67 (CIN) [P] Milford, OH Milford Spiritual Center.
Traub, Henry W. *s.j.* '66 (NY) [Z] New York, NY Jesuit Provincial's Office.
Traub, Robert L. '39 (FTW) [9] Fort Wayne, IN St. Jude Church.
Traudt, Robert *o.carm.* '82 (NEW) Leonia, NJ St. John the Evangelist's Church.
Traufler, John F. '57 (WIN) Winnebago, MN St. Mary's Church.
Trauger, Francis X. '72 (PH) Levittown, PA St. Michael the Archangel Church.
Traupman, Robert '69 (ORL) On Duty Outside the Diocese.
Trausch, Dennis '78 (DM) Carter Lake, IA Our Lady of Carter Lake Church; [C] Council Bluffs, IA Bergan Mercy Health System: Mercy Hospital.
Trautner, Kevin C. '74 (PH) [2] Norristown, PA St. Francis of Assisi Church.
Travaglione, Michael *o.f.m.* '66 (NY) [Z] New York, NY Franciscan Province of the Immaculate Conception.
Travassos, Horace J. '73 (FR) [1] Fall River, MA Cathedral of St. Mary of the Assumption.
Travers, Alan F. (NY) Yorktown Heights, NY St. Patrick Church.
Travers, David O. *s.j.* '68 (BO) [W] Boston, MA The Society of Jesus of New England-Provincial Offices.
Travers, David O. *s.s.* '68 (HON) [17] Honolulu, HI Saints Peter and Paul Church.
Travers, Gerard P. '65 (NY) Highland Mills, NY St. Patrick Church.
Travers, John J. *c.ss.r.* '59 (BRK) [107] Brooklyn, NY Our Lady of Perpetual Help Basilica.
Travers, Joseph A. *o.s.f.s.* '48 (CAM) [L] Pittsgrove, NJ Villa St. Joseph.
Travers, Luke *o.s.b.* '67 (PAT) [D] Morristown, NJ Delbarton School.
Travers, Luke L. *o.s.b.* '86 (PAT) [M] Morristown, NJ St. Mary's Abbey.
Travers, Patrick *ss.cc.* '62 (LA) [D] La Verne, CA Damien Boys High School; [R] La Verne, CA Congregation of the Sacred Hearts.
Travers, William *o.carm.* '45 (JOL) [J] Darien, IL Carmelite Fathers Provincial Office.
Traverso, Leonard '72 (SJ) San Jose, CA Notre Dame Villa; Saratoga, CA Our Lady of Fatima Villa; [I] Saratoga, CA Our Lady of Fatima Villa.
Travieso, Ernesto *s.j.* '73 (OM) [K] Omaha, NE Jesuit Community At Creighton University.
Travis, Francis J. '81 (CHR) Pickens, SC Holy Cross Church.
Travis, Herbert A. '42 (BRK) [10] Brooklyn, NY St. Anselm's Church; Retired.
Travis, Terrence A. '69 (STU) Absent on Leave.
Travnikar, Rick *o.f.m.* (IND) Oldenburg, IN Holy Family Church.
Travnikar, Rock *o.f.m.* (CIN) [M] Cincinnati, OH St. Francis Seraph Friary.
Trawick, Gregory '85 (OWN) Madisonville, KY Christ the King Church.
Trawinski, Joseph *o.f.m.conv.* '40 (BUF) [21] Buffalo, NY Corpus Christi Church.
Traxl, William L. '60 (HRT) Oakville, CT St. Mary Magdalen Church.
Trayers, Kevin '52 (WCH) Cherryvale, KS St. Francis Xavier's Church; Independence, KS St. Andrew Church.
Traylor, William A. '76 (EVN) On Duty Outside the Diocese.
Traynor, Anthony '58 (SAC) [6] Sacramento, CA Our Lady of Lourdes Church; Special Assignment.
Traynor, John '45 (RVC) Retired.
Traynor, Joseph P. '82 (GBG) Clymer, PA Church of the Resurrection.
Traynor, Patrick *c.s.p.* '68 (NY) [41] New York, NY Good Shepherd Church.
Traynor, Vincent dePaul *o.s.b.* '43 (OKL) Walters, OK St. Patrick Church; [I] Shawnee, OK St. Gregory's Abbey.
Treacy, Canice '52 (WDC) Olney, MD St. Peter Church; Retired.
Treacy, Jerome F. '61 (DET) [P] Clarkston, MI Colombiere Center.
Treacy, John R. *s.j.* '90 (SFR) [2] San Francisco, CA St. Agnes Church.
Treacy, William '44 (SEA) Retired.
Treanor, Boniface J. *o.s.b.* '56 (NEW) [N] Newark, NJ Newark Abbey.
Trebtoske, Everett (AUS) Wimberley, TX St. Mary Church.
Trejo, Ramario *o.f.m.cap.* '77 (AMA) Wellington, TX Our Mother of Mercy Church.
Trejo, Ramiro *o.f.m.cap.* '77 (AMA) Memphis, TX Sacred Heart Church.
Trela, Norman J. '42 (CHI) Brookfield, IL St. Barbara Church.
Trela, Tadeusz '82 (NEW) [19] Jersey City, NJ Our Lady of Czestochowa Church.
Treleaven, Michael *s.j.* '83 (SPK) [C] Spokane, WA Gonzaga University.
Treloar, John L. *s.j.* '70 (MIL) [P] Milwaukee, WI Arrupe House Jesuit Community.
Tremantozzi, Paul *o.c.d.* '55 (BO) [W] Brighton, MA Carmelite Monastery.
Tremblay, Eugene *o.m.i.* '74 (BUF) [27] Buffalo, NY Holy Angels Church.
Tremblay, J. Normand '53 (WOR) Charlton City, MA St. Joseph's Church.
Tremblay, Jean A. (MAN) Retired.
Tremblay, Leger '48 (SHP) Retired.
Tremblay, Marc P. '80 (FR) Somerset, MA St. Patrick's Church.
Tremblay, Nellis J. '54 (ALB) Warrensburg, NY St. Cecilia Church.
Tremie, Eugene R. '71 (LAF) Rayne, LA St. Joseph Church.
Tremmel, Benjamin *o.s.b.* '66 (KCK) [H] Atchison, KS St. Benedict's Abbey.
Tremmel, Michael B. '78 (TOL) Absent on Leave.
Tremonte, Pasquale T. *c.ss.r.* '81 (HBG) [H] Ephrata, PA St. Clement's Mission House.
Tremonti, Joseph B. '41 (CHI) [N] Arlington Heights, IL Viatorian Province Center-Clerics of St. Viator.
Trempe, James F. '96 (LC) [6] Eau Claire, WI St. Patrick Church; [D] Eau Claire, WI Eau Claire Coordinated Catholic Schools.
Trench, Msgr. Edmond J. '57 (RVC) Southampton, NY Sacred Hearts of Jesus and Mary Church.
Trenchard, Dawson D. '58 (HRT) Wallingford, CT Resurrection Church.
Trenchera, Manuel '80 (AGN) Malojlo, GU San Isidro Church.
Trenier, Anthony S. '66 (MIL) Retired; [Y] Milwaukee, WI Archdiocesan Marian Shrine.
Trenor, Msgr. Edward F. '58 (COL) [10] Columbus, OH Christ the King Church.
Trent, James F. '62 (DET) On Duty Outside the Archdiocese.
Trepanier, James *c.s.c.* '55 (FTW) [A] Notre Dame, IN Moreau Seminary.
Trepanier, Thomas A. '75 (MIL) [4] South Milwaukee, WI St. Sylvester's Church.
Trepanier, Thomas J. '64 (PRO) [16] Providence, RI Holy Name Church.
Treppa, Terence F. '67 (DET) Washington, MI SS. John and Paul Church.
Trese, John A. '48 (DET) [1] Birmingham, MI St. Columban Church.
Tresler, Carl D. '91 (LA) La Puente, CA St. Joseph Church.
Tresnak, Anthony J. '60 (OM) Retired.
Tressic, David L. '96 (ALB) Latham, NY Our Lady of the Assumption Church.
Tressler, Carl '91 (LA) [35] Los Angeles, CA Resurrection Church.
Tressler, David L. '85 (SCR) [4] Hazleton, PA Holy Trinity Church; [D] Hazleton, PA Bishop Hafey Junior/Senior High School.
Tressler, Robert '80 (ORG) Inactive Leave.
Treston, Msgr. James A. '60 (ALN) Sinking Spring, PA St. Ignatius Loyola Church.
Treston, Kevin *o.f.m.* '81 (WDC) [M] Washington, DC Commissariat of the Holy Land, Franciscan Monastery - Mount St. Sepulchre.
Trettel, Efrem *o.f.m.* '44 (SFR) [43] San Francisco, CA St. Paul of the Shipwreck Church.
Treu, Stanislaus K. *o.s.a.* '37 (NY) [Z] New York, NY Our Lady of Consolation Residence; [Z] New York, NY Our Lady of Consolation Residence.
Trevett, Msgr. Cyril I. '48 (BUF) [P] Orchard Park, NY Sisters of Mercy-Regional Community Offices.
Trevino, Alberto T., Jr. *m.s.f.* '84 (SAT) [B] San Antonio, TX MSF Formation Community.

Trevino, Richard *c.m.f.* '42 (SAT) [12] San Antonio, TX Immaculate Heart of Mary Church.
Trevizo, Raul P. '88 (TUC) [14] Tucson, AZ St. John the Evangelist Church.
Treyes, Reynaldo B. (CHI) Orland Park, IL St. Michael Church.
Trezza, Richard *o.f.m.* '87 (NEW) Wood-Ridge, NJ Our Lady of the Assumption Church.
Trezza, Richard *o.f.m.* '87 (NY) [48] New York, NY Holy Name of Jesus Church.
Tria, Celsus *c.m.* '81 (NY) [17] New York, NY St. Bernard Church.
Triano, Joseph A. *s.s.p.* '59 (DET) [K] Detroit, MI Society of St. Paul.
Triatmoko, Benedict *s.j.* '94 (BO) [W] Chestnut Hill, MA The Jesuit Community at Boston College.
Tribou, George W. '49 (LR) [B] Little Rock, AR Catholic High School.
Tribuiani, Raymond F. '73 (PH) Oreland, PA Holy Martyrs Church.
Tribunal, Hien Nguyen '57 (SJ) Special Assignment.
Trieu Ngoc Le, '58 (PIT) Verona, PA St. Joseph Church.
Triggs, Thomas J. '75 (TR) Cinnaminson, NJ St. Charles Borromeo Church.
Trigilio, John, Jr. '88 (HBG) Hershey, PA St. Joan of Arc Church.
Trigueros, Raul '69 (ELP) [7] El Paso, TX Cristo Rey Church.
Trimaglio, John *c.s.j.* '68 (LA) San Pedro, CA St. Peter Church; [R] Los Angeles, CA Congregation of St. Joseph Casa Nazareth.
Trimboli, Frank T. (KCK) [G] Kansas City, KS St. Joseph Care Center.
Trimbur, Edwin H. '51 (COV) Retired.
Trimbur, John S. '74 (Y) Campbell, OH St. John the Baptist Church.
Trimbur, Lee Francis '54 (LEX) Retired.
Trinchard, Paul '66 (NO) Retired.
Trindad, Mel *s.d.b.* '86 (OAK) [E] Richmond, CA Salesian High School.
Trindade, Leonard J. '95 (FRS) [4] Bakersfield, CA St. Francis Church.
Tringhese, James D. '74 (GBG) Trafford, PA St. Regis Church.
Trinh, Joseph T. '91 (PH) [11] Philadelphia, PA St. Anne Church; [156] Philadelphia, PA Visitation B.V.M. Church.
Trinh, Loc '92 (GR) [17] Grand Rapids, MI St. Mary Magdalen Church.
Trinh, Paul Hao '90 (CAM) Swedesboro, NJ St. Joseph's Church.
Trinh, Thai Q. '90 (SJ) San Jose, CA Alexian Brothers Hospital; [H] San Jose, CA Alexian Brothers Hospital.
Trinidad, Nelson '86 (LA) [33] Los Angeles, CA Precious Blood Church; Altadena, CA St. Elizabeth of Hungary Church.
Trinity, Msgr. Bernard J. '54 (PH) Southampton, PA Our Lady of Good Counsel Church.
Trinka, Joseph C. '59 (SUP) Clear Lake, WI St. John Church; Stanton, WI St. Bridget Church.
Trinkle, Clarence M. '92 (ARL) Culpeper, VA Precious Blood Church.
Trinkle, Donald F. '63 (CAM) [3] Cherry Hill, NJ St. Peter Celestine Church.
Tripi, Ronald R. *c.s.c.* '62 (FTW) [18] South Bend, IN St. Stanislaus Church.
Tripodi, Frank J. '88 (RCK) Absent on Leave.
Tripole, Martin R. *s.j.* '67 (PH) [C] Philadelphia, PA St. Joseph's University; [Z] Philadelphia, PA Jesuit Community at St. Joseph's University.
Tripp, Kevin F. '68 (FR) Absent on Leave.
Trippel, Jack '95 (LFT) Kokomo, IN St. Patrick Church.
Trisco, Msgr. Robert F. '54 (CHI) On Duty Outside the Archdiocese.
Trisco, Robert F. '54 (WDC) [C] Washington, DC Catholic University of America, The.
Trivison, Louis J. '48 (CLV) Retired.
Troche, Sigfried *m.ss.cc.* (CAM) [L] Linwood, NJ Villa Pieta.
Trocinski, LaVern E. '60 (WIN) [2] Rochester, MN Pax Christi Church.
Troha, Michael J. '80 (CLV) [34] Cleveland, OH Immaculate Conception Church.
Troiano, Leonard '79 (TR) [21] Trenton, NJ St. Raphael Church.
Troiano, Louis *o.f.m.* '57 (NY) [79] New York, NY Most Precious Blood Church.
Trojan, Columban *o.s.b.* (JOL) [J] Lisle, IL St. Procopius Abbey.
Trojanowski, Myroslav '87 (STF) Yonkers, NY St. Michael Church.
Trojcak, Ronald '62 (SFD) On Duty Outside the Diocese.
Troman, Richard (SPK) [B] Spokane, WA Mater Dei Institute.
Trombetta, Paul N. '79 (BRK) Released from Diocesan Assignment.
Trombley, Edward '50 (SAG) [F] Saginaw, MI St. Francis Nursing Home.
Trombley, J. Edward '50 (SAG) Retired.
Trombley, Joseph P. '65 (OG) Bloomingdale, NY St. Paul Church; Gabriels, NY Gabriel's Correctional Facility; [G] Ellenburg Center, NY Our Lady of the Adirondack's Inc. House of Prayer, Franciscan Sisters of the Atonement.
Trompeter, Arthur J. '33 (KCK) [7] Topeka, KS St. Joseph's Church.
Troncale, F. Charles '65 (MOB) Prattville, AL St. Joseph Church.
Trong, John T.B. '71 (ARL) [5] Arlington, VA Holy Martyrs of Vietnam Church.
Trong, Joseph '46 (SB) Retired.
Trongo, Nicholas '67 (GBG) Mount Pleasant, PA Visitation of the Blessed Virgin Mary Church; Connellsville, PA Highlands Hospital & Health Center; Mount Pleasant, PA Frick Community Health Center.
Trosch, David (MOB) On Leave from the Archdiocese.
Troska, Llewelyn J. '86 (CR) Leave of Absence.
Trosley, Anthony J. '78 (PEO) Oglesby, IL Holy Family Church.
Trott, William A. '57 (ROC) Livonia, NY St. Joseph Church.
Trotta, Louis P. *c.m.* '52 (BUF) [C] Niagara University, NY Niagara University; [O] Niagara University, NY Vincentian Community at Niagara University.
Trout, Richard W. '85 (ORL) Sanford, FL All Souls Church; Special Assignment.
Troutman, Richard E. '68 (TUC) [18] Tucson, AZ Saint Odilia Church.
Trovato, Joseph A. *c.s.b.* '56 (ROC) [13] Rochester, NY Christ the King Church.
Troxell, Christopher '92 (LA) Panorama City, CA St. Genevieve Church.
Troy, Gabriel '66 (BO) [70] Boston, MA St. Stephen Church; Society of St. James the Apostle; [W] Boston, MA The Society of St. James the Apostle, Inc.
Troy, Henry A. '41 (CHI) Retired.
Troy, Joseph F. *c.s.p.* '34 (NY) [104] New York, NY St. Paul the Apostle Church; [Z] Scarsdale, NY Paulist Fathers Generalate.
Troy, Leander *o.carm.* '42 (CHI) [D] Chicago, IL Mt. Carmel High School; [N] Chicago, IL Carmelite Priory of St. Cyril.
Troy, Thomas B. '73 (PH) Ambler, PA St. Anthony of Padua Church.
Troyan, Daniel '82 (PHU) Centralia, PA Assumption of B.V.M. Church; Mount Carmel, PA SS. Peter and Paul Church.
Trucksis, Frederick '64 (Y) Absent on Leave.
Trudeau, Marc V. '91 (LA) Pasadena, CA St. Philip the Apostle Church.
Trudel, Lionel G. *m.m.* '56 (NY) Kingston, NY Benedictine Hospital; [S] Kingston, NY Benedictine Hospital; [Z] Maryknoll, NY Maryknoll Fathers and Brothers.
True, David H. '88 (OKL) Sulphur, OK St. Francis Xavier Church.
True, Isaac *o.s.b.* '66 (KC) [A] Conception, MO Conception Seminary College; [J] Conception, MO Conception Abbey.
Truhan, Luke *o.c.s.o.* '82 (WOR) [A] Spencer, MA St. Joseph's Abbey School of Theology and Institute of Monastic Studies; [N] Spencer, MA St. Joseph's Abbey.
Trujillo, Amando *t.o.r.* '88 (FWT) [2] Fort Worth, TX All Saints Church.
Trujillo, Antonio *o.f.m.* '89 (GLP) Acoma, NM San Esteban, Indian Mission Church.
Trujillo, Carlos B. '76 (PBL) Center, CO St. Francis Jerome Church; Del Norte, CO Holy Name of Mary Church; Monte Vista, CO St. Joseph Church.
Trujillo, Daniel '53 (SJN) [7] Bayamon, PR Santa Elena Church.
Trujillo, Ivan R. '85 (BUF) [3] Batavia, NY St. Mary Church.
Trujillo, Vincent *o.s.b.* '82 (P) [L] St. Benedict, OR Mt. Angel Abbey.
Trunk, Dale (SFR) [B] San Francisco, CA Capuchi House of Studies.
Trunk, Vincent E. *c.m.* '52 (PH) [Z] Philadelphia, PA Congregation of the Mission.
Trupia, Msgr. Robert C. '73 (TUC) Absent on Leave.
Trussel, Christopher '92 (SCL) [8] St. Cloud, MN St. Paul Church; Special Assignment; [C] St. Cloud, MN Cathedral High and John XXIII Middle School.
Trutter, Carl B. *o.p.* '60 (NO) [25] New Orleans, LA St. Anthony Of Padua Church; [P] New Orleans, LA Dominican Fathers & Brothers, Southern Dominican Province; [P] New Orleans, LA Dominican Fathers & Brothers, Southern Dominican Province; [S] Metairie, LA Southern Dominican Foundation.
Trutter, Richard '57 (SFD) [H] Taylorville, IL St. Vincent Memorial Hospital.
Trzeciakowski, Edward J. '55 (PIT) McDonald, PA St. Alphonsus Church.
Trzecieski, Stephen *c.m.* '60 (MIA) [A] Miami, FL St. John Vianney College Seminary.
Trzecieski, Stephen P. *c.m.* '60 (PH) [Z] Philadelphia, PA Congregation of the Mission.
Trzil, Louis J. '50 (DUB) Harpers Ferry, IA St. Ann-St. Joseph Church; Wexford, IA Immaculate Conception Church.
Tsang, Peter '59 (LA) Rowland Heights, CA St. Elizabeth Ann Seton Church.
Tsau, Paul (WDC) [3] Rockville, MD St. Mary Church.
Tschakert, Gregory '82 (SFS) Hartford, SD St. George Church; [C] Sioux Falls, SD Sioux Falls Catholic School System.
Tscherne, David D. '77 (TOL) Junction, OH St. Mary Church; St. Michael's Ridge, OH St. Michael Church.
Tschudi, Michael '84 (PMB) North Palm Beach, FL St. Paul of the Cross Church.
Tseu, Msgr. Andrew '56 (LA) Pomona, CA St. Madeleine Church.
Tsoi, Peter '64 (NY) [64] New York, NY St. Joseph Church.
Tsong, Augustine *s.j.* '94 (SJ) [2] Santa Clara, CA St. Clare Church.
Tsung-Li-Chuen, Basil *o.f.m.* '53 (STL) [P] St. Louis, MO Franciscan Friary of St. Anthony of Padua.
Tu, Joachim Vu '63 (ORG) Absent on Sick Leave; [G] Santa Ana, CA Vietnamese Catholic Center.
Tu, Raymond '95 (KC) [15] Kansas City, MO Holy Cross Church; [17] Kansas City, MO Church of the Holy Martyrs.
Tuan, Bui quang *c.ss.r.* '96 (LA) [R] Baldwin Park, CA Vietnamese Redemptorist Mission.
Tubbs, Leo D. *o.p.* '66 (OAK) [N] Oakland, CA Dominican Order, Siena House.
Tubridy, James J. '53 (NY) Retired.
Tucceri, Robert A. '79 (TOL) Bellevue, OH Immaculate Conception Church.
Tucci, Bruno M. '71 (ALN) Nesquehoning, PA Immaculate Conception of B.V.M. Church; Nesquehoning, PA Our Lady of Mount Carmel Church.
Tucci, Italo '48 (DET) Retired.
Tuchalski, Stanley T. '90 (WH) Westover, WV St. Elizabeth Ann Seton Church.
Tuchols, Franklin J. '71 (BUF) [14] Buffalo, NY Blessed Sacrament Church; Absent on Leave.
Tuchscherer, Vincent J. '55 (FAR) Balta, ND Our Lady of Mount Carmel Church.
Tucker, James *s.s.* (SFR) [27] San Francisco, CA St. John the Evangelist Church.
Tucker, James *s.s.* '69 (SJ) Special Assignment.
Tucker, James S. '69 (LA) On Duty Outside the Archdiocese.
Tucker, John J. *s.j.* '55 (BO) [W] Weston, MA Campion Center.
Tucker, Mark *c.ss.r.* '89 (WDC) [M] Washington, DC Holy Redeemer College.
Tucker, Michael '77 (SEA) Unassigned.
Tucker, Patrick M. '74 (CHI) Forest Park, IL St. Bernardine Church.
Tucker, Richard '58 (ORL) [2] Lakeland, FL St. Anthony's Church; Retired.
Tucker, Richard '58 (SY) Retired.
Tucker, Robert F. '70 (HRT) Litchfield, CT St. Anthony's Church.
Tucker, Robert G. '89 (LIN) McCook, NE St. Patrick Church.
Tucker, Thomas J. *o.s.f.s.* '66 (WIL) [B] Wilmington, DE Salesianum School.
Tueth, Michael V. '71 (NY) [Z] New York, NY Jesuit Provincial's Office; [Z] New York, NY Xavier Jesuit Community.
Tufaro, Douglas J. '83 (BGP) [5] Danbury, CT St. Peter's Church.
Tufts, Donn P. '80 (GR) Brunswick, MI St. Michael's Church.
Tugwell, Michael W. '75 (PT) [1] Tallahassee, FL Co-Cathedral of St. Thomas More.
Tugwood, James C. '60 (BRK) [220] Queens, NY Our Lady of the Snows Church.
Tuisea, Setefano '92 (SPP) [1] Pago Pago, AS Cathedral of the Holy Family.
Tuite, Howard A. '54 (CHI) [47] Chicago, IL Corpus Christi Church.
Tuite, Thomas P. '86 (RVC) Massapequa, NY St. Rose of Lima Church.
Tulko, Richard *o.f.m.* '64 (GB) [I] Pulaski, WI Assumption of B.V.M. Friary.
Tull, Terry *c.ss.r.* (CGS) [B] Aguas Buenas, PR Casa Cristo Redentor.
Tuller, Eugene *o.f.m.cap.* '49 (MIL) [P] Mount Calvary, WI St. Lawrence Friary.
Tuller, Jerome '55 (GB) [I] Appleton, WI St. Fidelis Friary.
Tuller, Joel '51 (GB) [I] Appleton, WI St. Fidelis Friary.
Tulley, Edward M. '39 (CLV) Parma Heights, OH St. John Bosco Church.
Tullius, Richard F. '73 (DAL) Grand Prairie, TX St. Michael the Archangel Church.
Tully, Eugene D. '68 (BO) Billerica, MA St. Theresa Church.
Tully, Eugene M. '73 (PH) Morrisville, PA Holy Trinity Church.
Tully, Gerard *c.s.p.* '94 (NY) [41] New York, NY Good Shepherd Church.
Tully, Henry F. '77 (IND) [8] Indianapolis, IN Holy Spirit Church.
Tully, James J. '44 (BRK) Retired.
Tully, John '69 (Y) Absent on Leave.

Tully, Raymond M. *s.j.* '40 (STL) [P] St. Louis, MO Hallahan House.
Tully, Ronald J. '66 (PAT) Dover, NJ Sacred Heart Church.
Tully, Terence '42 (SPK) Retired.
Tully, Thomas S. '85 (R) [4] Durham, NC St. Matthew Church.
Tuma, Anthony F. '31 (OM) Retired.
Tumminelli, Lawrence *b.s.o.* '96 (NTN) [B] Methuen, MA Basilian Salvatorian Order.
Tumosa, John Joseph '69 (CAM) Newfield, NJ St. Rose of Lima Church.
Tumulty, Matt '59 (P) [Q] Portland, OR Franciscan Ministry Network.
Tumulty, Michael J. *c.m.* (BUF) [C] Niagara University, NY Niagara University; [O] Niagara University, NY Vincentian Community at Niagara University.
Tunesi, Enrico *o.s.j.* '48 (SAC) [16] Sacramento, CA St. Mary Church.
Tung, Paul Nguyen Van '79 (NO) Waggaman, LA Our Lady of the Angels Church.
Tungol, Eugene D. '75 (SFR) [3] South San Francisco, CA St. Augustine Church.
Tunink, Wilfrid *o.s.b.* '45 (SFE) [L] Pecos, NM Our Lady of Guadalupe Benedictine Abbey.
Tunney, Michael F. *s.j.* '88 (BUF) [O] Buffalo, NY Canisius Jesuit Community.
Tunny, John V. '58 (RVC) Hicksville, NY St. Ignatius Loyola Church.
Tunny, Kenneth J. '63 (ALB) [16] Schenectady, NY St. Paul the Apostle Church; Schoharie, NY St. Joseph Church; Special Assignment.
Tuoc, Ignatius '71 (SP) [3] Tampa, FL Epiphany Church.
Tuohey, John '81 (OKL) [E] Oklahoma City, OK Mercy Health Center.
Tuohey, John F. '81 (SPR) On Duty Outside the Diocese.
Tuohey, John J. '81 (WDC) [C] Washington, DC Catholic University of America, The.
Tuohig, Richard H. *s.j.* (DET) [K] Detroit, MI Jesuit Provincial Office-Detroit Province of the Society of Jesus.
Tuohy, Edward *s.v.d.* '58 (BO) [W] Duxbury, MA Society of the Divine Word.
Tuohy, Msgr. Francis R. '61 (IND) [3] Indianapolis, IN Christ The King Church.
Tuozzolo, Leonard *c.s.sp.* '59 (NY) [69] New York, NY St. Mark the Evangelist Church.
Tupa, Jerome *o.s.b.* '82 (SCL) [I] Collegeville, MN St. John's Abbey, of the Order of St. Benedict.
Tupa, Michael J. '91 (SUP) Bloomville, WI St. John the Baptist Church; Harrison, WI St. Augustine Church; Pier-Willow, WI St. Francis of Assisi Church; Tomahawk, WI St. Mary Church.
Tupper, Dale E. '67 (WIN) [1] Rochester, MN Holy Spirit Church.
Tupper, John B. '60 (GAY) Empire, MI St. Philip Neri Church.
Turati, Fortunato *s.c.* '67 (PRO) [4] East Providence, RI Sacred Heart Church.
Turbek, Aloysius *s.v.d.* '40 (TR) [M] Bordentown, NJ Society of the Divine Word.
Turci, Vitaliano *o.s.cam.* '44 (MIL) [P] Wauwatosa, WI St. Camillus Community House.
Turcich, Ronald R. *o.s.a.* '58 (CHI) Norridge, IL Divine Savior Church.
Turco, Alfredo *s.x.* '88 (MIL) [B] Franklin, WI Xaverian Missionary Fathers College Seminary.
Turcotte, Ulric *o.m.i.* '37 (MAN) [M] Hudson, NH Oblates of Mary Immaculate Retreat House.
Turczany, Christopher J. '83 (BRK) [235] Queens, NY St. Robert Bellarmine Church.
Turek, Michael E. '76 (STL) Clover Bottom, MO St. Ann's Church; [E] Washington, MO St. Francis Borgia Regional High School.
Turek, Ronald J. '74 (CLV) Mentor, OH St. Mary of the Assumption Church.
Tureman, Thomas *s.d.s.* (MIL) [P] Milwaukee, WI Salvatorian Formation Community.
Tureman, Thomas M. *c.s.p.* '88 (NY) [Z] Scarsdale, NY Paulist Fathers Generalate.
Turgeon, Armand A. '43 (MAN) Retired.
Turi, John J. '55 (SCR) Matamoras, PA St. Joseph's Church.
Turillo, B. Samuel '46 (PRO) Retired.
Turk, Damian C. *o.c.s.o.* '69 (ATL) [I] Conyers, GA The Monastery of the Holy Spirit.
Turk, John P. '50 (Y) [5] Warren, OH St. Joseph Church.
Turke, Francis X. '52 (BO) [1] Milton, MA St. Agatha Church.
Turley, Daniel T. *o.s.a.* '68 (CHI) [N] Olympia Fields, IL The Augustinian Provincialate Tolentine Center.
Turley, Sean F. '71 (WIL) On Duty Outside the Diocese.
Turlik, Andrew J. '46 (PIT) Retired; [N] Pittsburgh, PA St. John Vianney Manor.
Turlo, Walter J. '70 (CHI) Bridgeview, IL St. Fabian Church.
Turnbull, John B. *o.f.m.* '55 (CIN) Centerville, OH St. Francis of Assisi Church.
Turnbull, Paul E. '73 (ALT) [10] Altoona, PA St. John the Evangelist Church.
Turnbull, William D. '67 (ALB) [C] Troy, NY Catholic Central High School.
Turner, Bernard R. '77 (ALB) Johnsonville, NY St. Monica's Church; Special Assignment; [T] Albany, NY Diocesan HIV/AIDS Ministries.
Turner, David *o.s.b.* '63 (JOL) [J] Lisle, IL St. Procopius Abbey.
Turner, Edward '66 (HON) Retired.
Turner, George F. (LR) Retired.
Turner, James '84 (PHX) Flagstaff, AZ St. Pius X Church.
Turner, James M. *o.s.f.s.* '81 (ARL) Reston, VA St. John Neumann Church.
Turner, Jerome '64 (RIC) Norfolk, VA Depaul Medical Center; [E] Norfolk, VA Bon Secours - De Paul Medical Center, Inc.
Turner, Jerome R. '64 (MAD) Military Chaplains.
Turner, Joseph *s.d.s.* '58 (MIL) [P] Milwaukee, WI Salvatorian Provincial Residence.
Turner, Patrick A. '72 (BEA) Winnie, TX St. Louis Church.
Turner, Paul '79 (KC) [22] Kansas City, MO St. John Francis Regis Church.
Turner, Richard M. '80 (SPR) South Hadley, MA St. Patrick's Church.
Turner, Richard W. '91 (R) Wake Forest, NC St. Catherine of Siena Church.
Turner, Robert '62 (GR) On Duty Outside the Diocese.
Turner, Robert '88 (GLP) On Duty Outside of Diocese.
Turner, Robert D. '82 (SPK) Okanogan-Omak, WA Our Lady of the Valley Church.
Turner, Robert D. '88 (MIL) [13] Milwaukee, WI Blessed Sacrament Church.
Turner, Robert G. '59 (PIT) [4] West Mifflin, PA Resurrection Church.
Turner, Thomas W. '82 (KC) Leave of Absence; [O] Kansas City, MO Bishop Sullivan Center.
Turner, Wayne A. '50 (MAD) Retired.
Turner, William J. '75 (IND) New Alsace, IN St. Paul Church; Yorkville, IN St. Martin Church.
Turner, William J. '77 (LAN) [5] Lansing, MI Resurrection Church.
Turowski, William M. '85 (NY) Florida, NY St. Joseph Church.
Turro, Msgr. James C. *s.t.l., s.s.l., a.m.* '48 (BGP) [O] Stamford, CT St. John Fisher Seminary Residence.
Turro, Msgr. James C. *s.t.l., s.s.l., a.m.* '48 (NEW) Park Ridge, NJ Our Lady of Mercy Church; Retired; [A] South Orange, NJ Immaculate Conception Seminary; [B] South Orange, NJ Seton Hall University.
Turton, Derick *s.j.* '94 (STL) [P] St. Louis, MO Jesuit Community Corporation at St. Louis University - Jesuit Hall.
Turtora, Msgr. Dominic A. '48 (MET) [1] Metuchen, NJ Cathedral of St. Francis; Retired; [H] Somerset, NJ Maria Regina Residence.
Tushar, David (DUL) [1] Duluth, MN Cathedral of Our Lady of the Rosary; [G] Duluth, MN The Human Life and Development Fund of the Diocese of Duluth.
Tusky, Richard J. '73 (PIT) Burgettstown, PA Our Lady of Lourdes Church.
Tustin, Joseph E. *o.s.f.s.* '67 (R) Goldsboro, NC St. Mary Church.
Tutas, Stephen *s.m.* '53 (SJ) Special Assignment; [M] Cupertino, CA Villa Saint Joseph.
Tutko, Michael (PSC) Leave of Absence.
Tutokie, Msgr. Michael E. '45 (E) Winburne, PA SS. Cyril and Methodius Church; Retired.
Tutone, John J. '71 (RVC) Island Park, NY Sacred Heart Church.
Tuttle, Arthur *c.ss.r.* '65 (ALB) Saratoga Springs, NY St. Clement Church.
Tuttle, Charles W. '74 (BEL) Sandoval, IL St. Lawrence Church; [B] Breese, IL Mater Dei High School.
Tuttle, Patrick E. *o.f.m.* (R) [3] Durham, NC Immaculate Conception Church.
Tuttle, Richard '76 (STU) [2] Steubenville, OH Holy Family Church.
Tuugusamusu, Paulo '86 (HON) [10] Honolulu, HI Our Lady of the Mount Church; [F] Honolulu, HI St. Francis Healthcare System of Hawaii.
Tuxbury, James C. '63 (BIS) On Duty Outside the Diocese.
Tuxbury, James C. *o.f.m.* '63 (FR) Buzzards Bay, MA St. Margaret Church.
Tuyn, William R. '62 (BUF) North Evans, NY St. Vincent Church.
Tuzeneu, Kenard J. '79 (TR) Barnegat, NJ St. Mary Church
Tuzicka, Fred M. '51 (DOD) Retired.
Tuzik, Robert L. '73 (CHI) [2] Mt. Prospect, IL St. Emily Church.
Tvrdy, Julius '73 (LIN) [5] Lincoln, NE Sacred Heart Church
Twaddell, Gerald '67 (COV) [A] Covington, KY Thomas More College.
Twardzik, Francis M. *s.d.b.* '70 (PSC) Clarks Summit, PA Transfiguration Church; Scranton, PA St. Mary's Byzantine Catholic Church.
Twardzik, Michael W. '70 (SPR) South Deerfield, MA St. Stanislaus B. and M. Church.
Twarog, Jerome *c.r.* '82 (CHI) [D] Chicago, IL Weber High School.
Twarog, Theodore S. '50 (SD) Absent on Sick Leave.
Twele, Robert Augustine *ofm conv.* '81 (BUF) [D] Athol Springs, NY St. Francis High School; [O] Athol Springs, NY St. Francis of Assisi Friary.
Twiddy, Paul '52 (WDC) Retired.
Twigg-Porter, George M. *s.j.* '53 (SFR) [N] San Francisco, CA Jesuit Community at University of San Francisco; [U] San Francisco, CA Apostleship of Prayer.
Twiggs, Matthew J. '73 (PAT) Stockholm, NJ St. John Vianney Church.
Twiss, Francis *s.m.* '60 (HON) Kapaa, HI St. Catherine Church.
Twohig, Christopher T. '50 (WDC) On Duty Outside the Archdiocese.
Twohig, Michael J. '83 (SPR) West Springfield, MA Immaculate Conception Church.
Twohy, Patrick *s.j.* '70 (SEA) LaConner, WA St. Paul Church.
Twohy, Richard E. *s.j.* '42 (SPK) [C] Spokane, WA Gonzaga University.
Twomey, Daniel F. '75 (BO) Natick, MA St. Patrick Church.
Twomey, Dermot J. *s.c.j.* '76 (JKS) Southhaven, MS Christ the King Church; Walls, MS Sacred Heart Church; [E] Nesbit, MS St. Michael Community House.
Twomey, Gerald S. '81 (RVC) Brentwood, NY St. Anne's Church.
Twomey, John E. '52 (MIL) Retired.
Twomey, Msgr. John P. '63 (LA) [3] Long Beach, CA St. Barnabas Church. •
Twomey, Simon D. '70 (SAC) [7] Sacramento, CA Presentation of the Blessed Virgin Mary Church.
Twomey, Thomas G. '65 (NOR) East Hampton, CT St. Patrick Church.
Twomey, Timothy *s.a.c.* '60 (RNO) Sparks, NV Immaculate Conception Church.
Tyburski, Zbieniew '73 (PAT) [4] Wayne, NJ Our Lady of Consolation Church.
Tydlacka, Msgr. George '44 (AUS) Retired.
Tykohovytch, Ivan '94 (STF) Glen Spey, NY St. Volodymyr Church.
Tyl, Albert '54 (FWT) [1] Fort Worth, TX St. Patrick Cathedral.
Tylawskyj, Ivan '50 (SJP) North Port, FL Entrance of B.V.M. into the Temple Church.
Tylenda, Joseph N. *s.j.* '60 (WDC) [M] Washington, DC The Jesuit Community at Georgetown University; [V] Washington, DC Woodstock Theological Center.
Tyler, Benedict E. *o.s.b.* '52 (NEW) [N] Newark, NJ Newark Abbey.
Tyler, Bernard L. '61 (LAN) Dexter, MI St. Joseph Church.
Tyler, Thomas L. '79 (E) New Bethlehem, PA St. Charles Church.
Tylka, Louis J. '96 (CHI) Orland Park, IL St. Michael Church.
Tyma, John A. *o.s.a.* '59 (CHI) [N] Olympia Fields, IL The Augustinian Provincialate Tolentine Center.
Tyman, Gary L. '86 (ROC) [4] Rochester, NY St. Anne Church; [M] Rochester, NY Diocesan Office of Campus Ministry.
Tyminski, Joseph *s.d.b.* '49 (NEW) Mahwah, NJ Immaculate Heart of Mary Church.
Tymkiw, Msgr. Leo '48 (SJP) [2] Parma, OH St. Andrew Church.
Tynan, Desmond (BO) Society of St. James the Apostle.
Tynan, John C. *m.m.* '62 (NY) [Z] Maryknoll, NY Maryknoll Fathers and Brothers.
Tynan, Joseph F. *o.c.s.o.* '47 (ATL) [I] Conyers, GA The Monastery of the Holy Spirit.
Tyne, John J. *s.s.j.* '63 (HT) [8] Houma, LA St. Lucy Church; [6] Thibodaux, LA St. Luke Church.
Tynski, Robert M. '89 (TR) [12] Trenton, NJ St. Anthony Church.
Tyrasinski, Lucius *o.s.p.p.e.* (PH) [Z] Doylestown, PA Pauline Fathers Monastery, Shrine of Our Lady of Czestochowa.
Tyrell, Robert D. '67 (BO) Weston, MA St. Julia Church.
Tyrrell, Anthony *o.s.* '95 (PCE) [11] Ponce, PR San Jose Obrero Church.
Tyrrell, Bernard J. *s.j.* '65 (SPK) [C] Spokane, WA Gonzaga University.
Tyrrell, Joseph '89 (NY) [185] Bronx, NY St. Raymond Church.
Tyrrell, Michael A. *s.j.* '76 (P) [L] Portland, OR Jesuit Provincial Office (Oregon Prov.).
Tyrrell, Robert Mike *s.j.* (SPK) [E] Spokane, WA Gonzaga Preparatory School.
Tyrrell, Wilfred *s.a.* '94 (LA) [83] Los Angeles, CA St. Odilia Church.
Tysmans, Louis *c.i.c.m.* '47 (ARL) [J] Arlington, VA Missionhurst, C.I.C.M.-Central House and Provincialate; [J] Falls Church, VA Missionhurst-C.I.C.M.
Tyson, David T. *c.s.c.* '75 (P) [B] Portland, OR University of Portland; [L] Portland, OR Holy Cross Father

& Brother, C.S.C. - University of Portland.
Tyson, Joseph '89 (SEA) [8] Seattle, WA St. Edward Church.
Tyson, Michael *o.f.m.* '67 (WDC) [3] Silver Spring, MD St. Camillus Church.
Tyson, William F. *s.s.j.* (LAF) Eunice, LA St. Mathilda Church.
Tywoniak, Robert '83 (MIA) [10] Fort Lauderdale, FL St. Mark Church.
Tzanakas, George M. (AUS) Retired.

U

Ubalde, Ulysses L. '93 (NEW) Paramus, NJ Our Lady of the Visitation Church.
Ubel, John '89 (STP) [A] St. Paul, MN St. John Vianney Seminary; [C] St. Paul, MN University of St. Thomas.
Ubinger, Herman F. *o.s.b.* '58 (GBG) [H] Latrobe, PA Saint Vincent Archabbey.
Uboldi, Victor '45 (SD) Retired.
Ubowski, Chester '49 (CHI) Retired; [J] Chicago, IL Resurrection Medical Center.
Uchendu, Cajetan (NY) [3] New Rochelle, NY St. Joseph Church.
Ucker, Gerald L '70 (OKL) Calumet, OK Immaculate Heart of Mary Church; Retired.
Udick, William S. *s.j.* '55 (DEN) [M] Denver, CO Xavier Jesuit Center.
Udo, Emmanuel (MIL) [4] Wauwatosa, WI St. Jude the Apostle Church.
Udovic, Edward *c.m.* '84 (CHI) [N] Chicago, IL Vincentian Community, Congregation of the Mission, Midwest Province.
Udulutsch, Robert *o.f.m.cap.* '56 (GB) Kaukauna, WI St. Mary of the Annunciation Church.
Uebler, Michael G. '82 (BUF) Arcade, NY SS. Peter and Paul Church; East Arcade, NY St. Mary's Church; [D] Lancaster, NY St. Mary's High School.
Uecker, Joseph H. *c.pp.s.* '68 (SAN) [3] Abilene, TX St. Francis of Assisi Church; [4] Abilene, TX St. Vincent Pallotti Church.
Uehlein, Christopher *o.s.b.* '60 (SFS) [F] Marvin, SD Blue Cloud Abbey.
Uftring, Richard A. (BO) Awaiting Assignment.
Uglesic, Leopold '35 (SFR) Retired.
Ugliano, Bruno A. *o.s.b.* '67 (PAT) [M] Morristown, NJ St. Mary's Abbey.
Uglietto, Peter (BO) [A] Weston, MA Pope John XXIII National Seminary.
Ugochukwu, Sebastian (CHI) [8] Chicago, IL St. Aloysius Church.
Ugochukwu-Awka, John (BRK) [234] Queens, NY St. Rita Church.
Ugolik, Richard '54 (DET) Retired.
Ugomadi, Kevin '84 (CHI) [208] Chicago, IL Transfiguration of Our Lord Church.
Ugwuanya, Valentine '94 (NEW) [34] Newark, NJ Sacred Heart Church.
Uhde, Peter M. '81 (NEW) [13] Newark, NJ Epiphany Church; [16] Newark, NJ Holy Trinity Church.
Uhen, Cletus V. '42 (MIL) Retired.
Uhl, Anthony C. '68 (COS) Salida, CO St. Joseph Church.
Uhlenkott, Gary D. *s.j.* '80 (SPK) [C] Spokane, WA Gonzaga University.
Uhler, Carl A. '56 (CLV) West Salem, OH St. Stephen Church.
Uhlik, Charles R. '92 (OM) South Sioux City, NE St. Michael Church.
Uhlman, Laurence *t.o.r.* '90 (STU) [A] Steubenville, OH Franciscan University of Steubenville; [F] Steubenville, OH Holy Spirit Monastery.
Uhran, Vernon (ORL) Sabbatical.
Uhrig, A. Gregory '73 (MET) Somerville, NJ Immaculate Conception Church.
Uko, Joseph *m.s.p.* '88 (GAL) Barrett Station, TX St. Martin de Porres Church.
Ukwuoma, Augustine '83 (CLV) [1] Akron, OH Annunciation Church.
Ulak, Robert T. '70 (NEW) [3] Irvington, NJ Sacred Heart of Jesus Church.
Ulam, Richard *o.s.b.* '82 (GBG) [2] Greensburg, PA St. Bruno Church.
Ulatowski, Donald F. (CHI) Retired.
Ulincey, Andrew A. '66 (ALN) [6] Reading, PA Holy Rosary Church.
Uline, Cyprian *o.f.m.conv.* '70 (LAN) [3] Lansing, MI Holy Cross Church.
Ulkrickson, Brian L. *s.j.* '78 (P) [L] Portland, OR Jesuit Provincial Office (Oregon Prov.).
Ullery, Kirk '65 (SFR) [40] San Francisco, CA Our Lady of Lourdes Church.
Ullman, Earl L. '38 (SD) Retired.
Ulloa, Daniel *o.p.* '70 (GAL) [Q] Houston, TX Dominican Fathers and Brothers, St. Mark Priory, Inc.; [T] Houston, TX Rice University/Texas Medical Center Schools; Catholic Student Center.
Ullrich, David *o.m.i.* '71 (OAK) [N] Oakland, CA Oblate Provincial House & Procure.
Ullrich, John *o.f.m.* '76 (HRT) [14] Hartford, CT St. Patrick-St. Anthony Church.
Ullrich, Mark C. '78 (STL) St. Peters, MO All Saints Church.
Ullrich, Peter *o.s.b.* '59 (KC) [J] Conception, MO Conception Abbey.
Ullrich, Peter *o.s.b.* '87 (KC) [A] Conception, MO Conception Seminary College.
Ulm, John Francis '58 (GAL) [4] Spring, TX St. James the Apostle Church.
Ulman, Stanley A. '73 (DET) Hamtramck, MI St. Ladislaus Church.
Ulrich, Carl G. '43 (SCR) Retired; [N] Dunmore, PA Villa St. Joseph.
Ulrich, Eugene P. '74 (BUF) Almond, NY SS. Brendan and Jude Church; [R] Williamsville, NY Newman Club Chaplains.
Ulrich, Hugh *c.pp.s.* '36 (CIN) [B] Carthagena, OH St. Charles.
Ulrich, James E. '60 (CIN) [41] Cincinnati, OH St. James Church.
Ulrich, Stephen W. '90 (OWN) Clinton, KY St. Jude Church; Fulton, KY St. Edward Church; Hickman, KY Sacred Heart Church.
Ulrick, Stephen D. '82 (STP) Chanhassen, MN St. Hubert Church.
Ulses, Eugene '69 (SC) Schaller, IA St. Joseph's Church.
Ulshafer, Thomas *s.s.* '70 (WDC) On Duty Outside the Archdiocese.
Ulshafer, Thomas R. *s.s.* '70 (BAL) [A] Baltimore, MD St. Mary's Seminary and University; [M] Baltimore, MD Sulpician Provincial House.
Ulto, Victor A. (BRK) [120] Brooklyn, NY Queen of All Saints Church.
Umagu, Alfred *m.s.p.* '92 (GAL) [30] Houston, TX St. Francis Xavier Church.
Umana, Miguel '96 (WDC) [4] Rockville, MD St. Raphael Church.
Umana, Pedro *o.f.m.* '89 (OAK) [9] Oakland, CA St. Elizabeth's Church.
Umberg, Andrew J. '91 (CIN) On Duty Outside the Archdiocese.
Umberg, Andrew J. '91 (COL) [A] Columbus, OH Pontifical College Josephinum.
Umberger, Patrick A. '80 (LC) Plover, WI St. Bronislava Church.
Ume, Michael '93 (LA) Panorama City, CA St. Genevieve Church.
Umhoefer, Stephen J. '66 (MAD) Monroe, WI St. Victor Church.
Umrahn Kaleem '65 (BRK) [132] Brooklyn, NY St. Saviour Church.
Umwech, Adalbert '90 (CI) Lukunor, FM Sacred Heart Church.
Underdahl, Mark J. '96 (STP) Lake Elmo, MN Guardian Angels Church.
Underwood, Gary E. '80 (TUC) On Duty Outside the Diocese.
Underwood, Joseph '63 (BIR) Retired.
Underwood, O. Fred *c.s.c.* '56 (AUS) [H] Austin, TX Congregation of Holy Cross - Southern Province.
Underwood, Scott J. *o.s.b.* '76 (NO) [A] St. Benedict, LA St. Joseph's Seminary College; [P] St. Benedict, LA St. Joseph Abbey.
Ungashick, Thomas J. '76 (Y) Leetonia, OH St. Patrick's Church.
Unger, John M. '42 (PIT) Retired; [N] Pittsburgh, PA St. John Vianney Manor.
Unger, Msgr. John M. '65 (STL) [D] St. Louis, MO Paul VI Institute of Catechetical and Pastoral Studies; [R] St. Louis, MO Sancta Maria in Ripa.
Unger, Todd J. '82 (BAK) Madras, OR St. Patrick's Church.
Uniowski, Peter '75 (ORL) [3] Lakeland, FL St. John Neumann Church.
Universal, Patrick J. '75 (GLP) Crownpoint, NM St. Paul Church.
Unni, John J. '92 (BO) [74] Boston, MA St. William Church.
Unsworth, John E. '76 (PRO) Riverside, RI St. Brendan Church.
Unterreiner, Glennon T. '46 (STL) Retired.
Unterreiner, James J. '70 (SPC) Ironton, MO Ste. Marie Du Lac Church.
Unverdorben, Ernest *o.c.d.* '66 (MIL) [P] Holy Hill, WI Discalced Carmelite Monastery.
Unverferth, Steven R. '89 (BEL) Leave of Absence.
Unwin, Rick '79 (CIN) Piqua, OH St. Boniface Church.
Unz, Thomas E. '83 (CHI) Stickney, IL St. Pius X Church.
Uong, Luong *c.ss.r.* '95 (NO) [23] New Orleans, LA St. Alphonsus Church.
Uppena, James '68 (MAD) [I] Madison, WI Holy Name Catholic Center, Inc.
Upson, Michael G. '76 (BRK) Released from Diocesan Assignment.
Upson, Michael G. '76 (ROC) [27] Rochester, NY Immaculate Conception Church.
Upson, Wilfrid *o.m.i.* '56 (DUL) International Falls, MN St. Thomas Aquinas Church.
Upton, Edward F. '69 (CHI) Orland Park, IL St. Francis of Assisi Church.
Upton, John C. '83 (GAL) [40] Houston, TX St. John Vianney Church.
Uralikunnel, George '67 (BIS) Bowbells, ND St. Joseph Church.
Uram, Msgr. Kenneth '59 (STU) Richmond, OH St. John Fisher Church.
Urarte, Carmelo '59 (ARE) [11] Arecibo, PR Church of San Martin de Porres.
Urbain, Joseph V. '32 (CIN) Retired.
Urban, Anthony M. '73 (SCR) Bear Creek Township, PA St. Elizabeth Church.
Urban, Carl A. '66 (ALB) [1] Schenectady, NY Church of St. Adalbert.
Urban, Charles T. *o.praem.* '54 (PH) [Z] Paoli, PA Daylesford Abbey.
Urban, John L. '59 (MAD) Boscobel, WI Immaculate Conception Church.
Urban, Joseph '72 (NEW) Wallington, NJ Most Sacred Heart of Jesus Church.
Urban, Lawrence *s.d.b.* '77 (SP) [E] Tampa, FL Mary Help of Christians School.
Urban, Lonnie A. '67 (AUS) Taylor, TX St. Mary's Church.
Urban, Matthew J. '40 (MIL) Retired.
Urban, Peter '58 (DEN) Commerce City, CO Our Lady Mother of the Church.
Urban, Reginald A. '77 (GI) Loup City, NE St. Josaphat's Church.
Urban, Robert M. '60 (SUP) Glenwood City, WI St. John the Baptist Church; Wilson, WI St. Bridget Church.
Urbanek, Raymond '68 (LAN) Fenton, MI St. John Church.
Urbaniak, Msgr. Bernard J. '68 (E) [29] Erie, PA St. Stanislaus Church.
Urbaniak, Jan *c.m.* '71 (BRK) [134] Brooklyn, NY St. Stanislaus Kostka Church.
Urbaniak, Lawrence M. '61 (RCK) Hartland, IL St. Patrick Church.
Urbaniak, Lucian '85 (SY) [11] Utica, NY St. Mark Church.
Urbanic, James *c.pp.s.* '71 (KC) [3] St. Joseph, MO St. Francis Xavier Church.
Urbanik, Stanley J. '61 (NEW) Bloomfield, NJ St. Valentine Church.
Urbano, Claudio '84 (CHI) [W] Chicago, IL Northview University Center.
Urbanowicz, Msgr. Francis J. '39 (PH) Clifton Heights, PA Sacred Heart Church; Retired.
Urbanowski, Konrad *s.ch.* '23 (DET) [8] Sterling Heights, MI Our Lady of Czestochowa Church.
Urbanski, Louis J. '64 (P) [36] Portland, OR St. Therese of the Child Jesus Church.
Urbine, Gordon *o.f.m.* '42 (OAK) [9] Oakland, CA St. Elizabeth's Church; [N] Oakland, CA Franciscan Friars.
Urbine, Richard (FTW) Retired.
Urbonas, Msgr. Ignatius L. '35 (GRY) [9] Gary, IN St. Casimir Church.
Urdiain, Angelo *c.r.* '66 (DEN) [A] Denver, CO Provincial House at St. Andrew, Seminary (C.R.).
Ureel, Wayne G. '90 (DET) Dryden, MI St. Cornelius Church.
Urell, Msgr. John '78 (ORG) Laguna Hills, CA St. Nicholas Church.
Urian, Thomas R. '90 (PH) Secane, PA Our Lady of Fatima Church; [D] Springfield, PA Cardinal O'Hara High School.
Uribe, Arturo *c.ss.r.* '95 (LA) Whittier, CA St. Mary of the Assumption Church; [R] Whittier, CA Redemptorist Fathers Mission House.
Uribe, Saul de Jesus '80 (ELP) [34] El Paso, TX Sts. Peter and Paul Church.
Urizalqui, Richard '77 (FRS) Tulare, CA St. Aloysius Church.
Urlage, Robert J. '58 (COV) Retired.
Urmston, Benjamin J. *s.j.* '59 (CIN) [M] Cincinnati, OH Jesuit Community at Xavier Unversity.
Urnick, Charles B. '74 (NEW) Norwood, NJ Immaculate Conception Church.
Uroda, Stanley *s.v.d.* '74 (CHI) [B] Techny, IL Divine Word Residence; [N] Techny, IL Society of the Divine Word, Provincial Headquarter-Chicago Prov.; [N] Techny, IL Society of the Divine Word, Provincial Headquarter-Chicago Prov.
Urrea, Miguel '87 (SB) [2] San Bernardino, CA Christ the King Church.
Urriza, Luis *o.s.a.* '44 (BEA) [4] Beaumont, TX Cristo Rey Church.
Urtubia, Jorge *c.s.c.* '95 (FTW) [J] South Bend, IN Congregation of Holy Cross Indiana Province Provincial House.
Uschold, Raymond F. '64 (BUF) Delevan, NY Blessed Sacrament Church; Machias, NY Holy Family Church.
Useche, Teofilo '84 (CAM) Gloucester, NJ St. Mary's Church.
Useldinger, Karl J. '77 (COS) Woodland Park, CO Our Lady of the Woods Church.
Usenza, Robert J. '61 (BGP) Retired.
Ustaski, William '77 (LA) Canyon Country, CA St. Clare Church.

Ustaski, William B. *c.r.i.c.* '77 (LA) [B] Los Angeles, CA Canons Regular of the Immaculate Conception-Novitiate.
Ustaszewski, Thaddeus W. *o.s.b.* '49 (MAN) [K] Manchester, NH St. Anselm Abbey.
Utendorf, James M. *c.s.p.* '78 (NY) [Z] Scarsdale, NY Paulist Fathers Generalate.
Uter, Frank M. '69 (BR) [1] Baton Rouge, LA St. Joseph Cathedral.
Utrup, Eugene E. '59 (STL) Chesterfield, MO Incarnate Word Church.
Utz, Raymond Michael '63 (PIT) Penn Hills, PA St. Susanna Church.
Uvietta, Joseph *s.m.* '61 (STL) [T] Eureka, MO Marianist Retreat & Conference Center.
Uzdrowski, Mel R. *o.s.b.* '56 (JOL) [J] Lisle, IL St. Procopius Abbey.
Uzoh, Louis '73 (BRK) [163] Queens, NY St. Clare Church.
Uzzilio, Robert A. '65 (BGP) Brookfield, CT St. Marguerite Bourgeoys Church; [5] Stamford, CT St. Gabriel Church.

V

Vaca, Modesto *o.de.m.* '56 (PCE) [9] Ponce, PR La Merced Church.
Vacca, Bernard '52 (Y) Retired.
Vacca, Daniel L. '95 (WCH) [5] Wichita, KS Church of the Magdalen.
Vaccarella, Samuel *t.o.r.* '77 (WDC) [M] Washington, DC St. Louis Friary.
Vaccari, Andrew J. '86 (BRK) [215] Queens, NY Our Lady of the Miraculous Medal Church.
Vaccari, Peter I. '77 (BRK) Released from Diocesan Assignment.
Vaccari, Peter I. '77 (RVC) [A] Huntington, NY Diocesan Seminary of the Immaculate Conception.
Vaccaro, Guy '78 (JOL) Winfield, IL St. John the Baptist Church.
Vaccaro, Joseph V. '58 (NEW) On Duty Outside the Archdiocese.
Vaccaro, Joseph V. '58 (STP) [T] Lake Elmo, MN Hermits of the Most Blessed Virgin Mary of Mount Carmel.
Vacco, James *o.f.m.* '82 (BUF) [R] Williamsville, NY Newman Club Chaplains.
Vacco, James *o.f.m.* '82 (NY) [Z] New York, NY Franciscan Friars, Order of Friars Manor.
Vacek, Carl *t.o.r.* '79 (ORL) [D] Winter Park, FL San Pedro Spiritual Development Center; [F] Winter Park, FL San Pedro Center, Third Order Regular of St. Francis; [F] Winter Park, FL Franciscan Friars, T.O.R., Provincial Residence, San Pedro Friary.
Vacek, Edward V. *s.j.* '73 (BO) [W] Cambridge, MA Weston Jesuit Community.
Vacek, Edward V. *s.j.* '73 (MIL) [P] Milwaukee, WI Jesuit Provincial Office, Wisconsin Province.
Vachon, Robert *m.s.* '55 (FR) [K] Attleboro, MA La Salette Provincial House.
Vadakel, George T. '59 (NY) New City, NY St. Augustine Church.
Vadakethayil, Varghese '71 (BRK) [60] Brooklyn, NY Holy Spirit Church.
Vadakin, Msgr. Royale M. '64 (LA) [42] Los Angeles, CA St. Anastasia Church.
Vadakkedath, Vincent '72 (LKC) Grand Chenier, LA St. Eugene Church.
Vadakkekara, J. Philip '69 (MET) Bloomsbury, NJ Church of the Annunciation.
Vadakkekudy, Jacob '61 (HEL) Drummond, MT St. Michael Church; Philipsburg, MT St. Philip Church.
Vader, Anthony J. '52 (CHI) [83] Chicago, IL Holy Name of Mary Church; [190] Chicago, IL Sacred Heart Mission of Holy Name of Mary Church.
Vadino, Joseph A. '63 (PH) Center Square, PA St. Helena Church.
Vaeth, Paul *c.p.* '68 (MET) [H] South River, NJ Passionist Provincial Office.
Vaeth, Paul *c.p.* '68 (R) [H] Greenville, NC Catholic Student Center for Students at East Carolina University.
Vaghetto, Benedetto P. '78 (PIT) [10] New Castle, PA St. Vincent de Paul Church.
Vaghi, Msgr. Peter J. '85 (WDC) [36] Washington, DC St. Patrick Church; [V] Washington, DC The John Carroll Society.
Vago, John C. '70 (ALT) Bedford, PA St. Thomas Church.
Vail, John D. '67 (WDC) Leonardtown, MD St. Aloysius Church.
Vail, Nathan R. *f.s.s.p.* '94 (SCR) [M] Elmhurst, PA Priestly Fraternity of St. Peter (F.S.S.P.).
Vail, Thomas '51 (ALB) Retired.
Vaillancourt, Mark G. '94 (NY) [200] Staten Island, NY St. Charles Church.
Vaillancourt, Raymond *m.s.* '89 (FR) Brewster, MA Our Lady of the Cape Church.
Vaillancourt, Robert C. '82 (PRT) [1] Old Town, ME Holy Family Church.
Vainavicz, Anthony C. '61 (GR) Spring Lake, MI St. Mary's Church.
Vaisnoras, Boniface *m.i.c.* '47 (CHI) [N] Chicago, IL Congregation of Marian Fathers of the Immaculate Conception.
Vaisnoras, Boniface *m.i.c.* '47 (JOL) Plano, IL St. Mary Church.
Vaisnys, Juozas *s.j.* '43 (CHI) [N] Chicago, IL Lithuanian American Jesuits.
Vakoc, Henry T. '92 (STP) Military Chaplains.
Vakulskas, John A., Jr. '69 (SC) Milford, IA St. Joseph's Church.
Val, LaFrance *o.p.* '58 (MIA) [A] Miami, FL St. John Vianney College Seminary.
Vala, John B. '39 (NY) [Z] New York, NY Pope John Paul II Residence.
Vala, John B. '40 (NY) Retired.
Valades, Reuben '70 (RC) New Underwood, SD St. John the Evangelist Church.
Valainis, Vitolds '66 (DAV) Iowa City, IA State University of Iowa Hospital.
Valasek, Donald '74 (PBR) Barnesboro, PA St. John the Baptist Church; Patton, PA SS. Peter and Paul Church.
Valasek, Edward A. '46 (LIN) Retired.
Valastro, Msgr. George J. '56 (NY) Middletown, NY St. Joseph Church.
Valbuena, Luis *o.m.i.* '55 (LA) Pacoima, CA Mary Immaculate Church.
Valcovich, Giles *o.f.m.* '48 (OAK) [A] Berkeley, CA Franciscan School of Theology Student Residence.
Valcovich, Giles *o.f.m.* '48 (SFR) [U] San Francisco, CA St. Anthony Foundation.
Valdazo, Stephen '58 (BRK) [184] Queens, NY St. Joan of Arc Church.
Valdemaras, Valdas (DET) [3] Southfield, MI Divine Providence Church.
Valderrama, Viliulfo '96 (TUC) [17] Tucson, AZ St. Monica Church.
Valdes, Msgr. Angel (SJN) Resident Chaplains; [D] Rio Piedras, PR Hospital del Maestro.
Valdes, Bert W. '62 (WH) Charles Town, WV St. James Church.
Valdes, Luis '45 (SB) Retired.
Valdes, Nicanor '60 (SJN) [30] San Juan, PR San Juan Evangelista Church; [30] San Juan, PR San Juan Evangelista Church.
Valdez, Antonio *o.f.m.* '61 (SFE) [1] Santa Fe, NM The Cathedral of San Francisco de Asis.
Valdez, John '91 (AMA) [4] Amarillo, TX Our Lady of Guadalupe Church.
Valdez, Jose R. '89 (MIL) Retired.
Valdez, Max E. '44 (GI) Retired.
Valdez, Miguel Zamorano *o.s.b.* '69 (MIL) [P] Benet Lake, WI St. Benedict's Abbey.
Valdez, Patrick *c.r.* (DEN) [A] Denver, CO Provincial House at St. Andrew, Seminary (C.R.).
Valdez, Patrick M. *c.r.* '75 (PBL) San Luis, CO Sangre de Cristo Church.
Valdez, Paul R. '82 (MRY) [2] Salinas, CA Sacred Heart Church.
Valdez, Salvador *o.f.m.* (CHI) [D] Chicago, IL Hales Franciscan High School, Inc.
Valdivia, Adolfo A. '81 (SAT) [48] San Antonio, TX St. Lawrence Church.
Valdivia, Antonio A. '63 (OAK) Richmond, CA St. Cornelius Church; Richmond, CA St. Mark's Church.
Valdovinos, Francisco (SJN) [2] Canovanas, PR Resurreccion del Senior Church.
Valencia, Carlos D. '85 (BRK) [68] Brooklyn, NY St. John the Evangelist Church.
Valencia, Thaddeus T. *c.s.b.* '79 (GAL) Missouri City, TX Holy Family Church.
Valenciano, Luis C. '77 (SD) [23] San Diego, CA St. Charles Church.
Valenta, John (STL) [P] St. Louis, MO Jesuit Community Corporation at St. Louis University - Jesuit Hall.
Valente, John B. *o.f.m.* '41 (PRO) [P] Providence, RI St. Francis Friary.
Valente, Michael *o.s.* (JOL) Winfield, IL St. John the Baptist Church.
Valente, Palmo *s.f.* '52 (WDC) [B] Silver Spring, MD Holy Family Seminary.
Valenti, Thomas '77 (ROC) [M] Rochester, NY Diocesan Office of Campus Ministry.
Valentine, Charles R. '54 (TR) Englishtown, NJ Our Lady of Mercy Church.
Valentine, Daniel A. '74 (PIT) [2] West Mifflin, PA Holy Spirit Church.
Valentine, John C. '85 (WH) Benwood, WV St. John's Church; McMechen, WV St. James Church.
Valentine, Joseph R. '93 (CHL) Reidsville, NC Holy Infant Church.
Valentine, Lambert F. *o.f.m.* '43 (NY) [35] New York, NY St. Francis of Assisi Church.
Valentine, Leroy A. '77 (STL) Absent on Sick Leave.
Valentine, Richard A. '74 (PRO) Georgiaville, RI St. Michael's Church.
Valentine, Robert J. '69 (BGP) New Canaan, CT St. Aloysius Church.
Valentine, Timothy *s.j.* '85 (NY) [82] New York, NY Notre Dame Church.
Valentini, Francis M. '44 (CLV) Retired.
Valentino, Dominic '47 (JOL) Retired.
Valentino, Msgr. Frederick A. '50 (TR) Lavallette, NJ St. Bonaventure Church.
Valenzano, Arthur '75 (BAL) Westminster, MD St. John Church.
Valenzuela, Adolfo L. '80 (SAN) Big Spring, TX St. Thomas Church.
Valenzuela, Luciano '87 (SAC) Fairfield, CA Holy Spirit Church.
Valenzuela, Pablo '53 (SJN) [11] San Juan, PR Corpus Christi Church.
Valerio, Raymond A. '59 (MAR) Houghton, MI St. Ignatius Loyola Church.
Valerio, Thomas P. '92 (PAT) Prospect Park, NJ St. Paul's Church.
Valero, Isidro Giber '73 (SJN) [3] Trujillo Alto, PR San Francisco de Asis Church.
Valero, Pedro Ruiz *o.m.* '88 (CGS) Cayey, PR Nuestra Senora de la Asuncion Church.
Valiquette, Hilaire *o.f.m.* '64 (SFE) Pena Blanca, NM Nuestra Senora De Guadalupe Church.
Valit, Robert L. '61 (STP) Edina, MN Our Lady of Grace Church.
Valker, Richard J. '57 (CHI) Northbrook, IL St. Norbert Church.
Valko, George J. '77 (ALT) Cresson, PA St. Francis Xavier Church; [A] Cresson, PA Mount Aloysius College; [H] Huntingdon, PA Juniata College.
Valko, Robert A. '65 (PIT) Military Chaplains.
Valla, Dominic J. '63 (HRT) Oxford, CT St. Thomas the Apostle Church.
Valladares, Herman '48 (SAN) Retired.
Valle, Msgr. Fernando '56 (LA) Retired.
Vallecorsa, Daniel '93 (PIT) [10] New Castle, PA St. Vincent de Paul Church.
Vallee, Gerald A. '85 (STA) Branford, FL San Juan Mission (Independent) Church.
Vallee, Robert '87 (MIA) Higher Studies.
Vallejo, Jesus (SJN) [D] Santurce, PR Hospital de Diego.
Vallejos, Francisco '87 (BAK) Hermiston, OR Our Lady of Angels Church.
Vallelonga, J. Stephen '90 (WH) Weirton, WV Sacred Heart of Mary Church.
Vallely, James P. '49 (PRT) Retired.
Valleroy, Paul '74 (KNX) Signal Mountain, TN St. Augustine Church.
Valleroy, Rickey J. '93 (STL) [5] Florissant, MO St. Dismas Church.
Valles, Carlos *c.ss.r.* '67 (CGS) Aguas Buenas, PR Church of Tres Santos Reyes.
Valley, John '60 (CLV) Released from Diocesan Assignment.
Valley, Paul *s.p.* '64 (SFE) [J] Jemez Springs, NM The Jemez Program, Our Lady of Lourdes Novitiate.
Vallier, John F. '87 (GR) Rothbury, MI Our Lady of the Assumption Church; Shelby, MI Our Lady of Fatima Church.
Valliere, Romeo J. '63 (MAN) Absent on Sick Leave.
Valliere, Timothy C. '91 (NOR) Somersville, CT All Saints Church.
Vallina, Alfredo *o.p.* '57 (PCE) Yauco, PR Holy Rossary Church.
Vallina, Msgr. Emilio '52 (MIA) [22] Miami, FL St. John Bosco Church.
Vallocheril, George Sebastian '84 (MIL) [P] Milwaukee, WI Jesuit Community at Marquette University.
Vallone, Louis A. '48 (BUF) Retired.
Vallone, Louis F. '73 (PIT) [56] Pittsburgh, PA St. Mary of the Mount Church.
Vallooran, Joseph '59 (SR) Crescent City, CA Pelican Bay State Prison.
Vallor, Robert '55 (GBG) Retired.
Valls, Richard G. *sch.p.* '57 (KAL) [4] Kalamazoo, MI St. Monica Church.
Valois, Normand W. '46 (PRO) [1] Providence, RI Cathedral of SS. Peter and Paul; Retired.
Valone, Fred P. '94 (GAL) [49] Houston, TX St. Michael Church.
Valoret, Joseph '83 (MIA) Retired.
Valtierra, David D. *c.o.* '76 (CHR) [E] Rock Hill, SC Oratory of St. Philip Neri, Congregation of the Oratory of Pontifical Rite; [H] Rock Hill, SC Winthrop University, York Co. Tech Center Newman Center.
Valtierra, J. Antonio '79 (GRY) [1] Hammond, IN All Saints Church.
Vamos, Joseph E. '66 (GRY) [1] Merrillville, IN Our Lady of Consolation Church.
Vamos, Joseph L. '61 (TOL) [39] Toledo, OH St. Stephen Church.
Van Abel, John W. '72 (MIL) Whitewater, WI St. Patrick's Church.
Van Acker, Michael R. '81 (PEO) [J] Galesburg, IL St. Mary Medical Center.
van Ackeren, Leonard J. *o.s.b.* '38 (MIL) [P] Benet Lake, WI St. Benedict's Abbey.
Van Ackeren, Maurice E. *s.j.* '43 (KC) [B] Kansas City, MO Rockhurst College; [J] Kansas City, MO Rockhurst College - Jesuit Community.

Van Ban, Martin Tran *c.m.c.* '94 (BEA) [2] Port Arthur, TX Queen of Vietnam Church.
Van Beck, Alfred F. '50 (MIL) Retired.
van Beeck, Frans J. *s.j.* '63 (CHI) [C] Chicago, IL Jesuit Community at Loyola University of Chicago.
Van Beek, Alois R. '73 (MIL) Nabob, WI St. Matthias Church; St. Lawrence, WI St. Lawrence Church.
Van Beek, Dennis E. '69 (MIL) Waterford, WI St. Thomas Aquinas Church.
Van Bergen, Francis G. '56 (CLV) South Euclid, OH St. Gregory the Great Church.
Van Boxel, Msgr. W. H. '40 (LAF) Retired.
Van Breda, William C. *o.s.a.* '50 (PH) [Z] Villanova, PA St. Thomas Monastery.
Van Bui, Joseph Dung '95 (ORL) [7] Orlando, FL St. Charles Borromeo Church.
Van Cauwenburgh, Roger *c.i.c.m.* '51 (ARL) [J] Arlington, VA Missionhurst, C.I.C.M.-Central House and Provincialate.
Van Coillie, Paul *c.i.c.m.* '47 (SAT) [15] San Antonio, TX Our Lady of Good Counsel Church.
Van Damme, Larry P. '93 (MAR) DeTour, MI Sacred Heart Church; Goetzville, MI St. Stanislaus Kostka Church.
van de Crommert, Paul H. '88 (NU) Canby, MN St. Peter Church; St. Leo, MN St. Leo Church.
Van De Kreeke, William L. '63 (GB) [5] Oshkosh, WI St. John Church.
Van De Loo, Willard '55 (GB) [17] Green Bay, WI St. Willebrord Church; Special Assignment.
Van de Paer, John *c.i.c.m.* '47 (ARL) [J] Arlington, VA Missionhurst, C.I.C.M.-Central House and Provincialate.
Van De Ven, Kenneth A. '71 (PHX) [3] Glendale, AZ St. James Church.
Van De Voord, Simeon *o.s.b.* '61 (B) [1] Boise, ID Cathedral of St. John the Evangelist.
Van Den Boogaard, Henry '42 (RIC) Retired; [M] West Point, VA Missionaries of the Holy Family, General Mission Office—M.S.F., Inc.
Van den Bussche, Hugo *o.m.i.* '53 (BWN) Roma, TX Our Lady of Refuge Church.
Van den Eynde, Stephen *ss.cc.* '48 (HON) [H] Honolulu, HI St. Patrick's Monastery.
Van Der Horst, John G. '65 (GB) [13] Green Bay, WI SS. Peter and Paul Church.
Van Der Linden, Peter J. '55 (DET) Retired.
Van Der Paalen, Pieter *c.i.c.m.* '55 (SAT) [M] San Antonio, TX Missionhurst Community Residence.
Van Der Peet, Michael *s.c.j.* (GAL) Retired.
van der Peet, Michael *s.c.j.* (SP) [O] Pinellas Park, FL Priests of the Sacred Heart.
Van Der Poel, Cornelius *c.s.sp.* '47 (VEN) [G] Sarasota, FL Congregation of the Holy Ghost.
van der Werff, Msgr. Martin '50 (NO) Gretna, LA St. Cletus Church.
Van Der Zanden, Edmund '38 (P) Retired.
Van Derdys, Carlos Jimenez '67 (SJN) Dorado, PR San Antonio de Padua Church.
Van Deuren, John H. '59 (GB) [F] Green Bay, WI St. Mary's Hospital-Medical Center.
Van Doan, Vincent '86 (LAN) Ann Arbor, MI University of Michigan Hospitals; Ann Arbor, MI Veterans' Hospital.
Van Duren, Charles '52 (JOL) Retired.
Van Dyke, James R. *s.j.* '93 (BUF) [D] Buffalo, NY Canisius High School; [O] Buffalo, NY Canisius Jesuit Community.
Van Gastel, William '86 (LA) [9] Long Beach, CA St. Lucy Church.
van Gogh, James A. '50 (SEA) Retired.
Van Gorder, John '53 (KC) Retired.
Van Guilder, Alphonse *o.f.m.conv.* '64 (MRY) Pismo Beach, CA St. Paul the Apostle Church; San Luis Obispo, CA California Men's Colony East.
Van Handorf, Jay '75 (LEX) [5] Lexington, KY St. Elizabeth Ann Seton Church.
Van Hee, Francis *c.i.c.m.* '48 (SAT) [M] San Antonio, TX Missionhurst Community Residence.
Van Hoof, Achilles E. *o.praem.* '48 (GB) [I] De Pere, WI St. Norbert Abbey.
Van Hoof, Achilles E. *o.praem.* '48 (KAL) [4] Kalamazoo, MI St. Monica Church.
Van Hoof, Gordon *o.s.c.* '53 (CHI) [J] Chicago, IL Resurrection Medical Center.
Van Hoof, Gordon *o.s.c.* '53 (DET) [K] Riverview, MI Crosier Community of Riverview.
Van Hook, John E. *o.f.m.* '55 (ALB) [B] Loudonville, NY Siena College.
Van Horn, David J. *c.pp.s.* '54 (CIN) [M] Dayton, OH Provincial House of the Cincinnati Province of the Society of the Precious Blood.
van Kaam, Adrian *c.s.sp.* '46 (PIT) [B] Pittsburgh, PA Duquesne University of the Holy Ghost.
Van Kempen, Robert '93 (FTW) [9] Fort Wayne, IN St. Jude Church.
Van Kets, Raphael *o.p.* '50 (PRO) [P] Providence, RI St. Thomas Aquinas Priory at Providence College.
Van Kuren, Corey S. '86 (SY) [10] Binghamton, NY St. Paul Church.
Van Lai, Joseph Khuyen '74 (SD) [6] San Diego, CA Holy Family Church.
van Lare, John *c.m.* '47 (SAT) Cotulla, TX Sacred Heart Church.
Van Lente, Richard J. '66 (GR) Fremont, MI All Saints Church.
Van Liefde, Msgr. Christian M. '73 (LA) Los Angeles, CA L.A. City Fire Dept.
Van Linden, Phil *c.m.* '70 (FRS) [3] Fresno, CA The Catholic Community of Mt. Carmel/St. Alphonsus Church.
Van Mullekom, Richard '56 (SAG) Retired.
Van Nevel, Msgr. Albert H. '42 (GRY) Retired.
Van Nguyen, Joseph Huyen '95 (SAC) Chico, CA Our Divine Savior Church.
Van Nguyen, Peter Phan *c.s.s.r.* (CC) Rockport, TX St. Peter Indo-Chinese Parish Church.
Van Nguyen, Phuong '93 (WOR) [4] Worcester, MA Christ the King Church.
Van Nguyen, Thanh '90 (ORG) Stanton, CA St. Polycarp Church.
Van Ommeren, Msgr. William '52 (SPK) [M] Spokane, WA Immaculate Heart Retreat Center.
Van Oss, James R. '64 (BEL) Posen, IL Our Lady of Perpetual Help Church; Todd's Mill, IL St. Mary Magdalen Church; [K] Belleville, IL Catholic Committee on Scouting of the Diocese of Belleville.
van Oudheusden, Henry L. '79 (LA) [R] Los Angeles, CA Amat House.
Van Phuong, Msgr. Francis Pham '66 (ATL) Hapeville, GA St. John the Evangelist Church; Hapeville, GA St. John the Evangelist Church.
Van Raes, Michael T. '41 (PEO) Retired; [L] Peoria, IL St. Augustine Manor.
Van Roo, William A. *s.j.* '47 (MIL) [P] Milwaukee, WI Jesuit Community at Marquette University.
Van Sickler, Robert '93 (BAK) John Day, OR St. Elizabeth's Church.
van Sloun, Eugene G. '48 (DOD) Retired.
Van Sloun, Michael *o.s.c.* '95 (STP) Anoka, MN St. Stephen Church; [N] Anoka, MN Crosier Community of Anoka.
Van Snellenberg, John '59 (SAC) Retired and in Senior Ministry.
Van Stone, John J. '48 (PH) [20] Philadelphia, PA St. Barnabas Church.
van Straaten, Werenfried *o.praem.* '40 (ORG) [H] Silverado, CA Norbertine Fathers.
Van Tassel, Everell (JKS) Hernando, MS Holy Spirit Church.
Van Thanh, Louis '94 (NY) [1] Newburgh, NY St. Patrick Church.
Van Thuyne, Dennis G. '77 (PH) Glenside, PA St. Luke the Evangelist Church.
Van Ty, Nguyen '85 (HT) [2] Thibodaux, LA St. Charles Borromeo Church.
Van Vlaenderen, Leonard S. '88 (MIL) Special Assignment.
Van Vurst, James *o.f.m.* '61 (CIN) [L] Centerville, OH The Franciscan at St. Leonard.
Van Winkle, Charles E. *c.s.c.* '78 (AUS) Killeen, TX St. Joseph's Church; [H] Austin, TX Congregation of Holy Cross - Southern Province.
Van Wormer, Giles *o.f.m.conv.* '57 (ALB) [A] Rensselaer, NY Conventual Franciscan Friars; [L] Rensselaer, NY Provincialate, Immaculate Conception Friary - Order of Friars Minor Conventual; [L] Rensselaer, NY Provincialate, Immaculate Conception Friary - Order of Friars Minor Conventual.
van-Ackeren, Leonard *o.s.b.* '38 (MAD) [J] Baraboo, WI St. Marys Ringling Convent.
Van-Hoorn, Leo '55 (ALX) Retired.
Vanagas, Albeyro *c.s.v.* '90 (CHI) [N] Arlington Heights, IL Viatorian Province Center-Clerics of St. Viator.
VanAmburgh, Donald C. '61 (SY) Vestal, NY Our Lady of Sorrows Church.
Vanasse, Bernard '78 (FR) [1] Swansea, MA St. Dominic's Church.
Vanasse, Henry G. *f.i.c.* '85 (PRT) [I] Alfred, ME Notre Dame Institute.
Vanasse, Hervey '77 (SEA) Buckley, WA St. Aloysius Church.
Vanasse, Roman R. *o.praem.* '60 (GB) [I] De Pere, WI St. Norbert Abbey.
Vance, Charles P. '70 (PH) Lenni, PA St. Francis de Sales Church.
Vance, James *c.ss.r.* '35 (OM) [19] Omaha, NE Holy Name Church; [31] Omaha, NE Mother of Perpetual Help Church.
Vance, James L. '63 (SFE) Raton, NM St. Patrick/St. Joseph Church.
Vance, Leslie A. '76 (SAT) Kirby, TX St. Joan of Arc Church.
Vancik, Vladimir '34 (PRM) Retired.
Vandal, Roland *m.s.* '49 (FR) [K] Attleboro, MA La Salette Provincial House.
VanDane, Louis L. *m.s.* '45 (STL) [P] St. Louis, MO La Salette Missionaries.
Vande Castle, Louis J. *o.praem.* '50 (GB) [I] De Pere, WI St. Joseph Priory.
Vande Hey, Robert '49 (GB) [I] De Pere, WI St. Joseph Priory.
Vandeberg, Joseph '89 (SCL) Villard, MN St. Bartholomew's Church; West Union, MN St. Alexius Church.
Vandebroek, Felix J. *ss.cc.* '54 (HON) Koloa, HI St. Raphael Church.
Vandegrift, J. Raymond *o.p.* '60 (WDC) [B] Washington, DC Dominican House of Studies.
Vandegrift, William S. '80 (CAM) Ocean City, NJ St. Augustine's Church.
Vandehey, Ervin S. '46 (P) Retired.
Vandehey, Kelly '96 (P) Medford, OR Sacred Heart of Jesus Church.
Vandehey, Scott '66 (P) [3] Eugene, OR St. Mary Church.
Vandeloo, Melvin B. '53 (BEL) Mount Vernon, IL St. Mary Church.
Vanden Heuvel, Jeffrey M. '86 (GB) [7] Oshkosh, WI St. Raphael the Archangel Church; Special Assignment.
Vanden Hogen, Msgr. James '64 (GB) Little Chute, WI St. John Nepomucene Church; [O] Green Bay, WI The Diocesan Charismatic Renewal Center.
Vanden Hogen, Paul A. '54 (GB) King, WI St. George Church; King, WI Wisconsin Veterans Home.
Vandenberg, James '77 (PBL) Absent on Leave.
Vandenberg, Robert H. '58 (GB) Combined Locks, WI St. Paul Church.
Vandenberg, Thomas L. '62 (SEA) Federal Way, WA St. Vincent De Paul Church.
VanDenBogaard, Joseph E. *m.m.* '37 (NY) [Z] Maryknoll, NY Maryknoll Fathers and Brothers.
VandenBossche, John V. *c.s.c.* '51 (FTW) [J] South Bend, IN Congregation of Holy Cross Indiana Province Provincial House.
VandenBossche, John V. *c.s.c.* '51 (PHX) [F] Phoenix, AZ Holy Cross Congregation of Casa Santa Cruz.
Vander Heyden, William F. '70 (GB) On Duty Outside the Diocese.
Vander Woude, Thomas '92 (ARL) Great Falls, VA St. Catherine of Siena Church.
Vandergeest, Peter J. '40 (ALN) Retired.
Vanderholt, James '57 (BEA) Dayton, TX St. Joseph the Worker Church; Groves, TX Immaculate Conception Church.
Vanderkolk, Peter J. '83 (LFT) Delphi, IN St. Joseph Church.
Vanderlay, Louis *o.s.b.* (LA) Montebello, CA St. Benedict Church.
Vanderlin, Philip *o.s.b.* '70 (BIS) [A] Richardton, ND Assumption Abbey.
VanderVennet, Timothy *o.c.s.o.* '35 (SAC) [A] Vina, CA Abbey of New Clairvaux, Trappist Seminary.
VanderVennett, Timothy *o.c.s.o.* '35 (SAC) [H] Vina, CA Abbey of New Clairvaux, Trappist.
Vanderwall, Francis W. *s.j.* '76 (LAF) [A] Grand Coteau, LA St. Charles College.
VanderWeel, Richard L. *s.s.e.* '62 (BUR) [G] Colchester, VT Society of St. Edmund.
VandeVelde, J. Richard *s.j.* '68 (CHI) [C] Chicago, IL Jesuit Community at Loyola University of Chicago.
VanDeVoord, Simeon *o.s.b.* '61 (B) [C] Jerome, ID Ascension Priory.
VandeWalle, Victor '40 (OKL) Retired.
Vandreuil, Paul '64 (WOR) Fiskdale, MA St. Anne's and St. Patrick's Church.
Vandrovec, Jerry C. '78 (STP) Mahtomedi, MN St. Jude of the Lake Church.
Vanecko, William E. '65 (CHI) [114] Chicago, IL St. Kilian Church.
Vang, Chue Ying '92 (STP) [36] St. Paul, MN St. Vincent de Paul Church.
VanGorder, John '53 (KC) [28] Kansas City, MO Our Lady of Good Counsel Church.
VanHaverbeke, Kenneth S. '91 (WCH) [5] Wichita, KS Church of the Magdalen.
Vanhee, Francis '48 (SAT) Lytle, TX St. Andrew Church.
Vanhoomissen, Bernard *c.ss.r.* '42 (SEA) [32] Seattle, WA Sacred Heart of Jesus Church.
Vanin, Dino S. *p.i.m.e.* '72 (COL) [H] Newark, OH P.I.M.E. Mission & Prayer Center.
Vanissery, Matthew '64 (WIN) Le Roy, MN St. Patrick's Church.
Vanitvelt, Milton H. '49 (MAR) Retired.
Vankeirsbilck, Paul *e.c.* '90 (STU) [F] Bloomingdale, OH Holy Family Hermitage.
Vanleeuwen, Joseph *c.p.* '64 (CHI) [N] Chicago, IL Passionist Provincial Office.
VanLiefde, Msgr. Christian '73 (LA) Pico Rivera, CA St. Hilary Church.
VanLoon, Msgr. Neil J. *v.f.* '79 (SCR) Kingston, PA St. Ignatius Church.
Vann, Alfred *ss.cc.* '43 (HON) [H] Honolulu, HI St. Patrick's Monastery.
Vann, John C. '42 (MIA) Retired.
Vann, Kevin W. '81 (SFD) Bethany, IL St. Isidore Church; [2] Decatur, IL Our Lady of Lourdes Church.
VanNguyen, Peter '60 (PMB) Lake Worth, FL Sacred Heart Church.
VanNuffelen, Albert *c.i.c.m.* '41 (ARL) [J] Arlington, VA Missionhurst, C.I.C.M.-Central House and Provincialate.
VanNufflen, Albert *c.i.c.m.* '41 (ORL) Retired.

Vano, Roque P. '79 (SD) Brawley, CA St. Margaret Mary Church.
Vanoncini, Robert R. '63 (FRS) Dos Palos, CA Sacred Heart Church.
VanOverbeek, Gerald *o.s.a.* '65 (CHI) [N] Chicago, IL St. Rita Monastery.
VanSmoorenburg, Matthew *l.c.* (MAD) [I] Edgerton, WI Legion of Christ, Inc.
VanWiel, John E. *c.s.v.* '66 (CHI) [D] Arlington Heights, IL St. Viator High School.
Vanyo, Leo V. '52 (PIT) [1] Pittsburgh, PA St. Paul Cathedral.
Vanzillotta, Gino *o.m.* '54 (LA) [3] Los Angeles, CA All Saints Church; [R] Los Angeles, CA Minim Fathers.
Vap, Gerald F. '65 (LIN) Orleans, NE St. Mary's Church.
Vap, Msgr. Ivan F. '54 (LIN) Geneva, NE St. Joseph's Church.
Vaquero, Isaac *m.des.* '73 (ELP) Clint, TX San Lorenzo Church.
Varady, Michael *c.ss.r.* '87 (CHR) Sumter, SC St. Jude Church.
Varakukala, George *h.g.n.* '62 (TYL) Clarksville, TX St. Joseph Church.
Varano, Andrew R. '58 (BRK) [46] Brooklyn, NY St. Francis of Paola Church.
Varas, Felix '50 (SJN) [51] San Juan, PR Maria Reina del Mundo Church.
Varble, Edward F. '50 (Y) Middlebranch, OH St. Therese Little Flower Church; Retired.
Varela, Jose '90 (LA) Hacienda Heights, CA St. John Vianney Church; Pomona, CA Sacred Heart Church.
Varettoni, Msgr. Julian B. '55 (PAT) [1] Clifton, NJ Sacred Heart Church.
Varga, Andrew G. '78 (BGP) Brookfield, CT St. Joseph's Church.
Varga, George '42 (E) Retired.
Varga, Paul *o.f.m.conv.* '63 (TR) Holmdel, NJ St. Benedict Church.
Varga, Wayne F. '74 (PAT) [5] Passaic, NJ Holy Trinity Church.
Vargas, David (CC) Permanent Deacons.
Vargas, Eric P. *s.v.d.* '76 (SB) [7] San Bernardino, CA St. Anthony Church.
Vargas, Gabriel '90 (NEW) [7] Jersey City, NJ Assumption/All Saints Church; [17] Jersey City, NJ Mt. Carmel Church.
Vargas, German '63 (SJN) [60] San Juan, PR Santa Teresa Jornet Church.
Vargas, John '66 (DET) [4] Sterling Heights, MI St. Jane Frances de Chantal Church.
Vargas, John C. *c.ss.r.* '78 (BR) [H] Baton Rouge, LA Redemptorist Fathers Vice Provincialate.
Vargas, Jose Carlos '92 (PCE) Coamo, PR St. Blase Church.
Vargas, Roberto *o.s.a.* '55 (CC) [17] Laredo, TX St. Vincent de Paul Church.
Vargo, Robert B. '89 (HRT) Poquonock, CT St. Joseph's Church.
Varickamackal, Joseph '84 (HRT) [7] New Britain, CT St. Jerome's Church.
Varley, John J. '59 (SPR) [10] Pittsfield, MA St. Teresa Church.
Varna, Msgr. Leons '29 (BRK) [Y] Brooklyn, NY Latvian Roman Catholic Mission.
Varney, Lawrence F. '60 (TOL) Assumption, OH St. Mary of Assumption Church.
Varni, Msgr. Edward '39 (OAK) [3] Concord, CA St. Francis of Assisi Church; Retired.
Varno, John J. '66 (ALB) Wynantskill, NY St. Jude the Apostle Church.
Varnskuhler, Paschal *o.f.m.* '41 (CIN) [M] Cincinnati, OH St. Francis Seraph Friary.
Varo, Jose Luis *o.f.m.* '56 (FRS) McFarland, CA St. Elizabeth Church.
Varone, Normand G. '75 (SPC) Benton, MO St. Denis Church.
Varsany, Msgr. William I. (NY) [DD] New York, NY Hungarian Catholic League of America, Inc.
Varsanyi, Msgr. William I. '46 (PRO) [22] Providence, RI Our Lady of Charity Church; [M] Pawtucket, RI Jeanne Jugan Residence.
Vartzelis, George D. '53 (BO) Nahant, MA St. Thomas Aquinas Church.
Varvaro, Msgr. William A. '63 (BRK) [192] Queens, NY St. Margaret's Church.
Varvaro, Msgr. William A. '63 (NY) [DD] New York, NY National Italian Apostolate Conference.
Vas, Joseph S. '79 (OKL) Special Assignment; [E] Oklahoma City, OK St. Anthony Hospital.
Vasa, Msgr. Robert F. '76 (LIN) [13] Lincoln, NE Bishop Bonacum Chancery Church; [G] Lincoln, NE School Sisters of Christ the King, Villa Regina Motherhouse & Novitiate.
Vasaturo, Anthony J. '55 (BO) [5] Medford, MA Sacred Heart Church; Retired.
Vaschetto, Bernardo *o.f.m.cap.* '62 (BO) [60] Boston, MA St. Patrick Church.
Vascones, Hugo M. *c.m.* '48 (BUF) [O] Niagara University, NY Vincentian Community at Niagara University.
Vasek, Stephen *o.m.i.* '71 (BUF) [27] Buffalo, NY Holy Angels Church.
Vasil, James D. '74 (GBG) Smithton, PA St. Timothy Church.
Vasile, Louis A. '72 (ROC) Fairport, NY Church of the Resurrection.
Vasilj, Kvirin *o.f.m.* '40 (CHI) [N] Chicago, IL Croatian Franciscan Custody of the Holy Family.
Vaske, Martin O. *s.j.* '47 (OM) [K] Omaha, NE Jesuit Community At Creighton University.
Vasko, Christopher '83 (TOL) [4] Lima, OH St. Rose Church.
Vasquez, Joe '84 (SAN) Fort Stockton, TX St. Joseph's Church; Sanderson, TX St. James Church.
Vass, Robert *s.d.v.* '87 (PAT) [M] Florham Park, NJ Father Justin Vocationary.
Vasti, Michael *m.s.c.* '56 (ALN) [A] Center Valley, PA Missionaries of the Sacred Heart.
Vasti, Michael J. *m.s.c.* '56 (ALN) [G] Allentown, PA Sacred Heart Hospital.
Vater, Robert L. '45 (COV) Fort Thomas, KY St. Catherine of Siena Church; Retired.
Vath, Aloysius H. '40 (PH) [47] Philadelphia, PA St. Francis Xavier Church.
Vath, William R. '72 (LFT) [3] Lafayette, IN St. Boniface Church; Special Assignment.
Vattakudiyil, Francis P. '63 (RVC) Kings Park, NY St. Joseph's Church.
Vattakunnel, Jose '90 (LKC) Elton, LA St. Joseph's Church.
Vatter, Joseph E. (BUF) [2] Depew, NY St. Barnabas Church.
Vaughan, Brian S. '82 (WDC) Absent On Leave.
Vaughan, Gregory D. '72 (TR) New Monmouth, NJ St. Mary Church.
Vaughan, James '50 (ALB) [13] Troy, NY Sacred Heart Church.
Vaughan, Msgr. John J. '67 (MIA) [4] Miami Beach, FL St. Patrick Church.
Vaughan, John R. '74 (OWN) [1] Owensboro, KY St. Stephen Cathedral.
Vaughan, Richard P. *s.j.* '50 (LA) [C] Los Angeles, CA Loyola Marymount University.
Vaughan, Thomas *s.s.c.* '56 (OM) [K] St. Columbans, NE St. Columban's Foreign Mission Society.
Vaughan, William L. '95 (SFR) [3] San Rafael, CA St. Raphael Church.
Vaughey, Msgr. James K. (NY) On Special or Other (Arch)Diocesan Assignment.
Vaughey, Msgr. James K. '65 (NY) Briarcliff Manor, NY St. Theresa Church.
Vaughn, John *o.f.m.* '55 (MRY) [G] San Miguel, CA Franciscan Friars, O.F.M.; [G] San Miguel, CA Novitiate House for the Franciscan Friars, O.F.M.; [I] San Miguel, CA San Miguel Retreat House.
Vaughn, Mason L. '50 (SAG) Birch Run, MI Sacred Heart Church.
Vaughn, Robert William *o.p.* '71 (NY) [Z] New York, NY St. Vincent Ferrer Priory.
Vaughn, Roger *o.s.c.* '77 (NY) [Z] New Rochelle, NY Crosier (Canons Regular of the Order of the Holy Cross).
Vaughn, Roland '71 (LKC) Hackberry, LA St. Peter Apostle Church.
Vaught, Michael R. '73 (OKL) Clinton, OK St. Mary's Church.
Vavasseur, David A. '66 (BR) Baker, LA St. Isidore the Farmer Church; Baton Rouge, LA Nursing Homes not under Catholic auspices.
Vavasseur, Henry C. '58 (BR) Port Allen, LA Holy Family Church.
Vaverek, Gavin '90 (TYL) Longview, TX St. Mary Church.
Vaverek, Hayden J. '94 (CHR) Greenwood, SC Our Lady of Lourdes Church; [H] Greenwood, SC Lander College Newman Center.
Vaverek, Timothy V. '85 (AUS) [5] Waco, TX St. Joseph Church.
Vavonese, Charles S. '73 (SY) Special Assignment; [S] East Syracuse, NY Bishop Grimes Priests Residence.
Vavrick, Eugene '93 (TR) Lakewood, NJ St. Mary of the Lake Church.
Vavrina, Kenneth '62 (OM) Clarks, NE St. Peter Church; Silver Creek, NE St. Lawrence Church.
Vavro, Peter '50 (SB) [7] Riverside, CA St. Francis de Sales Church.
Vaz, Francis F. '61 (MET) Oxford, NJ St. Rose of Lima Church.
Vaz, Rock I. *s.j.* (AUS) [H] Austin, TX Jesuit Fathers and Brothers.
Vaz, Rock I. *s.j.* '71 (AUS) Belton, TX Christ the King Church.
Vaze Parampil, Thomas '69 (LUB) Retired.
Vazhapilly, Paul '61 (BRK) [55] Brooklyn, NY Holy Family Church; [T] Brooklyn, NY Catholic Migration & Refugee Office, Catholic Migration Services, Inc.
Vazhappily, Mathew *c.m.i.* '74 (SFS) Conde, SD St. John the Baptist Church.
Vazquez, Albert M. *c.m.f.* '55 (LA) [28] Los Angeles, CA Our Lady Queen of the Angels Church.
Vazquez, Antonio J. '91 (ARE) [4] Camuy, PR Our Lady of Monserrate Church.
Vazquez, Carlos R. '89 (WIL) New Castle, DE Delaware State Hospital.
Vazquez, Enrique '89 (SJN) [4] Bayamon, PR Cristo Salvador Church.
Vazquez, Harry Lopez '93 (MGZ) Sabana Grande, PR Church of San Isidro.
Vazquez, Jose '89 (Y) Absent on Leave.
Vazquez, Jose L. '95 (MIA) [18] Miami, FL St. Dominic Church.
Vazquez, Jose Natividad *m.sp.s.* '76 (LA) [3] Oxnard, CA Our Lady of Guadalupe Parish Church.
Vazquez, Luis A. '90 (ARE) Corozal-Padilla, PR Our Lady of the Seven Sorrows Church.
Vazquez, Msgr. Perfecto '56 (BRK) [52] Brooklyn, NY Guardian Angel Church.
Vazquez, Ramon Gomez *o.f.m.* '92 (CAM) [2] Camden, NJ St. Anthony of Padua Church.
Vazquez, Virginio '73 (TYL) Lovelady, TX Eastham Unit, Texas Department of Corrections.
Vazquez-Vega, Edwin '95 (PCE) Salinas, PR Our Lady of Monserrat Church.
Vead, Victor P. '92 (ALX) Isle Brevelle, LA St. Augustine's Church.
Vecchio, Egidio A. *m.s.* '55 (LKC) [1] Sulphur, LA Immaculate Conception of the B.V.M. Church.
Vecchio, Michael J. '50 (PIT) Retired.
Vecsey, Stephen N. '73 (LA) Retired.
Vedro, James A. *o.s.c.* '65 (DET) Trenton, MI St. Joseph Church; [K] Riverview, MI Crosier Community of Riverview.
Veeneman, Dismas J. *o.f.m.conv.* '69 (IND) Clarksville, IN St. Anthony of Padua Church.
Vega, Carlos '89 (MIA) [1] Miami, FL St. Mary's Cathedral.
Vega, Donald *s.j.* '65 (SJN) [22] San Juan, PR San Ignacio de Loyola Church.
Vega, Emilio *ss.cc.* '68 (BWN) [3] Harlingen, TX Queen of Peace Church.
Vega, Fernando *c.m.f.* '40 (FRS) [8] Fresno, CA St. Anthony Claret Church.
Vega, Hector *i.s.s.s.* '74 (CC) On Special Assignment.
Vega, Hector R. *c.c.* '74 (MIL) [T] Waukesha, WI Secular Institute of Schoenstatt Fathers.
Vega, John '74 (CC) Portland, TX Our Lady of Mount Carmel Church.
Vega, Jose Antonio Lopez '92 (PCE) Arroyo, PR Our Lady of Mt. Carmel Church.
Vega, Jose L. *o.m.* '69 (LA) [3] Los Angeles, CA All Saints Church; [R] Los Angeles, CA Minim Fathers.
Vega, Jose Luis '54 (FRS) Cutler, CA St. Mary Church.
Vega, Juan Ramon '55 (BR) Paincourtville, LA St. Elizabeth Church.
Vega, Raymond *s.c.j.* '73 (SP) [O] Pinellas Park, FL Priests of the Sacred Heart.
Vega, Richard '83 (LA) Lompoc, CA La Purisima Concepcion Church.
Vega, Roberto '87 (ARE) [1] Arecibo, PR Cathedral of San Felipe Apostol.
Vega (Vega-Montalbo), Jose (Giuseppe) '73 (SEA) Unassigned.
Vegvari, Basil *o.f.m.* '53 (PSC) New York, NY Exaltation of Holy Cross Church.
Vehovec, Valentine '43 (SB) Retired.
Veich, Vincent J. '71 (BGP) [1] Stamford, CT St. Benedict's Church.
Veigas, Albert '76 (CLV) [68] Cleveland, OH St. Rose Church.
Veik, Al *o.f.m.cap.* '67 (MIL) [Y] Milwaukee, WI House of Peace.
Veilleux, Dom Armand *o.c.s.o* (ATL) [I] Conyers, GA The Monastery of the Holy Spirit.
Veith, William E. '70 (CHI) [J] Elk Grove Village, IL Alexian Brothers Medical Center, Inc.
Vekemans, Roger *s.j.* (MIL) [Y] Milwaukee, WI International Institute of the Heart of Jesus.
Vela, Fabian '56 (MRY) Hollister, CA Sacred Heart Church; Tres Pinos, CA Immaculate Conception Church.
Vela, Rudy '84 (SAT) [B] San Antonio, TX Marianist Formation Community; [M] San Antonio, TX Marianist Formation Community.
Vela, William *c.s.b.* '90 (GAL) [F] Houston, TX St. Thomas High School.
Velas, Vincent '64 (PIT) [83] Pittsburgh, PA Risen Lord Church.
Velasco, Arturo '86 (LA) Norwalk, CA St. John of God Church.
Velasquez, Charles J. '85 (CHY) Wheatland, WY St. Patrick's Church.
Velasquez, Jose '67 (ELP) [9] El Paso, TX Holy Family Church.
Velasquez, Marcos C. '89 (TUC) Nogales, AZ Sacred Heart Church.
Velasquez, Rodrigo '58 (RVC) Great Neck, NY St. Aloysius Church.
Velazquez, David Mateo *m.sp.s.* '80 (LA) Huntington Park, CA St. Martha Church.
Velazquez, John Alicea '94 (CGS) Barranquitas, PR Church of St. Anthony of Padua.

Velazquez, Luis '75 (ARE) On Duty Outside the Diocese.
Velesz, Dunstan *o.f.m.* '35 (SFD) [B] Quincy, IL Quincy University.
Velez, Andrew '96 (PAT) Morristown, NJ St. Margaret's Church.
Velez, Msgr. Francisco '58 (PCE) Juana Diaz, PR St. Raymond Nonato Church.
Velie, Richard '79 (MIA) Absent on Leave.
Vella, Msgr. Desmond J. '59 (NY) [52] New York, NY Immaculate Conception Church.
Vella, Francis (OAK) On Special Assignment.
Vella, Francis M. (HRT) Newington, CT Department of Veteran Affairs Medical Center.
Vella, Joseph C. '68 (BRK) Military Chaplains.
Vellankal, James '58 (LAF) [2] Opelousas, LA Our Lady of Mercy Church; On Special Assignment.
Vellaramparampil, Aaron '71 (RVC) East Meadow, NY St. Raphael Church.
Vellenga, R. Stephen '81 (CLV) Northfield, OH St. Barnabas Church.
Velloorattil, George (CHI) [179] Chicago, IL Queen of All Saints Basilica.
Vellucci, Dennis C. '75 (LA) Walnut, CA St. Lorenzo Ruiz Church.
Velo, Msgr. Kenneth J. '73 (CHI) [U] Chicago, IL The Catholic Church Extension Society.
Velozo, Msgr. Donald D. '65 (CAM) Cape May Court House, NJ Our Lady of the Angels Church; Northfield, NJ St. Bernadette Church.
Velten, Robert *o.s.b.* '54 (SP) [O] St. Leo, FL St. Leo Abbey.
Veltri, Dennis J. '93 (E) [10] Erie, PA Our Lady of Peace Church.
Veltrie, James V. *s.j.* '65 (STL) [C] St. Louis, MO Saint Louis University; [P] St. Louis, MO Jesuit Community Corporation at St. Louis University - Jesuit Hall.
Velutis, John (CHI) Retired.
Vendetti, Michael A. '64 (BRK) Released from Diocesan Assignment.
Venditti, J. Michael '87 (MET) [7] Perth Amboy, NJ Holy Spirit Church; Perth Amboy, NJ Raritan Bay Medical Center.
Vendramin, Aldo *c.s.* '75 (CHI) [N] Stone Park, IL Scalabrini Mission Center.
Venegoni, John L. '95 (BEL) Pinckneyville, IL St. Bruno Church.
Veneklase, Michael G. *o.c.d.* '93 (GRY) [K] Munster, IN Discalced Carmelite Fathers Monastery.
Veneroso, Joseph R. *m.m.* '78 (NY) [Z] Maryknoll, NY Maryknoll Fathers and Brothers.
Veneto, Joseph P. '46 (BO) Retired.
Venette, Howard J. '84 (OG) Harrisville, NY St. Francis Solanus Church.
Venezia, Arthur '71 (PMB) North Palm Beach, FL St. Paul of the Cross Church.
Vengayil, Thomas '59 (PMB) Tequesta, FL St. Jude Church; Tequesta, FL St. Jude Church; [J] West Palm Beach, FL Our Lady Queen of Peace Catholic Cemetery, Inc.
Venglarik, Daniel M. '73 (Y) Boardman, OH St. Charles Borromeo's Church.
Venker, Josef V. *s.j.* '87 (SEA) [A] Seattle, WA Seattle University.
Venne, R. Thomas '62 (MIL) Pewaukee, WI St. Anthony's Church.
Venne, Samuel J. '78 (BUF) [46] Buffalo, NY St. Martin Church.
Venneri, Michael D. '82 (SPK) Special Ministry; [G] Spokane, WA Sacred Heart Medical Center.
Vennitti, Thomas A. '73 (STU) Cadiz, OH St. Teresa Church; Freeport, OH St. Matthias Mission Church; Jewett, OH Our Lady of Perpetual Help Mission Church.
Vennix, James F. '56 (GB) Waupaca, WI St. Mary Magdalene Church.
Venters, Darrell '89 (OWN) [5] Owensboro, KY Precious Blood Church.
Ventiquattro, Jude *t.o.r.* '88 (ALT) [F] Loretto, PA St. Francis Friary, Third Order Regular of St. Francis of Penance; [H] Huntingdon, PA Juniata College.
Ventre, Armand V. '57 (PRO) [K] North Providence, RI St. Joseph Health Services of Rhode Island - Our Lady of Fatima Hospital.
Ventresca, A. Andrew '57 (HRT) Retired.
Ventura, Anthony '78 (BUR) Newport, VT St. Mary Star of the Sea Church.
Ventura, Anthony C. '78 (HRT) Retired.
Ventura, Gennaro J. '43 (ROC) Retired.
Ventura, John '68 (BIR) Absent on Leave.
Ventura, Mauro '81 (STU) [F] Bloomingdale, OH Holy Family Hermitage.
Ventura, Thomas F. '61 (CHI) Winnetka, IL SS. Faith, Hope and Charity Church.
Venust Lobo, Mauro Raul '62 (NO) Violet, LA Our Lady of Lourdes Church.
Venuti, Angelo A. (BRK) [81] Brooklyn, NY St. Mary Mother of Jesus Church.
Venvertloh, Ken J. (SFD) Virginia, IL St. Luke Church.
Venvertloh, Ken J. '67 (SFD) Jacksonville, IL Our Saviour Church.
Venza, Felix F. '72 (TR) Florence, NJ St. Clare Church.
Venzor, Jesse C. '80 (FRS) Woodlake, CA St. Frances Cabrini Church.
Ver Bust, Richard M. '58 (GB) Special Assignment; [B] De Pere, WI St. Norbert College.
Ver-Schneider, Neil *s.j.* '66 (PH) [H] Philadelphia, PA The Gesu School.
Vera, Luis A. *o.s.a.* (NY) [216] Staten Island, NY Our Lady of Good Counsel Church.
Vera, Romulo E. *c.s.c.* '89 (FTW) [J] South Bend, IN Congregation of Holy Cross Indiana Province Provincial House.
Vera, Vincente (CHK) San Vicente Village, District 10, MP San Vicente Ferrer Parish Church; San Vicente Village, District 10, MP San Vicente Ferrer Parish Church.
Veras, Richard '96 (NY) [174] Bronx, NY Our Lady of Mt. Carmel Church.
Verbeke, Albert *c.i.c.m.* '46 (ARL) [J] Falls Church, VA Missionhurst-C.I.C.M.
Verberg, Richard R. '71 (MIL) Greenfield, WI St. John the Evangelist Church.
Verboomen, Willy *c.i.c.m.* '63 (BWN) McAllen, TX McAllen Medical Center.
Verbrugghe, Albert E. '50 (TUC) [F] Tucson, AZ Regina Cleri Center.
Verbryke, William L. *s.j.* '83 (CIN) [F] Cincinnati, OH St. Xavier High School; [M] Cincinnati, OH Jesuit Community at St. Xavier High School; [P] Milford, OH Milford Spiritual Center.
Vercek, Alphonse *sch.p.* '38 (BUF) [O] Derby, NY Piarist Fathers.
Vercellone, Anthony T. '80 (LAV) [8] Las Vegas, NV St. Elizabeth Ann Seton Church.
Verdegan, Albert L. '60 (SUP) Radisson, WI Sacred Heart Church; Winter, WI St. Peter Church.
Verdelotti, Anthony W. '86 (PRO) East Greenwich, RI Our Lady of Mercy Church.
Verdelotti, James J. '78 (PRO) Bristol, RI Our Lady of Mount Carmel Church.
Verdi, Ralph C. *c.pp.s.* '71 (LFT) [A] Rensselaer, IN Saint Joseph's College.
Verdia, Carlos *c.m.f.* '85 (SJN) [23] Bayamon, PR Santa Maria Church; [5] Toa Alta, PR N. Sra. de la Providencia Church.
Verdia, Francisco *c.m.f.* '87 (SJN) [2] Bayamon, PR San Antonio Maria Claret Church.
Verdick, James *o.f.m.* '40 (MIL) [P] Burlington, WI Queen of Peace Friary.
Verdick, Jerome F. '58 (WIN) Absent on Leave.
Verdoon, Cornelius '51 (SPK) Retired.
Verdun, Gerald J. '72 (PEO) Pekin, IL St. Joseph's Church.
Vereb, Jerome *c.p.* '72 (PIT) [N] Pittsburgh, PA St. Paul of the Cross Monastery.
Vereb, John '47 (PMB) [4] West Palm Beach, FL St. John Fisher Church; Retired.
VerEecke, Robert F. *s.j.* '78 (BO) [3] Newton, MA St. Ignatius Church.
Vereker, Tobias '58 (SAC) Vallejo, CA St. Vincent Ferrer Church.
Verespy, Joseph D. '79 (SCR) Hughestown, PA Blessed Sacrament Church.
Vergara, Armando '73 (STO) Linden, CA Holy Cross Church.
Vergauwen, Peter '42 (SAN) Retired.
Vergauwen, Peter '42 (SAT) [K] San Antonio, TX Padua Place.
Verhaeghe, Ronald '92 (KC) Leave of Absence.
Verhagen, Donald *s.d.s.* '45 (MIL) [P] Milwaukee, WI Salvatorians - Jordan Hall.
Verhagen, Norbert M. *m.m.* '39 (SJ) [M] Los Altos, CA Maryknoll.
Verhalen, Charles J. '47 (MIL) Theresa, WI St. Theresa's Church.
Verhalen, David H. *c.s.c.* '54 (FTW) [J] South Bend, IN Congregation of Holy Cross Indiana Province Provincial House.
Verhalen, David H. *c.s.c.* '54 (GRY) [E] Rolling Prairie, IN Le Mans Academy.
Verhalen, Peter *o.cist.* '81 (DAL) [D] Irving, TX Cistercian Preparatory School; [G] Irving, TX Cistercian Preparatory School; [M] Irving, TX Cistercian Abbey of Our Lady of Dallas.
Verhasselt, David A. '89 (MIL) Mapleton, WI St. Catherine Church.
Verheggen, Peter *o.f.m.* '49 (TUC) Topawa, AZ San Solano Missions - Tohono O'odham Indian Reservation Church.
Verhelst, Steven J. '90 (NU) Benson, MN St. Francis Church; Clontarf, MN St. Malachy Church; Danvers, MN Church of the Visitation; De Graff, MN St. Bridget Church; Murdock, MN Church of the Sacred Heart.
Verhoff, Melvin '91 (TOL) [19] Toledo, OH St. Catherine of Siena Church.
Verhoff, Werner F. *c.pp.s.* '43 (FTW) [11] Fort Wayne, IN Most Precious Blood Church.
Verhoye, Gerard A. '49 (PEO) Retired.
Verkamp, Bernard J. '64 (EVN) On Leave of Absence.
Verley, Jude *o.s.c.* '79 (DET) Riverview, MI St. Cyprian Church; [K] Riverview, MI Crosier Community of Riverview.
Vermiglio, Tom *m.c.c.j.* '72 (CHI) [N] La Grange Park, IL Comboni Mission Center.
Vernon, Donald B. '55 (LFT) Dunnington, IN St. Mary Church; Fowler, IN Sacred Heart of Jesus Church.
Vernon, John E. '54 (OM) [46] Omaha, NE St. Thomas More Church.
Verostko, Remigius B. *o.s.b.* '57 (GBG) [H] Latrobe, PA Saint Vincent Archabbey.
Verrecchia, James A. '83 (ARL) Manassas, VA All Saints Church.
Verrett, Joseph C. *s.s.j.* '55 (BAL) [M] Baltimore, MD St. Joseph Society of the Sacred Heart House of Central Administration.
Verrier, John M. '95 (PEO) [15] Peoria, IL St. Vincent De Paul Church.
Verrigni, Robert J. '77 (NY) Larchmont, NY SS. John and Paul Church.
Verrill, Wendell '63 (BO) [4] Waltham, MA St. Mary Church.
Verrill, William F. '79 (BGP) [3] Trumbull, CT St. Stephen Church.
Verruni, Samuel A. '86 (PH) Exton, PA SS. Philip and James Church; [DD] Philadelphia, PA Newman Apostolate.
Verschaeve, C. Michael '77 (DET) [1] Taylor, MI St. Alfred Church.
Verstreken, Alfred *c.j.* '73 (LA) [D] Santa Barbara, CA Bishop Garcia Diego High School.
Verstynen, Robert J. '47 (RCK) Retired.
Verzeletti, Mauro *c.s.* '93 (SD) Imperial, CA St. Anthony of Padua Church.
Vesbit, Thomas S. '64 (GR) [15] Grand Rapids, MI St. Jude Church.
Vescera, Giuseppe *c.p.* (BO) [53] Boston, MA Our Lady of the Assumption Church.
Veselenak, Stephen *o.s.b.* '67 (PBR) McKeesport, PA St. Nicholas Church.
Vesely, James J. '54 (CLV) Brooklyn, OH St. Thomas More Church.
Vesely, Stanley G. *o.s.b.* '40 (JOL) [A] Lisle, IL Benedictine University; [J] Lisle, IL St. Procopius Abbey.
Vesey, John E. '68 (BRK) Released from Diocesan Assignment.
Vesga, Mario '62 (SD) [2] Chula Vista, CA Our Lady of Guadalupe Church.
Vespa, Bauttista '34 (FRS) Faculties Only.
Vessels, John L. *s.j.* '57 (ATL) [K] Atlanta, GA Ignatius House.
Vessels, John L. *s.j.* '57 (NO) [C] New Orleans, LA Loyola University.
Vest, Joseph E. '81 (L) [14] Louisville, KY St. Bernard Church.
Veszelovszky, Albin V. *o.praem.* '44 (GB) [17] Green Bay, WI St. Willebrord Church; [I] De Pere, WI St. Norbert Abbey; [O] De Pere, WI Canons Regular of Magnovarad, Ltd.
Vetrano, Anthony *o.f.m.cap.* '92 (NY) [Z] Garrison, NY St. Francis Friary.
Vetrano, Michael A. '79 (RVC) Melville, NY St. Elizabeth Church.
Vetter, Austin A. '93 (BIS) Center, ND St. Martin Church.
Vetter, Joseph G. '73 (R) Southport, NC Sacred Heart Church.
Vetter, Msgr. Wendelyn '60 (FAR) [5] Fargo, ND St. Anthony of Padua Church.
Vettese, Donald *s.j.* '82 (TOL) [C] Toledo, OH St. John's Jesuit High School.
Vettiyankal, Abraham *c.m.i.* '70 (NY) Irvington-on-the-Hudson, NY Immaculate Conception Church.
Veverka, Floribert *o.f.m.* '48 (STL) [P] St. Louis, MO Franciscan Friary of St. Anthony of Padua.
Vevik, Paul '77 (SPK) [12] Spokane, WA St. Francis Xavier Church.
Vezhaparambil, Paul *c.m.i.* '64 (NY) Bronxville, NY St. Joseph Church; Bronxville, NY Lawrence Hospital.
Via, Anthony P. *s.j.* '62 (P) [L] Portland, OR Jesuit Provincial Office (Oregon Prov.).
Via, Anthony P. *s.j.* '62 (SPK) [C] Spokane, WA Gonzaga University.
Viale, Paul A. '67 (NEW) [2] Newark, NJ St. Patrick's Pro-Cathedral; [7] Newark, NJ St. Augustine's Church.
Viall, James A. '54 (CLV) [68] Cleveland, OH St. Rose Church.
Viall, John L. '59 (CLV) North Royalton, OH St. Albert the Great Church.
Viallis, Didier-Marie Dugas '94 (CC) [H] Laredo, TX St. John's Priory, (F.J.).
Vialpando, Kenneth '91 (SLC) Moab, UT St. Pius X Church; Monticello, UT St. Joseph Church.
Vianney, Peter J. '65 (NY) Hyde Park, NY Regina Coeli Church.
Viau, Msgr. Roger '43 (SPR) Retired; [H] Springfield, MA St. Michael's Residence.
Viberti, Victor L. *s.s.p.* '38 (NY) [B] New York, NY Society of St. Paul.

Vicente, Francisco '49 (OAK) Antioch, CA Holy Rosary Church.
Vicente, Isidore V. *o.p.* '64 (GAL) [Q] Houston, TX Dominican Fathers and Brothers, St. Mark Priory, Inc.; [T] Houston, TX University of Houston Central Campus Catholic Newman Association.
Vicente, Julian (SJN) On Duty Outside the Archdiocese.
Vichas, Walter A. '49 (HRT) [1] Waterbury, CT Blessed Sacrament Church.
Vichich, Michael T. '74 (MAR) Hermansville, MI St. John Neumann Church.
Vickery, Richard F. '48 (MAN) Retired.
Victor, Al '76 (PMB) Boynton Beach, FL St. Thomas More Church; Retired.
Victor, Ronald J. '78 (DET) [3] St. Clair Shores, MI St. Isaac Jogues Church.
Victoria, Anthony E. *s.m.* '69 (CIN) [M] Dayton, OH Marianist Provincialate.
Victoria, Robert '91 (LA) Rowland Heights, CA St. Elizabeth Ann Seton Church.
Vida, Msgr. George N. '57 (VNN) Anaheim, CA Annunciation Church.
Vidal, Robert S. '66 (ORG) Seal Beach, CA St. Anne's Church.
Vidiella, Felix '52 (CC) Retired.
Vidmar, John *o.p.* '80 (WDC) [B] Washington, DC Dominican House of Studies.
Vidra, Msgr. Thomas J. '63 (SD) El Centro, CA St. Mary Church.
Vidrine, Msgr. Curtis S. '45 (LKC) Cameron, LA Our Lady Star of the Sea Church.
Vieages, Harold '64 (RNO) Leave of Absence.
Vieck, Hilary F. '55 (EVN) Bloomfield, IN Holy Name Church; Linton, IN St. Peter Church.
Vieira, Victor M. '67 (PRO) Valley Falls, RI Our Lady of Fatima Church.
Vieites, Jesus *ss.cc.* '62 (SJN) [1] Guaynabo, PR Corazon de Jesus Church.
Vielgus, Thaddeus A. '54 (MET) Retired.
Vien, John R. '93 (STL) [14] St. Louis, MO Our Lady of Sorrows Church.
Vier, Msgr. Henry J. '40 (NY) [185] Bronx, NY St. Raymond Church; Retired.
Viera, Manuel *o.f.m.* '82 (SFE) [1] Santa Fe, NM The Cathedral of San Francisco de Asis.
Vierling, Ronald M. (NY) Suffern, NY Sacred Heart Church.
Viero, Carmine (LA) [D] Los Angeles, CA Bishop Mora Salesian High School.
Viero, James *c.s.* '45 (NY) [Z] Staten Island, NY Scalabrinian Missionaries.
Vierra, Theodore A. '60 (LA) [86] Los Angeles, CA St. Paul the Apostle Church; [BB] Los Angeles, CA Archdiocesan Office for Campus Ministry.
Vieson, Paul F. *s.m.* '84 (CIN) [D] Dayton, OH The University of Dayton; [M] Dayton, OH Marianist Provincialate.
Viet Tran, Bac-Hai '84 (NO) Pearl River, LA SS. Peter and Paul Church.
Viet-Chau, Joachim *s.s.s.* '72 (CLV) [P] Cleveland, OH Congregation of the Blessed Sacrament Provincial House.
Vieweg, Robert R. '64 (CLV) Grafton, OH Immaculate Conception Church.
Vigeant, Wilfred J. *s.j.* (BO) [W] Weston, MA Campion Center.
Vigil, Joe D. '80 (SFE) [5] Albuquerque, NM Holy Ghost Church.
Vigil, Michael A. '85 (GLP) Winslow, AZ St. Joseph's Church.
Vigil, Paul '91 (LA) Redondo Beach, CA St. Lawrence Martyr Church.
Vigilanti, John A. '72 (NY) Chappaqua, NY St. John and St. Mary Church; [CC] New York, NY University Apostolate.
Vigliotta, Thomas F. *o.f.m.* '85 (CHR) Anderson, SC St. Mary of the Angels Church.
Vigliotta, William J. *s.m.m.* '54 (RVC) [N] Eastport, NY Shrine of Our Lady of the Island.
Vignoe, Joseph M. '58 (BUR) Poultney, VT St. Raphael Church; [J] Burlington, VT University of Vermont-The Catholic Center at UVM.
Vignola, Robert R. *c.m.* '50 (BRK) [D] Queens and Staten Island, NY St. John's University; [U] Jamaica, NY St. Vincent's House.
Vignone, John J. '75 (CAM) Runnemede, NJ St. Teresa of the Infant Jesus Church.
Vigues, Gabriel '93 (MIA) Coral Springs, FL St. Andrew Church.
Vila, Manuel *c.m.* '35 (SJN) [47] San Juan, PR Nuestra Senora del Pilar Church.
Vila-Cha, Joao J. *s.j.* '91 (BO) [W] Chestnut Hill, MA The Jesuit Community at Boston College.
Viladesau, Richard R. *s.t.d.* '69 (BRK) [207] Queens, NY Our Lady of the Blessed Sacrament Church.
Viladesau, Richard R. *s.t.d.* '69 (RVC) Saltaire, NY Our Lady Star of the Sea, Mission Chapel; Priests Released from Diocesan Assignment.
Vilano, Anthony '96 (SAT) Kerrville, TX Notre Dame Church.
Vilaplana, Jose *s.j.* '63 (NY) [3] White Plains, NY St. Bernard Church.
Vilar, J. Juan Diaz *s.j.* '69 (NEW) [N] Jersey City, NJ Jesuits of Saint Peter's College, Inc.
Vileo, Stephen L. '87 (E) [16] Erie, PA St. George Church.
Vilkauskas, Edward J. *c.s.sp.* '73 (CHL) Monroe, NC Our Lady of Lourdes Church.
Villa, Angelo *p.i.m.e.* '51 (DET) [K] Detroit, MI P.I.M.E. Missionaries of SS. Peter and Paul.
Villa, Aurelio *o.f.m.* '64 (SR) Boyes Hot Springs, CA St. Leo Church; Sonoma, CA St. Francis Solano Church.
Villa, Eduardo '80 (BWN) Rio Grande City, TX Immaculate Conception Church.
Villa, James *o.f.m.* '69 (NY) [5] Mt. Vernon, NY Our Lady of Mount Carmel Church.
Villa, Leonard F. '86 (NY) [8] Yonkers, NY St. Eugene Church.
Villa Gomez, Nemorio '56 (LA) Retired.
Villabon, German *o.s.a.* '54 (RVC) [1] Rockville Centre, NY St. Agnes Cathedral.
Villacis, Jose H. '43 (LA) Retired.
Villada, Luis Eduardo '95 (SJN) Dorado, PR San Antonio de Padua Church.
Villafranca, Eugenio *c.m.* '62 (PCE) [14] Ponce, PR San Vicente-Cantera Church.
Villagomez, Jose *o.f.m.cap.* '74 (AGN) Merizo, GU San Dimas and Our Lady of the Rosary Church; Umatac, GU San Dionisio Church.
Villalba, Angel *o.m.i.* '39 (CC) Sarita, TX Our Lady of Guadalupe Church; [J] Sarita, TX Food Co-op of Sarita, Inc.
Villalobos, Alberto '85 (LA) Van Nuys, CA St. Elisabeth Church; [D] Mission Hills, CA Alemany High School.
Villalobos, David '96 (SR) Fort Bragg, CA Our Lady of Good Counsel Church.
Villalon, Jose M., Jr. '89 (BWN) San Isidro, TX St. Isidore Church.
Villalta, Moises *o.f.m.cap.* '95 (WDC) [39] Washington, DC Shrine of the Sacred Heart Church.
Villamide, Msgr. Aniceto '67 (BGP) [18] Bridgeport, CT St. Peter's Church; [W] Bridgeport, CT Hispanic Social Ministries of Fairfield County, Inc.
Villani, Ralph A. '68 (NY) Mt. Kisco, NY St. Francis of Assisi Church.
Villani, Msgr. Rocco D. '61 (BRK) [81] Brooklyn, NY St. Mary Mother of Jesus Church.
Villano, Mark A. '88 (LA) [86] Los Angeles, CA St. Paul the Apostle Church; [BB] Los Angeles, CA Archdiocesan Office for Campus Ministry.
Villano, Richard R. '58 (STP) [26] Minneapolis, MN St. Helena Church.
Villanova, Richard A. '67 (NEW) Hillside, NJ St. Catherine of Siena Church.
Villanueva, Alfred '96 (ELP) [1] El Paso, TX St. Patrick's Cathedral.
Villanueva, Camilo P. (SJ) [5] Santa Clara, CA Our Lady of Peace Church.
Villanueva, Felix Oliveras '82 (CGS) Humacao, PR Dulce Nombre de Jesus Church.
Villar, Msgr. Demetrio (RVC) Retired.
Villar, Vincent *s.d.b.* '55 (MIA) [25] Miami, FL St. Kieran Church.
Villaronga, Angel *o.f.m.* '51 (MIA) [H] Miami, FL Franciscan Fathers' Residence.
Villarreal, Louis J. *o.m.i.* '65 (BEA) Anahuac, TX Our Lady of Light Church.
Villarroya, Ernesto '63 (DAL) [1] Garland, TX Good Shepherd Church.
Villarroya, Pedro *c.m.* '59 (LA) [R] Los Angeles, CA Vincentian Fathers and Brothers.
Villaruel, Alvin M. '94 (SR) [B] Santa Rosa, CA Cardinal Newman High School.
Villaverde, Alberto *s.j.* '56 (SJN) [22] San Juan, PR San Ignacio de Loyola Church.
Villaverde, Antonio E. '55 (ALX) Retired.
Villaverde, Tirso S. '96 (CHI) [164] Chicago, IL St. Pascal Church.
Villegas, Efraim *o.s.b.* '88 (BIS) [A] Richardton, ND Assumption Abbey.
Villegas, Gonzalo J. '92 (TUC) [1] Tucson, AZ St. Augustine's Cathedral.
Villegas, Hernando '57 (MIA) Coral Gables, FL Little Flower Church.
Villegas, Jorge C. '66 (E) [30] Erie, PA St. Stephen Church.
Villegas, Juan C. *s.j.* '75 (NY) [Z] New York, NY Jesuit Provincial's Office.
Villegas, Miguel A. '69 (LA) [R] Azusa, CA Casa Comboni Mission Seminary.
Villegas, Rafael '90 (ORL) [1] Orlando, FL St. James Cathedral; [2] Orlando, FL Blessed Trinity Church.
Villegas, Robert *c.s.c.* '63 (LSC) Chamberino, NM San Luis Rey Church.
Villegas, Samuel '65 (LA) Huntington Park, CA St. Matthias Church.
Villegas, Samuel C. '56 (LA) Retired.
Villemaire, Arthur M. '51 (SP) St. Joseph, FL Sacred Heart Church; [F] Dade City, FL Sacred Heart Child Care Center.
Villerot, Henry E. '41 (DET) Retired.
Villerot, Msgr. Thomas H. '43 (DET) Royal Oak, MI St. Mary Church; Retired.
Vima, Amalar '71 (TLS) Cushing, OK SS. Peter and Paul Church.
Vincent, Msgr. Amos J. '49 (LKC) Westlake, LA St. John Bosco Church.
Vincent, David P. '64 (CIN) [3] Springfield, OH St. Mary Church.
Vincent, John F. '54 (WIN) Retired.
Vincent, John J. *o.s.c.* '58 (LIN) [A] Hastings, NE Crosier Monastery.
Vincent, Michael *s.j.* '82 (CLV) [E] Cleveland, OH St. Ignatius High School.
Vincent, Robert G. '57 (NO) La Place, LA St. Joan of Arc Church.
Vincenzo, Dennis J. '91 (HRT) [1] Hartford, CT Cathedral of St. Joseph.
Vinci, Msgr. Guy S. '59 (NY) [102] New York, NY St. Patrick Old Cathedral; Harrison, NY St. Gregory the Great Church; New York, NY New York Fire Department.
Vinci, Terzo *s.a.c.* '58 (NY) [13] Yonkers, NY Our Lady of Mt. Carmel Church.
Vincini, Andrea *s.j.* '96 (BO) [W] Chestnut Hill, MA The Jesuit Community at Boston College.
Vincze, Michael A. '40 (MET) Retired.
Vinklarek, Emil T. '41 (SAT) Retired.
Vinsko, John J. *m.m.* '62 (SJ) [M] Los Altos, CA Maryknoll.
Vinslauski, Robert '71 (SFS) Aberdeen, SD St. Mary Church.
Vinyard, Barry E. '75 (SD) [B] San Diego, CA University of San Diego.
Viola, William *s.s.* '84 (WDC) [A] Washington, DC Theological College of the Catholic University of America; [C] Washington, DC Catholic University of America, The.
Violette, Lawrence '93 (ARL) Annandale, VA St. Ambrose Church.
Violette, Tex '75 (HT) On Leave.
Virella, Miguel A. *s.v.d.* '96 (TR) Lakewood, NJ St. Anthony Claret Church.
Virgen, Javier G. '93 (SLC) Provo, UT St. Francis of Assisi Church; Gunnison, UT State Penitentiary.
Virgen, Jorge (ELP) [N] El Paso, TX Catholic Properties of El Paso, Inc.
Virgets, Edward J. *c.m.* '46 (STL) [P] St. Louis, MO Vincentian Bellerive Residence; [R] Normandy, MO Marillac Provincial House.
Virginia, Stephen '79 (COL) Leave of Absence.
Virnig, Laurn '63 (SCL) Royalton, MN Holy Trinity Church.
Virtue, William D. '75 (PEO) Earlville, IL St. Theresa's Church.
Virus, Keith M. '92 (GRY) Munster, IN St. Thomas More Church.
Visbisky, Richard W. '62 (BO) [Q] Brockton, MA Good Samaritan Medical Center.
Viscardi, Christopher J. *s.j.* '76 (MOB) [B] Mobile, AL Spring Hill College.
Viscardi, Robert *i.m.c.* '63 (MET) [H] Somerset, NJ Consolata Society for Foreign Missions.
Viscarra, Angel '46 (CC) [D] Laredo, TX Sacred Heart Children's Home.
Visconti, Luciano M. *c.r.s.p.* '42 (BUF) [B] Youngstown, NY St. Anthony Zaccaria Seminary.
Visich, Eduard C. '53 (BRK) Absent on Leave.
Viso, Jaime (SP) Plant City, FL St. Clement Church.
Vita, Mariano L. '42 (CHI) Bellwood, IL St. Simeon Church; Retired.
Vitacolonna, Xavier *c.p.* '74 (PIT) [N] Pittsburgh, PA St. Paul of the Cross Monastery.
Vitaglione, Robert '76 (BRK) [70] Brooklyn, NY St. Joseph's Church.
Vitale, Louis *o.f.m.* '63 (SFR) [7] San Francisco, CA St. Boniface Church.
Vitali, James V. *o.s.a.* '81 (VEN) Golden Gate, FL St. Elizabeth Seton Church.
Vitali, John *c.r.s.* '71 (MAN) [H] Allenstown, NH Pine Haven Boys Center.
Vitali, Theodore *c.p.* '69 (MET) [H] South River, NJ Passionist Provincial Office.
Vitaliano, Dominic '91 (PEO) Philo, IL St. Thomas Church.
Vitela, Francisco '68 (LA) Compton, CA Sagrado Corazon, Sacred Heart Church.
Vitillo, Robert J. '72 (PAT) On Duty Outside the Diocese.
Vitka, Stephen G. '41 (HRT) Retired.
Vito, Alfred J. '84 (SCR) Canadensis, PA St. Bernadette Church; [D] East Stroudsburg, PA Notre Dame Junior/Senior High School.
Vitro, Thomas J. '66 (CHI) Other Assignments.
Vitsas, John P. '46 (RVC) Wading River, NY St. John Baptist Church; Retired; [N] Uniondale, NY St. Pius X Residence.
Vitte, Jules '49 (NO) Retired.
Vitturino, Saverio T. '67 (WDC) Benedict, MD St. Francis de Sales Church.
Vitucci, James '72 (MIA) Pembroke Pines, FL St. Maximilian Kolbe Church.

Vitus, Frank K. '75 (JOL) Minooka, IL St. Mary Church.
Viveiros, Joseph F. '74 (FR) [1] Swansea, MA St. Dominic's Church; [N] Fall River, MA Special Apostolates, Department of.
Viviano, Benedict T. *o.p.* '66 (CHI) [N] Chicago, IL Dominicans (Provincial Office).
Viviano, Charles '89 (ORL) Titusville, FL St. Teresa Church.
Viviano, Nino '60 (SP) [5] Clearwater, FL St. Michael The Archangel Church.
Viviano, Nino '64 (ALX) On Duty Outside the Diocese.
Vivona, Francis '69 (VNN) Las Vegas, NV Our Lady of Wisdom Italo-Greek Mission Church.
Vizcaino, Mario B. *sch.p.* '60 (MIA) [K] Miami, FL Southeast Pastoral Institute; [K] Miami, FL Southeast Regional Office for Hispanic Ministry, Inc.; [M] Miami, FL SEPI Evangelization and Education Foundation, Inc.
Vizcaino, Mario B. *sch.p.* '60 (PH) [Z] Devon, PA Piarist Fathers (Order of the Pious Schools).
Vizcaino, Mario B. *sch.p.* '60 (WDC) [B] Washington, DC Queen of Pious Schools House of Studies-Piarist Fathers.
Vizcarra, Angel *o.p.* '46 (CC) [9] Laredo, TX San Martin De Porres Church; On Special Assignment.
Vizzard, Msgr. James J. '48 (PH) Bala-Cynwyd, PA St. Matthias Church; Retired.
Vjecha, Michael J. *s.j.* '87 (CLV) [C] Cleveland, OH John Carroll Jesuit Community.
Vjecha, Michael J. *s.j.* '87 (DET) [K] Detroit, MI Jesuit Provincial Office-Detroit Province of the Society of Jesus.
Vlasz, Melvyn J. '63 (RCK) On Disability Leave; [G] Rockford, IL Cor Mariae Center.
Vlaun, James C. (RVC) West Babylon, NY Our Lady of Grace Church; West Islip, NY Our Lady of Lourdes Church; [C] West Islip, NY St. John the Baptist.
Vo, Peter De Ta *s.v.d.* '87 (WDC) [M] Washington, DC Divine Word College.
Vodoklys, Edward J. *s.j.* '91 (WOR) [N] Worcester, MA Jesuits of Holy Cross College, Inc.
Voegele, Fridolin *o.f.m.* '58 (CIN) [24] Cincinnati, OH Corpus Christi Church.
Voelker, David A. '74 (BEL) Military Chaplains.
Voelker, Harold H. '54 (STL) Gardenville, MO St. George Church.
Voelker, James A. '69 (BEL) Beckemeyer, IL St. Anthony Church; [4] East St. Louis, IL St. Patrick Church; [5] East St. Louis, IL St. Philip Church.
Voelker, Karl *s.j.* '72 (WIN) [1] Mankato, MN SS. Peter and Paul's Church.
Voelker, Lawrence '66 (IND) [6] Indianapolis, IN Holy Cross Church; [7] Indianapolis, IN Holy Rosary Church; [36] Indianapolis, IN St. Patrick Church; Indianapolis, IN Indiana Women's Prison.
Voelker, Peter H. *c.ss.r.* '61 (GAL) [33] Houston, TX Holy Ghost Church.
Voellmecke, Francis W. '59 (CIN) [60] Cincinnati, OH Old St. Mary Church.
Vogan, Howard L. '69 (DET) South Lyon, MI St. Joseph Church.
Vogan, Robert C. '70 (PH) Aston, PA St. Joseph Church.
Vogel, Arthur '57 (SCL) Retired.
Vogel, Charles P. '43 (BRK) [137] Brooklyn, NY St. Sylvester Church; Retired.
Vogel, Edward A. '50 (MIL) [3] Racine, WI Holy Name Church.
Vogel, F. Philip *s.d.s.* '69 (BAL) Baltimore, MD Spring Grove Center Hospital.
Vogel, Gerhard *s.v.d.* '65 (TR) Asbury Park, NJ St. Peter Claver Church.
Vogel, J. Carl '50 (DAL) McKinney, TX St. Michael Church.
Vogel, John '86 (LA) Burbank, CA St. Robert Bellarmine Church.
Vogel, Joseph '87 (SFS) Westport, SD Sacred Heart of Westport Church; [H] Aberdeen, SD Diocesan Newman Apostolate; [H] Aberdeen, SD Aquinas Student Center.
Vogel, Murel R. *s.j.* '37 (CHI) [C] Chicago, IL Jesuit Community at Loyola University of Chicago.
Vogel, Philip *s.d.s.* '69 (WDC) [B] Silver Spring, MD Salvatorian Community.
Vogel, Walter J. '58 (MIL) Richfield, WI St. Mary Church; Thompson, WI St. Patrick's Church.
Vogel, Walter F. *o.s.a.* '63 (SD) [B] San Diego, CA Austin House - House of Formation; [C] San Diego, CA St. Augustine High School; [H] San Diego, CA Augustinian Community.
Vogel, William '49 (DOD) Kinsley, KS St. Nicholas Church; Offerle, KS St. Joseph Church.
Vogel, William *s.j.* '75 (SPK) [E] Spokane, WA Gonzaga Preparatory School.
Vogelgesang, John *s.v.d.* '42 (CHI) [B] Techny, IL Divine Word Residence.
Vogelpohl, Daniel J. '75 (COV) Fort Thomas, KY St. Catherine of Siena Church.
Vogelpohl, Msgr. Henry J. '39 (CIN) Retired.
Vogelpohl, Herbert '39 (LR) [A] Subiaco, AR Subiaco Monastery.
Vogelsang, Clifford R. '63 (IND) Jeffersonville, IN St. Augustine Church.
Vogl, Msgr. Robert R. '47 (DUB) Retired; [C] Dubuque, IA Loras College; [I] Dubuque, IA Marian Hall Infirmary.
Vogler, Harold *o.f.m.cap.* '28 (SAL) [D] Victoria, KS St. Fidelis Friary.
Vogler, Jean '70 (EVN) On Leave of Absence.
Vogler, John (STL) [G] Normandy, MO Mount Providence School.
Vogler, John E. (STL) Bellefontaine Neighbors, MO Our Lady of Good Counsel Church; Retired.
Voglio, John '87 (NY) Croton Falls, NY St. Joseph Church.
Vogrin, Joseph '44 (SCL) Retired.
Vogt, Daniel *c.m.f.* '89 (CHI) [N] Oak Park, IL Claretian Fathers Headquarters of U.S.A. Eastern Province.
Vogt, Emmerich *o.p.* (OAK) [N] Oakland, CA Dominican Order, Siena House.
Vogt, Eric T. *o.s.b.* '79 (GBG) [H] Latrobe, PA Saint Vincent Archabbey.
Vogt, Francis H. '38 (ROC) Palmyra, NY St. Anne Church; Retired.
Vogt, George '27 (ROC) [E] Rochester, NY St. Ann's Home for the Aged.
Vogt, John '62 (PHX) Wickenburg, AZ St. Anthony of Padua Church.
Vogt, Otto J. '50 (ROC) Retired.
Vogt, Richard J. *s.j.* '63 (CHI) [145] Chicago, IL Our Lady of Fatima Church; [D] Chicago, IL St. Ignatius Jesuit Community.
Vogt, Robert W. '62 (BUF) [4] Tonawanda, NY St. Francis of Assisi Church.
Vogt, William '56 (FRS) Faculties Only.
Vogt, William E. '46 (GRY) Retired.
Vohsing, William J. '78 (ORG) [4] Anaheim, CA San Antonio Church.
Voigt, Richard A. *s.d.b.* '78 (MRY) [D] Watsonville, CA St. Francis Youth Center.
Voiland, Msgr. George T. '50 (BRK) [203] Queens, NY Most Precious Blood Church; Retired.
Voiss, James K. *s.j.* '88 (P) [L] Portland, OR Jesuit Provincial Office (Oregon Prov.).
Voity, Maurice '79 (SAN) [1] San Angelo, TX Cathedral of the Sacred Heart.
Vojtek, John '76 (PIT) Etna, PA All Saints Church.
Vojtik, James '62 (MIL) [1] Sheboygan, WI St. Clement's Church.
Volino, Michael J. '92 (ROC) [57] Rochester, NY St. Theodore Church.
Volk, Edwin '56 (BIS) Beulah, ND St. Joseph Church.
Volk, Marvin C. '74 (BEL) [2] Belleville, IL Blessed Sacrament Church.
Volk, Michael '92 (MRY) Gonzales, CA St. Theodore Church.
Volk, Norman *o.m.i.* '68 (SUP) [G] River Falls, WI St. Thomas More Newman Center.
Volk, William A. *c.pp.s.* '50 (CIN) [M] Dayton, OH Provincial House of the Cincinnati Province of the Society of the Precious Blood.
Volker, Edward H. '41 (CIN) Retired.
Volkert, James T. '90 (MIL) [53] Milwaukee, WI St. Matthias Church.
Volkmer, Michael *c.pp.s.* '68 (JC) Sedalia, MO Sacred Heart Church.
Voll, Walter Urban *o.p.* '49 (NY) [Z] New York, NY St. Vincent Ferrer Priory; [DD] New York, NY St. Thomas Aquinas Foundation.
Vollenweider, Roy W. *s.j.* '47 (NO) [P] New Orleans, LA Ignatius Residence.
Vollkommer, Andrew J. '86 (CHR) Chapin, SC Our Lady of the Lake Church.
Vollmer, Anthony L. *c.pp.s.* '53 (SLC) Kanab, UT St. Christopher's Church.
Vollmer, Caron *o.f.m.* (GLP) Lukachukai, AZ St. Isabel Mission for Navajo Indians Church; [F] Gallup, NM Southwest Indian Foundation.
Vollmer, Gary '77 (LAV) [12] Las Vegas, NV St. Joseph, Husband of Mary Church.
Vollmer, Gary l. '77 (STL) On Duty Outside the Archdiocese.
Vollmer, Gene '78 (RVC) Floral Park, NY Our Lady of Victory Church.
Vollmer, Raymond A. '40 (PIT) Retired.
Vollmer, Msgr. Roman '45 (EVN) Retired.
Vollmer, William C. '58 (COS) Castle Rock, CO St. Francis of Assisi Church.
Vollor, John '79 (JKS) West Point, MS Immaculate Conception Church.
Vollor, William '63 (BLX) Hattiesburg, MS Holy Rosary Church.
Volmi, Dennis G. '75 (WIL) Military Chaplains.
Volpe, Al '83 (LKC) [5] Lake Charles, LA St. Margaret Church; Lake Charles, LA Lake Charles Memorial Hospital.
Volpe, Philip *o.f.m.cap.* '43 (NEW) [5] Hoboken, NJ St. Ann's Church.
Volpe, Rocco C. *c.s.b.* '57 (GAL) Retired; [Q] Houston, TX Dominican Fathers and Brothers, St. Mark Priory, Inc.; [Q] Houston, TX Dillon House.
Volpert, R. Cass '61 (L) [24] Louisville, KY Epiphany Church.
Volskis, Aloyzas '85 (LA) [54] Los Angeles, CA St. Casimir Church.
Voltaggio, Fred '71 (CAM) Pennsauken, NJ St. Cecilia's Church.
Volungis, Alphonse A. '45 (WOR) [15] Worcester, MA Our Lady of Vilna Church.
Volz, Anthony R. '85 (IND) [1] Terre Haute, IN Sacred Heart of Jesus Church; [2] Terre Haute, IN St. Ann Church.
Volz, Edward *o.s.p.p.e.* '88 (GBG) Cadogan, PA St. Lawrence Church; [H] Kittanning, PA Pauline Fathers Monastery.
Volz, Gerald '92 (KCK) Olathe, KS Prince of Peace Church; [B] Overland Park, KS Saint Thomas Aquinas High School.
Von Ah, Richard J. '58 (DAV) [L] Davenport, IA Kahl Home for the Aged and Infirm.
von Arx, Jeffrey *s.j.* '81 (WDC) [M] Washington, DC The Jesuit Community at Georgetown University.
von Behren, Thomas R. *c.s.v.* '83 (LAV) [D] Las Vegas, NV Clerics of St. Viator.
Von der Ahe, Karl E. *s.j.* '39 (LA) [C] Los Angeles, CA Loyola Marymount University.
von Dremle, James (DET) [H] Pontiac, MI St. Joseph Mercy - Oakland.
von Duerbeck, Julian *o.s.b.* '76 (JOL) [J] Lisle, IL St. Procopius Abbey.
Von Essen, Pacificus *s.a.* '53 (NY) [Z] Garrison, NY Generalate of the Franciscan Friars of the Atonement-St. James Friary.
Von Euw, Vincent P. '66 (BO) [4] Boston, MA St. Ambrose Church.
von Fauer, Stephen C. '41 (STF) [E] West Burke, VT Mary Theotokos Centre.
Von Fauer, Stephen C. '53 (BUR) Retired.
Von Hagel, Davin *o.f.m.* '47 (GLP) Kayenta, AZ Our Lady of Guadalupe Church.
von Hartleben, Msgr. Joseph A. '55 (CAM) [2] Vineland, NJ Sacred Heart Church.
Von Kaenel, George E. *s.j.* '58 (OM) [K] Omaha, NE Jesuit Community At Creighton University.
Von Kerssenbrock, Joachim *s.j.* '59 (NY) [DD] New York, NY American St. Boniface Society, Incorporated.
Von Kobs, Allan G. *o.f.m.* '82 (NY) [35] New York, NY St. Francis of Assisi Church.
Von Lehmen, Jeffrey D. '85 (COV) Edgewood, KY St. Pius X Church.
von Nell, Boniface *o.s.b.* '91 (WDC) [M] Washington, DC St. Anselm's Abbey.
von Phul Mouton, Msgr. Richard '55 (LAF) [16] Lafayette, LA St. Pius X Church.
Von Son, Msgr. Henry A. '49 (LA) Retired.
Von Tobel, James E. *s.j.* '67 (DET) [K] Detroit, MI Jesuit Provincial Office-Detroit Province of the Society of Jesus; [P] Clarkston, MI Colombiere Center.
Vona, Michael S. '68 (TR) Farmingdale, NJ St. Catherine of Siena Church.
vonBehren, Thomas R. *c.s.v.* '83 (LAV) [A] Las Vegas, NV Bishop Gorman High School.
Vonderhaar, Eugene F. '59 (CIN) Russia, OH St. Remy Church.
Vonderhaar, Ralph E. *s.j.* '57 (STL) [P] St. Louis, MO Hallahan House.
VonderHaar, Msgr. Roland '48 (LSC) Retired.
Vondras, John J. '85 (NY) [2] Newburgh, NY St. Francis of Assisi Church.
Vonnahmen, Robert J. '56 (BEL) Leave of Absence.
Voor, Joseph H. '50 (L) [16] Louisville, KY St. Brigid Church; [39] Louisville, KY St. James Church; Louisville, KY Vencor Veterans Hospital; Retired.
Voorhes, Msgr. Fred R. '71 (BUF) [P] Williamsville, NY Sisters of St. Francis of the Third Order Regular, St. Mary of the Angels.
Voorhies, Bennett J. '83 (LAF) On Duty Outside the Diocese.
Voorhies, Louis '67 (ALX) Retired.
Voorhies, Thomas P. '90 (LAF) Delcambre, LA Our Lady of the Lake Church; Delcambre, LA Saint Martin de Porres Church.
Voors, David W. '81 (FTW) Plymouth, IN St. Michael Church.
Voors, Msgr. William J. '39 (FTW) Retired.
Vorderlandwehr, Adrian *o.s.b.* '67 (OKL) Prague, OK St. Wenceslaus, National Shrine of the Infant Jesus of Prague Church.
Voris, Francis *o.f.m.cap.* '86 (SAG) Sanford, MI St. Agnes Church; [G] Saginaw, MI Queen of Angels Friary and Retreat House.
Vorisek, Rudolph T. *c.s.p.* '56 (NY) [104] New York, NY St. Paul the Apostle Church; [Z] Scarsdale, NY Paulist Fathers Generalate.
Vorwald, Aloysius J. '64 (DUB) Independence, IA St. John Evangelist Church; Rowley, IA All Saints Church.
Vorwerk, James *s.v.d.* '25 (TR) Neptune, NJ Our Lady of Providence Church.
Vorwoldt, James F. *s.j.* '71 (CHI) [D] Chicago, IL St. Ignatius Jesuit Community.

Vos, Jude F. '96 (FAR) [5] Fargo, ND St. Anthony of Padua Church; Devils Lake, ND St. Joseph's Church.
Vos, Thomas *o.f.m.* '61 (KNX) Mountain City, TN St. Anthony of Padua Catholic Church; [F] Mountain City, TN Franciscan Friars.
Vos, William (NY) [DD] Maryknoll, NY Maryknoll Mission Association of the Faithful.
Vos, William '64 (SCL) On Duty Outside the Diocese.
Vosen, Gerald P. '61 (MAD) Baraboo, WI St. Joseph Church.
Vosko, Richard '69 (ALB) Special Assignment.
Voss, Bernard L. '66 (BEL) [5] Belleville, IL St. Henry Church; [K] Belleville, IL Serra Club of St. Clair County.
Voss, Dennis F. '64 (BEL) [E] Belleville, IL St. Elizabeth Hospital.
Voss, Donald J. '93 (PBR) Clarence, PA St. Mary's Church; Hawk Run, PA St. John the Baptist Church.
Voss, Marcus J. *o.s.b.* '71 (BIR) [B] Cullman, AL St. Bernard Preparatory School, Inc.; [E] Cullman, AL St. Bernard Abbey.
Voss, Robert '70 (PHX) [4] Scottsdale, AZ St. Bernard of Clairvaux Church.
Vossler, Brian E. '91 (E) Clarion, PA Immaculate Conception Church; [P] Erie, PA Newman Centers and Campus Ministry; [P] Erie, PA Newman Centers and Campus Ministry.
Vota, Paul *m.j.* '85 (PCE) On Duty Outside the Diocese.
Votraw, Thomas G. '60 (OG) [1] Ogdensburg, NY St. Mary's Cathedral; Absent on Sick Leave.
Votraw, Wilbur J. '55 (SY) [24] Syracuse, NY St. Vincent de Paul Church; Syracuse, NY Loretto Geriatric Center; [P] Syracuse, NY Loretto; [P] Syracuse, NY Loretto Rest, Inc.
Votraw, William J. '55 (SY) Special Assignment.
Votruba, George L. '54 (SUP) [2] Superior, WI Assumption of the B.V.M. Church; Pattison Park, WI St. William Church.
Votta, Robert '79 (LAV) [6] Las Vegas, NV St. Anne Church.
Vouk, William, III '86 (SCL) St. Anthony, MN St. Anthony's Church; St. Francis, MN St. Francis of Assisi Church.
Vovk, Joseph '32 (DUL) Retired.
Vowells, John J. '90 (STL) [P] St. Louis, MO Leo Brown Jesuit Community.
Vowels, Donald M. '87 (L) Leave of Absence.
Vowels, G. Timothy '77 (STL) Hazelwood, MO St. Martin de Porres Church.
Voyt, Stephen A. '85 (PT) Military Chaplains.
Voytek, John Marion *o.f.m.conv.* '82 (HRT) [M] New Britain, CT Conventual Franciscans; [N] New Britain, CT Motherhouse of Daughters of Mary of the Immaculate Conception.
Voytek, Leonard E. '74 (ALT) [1] Windber, PA St. John Cantius Church; [4] Windber, PA St. Mary's Church.
Voytko, Geo. '49 (STU) Retired.
Vrabel, George A. '87 (CLV) North Olmsted, OH St. Richard Church.
Vrabely, George M. '53 (GRY) La Porte, IN St. Peter Church.
Vrablic, Cyril *o.s.b.* '51 (IND) [J] St. Meinrad, IN St. Meinrad Archabbey.
Vrana, Francis R. '53 (STP) Retired.
Vrana, John G. '67 (CLV) Maple Heights, OH St. Martin of Tours Church.
Vrana, John P. '56 (OKL) Ardmore, OK St. Mary Church.
Vrana, Joseph L. '65 (VIC) Wharton, TX Holy Family Church.
Vrazel, Edward '58 (CC) [5] Laredo, TX Our Lady of Guadalupe Church.
Vrba, James J. '77 (DAV) [2] Iowa City, IA St. Patrick's Church.
Vreteau, Robert *o.m.i.* '49 (SAN) [2] Midland, TX Our Lady of Guadalupe Church; [3] Midland, TX Our Lady of San Juan de Los Lagos Church.
Vu, An Ngoc '95 (WDC) Riverdale, MD St. Bernard Church.
Vu, Ignatius '94 (NY) [5] White Plains, NY Our Lady of Sorrows Church.
Vu, Joseph '90 (BRK) [10] Brooklyn, NY St. Anselm's Church.
Vu, Joseph Khai '96 (NEW) Newark, NJ St. James Hospital; Newark, NJ St. Michael Medical Center.
Vu, Joseph Thanh '90 (GAL) [27] Houston, TX St. Frances Cabrini Church.
Vu, Lieu '91 (SJ) Campbell, CA St. Lucy Church.
Vu, Louis Lam '85 (LAF) Youngsville, LA St. Anne Church.
Vu, Minh Xuan '94 (STP) Roseville, MN St. Rose of Lima Church.
Vu, Peter Duc '96 (ATL) [2] Atlanta, GA Holy Cross Church.
Vu, Than N. '84 (BR) [17] Baton Rouge, LA St. Patrick Church.
Vu, Toan '92 (HT) [1] Thibodaux, LA St. Joseph Co-Cathedral.
Vu dai Luong, James '73 (SB) [E] Corona, CA Congregation of the Mother Coredemptrix.
Vu Dinh Huyen, Leo M. *c.m.c.* (SPC) [E] Carthage, MO Congregation of the Mother Co-Redemptrix, United States Assumption Province.
Vu Han, John Baptist '65 (NO) [2] Marrero, LA St. Agnes Le Thi Thanh Church.
Vu Quang Huy, John Eudes M. *c.m.c.* (SPC) [E] Carthage, MO Congregation of the Mother Co-Redemptrix, United States Assumption Province.
Vu Thanh Thien, Cyril M. *c.m.c.* (SPC) [E] Carthage, MO Congregation of the Mother Co-Redemptrix, United States Assumption Province.
Vuatana, Viotri *s.m.* (BO) [59] Boston, MA Our Lady of Victories Church.
Vucinovich, Albert '64 (SFR) Fairfax, CA St. Rita Church.
Vuelvas-Arias, David '75 (ORG) [2] Anaheim, CA St. Boniface Church.
Vujs, Joseph E. '57 (HRT) [5] Meriden, CT St. Rose of Lima Church.
Vuketich, Donald F. *t.o.r.* '53 (PH) [Z] Fairless Hills, PA St. Anthony Friary.
Vukoja, Valentin *o.f.m.* '96 (NY) [29] New York, NY SS. Cyril and Methodius - St. Raphael Church.
Vuletic, Fetar '62 (LA) [45] Los Angeles, CA St. Anthony Church.
Vuoso, Pasquale *c.r.i.c.* '87 (LA) [64] Los Angeles, CA St. Francis of Assisi Church; [B] Los Angeles, CA Canons Regular of the Immaculate Conception-Novitiate; [R] Los Angeles, CA Canons Regular of the Immaculate Conception.
Vuturo, Paul '73 (MIA) Miramar, FL St. Bartholomew Church.
Vye, Francis W. *s.j.* '65 (BO) [W] Chestnut Hill, MA The Jesuit Community at Boston College.
Vyoral, Louis *s.d.b.* '50 (NY) [Z] New Rochelle, NY Salesian Provincial House.
Vyverman, Mark J. '93 (KAL) Gull Lake, MI St. Ann Church.

W

Wach, Anthony J. *s.j.* '72 (MIL) [P] Milwaukee, WI Jesuit Provincial Office, Wisconsin Province.
Wachdorf, Paul H. '75 (CHI) [A] Mundelein, IL University of St. Mary of the Lake-Mundelein Seminary.
Wachtel, Dominic *o.f.m.* (CIN) [K] Cincinnati, OH Franciscan Hospital, Mt. Airy Campus; [M] Cincinnati, OH St. Ann Friary.
Wachter, Robert B. '76 (WCH) Conway Springs, KS St. Joseph Church.
Wack, William *c.s.c.* '94 (COS) [9] Colorado Springs, CO Sacred Heart Church.
Wackenheim, Apollinaris *o.f.m.* (SFD) [K] Sherman, IL Our Lady of Angels Friary.
Waclawski, Msgr. Joseph P. '42 (BUF) [39] Buffalo, NY St. John Kanty Church; Retired.
Waczula, Michael F. '66 (GBG) On Duty Outside the Diocese.
Wadas, Msgr. Ignatius C. '53 (ALT) Central City, PA Sacred Heart Church; Central City, PA St. John the Baptist Church.
Wadas, Joseph S. (MOB) Eufaula, AL Holy Redeemer Church; Clayton, AL Ventress Correctional Institution; Union Springs, AL Bullock County Correctional Facility.
Wadas, Raymond J. '72 (WDC) [43] Washington, DC St. Thomas More Church.
Waddell, Chrysogonus *o.c.s.o.* '58 (L) [L] Trappist, KY Abbey of Our Lady of Gethsemani, of the Order of Cistercians of the Strict Observance.
Waddell, Paul M. '84 (NY) [159] Bronx, NY St. Lucy Church.
Waddill, Dale T. '64 (P) [27] Portland, OR St. Peter Church.
Wade, Edward C. '72 (CAM) On Duty Outside the Diocese.
Wade, Gerald T. *s.j.* '68 (SJ) [D] San Jose, CA Bellarmine College Preparatory.
Wade, Hubert '77 (SAN) Absent on Leave.
Wade, Msgr. James J. '33 (OAK) Pleasant Hill, CA Christ the King Church; Retired.
Wade, John '56 (TLS) [E] Tulsa, OK St. John Medical Center, Inc.
Wade, Michael J. (BAL) Absent on Leave.
Wadell, John '40 (SB) Retired.
Wadell, Paul *c.p.* '78 (CHI) [B] Chicago, IL The Catholic Theological Union at Chicago; [N] Chicago, IL Passionist Community-CTU.
Wadowicz, Msgr. Joseph M. '45 (STU) Retired.
Wadsworth, Msgr. James '41 (DM) Retired.
Waechter, Ernest *o.f.m.conv.* '59 (IND) Corydon, IN St. Joseph Church; New Middletown, IN Most Precious Blood Church; [I] Mount Saint Francis, IN Mount Saint Francis Friary and Retreat Center.
Wafzig, James E. '55 (L) [8] Louisville, KY St. Athanasius Church; Louisville, KY University Hospital; [O] Louisville, KY Catholic Charismatic Renewal.
Wageman, Msgr. Raymond L. '29 (LIN) Retired.
Wagener, Clarence M. *s.j.* '53 (OM) [K] Omaha, NE Jesuit Community At Creighton University.
Wagener, John M. '61 (NU) Military Chaplains.
Wagenhoffer, Msgr. Josef A. '65 (CAM) Somers Point, NJ St. Joseph's Church.
Wager, Terence J. *o.s.b.* '64 (SEA) Yelm, WA St. Columban Church.
Waggenor, William L. '52 (HEL) Retired.
Waggett, George *o.m.i.* '42 (BO) [Z] Tewksbury, MA Immaculate Heart of Mary Novitiate-Infirmary.
Wagman, Msgr. Cletus H. '42 (HBG) [5] Lancaster, PA St. Joseph Church.
Wagner, Alan *s.d.s.* '76 (TUC) Vail, AZ Shrine of St. Rita in the Desert Church.
Wagner, Alfred S. '48 (STP) Retired.
Wagner, Cyril J. *o.f.m.* '67 (MEM) [16] Memphis, TN St. Louis Church; Somerville, TN St. Philip the Apostle Church; [J] Memphis, TN Franciscan Friars (Sacred Heart Prov.) of Memphis.
Wagner, Dennis A. '76 (GR) On Special Assignment.
Wagner, Donald '87 (SCL) Special Assignment.
Wagner, Edward *o.s.s.t.* '80 (BAL) [M] Baltimore, MD Holy Trinity Monastery.
Wagner, Eugene L. '40 (BUF) Olcott, NY St. Charles Borromeo Church; Retired.
Wagner, Frank *o.m.i.* '57 (SD) [1] Chula Vista, CA Most Precious Blood Church.
Wagner, George J. '91 (TOL) [35] Toledo, OH St. Patrick of Heatherdowns Church.
Wagner, Greta (TOL) [H] Lima, OH St. Rita's Medical Center.
Wagner, Msgr. Harold '55 (BUF) [F] Buffalo, NY Cantalician Center for Learning, Inc.
Wagner, Jerome A. '72 (MIL) [2] Fond du Lac, WI St. Louis Church.
Wagner, John '49 (SAT) Charlotte, TX St. Rose of Lima Church.
Wagner, John '64 (SB) [4] Corona, CA St. Matthew Church.
Wagner, John C. '73 (MIL) On Leave.
Wagner, John J., III '87 (RIC) Williamsburg, VA St. Bede's Church.
Wagner, John P. '62 (SY) Baldwinsville, NY St. Elizabeth Ann Seton Church; On Duty Outside the Diocese.
Wagner, Joseph '65 (SFS) Military Chaplains.
Wagner, Joseph F. '44 (CLV) [46] Cleveland, OH St. Mark Church; Brunswick, OH St. Colette Church; Retired.
Wagner, Lawrence L. *o.s.b.* '54 (BIS) Lefor, ND St. Elizabeth Church; Lefor, ND St. Elizabeth Church.
Wagner, Leon R. '49 (CHI) Riverside, IL St. Mary Church; Retired.
Wagner, Mark '88 (STO) Ceres, CA St. Jude Church.
Wagner, Ralph J. '45 (MIL) Retired.
Wagner, Raymond J. '52 (LC) Retired.
Wagner, Richard '61 (DM) [8] Des Moines, IA Basilica of Saint John.
Wagner, Richard F. *s.s.j.* '59 (LAF) Breaux Bridge, LA St. Francis of Assisi Church.
Wagner, Robert *s.d.s.* '46 (BIR) [3] Huntsville, AL St. Joseph's Church.
Wagner, Robert F. '60 (SPR) Monson, MA State Hospital; [N] Holyoke, MA Bureau for Exceptional Children and Adults Inc.; [N] Pittsfield, MA Bureau for Exceptional Children and Adults.
Wagner, Robert J. '57 (LC) Trempealeau, WI St. Bartholomew Church.
Wagner, Ronald F. '79 (SAG) Palms, MI St. Patrick Church; Ruth, MI SS. Peter and Paul Church.
Wagner, Terence *o.s.b.* '64 (SEA) [M] Lacey, WA St. Martin's Abbey.
Wagner, Thomas A. '83 (PIT) Pleasant Hills, PA St. Elizabeth Church.
Wagner, Urban S. *o.f.m.conv.* '41 (STP) Bloomington, MN St. Bonaventure Church.
Wagner, Van A. '61 (TUC) [20] Tucson, AZ Saints Peter and Paul Church.
Wagner, Vernon *o.f.m.cap.* '53 (SAG) [G] Saginaw, MI Queen of Angels Friary and Retreat House.
Wagner, Walter C. *o.p.* '93 (PRO) [P] Providence, RI St. Thomas Aquinas Priory at Providence College.
Wagner, William C. '73 (CIN) Milford, OH St. Andrew Church.
Wagner, William F. '63 (L) [69] Louisville, KY SS. Simon and Jude Church.
Wagoner, Gordon P. (IND) Indianapolis, IN Veterans' Administration Hospital.
Waguespack, Clarence J. '62 (BR) Vacherie, LA Our Lady of Peace Church.
Wahl, Joseph A. *c.o.* '56 (CHR) [E] Rock Hill, SC Oratory of St. Philip Neri, Congregation of the Oratory of Pontifical Rite.
Wahl, Raymond J. '37 (ROC) Retired.
Wahl, Msgr. Raymond J. '52 (RCK) [4] Rockford, IL St. Edward Church.
Wahl, Richard A. *c.s.b.* (ROC) [B] Rochester, NY The Aquinas Institute; [I] Rochester, NY Residence of Basilian Fathers-The Aquinas Institute.
Wahl, Thomas *o.s.b.* '58 (SCL) [I] Collegeville, MN St. John's Abbey, of the Order of St. Benedict.
Wahmhoff, Andrew *o.s.b.* '58 (RCK) [H] Aurora, IL Marmion Abbey-St. Augustine's Abbey.
Waibel, Kenneth '84 (LEX) Richmond, KY St. Mark Church; Richmond, KY St. Stephen the Martyr

Church; [L] Richmond, KY Catholic Newman Center-St. Stephen the Martyr Parish.
Waibel, Philip *o.s.b.* '83 (P) [A] St. Benedict, OR Mount Angel Seminary; [L] St. Benedict, OR Mt. Angel Abbey.
Waickman, Thomas L. '84 (JC) Louisiana, MO St. Joseph Church.
Wainwright, Walter L. '65 (ROC) Canandaigua, NY St. Mary Church.
Wait, Dennis '72 (KCK) [8] Kansas City, KS St. Mary-St. Anthony Church.
Waite, Patrick J. '54 (SC) Retired.
Waitekus, Christopher '90 (SPR) [9] Chicopee, MA St. Rose de Lima Church.
Waiwood, Richard '73 (ELP) [37] El Paso, TX San Juan Bautista Church.
Wajda, Edward J. '56 (PHX) Retired.
Wajda, Joseph L. '73 (STP) Special Assignment.
Wake, John F. '74 (TR) Brick Town, NJ Epiphany Church.
Wakefield, Alan '75 (LAN) Special Assignment.
Wakefield, Christopher L. '96 (ALN) Shillington, PA St. John Baptist de la Salle Church.
Wakefield, Michael '81 (LA) [2] North Hollywood, CA St. Charles Borromeo Church.
Wakeman, Msgr. John J. '56 (ALX) Retired.
Wakim, Rodolphe W. (SAM) [A] Washington, DC Our Lady of Lebanon Maronite Seminary.
Wakitsch, Randal J. '89 (RCK) Absent on Leave.
Walas, Joseph '59 (RVC) Riverhead, NY St. Isidore's Church.
Walaszek, Luke A. *o.p.* '58 (NOR) Willimantic, CT St. Joseph Church.
Walbe, John '44 (LR) [A] Subiaco, AR Subiaco Monastery.
Walch, John '45 (OKL) Retired.
Walck, Edward F. *m.m.* '56 (NY) [Z] Maryknoll, NY Maryknoll Fathers and Brothers.
Walczak, Donald J. '63 (LC) [2] Stevens Point, WI St. Casimir Church; Torun, WI St. Mary Church.
Walczak, Melvin (ROC) Absent on Leave.
Walczyk, Florian A. *o.f.m.* '64 (PAT) [M] Butler, NJ St. Anthony Friary.
Wald, Edward *s.v.d.* '50 (STL) [53] St. Louis, MO St. Nicholas Church.
Wald, Jeffrey '92 (FAR) Devils Lake, ND St. Joseph's Church; Devils Lake, ND School for the Deaf; [I] Devils Lake, ND UND-Lake Region.
Wald, Kenneth '57 (BIS) Kenmare, ND St. Agnes Church.
Walden, Ellsworth R. '71 (RVC) Hauppauge, NY St. Thomas More Church.
Waldie, Paul *o.m.i.* '65 (OAK) [N] Oakland, CA Oblate Provincial House & Procure.
Waldie, Paul *o.m.i.* '65 (SEA) [4] Seattle, WA St. Benedict Church.
Waldie, Thomas E. *s.s.s.* '38 (CLV) [P] Cleveland, OH Blessed Sacrament Community.
Waldie, Thomas E. *s.s.s.* '38 (NY) [8] New York, NY St. Andrew Church.
Walding, Eugene F. '66 (SC) Fort Dodge, IA Trinity Regional Hospital; [E] Fort Dodge, IA The Marian Home.
Waldmann, Robert J. '46 (B) Retired.
Waldon, Clarence R. '64 (IND) [5] Indianapolis, IN Holy Angels Church.
Waldow, Msgr. Harold L. '70 (AMA) [F] Amarillo, TX St. Anthony's Hospital.
Waldrep, Jeffrey '90 (JKS) Greenville, MS St. Joseph Church.
Waldron, John '66 (P) Beaverton, OR Holy Trinity Church.
Waldron, Msgr. John E. '66 (BRK) [145] Brooklyn, NY Visitation of the Blessed Virgin Mary Church.
Waldron, John F. '62 (ALB) Colonie, NY Our Lady of Mercy Church.
Waldron, John R. '56 (NEW) Retired.
Waldron, Richard P. '61 (HBG) Mechanicsburg, PA St. Elizabeth Ann Seton Church.
Waldron, Robert J. '68 (BO) [3] Waltham, MA St. Jude Church.
Waldron, Walter J. '64 (BO) [36] Boston, MA St. Joseph Church; [60] Boston, MA St. Patrick Church.
Waldron, William '50 (PHX) Sun City, AZ St. Elizabeth Seton Church.
Waldruff, Stephen C. *t.o.r.* '53 (ALT) [F] Hollidaysburg, PA St. Joseph Friary.
Waldschmidt, Donald L. '55 (DAV) Retired; [M] Davenport, IA St. Vincent Center.
Waldschmidt, Valens J. *o.f.m.* '47 (CIN) [M] Cincinnati, OH St. Clement Friary; [V] Cincinnati, OH St. Dymphna Chapel.
Waldspurger, Daniel-Zachary *o.s.b.* '90 (GBG) [H] Latrobe, PA Saint Vincent Archabbey.
Walega, Stanley J. '64 (MET) Bound Brook, NJ St. Mary of Czestochowa Church.
Walick, Stephen J. '69 (CLV) [52] Cleveland, OH Our Lady of Angels Church; Cleveland, OH Fairview General Hospital.
Walijewski, Joseph A. '50 (LC) Foreign Missions.
Walk, Donald J. '67 (VEN) Priests Released from Diocesan Assignment.
Walk, Edward J. '78 (E) Du Bois, PA St. Catherine Church; [C] Du Bois, PA Du Bois Area Catholic Schools.
Walker, Anselm '56 (GAL) Retired.
Walker, Benjamin *o.s.b.* '60 (PIT) [81] Pittsburgh, PA St. Peter Church.
Walker, Brian G. *o.p.* '86 (CHI) [24] Chicago, IL St. Basil/Visitation Church.
Walker, Carlos '83 (BRK) [48] Brooklyn, NY St. Gabriel The Archangel Church.
Walker, Charles D. '81 (L) [65] Louisville, KY St. Pius X Church.
Walker, David M. '64 (HRT) [6] Hamden, CT St. Rita's Church.
Walker, Msgr. Dean P. '47 (SC) Retired.
Walker, Donald L. '58 (DET) Redford Township, MI St. Robert Bellarmine Church.
Walker, Earl G. '48 (LA) [2] Los Angeles, CA Cathedral Chapel.
Walker, Edmund *o.f.m. cap.* '63 (CHL) [8] Charlotte, NC St. Matthew Church.
Walker, Msgr. Edward J. '36 (BUF) Retired.
Walker, Gerald '55 (LA) Irwindale, CA Our Lady of Guadalupe Church.
Walker, Gerard T. '80 (BRK) [150] Queens, NY St. Andrew Avellino Church.
Walker, Gilbert R. *c.m.* '87 (NO) [60] New Orleans, LA St. Stephen Church.
Walker, J. Kenneth '81 (EVN) Newburgh, IN St. John the Baptist Church; Special Assignment.
Walker, J. Patrick '88 (STO) Turlock, CA Sacred Heart Church.
Walker, James '77 (Y) [4] Warren, OH St. James Church.
Walker, James B. '90 (SAV) Macon, GA St. Peter Claver Church.
Walker, John H. '53 (CLV) Sheffield, OH St. Teresa Church; Retired.
Walker, Kent A. '89 (ORL) Merritt Island, FL Divine Mercy Church.
Walker, Leonard *s.d.s.* '74 (MIL) [P] Milwaukee, WI Salvatorian Provincial Residence.
Walker, Michael '32 (KC) [E] Kansas City, MO St. Stephen's School.
Walker, Michael J. '62 (KC) [31] Kansas City, MO Our Lady of Peace Church.
Walker, Norbert J. '44 (PH) Retired.
Walker, Paul '72 (STU) McConnelsville, OH St. James Church.
Walker, Robert F. '65 (CAM) Margate, NJ Blessed Sacrament Church.
Walker, Robert L. *o.p.* '56 (WDC) [11] Washington, DC St. Dominic Church & Priory Church.
Walker, Thomas J. '89 (MIL) [1] Fond du Lac, WI St. Joseph's Church.
Walker, Thomas J. '90 (STP) Red Wing, MN St. Joseph Church.
Walkiewicz, Jacek *s.chr.* '93 (CHI) [87] Chicago, IL Holy Trinity Mission Church.
Walkowiak, David '79 (CLV) [A] Wickliffe, OH St. Mary Seminary.
Wall, Antoninus *o.p.* '50 (OAK) [N] Oakland, CA Dominican Order (Western Province), St. Albert's Priory.
Wall, Barry W. '62 (FR) Mattapoisett, MA St. Anthony's Church.
Wall, Damian '65 (CGS) [1] Caguas, PR Cathedral Dulce Nombre de Jesus Church.
Wall, G. Warren '76 (MOB) [7] Mobile, AL St. Ignatius Church.
Wall, Gus *s.v.d.* '91 (DUB) [B] Epworth, IA Divine Word College.
Wall, Msgr. James E. '63 (BUF) [Q] Derby, NY St. Columban's Center.
Wall, John A. '60 (R) Cary, NC St. Michael the Archangel Church.
Wall, John E. '57 (CIN) [56] Cincinnati, OH St. Margaret Mary Church.
Wall, John J. '68 (CHI) [165] Chicago, IL St. Patrick Church.
Wall, Malachy *o.c.s.o.* '55 (CHR) [E] Moncks Corner, SC Mepkin Abbey.
Wall, Patrick J. '92 (STP) Stillwater, MN St. Mary Church.
Wall, Sherman B. *o.m.i.* '57 (SPC) Willow Springs, MO Sacred Heart Church.
Wall, Warren (NY) [DD] New York, NY North American College of Rome, Alumni Assoc. of.
Wallace, Basil J. *o.s.b.* '78 (PAT) [M] Newton, NJ St. Paul's Abbey.
Wallace, Donald L. '62 (JC) Rolla, MO St. Patrick Church.
Wallace, Msgr. Francis T. '63 (LA) La Canada Flintridge, CA St. Bede the Venerable Church.
Wallace, Francis X. '47 (FR) Retired.
Wallace, George *s.m.* '57 (PH) [T] Langhorne, PA St. Mary Medical Center; [Z] Langhorne, PA Society of Mary, Marist Fathers.
Wallace, Harry C. '56 (ORL) Deltona, FL Our Lady of the Lakes Church.
Wallace, Harry C. '56 (SY) On Duty Outside the Diocese.
Wallace, James *c.ss.r.* '70 (WDC) [M] Washington, DC Holy Redeemer College.
Wallace, John *f.m.s.i.* '60 (BO) [B] Framingham, MA Sylva Maria.
Wallace, Joseph D. '85 (CAM) Haddon Heights, NJ St. Rose's Church.
Wallace, Leonard P. '55 (DET) Lakeport, MI St. Edward's on the Lake Church.
Wallace, Msgr. Murrough C. '60 (SAC) South Lake Tahoe, CA St. Theresa Church.
Wallace, Philip D. '65 (SEA) Seahurst, WA St. Francis of Assisi Church.
Wallace, Regis P. *o.s.b.* '60 (PAT) Cedar Knolls, NJ Notre Dame of Mt. Carmel Church; [M] Morristown, NJ St. Mary's Abbey.
Wallace, Richard '86 (P) Military Chaplains.
Wallace, Scott H. '92 (NSH) Absent on Leave.
Wallace, William J. *o.s.a.* '74 (NY) [168] Bronx, NY St. Nicholas of Tolentine Church.
Wallaik, William H. '49 (MIL) Mequon, WI St. James Church; Retired.
Walle, Msgr. Julius G. (ALX) Cheneyville, LA St. Joseph Church; Retired.
Walleman, Kenneth T. *s.j.* '59 (RC) St. Francis, SD Rosebud Reservation Church.
Wallen, Charles L. *c.s.c.* '54 (FR) [K] North Dartmouth, MA Holy Cross Mission House.
Wallen, Clarence J. *s.j.* '51 (LA) [C] Los Angeles, CA Loyola Marymount University.
Wallen, Michael J. '58 (CHI) Markham, IL St. Gerard Majella Church.
Wallenfelsz, Scott *s.d.s.* '69 (MIL) [P] Milwaukee, WI Salvatorian Provincial Residence.
Wallenhorst, George A. *s.j.* '39 (CHI) Chicago, IL Cook County Hospital; [D] Chicago, IL St. Ignatius Jesuit Community.
Waller, Charles J. '73 (PAT) East Hanover, NJ St. Rose of Lima Church.
Waller, Robert C. '75 (CIN) [48] Cincinnati, OH St. John Neumann Church.
Wallin, Msgr. Kevin W. '84 (BGP) [1] Bridgeport, CT St. Augustine Cathedral; [R] Bridgeport, CT Inner-City Foundation for Charity & Education.
Walling, Gerald C. *s.j.* (CHI) [C] Chicago, IL Jesuit Community at Loyola University of Chicago; [D] Chicago, IL St. Ignatius College Prep.
Walling, Lawrence *o.s.m.* '79 (P) Milwaukie, OR Christ the King Church.
Walling, Richard W. '78 (CIN) [5] Springfield, OH St. Teresa of the Child Jesus Church.
Wallis, William H. '82 (SPR) Great Barrington, MA St. Peter's Church.
Walljasper, Mark A. '55 (LC) Sparta, WI St. Patrick Church; [G] Sparta, WI Franciscan Skemp Healthcare, Mayo Health System, Sparta Campus Nursing Home.
Wallner, Francis A. *s.j.* '51 (ALN) [A] Wernersville, PA Novitiate of St. Isaac Jogues.
Wallner, Gerhard '89 (FBK) Leave of Absence.
Wallroth, Joseph *o.carm.* '70 (JOL) [J] Darien, IL Carmelite Fathers Provincial Office; [J] Darien, IL Carmelite Fathers Provincial Office.
Walls, Msgr. David E. '60 (PH) Bryn Mawr, PA St. John Neumann Church; Absent on Leave.
Walmesley, Jack '74 (SEA) Kent, WA St. John the Baptist Church.
Walmsley, Gerard *s.j.* '82 (BO) [W] Chestnut Hill, MA The Jesuit Community at Boston College.
Walpole, Donald *o.s.b.* '43 (IND) [B] St. Meinrad, IN St. Meinrad Seminary-College of Liberal Arts; [J] St. Meinrad, IN St. Meinrad Archabbey.
Walsh, Aidan J. (BO) Boston, MA V.A. Medical Centers.
Walsh, Al (GAL) Sugar Land, TX St. Laurence Church.
Walsh, Andrew J. '66 (NY) Carmel, NY St. James the Apostle Church.
Walsh, Arthur '85 (CC) On Duty Outside the Diocese.
Walsh, Austin *s.t.* (WDC) [M] Riverdale, MD Holy Spirit Missionary Cenacle.
Walsh, Bernard '55 (SY) Retired.
Walsh, Brendan J. '93 (LAN) [6] Lansing, MI St. Gerard Church.
Walsh, Broderick M. *c.s.p.* '92 (KNX) [3] Knoxville, TN Immaculate Conception Church.
Walsh, Msgr. Bryan O. '54 (MIA) Retired.
Walsh, Msgr. Charles F. '51 (WCH) El Dorado, KS St. John Church.
Walsh, Christopher J. '87 (BGP) [O] Stamford, CT St. John Fisher Seminary Residence.
Walsh, Clyde J. '51 (PRO) Retired; [P] Providence, RI St. John Vianney Residence.
Walsh, Dan *c.s.sp.* (PIT) Allegheny County, PA Allegheny County Jail.
Walsh, Daniel M. '59 (SHP) Vivian, LA St. Clement Church.
Walsh, Daniel P. '68 (BUF) Fredonia, NY St. Anthony Church.
Walsh, David *c.ss.r.* '47 (CC) [8] Corpus Christi, TX Our Lady of Perpetual Help Church; On Special Assignment.

Walsh, David I. *m.m.* '42 (NY) [Z] Maryknoll, NY Maryknoll Fathers and Brothers.
Walsh, David I. '46 (SFR) Retired; [K] San Francisco, CA Home for the Aged of the Little Sisters of the Poor.
Walsh, Denis '66 (TYL) [B] Palestine, TX Hermitage.
Walsh, Dennis *c.ss.r.* '92 (NY) [150] Bronx, NY Immaculate Conception Church.
Walsh, Donal C. '55 (SD) Julian, CA St. Elizabeth Church.
Walsh, E. Corbett *s.j.* '71 (BO) [W] Weston, MA Campion Center.
Walsh, Edward J. '64 (CAM) Woodlynne, NJ Immaculate Heart of Mary Church.
Walsh, Edward J. '91 (PH) On Duty Outside the Archdiocese.
Walsh, Edward J. '91 (RVC) Lindenhurst, NY Our Lady of Perpetual Help Church.
Walsh, Edward P. '93 (BIR) [3] Birmingham, AL St. Barnabas Church.
Walsh, Flannan J. (STA) On Duty Outside the Diocese.
Walsh, Flavian *o.f.m.* (PAT) Little Falls, NJ Our Lady of the Holy Angels Church.
Walsh, Francis (WDC) Cheverly, MD St. Ambrose Church.
Walsh, Francis *s.j.* '53 (SEA) [C] Tacoma, WA Bellarmine Preparatory School.
Walsh, Francis E. '66 (SPR) Military Chaplains.
Walsh, Francis M. *c.s.c.* '56 (FR) [B] North Easton, MA Stonehill College; [B] North Easton, MA Holy Cross Fathers Religious.
Walsh, Francis M. '67 (WDC) Hospital & Nursing Home Ministries.
Walsh, Francis P. '57 (CLV) [5] Lakewood, OH St. Luke Church.
Walsh, Frederick P. *o.s.b.* '38 (BR) [I] Tickfaw, LA Our Lady Queen Contemplative Monastery.
Walsh, Frederick P. *o.s.b.* '38 (IND) [J] St. Meinrad, IN St. Meinrad Archabbey.
Walsh, George J. '52 (PH) Retired.
Walsh, Gerald *c.s.sp.* '42 (PIT) [B] Pittsburgh, PA Duquesne University of the Holy Ghost.
Walsh, Gerald '95 (CHI) Tinley Park, IL St. George Church.
Walsh, Msgr. Gerald J. '55 (BIS) Special Assignment; [G] Bismarck, ND Emmaus Place.
Walsh, Gerald P. '74 (WOR) Oxford, MA St. Roch's Church.
Walsh, Msgr. Gerald T. '67 (NY) [53] New York, NY Incarnation Church.
Walsh, Msgr. Gerard W. '46 (NEW) Retired.
Walsh, Harry A. '60 (STP) Special Assignment.
Walsh, J. Daniel *c.s.c.* '60 (BR) Jackson, LA East Feliciana Chronic Disease Hospital and Rehabilitation Center.
Walsh, J. Patrick *s.j.* '63 (DEN) [30] Denver, CO St. Ignatius Loyola Church; [M] Denver, CO Loyola Parish - Jesuit Community.
Walsh, J. Thomas '89 (HRT) [5] New Britain, CT St. Ann Church.
Walsh, James '66 (DUL) Pequot Lakes, MN St. Alice's Church.
Walsh, James '69 (SJ) [11] San Jose, CA St. Christopher Church.
Walsh, James '73 (MAN) [3] Nashua, NH St. Christopher Church.
Walsh, James A. '54 (TOL) Milan, OH St. Anthony Church.
Walsh, James F. *s.j.* '72 (BO) [W] Boston, MA The Society of Jesus of New England-Provincial Offices.
Walsh, James G. *c.s.p.* '41 (NY) [Z] Scarsdale, NY Paulist Fathers Generalate.
Walsh, Msgr. James J. '36 (NY) Retired; [E] White Plains, NY Archbishop Stepinac High School.
Walsh, James J. '68 (CIN) On Duty Outside the Archdiocese.
Walsh, James J. '73 (SCR) Jermyn, PA Sacred Heart of Mary Church.
Walsh, James J. '93 (ALB) Delmar, NY St. Thomas the Apostle Church.
Walsh, James P. (MAN) [6] Manchester, NH St. Catherine Church.
Walsh, James P. *s.j.* '62 (BO) [W] Weston, MA Campion Center; [Y] Weston, MA Campion Renewal Center.
Walsh, James P. *s.j.* '66 (PBL) Springfield, CO Annunciation Church.
Walsh, James P.M. *s.j.* '70 (WDC) [M] Washington, DC The Jesuit Community at Georgetown University.
Walsh, Jeffrey J. '94 (SCR) [1] Scranton, PA St. Peter's Cathedral; [D] Scranton, PA Bishop Hannan High School.
Walsh, Jerome '69 (DET) On Duty Outside the Archdiocese.
Walsh, Jerome M. '58 (CHI) [N] Chicago, IL Dominicans (Provincial Office); [N] Chicago, IL Dominicans (Provincial Office).
Walsh, Joachim E. *o.s.b.* '37 (BR) [I] Tickfaw, LA Our Lady Queen Contemplative Monastery.
Walsh, Joachim E. *o.s.b.* '37 (IND) [J] St. Meinrad, IN St. Meinrad Archabbey.
Walsh, John '55 (SAL) Norton, KS St. Francis of Assisi Church.
Walsh, John A. '61 (SCR) On Duty Outside the Diocese.
Walsh, John A. '80 (E) Fryburg, PA St. Michael Church.
Walsh, John B. '57 (MAD) Lake Mills, WI St. Francis Xavier Church.
Walsh, John F. '70 (BRK) Absent on Leave.
Walsh, John F. '76 (PIT) [63] Pittsburgh, PA Prince of Peace Church.
Walsh, John F. '84 (BO) [8] Lowell, MA St. Margaret Church.
Walsh, John J. *c.s.sp.* (GAL) [B] Houston, TX Holy Ghost Fathers; [T] Houston, TX Texas Southern University Catholic Newman Hall.
Walsh, John J. *s.j.* '45 (STL) [P] St. Louis, MO Jesuit Community Corporation at St. Louis University - Jesuit Hall.
Walsh, John J. *s.j.* '46 (BO) Rockland, MA Holy Family Church; [W] Weston, MA Campion Health Center, Inc.
Walsh, John J. '57 (DUB) Webster City, IA St. Thomas Aquinas Church.
Walsh, John J. *m.m.* '61 (NY) [Z] Maryknoll, NY Maryknoll Fathers and Brothers.
Walsh, John Joseph *s.j.* '71 (BO) [E] Boston, MA Boston College High School & Jesuit Community; [W] Boston, MA The Society of Jesus of New England-Provincial Offices.
Walsh, John Kelly *m.m.* '33 (NY) [Z] Maryknoll, NY Maryknoll Fathers and Brothers.
Walsh, John M. '47 (PH) Retired.
Walsh, John P. (ATL) Peachtree City, GA Holy Trinity Catholic Church.
Walsh, John T. '44 (ROC) [43] Rochester, NY St. Margaret Mary Church; Retired.
Walsh, Joseph '64 (SFR) Special Assignment; [U] San Francisco, CA Spiritual Programs and Retreats.
Walsh, Joseph E. '47 (PH) Lenni, PA St. Francis de Sales Church; Retired.
Walsh, Joseph M. '86 (LIN) [11] Lincoln, NE St. Teresa's Church; [K] Lincoln, NE Catholic Social Services.
Walsh, Joseph R. '64 (SFR) [30] San Francisco, CA St. Kevin Church.
Walsh, Kenneth *c.p.* '50 (NEW) [3] Union City, NJ SS. Joseph and Michael Church.
Walsh, Kevin '78 (RVC) Priests Released from Diocesan Assignment.
Walsh, Kevin '92 (ARL) [8] Alexandria, VA St. Rita's Church.
Walsh, Kevin V. '78 (HRT) [17] Waterbury, CT SS. Peter and Paul Church.
Walsh, Laurence '45 (NO) Retired.
Walsh, Laurence E. *s.j.* '54 (STL) [P] St. Louis, MO Jesuit Community Corporation at St. Louis University - Jesuit Hall.
Walsh, Msgr. Lawrence F. '54 (SAT) [9] San Antonio, TX Holy Spirit Church.
Walsh, Msgr. Lawrence J. '63 (STL) [39] St. Louis, MO St. Joan of Arc Church.
Walsh, Leo A., Jr. '94 (ANC) [2] Anchorage, AK St. Anthony Church.
Walsh, Marion *o.s.b.* '42 (IND) [J] St. Meinrad, IN St. Meinrad Archabbey.
Walsh, Marion C. *o.s.b.* '42 (BR) [I] Tickfaw, LA Our Lady Queen Contemplative Monastery.
Walsh, Martin *o.m.i.* (BO) Tewksbury, MA St. William Church.
Walsh, Martin *o.p.* '50 (OAK) [N] Oakland, CA Dominican Order (Western Province), St. Albert's Priory.
Walsh, Martin *o.p.* '69 (OAK) [N] Oakland, CA Western Dominican Province.
Walsh, Msgr. Martin E. (OAK) Military Chaplains.
Walsh, Msgr. Martin E. '43 (OAK) Retired; [M] Oakland, CA Bishop Begin Villa.
Walsh, Martin J., Jr. '74 (BO) [3] Malden, MA Sacred Hearts Church.
Walsh, Michael (SFR) [43] San Francisco, CA St. Paul of the Shipwreck Church.
Walsh, Msgr. Michael '38 (LA) Retired.
Walsh, Michael '53 (DEN) [4] Englewood, CO St. Thomas More Church.
Walsh, Michael *o.f.m.cap.* '58 (BAK) Bend, OR St. Francis of Assisi Church.
Walsh, Michael '71 (SAC) Awaiting Assignment.
Walsh, Michael A. '72 (PAT) Military Chaplains.
Walsh, Michael E. *s.j.* '62 (SEA) [Q] Tacoma, WA Catholic Pastoral Care-Hospital Tacoma Ministry.
Walsh, Michael F. *c.m.* '72 (LA) [A] Camarillo, CA St. John's Seminary.
Walsh, Michael J. '38 (BRK) Retired.
Walsh, Michael J. '56 (CHI) Palos Hills, IL Sacred Heart Church.
Walsh, Michael J. '70 (BRK) [242] Queens, NY St. Stanislaus Kostka Church.
Walsh, Msgr. Michael J. '73 (TR) Lakewood, NJ St. Mary of the Lake Church.
Walsh, Michael L. '45 (PH) [U] Immaculata, PA Camilla Hall Nursing Home.
Walsh, Michael P. '88 (NY) [Z] Maryknoll, NY Maryknoll Fathers and Brothers.
Walsh, Miles D. (BR) Special Assignment.
Walsh, Milton T. '78 (SFR) [1] San Francisco, CA Cathedral of St. Mary (Assumption); San Francisco, CA Knights of Malta.
Walsh, Patrick *s.a.* '63 (NY) [Z] Garrison, NY Franciscan Friars of the Atonement.
Walsh, Patrick '72 (P) Springfield, OR St. Alice Church.
Walsh, Patrick *c.s.c.* '81 (PRT) Saco, ME Most Holy Trinity Church.
Walsh, Patrick *l.c.* '91 (MAN) [A] Center Harbor, NH Immaculate Conception Apostolic School.
Walsh, Patrick A. *s.m.a.* '65 (NY) Tuckahoe, NY Immaculate Conception Church.
Walsh, Patrick E. *s.j.* '60 (MIL) [29] Milwaukee, WI Gesu Parish Church.
Walsh, Patrick J. '58 (LA) [60] Los Angeles, CA St. Eugene Church.
Walsh, Patrick P. *o.p.* '34 (NY) Valhalla, NY Holy Name of Jesus Church.
Walsh, Patrick R. '69 (SC) [B] Fort Dodge, IA St. Edmond High School.
Walsh, Paul *c.s.b.* (ROC) Fairport, NY Assumption of the Blessed Virgin Mary Church.
Walsh, Paul '66 (RVC) Smithtown, NY St. Patrick Church.
Walsh, Paul F. *c.s.b.* '87 (ROC) [I] Rochester, NY Basilian Residence.
Walsh, Peter '59 (JC) Bonnots Mill, MO St. Louis Church; Frankenstein, MO Our Lady of Help Church.
Walsh, Peter *o.f.m.* '82 (NY) [Z] New York, NY Padua Friary.
Walsh, Peter *c.s.c.* '89 (BO) [18] Boston, MA St. Cecilia Church.
Walsh, Peter J. *c.s.c.* '89 (FR) [B] North Easton, MA Holy Cross Fathers Religious.
Walsh, Raymond D. '54 (BUR) West Rutland, VT St. Bridget Church.
Walsh, Richard '68 (ORL) Winter Park, FL St. Margaret Mary Church; Special Assignment.
Walsh, Richard '83 (JOL) Romeoville, IL St. Andrew the Apostle Church.
Walsh, Richard A. '62 (PRO) [6] Cranston, RI St. Matthew Church.
Walsh, Msgr. Richard J. '44 (ALT) Retired.
Walsh, Richard J. *c.s.p.* '44 (NY) [104] New York, NY St. Paul the Apostle Church; [Z] Scarsdale, NY Paulist Fathers Generalate.
Walsh, Msgr. Robert '46 (LA) Arcadia, CA Holy Angels Church; Retired.
Walsh, Robert A. '77 (CHI) [J] Chicago, IL St. Joseph Hospital.
Walsh, Robert J. '44 (RIC) Portsmouth, VA St. Paul Church; Retired.
Walsh, Robert T. *s.j.* '80 (LA) [F] Los Angeles, CA Loyola High School.
Walsh, Romuald *c.p.* '34 (BRK) [U] Jamaica, NY Immaculate Conception Monastery.
Walsh, Stephen M. *o.f.m.* '50 (BO) [Z] Boston, MA Saint Anthony Residence.
Walsh, Terrance G. *s.j.* '82 (BO) [W] Boston, MA The Society of Jesus of New England-Provincial Offices.
Walsh, Theodore *c.p.* '59 (BRK) [U] Jamaica, NY Immaculate Conception Monastery.
Walsh, Thomas '72 (STA) [20] Jacksonville, FL San Jose Church.
Walsh, Thomas *o.f.m.conv.* '80 (BAL) [M] Baltimore, MD Immaculate Heart of Mary Friary.
Walsh, Thomas '94 (LIN) McCook, NE St. Patrick Church.
Walsh, Thomas A. '42 (PHX) Retired.
Walsh, Thomas E. *o.f.m.conv.* '80 (BAL) [D] Baltimore, MD Archbishop Curley High School.
Walsh, Thomas F. *o.m.i.* '41 (BO) [Z] Tewksbury, MA Immaculate Heart of Mary Novitiate-Infirmary.
Walsh, Thomas F. '45 (PH) Retired.
Walsh, Thomas F. '46 (PH) Valley Forge, PA St. Teresa of Avila Church.
Walsh, Thomas F. *s.j.* '55 (PAT) [I] Morristown, NJ Loyola House of Retreats.
Walsh, Thomas J. *o.s.f.s.* '40 (WIL) [I] Childs, MD Oblates of St. Francis De Sales.
Walsh, Thomas J. *o.carm.* '50 (VEN) Englewood, FL St. Raphael Church.
Walsh, Thomas J. '67 (BO) Franklin, MA St. Mary Church.
Walsh, Thomas J. '94 (MET) East Brunswick, NJ St. Bartholomew Church.
Walsh, Thomas P. '86 (CHI) [175] Chicago, IL Presentation Church.
Walsh, Thomas R. (CHL) Retired.
Walsh, Thomas V. '67 (WOR) Clinton, MA St. John the Evangelist Church.
Walsh, Ulich (WCH) Retired.
Walsh, Vincent '64 (MRY) San Luis Obispo, CA San Luis Obispo Church; Atascadero, CA Atascadero State Hospital; [J] Monterey, CA Department of Campus Ministry.
Walsh, Vincent '64 (SY) On Duty Outside the Diocese.
Walsh, Msgr. Vincent M. '62 (PH) Wynnewood, PA Presentation B.V.M. Church.
Walsh, William D. '66 (BO) [13] Cambridge, MA St.

Peter Church.
Walsh, William F. *o.s.f.s.* '68 (ALN) [O] Kutztown, PA Christopher House; [O] Kutztown, PA Christopher House.
Walsh, William J. *s.j.* '54 (WDC) [M] Washington, DC Woodstock Jesuit Community; [V] Washington, DC Woodstock Theological Center.
Walsh, William K. '49 (SAC) Rio Vista, CA St. Joseph Church; Retired and in Senior Ministry.
Walsh, William M. '71 (BO) [3] Brockton, MA St. Edward Church.
Walsh, William P. *s.j.* '67 (PAT) [I] Morristown, NJ Loyola House of Retreats.
Walsman, Paul *o.f.m.* '58 (CIN) [K] Cincinnati, OH Franciscan Hospital, Western Hills Campus.
Walter, Anthony *o.f.m.* '59 (BR) [F] Baton Rouge, LA Our Lady of the Lake Regional Medical Center; [H] Baton Rouge, LA Franciscan Residence.
Walter, Charles *m.c.c.j.* '66 (CIN) [M] Cincinnati, OH Comboni Missionaries (Verona Fathers)-Comboni Mission Center.
Walter, Charles W. '74 (MIL) Sick Leave.
Walter, Chris B. '58 (BIS) [4] Minot, ND St. Leo Church.
Walter, David A. '63 (STL) Affton, MO St. Timothy Church.
Walter, Eugene *s.d.b.* (NY) [BB] West Haverstraw, NY Don Bosco Retreat Center and Marian Shrine; [BB] West Haverstraw, NY Marian Shrine.
Walter, Francis *o.f.m.* '77 (TR) Roebling, NJ Holy Assumption Church.
Walter, James A. '62 (COL) Sunbury, OH St. John Neumann Church.
Walter, James A. '69 (BUF) Springbrook, NY St. Vincent Church.
Walter, John F. '44 (MIL) Retired.
Walter, Joseph J. *s.j.* '45 (NY) [F] New York, NY Xavier High School; [Z] New York, NY Jesuit Provincial's Office; [Z] New York, NY Xavier Jesuit Community.
Walter, Joseph L. *c.s.c.* '61 (FTW) [B] Notre Dame, IN University of Notre Dame Du Lac; [J] Notre Dame, IN Holy Cross Community, Corby Hall, University of Notre Dame.
Walter, Raymond F. *c.ss.r.* '41 (STL) [P] Liguori, MO St. Clement Health Care Center.
Walter, Msgr. Robert J. '45 (DAV) Retired.
Walter, Steven P. '77 (CIN) [74] Cincinnati, OH Our Mother of Sorrows Church.
Walter, William P. *c.pp.s.* '61 (KC) Warrensburg, MO Sacred Heart Church; [A] Liberty, MO Society of the Precious Blood Provincial Offices.
Walters, Gary R. '79 (TOL) Bethlehem, OH Sacred Heart of Jesus Church; Crestline, OH St. Joseph Church.
Walters, James '59 (LR) Retired.
Walters, James *s.c.j.* '78 (SFS) Stephan, SD Immaculate Conception Church.
Walters, James L. *s.c.j.* '78 (RC) Lower Brule, SD St. Mary's Church; Lower Brule, SD Lower Brule Reservation Church; [B] Lower Brule, SD SCJ Community House.
Walters, John F. *s.j.* '71 (NY) [Z] New York, NY Jesuit Provincial's Office.
Walters, Michael M. '81 (NEW) Ridgefield, NJ St. Matthew's Church.
Walters, Neil G. '89 (CLV) [17] Akron, OH St. Sebastian Church.
Walters, Ronald F. *o.f.m.* '78 (GRY) [K] Cedar Lake, IN San Damiano Friary.
Walters, Theodore W. *s.j.* (DET) [K] Detroit, MI Jesuit Provincial Office-Detroit Province of the Society of Jesus.
Walters, Thomas J. *o.f.m.* '80 (NY) [35] New York, NY St. Francis of Assisi Church; [35] New York, NY St. Francis of Assisi Church.
Walters, Vincent '54 (SB) Retired.
Waltersheid, William '92 (HBG) [5] Steelton, PA Prince of Peace Church.
Walton, James *o.f.m.* '91 (CHI) [N] Countryside, IL St. Gratian Friary, Franciscan Friars.
Walton, James *o.f.m.* '91 (JOL) Hinsdale, IL Hinsdale Hospital.
Walton, Robert '74 (SAC) Elk Grove, CA St. Joseph Church.
Walz, Julius J. '46 (FAR) Retired.
Walz, Richard (SCL) On Duty Outside the Diocese.
Walz, Msgr. W. Dean (DUB) On Special or Other (Arch)Diocesan Assignment.
Wambach, John W. *s.j.* '64 (LC) Prairie du Chien, WI St. Gabriel Church; Prairie du Chien, WI St. John Nepomucene Church.
Wampach, Frank J. '84 (STP) Bellechester, MN St. Mary Church; Zumbrota, MN St. Paul Church.
Wanat, Edward *s.d.s.* '75 (SAT) Kosciuszko, TX St. Ann's Church.
Wanat, Mitchell J. *c.m.* '71 (MAN) [2] Concord, NH St. Peter Church.
Wanaurny, John '59 (OM) [K] St. Columbans, NE St. Columban's Foreign Mission Society.
Wancewicz, Walter G. '92 (OM) [25] Omaha, NE St. Joseph Church; [B] Omaha, NE Daniel J. Gross Catholic High School of Omaha.
Wanda, Michael J. '91 (CHI) La Grange Park, IL St. Louise de Marillac Church.
Wander, Paul H. '90 (B) St. Anthony, ID Mary Immaculate Church.
Wang, Barnabas '52 (BRK) Retired; [U] Douglaston, NY Bishop Mugavero Residence.
Wang, Francis X. *s.j.* '52 (SJ) [M] Los Gatos, CA California Province of the Society of Jesus, Jesuit Provincial Office; [M] Los Gatos, CA Sacred Heart Jesuit Center.
Wang, Msgr. Ignatius '59 (SFR) [23] San Francisco, CA Holy Name of Jesus Church; Special Assignment; [U] San Francisco, CA Holy Childhood Pontifical Association.
Wang, John '54 (HEL) Retired.
Wangler, Msgr. Alex '41 (SAT) Retired.
Wangler, Brian *o.s.b.* '69 (BIS) Richardton, ND St. Mary Church; [A] Richardton, ND Assumption Abbey.
Wangler, Msgr. Donald L. '43 (BUF) [2] Lockport, NY St. John the Baptist Church.
Wangler, Leonard '70 (LR) [A] Subiaco, AR Subiaco Monastery.
Wangler, Msgr. William O. '63 (BUF) Olean, NY St. John Church.
Wankerl, Gary A. '80 (MAD) Montello, WI St. John the Baptist Church.
Wannemuehler, Robert '51 (EVN) [15] Evansville, IN St. Boniface Church; Retired.
Wanser, George V. *s.j.* '76 (SAC) [C] Sacramento, CA Jesuit High School; [H] Carmichael, CA Jesuit High School Community of Sacramento.
Wanstreet, Msgr. Joseph W. '40 (WH) Retired.
Wantland, Thomas '67 (MAR) On Duty Outside the Diocese.
Wantland, Thomas '67 (VEN) Port Charlotte, FL St. Charles Borromeo Church.
Wanzong, Gary F. '82 (GAL) [31] Houston, TX St. Gregory the Great Church.
Wapen, Francis A. '70 (SY) Taberg, NY St. Patrick Church.
Waraksa, Alex '90 (KNX) Greeneville, TN Notre Dame Church; Newport, TN Good Shepherd Church; Rogersville, TN St. Henry Church.
Warburton, John C. *o.s.j.* '80 (SAC) [A] Loomis, CA Mount St. Joseph Novitiate and Seminary.
Warczynski, Leo '42 (BAL) [86] Baltimore, MD Sacred Heart of Mary Church.
Warczynski, Leon '42 (BAL) Retired.
Ward, Austin T. '70 (STP) Maplewood, MN Holy Redeemer Church.
Ward, Daniel *o.s.b.* '71 (SCL) [I] Collegeville, MN St. John's Abbey, of the Order of St. Benedict.
Ward, Donal '63 (BUR) Vergennes, VT St. Peter Church.
Ward, Donald *s.j.* '70 (CAM) [4] Camden, NJ Holy Name Church.
Ward, Edward *o.m.i.* '67 (CC) [5] Laredo, TX Our Lady of Guadalupe Church.
Ward, Edward *o.carm.* '73 (NEW) Bogota, NJ St. Joseph's Church.
Ward, Msgr. Edward F. '28 (PRT) Retired.
Ward, Gerald T. '79 (PEO) [4] Bloomington, IL St. Patrick Church of Merna; Downs, IL St. Mary's Church.
Ward, Guy *s.j.* '44 (P) [L] Portland, OR Jesuit Provincial Office (Oregon Prov.).
Ward, James Garcia *c.m.* '77 (NO) [60] New Orleans, LA St. Stephen Church.
Ward, James J. '48 (SFR) San Mateo, CA Serra Club of El Camino Real.
Ward, James J. '73 (ALN) Summit Hill, PA St. Joseph Church; Summit Hill, PA St. Stanislaus Church.
Ward, Jerome A. *o.m.i.* '67 (STP) [N] St. Paul, MN Oblate Provincial Offices; [N] St. Paul, MN Oblate Residence.
Ward, John *o.m.i.* (GAL) [S] Dickinson, TX Christian Renewal Center; [T] Houston, TX University of Houston, Clear Lake City Newman Center.
Ward, John '86 (BAL) [40] Baltimore, MD Immaculate Heart of Mary Church.
Ward, John A. *s.s.* '39 (BAL) [K] Baltimore, MD St. Charles Villa; [M] Baltimore, MD St. Charles Villa.
Ward, John B. '86 (BAL) Special Assignment.
Ward, Msgr. John C. '45 (NU) Retired.
Ward, John F. '58 (HEL) Three Forks, MT Holy Family Church.
Ward, John J. (SFR) [D] Kentfield, CA Marin Catholic College Preparatory (Coed).
Ward, John J. '55 (SFR) Retired.
Ward, John J. *c.s.b.* '70 (DET) [E] Redford, MI Catholic Central High School.
Ward, John P. '65 (CAM) Pine Hill, NJ St. Edward's Church.
Ward, Mark *c.p.* '76 (PIT) [N] Pittsburgh, PA St. Paul of the Cross Monastery; [N] Pittsburgh, PA St. Paul of the Cross Monastery; [P] Pittsburgh, PA St. Paul of the Cross Retreat Center.
Ward, Neal A. '57 (WDC) Morganza, MD St. Joseph Church.
Ward, Richard '93 (SEA) [1] Seattle, WA St. James Cathedral.
Ward, Richard E. '68 (PIT) Scott Township, PA SS. Simon and Jude Church.
Ward, Robert A. (BO) [4] Somerville, MA St. Catherine of Genoa Church.
Ward, Sebastian *o.f.m.cap.* '47 (LA) [B] Santa Ynez, CA San Lorenzo Novitiate and Seminary; [L] Ojai, CA St. Joseph's Health and Retirement Center.
Ward, Serge E. '75 (ATL) Eatonton, GA Christ Our Savior Mission Church.
Ward, Serge E. '95 (ATL) Greensboro, GA Christ Our King Parish Church.
Ward, Thomas '62 (KC) Retired.
Ward, Thomas R. '65 (OM) Bellevue, NE St. Mary Church.
Ward, William G. '50 (BUF) Elba, NY Our Lady of Fatima Church.
Ward, William J. '63 (STP) [10] Minneapolis, MN Our Lady of Lourdes Church.
Ward, Msgr. William P. '57 (SCR) Milford, PA St. Vincent de Paul Church.
Wardanski, Msgr. Joseph '67 (E) [K] Erie, PA St. Mary's Home of Erie.
Wardanski, Msgr. Joseph V. '67 (E) [27] Erie, PA St. Patrick/St. Hedwig Church.
Warden, Daniel L. '66 (GAL) Rosenberg, TX Holy Rosary Church.
Warden, T. Patrick *c.s.b.* '65 (GAL) [Q] Houston, TX Residence of the Basilian Fathers of the University of St. Thomas.
Wardenski, Robert W. '72 (BUF) Le Roy, NY St. Peter Church.
Ware, Donald *c.p.* '25 (NY) [BB] New York, NY Cardinal Spellman Retreat House.
Ware, Donald *c.p.* '72 (NY) [Z] New York, NY Passionist Spiritual Center.
Ware, Joseph F. '48 (ATL) Retired.
Ware, Joseph F. '48 (SAV) [7] Savannah, GA St. Frances Xavier Cabrini Church.
Warfel, Michael '80 (ANC) [6] Anchorage, AK Our Lady of Guadalupe Church.
Wargel, William '65 (EVN) [6] Evansville, IN Holy Redeemer Church.
Wargo, Msgr. Robert J. '72 (ALN) Orefield, PA St. Joseph The Worker Church.
Waris, Gerald R. '67 (KC) [35] Kansas City, MO St. Peter's Church.
Warman, William '64 (MET) Lyons, NJ U.S. Veterans Medical Center.
Warman, William C. '64 (BAL) On Duty Outside the Archdiocese.
Warnakula, Anthony B. (SAC) Carmichael, CA Our Lady of the Assumption Church.
Warner, Anthony '63 (RIC) Retired.
Warner, Carroll L. *o.f.m.cap.* '36 (WDC) [B] Washington, DC St. Francis Friary-Capuchin College.
Warner, J. Anthony '63 (RIC) [4] Richmond, VA Our Lady of Lourdes Church.
Warner, James L. '69 (GI) Ord, NE Our Lady of Perpetual Help Church.
Warner, John '70 (Y) North Canton, OH St. Paul's Church.
Warner, Richard V. *c.s.c.* (FTW) [B] Notre Dame, IN University of Notre Dame Du Lac.
Warner, Richard V. *c.s.c.* '66 (FTW) [B] Notre Dame, IN University of Notre Dame Du Lac; [J] Notre Dame, IN Holy Cross Community, Corby Hall, University of Notre Dame; [J] South Bend, IN Congregation of Holy Cross Indiana Province Provincial House.
Warnimont, Ronald R. '76 (TOL) [1] Toledo, OH Queen of the Most Holy Rosary Cathedral.
Warnken, Edward L. *m.div.* '88 (NY) [A] Yonkers, NY St. Joseph's Seminary.
Warnock, Damian J. *o.s.b.* '79 (GBG) [H] Latrobe, PA Saint Vincent Archabbey.
Warnstedt, Mark A. '96 (LA) Arcadia, CA Holy Angels Church.
Warosh, James *s.j.* '67 (MIL) [29] Milwaukee, WI Gesu Parish Church.
Warren, Anthony C. *s.s.p.* '85 (BUF) [O] Derby, NY Society of St. Paul Provincial Residence.
Warren, Arthur (LAF) Retired.
Warren, Clarence A. *s.s.p.* '85 (NY) [B] New York, NY Society of St. Paul.
Warren, Edward V. *s.j.* '52 (SJ) [B] Santa Clara, CA Santa Clara University.
Warren, Martin L. '78 (STP) [29] St. Paul, MN St. Matthew Church.
Warren, Paul F. *o.f.m.* '78 (OAK) [P] Danville, CA San Damiano Retreat.
Warren, Robert '64 (RIC) Retired.
Warren, Robert *s.a.* '81 (NY) [Z] Garrison, NY Franciscan Friars of the Atonement; [Z] Garrison, NY St. Christopher's Friary.
Warren, Ronald J. '62 (BAK) Chiloquin, OR Our Lady of Mt. Carmel Church.
Warren, Thomas '66 (LA) Sick Leave.
Warren, William E. '69 (NY) [161] Bronx, NY St. Margaret of Cortona Church.
Warrington, Bede (LA) [41] Los Angeles, CA St.

Ambrose Church.
Warsey, Robert M. *o.s.m.* '85 (CHI) [N] Chicago, IL Servite Friars - Eastern Province; [N] Chicago, IL Servite Friars - Eastern Province.
Warzocha, Frank S. '53 (BUR) West Rutland, VT St. Stanislaus Kostka Church.
Wasek, Stanislaus *c.p.* '53 (BRK) [U] Jamaica, NY Immaculate Conception Monastery.
Waseline, Nicholas R. *o.s.f.s.* (PH) [Z] Wyndmoor, PA Oblates of St. Francis de Sales (O.S.F.S.).
Waser, Frank A. '79 (RCK) Absent on Leave.
Wash, Pat J. '68 (WH) Absent on Leave.
Washington, Freddy *c.s.sp.* '92 (CIN) [16] Dayton, OH St. James Church; [26] Dayton, OH Resurrection of Our Lord Church.
Washira, Patrick Kanja '83 (SY) [3] Utica, NY Our Lady of Lourdes Church.
Washko, Robert M. '77 (GBG) Mount Pleasant, PA Transfiguration Church.
Washko, Stephen G. '78 (VNN) Las Vegas, NV St. Gabriel the Archangel Church.
Wasiel, Michael '33 (CHI) Harvey, IL St. John the Baptist Church.
Wasiel, Michael J. '33 (CHI) Retired.
Wasielewski, Henry R. '64 (PHX) Retired.
Wasikowski, Ronald S. '75 (OM) Constance, NE St. Joseph Church; Crofton, NE St. Rose of Lima Church.
Wasinger, Msgr. Alfred '44 (SAL) [E] Concordia, KS Nazareth Motherhouse for the Sisters of St. Joseph, Concordia.
Wasinger, Mark Shane '94 (STP) White Bear Lake, MN St. Pius X Church.
Waska, Raymond (FBK) Emmonak, AK Sacred Heart Church.
Wasko, Anthony J. *o.s.a.* '58 (LA) [31] Los Angeles, CA Mother of Good Counsel Church.
Waslo, Peter '86 (SJP) [2] Parma, OH St. Andrew Church.
Wasnewski, Richard P. '53 (BO) [3] Norwood, MA St. Peter Church.
Wasnie, Blane *o.s.b.* '66 (SCL) [I] Collegeville, MN St. John's Abbey, of the Order of St. Benedict.
Wasnie, Blane H. *o.s.b.* '66 (STP) Hastings, MN St. Elizabeth Ann Seton Church.
Wasowski, Ronald J. *c.s.c.* '73 (SCR) [C] Wilkes-Barre, PA Kings College.
Wassel, Msgr. Anthony F. '60 (ALN) [5] Mahanoy City, PA St. Joseph Church.
Wassel, Eugene A. '52 (PH) [30] Philadelphia, PA St. Casimir Church; Retired.
Wassel, Thomas W. '43 (PH) [11] Philadelphia, PA St. Anne Church; [124] Philadelphia, PA Our Lady of Mt. Carmel Church.
Wasser, James (SAT) New Braunfels, TX Holy Family Church.
Wassie, Stephen M. '79 (Y) Jefferson, OH St. Joseph Calasanctius Church.
Wassmuth, Dennis '73 (B) [4] Boise, ID Our Lady of the Rosary Church.
Waszak, Norbert J. '53 (CHI) Argo, IL St. Blase Church.
Waszczenko, Andrzej *s.d.s.* '89 (BRK) [187] Queens, NY St. Joseph Church.
Waszczenko, Andrzej *s.d.s.* '89 (NEW) [N] Verona, NJ The Salvatorian Fathers.
Watanabe, Philip '77 (KC) [39] (Kansas City North), MO St. Therese Parish Church.
Watanabe, Msgr. Terrence A.M. '77 (HON) [12] Honolulu, HI St. Philomena Church.
Waterfall, Richard A. '49 (SB) Retired.
Waterman, Thomas '56 (KC) Hirlingen, MO Seven Dolors Church.
Waters, J. Kevin *s.j.* '64 (SPK) [C] Spokane, WA Gonzaga University.
Waters, John J. *s.j.* '64 (DOD) Deerfield, KS Christ the King Church; Garden City, KS St. Mary Church.
Waters, Joseph '56 (CHL) Lenoir, NC St. Francis of Assisi Church.
Waters, Joseph '87 (MIA) [A] Miami, FL St. John Vianney College Seminary.
Waters, Joseph '87 (SP) On Duty Outside the Diocese.
Waters, Joseph L. *s.s.j.* '49 (BAL) [M] Baltimore, MD St. Joseph Society of the Sacred Heart House of Central Administration.
Waters, Mark S. '90 (STA) Fernandina Beach, FL St. Michael's Church.
Waters, Philip J. *o.s.b.* '72 (NEW) [23] Newark, NJ St. Mary's Church; [N] Newark, NJ Newark Abbey.
Waters, Robert E. '69 (BUF) Corfu, NY St. Francis of Assisi Church.
Waters, Robert J. '60 (SC) Absent on Leave.
Waters, Samuel M. '82 (PH) Absent on Leave.
Waters, William F. *o.s.a.* '71 (BRK) [205] Queens, NY St. Nicholas of Tolentine Church.
Wathen, Ambrose *o.s.b.* '65 (NO) [P] St. Benedict, LA St. Joseph Abbey.
Wathen, Ambrose G. *o.s.b.* '65 (NO) [A] St. Benedict, LA St. Joseph's Seminary College.
Wathier, Douglas O. (DUB) [A] Dubuque, IA Seminary of St. Pius X; [C] Dubuque, IA Loras College; [L] Dubuque, IA Mt. Loretto Convent.
Watkins, Clarence N. '67 (ARL) [8] Alexandria, VA St. Rita's Church.
Watkins, James D. '89 (WDC) [1] Washington, DC St. Matthew Cathedral.
Watkins, Jean (ORG) [F] Fullerton, CA St. Jude Medical Center.
Watkins, Mark T. '91 (CIN) [75] Cincinnati, OH Sts. Peter and Paul Church.
Watkins, Paul D. *o.p.* '90 (NO) [P] New Orleans, LA Dominican Fathers & Brothers, Southern Dominican Province.
Watkins, Thomas '64 (R) Lumberton, NC St. Francis De Sales Church.
Watkins, Thomas '96 (R) Awaiting Assignment.
Watrin, Bernardo *o.s.b.* '41 (CGS) [C] Humacao, PR San Antonio Abad Abbey of the Order of St. Benedict.
Watrin, Clarence E. *c.s.b.* '59 (GAL) [Q] Sugar Land, TX Basilian Mission Center.
Watroba, Boleslaus M. '35 (ALB) [2] Watervliet, NY Immaculate Conception Church; Retired.
Watry, Jerome R. '46 (GB) Retired.
Watson, Cletus M. *t.o.r.* '66 (STA) [4] Jacksonville, FL Crucifixion Church.
Watson, David *s.j.* '92 (TOL) [C] Toledo, OH St. John's Jesuit High School.
Watson, Douglas *s.c.j.* '83 (SAT) [M] San Antonio, TX Priests of the Sacred Heart-House of Formation.
Watson, Edwin P. *o.s.b.* (KCK) Basehor, KS Holy Angels Church; [H] Atchison, KS St. Benedict's Abbey; [K] Atchison, KS The Maur Hill Prep School Endowment Association, Inc.
Watson, J. Timothy *c.ss.r.* '90 (LA) Whittier, CA St. Mary of the Assumption Church.
Watson, James P. '54 (MAN) [1] Concord, NH St. John the Evangelist Church.
Watson, James Vincent *o.p.* '63 (COL) [36] Columbus, OH St. Patrick Church.
Watson, Joseph G. '92 (PH) Malvern, PA St. Patrick Church.
Watson, Joseph T. *s.j.* '52 (NEW) [C] Jersey City, NJ St. Peter's Preparatory School.
Watson, Mark A. '96 (SHP) [7] Shreveport, LA St. Elizabeth Ann Seton Church.
Watson, Michael B. '86 (COL) [29] Columbus, OH St. Mary Church.
Watson, Stephen *o.c.d.* '84 (LA) Alhambra, CA St. Therese Church.
Watson, Timothy *c.ss.r.* '90 (LA) [R] Whittier, CA Redemptorist Fathers Mission House.
Watson, Walter *s.j.* '70 (DEN) Arvada, CO St. Joan of Arc Church; [N] Boulder, CO Abbey of St. Walburga.
Watson, William *s.j.* '85 (WDC) [M] Washington, DC The Jesuit Community at Georgetown University.
Watson, William A. '62 (PEO) [14] Peoria, IL St. Thomas Church.
Watt, Gerald *c.r.* '67 (CHI) [N] Chicago, IL Provincial Office of the Congregation of the Resurrection.
Watt, Joseph '68 (MRY) Retired.
Watters, Joseph '88 (PT) Retired.
Watters, Timothy J. '71 (CHR) [B] Charleston, SC Bon Secours-St. Francis Xavier Hospital.
Watters, William J. *s.j.* '65 (BAL) [37] Baltimore, MD St. Ignatius Church; [F] Baltimore, MD St. Ignatius Loyola Academy; [Q] Baltimore, MD Radio Mass of Baltimore, Inc.
Watterson, John E. '62 (PRO) [9] Pawtucket, RI St. Mary's Church; Cranston, RI Rhode Island State Institutions.
Wattigny, Patrick B. '94 (NO) Covington, LA St. Peter Church.
Watts, Albert W. '59 (BGP) [L] Norwalk, CT Notre Dame Convalescent Home; [P] Norwalk, CT Regional House of Sisters of St. Thomas of Villanova.
Watts, Roger J. '59 (BGP) [3] Stamford, CT St. Cecilia's Church.
Watts, Thomas H. '57 (ROC) Van Etten, NY St. Pius the Tenth Church; Waverly, NY St. James Church.
Watts, Trent L. '93 (R) Dunn, NC Sacred Heart Church.
Watts, Wayne F. '90 (CHI) [179] Chicago, IL Queen of All Saints Basilica; [A] Chicago, IL Archbishop Quigley Preparatory Seminary.
Watzke, James N. *c.s.c.* '63 (FTW) [J] South Bend, IN Congregation of Holy Cross Indiana Province Provincial House.
Waudby, Lawrence '90 (BAL) [1] Baltimore, MD Cathedral of Mary Our Queen.
Waugh, John G. '55 (PEO) Wedron, IL St. Joseph's Church; Sheridan, IL Illinois Industrial School for Boys.
Wawerski, Msgr. Edward '61 (RVC) Hempstead, NY St. Ladislaus Church.
Wawiorka, Ray W. '56 (MIL) [1] Kenosha, WI St. Anthony's Church.
Wawrzycki, Andrew '70 (ORL) Clermont, FL Blessed Sacrament Church.
Wawrzyniakowski, Edward J. '57 (MIL) Cedarburg, WI St. Francis Borgia Church.
Wawrzynski, Edward A. '60 (YAK) Retired.
Way, Edmund J. *o.p.* '43 (WDC) [11] Washington, DC St. Dominic Church & Priory Church.
Wayda, Henry A. '41 (SCR) Retired.
Wayne, David A. *s.j.* '68 (DEN) [M] Aurora, CO Regis Jesuit High School - Jesuit Community.
Waywood, Frank *o.f.m.* (BO) [Z] Boston, MA Saint Anthony Residence.
Waznak, Robert J. *s.s.* '64 (SCR) On Duty Outside the Diocese.
Waznak, Robert P. *s.s.* '64 (BAL) [M] Baltimore, MD Sulpician Provincial House.
Wdowiak, Boleslaw '65 (SAC) Retired and in Senior Ministry.
Wdzieczny, Gilbert *o.f.m.conv.* '42 (BGP) [6] Danbury, CT Sacred Heart Church; Danbury, CT Danbury Hospital.
Wea, Raymundus Bhia *s.v.d.* (LA) [R] Los Angeles, CA Casa Guadalupe.
Weakley, Robert *o.f.m.* (PEO) Metamora, IL St. Mary of Lourdes Church.
Wearden, Msgr. Francis G. (GAL) Retired.
Wearsch, Ronald J. '92 (CLV) Medina, OH St. Francis Xavier Church.
Weary, William M. '84 (HBG) Danville, PA Geisinger Medical Center.
Weaver, Cyprian *o.s.b.* '72 (SCL) [I] Collegeville, MN St. John's Abbey, of the Order of St. Benedict.
Weaver, Jeffrey M. '82 (CLV) Willoughby, OH Immaculate Conception Church.
Weaver, John G. '70 (HRT) [1] Torrington, CT St. Francis of Assisi Church.
Weaver, Patrick '63 (CAM) On Leave of Absence.
Weaver, Richard '63 (DAL) [C] Dallas, TX Bishop Lynch High School.
Webb, Raymond J. '67 (CHI) [A] Mundelein, IL University of St. Mary of the Lake-Mundelein Seminary.
Webber, Donald A. *c.p.* '73 (SAC) [H] Citrus Heights, CA Christ the King Retreat; [J] Citrus Heights, CA Christ the King Retreat Center.
Webber, Msgr. Donald S. '62 (SB) Grand Terrace, CA Christ the Redeemer Church.
Weber, Alan (SP) [S] Tampa, FL Catholic Student Center, University of South Florida.
Weber, Allen *o.f.m.* '75 (BUF) [O] St. Bonaventure, NY St. Bonaventure Friary.
Weber, Arnold *o.s.b.* '52 (STP) Wayzata, MN Holy Name Church.
Weber, Charles A. *o.s.b.* '45 (GBG) [H] Latrobe, PA Saint Vincent Archabbey.
Weber, Charles E. '53 (COV) Covington, KY Children's Psychiatric Hospital of Northern Kentucky; Florence, KY St. Luke West; [I] Covington, KY St. Charles Care Center, Inc.
Weber, Charles P. '57 (BO) Permanent Disability.
Weber, Daniel C. *s.j.* '60 (SEA) [C] Tacoma, WA Bellarmine Preparatory School.
Weber, David C. '77 (CLV) [1] Cleveland, OH Cathedral of St. John the Evangelist.
Weber, Donald C. '53 (BUF) Sheldon, NY St. Cecilia Church.
Weber, Donald E. '58 (GR) [7] Grand Rapids, MI Holy Name Church.
Weber, Donald N. '47 (MIL) Retired.
Weber, Edward J. '76 (NY) West Nyack, NY St. Francis of Assisi Church.
Weber, Eugene J. '72 (WH) [1] Fairmont, WV St. Peter's Church.
Weber, Fidelis F. *t.o.r.* '55 (PH) [D] Fairless Hills, PA Conwell-Egan Catholic High School; [Z] Fairless Hills, PA St. Anthony Friary.
Weber, Msgr. Francis J. '59 (LA) Mission Hills, CA San Fernando Rey Mission Church.
Weber, Francis N. '72 (PH) On Duty Outside the Archdiocese.
Weber, Frank '72 (GB) Kimberly, WI Holy Name of Jesus Church.
Weber, Frank W. '62 (PAT) [3] Clifton, NJ St. Brendan Church.
Weber, Gabriel *o.s.m.* (ORG) Fullerton, CA St. Philip Benizi Church.
Weber, George A. '60 (CAM) Retired.
Weber, George J. *c.m.* '54 (DAL) [6] Dallas, TX Holy Trinity Church; [M] Dallas, TX Congregation of the Mission, Southern Province.
Weber, Gerard *o.m.i.* '62 (SAT) [M] San Antonio, TX Oblate Benson Residence (Southern Prov.).
Weber, Msgr. Gerard P. (CHI) [X] Chicago, IL Foundation for Adult Catechetical Teaching Aids.
Weber, Gerard P. '43 (CHI) Retired.
Weber, Gordon A. '52 (MIL) [2] Waukesha, WI St. Mary Church.
Weber, Herbert F. '74 (TOL) Mansfield, OH St. Peter Church.
Weber, James H. '43 (E) Retired.
Weber, Jerome '67 (HT) Galliano, LA St. Joseph Church.
Weber, Jerome F. '56 (SY) [3] Utica, NY Our Lady of Lourdes Church; Special Assignment.
Weber, Msgr. John A. '45 (BR) Retired.
Weber, Msgr. John George '43 (SAL) Retired.
Weber, John R. *c.s.sp.* '61 (PIT) [3] Millvale, PA Holy Spirit Church.
Weber, John S. *o.f.m.conv.* '73 (LSC) [D] Mesilla Park,

NM Holy Cross Retreat and Friary.
Weber, John-Benedict *o.carm.* '77 (CHI) [N] Mundelein, IL Carmelite Monastery.
Weber, Joseph A. '76 (PRM) St. Louis, MO St. Louis Mission Church.
Weber, Joseph A. '76 (STL) New Melle, MO Immaculate Heart of Mary Church.
Weber, Joseph J. '66 (BRK) [57] Brooklyn, NY Holy Innocents Church.
Weber, Joseph O. '57 (SCR) Carverton, PA St. Frances Cabrini Church.
Weber, Keith '83 (SAL) [3] Salina, KS St. Mary's Church.
Weber, Mark *s.v.d.* '82 (CHI) [B] Techny, IL Divine Word Residence; [N] Techny, IL Society of the Divine Word, Provincial Headquarter-Chicago Prov.
Weber, Mark E. *s.v.d.* '83 (CHI) [N] Chicago, IL Divine Word Theologate.
Weber, Michael '88 (TUC) Tucson, AZ Christ the King Chapel.
Weber, Michael J. *o.praem.* '77 (GB) [I] De Pere, WI St. Norbert Abbey.
Weber, Norbert *m.s.c.* '57 (ALN) Nazareth, PA Holy Family Church.
Weber, Randall D. '91 (SAL) Bird City, KS St. Joseph's Church; St. Francis, KS St. Francis Church.
Weber, Richard V. *o.p.* '63 (CHI) [N] Chicago, IL Dominicans (Provincial Office).
Weber, Robert C. '81 (SY) [2] Rome, NY St. Mary of the Assumption Church; Marcy, NY Mid-State Correctional Facility; Special Assignment.
Weber, Robert P. '65 (CAM) Cedarville, NJ St. Michael's Church; Delmont, NJ Southern State Correctional Facility; Leesburg, NJ New Jersey State Medium Security Prison.
Weber, Samuel *o.s.b.* '96 (IND) Greenwood, IN Our Lady of the Greenwood Church; [B] St. Meinrad, IN St. Meinrad Seminary-College of Liberal Arts; [J] St. Meinrad, IN St. Meinrad Archabbey.
Weber, Terry '85 (SFS) Humboldt, SD St. Ann Church; Montrose, SD St. Patrick Church.
Weber, Theodore R. '55 (P) Redland, OR St. Philip Benizi Church.
Weber, Thomas H. '57 (CLV) [A] Wickliffe, OH St. Mary Seminary.
Weber, Thomas L. '74 (CLV) [6] Parma, OH Holy Family Church.
Weber., Jacques *s.j.* '49 (GAL) [23] Houston, TX St. Cyril of Alexandria Church.
Webster, Robert '86 (ORL) Special Assignment.
Webster, Robert E. '86 (ORL) Daytona Beach, FL St. Paul's Church.
Wechter, David *o.c.s.o.* '58 (WIN) [G] Houston, MN Hermits of St. Mary of Carmel, H.S.M.C.
Weckbach, Hanford E. *s.j.* '43 (LA) [C] Los Angeles, CA Loyola Marymount University.
Weckerle, Leo F. '58 (BAK) Redmond, OR St. Thomas Church.
Wedeking, Patrick C. '88 (GLP) Aragon, NM Santo Nino Church.
Wedig, James '93 (CIN) [5] Dayton, OH Ascension Church.
Wedig, Mark *o.p.* '86 (MIA) [18] Miami, FL St. Dominic Church; [B] Miami, FL Barry University.
Weeg, Edmund J. '45 (DAV) Retired.
Weeke, James L. '86 (OM) [11] Omaha, NE St. Bridget Church; [41] Omaha, NE St. Rose Church.
Weeks, James M. *m.s.* '62 (HRT) [3] Hartford, CT Immaculate Conception Church; [7] Hartford, CT St. Anne Church; [M] Hartford, CT Missionaries of LaSalette Provincial Secretary.
Weeks, William H. *s.j.* '44 (BO) [W] Weston, MA Campion Health Center, Inc.
Weerakkody, Don Oliver '65 (AUS) [F] Austin, TX Seton Medical Center.
Weerasinghe, Felix (RVC) Islip Terrace, NY St. Peter the Apostle Church.
Weezorak, Dennis R. '86 (MET) South Amboy, NJ St. Mary Church.
Wegher, William F. '91 (LAN) [4] Ann Arbor, MI St. Mary Student Parish Church.
Wegierski, Blase *o.f.m.conv.* '71 (ALT) Boswell, PA All Saints Church; Boswell, PA St. Stanislaus Church.
Weglicki, Michael '79 (LEX) Lancaster, KY St. William Church; Ottenheim, KY St. Sylvester Church.
Wegman, Richard H. '90 (MAN) Alton, NH St. Joan of Arc Church.
Wegner, Gary *o.f.m.cap.* '89 (MIL) [B] Mount Calvary, WI St. Lawrence Seminary; [P] Mount Calvary, WI St. Lawrence Friary.
Wehage, Robert C. '71 (COV) Erlanger, KY St. Henry Church.
Wehby, Albert *b.a.o.* '63 (NTN) Northlake, IL St. John the Baptist Church.
Wehinger, Thomas '61 (TOL) [11] Toledo, OH Our Lady of Lourdes Church.
Wehman, Jack W. '80 (CIN) [70] Cincinnati, OH Our Lady of the Sacred Heart Church.
Wehn, Timothy C. *s.a.c.* '79 (LAV) Ely, NV Sacred Heart Church.
Wehner, Edwin P. '69 (BIS) [4] Bismarck, ND St. Anne Church.
Wehner, Eugene C. '75 (BIS) On Duty Outside the Diocese.
Wehnert, Donald *c.s.v.* (CHI) [210] Chicago, IL St. Viator Church.
Wehning, Jose *c.s.sp.* '37 (SJN) [E] Dorado, PR Santuario del Espiritu Santo.
Wehr, Arthur J. *s.j.* '90 (PHX) [11] Phoenix, AZ St. Francis Xavier Church.
Wehri, Francis *o.s.b.* '61 (BIS) [A] Richardton, ND Assumption Abbey.
Wehrle, Jonathan '78 (LAN) Okemos, MI St. Martha Church.
Wehrlen, Msgr. John B. '59 (PAT) Flanders, NJ St. Elizabeth Ann Seton Church.
Wehrlin, Leo J. '93 (Y) Ravenna, OH Immaculate Conception Church.
Wei, Luke '60 (BRK) [38] Brooklyn, NY St. Finbar's Church.
Weibel, George L. '48 (DEN) [1] Boulder, CO Sacred Heart of Jesus Church; Retired.
Weibel, John F. '72 (E) Coudersport, PA St. Eulalia Church.
Weibl, Nicholas '64 (TOL) Sandusky, OH Holy Angels Church.
Weible, Thomas C. '59 (LA) Retired.
Weibler, William (SP) St. Pete Beach, FL St. John Church.
Weibler, William F. '55 (DAV) On Duty Outside the Diocese.
Weider, Gregory (ALB) Special Assignment.
Weider, Gregory '63 (ALB) [9] Troy, NY Our Lady of Victory Church; Troy, NY Samaritan Hospital.
Weider, William *t.o.r.* '41 (TR) Marlboro, NJ St. Gabriel Church.
Weidert, Richard J. '95 (BEL) Beckemeyer, IL St. Anthony Church.
Weidman, Michael J. '95 (CHI) Orland Park, IL St. Francis of Assisi Church.
Weidner, Halbert *c.o.* '74 (CHR) [E] Rock Hill, SC Oratory of St. Philip Neri, Congregation of the Oratory of Pontifical Rite.
Weidner, Halbert *c.o.* '74 (HON) [8] Honolulu, HI Holy Trinity Church; [J] Honolulu, HI Leadership Association of Religious Congregation (LARC).
Weidner, Larry W. '80 (PHX) [14] Phoenix, AZ St. Joan of Arc Church.
Weidner, Mark *o.c.s.o.* '54 (P) [L] Lafayette, OR The Cistercian (Trappist) Abbey of Our Lady of Guadalupe.
Weidner, William F. '64 (OM) Madison, NE St. Leonard Church.
Weier, Msgr. John A. '43 (DET) Retired.
Weigand, Dom Peter *o.s.b.* '70 (WDC) [E] Washington, DC St. Anselm's Abbey School.
Weigand, John J. '67 (CLV) [4] Lakewood, OH St. James Church.
Weigand, Joseph C. '62 (CLV) [4] Elyria, OH St. Mary Church.
Weigand, Peter *o.s.b.* '70 (WDC) [M] Washington, DC St. Anselm's Abbey.
Weigel, Edmund *c.pp.s.* '58 (KC) [J] Liberty, MO Precious Blood Center.
Weigel, Jovian C. *o.f.m.* '48 (CIN) [L] Cincinnati, OH Archbishop Leibold Home for the Aged; [M] Cincinnati, OH Pleasant Street Friary.
Weiglein, John *s.m.* '79 (WH) [I] Wheeling, WV Good Shepherd Nursing Home.
Weigman, Joseph '91 (TOL) Bowling Green, OH St. Thomas More University Parish Church; [N] Bowling Green, OH Bowling Green State University Campus Ministry.
Weiher, Charles F. *c.s.c.* '53 (FTW) [B] Notre Dame, IN University of Notre Dame Du Lac; [J] Notre Dame, IN Holy Cross Community, Corby Hall, University of Notre Dame.
Weihrer, John A. (GAL) Retired.
Weihrer, John A. '83 (TYL) Retired.
Weik, Terence P. *s.m.* (BAL) Sykesville, MD St. Joseph Church.
Weiksnar, Jud *o.f.m.* '94 (WDC) [3] Silver Spring, MD St. Camillus Church.
Weiksner, Jerome M. '55 (GBG) Retired.
Weil, Frank *o.carm.* '67 (JOL) [J] Darien, IL Carmelite Fathers Provincial Office.
Weil, Msgr. H. Gil '56 (BUF) [1] Orchard Park, NY Nativity Church.
Weil, Robert L. '88 (MET) South River, NJ St. Mary of Ostrabrama Church.
Weiland, Duane J. '62 (DM) On Special Assignment.
Weiler, Michael F. *s.j.* '88 (LA) [C] Los Angeles, CA Loyola Marymount University.
Weimer, Allen '71 (CIN) [K] Dayton, OH St. Elizabeth Medical Center, Inc.
Weimer, Henry V. '39 (SC) Retired.
Weimer, John C. '58 (BUF) [R] Williamsville, NY Newman Club Chaplains.
Weinandy, Thomas *o.f.m.cap.* '72 (WDC) [39] Washington, DC Shrine of the Sacred Heart Church.
Weinberger, Paul L. '89 (DAL) [3] Dallas, TX Blessed Sacrament Church.
Weiner, James J. '88 (NEW) Glen Rock, NJ St. Catharine Church.
Weiner, Philip '91 (STF) Elmira Heights, NY St. Nicholas Church.
Weinert, Allan *c.ss.r.* '72 (STL) [P] Liguori, MO Liguori Mission House/Redemptorists.
Weingartz, Francis A. '54 (DET) [4] Warren, MI St. Dorothy Church.
Weinholtz, Bernard *o.f.m.* '40 (SP) [O] St. Petersburg, FL St. Anthony Friary.
Weinlader, Wayne T. *m.m.* '68 (NY) [Z] Maryknoll, NY Maryknoll Fathers and Brothers.
Weinlich, Alfred J. '35 (BRK) Retired; [R] Queens Village, NY Queen of Peace Residence.
Weinzapfel, Msgr. Thomas W. '45 (DAL) [25] Dallas, TX St. Pius X Church.
Weir, Bernard E. '86 (DAV) Columbus Junction, IA St. Joseph Church; Wapello, IA St. Mary's Church.
Weirauch, William P. '35 (PIT) Retired.
Weis, Denis P. '63 (MIL) [38] Milwaukee, WI Holy Spirit Church.
Weis, Earl A. *s.j.* '54 (CHI) [C] Chicago, IL Jesuit Community at Loyola University of Chicago.
Weis, Earl A. *s.j.* '54 (DET) [K] Detroit, MI Jesuit Provincial Office-Detroit Province of the Society of Jesus.
Weis, Eugene R. '94 (ROC) Owego, NY St. Patrick Church.
Weis, Ivan '80 (BLX) White Cypress, MS St. Matthew the Apostle Church.
Weis, John H. '66 (PAT) On Duty Outside the Diocese.
Weis, Paul L. '57 (DUB) Delhi, IA St. John's Church.
Weisbeck, Paul P. '70 (SJ) [9] San Jose, CA Holy Spirit Church.
Weisbecker, Thomas '96 (OM) Ralston, NE St. Gerald Church.
Weiscopf, Daniel '90 (BRK) [218] Queens, NY Our Lady, Queen of Martyrs Church.
Weise, Thomas (MOB) On Leave from the Archdiocese.
Weisenbaugh, Robert *s.j.* '71 (CHL) [L] Charlotte, NC Diocesan Office of Campus Ministry.
Weisenbaugh, Robert D. *s.j.* '71 (CHL) [J] Charlotte, NC Jesuit Community.
Weisenbeck, Jude *s.d.s.* '60 (MIL) [P] Milwaukee, WI Salvatorian Provincial Residence.
Weisenberger, Gary '77 (SEA) Gig Harbor, WA St. Nicholas Church.
Weisenberger, Leon *m.s.c.* '59 (RCK) [H] Aurora, IL Missionaries of the Sacred Heart Community.
Weisenberger, Raymond *s.v.d.* '39 (MIL) [P] East Troy, WI Divine Word Seminary.
Weisenberger, Richard J. '79 (LFT) [1] Lafayette, IN St. Mary Cathedral.
Weisenburger, Edward J. '87 (OKL) Okarche, OK Holy Trinity Church.
Weisensel, Cyril O. '67 (MAD) Hazel Green, WI St. Francis de Sales Church.
Weiser, Charles B. '66 (TR) [4] Long Branch, NJ St. Michael Church.
Weiser, Francis (SB) Soboba Indian Reservation, CA St. Joseph Church.
Weishaar, Berard *o.f.m.* '43 (LA) [R] Santa Barbara, CA Franciscan Friary, Order of Friars Minor (Old Mission).
Weishaar, Leo (MOB) [E] Mobile, AL Providence Hospital.
Weishaar, Ralph *o.f.m.* '44 (LA) [W] Malibu, CA Serra Retreat.
Weishar, John A. '43 (PEO) Retired.
Weishar, Paul M. '48 (MIL) Retired.
Weisman, Raymond F. '76 (WIL) Pocomoke City, MD Holy Name of Jesus Church.
Weisner, David E. '55 (DET) [54] Detroit, MI Our Lady of Good Counsel Church; [67] Detroit, MI St. Raymond Church.
Weiss, Charles W. *s.j.* '52 (P) Oakridge, OR St. Michael Church.
Weiss, James F. '90 (E) On Leave of Absence.
Weiss, Jerome P. '77 (DUL) [9] Duluth, MN St. John's Church.
Weiss, John '66 (SAG) Rapson, MI St. Joseph Church.
Weiss, John C. '67 (KC) [9] Kansas City, MO Christ the King Church.
Weiss, Joseph E. *s.j.* '85 (OM) [K] Omaha, NE Jesuit Community At Creighton University.
Weiss, Nicholas *o.f.m.conv.* '58 (ALB) [A] Rensselaer, NY Conventual Franciscan Friars.
Weiss, Peter C. *s.s.j.* '79 (NO) [38] New Orleans, LA St. Joan Of Arc Church.
Weiss, Richard (ELP) [38] El Paso, TX San Judas Tadeo Church.
Weiss, Robert *c.p.* '65 (CHI) [N] Chicago, IL Passionist Provincial Office.
Weiss, Robert E. '73 (BGP) Shelton, CT St. Joseph's Church.
Weiss, Robert F. *s.j.* '59 (STL) [P] St. Louis, MO Hallahan House; [P] St. Louis, MO The Jesuits of the Missouri Province.
Weissbeck, Reinhold B. '72 (DEN) Brighton, CO St. Augustine Church.

Weissler, John A. *o.m.i.* '43 (STP) [N] St. Paul, MN Oblate Provincial Offices.
Weisswange, Peter *o.f.m.cap.* '92 (WDC) [B] Washington, DC St. Francis Friary-Capuchin College.
Weist, Edward F. '69 (CLV) [43] Cleveland, OH St. Leo the Great Church.
Weitensteiner, Joseph M. '66 (SPK) [17] Spokane, WA St. Patrick Church; [H] Manito Station, WA Spokane Boys' Ranch, Inc.
Weithman, Martin V. '80 (COL) Lancaster, OH St. Mary Church.
Weithman, Raymond *c.ss.r.* '56 (NY) [Z] Esopus, NY Redemptorist Priests and Brothers C.Ss.R. (Province of Baltimore).
Weithman, Robert '74 (TOL) [3] Fremont, OH St. Casimir Church.
Weitzel, Eugene J. *c.s.v.* '59 (SFD) Arenzville, IL St. Fidelis Church; Beardstown, IL St. Alexius Church.
Weitzel, Stephen D. '90 (HBG) Hershey, PA St. Joan of Arc Church; Hershey, PA Milton J. Hershey Medical Center; [K] Harrisburg, PA Catholic Campus Ministry.
Weitzel, Theodore '68 (JOL) Hinsdale, IL St. Isaac Jogues Church.
Wekerle, Ronald '90 (B) On Duty Outside the Diocese.
Welbers, Thomas '68 (LA) Claremont, CA Our Lady of the Assumption Church.
Welch, Bernard J. '81 (PRT) Military Chaplains.
Welch, Christopher (DET) Detroit, MI Beaumont Hospital.
Welch, Christopher '94 (ALB) Loudonville, NY St. Francis de Sales Church.
Welch, D. Michael '70 (IND) [21] (Speedway City), IN St. Christopher Church.
Welch, Gregory T. '67 (STP) [18] Minneapolis, MN St. Austin Church.
Welch, J. Paul *s.s.* '39 (BAL) [K] Baltimore, MD St. Charles Villa; [M] Baltimore, MD St. Charles Villa.
Welch, John *o.carm.* '65 (WDC) [B] Washington, DC Whitefriars Hall; [V] Washington, DC Carmelite Institute.
Welch, John E. *m.s.* '60 (NOR) Jewett City, CT St. Mary Church.
Welch, Joseph '91 (OAK) [4] Concord, CA Queen of All Saints Church.
Welch, Paul *s.s.* '39 (SEA) Retired.
Welch, Robert J. *s.j.* '60 (LA) [C] Los Angeles, CA Loyola Marymount University.
Welch, Thomas David '56 (RIC) Retired.
Welch, William '55 (GLP) Winslow, AZ Madre de Dios Church.
Welch, William F. '36 (DET) Retired.
Weldgen, Msgr. Francis G. '59 (BUF) [2] Tonawanda, NY St. Christopher Church.
Welding, Brian J. '91 (PIT) Ross Township, PA St. Sebastian Church.
Weldishofer, Bernard J. '92 (CIN) [40] Cincinnati, OH St. James the Greater Church.
Weldon, Michael *o.f.m.* '81 (SFR) [5] San Francisco, CA St. Anthony Church.
Weligala, Joseph '59 (CHI) [98] Chicago, IL St. James Church.
Weling, John B. *s.j.* '81 (LA) [C] Los Angeles, CA Loyola Marymount University; [BB] Los Angeles, CA Archdiocesan Office for Campus Ministry.
Welk, Thomas *c.pp.s.* '69 (WCH) [H] Wichita, KS Provincialate of the Sisters Adorers of the Blood of Christ.
Welkie, Paul P. '57 (ALN) Nesquehoning, PA Sacred Heart Church; Retired.
Wellar, Thomas '80 (CC) Ingleside, TX Our Lady of the Assumption Church.
Welle, Jacob *m.s.c.* '50 (ALN) [A] Center Valley, PA Missionaries of the Sacred Heart; [B] Center Valley, PA Allentown College of St. Francis de Sales.
Wellein, Msgr. William G. '52 (CHL) Retired.
Weller, Arnold *o.c.s.o.* '38 (P) [L] Lafayette, OR The Cistercian (Trappist) Abbey of Our Lady of Guadalupe.
Weller, Msgr. Arnold J. '32 (DOD) Retired.
Weller, Harold E. '45 (LFT) Retired.
Weller, Joseph W. '64 (KAL) Buchanan, MI St. Anthony Church.
Wellisch, Robert B. '69 (STP) [C] St. Paul, MN University of St. Thomas.
Wellman, Msgr. Dale L. '64 (PEO) Milan, IL St. Ambrose Church.
Wellmeier, Herbert J. '56 (SAV) Richmond Hill, GA St. Anne Church.
Wells, Jack M. '72 (P) Newport, OR Sacred Heart Parish Church.
Wells, James *o.f.m.* '82 (NY) [Z] New York, NY Franciscan Province of the Immaculate Conception.
Wells, Morris *o.carm.* '64 (VEN) Grove City, FL St. Francis of Assisi Church.
Wells, Patrick R. '93 (GAL) [29] Houston, TX St. Francis of Assisi Church.
Wells, Peter B. '91 (TLS) On Duty Outside the Diocese.
Wells, Peter V.B. '84 (PAT) Absent on Leave.
Wells, Philip '83 (SAC) Elk Grove, CA Good Shepherd Catholic Church.
Wells, Robert P. '86 (MIL) [D] Waukesha, WI Catholic Memorial High School.
Wells, Msgr. Thomas M. '71 (WDC) [4] Bethesda, MD Our Lady of Lourdes Church.
Wells, Walter '31 (BUR) [F] Burlington, VT St. Joseph's Home for Aged.
Welna, Floyd '50 (SAG) Retired.
Welp, Msgr. Harry J. '45 (COV) Retired.
Welsch, Gerard R. '66 (STL) Manchester, MO St. Joseph Church.
Welsch, John '46 (Y) Retired.
Welsh, Msgr. Aloysius '40 (NEW) [N] Rutherford, NJ St. John Vianney Residence for Priests.
Welsh, Msgr. Aloysius J. '40 (NEW) Retired.
Welsh, Bartholomew *o.f.m.* '45 (MRY) Jolon, CA San Antonio Mission Church.
Welsh, Canice T. *o.s.b.* '47 (GBG) [H] Latrobe, PA Saint Vincent Archabbey.
Welsh, Msgr. David B. '37 (NY) [7] Yonkers, NY St. Denis Church; Retired.
Welsh, John *s.j.* '56 (LAF) Grand Coteau, LA St. Charles Borromeo Church.
Welsh, Peter J. *m.div., ph.d.* (ALN) [A] Northampton, PA Mary Immaculate Seminary.
Welsh, Peter J. '80 (PH) [A] Wynnewood, PA Theological Seminary of St. Charles Borromeo, Overbrook.
Welsh, Richard C. '60 (DET) [4] Roseville, MI Holy Innocents Church.
Welsh, Msgr. Robert E. '44 (BRK) [50] Brooklyn, NY Good Shepherd Church; Retired.
Welsh, Robert J. *s.j.* '67 (CLV) [E] Cleveland, OH St. Ignatius High School.
Welsh, Timothy L. *o.c.s.o.* '51 (DUB) [K] Peosta, IA New Melleray Abbey, Order of Cistercians of the Strict Observance.
Welsh, Vincent F. '89 (PH) [35] Philadelphia, PA St. Christopher Church.
Welsh, William P. '60 (CHI) Skokie, IL St. Lambert Church.
Welshons, Glendon R. *s.j.* '62 (RC) Norris, SD Sacred Heart Church; Parmelee, SD St. Agnes Church; St. Francis, SD Rosebud Reservation Church.
Welsmiller, Francis F. '44 (SAG) Retired.
Welstead, Flavian *o.f.m.cap.* '67 (SFR) [N] Burlingame, CA Capuchin Provincial House.
Welter, Charles J. *c.m.* '45 (CHI) [C] Chicago, IL Vincentian Community at DePaul University.
Weltin, Richard W. '83 (SFD) Oblong, IL Our Lady of Lourdes Church; Robinson, IL St. Elizabeth Church.
Welton, Arthur T. '69 (NY) [193] Bronx, NY Visitation Church
Welton, Paul D. '60 (STU) Shadyside, OH St. Mary Church
Weltzer, Arthur '32 (SAV) [1] Columbus, GA Holy Family Church; Retired.
Welzbacher, George A. '51 (STP) New Market, MN St. Nicholas Church.
Wempe, Michael '66 (LA) [41] Los Angeles, CA St. Ambrose Church; Los Angeles, CA Cedar Sinai Medical Center.
Wempe, Richard C. '52 (KCK) Retired.
Wendel, Fred '78 (CHY) Rock Springs, WY Our Lady of Sorrows Church; Rock Springs, WY SS. Cyril and Methodius Church; Rock Springs, WY Our Lady of Sorrows/Sts. Cyril & Methodius Church; [F] Rock Springs, WY Rock Springs Catholic School Foundation.
Wendel, Paul G. *c.s.c.* '55 (FTW) [L] Notre Dame, IN Holy Cross Mission House; [M] Notre Dame, IN Our Lady of Fatima Retreat Center.
Wendelken, Robert M. '61 (CLV) Solon, OH St. Rita Church.
Wenderoth, Joseph '84 (BAL) Special Assignment.
Wenderoth, Joseph R. '62 (BAL) Baltimore, MD Dismas House; [Q] Baltimore, MD Dismas House West; [Q] Baltimore, MD Dismas House East.
Wendland, Msgr. Thomas A. '52 (GAL) [72] Houston, TX St. Rose of Lima Church.
Wendling, Michael J. '85 (MAN) Absent on Leave.
Wendrychowicz, John B. '73 (PH) [109] Philadelphia, PA Mother of Divine Grace Church; [D] Philadelphia, PA Cardinal Dougherty High School.
Wendt, Anchim Gregory (PSC) [A] Miami, FL Holy Cross Community and Academy.
Wendt, Patrick R. '79 (MIL) West Bend, WI Immaculate Conception Church.
Wendzikowski, Msgr. Mecislaus S. '59 (BUF) Holland, NY St. Joseph Church.
Wenig, Laurin J. '73 (MIL) Neosho, WI St. Matthew's Church; Rubicon, WI St. John's Church; Woodland, WI St. Mary Church.
Wenke, Leonard C. '79 (CIN) On Duty Outside the Archdiocese.
Wenning, Grigion '54 (GB) [I] Appleton, WI St. Fidelis Friary.
Wenning, Paul A. '45 (SPK) Retired.
Wenninger, Magnus *o.s.b.* '45 (SCL) [I] Collegeville, MN St. John's Abbey, of the Order of St. Benedict.
Wenninger, William '54 (SUP) Retired.
Wenrick, Patrick *s.v.d.* '82 (TR) [M] Bordentown, NJ Society of the Divine Word.
Wensing, Michael G. '76 (SFS) [7] Sioux Falls, SD St. Michael Church.
Wenski, Thomas '76 (MIA) [10] Miami, FL Notre Dame d'Haiti Church.
Wenting, James J. '46 (JC) [A] Hannibal, MO St. Thomas Aquinas Seminary.
Wentink, William R. '70 (RCK) [10] Rockford, IL St. Rita Church; [D] Rockford, IL Saint Anthony Medical Center.
Wentz, Aelred W. '85 (ROC) [I] Piffard, NY Abbey of the Genesee.
Wenz, Robert F. '82 (CLV) Brecksville, OH St. Basil the Great Church.
Wenzel, Edward J. '51 (MAR) Retired.
Wenzel, Timothy '66 (SCL) Sauk Centre, MN St. Paul's Church.
Wenzinger, George E. '71 (TOL) Defiance, OH St. John the Evangelist Church.
Wenzinger, Mark *o.s.b.* '95 (GBG) Jeannette, PA Sacred Heart Church.
Wenzinger, Robert D. '82 (FRS) [5] Bakersfield, CA St. Joseph Church.
Werling, Norman G. *o.carm.* '41 (NEW) Paramus, NJ Carmelite Chapel of St. Therese Church.
Werner, Msgr. Cyril J. '45 (OM) Retired.
Werner, George J. *s.m.m.* '57 (RVC) [N] Bay Shore, NY Montfort Missionaries.
Werner, John P. '51 (COV) Retired; [H] Edgewood, KY St. Elizabeth Medical Center, South.
Werner, Jon K. '82 (SY) [1] Syracuse, NY The Cathedral of the Immaculate Conception.
Werner, Justin N. '58 (GB) Greenville, WI St. Mary Church.
Werner, Leo E. '51 (WH) Retired.
Werner, Msgr. Martin E. '35 (GF) Retired.
Wernert, Kurt *c.p.* '95 (CHI) [N] Chicago, IL Passionist Community-CTU.
Werr, Donald *o.f.m.* '46 (FWT) [G] Crowley, TX St. Francis Village, Inc.; [H] Crowley, TX St. Maximilian Kolbe Friary.
Werring, Edward J. '71 (RVC) Patchogue, NY Our Lady of Mt. Carmel Church; [Q] Rockville Centre, NY The Campus Parish of Long Island.
Wersing, Richard F. *c.s.sp.* '37 (PIT) [B] Pittsburgh, PA Duquesne University of the Holy Ghost.
Wert, William *o.carm.* '77 (LA) [F] Encino, CA Crespi Carmelite High School.
Werth, Alvin J. '59 (SAL) [1] Salina, KS Cathedral of the Sacred Heart.
Werth, Charles M. '53 (BUF) Retired.
Werth, Loren J. '56 (SAL) Clay Center, KS SS. Peter and Paul Church.
Werth, Robert '79 (ROC) [49] Rochester, NY Roman Catholic Community of the 19th Ward Church.
Werthman, Robert R. '60 (PIT) Brentwood, PA St. Sylvester Church.
Wertin, George P. '63 (STP) [27] Minneapolis, MN St. Joan of Arc Church.
Wertman, Raymond '72 (OG) Special Assignment.
Wertz, Gerald *s.d.b.* (SFR) [N] San Francisco, CA Salesian Provincial Residence.
Wesely, Eugene L. '57 (CR) Lake Eunice Township, MN St. Mary of the Lakes Church.
Wesely, Mark '93 (SAL) Manhattan, KS Seven Dolors Church.
Weseman, Alan R. '86 (NO) Chalmette, LA St. Mark Church.
Wesley, Andrew '80 (DET) [76] Detroit, MI Transfiguration Church.
Weslin, Norman U. *o.s.* '86 (PCE) On Duty Outside the Diocese.
Wesloh, Ferdinand J. '64 (STL) [3] Florissant, MO St. Angela Merici Church.
Wesnofske, Matthias *o.f.m.cap.* '67 (RVC) [N] Smithtown, NY St. Ann's Friary.
Wesolowski, Anthony P. *o.s.b.* '72 (SAV) [B] Savannah, GA Benedictine Military School; [F] Savannah, GA The Benedictine Priory.
Wesolowski, Edmund C. '48 (PH) [68] Philadelphia, PA Immaculate Conception Church; Absent on Sick Leave.
Wessel, John F. '57 (CLV) Avon, OH St. Mary of the Immaculate Conception Church.
Wessel, Stephen *o.m.i.* '40 (BEL) [G] Belleville, IL Missionary Oblates of Mary Immaculate - St. Henry's Oblate Residence.
Wessels, Cletus J. *o.p.* '57 (STP) [15] Minneapolis, MN St. Albert the Great Church.
Wesselsky, Msgr. Emil J. '56 (SAT) [40] San Antonio, TX St. Henry Church.
Wessling, Floyd A. '64 (OM) Columbus, NE St. Isidore Church.
Wessling, John E. '58 (CIN) [72] Cincinnati, OH Our Lady of Visitation Church; [F] Cincinnati, OH Ursuline Academy of Cincinnati.
West, David '65 (DET) [A] Orchard Lake, MI SS. Cyril and Methodius Seminary.
West, Gerald '59 (BAL) Retired; [N] Baltimore, MD Franciscan Sisters of Baltimore-General Motherhouse and Novitiate.

West, H. Gregory '93 (CHR) Bluffton, SC St. Andrew's Church.
West, James P. '86 (LR) Hot Springs National Park, AR St. John the Baptist Church.
West, John H. '80 (DET) Special Assignment.
West, Joseph *o.f.m.conv.* '92 (STP) Bloomington, MN St. Bonaventure Church.
West, Mauricio W. '79 (CHL) Special Assignment.
West, Norbert '56 (SUP) Retired.
West, Norbert R. '57 (Y) [I] Canton, OH House of Loreto.
West, Patrick J. '81 (BRK) [117] Brooklyn, NY St. Peter Claver Church.
West, Peter '91 (NEW) Bloomfield, NJ Sacred Heart Church.
West, Stephen C. '79 (GBG) [3] Latrobe, PA St. John the Evangelist Church; [I] Greensburg, PA Sisters of Charity.
West, Thomas *o.f.m.* '86 (OAK) [A] Berkeley, CA Franciscan School of Theology.
West, Tom *o.f.m.* '86 (OAK) [N] Oakland, CA Franciscan Friars.
West, Msgr. Willis W. '63 (NOR) Willimantic, CT St. Joseph Church.
Westbrook, James Severyn '62 (SPK) Cheney, WA St. Rose of Lima Church; [N] Cheney, WA Catholic Newman Center at Eastern Washington University.
Wester, Charles H. '59 (MIL) Mayville, WI St. Mary's Church.
Wester, Donald R. '78 (STL) Bellefontaine Neighbors, MO Our Lady of Good Counsel Church.
Wester, John C. '76 (SFR) [49] San Francisco, CA St. Stephen Church.
Wester, Kevin J. '90 (MIL) [1] Menomonee Falls, WI St. Anthony's Church.
Westerhoff, Ralph A. '62 (CIN) [52] Cincinnati, OH St. Lawrence Church.
Westfall, Joseph B. (LFT) On Duty Outside the Diocese.
Westfield, Carlton J. '71 (BUF) Falconer, NY Our Lady of Loreto Church; Frewsburg, NY Our Lady of Victory Church.
Westhoff, Donald F. '46 (STP) Retired.
Westhoff, Francis *m.s.c.* '35 (RCK) [H] Aurora, IL Missionaries of the Sacred Heart Community.
Westhoff, Frank D. '61 (SFD) On Duty Outside the Diocese.
Westhoven, Thomas *s.c.j.* '66 (RC) Eagle Butte, SD All Saints Church; Eagle Butte, SD Cheyenne River Reservation Church; [B] Eagle Butte, SD Sacred Heart Community House.
Westhues, Msgr. John H. '48 (SPC) Mount Vernon, MO St. Susanne Church.
Weston, Thomas C. *s.j.* '78 (OAK) [N] Oakland, CA Murray Residence Community.
Westray, Kenneth M. '81 (SFR) [47] San Francisco, CA Sacred Heart Church.
Wethington, Paul V. '47 (LEX) Retired.
Wetmore, John J. '73 (STL) [62] St. Louis, MO St. Stephen, Protomartyr Church.
Wetter, Msgr. Richard L. '57 (BUF) Clarence, NY Our Lady of Peace Church.
Wetterer, Msgr. Edward V. '64 (BRK) [201] Queens, NY St. Michael Church.
Wetterholm, Lawrence '56 (BO) Ipswich, MA St. Joseph Church; Ipswich, MA St. Stanislaus Church.
Wetzel, Leo *o.m.i.* '52 (BO) [16] Lowell, MA Sacred Heart Church.
Wetzel, William I. '55 (STL) Retired.
Wetzler, Daniel E. '63 (SPK) [16] Spokane, WA St. Paschal Church.
Wevita, Bede '91 (LAV) [4] Las Vegas, NV Our Lady of Las Vegas Church.
Wewer, Andrew '43 (LR) [A] Subiaco, AR Subiaco Monastery.
Wewers, Damian '37 (LR) [A] Subiaco, AR Subiaco Monastery.
Wewers, William '67 (LR) [A] Subiaco, AR Subiaco Monastery.
Wey, Richard '50 (SCL) Retired.
Weyand, John '62 (ALB) Greenfield Center, NY St. Joseph Church.
Weydert, Donald D. '43 (DUB) Retired.
Weyer, John T. (GAL) Sugar Land, TX St. Laurence Church.
Weyhing, John '51 (L) Retired.
Weyls, Richard '93 (COL) Newark, OH St. Francis de Sales Church.
Weymes, Gerald '74 (ARL) Stafford, VA St. William of York Church.
Weyrens, Ronald '82 (SCL) Waite Park, MN St. Joseph's Church.
Weyrmeyer, Richard L. '91 (PBL) Rocky Ford, CO St. Peter Church.
Whalen, Charles W. '44 (DUB) Retired.
Whalen, Msgr. Earl L. '40 (CIN) Princeton, OH St. Maximilian Kolbe Church; Retired.
Whalen, Edmund J. '84 (NY) [A] Yonkers, NY St. Joseph's Seminary; [DD] New York, NY North American College of Rome, Alumni Assoc. of.
Whalen, Frank J. '68 (CIN) Military Chaplains.
Whalen, James R. '47 (GI) Retired.
Whalen, James W. '58 (STP) Coates, MN St. Agatha Church; Retired.
Whalen, John J. '69 (DAV) North English, IA St. Joseph's Church; Parnell, IA St. Joseph's Church.
Whalen, John J. '94 (OM) [8] Sarpy Co., NE St. Bernadette Church.
Whalen, John P. '53 (ALB) Retired.
Whalen, John S. '39 (ROC) [60] Rochester, NY St. Thomas More Church; Retired.
Whalen, Joseph E. '89 (GI) On Duty Outside the Diocese.
Whalen, Joseph E. '89 (LEX) [D] Lexington, KY St. Joseph Hospital.
Whalen, Joseph F. *m.s.* '89 (NOR) Danielson, CT St. James Church.
Whalen, Joseph J. '71 (ALN) West Reading, PA Sacred Heart Church.
Whalen, Msgr. Joseph M. '66 (ALN) [J] Bethlehem, PA Holy Family Villa.
Whalen, Msgr. Leslie G. '38 (ROC) Retired; [E] Rochester, NY St. Ann's Home for the Aged.
Whalen, Norman M. '54 (TUC) Retired.
Whalen, Paul A. '82 (GBG) Farmington, PA St. Joan of Arc Church.
Whalen, Robert B. '51 (BUR) Castleton, VT St. John the Baptist Church; [J] Burlington, VT University of Vermont-The Catholic Center at UVM.
Whalen, Robert J. *s.j.* '62 (ALN) [A] Wernersville, PA Novitiate of St. Isaac Jogues.
Whalen, Msgr. Thomas J. '67 (BGP) Shelton, CT St. Margaret Mary Church.
Whalen, Timothy F. '78 (PIT) California, PA St. Thomas Aquinas Church; Roscoe, PA St. Joseph Church; [Q] Slippery Rock, PA Office for Campus Ministry.
Whalen, William C. '92 (HRT) On Duty Outside the Archdiocese.
Whalen, William H. '59 (MIL) [12] Milwaukee, WI St. Bernadette Church.
Wharton, Joseph E. '92 (WIL) Greenville, DE St. Joseph on the Brandywine Church.
Wharton, Paul J. '82 (WH) Hurricane, WV Catholic Church of the Ascension.
Wharton, Robert H. '54 (WDC) Retired; [L] Washington, DC Cardinal O'Boyle Residence for Priests.
Whatley, Christopher J. '70 (BAL) Glyndon, MD Sacred Heart Church; [M] Baltimore, MD Jesuit Fathers and Brothers Maryland Provincial Curia.
Whatley, Francis *o.ss.t.* '88 (NO) [16] New Orleans, LA Our Lady Of Good Counsel Church; [N] New Orleans, LA Mary-Joseph Residence for the Elderly.
Whealen, Martin *s.j.* '62 (DEN) [4] Englewood, CO St. Thomas More Church.
Whealen, Martin J. *s.j.* '62 (STL) [P] St. Louis, MO De Smet Jesuit High School Community.
Wheatley, Carroll '75 (OWN) Military Chaplains.
Wheatley, Charles J. '68 (MIL) Special Assignment.
Wheatley, Dennis *o.f.m.* '84 (BO) [W] Andover, MA St. Francis Friary.
Wheatley, Herbert *o.f.m.* '67 (P) [J] Portland, OR Providence Portland Medical Center.
Wheaton, William '92 (SLC) Price, UT Notre Dame de Lourdes Church; [C] Price, UT Notre Dame Regional School; [H] Price, UT College of Eastern Utah, Newman Club.
Whedbee, Dominic *o.c.s.o.* '77 (WOR) [A] Spencer, MA St. Joseph's Abbey School of Theology and Institute of Monastic Studies; [N] Spencer, MA St. Joseph's Abbey.
Whedbee, George *c.m.f.* '69 (LA) [K] Los Angeles, CA Queen of Angels-Hollywood Presbyterian Medical Center; [R] Los Angeles, CA Claretian Retreat Center Community.
Wheelahan, Michael '80 (OKL) Anadarko, OK St. Patrick's Church.
Wheeland, Thomas H. '66 (ROC) [21] Rochester, NY Holy Cross Church.
Wheeler, Ambrose J. *c.s.c.* '47 (PHX) [F] Phoenix, AZ Holy Cross Congregation of Casa Santa Cruz.
Wheeler, Arthur F. *c.s.c.* '84 (P) [B] Portland, OR University of Portland; [L] Portland, OR Holy Cross Father & Brother, C.S.C. - University of Portland.
Wheeler, Charles '79 (JOL) [3] Kankakee, IL St. Rose of Lima Church.
Wheeler, Clarence '54 (JC) Retired.
Wheeler, Daniel '75 (LAN) Tecumseh, MI St. Elizabeth Church.
Wheeler, Msgr. David A. '52 (DUB) [L] Dubuque, IA St. Joseph's Convent, Mount Carmel.
Wheeler, James D. *s.j.* '54 (KC) [B] Kansas City, MO Rockhurst College; [J] Kansas City, MO Rockhurst College - Jesuit Community.
Wheeler, James E. *o.f.m.* '88 (SFD) Belleview, IL St. Agnes Church; Hardin, IL St. Norbert Church; Kampsville, IL St. Anselm Church; Michael, IL St. Michael Church.
Wheeler, James J. *s.j.* '68 (NY) [Z] New York, NY Murray-Weigel Hall.
Wheeler, James J. *s.j.* '68 (RVC) [P] Melville, NY St. Joseph's Prayer Center.
Wheeler, John '47 (SD) Coronado, CA Sacred Heart Church; Retired.
Wheeler, Thomas F.X. *s.j.* '62 (PH) [AA] Merion Station, PA Religious Sisters of Mercy.
Wheeler, Wayne B., Jr. '79 (GR) Parnell, MI St. Patrick's Church.
Wheelock, Joseph '96 (OG) [5] Plattsburgh, NY St. Peter Church.
Wheelock, Robert *o.f.m.cap.* '64 (MIL) [25] Milwaukee, WI St. Francis of Assisi Church.
Whelan, Charles M. *s.j.* '58 (NY) [Z] New York, NY "America;" Residence and publication office of the America Press; [DD] New York, NY America Press, Inc., The.
Whelan, Dennis '65 (RVC) Franklin Square, NY St. Catherine of Sienna Church.
Whelan, Fintan *o.f.m.cap.* '60 (BAK) Bend, OR St. Francis of Assisi Church.
Whelan, Gerald J. *c.s.c.* '55 (FTW) [J] South Bend, IN Congregation of Holy Cross Indiana Province Provincial House.
Whelan, Harold *ss.cc.* '49 (FR) [K] Fairhaven, MA Sacred Hearts Provincial House.
Whelan, James J. '73 (PH) Manoa, PA Sacred Heart Church.
Whelan, James P. '93 (NEW) Midland Park, NJ Nativity Church.
Whelan, John F. '58 (RVC) Malverne, NY Our Lady of Lourdes Church.
Whelan, Michael (BRK) [169] Queens, NY St. Francis de Sales Church.
Whelan, Robert J. '83 (BRK) [14] Brooklyn, NY St. Augustine Church; [19] Brooklyn, NY St. Bernard's Church.
Whelan, Steven *s.d.b.* (SFR) [N] San Francisco, CA Salesian Provincial Residence.
Whelan, Thomas '45 (KC) Retired.
Whelan, Thomas J. (BO) Awaiting Assignment.
Whelan, Thomas J. *o.s.a.* '62 (P) [C] Medford, OR St. Mary's School; [L] Gold Hill, OR Augustinian Community; [N] Gold Hill, OR St. Rita's Retreat Center.
Whelan, William S. '57 (OM) Schuyler, NE St. Augustine Church.
Whelton, Daniel P. '70 (SR) Occidental, CA St. Philip Church.
Whetstone, Richard J. *j.c.o.l.* '83 (PBR) Uniontown, PA St. John the Baptist Church.
Whipkey, Robert G., Jr. '83 (DEN) Iliff, CO St. Catherine of Siena Church; Peetz, CO Sacred Heart Church; Sterling, CO St. Anthony Church; [P] Sterling, CO Northeastern Junior College (Sterling).
Whipple, Donald W. *c.s.c.* '57 (ORL) Retired; [F] Cocoa Beach, FL Holy Cross Fathers, Eastern Priests Province.
Whistle, J. Brad '81 (OWN) Hardinsburg, KY St. Romuald Church; Irvington, KY Holy Guardian Angels Church.
White, A. Paul '59 (BO) [25] Boston, MA Gate of Heaven Church.
White, Alan '81 (NSH) Military Chaplains.
White, Anthony J. '55 (NO) [49] New Orleans, LA St. Patrick Church.
White, Bernard C. '52 (CHI) Elmwood Park, IL St. Celestine Church; Retired.
White, Bernard L. '77 (ALT) West Salisbury, PA St. Michael's Church.
White, Cajetan *o.s.b.* '65 (IND) [A] St. Meinrad, IN St. Meinrad Seminary; [B] St. Meinrad, IN St. Meinrad Seminary-College of Liberal Arts; [J] St. Meinrad, IN St. Meinrad Archabbey.
White, Cavana '92 (SD) [5] San Diego, CA Good Shepherd Church.
White, Charles G. '55 (OKL) Retired.
White, Charles H. '65 (BRK) [248] Queens, NY St. Virgilius Church.
White, Charles S. *c.s.p.* '48 (NY) [104] New York, NY St. Paul the Apostle Church; [Z] Scarsdale, NY Paulist Fathers Generalate.
White, Clark S. '74 (OG) Brasher Falls, NY St. Patrick Church; North Lawrence, NY St. Lawrence Church.
White, Cosmas *o.s.b.* '61 (P) [2] Portland, OR St. Agatha Church.
White, Cosmos *o.s.b.* '61 (P) [L] St. Benedict, OR Mt. Angel Abbey.
White, David '52 (SEA) [7] Seattle, WA St. Catherine Church.
White, David F. *s.j.* '67 (NY) [F] New York, NY Xavier High School.
White, David P. (BO) [8] Quincy, MA Sacred Heart Church.
White, Denis E. '67 (JOL) Hopkins Park, IL Sacred Heart Church; Momence, IL St. Patrick Church.
White, Msgr. Francis A. '49 (OG) Elizabethtown, NY St. Elizabeth Church.
White, Francis P. *c.s.v.* '44 (LAV) [1] Las Vegas, NV Guardian Angel Cathedral.
White, Gale '56 (DAL) Retired.
White, George M. *o.m.i.* '45 (HRT) [2] Waterbury, CT Immaculate Conception Church.
White, George M. *o.m.i.* '45 (NY) [BB] Newburgh, NY Our Lady of Hope Center.
White, Gervase *o.f.m.* '54 (BUF) [O] St. Bonaventure,

NY St. Bonaventure Friary.
White, Gregory A. '96 (PAT) Sparta, NJ Blessed Kateri Tekakwitha Church.
White, Msgr. James (NY) [D] New York, NY Department of Education.
White, James D. '69 (TLS) [9] Tulsa, OK The Madalene Church; Special Assignment.
White, Msgr. James E. '83 (NY) [3] Newburgh, NY St. Mary Church; [Z] New York, NY St. John Neumann Residence.
White, James F. '55 (FTW) [B] Notre Dame, IN University of Notre Dame Du Lac.
White, James R. '80 (NEW) Mahwah, NJ Immaculate Conception Church; [C] Oradell, NJ Bergen Catholic.
White, James W. *c.ss.r.* '82 (WCH) [G] Wichita, KS Redemptorist Community; [I] Wichita, KS Spiritual Life Center.
White, Joanna (NY) [S] New York, NY Saint Vincent's Medical Center of Richmond.
White, John J. (BO) Retired.
White, John J. '55 (NOR) Rockville, CT St. Bernard Church.
White, John L. *s.m.* '45 (WDC) [M] Washington, DC Marist Provincial House.
White, John V. *s.j.* '65 (CLV) University Heights, OH Gesu Church.
White, John W. '83 (RVC) [H] Hicksville, NY Catholic Charities Central Administration.
White, Joseph L. *s.s.* '33 (BAL) [K] Baltimore, MD St. Charles Villa; [M] Baltimore, MD St. Charles Villa.
White, Joseph M. '92 (BO) Hull, MA St. Mary of the Assumption Church.
White, Kenneth R. '68 (PIT) Bethel Park, PA St. Thomas More Church.
White, Kris '41 (SB) Retired.
White, Lawrence E. '70 (CC) [14] Corpus Christi, TX SS. Cyril and Methodius Church.
White, Leland J. '65 (CHR) On Duty Outside the Diocese.
White, Msgr. Leo J. '56 (BRK) Released from Diocesan Assignment.
White, Leroy E. '56 (KAL) Retired.
White, Leroy E. '56 (LAN) Davison, MI St. John Church.
White, LLoyd W. '58 (SC) Retired.
White, Marcellus R. *c.p.* '34 (BO) [W] Brighton, MA St. Gabriel's Residence.
White, Michael J. '48 (BIR) [17] Birmingham, AL Our Lady of the Valley Church.
White, Michael J. '84 (BAL) Timonium, MD Church of the Nativity.
White, Michael T. *c.s.sp.* '83 (SD) [31] San Diego, CA St. Mary Magdalene Church; [C] San Diego, CA University of San Diego High School.
White, Paul *s.s.c.* '58 (LA) [66] Los Angeles, CA St. Gregory Nazianzen Church.
White, Paul C. '89 (RCK) St. Charles, IL St. Patrick Church.
White, Paul R. *c.pp.s.* '53 (LFT) Francesville, IN St. Francis Solano Church; Medaryville, IN St. Henry Church; [A] Rensselaer, IN Saint Joseph's College.
White, Peter H. '62 (WOR) Rochdale, MA St. Aloysius-St. Jude Church.
White, Ralph *o.f.m.conv.* '83 (SY) Bridgeport, NY St. Francis of Assisi Church.
White, Raymond F. *c.m.* '45 (CHI) [C] Chicago, IL Vincentian Community at DePaul University.
White, Robert E. '70 (SD) Leave of Absence.
White, Robert H. *o.f.m.* '51 (BUF) [O] St. Bonaventure, NY St. Bonaventure Friary.
White, Robert H. '60 (DEN) Absent on Leave.
White, Robert K. '61 (SFR) Tomales, CA Church of the Assumption.
White, Robert L. '74 (STP) Victoria, MN St. Victoria Church.
White, Robert S. *c.s.s.* '73 (BO) [W] Waltham, MA Stigmatine Fathers & Brothers Provincial House.
White, Stephen *m.s.c.* '46 (SAT) [M] San Antonio, TX Missionaries of the Sacred Heart.
White, Stephen C. '86 (PH) Absent on Sick Leave.
White, Thomas '64 (BLX) [3] Gulfport, MS St. John the Evangelist Church.
White, Thomas *l.c.* '78 (LA) [R] Pasadena, CA Legionaries of Christ; [BB] Los Angeles, CA Archdiocesan Office for Campus Ministry; [BB] Los Angeles, CA Archdiocesan Office for Campus Ministry.
White, Thomas J. '59 (JOL) Wheaton, IL St. Daniel the Prophet Church.
White, William (NY) On Duty Outside the Archdiocese.
White, Msgr. William '58 (PMB) [A] Boynton Beach, FL St. Vincent de Paul Regional Seminary.
White, William A. '90 (NY) [61] New York, NY St. Joseph Church.
White, William J. '52 (CHI) [2] Oak Lawn, IL St. Gerald Church.
White, William M. '58 (JOL) Braidwood, IL Immaculate Conception Church.
Whited, Msgr. Walter M. '66 (STL) Cottleville, MO St. Joseph Church.
Whiteing, Richard J. '80 (OM) Fullerton, NE St. Peter Church.
Whiteside, Daniel R. '92 (CHI) [109] Chicago, IL St. Josaphat Church.
Whitestone, David A. '89 (ARL) [6] Alexandria, VA St. Louis Church.
Whitley, Edward D. *c.s.p.* '51 (NY) [Z] Scarsdale, NY Paulist Fathers Generalate.
Whitley, John R. *c.s.b.* '54 (GAL) [Q] Sugar Land, TX Basilian Mission Center.
Whitley, Rufus J. *o.m.i.* '76 (SAT) [B] San Antonio, TX Joseph Gerard House of Studies; [C] San Antonio, TX Oblate School of Theology.
Whitlock Joseph E. '55 (PRT) Bridgton, ME St. Joseph Church.
Whitlow, Ronald F. '61 (NO) [28] New Orleans, LA St. Cecilia Church.
Whitman, Dan G. '83 (KNX) Clinton, TN St. Therese Church; Helenwood, TN St. Jude Parish Church; [K] Knoxville, TN Diocesan Council of Catholic Women.
Whitman, Glenn R. '75 (E) Girard, PA St. John the Evangelist Church.
Whitman, Mark G. '95 (STL) Des Peres, MO St. Clement Church.
Whitman, Thomas J. '87 (E) [21] Erie, PA St. Jude the Apostle Church.
Whitmore, James R. *m.m.* '59 (SJ) [M] Los Altos, CA Maryknoll.
Whitmore, Msgr. Paul E. '54 (OG) Port Leyden, NY St. Martin Church.
Whitney, A. Peter '84 (TYL) Fairfield, TX St. Bernard of Clarivaux Church; Fairfield, TX Boyd Unit, Texas Department of Criminal Justice.
Whitney, John D. *s.j.* '94 (SEA) [A] Seattle, WA Seattle University.
Whitney, Patrick J. '68 (RVC) Lake Ronkonkoma, NY St. Elizabeth Ann Seton Church.
Whitney, Msgr. Paul J. '58 (BUF) Medina, NY St. Mary Church.
Whitney, Philip '47 (HT) Retired.
Whitney, Richard P. '87 (RVC) Seaford, NY St. James Church.
Whitson, Robley E. '58 (NY) On Duty Outside the Archdiocese.
Whitt, D. Reginald *o.p.* '76 (FTW) [B] Notre Dame, IN University of Notre Dame Du Lac.
Whittaker, Kenneth '77 (MIA) Deerfield Beach, FL St. Ambrose Church.
Whitten, Carlton E. *s.j.* '61 (SAC) [C] Sacramento, CA Jesuit High School; [H] Carmichael, CA Jesuit High School Community of Sacramento.
Whittier, James E. (BO) Retired.
Whittier, William O. '61 (STP) Special Assignment.
Whittington, Kenneth L. '88 (CHL) Morganton, NC St. Charles Borromeo Church.
Whyte, Edmond F. '64 (MIA) [10] Fort Lauderdale, FL St. Mark Church.
Wiant, George '61 (ROC) Victor, NY St. Patrick Church.
Wiatrowski, Ralph E. '74 (CLV) [5] Lakewood, OH St. Luke Church.
Wible, Charles M. '96 (BAL) Hydes, MD St. John the Evangelist Church.
Wichlan, David L. '57 (STL) Vinita Park, MO St. Rita Church
Wichmann, Edward W. '52 (BWN) [E] Brownsville, TX El Rancho Grande Apartments.
Wichmann, Edward W. '52 (PBL) Retired.
Wichmanowski, Walter F. '52 (PIT) Retired; [N] Pittsburgh, PA St. John Vianney Manor.
Wicht, Robert *s.d.s.* '67 (TUC) Vail, AZ Shrine of St. Rita in the Desert Church.
Wicker, Paul F. '63 (COS) [4] Colorado Springs, CO Holy Apostles Church.
Wickers, Amideus M. *o.s.m.* '49 (CHI) [N] Chicago, IL Servite Friars - Eastern Province.
Wickey, Harold '55 (KCK) [14] Kansas City, KS St. Patrick's Church.
Wickham, William E. *c.s.c.* '81 (P) [13] Portland, OR St. Elizabeth of Hungary Church; Portland, OR Department of Veterans' Affairs Medical Center.
Wicki, Ted *c.r.* '88 (SB) [1] Fontana, CA Church of the Resurrection.
Wicklum, Paul R. '61 (LFT) De Motte, IN St. Cecilia Church.
Wickman, Robert (RVC) Retired.
Wickowski, Leroy '66 (CHI) [4] Oak Park, IL St. Giles Church.
Wickremasunge, Vernon '87 (NY) Monroe, NY Sacred Heart Church.
Wicks, W. Jared *s.j.* '62 (DET) [K] Detroit, MI Jesuit Provincial Office-Detroit Province of the Society of Jesus.
Widacki, Msgr. Roman '57 (AUS) Retired.
Widera, Siegfried '67 (ORG) Inactive Leave.
Widmann, Phillip A. '77 (FTW) Nix Settlement, IN St. Catharine Church; Roanoke, IN St. Joseph Church.
Widmer, Edward *c.m.f.* '51 (LA) [R] Rancho Dominguez, CA Dominguez Seminary Inc.
Widner, Thomas C. *s.j.* '69 (CHI) [N] Chicago, IL Chicago Province of the Society of Jesus-Provincial Office.
Wieber, Donald A. '57 (KAL) Watervliet, MI St. Joseph Church.
Wieber, Elmer F. '54 (KAL) Retired.
Wieber, Joseph E. '39 (LAN) Retired.
Wieber, Robert *o.s.b.* '67 (SCL) [I] Collegeville, MN St. John's Abbey, of the Order of St. Benedict.
Wiecek, Ronald P. *c.pp.s.* '71 (OAK) Newark, CA St. Edward's Church; [N] Berkeley, CA Society of the Precious Blood.
Wiecki, Donald J. '58 (MAD) Reedsburg, WI Sacred Heart Church.
Wieckowski, Msgr. John F. '38 (CAM) Retired.
Wieczorek, Anthony J. *o.praem.* '85 (GB) [A] De Pere, WI St. Norbert Abbey; [I] De Pere, WI St. Norbert Abbey; [M] De Pere, WI Ministry and Life Retreat Center.
Wieczorek, Edward R. '65 (Y) Randolph Township, OH St. Joseph Church.
Wieczorek, Matthew S. '57 (SY) [11] Binghamton, NY St. Stanislaus Kostka Church.
Wiedel, Thomas L. '90 (LIN) Alma, NE St. Joseph's Church.
Wieder, Henry '89 (OWN) Uniontown, KY St. Agnes Church.
Wiederholt, Clarence E. '55 (JC) St. Anthony, MO St. Anthony Church.
Wiederholt, Thomas W. '63 (KC) Gladstone, MO St. Andrew the Apostle Church.
Wiedmann, Paul A. '63 (PH) Levittown, PA Queen of the Universe Church.
Wieeichs, Paul *c.p.* '78 (NY) [DD] New York, NY Passionist Residence.
Wiegele, Lloyd *o.carm.* '56 (BO) [P] Peabody, MA Catholic Information Center; [BB] Peabody, MA St. Theresa Carmelite Chapel.
Wiegenstein, Francis J. '59 (HEL) Whitehall, MT St. Teresa Church.
Wieging, James F. '67 (DET) River Rouge, MI Our Lady of Lourdes Church.
Wiejata, Sylwester '96 (PH) [114] Philadelphia, PA Our Lady of Calvary Church.
Wiekierak, Joseph F. '46 (GAY) Retired.
Wieland, Bernard F. *m.m.* '38 (NY) [Z] Maryknoll, NY Maryknoll Fathers and Brothers.
Wieland, Dennis J. '91 (CR) Thief River Falls, MN St. Bernards Church.
Wieland, Edward R. '56 (MIL) New Berlin, WI Holy Apostles Church.
Wielebski, John T. '78 (BAL) Glyndon, MD Sacred Heart Church.
Wielgus, Bronislaw '62 (NEW) [7] Elizabeth, NJ St. Hedwig's Church.
Wieliczko, Christopher *o.s.p.* '87 (NY) [113] New York, NY St. Stanislaus Church.
Wieling, Raymond P. '49 (SC) Retired.
Wielinski, Alan '84 (SCL) Elizabeth, MN St. Elizabeth Church; Pelican Rapids, MN St. Leonard's Church.
Wielunski, Gregory '78 (BRK) [192] Queens, NY St. Margaret's Church.
Wiemeyer, Raymond G. '52 (CIN) Retired.
Wienhoff, Paul R. '78 (BEL) Dupo, IL Sacred Heart of Jesus Church.
Wiera, Stefan '68 (SAT) San Antonio, TX Methodist Hospital.
Wiercioch, Casimir '46 (DET) Maybee, MI St. Joseph Church.
Wierenga, Paul *o.p.* '63 (SFE) [M] Albuquerque, NM St. Thomas Aquinas.
Wierenge, Paul *o.p.* '63 (SFE) [29] Albuquerque, NM St. Thomas Aquinas University Parish Church.
Wiersgalla, Joseph '51 (SCL) Retired.
Wierzbicki, Melvin *o.f.m.* '53 (GB) [I] Pulaski, WI Assumption of B.V.M. Friary.
Wierzbinski, Zeno *o.f.m.conv.* '37 (SPR) [A] Granby, MA St. Hyacinth College and Seminary.
Wiese, Melvern A. '57 (OM) Dodge, NE St. Wenceslaus Church.
Wiese, Miro *o.f.m.* '57 (GAY) Klacking Creek, MI Holy Family Church.
Wiese, Steve *s.c.j.* '63 (MIL) [P] Milwaukee, WI St. Joseph House of Formation.
Wiese, Thomas *s.s.s.* (CLV) [P] Cleveland, OH Congregation of the Blessed Sacrament Provincial House.
Wieseler, Lawrence A. '69 (CR) On Duty Outside the Diocese.
Wiesenbaugh, Robert D. *s.j.* '71 (CHL) Mooresville, NC St. Therese Church.
Wieser, Francis (SB) Retired.
Wieser, Stanley '68 (SCL) Kent, MN St. Thomas Church; [G] Breckenridge, MN St. Francis Medical Center; [H] Breckenridge, MN St. Francis Home.
Wieslaw, Strzadala *s.d.s.* '90 (NEW) [N] Verona, NJ The Salvatorian Fathers.
Wiesler, Willard F. '47 (TUC) Apache Junction, AZ St. George Church; Florence, AZ Assumption of the Blessed Virgin Mary Church; Retired.
Wiesner, James F. *c.s.p.* '83 (STP) [29] Minneapolis, MN St. Lawrence Church; [N] Minneapolis, MN Paulist Fathers.
Wiesner, Louis *s.m.* '40 (CIN) [M] Cincinnati, OH Marianist Community.
Wiesner, Mark '95 (OAK) [1] Hayward, CA All Saints Church.

Wiest, Donald *o.f.m.cap.* '34 (DET) [K] Detroit, MI St. Bonaventure Friary.
Wiest, Msgr. John J. (RVC) Manhasset, NY St. Mary's Church; Retired.
Wiest, Robert E. '58 (GI) Retired.
Wieszczk, Rudolph *o.f.m.* '54 (TR) Trenton, NJ St. Francis Medical Center.
Wieszczek, Rudolph *o.f.m.* '54 (PH) [Z] Philadelphia, PA St. Pius X Friary.
Wieszczek, Rudolph *o.f.m.* '54 (TR) [I] Trenton, NJ St. Francis Medical Center.
Wiethe, Peter L. '89 (MEM) Humboldt, TN Sacred Heart Church; Milan, TN St. Matthew Mission Church.
Wigand, William J. '83 (STL) [1] Jennings, MO Corpus Christi/St.Lucy Church.
Wiggins, Charles W. '85 (WIL) Ogletown, DE Holy Family Church.
Wiggins, Frank '86 (RIC) [4] Richmond, VA Our Lady of Lourdes Church.
Wigginton, Ellsworth T. '76 (FWT) [13] Fort Worth, TX St. Paul Church.
Wiggs, Msgr. Joel M. '49 (MEM) Retired.
Wight, Jonathan C. '86 (TOL) [24] Toledo, OH St. Hyacinth Church.
Wightman, John H. '43 (NEW) Retired.
Wightman, Paul *o.m.i.* '41 (JUN) Sitka, AK St. Gregory of Nazianzen Church.
Wightman, William R. *s.m.* '59 (STL) [4] Creve Coeur, MO Our Lady of the Pillar Church.
Wijoyo, Alex Soesilo *s.j.* '82 (BRK) [T] Brooklyn, NY Catholic Migration & Refugee Office, Catholic Migration Services, Inc.
Wijoyo, Alex Soesilo *s.j.* '82 (NY) [Z] New York, NY West Side Jesuit Community.
Wiktor, Ronald A. *c.m.* '63 (HRT) Derby, CT St. Michael Church.
Wilber, Stewart A. '91 (ATL) Douglasville, GA St. Theresa Church.
Wilbers, Michael J. '72 (JC) [1] Jefferson City, MO St. Joseph Cathedral; Russellville, MO St. Michael Church.
Wilbur, David F. '36 (MIL) Retired.
Wilburn, Nathan *c.s.p.* '89 (NY) [Z] Scarsdale, NY Paulist Fathers Generalate.
Wilcox, C. Thomas *m.m.* '51 (NY) [Z] Maryknoll, NY Maryknoll Fathers and Brothers.
Wilcoxson, Thomas J. '89 (COV) Leave of Absence.
Wilczek, Walter *c.r.* '53 (CHI) [74] Chicago, IL St. Hedwig Church.
Wilczynski, Casimir J. *c.r.* '40 (MOB) [8] Montgomery, AL Resurrection Catholic Church.
Wilczynski, Richard J. '55 (SY) [2] Utica, NY Holy Trinity Church.
Wild, Alexander '89 (DUB) Unassigned.
Wild, David D. '53 (FAR) Retired.
Wild, J. Jerome '81 (PH) Maple Glen, PA St. Alphonsus Church.
Wild, Jon '82 (DUL) [6] Duluth, MN St. Benedict's Church.
Wild, Joseph C. *o.m.i.* '40 (BO) [Z] Tewksbury, MA Immaculate Heart of Mary Novitiate-Infirmary.
Wild, Michael L. '84 (MIL) Allenton, WI Sacred Heart Church; Allenton, WI St. Anthony Church; Nenno, WI SS. Peter and Paul Church.
Wild, Robert A. *s.j.* '57 (MIL) [C] Milwaukee, WI Marquette University.
Wild, Robert A. '67 (BUF) On Duty Outside the Diocese.
Wild, Robert A. *s.j.* '70 (MIL) [P] Milwaukee, WI Jesuit Community at Marquette University.
Wilde, Dennis G. *o.s.a.* '70 (PH) [C] Villanova, PA Villanova University; [Z] Villanova, PA St. Thomas Monastery.
Wildeman, Richard J. '77 (EVN) St. Joseph, IN St. Joseph's Church.
Wilder, Alfred W. *o.p.* '65 (NO) [P] New Orleans, LA Dominican Fathers & Brothers, Southern Dominican Province.
Wilder, Daniel '96 (PEO) Lincoln, IL Holy Family Church.
Wilder, Frank T. *o.a.r.* '91 (ORG) Fullerton, CA St. Mary's Church.
Wilderotter, Paul C. '74 (CHL) On Duty Outside the Diocese.
Wilderotter, Paul C. '74 (CHR) [B] Greenville, SC Franciscan Health System of South Carolina, Inc.
Wilders, Msgr. James G. '39 (NY) [96] New York, NY Our Lady of the Rosary Church; Retired.
Wildes, Kevin W. *s.j.* '86 (WDC) [M] Washington, DC The Jesuit Community at Georgetown University.
Wildgruber, Francis C. '60 (BRK) Absent on Sick Leave.
Wildonger, Lawrence H. *m.s.c.* '79 (ALN) [K] Reading, PA Missionaries of the Sacred Heart.
Wiles, Arthur W. '67 (COL) [11] Columbus, OH St. Christopher Church.
Wiley, James A. '58 (E) Grove City, PA Beloved Disciple Church; [P] Erie, PA Newman Centers and Campus Ministry.
Wiley, Joseph '44 (E) Retired.
Wiley, Leo A. '56 (OG) Croghan, NY St. Stephen Church.
Wilgenbusch, Lyle L. '66 (DUB) [11] Dubuque, IA St. Joseph the Worker Church.
Wilger, Donald F. '57 (LC) [E] Marshfield, WI St. Joseph's Hospital.
Wilger, John J. *t.o.r.* '48 (ALT) [F] Loretto, PA Mount Assisi Monastery.
Wilger, Norbert J. '49 (LC) Altoona, WI St. Mary Church.
Wilhelm, Chad '94 (FAR) Sanborn, ND Sacred Heart Church.
Wilhelm, Dean E. '88 (AUS) College Station, TX St. Mary's Church; [M] College Station, TX St. Mary's Catholic Center.
Wilhelm, Edward *c.ss.r.* '47 (CHI) [136] Chicago, IL St. Michael Church.
Wilhelm, H. Joseph *s.m.* '59 (WH) [11] Wheeling, WV St. Vincent de Paul's Church.
Wilhelm, Patrick R.C. '71 (NEW) Kearny, NJ St. Cecilia's Church; Kearny, NJ West Hudson Hospital.
Wilhelm, Paul W. *o.m.i.* '68 (LA) San Fernando, CA Santa Rosa Church.
Wilhelm, Paul W. *o.m.i.* '68 (STP) [N] St. Paul, MN Oblate Residence.
Wilhelm, Ray *o.m.i.* '58 (SAN) Colorado City, TX St. Ann's Church.
Wilhelm, Robert J. '59 (TOL) [27] Toledo, OH St. John the Baptist Church.
Wilhelm, Thomas *o.s.a.* '73 (NY) [168] Bronx, NY St. Nicholas of Tolentine Church.
Wilhelmi, Richard *o.s.b.* '55 (BIS) [A] Richardton, ND Assumption Abbey; [B] Bismarck, ND University of Mary.
Wilhite, Philip A. '90 (GAL) Pasadena, TX St. Pius the Fifth Church.
Wilimek, Louis J. '50 (MIL) Kohler, WI St. John Evangelist Church.
Wilk, Edward J. '47 (DET) [1] Clinton Twp., MI St. Claude Church.
Wilk, Joseph M. '87 (CHI) Schaumburg, IL St. Matthew Church.
Wilk, Mitchell S. '70 (SPC) Military Chaplains.
Wilke, David M. '95 (BEL) Fairmont City, IL Holy Rosary Church.
Wilke, James B. '89 (STL) Concord Village, MO St. Simon the Apostle Church.
Wilke, Peter B. '77 (RC) [1] Rapid City, SD Cathedral of Our Lady of Perpetual Help.
Wilkening, David F. '79 (DAV) Farmington, IA St. Boniface Church; West Point, IA Assumption of the Blessed Virgin Mary Church.
Wilkening, Henry '47 (JOL) Carol Stream, IL Corpus Christi Church; Retired.
Wilker, Ronald H. '71 (CIN) Coldwater, OH Holy Trinity Church.
Wilkerson, Msgr. Gerald E. '65 (LA) Encino, CA Our Lady of Grace Church.
Wilkerson, Msgr. Jerome F. '50 (STL) Clayton, MO St. Joseph Church.
Wilkes, Robert *o.s.b.* '47 (CLV) [P] Cleveland, OH Benedictine Order of Cleveland.
Wilkie, David *c.p.* '65 (ALT) [J] Bedford, PA St. Mary's House of Greater Solitude.
Wilkie, John '92 (SEA) Port Angeles, WA Queen of Angels Church.
Wilkie, William E. '54 (DUB) [C] Dubuque, IA Loras College; [I] Dubuque, IA Holy Family Hall Infirmary.
Wilkiemeyer, Philip '48 (OKL) Retired.
Wilkiemeyer, Victor L. '43 (SJ) [4] Santa Clara, CA St. Lawrence the Martyr Church; Retired.
Wilkins, Bernard J. '61 (STL) Brentwood, MO St. Mary Magdalen Church.
Wilkinson, Bruce W. '81 (ATL) [5] Atlanta, GA Most Blessed Sacrament Church.
Wilkinson, James '42 (WCH) [3] Wichita, KS Blessed Sacrament Church.
Wilkinson, John (NY) City, NY Adolescent Remand & Detention Center.
Wilkinson, John H. '59 (BRK) [24] Brooklyn, NY St. Brigid Church; Queens, NY Queens House of Detention.
Wilkinson, Msgr. John V. '48 (NY) Hartsdale, NY Sacred Heart Church.
Wilkosz, William '95 (CHI) [67] Chicago, IL St. Gall Church.
Wilks, Bede *o.p.* '62 (SAC) Benicia, CA St. Dominic Church.
Wilkuski, Leonard F. '63 (SAG) Midland, MI St. Brigid Church.
Will, Anthony *o.f.m.cap.* '47 (MIL) [P] Mount Calvary, WI St. Lawrence Friary.
Will, Carl G. '49 (CIN) Retired.
Will, Gerald T. '80 (STL) [56] St. Louis, MO St. Simon of Cyrene Church.
Will, Msgr. Irvin R. '37 (SFD) Retired.
Will, Lowell C. '68 (EVN) Montgomery, IN St. Peter Church.
Will, Ron *c.pp.s.* '75 (KC) Liberty, MO St. James Church.
Will, Ronald *c.pp.s.* '75 (KC) [A] Liberty, MO Society of the Precious Blood Provincial Offices; [J] Liberty, MO Precious Blood Society Provincial Office; [J] Liberty, MO Precious Blood Center.
Will, Tony *o.f.m.cap.* '47 (MIL) [Q] Fond du Lac, WI Convent of the Sisters of St. Agnes.
Willard, Stephen A. '93 (PEO) [1] Bloomington, IL Holy Trinity Church.
Willathgamuwa, Flavin *c.m.f.* '83 (LA) [R] Rancho Dominguez, CA Dominguez Seminary Inc.
Wille, Arthur H. *m.m.* '51 (SFR) [N] San Francisco, CA Maryknoll Fathers and Brothers, Catholic Foreign Mission Society of America, Inc.
Willemsen, Andrew J. '54 (AUS) On Duty Outside the Diocese.
Willenbring, Mark '57 (SCL) Princeton, MN St. Edward's Church.
Willenburg, Msgr. Francis J. '54 (SY) [5] Utica, NY St. Agnes Church.
Willett, Henry L. '45 (OWN) Retired.
Willett, John *c.ss.r.* '61 (CHI) [N] Bangkok, Thailand; [N] Parana, Brazil Rua Consulheiro Sinimbu.
Willett, John *c.ss.r.* '61 (DEN) [M] Denver, CO The Redemptorists/Denver Province.
Willett, Robert '68 (OWN) [1] Paducah, KY St. Francis de Sales Church; [2] Paducah, KY Rosary Chapel.
Willett, William D. '79 (OWN) Military Chaplains.
Willette, Donald '84 (DEN) Louisville, CO St. Louis Church.
Willey, Dennis B. '94 (CHR) [1] Charleston, SC Cathedral of St. John the Baptist; [H] Charleston, SC The College of Charleston Newman Center, Medical University of South Carolina.
Willger, Gerard I. '86 (SUP) Barron, WI St. Joseph Church; Cameron, WI St. Peter Church; Chetek, WI St. Boniface Church.
Willhite, Robert J. '63 (RCK) [8] Aurora, IL St. Rita of Cascia Church.
William, Noel *o.f.m.* '42 (CIN) [M] Cincinnati, OH St. Francis Center.
Williames, Lee (GAL) [C] Houston, TX University of St. Thomas.
Williams, Alfred '39 (P) Retired.
Williams, Anthony '83 (KCK) Military Chaplains.
Williams, Msgr. Charles M. '45 (NSH) Retired.
Williams, Clarence E. *c.pp.s.* '78 (CIN) [M] Dayton, OH Provincial House of the Cincinnati Province of the Society of the Precious Blood.
Williams, Clarence E. *c.pp.s.* '78 (DET) Special Assignment; [T] Detroit, MI The Black Catholic Televangelization Network.
Williams, Dennis P. '91 (NY) [170] Bronx, NY Our Lady of the Assumption Church.
Williams, Donald J. '83 (SCR) Shohola, PA St. Ann's Church.
Williams, Edward J. '93 (SCR) [I] Williamsport, PA Divine Providence Hospital of the Sisters of Christian Charity.
Williams, Edward T. '69 (CIN) Retired.
Williams, Francis '77 (LAN) Retired.
Williams, Gary (CC) Military Chaplains.
Williams, George J. '39 (BO) Retired.
Williams, George S. *s.j.* '72 (ALN) [A] Wernersville, PA Novitiate of St. Isaac Jogues; [N] Wernersville, PA Jesuit Center for Spiritual Growth.
Williams, George T. *s.j.* (BO) Suffolk County, MA South Bay House of Correction.
Williams, George W. '96 (DET) Grosse Pointe Farms, MI St. Paul Catholic Church.
Williams, Germain *o.f.m.conv.* '48 (ALB) [12] Albany, NY Our Lady of Angels Church.
Williams, Glenn F. *s.j.* '56 (CLV) [E] Cleveland, OH St. Ignatius High School.
Williams, H. Brendan '65 (TR) Howell Township, NJ St. Veronica Church.
Williams, Ian J. '96 (GRY) Munster, IN St. Thomas More Church.
Williams, J. Craig '83 (PT) Niceville, FL Christ Our Redeemer Church.
Williams, James '65 (SEA) Special Assignment.
Williams, James E. '89 (STL) [17] St. Louis, MO Visitation-St. Ann's Shrine Church.
Williams, James F. '69 (LA) La Mirada, CA Beatitudes of Our Lord Church.
Williams, James M. '70 (MAR) Mackinac Island, MI Ste. Anne de Michilimackinac Church.
Williams, Jerry *o.carm.* '80 (CHI) [N] Chicago, IL Carmelite Priory of St. Cyril.
Williams, John '78 (R) Clinton, NC Immaculate Conception Church.
Williams, John J. '91 (HRT) Wallingford, CT Holy Trinity Church.
Williams, John Mark '89 (PEO) [12] Peoria, IL St. Peter's Church.
Williams, Joseph *c.m.* (SPC) [2] Cape Girardeau, MO St. Vincent de Paul Church.
Williams, Kenneth '63 (SHP) Noble, LA St. Ann Church.
Williams, Manuel *c.r.* '87 (MOB) [8] Montgomery, AL Resurrection Catholic Church; [8] Montgomery, AL Resurrection Catholic Church; [F] Marbury, AL Resurrection Catholic Nursing Home; [F] Montgomery, AL Father Walter Memorial Center for Handicapped Children.

Williams, Matthew *o.c.d.* '90 (SEA) Stanwood, WA St. Cecilia's Church.
Williams, McKinley '83 (RIC) On Duty Outside the Diocese.
Williams, Michael A. *s.j.* '75 (MOB) [B] Mobile, AL Spring Hill College.
Williams, Michael J. '95 (LAN) East Lansing, MI St. Thomas Aquinas Church.
Williams, Michael S. '64 (STA) [2] Gainesville, FL Holy Faith Church.
Williams, Oliver F. *c.s.c.* '70 (FTW) [B] Notre Dame, IN University of Notre Dame Du Lac; [J] Notre Dame, IN Holy Cross Community, Corby Hall, University of Notre Dame.
Williams, Patrick J. '93 (NO) [A] New Orleans, LA Notre Dame Seminary Graduate School of Theology.
Williams, Paul D., Jr. '95 (ATL) Conyers, GA St. Pius X Catholic Church.
Williams, Paul M. *o.f.m.* '86 (CHR) Greenville, SC St. Anthony of Padua Church; [H] Greenville, SC Furman University Newman Center.
Williams, Peter '83 (SY) [13] Utica, NY St. Mary of Mt. Carmel Church.
Williams, Peter A. (SY) Special Assignment.
Williams, Peter G. '92 (WDC) Suitland, MD St. Bernardine Church.
Williams, Peter Y. '87 (BUR) [J] Burlington, VT University of Vermont-The Catholic Center at UVM.
Williams, Rayner F. *o.f.m.* '56 (NY) [35] New York, NY St. Francis of Assisi Church.
Williams, Rayner F. *o.f.m.* '56 (PAT) [P] Paterson, NJ St. Anthony's Guild.
Williams, Richard B. *o.p.* '71 (SAT) [26] San Antonio, TX St. Ann Church; [B] San Antonio, TX Dominican Priory of Juan Macias.
Williams, Richard C. '65 (PH) Chester Heights, PA St. Thomas the Apostle Church.
Williams, Robert '91 (DAL) Corsicana, TX Immaculate Conception Church.
Williams, Robert Hayes '82 (DET) Hazel Park, MI St. Justin Church; Special Assignment.
Williams, Robert L. '68 (LFT) Anderson, IN St. Mary Church.
Williams, Ronald R. '79 (DET) [49] Detroit, MI St. Mary's of Redford Church.
Williams, Steven T. (MOB) [12] Mobile, AL St. Mary Church; [C] Mobile, AL McGill-Toolen High School.
Williams, Thomas G. *s.j.* '60 (SPK) [6] Spokane, WA St. Aloysius Church; [K] Spokane, WA Regis Community.
Williams, Msgr. William E. '59 (NY) Centerville, NY St. John the Evangelist Church.
Williams, William G. '69 (BO) Hull, MA St. Mary of the Assumption Church.
Williams, William M. '96 (ATL) [3] Marietta, GA St. Joseph Church.
Williams, William W. *s.j.* '68 (COS) [E] Sedalia, CO Sacred Heart Retreat House - Jesuit Community; [G] Sedalia, CO Sacred Heart Jesuit Retreat House.
Williamson, Bruce *o.m.v.* '82 (BO) [B] Boston, MA Oblate Provincialate.
Williamson, Christopher '88 (ATL) Lawrenceville, GA St. Lawrence Church.
Williamson, G. Michael '86 (CLV) El Salvador, C.A., OH Senora del Pilar, Villa de Zaragoza.
Williamson, Harry A. *s.j.* '39 (BO) [W] Weston, MA Campion Center.
Williamson, Msgr. Robert J. '62 (BUF) Akron, NY St. Teresa of Avila Church.
Williamson, Thomas '96 (CHL) [1] Charlotte, NC St. Patrick Cathedral.
Willig, James M. '77 (CIN) [1] Cincinnati, OH St. Peter in Chains Cathedral.
Willingham, Charles W. *o.praem.* '95 (ORG) [D] Siverado, CA St. Michael's College Preparatory High School; [H] Silverado, CA Norbertine Fathers.
Willis, Eugene F. '55 (ALB) Walton, NY St. John the Baptist Church.
Willis, Glen *s.d.s.* '69 (WDC) [B] Silver Spring, MD Salvatorian Community; [G] Rockville, MD The Frost Center; [V] Silver Spring, MD Camp St. Charles, Inc.
Willis, John R. *s.j.* '62 (BO) [W] Chestnut Hill, MA The Jesuit Community at Boston College.
Willis, Kevin '93 (FAR) La Moure, ND Holy Rosary Church.
Willis, Lawrence R. *o.s.b.* '66 (CHL) [J] Belmont, NC Belmont Abbey.
Willis, Nathan S. '66 (Y) Conneaut, OH St. Mary's Church; Kingsville, OH St. Andrew Church.
Willis, Thomas S. '84 (STA) [10] Jacksonville, FL Most Holy Redeemer Church.
Willman, Herbert '57 (TOL) Norwalk, OH St. Paul Church.
Willmann, Robert E. '92 (COL) [8] Columbus, OH St. Catharine Church; Graduate Studies.
Willmes, Robert J. *s.j.* '40 (CHI) [C] Chicago, IL Jesuit Community at Loyola University of Chicago.
Willoughby, Malcolm S. *o.p.* '49 (DET) [21] Detroit, MI St. Dominic Church.
Wilmes, James J. '52 (CHL) Andrews, NC Holy Redeemer Church.
Wilmot, John P. *m.h.m.* '77 (WIN) Easton, MN Our Lady of Mount Carmel Church; Minnesota Lake, MN St. John the Baptist Church.
Wilmoth, James '65 (IND) Indianapolis, IN Indianapolis Fire Department.
Wilmoth, James R. '65 (IND) [34] Indianapolis, IN St. Michael the Archangel Church; Indianapolis, IN Marion County Sheriff Department.
Wilson, Alan *o.f.m.cap.* '69 (SFR) [28] San Francisco, CA St. John of God Church; [B] San Francisco, CA Capuchi House of Studies; [S] San Francisco, CA Newman Center, University of California Medical Center.
Wilson, Albert (L) Retired.
Wilson, Albert L. '51 (L) Rhodelia, KY St. Theresa Church.
Wilson, Brian *l.c.* '77 (LA) [R] Pasadena, CA Legionaries of Christ; [BB] Los Angeles, CA Archdiocesan Office for Campus Ministry; [BB] Los Angeles, CA Archdiocesan Office for Campus Ministry.
Wilson, Cedric M. *o.s.a.* '78 (WDC) [B] Silver Spring, MD Austin Friars Hall, Order of St. Augustine.
Wilson, Clarence E. *c.s.p.* '43 (NY) [Z] Scarsdale, NY Paulist Fathers Generalate.
Wilson, David J. '88 (E) Warren, PA St. Joseph Church.
Wilson, Dennis M. *o.f.m.* '92 (NY) [35] New York, NY St. Francis of Assisi Church; [115] New York, NY St. Stephen of Hungary Church.
Wilson, E. James '91 (DAV) [6] Davenport, IA St. Joseph's Church.
Wilson, Edward M. '56 (E) Retired.
Wilson, F. Philip *o.s.b.* '53 (PRO) [P] Portsmouth, RI Abbey of St. Gregory the Great.
Wilson, Gene *c.pp.s.* '60 (OAK) Newark, CA St. Edward's Church.
Wilson, George B. *s.j.* '59 (BAL) [M] Baltimore, MD Jesuit Fathers and Brothers Maryland Provincial Curia.
Wilson, George B. *s.j.* '59 (CIN) [M] Cincinnati, OH Jesuit Community at Xavier Unversity.
Wilson, George W. '92 (WDC) [7] Washington, DC St. Augustine Church; [34] Washington, DC Our Lady Queen of Peace Church.
Wilson, Guy B. *s.t.* '78 (LA) [4] Los Angeles, CA Ascension Church; Graduate Studies.
Wilson, James L., Jr. '90 (BO) Absent on Sick Leave.
Wilson, James R. '54 (B) Lapwai, ID Sacred Heart Church; Lewiston, ID Our Lady of Lourdes Church.
Wilson, Jerome *c.s.c.* '49 (FTW) [A] Notre Dame, IN Moreau Seminary.
Wilson, John F. '46 (CLV) Retired; [N] Fairlawn, OH St. Edward Home dba The Village at Saint Edward Nursing Care and Assisted Living; [N] Fairlawn, OH St. Edward Home dba The Village at Saint Edward Nursing Care and Assisted Living.
Wilson, Msgr. John F. '48 (BRK) [58] Brooklyn, NY Holy Name Church; Retired.
Wilson, John H. *c.s.c.* '41 (FTW) [L] Notre Dame, IN Holy Cross Mission House.
Wilson, Joseph B. '94 (SCR) [2] Williamsport, PA Ascension Church.
Wilson, Joseph C. '57 (BO) Billerica, MA St. Andrew Church.
Wilson, Joseph F. '86 (BRK) [191] Queens, NY St. Luke Church.
Wilson, Kent '90 (NY) Fishkill, NY Church of St. Mary, Mother of the Church.
Wilson, Leland '93 (LA) Covina, CA Sacred Heart Church.
Wilson, Method *o.f.m.* '52 (LFT) [F] Kokomo, IN Maria Regina Mater Monastery.
Wilson, Michael '75 (WDC) [4] Rockville, MD St. Raphael Church.
Wilson, Michael D. *s.s.j.* '89 (NO) [56] New Orleans, LA St. Raymond Church.
Wilson, Robert '57 (FWT) Colleyville, TX Good Shepherd Church.
Wilson, Ser Khu (WCH) Piqua, KS St. Martin Church; Yates Center, KS St. Joseph Church.
Wilson, Stuart T. '67 (BAL) Military Chaplains.
Wilson, Thomas R. '75 (PIT) Mt. Lebanon, PA St. Bernard Church.
Wilson, Thomas W. '96 (STP) Coon Rapids, MN Church of the Epiphany.
Wilson, William P. '69 (NEW) On Duty Outside the Archdiocese.
Wilson, William T. '45 (SD) La Jolla, CA All Hallows Church.
Wilt, George A. '59 (PIT) Mt. Lebanon, PA St. Bernard Church.
Wilt, John E. '57 (GBG) Seward, PA Holy Family Church.
Wiltgen, Ralph *s.v.d.* '50 (MIL) [P] East Troy, WI Divine Word Seminary.
Wilton, David '93 (OWN) [F] South Union, KY Fathers of Mercy.
Wiltz, George F. *s.j.* '65 (NO) [C] New Orleans, LA Loyola University.
Wiltz, George F. *s.j.* '76 (DAL) [26] Dallas, TX St. Rita Church.
Wilus, Msgr. John M. '37 (TR) Retired.
Wilutis, John P. '51 (RVC) [N] Uniondale, NY St. Pius X Residence.
Wilutis, John P. '55 (RVC) Retired.
Wilwerding, Anthony P. '46 (OM) Retired.
Wilwerding, James '92 (DM) [I] Panora, IA St. Thomas More Center.
Wilz, John C. '64 (PH) [3] Phoenixville, PA St. Mary of the Assumption Church.
Wimett, Leo J. '60 (SY) North Bay, NY St. John Church.
Wimmer, Joseph F. *o.s.a.* '64 (PH) [C] Villanova, PA Villanova University.
Wimmer, Joseph F. *o.s.a.* '64 (WDC) [B] Silver Spring, MD Austin Friars Hall, Order of St. Augustine.
Wimsett, Scott J. (L) On Duty Outside the Archdiocese.
Winance, Eleutherius *o.s.b.* '35 (LA) [R] Valyermo, CA St. Andrew's Abbey.
Winaski, William '76 (FWT) Wichita Falls, TX Our Lady Queen of Peace Church.
Winca, George F. '38 (Y) Retired.
Winca, Harry S. '45 (CLV) Middlefield, OH St. Lucy Church; Parkman, OH St. Edward Church.
Winchester, George P. *s.j.* '65 (BO) Boston, MA Brigham and Women's Hospital; [W] Boston, MA Jesuit Urban Center & Immaculate Conception Community.
Winczewski, Andrew *o.s.b.* '43 (SCL) [I] Collegeville, MN St. John's Abbey, of the Order of St. Benedict.
Wind, John F. '67 (DEN) Golden, CO St. Joseph Church.
Windbacher, Ambrose P. *o.p.* '54 (CHI) [N] Chicago, IL Dominicans (Provincial Office).
Windhaus, Edward A. '72 (PH) Hatfield, PA St. Maria Goretti Church.
Windholtz, Barry M. '88 (CIN) [54] Cincinnati, OH St. Louis Church.
Windisch, Adolf M. *s.m.* '60 (CIN) [M] Dayton, OH Marianist Provincialate.
Windisch, Adolf M. *s.m.* '60 (STL) [P] St. Louis, MO Provincialate of the Society of Mary, Province of St. Louis.
Windle, John J. '43 (CHI) Retired.
Windle, Raymond L. *s.j.* '59 (STL) [P] St. Louis, MO Jesuit Community Corporation at St. Louis University - Jesuit Hall.
Windolf, Michael *o.f.m.* '51 (CHI) Oak Forest, IL Oak Forest Hospital.
Windolph, George *o.f.m.* '48 (SFD) [B] Quincy, IL Quincy University.
Windolph, Joseph (CHI) [N] Chicago, IL St. Peter's Friary.
Windolph, Michael *o.f.m.* '51 (CHI) [N] Oak Forest, IL St. Roch Friary-Franciscan Fathers.
Windy, Jeffrey I. '96 (PEO) [10] Peoria, IL St. Mark's Church.
Winel, Msgr. Roland T. '39 (COL) Retired.
Wines, Frank (PT) Tiger Point, FL St. Sylvester Church.
Wing, Kenneth A. '59 (GR) Retired.
Wingate, Arthur K. '56 (FR) [J] Fall River, MA Catholic Memorial Home Inc.
Wingert, D. William '60 (SC) Retired.
Wingert, Gerald R. '47 (SC) Retired.
Wingert, La Vern '57 (DM) [I] Griswold, IA Wakonda Prayer House.
Wingfield, Harvey J. *o.s.b.* '81 (SEA) [M] Lacey, WA St. Martin's Abbey.
Winiarski, James *m.s.* '66 (MIL) [65] Milwaukee, WI St. Paul Church; [P] Milwaukee, WI La Salette Fathers.
Winkel, Thomas J. '71 (CLV) Bedford, OH St. Mary Church.
Winkelbauer, Phillip '75 (KCK) Baldwin, KS Annunciation Church.
Winkelbauer, Phillip J. '75 (KCK) Edgerton, KS Assumption of the Blessed Virgin Mary Church.
Winkels, Michael A. *o.p.* '76 (CHI) [N] Chicago, IL Dominicans (Provincial Office); [N] Chicago, IL Dominicans (Provincial Office); [N] River Forest, IL St. Thomas Aquinas Priory.
Winkels, Robert H. *m.m.* '41 (NY) [Z] Maryknoll, NY Maryknoll Fathers and Brothers.
Winkler, Clarence E. '38 (STL) Retired.
Winkler, Edward J. '86 (VIC) Eagle Lake, TX Parish of the Nativity Church.
Winkler, Eugene D. '50 (MIL) Lima, WI St. Rose Church; St. George, WI St. George Church; [W] Milwaukee, WI Council of Catholic Women.
Winkler, Jude *o.f.m.conv.* (BAL) [B] Ellicott City, MD Friary of St. Joseph Cupertino; [M] Ellicott City, MD St. Joseph Cupertino Friary, Friars Minor Conventual of St. Francis of Assisi.
Winkler, Kenneth H. '81 (RVC) Mineola, NY Corpus Christi Church.
Winkler, William '92 (KNX) On Duty Outside the Diocese.
Winkowski, Eugene R. '71 (CHI) [213] Chicago, IL St. Wenceslaus Church.
Winkowski, Michael J. *c.pp.s* '70 (FTW) Walkerton, IN St. Patrick Church.
Winne, George R. '83 (ALN) [9] Allentown, PA Sacred Heart of Jesus Church; [C] Allentown, PA Allentown

Central Catholic High School.
Winnenberg, John O. '55 (WDC) Retired.
Winnikates, Thomas '70 (CHI) Flossmoor, IL Infant Jesus of Prague Church.
Winrich, Walter W. *m.m.* '50 (NY) [Z] Maryknoll, NY Maryknoll Fathers and Brothers.
Winshman, Alfred O. *s.j.* '65 (BO) [W] Boston, MA Loyola House.
Winston, William L. '86 (PAT) Morristown, NJ Assumption of the Blessed Virgin Mary Church.
Winter, Donald *c.ss.r.* '55 (RIC) [2] Hampton, VA St. Joseph Church.
Winter, Harry *o.m.i.* '64 (WDC) [B] Washington, DC Cluster of Independent Theological School, The; [B] Washington, DC Oblate College/Oblate Center for Mission Studies.
Winterer, Michael J. '60 (SLC) Cedar City, UT Christ the King Church.
Wintergalen, Edward H. *s.j.* '37 (STL) [O] St. Louis, MO Fusz Pavilion.
Winterlin, John R. (GRY) [2] Hammond, IN Our Lady of Perpetual Help Church.
Wintermeyer, John S. '62 (WDC) [S] Washington, DC Archdiocesan Campus Ministry.
Wintermeyer, William P. '49 (CIN) Retired.
Wintermyer, John S. '62 (WDC) [13] Washington, DC St. Francis de Sales Church; Washington, DC Washington Hospital Center; Hospital & Nursing Home Ministries.
Winters, Alfred H. '62 (CLV) [1] Lakewood, OH St. Clement Church.
Winters, Arthur *s.v.d.* '45 (BLX) [A] Bay St. Louis, MS St. Augustine's.
Winters, Bartholomew S. *m. div.* '83 (CHI) [A] Mundelein, IL University of St. Mary of the Lake-Mundelein Seminary.
Winters, Daniel *s.m.* '63 (CIN) [M] Cincinnati, OH Marianist Community.
Winters, Francis X. *s.j.* '64 (BAL) [M] Baltimore, MD Jesuit Fathers and Brothers Maryland Provincial Curia.
Winters, Martin N. '52 (CHI) [O] Oak Forest, IL Our Lady of Sorrows Priory, Benedictine Sisters of Pontifical Jurisdiction.
Winters, Richard *s.v.d.* '41 (SB) [A] Riverside, CA Divine Word Seminary.
Winters, Sean G. '87 (MET) Bridgewater, NJ Holy Trinity Church; Somerville, NJ Somerset Medical Center.
Winters, Vaughn '93 (LA) Goleta, CA St. Raphael Church.
Winters, William *o.f.m.cap.* '64 (RVC) East Patchogue, NY St. Joseph the Worker Church.
Wintz, Gerald *o.f.m.cap.* (STL) [P] St. Louis, MO St. Crispin's Friary.
Wintz, Jack R. *o.f.m.* '63 (CIN) [M] Cincinnati, OH Pleasant Street Friary.
Winzenburg, George E. *s.j.* '74 (MIL) [29] Milwaukee, WI Gesu Parish Church.
Winzerling, James L. '61 (STL) St. Louis, MO Christian Hospital Northeast-Northwest.
Wippel, Msgr. John '60 (STU) On Duty Outside the Diocese.
Wippel, Msgr. John '60 (WDC) [C] Washington, DC Catholic University of America, The; [C] Washington, DC Catholic University of America, The.
Wirkes, Stephen E. '80 (SY) Mexico, NY St. Mary, Star of the Sea Church.
Wironen, John B. *c.s.c.* '79 (P) [13] Portland, OR St. Elizabeth of Hungary Church; Portland, OR Oregon Health Sciences University.
Wirth, Geoffrey '67 (RCK) Crystal Lake, IL St. Thomas the Apostle Church.
Wirth, Jerry E. '68 (BEL) Olney, IL St. Joseph Church.
Wirth, John J. '52 (STP) Retired.
Wirth, Richard P. '56 (STP) [35] St. Paul, MN St. Thomas The Apostle Church.
Wirth, Robert *c.ss.r.* '64 (CHI) [N] Bangkok, Thailand; [N] Parana, Brazil Rua Consulheiro Sinimbu.
Wirth, Robert *c.ss.r.* '64 (DEN) [M] Denver, CO The Redemptorists/Denver Province.
Wischmeyer, Amos H. '51 (LAN) Swartz Creek, MI St. Mary Church.
Wise, Carl A. *c.pp.s.* '56 (CIN) Montezuma, OH Our Lady of Guadalupe Church.
Wise, Joseph *c.r.* '41 (CHI) [88] Chicago, IL St. Hyacinth Church.
Wise, Kenneth '47 (COL) Retired.
Wise, Kenneth F. '47 (COL) Dennison, OH Immaculate Conception Church.
Wise, Marcos *c.ss.r.* '72 (CGS) [B] Aguas Buenas, PR Casa Cristo Redentor.
Wise, Neal *o.p.* '67 (AUS) [H] Austin, TX Dominican Fathers.
Wise, Paul C. '74 (CAM) [5] Atlantic City, NJ Our Lady Star of the Sea Church.
Wise, Richard P. '81 (ATL) Decatur, GA Sts. Peter and Paul Church.
Wise, Thomas F. *c.s.v.* '56 (SFD) Granite City, IL Holy Family Church.
Wiseman, James A. *o.s.b.* '70 (WDC) [C] Washington, DC Catholic University of America, The; [M] Washington, DC St. Anselm's Abbey.
Wiseman, Joseph F. '52 (BRK) [197] Queens, NY Mary's Nativity Church.
Wiseman, Robert *c.s.c.* '77 (ORL) Winter Park, FL St. Margaret Mary Church.
Wiseman, Robert A., C.S.C. (ORL) [E] Winter Park, FL Rollins College Campus Ministry.
Wiseman, Thomas '41 (P) Retired.
Wiseman, Vincent *o.p.* '71 (WDC) [B] Washington, DC Dominican House of Studies.
Wishard, John '62 (LA) Santa Maria, CA St. Mary of the Assumption Church.
Wiskirchen, George C. *c.s.c.* '55 (FTW) [B] Notre Dame, IN University of Notre Dame Du Lac; [J] Notre Dame, IN Holy Cross Community, Corby Hall, University of Notre Dame.
Wisner, John H. '72 (KCK) Roeland Park, KS St. Agnes Church.
Wisneske, S. Patrick '50 (MAR) Menominee, MI Holy Spirit Church.
Wisneski, Edward '67 (NOR) Retired.
Wisneski, John A. '57 (LC) Blenker, WI St. Kilian Church; Junction City, WI St. Michael Church; Milladore, WI St. Wenceslaus Church.
Wisneski, John J. '64 (GR) Alpine, MI Holy Trinity Church.
Wisniefski, Robert W. '80 (PAT) [9] Paterson, NJ St. Joseph's Church.
Wisniewski, David '81 (OG) Glenfield, NY St. Mary Church; Houseville, NY St. Hedwig Church; Lowville, NY St. Peter Church.
Wisniewski, Joseph *c.m.* '65 (BRK) [134] Brooklyn, NY St. Stanislaus Kostka Church.
Wisniewski, Robert W. '89 (CLV) North Royalton, OH St. Albert the Great Church.
Wisniewski, Stanley T. *s.j.* '64 (RNO) Fallon, NV St. Patrick Church.
Wisniewski, Theodore '47 (BAL) Retired.
Wisniewski, Theodore M. '47 (BAL) [Q] Baltimore, MD Johns Hopkins Hospital Apostolate.
Wisniewski, Thomas (NEW) Maplewood, NJ St. Joseph's Church.
Wisniewski, Thomas '76 (MIA) Parkland, FL Mary Help of Christians Church.
Wisniewski, Thomas J. '74 (PH) Penn Valley, PA St. Justin Martyr Church.
Wissel, Msgr. Francis C. '77 (BGP) [18] Bridgeport, CT St. Peter's Church; [T] Bridgeport, CT St. Peter's Parish, St. Maximillian Kolbe House of Studies.
Wissler, Thomas J. '83 (STL) Farmington, MO St. Joseph Church.
Wissman, J. Patrick '64 (SPC) Scott City, MO St. Joseph Church.
Wister, Msgr. Robert J. (NEW) [A] South Orange, NJ Immaculate Conception Seminary; [B] South Orange, NJ Seton Hall University.
Wisz, Dominic *o.f.m.conv.* '47 (RCK) [2] Rockford, IL St. Anthony of Padua Church.
Witalec, Dennis J. '82 (PH) [78] Philadelphia, PA St. John Cantius Church.
Witcoskie, Stanley '93 (CAM) Wildwood, NJ St. Ann's Church.
Witczak, Msgr. Edward '60 (GB) Absent on Leave.
Witczak, Michael G. '77 (MIL) [A] Milwaukee, WI Saint Francis Seminary.
Witek, John W. *s.j.* '65 (WDC) [M] Washington, DC The Jesuit Community at Georgetown University.
Witek, Stanley '87 (GRY) [13] East Chicago, IN St. Stanislaus Church.
With, William A. '72 (BRK) [214] Queens, NY Our Lady of Mercy Church.
Witherup, Ronald D. *s.s.* '76 (SFR) [A] Menlo Park, CA St. Patrick Seminary; [A] Menlo Park, CA St. Patrick Seminary.
Withrow, Justin *o.s.b.* '90 (GBG) Greensburg, PA Westmoreland Hospital; Latrobe, PA Latrobe Area Hospital; Jeannette, PA Jeannette District Memorial Hospital; Jeannette, PA Monsour Medical Center; [F] Jeannette, PA Jeannette District Memorial Hospital; [H] Latrobe, PA Saint Vincent Archabbey.
Witkowski, Msgr. Bernard E. '62 (PH) [78] Philadelphia, PA St. John Cantius Church.
Witkowski, Phillip J. '75 (GR) [7] Muskegon, MI St. Thomas the Apostle Church.
Witkowski, Raymond A. '42 (MIL) Retired.
Witkowski, Robert J. '61 (DET) [5] Warren, MI St. Edmund Church.
Witmer, Joseph W. '67 (Y) Aurora, OH Our Lady of Perpetual Help Church.
Witon, Russell F. '63 (MIL) [N] Milwaukee, WI St. Anne's Home for the Elderly.
Witsken, Gary J. '69 (CIN) [87] Cincinnati, OH St. Vincent de Paul Church.
Witt, Christopher P. *c.s.p.* '79 (NY) [Z] Scarsdale, NY Paulist Fathers Generalate.
Witt, Edward G. *s.j.* '91 (MIL) [E] Milwaukee, WI Marquette University High School; [P] Milwaukee, WI Pere Marquette House Jesuit Community.
Witt, Michael J. '90 (STL) [8] St. Louis, MO Most Blessed Sacrament Church.
Witt, Paul K. '71 (LIN) [8] Lincoln, NE St. Mary Church.
Witt, Robert G. '50 (COV) Retired.
Witt, William '49 (Y) Retired.
Wittbrod, Joseph *o.c.s.o.* '49 (SAC) [A] Vina, CA Abbey of New Clairvaux, Trappist Seminary.
Wittbrod, Joseph J. *o.c.s.o.* '49 (SAC) [H] Vina, CA Abbey of New Clairvaux, Trappist.
Witte, D. Steven '92 (BEL) Leave of Absence.
Witte, Msgr. John C. '45 (GRY) Retired.
Witte, Mark '95 (COV) [C] Covington, KY Academy of Notre Dame.
Witte, Mark G. '95 (COV) Fort Mitchell, KY Blessed Sacrament Church.
Wittemann, Paul J. '56 (MIL) Retired.
Wittenbrink, Boniface *o.m.i.* '41 (BEL) [G] Belleville, IL Shrine of Our Lady of the Snows.
Witterholt, Herbert M. '40 (BRK) Retired.
Witthauer, Paul G. (BAL) [68] Baltimore, MD Our Lady of Hope Church.
Witting, Martin *o.s.b.* '51 (RCK) [H] Aurora, IL Marmion Abbey-St. Augustine's Abbey.
Wittliff, Thomas F. '64 (MIL) [9] Milwaukee, WI St. Augustine's Church.
Wittman, Karl M. '46 (STP) [20] St. Paul, MN St. Francis De Sales Church; Retired.
Wittman, Michael A. '88 (CLV) Litchfield, OH Our Lady Help of Christians Parish Church.
Wittman, Peter C. (STP) Savage, MN St. John the Baptist Church.
Wittmann, Christopher T. *s.m.* '94 (CIN) [M] Dayton, OH Marianist Provincialate.
Wittosch, Paul '75 (JOL) Rockdale, IL St. Joseph Church.
Wittouck, Frank *s.c.j.* '65 (GAL) [26] Houston, TX St. Elizabeth Ann Seton Church.
Wittreich, John A. '47 (CLV) Norton, OH St. Andrew the Apostle Church; Retired.
Wittrock, Daniel L. '94 (OM) Bellevue, NE St. Mary Church.
Wittstock, John J. '36 (DET) Retired.
Wittstock, Joseph *o.c.s.o.* '84 (ARL) [J] Berryville, VA Cistercian Abbey of Our Lady of the Holy Cross.
Witz, Dennis M. '76 (MIL) [42] Milwaukee, WI Immaculate Conception Church.
Witzemann, B. Gerald '61 (COV) Taylor Mill, KY St. Patrick Church.
Witzmann, Hugh *o.s.b.* '55 (SCL) [I] Collegeville, MN St. John's Abbey, of the Order of St. Benedict.
Wixted, Matthew O. '62 (SLC) Tooele, UT St. Marguerite's Church.
Wladyka, Stanley *o.f.m.conv.* (BO) [5] Haverhill, MA St. Michael Church.
Wleczyk, Msgr. Leo '65 (GAL) Lake Jackson, TX St. Michael Church.
Wodarski, Msgr. John P. '31 (HRT) [5] Bristol, CT St. Stanislaus Church; Retired; Retired.
Wodniak, John L. '43 (CHI) [98] Chicago, IL St. James Church; Retired.
Wodziak, Michael (RVC) Retired.
Woefl, Paul A. *s.j.* '44 (TOL) [6] Toledo, OH Gesu Church.
Woempner, Michael A. '79 (MAR) White Pine, MI St. Jude Church.
Woerth, Thomas J. '66 (DEN) Denver, CO Veterans Hospital.
Woerz, Christian H. *s.d.b.* '76 (MRY) [D] Watsonville, CA St. Francis Youth Center.
Wohinc, Karl R. '63 (WH) Shinnston, WV St. Ann's Church.
Wohlrab, Paul G. '41 (ROC) Spencerport, NY St. John the Evangelist Church; Retired; [L] Spencerport, NY Legion of Mary.
Wohlwend, Paul W. *c.pp.s.* '54 (CIN) Fort Recovery, OH Mary Help of Christians Church.
Wohman, Andrew B. *c.s.c.* '44 (FTW) [J] South Bend, IN Congregation of Holy Cross Indiana Province Provincial House.
Wojcicki, Miroslaus A. '62 (PIT) East Pittsburgh, PA Holy Cross Church.
Wojcicki, Msgr. Ted L. '75 (STL) [61] St. Louis, MO St. Stanislaus Kostka Church.
Wojcicki, Wojciech '90 (DET) Hamtramck, MI Our Lady Queen of Apostles Church.
Wojciechowski, Christian *o.f.m.conv.* '53 (TR) [22] Trenton, NJ St. Stanislaus Church.
Wojciechowski, Edward C. '81 (PRM) Minneapolis, MN St. John the Baptist Church.
Wojciechowski, Richard P. '63 (BAL) [23] Baltimore, MD Christ the King Church.
Wojciechowski, Robert J. '83 (DET) [23] Detroit, MI St. Francis D'Assisi Church.
Wojciechowski, Thomas *o.f.m.* '75 (GB) [H] Manitowoc, WI St. Mary's Home for the Aged; [I] Pulaski, WI Assumption of B.V.M. Friary.
Wojciehowski, Msgr. Thaddeus J. (TR) [M] Trenton, NJ Villa Neumann.
Wojciehowski, Msgr. Thaddeus J. '36 (TR) Retired.
Wojcik, Eugene H. '74 (BEL) [1] Belleville, IL Cathedral of St. Peter.
Wojcik, Joseph J. '69 (CHI) Westchester, IL Divine

Providence Church.
Wojcik, Richard J. (CHI) Retired.
Wojcik, Richard J. '49 (CHI) [A] Mundelein, IL University of St. Mary of the Lake-Mundelein Seminary.
Wojcik, Roger L. *m.i.c.* '81 (WDC) [B] Washington, DC Marian Fathers Scholasticate.
Wojcinski, Anthony A. '85 (PBL) [1] Pueblo, CO Sacred Heart Cathedral.
Wojnicki, Richard J. *o.s.f.s.* '85 (VEN) [3] Fort Myers, FL St. Cecilia Church.
Wojtaszczyk, John '90 (CC) On Duty Outside the Diocese.
Wojtewicz, Eugene E. '57 (DET) Southgate, MI St. Hugh Church.
Wojtowicz, Edward L. '44 (NU) Retired.
Wojtowicz, John E. *o.f.m.* '80 (CHI) [N] Chicago, IL Holy Name Friary-Franciscan House of Formation.
Wojtunik, Henry *m.s.* '60 (MIL) [P] Twin Lakes, WI La Salette Missionaries Shrine.
Wojtus, Anthony '58 (WH) Retired.
Wojtycha, Msgr. Edward F. '38 (NEW) [2] Bayonne, NJ St. Andrew's Church; Retired.
Wolak, Edmund '92 (SY) Fairmount, NY Holy Family Church.
Wolan, Stephen J. '58 (WH) Retired.
Wolanski, Edward *c.p.* '72 (WOR) [N] Shrewsbury, MA Passionist Fathers of Shrewsbury, Inc., Calvary Retreat Center; [P] Shrewsbury, MA Calvary Retreat Center, Passionist Community.
Wolbach, Richard A. '56 (OM) Retired.
Wolbang, Charles A. *c.m.* '41 (MET) [H] Plainsboro, NJ Vincentian Residence.
Wolber, Ferdinand A. '40 (DET) Retired.
Wolbert, John R. '74 (CIN) Owensville, OH St. Louis Church; Stonelick, OH St. Philomena Church.
Wolensky, Paul '94 (STF) [5] Glastonbury, CT St. John The Baptist Church; [A] Stamford, CT St. Basil College.
Wolesky, John A. '67 (SAL) Gypsum, KS St. Patrick's Church.
Wolf, Anthony J. '96 (LC) Graduate Studies.
Wolf, Benedict L. '41 (ALT) Retired.
Wolf, David *o.s.b.* '52 (BIS) [A] Richardton, ND Assumption Abbey.
Wolf, Dennis G. '72 (BUF) Wellsville, NY Immaculate Conception Church.
Wolf, Don '81 (OKL) [17] Oklahoma City, OK Sacred Heart Church.
Wolf, Eugene *o.f.m.cap.* '54 (MIL) [P] Mount Calvary, WI St. Lawrence Friary.
Wolf, Eugene J. '63 (LC) Seneca, WI St. Patrick Church; Wauzeka, WI Sacred Heart Church.
Wolf, George '44 (SCL) [I] Collegeville, MN St. John's Abbey, of the Order of St. Benedict.
Wolf, George '80 (P) Salem, OR Queen of Peace Church.
Wolf, George C. '63 (RNO) Sparks, NV Holy Cross Catholic Community Church.
Wolf, James '48 (SFS) Retired.
Wolf, James *o.f.m.cap.* '57 (DET) [K] Detroit, MI St. Bonaventure Friary; [K] Detroit, MI St. Bonaventure Friary.
Wolf, Msgr. James J. '69 (FTW) [1] Fort Wayne, IN Cathedral of the Immaculate Conception.
Wolf, John *c.pp.s.* '69 (KC) [8] Kansas City, MO St. Charles Borromeo Church.
Wolf, Msgr. John V. '45 (COL) Retired.
Wolf, John W. '38 (CLV) Chagrin Falls, OH St. Joan of Arc Church; Retired.
Wolf, Joseph A. '68 (MIL) [58] Milwaukee, WI Our Lady of Good Hope Church.
Wolf, Joseph B. '54 (STL) Retired.
Wolf, Joseph D. (BUF) East Aurora, NY Immaculate Conception Church.
Wolf, Joseph M. '94 (DAV) Clinton, IA Jesus Christ, Prince of Peace Church.
Wolf, Lawrence *o.s.b.m.* '75 (PSC) Trenton, NJ St. Nicholas Church.
Wolf, Lawrence Robert *o.s.b.m.* '75 (PSC) [B] Matawan, NJ Basilian Fathers of Mariapoch.
Wolf, Matthias J. '41 (BRK) Retired.
Wolf, Michael H. '42 (SAG) Essexville, MI St. John the Evangelist Church; Retired.
Wolf, Msgr. Michael O.J. '38 (EVN) [1] Evansville, IN Pro-Cathedral of the Most Holy Trinity.
Wolf, Norbert K. '47 (E) Wilcox, PA St. Anne Church.
Wolf, Paul L. '83 (NU) Seaforth, MN St. Mary Church; Wabasso, MN St. Anne Church.
Wolf, Peter (BO) [6] Newton, MA Our Lady Help of Christians Church.
Wolf, Robert J. '44 (MIL) Retired.
Wolf, Ronald D. *s.j.* '74 (SJ) [M] Los Gatos, CA California Province of the Society of Jesus, Jesuit Provincial Office; [M] Los Gatos, CA Sacred Heart Jesuit Center.
Wolf, Theodore J. *s.j.* '38 (P) [L] Portland, OR Jesuit Provincial Office (Oregon Prov.).
Wolf, Msgr. Vincent J. '38 (FWT) Retired.
Wolf, Werner *o.f.m.cap.* '58 (GB) [M] Appleton, WI Monte Alverno Retreat Center.
Wolfe, Allen F. '92 (HBG) [6] Lancaster, PA Sacred Heart of Jesus Church.
Wolfe, James T. '55 (ROC) Avon, NY St. Agnes Church.
Wolfe, Joseph M. *m.f.v.a.* '93 (BIR) [E] Birmingham, AL Franciscan Missionaries of the Eternal Word, A Public Association of the Christian Faithful.
Wolfe, Robert *o.carm.* '75 (NEW) Bogota, NJ St. Joseph's Church.
Wolfe, William P. '70 (LA) La Mirada, CA St. Paul of the Cross Church.
Wolfel, Daniel C. *o.s.b.* '54 (ALT) Summerhill, PA St. John Church.
Wolfer, Paul J. '45 (CIN) [68] Cincinnati, OH Our Lady of Lourdes Church; Retired.
Wolfer, Robert R. '48 (CIN) [68] Cincinnati, OH Our Lady of Lourdes Church; Retired.
Wolff, Alec J. '81 (CHI) Highland Park, IL Immaculate Conception Church; [X] Wilmette, IL Musica Pacis.
Wolff, Msgr. Robert C. '50 (CLV) Copley, OH Guardian Angels Church; Retired.
Wolford, Charles '80 (OWN) Retired.
Wolford, Donald L. '79 (SFD) [3] Decatur, IL St. Patrick Church.
Wolfram, Frank R. *s.d.b.* '62 (SP) [E] Tampa, FL Mary Help of Christians School.
Wolfzorn, Eugene E. '58 (COV) [2] Newport, KY St. Stephen Church; [3] Newport, KY St. Francis de Sales Church.
Wolken, Gary '93 (STL) Chesterfield, MO Ascension Church.
Wolkovich, William L. '53 (BO) [2] Norwood, MA St. George Church.
Wolkovits, Paul D. '93 (LA) Manhattan Beach, CA American Martyrs Church.
Woll, Peter J. '44 (CLV) [31] Cleveland, OH Holy Trinity - St. Edward Church; [5] Euclid, OH St. Robert Bellarmine Church; Retired.
Wollering, Carl J. '66 (CIN) [32] Cincinnati, OH Guardian Angels Church; [42] Cincinnati, OH St. Jerome Church.
Wollersheim, David '77 (GLP) Absent on Leave.
Wollesen, Charles A. *s.j.* '52 (P) [L] Portland, OR Jesuit Provincial Office (Oregon Prov.).
Wollet, George H. '32 (MIL) Retired.
Wollmering, Bruce *o.s.b.* '67 (SCL) [I] Collegeville, MN St. John's Abbey, of the Order of St. Benedict.
Wolnik, James G. '79 (STP) Excelsior, Lake Minnetonka, MN St. John the Baptist Church.
Wolnowski, Kenneth J. '65 (CLV) [10] Lorain, OH St. Peter Church.
Woloszczuk, Wolodymyr '81 (SJP) Retired.
Woloszyk, Ignatius J. '38 (SAG) Retired.
Wolsin, Msgr. Carl J. '45 (PAT) Retired; [P] Chester, NJ Nazareth Village.
Wolski, Adalbert *t.o.r.* '59 (ALT) [F] Hollidaysburg, PA St. Joseph Friary.
Wolski, Mark J. '67 (BUF) [38] Buffalo, NY St. John the Evangelist Church.
Wolter, Allan *o.f.m.* '40 (LA) [R] Santa Barbara, CA Franciscan Friary, Order of Friars Minor (Old Mission).
Wolter, Allan *o.f.m.* '40 (STL) [P] St. Louis, MO Franciscan Friary of St. Anthony of Padua.
Wolter, Martin *o.f.m.* '46 (STL) [P] St. Louis, MO Franciscan Friary of St. Anthony of Padua.
Wolter, Richard J. '59 (STP) Centerville, MN St. Genevieve Church.
Wolter, Thomas '66 (JOL) Elmhurst, IL Mary, Queen of Heaven Church; Elmhurst, IL Elmhurst Memorial Hospital.
Wolters, Gilbert *o.s.b.* '34 (KCK) [H] Atchison, KS St. Benedict's Abbey.
Wolverton, R. Ambrose *o.s.b.* '65 (PRO) [P] Portsmouth, RI Abbey of St. Gregory the Great.
Womack, Emil *c.p.* '44 (DET) [K] Detroit, MI St. Paul of the Cross Community, Congregation of the Passion.
Womack, Warren *c.p.* '49 (CHI) [N] Chicago, IL Passionist Provincial Office.
Won, Msgr. John P. '58 (LA) West Covina, CA St. Christopher Church.
Won, Luke J. '86 (PH) [56] Philadelphia, PA Holy Angels Church.
Wondolowski, Robert '76 (WOR) Absent on Leave.
Wong, Andrew *o.f.m.cap.* '92 (HBG) [2] York, PA St. Joseph Church.
Wong, Christopher '75 (CHI) [203] Chicago, IL St. Therese Catholic Chinese Church.
Wong, George *s.j.* '51 (SJ) [M] Los Gatos, CA California Province of the Society of Jesus, Jesuit Provincial Office; [M] Los Gatos, CA Sacred Heart Jesuit Center.
Wong, Maurice *s.j.* '67 (BGP) [A] Fairfield, CT Fairfield University; [O] Fairfield, CT The Fairfield Jesuit Community-Fairfield University.
Wong, Victor '50 (WDC) [5] Washington, DC St. Anthony Church.
Woo, Henry *s.d.b.* '93 (OAK) [N] Berkeley, CA Salesian Community.
Wood, Dennis A. '68 (SEA) Des Moines, WA St. Philomena Church.
Wood, Drew '73 (GAL) [A] Houston, TX St. Mary's Seminary.
Wood, Edson J. *o.s.a.* '72 (NY) West Point, NY Catholic Chapel of the Most Holy Trinity Church.
Wood, Edson J. *o.s.a.* '72 (PH) [C] Villanova, PA Villanova University.
Wood, Gregg D. *s.j.* '75 (FBK) Chevak, AK Sacred Heart Church; Scammon Bay, AK Blessed Sacrament Church.
Wood, Gregg D. *s.j.* '75 (SEA) [A] Seattle, WA Seattle University.
Wood, Gregg D. *s.j.* '95 (FBK) Hooper Bay, AK Little Flower of Jesus Church.
Wood, James L. '72 (RVC) Bohemia, NY St. John Nepomucene Church.
Wood, John K. *s.j.* '50 (SPK) [K] Spokane, WA Regis Community.
Wood, John M. '83 (SY) [1] Rome, NY St. John the Baptist Church.
Wood, Joseph *o.s.b.* '56 (B) [C] Jerome, ID Ascension Priory.
Wood, Kenneth E. '89 (RIC) Harrisonburg, VA Blessed Sacrament Church.
Wood, Mark '87 (LR) Fayetteville, AR St. Joseph's Church; Fayetteville, AR St. Thomas Aquinas University Parish Church; [J] Little Rock, AR Catholic Campus Ministries.
Wood, Michael '84 (AMA) Absent on Leave.
Wood, Norbert *o.praem.* '81 (ORG) [H] Silverado, CA Norbertine Fathers.
Wood, Paul A. '80 (BRK) [189] Queens, NY St. Kevin Church; [E] Brooklyn, NY Office of the Superintendent of Schools.
Wood, Paul F. '58 (BRK) Absent on Leave.
Wood, Peter N. '82 (PT) On Leave of Absence.
Wood, Raymond B. '64 (SY) Jamesville, NY St. Mary Church.
Wood, Robert J. '44 (NOR) Retired.
Wood, Robert T. '87 (OKL) Ada, OK St. Joseph Church; [K] Norman, OK Campus Ministry for the Archdiocese of Oklahoma City.
Wood, Robert T. '87 (TLS) Coalgate, OK Blessed Sacrament Church.
Wood, Robert W. '74 (BUF) Elma, NY Annunciation of the Blessed Virgin Mary Church.
Wood, Simon *c.p.* '43 (BAL) [M] Baltimore, MD St. Joseph's Passionist Community.
Wood, William J. *s.j.* '65 (SJ) [B] Santa Clara, CA Santa Clara University.
Wood, William T. *s.j.* '48 (NY) [Z] New York, NY Jesuit Provincial's Office; [Z] New York, NY St. Ignatius Loyola Residence; [DD] New York, NY Catholic Medical Mission Board, Inc.
Woodarek, Richard *c.s.s.* '57 (BO) [W] Waltham, MA Stigmatine Fathers & Brothers Provincial House.
Woodcock, Michael '73 (PMB) Royal Palm Beach, FL Our Lady Queen of the Apostles Church.
Woodeshick, Martin E. '69 (PH) Sharon Hill, PA Holy Spirit Church.
Woodka, Raymond A. *s.s.j.* (GAL) [65] Houston, TX St. Peter the Apostle Church.
Woodland, Stephen '88 (LA) Santa Monica, CA St. Clement Church.
Woodman, Gerald '78 (SEA) Renton, WA St. Anthony's Church.
Woodruff, Mark '72 (SAN) [3] Odessa, TX St. Elizabeth Ann Seton Church.
Woodruff, William F. '82 (NY) Mahopac, NY St. John the Evangelist Church.
Woods, Curtis '80 (SHP) [8] Shreveport, LA St. Joseph Church.
Woods, Msgr. Earl C. '57 (NO) Retired.
Woods, James A. *s.j.* '61 (BO) [C] Chestnut Hill, MA Boston College; [C] Chestnut Hill, MA Boston College; [W] Chestnut Hill, MA The Jesuit Community at Boston College.
Woods, Joseph E. *o.s.f.s.* '44 (WIL) [I] Childs, MD Oblates of St. Francis De Sales.
Woods, Keith A. '95 (WDC) La Plata, MD Sacred Heart Church.
Woods, Lawrence H. '56 (KAL) Retired.
Woods, Michael A. '66 (ATL) On Duty Outside the Archdiocese.
Woods, Michael A. '66 (KNX) Oak Ridge, TN St. Mary Church.
Woods, Patrick F. *c.ss.r.* '75 (BRK) [U] Brooklyn, NY Our Lady of Good Counsel Residence.
Woods, Msgr. Patrick J. '42 (BUF) Arcade, NY SS. Peter and Paul Church; Retired.
Woods, Randall *s.t.* (WDC) [M] University Park, MD Holy Trinity Missionary Cenacle.
Woods, Richard J. *o.p.* '69 (CHI) [N] Chicago, IL Dominicans (Provincial Office).
Woods, Walter J. '69 (BO) [A] Boston, MA St. John's Seminary School of Theology.
Woods, Warren L. '50 (SFR) [34] San Francisco, CA St. Monica Church.
Woodward, John B. *s.j.* '58 (WDC) [E] Washington, DC Gonzaga College High School.
Woolever, James '74 (SY) On Duty Outside the Diocese.
Woollett, D. Mathew '82 (ALX) Pineville, LA Sacred Heart Church.
Woolsey, Msgr. John G. '65 (NY) [60] New York, NY St. John the Martyr Church; [190] Bronx, NY St.

Theresa of the Infant Jesus Church.
Woolson, Herbert *c.pp.s.* '82 (LFT) Winamac, IN St. Peter Church.
Woolway, John S. '80 (LA) Los Nietos, CA Our Lady of Perpetual Help Church.
Woost, David G. (CLV) Concord Twp., OH St. Gabriel Church; [D] Mentor, OH Lake Catholic High.
Woost, Michael G. '84 (CLV) Graduate Studies.
Wooton, Jerry A. '96 (ARL) Leesburg, VA St. John the Apostle Church.
Wopperer, Thomas J. '64 (BUF) [4] Dunkirk, NY St. Elizabeth Ann Seton Church.
Woracek, Msgr. Thomas J. '46 (STL) Webster Groves, MO Mary, Queen of Peace Church.
Worcester, Thomas W. *s.j.* '91 (WOR) [N] Worcester, MA Jesuits of Holy Cross College, Inc.
Worch, Donald P. '67 (WDC) Derwood, MD St. Francis of Assisi Church.
Worczak, Paul F. '68 (OG) Norwood, NY St. Andrew Church.
Wordekemper, Thomas *o.s.b.* '94 (BIS) [A] Richardton, ND Assumption Abbey.
Wordeman, John J. '57 (LEX) Ashland, KY Holy Family Church.
Worland, T. Vincent '56 (SFD) Altamont, IL St. Clare Church; Edgewood, IL St. Anne Church; St. Elmo, IL St. Bonaventure Church; St. Elmo, IL St. Mary Church.
Worm, Paul F. '88 (LR) West Memphis, AR St. Michael's Church.
Worman, Jeremiah F. '67 (GB) Antigo, WI St. Mary Church; Neva, WI St. Wenceslaus Church.
Wormek, Joseph E. '76 (STL) Manchester, MO Christ, Prince of Peace Church.
Worn, G. Peter '77 (SY) Special Assignment; [V] Oswego, NY Newman Foundation, Inc., State University of New York.
Worner, William H. '45 (SFR) Special Assignment; Retired.
Woroniewicz, Michael A. '85 (DET) Royal Oak, MI St. Mary Church.
Worry, Benedict Michael *o.s.b.* (PAT) [M] Morristown, NJ St. Mary's Abbey.
Worry, Benedict Michael *o.s.b.* (TR) Pennington, NJ St. James Church; [R] Princeton, NJ Campus Ministry for the Diocese of Trenton; [R] Princeton, NJ Campus Ministry for the Diocese of Trenton.
Worschak, George D. '78 (PHU) Absent on Leave.
Worsley, Stephen C. '84 (R) New Bern, NC St. Paul Church.
Worster, John '87 (B) Soda Springs, ID St. Mary's Church.
Worthley, John '90 (RVC) Selden, NY St. Margaret of Scotland Church.
Worthy, Donald *o.s.c.* '62 (DET) [H] Pontiac, MI St. Joseph Mercy - Oakland.
Wortmann, Edgar J. '48 (OM) [10] Omaha, NE Blessed Sacrament Church.
Wortmann, Joseph F. '58 (NEW) [B] South Orange, NJ Seton Hall University; [C] West Orange, NJ Seton Hall Preparatory School.
Worzalla, Dennis A. '50 (GB) Retired.
Worzalla, Dennis A. '50 (LC) [4] Stevens Point, WI St. Peter Church.
Wosman, Richard *s.m.* '92 (STL) [F] Kirkwood, MO Vianney High School.
Woster, Msgr. Michael '82 (RC) [D] Rapid City, SD Priest Retirement and Aid Association.
Wotelko, Matthew S. *o.s.b.* '67 (NEW) [N] Newark, NJ Newark Abbey.
Woulfe, Cornelius C. *c.s.sp.* '44 (NY) [4] Kingston, NY St. Mary Church; Kingston, NY Kingston City Hospital.
Woy, Richard '79 (BAL) [51] Baltimore, MD St. Lawrence Church; Special Assignment.
Woytyna, Chistopher *o.s.b.m.* '61 (STF) Long Island City, NY Holy Cross Church; [E] New York, NY Provincialate of Basilian Fathers.
Wozniak, Aloysius A. '52 (LC) Retired.
Wozniak, Anthony A. '59 (GBG) Fairchance, PA SS. Cyril and Methodius Church.
Wozniak, Casimir J. '68 (E) [B] Erie, PA Gannon University.
Wozniak, Louis B. '49 (GRY) Retired.
Wozniak, Msgr. Louis J. '51 (AUS) Georgetown, TX St. Helen's Church.
Wozniak, Philip *o.f.m.conv.* '58 (CHI) [O] Chicago, IL Mother of Good Counsel Convent.
Wozniak, Richard *c.m.f.* '52 (ORG) [2] Orange, CA La Purisima Church.
Wozniak, Robert A. '88 (BUF) Amherst, NY St. Leo Church; [4] Cheektowaga, NY St. Josaphat Church.
Wozniak, Ronald E. *s.j.* '77 (BO) [W] Boston, MA The Society of Jesus of New England-Provincial Offices.
Wozniak, Timothy J. '74 (STP) St. Paul Park, MN St. Thomas Aquinas Church.
Woznick, Michael *o.f.m.conv.* '72 (LA) Hermosa Beach, CA Our Lady of Guadalupe Church.
Wozniczka, Stephen Z. *o.s.p.p.e.* '60 (PH) [Z] Doylestown, PA Pauline Fathers Monastery, Shrine of Our Lady of Czestochowa.
Wozny, William J. '48 (CHI) Retired.
Wraszczak, Chester '43 (P) Retired.
Wray, Joseph M. '96 (OM) [1] Omaha, NE St. Cecilia's Cathedral.
Wreisner, Hugh *o.p.* '88 (MAD) [3] Madison, WI Blessed Sacrament Church.
Wreisner, Hugo *o.p.* '88 (MAD) [G] Madison, WI St. Marys Hospital Medical Center.
Wren, Benjamin L. *s.j.* '61 (NO) [C] New Orleans, LA Loyola University.
Wrenn, Lawrence '77 (WH) Princeton, WV Sacred Heart Church; [Q] Athens, WV Concord College Newman Center.
Wrenn, Lawrence G. '53 (HRT) Special and other (Arch)Diocesan Assignment.
Wrenn, Msgr. Michael J. '61 (NY) [58] New York, NY St. John the Evangelist Church.
Wright, Addison G. *s.s.* '60 (BAL) [M] Baltimore, MD Sulpician Provincial House.
Wright, Arthur F. '67 (BO) [7] Cambridge, MA Immaculate Conception Church.
Wright, Charles *o.s.b.* '70 (SD) [H] Oceanside, CA Prince of Peace Abbey, Benet Hill.
Wright, D. Ralph *o.s.b.* '70 (STL) [1] Creve Coeur, MO St. Anselm Church; [F] Creve Coeur, MO St. Louis Priory School; [P] St. Louis, MO The Abbey of St. Mary and St. Louis.
Wright, David F. *o.p.* '68 (CHI) [N] Chicago, IL Dominicans (Provincial Office); [N] Chicago, IL Dominicans (Provincial Office); [N] Chicago, IL Dominicans (Provincial Office).
Wright, Msgr. Edward S. '54 (RCK) North Aurora, IL Blessed Sacrament Church.
Wright, Francis W. *c.s.sp.* (WDC) [V] Washington, DC Holy Childhood Association.
Wright, Gerald *o.m.v.* '80 (BO) [B] Boston, MA Oblate Provincialate.
Wright, James B. '69 (DET) Farmington Hills, MI St. Alexander Church.
Wright, John '56 (CHY) [E] Powell, WY NorthWest College.
Wright, John A. '56 (CHY) Powell, WY St. Barbara Church.
Wright, John A. '82 (MAN) Hillsborough, NH St. Mary Church.
Wright, John C. *s.j.* '55 (SJ) [M] Los Gatos, CA Sacred Heart Jesuit Center.
Wright, John H. *s.j.* '52 (OAK) [A] Berkeley, CA The Jesuit School of Theology at Berkeley; [N] Berkeley, CA Jesuit Community at Jesuit School of Theology at Berkeley.
Wright, John H. '62 (HBG) [H] Ephrata, PA St. Clement's Mission House.
Wright, John J. '78 (CLV) [Q] Cleveland, OH Motherhouse and Novitiate of the Sisters of the Holy Spirit; [AA] Cleveland, OH The Greater Cleveland/Akron Corporation United for Education.
Wright, Msgr. John M. '62 (IND) Military Chaplains.
Wright, Joseph R. *c.m.* (BAL) Emmitsburg, MD St. Joseph Church; [M] Emmitsburg, MD Vincentian House.
Wright, Michael '95 (SEA) [2] Tacoma, WA St. Charles Borromeo Church.
Wright, Patrick J. *v.f.* '54 (SFD) [5] Springfield, IL St. Agnes Church.
Wright, Richard J. '45 (PH) Ardmore, PA St. Colman Church; Retired.
Wright, Robert '54 (SY) Retired.
Wright, Robert E. *o.m.i.* '74 (SAT) [B] San Antonio, TX George Sexton House of Studies; [C] San Antonio, TX Oblate School of Theology.
Wright, Robert P. '54 (SY) [S] Syracuse, NY St. Pius X Home, Inc.
Wright, Msgr. Rupert A. '56 (BUF) Williamsville, NY St. Gregory the Great Church.
Wright, Tennant C. *s.j.* '62 (SJ) [B] Santa Clara, CA Santa Clara University.
Wright, Thomas E. '55 (RNO) Yerington, NV Holy Family Church.
Wright, Vincent L. '57 (BUF) Retired.
Wright, Warren J. *s.j.* '82 (SFR) [E] San Francisco, CA St. Ignatius College Preparatory (Coed); [N] San Francisco, CA Jesuit Community at St. Ignatius College Preparatory.
Wright, William A. '65 (PH) [2] Drexel Hill, PA St. Bernadette Church.
Wrightson, Mark J. *o.s.f.s.* '86 (WIL) [B] Wilmington, DE Salesianum School.
Wrigley, Franklin '52 (OKL) Special Assignment; [I] Oklahoma City, OK House of Prayer for Priests.
Wrobel, Julian *c.s.sp.* '43 (ALX) Natchitoches, LA St. Anthony Church.
Wrobleski, Edward D. *c.s.p.* '62 (LA) [86] Los Angeles, CA St. Paul the Apostle Church.
Wroblewski, Anthony *o.m.i.* '95 (DUL) [3] Duluth, MN Holy Family, Church.
Wroblewski, Edward D. *c.s.p.* '62 (NY) [Z] Scarsdale, NY Paulist Fathers Generalate.
Wroblewski, Edward M. *m.m.* '52 (NY) [Z] Maryknoll, NY Maryknoll Fathers and Brothers.
Wroblewski, John J. '92 (NY) [227] Staten Island, NY Sacred Heart Church.
Wroblewski, Lawrence J. *s.j.* '74 (ROC) [B] Rochester, NY McQuaid Jesuit High School.
Wroblewski, Marion *c.r.* '65 (CHI) [192] Chicago, IL St. Stanislaus, Bishop and Martyr Church.
Wronski, John C. *s.j.* (CHI) [C] Chicago, IL Jesuit Community at Loyola University of Chicago.
Wrozek, Timothy A. '88 (FTW) Wabash, IN St. Bernard Church.
Wrynn, John '70 (NEW) [B] Jersey City, NJ Saint Peter's College.
Wrynn, John F. *s.j.* '70 (NEW) [N] Jersey City, NJ Jesuits of Saint Peter's College, Inc.
Wtorek, Krzysztof '94 (CAM) Haddon Heights, NJ St. Rose's Church.
Wtulich, John S. '72 (BRK) [26] Brooklyn, NY St. Catharine of Alexandria Church.
Wu, Stanley '76 (SFR) [51] San Francisco, CA St. Thomas, The Apostle Church.
Wudarski, Dariusz '96 (SPR) Longmeadow, MA St. Mary's Church.
Wuellner, Bernard J. *s.j.* '33 (DET) [P] Clarkston, MI Colombiere Center.
Wuellner, George E. '54 (PEO) Seymour, IL St. Boniface Church; Retired.
Wuerth, James E. *m.s.f.* '71 (SAT) Seguin, TX Our Lady of Guadalupe Church.
Wuertz, Richard A. '68 (YAK) Richland, WA Christ the King Church.
Wuest, George *s.j.* '58 (PHX) El Mirage, AZ Santa Teresita Church.
Wueste, Andy *o.m.i.* '54 (SAN) [E] San Angelo, TX Christ the King Retreat Center.
Wulinski, Stanley F. '80 (BRK) Released from Diocesan Assignment.
Wulsch, Michael A. '72 (CHI) [140] Chicago, IL St. Monica Church.
Wummer, Robert P. '56 (WDC) Fort Washington, MD St. Ignatius Church.
Wunderlich, Dale P. '74 (STL) [2] St. Louis, MO Epiphany of Our Lord Church.
Wunderlich, Daniel F. '87 (LAN) On Duty Outside the Diocese.
Wunderlich, Donulus *o.f.m.* (SFD) [K] Sherman, IL Our Lady of Angels Friary.
Wurm, Robert L. '60 (DET) Ferndale, MI St. James Church.
Wurm, William *o.s.b.* '79 (GBG) [H] Latrobe, PA Saint Vincent Archabbey.
Wurst, Wayne H. '80 (CHI) Other Assignments.
Wurth, M. Philip *o.c.d.* '59 (DAL) [K] Dallas, TX Mount Carmel Center.
Wurtz, Camillus *o.s.b.* '52 (KCK) [E] Atchison, KS Maur Hill Prep School.
Wurtz, Msgr. Robert C. '58 (BUF) [1] Lackawanna, NY Basilica of Our Lady of Victory; [J] Lackawanna, NY Baker Victory Services; [J] Lackawanna, NY Our Lady of Victory Infant Home; [K] Lackawanna, NY Our Lady of Victory Hospital; [T] Lackawanna, NY Our Lady of Victory Homes of Charity.
Wurz, George E. '60 (SY) [3] Oswego, NY St. Louis Church; [6] Oswego, NY St. Peter Church.
Wurzel, Richard T. '59 (TOL) Sylvania, OH St. Joseph Church.
Wutscheck, John J. '61 (MIL) [2] Milwaukee, WI St. Adalbert Church.
Wyckoff, Eric T. *s.d.b.* '92 (NO) [D] Marrero, LA Archbishop Shaw High School.
Wyczawski, Stanley '73 (DET) Port Huron, MI St. Mary Church.
Wydeven, John (OAK) Military Chaplains.
Wyen, Larry *c.pp.s.* '69 (CIN) St. Henry, OH St. Henry Church.
Wyffels, Robert J. '60 (NU) Winsted, MN Holy Trinity Church; Winsted, MN Holy Trinity Church.
Wylie, Stephen '41 (DOD) Retired.
Wymelenberg, M. John *s.j.* '60 (OM) [K] Omaha, NE Jesuit Community At Creighton University.
Wymes, John F. *m.m.* '54 (NY) [Z] Maryknoll, NY Maryknoll Fathers and Brothers.
Wymes, John F. *m.m.* '54 (RVC) Malverne, NY Our Lady of Lourdes Church.
Wynants, Paul G. *c.i.c.m.* (ARL) [N] Vienna, VA Mount Tabor Society, Inc.
Wyndaele, Bill *c.i.c.m.* '59 (ARL) [J] Arlington, VA Missionhurst, C.I.C.M.-Central House and Provincialate.
Wyndham, Thomas F. '69 (BO) [4] Weymouth, MA St. Jerome Church.
Wynne, James J. *o.m.i.* '55 (STP) [N] St. Paul, MN Oblate Provincial Offices; [N] St. Paul, MN Oblate Residence.
Wynne, Robert F. *m.m.* '68 (HON) Kamuela, HI Church of the Annunciation; [H] Honolulu, HI Maryknoll Fathers House.
Wynne, William J. *o.s.a.* '44 (BO) [C] North Andover, MA Merrimack College.
Wynnycky, John P. '92 (DET) Pontiac, MI St. Michael Church; Pontiac, MI St. Vincent de Paul Church.
Wypych, Andrew P. (CHI) [60] Chicago, IL Five Holy

Martyrs Church; [163] Chicago, IL St. Pancratius Church.
Wyrsch, Thomas W. '78 (STL) [16] St. Louis, MO Resurrection of Our Lord Church.
Wyse, Alexander *o.f.m.* '43 (BO) [BB] Boston, MA St. Anthony Shrine.
Wyse, James B. '87 (GR) [3] Muskegon, MI St. Jean Baptiste Church.
Wysochansky, Constantine *o.s.b.m.* '62 (STN) Hamtramck, MI Immaculate Conception of B.V.M. Church.
Wysochansky, Demetrius *o.s.b.m.* '59 (STN) [7] Palos Park, IL Nativity of B. V. M. Church.
Wysochansky, John '57 (PHU) St. Clair, PA St. Nicholas Church; St. Clair, PA Holy Trinity Church.
Wysochansky, Walter J. '64 (SJP) [5] Austintown, OH St. Anne Church.
Wysocki, James R. '67 (DET) Marine City, MI Holy Cross Church.
Wysocki, Joseph A. '71 (SCR) On Duty Outside the Diocese.
Wysocki, Marek (NEW) [2] Elizabeth, NJ St. Adalbert's Church.
Wysocki, Paul J. '64 (CLV) Orrville, OH St. Agnes Church.
Wysocki, Paul P. '54 (HRT) [3] New Britain, CT Sacred Heart of Jesus Church.
Wysong, William H. '72 (CIN) [J] Cincinnati, OH St. Rita School for the Deaf.
Wyszynski, Darius W. '58 (LAN) [5] Jackson, MI St. Stanislaus Kostka Church.
Wytish, Michael Jude '90 (PBR) Monroeville, PA Church of the Resurrection.
Wytrwal, Alexander J. '50 (DET) New Boston, MI St. Stephen Church.
Wyvill, Christopher *o.s.b.* '65 (WDC) [M] Washington, DC St. Anselm's Abbey.
Wyzgoski, Richard F. '59 (DET) [3] Birmingham, MI Our Lady Queen of Martyrs Church.
Wyzykiewicz, Richard *sch.p.* (PH) [Z] Devon, PA Piarist Fathers (Order of the Pious Schools).
Wyzykiewicz, Richard S. *sch.p.* (PH) [G] Devon, PA Devon Preparatory School; [Z] Devon, PA Piarist Fathers (Order of the Pious Schools).

X

Xavier, Antony '60 (RVC) Manhasset, NY North Shore Univ. Hospital.
Xavier, Francis '41 (WOR) [N] Still River, MA Benedictine Monks, St. Benedict Abbey.
Xavier, Goodwin (SAC) Downieville, CA Immaculate Conception Church.
Xuereb, Paul '45 (DET) Armada, MI St. Mary Mystical Rose Church.
Xuereb, Publius '68 (FWT) The Colony, TX Holy Cross Church.

Y

Yabes, Arthur *s.v.d.* (SJ) [15] San Jose, CA St. Maria Goretti Church.
Yablonsky, Gabriel '59 (Y) Retired.
Yackanich, Eugene P. '65 (PBR) Munhall, PA St. Elias Church.
Yacobi, Francis *o.f.m.cap.* '90 (WDC) [B] Washington, DC St. Francis Friary-Capuchin College.
Yadrich, John B. '51 (KCK) Retired.
Yadron, Michael J. '83 (GRY) [3] Michigan City, IN Queen of All Saints Church.
Yadron, Raymond A. '63 (CHI) Palatine, IL St. Thomas of Villanova Church.
Yaeger, Gerald '66 (PHX) Prescott Valley, AZ St. Germaine Church.
Yaeger, Joseph J. (R) Newton Grove, NC Our Lady of Guadalupe Church.
Yagaza, Severine (ROC) [M] Rochester, NY Diocesan Office of Campus Ministry.
Yager, James P. '41 (GR) Retired.
Yagesh, Richard C. '78 (PIT) Military Chaplains.
Yaghi, Milad T. *m.l.m.* '88 (OLL) Houston, TX Our Lady of the Cedars Mission Church; [A] San Antonio, TX The Congregation of Maronite Lebanese Missionaries.
Yagley, Carl J. '53 (DET) Centerline, MI St. Clement Church.
Yahn, George '50 (SB) Retired.
Yahner, Gordon A. '63 (CLV) [7] Akron, OH St. Hilary Church.
Yakaitis, Michael T. '78 (CHI) [21] Chicago, IL St. Barbara Church.
Yaksick, Michael L. '94 (PIT) Castle Shannon, PA St. Anne Church.
Yallaly, Jules G. *c.m.* '36 (STL) [K] Bridgeton, MO De Paul Health Center; [P] St. Louis, MO Vincentian Bellerive Residence.
Yamada, John *ss.cc.* '71 (FR) [K] Fairhaven, MA Sacred Hearts Provincial House.
Yanas, John '84 (ALB) [5] Albany, NY St. Catherine of Siena Church; Special Assignment; [H] Albany, NY Mercycare Corporation, St. Peter's Hospital.
Yandrisevits, Philip *m.s.c.* '42 (ALN) [K] Reading, PA Missionaries of the Sacred Heart.
Yanez, Horacio V. '75 (SEA) Bellevue, WA St. Louise Church.
Yanez, Jaime *o.f.m.* '47 (ELP) [B] El Paso, TX St. Anthony's School of Theology.
Yanez, Jose *c.m.* (SJN) [55] San Juan, PR Sagrado Corazon de Jesus Church.
Yang, Paul '48 (RVC) Retired.
Yangas, Peter M. '64 (CHI) Schaumburg, IL St. Marcelline Church.
Yaniak, Frank J. '49 (MIL) [51] Milwaukee, WI St. Mary Magdalen Church.
Yankauskas, Albin J. '51 (WOR) Retired.
Yankevitch, Robert *s.j.* '69 (PH) [82] Philadelphia, PA Old St. Joseph's Church.
Yannarell, James J. *s.j.* '71 (NY) [Z] New York, NY Jesuit Provincial's Office; [Z] New York, NY Xavier Jesuit Community.
Yanos, Richard M. '83 (CHI) Lake Zurich, IL St. Francis de Sales Church.
Yanovski, Stepan '90 (STF) Amsterdam, NY St. Nicholas Church; Little Falls, NY St. Nicholas Church.
Yanus, Gary D. '81 (CLV) [33] Cleveland, OH St. Ignatius Church.
Yaoch, Felix K. *s.j.* '67 (CI) Koror, FM Sacred Heart Church; [C] Koror, Palau, PW Manresa Jesuit House.
Yarbrough, Michael H. '80 (SAT) Jourdanton, TX St. Matthew's Church.
Yarce, Eugenio '92 (SLC) Milford, UT St. Bridget Church.
Yardemian, Dadjad (ARM) [C] Glendale, CA Mekhitarian Educational Foundation.
Yargeau, Ronald G. '73 (SPR) Haydenville, MA St. Mary's Church.
Yarno, Kenneth *c.s.v.* '59 (JOL) St. George, IL St. George Church.
Yarnovitz, Msgr. Robert '57 (PRM) Parma, OH Saint John the Baptist, Cathedral.
Yaroch, Kenneth E. '67 (SAG) Albee, MI St. Mary Church.
Yaroch, Paul *o.f.m.cap.* '64 (MIL) [P] Mount Calvary, WI St. Lawrence Friary.
Yarrish, Msgr. Bernard E. '76 (SCR) On Duty Outside the Diocese.
Yarrosh, Ronald J. '74 (ALN) [8] Reading, PA St. Margaret Church; [O] Kutztown, PA Christopher House.
Yasso, Jacob O. '60 (DET) [69] Detroit, MI Sacred Heart-Chaldean Parish Church.
Yasso, Jacob O. '60 (EST) Detroit, MI Sacred Heart Chaldean Parish Church.
Yast, Robert A. '56 (FTW) [2] Mishawaka, IN St. Joseph Church.
Yastishock, Charles '77 (PSC) Toms River, NJ Our Lady of Perpetual Help Church.
Yaszcz, Thomas A. '75 (SCR) Special Assignment.
Yates, John *c.ss.p.* '54 (SB) Beaumont, CA San Gorgonio Church; [E] Hemet, CA Holy Ghost Fathers.
Yates, Msgr. Robert J. '41 (MIA) Hollywood, FL St. Bernadette Church.
Yates, Msgr. Robert J. '41 (TOL) Retired.
Yates, Simeon *o.f.m.conv.* '63 (STP) [Q] Prior Lake, MN Franciscan Retreat House.
Yatkauskas, Matthew '89 (NY) Croton-on-Hudson, NY Holy Name of Mary Church.
Yavorsky, James A. '34 (CLV) [2] Barberton, OH SS. Cyril and Methodius Church; Retired.
Yavorsky, Stephen T. *s.j.* '77 (DEN) [30] Denver, CO St. Ignatius Loyola Church; [M] Denver, CO Loyola Parish - Jesuit Community.
Ybarra, Manuel *o.f.m.* '86 (WDC) [M] Washington, DC Commissariat of the Holy Land, Franciscan Monastery - Mount St. Sepulchre.
Ycoback, John D. '60 (PBR) [1] Youngstown, OH Assumption of the Blessed Virgin Church.
Yeager, Robert J. '62 (TOL) [B] Oregon, OH Cardinal Stritch High School.
Yeaglin, Armand *o.f.m.cap.* '38 (PIT) Monongahela, PA St. Anthony Church; Washington County, PA Mon Valley Hospital.
Yeazel, J. Robert (SY) Special Assignment; [S] East Syracuse, NY Bishop Grimes Priests Residence.
Yee Mon, Ronald '85 (FAR) Towner, ND St. Cecilia's Church.
Yehl, Msgr. Addison *m.s.* '51 (E) [B] Erie, PA Gannon University.
Yelinko, Flavian G. *o.s.b.* '33 (GBG) [H] Latrobe, PA Saint Vincent Archabbey.
Yelle, Ronald R. '79 (HRT) Granby, CT St. Therese's Church.
Yelovich, Columban *o.f.m.* '47 (STL) [P] St. Louis, MO Franciscan Friary of St. Anthony of Padua.
Yender, Basil *o.s.b.* '71 (RCK) [C] Aurora, IL Marmion Academy; [H] Aurora, IL Marmion Abbey-St. Augustine's Abbey.
Yenkevich, Daniel J. '90 (SCR) On Duty Outside the Diocese.
Yennock, Msgr. Eugene M. '50 (SY) [15] Syracuse, NY St. Daniel Church.
Yenushosky, Daniel J. '77 (ALN) [1] Minersville, PA St. Barbara Church; [2] Minersville, PA St. Francis of Assisi Church.
Yeo, William '58 (NEW) Hackensack, NJ Hackensack Medical Center.
Yesalonia, Dennis J. *s.j.* '85 (BO) [W] Chestnut Hill, MA The Jesuit Community at Boston College.
Yescas, Higinio M. *s.v.d.* '87 (CHI) [B] Techny, IL Divine Word Residence; [N] Chicago, IL Divine Word Theologate.
Yescas, Higinlo M. *s.v.d.* '87 (CHI) [N] Techny, IL Society of the Divine Word, Provincial Headquarter-Chicago Prov.
Yetmar, J. Charles '57 (SC) Sioux Rapids, IA St. Joseph's Church.
Yetsko, Robert K. *t.o.r.* '84 (PIT) [27] Pittsburgh, PA St. Matthew Church.
Yetter, Robert M. '73 (BUF) Swormville, NY St. Mary Church.
Yiengst, Msgr. George B. '62 (BUF) Getzville, NY St. Pius X Church.
Yifthog, Cuthbert '89 (CI) [B] Chuuk, FM Saramen Chuuk Academy.
Yim, Louis H. '57 (HON) [16] Honolulu, HI St. Pius X Church.
Yncierto, Frank S. '75 (LAV) [9] Las Vegas, NV St. Francis de Sales Church.
Yocis, David A. '87 (BGP) [7] Norwalk, CT St. Thomas the Apostle Church; Leave of Absence.
Yock, Peter *o.s.b.* '95 (IND) [J] St. Meinrad, IN St. Meinrad Archabbey.
Yockey, Gregory *o.s.b.* '93 (CC) [H] Sandia, TX Corpus Christi Abbey.
Yockey, John G. '70 (MIL) [67] Milwaukee, WI St. Philip Neri Church; [B] Hales Corners, WI Sacred Heart School of Theology.
Yoelker, James A. '69 (BEL) Washington Park, IL St. Martin of Tours Church.
Yogus, Ronald B. '75 (ALT) [4] Portage, PA St. John the Baptist Church; Cresson, PA State Correctional Institution.
Yohe, Robert A. '89 (HBG) [1] Mount Carmel, PA Divine Redeemer Church.
Yonkovig, John R. '77 (OG) [5] Plattsburgh, NY St. Peter Church.
Yonson, Wenceslaus '46 (BRK) Retired.
Yontz, Msgr. George W. '59 (STU) [7] Steubenville, OH St. Peter's Church; [9] Steubenville, OH St. Stanislaus Church.
Yontz, Msgr. William C. '50 (STU) Byesville, OH Holy Trinity Church.
Yore, Lambert *o.carm.* '45 (WDC) [B] Washington, DC Whitefriars Hall.
Yori, Robert '61 (CAM) Woodbine, NJ St. Casimir's Church; Woodbine, NJ State Colony.
York, Edward '47 (WCH) Retired.
York, James E. '40 (PH) Retired.
York, Kenneth J. *j.c.l.* '88 (BEL) Smithton, IL St. John the Baptist Church.
York, Patrick G. '90 (WCH) Frontenac, KS Sacred Heart Church; [K] Pittsburg, KS St. Pius X Center (Pittsburg State University).
York, Paul H. '64 (LIN) Plattsmouth, NE Church of the Holy Spirit.
York, Richard R. '73 (PH) [27] Philadelphia, PA St. Bridget Church; [DD] Philadelphia, PA Newman Apostolate; [DD] Philadelphia, PA Newman Apostolate.
York, Vincent P. '68 (ALN) Fountain Hill, PA St. Ursula Church.
Yossa, Kenneth F. '88 (ROM) Special Assignment.
Yost, Charles *s.c.j.* '58 (JKS) Hernando, MS Holy Spirit Church; [E] Nesbit, MS St. Michael Community House.
Yost, Herbert C. *c.s.c.* '75 (FTW) [J] South Bend, IN Congregation of Holy Cross Indiana Province Provincial House.
Yost, Richard J. *o.s.f.s.* '76 (DET) Royal Oak, MI St. Mary Church; [Q] Warren, MI St. John's Deaf Center.
Young, Anthony J. '44 (MAD) Retired.
Young, Arthur *o.f.m.conv.* (LSC) [D] Mesilla Park, NM Holy Cross Retreat and Friary.
Young, Bernard L. '63 (NO) Military Chaplains.
Young, Bernard L. '63 (PHX) Phoenix, AZ United States Veterans Affairs Medical Center.
Young, Carl A. '53 (NEW) Retired.
Young, Charles H., Jr. '43 (BAL) [68] Baltimore, MD Our Lady of Hope Church.
Young, Msgr. Charles P. '50 (SD) [4] Chula Vista, CA St. Rose of Lima Church; Retired.
Young, Clyde *o.f.m.* '54 (CIN) [C] Cincinnati, OH St. Anthony Shrine, Francisan Candidacy.
Young, Daniel A. '95 (BUF) Harris Hill, NY Nativity of the Blessed Virgin Mary Church.
Young, David (MI) Special Assignment.
Young, David E. '95 (COL) [37] Columbus, OH St. Peter Church.
Young, Dennis M. (HBG) Lebanon, PA Veterans Administration Hospital.
Young, Dennis M. '80 (HBG) Annville, PA St. Paul the Apostle Church.

Young, Dennis M. '80 (STA) On Duty Outside the Diocese.
Young, DeSales *o.f.m.cap.* '48 (PIT) [N] Pittsburgh, PA St. Augustine Friary.
Young, Dismas *o.f.m.cap.* '66 (GBG) Export, PA St. Mary Church.
Young, Dominic '79 (LFT) Monterey, IN St. Anne Church.
Young, Edward '83 (STF) [A] Stamford, CT St. Basil College.
Young, Edward J. '53 (SC) Retired.
Young, Eugene '86 (PHX) [1] Scottsdale, AZ Blessed Sacrament Church.
Young, Frank '70 (SY) North Syracuse, NY St. Rose of Lima Church.
Young, Gary *c.r.* '76 (CHI) [D] Chicago, IL Weber High School.
Young, Gary *c.r.* '76 (L) [M] Nazareth, KY Generalate, Motherhouse and Novitiate of the Sisters of Charity of Nazareth.
Young, Gerald A. '72 (DEN) Wray, CO St. Andrew Church; Yuma, CO St. John Church.
Young, Gerald A. '72 (LA) On Duty Outside the Archdiocese.
Young, Gerard F. '63 (BR) [15] Baton Rouge, LA Most Blessed Sacrament Church.
Young, James *s.m.* '45 (FWT) [A] Fort Worth, TX Nolan Catholic High School; [I] Fort Worth, TX Provincialate, Our Lady of Victory Center.
Young, Msgr. James E. '74 (TYL) Nacogdoches, TX Sacred Heart Church.
Young, James G. '69 (PIT) Washington, PA Immaculate Conception Church.
Young, Jerome *o.s.b.* '86 (P) [L] St. Benedict, OR Mt. Angel Abbey.
Young, John *s.c.j.* '74 (JKS) Olive Branch, MS Queen of Peace Church.
Young, John E. '57 (KAL) South Haven, MI St. Basil Church.
Young, Msgr. John M. '47 (LA) Retired.
Young, Larry '81 (OAK) Pittsburg, CA Good Shepherd Church.
Young, Peter '70 (SP) [5] St. Petersburg, FL St. Joseph Church; [5] St. Petersburg, FL St. Joseph Church.
Young, Peter G. '47 (PRO) [2] North Providence, RI St. Lawrence's Church; Retired.
Young, Peter G. '59 (ALB) Bolton Landing, NY Blessed Sacrament Church.
Young, Richard *o.f.m.* '95 (ATL) [1] Atlanta, GA Cathedral of Christ the King.
Young, Richard *o.f.m.* '95 (LSC) Roswell, NM St. Peter Church; Roswell, NM St. John's Church.
Young, Robert (BRK) [U] Douglaston, NY Bishop Mugavero Residence.
Young, Robert '94 (SP) [12] Tampa, FL St. Mary Church.
Young, Robert F. *s.j.* '58 (SCR) [C] Scranton, PA University of Scranton.
Young, Ronald *o.m.i.* '88 (SAT) [M] San Antonio, TX De Mazenod House.
Young, Ronald E. '75 (DAV) Clinton, IA Jesus Christ, Prince of Peace Church.
Young, Ronald W. *o.m.i.* '88 (SAT) [C] San Antonio, TX Oblate School of Theology.
Young, Samuel V., Jr. '90 (BAL) [68] Baltimore, MD Our Lady of Hope Church.
Young, Msgr. Terry W. '72 (ATL) Duluth, GA St. Benedict Church.
Young, Valentine *o.f.m.cap.* '49 (STL) [54] St. Louis, MO St. Patrick Church; [P] St. Louis, MO St. Patrick Friary; [W] St. Louis, MO Catholic Information Center.
Young, Valentine *o.f.m.* '56 (GLP) Houck, AZ St. John Church.
Young, Vincent J. *o.m.v.* '78 (SCR) [M] Little Meadows, PA St. Joseph's House.
Young, Walter J. *s.j.* '65 (BGP) [O] Fairfield, CT The Fairfield Jesuit Community-Fairfield University.
Young, William *s.s.s.* '64 (CLV) Highland Heights, OH St. Paschal Baylon Church.
Young, William '76 (SFR) Absent on Leave.
Young, William E. '90 (NY) On Duty Outside the Archdiocese.
Young, William E. '90 (SFE) Questa, NM St. Anthony Church.
Young, William J. *c.s.b.* '51 (GAL) [C] Houston, TX University of St. Thomas; [Q] Houston, TX Residence of the Basilian Fathers of the University of St. Thomas.
Young, William L., III '70 (GAL) [76] Houston, TX St. Thomas More Church.
Young, William T. *s.s.s.* '64 (CLV) [P] Cleveland, OH Blessed Sacrament Community.
Young, William W. '76 (SFR) [35] San Francisco, CA Most Holy Redeemer Church.
Youngberg, Vincent *c.p.* '67 (NY) [Z] Pelham Manor, NY St. Vincent's Residence.
Youngs, Fred '90 (BR) Baker, LA St. Isidore the Farmer Church.
Youtz, Msgr. Richard A. '66 (HBG) [4] Lancaster, PA St. John Neumann Church.
Yrarrazaval, Diego J. *c.s.c.* '84 (FTW) [J] South Bend, IN Congregation of Holy Cross Indiana Province Provincial House.
Yrigan, Msgr. Pedro '47 (ORG) Retired.
Yslas, Martin *o.s.b.* '87 (LA) [R] Valyermo, CA St. Andrew's Abbey.
Ytsen, Robert A. *s.j.* '82 (CHI) [D] Wilmette, IL Loyola Academy.
Yu, Reynaldo '83 (SEA) [4] Vancouver, WA St. Joseph Church.
Yudin, Raynald E. *o.f.m.conv.* '62 (SY) [2] Syracuse, NY Assumption B.V.M. Church.
Yuen, Thomas '58 (SCR) [21] Scranton, PA St. Patrick's Church.
Yuhaus, Cassian J. *c.p.* '51 (SCR) [M] Scranton, PA Saint Ann's Passionist Monastery; [R] Clarks Summit, PA Ministry for Religious Research and Consultancy.
Yulfo, Nestor '92 (SJN) [26] Bayamon, PR Santo Domingo De Guzman Church.
Yunk, Msgr. Michael J. '57 (BUF) [4] Lockport, NY St. Mary Church.
Yurchak, Thomas D. '76 (P) Canby, OR St. Patrick Church.
Yurco, Roy *ss.cc.* '62 (FR) [J] Fairhaven, MA Our Lady's Haven of Fairhaven Inc.; [K] Fairhaven, MA Sacred Hearts Provincial House.
Yurgel, Robert *o.f.m.cap.* '96 (NY) [Z] New York, NY Immaculate Conception Friary.
Yurista, Michael (PSC) Absent on Sick Leave.
Yurko, William '48 (Y) [4] Youngstown, OH Immaculate Heart of Mary Church; Retired.
Yurkovic, Dale E. '91 (GF) Livingston, MT St. Mary's Church.
Yuse, Raymond B. '58 (HRT) Retired.

Z

Zabala, Efrain '67 (CGS) [12] Barrio Rio Canas, PR Santisima Trinidad Church.
Zabala, Luis *o.f.m.* (SJN) [52] San Juan, PR Resurreccion del Senor Church; [5] Toa Alta, PR N. Sra. de la Providencia Church.
Zaballa, Pedro L. (SJN) [D] San Juan, PR Centro Medico de P.R.
Zabelskas, John A. '56 (GAL) Highlands, TX St. Jude Thaddeus Church.
Zabicki, Paul '53 (BAL) [M] Ellicott City, MD Order of Friars Minor Conventual.
Zabinski, Claude A. *o.f.m.* '40 (GB) Eland, WI St. William Church; Wittenberg, WI Holy Family Church.
Zabler, Charles G. '77 (MIL) West Allis, WI West Allis Memorial Hospital.
Zablotny Carl '81 (SJP) Absent on Leave.
Zaborowski, Edward (CC) [1] Beeville, TX Our Lady of Victory Church; [3] Beeville, TX St. James Church.
Zabowski, Theodore P. '70 (PIT) Washington, PA Immaculate Conception Church.
Zabrocki, Patrick '88 (GF) Havre, MT St. Jude Thaddeus Church.
Zabrocki, Stephen J. '89 (GF) Wolf Point, MT Immaculate Conception Church.
Zaccagnini, Kenneth G. '82 (GBG) Derry, PA St. Joseph Church.
Zaccardo Peter J. '64 (NEW) Scotch Plains, NJ St. Bartholomew Church.
Zaccone, Paul C. '87 (OM) St. James, NE SS. Philip and James Church; Wynot, NE Sacred Heart Church.
Zach, Charles *o.s.b.* '73 (OM) [C] Elkhorn, NE Mount Michael High School; [K] Elkhorn, NE Mount Michael Abbey.
Zach, Hilary *o.f.m.cap.* '49 (MIL) [K] Fond du Lac, WI Genesys HealthCare of Fond du Lac, Inc.; [P] Mount Calvary, WI St. Lawrence Friary.
Zach, Kenneth M. '81 (RVC) Absent on Leave.
Zach, Placidus *o.s.b.* '56 (P) [L] St. Benedict, OR Mt. Angel Abbey.
Zach, Roger *o.f.m.cap.* '48 (MIL) [P] Mount Calvary, WI St. Lawrence Friary.
Zachar, Msgr. Albert L. '39 (DUB) Retired.
Zachariadis, Nicholas '86 (VNN) [A] Newberry Springs, CA Holy Resurrection Monastery.
Zacheis, Dennis B. '75 (STL) Krakow, MO St. Gertrude's Church.
Zachman, Clarence *o.m.i.* '48 (BEL) [G] Belleville, IL Shrine of Our Lady of the Snows.
Zack, Timothy '91 (NEW) [N] South Orange, NJ Don Bosco Residence.
Zacker, Mark A. *m.s.c.* '96 (OG) [2] Watertown, NY Our Lady of the Sacred Heart, Missionaries of the Sacred Heart Church.
Zadora, Bill *s.d.s.* '74 (SAT) St. Hedwig, TX Annunciation of the Blessed Virgin Mary Church.
Zadora, Charles J. '67 (BUF) Springville, NY St. Aloysius Church.
Zagar, Janko *o.p.* '48 (OAK) [N] Oakland, CA Dominican Order (Western Province), St. Albert's Priory.
Zagar, John T. '61 (OKL) Retired.
Zagarella, John *o.praem* '86 (PH) [D] Philadelphia, PA St. John Neumann High School.
Zagarella, John C. *o.praem.* '88 (PH) [Z] Philadelphia, PA St. Norbert Priory.
Zagari, Joseph '52 (CC) Retired.
Zagone, Frederick P. *s.j.* '93 (SCR) [C] Scranton, PA University of Scranton.
Zagorc, Francis D. *c.s.c.* '58 (PHX) Grand Canyon, AZ El Cristo Rey Church.
Zagorski, Thomas *o.f.m.conv.* '51 (RNO) Lovelock, NV St. John the Baptist Church.
Zagst, Bernard L. '61 (ALX) Boyce, LA St. Margaret Church.
Zahler, Paul *o.s.b.* '40 (OKL) [L] Shawnee, OK Oklahoma Benedictine Institute on Mental Retardation, Inc.
Zahler, Paul J. *o.s.b.* '62 (OKL) [I] Shawnee, OK St. Gregory's Abbey.
Zahn, George E. '68 (RIC) [14] Richmond, VA St. Paul Church; Richmond, VA MCV Hospital.
Zahn, John H. (LFT) Kewanna, IN St. Ann Church; Rochester, IN St. Joseph Church.
Zahner, William (L) Retired; [L] Louisville, KY Bishop David Apartments.
Zahorchak, Michael '56 (STU) Retired.
Zaiats, Volodymyr '74 (STF) Kerhonkson, NY Holy Trinity Church.
Zaidan, Abdallah E. *m.l.m.* '86 (OLL) Los Angeles, CA Our Lady of Mt. Lebanon-St. Peter Cathedral; Denver, CO Maronite Catholic Community Church; [A] San Antonio, TX The Congregation of Maronite Lebanese Missionaries.
Zajac, Jesse *o.f.m.* '61 (GB) [I] Pulaski, WI Assumption of B.V.M. Friary.
Zajac, Richard E. '76 (BUF) [K] Buffalo, NY Sisters of Charity Hospital of Buffalo, NY.
Zajac, Msgr. Stephen '54 (PSC) Old Forge, PA St. Nicholas Church.
Zajdel, Adam *o.f.m.conv.* '38 (BGP) [6] Danbury, CT Sacred Heart Church.
Zajdel, Bernard *o.f.m.conv.* '64 (GR) [4] Grand Rapids, MI St. Anthony of Padua Church.
Zajdel, Robert J. '80 (PIT) Braddock, PA Good Shepherd Church.
Zak, Msgr. Casimir A. '45 (BUF) Retired; [O] Tonawanda, NY O'Hara Residence.
Zak, Daniel (TOL) Bowling Green, OH St. Thomas More University Parish Church; [N] Bowling Green, OH Bowling Green State University Campus Ministry.
Zak, Steven B. '88 (LA) On Duty Outside the Archdiocese.
Zak, Timothy *s.d.b.* (NEW) [S] South Orange, NJ Salesians of Don Bosco, S.D.B.
Zak, Timothy *s.d.b.* (NY) [Z] New Rochelle, NY Salesian Cooperators of St. John Bosco.
Zakarauskas, Anthony J. '41 (CHI) [141] Chicago, IL Nativity of the Blessed Virgin Mary Church; Retired.
Zakarauskas, Vaclovas '31 (CHI) [141] Chicago, IL Nativity of the Blessed Virgin Mary Church; Retired.
Zake, Louis J. '60 (CHI) [14] Chicago, IL St. Ann Church; [A] Chicago, IL Archbishop Quigley Preparatory Seminary.
Zakens, Michael '45 (ALB) [12] Schenectady, NY St. Mary Church.
Zakowicz, Giles *o.f.m.conv.* '75 (BAL) [M] Ellicott City, MD Order of Friars Minor Conventual.
Zakshesky, Francis '81 (TYL) Absent on Sick Leave.
Zalecki, Dennis M. '76 (CHI) [A] Mundelein, IL University of St. Mary of the Lake-Mundelein Seminary.
Zalecki, Marian *o.s.p.p.e.* '62 (PH) [Z] Doylestown, PA Pauline Fathers Monastery, Shrine of Our Lady of Czestochowa.
Zalenski, Gary '77 (STU) Absent on Leave.
Zaleski, Daniel '80 (DET) Eastpointe, MI St. Veronica Church.
Zalewski, Francis '78 (TR) [20] Trenton, NJ SS. Peter and Paul Church; [23] Trenton, NJ St. Stephen Church.
Zalewski, Thomas *o.carm.* '79 (PMB) [B] Boca Raton, FL Pope John Paul II High School; [G] Boca Raton, FL St. Elias Priory-Order of Carmelites, NY.
Zaloga, Daniel S. '67 (MAR) Iron Mountain, MI St. Mary and St. Joseph Church.
Zalonis, Jerome *m.i.c.* '59 (JOL) Plano, IL St. Mary Church.
Zalonis, John A. '59 (HRT) [1] East Hartford, CT Blessed Sacrament Church.
Zalotay, Joseph '51 (WDC) Derwood, MD St. Francis of Assisi Church.
Zambanini, Julian *o.f.m.conv.* '65 (ALB) [A] Rensselaer, NY Conventual Franciscan Friars.
Zamborsky, Bill '74 (ORL) Mims, FL Holy Spirit Church.
Zamborsky, Leonard J. '76 (CLV) Cleveland Heights, OH St. Louis Church.
Zamborsky, Stephen A. *c.s.sp.* '36 (PH) [Z] Bensalem, PA Congregation of the Holy Ghost Fathers and Brothers.
Zammit, Francis X. '66 (ORL) Bushnell, FL St. Lawrence Church; Special Assignment.
Zammit, Msgr. Joseph J. '56 (NY) [105] New York, NY St. Peter Church; New York, NY New York Police Department.

Zamora, Marcos *c.s.p.* '90 (NY) [41] New York, NY Good Shepherd Church; [104] New York, NY St. Paul the Apostle Church.
Zamorano, Richard '93 (ELP) Pecos, TX Santa Rosa Church.
Zamorski, Msgr. Robert J. '72 (MET) Fords, NJ Our Lady of Peace Church.
Zampelli, Michael *s.j.* '93 (BO) [W] Chestnut Hill, MA The Jesuit Community at Boston College.
Zampino, Ignatius *o.f.m.cap.* '61 (CHL) [10] Charlotte, NC St. Thomas Aquinas Church.
Zamudio, Ruben *o.s.a.* '73 (CC) [4] Laredo, TX Holy Redeemer Church.
Zanatta, Albert *c.r.s.* '74 (HRT) [6] Hartford, CT Sacred Heart Church.
Zanavich, Albert J. '41 (HRT) [1] Ansonia, CT Assumption Church; Retired.
Zancan, Robert D. '82 (BUF) Retired.
Zandri, William A. '45 (RC) Lead, SD St. Patrick's Church.
Zandy, Edward J. '70 (SY) [4] Binghamton, NY St. Christopher Church.
Zanetti, Humberto C. *o.f.m.* '55 (SD) Oceanside, CA St. Mary Star of the Sea Church.
Zang, Richard P. *c.s.c.* (FTW) [J] South Bend, IN Congregation of Holy Cross Indiana Province Provincial House.
Zangari, Salvatore V. '44 (HBG) Retired.
Zaniewski, Jaroslaw *s.d.b.* '93 (NY) [2] Port Chester, NY Corpus Christi Church.
Zaniolo, Michael G. '88 (CHI) [214] Chicago, IL St. William Church; Calumet City, IL St. Andrew the Apostle Church.
Zankl, Angelo *o.s.b.* '26 (SCL) [I] Collegeville, MN St. John's Abbey, of the Order of St. Benedict.
Zanni, Frank '90 (Y) Girard, OH St. Rose Church.
Zanni, James '96 (Y) [8] Canton, OH St. Joseph's Church.
Zanon, Romano '66 (BRK) [239] Queens, NY Sacred Heart Church; [Y] Flushing, NY Mount St. Mary.
Zanon, Salvino *c.s.* '24 (LA) [Q] Sun Valley, CA Villa Scalabrini.
Zanoni, Charles *c.s.* (WDC) [19] Washington, DC Holy Rosary Church.
Zanoni, John '60 (JOL) Lombard, IL Sacred Heart Church.
Zanoni, Richard J. *s.j.* '75 (BUF) [50] Buffalo, NY St. Michael Church; [D] Buffalo, NY Canisius High School.
Zanotti, Charles F. '53 (NY) Glasco, NY St. Joseph Church.
Zanotti, Richard *c.s.* '80 (GAL) [43] Houston, TX St. Leo the Great Church.
Zanotto, Luigi *m.c.c.j.* '68 (LA) Compton, CA St. Albert the Great Church.
Zans, Florentino (SJN) [D] San Juan, PR Centro Medico de P.R.
Zaorski, Edward F. '90 (DET) [2] Detroit, MI All Saints Church; [5] Detroit, MI SS. Andrew and Benedict Church.
Zaorski, Thaddeus L. '40 (MET) [G] Woodbridge, NJ St. Joseph Senior Residence.
Zaorski, Thaddeus L. '40 (NEW) [6] Bayonne, NJ Mt. Carmel Church; Retired.
Zapalac, David J. *c.s.b.* '93 (GAL) [7] Houston, TX St. Anne Church.
Zapalac, William '70 (BWN) Weslaco, TX St. Pius X Church.
Zapata, Antonio '68 (ORG) [3] Anaheim, CA St. Justin Martyr Church.
Zapata, Emiliano *o.p.* '95 (MIA) [18] Miami, FL St. Dominic Church; [B] Miami, FL Barry University.
Zape, Juan de la Cruz '85 (STO) Riverbank, CA St. Frances of Rome Church.
Zapf, Albert L. (PIT) Braddock, PA Good Shepherd Church; Braddock Hills, PA Sacred Heart Church.
Zapfel, Robert E. (BUF) On Duty Outside the Diocese.
Zapotocki, Henry E. '48 (SCR) Tannersville, PA Our Lady of Victory Church.
Zapp, John '72 (Y) Uniontown, OH Holy Spirit Church.
Zappa, James C., Jr. '76 (STP) Burnsville, MN Mary, Mother of the Church.
Zappitelli, Francis R. '62 (PHX) [5] Scottsdale, AZ St. Daniel the Prophet Church.
Zarama, Luis (ATL) Clarkesville, GA St. Mark's Church.
Zarate, Raymond J. *c.pp.s.* '79 (CIN) [57] Cincinnati, OH St. Mark Church.
Zarate-Suarez, Jose Edmundo '96 (SD) Escondido, CA Church of the Resurrection.
Zaratti, Elio '40 (SB) Retired.
Zaratti, Filiberto '40 (CHR) On Duty Outside the Diocese.
Zareski, Joseph S. '80 (SY) Norwich, NY St. Bartholomew the Apostle Church; Oxford, NY St. Joseph Church.
Zarichny, Steven '78 (SJP) [7] Cleveland, OH Ss. Peter and Paul Church.
Zarkoski, Donald *s.d.b.* '62 (MIA) [25] Miami, FL St. Kieran Church.
Zarlenga, Vincent I. *o.p.* '51 (CHI) River Forest, IL St. Vincent Ferrer Priory Church; [N] Chicago, IL Dominicans (Provincial Office).
Zarrilli, Frederick B. '54 (LR) Forrest City, AR St. Francis of Assisi Church.
Zasacki, Robert E. '67 (STP) Robbinsdale, MN Sacred Heart Church.
Zastawny, Kazimierz '57 (BO) [5] Lynn, MA St. Michael Church.
Zastoupil, Stephen R. '61 (BIS) [3] Bismarck, ND Corpus Christi Church.
Zastrow, John A. '56 (LIN) Holdrege, NE All Saints Church.
Zatalava, James D. '70 (ALT) State College, PA Our Lady of Victory Church.
Zatarga, George F. '68 (BRK) [162] Queens, NY Christ the King Church.
Zatina, Gregory E.J. '87 (SPC) Bolivar, MO Sacred Heart Church.
Zaucha, Finian *o.f.m.* '68 (GB) [10] Green Bay, WI St. Mary Church; [I] Green Bay, WI St. Mary of the Angels Friary.
Zavacki, Richard A. '58 (SCR) Kingston, PA St. Hedwig's Church.
Zavaski, William J. '69 (CHI) Arlington Heights, IL St. James Church.
Zavattaro, Gabriel J. *s.d.b.* '34 (SFR) [45] San Francisco, CA SS. Peter and Paul Church.
Zavell, Edward '61 (PRM) Fairview Park, OH St. Mary Magdalene Church.
Zavodny, Msgr. Francis J. '51 (ALN) [4] Allentown, PA St. John the Baptist Church.
Zawacki, Casimir J. '50 (GAY) Retired.
Zawacki, Robert *s.s.j.* (GAL) Huntsville, TX Ellis II Unit; Huntsville, TX Walls Unit; Huntsville, TX Wynne Unit.
Zawacki, Robert P. *s.s.j.* '77 (GAL) Huntsville, TX St. Thomas the Apostle Church.
Zawada, Jerome *o.f.m.* '64 (MIL) [P] Milwaukee, WI Francis and Clare House.
Zawada, Joseph F. *o.c.d.* '64 (STA) [J] Korona, FL Carmelite Fathers House of Prayer.
Zawadzki, Justin '68 (SJ) Los Gatos, CA St. Mary of the Immaculate Conception Church.
Zawadzki, Victor C. '50 (SCR) Hudson, PA St. Joseph's Church.
Zawistanowicz, Norbert J. '49 (CHI) [94] Chicago, IL Immaculate Heart of Mary Church; [161] Chicago, IL Our Lady of Victory Church; Retired.
Zawodniak, Edward J. '47 (SCR) Retired.
Zayas, Antonio '59 (PCE) On Duty Outside the Diocese.
Zayas, Hector '93 (ARE) [3] Utuado, PR Our Lady of Angels Church.
Zazella, Msgr. Thomas J. (PAT) [5] Clifton, NJ SS. Cyril and Methodius Church.
Zbieranski, Roman *o.f.m.* '61 (GB) [3] Manitowoc, WI St. Mary Church.
Zbin, Raphael *o.s.b.* '47 (CLV) [5] Cleveland, OH St. Andrew Church; [P] Cleveland, OH Benedictine Order of Cleveland.
Zborowski, Richard M. '78 (CHI) Ingleside, IL St. Bede Church.
Zdancewicz, Carl *o.f.m.conv.* '77 (ATL) Lithia Springs, GA St. John Vianney Church.
Zdilla, Valentine D. '96 (LA) [2] Oxnard, CA Santa Clara Church.
Zdrodowski, Francis '43 (DET) Retired.
Zebron, Samuel *o.f.m.* '58 (CIN) [L] Centerville, OH The Franciscan at St. Leonard.
Zebrowski, Arnold '73 (VEN) Cape Coral, FL St. Andrew Church.
Zebrowski, Roy *o.f.m.* '58 (GAY) Mio, MI St. Mary Church.
Zec, John J. '70 (BAL) [C] Emmitsburg, MD Mount Saint Mary's College.
Zec, John J. '70 (TR) On Duty Outside the Diocese.
Zeck, George '70 (DUL) Two Harbors, MN Holy Spirit Church.
Zedar, Thomas J. '65 (VEN) Port Charlotte, FL San Antonio Church.
Zeder, Msgr. John M. '54 (SY) Parish, NY St. Ann Church.
Zee, Louis C. '59 (DUB) Blairstown, IA St. John Church; Newhall, IA St. Paul's Church; Van Horne, IA Immaculate Conception Church.
Zeeb, Charles '56 (DET) Retired.
Zega, Eugene M. *o.s.a.* '36 (PH) [111] Philadelphia, PA St. Nicholas of Tolentine Church.
Zegar, David '79 (P) Woodburn, OR St. Luke Church.
Zegers, Msgr. James J. '40 (CAM) Retired.
Zegers, Paul A. *ss.cc.* (HON) Hana, HI St. Mary Church.
Zehe, Ralph *o.f.m.cap.* '50 (PIT) [29] Pittsburgh, PA Our Lady of the Angels Church; Allegheny County, PA Veterans Administration - Aspinwall; Allegheny County, PA Veterans Administration - Oakland.
Zeihen, Joseph N. '50 (MIL) Retired.
Zeis, Gabriel *t.o.r.* '80 (PH) [D] Fairless Hills, PA Conwell-Egan Catholic High School; [Z] Fairless Hills, PA St. Anthony Friary.
Zeisig, B. Thomas '57 (CLV) Cuyahoga Falls, OH St. Eugene Church.
Zeisler, Warren *o.f.m.* '50 (CIN) [M] Cincinnati, OH St. Clement Friary.
Zeitler, Msgr. Edward J. '58 (E) Hermitage, PA Church of Notre Dame.
Zeitler, Msgr. John W. '64 (BUF) Lake View, NY Our Lady of Perpetual Help Church.
Zekas, Msgr. Stanley '49 (STU) Retired.
Zeleznik, Clement *o.s.b.* '59 (CLV) [E] Cleveland, OH Benedictine High School; [P] Cleveland, OH Benedictine Order of Cleveland.
Zelik, Richard J. *o.f.m.cap.* (WH) [2] Charleston, WV St. Anthony's Church; [N] Charleston, WV Capuchins-St. Anthony Friary.
Zelinski, James *o.f.m.cap.* (DET) [K] Detroit, MI St. Mary's Friary.
Zelinski, Thomas *o.f.m.cap.* '72 (FTW) Huntington, IN SS. Peter and Paul Church.
Zelker, Thomas '83 (ALB) Granville, NY Roman Catholic Community of Granville Church.
Zell, Charles Felix *o.c.s.o.* '80 (ATL) [I] Conyers, GA The Monastery of the Holy Spirit.
Zeller, Joseph E. '58 (RC) Timber Lake, SD Holy Cross Church.
Zeller, Leonard H. '73 (BAL) Military Chaplains.
Zelonis, Richard *s.c.j.* '79 (MIL) [N] Racine, WI St. Monica's Senior Citizens Home, Inc.; [P] Hales Corners, WI Sacred Heart Monastery.
Zemaitis, Kestutis '65 (CLV) [N] Cleveland, OH Jennings Hall Inc.
Zeman, Gerald L. '63 (SC) Sutherland, IA Sacred Heart Church.
Zemanick, Peter *o.c.s.o.* '44 (SP) [L] St. Petersburg, FL Bon Secours-Maria Manor Nursing Care Center, Inc.
Zemanick, Peter *o.c.s.o.* '44 (WOR) [N] Spencer, MA St. Joseph's Abbey.
Zemanik, Edward S. '81 (ALN) [1] Easton, PA St. Anthony of Padua Church.
Zembal, Theodore E. *s.j.* '68 (SEA) [A] Seattle, WA Seattle University.
Zembrzuski, Michael *o.s.p.p.e.* '34 (PH) [Z] Doylestown, PA Pauline Fathers Monastery, Shrine of Our Lady of Czestochowa.
Zemeikis, Alfred '36 (NEW) [13] Elizabeth, NJ SS. Peter and Paul's Church.
Zemelko, Edward A. *c.s.b.* '86 (GRY) [K] Merrillville, IN Basilian Fathers Residence.
Zemelko, John J. '87 (GRY) Chesterton, IN St. Patrick Church.
Zemites, Joseph '54 (KCK) On Duty Outside the Archdiocese.
Zemula, Anthony *s.a.c.* '78 (BUF) [O] North Tonawanda, NY Society of the Catholic Apostolate.
Zender, Gary M. '86 (SEA) Enumclaw, WA Sacred Heart of Jesus Church.
Zendzian, Peter W. '79 (BRK) [94] Brooklyn, NY Our Lady of Czestochowa-St. Casimir Church; [T] Brooklyn, NY Catholic Migration & Refugee Office, Catholic Migration Services, Inc.
Zengierski, Patrick '91 (BUF) [2] Cheektowaga, NY Infant of Prague Church.
Zeni, Msgr. Dino M. '59 (BRK) [126] Brooklyn, NY St. Rosalia-Regina Pacis Church.
Zenk, Donald W. '54 (WIN) Twin Lakes, MN St. James Church; Retired.
Zenk, Richard E. '54 (SC) Akron, IA St. Patrick's Church.
Zenkel, Edward B. '62 (ROC) Honeoye, NY St. Mary, Our Lady of the Hills Church.
Zenorini, Henry J. *s.j.* '61 (NY) [Z] New York, NY Xavier Jesuit Community.
Zenozian, Peter (SAT) [T] San Antonio, TX Polish American Priest Association (P.A.P.A.).
Zens, Roger A. '57 (MIL) Retired.
Zensen, Gerald '24 (SC) Mapleton, IA St. Mary's Church.
Zensen, Gerald F. '49 (SC) Retired.
Zenz, Msgr. John P. (DET) Special Assignment; [Q] Detroit, MI Catholic Community Services of the Archdiocese of Detroit, Inc.; [T] Detroit, MI Christ Child Society.
Zenz, Louis '39 (FTW) Retired; [H] Fort Wayne, IN Saint Anne Home & Retirement Community.
Zepczyk, Gabriel C. '62 (SUP) Ino, WI St. Florian Church; Moquah, WI Ss. Peter and Paul Church.
Zepecki, Ronald P. '95 (HRT) [9] Hartford, CT SS. Cyril and Methodius Church.
Zepeda, Luis '94 (SAN) [2] Odessa, TX St. Anthony Church; [4] Odessa, TX St. Joseph Church.
Zepp, Anthony W. '56 (CLV) [2] Garfield Heights, OH SS. Peter and Paul Church.
Zeps, Michael J. *s.j.* '71 (MIL) [P] Milwaukee, WI Jesuit Community at Marquette University.
Zercie, David '75 (NOR) [F] Cromwell, CT Missionaries of the Holy Apostles.
Zerfas, Msgr. Herman H. '47 (GR) Retired.
Zerhusen, Msgr. Henry F. '53 (BAL) [55] Baltimore, MD St. Mark Church.
Zeringue, Guy P. '75 (HT) Bourg, LA St. Ann Church.
Zerkel, Donald F. '57 (MIL) Byron, WI St. John's Church; Oakfield, WI St. James Church.
Zermeno, Joseph *o.f.m.* '68 (LSC) Tularosa, NM St. Francis de Paula Church.

Zerner, Harry B. *s.j.* '63 (R) Chapel Hill, NC St. Thomas More Church; [1] Durham, NC Holy Cross Church; [E] Durham, NC Jesuit Community.
Zerwas, Rick '91 (SFE) Los Lunas, NM St. Clement Church.
Zeth, Allen P. '86 (ALT) [13] Altoona, PA St. Therese of the Child Jesus Church; [H] Huntingdon, PA Juniata College; [H] Huntingdon, PA Juniata College.
Zettel, David H. '66 (L) [B] Louisville, KY Trinity High School.
Zetzl, Ralph (SFD) [K] Sherman, IL Our Lady of Angels Friary.
Zeugner, Raymond J. '67 (MAR) Nadeau, MI St. Bruno Church; Stephenson, MI Precious Blood Church.
Zeuner, Karl A. '71 (PH) [3] Philadelphia, PA St. Agatha-St. James Church.
Zewe, M. Donald *s.j.* '56 (SY) [S] Syracuse, NY Jesuits at LeMoyne, Inc.
Zeyack, John *s.t.l.* '65 (PSC) Rahway, NJ St. Thomas the Apostle Church.
Zeyen, Thomas E. *s.j.* '54 (P) [L] Portland, OR Jesuit Provincial Office (Oregon Prov.).
Zglejszewski, Andrzej '90 (RVC) West Hempstead, NY St. Thomas, the Apostle Church.
Zgunda, Ronald S. '77 (EVN) Washington, IN Immaculate Conception Church.
Zhang, Dehua *c.s.j.b.* '76 (BRK) [U] Elmhurst, NY Congregation of St. John the Baptist of China.
Zibert, Jack *o.f.m.* '78 (BUF) [O] St. Bonaventure, NY St. Bonaventure Friary.
Zicarelli, Mario '47 (NY) Haverstraw, NY St. Mary Church.
Ziccardi, C. Anthony '90 (NEW) [A] South Orange, NJ Immaculate Conception Seminary; [B] South Orange, NJ Seton Hall University.
Zich, John S. '57 (WCH) Chetopa, KS Sacred Heart Church; Oswego, KS Mother of God Church.
Zickert, John '68 (GB) Kimberly, WI Holy Name of Jesus Church.
Zidek, Vincent E. *o.s.b.* '91 (GBG) [2] Latrobe, PA St. Vincent Basilica; [H] Latrobe, PA Saint Vincent Archabbey.
Zieba, Jerzy *c.r.* (CHI) [88] Chicago, IL St. Hyacinth Church.
Zieba, Wojtech '82 (CHI) [201] Chicago, IL St. Thecla Church.
Ziebacz, Wieslaw '92 (SCR) Honesdale, PA St. John the Evangelist Church.
Ziebowicz, Dariusz (NEW) [2] Elizabeth, NJ St. Adalbert's Church.
Ziegelmaier, David A. '60 (LC) Alma Center, WI Immaculate Conception Church; Fairchild, WI St. John Cantius Church; Fairview, WI St. Joseph Church.
Ziegler, Ambrose M. '61 (LFT) [2] Lafayette, IN St. Ann Church.
Ziegler, Anthony '59 (OWN) Waverly, KY Sacred Heart Church; Waverly, KY St. Peter Church.
Ziegler, Francis G. *s.j.* '54 (MIL) [P] Milwaukee, WI Jesuit Community at Marquette University.
Ziegler, John '96 (ARL) [5] Alexandria, VA St. Lawrence Church.
Ziegler, Thomas G. '69 (Y) Columbiana, OH St. Jude Church.
Ziegmann, Msgr. Leonard M. '59 (SC) Laurens, IA Sacred Heart Church.
Zielezienski, Ray '81 (OAK) [4] Hayward, CA St. Joachim Church.
Zielinski, Brian A. *o.praem.* '71 (WIL) [B] Claymont, DE Archmere Academy; [I] Claymont, DE Immaculate Conception Priory of the Canons Regular of Premontre.
Zielinski, Chad W. '96 (GAY) Traverse City, MI Immaculate Conception Church.
Zielinski, Francis A. '62 (DET) Columbus, MI St. Philip Neri Church.
Zielinski, Martin A. '78 (CHI) [A] Mundelein, IL University of St. Mary of the Lake-Mundelein Seminary.
Zielinski, Thomas J. '41 (DET) Retired.
Zielke, Michael *o.f.m.conv.* '89 (BAL) [D] Baltimore, MD Archbishop Curley High School; [M] Baltimore, MD Immaculate Heart of Mary Friary.
Zielonka, Darius J. '95 (BGP) [2] Stratford, CT St. James Church.
Ziemba, Anthony F. '43 (PH) [86] Philadelphia, PA St. Laurentius Church; Retired.
Ziemba, Herman J. *o.f.m.* '48 (GB) [I] Pulaski, WI Assumption of B.V.M. Friary.
Ziemba, Howard '79 (Y) Absent on Leave.
Ziemba, Walter J. '51 (DET) Retired; [A] Orchard Lake, MI SS. Cyril and Methodius Seminary.
Ziemkiewicz, Frank E. *o.s.b.* '84 (GBG) [H] Latrobe, PA Saint Vincent Archabbey.
Ziemnicki, Edward M. (HRT) Union City, CT St. Hedwig Church.
Zientek, Msgr. Benedict '58 (SAN) Brownwood, TX St. Mary's Church.
Zientek, Msgr. Boleslaus J. '59 (GAL) Sealy, TX Immaculate Conception Church.
Zientek, Timothy *o.f.m.conv.* '49 (BAL) [20] Baltimore, MD St. Casimir Church.
Ziezulewicz, George F. '64 (HRT) Union City, CT St. Hedwig Church; [18] Waterbury, CT St. Stanislaus Kostka Church.
Zigmond, Kenneth *o.s.b.* '57 (JOL) Lisle, IL St. Joan of Arc Church; [J] Lisle, IL St. Procopius Abbey.
Zigrang, Stephen P. '78 (GAL) On Special Assignment.
Zilbert, Jack *o.f.m.* '78 (BUF) [C] St. Bonaventure, NY St. Bonaventure University.
Ziliak, Joseph L. '62 (EVN) Newburgh, IN St. John the Baptist Church.
Zilonka, Paul *c.p.* '71 (NEW) [N] Union City, NJ Congregation of the Passion (Passionists)-St. Michael's Residence.
Zilonka, Paul *c.p.* '71 (NY) [A] Yonkers, NY St. Joseph's Seminary.
Ziminski, James C. '91 (MAR) [5] Marquette, MI St. Michael Church; Special Assignment; [G] Marquette, MI Catholic Campus Ministry-Northern Michigan University.
Zimmer, Anthony S. '86 (MIL) [D] Milwaukee, WI Pius XI High School.
Zimmer, David L. '88 (BIS) New Salem, ND St. Pius V Church.
Zimmer, Edward A. '47 (ROC) [29] Rochester, NY St. John Evangelist Church; Retired.
Zimmer, Ellis *o.f.m.cap.* '55 (GB) [M] Appleton, WI Monte Alverno Retreat Center.
Zimmer, Eric A. *s.j.* (DET) [K] Detroit, MI Jesuit Provincial Office-Detroit Province of the Society of Jesus.
Zimmer, James '76 (SFS) [1] Sioux Falls, SD St. Joseph Cathedral.
Zimmer, Joseph H. *s.a.c.* '56 (FAR) Dunseith, ND St. Louis Church.
Zimmer, Luke *ss.cc.* '54 (LA) [R] Fillmore, CA Apostolate of Christian Renewal Holy Family; [CC] Fillmore, CA Apostolate of Christian Renewal/Holy Family Home of Peace.
Zimmer, Nicholas M. '57 (SCL) Braham, MN St. Peter & Paul Church.
Zimmer, William '91 (CHI) [143] Chicago, IL St. Nicholas of Tolentine Church.
Zimmer, William H. '60 (GB) [4] Manitowoc, WI Sacred Heart Church.
Zimmerman, Albert J. '45 (GRY) Retired.
Zimmerman, David M. *o.f.m.cap.* '95 (GB) [2] Manitowoc, WI Holy Innocents Church.
Zimmerman, Donald D. '73 (SAL) Hays, KS Immaculate Heart of Mary Church.
Zimmerman, Msgr. Donald F. '73 (DAL) [4] Dallas, TX Christ the King Church.
Zimmerman, Eugene *s.j.* '51 (CHY) St. Stephens, WY St. Stephen's Church; [C] St. Stephens, WY St. Stephens Mission - Jesuit Community; [F] St. Stephens, WY St. Stephens Indian Mission Foundation.
Zimmerman, John F. *c.m.* '34 (STL) [P] Perryville, MO Congregation of The Mission.
Zimmerman, Joseph *o.f.m.* '62 (SFD) [B] Quincy, IL Quincy University.
Zimmerman, Lee B. *c.m.* '41 (NO) [P] New Orleans, LA Vincentian Fathers.
Zimmerman, Ralph G. '76 (SCL) Melrose, MN St. Mary's Church.
Zimmerman, Rex A. '67 (LC) Bevent, WI St. Ladislaus Church; Galloway, WI St. Joseph Church.
Zimmerman, Msgr. Roland G. '51 (LA) Arcadia, CA Annunciation Church.
Zimmermann, P. Francis *c.m.* '39 (NO) [P] New Orleans, LA Vincentian Fathers.
Zimmers, Eugene R. *s.j.* '51 (OAK) [A] Oakland, CA Graduate School of Theology, School of Applied Theology; [R] Oakland, CA Institute of Lay Theology.
Zimmers, Eugene R. *s.j.* '51 (SFR) [N] San Francisco, CA Jesuit Community at University of San Francisco.
Zimmers, Michael J. *s.j.* '54 (OAK) [R] Oakland, CA Institute of Lay Theology.
Zimmers, Michael J. *s.j.* '54 (SFR) [N] San Francisco, CA Jesuit Community at University of San Francisco.
Zimney, Robert J. *c.m.* '42 (STL) [P] Perryville, MO Congregation of The Mission.
Zimpfer, Eugene A. *s.j.* '65 (BUF) [D] Buffalo, NY Canisius High School; [O] Buffalo, NY Canisius Jesuit Community.
Zina, George '68 (SAM) Orlando, FL St. Jude Mission Church.
Zingales, A. Jonathan '76 (CLV) [10] Lorain, OH St. Peter Church; [D] Lorain, OH Lorain Catholic High School.
Zingaro, Joseph J. '78 (PH) Swedesburg, PA Sacred Heart Church.
Zink, David L. '90 (CIN) Sidney, OH Holy Angels Church.
Zink, Harold G. *c.s.c.* '51 (AUS) [13] Austin, TX St. Ignatius Martyr Church.
Zink, William F. '68 (GR) Remus, MI St. Michael's Church.
Zinkan, Matthias *o.s.b.* '40 (RCK) [H] Aurora, IL Marmion Abbey-St. Augustine's Abbey.
Zinkle, Ronald T. *s.j.* '59 (LC) Lyndon Station, WI St. Mary Church.
Zinkula, Thomas R. '90 (DUB) Graduate Studies.
Zinn, Donald *c.r.* '72 (CHI) [D] Chicago, IL Gordon Technical High School.
Zinnamon, Brian F. *s.j.* '79 (GAL) [F] Houston, TX Strake, Jesuit College Preparatory Inc.
Zinno, Henry P., Jr. '82 (PRO) Bristol, RI Our Lady of Mount Carmel Church; [S] Bristol, RI Roger Williams University.
Zins, Charles '77 (BIS) Bowman, ND St. Charles Church.
Zinser, Robert E. (STL) [63] St. Louis, MO St. Teresa of Avila Church.
Zinthefer, Neil G. '69 (MIL) Fredonia, WI St. Rose of Lima Church; Holy Cross, WI Holy Cross Church; Little Kohler, WI Mother of Sorrows Church.
Zinzer, Walter A. '64 (STL) Military Chaplains.
Ziobro, Joseph M. '73 (SCR) [18] Wilkes-Barre, PA Sacred Heart of Jesus Church.
Ziolkowski, Adam *o.f.m.conv.* '72 (SPR) [5] Holyoke, MA Mater Dolorosa Church.
Ziolkowski, Waldek *m.i.c.* '90 (CHL) [1] Greensboro, NC Our Lady of Grace Church.
Ziomek, David F. '94 (BO) Franklin, MA St. Mary Church.
Ziomek, Dennis A. '78 (CHI) [158] Chicago, IL Our Lady of the Snows Church; [A] Chicago, IL Archbishop Quigley Preparatory Seminary.
Ziotkowski, Francis T. *c.s.c.* (BO) Boston, MA Brigham and Women's Hospital.
Zipay, Michael J. '68 (SCR) Swoyersville, PA Holy Trinity Church.
Zipple, Francis '49 (LAN) Absent on Leave.
Zirnheld, Matthew J. '93 (BUF) [1] Lackawanna, NY Basilica of Our Lady of Victory.
Zitek, Bradley J. '89 (LIN) Steinauer, NE St. Anthony Church.
Ziter, Nelson B. *s.s.e.* '47 (MOB) [H] Selma, AL Edmundite Fathers.
Zitko, Msgr. Aloysius '28 (OAK) Retired.
Zitz, Nicholas *c.p.* '56 (BRK) [U] Jamaica, NY Immaculate Conception Monastery.
Ziuraitis, Gary *c.ss.r.* '78 (DEN) Fort Lupton, CO St. William Church.
Zivjak, John *c.pp.s.* (CLV) [53] Cleveland, OH Our Lady of Good Counsel Church.
Zivkovic, Robert M. *o.s.m.* '66 (ORG) [H] Buena Park, CA Servite Fathers And Brothers.
Zizka, Peter J. '75 (HRT) [2] Manchester, CT St. Bartholomew's Church.
Zlock, Charles J. '94 (PH) [94] Philadelphia, PA St. Martin of Tours Church.
Zlotkowski, Francis T. *c.s.c* '76 (BGP) [O] Bridgeport, CT Provincial Offices of the Priests and Brothers of Holy Cross, Eastern Province.
Zlotkowski, Francis T. *c.s.c.* '76 (FR) [B] North Easton, MA Holy Cross Fathers Religious.
Zmerlicki, Andrew '92 (NEW) Hasbrouck Heights, NJ Corpus Christi Church.
Zmija, Walter J. '42 (CHI) [115] Chicago, IL St. Ladislaus Church; Retired.
Zmozynski, Francis J. '57 (BUF) [60] Buffalo, NY St. Rose of Lima Church.
Znotinas, John '40 (WDC) Retired.
Zocco, Salvatore (HRT) [3] New Haven, CT St. Anthony's Church.
Zodrow, Nathan *o.s.b.* '88 (P) [A] St. Benedict, OR Mount Angel Seminary; [L] St. Benedict, OR Mt. Angel Abbey.
Zoeller, Ben '65 (OKL) Yukon, OK St. John Nepomuk Church.
Zoeller, Eugene L. '58 (L) [A] Louisville, KY Bellarmine College.
Zoellner, Michael *o.s.b.* '80 (KCK) [H] Atchison, KS St. Benedict's Abbey.
Zogby, Edward G. *s.j.* '67 (NY) [Z] New York, NY West Side Jesuit Community.
Zoghby, James F. '71 (MOB) [3] Mobile, AL Corpus Christi Church.
Zoghby, Paul G. '93 (MOB) [12] Mobile, AL St. Mary Church.
Zogheib, Hares '54 (SAM) Retired.
Zohlen, Raym J. '53 (SFR) [23] San Francisco, CA Holy Name of Jesus Church.
Zollinger, Msgr. Richard F. '55 (GRY) Knox, IN St. Thomas Aquinas Church.
Zolnerowich, Nicholas *s.s.s.* '62 (NY) [55] New York, NY St. Jean Baptiste Church.
Zolnierzak, Stanislaus J. '36 (PIT) Retired; [N] Pittsburgh, PA St. John Vianney Manor.
Zona, James '73 (BRK) [210] Queens, NY Our Lady of Fatima Church.
Zonneveld, Leo J. *c.i.c.m.* '58 (ARL) Culpeper, VA Precious Blood Church; [J] Arlington, VA Missionhurst, C.I.C.M.-Central House and Provincialate.
Zonta, Angelo *c.s.j.* (LA) Lancaster, CA Blessed Junipero Serra Church; San Pedro, CA St. Peter Church; [D] Lancaster, CA Paraclete High School.
Zoph, John L. '36 (SFR) Retired; [D] San Mateo, CA

Junipero Serra High School (Boys).
Zorbach, Msgr. Francis X. '52 (BAL) Linthicum Heights, MD St. Philip Neri Church.
Zore, Richard I. '57 (IND) Plainfield, IN St. Susanna Church.
Zorichak, William '39 (DUL) Retired.
Zorman, Fortunat *o.f.m.* '40 (CHI) [N] Lemont, IL The Slovene Franciscan Fathers, Order of Friars Minor, Commissariat of the Holy Cross.
Zoromski, Herbert P. '51 (LC) Retired.
Zoshak, William H. '62 (NY) Military Chaplains.
Zotter, Thomas A. '76 (SFE) [22] Albuquerque, NM St. Bernadette Church.
Zoubek, Ronald '89 (BAL) [55] Baltimore, MD St. Mark Church.
Zoufal, Michael L. '87 (CHI) Calumet City, IL Our Lady of Knock Church; [G] Chicago, IL Catholic Charities of the Archdiocese of Chicago-Archdiocesan Offices.
Zsolczai, Raymond *o.f.m.* '83 (CHI) [J] Oak Park, IL Oak Park Hospital.
Zube, Joseph '53 (PEO) Special Residence.
Zuber, Marti G. '76 (BWN) Absent.
Zuber, Thaddeus F. '50 (NEW) Retired; [N] Rutherford, NJ St. John Vianney Residence for Priests.
Zuberbueler, Matthew H. '96 (ARL) Chantilly, VA St. Timothy Church.
Zubik, David A. '75 (PIT) [O] Ross Township, PA Motherhouse, Sisters of the Holy Spirit (S.H.S.).
Zubik, Rudolf '64 (NEW) Harrison, NJ Our Lady of Czestochowa Church.
Zuchowski, Robert J. '72 (GAY) Manistee, MI St. Joseph Church.
Zudaire, Claudio *o.f.m.cap.* '54 (FWT) [6] Fort Worth, TX Our Lady of Guadalupe Church.
Zuelke, Michael *o.f.m.cap.* '74 (MIL) [25] Milwaukee, WI St. Francis of Assisi Church.
Zuercher, John D. *s.j.* '59 (OM) [K] Omaha, NE Jesuit Community At Creighton University.
Zuerlein, Damian J. '81 (OM) [32] Omaha, NE Our Lady of Guadalupe Church.
Zuern, Theodore F. *s.j.* '57 (MIL) [P] Milwaukee, WI Jesuit Provincial Office, Wisconsin Province.
Zuern, Theodore F. *s.j.* '57 (WDC) [M] Washington, DC Leonard Neale House.
Zuffoletto, Michael P. '72 (BUF) Military Chaplains.
Zugelter, Alvin T. '46 (CIN) Retired.
Zugger, Christopher L. '81 (VNN) Albuquerque, NM Our Lady of Perpetual Help Church.
Zukas, Stephen P. '92 (BO) [43] Boston, MA St. Margaret Church.
Zukowski, John A. '36 (CHI) Retired.
Zukowski, Nicholas '82 (DET) New Baltimore, MI St. Mary Church.
Zuleger, Donald M. '76 (GB) [5] Appleton, WI St. Pius X Church.
Zuleta, Nondier '92 (B) Idaho Falls, ID Holy Rosary Church.
Zuliani, Vincent *s.d.b.* '56 (NEW) [3] Elizabeth, NJ St. Anthony's Church.
Zuluaga, Jose Omar '84 (PRO) [5] Pawtucket, RI St. John the Baptist Church.
Zumaya, David G. '77 (SAT) Nixon, TX St. Joseph's Church; Smiley, TX St. Philip Benizi Church.
Zummach, Jerome A. *s.j.* '45 (STL) [O] St. Louis, MO Fusz Pavilion.
Zuniga, Domingo *c.m.f.* (LA) [28] Los Angeles, CA Our Lady Queen of the Angels Church.
Zuniga, Juan M. *m.m.* '88 (SFR) [N] San Francisco, CA Maryknoll Fathers and Brothers, Catholic Foreign Mission Society of America, Inc.
Zupa, Msgr. Emil P. '48 (BUF) Le Roy, NY St. Joseph Church.
Zupka, Anselm *o.s.b.* '67 (CLV) [E] Cleveland, OH Benedictine High School; [P] Cleveland, OH Benedictine Order of Cleveland.
Zurat, Hugh *o.f.m.* '62 (MIL) [P] Milwaukee, WI Francis and Clare House.
Zuraw, John '87 (Y) [1] Warren, OH Blessed Sacrament Church.
Zurawski, Lawrence '85 (DET) Berkley, MI Our Lady of La Salette Church.
Zurek, Lawrence W. *o.f.m.* '85 (DET) [5] Southfield, MI St. Michael Church.
Zurek, Patrick J. '75 (AUS) [14] Austin, TX St. John Neumann Church.
Zuromskis, John D. '41 (BO) Retired.
Zurovetz, Jerome '67 (CC) [21] Corpus Christi, TX St. Pius X Church.
Zurutuza, Juan Maria *c.m.* '58 (SJN) [47] San Juan, PR Nuestra Senora del Pilar Church.
Zuscak, Richard T. '84 (WOR) Clinton, MA Our Lady of Jasna Gora Church; [1] Southbridge, MA St. Hedwig's Church.
Zuschmidt, Joseph C. *o.s.f.s.* '65 (CHL) High Point, NC Immaculate Heart of Mary Church.
Zusy, Dennis R. *o.p.* '55 (CHI) [N] Chicago, IL Dominicans (Provincial Office).
Zusy, James *o.p.* '59 (LEX) [6] Lexington, KY St. Paul Church.
Zuziak, Joseph R. *s.d.s.* '66 (GRY) [K] Merrillville, IN Salvatorian Fathers (Society of the Divine Savior).
Zuzik, John E. '91 (Y) [2] Canton, OH Our Lady of Peace Church.
Zvinklys, Antanas '39 (LC) Retired; [I] La Crosse, WI Holy Cross (Seminary) Diocesan Center.
Zvirblis, John '38 (GR) Retired.
Zwack, Jeffrey A. '84 (BIS) Hazelton, ND St. Paul Church; Linton, ND St. Anthony Church.
Zwahl, Eugene *o.f.m.conv.* '42 (TR) Seaside Park, NJ St. Catharine of Siena Church.
Zwaska, Victor L. '56 (MIL) Retired.
Zweber, Benedict A. *m.m.* '60 (CHI) [N] Chicago, IL Maryknoll Fathers & Brothers.
Zweber, Clement J. '49 (STP) Retired.
Zweber, Raymond J. '54 (STP) South St. Paul, MN St. Augustine Church.
Zwers, John B. '50 (DET) Redford Township, MI St. Robert Bellarmine Church.
Zwicky, Richard C. '44 (NU) Retired.
Zwiefka, William L. '83 (GAY) Mancelona, MI St. Anthony Church.
Zwifka, David *m.a., j.c.d.* (BUF) [A] East Aurora, NY Christ the King Seminary.
Zwinger, Msgr. Leonard '51 (SFS) Retired.
Zwirn, Ralph H. '85 (CHI) [131] Chicago, IL St. Mary, Star of the Sea Church.
Zwolenkiewicz, Raphael *o.f.m.conv.* '79 (SPR) [5] Holyoke, MA Mater Dolorosa Church.
Zych, Janusz *s.chr.* '90 (LA) [22] Los Angeles, CA Our Lady of the Bright Mount Church.
Zygadlo, Mitchell '82 (ROC) [56] Rochester, NY St. Stanislaus Church; [58] Rochester, NY St. Theresa Church.
Zyla, Jeffrey L. '92 (OM) [26] Omaha, NE St. Leo Church.
Zylla, Paul '45 (SCL) Retired.
Zylla, Robert V. *o.s.c.* '51 (BAL) [A] Emmitsburg, MD Mount St. Mary's Seminary.
Zylla, Robert V. *o.s.c.* '51 (PHX) [F] Phoenix, AZ Crosier Community of Phoenix (Canons Regular of the Order of the Holy Cross).
Zywan, Paul J. '86 (PIT) [1] Pittsburgh, PA St. Paul Cathedral.
Zywicki, Francis S. '53 (ALT) Retired.

Necrology

CARDINALS

✠ Bernardin, His Eminence Joseph (CHI). —Died Nov. 14, 1996

✠ Krol, His Eminence John (PH) (Retired). —Died March 3, 1996

BISHOPS

✠ Arliss, Most Rev. Reginald, *c.p.* (FgM) Retired Bishop of Marbel, Philippines. —Died April 26, 1996

✠ Dempsey, Most Rev. Michael J., *o.p.* (FgM) Retired Bishop of Sokoto, Nigeria. —Died March 19, 1996

✠ Gerbermann, Most. Rev. Hugo M., *m.m.* (SAT) Former Auxiliary Bishop of San Antonio. —Died Oct. 19, 1996

✠ Markiewicz, Most Rev. Alfred J. (KAL) Kalamazoo, MI Bishop of Kalamazoo. —Died Jan. 9, 1997

✠ Moran, Most Rev. William J. (SFR) San Rafael, CA Nazareth House. —Died Aug. 23, 1996

✠ Schladweiler, Most Rev. Alphonse J. (NU) (Retired). —Died April 3, 1996

ABBOTS

✠ Dworschak, Rt. Rev. Baldwin, *o.s.b.* (SCL) Collegeville, MN St. John's Abbey, of the Order of St. Benedict. —Died June 16, 1996

✠ Hartman, Rt. Rev. Thomas, *o.s.b.* (KCK) Atchison, KS St. Benedict's Abbey. —Died March 17, 1996

PRIESTS

† Achatz, Elias, *o.s.b.* (SCL) Collegeville, MN St. John's Abbey, of the Order of St. Benedict. —Died Dec. 4, 1995

† Adams, Rev. Msgr. Donald E. (HBG) (On Special Assignment). —Died April 18, 1996

† Adams, Hubert W., *s.j.* (SPK) Spokane, WA Gonzaga University. —Died Sept. 21, 1995

† Aleckna, Conrad (Y) (Retired). —Died Nov. 3, 1996

† Anderson, James R. (SD) (Retired). —Died Feb. 3, 1996

† Anderson, John M. (PRT) (Retired). —Died April 19, 1996

† Andrade, Manuel (FR) (Retired). —Died Dec. 27, 1995

† Andrecic, John (Y) Boardman, OH St. Charles Parish. —Died Jan. 21, 1996

† Andres, Anthony G. (CIN) (Retired). —Died Sept. 29, 1996

† Angelaitis, Joseph F. (CLV) Cleveland, OH Our Lady of Perpetual Help. —Died Oct. 6, 1996

† Angelo, Mark, *o.f.m.* (SP) St. Petersburg, FL St. Anthony. —Died Oct. 12, 1995

† Arand, Louis A., *s.s.* (BAL) Retired. —Died Nov. 22, 1995

† Aranda, Sofronio A. (GAL) Houston, TX Catholic Chaplain Corps, Texas Medical Center. —Died March 24, 1996

† Arkle, Robert V. (WH) Wheeling, WV St. Joseph's Cathedral. —Died May 24, 1996

† Armigo, Walter, *o.f.m.* (SP) St. Petersburg, FL St. Anthony. —Died Aug. 9, 1996

† Aron, Iuliu (ROM) Dearborn, MI St. Mary Church. —Died June 2, 1994

† Asturias, Joseph L., *o.p.* (SFR) San Francisco, CA St. Dominic Priory. —Died Nov. 15, 1995

† Atwood, J. Clifford, *c.s.c.* (FTW) South Bend, IN Congregation of Holy Cross Indiana Province Provincial House. —Died April 6, 1996

† Aufderheide, Edwin J. (CIN) (Retired). —Died Jan. 16, 1996

† Aumann, Peter A. (NY) New Rochelle, NY Blessed Sacrament. —Died Jan. 12, 1996

† Baird, Richard P., *c.pp.s.* (CIN) Retired. —Died Jan. 13, 1996

† Bajo, Philip (RCK) (Retired). —Died Feb. 5, 1996

† Ballouz, Marcel A. (WH) Hutington, WV Sacred Heart. —Died June 21, 1996

† Banahan, John S. (CHI) (Retired). —Died Jan. 5, 1996

† Bankowski, John A. (IND) (Retired). —Died May 18, 1996

† Barandiaran, Jose, *s.s.s.* (GAL) Houston, TX Corpus Christi. —Died May 15, 1996

† Barder, Patrick, *s.v.d.* (BO) Duxbury, MA Society of the Divine Word. —Died Jan. 21, 1996

† Bares, Elmer J. (MAR) (Retired). —Died Oct. 17, 1996

† Barrett, Brian P. (NY) Yonkers, NY St. Joseph's Seminary. —Died July 13, 1996

† Barrett, Rev. Msgr. Francis G. (SCR) (Retired). —Died May 29, 1996

† Barrett, Michael F. (HBG) Lancaster, PA St. Joseph Church. —Died Nov. 1, 1996

† Barry, Dominic, *f.s.c.* (SR) Retired. —Died Nov. 22, 1995

† Barthel, Aloysius A. (IND) (Retired). —Died Nov. 30, 1996

† Bartley, William J. (BRK) Brooklyn, NY Holy Name. —Died Aug. 18, 1996

† Bartnikowski, Francis G. (CLV) Grafton, OH Assumption. —Died Jan. 6, 1996

† Bass, Gerald C., *c.ss.r.* (CHI) Glenview, IL The Redemptorists/St. Louis Province. —Died March 12, 1996

† Basterra, Ignacio, *o.a.r.* (NY) Bronx, NY St. Roch. —Died Dec. 24, 1995

† Baudo, Rev. Msgr. Francis J. (STU) (Retired). —Died June 21, 1996

† Bauer, Vincent Louis (CHY) (Retired). —Died Sept. 27, 1996

† Bauer, Rev. Msgr. W. B. (SC) (Retired). —Died Jan. 24, 1996

† Baum, John (GB) (Retired). —Died Oct. 20, 1996

† Baur, Francis G., *o.f.m.* (OAK) Berkeley, CA Franciscan School of Theology. —Died Sept. 30, 1996

† Becker, Rev. Msgr. Edmund J. (DUB) (Retired). —Died Nov. 23, 1996

† Beckius, Donald J. (MAD) Baraboo, WI St. Clare Hospital & Health Services. —Died June 2, 1996

† Beckman, Peter, *o.s.b.* (KCK) Atchison, KS St. Benedict's Abbey. —Died March 27, 1996

† Beckmann, John M. (GRY) (Retired). —Died Feb. 4, 1996

† Beger, Leo F., *o.s.b.* (PAT) Morristown, NJ St. Mary's Abbey. —Died April 8, 1996

† Bellerose, Joseph A. (FAR) San Antonio, TX Padua Place. —Died Jan. 9, 1996

† Benincasa, Albert E. (BRK) Brooklyn, NY St. Mary Mother of Jesus. —Died May 28, 1996

† Benvegnu, Mark O. (SLC) (Retired). —Died Dec. 17, 1995

† Bergan, William A. (SJ) (Retired). —Died Dec. 7, 1995

† Bergan, William A., *m.m.* (SJ) Los Altos, CA Maryknoll. —Died Dec. 7, 1995

† Bergeron, Arthur I. (BO) Groton, MA St. James. —Died Oct. 25, 1996

† Berkbigler, Donald L., *c.m.* (STL) Perryville, MO St. Mary's of the Barrens. —Died Sept. 7, 1996

† Berst Theodore (JOL) Coal City, IL Assumption Parish. —Died Aug. 2, 1996

† Berton, Joseph, *c.ss.r.* (ALB) Saratoga Springs, NY St. John Neumann Residence. —Died Dec. 26, 1995

† Betrand, Louis N. (LAF) (Retired). —Died July 19, 1996

† Beznoska, Kenneth, *m.s.c.* (Y) Retired. —Died June 27, 1996

† Bialek, Rev. Msgr. Joseph L. (BUF) Buffalo, NY St. Adalbert Basilica. —Died March 3, 1996

† Bianco, Bernard (CHY) (Retired). —Died July 21, 1996

† Biehler, Rev. Msgr. Joseph E. (KCK) Flush, KS St. Joseph Parish. —Died April 11, 1996

† Biever, Bruce F., *s.j.* (MIL) Milwaukee, WI Jesuit Community at Marquette University. —Died July 28, 1996

† Biscardi, Pasquale D. (WOR) Fitchburg, MA Madonna of the Holy Rosary. —Died June 22, 1996

† Blackledge, Dennis C., *c.s.sp.* (OKL) Enid, OK St. Mary Hospital. —Died Nov. 12, 1995

† Blackledge, Michael R. (WCH) (Retired). —Died Nov. 29, 1995

† Blair, Rev. Msgr. Robert C. (CLV) Cleveland, OH Cathedral of St. John the Evangelist. —Died June 5, 1996

† Blaney, Joseph E., *o.m.i.* (GR) Grand Rapids, MI Immaculate Heart of Mary. —Died Nov. 4, 1995

† Bloemer, Charles C., *s.m.* (CIN) Retired. —Died March 19, 1996

† Bloms, Romuald, *o.s.b.* (SCL) Retired. —Died Dec. 2, 1995

† Bober, Edward, *c.ss.r.* (ALB) Saratoga Springs, NY St. John Neumann Residence. —Died Aug. 14, 1996

† Boeckmann, Walter F. (DAV) (Retired). —Died July 19, 1996

† Boehmicke, George (OWN) (Retired). —Died Nov. 6, 1996

† Boesflug, Clement P., *m.m.* (NY) Maryknoll, NY Maryknoll Fathers and Brothers. —Died Oct. 18, 1995

† Boeynaems, Louis, *ss.cc.* (HON) Honolulu, HI St. Patrick's Monastery. —Died March 13, 1996

† Bogus, Daniel (DET) (Retired). —Died Oct. 4, 1996

† Bollich, Ronald (BEA) (Retired). —Died Aug. 7, 1996

† Borcino, Raymond F. (RVC) (Retired). —Died March 2, 1996

† Bordenave, Marius F. (MAN) (Retired). —Died Jan. 4, 1996

† Borgola, Bonaventure, *o.f.m.* (ALT) Johnstown, PA St. Therese of the Child Jesus. —Died Jan. 19, 1996

† Borkowicz, Rev. Msgr. Vincent P. (DET) (Retired). —Died July 27, 1996

† Borovec, Peter J. (LR) (On Leave). —Died November 25, 1995

† Bottoni, Samuel A. (MAR) Watersmeet, MI Immaculate Conception Church. —Died July 5, 1996

† Bower, Rene, *o.f.m.cap.* (DEN) Denver, CO St. Francis of Assisi Friary. —Died Dec. 15, 1995

† Bowling, Chester B. (L) (Retired). —Died Oct. 26, 1996

† Bradley, Edward A., *s.j.* (DET) Clarkston, MI Colombiere Jesuit Community. —Died April 15, 1996

† Brandley, Theodore E., *m.s.* (STL) Retired. —Died March 10, 1996

† Brauner, Omer H. (STL) (Retired). —Died Feb. 2, 1996

† Brehm, David W., *s.j.* (STP) Minneapolis, MN La Storta Jesuit Community. —Died Feb. 9, 1996

† Breines, Andrew R. (MAD) (Retired). —Died May 2, 1996

† Brennan, John J., *s.j.* (DET) Clarkston, MI Colombiere Center. —Died Nov. 10, 1995

† Brennan, Robert O., *s.j.* (NY) New York, NY Murray-Weigel Hall. —Died Dec. 6, 1996

† Brennan, Thomas F. (ROC) Corning, NY St. Mary's Church. —Died July 30, 1996

† Breslin, Robert, *o.f.m.* (SFR) San Francisco, CA Immaculate Conception. —Died Jan. 12, 1996

† Brickl, Frank C. (LC) (Retired). —Died Oct. 12, 1996

† Brockman, Vaughn W. (LC) Menomonie, WI St. Joseph Parish. —Died Dec. 5, 1995

† Brodeur, Robert (HON) Hana, Maui, HI St. Mary. —Died May 1, 1996

† Brodie, Paul S., *o.f.m.cap.* (SJN) Rio Piedras, PR San Antonio Friary. —Died April 17, 1996

† Brown, Rev. Msgr. Douglas L. (BRK) Brooklyn, NY St. Ephrem's Church. —Died Dec. 10, 1996

† Brown, Stewart R. (BRK) Glendale, NY St. Pancras. —Died Feb. 26, 1996

† Broyles, Henry J. (TLS) Vinita, OK Holy Ghost Church. —Died Oct. 16, 1996

† Bruder, Rev. Msgr. James I. (PH) (Retired). —Died Dec. 22, 1995

† Brueggeman, Edward B., *s.j.* (CIN) Cincinnati, OH Xavier University. —Died Dec. 28, 1995

† Bryce, Philip (OKL) Yukon, OK St. John Nepomuk. —Died May 6, 1996

† Bryda, Richard (STF) Staten Island, NY Holy Trinity. —Died March 5, 1996

† Bucciero, Angelo, *o.f.m.* (BO) Lynn, MA Franciscan Community (Province of Immaculate Conception). —Died Feb. 15, 1996

† Buchman, William J. (LC) (Retired). —Died Sept. 19, 1996

† Buckley, Albert J. (CHI) (Retired). —Died Oct. 3, 1996

† Buday, Robert (JOL) Lisle, IL St. Procopius Abbey. —Died May 17, 1996

† Buhler, Joseph L., *c.ss.r.* (NO) New Orleans, LA Redemptorist Fathers Vice-Provincialate. —Died April 8, 1996
† Bujarski, Edward (GB) (Retired). —Died Dec. 8, 1995
† Bujarski, Paul R. (LR) (Retired). —Died Dec. 23, 1995
† Bulla, Charles A. (TR) (Retired). —Died Jan. 10, 1996
† Bumstead, Rev. Msgr. John Joseph (BGP) Danbury, CT St. Peter Parish. —Died June 20, 1996
† Burggraff, Alvin R., *c.s.p.* (STP) Retired. —Died Sept. 25, 1996
† Burke, Rev. Msgr. Edward T. (BRK) Brooklyn, NY Monastery of the Sisters Adorers of the Precious Blood. —Died Dec. 25, 1996
† Burke, James T. (SFE) Socorro, NM San Miguel. —Died Feb. 11, 1996
† Burke, Redmond A., *c.s.v.* (CHI) Retired. —Died May 14, 1996
† Burlage, Carl J., *s.j.* (CHI) Clarkston, MI Colombiere Jesuit Community. —Died Sept. 1, 1996
† Burns, Rev. Msgr. John P. (STA) Jacksonville, FL St. Matthews. —Died April 25, 1996
† Bussieres, Francois (LAF) (Retired). —Died July 5, 1996
† Byrne, Most Rev. James J. (DUB) (Retired). —Died Aug. 2, 1996
† Cabral, Kenneth (OAK) (Retired). —Died March 3, 1996
† Caglioti, Ralph V. (SCR) (Retired). —Died May 21, 1996
† Caldarola, Rev. Msgr. John B. (NY) (Retired). —Died Aug. 26, 1996
† Calhoun, James R. (BEL) (Retired). —Died May 26, 1996
† Callaghan, Philip P., *s.j.* (SFR) San Francisco, CA University of San Francisco. —Died Dec. 7, 1996
† Callan, Thomas, *t.o.r.* (ARL) Winchester, VA Sacred Heart Monastery. —Died April 30, 1996
† Campbell, Rev. Msgr. Arthur A. (NY) Nyack, NY St. Ann. —Died Sept. 10, 1996
† Canaan, Joseph A. (DET) (Retired). —Died Feb. 8, 1996
† Cannizzaro, Francis J. (RVC) Inwood, NY Our Lady of Good Counsel. —Died June 16, 1996
† Cantwell, Rev. Msgr. Daniel M. (CHI) (Retired). —Died Jan. 2, 1996
† Capros, Rev. Msgr. Carol (ROM) (Retired). —Died Dec. 28, 1995
† Carberry, Francis J. (WOR) Sterling, MA St. Richard of Chichester. —Died Feb. 6, 1996
† Carberry, Paul A. (SPR) (Retired). —Died Jan. 1, 1996
† Cardoza, Joseph A. (PRO) Newport, RI Jesus Savior Church. —Died Oct. 9, 1996
† Carey, William V. (PEO) Wenona, IL St. Mary's. —Died Nov. 3, 1996
† Cariglia, Michael W. (FRS) (Retired). —Died June 3, 1996
† Carney, John J. (SAC) (Retired). —Died Dec. 12, 1996
† Carr, Frank M. (TUC) Yuma, AZ St. Francis of Assisi. —Died Feb. 7, 1996
† Carroll, Rev. Msgr. Joseph A. (NEW) Kearny, NJ St. Cecilia. —Died Dec. 29, 1996
† Cartmell, J. Richard (CLV) (Retired). —Died May 29, 1996
† Caselli, Joseph, *s.d.b.* (NY) West Haverstraw, NY Don Bosco Retreat Center and Marian Shrine. —Died Oct. 20, 1995
† Casey, Jeremiah, *ss.cc.* (FR) Fairhaven, MA Damien Residence. —Died May 6, 1996
† Casey, Raymond J., *c.s.sp.* (VEN) Sarasota, FL Stella Maris Community. —Died Oct. 28, 1995
† Casey, Thomas A. (ARL) Fairfax, VA St. Mary of Sorrows. —Died Feb. 29, 1996
† Casey, Thomas F. (BO) Braintree, MA St. Clare. —Died July 20, 1995
† Cassidy, Francis P. (DUB) Corwith, IA St. Mary Parish. —Died June 19, 1996
† Cassidy, James J. (PRO) Cumberland, RI Mt. St. Rita Health Centre. —Died Feb. 4, 1996
† Chaisson, Paul A., *s.m.* (BO) Boston, MA Marist Fathers of Our Lady of Victories (Boston Prov.). —Died Nov. 19, 1995
† Chapman, Francis, *c.ss.r.* (ALB) Saratoga Springs, NY St. John Neumann Residence. —Died Oct. 8, 1995
† Chassagne, Rt. Rev. M. Anthony (CHR) (Retired). —Died Oct. 9, 1996
† Chavez, Angelico Manuel E., *o.f.m.* (SFE) Santa Fe, NM St. Francis Cathedral. —Died March 18, 1996
† Chen, Matthew F., *o.p.* (NY) New York, NY St. Catherine of Siena. —Died Aug. 14, 1996
† Chenier, Roland J. (WOR) Millville, MA St. Augustine. —Died Jan. 11, 1996
† Chevalier, Alfred J. (OG) (Retired). —Died April 15, 1996
† Chmielewski, Edward A. (GR) (Retired). —Died Sept. 24, 1996
† Choquette, John Paul, *s.s.s.* (CLV) Retired. —Died Dec. 22, 1995
† Cisek, Ferdinand, *o.f.m.conv.* (BRK) Elmhurst, NY St. Adalbert. —Died April 2, 1996
† Cizek, Rev. Msgr. Robert W. (DUB) Greene, IA St. Mary Parish. —Died April 27, 1996
† Cizmar, John S. (E) (Retired). —Died July 16, 1996
† Clarke, Martin, *o.f.m.cap.* (NY) Yonkers, NY St. Clare Friary. —Died Dec. 14, 1995
† Clonan, Edward L., *s.m.* (BO) Retired. —Died Sept. 17, 1996
† Cloonan, John Henry (SD) (Retired). —Died May 16, 1996
† Cockerill, Rev. Msgr. James (NY) Manchester, NY St. Veronica. —Died Oct. 18, 1996
† Codd, Rembert J., *o.s.b.* (RIC) Richmond, VA St. Benedict's. —Died June 11, 1995
† Collins, Clement E., *o.p.* (SAT) San Antonio, TX St. Ann's. —Died Dec. 10, 1995
† Condon, John P. (PRO) Newport, RI St. Augustin Rectory. —Died Jan. 3, 1996
† Conger, Donald W. (SEA) (Retired). —Died June 7, 1996
† Conlin, Rev. Msgr. Norman R. (BUF) (Retired). —Died March 26, 1996
† Conlon, Rev. Msgr. Joseph E. (CAM) (Retired). —Died Dec. 11, 1996
† Connors, Francis J. (BO) Needham, MA St. Joseph. —Died Oct. 7, 1996
† Conrad, Adrian, *o.f.m.cap.* (PIT) Pittsburgh, PA Vincentian Home. —Died April 18, 1996
† Considine, Rev. Msgr. Raymond T., P.A. (FR) (Retired). —Died Oct. 15, 1996
† Conti, Rev. Msgr. Richard E. (ALT) Johnstown, PA St. Gregory. —Died May 10, 1996
† Conway, John William (NEW) Montclair, NJ Immaculate Conception. —Died Feb. 4, 1996
† Conway, Rev. Msgr. Paul E. (ALX) (Retired). —Died Jan. 15, 1996
† Cooley, Richard A. (LFT) (On Duty Outside the Diocese). —Died June 6, 1996
† Cooney, Robert E. (DUB) Marion, IA St. Joseph Parish. —Died May 12, 1996
† Cooper, Rev. Msgr. Daniel E. (LIN) (Retired). —Died Jan. 30, 1996
† Corcoran, Daniel J. (WIN) (Retired). —Died Dec. 7, 1995
† Corcoran, Francis P. (SCR) Williamsport, PA St. Boniface's Church. —Died Aug. 11, 1996
† Cornea, Very Rev. Teodor (ROM) Aurora, IL St. Michael Church. —Died Feb. 20, 1995
† Cortes, Augustine, *s.f.* (WDC) Retired. —Died Feb. 26, 1996
† Costello, Joseph, *s.m.* (WDC) Washington, DC Marist Provincial House. —Died July 11, 1996
† Cote, Owen, *o.carm.* (JOL) Darien, IL Carmelite Fathers Provincial Office. —Died June 3, 1996
† Courtney, Thomas M. (ALN) (Retired). —Died Aug. 26, 1996
† Coveney, Edwin J. (BUF) (Retired). —Died Jan. 21, 1996
† Craddock, William T., *c.s.c.* (FTW) South Bend, IN Congregation of Holy Cross Indiana Province Provincial House. —Died May 24, 1996
† Craven, Aloysius, *s.a.* (NY) Garrison, NY Graymoor Infirmary. —Died June 5, 1996
† Crocchiola, Rev. Msgr. Stanley (AMA) (Retired). —Died Feb. 6, 1996
† Cronin, Charles E. (CHI) Chicago, IL Queen of All Saints. —Died Jan. 9, 1996
† Cronin, Peter F. (PH) (Retired). —Died May 24, 1996
† Crowe James Edward (P) (Retired). —Died March 20, 1996
† Cukuras, Valdemar (NOR) Putnam, CT Immaculate Conception Convent. —Died July 17, 1996
† Cullen, Leo (SJ) (Retired). —Died Oct. 21, 1995
† Cummings, Frederick F. (SY) (Retired). —Died Oct. 16, 1996
† Cunningham, James J., *o.p.* (RIC) Charlottesville, VA St. Thomas. —Died Oct. 1, 1996
† Cunningham, John P. (CHI) (Retired). —Died Nov. 13, 1996
† Cure, Laverne J. (CHI) (Retired). —Died Oct. 2, 1996
† Curran, Alphonsus B., *i.c.* (PEO) Peoria, IL Rosminian Novitiate. —Died June 4, 1996
† Curtin, Rev. Msgr. William T. (KCK) Kansas City, KS St. Peter's Cathedral. —Died May 26, 1996
† Curtis, Leonard E., *o.p.* (NO) New Orleans, LA Dominican Fathers and Brothers, Southern Dominican Province. —Died Nov. 17, 1995
† Cusack, Donald E. (CHI) Chicago, IL St. Therese Medical Center. —Died Nov. 17, 1996
† Cusack, Joseph P. (NY) (Retired). —Died Sept. 11, 1996
† Cutler S. Oley, *s.j.* (NY) New York, NY Murray-Weigel Hall. —Died Dec. 11, 1996
† Cutter, James R., *o.s.f.s.* (TOL) Toledo, OH St. Francis de Sales High School. —Died Sept. 23, 1995
† D'Alessandro, Patrick A. (HBG) (Retired). —Died April 28, 1996
† D'Amico, Joseph (FR) (Retired). —Died May 1, 1996
† D'Argenio, Herbert F. (NY) Bronx, NY St. Lucy. —Died March 9, 1996
† D'Auria, Martin J. (PAT) Paterson, NJ Out Lady of Pompei. —Died Sept. 18, 1996
† Dabrowski, Robert H., *o.f.m.cap.* (TLS) Broken Arrow, OK St. Anne. —Died Sept. 27, 1996
† Daley, John M. (CHI) Chicago, IL Archbishop Quigley Seminary. —Died March 14, 1996
† Daly, Joseph M. (HRT) (Retired). —Died March 30, 1996
† Danagher, John J., *c.m.* (LA) Retired. —Died April 11, 1996
† Danahy, William F., *s.s.j.* (LAF) Eunice, LA St. Mathilda. —Died Feb. 1, 1996
† Darnieder, Leslie A. (MIL) (Retired). —Died Dec. 23, 1995
† Daugiello, Conrad (SPR) (Retired). —Died Oct. 12, 1996
† Daunhauer, Richard J. (L) (Retired). —Died March 6, 1996
† Davis, Rev. Msgr. Russell H. (BO) Wellesley, MA St. Paul. —Died Sept. 26, 1995
† De Wilde, Albert H., *o.s.b.* (SPK) Pasco, WA Our Lady of Lourdes Health Center. —Died April 27, 1996
† Dean, Rev. Msgr. Michael J. (PH) (Retired). —Died Jan. 18, 1996
† DeAngelis, Nazareno (CLV) Cleveland, OH Our Lady of Mount Carmel (East). —Died July 1, 1996
† Deasy, Thomas (SJ) (Retired). —Died Feb. 23, 1995
† Debski, John (TUC) Solomon, AZ Our Lady of Guadalupe. —Died Oct. 7, 1996
† deCampos, Jacinto A. (PRO) Providence, RI Our Lady of Rosary Church. —Died March 18, 1996
† DeDominicis, Daniel B., *c.s.sp.* (PIT) Retired. —Died June 24, 1996
† Degan, David Arthur (CHR) (Retired). —Died Feb. 5, 1996
† Delli Veneri, Leander, *c.p.* (SCR) Scranton, PA Saint Ann's Passionist Monastery. —Died Dec. 15, 1995
† Dembeck, Joachim, *o.f.m.conv.* (BO) Chelsea, MA St. Stanislaus. —Died Jan. 7, 1996
† Dempsey, Joseph G. (PIT) Harmarville, PA St. Francis. —Died June 11, 1996
† Dende, Cornelian, *o.f.m.conv.* (BUF) Athol Springs, NY St. Francis Friary. —Died Aug. 31, 1996
† Dermody, Ralph R. (COL) (Retired). —Died Jan. 31, 1996
† Desmond, Joseph R., *o.p.* (PRO) Retired. —Died Jan. 25, 1996
† Deters, Henry R., *o.s.b.* (KCK) St. Benedict, KS St. Mary's. —Died Jan. 3, 1996
† Devlin, James J. (SJ) (Retired). —Died Feb. 13, 1996
† Devlin, Rev. Msgr. Joseph A. (DM) (Retired). —Died July 22, 1996
† Dewey, Rev. Msgr. Charles F. (BO) Dedham, MA St. Mary. —Died Sept. 15, 1996
† DeWitte, Charles F. (PEO) (Retired). —Died May 18, 1996
† Diamond, Raphael, *o.cart.* (BUR) Arlington, VT Carthusian Foundation, Charterhouse of the Transfiguration. —Died June 16, 1996
† DiBenedetto, Rev. Msgr. Peter Paul (AMA) Amarillo, TX St. Hyacinth's. —Died Nov. 28, 1995
† Dick, C. Norbert (ALN) (Retired). —Died Feb. 7, 1996
† Dlugosz, John M., *o.f.m.* (GB) Manitowoc, WI St. Mary's Home for the Aged. —Died Feb. 5, 1996
† Dobkiewicz, Stanley A., *o.s.f.s.* (PH) Retired. —Died Jan. 14, 1996
† Doherty, Rev. Msgr. John C. (SC) (Retired). —Died May 24, 1996
† Doherty, Sean B., *o.p.* (P) Ashland, OR Our Lady of the Mountain Church. —Died July 15, 1996
† Doherty, Thomas (JOL) San Pierre, IN Little Co. of Mary. —Died Aug. 25, 1996
† Dohony, Rev. Msgr. Nicholas (BAL) (Retired). —Died May 25, 1996
† Doiron, James Wilson (LAF) Lafayette, LA St. Mary. —Died Jan. 16, 1996
† Donachie, Joseph (NY) Bronx, NY St. Vincent de Paul Residence. —Died May 6, 1996
† Donahue, James C., *o.s.f.s.* (CAM) Retired. —Died Oct. 7, 1996
† Donega, Carl D. (WOR) Worcester, MA Our Lady of Mt. Carmel-St. Ann. —Died Dec. 31, 1995
† Donnelly, John R. (MEM) Memphis, TN Blessed Sacrament Church. —Died April 19, 1996
† Dorsch, Rev. Msgr. David (BAL) (Retired). —Died July 2, 1996
† Dougherty, Harold Gene (SD) (Retired). —Died Aug. 18, 1996
† Dougherty, Rev. Msgr. T. David (BRK) Brooklyn, NY St. Athanasius Church. —Died Dec. 12, 1996
† Dowling, Edward J., *s.j.* (DET) Clarkston, MI Colombiere Jesuit Community. —Died May 18, 1996
† Downey, John P. (OM) (Retired). —Died Aug. 8, 1996
† Doyle, Howard (MEM) Memphis, TN St. Louis Church. —Died Feb. 5, 1996
† Doyle, Thomas A. (TUC) Tombstone, AZ Sacred Heart. —Died May 4, 1996
† Draeger, Robert R. (MIL) Milwaukee, WI St. Joseph

Hospital. —Died March 20. 1996
† Dressel, Rev. Msgr. John J. (WDC) Silver Spring, MD Christ the King Church. —Died April 5, 1996
† Drewes, Robert F. (IND) North Vernon, IN St. Mary. —Died June 15, 1996
† Driscoll, John J., *m.m.* (NY) Maryknoll, NY Maryknoll Fathers and Brothers. —Died Jan. 2, 1996
† Droney, James A., *m.s.* (LKC) Sulphur, LA St. Theresa. —Died March 28, 1996
† Droziak, Cyril, *o.f.m.* (PSC) Sybertsville, PA Holy Dormition Monastery. —Died Dec. 15, 1996
† Duda, Thaddeus Z. (CHI) Chicago, IL St. Constance. —Died April 25, 1996
† Dudek, Anthony A. (CHI) (Retired). —Died March 1, 1996
† Duffy, Finian, *o.f.m.* (PAT) Ringwood, NJ Holy Name. —Died Feb. 24, 1996
† Duffy, Joseph F. (PH) Linfield, PA St. Clare. —Died Dec. 7, 1995
† Duggan, Rev. Msgr. John J. (BAL) (Retired). —Died March 28, 1996
† Duggan, John P. (BUF) (Retired). —Died Dec. 29, 1996
† Dullea, Rev. Msgr. Edward M. (SFR) Mill Valley, CA Our Lady of Mount Carmel. —Died Aug. 8, 1996
† Dunfey, Kenneth (JUN) (Retired). —Died April 13, 1996
† Dunn, Edward J. (SFD) (On Duty Outside the Diocese). —Died Aug. 28, 1996
† Dunn, Robert T. (NY) (Retired). —Died March 31, 1996
† Dunne, John R., *o.s.a.* (PH) Villanova, PA Saint Thomas Monastery. —Died April 4, 1996
† Dunne, Rev. Msgr. Kevin (CC) (Retired). —Died April 8, 1996
† Durbin, Ambrose A., *c.m.* (STL) Perryville, MO St. Mary's of the Barrens. —Died Dec. 7, 1995
† Dwyer, Cormac, *s.d.s.* (MIL) Retired. —Died April 4, 1996
† Dziemian, Rev. Msgr. Anthony Bernard (DOD) (Retired). —Died April 24, 1996
† Ebel, Alfred (GB) (Special Assignment). —Died May 2, 1996
† Eckhoff, Rev. Msgr. Frederick C. (STL) (Retired). —Died Nov. 10, 1996
† Effinger, William J. (MIL) (On Leave). —Died Dec. 4, 1996
† Egan, Sebastian, *o.f.m.* (PAT) Ringwood, NJ Holy Name. —Died Feb. 22, 1996
† Eilerman, Herbert, *c.pp.s.* (CIN) Carthagena, OH St. Charles Center. —Died July 5, 1996
† Eimers, Robert J. (OM) Atkinson, NE St. Joseph Church. —Died April 24, 1996
† Elliott, William G., *s.j.* (SPK) Spokane, WA Gonzaga University. —Died July 8, 1996
† Ellis, William, *m.s.c.* (Y) Sebring, OH St. Ann. —Died Dec. 31, 1995
† Elsaesser, John Severin (COV) (Retired). —Died Aug. 17, 1996
† Endres, LeRoy E., *s.j.* (MIL) Wauwatosa, WI Jesuit Community at St. Camillus. —Died Dec. 5, 1995
† Engle, Robert B., *c.p.* (SCR) Scranton, PA Saint Ann's Passionist Monastery. —Died Dec. 12, 1995
† Enright, Neil, *o.m.i.* (BO) Tewksbury, MA Immaculate Heart of Mary Novitiate-Infirmary. —Died Sept. 4, 1996
† Essig, Robert G. (SJ) (Retired). —Died Nov. 20, 1996
† Estes, Ignatius, *o.ss.t.* (BAL) Retired. —Died Feb. 13, 1996
† Evers, Robert T., *s.s.* (TR) Retired. —Died Aug. 31, 1996
† Ewing, Robert J. (MEM) Memphis, TN St. Therese Church. —Died Sep. 14, 1996
† Eye, Rev. Msgr. Sylvester J., P.A. (RCK) (Retired). —Died April 4, 1996
† Fabisinski, Rev. Msgr. Edmund J. (NY) Hastings-on-Hudson, NY St. Stanislaus. —Died July 19, 1996
† Fagundes, Rev. Msgr. Valdemiro M. (SAC) Rio Vista, CA St. Elizabeth Parish. —Died Sept. 22, 1996
† Fahey, Cieran James (ORL) (Retired). —Died Nov. 15, 1995
† Fallon, Joseph M., *s.j.* (BO) Weston, MA Campion Health Center, Inc. —Died Jan. 29, 1997
† Farrant, James J. (PH) Philadelphia, PA St. Martin de Porres. —Died Aug. 14, 1996
† Farrell, Victor (MRY) (Retired). —Died April 13, 1996
† Farrell, William, *s.m.m.* (BRK) Ozone Park, NY Montfort Missionaries Provincialate. —Died Oct. 29, 1995
† Farren, Michael V., *c.m.* (PH) Philadelphia, PA St. Vincent's Seminary. —Died June 28, 1996
† Fasnacht, James P. (WIN) (Retired). —Died Jan. 16, 1996
† Fay, John P. (PRO) (Retired). —Died March 24, 1996
† Fearson, Alexander (ELP) El Paso, TX Nazareth Hall. —Died Dec. 30, 1995
† Fedewa, Rev. Msgr. Stanley (DET) (Retired). —Died Sept. 7, 1996
† Fedorchuck, Rev. Msgr. Peter (STF) (Retired). —Died April 27, 1996
† Feeney, John T. (BO) Newton, MA Corpus Christi. —Died Aug. 22, 1996
† Fell, Arnold A., *c.s.c.* (FTW) South Bend, IN Congregation of Holy Cross Indiana Province Provincial House. —Died June 18, 1996
† Ferrari, Adolph, *c.s.s.* (BO) Retired. —Died Jan. 25, 1996
† Ferrazzi, Thomas M., *o.s.m.* (CHI) Retired. —Died Oct. 21, 1995
† Ferris, Rev. Msgr. Richard W. (BRK) Rockaway Point, NY St. Genevieve. —Died April 21, 1996
† Fettig, Matthew, *o.s.b.* (BIS) Richardton, ND Assumption Abbey. —Died May 21, 1996
† Feyereisen, Nicholas J. (MAD) (Retired). —Died March 23, 1996
† Finan, Arthur, *c.ss.r.* (ALB) Saratoga Springs, NY St. John Neumann Residence. —Died June 20, 1996
† Finley, James F., *c.s.p.* (PAT) Retired. —Died Sept. 7, 1996
† Finn, Daniel E. (CHI) (Retired). —Died June 21, 1996
† Fisher, Marcellus, *o.s.b.* (IND) St. Meinrad, IN St. Meinrad Archabbey. —Died April 6, 1996
† Fitzgerald, A. Thomas (LAN) (Retired). —Died July 5, 1996
† Fitzgerald, Cyril, *o.carm.* (JOL) Darien, IL Carmelite Fathers Provincial Office. —Died Aug. 25, 1996
† Fitzpatrick, Rev. Msgr. David K. (PRT) Lewiston, ME St. Patrick's Church. —Died Aug. 12, 1996
† Fitzpatrick, Rev. Msgr. Michael J. (NEW) (Retired). —Died May 6, 1996
† Fitzsimons, Rev. Msgr. Edward J. (BUR) (Retired). —Died Aug. 6, 1996
† Flaherty, James A. (SJ) (Retired). —Died Sept. 28, 1995
† Flaherty, Patrick A., *c.m.* (PH) Philadelphia, PA St. Vincent's Seminary. —Died Aug. 30, 1996
† Flavin, Rev. Msgr. Cornelius J. (STL) (Retired). —Died Oct. 18, 1996
† Fleming, Edward B., *m.m.* (NY) Maryknoll, NY Maryknoll Fathers and Brothers. —Died Nov. 13, 1995
† Fleming, Rev. Msgr. John M. (NY) (Retired). —Died Oct. 17, 1996
† Flinn, John R. (NY) Maryknoll, NY Maryknoll Fathers and Brothers. —Died Aug. 6, 1996
† Flynn, Rev. Msgr. Cornelius P. (GAL) (Retired). —Died Feb. 9, 1996
† Flynn, John (TOL) (Retired). —Died Aug. 21, 1996
† Flynn, William C. (BO) Rockland, MA Holy Family. —Died Nov. 25, 1995
† Fogarty, Rev. Msgr. Edmund F. (NY) Shrub Oak, NY St. Elizabeth Ann Seton. —Died Aug. 2, 1996
† Foley, John J. (WOR) Worcester, MA Sacred Heart of Jesus. —Died July 26, 1996
† Follett, John E. (CAM) Runnemede, NJ St. Maria Goretti. —Died Feb. 4, 1996
† Forliti, Rev. Msgr. Robert Q. (DAL) (Retired). —Died May 10, 1996
† Fos, Rev. Msgr. John L. (GAL) (Retired). —Died March 13, 1996
† Fournier, Roger F. (MAN) (On Leave of Absence). —Died Nov. 10, 1995
† Fowlie, John, *o.f.m.* (SFR) San Francisco, CA St. Boniface. —Died Aug. 10, 1996
† Fox, John (BIR) (Retired). —Died Oct. 1, 1996
† Frank, Clement, *o.s.b.* (P) St. Benedict, OR Mt. Angel Abbey. —Died April 28, 1996
† Freegard, Charles E. (SLC) (Retired). —Died April 9, 1996
† French, Gregory E., *s.t.* (JKS) Philadelphia, MS Holy Cross. —Died Aug. 8, 1996
† Fruth, Alban, *o.s.b.* (SCL) Collegeville, MN St. John's Abbey, of the Order of St. Benedict. —Died March 15, 1996
† Fullam, Brendan J. (FgM) Maryknoll Foreign Missions. —Died March 20, 1996
† Fuller, Gregory J. (MEM) Memphis, TN St. Louis Church. —Died Sep. 10, 1996
† Fundalewicz, Edward L. (SCR) Scranton, PA St. Michael's Church. —Died Nov. 22, 1995
† Funk, Hubert J. (NEW) South Orange, NJ Seton Hall University. —Died Oct. 1, 1996
† Gacquin, Rev. Msgr. James (PAT) Montague, NJ St. James the Greater. —Died March 31, 1996
† Gaiero, Michael R., *m.m.* (NY) Maryknoll, NY Maryknoll Fathers and Brothers. —Died Nov. 12, 1995
† Galla, Rev. Msgr. Francis George (BGP) Monroe, CT Provincial House, Immaculate Heart of Mary Province, Sisters of the Holy Family of Nazareth. —Died Jan. 27, 1996
† Gallagher, Jerome, *o.f.m.* (PAT) Ringwood, NJ Holy Name. —Died Jan. 3, 1996
† Gallagher, Michael (BRK) (Retired). —Died June 24, 1996
† Gallagher, Rev. Msgr. Vincent B. (PH) (Retired). —Died April 26, 1996
† Gallivan, A. Paul (BO) Braintree, MA St. Clare. —Died Oct. 16, 1995
† Gallo, Marion R., *o.s.b.* (GBG) Vandergrift, PA Saint Gertrude. —Died July 31, 1996
† Galvin, Rev. Msgr. William E. (LR) Fort Smith, AK Immaculate Conception. —Died June 1, 1996
† Gamache, Flavius, *s.m.m.* (HRT) Litchfield, CT Montfort Missionaries. —Died Sept. 26, 1996
† Ganel, Stephen J., *c.m.* (NO) New Orleans, LA St. Stephen. —Died Oct. 23, 1995
† Garber, George T. (PIT) Bulger, PA St. Ann. —Died Jan. 18, 1996
† Garcia, Bienvenido, *o.f.m.cap.* (DAL) Dallas, TX Our Lady of Lourdes. —Died Aug. 5, 1996
† Gardzalla, Robert J. (SCR) (Retired). —Died April 19, 1996
† Gately, Thomas A. (BRK) Brooklyn, NY St. Francis of Assisi-St. Blaise Church. —Died Sept. 4, 1996
† Gauthier, Raphael (LAF) (Retired). —Died Dec. 30, 1996
† Gavin, Justin H. (TLS) Langley, OK St. Frances of Rome Church. —Died Oct. 24, 1996
† Gawinek, Walter J. (MIL) (Retired). —Died June 24, 1996
† Gendreau, Rev. Msgr. Alfred J. (FR) (Retired). —Died April 12, 1996
† Gerber, Francis W., *s.m.* (CIN) Retired. —Died Sept. 1, 1996
† Gerhart, Rudolph (SPK) (Retired). —Died April 28, 1996
† Ghirlando, Gabriel, *s.j.* (BO) Weston, MA Campion Center. —Died Feb. 9, 1997
† Ghirlando, Roland J. (BRK) Brooklyn, NY Assumption of the Blessed Virgin Mary Church. —Died Dec. 27, 1996
† Giammarino, Rev. Msgr. Vincent J. (CAM) (Retired). —Died Feb. 14, 1996
† Giblin, Gerard F., *s.j.* (NY) New York, NY Murray-Weigel Hall. —Died Dec. 31, 1995
† Gildea, Thomas, *c.ss.r.* (ALB) Saratoga Springs, NY St. John Neumann Residence. —Died Jan. 21, 1996
† Giltinan, William P. (ALT) (Medical Leave). —Died Dec. 21, 1995
† Gontek, Joseph C., *o.s.f.s.* (CAM) Retired. —Died Dec. 13, 1995
† Goodwin, Justin Leo (CHR) (Retired). —Died Dec.25, 1995
† Gorczyca, Benvenute, *o.f.m.conv.* (BUF) Buffalo, NY Corpus Christi. —Died April 12, 1996
† Gordon, Rev. Msgr. Bernard (PHX) (Retired). —Died June 24, 1996
† Gordon, Raymond P. (RCK) (Retired). —Died May 15, 1996
† Gordon, Thomas (STA) Keystone Heights, FL St. William. —Died May 6, 1996
† Gorman, Charles D. (WDC) (Retired). —Died Nov. 20, 1995
† Gosselin, Antonio A. (PRT) (Retired). —Died Feb. 14, 1996
† Gottenbos, Gerard J., *o.m.i.* (JUN) Wrangell, AK St. Rose of Lima. —Died June 15, 1996
† Gottschalk, Andrew E. (DEN) (Retired). —Died April 1, 1996
† Gough, Joseph F. (BO) Sudbury, MA Our Lady of Fatima. —Died Dec. 10, 1995
† Grace, John A. (NY) (Retired). —Died Dec. 3, 1996
† Gracias, Edward (OAK) Alameda, CA St. Albert. —Died Sept. 7, 1996
† Graf, John H. (COL) (Retired). —Died Dec. 16, 1996
† Greco, Amalio E., *s.a.c.* (BAL) Baltimore, MD St. Jude Shrine. —Died Nov. 1, 1995
† Green, John J. (SCR) (Retired). —Died Sept. 23, 1996
† Greene, James E. (DAV) (Retired). —Died June 21, 1996
† Grey, Thomas J., *s.j.* (BO) Chestnut Hill, MA The Jesuit Community at Boston College. —Died March 27, 1997
† Griffin, Rev. Msgr. W. Robert (E) (Retired). —Died May 18, 1996
† Griffith, J. William (DET) (Retired). —Died Feb. 12, 1996
† Grimmel, Richard R. (CHI) Oak Forest, IL St. Damian. —Died Dec. 30, 1995
† Grochowski, Edwin A. (MIL) (Retired). —Died Sept. 4, 1996
† Grogan, Francis J., *s.j.* (NY) New York, NY Murray-Weigel Hall. —Died Sept. 16, 1996
† Gryzik, Charles P. (CHI) (Retired). —Died July 28, 1996
† Guido, Rev. Msgr. John L. (NY) New York, NY Our Lady of Consolation Residence. —Died May 22, 1996
† Gunther, Carroll A. (MIL) (Retired). —Died March 11, 1996
† Haddican, Bernard Christopher (JKS) (Retired). —Died Jan. 28, 1996
† Haen, John (GB) (Retired). —Died Oct. 23, 1996
† Hafemann, Sigmund, *o.f.m.cap.* (SP) Seminole, FL Pope John XXIII Residence. —Died March 13, 1996
† Haile, Donald, *o.m.i.* (SAT) San Antonio, TX Oblate Madonna Residence. —Died April 1, 1996
† Hajjar, Peter, *b.s.o.* (NTN) Methuen, MA Basilian Salvatorian Order. —Died June 15, 1996
† Hakalski, Benvenute, *o.f.m.conv.* (TR) Trenton, NJ

St. Stanislaus. —Died March 1, 1996
† Halpin, Rev. Msgr. George C. (CHI) (Retired). —Died April 28, 1996
† Hammel, James T. (WIL) (Retired). —Died Aug. 4, 1996
† Hanna, Rev. Msgr. Francis J. (BUF) (Retired). —Died March 28, 1996
† Hanzel, Louis, *s.v.d.* (FgM) Society of the Divine Word Foreign Missions. —Died May 16, 1996
† Hardiman, Francis J. (BO) Saugus, MA Blessed Sacrament. —Died April 15, 1996
† Harrington, Rayner, *o.f.m.* (OAK) Oakland, CA St. Elizabeth's. —Died July 26, 1996
† Harris, Yates (MIA) (Retired). —Died Nov. 1, 1996
† Hartman, Robert J. (HEL) (Retired). —Died Aug. 12, 1996
† Hartmann, Jerome J. (CHI) (Retired). —Died Nov. 12, 1996
† Hayden, Jerry, *s.t.* (LKC) Retired. —Died Feb. 19, 1996
† Hayes, Damien J. (CC) (Retired). —Died Oct. 4, 1996
† Hearn, Robert J. (NY) (Retired). —Died May 16, 1996
† Heckathorn, Matthew, *o.s.c.* (LIN) Hastings, NE Crosier Monastery. —Died March 4, 1996
† Heery, Cornelius J. (BO) Quincy, MA Sacred Heart. —Died Jan. 12, 1996
† Heim, Henry L., *c.ss.r.* (BLX) Biloxi, MS St. John Neumann Residence. —Died Feb. 28, 1996
† Heinrichs, Joseph L., *s.a.c.* (MIL) Milwaukee, WI Mother of God Province. —Died June 26, 1996
† Hellmer, Rev. Msgr. Michael D. (STU) (Absent on Leave). —Died Aug. 11, 1996
† Hemenway, Richard F. (HT) Houma, LA Maria Immaculata. —Died March 30, 1996
† Henighan, Walter, *c.ss.r.* (ALB) Saratoga Springs, NY St. John Neumann Residence. —Died Jan. 22, 1996
† Herbst, Herman, *c.pp.s.* (CIN) Carthagena, OH St. Charles Center. —Died Nov. 14, 1995
† Hernandez, Manuel (PAT) Morristown, NJ Morristown Memorial Hospital. —Died Sept. 27, 1996
† Herrero, Bernardino (CC) (Retired). —Died Aug. 3, 1996
† Herrero, Fortunato, *o.m.i.* (SAT) San Antonio, TX Oblate Madonna Residence. —Died May 3, 1996
† Hesnan, Thomas F. (SFE) Albuquerque, NM Annunciation. —Died Dec. 4, 1996
† Hicks, Rev. Msgr. Harold E. (NY) Hyde Park, NY Regina Coeli. —Died April 9, 1996
† Higgins, Clement (FRS) (Retired). —Died Feb. 18, 1996
† Hill, John H. (SY) (Retired). —Died Nov. 11, 1996
† Hiller, George P. (PH) (Retired). —Died Sept. 10, 1996
† Hines, Vincent J. (KNX) (Retired). —Died Jan. 23, 1996
† Hlavac, Wencelaus M. (BAL) (Retired). —Died April 30, 1996
† Hoban, Michael J. (CHL) (Retired). —Died Dec. 29, 1995
† Hobbs, Frederick J. (BO) Wayland, MA St. Zepherin. —Died April 11, 1995
† Hoffman, Rev. Msgr. Leo A. (FTW) (Retired). —Died July 28, 1996
† Hogan, James P. (FAR) (Retired). —Died Nov. 11, 1996
† Hogan, Joseph F. (ROC) (Retired). —Died March 22, 1996
† Hohn, Francis (SCL) (Retired). —Died Dec. 31, 1995
† Hollerich, Cornelius J. (PEO) Orion, IL Mary, Our Lady of Peace. —Died Jan. 25, 1996
† Holmes, Richard H. (PH) Primos, PA St. Eugene. —Died Feb. 10, 1996
† Hoorman, John E., *c.pp.s.* (SAN) Winters, TX Our Lady of Mt. Carmel. —Died Dec. 30, 1995
† Hoover, William R. (FWT) (Retired). —Died Oct. 19, 1996
† Hopkins, Joseph P., *s.j.* (DET) Clarkston, MI Colombiere Center. —Died Oct. 31, 1995
† Hopkins, Thomas J., *o.s.f.s.* (VEN) Fort Myers, FL Our Lady of Light. —Died July 16, 1996
† Horan, John, *i.c.* (VEN) Bradenton, FL Sacred Heart. —Died Aug. 9, 1996
† Horner, Thomas P. (PH) Philadelphia, PA St. Mary Assumption. —Died Feb. 25, 1996
† Houlehin, John J. (STL) (Retired). —Died Oct. 24, 1996
† Howatt, William F. (BO) Revere, MA Our Lady of Lourdes. —Died Sept. 1, 1995
† Howe, Christian F., *o.carm.* (NY) Tappan, NY St. Eliseus Priory. —Died Dec. 5, 1995
† Hresko, George (NEW) (Retired). —Died May 16, 1996
† Huag, Rev. Msgr. William (SFD) Springfield, IL Sacred Heart Convent. —Died April 17, 1996
† Hudson, Frank, *s.c.j.* (MIL) Retired. —Died Jan. 5, 1996
† Hug, Edward O. (TOL) (Retired). —Died Aug. 21, 1996
† Hurley, John D. (HRT) (Retired). —Died April 21, 1996
† Hynes, Francis J., *c.m.* (SAN) Sweetwater, TX Holy Family. —Died May 28, 1996
† Iannetta, Vincent T. (HRT) (Retired). —Died Sept. 8, 1996
† Iannucci, Edward L. (PH) (Retired). —Died Feb. 29, 1996
† Ingoldsby, Gervase W. (SPC) (Retired). —Died June 9, 1996
† Isaacs, John S. (SFR) San Francisco, CA St. Peter. —Died Dec. 29, 1996
† Isabelle, Raymond, *m.s.* (LKC) Retired. —Died May 6, 1996
† Izabal, Juan B., *o.carm.* (LA) Los Angeles, CA St. Raphael. —Died Jan. 31, 1996
† James, Gerard A. (WH) Buckhannon, WV Holy Rosary. —Died Feb. 9, 1996
† James, Gerard A., *s.m.* (WH) Buckhannon, WV Holy Rosary. —Died Feb. 9, 1996
† Janak, Rev. Msgr. Hubert (SAT) (Retired). —Died June 26, 1996
† Janas, Edward, *c.r.* (MIL) Retired. —Died Nov. 15, 1995
† Janik, Walter T., *o.f.m.* (GR) Grand Rapids, MI St. Bernardine Friary. —Died June 1, 1996
† Jankowski, John, *c.m.* (HRT) Enfield, CT St. Joseph's Residence. —Died Jan. 3, 1996
† Jarosz, Alfred J., *o.c.d.* (GRY) Munster, IN Discalced Carmelite Fathers Monastery. —Died March 27, 1996
† Jaskievicz, Walter C., *s.j.* (NY) New York, NY Jesuit Community at Fordham University. —Died July 6, 1996
† Jenco, Martin (Lawrence), *o.s.m.* (CHI) Hillside, IL St. Domitilla. —Died July 19, 1996
† Jones, Fred B. (BEL) (Retired). —Died March 12, 1996
† Jones, William (BIR) (Retired). —Died Oct. 30, 1996
† Jordick, Leonard J. (NEW) Newark, NJ St. Antoninus. —Died July 24, 1996
† Joyce, Walter Joseph (SPR) (Retired). —Died July 16, 1996
† Julien, Rene E. (BO) Shirley, MA St. Anthony. —Died May 3, 1996
† Kakizaki, John T. (BRK) Rockaway Beach, NY St. Camillus. —Died May 15, 1996
† Kaleth, Marian, *c.r.* (MIL) Twin Lakes, WI St. John's. —Died Jan. 17, 1996
† Kalina, Francis (SAT) (Absent on Sick Leave). —Died March 5, 1996
† Kammer, Arthur C. (BRK) (Retired). —Died Feb. 1, 1996
† Kane, Eugene C. (CLV) (Retired). —Died Jan. 3, 1996
† Kane, Joseph R., *m.m.* (NY) Maryknoll, NY Maryknoll Fathers and Brothers. —Died Jan. 11, 1996
† Kane, William Francis Edward (LR) (Retired). —Died April 19, 1996
† Kapellen, John A. (MIL) (Retired). —Died Nov. 22, 1995
† Karaba, Joseph, *o.s.b.* (CLV) Cleveland, OH Benedictine Order of Cleveland. —Died Feb. 25, 1996
† Karas, Wenceslaus, *o.f.m.cap.* (TLS) Broken Arrow, OK St. Anne. —Died Aug. 26, 1994
† Karpowicz, Boleslaus P. (CHI) (Retired). —Died June 21, 1996
† Kauffman, Paul D., *s.s.j.* (MOB) Chastang, AL St. Peter the Apostle. —Died July 14, 1996
† Kazlauskas, John J. (SCR) (Retired). —Died Dec. 17, 1995
† Kealy, Rev. Msgr. Thomas M. (LIN) (Retired). —Died May 16, 1996
† Kean, David J., *c.j.* (LA) Santa Maria, CA St. Louis de Montfort. —Died March 5, 1996
† Keating, Rev. Msgr. James J. (BO) (Retired). —Died Nov. 15, 1995
† Keating, Robert J. (BEL) (Retired). —Died Sept. 26, 1996
† Keefe, Ambrose J., *o.s.b.* (RIC) Richmond, VA St. Benedict's. —Died April 11, 1994
† Keen, Robert J. (HRT) (Medical Leave). —Died Nov. 12, 1996
† Keever, Edward T. (FTW) (Retired). —Died July 8, 1996
† Keilen, Ernest, *s.v.d.* (FgM) Society of the Divine Word Foreign Missions. —Died July 25, 1996
† Keis, Rev. Msgr. Gottfried (CAM) (Retired). —Died March 4, 1996
† Kelley, Rev. Msgr. James F. (NEW) (Retired). —Died Sept. 11, 1996
† Kelly, James J., *s.j.* (CHI) Chicago, IL Loyola University. —Died Aug. 6, 1996
† Kelly, Laurence D. (CHI) (Retired). —Died May 23, 1996
† Kelly, Michael Joseph (GF) (Retired). —Died May 4, 1996
† Kenny, Dominic, *s.a.* (NY) Garrison, NY Graymoor Infirmary. —Died Jan. 1, 1996
† Kenny, Patrick J., *s.j.* (SEA) Mercer Island, WA St. Monica. —Died June 24, 1996
† Keohane, John J. (BO) Cohasset, MA St. Anthony. —Died May 31, 1996
† Kerwan, Rev. Msgr. James P. (HRT) (Retired). —Died July 4, 1996
† Kiely, John J. (HRT) West Hartford, CT St. Peter Claver. —Died Dec. 7, 1996
† Kilduff, John J. (RCK) (Retired). —Died Dec. 10, 1995
† Kim, Joseph (TR) Eatontown, NJ Immaculate Conception. —Died Aug. 29, 1996
† Kimmett, Rev. Msgr. Frederick J. (CHY) (Retired). —Died April 2, 1996
† King, Edward F. (BO) Concord, MA Our Lady. —Died Dec. 27, 1995
† King, Ronald, *o.f.m.* (PAT) Ringwood, NJ Holy Name. —Died Dec. 11, 1995
† Kirk, Martin J., *c.m.f.* (CHI) Oak Park, IL Claretian Fathers Headquarters of U.S.A. Eastern Province. —Died Sept. 15, 1996
† Kirn, Brian, *o.f.m.* (CHI) Chicago, IL Saint Peter's. —Died June 13, 1996
† Kittredge, Austin F., *s.a.* (LUB) Rotan, TX St. Joseph. —Died Jan. 21, 1995
† Klein, Robert J. (IND) (On Disability Leave). —Died Jan. 1, 1997
† Kline, John L. (PH) Scoventry, PA St. Thomas More. —Died Jan. 5, 1996
† Klinec, Rev. Msgr. Julius G. (COL) (Retired). —Died Dec. 20, 1996
† Klug, Elmer C. (CHI) (Retired). —Died Jan. 7, 1996
† Knopke, Kenneth, *o.f.m.* (SP) St. Petersburg, FL St. Anthony. —Died April 10, 1996
† Knuff, Robert C. (CLV) Euclid, OH St. Robert Bellarmine. —Died May 17, 1996
† Kochanowski, John P. (WOR) West Warren, MA St. Stanislaus. —Died March 31, 1996
† Kolk, Raymond, *s.v.d.* (TR) Bordentown, NJ Society of the Divine Word. —Died Jan. 3, 1996
† Kolodziejcsyk, Joseph (LUB) (Retired). —Died Jan. 22, 1996
† Kopsca, Andrew (FTW) (Retired). —Died Nov. 3, 1996
† Kormann, Joseph, *s.d.b.* (SP) Tampa, FL Mary Help of Christians School. —Died March 15, 1996
† Korth, Francis N., *s.j.* (MIL) Wauwatosa, WI Jesuit Community at St. Camillus. —Died Oct. 16, 1995
† Kosarchyn, Mykola (STN) Chicago, IL SS. Volodymyr ans Olha Parish. —Died Oct. 23, 1996
† Kosin, Wallace W. (Y) (Retired). —Died Oct. 6, 1996
† Kostrzewski, Daniel, *o.f.m. conv.* (FAR) Grafton, ND Sacred Heart of Oakwood. —Died Oct. 6, 1996
† Kostrzewski, Daniel, *o.f.m.conv.* (FAR) Grafton, ND Sacred Heart. —Died Oct. 5, 1996
† Koziol, Thaddeus R. (STP) (Retired). —Died April 7, 1996
† Kozlowski, Rev. Msgr. Raymond J. (BUF) Buffalo, NY Immaculate Heart of Mary. —Died June 22, 1996
† Kraft, George, *c.pp.s.* (CIN) Carthagena, OH St. Charles Center. —Died July 28, 1996
† Kranak, Donald (PSC) Minersville, PA SS. Peter and Paul Church. —Died April 21, 1996
† Kreger, Rev. Msgr. Edmund W. (TR) Normandy Beach, NJ Our Lady of Peace. —Died Aug. 28, 1996
† Kreidermacher, Andrew L. (WIN) (Retired). —Died Dec. 24, 1995
† Kress, Sylvester J. (PIT) Carnegie, PA St. Joseph. —Died March 20, 1996
† Krol, Michael (AUS) (Retired). —Died Sept. 18, 1996
† Krol, Michael F. (GAL) (Retired). —Died Sept. 18, 1996
† Kubsz, Charles J., *er.cam.* (STU) Bloomingdale, OH Holy Family Hermitage. —Died June 1, 1996
† Kuenz, Robert B. (STL) (Retired). —Died Jan. 2, 1996
† Kuppens, William J., *c.i.c.m.* (SAT) Lytle, TX St. Andrew. —Died Sept. 22, 1996
† Kwaaitaal, Rev. Msgr. William (SHP) (Retired). —Died Jan. 16, 1996
† Laketek, Victor J., *o.s.b.* (JOL) Lisle, IL St. Procopius Abbey. —Died July 19, 1996
† Lamontagne, Maurice H. (FR) (Retired). —Died July 2, 1996
† Lamping, Stephen (JC) Wellsville, MO Church of the Resurrection. —Died Dec. 7, 1995
† Lana, Francis A. (DUB) Cascade, IA St. Mary Parish. —Died June 14, 1996
† Lanning, George B. (LFT) (Retired). —Died Oct. 1, 1996
† LaPiezo, Rev. Msgr. Francisco (ELP) El Paso, TX Holy Family. —Died Jan. 1, 1996
† Lapinski, Joseph S., *c.pp.s.* (CIN) Retired. —Died Feb. 17, 1996
† LaRiviere, Earl W. (SD) (Retired). —Died June 24, 1996
† Larkin, James A. (SP) Dunedin, FL Our Lady of Lourdes Church. —Died July 1, 1996
† Las Heras, Segundo (HRT) Poquonock, CT St. Joseph Church. —Died Feb. 12, 1996
† LaSalle, John, *o.f.m.* (SFR) Retired. —Died Aug. 10, 1996
† Lauer, Severin, *o.s.b.* (SCL) Collegeville, MN St. John's Abbey, of the Order of St. Benedict. —Died

July 11, 1996
† Lauters, Harry J. (MAD) (Retired). —Died Jan. 31, 1996
† Lawler, Phillip (DM) Cumming, IA St. John's Church. —Died Dec. 16, 1995
† Lawrie, Edward A. (BRK) (Retired). —Died Aug. 8, 1996
† Leach, Cyril V. (SFR) Greenbrae, CA St. Sebastian. —Died March 19, 1996
† Leahy, Edward, *o.c.d.* (SR) Oakville, CA Carmelite House of Prayer. —Died Dec. 29, 1995
† Ledbetter, Dominic, *b.s.o.* (NTN) Retired. —Died May 19, 1996
† Lee, Lawrence J. (LA) Los Angeles, CA St. John of God. —Died Dec. 5, 1996
† Lees, Charles J., *s.m.* (CIN) Dayton, OH Marianist Provincialate. —Died Oct. 16, 1996
† Lehane, James A. (WOR) Fitchburg, MA St. Bernard's. —Died Jan. 4, 1996
† Leonard, Francis J. (CAM) Audubon, NJ Holy Maternity. —Died Oct. 3, 1996
† Lesniewski, Eldred B. (MIL) (Retired). —Died Aug. 22, 1996
† Lettau, Rev. Msgr. John J. (Y) Youngstown, OH St. Edward. —Died May 25, 1996
† Licari, John (PT) (Retired). —Died May 4, 1996
† Lievens, Joseph J. (DEN) (Retired). —Died Nov. 3, 1995
† Lima, Rev. Msgr. Joseph (FRS) (Retired). —Died April 11, 1996
† Lingenfelser, Angelus, *o.s.b.* (KCK) Atchison, KS St. Benedict's Abbey. —Died Nov. 11, 1996
† Lis, Edward (DET) (Retired). —Died June 11, 1996
† Loeper, Frederick J. (ALN) (Retired). —Died Aug. 31, 1996
† Loftus, Robert J. (CHI) Chicago, IL St. Raymond de Penafort. —Died April 27, 1996
† Long, Florent, *o.f.m.* (NY) New York, NY Franciscan Friars, Order of Friars Minor. —Died April 27, 1996
† Long, Jeremiah (NEW) Secaucus, NJ Immaculate Conception. —Died Oct. 16, 1996
† LoPresto, James, *s.d.s.* (MIL) Retired. —Died Oct. 14, 1995
† Lucas, Eugene (SAC) Rio Vista, CA St. Joseph Parish. —Died Dec. 10, 1996
† Lucas, Joseph R. (Y) (Retired). —Died Dec. 2, 1995
† Luger, Arnold E. (STP) (Retired). —Died Nov. 19, 1995
† Lukach, John P. (BIS) New Town, ND Church of St. Anthony. —Died Jan. 31, 1996
† Lukan, Kenneth J. (DUB) (Retired). —Died Feb. 18, 1996
† Lutz, Eugene J., *c.s.v.* (RCK) McHenry, IL Villa Desiderata Retreat House. —Died June 11, 1996
† Lux, Michael J., *c.s.p.* (CHI) Retired. —Died June 12, 1996
† Lynch, Rev. Msgr. John J. (RVC) Southampton, NY Sacred Hearts of Jesus and Mary. —Died April 11, 1996
† Lyons, Rev. Msgr. Joseph G. (PH) (Retired). —Died Dec. 24, 1995
† MacDonald, John H. (MET) (On Leave). —Died July 29, 1996
† Macher, F. Stephen, *c.m.* (MET) Plainsboro, NJ Vincentian Renewal Center. —Died May 6, 1996
† Macholz, Ignatius M. (CHI) (Retired). —Died March 15, 1996
† Mack, Thaddeus, *o.s.c.* (LIN) Hastings, NE Crosier Monastery. —Died Dec. 20, 1995
† Mackesy, William M., *m.m.* (NY) Maryknoll, NY Maryknoll Fathers and Brothers. —Died Aug. 27, 1996
† Mackey, Daniel P. (DAV) Davenport, IA St. Vincent Center. —Died Feb. 20, 1996
† Mackey, John J. (BAL) (Retired). —Died July 6, 1996
† Maco, Joseph P. (HRT) (Retired). —Died July 15, 1996
† Maguire, Bernard F. (SHP) (Retired). —Died April 10, 1996
† Maguire, Francis X. (SP) St. Petersburg, FL Transfiguration Church. —Died Nov. 8, 1996
† Maguire, Peter J. (PRO) (Retired). —Died July 8, 1996
† Mahaffey, Neal R., *o.f.m.cap.* (SAL) Victoria, KS St. Fidelis Friary. —Died Oct. 22, 1995
† Maher, Thomas J., *c.ss.r.* (BRK) Brooklyn, NY Our Lady of Perpetual Help Basilica. —Died July 7, 1996
† Mahoney, Rev. Msgr. Charles A. (SAG) (Retired). —Died Oct. 28, 1996
† Mahoney, John P., *o.p.* (BO) Hanover, MA St. Mary of the Sacred Heart. —Died July 7, 1996
† Mahoney, Rev. Msgr. John T. (BRK) (Retired). —Died Oct. 14, 1996
† Maier, Raymond P. (MAD) (Absent On Sick Leave). —Died Feb. 23, 1996
† Malik, Joseph A. (Y) Jefferson, OH St. Joseph Parish. —Died Jan. 2, 1996
† Mamo, Henry (HT) (Retired). —Died Dec. 8, 1996
† Mannion, John J. (NEW) South Orange, NJ Seton Hall University. —Died Nov. 20, 1996
† Marco, LeRoy (JOL) Napperville, IL St. Patrick Residence. —Died June 22, 1996
† Marien, Jerome E., *o.m.i.* (BO) Tewksbury, MA Immaculate Heart of Mary Novitiate-Infirmary. —Died Dec. 25, 1995
† Marinak, Rev. Msgr. Thomas A. (NY) Staten Island, NY Holy Family. —Died Aug. 14, 1996
† Mark, Albert Andrew (NEW) Midland Park, NJ Nativity. —Died April 4, 1996
† Markowski, Rev. Msgr. Alexander F. (NY) Newburgh, NY St. Francis of Assisi. —Died March 16, 1996
† Marleau, Floyd J., *s.m.m.* (RVC) Bay Shore, NY Montfort Missionaries. —Died Aug. 9, 1996
† Martel, Leo A., *s.s.e.* (MOB) Selma, AL Edmundite Fathers. —Died Jan. 30, 1996
† Martell, Ceferino (PCE) (Retired). —Died Aug. 25, 1996
† Martens, John, *c.m.f.* (PHX) Prescott, AZ Sacred Heart Parish Center. —Died Sept. 1, 1995
† Martin, Jerome (MIA) Fort Lauderdale, FL Blessed Sacrament Church. —Died May 12, 1996
† Martocchi, Felix J., *s.d.b.* (SFR) Retired. —Died Oct. 22, 1995
† Marum, Rev. Msgr. Kieran (LA) Burbank, CA St. Finbar. —Died Dec. 5. 1995
† Marx, Joseph B. (LC) (Retired). —Died Nov. 27, 1996
† Marzan, Miguel A., *s.t.* (FgM) Trinity Missions. —Died Dec. 17, 1995
† Masalewicz, Edward A. (LC) (Retired). —Died Oct. 26, 1996
† Mason, John, *o.s.b.* (PRO) Portsmouth, RI Abbey of St. Gregory the Great. —Died April 26, 1995
† Masterson, Reginald R., *o.p.* (NO) New Orleans, LA St. Dominic. —Died March 28, 1996
† Mathieu, Georges P. (LC) (Retired). —Died Feb. 28, 1996
† Matircho, George J. (SCR) (Retired). —Died March 24, 1996
† Matt, Irwin H. (DUB) LaMotte, IA Holy Rosary Parish. —Died Dec. 4, 1995
† Matteo, Francis G., *o.s.a.* (BO) Lawrence, MA Holy Rosary. —Died Feb. 24, 1996
† Matters, William F. (BRK) Elmhurst, NY Ascension. —Died April 23, 1996
† Matuszewski, Leo J. (ROC) (Retired). —Died Nov. 8, 1996
† Matz, Leroy A. (WCH) (Retired). —Died Dec. 12, 1995
† Maus, Lawrence Dennis (LR) Clinton, AR St. Mary-St. Vincent. —Died June 9, 1996
† May, Alois B. (DUB) Waterloo, IA St. Edward Parish. —Died Aug. 1, 1996
† Mayer, Arthur, *o.s.b.* (TR) Pennington, NJ St. James. —Died Feb. 1, 1996
† Mayer, John F., *o.f.m.* (FgM) Franciscan Foreign Missions. —Died March 28, 1996
† Mayfield, Gerald K. (OKL) Mustang, OK Holy Spirit Church. —Died Jan. 10, 1996
† Maziarz, Emil J. (BEL) (Retired). —Died Sept. 24, 1996
† McAllister, Rev. Msgr. Joseph B. (WDC) Garrett Park, MD Holy Cross Church. —Died Dec. 16, 1995
† McAndrew, Anthony D. (PH) (Retired). —Died July 25, 1996
† McAndrews, Arthur J. (SCR) (Retired). —Died April 25, 1996
† McAndrews, Dunstan, *o.s.b.* (IND) St. Meinrad, IN St. Meinrad Archabbey. —Died Sept. 18, 1996
† McAuley, Gary, *o.f.m.cap.* (NY) Retired. —Died April 22, 1995
† McBride, James J. (DUB) Peosta, IA St. John the Baptist Church. —Died Dec. 27, 1995
† McCarrick, Paul F. (FR) Fall River, MA Saint Joseph's Church. —Died Dec. 12, 1996
† McCarthy, Edward J., *o.s.a.* (ORL) Casselberry, FL Saint Augustine. —Died April 8, 1996
† McCloskey, George P. (SCR) (Military Chaplains). —Died Aug. 20, 1996
† McCloskey, James V., *m.m.* (FgM) Maryknoll Foreign Missions. —Died Nov. 11, 1995
† McCloskey, Kevin, *c.p.* (SCR) Scranton, PA Saint Ann's Passionist Monastery. —Died March 6, 1996
† McCool, Francis (NY) New York, NY Murray-Weigal Hall. —Died April 20, 1996
† McCool, Francis J., *s.j.* (NY) New York, NY Murray-Weigel Hall. —Died April 20, 1996
† McCormack, Francis J., *c.m.* (PH) Philadelphia, PA St. Vincent's Seminary. —Died June 13, 1996
† McCormick, Most Rev. J. Carroll (SCR) (Retired). —Died Nov. 2, 1996
† McCullough, Francis, *o.m.i.* (SAT) San Antonio, TX Oblate Madonna Residence. —Died March 5, 1996
† McDonnell, Joseph A., *o.s.f.s.* (PH) Retired. —Died June 13, 1996
† McEnrue, James R., *s.m.* (BO) Framingham Centre, MA The Marist House. —Died Aug. 22, 1996
† McGavin, William, *o.f.m.* (PAT) Ringwood, NJ Holy Name. —Died Jan. 14, 1996
† McGill, Rev. Msgr. Henry (DAL) (Retired). —Died Dec. 29, 1996
† McGinnis, Daniel P. (COL) Columbus, OH Holy Trinity Church. —Died Oct. 21, 1996
† McGinty, Michael J. (OAK) (Retired). —Died March 3, 1996
† McGivern, Carroll A. (DAV) (Retired). —Died April 2, 1996
† McGoldrick, Frances E. (TLS) (Retired). —Died Aug. 20, 1996
† McGovern, William H. (ALT) (Retired). —Died Dec. 29, 1995
† McGowan, Thomas C., *o.p.* (BO) Dover, MA St. Stephen Priory. —Died Sept. 13, 1996
† McGrath, Daniel E., *c.ss.r.* (ALB) Saratoga Springs, NY St. John Neumann Residence. —Died Sept. 25, 1995
† McGrath, John (PBL) (Retired). —Died Aug. 18, 1996
† McGraw, John B., *s.j.* (NEW) Jersey City, NJ Jesuits of Saint Peter's College, Inc. —Died Feb. 21, 1996
† McGuire, Bernard F., *o.carm.* (NEW) Cresskill, NJ St. Therese of Lisieux. —Died July 23, 1996
† McHale, Michael A. (ROC) Rochester, NY Rochester Institute of Technology. —Died Dec. 25, 1995
† McHugh, Rev. Msgr. Neil (PHX) (Retired). —Died Nov. 29, 1995
† McKenzie, John J. (PH) (Retired). —Died April 7, 1996
† McMahon, Donald A. (DEN) (Retired). —Died Nov. 18, 1995
† McManamon, John, *o.f.m.* (CLV) Parma, OH Holy Family Home. —Died April 11, 1996
† McNaboe, Charles (CC) Laredo, TX St. Patrick Church. —Died Jan. 26, 1996
† McPartland, Thomas, *c.ss.r.* (ALB) Saratoga Springs, NY St. John Neumann Residence. —Died Dec. 19, 1995
† McSherry, Hugh E. (PH) (Retired). —Died Dec. 27, 1995
† McTernan, Frederick J. (NEW) (Retired). —Died Sept. 2, 1996
† Meinen, Myron J. (LC) (Retired). —Died May 13, 1996
† Melancon, David, *o.s.b.* (NO) St. Benedict, LA St. Joseph Abbey. —Died Nov. 25, 1995
† Melican, Thomas J. (NY) Sloatsburg, NY St. Joseph's Home. —Died Feb. 14, 1996
† Memmolo, Louis, *c.s.* (WDC) Bowie, MD Villa Rosa Nursing Home. —Died June 24, 1996
† Menard, Anthony J. (SPR) (Retired). —Died Jan. 22, 1996
† Meyer, Theophilus, *o.f.m.cap.* (DET) Detroit, MI St. Bonaventure Friary. —Died Sept. 15, 1996
† Midura, Anthony, *s.d.b.* (NY) West Haverstraw, NY Don Bosco Retreat Center and Marian Shrine. —Died March 10, 1996
† Mielechowski, James, *c.m.* (HRT) Enfield, CT St. Joseph's Residence. —Died April 8, 1996
† Mierzwinski, Eugene A., *c.s.v.* (CHI) Retired. —Died Oct. 16, 1995
† Mihouich, George R. (BRK) (Retired). —Died Dec. 8, 1996
† Minnich, John C. (CLV) Bedford Heights, OH Holy Trinity. —Died July 9, 1996
† Missenda, Rev. Msgr. Edward S. (GAL) Crosby, TX Sacred Heart Church. —Died Dec. 19, 1995
† Mitchell, John E. (FWT) St. Antonio, TX St. Henry's Church. —Died Oct. 1, 1996
† Mitchell, John D., *c.s.p.* (NY) New York, NY St. John the Apostle. —Died Dec. 18, 1996
† Mohler, James A., *s.j.* (DET) Clarkston, MI Colombiere Center. —Died Aug. 19, 1996
† Molloy, William J. (CIN) (Retired). —Died Nov. 14, 1996
† Monahan, John, *c.s.v.* (JOL) St. Anne, IL St. Anne. —Died Oct. 6, 1996
† Moncrief, Justin, *o.f.m.* (TUC) Tucson, AZ Mission San Xavier del Bac. —Died Dec. 31, 1995
† Monroe, Lee J. (CLV) Wickliffe, OH Borromeo Seminary. —Died Nov. 2, 1996
† Montague, Vincent H., *m.m.* (FgM) Maryknoll Foreign Missions. —Died July 29, 1996
† Montano, Benjamin (FRS) Delano, CA St. Mary's. —Died Oct. 19, 1996
† Monte, Alfred J., *o.s.a.* (BO) Chestnut Hill, MA Our Mother of Consolation. —Died March 7, 1996
† Montgomery, Leo F. (WIL) (Retired). —Died Nov. 27, 1996
† Monty, Raymond P. (FR) (Retired). —Died Feb. 8, 1996
† Moore, John D. (SFD) Macon, IL St. Stanislaus Church. —Died May 15, 1996
† Morais, Stephen G., *s.m.* (BO) Lawrence, MA Sacred Heart. —Died Sept. 16, 1996
† Morgan, Harry (PHX) (Retired). —Died Nov. 18, 1995
† Morris, Edward V. (MET) (Retired). —Died Aug. 30, 1996
† Morrissey, William J., *m.m.* (NY) Maryknoll, NY Maryknoll Fathers and Brothers. —Died April 20, 1996
† Mott, Charles, *o.f.m.cap.* (NEW) Union City, NJ Our Lady of Guadalupe Friary. —Died March 28, 1996

† Muench, Richard F., *s.a.c.* (MIL) Milwaukee, WI Mother of God Province. —Died Oct. 17, 1995
† Mulcahy, Rev. Msgr. Philip M. (NY) Bronx, NY St. Helena. —Died April 3, 1996
† Muldoon, Charles (SFR) (On Duty Outside the Diocese). —Died Oct. 16, 1995
† Mullen, Lawrence P. (JC) Edina, MO St. Joseph. —Died March 1, 1996
† Mullen, Rev. Msgr. Timothy M. (BAL) (Retired). —Died March 11, 1996
† Muller, Liguori, *o.f.m.* (PAT) Ringwood, NJ Holy Name. —Died Dec. 3, 1995
† Mulligan, Eugene (SPK) (Retired). —Died Sept. 20, 1996
† Mulligan, Rev. Msgr. Robert T. (RVC) Rockville Center, NY St. Agnes Cathedral. —Died Nov. 4, 1996
† Mulvaney, Bernard G., *c.s.v.* (CHI) Retired. —Died Sept. 25, 1995
† Munnelly, James (SB) Sun City, CA St. Vincent Ferrer Church. —Died April 15, 1996
† Muresan, Very Rev. George (ROM) (Retired). —Died March 22, 1996
† Murphy, Cornelius, *o.f.m.cap.* (DET) Detroit, MI St. Bonaventure Friary. —Died July 8, 1996
† Murphy, Cronan, *o.f.m.* (GB) Manitowoc, WI St. Mary's Home for the Aged. —Died March 16, 1996
† Murphy, Edward J. (CLV) (Retired). —Died Nov. 10, 1996
† Murphy, Rev. Msgr. Francis J. (BRK) Brooklyn, NY St. Anselm. —Died Jan. 24, 1996
† Murphy, Rev. Msgr. Francis H. (PAT) Clifton, NJ St. Philip the Apostle. —Died May 9, 1996
† Murphy, J. Dennis, *o.s.b.* (SP) San Antonio, FL St. Anthony. —Died Dec. 6, 1995
† Murphy, James (DET) (Retired). —Died June 17, 1996
† Murphy, James D. (NY) Staten Island, NY St. Joseph-St. Thomas. —Died July 17, 1996
† Murphy, Robert M. (PIT) Wilkinsburg, PA St. James. —Died May 2, 1996
† Murray, Edward F. (LEX) (Retired). —Died April 13, 1996
† Murray, Eugene J., *s.j.* (NY) New York, NY Murray-Weigel Hall. —Died May 26, 1996
† Murray, James (JOL) Clarendon Hills, IL Notre Dame. —Died April 3, 1996
† Murray, Sylvester J., *s.m.a.* (NEW) Tenafly, NJ Society of African Missions. —Died May 17, 1996
† Mylin, Edwin B. (BAL) (Retired). —Died Dec. 31, 1995
† Nadeau, Armand G., *m.s.* (WOR) Retired. —Died Oct. 3, 1996
† Nadeau, Henry E., *s.s.e.* (MOB) Selma, AL Edmundite Fathers. —Died March 17, 1996
† Nadeau, Leon (SPR) (Retired). —Died Nov. 14, 1996
† Nagele, Joseph, *glmy.* (CIN) Retired. —Died Nov. 22, 1995
† Nakonechny, Emilian (SJP) (Retired). —Died Jan. 4, 1997
† Nardone, Michael (DET) Sterling Heights, MI St. Malachy Parish. —Died May 2, 1996
† Naughton, Joseph J. (WDC) (Retired). —Died Sept. 12, 1996
† Nawn, Henry J. (PH) (Retired). —Died Jan. 20, 1996
† Neal, Leo G., *o.f.m.conv.* (MIL) Retired. —Died Oct. 4, 1996
† Nedd, Edward S. (RVC) (Retired). —Died Nov. 22, 1995
† Nees, John F., *o.s.f.s.* (PH) Retired. —Died Feb. 2, 1995
† Neill, Rev. Msgr. Christopher C. (BO) Woburn, MA St. Charles. —Died Dec. 4, 1995
† Neverauskas, Rev. Msgr. Joseph A. (ALN) (Retired). —Died Jan. 13, 1996
† Nichols, Richard W. (MIL) (Retired). —Died July 25, 1996
† Niebling, Howard V. (E) Curwensville, PA St. Timothy Church. —Died Sept. 14, 1996
† Niedermaier, Joseph F., *o.s.f.s.* (WIL) Retired. —Died Dec. 2, 1995
† Nijenhius, John, *o.carm.* (GAL) Baytown, TX St. John the Evangelist. —Died July 18, 1996
† Noonan, Timothy, *o.f.m.* (SFE) Retired. —Died Sept. 25, 1995
† North, Orlis F. (KC) (Retired). —Died May 6, 1996
† Norton, Paul P. (WDC) (Retired). —Died Aug. 16, 1996
† Novak, Emilian E. (TYL) (Retired). —Died Aug. 27, 1996
† Nowak, Evarist, *o.f.m.conv.* (BUF) Batavia, NY St. Jerome Hospital. —Died Jan. 23, 1996
† Nuevo, Joseph, *c.m.f.* (PHX) Prescott, AZ Sacred Heart Parish Center. —Died April 26, 1996
† Nugent, Edmund B., *o.s.b.* (PAT) Morristown, NJ St. Mary's Abbey. —Died Aug. 2, 1995
† O'Brien, Michael J. (NY) Mamaroneck, NY Holy Trinity. —Died Dec. 3, 1996
† O'Connell, Thomas, *c.ss.r.* (NY) New York, NY Our Lady of Perpetual Help. —Died Dec. 8, 1995
† O'Connor, Colm (MRY) (Retired). —Died March 6, 1996
† O'Connor, James (OAK) (Retired). —Died May 24, 1996
† O'Connor, Kyran, *c.p.* (CHI) Chicago, IL Passionist Community - Daneo Hall. —Died April 13, 1996
† O'Connor, Patrick J. (RC) Burkw, SD Sacred Heart Church. —Died Sept. 22, 1996
† O'Day, Thomas J., *s.j.* (NY) New York, NY Murray-Weigel Hall. —Died Aug. 22, 1996
† O'Donnell, Rev. Msgr. Michael F. (NY) Bronx, NY Our Lady of Assumption. —Died Sept. 26, 1996
† O'Donnell, Ralph M. (OM) (Retired). —Died Nov. 14, 1996
† O'Donnell, Thomas (ORG) Newport Beach, CA Our Lady of Mt. Carmel. —Died Aug. 3, 1996
† O'Grady, James B. (BRK) (Retired). —Died Dec. 12, 1996
† O'Hara, Philbert J., *m.s.* (HRT) Retired. —Died March 17, 1996
† O'Hare, John, *o.f.m.cap.* (ROC) Trumansburg, NY St. James the Apostle. —Died July 20, 1996
† O'Keefe, Joseph, *o.m.i.* (MIA) Miami, FL Holy Redeemer. —Died Jan. 22, 1996
† O'Malley, James Joseph (BGP) St. Rose Parish. —Died June 9, 1996
† O'Neil, John J., *s.s.* (BAL) Retired. —Died Jan. 26, 1996
† O'Neill, Emmet P. (HEL) (Retired). —Died July 26, 1996
† O'Neill, Rev. Msgr. John J. (PH) (Retired). —Died Feb. 27, 1996
† O'Neill, John J. (SCR) (Retired). —Died Dec. 19, 1995
† O'Neill, John J. (SJ) (Retired). —Died Oct. 24, 1995
† O'Nolan, Gerald M. (OKL) (Retired). —Died Dec. 20, 1996
† O'Reilly, Daniel J. (LC) (Retired). —Died Dec. 20, 1995
† O'Reilly, James (BIR) (Retired). —Died May 5, 1996
† O'Reilly, Michael, *o.s.b.* (SFS) Retired. —Died Aug. 28, 1996
† O'Shea, Daniel (ROC) New York, NY General Theological Seminary. —Died Sept. 1, 1996
† O'Sullivan, Carroll (SJ) (Retired). —Died Oct. 24, 1996
† O'Toole, Eugene J. (R) Bordentown, NJ Bordentown Correctional Center. —Died March 5, 1996
† O'Toole, Eugene J. (TR) Bordentown, NJ NJ Bordentown Correction Center. —Died March 5, 1996
† Oates, John (NEW) Linden, NJ St. Elizabeth. —Died June 2, 1996
† Oborny, Francis J. (OM) (Retired). —Died Nov. 12, 1995
† Ochoa, Javier G., *o.s.b.* (CC) Sandia, TX Corpus Christi Abbey. —Died May 28, 1996
† Okruhlik, Theophil, *o.m.i.* (SAT) San Antonio, TX Oblate Madonna Residence. —Died May 2, 1996
† Olson, Donald J. (WIN) (Retired). —Died Jan. 30, 1996
† Oman, Richard B. (MIL) (Retired). —Died May 27, 1996
† Opdenaker, Rev. Msgr. Theodore A. (TR) (Retired). —Died May 7, 1996
† Orso-Manzonetta, Aldo (P) (Retired). —Died March 22, 1996
† Orta-Colomo, Antonio (SFR) San Francisco, CA St. Peter. —Died Sept. 22, 1996
† Ozimec, Joseph J. (CLV) Barberton, OH Sacred Heart. —Died Nov. 10, 1996
† Page, Russell B. (PRO) Chepachet, RI St. Eugene Rectory. —Died Oct. 10, 1996
† Pallas, Raymond A. (SJ) (Retired). —Died March 17, 1996
† Palumbo, Louis (MOB) (Retired). —Died Sept. 6, 1996
† Parrott, Thomas W. (SPC) (Retired). —Died Jan. 31, 1996
† Parulis, Vincent J., *m.i.c.* (WOR) Worcester, MA St. Casimir. —Died March 23, 1996
† Patacconi, Noel, *o.s.b.* (DET) Detroit, MI Holy Family. —Died Sept. 26, 1996
† Patnode, Keough (CR) (Retired). —Died Dec. 14, 1995
† Paul, Harry (DET) (Retired). —Died March 20, 1996
† Paulmichi, John (GLP) (Retired). —Died Jan. 8, 1996
† Pavel, John (ROM) (Retired). —Died May 5, 1994
† Pegnam, John W. (FR) (Retired). —Died April 16, 1996
† Penley, W. Dunstan, *o.s.b.* (PRO) Portsmouth, RI Abbey of St. Gregory the Great. —Died June 15, 1996
† Peradotto, Richard (SFD) Carlinville, IL SS. Mary & Joseph Church. —Died Dec. 28, 1995
† Perfetto, Anthony R., *s.m.* (CIN) Centerville, OH St. Leonard Center, Inc. —Died May 3, 1996
† Perhach, Ernest (GAL) (Retired). —Died Oct. 14, 1996
† Peters, Rev. Msgr. Robert (PEO) (Retired). —Died Sept. 7, 1996
† Petramale, Dennis, *o.f.m.* (ALB) Catskill, NY St. Anthony Friary. —Died Feb. 22, 1996
† Petricek, Irenes, *o.f.m.* (CHI) Retired. —Died Feb. 26, 1996
† Petz, Norman (JOL) Lockport, IL St. John Vianney. —Died June 20, 1996
† Peyton, Thomas F., *c.s.c.* (FTW) South Bend, IN Congregation of Holy Cross Indiana Province Provincial House. —Died June 30, 1996
† Pfeil, Elmer F. (MIL) (Retired). —Died Jan. 7, 1996
† Pfeilschifter, Daniel, *o.f.m.* (IND) Indianapolis, IN Sacred Heart. —Died May 22, 1996
† Phelan, Edward J. (PEO) (Retired). —Died June 25, 1996
† Phillips, Salvator, *o.f.m.* (PAT) Ringwood, NJ Holy Name. —Died Dec. 11, 1995
† Pichla, John H. (PH) (Absent On Leave). —Died Aug. 23, 1996
† Pickla, John (CR) (Retired). —Died Aug. 23, 1996
† Pietrzyk, Rev. Msgr. Stanley (NY) (Retired) Poughkeepsie, NY St. Joseph's. —Died Oct. 31, 1996
† Pikus, Edward, *o.f.m.cap.* (PIT) Pittsburgh, PA Vincentian Home. —Died April 11, 1996
† Pitaro, Rev. Msgr. Mimie B. (BO) Stoughton, MA Immaculate Conception. —Died Sept. 3, 1995
† Pitoniak, Mark, *o.s.b.* (CLV) Cleveland, OH Benedictine Order of Cleveland. —Died May 13, 1996
† Pluhacek, Anthony (OM) (Retired). —Died June 6, 1996
† Podowski, Rev. Msgr. Henry A. (GBG) (Retired). —Died Sept. 19, 1996
† Poirier, Philip (PHX) (Retired). —Died Aug. 5, 1996
† Popell, Rev. Msgr. Charles W. (GR) (Retired). —Died Sept. 18, 1996
† Pouget, Richard A. (DET) Allenton, MI St. John the Evangelist Parish. —Died Feb. 14, 1996
† Poulin, Donald J. (NY) Beacon, NY St. Joachim. —Died Sept. 27, 1996
† Powell, George C. (PSC) (Retired). —Died March 13, 1996
† Powell, Rev. Msgr. John K. (PSC) (Retired). —Died Feb. 21, 1996
† Powell, Thomas M. (CC) Corpus Christi, TX Most Precious Blood Church. —Died June 7, 1996
† Powers, James E., *s.j.* (BO) Weston, MA Campion Health Center, Inc. —Died Jan. 17, 1997
† Prefontaine, Maurice A., *s.s.s.* (SLC) Taylorsville, UT St. Martin de Porres. —Died Aug. 12, 1996
† Preske, Felix J. (FAR) (Retired). —Died July 25, 1996
† Price, Rev. Msgr. L. J. (GAL) (Retired). —Died Sept. 29, 1995
† Principe, Walter H., *c.s.b.* (GAL) Houston, TX Dillon House. —Died May 8, 1996
† Pronovost, Raoul (NOR) Moosup, CT All Hallows Church. —Died Nov. 2, 1996
† Prusko, Edwin (ALB) (Retired). —Died May 7, 1996
† Przyborowski, Brian T., *o.f.m.* (SUP) Tomahawk, WI St. Mary. —Died Sept. 23, 1996
† Pulvirenti, Paul F. (PAT) Paterson, NJ St. John the Baptist Cathedral. —Died March 3, 1996
† Quinn, Justin J. (FR) (Retired). —Died June 14, 1996
† Quinn, Timothy, *o.f.m.* (PAT) Ringwood, NJ Holy Name. —Died Nov. 3, 1995
† Quintana, Rev. Msgr. Eusebio (YAK) White Swan, WA St. Mary's Church. —Died Sept. 24, 1996
† Rabatsky, Raymond (SB) Yucca Valley, CA St. Mary of the Valley. —Died June 12, 1996
† Radvina, Vincent (SR) (Retired). —Died Nov. 30, 1995
† Radziecki, Sylvester L. (DET) (Retired). —Died April 16, 1996
† Rail, Damian, *c.p.* (SCR) Scranton, PA Saint Ann's Passionist Monastery. —Died Feb. 17, 1996
† Rakowski, Emil A., *o.f.m.* (GB) Manitowoc, WI St. Mary's Home for the Aged. —Died July 28, 1996
† Rastatter, Rev. Msgr. Rowan (MIA) (Retired). —Died Jan. 8, 1996
† Rathke, Jerome J. (MIL) (Retired). —Died Nov. 27, 1995
† Reilly, Joseph W., *s.j.* (NY) New York, NY Murray-Weigel Hall. —Died Feb. 14, 1996
† Remias, Joseph L. (TR) North Plainfield, NJ St. Luke's. —Died Aug. 7, 1996
† Rey, Antonio R. (SFR) Daly City, CA Our Lady of Perpetual Help. —Died Feb. 6, 1996
† Reynolds, Rev. Msgr. William J. (CAM) Raymond, NJ St. Villas. —Died April 22, 1996
† Rice, George (SB) (Retired). —Died March 3, 1996
† Richards, Willaim G. (MAR) (Retired). —Died April 1, 1996
† Richardson, James W., *c.m.* (STL) Perryville, MO St. Mary's of the Barrens. —Died July 8, 1996
† Richmond, Joseph J. (STL) (Retired). —Died March 25, 1996
† Ried, Robert N., *o.p.* (PH) Philadelphia, PA Holy Name Priory. —Died Aug. 18, 1996
† Riedmueller, Robert F. (SUP) (Retired). —Died Oct. 2, 1996
† Rigovsky, Ronald R., *o.s.b.* (JOL) Lisle, IL St. Procopius Abbey. —Died March 3, 1996

† Ring, John M. (SFR) (Retired). —Died April 15, 1996
† Ringwelski, Raymond (SCL) (Retired). —Died Nov. 4, 1996
† Rittenhouse, David A. (BO) Cambridge, MA Blessed Sacrament. —Died Sept. 17, 1996
† Roczen, Edward A. (GAY) (Retired). —Died Jan. 2, 1996
† Rodak, Roman, *c.pp.s.* (TOL) Bellevue, OH Sorrowful Mother Shrine. —Died July 3, 1996
† Rodriguez, Jose (SFE) Santa Fe, NM St. Anne. —Died Feb. 22, 1996
† Rodriquez, Victor J. (ARE) Hatillo, Perpetual Help Church. —Died Dec. 30, 1995
† Roethler, Michael, *o.s.b.* (OKL) Shawnee, OK St. Benedict. —Died June 26, 1995
† Rogers, Alfred J. (RVC) (Retired). —Died Jan. 13, 1996
† Rogers, John (SR) (Graduate Studies). —Died Nov. 8, 1995
† Rogers, William J. (CHI) (Retired). —Died April 30, 1996
† Rohr, Vincent, *o.f.m.cap.* (SAL) Victoria, KS St. Fidelis Friary. —Died Nov. 5, 1995
† Rokicki, Stanley C. (DET) (Retired). —Died July 16, 1996
† Romb, Anselm, *o.f.m.conv.* (CHI) Libertyville, IL Our Lady of Fatima Friary. —Died Oct. 10, 1996
† Romero, Tobias, *c.m.f.* (LA) San Gabriel, CA San Gabriel Mission. —Died Aug. 4, 1996
† Rooney, John E. (NY) Port Jervis, NY NY Immaculate Conception. —Died June 23, 1996
† Rosario, Jorge del Valle (CGS) Caguas, PR Movimiento Juan XX111. —Died Oct. 24, 1995
† Rosing, Fred, *s.d.s.* (MIL) Milwaukee, WI Milwaukee Archdiocesan Campus Ministry. —Died Oct. 6, 1996
† Rowe, Stephen, *o.f.m.cap.* (PIT) Pittsburgh, PA Vincentian Home. —Died July 16, 1996
† Rowley, Charles, *o.f.m.* (BO) Boston, MA St. Anthony Shrine. —Died Nov. 20, 1996
† Royce, James E., *s.j.* (SEA) Seattle, WA Jesuit House. —Died Jan. 6, 1996
† Rudden, Victor (JOL) Elmhurst, IL Mary Queen of Heaven. —Died March 6, 1996
† Rumery, Roger, *o.s.b.* (KCK) Atchison, KS Sacred Heart. —Died March 29, 1996
† Rusu, Rev. Dr. Gheorge (ROM) (Retired). —Died Feb. 25, 1996
† Ryan, Brice T., *o.s.b.* (GBG) Latrobe, PA Saint Vincent Archabbey. —Died March 19, 1996
† Ryan, Frederick I., *o.s.a.* (PH) Villanova, PA Saint Thomas Monastery. —Died Aug. 24, 1996
† Ryan, Rev. Msgr. Philip F. (SFR) (Retired). —Died May 2, 1996
† Ryan, Richard R., *c.s.p.* (NY) Retired. —Died Nov. 25, 1995
† Ryan, Rev. Msgr. William G. (BRK) Bayside, NY Queen of Peace Residence. —Died June 21, 1996
† Rybka, Damian A., *o.f.m.* (GB) Manitowoc, WI St. Mary's Home for the Aged. —Died Sept. 27, 1996
† Ryzner, Stanley L. (CHI) (Retired). —Died Dec. 24, 1995
† Sabas, John Paul (ALN) (Retired). —Died July 18, 1996
† Sabo, William Robert (PBR) Johnstown, PA St. Mary's Church. —Died Jan. 2, 1996
† Saghy, Paul (MIA) (Retired). —Died Sept. 19, 1996
† Sakalauskas, Kajetonas (PH) Philadelphia, PA Our Lady Calvary. —Died June 8, 1996
† Salazar, Mario Arias (NEW) (Retired). —Died July 21, 1996
† Saldutti, Soccorso J. (PH) Croydon, PA St. Thomas Aquinas. —Died April 21, 1996
† Sampson, Rev. Msgr. Francis (SFS) (Retired). —Died Jan. 28, 1996
† Sander, Rev. Msgr. Edward (SAL) Lincoln, KS St. Patrick's. —Died Jan. 3, 1996
† Santen, Raymond (STL) (Retired). —Died March 22, 1996
† Satterlee, John A. (MAD) (Absent On Sick Leave). —Died June 15, 1996
† Saunders, Rev. Msgr. Kenneth W. (CLV) Middleburg Heights, OH St. Bartholomew. —Died Oct. 19, 1996
† Sauter, John D. (CIN) (Retired). —Died Sept. 28, 1996
† Sauve, James W., *s.j.* (WDC) Washington, DC Vice President of AJCU. —Died Sept. 23, 1996
† Savage, John H. (BRK) Brooklyn, NY St. Saviour. —Died Aug. 15, 1996
† Savage, William D. (JC) Slater, MO St. Joseph. —Died March 11, 1996
† Scallan, Rev. Msgr. Belton A. (ALX) (Retired). —Died Aug. 7, 1996
† Scanlon, Thomas, *o.m.i.* (HBG) Harrisburg, PA St. Margaret Mary Alacoque. —Died April 20, 1996
† Scannell, Joseph F., *c.ss.r.* (BO) Boston, MA Our Lady of Perpetual Help. —Died Nov. 26, 1995
† Schaefer, Rev. Msgr. Frederick F. (RVC) Patchogue, NY St. Francis de Sales. —Died Aug. 20, 1996
† Schauer, Blase W., *o.p.* (OAK) Oakland, CA St. Albert Priory. —Died June 4, 1996
† Scheets, Thomas (PBL) Pueblo, CO St. Leander's Parish. —Died Aug. 7, 1996
† Scheljens, Alphonse C., *c.j.* (LA) Santa Maria, CA St. Elizabeth Ann Seton. —Died Aug. 14, 1996
† Schellhase, Owen, *o.f.m.cap.* (SAL) Victoria, KS St. Fidelis Friary. —Died Feb. 20, 1996
† Schendel, Alfred, *t.o.r.* (ALT) Johnstown, PA Sacred Heart Monastery. —Died April 16, 1996
† Schick, William F. (MAR) (Retired). —Died Jan. 9, 1996
† Schieder, Rev. Msgr. Joseph E. (BUF) (Retired). —Died June 12, 1996
† Schmidt, Rev. Msgr. John J. (BRK) Brooklyn, NY St. Mary's. —Died Jan. 31, 1996
† Schmidt, John J. (BRK) Brooklyn, NY St. Mark's Church. —Died Jan. 31, 1996
† Schneider, Albert A. (SFE) Espanola, NM Sacred Heart. —Died June 1, 1996
† Schneider, Herman, *o.f.m.* (LA) Santa Barbara, CA Franciscan Friary, Order of Friars Minor (Old Mission). —Died June 29, 1996
† Schoenberg, Martin W., *o.s.c.* (LIN) Hastings, NE Crosier Monastery. —Died Nov. 11, 1996
† Schreifels, Ferdinand, *o.s.b.* (SCL) Collegeville, MN St. John's Abbey, of the Order of St. Benedict. —Died Jan. 29, 1996
† Schuh, Joseph E., *s.j.* (NY) New York, NY Murray-Weigel Hall. —Died July 8, 1996
† Schulte, Rev. Msgr. George N. (DUB) Dubuque, IA Loras College. —Died April 23, 1996
† Schultz, Henry J., *c.ss.r.* (STL) Liguori, MO St. Clement Health Care Center. —Died Oct. 4, 1996
† Schwarten, Paul J. (WH) (Retired). —Died Dec. 5, 1995
† Schwartz, James A. (KC) (Retired). —Died April 29, 1996
† Sclafani, Rev. Msgr. Dominic A. (BRK) Brooklyn, NY Our Lady of Grace. —Died May 4, 1996
† Scyocurka, Peter Joseph Dionysius (PSC) Trenton, NJ St. Mary of the Assumption. —Died Oct. 29, 1996
† Seitz, Aloys (CR) (Retired). —Died May 29, 1996
† Selbert, Rev. Msgr. Eugene H. (BUF) (Retired). —Died July 16, 1996
† Seliskar, David R., *s.j.* (DET) Clarkston, MI Colombiere Center. —Died Feb. 3, 1996
† Severin, Gustav, *o.s.j.* (SAC) Sacramento, CA St. Mary's. —Died March 18, 1996
† Sexton, Rev. Msgr. Francis J. (BO) Brookline, MA St. Mary. —Died Aug. 25, 1996
† Shanahan, James J., *s.j.* (NY) New York, NY Murray-Weigel Hall. —Died Feb. 12, 1996
† Shanahan, Patrick E. (RVC) West Babylon, NY Our Lady of Grace. —Died Nov. 26, 1995
† Shanahan, William J. (SY) (Retired). —Died Sept. 20, 1996
† Shea, Joseph Thomas (NEW) (Retired). —Died March 14, 1996
† Shea, Louis C. (SFD) Quincy, IL St. Dominic Church. —Died Nov. 15, 1996
† Shea, Thomas F. (HRT) (Retired). —Died Feb. 11, 1996
† Shedivy, Leo F., *o.s.c.* (LIN) Hastings, NE Crosier Monastery. —Died June 2, 1996
† Sheehan, Robert L. (WIN) (Retired). —Died Dec. 15, 1995
† Sherer, Joseph M., *o.p.* (WDC) Retired. —Died June 28, 1996
† Sheridan, Stephen Edward (NEW) Jersey City, NJ St. Aloysius. —Died April 10, 1996
† Sherman, Rev. Msgr. James E. (CIN) (Retired). —Died July 20, 1996
† Sherman, John T. (BRK) Douglaston, NY Bishop Mugavero Residence. —Died Oct. 1, 1996
† Shields, Thomas M., *s.j.* (CLV) Clinton, OH Loyola Lakes Retreat House. —Died Aug. 18, 1996
† Shimalonis, Albert L. (COS) (Retired). —Died Nov. 30, 1996
† Shine, Cornelius (LA) Los Angeles, CA Immaculate Heart of Mary Church. —Died Dec. 4, 1996
† Shreve, Robert (LKC) (Retired). —Died Feb. 24, 1996
† Sickler, James G. (BRK) Brooklyn, NY St. Finbar. —Died Oct. 14, 1996
† Sievers, V. Paul (STL) (Retired). —Died April 5, 1996
† Sikora, Joseph F. (PH) (Retired). —Died July 12, 1996
† Silva, John C. (STO) Modesto, CA St. Stanislaus Church. —Died Feb. 25, 1996
† Simms, Russell J. (DOD) (Retired). —Died Sept. 25, 1996
† Simon, Francis R., *o.s.b.* (OKL) Shawnee, OK St. Gregory's Abbey. —Died Dec. 18, 1995
† Sinnige, Joannes Cornelius (LAF) (Retired). —Died Oct. 7, 1996
† Skoyles, Arthur W. (SFR) San Mateo, CA Serra Clergy House. —Died Sept. 4, 1996
† Skupien, James F. (ALT) Bellwood, PA St. Joseph. —Died Feb. 11, 1996
† Skurski, Herbert, *o.f.m.conv.* (SPR) Granby, MA St. Hyacinth Friary. —Died Jan. 16, 1996
† Sliben, Robert J., *o.praem.* (PH) Retired. —Died Aug. 5, 1996
† Smaza, Rev. Msgr. Edward J. (CHI) (Retired). —Died Nov. 28, 1995
† Smith, Gregory L. (BUF) Clarence, NY Clarence Residence. —Died Jan. 2, 1996
† Smith, James F., *m.m.* (NY) Maryknoll, NY Maryknoll Fathers and Brothers. —Died Nov. 6, 1996
† Smith, Raymond J. (MAR) South Range, MI Holy Family Church. —Died Sept. 16, 1996
† Snell, George E. (DAV) (Retired). —Died Jan. 1, 1996
† Snyder, Sigmund, *o.f.m.* (LA) Santa Barbara, CA Franciscan Friary, Order of Friars Minor (Old Mission). —Died May 17, 1996
† Sodja, Max F. (CLV) (Retired). —Died Feb. 16, 1996
† Sorokowski, Vincent (NEW) Little Ferry, NJ St. Margaret. —Died May 7, 1996
† Souza, Rev. Msgr. Maurice (FR) (Retired). —Died Aug. 17, 1996
† Spriggs, John, *c.s.sp.* (BR) Baton Rouge, LA St. Agnes. —Died Jan. 1996
† Squier, Andrew J. (SEA) (Retired). —Died Aug. 7, 1996
† Stamborski, James (GB) Manitowoc, WI St. Andrew. —Died Dec. 31, 1995
† Stanek, Edwin J. (LC) (Retired). —Died Aug. 12, 1996
† Starc, Rev. Msgr. Martin, *s.t.d.* (STO) San Andreas, CA St. Andrew. —Died Oct. 30, 1996
† Statham, Dennis, *o.s.b.* (OKL) Shawnee, OK St. Gregory's Abbey. —Died April 11, 1996
† Stebelsky, Reverend Canons Basil (PHU) (Retired). —Died May 25, 1996
† Stern, Sylvester (GB) (Retired). —Died April 13, 1996
† Stim, Rev. Msgr. John A. (PSC) (Retired). —Died Jan. 21, 1996
† Stock, Michael E., *o.p.* (BO) Dover, MA St. Stephen Priory. —Died May 8, 1996
† Stockmeyer, Timothy, *c.p.* (HRT) West Hartford, CT Holy Family Monastery. —Died June 25, 1996
† Stout, Dunstan, *c.p.* (SCR) Scranton, PA Saint Ann's Passionist Monastery. —Died Sept. 6, 1996
† Stovik, Louis C. (PBL) Pueblo, CO St. Leander's Parish. —Died Aug. 7, 1996
† Straka, William, *o.s.c.* (SCL) Onamia, MN Crosier Monastery. —Died Nov. 14, 1995
† Stremel, Rev. Msgr. Joseph A. (DOD) (Retired). —Died Feb. 28, 1996
† Strzelewicz, Joseph (LAN) (Retired). —Died May 18, 1996
† Sudock, Joseph (TOL) (Retired). —Died Dec. 30, 1995
† Suelzer, Anthony J. (GRY) (Retired). —Died Dec. 5, 1996
† Sullivan, Charles E., *s.j.* (TOL) Toledo, OH Gesu. —Died Sept. 3, 1996
† Sullivan, Francis P., *o.s.a.* (CHI) Olympia Fields, IL St. Nicholas of Tolentine Monastery. —Died Nov. 4, 1995
† Sullivan, Jeremiah (CR) (Retired). —Died June 24, 1996
† Sullivan, Robert J. (SY) Binghamton, NY St. Paul. —Died June 8, 1996
† Sullivan, William J. (DAV) Fairfield, IA St. Mary Church. —Died May 28, 1996
† Suttmiller, Francis, *o.s.b.* (SFS) Retired. —Died Sept. 7, 1996
† Svetinsky, Ludvik F. (FAR) (Retired). —Died Jan. 6, 1996
† Swain, Arthur E., *s.j.* (SFR) Retired. —Died July 18, 1996
† Sweeney, Joseph F., *c.s.sp.* (SB) Retired. —Died Jan. 17, 1996
† Sweeney, Rev. Msgr. William J. (YAK) (Retired). —Died Jan. 9, 1996
† Swiatecki, Jerome (TOL) (Retired). —Died Jan. 5, 1996
† Swick, Robert J. (BUF) (Retired). —Died June 23, 1996
† Sypneski, John (FRS) (Retired). —Died June 8, 1996
† Szamocki, John A. (WOR) Dudley, MA St. Andrew Bobola. —Died Aug. 16, 1996
† Tait, Alexander A. (SJ) (Retired). —Died Oct. 1, 1996
† Talbott, Raymond L., *s.j.* (P) Portland, OR Colombiere Community. —Died Nov. 22, 1995
† Tallon, William F. (PH) (Retired). —Died Dec. 14, 1995
† Tamayo, Santiago L. (LA) (Unassigned). —Died Jan. 22, 96
† Tarnowski, Cajetan, *o.f.m.conv.* (MIL) Retired. —Died Oct. 2, 1996
† Taxter, John F. (CAM) Waterford, NJ St. Anthony. —Died May 16, 1996
† Temaat, Norbert C. (DOD) Garden City, KS St. Mary Parish. —Died Feb. 16, 1996
† Teolis, Anthony, *c.pp.s.* (TOL) Bellevue, OH Sorrowful Mother Shrine. —Died March 3, 1996
† Terpstra, John R. (SC) (On Leave). —Died Oct. 10, 1996
† Teske, Lloyd W., *c.s.c.* (FTW) South Bend, IN

Congregation of Holy Cross Indiana Province Provincial House. —Died Sept. 29, 1995
† Tessier, Henri (ALB) (Retired). —Died May 4, 1996
† Tessier, Victor J. (BRK) Far Rockaway, NY St. Gertrude. —Died June 26, 1996
† Thompson, Mark (LAN) (Retired). —Died Feb. 14, 1996
† Thompson, William G., *s.j.* (CHI) Chicago, IL Loyola University. —Died Sept. 24, 1996
† Timm, James D. (WIN) Adrian, MN St. Adrian Church. —Died Feb. 29, 1996
† Tinney, Rev. Msgr. William L. (GAL) (Retired). —Died April 3, 1996
† Tobin, William (ROC) Elmira Heights, NY St. Charles Borromeo Rectory. —Died Oct. 29, 1996
† Tockert, Joseph V. (WCH) Yates Center, KS St. Joseph Church. —Died Nov. 23, 1995
† Tomlinson, Donald F. (STP) (Retired). —Died Nov. 9, 1995
† Toner, Richard J. (HRT) (Retired). —Died Oct. 28, 1996
† Tong, Paul J., *c.ss.r.* (BLX) Biloxi, MS St. John Neumann Residence. —Died July 18, 1996
† Topic, Peter, *o.f.m.* (SJ) San Jose, CA Croatian Center. —Died Jan. 8, 1996
† Torres-Frias, Rev. Msgr. Victor Joseph (BGP) (Retired). —Died Nov. 10, 1995
† Torresan, Adam, *c.s.* (LA) Retired. —Died Aug. 13, 1996
† Tortorice, John (BEA) (Retired). —Died May 7, 1996
† Tracy, Melvin, *s.d.s.* (GB) St. Nazianz, WI St. Mary's Convent. —Died March 15, 1996
† Trapp, Donald G. (BUF) (Retired). —Died March 24, 1996
† Trapp, Raymond A. (CLV) Brook Park, OH Assumption of Mary. —Died April 11, 1996
† Treinen, Most Rev. Sylvester William (B) (Retired). —Died Sept. 30, 1996
† Troch, Louis G. (WDC) (Retired). —Died June 22, 1996
† Trott, William (ROC) Livonia, NY St. Joseph. —Died Oct. 2, 1996
† Truesdell, William H., *s.j.* (CHI) Chicago, IL V.A. Lakeside Medical Center. —Died Nov. 3, 1995
† Truoy, Lucien, *o.f.m.* (GB) Manitowoc, WI St. Mary's Home for the Aged. —Died Sept. 14, 1996
† Tuchlinsky, John F. (RCK) (Retired). —Died July 24, 1996
† Tucke, Charles L. (BO) (Retired). —Died Dec. 2, 1995
† Urbanek, Sylvester M. (CHI) (Retired). —Died Feb. 8, 1996
† Ustaszewski, Thaddeus W., *o.s.b.* (Man) (MAN) St. Anselm Abbey. —Died Oct. 21, 1995
† Van De Casteele, Henry, *o.m.i.* (SAT) San Antonio, TX Oblate Madonna Residence. —Died May 25, 1996
† Vanecko, Martin, *o.s.b.* (CLV) Cleveland, OH Benedictine Order of Cleveland. —Died Nov. 6, 1995
† VanWolvlear, John L., *c.s.c.* (FTW) Granger, IN St. Pius X. —Died Dec. 21, 1995
† Varna, Rev. Msgr. Leons (DM) (Retired). —Died Feb. 15, 1996
† Varriale, Rev. Msgr. Alfred A. (BRK) Brooklyn, NY Our Lady of Guadalupe. —Died Jan. 18, 1996
† Vega, Manuel de Jesus, *f.s.c.* (OAK) Moraga, CA Saint Mary's College. —Died Nov. 28, 1995
† Verbrugge, Bernard, *o.m.i.* (AUS) Kingsland, TX St. Charles Borromeo. —Died Aug. 24, 1996
† Verhelle, Joseph C., *s.j.* (DET) Bloomfield Hills, MI Manresa Jesuit Retreat House. —Died April 29, 1996
† Viater, Rev. Msgr. John J. (GRY) Hammond, IN St. Margaret Mary Parish. —Died Nov. 7, 1996
† Vinklarek, Emil Thomas (SAT) (Retired). —Died Oct. 31, 1996
† Vogt, George (ROC) (Retired). —Died June 27, 1996
† VonArx, William A. (KC) (Retired). —Died July 6, 1996
† Vossberg, Roger (SCL) (Retired). —Died May 1, 1996
† Vrabely, John A. (FTW) Garrett, IN St. Joseph. —Died Sept. 18, 1996
† Wade, Rev. Msgr. Francis J. (BIR) (Retired). —Died Oct. 21, 1996
† Wagner, Elmer A., *o.f.m.* (ALB) Loudonville, NY Siena College. —Died May 21, 1996
† Wagner, George H. (OKL) (Retired). —Died Jan. 7, 1996
† Wahl, Edward V., *c.o.* (CHR) Rock Hill, SC The Oratory of Rock Hill. —Died June 25, 1995
† Walbaum, Dean L. (DUB) Andrew, IA St. John Parish. —Died April 4, 1996
† Waldie, George J. (L) (Retired). —Died June 11, 1996
† Waldron, John (SAN) Midland, TX St. Stephen. —Died Dec. 20, 1995
† Walling, Edward (DET) (Retired). —Died Sept. 14, 1996
† Wallis, Anthony I. (DET) (Retired). —Died Sept. 4, 1996
† Walsh, Edmond W. (PH) (Retired) —Died June 5, 1996
† Walsh, James G., *c.s.p.* (NY) New York, NY Murray-Weigel Hall. —Died Nov. 3, 1996
† Walsh, Romuald, *c.p.* (BRK) Jamaica, NY Immaculate Conception Monastery. —Died Dec. 22, 1996
† Wassel Thomas W. (PH) (Retired). —Died April 22, 1996
† Waterhouse, Rev. Msgr. John M. (OG) (Retired). —Died Dec. 28, 1995
† Waters, James E. (R) (Retired). —Died March 29, 1996
† Watterson, Peter F. (PMB) Palm Beach Gardens, FL Prison Ministry. —Died Sep. 12, 1996
† Webber, Bernard F. (E) (Retired). —Died Aug. 15, 1996
† Weber, Richard V., *o.p.* (DET) Farmington Hills, MI Monastery of the Blessed Sacrament. —Died Jan. 7, 1996
† Webster, Giles, *o.f.m.* (PAT) Ringwood, NJ Holy Name. —Died Feb. 10, 1996
† Weiker, Clemens J. (L) (Retired). —Died May 15, 1996
† Weimer, Henry V. (SC) (Retired). —Died Nov. 20, 1995
† Weinzapel, Joseph J. (DAL) (Retired). —Died May 1, 1996
† Weishaar, Michael, *o.f.m.* (LA) Santa Barbara, CA Franciscan Friary, Order of Friars Minor (Old Mission). —Died Feb. 20, 1996
† Weiss, Bernard A. (BUF) (Retired). —Died March 3, 1996
† Weltin, Roman G., *s.j.* (DET) Clarkston, MI Colombiere Center. —Died Dec. 31, 1995
† Wenz, Hyacinth, *o.f.m.* (BO) Boston, MA St. Anthony Residence. —Died Oct. 22, 1995
† Werenski, Robert J. (DET) Oakland, CO Hospice of Southeastern Michigan. —Died Dec. 10, 1996
† Wheeler, Raymond P., *o.s.a.* (CHI) Olympia Fields, IL St. Nicholas of Tolentine Monastery. —Died Dec. 30, 1995
† White, Norman R. (DUB) (Retired). —Died Aug. 28, 1996
† Wieber, Edward L., *s.j.* (DET) Clarkston, MI Colombiere Jesuit Community. —Died May 13, 1996
† Wiewell, Rev. Msgr. John M. (FWT) (Retired). —Died April 1, 1996
† Wild, Philip T. (CHI) (Retired). —Died Feb. 3, 1996
† Wilde, Rev. Msgr. Alvin (SAN) Midland, TX Our Lady of San Juan Church. —Died June 22, 1996
† Williams, Brian J. (CIN) St. Martin, OH St. Martin Church. —Died Aug. 1, 1996
† Willis, Charles J., *s.m.* (STP) White Bear Lake, MN St. Mary of the Lake. —Died Jan. 27, 1996
† Wilson, Francis M., *s.j.* (DET) Clarkston, MI Colombiere Jesuit Community. —Died Jan. 6, 1996
† Winkler, Raymond J. (MIL) (Retired). —Died July 19, 1996
† Wisniewski, Robert E. (CHI) Tinley Park, IL St. George. —Died April 19, 1996
† Wixted, John W., *o.s.f.s.* (WIL) Retired. —Died May 22, 1996
† Wolf, Adam, *o.f.m.* (SFD) Sherman, IL Villa Health Care. —Died Jan. 3, 1996
† Wolf, Jerry, *c.pp.s.* (CIN) Carthagena, OH St. Charles Center. —Died Jan. 4, 1996
† Wyse, Gregory, *o.f.m.* (PAT) Ringwood, NJ Holy Name. —Died May 6, 1996
† Yanez-Moreno, Eduardo (BWN) Brownsville, TX Saint Mary, Mother of the Church. —Died Feb. 18, 1996
† Yashkas, Rev. Msgr. Frank L. (SCR) (Retired). —Died March 26, 1996
† Zahorsky, Julius (CLV) Cleveland, OH St. Elizabeth. —Died Dec. 4, 1995
† Zalonis, John A. (HRT) East Hartford, CT Blessed Sacrament Rectory. —Died June 14, 1996
† Zaunbrecher, Charles (LAF) (Retired). —Died June 19, 1996
† Zawacki, Carl E. (KCK) Overland Park, KS Queen of Holy Rosary Parish. —Died July 24, 1996
† Zawistowski, Stanley J. (PAT) Prospect Park, NJ St. Paul. —Died Jan. 13, 1996
† Zehnder, Victor R., *s.j.* (SPK) Spokane, WA Manresa Jesuit Community. —Died March 19, 1996
† Zemrowski, Rev. Msgr. Anthony (CAM) (Retired). —Died Feb. 14, 1996
† Zenns, Rev. Msgr. William C. (BUF) (Retired). —Died Aug. 7, 1996
† Zlotkowski, Clarence L. (STP) (Retired). —Died Oct. 3, 1996
† Zukowski, Edward, *c.pp.s.* (CIN) Carthagena, OH St. Charles Center. —Died April 14, 1996

ALPHABETICAL LIST OF INSTITUTIONS

(Letters in brackets designate categories in the Institutions section; followed by the (Arch)Diocesan abbreviation code.)

A

A.B.L.E. Families, Inc., [L], (WH), Naugatuck, WV.
A.C.T. Child Case Management, [I], (CIN). See St. Joseph Orphanage.
A.I.I.L.S., [U], (GAL), Houston, TX.
AAmethyst House, [E], (WIN). See St. Francis Community Programs of Minnesota, Inc.
ABBA House, [F], (LR), Little Rock, AR.
Abba House of Prayer, [O], (ALB), Albany, NY.
Abbey Christian Life Center, [R], (NO), St. Benedict, LA.
Abbey of New Clairvaux, Trappist, [H], (SAC), Vina, CA.
Abbey of New Clairvaux, Trappist Seminary, [A], (SAC), Vina, CA.
Abbey of Our Lady of Gethsemani, of the Order of Cistercians of the Strict Observance, [L], (L), Trappist, KY.
Abbey of Our Lady of the Holy Trinity, [A], (SLC), Huntsville, UT.
Abbey of Our Lady of the Holy Trinity of the Order of Cistercians, [F], (SLC), Huntsville, UT.
Abbey of Regina Laudis, [N], (HRT), Bethlehem, CT.
Abbey of St. Gregory the Great, [P], (PRO), Portsmouth, RI.
The Abbey of St. Mary and St. Louis, [P], (STL), St. Louis, MO.
Abbey of St. Walburga, [N], (DEN), Boulder, CO.
Abbey of the Genesee, [I], (ROC), Piffard, NY.
The ABC's, Associates for Breast Cancer Studies, [K], (LA). See Saint John's Hospital and Health Center.
Aberdeen Catholic Schools Education Office, [C], (SFS), Aberdeen, SD.
Aberdeen Living Center, [E], (SFS), Aberdeen, SD.
Abraham House, Inc., [DD], (NY), Bronx, NY.
Academia Cristo de los Milagros, [A], (CGS), Caguas, PR.
Academia Sagrado Corazon, [A], (SJN), Santurce, PR.
Academia San Alfonso, [A], (CGS), Aguas Buenas, PR.
Academia Santa Teresita, [A], (CGS), Naranjito, PR.
Academy and Boarding-School of the Holy Family, [C], (NOR), Baltic, CT.
Academy of American Franciscan History, [R], (OAK), Berkeley, CA.
Academy of Holy Angels, [F], (STP), Richfield, MN.
Academy of Mount St. Ursula, [F], (NY), New York, NY.
Academy of Notre Dame, [E], (BO), Tyngsboro, MA.
Academy of Notre Dame, [C], (COV), Covington, KY.
Academy of Notre Dame at Tyngsboro, [H], (BO), Tyngsboro, MA.
Academy of Notre Dame de Namur, [G], (PH), Villanova, PA.
Academy of Our Lady, [D], (CHI), Chicago, IL.
Academy of Our Lady of Good Counsel, [F], (NY), White Plains, NY.
Academy of Our Lady of Good Counsel, [H], (NY), White Plains, NY.
Academy of Our Lady of Guam, [B], (AGN), Agana, GU.
Academy of Our Lady of Mercy, [E], (HRT), Milford, CT.
Academy of Our Lady of Mercy, [C], (L), Louisville, KY.
Academy of Our Lady of Peace, [C], (SD), San Diego, CA.
Academy of St. Aloysius, [C], (NEW), Jersey City, NJ.
Academy of St. Dorothy, [H], (NY), New York, NY.
Academy of St. Dorothy, [AA], (NY), New York, NY.
Academy of St. Elizabeth, [D], (PAT), Convent Station, NJ.
Academy of St. Joseph, [D], (RVC), Brentwood, NY.
Academy of the Holy Angels, [C], (NEW), Demarest, NJ.
Academy of the Holy Cross Convent, [O], (WDC). See Sisters of the Holy Cross.
The Academy of the Holy Cross, Inc., [E], (WDC), Kensington, MD.
Academy of the Holy Names Elementary, [E], (SP), Tampa, FL.
Academy of the Holy Names High School, [C], (SP), Tampa, FL.
Academy of the Holy Names of New York, [M], (ALB). See Holy Name.
Academy of the Holy Names Upper, Middle and Lower Schools, [D], (ALB), Albany, NY.
Academy of the Incarnate Word, [F], (GAL), Houston, TX.
Academy of the Sacred Heart, [E], (DET), Bloomfield Hills, MI.
Academy of the Sacred Heart, [G], (DET), Bloomfield Hills, MI.
Academy of the Sacred Heart, [E], (LAF), Grand Coteau, LA.
Academy of the Sacred Heart, [C], (NEW), Hoboken, NJ.
Academy of the Sacred Heart, [H], (NO), New Orleans, LA.
Academy of the Sacred Heart, [G], (STL), St. Charles, MO.
Academy of the Sacred Heart "The Rosary", [F], (NO), New Orleans, LA.
Academy of the Visitation, [E], (BAL), Frederick, MD.
The Achievement Center-St. Vincent's Home, Inc., [F], (RIC), Roanoke, VA.
Acorn Apartments (Crandon), [E], (SUP). See Catholic Charities Bureau, Inc.
Acorn Apartments (Minong), [E], (SUP). See Catholic Charities Bureau, Inc.
Acorn Apartments (Wisconsin Rapids), [E], (SUP). See Catholic Charities Bureau, Inc.
Ada S. Niles Senior Center and Adult Day Care Services, [G], (CHI). See Catholic Charities of the Archdiocese of Chicago-Archdiocesan Offices.
Addiction Consultation and Educational Services, [G], (CHI). See Catholic Charities of the Archdiocese of Chicago-Archdiocesan Offices.
Addiction Services, [D], (WIL). See Catholic Charities, Inc.
Addolorata Villa, Inc., [M], (CHI), Wheeling, IL.
Adirondack Community College, [S], (ALB), Glens Falls, NY.
Administration, [V], (WDC). See Spanish Catholic Center.
Administrative Center of the Sisters of Mercy of the Americas, [O], (CHI), Chicago, IL.
Administrative Services, [H], (RVC). See Catholic Charities Central Administration.
Admission & Family Services, [N], (NY). See Pius XII Youth and Family Services.
Adoption, [G], (RNO), Reno, NV.
Adoption Program, [G], (BGP). See Catholic Charities of Fairfield County.
Adoption Services, [E], (HBG). See Department for Catholic Charities Counseling/Field Services.
Adoption Services, Inc., [L], (LR), Little Rock, AR.
Adoptions and Foster Care, [Q], (SFR). See Catholic Charities of the Archdiocese of San Francisco.
Adoptions, Child Care Division, and Young Parents Program, [H], (BUF). See The Catholic Charities of the Diocese of Buffalo.
Adoration Convent and Church of Christ the King, [G], (LIN), Lincoln, NE.
Adorers of the Blood of Christ, [I], (HBG), Columbia, PA.
Adorers of the Blood of Christ, [C], (LSC), Carlsbad, NM.
Adorers of the Blood of Christ, [B], (SAN), Coleman, TX.
Adorers of the Blood of Christ (A.S.C.), [K], (ELP), El Paso, TX.
Adorers of the Blood of Christ Charitable Trust Fund, [M], (WCH), Wichita, KS.
Adrian Dominican Office of Development, [L], (LAN), Adrian, MI.
Adrian Dominican Sisters, [I], (AUS), Austin, TX.
Adrian Dominican Sisters, [H], (MRY), Santa Cruz, CA.
Adrian Dominican Sisters - Great Lakes Mission Chapter, [L], (DET), Detroit, MI.
Adrian Dominican Sisters (O.P.), [K], (ELP), El Paso, TX.
Adrian Dominican Sisters, Florida Mission Chapter, [H], (PMB), West Palm Beach, FL.
Adrian Dominican Sisters, Mid-Atlantic Mission Chapter, [J], (ATL), Gainesville, GA.
Adrian Dominican Sisters, Midwest Dominican Mission Chapter, [O], (CHI). See Adrian Dominican Sisters, Upper Midwest Mission Chapter.
Adrian Dominican Sisters, Nokomis Mission Chapter, [L], (DET), Dearborn Heights, MI.
Adrian Dominican Sisters, Southeast Adrian Mission Chapter, [L], (DET), Farmington Hills, MI.
Adrian Dominican Sisters, Upper Midwest Mission Chapter, [O], (CHI), Hometown, IL.
Adrian Dominicans, [I], (ORG), Orange, CA.
Adrian Dominicans, [I], (ORG), Tustin, CA.
Adrian Dominicans of the Most Holy Rosary, [F], (R), Fuquay-Varina, NC.
Adult Day Health Center, [U], (BO). See St. Joseph Manor Nursing & Extended Care Facility.
Adult Day Services, [J], (WCH). See Catholic Charities.
Adult Day Services, [L], (WCH). See Catholic Charities, Inc.
Adult Reading Program, [L], (SAC). See Catholic Charities of Sacramento, Inc.
Adult Treatment Services, [O], (P). See De Paul Treatment Centers, Inc.
Adventus, [R], (OAK), Oakland, CA.
Affiliated Health Services, Inc., Detroit, [H], (DET). See St. John Hospital and Medical Center.
Affinity Health System, [O], (GB), Oshkosh, WI.
Affirmation Counseling Center, [J], (NOR), Portland, CT.
African Mission House and African Cultural Center, [W], (BO), Dedham, MA.
After School Programs, [N], (NY). See Pius XII Youth and Family Services.
Agape Community Center of Milwaukee, Inc., [Y], (MIL), Milwaukee, WI.
Agape Convent, [AA], (PH). See Religious Sisters of Mercy.
Agape Institute of St. Teresa of Jesus, [I], (BIR), Birmingham, AL.
*Aid for Women, [X], (CHI), Chicago, IL.
Aid to the Church in Need, [R], (RVC), Deer Park, NY.
Aid to the Church In Need, Inc., [M], (ORG), El Toro, CA.
"Aimin' High" Family Service Center, [N], (NY). See Pius XII Youth and Family Services.
Aina Kupaa O Maili, [J], (HON), Honolulu, HI.
Air Force Base, [I], (FAR), Grand Forks, ND.
AJT, Inc., [W], (STL), Arnold, MO.
Akron District Council, [V], (CLV). See Society of St. Vincent de Paul, Diocesan Central Council.
Alabama Southern Community College Newman Center, [K], (MOB), Monroeville, AL.
Alabama State University Newman Center, [K], (MOB), Montgomery, AL.
Alameda, [H], (OAK). See Catholic Charities of the Diocese of Oakland, Inc.
Alameda County Area Supervisor, Marguerite Dean, [H], (OAK). See Catholic Charities of the Diocese of Oakland, Inc.
Alamo Catholic High School and Amarillo Catholic Middle School, [A], (AMA), Amarillo, TX.
Alaska Radio Mission, Station KNOM, [E], (FBK), Nome, AK.
Albany Area Hospital, [G], (SCL), Albany, MN.
Albergue La Providencia, Inc., [H], (PCE), Ponce, PR.
Alberta Health Center, [I], (MOB), Alberta, AL.
Albertine Home, [I], (GRY), Hammond, IN.
Albertine Sisters (Prov. of Krakow, Poland), [L], (GRY), Hammond, IN.
Albertson's College of Idaho, [F], (B), Caldwell, ID.
Albertus Magnus, [F], (NY), Bardonia, NY.
Albertus Magnus College, [C], (HRT), New Haven, CT.
Albertus Magnus College, [N], (HRT). See St. Joseph Convent.
Alcohol Clinic, [N], (NY). See Pius XII Youth and Family Services.
Alee Shelter Program for Spouse Abuse, [E], (AGN). See Catholic Social Services of Guam.
Alegent Health, [G], (OM), Omaha, NE.
*Alegent Health - Bergan Mercy Health System dba Alegent Health - Mercy Care Center, [H], (OM), Omaha, NE.
*Alegent Health - Bergan Mercy Health System dba Algent Health - Bergan Mercy Medical Center, [G], (OM), Omaha, NE.
Alemany High School, [D], (LA), Mission Hills, CA.
Alexian Brothers, [F], (KNX), Signal Mountain, TN.
Alexian Brothers Community, [P], (MIL), Milwaukee, WI.
Alexian Brothers Health Management, Inc., (ABHM), [X], (CHI), Elk Grove Village, IL.
Alexian Brothers Health System Inc., [X], (CHI), Elk Grove Village, IL.
Alexian Brothers Hospital, [H], (SJ), San Jose, CA.
Alexian Brothers Hospital, [K], (STL), St. Louis, MO.
Alexian Brothers Lansdowne Village, [O], (STL), St. Louis, MO.
Alexian Brothers Medical Center, Inc., [J], (CHI), Elk Grove Village, IL.
Alexian Brothers of America, Inc., [X], (CHI), Elk Grove Village, IL.
Alexian Brothers of Elizabeth, Inc., [S], (NEW), Elizabeth, NJ.
Alexian Brothers of Missouri, Inc., [W], (STL), St. Louis, MO.
Alexian Brothers of New Jersey, Inc., [S], (NEW), Elizabeth, NJ.
Alexian Brothers of St. Louis, Inc., [W], (STL), St. Louis, MO.
Alexian Brothers Services, Inc., [W], (STL), St. Louis, MO.
Alexian Brothers Sherbrooke Village, [O], (STL), St. Louis, MO.
Alexian Court Apartments, [I], (STL). See Cardinal Ritter Institute.
Alexian Village Health Care Center, [C], (KNX), Signal Mountain, TN.
Alexian Village of Milwaukee, Inc., [N], (MIL), Milwaukee, WI.

Alexian Village of Tennessee, Inc., [D], (KNX), Signal Mountain, TN.
Alexis Apartments of St. Patrick's Parish, [K], (SFR), San Francisco, CA.
Alfred E. Smith Memorial Foundation, Inc., The, [DD], (NY), New York, NY.
Alfred Fortin Villa and Day Care Learning Center, [F], (JOL), Bourbonnais, IL.
Alhambra, International Order of, [Q], (BAL), Baltimore, MD.
*All Hallows Community, Inc., [U], (SFR), San Francisco, CA.
All Hallows Institute, [F], (NY), New York, NY.
All Hallows Mission Fund, Inc., [V], (WDC), Silver Spring, MD.
All Saints Academy, [C], (BEL), Breese, IL.
All Saints Academy, The Newport County Catholic Regional School, [G], (PRO), Portsmouth, RI.
All Saints Catholic East School System, Inc., [H], (MIL), Milwaukee, WI.
All Saints Catholic Elementary, [H], (MIL), Milwaukee, WI.
All Saints Catholic Jr. High, [C], (ROC), Rochester, NY.
All Saints Catholic School, [C], (ALT), Cresson, PA.
All Saints Catholic School, [D], (CHL). See Mecklenburg Area Catholic Schools (M.A.C.S.).
All Saints Catholic School, [D], (OKL), Norman, OK.
All Saints Catholic School, [D], (OM), Omaha, NE.
All Saints Catholic School, [D], (TOL), Rossford, OH.
All Saints Catholic School Endowment, [N], (OM). See The Omaha Archdiocesan Educational Foundation, Inc.
All Saints Central High School, [A], (SAG), Bay City, MI.
All Saints Elementary School, [D], (ALN), Pottsville, PA.
All Saints Healthcare Foundation, Inc., [Y], (MIL), Racine, WI.
All Saints Healthcare System, Inc., [Y], (MIL), Racine, WI.
All Saints High School, [B], (LEX), Corbin, KY.
All Saints Home, [F], (STA), Jacksonville, FL.
All Saints Interfaith Center of Concern, [G], (BIR), Anniston, AL.
All Saints Junior High School, [E], (SY), Syracuse, NY.
All Saints Medical Group-Northwestern Campus, [K], (MIL). See St. Mary's Medical Center.
All Saints Medical Group-Spring St. Campus, [K], (MIL). See St. Mary's Medical Center.
All Saints of St. John Vianney School, [G], (CLV), Wickliffe, OH.
All Saints Primary, [F], (SPK). See All Saints School.
All Saints Regional Catholic School, [E], (RVC), Glen Cove, NY.
All Saints Regional School, [F], (DET), Canton, MI.
All Saints Regional School, [C], (MET), Phillipsburg, NJ.
All Saints School, [C], (KCK), Kansas City, KS.
All Saints School, [F], (SPK), Spokane, WA.
All Saints School, [C], (TLS), Broken Arrow, OK.
All Saints Visiting Nurse Association and Hospice of Racine, Inc., [Y], (MIL), Racine, WI.
Allegany Health System, [J], (ALB). See Villa Mary Immaculate.
Allegany Health System Foundation, Inc., [T], (SP). See Chancery Office.
Alleman High School, [B], (PEO), Rock Island, IL.
Allen Memorial Home Skilled Nursing Facility, [F], (MOB), Mobile, AL.
Allen University, Benedict College Newman Center, [H], (CHR), Columbia, SC.
Allentown Central Catholic High School, [C], (ALN), Allentown, PA.
Allentown College of St. Francis de Sales, [B], (ALN), Center Valley, PA.
Alliance Division, Catholic Charities, [K], (SY), Syracuse, NY.
Alliance for Access dba Medical Center South, [AA], (CLV), Broadview Heights, OH.
Alliance for International Monasticism (AIM), [Q], (E), Erie, PA.
Almost Home, [W], (STL), St. Louis, MO.
Alpha House Adult Day Health Care Center, [M], (NO), Covington, LA.
Alpha House I, [E], (SUP). See Catholic Charities Bureau, Inc.
Alpha House II, [E], (SUP). See Catholic Charities Bureau, Inc.
Alpha House Kindergarten, [EE], (PH), Philadelphia, PA.
Alpha Omega Family Center, Inc., [DD], (NY), Rye, NY.
Alpha Omege, Inc. The Legion of Christ Inc., [V], (WDC), Bethesda, MD.
Alpha-Omega, [O], (BO), Boston, MA.
Altercrest, [I], (CIN). See St. Joseph Orphanage.
Alternative Residential Arrangements, Inc., [Y], (MIL), Milwaukee, WI.
Alternatives, [N], (NY). See Pius XII Youth and Family Services.
Althoff Catholic High School, [B], (BEL), Belleville, IL.
Althoff Catholic High School Educational Endowment Trust, [K], (BEL), Belleville, IL.
Alumni Association of the Apostolate of Cuba (in Exile), Inc., [M], (MIA), Miami, FL.
Alumni of Apostolate Charity Foundation, Inc., [M], (MIA), Miami, FL.
Alumni Office, [V], (WDC). See Archbishop Carroll High School.
Alverna Apartments, [H], (SCL), Little Falls, MN.
Alvernia Center for Environmental Studies, [R], (RVC). See Mt. Alvernia, Inc.
Alvernia College, [B], (ALN), Reading, PA.
Alvernia College Convent, [L], (ALN), Reading, PA.
Alvernia Manor, [M], (CHI), Lemont, IL.
Alvernia Montessori School, [E], (ALN), Reading, PA.
Alverno Administrative Services, Inc., [O], (FTW), Mishawaka, IN.
Alverno Administrative Services, Inc., [O], (IND), Beech Grove, IN.
Alverno College, [C], (MIL), Milwaukee, WI.
Alverno Community, [J], (OKL), Oklahoma City, OK.
The Alverno Health Care Facility, [L], (DAV), Clinton, IA.
Alverno Health Corporation, [O], (FTW). See Alverno Administrative Services, Inc.
Alverno High School, [F], (LA), Sierra Madre, CA.
Alverno Lakeside Corporation, [J], (CHI), Chicago Heights, IL.
Alverno Memphis Corporation, [O], (FTW). See Alverno Administrative Services, Inc.
Alverno-Beech Grove Corp., [O], (IND), Beech Grove, IN.
Alverno-Hammond Corporation, [P], (GRY), Hammond, IN.
Alverno-Lafayette Corporation, [I], (LFT), Mishawaka, IN.
Alverno-Louisville Corporation, [O], (FTW). See Alverno Administrative Services, Inc.
Alverno-Michigan City Corp., [P], (GRY), Michigan City, IN.
Alvin Community College Newman Center, [T], (GAL), Alvin, TX.
Alzheimer's Respite/Resource Center, [E], (SR). See Diocese of Santa Rosa, Catholic Charities.
Amarillo Catholic Children's Development Centers, [C], (AMA), Amarillo, TX.
Amarillo Catholic Education Foundation, [L], (AMA), Amarillo, TX.
Amarillo Catholic School System, [L], (AMA), Amarillo, TX.
Amarillo Scholarship Endowment and Assistance Fund, [L], (AMA), Amarillo, TX.
Amat House, [R], (LA), Los Angeles, CA.
Amelia House, [I], (PIT). See Providence Connections, Inc.
America Press, Inc., The, [DD], (NY), New York, NY.
"America"; Residence and publication office of the America Press, [Z], (NY), New York, NY.
*American Academy of Natural Family Planning, [W], (STL), St. Louis, MO.
American Catholic Philosophical Association, [V], (WDC), Washington, DC.
American Committee on Italian Immigration, Inc., [DD], (NY), New York, NY.
American Dominican Friars Serving in Canada, [I], (PRT). See SS. Peter and Paul Priory.
*American Friends of the Ecole Biblique, [U], (CHI), River Forest, IL.
American Friends of the Vatican Library, [T], (DET), Grosse Pointe Farms, MI.
American Life League, Inc., [N], (ARL), Stafford, VA.
American Lithuanian Catholic Archives, [D], (LIT), Putnam, IL.
American Martyrs Retreat House, [M], (DUB), Cedar Falls, IA.
American Province Archives, [AA], (FH). See Sisters of the Holy Child.
American Province of Little Company of Mary Sisters, [O], (CHI), Evergreen Park, IL.
American Province of Little Company of Mary Sisters Charitable Trust, [X], (CHI), Evergreen Park, IL.
American St. Boniface Society, Incorporated, [DD], (NY), New York, NY.
American University, [S], (WDC). See Archdiocesan Campus Ministry.
American-Innsbruck Alumni Association, [J], (EVN), Loogootee, IN.
American-International-Agrimissio, [I], (DM), Des Moines, IA.
"The Americas," [V], (WDC), Washington, DC.
Amicare Home Health Care - Metro Detroit, [T], (DET), Bloomfield Hills, MI.
Amicare Home Health Services, [P], (DAV), Clinton, IA.
*Amicare Home Health Services, Inc., [T], (DET), Farmington Hills, MI.
Amicare Home Health Services, Inc., [P], (GRY), Dyer, IN.
Amicare Home Health Services-Western Michigan, Inc., [E], (GR). See Mercy Hospital.
*Amicare Hospice Services, Inc., [T], (DET), Farmington Hills, MI.
Amityville Dominican Sisters, Inc., [R], (RVC), Amityville, NY.
Ammendale Normal Institute of Prince George's County-LaSalle Hall (1880), [B], (WDC), Beltsville, MD.
Anawim Community, [N], (HRT), Waterbury, CT.
The Anawim Community, [L], (MET), Phillipsburg, NJ.
Anawim Community Center, [K], (ROC), Corning, NY.
Ancient Order of Hibernians, [K], (BEL), Belleville, IL.
Ancient Order of Hibernians (LAOH), [K], (BEL), Belleville, IL.
Ancilla College, [K], (FTW). See Convent Ancilla Domini.
Ancilla Convent, [Q], (MIL), Milwaukee, WI.
Ancilla Domini College, [B], (FTW), Donaldson, IN.
Ancilla Domini Hospitals Insurance Trust, [K], (FTW). See Convent Ancilla Domini.
Ancilla Health Care, Incorporated, [O], (FTW), Mishawaka, IN.
Ancilla Medical Foundation, Inc., [P], (GRY). See Ancilla Systems, Inc.
Ancilla Systems Foundation, Inc., [P], (GRY). See Ancilla Systems, Inc.
Ancilla Systems, Inc., [P], (GRY), Hobart, IN.
Ancillae-Assumpta Academy, [H], (PH), Wyncote, PA.
Anderson Center of Saint John's, [C], (LFT). See Saint John's Health System.
Anderson College Newman Center, [H], (CHR), Anderson, SC.
Andre House of Arizona, [J], (PHX), Phoenix, AZ.
Andre House-East, [K], (FTW). See Saint Mary's of the Immaculate Conception.
Andre House-West, [K], (FTW). See Saint Mary's of the Immaculate Conception.
Andrean High School, [B], (GRY), Merrillville, IN.
Angel Guardian German Catholic Orphan Society of Chicago, [X], (CHI), Chicago, IL.
The Angel Guardian Homes, [O], (BRK), Brooklyn, NY.
Angela Center, [L], (SR), Santa Rosa, CA.
Angela Hall, [E], (SFS). See St. William Home for the Aged.
*Angela Hospice Home Care, Inc., [T], (DET), Livonia, MI.
Angela House, [M], (GRY), Michigan City, IN.
Angela House, Inc., [G], (NY), New Rochelle, NY.
Angela Merici House, [F], (WIL). See Ministry of Caring, Inc.
Angelicum Fund, [V], (HRT), New Haven, CT.
Ann Arbor Catholic Forum, [L], (LAN), Ann Arbor, MI.
Anna Maria College, [B], (WOR), Paxton, MA.
Anna Maria College, [Q], (WOR), Paxton, MA.
Anna Trust, [W], (STL), St. Louis, MO.
Annual Catholic Appeal Foundation of the Archdiocese of Santa Fe, [N], (SFE), Albuquerque, NM.
Annunciata Regional Priory, [N], (CHI). See Servite Friars - Eastern Province.
Annunciation Community, [AA], (PH), Philadelphia, PA.
Annunciation Convent, [I], (HBG), McSherrystown, PA.
Annunciation Friary, [M], (DEN), Denver, CO.
Annunciation House, [N], (ELP), El Paso, TX.
Annunciation Inn, [N], (NO), New Orleans, LA.
Annunciation Priory, [H], (BIS), Bismarck, ND.
Annunciation School, [B], (STA), Middleburg, FL.
*Another Chance Houses, Inc., [E], (AMA). See Catholic Family Service, Inc.
Anthonian Hall, Inc., [L], (BRK). See Catholic Charities.
Anthony Family Shelter (and Emergency Services), [J], (WCH). See Catholic Charities.
Anthony Family Shelter (and Emergency Services), [L], (WCH). See Catholic Charities, Inc.
Antioch, [H], (OAK). See Catholic Charities of the Diocese of Oakland, Inc.
Antioch College Campus Ministry, [Q], (CIN), Yellow Springs, OH.
The Antonian, [G], (WIL), Wilmington, DE.
Antonian College Prep, [D], (SAT), San Antonio, TX.
Antonian Towers, [I], (ALN), Easton, PA.
Antonine Maronite Sisters of Youngstown, Inc., [B], (OLL), North Jackson, OH.
Apostles in the Marketplace (A.I.M.), [Q], (BAL), Baltimore, MD.
Apostles of the Sacred Heart of Jesus, [I], (GBG), Greensburg, PA.
Apostles of the Sacred Heart of Jesus, [G], (NOR), Higganum, CT.
Apostles of the Sacred Heart of Jesus, [I], (SAC), Sacramento, CA.
Apostleship of Prayer, [V], (CIN), Cincinnati, OH.
Apostleship of Prayer, [P], (DAL), Commerce, TX.
Apostleship of Prayer, [L], (MOB), Daphne, AL.
Apostleship of Prayer, [EE], (PH), Philadelphia, PA.

B

Basilian Residence, [I], (ROC), Rochester, NY.
Basilian Salvatorian Order, [B], (NTN), Methuen, MA.
Basilica of St. Mary, [L], (RIC). See Ethnic and Special Ministries.
Basilica of the Assumption Historic Trust, Inc., [P], (BAL). See Chancery Office.
Basilica of the National Shrine of the Immaculate Conception, [Q], (WDC), Washington, DC.
Batavia, [H], (BUF). See The Catholic Charities of the Diocese of Buffalo.
Bates College, [M], (PRT), Lewiston, ME.
Batesville Deanery Counseling & Family Mediations, [L], (IND), Greensburg, IN.
Bath County Medical Clinic, [E], (LEX), Owingsville, KY.
Baton Rouge Chancery Office, [M], (BR), Baton Rouge, LA.
Baton Rouge/Southwest Regional Office, [I], (BR), Baton Rouge, LA.
Battle Creek Health System, [D], (KAL), Battle Creek, MI.
Bay County Jail Ministry, [I], (SAG), Bay City, MI.
Bay View Community, [J], (PRT), Saco, ME.
Bay View Villa, Guest and Retreat House, [L], (PRT), Saco, ME.
Bay Webster Corporation, Inc., [Y], (BRK), Brooklyn, NY.
Bayley Seton Hospital, [S], (NY), New York, NY.
Bayley-Ellard High School, [C], (PAT), Madison, NJ.
Bayside Linda Vista, [J], (SD). See Bayside Settlement House.
*Bayside Settlement House, [J], (SD), San Diego, CA.
Bayview Detention Center Ministry, [C], (BWN), Brownsville, TX.
BCACS Foundation, Inc., [I], (KAL), Battle Creek, MI.
Beacon House, House of Prayer, [O], (DAV), Burlington, IA.
Beacon of Hope House, [K], (NY), New York, NY.
Beatitude House, [M], (Y), Youngstown, OH.
Beaumont School, [E], (CLV), Cleveland, OH.
Beaven Kelly Home, [H], (SPR). See Sisters of Providence Care Centers, Inc.
Becker College, [Q], (WOR). See Campus Ministry.
Becker College at Leicester, [Q], (WOR). See Campus Ministry.
Becket Hall, [I], (ROC), Rochester, NY.
Becket House Apartments, [D], (PHX), Lake Havasu City, AZ.
Beckman High School, [D], (DUB), Dyersville, IA.
BECOMING, [O], (SPK), Spokane, WA.
Bede House, Trenton State College, [R], (TR). See Campus Ministry for the Diocese of Trenton.
Beginning Experience, [K], (FWT). See The Catholic Renewal Center of North Texas, Inc.
Beginning Experience, [O], (OM), Omaha, NE.
Belen Jesuit Preparatory School, [D], (MIA), Miami, FL.
Belhaven, [F], (CHL). See Holy Angels, Inc.
Belhaven College Newman Center, [G], (JKS), Jackson, MS.
Bell Tower Residence, Inc., [D], (SUP). See Holy Cross Provincial Office.
Bellarmine College, [A], (L), Louisville, KY.
Bellarmine College Preparatory, [D], (SJ), San Jose, CA.
Bellarmine Hall, [T], (CHI), Barrington, IL.
Bellarmine House, [W], (BO), Cohasset, MA.
Bellarmine House of Studies, [P], (STL), St. Louis, MO.
Bellarmine Jefferson High School, [D], (LA), Burbank, CA.
Bellarmine Preparatory School, [C], (SEA), Tacoma, WA.
Bellerose Senior Housing Development Fund Company, Inc., [Y], (BRK), Brooklyn, NY.
Bellevue Area Catholic Elementary School, [F], (DUB), Bellevue, IA.
Bellmore Campus, [E], (RVC). See St. Elizabeth Ann Seton Regional School.
Belmont Abbey, [J], (CHL), Belmont, NC.
*Belmont Abbey College, [A], (CHL), Belmont, NC.
Belmont House Aids Hospice, [Q], (SFR). See Catholic Charities of the Archdiocese of San Francisco.
Beloit District Office, [K], (MAD). See Catholic Charities, Inc.
Bend Social Services Conference, [D], (BAK). See Saint Vincent de Paul Society - District Council of Central Oregon.
Bender Memorial Academy, [E], (NEW), Elizabeth, NJ.
Benedict Court, [H], (SCL). See St. Benedict's Center.
Benedict Homes, [H], (SCL). See St. Benedict's Center.
Benedict Inn Retreat & Conference Center, [I], (IND), Beech Grove, IN.
Benedict Village, [H], (SCL). See St. Benedict's Center.
Benedictine Academy, [C], (NEW), Elizabeth, NJ.
Benedictine Center - St. Paul's Priory, [Q], (STP), St. Paul, MN.
Benedictine Center, Inc., [O], (PIT). See St. Benedict Monastery.
Benedictine Center, Inc., [I], (SFS), Yankton, SD.
Benedictine Chinese Mission, [J], (JOL). See St. Procopius Abbey.
Benedictine College, [A], (KCK), Atchison, KS.
Benedictine Convent of Perpetual Adoration, [K], (KC), Clyde, MO.
Benedictine Convent of Perpetual Adoration, [R], (STL), St. Louis, MO.
*Benedictine Convent of St. Martin, [C], (RC), Rapid City, SD.
Benedictine Convent of St. Martin Retirement Trust, [C], (RC). See Benedictine Convent of St. Martin.
Benedictine Counseling and Consulting Institute, [O], (KC), Kansas City, MO.
Benedictine Early Learning Center, [C], (PBR), Warren, OH.
Benedictine Foundation of Oregon, [Q], (P), Mt. Angel, OR.
Benedictine Foundation, Inc., [G], (DUL). See Benedictine Sisters Benevolent Association.
The Benedictine Grange, [N], (BGP), West Redding, CT.
Benedictine Health Center, [D], (DUL), Duluth, MN.
Benedictine Health Center, [G], (DUL). See Benedictine Sisters Benevolent Association.
Benedictine Health Foundation, Inc., [I], (SFS), Yankton, SD.
Benedictine Health System, [G], (DUL). See Benedictine Sisters Benevolent Association.
Benedictine Health System, [I], (SFS), Yankton, SD.
Benedictine High School, [E], (CLV), Cleveland, OH.
Benedictine High School, [B], (RIC), Richmond, VA.
Benedictine Hospital, [S], (NY), Kingston, NY.
Benedictine Manor, [G], (LR), Hot Springs, AR.
Benedictine Manor Retirement Home, Inc., [I], (BIR), Cullman, AL.
Benedictine Military School, [B], (SAV), Savannah, GA.
Benedictine Mission House, [K], (OM), Schuyler, NE.
Benedictine Monastery, [G], (NOR), Ashford, CT.
Benedictine Monastery, [H], (NOR), Ashford, CT.
Benedictine Monastery, [G], (TUC), Tucson, AZ.
The Benedictine Monastery of Erlac in Sonoita, [F], (TUC), Sonoita, AZ.
Benedictine Monastery of Hawaii, [H], (HON), Waialua, Oahu, HI.
Benedictine Monks, St. Benedict Abbey, [N], (WOR), Still River, MA.
Benedictine Monks, St. Benedict Abbey, [P], (WOR), Still River, MA.
Benedictine Nursing Center, [K], (P), Mt. Angel, OR.
Benedictine Order of Cleveland, [P], (CLV), Cleveland, OH.
The Benedictine Priory, [F], (SAV), Savannah, GA.
Benedictine Resource Center, [T], (SAT), San Antonio, TX.
Benedictine Retreat Center, [G], (CC), Sandia, TX.
The Benedictine School for Exceptional Children, [C], (WIL), Ridgely, MD.
Benedictine School for Exceptional Children Foundation, Inc., [C], (WIL), Ridgely, MD.
The Benedictine School Habilitation Center, [B], (WIL), Ridgely, MD.
Benedictine Sisters (Eichstatt, Bavaria), [I], (GBG), Greensburg, PA.
Benedictine Sisters Benevolent Association, [E], (DUL), Duluth, MN.
Benedictine Sisters Benevolent Association, [G], (DUL), Duluth, MN.
Benedictine Sisters of Crookston, MN, [F], (BWN), Rio Grande City, TX.
Benedictine Sisters of Denver, Inc., [N], (DEN), Lakewood, CO.
The Benedictine Sisters of Elizabeth, NJ, [M], (CAM), Ventnor, NJ.
Benedictine Sisters of Elk County O.S.B. St. Joseph Monastery, [M], (E), St. Marys, PA.
Benedictine Sisters of Glendora, [I], (SD), Chula Vista, CA.
Benedictine Sisters of Perpetual Adoration, [D], (CHY), Dayton, WY.
Benedictine Sisters of Perpetual Adoration, [H], (TLS), Sand Springs, OK.
Benedictine Sisters of the Good Shepherd, [F], (BWN), Rio Grande City, TX.
Benedictine Sisters of the Sacred Heart, Sacred Heart Monastery, [K], (JOL), Lisle, IL.
Benedictine Sisters of Virginia, [N], (RIC), Richmond, VA.
Benedictine Sisters Shalom Prayer Center, [N], (P), Mt. Angel, OR.
Benedictine Spirituality and Conference Center, [I], (BIR), Cullman, AL.
Benedictine Spirituality Center, [L], (OKL), Piedmont, OK.
Benedictine University, [A], (JOL), Lisle, IL.
Benedictine University, [J], (JOL). See St. Procopius Abbey.
Benedictines of Jesus Crucified, [Q], (PRO), Newport, RI.
Benedictines, Grand Terrace, [I], (ORG), Huntington Beach, CA.
Benedictines, Grand Terrace and Rapid City, [I], (ORG), Laguna Beach, CA.
Benedictines-at-Innisfail Spirituality and Conference Center, [M], (WIL), Hockessin, DE.
*Benedictus, [N], (SD), Escondido, CA.
Benefis Health Care, [G], (GF), Great Falls, MT.
Benefit Trust for Non-Incardinated Priests, [DD], (BO). See Chancery Office.
Benefit Trust of the Adrian Dominican Congregation (Adrian), [K], (LAN). See Chancery Office.
Benet Academy, [C], (JOL), Lisle, IL.
Benet Academy, [J], (JOL). See St. Procopius Abbey.
*Benet Hill Monastery, [F], (COS), Colorado Springs, CO.
*Benet Pines, [G], (COS), Colorado Springs, CO.
*Benet Place, [H], (SCL). See St. Benedict's Center.
Benet Place, [I], (SFS). See St. Ann's Corporation.
*Benetwood Apartments for Persons Elderly and Handicapped, [I], (E), Harborcreek, PA.
The Benilde Religious & Charitable Trust, [R], (OAK), Oakland, CA.
Benilde-St. Margaret's Jr. & Sr. High School, [E], (STP), St. Louis Park, MN.
Benincasa-Dominican Renewal Center, [N], (SFD), Riverton, IL.
Benitia Family Center, [T], (SAT), San Antonio, TX.
Bentley College Campus Ministry, [CC], (BO), Waltham, MA.
Berakah, [L], (MAN), Pittsfield, NH.
Berakah Alternative Investment Fund, [U], (GAL), Houston, TX.
The Berakkah House, [I], (SFS), Sioux Falls, SD.
Berg Retreat Center, [M], (WIL), Ridgely, MD.
Bergamo, [P], (CIN), Dayton, OH.
*Bergan Mercy Foundation, Inc., [O], (OM), Omaha, NE.
Bergan Mercy Health System: Mercy Hospital, [C], (DM), Council Bluffs, IA.
Bergen Catholic, [C], (NEW), Oradell, NJ.
Berkley, [H], (OAK). See Catholic Charities of the Diocese of Oakland, Inc.
Berlin Catholic School, [E], (MAD), Berlin, WI.
Berlin Regional Catholic School, [E], (MAN), Berlin, NH.
Bernadine Franciscan Sisters, [N], (SAT), San Antonio, TX.
Bernard & Caroline Cobb Memorial School, [G], (ALB), Altamont, NY.
Bernardine Apartments, Inc., [P], (SY), Syracuse, NY.
Bernardine Center, [R], (PH), Chester, PA.
Bernardine Franciscan Sisters, [L], (DET), Farmington Hills, MI.
Bernardine Franciscan Sisters, [AA], (PH), Philadelphia, PA.
Bernardine Franciscan Sisters, [AA], (PH), King of Prussia, PA.
Bernardine Franciscan Sisters Foundation, Inc., [E], (RIC). See Mary Immaculate Hospital.
Bernardine Franciscans, Delaware County, [EE], (PH), King of Prussia, PA.
Bernardine Sisters of St. Francis, [AA], (PH), Chester, PA.
Bernardine Sisters of St. Francis, [AA], (PH), Essington, PA.
Bernardine Sisters of St. Francis, [AA], (PH), Sellersville, PA.
Bernardine Sisters of the Third Order of St. Francis, [N], (RIC), Newport News, VA.
Bethania Regional Health Care Center, [F], (FWT), Wichita Falls, TX.
Bethany, [H], (MRY), Salinas, CA.
Bethany, [Q], (PRO). See Franciscan Missionaries of Mary.
The Bethany Community, Inc., [P], (BAL). See Chancery Office.
Bethany Community/Formation Center, [N], (HRT). See Spirit of Mercy Community.
Bethany Convent, [I], (CC), Corpus Christi, TX.
Bethany Convent for Retired Sisters, [M], (STP), St. Paul, MN.
Bethany Health Care Center, Inc., [FF], (BO), Framingham, MA.
Bethany Home, [F], (SCL), Cold Springs, MN.
Bethany House, [N], (DAL), Dallas, TX.
Bethany House, [K], (FTW). See Saint Mary's of the Immaculate Conception.
Bethany House, [L], (IND). See Catholic Charities.
Bethany House, [U], (LA), Los Angeles, CA.
Bethany House Adult Day Care, [J], (FR), Taunton, MA.
Bethany House of Beutel, [F], (ORL), Orlando, FL.
Bethany M.H.S. Health Care Center, [G], (LAF), Lafayette, LA.
Bethany on the Rio Grande, [J], (SFE), Albuquerque, NM.
Bethany Renewal Center, [R], (PRO), North Providence, RI.

Bethany Residence, [L], (PAT), Wayne, NJ.
Bethany Retreat House, [M], (GRY), East Chicago, IN.
Bethany Retreat House, [BB], (NY), Highland Mills, NY.
Bethany Ridge, [J], (MET), Little York, NJ.
Bethany Spring, [O], (L), New Haven, KY.
Bethany-St. Joseph Care Center, [G], (LC), La Crosse, WI.
Bethesda House, [L], (VEN), Sarasota, FL.
Bethlehem, [L], (BRK). See Catholic Charities.
Bethlehem Academy, [F], (STP), Faribault, MN.
Bethlehem Catholic High School, [C], (ALN), Bethlehem, PA.
Bethlehem Centre, Inc., [N], (SP), Largo, FL.
Bethlehem Community Housing Development Fund Company, Inc., [Y], (BRK), Brooklyn, NY.
Bethlehem Convent, [M], (L), Bardstown, KY.
Bethlehem High School, [B], (L), Bardstown, KY.
Bethlehem Monastery of the Poor Clare Nuns, [N], (RIC), Newport News, VA.
Bethlehem Retirement Village, [X], (PH), Flourtown, PA.
Bethlehem Woods Retirement Living Center, [G], (CHI). See Catholic Charities of the Archdiocese of Chicago-Archdiocesan Offices.
Bethpage Campus, [E], (RVC). See St. John Baptist de LaSalle Regional School.
Bhrags, Inc., [L], (BRK). See Catholic Charities.
BHS Long Term Care, Inc., [G], (DUL). See Benedictine Sisters Benevolent Association.
Big Sisters, [L], (CHI), Chicago, IL.
Big Sky Cum Christo, [K], (GF), Great Falls, MT.
Billings Area Catholic Education Trust, [K], (GF), Billings, MT.
Binghamton University Newman Center, [V], (SY), Vestal, NY.
Birchview Group Home (Siren), [E], (SUP). See Catholic Charities Bureau, Inc.
Birthline Pregnancy Support Services, [E], (PRT). See Catholic Charities Maine.
Birthright, [W], (STL), St. Louis, MO.
Birthright of Albany, [T], (ALB), Albany, NY.
Birthright of Jackson, Inc., [M], (MEM), Jackson, TN.
Birthright of Memphis, Inc., [M], (MEM), Memphis, TN.
Bishop Ahr High School, [A], (MET), Edison, NJ.
Bishop Amat Memorial High School, [D], (LA), La Puente, CA.
Bishop Baraga Elementary, [A], (GAY), Cheboygan, MI.
Bishop Baraga Preschool, [A], (GAY), Cheboygan, MI.
Bishop Baumgartner Memorial School, [C], (AGN), Sinajana, GU.
Bishop Begin Villa, [M], (OAK), Oakland, CA.
Bishop Boardman Apartments, HDFC, Inc., [L], (BRK). See Catholic Charities.
Bishop Borgess High School, [D], (DET), Detroit, MI.
Bishop Bradley Apartments, [J], (MAN), Laconia, NH.
Bishop Brady High School, [C], (MAN), Concord, NH.
Bishop Broderick Apartments Housing Development Fund Co., Inc., [K], (ALB), Albany, NY.
Bishop Brossart High School, [B], (COV), Alexandria, KY.
Bishop Byrne High School, [B], (MEM), Memphis, TN.
Bishop Carroll High School, [B], (ALT), Ebensburg, PA.
Bishop Chatard High School, [C], (IND), Indianapolis, IN.
Bishop Conaty-Our Lady of Loretto High School, [D], (LA), Los Angeles, CA.
Bishop Connolly High School, [C], (FR), Fall River, MA.
Bishop Conroy School of Religion, [D], (OG), Ogdensburg, NY.
Bishop David Apartments, [L], (L), Louisville, KY.
Bishop DeFalco Retreat Center, [H], (AMA), Amarillo, TX.
Bishop DeFalco Retreat Center Foundation, [H], (AMA). See Bishop DeFalco Retreat Center.
Bishop Denis J. O'Connell High School, [D], (ARL), Arlington, VA.
Bishop Donahue Memorial High School, [B], (WH), McMechen, WV.
Bishop Drumm Foundation - Affiliate of Catholic Health Initiatives, [I], (DM), Johnston, IA.
Bishop Drumm Retirement Center, [D], (DM), Johnston, IA.
Bishop DuBourg High School, [E], (STL), St. Louis, MO.
Bishop Dunn Memorial School, [H], (NY), Newburgh, NY.
Bishop Dunne High School, [C], (DAL), Dallas, TX.
Bishop Dwenger High School, [C], (FTW), Fort Wayne, IN.
Bishop England High School, [A], (CHR), Charleston, SC.
Bishop Eustace Prep School, [C], (CAM), Pennsauken, NJ.
Bishop Feehan High School, [C], (FR), Attleboro, MA.
Bishop Fenwick High School, [D], (BO), Peabody, MA.
Bishop Foery Foundation, [I], (SY), Syracuse, NY.
Bishop Foley High School, [D], (DET), Madison Heights, MI.
Bishop Foley Venture Fund, [D], (DET). See Bishop Foley High School.
Bishop Ford Central Catholic High School, [G], (BRK), Brooklyn, NY.
Bishop Ford Residence, [A], (NY). See Cathedral Preparatory Seminary.
Bishop Francis J. Mugavero Center for Geriatric Care, Inc., [R], (BRK), Brooklyn, NY.
Bishop Francis J. Mugavero, HDFC, Inc., [L], (BRK). See Catholic Charities.
Bishop Francis P. Keough Regional High School, [D], (PRO), Pawtucket, RI.
Bishop Gallagher High School, [D], (DET), Harper Woods, MI.
Bishop Garcia Diego High School, [D], (LA), Santa Barbara, CA.
Bishop Garriga Middle School, [B], (CC), Corpus Christi, TX.
Bishop Garrigan Catholic High School, [B], (SC), Algona, IA.
Bishop Gorman High School, [A], (LAV), Las Vegas, NV.
Bishop Grimes Jr./Sr. High School, [C], (SY), East Syracuse, NY.
Bishop Grimes Priests Residence, [S], (SY), East Syracuse, NY.
Bishop Guertin High School, [D], (MAN), Nashua, NH.
Bishop Guilfoyle High School, [B], (ALT), Altoona, PA.
Bishop Hafey Junior/Senior High School, [D], (SCR), Hazleton, PA.
Bishop Hannan High School, [D], (SCR), Scranton, PA.
Bishop Harrison Education Foundation, [W], (SY), Endicott, NY.
The Bishop Harry J. Flynn Hospitality Center, [N], (LAF). See Lafayette Catholic Service Centers, Inc.
Bishop Hartley High School, [C], (COL), Columbus, OH.
Bishop Heelan Catholic High School, [B], (SC), Sioux City, IA.
Bishop Hendricken High School, [C], (PRO), Warwick, RI.
Bishop Hoban High School, [D], (SCR), Wilkes-Barre, PA.
Bishop Hoch Villa, [E], (SFS). See Brady Memorial Home.
Bishop Hodges Pastoral Center, [F], (WH), Huttonsville, WV.
Bishop Hogan High School, [C], (KC), Kansas City, MO.
Bishop Ireton High School, [D], (ARL), Alexandria, VA.
Bishop John Neumann School, [F], (BAL), Baltimore, MD.
Bishop Joseph H. Hodges Continuous Care Center, [H], (WH), Wheeling, WV.
Bishop Joseph John Ruocco House, [O], (BO), Lakeville, MA.
Bishop Joseph V. Sullivan Diocesan Regional Catholic High School, [B], (BR), Baton Rouge, LA.
Bishop Kearney, [G], (BRK), Brooklyn, NY.
Bishop Kearney High School, [B], (ROC), Rochester, NY.
Bishop Kelley High School, [A], (TLS), Tulsa, OK.
Bishop Kelley High School Endowment Trust, [J], (TLS), Tulsa, OK.
Bishop Kelly High School, [A], (B), Boise, ID.
Bishop Kenny High School, [A], (STA), Jacksonville, FL.
Bishop Lane Retreat House, [K], (RCK), Rockford, IL.
Bishop Larkin Interparochial School, [D], (SP), Hudson, FL.
Bishop LeBlond High School, [C], (KC), St. Joseph, MO.
Bishop Leibold School, [G], (CIN), Dayton, OH.
Bishop Loughlin Memorial High School, [F], (BRK), Brooklyn, NY.
Bishop Ludden Junior/Senior High School, [C], (SY), Syracuse, NY.
Bishop Luers High School, [C], (FTW), Fort Wayne, IN.
Bishop Lynch High School, [C], (DAL), Dallas, TX.
Bishop Maginn High School, [C], (ALB), Albany, NY.
Bishop Maher Men's Center, [J], (SD). See St. Vincent de Paul Village.
Bishop Manogue High School, [A], (RNO), Reno, NV.
Bishop Mark K. Carroll High School, [B], (WCH), Wichita, KS.
Bishop McCarthy Residence, [H], (CAM), Vineland, NJ.
Bishop McCarthy Residence Convent, [M], (CAM), Vineland, NJ.
Bishop McCort High School, [B], (ALT), Johnstown, PA.
Bishop McDevitt High School, [A], (HBG), Harrisburg, PA.
Bishop McDevitt High School, [D], (PH), Wyncote, PA.
Bishop McDonnell Camp, [Q], (BRK), Brooklyn, NY.
Bishop McGuinness High School, [B], (CHL), Winston-Salem, NC.
Bishop McGuinness High School, [B], (OKL), Oklahoma City, OK.
Bishop McNamara High School, [B], (JOL), Kankakee, IL.
Bishop McNamara High School, [E], (WDC), Forestville, MD.
Bishop McVinney Regional School, [G], (PRO), Providence, RI.
Bishop Michael J. Murphy Residence for Retired Priests, [J], (E), Erie, PA.
Bishop Miege High School, [B], (KCK), Kansas City, KS.
Bishop Molloy Retreat House for Laymen, [W], (BRK), Jamaica, NY.
Bishop Montgomery High School, [D], (LA), Torrance, CA.
Bishop Moore High School, [A], (ORL), Orlando, FL.
Bishop Mora Salesian High School, [D], (LA), Los Angeles, CA.
Bishop Morrow Personal Care Home, [K], (GBG), Leechburg, PA.
Bishop Mugavero Residence, [U], (BRK), Douglaston, NY.
Bishop Neumann High School Endowment Fund, [K], (LIN), Wahoo, NE.
Bishop Neumann Junior/Senior High School, [D], (SCR), Williamsport, PA.
Bishop Noa Home for Senior Citizens, [D], (MAR), Escanaba, MI.
Bishop Noll Institute, [B], (GRY), Hammond, IN.
Bishop O'Dowd High School, [C], (OAK), Oakland, CA.
Bishop O'Hara High School, [D], (SCR), Dunmore, PA.
Bishop O'Reilly High School, [D], (SCR), Kingston, PA.
Bishop Perry Middle School, [I], (NO), New Orleans, LA.
Bishop Quinn High School, [B], (SAC), Palo Cedro, CA.
Bishop Ready High School, [C], (COL), Columbus, OH.
Bishop Rene H. Gracida Retreat House, [G], (CC), Corpus Christi, TX.
Bishop Robert E. Tracy Center, [J], (BR), Baton Rouge, LA.
Bishop Rosecrans High School, [C], (COL), Zanesville, OH.
Bishop Rosecrans High School Foundation, [K], (COL), Zanesville, OH.
Bishop Ryan High School, [C], (BIS), Minot, ND.
Bishop Ryan High School, [J], (BIS). See Minot Catholic Schools Corporation.
Bishop Scully High School, [C], (ALB), Amsterdam, NY.
Bishop Shanahan High School, [D], (PH), West Chester, PA.
Bishop Soenneker Home, [E], (OWN), Knottsville, KY.
Bishop Stang High School, [C], (FR), North Dartmouth, MA.
Bishop Stanley J. Ott Shelter, [L], (BR), Baton Rouge, LA.
Bishop Stanley J. Ott Works of Mercy Trust, [M], (BR). See Baton Rouge Chancery Office.
*Bishop Sullivan Center, [O], (KC), Kansas City, MO.
Bishop Thomas J. Drury Retreat Center, [G], (CC), Corpus Christi, TX.
Bishop Timon-St. Jude High School, [D], (BUF), Buffalo, NY.
Bishop Verot High School, [A], (VEN), Fort Myers, FL.
The Bishop Verot High School Foundation, [K], (VEN), Fort Myers, FL.
Bishop Walsh Middle-High School, [D], (BAL), Cumberland, MD.
Bishop Ward High School, [B], (KCK), Kansas City, KS.
Bishop Watterson High School, [C], (COL), Columbus, OH.
Bishop White Seminary, [A], (SPK), Spokane, WA.
Bishop William M. Cosgrove Center, [V], (CLV). See Catholic Charities Services Corporation.
Bishop William M. Cosgrove Center, [V], (CLV), Cleveland, OH.
Bishop's Attic, III, [E], (FBK), Fairbanks, AK.
Bishop's Education Endowment Trust, [M], (LC), La Crosse, WI.
The Bishop's Educational Foundation, Diocese of Stockton, [G], (STO), Stockton, CA.
Bishop's Endowment Fund Foundation, [I], (DM), Des Moines, IA.
Bishop's House, [L], (MAN), Manchester, NH.
Bishop's Residence, [O], (BUF), Buffalo, NY.
Bishop's Residence, [L], (CAM), Blackwood, NJ.
Bishop's Residence Convent, [L], (FR), Fall River, MA.
Bishops Retirement Trust Fund, [E], (SAM), Staten Island, NY.
Bishops' Housing Corporation, [L], (GR), Grand Rapids, MI.
Bishops' Residence, [I], (HBG), Harrisburg, PA.

C

Carmel of St. Joseph Discalced Carmelite Nuns, [S], (LA), Solvang, CA.
Carmel of St. Teresa, [S], (LA), Alhambra, CA.
Carmel of St. Therese of Lisieux Monastery, [G], (ALT), Loretto, PA.
Carmel of the Holy Family, [Q], (CLV), Cleveland, OH.
Carmel of the Holy Trinity (Carmelite Monastery), [I], (HON), Kaneohe, HI.
Carmel of the Immaculate Heart of Mary, [N], (PAT), Chester, NJ.
*Carmel of the Immaculate Heart of Mary Monastery, [G], (SLC), Salt Lake City, UT.
Carmel of the Mother of God, [Q], (MIL), Pewaukee, WI.
Carmel of the Queen of Heaven Discalced Carmelite Nuns, [N], (DAV), Eldridge, IA.
Carmel of the Sacred Heart, [D], (SUP), Hudson, WI.
Carmel Retreat House, [P], (NEW), Mahwah, NJ.
Carmel Richmond Nursing Home, Inc., [V], (NY), Staten Island, NY.
Carmel Ridge, [K], (BGP), Trumbull, CT.
Carmel Terrace, [U], (BO), Framingham, MA.
Carmel West Community, [B], (LA), North Hills, CA.
Carmelitas del Sagrado Corazon-OCD, [N], (SAT), Big Wells, TX.
Carmelite (Discalced) House of Studies, [N], (OAK), Berkeley, CA.
Carmelite Carefree Retirement Village, [I], (JOL), Darien, IL.
Carmelite Child Development Center, [M], (STL), Kirkwood, MO.
Carmelite Communities Assoc., [Q], (BAL), Baltimore, MD.
Carmelite Community, [J], (JOL), Darien, IL.
Carmelite Community, [F], (PHX), Phoenix, AZ.
Carmelite Community, [M], (WDC), Washington, DC.
The Carmelite Community of The St. Francis DeSales Priory, [B], (L). See St. Francis DeSales High School.
Carmelite Community of the Word, [G], (ALT), Johnstown, PA.
Carmelite Community of the Word, [G], (ALT), McConnellsburg, PA.
Carmelite Community of the Word, [G], (ALT), Ebensburg, PA.
Carmelite Community of the Word, [G], (ALT), Altoona, PA.
Carmelite Community of the Word, [G], (ALT), Hastings, PA.
Carmelite Community of the Word Motherhouse and Diocesan Pastoral Center, [G], (ALT), Altoona, PA.
Carmelite Convent, [N], (SAT), San Antonio, TX.
Carmelite Convent of Dartmouth, Inc., [Q], (FR), Fall River, MA.
Carmelite Fathers House of Prayer, [J], (STA), Korona, FL.
Carmelite Fathers Provincial Office, [J], (JOL), Darien, IL.
Carmelite Fathers Residence, [N], (CHI), Chicago, IL.
Carmelite Fathers, NY Prov. of St. Elias, [Z], (NY), Scarborough, NY.
Carmelite Hermits of Adoration, Inc., [M], (SCL), Alexandria, MN.
Carmelite Home for Boys, [H], (GRY), Hammond, IN.
Carmelite Home for Girls, [H], (GRY), East Chicago, IN.
Carmelite Home, Inc., [J], (MIL), Wauwatosa, WI.
Carmelite House of Prayer, [L], (SR), Oakville, CA.
Carmelite House of Prayer, [M], (SR), Oakville, CA.
Carmelite Institute, [V], (WDC), Washington, DC.
Carmelite Learning Center, [J], (SAT), San Antonio, TX.
Carmelite Learning Center of Corpus Christi, [C], (CC), Corpus Christi, TX.
Carmelite Mission Office, [M], (JOL), Darien, IL.
Carmelite Monastery, [L], (ALN), Coopersburg, PA.
Carmelite Monastery, [N], (BAL), Baltimore, MD.
Carmelite Monastery, [W], (BO), Brighton, MA.
Carmelite Monastery, [N], (CHI), Mundelein, IL.
Carmelite Monastery, [D], (GLP), Gallup, NM.
Carmelite Monastery, [I], (HBG), Elysburg, PA.
Carmelite Monastery, [AA], (NY), Beacon, NY.
Carmelite Monastery, [AA], (PH), Philadelphia, PA.
Carmelite Monastery, [G], (SAV), Savannah, GA.
Carmelite Monastery (O.C.D.), [E], (RNO), Reno, NV.
Carmelite Monastery of Cristo Rey, Discalced Carmelite Nuns, [O], (SFR), San Francisco, CA.
Carmelite Monastery of Jesus, Mary and Joseph (O.C.D.), [E], (LAV), Las Vegas, NV.
Carmelite Monastery of Our Lady and St. Therese, [H], (MRY), Carmel, CA.
Carmelite Monastery of San Diego, California, [I], (SD), San Diego, CA.
Carmelite Monastery of the Infant Jesus, Discalced Carmelite Nuns, [N], (SJ), Santa Clara, CA.
Carmelite Monastery of the Mother of God, Discalced Carmelite Nuns, [O], (SFR), San Rafael, CA.
Carmelite Monastery of Wheeling, [P], (WH), Wheeling, WV.
Carmelite Monastery, Novitiate, [M], (SJ), San Jose, CA.
Carmelite Nuns of the Ancient Observance, [B], (SAN), San Angelo, TX.
Carmelite Nuns, Discalced, O.C.D., Monastery of St. Joseph and St. Theresa, [Q], (NO), Covington, LA.
Carmelite Priory, [Q], (GAL), Houston, TX.
Carmelite Priory, [F], (TUC), Tucson, AZ.
Carmelite Priory of St. Cyril, [N], (CHI), Chicago, IL.
Carmelite Sisters for the Aged and Infirm (O.Carm.), [AA], (PH), Philadelphia, PA.
Carmelite Sisters of Charity, [O], (WDC), Silver Spring, MD.
Carmelite Sisters of Mary, [L], (SPK), Newport, WA.
Carmelite Sisters of St. Therese of the Infant Jesus Motherhouse, Villa Teresa, [J], (OKL), Oklahoma City, OK.
Carmelite Sisters of the Divine Heart of Jesus, [I], (SD), La Mesa, CA.
Carmelite Sisters of the Divine Heart of Jesus Provincial House and Novitiate, [R], (STL), Kirkwood, MO.
Carmelite Sisters of the Eucharist, [G], (NOR), Windham, CT.
Carmelite Sisters of the Eucharist, [H], (NOR), Windham, CT.
Carmelite Sisters of the Most Sacred Heart of Los Angeles, [S], (LA), Alhambra, CA.
Carmelite Sisters of the Most Sacred Heart of Los Angeles, [S], (LA). See Carmelite Sisters of the Most Sacred Heart of Los Angeles.
Carmelite Sisters of the Sacred Heart (O.C.D.), [R], (GAL), Houston, TX.
Carmelite Sisters Teresas of St. Joseph, Inc., [AA], (NY), New York, NY.
Carmelite Spiritual Center, [L], (JOL), Darien, IL.
Carmelite Visitor Center (National Shrine & Museum of St. Therese), [M], (JOL), Darien, IL.
Carmelites of Mary Immaculate Center of Spirituality, [K], (NSH), Liberty, TN.
Carmelites of Mary Immaculate, Inc., [U], (BRK), Brooklyn, NY.
Carney Hospital, [Q], (BO), Boston, MA.
The Carney Hospital Foundation, Inc., [DD], (BO). See Chancery Office.
The Caroline Center, [Q], (BAL), Baltimore, MD.
Caroline Conference and Retreat Center, [R], (STL). See Sancta Maria in Ripa.
Caroline House, Inc., [W], (BGP), Wilton, CT.
The Caroline Trust, [W], (STL), St. Louis, MO.
Carondelet Behavioral Health Center, [B], (YAK), Richland, WA.
Carondelet Community, [I], (HON). See Sisters of St. Joseph of Carondelet CSJ, Hawaii Vice-Province.
Carondelet Community, [G], (TUC), Tucson, AZ.
Carondelet Foundation, [E], (TUC) See Carondelet Health Care Corporation of Arizona, Inc.
Carondelet Foundation, [J], (TUC), Tucson, AZ.
Carondelet Health Care Corporation of Arizona, Inc., [E], (TUC), Tucson, AZ.
Carondelet Health Corporation, [G], (KC). See Saint Joseph Health Center.
Carondelet Health System, [W], (STL), St. Louis, MO.
Carondelet High School, [E], (OAK), Concord, CA.
Carondelet Home Care Services Inc., [G], (KC). See Saint Joseph Health Center.
Carondelet Lifecare Ministries/St. Mary's Health Clinics, [W], (STP), St. Paul, MN.
Carondelet Manor, [G], (KC). See Saint Joseph Health Center.
Carpenter Center, Inc., [J], (MAN), Manchester, NH.
Carriage House Apartments, Pontchartrain Housing Corp. I, [N], (NO), New Orleans, LA.
Carrington Health Center, [D], (FAR), Carrington, ND.
Carroll Children's Center, [C], (YAK), Yakima, WA.
Carroll College, [A], (HEL), Helena, MT.
Carroll College, [B], (HEL), Helena, MT.
Carroll High School, [E], (CIN), Dayton, OH.
Carroll House, [M], (WDC), Washington, DC.
Carroll Manor Inc., [K], (WDC). See Providence Hospital.
Carroll Manor Nursing and Rehabilitation, [K], (WDC). See Providence Hospital.
Carroll Manor Nursing & Rehabilitation Center, [V], (WDC), Washington, DC.
Carrollton School of the Sacred Heart, [D], (MIA), Miami, FL.
The Carron Center, [G], (DEN), Denver, CO.
The Carron Center, [L], (DEN). See Catholic Charities and Community Services of the Archdiocese of Denver, Inc.
Carter County Medical Clinic, [E], (LEX), Olive Hill, KY.
Carter-May Home, [D], (CHR), Charleston, SC.
Carthusian Foundation, Charterhouse of the Transfiguration, [G], (BUR), Arlington, VT.
Casa Angelica, [I], (SFE), Albuquerque, NM.
Casa Belen, [L], (ALN), Bethlehem, PA.
CASA Brendan and CASA II, Inc. Catholic Charities, [G], (FWT), Stephenville, TX.
Casa Calderon, Inc., [E], (PT), Tallahassee, FL.
Casa Charlie Rodriguez, [B], (CGS), San Lorenzo, P.R.
Casa Chiara Community, [O], (SFR), Redwood City, CA.
Casa Comboni Mission Seminary, [R], (LA), Azusa, CA.
Casa Cristo Redentor, [B], (CGS), Aguas Buenas, PR.
Casa Cristo Rey, [M], (SPR), Springfield, MA.
Casa Cursillos de Cristiandad de Caguas, [B], (CGS), Juncos, PR.
Casa de Esperanza, [R], (GAL), Houston, TX.
Casa de Esperanza, De Los Ninos, Inc., [M], (GAL), Houston, TX.
Casa de los Ninos Crisis Center, [J], (TUC), Tucson, AZ.
Casa De Merced, [J], (PHX), Phoenix, AZ.
Casa De Padres, [K], (SAT), San Antonio, TX.
Casa de Padres Endowment Fund, [S], (SAT), San Antonio, TX.
Casa de San Jose, [D], (LUB), Lubbock, TX.
Casa de San Jose - Franciscan Sisters of Our Lady of the Sacred Heart, [J], (WIL), Wilmington, DE.
Casa del Carmen, [R], (PH), Philadelphia, PA.
Casa del Cor, Inc., [G], (FWT), Fort Worth, TX.
Casa Generalizia di Suore di Nostra Signora di Namur, [X], (BO). See Sisters of Notre Dame de Namur Generalate Office of the General Treas.
Casa Guadalupe, [R], (LA), Los Angeles, CA.
Casa Guadalupe, Family Growth Center, [J], (SPC), Ellington, MO.
Casa Juan Diego, [M], (GAL), Houston, TX.
Casa Juan Diego Centro de Evangelization, [K], (KCK), Kansas City, KS.
Casa Linda Lodge, [J], (PHX). See Catholic Social Services of Central and Northern Arizona, Inc.
Casa Manana Inn, [D], (STO), Stockton, CA.
Casa Manresa, [B], (CGS), Aibonito, PR.
Casa Maria, [J], (DET). See Ryan Senior Residences of the Archdiocese of Detroit. Inc.
Casa Maria, [M], (SPR), Holyoke, MA.
Casa Maria, [J], (TUC), Tucson, AZ.
Casa Maria de Guadalupe Medical Clinic and Social Service Center, [M], (GAL), Houston, TX.
Casa Maria Marianist Community, [M], (SAT), San Antonio, TX.
Casa Maria Montessori, Preschool & Kindergarten, [E], (SJ), Los Gatos, CA.
Casa Maryknoll, [N], (SFR). See Maryknoll Fathers and Brothers, Catholic Foreign Mission Society of America, Inc.
Casa Merced, Sisters of Mercy Convent, [D], (LUB), Lubbock, TX.
Casa Pasionista Guadalupe, [M], (SAT), San Antonio, TX.
Casa Reina, [D], (GLP), Gallup, NM.
Casa Salesiana de Retiros, [C], (CGS), Aibonito, PR.
Casa San Basilio, [B], (GAL), Houston, TX.
Casa San Carlo, [G], (CHI). See Catholic Charities of the Archdiocese of Chicago-Archdiocesan Offices.
Casa San Jose, [F], (GLP), Grants-Milan, NM.
Casa San Lorenzo, [H], (MIA), Miami, FL.
Casa San Martin, [F], (GLP), Gallup, NM.
Casa San Pablo, [C], (ORL), Daytona Beach, FL.
Casa Santa Maria del Camino, Inc., [R], (WOR), Worcester, MA.
Casa Stella Maris, [H], (PT), Navarre, FL.
Casa Teresa, [R], (LA). See Missionaries of Charity Brothers.
"Casa Teresa," Missionary Brothers of Charity, [V], (LA), Los Angeles, CA.
Casa Venegas, [I], (SB), Victorville, CA.
Casa Vides, [N], (ELP), El Paso, TX.
Casa Vincentia, [R], (OAK), Oakland, CA.
Casa, Inc. Housing for the Elderly and Handicapped, [G], (FWT), Fort Worth, TX.
Cascade County Council of the St. Vincent de Paul Society, [K], (GF), Great Falls, MT.
Cascades Apartments, Walmsley Housing Corp., [N], (NO), Metairie, LA.
Cascia Hall Preparatory School, [B], (TLS), Tulsa, OK.
Case Management Services, [H], (SY). See Catholic Charities of Cortland County.
Casita Maria Inc., [Y], (NY), New York, NY.
Casita Maria-Carver Community Center, [Y], (NY), New York, NY.
Casper Community College, [E], (CHY), Casper, WY.
Cassata Learning Center, [A], (FWT), Fort Worth, TX.
Castle College, [B], (MAN), Windham, NH.
Cataldo Catholic School, [F], (SPK), Spokane, WA.
Catechetical Regional Offices, [D], (NY). See Department of Education.
Cathedral - Religious Education/Faith Formation, [B], (CR), Crookston, MN.
Cathedral Academy, [F], (ALB), Albany, NY.
Cathedral Arts Project, Inc., [O], (OM), Omaha, NE.
Cathedral Camp Retreat Center, [M], (FR), East Freetown, MA.
Cathedral Convent, [G], (TUC), Tucson, AZ.
Cathedral Convent-Ursuline Sisters, [F], (R), Raleigh, NC.
Cathedral Diocesan Elementary School, [D], (TR), Trenton, NJ.

Cathedral Elementary School, [C], (WIN). See Winona Area Catholic Schools.
Cathedral Health Services, Inc., [F], (NEW). See Cathedral Healthcare System, Inc.
Cathedral Healthcare System, Inc., [F], (NEW), Newark, NJ.
Cathedral Heritage Foundation, Inc., [Q], (L), Louisville, KY.
Cathedral High and John XXIII Middle School, [C], (SCL), St. Cloud, MN.
Cathedral High School, [D], (BO), Boston, MA.
Cathedral High School, [C], (ELP), El Paso, TX.
Cathedral High School, [F], (LA), Los Angeles, CA.
Cathedral High School, [A], (NU). See New Ulm Area Catholic Schools.
Cathedral High School, [E], (NY), New York, NY.
Cathedral High School, [C], (SPR), Springfield, MA.
Cathedral High School (Cathedral Trustees, Inc.), [D], (IND), Indianapolis, IN.
Cathedral High School Education Foundation, [C], (SCL). See Cathedral High and John XXIII Middle School.
Cathedral Library, [Q], (BAL), Baltimore, MD.
Cathedral Mercy Convent, [G], (AGN), Agana, GU.
Cathedral of St. Joseph the Workman Endowment Trust, [M], (LC), La Crosse, WI.
Cathedral Place, [G], (MOB), Mobile, AL.
Cathedral Plaza, [G], (SD), San Diego, CA.
Cathedral Plaza Apartments, [I], (SPK), Spokane, WA.
Cathedral Plaza Inc., [K], (DEN). See Archdiocesan Housing Committee.
Cathedral Preparatory School, [C], (E), Erie, PA.
Cathedral Preparatory Seminary, [A], (NY), New York, NY.
Cathedral Preparatory Seminary of the Immaculate Conception, [B], (BRK), Elmhurst, NY.
Cathedral Preschool, [J], (OWN), Owensboro, KY.
Cathedral Preservation Fund, Inc., [P], (DAL), Dallas, TX.
Cathedral Rectory, [L], (MAN), Manchester, NH.
Cathedral Residence of the Immaculate Conception, [B], (BRK), Douglaston, NY.
Cathedral School, [B], (HBG), Harrisburg, PA.
The Cathedral Soup Kitchen, Inc., [T], (CAM), Camden, NJ.
Cathedral Square Housing, Inc., [L], (TR), Trenton, NJ.
Cathedral Square Towers, [I], (KC), Kansas City, MO.
Cathedral Tower, [S], (STL), St. Louis, MO.
Cathedral Unit School, [A], (JKS), Natchez, MS.
Catherine Kasper Home, [K], (FTW). See Convent Ancilla Domini.
Catherine Marian Housing, Inc., [Y], (MIL), Racine, WI.
Catherine McAuley, [G], (BRK), Brooklyn, NY.
The Catherine McAuley Center, [R], (SCR), Scranton, PA.
The Catherine McAuley Center - Bridge Program, [R], (SCR), Scranton, PA.
The Catherine McAuley Center - Maple Street House, [R], (SCR), Scranton, PA.
The Catherine McAuley Center - Swetland Street House, [R], (SCR), Scranton, PA.
Catherine McAuley Convent of Mercy, [I], (LR), Barling, AR.
Catherine McAuley Health Services Corporation, [F], (LAN), Ann Arbor, MI.
Catherine McAuley Health System, [F], (LAN), Ann Arbor, MI.
Catherine McAuley High School, [C], (PRT), Portland, ME.
The Catherine McAuley House, [R], (SCR), Plymouth, PA.
The Catherine McAuley House Annex, [R], (SCR), Scranton, PA.
Catherine McAuley Housing, [L], (ROC), Rochester, NY.
Catherine McAuley Unit, [N], (HRT). See Sisters of Mercy of the Americas of Connecticut.
Catherine St. Housing Development Fund Company, Inc., [Q], (SY), Utica, NY.
Catherine Sheridan Houses, [L], (BRK). See Catholic Charities.
Catherine Spalding Center, [O], (L), Nazareth, KY.
Catherine Spalding School, [C], (OWN), Owensboro, KY.
Catherine's Early Childhood Center, [O], (TOL), Toledo, OH.
*Catherine's House, [Q], (CHL), Belmont, NC.
Catherine's House c/o Sisters of Mercy Health System, [F], (LR), Little Rock, AR.
Catholic Community Services Inc., [K], (KCK), Topeka, KS.
Catholic Academy of West Buffalo, [G], (BUF), Buffalo, NY.
Catholic Action Fund, [D], (LIT), Chicago, IL.
Catholic Actors Guild of America, Inc., The, [DD], (NY), New York, NY.
Catholic Agency-Migration & Refugee Service, [F], (DOD), Garden City, KS.
Catholic Alumni Club, [Q], (BAL), Baltimore, MD.
Catholic Alumni Club, [L], (COL), Columbus, OH.
Catholic Alumni Club, [P], (DAL), Dallas, TX.
Catholic Alumni Club (Cincinnati Chapter), [V], (CIN), Cincinnati, OH.
Catholic Alumni Club (Dayton Chapter), [V], (CIN), Centerville, OH.
Catholic Alumni Club of Denver, Inc., [Q], (DEN), Denver, CO.
Catholic Alumni Club of Orange County, [M], (ORG), Anaheim, CA.
Catholic Alumni Club of the Archdiocese of New York, [DD], (NY), New York, NY.
*Catholic Answers, Inc., [N], (SD), San Diego, CA.
Catholic Apostolic Center: Ajeltake, [A], (MI), Majuro, MH.
Catholic Archives of Texas, [N], (AUS), Austin, TX.
Catholic Association for Regional Education, [G], (PRO), Providence, RI.
Catholic Biblical Association, [V], (WDC), Washington, DC.
Catholic Big Brothers of New York, Inc., [DD], (NY), New York, NY.
Catholic Big Brothers, Inc., [CC], (LA), Los Angeles, CA.
The Catholic Big Sisters, [DD], (NY), New York, NY.
Catholic Business Alliance, [R], (PIT), Pittsburgh, PA.
The Catholic Camp Association Inc., [X], (NY), New York, NY.
The Catholic Campaign of America, Inc., [J], (CC), Corpus Christi, TX.
Catholic Campus Center of Washburn University, [J], (KCK), Topeka, KS.
Catholic Campus Ministers Association, [T], (DET), Warren, MI.
Catholic Campus Ministries, [J], (LR), Little Rock, AR.
Catholic Campus Ministry, [M], (FWT), Wichita Falls, TX.
Catholic Campus Ministry, [K], (HBG), Harrisburg, PA.
Catholic Campus Ministry, [Q], (SAT), San Antonio, TX.
Catholic Campus Ministry at Central Washington University, [G], (YAK), Ellensburg, WA.
Catholic Campus Ministry at Northeast Louisiana University, [G], (SHP), Monroe, LA.
Catholic Campus Ministry-Northern Michigan University, [G], (MAR), Marquette, MI.
Catholic Care Center, Inc., [N], (SFD), Springfield, IL.
Catholic Care Center, Inc., [F], (WCH), Wichita, KS.
Catholic Center, [L], (WH), Ghent, WV.
Catholic Center at Rutgers University, [M], (MET), New Brunswick, NJ.
Catholic Center for the Deaf and Hard of Hearing, [R], (PH), Philadelphia, PA.
Catholic Center of Concern, [G], (BIR), Birmingham, AL.
Catholic Center of Concern, [G], (BIR), Gadsden, AL.
Catholic Center of Concern, [G], (BIR), Huntsville, AL.
The Catholic Center U Mass, Lowell, [CC], (BO), Lowell, MA.
The Catholic Central Endowment Trust, [E], (DET), Redford, MI.
Catholic Central High School, [C], (ALB), Troy, NY.
Catholic Central High School, [E], (CIN), Springfield, OH.
Catholic Central High School, [E], (DET), Redford, MI.
Catholic Central High School, [C], (GR), Grand Rapids, MI.
Catholic Central High School, [D], (MIL), Burlington, WI.
Catholic Central High School, [B], (STU), Steubenville, OH.
Catholic Central School, [G], (BUF), Buffalo, NY.
Catholic Chair of Religion, [C], (DAV), Iowa City, IA.
The Catholic Chaplain Corps, [K], (GAL), Houston, TX.
Catholic Chaplain Corps, Texas Medical Center, [K], (GAL). See The Catholic Chaplain Corps.
Catholic Chaplaincy at O'Hare, [X], (CHI), Chicago, IL.
Catholic Charismatic Center, [U], (GAL), Houston, TX.
Catholic Charismatic Center, [N], (SFE), Albuquerque, NM.
Catholic Charismatic Renewal, [O], (L), Louisville, KY.
Catholic Charismatic Renewal, [L], (ROC), Rochester, NY.
The Catholic Charismatic Renewal in Atlanta, [M], (ATL), Atlanta, GA.
Catholic Charismatic Renewal Liaison, [V], (CIN), Cincinnati, OH.
Catholic Charismatic Renewal Office, [DD], (NY), Scarsdale, NY.
The Catholic Charismatic Renewal Office of Southeastern Wisconsin, Inc., [Y], (MIL), Milwaukee, WI.
Catholic Charismatic Renewal Services, [H], (COS), Colorado Springs, CO.
Catholic Charitable Bureau of the Archdiocese of Boston, Inc., [J], (BO), Boston, MA.
Catholic Charities, [L], (BRK), Brooklyn, NY.
Catholic Charities, [C], (BWN), Brownsville, TX.
Catholic Charities, [J], (DAL), Dallas, TX.
Catholic Charities, [G], (ELP), El Paso, TX.
Catholic Charities, [N], (FTW), Fort Wayne, IN.
Catholic Charities, [N], (FTW), South Bend, IN.
Catholic Charities, [N], (FTW), Elkhart, IN.
Catholic Charities, [I], (GAL). See Associated Catholic Charities of the Diocese of Galveston-Houston.
Catholic Charities, [N], (GRY), Gary, IN.
Catholic Charities, [L], (IND), New Albany, IN.
Catholic Charities, [L], (IND), Tell City, IN.
Catholic Charities, [L], (IND), Terre Haute, IN.
Catholic Charities, [D], (JOL), Joliet, IL.
Catholic Charities, [D], (JOL), Kankakee, IL.
Catholic Charities, [D], (JOL), Lombard, IL.
Catholic Charities, [J], (OM), Omaha, NE.
Catholic Charities, [J], (OM), Columbus, NE.
Catholic Charities, [J], (OM), Norfolk, NE.
Catholic Charities, [J], (SD), San Diego, CA.
Catholic Charities, [K], (SY), Syracuse, NY.
Catholic Charities, [F], (TR), Trenton, NJ.
Catholic Charities, [J], (WCH), Wichita, KS.
Catholic Charities, [H], (WOR), Worcester, MA.
Catholic Charities Activity Center, [G], (CHI). See Catholic Charities of the Archdiocese of Chicago-Archdiocesan Offices.
Catholic Charities Administration, [G], (MAN), Manchester, NH.
Catholic Charities Adolescent Group Home, [H], (SY), Binghamton, NY.
Catholic Charities and Community Services East Office, [L], (DEN). See Catholic Charities and Community Services of the Archdiocese of Denver, Inc.
Catholic Charities & Community Services Farm Labor Housing Corp., [L], (DEN). See Catholic Charities and Community Services of the Archdiocese of Denver, Inc.
Catholic Charities and Community Services Northern, [L], (DEN). See Catholic Charities and Community Services of the Archdiocese of Denver, Inc.
Catholic Charities and Community Services of the Archdiocese of Denver, Inc., [L], (DEN), Denver, CO.
Catholic Charities Annex, Inc., [G], (LAV), Las Vegas, NV.
Catholic Charities Appeal, [H], (BUF). See The Catholic Charities of the Diocese of Buffalo.
Catholic Charities Auxiliary of San Mateo, [Q], (SFR). See Catholic Charities of the Archdiocese of San Francisco.
Catholic Charities Bureau, Inc., [C], (STA), Jacksonville, FL.
Catholic Charities Bureau, Inc., [E], (SUP), Superior, WI.
Catholic Charities Central Administration, [H], (RVC), Hicksville, NY.
Catholic Charities Central Office, [E], (MET), Metuchen, NJ.
Catholic Charities Child Care, Inc., [Y], (MIL), Milwaukee, WI.
Catholic Charities Children's Services, [E], (FTW), Fort Wayne, IN.
Catholic Charities Community Development Corporation, Inc., [CC], (LA), Los Angeles, CA.
Catholic Charities Community Services, [F], (SFD), Decatur, IL.
Catholic Charities Community Services Odessa, Inc., [C], (SAN), Odessa, TX.
Catholic Charities Counseling Office, [G], (SPR), Pittsfield, MA.
Catholic Charities Department of Social Development, [J], (NY), New York, NY.
Catholic Charities District I, [J], (VEN), Sarasota, FL.
*Catholic Charities Foundation, [O], (OM), Omaha, NE.
Catholic Charities Foundation, [W], (STL), St. Louis, MO.
Catholic Charities Foundation of Tampa Bay, Inc., [T], (SP). See Chancery Office.
Catholic Charities Foundation, Inc., [Y], (MIL), Milwaukee, WI.
Catholic Charities Housing Development Corp., [G], (CHI). See Catholic Charities of the Archdiocese of Chicago-Archdiocesan Offices.
Catholic Charities Housing Opportunities Corporation, [P], (Y), Youngstown, OH.
Catholic Charities Housing, Inc., [T], (SP), St. Petersburg, FL.
Catholic Charities Housing, Inc., [T], (SP). See Chancery Office.
Catholic Charities in Collier County, [J], (VEN), Naples, FL.
Catholic Charities Inc., [K], (LC), La Crosse, WI.
Catholic Charities Intensive Treatment Unit, [F], (SCL), Fergus Falls, MN.
Catholic Charities Maine, [E], (PRT), Falmouth, ME.
Catholic Charities Maine Adult and Family Services,

[E], (PRT). See Catholic Charities Maine.
Catholic Charities Maine Counseling Services, [E], (PRT). See Catholic Charities Maine.
Catholic Charities Maine Family Child Care, [E], (PRT). See Catholic Charities Maine.
Catholic Charities Manpower Services, [H], (BUF). See The Catholic Charities of the Diocese of Buffalo.
Catholic Charities Mojave Project, Inc., [G], (LAV), Las Vegas, NV.
Catholic Charities Neighborhood Center, [L], (WH), Wheeling, WV.
Catholic Charities of Alton and Wood River, [F], (SFD), Alton, IL.
Catholic Charities of Buffalo, NY, Foundation, Inc., [T], (BUF), Buffalo, NY.
Catholic Charities of California, Inc., [P], (SAC), Sacramento, CA.
Catholic Charities of Central Maryland, Inc., [P], (BAL). See Chancery Office.
Catholic Charities of Cortland County, [H], (SY), Cortland, NY.
Catholic Charities of De Soto County, [J], (VEN), Arcadia, FL.
Catholic Charities of Effingham, [F], (SFD), Effingham, IL.
Catholic Charities of Fairfield County, [G], (BGP), Bridgeport, CT.
Catholic Charities of Hampton Roads, Inc., [K], (RIC), Virginia Beach, VA.
Catholic Charities of Los Angeles, Inc., [Y], (LA), Los Angeles, CA.
Catholic Charities of Orange County, Inc., [J], (ORG), Santa Ana, CA.
Catholic Charities of Oswego County, [H], (SY), Fulton, NY.
Catholic Charities of Quad Cities, [F], (SFD), Granite City, IL.
Catholic Charities of Rome, [H], (SY), Rome, NY.
Catholic Charities of Sacramento, Inc., [L], (SAC), Sacramento, CA.
Catholic Charities of Santa Clara County, [F], (SJ), San Jose, CA.
Catholic Charities of Southern Nevada, [G], (LAV), Las Vegas, NV.
Catholic Charities of Springfield, [F], (SFD), Springfield, IL.
Catholic Charities of the Archdiocese of Chicago-Archdiocesan Offices, [G], (CHI), Chicago, IL.
Catholic Charities of the Archdiocese of Milwaukee, Inc., [Y], (MIL), Milwaukee, WI.
The Catholic Charities of the Archdiocese of New York, [I], (NY), New York, NY.
Catholic Charities of the Archdiocese of Portland in Oregon, [G], (P), Portland, OR.
Catholic Charities of the Archdiocese of San Francisco, [Q], (SFR), San Francisco, CA.
Catholic Charities of the Archdiocese of Washington, Inc., [H], (WDC), Washington, DC.
The Catholic Charities of the Diocese of Buffalo, [H], (BUF), Buffalo, NY.
Catholic Charities of the Diocese of Charleston, [G], (CHR), Charleston, SC.
Catholic Charities of the Diocese of Fresno, [E], (FRS), Fresno, CA.
Catholic Charities of the Diocese of Oakland, Inc., [H], (OAK), Oakland, CA.
Catholic Charities of the Diocese of Palm Beach, Inc., [J], (PMB), West Palm Beach, FL.
The Catholic Charities of the Diocese of Stockton, [B], (STO), Stockton, CA.
Catholic Charities of the Diocese of Yakima, [C], (YAK), Yakima, WA.
Catholic Charities of the Roman Catholic Diocese of Syracuse, [H], (SY), Syracuse, NY.
Catholic Charities Regional Office, [C], (STA), St. Augustine, FL.
Catholic Charities Regional Office, [C], (STA), Gainesville, FL.
Catholic Charities Regional Office, [C], (STA), Jacksonville, FL.
Catholic Charities Senior Daycare Center, [N], (MIL), Milwaukee, WI.
Catholic Charities Services Corporation, [V], (CLV), Cleveland, OH.
Catholic Charities Social Service Division of Portland, [G], (P). See Catholic Charities of the Archdiocese of Portland in Oregon.
Catholic Charities Thrift Shop, [D], (WIL). See Catholic Charities, Inc.
Catholic Charities Thrift Shop, [D], (WIL). See Catholic Charities, Inc.
Catholic Charities Volunteer Department, [W], (STL), St. Louis, MO.
Catholic Charities, Archdiocese of San Antonio, [P], (SAT), San Antonio, TX.
Catholic Charities, Diocese of St. Petersburg, Inc., [J], (SP), St. Petersburg, FL.
Catholic Charities, Eastern Region, [H], (SY), Utica, NY.
Catholic Charities, Inc., [E], (FWT), Fort Worth, TX.
Catholic Charities, Inc., [K], (MAD), Madison, WI.
Catholic Charities, Inc., [H], (SPK), Spokane, WA.
Catholic Charities, Inc., [L], (WCH), Wichita, KS.
Catholic Charities, Inc., [D], (WIL), Wilmington, DE.
Catholic Charities, Youth Services Division, [K], (SY), Utica, NY.
Catholic Charities-Catholic Family Services (Archdiocese of Hartford), [S], (HRT), Hartford, CT.
Catholic Charities-STEPS-TASA, [H], (SY), Cortland, NY.
Catholic Charity Fund, [T], (PRO). See Miscellaneous Listings for the Diocese of Providence.
Catholic Child Care Society of the Diocese of Brooklyn, [C], (BRK), Brooklyn, NY.
Catholic Children and Family Services, [H], (SPK), Walla Walla, WA.
Catholic Children's Home, [G], (SFD), Alton, IL.
Catholic Chinese Cultural Center, [N], (CHI). See Society of the Divine Word, Provincial Headquarter-Chicago Prov.
Catholic Chinese Cultural Center, [S], (CHI), Chicago, IL.
Catholic Christian Newman Association, [I], (SPC), Branson, MO.
The Catholic Church Extension Society, [U], (CHI), Chicago, IL.
Catholic Clerical Student Fund, [U], (GAL), Houston, TX.
Catholic Club, The, [O], (TOL), Toledo, OH.
Catholic Commission on Housing, [W], (STL), St. Louis, MO.
The Catholic Committee of Appalachia, [R], (WH), Webster Springs, WV.
Catholic Committee of the South, Inc., [H], (JKS), Aberdeen, MS.
Catholic Committee on Scouting, [L], (ROC), Rochester, NY.
Catholic Committee on Scouting, [M], (SAC), Orangevale, CA.
Catholic Committee on Scouting, [N], (SD), San Diego, CA.
Catholic Committee on Scouting of the Diocese of Belleville, [K], (BEL), Belleville, IL.
Catholic Community Appeal, Inc., [P], (DAL), Dallas, TX.
Catholic Community at Quinnipiac College, [R], (HRT), Hamden, CT.
Catholic Community at Relay, [Q], (BAL), Baltimore, MD.
Catholic Community Center, [J], (STU), Steubenville, OH.
Catholic Community of the Korean Martyrs, [L], (RIC). See Ethnic and Special Ministries.
Catholic Community School of South Baltimore, [F], (BAL), Baltimore, MD.
Catholic Community Service of Southern Arizona, Inc., [D], (TUC), Tucson, AZ.
Catholic Community Services, [I], (ALX), Alexandria, LA.
Catholic Community Services, [V], (CLV). See Catholic Social Services of Lorain County.
Catholic Community Services, [J], (SLC), Salt Lake City, UT.
Catholic Community Services (C.C.S.) Mt. Carmel Guild Hospital, [G], (NEW), Newark, NJ.
Catholic Community Services Administration, [W], (STL), St. Louis, MO.
Catholic Community Services in Western Arizona, [D], (TUC). See Social Service Agencies: Pima County.
Catholic Community Services of Cochise County, [D], (TUC). See Social Service Agencies: Pima County.
Catholic Community Services of Lane County, [G], (P). See Catholic Charities of the Archdiocese of Portland in Oregon.
Catholic Community Services of Mid-Willamette Valley and the Central Coast, [G], (P). See Catholic Charities of the Archdiocese of Portland in Oregon.
Catholic Community Services of Southern Oregon, [G], (P). See Catholic Charities of the Archdiocese of Portland in Oregon.
Catholic Community Services of Stark County, Inc., [L], (Y), Canton, OH.
Catholic Community Services of the Archdiocese of Detroit, Inc., [Q], (DET), Detroit, MI.
Catholic Community Services of Western Washington, [E], (SEA), Seattle, WA.
Catholic Community Services, Inc. of Trumbull County, [L], (Y), Warren, OH.
Catholic Conference Center, [P], (CHL), Hickory, NC.
Catholic Conference of Illinois, [X], (CHI), Chicago, IL.
Catholic Counseling Services, [J], (DAL), Dallas, TX.
Catholic Counseling Services, Inc., [N], (ELP), El Paso, TX.
Catholic County Jail Ministry, [O], (OM), Omaha, NE.
Catholic Cursillo of Cincinnati, [V], (CIN), Cincinnati, OH.
Catholic Daughters of the America, [J], (STU), Martins Ferry, OH.
Catholic Daughters of the Americas, [Q], (BAL), Baltimore, MD.
Catholic Daughters of the Americas, [K], (BEL), Belleville, IL.
Catholic Daughters of the Americas, [B], (STV). See Miscellaneous Organizations.
Catholic Daughters of the Americas and Its Courts, [DD], (NY), New York, NY.
Catholic Day Care Center, [D], (BEL), East St. Louis, IL.
Catholic Deaf Center, [V], (WDC), Landover Hills, MD.
Catholic Deaf Ministry, [W], (STL), St. Louis, MO.
Catholic Deaf of Baltimore, [Q], (BAL), Baltimore, MD.
Catholic Development Foundation, [I], (FAR), Fargo, ND.
The Catholic Diocese of El Paso Foundation, [N], (ELP), El Paso, TX.
The Catholic Diocese of Knoxville Foundation, Inc., [K], (KNX), Knoxville, TN.
Catholic Diocese of Las Cruces Foundation, Inc., [E], (LSC), Las Cruces, NM.
Catholic Diocese of Pittsburgh Foundation, [R], (PIT), Pittsburgh, PA.
*Catholic Diocese of Pueblo Foundation, [H], (PBL), Pueblo, CO.
The Catholic Distance University, [C], (ARL), Paeonian Springs, VA.
Catholic East Elementary, [H], (MIL), Milwaukee, WI.
Catholic Eastside Apostolate, [T], (SAT), San Antonio, TX.
Catholic Education Association, [O], (OM), Omaha, NE.
Catholic Education Foundation, Inc., [J], (EVN), Evansville, IN.
Catholic Education Foundation, Inc., [T], (SP). See Chancery Office.
The Catholic Education Fund, Inc., [D], (RC), Rapid City, SD.
Catholic Education Ministries of Western Maryland, [Q], (BAL), Cumberland, MD.
Catholic Eldercare, Inc., [W], (STP), Minneapolis, MN.
Catholic Elementary Education Foundation of Hampton Roads, [P], (RIC), Portsmouth, VA.
Catholic Elementary School of Pointe Coupee, [D], (BR), New Roads, LA.
Catholic Elementary Schools-Region I, [E], (BGP), Greenwich, CT.
Catholic Elementary Schools-Region II, [E], (BGP), Stamford, CT.
Catholic Elementary Schools-Region III, [E], (BGP), Norwalk, CT.
Catholic Elementary Schools-Region IV, [E], (BGP), Wilton, CT.
Catholic Elementary Schools-Region V, [E], (BGP), Fairfield, CT.
Catholic Elementary Schools-Region VI, [E], (BGP), Stratford, CT.
Catholic Elementary Schools-Region VII, [E], (BGP), Trumbull, CT.
Catholic Elementary Schools-Region VIII, [E], (BGP), Shelton, CT.
Catholic Elementary Schools-Region IX, [E], (BGP), Danbury, CT.
Catholic Elementary Schools-Region X, [E], (BGP), Bridgeport, CT.
Catholic Engaged Encounter of Oregon, Inc., [Q], (P), Gresham, OR.
*The Catholic Evidence Guild, [L], (LAN), Ann Arbor, MI.
Catholic Evidence League, [Q], (BAL), Baltimore, MD.
Catholic Family and Child Service, [C], (YAK), Yakima, WA.
Catholic Family and Child Service, [C], (YAK), Ephrata, WA.
Catholic Family and Child Service, [C], (YAK), Grandview, WA.
Catholic Family and Child Service, [C], (YAK), Moses Lake, WA.
Catholic Family and Child Service, [C], (YAK), Richland, WA.
Catholic Family and Child Service, [C], (YAK), Wenatchee, WA.
Catholic Family Fraternal of Texas. KJZT, [N], (AUS), Austin, TX.
Catholic Family Service, [I], (FAR), Fargo, ND.
Catholic Family Service, [N], (GRY). See Catholic Charities.
Catholic Family Service, [H], (SPK), Spokane, WA.
*Catholic Family Service, Inc., [E], (AMA), Amarillo, TX.
Catholic Family Services, [G], (BIR), Birmingham, AL.
Catholic Family Services, [G], (BIR), Huntsville, AL.
Catholic Family Services, [G], (BIR), Tuscaloosa, AL.
Catholic Family Services, [C], (KAL), Kalamazoo, MI.
Catholic Family Services, [W], (STL), St. Louis, MO.
Catholic Family Services, Bridgeport, [G], (BGP). See Catholic Charities of Fairfield County.
Catholic Family Services, Danbury, [G], (BGP). See Catholic Charities of Fairfield County.

Catholic Family Services, Norwalk, [G], (BGP). See Catholic Charities of Fairfield County.
Catholic Family Services, Stamford, [G], (BGP). See Catholic Charities of Fairfield County.
The Catholic Foreign Mission Society of America, Inc., [M], (CIN), Cincinnati, OH.
The Catholic Foundation for Eastern South Dakota, [I], (SFS), Sioux Falls, SD.
Catholic Foundation for the Dominican Republic, [DD], (NY), New York, NY.
The Catholic Foundation for the People of the Diocese of Rockford, [L], (RCK), Rockford, IL.
The Catholic Foundation of Broome County, [H], (SY), Binghamton, NY.
Catholic Foundation of East Tennessee, [K], (KNX), Knoxville, TN.
Catholic Foundation of Eastern Oklahoma, Inc., [J], (TLS), Tulsa, OK.
Catholic Foundation of North Georgia, Inc., [M], (ATL), Atlanta, GA.
Catholic Foundation of Northcentral Indiana, Inc., [I], (LFT), Lafayette, IN.
Catholic Foundation of Tennessee, Inc., [L], (NSH), Nashville, TN.
Catholic Foundation of the Archdiocese of Boston, [DD], (BO). See Chancery Office.
The Catholic Foundation of the Diocese of Colorado Springs, Inc., [H], (COS), Colorado Springs, CO.
Catholic Foundation of the Diocese of Toledo, [O], (TOL), Toledo, OH.
The Catholic Foundation of the Spokane Diocese, [O], (SPK), Spokane, WA.
The Catholic Foundation of West Michigan, [L], (GR), Grand Rapids, MI.
The Catholic Foundation of Western Kentucky, [J], (OWN), Owensboro, KY.
Catholic Foundation, Diocese of Lubbock, [E], (LUB), Lubbock, TX.
Catholic Fraternity, [Q], (BAL), Baltimore, MD.
Catholic Fraternity for Restoration, [J], (FRS), Clovis, CA.
Catholic Guardian Society, [P], (NY), New York, NY.
Catholic Guidance Center, [H], (STL), St. Louis, MO.
Catholic Guild for the Blind, [H], (BUF). See The Catholic Charities of the Diocese of Buffalo.
*The Catholic Guild for the Blind, [U], (CHI), Chicago, IL.
Catholic Guild for the Blind, Diocese of Brooklyn, Inc., [L], (BRK). See Catholic Charities.
Catholic Health Alliance for Metropolitan Chicago, [X], (CHI), Chicago, IL.
Catholic Health Association of Kansas, [K], (KCK), Topeka, KS.
The Catholic Health Association of the United States, [W], (STL), St. Louis, MO.
Catholic Health Association of Wisconsin, Inc., [M], (MAD), Madison, WI.
Catholic Health Care Federation, [G], (OM). See Catholic Health Corp.
Catholic Health Care Network, [DD], (NY), New York, NY.
Catholic Health Care West-Southern California, [K], (LA), Lynwood, CA.
Catholic Health Corp., [G], (OM), Omaha, NE.
Catholic Health Corporation Retirement Plan, [G], (OM). See Catholic Health Corp.
Catholic Health Partners Services, [X], (CHI), Chicago, IL.
Catholic Healthcare West, [U], (SFR), San Francisco, CA.
Catholic Healthcare West Southern California, [CC], (LA), Los Angeles, CA.
Catholic High School, [A], (BIR), Huntsville, AL.
Catholic High School, [C], (BR), Baton Rouge, LA.
Catholic High School, [B], (LAF), New Iberia, LA.
Catholic High School, [B], (LR), Little Rock, AR.
Catholic High School, [C], (MAD), Beloit, WI.
Catholic High School, [A], (RIC), Virginia Beach, VA.
Catholic High School Association, [W], (STL), St. Louis, MO.
Catholic High School Association of New York, [DD], (NY), New York, NY.
The Catholic High School of Baltimore, [D], (BAL), Baltimore, MD.
Catholic High School of Pointe Coupee, [B], (BR), New Roads, LA.
Catholic High Schools Alumni Association of Mobile, [L], (MOB), Mobile, AL.
Catholic High Schools' Athletic Association of the Archdiocese of New York, [DD], (NY), New York, NY.
Catholic Hispanic Center, [L], (VEN), Naples, FL.
Catholic Hispanic Community of Memphis (Comunidad Catolica Hispana de Memphis), [M], (MEM), Memphis, TN.
Catholic Hispanic Social Services, [J], (VEN), Fort Myers, FL.
Catholic Historical Society of the Roanoke Valley, [P], (RIC), Roanoke, VA.
Catholic Historical Society of Washington, [V], (WDC), Washington, DC.
The Catholic Historical Society of Western Pennsylvania, [R], (PIT), Pittsburgh, PA.
Catholic Home Bureau, [P], (NY), New York, NY.
Catholic Home Care, [R], (CHI), Chicago, IL.
Catholic Home Care Home Services, [R], (CHI), Chicago, IL.
Catholic Home Care, Inc., [G], (CHI). See Catholic Charities of the Archdiocese of Chicago-Archdiocesan Offices.
Catholic Home for Girls, [K], (PH), Philadelphia, PA.
Catholic Home Study Service, [W], (STL), Perryville, MO.
Catholic Horizons, Inc., [I], (BIR), Birmingham, AL.
Catholic Hospital Ministries, [Q], (SEA), Seattle, WA.
Catholic Housing Corporation, [I], (R), Raleigh, NC.
Catholic Housing Initiatives, Inc., [F], (ATL). See Catholic Social Services, Inc.
Catholic Housing of Birmingham, Inc., [I], (BIR), Birmingham, AL.
Catholic Housing Service, Inc., [K], (KCK), Kansas City, KS.
The Catholic Housing, Inc., [P], (BAL). See Chancery Office.
Catholic Human Services, [G], (GAY), Gaylord, MI.
Catholic Immigrant Ministries, Inc., [T], (BRK). See Catholic Migration & Refugee Office, Catholic Migration Services, Inc.
Catholic Information Center, [P], (BO), Peabody, MA.
Catholic Information Center, [Y], (MIL), Milwaukee, WI.
Catholic Information Center, [W], (STL), St. Louis, MO.
Catholic Information Center, [V], (WDC), Washington, DC.
Catholic Information Center of Newport, [T], (PRO). See Miscellaneous Listings for the Diocese of Providence.
Catholic Interracial Council of N.Y., The, [DD], (NY), New York, NY.
Catholic Investment Trust, Inc., [T], (PRO). See Miscellaneous Listings for the Diocese of Providence.
Catholic Junior-Senior High School, [A], (HBG), Lebanon, PA.
Catholic Knights and Ladies of Illinois, [K], (BEL), Belleville, IL.
Catholic Kolping House, [V], (LA), Los Angeles, CA.
Catholic Kolping Society, [EE], (PH), Philadelphia, PA.
Catholic Kolping Society, [U], (SFR), San Francisco, CA.
Catholic Kolping Society of America, [W], (STL), St. Louis, MO.
Catholic Kolping Society of America, Detroit Branch, Inc., [T], (DET), St. Clair Shores, MI.
Catholic Kolping Society of America-National Endowment Fund, [U], (CHI), Chicago, IL.
Catholic Ladies' Aid Society, Grand Chaplain, [R], (OAK), Oakland, CA.
Catholic Lawyers Guild, [L], (LAN), Lansing, MI.
The Catholic Lawyers Guild of the Archdiocese of Boston, Inc., [FF], (BO), Boston, MA.
The Catholic Lawyers Guild of the Diocese of Metuchen, Inc., [N], (MET), Metuchen, NJ.
Catholic Leadership Development, [W], (STL), St. Louis, MO.
Catholic League For Persons With Disabilities, [EE], (PH), Philadelphia, PA.
*The Catholic League for Religious and Civil Rights, [DD], (NY), New York, NY.
Catholic League for Religious Assistance to Poland, [U], (CHI), Chicago, IL.
Catholic Legal Immigration Network, Inc. (CLINIC), [N], (ELP), El Paso, TX.
Catholic Media Ministry, Inc., [T], (SP). See Chancery Office.
*Catholic Media Productions, [L], (NSH), Nashville, TN.
Catholic Medical Center Catholic Hospital Administration Personnel (CHAP) Program, [N], (BRK). See Catholic Medical Center of Brooklyn & Queens.
Catholic Medical Center Emergency Medical Services Institute, [N], (BRK). See Catholic Medical Center of Brooklyn & Queens.
Catholic Medical Center of Brooklyn & Queens, [N], (BRK), Jamaica, NY.
Catholic Medical Center of Manchester, NH, Inc., [I], (MAN), Manchester, NH.
Catholic Medical Center Pathology Assistants Program, [N], (BRK). See Catholic Medical Center of Brooklyn & Queens.
Catholic Medical Center Physician Assistant Program, [N], (BRK). See Catholic Medical Center of Brooklyn & Queens.
Catholic Medical Center Program of Medical Technology, [N], (BRK). See Catholic Medical Center of Brooklyn & Queens.
Catholic Medical Center Program of Radiography, [N], (BRK). See Catholic Medical Center of Brooklyn & Queens.
Catholic Medical Center School of Nursing, [N], (BRK). See Catholic Medical Center of Brooklyn & Queens.
Catholic Medical Mission Board, Inc., [DD], (NY), New York, NY.
Catholic Memorial High School, [D], (MIL), Waukesha, WI.
Catholic Memorial High School and Lower School, [E], (BO), Boston, MA.
Catholic Memorial Home Inc., [J], (FR), Fall River, MA.
The Catholic Migrant Farmworker Network, [O], (TOL), Toledo, OH.
Catholic Migration & Refugee Office, Catholic Migration Services, Inc., [T], (BRK), Brooklyn, NY.
Catholic Near East Welfare Association, [DD], (NY), New York, NY.
Catholic Newman Center, [D], (SAN), San Angelo, TX.
Catholic Newman Center - Northern Kentucky University, [Q], (COV), Highland Heights, KY.
Catholic Newman Center at Eastern Washington University, [N], (SPK), Cheney, WA.
Catholic Newman Center, Truman State University, [F], (JC), Kirksville, MO.
Catholic Newman Center-St. Stephen the Martyr Parish, [L], (LEX), Richmond, KY.
Catholic Newman Community of Colgate University, [V], (SY), Hamilton, NY.
Catholic Office of Disability Ministry, [W], (STL), St. Louis, MO.
Catholic Office of the Deaf, [X], (CHI), Chicago, IL.
Catholic Office of the Deaf, [N], (RCK), Rockford, IL.
Catholic Outreach, [D], (LAN), Flint, MI.
Catholic Outreach Services, [C], (SAN), San Angelo, TX.
Catholic Parent Teacher Groups, [R], (OAK), Oakland, CA.
Catholic Parish Association Contingency Fund, Inc., [D], (RC), Rapid City, SD.
Catholic Parish Outreach, [I], (R), Raleigh, NC.
Catholic Pastoral Care-Hospital Tacoma Ministry, [Q], (SEA), Tacoma, WA.
Catholic Personal Care Homes, Inc., [F], (ATL). See Catholic Social Services, Inc.
Catholic Press Association of the United States and Canada, Inc., [R], (RVC), Ronkonkoma, NY.
Catholic Press Council, [CC], (LA), La Crescenta, CA.
Catholic Professional & Business Breakfast Club of the Fresno Diocese, [J], (FRS), Clovis, CA.
Catholic Properties of El Paso, Inc., [N], (ELP), El Paso, TX.
Catholic Relief Services, [Q], (SFR). See Catholic Charities of the Archdiocese of San Francisco.
Catholic Relief Services (CRS), [H], (OAK). See Catholic Charities of the Diocese of Oakland, Inc.
Catholic Relief Services, U.S.C.C. World Headquarters, [Q], (BAL), Baltimore, MD.
The Catholic Renewal Center of North Texas, Inc., [K], (FWT), Fort Worth, TX.
Catholic Residential Services with People with Mental Retardation, [O], (CIN), Cincinnati, OH.
Catholic Retirement Facilities, Inc., [F], (ATL). See Catholic Social Services, Inc.
Catholic School Administrators' Association of New York State, [T], (ALB), Troy, NY.
Catholic School Foundation of the Leavenworth Region, Inc., [K], (KCK), Leavenworth, KS.
Catholic School Network Foundation, [I], (FAR), Fargo, ND.
Catholic Schools Endowment Trust in Portage County, Wisconsin, [M], (LC), Stevens Point, WI.
The Catholic Schools Foundation of the Diocese of Sioux City, [H], (SC), Sioux City, IA.
*Catholic Schools Foundation, Inc., [DD], (BO). See Chancery Office.
Catholic Schools of Chicopee, [D], (SPR), Springfield, MA.
Catholic Schools of Mission, [L], (MRY), San Luis Obispo, CA.
Catholic Scouting, [U], (SFR), San Rafael, CA.
Catholic Seamen's Club, [L], (SEA), Seattle, WA.
Catholic Service Board, [P], (DAV), Davenport, IA.
Catholic Service Center, [G], (LKC), Lake Charles, LA.
Catholic Service League, [L], (Y), Ashtabula, OH.
Catholic Services for Children and Youth, [W], (STL), St. Louis, MO.
Catholic Services of Geauga County, [V], (CLV). See Catholic Charities Services Corporation.
Catholic Services of Macomb, [N], (DET), Mount Clemens, MI.
Catholic Social Agency, [M], (ALN). See St. Francis Center.
Catholic Social Agency-Catholic Charities Administrative Office, [F], (ALN), Allentown, PA.
Catholic Social Ministries of the Diocese of Raleigh, Inc., [D], (R), Raleigh, NC.
Catholic Social Policy Coalition of the Archdiocese of New York, The, [DD], (NY), New York, NY.
Catholic Social Service Counseling, [G], (PEO). See Catholic Social Service of Peoria.
Catholic Social Service Flagstaff, [J], (PHX). See Catholic Social Services of Central and Northern Arizona, Inc.
Catholic Social Service Foster Care Placement, [H],

(PEO), Peoria, IL.
Catholic Social Service Institutions, [G], (PEO). See Catholic Social Service of Peoria.
Catholic Social Service of Mohave, [J], (PHX). See Catholic Social Services of Central and Northern Arizona, Inc.
Catholic Social Service of Peoria, [G], (PEO), West Peoria, IL.
Catholic Social Service of Phoenix, [J], (PHX). See Catholic Social Services of Central and Northern Arizona, Inc.
Catholic Social Service of Solano County, [L], (SAC), Vallejo, CA.
Catholic Social Service of the Diocese of Rapid City, [D], (RC), Rapid City, SD.
Catholic Social Service of Yavapai, [J], (PHX). See Catholic Social Services of Central and Northern Arizona, Inc.
Catholic Social Service West, [G], (PEO). See Catholic Social Service of Peoria.
Catholic Social Service, Sacramento, [L], (SAC), Sacramento, CA.
Catholic Social Services, [P], (CAM), Camden, NJ.
Catholic Social Services, [P], (CAM), Atlantic City, NJ.
Catholic Social Services, [P], (CAM), Pleasantville, NJ.
Catholic Social Services, [P], (CAM), Rio Grande, NJ.
Catholic Social Services, [P], (CAM), Salem, NJ.
Catholic Social Services, [O], (COV), Covington, KY.
Catholic Social Services, [E], (FRS), Fresno, CA.
Catholic Social Services, [E], (FRS), Bakersfield, CA.
Catholic Social Services, [E], (FRS), Merced, CA.
Catholic Social Services, [E], (FRS), Visalia, CA.
Catholic Social Services, [E], (FRS), Porterville, CA.
Catholic Social Services, [K], (LIN), Lincoln, NE.
Catholic Social Services, [I], (SAV), Augusta, GA.
Catholic Social Services, [F], (SFD), Quincy, IL.
Catholic Social Services, [B], (STV). See Miscellaneous Organizations.
Catholic Social Services - Clarksville Branch, [L], (NSH). See Mid-Tennessee Rural Outreach Association.
Catholic Social Services Branch Office, [C], (BWN), Brownsville, TX.
Catholic Social Services Center, [F], (ANC), Anchorage, AK.
Catholic Social Services Central Office, [P], (CAM), Pennsauken, NJ.
Catholic Social Services Endowment Fund, [C], (DOD), Great Bend, KS.
Catholic Social Services of Ashland, Medina, and Wayne Counties, [V], (CLV). See Catholic Charities Services Corporation.
Catholic Social Services of Ashland, Medina, and Wayne Counties, [V], (CLV), Cleveland, OH.
Catholic Social Services of Attleboro, [N], (FR). See Catholic Social Services of Fall River.
Catholic Social Services of Broome County, [H], (SY), Binghamton, NY.
Catholic Social Services of Cape Cod, [N], (FR). See Catholic Social Services of Fall River.
Catholic Social Services of Central and Northern Arizona, Inc., [J], (PHX), Phoenix, AZ.
Catholic Social Services of Central Indiana, [L], (IND), Indianapolis, IN.
Catholic Social Services of Cuyahoga County, [V], (CLV), Cleveland, OH.
Catholic Social Services of Cuyahoga County, [V], (CLV). See Catholic Charities Services Corporation.
Catholic Social Services of Fall River, [N], (FR), Fall River, MA.
Catholic Social Services of Flint, [D], (LAN), Flint, MI.
Catholic Social Services of Geauga County, [V], (CLV), Cleveland, OH.
Catholic Social Services of Guam, [E], (AGN), Agana, GU.
Catholic Social Services of Jackson, [D], (LAN), Jackson, MI.
Catholic Social Services of Lake County, [V], (CLV), Cleveland, OH.
Catholic Social Services of Lake County, [V], (CLV). See Catholic Charities Services Corporation.
Catholic Social Services of Lenawee County, [D], (LAN), Adrian, MI.
Catholic Social Services of Lorain County, [V], (CLV), Elyria, OH.
Catholic Social Services of Lorain County, [V], (CLV). See Catholic Charities Services Corporation.
Catholic Social Services of Monroe County, [N], (DET), Monroe, MI.
Catholic Social Services of Montgomery, [J], (MOB), Montgomery, AL.
Catholic Social Services of New Bedford, [N], (FR). See Catholic Social Services of Fall River.
Catholic Social Services of Oakland County, [N], (DET), Pontiac, MI.
Catholic Social Services of St. Clair County, Inc., [N], (DET), Port Huron, MI.
Catholic Social Services of Shiawassee County, [D], (LAN), Owosso, MI.
Catholic Social Services of Summit County, [V], (CLV). See Catholic Charities Services Corporation.
Catholic Social Services of Summit County, Inc., [V], (CLV), Akron, OH.
Catholic Social Services of Taunton, [N], (FR). See Catholic Social Services of Fall River.
The Catholic Social Services of the Archdiocese of Philadelphia, [J], (PH), Philadelphia, PA.
Catholic Social Services of the Diocese of Charlotte, Inc., [G], (CHL), Charlotte, NC.
Catholic Social Services of Utica, [H], (SY), Utica, NY.
Catholic Social Services of Vineland, [P], (CAM), Vineland, NJ.
Catholic Social Services of Wayne County, [N], (DET), Detroit, MI.
Catholic Social Services Office, [C], (BWN), San Juan, TX.
Catholic Social Services Regional Counseling Center, [P], (CAM), Newfield, NJ.
Catholic Social Services Senior Center, [P], (CAM), Cape May, NJ.
Catholic Social Services, Archdiocese of Mobile, [J], (MOB), Mobile, AL.
Catholic Social Services, Camden/Gloucester Regional Counseling Center, [P], (CAM), Gibbstown, NJ.
Catholic Social Services, Gloucester County Office, [P], (CAM), Woodbury, NJ.
Catholic Social Services, Inc., [F], (ATL), Atlanta, GA.
Catholic Social Services, Inc., [E], (SPP), Pago Pago, AS.
Catholic Social Services, Inc. (St. Vincent de Paul), [G], (B), Twin Falls, ID.
Catholic Social Services-St. Vincent Home for Children, Inc., [D], (LAN), Lansing, MI
Catholic Solitudes, [H], (CC), Hebbronville, TX.
Catholic Southwest, [N], (AUS), Austin, TX.
Catholic Student Center, [M], (AUS), San Marcos, TX.
Catholic Student Center, [I], (BIS), Dickinson, ND.
Catholic Student Center, [I], (BIS), Minot, ND.
Catholic Student Center, [F], (LKC), Lake Charles, LA.
Catholic Student Center, [H], (R), Raleigh, NC.
Catholic Student Center, [H], (R), Wilmington, NC.
Catholic Student Center, [G], (VIC), Victoria, TX.
Catholic Student Center at Baylor University, [M], (AUS), Waco, TX.
The Catholic Student Center at Dartmouth, Aquinas House, Aquinas at Dartmouth, Inc., [N], (MAN), Hanover, NH.
Catholic Student Center at West Texas A & M University, [K], (AMA), Canyon, TX.
Catholic Student Center for Students at Duke University, [H], (R), Durham, NC.
Catholic Student Center for Students at East Carolina University, [H], (R), Greenville, NC.
Catholic Student Center, S.H.S.U., [T], (GAL), Huntsville, TX.
Catholic Student Center, University of South Florida, [S], (SP), Tampa, FL.
Catholic Student Center-Louisiana State Univ., [L], (LAF), Eunice, LA.
Catholic Student Center-Morehead State University, [L], (LEX), Morehead, KY.
Catholic Teachers' College of Providence, [T], (PRO). See Miscellaneous Listings for the Diocese of Providence.
The Catholic Theological Union at Chicago, [B], (CHI), Chicago, IL.
Catholic Thrift Shop, [I], (SAV), Millen, GA.
Catholic Tours of Ohio, Inc., [AA], (CLV), Cleveland, OH.
Catholic Truth International, [J], (FRS), Fresno, CA.
Catholic Union of Texas, [N], (AUS), LaGrange, TX.
Catholic Union Store, [T], (BUF), Buffalo, NY.
Catholic University of America, The, [C], (WDC), Washington, DC.
Catholic University Parish at Arkansas State University, [J], (LR). See Catholic Campus Ministries.
Catholic University Parish at Arkansas Tech University, [J], (LR). See Catholic Campus Ministries.
*Catholic Volunteers in Florida, Inc., [G], (ORL), Goldenrod, FL.
Catholic War Veterans, [K], (BEL), Belleville, IL.
Catholic War Veterans, Inc., [Q], (BAL), Baltimore, MD.
Catholic Woman's Club, [O], (KC), Kansas City, MO.
Catholic Women's Union, [DD], (NY), New York, NY.
Catholic Worker Center, [O], (BUF), Niagara Falls, NY.
The Catholic Worker Community, [U], (SFR), Redwood City, CA.
Catholic Worker Hospitality House, [P], (RIC), Norfolk, VA.
Catholic Youth Camps, Inc., [U], (STP), McGregor, MN.
Catholic Youth Center, [Q], (SCR), Scranton, PA.
Catholic Youth Center, [Q], (SCR), Wilkes-Barre, PA.
Catholic Youth Center, [O], (SPR), Pittsfield, MA.
Catholic Youth Ministries of Fort Smith, Inc., [L], (LR), Fort Smith, AR.
Catholic Youth Ministry Services, [Q], (STP), St. Paul, MN.
Catholic Youth Ministry Services, [U], (STP), St. Paul, MN.
Catholic Youth Organization, [M], (IND), Indianapolis, IN.
Catholic Youth Organization of the Archdiocese of New York Inc., [L], (NY), New York, NY.
Catholic Youth Organization of the Archdiocese of San Francisco, [R], (SFR), San Francisco, CA.
Catholic Youth Organization of the Diocese of Brooklyn, Inc., [L], (BRK). See Catholic Charities.
Catholic Youth Organization/Camp Howard, [G], (P). See Catholic Charities of the Archdiocese of Portland in Oregon.
Catholic Youth, Archdiocese of Chicago, [X], (CHI), Chicago, IL.
CatholiCare, Inc., [S], (NEW), Newark, NJ.
Catholic-Presbyterian Apts., Inc., [L], (BR), Baton Rouge, LA.
Catholics Committed to Support the Pope, [V], (WDC), Silver Spring, MD.
Catholics for Truth & Justice, [U], (SFR), San Francisco, CA.
*Catholics United for Spiritual Action, Inc., [DD], (NY), New York, NY.
Catholics United for the Faith, [EE], (PH), Philadelphia, PA.
*Catholics United for the Faith, Inc., [J], (STU), Steubenville, OH.
Catlin Family Practice, [J], (PEO). See United Samaritans Medical Center.
Cazenovia College Newman Center, [V], (SY), Cazenovia, NY.
CCS Athens, [F], (ATL). See Catholic Social Services, Inc.
CCS Holding Corporation, Inc., [S], (NEW). See New Jersey Caritas Corporation, Inc.
CCS North-Loveland, [L], (DEN). See Catholic Charities and Community Services of the Archdiocese of Denver, Inc.
Cecilian Academy, [H], (PH), Philadelphia, PA.
Cedar Catholic High School, [B], (OM), Hartington, NE.
Cedar Catholic High School Endowment (Halemba), [N], (OM). See The Omaha Archdiocesan Educational Foundation, Inc.
Cedar Court School, Inc., [F], (HRT), West Hartford, CT.
Cedar Hill Enrichment Center, Inc., [K], (ATL), Gainesville, GA.
Cedar Holdings, Inc., [E], (SAM), New Bedford, MA.
Cedar Park Place, Inc., [E], (DOD), Great Bend, KS.
Cedar Pines - Augustinian Community, [H], (SD), Boulevard, CA.
Cedar Rapids Council, [O], (DUB). See St. Vincent de Paul Society of the Archdiocese of Dubuque.
Cedarbrake Renewal Center, [L], (AUS), Belton, TX.
*Celebrate Life Ministries, [T], (DET), St. Clair Shores, MI.
Cemeteries Trust, [E], (HT), Thibodaux, LA.
Cemetery Continuing Care Trust, [P], (BAL). See Chancery Office.
The Cenacle, [T], (STL), St. Louis, MO.
Cenacle Center for Spiritual Renewal, [W], (BRK), Flushing, NY.
Cenacle Formation House, [O], (RVC). See Religious of Our Lady of the Retreat in the Cenacle.
The Cenacle of Our Lady of Divine Providence, [H], (SP), Clearwater, FL.
The Cenacle of Our Lady of Divine Providence School of Spirituality, [Q], (SP). See Our Lady of Divine Providence, House of Prayer, Inc.
Cenacle Retreat House, [S], (GAL), Houston, TX.
Cenacle Retreat House, [J], (MET), Highland Park, NJ.
Cenacle Retreat House, [R], (NO), Metairie, LA.
Cenacle Retreat House, [BB], (NY), Bedford Village, NY.
Cenacle Retreat House, [O], (RVC). See Religious of Our Lady of the Retreat in the Cenacle.
Cenacle Retreat House, [P], (RVC), Ronkonkoma, NY.
Cenacle Retreat House, [Q], (STP), Wayzata, MN.
Cenacle Retreat House, [G], (WH), Charleston, WV.
Cenacle Retreat League, [M], (MEM), Memphis, TN.
Cenacle Youth Shelter, [E], (HBG). See Department for Catholic Charities Counseling/Field Services.
The Cenacle, Spiritual Life Center, [I], (PMB), Lantana, FL.
Censores Librorum, [L], (ROC), Rochester, NY.
*The Center at Benet Hill Monastery, [A], (COS), Colorado Springs, CO.
Center for Action and Contemplation, [N], (SFE), Albuquerque, NM.
Center for Adult Services, [Y], (LA). See Catholic Charities of Los Angeles, Inc.
The Center for AIDS Services, [R], (OAK), Oakland, CA.
Center for Eastern Christian Studies, [C], (SCR). See University of Scranton.
Center for Gerontology, [F], (LAN), Flint, MI.
Center for International Resources, Inc. (CIRIMEX), [V], (WDC), Bethesda, MD.

Chestnut Hill College, [C], (PH), Philadelphia, PA.
Cheverus High School, [C], (PRT), Portland, ME.
Chiara Center, [M], (TOL), Sylvania, OH.
Chiara Corporation, [W], (STL), St. Louis, MO.
Chiara Home, Inc., [K], (FTW). See The Sisters of St. Joseph of the Third Order of St. Francis Central Offices, S.S.J.-T.O.S.F.
Chiara Home, Inc., [O], (FTW), South Bend, IN.
*Chicago Catholic Healthcare System, Inc., [X], (CHI), Elk Grove Village, IL.
The Chicago Center for Peace Studies, [X], (CHI), Chicago, IL.
Chicago Institute for Neuro Surgery & Neuro Research, [J], (CHI). See Columbus Hospital.
The Chicago Marian Center, [X], (CHI), Chicago, IL.
Chicago Province of the Society of Jesus-Provincial Office, [N], (CHI), Chicago, IL.
Child & Adult Care Food Program, [D], (WIL). See Catholic Charities, Inc.
Child & Family Services, [H], (WOR). See Catholic Charities.
Child Care Center, [D], (HEL). See St. Joseph Elementary School.
Child Care Center, [F], (WIL). See Ministry of Caring, Inc.
Child Care Service Center, [E], (MET), Manville, NJ.
Child Center Foundation, [W], (STL), St. Louis, MO.
Child Center of Our Lady, [J], (STL), St. Louis, MO.
Child Development Center, [F], (SAT). See Blessed Sacrament Academy.
Child Development Center - Peaks Island, [E], (PRT). See Catholic Charities Maine.
Child Development Services Department (ADESTE), [Y], (LA). See Catholic Charities of Los Angeles, Inc.
Child Jesus Convent, [N], (HRT). See Felician Sisters - Our Lady of the Angels.
Child Protective Services, [G], (CHI). See Catholic Charities of the Archdiocese of Chicago-Archdiocesan Offices.
Child Space, [F], (SEA), Everett, WA.
Child Welfare Program, [D], (LAN). See Catholic Social Services-St. Vincent Home for Children, Inc.
Childcare Center, [I], (SY). See Bishop Foery Foundation.
Children & Adolescent Parent Program, [G], (CHI). See Catholic Charities of the Archdiocese of Chicago-Archdiocesan Offices.
The Children's Cottage, [E], (FTW), Fort Wayne, IN.
Children's Counseling Center, [F], (SJ). See Catholic Charities of Santa Clara County.
The Children's Fund, Inc., [P], (BAL). See Chancery Office.
Children's Health Care, Inc., [K], (WH), Wheeling, WV.
Children's Health Care, Inc., [K], (WH), Pineville, WV.
Children's Home, [D], (WIL). See Catholic Charities, Inc.
Children's Home, Inc., [E], (WIL), Claymont, DE.
Children's Hospital Foundation of Austin, [N], (AUS), Austin, TX.
Children's Placement Services, [I], (GAL). See Associated Catholic Charities of the Diocese of Galveston-Houston.
Children's Services (adoption and foster care), [D], (WIL). See Catholic Charities, Inc.
Children's Vacation House/Catholic Charities, [N], (BO), Hull, MA.
Chimbote Foundation, [R], (PIT), Pittsburgh, PA.
Chinese Apostolate-Brooklyn, [T], (BRK). See Catholic Migration & Refugee Office, Catholic Migration Services, Inc.
Chinese Apostolate-Queens, [T], (BRK). See Catholic Migration & Refugee Office, Catholic Migration Services, Inc.
Chinese Catholic Bishops Conference Vocations Center, [CC], (LA), Granada Hills, CA.
Chinese Catholic Information Center, [DD], (NY), New York, NY.
Chinese Catholic Pastoral Center, [N], (BO), Boston, MA.
Chinese Clergy & Religious Association in North America, [DD], (NY), New York, NY.
Chippewa Area Catholic Schools, [D], (LC), Chippewa Falls, WI.
The Chippewa Area Catholic Schools Endowment Trust, [M], (LC), Chippewa Falls, WI.
CHIRO, [L], (LAN), Ann Arbor, MI.
Choix de Vie, [E], (SR). See Diocese of Santa Rosa, Catholic Charities.
Choose Life Program, [J], (BUF). See Our Lady of Victory Infant Home.
Chrisman Clinic, [J], (PEO). See United Samaritans Medical Center.
Christ Child - DePaul Day Care Center, [M], (CLV), Cleveland, OH.
Christ Child Day Nursery, [J], (OG), Plattsburgh, NY.
Christ Child House, [O], (DET), Detroit, MI.
Christ Child Society, [T], (DET), Detroit, MI.
Christ Child Society, [N], (ELP), El Paso, TX.
Christ Child Society, [H], (GAY), Harbor Springs, MI.
Christ Child Society, [J], (PHX), Phoenix, AZ.
Christ Child Society of Boca Raton, [J], (PMB), Palm Beach Gardens, FL.
The Christ Child Society of Columbus, Inc., [L], (COL), Columbus, OH.
Christ Child Society of Omaha, [O], (OM), Omaha, NE.
Christ Child Society of Palm Beach, [J], (PMB), North Palm Beach, FL.
Christ Child Society of Pittsburgh, [R], (PIT), Wildwood, PA.
Christ Child Society of South Bend, [O], (FTW), South Bend, IN.
Christ Child Society of Toledo, [O], (TOL), Toledo, OH.
Christ Child Society of Tucson, [J], (TUC), Tucson, AZ.
Christ Child Society of Washington, DC, Inc., [V], (WDC), Washington, DC.
Christ Child Society-Geauga Chapter, [AA], (CLV), Chardon, OH.
Christ House, Inc., [DD], (NY), New York, NY.
Christ in the Wilderness, [N], (RCK), Stockton, IL.
Christ of the Desert Newman Center, [H], (SB), Palm Desert, CA.
Christ the Divine Teacher School, [D], (GBG), Latrobe, PA.
Christ the King, [G], (BRK), Middle Village, NY.
Christ The King, [C], (BUR), Burlington, VT.
Christ the King, [C], (BUR), Rutland, VT.
Christ the King (FOCUS), [I], (SAV), Hamilton, GA.
Christ the King Cathedral School Foundation, [E], (LUB), Lubbock, TX.
Christ the King Catholic Center, [L], (LAN), Ann Arbor, MI.
Christ the King Community, [I], (HON). See Sisters of St. Joseph of Carondelet CSJ, Hawaii Vice-Province.
Christ the King Educational Endowment Trust, [N], (OM). See The Omaha Archdiocesan Educational Foundation, Inc.
Christ the King Elementary School, [C], (SFS). See Sioux Falls Catholic School System.
Christ the King Extended Care, [G], (RIC), Norfolk, VA.
Christ the King Housing II, Inc. dba Kings Manor, [M], (SP), Tampa, FL.
Christ the King Housing, Inc. dba Kings Arms, [M], (SP), Tampa, FL.
Christ the King Learning Center, [C], (CC), Laredo, TX.
Christ the King Manor, Inc., [K], (E), Du Bois, PA.
Christ the King Monastery of St. Clare, [H], (PMB), Delray Beach, FL.
Christ the King Parish and Catholic Student Center, [K], (BR), Baton Rouge, LA.
Christ the King Parish Conference, [E], (YAK), Richland, WA.
Christ the King Regional School, [D], (CAM), Haddonfield, NJ.
Christ the King Retreat, [H], (SAC), Citrus Heights, CA.
Christ the King Retreat Center, [J], (SAC), Citrus Heights, CA.
Christ the King Retreat Center, [E], (SAN), San Angelo, TX.
Christ the King Retreat Center, [Q], (STP), Buffalo, MN.
Christ the King Retreat House, [U], (SY), Syracuse, NY.
Christ the King School, [D], (ALN), Coplay, PA.
Christ the King School, [B], (CC), Corpus Christi, TX.
Christ the King Seminary, [A], (BUF), East Aurora, NY.
Christ the King University Parish - Ohio University, [I], (STU), Athens, OH.
Christa Center, [AA], (CLV), Cleveland, OH.
Christa House, Inc., [R], (RVC), West Babylon, NY.
*Christamore House Incorporated, [I], (DAV). See Young House Family Services, Inc.
Christendom College, [A], (ARL), Front Royal, VA.
Christian Brothers, [J], (ELP), El Paso, TX.
Christian Brothers (F.S.C.), [Z], (PH), Audubon, PA.
Christian Brothers (F.S.C.), [Z], (PH), Wyndmoor, PA.
Christian Brothers (F.S.C.)- St. Joseph Community, [M], (DEN), Denver, CO.
Christian Brothers Academy, [D], (SY), Syracuse, NY.
Christian Brothers Academy, [F], (SY), Syracuse, NY.
Christian Brothers Academy, [C], (TR), Lincroft, NJ.
Christian Brothers Center, [J], (JOL), Romeoville, IL.
Christian Brothers College High School (C.B.C.), [F], (STL), St. Louis, MO.
Christian Brothers Community Support Charitable Trust, [P], (BAL). See Chancery Office.
Christian Brothers Counseling Center, Inc., [X], (CHI), Westchester, IL.
Christian Brothers Employee Benefit Trust, [M], (JOL), Romeoville, IL.
Christian Brothers Employee Retirement Plan Trust, [M], (JOL), Romeoville, IL.
Christian Brothers Foundation, [S], (NO), New Orleans, LA.
Christian Brothers Fund, Inc., [M], (JOL), Romeoville, IL.
*Christian Brothers High School, [C], (MEM), Memphis, TN.
Christian Brothers High School of Sacramento, Inc., [C], (SAC), Sacramento, CA.
Christian Brothers Institute of California, Inc., [B], (MRY), Salinas, CA.
Christian Brothers Provincial Office (Midwest Province), [J], (JOL), Burr Ridge, IL.
Christian Brothers Provincialate, [M], (BAL), Adamstown, MD.
Christian Brothers Religious Comprehensive Trust, [M], (JOL), Romeoville, IL.
Christian Brothers Religious Deductible Trust, [M], (JOL), Romeoville, IL.
Christian Brothers Residence, [U], (BRK), Brooklyn, NY.
Christian Brothers Retreat and Conference Center, [L], (SR), Napa, CA.
Christian Brothers Retreat Center, [Q], (STP), Marine on St. Croix, MN.
Christian Brothers School, [H], (NO), New Orleans, LA.
*Christian Brothers Services, [M], (JOL), Romeoville, IL.
Christian Brothers Spiritual Center, [L], (BAL), Adamstown, MD.
*Christian Brothers University, [A], (MEM), Memphis, TN.
Christian Brothers Youth Home, [W], (STP), St. Paul, MN.
Christian Brothers' Academy, [D], (ALB), Albany, NY.
Christian Brothers' Center, [P], (PRO), Narragansett, RI.
Christian Brothers, St. La Salle Auxiliary, [M], (TR), Lincroft, NJ.
Christian Care and Share Center, [N], (LAF), Ville Platte, LA.
Christian Center of Concern, [G], (BIR), Hamilton, AL.
Christian Center of Concern, [G], (BIR), Winfield, AL.
Christian Center of Concern, [G], (BIR), Sulligent, AL.
Christian Center of Concern, [G], (BIR), Fayette, AL.
Christian Community Center, [L], (GR), Muskegon Heights, MI.
Christian Community of God's Delight, [P], (DAL), Dallas, TX.
Christian Family Movement (CFM), [O], (OM), Omaha, NE.
Christian Family School, [E], (DUB), Calmar, IA.
Christian Family Services of Lapeer County, Inc., [N], (DET), Lapeer, MI.
The Christian Institute for the Study of Human Sexuality, [FF], (BO), Brighton, MA.
Christian Life Center, [P], (MAN), Berlin, NH.
Christian Life Center, [P], (MAN), Durham, NH.
Christian Life Center, [P], (MAN), Keene, NH.
Christian Life Center, [P], (MAN), Laconia, NH.
Christian Life Center, [P], (MAN), Salem, NH.
Christian Life Center, [L], (PRT), Upper Frenchville, ME.
Christian Life Center, [G], (SPR), Northampton, MA.
Christian Life Communities, [V], (WDC), Washington, DC.
Christian Life Community Regional Information Center, [Q], (BAL), Silver Spring, MD.
Christian Live Communities (Sodalities), [U], (SFR), Los Angeles, CA.
Christian Renewal Center, [S], (GAL), Dickinson, TX.
Christian Renewal Center, [A], (LUB), Lubbock, TX.
Christian Service Center, [N], (LAF), Abbeville, LA.
The Christian Sisters, [U], (MIL), Milwaukee, WI.
Christian Urban Education Service, [O], (OM), Omaha, NE.
Christian Urban Education Service Foundation, [F], (OM), Omaha, NE.
Christians Encounter Christ, [O], (OM), Omaha, NE.
Christina House, [M], (WCH), Wichita, KS.
Christlife, Inc., [Q], (BAL), Baltimore, MD.
Christmas House, [L], (IND). See Catholic Charities.
Christopher Assurance, Inc., [T], (SP). See Chancery Office.
Christopher Columbus High School, [D], (MIA), Miami, FL.
Christopher Community, Inc., [Q], (SY), Syracuse, NY.
The Christopher Home, [E], (PRT). See Catholic Charities Maine.
Christopher Homes of Arkansas, Inc., [L], (LR). See Adoption Services, Inc.
Christopher Homes of Augusta, Inc., [L], (LR). See Adoption Services, Inc.
Christopher Homes of Brinkley, Inc., [L], (LR). See Adoption Services, Inc.
Christopher Homes of Camden, Inc., [L], (LR). See Adoption Services, Inc.
Christopher Homes of Clarendon, Inc., [L], (LR). See Adoption Services, Inc.
Christopher Homes of El Dorado, Inc., [L], (LR). See Adoption Services, Inc.
Christopher Homes of Elaine, Inc., [L], (LR). See Adoption Services, Inc.
Christopher Homes of Forrest City, Inc., [L], (LR). See

College of St. Joseph in Vermont, [A], (BUR), Rutland, VT.
College of St. Mary, [A], (OM), Omaha, NE.
The College of Saint Rose, [B], (ALB), Albany, NY.
College of St. Scholastica, [A], (DUL), Duluth, MN.
College of Santa Fe, [C], (SFE), Santa Fe, NM.
College of Southern Idaho, [F], (B), Twin Falls, ID.
College of the Holy Cross, Inc, [B], (WOR), Worcester, MA.
College of the Queen of Peace, [B], (LA), Santa Barbara, CA.
College Seminary, [B], (NEW). See Seton Hall University.
Colleges of Business Administration, [D], (BRK). See St. John's University.
Collegiate Religious Center, [Q], (WOR). See Campus Ministry.
Collegio San Benito, [A], (CGS), Humacao, PR.
Collier Group Home, [K], (TR), Red Bank, NJ.
Collier Services, [K], (TR), Wickatunk, NJ.
Collin County Catholic High School Campaign, Inc., [P], (DAL), Dallas, TX.
Colombiere Center, [P], (DET), Clarkston, MI.
Colorado Affordable Catholic Housing Corporation, [K], (DEN). See Archdiocesan Housing Committee.
Colorado Mountain College, [P], (DEN), Steamboat Springs, CO.
Colorado Northwestern Community College (Rangely), [P], (DEN), Rangely, CO.
Colorado School of Mines (Golden), [P], (DEN), Golden, CO.
Colorado Springs Council of Black Catholics, [H], (COS), Colorado Springs, CO.
Colorado Springs Diocesan Council of Catholic Women, [H], (COS), Colorado Springs, CO.
Colorado State University (Fort Collins), [P], (DEN), Fort Collins, CO.
*Colorado Vincentian Volunteers, [Q], (DEN), Denver, CO.
Columba Hall, [J], (FTW), Notre Dame, IN.
Columban Fathers, [H], (ORG), Westminster, CA.
Columban Fathers Mission Center, [N], (CHI), Chicago, IL.
Columban Fathers Regional Administration, [N], (OM), St. Columbans, NE.
Columban Fathers Theologate, [N], (CHI), Chicago, IL.
Columban Fathers, Procure House, [R], (LA), Los Angeles, CA.
Columban Medical and Retirement Trust, [N], (OM). See Columban Fathers Regional Administration.
Columban Sisters, [X], (BO), Boston, MA.
Columbia Nursing Home Ministry, [D], (JC), Columbia, MO.
Columbia University, [CC], (NY). See University Apostolate.
Columbia-Greene Community College, [S], (ALB), Hudson, NY.
Columbian House, [J], (ORG). See Catholic Charities of Orange County, Inc.
Columbiere House, [R], (LA), Los Angeles, CA.
Columbus High School, [D], (DUB), Waterloo, IA.
Columbus High School, [C], (LC), Marshfield, WI.
Columbus High School Foundation, [M], (LC), Marshfield, WI.
Columbus Home, Inc., [E], (KNX), Knoxville, TN.
Columbus Hospital, [J], (CHI), Chicago, IL.
Columbus Park Plaza, [I], (KC), Kansas City, MO.
The Comboni Lay Missionaries Association, [V], (CIN), Cincinnati, OH.
Comboni Mission Center, [N], (CHI), La Grange Park, IL.
Comboni Missionaries, [CC], (LA), Covina, CA.
Comboni Missionaries (Verona Fathers)-Comboni Mission Center, [M], (CIN), Cincinnati, OH.
The Comboni Missionaries Auxiliary, Inc., [V], (CIN), Cincinnati, OH.
Comboni Missionaries of the Heart of Jesus (Verona Fathers), [N], (NEW), Montclair, NJ.
Comboni Missionaries Theologate (M.C.C.J.), Verona Fathers, [N], (CHI), Chicago, IL.
Comboni Missionary Sisters, [O], (CHI), Chicago, IL.
Comboni Missionary Sisters, [AA], (PH), Coatsville, PA.
Comboni Missionary Sisters, Provincial House, [N], (RIC), Richmond, VA.
Comeau Catholic Campus Center at Fort Hays State University, [H], (SAL), Hays, KS.
Commissariat of the Holy Land, Franciscan Monastery - Mount St. Sepulchre, [M], (WDC), Washington, DC.
Commission on Ecumenism, [P], (DAL), Dallas, TX.
Commission on Education for Jordan Catholic School, [E], (PEO). See Jordan Catholic School of Rock Island, Inc.
Commitment, [P], (DAV), Davenport, IA.
Common Fund for Schools, [P], (WH), Wheeling, WV.
Common Ground Center for Community Renewal, Inc., [AA], (CLV), Oberlin, OH.
Common Sense Parenting, [I], (SAT). See Father Flanagan's Boys' Town of San Antonio.
The Common-St. Joseph Monastery, [M], (MAN), Peterborough, NH.
Commonwealth Catholic Charities, [K], (RIC), Richmond, VA.
Communio: International Catholic Review, [V], (WDC), Washington, DC.
Community, [N], (HRT). See Sisters of Notre Dame de Namur.
Community Action for Better Housing, Inc., [Q], (FR), Fall River, MA.
Community and Family Support Services, [D], (WIL). See Catholic Charities, Inc.
Community Catholic School, [D], (L), Louisville, KY.
Community College of Denver, [P], (DEN). See Auraria Campus.
Community College of R.I., [S], (PRO), Warwick, RI.
Community Counseling & Education Svcs., [F], (SJ). See Catholic Charities of Santa Clara County.
Community Family Service Center, [G], (CHI). See Catholic Charities of the Archdiocese of Chicago-Archdiocesan Offices.
Community Food Depots, [Q], (DET), Detroit, MI.
Community Foundation of St. Joseph's Hospital of Marshfield, Inc., [M], (LC), Marshfield, WI.
Community Foundation of St. Michael's Hospital, [M], (LC), Stevens Point, WI.
Community Hospice of Texas, [N], (FWT), Fort Worth, TX.
Community House at St. Thomas, [N], (MET), East Brunswick, NJ.
Community House Inc., [L], (E), Erie, PA.
Community Integration Program, [L], (OKL). See Oklahoma Benedictine Institute on Mental Retardation, Inc.
Community of the Resurrection, [J], (PRT), Casco, ME.
Community of Christ, [U], (WDC), Washington, DC.
Community of Christ the Redeemer, [T], (STP), West St. Paul, MN.
The Community of God's Love, [S], (NEW), Rutherford, NJ.
Community of Hope, [J], (MAD), Baraboo, WI.
Community of Jesus Crucified, [M], (LAF), Lafayette, LA.
Community of Little Brothers and Sisters of the Eucharist, Inc., [T], (CLV), Cleveland, OH.
Community of Our Lady, [I], (GB), Oshkosh, WI.
The Community of St. John, [V], (WDC), Washington, DC.
Community of Teresian Carmelites, [P], (WOR), Worcester, MA.
Community of the Holy Spirit, [I], (ORG), Newport Beach, CA.
Community of the Holy Spirit, [I], (SD), San Diego, CA.
Community of the Holy Spirit, [N], (SJ), San Jose, CA.
Community of the Mother of God of Tenderness, [C], (NTN), Danbury, CT.
Community of the Sisters of Saint Anne, [X], (BO). See Sisters of St. Anne, Provincialate.
Community of the Way, [I], (NOR), Hampton, CT.
Community Outreach, [I], (SFS), Sioux Falls, SD.
Community Outreach Program for the Deaf, [D], (TUC). See Social Service Agencies: Pima County.
Community Residence Program, [H], (SY), Norwich, NY.
Community Service Center, [K], (KCK), Kansas City, KS.
Community Service Center, [K], (KCK), Emporia, KS.
Community Service Center, [K], (KCK), Lawrence, KS.
Community Service Center, [K], (KCK), Leavenworth, KS.
Community Service Center, [K], (KCK), Olathe, KS.
Community Services Department, [Y], (LA). See Catholic Charities of Los Angeles, Inc.
Community Services Department, [Y], (LA). See Catholic Charities of Los Angeles, Inc.
Community Services of Catholic Charities, [F], (SCL), St. Cloud, MN.
Community Support Charitable Trust, [U], (CIN), Cincinnati, OH.
Community Support Charitable Trust, [U], (CIN), Dayton, OH.
Companions of Christ, [J], (PRT), Auburn, ME.
The Companions of Christ, [T], (STP), St. Paul, MN.
Companions of Christ the Lamb, [T], (DET), Newport, MI.
Company of St. Paul, [DD], (NY), White Plains, NY.
Comtemplative Sisters of the Good Shepherd, [O], (WDC), Baltimore, MD.
Comunidad Catolica Hispana Santiago Apostol Mission, [L], (VEN), Lake Placid, FL.
Con El, Inc., [J], (PMB), Palm Beach Gardens, FL.
Conception Abbey, [J], (KC), Conception, MO.
Conception Benedictine Trust, [O], (KC), Conception, MO.
Conception Seminary College, [A], (KC), Conception, MO.
Concord, [H], (OAK). See Catholic Charities of the Diocese of Oakland, Inc.
Concord College Newman Center, [Q], (WH), Athens, WV.
Conference of Permanent Deacons, [S], (NEW), Newark, NJ.
Conference of Regional Treasurers, [T], (PRO), Pascoag, RI.
Congration of the Humility of Mary, CHM, [B], (SAN), Midland, TX.
Congregacion de Santa Cruz, [J], (FTW). See Congregation of Holy Cross Indiana Province Provincial House.
Congregation of Alexian Brothers Immaculate Conception Province, Inc., [N], (CHI), Elk Grove Village, IL.
Congregation of Alexian Brothers-Alexian Brothers Novitiate, [N], (CHI), Chicago, IL.
Congregation of Armenian Catholic Sisters of Immaculate Conception, Inc., [X], (BO), Lexington, MA.
Congregation of Christian Brothers, [H], (HON), Honolulu, HI.
Congregation of Christian Brothers, [N], (NEW), East Orange, NJ.
Congregation of Christian Brothers, [N], (NEW), Oradell, NJ.
Congregation of Christian Brothers, [Z], (NY), West Park, NY.
Congregation of Christian Brothers, [M], (SEA), Seattle, WA.
Congregation of Christian Brothers, Brother Rice Community, [N], (CHI), Chicago, IL.
Congregation of Christian Brothers, Brother Rice Community, [K], (DET), Bloomfield Hills, MI.
Congregation of Christian Brothers, Brother Rice Provincialate, [J], (JOL), Joliet, IL.
Congregation of Divine Providence, [F], (BWN), Pharr, TX.
Congregation of Divine Providence, [I], (FWT), Lindsay, TX.
Congregation of Divine Providence (C.D.P.), [R], (GAL), Houston, TX.
Congregation of Divine Providence, C.D.P., [Q], (NO), New Orleans, LA.
Congregation of Holy Cross - Formation Community, [B], (SAT), San Antonio, TX.
Congregation of Holy Cross - Southern Province, [H], (AUS), Austin, TX.
Congregation of Holy Cross Indiana Province Provincial House, [J], (FTW), South Bend, IN.
Congregation of Holy Cross, Midwest Province, [J], (FTW), Notre Dame, IN.
Congregation of Holy Faith, [I], (ORG), Cypress, CA.
Congregation of Humility of Mary, [F], (BLX), Biloxi, MS.
Congregation of Jesus and Mary, Provincialate, [O], (WDC), Mount Rainier, MD.
Congregation of Marian Fathers of the Immaculate Conception, [N], (CHI), Chicago, IL.
Congregation of Marians, [I], (SPR), Stockbridge, MA.
The Congregation of Maronite Lebanese Missionaries, [A], (OLL), San Antonio, TX.
Congregation of Mary Queen, [F], (SPC), Springfield, MO.
Congregation of Mary Queen (Vietnam), [G], (LIN), Lincoln, NE.
Congregation of Mary, Queen of the World Community, [R], (STL), St. Louis, MO.
Congregation of Mother Co-Redemptrix, Our Lady of the Rosary House, [E], (SPC), Springfield, MO.
Congregation of Notre Dame, [M], (ALB), Latham, NY.
Congregation of Notre Dame, [N], (HRT), Southington, CT.
Congregation of Notre Dame of Montreal, [F], (BWN), La Feria, TX.
The Congregation of Our Lady of Charity of the Good Shepherd, Community Support Trust, [U], (CIN), Cincinnati, OH.
Congregation of Our Lady of Mount Carmel, O.Carm., [Q], (NO), Lacombe, LA.
Congregation of Our Lady of the Retreat in the Cenacle, [T], (CHI), Chicago, IL.
Congregation of Our Lady of the Retreat in the Cenacle, [L], (JOL), Warrenville, IL.
Congregation of St. Agnes, [F], (R), Tarboro, NC.
Congregation of Saint Basil, [A], (VNN), Phoenix, AZ.
Congregation of St. Dominic General Motherhouse of the Sisters of St. Dominic of Blauvelt, [AA], (NY), Blauvelt, NY.
Congregation of St. John the Baptist, [CC], (LA), Monterey Park, CA.
Congregation of St. John the Baptist of China, [U], (BRK), Elmhurst, NY.
Congregation of St. Joseph, [P], (CLV), Avon, OH.
Congregation of St. Joseph Casa Nazareth, [R], (LA), Los Angeles, CA.
Congregation of the Benedictines of Jesus Crucified, O.S.B., [AA], (PH), Devon, PA.
Congregation of the Blessed Sacrament Provincial House, [P], (CLV), Cleveland, OH.
Congregation of the Brothers of St. Francis Xavier, [F], (NOR), Middletown, CT.

Heights, MN.
The Convent Project, Inc., [G], (GB), Oshkosh, WI.
Convent Sisters of Mercy, [AA], (PH), Philadelphia, PA.
Convent, Franciscan Missionary Sisters of Our Lady of Sorrows, [M], (P), Beaverton, OR.
Convent, Franciscan Sisters of the Eucharist, [M], (P), Bridal Veil, OR.
Conventual Franciscan Friars, [A], (ALB), Rensselaer, NY.
Conventual Franciscan Friars of Marytown, [N], (CHI). See Marytown, Our Lady of Fatima Friary.
Conventual Franciscan Friars, St. Anthony of Padua Province, [Q], (BAL), Ellicott City, MD.
Conventual Franciscans, [M], (HRT), New Britain, CT.
Conventual Franciscans, [E], (R), Burlington, NC.
Conventual Franciscans O.F.M.Conv., [E], (R), Wilmington, NC.
Conventual Franciscans of St. Bonaventure Province, [N], (CHI), Chicago, IL.
The Conventual Franciscans of Saint Bonaventure Province Corporation, [N], (CHI). See Conventual Franciscans of St. Bonaventure Province.
Convergence, Inc., [Y], (MIL), Milwaukee, WI.
Converse College, Wofford College, Spartanburg Methodist College Newman Center, [H], (CHR), Spartanburg, SC.
Conway County Hospital, [E], (LR), Morrilton, AR.
Conwell-Egan Catholic High School, [D], (PH), Fairless Hills, PA.
Cook County Senior Community Services, [G], (CHI). See Catholic Charities of the Archdiocese of Chicago-Archdiocesan Offices.
Cooke's Manor Transitional Housing For Men, [G], (CHI). See Catholic Charities of the Archdiocese of Chicago-Archdiocesan Offices.
Coolock House, [K], (CHL), Charlotte, NC.
Cooperative Ministries Interfaith Center, [L], (MEM), Martin, TN.
COR (Christ in Others Retreat), [B], (STV). See Miscellaneous Organizations.
Cor Jesu Academy, [F], (STL), St. Louis, MO.
Cor Jesu Monastery, [K], (SFE), Jemez Springs, NM.
Cor Mariae, [W], (NY), New York, NY.
Cor Mariae Center, [G], (RCK), Rockford, IL.
CORA Services, [EE], (PH), Philadelphia, PA.
Corcoran House/Boysville of Michigan, Inc., [E], (LAN), Mount Morris, MI.
Cordi-Marian Center, [I], (CHI), Chicago, IL.
Cordi-Marian Missionary Sisters, [N], (SAT), San Antonio, TX.
Cordi-Marian Missionary Sisters Convent and Formation House, [N], (SAT), San Antonio, TX.
Cordi-Marian Sisters, [I], (AUS), San Marcos, TX.
Cordis House, [G], (SPC), Republic, MO.
Cormaria Retreat House, [P], (RVC), Sag Harbor, NY.
Cornelia Connelly Convent, [I], (ORG), Anaheim, CA.
*Cornelia Connelly Pastoral Counseling Center, [Q], (P), Marylhurst, OR.
Cornelia Connelly School of the Holy Child, [D], (ORG), Anaheim, CA.
Corporate Action for the Care of the Elderly, Inc., [I], (STL), St. Louis, MO.
Corpus Christi Abbey, [H], (CC), Sandia, TX.
Corpus Christi Academy, [A], (CC), Corpus Christi, TX.
Corpus Christi Academy Convent, [I], (CC), Corpus Christi, TX.
Corpus Christi Academy Middle School, [B], (CC), Corpus Christi, TX.
Corpus Christi Carmel, [Q], (PRO), Newport, RI.
Corpus Christi Child Development Center, [S], (HRT). See Catholic Charities-Catholic Family Services (Archdiocese of Hartford).
Corpus Christi Early Childhood Center, [H], (ARL), Falls Church, VA.
Corpus Christi Jenkins Memorial Trust, Inc., [P], (BAL). See Chancery Office.
Corpus Christi Monastery, [AA], (NY), New York, NY.
Corpus Christi Monastery, [O], (SFR), Menlo Park, CA.
Corpus Christi School, [G], (ARL), Falls Church, VA.
Corpus Christi School, [D], (ROC), Rochester, NY.
Corryville Catholic Elementary School, [G], (CIN), Cincinnati, OH.
Cortland Manor, [G], (CHI). See Catholic Charities of the Archdiocese of Chicago-Archdiocesan Offices.
Cortland Manor Retirement Home, [M], (CHI), Chicago, IL.
Coterie of St. Augustine Manor, The, [N], (CLV). See St. Augustine Manor.
Cottage 8 - St. Cloud Children's Home, [F], (SCL). See St. Cloud Children's Home of the Diocese of St. Cloud.
Cotter High School, [C], (WIN), Winona, MN.
Council Bluffs Area Catholic Education Systems, Inc., [A], (DM), Council Bluffs, IA.
Council for Research in Values and Philosophy, [V], (WDC), Washington, DC.
Council of Catholic Women, [T], (DET), Detroit, MI.
Council of Catholic Women, [W], (MIL), Milwaukee, WI.
Council of Catholic Women, DDCCW, [P], (DAL), Carrollton, TX.
Council of Rockland County, [M], (NY). See Society of St. Vincent De Paul, Archdiocesan Central Council of New York.
The Counseling Center, [J], (CC), Corpus Christi, TX.
Counseling Center at St. Luke's, [EE], (PH), Glenside, PA.
The Counseling Program, [H], (SY). See Chenango County Catholic Charities.
The Counseling Program, [H], (SY), Norwich, NY.
Counseling Referral, [E], (SR). See Diocese of Santa Rosa, Catholic Charities.
Counseling Services, [J], (ORG). See Catholic Charities of Orange County, Inc.
Counseling Services, [J], (WCH). See Catholic Charities.
Counterpoint Communications, Inc., [V], (HRT), Hartford, CT.
Country Day School of the Holy Union, [H], (BO), Groton, MA.
Country Day School of the Sacred Heart, [E], (BO), Newton, MA.
Country Day School of the Sacred Heart, [G], (PH), Bryn Mawr, PA.
Couple to Couple League, [K], (BEL), Dahlgren, IL.
*The Couple to Couple League International, [V], (CIN), Cincinnati, OH.
Courage, [DD], (NY), New York, NY.
*Coursey Station Apartments, Inc., [Q], (BAL), Lansdowne, MD.
Court Diversion Project, [N], (NY). See Pius XII Youth and Family Services.
Court of Appeals-Province of Chicago, [X], (CHI), Chicago, IL.
Covenant Community Foundation, Inc., [Y], (MIL), Milwaukee, WI.
Covenant Corporation of Suffern, NY, [DD], (NY), Suffern, NY.
Covenant Foundation, Inc., [H], (DUB). See Covenant Medical Center.
Covenant Health System, Inc., [H], (DUB). See Covenant Medical Center.
Covenant Health Systems, Inc., [FF], (BO), Lexington, MA.
Covenant Healthcare System, Inc., [Y], (MIL), Milwaukee, WI.
Covenant Home Health, Inc., [Y], (MIL), Milwaukee, WI.
*Covenant House, [K], (NO), New Orleans, LA.
Covenant House Alaska, [K], (ANC), Anchorage, AK.
Covenant House Texas, [M], (GAL), Houston, TX.
Covenant House Under 21, [N], (NY), New York, NY.
Covenant Medical Center, [H], (DUB), Waterloo, IA.
Covenant Medical Center of Champaign/Urbana, [J], (PEO), Urbana, IL.
Covington Catholic High School, [B], (COV), Covington, KY.
Covington Latin School, [B], (COV), Covington, KY.
Coyle and Cassidy High School, [C], (FR), Taunton, MA.
Cranston-Johnston Catholic Regional School, [G], (PRO), Cranston, RI.
Crazy Quilt Friendship Center, [I], (KNX), Newcomb, TN.
Creative Acting, [V], (HRT). See Franciscan Life Center Network, Incorporated.
Creighton Preparatory School, [C], (OM), Omaha, NE.
*Creighton University, [A], (OM), Omaha, NE.
Crescent House, [L], (NO), New Orleans, LA.
Crespi Carmelite High School, [F], (LA), Encino, CA.
Cretin-Derham Hall, [F], (STP), St. Paul, MN.
Crime Victims-Witness Assistance Program, [H], (SY), Norwich, NY.
Crisis Alleviation, [D], (WIL). See Catholic Charities, Inc.
Cristo Rey Catholic Hispanic Center, [K], (LIN), Lincoln, NE.
Cristo Rey Community Center, [D], (LAN), Lansing, MI.
Cristo Rey Jesuit High School, Inc., [D], (CHI), Chicago, IL.
Cristo Rey Mission, [X], (CLV). See Diocesan Hispanic Office.
Cristo Rey Monastery of Perpetual Adoration, [K], (ELP). See Sisters of Perpetual Adoration (A.P.).
Cristo Rey Provincial House, [K], (SFE), Albuquerque, NM.
Cristo Rey Ranch, Inc., [M], (MIL), Mount Calvary, WI.
Cristo Rey Work/Study Program, Inc., [D], (CHI). See Cristo Rey Jesuit High School, Inc.
Croatian Commissariate, T.O.R., [N], (PIT), Pittsburgh, PA.
Croatian Dominican Fathers, [N], (CHI), Chicago, IL.
Croatian Franciscan Custody of the Holy Family, [N], (CHI), Chicago, IL.
Croation Apostolate, [T], (BRK). See Catholic Migration & Refugee Office, Catholic Migration Services, Inc.
Crosier (Canons Regular of the Order of the Holy Cross), [Z], (NY), New Rochelle, NY.
Crosier Community of Anoka, [N], (STP), Anoka, MN.
Crosier Community of Chicago, [N], (CHI), Chicago, IL.
Crosier Community of Phoenix (Canons Regular of the Order of the Holy Cross), [F], (PHX), Phoenix, AZ.
Crosier Community of Riverview, [K], (DET), Riverview, MI.
Crosier Community of St. Cloud, [I], (SCL), St. Cloud, MN.
Crosier Community of Shoreview, [N], (STP), Shoreview, MN.
Crosier Fathers of Fort Wayne, [O], (FTW), Fort Wayne, IN.
Crosier Missions, [W], (STP), Shoreview, MN.
Crosier Monastery, [A], (LIN), Hastings, NE.
Crosier Monastery, [I], (SCL), Onamia, MN.
Crosier Provincial House Province of St. Odilia, [N], (STP), Shoreview, MN.
Cross Apartments, [R], (SCR), Scranton, PA.
Crossbridge Adolescent Home, [H], (SY). See Chenango House.
Crossroads Family Shelter, [G], (LAV), Las Vegas, NV.
Crossroads Shelter, [J], (PHX). See Catholic Social Services of Central and Northern Arizona, Inc.
The Crotona-Thorpe Housing Development Fund Corporation, [W], (NY). See Thorpe Family Residence, Inc.
Crowley Christian Care Center, [N], (LAF), Crowley, LA.
Crozier House, [H], (WOR). See Catholic Charities.
Crusade for Family Prayer, Inc., [T], (ALB). See The Family Rosary Worldwide Office.
Crystal City/Festus, [W], (STL). See Catholic Family Services.
CSA Providence Ministries, [J], (CHR), Columbia, SC.
CSA St. John Ministries fka St. John West Shore Hospital, [AA], (CLV), Cleveland, OH.
CSA St. Vincent Charity Ministries fka St. Vincent Charity Hospital, [AA], (CLV), Cleveland, OH.
Curial Residence, [U], (BRK), Brooklyn, NY.
Cursillo, [U], (SFR), Pacifica, CA.
Cursillo Center, [K], (LAF), Opelousas, LA.
Cursillo Moderator, [J], (STU), Bridgeport, OH.
Cursillo Movement, [Q], (BAL), Baltimore, MD.
Cursillo Movement, [Q], (SEA), Seattle, WA.
Cursillo Movement, [B], (STV). See Miscellaneous Organizations.
Cursillo Trust, [L], (LR). See Adoption Services, Inc.
Cursillos, [I], (BWN), Edinburg, TX.
Cursillos in Christianity, [K], (BEL), Belleville, IL.
Cursillos in Christianity, [W], (MIL), Milwaukee, WI.
Cursillos in Christianity Movement of the Archdiocese of Detroit, [T], (DET), Roseville, MI.
Curtis House, [D], (SAG). See St. Vincent Home-Boysville of Michigan, Inc.
Custer County Conference of the Society of Saint Vincent de Paul and Thrift Store, [K], (GF), Miles City, MT.
Cuvilly Arts and Earth Center, Inc., [FF], (BO), Ipswich, MA.
CYO Adult Day Care Services, [V], (CLV). See CYO & Community Services.
CYO & Community Services, [V], (CLV), Akron, OH.
CYO & Community Services of Summit County, [V], (CLV). See Catholic Charities Services Corporation.
CYO Archbishop McGucken Youth Retreat and Conference Center, [R], (SFR). See Catholic Youth Organization of the Archdiocese of San Francisco.
CYO Camp Armstrong, [R], (SFR). See Catholic Youth Organization of the Archdiocese of San Francisco.
CYO Caritas Creek Environmental Education Program, [R], (SFR). See Catholic Youth Organization of the Archdiocese of San Francisco.
CYO Fulton, [K], (SY), Fulton, NY.
CYO Mission Day Care, [R], (SFR). See Catholic Youth Organization of the Archdiocese of San Francisco.
CYO San Francisco Boys and Girls Home, [R], (SFR). See Catholic Youth Organization of the Archdiocese of San Francisco.
CYO Sports & Recreation, [R], (SFR). See Catholic Youth Organization of the Archdiocese of San Francisco.
CYO Transportation Services, [R], (SFR). See Catholic Youth Organization of the Archdiocese of San Francisco.
CYO Youth Athletics, [Y], (LA). See Catholic Charities of Los Angeles, Inc.
CYO Youth Ministry Services, [R], (SFR). See Catholic Youth Organization of the Archdiocese of San Francisco.
Cypress House, [E], (SUP). See Catholic Charities Bureau, Inc.
Czech Catholic Home For The Aged, [C], (VIC), Hillje, TX.

D

D'Evereaux Hall Home, Inc., [D], (JKS), Jackson, MS.
*D'Youville College, [C], (BUF), Buffalo, NY.
D'Youville College, [K], (BUF). See Our Lady of Victory Hospital.
D'Youville House, Grey Nuns of the Sacred Heart, [G], (OG), Ogdensburg, NY.
D'Youville Manor, [U], (BO), Lowell, MA.
D'Youville Manor, [X], (PH), Yardley, PA.
Daemen College, [K], (BUF). See Our Lady of Victory Hospital.
Dainava Conference Center and Camp, [D], (LIT), Manchester, MI.
Dakota State University Newman Center, [H], (SFS), Madison, SD.
Dalton Center for Mission and Peace, [AA], (NY), New York, NY.
Daly City Counseling, [Q], (SFR). See Catholic Charities of the Archdiocese of San Francisco.
Damen House, [K], (DEN), Denver, CO.
Damien Boys High School, [D], (LA), La Verne, CA.
Damien House, [B], (WDC), Cheverly, MD.
Damien Memorial High School, [D], (HON), Honolulu, HI.
Damien-Dutton Society for Leprosy Aid, Inc., [R], (RVC), Bellmore, NY.
Daneo Hall, [N], (CHI), Chicago, IL.
Daniel Freeman Marina Hospital, [K], (LA), Marina Del Rey, CA.
Daniel Freeman Memorial Hospital, [K], (LA), Inglewood, CA.
Daniel J. Gross Catholic High School of Omaha, [B], (OM), Omaha, NE.
Daniel Murphy Catholic High School, [D], (LA), Los Angeles, CA.
*Daniel Pitino Shelter, Inc., [J], (OWN), Owensboro, KY.
Daraja House, [S], (NO). See Caritas.
The Darlington Fund, [A], (NEW). See Immaculate Conception Seminary.
Dart, Inc., [P], (BAL). See Chancery Office.
Daughters of Charity, [N], (BAL), Baltimore, MD.
Daughters of Charity, [I], (MOB), Montgomery, AL.
Daughters of Charity, [F], (R), Fayetteville, NC.
Daughters of Charity, [N], (RIC), Richmond, VA.
Daughters of Charity, [N], (RIC), Petersburg, VA.
Daughters of Charity, [B], (SAN), Odessa, TX.
Daughters of Charity Convent, [N], (SAT), San Antonio, TX.
Daughters of Charity Healthcare Foundation of St. Louis, [W], (STL), St. Louis, MO.
Daughters of Charity National Health System, [C], (LFT). See St. Vincent Mercy Hospital, Inc.
Daughters of Charity National Health System, [W], (STL), St. Louis, MO.
Daughters of Charity National Health System East, Inc., [Q], (BAL), Baltimore, MD.
Daughters of Charity National Health System-East Central, Inc., [J], (EVN), Evansville, IN.
Daughters of Charity National Health System-West Central Inc., [W], (STL), St. Louis, MO.
Daughters of Charity of St. Vincent de Paul, [J], (AMA), Amarillo, TX.
Daughters of Charity of St. Vincent de Paul, [K], (ARL), Spotsylvania, VA.
Daughters of Charity of St. Vincent De Paul, [I], (AUS), Austin, TX.
Daughters of Charity of St. Vincent De Paul, [I], (AUS), Waco, TX.
Daughters of Charity of St. Vincent de Paul, [I], (MIA), Miami, FL.
Daughters of Charity of St. Vincent de Paul, [J], (SFR). See Seton Medical Center.
Daughters of Charity of St. Vincent de Paul, [N], (SJ), San Jose, CA.
Daughters of Charity of St. Vincent De Paul (D.C.), [K], (ELP), El Paso, TX.
Daughters of Charity of St. Vincent de Paul (Laboure Residence), Seton Provincialate, [N], (SJ), Los Altos Hills, CA.
Daughters of Charity of St. Vincent de Paul of Indiana, Inc., [H], (EVN), Evansville, IN.
Daughters of Charity of St. Vincent de Paul, D.C., [K], (FTW), Fort Wayne, IN.
Daughters of Charity of St. Vincent de Paul, D.C., [Q], (NO), New Orleans, LA.
Daughters of Charity of St. Vincent de Paul, Emmitsburg Province, [N], (BAL), Emmitsburg, MD.
Daughters of Charity of the Most Precious Blood, [N], (PAT), Paterson, NJ.
Daughters of Charity of the Most Precious Blood Convent, [P], (BGP), Bridgeport, CT.
Daughters of Charity of the Most Precious Blood Day Nursery, [H], (BGP), Bridgeport, CT.
Daughters of Charity Residence, [F], (BLX), Gulfport, MS.
Daughters of Charity Services of New Orleans, [O], (NO), New Orleans, LA.
Daughters of Charity Services of San Antonio, [P], (SAT), San Antonio, TX.
Daughters of Charity West Central Region Foundation, [W], (STL), St. Louis, MO.
Daughters of Divine Charity, [I], (SD), San Diego, CA.
Daughters of Divine Charity - Holy Trinity Province, [L], (DET), Bloomfield Hills, MI.
The Daughters of Divine Charity, St. Mary Province, Charitable Trust, [Z], (CLV), Akron, OH.
Daughters of Divine Love Congregation, [O], (CHI), Highwood, IL.
Daughters of Divine Providence, [G], (ALX), Bunkie, LA.
Daughters of Divine Providence, F.D.P., [Q], (NO), Chalmette, LA.
Daughters of Divine Zeal, Inc., [L], (ALN), Reading, PA.
Daughters of Isabella, [K], (BEL), Breese, IL.
Daughters of Mary and Joseph, [S], (LA), Los Angeles, CA.
Daughters of Mary and Joseph, [I], (ORG), Orange, CA.
Daughters of Mary and Joseph, [I], (SD), Lake San Marcos, CA.
Daughters of Mary & Joseph, D.M.J., [S], (LA), Rancho Palos Verdes, CA.
Daughters of Mary Help of Christians, [H], (MRY), Corralitos, CA.
Daughters of Mary Help of Christians, [N], (PAT), Paterson, NJ.
Daughters of Mary Help of Christians (Salesian Sisters of St. John Bosco), [I], (AUS), Austin, TX.
Daughters of Mary Immaculate, [AA], (NY), New York, NY.
Daughters of Mary Immaculate, [AA], (NY), Newburgh, NY.
Daughters of Mary, Mother of Mercy, D.M.M.M., [S], (LA), Lynwood, CA.
Daughters of Our Lady of the Holy Rosary, [F], (BLX), Biloxi, MS.
Daughters of Our Lady of the Holy Rosary Provincial House, F.M.S.R., [Q], (NO), New Orleans, LA.
Daughters of Our Lady of the Sacred Heart, [AA], (PH), Cheltenham, PA.
Daughters of Our Mother of Peace, [R], (STL), St. Louis, MO.
Daughters of St. Mary of Providence, [O], (CHI), Chicago, IL.
Daughters of St. Mary of Providence, [O], (CHI), Lake Zurich, IL.
Daughters of St. Mary of Providence, [AA], (PH), Springfield, PA.
Daughters of St. Mary of Providence (D.S.M.P.), [AA], (PH), Elverson, PA.
Daughters of St. Mary of Providence (D.S.M.P.), [AA], (PH), Rosemont, PA.
Daughters of St. Paul, [H], (ANC), Anchorage, AK.
Daughters of St. Paul, [O], (CHI), Chicago, IL.
Daughters of St. Paul, [S], (LA), Culver City, CA.
Daughters of St. Paul, [I], (MIA), Miami, FL.
Daughters of St. Paul, [AA], (PH), Philadelphia, PA.
Daughters of St. Paul, [O], (SFR), San Francisco, CA.
Daughters of St. Paul Convent, [F], (CHR), Charleston, SC.
Daughters of St. Paul Convent, [AA], (PH), Philadelphia, PA.
The Daughters of St. Paul Convent, [N], (SAT), San Antonio, TX.
Daughters of St. Paul Convent, [R], (STL), St. Louis, MO.
Daughters of St. Paul Convent, F.S.P., [Q], (NO), Metairie, LA.
Daughters of St. Paul Inc., [X], (BO), Boston, MA.
Daughters of St. Paul, Pious Society, [AA], (NY), Staten Island, NY.
Daughters of the Charity of the Sacred Heart of Jesus, [J], (PRT), Sanford, ME.
The Daughters of the Cross, [E], (STO), Stockton, CA.
The Daughters of the Cross, [E], (STO), Tracy, CA.
Daughters of the Heart of Mary, [C], (LSC), Deming, NM.
Daughters of the Heart of Mary Provincial Residence, [J], (SPR), Holyoke, MA.
Daughters of the Holy Spirit, [N], (HRT), Manchester, CT.
Daughters of the Holy Spirit, [N], (HRT), New Britain, CT.
Daughters of the Holy Spirit, [I], (MOB), Hayneville, AL.
Daughters of the Holy Spirit, [I], (SAC), West Sacramento, CA.
Daughters of the Holy Spirit, [E], (STO), Stockton, CA.
Daughters of the Holy Spirit, [E], (STO), Patterson, CA.
The Daughters of the Holy Spirit Charitable Trust, [M], (NOR), Putnam, CT.
Daughters of the Holy Spirit, Nazareth of the Good Shepherd, [G], (LIN), Lincoln, NE.
Daughters of Wisdom, [N], (HRT), Forestville, CT.
Daughters of Wisdom, [N], (HRT), Hamden, CT.
Daughters of Wisdom, [N], (HRT), Litchfield, CT.
Daughters of Wisdom, [N], (HRT), Terryville, CT.
Daughters of Wisdom, [N], (HRT), Wethersfield, CT.
Daughters of Wisdom, [N], (HRT), Wolcott, CT.
Daughters of Wisdom, [J], (PRT), Lewiston, ME.
Daughters of Wisdom, [F], (R), Greenville, NC.
Daughters of Wisdom, [O], (RVC), Coram, NY.
Daughters of Wisdom, [O], (WDC), Washington, DC.
Daughters of Wisdom (Provincial House), [O], (RVC), Islip, NY.
Daughters of Wisdom Islip Community, [O], (RVC), Islip, NY.
David Minkin Residence, HDFC, Inc., [L], (BRK). See Catholic Charities.
*David W. Barry Foundation, [W], (SY), Syracuse, NY.
Day Break, [H], (SCL). See St. Benedict's Center.
Day Break II, [H], (SCL). See St. Benedict's Center.
Day Care Center, [D], (HEL). See St. Matthew School.
Day Care Center, [E], (NEW). See Sacred Heart School.
Day Care Nutrition, [C], (YAK), Yakima, WA.
Day Care Services, [H], (BUF). See The Catholic Charities of the Diocese of Buffalo.
Day Care Services, [G], (CHI). See Catholic Charities of the Archdiocese of Chicago-Archdiocesan Offices.
Day Care Services, [G], (CHI). See Catholic Charities of the Archdiocese of Chicago-Archdiocesan Offices.
Day Program, [E], (NEW). See The Felician School for Exceptional Children.
Day Treatment Services, [F], (SCL), St. Cloud, MN.
Daylesford Abbey, [B], (PH), Paoli, PA.
Daylesford Abbey, [Z], (PH), Paoli, PA.
Dayspring Villa, Inc., [K], (DEN), Denver, CO.
Daystar, Inc., [M], (MIL), Milwaukee, WI.
Dayton Catholic Elementary School, [G], (CIN), Dayton, OH.
DBH Management, Inc., [J], (MAN). See Carpenter Center, Inc.
DBH Shelter II, Inc., [J], (MAN). See Carpenter Center, Inc.
DBH Shelter III, Inc., [J], (MAN). See Carpenter Center, Inc.
DBH Shelter, Inc., [J], (MAN). See Carpenter Center, Inc.
De Chappotin Community, [Q], (PRO). See Franciscan Missionaries of Mary.
De La Salle Academy, [D], (KC), Kansas City, MO.
De La Salle Christian Brothers, [H], (LAF), Lafayette, LA.
De La Salle Christian Brothers Provincialate, [H], (LAF), Lafayette, LA.
De La Salle Collegiate for Boys, [E], (DET), Warren, MI.
De La Salle Hall, Inc., [M], (TR), Lincroft, NJ.
De La Salle Hall, Lewis University Student Res., [J], (JOL), Romeoville, IL.
De La Salle High School, [D], (CHI), Chicago, IL.
De La Salle High School, [E], (STP), Minneapolis, MN.
De La Salle High School of Concord, Inc. dba De La Salle High School, [E], (OAK), Concord, CA.
De La Salle Institute/Provincial Office, [M], (SR), Napa, CA.
De La Salle Junior High School, [H], (NO), New Orleans, LA.
De La Salle Senior High School, [F], (NO), New Orleans, LA.
De La Salle Vocational Day Treatment Center, [O], (PH), Bensalem, PA.
De La Salle-In-Towne Day Treatment Center, [O], (PH), Philadelphia, PA.
De LaSalle Academy Corporation, [T], (PRO). See Miscellaneous Listings for the Diocese of Providence.
De Matha Catholic High School, [E], (WDC), Hyattsville, MD.
De Mazenod House, [M], (SAT), San Antonio, TX.
De Paul Apartments, [P], (L). See Society of St. Vincent de Paul, Council of Louisville.
De Paul Center, [R], (LA). See Amat House.
De Paul Community Development Centers, Inc., [L], (LR), Stamps, AR.
De Paul Family Services, Inc., [F], (RIC), Roanoke, VA.
De Paul Foundation, Inc., [K], (WDC), Washington, DC.
De Paul Health Center, [K], (STL), Bridgeton, MO.
De Paul High School, [C], (PAT), Wayne, NJ.
De Paul Industries, [S], (CIN). See Archdiocesan Central Council of Cincinnati.
The De Paul Institute, [H], (PIT), Pittsburgh, PA.
De Paul Novitiate, [Z], (PH). See Congregation of the Mission.
De Paul Provincial House, [M], (ALB), Menands, NY.
De Paul Thrift Stores, [P], (L). See Society of St. Vincent de Paul, Council of Louisville.
De Paul Treatment Centers, Inc., [O], (P), Portland, OR.
De Paul University, [C], (CHI), Chicago, IL.
De Paul University, Campus Ministry Department, [V], (CHI). See Ministry in Higher Education.
De Paul University, Campus Ministry-Stewart Center, [V], (CHI). See Ministry in Higher Education.

Discalced Carmelite Monastery, [X], (BO), Danvers, MA.
Discalced Carmelite Monastery, [H], (BUR), Barre, VT.
Discalced Carmelite Monastery, [E], (JC), Jefferson City, MO.
Discalced Carmelite Monastery, [P], (MIL), Holy Hill, WI.
Discalced Carmelite Monastery, [K], (SFE), Santa Fe, NM.
Discalced Carmelite Monastery of St. Teresa of the Child Jesus, [P], (BUF), Buffalo, NY.
Discalced Carmelite Nuns, [V], (BRK), Brooklyn, NY.
Discalced Carmelite Nuns, [I], (GBG), Latrobe, PA.
Discalced Carmelite Nuns, [I], (LR), Little Rock, AR.
Discalced Carmelite Nuns, [O], (OAK), Kensington, CA.
Discalced Carmelite Nuns, [I], (SAC), Georgetown, CA.
Discalced Carmelite Nuns (O.C.D.) Carmel of the Holy Trinity, [R], (GAL), New Caney, TX.
Discalced Carmelite Nuns, Monastery of Our Lady of Guadalupe, [I], (GR), Ada, MI.
Discalced Carmelites, [I], (LAF), Lafayette, LA.
Discalced Carmelites (Prov. of St. Therese), [M], (SAT), San Antonio, TX.
Discalced Order Of Carmelites Monastery, [G], (AGN), Malojlo, GU.
Disciples of the Holy Spirit, Inc., [B], (STV). See Miscellaneous Organizations.
Disciples of the Lord Jesus Christ, [G], (ALX), Alexandria, LA.
Disciples of the Lord Jesus Christ, [J], (AMA), Channing, TX.
Dismas House East, [Q], (BAL), Baltimore, MD.
Dismas House of St. Louis, [W], (STL), St. Louis, MO.
Dismas House West, [Q], (BAL), Baltimore, MD.
*Dismas, Inc., [L], (NSH), Nashville, TN.
Disruptive Behavior Intervention, [G], (CHI). See Catholic Charities of the Archdiocese of Chicago-Archdiocesan Offices.
District Council of Cincinnati and Subordinate Parish Conferences, [S], (CIN). See Archdiocesan Central Council of Cincinnati.
District Council of Dayton and Subordinate Parish Conferences, [S], (CIN). See Archdiocesan Central Council of Cincinnati.
District Council of Hamilton and Subordinate Parish Conferences, [S], (CIN). See Archdiocesan Central Council of Cincinnati.
District Council of Manhattan, [M], (NY). See Society of St. Vincent De Paul, Archdiocesan Central Council of New York.
District Council of Saint Martin and Subordinate Parish Conferences, [S], (CIN). See Archdiocesan Central Council of Cincinnati.
District Council of Springfield and Subordinate Parish Conferences, [S], (CIN). See Archdiocesan Central Council of Cincinnati.
District Council of Staten Island, [M], (NY). See Society of St. Vincent De Paul, Archdiocesan Central Council of New York.
District Council of the Bronx, [M], (NY). See Society of St. Vincent De Paul, Archdiocesan Central Council of New York.
District Council of the Bronx, [M], (NY), Bronx, NY.
District of Columbia Detention Facility, [V], (WDC), Washington, DC.
District of Columbia Health Center, [V], (WDC). See Spanish Catholic Center.
District of Columbia Social Services, [V], (WDC). See Spanish Catholic Center.
District of San Francisco Christian Brothers Charitable Trust, [M], (SR). See De La Salle Institute/ Provincial Office.
Diversified Services, Inc., [E], (SUP). See Catholic Charities Bureau, Inc.
Divine Mercy Hermitage, [K], (PRT), St. Albans, ME.
Divine Providence Community Home & Lake Villa Maria Senior Apts., [C], (NU), Sleepy Eye, MN.
Divine Providence Convent, [I], (MET), Piscataway, NJ.
Divine Providence Foundation, [R], (PIT), Allison Park, PA.
Divine Providence Health Center, [B], (NU), Ivanhoe, MN.
Divine Providence Hospital of the Sisters of Christian Charity, [I], (SCR), Williamsport, PA.
Divine Providence Pre-school and Kindergarten, [J], (LA), Los Angeles, CA.
Divine Providence Village, [L], (PH), Springfield, PA.
Divine Redeemer Health Care Ministeries Corp., [R], (PIT), Elizabeth, PA.
Divine Redeemer Motherhouse, [O], (PIT), Elizabeth, PA.
Divine Savior Holy Angels High School, [E], (MIL), Milwaukee, WI.
Divine Savior Holy Angels High School Endowment Foundation, Inc., [Y], (MIL), Milwaukee, WI.
Divine Savior Hospital & Nursing Home, Inc., [G], (MAD), Portage, WI.
Divine Savior Nursing Home, [H], (MAD), Portage, WI.
Divine Word, [H], (ORG), Santa Ana, CA.
Divine Word College, [B], (DUB), Epworth, IA.
Divine Word College, [M], (WDC), Washington, DC.
Divine Word International, [N], (CHI). See Society of the Divine Word, Provincial Headquarter-Chicago Prov.
Divine Word Missionaries, [W], (BO), Boston, MA.
Divine Word Missionaries, Augustine Tolton House of Studies, [B], (NO), New Orleans, LA.
Divine Word Missionaries, Inc., Divine Word Funds, Inc., [U], (CHI), Techny, IL.
Divine Word Novitiate, [N], (CHI). See Society of the Divine Word, Provincial Headquarter-Chicago Prov.
Divine Word Residence, [B], (CHI), Techny, IL.
Divine Word Residence, [N], (CHI). See Society of the Divine Word, Provincial Headquarter-Chicago Prov.
Divine Word Retreat Center, [G], (SB), Riverside, CA.
Divine Word Seminary, [P], (MIL), East Troy, WI.
Divine Word Seminary, [A], (SB), Riverside, CA.
Divine Word Theologate, [B], (CHI). See Divine Word Residence.
Divine Word Theologate, [N], (CHI), Chicago, IL.
Division of Community Development Services, [G], (CHI). See Catholic Charities of the Archdiocese of Chicago-Archdiocesan Offices.
Division of Family and Parish Support Services, [G], (CHI). See Catholic Charities of the Archdiocese of Chicago-Archdiocesan Offices.
Division of Non-Residential Services for Children and Youth for Cook and Lake Counties, [G], (CHI). See Catholic Charities of the Archdiocese of Chicago-Archdiocesan Offices.
Div. of Residential Child-Adult Care Services, [G], (CHI). See Catholic Charities of the Archdiocese of Chicago-Archdiocesan Offices.
Division of Senior Residential Services, [G], (CHI). See Catholic Charities of the Archdiocese of Chicago-Archdiocesan Offices.
Division of Senior Social Services, [G], (CHI). See Catholic Charities of the Archdiocese of Chicago-Archdiocesan Offices.
Dixie College, Newman Center, [H], (SLC), St. George, UT.
Dmitri Manor Priests' Residence, [E], (ALT), Hollidaysburg, PA.
D-M-P Trust, [N], (OM). See Columban Fathers Regional Administration.
The Doane Stuart School, [D], (ALB), Albany, NY.
Dr. White Community Center, [L], (BRK). See Catholic Charities.
Dogwood Foundation, Inc., [U], (GAL), Conroe, TX.
Dolores Vipond Memorial Endowment, [N], (OM). See The Omaha Archdiocesan Educational Foundation, Inc.
DOM, Inc., [M], (MIA), Miami Shores, FL.
Domestic Department, [E], (KCK). See Maur Hill Prep School.
Dominguez Seminary Inc., [R], (LA), Rancho Dominguez, CA.
Dominguez Seminary, Inc., [R], (LA). See Missionary Sons of the Immaculate Heart of Mary.
Dominican Academy, [D], (AUS), Austin, TX.
Dominican Academy, [E], (FR), Fall River, MA.
Dominican Academy, [F], (NY), New York, NY.
Dominican Center, [I], (GR), Grand Rapids, MI.
Dominican Center for Religious Development, [T], (DET), Dearborn Heights, MI.
Dominican Center Hawaii, [I], (HON), Waipahu, HI.
Dominican Center, Sinsinawa Dominican Sisters, [L], (SPK), Spokane, WA.
Dominican Child Development Center, [D], (AGN), Ordot, GU.
Dominican College, [CC], (NY). See University Apostolate.
Dominican College, [C], (SFR), San Rafael, CA.
Dominican College of Blauvelt, [C], (NY), Orangeburg, NY.
Dominican College of Racine, Inc., [Y], (MIL), Racine, WI.
Dominican Commercial, [G], (BRK), Jamaica, NY.
Dominican Community, [N], (CHI), Chicago, IL.
Dominican Community, [N], (OAK), Moraga, CA.
Dominican Community, [E], (R), Raleigh, NC.
Dominican Community of St. Louis, [P], (STL), St. Louis, MO.
Dominican Community of St. Martin de Porres, [N], (CHI), Oak Park, IL.
Dominican Community Support Charitable Trust, [R], (OAK), Oakland, CA.
Dominican Conference Center, [R], (NO), New Orleans, LA.
Dominican Congregation of St. Catherine DeRicci, [F], (R), Durham, NC.
Dominican Consultation Center, [T], (DET), St. Clair Shores, MI.
Dominican Convent, [I], (CC). See Religious Missionaries of St. Dominic, Inc.
Dominican Convent, [O], (SFR). See Dominican Sisters of San Rafael Generalate & Convent.
Dominican Convent of Our Lady of the Rosary, [AA], (NY), Sparkill, NY.
Dominican Daughters of the Immaculate Mother, [L], (ALN), Pen Argyl, PA.
Dominican Ecclesial Institute, [N], (SFE), Albuquerque, NM.
Dominican Fathers, [H], (AUS), Austin, TX.
Dominican Fathers and Brothers, St. Mark Priory, Inc., [Q], (GAL), Houston, TX.
Dominican Fathers & Brothers, Southern Dominican Province, [P], (NO), New Orleans, LA.
Dominican Fathers of Miami, Inc., [M], (MIA), Miami, FL.
Dominican Friar Residence - Southern Dominican Province, [V], (WDC), Takoma Park, MD.
Dominican Friars, [H], (GR), Muskegan, MI.
Dominican Friars, [H], (NSH), Nashville, TN.
Dominican Friars Residence, [H], (MIA), Bal Harbour, FL.
Dominican Friars' Guild, [DD], (NY), New York, NY.
Dominican Fund of Kenosha, Inc., [Y], (MIL), Kenosha, WI.
Dominican Health Care, Inc., [Y], (MIL), Kenosha, WI.
Dominican Health Services, [F], (MRY), Santa Cruz, CA.
Dominican Health Services, [O], (SPK), Spokane, WA.
Dominican High School, [E], (MIL), Whitefish Bay, WI.
Dominican High School and Academy, [E], (DET), Detroit, MI.
Dominican House, [F], (CHR), Columbia, SC.
Dominican House, [K], (FR), Fall River, MA.
Dominican House, [L], (SPK), Spokane, WA.
Dominican House of Studies, [H], (WCH), Wichita, KS.
Dominican House of Studies, [B], (WDC), Washington, DC.
Dominican Kindergarten, [F], (OAK), Mission San Jose, CA.
*Dominican Land Company, [L], (GR), Grand Rapids, MI.
Dominican Leadership Conference, [U], (CHI), River Forest, IL.
Dominican Life Center, [H], (LAN). See Motherhouse of the Sisters of St. Dominic.
Dominican Literacy Center, [T], (DET), Detroit, MI.
Dominican Monastery of St. Jude (St. Jude Monastery), [I], (MOB), Marbury, AL.
Dominican Monastery of the Perpetual Rosary, [T], (SY), Syracuse, NY.
Dominican Motherhouse, [J], (MAD), Sinsinawa, WI.
Dominican Motherhouse, Congregation of St. Catherine de Ricci, [AA], (PH), Elkins Park, PA.
Dominican Network, [O], (SPK), Spokane, WA.
Dominican Novitiate, [C], (CIN), Cincinnati, OH.
Dominican Oaks Corporation, [K], (MRY), Santa Cruz, CA.
Dominican Oblates of Jesus, [N], (HRT), Hartford, CT.
Dominican Order (Western Province), St. Albert's Priory, [N], (OAK), Oakland, CA.
Dominican Order, Siena House, [N], (OAK), Oakland, CA.
Dominican Outreach Foundation, [O], (SPK), Spokane, WA.
Dominican Pastoral Counseling Center, [Q], (BAL), Westminster, MD.
Dominican Priory of Juan Macias, [B], (SAT), San Antonio, TX.
Dominican Priory of St. Albert the Great, [M], (DAL), Irving, TX.
Dominican Reflection Center, [O], (SEA), Edmonds, WA.
Dominican Retreat, [L], (ARL), McLean, VA.
Dominican Retreat House, [BB], (PH), Elkins Park, PA.
Dominican Retreat House, [L], (SFE), Albuquerque, NM.
Dominican Retreat House, Convent of Our Lady of Prouille, [AA], (PH), Elkins Park, PA.
Dominican Retreat House, Mary Queen of Apostles, [J], (MIA), Miami, FL.
Dominican Rosary Apostolate, [DD], (NY). See Dominican Friars' Guild.
Dominican Rural Missionaries, [I], (LAF), New Iberia, LA.
Dominican Santa Cruz Hospital, [E], (MRY), Santa Cruz, CA.
Dominican School, [C], (AGN), Yigo, GU.
Dominican School of Philosophy and Theology, [A], (OAK), Berkeley, CA.
Dominican Shrine of St. Jude, Inc., [DD], (NY), New York, NY.
Dominican Sisters, [N], (CIN), Cincinnati, OH.
Dominican Sisters, [N], (DAV), Iowa City, IA.
Dominican Sisters, [N], (HRT), Ansonia, CT.
Dominican Sisters, [N], (HRT), East Haven, CT.
Dominican Sisters, [N], (HRT), Manchester, CT.
Dominican Sisters, [V], (HRT), West Hartford, CT.
Dominican Sisters, [G], (KNX), Newport, TN.
Dominican Sisters, [I], (LAF), Lafayette, LA.

Dominican Sisters, [J], (PRT), Sabattus, ME.
Dominican Sisters, [I], (SAC), Carmichael, CA.
Dominican Sisters, [B], (SAN), San Angelo, TX.
Dominican Sisters, [L], (SPK), Spokane, WA.
Dominican Sisters (Adrian), O.P., [Q], (NO), Slidell, LA.
Dominican Sisters (Cabra, Ireland) O.P., [Q], (NO), New Orleans, LA.
Dominican Sisters (St. Cecilia Congregation), [G], (KNX), Oak Ridge, TN.
Dominican Sisters Community Support Corp., [R], (RVC), Amityville, NY.
Dominican Sisters Convent, [K], (ARL), Woodbridge, VA.
Dominican Sisters Family Health Service, [M], (RVC), Hampton Bays, NY.
Dominican Sisters Family Health Services, Inc., [U], (NY), Ossining, NY.
Dominican Sisters of Adrian, [I], (SD), La Jolla, CA.
Dominican Sisters of Adrian, MI, [O], (OAK), Hayward, CA.
Dominican Sisters of Charity of the Presentation, [F], (BWN), Brownsville, TX.
Dominican Sisters of Charity of the Presentation of the Blessed Virgin, [L], (FR), Dighton, MA.
Dominican Sisters of Divine Providence, [L], (MET), Piscataway, NJ.
Dominican Sisters of Hope, [N], (DEN), Denver, CO.
Dominican Sisters of Hope, [L], (FR), North Dartmouth, MA.
Dominican Sisters of Hope, [N], (HRT), New Britain, CT.
Dominican Sisters of Hope, [N], (HRT), Litchfield, CT.
Dominican Sisters of Hope, [N], (HRT), Hamden, CT.
Dominican Sisters of Hope, [AA], (NY), Ossining, NY.
Dominican Sisters of Hope Ministry Trust, [DD], (NY), Ossining, NY.
Dominican Sisters of Hope, Ossining, [G], (OG), Tupper Lake, NY.
Dominican Sisters of Houston, [I], (AUS), Austin, TX.
Dominican Sisters of Houston, [I], (AUS), Taylor, TX.
Dominican Sisters of Houston, [R], (GAL), Houston, TX.
Dominican Sisters of Mission San Jose, [O], (OAK), Oakland, CA.
Dominican Sisters of Mission San Jose, [O], (OAK), Berkeley, CA.
Dominican Sisters of Mission San Jose, [O], (OAK), Mission San Jose, CA.
Dominican Sisters of Mission San Jose, [O], (OAK), Newark, CA.
Dominican Sisters of Mission San Jose Foundation (A Non-Profit Corp.), [R], (OAK), Mission San Jose, CA.
Dominican Sisters of Oakford, [O], (OAK), Oakland, CA.
Dominican Sisters of Oakford, [O], (OAK), San Leandro, CA.
Dominican Sisters of Oakford (Dedicated to St. Catherine of Siena), [N], (SJ), Mountain View, CA.
Dominican Sisters of Our Lady of the Rosary, O.P., [AA], (PH), Philadelphia, PA.
Dominican Sisters of San Rafael, [O], (OAK), Oakland, CA.
Dominican Sisters of San Rafael, [O], (OAK), Berkeley, CA.
Dominican Sisters of San Rafael, [O], (OAK), Livermore, CA.
Dominican Sisters of San Rafael, [N], (SJ), Santa Clara, CA.
Dominican Sisters of San Rafael Generalate & Convent, [O], (SFR), San Rafael, CA.
Dominican Sisters of San Rafael, California, [E], (STO), Stockton, CA.
Dominican Sisters of the Perpetual Rosary Chaplain's Residence, [L], (CAM), Camden, NJ.
Dominican Sisters of the Roman Congregation, [J], (PRT), Lewiston, ME.
Dominican Sisters, Congregation of St. Catharine of Siena, KY O.P., [K], (MEM), Memphis, TN.
Dominican Sisters, Congregation of St. Cecila, [K], (MEM), Memphis, TN.
Dominican Sisters, Congregation of St. Rose of Lima, St. Joseph Convent, [L], (DET), Oxford, MI.
Dominican Sisters, Congregation of the Sacred Heart, Houston, [N], (SJ), San Jose, CA.
Dominican Sisters, O.P., [D], (LUB), Lubbock, TX.
Dominican Sisters-Vietnamese (O.P.), Inc., [R], (GAL), Houston, TX.
Dominican Spiritual Life Center, [O], (ALB), Schenectady, NY.
Dominican University (Formerly Rosary College), [C], (CHI), River Forest, IL.
Dominican Village, Inc., [J], (RVC), Amityville, NY.
Dominican Vocation Sponsors, [P], (NO). See Dominican Fathers & Brothers, Southern Dominican Province.
Dominicans (Dominican Community-Jordan House), [F], (PHX), Tempe, AZ.
Dominicans (Provincial Office), [N], (CHI), Chicago, IL.
Dominicans, Mission San Jose, [I], (ORG), Anaheim, CA.
Dominicans, Mission San Jose, [I], (ORG), Santa Ana, CA.
Dominicare, [H], (SPK), Chewelah, WA.
Dominicas De La Doctrina Cristiana, [C], (LSC), Chapparal, NM.
Dominicas de la Inmaculada Concepcion, [M], (MIA), Hialeah, FL.
Domus Corporation, Inc., [S], (NEW). See New Jersey Caritas Corporation, Inc.
Domus Transitional Housing of Catholic Charities, [M], (SCL), St. Cloud, MN.
Don Bosco Annex, [S], (NEW). See Salesians of Don Bosco, S.D.B.
Don Bosco Camp, [U], (STL), Hillsboro, MO.
Don Bosco Hall, Inc., [O], (DET), Detroit, MI.
*Don Bosco Harlem Association, Inc., [DD], (NY), New York, NY.
Don Bosco High School, [D], (DUB), Gilbertville, IA.
Don Bosco High School, [C], (LA). See Don Bosco Technical Institute.
Don Bosco Home Children's Center, [D], (BEL), Belleville, IL.
Don Bosco Preparatory High School for Boys, [C], (NEW), Ramsey, NJ.
Don Bosco Preparatory School of Technology, [E], (BO), Boston, MA.
Don Bosco Residence, [N], (NEW), South Orange, NJ.
Don Bosco Retreat Center and Marian Shrine, [BB], (NY), West Haverstraw, NY.
Don Bosco Technical High School, [D], (PAT), Paterson, NJ.
Don Bosco Technical Institute, [C], (LA), Rosemead, CA.
Don Bosco Technical Institute, [D], (LA), Rosemead, CA.
Don Bosco Volunteers, Inc., [D], (PAT). See Don Bosco Technical High School.
Don Guanella Center, Inc., Daughters of St. Mary of Providence, [X], (BO), Chelsea, MA.
Don Guanella House of Formation, [B], (PH), Springfield, PA.
Don Guanella School for Retarded Boys, [L], (PH), Springfield, PA.
Don Orione Center, [Y], (BO), Bradford, MA.
Don Orione Nursing Home, [U], (BO), Boston, MA.
Donnelly College, [A], (KCK), Kansas City, KS.
Donovan-Mayotte Catholic School, [C], (LAN), Flint, MI.
Dooley Center, Inc., [I], (KCK), Atchison, KS.
Doran Hall, [J], (GBG), Greensburg, PA.
Dorn Day Care Center (dba Gingerbread House Day Care Center), [L], (SY). See Sister Patricia Ann's Preschool dba Gingerbread House Preschool.
Dorothy Day Catholic Worker, [V], (WDC), Washington, DC.
Dothan Office of Catholic Social Services, [J], (MOB), Dothan, AL.
Douglas County Correction Center, [O], (OM). See Omaha Catholic Jail Ministry.
The Dove, Inc., [E], (SUP). See Catholic Charities Bureau, Inc.
Dover General Campus, [J], (PAT). See Sisters of the Sorrowful Mother Health Care Ministry Corp.
Dowagiac Nursing Home, [F], (KAL), Dowagiac, MI.
Dowling High School, [B], (DM), West Des Moines, IA.
Dowling-St. Joseph Alumni Foundation, [I], (DM), Des Moines, IA.
Downeast Big Brothers - Big Sisters, [E], (PRT). See Catholic Charities Maine.
*Downtown Women's Center and Abba House, Inc., [E], (AMA). See Catholic Family Service, Inc.
Drake Newman Center, [H], (DM), Des Moines, IA.
Drew University Catholic Campus Ministry, [O], (PAT), Madison, NJ.
Drew-Hamilton CYO Center, [Y], (NY), New York, NY.
Driscoll Catholic High School, [C], (JOL), Addison, IL.
Drueding Center, [R], (PH), Philadelphia, PA.
Du Bois Area Catholic Schools, [C], (E), Du Bois, PA.
Dubuque Council, [O], (DUB). See St. Vincent de Paul Society of the Archdiocese of Dubuque.
Duchesne Academy of the Sacred Heart, [F], (GAL), Houston, TX.
Duchesne Academy of the Sacred Heart, [G], (GAL), Houston, TX.
Duchesne Academy of the Sacred Heart, [C], (OM), Omaha, NE.
Duchesne Clinic, [K], (KCK), Kansas City, KS.
Duchesne High School, [E], (STL), St. Charles, MO.
Duchesne High School Endowment Fund Inc., [W], (STL), St. Charles, MO.
Dujarie House, [J], (FTW). See Holy Cross Brother Center.
Dukette Catholic School, [C], (LAN), Flint, MI.
Dukette Intercultural Center for Black Catholic Ministry, [L], (LAN), Flint, MI.
Dunkirk, [H], (BUF). See The Catholic Charities of the Diocese of Buffalo.
Dunn Tower Apartments, Inc., [L], (ROC), Rochester, NY.
Duns Scotus, [B], (DET), Detroit, MI.
Duquesne Catholic School, [F], (PIT), Duquesne, PA.
Duquesne University of the Holy Ghost, [B], (PIT), Pittsburgh, PA.
Dutchess, [D], (NY). See Department of Education.
The Dwelling Place, [F], (JKS), Brooksville, MS.
The Dwelling Place, [S], (MIL), Milwaukee, WI.
The Dwelling Place, [W], (NY), New York, NY.
The Dwelling Place, [O], (RIC), Richmond, VA.
The Dwelling Place of New York, Inc., [AA], (NY), New York, NY.

E

E. Donn Piatt Catholic Student Center at Louisiana Tech University, [G], (SHP), Ruston, LA.
E.D. White Catholic High School Alumni Association, [A], (HT). See Edward Douglas White Catholic High.
E.D. White Catholic High School Foundation, Inc., [A], (HT). See Edward Douglas White Catholic High.
Earlham College Newman Center, [N], (IND), Richmond, IN.
Earthworks, Inc., [O], (FTW), Plymouth, IN.
East & South Manhattan, [D], (NY). See Department of Education.
East Bay C.Y.O. Center, [N], (PRO), Riverside, RI.
East Bay Services to the Developmentally Disabled, [R], (OAK), Concord, CA.
East Catholic Elementary, [D], (OM), Hartington, NE.
East Catholic Elementary School Endowment, [N], (OM). See The Omaha Archdiocesan Educational Foundation, Inc.
East Catholic High School, [D], (DET), Detroit, MI.
East Catholic High School, [D], (HRT), Manchester, CT.
East Central Community College Newman Center, [G], (JKS), Forest, MS.
East Greenbush Housing Development Fund Co., Inc. dba Branson Manor Senior Apartment, [K], (ALB), Rensselaer, NY.
East Main Family Practice, [J], (PEO). See United Samaritans Medical Center.
East Meadow Campus, [E], (RVC). See St. Elizabeth Ann Seton Regional School.
East Oakland, [H], (OAK). See Catholic Charities of the Diocese of Oakland, Inc.
East Side Service for Senior Citizens, [Y], (MIL), Milwaukee, WI.
East Valley Catholic Social Service, [J], (PHX). See Catholic Social Services of Central and Northern Arizona, Inc.
Eastern Arizona Junior College, [I], (TUC), Thatcher, AZ.
Eastern Catholic Associates, [D], (PSC), Passaic, NJ.
Eastern Illinois University Newman Center, [M], (SFD), Charleston, IL.
*Eastern Mercy Health System, [EE], (PH), Radnor, PA.
Eastern Point Retreat House, [Y], (BO), Gloucester, MA.
Eastern Province of the Oblates of St. Joseph, [M], (SCR), Pittston, PA.
Eastern Region, [N], (SY), Syracuse, NY.
Eastern Shore Co-op, [J], (WIL), Easton, MD.
Easton Catholic Elementary School, [D], (ALN), Easton, PA.
Eastside Catholic Community of Great Falls, [K], (GF), Great Falls, MT.
Eastside Catholic High School, [C], (SEA), Bellevue, WA.
Eastside Neighborhood Center, [F], (SJ). See Catholic Charities of Santa Clara County.
Eastside Nutrition Site, [F], (SJ). See Catholic Charities of Santa Clara County.
Eastwood-Oxford Network of Care, Detroit, [H], (DET). See St. John Hospital and Medical Center.
Eau Claire Coordinated Catholic Schools, [D], (LC), Eau Claire, WI.
Ecclesia Center, [O], (E), Erie, PA.
Ecclesial Consultants, Inc., [L], (BRK). See Catholic Charities.
Echo House-Inner City Apostolate, [G], (CHR), Charleston, SC.
Ecumenical Institute of Spirituality, [P], (WOR), Spencer, MA.
The Ecumenical Institute of Wake Forest University and Belmont Abbey College, [A], (CHL). See Belmont Abbey College.
Edgewood Campus School, [F], (MAD), Madison, WI.
Edgewood College, [B], (MAD), Madison, WI.
Edgewood High School, [D], (MAD), Madison, WI.
Edgewood Incorporated, [M], (MAD), Madison, WI.
Edinboro University of PA, [K], (BUF). See Our Lady of Victory Hospital.
Edith Stein House of Studies, [N], (CHI), Chicago, IL.
Edmundite Apostolate Center, [I], (NOR), Enders Island, CT.
Edmundite Fathers, [H], (MOB), Selma, AL.
Edmundite House of Formation, [A], (MOB), Selma, AL.

Edmundite Seminary Guild, [A], (NOR), Mystic, CT.
Edu Care Pre-School and Daycare, [A], (NU). See New Ulm Area Catholic Schools.
*Education for Parish Service Programs, [V], (WDC), Washington, DC.
Education Foundation of the Diocese of Galveston-Houston, [U], (GAL), Houston, TX.
Education Through the 90's Foundation, [L], (RCK), Freeport, IL.
The Education/Sustaining Endowment Trust, [M], (LC), Chippewa Falls, WI.
Educational Endowment Trust of Eau Claire Coordinated Catholic Schools, [M], (LC), Eau Claire, WI.
Educational Foundation of St. Francis Xavier School, Inc., [L], (GR), Grand Rapids, MI.
Educational Services for Blind and Visually Impaired Children, [E], (PRT). See Catholic Charities Maine.
Educational Services for Blind and Visually Impaired Children-Satellite Office, [E], (PRT). See Catholic Charities Maine.
Educational Trust, [N], (OM). See Columban Fathers Regional Administration.
Edward Douglas White Catholic High, [A], (HT), Thibodaux, LA.
Edward McGuinn House of Studies, [N], (CHI). See Society of the Divine Word, Provincial Headquarter-Chicago Prov.
Efharisto Studio, Inc., [Q], (BAL), Baltimore, MD.
El Carmelo Residence, [W], (NY), New York, NY.
El Carmelo Retreat House, [G], (SB), Redlands, CA.
El Carmen Sister's Residence, [N], (SAT), San Antonio, TX.
El Centro de Servicios Para Hispanos, [K], (KCK), Topeka, KS.
El Centro Del Cardenal/Catholic Charities, [N], (BO), Boston, MA.
El Centro Drop-In Center, [G], (CHI). See Catholic Charities of the Archdiocese of Chicago-Archdiocesan Offices.
El Centro, Inc., [K], (KCK), Kansas City, KS.
El Rancho Grande Apartments, [E], (BWN), Brownsville, TX.
El Rosario Charitable Trust, [I], (BWN), Mission, TX.
El Yo Yo Bilingual Day Care Center, [J], (NO), New Orleans, LA.
Elbert House, [K], (SEA), Bellevue, WA.
Elder Abuse Program, [B], (STO). See The Catholic Charities of the Diocese of Stockton.
Elder Care of North La Crosse, Inc. (Village Apts. of St. James), [G], (LC), La Crosse, WI.
Elder Care of Sparta, Inc., [G], (LC), Sparta, WI.
Elder High School, [E], (CIN), Cincinnati, OH.
Elder Hospitality of Iowa II, Inc., [J], (DUB). See Elder Hospitality of Iowa, Inc.
Elder Hospitality of Iowa, Inc., [J], (DUB), Cresco, IA.
Eldercare Foundation, Inc. c/o CHI Services, [U], (CIN), Cincinnati, OH.
Eldercare Management, [B], (STO). See The Catholic Charities of the Diocese of Stockton.
Elementary Education Fund, [Q], (DEN), Denver, CO.
Elementary School, [C], (PBL). See John Neumann Catholic Schools.
Elementary Schools: Shelby County Catholic Schools, [A], (DM). See Shelby County Board of Catholic Education.
Elizabeth Ann Seton Catholic School, [C], (BEL), Fairview Heights, IL.
Elizabeth Ann Seton Center, [K], (RIC), Richmond, VA.
Elizabeth Ann Seton Center, [K], (RIC), Charlottesville, VA.
Elizabeth Seton Center Inc., [R], (PIT), Pittsburgh, PA.
The Elizabeth Seton Federation, Inc., [AA], (NY). See Sisters of Charity Center.
Elizabeth Seton High School, [E], (WDC), Bladensburg, MD.
*The Elizabeth Seton Housing Development Fund Corporation, [DD], (NY), New York, NY.
Elizabeth Seton Montessori School of Westmoreland County, Inc., [E], (GBG), Greensburg, PA.
Elizabeth Seton Residence, Health Care Facility, [X], (BO). See Mount Saint Vincent.
Elizabeth Seton Residence, Inc., [X], (BO), Wellesley, MA.
Elizabethport Catholic School, [E], (NEW), Elizabeth, NJ.
Elk County Christian High School, [C], (E), Saint Marys, PA.
Ellendale Nursing Center, [E], (FAR), Ellendale, ND.
Elliot County Medical Clinic, [E], (LEX), Sandy Hook, KY.
Elmbrook Memorial Hospital, Inc., [K], (MIL), Brookfield, WI.
Elmwood Apartments, [E], (SUP). See Catholic Charities Bureau, Inc.
Elon College, [H], (R), Elon College, NC.
Elyria Catholic High School, [D], (CLV), Elyria, OH.
Embry-Riddle Aeronautical University, [E], (ORL), Daytona Beach, FL.
Emergency Assistance, [G], (LAV), Las Vegas, NV.
Emergency Assistance, [G], (RNO), Reno, NV.
Emergency Assistance, [J], (VEN). See Catholic Charities in Collier County.
Emergency Assistance Program, [G], (CHI). See Catholic Charities of the Archdiocese of Chicago-Archdiocesan Offices.
Emergency Foster Care, [E], (PRT). See Catholic Charities Maine.
Emergency Services, [H], (OAK). See Catholic Charities of the Diocese of Oakland, Inc.
Emergency Services Division, [F], (TR). See Catholic Charities.
Emergency Shelter for Women, [D], (LAN). See Shelter of Flint, Inc.
Emma McRedmond Manor, [K], (SEA), Redmond, WA.
Emmanuel College, [C], (BO), Boston, MA.
Emmanuel College Campus Ministry, [CC], (BO), Boston, MA.
Emmanuel Community, [I], (MOB), Vredenburgh, AL.
Emmanuel House, [X], (BO), Wayland, MA.
Emmanuel House, [E], (JKS), Greenville, MS.
Emmanuel House, [Q], (PRO), Woonsocket, RI.
Emmanuel House Family Shelter, [N], (LAF). See Lafayette Catholic Service Centers, Inc.
Emmanuel House Kindergarten, [I], (BO), Boston, MA.
Emmanuel House of Prayer Country Retreat and Solitude Center, [O], (DAV), Iowa City, IA.
Emmanuel House/Catholic Charities - Community Social Service Center, [N], (BO), Boston, MA.
Emmanuel Monastery, [N], (BAL), Lutherville, MD.
Emmanuel, Inc., [V], (WDC), Gaithersburg, MD.
Emmaus Community, [F], (BLX), Pascagoula, MS.
Emmaus Community, [M], (CAM), Maple Shade, NJ.
Emmaus Community, [F], (CHR), Dillon, SC.
Emmaus Community, [G], (NOR), Uncasville, CT.
Emmaus Conference Center, [AA], (CLV), Bedford, OH.
Emmaus Convent, [AA], (PH), Philadelphia, PA.
Emmaus East Harlem, [D], (NTN), New York, NY.
Emmaus House, [T], (ALB), Albany, NY.
Emmaus House, [G], (DM), Des Moines, IA.
Emmaus House, [F], (DOD), Garden City, KS.
Emmaus House, [E], (LFT), Lafayette, IN.
Emmaus House, [M], (MAN), Manchester, NH.
Emmaus House, [J], (MET), Perth Amboy, NJ.
Emmaus House, [I], (SAG), Saginaw, MI.
Emmaus House, [S], (TR), Elberon, NJ.
Emmaus House, [I], (Y), Louisville, OH.
Emmaus House, Rider College, [R], (TR). See Campus Ministry for the Diocese of Trenton.
Emmaus House/Harlem, [D], (NTN), New York, NY.
Emmaus Inns, AIDS Ministry, [D], (NTN), New York, NY.
Emmaus Ministries, [N], (E), Erie, PA.
*Emmaus Ministries, [I], (LAN), Howell, MI.
Emmaus of the Diocese of Brooklyn, Inc., [L], (BRK). See Catholic Charities.
Emmaus Place, [G], (BIS), Bismarck, ND.
Emmaus Residence, [J], (PMB), West Palm Beach, FL.
Emmaus Spirituality Program for Priests, [R], (SCR), Plymouth, PA.
Emmaus-Diocesan Spiritual Life Center, [J], (NOR), Uncasville, CT.
Employee Assistance Services Office, [N], (NY). See Pius XII Youth and Family Services.
Employment and Education Program & Career Center, [F], (SJ). See Catholic Charities of Santa Clara County.
Employment Integration Program, [L], (OKL). See Oklahoma Benedictine Institute on Mental Retardation, Inc.
Employment Services, [G], (CHI). See Catholic Charities of the Archdiocese of Chicago-Archdiocesan Offices.
Employment Services, [J], (ORG). See Catholic Charities of Orange County, Inc.
Employment Training and Job Placement, [N], (NY). See Pius XII Youth and Family Services.
En El, Inc., [Y], (BRK), Brooklyn, NY.
Endowment Foundation of Thomas More Prep-Marian, Inc., [B], (SAL). See Thomas More Prep-Marian.
Endowment Fund for the Catholic Diocese of Victoria in Texas, [H], (VIC), Victoria, TX.
Endowment Trust of the Friends and Parishioners of St. Patrick Parish, [M], (LC), Sparta, WI.
Energy Assistance, [D], (WIL). See Catholic Charities, Inc.
Enfield Montessori School, [N], (HRT). See Felician Sisters - Our Lady of the Angels.
Enfield Montessori School, [N], (HRT), Enfield, CT.
Engaged Encounter, [L], (AMA), Amarillo, TX.
Engaged Encounter, [K], (BEL), Belleville, IL.
Engaged Encounter of North Texas, [K], (FWT). See The Catholic Renewal Center of North Texas, Inc.
English Action Center, [H], (OAK). See Catholic Charities of the Diocese of Oakland, Inc.
English Action Center-Verde School, [H], (OAK). See Catholic Charities of the Diocese of Oakland, Inc.
Enserv Inc., [EE], (PH), Immaculata, PA.
Ephpheta Center and Hearing Conservation Service, [L], (CHI), Oak Park, IL.
Ephphetha - Be Opened, [P], (PEO), Peoria, IL.
Ephrata House, [D], (NTN), Steubenville, OH.
The Epiphany Association, [R], (PIT), Pittsburgh, PA.
Epiphany Center for Families in Recovery, [L], (SFR). See Mount St. Joseph-St. Elizabeth.
Epiphany Housing of Tampa, Inc., [T], (SP), St. Petersburg, FL.
Epiphany Manor, [C], (ORL), Port Orange, FL.
Epiphany Monastery, [F], (HEL), Columbia Falls, MT.
Epiphany Monastery, [M], (MAN), New Boston, NH.
Episcopal Catholic Apartments, [C], (ORL), Winter Haven, FL.
Equestrian Order of the Holy Sepulcher of Jerusalem, [CC], (LA), Los Angeles, CA.
Equestrian Order of the Holy Sepulchre, [S], (NO), New Orleans, LA.
Equestrian Order of the Holy Sepulchre of Jerusalem, [FF], (BO), Boston, MA.
Equestrian Order of the Holy Sepulchre of Jerusalem, [S], (CHI), Chicago, IL.
Equestrian Order of the Holy Sepulchre of Jerusalem, [U], (GAL), Houston, TX.
Equestrian Order of the Holy Sepulchre of Jerusalem - Middle Atlantic Lieutenancy of the U.S., [V], (WDC), Washington, DC.
Equestrian Order of the Holy Sepulchre of Jerusalem - Northwest Lieutenancy, [U], (SFR), San Francisco, CA.
Erie Community College, [K], (BUF). See Our Lady of Victory Hospital.
Erie Dawn, [M], (E), Erie, PA.
Erie East Coast Migrant Programs, [F], (E), Erie, PA.
Erskine College Newman Center, [H], (CHR), Due West, SC.
Escuela Nuestra Sra. de la Providencia, [A], (CGS), Caguas, PR.
Escuela Superior Catolica de Bayamon, Jazmin Esq. Millones, [A], (SJN), Bayamon, PR.
Espousal Retreat House and Conference Center, [Y], (BO), Waltham, MA.
Essex Catholic Boys High School, [D], (NEW), East Orange, NJ.
Essex County College, Rutgers University/Newark, NJIT, [Q], (NEW), Newark, NJ.
Establishing Mission Churches with Lay Leaders, [L], (NSH). See Glenmary Department of Pastoral Services.
Estrella del Mar, Inc. dba Regis House, [U], (LA), Los Angeles, CA.
Ethiopian and Eritrean Catholic Mission, USA, [V], (WDC), Washington, DC.
Ethnic and Special Ministries, [L], (RIC), Richmond, VA.
ETSU-Catholic Center, [J], (KNX), Johnson City, TN.
Eucharistic Franciscan Missionary Sisters, [S], (LA), Los Angeles, CA.
Eucharistic Franciscan Missionary Sisters, [N], (SAT), San Antonio, TX.
Eucharistic Franciscan Missionary Sisters, [E], (STO), Stockton, CA.
Eucharistic Franciscan Missionary Sisters of Los Angeles, [S], (LA). See Eucharistic Franciscan Missionary Sisters.
Eucharistic Missionaries of St. Dominic, [F], (BLX), Gulfport, MS.
Eucharistic Missionaries of St. Dominic, [I], (LAF), Lafayette, LA.
Eucharistic Missionaries of St. Dominic, [I], (LAF), Duson, LA.
Eucharistic Missionaries of St. Dominic, [E], (PHX), Glendale, AZ.
Eucharistic Missionaries of St. Dominic, O.P., [Q], (NO), New Orleans, LA.
Eucharistic Missionaries of St. Theresa, [W], (STL), St. Louis, MO.
Eucharistic Missionaries of St. Theresa-Mexico (M.E.S.T.), [R], (GAL), Houston, TX.
Eucharistic Missionaries of the Most Holy Trinity, [I], (ORG), Garden Grove, CA.
Eucharistic Missionaries of the Most Holy Trinity, [N], (SJ), San Jose, CA.
Eucharistic Shrine of the Adorable Face of Jesus, [R], (NEW), Kearny, NJ.
Eugene Kennedy Residence, [L], (PAT), Pompton Lakes, NJ.
Euphrasia Hall, [N], (HRT). See Convent of Mary Immaculate, Provincial House of the Sisters of St. Joseph of Chambery.
Euphrasia House, Inc., [EE], (PH), Philadelphia, PA.
Evelyn Malloy Education Fund for the Sisters of Charity of the Incarnate Word, [R], (GAL). See Congregation of the Sisters of Charity of the Incarnate Word (C.C.V.I.).
Evergreen Apartments (Chetek), [E], (SUP). See Catholic Charities Bureau, Inc.
Evergreen Apartments (Shell Lake), [E], (SUP). See Catholic Charities Bureau, Inc.
Evergreen Court for Retirement Living, Inc., [K], (P),

North Bend, OR.
Evergreen House and Day Care Program, [E], (HBG). See Department for Catholic Charities Counseling/ Field Services.
Everitt Academy, [N], (MET), Peapack, NJ.
Evodia House, [E], (PRT). See Catholic Charities Maine.

F

F.A.I.T.H. Services Inc., [S], (NEW), Hoboken, NJ.
F.A.I.T.H. Services., [N], (NEW), Hoboken, NJ.
F.I.R.E., [J], (STU), Steubenville, OH.
Fa'asao High School, [C], (SPP), Lepuapua, AS.
Faber House, [W], (BO), Cambridge, MA.
Faber Jesuit Community, [M], (CIN), Cincinnati, OH.
Faces-St. Joseph Campus & Faces Preschool, [H], (MIL). See Fond du Lac Area Catholic Education System (FACES).
Faces-St. Mary Middle School Campus, [H], (MIL). See Fond du Lac Area Catholic Education System (FACES).
Faces-St. Patrick Campus, [H], (MIL). See Fond du Lac Area Catholic Education System (FACES).
Facilities Operations, [G], (CHI). See Catholic Charities of the Archdiocese of Chicago-Archdiocesan Offices.
Fahy Garden Apartments, [I], (SPK), Spokane, WA.
Fahy West Apartments, [I], (SPK), Spokane, WA.
Fairfield College Preparatory School, [D], (BGP), Fairfield, CT.
Fairfield Foundation of the Diocese of Bridgeport, Inc., [R], (BGP), Bridgeport, CT.
The Fairfield Jesuit Community-Fairfield University, [O], (BGP), Fairfield, CT.
*Fairfield University, [A], (BGP), Fairfield, CT.
Fairleigh Dickinson Univ.-Teaneck Campus, [Q], (NEW), Teaneck, NJ.
Fairleigh Dickinson University and Drew University, [O], (PAT), Madison, NJ.
Fairmont Catholic Grade School, [D], (WH), Fairmont, WV.
Fairmont State College Newman Center, [Q], (WH), Fairmont, WV.
Faith and Light U.S.A., Inc., [AA], (CLV), Euclid, OH.
Faith House, Inc., [V], (WDC), Hyattsville, MD.
Faith in the Future Fund, Inc., [W], (BGP), Bridgeport, CT.
Fall River Area Catholic Youth Organization, [O], (FR). See Diocesean Catholic Youth Organization.
Families Together, [L], (BRK). See Catholic Charities.
Family and Children's Services, [K], (NY), New York, NY.
Family and Community Services of Catholic Charities, [L], (Y), Kent, OH.
Family & Community Services, Inc. of Catholic Charities of Columbiana County, [L], (Y), Lisbon, OH.
Family & Individual Services (including Family Life Bureau), [D], (WIL). See Catholic Charities, Inc.
Family Based Services, [G], (CHI). See Catholic Charities of the Archdiocese of Chicago-Archdiocesan Offices.
Family Care Center, [J], (PEO). See United Samaritans Medical Center.
The Family Center, [L], (DEN). See Catholic Charities and Community Services of the Archdiocese of Denver, Inc.
Family Counseling, [I], (GAL). See Associated Catholic Charities of the Diocese of Galveston-Houston.
Family Counseling and Guidance Centers, [K], (BO), Boston, MA.
Family Counseling Endowment Fund, Inc., [DD], (BO). See Chancery Office.
Family Counseling Service, [S], (HRT). See Catholic Charities-Catholic Family Services (Archdiocese of Hartford).
Family Crisis Center, [F], (DOD), Great Bend, KS.
Family Division, Catholic Charities, [K], (SY), Syracuse, NY.
Family Focus, [P], (RIC), Newport News, VA.
Family Focus Program, [H], (BUF). See The Catholic Charities of the Diocese of Buffalo.
Family Growth Division, [F], (TR). See Catholic Charities.
Family Health Service, Inc.; Little Sisters of the Assumption, [U], (NY), New York, NY.
Family Life Education, [N], (SY), Syracuse, NY.
Family Life Ministry, [G], (BGP). See Catholic Charities of Fairfield County.
Family Life Ministry, [N], (GRY). See Catholic Charities.
Family Life Ministry, [K], (MIA), Miami, FL.
Family Life Office, [G], (ALT), Ebensburg, PA.
Family Life/Respect Life Catholic Center, [G], (BGP). See Catholic Charities of Fairfield County.
Family Mental Health Clinic, [D], (LAN). See Catholic Social Services-St. Vincent Home for Children, Inc.
The Family of Nazareth, Inc., [S], (NEW), Kearny, NJ.
Family of the Americas Foundation, Inc., [Q], (BAL), Dunkirk, MD.
Family Practice Associates of Kenosha, [K], (MIL). See St. Mary's Medical Center.
Family Practice Center, [J], (PEO). See United Samaritans Medical Center.
Family Preservation Services, [I], (SAT). See Father Flanagan's Boys' Town of San Antonio.
Family Resource Center, [J], (ORG). See Catholic Charities of Orange County, Inc.
Family Rosary For Peace, Inc., [L], (ROC), Rochester, NY.
The Family Rosary Worldwide Office, [T], (ALB), Albany, NY.
Family Service Center, [J], (ORG). See Catholic Charities of Orange County, Inc.
Family Service Office, [E], (MET), Bridgewater, NJ.
Family Service Office, [E], (MET), Edison, NJ.
Family Service Office, [E], (MET), Milford, NJ.
Family Service Office, [E], (MET), Perth Amboy, NJ.
Family Service Office, [E], (MET), Phillipsburg, NJ.
Family Support Center, [J], (ORG). See Catholic Charities of Orange County, Inc.
Family Support Center, [E], (SR). See Diocese of Santa Rosa, Catholic Charities.
Family Theater Productions, [CC], (LA), Hollywood, CA.
Family Ties Therapeutic Foster Care, [I], (CIN). See St. Joseph Orphanage.
Family Unity International, Inc., [V], (MIL), Elm Grove, WI.
Fanny Allen Hospital, [E], (BUR), Colchester, VT.
Fargo Catholic Schools Network, [E], (FAR), Fargo, ND.
Faribault B.A., Inc., [F], (STP), Faribault, MN.
Farley Health Care Corp., [O], (TOL), Toledo, OH.
Farmingdale Campus, [E], (RVC). See St. John Baptist de LaSalle Regional School.
Farren Care Center, Inc., [F], (SPR), Turners Falls, MA.
Father Al Miller Educational Trust Fund (St. Mary Parish, Westphalia), [K], (LAN). See Chancery Office.
Father Andre Coindre Charitable Trust, [T], (PRO), Pascoag, RI.
Father Barry CYO Center, [N], (PRO), Pawtucket, RI.
Father Dempsey's Hotel, Inc., [S], (STL), St. Louis, MO.
The Father Duenas Memorial School, [B], (AGN), Agana, GU.
Father Duenas Minor Seminary, [A], (AGN), Agana, GU.
Father Dunne's News Boys Home, [N], (STL), Florissant, MO.
Father Farrell Spiritual Life Center, [K], (LEX), Hazard, KY.
Father Flanagan High School, [B], (OM), Omaha, NE.
Father Flanagan High School, [I], (OM). See Father Flanagan's Boys' Home.
Father Flanagan's Boys' Home, [C], (OM), Boys Town, NE.
Father Flanagan's Boys' Home, [E], (OM), Boys Town, NE.
*Father Flanagan's Boys' Home, [I], (OM), Boys Town, NE.
Father Flanagan's Boys' Town of San Antonio, [I], (SAT), San Antonio, TX.
The Father Flohe Foundation, [L], (GR), Portland, MI.
Father Gabriel Richard High School, [B], (LAN), Ann Arbor, MI.
Father Gabriel Richard High School Trust Fund (Fr. Gabriel Richard H.S., Ann Harbor), [K], (LAN). See Chancery Office.
Fr. Hannibal House Social Service Center, [J], (FRS), Sanger, CA.
Father Holland Catholic Regional Elementary School, [H], (PRO), Woonsocket, RI.
Fr. James E. Fitzgerald Educational Memorial, [N], (OM). See The Omaha Archdiocesan Educational Foundation, Inc.
Father James Fitton House of Priestly Formation, [N], (WOR), Leicester, MA.
Father Jim's Home, [S], (STL), St. Louis, MO.
Father John C. Silva Education Foundation, [G], (STO), Modesto, CA.
Father John Rossiter and Friends Endowment Trust of St. Patrick Parish, [M], (LC), Onalaska, WI.
Father Judge Apostolic Center, [P], (PAT), Stirling, NJ.
Father Judge Faculty House, [Z], (PH), Philadelphia, PA.
Father Judge High School for Boys, [D], (PH), Philadelphia, PA.
Father Justin Rosary Hour Radio Apostolate, [O], (BUF), Athol Springs, NY.
Father Justin Vocationary, [M], (PAT), Florham Park, NJ.
Father Kolbe Interparochial School, [F], (BAL), Baltimore, MD.
Fr. Kolbe Missionaries of the Immaculata, [CC], (LA), West Covina, CA.
Father Lopez High School, [A], (ORL), Daytona Beach, FL.
Fr. Marot CYO Center, [N], (PRO), Woonsocket, RI.
Fr. Marquette Catholic Central Schools System, [A], (MAR), Marquette, MI.
Fr. McKenna St. Vincent de Paul Shoppe, [W], (BGP), Shelton, CT.
Father Purcell Memorial Exceptional Children Center, [F], (MOB), Montgomery, AL.
Father Raphael Piperni Charitable Trust, [U], (SFR), San Francisco, CA.
Father Ryan Board of Trust, [B], (NSH), Nashville, TN.
Father Ryan High School, [B], (NSH), Nashville, TN.
Father Sweeney School, [D], (PEO), Peoria, IL.
Father Thomas O'Keeffe Missionary Cenacle, [M], (WDC), Adelphi, MD.
Father Thomas Scecina Memorial High School, [C], (IND), Indianapolis, IN.
Father Tolton Catholic Community Services, [W], (STL). See Catholic Community Services Administration.
Father Toubia Retirement Home, [E], (OLL), North Jackson, OH.
Father Walter J. Ciszek Elementary School, [D], (ALN), Shenandoah, PA.
Father Walter Memorial Center for Handicapped Children, [F], (MOB), Montgomery, AL.
Father Yermo Elementary School, [E], (ELP), El Paso, TX.
Father Yermo High School, [D], (ELP), El Paso, TX.
Fathers and Brothers of Holy Cross, [G], (ANC), Anchorage, AK.
Fathers of Mercy, [F], (OWN), South Union, KY.
Fatima Community Center, [V], (CLV). See Catholic Charities Services Corporation.
Fatima Family Apostolate, [I], (SFS), Alexandria, SD.
Fatima Renewal Center, [H], (SCR), Dalton, PA.
Faulkner State Jr. College Newman Center, [K], (MOB), Bay Minette, AL.
Faulkner University Newman Center, [K], (MOB), Montgomery, AL.
Featherbed Lane Day Care Center, [R], (NY), New York, NY.
Federation of Catholic Parent Teacher Clubs of the Archdiocese of San Antonio, [T], (SAT), San Antonio, TX.
Federation of Catholic School Parents, Diocese of Buffalo, NY, [T], (BUF), Buffalo, NY.
Felician Adult Day Care, [N], (HRT). See Felician Sisters - Our Lady of the Angels.
Felician College, [B], (NEW), Lodi, NJ.
Felician Retreat House, [I], (PAT), Mount Arlington, NJ.
The Felician School for Exceptional Children, [E], (NEW), Lodi, NJ.
Felician Sisters, [I], (AUS), Bremond, TX.
Felician Sisters, [N], (SAT), San Antonio, TX.
Felician Sisters, [K], (SFE), Rio Rancho, NM.
Felician Sisters - Our Lady of the Angels, [N], (HRT), Enfield, CT.
Felician Sisters Infirmary, [N], (HRT). See Felician Sisters - Our Lady of the Angels.
Felician Sisters of St. Francis of Assisi Convent, [N], (PAT), Mount Arlington, NJ.
Felician Village Inc., [H], (GB), Manitowoc, WI.
Felix Varela Foundation, Inc., The, [DD], (NY), New York, NY.
The Fellowship House, [E], (PRT). See Catholic Charities Maine.
Fellowship of Catholic Scholars, [V], (WDC), Washington, DC.
The Fellowship of the Beloved Disciple, [DD], (NY), Chelsea, NY.
Fenwick High School, [D], (CHI), Oak Park, IL.
Fenwick High School, [E], (CIN), Middletown, OH.
Ferdinand Wheeler House, [M], (BAL), Baltimore, MD.
Ferncliff Nursing Home, [V], (NY), Rhinebeck, NY.
Ferrini Welfare League, [L], (BRK). See Catholic Charities.
Field Neurosciences Institute, [E], (SAG). See St. Mary's Medical Center of Saginaw, Inc.
Fields-Wright Medical Facility, Inc., [N], (SFD), Springfield, IL.
The 1540 House, [N], (NO), New Orleans, LA.
Filipino Apostolate, [T], (BRK). See Catholic Migration & Refugee Office, Catholic Migration Services, Inc.
Filipino Apostolate, [L], (RIC). See Ethnic and Special Ministries.
Filipino Cursillo Secretariat, [U], (SFR), San Francisco, CA.
Filipino Pastoral Ministry, [CC], (LA), Los Angeles, CA.
Finance, [H], (RVC). See Catholic Charities Central Administration.
Finance Dept., [H], (BUF). See The Catholic Charities of the Diocese of Buffalo.
Financial Services, [G], (CHI). See Catholic Charities of the Archdiocese of Chicago-Archdiocesan Offices.
*First Care North, Inc., [O], (GB), Appleton, WI.
Fitchburg State College (Fitchburg), [Q], (WOR). See Campus Ministry.

Fitzgerald Charitable Trust, [N], (SFE), Jemez Springs, NM.
Fitzgerald Middle School, [C], (WIN). See Mankato Area Catholic Schools.
572 Sterling Place, [L], (BRK). See Catholic Charities.
Flaget Center for Spirituality and Ministry Formation, [O], (L), Louisville, KY.
Flaget Memorial Hospital, [H], (L), Bardstown, KY.
Flagler College Newman Center, [L], (STA), St. Augustine, FL.
Flint-Goodridge Day Care Center, [J], (NO), New Orleans, LA.
Flintridge Sacred Heart Academy, [F], (LA), La Canada Flintridge, CA.
The Florida Catholic Aids Network, [K], (STA), Orlando, FL.
The Florida Catholic of Palm Beach, Inc., [J], (PMB), Palm Beach Gardens, FL.
Florida Head Start, [J], (NO), New Orleans, LA.
Florida Institute of Technology Campus Ministry, [E], (ORL), Melbourne, FL.
Florida Southern College Newman Center, [E], (ORL), Lakeland, FL.
Flowers With Care Youth Services, Diocese of Brooklyn, Inc., [Y], (BRK), Astoria, NY.
Flowers with Care, Diocese of Brooklyn, Inc., [L], (BRK). See Catholic Charities.
FMOL Health Systems, Inc., [L], (BR), Baton Rouge, LA.
Focolare Movement, [FF], (BO), Newton, MA.
Focolare Movement, [Y], (BRK), Queens, NY.
Focolare Movement, [X], (CHI), Chicago, IL.
Focolare Movement, [DD], (NY), New York, NY.
Focolare Movement, [T], (SAT), San Antonio, TX.
Focolare Movement, Men's Branch, [DD], (NY). See Focolare Movement.
The Focolare Movement, Men's Branch (California) (Work of Mary), [CC], (LA), Los Angeles, CA.
Focolare Movement, Women's Branch, [DD], (NY). See Focolare Movement.
Focolare Movement-Mariapolis Center, [T], (CHI), Chicago, IL.
Focus for Work, [F], (SJ). See Catholic Charities of Santa Clara County.
Focus Foundation (Federation of Catholic Urban Schools), [W], (STL). See Catholic High School Association.
*Focus Syndicate, Inc., [S], (NO), New Orleans, LA.
Fond du Lac Area Catholic Education System (FACES), [H], (MIL), Fond du Lac, WI.
Fontbonne Academy, [E], (BO), Milton, MA.
Fontbonne College, [C], (STL), St. Louis, MO.
Fontbonne Hall, [X], (BO), Framingham, MA.
Fontbonne Hall, [G], (BRK), Brooklyn, NY.
Food Co-op of Sarita, Inc., [J], (CC), Sarita, TX.
Food Distribution Center, [G], (ORG). See St. Vincent de Paul Society.
Food Distribution Center Program, [L], (SAC). See Catholic Charities of Sacramento, Inc.
Food for the Starving, [J], (LIN). See Chancery.
Food for Thought, Inc., [Q], (BAL), Baltimore, MD.
Food Pantry, [H], (SY). See Catholic Charities of Cortland County.
Ford City Catholic, [D], (GBG), Ford City, PA.
Fordham Preparatory School, [F], (NY), New York, NY.
*Fordham University, [C], (NY), Bronx, NY.
Fordham University at Lincoln Center, [CC], (NY). See University Apostolate.
Fordham University at Rosemill, [CC], (NY). See University Apostolate.
Forest Ridge School of the Sacred Heart, [C], (SEA), Bellevue, WA.
Forever Free Phase II-Transitional Housing For Women, [G], (CHI). See Catholic Charities of the Archdiocese of Chicago-Archdiocesan Offices.
Forever Free-Women's Wholistic Recovery Home, [G], (CHI). See Catholic Charities of the Archdiocese of Chicago-Archdiocesan Offices.
Formation Center, [P], (BUF). See Franciscan Missionary Sisters of the Divine Child, Inc.
Formation Community, Religious of the Sacred Heart of Mary, [S], (LA), Los Angeles, CA.
Formation House, [A], (CHK), Saipan, MP.
Formation House, [Q], (NO). See Teresian Sisters (Society of St. Teresa of Jesus), S.T.J.
Fort Atkinson-St. Lucas Catholic School, [F], (DUB), St. Lucas, IA.
Foster Boarding Home and Adoption Services, [O], (BRK). See The Angel Guardian Homes.
Foster Boarding Homes & Adoption, [N], (NY). See Pius XII Youth and Family Services.
Foster G. McGaw Hospital of Loyola University of Chicago, [J], (CHI), Maywood, IL.
Foster Grandparent Program, [F], (SJ). See Catholic Charities of Santa Clara County.
Foster Grandparent Program, [E], (SUP). See Catholic Charities Bureau, Inc.
Foster Grandparent Program, [J], (WCH), Wichita, KS.
Foster Grandparents Program, [H], (BUF). See The Catholic Charities of the Diocese of Buffalo.
Foster Grandparents Program, [D], (LAN). See Catholic Social Services-St. Vincent Home for Children, Inc.
Foster Parents Mission Club, [T], (DET), Detroit, MI.
Foundation for Adult Catechetical Teaching Aids, [X], (CHI), Chicago, IL.
The Foundation for Catholic Education, [N], (MET), Metuchen, NJ.
The Foundation for Catholic Education of Greater Grand Rapids, Inc., [L], (GR), Grand Rapids, MI.
Foundation For Catholic Secondary Schools of Fort Wayne, Inc., [O], (FTW), Fort Wayne, IN.
Foundation for Christian Education, S.T.J., [S], (NO), New Orleans, LA.
Foundation for Religious Retirement, Inc., [Y], (MIL), Milwaukee, WI.
The Foundation for St. Catherine's Center for Children, [G], (ALB). See Saint Catherine's Center for Children.
Foundation for Senior Adult Living, Inc., [J], (PHX). See Foundation for Senior Living.
Foundation for Senior Living, [J], (PHX), Phoenix, AZ.
Foundation for the Advancement of Catholic Schools, [V], (HRT), Bloomfield, CT.
Foundation for the Care of the Migrant Poor, [K], (VEN), Venice, FL.
Foundation for the People of the Diocese of Springfield in Illinois, [N], (SFD), Springfield, IL.
The Foundation of Ancilla Health Care, [O], (FTW), South Bend, IN.
Foundation of Christ the Redeemer & Institute Id, [DD], (NY), Bronx, NY.
*The Foundation of the Catholic Diocese of Columbus, [K], (COL), Columbus, OH.
The Foundation of the Roman Catholic Diocese of Albany, New York, Inc., [T], (ALB), Albany, NY.
The Foundation of the Roman Catholic Diocese of Buffalo, NY, Inc., [T], (BUF), Buffalo, NY.
Fourth Street Bridge Youth Shelter, [J], (RCK), Rockford, IL.
Fox Knoll (Retirement Community), [G], (RCK), Aurora, IL.
Fox Manor, Inc., [J], (DET), Waterford, MI.
Fox Run ICF/MR Group Homes, [F], (CHL). See Holy Angels, Inc.
Foyer of Charity, [Y], (BO), Scituate, MA.
Framingham State College Campus Ministry, [CC], (BO), Framingham, MA.
*Frances Warde Health Service, [H], (CHL), Rosman, NC.
Frances Warde House, [R], (SCR), Scranton, PA.
Frances Warde House, Inc., [J], (MAN), Manchester, NH.
Francesca Residence, [N], (CLV), Akron, OH.
Francis and Clare House, [P], (MIL), Milwaukee, WI.
Francis F. Reh Academy, [C], (SAG), Saginaw, MI.
Francis Heights, [K], (DEN), Denver, CO.
Francis Heights, Inc., [I], (DEN), Denver, CO.
Francis House, [O], (OM), Omaha, NE.
Francis House of Prayer, [P], (TR), Mount Holly, NJ.
Francis House, Inc., [Q], (BAL), Baltimore, MD.
Francis Marion University Newman Center, [H], (CHR), Florence, SC.
Francis of Assisi Foundation of Colorado, Inc., [Q], (DEN), Denver, CO.
Francis R. Cotton School, [C], (OWN), Owensboro, KY.
Francis Realty Corporation, [M], (MIA), Miami Shores, FL.
Francis X. Gallagher Services, [H], (BAL), Timonium, MD.
Francis X. Singleton Emergency Food Assistance Program, [E], (FRS), Fresno, CA.
The Franciscan, [K], (SEA), Seattle, WA.
Franciscan Apostolic Sisters, [Q], (PRO), Woonsocket, RI.
The Franciscan at St. Clare, [L], (CIN), Cincinnati, OH.
The Franciscan at St. John, [R], (CIN), Cincinnati, OH.
The Franciscan at St. Leonard, [L], (CIN), Centerville, OH.
The Franciscan at St. Leonard, Assisted Living & Nursing Assistance, [M], (CIN). See Marianist Provincialate.
Franciscan at St. Raphael, Inc., [N], (CIN), Hamilton, OH.
The Franciscan at St. Raphael, Inc., [R], (CIN), Hamilton, OH.
The Franciscan at Schroder, [L], (CIN), Hamilton, OH.
The Franciscan at West Park, [L], (CIN), Cincinnati, OH.
Franciscan Brothers House of Studies, [P], (STL), Eureka, MO.
Franciscan Brothers of Brooklyn, [M], (HRT), West Haven, CT.
Franciscan Brothers of Peace, Inc., [T], (STP), St. Paul, MN.
Franciscan Brothers of the Holy Cross, [K], (SFD), Springfield, IL.
Franciscan Brothers of the Third Order Regular, [R], (LA), Los Angeles, CA.
Franciscan Brothers Work Crew, [V], (CIN), Cincinnati, OH.
Franciscan Brothers, of the St. Francis Monastery-Brooklyn, New York, at St. John the Baptist Parish, [P], (STL), St. Louis, MO.
Franciscan Care Center, Inc., [H], (GB), Appleton, WI.
Franciscan Care Services, Inc., (d.b.a. St. Francis Memorial Hospital, [G], (OM), West Point, NE.
Franciscan Care Services, Inc., (d.b.a. St. Joseph Retirement Community), [H], (OM), West Point, NE.
Franciscan Center, [Q], (BAL), Baltimore, MD.
Franciscan Center, [P], (BO), Andover, MA.
Franciscan Center, [F], (CHR), St. Helena Island, SC.
Franciscan Center, [G], (COS), Colorado Springs, CO.
Franciscan Center, [O], (TOL), Sylvania, OH.
The Franciscan Center, [N], (WIL), Wilmington, DE.
Franciscan Center - Retreat House, [Y], (BO), Andover, MA.
The Franciscan Center, Inc., [J], (BUF), Buffalo, NY.
Franciscan Center, Retreat House, [Q], (SP), Tampa, FL.
Franciscan Central Purchasing, [V], (CIN), Cincinnati, OH.
Franciscan Child Day Care Center, [I], (PIT), Pittsburgh, PA.
Franciscan Children's Hospital and Rehabilitation Center, [R], (BO), Boston, MA.
Franciscan Clarist Congregation, F.C.C., [O], (STP), Wayzata, MN.
Franciscan Communications, [CC], (LA), Los Angeles, CA.
Franciscan Community (Province of Immaculate Conception), [W], (BO), Lynn, MA.
Franciscan Cre-Act School, [V], (HRT). See Franciscan Life Center Network, Incorporated.
Franciscan Cultural Center, [D], (LIT), Brooklyn, NY.
Franciscan Elder Care, Inc., [G], (LC), La Crosse, WI.
*Franciscan Enterprise of Oregon, Inc., [Q], (P), Portland, OR.
Franciscan Family Care Center, [P], (HRT), Meriden, CT.
Franciscan Family Life Center, [V], (HRT). See Franciscan Life Center Network, Incorporated.
Franciscan Family Wellness Program, Inc., [H], (COS), Colorado Springs, CO.
Franciscan Fathers, [H], (ORG), Huntington Beach, CA.
Franciscan Fathers, [H], (ORG), Santa Ana, CA.
Franciscan Fathers' Residence, [H], (MIA), Miami, FL.
Franciscan Fathers, T.O.R., Tau Fraternity, [B], (WDC), Washington, DC.
Franciscan Formation Community, [A], (P), Portland, OR.
Franciscan Formation House, [T], (SY), Syracuse, NY.
Franciscan Formation Program in San Jose Friary (Casa Juan Diego), [B], (SAT), San Antonio, TX.
The Franciscan Foundation of Colorado Springs, [H], (COS), Colorado Springs, CO.
The Franciscan Foundation, Inc., [Q], (L), Pleasure Ridge Park, KY.
Franciscan Fraternity, [P], (NO), New Orleans, LA.
Franciscan Friars, [Q], (GAL), Houston, TX.
Franciscan Friars, [F], (KNX), Mountain City, TN.
Franciscan Friars, [N], (OAK), Oakland, CA.
Franciscan Friars, [N], (OAK). See Franciscan Friars Provincial Office, Province of St. Barbara.
Franciscan Friars, [N], (PIT), McKeesport, PA.
Franciscan Friars - O.F.M., [H], (CC), Hebbronville, TX.
Franciscan Friars (Sacred Heart Prov.) of Memphis, [J], (MEM), Memphis, TN.
Franciscan Friars Educational Corporation, [N], (CHI). See Conventual Franciscans of St. Bonaventure Province.
Franciscan Friars of California, Office of Communications, [U], (SFR), San Francisco, CA.
Franciscan Friars of the Atonement, [Z], (NY), Garrison, NY.
Franciscan Friars Provincial Office, Province of St. Barbara, [N], (OAK), Oakland, CA.
Franciscan Friars Retirement Corporation, [X], (CHI), Chicago, IL.
Franciscan Friars' Vacation Home, [L], (CAM), Margate, NJ.
Franciscan Friars, O.F.M., [G], (MRY), San Miguel, CA.
Franciscan Friars, Order of Friars Manor, [Z], (NY), New York, NY.
Franciscan Friars, St. Bonaventure Friary, [R], (LA), Torrance, CA.
Franciscan Friars, T.O.R., [N], (PIT), Pittsburgh, PA.
Franciscan Friars, T.O.R., Provincial Residence, San Pedro Friary, [F], (ORL), Winter Park, FL.
Franciscan Friary, [O], (SP), Kennebunkport, ME.
Franciscan Friary of St. Anthony of Padua, [P], (STL), St. Louis, MO.

Franciscan Friary, Order of Friars Minor (Old Mission), [R], (LA), Santa Barbara, CA.
Franciscan Handmaids of Mary Convent, [AA], (NY), New York, NY.
Franciscan Health & Education Corp., Inc., [M], (JOL), Wheaton, IL.
The Franciscan Health Care Center at Tacoma, [K], (SEA), Tacoma, WA.
The Franciscan Health Care Center at University Place, [K], (SEA), Tacoma, WA.
Franciscan Health Care Center/Retirement Center, [K], (L), Louisville, KY.
Franciscan Health Center, [L], (LA), Los Angeles, CA.
Franciscan Health Community, [M], (STP), St. Paul, MN.
Franciscan Health System of Kentucky, Inc., [M], (LEX), Ashland, KY.
Franciscan Health System of New Jersey, Inc., [S], (NEW), Jersey City, NJ.
Franciscan Health System of New York, Inc., [V], (NY), Bronx, NY.
*Franciscan Health System of South Carolina, Inc., [B], (CHR), Greenville, SC.
Franciscan Health System of the Ohio Valley, [T], (CIN), Cincinnati, OH.
Franciscan Health System of the Ohio Valley (FHSOV), [T], (CIN), Cincinnati, OH.
Franciscan Health System of the Ohio Valley operations in Dayton, OH, [T], (CIN), Dayton, OH.
Franciscan Health System/Care at Brackenville, [G], (WIL), Hockessin, DE.
Franciscan Health System/Care at Wilmington, [G], (WIL), Wilmington, DE.
The Franciscan Healthcare Center at Bothell, [K], (SEA), Bothell, WA.
The Franciscan Healthcare Center at Enumclaw, [K], (SEA), Enumclaw, WA.
Franciscan Home Development, Inc., [V], (CIN), Cincinnati, OH.
Franciscan Home Health, [G], (JOL). See St. Joseph Medical Center.
Franciscan Home Health, [J], (PEO). See United Samaritans Medical Center.
Franciscan Home Health of St. Joseph Hospital, [D], (RCK). See St. Joseph Hospital.
Franciscan Hospital, Mt. Airy Campus, [K], (CIN), Cincinnati, OH.
Franciscan Hospital, Western Hills Campus, [K], (CIN), Cincinnati, OH.
Franciscan Hospitaller Sisters of the Immaculate Conception, [H], (MRY), Santa Cruz, CA.
Franciscan Hospitallers, [F], (FRS), Fresno, CA.
Franciscan House of Studies, [N], (CHI), Chicago, IL.
Franciscan House, Mill Hill Sisters, [M], (ALB), Albany, NY.
Franciscan Learning Center, [F], (JOL), Joliet, IL.
Franciscan Life Center, [O], (HRT), Meriden, CT.
Franciscan Life Center, [V], (HRT). See Franciscan Life Center Network, Incorporated.
Franciscan Life Center Network, Incorporated, [V], (HRT), Meriden, CT.
Franciscan Life Process Center, [V], (HRT). See Franciscan Life Center Network, Incorporated.
Franciscan Life Process Child Development Center, [L], (GR), Lowell, MI.
Franciscan Ministries Foundation, Inc., [EE], (PH), Aston, PA.
Franciscan Ministries, Inc., [K], (DEN), Denver, CO.
Franciscan Ministries, Inc., [M], (JOL), Wheaton, IL.
*Franciscan Ministry Network, [Q], (P), Portland, OR.
Franciscan Mission Associates, [DD], (NY), Mount Vernon, NY.
Franciscan Mission Association, [K], (TOL), Carey, OH.
Franciscan Mission House, [L], (ALB), Rensselaer, NY.
Franciscan Mission Service of North America, [B], (WDC), Washington, DC.
Franciscan Missionaries of Mary, [X], (BO), Cambridge, MA.
Franciscan Missionaries of Mary, [O], (CHI), Waukegan, IL.
Franciscan Missionaries of Mary, [C], (LSC), Chamberino, NM.
Franciscan Missionaries of Mary, [C], (LSC), Garfield, NM.
Franciscan Missionaries of Mary, [AA], (NY), New York, NY.
Franciscan Missionaries of Mary, [AA], (NY), Millbrook, NY.
Franciscan Missionaries of Mary, [O], (OAK), Oakland, CA.
Franciscan Missionaries of Mary, [Q], (PRO), North Providence, RI.
Franciscan Missionaries of Mary, [Q], (PRO), North Smithfield, RI.
Franciscan Missionaries of Mary, [T], (PRO), North Providence, RI.
Franciscan Missionaries of Mary (F.M.M.), [O], (SFR), San Francisco, CA.
Franciscan Missionaries of Mary, Mary of Nazareth Novitiate, [L], (FR), Fall River, MA.
Franciscan Missionaries of Our Lady, [I], (LAF), Lafayette, LA.
Franciscan Missionaries of the Eternal Word, A Public Association of the Christian Faithful, [E], (BIR), Birmingham, AL.
Franciscan Missionary Sisters for Africa, [X], (BO), Boston, MA.
Franciscan Missionary Sisters of the Divine Child, Inc., [P], (BUF), Williamsville, NY.
Franciscan Missionary Sisters of the Immaculate Conception, [I], (ORG), Santa Ana, CA.
Franciscan Missionary Sisters of the Infant Jesus, [M], (CAM), Cherry Hill, NJ.
Franciscan Missionary Union, [V], (CIN), Cincinnati, OH.
Franciscan Missionary Union, Province of the Most Holy Name, [DD], (NY), New York, NY.
Franciscan Monastery of Saint Clare, [N], (TR), Bordentown, NJ.
Franciscan Monastery of St. Clare, [E], (VIC), Victoria, TX.
Franciscan Monastery of St. Clare (Poor Clares), [N], (CIN), Cincinnati, OH.
Franciscan Monastery of St. Clare, The, [X], (BO), Boston, MA.
Franciscan Montessori Earth School, [V], (HRT). See Franciscan Life Center Network, Incorporated.
Franciscan Montessori Earth School, [F], (P), Portland, OR.
Franciscan Northwoods Computer Center, [V], (HRT). See Franciscan Life Center Network, Incorporated.
Franciscan Oaks Independent Living Units & Health Center, [K], (PAT), Denville, NJ.
Franciscan Outreach Assoc., [X], (CHI), Chicago, IL.
Franciscan Pilgrimage Programs, Inc., [Y], (MIL), Milwaukee, WI.
Franciscan Properties, Inc., [O], (TOL), Sylvania, OH.
Franciscan Province of the Immaculate Conception, [Z], (NY), New York, NY.
Franciscan Publishers, [I], (GB). See Assumption of B.V.M. Friary.
Franciscan Renewal Center, [M], (P), Portland, OR.
Franciscan Renewal Center, Inc. (Casa de Paz Y Bien), [G], (PHX), Scottsdale, AZ.
Franciscan Renewal Center/Pilgrim House, [L], (TOL), Carey, OH.
Franciscan Residence, [H], (BR), Baton Rouge, LA.
Franciscan Retreat Center, Inc., [S], (MIL), Burlington, WI.
Franciscan Retreat House, [Q], (STP), Prior Lake, MN.
Franciscan School of Theology, [A], (OAK), Berkeley, CA.
Franciscan School of Theology Student Residence, [A], (OAK), Berkeley, CA.
Franciscan Seniors, Kenosha, Inc., [Y], (MIL), Milwaukee, WI.
Franciscan Services Corporation, [O], (TOL), Sylvania, OH.
Franciscan Shared Laboratory, Inc., [Y], (MIL), Wauwatosa, WI.
Franciscan Shelters-Bethany House, [O], (TOL), Sylvania, OH.
Franciscan Sisters, [I], (HON). See St. Francis Convent.
Franciscan Sisters, [N], (PEO), Streator, IL.
Franciscan Sisters Daughters of Mercy, [I], (AUS), Waco, TX.
Franciscan Sisters Daughters of Mercy (Hermanas Franciscanas Hijas de la Misericordia), [I], (AUS), Austin, TX.
Franciscan Sisters Health Care Corp., [J], (CHI). See Saint Therese Medical Center.
Franciscan Sisters Health Care Corporation, [M], (JOL), Frankfort, IL.
Franciscan Sisters Health Care, Inc., [M], (SCL), Little Falls, MN.
Franciscan Sisters of Allegany, [I], (MIA), Miami Shores, FL.
Franciscan Sisters of Allegany (O.S.F.), [AA], (PH), Philadelphia, PA.
Franciscan Sisters of Allegany Health System, Inc., [T], (SP). See Chancery Office.
Franciscan Sisters of Allegany, New York-Blessed Sacrament Mission Center, [P], (BUF), Delevan, NY.
Franciscan Sisters of Allegany, NY, [M], (MIA), St. Petersburg, FL.
Franciscan Sisters of Allegheny, NY, [N], (HRT), Waterbury, CT.
Franciscan Sisters of Atonement, [O], (WDC), Washington, DC.
Franciscan Sisters of Baltimore, Inc., Trust, [P], (BAL). See Chancery Office.
Franciscan Sisters of Baltimore-General Motherhouse and Novitiate, [N], (BAL), Baltimore, MD.
Franciscan Sisters of Christ the Divine Teacher, [N], (DAV), Davenport, IA.
Franciscan Sisters of Christian Charity (O.S.F.), [Q], (MIL), Slinger, Wi.
Franciscan Sisters of Christian Charity Healthcare Ministry, Inc., [O], (GB), Manitowoc, WI.
Franciscan Sisters of Little Falls (Little Falls, MN), [K], (MEM), Huntingdon, TN.
Franciscan Sisters of Little Falls, Minn., [AA], (NY), New York, NY.
Franciscan Sisters of Little Falls, MN, [O], (OAK), Berkeley, CA.
Franciscan Sisters of Little Falls, MN, [N], (SAT), San Antonio, TX.
Franciscan Sisters of Little Falls, MN (O.S.F.), [O], (STP), St. Paul, MN.
Franciscan Sisters of Little Falls, MN Charitable Trust, [M], (SCL), Little Falls, MN.
Franciscan Sisters of Mary, [M], (ALB), Albany, NY.
Franciscan Sisters of Mary, [M], (ALB), Glen Falls, NY.
Franciscan Sisters of Mary, [F], (BWN), Harlingen, TX.
Franciscan Sisters of Mary, [O], (CHI), Blue Island, IL.
Franciscan Sisters of Mary, [E], (JC), Jefferson City, MO.
Franciscan Sisters of Mary, [J], (MAD), Madison, WI.
Franciscan Sisters of Mary, [P], (SP), Tampa, FL.
Franciscan Sisters of Mary, [R], (STL), St. Charles, MO.
Franciscan Sisters of Mary, [W], (STL), St. Louis, MO.
Franciscan Sisters of Mary Administrative Offices, [R], (STL), St. Louis, MO.
Franciscan Sisters of Mary Convent, [H], (BEL), Mount Vernon, IL.
Franciscan Sisters of Mary Novitiate, [R], (STL), St. Louis, MO.
Franciscan Sisters of Our Lady, [U], (MIL), Beloit, WI.
Franciscan Sisters of Our Lady of Perpetual Help, [C], (LSC), Mescalero, NM.
Franciscan Sisters of Our Lady of Perpetual Help, [R], (STL), St. Louis, MO.
Franciscan Sisters of Our Lady of Perpetual Help (O.S.F.), [K], (ELP), El Paso, TX.
Franciscan Sisters of Peace, [V], (BRK), Long Island City, NY.
Franciscan Sisters of Peace, [AA], (PH), Philadelphia, PA.
Franciscan Sisters of Perpetual Adoration, [E], (RNO), Gardnerville, NV.
Franciscan Sisters of Perpetual Adoration (FSPA), [O], (OAK), El Cerrito, CA.
Franciscan Sisters of Poor Mt. Alverno Center, Inc. Franciscan Health Systems of Warwick, Inc., [AA], (NY), Warwick, NY.
Franciscan Sisters of St. Clare, F.S.S.C., [H], (SAG), Saginaw, MI.
Franciscan Sisters of Saint Clare, Inc., [U], (MIL), Franklin, WI.
Franciscan Sisters of St. Francis of Penance and Christian Charity, [O], (OAK), Oakland, CA.
Franciscan Sisters of St. Joseph (Mexico City), [I], (COL), Newark, OH.
Franciscan Sisters of St. Joseph (Mexico City), [L], (DET), Detroit, MI.
Franciscan Sisters of St. Paul, [O], (STP), St. Paul, MN.
Franciscan Sisters of the Atonement, [N], (HRT), Hamden, CT.
Franciscan Sisters of the Atonement, [N], (HRT), Milford, CT.
Franciscan Sisters of the Atonement, [H], (MRY), San Juan Bautista, CA.
Franciscan Sisters of the Atonement, [G], (OG), Plattsburgh, NY.
Franciscan Sisters of the Atonement, [F], (R), Wilson, NC.
Franciscan Sisters of the Atonement, [I], (SAC), Placerville, CA.
Franciscan Sisters of the Eucharist, [N], (SEA), Shaw Island, WA.
Franciscan Sisters of the Immaculate, [L], (FR), Fairhaven, MA.
Franciscan Sisters of the Immaculate Conception, [S], (LA), San Fernando, CA.
Franciscan Sisters of the Immaculate Conception, St. Francis Community, [X], (BO), Newton, MA.
Franciscan Sisters of the Immaculate Conception, St. Mary of the Hills, [X], (BO), Milton, MA.
Franciscan Sisters of the Poor, [V], (BRK), Brooklyn, NY.
Franciscan Sisters of the Poor Foundation, Inc., [V], (NY). See Franciscan Health System of New York, Inc.
Franciscan Sisters of the Poor Foundation, Inc., [AA], (NY), New York, NY.
Franciscan Sisters of the Poor Health System, Inc., [V], (BRK). See Franciscan Sisters of the Poor.
Franciscan Sisters of the Poor Health System, Inc., [V], (NY). See Franciscan Health System of New York, Inc.
Franciscan Sisters of the Poor Health System, Inc., [AA], (NY), New York, NY.
Franciscan Sisters of the Sacred Heart, [S], (LA),

G

Ministry for the Diocese of Trenton.
Gerald J. Ryan Outreach Center, Inc., [R], (RVC), Wyandanch, NY.
Gerard Hall, [F], (LC). See St. Francis Community Programs, Inc.
Gerard House, Inc., [M], (WCH), Wichita, KS.
Geriatrics Outreach Treatment Team, [H], (BUF). See The Catholic Charities of the Diocese of Buffalo.
German Roman Catholic Orphan Home, [I], (BUF), Buffalo, NY.
Gertrude C. Luther, M.D. Charitable Trust, [I], (BIR), Anniston, AL.
The Gesu School, [H], (PH), Philadelphia, PA.
Gesu School Jesuit Community and Outreach Center(S.J.), [Z], (PH), Philadelphia, PA.
Gettysburg Day Care Center, [D], (SFS). See Gettysburg Medical Center.
Gettysburg Medical Center, [D], (SFS), Gettysburg, SD.
Gibault Catholic High School, [B], (BEL), Waterloo, IL.
Gibault School for Boys, [G], (IND), Terre Haute, IN.
Gift Annuity Trust, [N], (OM). See Columban Fathers Regional Administration.
Gift of Hopė, Missionaries of Charity, [F], (MIA), Miami, FL.
Gila County Case Management, [D], (TUC). See Social Service Agencies: Pima County.
Gilbert Straub Plaza, [K], (GBG), Greensburg, PA.
Gilead, Inc., [O], (ALB), Unadilla, NY.
Gillen Property Holding Corporation, [J], (PAT). See St. Mary's Hospital.
Gilmary Diocesan Center, [P], (PIT), Coraopolis, PA.
Gilmour Academy, [E], (CLV), Gates Mills, OH.
Gilroy Nutrition Site, [F], (SJ). See Catholic Charities of Santa Clara County.
Giovanni Center, Inc., [P], (SJ), San Jose, CA.
*Girls Hope of Pittsburgh, Inc., [R], (PIT), Baden, PA.
Glastonbury Abbey, [W], (BO), Hingham, MA.
The Glenmary Center, [G], (OWN), Owensboro, KY.
The Glenmary Center for Mission Training, [G], (OWN), Livermore, KY.
Glenmary Co-Missioners, [L], (NSH). See Glenmary Department of Pastoral Services.
Glenmary Department of Pastoral Services, [L], (NSH), Nashville, TN.
Glenmary Home Missioners Charitable Trust, [U], (CIN), Fairfield, OH.
Glenmary House, [F], (OWN), Hartford, KY.
Glenmary House of Studies, [M], (WDC), Washington, DC.
Glenmary Personnel Office, [L], (NSH). See Glenmary Department of Pastoral Services.
Glenwood, [F], (PIT), Ambridge, PA.
Glinodo Center, [O], (E), Erie, PA.
Global Outreach, Inc., [O], (GB), Neenah, WI.
Gloucester Catholic High School, [B], (CAM), Gloucester, NJ.
Golden Age Clubs, [L], (BRK). See Catholic Charities.
Gonzaga College High School, [E], (WDC), Washington, DC.
Gonzaga Jesuit Community, [O], (ALB), Auriesville, NY.
Gonzaga Preparatory School, [E], (SPK), Spokane, WA.
Gonzaga University, [C], (SPK), Spokane, WA.
Good Counsel, [K], (NY). See Good Counsel/The Cardinal Cooke Residence.
Good Counsel, [K], (NY), Staten Island, NY.
Good Counsel Apartments, [T], (BUF), Buffalo, NY.
Good Counsel Education Center, [H], (WIN), Mankato, MN.
Good Counsel High School, [E], (WDC), Wheaton, MD.
Good Counsel High School, Inc., [D], (CHI), Chicago, IL.
Good Counsel, Inc., [K], (NEW). See Good Counsel, Inc. (St. Francis Home).
Good Counsel, Inc. (St. Francis Home), [K], (NEW), Hoboken, NJ.
Good Counsel/The Cardinal Cooke Residence, [K], (NY), Spring Valley, NY.
Good Counsel/The Paraclete Foundation, [K], (NY). See Good Counsel/The Cardinal Cooke Residence.
Good News Center (Sr. Ursula's Kitchen & Thrift Store), [E], (FRS). See Catholic Social Services.
The Good News Foundation of Central New York, [W], (SY), Utica, NY.
Good News Inn (Shelter), [E], (FRS). See Catholic Social Services.
Good News Medical Clinic, [E], (FRS). See Catholic Social Services.
Good Samaritan Foundation for Better Health, Inc., [DD], (NY), Suffern, NY.
Good Samaritan Foundation, Inc., [G], (ALN). See Good Samaritan Regional Medical Center.
Good Samaritan Health Center Foundation of Merrill, Wisconsin, Inc., [A], (SUP). See Good Samaritan Health Center of Merrill, Wisconsin, Inc.
Good Samaritan Health Center Foundation of Merrill, Wisconsin, Inc., [I], (SUP), Merrill, WI.
Good Samaritan Health Center of Merrill, Wisconsin, Inc., [A], (SUP), Merrill, WI.
Good Samaritan Health Corporation, [G], (ALN). See Good Samaritan Regional Medical Center.
Good Samaritan Health Systems dba Good Samaritan Hospital, [B], (GI), Kearney, NE.
Good Samaritan Hospice, [FF], (BO). See Caritas Christi - A Catholic Health Care System.
Good Samaritan Hospice, [K], (RVC), West Islip, NY.
Good Samaritan Hospital, [K], (CIN), Cincinnati, OH.
Good Samaritan Hospital, [K], (CIN), Dayton, OH.
Good Samaritan Hospital Foundation of Cincinnati, Inc., [U], (CIN), Cincinnati, OH.
Good Samaritan Hospital Medical Center, [I], (RVC). See The Samaritan Corporation.
Good Samaritan Hospital of Suffern, [S], (NY), Suffern, NY.
Good Samaritan Medical Center, [D], (ALT), Johnstown, PA.
Good Samaritan Medical Center, [Q], (BO), Brockton, MA.
Good Samaritan Medical Center and Rehabilitation Center, [E], (COL), Zanesville, OH.
Good Samaritan Nursing Home, [K], (RVC), Sayville, NY.
Good Samaritan Regional Health Center, [E], (BEL), Mount Vernon, IL.
Good Samaritan Regional Medical Center, [G], (ALN), Pottsville, PA.
Good Samaritan Regional Medical Center Auxiliary, [G], (ALN). See Good Samaritan Regional Medical Center.
Good Samaritan Village, [M], (MEM), Camden, TN.
Good Shepherd Association of Springfield Mass., [Q], (SPR), Springfield, MA.
Good Shepherd Catholic Regional Middle School, [H], (PRO), Woonsocket, RI.
Good Shepherd Center, [H], (BAL), Baltimore, MD.
Good Shepherd Center, [I], (SFS), Sioux Falls, SD.
Good Shepherd Center for Homeless Women, [U], (LA), Los Angeles, CA.
Good Shepherd Center for Homeless Women, [Y], (LA). See Catholic Charities of Los Angeles, Inc.
Good Shepherd Center, Inc., [H], (SFE), Albuquerque, NM.
Good Shepherd Center, Inc. of New Mexico, [N], (SFE), Albuquerque, NM.
Good Shepherd Convent, [G], (SLC), East Carbon City, UT.
Good Shepherd Corporation of Orlando, Inc., [G], (ORL), Orlando, FL.
Good Shepherd Counseling Center, [M], (ATL). See Good Shepherd Services.
The Good Shepherd Gracenter, [L], (SFR), San Francisco, CA.
Good Shepherd Home Health & Hospice Agency, Inc., [H], (CHL), Hayesville, NC.
Good Shepherd Manor, [E], (JOL), Momence, IL.
Good Shepherd Manor, [H], (SFE), Albuquerque, NM.
Good Shepherd Mother/Child Center, [Y], (LA). See Catholic Charities of Los Angeles, Inc.
Good Shepherd Neighborhood House, [EE], (PH), Philadelphia, PA.
Good Shepherd Nursing Home, [J], (MAN), Jaffrey, NH.
Good Shepherd Nursing Home, [I], (WH), Wheeling, WV.
Good Shepherd Outreach Center, [M], (ATL). See Good Shepherd Services.
Good Shepherd Programs, Inc., [W], (STL), St. Louis, MO.
Good Shepherd Provincialate, [R], (STL), Normandy, MO.
Good Shepherd Provincialate, [O], (WDC), Silver Spring, MD.
Good Shepherd Regional School, [D], (ALN), Minersville, PA.
Good Shepherd Residence, [G], (RVC). See St. Christopher-Ottilie Corp.
Good Shepherd Retreat Center, [I], (PAT), Morristown, NJ.
Good Shepherd Services, [M], (ATL), Atlanta, GA.
Good Shepherd Services, [O], (BRK), Brooklyn, NY.
Good Shepherd Services, [O], (NY), New York, NY.
Good Shepherd Volunteers, Saint Germaines Services, [Y], (BRK), Brooklyn, NY.
The Good Shepherd: Maria Droste Services, [K], (BO), Quincy, MA.
Good Shepherd-Marycrest Endowment Fund, [Z], (CLV), Cleveland, OH.
Gordon Technical High School, [D], (CHI), Chicago, IL.
Goshen Day Care, [N], (NY). See Pius XII Youth and Family Services.
Governmental Relations, [G], (CHI). See Catholic Charities of the Archdiocese of Chicago-Archdiocesan Offices.
Grace Day Home, [E], (SAC), Sacramento, CA.
Grace Institute, [G], (NY), New York, NY.
Grace Mansion Personal Care Residence of Holy Manor, [I], (ALN), Bethlehem, PA.
Graceville Health Center dba Holy Trinity Hospital and Grace Home, [B], (NU), Graceville, MN.
Graceville Missionary Benedictine Sisters, Inc., [F], (NU), Graceville, MN.
The Graduate School, [C], (CHI). See Loyola University-Chicago.
Graduate School of Arts and Sciences, [D], (BRK). See St. John's University.
Graduate School of Library and Information Science, [C], (CHI). See Dominican University (Formerly Rosary College).
Graduate School of Theology, School of Applied Theology, [A], (OAK), Oakland, CA.
Graduate Studies and Research, [D], (CIN). See The University of Dayton.
Grailville, [P], (CIN), Loveland, OH.
*Grampian Health Services, Inc., [I], (SCR), Williamsport, PA.
Grand Council, Catholic Ladies Relief Society of the Sacramento Diocese, [L], (SAC), Chico, CA.
Grand Forks Catholic Schools Association, [I], (FAR), Grand Forks, ND.
Grand Traverse Area Catholic Schools, [A], (GAY), Traverse City, MI.
Grand Valley Catholic Outreach, [H], (PBL), Grand Junction, CO.
Grand Valley Peace and Justice, [H], (PBL), Grand Junction, CO.
Grand Valley State University Catholic Campus Ministry, [K], (GR), Coopersville, MI.
Grande Apartments-Los Angeles, [R], (LA). See Brothers of John of God, Inc., The.
Graymoor Ecumenical and Interreligious Institute, [Z], (NY). See Franciscan Friars of the Atonement.
Great Adventures Social Club, [F], (CHL). See Holy Angels, Inc.
Great Bend Dominican Sisters Office of Mission and Ministry, [D], (DOD). See Immaculate Conception Convent.
Great Falls City-Wide Ministry to Native Americans, [K], (GF), Great Falls, MT.
The Greater Cleveland/Akron Corporation United for Education, [AA], (CLV), Cleveland, OH.
Greater Lansing Catholic Education Foundation (Lansing), [K], (LAN). See Chancery Office.
"The Greatest of These is Love" Fund, [L], (OKL). See Oklahoma Benedictine Institute on Mental Retardation, Inc.
Green Bay Area Catholic High School Foundation, L.T.D., [O], (GB), Green Bay, WI.
Greensburg Central Catholic High School, [C], (GBG), Greensburg, PA.
The Greenwalt Center for Alzheimer's Day Care and Research, [M], (NO), Kenner, LA.
Gregorian University Foundation, [W], (STL), St. Louis, MO.
Gregorian University Foundation, The, [DD], (NY), New York, NY.
Grey Nun Academy, [H], (PH), Yardley, PA.
Grey Nuns Adult Day Health Center, Inc., [S], (BO), Lexington, MA.
Grey Nuns of Montreal Residence, [J], (PRT), Lewiston, ME.
Grey Nuns of the Sacred Heart, [G], (OG), Watertown, NY.
Grey Nuns of the Sacred Heart, [AA], (PH), Philadelphia, PA.
Grey Nuns of the Sacred Heart, [AA], (PH), Bensalem, PA.
Grey Nuns of the Sacred Heart, [AA], (PH), Feasterville, PA.
Grey Nuns of the Sacred Heart, [AA], (PH), Jenkintown, PA.
Grey Nuns of the Sacred Heart, [AA], (PH), Newtown, PA.
Grey Nuns of the Sacred Heart (G.N.S.H.), [AA], (PH), Yardley, PA.
Grey Nuns Provincial House, [X], (BO), Lexington, MA.
Grief Care, [Q], (SFR). See Catholic Charities of the Archdiocese of San Francisco.
Grimes Foundation, [W], (SY), Syracuse, NY.
Grotto of the Redemption, [H], (SC), West Bend, IA.
The Grotto, The National Sanctuary of Our Sorrowful Mother, [L], (P), Portland, OR.
Group Home, [G], (RVC). See St. Christopher-Ottilie Corp.
Group Home After Care, [E], (PRT). See Catholic Charities Maine.
Group Home for Adolescent Boys, [I], (PRO), Providence, RI.
Group Homes, [N], (NY). See Pius XII Youth and Family Services.
Guadalupan Missionaries of the Holy Spirit, [I], (MIA), Miami, FL.
Guadalupanas Missionaries of the Holy Spirit, [S], (LA), Los Angeles, CA.
Guadalupe Area Social Services, [I], (GAL). See Associated Catholic Charities of the Diocese of Galveston-Houston.
Guadalupe Arms, [H], (ANC), Anchorage, AK.
The Guadalupe Center, [L], (VEN), Immokalee, FL.

H

HeartShare Human Services - Russo First Step Early Childhood Center, [O], (BRK). See HeartShare Human Services of New York, Roman Catholic Diocese of Brooklyn.
HeartShare Human Services - South Brooklyn Family Services, [O], (BRK). See HeartShare Human Services of New York, Roman Catholic Diocese of Brooklyn.
HeartShare Human Services - Surfside Beacon Program and Surfside Family Services, [O], (BRK). See HeartShare Human Services of New York, Roman Catholic Diocese of Brooklyn.
HeartShare Human Services - Thomas J. Cuite Residence, [O], (BRK). See HeartShare Human Services of New York, Roman Catholic Diocese of Brooklyn.
HeartShare Human Services of New York, Roman Catholic Diocese of Brooklyn, [O], (BRK), Brooklyn, NY.
The Heenan Spiritual Program for the Handicapped, Inc., [R], (SY), Yorkville, NY.
Heidelberg College Campus Ministry, [N], (TOL), Tiffin, OH.
The Heights School, [E], (WDC), Potomac, MD.
Heisey Memorial Trust Fund, [K], (GF), Great Falls, MT.
Heisey Memorial Youth Center, [K], (GF), Great Falls, MT.
Helen Clark Auxiliary, [P], (LA). See St. Anne's.
Helias High School, [B], (JC), Jefferson City, MO.
Helper's Club, Inc., [R], (LA). See Brothers of John of God, Inc., The.
Helpers Club of St. John of God, [CC], (LA). See Hospitaller Foundation of California, Inc., The.
Helping Hand Investments, Inc, [V], (HRT), Orange, CT.
Henderson State Teachers College and Ouchita Baptist University Campus Ministry, [J], (LR). See Catholic Campus Ministries.
Hennessy Charitable Trust, [O], (DUB), Dubuque, IA.
Henry J. Soenneker School, [C], (OWN), Owensboro, KY.
*Herald of Good News, Inc., [D], (LKC), Elton, LA.
Herbert H. Lehman College, [CC], (NY). See University Apostolate.
*Heritage College, [A], (YAK), Toppenish, WA.
Hermanas Catequistas Guadalupanas, [I], (FWT), Fort Worth, TX.
Hermanas Catequistas Guadalupanas Convent, [N], (SAT), San Antonio, TX.
Hermanas Contemplativas del Buen Pastor (H.B.P.), [K], (ELP), El Paso, TX.
Hermanas del Servicio Social, [K], (ELP), El Paso, TX.
Hermanas Dominicas de la Doctrinia Cristiana (O.P.), [K], (ELP), El Paso, TX.
Hermanas Josefinas - St. Charles Seminary, [K], (ELP), El Paso, TX.
Hermanas Missionaras del Corazon de Jesus, [O], (NEW), Newark, NJ.
Hermitage, [B], (TYL), Palestine, TX.
Hermitage of Christ the King, [N], (SR), Sebastopol, CA.
Hermitage of St. Joseph, [C], (B), Lemhi, ID.
Hermitage of the Trinity, [R], (MIL), Campbellsport, WI.
Hermits of Bethlehem of the Heart of Jesus, [I], (PAT), Chester, NJ.
Hermits of Jesus The Eternal Priest, [B], (SAM), North Brookfield, MA.
Hermits of Mt. Carmel, [F], (STU), Bloomingdale, OH.
Hermits of Mt. Carmel, [H], (SUP), Amery, WI.
Hermits of St. Mary of Carmel, H.S.M.C., [G], (WIN), Houston, MN.
Hermits of the Most Blessed Virgin Mary of Mount Carmel, [T], (STP), Lake Elmo, MN.
Hesed Community, [R], (OAK), Oakland, CA.
Hesed House, Inc., [J], (RCK), Aurora, IL.
Hesychia House of Prayer, [K], (LR), Shoal Creek, AR.
Hiawatha Hall, [E], (WIN). See St. Francis Community Programs of Minnesota, Inc.
Higgins Plaza, Inc., [K], (DEN). See Archdiocesan Housing Committee.
Highbridge Neighborhood Supported Housing Program, [K], (NY). See Beacon of Hope House.
Highland Catholic School, [H], (STP), St. Paul, MN.
Highland School, [D], (DAL), Irving, TX.
Highland School, [G], (DAL), Irving, TX.
Highwood Learning Center, [P], (PEO). See St. Augustine Community.
Hilbert College, [C], (BUF), Hamburg, NY.
Hill Camp, [X], (NY). See The Catholic Camp Association Inc.
Hill College Newman Center, [M], (FWT), Hillsboro, TX.
Hillcrest Health Center, Inc., [E], (OKL), Oklahoma City, OK.
Hill-Murray School, [E], (STP), St. Paul, MN.
Hinds Community College Catholic Student Organization, [G], (JKS), Raymond, MS.
Hispanic Catholic Center, [P], (GRY). See Hispanic Ministry Office.
Hispanic Catholic Charismatic Center of the Archdiocese of New York, [DD], (NY), New York, NY.
The Hispanic Child Guidance Clinic, [S], (HRT). See Catholic Charities-Catholic Family Services (Archdiocese of Hartford).
Hispanic Ministry of the Archdiocese of St. Louis, [W], (STL), St. Louis, MO.
Hispanic Ministry Office, [T], (BRK). See Catholic Migration & Refugee Office, Catholic Migration Services, Inc.
Hispanic Ministry Office, [P], (GRY), East Chicago, IN.
Hispanic Parishes: San Juan Bautista Parish, [X], (CLV). See Diocesan Hispanic Office.
Hispanic Senior Center, [V], (CLV). See Catholic Charities Services Corporation.
Hispanic Social Ministries of Fairfield County, Inc., [W], (BGP), Bridgeport, CT.
Hispanic Telecommunications Network, Inc., [T], (SAT), San Antonio, TX.
Historic Missions Restoration, Inc., [N], (ELP), El Paso, TX.
Historic St. Mary's Mission, [I], (HEL), Stevensville, MT.
Hitchcock Center/Boysville of Michigan, Inc., [O], (DET). See Boysville of Michigan, Inc.
HIV Direct Services, [Q], (SFR). See Catholic Charities of the Archdiocese of San Francisco.
HIV Food & Emergency Services, [Q], (SFR). See Catholic Charities of the Archdiocese of San Francisco.
HIV Housing Services, [Q], (SFR). See Catholic Charities of the Archdiocese of San Francisco.
HIV Money Management, [Q], (SFR). See Catholic Charities of the Archdiocese of San Francisco.
HIV Prison Project, [H], (OAK). See Catholic Charities of the Diocese of Oakland, Inc.
HIV/AIDS Ministry Team, [V], (CIN), Cincinnati, OH.
HIV/AIDS Services, [H], (OAK). See Catholic Charities of the Diocese of Oakland, Inc.
HM Health Services, [G], (Y), Youngstown, OH.
HM Health Services, St. Elizabeth Health Center, [G], (Y), Youngstown, OH.
Hmong Catholic Community, [Q], (DEN), Denver, CO.
Ho'omaluhia Community, [I], (HON). See Sisters of St. Joseph of Carondelet CSJ, Hawaii Vice-Province.
Hocking Technical College, [I], (STU), Nelsonville, OH.
Hogar Carmelitano, [E], (SJN), Rio Piedras, PR.
Hogar de Ancianos San Vicente, [B], (ARE), Arecibo, PR.
Hogar Infantil Jesus Nazareno, Inc., [B], (ARE), Isabela, P.R.
Hogar Santa Teresa Jornet for the Aged, [E], (SJN), Rio Piedras, PR.
Hogar Sta. Maria Eufrasia, [B], (ARE), Arecibo, PR.
Holbrook Center for Counseling and Psychotherapy, [G], (CHI). See Catholic Charities of the Archdiocese of Chicago-Archdiocesan Offices.
Holistic Spirituality and Wellness Center, [AA], (CLV). See Christa Center.
Holland House, [D], (SAG). See St. Vincent Home-Boysville of Michigan, Inc.
Hollidaysburg Consolidated Catholic Elementary School, [C], (ALT), Hollidaysburg, PA.
Hollybrook I & II, [J], (RIC), Richmond, VA.
Holmes Community College Newman Center, [G], (JKS), Lexington, MS.
Holy Angels, [G], (RIC), Richmond, VA.
Holy Angels Academy, Inc., [E], (L), Louisville, KY.
Holy Angels Convent, [G], (TUC), Globe, AZ.
Holy Angels Convent-Motherhouse, [I], (LR), Jonesboro, AR.
Holy Angels Elementary, [C], (OWN), Owensboro, KY.
Holy Angels Regional School, [E], (RVC), Patchogue, NY.
Holy Angels Residential Facility, [C], (SHP), Shreveport, LA.
*Holy Angels School Foundation, Inc., [I], (KAL), Sturgis, MI.
Holy Angels Specialized Community Residential Center, [F], (CHL). See Holy Angels, Inc.
Holy Angels' Academy, [D], (BUF), Buffalo, NY.
*Holy Angels, Inc., [F], (CHL), Belmont, NC.
Holy Annunciation Monastery, [C], (PSC), Sugarloaf, PA.
Holy Apostles College and Seminary, [A], (NOR), Cromwell, CT.
Holy Apostles Parish Conference, [E], (YAK), East Wenatchee, WA.
Holy Assumption School for the Blind, [I], (MIL), West Allis, WI.
Holy Child Convent, [AA], (PH), Drexel Hill, PA.
Holy Child Day Home, [C], (RNO), Reno, NV.
Holy Child Day Home, [G], (RNO), Reno, NV.
Holy Child Elementary School, [F], (SCR), Plymouth, PA.
Holy Child Infirmary, [AA], (PH), Rosemont, PA.
Holy Child Nursery, [C], (HBG), York, PA.
Holy Child School, [D], (ALN), Bethlehem, PA.
Holy Childhood Association, [L], (ROC), Rochester, NY.
Holy Childhood Association, [V], (WDC), Washington, DC.
Holy Childhood Nursery & Kindergarten, [I], (BO), Peabody, MA.
Holy Childhood Pontifical Association, [U], (SFR), San Francisco, CA.
Holy City Community, [C], (LKC), Lake Charles, LA.
Holy Cross, [G], (BRK), Flushing, NY.
Holy Cross, [J], (PRT), Lewiston, ME.
Holy Cross (Seminary) Diocesan Center, [I], (LC), La Crosse, WI.
Holy Cross Abbey, [E], (PBL), Canon City, CO.
Holy Cross Associates, [O], (FTW), Notre Dame, IN.
Holy Cross Brother Center, [J], (FTW), Notre Dame, IN.
Holy Cross Brothers, [M], (SAT). See Holy Cross Community.
Holy Cross Brothers Residence, [D], (BEA), Beaumont, TX.
Holy Cross Brothers, Eastern Province, Charitable Trust, [Z], (NY), New Rochelle, NY.
Holy Cross Camp Grounds, [O], (SPR), Goshen, MA.
Holy Cross Care Services dba Little Company of Mary Health Facility, Inc., [I], (GRY), San Pierre, IN.
Holy Cross Care Services, Inc., [O], (FTW), South Bend, IN.
Holy Cross Care Services, Inc. dba Northland Terrace Medical Center, [E], (COL), Columbus, OH.
Holy Cross Cemetery Trust, Inc., [Q], (L), Loretto, KY.
Holy Cross Center/Boysville of Michigan, Inc., [O], (DET). See Boysville of Michigan, Inc.
*Holy Cross Chapter of St. Vincent De Paul Food Pantry, Inc., [O], (IND), Indianapolis, IN.
Holy Cross College, [Q], (WOR). See Campus Ministry.
Holy Cross College, Holy Cross College, Inc., [B], (FTW), Notre Dame, IN.
Holy Cross Community, [M], (SAT), San Antonio, TX.
*Holy Cross Community and Academy, [A], (PSC), Miami, FL.
Holy Cross Community Services, Inc., [O], (FTW), South Bend, IN.
Holy Cross Community, Corby Hall, University of Notre Dame, [J], (FTW), Notre Dame, IN.
Holy Cross Congregation of Casa Santa Cruz, [F], (PHX), Phoenix, AZ.
Holy Cross Convent, [N], (HRT), New Britain, CT.
Holy Cross Convent, [M], (P), Portland, OR.
Holy Cross Convent, [J], (PRT), South Portland, ME.
Holy Cross Convent, [I], (SAC). See Institute of the Sisters of Mercy of the Americas.
Holy Cross Elementary School, [D], (ALN), New Philadelphia, PA.
Holy Cross Father & Brother, C.S.C. - University of Portland, [L], (P), Portland, OR.
Holy Cross Fathers, [M], (SAT). See Holy Cross Community.
Holy Cross Fathers Religious, [B], (FR), North Easton, MA.
Holy Cross Fathers Retreat House, [M], (FR), North Easton, MA.
Holy Cross Fathers, Eastern Priests Province, [F], (ORL), Cocoa Beach, FL.
Holy Cross Fathers-Holy Cross Center, [N], (OAK), Berkeley, CA.
Holy Cross Florida Regional Center, [G], (VEN), Sarasota, FL.
*Holy Cross Food Center, Inc., [F], (CHY), Casper, WY.
Holy Cross Geriatric Center, [E], (TUC). See Holy Cross Hospital, Inc.
Holy Cross Hall, [K], (FTW). See Saint Mary's of the Immaculate Conception.
Holy Cross Health Center, Inc., [O], (MAN), Manchester, NH.
Holy Cross Health System Corporation, [O], (FTW), South Bend, IN.
Holy Cross High School, [D], (CHI), River Grove, IL.
Holy Cross High School, [B], (COV), Covington, KY.
Holy Cross High School, [E], (HRT), Waterbury, CT.
Holy Cross High School, [B], (L), Louisville, KY.
Holy Cross High School, [D], (SAT), San Antonio, TX.
Holy Cross High School, [C], (SEA), Everett, WA.
Holy Cross High School, [B], (TR), Delran, NJ.
Holy Cross Hospital, [J], (CHI), Chicago, IL.
Holy Cross Hospital, [H], (DET), Detroit, MI.
Holy Cross Hospital, [B], (LIT), Chicago, IL.
Holy Cross Hospital, [G], (MIA), Fort Lauderdale, FL.
Holy Cross Hospital and Sisters of St. Casimir Foundation, [J], (CHI). See Holy Cross Hospital.
Holy Cross Hospital Convent, [O], (WDC). See Sisters of the Holy Cross.
Holy Cross Hospital of Silver Spring, Inc., [K], (WDC), Silver Spring, MD.
Holy Cross Hospital, Inc., [E], (TUC), Nogales, AZ.
Holy Cross Hospital, Inc., [E], (TUC). See Holy Cross Hospital, Inc.
Holy Cross House, [J], (FTW). See Congregation of Holy Cross Indiana Province Provincial House.
Holy Cross Housing dba Casa Santa Cruz, [M], (SP),

St. Petersburg, FL.
Holy Cross Kindergarten, [F], (MAN), Manchester, NH.
Holy Cross Middle School, [G], (LA), Los Angeles, CA.
Holy Cross Ministries, [D], (SLC), Murray, UT.
Holy Cross Mission House, [K], (FR), North Dartmouth, MA.
Holy Cross Mission House, [L], (FTW), Notre Dame, IN.
Holy Cross Novitiate, [E], (COS), Cascade, CO.
Holy Cross Parish, [J], (FTW). See Congregation of Holy Cross Indiana Province Provincial House.
Holy Cross Provincial Office, [D], (SUP), Merrill, WI.
Holy Cross Regional School, [A], (RIC), Lynchburg, VA.
Holy Cross Retreat and Friary, [D], (LSC), Mesilla Park, NM.
Holy Cross School, [H], (MIL), South Milwaukee, WI.
Holy Cross School, [F], (NO), New Orleans, LA.
Holy Cross School, [H], (NO), New Orleans, LA.
Holy Cross School/Clete and Claire Haney Memorial, [N], (OM). See The Omaha Archdiocesan Educational Foundation, Inc.
Holy Cross Seminary Education Fund Endowment Trust, [M], (LC), La Crosse, WI.
Holy Cross Seminary House of Formation, [A], (LC), La Crosse, WI.
Holy Cross Services Corp., [O], (FTW), Notre Dame, IN.
Holy Cross Sisters, [E], (STO), Stockton, CA.
Holy Dormition Monastery, [E], (PHU), Sybertsville, PA.
Holy Dormition Monastery, [B], (PSC), Sybertsville, PA.
The Holy Evangelists Friary, [N], (CHI), Chicago, IL.
Holy Face of Jesus Monastery, [M], (PAT), Clifton, NJ.
Holy Family, [J], (PRT), Lewiston, ME.
Holy Family (Middle) School, [C], (OWN), Owensboro, KY.
Holy Family Academy, [C], (MET), Bound Brook, NJ.
Holy Family Academy, [C], (NEW), Bayonne, NJ.
Holy Family Adoption Foundation, Inc., [N], (LA). See Holy Family Services, Adoption & Foster Care.
Holy Family Adult Day Care, [I], (ALN), Bethlehem, PA.
Holy Family Adult Day Care, [M], (ALN). See St. Francis Center.
Holy Family Adult Day Care at St. Francis Center, [I], (ALN), Orwigsburg, PA.
Holy Family Apartments, [I], (ALN), Bethlehem, PA.
Holy Family Apartments, [I], (ALN), New Philadelphia, PA.
Holy Family Catholic Consolidated School, [F], (DUB), Cedar Rapids, IA.
Holy Family Catholic School, [D], (COV), Covington, KY.
Holy Family Catholic School of Coeur d'Alene, [A], (B), Coeur d'Alene, ID.
Holy Family Catholic School System-Diocese of Rochester, [D], (ROC), Rochester, NY.
Holy Family Center, [P], (OAK), Pleasant Hill, CA.
Holy Family Center, [J], (PH). See The Catholic Social Services of the Archdiocese of Philadelphia.
Holy Family Center, Inc., [E], (TUC). See Carondelet Health Care Corporation of Arizona, Inc.
Holy Family Child Care Center, [S], (WH), Wheeling, WV.
Holy Family Church Inc., [X], (CHI), Chicago, IL.
Holy Family College, [C], (PH), Philadelphia, PA.
Holy Family Community, [Q], (PRO). See Franciscan Missionaries of Mary.
Holy Family Community, [M], (SR), Napa, CA.
Holy Family Convent, [E], (LAV), Las Vegas, NV.
Holy Family Convent, [Q], (PRO), North Kingstown, RI.
Holy Family Convent, [O], (SFR), South San Francisco, CA.
Holy Family Convent, [N], (SR), Crescent City, CA.
Holy Family Convent and Infirmary, [G], (HBG), Danville, PA.
Holy Family Convent of Franciscan Sisters of Christian Charity, [J], (GB), Manitowoc, WI.
Holy Family Day Care Center, [C], (LAV), Las Vegas, NV.
Holy Family Day Home, [I], (SFR), San Francisco, CA.
Holy Family Day Nursery and Convent, [J], (NEW), Nutley, NJ.
Holy Family Educational Foundation, [I], (BIR), Birmingham, AL.
Holy Family Emergency Shelter, [L], (IND), Indianapolis, IN.
Holy Family Endowment Trust Fund, [M], (LC), St. Mary's Ridge, WI.
Holy Family Foundation, [R], (PIT), Pittsburgh, PA.
Holy Family Friary, [N], (PIT), Avalon, PA.
Holy Family Hall Infirmary, [I], (DUB), Dubuque, IA.
Holy Family Health Center, [M], (CHI), Des Plaines, IL.
Holy Family Hermitage, [F], (STU), Bloomingdale, OH.
Holy Family High School, [B], (BIR), Birmingham, AL.
Holy Family High School, [C], (DEN), Denver, CO.
Holy Family Home, [R], (BRK), Brooklyn, NY.
Holy Family Home, [M], (BUF), Williamsville, NY.
Holy Family Home, [L], (CLV), Cleveland, OH.
Holy Family Home, [M], (COV), Melbourne, KY.
Holy Family Home, [X], (PH), Philadelphia, PA.
Holy Family Home, [G], (PT), Tallahassee, FL.
Holy Family Home and Shelter, Inc., [E], (NOR), Willimantic, CT.
Holy Family Home Health and Hospice Care, [H], (ALN), Orwigsburg, PA.
Holy Family Home Health Care, [M], (ALN). See St. Francis Center.
Holy Family Hospital, [D], (SC), Estherville, IA.
Holy Family Hospital, [G], (SPK), Spokane, WA.
Holy Family Hospital, [A], (SUP), New Richmond, WI.
Holy Family Hospital Adult Day Health, [G], (SPK), Spokane, WA.
Holy Family Hospital and Medical Center, [Q], (BO), Methuen, MA.
Holy Family Hospital Foundation, Inc., [DD], (BO), Methuen, MA.
Holy Family Hospital Foundation, Inc., [FF], (BO). See Valley Regional Health System, Inc.
Holy Family Hospital Foundation, Inc., [I], (SUP), New Richmond, WI.
Holy Family Hospital Foundation., [D], (SC). See Holy Family Hospital.
Holy Family Hospital Men's Guild, [R], (BO), Methuen, MA.
Holy Family Hospital Men's Guild, [FF], (BO), Methuen, MA.
Holy Family Hospital, Inc., [FF], (BO). See Valley Regional Health System, Inc.
Holy Family House Convent, S.S.J., [K], (ARL), Falls Church, VA.
Holy Family Institute, [I], (PIT), Emsworth, PA.
Holy Family Manor, [H], (ALN), Bethlehem, PA.
Holy Family Manor, [O], (PIT), Pittsburgh, PA.
Holy Family Medical Center, [J], (CHI), Des Plaines, IL.
Holy Family Memorial, Inc., [F], (GB), Manitowoc, WI.
Holy Family Middle School, [D], (LC), Marshfield, WI.
Holy Family Middle School, [B], (SAG), Bay City, MI.
Holy Family Monastery, [M], (E), Erie, PA.
Holy Family Monastery/Retreat, [M], (HRT), West Hartford, CT.
Holy Family Monastery/Retreat, [N], (HRT), West Hartford, CT.
Holy Family Motherhouse, [G], (NOR), Baltic, CT.
Holy Family Parish Conference, [E], (YAK), Yakima, WA.
Holy Family Plaza, Inc., [K], (DEN). See Archdiocesan Housing Committee.
Holy Family Priory, [Q], (MIL), Benet Lake, WI.
Holy Family Regional School, [F], (DET), Rochester, MI.
Holy Family Regional School, [E], (RVC), Commack, NY.
Holy Family Regional School Foundation, [I], (BIR), Huntsville, AL.
Holy Family Residence, [I], (ALN), Orwigsburg, PA.
Holy Family Residence, [M], (ALN). See St. Francis Center.
Holy Family Residence, [L], (PAT), West Paterson, NJ.
Holy Family Residence, [M], (STP), St. Paul, MN.
Holy Family Retreat Center, [F], (BEA), Beaumont, TX.
Holy Family Retreat House, [Q], (HRT), Farmington, CT.
Holy Family Retreat House, [O], (RIC), Hampton, VA.
Holy Family School, [D], (ALN), Frackville, PA.
Holy Family School, [B], (CC), Corpus Christi, TX.
Holy Family School, [C], (LAF), Lafayette, LA.
Holy Family School, [C], (PCE), Ponce, PR.
Holy Family School, [E], (SCL), Sauk Centre, MN.
Holy Family School, [D], (SEA), Lacey, WA.
Holy Family School, [G], (SY), Norwich, NY.
Holy Family School, [C], (TLS), Tulsa, OK.
Holy Family School Endowment Fund, Inc., [B], (MAR), Sault Ste. Marie, MI.
Holy Family Seminary, [B], (WDC), Silver Spring, MD.
Holy Family Services, Adoption & Foster Care, [N], (LA), Pasadena, CA.
Holy Family Services, Adoption and Foster Care, [G], (ORG), Santa Ana, CA.
Holy Family Services-Birth Center, [I], (BWN), Weslaco, TX.
Holy Family Sisters, [O], (OAK), Pleasant Hill, CA.
Holy Family Sisters, [E], (STO), Stockton, CA.
Holy Family Soup Kitchen, [I], (SAV), Columbus, GA.
Holy Family Spiritual Renewal Center, [H], (SCR), Nanticoke, PA.
Holy Family Villa, [J], (ALN), Bethlehem, PA.
Holy Family Villa, [M], (CHI), Lemont, IL.
Holy Family Villa, [C], (LIT), Lemont, IL.
Holy Family, Seaside Convent, [M], (CAM), Ventnor, NJ.
Holy Ghost, [D], (LC). See Chippewa Area Catholic Schools.
Holy Ghost Animation Center, [P], (PIT), Bethel Park, PA.
Holy Ghost Educational Endowment, [N], (OM). See The Omaha Archdiocesan Educational Foundation, Inc.
Holy Ghost Fathers, [B], (GAL), Houston, TX.
Holy Ghost Fathers, [Z], (PH), Philadelphia, PA.
Holy Ghost Fathers, [E], (SB), Hemet, CA.
Holy Ghost Fathers and Brothers Provincialate, [N], (PIT), Bethel Park, PA.
Holy Ghost Fathers Development Office, [B], (WDC), Wheaton, MD.
Holy Ghost Fathers Home, Maison Brothier, [F], (ALX), Natchitoches, LA.
Holy Ghost Fathers of Ireland, [U], (BRK), Long Island City, NY.
Holy Ghost Preparatory School, [G], (PH), Bensalem, PA.
Holy Heart of Mary Novitiate, [I], (RCK), Batavia, IL.
Holy Hill National Shrine of Mary Help of Christians, [P], (MIL). See Discalced Carmelite Monastery.
Holy Infant Apartments, Inc., [I], (STL). See Cardinal Ritter Institute.
Holy Infant Jesus School, [E], (MAN), Nashua, NH.
Holy Innocents Day Care Center, [N], (BUF), Buffalo, NY.
Holy Innocents Foundation, [DD], (NY), Riverdale, NY.
Holy Innocents House, [N], (HRT). See Sisters of Notre Dame de Namur.
Holy Innocents' Adult and Family Services, [E], (PRT). See Catholic Charities Maine.
Holy Land Convent, [N], (HRT), Waterbury, CT.
Holy Martyrs of Vietnam Church Child Enrichment Day Care Center, [H], (ARL), Arlington, VA.
Holy Name, [M], (ALB), Albany, NY.
Holy Name, [D], (LC). See Wausau Area Catholic Schools.
Holy Name Academy Child Care Center dba Bendictine Sisters of Florida, [F], (SP), San Antonio, FL.
Holy Name Catholic Center, Inc., [I], (MAD), Madison, WI.
Holy Name Central Catholic High School, [C], (WOR), Worcester, MA.
Holy Name Central Endowment Fund, Inc., [B], (MAR), Escanaba, MI.
Holy Name Central Grade School, [A], (MAR), Escanaba, MI.
Holy Name College, [B], (WDC), Silver Spring, MD.
Holy Name Friary, [M], (PAT), Ringwood, NJ.
Holy Name Friary-Franciscan House of Formation, [N], (CHI), Chicago, IL.
Holy Name Health Care Foundation, [S], (NEW), Teaneck, NJ.
Holy Name High School, [C], (ALN), Reading, PA.
Holy Name High School, [D], (CLV), Cleveland, OH.
Holy Name High School, [E], (OAK), Oakland, CA.
Holy Name Hospital, [G], (NEW), Teaneck, NJ.
Holy Name Housing Corp., [O], (OM), Omaha, NE.
Holy Name Loaves and Fishes Community Meal, [L], (NSH), Nashville, TN.
Holy Name Monastery, [P], (SP), St. Leo, FL.
Holy Name of Jesus Hospital Trust, [I], (BIR), Birmingham, AL.
Holy Name Priory, Dominican Friars, [Z], (PH), Philadelphia, PA.
Holy Name Retreat Center, [S], (GAL), Houston, TX.
Holy Name Retreat House, [M], (GB), Chambers Island, WI.
Holy Name Scholarship Foundation, [B], (MAR). See Holy Name Central Endowment Fund, Inc.
Holy Name Society, [Q], (BAL), Baltimore, MD.
Holy Name Society, [P], (DAL), Ferris, TX.
Holy Name Society, [J], (STU), Steubenville, OH.
Holy Names Academy, [C], (SEA), Seattle, WA.
Holy Names College, [B], (OAK), Oakland, CA.
Holy Names College, [G], (OAK), Oakland, CA.
Holy Names College Campus Ministry, [Q], (OAK), Oakland, CA.
Holy Names Foundation, [L], (SPK), Spokane, WA.
Holy Names Music Center, [O], (SPK), Spokane, WA.
Holy Names Preschool & After School Program, [G], (MEM), Memphis, TN.
Holy Names Sisters, [O], (OAK), Oakland, CA.
Holy Names Sisters, [O], (OAK), Hayward, CA.
Holy Names Sisters, [O], (OAK), Kensington, CA.
Holy Names Sisters, [O], (OAK), San Leandro, CA.
Holy Nativity Monastery, [B], (RC), Bethlehem, SD.
Holy Nativity Monastery, [C], (SAM), Bethlehem, SD.
Holy Redeemer College, [M], (WDC), Washington, DC.
Holy Redeemer Educational Trust Fund (Holy Redeemer Parish, Burton), [K], (LAN). See Chancery Office.
Holy Redeemer Foundation, [T], (PH), Huntingdon Valley, PA.
*Holy Redeemer Health System, Inc., [EE], (PH), Huntingdon Valley, PA.

Holy Redeemer Hospital and Medical Center, [T], (PH), Meadowbrook, PA.
*Holy Redeemer Multi-Care, Inc., [EE], (PH), Swainton, NJ.
Holy Redeemer Parish Conference, [E], (YAK), Yakima, WA.
*Holy Redeemer Physician Services, [EE], (PH), Huntingdon Valley, PA.
*Holy Redeemer Physician Services, [EE], (PH), Philadelphia, PA.
Holy Redeemer Rehabilitation Center, [I], (CAM), Cape May, NJ.
Holy Redeemer Rehabilitation Center, [S], (TR). See Holy Redeemer Visiting Nurse Agency, Inc.
Holy Redeemer Retreat and Conference Center, [N], (OAK). See Redemptorists.
*Holy Redeemer Support Services, [V], (PH). See Holy Redeemer, Nazareth & St. Mary Home Health Services.
Holy Redeemer Visiting Nurse Agency, Inc., [I], (CAM), Swainton, NJ.
*Holy Redeemer Visiting Nurse Agency, Inc., [EE], (PH), Swainton, NJ.
Holy Redeemer Visiting Nurse Agency, Inc., [S], (TR), Swainton, NJ.
*Holy Redeemer, Nazareth & St. Mary Home Health Services, [V], (PH), Philadelphia, PA.
Holy Resurrection Monastery, [A], (VNN), Newberry Springs, CA.
Holy Rosary Academy, [B], (ANC), Anchorage, AK.
Holy Rosary Academy, [C], (L), Louisville, KY.
Holy Rosary Academy, [E], (NEW), Union City, NJ.
Holy Rosary Academy, [I], (NO), New Orleans, LA.
Holy Rosary Catholic School "Vision 2000" Educational Trust Fund, [L], (LR), Stuttgart, AR.
Holy Rosary Child Care Center, [G], (RIC), Richmond, VA.
Holy Rosary Convent, [F], (JKS), Philadelphia, MS.
Holy Rosary Convent, [O], (NEW), Jersey City, NJ.
Holy Rosary Convent, [N], (SAT), San Antonio, TX.
Holy Rosary Elementary, [B], (GAY), Cedar, MI.
Holy Rosary Health Center, [G], (GF), Miles City, MT.
Holy Rosary Institute, [M], (LAF), Lafayette, LA.
Holy Rosary Marianist Community, [M], (SAT), San Antonio, TX.
Holy Rosary Medical Center, [A], (BAK), Ontario, OR.
Holy Rosary Parish Endowment Fund, [G], (DUL), Duluth, MN.
Holy Rosary Parish, R.E. Program, [B], (CR), Detroit Lakes, MN.
Holy Rosary Priory, [L], (P), Portland, OR.
Holy Rosary School, [C], (WIN). See Mankato Area Catholic Schools.
Holy Rosary Villa, [O], (NEW), Union City, NJ.
Holy Savior Menard Central, [A], (ALX), Alexandria, LA.
Holy Shroud Guild, [DD], (NY), Esopus, NY.
Holy Spirit Academy, [F], (SCR), Hazleton, PA.
Holy Spirit Campus, [C], (MET), Perth Amboy, NJ.
Holy Spirit Central School Educational Fund, [A], (MAR), Norway, MI.
Holy Spirit Central School Educational Fund, [B], (MAR), Norway, MI.
Holy Spirit Community, [L], (SPK), Spokane, WA.
Holy Spirit Consolidated School, [B], (HBG), Mount Carmel, PA.
Holy Spirit Convent, [G], (OG), Tupper Lake, NY.
Holy Spirit Convent, [L], (PRO), Providence, RI.
Holy Spirit Convent, [F], (R), Jacksonville, NC.
Holy Spirit Convent, [I], (SAC). See Institute of the Sisters of Mercy of the Americas.
Holy Spirit Convent, Daughters of the Holy Spirit, [P], (BGP), Bridgeport, CT.
Holy Spirit Elementary School, [D], (COV), Newport, KY.
Holy Spirit Friary, [D], (CHI). See Hales Franciscan High School, Inc.
The Holy Spirit Health Care Center, Inc., [M], (NOR), Putnam, CT.
Holy Spirit Hermitage, [G], (WH), Old Fields, WV.
Holy Spirit High School, [A], (BIR), Tuscaloosa, AL.
Holy Spirit High School, [A], (CAM), Absecon, NJ.
Holy Spirit Hospital and Community Mental Health Center, [F], (HBG), Camp Hill, PA.
Holy Spirit Junior High School, [D], (COV), Newport, KY.
Holy Spirit Missionary Cenacle, [I], (MOB), Dothan, AL.
Holy Spirit Missionary Cenacle, [M], (PAT), Stirling, NJ.
Holy Spirit Missionary Cenacle, [M], (WDC), Riverdale, MD.
Holy Spirit Missonary Cenacle, [Z], (PH), Philadelphia, PA.
Holy Spirit Monastery, [F], (STU), Steubenville, OH.
Holy Spirit Motherhouse, [N], (SAT), San Antonio, TX.
Holy Spirit Newman Center, [F], (CR), Bemidji, MN.
Holy Spirit Parish, University of California, Newman Hall, [Q], (OAK), Berkeley, CA.
Holy Spirit Provincial House, [G], (NOR), Putnam, CT.
Holy Spirit Regional School Foundation, [I], (BIR), Huntsville, AL.
Holy Spirit Retirement Home, [E], (SC), Sioux City, IA.
Holy Spirit Retirement Home Foundation, Inc., [H], (SC), Sioux City, IA.
Holy Spirit Retreat and Conference Center, [G], (CC), Laredo, TX.
Holy Spirit Retreat Center, [W], (LA), Encino, CA.
Holy Spirit Retreat House, [G], (ANC), Anchorage, AK.
Holy Spirit Retreat House, [I], (ANC), Anchorage, AK.
Holy Spirit School, [D], (ALN), Allentown, PA.
Holy Spirit School, [C], (WIN). See Rochester Catholic Schools.
Holy Spirit School of Tuscaloosa Endowment Foundation, [I], (BIR), Tuscaloosa, AL.
Holy Spirit Sisters Charitable Trust, [I], (SAG), Saginaw, MI.
Holy Spirit Trust, [S], (SAT), San Antonio, TX.
Holy Spirit/Rego Park, [L], (BRK). See Catholic Charities.
Holy Transfiguration Monastery, [A], (STN), Redwood Valley, CA.
Holy Trinity, [E], (MAN), Laconia, NH.
Holy Trinity, [C], (RVC), Hicksville, NY.
Holy Trinity, [D], (TOL), Swanton, OH.
Holy Trinity Catholic, [D], (GBG), Mount Pleasant, PA.
Holy Trinity Catholic Church Endowment Trust, [M], (LC), La Crosse, WI.
Holy Trinity Catholic Mission School, [G], (DAV), Davenport, IA.
Holy Trinity Catholic School, [G], (CIN), Springfield, OH.
Holy Trinity Catholic School, [C], (FWT), Grapevine, TX.
Holy Trinity Community, [I], (HON). See Sisters of St. Joseph of Carondelet CSJ, Hawaii Vice-Province.
Holy Trinity Convent, [N], (HRT), Wallingford, CT.
Holy Trinity Convent, [N], (PAT), Stirling, NJ.
Holy Trinity Friary, [M], (DEN), Denver, CO.
Holy Trinity High School, [D], (CHI), Chicago, IL.
Holy Trinity Manor, [B], (CHY), Cheyenne, WY.
Holy Trinity Middle School, [D], (CHL). See Mecklenburg Area Catholic Schools (M.A.C.S.).
Holy Trinity Middle School, [A], (NU). See New Ulm Area Catholic Schools.
Holy Trinity Mission Seminary (1926), [B], (WDC), Silver Spring, MD.
Holy Trinity Missionary Cenacle, [M], (WDC), University Park, MD.
Holy Trinity Monastery, [M], (BAL), Baltimore, MD.
Holy Trinity Monastery, [D], (PBR), Butler, PA.
Holy Trinity Monastery, [F], (TUC), St. David, AZ.
Holy Trinity Parish Endowment, [N], (OM). See The Omaha Archdiocesan Educational Foundation, Inc.
Holy Trinity Place - Adult Day Care Center, [L], (IND), Indianapolis, IN.
Holy Trinity School, [E], (SCL), Pierz, MN.
Holy Trinity Seminary, [A], (DAL), Irving, TX.
Holy Trinity Spiritual Center, [L], (BAL), Baltimore, MD.
Holy Trinity Student Chapel, [J], (LAN), Ypsilanti, MI.
Holy Trinity-Sacred Heart Consolidation, [F], (DUB), Dubuque, IA.
Holy Union Provincialate, [L], (FR), Fall River, MA.
Holyoke Catholic High School, [C], (SPR), Holyoke, MA.
Hombre Nueva (RI), Inc., [T], (PRO), South Kingston, RI.
Hombre Nuevo, [CC], (LA), El Monte, CA.
Home Care Services, [H], (BUF). See The Catholic Charities of the Diocese of Buffalo.
Home Care Services, [H], (WOR). See Catholic Charities.
Home for Aged and Infirm, [D], (PCE), Ponce, PR.
Home for Aged of the Little Sisters of the Poor, Holy Family Residence, [L], (SCR), Scranton, PA.
The Home for the Aged of the Little Sisters of the Poor, [K], (HRT), Enfield, CT.
Home for the Aged of the Little Sisters of the Poor, [L], (PIT), Pittsburgh, PA.
Home for the Aged of the Little Sisters of the Poor, [K], (SFR), San Francisco, CA.
Home Integration Program, [L], (OKL). See Oklahoma Benedictine Institute on Mental Retardation, Inc.
Home of Divine Providence, [D], (PHU), Philadelphia, PA.
Home of Divine Providence, Inc.-Bayard House, [F], (WIL), Wilmington, DE.
Home of the Daughters of Charity, [G], (SLC), Price, UT.
Home of the Good Shepherd, [L], (STP), St. Paul, MN.
Home on the Range, [F], (BIS), Sentinel Butte, ND.
Home Start Program, [L], (OKL). See Oklahoma Benedictine Institute on Mental Retardation, Inc.
Homeless Haven (Transitional Housing Program), [L], (SAC). See Catholic Charities of Sacramento, Inc.
Homeless Service Center, [E], (SR). See Diocese of Santa Rosa, Catholic Charities.
Homeless Services, [H], (SFR). See San Mateo County District Council.
Homemaker-Companion Program, [B], (STO). See The Catholic Charities of the Diocese of Stockton.
Homes Again Program, [Q], (DEN). See Mercy Housing, Inc.
Homes for Hope Foundation, [T], (PRO). See Miscellaneous Listings for the Diocese of Providence.
Homes of Hope, Inc., [P], (PEO), Bloomington, IL.
Hood College, [O], (BAL). See Archdiocesan Office-Newman Center.
Hoosier Boys' Town, [H], (GRY), Schererville, IN.
Hope Community of Hicksville, Inc., [R], (RVC), Hicksville, NY.
The Hope Guild, [K], (LA). See Saint John's Hospital and Health Center.
Hope Haven Center, [I], (NO), Marrero, LA.
Hope Haven Center, [K], (NO), Marrero, LA.
HOPE House, [E], (HBG). See Department for Catholic Charities Counseling/Field Services.
Hope House, [J], (SPC), Springfield, MO.
Hope in Youth, [Y], (LA). See Catholic Charities of Los Angeles, Inc.
Hope Manor, [O], (TOL), Toledo, OH.
Hope Nursing Home, Inc., [N], (MIL), Lomira, WI.
Hope of Buffalo, Inc., [T], (BUF), Buffalo, NY.
Hope Rural School, [C], (PMB), Indiantown, FL.
Hope, Faith & Love, Inc., [J], (CC), Corpus Christi, TX.
Horizons Institute, Inc., [V], (HRT), Orange, CT.
Horizons Institute, Inc., [V], (HRT), Hamden, CT.
Hospice, [H], (ALB). See Mercycare Corporation, St. Peter's Hospital.
Hospice of Peace, [J], (DEN), Denver, CO.
Hospice of Rensselaer Co., [H], (ALB). See Mercycare Corporation, St. Peter's Hospital.
Hospital and Health Services Liaison, [U], (SFR), Mountain View, CA.
Hospital de Diego, [D], (SJN), Santurce, PR.
Hospital del Maestro, [D], (SJN), Rio Piedras, PR.
Hospital of St. Raphael, [I], (HRT), New Haven, CT.
Hospital of the Immaculate Conception, [A], (MGZ), San German, PR.
Hospital Sisters Health Care-West, Inc., [P], (LC), Eau Claire, WI.
Hospital Sisters Health System, [N], (SFD), Springfield, IL.
Hospital Sisters of St. Francis, [H], (BEL), Belleville, IL.
Hospital Sisters of St. Francis Foundation, Inc., [N], (SFD), Springfield, IL.
Hospital Sisters of the Third Order of St. Francis, [O], (CHI), Alsip, IL.
Hospital Sisters of the Third Order of St. Francis, [J], (GB), Green Bay, WI.
Hospital Sisters of the Third Order of St. Francis, [Q], (MIL), Sheboygan, WI.
Hospital Sisters Services, Inc., [N], (SFD), Springfield, IL.
Hospitaler Sisters of Mercy Novitiate, [M], (CAM), Pleasantville, NJ.
Hospitality Center, Inc., [G], (BEA), Port Arthur, TX.
Hospitality House, [D], (LAN). See Shelter of Flint, Inc.
Hospitality House Therapeutic Community Inc., [Q], (ALB), Albany, NY.
Hospitaller Brothers Healthcare, Inc., [R], (LA). See Brothers of John of God, Inc., The.
Hospitaller Brothers of St. John of God, [R], (LA), Los Angeles, CA.
Hospitaller Brothers St. John of God, [E], (SB), Victorville, CA.
Hospitaller Foundation of California, Inc., [R], (LA). See Brothers of John of God, Inc., The.
Hospitaller Foundation of California, Inc., The, [CC], (LA), Los Angeles, CA.
Hospitaller Order of St. John of God, [L], (CAM), Westville Grove, NJ.
Hostos Community College, [CC], (NY). See University Apostolate.
House of Charity, [H], (SPK), Spokane, WA.
House of Discernment, [J], (PRT), Lewiston, ME.
House of Formation, [R], (LA). See Missionaries of Charity Brothers.
House of Formation, [J], (PRT), Portland, ME.
House of Joseph II, [F], (WIL). See Ministry of Caring, Inc.
House of Joseph Transitional Residence, [F], (WIL). See Ministry of Caring, Inc.
House of Loreto, [I], (Y), Canton, OH.
The House of Mary Shrine, Inc., [I], (SFS), Yankton, SD.
House of Mercy - Affiliate of Catholic Health Initiatives, [E], (DM), Des Moines, IA.
House of Mercy, Inc., [Q], (CHL), Belmont, NC.
House of Nazareth (Casa Nazaret), [L], (ALN), Reading, PA.
House of Nazareth Life Institute Ltd. (Nazareth Life Center), [DD], (NY), Garrison, NY.

House of Peace, [Y], (MIL), Milwaukee, WI.
House of Peace & Education, Inc., [R], (WOR), Gardner, MA.
House of Peace, Inc., [DD], (NY), New York, NY.
House of Prayer, [E], (FBK), Fairbanks, AK.
House of Prayer for Priests, [I], (OKL), Oklahoma City, OK.
House of Prayer for Priests, [K], (ORG), Orange, CA.
House of Providence, [L], (SY), Syracuse, NY.
House of Religious Men: Divine Word Theologate, [N], (CHI). See Society of the Divine Word, Provincial Headquarter-Chicago Prov.
House of the Good Shepherd, [L], (CHI), Chicago, IL.
House of the Good Shepherd of Columbus, [I], (COL), Columbus, OH.
House of the Good Shepherd of Providence, [T], (PRO). See Miscellaneous Listings for the Diocese of Providence.
House of the Holy Family School, [I], (NO), New Orleans, LA.
House of the Holy Innocents, Inc., [P], (RVC), Mount Sinai, NY.
House of the Holy Shroud, [H], (GAY), Prescott, MI.
House of the Lord Retreat Center, Inc., [M], (SPK), Tum Tum, WA.
House of Theological Studies and Provincialate, [W], (BO), Milton, MA.
House of Welcome, [I], (GBG), Greensburg, PA.
Household Exchange, [L], (IND). See Catholic Charities.
Housing and Supportive Services, [H], (BUF). See The Catholic Charities of the Diocese of Buffalo.
The Housing Fund of the Archdiocese of New York, [DD], (NY), New York, NY.
Housing Services, [H], (OAK). See Catholic Charities of the Diocese of Oakland, Inc.
Housing Services, [H], (RVC). See Catholic Charities Central Administration.
Howard Univ. Newman Center, [S], (WDC). See Archdiocesan Campus Ministry.
Howells Community Catholic School, [D], (OM), Howells, NE.
HRH Management Corporation, [T], (PH), Huntingdon Valley, PA.
Hudson Catholic High School, [D], (NEW), Jersey City, NJ.
Hudson Day Care Center (Hudson), [E], (SUP). See Catholic Charities Bureau, Inc.
Hudson Valley Community College, [S], (ALB), Troy, NY.
The Human Life and Development Fund of the Diocese of Duluth, [G], (DUL), Duluth, MN.
Human Life International, [V], (WDC), Front Royale, VA.
Human Resources, [G], (CHI). See Catholic Charities of the Archdiocese of Chicago-Archdiocesan Offices.
Human Services, [H], (RVC). See Catholic Charities Central Administration.
Human Services Division/Pierre Toussaint Haitian Catholic Center, Inc., [M], (MIA), Miami, FL.
Humility Convent, [N], (DAV), Davenport, IA.
Humility of Mary Center-Motherhouse of the Congregation of the Humility of Mary, [N], (DAV), Davenport, IA.
Humility of Mary Health Care Corporation, [AA], (CLV), Middleburg Heights, OH.
Humility of Mary Housing, Inc., [AA], (CLV), Akron, OH.
Humility of Mary Information Systems, Inc., [P], (Y), Youngstown, OH.
Humility of Mary Novitiate, [N], (DAV), Davenport, IA.
Hungarian Catholic League of America, Inc., [DD], (NY), New York, NY.
Hunger, Inc., [N], (SFD), Springfield, IL.
Hunter/Baruch College, [CC], (NY). See University Apostolate.
Hunterdon County Services, [E], (MET), Flemington, NJ.
Huntington College Newman Center, [K], (MOB), Montgomery, AL.
Hurley Manor I, [G], (STA). See Jacksonville, Family Housing Management Co.
Hurley Manor II, [G], (STA). See Jacksonville, Family Housing Management Co.
Huron House/Boysville of Michigan, Inc., [E], (GAY), Alpena, MI.

I

I'm Home Alone, [E], (SR). See Diocese of Santa Rosa, Catholic Charities.
I.H.M. Congregation Charitable Trust, [R], (SCR), Scranton, PA.
Idaho State University, St. John's Community, [F], (B), Pocatello, ID.
Idente Missionaries of Santa Maria Residence, [Z], (NY), Bronx, NY.
Iglesia de San Juan Bautista, [J], (HBG), Lancaster, PA.
Ignatian Lay Volunteer Corps, [Q], (BAL), Baltimore, MD.
Ignatius House, [K], (ATL), Atlanta, GA.
Ignatius House, The Novitiate of the California Province, Society of Jesus, [R], (LA), Culver City, CA.
Ignatius Residence, [P], (NO), New Orleans, LA.
IHM Center for Literacy and GED Programs, [EE], (PH), Philadelphia, PA.
IHM/St. Luke's Consolidated School, [H], (STP), St. Paul, MN.
III Order of St. Dominic, [N], (SEA), Tacoma, WA.
Il Ritiro-The Little Retreat, [T], (STL), Dittmer, MO.
Illinois College Newman Center, [M], (SFD), Jacksonville IL.
Immacolata Manor Foundation, [H], (KC), Liberty, MO.
Immacolata Retreat Center, [O], (KC), Kansas City, MO.
Immaculata Academy, [D], (BUF), Hamburg, NY.
Immaculata College, [C], (PH), Immaculata, PA.
Immaculata Congretional Home, [O], (CHI), Bartlett, IL.
Immaculata Convent, [L], (OM), Norfolk, NE.
Immaculata Hall Convent, [K], (FTW). See Saint Mary's of the Immaculate Conception.
Immaculata High School, [B], (KCK), Leavenworth, KS.
Immaculata High School, [E], (NO), Marrero, LA.
Immaculata Retreat House, [I], (NOR), Willimantic, CT.
Immaculate Care Preschool, [G], (SCR), Scranton, PA.
Immaculate Conception Academy, [E], (PRO), Greenville, RI.
Immaculate Conception Academy, (Girls), [E], (SFR), San Francisco, CA.
Immaculate Conception Apostolic School, [A], (MAN), Center Harbor, NH.
Immaculate Conception Cathedral Middle and High School, [C], (MEM), Memphis, TN.
Immaculate Conception Catholic School, [C], (FWT), Denton, TX.
Immaculate Conception Convent, [X], (BO), Boston, MA.
Immaculate Conception Convent, [P], (BUF), Belmont, NY.
Immaculate Conception Convent, [P], (BUF), Hamburg, NY.
Immaculate Conception Convent, [D], (DOD), Great Bend, KS.
Immaculate Conception Convent, [D], (FBK), Fairbanks, AK.
Immaculate Conception Convent, [O], (NEW), Irvington, NJ.
Immaculate Conception Convent, [O], (NEW), Lodi, NJ.
Immaculate Conception Convent, [N], (PEO), Peoria, IL.
Immaculate Conception Convent, [G], (TUC), Yuma, AZ.
Immaculate Conception Convent, Spiritual Renewal Center and Novitiate, [G], (NOR), Putnam, CT.
Immaculate Conception Friary, [Z], (NY), New York, NY.
Immaculate Conception Friary, [P], (STL), Arnold, MO.
Immaculate Conception Grade School, [B], (FBK), Fairbanks, AK.
Immaculate Conception High School, [C], (NEW), Lodi, NJ.
Immaculate Conception Home for Girls, [P], (LA), Los Angeles, CA.
Immaculate Conception Kindergarten and Nursery, [J], (SAT), San Antonio, TX.
Immaculate Conception Middle School, [A], (GAY), Traverse City, MI.
Immaculate Conception Monastery, [U], (BRK), Jamaica, NY.
Immaculate Conception Monastery, [N], (CHI), Chicago, IL.
Immaculate Conception Monastery Passionist Nuns, [R], (STL), Ellisville, MO.
Immaculate Conception Pastoral Center, [A], (BRK), Douglaston, NY.
Immaculate Conception Pre-Kindergarten, [E], (PEO), Peoria, IL.
Immaculate Conception Pre-School, [F], (SP), St. Petersburg, FL.
Immaculate Conception Priory, [I], (LC), St. Mary's Ridge, WI.
Immaculate Conception Priory of the Canons Regular of Premontre, [I], (WIL), Claymont, DE.
Immaculate Conception Prov. House and Novitiate of the Dominican Sisters, [O], (CHI), Justice, IL.
Immaculate Conception Provincialate, [X], (BO), Newton, MA.
Immaculate Conception Provincialate, [F], (STF), Sloatsburg, NY.
Immaculate Conception Rectory, [M], (HRT). See Missionaries of LaSalette Provincial Secretary.
Immaculate Conception Rectory, [M], (HRT), Waterbury, CT.
Immaculate Conception Regional School, [D], (CAM), Bridgeton, NJ.
Immaculate Conception Regional School, [F], (PAT), Franklin, NJ.
Immaculate Conception School, [D], (ALN), Pen Argyl, PA.
Immaculate Conception School, [C], (GLP), Cuba, NM.
Immaculate Conception School Endowment-Heine Memorial, [N], (OM). See The Omaha Archdiocesan Educational Foundation, Inc.
Immaculate Conception School Foundation, Inc., [I], (SFS), Watertown, SD.
Immaculate Conception Seminary, [A], (NEW), South Orange, NJ.
Immaculate Conception Trust Fund, [L], (LR), Blytheville, AR.
Immaculate Conception-St. Joseph School, [F], (DUB), Gilbertville, IA.
Immaculate Heart Academy, [D], (NEW), Washington Township, NJ.
Immaculate Heart Academy, [C], (TUC), Tucson, AZ.
Immaculate Heart Central High School, [C], (OG), Watertown, NY.
Immaculate Heart Claretian Seminary, [B], (SAT), San Antonio, TX.
Immaculate Heart Convent, [AA], (PH), Philadelphia, PA.
Immaculate Heart Convent, [AA], (PH), Norristown, PA.
Immaculate Heart Elementary School, [D], (ALN), Girardville, PA.
Immaculate Heart High School, [F], (LA), Los Angeles, CA.
Immaculate Heart High School, [B], (TUC), Tucson, AZ.
Immaculate Heart Lodge Convent, [G], (TUC), Tucson, AZ.
Immaculate Heart Monastery of the Poor Clares, [N], (SJ), Los Altos Hills, CA.
Immaculate Heart Novitiate, [AA], (NY). See Sisters of St. John the Baptist.
Immaculate Heart Novititate, [G], (TUC), Tucson, AZ.
Immaculate Heart of Mary Center, Marywood, [O], (SCR), Scranton, PA.
Immaculate Heart of Mary Convent, [I], (HBG), Harrisburg, PA.
Immaculate Heart of Mary Convent, [AA], (PH), Springfield, PA.
Immaculate Heart of Mary Convent, [AA], (PH), Warminster, PA.
Immaculate Heart of Mary Convent, [F], (SCR). See Monsignor McHugh Elementary School.
Immaculate Heart of Mary Convent, [G], (TUC), Somerton, AZ.
Immaculate Heart of Mary Friary, [M], (BAL), Baltimore, MD.
Immaculate Heart of Mary High School, [D], (CHI), Westchester, IL.
Immaculate Heart of Mary Novitiate, [A], (SFD), Godfrey, IL.
Immaculate Heart of Mary Novitiate-Infirmary, [Z], (BO), Tewksbury, MA.
Immaculate Heart of Mary Nursery, School & Kindergarten, [J], (NEW), Elizabeth, NJ.
Immaculate Heart of Mary Provincial House, [G], (TUC), Tucson, AZ.
Immaculate Heart of Mary Provincial House and Convent, [P], (BUF), Buffalo, NY.
Immaculate Heart of Mary St. Casimir School Mary Goeddeke Educational Trust Fund, [K], (LAN). See Chancery Office.
Immaculate Heart of Mary Seminary, [A], (SFE), Santa Fe, NM.
Immaculate Heart of Mary Seminary, Saint Mary's University of MN #43, [A], (WIN), Winona, MN.
The Immaculate Heart of Mary Spiritual Renewal Center, [H], (SCR), Cresco, PA.
Immaculate Heart Religious Center, [G], (TUC), Tucson, AZ.
Immaculate Heart Retreat Center, [M], (SPK), Spokane, WA.
Immaculate Heart Retreat Center Foundation, [O], (SPK), Spokane, WA.
Immaculate Heart Retreat House, [W], (LA), Los Angeles, CA.
Immaculate High School, [C], (BGP), Danbury, CT.
Immaculate Mary Home, [X], (PH), Philadelphia, PA.
Immigrant and Refugee Services, [J], (NY), New York, NY.
Immigration & Naturalization Services and Refuge Resettlement Program, [G], (CHI). See Catholic Charities of the Archdiocese of Chicago-Archdiocesan Offices.
Immigration and Refugee Department, [Y], (LA). See Catholic Charities of Los Angeles, Inc.
Immigration & Refugee Program, [D], (WIL). See Catholic Charities, Inc.
Immigration & Refugee Services, [E], (FRS), Fresno, CA.
Immigration & Refugee Services, [E], (FRS), Bakersfield, CA.

Immigration and Refugee Services, [E], (HBG). See Department for Catholic Charities Counseling/Field Services.
Immigration and Resettlement, [L], (DEN). See Catholic Charities and Community Services of the Archdiocese of Denver, Inc.
Immigration Counseling Service, [D], (TUC). See Social Service Agencies: Pima County.
Immigration Counseling Services, [J], (DAL), Dallas, TX.
Immigration Counseling Services, [G], (P). See Catholic Charities of the Archdiocese of Portland in Oregon.
Immigration Program, [F], (SJ). See Catholic Charities of Santa Clara County.
Immigration Services, [E], (SR). See Diocese of Santa Rosa, Catholic Charities.
Immigration Services & Citizenship Dept., [L], (SAC). See Catholic Social Service, Sacramento.
Incarnate Word Academy, [F], (CLV), Cleveland, OH.
Incarnate Word Academy, [F], (STL), St. Louis, MO.
Incarnate Word Academy Elementary and Middle School, [B], (BWN), Brownsville, TX.
Incarnate Word Academy Foundation, [J], (CC), Corpus Christi, TX.
Incarnate Word Academy High School, [A], (CC), Corpus Christi, TX.
Incarnate Word and Blessed Sacrament Convent, [N], (SAT), San Antonio, TX.
Incarnate Word and Blessed Sacrament Sisters, [R], (GAL), Danbury, TX.
Incarnate Word Charitable Trust, [R], (GAL). See Congregation of the Sisters of Charity of the Incarnate Word (C.C.V.I.).
Incarnate Word Convent, [F], (BWN), Brownsville, TX.
Incarnate Word Convent, [I], (CC), Corpus Christi, TX.
Incarnate Word Convent, [R], (GAL), Houston, TX.
Incarnate Word Convent, [R], (STL), St. Louis, MO.
Incarnate Word Convent, [E], (VIC), Victoria, TX.
Incarnate Word Elementary, [B], (CC), Corpus Christi, TX.
Incarnate Word Endowment Trust, [Z], (CLV), Parma Heights, OH.
Incarnate Word Generalate, [N], (SAT), San Antonio, TX.
Incarnate Word Health System, [H], (SAT), San Antonio, TX.
Incarnate Word High School, [F], (SAT), San Antonio, TX.
Incarnate Word Hospital, [K], (STL), St. Louis, MO.
Incarnate Word Middle School, [B], (CC), Corpus Christi, TX.
Incarnate Word Motherhouse and Retirement Center, [K], (SAT), San Antonio, TX.
Incarnate Word Motherhouse and Retirement Community, [N], (SAT), San Antonio, TX.
Incarnate Word Preschool Program, [J], (NO), New Orleans, LA.
Incarnate Word Sisters, C.C.V.I., [Q], (NO), Metairie, LA.
Incarnation Children's Center Fund, Inc., [DD], (NY), New York, NY.
Incarnation Monastery, Camaldolese Benedictines, [R], (OAK), Berkeley, CA.
Incarnation School Foundation, [K], (VEN), Sarasota, FL.
Incarnational Consecration Mission, [H], (BR), Baton Rouge, LA.
Independent Aging Program, [F], (SJ). See Catholic Charities of Santa Clara County.
Independent Allied Community Agencies Mobile Meals of Tucson, [D], (TUC). See Social Service Agencies: Pima County.
Indian Apostolate, [T], (BRK). See Catholic Migration & Refugee Office, Catholic Migration Services, Inc.
Indiana Harbor Catholic Elementary School, [F], (GRY), East Chicago, IN.
Indiana State University, Rose Hulman Institute Newman Center, [N], (IND), Terre Haute, IN.
Indiana University Northwest, [O], (GRY), Gary, IN.
Indiana University, Bloomington Newman Center, [N], (IND), Bloomington, IN.
Indiana University-Purdue University, Indianapolis Newman Center, [N], (IND), Indianapolis, IN.
Individual, Group, and Family Counseling, [Y], (LA). See Catholic Charities of Los Angeles, Inc.
Individualized Services, [I], (CIN). See St. Joseph Orphanage.
Indonesian Apostolate, [T], (BRK). See Catholic Migration & Refugee Office, Catholic Migration Services, Inc.
Industrial Rehab Center, [G], (JOL). See St. Joseph Medical Center.
Infant Jesus of Prague Monastery, [D], (GAY), Traverse City, MI.
Infant of Prague Adoption and Counseling Services, [E], (FRS), Fresno, CA.
Infant of Prague Manor, [B], (PBR), Warren, OH.
Infant of Prague Nursery School, [D], (AGN), Tai, GU.
Infirmary of St. Joseph Hall, [O], (PIT). See Our Lady of the Sacred Heart Convent.
Information & Referral, [J], (STU), Steubenville, OH.
In-Home Family Services, Catholic Charities Community Services, [F], (SCL), St. Cloud, MN.
Inner City House, [Z], (PH), Philadelphia, PA.
Inner-City Foundation for Charity & Education, [R], (BGP), Bridgeport, CT.
Innovative Teen Services, Inc., [N], (ALB), Guilderland, NY.
The Institute for Pastoral Ministry, [A], (DET). See Sacred Heart Major Seminary, Inc.
*Institute for Pastoral Renewal, Inc., [V], (WDC), Washington, DC.
*The Institute for Priestly Formation, [O], (OM), Omaha, NE.
Institute for Religious Education and Pastoral Studies, [A], (BGP). See Sacred Heart University.
The Institute for Religious Education and Pastoral Studies (REAPS), [W], (BGP), Fairfield, CT.
Institute for Spiritual Development, [H], (BUR). See Mount St. Mary Convent.
Institute for Spiritual Development, [K], (BUR), Burlington, VT.
Institute for Spiritual Leadership, [N], (CHI), Chicago, IL.
Institute for Spiritual Leadership, [X], (CHI), Chicago, IL.
Institute for the Hispanic Family, [S], (HRT). See Catholic Charities-Catholic Family Services (Archdiocese of Hartford).
Institute for the Study of Bibliotherapy, [O], (FTW), Fort Wayne, IN.
Institute for Theological Encounter with Science & Technology (ITEST), [W], (STL), St. Louis, MO.
The Institute of Apostolic Oblates, [X], (BRK), Brooklyn, NY.
Institute of Blessed Virgin Mary (I.B.V.M.), [E], (PHX), Phoenix, AZ.
Institute of Carmelite Studies and ICS Publications, [V], (WDC), Washington, DC.
Institute of Catechists of the Heart of Jesus, [G], (STF), Stamford, CT.
Institute of Christ the King-Sovereign Priest, [O], (LC), Cashton, WI.
The Institute of Divine Mercy Convent, [N], (DAL), Dallas, TX.
The Institute of Divine Mercy, Inc., [P], (DAL), Dallas, TX.
Institute of Jesuit Sources, [W], (STL), St. Louis, MO.
Institute of Lay Theology, [R], (OAK), Oakland, CA.
Institute of Notre Dame, [D], (BAL), Baltimore, MD.
Institute of Our Lady of Mount Carmel, [O], (WDC), Washington, DC.
Institute of St. Joseph, [N], (LC), Tilden, WI.
Institute of the Apostolic Oblates, [M], (OM), Omaha, NE.
Institute of the Blessed Virgin Mary Charitable Trust, [M], (JOL), Wheaton, IL.
Institute of the Daughters of Mary Help of Christians, [N], (PAT), Haledon, NJ.
Institute of the Daughters of Mary Help of Christians, [N], (SAT), San Antonio, TX.
Institute of the Heart of Jesus, [F], (DM), Des Moines, IA.
Institute of the Helpers, [DD], (NY), New York, NY.
The Institute of the Incarnate Word, Inc., [Q], (FR), New Bedford, MA.
Institute of the Sisters of Mercy of the Americas, [I], (SAC), Auburn, CA.
Institute of the Sisters of Mercy of the Americas, Regional Community of New York, [AA], (NY), Hartsdale, NY.
Institute of Vocation Awareness, [A], (CHI), Chicago, IL.
*The Institute on Religious Life, [X], (CHI), Chicago, IL.
Institutional Services Residence, [U], (BRK), Douglaston, NY.
Instituto de Estudios Aymaras, [J], (FTW). See Congregation of Holy Cross Indiana Province Provincial House.
Instituto Fe y Vida, [G], (STO), Stockton, CA.
Instituto Psicopedagogico De P.R., [B], (SJN), San Juan, PR.
Instituto Secular de Ntra. Sra. de la Altagracia, [E], (CGS), Caguas, PR.
Integrated Auxiliaries The Friends of John Paul II Foundation, [J], (TUC), Tucson, AZ.
Intensive Day Treatment, [E], (HBG). See Department for Catholic Charities Counseling/Field Services.
Intensive Supportive Apartment Program, [H], (SY). See Chenango House.
Inter Mirifica, [V], (WDC), Kensington, MD.
Inter-Community, [J], (PRT), Winslow, ME.
Inter-Community, [O], (RVC), Medford, NY.
Intercommunity Center for Justice & Peace, [DD], (NY), New York, NY.
Intercommunity Convent, [N], (SJ), Cupertino, CA.
Intercommunity Housing, [Q], (SEA), Seattle, WA.
Intercommunity Housing Association, [W], (STL), St. Louis, MO.
Intercommunity Housing Corporation, [X], (CHI), Chicago, IL.
Intercommunity Housing Ferndale, [Q], (SEA), Seattle, WA.
Intercommunity Ministry Volunteer Program, [Q], (SEA), Edmonds, WA.
*Intercommunity Peace & Justice Center, [Q], (SEA), Seattle, WA.
Intercommunity Properties, [Q], (SEA), Seattle, WA.
Intercongregational Justice & Peace Office, [T], (SAT), San Antonio, TX.
Interfaith Commission of Northern Kentucky, [R], (COV), Covington, KY.
Interfaith Housing, Ltd., [P], (DAV), Davenport, IA.
Interfaith Shelter for Homeless Families, [E], (HBG). See Department for Catholic Charities Counseling/ Field Services.
Interfaith Volunteer Caregiver Program, [E], (SR). See Diocese of Santa Rosa, Catholic Charities.
Inter-Friendship House Association, Friendship Center, [R], (OAK), Berkeley, CA.
Intergenerational Daycare Center, [D], (LAN). See Catholic Social Services-St. Vincent Home for Children, Inc.
International Catholic Child Bureau/North America, Inc., [DD], (NY), New York, NY.
International Catholic Deaf Association (Chapter No. 38), [O], (IND), Indianapolis, IN.
International Catholic Network, [P], (DAL), Dallas, TX.
International Federation of Catholic Alumnae, Maryland Chapter, [Q], (BAL), Baltimore, MD.
International Institute of the Heart of Jesus, [T], (BUF), Bowmansville, NY.
International Institute of the Heart of Jesus, [Y], (MIL), Milwaukee, WI.
International Institute on Mental Retardation, [L], (OKL). See Oklahoma Benedictine Institute on Mental Retardation, Inc.
Interparish Deposit Loan Fund Corp., [J], (OWN), Owensboro, KY.
Inter-Parish Loan Fund, Inc., [T], (PRO). See Miscellaneous Listings for the Diocese of Providence.
Interval Brotherhood Home Alcohol-Drug Rehabilitation Center, [V], (CLV), Akron, OH.
Iona College, [C], (NY), New Rochelle, NY.
Iona College, [CC], (NY). See University Apostolate.
Iona Grammar School, [H], (NY), New Rochelle, NY.
Iona Preparatory School, [F], (NY), New Rochelle, NY.
The Irene Dunne Guild, [K], (LA). See Saint John's Hospital and Health Center.
Irish Apostolate, [T], (BRK). See Catholic Migration & Refugee Office, Catholic Migration Services, Inc.
ISECP, Inc., [R], (SCR), Scranton, PA.
Island View Nursing Home, [B], (JUN). See Ketchikan General Hospital.
Issenmann Place, [O], (CLV), Brooklyn, OH.
Italian Apostolate, [T], (BRK). See Catholic Migration & Refugee Office, Catholic Migration Services, Inc.
Italian Board of Guardians, [L], (BRK). See Catholic Charities.
Italian Catholic Federation, [X], (CHI), Northlake, IL.
Italian Catholic Federation, [R], (OAK), Oakland, CA.
Italian Cultural Center, [N], (CHI). See Missionaries of Saint Charles.
Italian Seamen's Club, The, [DD], (NY), New York, NY.
Italian-American Housing Development Fund Co., Inc. dba Cabrini Acers Senior Apts., [K], (ALB), Watervliet, NY.
ITP Paulist Communications, [V], (WDC), Washington, DC.
Ittawamba Community College Newman Center, [G], (JKS), Fulton, MS.
Ivrea Sisters of Charity of the Immaculate Conception, [I], (GBG), Mount Pleasant, PA.
IWHS Forth Worth Health Care Corporation, [H], (SAT). See Incarnate Word Health System.

J

J.K. Mullen High School, Corp., [D], (DEN), Denver, CO.
Jackson Catholic Middle School, [C], (LAN), Jackson, MI.
Jackson County Junior College, [G], (BLX), Gautier, MS.
Jackson School Elementary, [H], (BO), Newton, MA.
Jackson State University Newman Center, [G], (JKS), Jackson, MS.
Jacksonville State University, [H], (BIR), Jacksonville, AL.
Jacksonville University and University of North Florida Catholic Campus Ministry, [L], (STA), Jacksonville, FL.
Jacksonville, Family Housing Management Co., [G], (STA), Jacksonville, FL.
Jail Ministries, [H], (COS), Colorado Springs, CO.
Jail Ministry, [I], (SAG). See Emmaus House.

Jail Ministry, [H], (SY), Syracuse, NY.
Jamestown, [H], (BUF). See The Catholic Charities of the Diocese of Buffalo.
Jamestown College, [I], (FAR), Jamestown, ND.
Jan Beyzym Society, Inc., [N], (CHI). See Sacred Heart Mission House.
Jan Beyzym Society, Inc., [U], (CHI), Chicago, IL.
Janesville District Office, [K], (MAD). See Catholic Charities, Inc.
Jean Francois Rivet High School, [A], (EVN), Vincennes, IN.
Jeanne d'Arc Convent, [H], (BO), Milton, MA.
Jeanne d'Arc Manor, [J], (SJ), San Jose, CA.
The Jeanne d'Arc Residence, [W], (NY), New York, NY.
Jeanne Jugan Apartments, [M], (PRO), Pawtucket, RI.
Jeanne Jugan Center, [I], (KC), Kansas City, MO.
Jeanne Jugan Pavilion, [U], (BO), Somerville, MA.
Jeanne Jugan Residence, [U], (BO), Somerville, MA.
Jeanne Jugan Residence, [V], (NY), Bronx, NY.
Jeanne Jugan Residence, [M], (PRO), Pawtucket, RI.
Jeanne Jugan Residence, [G], (WIL), Newark, DE.
Jeanne Jugan Residence-St. Joseph's Villa, [L], (WDC), Washington, DC.
Jeannette District Memorial Hospital, [F], (GBG), Jeannette, PA.
Jefferson Care Center, [L], (NO), Marrero, LA.
Jefferson County Technical Institute, [I], (STU), Steubenville, OH.
Jefferson House, [Q], (DET). See Capuchin Soup Kitchen.
The Jemez Program, Our Lady of Lourdes Novitiate, [J], (SFE), Jemez Springs, NM.
Jenkins Apartments, Inc., [P], (BAL). See Chancery Office.
Jenkins Housing, Inc., [P], (BAL). See Chancery Office.
Jennings Hall Inc., [N], (CLV), Cleveland, OH.
Jennings Hall, Inc., [V], (CLV). See Catholic Charities Services Corporation.
Jersey City State College, [Q], (NEW), Jersey City, NJ.
Jessie Albert Memorial Dental Center, [E], (PRT). See Catholic Charities Maine.
Jesu Children's Enrichment Center, III, [I], (PEO), Peoria, IL.
Jesuit Center for Spiritual Growth, [N], (ALN), Wernersville, PA.
Jesuit College Preparatory School, [D], (DAL), Dallas, TX.
Jesuit Community, [J], (CHL), Charlotte, NC.
Jesuit Community, [O], (FTW), Granger, IN.
Jesuit Community, [C], (LA). See Loyola Marymount University.
Jesuit Community, [Z], (NY). See Jesuit Provincial's Office.
Jesuit Community, [E], (R), Durham, NC.
Jesuit Community, [B], (SJ). See Santa Clara University.
Jesuit Community - Casa Claver, [E], (SJN), Hato Rey, PR.
The Jesuit Community at Boston College, [W], (BO), Chestnut Hill, MA.
Jesuit Community At Creighton University, [K], (OM), Omaha, NE.
Jesuit Community at Fordham University, [Z], (NY), New York, NY.
The Jesuit Community at Georgetown University, [M], (WDC), Washington, DC.
Jesuit Community at Jesuit School of Theology at Berkeley, [N], (OAK), Berkeley, CA.
Jesuit Community at Loyola University of Chicago, [C], (CHI), Chicago, IL.
Jesuit Community at Marquette University, [P], (MIL), Milwaukee, WI.
Jesuit Community at St. Camillus, [P], (MIL), Wauwatosa, WI.
Jesuit Community at St. Ignatius College Preparatory, [N], (SFR), San Francisco, CA.
Jesuit Community at St. Joseph's University, [Z], (PH), Philadelphia, PA.
Jesuit Community at St. Xavier High School, [M], (CIN), Cincinnati, OH.
Jesuit Community at the University of Detroit, [K], (DET), Detroit, MI.
Jesuit Community at University of San Francisco, [N], (SFR), San Francisco, CA.
Jesuit Community at Xavier Unversity, [M], (CIN), Cincinnati, OH.
Jesuit Community Corporation at St. Louis University - Jesuit Hall, [P], (STL), St. Louis, MO.
Jesuit Community of Holy Rosary Mission, [B], (RC), Pine Ridge, SD.
Jesuit Community of Loyola College, Inc., [C], (BAL). See Loyola College.
Jesuit Community of Loyola College, Inc., [M], (BAL), Baltimore, MD.
Jesuit Community of Pittsburgh, [R], (PIT), Pittsburgh, PA.
Jesuit Community of the Vatican Observatory, [F], (TUC), Tucson, AZ.
Jesuit Conference, Inc., [V], (WDC), Washington, DC.
Jesuit Development & Communications Office, [Q], (P), Portland, OR.
Jesuit Development Office, [V], (CIN), Cincinnati, OH.
Jesuit Educational Association of Maryland, Inc., [Q], (BAL), Baltimore, MD.
The Jesuit Educational Center for Human Development, [FF], (BO), Brighton, MA.
Jesuit Fathers and Brothers, [H], (AUS), Austin, TX.
Jesuit Fathers and Brothers Maryland Provincial Curia, [M], (BAL), Baltimore, MD.
Jesuit Fathers House, [H], (HON), Honolulu, HI.
Jesuit Fathers of the Province of the Antilles, Inc., [H], (MIA), Miami, FL.
Jesuit Health Trust, [P], (NO). See Jesuit Provincial Office.
Jesuit High School, [F], (NO), New Orleans, LA.
Jesuit High School, [H], (NO), New Orleans, LA.
Jesuit High School, [D], (P), Portland, OR.
Jesuit High School, [C], (SAC), Sacramento, CA.
Jesuit High School, [C], (SP), Tampa, FL.
Jesuit High School Community of Sacramento, [H], (SAC), Carmichael, CA.
Jesuit House, [G], (ANC), Anchorage, AK.
Jesuit House, [C], (CI), Kolonia, Pohnpei, FM.
*Jesuit House of Prayer, [M], (CHL), Hot Springs, NC.
Jesuit Institute for Family Life, [P], (SJ), Los Altos, CA.
Jesuit International Missions, [T], (DET). See Jesuit Seminary Association.
Jesuit International Missions, Inc., [X], (CHI), Chicago, IL.
Jesuit Jamshedpur Mission Society, Inc., [Q], (BAL), Baltimore, MD.
Jesuit Lithuanian Center, [D], (LIT), Chicago, IL.
The Jesuit Middle School of Omaha, [F], (OM), Omaha, NE.
Jesuit Missions, Inc., [V], (WDC), Washington, DC.
Jesuit Novitiate, [B], (SJN), Rio Piedras, PR.
Jesuit Novitiate, [B], (STP), St. Paul, MN.
Jesuit Novitiate of St. Francis Xavier, [A], (P), Portland, OR.
The Jesuit Partnership, [Y], (MIL), Milwaukee, WI.
Jesuit Program for Living and Learning of New Orleans, Inc., [S], (NO), New Orleans, LA.
Jesuit Provincial Office, [P], (NO), New Orleans, LA.
Jesuit Provincial Office (Oregon Prov.), [L], (P), Portland, OR.
Jesuit Provincial Office, Wisconsin Province, [P], (MIL), Milwaukee, WI.
Jesuit Provincial Office-Detroit Province of the Society of Jesus, [K], (DET), Detroit, MI.
Jesuit Provincial's Office, [Z], (NY), New York, NY.
Jesuit Refugee Service, [V], (WDC), Washington, DC.
Jesuit Residence, [G], (ANC), Anchorage, AK.
Jesuit Residence, [C], (FBK), Fairbanks, AK.
Jesuit Residence, [Z], (NY). See Jesuit Provincial's Office.
Jesuit Residence, [Z], (NY). See Xavier Jesuit Community.
Jesuit Residence, Robert Southwell House, [E], (R), Chapel Hill, NC.
Jesuit Retreat House, [U], (CLV), Cleveland, OH.
Jesuit Retreat House, [M], (GB), Oshkosh, WI.
Jesuit Retreat House, [L], (SJ), Los Altos, CA.
Jesuit Retreat House, [Q], (STP), Lake Elmo, MN.
Jesuit Retreat House for Priests, Religious and Lay People, [O], (ALB), Auriesville, NY.
The Jesuit School of Theology at Berkeley, [A], (OAK), Berkeley, CA.
Jesuit Secondary Education Association, [V], (WDC), Washington, DC.
Jesuit Seminary and Mission Bureau, [S], (NO), New Orleans, LA.
Jesuit Seminary and Mission Bureau, Inc., [DD], (NY), New York, NY.
Jesuit Seminary and Mission Bureau, Inc. (Jesuit Deferred Funds), [Z], (NY), New York, NY.
Jesuit Seminary Association, [T], (DET), Detroit, MI.
Jesuit Seminary Guild & Jesuit Mission Bureau, Maryland Province, Inc., [Q], (BAL), Baltimore, MD.
Jesuit Social Ministries-National Office, [V], (WDC), Washington, DC.
Jesuit Urban Center & Immaculate Conception Community, [W], (BO), Boston, MA.
Jesuit Volunteer Corps Southwest, [P], (OAK), Berkeley, CA.
Jesuit Volunteer Corps. Midwest, Inc., [T], (DET), Detroit, MI.
*Jesuit Volunteer Corps: Northwest, [Q], (P), Portland, OR.
Jesuit Volunteer Corps: South, [U], (GAL), Houston, TX.
Jesuit Volunteers: International, [V], (WDC), Washington, DC.
Jesuits, [H], (ORG), Laguna Niguel, CA.
Jesuits, [H], (ORG), Orange, CA.
Jesuits at LeMoyne, Inc., [S], (SY), Syracuse, NY.
Jesuits of Holy Cross College, Inc., [N], (WOR), Worcester, MA.
Jesuits of Saint Peter's College, Inc., [N], (NEW), Jersey City, NJ.
The Jesuits of the Missouri Province, [P], (STL), St. Louis, MO.
The Jesuits of the Missouri Province, [W], (STL), St. Louis, MO.
Jesus and Mary Mission Center, [X], (BO), Plainville, MA.
Jesus Redeemer Convent, [O], (PIT), Pittsburgh, PA.
The Jesus School, [N], (MET), Lambertville, NJ.
Joan Ann Kennedy Memorial Preschool, [D], (NY). See Department of Education.
Joan Kroc Homeless Center, [J], (SD). See St. Vincent de Paul Village.
Joan of Arc Residence, [J], (SD), San Diego, CA.
Jogues Retreat, [Z], (NY), Cornwall, NY.
John A. Coleman Catholic High School, [E], (NY), Hurley, NY.
John Cardinal Wright Vocation and Prayer Center, [P], (PIT), Gibsonia, PA.
John Carroll Education Foundation, [I], (BIR), Birmingham, AL.
John Carroll Foundation of the Roman Catholic Archdiocese of Baltimore, [P], (BAL). See Chancery Office.
John Carroll High School, [A], (BIR), Birmingham, AL.
John Carroll High School, [B], (PMB), Fort Pierce, FL.
John Carroll Jesuit Community, [C], (CLV), Cleveland, OH.
The John Carroll School, [D], (BAL), Bel Air, MD.
The John Carroll Society, [V], (WDC), Washington, DC.
John Carroll University, [C], (CLV), Cleveland, OH.
John Courtney Murray Newman Center, [S], (DET), Port Huron, MI.
John F. Kennedy Catholic High School, [E], (STL), Manchester, MO.
John F. Kennedy High School, [E], (NY), Somers, NY.
John F. Kennedy High School, [C], (Y), Warren, OH.
John F. Kennedy Memorial High School, [B], (SEA), Seattle, WA.
John Flynn Family Endowment Trust, [N], (OM). See The Omaha Archdiocesan Educational Foundation, Inc.
John Gazzola Trust Estate, [L], (LR), Little Rock, AR.
John Ireland Schools, [H], (STP), Hopkins, MN.
John LaFarge Institute, The, [DD], (NY), New York, NY.
John Lewis Coffee Shop/Miriam House, [K], (DAV), Davenport, IA.
John Neumann Catholic School (Administration & Middle School), [H], (PBL), Pueblo, CO.
John Neumann Catholic Schools, [C], (PBL), Pueblo, CO.
John of the Cross Monastery Hermitage, [K], (PRT), Orland, ME.
John Paul Apartments, [H], (SCL), Cold Spring, MN.
John Paul II Catholic School, [G], (GAL), Houston, TX.
John Paul II Center for Special Learning, [E], (ALN), Reading, PA.
John Paul II Foundation for Peace, Justice & Human Rights, [EE], (PH), Fort Washington, PA.
John Paul II Foundation of Michigan, Inc., [T], (DET), Grosse Pointe, MI.
John Paul II Nursing Home, [K], (SAT), Kenedy, TX.
John Paul II Regional School, Inc., [P], (BAL). See Chancery Office.
John Paul II Retreat House, [J], (MIA), Miami, FL.
John Paul Regional Catholic School, Inc., [F], (BAL), Baltimore, MD.
John S. Burke Catholic High School, [E], (NY), Goshen, NY.
John S. Duss Memorial Music Center, [V], (HRT). See Franciscan Life Center Network, Incorporated.
John S. Duss Memorial Music Conservatory, [G], (DUL), Duluth, MN.
John V. Mara CYO Camps, [X], (NY). See The Catholic Camp Association Inc.
John W. Hallahan Catholic Girls High School, [D], (PH), Philadelphia, PA.
John Wayne Cancer Institute Auxiliary, [K], (LA). See Saint John's Hospital and Health Center.
John Wayne Cancer Institute Benefactors, [K], (LA). See Saint John's Hospital and Health Center.
John XXIII Center, [G], (LFT), Hartford City, IN.
John XXIII Center, [L], (MOB), Hurtsboro, AL.
John XXIII Elementary School, [G], (CIN), Middletown, OH.
John XXIII Home, [K], (E), Hermitage, PA.
John XXIII Neighborhood Center, [F], (SJ). See Catholic Charities of Santa Clara County.
John XXIII Nutrition Site, [F], (SJ). See Catholic Charities of Santa Clara County.
John XXIII Pastoral Center, [F], (WH), Charleston, WV.
John XXIII Regional School, [F], (DAL), Dallas, TX.
Johns Hopkins Hospital Apostolate, [Q], (BAL), Baltimore, MD.

K

L

M

Marian Hall, [J], (PRT), Standish, ME.
Marian Hall Agencies, [N], (STL), St. Louis, MO.
Marian Hall Emergency Shelter, [N], (STL), St. Louis, MO.
Marian Hall Home, Inc., [L], (PIT), Pittsburgh, PA.
Marian Hall Infirmary, [I], (DUB), Dubuque, IA.
Marian Health Center, [D], (SC), Sioux City, IA.
Marian Heights Academy, [B], (EVN), Ferdinand, IN.
Marian Heights Apartments, [J], (SFD), Alton, IL.
Marian High School, [D], (BO), Framingham, MA.
Marian High School, [C], (FTW), Mishawaka, IN.
Marian High School, [C], (OM), Omaha, NE.
Marian High School for Young Women, [E], (DET), Bloomfield Hills, MI.
Marian High School, Inc. Endowment Trust, [N], (OM). See The Omaha Archdiocesan Educational Foundation, Inc.
Marian High School, Inc. Scholarship Endowment Trust, [N], (OM). See The Omaha Archdiocesan Educational Foundation, Inc.
Marian Home, [K], (L), Louisville, KY.
The Marian Home, [E], (SC), Fort Dodge, IA.
Marian House Apartments, [H], (ANC), Anchorage, AK.
Marian House, Inc., [P], (BAL). See Chancery Office.
Marian Housing Center, Inc, [N], (MIL), Racine, WI.
The Marian Library/International Marian Research Institute (IMRI), [D], (CIN). See The University of Dayton.
Marian Manor, [U], (BO), Boston, MA.
Marian Manor, [H], (RIC), Virginia Beach, VA.
Marian Manor Corp., [L], (PIT), Pittsburgh, PA.
Marian Manor Inc., [J], (FR), Taunton, MA.
Marian Manor, Inc., [J], (STU), Steubenville, OH.
Marian Medical Center, [K], (LA), Santa Maria, CA.
Marian Medical Center Day Care Facility for Children, [K], (LA). See Marian Medical Center.
Marian Medical Center Extended Care Facility, [K], (LA). See Marian Medical Center.
Marian Medical Center Foundation, [K], (LA). See Marian Medical Center.
Marian Novitiate, [B], (WDC), Brookeville, MD.
Marian Oakland-West, [J], (DET). See Ryan Senior Residences of the Archdiocese of Detroit. Inc.
Marian Park, Inc., [I], (JOL), Wheaton, IL.
Marian Place, [J], (DET). See Ryan Senior Residences of the Archdiocese of Detroit. Inc.
Marian Plaza, Inc., [K], (DEN). See Archdiocesan Housing Committee.
Marian Residence, [J], (CAM), Cherry Hill, NJ.
Marian Residence, [Q], (LA), Santa Maria, CA.
Marian Residence, [J], (SPR), Holyoke, MA.
Marian Residence Retirement Home, [K], (LA). See Marian Medical Center.
Marian Retreat Center, [J], (SAC), Auburn, CA.
Marian Servants of the Holy Spirit, [L], (DAL), Dallas, TX.
Marian Shrine, [BB], (NY), West Haverstraw, NY.
Marian Sisters of the Diocese of Lincoln Motherhouse and Novitiate, [G], (LIN), Waverly, NE.
Marian Spiritual Center, [B], (WDC), Brookeville, MD.
Marian Village Corporation, [H], (DET), Livonia, MI.
Marianapolis Preparatory School, [C], (NOR), Thompson, CT.
The Marianist Center, [BB], (PH), Folsom, PA.
*Marianist Center of Hawaii, [H], (HON), Honolulu, HI.
Marianist Community, [M], (BAL), Baltimore, MD.
Marianist Community, [M], (CIN), Cincinnati, OH.
Marianist Community, [M], (CIN). See Marianist Provincialate.
Marianist Community, [P], (CLV), Cleveland, OH.
Marianist Community, [Q], (GAL), Houston, TX.
Marianist Community, [F], (LA). See Chaminade College Preparatory.
Marianist Community, [N], (PIT), Pittsburgh, PA.
Marianist Community, [N], (RVC), Hewlett, NY.
Marianist Community, [N], (SFR), San Francisco, CA.
Marianist Community, [M], (SJ), San Jose, CA.
Marianist Community, [M], (SJ), Santa Clara, CA.
Marianist Community, [P], (STL), St. Louis, MO.
Marianist Community, Novitiate, [M], (CIN). See Marianist Provincialate.
Marianist Conference, [Q], (BAL), Baltimore, MD.
Marianist Environmental Education Center, [M], (CIN). See Marianist Provincialate.
Marianist Family Ministry, Inc., [I], (R), North Topsail Beach, NC.
Marianist Family Retreat Center, [O], (CAM), Cape May Point, NJ.
Marianist Formation Community, [B], (SAT), San Antonio, TX.
Marianist Formation Community, [M], (SAT), San Antonio, TX.
Marianist Hall Community, [H], (HON), Honolulu, HI.
Marianist Lay Network, [T], (SAT), San Antonio, TX.
The Marianist Mission, [M], (CIN). See Marianist Provincialate.
Marianist Mission, [M], (CIN). See Marianist Provincialate.
The Marianist Mission, [M], (SJ), Cupertino, CA.
Marianist Network for the Arts, [M], (CIN). See Marianist Provincialate.
Marianist Novitiate, [C], (CIN), Dayton, OH.
Marianist Novitiate Corporation, [M], (SJ). See Marianist Provincial Residence.
Marianist Press, [M], (CIN). See Marianist Provincialate.
Marianist Provincial Residence, [M], (SJ), Cupertino, CA.
Marianist Provincialate, [M], (CIN), Dayton, OH.
Marianist Residence, [M], (SAT), San Antonio, TX.
Marianist Retreat & Conference Center, [T], (STL), Eureka, MO.
Marianist Retreat Center, [M], (SJ), Cupertino, CA.
Marianist Seminary, [B], (SFR), San Francisco, CA.
Marianist Vocation Ministry, [M], (SAT), San Antonio, TX.
Marianist Voluntary Service Communities, [M], (CIN). See Marianist Provincialate.
Marianist Voluntary Service Communities, MVSC, [V], (CIN), Dayton, OH.
Marianists, [H], (ORG), Orange, CA.
Marianists, [M], (SJ), Los Gatos, CA.
Marianists Community (New York Province), [M], (BAL), Baltimore, MD.
Marianites of Holy Cross, [I], (LAF), Lafayette, LA.
Marianites of Holy Cross, M.S.C., [Q], (NO), New Orleans, LA.
Marianites of the Holy Cross, [I], (LAF), Franklin, LA.
Marianites of the Holy Cross, [I], (LAF), Crowley, LA.
Marianjoy Rehabilitation Hospital & Clinics, [H], (JOL), Wheaton, IL.
Marianne Cope Convent, [I], (HON). See St. Francis Convent.
Marianwood, [I], (SEA), Issaquah, WA.
Mariawald Renewal Center-Precious Blood Convent, [M], (ALN), Shillington, PA.
Marie Amadea Shelter for Unwed Mothers, [H], (SFE), Albuquerque, NM.
Marie Claire Residence, [J], (PRT), Houlton, ME.
Marie Esther Health Center, Inc., [U], (BO), Marlboro, MA.
Marie Fitzbach Convent, [J], (PRT), Biddeford, ME.
Marie Joseph Spiritual Center, [J], (PRT), Biddeford, ME.
Marie Joseph Spiritual Center, [L], (PRT), Biddeford, ME.
Marie's Family Home, [L], (NO), New Orleans, LA.
Marie-Rose Manor HDFCI, [K], (ALB), Slingerlands, NY.
Marietta College, [I], (STU), Marietta, OH.
Marillac Clinic, Inc., [D], (PBL), Grand Junction, CO.
Marillac Home for Children, [O], (KC), Kansas City, MO.
Marillac House, [J], (SLC). See Catholic Community Services.
Marillac Manor, [G], (BIS), Bismarck, ND.
Marillac Programs, [O], (DET), Farmington Hills, MI.
Marillac Provincial House, [R], (STL), Normandy, MO.
Marillac Social Center, [I], (CHI), Chicago, IL.
Marillac Social Center, [J], (DAL), Dallas, TX.
Marillac Social Center Residence, [N], (DAL), Dallas, TX.
Marillac Transitional Housing Services, Inc., [J], (SLC). See Catholic Community Services.
Marin Catholic College Preparatory (Coed), [D], (SFR), Kentfield, CA.
Marin Counseling, [Q], (SFR). See Catholic Charities of the Archdiocese of San Francisco.
Marin County Vincentian Life, [H], (SFR). See St. Vincent de Paul Society Marin County District Council.
Marin Family Services, [Q], (SFR). See Catholic Charities of the Archdiocese of San Francisco.
Marine Senior Services, [Q], (SFR). See Catholic Charities of the Archdiocese of San Francisco.
Marinette Catholic Central High School, [C], (GB), Marinette, WI.
The Marion Burk Knott Scholarship Fund, Educational Trust, [P], (BAL). See Chancery Office.
Marion Catholic High School, [C], (COL), Marion, OH.
Marion Catholic High School Endowment Fund, [K], (COL), Marion, OH.
Marion Institute Newman Center, [K], (MOB), Selma, AL.
Marionapolis Prep School, [A], (LIT), Thompson, CT.
Maris Stella, [Q], (TR), Harvey Cedars, NJ.
Maris Stella Retreat House, [N], (TR), Harvey Cedars, NJ.
Marist Brothers, [Z], (BO), Lawrence, MA.
Marist Brothers, [H], (CC), Laredo, TX.
Marist Brothers, [N], (CHI), Aslip, IL.
Marist Brothers, [N], (CHI), Blue Island, IL.
Marist Brothers, [N], (CHI), Chicago, IL.
Marist Brothers, [N], (NEW), Newark, NJ.
Marist Brothers, [N], (NEW), Bayonne, NJ.
Marist Brothers, [Z], (NY). See Marist Brothers Residence.
Marist Brothers Champagnat Hall Community, [Z], (NY). See Marist Brothers Residence.
Marist Brothers F.M.S. (Province of St. Joseph), [Z], (NY), Esopus, NY.
Marist Brothers of the Schools, [E], (BWN), Brownsville, TX.
Marist Brothers of Ulster County, [BB], (NY), Esopus, NY.
Marist Brothers Residence, [W], (BO), Lawrence, MA.
Marist Brothers Residence, [N], (NEW), Roselle, NJ.
Marist Brothers Residence, [Z], (NY), New York, NY.
Marist Brothers Residences, [H], (MIA), Miami, FL.
Marist Brothers Support Trust, [S], (NEW), Bayonne, NJ.
Marist Brothers, St. Joseph Academy, [E], (BWN), Brownsville, TX.
Marist Capital Trust Fund, [DD], (BO). See Chancery Office.
Marist College, [C], (NY), Poughkeepsie, NY.
Marist College, [CC], (NY). See University Apostolate.
Marist College, The-Scholasticate, [B], (WDC), Washington, DC.
Marist Fathers and Brothers, [N], (OAK), Berkeley, CA.
Marist Fathers and Brothers Provincial House, [W], (BO), Boston, MA.
Marist Fathers Lourdes Residence, [W], (BO), Boston, MA.
Marist Fathers of Our Lady of Victories (Boston Prov.), [W], (BO), Boston, MA.
Marist Foreign Missions, [C], (NY). See Marist College.
Marist High School, [D], (CHI), Chicago, IL.
Marist High School, [D], (P), Eugene, OR.
Marist High School, [C], (SPP), Malaeloa, AS.
Marist High Schoool, [C], (NEW), Bayonne, NJ.
The Marist House, [Y], (BO), Framingham Centre, MA.
Marist Missionary Sisters, [X], (BO), Waltham, MA.
Marist Provincial House, [Z], (NY). See Marist Brothers Residence.
Marist Provincial House, [M], (WDC), Washington, DC.
Marist Residence, [Z], (NY). See Marist Brothers Residence.
Marist School, [C], (ATL), Atlanta, GA.
Marist Sisters, [B], (SAN), Abilene, TX.
Marist Volunteer Program, [X], (CHI), Chicago, IL.
Maristhill Nursing Home, [U], (BO), Waltham, MA.
Mark Seven - DePaul House of Studies, [A], (NY). See St. Joseph's Seminary.
Marksville Catholic School, [B], (ALX), Marksville, LA.
Marlborough Manor, [I], (KC), Kansas City, MO.
Marmion Abbey, [A], (RCK), Aurora, IL.
Marmion Abbey-St. Augustine's Abbey, [H], (RCK), Aurora, IL.
Marmion Academy, [C], (RCK), Aurora, IL.
The Marnee and John DeVine Foundation, [L], (LAN), Ann Arbor, MI.
Marquette Area Catholic Education Fund, [B], (MAR), Marquette, MI.
Marquette Catholic High School, [B], (GRY), Michigan City, IN.
Marquette Catholic High School, [D], (SFD), Alton, IL.
Marquette Catholic School, [B], (DUL), Virginia, MN.
Marquette Foundation, [P], (DAV), West Point, IA.
Marquette High School, [D], (DUB), Bellevue, IA.
Marquette High School, [B], (PEO), Ottawa, IL.
Marquette School System: Marquette Intermediate, [G], (DAV). See Marquette School, Inc.
Marquette School System: Marquette Jr./Sr. High, [G], (DAV). See Marquette School, Inc.
Marquette School System: Marquette Primary, [G], (DAV). See Marquette School, Inc.
Marquette School, Inc., [E], (DAV), West Point, IA.
Marquette School, Inc., [G], (DAV), West Point, IA.
*Marquette University, [C], (MIL), Milwaukee, WI.
Marquette University High School, [E], (MIL), Milwaukee, WI.
Marquette University Ministry, [X], (MIL), Milwaukee, WI.
Marriage Counseling Center, [H], (BUF). See The Catholic Charities of the Diocese of Buffalo.
Marriage Counseling Service, [G], (SPR), Springfield, MA.
Marriage Encounter, [L], (AMA), Amarillo, TX.
Marriage Encounter, [O], (OM), Omaha, NE.
Marriage Encounter, [J], (STU), Beverly, OH.
Marriage Encounter Apostolate, [L], (ROC), Rochester, NY.
Marriage Preparation Program, [M], (MEM), Memphis, TN.
Marshall Newman Center, [Q], (WH), Huntington, WV.
Marshalltown Area Consolidated Catholic School, [F], (DUB), Marshalltown, IA.
Martha Mary House for Women and Children, [L], (LR), Berryville, AR.

Martha W. Davis Cancer Center, [H], (RIC). See Bon Secours-Maryview Nursing Care.
Martha's Kitchen, [F], (SJ). See Catholic Charities of Santa Clara County.
Martha's Kitchen, [F], (SJ). See Catholic Charities of Santa Clara County.
The Martin Center, [H], (SEA), Bellingham, WA.
Martin De Porres Brothers Community, [U], (BRK), Springfield Gardens, NY.
Martin De Porres Group Homes, [P], (BRK), Springfield Gardens, NY.
Martin de Porres House, [X], (CHI), Chicago, IL.
Martin de Porres School, [I], (BRK), Springfield Gardens, NY.
Martin de Porres Village Corporation, [P], (PAT), Paterson, NJ.
Martin House, [F], (PT), Apalachicola, FL.
Martin House, [J], (RCK), Rockford, IL.
Martin House, [S], (TR), Trenton, NJ.
Martin Luther King, Jr. Student Center, [K], (BR), Baton Rouge, LA.
Martin Luther King. Jr., Day Home Center, [F], (SEA), Seattle, WA.
Martina Spiritual Renewal Center, Inc., [P], (PIT), Pittsburgh, PA.
Mary and Joseph Retreat Center, [W], (LA), Rancho Palos Verdes, CA.
Mary and Joseph Trust, [W], (STL), St. Louis, MO.
*Mary Conrad Center, [E], (ANC), Anchorage, AK.
Mary Health of the Sick Convalescent and Nursing Hospital, [L], (LA), Newbury Park, CA.
Mary Help of Christians Academy, [D], (PAT), North Haledon, NJ.
Mary Help of Christians School, [B], (CC), Laredo, TX.
Mary Help of Christians School, [E], (SP), Tampa, FL.
Mary House, Benedictine Grange Guest House, [N], (BGP). See The Benedictine Grange.
Mary House, Inc., [P], (WOR), Spencer, MA.
Mary Immaculate Academy, [E], (HRT), New Britain, CT.
Mary Immaculate Convent, [AA], (PH), Philadelphia, PA.
Mary Immaculate Hospital, [E], (RIC), Newport News, VA.
Mary Immaculate Hospital Division, [N], (BRK). See Catholic Medical Center of Brooklyn & Queens.
Mary Immaculate Hospital Home Health Agency, [N], (BRK). See Catholic Medical Center of Brooklyn & Queens.
Mary Immaculate School, [F], (TOL), Toledo, OH.
Mary Immaculate Seminary, [A], (ALN), Northampton, PA.
Mary Immaculate Seminary, [M], (ALN), Northhampton, PA.
Mary Immaculate Star of the Sea, [E], (MIA), Key West, FL.
Mary Immaculate, Inc., [Y], (BRK), Jamaica, NY.
Mary Katherine Convent, Poor Handmaids of Jesus Christ, [H], (BEL), Cairo, IL.
*Mary Lay Center, [O], (TOL), Bellevue, OH.
The Mary Louis Academy (College Preparatory), [G], (BRK), Jamaica Estates, NY.
The Mary Magdalen Foundation, [M], (WCH), Wichita, KS.
Mary Manning Walsh Home, [V], (NY), New York, NY.
Mary Martha House Convent, [X], (BO), Marlboro, MA.
Mary Mother of Hope House Transitional Residence, [F], (WIL). See Ministry of Caring, Inc.
Mary Mother of the Church Abbey, [M], (RIC), Richmond, VA.
Mary of Lourdes Elementary and Middle School, [E], (SCL), Little Falls, MN.
Mary of the Angels Convent, [L], (SPK), Spokane, WA.
Mary Our Queen Educational Endowment Trust, [N], (OM). See The Omaha Archdiocesan Educational Foundation, Inc.
Mary Queen of Peace Child Development Center, [J], (NO), New Orleans, LA.
Mary Queen of Peace School, [S], (NO), Mandeville, LA.
Mary Rondorf Retirement Home of Sacred Heart Parish, [H], (SCL), Staples, MN.
Mary Star of the Sea Apartments, HFDC, Inc., [L], (BRK). See Catholic Charities.
Mary The Mother Montesorri Pre-School, [A], (SPP), Pago Pago, American Samoa.
Mary Theotokos Centre, [E], (STF), West Burke, VT.
Mary's Center, [Q], (BAL), Pasadena, MD.
Mary's Hall, Inc., [L], (BRK). See Catholic Charities.
Mary's Home, Transitional Housing, La Habra, [G], (ORG). See St. Vincent de Paul Society.
Mary's House, [H], (ANC), Anchorage, AK.
Mary's Solitude, [K], (FTW). See Saint Mary's of the Immaculate Conception.
Mary's Solitude-Prayer Center, [M], (FTW), Notre Dame, IN.
Mary, Help of Christians Convent, [I], (CC), Laredo, TX.
Mary, Mother of the Church Convent, [N], (HRT), Hamden, CT.
Mary, Queen and Mother Nursing Center, [O], (STL), St. Louis, MO.
Mary, Queen of the Universe Convent, [N], (PEO), Alton, IL.
Marybrook Manor, [J], (DET), Livonia, MI.
Marycrest, [M], (CLV), Independence, OH.
Marycrest Convent Franciscan Sisters, [N], (DEN), Denver, CO.
Marycrest Health System, [Q], (DEN), Denver, CO.
Marycrest Manor, [I], (DET), Livonia, MI.
Marycrest Manor, Convalescent Home, [L], (LA), Culver City, CA.
Marydale, [G], (RVC). See St. Christopher-Ottilie Corp.
Marydale Center, [J], (DET). See Ryan Senior Residences of the Archdiocese of Detroit. Inc.
Marydale Retirement Village, [G], (WIL), Newark, DE.
Marydale Retreat Center, [P], (COV), Erlanger, KY.
Maryfield Nursing Home, [I], (CHL), High Point, NC.
Marygrove College, [C], (DET), Detroit, MI.
Marygrove College Campus Ministry, [S], (DET), Detroit, MI.
Marygrove Retreat Center, [F], (MAR), Garden, MI.
Marygrove Services, Inc., [N], (STL), Florissant, MO.
Marygrove, Inc., [W], (STL), Florissant, MO.
Maryhaven, [J], (DET). See Ryan Senior Residences of the Archdiocese of Detroit. Inc.
Maryhaven Center of Hope, [G], (RVC), Port Jefferson, NY.
Maryhaven Inc., [M], (CHI), Glenview, IL.
Maryhill Hermitage, [G], (WH), Wheeling, WV.
Maryhill Manor Nursing Home (SNF), [H], (GB), Niagara, WI.
Maryhill Renewal Center, [H], (ALX), Pineville, LA.
Maryhill Retreat Center, [Q], (STP), St. Paul, MN.
Maryhouse, [N], (HRT), Newington, CT.
Maryhouse, [P], (SAC). See Loaves & Fishes.
Maryhouse Residence for Women, [R], (PIT). See St. Joseph's House of Hospitality, Inc.
Maryhouse Residential Nursing Facility, [D], (SFS). See St. Mary's Healthcare Center of Pierre, South Dakota.
Maryhurst, [J], (L), Louisville, KY.
Mary-Joseph Residence for the Elderly, [N], (NO), New Orleans, LA.
Maryknoll, [M], (HRT), Wolcott, CT.
Maryknoll, [M], (SJ), Los Altos, CA.
Maryknoll Department of Development, [W], (BO), East Walpole, MA.
Maryknoll Fathers, [P], (CLV), Cleveland, OH.
Maryknoll Fathers, [N], (NEW), South Orange, NJ.
Maryknoll Fathers, [M], (SEA), Seattle, WA.
Maryknoll Fathers & Brothers, [N], (CHI), Chicago, IL.
Maryknoll Fathers and Brothers, [K], (DET), Detroit, MI.
Maryknoll Fathers and Brothers, [Q], (GAL), Houston, TX.
Maryknoll Fathers and Brothers, [R], (LA), Los Angeles, CA.
Maryknoll Fathers and Brothers, [Z], (NY), Maryknoll, NY.
Maryknoll Fathers and Brothers, [Z], (NY). See Maryknoll Fathers and Brothers.
Maryknoll Fathers & Brothers, [H], (STA), Jacksonville, FL.
Maryknoll Fathers and Brothers, [B], (WDC), Washington, DC.
The Maryknoll Fathers & Brothers Charitable Trust, [Z], (NY). See Maryknoll Fathers and Brothers.
Maryknoll Fathers and Brothers, Catholic Foreign Mission Society of America, [N], (STP), Minneapolis, MN.
Maryknoll Fathers and Brothers, Catholic Foreign Mission Society of America, Inc., [N], (SFR), San Francisco, CA.
Maryknoll Fathers House, [H], (HON), Honolulu, HI.
Maryknoll Fathers, Catholic Foreign Mission Society of America (Legal Title), [M], (DEN), Denver, CO.
Maryknoll House, [O], (BUF), Buffalo, NY.
Maryknoll House, [Z], (NY), New York, NY.
Maryknoll House, [Z], (PH), Philadelphia, PA.
Maryknoll House, [P], (STL), St. Louis, MO.
Maryknoll Mission Association of the Faithful, [DD], (NY), Maryknoll, NY.
Maryknoll Mission Association of the Faithful, Inc., [DD], (NY). See Maryknoll Mission Association of the Faithful.
Maryknoll Missioners, [N], (SJ), Gilroy, CA.
Maryknoll Residence, [N], (RVC), West Hempstead, NY.
Maryknoll Residential Care, [AA], (NY), Maryknoll, NY.
Maryknoll St. Teresa's Residence, [Z], (NY). See Maryknoll Fathers and Brothers.
Maryknoll Schools, [C], (HON), Honolulu, HI.
Maryknoll Sisters, [D], (CI), Colonia, Yap, FM.
Maryknoll Sisters, [I], (HON). See Maryknoll Sisters of St. Dominic M.M.
Maryknoll Sisters, [I], (HON). See Maryknoll Sisters of St. Dominic M.M.
Maryknoll Sisters, [C], (LSC), Las Cruces, NM.
Maryknoll Sisters, [I], (SD), San Diego, CA.
Maryknoll Sisters, [E], (STO), Stockton, CA.
Maryknoll Sisters Charitable Trust, [AA], (NY), Maryknoll, NY.
Maryknoll Sisters Cloister, [AA], (NY), Maryknoll, NY.
Maryknoll Sisters of St. Dominic, [N], (HRT), Wethersfield, CT.
Maryknoll Sisters of St. Dominic, [N], (HRT), New Britain, CT.
Maryknoll Sisters of St. Dominic, [N], (HRT), Terryville, CT.
Maryknoll Sisters of St. Dominic, [N], (HRT), Waterbury, CT.
Maryknoll Sisters of St. Dominic (M.M.), [R], (GAL), Houston, TX.
Maryknoll Sisters of St. Dominic Inc., [AA], (NY), Maryknoll, NY.
Maryknoll Sisters of St. Dominic M.M., [I], (HON), Honolulu, HI.
Maryknoll Sisters of St. Dominic, Inc., [F], (BWN), McAllen, TX.
Marylake - Carmelite Novitiate, [A], (LR), Little Rock, AR.
Maryland Catholic Health Care Consortium, Inc., [Q], (BAL), Baltimore, MD.
Maryland Health Center, [V], (WDC). See Spanish Catholic Center.
Maryland Province Center, [N], (BAL), Stevenson, MD.
Marylawn of the Oranges Convent, [O], (NEW), South Orange, NJ.
Marylawn of the Oranges, High School for Girls, [C], (NEW), South Orange, NJ.
Marylhurst College, [B], (P), Marylhurst, OR.
Marymount Academy, [H], (LA), Santa Barbara, CA.
Marymount Child Care Center, [I], (CLV), Garfield Heights, OH.
Marymount College, [C], (NY), Tarrytown, NY.
Marymount College, [CC], (NY). See University Apostolate.
Marymount College, Palos Verdes, California, [C], (LA), Rancho Palos Verdes, CA.
Marymount Congregational Home, [Q], (CLV), Cleveland, OH.
Marymount Diocesan Activities Center, Inc., [I], (SAL), Salina, KS.
Marymount Health Care Systems, [AA], (CLV), Garfield Heights, OH.
Marymount Hermitage, Inc., Hermit Sisters of Mary, [D], (B), Mesa, ID.
Marymount High School, [F], (LA), Los Angeles, CA.
Marymount Hospital, Inc., [J], (CLV), Cleveland, OH.
Marymount Manhattan College, [C], (NY), New York, NY.
Marymount Manhattan College, [CC], (NY). See University Apostolate.
Marymount Memorial Educational Trust Fund, [I], (SAL), Salina, KS.
Marymount School, [H], (NY), New York, NY.
Marymount School of Practical Nursing, [K], (CLV), Cleveland, OH.
Marymount University, [A], (ARL), Arlington, VA.
Marytown, Our Lady of Fatima Friary, [N], (CHI), Libertyville, IL.
Marytown, U.S. National Center of the Militia of the Immaculata Movement, [Q], (CHI), Libertyville, IL.
Maryvale, [I], (LA), Rosemead, CA.
Maryvale Educational Fund, Inc., [P], (BAL). See Chancery Office.
Maryvale Motherhouse, [K], (CHL), Vale, NC.
Maryvale Preparatory School, [D], (BAL), Brooklandville, MD.
Maryview Employee Assistance Program, [H], (RIC). See Bon Secours-Maryview Nursing Care.
Maryview Hospice Program, [H], (RIC). See Bon Secours-Maryview Nursing Care.
Maryview MedCare Centers (Urgent Care), [H], (RIC). See Bon Secours-Maryview Nursing Care.
Maryview Medical Center, [E], (RIC), Portsmouth, VA.
Maryview Psychiatric Hospital, [P], (RIC), Portsmouth, VA.
Maryview Wellspring Home Health Agency, [H], (RIC). See Bon Secours-Maryview Nursing Care.
Maryville Academy, [H], (CHI), Des Plaines, IL.
Maryville Novitiate and Provincial House, [I], (BR), Baton Rouge, LA.
Maryville Nursing Home, [K], (P), Beaverton, OR.
Marywood Academy, [L], (GR), Grand Rapids, MI.
Marywood Apartments, [H], (RIC), Richmond, VA.
Marywood Center for Spirituality and Ministry Formation, [J], (STA), Jacksonville, FL.
Marywood Children & Family Services, [E], (AUS), Austin, TX.
Marywood College, [C], (SCR), Scranton, PA.
Marywood Convalescent Center, [G], (LC), Wausau, WI.

Mercy Convent, [J], (PRT), Portland, ME.
Mercy Convent, [I], (SAC). See Institute of the Sisters of Mercy of the Americas.
Mercy Convent, [G], (SAV), Savannah, GA.
Mercy Convent and Formation House, [G], (AGN), Tai, GU.
Mercy Court, [C], (DM). See Mercy Hospital Medical Center.
Mercy Court, [EE], (PH), Yeadon, PA.
Mercy Crest of Arkansas, Inc., [G], (LR), Barling, AR.
Mercy Crestview Village, [O], (OM). See Mercy Housing dba Mercy House.
Mercy Cross Inter-Parochial High School, [B], (BLX), Biloxi, MS.
Mercy Diagnostic & Treatment Center, [J], (CHI). See Mercy Hospital and Medical Center.
Mercy Education Resource Center, [L], (SAC), Sacramento, CA.
Mercy Family Care Program Unit, [H], (DET), Detroit, MI.
Mercy Family Plaza, [U], (SFR). See Mercy/Charities Housing California.
Mercy Foundation - Bakersfield, [C], (FRS). See Mercy Healthcare Bakersfield.
Mercy Foundation of Des Moines - Affiliate of Catholic Health Initiatives, [I], (DM), Des Moines, IA.
Mercy Foundation, Inc., [J], (CHI). See Mercy Hospital and Medical Center.
Mercy Foundation, Inc., [J], (P). See Mercy Medical Center, Inc.
Mercy General Hospital, [G], (SAC), Sacramento, CA.
Mercy Geriatric Service, [C], (DM). See Mercy Hospital Medical Center.
Mercy Green Mountain Manor, [Q], (DEN). See Mercy Properties, Inc.
Mercy Hall, [N], (CIN), Cincinnati, OH.
Mercy Haverford Hospital, [T], (PH), Haverford, PA.
Mercy Health and Human Services, [C], (DM). See Mercy Hospital Medical Center.
Mercy Health & Rehabilitation Center Nursing Home Co., Inc., [H], (ROC), Auburn, NY.
Mercy Health Care & Rehabilitation Center, [J], (CHI). See Mercy Hospital and Medical Center.
Mercy Health Care and Rehabilitation Center, [M], (CHI), Homewood, IL.
Mercy Health Care Center, [J], (SCR), Nanticoke, PA.
Mercy Health Care Corp., [J], (CHI). See Mercy Hospital and Medical Center.
Mercy Health Center, [E], (OKL), Oklahoma City, OK.
Mercy Health Center of Central Iowa, [C], (DM). See Mercy Hospital Medical Center.
Mercy Health Center St. Mary's Unit-Oakcrest Manor, [J], (DUB), Dyersville, IA.
Mercy Health Center-St. Joseph's Unit, [H], (DUB), Dubuque, IA.
Mercy Health Center-St. Mary's Unit, [H], (DUB), Dyersville, IA.
Mercy Health Corp. of Southeastern PA, [EE], (PH), Bala Cynwyd, PA.
Mercy Health Corporation, [D], (RCK), Aurora, IL.
Mercy Health Foundation, [T], (DET), Farmington Hills, MI.
Mercy Health Foundation, [H], (PBL), Durango, CO.
Mercy Health Plaza, [K], (CIN), Fairfield, OH.
Mercy Health Promotion, Inc., [J], (P). See Mercy Medical Center, Inc.
Mercy Health Services (Formerly Sisters of Mercy Health Corporation), [T], (DET), Farmington Hills, MI.
Mercy Health System, [T], (CIN), Cincinnati, OH.
Mercy Health System - Western Ohio, Sisters of Mercy, [T], (CIN), Springfield, OH.
Mercy Health System of Western New York, [K], (BUF), Buffalo, NY.
Mercy Health System of Western New York, [T], (BUF), Buffalo, NY.
Mercy Healthcare Bakersfield, [C], (FRS), Bakersfield, CA.
Mercy Healthcare Center, Inc., [E], (OG), Tupper Lake, NY.
Mercy Healthcare North dba St. Elizabeth Community Hospital, [G], (SAC), Red Bluff, CA.
Mercy Healthcare Sacramento, [G], (SAC), Rancho Cordova, CA.
Mercy Healthcare, Inc., [J], (P). See Mercy Medical Center, Inc.
Mercy Heights Convent, [G], (AGN), Perezville-Tamuning, GU.
Mercy Heights Nursery and Kindergarten, [D], (AGN), Perezville-Tamuning, GU.
Mercy High School, [D], (BAL), Baltimore, MD.
Mercy High School, [B], (NOR), Middletown, CT.
Mercy High School, [C], (OM), Omaha, NE.
Mercy High School, [D], (RVC), Riverhead, NY.
Mercy High School, [B], (SAC), Red Bluff, CA.
Mercy High School (Girls), [E], (SFR), San Francisco, CA.
Mercy High School (Girls), [E], (SFR), Burlingame, CA.
Mercy High School for Girls, [E], (DET), Farmington Hills, MI.
Mercy High, Private School for Girls, [D], (ALB), Albany, NY.
Mercy Holly Park East, [Q], (DEN), See Mercy Properties, Inc.
Mercy Holly Park West, [Q], (DEN). See Mercy Properties, Inc.
The Mercy Home and School, [T], (PRO). See Miscellaneous Listings for the Diocese of Providence.
Mercy Home Care, [T], (CIN), Cincinnati, OH.
Mercy Home Care, [C], (FRS). See Mercy Hospital & Health Services.
Mercy Home for Children, [O], (BRK), Brooklyn, NY.
Mercy Home Health Services, Inc., [Q], (BAL), Baltimore, MD.
Mercy Hospice, [R], (PH), Philadelphia, PA.
Mercy Hospice, [K], (RVC), Uniondale, NY.
Mercy Hospice of Horry County, [C], (CHR), Myrtle Beach, SC.
Mercy Hospital, [D], (BIS), Williston, ND.
Mercy Hospital, [K], (BUF), Buffalo, NY.
Mercy Hospital, [J], (DAV), Iowa City, IA.
Mercy Hospital, [H], (DET), Detroit, MI.
Mercy Hospital, [D], (FAR), Devils Lake, ND.
Mercy Hospital, [D], (FAR), Valley City, ND.
Mercy Hospital, [C], (GAY), Cadillac, MI.
Mercy Hospital, [C], (GAY), Grayling, MI.
Mercy Hospital, [E], (GR), Muskegon, MI.
Mercy Hospital, [G], (MIA), Miami, FL.
*Mercy Hospital, [H], (PRT), Portland, ME.
Mercy Hospital, [I], (SCR), Scranton, PA.
Mercy Hospital, [I], (SCR), Wilkes-Barre, PA.
Mercy Hospital, [F], (SPR), Springfield, MA.
Mercy Hospital, [H], (TOL), Toledo, OH.
Mercy Hospital, [H], (TOL), Tiffin, OH.
Mercy Hospital, [E], (WCH), Fort Scott, KS.
Mercy Hospital & Health Services, [C], (FRS), Merced, CA.
Mercy Hospital and Medical Center, [J], (CHI), Chicago, IL.
Mercy Hospital and Medical Center dba Mercy Healthcare San Diego, [F], (SD), San Diego, CA.
Mercy Hospital Anderson, [K], (CIN), Cincinnati, OH.
Mercy Hospital Anderson Foundation, [U], (CIN), Cincinnati, OH.
Mercy Hospital Convent, [Q], (NO). See Sisters of Mercy of the Americas, R.S.M.
Mercy Hospital Convent, Sisters' Retirement Center, [I], (SC). See Sisters of Mercy of the St. Louis Regional Community, Inc.
Mercy Hospital Foundation, [P], (DAV), Iowa City, IA.
Mercy Hospital Foundation, [F], (SD). See Mercy Hospital and Medical Center dba Mercy Healthcare San Diego.
Mercy Hospital Foundation, Council Bluffs, [I], (DM), Council Bluffs, IA.
Mercy Hospital Guild of Iowa City, Iowa, [P], (DAV). See Mercy Hospital Foundation.
Mercy Hospital Medical Center, [C], (DM), Des Moines, IA.
Mercy Hospital of Folsom, [G], (SAC), Folsom, CA.
Mercy Hospital of Franciscan Sisters, [H], (DUB), Oelwein, IA.
Mercy Hospital of Hamilton-Fairfield, [K], (CIN), Hamilton, OH.
Mercy Hospital of Pittsburgh, [J], (PIT), Pittsburgh, PA.
The Mercy Hospital of Pittsburgh, [J], (PIT). See Pittsburgh Mercy Health System, Inc.
Mercy Hospital of Port Huron, [H], (DET), Port Huron, MI.
Mercy Hospital, Iowa City, Iowa, [P], (DAV). See Mercy Hospital Foundation.
Mercy Hospital, Willard, [H], (TOL), Willard, OH.
Mercy Hospitals of Kansas-Independence, [E], (WCH), Independence, KS.
Mercy Housing & Shelter Corporation, [V], (HRT), Hartford, CT.
Mercy Housing Arizona, [J], (PHX), Phoenix, AZ.
Mercy Housing Colorado, [Q], (DEN). See Mercy Housing, Inc.
Mercy Housing Corporation, [X], (CHI), Chicago, IL.
Mercy Housing dba Mercy House, [O], (OM), Omaha, NE.
Mercy Housing Development Fund Co., Inc., [Q], (SY), Auburn, NY.
Mercy Housing Idaho Properties, Inc., [G], (B). See Mercy Housing Idaho, Inc.
Mercy Housing Idaho, Inc., [G], (B), Nampa, ID.
*Mercy Housing Midwest, [O], (OM). See Mercy Housing dba Mercy House.
Mercy Housing, Inc., [Q], (DEN), Denver, CO.
Mercy Information Systems, [T], (DET), Farmington Hills, MI.
Mercy International Health Services, [T], (DET), Farmington Hills, MI.
Mercy Life Center Corporation, [J], (PIT). See Pittsburgh Mercy Health System, Inc.
Mercy Long Term Care Initiatives dba Providence Retirement Home, [H], (IND), New Albany, IN.
Mercy McAuley Center-Mercy Health Systems, [L], (CIN), Urbana, OH.
Mercy Med-Care, Inc., [I], (SCR), Wilkes-Barre, PA.
Mercy Medical, [F], (MOB), Daphne, AL.
Mercy Medical at Presidential Towers, [J], (CHI). See Mercy Hospital and Medical Center.
Mercy Medical Center, [B], (B), Nampa, ID.
Mercy Medical Center, [D], (BIS), Williston, ND.
Mercy Medical Center, [K], (CIN), Springfield, OH.
Mercy Medical Center, [F], (GB), Oshkosh, WI.
Mercy Medical Center, [D], (PBL), Durango, CO.
Mercy Medical Center, [I], (RVC), Rockville Centre, NY.
Mercy Medical Center, [G], (SAC), Mt. Shasta, CA.
Mercy Medical Center, [G], (SAC), Redding, CA.
Mercy Medical Center, Cedar Rapids, Iowa, [H], (DUB), Cedar Rapids, IA.
Mercy Medical Center, Cedar Rapids, Iowa, Endowment Foundation, Inc., [H], (DUB), Cedar Rapids, IA.
Mercy Medical Center, Inc., [I], (BAL), Baltimore, MD.
Mercy Medical Center, Inc., [J], (P), Roseburg, OR.
Mercy Medical Center, Wittenberg University Campus Ministry, [Q], (CIN), Springfield, OH.
Mercy Medical Foundation, [D], (BIS), Williston, ND.
Mercy Medical in Chatham, [J], (CHI). See Mercy Hospital and Medical Center.
Mercy Medical in Chicago Ridge, [J], (CHI). See Mercy Hospital and Medical Center.
Mercy Medical in Chinatown, [J], (CHI). See Mercy Hospital and Medical Center.
Mercy Medical in Justice, [J], (CHI). See Mercy Hospital and Medical Center.
Mercy Medical in Lincoln Park, Chicago, [J], (CHI). See Mercy Hospital and Medical Center.
Mercy Medical in Little Village, [J], (CHI). See Mercy Hospital and Medical Center.
Mercy Medical in Mt. Greenwood, Chicago, [J], (CHI). See Mercy Hospital and Medical Center.
Mercy Medical Office Bldgs., Inc., [C], (DM). See Bergan Mercy Health System: Mercy Hospital.
Mercy Medical on Michigan, [J], (CHI). See Mercy Hospital and Medical Center.
Mercy Medical on Pulaski, [J], (CHI). See Mercy Hospital and Medical Center.
Mercy Memorial Hospital, [K], (CIN), Urbana, OH.
Mercy Midlands: Mercy Hospital, [C], (DM), Corning, IA.
Mercy Midwest Properties, [O], (KC), Lee's Summit, MO.
Mercy Mission Services, [G], (MIA). See Mercy Hospital.
Mercy Montessori School, [Y], (BRK), Brooklyn, NY.
Mercy Montessori School, [E], (L), Louisville, KY.
Mercy Moscow, Inc., [G], (B), Nampa, ID.
Mercy Mount Clemens Corporation, [H], (DET), Clinton Township, MI.
Mercy North, Inc., [G], (MIA). See Mercy Hospital.
Mercy Northglen, [O], (OM). See Mercy Housing dba Mercy House.
Mercy Outreach Iowa City, Inc., [P], (DAV). See Mercy Hospital Foundation.
Mercy Pavilion Skilled Nursing Home and Senior Care Residence, [F], (KAL), Battle Creek, MI.
Mercy Prayer Center, [K], (ROC), Rochester, NY.
Mercy Primary Care Group, Inc., [P], (BAL). See Chancery Office.
Mercy Properties, [C], (DM). See Mercy Hospital Medical Center.
Mercy Properties Arizona, [J], (PHX), Phoenix, AZ.
Mercy Properties II, Inc., [G], (B). See Mercy Housing Idaho, Inc.
Mercy Properties, Inc., [Q], (DEN), Denver, CO.
Mercy Providence Hospital, [J], (PIT), Pittsburgh, PA.
Mercy Providence Hospital, Inc., [J], (PIT). See Pittsburgh Mercy Health System, Inc.
Mercy Recovery Center, [D], (BIS), Williston, ND.
Mercy Regional Health Foundation, Inc., [C], (SPC). See St. John's Regional Medical Center; Mercy Lifecare Systems, Inc.
Mercy Regional Health System, [D], (ALT), Altoona, PA.
Mercy Regional Medical Center, [E], (CC), Laredo, TX.
Mercy Residence, [I], (SAC). See Institute of the Sisters of Mercy of the Americas.
Mercy Residence at Tolentine Center, [M], (CHI), Olympia Fields, IL.
Mercy Retirement and Care Center, [M], (OAK), Oakland, CA.
Mercy Retreat Center, [Y], (MIL), Bristol, WI.
Mercy St. Theresa Center, [L], (CIN), Cincinnati, OH.
Mercy San Juan, [I], (SAC). See Institute of the Sisters of Mercy of the Americas.
Mercy San Juan Hospital/Mercy American River Hospital, [G], (SAC). See Mercy American River Hospital.
Mercy School of Health Sciences, [C], (DM). See Mercy Hospital Medical Center.
Mercy Services Corp., [J], (CHI). See Mercy Hospital and Medical Center.
Mercy Services Corp., [Q], (DEN). See Mercy Housing, Inc.
Mercy Services Corporation, [C], (PHX), Phoenix, AZ.

Mercy Services for Aging, [J], (DET), Farmington Hills, MI.
Mercy Services for Aging, [T], (DET), Farmington Hills, MI.
Mercy Services for Aging, Non-profit Housing Corporation, [T], (DET), Farmington Hills, MI.
Mercy Services Foundation of Aurora, [L], (RCK), Aurora, IL.
Mercy Siena Woods, [L], (CIN), Dayton, OH.
Mercy Sisters, Ireland, [O], (OAK), El Cerrito, CA.
Mercy Southeast Idaho, Inc., [G], (B), Nampa, ID.
Mercy Southwest Hospital, [C], (FRS). See Mercy Healthcare Bakersfield.
Mercy Special Care Hospital, [I], (SCR), Nanticoke, PA.
Mercy Special Learning Center, [E], (ALN), Allentown, PA.
Mercy Surgical & Diagnostic Center, [C], (FRS). See Mercy Hospital & Health Services.
Mercy Terrace Apartments, [I], (E), Erie, PA.
Mercy Terrace Corporation, [U], (SFR). See MSC Psychiatric Services.
Mercy Terrace Corporation Apartments, [K], (SFR), San Francisco, CA.
Mercy Tiffin Health Foundation, [O], (TOL), Tiffin, OH.
Mercy Twin Cities - Mercy Oakwood Gardens, [O], (OM), Omaha, NE.
Mercy Twin Falls, Inc., [G], (B). See Mercy Housing Idaho, Inc.
Mercy Villa, [M], (CAM), Ventnor, NJ.
Mercy Villa, [H], (OM), Omaha, NE.
Mercy Village (Assisted Living), [E], (LR). See St. Edward Health Facilities of Scott County dba Mercy Hospital.
Mercy Vocational High School, [E], (PH), Philadelphia, PA.
Mercy Western Manor, [O], (OM). See Mercy Housing dba Mercy House.
Mercy Works on Ashland, [J], (CHI). See Mercy Hospital and Medical Center.
Mercy/Charities Housing California, [L], (SAC), Sacramento, CA.
Mercy/Charities Housing California, [Q], (SFR). See Catholic Charities of the Archdiocese of San Francisco.
Mercy/Charities Housing California, [U], (SFR), San Francisco, CA.
Mercycare Corporation, [H], (ALB), Albany, NY.
Mercycare Corporation, St. Peter's Hospital, [H], (ALB), Albany, NY.
Mercycare Service Corporation, [H], (DUB), Cedar Rapids, IA.
MercyClinic, [P], (SAC). See Loaves & Fishes.
Mercyhurst College, [B], (E), Erie, PA.
Mercyhurst Preparatory School, [D], (E), Erie, PA.
Mercyknoll, Incorporated, [N], (HRT), West Hartford, CT.
Mercy-McMahon Terrace, [F], (SAC), Sacramento, CA.
Mercymount Country Day School, [F], (PRO), Cumberland, RI.
Mercy-St. John's Center, [R], (CIN), Springfield, OH.
Mercy-Xavier Fund Corporation, [M], (NOR), Middletown, CT.
Meredith Memorial Home, [F], (BEL), Belleville, IL.
Meriden, [S], (HRT). See Catholic Charities-Catholic Family Services (Archdiocese of Hartford).
Merilac Lodge and Casa de Crianza, [D], (TUC). See Social Service Agencies: Pima County.
Merion Mercy Academy, [G], (PH), Merion, PA.
Merkle-Knipprath Countryside Home, [I], (JOL), Clifton, IL.
Merrimack College, [C], (BO), North Andover, MA.
Merrimack College Campus Ministry Center, [CC], (BO), North Andover, MA.
The Merrimack Montessori School, [G], (BO), Haverhill, MA.
Metairie Manor, Metairie II, and Metairie III, [N], (NO), Metairie, LA.
Metro Catholic Broadcasting, KBVM-FM, 88.3, [Q], (P), Portland, OR.
Metropolitan Boston, [K], (BO). See Family Counseling and Guidance Centers.
Metropolitan Boston Dialysis Center, [FF], (BO). See Caritas Christi - A Catholic Health Care System.
Metropolitan Boston Dialysis Center, Inc., [DD], (BO). See Chancery Office.
Metropolitan Office of Catholic Education, [D], (DUB), Cedar Rapids, IA.
Metropolitan State College, [P], (DEN). See Auraria Campus.
Metuchen Community Services Corporation, [N], (MET), East Brunswick, NJ.
MI Management, Inc., [FF], (BO), Boston, MA.
Miami University Catholic Campus Ministry, [Q], (CIN), Oxford, OH.
The Michael Burke Foundation, [K], (LA). See Saint John's Hospital and Health Center.
Michaelmas Manor, Inc., [O], (TOL), Toledo, OH.
Michaud Memorial Manor, [F], (BUR), Derby Line, VT.
Michigan Catholic Conference, [L], (LAN), Lansing, MI.
Micronesia Seminar, [A], (CI), Pohnpei, FM.
Mid Ohio Valley - S.J. Health Service, Inc, [R], (WH), Wheeling, WV.
Mid-America Catholic Colleges, [M], (MAD), Madison, WI.
Mid-County Medical Center, Inc., [D], (PMB). See St. Mary's Hospital, Inc.
Middle Building, [D], (Y). See Ashtabula Catholic Elementary School.
Middle Division, [G], (PRO). See Bishop McVinney Regional School.
Middle School, [D], (ALN). See Holy Spirit School.
Middle School, [C], (PBL). See John Neumann Catholic Schools.
Middlesex County Office, [E], (MET), Edison, NJ.
Mid-Life Directions, [S], (TR), Brick, NJ.
Mid-Tennessee Rural Outreach Association, [L], (NSH), Nashville, TN.
Midtown Catholic Community Services, [W], (STL). See Catholic Community Services Administration.
Midtown Center, [W], (CHI), Chicago, IL.
Midwest Hispanic Catholic Commission, N.C.C.B., [O], (FTW), Notre Dame, IN.
The Midwest Patrons of the Arts in the Vatican Museums, [X], (CHI), Chicago, IL.
Migrant and Refugee Services, [E], (FRS), Merced, CA.
Migrant Education Apostolate, Los Hermanos, [C], (VEN), Bonita Springs, FL.
Migrant Program-Cristo Rey Community Center, [D], (LAN), Lansing, MI.
Migration and Refugee Resettlement Dept., [J], (PH). See The Catholic Social Services of the Archdiocese of Philadelphia.
Migration and Refugee Service, [S], (HRT). See Catholic Charities-Catholic Family Services (Archdiocese of Hartford).
Migration and Refugee Services, [G], (LAV), Las Vegas, NV.
Migration and Refugee Services, [W], (STL), St. Louis, MO.
Migration and Refugee Services, [D], (TUC). See Social Service Agencies: Pima County.
Migration Refugee Services; Refugee Resettlement; Refugee Job Placement, [J], (DAL), Dallas, TX.
Mike Foye Apartments, [I], (SPK), Walla Walla, WA.
Miles Jesu, [H], (PCE), Ponce, PR.
Milford, [S], (HRT). See Catholic Charities-Catholic Family Services (Archdiocese of Hartford).
Milford Catholic Elementary School, [F], (WOR), Milford, MA.
Milford Spiritual Center, [P], (CIN), Milford, OH.
Mill Hill Fathers Residence, [Z], (NY), Hartsdale, NY.
Mill Hill Missionaries Procure, [R], (LA), Los Angeles, CA.
Mill Hill Sisters, [G], (NOR), Middletown, CT.
Millbrook Village Senior Citizens Development, [N], (HRT). See Sisters of Notre Dame de Namur.
Miller Road Housing Development Co., Inc., [Q], (SY), Syracuse, NY.
Millikin University Newman Catholic Community, [M], (SFD), Decatur, IL.
Mills College Newman Center, [Q], (OAK), Oakland, CA.
Millsaps College Newman Center, [G], (JKS), Jackson, MS.
Milwaukee Achiever Program, Inc., [Y], (MIL), Milwaukee, WI.
Milwaukee Archdiocesan Campus Ministry, [X], (MIL), Milwaukee, WI.
Milwaukee Archdiocesan Council of Deacons, [Y], (MIL), Milwaukee, WI.
Milwaukee Archdiocesan Elementary Principal's Association, [Y], (MIL), Milwaukee, WI.
Milwaukee Archdiocesan Holy Name Society, [W], (MIL), Wauwatosa, WI.
Milwaukee Archdiocesan Office for World Mission, [V], (MIL), Milwaukee, WI.
*Milwaukee Catholic Home, [N], (MIL), Milwaukee, WI.
Mindszenty High School, [B], (CI), Palau, PW.
Minim Fathers, [R], (LA), Los Angeles, CA.
Ministerio Nueva Vida, [H], (YAK), Sunnyside, WA.
Ministers of Service, [V], (CIN), Cincinnati, OH.
Ministr-O-Media, Inc., [V], (WDC), Pomfret, MD.
Ministry and Life Retreat Center, [M], (GB), De Pere, WI.
The Ministry Development Center for Women Religious, Inc., [FF], (BO), Newton, MA.
Ministry for Religious Research and Consultancy, [R], (SCR), Clarks Summit, PA.
Ministry in Higher Education, [V], (CHI), Chicago, IL.
Ministry of Caring, Inc., [F], (WIL), Wilmington, DE.
Ministry of Evangelization and Catechesis, [FF], (BO), Boston, MA.
Ministry of His Able People, [I], (NOR), Wauregan, CT.
Ministry of the Word, [W], (BO), Boston, MA.
Ministry Potential Discerner, [I], (FAR), Fargo, ND.
Ministry Resource Center for Women Religious, [S], (NEW), Scotch Plains, NJ.
Ministry to Nursing Homes, [K], (GF), Billings, MT.
The Ministry to the University of Wisconsin-Stout, [L], (LC), Menomonie, WI.
Ministry with Persons with Disabilities, [M], (LA), Los Angeles, CA.
Minnesota Catholic Conference, [S], (STP), St. Paul, MN.
Minot Catholic Schools Corporation, [J], (BIS), Minot, ND.
Minot State University-Bottineau, [I], (FAR), Bottineau, ND.
Miramar Retreat Center, [Y], (BO), Duxbury, MA.
Miryam's House, [H], (SPK), Spokane, WA.
Miryam's House of Transition, [O], (SPK). See Transitional Program for Women dba Transitions.
Miscellaneous Listings for the Diocese of Providence, [T], (PRO), Providence, RI.
Miscellaneous Organizations, [B], (STV), St. Thomas, VI.
Misericordia Convalescent Home, [G], (HBG), York, PA.
Misericordia Home South, [L], (CHI), Chicago, IL.
Misericordia/Heart of Mercy Center, [L], (CHI), Chicago, IL.
Misioneras Catequistas de los Pobres, [F], (BWN), Mission, TX.
Misioneras Eucaristicas Franciscanas, [F], (BWN), Mission, TX.
Misioneras Guadalupanas del Espiritu Santo, [L], (FR), New Bedford, MA.
Misioneros Hijos del Immaculado Corazon de Maria (Claretianos), [C], (CGS), Caguas, PR.
Mission College Preparatory Catholic High School, [C], (MRY), San Luis Obispo, CA.
*Mission Health Corporation, [T], (DET), Novi, MI.
Mission Helper Center, [N], (BAL), Baltimore, MD.
Mission Helper Productions, Inc., [Q], (BAL), Baltimore, MD.
Mission Helpers of the Sacred Heart, [O], (WDC), Lanham-Seabrook, MD.
Mission Helpers of the Sacred Heart Convent, [F], (PT), Marianna, FL.
Mission Helpers of the Sacred Heart-Our Lady of Pompei Convent, [N], (BAL), Baltimore, MD.
Mission Holding Corporation, [U], (SFR), San Rafael, CA.
Mission Hospital Regional Medical Center, [F], (ORG), Mission Viejo, CA.
Mission International, Inc., [N], (MET), Somerset, NJ.
Mission of Our Lady of Mercy-Mercy Home for Boys and Girls, [H], (CHI), Chicago, IL.
Mission of the Holy Cross, [G], (CHI). See Catholic Charities of the Archdiocese of Chicago-Archdiocesan Offices.
Mission of the Immaculate Virgin, [O], (NY), New York, NY.
Mission Project Service, [J], (OG), Watertown, NY.
Mission Promotion, [DD], (BO). See Chancery Office.
Mission Resource Center, [T], (PRO). See Franciscan Missionaries of Mary.
Mission San Luis Rey Retreat, [K], (SD), San Luis Rey, CA.
Mission Share, [S], (COV), Fort Thomas, KY.
Missionaries of Africa, [N], (CHI), Chicago, IL.
Missionaries of Africa, [H], (ORG), Orange, CA.
Missionaries of Africa, [O], (SP), St. Petersburg, FL.
Missionaries of Africa, [M], (WDC), Washington, DC.
Missionaries of Charity, [J], (ATL), Atlanta, GA.
Missionaries of Charity, [N], (BAL), Baltimore, MD.
Missionaries of Charity, [O], (CHI), Chicago, IL.
Missionaries of Charity, [K], (CHL), Charlotte, NC.
Missionaries of Charity, [N], (DAL), Dallas, TX.
Missionaries of Charity, [N], (DEN), Denver, CO.
Missionaries of Charity, [L], (DET), Detroit, MI.
Missionaries of Charity, [Q], (FR), New Bedford, MA.
Missionaries of Charity, [I], (LAF), Lafayette, LA.
Missionaries of Charity, [K], (MEM), Memphis, TN.
Missionaries of Charity, [I], (MIA), Miami, FL.
Missionaries of Charity, [AA], (PH), Norristown, PA.
Missionaries of Charity, [E], (PHX), Phoenix, AZ.
Missionaries of Charity, [I], (SD), San Diego, CA.
Missionaries of Charity, [O], (SFR), San Francisco, CA.
Missionaries of Charity, [R], (STL), St. Louis, MO.
Missionaries of Charity, [O], (WDC), Washington, DC.
Missionaries of Charity Brothers, [R], (LA), Los Angeles, CA.
Missionaries of Charity Brothers, House of Formation, [V], (LA), Los Angeles, CA.
Missionaries of Charity Brothers, Regional Center and Novitiate, [V], (LA), Los Angeles, CA.
Missionaries of Charity Convent, [N], (PEO), Peoria, IL.
Missionaries of Charity, Contemplative Our Lady of Lourdes Convent, [V], (BRK), Brooklyn, NY.
Missionaries of Charity, Gift of Mary, [AA], (PH), Chester, PA.

Missionaries of Charity, Gift of Peace Convent, [O], (WDC), Washington, DC.
Missionaries of Charity, Inc., [AA], (NY), New York, NY.
Missionaries of Jesus, [F], (BWN), Brownsville, TX.
Missionaries of LaSalette, [M], (HRT). See Missionaries of LaSalette Provincial Secretary.
Missionaries of LaSalette Provincial Secretary, [M], (HRT), Hartford, CT.
The Missionaries of Our Lady of La Salette, Provincialate, [W], (STL), St. Louis, MO.
Missionaries of Our Lady of LaSalette Corp., [W], (BO), Ipswich, MA.
Missionaries of Pastoral Charity Society, [T], (SAT), San Antonio, TX.
Missionaries of Saint Charles, [N], (CHI), Oak Park, IL.
Missionaries of the Company of Mary-Montfort Missionaries, [M], (WDC), Washington, DC.
Missionaries of the Holy Apostles, [F], (NOR), Cromwell, CT.
Missionaries of the Holy Family, General Mission Office—M.S.F., Inc., [M], (RIC), West Point, VA.
Missionaries of the Kingship of Christ, [R], (OAK), Oakland, CA.
Missionaries of the Kingship of Christ, [P], (SFR), San Francisco, CA.
Missionaries of the Kingship of Christ, [W], (STL), St. Louis, MO.
Missionaries of the Kingship of Christ, [P], (STP), St. Paul, MN.
Missionaries of the Kingship of Christ, [U], (WDC), West Bethesda, MD.
Missionaries of the Sacred Heart, [A], (ALN), Center Valley, PA.
Missionaries of the Sacred Heart, [K], (ALN), Reading, PA.
Missionaries of the Sacred Heart, [M], (SAT), San Antonio, TX.
Missionaries of the Sacred Heart Community, [H], (RCK), Aurora, IL.
Missionaries of the Sacred Heart of Jesus and Our Lady of Guadalupe M.S.C.Gpe., [O], (CHI), Arlington Heights, IL.
Missionary Association of Catholic Women, [V], (MIL), Milwaukee, WI.
Missionary Association of Mary Immaculate-Mission Oblates of Mary Immaculate, [K], (BEL), Belleville, IL.
Missionary Brothers of Charity, [P], (LA), Los Angeles, CA.
Missionary Carmelites of St. Teresa (C.M.S.T.), [R], (GAL), Houston, TX.
Missionary Catechist of the Poor, [N], (DAL), Dallas, TX.
Missionary Catechists of Divine Providence, [F], (BWN), Pharr, TX.
Missionary Catechists of Divine Providence, [B], (SAN), Odessa, TX.
Missionary Catechists of Divine Providence, [N], (SAT), San Antonio, TX.
Missionary Catechists of Divine Providence (M.C.D.P.) Casa Providencia, [R], (GAL), Houston, TX.
The Missionary Catechists of St. Therese of the Infant Jesus, Inc., [O], (WDC), Fort Washington, MD.
Missionary Catechists of the Sacred Hearts of Jesus and Mary, [I], (FWT), Fort Worth, TX.
Missionary Catechists of the Sacred Hearts of Jesus and Mary, [E], (VIC), Victoria, TX.
Missionary Catechists of the Sacred Hearts of Jesus and Mary (M.C.S.H.S.M.), [R], (GAL), Houston, TX.
Missionary Cathechists of Divine Providence, [I], (AUS), Austin, TX.
Missionary Community of St. Paul the Apostle and Mary, Mother of the Church, Inc., [Y], (MIL), Racine, WI.
Missionary Daughters of the Most Pure Virgin Mary, [I], (CC), Kingsville, TX.
Missionary Ecumenical, [I], (AUS), Somerville, TX.
Missionary Franciscan Sisters of the Immaculate Conception, [N], (HRT), New Haven, CT.
Missionary Franciscan Sisters of the Immaculate Conception, [N], (HRT), East Haven, CT.
Missionary Fraternity of Mary, USA, Ltd., [I], (WIL), Seaford, DE.
Missionary Oblates of Mary Immaculate, [W], (BO), Lowell, MA.
Missionary Oblates of Mary Immaculate, [K], (MAN), Hudson, NH.
Missionary Oblates of Mary Immaculate, [W], (STP), St. Paul, MN.
Missionary Oblates of Mary Immaculate, [M], (WDC), Washington, DC.
Missionary Oblates of Mary Immaculate - St. Henry's Oblate Residence, [G], (BEL), Belleville, IL.
Missionary Oblates of Mary Immaculate of Texas Continuing Care Foundation, [S], (SAT), San Antonio, TX.
Missionary Oblates of Mary Immaculate, Western Province, Inc., [DD], (LA). See Chancery Office.
Missionary Oblates of St. Benedict, [K], (JOL), Naperville, IL.
Missionary Servant of the Most Blessed Trinity, [AA], (PH), Philadelphia, PA.
The Missionary Servants of Pope John Paul I, [O], (MAN), Gilford, NH.
Missionary Servants of the Most Blessed Trinity, [N], (HRT), Bloomfield, CT.
Missionary Servants of the Most Blessed Trinity, [N], (HRT), New Hartford, CT.
Missionary Servants of the Most Blessed Trinity, [F], (R), Southern Pines, NC.
Missionary Servants of the Most Blessed Trinity Ascension Missionary Cenacle, [S], (LA), Los Angeles, CA.
Missionary Servants of the Most Holy Trinity, [P], (CLV), Cleveland, OH.
Missionary Servants of the Most Holy Trinity, [M], (WDC), Adelphi, MD.
Missionary Servants of the Most Holy Trinity, S.T., [J], (ARL), Arlington, VA.
Missionary Sisters of Christ the King, [O], (CHI), Chicago, IL.
Missionary Sisters of Christ the King (Poland), [S], (LA), Los Angeles, CA.
Missionary Sisters of Divine Providence, [N], (PAT), Passaic, NJ.
Missionary Sisters of Jesus, Mary & Joseph, [K], (ELP), Marfa, TX.
Missionary Sisters of Jesus, Mary & Joseph (M.J.M.J.), [K], (ELP), El Paso, TX.
Missionary Sisters of Mother of God, [F], (STF), Stamford, CT.
Missionary Sisters of Our Lady of Africa, [O], (WDC), Chevy Chase, MD.
Missionary Sisters of Our Lady of Africa (M.S.O.L.A.), [H], (BUR), Winooski, VT.
Missionary Sisters of St. Benedict, [O], (RVC), Huntington, NY.
Missionary Sisters of St. Columbans, St. Columban's on the Lake, [P], (BUF), Silver Creek, NY.
Missionary Sisters of St. Peter Claver, [R], (STL), Chesterfield, MO.
Missionary Sisters of the Holy Family, [Q], (MIL), West Allis, WI.
Missionary Sisters of the Holy Rosary, [AA], (PH), Philadelphia, PA.
Missionary Sisters of the Holy Rosary, [AA], (PH), Bryn Mawr, PA.
Missionary Sisters of the Holy Rosary (M.S.H.R.), [AA], (PH), Ardmore, PA.
Missionary Sisters of the Immaculate Conception, [J], (PRT), Orland, ME.
Missionary Sisters of the Immaculate Conception, [F], (SB), Calimesa, CA.
Missionary Sisters of the Immaculate Conception (S.M.I.C.), [R], (GAL), Houston, TX.
Missionary Sisters of the Immaculate Conception of the Mother of God, [I], (AUS), Austin, TX.
Missionary Sisters of the Immaculate Conception of the Mother of God, [N], (PAT), West Paterson, NJ.
Missionary Sisters of the Immaculate Conception of the Mother of God, [N], (PAT), Paterson, NJ.
Missionary Sisters of the Immaculate Conception, Convent of the Immaculate Conception, [N], (PAT), West Paterson, NJ.
Missionary Sisters of the Immaculate Conception, Peace Community, [N], (PAT), West Paterson, NJ.
Missionary Sisters of the Immaculate Heart of Mary, [F], (BWN), Alamo, TX.
Missionary Sisters of the Immaculate Heart of Mary, [F], (BWN), McAllen, TX.
Missionary Sisters of the Immaculate Heart of Mary, [F], (BWN), San Benito, TX.
Missionary Sisters of the Immaculate Heart of Mary, [F], (BWN), La Feria, TX.
Missionary Sisters of the Immaculate Heart of Mary, [AA], (NY), New York, NY.
Missionary Sisters of the Immaculate of the Mother of God, [N], (PAT), Paterson, NJ.
Missionary Sisters of the Lady of the Holy Rosary, [B], (SAN), Ft. Stockton, TX.
Missionary Sisters of the Most Blessed Sacrament and Mary Immaculate, [O], (NEW), Newark, NJ.
Missionary Sisters of the Most Sacred Heart of Jesus, [L], (ALN), Allentown, PA.
Missionary Sisters of the Most Sacred Heart, Trinity House, [AA], (PH), Philadelphia, PA.
Missionary Sisters of the Sacred Heart (Cabrini Sisters), [AA], (PH), Philadelphia, PA.
Missionary Sisters of the Sacred Heart (Cabrini) M.S.C., [Q], (NO), New Orleans, LA.
Missionary Sisters of the Sacred Heart "ad Gentes", [J], (ATL), Chamblee, GA.
Missionary Sisters of the Sacred Heart of Jesus, [O], (CHI), Chicago, IL.
Missionary Sisters of the Sacred Heart of Jesus (Cabrini Sisters), [AA], (PH), Radnor, PA.
Missionary Sisters of the Sacred Heart of Jesus "Ad Gentes", [G], (KNX), Chattanooga, TN.
Missionary Sisters Of The Society Of Mary (Waltham, MA) S.M.S.M., [K], (MEM), Memphis, TN.
Missionary Society of St. Paul, Inc. - U.S. Region, [Q], (GAL), Barrette Station, TX.
Missionary Sons of the Immaculate Heart of Mary, [R], (LA), Los Angeles, CA.
*Missionary Vehicle Association, Inc., [V], (WDC), Washington, DC.
Missionhurst Community Residence, [M], (SAT), San Antonio, TX.
Missionhurst Formation Community, [B], (SAT), San Antonio, TX.
Missionhurst, C.I.C.M.-Central House and Provincialate, [J], (ARL), Arlington, VA.
Missionhurst-C.I.C.M., [J], (ARL), Falls Church, VA.
Mississippi College Newman Center, [G], (JKS), Clinton, MS.
Mississippi Gulf Coast Community College, [G], (BLX), Gulfport, MS.
Mississippi State University Catholic Student Association, [G], (JKS), Starkville, MS.
Mississippi State University for Women Student Center, [G], (JKS), Columbus, MS.
Missouri Catholic Conference, [G], (JC), Jefferson City, MO.
Mobile Podiatry, Dentures and Eyeglasses Clinic, [D], (TUC). See Social Service Agencies: Pima County.
Moeller High School, [E], (CIN), Cincinnati, OH.
Mohawk Valley Community College, [V], (SY), Utica, NY.
Mohun Health Care Center, [E], (COL), Columbus, OH.
Mohun Health Care Center, [I], (COL). See St. Mary of the Springs.
Mokena Family Health Center, [G], (JOL). See St. Joseph Medical Center.
Molloy College, [B], (RVC), Rockville Centre, NY.
Molokai Catholic Community, [I], (HON). See St. Francis Convent.
Monastery of Christ in the Desert, [J], (SFE), Abiquiu, NM.
Monastery of Christ in the Mountains, [F], (LAV), Caliente, NV.
Monastery of Christ on the Mountain, [N], (WH), Hinton, WV.
Monastery of Discalced Carmelite Nuns, [I], (MOB), Mobile, AL.
Monastery of Discalced Carmelites, [X], (BO), Boston, MA.
Monastery of Discalced Carmelites, [N], (DAL), Dallas, TX.
Monastery of Discalced Carmelites, [L], (MAN), Concord, NH.
Monastery of Discalced Carmelites, [Q], (PRO), Barrington, RI.
Monastery of Discalced Carmelities, [O], (CHI), Des Plaines, IL.
Monastery of Mary the Queen, Dominican Nuns, [J], (ROC), Elmira, NY.
Monastery of Our Lady and St. Joseph Carmelite Monastery, [J], (ROC), Pittsford, NY.
Monastery of Our Lady of Charity of Refuge, [I], (LR), Hot Springs, AR.
Monastery of Our Lady of Charity of Refuge (Good Shepherd), [F], (LR), Hot Springs National Park, AR.
Monastery of Our Lady of Grace, [N], (HRT), North Guilford, CT.
Monastery of Our Lady of Light (Capuchin Poor Clares), [N], (DEN), Denver, CO.
Monastery of Our Lady of Little Citeaux, [F], (KNX), Copperhill, TN.
Monastery of Our Lady of Mercy, [Z], (PH), Philadelphia, PA.
Monastery of Our Lady of Mount Carmel, [B], (WDC), Washington, DC.
Monastery of Our Lady of Mount Carmel and Little Flower, [I], (OKL), Oklahoma City, OK.
Monastery of Our Lady of Sorrows, [N], (CHI). See Servite Friars - Eastern Province.
Monastery of Our Lady of the Desert, [K], (SFE), Santa Cruz, NM.
Monastery of Our Lady of the Mountains, [E], (RNO), Reno, NV.
Monastery of Our Lady of the Rosary, [P], (BUF), Buffalo, NY.
Monastery of Our Lady of the Rosary, [O], (NEW), Summit, NJ.
Monastery of Perpetual Adoration, Nuns of Perpetual Adoration, [O], (SFR), San Francisco, CA.
Monastery of Poor Clares, [S], (LA), Santa Barbara, CA.
Monastery of St. Alphonsus, [R], (STL), Liguori, MO.
Monastery of St. Benedict Center, [J], (MAD), Madison, WI.
Monastery of St. Clare, [I], (AUS), Brenham, TX.
Monastery of St. Clare, [P], (BGP), Stamford, CT.
Monastery of St. Clare, [X], (BO), Andover, MA.
Monastery of St. Clare, [F], (CHR), Greenville, SC.
Monastery of St. Clare, [H], (EVN), Evansville, IN.
Monastery of St. Clare, [AA], (NY), New York, NY.
Monastery of St. Clare, [L], (OM), Omaha, NE.
Monastery of St. Clare, [L], (SPK), Spokane, WA.
Monastery Of St. Clare O.S.C., [K], (MEM), Memphis, TN.

Monastery of St. Clare of the Immaculate Conception, [R], (STL), St. Louis, MO.
Monastery of St. Clare, Poor Clares, [AA], (PH), Langhorne, PA.
Monastery of St. Dominic, [O], (NEW), Newark, NJ.
Monastery of St. Gertrude, Motherhouse and Novitiate, [D], (B), Cottonwood, ID.
Monastery of St. Joseph, Discalced Carmelites, [K], (IND), Terre Haute, IN.
Monastery of St. Teresa of Jesus of Discalced Carmelites, [M], (ALB), Schenectady, NY.
Monastery of St. Therese of the Child Jesus, [L], (DET), Clinton Twp., MI.
Monastery of St. Veronica Giuliani, [J], (WIL), Wilmington, DE.
Monastery of the Angels (Contemplative), [S], (LA), Los Angeles, CA.
Monastery of the Blessed Sacrament, [L], (DET), Farmington Hills, MI.
Monastery of the Discalced Carmelite Nuns, [M], (L), Louisville, KY.
Monastery of the Discalced Carmelite Nuns, [N], (SAT), San Antonio, TX.
Monastery of the Discalced Carmelite Nuns, [F], (SC), Sioux City, IA.
Monastery of the Dominican Nuns of the Perpetual Rosary, [M], (CAM), Camden, NJ.
Monastery of the Dominican Nuns of the Perpetual Rosary, [I], (HBG), Lancaster, PA.
Monastery of the Dominican Nuns of the Perpetual Rosary, [O], (NEW), Union City, NJ.
Monastery of the Heart of Jesus, [D], (HT), Lockport, LA.
Monastery of the Holy Cross, [N], (CHI), Chicago, IL.
Monastery of the Holy Cross, [E], (MAR), Iron Mountain, MI.
Monastery of the Holy Name of Jesus, Ltd., [J], (GB), New Franken, WI.
The Monastery of the Holy Spirit, [I], (ATL), Conyers, GA.
Monastery of the Immaculate Heart of Mary, [H], (BUR), Westfield, VT.
Monastery of the Infant Jesus, [C], (TYL), Lufkin, TX.
Monastery of the Most Holy Trinity, Discalced Carmelites, [I], (FWT), Arlington, TX.
Monastery of the Mother of God, Dominican Nuns (Contemplative), [J], (SPR), West Springfield, MA.
Monastery of the Perpetual Rosary, [Q], (MIL), Milwaukee, WI.
Monastery of the Poor Clares, [Q], (CLV), Cleveland, OH.
Monastery of the Precious Blood, [F], (LFT), Lafayette, IN.
Monastery of the Precious Blood, [L], (MAN), Manchester, NH.
Monastery of the Precious Blood, [J], (PRT), Portland, ME.
Monastery of the Risen Christ, [G], (MRY), San Luis Obispo, CA.
Monastery of the Risen Christ, [H], (MRY), San Luis Obispo, CA.
Monastery of the Sacred Passion, [M], (COV), Erlanger, KY.
Monastery of the Sisters Adorers of the Precious Blood, [V], (BRK), Brooklyn, NY.
Monastery of the Visitation, [J], (ATL), Snellville, GA.
Monastery of the Visitation, [V], (BRK), Brooklyn, NY.
Monastery of the Visitation, [O], (STP), St. Paul, MN.
Monastery of the Visitation, [L], (TOL), Toledo, OH.
Monastery of the Visitation Monte Maria, [N], (RIC), Rockville, VA.
Monastery of the Visitation Nuns, [AA], (PH), Philadelphia, PA.
Monastery of the Visitation, St. Louis, [R], (STL), Town and Country, MO.
The Monastic Family of Bethlehem, [DD], (NY), Livingston Manor, NY.
Monastic Interreligious Dialogue, [M], (SCL), St. Joseph, MN.
Monastic Sisters of Bethlehem and of the Assumption of the Virgin, [AA], (NY), Livingston Manor, NY.
Monica House - Augustinian Community, [H], (SD), San Diego, CA.
Monmouth University, [R], (TR). See Campus Ministry for the Diocese of Trenton.
Monmouth/Ocean Behavioral Healthcare Division, [F], (TR). See Catholic Charities.
Monocacy Manor, [L], (ALN), Bethlehem, PA.
Monroe Catholic Junior-Senior High School, [A], (FBK), Fairbanks, AK.
Monroe County Catholic Schools, [C], (ROC), Rochester, NY.
*Monroe Foundation, Inc., [E], (FBK), Fairbanks, AK.
Msgr. A. O. Sigur Service Center, [N], (LAF). See Lafayette Catholic Service Centers, Inc.
Monsignor Adamski Village Housing Development Fund Company, Inc., [T], (BUF), Buffalo, NY.
Monsignor Adamski Village, Inc., [T], (BUF), Buffalo, NY.
Monsignor Bishop Manor Apts., Inc., [C], (ORL), Orlando, FL.
Msgr. Bojnowski Manor, [N], (HRT). See Motherhouse of Daughters of Mary of the Immaculate Conception.
Monsignor Bojnowski Manor, Inc., [K], (HRT), New Britain, CT.
Monsignor Bonner High School, [D], (PH), Drexel Hill, PA.
Monsignor Carr Institute, [T], (BUF), Buffalo, NY.
Msgr. Clare J. O'Dwyer Retreat House, [L], (BAL), Sparks, MD.
Monsignor Donovan High School, [B], (TR), Toms River, NJ.
Msgr. Edward Pace High School, [C], (MIA), Miami, FL.
Monsignor Farrell High School, [E], (NY), New York, NY.
Monsignor Gadoury Regional Primary School, [H], (PRO), Woonsocket, RI.
Monsignor Gambino Tower, Ltd., [T], (BUF). See Santa Maria Towers.
Msgr. Hackett Catholic Central High School, [A], (KAL), Kalamazoo, MI.
Msgr. James H. Fitzpatrick Pavilion for Skilled Nursing Care, [R], (BRK), Jamaica, NY.
Msgr. John O'Brien Apts., HDFC, Inc., [L], (BRK). See Catholic Charities.
Monsignor John P. Brady Center, [J], (DAL), Dallas, TX.
Monsignor Julian Benoit Academy, [D], (FTW), Fort Wayne, IN.
Monsignor Kelly Catholic High School, [A], (BEA), Beaumont, TX.
Monsignor Kelly Catholic High School Foundation, Inc., [G], (BEA), Beaumont, TX.
Monsignor Kirby Apartments Housing Development Fund Company, Inc., [T], (BUF), Buffalo, NY.
Msgr. Lawrence H. Soest Educational Trust Fund (St. Mary Parish, Flint), [K], (LAN). See Chancery Office.
Monsignor Matthew F. Clarke Regional School, [G], (PRO), Wakefield, RI.
Monsignor McClancy, [G], (BRK), East Elmhurst, NY.
Monsignor McHugh Elementary School, [F], (SCR), Cresco, PA.
Msgr. Mullaney Apartments, [L], (BRK). See Catholic Charities.
*Monsignor Robert Fox Memorial Shelter Housing Development, Inc., [DD], (NY), New York, NY.
Monsignor Thomas Griffin Foundation, [R], (WOR), Worcester, MA.
The Monsignor William P. Kennedy Education Foundation, [G], (STO), Modesto, CA.
Mont La Salle Novitiate, [A], (SR), Napa, CA.
Mont Marie, [J], (SPR), Holyoke, MA.
Mont Marie Child Care Center, Inc., [G], (SPR), Holyoke, MA.
Mont Marie Conference Center, [Q], (SPR), Holyoke, MA.
Mont Marie Health Care Center, Inc., [H], (SPR), Holyoke, MA.
Montague Catholic Social Ministries, Inc., [G], (SPR), Turners Falls, MA.
Montana College of Mineral Science and Technology, [H], (HEL), Butte, MT.
Montana State University, [H], (HEL), Bozeman, MT.
Montcalm Community College Newman Center, [K], (GR), Edmore, MI.
Montclair State University, [Q], (NEW), Upper Montclair, NJ.
Monte Alverno Retreat Center, [M], (GB), Appleton, WI.
Monte Cassino School, [D], (TLS), Tulsa, OK.
Montessori Community, Inc., [DD], (NY), Thornwood, NY.
Montfort Academy, Inc., [F], (ARL), Fredericksburg, VA.
Montfort Missionaries, [M], (HRT), Litchfield, CT.
Montfort Missionaries, [N], (RVC), Bay Shore, NY.
Montfort Missionaries - Retreat Center, [N], (RVC). See Montfort Missionaries.
Montfort Missionaries Provincialate, [U], (BRK), Ozone Park, NY.
Montgomery Catholic High School, [C], (MOB), Montgomery, AL.
Montgomery County Regional Office, [H], (WDC). See Catholic Charities of the Archdiocese of Washington, Inc.
Montini Catholic High School, [C], (JOL), Lombard, IL.
Montserrat Jesuit Retreat House, [J], (FWT), Lake Dallas, TX.
Moody Manor, [O], (TOL), Toledo, OH.
Moore Catholic High School, [E], (NY), New York, NY.
Moreau Catholic High School, [E], (OAK), Hayward, CA.
Moreau Center/Boysville of Michigan, Inc., [O], (DET). See Boysville of Michigan, Inc.
Moreau Convent, [K], (FTW). See Saint Mary's of the Immaculate Conception.
Moreau House, [H], (AUS), Austin, TX.
Moreau House, [M], (SCR), Wilkes-Barre, PA.
Moreau Seminary, [A], (FTW), Notre Dame, IN.
Moreland Notre Dame Convent, [H], (MRY), Watsonville, CA.
Moreland Notre Dame School, [D], (MRY), Watsonville, CA.
Morgan Hill Nutrition Site, [F], (SJ). See Catholic Charities of Santa Clara County.
Morgan State College, [O], (BAL). See Archdiocesan Office-Newman Center.
*The Morley Institute, [V], (WDC), Washington, DC.
Morning Star Community, [G], (RVC). See St. Christopher-Ottilie Corp.
Morning Star Hostel and Mark Schupp Center, [E], (AMA). See Catholic Family Service, Inc.
Morning Star House of Prayer, [P], (TR), Trenton, NJ.
Morning Star School, [B], (ORL), Orlando, FL.
Morning Star School, [G], (SP), Pinellas Park, FL.
Morning Star School, [G], (SP), Tampa, FL.
Morning Star School, [D], (STA), Jacksonville, FL.
Morris Catholic High School, [C], (PAT), Denville, NJ.
Morris Hall/Saint Lawrence, Inc., [J], (TR), Lawrenceville, NJ.
Morris Hall/St. Lawrence, Inc., [S], (TR), Lawrenceville, NJ.
Morris Hall-Saint Lawrence, Inc., [L], (TR), Lawrenceville, NJ.
Most Holy Redeemer Interparochial School, [D], (SP), Tampa, FL.
Most Holy Trinity Educational Trust Fund (Most Holy Trinity Church, Fowler), [K], (LAN). See Chancery Office.
Most Holy Trinity Monastery, [C], (SAM), Petersham, MA.
Most Precious Blood School, [B], (CC), Corpus Christi, TX.
Mother and Child Food and Nurtition Program, [G], (CHI). See Catholic Charities of the Archdiocese of Chicago-Archdiocesan Offices.
Mother Angela Residence, [N], (HRT). See Felician Sisters - Our Lady of the Angels.
Mother Boniface Center, [BB], (PH), Philadelphia, PA.
Mother Cabrini High School, [F], (NY), New York, NY.
Mother Cabrini League, [X], (CHI), Chicago, IL.
Mother Cabrini Shrine, [N], (DEN), Golden, CO.
Mother Caroline Academy, [H], (BO), Dorchester, MA.
Mother Frances Convent, [O], (PIT), Emsworth, PA.
Mother Gertrude Home for Senior Citizens, [Q], (LA), San Fernando, CA.
Mother Joseph Manor, Nursing Care Facility, [E], (SFS), Aberdeen, SD.
Mother Lurana House, [AA], (NY), Graymoor, NY.
Mother Marianne Cope Housing Development Fund Co., Inc., [Q], (SY), Syracuse, NY.
Mother McAuley Liberal Arts High School, [D], (CHI), Chicago, IL.
Mother of Divine Grace Housing Development Fund Company, Inc., [T], (BUF), Buffalo, NY.
Mother of God Community School, [E], (WDC), Gaithersburg, MD.
Mother of God House of Prayer, [I], (VEN), Alva, FL.
Mother of God Monastery, [G], (SFS), Watertown, SD.
Mother of Good Counsel Convent, [O], (CHI), Chicago, IL.
Mother of Good Counsel Home, [O], (STL), St. Louis, MO.
Mother of Hope Novitiate, [T], (PRO). See Miscellaneous Listings for the Diocese of Providence.
Mother of Light Community, Our Lady of Guadalupe Convent, [B], (SAM), Rutland, MA.
Mother of Mercy Convent, [S], (LA), Northridge, CA.
Mother of Mercy High School, [E], (CIN), Cincinnati, OH.
Mother of Mercy Nursing Home and Retirement Center, [H], (SCL), Albany, MN.
Mother of Peace Home, [N], (PEO), West Peoria, IL.
Mother of Peace House, [AA], (PH), Philadelphia, PA.
Mother of Perpetual Help Home, [D], (BWN), Brownsville, TX.
Mother of Perpetual Help Monastery, [AA], (NY), Esopus, NY.
Mother of Perpetual Help Nursing Home, [F], (BWN), Brownsville, TX.
Mother of Sorrows Convent, [O], (CHI), Blue Island, IL.
Mother of the Good Shepherd Monastery by the Sea, [L], (PRT), Peaks Island, ME.
Mother of the Redeemer Monastery, [H], (LAF), Opelousas, LA.
Mother Seton (Girls) Regional High School, [D], (NEW), Clark, NJ.
Mother Seton Academy, [F], (BAL), Baltimore, MD.
The Mother Seton Guild of Sacred Heart Hospital, Inc., [C], (PT), Pensacola, FL.
Mother Seton House on Paca Street, Inc., [Q], (BAL), Baltimore, MD.
*Mother Seton Housing, Inc., [F], (CHY), Casper, WY.
Mother Seton Residence, [H], (NEW), Montclair, NJ.
Mother Seton School, [E], (BAL), Emmitsburg, MD.
Mother Teresa Home, [F], (SCL), Cold Spring, MN.
Mother Theodore Guerin High School, [D], (CHI), River Grove, IL.

Mother Theresa, [G], (AGN). See S.S.N.D. Regional House.
Mother Theresa Home, [M], (CHI), Lemont, IL.
Mother-Baby Program, [L], (SAC). See Catholic Charities of Sacramento, Inc.
Mother-Child, [U], (LA). See Good Shepherd Center for Homeless Women.
Motherhouse and Convent of Infant Jesus, [V], (BRK), Brooklyn, NY.
Motherhouse and Convent of the Sisters of Mercy of the Americas, [V], (BRK), Brooklyn, NY.
Motherhouse and Educational Center of the Ursuline Sisters, [K], (Y), Canfield, OH.
Motherhouse and Novitiate, [A], (PRM), North Royalton, OH.
Motherhouse and Novitiate of Sisters of Our Lady of Charity, [G], (STU), Carrollton, OH.
Motherhouse and Novitiate of Sisters of St. Dominic, [O], (NEW), Caldwell, NJ.
Motherhouse and Novitiate of the Franciscan Sisters of the Atonement, [AA], (NY), Graymoor, NY.
Motherhouse and Novitiate of the Mission Sisters of the Holy Spirit, [H], (SAG), Saginaw, MI.
Motherhouse and Novitiate of the Religious Sisters of Mercy of Alma, Michigan, [H], (SAG), Alma, MI.
Motherhouse and Novitiate of the Sisters of Loretto at the Foot of the Cross, [M], (L), Nerinx, KY.
Motherhouse and Novitiate of the Sisters of St. Basil the Great, [E], (PBR), Mount St. Macrina, PA.
Motherhouse and Novitiate of the Sisters of Saint Benedict, [E], (DUL), Duluth, MN.
Motherhouse & Novitiate of the Sisters of St. Dominic, Congregation of St. Rose of Li, [AA], (NY), Hawthorne, NY.
Motherhouse and Novitiate of the Sisters of St. Joseph, [G], (KAL), Nazareth, MI.
Motherhouse and Novitiate of the Sisters of the Holy Spirit, [Q], (CLV), Cleveland, OH.
Motherhouse and Novitiate of the Ursuline Nuns, [Q], (CLV), Cleveland, OH.
Motherhouse and Novitiate of the Vincentian Sisters of Charity, [Q], (CLV), Bedford, OH.
Motherhouse and Novitiate of the Vincentian Sisters of Charity, [O], (PIT), Pittsburgh, PA.
Motherhouse and Novitiate of Ursuline Sisters of Belleville, [H], (BEL), Belleville, IL.
Motherhouse Mission Chapter, [H], (LAN). See Motherhouse of the Sisters of St. Dominic.
Motherhouse Oblate Sisters of the Blessed Sacrament, [G], (SFS), Marty, SD.
Motherhouse of Daughters of Mary of the Immaculate Conception, [N], (HRT), New Britain, CT.
Motherhouse of the Congregation of the Sisters of the Third Order of St. Francis, [K], (IND), Oldenburg, IN.
Motherhouse of the Consolata Missionary Sisters, [I], (GR), Belmont, MI.
Motherhouse of the Daughters of the Cross in America, [F], (SHP), Shreveport, LA.
Motherhouse of the Dominican Sisters, [I], (GR), Grand Rapids, MI.
Motherhouse of the Grey Nuns of the Sacred Heart, [AA], (PH), Yardley, PA.
Motherhouse of the Missionary Sisters of Mother of God, [F], (PHU), Philadelphia, PA.
Motherhouse of the Servants of Mary, [L], (OM), Omaha, NE.
Motherhouse of the Sisters of Charity, [N], (PAT), Convent Station, NJ.
Motherhouse of the Sisters of Charity of Leavenworth, [I], (KCK), Leavenworth, KS.
Motherhouse of the Sisters of Mercy of the Americas, [J], (PRT), Portland, ME.
Motherhouse of the Sisters of St. Dominic, [H], (LAN), Adrian, MI.
Motherhouse of the Sisters of St. Dominic of the Immaculate Heart of Mary, [Q], (CLV), Akron, OH.
Motherhouse of the Sisters of St. Joseph, [Q], (CLV), Cleveland, OH.
Motherhouse of the Sisters of St. Joseph of Boston, [X], (BO), Boston, MA.
Motherhouse of the Sisters of St. Joseph of St. Augustine, Florida, [I], (STA), St. Augustine, FL.
Motherhouse, Novitiate, Sacred Heart Residence, Portiuncula, Center for Prayer, [K], (JOL), Frankfort, IL.
Motherhouse, Sisters of the Holy Spirit (S.H.S.), [O], (PIT), Ross Township, PA.
Motherhouse, The Sisters of the Third Order of St. Francis, [N], (PEO), East Peoria, IL.
Mount Aloysius College, [A], (ALT), Cresson, PA.
Mt. Aloysius Jr. College (Cresson), [H], (ALT). See Juniata College.
Mount Alverna Home, Inc. & Mount Alverna Home Annex, Inc., [N], (CLV), Cleveland, OH.
Mount Alvernia Academy, [H], (BO), Newton, MA.
Mt. Alvernia Convent, [X], (BO), Newton, MA.
Mt. Alvernia Convent, [AA], (PH), Aston, PA.
Mt. Alvernia Day Care & Learning Center, Kindergarten, [I], (PIT), Pittsburgh, PA.
Mt. Alvernia Friary, [J], (Y), Youngstown, OH.
Mount Alvernia High School, [E], (BO), Newton, MA.
Mt. Alvernia High School, [D], (PIT), Pittsburgh, PA.
Mt. Alvernia Retreat House, [BB], (NY), Wappingers Falls, NY.
Mt. Alvernia, Inc., [R], (RVC), Centerport, NY.
Mount Alverno Center and Convent, [BB], (NY), Warwick, NY.
Mount Alverno Conference and Retreat Center, [M], (SFR), Redwood City, CA.
Mt. Alverno Novitiate, [N], (PEO), East Peoria, IL.
Mt. Angel Abbey, [L], (P), St. Benedict, OR.
Mount Angel Abbey Retreat House, [N], (P), St. Benedict, OR.
Mount Angel Seminary, [A], (P), St. Benedict, OR.
Mt. Assisi Academy for Girls, [D], (CHI), Lemont, IL.
Mount Assisi Convent, [O], (PIT), Bellevue, PA.
Mount Assisi Convent, Sisters of St. Francis of Christ the King, [O], (CHI), Lemont, IL.
Mount Assisi Monastery, [F], (ALT), Loretto, PA.
Mount Augustine, Motherhouse of the Sisters of Charity of St. Augustine, [Q], (CLV), Richfield, OH.
Mount Aviat Academy, [C], (WIL), Childs, MD.
Mount Benedict Priory, [G], (SLC), Ogden, UT.
Mount Carmel Academy, [F], (NO), New Orleans, LA.
Mount Carmel Center, [K], (DAL), Dallas, TX.
Mt. Carmel Community, [G], (AGN), Agat, GU.
Mt. Carmel Convent, [N], (HRT), Meriden, CT.
Mt. Carmel Elementary School, [D], (LAF), Abbeville, LA.
Mount Carmel Health, [E], (COL). See Mount Carmel Health System.
Mount Carmel Health System, [E], (COL), Columbus, OH.
Mount Carmel Health System Foundation, [E], (COL). See Mount Carmel Health System.
Mount Carmel Hermitage, [H], (GBG), New Florence, PA.
Mount Carmel Hermitage, [A], (SAN), Christoval, TX.
Mount Carmel Hermitage, [F], (SUP), Amery, WI.
Mt. Carmel High School, [D], (CHI), Chicago, IL.
Mt. Carmel High School, [D], (GAL), Houston, TX.
Mount Carmel Home, [F], (CC), Corpus Christi, TX.
Mount Carmel Home Convent, [I], (CC), Corpus Christi, TX.
Mt. Carmel Home Nursing Service, [N], (MET), Woodbridge, NJ.
Mount Carmel Home-Keens' Memorial, [C], (GI), Kearney, NE.
Mount Carmel Hospital, [G], (SPK), Colville, WA.
Mount Carmel House, [V], (WDC), Washington, DC.
Mount Carmel Medical Center; Mount Carmel Foundation, [E], (WCH), Pittsburg, KS.
Mt. Carmel Nursing Home, [J], (MAN), Manchester, NH.
Mount Carmel Priory, Carmelite Fathers and Brothers, [R], (LA), Los Angeles, CA.
Mount Carmel Retreat Center, [K], (SPR), Williamstown, MA.
Mt. Claret Retreat Center, [G], (PHX), Phoenix, AZ.
The Mount Community Center, Inc., [K], (KCK), Atchison, KS.
Mount de Chantal Visitation Academy, Inc., [C], (WH), Wheeling, WV.
Mount de Sales Academy, [D], (BAL), Baltimore, MD.
Mount de Sales Academy, [B], (SAV), Macon, GA.
Mt. Gallitzin Academy, [G], (PIT), Baden, PA.
Mount Gallitzin Academy, [G], (PIT), Pittsburgh, PA.
Mount Grace Convent and Chapel of Perpetual Adoration, [R], (STL), St. Louis, MO.
Mount Irenaeus, Franciscan Mountain Retreat & Holy Peace Friary, [Q], (BUF), West Clarksville, NY.
Mount Joseph Senior Community, [C], (SAL), Concordia, KS.
Mt. Loretto Convent, [L], (DUB), Dubuque, IA.
Mt. Loretto Nursing Home, [J], (ALB), Amsterdam, NY.
Mount Macrina Manor Nursing Home, [B], (PBR), Uniontown, PA.
Mount Manresa Jesuit Retreat House, [BB], (NY), Staten Island, NY.
Mount Marty College, [A], (SFS), Yankton, SD.
Mount Mary College, [C], (MIL), Milwaukee, WI.
Mt. Mercy Academy, [D], (BUF), Buffalo, NY.
Mount Mercy College, [C], (DUB), Cedar Rapids, IA.
Mount Mercy Convent, [P], (BUF), Buffalo, NY.
Mt. Merici Convent, [J], (PRT), Waterville, ME.
Mount Merici Elementary School, [D], (PRT), Waterville, ME.
Mount Michael Abbey, [K], (OM), Elkhorn, NE.
Mt. Michael Foundation, Inc., [N], (OM). See The Omaha Archdiocesan Educational Foundation, Inc.
Mount Michael High School, [C], (OM), Elkhorn, NE.
Mount Nazareth, [U], (PH), Philadelphia, PA.
Mount Nazareth Center, Inc., [R], (PIT), Pittsburgh, PA.
Mt. Nazareth Learning Center, [R], (PIT). See Mount Nazareth Center, Inc.
Mt. Notre Dame High School, [E], (CIN), Cincinnati, OH.
Mount Pleasant Catholic Elementary Education Center, [G], (CLV), Cleveland, OH.
Mount Providence, [R], (STL), Normandy, MO.
Mount Providence Child Development Center, [Q], (BAL), Baltimore, MD.
Mount Providence Reading Center, [Q], (BAL), Baltimore, MD.
Mount Providence School, [G], (STL), Normandy, MO.
Mt. Sacred Heart College, [C], (HRT), Hamden, CT.
Mount Sacred Heart Convent, [N], (SAT), San Antonio, TX.
Mount Sacred Heart Provincial House and Novitiate, [N], (HRT), Hamden, CT.
Mount Sacred Heart School, [G], (SAT), San Antonio, TX.
Mount St. Agnes College, [C], (BAL). See Loyola College.
Mount St. Alphonsus Redemptorist Retreat Center, [BB], (NY), Esopus, NY.
Mount St. Andrew Villa, [H], (NEW), Paramus, NJ.
Mount St. Ann Retreat House and Novitiate, [G], (ALT), Ebensburg, PA.
*Mount Saint Benedict Foundation, [G], (CR), Crookston, MN.
Mount St. Benedict Monastery, [E], (CR), Crookston, MN.
Mount Saint Benedict Monastery, [M], (E), Erie, PA.
Mt. St. Charles Academy, [E], (PRO), Woonsocket, RI.
Mt. St. Clare College, [B], (DAV), Clinton, IA.
Mount St. Clare Convent, [N], (DAV), Clinton, IA.
Mount St. Clare Speech & Hearing Center, [P], (DAV), Clinton, IA.
Mount St. Dominic Academy, [C], (NEW), Caldwell, NJ.
Mount St. Francis, [F], (COS), Colorado Springs, CO.
Mt. St. Francis, [L], (DUB), Dubuque, IA.
Mt. St. Francis, [N], (PAT), Ringwood, NJ.
Mount St. Francis Day Care Center, [J], (PRO), Manville, RI.
Mount Saint Francis Friary and Retreat Center, [I], (IND), Mount Saint Francis, IN.
Mount St. Francis Hermitage, [W], (SY), Maine, NY.
Mt. St. Francis Infirmary, [AA], (NY). See Mt. St. Francis, Motherhouse & Infirm of Franciscan Missionary Sisters of Sacred Heart.
Mt. St. Francis Retreat Center, [I], (PAT), Ringwood, NJ.
Mount Saint Francis Sanctuary, Inc., [O], (IND), Mount Saint Francis, IN.
Mt. St. Francis, Motherhouse & Infirm of Franciscan Missionary Sisters of Sacred Heart, [AA], (NY), Peekskill, NY.
Mount St. James Corporation, [Q], (SY), Syracuse, NY.
Mount St. John, [D], (NOR), Deep River, CT.
Mt. St. John Convent, [AA], (NY). See Sisters of St. John the Baptist.
Mt. St. John Convent, [N], (PAT), Gladstone, NJ.
Mount St. Joseph, [N], (CLV), Cleveland, OH.
Mt. St. Joseph, [AA], (NY), New Windsor, NY.
Mount St. Joseph, [G], (OWN), Maple Mount, KY.
Mount St. Joseph, [L], (SPK), Spokane, WA.
Mt. St. Joseph, [O], (WH), Wheeling, WV.
Mt. St. Joseph Academy, [E], (BO), Brighton, MA.
Mount St. Joseph Academy, [E], (BUF), Buffalo, NY.
Mt. St. Joseph Academy, [B], (BUR), Rutland, VT.
Mt. St. Joseph Academy, [G], (PH), Flourtown, PA.
Mt. St. Joseph Children's Center, [H], (PAT), Paterson, NJ.
Mt. St. Joseph College High School, [D], (BAL), Baltimore, MD.
Mt. St. Joseph Convent, [AA], (PH), Philadelphia, PA.
Mt. St. Joseph Fontbonne Community, [J], (PRT), Waterville, ME.
Mt. St. Joseph Holistic Care Community, [G], (PRT), Waterville, ME.
Mt. St. Joseph Home, [L], (CHI), Lake Zurich, IL.
Mount St. Joseph Novitiate and Seminary, [A], (SAC), Loomis, CA.
Mt. St. Joseph Priest Retirement Home, [I], (PRT), Waterville, ME.
Mount St. Joseph Program-Benita House, [L], (SFR). See Mount St. Joseph-St. Elizabeth.
Mt. St. Joseph Provincialate, [Q], (PRO), Bristol, RI.
Mt. St. Joseph Residence and Extended Care Center, [K], (P), Portland, OR.
Mt. St. Joseph Retreat Center, [H], (OWN), Maple Mount, KY.
Mt. St. Joseph Sisters' Residence, [J], (PRT), Waterville, ME.
Mount St. Joseph-St. Elizabeth, [L], (SFR), San Francisco, CA.
Mount St. Mary, [I], (MET), Watchung, NJ.
Mt. St. Mary Academy, [D], (BUF), Kenmore, NY.
Mount St. Mary Academy, [C], (LR), Little Rock, AR.
Mount St. Mary Academy, [B], (MET), Watchung, NJ.
Mount St. Mary Academy Endowment and Scholarship Fund, [C], (LR). See Mount St. Mary Academy.
Mt. St. Mary College, [C], (NY), Newburgh, NY.
Mt. St. Mary College, [CC], (NY). See University Apostolate.
Mount St. Mary Convent, [H], (BUR), Burlington, VT.
Mt. St. Mary Convent, Motherhouse and Novitiate of

the Sisters of St. Joseph, [H], (WCH), Wichita, KS.
Mount Saint Mary Corporation of the Sisters of Mercy, [L], (MAN). See Sisters of Mercy of the Americas.
Mount Saint Mary Early Childhool Center, [E], (MAN), Manchester, NH.
Mount St. Mary High School, [C], (OKL), Oklahoma City, OK.
Mt. St. Mary House of Prayer, [I], (MET), Watchung, NJ.
Mount St. Mary's Abbey, [X], (BO), Wrentham, MA.
Mount Saint Mary's College, [C], (BAL), Emmitsburg, MD.
Mount St. Mary's College, [C], (LA), Los Angeles, CA.
Mt. St. Mary's Convent, [I], (LR), Little Rock, AR.
Mount St. Mary's Hospital of Niagara Falls, [K], (BUF), Lewiston, NY.
Mount St. Mary's LTC Facility, Inc., [M], (BUF), Niagara Falls, NY.
Mount St. Mary's Seminary, [A], (BAL), Emmitsburg, MD.
Mt. St. Mary's Seminary of the West, [B], (CIN), Cincinnati, OH.
Mount St. Michael Academy, [F], (NY), Bronx, NY.
Mount St. Michael Spiritual Life Center, [K], (DAL), Dallas, TX.
Mount St. Rita Health Centre, [M], (PRO), Cumberland, RI.
Mount St. Scholastica, [I], (KCK), Atchison, KS.
Mount St. Scholastica Academy, [E], (KCK), Atchison, KS.
Mount St. Ursula Speech Center, [G], (NY), New York, NY.
Mount Saint Vincent, [X], (BO), Wellesley, MA.
Mount St. Vincent Nursing Home, [H], (SPR). See Sisters of Providence Care Centers, Inc.
Mt. St. Vincent's Home, [F], (DEN), Denver, CO.
Mount Saviour Monastery, [I], (ROC), Pine City, NY.
Mount Tabor Convent, [I], (CC), Corpus Christi, TX.
Mount Tabor Society, Inc., [N], (ARL), Vienna, VA.
Mt. Wachusett Community College (Gardner), [Q], (WOR). See Campus Ministry.
Mountain View Serra Club, [P], (SJ), Mountain View, CA.
The Mountaincrest, [H], (KNX), Knoxville, TN.
Movimiento Juan XXIII, [E], (CGS), Caguas, PR.
Moye Center, [O], (SAT), Castroville, TX.
MSC Province Center, [L], (ALN), Reading, PA.
MSC Psychiatric Services, [U], (SFR). See MSC Psychiatric Services.
MSF Center & Provincialate, [M], (SAT), San Antonio, TX.
MSF Formation Community, [B], (SAT), San Antonio, TX.
Mullen Home, [I], (DEN), Denver, CO.
Mulroy Neighborhood Center, [L], (DEN). See Catholic Charities and Community Services of the Archdiocese of Denver, Inc.
Multicultural Institute, [R], (OAK), Berkley, CA.
Multi-Service Senior Center Programming, [F], (SJ). See Catholic Charities of Santa Clara County.
Muncy Valley Hospital, [I], (SCR), Muncy, PA.
Mundelein College of Loyola, [C], (CHI). See Loyola University-Chicago.
Murphy Branch, [H], (CHL). See Good Shepherd Home Health & Hospice Agency, Inc.
Murray Residence Community, [N], (OAK), Oakland, CA.
Murray State University Newman House, [I], (OWN), Murray, KY.
Murray-Weigel Hall, [Z], (NY), New York, NY.
The Museum of Western Jesuit Missions, [W], (STL), St. Louis, MO.
Music at Kohl Mansion, Inc., [U], (SFR), Burlingame, CA.
Music in Catholic Schools, [N], (OM). See The Omaha Archdiocesan Educational Foundation, Inc.
Musica Pacis, [X], (CHI), Wilmette, IL.
Muskegon Catholic Central Junior High and High School, [C], (GR), Muskegon, MI.
Mustard Seed., [P], (SAC). See Loaves & Fishes.
My Father's House, [I], (NOR), Moodus, CT.
My Father's House, Inc., [DD], (NY), Peekskill, NY.
My Sister's Place, [J], (PHX). See Catholic Social Services of Central and Northern Arizona, Inc.
Myriam's House, Inc., [L], (BR), Baton Rouge, LA.

N

Na Leo Ho'onani Community, [I], (HON). See Congregation of the Sacred Hearts and of Perpetual Adoration.
NAAS House of Mercy, [I], (LR), Ozark, AR.
Namaste Alzheimer Center, [D], (COS), Colorado Springs, CO.
The Nancy McGregor House, Southwest MO State University, Drury College, Ozark Technical College, [I], (SPC), Springfield, MO.
Naomi House, [G], (PT), Panama City, FL.
Nardin Academy, [E], (BUF), Buffalo, NY.
Nardin Academy High School, [D], (BUF), Buffalo, NY.
Narnia Catechetical & Cultural Centre, Inc., [DD], (NY), New York, NY.
Nashua Catholic Regional Junior High, [E], (MAN), Nashua, NH.
Nashua Deanery Toward Marriage Program, [P], (MAN), Nashua, NH.
National Alliance of Parishes Restructuring into Communities, [T], (DET), Marysville, MI.
National Association for Treasurers of Religious Institutes, [V], (WDC), Silver Spring, MD.
National Association of Catholic Chaplains, [Y], (MIL), Milwaukee, WI.
National Association of Catholic Home Educators (NACHE), [N], (ARL), Broad Run, VA.
National Association of Catholic Nurses-U.S.A., [M], (JOL), Lisle, IL.
National Association of Diaconate Directors (NADD), [U], (CHI), Chicago, IL.
The National Black Catholic Congress, Inc., [P], (BAL). See Chancery Office.
National Black Sisters' Conference, [V], (WDC), Washington, DC.
National Catholic AIDS Network, [O], (SR), Sebastopol, CA.
National Catholic Association of Diocesan Directors for Hispanic Ministry, Inc., [M], (ATL), Atlanta, GA.
National Catholic Conference for Interracial Justice, [V], (WDC), Washington, DC.
National Catholic Council for Hispanic Ministry, Inc. (NCCHM), [CC], (LA), Los Angeles, CA.
National Catholic Group Purchasing Association, Inc., [FF], (BO), Boston, MA.
National Catholic Ministry to the Bereaved, Inc., [AA], (CLV), Cleveland, OH.
National Catholic Resettlement Council, [DD], (NY), New York, NY.
National Catholic Rural Life Conference, [I], (DM), Des Moines, IA.
National Center of the Enthronement, [K], (FR), Fairhaven, MA.
National Center of the Haitian Apostolate, [Y], (BRK), Cambria Heights, NY.
National Christ Child Society, [N], (AUS), Austin, TX.
National Christ Child Society, [V], (WDC), Washington, DC.
The National Christ Child Society, Inc., [U], (CAM), North Cape May, NJ.
National Christian Life Community of the United States of America (CLC), [W], (STL), St. Louis, MO.
National Coalition for Church Vocations, [U], (CHI), Chicago, IL.
National Communicators Network for Women Religious, [O], (DUB), Dubuque, IA.
The National Cursillo Center and Office of the National Secretariat, [P], (DAL), Dallas, TX.
National Federation for Life, [DD], (NY), New York, NY.
National Foundation for Mexican-American Vocations, [S], (SAT), San Antonio, TX.
National Institute for the Family, Inc., [V], (WDC), Washington, DC.
National Italian Apostolate Conference, [DD], (NY), New York, NY.
National LEARNING CLUB Ministry, [E], (ALN), Whitehall, PA.
National Marriage Encounter of North Texas, [K], (FWT). See The Catholic Renewal Center of North Texas, Inc.
National Office of Post-Abortion Reconciliation and Healing, Inc., [Y], (MIL), Milwaukee, WI.
National Organization for Continuing Education of Roman Catholic Clergy, Inc., [U], (CHI), Chicago, IL.
National Religious Vocation Conference, [U], (CHI), Chicago, IL.
The National Shrine of Blessed Kateri Tekakwitha and Friary, [R], (ALB), Fonda, NY.
National Shrine of Our Lady of La Salette, [BB], (BO), Ipswich, MA.
National Shrine of Our Lady of Lebanon, [C], (OLL), North Jackson, OH.
National Shrine of Our Lady of Mount Carmel, [BB], (NY), Middletown, NY.
National Shrine of St. Elizabeth Ann Seton, [Q], (BAL), Emmitsburg, MD.
National Shrine of St. George, [E], (NTN), Birmingham, AL.
National Shrine of St. Odilia, [M], (SCL), Onamia, MN.
Native American Lay Ministry and Diaconate Program, [A], (GLP), Chinle, AZ.
Native Ministry Training Program, [E], (FBK), St. Marys, AK.
Nativity B.V.M. Convent, [AA], (PH), Philadelphia, PA.
Nativity B.V.M. High School, [C], (ALN), Pottsville, PA.
Nativity Convent, [O], (PIT), Pittsburgh, PA.
Nativity Housing Development Fund Company, Inc., [T], (BUF), Buffalo, NY.
Nativity Jesuit Middle School, Inc., [G], (MIL), Milwaukee, WI.
Nativity Mission Center, Inc., [DD], (NY), New York, NY.
Nativity of Our Lord Endowment Fund, [W], (STP), St. Paul, MN.
Nativity of the Blessed Virgin (German Mission), [V], (WDC), Washington, DC.
Nativity Preparatory School, [H], (BO), Boston, MA.
*Natural Family Planning, [J], (PHX), Phoenix, AZ.
Natural Family Planning, [J], (STU), Steubenville, OH.
Natural Family Planning Center of Washington, DC, Inc., [V], (WDC), Bethesda, MD.
Nazareth, [E], (B), Boise, ID.
Nazareth Academy, [X], (CHI), LaGrange Park, IL.
Nazareth Academy, [B], (VIC), Victoria, TX.
Nazareth Academy Grade School, [H], (PH), Philadelphia, PA.
Nazareth Academy High School, [G], (PH), Philadelphia, PA.
Nazareth Arts For Life, Inc., [Q], (L), Nazareth, KY.
Nazareth Convent, [AA], (PH), Philadelphia, PA.
Nazareth Convent, [J], (ROC), Rochester, NY.
Nazareth Day Care, [M], (BO), Jamaica Plain, MA.
Nazareth Family Center, [M], (BO), Jamaica Plain, MA.
Nazareth Family Services, [R], (PIT). See Mount Nazareth Center, Inc.
Nazareth Farm, [L], (WH), Salem, WV.
Nazareth Group Home, [M], (BO), Brighton, MA.
Nazareth Hall, [I], (ELP), El Paso, TX.
Nazareth Hall Elementary School, [D], (ROC), Rochester, NY.
Nazareth Hall Middle School, [D], (ROC). See Nazareth Hall Elementary School.
Nazareth Heights, Inc., [Q], (MIL), Fond du Lac, WI.
Nazareth Hermitage, [F], (SPC), Ava, MO.
Nazareth Home, [G], (GRY). See St. Catherine Hospital.
Nazareth Home, [K], (L), Louisville, KY.
Nazareth Home, Residence for Single Pregnant Women, [D], (SAV), Macon, GA.
The Nazareth Home-Carter Day Nursery, [J], (PRO), Providence, RI.
Nazareth Hospital, [T], (PH), Philadelphia, PA.
Nazareth House, [D], (FRS), Fresno, CA.
Nazareth House, [Q], (LA), Los Angeles, CA.
Nazareth House, [H], (MAD), Stoughton, WI.
Nazareth House, [N], (MET), Perth Amboy, NJ.
Nazareth House, [E], (SD), San Diego, CA.
Nazareth House, [K], (SFR), San Rafael, CA.
Nazareth House, [D], (SPP), Pago Pago, American Samoa.
Nazareth House of Prayer, [O], (RIC), Gate City, VA.
Nazareth House Retirement Home, [G], (SD), San Diego, CA.
Nazareth Housing Services, [R], (PIT). See Mount Nazareth Center, Inc.
*Nazareth Housing, Inc., [DD], (NY), New York, NY.
Nazareth II, [N], (NO), New Orleans, LA.
Nazareth In The Woods, Inc., [O], (E), Du Bois, PA.
Nazareth Inn, [N], (NO), New Orleans, LA.
Nazareth Living Center, [O], (STL), Mehlville, MO.
Nazareth Montessori Children's Center, [E], (L), Nazareth, KY.
Nazareth Motherhouse for the Sisters of St. Joseph, Concordia, [E], (SAL), Concordia, KS.
Nazareth Nursery, [R], (NY), New York, NY.
Nazareth Nursing Home, [M], (BUF), Buffalo, NY.
Nazareth Regional, [G], (BRK), Brooklyn, NY.
Nazareth Schools: The Hall; The Academy, [B], (ROC), Rochester, NY.
Nazareth Spiritual Enrichment Center, [R], (PRO), Newport, RI.
Nazareth Towers, [G], (COL), Columbus, OH.
Nazareth Village, [P], (PAT), Chester, NJ.
Nazarethville, [M], (CHI), Des Plaines, IL.
Near East Side Adventures Program, [K], (SY), Syracuse, NY.
Needle Fund, Inc., [W], (BGP), Bridgeport, CT.
Negaunee St. Paul Endowment Fund, [B], (MAR), Negaunee, MI.
Neighborhood Division, Catholic Charities, [K], (SY), Syracuse, NY.
Neighborhood House-Inner City Apostolate, [G], (CHR), Charleston, SC.
Neighbors Together, [Y], (BRK), Brooklyn, NY.
Nerinx Hall High School, [F], (STL), Webster Groves, MO.
Nestucca Sanctuary, [N], (P), Pacific City, OR.
NET Ministries, Inc., [T], (STP), West St. Paul, MN.
Network of Sacred Heart Schools, Inc., [W], (STL), St. Louis, MO.
Neumann Apartments, [I], (ALN), Saint Clair, PA.
Neumann College, [C], (PH), Aston, PA.
Neumann Convent Sisters of St. Francis of Philadelphia (Glen Riddle), [L], (ALN), Reading, PA.
Neumann Early Childhood Center, Inc., [P], (BAL). See Chancery Office.
Neumann Early Childhood Center, Inc., [Q], (BAL),

Cumberland, MD.
Neumann High School, [C], (LIN), Wahoo, NE.
Neumann House, [G], (GBG), Greensburg, PA.
Neumann House, Village of St. Mary, [L], (CAM), Cherry Hill, NJ.
Neumann Services, Inc., [L], (HBG), Lancaster, PA.
New Albany Deanery/Catholic Youth Ministry, [E], (IND). See Aquinas Center for Continuing Religious Education.
New Albany Deanery-Catholic Youth Ministry, [O], (IND), New Albany, IN.
New Bedford Area Catholic Youth Organization, [O], (FR). See Diocesean Catholic Youth Organization.
New Britain, [S], (HRT). See Catholic Charities-Catholic Family Services (Archdiocese of Hartford).
New Camaldoli, [A], (MRY), Big Sur, CA.
New Camaldoli Hermitage, [G], (MRY), Big Sur, CA.
New Camaldoli Hermitage, [I], (MRY), Big Sur, CA.
New Cassel Retirement Center, [H], (OM), Omaha, NE.
New Covenant Center: Education for Justice and Peace, [O], (OM), Omaha, NE.
New Covenant House of Hospitality (Yerwood Center), [G], (BGP). See Catholic Charities of Fairfield County.
New Directions Adult Day Health Care Center, [M], (NO), New Orleans, LA.
New England College Newman Center, [N], (MAN), Henniker, NH.
New England Conference of Diocesan Directors of Religious Education, [T], (PRO). See Miscellaneous Listings for the Diocese of Providence.
New Hampshire Catholic Charities, [G], (MAN), Manchester, NH.
New Hampshire Food Bank, [G], (MAN), Manchester, NH.
New Haven, [S], (HRT). See Catholic Charities-Catholic Family Services (Archdiocese of Hartford).
New Hope Manor, [K], (NY), Barryville, NY.
New Hope Manor, [DD], (NY), Barryville, NY.
New Hope Program, [C], (STA), Jacksonville, FL.
New Horizons Adult Education Program, Inc., [Y], (BRK), Brooklyn, NY.
New Horizons of Faith, Inc., [D], (DAV), Davenport, IA.
New Jersey Boystown, [K], (NEW), Kearny, NJ.
New Jersey Caritas Corporation, Inc., [S], (NEW), Newark, NJ.
New Jerusalem, [O], (RVC), Bay Shore, NY.
New Jerusalem Community, [V], (CIN), Cincinnati, OH.
New Lenox Family Health Center, [G], (JOL). See St. Joseph Medical Center.
New Melleray Abbey, Order of Cistercians of the Strict Observance, [K], (DUB), Peosta, IA.
New Melleray Guest House, [M], (DUB), Dubuque, IA.
New Ulm Area Catholic Schools, [A], (NU), New Ulm, MN.
The New World, [X], (CHI), Chicago, IL.
New York Catholic Forum, [DD], (NY), New York, NY.
New York Foundling Charitable Corp., [O], (NY), New York, NY.
New York Foundling Charitable Corp., [DD], (NY), New York, NY.
New York Foundling Hospital for Pediatric, Medical and Rehabilitative Care, Inc., The, [O], (NY), New York, NY.
New York Foundling Hospital, The, [O], (NY), New York, NY.
New York Institute for Human Development, Inc., [J], (NY), New York, NY.
New York Maritime College, [CC], (NY). See University Apostolate.
New York State Catholic Conference, [T], (ALB), Albany, NY.
New York State Catholic Healthcare Council, [T], (ALB), Albany, NY.
New York State Council of Catholic Charities Directors, [T], (ALB), Albany, NY.
New York State Council of Catholic School Superintendents, [T], (ALB), Albany, NY.
New York State University at Albany, [S], (ALB), Albany, NY.
New York State University at Oneonta and Hartwick College, [S], (ALB), Oneonta, NY.
New York University, [CC], (NY). See University Apostolate.
Newark Abbey, [N], (NEW), Newark, NJ.
Newark Catholic High School, [C], (COL), Newark, OH.
*Newark Catholic High School Endowment Fund, [K], (COL), Newark, OH.
Newberry College Newman Center, [H], (CHR), Newberry, SC.
*Newburgh Ministry, [DD], (NY), Newburgh, NY.
Newman Apostolate, [DD], (PH), Philadelphia, PA.
Newman Apostolate Center, [T], (GAL), Galveston, TX.
Newman Apostolate-Valparaiso University, [O], (GRY), Valparaiso, IN.
Newman Association at SUNY Morrisville, [V], (SY), Morrisville, NY.
Newman Catholic, [G], (DUB), Mason City, IA.
Newman Catholic Fellowship, [H], (SB), San Bernardino, CA.
Newman Catholic Student Center, [H], (DAV), Iowa City IA.
Newman Catholic Student Center, [H], (R), Chapel Hill, NC.
Newman Catholic Student Center, [L], (SCL), Morris, MN.
The Newman Center, [J], (BEL), Carbondale, IL.
Newman Center, [K], (GF), Billings, MT.
Newman Center, [I], (WIN), Mankato, MN.
Newman Center Alderson-Broaddus College, [Q], (WH), Philippi, WV.
Newman Center at Wabash College, [H], (LFT), Crawfordsville, IN.
Newman Center at Youngstown State University, [O], (Y), Youngstown, OH.
Newman Center for the University of Evansville, [I], (EVN), Evansville, IN.
The Newman Center Holy Spirit Parish University of Kentucky, [L], (LEX), Lexington, KY.
Newman Center of Northern Illinois University Educational Program, [L], (RCK), DeKalb, IL.
Newman Center, Catholic Community at Stanford, [O], (SJ), Palo Alto, CA.
Newman Center, Inc., [L], (SCL), St. Cloud, MN.
Newman Center, San Francisco State University, [S], (SFR), San Francisco, CA.
Newman Center, University of California Medical Center, [S], (SFR), San Francisco, CA.
The Newman Center/Catholic Campus Ministry, [O], (SJ), San Jose, CA.
Newman Centers, [V], (BGP), Bridgeport, CT.
Newman Centers and Campus Ministry, [P], (E), Erie, PA.
Newman Central Catholic High School; Newman Middle School, [B], (RCK), Sterling, IL.
Newman Club Chaplains, [R], (BUF), Williamsville, NY.
Newman Club, Missouri Southern College, [I], (SPC), Webb City, MO.
Newman Community, Humboldt State University, [K], (SR), Arcata, CA.
Newman Foundation at Bradley University & Illinois Central College, [O], (PEO), Peoria, IL.
Newman Foundation for Catholic Students of Northern Illinois University, [M], (RCK), DeKalb, IL.
Newman Foundation of Chattanooga, Inc., [J], (KNX), Chattanooga, TN.
Newman Foundation of Cortland, Inc. at the State University College of New York, [V], (SY), Cortland, NY.
Newman Foundation, Inc., State University of New York, [V], (SY), Oswego, NY.
Newman Hall, Sonoma State University, Intercollegiate Catholic Ministries, [K], (SR), Penngrove, CA.
Newman High School, [C], (LC), Wausau, WI.
Newman House Catholic Center at Boston University, [CC], (BO), Boston, MA.
Newman Institute for Historical and Religious Studies, [L], (MRY), Monterey, CA.
Newman Parish, [L], (LC), Eau Claire, WI.
The Newman Parish - Eau Claire Endowment Trust, [M], (LC), Eau Claire, WI.
Newman University Parish, [L], (LC), Stevens Point, WI.
Newport Central Catholic High School, [B], (COV), Newport, KY.
Newport County C.Y.O. Center, [N], (PRO), Portsmouth, RI.
Next Step Learning Center, [R], (OAK), Oakland, CA.
NH Catholic Charities, [G], (MAN), Berlin, NH.
NH Catholic Charities, [G], (MAN), Concord, NH.
NH Catholic Charities, [G], (MAN), Keene, NH.
NH Catholic Charities, [G], (MAN), Laconia, NH.
NH Catholic Charities, [G], (MAN), Lebanon, NH.
NH Catholic Charities, [G], (MAN), Littleton, NH.
NH Catholic Charities, [G], (MAN), Nashua, NH.
NH Catholic Charities, [G], (MAN), Rochester, NH.
NH Catholic Charities, [G], (MAN), Salem, NH.
Niagara Catholic Junior-Senior School, [D], (BUF), Niagara Falls, NY.
Niagara Community College, [K], (BUF). See Our Lady of Victory Hospital.
Niagara Health Corporation, [E], (COL). See Mount Carmel Health System.
Niagara Homemaker Services, dba Mercy Home Care of Western New York, [K], (BUF), Lockport, NY.
Niagara University, [C], (BUF), Niagara University, NY.
Niagra Falls, [H], (BUF). See The Catholic Charities of the Diocese of Buffalo.
Nichols College (Dudley), [Q], (WOR). See Campus Ministry.
Nim Fecquet Holy Family School Foundation, [M], (BR) See Baton Rouge Chancery Office.
Niobrara Valley House of Renewal, [O], (OM), Lynch, NE.
Noah Homes, [E], (SD), Spring Valley, CA.
Nocturnal Adoration Society of the United States, [DD], (NY), New York, NY.
Nolan Catholic High School, [A], (FWT), Fort Worth, TX.
Nolan School Trust, [A], (FWT). See Nolan Catholic High School.
Non-Secure Detention/Boysville of Michigan, Inc., [E], (GAY), Traverse City, MI.
NORBERT & CO., [O], (GB), De Pere, WI.
Norbertine Community of New Mexico, Inc., [N], (SFE), Albuquerque, NM.
Norbertine Fathers, [H], (ORG), Silverado, CA.
Norbertine Generalate, Inc., [O], (GB), De Pere, WI.
Norbertine Retirement Fund Trust, [O], (GB), De Pere, WI.
Norco Adult Day Care, [M], (NO), Norco, LA.
Noreen McKeen Residence for Geriatric Care, [E], (PMB), West Palm Beach, FL.
Norfolk Catholic High School, [B], (OM), Norfolk, NE.
Noriega Adult Day Support Center, [Q], (SFR). See Catholic Charities of the Archdiocese of San Francisco.
Norm Fournier Court, [K], (SEA), Tacoma, WA.
Norris Square Senior Citizens Center, [Q], (PH), Philadelphia, PA.
North America Union Sisters of Our Lady of Charity, Inc., [O], (WH), Wheeling, WV.
North American Center for Marianist Studies, [M], (CIN). See Marianist Provincialate.
North American College of Rome, Alumni Assoc. of, [DD], (NY), New York, NY.
North American La Salette Mission Center, [M], (HRT). See Missionaries of LaSalette Provincial Secretary.
North American Union of the Sisters of Our Lady of Charity, [P], (BUF), Hamburg, NY.
North American Union of the Sisters of Our Lady of Charity, Inc., [J], (MAD), Wisconsin Dells, WI.
North American Union Sisters of Our Lady of Charity, [M], (E), Erie, PA.
North American Union Sisters of Our Lady of Charity, [K], (ELP), El Paso, TX.
North American Union, Sisters of Our Lady of Charity, [N], (SAT), San Antonio, TX.
North American Union-Sisters of Our Lady of Charity, OLC Holy Angels Convent, [J], (ROC), Rochester, NY.
North American Ursuline Education Services, [V], (CIN), Cincinnati, OH.
North & West Manhattan, Harlem, East Bronx, [D], (NY). See Department of Education.
North Area Cares Emergency Assistance, [L], (DEN). See Catholic Charities and Community Services of the Archdiocese of Denver, Inc.
North Bronx Family Service Center, [N], (NY). See Pius XII Youth and Family Services.
North Cambridge Catholic High School, [D], (BO), Cambridge, MA.
North Carolina Central University, [H], (R), Durham, NC.
North Catholic Endowment Fund, [R], (PIT), Pittsburgh, PA.
North Catholic High School, [C], (PIT), Pittsburgh, PA.
North Central Catholic School Corp., [N], (AUS), Austin, TX.
North City, [W], (STL). See Catholic Family Services.
North Country Independent Living, Inc., [E], (SUP). See Catholic Charities Bureau, Inc.
North County, [H], (SFR). See San Mateo County District Council.
North East Hispanic Catholic Center, Inc., [DD], (NY), New York, NY.
North End Soup Kitchen, [D], (LAN), Flint, MI.
North Harris College Newman Center, [T], (GAL), Spring, TX.
North Idaho College, [F], (B), Coeur D'Alene, ID.
North Iowa Mercy Health Center, [H], (DUB), Mason City, IA.
North Shore-Danvers, [K], (BO). See Family Counseling and Guidance Centers.
North Tonawanda Catholic, [G], (BUF), North Tonawanda, NY.
Northeast Catholic Counseling Center, [Q], (P), Portland, OR.
Northeast Catholic High School for Boys, [D], (PH), Philadelphia, PA.
Northeast E.A. Center, [L], (DEN). See Catholic Charities and Community Services of the Archdiocese of Denver, Inc.
Northeast Hispanic Catholic Center, [DD], (NY), New York, NY.
Northeast Mississippi Community College Catholic Student Center, [G], (JKS), Booneville, MS.
Northeast Regional Catholic School, [H], (STP), Minneapolis, MN.
Northeast, Northwest, & South Bronx, [D], (NY). See Department of Education.
Northeastern Catholic Jr. High, [C], (ROC), Rochester, NY.
Northeastern Junior College (Sterling), [P], (DEN),

Sterling, CO.
Northeastern Maine Adult and Family Services, [E], (PRT). See Catholic Charities Maine.
Northeastern Maine Adult and Family Services-Satellite Office, [E], (PRT). See Catholic Charities Maine.
Northeastern Oklahoma A & M College Newman Center, [I], (TLS), Miami, OK.
Northeastern State University Catholic Student Organization, [I], (TLS), Tahlequah, OK.
Northern Cambria Catholic School, [C], (ALT), Nicktown, PA.
Northern Chautauqua Catholic, [G], (BUF), Dunkirk, NY.
Northern Koolau Health Education Center, [F], (HON). See St. Francis Healthcare System of Hawaii.
Northern Office, [E], (HBG). See Department for Catholic Charities Counseling/Field Services.
Northern Region, [N], (SY), Syracuse, NY.
Northern Region Religious Education Office & Special Education for Catholics, [N], (SY), Syracuse, NY.
Northern San Joaquin Region, [C], (STO). See St. Joseph's Regional Health System of Northern San Joaquin Valley.
Northern Valley Catholic Social Service, [L], (SAC), Redding, CA.
Northern Wisconsin Center for the Developmentally Disabled, [P], (LC), Chippewa Falls, WI.
Northern Worcester Co., [H], (WOR). See Catholic Charities.
Northland House, [K], (LC), Wausau, WI.
Northside Community Health Center, [E], (LR), Fort Smith, AR.
Northside CYO, [K], (SY), Syracuse, NY.
Northside Office of Christian Response, [P], (PEO), Peoria, IL.
Northview University Center, [W], (CHI), Chicago, IL.
Northwest, [W], (STL). See Catholic Family Services.
Northwest Catholic High School, [D], (HRT), West Hartford, CT.
NorthWest College, [E], (CHY), Powell, WY.
Northwest Covenant Medical Center, Inc., [J], (PAT). See Sisters of the Sorrowful Mother Health Care Ministry Corp.
Northwest Mississippi Community College Newman Center, [G], (JKS), Senatobia, MS.
Northwest Missouri State University Newman House, [N], (KC), Maryville, MO.
Northwest Suburban Family Shelter, [G], (CHI). See Catholic Charities of the Archdiocese of Chicago-Archdiocesan Offices.
Northwest Suburban Senior Services, [G], (CHI). See Catholic Charities of the Archdiocese of Chicago-Archdiocesan Offices.
Northwestern State University, [J], (ALX), Natchitoches, LA.
Northwood Park Apartments, [I], (MEM), Memphis, TN.
Norwood-Fontbonne Academy for Boys and Girls, [H], (PH), Philadelphia, PA.
Notre Dame Academy, [E], (BO), Hingham, MA.
Notre Dame Academy, [F], (LA), Los Angeles, CA.
Notre Dame Academy, [C], (TOL), Toledo, OH.
Notre Dame Academy, [E], (WOR), Worcester, MA.
Notre Dame Academy (Elementary), [H], (LA), Los Angeles, CA.
Notre Dame Academy High School, [F], (NY), New York, NY.
Notre Dame Academy, Middleburg, VA, [E], (ARL), Middleburg, VA.
Notre Dame Academy-Elementary School, [H], (NY), New York, NY.
Notre Dame Catholic High School, [C], (BGP), Fairfield, CT.
Notre Dame Children's Class, [G], (BO), Wenham, MA.
Notre Dame Children's Endowment Trust, [M], (LC), Chippewa Falls, WI.
Notre Dame College, [D], (BRK). See St. John's University.
Notre Dame College, [B], (MAN), Manchester, NH.
Notre Dame College of Ohio, [C], (CLV), Cleveland, OH.
Notre Dame Community, [G], (AGN), Talofofo, GU.
Notre Dame Convalescent Home, [L], (BGP), Norwalk, CT.
Notre Dame Convent, [I], (FWT), Wichita Falls, TX.
Notre Dame Convent, [N], (HRT), Waterbury, CT.
Notre Dame Convent, [L], (TOL), Toledo, OH.
Notre Dame Convent, Sisters of the Congregation of Notre Dame, [F], (PT), Pensacola, FL.
Notre Dame de la Baie Academy, [D], (GB), Green Bay, WI.
Notre Dame de la Mer Retirement Apartments, [D], (BLX), Bay St. Louis, MS.
Notre Dame de Lourdes, [J], (PRT), Saco, ME.
Notre Dame de Sion Elementary & Middle School, [F], (KC), Kansas City, MO.
Notre Dame de Sion High School, [D], (KC), Kansas City, MO.
Notre Dame Development Fund, Inc., [X], (BO), Lowell, MA.
Notre Dame Diocesan Convent, [N], (TR), Trenton, NJ.
Notre Dame Education Center, [D], (BO), Boston, MA.
*Notre Dame Education Center, [V], (WDC), Washington, DC.
Notre Dame Elementary School, [F], (CLV), Chardon, OH.
Notre Dame Elementary School, [C], (FWT), Wichita Falls, TX.
Notre Dame Elementary School, [F], (SCR), East Stroudsburg, PA.
Notre Dame Elementary School, [G], (SFR), Belmont, CA.
Notre Dame Hall, [R], (STL), St. Louis, MO.
Notre Dame High School, [B], (AGN), Talofofo, GU.
Notre Dame High School, [C], (ALN), Easton, PA.
Notre Dame High School, [D], (CHI), Chicago, IL.
Notre Dame High School, [D], (CHI), Niles, IL.
Notre Dame High School, [C], (COL), Portsmouth, OH.
Notre Dame High School, [E], (DAV), Burlington, IA.
Notre Dame High School, [E], (DET), Harper Woods, MI.
Notre Dame High School, [E], (HRT), West Haven, CT.
Notre Dame High School, [A], (KNX), Chattanooga, TN.
Notre Dame High School, [F], (LA), Sherman Oaks, CA.
Notre Dame High School, [C], (MRY), Salinas, CA.
Notre Dame High School, [B], (PEO), Peoria, IL.
Notre Dame High School, [B], (ROC), Elmira, NY.
Notre Dame High School, [B], (SB), Riverside, CA.
Notre Dame High School, [D], (SJ), San Jose, CA.
Notre Dame High School, [F], (STL), St. Louis, MO.
Notre Dame High School, [B], (TR), Trenton, NJ.
Notre Dame High School (Girls), [E], (SFR), Belmont, CA.
Notre Dame High School Financial Board of Trustees, [A], (KNX). See Notre Dame High School.
Notre Dame High School of Acadia Parish, [B], (LAF), Crowley, LA.
Notre Dame High School of Batavia, [D], (BUF), Batavia, NY.
Notre Dame Housing, Inc., [O], (OM), Omaha, NE.
Notre Dame Institute, [I], (PRT), Alfred, ME.
Notre Dame Institute for Catechetics, [B], (ARL), Arlington, VA.
Notre Dame Interparochial School, [D], (SP), Spring Hill, FL.
Notre Dame Jr./Sr. High School, [C], (SY), Utica, NY.
Notre Dame Junior/Senior High School, [D], (SCR), East Stroudsburg, PA.
Notre Dame Living Center, Inc., [O], (OM), Omaha, NE.
Notre Dame Long Term Care Center, [K], (WOR), Worcester, MA.
Notre Dame Loyalty & Endowment Fund, Inc., [E], (HRT). See Notre Dame High School.
Notre Dame Middle School, [D], (LC). See Chippewa Area Catholic Schools.
Notre Dame Middle School, Inc., [G], (MIL), Milwaukee, WI.
Notre Dame Middle-High School, [A], (FWT), Wichita Falls, TX.
Notre Dame Ministry Corporation, [W], (STL), St. Louis, MO.
Notre Dame Mission Volunteer Corporation, [FF], (BO), Cambridge, MA.
Notre Dame Montessori School, [F], (CLV), Chardon, OH.
Notre Dame of Dallas Schools, Inc., [H], (DAL), Dallas, TX.
Notre Dame of Elm Grove, [Q], (MIL), Elm Grove, WI.
Notre Dame Parish Endowment Trust, [M], (LC), Chippewa Falls, WI.
Notre Dame Plaza Corporation, [P], (SJ), Saratoga, CA.
Notre Dame Preparatory High School and Marist Academy, [D], (DET), Pontiac, MI.
Notre Dame Preparatory School, [D], (BAL), Towson, MD.
Notre Dame Preparatory School, [E], (WOR), Fitchburg, MA.
Notre Dame Provincialate, [L], (TOL), Toledo, OH.
Notre Dame Regional High School, [B], (SPC), Cape Girardeau, MO.
Notre Dame Regional School, [D], (CAM), Newfield, NJ.
Notre Dame Regional School, [G], (PRO), West Warwick, RI.
Notre Dame Regional School, [C], (SLC), Price, UT.
Notre Dame Residence, [O], (SP), St. Petersburg, FL.
Notre Dame Retreat House, [K], (ROC), Canandaigua, NY.
Notre Dame School of Manhattan, [F], (NY), New York, NY.
Notre Dame Seminary Graduate School of Theology, [A], (NO), New Orleans, LA.
Notre Dame Spiritual Center, [L], (PRT), Alfred, ME.
Notre Dame System of Education, [F], (DUB), Cresco, IA.
Notre Dame-Bishop Gibbons School, [C], (ALB), Schenectady, NY.
Notre Dame-Cathedral Latin School, [E], (CLV), Chardon, OH.
Nott Homes, Inc., [H], (RIC), Lynchburg, VA.
Nouvel Catholic Central High School, [A], (SAG), Saginaw, MI.
Novitiate, [AA], (NY). See Mt. St. Francis, Motherhouse & Infirm of Franciscan Missionary Sisters of Sacred Heart.
Novitiate House for the Franciscan Friars, O.F.M., [G], (MRY), San Miguel, CA.
Novitiate of St. Isaac Jogues, [A], (ALN), Wernersville, PA.
Novitiate of the Immaculate Conception Province of the T.O.R. of St. Francis, [F], (ALT). See St. Bernardine Monastery.
Novitiate of the Legion of Christ, [B], (HRT), Cheshire, CT.
"Now and at the Hour" Magazine, [L], (LAN). See The Pious Union of St. Joseph.
Nowe Zycie Association, [X], (CHI), Chicago, IL.
"Nuestra Hogar" Missionaries of Charity Brothers, [V], (LA), Los Angeles, CA.
Nuestra Senora de Guadalupe Convent, [I], (CC). See Religious Missionaries of St. Dominic, Inc.
Nuestra Senora Del Perpetuo Socorro, [H], (JKS), Jackson, MS.
Nuestro Hogar, [R], (LA). See Missionaries of Charity Brothers.
Nuestro Hogar, Inc. Catholic Charities, [G], (FWT), Arlington, TX.
Nuns of St. Basil the Great, [F], (STF), Middletown, NY.
Nursery School, [F], (PHU). See Motherhouse of the Missionary Sisters of Mother of God.
Nurses School, [I], (HRT). See Saint Francis Hospital and Medical Center.
Nursing School, [E], (RIC). See Bon Secours - De Paul Medical Center, Inc.
Nursing Sisters Home Visiting Service, Inc., [M], (BRK), Brooklyn, NY.
Nursing Sisters Home Visiting Service, Inc., [M], (RVC), Westbury, NY.
Nursing Sisters of the Sick Poor, [V], (BRK), Brooklyn, NY.
The Nurturing Place, [K], (NEW). See St. Joseph's Home.
Nurturing Place Day Care, [O], (NEW). See St. Joseph Province Shalom Center.
Nutrition and Aging Services, [G], (BGP). See Catholic Charities of Fairfield County.

O

O'Connell High School, [D], (GAL), Galveston, TX.
O'Connor Foundation, [H], (SJ). See O'Connor Hospital.
O'Connor Hospital, [H], (SJ), San Jose, CA.
O'Connor Hospital dba Saint Louise Hospital & Health Center, [H], (SJ), Morgan Hill, CA.
O'Connor Woods Housing Corp. dba Garden Oaks, [D], (STO). See St. Joseph's Regional Housing Corp.
O'Connor Woods, A Calif. Corp., [D], (STO). See St. Joseph's Regional Housing Corp.
O'Dea High School, [B], (SEA), Seattle, WA.
O'Gorman High School, [C], (SFS). See Sioux Falls Catholic School System.
O'Hara Area Elementary Catholic School, [E], (P), Eugene, OR.
O'Hara Residence, [O], (BUF), Tonawanda, NY.
O'Keefe Hall, [M], (DAV), Iowa City, IA.
The O'Malley, [I], (SPK), Spokane, WA.
The O'Neill Brothers Foundation, [AA], (CLV), Pepper Pike, OH.
O.S.F. St. Francis Hospital, [C], (MAR), Escanaba, MI.
O.S.F. Services, Inc., [Y], (MIL), Milwaukee, WI.
OACES-Oshkosh Area Catholic Educational System, [E], (GB), Oshkosh, WI.
OAEF, Inc.- C.J. Miller Trust, [N], (OM). See The Omaha Archdiocesan Educational Foundation, Inc.
Oak Hill School, [G], (STL), Frontenac, MO.
Oak Knoll School of the Holy Child Upper School, [C], (NEW), Summit, NJ.
Oak Knoll School of The Holy Child, Lower School, [E], (NEW), Summit, NJ.
Oak Park Hospital, [J], (CHI), Oak Park, IL.
Oak Park Hospital Endowment Fund, [J], (CHI). See Oak Park Hospital.
Oak Park Study Center, [W], (CHI), Oak Park, IL.
Oakcrest School, [E], (WDC), Washington, DC.
Oakes Community Hospital, [D], (FAR), Oakes, ND.
Oakland Catholic High School, [C], (PIT), Pittsburgh, PA.
Oakland City College Newman Center, [I], (EVN), Oakland City, IN.
Oaklawn Academy, [M], (MAD), Edgerton, WI.
Oaklawn Incorporated, [M], (MAD), Edgerton, WI.

Oakwood Apartments (Superior), [E], (SUP). See Catholic Charities Bureau, Inc.
Oakwood Village Retirement Community, [L], (CIN), Springfield, OH.
Oasis, [F], (SJ). See Catholic Charities of Santa Clara County.
OASIS (Older Adult Services & Intervention System), [Y], (LA). See Catholic Charities of Los Angeles, Inc.
Oblate Benson Residence (Southern Prov.), [M], (SAT), San Antonio, TX.
Oblate College/Oblate Center for Mission Studies, [B], (WDC), Washington, DC.
Oblate Conference, [V], (WDC), Silver Spring, MD.
Oblate Fathers of St. Francis De Sales, Inc., [L], (LAN), Brooklyn, MI.
Oblate Fathers-Oblate World/Missionary Association of Mary Immaculate, [W], (BO), Tewksbury, MA.
Oblate Fathers-Office of the Provincial Treasurer, [W], (BO), Tewksbury, MA.
Oblate House, [F], (SLC), Salt Lake City, UT.
Oblate House of Studies, [W], (STL), St. Louis, MO.
The Oblate House of Theology, [N], (CHI), Chicago, IL.
Oblate Lourdes Grotto Shrine of the Southwest, [T], (SAT), San Antonio, TX.
Oblate Madonna Residence, [K], (SAT), San Antonio, TX.
Oblate Media and Communication Corporation, [W], (STP), St. Paul, MN.
Oblate Ministry Development Service, [FF], (BO), Lowell, MA.
Oblate Missions, [T], (SAT), San Antonio, TX.
Oblate Preaching Team, [K], (BEL), Belleville, IL.
Oblate Provincial House & Procure, [N], (OAK), Oakland, CA.
Oblate Provincial Offices, [N], (STP), St. Paul, MN.
Oblate Provincialate, [B], (BO), Boston, MA.
Oblate Renewal Center, [O], (SAT), San Antonio, TX.
Oblate Residence, [N], (STP), St. Paul, MN.
Oblate Residences, [O], (TOL), Toledo, OH.
Oblate School of Theology, [C], (SAT), San Antonio, TX.
Oblate Seminary Residence, [B], (BO), Brighton, MA.
Oblate Sisters of the Most Holy Eucharist, [O], (WDC), Brookville, MD.
Oblate Sisters of the Most Holy Redeemer, [AA], (NY), New York, NY.
Oblate Sisters of the Most Holy Redeemer, [O], (RVC), Roosevelt, NY.
Oblate Sisters' Kindergarten and Nursery, Villa Aviat, [C], (WIL), Childs, MD.
Oblates of Mary Immaculate, [M], (HRT), Hamden, CT.
Oblates of Mary Immaculate, [F], (NOR), Willimantic, CT.
Oblates of Mary Immaculate Retreat House, [M], (MAN), Hudson, NH.
Oblates of Mary Immaculate, De Mazenod Residence, [B], (WDC), Washington, DC.
Oblates of Notre Dame, [B], (SAN), Midland, TX.
Oblates of St. Francis de Sales, [K], (ALN), Center Valley, PA.
Oblates of St. Francis De Sales, [Z], (PH), Philadelphia, PA.
Oblates of St. Francis de Sales, [K], (TOL), Toledo, OH.
Oblates of St. Francis de Sales, [G], (VEN), Fort Myers, FL.
Oblates of St. Francis De Sales, [I], (WIL), Wilmington, DE.
Oblates of St. Francis De Sales, [I], (WIL), Childs, MD.
Oblates of St. Francis de Sales (O.S.F.S.), [Z], (PH), Wyndmoor, PA.
Oblates of St. Francis de Sales House of Studies, [B], (WDC), Washington, DC.
Oblates of St. Francis de Sales Residence, [J], (ARL), Alexandria, VA.
Oblates of St. Francis de Sales Residence, [J], (ARL), Fairfax, VA.
Oblates of St. Joseph Provincial House and Shrine, [G], (MRY), Santa Cruz, CA.
Oblates of the Mother of Orphans, [AA], (NY), New York, NY.
Oblates of Wisdom, [H], (PCE), Ponce, PR.
Oblates Sisters of the Most Holy Eucharist, [O], (WDC), Washington, DC.
Ocean Avenue Community Home, [L], (NO), Gretna, LA.
Ocean County Community College, [R], (TR). See Campus Ministry for the Diocese of Trenton.
Ocean County Office, [S], (TR). See Holy Redeemer Visiting Nurse Agency, Inc.
Ocean Rest Summer School and Retreat House, [L], (CAM), Ocean City, NJ.
Ocean Tides, [I], (PRO), Narragansett, RI.
Office for Adolescent Formation & Youth Ministry, [P], (PIT). See Gilmary Diocesan Center.
Office for Campus Ministry, [Q], (PIT), Slippery Rock, PA.
Office for Cursillo Movement, [A], (LUB). See Christian Renewal Center.
Office for Disabled Persons, [L], (BRK). See Catholic Charities.
Office for Hispanic Catholics of Tidewater - Cristo Rey Hispanic Apostolate, [L], (RIC). See Ethnic and Special Ministries.
Office for Justice and Peace, [J], (NY), New York, NY.
Office for Parish Social Ministry, [D], (WIL). See Catholic Charities, Inc.
Office for the Homeless and Hungry, [J], (NY), New York, NY.
Office of Aging Services, [C], (STA), Jacksonville, FL.
Office of AIDS Ministry, Inc., [Q], (FR), Fall River, MA.
Office of Annual and Deferred Giving, [G], (CHI). See Catholic Charities of the Archdiocese of Chicago-Archdiocesan Offices.
Office of Archdiocesan Council, [I], (WDC). See Society of St. Vincent de Paul.
Office of Board Relations and Major Events, [G], (CHI). See Catholic Charities of the Archdiocese of Chicago-Archdiocesan Offices.
Office of Campus and Young Adult Ministry, [P], (SEA), Seattle, WA.
Office of Chaplaincies, [Q], (PIT), Pittsburgh, PA.
Office of Criminal Justice, [J], (NY), New York, NY.
Office of Evangelization, [A], (LUB). See Christian Renewal Center.
Office of Family Ministries, [G], (MAN), Manchester, NH.
Office of Global Concerns, [O], (TOL), Toledo, OH.
Office of Guest House, Inc., [I], (DET). See Guest House for Women Religious.
Office of Justice and Peace, [C], (STA), Jacksonville, FL.
Office of Lay Carmelites, [Z], (NY). See St. Eliseus Priory.
Office of Major Gifts, [G], (CHI). See Catholic Charities of the Archdiocese of Chicago-Archdiocesan Offices.
The Office of Migrant and Refugee Services, [N], (ELP), El Paso, TX.
Office of Newman Campus Ministry, [Y], (CLV), Cleveland, OH.
Office of Pastoral Ministry With Handicapped Persons, [H], (BUF). See The Catholic Charities of the Diocese of Buffalo.
Office of Peace & Justice, [J], (PHX). See Catholic Social Services of Central and Northern Arizona, Inc.
Office of Religious Education: Evangelization and Catholic Formation, [E], (BRK), Brooklyn, NY.
Office of Senior Affairs, [E], (FRS), Fresno, CA.
Office of Social Justice and Peace, [E], (PRT). See Catholic Charities Maine.
Office of Social Ministry, [I], (SAV), Savannah, GA.
Office of Substance Abuse and AIDS Ministry, [J], (STU), Steubenville, OH.
Office of the Carmelite Midwest Commissary Provincial, [M], (JOL), Darien, IL.
Office of the Immaculate Heart of Mary Shrine, [J], (SPC), Carthage, MO.
Office of the Marginalized, [O], (E), Erie, PA.
Office of the Superintendent of Schools, [E], (BRK), Brooklyn, NY.
Office of Youth and Young Adult Ministries, [H], (PHX), Phoenix, AZ.
Offices of The Vatican Observatory, [F], (TUC). See Jesuit Community of the Vatican Observatory.
Ohio Conference Advisory Council, [J], (STU), Steubenville, OH.
Ohio Dominican College, [B], (COL), Columbus, OH.
Ohio University - Eastern, [I], (STU), St. Clairsville, OH.
Oklahoma Benedictine Institute on Mental Retardation, [L], (OKL). See Oklahoma Benedictine Institute on Mental Retardation, Inc.
Oklahoma Benedictine Institute on Mental Retardation, Inc., [L], (OKL), Shawnee, OK.
Oklahoma Benedictine Institute TV Network for Success, [L], (OKL). See Oklahoma Benedictine Institute on Mental Retardation, Inc.
OLA/St. Joseph Center, [V], (CLV). See Catholic Charities Services Corporation.
OLA-St. Joseph Center, [H], (CLV), Cleveland, OH.
Old Cathedral Library & Museum, Inc., [J], (EVN), Vincennes, IN.
Old College, [A], (FTW), Notre Dame, IN.
The Old Convent, [F], (MOB). See City of St. Jude, Inc., The.
Oldenburg Academy of the Immaculate Conception, [D], (IND), Oldenburg, IN.
Olean, [H], (BUF). See The Catholic Charities of the Diocese of Buffalo.
Ollie Steele Burden Manor, [G], (BR), Baton Rouge, LA.
Om Shanti, [M], (E), Erie, PA.
The Omaha Archdiocesan Community Foundation and Donor Directed Depository, [O], (OM), Omaha, NE.
The Omaha Archdiocesan Educational Foundation, Inc., [N], (OM), Omaha, NE.
Omaha Archdiocesan Educational Foundation, Inc., [O], (OM), Omaha, NE.
Omaha Catholic Jail Ministry, [O], (OM), Omaha, NE.
Ombudsman & Meals on Wheels, [Q], (SFR). See Catholic Charities of the Archdiocese of San Francisco.
Omega Retreat Center, [O], (SAT), Boerne, TX.
OMI Senior Center, [Q], (SFR). See Catholic Charities of the Archdiocese of San Francisco.
1-800-Mass-Times Trust, [M], (MIA), Key Largo, FL.
ONE (Opportunity Network in Economics), [W], (SY), Syracuse, NY.
One sixty one 161-01 89th Avenue Corp., [L], (BRK). See Catholic Charities.
The One Thousand Corporation, [I], (HRT). See Saint Francis Hospital and Medical Center.
One Thousand One Corporation, [I], (HRT). See Saint Francis Hospital and Medical Center.
Oneness in Peace Spiritual Center, [T], (ALB), Germantown, NY.
Onondaga Community College Newman Center, [V], (SY), Syracuse, NY.
Onondaga County Catholic School Foundation (Western Region Catholic School Foundation), [W], (SY), Syracuse, NY.
Opdyke, Inc., [T], (DET), Bloomfield Hills, MI.
Opelousas Catholic School, [B], (LAF), Opelousas, LA.
Opelousas Housing Corporation, [N], (LAF), Opelousas, LA.
Open Hand Kitchen, [P], (L). See Society of St. Vincent de Paul, Council of Louisville.
Open Window Book and Gift Shop of the Diocese of Springfield, Inc., [L], (SPR), Chicopee, MA.
The Opening Word Program, Inc., [R], (RVC), Wyandanch, NY.
Operarios Del Reino De Cristo, O.R.C., [E], (SB), Riverside, CA.
Opportunity for Parochial Education Network (OPEN), [Q], (E), St. Marys, PA.
Opus Dei, [V], (BO), Chestnut Hill, MA.
Opus Dei, [K], (BUR), Randolph, VT.
Opus Dei, [W], (CHI), Chicago, IL.
Opus Dei, [L], (DAL), Irving, TX.
Opus Dei, [P], (GAL), Houston, TX.
Opus Dei, [J], (GRY), Valparaiso, IN.
Opus Dei, [M], (NEW), South Orange, NJ.
Opus Dei, [M], (PIT), Pittsburgh, PA.
Opus Dei, [F], (PMB), Delray Beach, FL.
Opus Dei, [T], (SFR), San Francisco, CA.
Opus Dei, [F], (SJN), Guaynabo, PR.
Opus Dei, [Q], (STL), Kirkwood, MO.
Opus Dei, [D], (VIC), Schulenburg, TX.
Opus Dei, [T], (WDC), Washington, DC.
Opus Dei (Prelature of the Holy Cross and Opus Dei), [C], (MGZ), Mayaguez, PR.
Opus Dei (Prelature of the Holy Cross and Opus Dei), [EE], (NY), New Rochelle, NY.
Opus Dei (Prelature of the Holy Cross and Opus Dei), [R], (SAT), San Antonio, TX.
Opus Dei, Mathewson House, [O], (PRO), Providence, RI.
Opus Dei, Prelature of the Holy Cross and Opus Dei, [V], (BO), Cambridge, MA.
Opus Dei. Prelature of the Holy Cross and Opus Dei, [X], (LA), Los Angeles, CA.
Opus Dei-Prelature of the Holy Cross and Opus Dei., [O], (MIL), Brookfield, WI.
Opus Spiritus Sancti, [G], (SC), Pocahontas, IA.
Orange, [D], (NY). See Department of Education.
Oratorian Community-Congregation of the Oratory of Pontifical Right, [G], (MRY), Monterey, CA.
The Oratory, [J], (HON), Honolulu, HI.
Oratory Academy, [B], (BWN), Pharr, TX.
The Oratory Catholic Preparatory School, [D], (NEW), Summit, NJ.
Oratory of St. Philip Neri, Congregation of the Oratory of Pontifical Rite, [E], (CHR), Rock Hill, SC.
Oratory of Saint Philip Neri, Congregation Pontifical Rite, [U], (BRK), Brooklyn, NY.
Oratory of St. Philip Neri, of Pontifical Right, [E], (BWN), Pharr, TX.
Orchard View, Inc., [D], (SC). See St. Anthony Regional Hospital.
Orchard View, Inc., [H], (SC), Carroll, IA.
Order of Friars Minor, [H], (AUS), Brenham, TX.
Order of Friars Minor Conventual, [M], (BAL), Ellicott City, MD.
Order of Friars Minor Conventual Immaculate Conception Province Charitable Trust, [T], (ALB), Rensselaer, NY.
Order of Friars Minor, Holy Name Province, [Z], (PH), Philadelphia, PA.
Order Of Preachers (Southern Dominican Prov.), [J], (MEM), Memphis, TN.
Order of Preachers (Southern Province), [N], (OAK), Oakland, CA.
Order of St. Augustine, [E], (KAL), Douglas, MI.
Order of St. Augustine, [Z], (PH), Villanova, PA.
Order of St. Augustine, [Z], (PH), Willowburn, PA.
Order of St. Sharbel Trust Fund, [E], (SAM), Staten Island, NY.

Order of the BVM of Mercy/Mercedarian Friars, [O], (BUF), LeRoy, NY.
Order of The Holy Trinity, [J], (MEM), Memphis, TN.
The Order of the Legion of Little Souls of the Merciful Heart of Jesus, [P], (PEO), Moline, IL.
Order of the Visitation of Holy Mary, [J], (SPR), Tyringham, MA.
*The Ordinary Mutual, RRG, [U], (SFR), San Francisco, CA.
Oregon Catholic Conference, [Q], (P), Portland, OR.
Osborn Family Health Center, Inc., [G], (CAM). See Our Lady of Lourdes Medical Center, Inc.
OSF Healthcare Foundation, [J], (PEO). See OSF Healthcare System.
OSF Healthcare System, [J], (PEO), Peoria, IL.
Osmund Program, [V], (WDC), Seat Pleasant, MD.
Ostrich Outreach Program, [L], (OKL). See Oklahoma Benedictine Institute on Mental Retardation, Inc.
Other Jesuit Residences, [Z], (NY). See Jesuit Provincial's Office.
Otsego Senior Apts., Inc., [F], (KAL), Otsego, MI.
Our Blessed Lady of Victory Mission, Inc., [V], (MIL), Milwaukee, WI.
Our House of Minnesota, Inc. I, [R], (STP), St. Paul, MN.
Our House of Minnesota, Inc. II, [R], (STP), St. Paul, MN.
Our Lady of Angels Association, [T], (BUF), Niagara University, NY.
Our Lady of Angels Friary, [K], (SFD), Sherman, IL.
Our Lady of Angels Retirement Home, [I], (JOL), Joliet, IL.
Our Lady of Bellefonte Hospital, Inc., [D], (LEX), Ashland, KY.
Our Lady of Bethlehem Convent, [I], (COL), Columbus, OH.
Our Lady of Bethlehem Early Child Education Center, [I], (COL). See Our Lady of Bethlehem Convent.
Our Lady of Black Rock, [G], (BUF), Buffalo, NY.
Our Lady of Calvary Retreat House, [Q], (HRT), Farmington, CT.
Our Lady of Charity Center, Inc., [G], (GB), Green Bay, WI.
Our Lady of Charity, Inc., [CC], (LA), Lancaster, CA.
Our Lady of Comfort Women's Center, [DD], (NY), Newburgh, NY.
Our Lady of Compassion, [D], (KCK), Spring Hill, MO.
Our Lady of Confidence Day School, [I], (PH), Philadelphia, PA.
Our Lady of Consolation Geriatric Care Center, [J], (RVC), West Islip, NY.
Our Lady of Consolation Residence, [Z], (NY), New York, NY.
Our Lady of Consolation, Early Childhood School, [EE], (PH), Gap, PA.
Our Lady of Creek Bend, [I], (RCK), St. Charles, IL.
Our Lady of Czestochowa, [N], (SAT), San Antonio, TX.
Our Lady of Czestochowa Shrine, [W], (CLV), Garfield Heights, OH.
Our Lady of Divine Providence House of Prayer, [Q], (SP). See Our Lady of Divine Providence, House of Prayer, Inc.
Our Lady of Divine Providence, House of Prayer, Inc., [Q], (SP), Clearwater, FL.
Our Lady of Elms Elementary School, [F], (CLV), Akron, OH.
Our Lady of Elms Pre-School, [I], (CLV), Akron, OH.
Our Lady of Fatima Apts., HDFC, Inc., [L], (BRK). See Catholic Charities.
Our Lady of Fatima Convent, [F], (BLX), Biloxi, MS.
Our Lady of Fatima Convent, [I], (ORG), San Clemente, CA.
Our Lady of Fatima Convent, [I], (SAC). See Institute of the Sisters of Mercy of the Americas.
Our Lady of Fatima Convent, [J], (WIL), New Castle, DE.
Our Lady of Fatima High School, [E], (PRO), Warren, RI.
Our Lady of Fatima Parish Conference, [E], (YAK), Moses Lake, WA.
Our Lady of Fatima Retreat Center, [M], (FTW), Notre Dame, IN.
Our Lady of Fatima Retreat House, Inc., [I], (IND), Indianapolis, IN.
Our Lady of Fatima Shrine, [BB], (BO), Holliston, MA.
Our Lady of Fatima Shrine, [H], (STU), Fatima, OH.
Our Lady of Fatima Villa, [I], (SJ), Saratoga, CA.
Our Lady of Fatima Villa Convent, [N], (SJ), Saratoga, CA.
Our Lady of Florida Spiritual Center, [G], (PMB), North Palm Beach, FL.
Our Lady of Florida Spiritual Center, [I], (PMB), North Palm Beach, FL.
Our Lady of Good Counsel Camp, [R], (SP), St. Petersburg, FL.
Our Lady of Good Counsel Conference, St. Vincent de Paul Society, [G], (B), Mountain Home, ID.
Our Lady of Good Counsel Franciscan Friary, [G], (WH), Morgantown, WV.
Our Lady of Good Counsel Historic Trust, Inc., [P], (BAL). See Chancery Office.
Our Lady of Good Counsel Home, [K], (STP), St. Paul, MN.
Our Lady of Good Counsel Residence, [U], (BRK), Brooklyn, NY.
Our Lady of Good Counsel Retreat House, [F], (LIN), Waverly, NE.
Our Lady of Good Voyage Chapel, [BB], (BO), Boston, MA.
Our Lady of Grace Convent, [P], (BGP), Stamford, CT.
Our Lady of Grace Convent, [D], (LUB), Lubbock, TX.
Our Lady of Grace Day Nursery, [H], (BGP), Stamford, CT.
Our Lady of Grace Home for Children, Inc., [F], (WIL), Newark, DE.
Our Lady of Grace Monastery, [K], (DET), Dearborn Heights, MI.
Our Lady of Grace Monastery, [M], (HRT), North Guilford, CT.
Our Lady of Grace Monastery for Sisters of St. Benedict of Beech Grove, IN, Inc., [K], (IND), Beech Grove, IN.
Our Lady of Grace Montessori School and Center, [F], (RVC), Manhasset, NY.
Our Lady of Grace School, [D], (CAM), Somerdale, NJ.
Our Lady of Grace Seminary, [B], (BO), Boston, MA.
Our Lady of Guadalupe, [I], (SFS), Sioux Falls, SD.
Our Lady of Guadalupe Benedictine Abbey, [L], (SFE), Pecos, NM.
Our Lady of Guadalupe Campus, [C], (AMA). See Amarillo Catholic Children's Development Centers.
Our Lady of Guadalupe Convent, [K], (CHL), Cherokee, NC.
Our Lady of Guadalupe Convent, [O], (OAK). See Dominican Sisters of Mission San Jose.
Our Lady of Guadalupe Mission, [D], (ALX), Forest Hill, LA.
Our Lady of Guadalupe Prayer Center, Inc., [E], (LSC), Las Cruces, NM.
Our Lady of Guadalupe Renewal Center, [L], (BAL), Catonsville, MD.
Our Lady of Guadalupe School, [B], (AMA), Amarillo, TX.
Our Lady of Guadalupe School, [B], (CC), Laredo, TX.
Our Lady of Guadalupe School, [E], (KC), Kansas City, MO.
Our Lady of Holy Cross College, [C], (NO), New Orleans, LA.
Our Lady of Holy Cross Convent, [K], (FTW), South Bend, IN.
Our Lady of Hope Center, [BB], (NY), Newburgh, NY.
Our Lady of Hope Health Center, Inc., [H], (RIC), Richmond, VA.
Our Lady of Hope Residence, [J], (ALB), Latham, NY.
Our Lady of Hope, House of Prayer, [L], (MAN), New Ipswich, NH.
Our Lady of Hungary Regional School, [D], (ALN), Northampton, PA.
Our Lady of Kazan Russian Greek Catholic Mission, [FF], (BO), Braintree, MA.
Our Lady of Lavang Vietnamese Community of Tidewater, [L], (RIC). See Ethnic and Special Ministries.
Our Lady of Lebanon Maronite Seminary, [A], (SAM), Washington, DC.
Our Lady of Levocha, [W], (CLV), Bedford, OH.
Our Lady of Life Apartments, Inc., [I], (STL). See Cardinal Ritter Institute.
Our Lady of Light Chapel, [F], (TR), Trenton, NJ.
Our Lady of Light Chapel, [O], (TR), Trenton, NJ.
Our Lady of Loretto, [G], (ALT), Loretto, PA.
Our Lady of Lourdes, [W], (CLV), Cleveland, OH.
Our Lady of Lourdes, [L], (RIC). See Ethnic and Special Ministries.
Our Lady of Lourdes, [I], (SAV), Columbus, GA.
Our Lady of Lourdes, [G], (SY), Utica, NY.
Our Lady of Lourdes Academy, [C], (MIA), Miami, FL.
Our Lady of Lourdes Associates Foundation, Inc., [G], (CAM). See Our Lady of Lourdes Medical Center, Inc.
Our Lady of Lourdes Convent, [L], (FR), Taunton, MA.
Our Lady of Lourdes Convent, [H], (GF), Great Falls, MT.
Our Lady of Lourdes Convent, [I], (KCK), Paola, KS.
Our Lady of Lourdes Convent, [L], (MAN), Portsmouth, NH.
Our Lady of Lourdes Convent, [G], (SLC), Salt Lake City, UT.
Our Lady of Lourdes Convent, [O], (WDC). See Sisters of the Holy Cross.
Our Lady of Lourdes Convent (Infirmary), [O], (SFR). See Dominican Sisters of San Rafael Generalate & Convent.
Our Lady of Lourdes Educational Endowment Trust, [N], (OM). See The Omaha Archdiocesan Educational Foundation, Inc.
Our Lady of Lourdes Friary, [K], (GRY), Cedar Lake, IN.
Our Lady of Lourdes Health Care Services, Inc., [G], (CAM). See Our Lady of Lourdes Medical Center, Inc.
Our Lady of Lourdes Health Center, [G], (SPK), Pasco, WA.
Our Lady of Lourdes High School, [E], (NY), Poughkeepsie, NY.
Our Lady of Lourdes High School, [B], (TUC), Nogales, AZ.
Our Lady of Lourdes High School, [G], (TUC), Nogales, AZ.
Our Lady of Lourdes Hospital, [G], (OM), Norfolk, NE.
Our Lady of Lourdes Medical Center, Inc., [G], (CAM), Camden, NJ.
Our Lady of Lourdes Medical Center, Inc. Auxiliary, [G], (CAM). See Our Lady of Lourdes Medical Center, Inc.
Our Lady of Lourdes Memorial Hospital, [O], (SY), Binghamton, NY.
Our Lady of Lourdes Regional High School, [A], (HBG), Coal Township, PA.
Our Lady of Lourdes Regional Medical Center, Inc., [F], (LAF), Lafayette, LA.
Our Lady of Lourdes School Convent, [C], (RC), Porcupine, SD.
Our Lady of Lourdes School of Nursing, Inc., [G], (CAM). See Our Lady of Lourdes Medical Center, Inc.
Our Lady of Mattaponi Youth Retreat and Conference Center, [P], (WDC), Upper Marlboro, MD.
Our Lady of Mercy Academy, [C], (CAM), Newfield, NJ.
Our Lady of Mercy Academy, [D], (RVC), Syosset, NY.
Our Lady of Mercy Community Outreach Services, Inc., [J], (CHR), Johns Island, SC.
Our Lady of Mercy Convent, [C], (FR). See Bishop Feehan High School.
Our Lady of Mercy Convent, [L], (FR), Attleboro, MA.
Our Lady of Mercy Convent, [AA], (PH), Springfield, PA.
Our Lady of Mercy Convent, [J], (PRT), South Portland, ME.
Our Lady of Mercy Convent, [O], (SFR). See Dominican Sisters of San Rafael Generalate & Convent.
Our Lady of Mercy Country Home, [I], (KC), Liberty, MO.
Our Lady of Mercy Health Care Center, Inc., [L], (WOR), Worcester, MA.
Our Lady of Mercy High School, [B], (ROC), Rochester, NY.
Our Lady of Mercy Home, [O], (KC), Liberty, MO.
Our Lady of Mercy Life Center, [H], (ALB). See Mercycare Corporation, St. Peter's Hospital.
Our Lady of Mercy Marist Novitiate, [W], (BO), Cambridge, MA.
Our Lady of Mercy Medical Center, [S], (NY), New York, NY.
Our Lady of Mercy Rectory, [M], (HRT), Plainville, CT.
Our Lady of Mercy Regional School, [G], (PRO), East Greenwich, RI.
Our Lady of Mercy Regional School, [E], (RVC), Cutchogue, NY.
Our Lady of Mercy Retreat Center, [C], (LUB), Slaton, TX.
Our Lady of Mercy School, Incorporated, [F], (HRT), Madison, CT.
Our Lady of Mercy Vocational Training School, [B], (CI), Pohnpei, FM.
Our Lady of Mt. Carmel, [D], (CAM), Berlin, NJ.
Our Lady of Mt. Carmel, [D], (GLP), Gallup, NM.
Our Lady of Mt. Carmel, [L], (RIC). See Ethnic and Special Ministries.
Our Lady of Mount Carmel and Little Flower Monastery, [F], (JKS), Jackson, MS.
Our Lady of Mount Carmel Convent, [X], (BO), Methuen, MA.
Our Lady of Mt. Carmel Convent, [Q], (MIL), Mount Calvary, WI.
Our Lady of Mt. Carmel Convent, [O], (SFR). See Dominican Sisters of San Rafael Generalate & Convent.
Our Lady of Mt. Carmel Convent, Franciscan Sisters of Ringwood, [N], (PAT), Passaic, NJ.
Our Lady of Mount Carmel Parochial School Trust, [I], (LFT), Mt. Carmel, IN.
Our Lady of Mt. Carmel School, [C], (AGN), Agat, GU.
Our Lady of Mt. Carmel School, [D], (ALN), Roseto, PA.
Our Lady of Mt. Providence Convent-Motherhouse, [N], (BAL), Baltimore, MD.
Our Lady of Mt. Thabor Monastery, [L], (DET), Ortonville, MI.
Our Lady of Nazareth Academy, [E], (BO), Wakefield, MA.
Our Lady of Peace, [H], (RIC), Charlottesville, VA.
Our Lady of Peace Catholic School Endowment Fund, [B], (MAR), Ironwood, MI.
Our Lady of Peace Convent, [J], (WIL), Wilmington, DE.
Our Lady of Peace Elementary School, [F], (SCR),

Clarks Green, PA.
The Our Lady of Peace Endowment Trust, [M], (LC), Marshfield, WI.
Our Lady of Peace Gift Shop, [A], (SJ). See Shrine of Our Lady of Peace.
Our Lady of Peace Institute in Catholic Teaching, [Q], (P), Beaverton, OR.
Our Lady of Peace Monastery, [E], (JC), Columbia, MO.
Our Lady of Peace Monastery, [N], (PIT), Beaver Falls, PA.
Our Lady of Peace Retreat, [N], (P), Beaverton, OR.
Our Lady of Peace School, [E], (KC), Kansas City, MO.
Our Lady of Peace Spiritual Life Center, [R], (PRO), Narragansett, RI.
Our Lady of Perpetual Help, [H], (BRK), Brooklyn, NY.
Our Lady of Perpetual Help Charitable Trust, [O], (KC), Kansas City, MO.
Our Lady of Perpetual Help Convent, [G], (ALT), Altoona, PA.
Our Lady of Perpetual Help Convent, [F], (R), Rocky Mount, NC.
Our Lady of Perpetual Help Convent, [O], (RVC), Sound Beach, NY.
Our Lady of Perpetual Help Day Nursery, [J], (NEW), Newark, NJ.
Our Lady of Perpetual Help Home, [H], (ATL), Atlanta, GA.
Our Lady of Perpetual Help House of Prayer, [L], (ALN), Nesquehoning, PA.
Our Lady of Perpetual Help Retreat and Spirituality Center, [I], (VEN), Venice, FL.
Our Lady of Perpetual Help School, [B], (CC), Corpus Christi, TX.
Our Lady of Perpetual Help Trust, [M], (BR). See Baton Rouge Chancery Office.
Our Lady of Princeton, [N], (TR), Princeton, NJ.
Our Lady of Prompt Succor Child Care Center, [J], (NO), Chalmette, LA.
Our Lady of Prompt Succor Home, [G], (LAF), Opelousas, LA.
Our Lady of Providence, [C], (IND), Clarksville, IN.
Our Lady of Providence, [J], (MET), Flemington, NJ.
Our Lady Of Providence, [D], (SJN), San Juan, PR.
Our Lady of Providence Center, [O], (DET), Northville, MI.
Our Lady of Providence Center, [N], (PRO), Warwick, RI.
Our Lady of Providence Convent, [H], (BUR), Winooski, VT.
Our Lady of Providence Regional School, [E], (RVC), Central Islip, NY.
Our Lady of Rose Hill Day Care Center, [N], (HRT). See Motherhouse of Daughters of Mary of the Immaculate Conception.
Our Lady of Rosehill Day Care Center, [H], (HRT), New Britain, CT.
Our Lady of Solitude Hermitage, [D], (OLL), Philippi, WV.
Our Lady of Sorrows, [G], (SY), Vestal, NY.
Our Lady of Sorrows Convent, [X], (BO), Brockton, MA.
Our Lady of Sorrows Convent, [O], (NEW), Kearny, NJ.
Our Lady of Sorrows Convent of the Passionist Nuns, [O], (PIT), Pittsburgh, PA.
Our Lady of Sorrows Convent, Sisters of Sorrowful Mother, [N], (PAT), Denville, NJ.
Our Lady of Sorrows Educational School Foundation, [I], (BIR), Birmingham, AL.
Our Lady of Sorrows Priory, Benedictine Sisters of Pontifical Jurisdiction, [O], (CHI), Oak Forest, IL.
Our Lady of Sorrows Rectory, [M], (HRT). See Missionaries of LaSalette Provincial Secretary.
Our Lady of Spring Bank, Cistercian Abbey, [I], (LC), Sparta, WI.
Our Lady of Tenderness Hermitage, [E], (BWN), San Benito, TX.
*Our Lady of Tenderness, Poustinia, [Q], (DEN), Estes Park, CO.
Our Lady of the Adirondack's Inc. House of Prayer, Franciscan Sisters of the Atonement, [G], (OG), Ellenburg Center, NY.
Our Lady of the Airways Chapel, [BB], (BO), East Boston, MA.
Our Lady of the Angels Convent, [K], (FTW), Mishawaka, IN.
Our Lady of the Angels Metro Region, [Y], (LA). See Catholic Charities of Los Angeles, Inc.
Our Lady of the Angels Monastery, [P], (STL), Eureka, MO.
Our Lady of the Angels Monastery, Inc., [F], (BIR), Birmingham, AL.
Our Lady of the Angels Western Region, [Y], (LA). See Catholic Charities of Los Angeles, Inc.
Our Lady of the Assumption Convent, [L], (ALN), Reading, PA.
Our Lady of the Assumption Convent, [AA], (PH), Strafford, PA.
Our Lady of the Assumption School, [D], (CHL). See Mecklenburg Area Catholic Schools (M.A.C.S.).
Our Lady of the Atonement Convent, [F], (FRS), Atwater, CA.
Our Lady of the Cenacle (R.C.), [R], (GAL), Houston, TX.
Our Lady of the Elms High School, [E], (CLV), Akron, OH.
Our Lady of the Elms/Our Lady of the Elms Foundation, [Z], (CLV), Akron, OH.
Our Lady of the Hamptons Regional School, [E], (RVC), Southampton, NY.
Our Lady of the Lake College, [A], (BR), Baton Rouge, LA.
Our Lady of the Lake Convent, [N], (SAT), San Antonio, TX.
Our Lady of the Lake Elementary, [B], (GAY), Prudenville, MI.
Our Lady of the Lake Foundation, [M], (BR). See Baton Rouge Chancery Office.
Our Lady of the Lake Regional Medical Center, [F], (BR), Baton Rouge, LA.
Our Lady of the Lake University, [C], (SAT), San Antonio, TX.
Our Lady of the Lakes Corporation, [V], (HRT), New Milford, CT.
Our Lady of the Lourdes Convent, [Q], (PRO). See Franciscan Missionaries of Mary.
Our Lady of the Mississippi Abbey, [L], (DUB), Dubuque, IA.
Our Lady of the Most Holy Trinity Convent, [I], (CC), Skidmore, TX.
Our Lady of the Mountains, [I], (SLC), Ogden, UT.
Our Lady of the Mystical Rose Chapel, [J], (HON), Honolulu, HI.
Our Lady of the Oaks Retreat House, [J], (LAF), Grand Coteau, LA.
Our Lady of the Oaks Villa, [J], (SAC), Applegate, CA.
Our Lady of the Osage Hills Center, [J], (TLS), Tulsa, OK.
Our Lady of the Pillar Convent, [N], (SAT), San Antonio, TX.
Our Lady of the Pines Convent, [L], (TOL), Fremont, OH.
Our Lady of the Pines Prayer House, Inc., [J], (OWN), Paducah, KY.
Our Lady of the Pines Retreat Center, [M], (TOL), Fremont, OH.
Our Lady of the Prairie Retreat, [O], (DAV), Wheatland, IA.
Our Lady of the Redwoods Abbey, [N], (SR), Whitethorn, CA.
*Our Lady of the Resurrection Medical Center, [J], (CHI), Chicago, IL.
Our Lady of the Rock Priory, [N], (SEA), Shaw Island, WA.
Our Lady of the Rosary, [E], (JC), Marceline, MO.
Our Lady of the Rosary Chapel, [O], (TR), Lawrenceville, NJ.
Our Lady of the Rosary Learning Center, [C], (CC), Corpus Christi, TX.
Our Lady of the Rosary Learning Center, [I], (CC). See Religious Missionaries of St. Dominic, Inc.
Our Lady of the Sacred Heart Convent, [L], (MAN), West Franklin, NH.
Our Lady of the Sacred Heart Convent, [O], (PIT), Coraopolis, PA.
Our Lady of the Sacred Heart High School, [D], (PIT), Coraopolis, PA.
Our Lady of the Snows Apartment Community Retirement Home, [F], (BEL), Belleville, IL.
Our Lady of the Snows Catholic Shrine, [K], (KCK), Mayetta, KS.
Our Lady of the Snows Layman's Association, [K], (BEL), Belleville, IL.
Our Lady of the Springs Community, [K], (KC), Blue Springs, MO.
Our Lady of the Valley, [F], (SPC), Pilot Knob, MO.
Our Lady of the Valley Educational Foundation, [I], (BIR), Birmingham, AL.
Our Lady of the Valley Retirement Community, [H], (RIC), Roanoke, VA.
Our Lady of the Valley School, [D], (ALN), Lansford-Summit Hill, PA.
Our Lady of the Valley School, [B], (HBG), Lebanon, PA.
Our Lady of the Wasatch Convent, [G], (SLC), Salt Lake City, UT.
Our Lady of the Waters House of Prayer, [H], (AGN), Agana, GU.
Our Lady of the Way Hospital, Inc., [D], (LEX), Martin, KY.
Our Lady of the Way Residence, [AA], (BO), Boston, MA.
Our Lady of the Woods, [O], (WDC). See Sisters of the Holy Cross.
Our Lady of Unity School, [C], (KCK), Kansas City, KS.
Our Lady of Valley Regional Elementary School, [F], (WOR), Uxbridge, MA.
Our Lady of Victories Regional Primary School, [H], (PRO), Woonsocket, RI.
Our Lady of Victory Academy High School, [F], (NY), Dobbs Ferry, NY.
Our Lady of Victory Convent, [O], (CHI), Lemont, IL.
Our Lady of Victory Convent, [N], (HRT), West Haven, CT.
Our Lady of Victory Convent, [I], (SD), El Centro, CA.
Our Lady of Victory Elementary, [D], (FWT), Fort Worth, TX.
Our Lady of Victory Homes of Charity, [T], (BUF), Lackawanna, NY.
Our Lady of Victory Hospital, [K], (BUF), Lackawanna, NY.
Our Lady of Victory Hospital Auxiliary, [K], (BUF), Lackawanna, NY.
Our Lady of Victory Infant Home, [J], (BUF), Lackawanna, NY.
Our Lady of Victory Missionary Sisters, [I], (AUS), Luling, TX.
Our Lady of Victory Missionary Sisters, [F], (SB), Coachella, CA.
Our Lady of Victory Missionary Sisters, [F], (SB), Yucaipa, CA.
Our Lady of Victory Missionary Sisters Convent, [N], (SAT), San Antonio, TX.
Our Lady of Victory Nursing Home, [I], (JOL), Bourbonnais, IL.
Our Lady of Victory School, [I], (CC). See Religious Missionaries of St. Dominic, Inc.
Our Lady of Viet Nam Chapel, [L], (RIC). See Ethnic and Special Ministries.
Our Lady of Wisdom Catholic Student Center, [L], (LAF), Lafayette, LA.
Our Lady of Wisdom Convent, [J], (PRT), St. Agatha, ME.
Our Lady of Wisdom Regional School, [E], (RVC), Port Jefferson, NY.
Our Lady Preschool Learning Center, [H], (BO), Marlboro, MA.
Our Lady Queen Contemplative Monastery, [I], (BR), Tickfaw, LA.
Our Lady Queen of Heaven Manor, [E], (LKC), Lake Charles, LA.
Our Lady Queen of Peace, [H], (GAL), Richwood, TX.
Our Lady Queen of the Clergy Home, [O], (BGP), Stamford, CT.
Our Lady's Academy, [B], (BLX), Bay St. Louis, MS.
Our Lady's Family Center, [N], (AUS), Austin, TX.
Our Lady's Guest and Retreat House, [AA], (NY), Graymoor, NY.
Our Lady's Guild House, [AA], (BO), Boston, MA.
Our Lady's Haven of Fairhaven Inc., [J], (FR), Fairhaven, MA.
Our Lady's House of Peace, [Q], (SP). See Our Lady of Divine Providence, House of Prayer, Inc.
Our Lady's Inn, [W], (STL), St. Louis, MO.
Our Lady's Manor, Inc., [E], (ALX), Alexandria, LA.
Our Lady's Residence, [H], (CAM), Pleasantville, NJ.
Our Lady's Rosary Makers, [Q], (L), Louisville, KY.
Our Lady's Youth Center, [N], (ELP), El Paso, TX.
Our Lady, Queen of Apostles Regional School, [E], (RVC), Center Moriches, NY.
Our Lady, Queen of Peace, Assisted Living Community, [Q], (PRO). See Franciscan Missionaries of Mary.
Our Lady, Queen of the Clergy, [T], (PRO). See Miscellaneous Listings for the Diocese of Providence.
Our Lady, Queen of the Holy Rosary, [W], (CLV), Parma, OH.
Our Lady, Star of the Sea, [D], (CAM), Cape May, NJ.
Our Mother of Mercy School Foundation, [G], (BEA), Beaumont, TX.
Our Mother's House, [J], (VEN), Venice, FL.
Our Place Day Care, [F], (SEA), Seattle, WA.
Our Sunday Visitor, Inc., [O], (FTW), Huntington, IN.
The Outpost, [J], (EVN), Santa Claus, IN.
Outreach East, [L], (LAN), Davison, MI.
Outreach in Love, [J], (RIC), Richmond, VA.
Outreach Office, [S], (HRT). See Catholic Charities-Catholic Family Services (Archdiocese of Hartford).
Overbrook Academy at Our Lady of Providence Center, [G], (PRO), Warwick, RI.
Overbrook School, [D], (NSH), Nashville, TN.
Overbrook, Incorporated, [T], (PRO), Wakefield, RI.
Owensboro Catholic Consolidated School System, [J], (OWN), Owensboro, KY.
Owensboro Catholic High School, [B], (OWN), Owensboro, KY.
Ozanam Center, [S], (CIN). See Archdiocesan Central Council of Cincinnati.
Ozanam Center, [H], (SFR). See Society of St. Vincent de Paul Archdiocesan Council.
Ozanam Hall of Queens Nursing Home, Inc., [R], (BRK), Bayside, NY.
Ozanam Inn, [P], (L). See Society of St. Vincent de Paul, Council of Louisville.
Ozanam Inn, [L], (NO), New Orleans, LA.
The Ozanam Shelter for Families and Single Women, [N], (MET), Edison, NJ.
The Ozanam Shelter for Men, [N], (MET), New Brunswick, NJ.

P

P.I.M.E. College Community, [K], (DET), Detroit, MI.
P.I.M.E. Mission & Prayer Center, [H], (COL), Newark, OH.
P.I.M.E. Missionaries, [G], (PMB), Tequesta, FL.
P.I.M.E. Missionaries of SS. Peter and Paul, [K], (DET), Detroit, MI.
P.I.M.E. Missionaries Residence, [M], (PAT), Wayne, NJ.
P.O.M., Inc., [M], (MIA), Miami Shores, FL.
P.S. 91, [N], (NY). See Pius XII Youth and Family Services.
PACE - Parents Alliance for Catholic Education, [R], (WOR), Worcester, MA.
Pace University, [CC], (NY). See University Apostolate.
Pace University-Westchester, Suny, Purchase, [CC], (NY). See University Apostolate.
Pacelli High School, [C], (LC), Stevens Point, WI.
Pacelli High School, [A], (SAV), Columbus, GA.
Pacelli High School Foundation, [M], (LC), Stevens Point, WI.
Pacelli Junior/Senior High School, [C], (WIN). See Austin Area Catholic Schools.
Pacem in Terris Center for Spirituality, [K], (SCL), St. Francis, MN.
Pacific Institute for Community Organization, [R], (OAK), Oakland, CA.
Padre Pio Health Care Center, Inc. dba Stonehill Care Center, [J], (DUB), Dubuque, IA.
Padre Pio Shelter for Homeless Men, [W], (NY), New York, NY.
Padua Community Services Pediatric Residential Program, [K], (NO), Belle Chasse, LA.
Padua Franciscan Friary, [P], (CLV), Cleveland, OH.
Padua Franciscan High School, [E], (CLV), Cleveland, OH.
Padua Friary, [Z], (NY), New York, NY.
Padua Hills Apartments, [D], (PHX), Wickenburg, AZ.
Padua Place, [K], (SAT), San Antonio, TX.
Paewalani Community, [I], (HON). See Congregation of the Sacred Hearts and of Perpetual Adoration.
Pakistan Apostolate, [T], (BRK). See Catholic Migration & Refugee Office, Catholic Migration Services, Inc.
Pala Rey Youth Camp & Retreat Center, [K], (SD), Pala, CA.
Pala Rey Youth Camp and Retreat Center, [L], (SD). See Pala Rey Youth Camp and Retreat Center.
Palisades Retreat House, [O], (SEA), Federal Way, WA.
Pallotti Convent, [O], (WDC), Laurel, MD.
Pallotti House, [P], (MIL), Milwaukee, WI.
Pallottine Apostolic Associates, [Y], (MIL), Milwaukee, WI.
Pallottine Center for Apostolic Causes, [M], (BAL), Baltimore, MD.
Pallottine Fathers, [K], (DET), Wyandotte, MI.
Pallottine Fathers, [Z], (NY), New York, NY.
Pallottine Fathers and Brothers, Inc., Disability Trust, [Y], (MIL), Milwaukee, WI.
Pallottine Fathers and Brothers, Inc., Educational and Apostolic Ministry Trust, [Y], (MIL), Milwaukee, WI.
Pallottine Health Services, Inc., [K], (WH), Huntington, WV.
Pallottine Missionary Sisters-Frascati Community, [R], (STL), Lonedell, MO.
Pallottine Missionary Sisters-Queen of Apostles Province, [R], (STL), Florissant, MO.
Pallottine Renewal Center, [T], (STL), Florissant, MO.
Pallottine Seminary at Green Hill, [B], (WDC), West Hyattsville, MD.
The Pallottines of South Orange, Inc., [S], (NEW), South Orange, NJ.
Palma Community, [G], (MRY), Salinas, CA.
Palmetto Catholic Charities, [J], (VEN), Palmetto, FL.
Palo Alto/Los Altos Auxiliary, [F], (SJ). See Catholic Charities of Santa Clara County.
Pamphile and Mabyn Donaldson Trust for St. Louis King of France Church, [M], (BR). See Baton Rouge Chancery Office.
Paraclete High School, [D], (LA), Lancaster, CA.
Paradise School, [E], (HBG). See Department for Catholic Charities Counseling/Field Services.
Paramus Catholic High School, [D], (NEW), Paramus, NJ.
Paris Foreign Mission Society Residence, [N], (SFR), San Francisco, CA.
Parish Conferences, [P], (L). See Society of St. Vincent de Paul, Council of Louisville.
Parish Endowment Trust Fund of St. Michael Catholic Church, [N], (OM). See The Omaha Archdiocesan Educational Foundation, Inc.
Parish Kitchen, [O], (COV), Covington, KY.
Parish Mission Team Res., [Z], (NY), Suffern, NY.
Parish Outreach Program, [H], (BUF). See The Catholic Charities of the Diocese of Buffalo.
Parish Social Ministry, [I], (GAL). See Associated Catholic Charities of the Diocese of Galveston-Houston.
Parish Social Ministry, [D], (LAN). See Catholic Social Services-St. Vincent Home for Children, Inc.
Parish Social Ministry, [E], (PRT). See Catholic Charities Maine.
Parish Social Ministry, [H], (RVC). See Catholic Charities Central Administration.
Parish Social Ministry, [O], (SR), Santa Rosa, CA.
Parish Social Ministry Consultation Services, [G], (CHI). See Catholic Charities of the Archdiocese of Chicago-Archdiocesan Offices.
Parish Social Ministry Outreach, [Q], (BAL), Baltimore, MD.
Parish Social Work Program, [H], (BUF). See The Catholic Charities of the Diocese of Buffalo.
Parish Visitors of Mary Immaculate, [AA], (NY), New York, NY.
Parish Visitors of Mary Immaculate, [O], (SCR), Scranton, PA.
Parish Visitors of Mary Immaculate (P.V.M.I.), [AA], (NY), Monroe, NY.
Parish/Family Services, [E], (SR). See Diocese of Santa Rosa, Catholic Charities.
Parishes with Ministry to Spanish Speaking: St. Bernard, [X], (CLV). See Diocesan Hispanic Office.
Park Performing Arts, Inc., [S], (NEW), Union City, NJ.
Park Village Day Care Center, Inc., [H], (HRT), West Hartford, CT.
Parkersburg Catholic Elementary School, [D], (WH), Parkersburg, WV.
Parkersburg Catholic Junior-Senior High School, [B], (WH), Parkersburg, WV.
Parkersburg Catholic Schools Foundation, Inc., [P], (WH), Parkersburg, WV.
Parkland Hospital, [I], (DAL), Dallas, TX.
Parks College of Saint Louis University, [A], (BEL), Cahokia, IL.
Parkville, HDFC, [L], (BRK). See Catholic Charities.
Parkway Medical Buildings, Inc., [J], (P). See Mercy Medical Center, Inc.
Parkwood Retirement Apartments, [D], (SFS). See St. Mary's Healthcare Center of Pierre, South Dakota.
Parmadale, [M], (CLV), Parma, OH.
Parmadale, [V], (CLV). See Catholic Charities Services Corporation.
Parsons Catholic Elementary School, [C], (WCH), Parsons, KS.
Parsons Manor, [U], (BRK), Jamaica, NY.
Particular Council of Flint, [L], (LAN), Flint, MI.
Particular Council of Gary, [N], (GRY). See Catholic Charities.
Particular Council of Staten Island, [M], (NY), Staten Island, NY.
Particular Council of the St. Vincent de Paul Society, [U], (HRT), Hartford, CT.
Particular Council of Wichita Falls, St. Vincent de Paul Society, [L], (FWT), Wichita Falls, TX.
Partnership for Quality Education, Inc., [DD], (NY), New York, NY.
Passaic Catholic Regional School, [F], (PAT), Passaic, NJ.
Passionist Communications Center, [DD], (NY). See Passionist Communications, Inc.
Passionist Communications, Inc., [DD], (NY), Pelham, NY.
Passionist Community, [R], (LA), Pasadena, CA.
Passionist Community-CTU, [N], (CHI), Chicago, IL.
Passionist Fathers of Shrewsbury, Inc., Calvary Retreat Center, [N], (WOR), Shrewsbury, MA.
Passionist Lay Missioners, [N], (CHI). See Passionist Provincial Office.
Passionist Missionaries, Inc., [N], (NEW). See Congregation of the Passion (Passionists)-St. Michael's Residence.
Passionist Missions of India, [N], (CHI). See Passionist Provincial Office.
Passionist Missions, Inc., [N], (CHI). See Passionist Provincial Office.
Passionist Provincial Office, [N], (CHI), Chicago, IL.
Passionist Provincial Office, [H], (MET), South River, NJ.
Passionist Residence, [DD], (NY), New York, NY.
Passionist Retreat House, [R], (LA). See Passionist Community.
Passionist Spiritual Center, [Z], (NY), New York, NY.
Pastoral Care of the Sick, [H], (PCE), Ponce, PR.
Pastoral Center, [D], (SAM), Staten Island, NY.
Pastoral de Ecuadores, [E], (CGS), Caguas, P.R.
Pastoral Hispana Office (Hispanic Pastoral Ministry), [T], (HRT), Bloomfield, CT.
Pastoral Institute of the Diocese of St. Petersburg, [H], (SP), St. Petersburg, FL.
The Pastoral Theological Institute Inc., [V], (HRT), Hamden, CT.
Paterson Catholic Regional High School, [C], (PAT), Paterson, NJ.
Pathways (Employee Assistance Program), [G], (CHI). See Catholic Charities of the Archdiocese of Chicago-Archdiocesan Offices.
The Patrician Movement, [T], (SAT), San Antonio, TX.
Patrons of the Arts in the Vatican Museum, [P], (DAL), Dallas, TX.
Patrons of the Arts in the Vatican Museums, [DD], (NY), New York, NY.
The Patrons of the Vatican Museums in the South, Inc., [S], (NO), New Orleans, LA.
PATS (Pohnpei Agriculture and Trade School), [B], (CI), Pohnpei, FM.
Paul A. Dever State School (For Retarded) Newman Center, [P], (FR), Taunton, MA.
Paul VI High School, [D], (ARL), Fairfax, VA.
Paul VI High School, [A], (CAM), Haddonfield, NJ.
Paul VI Institute for the Arts, [V], (WDC), Washington, DC.
Paul VI Institute of Catechetical and Pastoral Studies, [D], (STL), St. Louis, MO.
Paul VI Pastoral Center, [F], (WH), Wheeling, WV.
Pauline Auberle Foundation, [R], (PIT), McKeesport, PA.
Pauline Book and Media, [CC], (LA), Culver City, CA.
Pauline Book & Media Center, [X], (BO). See Daughters of St. Paul Inc.
Pauline Book and Media Center, [T], (SAT), San Antonio, TX.
Pauline Book and Media Center, [N], (SD), San Diego, CA.
Pauline Books & Media, [K], (ANC), Anchorage, AK.
Pauline Books & Media, [J], (CHR), Charleston, SC.
Pauline Books & Media, [DD], (NY), New York, NY.
Pauline Books & Media, [U], (SFR), San Francisco, CA.
Pauline Fathers Monastery, [H], (GBG), Kittanning, PA.
Pauline Fathers Monastery, Shrine of Our Lady of Czestochowa, [Z], (PH), Doylestown, PA.
Paulist Center, [P], (BO), Boston, MA.
Paulist Fathers, [N], (STP), Minneapolis, MN.
Paulist Fathers - Generalate, [U], (BRK), Jamaica Estates, NY.
Paulist Fathers (New York), [J], (MEM), Memphis, TN.
Paulist Fathers Catholic Center for Evangelization, [Q], (P), Portland, OR.
Paulist Fathers Generalate, [Z], (NY), Scarsdale, NY.
Paulist Fathers Residence, [W], (BO), Boston, MA.
Paulist Fathers Retirement Home, [G], (PMB), Vero Beach, FL.
Paulist National Catholic Evangelization Assoc., [V], (WDC), Washington, DC.
Paulist Novitiate, [A], (PAT), Oak Ridge, NJ.
Paulist Pictures, [CC], (LA), Pacific Palisades, CA.
Paulist Press, [S], (NEW), Mahwah, NJ.
Paulist Productions, [CC], (LA), Pacific Palisades, CA.
Pawtuxet Valley C.Y.O. Center, [N], (PRO), Coventry, RI.
Pax Christi Florida, Inc., [K], (STA), St. Petersburg, FL.
Pax Christi Hospice, [U], (NY), Staten Island, NY.
Pax Christi Metro New York, [DD], (NY), New York, NY.
Pax Christi Residence, [I], (CC), Corpus Christi, TX.
Pax Christi-Franciscan, [H], (JKS), Greenwood, MS.
Pax Christi-Franciscan, [H], (JKS), Jackson, MS.
Pax Priory, [N], (E), Erie, PA.
Payson Senior Living, Inc., [J], (PHX). See Foundation for Senior Living.
Peace and Justice Office, [D], (R). See Catholic Social Ministries of the Diocese of Raleigh, Inc.
Peace Harbor Hospital, [J], (P), Florence, OR.
Peace Hermitage, [AA], (PH), Philadelphia, PA.
Peace House-Casa de Paz, [G], (SLC), Richfield, UT.
Pearl River Junior College, St. Joseph Catholic Center, [G], (BLX), Lumberton, MS.
Peconic Heights, [G], (RVC). See St. Christopher-Ottilie Corp.
Pelletier School & Services, [P], (NY), New York, NY.
Pelletier Trust, a Charitable Trust of the Sisters of the Good Shepherd, [R], (STL). See Good Shepherd Provincialate.
Pendola Center, [J], (SAC), Sacramento, CA.
Pendola Center, [N], (SAC), Sacramento, CA.
Peninsula Catholic High School, [A], (RIC), Newport News, VA.
Peninsula Family Resource Center (PFRC), [Q], (SFR). See Catholic Charities of the Archdiocese of San Francisco.
Penn State Catholic Community, [I], (ALT), University Park, PA.
Penn State University - Altoona Campus, [H], (ALT). See Juniata College.
Pennsylvania Catholic Conference, [L], (HBG), Harrisburg, PA.
Pennsylvania Catholic Health Association, [L], (HBG), Harrisburg, PA.
Penrose Community Hospital, [B], (COS). See Penrose-St. Francis Health Services.
The Penrose Foundation, [B], (COS), Colorado Springs, CO.
Penrose Hospital, [B], (COS). See Penrose-St. Francis Health Services.

Adorers of the Blood of Christ.
Pregnancy Counseling / Adoption Services, [Q], (SFR). See Catholic Charities of the Archdiocese of San Francisco.
Pregnancy Crisis Careline, Inc., [L], (VEN), Port Charlotte, FL.
Pregnancy Parenting & Adoption Services, [J], (PHX). See Catholic Social Services of Central and Northern Arizona, Inc.
Prelature of the Holy Cross and Opus Dei, [I], (FTW), South Bend, IN.
Prelature of the Holy Cross and Opus Dei, [G], (PCE), Alhambra, Ponce, PR.
Premonstratensian Fathers and Brothers (Norbertines), [N], (CHI), Chicago, IL.
Presbyterian College Newman Center, [H], (CHR), Clinton, SC.
Preschool, [D], (ALN). See Christ the King School.
Pre-School, [C], (PBL). See John Neumann Catholic Schools.
Preschool Activity and Learning Sessions, Inc., [I], (CLV), Twinsburg, OH.
Presentation Academy, [C], (L), Louisville, KY.
Presentation Care Center, [E], (FAR), Rolette, ND.
Presentation Center-Sacred Heart Convent, [F], (FAR), Fargo, ND.
Presentation College, [A], (SFS), Aberdeen, SD.
Presentation Convent, [F], (BLX), Long Beach, MS.
Presentation Convent, [N], (SAT), San Antonio, TX.
Presentation Convent, [G], (SFS), Aberdeen, SD.
Presentation Convent, [N], (SJ), Los Gatos, CA.
Presentation Convent, [O], (WOR), Leominster, MA.
Presentation Convent, Motherhouse of the Sisters of the Presentation of B.V.M., [O], (SFR), San Francisco, CA.
Presentation Education and Retreat Center, [L], (SJ), Los Gatos, CA.
The Presentation Foundation, [I], (FAR), Fargo, ND.
Presentation Health Care Center, [M], (WOR), Leominster, MA.
Presentation High School, [D], (SJ), San Jose, CA.
Presentation Medical Center, [D], (FAR), Rolla, ND.
Presentation of Mary Academy, [E], (BO), Methuen, MA.
Presentation of Mary Academy, [F], (MAN), Hudson, NH.
Presentation Prayer Center, [G], (FAR), Fargo, ND.
Presentation Sisters, [O], (OAK), Oakland, CA.
Presentation Sisters, [I], (SAC), Sacramento, CA.
Presentation Sisters of B.V.M., [G], (KNX), Jacksboro, TN.
Presentation Sisters of the Blessed Virgin Mary, Union of, P.B.V.M. (United States Province), [Q], (NO), New Orleans, LA.
Presentation Sisters, Kildare, Ireland, [O], (OAK), San Lorenzo, CA.
Preston High School, [F], (NY), New York, NY.
Pretty Eagle Catholic School, [E], (GF), St. Xavier, MT.
Preventative Services & Batterer's Intervention Program, [H], (BUF). See The Catholic Charities of the Diocese of Buffalo.
Prevention Services, [I], (GAL). See Associated Catholic Charities of the Diocese of Galveston-Houston.
Price Memorial, [O], (STL), Eureka, MO.
Priest Field Pastoral Center, [F], (WH), Kearneysville, WV.
Priest Retirement and Aid Association, [D], (RC), Rapid City, SD.
Priest Retirement Committee, [J], (STU), Steubenville, OH.
Priest Retirement Trust Fund, [E], (SAM), Staten Island, NY.
Priest's Retirement Fund, [F], (OLL), Los Angeles, CA.
Priest's Retirement Home, [F], (OLL), El Monte, California.
The Priestly Education Fund, Inc., [N], (MET), Metuchen, NJ.
Priestly Fraternity of St. Peter, [L], (LR), Little Rock, AR.
Priestly Fraternity of St. Peter (F.S.S.P.), [M], (SCR), Elmhurst, PA.
Priestly Fraternity of the Missionaries of St. Charles Borromeo, Inc., [Q], (FR), Fall River, MA.
Priestly Life and Ministry, [L], (LAN), Lansing, MI.
Priests Eucharistic League, [V], (CIN), Cincinnati, OH.
Priests Eucharistic League, [L], (NSH), Hendersonville, TN.
Priests Health and Retirement Plan Trust, [N], (OM). See Columban Fathers Regional Administration.
Priests of the Congregation of Holy Cross, [M], (HRT), New Haven, CT.
Priests of the Sacred Heart, [E], (BWN), Harlingen, TX.
Priests of the Sacred Heart, [N], (CHI), Chicago, IL.
Priests of the Sacred Heart, [P], (MIL), Hales Corners, WI.
Priests of the Sacred Heart, [F], (SFS), Chamberlain, SD.
Priests of the Sacred Heart, [O], (SP), Pinellas Park, FL.
Priests of the Sacred Heart-House of Formation, [M], (SAT), San Antonio, TX.
Priests Residence, [P], (PAT), Morristown, NJ.
Priests Retirement Center, [G], (WCH), Wichita, KS.
Priests' Benefit Plan of the Diocese of Pittsburgh, [R], (PIT), Pittsburgh, PA.
Priests' Hostel, [K], (FR), Fall River, MA.
Priests' Purgatorial Society, [W], (MIL), Milwaukee, WI.
Priests' Purgatorial Society, [K], (SFD), Springfield, IL.
Priests' Retirement Facility, [K], (SFD), Springfield, IL.
The Priests' Retirement Plan of the Catholic Diocese of Las Cruces, Inc., [E], (LSC), Las Cruces, NM.
Primary Building, [D], (Y). See Ashtabula Catholic Elementary School.
Primary Care Clinic, [G], (BEA), Beaumont, TX.
Primary School, [D], (ALN). See Holy Spirit School.
Primary School, [E], (RVC). See All Saints Regional Catholic School.
Prime E.A.P., Inc., [P], (BAL). See Chancery Office.
Primrose House of Catholic Charities of San Mateo, [Q], (SFR). See Catholic Charities of the Archdiocese of San Francisco.
Prince Gallitzin Chapel House (Diocesan), [J], (ALT), Loretto, PA.
Prince George's County Regional Office, [H], (WDC). See Catholic Charities of the Archdiocese of Washington, Inc.
Prince of Peace - Dallas, [E], (DAL), Dallas, TX.
Prince of Peace Abbey, Benet Hill, [H], (SD), Oceanside, CA.
Prince of Peace Catholic School, [F], (PIT), Pittsburgh, PA.
Prince of Peace Regional School, [E], (RVC), Sayville, NY.
Prince of Peace Religious Education, [O], (IND), Madison, IN.
Prince of Peace Retirement Community, Inc., [E], (SFS), Sioux Falls, SD.
Prince of Peace Retreat Center, [K], (SD), Oceanside, CA.
Prince of Peace School, [D], (COV), Covington, KY.
Prince of Peace Villas, Inc., [C], (ORL), Ormond Beach, FL.
The Priory, [O], (ALB), Chestertown, NY.
Priory of Benedictine Monks, [G], (BUR), Weston, VT.
Priory of St. Moses the Black, [E], (JKS), Jackson, MS.
Prison Outreach Ministry, [V], (WDC), Hyattsville, MD.
Private Kindergarten, [P], (BUF). See Franciscan Missionary Sisters of the Divine Child, Inc.
Pro Maria Committee, [FF], (BO), Lowell, MA.
Pro Sanctity Movement, [Y], (BRK), Brooklyn, NY.
Pro Sanctity Movement, [M], (OM), Elkhorn, NE.
Pro Sanctity Movement, [K], (ORG). See Pro Sanctity Spirituality Center, Retreat House.
Pro Sanctity Spirituality Center, Retreat House, [K], (ORG), Fullerton, CA.
Professional Counseling Services of Humboldt/Del Norte, [E], (SR). See Diocese of Santa Rosa, Catholic Charities.
Professional Foster Care, [E], (SR). See Diocese of Santa Rosa, Catholic Charities.
Professional Office Corporation, [C], (FRS). See Saint Agnes' Medical Center.
Program for the Medically Underserved of Cincinnati, [R], (CIN), Cincinnati, OH.
Progress for the Diocese of El Paso, [N], (ELP), El Paso, TX.
Progress of Peoples Development Corporation, [L], (BRK). See Catholic Charities.
Progress of Peoples Managment Corporation, [L], (BRK). See Catholic Charities.
PROJECT AIMM, [Q], (L), Louisville, KY.
Project Ayuda, [D], (TUC). See Social Service Agencies: Pima County.
Project Hope, Inc., [V], (HRT), West Hartford, CT.
Project Lazarus, [L], (NO), New Orleans, LA.
Project REMAIN, [R], (SCR), Wilkes-Barre, PA.
Project Renewal of Davenport, Inc., [K], (DAV), Davenport, IA.
Project Timothy: Christian Service Center, [O], (SPK), Dayton, WA.
*The Promise Outreach, Inc., [S], (NEW), Lodi, NJ.
Pronto of Long Island, Inc., [R], (RVC), Bay Shore, NY.
Propagation of the Faith and Holy Childhood Association & Society of St. Peter the Apostle, [FF], (BO), Boston, MA.
Propagation of the Faith Holy Childhood Association, [J], (STU), Steubenville, OH.
Propagation of the Faith/Holy Childhood, [B], (STV). See Miscellaneous Organizations.
The Prout School, [C], (PRO), Wakefield, RI.
Providence Alaska Foundation, [C], (ANC), Anchorage, AK.
Providence Alaska Medical Center, [C], (ANC), Anchorage, AK.
Providence Alaska Medical Center, [H], (ANC), Anchorage, AK.
*Providence Building Corporation, [L], (MOB), Mobile, AL.
Providence Care Center, [K], (LA). See Providence Health System.
Providence Catholic High School, [C], (JOL), New Lenox, IL.
Providence Center, [BB], (PH), Yardley, PA.
Providence Center, [G], (STA). See Jacksonville, Family Housing Management Co.
Providence Centralia Hospital, [G], (SEA), Centralia, WA.
Providence Child Care Center, [I], (PIT), Pittsburgh, PA.
Providence Child Care Center, South, [I], (PIT). See Providence Connections, Inc.
*Providence Child Center, [H], (P), Portland, OR.
Providence College, [B], (PRO), Providence, RI.
*Providence Community Health Foundation, Medford, [J], (P). See Providence Medford Medical Center.
Providence Connections, Inc., [I], (PIT), Allison Park, PA.
Providence County C.Y.O. Center, [N], (PRO), Cranston, RI.
Providence Day Care Center, North, [I], (PIT). See Providence Connections, Inc.
Providence Extended Care Center, [D], (ANC), Anchorage, AK.
Providence Extended Care Center, [K], (WOR), Worcester, MA.
Providence Family Support Center, [I], (PIT). See Providence Connections, Inc.
Providence Foundation, [E], (MOB), Mobile, AL.
Providence Foundation, [I], (SCR), Williamsport, PA.
The Providence Fund, [O], (TOL), Sandusky, OH.
Providence General Medical Center, [G], (SEA), Everett, WA.
Providence Health Center, [F], (AUS), Waco, TX.
Providence Health Foundation, [K], (WDC). See De Paul Foundation, Inc.
*Providence Health Services, [I], (NY), New York, NY.
Providence Health Services Inc., [K], (WDC). See Providence Hospital.
Providence Health System, [K], (LA), Burbank, CA.
Providence Health System, Inc., [I], (SCR), Williamsport, PA.
Providence Healthcare Services, [E], (MOB), Mobile, AL.
Providence Heights Alpha School, [G], (PIT), Allison Park, PA.
Providence High School, [F], (LA), Burbank, CA.
Providence High School, [F], (SAT), San Antonio, TX.
Providence Home & Family Services, Inc., [I], (SAT), San Antonio, TX.
Providence Home Care and Hospice of Snohomis County, [J], (SEA), Everett, WA.
Providence Home Services, [J], (SEA), Seattle, WA.
Providence Home, Nursing Home for the Needy, [F], (EVN), Jasper, IN.
Providence Hospital, [H], (DET), Southfield, MI.
Providence Hospital, [E], (MOB), Mobile, AL.
Providence Hospital, [Z], (PH). See Congregation of the Mission.
Providence Hospital, [K], (WDC). See Providence Hospital.
Providence Hospital, [K], (WDC), Washington, DC.
Providence Hospital, [B], (YAK), Toppenish, WA.
Providence Hospital Inc., [H], (TOL), Sandusky, OH.
Providence Hospital School of Nursing, [H], (TOL). See Providence Hospital Inc.
Providence Hospital School of Radiology, [H], (TOL). See Providence Hospital Inc.
Providence Hospital, Inc., [F], (SPR), Holyoke, MA.
Providence Hospitality House, [L], (SEA), Seattle, WA.
Providence House, [DD], (NY), Newburgh, NY.
Providence House, [Q], (SP). See Our Lady of Divine Providence, House of Prayer, Inc.
Providence House Apartments, [Q], (SY), Syracuse, NY.
Providence House Division, [F], (TR). See Catholic Charities.
Providence House Nursing Home of Millbury, [K], (WOR), Millbury, MA.
Providence House Nursing Home of Southbridge, [K], (WOR), Southbridge, MA.
Providence House, Inc., [L], (BRK). See Catholic Charities.
Providence Housing Development Corporation, [L], (ROC), Rochester, NY.
Providence Medford Medical Center, [J], (P), Medford, OR.
Providence Medical Center, [F], (KCK), Kansas City, KS.
Providence Medical Center, [G], (OM), Wayne, NE.
Providence Medical Center Foundation, [K], (KCK), Kansas City, KS.

Providence Medical Foundation, [J], (P). See Providence Portland Medical Center.
*Providence Milwaukie Foundation, Milwaukie, [J], (P). See Providence Milwaukie Hospital.
*Providence Milwaukie Hospital, [J], (P), Milwaukie, OR.
Providence Ministries for the Needy, Inc., [G], (SPR), Holyoke, MA.
Providence Ministries for the Needy, Inc., [J], (SPR). See Providence Motherhouse - Sisters of Providence.
Providence Montessori School, [H], (P). See Providence Child Center.
Providence Mother Joseph Care Center, [J], (SEA), Olympia, WA.
Providence Motherhouse - Sisters of Providence, [J], (SPR), Holyoke, MA.
Providence Mount St. Vincent, [I], (SEA), Seattle, WA.
Providence Mount St. Vincent, [K], (SEA), Seattle, WA.
Providence Newberg Hospital, [J], (P), Newberg, OR.
Providence Newman Center, [O], (RVC), Selden, NY.
Providence Place, [G], (KCK), Kansas City, KS.
Providence Place, [K], (SEA), Chehalis, WA.
Providence Portland Medical Center, [J], (P), Portland, OR.
Providence Rest, [V], (NY), Bronx, NY.
Providence Rest Child Day Care Center, Inc., [R], (NY), New York, NY.
Providence Saint Joseph Medical Center, [K], (LA), Burbank, CA.
Providence St. Joseph Medical Center, [K], (LA). See Providence Health System.
Providence St. Peter Hospital, [G], (SEA), Olympia, WA.
Providence St. Vincent Medical Center, [J], (P), Portland, OR.
Providence Seaside Hospital, [J], (P), Seaside, OR.
*Providence Seaside Hospital Foundation, [J], (P). See Providence Seaside Hospital.
Providence Seattle Medical Center, [G], (SEA), Seattle, WA.
Providence Self-Sufficiency Ministries, Inc., [K], (IND). See Sisters of Providence General Administration.
Providence Services, [O], (SPK), Spokane, WA.
Providence Sisters, [O], (OAK), Oakland, CA.
Providence SoundHomeCare and Hospice, [J], (SEA), Olympia, WA.
Providence Trust, [S], (SAT), Helotes, TX.
Providence Yakima Medical Center, [B], (YAK), Yakima, WA.
Province Development Office, [E], (BLX). See Southern Province of St. Augustine - Provincial Residence.
Province House for Homeless Men, [DD], (NY), Newburgh, NY.
Province of Our Lady of Consolation, Inc., [I], (IND). See Mount Saint Francis Friary and Retreat Center.
Provincial Administration Office, Oblates of Mary Immaculate (Southern Prov.), [M], (SAT), San Antonio, TX.
Provincial Center, Religious Sacred Heart of Mary, [AA], (NY), Tarrytown, NY.
Provincial Definitors of the Province of Saint Barbara, [CC], (LA). See St. Francis Center.
Provincial Headquarters for the Conventual Franciscan Province, [J], (IND), Mount Saint Francis, IN.
Provincial House, [X], (BO), Methuen, MA.
Provincial House, [N], (HRT), East Haven, CT.
Provincial House, [P], (PRO), Harrisville, RI.
Provincial House, [O], (RVC). See Religious of Our Lady of the Retreat in the Cenacle.
Provincial House and Formation House, [J], (SPR), Holyoke, MA.
Provincial House and Novitiate, [N], (HRT). See Felician Sisters - Our Lady of the Angels.
Provincial House and Novitiate of the Sisters of St. Felix, [L], (DET), Livonia, MI.
Provincial House at St. Andrew, Seminary (C.R.), [A], (DEN), Denver, CO.
Provincial House of Daughters of the Charity of the Sacred Heart of Jesus, [L], (MAN), Littleton, NH.
Provincial House of the Cincinnati Province of the Society of the Precious Blood, [M], (CIN), Dayton, OH.
Provincial House of the Dallas Province, [N], (DAL). See School Sisters of Notre Dame.
Provincial House of the School Sisters of Notre Dame, [G], (WIN), Mankato, MN.
Provincial House of the Sisters of Notre Dame, Juniorate, Novitiate, [Q], (CLV), Chardon, OH.
Provincial House of the Sisters of St. Francis of Penance and Christian Charity, [O], (SFR), Redwood City, CA.
Provincial House of the Sisters of St. Joseph of Carondelet, [S], (LA), Los Angeles, CA.
Provincial House of the Sisters of St. Joseph of Carondelet (Albany Province), [M], (ALB), Latham, NY.
Provincial House of the Sisters of the Holy Family of Nazareth, [O], (CHI), Des Plaines, IL.
Provincial House of the Sisters of the Holy Family of Nazareth, [AA], (PH), Philadelphia, PA.
Provincial House, Adorers of the Blood of Christ, Province of Ruma, [H], (BEL), Ruma, IL.
Provincial House, Congregation de Notre Dame, [P], (BGP), Ridgefield, CT.
Provincial House, Health Center of Sisters of Notre Dame de Namur, [N], (CIN), Cincinnati, OH.
Provincial House, Immaculate Heart of Mary Province, Sisters of the Holy Family of Nazareth, C.S.F.N., [P], (BGP), Monroe, CT.
Provincial House, Juniorate and Novitiate of the Sisters of Resurrection, [M], (ALB), Castleton-on-Hudson, NY.
Provincial House, Society of the Sacred Heart-United States Province, [R], (STL), St. Louis, MO.
Provincial Motherhouse and Novitiate of the Daughters of Divine Charity, [Q], (CLV), Akron, OH.
Provincial Motherhouse and Novitiate of the Notre Dame Sisters, [L], (OM), Omaha, NE.
Provincial Motherhouse of Brothers of Mercy, [O], (BUF), Clarence, NY.
Provincial Motherhouse of the Carmelite Sisters of the Divine Heart of Jesus, [Q], (MIL), Wauwatosa, WI.
Provincial Motherhouse of the Missionary Sisters Servants of the Holy Spirit, [O], (CHI), Techny, IL.
Provincial Motherhouse of the Sisters of St. Basil the Great, [F], (PHU), Fox Chase Manor, PA.
Provincial Office of Lay Carmelites and Scapular Confraternity, [M], (JOL), Darien, IL.
Provincial Office of the Congregation of the Resurrection, [N], (CHI), Chicago, IL.
Provincial Offices - Discalced Carmelites, [P], (MIL), Milwaukee, WI.
Provincial Offices of the Order of St. Augustine, Province of St. Thomas of Villanova, [Z], (PH), Villanova, PA.
Provincial Offices of the Priests and Brothers of Holy Cross, Eastern Province, [O], (BGP), Bridgeport, CT.
Provincial Realty Associates, Inc., [M], (MIA), Miami Shores, FL.
Provincial Residence, [J], (PRT), Saco, ME.
Provincial Residence, [N], (SFR), San Francisco, CA.
Provincial Residence and Novitiate, [N], (RVC), Mineola, NY.
Provincial Residence of the Handmaids of the Sacred Heart of Jesus, [AA], (PH), Haverford, PA.
Provincial Residence, Sisters of Divine Providence, [X], (BO), Kingston, MA.
Provincial Vocation Office, [P], (STL). See La Salette Missionaries.
Provincialate Community, [M], (SR), Napa, CA.
Provincialate Community of the Daughters of the Holy Spirit, [G], (NOR), Woodstock, CT.
Provincialate of Basilian Fathers, [E], (STF), New York, NY.
Provincialate of the Sisters Adorers of the Blood of Christ, [H], (WCH), Wichita, KS.
Provincialate of the Sisters of St. Joseph, [J], (PRT), Winslow, ME.
Provincialate of the Sisters of St. Paul de Chartres, [E], (MAR), Marquette, MI.
Provincialate of the Sisters of the Good Shepherd, [V], (BRK), Jamaica, NY.
Provincialate of the Sisters of the Holy Names, [N], (SJ), Los Gatos, CA.
Provincialate of the Society of Mary, Province of St. Louis, [P], (STL), St. Louis, MO.
Provincialate of Ursuline Nuns, [N], (SR), Santa Rosa, CA.
Provincialate, Immaculate Conception Friary - Order of Friars Minor Conventual, [L], (ALB), Rensselaer, NY.
Provincialate, Our Lady of Victory Center, [I], (FWT), Fort Worth, TX.
Provincialate, Southern Province, Sisters of Charity of St. Elizabeth, [O], (NEW), West Orange, NJ.
Provincialhouse of Sisters of the Most Holy Trinity, [Q], (CLV), Cleveland, OH.
Psychological Services Department, [Y], (LA). See Catholic Charities of Los Angeles, Inc.
Public Action to Deliver Shelter, Inc. (PADS), [J], (RCK), Aurora, IL.
Publication: "The Record", [Q], (L), Louisville, KY.
Pueblo Community Soup Kitchen, Inc., [H], (PBL), Pueblo, CO.
Purcell Marian High School, [E], (CIN), Cincinnati, OH.
Putnam & Northern Westchester, [D], (NY). See Department of Education.
Pyramid Life Center, [O], (ALB), Paradox, NY.

Q

Quad Cities Catholic Deaf Ministry, [P], (DAV), Davenport, IA.
Queen of Americas Guild, [N], (RCK), St. Charles, IL.
Queen of Angels, [C], (WIN). See Austin Area Catholic Schools.
Queen of Angels Academy, [D], (LA), Compton, CA.
Queen of Angels Apartment, [I], (ALN), Reading, PA.
Queen of Angels Center, [H], (WIN), Austin, MN.
Queen of Angels DayCare Center, [J], (SPC), Springfield, MO.
Queen of Angels Friary and Retreat House, [G], (SAG), Saginaw, MI.
Queen of Angels Hospital, [CC], (LA), Los Angeles, CA.
Queen of Angels Monastery, [M], (P), Mt. Angel, OR.
Queen of Angels Monastery - Benedictine Sisters, [K], (KC), Liberty, MO.
Queen of Angels Regional Catholic School, [D], (GBG), North Huntingdon, PA.
Queen of Angels Residence for College Girls and Business Women, [L], (ELP), El Paso, TX.
Queen of Angels-Hollywood Presbyterian Medical Center, [K], (LA), Los Angeles, CA.
Queen of Apostles, [D], (TOL), Toledo, OH.
Queen of Apostles Center, [M], (STL), Imperial, MO.
Queen of Apostles Philosophy Center, [J], (FTW). See Congregation of Holy Cross Indiana Province Provincial House.
Queen of Apostles Provincial House, [N], (HRT), Bristol, CT.
Queen of Heaven Convent, [M], (CAM), Cherry Hill, NJ.
Queen of Heaven Monastery, [E], (PBR), Warren, OH.
Queen of Peace, [K], (NEW), Newark, NJ.
Queen of Peace Apartments, [I], (ALN), Pottsville, PA.
Queen of Peace Centennial House, [J], (SPR). See Providence Motherhouse - Sisters of Providence.
Queen of Peace Center, [I], (JOL), Lisle, IL.
Queen of Peace Center, [S], (STL), St. Louis, MO.
Queen of Peace Community, [O], (OAK). See Dominican Sisters of Mission San Jose.
Queen of Peace Consolidated School, [B], (HBG), Shamokin, PA.
Queen of Peace Convent, [N], (DEN), Denver, CO.
Queen of Peace Convent, [K], (ELP). See Servants of the Sacred Heart of Jesus and of the Poor (S.S.H.J.P.).
Queen of Peace Convent, [K], (FTW). See Saint Mary's of the Immaculate Conception.
Queen of Peace Convent, [G], (SLC), Salt Lake City, UT.
Queen of Peace Elementary Cluster, St. James and St. John School, [F], (BAL), Baltimore, MD.
Queen of Peace Friary, [P], (MIL), Burlington, WI.
Queen of Peace High School, [D], (CHI), Burbank, IL.
Queen of Peace Home and Soup Kitchen, [L], (BR), Baton Rouge, LA.
Queen of Peace Hospital, [D], (SFS), Mitchell, SD.
Queen of Peace Hospital, [J], (STP), New Prague, MN.
Queen of Peace Monastery, [F], (FAR), Belcourt, ND.
Queen of Peace Residence, [R], (BRK), Queens Village, NY.
Queen of Peace Retreat Center, [G], (FAR), Fargo, ND.
Queen of Peace Retreat House, [I], (PAT), Newton, NJ.
Queen of Pious Schools House of Studies-Piarist Fathers, [B], (WDC), Washington, DC.
Queen of Saints, The Catholic Center, [B], (BGP), Bridgeport, CT.
Queen of the Apostles Mission Association, Inc., [Q], (DEN), Englewood, CO.
Queen of the Holy Rosary College, [B], (OAK), Fremont, CA.
Queen of the Holy Rosary College, [G], (OAK), Mission San Jose, CA.
Queen of the Resurrection House of Prayer, [O], (CHI), Chicago, IL.
Queen of the Rosary, Motherhouse, [O], (RVC), Amityville, NY.
Queen of the Universe Day Center, [I], (PH), Levittown, PA.
Queen of the Valley Convent, [N], (SR), Napa, CA.
Queen of the Valley Hospital, [K], (LA), West Covina, CA.
Queen of the Valley Hospital of Napa, [G], (SR), Napa, CA.
Queen's Court I Apartments, [G], (MOB), Prichard, AL.
The Queen's Daughters, [W], (BGP), Bridgeport, CT.
Queen's Daughters Day Care Center, Inc., [R], (NY), Yonkers, NY.
Queens East, [L], (BRK). See Catholic Charities.
Queens Rehab, [L], (BRK). See Catholic Charities.
Queens West, [L], (BRK). See Catholic Charities.
Quigley Catholic High School, [C], (PIT), Baden, PA.
Quincy Notre Dame High School, [D], (SFD), Quincy, IL.
Quincy University, [B], (SFD), Quincy, IL.
Quinhon Missionary Sisters of the Holy Cross, [O], (SFR), Daly City, CA.
Quinhon Missionary Sisters of the Holy Cross, [N], (SJ), San Jose, CA.
Quinsigamond Community College, [Q], (WOR). See Campus Ministry.

R

R.E.B.A. (Religious Education Burlington Area) Trust

Religious of the Sacred Heart, [R], (STL), St. Louis County, MO.
Religious of the Sacred Heart, [R], (STL), St. Louis County, MO.
Religious of the Sacred Heart, [R], (STL), St. Charles, MO.
Religious of the Sacred Heart, [R], (STL), St. Charles, MO.
Religious of the Sacred Heart, [O], (WDC), Washington, DC.
Religious of the Sacred Heart (R.S.C.J.), [R], (GAL), Houston, TX.
Religious of the Sacred Heart Convent, [R], (STL), Frontenac, MO.
Religious of the Sacred Heart Oakwood, [O], (SFR), Atherton, CA.
Religious of the Sacred Heart of Mary, [K], (ARL), Arlington, VA.
Religious of the Sacred Heart of Mary, [S], (LA), Montebello, CA.
Religious of the Sacred Heart of Mary Charitable Trust, [DD], (NY), Tarrytown, NY.
Religious of the Sacred Heart Regis Hall, [R], (STL), St. Charles, MO.
Religious of the Sacred Heart, R.S.C.J., [Q], (NO), New Orleans, LA.
Religious of the Virgin Mary, [I], (SAC), Sacramento, CA.
Religious Sisters of Charity, [S], (LA), San Fernando, CA.
Religious Sisters of Charity, [I], (ORG), Garden Grove, CA.
Religious Sisters of Charity, [I], (ORG), Long Beach, CA.
Religious Sisters of Charity Regional, [S], (LA), Los Angeles, CA.
Religious Sisters of Mercy, [D], (CI), Neepwukos, Chuuk, FM.
Religious Sisters of Mercy, [I], (ORG), Dana Point, CA.
Religious Sisters of Mercy, [AA], (PH), Darby, PA.
Religious Sisters of Mercy, [AA], (PH), Merion Station, PA.
Religious Sisters of Mercy Convent, [AA], (PH), Merion, PA.
Religious Sisters of Mercy of Alma Corporation, [I], (SAG), Alma, MI.
Religious Sisters of Mercy of the Americas, [I], (ORG), Anaheim, CA.
Religious Sisters of Mercy, Agape, [AA], (PH), Merion, PA.
Religious Sisters of Mercy, Bethany House of Prayer, [AA], (PH). See Religious Sisters of Mercy.
Religious Sisters of Mercy, Justice Ministry, [AA], (PH). See Religious Sisters of Mercy.
Religious Sisters of Mercy, McAuley Convent (Infirmary), [AA], (PH). See Religious Sisters of Mercy.
Religious Sisters of Mercy, St. Joseph Convent, [AA], (PH). See Sisters of Mercy of the Americas, Annunciation Convent.
Religious Sisters of Mercy, Treweryn Convent, [AA], (PH). See Sisters of Mercy of the Americas, Annunciation Convent.
Religious Sisters of the Assumption, [AA], (PH), Philadelphia, PA.
Religious Trust (RETA), [U], (SFR), San Francisco, CA.
Religious Trust of the Missionaries of Our Lady of LaSalette, [V], (HRT), Hartford, CT.
Religious Trust of the Sisters of St. Joseph of Chambery (the "Trust"), [N], (HRT). See Convent of Mary Immaculate, Provincial House of the Sisters of St. Joseph of Chambery.
Religious Venerini Sisters Provincial Office, [O], (WOR), Worcester, MA.
Renewal Ministries Inc., [L], (LAN), Ann Arbor, MI.
Renovacion Conyugal, [C], (SJN), Hato Rey, PR.
The Rensselaer Newman Foundation, [S], (ALB). See Rensselaer Polytechnic Institute.
Rensselaer Polytechnic Institute, [S], (ALB), Troy, NY.
Reparation Society of the Immaculate Heart of Mary, [Q], (BAL), Baltimore, MD.
Research and Planning Services, [G], (CHI). See Catholic Charities of the Archdiocese of Chicago-Archdiocesan Offices.
Resettlement, Immigration & Citizenship Services, [J], (ORG). See Catholic Charities of Orange County, Inc.
Residence for Retired Sisters, [AA], (PH). See Missionary Sisters of the Sacred Heart (Cabrini Sisters).
Residence for the Aged, San Jose, [B], (MGZ), Hormigueros, PR.
Residence of Basilian Fathers-The Aquinas Institute, [I], (ROC), Rochester, NY.
Residence of the Basilian Fathers of the University of St. Thomas, [Q], (GAL), Houston, TX.
Residence of the Sisters of the Sacred Hearts, [L], (FR), Fall River, MA.
Residencia Asis, [E], (PCE), Ponce, PR.
Residential Center, [I], (SAT). See Father Flanagan's Boys' Town of San Antonio.
Residential Services, [H], (SY). See Catholic Charities of Cortland County.
Residential Services, [D], (WIL). See Catholic Charities, Inc.
Residents Encounter Christ, [G], (JC), St. Louis, MO.
*The Resource Center for Community Development, Inc., [DD], (NY), Bronx, NY.
Resource Development, [R], (STL). See Sancta Maria in Ripa.
Resources, Inc., [T], (BRK). See Catholic Migration & Refugee Office, Catholic Migration Services, Inc.
Respect Life Office, [K], (MIA), Miami, FL.
Respite Care Program, [B], (STO). See The Catholic Charities of the Diocese of Stockton.
Respond Now, [G], (CHI). See Catholic Charities of the Archdiocese of Chicago-Archdiocesan Offices.
Response-Ability Residence, [AA], (PH). See Sisters of the Holy Child.
Resurrection Ambulatory Care Services, [J], (CHI). See Resurrection Medical Center.
Resurrection Catholic Nursing Home, [F], (MOB), Marbury, AL.
Resurrection Center Retreat House, [A], (RCK), Woodstock, IL.
Resurrection Day Care Center, [I], (CHI), Chicago, IL.
Resurrection Development Foundation, [J], (CHI). See Resurrection Medical Center.
Resurrection Early Childhood Center, [G], (SCR), Muncy, PA.
Resurrection Health Care Corporation, [J], (CHI). See Resurrection Medical Center.
Resurrection High School, [D], (CHI), Chicago, IL.
Resurrection Medical Center, [J], (CHI), Chicago, IL.
Resurrection Nursing Home, [J], (ALB), Castleton, NY.
Resurrection Nursing and Rehabilitation Center, [M], (CHI), Park Ridge, IL.
Resurrection Retirement Community, [M], (CHI), Chicago, IL.
Resurrection School-Jr./Sr. School, [B], (BLX), Pascagoula, MS.
Retired and Senior Volunteer Program, [D], (LAN). See Catholic Social Services-St. Vincent Home for Children, Inc.
Retired Senior Volunteer Program, [G], (LAV), Las Vegas, NV.
Retired Senior Volunteer Program, [E], (SUP). See Catholic Charities Bureau, Inc.
Retirement Facility for Priests in the Oakland Diocese, [M], (OAK). See Mercy Retirement and Care Center.
Retirement Trust, [I], (SFS), Watertown, SD.
Retorno, [K], (FWT). See The Catholic Renewal Center of North Texas, Inc.
Retreat and Renewal Center, [I], (BEL), Belleville, IL.
Retreat Center, [Y], (BO), Cohasset, MA.
Retreat House of the Immaculate Heart of Mary, [T], (PRO). See Miscellaneous Listings for the Diocese of Providence.
Retreat House of the Sacred Heart, [W], (LA), Alhambra, CA.
Retreat House, Holy Cross Abbey, [L], (ARL), Berryville, VA.
Retrouvaille Program of the Saginaw Diocese, [I], (SAG), Bay City, MI.
Rev. Herman Vincent Scholarship Fund, [G], (BEA), Beaumont, TX.
Rev. Joseph R. Robb Educational Trust Fund (Holy Rosary Parish, Flint), [K], (LAN). See Chancery Office.
Review for Religious, [W], (STL), St. Louis, MO.
Rhinecliff Campus, [N], (NY). See Pius XII Youth and Family Services.
Rhinecliff Union Free School District, [N], (NY). See Pius XII Youth and Family Services.
The Rhode Island Catholic Orphan Asylum (St. Aloysius Home), [T], (PRO). See Miscellaneous Listings for the Diocese of Providence.
Rhode Island College, [S], (PRO), Providence, RI.
Rhodell Health Clinic, [K], (WH), Rhodell, WV.
The Rhodena, A Washington Non-profit Organization, [H], (SPK), Colville, WA.
The Ricci Institute for Chinese-Western Cultural History at the Center for the Pacific Rim, [U], (SFR), San Francisco, CA.
Rice High School, [F], (NY), New York, NY.
Rice Memorial High School, [B], (BUR), South Burlington, VT.
Rice University/Texas Medical Center Schools; Catholic Student Center, [T], (GAL), Houston, TX.
Richard H. Young Hospital, [B], (GI). See Good Samaritan Health Systems dba Good Samaritan Hospital.
Richard Stockton College of New Jersey, [Q], (CAM), Pomona, NJ.
Richmond, [H], (OAK). See Catholic Charities of the Diocese of Oakland, Inc.
Richmond Hill, [O], (RIC), Richmond, VA.
Richmond Hills Family Center, [Q], (SFR). See Catholic Charities of the Archdiocese of San Francisco.
Rickardsville-Holy Cross-Luxemburg (RHCL) Catholic School, [F], (DUB), Holy Cross, IA.
Ridgeway Place, Inc., [O], (DUB), Waterloo, IA.
Riese Corporation, [P], (PAT), Paterson, NJ.
Riley Center Community Office, [H], (SFR). See Society of St. Vincent de Paul Archdiocesan Council.
Rio Grande University, [I], (STU), Rio Grande, OH.
Risen Christ Catholic School, [H], (STP), Minneapolis, MN.
River Road Apartments, Pontchartrain Housing Corp. II, [N], (NO), St. Rose, LA.
Riverdale Clinic, [K], (LC), La Crosse, WI.
Riverdale Clinic, [K], (LC), Eau Claire, WI.
Riverdale Clinic, [K], (LC), Stevens Point, WI.
Riverside Hospital, Inc., [E], (STA). See St. Vincent's Medical Center, Inc.
Riverview Place, Inc., [E], (FAR), Fargo, ND.
Rivier College, [B], (MAN), Nashua, NH.
Rivier-St. Joseph School of Nursing, [I], (MAN). See St. Joseph Hospital.
Road to Emmaus (Catholic Home for Girls of all Faith), [N], (AUS), Austin, TX.
Roanoke Catholic School, [A], (RIC), Roanoke, VA.
Robert F. Kennedy Incentive Program, [I], (BRK), Brooklyn, NY.
Robert F. Kennedy Medical Center, [K], (LA). See Catholic Health Care West-Southern California.
Robert F. Kennedy Medical Center, [CC], (LA). See Catholic Healthcare West Southern California.
Robert G. Cunningham Endowment Trusts, [N], (OM). See The Omaha Archdiocesan Educational Foundation, Inc.
Roberts Hall, [P], (L). See Society of St. Vincent de Paul, Council of Louisville.
Robertsdale Office of Catholic Social Services, [J], (MOB), Robertsdale, AL.
Rochester Catholic Schools, [C], (WIN), Rochester, MN.
Rochester Catholic Worker Bethany House, [L], (ROC), Rochester, NY.
Rock Creek Apartments, Walmsley Housing Corp., [N], (NO), Metairie, LA.
Rock Springs Catholic School Foundation, [F], (CHY), Rock Springs, WY.
Rockhurst College, [B], (KC), Kansas City, MO.
Rockhurst College - Jesuit Community, [J], (KC), Kansas City, MO.
Rockhurst High School, [D], (KC), Kansas City, MO.
Rockhurst High School - Jesuit Community, [J], (KC), Kansas City, MO.
Rockland, [D], (NY). See Department of Education.
Rockland Community College, [CC], (NY). See University Apostolate.
Rockwood Lane/Court, [I], (SPK), Spokane, WA.
Rogationist Fathers, [R], (LA), North Hills, CA.
Rogationist Fathers, [R], (LA), Oxnard, CA.
Roger Bacon College, [B], (ELP), El Paso, TX.
Roger Bacon High School, [E], (CIN), Cincinnati, OH.
Roger Bacon High School Endowment, [U], (CIN), Cincinnati, OH.
Roger Williams University, [S], (PRO), Bristol, RI.
Rollins College Campus Ministry, [E], (ORL), Winter Park, FL.
Roman Catholic Archdiocese of Boston Common Investment Fund, [DD], (BO). See Chancery Office.
Roman Catholic Archdiocese of Boston Fixed Income Investment Fund, [DD], (BO). See Chancery Office.
Roman Catholic Archdiocese of Boston Health Benefit Trust, [DD], (BO). See Chancery Office.
Roman Catholic Archdiocese of Boston Insurance Trust, [DD], (BO). See Chancery Office.
Roman Catholic Archdiocese of Boston Long Term Disability Trust, [DD], (BO). See Chancery Office.
Roman Catholic Archdiocese of Boston Pension Trust, [DD], (BO). See Chancery Office.
Roman Catholic Bishop of Providence, [T], (PRO). See Miscellaneous Listings for the Diocese of Providence.
The Roman Catholic Communications Corporation of the Bay Area, [R], (OAK), Menlo Park, CA.
Roman Catholic Communications Corporation of the Bay Area, [P], (SJ), Menlo Park, CA.
Roman Catholic Community Center, Inc. (Kateri Tekakwitha Center), [J], (OG). See St. Regis Mission.
Roman Catholic Daughters of the King, [I], (LEX), Ashland, KY.
*The Roman Catholic Diocese of Owensboro Kentucky Charitable Trust Fund, Inc., [J], (OWN), Owensboro, KY.
Roman Catholic High School for Boys, [D], (PH), Philadelphia, PA.
Roman Catholic Pastoral Center Foundation, [I], (DM), Des Moines, IA.
The Roman Catholic Pontifical Lay Association Memores Domini, [Y], (BRK), Brooklyn, NY.
Roman Catholic Priests' Medical Fund Foundation, [I], (DM), Des Moines, IA.
Roman Catholic Seminary Fund Foundation, [I], (DM), Des Moines, IA.
The Roman Catholic Welfare Corporation of San Jose, [P], (SJ), Santa Clara, CA.

S

Sacred Heart Medical Center, [G], (SPK), Spokane, WA.
Sacred Heart Mercy Health Care Center, [I], (SAG), Alma, MI.
Sacred Heart Mercy Health Care Center, [J], (WIN), Jackson, MN.
Sacred Heart Mission House, [N], (CHI), Chicago, IL.
Sacred Heart Missions, Inc., [H], (JKS), Walls, MS.
Sacred Heart Model School, [E], (L), Louisville, KY.
Sacred Heart Monastery, [F], (BIR), Cullman, AL.
Sacred Heart Monastery, [H], (BIS), Richardton, ND.
Sacred Heart Monastery, [P], (MIL), Hales Corners, WI.
Sacred Heart Monastery, [G], (SFS), Yankton, SD.
Sacred Heart of Jesus Charitable Trust, [I], (BIR), Anniston, AL.
The Sacred Heart of Mary and Sisters of St. Joseph of Orange, [C], (LA). See Loyola Marymount University.
Sacred Heart of the Lake Chalet, [Q], (MIL), Cedar Grove, WI.
Sacred Heart Parish Educational Endowment Trust, [N], (OM). See The Omaha Archdiocesan Educational Foundation, Inc.
Sacred Heart Parish Endowment Fund, [M], (BR). See Baton Rouge Chancery Office.
Sacred Heart Parish Endowment Fund, [N], (OM). See The Omaha Archdiocesan Educational Foundation, Inc.
The Sacred Heart Parish Endowment Trust, [M], (LC), Eau Claire, WI.
Sacred Heart Parish, R.E. Program, [B], (CR), East Grand Forks, MN.
Sacred Heart Preparatory (Convent of the Sacred Heart)(Girls), [E], (SFR), Atherton, CA.
Sacred Heart Pre-Primary School, [H], (BO), Kingston, MA.
Sacred Heart Private Elementary School, Inc., [H], (NY), New York, NY.
Sacred Heart Program, Inc., [W], (STL), St. Louis, MO.
Sacred Heart Provincialate, [H], (MET), Belvidere, NJ.
Sacred Heart Rectory, [M], (HRT), Hartford, CT.
Sacred Heart Rectory, [M], (HRT), New Haven, CT.
Sacred Heart Rehabilitation Center, Inc., [Q], (DET), Detroit, MI.
Sacred Heart Rehabilitation Institute, Inc., [L], (MIL), Milwaukee, WI.
Sacred Heart Residence, [W], (NY), New York, NY.
Sacred Heart Retreat, [F], (GLP), Gallup, NM.
Sacred Heart Retreat, [L], (L), Louisville, KY.
Sacred Heart Retreat and Renewal Center, [N], (Y), Youngstown, OH.
Sacred Heart Retreat Camp, [Z], (LA). See Scouting and Camp Fire Ministry/Catholic Youth Camps.
Sacred Heart Retreat Camp, [G], (SB), Big Bear, CA.
Sacred Heart Retreat Center, [Y], (BO), Ipswich, MA.
Sacred Heart Retreat Center, [I], (GF), Billings, MT.
Sacred Heart Retreat Center, [I], (PAT), Newton, NJ.
Sacred Heart Retreat House - Jesuit Community, [E], (COS), Sedalia, CO.
Sacred Heart Retreat House & Renewal Center, [A], (Y), Youngstown, OH.
Sacred Heart School, [D], (ALN), Allentown, PA.
Sacred Heart School, [D], (CAM), Mount Ephraim, NJ.
Sacred Heart School, [B], (CC), Rockport, TX.
Sacred Heart School, [B], (FWT), Muenster, TX.
Sacred Heart School, [C], (GLP), Farmington, NM.
Sacred Heart School, [E], (MAN), Hampton, NH.
Sacred Heart School, [E], (NEW), Kearny, NJ.
Sacred Heart School, [D], (SPR), Springfield, MA.
The Sacred Heart School Education Endowment, Inc., [C], (DOD), Pratt, KS.
The Sacred Heart School Endowment, [C], (DOD), Dodge City, KS.
Sacred Heart School Endowment Fund, [B], (MAR), L'Anse, MI.
Sacred Heart School of Theology, [B], (MIL), Hales Corners, WI.
Sacred Heart Schools (Academy of the Sacred Heart for Girls, Hardey Prep. for Boys), [E], (CHI), Chicago, IL.
Sacred Heart Schools, Inc., [C], (BUR), Newport, VT.
Sacred Heart Seminary, Inc., [O], (GB), Green Bay, WI.
Sacred Heart Southern Missions Housing Corporation, [H], (JKS), Walls, MS.
*Sacred Heart Teachers Trust Fund, [B], (FWT). See Sacred Heart School.
Sacred Heart Trust Fund, [DD], (BO). See Chancery Office.
*Sacred Heart University, [A], (BGP), Fairfield, CT.
Sacred Heart Villa, [M], (STL), St. Louis, MO.
Sacred Heart Villa, [G], (STU), Steubenville, OH.
Sacred Heart Villa School, [E], (BUF), Lewiston, NY.
Sacred Heart-Griffin, [D], (SFD), Springfield, IL.
Sacred Hearts Academy, [D], (HON), Honolulu, HI.
Sacred Hearts Center, [H], (HON), Kaneohe, HI.
Sacred Hearts Convent, [X], (BO), Bradford, MA.
Sacred Hearts Convent, [I], (HON). See St. Francis Convent.
Sacred Hearts Convent, [I], (HON). See Sisters of Charity of the Blessed Virgin Mary.
Sacred Hearts Provincial House, [K], (FR), Fairhaven, MA.
Sacred Hearts Retreat Center, [A], (FR), Wareham, MA.
Sacred Heart-St. Mary's Hospitals, Inc., [A], (SUP), Rhinelander, WI.
Sacred Heart-St. Mary's Hospitals, Inc., [A], (SUP), Tomahawk, WI.
Sacred Military Constantinian Order of Saint George, American Delegation, [U], (GAL), Houston, TX.
Sacred Music Inc. of the Diocese of St. Cloud, [M], (SCL), St. Cloud, MN.
Sacro Costato Missionary Sisters, [E], (STO), Stockton, CA.
Sagrado Corazon de Jesus, Inc. of Windham, [M], (NOR), Windham, CT.
St. Adalbert Campus Lower School, [E], (NEW). See Elizabethport Catholic School.
St. Adalbert Church Educational Endowment Fund, [N], (OM). See The Omaha Archdiocesan Educational Foundation, Inc.
St. Adalbert Convent, [N], (HRT). See Felician Sisters - Our Lady of the Angels.
St. Agatha Home of the New York Foundling Hospital, [N], (NY), Nanuet, NY.
St. Agnes, [D], (CAM), Blackwood, NJ.
St. Agnes, [J], (PRT), Pittsfield, ME.
St. Agnes Academic, [G], (BRK), College Point, NY.
St. Agnes Academy, [F], (GAL), Houston, TX.
St. Agnes Academy, [C], (MEM), Memphis, TN.
St. Agnes Academy, [D], (MEM), Memphis, TN.
St. Agnes Apartments, [D], (PHX), Williams, AZ.
St. Agnes Apartments, Inc., [I], (STL). See Cardinal Ritter Institute.
St. Agnes Clinical Practice Group, Inc., [P], (BAL). See Chancery Office.
St. Agnes Clinical Practice Group, Inc., [Q], (BAL), Baltimore, MD.
St. Agnes Diocesan School, [E], (PIT), Pittsburgh, PA.
St. Agnes Foundation, [EE], (PH), Philadelphia, PA.
St. Agnes Foundation, Inc., [I], (BAL). See St. Agnes HealthCare, Inc.
St. Agnes HealthCare, Inc., [I], (BAL), Baltimore, MD.
St. Agnes Home for the Elderly, [O], (STL), Kirkwood, MO.
Saint Agnes Home, Inc., [J], (HRT), West Hartford, CT.
St. Agnes Hospital and Children's Rehabilitation Center, [S], (NY), White Plains, NY.
St. Agnes Hospital Convent, [F], (FRS), Fresno, CA.
St. Agnes Hospital Foundation, Inc., [P], (BAL). See Chancery Office.
St. Agnes Medical Center, [T], (PH), Philadelphia, PA.
St. Agnes Seminary, [J], (BRK), Brooklyn, NY.
Saint Agnes' Medical Center, [C], (FRS), Fresno, CA.
St. Agnes' Residence, [W], (NY), New York, NY.
Saint Albert Catholic Schools, [B], (DM), Council Bluffs, IA.
St. Albert Educational Foundation, [I], (DM), Council Bluffs, IA.
St. Albert Hall dba St. Albert Early Learning Center, [J], (SAT), Boerne, TX.
St. Albert Intermediate School, [A], (DM). See Council Bluffs Area Catholic Education Systems, Inc.
St. Albert Junior High School, [A], (DM). See Council Bluffs Area Catholic Education Systems, Inc.
St. Albert Primary School, [A], (DM). See Council Bluffs Area Catholic Education Systems, Inc.
St. Albert School, [E], (MAN), West Stewartstown, NH.
St. Albert the Great Catholic Center, [K], (BR), Hammond, LA.
St. Albert the Great House of Studies, [H], (LAN), De Witt, MI.
St. Albert the Great Priory, [N], (STP), Minneapolis, MN.
St. Albert the Great, University Parish, [G], (MAR), Houghton, MI.
St. Albert's Priory, [Z], (NY), Middletown, NY.
St. Alexius Medical Center, [D], (BIS), Bismarck, ND.
St. Alice Convent, [D], (LUB), Plainview, TX.
St. Aloisius Medical Center, [D], (FAR), Harvey, ND.
St. Aloysius Academy, [H], (PH), Bryn Mawr, PA.
St. Aloysius Educational Foundation, [I], (BIR), Bessemer, AL.
St. Aloysius Novitiate, [AA], (NY), Hopewell Junction, NY.
St. Aloysius Orphanage, [I], (CIN), Cincinnati, OH.
St. Aloysius Parish Conference, [E], (YAK), Toppenish, WA.
St. Aloysius School Endowment Fund, [M], (BR). See Baton Rouge Chancery Office.
St. Alphonsus Formation Residence, [C], (BRK), Whitestone, NY.
St. Alphonsus House, [Z], (PH). See Jesuit Community at St. Joseph's University.
St. Alphonsus House, [Z], (PH), Philadelphia, PA.
St. Alphonsus Rectory of the Redemptorist, [P], (STL), St. Louis, MO.
St. Alphonsus Regional Medical Center Convent-Sisters of Holy Cross, [D], (B), Boise, ID.
St. Alphonsus Regional Medical Center, Inc., [B], (B), Boise, ID.
St. Alphonsus Residence, [G], (VEN), Venice, FL.
St. Alphonsus Villa-Redemptorist Fathers and Brothers, [F], (ORL), New Smyrna Beach, FL.
St. Ambrose, [E], (BGP). See Catholic Elementary Schools-Region X.
St. Ambrose University, [B], (DAV), Davenport, IA.
St. Ambrose University Seminary, [A], (DAV), Davenport, IA.
St. Andre Health Care Facility, [G], (PRT), Biddeford, ME.
St. Andre Home, Inc., [F], (PRT), Biddeford, ME.
St. Andre's Group Home for Pregnant and Parenting Young Women, [F], (PRT), Biddeford, ME.
St. Andre's Group Home for Single Mothers with Infants, [F], (PRT), Bangor, ME.
St. Andre's Group Home for Troubled Girls, [F], (PRT), Lewiston, ME.
Saint Andrew Early Childhood Center, [B], (R), Apex, NC.
Saint Andrew Hall, [A], (SY), Syracuse, NY.
St. Andrew Home for the Aged, [M], (CHI), Niles, IL.
St. Andrew Kim Korean Catholic Society, [V], (CIN), Cincinnati, OH.
St. Andrew Kim Roman Catholic Church Society of Amherst, NY, Diocese of Buffalo, [T], (BUF), Amherst, NY.
St. Andrew Legal Clinic, [Q], (P), Portland, OR.
St. Andrew's Abbey, [R], (LA), Valyermo, CA.
St. Andrew's Abbey Retreat House (All Groups), [W], (LA), Valyermo, CA.
St. Andrew's Health Center, [D], (FAR), Bottineau, ND.
St. Andrew's Retreat House, [BB], (NY), Walden, NY.
St. Andrews Newman Center, [H], (SB), Riverside, CA.
St. Angela Convent, [O], (RVC), Seaford, NY.
St. Angela Education Center, [F], (L), Louisville, KY.
St. Angela Hall Academy, [J], (BRK), Brooklyn, NY.
St. Angela Merici School, [C], (OWN), Owensboro, KY.
St. Ann, [J], (MAN), Dover, NH.
St. Ann Adult Day Care, Inc., [N], (MIL), St. Francis, WI.
St. Ann Convent, [N], (HRT), New Britain, CT.
St. Ann Convent, [G], (TUC), Tucson, AZ.
St. Ann Day Care, [O], (NEW). See St. Joseph Province Shalom Center.
St. Ann Elementary, [B], (GAY), Cadillac, MI.
St. Ann Friary, [M], (CIN), Cincinnati, OH.
St. Ann Interparochial School, [C], (OWN), Morganfield, KY.
St. Ann Mission Center, [K], (AUS), Somerville, TX.
St. Ann Rest Home, [N], (MIL), Milwaukee, WI.
St. Ann School, [D], (CHL). See Mecklenburg Area Catholic Schools (M.A.C.S.).
*St. Ann School Foundation, Inc., [K], (VEN), Naples, FL.
St. Ann's Care Center, Inc., [A], (JUN), Juneau, AK.
St. Ann's Convent, [J], (PRT), Indian Island, ME.
St. Ann's Convent, [J], (PRT), Pleasant Point, ME.
St. Ann's Corporation, [I], (SFS), Watertown, SD.
St. Ann's Educational Foundation, [I], (BIR), Decatur, AL.
St. Ann's Friary, [N], (RVC), Smithtown, NY.
St. Ann's Home, [G], (GR), Grand Rapids, MI.
St. Ann's Home, [F], (SCL), Cold Spring, MN.
St. Ann's Home for the Aged, [H], (NEW), Jersey City, NJ.
St. Ann's Home for the Aged, [O], (NEW). See St. Joseph Province Shalom Center.
St. Ann's Home for the Aged, [E], (ROC), Rochester, NY.
St. Ann's Home Special Needs School, [I], (BO), Methuen, MA.
St. Ann's Home, Inc., [M], (BO), Methuen, MA.
St. Ann's Home, Inc., [H], (OKL), Oklahoma City, OK.
St. Ann's Hospital, [E], (COL). See Mount Carmel Health System.
St. Ann's Infant and Maternity Home, [J], (WDC), Hyattsville, MD.
Saint Ann's Media, Inc., [R], (SCR), Scranton, PA.
St. Ann's Novitiate, Little Sisters of the Poor, [V], (BRK), Queens Village, NY.
St. Ann's Nursery School, [C], (STF), Stamford, CT.
St. Ann's Nursing Home, [D], (AMA), Panhandle, TX.
St. Ann's Nursing Home Co., Inc., [E], (ROC), Rochester, NY.
Saint Ann's Passionist Monastery, [M], (SCR), Scranton, PA.
St. Ann's Place-East, [L], (IND), Indianapolis, IN.
St. Ann's Place-North, [L], (IND), Indianapolis, IN.
St. Ann's Senior Residence, [D], (DUL), Duluth, MN.
St. Ann's University Parish, [CC], (BO), Boston, MA.
St. Anne Center, [G], (RCK), Rockford, IL.
St. Anne Church, [G], (TLS), Broken Arrow, OK.
St. Anne Convent, [M], (COV), Melbourne, KY.

St. Benedict the Moor Center, [DD], (NY), New York, NY.
St. Benedict the Moor Friary, [M], (PAT), Paterson, NJ.
St. Benedict Thrift Shop, [V], (PH), Philadelphia, PA.
St. Benedict's Abbey, [H], (KCK), Atchison, KS.
St. Benedict's Abbey, [P], (MIL), Benet Lake, WI.
St. Benedict's Center, [H], (SCL), St. Cloud, MN.
St. Benedict's Convent, [AA], (NY), New York, NY.
St. Benedict's Convent, [N], (TR), Hazlet, NJ.
St. Benedict's Day Nursery, Day Care Center, [R], (NY), New York, NY.
The St. Benedict's Foundation, [D], (SLC), Ogden, UT.
St. Benedict's Health Center, [E], (BIS), Dickinson, ND.
St. Benedict's Hearth Corporation, East Providence., [T], (PRO). See Miscellaneous Listings for the Diocese of Providence.
St. Benedict's Monastery, [J], (AMA), Canyon, TX.
St. Benedict's Monastery, [M], (DEN), Snowmass, CO.
St. Benedict's Monastery, [J], (SCL), St. Joseph, MN.
St. Benedict's Preparatory School, [C], (NEW), Newark, NJ.
St. Benedict-at-Innisfail, [J], (WIL), Hockessin, DE.
Saint Benilde Community Support Charitable Trust, [T], (PRO), Narragansett, RI.
*St. Bernadette Institute of Sacred Art, [N], (SFE), Albuquerque, NM.
St. Bernadine Medical Center, [K], (LA). See Catholic Health Care West-Southern California.
St. Bernard Abbey, [E], (BIR), Cullman, AL.
*St. Bernard Academy and After School Program, [D], (NSH), Nashville, TN.
St. Bernard After School Program, [E], (NSH), Nashville, TN.
St. Bernard Convent, [N], (HRT). See Felician Sisters - Our Lady of the Angels.
St. Bernard High School, [D], (LA), Playa Del Rey, CA.
St. Bernard High School, [B], (NOR), Uncasville, CT.
St. Bernard Hospital, [J], (CHI), Chicago, IL.
St. Bernard Manor, St. Bernard II, and St. Bernard III, [N], (NO), Meraux, LA.
St. Bernard Memorial Endowment Fund, [N], (OM). See The Omaha Archdiocesan Educational Foundation, Inc.
St. Bernard Preparatory School, Inc., [B], (BIR), Cullman, AL.
St. Bernard Providence Hospital, [D], (SFS), Milbank, SD.
St. Bernard Religious Educational Endowment Fund, [N], (OM). See The Omaha Archdiocesan Educational Foundation, Inc.
St. Bernard's Central Catholic High School, [C], (WOR), Fitchburg, MA.
St. Bernard's Convent, [J], (PRT), Rockland, ME.
St. Bernard's Convent, [N], (SR), Eureka, CA.
St. Bernard's Convent, Servants of Mary-Omaha, [G], (OG), Saranac Lake, NY.
St. Bernard's High School, [B], (SR), Eureka, CA.
St. Bernard's Institute, [A], (ROC), Rochester, NY.
St. Bernard's Institute at Albany, [B], (ALB), Albany, NY.
St. Bernard's Regional Medical Center, [E], (LR), Jonesboro, AR.
St. Bernard's Senior Adult Program, [Q], (PH), Philadelphia, PA.
St. Bernardine Home, [L], (TOL), Fremont, OH.
St. Bernardine Medical Center, [CC], (LA). See Catholic Healthcare West Southern California.
St. Bernardine Medical Center, [D], (SB), San Bernardino, CA.
St. Bernardine Monastery, [F], (ALT), Newry, PA.
St. Bernardine of Siena Friary, [Z], (NY), Mount Vernon, NY.
St. Bernardine Plaza, [C], (SB), San Bernardino, CA.
St. Bonaventure, [O], (BUF), West Seneca, NY.
St. Bonaventure Church Endowment Trust, [N], (OM). See The Omaha Archdiocesan Educational Foundation, Inc.
St. Bonaventure Friary, [F], (ALT), Loretto, PA.
St. Bonaventure Friary, [O], (BUF), St. Bonaventure, NY.
St. Bonaventure Friary, [K], (DET), Detroit, MI.
St. Bonaventure Friary, [B], (WDC), Washington, DC.
St. Bonaventure Friary (Province of Our Lady of Consolation), [P], (STL), St. Louis, MO.
St. Bonaventure Friary, Franciscan Friars, [W], (BO), Brighton, MA.
St. Bonaventure High School, [D], (LA), Ventura, CA.
St. Bonaventure Indian Mission & School, [F], (GLP), Thoreau, NM.
St. Bonaventure University, [C], (BUF), St. Bonaventure, NY.
St. Bonaventure's Friary, [D], (SAL), Hays, KS.
St. Bonfilius Priory, [N], (CHI). See Servite Friars - Eastern Province.
Saint Boniface Elementary School, [F], (SCR), Wilkes-Barre, PA.
St. Boniface Elementary School Endowment Fund, [N], (OM). See The Omaha Archdiocesan Educational Foundation, Inc.
St. Boniface Friary, [L], (L), Louisville, KY.
St. Boniface Mission League, Inc., [V], (MIL), Milwaukee, WI.
St. Boniface Parish Catholic School Endowment Trust Fund, [M], (LC), Waumandee, WI.
St. Boniface Parish Endowment, [N], (OM). See The Omaha Archdiocesan Educational Foundation, Inc.
St. Boniface Parish Endowment Trust, [N], (OM). See The Omaha Archdiocesan Educational Foundation, Inc.
St. Boniface School, [G], (CIN), Cincinnati, OH.
St. Boniface School Endowment Trust, [N], (OM). See The Omaha Archdiocesan Educational Foundation, Inc.
St. Brendan Apartments, [G], (CHI). See Catholic Charities of the Archdiocese of Chicago-Archdiocesan Offices.
St. Brendan Convent, [N], (HRT), New Haven, CT.
St. Brendan High School, [C], (MIA), Miami, FL.
St. Brendans Apartments, HDFC, Inc., [L], (BRK). See Catholic Charities.
St. Bridget Regional School, [D], (CAM), Glassboro, NJ.
St. Bridget's Convent, [K], (FTW). See Saint Mary's of the Immaculate Conception.
St. Brigid Elementary School, [F], (SFR), San Francisco, CA.
St. Brigid's Convent, [N], (SAT), San Antonio, TX.
St. Brigid's Kindergarten, [J], (SAT), San Antonio, TX.
St. Bronislava, [D], (LC). See Stevens Point Area Catholic Schools.
St. Bruno Convent, [J], (PRT), Van Buren, ME.
St. Cabrini Home, [N], (NY), West Park, NY.
St. Cabrini Nursing Home, [V], (NY), Dobbs Ferry, NY.
St. Callistus Convent, [AA], (PH), Philadelphia, PA.
St. Camillus Academy, [C], (LEX), Corbin, KY.
St. Camillus Adult Day Care, [J], (BGP). See St. Camillus Health Center.
St. Camillus Auxiliary Committee, [J], (BGP). See St. Camillus Health Center.
St. Camillus Communities, Inc., [Y], (MIL), Wauwatosa, WI.
St. Camillus Community, [N], (WOR), Whitinsville, MA.
St. Camillus Community House, [P], (MIL), Wauwatosa, WI.
St. Camillus Formation Community, [P], (MIL), St. Francis, WI.
St. Camillus Foundation, [P], (SY). See St. Camillus Health & Rehabilitation Center.
St. Camillus Health & Rehabilitation Center, [P], (SY), Syracuse, NY.
St. Camillus Health Center, [J], (BGP), Stamford, CT.
St. Camillus Health Center, Inc., [N], (MIL), Wauwatosa, WI.
St. Camillus Home Foundation, Inc., [J], (BGP), Bridgeport, CT.
St. Camillus Institute, [K], (WOR). See St. Camillus Nursing Home Inc.
St. Camillus Institute, Inc., [Y], (MIL), Wauwatosa, WI.
St. Camillus Institute, Inc., [R], (WOR), Whitinsville, MA.
St. Camillus Ministries, Inc., [Y], (MIL), Wauwatosa, WI.
St. Camillus Monastery and Retreat Center, [A], (MAD), Durward's Glen, WI.
St. Camillus Nursing Home Inc., [K], (WOR), Whitinsville, MA.
St. Camillus Place, [F], (SCL), Little Falls, MN.
St. Camillus Provincialate, [P], (MIL), Wauwatosa, WI.
St. Camillus Rectory, [K], (WOR). See St. Camillus Nursing Home Inc.
St. Casimir Elementary, [B], (GAY), Posen, MI.
St. Casimir School, [E], (MAN), Manchester, NH.
St. Casimir's Monastery, Printing Plant and Cultural Center, [U], (BRK), Brooklyn, NY.
St. Catharine Academy, [F], (NY), New York, NY.
St. Catharine College, [A], (L), St. Catharine, KY.
St. Catharine of Siena Convent, [M], (L), St. Catharine, KY.
St. Catharine of Siena School, [D], (ALN), Reading, PA.
St. Catherine, [G], (SY), Binghamton, NY.
St. Catherine Community Center, [E], (SHP), Shreveport, LA.
St. Catherine Convent, [L], (GRY), East Chicago, IN.
St. Catherine Convent, [M], (L), Louisville, KY.
St. Catherine Convent, [L], (MAN), Manchester, NH.
St. Catherine Convent, [G], (TUC), Topawa, AZ.
St. Catherine Hall, [AA], (PH), Elkins Park, PA.
St. Catherine Hospital, [A], (DOD), Garden City, KS.
St. Catherine Hospital, [G], (GRY), East Chicago, IN.
St. Catherine Hospital Foundation, Inc., [G], (GRY). See St. Catherine Hospital.
St. Catherine Indian Boarding School, Inc., Junior-Senior High Boarding School, [E], (SFE), Santa Fe, NM.
St. Catherine Infirmary, [Z], (PH). See Congregation of the Mission.
St. Catherine Laboure Manor, [F], (STA), Jacksonville, FL.
St. Catherine Laboure Manor, Inc., [E], (STA). See St. Vincent's Medical Center, Inc.
St. Catherine Nursing Home, [N], (BAL). See Villa Julie at Seven Oaks.
St. Catherine of Siena Convent, [O], (SFR). See Dominican Sisters of San Rafael Generalate & Convent.
St. Catherine of Siena Priory, [Z], (NY), New York, NY.
St. Catherine of Siena Supervised Apartment, [L], (NO), Harvey, LA.
St. Catherine Preschool, [G], (SCR), Moscow, PA.
St. Catherine Residence For Women, [Y], (MIL), Milwaukee, WI.
St. Catherine School, [E], (MAN), Manchester, NH.
St. Catherine School Foundation, [G], (BEA), Port Arthur, TX.
Saint Catherine's Center for Children, [G], (ALB), Albany, NY.
St. Catherine's Convent of Mercy, [N], (HRT), Bethlehem, CT.
St. Catherine's High School, [E], (MIL), Racine, WI.
St. Catherine's High School Corporation, [Y], (MIL), Racine, WI.
St. Catherine's High School of Racine, Inc., [Y], (MIL), Racine, WI.
St. Catherine's Hospital, [K], (MIL), Kenosha, WI.
St. Catherine's House, [J], (DET), Detroit, MI.
St. Catherine's Infirmary, Inc., [Y], (MIL), Racine, WI.
St. Catherine's Military School, [E], (ORG), Anaheim, CA.
St. Catherine's Montessori, [G], (GAL), Houston, TX.
St. Catherine's Residence, [J], (PRT), Portland, ME.
St. Catherine's Residence and Nursing Center, [K], (P), North Bend, OR.
St. Cecelia Interparochial School, [D], (SP), Clearwater, FL.
St. Cecilia Academy, [C], (NSH), Nashville, TN.
St. Cecilia Cathedral Endowment Trust, [N], (OM). See The Omaha Archdiocesan Educational Foundation, Inc.
St. Cecilia Convent, [I], (NSH), Nashville, TN.
St. Cecilia Friary, [N], (PIT), Rochester, PA.
St. Cecilia High School Endowment Fund, [K], (LIN), Hastings, NE.
St. Cecilia House/Boysville of Michigan, Inc., [O], (DET). See Boysville of Michigan, Inc.
St. Cecilia's Convent, [O], (WOR), Leominster, MA.
St. Cecilia's Day Nursery, [R], (NY), New York, NY.
St. Cecilia's Middle School/High School, [C], (LIN), Hastings, NE.
St. Charles, [B], (CIN), Carthagena, OH.
St. Charles, [W], (STL). See Catholic Family Services.
St. Charles Borromeo, [D], (LC). See Chippewa Area Catholic Schools.
St. Charles Borromeo Convent, [N], (SEA), Tacoma, WA.
St. Charles Borromeo Educational Foundation, Inc., [DD], (BO). See Chancery Office.
St. Charles Care Center, Inc., [I], (COV), Covington, KY.
St. Charles Catholic High School, [D], (NO), La Place, LA.
St. Charles Cemetery, [Y], (MIL), Taycheedah, WI.
St. Charles Center, [C], (LKC), Moss Bluff, LA.
St. Charles Children's Home, [H], (MAN), Rochester, NH.
St. Charles College, [A], (LAF), Grand Coteau, LA.
The St. Charles Corporation, [I], (RVC), Port Jefferson, NY.
St. Charles County Catholic Community Services, [W], (STL). See Catholic Community Services Administration.
St. Charles Future Fund Trust, [M], (LC), Chippewa Falls, WI.
St. Charles Hospital, [H], (TOL), Oregon, OH.
St. Charles Hospital, Port Jefferson, New York, [I], (RVC), Port Jefferson, NY.
Saint Charles House of Studies, [U], (BRK), Jamaica, NY.
St. Charles House, Inc., [Q], (BAL), Pikesville, MD.
St. Charles Housing I, Inc., [F], (VEN), Port Charlotte, FL.
St. Charles Housing II, Inc., [F], (VEN), Port Charlotte, FL.
St. Charles Lwanga Center, [W], (STL), St. Louis, MO.
St. Charles Medical Center, [A], (BAK), Bend, OR.
St. Charles Mission School, [E], (GF), Pryor, MT.
St. Charles Preparatory School, [C], (COL), Columbus, OH.
St. Charles Seminary College Program, [A], (ELP), El Paso, TX.
St. Charles Villa, [K], (BAL), Baltimore, MD.
St. Charles Villa, [M], (BAL), Baltimore, MD.
St. Charles Youth and Family Services, [M], (MIL), Milwaukee, WI.
St. Chretienne Convent, [X], (BO), Salem, MA.
St. Chretienne Novitiate, [X], (BO), Lynn, MA.

(HRT), Hartford, CT.
St. Francis Hospital and Medical Center, [F], (KCK), Topeka, KS.
Saint Francis Hospital and Medical Center Foundation, Inc., [I], (HRT). See Saint Francis Hospital and Medical Center.
St. Francis Hospital Foundation, [O], (KC), Maryville, MO.
St. Francis Hospital Foundation, [K], (KCK), Topeka, KS.
St. Francis Hospital Foundation, [O], (TOL), Green Springs, OH.
Saint Francis Hospital of Evanston, [J], (CHI), Evanston, IL.
St. Francis Hospital of Federal Way, [G], (SEA), Federal Way, WA.
St. Francis Hospital of Franciscan Sisters, [C], (SPC). See St. Francis' Medical Center.
St. Francis Hospital of New Castle, [J], (PIT), New Castle, PA.
St. Francis Hospital of New Castle, [J], (PIT). See St. Francis Health System.
Saint Francis Hospital, Beacon, [S], (NY). See St. Francis Hospital.
*St. Francis Hospital, Inc., [B], (CHR). See Franciscan Health System of South Carolina, Inc.
Saint Francis Hospital, Inc., [E], (TLS), Tulsa, OK.
Saint Francis Hospital, Inc., [R], (WH), Wheeling, WV.
St. Francis Hospital, Inc., [H], (WIL), Wilmington, DE.
Saint Francis House, [M], (PRO), Woonsocket, RI.
St. Francis House, [E], (PRT). See Catholic Charities Maine.
St. Francis House, [L], (SEA), Seattle, WA.
St. Francis House, [I], (SFS), Sioux Falls, SD.
St. Francis House, Inc., [P], (RIC), Roanoke, VA.
St. Francis Housing Alternatives, Inc., [F], (LC). See St. Francis Community Programs, Inc.
St. Francis Housing Corporation, [P], (BAL). See Chancery Office.
St. Francis Inn, [V], (PH), Philadelphia, PA.
St. Francis Intermediate School, [D], (GF), Billings, MT.
St. Francis Life Care Corporation, [J], (PAT). See Sisters of the Sorrowful Mother Health Care Ministry Corp.
St. Francis Medical & Health Care Foundation, Inc., [M], (MIA). See Franciscan Sisters of Allegany, NY.
St. Francis Medical & Health Care Services, Inc., [M], (MIA). See Franciscan Sisters of Allegany, NY.
Saint Francis Medical Center, [B], (GI), Grand Island, NE.
St. Francis Medical Center, [F], (HON). See St. Francis Healthcare System of Hawaii.
St. Francis Medical Center, [K], (LA), Lynwood, CA.
St. Francis Medical Center, [K], (LA). See Catholic Health Care West-Southern California.
St. Francis Medical Center, [CC], (LA). See Catholic Healthcare West Southern California.
St. Francis Medical Center, [J], (PIT). See St. Francis Health System.
St. Francis Medical Center, [J], (PIT), Pittsburgh, PA.
St. Francis Medical Center, [G], (SCL), Breckenridge, MN.
St. Francis Medical Center, [B], (SHP), Monroe, LA.
St. Francis Medical Center, [C], (SPC). See St. Francis' Medical Center.
St. Francis Medical Center, [I], (TR), Trenton, NJ.
St. Francis Medical Center - West, [F], (HON). See St. Francis Healthcare System of Hawaii.
St. Francis Medical Center - West, [I], (HON). See St. Francis Convent.
St. Francis Medical Center Hospital - Convent, [N], (PEO), Peoria, IL.
St. Francis Medical Center of Santa Barbara, [K], (LA), Santa Barbara, CA.
Saint Francis Middle School, [D], (SAC), Palo Cedro, CA.
St. Francis Mission Center, [K], (AUS), Waco, TX.
St. Francis Mission Community Central House, [D], (LUB), Lubbock, TX.
St. Francis Mission Community, O.S.F., [J], (AMA), Amarillo, TX.
St. Francis Monastery, Novitiate and Apostolic Center, [N], (RVC), Oyster Bay, NY.
St. Francis Monastery-Generalate Offices of Franciscan Brothers, [U], (BRK), Brooklyn, NY.
St. Francis Novitiate, [B], (NY), New York, NY.
*St. Francis Nursing Center, [C], (COS), Colorado Springs, CO.
St. Francis Nursing Center, [H], (RIC), Newport News, VA.
St. Francis Nursing Center-East, [J], (PIT). See St. Francis Health System.
St. Francis Nursing Center-East, [J], (PIT), Pittsburgh, PA.
St. Francis Nursing Center-North, [J], (PIT). See St. Francis Health System.
St. Francis Nursing Center-North, [J], (PIT), Cranberry Twp., PA.
St. Francis Nursing Home, [F], (SAG), Saginaw, MI.
St. Francis Nursing Home, [K], (SAT), San Antonio, TX.
St. Francis of Assisi, [L], (RIC). See Ethnic and Special Ministries.
St. Francis of Assisi Chapel and Catholic Information Center, [L], (SPR), Springfield, MA.
St. Francis of Assisi Church of South Omaha Educational Endowment Fund, [N], (OM). See The Omaha Archdiocesan Educational Foundation, Inc.
St. Francis of Assisi Conference, St. Vincent de Paul, [G], (B), Boise, ID.
St. Francis of Assisi Convent, [N], (HRT), Torrington, CT.
St. Francis of Assisi Convent, School Sisters of Notre Dame, [N], (HRT), New Britain, CT.
St. Francis of Assisi Educational Trust Fund (St. Francis of Assisi Parish, Ann Harbor), [K], (LAN). See Chancery Office.
St. Francis of Assisi Friary, [O], (BUF), Athol Springs, NY.
St. Francis of Assisi Friary, [M], (DEN), Denver, CO.
St. Francis of Assisi Kitchen, [R], (SCR), Scranton, PA.
St. Francis of Assisi Newman Center, [O], (PEO), Macomb, IL.
St. Francis of Assisi Novitiate, [Z], (NY). See Franciscan Friars of the Atonement.
St. Francis of Assisi Novitiate-Franciscan Sisters of St. Elizabeth, [N], (PAT), Parsippany, NJ.
St. Francis of Assisi School, [E], (MAN), Manchester, NH.
St. Francis of Assisi University Church, [H], (LFT), Muncie, IN.
The St. Francis Parish Endowment Trust, [M], (LC), Ellsworth, WI.
*St. Francis Plaza, Inc., [J], (PIT). See St. Francis Health System.
*St. Francis Plaza, Inc., [L], (PIT), Pittsburgh, PA.
St. Francis Preparatory School, [G], (BRK), Fresh Meadows, NY.
St. Francis Primary School, [D], (GF), Billings, MT.
St. Francis Provincialate, [K], (FTW), Mishawaka, IN.
St. Francis R.C.I.A. Residence, [I], (MET), Metuchen, NJ.
St. Francis Regional Medical Center, [G], (DUL). See Benedictine Sisters Benevolent Association.
St. Francis Regional Medical Center, [J], (STP), Shakopee, MN.
St. Francis Renewal Center, [L], (WIL), Wilmington, DE.
St. Francis Residence, [P], (MIL), Franklin, WI.
St. Francis Residence, Inc., [K], (SP). See St. Joseph's Hospital, Inc.
St. Francis Respite Program, Inc., [T], (BUF), Buffalo, NY.
St. Francis Retreat Center, [I], (LAN), De Witt, MI.
St. Francis Retreat Center, [I], (MRY), San Juan Bautista, CA.
St. Francis Retreat House, [M], (ALN), Easton, PA.
St. Francis School, [C], (AGN), Yona, GU.
St. Francis School, [C], (GLP), Lumberton, NM.
St. Francis School, [D], (HON), Honolulu, HI.
St. Francis School, [F], (SPK), Spokane, WA.
St. Francis School, [C], (WIN). See Rochester Catholic Schools.
Saint Francis School for Exceptional Children, [F], (RCK), Freeport, IL.
St. Francis School for Special Education, [G], (BAL), Baltimore, MD.
St. Francis School of Nursing, [J], (CHI). See Saint Francis Hospital of Evanston.
Saint Francis Seminary, [A], (MIL), Milwaukee, WI.
St. Francis Seminary, [A], (SD), San Diego, CA.
St. Francis Seraph Friary, [M], (CIN), Cincinnati, OH.
St. Francis Social Adult Day Service, [W], (SY), Syracuse, NY.
St. Francis Solanus Friary, [K], (SFD), Quincy, IL.
*St. Francis Specialty Hospital, [B], (SHP), Monroe, LA.
St. Francis Thrift Shop, [K], (BEL), Belleville, IL.
St. Francis Transitional Residence, [F], (WIL). See Ministry of Caring, Inc.
St. Francis Upper School, [D], (GF), Billings, MT.
St. Francis Villa Custody House, [P], (BGP). See Sisters Minor of Mary Immaculate.
St. Francis Village, Inc., [G], (FWT), Crowley, TX.
St. Francis Villas, Inc., [O], (TOL), Tiffin, OH.
St. Francis Xavier, [C], (BUR), Winooski, VT.
St. Francis Xavier - Jesuit Community, [J], (KC), Kansas City, MO.
St. Francis Xavier Catholic School Education Foundation, [I], (BIR), Birmingham, AL.
St. Francis Xavier Elementary, [B], (GAY), Petoskey, MI.
*St. Francis Xavier Home Health Care, Inc., [B], (CHR). See Bon Secours-St. Francis Xavier Hospital.
St. Francis Xavier Regional School, [C], (SLC), Kearns, UT.
St. Francis Xavier School, [E], (GB). See Manitowoc Area Catholic System (MACS).
St. Francis Xavier School Foundation, [K], (VEN), Fort Myers, FL.
St. Francis Youth Center, [D], (MRY), Watsonville, CA.
St. Francis' Medical Center, [J], (PEO), Peoria, IL.
*St. Francis' Medical Center, [C], (SPC), Cape Girardeau, MO.
St. Francis' Residence, [Q], (FR), Fall River, MA.
St. Francis/Marist, [B], (SPP), Lepua, AS.
The St. Francis-Mercy Corporation, [I], (RVC), Old Brookville, NY.
St. Frederick High School, [A], (SHP), Monroe, LA.
St. Gabriel, [G], (CIN), Cincinnati, OH.
St. Gabriel House, [N], (HRT), Farmington, CT.
St. Gabriel School, [D], (CHL). See Mecklenburg Area Catholic Schools (M.A.C.S.).
St. Gabriel's, [H], (ARL), Alexandria, VA.
St. Gabriel's Convent, [K], (ARL), Alexandria, VA.
The St. Gabriel's Endowment Trust, [M], (LC), Prairie du Chien, WI.
St. Gabriel's Hall, [N], (PH), Audubon, PA.
St. Gabriel's Hospital, [G], (SCL), Little Falls, MN.
St. Gabriel's Monastery, [O], (SCR), Clarks Summit, PA.
St. Gabriel's Passionist Community, [W], (BO), Brighton, MA.
St. Gabriel's Residence, [W], (BO), Brighton, MA.
St. Gabriel's Retreat Center, [P], (SCR), Clarks Summit, PA.
St. Gabriel's System, [N], (PH), Philadelphia, PA.
St. Gabriel's Youth House, [P], (RVC), Shelter Island Heights, NY.
*St. Gaspar Society, [O], (KC), Liberty, MO.
St. Genevieve of the Pines, [K], (CHL), Asheville, NC.
St. George Chapel of Marianist Community, [M], (CIN), Huntsville, OH.
St. George Hall, [J], (PRT), Windham, ME.
St. George Manor, [L], (MAN), Manchester, NH.
St. George's Rectory, [I], (ROC), Rochester, NY.
St. Gerard Catholic High School, [E], (SAT), San Antonio, TX.
St. Gerard Community Nursing Home, [E], (FAR), Hankinson, ND.
St. Gerard Educational Trust Fund (St. Gerard Parish, Lansing), [K], (LAN). See Chancery Office.
St. Gerard Majella Alternative School, [I], (NO), New Orleans, LA.
Saint Gertrude High School, [B], (RIC), Richmond, VA.
St. Gertrude Priory, [M], (CIN), Cincinnati, OH.
St. Gertrude School, [B], (CC), Kingsville, TX.
St. Gertrude's Convent, Benedictine Sisters, [Q], (NO), Mandeville, LA.
St. Gertrude's Health Center, [W], (STP), Shakopee, MN.
St. Gertrude's Monastery, Motherhouse and Novitiate of the Sisters of St. Benedict, [J], (WIL), Ridgely, MD.
St. Gratian Friary, Franciscan Friars, [N], (CHI), Countryside, IL.
St. Gregory Church-Union College, [L], (LEX), Barbourville, KY.
Saint Gregory Early Childhood Center, [F], (SCR), Clarks Green, PA.
The St. Gregory Seminary Trust, [A], (CIN). See The Athenaeum of Ohio.
St. Gregory the Great Housing Committee, Inc., [P], (BAL). See Chancery Office.
St. Gregory's Abbey, [I], (OKL), Shawnee, OK.
St. Gregory's Academy, [E], (SCR), Moscow, PA.
St. Gregory's College, [A], (OKL), Shawnee, OK.
St. Gregory's Priory (Priestly Fraternity of St. Peter), [M], (SCR), Scranton, PA.
Saint Gregory's School, [E], (ALB), Loudonville, NY.
St. Hedwig Cemetery and Mausoleum Corporation, [N], (CHI). See Conventual Franciscans of St. Bonaventure Province.
Saint Hedwig's Church Corporation, Providence, [T], (PRO). See Miscellaneous Listings for the Diocese of Providence.
St. Hedwig's Industrial School for Girls, [X], (CHI), Chicago, IL.
St. Helen's, Sisters of St. Joseph, [G], (OG), Chasm Falls, NY.
The St. Helena Cathedral Foundation, Inc., [I], (HEL), Helena, MT.
St. Helena Convent, [N], (SR), St. Helena, CA.
St. Helena House, [AA], (BO), Boston, MA.
St. Henry Day Care Center, [D], (BEL), Belleville, IL.
St. Henry District High School, [B], (COV), Erlanger, KY.
*St. Henry Property Development, Inc. dba The Cloister, [L], (NSH), Nashville, TN.
*St. Hilary Parish Foundation, [Z], (CLV), Akron, OH.
St. Hubert's Catholic High School for Girls, [D], (PH), Philadelphia, PA.
St. Hyacinth College and Seminary, [A], (SPR), Granby, MA.
St. Ignatius, [J], (PRT), Sanford, ME.
St. Ignatius College Prep, [D], (CHI), Chicago, IL.
St. Ignatius College Preparatory (Coed), [E], (SFR), San Francisco, CA.

St. Ignatius Early Childhood Center, [F], (SP), Tarpon Springs, FL.
St. Ignatius Elementary, [B], (GAY), Rogers City, MI.
St. Ignatius High School, [E], (CLV), Cleveland, OH.
St. Ignatius Jesuit Community, [D], (CHI), Chicago, IL.
St. Ignatius Loyola Academy, [F], (BAL), Baltimore, MD.
St. Ignatius Loyola Residence, [Z], (NY), New York, NY.
St. Ignatius Loyola School, [D], (ALN), Sinking Spring, PA.
St. Ignatius Nursing Home, [W], (PH), Philadelphia, PA.
St. Ignatius Residence, [I], (PRT), Portland, ME.
St. Ignatius Retreat House, Inisfada, [P], (RVC), Manhasset, NY.
St. Isaac House, Society of the Daughters of the Heart of Mary, [AA], (PH), Philadelphia, PA.
St. Isidore Church Endowment Trust, [N], (OM). See The Omaha Archdiocesan Educational Foundation, Inc.
St. Isidore Elementary School Endowment Trust, [N], (OM). See The Omaha Archdiocesan Educational Foundation, Inc.
St. Isidore's Catholic Student Center, [H], (SAL), Manhattan, KS.
St. James, [D], (CAM), Penns Grove, NJ.
St. James, [D], (LC). See Eau Claire Coordinated Catholic Schools.
St. James Cathedral Foundation, Inc., [Y], (BRK), Brooklyn, NY.
St. James Church, [DD], (PH). See Newman Apostolate.
St. James Community Hospital, Inc., [E], (HEL), Butte, MT.
St. James Convent, [N], (HRT). See Sisters of Mercy of the Americas of Connecticut.
St. James Convent, [O], (NEW), Springfield, NJ.
St. James Convent, [N], (SAT), San Antonio, TX.
St. James Convent, Sisters of St. Joseph, [G], (OG), Carthage, NY.
St. James Educational Foundation, [I], (BIR), Gadsden, AL.
St. James Friary, [O], (SP), Belleair Bluffs, FL.
St. James High School, [A], (CAM), Carneys Point, NJ.
St. James Hospital, [G], (NEW), Newark, NJ.
Saint James Hospital, [J], (PEO), Pontiac, IL.
St. James Hospital and Health Centers, [J], (CHI), Chicago Heights, IL.
St. James Hospital Division, Newark, [F], (NEW). See Cathedral Healthcare System, Inc.
St. James Manor, [I], (JOL), Crete, IL.
St. James Manor, Inc., [O], (OM), Omaha, NE.
St. James Mercy Hospital, [H], (ROC), Hornell, NY.
St. James Middle School, [G], (SY), Johnson City, NY.
St. James Parish Endowment Trust, [M], (LC), La Crosse, WI.
St. James Residence, [P], (PRO), Manville, RI.
The St. James the Greater Catholic Church Endowment Trust, [M], (LC), Eau Claire, WI.
St. James' Convent, Sisters of St. Joseph, [G], (OG), Gouverneur, NY.
St. James/Seton School Endowment Fund, [N], (OM). See The Omaha Archdiocesan Educational Foundation, Inc.
St. James-Seton School, [D], (OM), Omaha, NE.
St. Jane Catholic Community Services, [W], (STL). See Catholic Community Services Administration.
St. Jeanne de Lestonnac Kindergarten and Day Nursery, [J], (LA), Los Angeles, CA.
St. Jeanne de Lestonnac Preschool/Kindergarten & First Grade, [F], (SB). See Sisters of the Company of Mary (O.D.N.).
Saint Jeanne de Lestonnac School, [E], (ORG), Tustin, CA.
St. Jerome Early Childhood Center, [F], (SP), Largo, FL.
St. Jerome Hospital, [K], (BUF), Batavia, NY.
St. Jerome Housing Corporation, Inc., [P], (BAL). See Chancery Office.
St. Jerome Regional School, [D], (ALN), Tamaqua, PA.
St. Joachin & St. Anne Retreat Center, [G], (SB), Running Springs, CA.
St. Joan Antida Day Care Center, Inc., [J], (MIL), West Allis, WI.
*St. Joan Antida High School Foundation, Ltd., [Y], (MIL), Milwaukee, WI.
St. Joan Antida High School, Inc., [E], (MIL), Milwaukee, WI.
St. Joan Antida Home, Inc., [N], (MIL), West Allis, WI.
St. Joan of Arc Parish Educational Endowment Fund, [N], (OM). See The Omaha Archdiocesan Educational Foundation, Inc.
St. Joan of Arc Parish Endowment, [N], (OM). See The Omaha Archdiocesan Educational Foundation, Inc.
St. John, [D], (CAM), Collingswood, NJ.
St. John Ambulatory Care, Detroit, [H], (DET). See St. John Hospital and Medical Center.
St. John and St. Joseph Home, Inc., [R], (SY), Utica, NY.
St. John Baptist de LaSalle Regional School, [E], (RVC), Bethpage, NY.
St. John Berchmans Child Development Center, [J], (NO), New Orleans, LA.
St. John Berchmans Manor, [N], (NO), New Orleans, LA.
St. John Bosco Church, [DD], (PH). See Newman Apostolate.
St. John Bosco Convent, [N], (SAT), San Antonio, TX.
St. John Bosco High School, [F], (LA), Bellflower, CA.
St. John Bosco School, [G], (SAT), San Antonio, TX.
St. John Cathedral Endowment Trust, [Z], (CLV), Cleveland, OH.
St. John Center, [G], (DAV). See Burlington Catholic School System: St. Paul Center.
St. John Central High School, [B], (STU), Bellaire, OH.
St. John Children's Home, [D], (BEL), Belleville, IL.
St. John Day Care Center, [D], (BEL), Belleville, IL.
Saint John De La Salle of New York, Inc., [R], (RVC), Oakdale, NY.
St. John de Matha Monastery, Order of Most Holy Trinity, [M], (WDC), Hyattsville, MD.
St. John Dialysis Center, Detroit, [H], (DET). See St. John Hospital and Medical Center.
St. John Fisher Catholic Chapel, [Q], (WH), Bethany, WV.
St. John Fisher Chapel University Parish, [S], (DET), Auburn Hills, MI.
St. John Fisher Seminary Residence, [O], (BGP), Stamford, CT.
Saint John Hall-Long Crandon, [K], (BAL). See Stella Maris Operating Corporation.
St. John Health System, [T], (DET), Detroit, MI.
St. John High School, [C], (Y), Ashtabula, OH.
St. John Hospice for Men, [R], (PH), Philadelphia, PA.
St. John Hospital, [J], (CLV), Cleveland, OH.
St. John Hospital, [J], (GAL), Nassau Bay, TX.
St. John Hospital, [F], (KCK), Leavenworth, KS.
St. John Hospital and Medical Center, [H], (DET), Detroit, MI.
St. John Hospital-Macomb Center, Morrison Township, [H], (DET). See St. John Hospital and Medical Center.
St. John Interparochial Elementary/Middle School, [D], (BR), Plaquemine, LA.
St. John Inter-Parochial High School, [B], (BLX), Gulfport, MS.
St. John Interparochial High School, [B], (BR), Plaquemine, LA.
St. John Manor, [H], (LR), Little Rock, AR.
St. John Medical Center, [G], (SEA), Longview, WA.
St. John Medical Center Foundation, Inc., [J], (TLS), Tulsa, OK.
St. John Medical Center, Inc., [E], (TLS), Tulsa, OK.
St. John Montessori Center, [E], (HON), Mililani Town, HI.
St. John Neumann, [K], (BRK), Brooklyn, NY.
St. John Neumann Apartments, Inc., [I], (STL). See Cardinal Ritter Institute.
St. John Neumann High School, [D], (PH), Philadelphia, PA.
St. John Neumann High School, [A], (VEN), Naples, FL.
St. John Neumann High School Faculty Residence, [G], (VEN), Naples, FL.
St. John Neumann House, [B], (STL), St. Louis, MO.
St. John Neumann Nursing Home, [W], (PH), Philadelphia, PA.
St. John Neumann Regional School, [D], (ALN), Palmerton-Slatington, PA.
St. John Neumann Regional, Catholic Elementary, [F], (PIT), Pittsburgh, PA.
St. John Neumann Residence, [L], (ALB), Saratoga Springs, NY.
St. John Neumann Residence, [E], (BLX), Biloxi, MS.
St. John Neumann Residence, [Z], (NY), New York, NY.
St. John Neumann School, [F], (BAL), Cumberland, MD.
The Saint John Neumann Spiritual Renewal Center, [H], (PT), Tallahassee, FL.
St. John Neuwmann Regional School, Inc., [P], (BAL). See Chancery Office.
St. John Newco, [T], (DET), Detroit, MI.
St. John of God Community Health Center, [N], (MET), New Brunswick, NJ.
St. John of God Health Care Services, [R], (LA). See Brothers of John of God, Inc., The.
St. John of God Hospital, [R], (BO), Brighton, MA.
St. John of God Retirement and Care Center, [Q], (LA), Los Angeles, CA.
St. John of God Retirement and Care Center, [R], (LA). See Brothers of John of God, Inc., The.
St. John of God Retirement and Care Center, [R], (LA), Los Angeles, CA.
St. John of God School, [F], (PIT), McKees Rocks, PA.
St. John of the Cross, Discalced Carmelite House of Studies, [B], (NO), New Orleans, LA.
St. John Parish Endowment Trust, [M], (LC), Whitehall, WI.
St. John Parish Foundation, Inc., [O], (TOL), Delphos, OH.
St. John Preparatory School, [G], (BRK), Astoria, NY.
St. John Regional Catholic School, [F], (BAL), Frederick, MD.
St. John Regional School, [E], (MAN), Concord, NH.
St. John Resurrection Early Childhood Center, [F], (MOB), Montgomery, AL.
St. John School, [C], (WIN). See Rochester Catholic Schools.
St. John Stone Friary, [N], (CHI), Chicago, IL.
St. John Stone Friary, [Z], (PH), Villanova, PA.
St. John Student Parish, [J], (LAN), East Lansing, MI.
St. John the Baptist, [C], (RVC), West Islip, NY.
St. John the Baptist Church Educational Endowment Trust, [N], (OM). See The Omaha Archdiocesan Educational Foundation, Inc.
St. John the Baptist Convent, [Q], (PRO), Pawtucket, RI.
St. John the Baptist Convent, [J], (PRT), Brunswick, ME.
St. John the Baptist Educational Endowment Trust, [M], (LC), Marshfield, WI.
St. John the Baptist Family Center, [G], (TR), Long Branch, NJ.
St. John the Baptist Friary, [J], (JOL), Joliet, IL.
St. John the Baptist Maintenance Endowment Trust, [M], (LC), Marshfield, WI.
St. John the Baptist Pre-Natal Clinic, [P], (CAM), Camden, NJ.
St. John the Baptist Pre-School Program, [J], (NO), New Orleans, LA.
St. John the Baptist Rectory, [U], (BRK), Brooklyn, NY.
St. John The Baptist Retreat Center, [J], (ALT), New Baltimore, PA.
St. John the Evangelist, [G], (SY), Binghamton, NY.
St. John the Evangelist Convent, [N], (HRT), Watertown, CT.
St. John the Evangelist Convent, [J], (PRT), South Portland, ME.
St. John the Evangelist Parish Educational Trust Fund (St. John the Evangelist Parish, Jackson), [K], (LAN). See Chancery Office.
St. John Vianney Church of Millard Parish Endowment Trust, [N], (OM). See The Omaha Archdiocesan Educational Foundation, Inc.
St. John Vianney College Seminary, [A], (MIA), Miami, FL.
St. John Vianney Educational Trust Fund (St. John Vianney Parish, Flint), [K], (LAN). See Chancery Office.
St. John Vianney High School, [B], (TR), Holmdel, NJ.
St. John Vianney Hospital, [U], (PH), Downingtown, PA.
St. John Vianney House, [K], (FR), Fall River, MA.
St. John Vianney House, [N], (WDC), Kensington, MD.
St. John Vianney Manor, [N], (PIT), Pittsburgh, PA.
St. John Vianney Residence, [P], (PRO), Providence, RI.
St. John Vianney Residence for Priests, [N], (NEW), Rutherford, NJ.
St. John Vianney School Development Fund, [J], (PHX), Goodyear, AZ.
St. John Vianney Seminary, [A], (STP), St. Paul, MN.
St. John Vianney Villa, [I], (JOL), Naperville, IL.
St. John Villa, [D], (STU), Carrollton, OH.
St. John Villa Academy Elementary School, [H], (NY), New York, NY.
St. John Villa Academy High School, [F], (NY), New York, NY.
St. John's Abbey, of the Order of St. Benedict, [I], (SCL), Collegeville, MN.
St. John's Area School, [E], (SCL), Foley, MN.
St. John's Bread & Life Program, Inc., [Y], (BRK), Brooklyn, NY.
St. John's Breadline, [F], (SFD), Springfield, IL.
St. John's Catholic Student Chapel and Newman Foundation, University of Illinois, [O], (PEO), Champaign, IL.
Saint John's Child Study Center, Saint John's Hospital & Health Center, [M], (LA), Santa Monica, CA.
St. John's Church of Providence, [T], (PRO). See Miscellaneous Listings for the Diocese of Providence.
St. John's College High School, [E], (WDC), Washington, DC.
St. John's College of Nursing, [H], (SFD). See St. John's Hospital.
St. John's College, Queens Campus, [D], (BRK). See St. John's University.
St. John's Convent, [J], (AMA), Borger, TX.
St. John's Convent, [K], (FTW). See Saint Mary's of the Immaculate Conception.
St. John's Convent, [G], (OG), Plattsburgh, NY.
St. John's Deaf Center, [Q], (DET), Warren, MI.

St. John's Diocesan Center, [L], (KC), Kansas City, MO.
St. John's Educational Foundation, [I], (BIR), Madison, AL.
St. John's Elementary School, [A], (NU). See New Ulm Area Catholic Schools.
The St. John's Endowment Trust, [M], (LC), Prairie du Chien, WI.
Saint John's Health System, [C], (LFT), Anderson, IN.
*St. John's Health System, Inc., [J], (SPC), Springfield, MO.
St. John's High School, [E], (WOR), Shrewsbury, MA.
St. John's Home for Children, [M], (WH), Wheeling, WV.
St. John's Home for the Aged, [F], (EVN), Evansville, IN.
St. John's Home Missions Seminary, Inc., [L], (LR), Little Rock, AR.
St. John's Hospital, [H], (SFD), Springfield, IL.
Saint John's Hospital and Health Center, [K], (LA), Santa Monica, CA.
St. John's Hospital and Health Center, [H], (SAT). See Incarnate Word Health System.
Saint John's Hospital and Health Center Foundation, [K], (LA). See Saint John's Hospital and Health Center.
St. John's Jesuit High School, [C], (TOL), Toledo, OH.
St. John's Literary Institution at Prospect Hall, [D], (BAL), Frederick, MD.
St. John's Mercy Hospital, [K], (STL), Washington, MO.
St. John's Mercy Medical Center, [K], (STL), Creve Coeur, MO.
St. John's Mercy Villa, [D], (SPC), Springfield, MO.
St. John's Mission, [W], (STL), St. Louis, MO.
St. John's New Horizons, [C], (SAL), Hays, KS.
St. John's Place of New Orleans, Inc. dba Mercy Family Center, [O], (NO), New Orleans, LA.
St. John's Plaza, [G], (SD), San Diego, CA.
St. John's Pleasant Valley Hospital, [K], (LA). See St. John's Regional Medical Center.
St. John's Preparatory School, [E], (BO), Danvers, MA.
St. John's Preparatory School, [D], (SCL), Collegeville, MN.
St. John's Priory, (F.J.), [H], (CC), Laredo, TX.
St. John's Queens Hospital Division, [N], (BRK). See Catholic Medical Center of Brooklyn & Queens.
St. John's Regional Health Center, [C], (SPC), Springfield, MO.
St. John's Regional Medical Center, [K], (LA), Oxnard, CA.
St. John's Regional Medical Center; Mercy Lifecare Systems, Inc., [C], (SPC), Joplin, MO.
St. John's Residence, [P], (PRO), Woonsocket, RI.
St. John's Residence and School for Boys, [O], (BRK), Rockaway Park, NY.
St. John's Rest Home, [C], (SAL), Victoria, KS.
St. John's Retreat House and Rest Home, [M], (CAM), Atlantic City, NJ.
St. John's School, [E], (DUB), New Hampton, IA.
St. John's Seminary, [A], (BO), Boston, MA.
St. John's Seminary, [A], (LA), Camarillo, CA.
St. John's Seminary, [A], (SCL), Collegeville, MN.
St. John's Seminary College of the Archdiocese of Los Angeles, [A], (LA), Camarillo, CA.
St. John's Seminary School of Theology, [A], (BO), Boston, MA.
St. John's Seminary, Inc., [O], (KC), Kansas City, MO.
St. John's Soup Kitchen, Inc., [L], (MOB), Montgomery, AL.
St. John's University, [D], (BRK), Queens and Staten Island, NY.
St. John's University, [D], (BRK), Jamaica, NY.
St. John's University, [CC], (NY). See University Apostolate.
St. John's University, [B], (SCL), Collegeville, MN.
St. John's University Parish and Catholic Student Center, [I], (TLS), Stillwater, OK.
St. John's University Staten Island Campus, [C], (NY), Staten Island, NY.
St. John's Village, [E], (ALX), Moreauville, LA.
St. John/Holy Family School, [C], (KCK), Kansas City, KS.
St. John-Bon Secour Senior Community, Detroit, [H], (DET). See St. John Hospital and Medical Center.
St. Josaphat, [X], (CLV). See Diocesan Hispanic Office.
*St. Josaphat Basilica Foundation, Inc., [Y], (MIL), Milwaukee, WI.
St. Josaphat Convent, [A], (SJP), Parma, OH.
St. Josaphat Seminary, [A], (PHU), Washington, DC.
St. Josaphatis Monastery, Novitiate and Retreat House, [N], (RVC), Glen Cove, NY.
St. Joseph, [L], (ALB), Valatie, NY.
St. Joseph, [G], (BRK), Brooklyn, NY.
St. Joseph, [C], (BUR), Burlington, VT.
St. Joseph, [A], (CAM), Hammonton, NJ.
St. Joseph, [D], (CAM), Hammonton, NJ.
St. Joseph, [D], (CAM), Sea Isle City, NJ.
St. Joseph, [D], (LC). See Stevens Point Area Catholic Schools.
St. Joseph, [L], (RIC). See Ethnic and Special Ministries.
St. Joseph - St. John School, [C], (WIN). See Mankato Area Catholic Schools.
St. Joseph Abbey, [P], (NO), St. Benedict, LA.
St. Joseph Abbey, [P], (WOR), Spencer, MA.
St. Joseph Academy, [A], (BWN), Brownsville, TX
St. Joseph Academy, [E], (CLV), Cleveland, OH.
St. Joseph Academy, [F], (COV), Walton, KY.
St. Joseph Academy, [C], (HBG), McSherrystown, PA.
St. Joseph Academy, [A], (STA), St. Augustine, FL.
St. Joseph Academy Montessori Children's House, [C], (LAN), Adrian, MI.
St. Joseph Addictions Recovery Program, [Q], (CHL), Asheville, NC.
St. Joseph Adolescent & Family Counseling Center, [J], (DAL), Dallas, TX.
St. Joseph Adoration Monastery, Poor Clares of Perpetual Adoration, [I], (COL), Portsmouth, OH.
St. Joseph Adult Day Care Center, [G], (RCK), Freeport, IL.
St. Joseph Alpha Montessori Preschool, [J], (NO), New Orleans, LA.
St. Joseph and St. Mary Hospitals and Health Centers, [E], (TUC). See Carondelet Health Care Corporation of Arizona, Inc.
St. Joseph Apartments, Inc., [I], (STL). See Cardinal Ritter Institute.
St. Joseph Assisted Living Residence/Kervick Home, [F], (BUR), Rutland, VT.
St. Joseph Bohemian Orphanage, [X], (CHI), Chicago, IL.
St. Joseph by the Sea Retreat House, [Q], (TR), South Mantoloking, NJ.
St. Joseph by the Sea, High School, [F], (NY), New York, NY.
St. Joseph Camp, [J], (SR), Duncan Mills, CA.
St. Joseph Campus, [C], (AMA). See Amarillo Catholic Children's Development Centers.
St. Joseph Campus, [H], (MIL). See Waukesha Catholic School System, Inc.
St. Joseph Care Center, [G], (KCK), Kansas City, KS.
St. Joseph Care Center, [J], (SPK), Spokane, WA.
St. Joseph Care Center, [I], (Y), Louisville, OH.
St. Joseph Carmelite Home, [O], (STL), St. Charles, MO.
St. Joseph Cathedral Cemetery Fund, [M], (BR). See Baton Rouge Chancery Office.
St. Joseph Cathedral Elementary & Junior High School, [C], (SFS). See Sioux Falls Catholic School System.
St. Joseph Cathedral Trust, [M], (BR). See Baton Rouge Chancery Office.
St. Joseph Catholic Cemetery Association, [I], (DM), Council Bluffs, IA.
St. Joseph Catholic Community Services, [W], (STL). See Catholic Community Services Administration.
St. Joseph Catholic High School, [B], (SLC), Ogden, UT.
St. Joseph Catholic Housing - Heritage, Inc., [I], (SFS). See St. Joseph Catholic Housing, Inc.
St. Joseph Catholic Housing - Northridge, Inc., [I], (SFS). See St. Joseph Catholic Housing, Inc.
St. Joseph Catholic Housing - Rolling Hills, Inc., [I], (SFS). See St. Joseph Catholic Housing, Inc.
St. Joseph Catholic Housing - West Creek Woods, Inc., [I], (SFS). See St. Joseph Catholic Housing, Inc.
St. Joseph Catholic Housing, Inc., [I], (SFS), Sioux Falls, SD.
St. Joseph Catholic Orphan Society, [G], (L), Louisville, KY.
St. Joseph Catholic School, [A], (JKS), Jackson, MS.
St. Joseph Center, [E], (ALN), Pottsville, PA.
St. Joseph Center, [G], (CHI). See Catholic Charities of the Archdiocese of Chicago-Archdiocesan Offices.
St. Joseph Center, [N], (CIN), Cincinnati, OH.
St. Joseph Center, [K], (GBG), Greensburg, PA.
St. Joseph Center, [CC], (LA), Venice, CA.
St. Joseph Center for Health & Human Services, [K], (PRO). See St. Joseph Health Services of Rhode Island - St. Joseph Hospital for Specialty Care.
St. Joseph Center For Life, Inc., [E], (SAV), Augusta, GA.
St. Joseph Center for Poor and Needy, Inc., [G], (BGP). See Catholic Charities of Fairfield County.
St. Joseph Center for Psychiatric Services, [K], (PRO). See St. Joseph Health Services of Rhode Island - St. Joseph Hospital for Specialty Care.
St. Joseph Center: Sisters of St. Joseph, [F], (LFT), Tipton, IN.
St. Joseph Center-Mount St. Joseph, [G], (WH), Wheeling, WV.
St. Joseph Central, [C], (STU), Ironton, OH.
St. Joseph Central Catholic High School, [B], (TOL), Fremont, OH.
St. Joseph Central Catholic High School, [B], (WH), Huntington, WV.
St. Joseph Central High School, [C], (SPR), Pittsfield, MA.
St. Joseph Child Care Center, [F], (PRT), Auburn, ME.
St. Joseph Child Development Center, [F], (L), Louisville, KY.
St. Joseph Children's Home, [G], (L), Louisville, KY.
St. Joseph Christian Life Center, [U], (CLV), Cleveland, OH.
St. Joseph Church Educational Endowment Trust, [N], (OM). See The Omaha Archdiocesan Educational Foundation, Inc.
St. Joseph Church of Howell Trust Fund (St. Joseph Church, Howell), [K], (LAN). See Chancery Office.
Saint Joseph College, [C], (HRT), West Hartford, CT.
St. Joseph College, [N], (HRT). See Sisters of Mercy of the Americas of Connecticut.
Saint Joseph College of Nursing, [A], (JOL), Joliet, IL.
St. Joseph College of Nursing, [G], (JOL). See St. Joseph Medical Center.
St. Joseph College, Orange, [B], (ORG), Orange, CA.
St. Joseph Community, [G], (TUC), Tucson, AZ.
St. Joseph Community Hospital, [H], (DUB), New Hampton, IA.
*St. Joseph Community Hospital, [F], (FTW), Mishawaka, IN.
St. Joseph Congregational Home, [J], (LC), Stevens Point, WI.
St. Joseph Consolidated School, [G], (CIN), Hamilton, OH.
St. Joseph Convent, [L], (ALN), Bethlehem, PA.
St. Joseph Convent, [L], (ALN), Mahanoy City, PA.
St. Joseph Convent, [I], (BR), Baton Rouge, LA.
St. Joseph Convent, [I], (HBG), Harrisburg, PA.
St. Joseph Convent, [I], (HON). See St. Francis Convent.
St. Joseph Convent, [N], (HRT), Suffield, CT.
St. Joseph Convent, [N], (HRT), New Haven, CT.
St. Joseph Convent, [N], (HRT). See Sisters of Mercy of the Americas of Connecticut.
St. Joseph Convent, [N], (HRT), Meriden, CT.
St. Joseph Convent, [J], (LC), Chippewa Falls, WI.
St. Joseph Convent, [D], (LUB), Lubbock, TX.
St. Joseph Convent, [I], (MET), Woodbridge, NJ.
St. Joseph Convent, [Q], (MIL), Campbellsport, WI.
St. Joseph Convent, [N], (PAT), Passaic, NJ.
St. Joseph Convent, [AA], (PH), Philadelphia, PA.
St. Joseph Convent, [AA], (PH), Drexel Hill, PA.
St. Joseph Convent, [AA], (PH), Springfield, PA.
St. Joseph Convent, [O], (PIT), Baden, PA.
St. Joseph Convent, [J], (PRT), Bangor, ME.
Saint Joseph Convent, [O], (RVC), Brentwood, NY.
St. Joseph Convent, [G], (TUC), Nogales, AZ.
St. Joseph Convent, [O], (WOR), Webster, MA.
St. Joseph Convent Infirmary, [J], (ROC), Rochester, NY.
St. Joseph Convent, General Motherhouse of the School Sisters of St. Francis, [Q], (MIL), Milwaukee, WI.
St. Joseph Corporate Care, [K], (PRO), Providence, RI.
St. Joseph Corporation, [O], (GB), Green Bay, WI.
St. Joseph Cupertino Friary, Friars Minor Conventual of St. Francis of Assisi, [M], (BAL), Ellicott City, MD.
St. Joseph Cupertino Province, Provincial Center, [G], (MRY), Arroyo Grande, CA.
St. Joseph dba St. Brendan Continuing Care Center, [J], (SPK), Spokane, WA.
St. Joseph Development Foundation, [P], (Y), Warren, OH.
St. Joseph Diner, [N], (LAF). See Lafayette Catholic Service Centers, Inc.
St. Joseph Diocesan Regional Junior High Building, [E], (MAN), Manchester, NH.
St. Joseph Distribution Center, [N], (LAF). See Lafayette Catholic Service Centers, Inc.
St. Joseph Educational Center, [A], (DM), West Des Moines, IA.
St. Joseph Educational Child Care Center, [M], (STL), Kirkwood, MO.
St. Joseph Educational Trust Fund (St. Joseph Church, Owosso), [K], (LAN). See Chancery Office.
St. Joseph Educational Trust Fund (St. Joseph Church, St Johns), [K], (LAN). See Chancery Office.
St. Joseph Elementary, [B], (GAY), East Tawas, MI.
St. Joseph Elementary, [B], (GAY), West Branch, MI.
St. Joseph Elementary School, [D], (HEL), Missoula, MT.
St. Joseph Emergency Shelter, [I], (DM), Des Moines, IA.
St. Joseph Endowment Trust, [M], (LC), St. Joseph Ridge, WI.
Saint Joseph Foundation for Apostolic and Charitable Purposes, [E], (SAL). See Nazareth Motherhouse for the Sisters of St. Joseph, Concordia.
Saint Joseph Foundation of Kokomo, Indiana, Inc., [C], (LFT). See Saint Joseph Hospital & Health Center of Kokomo, Indiana, Inc.
St. Joseph Friary, [F], (ALT), Hollidaysburg, PA.
St. Joseph Friary, [N], (CHI), Chicago, IL.
St. Joseph Friary, [I], (GB), Appleton, WI.
St. Joseph Friary, [Z], (NY), New Paltz, NY.

Saint Joseph Guild, [EE], (PH), Flourtown, PA.
St. Joseph Hall, [H], (AUS), Austin, TX.
St. Joseph Hall, [K], (FTW). See Our Lady of Holy Cross Convent.
St. Joseph Health Care Foundation, Inc., [AA], (CLV), Lorain, OH.
Saint Joseph Health Center, [G], (KC), Kansas City, MO.
St. Joseph Health Center, [K], (STL), St. Charles, MO.
St. Joseph Health Center, [G], (Y), Warren, OH.
St. Joseph Health Center and St. Joseph Hospital West Foundation, [W], (STL), St. Charles, MO.
Saint Joseph Health Center Foundation, [G], (KC). See Saint Joseph Health Center.
St. Joseph Health Corporation, [E], (WCH), Wichita, KS.
St. Joseph Health Services of Rhode Island - Our Lady of Fatima Hospital, [K], (PRO), North Providence, RI.
St. Joseph Health Services of Rhode Island - St. Joseph Hospital for Specialty Care, [K], (PRO), Providence, RI.
St. Joseph Health System, [F], (ORG), Orange, CA.
St. Joseph Health System, [D], (SB). See St. Mary Regional Medical Center.
St. Joseph Health System, A Sisters of St. Joseph of Orange Corporation, [F], (ORG), Orange, CA.
St. Joseph Healthcare System, [F], (SFE), Albuquerque, NM.
St. Joseph Heights Provincialate and Novitiate of the Sisters of Notre Dame, [M], (COV), Covington, KY.
St. Joseph High School, [C], (BGP), Trumbull, CT.
St. Joseph High School, [D], (CHI), Westchester, IL.
Saint Joseph High School, [D], (LA), Lakewood, CA.
St. Joseph High School, [D], (LA), Santa Maria, CA.
St. Joseph High School, [B], (LR), Conway, AK.
St. Joseph High School, [B], (MET), Metuchen, NJ.
St. Joseph High School, [D], (MIL), Kenosha, WI.
St. Joseph High School, [A], (STV), St. Croix, VI.
St. Joseph High School, [A], (VIC), Victoria, TX.
St. Joseph High School Convent, [K], (FTW). See Our Lady of Holy Cross Convent.
St. Joseph High School Endowment Trust, [N], (OM). See The Omaha Archdiocesan Educational Foundation, Inc.
St. Joseph Hill Academy, [F], (NY), Staten Island, NY.
St. Joseph Hill Academy Elementary, [H], (NY), New York, NY.
St. Joseph Hill Infirmary, Inc., [O], (STL), Eureka, MO.
St. Joseph Home, [O], (NEW). See St. Joseph Province Shalom Center.
St. Joseph Home, [D], (SHP), Monroe, LA.
St. Joseph Home Convent, [I], (CC), Corpus Christi, TX.
St. Joseph Home for Children, Inc., [E], (LAN), Jackson, MI.
St. Joseph Home for the Aged, [K], (L), Louisville, KY.
St. Joseph Home for the Aged, [X], (PH), Holland, PA.
St. Joseph Home for the Aged, [G], (RCK), Freeport, IL.
St. Joseph Home for the Blind, [O], (NEW). See St. Joseph Province Shalom Center.
St. Joseph Home of Chicago, Inc., [M], (CHI), Chicago, IL.
St. Joseph Hospital, [E], (BEL), Breese, IL.
St. Joseph Hospital, [K], (BUF), Cheektowaga, NY.
St. Joseph Hospital, [J], (CHI), Chicago, IL.
St. Joseph Hospital, [H], (DEN), Denver, CO.
St. Joseph Hospital, [J], (GAL), Houston, TX.
St. Joseph Hospital, [F], (HBG), Lancaster, PA.
St. Joseph Hospital, [D], (LEX), Lexington, KY.
St. Joseph Hospital, [I], (MAN), Nashua, NH.
St. Joseph Hospital, [F], (MEM), Memphis, TN.
St. Joseph Hospital, [H], (PRT), Bangor, ME.
Saint Joseph Hospital, [D], (RCK), Belvidere, IL.
St. Joseph Hospital, [D], (RCK), Elgin, IL.
St. Joseph Hospital, [G], (SEA), Bellingham, WA.
St. Joseph Hospital, [E], (TUC). See Carondelet Health Care Corporation of Arizona, Inc.
St. Joseph Hospital and Health Center, [A], (TYL), Paris, TX.
St. Joseph Hospital and Health Center of Bryan, Inc., [F], (AUS), Bryan, TX.
Saint Joseph Hospital & Health Center of Kokomo, Indiana, Inc., [C], (LFT), Kokomo, IN.
St. Joseph Hospital Auxiliary, [D], (RCK). See St. Joseph Hospital.
St. Joseph Hospital Convent, [K], (CHL), Asheville, NC.
St. Joseph Hospital Corporation, [E], (HEL), Polson, MT.
Saint Joseph Hospital Foundation, [Q], (DEN), Denver, CO.
St. Joseph Hospital Foundation, [D], (RCK). See St. Joseph Hospital.
St. Joseph Hospital of Eureka, [G], (SR), Eureka, CA.
St. Joseph Hospital of Kirkwood, [K], (STL), Kirkwood, MO.
St. Joseph Hospital of Kirkwood Foundation, [W], (STL), Kirkwood, MO.
St. Joseph Hospital of Mishawaka Foundation, Inc., [O], (FTW), Mishawaka, IN.
St. Joseph Hospital of Orange, [F], (ORG), Orange, CA.
St. Joseph Hospital West, [K], (STL), Lake St. Louis, MO.
St. Joseph Hospital, Augusta, GA, Inc., [E], (SAV), Augusta, GA.
St. Joseph House by the Sea, [M], (CAM), Ventnor, NJ.
St. Joseph House of Formation, [P], (MIL), Milwaukee, WI.
St. Joseph Housing Corporation, [X], (PH), Philadelphia, PA.
*Saint Joseph Huron Home Health and Hospice, [C], (GAY), Tawas City, MI.
St. Joseph Indian School, [B], (SFS), Chamberlain, SD.
St. Joseph Indian School, [F], (SFS). See Priests of the Sacred Heart.
St. Joseph Infant and Maternity Home dba St. Joseph Home, [I], (CIN), Cincinnati, OH.
St. Joseph Institute for the Deaf, [H], (STL), University City, MO.
St. Joseph Intermediate Regional School, [H], (PRO), Woonsocket, RI.
St. Joseph Junior-Senior High School, [C], (HON), Hilo, HI.
St. Joseph Junior-Senior High School, [A], (JKS), Greenville, MS.
St. Joseph Living Center, [E], (NOR), Windham, CT.
St. Joseph Living Center, [M], (PRO), Providence, RI.
St. Joseph Manor, [M], (BUF), Olean, NY.
St. Joseph Manor, [E], (HT), Thibodaux, LA.
St. Joseph Manor, [I], (MEM), Dyersburg, TN.
St. Joseph Manor, [D], (PBL), Florence, CO.
St. Joseph Manor Nursing & Extended Care Facility, [U], (BO), Brockton, MA.
St. Joseph Manor Nursing Home, [C], (LIT), Brockton, MA.
Saint Joseph Medical Center, [G], (ALN), Reading, PA.
St. Joseph Medical Center, [I], (BAL), Baltimore, MD.
St. Joseph Medical Center, [I], (BGP), Stamford, CT.
St. Joseph Medical Center, [F], (FTW), Fort Wayne, IN.
St. Joseph Medical Center, [G], (JOL), Joliet, IL.
St. Joseph Medical Center, [J], (PEO), Bloomington, IL.
St. Joseph Medical Center, [G], (SEA), Tacoma, WA.
St. Joseph Medical Center, [F], (SFE), Albuquerque, NM.
St. Joseph Medical Center Corporation, [I], (BGP), Stamford, CT.
St. Joseph Medical Center Foundation, [G], (JOL). See St. Joseph Medical Center.
St. Joseph Medical Center Foundation, Inc., [I], (BGP), Stamford, CT.
St. Joseph Medical Center of Fort Wayne, Inc., [O], (FTW), Fort Wayne, IN.
St. Joseph Medical Center Physical Rehabilitation and Sports Injury Center, [G], (JOL). See St. Joseph Medical Center.
St. Joseph Medical Center Women Auxiliary, [G], (JOL). See St. Joseph Medical Center.
St. Joseph Memorial Hospital, [E], (BEL), Murphysboro, IL.
St. Joseph Mercy - Oakland, [H], (DET), Pontiac, MI.
St. Joseph Mercy Hospital, [F], (LAN), Ann Arbor, MI.
St. Joseph Mercy Living Care Center, [I], (DET), Mount Clemens, MI.
St. Joseph Monastery, [H], (TLS), Tulsa, OK.
St. Joseph Montessori School, [D], (COL), Columbus, OH.
St. Joseph Motherhouse and Novitiate, [N], (PEO), Lacon, IL.
St. Joseph Nazareth Residence, [E], (SR). See Diocese of Santa Rosa, Catholic Charities.
St. Joseph Nazareth Residence, [I], (SR), Fortuna, CA.
St. Joseph Northeast Heights Hospital, [F], (SFE), Albuquerque, NM.
Saint Joseph Notre Dame High School, [D], (OAK), Alameda, CA.
Saint Joseph Novitiate, [O], (RVC), Brentwood, NY.
St. Joseph Novitiate-Franciscan Friars, [K], (FR), Onset, MA.
St. Joseph Nursing and Health Care Center, Inc., [J], (PIT). See Pittsburgh Mercy Health System, Inc.
St. Joseph Nursing and Health Care Center, Inc., [L], (PIT), Pittsburgh, PA.
St. Joseph Nursing Care Center, [U], (BO), Boston, MA.
St. Joseph Nursing Home, [C], (LIT), Holland, PA.
St. Joseph Nursing Home, [H], (OM), Norfolk, NE.
St. Joseph Nursing Home, [P], (SY), Utica, NY.
St. Joseph of Arimathia Guild, [G], (SPR). See Providence Ministries for the Needy, Inc.
St. Joseph of Cluny Sisters' School, Inc., [F], (PRO), Newport, RI.
St. Joseph of the Pines Convent, [F], (R), Southern Pines, NC.
St. Joseph of the Pines Home Health Agency, [I], (R), Pinehurst, NC.
St. Joseph of the Pines Hospital, [C], (R), Southern Pines, NC.
St. Joseph of the Pines Retirement Villa, [I], (R), Southern Pines, NC.
St. Joseph of the Valley, [H], (ELP), El Paso, TX.
St. Joseph Orphanage, [I], (CIN), Cincinnati, OH.
St. Joseph Parish Conference, [E], (YAK), Kennewick, WA.
St. Joseph Parish Conference, [E], (YAK), White Salmon, WA.
St. Joseph Parish Conference, St Vincent de Paul, [E], (YAK), Wenatchee, WA.
St. Joseph Parish Endowment Trust, [M], (LC), Stratford, WI.
St. Joseph Parish, R.E. Program, [B], (CR), Ada, MN.
St. Joseph Pre-School, [J], (NEW), Ramsey, NJ.
St. Joseph Pre-School, [B], (R), Raleigh, NC.
St. Joseph Priory, [I], (GB), De Pere, WI.
St. Joseph Priory, [O], (OAK). See Dominican Sisters of Mission San Jose.
St. Joseph Province Shalom Center, [O], (NEW), Englewood Cliffs, NJ.
St. Joseph Provincial House, [X], (BO), Lowell, MA.
St. Joseph Provincialate, [AA], (NY), New York, NY.
St. Joseph Rectory, [M], (HRT). See DePaul Provincial Residence.
St. Joseph Rectory, [M], (HRT). See St. Patrick-St. Anthony Friary.
St. Joseph Rectory, [M], (HRT), New Haven, CT.
St. Joseph Rectory, [M], (HRT), New Haven, CT.
St. Joseph Regional Academy, [D], (ALN), Jim Thorpe, PA.
St. Joseph Regional High School, [D], (NEW), Montvale, NJ.
St. Joseph Regional Medical Center, [B], (B), Lewiston, ID.
St. Joseph Regional Medical Center, [E], (OKL), Ponca City, OK.
St. Joseph Regional School, [E], (MAN), Salem, NH.
St. Joseph Regional School, [F], (PAT), Newton, NJ.
St. Joseph Regional School, [F], (PIT), Port Vue, PA.
St. Joseph Regional School, [C], (SLC), Ogden, UT.
St. Joseph Rehabilitation Hospital, [F], (SFE), Albuquerque, NM.
St. Joseph Renewal Center, [M], (TOL), Tiffin, OH.
St. Joseph Residence, [J], (DAL), Dallas, TX.
St. Joseph Residence, [G], (RVC). See St. Christopher-Ottilie Corp.
St. Joseph Residence for Mother and Child, [G], (BGP). See Catholic Charities of Fairfield County.
St. Joseph Residence, Inc., [J], (TLS), Tulsa, OK.
St. Joseph Residence, Inc., New London, [H], (GB), New London, WI.
St. Joseph Rest Home for Aged Women, [K], (PAT), Paterson, NJ.
St. Joseph Retreat Center, [M], (GB), Baileys Harbor, WI.
St. Joseph School, [B], (CC), Alice, TX.
St. Joseph School, [I], (CC). See Religious Missionaries of St. Dominic, Inc.
St. Joseph School, [I], (CC). See Religious Missionaries of St. Dominic, Inc.
St. Joseph School, [C], (GLP), San Fidel, NM.
St. Joseph School, [E], (MAN), Keene, NH.
St. Joseph School, [C], (OWN), Bowling Green, KY.
The St. Joseph School at Menomonie Endowment Trust, [M], (LC), Menomonie, WI.
St. Joseph School Education Endowment Fund, [C], (DOD), Ellinwood, KS.
St. Joseph School Endowment Trust, [J], (TLS), Muskogee, OK.
St. Joseph School for the Blind, [O], (NEW). See St. Joseph Province Shalom Center.
St. Joseph School Foundation, Florence, [I], (BIR), Florence, AL.
St. Joseph Seminary, [A], (CHI), Chicago, IL.
St. Joseph Seminary (Josephite Fathers' Novitiate), [B], (LA), Santa Maria, CA.
St. Joseph Seminary Corporation, [P], (SJ), Santa Clara, CA.
St. Joseph Senior Community, Inc., [C], (SAL), Manhattan, KS.
St. Joseph Senior Residence, [G], (MET), Woodbridge, NJ.
St. Joseph Services for Children and Families, [O], (BRK), Brooklyn, NY.
St. Joseph Shelter for Men, [N], (LAF). See Lafayette Catholic Service Centers, Inc.
St. Joseph Society of the Sacred Heart House of Central Administration, [M], (BAL), Baltimore, MD.
St. Joseph Spiritual Life Center, [O], (ALB), Valatie, NY.
St. Joseph the Worker, [J], (PHX), Phoenix, AZ.
St. Joseph the Worker Center, [P], (SJ), Mountain View, CA.
St. Joseph the Worker Community, [I], (HON). See Sisters of St. Joseph of Carondelet CSJ, Hawaii Vice-Province.

St. Joseph the Worker Convent, [AA], (PH), Philadelphia, PA.
St. Joseph the Worker Convent, [G], (SLC), West Jordan, UT.
St. Joseph Tridentine Chapel, [L], (RIC). See Ethnic and Special Ministries.
St. Joseph Villa, [L], (ALN), Reading, PA.
St. Joseph Villa, [I], (CIN). See St. Joseph Orphanage.
St. Joseph Villa, [U], (PH), Flourtown, PA.
St. Joseph Villa, [E], (SLC), Salt Lake City, UT.
St. Joseph Villa Convent, [G], (SLC), Salt Lake City, UT.
St. Joseph West Mesa Hospital, [F], (SFE), Albuquerque, NM.
St. Joseph's Mercy Foundation, [H], (DET). See Mercy Mount Clemens Corporation.
St. Joseph's Abbey, [N], (WOR), Spencer, MA.
St. Joseph's Abbey School of Theology and Institute of Monastic Studies, [A], (WOR), Spencer, MA.
St. Joseph's Academy, [C], (BR), Baton Rouge, LA.
St. Joseph's Academy, [F], (STL), St. Louis, MO.
St. Joseph's Adult Day Care Center, Inc., [N], (MIL), Kenosha, WI.
St. Joseph's Apartment, Inc., [M], (SCL), St. Cloud, MN.
St. Joseph's Area Health Services, [C], (CR), Park Rapids, MN.
St. Joseph's Behavioral Health Center, [C], (STO), Stockton, CA.
Saint Joseph's Care Foundation, Inc., [O], (FTW), South Bend, IN.
Saint Joseph's Care Group, Inc., [O], (FTW), South Bend, IN.
St. Joseph's Carmelite Monastery, [N], (SEA), Seattle, WA.
St. Joseph's Carmelite Monastery, Discalced Carmelite Nuns, [G], (OG), Saranac Lake, NY.
St. Joseph's Carondelet Child Center, [L], (CHI), Chicago, IL.
St. Joseph's Center, [A], (DM). See Shelby County Board of Catholic Education.
St. Joseph's Center, [BB], (NY), Bronx, NY.
St. Joseph's Center, [DD], (NY), Bronx, NY.
St. Joseph's Center, [J], (SCR), Scranton, PA.
St. Joseph's Center for Deaf and Hard of Hearing, [L], (OAK), Union City, CA.
St. Joseph's Children's Home, [A], (CHY), Torrington, WY.
*St. Joseph's College, [D], (BRK), Brooklyn, NY.
Saint Joseph's College, [A], (LFT), Rensselaer, IN.
Saint Joseph's College, [A], (PRT), Standish, ME.
Saint Joseph's College, [M], (PRT), Standish, ME.
St. Joseph's College, [B], (RVC), Patchogue, NY.
St. Joseph's Collegiate Institute, [D], (BUF), Buffalo, NY.
St. Joseph's Community, [K], (SAT), San Antonio, TX.
St. Joseph's Convent, [F], (CHR), Conway, SC.
St. Joseph's Convent, [L], (DET), Ida, MI.
St. Joseph's Convent, [K], (FTW). See Saint Mary's of the Immaculate Conception.
St. Joseph's Convent, [C], (JUN), Juneau, AK.
St. Joseph's Convent, [N], (PAT), Hewitt, NJ.
St. Joseph's Convent, [J], (PRT), Biddeford, ME.
St. Joseph's Convent, [O], (WH), Wheeling, WV.
St. Joseph's Convent - S.S.N.D. House of Formation, [N], (SAT), San Antonio, TX.
St. Joseph's Convent - Sisters of St. Mary of Namur, [P], (BUF), Lockport, NY.
St. Joseph's Convent of Mercy, [R], (STL), St. Louis, MO.
St. Joseph's Convent of Mercy of St. Louis, [R], (STL). See Sisters of Mercy of the Americas, Regional Community of St. Louis.
St. Joseph's Convent, Grey Nuns of the Sacred Heart, [G], (OG), Ogdensburg, NY.
St. Joseph's Convent, Mount Carmel, [L], (DUB), Dubuque, IA.
St. Joseph's Convent, Sisters of St. Joseph, [G], (OG), Massena, NY.
St. Joseph's Convent-Day Care Center, [AA], (NY), Monroe, NY.
St. Joseph's Counseling Center, [H], (SPK), Spokane, WA.
St. Joseph's Cupertino Novitiate, [G], (MRY), Arroyo Grande, CA.
St. Joseph's Day Care Center, [D], (LR), North Little Rock, AR.
St. Joseph's Day Nursery & Kindergarten, [H], (ARL), Falls Church, VA.
St. Joseph's Day Training Center, [H], (BUF). See The Catholic Charities of the Diocese of Buffalo.
St. Joseph's Education Trust, [K], (GF), Great Falls, MT.
St. Joseph's Farm, [O], (FTW), Granger, IN.
St. Joseph's Foundation of Buckhannon, Inc., [H], (WH). See St. Joseph's Hospital of Buckhannon, Inc.
St. Joseph's Foundation of Paris, Texas, [A], (TYL). See St. Joseph Hospital and Health Center.
St. Joseph's Foundation, Inc., [J], (OG), Ogdensburg, NY.
St. Joseph's Friary, [Z], (NY). See Saint Felix Friary.
St. Joseph's Friary, [Z], (NY), New York, NY.
St. Joseph's Friary, [F], (OG), Saranac Lake, NY.
St. Joseph's Friary, [D], (SAL), Hays, KS.
St. Joseph's Friary, [M], (SCR), Wilkes-Barre, PA.
St. Joseph's Group Home, [D], (BUR), Burlington, VT.
St. Joseph's Guest Home for the Aged, Inc., [J], (RVC), Huntington, NY.
St. Joseph's Hall, [K], (FR), North Dartmouth, MA.
St. Joseph's Health and Retirement Center, [L], (LA), Ojai, CA.
St. Joseph's Health and Retirement Center, [R], (LA). See Brothers of John of God, Inc., The.
St. Joseph's Health Foundation, Inc., [O], (FTW), Fort Wayne, IN.
St. Joseph's Health Services Corporation, [E], (CHL), Asheville, NC.
Saint Joseph's Health System, Inc., [M], (ATL), Atlanta, GA.
Saint Joseph's High School, [C], (FTW), South Bend, IN.
St. Joseph's Home, [J], (DET), Detroit, MI.
St. Joseph's Home, [D], (JC), Jefferson City, MO.
St. Joseph's Home, [H], (MAD), Watertown, WI.
St. Joseph's Home, [K], (NEW), Jersey City, NJ.
St. Joseph's Home, [E], (OG), Ogdensburg, NY.
St. Joseph's Home, [J], (SFD), Springfield, IL.
St. Joseph's Home, [D], (STF), Sloatsburg, NY.
St. Joseph's Home (Residence for Women), [O], (WOR), Worcester, MA.
St. Joseph's Home for Aged, [F], (BUR), Burlington, VT.
St. Joseph's Home for Boys, [N], (STL), St. Louis, MO.
St. Joseph's Home for Children, [I], (STP), Minneapolis, MN.
St. Joseph's Home for Retired Priests, [D], (AMA), Panhandle, TX.
St. Joseph's Home for the Aged, [N], (MIL), Kenosha, WI.
St. Joseph's Home for the Aged, [M], (NOR), Willimantic, CT.
St. Joseph's Home for the Aged, [H], (RIC), Richmond, VA.
St. Joseph's Home for the Blind, [I] (NEW), Jersey City, NJ.
St. Joseph's Home for the Elderly, [M], (CHI), Palatine, IL.
St. Joseph's Home for the Elderly, [K], (PAT), Totowa, NJ.
St. Joseph's Home of Peoria, [L], (PEO), Peoria, IL.
St. Joseph's HomeCare, [H], (DET). See Mercy Mount Clemens Corporation.
St. Joseph's Hospital, [E], (CHL), Asheville, NC.
St. Joseph's Hospital, [E], (LC), Chippewa Falls, WI.
St. Joseph's Hospital, [E], (LC), Marshfield, WI.
St. Joseph's Hospital, [H], (ROC), Elmira, NY.
St. Joseph's Hospital, [E], (SAV), Savannah, GA.
St. Joseph's Hospital, [H], (SFD), Highland, IL.
St. Joseph's Hospital and Health Center, [D], (BIS), Dickinson, ND.
St. Joseph's Hospital and Medical Center, [J], (PAT), Paterson, NJ.
St. Joseph's Hospital and Medical Center, [C], (PHX), Phoenix, AZ.
St. Joseph's Hospital dba UniMed Medical Center, [D], (BIS), Minot, ND.
St. Joseph's Hospital Division, [N], (BRK). See Catholic Medical Center of Brooklyn & Queens.
St. Joseph's Hospital Foundation, Inc., [H], (ROC), Elmira, NY.
St. Joseph's Hospital Health Center, [O], (SY), Syracuse, NY.
Saint Joseph's Hospital of Atlanta, Inc., [G], (ATL), Atlanta, GA.
St. Joseph's Hospital of Buckhannon, Inc., [H], (WH), Buckhannon, WV.
St. Joseph's Hospital of Chewelah, [G], (SPK), Chewelah, WA.
St. Joseph's Hospital of Franciscan Sisters, Milwaukee, Inc., [K], (MIL), Milwaukee, WI.
Saint Joseph's Hospital of Marshall County, Inc., [F], (FTW), Plymouth, IN.
St. Joseph's Hospital of Parkersburg, Inc., [R], (WH), Wheeling, WV.
St. Joseph's Hospital Sponsor, Inc., [W], (STP), St. Paul, MN.
St. Joseph's Hospital, Inc., [K], (SP), Tampa, FL.
St. Joseph's House, [M], (SCR), Little Meadows, PA.
St. Joseph's House for Boys, [K], (PH), Philadelphia, PA.
St. Joseph's House of Hospitality, [L], (ROC), Rochester, NY.
St. Joseph's House of Hospitality, Inc., [R], (PIT), Pittsburgh, PA.
St. Joseph's Housing Corporation, [K], (BGP), Trumbull, CT.
St. Joseph's Immigrant Home, [W], (NY), New York, NY.
St. Joseph's in the Hills, [BB], (PH), Malvern, PA.
St. Joseph's Inn, [I], (GAL). See Associated Catholic Charities of the Diocese of Galveston-Houston.
St. Joseph's Manor, [M], (BAL), Baltimore, MD.
St. Joseph's Manor, [K], (BGP), Trumbull, CT.
St. Joseph's Manor, [X], (PH). See Redeemer Long Term Care & Elder Services.
St. Joseph's Manor, [G], (PRT), Portland, ME.
St. Joseph's Medical Center, [C], (DUL), Brainerd, MN.
St. Joseph's Medical Center, [S], (NY), Yonkers, NY.
St. Joseph's Medical Center of Stockton, [C], (STO), Stockton, CA.
St. Joseph's Medical Center, Brainerd, [G], (DUL). See Benedictine Sisters Benevolent Association.
Saint Joseph's Medical Center, Inc., [F], (FTW), South Bend, IN.
St. Joseph's Medical Centers, [H], (DET). See Mercy Mount Clemens Corporation.
St. Joseph's Memorial Hospital, Inc., [E], (LC), Hillsboro, WI.
St. Joseph's Mercy - East, [H], (DET). See Mercy Mount Clemens Corporation.
St. Joseph's Mercy - North, [H], (DET). See Mercy Mount Clemens Corporation.
St. Joseph's Mercy - West, [H], (DET). See Mercy Mount Clemens Corporation.
Saint Joseph's Mercy Care Services, [H], (ATL), Atlanta, GA.
Saint Joseph's Mercy Foundation, [M], (ATL), Atlanta, GA.
St. Joseph's Mercy Healthier Image, [H], (DET). See Mercy Mount Clemens Corporation.
St. Joseph's Mercy Hospital, [J], (DAV), Centerville, IA.
St. Joseph's Monastery, [G], (OWN), Whitesville, KY.
St. Joseph's Monastery of the Poor Clares (Colettines), [H], (MRY), Aptos, CA.
St. Joseph's Novitiate, [B], (LA), Los Angeles, CA.
St. Joseph's Novitiate, Franciscan Hospitaller Sisters of the Immaculate Conception, [N], (SJ), San Jose, CA.
St. Joseph's Nursery School, [K], (CAM), Camden, NJ.
St. Joseph's Nursing Home, [K], (BAL), Baltimore, MD.
St. Joseph's Nursing Home, [G], (LC), La Crosse, WI.
St. Joseph's Nursing Home, [G], (LC), Hillsboro, WI.
St. Joseph's Nursing Home, [K], (PEO), Lacon, IL.
St. Joseph's Oblate Seminary, [B], (SCR), Pittston, PA.
St. Joseph's of Buckhannon, Inc., [K], (WH). See Pallottine Health Services, Inc.
St. Joseph's Parish Conference, [E], (YAK), Yakima, WA.
St. Joseph's Parish School Fund, Inc., Needham, [DD], (BO), Needham, MA.
St. Joseph's Passionist Community, [M], (BAL), Baltimore, MD.
St. Joseph's Plains Community Center, [E], (NTN), Lawrence, MA.
St. Joseph's Prayer Center, [P], (RVC), Melville, NY.
St. Joseph's Preparatory School, [G], (PH), Philadelphia, PA.
St. Joseph's Preparatory School Jesuit Community, Arrupe House, [Z], (PH), Philadelphia, PA.
St. Joseph's Priest Residence, [U], (BRK), Brooklyn, NY.
St. Joseph's Provincial House, [R], (STL), St. Louis, MO.
St. Joseph's Rectory, [H], (COL), Somerset, OH.
St. Joseph's Regional Health Center, [E], (LR), Hot Springs National Park, AR.
St. Joseph's Regional Health System of Northern San Joaquin Valley, [C], (STO), Stockton, CA.
St. Joseph's Regional Housing Corp., [D], (STO), Stockton, CA.
St. Joseph's Rehabilitation Center, Inc., [Z], (NY). See Generalate of the Franciscan Friars of the Atonement-St. James Friary.
St. Joseph's Rehabilitation Center, Inc., [E], (OG), Saranac Lake, NY.
St. Joseph's Residence, [U], (LA), Los Angeles, CA.
St. Joseph's Residence, [N], (SEA), Seattle, WA.
Saint Joseph's Residence, Inc., [Z], (NY), New Rochelle, NY.
St. Joseph's Salesian Youth Renewal Center, [W], (LA), Rosemead, CA.
St. Joseph's School, [B], (AMA), Amarillo, TX.
St. Joseph's School, [G], (SFR), Atherton, CA.
St. Joseph's School for the Blind, [E], (NEW), Jersey City, NJ.
St. Joseph's School for the Deaf, [H], (NY), Bronx, NY.
St. Joseph's School for the Deaf Development, Inc., [DD], (NY), Bronx, NY.
St. Joseph's Seminary, [C], (CHI). See Loyola University-Chicago.
St. Joseph's Seminary, [A], (NY), Yonkers, NY.
St. Joseph's Seminary, [B], (WDC), Washington, DC.
St. Joseph's Seminary College, [A], (NO), St. Benedict, LA.
St. Joseph's Shelter, [Q], (P), Mt. Angel, OR.
St. Joseph's Social Service Center, [S], (NEW), Elizabeth, NJ.
St. Joseph's Texas, School Endowment Trust, [P], (BAL). See Chancery Office.
St. Joseph's Union of Staten Island, New York Inc.,

[DD], (NY), New York, NY.
St. Joseph's University, [C], (PH), Philadelphia, PA.
St. Joseph's Urgent Care, Inc., [E], (CHL), Asheville, NC.
St. Joseph's Ursuline Academy, [D], (SFD), Springfield, IL.
St. Joseph's Ursuline Convent, Ursuline Nuns, [G], (OG), Malone, NY.
St. Joseph's Villa, [J], (ALB), Catskill, NY.
St. Joseph's Villa, [F], (RIC), Richmond, VA.
St. Joseph's Villa, [O], (RVC), Rockville Centre, NY.
St. Joseph's Villa Foundation, [L], (ROC), Rochester, NY.
St. Joseph's Villa Housing Corp, [I], (RIC), Richmond, VA.
St. Joseph's Villa Housing Corp., II, [I], (RIC). See St. Joseph's Villa Housing Corp.
St. Joseph's Villa of Rochester, [F], (ROC), Rochester, NY.
St. Joseph's Villa Retreat and Renewal Center, [O], (RVC), Hampton Bays, NY.
St. Joseph's Villa, Inc., [E], (LIN), David City, NE.
St. Joseph's Village, [Q], (SFR). See Catholic Charities of the Archdiocese of San Francisco.
St. Joseph's Vocational Center, [H], (STL), St. Louis, MO.
St. Joseph's-St. Patrick's College Alumni Association, [U], (SFR), Menlo Park, CA.
St. Joseph, Foster Parent, Friary, [J], (BUF). See The Franciscan Center, Inc.
St. Jude, [D], (CAM), Blackwood, NJ.
St. Jude Administration Building, [F], (MOB). See City of St. Jude, Inc., The.
St. Jude Apartments, [F], (MOB). See City of St. Jude, Inc., The.
St. Jude Baby Village, [J], (NO), New Orleans, LA.
St. Jude Center, [F], (DUB). See Holy Family Catholic Consolidated School.
St. Jude Church and Rectory, [F], (MOB). See City of St. Jude, Inc., The.
St. Jude Dominican Missions, [DD], (NY). See Dominican Friars' Guild.
St. Jude Elementary and High School, [F], (MOB). See City of St. Jude, Inc., The.
St. Jude Exceptional Children's Center, [F], (MOB). See City of St. Jude, Inc., The.
St. Jude Friary, [P], (CLV), Cleveland, OH.
St. Jude Head Start, [F], (MOB). See City of St. Jude, Inc., The.
St. Jude High School, [C], (MOB), Montgomery, AL.
St. Jude Home, Inc., [J], (DET), Waterford, MI.
St. Jude House, [P], (L). See Society of St. Vincent de Paul, Council of Louisville.
St. Jude Media Ministries, [P], (PAT), Passaic, NJ.
St. Jude Medical Center, [F], (ORG), Fullerton, CA.
St. Jude Memorial Foundation, [F], (ORG), Fullerton, CA.
St. Jude Mission, [H], (SLC), Ephraim, UT.
St. Jude Shrine Corporation, [P], (BAL). See Chancery Office.
St. Jude Social Services Center, [F], (MOB). See City of St. Jude, Inc., The.
St. Jude Thaddeus Convent, [G], (AGN), Sinajana, GU.
St. Jude the Apostle, [L], (NO), Gretna, LA.
St. Jude's Center, [G], (SPR). See Providence Ministries for the Needy, Inc.
St. Jude's Education Trust, [K], (GF), Havre, MT.
St. Jude, Inc., [J], (DAL), Dallas, TX.
St. Julie Convent, [O], (WOR), Leominster, MA.
Saint Jutta Foundation, Inc., [DD], (NY), Bronx, NY.
St. Katharine Convent, [F], (CHR), Charleston, SC.
St. Katherine Day School, [I], (PH), Wynnewood, PA.
St. Katherine of Sienna School, [F], (BAL). See Queen of Peace Elementary Cluster, St. James and St. John School.
St. Kim Taegon Church, [L], (RIC). See Ethnic and Special Ministries.
St. La Salle Auxiliary, [M], (LAF), Lafayette, LA.
St. Labre Home for Indian Children and Youth, [K], (GF), Ashland, MT.
St. Labre Indian Catholic Elementary School, [E], (GF), Ashland, MT.
St. Labre Indian Catholic High School, [C], (GF), Ashland, MT.
St. Labre Indian School Educational Association, [K], (GF), Ashland, MT.
St. Lambert Elementary School, [C], (SFS). See Sioux Falls Catholic School System.
The Saint LaSalle Auxiliary, [B], (WDC), Beltsville, MD.
St. Laurence Campus, [C], (AMA). See Amarillo Catholic Children's Development Centers.
St. Laurence Cathedral School, [B], (AMA), Amarillo, TX.
St. Laurence High School, Inc., [D], (CHI), Burbank, IL.
Saint Lawrence Academy, [C], (SJ), Santa Clara, CA.
St. Lawrence Catholic Campus Center at the University of Kansas and Residence, [J], (KCK), Lawrence, KS.
St. Lawrence Dimondale Center, [G], (LAN), Dimondale, MI.
St. Lawrence Friary, [P], (MIL), Mount Calvary, WI.
St. Lawrence Hospital and Healthcare Services, [F], (LAN), Lansing, MI.
St. Lawrence O'Toole Convent, [O], (OAK), Oakland, CA.
St. Lawrence of Brindisi Friary, [B], (NY), Beacon, NY.
St. Lawrence Seminary, [B], (MIL), Mount Calvary, WI.
St. Lawrence the Martyr Child Care Center, [J], (NO), Metairie, LA.
St. Lazare Retreat House, [J], (GR), Spring Lake, MI.
St. Lazare Retreat House, [Z], (PH). See Congregation of the Mission.
St. Leo Abbey, [O], (SP), St. Leo, FL.
St. Leo Abbey Retreat Center, [Q], (SP), St. Leo, FL.
Saint Leo College, [A], (SP), St. Leo, FL.
St. Leo School, Inc., [F], (MIL), Milwaukee, WI.
St. Leo's Catholic Education Trust, [K], (GF), Lewistown, MT.
St. Leo's School, [J], (BIS). See Minot Catholic Schools Corporation.
St. Leonard Faith Community, [V], (CIN), Centerville, OH.
St. Leonard Parish Endowment Trust, [N], (OM). See The Omaha Archdiocesan Educational Foundation, Inc.
St. Leonard's Home, Inc., [E], (ALT), Hollidaysburg, PA.
St. Louis, [J], (PRT), Fort Kent, ME.
St. Louis Catholic Charismatic Renewal, [W], (STL), St. Louis, MO.
St. Louis Center for Exceptional Children & Adults, [E], (LAN), Chelsea, MI.
St. Louis Center for Exceptional Children & Adults Endowment Trust Agreement (St. Louis Center, Chelsea), [K], (LAN). See Chancery Office.
St. Louis Child Care Center, [E], (PRT). See Catholic Charities Maine.
St. Louis Child Care Center, [E], (PRT). See Catholic Charities Maine.
St. Louis Community, Sisters of Charity of St. Louis, [G], (OG), Plattsburgh, NY.
St. Louis Extended, [G], (MEM), Memphis, TN.
St. Louis Friary, [M], (WDC), Washington, DC.
St. Louis Health Care Network, [W], (STL), St. Louis, MO.
St. Louis High School, [A], (LKC), Lake Charles, LA.
St. Louis Priory School, [F], (STL), Creve Coeur, MO.
St. Louis Priory School, [G], (STL), Creve Coeur, MO.
St. Louis Roman Catholic Landmark Corp., [W], (STL), St. Louis, MO.
*St. Louis School, [D], (HON), Honolulu, HI.
Saint Louis University, [C], (STL), St. Louis, MO.
St. Louis University High School Jesuit Community, [P], (STL), St. Louis, MO.
St. Louis University High School, George H. Backer Memorial, [F], (STL), St. Louis, MO.
Saint Louis University Hospital, [K], (STL), St. Louis, MO.
St. Louise Missionary Cenacle, [I], (MOB), Auburn, AL.
St. Lucian Home, [N], (HRT). See Motherhouse of Daughters of Mary of the Immaculate Conception.
St. Lucian's Home for the Aged, [K], (HRT), New Britain, CT.
St. Lucy Day School for Children with Visual Impairments, [I], (PH), Upper Darby, PA.
St. Lucy Filippini Academy, [E], (NEW), Newark, NJ.
St. Lucy's Day Care and Child Development Center, [B], (HT), Houma, LA.
St. Lucy's Priory, [S], (LA), Glendora, CA.
St. Lucys's Priory High School, [F], (LA), Glendora, CA.
St. Ludger Parish Endowment Trust, [N], (OM). See The Omaha Archdiocesan Educational Foundation, Inc.
St. Ludmila Center, [F], (DUB). See Holy Family Catholic Consolidated School.
St. Luke Early Childhood Center, [F], (SP), Palm Harbor, FL.
Saint Luke Institute, Inc., [V], (WDC), Silver Spring, MD.
St. Luke Manor, [M], (BUF), Batavia, NY.
St. Luke Rectory, [R], (TR). See Campus Ministry for the Diocese of Trenton.
Saint Luke's Catholic Medical Services, Inc., [R], (CAM), Camden, NJ.
St. Luke's Center, Inc., [M], (MIA), Miami, FL.
St. Luke's Guild, [T], (ALB), Schenectady, NY.
St. Luke's Home, [F], (SCL), Cold Spring, MN.
St. Luke's Home, [H], (SPR). See Sisters of Providence Care Centers, Inc.
St. Luke's Housing Development Fund Co., Inc., [Q], (SY), Oswego, NY.
St. Luke's Midland Regional Medical Center, [D], (SFS), Aberdeen, SD.
Saint Luke's Residential Health Care Facility Co., Inc., [P], (SY), Oswego, NY.
St. Madeleine Sophie's Center for Developmentally Disabled Adults, [D], (SD), El Cajon, CA.
St. Malachi Center, Inc., [V], (CLV), Cleveland, OH.
St. Malo Conference, Retreat Center, [O], (DEN), Allenspark, CO.
St. Margaret, [D], (CAM), Woodbury Heights, NJ.
St. Margaret Convent, [E], (OG), Lake Placid, NY.
St. Margaret Hall, [L], (CIN), Cincinnati, OH.
St. Margaret Mary Church Educational Endowment Trust, [N], (OM). See The Omaha Archdiocesan Educational Foundation, Inc.
Saint Margaret Mary Convent, [I], (HBG), Harrisburg, PA.
*St. Margaret Mercy Health Care Center, Inc., [O], (FTW), Mishawaka, IN.
St. Margaret Mercy Healthcare Centers - North Campus, [G], (GRY), Hammond, IN.
St. Margaret Mercy Healthcare Centers, South Campus, [G], (GRY), Dyer, IN.
St. Margaret's Daughters' Home for Aged Women, [N], (NO), New Orleans, LA.
St. Margaret's Foundation, [L], (MOB), Montgomery, AL.
Saint Margaret's Home, [T], (PRO). See Miscellaneous Listings for the Diocese of Providence.
St. Margaret's Hospital, [J], (PEO), Spring Valley, IL.
St. Margaret's Services, [L], (MOB), Montgomery, AL.
St. Margaret's Shelter, [H], (SPK), Spokane, WA.
St. Marguerite Convent, [N], (SEA), Tacoma, WA.
St. Maria Goretti High School, [D], (BAL), Hagerstown, MD.
St. Maria Goretti High School, [D], (PH), Philadelphia, PA.
Saint Maria Society, [T], (PRO). See Miscellaneous Listings for the Diocese of Providence.
The St. Mark Catholic Parish Endowment Trust, [M], (LC), Rothschild, WI.
St. Mark Latin American Center, [Y], (MIL), Kenosha, WI.
St. Mark Village Apartments, [I], (MEM), Moscow, TN.
St. Mark's Center, [N], (GRY). See Catholic Charities.
St. Mark's Convent, [F], (R), Sanford, NC.
St. Mark's Faculty Residence, [J], (WIL), Wilmington, DE.
St. Mark's High School, [A], (WIL), Wilmington, DE.
St. Mark's Seminary, [A], (E), Erie, PA.
St. Mark, Rothschild, [D], (LC). See Wausau Area Catholic Schools.
St. Martha Manor, [W], (PH), Downingtown, PA.
St. Martha's Hall, [S], (STL), St. Louis, MO.
St. Martha's Hall, [W], (STL), St. Louis, MO.
St. Martha's Housing II, Inc., [F], (VEN), Sarasota, FL.
St. Martha's Housing, Inc., [P], (BAL). See Chancery Office.
St. Martha's Housing, Inc., [F], (VEN), Sarasota, FL.
St. Martin Catholic School, [B], (CC), Kingsville, TX.
St. Martin de Porres Academy, [D], (CHI), Chicago, IL.
St. Martin de Porres Center, [V], (CLV). See Catholic Charities Services Corporation.
St. Martin de Porres Convent, [N], (PEO), Peoria, IL.
St. Martin de Porres Guild, [DD], (NY). See Dominican Friars' Guild.
St. Martin de Porres High, [D], (DET), Detroit, MI.
St. Martin De Porres Lay Dominican Community, [Q], (L), New Hope, KY.
St. Martin de Porres Multi-Purpose Center, [N], (PRO), Providence, RI.
St. Martin de Porres Regional School, [E], (RVC), Uniondale, NY.
St. Martin de Porres, Inc., [J], (DAL), Coppell, TX.
St. Martin Family Service Center, Inc., [J], (DAL), Dallas, TX.
St. Martin Hall, Our Lady of the Lake University of San Antonio, [G], (SAT), San Antonio, TX.
Saint Martin House, [K], (MAD), Madison, WI.
St. Martin Infirmary, [O], (OAK). See Dominican Sisters of Mission San Jose.
St. Martin Manor, [N], (NO), New Orleans, LA.
St. Martin Plaza, Inc., [K], (DEN). See Archdiocesan Housing Committee.
St. Martin's Abbey, [M], (SEA), Lacey, WA.
St. Martin's Barn, [F], (WIL). See St. Martin's Ministries.
St. Martin's Child Center, [M], (STL), Kinloch, MO.
St. Martin's College, [A], (SEA), Lacey, WA.
St. Martin's Community Center, [D], (RC), Rapid City, SD.
St. Martin's Convent, [J], (AMA), Amarillo, TX.
St. Martin's Home for Aged, Little Sisters of the Poor, [K], (BAL), Baltimore, MD.
St. Martin's House, [F], (WIL). See St. Martin's Ministries.
St. Martin's Learning Center, [D], (RC), Rapid City, SD.
St. Martin's Ministries, [F], (WIL), Ridgely, MD.
St. Mary, [D], (CAM), Salem, NJ.
St. Mary, [D], (CAM), Vineland, NJ.
St. Mary, [J], (PRT), Augusta, ME.
St. Mary, [B], (SPC), Joplin, MO.

St. Mary Academy, [E], (MAN), Dover, NH.
St. Mary Academy, [E], (PRO), East Providence, RI.
St. Mary Academy, [F], (PRO), East Providence, RI.
St. Mary Academy of the Visitation, [T], (PRO). See Miscellaneous Listings for the Diocese of Providence.
St. Mary and St. Scholastica Church, Inc., [R], (WOR), Petersham, MA.
St. Mary Campus, [C], (MET). See Holy Family Academy.
St. Mary Campus, [C], (MET), Perth Amboy, NJ.
St. Mary Campus, [H], (MIL). See Waukesha Catholic School System, Inc.
St. Mary Cathedral Elementary School, [B], (GAY), Gaylord, MI.
St. Mary Cathedral High School, [B], (GAY), Gaylord, MI.
St. Mary Catholic Central High School, [D], (DET), Monroe, MI.
St. Mary Catholic Church Endowment, [N], (OM). See The Omaha Archdiocesan Educational Foundation, Inc.
The St. Mary Catholic Education Endowment Fund, [C], (DOD), Garden City, KS.
St. Mary Catholic Housing Corp., [CC], (LA), Long Beach, CA.
St. Mary Catholic School Endowment Trust, [M], (LC), Durand, WI.
St. Mary Central High School, [C], (BIS), Bismarck, ND.
St. Mary Central High School, [C], (GB), Menasha, WI.
St. Mary Child Development Center, [B], (R), Garner, NC.
St. Mary Church Educational Endowment Trust, [N], (OM). See The Omaha Archdiocesan Educational Foundation, Inc.
Saint Mary College, [A], (KCK), Leavenworth, KS.
St. Mary Community Hospital, [F], (FTW), South Bend, IN.
St. Mary Conference Center, [O], (SEA), Toledo, WA.
St. Mary Convent, [K], (FTW), Avilla, IN.
St. Mary Convent, [N], (HRT). See Sisters of Mercy of the Americas of Connecticut.
St. Mary Convent, [N], (HRT), Newington, CT.
St. Mary Convent, [D], (LUB), Lubbock, TX.
St. Mary Convent, [Q], (PRO), Riverside, RI.
Saint Mary Convent, [A], (VNN), Van Nuys, CA.
St. Mary Convent, Poor Handmaids of Jesus Christ, [H], (BEL), East St. Louis, IL.
St. Mary Desert Valley Hospital Foundation, [D], (SB). See St. Mary Regional Medical Center.
St. Mary Education Endowment Trust, [M], (LC), Auburndale, WI.
St. Mary Educational Endowment Fund, [N], (OM). See The Omaha Archdiocesan Educational Foundation, Inc.
St. Mary Educational Trust Fund (St. Mary Parish, Mt. Morris), [K], (LAN). See Chancery Office.
St. Mary Elementary, [B], (GAY), Alpena, MI.
St. Mary Elementary, [B], (GAY), Charlevoix, MI.
St. Mary Elementary, [C], (OWN), Paducah, KY.
St. Mary Elementary & Junior High School, [C], (SFS). See Sioux Falls Catholic School System.
St. Mary Elementary Day School Endowment Trust, [Z], (CLV), Wooster, OH.
St. Mary Family Center, [I], (DM), Des Moines, IA.
St. Mary Health Corporation, [J], (PAT). See St. Mary's Hospital.
St. Mary High School, [B], (OWN), Paducah, KY.
St. Mary High School Benefit Fund, [J], (OWN), Paducah, KY.
St. Mary High School Foundation, Inc., [O], (GB), Menasha, WI.
Saint Mary Home, [K], (HRT), West Hartford, CT.
St. Mary Home, [N], (HRT), West Hartford, CT.
St. Mary Home, II, Inc., [K], (HRT). See Saint Mary Home.
St. Mary Hospital, [C], (BEA), Port Arthur, TX.
St. Mary Hospital, [H], (DET), Livonia, MI.
St. Mary Hospital, [I], (HRT), Waterbury, CT.
St. Mary Hospital, [N], (HRT), Waterbury, CT.
St. Mary Hospital, [G], (NEW), Hoboken, NJ.
St. Mary Hospital and Medical Center, [D], (PBL), Grand Junction, CO.
St. Mary Hospital Foundation, [E], (LR). See St. Mary-Rogers Memorial Hospital.
St. Mary Hospital Foundation of Port Arthur, [G], (BEA), Port Arthur, TX.
St. Mary Hospital of East St. Louis, Illinois Volunteers, [K], (BEL), East St. Louis, IL.
St. Mary Hospitality House, [C], (PRM), Cleveland, OH.
St. Mary Kewaunee Area Memorial Hospital, [F], (GB), Kewaunee, WI.
Saint Mary Life Center, Inc. - Pope John Paul II Pavillion, [G], (NEW), Orange, NJ.
St. Mary Magdalen Catholic Community, [T], (DET), Detroit, MI.
St. Mary Magdalen Early Childhood Development Center, [J], (NO), Metairie, LA.
St. Mary Magdalene Friary, [N], (CHI), Chicago, IL.
St. Mary Magdelen Convent, [O], (OAK). See Dominican Sisters of Mission San Jose.
St. Mary Manor, [I], (MEM), Jackson, TN.
St. Mary Manor, [X], (PH), Lansdale, PA.
St. Mary Medical Center, [G], (GRY), Hobart, IN.
St. Mary Medical Center, [K], (LA), Long Beach, CA.
St. Mary Medical Center, [K], (LA). See Catholic Health Care West-Southern California.
St. Mary Medical Center, [CC], (LA). See Catholic Healthcare West Southern California.
St. Mary Medical Center, [A], (LSC), Hobbs, NM.
St. Mary Medical Center, [J], (PEO), Galesburg, IL.
St. Mary Medical Center, [T], (PH), Langhorne, PA.
St. Mary Medical Center, [G], (SPK), Walla Walla, WA.
St. Mary Medical Center Foundation, [K], (LA), Long Beach, CA.
St. Mary Medical Center Foundation, [CC], (LA), Long Beach, CA.
St. Mary Medical Center Foundation, Inc., [G], (GRY). See St. Mary Medical Center.
St. Mary Mercy Hospital, [E], (OKL), Enid, OK.
St. Mary Middle School, [C], (OWN), Paducah, KY.
St. Mary Monastery, Motherhouse and Novitiate, [N], (PEO), Nauvoo, IL.
St. Mary of Nazareth Hospital Center, [J], (CHI), Chicago, IL.
St. Mary of Providence, [L], (CHI), Chicago, IL.
St. Mary of Providence Center, [X], (PH), Elverson, PA.
St. Mary of the Angels Convent, [M], (CAM), Haddonfield, NJ.
St. Mary of the Angels Convent, [N], (PEO), Rock Island, IL.
St. Mary of the Angels Friary, [A], (GB), Green Bay, WI.
St. Mary of the Angels Friary, [I], (GB), Green Bay, WI.
St. Mary of the Annunciation School, [F], (BO), Danvers, MA.
St. Mary of the Assumption Parish Endowment Trust, [Z], (CLV), Mentor, OH.
St. Mary of the Lake, [L], (ALB), Lake George, NY.
St. Mary of the Pines, [F], (JKS), Chatawa, MS.
St. Mary of the Plains Hospital, [B], (LUB), Lubbock, TX.
St. Mary of the Springs, [I], (COL), Columbus, OH.
St. Mary of the Springs Montessori School, [D], (COL), Columbus, OH.
St. Mary of the Springs Montessori School, [I], (COL). See St. Mary of the Springs.
St. Mary of the Valley Convent, [M], (P), Beaverton, OR.
St. Mary of the Valley Grade School, [F], (P), Beaverton, OR.
St. Mary Orphan Home, Inc., [D], (JKS), Jackson, MS.
St. Mary Orphanage, Inc. dba St. Mary Villa, [E], (NSH), Nashville, TN.
St. Mary Parish Educational Trust Fund (St. Mary Parish, Charlotte), [K], (LAN). See Chancery Office.
St. Mary Playschool, [G], (SCR), Mount Pocono, PA.
St. Mary Priory, [M], (HRT), New Haven, CT.
St. Mary Professional Building, Inc., [K], (LA), Long Beach, CA.
Saint Mary Rectory, [M], (BAL), Annapolis, MD.
St. Mary Regional High School, [A], (MET), South Amboy, NJ.
St. Mary Regional Medical Center, [D], (SB), Apple Valley, CA.
St. Mary Regional Medical Center Auxiliary, [D], (SB). See St. Mary Regional Medical Center.
St. Mary School, [B], (AMA), Amarillo, TX.
St. Mary School, [E], (MAN), Claremont, NH.
St. Mary School Foundation, [G], (BEA), Orange, TX.
St. Mary School Foundation, [P], (DAV), Centerville, IA.
St. Mary Seminary, [A], (CLV), Wickliffe, OH.
St. Mary Star of the Sea Educational Trust Fund (St. Mary Star of the Sea Parish, Jackson), [K], (LAN). See Chancery Office.
St. Mary Student Parish, [J], (LAN), Ann Arbor, MI.
St. Mary Villa Child Development Center, [E], (NSH), Nashville, TN.
St. Mary Villa Retirement Community, Inc., [G], (NSH), Nashville, TN.
St. Mary Wood's, [H], (RIC), Richmond, VA.
St. Mary Youth Minister Residence, [F], (PBL), Montrose, CO.
St. Mary's, [A], (ANC), Kodiak, AK.
St. Mary's - Painesville, [X], (CLV). See Diocesan Hispanic Office.
St. Mary's A.S.C., Inc., [D], (PMB). See St. Mary's Hospital, Inc.
St. Mary's Abbey, [M], (PAT), Morristown, NJ.
St. Mary's Abbey Retreat Center, [I], (PAT), Morristown, NJ.
St. Mary's Academy, [F], (LA), Inglewood, CA.
St. Mary's Academy, [H], (NO), New Orleans, LA.
St. Mary's Academy, [D], (P), Portland, OR.
St. Mary's Academy, [C], (PEO), Nauvoo, IL.
St. Mary's Academy Elementary School, [B], (CC), Beeville, TX.
St. Mary's Academy High School, [D], (DEN), Denver, CO.
St. Mary's Academy Lower School, [E], (DEN), Denver, CO.
St. Mary's Academy Middle School, [B], (CC), Beeville, TX.
St. Mary's Academy of the Holy Family, [F], (NO), New Orleans, LA.
St. Mary's Academy, Middle School, [E], (DEN), Englewood, CO.
St. Mary's Ancillary Services, Inc., [D], (PMB). See St. Mary's Hospital, Inc.
St. Mary's Care Center, [B], (NU), Winsted, MN.
St. Mary's Care Services, Inc., [D], (PMB). See St. Mary's Hospital, Inc.
St. Mary's Catholic Center, [M], (AUS), College Station, TX.
The St. Mary's Catholic Church Educational Endowment Trust, [M], (LC), Tomah, WI.
The St. Mary's Catholic Church Endowment Trust, [M], (LC), Neillsville, WI.
St. Mary's Catholic Education Trust, [K], (GF), Malta, MT.
St. Mary's Center, [A], (DM). See Shelby County Board of Catholic Education.
St. Mary's Center, [R], (LA). See Amat House.
St. Mary's Center, [R], (OAK), Oakland, CA.
St. Mary's Child Development Center, [V], (PH), Langhorne, PA.
St. Mary's Children and Family Services, [G], (RVC), Syosset, NY.
St. Mary's Church Educational Endowment Foundation, [O], (TOL), Vermilion, OH.
Saint Mary's College, [C], (DET), Orchard Lake, MI.
Saint Mary's College, [B], (FTW), Notre Dame, IN.
Saint Mary's College, [B], (OAK), Moraga, CA.
St. Mary's College, [G], (OAK), Moraga, CA.
St. Mary's College Campus Ministry, [Q], (OAK), Moraga, CA.
St. Mary's College Campus Ministry, [S], (WDC). See Archdiocesan Campus Ministry.
Saint Mary's College High School of Berkeley, Inc., [E], (OAK), Berkeley, CA.
St. Mary's College, Assumption Hall Vocation Office, [A], (OAK), Moraga, CA.
St. Mary's Convent, [H], (ANC), Kodiak, AK.
St. Mary's Convent, [P], (BUF), Buffalo, NY.
Saint Mary's Convent, [K], (FTW). See Saint Mary's of the Immaculate Conception.
St. Mary's Convent, [G], (OG), Champlain, NY.
St. Mary's Convent, [J], (PRT), Presque Isle, ME.
St. Mary's Convent, [F], (R), Goldsboro, NC.
St. Mary's Convent, [N], (SR), Arcata, CA.
St. Mary's Convent (O.P.), [E], (RNO), Reno, NV.
St. Mary's Convent, Grey Nuns of the Sacred Heart, [G], (OG), Potsdam, NY.
St. Mary's Convent, Sisters of St. Joseph, [G], (OG), Ticonderoga, NY.
St. Mary's Convent: Residence for Women, [Y], (PH), Philadelphia, PA.
St. Mary's Convent-Sisters of the Divine Savior, [J], (GB), St. Nazianz, WI.
St. Mary's Diocesan High School-Bundschu Memorial, [C], (KC), Independence, MO.
St. Mary's Dominican High School, [F], (NO), New Orleans, LA.
St. Mary's Dominican High School, [H], (NO), New Orleans, LA.
St. Mary's Early Childhood Learning Center, [G], (SCR), Pittston, PA.
Saint Mary's Education Fund, Inc., [Q], (FR), Fall River, MA.
St. Mary's Elementary School, [A], (NU). See New Ulm Area Catholic Schools.
St. Mary's EMS, [C], (CR). See St. Mary's Regional Health Center.
The St. Mary's Endowment Trust, [W], (BGP), Ridgefield, CT.
St. Mary's Family Health Care Center, [A], (LSC), Hobbs, NM.
St. Mary's Food Bank, [Q], (SEA), Seattle, WA.
St. Mary's Foundation, [D], (SFS), Pierre, SD.
St. Mary's Foundation Ozaukee, Inc., [Y], (MIL), Mequon, WI.
St. Mary's Foundation, Inc., [B], (KNX). See St. Mary's Medical Center, Inc.
St. Mary's Franciscan Shelter, [V], (PH), Phoenixville, PA.
St. Mary's Friary, [K], (DET), Detroit, MI.
St. Mary's Friary, [N], (PIT), Herman, PA.
St. Mary's Goods Bookstore, [F], (CHY), Cheyenne, WY.
St. Mary's Hannah School, [B], (GAY), Hannah, MI.
St. Mary's Health Care Center, [A], (LSC), Carlsbad, NM.
St. Mary's Health Center, [K], (STL), St. Louis, MO.
St. Mary's Health Center Foundation, [G], (JC), Jefferson City, MO.

St. Michael Rectory, [M], (HRT). See St. Anthony Rectory.
St. Michael Rectory, [M], (HRT), Waterbury, CT.
St. Michael Rehabilitation Hospital, [A], (TYL), Texarkana, TX.
St. Michael School, [D], (ALN), Lansford, PA.
St. Michael School, [D], (COV), Bellevue, KY.
St. Michael School, [E], (ELP), El Paso, TX.
St. Michael Schools Educational Foundation, [O], (TOL), Findlay, OH.
St. Michael the Archangel Rectory, [M], (HRT). See DePaul Provincial Residence.
St. Michael the Archangel School, [D], (ALN), Bethlehem, PA.
St. Michael Villa, [O], (NEW), Englewood Cliffs, NJ.
St. Michael's, [C], (BUR), Brattleboro, VT.
St. Michael's Hospital, [D], (SFS), Tyndall, SD.
St. Michael's Center, [A], (DM). See Shelby County Board of Catholic Education.
St. Michael's Center, [N], (PRT), Bangor, ME.
St. Michael's Center Emergency Foster Care, [E], (PRT). See Catholic Charities Maine.
St. Michael's Church, [M], (ROC), Penn Yan, NY.
St. Michael's College, [A], (BUR), Colchester, VT.
St. Michael's College Preparatory High School, [D], (ORG), Siverado, CA.
St. Michael's Convent, [O], (NEW), Newark, NJ.
St. Michael's Elementary, Hastings Catholic Schools, [B], (LIN), Hastings, NE.
St. Michael's Friary, [U], (BRK), Brooklyn, NY.
St. Michael's Group Home, [K], (SCR), Falls, PA.
St. Michael's Group Home, [K], (SCR), Tunkhannock, PA.
St. Michael's Group Home, [K], (SCR), West Pittston, PA.
St. Michael's Group Home, [K], (SCR), Williamsport, PA.
St. Michael's High School, [E], (SFE), Santa Fe, NM.
St. Michael's High School Foundation, [N], (SFE), Santa Fe, NM.
St. Michael's Home, [L], (BR), Baton Rouge, LA.
St. Michael's Hospital and School for Med. Technology, [E], (LC), Stevens Point, WI.
Saint Michael's Hospital Auxiliary, [P], (LC), Stevens Point, WI.
St. Michael's Housing Corporation dba Casa Miguel, [M], (SP), Clearwater, FL.
St. Michael's Institute, [B], (SPK), Spokane, WA.
Saint Michael's Medical Center, [G], (NEW), Newark, NJ.
St. Michael's Medical Center Division, Newark, [F], (NEW). See Cathedral Healthcare System, Inc.
St. Michael's Norbertine Postulancy, Novitiate and Juniorate, [A], (ORG), Silverado, CA.
St. Michael's of Morongo Valley, Inc., [E], (SB), Morongo Valley, CA.
St. Michael's Orphanage and Industrial School, [H], (TR), Hopewell, NJ.
St. Michael's Passionist Residence, [Z], (PH), Philadelphia, PA.
St. Michael's Residence, [H], (SPR), Springfield, MA.
St. Michael's School, [C], (BUR), Montpelier, VT.
St. Michael's School, [F], (LR), Hot Springs National Park, AR.
St. Michael's School, [K], (SCR), Hoban Heights, PA.
St. Michael's School Endowment Fund Policy (St. Michael School, Grand Ledge), [K], (LAN). See Chancery Office.
St. Michael's Summer Camp, [G], (ORG), Silverado, CA.
St. Michaels's Catholic Academy, [C], (AUS), Austin, TX.
St. Mike's Tikes, [F], (SEA), Olympia, WA.
St. Monica Day Care Center, [S], (PH), Philadelphia, PA.
St. Monica School, [E], (KC), Kansas City, MO.
St. Monica's, [C], (BUR), Barre, VT.
St. Monica's Center, [I], (SFD), Springfield, IL.
St. Monica's Parish, [J], (FTW). See Congregation of Holy Cross Indiana Province Provincial House.
St. Monica's Senior Citizens Home, Inc., [N], (MIL), Racine, WI.
St. Nicholas Convent, [O], (NEW), Jersey City, NJ.
St. Nicholas Foundation, [L], (COL), Zanesville, OH.
St. Nicholas Hospital, [K], (MIL), Sheboygan, WI.
St. Nicholas Indian Center, [J], (TUC), Tucson, AZ.
St. Nicholas of Myra Adoption Program, [D], (TUC). See Social Service Agencies: Pima County.
Saint Nicholas-Saint Mary Elementary School, [F], (SCR), Wilkes-Barre, PA.
St. Norbert Abbey, [A], (GB), De Pere, WI.
St. Norbert Abbey, [I], (GB), De Pere, WI.
St. Norbert Abbey Seminary and Education Fund Trust, [O], (GB), De Pere, WI.
St. Norbert College, [B], (GB), De Pere, WI.
St. Norbert Priory, [Z], (PH), Philadelphia, PA.
St. Olaf, [D], (LC). See Eau Claire Coordinated Catholic Schools.
St. Olaf Parish Endowment Trust, [M], (LC), Eau Claire, WI.
St. Olaf's Daycare, [F], (SEA), Poulsbo, WA.
St. Otto's Care Center, [H], (SCL), Little Falls, MN.
St. Patrick, [E], (MAN), Portsmouth, NH.
St. Patrick, [J], (PRT), Portland, ME
St. Patrick Academy, [G], (SY), Binghamton, NY.
St. Patrick Apartments, Inc., [I], (STL). See Cardinal Ritter Institute.
St. Patrick Campus Upper School, [E], (NEW). See Elizabethport Catholic School.
St. Patrick Catholic Church Endowment Trust, [N], (OM). See The Omaha Archdiocesan Educational Foundation, Inc.
St. Patrick Center, [F], (DUB). See Holy Family Catholic Consolidated School.
St. Patrick Center, [W], (STL), St. Louis, MO.
St. Patrick Children's Home, Inc., [E], (SAC), Sacramento, CA.
St. Patrick Church Educational Endowment Trust, [N], (OM). See The Omaha Archdiocesan Educational Foundation, Inc.
St. Patrick Church Endowment Trust, [Z], (CLV), Wellington, OH.
Saint Patrick Convent, [L], (GRY), East Chicago, IN.
St. Patrick Convent, [N], (HRT), Enfield, CT.
St. Patrick Ecumenical Shelter for the Homeless, [L], (NSH), Nashville, TN.
St. Patrick Endowment Trust, [O], (IND), Terre Haute, IN.
St. Patrick Foundation, [N], (OM). See The Omaha Archdiocesan Educational Foundation, Inc.
St. Patrick Friary, [N], (PIT), Pittsburgh, PA.
St. Patrick Friary, [P], (STL), St. Louis, MO.
The St. Patrick Grade School Education Endowment Fund, [C], (DOD), Great Bend, KS.
St. Patrick Haven, Inc., [L], (E), Erie, PA.
St. Patrick High School, [D], (CHI), Chicago, IL.
St. Patrick High School, [B], (COV), Maysville, KY.
St. Patrick Hospital Corporation, [E], (HEL), Missoula, MT.
St. Patrick Hospital of Lake Charles, [B], (LKC), Lake Charles, LA.
St. Patrick Middle School, [D], (LC). See Eau Claire Coordinated Catholic Schools.
St. Patrick Parish Educational Endowment (Lauer), [N], (OM). See The Omaha Archdiocesan Educational Foundation, Inc.
St. Patrick Parish Educational Trust Fund (St. Patrick Parish, Brighton), [K], (LAN). See Chancery Office.
St. Patrick Parish Endowment Trust, [N], (OM). See The Omaha Archdiocesan Educational Foundation, Inc.
St. Patrick Parish Endowment Trust, [N], (OM). See The Omaha Archdiocesan Educational Foundation, Inc.
St. Patrick Parish Foundation, [P], (DAV), Brooklyn, IA.
St. Patrick Parish of Eau Claire Endowment Trust, [M], (LC), Eau Claire, WI.
St. Patrick Parish/St. Mary School Endowment, [N], (OM). See The Omaha Archdiocesan Educational Foundation, Inc.
St. Patrick Preschool, [G], (SCR), Milford, PA.
St. Patrick Rectory, [M], (HRT), Enfield, CT.
St. Patrick School, [B], (CC), Corpus Christi, TX.
St. Patrick School, [D], (CHL). See Mecklenburg Area Catholic Schools (M.A.C.S.).
St. Patrick School, [E], (MAN), Pelham, NH.
St. Patrick School, [E], (MAN), Jaffrey, NH.
St. Patrick School Annex, [K], (FTW), Walkerton, IN.
St. Patrick School Endowment Trust, [N], (OM). See The Omaha Archdiocesan Educational Foundation, Inc.
*St. Patrick School Fund, [E], (TYL), Lufkin, TX.
St. Patrick School Tuition Assistance Endowment Trust, [N], (OM). See The Omaha Archdiocesan Educational Foundation, Inc.
St. Patrick Seminary, [A], (SFR), Menlo Park, CA.
St. Patrick Villa, [AA], (NY), Nanuet, NY.
St. Patrick's Center, [M], (MEM), Memphis, TN.
St. Patrick's Congregation Trust, [M], (LC), Mauston, WI.
St. Patrick's Convent, [L], (FR), Fall River, MA.
St. Patrick's Convent, [G], (LIN), McCook, NE.
St. Patrick's Convent, Sisters of Charity of St. Louis, [G], (OG), Rouses Point, NY.
St. Patrick's Day Care, [M], (STL). See Guardian Angel Settlement Association.
St. Patrick's Family Health Center, [J], (CHI). See Mercy Hospital and Medical Center.
St. Patrick's Home for the Aged and Infirm, [V], (NY), Bronx, NY.
St. Patrick's House, Inc., [G], (WIL), Wilmington, DE.
St. Patrick's Housing Corporation dba Patrician Arms, [M], (SP), Tampa, FL.
St. Patrick's Manor, Inc., [U], (BO), Framingham, MA.
St. Patrick's Missionary Cenacle, [L], (FR), Wareham, MA.
St. Patrick's Missionary Cenacle, [I], (MOB), Phenix City, AL.
St. Patrick's Missionary Society, [N], (CHI), Chicago, IL.
St. Patrick's Missionary Society, [N], (NEW), Cliffside Park, NJ.
St. Patrick's Missionary Society, [M], (SJ), Saratoga, CA.
St. Patrick's Monastery, [H], (HON), Honolulu, HI.
St. Patrick's Novitiate and Scholasticate, [A], (ORG), Midway City, CA.
St. Patrick's Provincial House (Congregation of Christian Brothers), [Z], (NY), New Rochelle, NY.
St. Patrick's Residence, [I], (JOL), Naperville, IL.
St. Patrick's Retreat, [Q], (DET), Onsted, MI.
St. Patrick's Senior Center, Inc., [Q], (DET), Detroit, MI.
St. Patrick's Villa, [AA], (NY), Harriman, NY.
St. Patrick-St. Anthony Friary, [M], (HRT), Hartford, CT.
St. Patrick-St. Vincent High School, [B], (SAC), Vallejo, CA.
St. Paul Book and Media Center, [J], (HON), Honolulu, HI.
St. Paul Book and Media Center, [N], (MET), Edison, NJ.
St. Paul Book and Media Center, [K], (MIA), Miami, FL.
St. Paul Book and Media Center (Daughters of St. Paul), [N], (ARL), Alexandria, VA.
St. Paul Books and Media, [W], (STL), St. Louis, MO.
St. Paul Cathedral School Education Foundation, [I], (BIR), Birmingham, AL.
St. Paul Catholic High School, [D], (HRT), Bristol, CT.
St. Paul Center, [W], (BRK), Astoria, NY.
St. Paul Convent, [N], (HRT), Kensington, CT.
St. Paul Convent, [N], (HRT), West Haven, CT.
St. Paul Convent, [N], (HRT). See Sisters of Mercy of the Americas of Connecticut.
St. Paul Convent, [F], (R), New Bern, NC.
St. Paul Friary, [P], (CLV), Cleveland, OH.
St. Paul Friary, [M], (HRT). See Conventual Franciscans.
St. Paul Hermitage, [H], (IND), Beech Grove, IN.
St. Paul High School, [D], (LA), Santa Fe Springs, CA.
St. Paul Home, Inc., [H], (GB), Kaukauna, WI.
St. Paul Interparochial School, [D], (SP), St. Petersburg, FL.
St. Paul Jung-Ha-Sang, [G], (LAV), Las Vegas, NV.
St. Paul Manor, [H], (GB). See St. Paul Home, Inc.
St. Paul Manor, [L], (PIT), Pittsburgh, PA.
St. Paul Medical Center, [I], (DAL), Dallas, TX.
St. Paul Medical Center, [I], (DAL), Dallas, TX.
St. Paul Medical Center Foundation Inc., [I], (DAL), Dallas, TX.
St. Paul Newman Center, [H], (FRS), Fresno, CA.
St. Paul of the Cross Community, Congregation of the Passion, [K], (DET), Detroit, MI.
St. Paul of the Cross Monastery, [N], (PIT), Pittsburgh, PA.
St. Paul of the Cross Retreat Center, [P], (DET), Detroit, MI.
St. Paul of the Cross Retreat Center, [P], (PIT), Pittsburgh, PA.
St. Paul Parish Endowment Trust, [M], (LC), Mosinee, WI.
St. Paul Preschool, [F], (SP), Tampa, FL.
St. Paul Priory Guest House, [R], (PRO), Newport, RI.
St. Paul Retreat House and Cursillo Center, [I], (PRT), Augusta, ME.
St. Paul Retreat House and Cursillo Center, [L], (PRT), Augusta, ME.
Saint Paul Seminary, [A], (PIT), Pittsburgh, PA.
The Saint Paul Seminary, [A], (STP), St. Paul, MN.
St. Paul's, [C], (BUR), Barton, VT.
St. Paul's Abbey, [M], (PAT), Newton, NJ.
St. Paul's Catholic Chapel, [H], (FAR), Fargo, ND.
St. Paul's College, [B], (WDC), Washington, DC.
St. Paul's Guild, Inc., [DD], (NY), New York, NY.
St. Paul's Outreach, Inc., [W], (STP), West St. Paul, MN.
St. Paul's Parish Conference, [E], (YAK), Yakima, WA.
St. Paul's Priory, [O], (STP), St. Paul, MN.
The St. Paul's School, [F], (NO), Covington, LA.
The St. Paul's School, [H], (NO), Covington, LA.
St. Paul's School Education Trust Fund (St. Paul Parish, Owosso), [K], (LAN). See Chancery Office.
St. Paul's School of Religion, [E], (DUB), Manchester, IA.
St. Paul, Highlands University Newman Center, [M], (SFE), Las Vegas, NM.
St. Paulene Book and Media Center, [FF], (BO), Dedham, MA.
St. Peter, [G], (SY), Rome, NY.
St. Peter & Joseph Childrens Home, [I], (SAT), San Antonio, TX.
St. Peter and Joseph Childrens' Home Endowment Fund, [S], (SAT), San Antonio, TX.
St. Peter and Paul House, [N], (MET), Phillipsburg, NJ.
St. Peter Catholic Church Endowment Trust, [N], (OM). See The Omaha Archdiocesan Educational Foundation, Inc.
St. Peter Chanel High School, [D], (CLV), Bedford, OH.

St. Peter Chanel Interparochial School, [D], (BR), Paulina, LA.
St. Peter Chanel Seminary, [B], (SFR), San Francisco, CA.
St. Peter Chapel & Activity Center, [I], (MEM). See St. Peter Manor.
St. Peter Claver Center, [CC], (LA), Los Angeles, CA.
St. Peter Convent, [N], (HRT), Hartford, CT.
St. Peter Convent, [N], (HRT), Torrington, CT.
St. Peter Friary, [E], (R), Greenville, NC.
St. Peter Home for Children, [E], (MEM), Memphis, TN.
St. Peter Manor, [I], (MEM), Memphis, TN.
St. Peter Middle School, [D], (LC). See Stevens Point Area Catholic Schools.
St. Peter Nolasco Residence, [O], (SP), St. Petersburg, FL.
St. Peter Nolasco Spiritual Center, [Q], (BUF), LeRoy, NY.
St. Peter Parish Endowment Trust, [M], (LC), Tilden, WI.
St. Peter Parish Endowment Trust, [N], (OM). See The Omaha Archdiocesan Educational Foundation, Inc.
St. Peter Regional Treatment Center, [G], (NU), St. Peter, MN.
St. Peter the Apostle, [L], (RIC). See Ethnic and Special Ministries.
St. Peter the Apostle Convent, [F], (BLX), Pascagoula, MS.
St. Peter the Apostle Retreat Center, [F], (YAK), Cowiche, WA.
St. Peter the Fisherman, [L], (NO), Slidell, LA.
St. Peter Villa, [I], (MEM), Memphis, TN.
St. Peter's Adult Learning Center, [G], (BAL), Baltimore, MD.
St. Peter's Cemetery Restoration Fund, Inc., [P], (BAL). See Chancery Office.
St. Peter's Central Catholic Elementary School, [F], (WOR), Worcester, MA.
Saint Peter's College, [B], (NEW), Jersey City, NJ.
St. Peter's College Jesuit Community, [B], (NEW). See Saint Peter's College.
St. Peter's Convent, Dominican Sisters of Hope, [G], (OG), Plattsburgh, NY.
St. Peter's Convent, Sisters of St. Joseph, [G], (OG), Lowville, NY.
St. Peter's Endowment Foundation, [I], (BIR), Birmingham, AL.
St. Peter's Friary, [N], (CHI), Chicago, IL.
St. Peter's Home, [H], (MAN), Manchester, NH.
St. Peter's Italian Church Housing Development Fund Co., Inc. Villa Scalabrini Apts., [Q], (SY), Syracuse, NY.
St. Peter's Junior High School, [B], (SPC), Joplin, MO.
St. Peter's Medical Center, [F], (MET), New Brunswick, NJ.
St. Peter's Memorial School, [B], (CC), Laredo, TX.
St. Peter's Parish, St. Maximilian Kolbe House of Studies, [T], (BGP), Bridgeport, CT.
St. Peter's Preparatory School, [C], (NEW), Jersey City, NJ.
St. Peter's Village, [H], (PAT), Denville, NJ.
St. Peter's, Westernport, School Endowment Trust, [P], (BAL). See Chancery Office.
St. Peter-Marian Central Catholic Junior-Senior High School, [C], (WOR), Worcester, MA.
St. Petersburg Catholic High School, [B], (SP), St. Petersburg, FL.
St. Petersburg Eckerd College, [S], (SP), St. Petersburg, FL.
St. Philip Catholic Central High School, [A], (KAL), Battle Creek, MI.
St. Philip Neri Church of Omaha Endowment Trust, [N], (OM). See The Omaha Archdiocesan Educational Foundation, Inc.
St. Philip Preschool, [J], (NO), New Orleans, LA.
St. Philippine Duchesne Shelter, [S], (STL), St. Louis, MO.
St. Philips Parish, R. Formation Program, [B], (CR), Bemidji, MN.
St. Philomena Early Learning Center, [E], (HON), Honolulu, HI.
St. Philomena School, [F], (PRO), Portsmouth, RI.
St. Pius Priory, [P], (PRO), Providence, RI.
St. Pius V Housing Committee, Inc., [P], (BAL). See Chancery Office.
St. Pius V Priory, [N], (CHI). See Dominicans (Provincial Office).
St. Pius X Catholic High School, [B], (ATL), Atlanta, GA.
St. Pius X Center (Pittsburg State University), [K], (WCH), Pittsburg, KS.
St. Pius X Church Educational Trust Fund (St. Pius X Church, Flint), [K], (LAN). See Chancery Office.
St. Pius X Convent, [G], (SLC), Moab, UT.
St. Pius X Friary, [Z], (PH), Philadelphia, PA.
St. Pius X High School, [C], (KC), Kansas City, MO.
St. Pius X High School, [D], (PH), Pottstown, PA.
St. Pius X High School, [D], (SFE), Albuquerque, NM.
St. Pius X High School, [E], (STL), Festus, MO.
St. Pius X High School Foundation, Inc., [U], (GAL), Houston, TX.
St. Pius X High School Foundation, Inc., [N], (SFE), Albuquerque, NM.
St. Pius X High School, Inc., [F], (GAL), Houston, TX.
St. Pius X Home, Inc., [S], (SY), Syracuse, NY.
St. Pius X Parish Endowment Trust, [M], (LC), La Crosse, WI.
St. Pius X Residence, [N], (RVC), Uniondale, NY.
St. Pius X Residence, Inc., [J], (PIT). See Pittsburgh Mercy Health System, Inc.
St. Pius X Residence, Inc., [L], (PIT), Pittsburgh, PA.
St. Pius X School, [B], (CC), Corpus Christi, TX.
St. Pius X School, [C], (WIN). See Rochester Catholic Schools.
Saint Pius X Seminary, [A], (SCR), Dalton, PA.
St. Pius X Spiritual Life Center, [N], (CAM), Blackwood, NJ.
St. Pius X-St. Leo School, [D], (OM), Omaha, NE.
St. Placid Priory, [N], (SEA), Lacey, WA.
St. Procopius Abbey, [J], (JOL), Lisle, IL.
St. Raphael Academy, [C], (PRO), Pawtucket, RI.
St. Raphael Catholic School and Early Childhood Center, [B], (R), Raleigh, NC.
St. Raphael Convent, [J], (PRT), Kittery, ME.
St. Raphael Family Life Center, [J], (PMB), Palm City, FL.
St. Raphael Home for the Aged, Inc., [G], (COL), Columbus, OH.
Saint Raphael's Industrial Home and School, [T], (PRO). See Miscellaneous Listings for the Diocese of Providence.
Saint Raphaela Center, [BB], (PH), Haverford, PA.
St. Raymond, [D], (CAM), Villas, NJ.
St. Raymond Nonnatus Novitiate, [O], (BUF), LeRoy, NY.
Saint Regis Health Center, Inc., [I], (HRT), New Haven, CT.
St. Regis Mission, [J], (OG), Hogansburg (Akwesasne), NY.
St. Regis Residence for Ladies, [R], (PIT), Pittsburgh, PA.
St. Richard's School Endowment Foundation, [O], (TOL), Swanton, OH.
St. Richard's Special Kids Program, [B], (JKS), Jackson, MS.
St. Rita Convent, [N], (HRT), Hamden, CT.
St. Rita Convent, [AA], (PH), Flourtown, PA.
St. Rita High School, [D], (CHI), Chicago, IL.
St. Rita Home, [G], (COL), Columbus, OH.
St. Rita Monastery, [N], (CHI), Chicago, IL.
St. Rita School for the Deaf, [J], (CIN), Cincinnati, OH.
St. Rita's Medical Center, [H], (TOL), Lima, OH.
St. Rita's Retreat Center, [N], (P), Gold Hill, OR.
St. Rita's Senior Citizen Center, [Q], (PH), Philadelphia, PA.
St. Robert Bellarmine Chapel, [M], (ARL). See George Mason University, Catholic Campus Ministry House.
St. Robert Bellarmine Church Educational Endowment Trust, [N], (OM). See The Omaha Archdiocesan Educational Foundation, Inc.
St. Robert Bellarmine Newman Center, Illinois State University, [O], (PEO), Normal, IL.
St. Robert Bellarmine Parish Endowment Trust, [N], (OM). See The Omaha Archdiocesan Educational Foundation, Inc.
St. Robert Bellarmine/Fr. Jacob Educational Trust Fund (St, Robert Bellarmine Parish, Flushing), [K], (LAN). See Chancery Office.
St. Robert's Holy Name Society Boosters, [AA], (CLV), Euclid, OH.
St. Roch Friary-Franciscan Fathers, [N], (CHI), Oak Forest, IL.
St. Romuald School, [C], (OWN), Hardinsburg, KY.
St. Rosalie, [L], (NO), Gretna, LA.
St. Rose Academy Corporation, [U], (SFR), San Francisco, CA.
St. Rose Catholic Urban Academy, [F], (MIL), Milwaukee, WI.
St. Rose Center, [I], (CHI), Chicago, IL.
St. Rose Convent, [N], (CIN), Cincinnati, OH.
St. Rose Convent, [J], (LC), La Crosse, WI.
St. Rose Dominican Hospital, [B], (LAV), Henderson, NV.
Saint Rose High School, [B], (TR), Belmar, NJ.
St. Rose Hospital, [K], (OAK), Hayward, CA.
St. Rose Hospital Foundation, [K], (OAK). See St. Rose Hospital.
St. Rose Lima Trust Fund, [I], (KAL), Hastings, MI.
St. Rose Medical Office Bldg., [K], (OAK). See St. Rose Hospital.
St. Rose of Lima Academy, [C], (BIR), Birmingham, AL.
St. Rose of Lima Catholic Church Endowment Trust, [M], (LC), Cadott, WI.
The St. Rose of Lima Grade School Education Endowment Fund, [C], (DOD), Great Bend, KS.
St. Rose of Lima Parish Endowment, [N], (OM). See The Omaha Archdiocesan Educational Foundation, Inc.
St. Rose Parish Endowment, [N], (OM). See The Omaha Archdiocesan Educational Foundation, Inc.
St. Rose Parish, R.E. Program, [B], (CR), Argyle, MN.
St. Rose's Home, [T], (NY), New York, NY.
St. Rose's Settlement, [DD], (NY), New York, NY.
St. Saviour, [H], (BRK), Brooklyn, NY.
St. Saviour's Day Nursery, [G], (FR), New Bedford, MA.
St. Scholastica Academy, [D], (CHI), Chicago, IL.
St. Scholastica Academy, [D], (NO), Covington, LA.
St. Scholastica Academy, [B], (PBL), Canon City, CO.
St. Scholastica Center, [K], (LR), Fort Smith, AR.
St. Scholastica Monastery, [N], (SAT), Boerne, TX.
St. Scholastica Monastery-Motherhouse, [I], (LR), Fort Smith, AR.
St. Scholastica Priory, [M], (E), Erie, PA.
St. Scholastica Priory, [O], (WOR), Petersham, MA.
St. Scholastica Priory and Academy, Benedictine Sisters of Chicago, [O], (CHI), Chicago, IL.
St. Sebastian School Endowment Fund, Inc., [B], (MAR), Bessemer, MI.
St. Sebastian's Country Day School, Inc., [E], (BO), Needham, MA.
St. Stanislaus, [D], (LC). See Stevens Point Area Catholic Schools.
St. Stanislaus B. M. Friary, [M], (PAT), Oak Ridge-Milton, NJ.
St. Stanislaus Church Educational Endowment Trust, [N], (OM). See The Omaha Archdiocesan Educational Foundation, Inc.
St. Stanislaus College, [C], (BLX), Bay St. Louis, MS.
Saint Stanislaus Community, [E], (BLX), Bay St. Louis, MS.
St. Stanislaus Convent, [N], (HRT), Meriden, CT.
St. Stanislaus Convent, [G], (OG), Keeseville, NY.
St. Stanislaus Friary, [P], (CLV), Cleveland, OH.
St. Stanislaus Kostka Soup Kitchen, [G], (CHI). See Catholic Charities of the Archdiocese of Chicago-Archdiocesan Offices.
St. Stanislaus Middle School, [C], (WIN). See Winona Area Catholic Schools.
St. Stanislaus Parish Endowment Trust, [N], (OM). See The Omaha Archdiocesan Educational Foundation, Inc.
St. Stanislaus Rectory, [M], (HRT). See DePaul Provincial Residence.
St. Stanislaus Rectory, [M], (HRT). See DePaul Provincial Residence.
St. Stanislaus School and Educational Endowment Trust, [N], (OM). See The Omaha Archdiocesan Educational Foundation, Inc.
St. Stephen, [D], (LC). See Stevens Point Area Catholic Schools.
St. Stephen Campus, [C], (MET), Perth Amboy, NJ.
St. Stephen Convent, [N], (HRT). See Sisters of Mercy of the Americas of Connecticut.
St. Stephen Convent, [A], (VNN), Phoenix, AZ.
St. Stephen Parish Endowment Trust, [M], (LC), Stevens Point, WI.
St. Stephen Priory, [W], (BO), Dover, MA.
St. Stephen Priory Spiritual Life Center, [Y], (BO), Dover, MA.
St. Stephen Regional School, [D], (ALN), Port Carbon, PA.
St. Stephen the Witness Catholic Student Center, University of Northern Iowa, [N], (DUB), Cedar Falls, IA.
St. Stephen University Parish, [H], (BIR), Birmingham, AL.
St. Stephen's Community House, [L], (COL), Columbus, OH.
St. Stephen's Diocesan Center, [A], (HON), Kaneohe, HI.
St. Stephen's League, [Y], (MIL), Milwaukee, WI.
St. Stephen's School, [E], (KC), Kansas City, MO.
St. Stephen, Inc., [J], (DAL), Dallas, TX.
St. Stephens Indian Mission Foundation, [F], (CHY), St. Stephens, WY.
St. Stephens Mission - Jesuit Community, [C], (CHY), St. Stephens, WY.
St. Sylvester Monastery, [K], (DET), Detroit, MI.
St. Teresa, [D], (CAM), Runnemede, NJ.
St. Teresa High School, [D], (SFD), Decatur, IL.
St. Teresa of Avila School, [C], (GLP), Grants, NM.
St. Teresa's Academy, [D], (KC), Kansas City, MO.
St. Teresa's Convent, [N], (SAT), San Antonio, TX.
St. Teresa's Motherhouse, [M], (ALB), Germantown, NY.
St. Teresa's Nursing Home, [V], (NY), Middletown, NY.
St. Teresas Manor & Bishop Primeau Apartments, [J], (MAN), Manchester, NH.
St. Thecla's Retreat House, [Y], (BO), Billerica, MA.
St. Theodore Apartments, [G], (CHI). See Catholic Charities of the Archdiocese of Chicago-Archdiocesan Offices.
St. Theodore Catholic School Endowment, [J], (WIN), Albert Lea, MN.
St. Theodore School, [C], (WIN), Albert Lea, MN.
St. Theodore's Apartment Housing Development Fund

Co., Inc. (Dunn Tower II Apts.), [L], (ROC), Rochester, NY.
St. Theresa, [B], (SPP), Leone, AS.
St. Theresa Carmelite Chapel, [BB], (BO), Peabody, MA.
St. Theresa Community, [I], (HON). See Sisters of St. Joseph of Carondelet CSJ, Hawaii Vice-Province.
St. Theresa Community, [J], (PRT), Oakland, ME.
St. Theresa House, [X], (BO), Boston, MA.
St. Theresa of Avila Catholic School Educational Foundation, [M], (BR). See Baton Rouge Chancery Office.
St. Theresa's Camp, [J], (ANC), Anchorage, AK.
St. Therese Catholic Church Endowment Fund, [M], (LC), Rothschild, WI.
St. Therese Center for Special Ministry, [M], (SCL), St. Cloud, MN.
St. Therese Convent, [G], (KNX), Clinton, TN.
St. Therese Educational Trust Fund (St. Therese Parish, Lansing), [K], (LAN). See Chancery Office.
St. Therese Little Flower Day Care Center, [G], (MEM), Memphis, TN.
Saint Therese Medical Center, [J], (CHI), Waukegan, IL.
St. Therese, Schofield, [D], (LC). See Wausau Area Catholic Schools.
The Saint Thomas Academy, [E], (STP), St. Paul, MN.
St. Thomas Aquinas, [CC], (NY). See University Apostolate.
St. Thomas Aquinas, [M], (SFE), Albuquerque, NM.
St. Thomas Aquinas, [G], (SY), Binghamton, NY.
St. Thomas Aquinas Church and Catholic Student Center (Iowa State University), [N], (DUB), Ames, IA.
St. Thomas Aquinas College, [C], (NY), Sparkill, NY.
St. Thomas Aquinas Convent, [I], (MET), Edison, NJ.
St. Thomas Aquinas Early Childhood Center, [F], (SP), New Port Richey, FL.
St. Thomas Aquinas Educational Foundation Trust (St. Thomas Aquinas Parish, East Lansing), [K], (LAN). See Chancery Office.
St. Thomas Aquinas Foundation, [X], (CHI), Chicago, IL.
St. Thomas Aquinas Foundation, [DD], (NY), New York, NY.
St. Thomas Aquinas High School, [E], (HRT), New Britain, CT.
Saint Thomas Aquinas High School, [B], (KCK), Overland Park, KS.
St. Thomas Aquinas High School, [C], (MAN), Dover, NH.
St. Thomas Aquinas High School, [C], (MIA), Fort Lauderdale, FL.
St. Thomas Aquinas High School, [C], (Y), Louisville, OH.
St. Thomas Aquinas High School Endowment Fund, [P], (Y), Louisville, OH.
St. Thomas Aquinas House, [N], (OAK), Berkeley, CA.
St. Thomas Aquinas Newman Center, [I], (WIN), Winona, MN.
St. Thomas Aquinas Parish and Foundation for Catholic Students attending Purdue Univ., [H], (LFT), West Lafayette, IN.
St. Thomas Aquinas Priory, [N], (CHI), River Forest, IL.
St. Thomas Aquinas Priory at Providence College, [P], (PRO), Providence, RI.
St. Thomas Aquinas Regional Catholic High School, [B], (BR), Tangipahoa, LA.
St. Thomas Aquinas School, [E], (MAN), Derry, NH.
St. Thomas Aquinas Seminary, [A], (JC), Hannibal, MO.
St. Thomas Aquinas, Newman Center, [H], (SLC), Logan, UT.
St. Thomas Aquinas-Mercy High School, [E], (STL), Florissant, MO.
St. Thomas Assessment Center/Boysville of Michigan, Inc., [O], (DET). See Boysville of Michigan, Inc.
St. Thomas Center, [O], (SEA), Bothell, WA.
St. Thomas Child and Family Center, [F], (GF), Great Falls, MT.
St. Thomas Child Development Center, [B], (R), Wilmington, NC.
Saint Thomas Foundation, [F], (NSH). See St. Thomas Hospital.
St. Thomas Grade School Trust Agreement (St. Thomas the Apostle Parish, Ann Arbor), [K], (LAN). See Chancery Office.
St. Thomas High School, [F], (GAL), Houston, TX.
St. Thomas High School, Inc., [Y], (MIL), Sheboygan, WI.
St. Thomas Hospital, [F], (NSH), Nashville, TN.
St. Thomas Korean Catholic Center, [G], (ORG), Anaheim, CA.
St. Thomas Medical Plaza East, [F], (NSH). See St. Thomas Hospital.
St. Thomas Monastery, [Z], (PH), Villanova, PA.
St. Thomas More, [B], (LAF), Lafayette, LA.
St. Thomas More Academy, [C], (LAN), Burton, MI.
St. Thomas More Catholic Newman Center, [H], (SFS), Vermillion, SD.
St. Thomas More Catholic Student Center at the University of New Hampshire, [N], (MAN), Durham, NH.
St. Thomas More Center, [I], (DM), Panora, IA.
St. Thomas More Center, [G], (WH), Wheeling, WV.
St. Thomas More Chapel, [BB], (BO), Boston, MA.
St. Thomas More Friary, Third Order Regular of St. Francis, [B], (WDC), Wheaton, MD.
St. Thomas More High School, [A], (RC), Rapid City, SD.
St. Thomas More High-Boysville, [B], (LAN), Clinton, MI.
St. Thomas More Hospital and Progressive Care Center, [D], (PBL), Canon City, CO.
St. Thomas More Lawyers Society, [Y], (MIL), Milwaukee, WI.
St. Thomas More Newman Center, [G], (SUP), River Falls, WI.
St. Thomas More Parish Endowment Trust, [M], (LC), La Crosse, WI.
St. Thomas More School, [F], (SFR), San Francisco, CA.
St. Thomas More School Endowment Trust, [M], (BR). See Baton Rouge Chancery Office.
St. Thomas More School Endowment Trust, [N], (OM). See The Omaha Archdiocesan Educational Foundation, Inc.
St. Thomas More Sisters' Residence, [F], (R), Chapel Hill, NC.
St. Thomas More Society, [Q], (E), Erie, PA.
St. Thomas More Society, [L], (MRY), Watsonville, CA.
Saint Thomas More Society, [R], (PIT), Pittsburgh, PA.
St. Thomas More Society of Maryland, [Q], (BAL), Baltimore, MD.
St. Thomas More Society of Southeast Texas, [G], (BEA), Beaumont, TX.
St. Thomas Newman Center, [F], (CR), Moorhead, MN.
St. Thomas Orphan Society, Inc., [G], (L), Louisville, KY.
Saint Thomas Preparatory Seminary Fund, [W], (SY), Syracuse, NY.
St. Thomas Regional School, [G], (PRO), Providence, RI.
St. Thomas Seminary, [A], (HRT), Bloomfield, CT.
St. Thomas the Apostle Church, [J], (FTW). See Congregation of Holy Cross Indiana Province Provincial House.
St. Thomas the Apostle School Foundation, Inc., [L], (RCK), Crystal Lake, IL.
St. Thomas University, [B], (MIA), Opa Locka, FL.
St. Thomas Villa, [AA], (NY), Monticello, NY.
St. Timothy Preschool, [F], (SP), Tampa, FL.
St. Timothy's Park Villa Housing Development Fund Company, Inc., [T], (BUF), Buffalo, NY.
St. Ursula Academy, [C], (TOL), Toledo, OH.
St. Ursula Academy High School, [F], (CIN), Cincinnati, OH.
St. Ursula Retreat Center, Inc., [P], (RVC), Blue Point, NY.
St. Ursula Villa, [H], (CIN), Cincinnati, OH.
St. Valerians Catholic Indian Center, [D], (GLP), Gallup, NM.
St. Veronica Giuliani Friary, Capuchin Franciscan Friars, [N], (NEW), Orange, NJ.
St. Veronica's Headstart Center, [Q], (BAL), Baltimore, MD.
St. Viator High School, [D], (CHI), Arlington Heights, IL.
St. Vincent Academy, [C], (NEW), Newark, NJ.
St. Vincent and Sarah Fisher Center, [O], (DET), Farmington Hills, MI.
St. Vincent Apartments Housing Development Fund Co., Inc., [K], (ALB), Albany, NY.
Saint Vincent Archabbey, [H], (GBG), Latrobe, PA.
*St. Vincent Cardiac Services, Inc., [F], (IND). See Seton Health Corporation of Central Indiana.
St. Vincent Center, [K], (DAV), Davenport, IA.
St. Vincent Center, [M], (DAV), Davenport, IA.
St. Vincent Church, [W], (STL). See Catholic Family Services.
St. Vincent College, [B], (GBG), Latrobe, PA.
St. Vincent Community, [P], (MIL), Milwaukee, WI.
St. Vincent Day Care Center, [D], (EVN), Evansville, IN.
St. Vincent Day Care Center, [J], (PRO), Providence, RI.
St. Vincent de Paul Camp, [S], (BUF), Angola, NY.
St. Vincent de Paul Center, [I], (CHI), Chicago, IL.
St. Vincent de Paul Center, [E], (FRS), Farmersville, CA.
St. Vincent de Paul Center, [N], (LAF), Abbeville, LA.
St. Vincent de Paul Center, [J], (SLC). See Catholic Community Services.
St. Vincent de Paul Center, [E], (YAK), Toppenish, WA.
St. Vincent de Paul Center for Community Reconciliation, [G], (ORG). See St. Vincent de Paul Society.
St. Vincent de Paul Convent, [G], (SLC), Salt Lake City, UT.
St. Vincent de Paul Dining Room, [H], (SFR). See St. Vincent de Paul Society Marin County District Council.
St. Vincent de Paul Dining Room at St. Francis of Assisi Church, [H], (SFR). See San Mateo County District Council.
St. Vincent de Paul Diocesan Council of Fort Worth, [L], (FWT), Fort Worth, TX.
St. Vincent de Paul Educational Foundation, [W], (STL), St. Louis, MO.
St. Vincent de Paul Furniture and Clothing Inc., [J], (SY), Syracuse, NY.
St. Vincent de Paul High School, [A], (RIC), Petersburg, VA.
St. Vincent De Paul Historic Trust, Inc., [P], (BAL). See Chancery Office.
St. Vincent de Paul Home, Woonsocket, [T], (PRO). See Miscellaneous Listings for the Diocese of Providence.
St. Vincent De Paul Kitchen, [R], (SCR), Wilkes-Barre, PA.
St. Vincent de Paul Nursing Home, [J], (MAN), Berlin, NH.
St. Vincent de Paul Parish Conference, [H], (SPK), Spokane, WA.
St. Vincent de Paul Particular Council, [L], (LAN), Lansing, MI.
St. Vincent de Paul Preschool, [G], (SCR), Milford, PA.
St. Vincent de Paul Ranch Camp & Retreat Center, [AA], (LA). See St. Vincent de Paul Society.
St. Vincent de Paul Referral Services, [O], (FTW), South Bend, IN.
St. Vincent de Paul Regional Seminary, [Z], (PH). See Congregation of the Mission.
St. Vincent de Paul Regional Seminary, [A], (PMB), Boynton Beach, FL.
St. Vincent de Paul Regional Seminary Endowment Trust, [J], (PMB), Boynton Beach, FL.
St. Vincent de Paul Rehabilitation Service, Inc., [O], (P), Portland, OR.
St. Vincent de Paul Social Service Office, [H], (SPK), Spokane, WA.
Saint Vincent de Paul Society, [H], (AGN), Agana, GU.
St. Vincent de Paul Society, [K], (ANC), Anchorage, AK.
St. Vincent de Paul Society, [G], (B), Idaho Falls, ID.
St. Vincent de Paul Society, [G], (B), Boise, ID.
St. Vincent de Paul Society, [Q], (DET), Detroit, MI.
St. Vincent de Paul Society, [G], (DUL), Duluth, MN.
St. Vincent de Paul Society, [AA], (LA), Los Angeles, CA.
St. Vincent de Paul Society, [L], (LR), Eureka Springs, AR.
St. Vincent de Paul Society, [L], (LR), Horseshoe Bend, AR.
St. Vincent De Paul Society, [H], (MAR), Marquette, MI.
St. Vincent de Paul Society, [W], (MIL), Milwaukee, WI.
St. Vincent de Paul Society, [G], (ORG), Orange, CA.
St. Vincent De Paul Society, [P], (PEO), Peoria, IL.
St. Vincent de Paul Society, [EE], (PH), Conshohocken, PA.
St. Vincent De Paul Society, [J], (PHX), Phoenix, AZ.
St. Vincent de Paul Society, [R], (PIT), Pittsburgh, PA.
St. Vincent De Paul Society, [C], (SAN), Abilene, TX.
St. Vincent De Paul Society, [C], (SAN), Big Spring, TX.
St. Vincent De Paul Society, [C], (SAN), Midland, TX.
St. Vincent De Paul Society, [C], (SAN), Stanton, TX.
St. Vincent de Paul Society, [H], (SPK), Spokane, WA.
St. Vincent de Paul Society, [G], (STO), Manteca, CA.
St. Vincent de Paul Society, [B], (STV). See Miscellaneous Organizations.
St. Vincent de Paul Society, [J], (SY), Syracuse, NY.
Saint Vincent de Paul Society - District Council of Central Oregon, [D], (BAK), Bend, OR.
Saint Vincent de Paul Society - Prineville Conference, [D], (BAK), Prineville, OR.
Saint Vincent de Paul Society - Redmond Conference, [D], (BAK), Redmond, OR.
Saint Vincent de Paul Society - The Dalles Conference, [D], (BAK), The Dalles, OR.
St. Vincent De Paul Society Archdiocese Council of Indianapolis, Inc., [O], (IND), Indianapolis, IN.
St. Vincent de Paul Society Marin County District Council, [H], (SFR), San Rafael, CA.
St. Vincent de Paul Society of St. Joseph County, Inc., [O], (FTW), South Bend, IN.
St. Vincent de Paul Society of the Archdiocese of Dubuque, [O], (DUB), Dubuque, IA.
St. Vincent de Paul Society of Yellowstone County, [K], (GF), Billings, MT.
St. Vincent de Paul Society Store, [O], (FTW), Fort Wayne, IN.
St. Vincent de Paul Society, District Council of Santa Clara County, [P], (SJ), San Jose, CA.
St. Vincent De Paul Society, St. John the Baptist Church Conference, [P], (DAV). See Burlington Notre Dame Foundation.
Saint Vincent de Paul Society-Baraboo, [M], (MAD),

Salesian High School, [E], (OAK), Richmond, CA.
Salesian Monastery, [M], (SCR), Brodheadsville, PA.
Salesian Provincial House, [Z], (NY), New Rochelle, NY.
Salesian Provincial Residence, [N], (SFR), San Francisco, CA.
Salesian Residence, [N], (NEW), South Orange, NJ.
Salesian Sisters (Daughters of Mary Help of Christians) F.M.A., [Q], (NO), Marrero, LA.
Salesian Sisters' School: Mary Help of Christians Youth Center, [D], (MRY), Corralitos, CA.
Salesians of Don Bosco, [H], (AUS), Waco, TX.
Salesians of Don Bosco, [A], (VNN), Phoenix, AZ.
Salesians of Don Bosco, S.D.B., [S], (NEW), South Orange, NJ.
Salesianum School, [B], (WIL), Wilmington, DE.
Salina Catholic Diocese Education Endowment, Inc., [I], (SAL), Salina, KS.
Salina Catholic Diocese Gift & Annuity Fund, Inc., [I], (SAL), Salina, KS.
Salina Catholic Diocese Seminary Burses, Inc., [I], (SAL), Salina, KS.
Salina Civic Center, [K], (SY), Syracuse, NY.
Saline Community Hospital, [F], (LAN), Saline, MI.
Salisbury State College, [O], (WIL). See Univ. of Delaware Newman Center.
Salpointe Catholic High School, [A], (TUC), Tucson, AZ.
Salvatorian Center Residence, [I], (GB), New Holstein, WI.
Salvatorian Community, [B], (WDC), Silver Spring, MD.
The Salvatorian Fathers, [N], (NEW), Verona, NJ.
Salvatorian Fathers (Society of the Divine Savior), [K], (GRY), Merrillville, IN.
Salvatorian Formation Community, [P], (MIL), Milwaukee, WI.
Salvatorian Heights Assisted Living Unit, [Q], (MIL). See Sisters of the Divine Savior.
Salvatorian Mission Warehouse, [I], (GB). See Salvatorian Center Residence.
Salvatorian Provincial Residence, [P], (MIL), Milwaukee, WI.
Salvatorian Public Relations, [I], (GB). See Salvatorian Center Residence.
Salvatorians - Jordan Hall, [P], (MIL), Milwaukee, WI.
Salve Regina University, [B], (PRO), Newport, RI.
The Samaritan Corporation, [I], (RVC), West Islip, NY.
*Samaritan Health Foundation, [U], (CIN), Dayton, OH.
Samaritan Health Partners, [T], (CIN), Dayton, OH.
Samaritan Health System, Inc., [J], (DAV), Clinton, IA.
Samaritan Homecare/Hospice, [N], (RCK), Mount Carroll, IL.
*Samaritan Homes, Inc., [W], (STP), Minneapolis, MN.
Samaritan Hospital North, [J], (DAV). See Samaritan Health System, Inc.
Samaritan Hospital South, [J], (DAV). See Samaritan Health System, Inc.
Samaritan House, [D], (BLX), Ocean Springs, MS.
Samaritan House, [G], (CHI). See Catholic Charities of the Archdiocese of Chicago-Archdiocesan Offices.
Samaritan House, [L], (DEN). See Catholic Charities and Community Services of the Archdiocese of Denver, Inc.
Samaritan Manor at Tuxedo, Inc., [W], (NY), Tuxedo, NY.
Samaritan Outreach, [F], (WIL). See Ministry of Caring, Inc.
Samaritan Services for Aging, [J], (DAV). See Samaritan Health System, Inc.
San Alfonso Retreat House, [Q], (TR), Long Branch, NJ.
San Antonio Abad Abbey of the Order of St. Benedict, [C], (CGS), Humacao, PR.
San Antonio Community Law Center, [T], (SAT), San Antonio, TX.
San Antonio Intercommunity Finance Office, [T], (SAT), San Antonio, TX.
San Antonio Parish Convent, [A], (CHK), Saipan, MP.
San Antonio Provincial Friary Franciscan Friars, [J], (SFE), Albuquerque, NM.
San Augustin Historical Preservation & Restoration Society, Inc., [J], (CC), Laredo, TX.
San Camillo, Inc., [N], (MIL), Wauwatosa, WI.
San Carlos Adult Day Care, [Q], (SFR). See Catholic Charities of the Archdiocese of San Francisco.
San Damiano Convent, [I], (MET), North Plainfield, NJ.
San Damiano Convent, [AA], (PH), Langhorne, PA.
San Damiano Friary, [K], (GRY), Cedar Lake, IN.
San Damiano Friary, [M], (MAD), Madison, WI.
San Damiano Friary, [B], (SAT), San Antonio, TX.
San Damiano Friary, [M], (SAT), San Antonio, TX.
San Damiano Monastery of St. Clare., [H], (VEN), Fort Myers Beach, FL.
San Damiano Retreat, [P], (OAK), Danville, CA.
San Diego Catholic Worker, [N], (SD), San Diego, CA.
San Diego Central Magnificat, [N], (SD), San Diego, CA.
San Diego Mercy Hospital Auxiliary, [F], (SD). See Mercy Hospital and Medical Center dba Mercy Healthcare San Diego.
San Diego State University Newman Center, [M], (SD), San Diego, CA.
San Domenico Community, [O], (OAK). See Dominican Sisters of Mission San Jose.
San Domenico Convent, [O], (SFR). See Dominican Sisters of San Rafael Generalate & Convent.
San Domenico Early Ed., Lower and Middle School, [G], (SFR), San Anselmo, CA.
San Domenico School, [E], (SFR), San Anselmo, CA.
San Fernando Pastoral Region, [Y], (LA). See Catholic Charities of Los Angeles, Inc.
San Francisco Counseling, [Q], (SFR). See Catholic Charities of the Archdiocese of San Francisco.
San Francisco District Council of the St. Vincent de Paul Society, [H], (SFR). See Society of St. Vincent de Paul Archdiocesan Council.
San Francisco Family Services, [Q], (SFR). See Catholic Charities of the Archdiocese of San Francisco.
San Francisco Heart Institute, [J], (SFR). See Seton Medical Center.
San Francisco Senior Services, [Q], (SFR). See Catholic Charities of the Archdiocese of San Francisco.
San Francisco Vincentian Desk, [H], (SFR). See Society of St. Vincent de Paul Archdiocesan Council.
San Francisco Vincentian Life, [H], (SFR). See Society of St. Vincent de Paul Archdiocesan Council.
San Gabriel Pastoral Region, [Y], (LA). See Catholic Charities of Los Angeles, Inc.
San Jacinto Community College North Campus Newman Center, [T], (GAL), Houston, TX.
San Jacinto Community College South Campus, Catholic Newman Association, [T], (GAL), Houston, TX.
San Joaquin Memorial Convent, [F], (FRS), Fresno, CA.
The San Joaquin Memorial High School of Fresno, Inc., [A], (FRS), Fresno, CA.
San Jose Cathedral Foundation, [P], (SJ), Santa Clara, CA.
San Jose Clinic, [L], (GAL), Houston, TX.
San Jose Day Nursery, [R], (NY), New York, NY.
San Jose Serra Club, [P], (SJ), Los Gatos, CA.
San Juan Day Care Center, [K], (ELP). See North American Union Sisters of Our Lady of Charity.
San Juan del Rio Catholic School, [A], (STA), Jacksonville, FL.
San Juan Diocesan Retreat Center, [G], (BWN), San Juan, TX.
San Juan Home Health and Hospice, [D], (BWN), San Juan, TX.
San Juan Nursing Home, [D], (BWN), San Juan, TX.
San Juan Pilgrim House/Hotel, [I], (BWN). See Virgen de San Juan del Valle Shrine.
San Juan Print Shop, [I], (BWN). See Virgen de San Juan del Valle Shrine.
San Juan Retreat Center, [I], (BWN). See Virgen de San Juan del Valle Shrine.
San Lorenzo Novitiate and Seminary, [B], (LA), Santa Ynez, CA.
San Lorenzo Ruiz De Manila, [G], (STO), Stockton, CA.
San Luis Apartments, Inc., [I], (STL). See Cardinal Ritter Institute.
San Luis Rey, [H], (SD), San Luis Rey, CA.
San Martin Center, [H], (JKS). See DePorres Delta Ministries, Inc.
San Mateo Counseling, [Q], (SFR). See Catholic Charities of the Archdiocese of San Francisco.
San Mateo County District Council, [H], (SFR), San Mateo, CA.
San Mateo Vincentian Life, [H], (SFR). See San Mateo County District Council.
*San Miguel Center, Inc., [I], (CHI), Chicago, IL.
San Miguel Retreat House, [I], (MRY), San Miguel, CA.
San Miguel School, [F], (PRO), Providence, RI.
San Pedro Center, Third Order Regular of St. Francis, [F], (ORL), Winter Park, FL.
San Pedro Pastoral Region, [Y], (LA). See Catholic Charities of Los Angeles, Inc.
San Pedro Peninsula Hospital, [K], (LA). See Little Company of Mary Health Services.
San Pedro Peninsula Hospital, [K], (LA), San Pedro, CA.
San Pedro Spiritual Development Center, [D], (ORL), Winter Park, FL.
San Pedro Valley Center for the Arts, [J], (TUC), St. David, AZ.
San Rafael Home for Aged, [B], (ARE), Arecibo, PR.
San Ramon, [H], (OAK). See Catholic Charities of the Diocese of Oakland, Inc.
San Tomas/Charities Housing Corporation, [P], (SJ), San Jose, CA.
San Vicente Community, [G], (AGN), Barrigada, GU.
San Vicente School, [C], (AGN), GMF, GU.
San Xavier Mission, [G], (TUC), Tucson, AZ.
Sancta Clara Monastery, [K], (Y), Canton, OH.
Sancta Maria Convent, [X], (BO), Cambridge, MA.
Sancta Maria Convent (North American Region and Novitiate), [J], (AMA), Panhandle, TX.
Sancta Maria in Ripa, [R], (STL), St. Louis, MO.
Sancta Maria Nursing Facility, [FF], (BO), Cambridge, MA.
Sanctuary of Mary-Our Lady of the Holy Spirit, [I], (PAT), Branchville, NJ.
Sangre de Cristo Center, [B], (SFE), Santa Fe, NM.
Sansbury Memorial Infirmary, [M], (L), St. Catharine, KY.
Santa Ana Apartments, Inc., [I], (STL). See Cardinal Ritter Institute.
Santa Ana Chapel, [C], (SJN), San Juan, PR.
Santa Barbara Convent, [G], (AGN), Dededo, GU.
Santa Barbara Pastoral Region, [Y], (LA). See Catholic Charities of Los Angeles, Inc.
Santa Barbara School, [C], (AGN), Dededo, GU.
Santa Catalina Lower School, [D], (MRY), Monterey, CA.
Santa Catalina Upper School, [B], (MRY), Monterey, CA.
Santa Clara Day Nursery and Kindergarten, [E], (ORG), Santa Ana, CA.
Santa Clara High School, [D], (LA), Oxnard, CA.
Santa Clara University, [B], (SJ), Santa Clara, CA.
Santa Cruz Project, [D], (TUC). See Social Service Agencies: Pima County.
Santa Fe Catholic High School, [A], (ORL), Lakeland, FL.
Santa Fe Communications, Inc., [Y], (MIL), Milwaukee, WI.
Santa Margarita Catholic High School, [C], (ORG), Rancho Santa Margarita, CA.
Santa Maria de la Vid Priory, [J], (SFE), Albuquerque, NM.
Santa Maria Hostel, [M], (GAL), Houston, TX.
Santa Maria Retirement Apartments, [D], (BLX), Biloxi, MS.
Santa Maria Towers, [T], (BUF), Buffalo, NY.
Santa Marta Hospital, [K], (LA), Los Angeles, CA.
Santa Marta Hospital Foundation, [CC], (LA), Los Angeles, CA.
Santa Monica Youth Employment & Training Program, [Y], (LA). See Catholic Charities of Los Angeles, Inc.
Santa Rita Abbey, [G], (TUC), Sonoita, AZ.
Santa Rosa Children's Hospital, [H], (SAT), San Antonio, TX.
Santa Rosa Health Care System, [H], (SAT), San Antonio, TX.
Santa Rosa Home Health, [H], (SAT). See Santa Rosa Health Care System.
Santa Rosa Hospice, [H], (SAT). See Santa Rosa Health Care System.
Santa Rosa Hospital, [H], (SAT), San Antonio, TX.
Santa Rosa Memorial Hospital, [G], (SR), Santa Rosa, CA.
Santa Rosa Northwest Hospital, [H], (SAT), San Antonio, TX.
Santa Rosa Rehabilitation Hospital, [H], (SAT). See Santa Rosa Northwest Hospital.
Santa Rosa Skilled Nursing Facility, [H], (SAT), San Antonio, TX.
Santa Sabina Center, [M], (SFR), San Rafael, CA.
Santa Teresita Hospital, [K], (LA), Duarte, CA.
Santo Domingo, [A], (SJN), Bayamon, PR.
Santo Domingo de Guzman Priory, [B], (SJN), Toa Alta, PR.
Santo Tomas de Aquino, [A], (SJN), Bayamon, PR.
Santuario del Espiritu Santo, [E], (SJN), Dorado, PR.
Saramen Chuuk Academy, [B], (CI), Chuuk, FM.
Saratoga Central Catholic High School, [C], (ALB), Saratoga Springs, NY.
Sarto Retreat House, [G], (EVN), Evansville, IN.
Sauk Valley Area Religious Education Center, [L], (RCK). See Sauk Valley Catholic Education Foundation.
Sauk Valley Catholic Education Foundation, [L], (RCK), Sterling, IL.
Savannah State College Newman Group, [H], (SAV), Savannah, GA.
Savio Preparatory High School, [E], (BO), Boston, MA.
Scalabrini House of Theology, [N], (CHI), Chicago, IL.
Scalabrini Mission Center, [N], (CHI), Stone Park, IL.
Scalabrini Villa, [M], (PRO), North Kingstown, RI.
Scalabrini Village, [X], (CHI), Northlake, IL.
Scalabrinian Missionaries, [Z], (NY), Staten Island, NY.
Scalabrinians Community Formation Corporation, Oak Park, [N], (CHI). See Missionaries of Saint Charles.
Scalabrinians Community Support Corporation, Oak Park, [N], (CHI). See Missionaries of Saint Charles.
SCH Corporate Offices, [J], (GAL). See Sisters of Charity of the Incarnate Word, Houston, Texas.
SCH Employee Benefit Plans, [J], (GAL). See Sisters of Charity of the Incarnate Word, Houston, Texas.

Seraphic Sisters Boarding Home for the Aged, [L], (SAT), San Antonio, TX.
Seraphic Sisters of Our Lady of Sorrows Convent, [N], (SAT), San Antonio, TX.
Serenity House, [I], (GAL). See Associated Catholic Charities of the Diocese of Galveston-Houston.
Serenity Retreat League, [M], (PAT), Stirling, NJ.
Serra Ancillary Care, [CC], (LA), Los Angeles, CA.
Serra Catholic Elementary School, [E], (ORG), Rancho Santa Margarita, CA.
Serra Catholic High School, [C], (PIT), McKeesport, PA.
Serra Club, [Q], (BAL), Baltimore, MD.
Serra Club, [M], (MEM), Cordova, TN.
Serra Club #120, Dis. 18, [M], (ATL), Atlanta, GA.
Serra Club #684, Dis. 18, [M], (ATL), Atlanta, GA.
Serra Club of Pueblo, [H], (PBL), Pueblo, CO.
Serra Club of St. Clair County, [K], (BEL), Belleville, IL.
Serra Club of San Antonio, Inc., [T], (SAT), San Antonio, TX.
Serra Club of Spokane, [O], (SPK), Spokane, WA.
Serra Club of Wichita - Downtown, [M], (WCH), Wichita, KS.
Serra Club of Wichita - Metro, [M], (WCH), Wichita, KS.
Serra Clubs District 31, [P], (SJ), San Jose, CA.
Serra Institute, [CC], (LA), Glendora, CA.
Serra International, [X], (CHI), Chicago, IL.
Serra Retreat, [W], (LA), Malibu, CA.
Servants of Charity (S.C.), [Z], (PH), Springfield, PA.
Servants of Jesus, [L], (DET), Clarkston, MI.
Servants of Mary, [I], (ORG), Orange, CA.
Servants of Mary, [D], (SUP), Ladysmith, WI.
Servants of Mary, Inc., [X], (CHI), Berwyn, IL.
Servants of St. Joseph Convent, [K], (ARL), Falls Church, VA.
Servants of St. Joseph Convent, [O], (NEW), Elizabeth, NJ.
Servants of the Blessed Sacrament, [F], (PBL), Pueblo, CO.
Servants of the Holy Heart of Mary, [K], (JOL), Kankakee, IL.
Servants of the Immaculate Child Mary, [CC], (LA), Los Angeles, CA.
Servants of the Paraclete, [P], (STL), St. Louis, MO.
Servants of the Paraclete, [N], (Y), Canton, OH.
Servants of the Paraclete Guadalupe Retreat Center, [G], (SB), Cherry Valley, CA.
Servants of the Sacred Heart of Jesus and of the Poor (S.S.H.J.P.), [K], (ELP), El Paso, TX.
Service Center of Catholic Social Services, [J], (MOB), Mobile, AL.
Service Units-Dept. of Family & Children's Services, [I], (NY). See The Catholic Charities of the Archdiocese of New York.
Services for the Incarcerated - Hope in Action Ministry, [H], (SFR). See San Mateo County District Council.
Services to Aging of Catholic Charities, [M], (SCL), St. Cloud, MN.
Services to Gays & Lesbians & Their Families, [H], (OAK). See Catholic Charities of the Diocese of Oakland, Inc.
Services to Parish Schools, [H], (OAK). See Catholic Charities of the Diocese of Oakland, Inc.
Services to Pregnant Adolescents and Their Families, [I], (GAL). See Associated Catholic Charities of the Diocese of Galveston-Houston.
Services to the Aging, Retired Senior Volunteer Program, [N], (GRY). See Catholic Charities.
Services to the Alone and Frail Elderly, [I], (GAL). See Associated Catholic Charities of the Diocese of Galveston-Houston.
Services to the St. Anthony's Residence, [K], (NY). See Beacon of Hope House.
Servite Community, Sarpi Priory, [N], (OAK), Berkeley, CA.
Servite Development Office, [N], (CHI). See Servite Friars - Eastern Province.
Servite Fathers and Brothers, [H], (ORG), Anaheim, CA.
Servite Fathers And Brothers, [H], (ORG), Buena Park, CA.
Servite Fathers and Brothers, [H], (ORG), Fullerton, CA.
Servite Fathers and Brothers, [H], (ORG), Orange, CA.
Servite Friars - Eastern Province, [N], (CHI), Chicago, IL.
Servite Friars-Eastern Province Retirement Trust, [X], (CHI), Chicago, IL.
Servite Friars-Eastern Province, Inc., [X], (CHI), Chicago, IL.
Servite High School; Servite High School Development Fund, [D], (ORG), Anaheim, CA.
Seton Academy, [D], (CHI), South Holland, IL.
Seton Catholic Central, [C], (OG), Plattsburgh, NY.
Seton Catholic Central High School of Broome County, [C], (SY), Binghamton, NY.
Seton Catholic Elementary School, [F], (DUB), Epworth, IA.
Seton Catholic High School, [A], (PHX), Phoenix, AZ.
Seton Catholic High School, [D], (SCR), Pittston, PA.
Seton Catholic Jr. High School, [E], (GAL), Houston, TX.
Seton Catholic Middle School, [G], (SY), Endicott, NY.
Seton Catholic School, [G], (DAV), Ottumwa, IA.
Seton Catholic School, [E], (PEO), Moline, IL.
*Seton Center, [M], (KC), Kansas City, MO.
Seton Center, [D], (WIL). See Catholic Charities, Inc.
Seton Center, Inc., [Q], (BAL), Emmitsburg, MD.
Seton Center, Sisters of Charity, [J], (WIL), Princess Anne, MD.
Seton Centers, Inc., [I], (ARL), Falls Church, VA.
Seton Children's School, Inc., [J], (MIL), Milwaukee, WI.
Seton Coshocton, Inc., [G], (COL), Coshocton, OH.
The Seton Cove - A Spirituality Center, [N], (AUS), Austin, TX.
Seton East Community Health Center, [F], (AUS), Austin, TX.
Seton Foundation for Learning, Inc., [G], (NY), New York, NY.
Seton Hall Preparatory School, [C], (NEW), West Orange, NJ.
Seton Hall University, [B], (NEW), South Orange, NJ.
Seton Hall University College Seminary, [A], (NEW), South Orange, NJ.
Seton Haven, [G], (MOB), Montgomery, AL.
Seton Health Care of Northern Illinois, [J], (CHI). See St. Joseph Hospital.
Seton Health Care Services, Inc., [Y], (MIL), Milwaukee, WI.
Seton Health Care, Inc., [P], (PAT), Convent Station, NJ.
Seton Health Corp. of South Alabama, [E], (MOB), Mobile, AL.
Seton Health Corporation of Central Indiana, [F], (IND), Indianapolis, IN.
Seton Health Corporation of East Central Michigan, [I], (SAG), Saginaw, MI.
Seton Health Corporation of North Alabama, [D], (BIR), Birmingham, AL.
Seton Health Corporation of Southeast Michigan, [T], (DET), Southfield, MI.
Seton Health Corporation of Southern Indiana, [J], (EVN), Evansville, IN.
Seton Health Corporation of Tennessee, Inc., [F], (NSH). See St. Thomas Hospital.
Seton Health Corporation of Wisconsin, [Y], (MIL), Milwaukee, WI.
Seton Health Services Foundation, [J], (SFR). See Seton Medical Center.
Seton Health System, Inc., [H], (ALB), Troy, NY.
Seton High School, [E], (CIN), Cincinnati, OH.
Seton High School Foundation, [U], (CIN), Cincinnati, OH.
Seton Hill College, [B], (GBG), Greensburg, PA.
Seton Home Endowment Fund, [S], (SAT), San Antonio, TX.
Seton Home for Homeless, Pregnant Young Women, [I], (SAT), San Antonio, TX.
Seton Home Study School, [N], (ARL), Front Royal, VA.
Seton Housing, Inc., [G], (COL), Zanesville, OH.
Seton Institute for International Development, [J], (SFR). See Seton Medical Center.
Seton Kenton, Inc., [G], (COL), Kenton, OH.
The Seton Keough High School, [D], (BAL), Baltimore, MD.
Seton Lancaster, Inc., [G], (COL), Lancaster, OH.
Seton London, Inc., [G], (COL), Columbus, OH.
Seton Manor, [H], (RIC), Hampton, VA.
Seton Medical Center, [F], (AUS), Austin, TX.
Seton Medical Center, [J], (SFR), Daly City, CA.
Seton Medical Center, [J], (SFR). See Seton Medical Center.
Seton Medical Center Coastside, [J], (SFR), Moss Beach, CA.
Seton Medical Management, Inc., [E], (MOB), Mobile, AL.
Seton Northwest Hospital, [F], (AUS), Austin, TX.
Seton Nursery School and Infant-Toddler Child Care Center, [O], (DET), Farmington Hills, MI.
Seton Regional Foundation, Inc., [P], (BAL). See Chancery Office.
Seton Regional Health System, Inc., [P], (BAL). See Chancery Office.
Seton Residence, [F], (EVN), Evansville, IN.
Seton Retreat Center, [L], (BAL), Emmitsburg, MD.
Seton South Columbus, Inc., [G], (COL), Columbus, OH.
Seton South Community Health Center, [F], (AUS), Austin, TX.
Seton Square Dover, I, Inc., [G], (COL), Dover, OH.
Seton Square Dover, II, Inc., [G], (COL), Dover, OH.
Seton Square East, Inc., [G], (COL), Reynoldsburg, OH.
Seton Square Marion, Inc., [G], (COL), Marion, OH.
Seton Square North, [G], (COL), Columbus, OH.
Seton Square Wellston, Inc., [G], (COL), Wellston, OH.
Seton Villa, Inc., [E], (WIL), Wilmington, DE.
Seton Village Inc., [G], (PRT), Waterville, ME.
Seton Washington Court House, Inc., [G], (COL), Columbus, OH.
Seton-LaSalle Catholic High School, [C], (PIT), Mt. Lebanon, PA.
Seymour Deanery Counseling, [L], (IND), Columbus, IN.
Shade Tree Family Resource Center, Inc., [Y], (MIL), Milwaukee, WI.
Shakopee Area Catholic School, [H], (STP), Shakopee, MN.
Shalem House, [K], (FTW). See Saint Mary's of the Immaculate Conception.
Shalom Catholic Worker House, [K], (KCK), Kansas City, KS.
Shalom Center, Inc., [O], (GAL), Splendora, TX.
Shalom Community, [N], (HRT). See Sisters of St. Joseph.
Shalom Convent, [AA], (NY), New York, NY.
Shalom Convent, [AA], (PH), Philadelphia, PA.
Shalom Convent, [O], (SFR), San Francisco, CA.
Shalom House, [O], (RIC), Montpelier, VA.
Shalom House Family Shelter, [N], (LAF). See Lafayette Catholic Service Centers, Inc.
Shalom House of Prayer, [S], (GAL), Houston, TX.
Shalom Retreat Center, [M], (DUB), Dubuque, IA.
Shanley High School, [B], (FAR), Fargo, ND.
Shantivanam Archdiocesan House of Prayer, [K], (KCK), Easton, KS.
SHARE Colorado, [L], (DEN). See Catholic Charities and Community Services of the Archdiocese of Denver, Inc.
SHARE Food Program of Central Illinois, Inc., [P], (PEO), Peoria, IL.
SHARE Southern California, [J], (SD). See St. Vincent de Paul Village.
Shared Housing Exchange, [E], (SR). See Diocese of Santa Rosa, Catholic Charities.
Shared Housing Program, [F], (SJ). See Catholic Charities of Santa Clara County.
Shared Therapeutic Services, Inc., [Y], (MIL), Milwaukee, WI.
The Sharkey Family Charitable Trust, [F], (CAM), Ocean City, NJ.
Shawe Memorial Junior-Senior High School, [C], (IND), Madison, IN.
Sheehan Residence for Priests, [O], (BUF), Buffalo, NY.
Shelby County Board of Catholic Education, [A], (DM), Panama, IA.
Shelby County Catholic Education Foundation, [I], (DM), Harlan, IA.
Shelter for Homeless, [L], (DEN). See Catholic Charities and Community Services of the Archdiocese of Denver, Inc.
Shelter for the Homeless, [H], (PCE), Ponce, PR.
Shelter Nursery for Drug Exposed Babies, [L], (SFR). See Mount St. Joseph-St. Elizabeth.
Shelter of Flint, Inc., [D], (LAN), Flint, MI.
Shelter Plus Housing, [J], (SLC). See Catholic Community Services.
Sheltering Arms, [J], (DET), Southfield, MI.
Sheltering Arms Adult Day Care, [N], (DET). See Catholic Social Services of Oakland County.
Shelters for the Homeless, Inc., [X], (CHI), Chicago, IL.
Sheptytsky Arms, [B], (SJP), Pittsburgh, PA.
Sherri Lyn Shaffer Trust for St. Thomas More Church, [M], (BR). See Baton Rouge Chancery Office.
Shevchenko Manor, [B], (SJP), Parma, OH.
Shoreless Lake School, [B], (MET), New Brunswick, NJ.
Short Journey Center, [I], (R), Smithfield, NC.
Shrine Chapel of the Blessed Sacrament, [K], (MET), Raritan, NJ.
Shrine High School, [D], (DET), Royal Oak, MI.
Shrine of Immaculate Heart of Mary, [H], (SPC), Carthage, MO.
Shrine of Our Lady of Charity, [K], (MIA), Miami, FL.
Shrine of Our Lady of Grace, [K], (MAN), Colebrook, NH.
Shrine of Our Lady of La Salette, [K], (MAN), Enfield, NH.
Shrine of Our Lady of Martyrs, [O], (ALB), Auriesville, NY.
Shrine of Our Lady of Peace, [A], (SJ), Santa Clara, CA.
Shrine of Our Lady of the Island, [N], (RVC), Eastport, NY.
Shrine of Our Lady of the Snows, [G], (BEL), Belleville, IL.
Shrine of Our Lady of Victories at St. Peter Claver, [EE], (PH), Philadelphia, PA.
Shrine of St. Joseph, [M], (PAT), Stirling, NJ.
Shrine of St. Jude Thaddeus, [U], (SFR), San Francisco, CA.
Shrine of St. Jude, Inc., [DD], (NY), New York, NY.

Shrine of St. Maximilian Kolbe, [N], (CHI). See Marytown, Our Lady of Fatima Friary.
Shrine of the Immaculate Heart of Mary, [K], (MET), Washington, NJ.
Shrine of the Infant Jesus, [T], (BUF), North Tonawanda, NY.
Shrine of the Sacred Heart, [R], (SCR), Harleigh, PA.
Shrine of the Weeping Madonna of Mariapoch, [B], (PRM), Burton, OH.
Siegfried Hall, Notre Dame, [K], (FTW). See Saint Mary's of the Immaculate Conception.
Siena - Francis House, Inc., [O], (OM), Omaha, NE.
Siena Club, [O], (KC), Kansas City, MO.
Siena College, [B], (ALB), Loudonville, NY.
Siena College, [S], (ALB), Loudonville, NY.
Siena Convent, [N], (SR), Napa, CA.
Siena Hall, Inc., [E], (WIL), Wilmington, DE.
Siena Heights College - President, [A], (LAN), Adrian, MI.
Siena Heights College Newman Center, [J], (LAN), Adrian, MI.
Siena House, [O], (OAK). See Dominican Sisters of Mission San Jose.
Siena House, [O], (OM), Omaha, NE.
Siena Literacy Center, [T], (DET), Redford, MI.
Siena Retreat Center - A Small Part of the Holy Cross, [I], (MRY), Santa Cruz, CA.
Siena Senior Citizen Housing Corp., [S], (NEW), Caldwell, NJ.
Siena Spirituality Center, [O], (RVC), Water Mill, NY.
Siena Springs, [L], (CIN), Dayton, OH.
Siena Village, [P], (PAT), Wayne, NJ.
Silva Pediatric Clinic, [K], (OAK). See St. Rose Hospital.
Silver Lake College of the Holy Family, [B], (GB), Manitowoc, WI.
Silver Penny Farm Retreat Center, [M], (SFR), Petaluma, CA.
Simeon House I (St. Patrick Parish), [L], (IND). See Catholic Charities.
Simeon House II (Sacred Heart Parish), [L], (IND). See Catholic Charities.
Simon Hall, [P], (L). See Society of St. Vincent de Paul, Council of Louisville.
Simpatico School, [L], (SFR). See Mount St. Joseph-St. Elizabeth.
Sinclair Community College Campus Ministry, [Q], (CIN), Dayton, OH.
Sinsinawa Dominican Community Support Trust, [M], (MAD), Sinsinawa, WI.
Sinsinawa Dominican Congregation of the Most Holy Rosary, [N], (SJ), San Jose, CA.
Sinsinawa Dominican Congregation of the Most Holy Rosary, O.P., [Q], (NO), Harvey, LA.
Sinsinawa Dominican Sisters, [I], (AUS), Austin, TX.
Sinsinawa Dominican Sisters, [K], (MEM), Somerville, TN.
Sinsinawa Dominican Sisters, [I], (MOB), Ozark, AL.
Sioux Falls Catholic School Corporation, [I], (SFS), Sioux Falls, SD.
Sioux Falls Catholic School System, [C], (SFS), Sioux Falls, SD.
Sister Disciples of the Divine Master, [X], (BO), Boston, MA.
Sister Disciples of the Divine Master, [F], (FRS), Fresno, CA.
Sr. Elizabeth Boyle Child Learning Center, Inc., [R], (NY), New York, NY.
Sister Georgine School, [H], (TR), Trenton, NJ.
Sister Joanna House of Formation, [N], (PAT), Florham Park, NJ.
Sr. Lucian Apartments, HDFC, Inc., [L], (BRK). See Catholic Charities.
The Sister Maureen Keleher Center (Hospice), [F], (HON). See St. Francis Healthcare System of Hawaii.
Sister of Charity of St. Charles Borromeo, Inc., [O], (WDC), Silver Spring, MD.
Sister of Charity, Franciscan Sister, Sister of the Incarnate Word, [C], (LSC), Sunland Park, NM.
Sister of Notre Dame de Namur, [N], (HRT), Hartford, CT.
Sister of St. Francis of Philadelphia, [N], (SEA), Tacoma, WA.
Sister of St. Mary of Namur Marion House, [N], (FWT), Fort Worth, TX.
Sister of the Sorrowful Mother, [C], (LSC), Truth or Consequences, NM.
Sister Patricia Ann's Preschool dba Gingerbread House Preschool, [L], (SY), Syracuse, NY.
Sister Servants of the Blessed Sacrament, [I], (SAC), Sacramento, CA.
Sister Servants of the Blessed Sacrament, [I], (SD), Calexico, CA.
Sister Servants of the Blessed Sacrament, [I], (SD), San Ysidro, CA.
Sister Servants of the Eternal Word, A Public Association of the Christian Faithful, [F], (BIR), Birmingham, AL.
Sister Servants of the Holy Spirit of Perpetual Adoration (S.Sp.S.A.P.), [AA], (PH), Philadelphia, PA.
Sr. Thea Bowman Academy, [B], (BEA), Port Arthur, TX.
Sister Thea Bowman Catholic School, [C], (BEL), East St. Louis, IL.
Sr. Thea Bowman Elementary School, [D], (GRY), Gary, IN.
Sister Winifred Auxiliary, [P], (LA). See St. Anne's.
Sisters de L'Union-Chretienne de Chaumond, [I], (ORG), Tustin, CA.
Sisters for Christian Community, [L], (ALN), Whitehall, PA.
Sisters For Christian Community, [F], (BLX), Hattiesburg, MS.
Sisters for Christian Community, [H], (PBL), Pueblo, CO.
Sisters For Christian Community, [F], (R), Rolesville, NC.
Sisters for Christian Community (S.F.C.C.), [R], (GAL), Houston, TX.
Sisters Hospital Foundation, Inc., [K], (BUF), Buffalo, NY.
Sisters House, [L], (ALN), Pottsville, PA.
Sisters Minor of Mary Immaculate, [P], (BGP), Stamford, CT.
Sisters Minor of Mary Immaculate, [F], (FAR), Fargo, ND.
Sisters of A New Genesis (ANG), [O], (GB), Green Bay, WI.
Sisters of Benedict of Colorado, Inc., [N], (DEN), Littleton, CO.
Sisters of Benedict Red Plains Monastery, [J], (OKL), Piedmont, OK.
Sisters of Bon Secours, [AA], (PH), Lansdowne, PA.
Sisters of Bon Secours, [N], (RIC), Portsmouth, VA.
Sisters of Bon Secours Convent, [F], (CHR), Charleston, SC.
Sisters of Bon Secours Nursing Care Center, [I], (DET), St. Clair Shores, MI.
Sisters of Bon Secours Nursing Care Center, [J], (DET), St. Clair Shores, MI.
Sisters of Bon Secours, C.B.S., Provincial House, [N], (BAL), Marriottsville, MD.
Sisters of Charity, [G], (ALT), Altoona, PA.
Sisters of Charity, [I], (GBG), Greensburg, PA.
Sisters of Charity, [E], (PHX), Tempe, AZ.
Sisters of Charity, [J], (PRT), Portland, ME.
Sisters of Charity, [F], (R), Kill Devil Hills, NC.
Sisters of Charity Center, [AA], (NY), New York, NY.
Sisters of Charity Formation House, [I], (GBG), Greensburg, PA.
Sisters of Charity Foundation of South Carolina, [J], (CHR), Columbia, SC.
Sisters of Charity Foundation, Inc., [U], (CIN), Cincinnati, OH.
Sisters of Charity Health Care System Corp., [DD], (NY), New York, NY.
Sisters of Charity Health Care Systems, Inc., [T], (CIN), Cincinnati, OH.
Sisters of Charity Hospital of Buffalo, NY, [K], (BUF), Buffalo, NY.
Sisters of Charity of Cincinnati, [G], (KNX), Cleveland, TN.
Sisters of Charity of Cincinnati, [O], (OAK), Oakland, CA.
Sisters of Charity of Cincinnati, Ohio, [N], (CIN), Cincinnati, OH.
Sisters of Charity of Cincinnati-Charitable Trust, [U], (CIN), Cincinnati, OH.
Sisters of Charity of Leavenworth, [F], (BWN), Mission, TX.
Sisters of Charity of Leavenworth, [H], (GF), Billings, MT.
Sisters of Charity of Leavenworth, [I], (ORG), Orange, CA.
Sisters of Charity of Leavenworth Health Services Corporation, [K], (KCK), Leavenworth, KS.
Sisters of Charity of Nazareth, [G], (KNX), Chattanooga, TN.
Sisters of Charity of Nazareth, [AA], (PH), Philadelphia, PA.
Sisters of Charity of Nazareth, [N], (SJ), San Jose, CA.
Sisters Of Charity Of Nazareth (KY) S.C.N., [K], (MEM), Memphis, TN.
Sisters of Charity of Nazareth Health System, [Q], (L), Nazareth, KY.
Sisters of Charity of Nazareth Regional House, [X], (BO), Quincy, MA.
Sisters of Charity of New York Charitable Trust, [DD], (NY), New York, NY.
The Sisters of Charity of Our Lady of Mercy Charitable Trust, [J], (CHR), Charleston, SC.
Sisters of Charity of Our Lady, Mother of the Church, [N], (HRT), West Hartford, CT.
Sisters of Charity of Our Lady, Mother of the Church, [G], (NOR), Willimantic, CT.
Sisters of Charity of Rolling Hills, [S], (LA), Rolling Hills, CA.
Sisters of Charity of St. Augustine Health Network, [AA], (CLV), Cleveland, OH.
Sisters of Charity of St. Augustine Health System, [AA], (CLV), Cleveland, OH.
Sisters of Charity of St. Elizabeth (Convent, NJ) Northern Provincial House, [O], (NEW), Jersey City, NJ.
Sisters of Charity of St. Elizabeth, Convent Station, [N], (HRT), New Haven, CT.
Sisters of Charity of St. Elizabeth, Convent Station, [N], (HRT), Waterbury, CT.
Sisters of Charity of St. Elizabeth, Convent Station, [N], (HRT), Watertown, CT.
Sisters of Charity of St. Joan Antida, [Q], (MIL), Milwaukee, WI.
Sisters of Charity of St. Joan Antida Convent, [Q], (MIL), West Allis, WI.
Sisters of Charity of St. Joan Antida Convent (Emmanuel), [Q], (MIL), Milwaukee, WI.
Sisters of Charity of St. Joan Antida Convent (Maranatha), [Q], (MIL), Milwaukee, WI.
Sisters of Charity of St. Joan Antida Convent (Presentation), [Q], (MIL), Milwaukee, WI.
Sisters of Charity of St. Joan Antida Regina Mundi Provincial House and Novitiate, [Q], (MIL), Milwaukee, WI.
Sisters of Charity of St. Louis Convent, [M], (ALB), Clifton Park, NY.
Sisters of Charity of St. Vincent de Paul of Zagreb, Croatia, [P], (BUF), Lackawanna, NY.
Sisters of Charity of St. Vincent de Paul of Zagreb, Croatia, [P], (BUF), West Seneca, NY.
Sisters of Charity of Seton Hill, [F], (R), Raleigh, NC.
Sisters of Charity of Seton Hill, [F], (R), New Bern, NC.
Sisters of Charity of the Blessed Virgin Mary, [I], (HON), Waipahu, HI.
Sisters of Charity of the Blessed Virgin Mary, [G], (KNX), Chattanooga, TN.
Sisters of Charity of the Blessed Virgin Mary, [O], (OAK), Union City, CA.
Sisters of Charity of the Blessed Virgin Mary, [I], (ORG), Cypress, CA.
Sisters of Charity of the Blessed Virgin Mary, [I], (ORG), Huntington Beach, CA.
Sisters of Charity of the Blessed Virgin Mary, [I], (ORG), Tustin, CA.
Sisters of Charity of the Blessed Virgin Mary, [E], (PHX), Phoenix, AZ.
Sisters of Charity of the Blessed Virgin Mary, [I], (SD), Carlsbad, CA.
Sisters of Charity of the Blessed Virgin Mary, [N], (SJ), San Jose, CA.
Sisters of Charity of the Blessed Virgin Mary, [N], (SJ), San Jose, CA.
Sisters of Charity of the Blessed Virgin Mary, [N], (SJ), Santa Clara, CA.
Sisters of Charity of the Blessed Virgin Mary, [E], (STO), Stockton, CA.
Sisters Of Charity Of The Blessed Virgin Mary (Dubuque, IA) B.V.M., [K], (MEM), Memphis, TN.
Sisters of Charity of the Blessed Virgin Mary, BVM Center, Mount Carmel, [L], (DUB), Dubuque, IA.
Sisters of Charity of the Incarnate Word, [I], (AUS), Waco, TX.
Sisters of Charity of the Incarnate Word, [F], (BWN), Brownsville, TX.
Sisters of Charity of the Incarnate Word, [D], (LUB), Levelland, TX.
Sisters of Charity of the Incarnate Word, [B], (SAN), San Angelo, TX.
Sisters of Charity of the Incarnate Word (Houston), [F], (BWN), Harlingen, TX.
Sisters of Charity of the Incarnate Word (San Antonio), [F], (BWN), Brownsville, TX.
Sisters of Charity of the Incarnate Word Retirement Trust, [J], (GAL). See Sisters of Charity of the Incarnate Word, Houston, Texas.
Sisters of Charity of the Incarnate Word, Houston, Texas, [J], (GAL), Houston, TX.
Sisters of Charity of the Infant Mary Community of Formation, [H], (MRY), Gonzales, CA.
Sisters of Charity Senior Care Corp., dba Bayley Place, [L], (CIN), Cincinnati, OH.
Sisters of Charity, B.V.M., [O], (OAK), Berkeley, CA.
Sisters of Charity, Sisters' Residence, [J], (PRT), Lewiston, ME.
Sisters of Charity/City of Houston Southwest Community Health Clinic, [J], (GAL). See Sisters of Charity of the Incarnate Word, Houston, Texas.
Sisters of Christian Charity Healthcare Corporation, [I], (SCR), Williamsport, PA.
Sisters of Divine Providence, [G], (ALX), Natchez, LA.
Sisters of Divine Providence, [I], (AUS), Austin, TX.
Sisters of Divine Providence, [I], (AUS), Fayetteville, TX.
Sisters of Divine Providence, [I], (LAF), Lafayette, LA.
Sisters of Divine Providence, [I], (LAF), Arnaudville, LA.
Sisters of Divine Providence, [I], (LAF), Iota, LA.
Sisters of Divine Providence, [I], (LAF), Crowley, LA.

The Sisters of Divine Providence, [O], (PIT), Allison Park, PA.
Sisters of Divine Providence, [F], (R), Raleigh, NC.
Sisters of Divine Providence, [B], (SAN), Rowena, TX.
Sisters of Divine Providence Charitable Trust, [R], (PIT), Allison Park, PA.
Sisters of Divine Providence of San Antonio, Texas, [G], (ALX), Alexandria, LA.
Sisters of Divine Redeemer Charitable Trust, [R], (PIT), Elizabeth, PA.
Sisters of Divine Savior, [E], (PHX), Phoenix, AZ.
Sisters of Holy Cross, [G], (KNX), Lancing, TN.
Sisters of Holy Cross, [L], (MAN), Londonderry, NH.
Sisters of Holy Cross, [L], (MAN), Manchester, NH.
Sisters of Holy Cross, [L], (MAN), West Franklin, NH.
Sisters of Holy Cross, [G], (OG), Clayton, NY.
Sisters of Holy Family of Nazareth, [N], (HRT), Ansonia, CT.
Sisters of Immaculate Heart of Mary, [O], (OAK), Rodeo, CA.
Sisters of Jesus Our Hope, [I], (MET), Bound Brook, NJ.
Sisters of Jesus Our Hope, [I], (MET), Hampton, NJ.
Sisters of Jesus Our Hope, [I], (MET), Carteret, NJ.
Sisters of Jesus Our Hope, [L], (MET), Bound Brook, NJ.
Sisters of LaSalle, [N], (SJ), San Jose, CA.
Sisters of Little Company of Mary, [I], (ORG), Laguna Hills, CA.
Sisters of Loretto, [G], (KNX), Lake City, TN.
Sisters of Loretto, [I], (MOB), Mobile, AL.
Sisters of Loretto, [I], (MOB), Montgomery, AL.
Sisters of Loretto, [I], (SD), San Diego, CA.
Sisters of Loretto (S.L.), [R], (GAL), Houston, TX.
Sisters of Loretto at the Foot of the Cross, [N], (SJ), San Jose, CA.
Sisters of Loretto at the Foot of the Cross (S.L.), [K], (ELP), El Paso, TX.
Sisters of Loretto at the Foot of the Hill, [N], (SJ), Palo Alto, CA.
Sisters of Loretto Charitable Trust, [Q], (L), Louisville, KY.
Sisters of Marie Auxiliatrice, [D], (CI), Awak, Pohnpei, FM.
Sisters of Mary Immaculate (Krishnagar, India), [I], (GBG), Greensburg, PA.
Sisters of Mary Immaculate (West Bengal, India), [I], (GBG), Leechburg, PA.
Sisters of Mary Mother of the Church, [S], (LA), Beverly Hills, CA.
Sisters of Mary of the Presentation, [F], (FAR), Valley City, ND.
Sisters of Mary Reparatrix, [L], (DET), Port Huron, MI.
Sisters of Mary Reparatrix, [BB], (NY), New York, NY.
Sisters of Mercy, [G], (ALT), Johnstown, PA.
Sisters of Mercy, [N], (BAL), Baltimore, MD.
Sisters of Mercy, [N], (CIN), Cincinnati, OH.
Sisters of Mercy, [N], (CIN), Batavia, OH.
Sisters of Mercy, [L], (FR), Fall River, MA.
Sisters of Mercy, [L], (FR), New Bedford, MA.
Sisters of Mercy, [F], (JKS), Vicksburg, MS.
Sisters of Mercy, [G], (KNX), Knoxville, TN.
Sisters of Mercy, [G], (KNX), Helenwood, TN.
Sisters of Mercy, [G], (NOR), Middletown, CT.
Sisters of Mercy, [Q], (PRO), Cumberland, RI.
Sisters of Mercy, [F], (R), Kinston, NC.
Sisters of Mercy, [N], (RIC), Williamsburg, VA.
Sisters of Mercy, [I], (SAC). See Institute of the Sisters of Mercy of the Americas.
Sisters of Mercy, [I], (SAC), Fair Oaks, CA.
Sisters of Mercy, [N], (SJ), Los Altos Hills, CA.
Sisters of Mercy, [O], (WOR), Worcester, MA.
Sisters of Mercy - ARISE, Las Milpas, Inc., [R], (STL). See Sisters of Mercy of the Americas, Regional Community of St. Louis.
Sisters of Mercy - New Jersey Region, [C], (LSC), LaUnion, NM.
Sisters of Mercy - St. James Convent, [F], (BLX), Gulfport, MS.
Sisters of Mercy (Ireland & South Africa), [I], (SD), San Diego, CA.
Sisters of Mercy (Ireland & South Africa), [I], (SD), El Cajon, CA.
Sisters of Mercy Continuing Support Trust Fund, [R], (PIT), Pittsburgh, PA.
Sisters of Mercy Convent, [F], (BLX), Biloxi, MS.
Sisters of Mercy Convent, [F], (JKS), Vicksburg, MS.
Sisters of Mercy Convent, [M], (P), Portland, OR.
Sisters of Mercy Convent, [O], (WDC), Silver Spring, MD.
Sisters of Mercy Education System, Inc., [W], (STL), St. Louis, MO.
Sisters of Mercy Education System, St. Louis, Inc., Begin Literacy Program, [R], (STL). See Sisters of Mercy of the Americas, Regional Community of St. Louis.
Sisters of Mercy Health Foundation, [O], (TOL), Toledo, OH.
Sisters of Mercy Health System, North, [O], (TOL), Toledo, OH.
Sisters of Mercy Health System, St. Louis, Inc., [R], (STL). See Sisters of Mercy of the Americas, Regional Community of St. Louis.
Sisters of Mercy Ministry Corporation, [I], (MIA), Fort Lauderdale, FL.
Sisters of Mercy Motherhouse, [M], (E), Erie, PA.
Sisters of Mercy of Americas (Burlingame), [N], (SJ), Mountain View, CA.
Sisters of Mercy of Ireland, [I], (ORG), Costa Mesa, CA.
Sisters of Mercy of North Carolina Foundation, Inc., [Q], (CHL), Charlotte, NC.
Sisters of Mercy of North Carolina on Guam - Mercy Administration Center, [Q], (CHL), Belmont, NC.
Sisters of Mercy of North Carolina on Guam - Sacred Heart Convent, [K], (CHL), Belmont, NC.
Sisters of Mercy of St. Joseph Convent of Hot Springs, Arkansas, Inc., [E], (LR). See St. Joseph's Regional Health Center.
Sisters of Mercy of the Americas, [F], (BWN), McAllen, TX.
Sisters of Mercy of the Americas, [F], (BWN), McAllen, TX.
Sisters of Mercy of the Americas, [F], (BWN), Pharr, TX.
Sisters of Mercy of the Americas, [F], (BWN), Raymondville, TX.
Sisters of Mercy of the Americas, [L], (DET). See Sisters of Mercy-Regional Community of Detroit, Inc.
Sisters of Mercy of the Americas, [I], (LAF), St. Martinville, LA.
Sisters of Mercy of the Americas, [L], (MAN), Windham, NH.
Sisters of Mercy of the Americas, [G], (OG), Saranac Lake, NY.
Sisters of Mercy of the Americas, [J], (OKL), Oklahoma City, OK.
Sisters of Mercy of the Americas, [J], (OKL), Oklahoma City, OK.
Sisters of Mercy of the Americas, [I], (ORG), Santa Ana, CA.
Sisters of Mercy of the Americas, [N], (PEO), Ottawa, IL.
Sisters of Mercy of the Americas, [AA], (PH), Philadelphia, PA.
Sisters of Mercy of the Americas, [J], (PRT), Portland, ME.
Sisters of Mercy of the Americas, [J], (PRT), Hampden, ME.
Sisters of Mercy of the Americas, [F], (R), Cary, NC.
Sisters of Mercy of the Americas, [F], (SPC), Springfield, MO.
Sisters of Mercy of the Americas (Burlingame), [I], (SD), San Diego, CA.
Sisters of Mercy of the Americas (Omaha Region & Vermont Region), [C], (LSC), Anthony, NM.
Sisters of Mercy of the Americas Administrative Center, [O], (WDC), Silver Spring, MD.
Sisters of Mercy of the Americas of Albany, [N], (HRT), West Hartford, CT.
Sisters of Mercy of the Americas of Albany, [N], (HRT), Bloomfield, CT.
Sisters of Mercy of the Americas of Connecticut, [N], (HRT), Bloomfield, CT.
Sisters of Mercy of the Americas of Connecticut, [N], (HRT), Bristol, CT.
Sisters of Mercy of the Americas of Connecticut, [N], (HRT), Guilford, CT.
Sisters of Mercy of the Americas of Connecticut, [N], (HRT), Hamden, CT.
Sisters of Mercy of the Americas of Connecticut, [N], (HRT), Hartford, CT.
Sisters of Mercy of the Americas of Connecticut, [N], (HRT), Madison, CT.
Sisters of Mercy of the Americas of Connecticut, [N], (HRT), Manchester, CT.
Sisters of Mercy of the Americas of Connecticut, [N], (HRT), Milford, CT.
Sisters of Mercy of the Americas of Connecticut, [N], (HRT), Naugatuck, CT.
Sisters of Mercy of the Americas of Connecticut, [N], (HRT), New Britain, CT.
Sisters of Mercy of the Americas of Connecticut, [N], (HRT), New Haven, CT.
Sisters of Mercy of the Americas of Connecticut, [N], (HRT), Waterbury, CT.
Sisters of Mercy of the Americas of Connecticut, [N], (HRT), West Hartford, CT.
Sisters of Mercy of the Americas of Connecticut, [N], (HRT), Wallingford, CT.
Sisters of Mercy of the Americas of Detroit, [N], (HRT), North Branford, CT.
Sisters of Mercy of the Americas of Vermont, [N], (HRT), Farmington, CT.
Sisters of Mercy of the Americas of Vermont, [N], (HRT), West Hartford, CT.
Sisters of Mercy of the Americas Regional Community of Dallas, [O], (SCR), Dallas, PA.
Sisters of Mercy of the Americas Regional Community of Rochester, [J], (ROC), Rochester, NY.
Sisters of Mercy of the Americas, Annunciation Convent, [AA], (PH), Gwynedd Valley, PA.
Sisters of Mercy of the Americas, R.S.M., [Q], (NO), New Orleans, LA.
Sisters of Mercy of the Americas, Regional Community of Chicago Charitable Trust, [O], (CHI). See Administrative Center of the Sisters of Mercy of the Americas.
Sisters of Mercy of the Americas, Regional Community of Providence, [Q], (PRO), Cumberland, RI.
Sisters of Mercy of the Americas, Regional Community of St. Louis, [R], (STL), St. Louis, MO.
Sisters of Mercy of the Americas, St. Louis Regional Community, [I], (MOB), Mobile, AL.
Sisters of Mercy of the Blessed Sacrament, [I], (SD), Lemon Grove, CA.
Sisters of Mercy of the Buffalo Diocese Retirement Corp., [P], (BUF), Orchard Park, NY.
Sisters of Mercy of the Holy Cross Community Support Charitable Trust, [D], (SUP). See Holy Cross Provincial Office.
Sisters of Mercy of the Holy Cross Community Support Charitable Trust, [I], (SUP), Merrill, WI.
Sisters of Mercy of the St. Louis Regional Community, Inc., [I], (CC), Laredo, TX.
Sisters of Mercy of the St. Louis Regional Community, Inc., [R], (STL). See Sisters of Mercy of the Americas, Regional Community of St. Louis.
Sisters of Mercy, Burlingame, [O], (OAK), Oakland, CA.
Sisters of Mercy, U.S. Province, [F], (SB), Redlands, CA.
Sisters of Mercy, Watertown, NY, [G], (OG), Watertown, NY.
Sisters of Mercy-Regional Community of Detroit, Inc., [L], (DET), Farmington Hills, MI.
Sisters of Mercy-Regional Community Offices, [P], (BUF), Orchard Park, NY.
Sisters of Mt. Carmel, [I], (LAF), Lafayette, LA.
Sisters of Mt. Carmel, [I], (LAF), Abbeville, LA.
Sisters of Mt. Carmel, [I], (LAF), Grand Coteau, LA.
Sisters of Mt. Carmel, [I], (LAF), Rayne, LA.
Sisters of Notre Dame, [S], (LA), Thousand Oaks, CA.
Sisters of Notre Dame, [J], (PRT), Scarborough, ME.
Sisters of Notre Dame, [F], (R), Wilson, NC.
Sisters of Notre Dame, [F], (R), Raleigh, NC.
Sisters of Notre Dame, [F], (R), Carrboro, NC.
Sisters of Notre Dame, [G], (SLC), Salt Lake City, UT.
The Sisters of Notre Dame Charitable Trust, [Z], (CLV), Chardon, OH.
Sisters of Notre Dame de Namur, [I], (AUS), Austin, TX.
Sisters of Notre Dame de Namur, [I], (COL), Columbus, OH.
Sisters of Notre Dame de Namur, [I], (HON), Honolulu, HI.
Sisters of Notre Dame de Namur, [N], (HRT), Bloomfield, CT.
Sisters of Notre Dame de Namur, [N], (HRT), Windsor, CT.
Sisters of Notre Dame de Namur, [N], (HRT), Hartford, CT.
Sisters of Notre Dame de Namur, [N], (HRT), East Hartford, CT.
Sisters of Notre Dame de Namur, [N], (HRT), East Haven, CT.
Sisters of Notre Dame de Namur, [N], (HRT), Hartford, CT.
Sisters of Notre Dame de Namur, [N], (HRT), Manchester, CT.
Sisters of Notre Dame de Namur, [N], (HRT), New Haven, CT.
Sisters of Notre Dame de Namur, [N], (HRT), Newington, CT.
Sisters of Notre Dame de Namur, [N], (HRT), Waterbury, CT.
Sisters of Notre Dame de Namur, [N], (HRT), West Hartford, CT.
Sisters of Notre Dame de Namur, [N], (HRT), Wethersfield, CT.
Sisters of Notre Dame de Namur, [N], (HRT), Windsor Locks, CT.
Sisters of Notre Dame de Namur, [G], (KNX), Kingsport, TN.
Sisters of Notre Dame de Namur, [O], (OAK), Alameda, CA.
Sisters of Notre Dame de Namur, [O], (OAK), Berkeley, CA.
Sisters of Notre Dame de Namur, [AA], (PH), Philadelphia, PA.
Sisters of Notre Dame de Namur, [AA], (PH), Drexel Hill, PA.
Sisters of Notre Dame de Namur, [AA], (PH), Villanova, PA.
Sisters of Notre Dame de Namur, [E], (PHX), Mesa, AZ.
Sisters of Notre Dame de Namur, [N], (SJ), San Jose, CA.

Provincial House of the Sisters of St. Joseph of Carondelet.
Sisters of St. Joseph in the Third Order of St. Francis, [O], (OAK), Castro Valley, CA.
Sisters of St. Joseph Ministerial Services, [S], (LA). See Provincial House of the Sisters of St. Joseph of Carondelet.
Sisters of St. Joseph Motherhouse, [G], (OG), Watertown, NY.
Sisters of St. Joseph of Brentwood, [N], (HRT), Madison, CT.
Sisters of St. Joseph of Carondelet, [F], (BWN), Brownsville, TX.
Sisters of St. Joseph of Carondelet, [F], (BWN), Mission, TX.
Sisters of St. Joseph of Carondelet, [F], (BWN), Edinburg, TX.
Sisters of St. Joseph of Carondelet, [I], (LAF), Lafayette, LA.
Sisters of St. Joseph of Carondelet, [O], (OAK), Berkeley, CA.
Sisters of St. Joseph of Carondelet, [O], (OAK), Concord, CA.
Sisters of St. Joseph of Carondelet, [O], (OAK), Lafayette, CA.
Sisters of St. Joseph of Carondelet, [O], (OAK), Martinez, CA.
Sisters of St. Joseph of Carondelet, [O], (OAK), Pleasant Hill, CA.
Sisters of St. Joseph of Carondelet, [I], (ORG), La Habra, CA.
Sisters of St. Joseph of Carondelet, [I], (ORG), Newport Beach, CA.
Sisters of St. Joseph of Carondelet, [I], (ORG), Santa Ana, CA.
Sisters of St. Joseph of Carondelet, [I], (SD), San Diego, CA.
Sisters of St. Joseph of Carondelet, [I], (SD), Solana Beach, CA.
Sisters of St. Joseph of Carondelet, [N], (SJ), San Jose, CA.
Sisters of St. Joseph of Carondelet, [E], (STO), Stockton, CA.
Sisters of St. Joseph of Carondelet, [O], (STP), St. Paul, MN.
Sisters of St. Joseph of Carondelet (C.S.J.), [K], (ELP), El Paso, TX.
Sisters of St. Joseph of Carondelet CSJ, Hawaii Vice-Province, [I], (HON), Honolulu, HI.
Sisters of St. Joseph of Carondelet Ministries Foundation, St. Paul Province, [W], (STP), St. Paul, MN.
Sisters of St. Joseph of Carondelet, Albany Province, [I], (ORG), Trabuco Canyon, CA.
Sisters of St. Joseph of Carondelet, Sisters of St. Joseph of Cluny, [I], (ORG), Orange, CA.
Sisters of St. Joseph of Chambery, [N], (HRT), Windsor, CT.
Sisters of St. Joseph of Chambery, [N], (HRT), Northford, CT.
Sisters of St. Joseph of Chambery, [N], (HRT), New Haven, CT.
Sisters of St. Joseph of Chambery, [N], (HRT), Manchester, CT.
Sisters of St. Joseph of Chambery, [N], (HRT), Bristol, CT.
Sisters of St. Joseph of Chambery, [N], (HRT), Cheshire, CT.
Sisters of St. Joseph of Chambery, [G], (NOR), Moodus, CT.
Sisters of St. Joseph of Chestnut Hill, Thea House, [O], (NEW), Newark, NJ.
Sisters of St. Joseph of La Grange, [O], (CHI), La Grange Park, IL.
Sisters of St. Joseph of LaGrange Charitable Trust, [X], (CHI), LaGrange Park, IL.
Sisters of St. Joseph of Medaille, [K], (FTW), Mishawaka, IN.
Sisters of St. Joseph of Medaille, New Orleans, C.S.J., [Q], (NO), New Orleans, LA.
Sisters of St. Joseph of Orange, [S], (LA), Los Angeles, CA.
Sisters of St. Joseph of Orange, [I], (ORG), Fullerton, CA.
Sisters of St. Joseph of Orange, [I], (ORG), Santa Ana, CA.
Sisters of St. Joseph of Orange, [I], (ORG), Dana Point, CA.
Sisters of St. Joseph of Orange, [I], (ORG), La Habra, CA.
Sisters of St. Joseph of Orange, [I], (SD), Spring Valley, CA.
Sisters of St. Joseph of Orange, [O], (SFR), San Francisco, CA.
Sisters of St. Joseph of Orange, [O], (SFR), San Francisco, CA.
Sisters of St. Joseph of Orange Motherhouse Community, [I], (ORG), Orange, CA.
Sisters of St. Joseph of Peace, [H], (ANC), Anchorage, AK.
Sisters of St. Joseph of Peace, [C], (JUN), Ketchikan, AK.
Sisters of St. Joseph of Peace, [I], (MET), New Brunswick, NJ.
Sisters of St. Joseph of Peace, [O], (NEW), Jersey City, NJ.
Sisters of St. Joseph of Peace, [I], (SD), San Diego, CA.
Sisters of St. Joseph of Peace, [N], (SEA), Seattle, WA.
Sisters of St. Joseph of Peace, Our Lady Province, Charitable Trust, [Q], (SEA), Bellevue, WA.
Sisters of St. Joseph of Peace, PeaceHealth, [Q], (SEA), Bellevue, WA.
Sisters Of St. Joseph Of Pennsylvania (Erie, PA) S.S.J., [K], (MEM), Memphis, TN.
Sisters of St. Joseph of Philadelphia, [I], (MOB), Camden, AL.
Sisters of St. Joseph of Philadelphia, [AA], (PH), Philadelphia, PA.
Sisters of St. Joseph of Philadelphia, [AA], (PH), Philadelphia, PA.
Sisters of St. Joseph of Philadelphia, [AA], (PH), Warminster, PA.
Sisters of St. Joseph of Philadelphia, Cecilian Academy, [AA], (PH), Philadelphia, PA.
Sisters of St. Joseph of Philadelphia, Fournier Community, [AA], (PH), Philadelphia, PA.
Sisters of St. Joseph of Philadelphia, Mt. St. Joseph Academy, [AA], (PH), Flourtown, PA.
Sisters of St. Joseph of Philadelphia, Nazareth House, [AA], (PH), Philadelphia, PA.
Sisters of St. Joseph of Philadelphia, St. Joseph Villa Staff, [W], (PH), Flourtown, PA.
Sisters of St. Joseph of St. Mark, [Q], (CLV), Cleveland, OH.
Sisters of St. Joseph of the Third Order of St. Francis, [N], (HRT), Beacon Falls, CT.
Sisters of St. Joseph of the Third Order of St. Francis, [N], (HRT), Forestville, CT.
Sisters of St. Joseph of the Third Order of St. Francis, [O], (OAK), Concord, CA.
Sisters of St. Joseph of the Third Order of St. Francis, [O], (OAK), Dublin, CA.
The Sisters of St. Joseph of the Third Order of St. Francis Central Offices, S.S.J.-T.O.S.F., [K], (FTW), South Bend, IN.
Sisters of St. Joseph of the Third Order of St. Francis Residences, [K], (FTW). See The Sisters of St. Joseph of the Third Order of St. Francis Central Offices, S.S.J.-T.O.S.F.
Sisters of St. Joseph of the Third Order of St. Francis Residences S.S.J.-T.O.S.F., [K], (FTW), Fort Wayne, IN.
Sisters of St. Joseph of the Third Order of St. Francis, S.S.J.-T.O.S.F., [O], (OAK), El Sobrante, CA.
Sisters of St. Joseph of Wheeling Foundation, Inc., [P], (WH), Wheeling, WV.
Sisters of St. Joseph of Wichita, [O], (OAK), San Leandro, CA.
Sisters of St. Joseph of Wichita, [J], (OKL), Ponca City, OK.
Sisters of St. Joseph of Wichita, KS., [O], (OAK), Hayward, CA.
Sisters of St. Joseph Society, Inc., [H], (BUR), Rutland, VT.
Sisters of St. Joseph's Architectural Stained Glass, [G], (ORL), Winter Garden, FL.
Sisters of St. Joseph, Concordia, KS, [C], (LSC), Las Cruces, NM.
Sisters of St. Joseph, S.S.J., [O], (WOR), Worcester, MA.
Sisters of St. Joseph, T.O.S.F., [G], (NOR), Middletown, CT.
Sisters of St. Joseph, Third Order of St. Francis, [G], (KNX), Butler, TN.
Sisters of St. Joseph, Third Order of St. Francis, [G], (KNX), Jonesborough, TN.
Sisters of St. Joseph-St. Benedict's Convent, [J], (AMA), Amarillo, TX.
Sisters of St. Louis, [S], (LA), Encino, CA.
Sisters of St. Louis, [I], (ORG), Tustin, CA.
Sisters of St. Louis Monaghan, Inc., [DD], (LA). See Chancery Office.
Sisters of St. Louis, Louisville Convent, [S], (LA), Woodland Hills, CA.
Sisters of St. Louis—California Region, [F], (R), Ahoskie, NC.
Sisters of St. Mary, [P], (BUF), Buffalo, NY.
Sisters of St. Mary Convent, [F], (CHR), Charleston, SC.
Sisters of St. Mary Namur, [I], (FWT), Fort Worth, TX.
Sisters of St. Mary of Namur, [P], (BUF), Derby, NY.
Sisters of St. Mary of Namur (S.S.M.N.), [R], (GAL), Houston, TX.
Sisters of St. Mary of Oregon, [I], (SAC), Marysville, CA.
Sisters of St. Mary of Washington, [O], (WDC), Washington, DC.
Sisters of St. Paul de Chartres, [H], (ANC), Anchorage, AK.
Sisters of St. Philip Neri, [E], (RNC), Sparks, NV.
Sisters of St. Ursula, [F], (R), Wilmington, NC.
Sisters of Sion Residence-Congregation of Our Lady of Sion, [V], (BRK), Brooklyn, NY.
Sisters of Social Service, [I], (ORG), Fountain Valley, CA.
Sisters of Social Service, [I], (SAC), Sacramento, CA.
Sisters of Social Service, [I], (SD), San Diego, CA.
Sisters of Social Service, [O], (SFR), San Francisco, CA.
Sisters of Social Service District Residence, [P], (BUF), Buffalo, NY.
Sisters of Social Service of Los Angeles, [S], (LA), Los Angeles, CA.
Sisters of Social Srvice, [I], (ORG), Dana Point, CA.
Sisters of St Joseph of Carondelet, Casa Viriditas, [H], (MRY), San Luis Obispo, CA.
Sisters of Ste. Chretienne, [X], (BO), Marlboro, MA.
Sisters of Ste. Chretienne, [X], (BO). See Sisters of Ste. Chretienne.
Sisters of the Annunciation of the Archdiocese of Omaha, [L], (OM), Omaha, NE.
Sisters of the Assumption, [N], (HRT), West Haven, CT.
Sisters of the Assumption of the Blessed Virgin Provincial Administration, [O], (WOR), Worcester, MA.
Sisters of the Blessed Sacrament, [I], (LAF), Church Point, LA.
Sisters of the Blessed Sacrament, [I], (LAF), Rayne, LA.
Sisters of the Blessed Sacrament, [I], (LAF), St. Martinville, LA.
Sisters of the Blessed Sacrament, [AA], (PH), Philadelphia, PA.
Sisters of the Blessed Sacrament Novitiate, [AA], (PH), Bensalem, PA.
Sisters of the Blessed Sacrament, S.B.S., [Q], (NO), New Orleans, LA.
Sisters of the Blessed Virgin Mary, [I], (ORG), Cypress, CA.
Sisters of the Cenacle, [K], (ARL), Great Falls, VA.
Sisters of the Cenacle, [K], (ATL), Hoschton, GA.
Sisters of the Company of Mary, [S], (LA), Los Angeles, CA.
Sisters of the Company of Mary, [I], (ORG), Costa Mesa, CA.
Sisters of the Company of Mary, [I], (ORG), Orange, CA.
Sisters of the Company of Mary, [I], (ORG), Santa Ana, CA.
Sisters of the Company of Mary, [I], (ORG), Tustin, CA.
Sisters of the Company of Mary (O.D.N.), [F], (SB), Tustin, CA.
Sisters of the Company of the Savior, [P], (BGP), Bridgeport, CT.
Sisters of the Cross and Passion, [N], (HRT), Hartford, CT.
Sisters of the Cross and Passion, [N], (HRT), New Britain, CT.
Sisters of the Cross and Passion, [N], (HRT), Farmington, CT.
Sisters of the Cross and Passion, [Q], (PRO), Peace Dale, RI.
Sisters of the Cross & Passion Convent, [Q], (PRO), Narragansett, RI.
Sisters of the Cross & Passion, C.P., [S], (LA), San Gabriel, CA.
Sisters of the Cross of the Sacred Heart of Jesus, [E], (STO), Modesto, CA.
Sisters of the Divine Compassion, [G], (KNX), Knoxville, TN.
Sisters of the Divine Redeemer, [AA], (PH), Darby, PA.
Sisters of the Divine Savior, [Q], (MIL), Milwaukee, WI.
Sisters of the Eucharistic Covenant, [M], (LAF), Lafayette, LA.
Sisters of the Good Shepherd, [N], (BAL), Baltimore, MD.
Sisters of the Good Shepherd, [X], (BO), Boston, MA.
Sisters of the Good Shepherd, [X], (BO), Marlboro, MA.
Sisters of the Good Shepherd, [V], (BRK), Brooklyn, NY.
Sisters of the Good Shepherd, [N], (CIN), Cincinnati, OH.
Sisters of the Good Shepherd, [N], (CIN), Cincinnati, OH.
Sisters of the Good Shepherd, [M], (COV), Fort Thomas, KY.
Sisters of the Good Shepherd, [M], (L), Louisville, KY.
Sisters of the Good Shepherd, [S], (LA), Los Angeles, CA.
Sisters of the Good Shepherd, [AA], (NY), New York, NY.
Sisters of the Good Shepherd, [AA], (NY), Peekskill, NY.
Sisters of the Good Shepherd, [AA], (PH), Philadelphia, PA.
Sisters of the Good Shepherd, [O], (RVC), Dix Hills, NY.
Sisters of the Good Shepherd, [N], (SEA), Seattle, WA.

Sisters of the Good Shepherd, [O], (SFR), San Francisco, CA.
Sisters of the Good Shepherd - St. Paul Province, [O], (STP), St. Paul, MN.
Sisters of the Good Shepherd (Contemplative), [AA], (PH), Philadelphia, PA.
Sisters of the Good Shepherd (R.G.S.), [L], (OM), Omaha, NE.
Sisters of the Good Shepherd (R.G.S.), [AA], (PH), Philadelphia, PA.
Sisters of the Good Shepherd (R.G.S.), [AA], (PH), Philadelphia, PA.
Sisters of the Good Shepherd Convent, [G], (AGN), Ordot, GU.
Sisters of the Good Shepherd, Marycrest, [Q], (CLV), Independence, OH.
Sisters of the Good Shepherd-St. Joseph Residence, [N], (BAL), Baltimore, MD.
Sisters of the Guardian Angel, [S], (LA), Los Angeles, CA.
The Sisters of the Handmaids of the Holy Child Jesus (of Nigeria, Africa), [G], (ALX), Alexandria, LA.
Sisters of the Heart of Jesus in the Blessed Sacrament, [I], (SD), National City, CA.
Sisters of the Holy Child, [AA], (PH), Philadelphia, PA.
Sisters of the Holy Child, [AA], (PH), Bryn Mawr, PA.
Sisters of the Holy Child Jesus, [AA], (PH), Bryn Mawr, PA.
Sisters of the Holy Child Jesus, [AA], (PH), Wynnewood, PA.
Sisters of the Holy Child Jesus, [O], (RVC), Old Westbury, NY.
Sisters of the Holy Child Jesus, [O], (WDC), Washington, DC.
Sisters of the Holy Child Jesus (S.H.C.J.), [AA], (PH), Rosemont, PA.
Sisters of the Holy Child Jesus (S.H.C.J.), [AA], (PH), Sharon Hill, PA.
Sisters of the Holy Child Jesus (S.H.C.J.), [AA], (PH), Drexel Hill, PA.
Sisters of the Holy Child Jesus-African Province Office, [DD], (NY), New York, NY.
Sisters of the Holy Cross, [K], (ARL), Alexandria, VA.
Sisters of the Holy Cross, [I], (AUS), Austin, TX.
Sisters of the Holy Cross, [I], (AUS), Waco, TX.
Sisters of the Holy Cross, [N], (BAL), Baltimore, MD.
Sisters of the Holy Cross, [X], (BO), Boston, MA.
Sisters of the Holy Cross, [F], (BWN), Raymondville, TX.
Sisters of the Holy Cross, [O], (CHI), Chicago, IL.
Sisters of the Holy Cross, [K], (FTW), Elkhart, IN.
Sisters of the Holy Cross, [M], (L), Tompkinsville, KY.
Sisters of the Holy Cross, [M], (L), Columbia, KY.
Sisters of the Holy Cross, [S], (LA), Mission Hills, CA.
Sisters of the Holy Cross, [S], (LA), Ventura, CA.
Sisters of the Holy Cross, [F], (LFT), Anderson, IN.
Sisters of the Holy Cross, [G], (NOR), Baltic, CT.
Sisters of the Holy Cross, [I], (ORG), Orange, CA.
Sisters of the Holy Cross, [I], (ORG), Rancho Santa Margarita, CA.
Sisters of the Holy Cross, [F], (R), Raleigh, NC.
The Sisters of the Holy Cross, [N], (SAT), San Antonio, TX.
Sisters of the Holy Cross, [I], (SD), La Jolla, CA.
Sisters of the Holy Cross, [P], (SP), Tampa, FL.
Sisters of the Holy Cross, [P], (SP), Tampa, FL.
Sisters of the Holy Cross, [E], (STO), Modesto, CA.
Sisters of the Holy Cross, [G], (TUC), Tucson, AZ.
Sisters of the Holy Cross, [O], (WDC), Kensington, MD.
Sisters of the Holy Cross, [O], (WDC). See Sisters of the Holy Cross.
Sisters of the Holy Cross Convents, [K], (FTW). See Our Lady of Holy Cross Convent.
Sisters of the Holy Cross, C.S.C., [Q], (NO), Marrero, LA.
Sisters of the Holy Cross, Inc., [F], (LFT). See Sisters of the Holy Cross.
Sisters of the Holy Cross, Our Lady of Mount Carmel Convent, [I], (COL), Columbus, OH.
Sisters of the Holy Faith, [I], (SAC), Fairfield, CA.
Sisters of the Holy Faith in California, [S], (LA), Downey, CA.
Sisters of the Holy Family, [I], (LAF), Opelousas, LA.
Sisters of the Holy Family, [O], (OAK), Oakland, CA.
Sisters of the Holy Family, [O], (OAK), Castro Valley, CA.
Sisters of the Holy Family, [O], (OAK), Fremont, CA.
Sisters of the Holy Family, [I], (SD), San Diego, CA.
Sisters of the Holy Family, [O], (SFR), San Francisco, CA.
Sisters of the Holy Family, [N], (SJ), Palo Alto, CA.
Sisters of the Holy Family (S.S.F.), [R], (GAL), Houston, TX.
Sisters of the Holy Family Convent, S.H.F., [E], (RNO), Reno, NV.
Sisters of the Holy Family Development Office, [Q], (NO). See Sisters of the Holy Family Motherhouse and Novitiate, S.S.F.
Sisters of the Holy Family Motherhouse and Novitiate, S.S.F., [Q], (NO), New Orleans, LA.
Sisters of the Holy Family of Nazareth, [N], (DAL), Grand Prairie, TX.
Sisters of the Holy Family of Nazareth, [AA], (PH), Philadelphia, PA.
Sisters of the Holy Family of Nazareth, [O], (WOR), Worcester, MA.
Sisters of the Holy Family of Nazareth (C.S.F.N.), [AA], (PH), Ambler, PA.
Sisters of the Holy Family of Nazareth of Western Pennsylvania, [O], (PIT), Pittsburgh, PA.
Sisters of the Holy Family Residences, [I], (HON), Mountain View, HI.
Sisters of the Holy Family, Holy Family Convent, [N], (SJ), San Jose, CA.
Sisters of the Holy Names (S.N.J.M.), [O], (WDC), Silver Spring, MD.
Sisters of the Holy Names of Jesus and Mary, [T], (ALB), Albany, NY.
Sisters of the Holy Names of Jesus and Mary, [N], (SJ), San Jose, CA.
Sisters of the Holy Names, Santa Clara Residence, [N], (SJ), Santa Clara, CA.
Sisters of the Holy Names, Stella Kennedy Residence, [N], (SJ), Santa Clara, CA.
Sisters of the Holy Redeemer, [AA], (PH), Philadelphia, PA.
Sisters of the Holy Redeemer, [AA], (PH), Philadelphia, PA.
Sisters of the Holy Redeemer, [AA], (PH), Meadowbrook, PA.
Sisters of the Holy Redeemer Provincialate, [AA], (PH), Huntingdon Valley, PA.
Sisters of the Holy Redeemer, C.S.R., [M], (CAM), Swainton, NJ.
Sisters of the Holy Redeemer, C.S.R., [AA], (PH), Jenkintown, PA.
Sisters of the Holy Rosary of Fatima, [I], (SAC), Sacramento, CA.
Sisters of the Holy Spirit, [I], (LAF), Crowley, LA.
Sisters of the Holy Spirit, [I], (LAF), Lebeau, LA.
Sisters of the Holy Spirit and Mary Immaculate (S.H.Sp.), [R], (GAL), Houston, TX.
Sisters of the Holy Union Provincial House, [X], (BO), Groton, MA.
Sisters of the Humility of Mary, [O], (PIT), Villa Maria, PA.
Sisters of the Humility of Mary, [N], (TR), Trenton, NJ.
Sisters of the Humility of Mary Charitable Trust, [R], (PIT), Villa Maria, PA.
Sisters of the Immaculate Heart of Mary at Mirinae, I.H.M., [S], (LA), Los Angeles, CA.
Sisters of the Immaculate Heart of Mary of Wichita, Inc. (I.H.M.), [H], (WCH), Wichita, KS.
Sisters of the Incarnate Word and Blessed Sacrament, [I], (AUS), La Grange, TX.
Sisters of the Incarnate Word and Blessed Sacrament, [F], (BWN), Brownsville, TX.
Sisters of the Incarnate Word and Blessed Sacrament, [F], (BWN), Brownsville, TX.
Sisters of the Incarnate Word and Blessed Sacrament, [Q], (CLV), Cleveland, OH.
Sisters of the Incarnate Word and Blessed Sacrament of Victoria, [H], (VIC), Victoria, TX.
Sisters of the Incarnate Word Casa de Vida, [G], (BWN), Brownsville, TX.
Sisters of the Korean Martyrs, S.K.M., [S], (LA), Carson, CA.
Sisters of the Living Word, [O], (CHI), Arlington Heights, IL.
Sisters of the Living Word, [B], (SAN), San Angelo, TX.
Sisters of the Living Word, S.L.W., [Q], (NO), Gretna, LA.
Sisters of the Most Holy Sacrament, [I], (LAF), Lafayette, LA.
Sisters of the Most Holy Sacrament, [I], (LAF), Breaux Bridge, LA.
Sisters of the Most Holy Sacrament, [I], (LAF), Crowley, LA.
Sisters of the Most Holy Sacrament, M.H.S., [Q], (NO), Metairie, LA.
Sisters of the Most Precious Blood of O'Fallen, Missouri, [K], (ELP), Presidio, TX.
Sisters of the New Covenant, [N], (DEN), Denver, CO.
Sisters of the Precious Blood, [E], (PHX), Phoenix, AZ.
Sisters of the Precious Blood, [I], (SD), Oceanside, CA.
Sisters of the Precious Blood, [I], (SD), San Diego, CA.
Sisters of the Precious Blood, [O], (SFR), San Francisco, CA.
Sisters of the Precious Blood Generalate, [N], (CIN), Dayton, OH.
Sisters of the Precious Blood, Salem Heights Convent, [N], (CIN), Dayton, OH.
Sisters of the Presentation Community Support Trust Fund, [U], (SFR), San Francisco, CA.
Sisters of the Presentation of Mary Provincial House, [L], (MAN), Manchester, NH.
Sisters of the Presentation of the B.V.M., San Jose, [N], (SJ), San Jose, CA.
Sisters of the Presentation of the Blessed Virgin Mary, [I], (AUS), Cameron, TX.
Sisters of the Presentation of the Blessed Virgin Mary, [G], (KNX), Jellico, TN.
Sisters of the Presentation of the Blessed Virgin Mary, [I], (ORG), Garden Grove, CA.
Sisters of the Presentation of the Blessed Virgin Mary, [I], (ORG), Huntington Beach, CA.
Sisters of the Presentation of the Blessed Virgin Mary, [I], (ORG), Orange, CA.
Sisters of the Presentation of the Blessed Virgin Mary, [N], (SJ), Morgan Hill, CA.
Sisters of the Presentation, B.V.M., [G], (KNX), Harriman, TN.
Sisters of the Resurrection Provincial House and Novitiate, [O], (CHI), Chicago, IL.
Sisters of the Sacred Heart (S.S.C.J.), [R], (GAL), Houston, TX.
Sisters of the Sacred Heart of Jesus, [F], (BWN), San Juan, TX.
Sisters of the Sacred Heart of Jesus (S.S.H.J.), [P], (BUF), Lewiston, NY.
Sisters of the Sacred Heart of Jesus, H.C.J.S., [S], (LA), Whittier, CA.
Sisters of the Sacred Hearts of Jesus & Mary, [I], (SAC), Sacramento, CA.
Sisters of the Sacred Hearts of Jesus and Mary, [E], (STO), Turlock, CA.
Sisters of the Sacred Hearts of Jesus and Mary and of Perpetual Adoration, SS.CC, [L], (FR), Fairhaven, MA.
Sisters of the Society Devoted to the Sacred Heart, [S], (LA), Los Angeles, CA.
Sisters of the Society Devoted to the Sacred Heart, [S], (LA), Los Angeles, CA.
Sisters of the Society Devoted to the Sacred Heart, [S], (LA), Northridge, CA.
Sisters of the Society Devoted to the Sacred Heart, [S], (LA), Solvang, CA.
Sisters of the Society of Our Lady of the Most Holy Trinity, [K], (KC), Kansas City, MO.
Sisters of the Sorrowful Mother - Our Lady of Sorrows Convent, [H], (TLS), Broken Arrow, OK.
Sisters of the Sorrowful Mother - U.S./Caribbean Province, Inc., [H], (TLS), Broken Arrow, OK.
Sisters of the Sorrowful Mother Ambulatory Care Corporation, [J], (PAT). See Sisters of the Sorrowful Mother Health Care Ministry Corp.
Sisters of the Sorrowful Mother Charitable Trust, [Y], (MIL), Brown Deer, WI.
Sisters of the Sorrowful Mother Health Care Ministry Corp., [J], (PAT), Denville, NJ.
Sisters of the Sorrowful Mother Housing Corporation I, Inc., [J], (PAT). See Sisters of the Sorrowful Mother Health Care Ministry Corp.
Sisters of the Sorrowful Mother Housing Corporation II, Inc., [J], (PAT). See Sisters of the Sorrowful Mother Health Care Ministry Corp.
Sisters of the Sorrowful Mother International Finance, Inc., [Y], (MIL), Brown Deer, WI.
Sisters of the Sorrowful Mother, Novitiate House, [Q], (MIL), Mequon, WI.
Sisters of the Sorrowful Mother-Generalate, Inc., [Q], (MIL), Brown Deer, WI.
Sisters of the Sorrowful Mother-Ministry Corporation, [Y], (MIL), Milwaukee, WI.
Sisters of the Sorrowful Mother-St. John Ministry Corporation, [E], (TLS), Tulsa, OK.
Sisters of the Sorrowful Mother-US Health System, Inc., [E], (TLS), Tulsa, OK.
Sisters of the Third Franciscan Order, [K], (KC), Parkville, MO.
Sisters of the Third Franciscan Order-Retirement Trust Fund, [W], (SY), Syracuse, NY.
Sisters of the Third Franciscan Order-Syracuse, NY, [O], (WDC), Washington, DC.
Sisters of the Third Order of St. Dominic, [F], (FRS), Merced, CA.
Sisters of the Visitation, [G], (WH), Wheeling, WV.
Sisters of the Visitation, [O], (WH), Wheeling, WV.
Sisters of the Visitation of Japan, [O], (SFR), San Francisco, CA.
Sisters of the Visitation-Stella Maris Hospice, [N], (BAL), Baltimore, MD.
Sisters Place, Inc., [R], (PIT), Clairton, PA.
Sisters Residence, [K], (CHL), Rosman, NC.
Sisters Residence, [I], (MOB), Selma, AL.
Sisters Residence for Holy Family School, [G], (OG), Malone, NY.
Sisters St. Joseph Motherhouse, [J], (ROC), Rochester, NY.
Sisters Servants of I.H.M., [N], (RIC), Virginia Beach, VA.
Sisters Servants of Mary, [S], (LA), Oxnard, CA.
Sisters Servants of Mary Immaculate Day Nursery & Convent, [H], (BAL), Baltimore, MD.
Sisters Servants of Mary Immaculate, Home of Divine Providence, [F], (PHU), Philadelphia, PA.
Sisters Servants of Mary Immaculate, Inc., [N],

(BAL), Baltimore, MD.
Sisters Servants of Mary, Ministers of the Sick, [O], (LA), Los Angeles, CA.
Sisters Servants of the Blessed Sacrament, [S], (LA), El Segundo, CA.
Sisters Servants of the Immaculate Heart of Mary, [K], (ARL), Arlington, VA.
Sisters Servants of the Immaculate Heart of Mary, [N], (RIC), Norfolk, VA.
Sisters Servants of the Sacred Heart, [G], (ALT), Cresson, PA.
Sisters Servants of the Sacred Heart Novitiate, [G], (ALT), Portage, PA.
Sisters Treatment Group Home, [G], (GB), Two Rivers, WI.
Sisters' Residence, [K], (CHL), Charlotte, NC.
Sisters, Home Visitors of Mary Convent, [L], (DET), Detroit, MI.
Sisters, Lovers of the Holy Cross, [R], (RVC), Brookville, NY.
Sisters, Servants of Mary, S.M., [Q], (NO), New Orleans, LA.
Sisters, Servants of the Immaculate Heart of Mary, [I], (AUS), Austin, TX.
Sisters, Servants of the Immaculate Heart of Mary, [F], (R), Chapel Hill, NC.
Sisters, Servants of the Immaculate Heart of Mary, [F], (R), Plymouth, NC.
Sisters, Servants of the Immaculate Heart of Mary, [F], (R), Williamston, NC.
Sisters, Servants of the Immaculate Heart of Mary, [F], (R), Farmville, NC.
Sisters, Servants of the Immaculate Heart of Mary, [N], (SAT), San Antonio, TX.
Sisters, Servants of the Immaculate Heart of Mary, [N], (SJ), Los Altos, CA.
Sisters, Servants of the Immaculate Heart of Mary (I.H.M.), [AA], (PH), Immaculata, PA.
Sisters, Servants of the Immaculate Heart of Mary (I.H.M.), [AA], (PH), Immaculata, PA.
Sisters, Servants of the Immaculate Heart of Mary (I.H.M.), [AA], (PH), Immaculata, PA.
Sisters, Servants of the Immaculate Heart of Mary, Leadership Council, [L], (DET), Monroe, MI.
Skagit Valley Regional Ministry, [Q], (SEA), LaConner, WA.
Skidmore College, [S], (ALB), Saratoga, NY.
Skutt Catholic High School Endowment Trust, [N], (OM). See The Omaha Archdiocesan Educational Foundation, Inc.
Slav Missions, [J], (JOL). See St. Procopius Abbey.
Slovak Department, [N], (CHI). See Society of the Divine Word, Provincial Headquarter-Chicago Prov.
The Slovene Franciscan Fathers, Order of Friars Minor, Commissariat of the Holy Cross, [N], (CHI), Lemont, IL.
SMILE, Independent Living Services, Inc. at Catholic Charities, [I], (ALB), Albany, NY.
Smokey Hollow Housing Development Fund Company, Inc., [Q], (SY), Baldwinsville, NY.
SOAR, [V], (WDC), Silver Spring, MD.
Social Action-Campaign for Human Needs, Catholic Relief Services, [G], (BGP). See Catholic Charities of Fairfield County.
Social Apostolate, [I], (SAV), Savannah, GA.
Social Concern Ministries, [G], (BGP). See Catholic Charities of Fairfield County.
Social Issues Advocacy, [G], (BGP). See Catholic Charities of Fairfield County.
Social Issues Advocate-Parish Social Concerns, [M], (BGP), Bridgeport, CT.
Social Justice, [E], (SR). See Diocese of Santa Rosa, Catholic Charities.
Social Justice Resource Center, [H], (OAK). See Catholic Charities of the Diocese of Oakland, Inc.
Social Service Agencies: Pima County, [D], (TUC), Tucson, AZ.
Social Service Center, [N], (LAF), New Iberia, LA.
Social Service Center, [E], (MET), Phillipsburg, NJ.
Social Service Center, [E], (MET), Woodbridge, NJ.
Social Service Counseling Centers, [D], (WIL). See Catholic Charities, Inc.
Social Service Sisters, [O], (OAK), Oakland, CA.
Social Services, [M], (STL). See Guardian Angel Settlement Association.
Sociedad San Martin de Porres, [U], (GAL), Houston, TX.
Societies of St. Vincent de Paul, [L], (VEN), Fort Myers, FL.
Society Devoted to the Sacred Heart, [I], (ORG), Santa Ana, CA.
Society for Religious Vocations, [P], (PEO), Peoria, IL.
The Society for the Propagation of the Faith & Holy Childhood Assn., [J], (ALT). See Prince Gallitzin Chapel House (Diocesan).
Society for the Propagation of the Faith, Holy Childhood Association, [V], (MIL), Milwaukee, WI.
Society for the Renewal of Christian Art, The, [DD], (NY), New York, NY.
Society of African Missions (S.M.A.), [M], (WDC), Takoma Park, MD.
Society of African Missions, Provincialate, S.M.A. Fathers, [N], (NEW), Tenafly, NJ.
Society of Catholic Medical Missionaries Generalate, Inc., [EE], (PH), Philadelphia, PA.
Society of Christ Provincial Home, [K], (DET), Sterling Heights, MI.
Society of Friends of Madonna High School, Inc., [P], (WH), Weirton, WV.
Society of Helpers, [O], (CHI), Chicago, IL.
Society of Helpers, [AA], (NY), New York, NY.
Society of Helpers, [DD], (NY), New York, NY.
Society of Helpers, [N], (SJ), San Jose, CA.
Society of Helpers (Helpers of the Holy Souls), [O], (SFR), San Francisco, CA.
Society of Jesus Christ the Priest, [H], (MET), New Village, NJ.
The Society of Jesus of New England-Provincial Offices, [W], (BO), Boston, MA.
Society of Mary, [E], (KAL), Portage, MI.
Society of Mary (Marianists), [M], (HRT), Bloomfield, CT.
Society of Mary, Marianists, [G], (MRY), Santa Cruz, CA.
Society of Mary, Marist Fathers, [Z], (PH), Langhorne, PA.
Society of Mary, Marists, [G], (MRY), Santa Cruz, CA.
The Society of Oblate Fathers Continuing Support Fund, [DD], (BO), Tewksbury, MA.
The Society of Oblate Fathers for Missions Among the Poor Formation Charitable Trust, [DD], (BO), Tewksbury, MA.
Society of Our Lady of the Most Holy Trinity, [H], (CC), Robstown, TX.
Society of Our Lady of the Most Holy Trinity, [M], (HRT), East Hartford, CT.
Society of Our Lady of the Most Holy Trinity, [O], (KC), Kansas City, MO.
The Society of Our Lady of the Way, [Q], (BGP), Bridgeport, CT.
Society of Our Lady of the Way, [R], (CLV), Cleveland Heights, OH.
Society of Our Lady of the Way, [T], (LA), Los Angeles, CA.
Society of Our Lady of the Way, [S], (NO), New Orleans, LA.
The Society of Our Lady of the Way, [P], (SFR), San Francisco, CA.
Society of Our Mother of Peace, [P], (STL), High Ridge, MO.
The Society of Our Mother of Peace, Daughters of Our Mother of Peace, [G], (SPC), Marionville, MO.
Society of Our Mother of Peace, Daughters of Our Mother of Peace, [R], (STL), High Ridge, MO.
The Society of Our Mother of Peace, Daughters of Our Mothers of Peace, [F], (SPC), Marionville, MO.
The Society of Our Mother of Peace, Sons of Our Mother of Peace, [E], (SPC), Marionville, MO.
Society of Our Mother of Peace-Maria Fonte Solitude, [T], (STL), High Ridge, MO.
Society of St. Edmund, [G], (BUR), Colchester, VT.
Society of St. Edmund, [G], (BUR). See Society of St. Edmund.
Society of St. Edmund, [F], (NOR), Mystic, CT.
Society of St. Edmund Residence, [G], (VEN), Englewood, FL.
Society of St. Francis De Sales, [M], (JOL), Glen Ellyn, IL.
The Society of St. James the Apostle, Inc., [W], (BO), Boston, MA.
Society of St. John (Brothers of Saint Benedict), [I], (DM), Des Moines, IA.
The Society of St. John Vianney, [A], (PRO), Coventry, RI.
Society of St. Joseph the Worker, [AA], (CLV), Parma, OH.
Society of St. Paul, [K], (DET), Detroit, MI.
Society of St. Paul, [R], (LA), Los Angeles, CA.
Society of St. Paul, [B], (NY), New York, NY.
Society of St. Paul, [A], (Y), Canfield, OH.
Society of St. Paul Provincial Residence, [O], (BUF), Derby, NY.
Society of St. Teresa of Jesus, [N], (SAT), Uvalde, TX.
Society of St. Vincent de Paul, [N], (AUS), Austin, TX.
Society of St. Vincent de Paul, [G], (B), Kellogg, ID.
Society of St. Vincent de Paul, [G], (B), Caldwell, ID.
Society of St. Vincent de Paul, [I], (BIR), Huntsville, AL.
Society of St. Vincent de Paul, [H], (BUF). See The Catholic Charities of the Diocese of Buffalo.
Society of St. Vincent de Paul, [N], (COV), Covington, KY.
Society of St. Vincent de Paul, [P], (DAL), Dallas, TX.
Society of Saint Vincent de Paul, [I], (DM), Des Moines, IA.
Society of St. Vincent de Paul, [I], (FRS), Fresno, CA.
Society of St. Vincent de Paul, [M], (JOL), West Chicago, IL.
Society of St. Vincent de Paul, [L], (LAN), Lansing, MI.
Society of St. Vincent de Paul, [L], (LAN), Jackson, MI.
Society of St. Vincent de Paul, [I], (LEX), Lexington, KY.
Society of St. Vincent de Paul, [K], (MAD), Madison, WI.
Society of St. Vincent de Paul, [L], (MOB), Mobile, AL.
Society of St. Vincent de Paul, [O], (P), Portland, OR.
Society of St. Vincent de Paul, [O], (P), Medford, OR.
*Society of St. Vincent de Paul, [O], (P), Salem, OR.
Society of St. Vincent de Paul, [O], (P), Eugene, OR.
Society of Saint Vincent de Paul, [R], (PIT), Pittsburgh, PA.
Society of St. Vincent de Paul, [I], (SAG), Bay City, MI.
Society of St. Vincent de Paul, [P], (SAT), San Antonio, TX.
Society of St. Vincent de Paul, [I], (SAV), Brunswick, GA.
Society of St. Vincent de Paul, [L], (SEA), Everett, WA.
Society of St. Vincent de Paul, [J], (TUC), Tucson, AZ.
Society of St. Vincent de Paul, [I], (WDC), Riverdale, MD.
Society of St. Vincent de Paul, [L], (WH), Wheeling, WV.
Society of St. Vincent de Paul - Archdiocesan Council, [L], (SEA), Bellevue, WA.
Society of St. Vincent de Paul - Particular Council of Tacoma, [L], (SEA), Tacoma, WA.
Society of St. Vincent de Paul - Stores, [L], (SEA). See Society of St. Vincent de Paul - Archdiocesan Council.
Society of St. Vincent de Paul (Diocesan Central Council), [F], (SFD), Springfield, IL.
The Society of St. Vincent de Paul (not under membership structure), [V], (CLV). See Catholic Charities Services Corporation.
Society of St. Vincent de Paul and Related Stores, [L], (SEA), Manchester, WA.
Society of St. Vincent de Paul Archdiocesan Council, [H], (SFR), San Francisco, CA.
Society of St. Vincent de Paul District - Council of Seattle Area, [L], (SEA). See Society of St. Vincent de Paul - Archdiocesan Council.
Society of St. Vincent De Paul District Council, [I], (BWN), Brownsville, TX.
Society of St. Vincent de Paul in Diocese of Brooklyn, [L], (BRK). See Catholic Charities.
Society of St. Vincent de Paul of Alameda County, [I], (OAK), Oakland, CA.
Society of St. Vincent de Paul of Alameda County, [I], (OAK). See Society of St. Vincent de Paul of Alameda County.
Society of St. Vincent De Paul of Chicago, [G], (CHI). See Catholic Charities of the Archdiocese of Chicago-Archdiocesan Offices.
Society of St. Vincent de Paul Solano District Council, [L], (SAC), Vallejo, CA.
Society of St. Vincent de Paul Stores and Workshop, [L], (SEA), Tacoma, WA.
Society of St. Vincent De Paul, Archdiocesan Central Council of New York, [M], (NY), New York, NY.
Society of St. Vincent de Paul, Council of Louisville, [P], (L), Louisville, KY.
Society of St. Vincent de Paul, Diocesan Central Council, [V], (CLV), Cleveland, OH.
Society of St. Vincent de Paul, District Council, [J], (PMB), Riviera Beach, FL.
Society of St. Vincent de Paul, District Council of Napa County, [F], (SR), Napa, CA.
Society of St. Vincent de Paul, District Council of Sonoma County, [F], (SR), Rohnert Park, CA.
Society of St. Vincent de Paul, District Council of the Redwood Region, [F], (SR), Eureka, CA.
Society of St. Vincent de Paul, Particular Council of Yakima, [E], (YAK), Yakima, WA.
Society of St. Vincent de Paul, Sacramento District Council, [L], (SAC), Sacramento, CA.
Society of St. Vincent de Paul, St. Sebastian Conference, [J], (PMB), Vero Beach, FL.
Society of St. Vincent de Paul-Family Welfare Office, [L], (SEA). See Society of St. Vincent de Paul - Archdiocesan Council.
Society of St. Vincent DePaul, [N], (GRY). See Catholic Charities.
Society of St. Vincent DePaul, [L], (SAC), Roseville, CA.
Society of St. Vincent DePaul, Central Office, [L], (BO), Boston, MA.
Society of St. Vincent DePaul, Council of the United States, [W], (STL), St. Louis, MO.
The Society of Sisters for the Church, [N], (PAT), West Paterson, NJ.
Society of the Brothers of the Holy Spirit (B.H.S.), [Z], (PH), Philadelphia, PA.
Society of the Catholic Apostolate, [O], (BUF), North Tonawanda, NY.
Society of the Divine Word, [W], (BO), Duxbury, MA.
Society of The Divine Word, [N], (PIT), Pittsburgh, PA.
Society of the Divine Word, [M], (TR), Bordentown, NJ.

T

Towson State University, [O], (BAL). See Archdiocesan Office-Newman Center.
Traditional and Specialized Foster Care Services, [G], (CHI). See Catholic Charities of the Archdiocese of Chicago-Archdiocesan Offices.
Training School for the Lay Apostolate (Hermanos Cheos), [H], (PCE), Penuelas, PR.
Tranquil House, [P], (L). See Society of St. Vincent de Paul, Council of Louisville.
Transfiguration Convent, [AA], (PH). See Sisters of Mercy of the Americas, Annunciation Convent.
Transfiguration Hermitage, [K], (PRT), Thorndike, ME.
Transfiguration Monastery, [T], (SY), Windsor, NY.
Transitional Care Unit (TCU), [G], (GRY). See St. Catherine Hospital.
Transitional Housing, [L], (DEN). See Catholic Charities and Community Services of the Archdiocese of Denver, Inc.
Transitional Housing, [P], (RIC), Richmond, VA.
Transitional Living Center, [H], (SPK), Spokane, WA.
Transitional Living Center, [O], (SPK). See Transitional Program for Women dba Transitions.
Transitional Program for Women dba Transitions, [O], (SPK), Spokane, WA.
Transitional Shelter Program for Families and Individuals, [G], (CHI). See Catholic Charities of the Archdiocese of Chicago-Archdiocesan Offices.
Transitions, [O], (SPK). See Transitional Program for Women dba Transitions.
Transitus House, [F], (LC), Chippewa Falls, WI.
Travelers Aid, [S], (HRT). See Catholic Charities-Catholic Family Services (Archdiocese of Hartford).
Tremont Place, [I], (KC), Kansas City, MO.
Trexler Pavilion, Personal Care Residence of Holy Family Manor, [I], (ALN), Bethlehem, PA.
Tri-Cities Preparatory School, [O], (SPK), Pasco, WA.
Trinidad Area Catholic Community, [E], (PBL), Trinidad, CO.
Trinidad Catholic Schools, [A], (PBL), Trinidad, CO.
Trinita, [Q], (HRT), New Hartford, CT.
Trinitarian Counseling Services, Inc., [Q], (BAL), Baltimore, MD.
Trinitarian Missionaries/Missionary Servants of the Most Holy Trinity, [H], (ORG), Santa Ana, CA.
Trinity Catholic Academy, [C], (WOR), Southbridge, MA.
Trinity Catholic High School, [C], (BGP), Stamford, CT.
Trinity Catholic School, [C], (LAF), St. Martinville, LA.
Trinity Catholic School, [H], (NY), Port Jervis, NY.
Trinity Catholic School, [H], (STP), St. Paul, MN.
Trinity College, [C], (WDC), Washington, DC.
Trinity College of Vermont, [A], (BUR), Burlington, VT.
Trinity Community Medical Center of Brenham, [F], (AUS), Brenham, TX.
Trinity Community, Assisted Living Community, [Q], (PRO). See Franciscan Missionaries of Mary.
Trinity Early Learning Center, [F], (DAV), Clinton, IA.
Trinity Educational Trust Fund, [B], (LR). See Trinity Junior High.
Trinity Elementary, [F], (DAV). See Trinity Early Learning Center.
Trinity Health System, [E], (STU), Steubenville, OH.
Trinity High School, [C], (BIS), Dickinson, ND.
Trinity High School, [D], (CHI), River Forest, IL.
Trinity High School, [E], (CLV), Cleveland, OH.
Trinity High School, [A], (HBG), Camp Hill, PA.
Trinity High School, [D], (HBG), Camp Hill, PA.
Trinity High School, [B], (L), Louisville, KY.
Trinity High School, [C], (MAN), Manchester, NH.
Trinity High School, [B], (OWN), Whitesville, KY.
Trinity High School, [B], (WCH), Hutchinson, KS.
The Trinity High School Education Endowment Fund, [B], (WCH), Hutchinson, KS.
*Trinity House, [U], (CHI), Chicago, IL.
Trinity House, [F], (VIC), Victoria, TX.
Trinity House of Prayer, [M], (TOL). See Chiara Center.
Trinity Junior High, [B], (LR), Fort Smith, AR.
Trinity Medical Center, East, [E], (STU). See Trinity Health System.
Trinity Medical Center, West, [E], (STU). See Trinity Health System.
Trinity Missions House of Studies, [A], (ORG), Santa Ana, CA.
Trinity Montessori School, [D], (ROC), East Rochester, NY.
Trinity Mother Frances Health System, [A], (TYL), Tyler, TX.
Trinity Place Apartments, [L], (OKL), Oklahoma City, OK.
Trinity Regional School, [E], (RVC), East Northport, NY.
Trinity Retreat, [BB], (NY), Larchmont, NY.
Trinity School, [E], (BAL), Ellicott City, MD.
Trinity School, [F], (SPK), Spokane, WA.
Trinity Spiritual Center, [L], (HBG), Shiremanstown, PA.
Trinity Villas I, Inc., [C], (ORL), Ocala, FL.
Trinity Villas II, Inc., [C], (ORL), Ocala, FL.
Tri-State Coalition for Responsible Investment, [DD], (NY), New York, NY.
Trocaire, [N], (HRT). See Sisters of Mercy of the Americas of Connecticut.
Trocaire College, [C], (BUF), Buffalo, NY.
Trocaire College, [K], (BUF). See Our Lady of Victory Hospital.
Troy CYO Day Camp, [U], (ALB), Troy, NY.
Troy Quasi-Endowment Trust, [M], (LC), Lyndon Station, WI.
Troy State University Newman Center, [K], (MOB), Troy, AL.
Trust for Theological Studies, [R], (PIT), Pittsburgh, PA.
Trustees, [N], (AUS), Austin, TX.
Tufts University Catholic Center, [CC], (BO), Medford, MA.
The Tuition Assistance Fund, Inc., [F], (CAM), Camden, NJ.
Tumwater Apartments, [K], (SEA), Tumwater, WA.
Turner Carroll High School, [D], (BUF), Buffalo, NY.
Tuscarawas Central Catholic High School Endowment Fund, [K], (COL), New Philadelphia, OH.
Tusculum College Newman Center, [J], (KNX), Greeneville, TN.
Tuskegee University Newman Center, [K], (MOB), Tuskegee Institute, AL.
Tutwiler Clinic, Inc., [C], (JKS), Tutwiler, MS.
Twin Cities Catholic Alumni Club, [W], (STP), Minneapolis, MN.
Twin Cities Catholic Educational System (TCCES), [E], (GB), Menasha, WI.
Twin-City Area Catholic School Fund, Inc., [I], (KAL), St. Joseph, MI.
*Tyler Catholic School Foundation, [E], (TYL), Tyler, TX.
Tyler Junior College and The University of Texas at Tyler Newman Center, [D], (TYL), Tyler, TX.
*Tyme Out Youth Ministry Center, Inc., [Y], (MIL), Nashotah, WI.
Tyson Place Housing Development Fund Company, Inc., [Q], (SY), Syracuse, NY.

U

U.P. Catholic Education Endowment Fund, [B], (MAR), Marquette, MI.
Uihlein Mercy Center, [E], (OG), Lake Placid, NY.
*Ukrainian Catholic Relief, Inc., [G], (STF), Stamford, CT.
Ulster, [D], (NY). See Department of Education.
Unaccompanied Juvenile Foster Care Program, [I], (GAL). See Associated Catholic Charities of the Diocese of Galveston-Houston.
UND-Lake Region, [I], (FAR), Devils Lake, ND.
Unified Catholic Parish Schools of Beaver Dam, [H], (MIL), Beaver Dam, WI.
UniMed Medical Center Foundation, [D], (BIS), Minot, ND.
Union Catholic Convent, [O], (NEW), Scotch Plains, NJ.
Union Catholic Regional High School, [D], (NEW), Scotch Plains, NJ.
Union College, Catholic Campus Ministry, [S], (ALB), Schenectady, NY.
Union County College, [Q], (NEW), Cranford, NJ.
Union of the Sisters of the Presentation of the Blessed Virgin Mary, [E], (PHX), Phoenix, AZ.
United Catholic Schools Foundation of Austin, MN, Inc., [C], (WIN). See Austin Area Catholic Schools.
The United Colleges of San Antonio, [C], (SAT), San Antonio, TX.
United Day Care, Inc., [E], (SUP). See Catholic Charities Bureau, Inc.
United Medical Management, [D], (PMB). See St. Mary's Hospital, Inc.
United Samaritans Medical Center, [J], (PEO), Danville, IL.
United Samaritans Medical Center Apothecary, [J], (PEO). See United Samaritans Medical Center.
United Samaritans Medical Center Apothecary, [J], (PEO). See United Samaritans Medical Center.
United Samaritans Medical Center Foundation, [J], (PEO). See United Samaritans Medical Center.
United Stand Family Center, [X], (CHI), Chicago, IL.
U.S. Catholic China Bureau, [S], (NEW), South Orange, NJ.
United States Catholic Historical Society, The, [DD], (NY), New York, NY.
The United States Catholic Widows and Widowers Association, Inc., [DD], (NY), Scarsdale, NY.
United States Military Academy, [CC], (NY). See University Apostolate.
United States Province, [Q], (MIL), Milwaukee, WI.
Univ. of Arkansas at Little Rock Campus Ministry, [J], (LR). See Catholic Campus Ministries.
Univ. of Delaware Newman Center, [O], (WIL), Newark, DE.
Univ. of Michigan, Dearborn, Henry Ford Community College Newman Center, [S], (DET), Dearborn, MI.
Univ. of North Dakota Newman Center, [H], (FAR), Grand Forks, ND.
University Apostolate, [CC], (NY), New York, NY.
University Catholic Center, [M], (AUS), Austin, TX.
University Catholic Center - St. Thomas More Chapel, [M], (SFE), Portales, NM.
University College, [B], (NEW). See Seton Hall University.
University Health Services, [G], (FTW), Notre Dame, IN.
University Health Services, Notre Dame, [K], (FTW). See Saint Mary's of the Immaculate Conception.
University Heights Day Care, [N], (NY). See Pius XII Youth and Family Services.
University of Alabama in Tuscaloosa, [H], (BIR), Tuscaloosa, AL.
University of Arizona, [I], (TUC), Tucson, AZ.
University of Arkansas, St. Thomas Aquinas University Parish, [J], (LR). See Catholic Campus Ministries.
University of California at San Diego (Campus Ministry), [M], (SD), San Diego, CA.
University of California, Irvine, [L], (ORG). See Campus Ministry-Diocese of Orange.
University of Central Arkansas & Hendrix College Campus Ministry, [J], (LR). See Catholic Campus Ministries.
University of Central Florida Newman Center, [E], (ORL), Orlando, FL.
University of Charleston Newman Center, [Q], (WH), Charleston, WV.
University of Cincinnati Newman Center, [Q], (CIN), Cincinnati, OH.
University of Colorado (Boulder), [P], (DEN), Boulder, CO.
University of Colorado at Denver, [P], (DEN). See Auraria Campus.
University of Dallas, [B], (DAL), Irving, TX.
The University of Dayton, [D], (CIN), Dayton, OH.
University of Dayton Campus Ministry, [Q], (CIN), Dayton, OH.
University of Denver, [P], (DEN), Denver, CO.
University of Detroit Jesuit High School and Academy, [E], (DET), Detroit, MI.
University of Detroit Mercy, [C], (DET), Detroit, MI.
University of Detroit Mercy Campus Ministry, [S], (DET), Detroit, MI.
University of Detroit-Mercy Campus Ministry, [S], (DET), Detroit, MI.
University of Findlay Campus Ministry, [N], (TOL), Findlay, OH.
University of Florida-St. Augustine Parish and Student Center, [L], (STA), Gainesville, FL.
University of Great Falls, [A], (GF), Great Falls, MT.
University of Hartford Newman Center, [R], (HRT), Hartford, CT.
University of Houston Central Campus Catholic Newman Association, [T], (GAL), Houston, TX.
University of Houston Downtown Catholic Campus Ministry, [T], (GAL), Houston, TX.
University of Houston, Clear Lake City Newman Center, [T], (GAL), Houston, TX.
University of Idaho, St. Augustine Catholic Center, [F], (B), Moscow, ID.
University of Indianapolis Newman Center, [N], (IND), Indianapolis, IN.
University of Maine, [M], (PRT), Orono, ME.
University of Maine at Farmington, [M], (PRT), Farmington, ME.
University of Maine at Fort Kent, [M], (PRT), Fort Kent, ME.
University of Maine at Machias, [M], (PRT), Machias, ME.
University of Maine at Presque Isle, [M], (PRT), Presque Isle, ME.
University of Mary, [B], (BIS), Bismarck, ND.
University of Maryland Catholic Student Center, [S], (WDC). See Archdiocesan Campus Ministry.
University of Maryland-Baltimore County, [O], (BAL). See Archdiocesan Office-Newman Center.
University of Massachusetts and Amherst College, Newman Center, [P], (SPR), Amherst, MA.
University of Massachusetts at Boston Campus Ministry, [CC], (BO), Dorchester, MA.
University of Massachusetts Dartmouth Catholic Campus Ministry, [P], (FR), North Dartmouth, MA.
University of Massachusetts Medical School, [Q], (WOR). See Campus Ministry.
University of Minnesota Cooperative Campus Ministry, [F], (CR), Crookston, MN.
University of Minnesota Newman Center and Chapel, [V], (STP), Minneapolis, MN.
University of Mississippi Medical Center - Newman Center, [G], (JKS), Jackson, MS.
University of Mississippi Newman Center, [G], (JKS), Oxford, MS.
University of Missouri, St. Louis, Newman House, [V], (STL), St. Louis, MO.
University of Missouri-Columbia, Campus Ministry,

V

W

X

Y

Z

	*Mobile AL	Birmingham AL	ALABAMA TOTAL	*Anchorage AK	Fairbanks AK	Juneau AK	1997 U.S. GRAND TOTAL
Cardinals	–	–	–	–	–	–	**9**
Archbishops	1	–	1	1	–	–	**50**
Bishops	–	1	1	–	2	1	**358**
Abbots	1	4	5	–	–	–	**112**
Diocesan Priests	107	65	172	19	9	16	**31,977**
Religious Priests	44	49	93	12	23	3	**16,120**
Total Priests in Diocese	151	114	265	31	32	19	**48,097**
Newly Ordained Priests	2	–	2	1	–	–	**521**
Total Permanent Deacons	41	24	65	12	42	9	**11,788**
Total Brothers	15	31	46	1	4	–	**6,293**
Total Sisters	223	171	394	47	19	7	**87,644**
Number of Parishes	77	62	139	20	41	8	**19,677**
Missions	15	13	28	8	7	4	**3,051**
Pastoral Centers	3	–	3	–	1	–	**1,229**
New Parishes	–	–	–	–	–	–	**39**
Catholic Hospitals	1	1	2	1	–	1	**590**
Patients Assisted Annually	153,924	119,158	273,082	287,000	–	70,081	**61,489,163**
Health Care Centers	4	2	6	1	–	–	**366**
Patients Assisted Annually	3,971	893,390	897,361	380	–	–	**4,861,384**
Specialized Homes	5	–	5	1	–	1	**1,252**
Total Assisted Annually	435	–	435	89	–	68	**946,572**
Residential Care of Children (Orphanages)	1	–	1	–	–	–	**178**
Total Assisted Annually	200	–	200	–	–	–	**74,324**
Day Care and Extended Day Care Centers	4	–	4	–	–	1	**1,110**
Total Assisted Annually	232	–	232	–	–	8,628	**126,432**
Special Centers for Social Services	9	12	21	4	1	1	**2,014**
Total Assisted Annually	89,762	66,474	156,236	27,697	4,400	6,030	**18,262,444**
Diocesan Seminaries	–	–	–	–	–	–	**77**
Students	–	–	–	–	–	–	**3,149**
Religious Seminaries	–	–	–	–	–	–	**129**
Students	–	–	–	–	–	–	**1,496**
Colleges and Universities	1	–	1	–	–	–	**241**
Total Students	946	–	946	–	–	–	**690,826**
High Schools, Diocesan and Parish	3	3	6	–	1	–	**794**
Total Students	1,618	1,043	2,661	–	225	–	**369,281**
High Schools, Private	–	2	2	1	–	–	**563**
Total Students	–	300	300	40	–	–	**283,406**
Elementary Schools, Diocesan and Parish	21	20	41	2	1	1	**6,822**
Total Students	7,688	4,907	12,595	379	261	100	**1,960,274**
Elementary Schools, Private	–	1	1	1	–	–	**343**
Total Students	–	190	190	140	–	–	**93,545**
Non–residential Schools for the Disabled	–	1	1	–	–	–	**80**
Total Students	–	143	143	–	–	–	**19,198**
Religious Education High School Students	832	1,763	2,595	1,067	381	143	**804,759**
Religious Education Elementary Students	3,551	6,003	9,554	2,932	1,542	574	**3,445,153**
Priests Teaching	–	7	7	–	1	–	**2,174**
Scholastics Teaching	–	1	1	–	–	–	**51**
Brothers Teaching	1	–	1	–	–	–	**1,191**
Sisters Teaching	16	22	38	3	2	–	**11,217**
Lay Teachers	396	395	791	43	36	9	**152,165**
Infant Baptisms	1,218	1,210	2,428	538	519	86	**1,044,304**
Adult Baptisms	191	180	371	60	19	15	**75,645**
Received into Full Communion	359	445	804	97	38	17	**85,970**
First Communions	1,273	1,159	2,432	545	399	111	**846,104**
Confirmations	1,271	1,002	2,273	341	141	39	**592,399**
Marriages	476	405	881	135	72	52	**300,582**
Deaths	667	495	1,162	132	139	19	**472,126**
Totals Catholics	67,205	68,979	136,184	27,019	17,181	5,816	**61,207,914**
Total Population	1,452,506	2,682,886	4,135,392	373,019	152,194	86,870	**268,299,833**
Catholic Population Percentage	5	3	3	7	11	7	**23**

Archdioceses = 36; Dioceses = 164; Apostolates = 3

1997 GENERAL SUMMARY

	ALASKA TOTAL	Samoa-Pago Pago AS	Phoenix AZ	Tucson AZ	ARIZONA TOTAL	Little Rock AR	1997 U.S. GRAND TOTAL
Cardinals	–	–	–	–	–	–	**9**
Archbishops	1	–	1	–	1	–	**50**
Bishops	3	1	2	1	3	1	**358**
Abbots	–	–	–	–	–	2	**112**
Diocesan Priests	44	10	144	111	255	87	**31,977**
Religious Priests	38	1	110	76	186	67	**16,120**
Total Priests in Diocese	82	11	254	187	441	154	**48,097**
Newly Ordained Priests	1	–	2	2	4	1	**521**
Total Permanent Deacons	63	19	178	123	301	65	**11,788**
Total Brothers	5	–	7	8	15	47	**6,293**
Total Sisters	73	16	232	289	521	364	**87,644**
Number of Parishes	69	8	87	64	151	90	**19,677**
Missions	19	1	28	31	59	45	**3,051**
Pastoral Centers	1	–	–	15	15	–	**1,229**
New Parishes	–	–	–	–	–	–	**39**
Catholic Hospitals	2	–	1	3	4	10	**590**
Patients Assisted Annually	357,081	–	212,853	281,129	493,982	694,164	**61,489,163**
Health Care Centers	1	–	2	1	3	–	**366**
Patients Assisted Annually	380	–	98,628	23,000	121,628	–	**4,861,384**
Specialized Homes	2	1	15	–	15	7	**1,252**
Total Assisted Annually	157	31	921	–	921	392	**946,572**
Residential Care of Children (Orphanages)	–	–	–	–	–	–	**178**
Total Assisted Annually	–	–	–	–	–	–	**74,324**
Day Care and Extended Day Care Centers	1	1	26	–	26	11	**1,110**
Total Assisted Annually	8,628	120	882	–	882	521	**126,432**
Special Centers for Social Services	6	1	11	1	12	25	**2,014**
Total Assisted Annually	38,127	663	2,106,076	385,000	2,491,076	13,522	**18,262,444**
Diocesan Seminaries	–	–	–	–	–	–	**77**
Students	–	–	–	–	–	–	**3,149**
Religious Seminaries	–	–	–	–	–	–	**129**
Students	–	–	–	–	–	6	**1,496**
Colleges and Universities	–	–	–	–	–	–	**241**
Total Students	–	–	–	–	–	–	**690,826**
High Schools, Diocesan and Parish	1	2	4	1	5	3	**794**
Total Students	225	320	2,417	1,212	3,629	996	**369,281**
High Schools, Private	1	–	1	2	3	2	**563**
Total Students	40	–	1,159	371	1,530	780	**283,406**
Elementary Schools, Diocesan and Parish	4	2	23	18	41	30	**6,822**
Total Students	740	454	7,642	4,680	12,322	6,676	**1,960,274**
Elementary Schools, Private	1	–	–	2	2	1	**343**
Total Students	140	–	–	352	352	82	**93,545**
Non–residential Schools for the Disabled	–	–	–	–	–	–	**80**
Total Students	–	–	–	–	–	–	**19,198**
Religious Education High School Students	1,591	360	5,653	3,212	8,865	2,293	**804,759**
Religious Education Elementary Students	5,048	1,686	27,996	15,141	43,137	5,296	**3,445,153**
Priests Teaching	1	1	15	7	22	9	**2,174**
Scholastics Teaching	–	–	2	–	2	–	**51**
Brothers Teaching	–	–	1	2	3	10	**1,191**
Sisters Teaching	5	7	39	44	83	40	**11,217**
Lay Teachers	88	44	530	272	802	516	**152,165**
Infant Baptisms	1,143	310	10,443	7,203	17,646	1,815	**1,044,304**
Adult Baptisms	94	47	506	376	882	255	**75,645**
Received into Full Communion	152	19	845	721	1,566	460	**85,970**
First Communions	1,055	248	6,527	4,326	10,853	1,688	**846,104**
Confirmations	521	205	2,800	2,802	5,602	1,349	**592,399**
Marriages	259	54	1,798	1,292	3,090	601	**300,582**
Deaths	290	56	3,453	2,259	5,712	861	**472,126**
Totals Catholics	50,016	6,676	386,821	291,230	678,051	85,992	**61,207,914**
Total Population	612,083	58,070	2,915,165	1,106,076	4,021,241	2,483,769	**268,299,833**
Catholic Population Percentage	8	12	13	26	17	3	**23**

*Indicates Archdioceses.

†Certain Dioceses traverse state lines.

1997 GENERAL SUMMARY

	*Los Angeles CA	*San Francisco CA	Fresno CA	Monterey in California CA	Oakland CA	Orange in California CA	1997 U.S. GRAND TOTAL
Cardinals	1	–	–	–	–	–	**9**
Archbishops	–	2	–	–	–	–	**50**
Bishops	6	3	1	3	1	2	**358**
Abbots	1	–	–	–	–	2	**112**
Diocesan Priests	572	223	114	84	228	165	**31,977**
Religious Priests	593	207	38	22	78	94	**16,120**
Total Priests in Diocese	1,165	430	152	106	306	259	**48,097**
Newly Ordained Priests	20	9	1	4	1	5	**521**
Total Permanent Deacons	144	53	6	2	80	50	**11,788**
Total Brothers	220	47	10	29	16	9	**6,293**
Total Sisters	1,980	873	127	114	330	407	**87,644**
Number of Parishes	285	89	84	46	86	54	**19,677**
Missions	17	6	40	10	3	5	**3,051**
Pastoral Centers	1	4	–	–	11	4	**1,229**
New Parishes	–	–	–	1	–	1	**39**
Catholic Hospitals	18	3	3	1	1	1	**590**
Patients Assisted Annually	1,514,263	451,997	513,646	166,586	29,000	47,546	**61,489,163**
Health Care Centers	2	–	2	–	1	2	**366**
Patients Assisted Annually	13,200	–	–	–	6	247,005	**4,861,384**
Specialized Homes	12	17	2	4	7	6	**1,252**
Total Assisted Annually	1,181	7,217	205	444	17,219	15,807	**946,572**
Residential Care of Children (Orphanages)	3	2	–	–	–	–	**178**
Total Assisted Annually	379	368	–	–	–	–	**74,324**
Day Care and Extended Day Care Centers	80	2	–	–	5	1	**1,110**
Total Assisted Annually	13,189	154	–	–	1,400	100	**126,432**
Special Centers for Social Services	82	35	5	–	5	3	**2,014**
Total Assisted Annually	356,920	70,000	561,742	–	25,017	336,292	**18,262,444**
Diocesan Seminaries	2	1	–	–	–	–	**77**
Students	135	47	–	–	–	–	**3,149**
Religious Seminaries	15	–	–	–	–	2	**129**
Students	24	12	–	9	71	13	**1,496**
Colleges and Universities	6	3	–	–	3	1	**241**
Total Students	9,977	10,930	–	–	4,500	100	**690,826**
High Schools, Diocesan and Parish	29	4	1	2	3	3	**794**
Total Students	17,585	3,473	727	625	1,922	4,605	**369,281**
High Schools, Private	22	9	1	2	6	3	**563**
Total Students	12,892	4,105	699	750	4,090	1,030	**283,406**
Elementary Schools, Diocesan and Parish	221	60	23	12	51	35	**6,822**
Total Students	67,538	19,297	5,715	3,336	14,419	13,030	**1,960,274**
Elementary Schools, Private	9	6	–	3	–	2	**343**
Total Students	2,586	1,817	–	536	–	706	**93,545**
Non–residential Schools for the Disabled	–	–	–	–	–	–	**80**
Total Students	–	–	–	–	–	–	**19,198**
Religious Education High School Students	24,000	2,083	6,193	1,658	1,700	6,669	**804,759**
Religious Education Elementary Students	200,000	14,967	22,393	9,721	8,000	29,611	**3,445,153**
Priests Teaching	69	35	–	–	–	8	**2,174**
Scholastics Teaching	–	4	–	–	–	–	**51**
Brothers Teaching	32	10	5	8	16	4	**1,191**
Sisters Teaching	439	128	36	32	20	55	**11,217**
Lay Teachers	3,963	1,759	333	264	850	889	**152,165**
Infant Baptisms	95,611	8,424	16,818	5,532	9,265	17,833	**1,044,304**
Adult Baptisms	2,023	447	507	216	463	885	**75,645**
Received into Full Communion	2,661	337	348	750	768	803	**85,970**
First Communions	40,086	5,172	10,275	3,478	6,864	9,825	**846,104**
Confirmations	15,180	2,994	3,687	978	2,444	3,990	**592,399**
Marriages	14,178	2,072	2,364	1,048	1,634	3,593	**300,582**
Deaths	13,737	3,567	3,134	1,111	3,110	2,510	**472,126**
Totals Catholics	3,672,763	420,000	323,191	170,321	431,272	603,589	**61,207,914**
Total Population	11,689,801	1,700,000	2,171,617	851,604	2,195,411	2,624,300	**268,299,833**
Catholic Population Percentage	31	25	15	20	20	23	**23**

Archdioceses = 36; Dioceses = 164; Apostolates = 3

1997 GENERAL SUMMARY

	Sacramento CA	San Bernardino CA	San Diego CA	San Jose in California CA	Santa Rosa in California CA	Stockton CA	1997 U.S. GRAND TOTAL
Cardinals	–	–	–	–	–	–	9
Archbishops	–	–	–	–	–	–	50
Bishops	2	1	2	1	2	1	358
Abbots	1	–	2	–	–	–	112
Diocesan Priests	163	143	212	118	82	64	31,977
Religious Priests	73	75	93	211	19	20	16,120
Total Priests in Diocese	236	218	305	329	101	84	48,097
Newly Ordained Priests	2	1	3	1	3	1	521
Total Permanent Deacons	106	–	95	8	21	27	11,788
Total Brothers	35	20	21	76	42	4	6,293
Total Sisters	208	156	355	440	101	69	87,644
Number of Parishes	98	97	98	46	43	32	19,677
Missions	43	13	20	5	20	16	3,051
Pastoral Centers	–	–	2	1	13	2	1,229
New Parishes	–	–	–	1	–	–	39
Catholic Hospitals	8	2	1	3	4	3	590
Patients Assisted Annually	442,028	308,361	487,930	245,343	265,535	325,164	61,489,163
Health Care Centers	3	–	1	1	–	–	366
Patients Assisted Annually	11,303	–	32,727	85	–	–	4,861,384
Specialized Homes	1	–	13	1	3	2	1,252
Total Assisted Annually	118	–	3,577	66	79	448	946,572
Residential Care of Children (Orphanages)	2	–	1	–	1	–	178
Total Assisted Annually	–	–	9	–	107	–	74,324
Day Care and Extended Day Care Centers	3	–	1	–	–	–	1,110
Total Assisted Annually	341	–	18,021	270	–	–	126,432
Special Centers for Social Services	7	–	16	41	23	1	2,014
Total Assisted Annually	951,089	–	185,463	66,769	255,000	25,000	18,262,444
Diocesan Seminaries	–	1	1	–	–	–	77
Students	–	8	22	–	–	–	3,149
Religious Seminaries	2	–	–	–	–	–	129
Students	–	–	–	–	–	–	1,496
Colleges and Universities	–	–	1	1	–	–	241
Total Students	–	–	6,603	7,863	–	–	690,826
High Schools, Diocesan and Parish	4	2	3	2	3	2	794
Total Students	1,688	894	1,820	1,631	1,034	1,324	369,281
High Schools, Private	3	–	2	4	4	–	563
Total Students	2,364	–	1,312	3,965	1,041	–	283,406
Elementary Schools, Diocesan and Parish	48	30	43	30	13	12	6,822
Total Students	13,710	8,351	12,934	10,974	2,991	3,439	1,960,274
Elementary Schools, Private	–	1	1	1	2	–	343
Total Students	–	51	353	152	102	–	93,545
Non–residential Schools for the Disabled	–	–	1	–	–	–	80
Total Students	–	–	165	–	–	–	19,198
Religious Education High School Students	1,739	8,299	7,357	2,629	1,655	1,927	804,759
Religious Education Elementary Students	14,356	24,897	26,023	14,687	5,744	9,909	3,445,153
Priests Teaching	8	1	15	57	4	4	2,174
Scholastics Teaching	2	–	–	2	–	–	51
Brothers Teaching	7	–	–	6	–	2	1,191
Sisters Teaching	27	45	49	8	14	28	11,217
Lay Teachers	685	438	1,101	594	308	195	152,165
Infant Baptisms	8,401	9,001	12,435	8,818	3,097	5,124	1,044,304
Adult Baptisms	705	1,539	566	498	205	315	75,645
Received into Full Communion	640	678	642	497	118	438	85,970
First Communions	6,045	8,230	9,149	5,053	2,431	3,268	846,104
Confirmations	4,788	2,644	3,665	2,272	686	2,345	592,399
Marriages	1,568	1,871	2,357	1,871	792	800	300,582
Deaths	2,626	2,331	2,697	2,049	1,052	1,396	472,126
Totals Catholics	425,000	626,236	690,783	391,313	137,391	161,437	61,207,914
Total Population	2,854,000	3,037,303	2,782,204	1,565,253	772,859	1,035,972	268,299,833
Catholic Population Percentage	15	21	25	25	18	16	23

*Indicates Archdioceses.
†Certain Dioceses traverse state lines.

	CALIFORNIA TOTAL	Caroline Islands	*Denver CO	Colorado Springs CO	Pueblo CO	COLORADO TOTAL	1997 U.S. GRAND TOTAL
Cardinals	1	–	–	–	–	–	**9**
Archbishops	2	–	2	–	–	2	**50**
Bishops	25	2	–	1	2	3	**358**
Abbots	6	–	1	–	–	1	**112**
Diocesan Priests	2,168	12	151	31	76	258	**31,977**
Religious Priests	1,523	16	133	18	40	191	**16,120**
Total Priests in Diocese	3,691	28	284	49	116	449	**48,097**
Newly Ordained Priests	51	–	1	–	–	1	**521**
Total Permanent Deacons	592	42	117	21	6	144	**11,788**
Total Brothers	529	2	19	3	13	35	**6,293**
Total Sisters	5,160	33	433	145	93	671	**87,644**
Number of Parishes	1,058	21	112	30	54	196	**19,677**
Missions	198	18	39	9	61	109	**3,051**
Pastoral Centers	38	–	–	–	–	–	**1,229**
New Parishes	3	2	–	–	–	–	**39**
Catholic Hospitals	48	–	3	3	5	11	**590**
Patients Assisted Annually	4,797,399	–	412,832	265,000	877,712	1,555,544	**61,489,163**
Health Care Centers	12	–	2	2	–	4	**366**
Patients Assisted Annually	304,326	–	31,950	113	–	32,063	**4,861,384**
Specialized Homes	68	–	9	2	4	15	**1,252**
Total Assisted Annually	46,361	–	1,125	103	–	1,228	**946,572**
Residential Care of Children (Orphanages)	9	–	1	–	–	1	**178**
Total Assisted Annually	863	–	40	–	–	40	**74,324**
Day Care and Extended Day Care Centers	92	–	28	–	–	28	**1,110**
Total Assisted Annually	33,475	–	1,950	–	–	1,950	**126,432**
Special Centers for Social Services	218	–	4	–	1	5	**2,014**
Total Assisted Annually	2,833,292	–	7,550	–	2,997	10,547	**18,262,444**
Diocesan Seminaries	5	–	–	–	–	–	**77**
Students	212	–	–	–	–	–	**3,149**
Religious Seminaries	19	–	2	–	–	2	**129**
Students	129	–	13	–	–	13	**1,496**
Colleges and Universities	15	–	1	–	–	1	**241**
Total Students	39,973	–	9,648	–	–	9,648	**690,826**
High Schools, Diocesan and Parish	58	3	2	–	1	3	**794**
Total Students	37,328	380	559	–	225	794	**369,281**
High Schools, Private	56	2	3	–	1	4	**563**
Total Students	32,248	321	1,714	–	100	1,814	**283,406**
Elementary Schools, Diocesan and Parish	578	5	36	4	4	44	**6,822**
Total Students	175,734	1,644	10,959	1,212	1,027	13,198	**1,960,274**
Elementary Schools, Private	25	–	1	–	1	2	**343**
Total Students	6,303	–	469	–	223	692	**93,545**
Non–residential Schools for the Disabled	1	–	2	–	–	2	**80**
Total Students	165	–	465	–	–	465	**19,198**
Religious Education High School Students	65,909	450	5,716	1,785	2,203	9,704	**804,759**
Religious Education Elementary Students	380,308	3,250	22,171	4,936	5,137	32,244	**3,445,153**
Priests Teaching	201	8	3	–	–	3	**2,174**
Scholastics Teaching	8	5	–	–	–	–	**51**
Brothers Teaching	90	1	3	–	–	3	**1,191**
Sisters Teaching	881	26	31	–	12	43	**11,217**
Lay Teachers	11,379	129	726	74	102	902	**152,165**
Infant Baptisms	200,359	1,895	9,389	1,312	2,072	12,773	**1,044,304**
Adult Baptisms	8,369	98	735	140	138	1,013	**75,645**
Received into Full Communion	8,680	71	968	269	377	1,614	**85,970**
First Communions	109,876	1,501	6,686	1,406	1,482	9,574	**846,104**
Confirmations	45,673	656	4,187	618	875	5,680	**592,399**
Marriages	34,148	273	2,254	331	478	3,063	**300,582**
Deaths	39,320	–	2,661	370	1,224	4,255	**472,126**
Totals Catholics	8,053,296	64,089	358,600	36,462	104,592	549,654	**61,207,914**
Total Population	33,280,324	122,027	2,628,800	593,175	487,615	3,709,590	**268,299,833**
Catholic Population Percentage	24	53	14	15	21	15	**23**

Archdioceses = 36; Dioceses = 164; Apostolates = 3

1997 GENERAL SUMMARY

	*Hartford CT	Bridgeport CT	† Norwich CT	CONNECTICUT TOTAL	† Wilmington DE	*† Washington DC	1997 U.S. GRAND TOTAL
Cardinals	–	–	–	–	–	1	**9**
Archbishops	1	–	–	1	–	1	**50**
Bishops	1	2	1	4	1	3	**358**
Abbots	–	–	–	–	–	3	**112**
Diocesan Priests	432	258	142	832	129	336	**31,977**
Religious Priests	146	82	83	311	86	495	**16,120**
Total Priests in Diocese	578	340	225	1,143	215	831	**48,097**
Newly Ordained Priests	5	6	1	12	4	7	**521**
Total Permanent Deacons	333	77	50	460	45	245	**11,788**
Total Brothers	78	2	33	113	35	125	**6,293**
Total Sisters	1,069	523	326	1,918	297	885	**87,644**
Number of Parishes	222	88	78	388	55	139	**19,677**
Missions	4	2	10	16	21	9	**3,051**
Pastoral Centers	–	–	23	23	10	1	**1,229**
New Parishes	–	–	–	–	–	–	**39**
Catholic Hospitals	3	2	–	5	1	3	**590**
Patients Assisted Annually	498,190	200,000	–	698,190	298,000	452,959	**61,489,163**
Health Care Centers	–	–	–	–	2	5	**366**
Patients Assisted Annually	–	–	–	–	200	92,143	**4,861,384**
Specialized Homes	10	17	3	30	5	17	**1,252**
Total Assisted Annually	2,167	749	249	3,165	785	1,941	**946,572**
Residential Care of Children (Orphanages)	2	–	–	2	4	1	**178**
Total Assisted Annually	164	–	–	164	113	447	**74,324**
Day Care and Extended Day Care Centers	10	21	–	31	1	5	**1,110**
Total Assisted Annually	894	340	–	1,234	147	781	**126,432**
Special Centers for Social Services	6	20	1	27	15	68	**2,014**
Total Assisted Annually	37,401	13,675	130	51,206	321,546	109,220	**18,262,444**
Diocesan Seminaries	1	1	–	2	–	1	**77**
Students	–	21	–	21	–	60	**3,149**
Religious Seminaries	1	–	1	2	–	33	**129**
Students	123	–	5	128	–	190	**1,496**
Colleges and Universities	3	3	–	6	–	3	**241**
Total Students	2,833	10,868	–	13,701	–	20,958	**690,826**
High Schools, Diocesan and Parish	4	5	3	12	4	1	**794**
Total Students	1,751	2,448	1,713	5,912	2,845	704	**369,281**
High Schools, Private	7	3	2	12	4	16	**563**
Total Students	3,116	989	307	4,412	1,867	7,154	**283,406**
Elementary Schools, Diocesan and Parish	70	32	22	124	25	79	**6,822**
Total Students	19,183	9,682	4,646	33,511	9,720	22,665	**1,960,274**
Elementary Schools, Private	3	2	–	5	5	9	**343**
Total Students	388	419	–	807	996	1,418	**93,545**
Non–residential Schools for the Disabled	–	–	–	–	1	1	**80**
Total Students	–	–	–	–	104	71	**19,198**
Religious Education High School Students	8,827	3,257	4,204	16,288	910	3,230	**804,759**
Religious Education Elementary Students	47,744	26,423	15,559	89,726	8,247	24,150	**3,445,153**
Priests Teaching	5	17	1	23	18	29	**2,174**
Scholastics Teaching	–	–	–	–	–	3	**51**
Brothers Teaching	8	2	1	11	6	23	**1,191**
Sisters Teaching	117	46	15	178	38	124	**11,217**
Lay Teachers	1,181	699	23	1,903	806	2,329	**152,165**
Infant Baptisms	11,561	6,090	3,391	21,042	2,886	6,924	**1,044,304**
Adult Baptisms	373	202	144	719	228	568	**75,645**
Received into Full Communion	489	157	336	982	311	662	**85,970**
First Communions	10,133	5,425	2,932	18,490	2,701	6,998	**846,104**
Confirmations	6,738	3,741	2,065	12,544	1,887	4,609	**592,399**
Marriages	3,867	2,533	994	7,394	1,161	2,167	**300,582**
Deaths	8,779	3,526	2,009	14,314	1,371	2,646	**472,126**
Totals Catholics	778,856	359,455	221,599	1,359,910	164,973	440,000	**61,207,914**
Total Population	1,814,610	830,728	625,450	3,270,788	1,049,769	2,388,506	**268,299,833**
Catholic Population Percentage	43	43	35	42	16	18	**23**

*Indicates Archdioceses.
†Certain Dioceses traverse state lines.

1997 GENERAL SUMMARY

	*Miami FL	Orlando FL	Palm Beach FL	Pensacola-Tallahassee FL	St. Augustine FL	St. Petersburg FL	1997 U.S. GRAND TOTAL
Cardinals	–	–	–	–	–	–	9
Archbishops	2	–	–	–	–	–	50
Bishops	1	2	1	1	1	3	358
Abbots	–	–	–	–	–	1	112
Diocesan Priests	253	123	93	74	90	130	31,977
Religious Priests	122	54	41	10	20	147	16,120
Total Priests in Diocese	375	177	134	84	110	277	48,097
Newly Ordained Priests	8	5	2	2	3	2	521
Total Permanent Deacons	113	109	37	53	22	71	11,788
Total Brothers	56	10	5	7	2	50	6,293
Total Sisters	346	142	178	61	119	350	87,644
Number of Parishes	108	70	46	49	50	72	19,677
Missions	3	9	5	9	9	5	3,051
Pastoral Centers	1	–	–	–	–	1	1,229
New Parishes	–	–	–	–	–	1	39
Catholic Hospitals	2	–	1	1	1	2	590
Patients Assisted Annually	527,144	–	640,000	106,560	254,166	589,704	61,489,163
Health Care Centers	3	–	–	–	–	7	366
Patients Assisted Annually	35,000	–	–	–	–	38,129	4,861,384
Specialized Homes	7	–	2	3	2	9	1,252
Total Assisted Annually	32,255	–	139	247	1,034	1,818	946,572
Residential Care of Children (Orphanages)	2	–	–	–	–	–	178
Total Assisted Annually	380	–	–	–	–	–	74,324
Day Care and Extended Day Care Centers	6	12	2	–	–	13	1,110
Total Assisted Annually	2,300	900	101	–	–	1,432	126,432
Special Centers for Social Services	31	6	23	7	6	36	2,014
Total Assisted Annually	528,655	21,000	19,268	50,362	40,000	396,211	18,262,444
Diocesan Seminaries	1	–	1	–	–	–	77
Students	35	–	67	–	–	–	3,149
Religious Seminaries	–	–	–	–	–	–	129
Students	–	–	–	–	–	–	1,496
Colleges and Universities	2	–	–	–	–	1	241
Total Students	10,378	–	–	–	–	7,179	690,826
High Schools, Diocesan and Parish	7	4	3	1	2	5	794
Total Students	6,706	2,387	1,897	570	1,720	1,847	369,281
High Schools, Private	5	–	–	–	–	2	563
Total Students	2,905	–	–	–	–	978	283,406
Elementary Schools, Diocesan and Parish	49	32	14	8	23	40	6,822
Total Students	21,705	11,531	5,176	2,610	6,985	10,792	1,960,274
Elementary Schools, Private	3	–	2	–	–	4	343
Total Students	1,264	–	570	–	–	1,239	93,545
Non–residential Schools for the Disabled	2	1	–	1	1	2	80
Total Students	11,641	65	–	16	110	133	19,198
Religious Education High School Students	2,543	4,058	2,574	1,307	1,090	2,443	804,759
Religious Education Elementary Students	41,891	20,538	14,360	5,051	8,350	18,891	3,445,153
Priests Teaching	10	4	9	–	1	14	2,174
Scholastics Teaching	–	–	–	–	–	–	51
Brothers Teaching	21	–	2	–	1	4	1,191
Sisters Teaching	51	38	26	10	17	60	11,217
Lay Teachers	1,733	741	394	195	386	803	152,165
Infant Baptisms	18,644	5,482	4,450	1,068	2,000	4,423	1,044,304
Adult Baptisms	986	454	338	164	258	712	75,645
Received into Full Communion	1,256	779	377	295	462	567	85,970
First Communions	13,003	5,456	3,681	1,201	2,230	4,963	846,104
Confirmations	7,734	3,317	1,966	824	1,803	3,403	592,399
Marriages	3,822	1,694	1,320	336	743	2,055	300,582
Deaths	4,856	3,356	2,380	458	907	4,319	472,126
Totals Catholics	760,078	301,958	215,907	62,735	115,975	353,117	61,207,914
Total Population	3,525,351	2,955,200	1,415,520	1,256,474	1,502,699	2,287,817	268,299,833
Catholic Population Percentage	22	10	15	5	8	15	23

Archdioceses = 36; Dioceses = 164; Apostolates = 3

1997 GENERAL SUMMARY

	Venice FL	FLORIDA TOTAL	*Atlanta GA	Savannah GA	GEORGIA TOTAL	*Agana GUAM	1997 U.S. GRAND TOTAL
Cardinals	–	–	–	–	–	–	**9**
Archbishops	–	2	2	–	2	1	**50**
Bishops	1	10	–	2	2	–	**358**
Abbots	–	1	2	–	2	–	**112**
Diocesan Priests	86	849	117	64	181	29	**31,977**
Religious Priests	65	459	94	30	124	19	**16,120**
Total Priests in Diocese	151	1,308	211	94	305	48	**48,097**
Newly Ordained Priests	2	24	11	1	12	–	**521**
Total Permanent Deacons	60	465	105	37	142	9	**11,788**
Total Brothers	20	150	1	18	19	1	**6,293**
Total Sisters	155	1,351	125	146	271	120	**87,644**
Number of Parishes	50	445	69	53	122	24	**19,677**
Missions	12	52	22	26	48	2	**3,051**
Pastoral Centers	–	2	2	1	3	–	**1,229**
New Parishes	–	1	1	–	1	–	**39**
Catholic Hospitals	2	9	2	3	5	–	**590**
Patients Assisted Annually	198,083	2,315,657	226,691	305,276	531,967	–	**61,489,163**
Health Care Centers	6	16	2	8	10	–	**366**
Patients Assisted Annually	72,721	145,850	262	163,172	163,434	–	**4,861,384**
Specialized Homes	8	31	4	1	5	2	**1,252**
Total Assisted Annually	3,658	39,151	148	30	178	240	**946,572**
Residential Care of Children (Orphanages)	–	2	–	1	1	–	**178**
Total Assisted Annually	–	380	–	42	42	–	**74,324**
Day Care and Extended Day Care Centers	–	33	1	–	1	4	**1,110**
Total Assisted Annually	–	4,733	55	–	55	525	**126,432**
Special Centers for Social Services	11	120	5	21	26	1	**2,014**
Total Assisted Annually	18,922	1,074,418	37,430	280,640	318,070	120	**18,262,444**
Diocesan Seminaries	–	2	–	–	–	–	**77**
Students	–	102	–	–	–	–	**3,149**
Religious Seminaries	–	–	–	–	–	–	**129**
Students	–	–	–	–	–	1	**1,496**
Colleges and Universities	–	3	–	–	–	–	**241**
Total Students	–	17,557	–	–	–	–	**690,826**
High Schools, Diocesan and Parish	3	25	1	2	3	3	**794**
Total Students	1,577	16,704	1,010	613	1,623	1,058	**369,281**
High Schools, Private	–	7	1	3	4	–	**563**
Total Students	–	3,883	1,025	2,023	3,048	–	**283,406**
Elementary Schools, Diocesan and Parish	9	175	13	15	28	7	**6,822**
Total Students	3,999	62,798	4,617	4,509	9,126	2,699	**1,960,274**
Elementary Schools, Private	–	9	2	–	2	–	**343**
Total Students	–	3,073	195	–	195	–	**93,545**
Non–residential Schools for the Disabled	–	7	–	–	–	–	**80**
Total Students	–	11,965	–	–	–	–	**19,198**
Religious Education High School Students	2,635	16,650	3,882	5,105	8,987	2,250	**804,759**
Religious Education Elementary Students	8,618	117,699	24,194	1,079	25,273	4,589	**3,445,153**
Priests Teaching	3	41	6	5	11	2	**2,174**
Scholastics Teaching	–	–	–	–	–	–	**51**
Brothers Teaching	2	30	1	1	2	–	**1,191**
Sisters Teaching	16	218	7	30	37	28	**11,217**
Lay Teachers	274	4,526	383	366	749	191	**152,165**
Infant Baptisms	2,663	38,730	5,539	1,408	6,947	2,289	**1,044,304**
Adult Baptisms	204	3,116	494	207	701	35	**75,645**
Received into Full Communion	279	4,015	932	412	1,344	54	**85,970**
First Communions	2,483	33,017	4,468	1,406	5,874	1,223	**846,104**
Confirmations	2,067	21,114	3,419	1,203	4,622	785	**592,399**
Marriages	778	10,748	1,630	439	2,069	241	**300,582**
Deaths	2,266	18,542	888	584	1,472	474	**472,126**
Totals Catholics	172,906	1,982,676	256,049	73,853	329,902	114,906	**61,207,914**
Total Population	1,367,235	14,310,296	4,712,254	2,439,868	7,152,122	136,421	**268,299,833**
Catholic Population Percentage	13	14	5	3	5	84	**23**

*Indicates Archdioceses.

†Certain Dioceses traverse state lines.

	Honolulu HI	Boise ID	*Chicago IL	Belleville IL	Joliet in Illinois IL	Peoria IL	1997 U.S. GRAND TOTAL
Cardinals	–	–	–	–	–	–	**9**
Archbishops	–	–	–	–	–	–	**50**
Bishops	3	1	9	1	2	2	**358**
Abbots	–	–	–	–	3	2	**112**
Diocesan Priests	75	95	958	148	204	246	**31,977**
Religious Priests	77	16	359	45	113	57	**16,120**
Total Priests in Diocese	152	111	1,317	193	317	303	**48,097**
Newly Ordained Priests	–	1	16	3	3	12	**521**
Total Permanent Deacons	36	30	595	25	117	83	**11,788**
Total Brothers	45	8	444	10	92	10	**6,293**
Total Sisters	243	121	3,434	263	757	303	**87,644**
Number of Parishes	69	73	378	128	119	165	**19,677**
Missions	29	40	11	1	10	39	**3,051**
Pastoral Centers	–	–	8	7	–	5	**1,229**
New Parishes	–	–	2	–	1	1	**39**
Catholic Hospitals	2	5	19	7	3	8	**590**
Patients Assisted Annually	343,985	485,821	2,680,658	354,669	433,605	898,592	**61,489,163**
Health Care Centers	3	–	1	–	–	–	**366**
Patients Assisted Annually	38,487	–	4,500	–	–	–	**4,861,384**
Specialized Homes	45	–	48	5	12	4	**1,252**
Total Assisted Annually	1,575	–	16,200	644	3,735	304	**946,572**
Residential Care of Children (Orphanages)	–	–	–	–	–	1	**178**
Total Assisted Annually	–	–	–	–	–	58	**74,324**
Day Care and Extended Day Care Centers	–	4	11	4	3	3	**1,110**
Total Assisted Annually	–	135	2,100	550	662	315	**126,432**
Special Centers for Social Services	13	12	45	3	5	1	**2,014**
Total Assisted Annually	5,955	51,116	93,000	43,856	39,196	18,761	**18,262,444**
Diocesan Seminaries	–	–	3	–	–	–	**77**
Students	–	–	471	–	–	–	**3,149**
Religious Seminaries	–	–	1	–	–	–	**129**
Students	1	–	93	–	–	–	**1,496**
Colleges and Universities	1	–	6	1	4	1	**241**
Total Students	2,528	–	40,599	632	8,171	152	**690,826**
High Schools, Diocesan and Parish	3	1	9	3	4	6	**794**
Total Students	1,230	713	2,727	1,641	2,474	2,604	**369,281**
High Schools, Private	4	–	39	–	4	1	**563**
Total Students	2,445	–	30,698	–	3,128	70	**283,406**
Elementary Schools, Diocesan and Parish	25	13	274	39	63	48	**6,822**
Total Students	6,216	2,388	100,842	7,574	19,372	12,517	**1,960,274**
Elementary Schools, Private	1	–	2	–	–	–	**343**
Total Students	358	–	1,182	–	–	–	**93,545**
Non–residential Schools for the Disabled	–	–	7	–	–	–	**80**
Total Students	–	–	600	–	–	–	**19,198**
Religious Education High School Students	2,123	2,787	10,797	1,286	6,906	3,697	**804,759**
Religious Education Elementary Students	7,292	6,595	93,812	7,174	47,194	13,319	**3,445,153**
Priests Teaching	6	–	55	–	14	6	**2,174**
Scholastics Teaching	–	–	–	–	–	–	**51**
Brothers Teaching	19	–	67	–	10	–	**1,191**
Sisters Teaching	83	5	357	12	39	51	**11,217**
Lay Teachers	793	152	5,710	382	1,029	875	**152,165**
Infant Baptisms	3,603	2,579	39,989	1,655	11,156	3,124	**1,044,304**
Adult Baptisms	445	202	1,804	280	383	510	**75,645**
Received into Full Communion	488	261	1,544	251	871	596	**85,970**
First Communions	2,725	1,913	29,219	1,901	13,978	3,233	**846,104**
Confirmations	1,482	1,014	19,827	2,102	6,538	3,492	**592,399**
Marriages	1,016	576	11,315	733	2,741	1,341	**300,582**
Deaths	1,714	671	18,948	1,267	6,052	2,324	**472,126**
Totals Catholics	232,780	116,500	2,342,000	109,985	512,609	234,298	**61,207,914**
Total Population	1,178,600	1,163,000	5,712,000	855,010	1,494,976	1,436,088	**268,299,833**
Catholic Population Percentage	20	10	41	13	34	16	**23**

Archdioceses = 36; Dioceses = 164; Apostolates = 3

1997 GENERAL SUMMARY

	Rockford IL	Springfield in Illinois IL	ILLINOIS TOTAL	*Indianapolis IN	Evansville IN	Fort Wayne - South Bend IN	1997 U.S. GRAND TOTAL
Cardinals	–	–	–	–	–	–	**9**
Archbishops	–	–	–	1	–	–	**50**
Bishops	2	1	17	–	1	4	**358**
Abbots	3	–	8	3	–	–	**112**
Diocesan Priests	145	149	1,850	168	106	104	**31,977**
Religious Priests	61	69	1,204	127	10	159	**16,120**
Total Priests in Diocese	206	218	3,054	295	116	263	**48,097**
Newly Ordained Priests	2	1	37	2	1	1	**521**
Total Permanent Deacons	100	2	922	–	22	25	**11,788**
Total Brothers	15	19	590	60	2	129	**6,293**
Total Sisters	366	717	5,840	806	318	697	**87,644**
Number of Parishes	101	166	1,057	138	73	88	**19,677**
Missions	6	–	67	13	–	–	**3,051**
Pastoral Centers	48	–	68	–	6	2	**1,229**
New Parishes	–	1	5	–	–	–	**39**
Catholic Hospitals	4	8	49	2	2	5	**590**
Patients Assisted Annually	477,646	870,661	5,715,831	1,007,174	332,475	361,160	**61,489,163**
Health Care Centers	1	–	2	1	1	1	**366**
Patients Assisted Annually	375	–	4,875	185	60	20,000	**4,861,384**
Specialized Homes	5	4	78	8	3	7	**1,252**
Total Assisted Annually	750	535	22,168	828	251	20,547	**946,572**
Residential Care of Children (Orphanages)	–	1	2	–	–	–	**178**
Total Assisted Annually	–	130	188	–	–	–	**74,324**
Day Care and Extended Day Care Centers	1	1	23	5	1	2	**1,110**
Total Assisted Annually	56	126	3,809	202	436	600	**126,432**
Special Centers for Social Services	10	–	64	12	15	6	**2,014**
Total Assisted Annually	285,345	–	480,158	117,512	23,000	–	**18,262,444**
Diocesan Seminaries	–	–	3	–	–	–	**77**
Students	–	–	471	–	–	–	**3,149**
Religious Seminaries	–	1	2	1	–	2	**129**
Students	–	5	98	113	–	33	**1,496**
Colleges and Universities	–	2	14	3	–	5	**241**
Total Students	–	1,677	51,231	2,573	–	13,805	**690,826**
High Schools, Diocesan and Parish	6	3	31	6	4	4	**794**
Total Students	3,462	742	13,650	3,306	1,722	3,045	**369,281**
High Schools, Private	2	4	50	3	1	–	**563**
Total Students	761	1,949	36,606	1,879	101	–	**283,406**
Elementary Schools, Diocesan and Parish	41	54	519	62	24	40	**6,822**
Total Students	11,451	12,692	164,448	18,767	5,745	11,542	**1,960,274**
Elementary Schools, Private	–	–	2	–	–	–	**343**
Total Students	–	–	1,182	–	–	–	**93,545**
Non–residential Schools for the Disabled	–	–	7	–	1	–	**80**
Total Students	–	–	600	–	17	–	**19,198**
Religious Education High School Students	4,959	2,777	30,422	3,256	1,929	1,601	**804,759**
Religious Education Elementary Students	21,105	11,464	194,068	10,429	8,049	7,875	**3,445,153**
Priests Teaching	13	9	97	5	2	–	**2,174**
Scholastics Teaching	–	–	–	–	–	–	**51**
Brothers Teaching	–	4	81	9	2	2	**1,191**
Sisters Teaching	30	54	543	48	36	23	**11,217**
Lay Teachers	754	924	9,674	1,576	440	694	**152,165**
Infant Baptisms	6,411	2,588	64,923	4,106	1,596	2,534	**1,044,304**
Adult Baptisms	356	387	3,720	650	122	440	**75,645**
Received into Full Communion	457	462	4,181	741	143	455	**85,970**
First Communions	6,290	2,906	57,527	3,507	1,558	2,956	**846,104**
Confirmations	3,535	2,596	38,090	2,379	1,305	2,532	**592,399**
Marriages	1,610	1,190	18,930	1,512	653	1,000	**300,582**
Deaths	2,153	1,745	32,489	1,963	859	1,404	**472,126**
Totals Catholics	280,652	170,478	3,650,022	213,252	89,203	159,659	**61,207,914**
Total Population	1,201,303	1,106,124	11,805,501	2,201,503	475,953	1,960,876	**268,299,833**
Catholic Population Percentage	23	15	31	10	19	8	**23**

*Indicates Archdioceses.

†Certain Dioceses traverse state lines.

	Gary IN	Lafayette in Indiana IN	INDIANA TOTAL	*Dubuque IA	Davenport IA	Des Moines IA	1997 U.S. GRAND TOTAL
Cardinals	–	–	–	–	–	–	**9**
Archbishops	–	–	1	2	–	–	**50**
Bishops	2	1	8	–	2	1	**358**
Abbots	–	–	3	5	–	–	**112**
Diocesan Priests	131	120	629	268	146	115	**31,977**
Religious Priests	50	19	365	32	7	7	**16,120**
Total Priests in Diocese	181	139	994	300	153	122	**48,097**
Newly Ordained Priests	2	–	6	1	1	4	**521**
Total Permanent Deacons	30	5	82	63	50	53	**11,788**
Total Brothers	20	2	213	28	2	4	**6,293**
Total Sisters	137	112	2,070	1,054	214	128	**87,644**
Number of Parishes	79	62	440	213	93	87	**19,677**
Missions	3	1	17	2	–	1	**3,051**
Pastoral Centers	7	–	15	1	1	–	**1,229**
New Parishes	–	–	–	–	1	–	**39**
Catholic Hospitals	6	4	19	6	3	3	**590**
Patients Assisted Annually	401,469	501,103	2,603,381	781,597	275,966	583,890	**61,489,163**
Health Care Centers	–	2	5	3	–	1	**366**
Patients Assisted Annually	–	–	20,245	391	–	5,389	**4,861,384**
Specialized Homes	3	2	23	5	3	2	**1,252**
Total Assisted Annually	478	693	22,797	399	441	442	**946,572**
Residential Care of Children (Orphanages)	4	–	4	–	–	–	**178**
Total Assisted Annually	184	–	184	–	–	–	**74,324**
Day Care and Extended Day Care Centers	1	–	9	1	–	–	**1,110**
Total Assisted Annually	200	–	1,438	61	–	–	**126,432**
Special Centers for Social Services	–	–	33	–	–	4	**2,014**
Total Assisted Annually	–	–	140,512	–	–	31,970	**18,262,444**
Diocesan Seminaries	–	–	–	1	1	–	**77**
Students	–	–	–	12	5	–	**3,149**
Religious Seminaries	1	–	4	1	–	–	**129**
Students	5	–	151	115	–	–	**1,496**
Colleges and Universities	1	3	12	3	2	–	**241**
Total Students	1,022	7,700	25,100	4,198	3,119	–	**690,826**
High Schools, Diocesan and Parish	3	1	18	8	7	2	**794**
Total Students	2,093	368	10,534	3,189	1,278	1,380	**369,281**
High Schools, Private	1	–	5	–	–	–	**563**
Total Students	105	–	2,085	–	–	–	**283,406**
Elementary Schools, Diocesan and Parish	30	18	174	54	45	15	**6,822**
Total Students	7,911	4,013	47,978	12,447	4,627	4,673	**1,960,274**
Elementary Schools, Private	1	–	1	–	–	–	**343**
Total Students	110	–	110	–	–	–	**93,545**
Non–residential Schools for the Disabled	–	–	1	–	–	–	**80**
Total Students	–	–	17	–	–	–	**19,198**
Religious Education High School Students	948	2,626	10,360	7,058	3,200	2,064	**804,759**
Religious Education Elementary Students	10,996	7,938	45,287	16,726	9,600	9,232	**3,445,153**
Priests Teaching	6	–	13	10	29	1	**2,174**
Scholastics Teaching	–	–	–	–	–	–	**51**
Brothers Teaching	3	–	16	1	–	1	**1,191**
Sisters Teaching	20	–	127	44	18	11	**11,217**
Lay Teachers	504	234	3,448	1,015	538	305	**152,165**
Infant Baptisms	2,638	1,893	12,767	3,564	1,543	1,801	**1,044,304**
Adult Baptisms	181	252	1,645	158	236	238	**75,645**
Received into Full Communion	282	310	1,931	405	221	544	**85,970**
First Communions	2,336	1,804	12,161	3,639	2,110	1,852	**846,104**
Confirmations	2,134	1,450	9,800	3,127	1,928	1,628	**592,399**
Marriages	880	631	4,676	1,770	730	654	**300,582**
Deaths	1,824	792	6,842	2,151	1,117	709	**472,126**
Totals Catholics	184,516	92,454	739,084	206,199	106,460	97,105	**61,207,914**
Total Population	759,673	1,101,765	6,499,770	923,000	707,123	671,091	**268,299,833**
Catholic Population Percentage	24	8	11	22	15	14	**23**

Archdioceses = 36; Dioceses = 164; Apostolates = 3

1997 GENERAL SUMMARY

	Sioux City IA	IOWA TOTAL	*Kansas City in Kansas KS	Dodge City KS	Salina KS	Wichita KS	1997 U.S. GRAND TOTAL
Cardinals	–	–	–	–	–	–	**9**
Archbishops	–	2	2	–	–	–	**50**
Bishops	1	4	1	2	2	1	**358**
Abbots	–	5	3	–	–	–	**112**
Diocesan Priests	179	708	98	51	68	129	**31,977**
Religious Priests	–	46	66	3	19	8	**16,120**
Total Priests in Diocese	179	754	164	54	87	137	**48,097**
Newly Ordained Priests	2	8	–	–	1	1	**521**
Total Permanent Deacons	35	201	–	6	–	2	**11,788**
Total Brothers	–	34	20	–	1	–	**6,293**
Total Sisters	128	1,524	840	122	213	414	**87,644**
Number of Parishes	118	511	119	57	92	95	**19,677**
Missions	10	13	–	–	–	–	**3,051**
Pastoral Centers	–	2	–	–	–	–	**1,229**
New Parishes	–	1	–	–	–	–	**39**
Catholic Hospitals	3	15	3	3	–	5	**590**
Patients Assisted Annually	318,297	1,959,750	327,154	97,722	–	477,751	**61,489,163**
Health Care Centers	–	4	2	–	–	2	**366**
Patients Assisted Annually	–	5,780	13,378	–	–	25,581	**4,861,384**
Specialized Homes	4	14	4	–	4	3	**1,252**
Total Assisted Annually	300	1,582	573	–	326	294	**946,572**
Residential Care of Children (Orphanages)	4	4	–	–	–	–	**178**
Total Assisted Annually	7	7	–	–	–	–	**74,324**
Day Care and Extended Day Care Centers	–	1	1	–	–	–	**1,110**
Total Assisted Annually	–	61	125	–	–	–	**126,432**
Special Centers for Social Services	4	8	10	4	–	1	**2,014**
Total Assisted Annually	6,280	38,250	15,245	62,737	–	14,022	**18,262,444**
Diocesan Seminaries	–	2	–	–	–	–	**77**
Students	–	17	–	–	–	–	**3,149**
Religious Seminaries	–	1	–	–	–	–	**129**
Students	–	115	2	–	–	–	**1,496**
Colleges and Universities	1	6	3	–	–	1	**241**
Total Students	1,116	8,433	2,430	–	–	1,984	**690,826**
High Schools, Diocesan and Parish	8	25	5	–	4	4	**794**
Total Students	2,380	8,227	3,083	–	397	1,919	**369,281**
High Schools, Private	–	–	2	–	1	–	**563**
Total Students	–	–	338	–	305	–	**283,406**
Elementary Schools, Diocesan and Parish	28	142	39	10	12	33	**6,822**
Total Students	6,540	28,287	12,097	1,378	1,887	7,524	**1,960,274**
Elementary Schools, Private	–	–	1	–	–	–	**343**
Total Students	–	–	40	–	–	–	**93,545**
Non–residential Schools for the Disabled	–	–	–	–	–	–	**80**
Total Students	–	–	–	–	–	–	**19,198**
Religious Education High School Students	4,086	16,408	3,418	2,453	2,142	2,887	**804,759**
Religious Education Elementary Students	8,764	44,322	14,790	4,311	6,171	8,311	**3,445,153**
Priests Teaching	7	47	3	–	9	–	**2,174**
Scholastics Teaching	–	–	–	–	–	–	**51**
Brothers Teaching	–	2	1	–	–	–	**1,191**
Sisters Teaching	26	99	45	4	6	43	**11,217**
Lay Teachers	518	2,376	1,012	120	205	487	**152,165**
Infant Baptisms	1,784	8,692	3,678	944	983	2,447	**1,044,304**
Adult Baptisms	80	712	409	219	111	353	**75,645**
Received into Full Communion	480	1,650	588	264	211	381	**85,970**
First Communions	1,689	9,290	3,487	1,060	978	2,348	**846,104**
Confirmations	1,529	8,212	2,693	658	693	1,876	**592,399**
Marriages	703	3,857	1,297	301	460	793	**300,582**
Deaths	1,206	5,183	1,354	303	588	794	**472,126**
Totals Catholics	99,377	509,141	181,638	44,504	52,114	105,172	**61,207,914**
Total Population	472,136	2,773,350	952,000	212,147	328,480	910,544	**268,299,833**
Catholic Population Percentage	21	18	19	21	16	12	**23**

*Indicates Archdioceses.
†Certain Dioceses traverse state lines.

	KANSAS TOTAL	*Louisville KY	Covington KY	Lexington KY	Owensboro KY	KENTUCKY TOTAL	1997 U.S. GRAND TOTAL
Cardinals	–	–	–	–	–	–	**9**
Archbishops	2	2	–	–	–	2	**50**
Bishops	6	1	2	1	1	5	**358**
Abbots	3	1	–	–	–	1	**112**
Diocesan Priests	346	197	119	50	82	448	**31,977**
Religious Priests	96	62	1	21	10	94	**16,120**
Total Priests in Diocese	442	259	120	71	92	542	**48,097**
Newly Ordained Priests	2	2	3	–	1	6	**521**
Total Permanent Deacons	8	103	17	28	–	148	**11,788**
Total Brothers	21	94	7	5	1	107	**6,293**
Total Sisters	1,589	1,083	464	186	242	1,975	**87,644**
Number of Parishes	363	113	51	61	79	304	**19,677**
Missions	–	13	5	6	–	24	**3,051**
Pastoral Centers	–	3	–	–	2	5	**1,229**
New Parishes	–	–	–	–	1	1	**39**
Catholic Hospitals	11	2	3	6	1	12	**590**
Patients Assisted Annually	902,627	130,642	220,722	253,840	85,000	690,204	**61,489,163**
Health Care Centers	4	1	–	4	2	7	**366**
Patients Assisted Annually	38,959	2,000	–	60,002	8,000	70,002	**4,861,384**
Specialized Homes	11	6	4	1	2	13	**1,252**
Total Assisted Annually	1,193	955	579	86	176	1,796	**946,572**
Residential Care of Children (Orphanages)	–	1	2	–	–	3	**178**
Total Assisted Annually	–	22	78	–	–	100	**74,324**
Day Care and Extended Day Care Centers	1	1	1	3	3	8	**1,110**
Total Assisted Annually	125	200	81	148	136	565	**126,432**
Special Centers for Social Services	15	1	4	1	2	8	**2,014**
Total Assisted Annually	92,004	3,521	24,383	8,240	16,000	52,144	**18,262,444**
Diocesan Seminaries	–	–	–	–	–	–	**77**
Students	–	–	–	–	–	–	**3,149**
Religious Seminaries	–	–	–	–	–	–	**129**
Students	2	–	–	–	–	–	**1,496**
Colleges and Universities	4	3	1	–	1	5	**241**
Total Students	4,414	3,940	1,426	–	760	6,126	**690,826**
High Schools, Diocesan and Parish	13	4	7	1	3	15	**794**
Total Students	5,399	2,095	2,391	664	1,034	6,184	**369,281**
High Schools, Private	3	6	2	2	–	10	**563**
Total Students	643	3,849	773	78	–	4,700	**283,406**
Elementary Schools, Diocesan and Parish	94	56	30	14	19	119	**6,822**
Total Students	22,886	17,740	7,972	2,975	4,415	33,102	**1,960,274**
Elementary Schools, Private	1	3	2	1	–	6	**343**
Total Students	40	540	492	210	–	1,242	**93,545**
Non–residential Schools for the Disabled	–	1	–	–	–	1	**80**
Total Students	–	74	–	–	–	74	**19,198**
Religious Education High School Students	10,900	1,282	416	744	1,326	3,768	**804,759**
Religious Education Elementary Students	33,583	8,248	4,207	2,729	3,703	18,887	**3,445,153**
Priests Teaching	12	12	1	2	1	16	**2,174**
Scholastics Teaching	–	–	–	–	–	–	**51**
Brothers Teaching	1	28	1	–	1	30	**1,191**
Sisters Teaching	98	55	57	24	12	148	**11,217**
Lay Teachers	1,824	1,262	584	215	273	2,334	**152,165**
Infant Baptisms	8,052	2,912	1,603	701	976	6,192	**1,044,304**
Adult Baptisms	1,092	313	174	143	203	833	**75,645**
Received into Full Communion	1,444	523	153	287	233	1,196	**85,970**
First Communions	7,873	3,125	1,473	707	1,086	6,391	**846,104**
Confirmations	5,920	2,654	1,375	702	1,143	5,874	**592,399**
Marriages	2,851	1,259	609	263	509	2,640	**300,582**
Deaths	3,039	1,719	703	193	523	3,138	**472,126**
Totals Catholics	383,428	181,570	82,341	41,905	51,339	357,155	**61,207,914**
Total Population	2,403,171	1,139,022	401,127	1,376,114	778,235	3,694,498	**268,299,833**
Catholic Population Percentage	16	16	21	3	7	10	**23**

Archdioceses = 36; Dioceses = 164; Apostolates = 3

1997 GENERAL SUMMARY

	*New Orleans LA	Alexandria LA	Baton Rouge LA	Houma–Thibodaux LA	Lafayette LA	Lake Charles LA	1997 U.S. GRAND TOTAL
Cardinals	–	–	–	–	–	–	**9**
Archbishops	2	–	1	–	–	–	**50**
Bishops	3	1	–	2	2	1	**358**
Abbots	1	–	–	–	–	–	**112**
Diocesan Priests	231	64	93	73	146	50	**31,977**
Religious Priests	227	15	47	7	52	18	**16,120**
Total Priests in Diocese	458	79	140	80	198	68	**48,097**
Newly Ordained Priests	5	3	1	3	4	1	**521**
Total Permanent Deacons	198	7	27	25	52	19	**11,788**
Total Brothers	141	3	15	12	30	4	**6,293**
Total Sisters	873	69	120	34	175	32	**87,644**
Number of Parishes	147	48	70	40	121	36	**19,677**
Missions	8	23	–	6	35	25	**3,051**
Pastoral Centers	1	1	–	–	–	–	**1,229**
New Parishes	–	–	–	–	–	–	**39**
Catholic Hospitals	–	1	1	–	1	1	**590**
Patients Assisted Annually	–	73,946	230,000	–	81,000	104,497	**61,489,163**
Health Care Centers	3	1	–	–	1	–	**366**
Patients Assisted Annually	1,059	400	–	–	16,000	–	**4,861,384**
Specialized Homes	21	2	9	2	6	–	**1,252**
Total Assisted Annually	6,596	164	809	–	2,200	–	**946,572**
Residential Care of Children (Orphanages)	3	–	–	–	–	–	**178**
Total Assisted Annually	318	–	–	–	–	–	**74,324**
Day Care and Extended Day Care Centers	18	–	–	1	–	1	**1,110**
Total Assisted Annually	1,159	–	–	65	–	57	**126,432**
Special Centers for Social Services	79	16	6	3	6	1	**2,014**
Total Assisted Annually	447,133	125,150	104,733	8,936	180,000	2,437	**18,262,444**
Diocesan Seminaries	2	–	–	–	–	–	**77**
Students	154	–	–	–	–	–	**3,149**
Religious Seminaries	4	–	–	–	1	–	**129**
Students	22	–	–	–	10	–	**1,496**
Colleges and Universities	3	–	1	–	–	–	**241**
Total Students	10,296	–	869	–	–	–	**690,826**
High Schools, Diocesan and Parish	10	3	6	3	9	1	**794**
Total Students	6,580	514	2,482	1,866	3,383	483	**369,281**
High Schools, Private	13	–	2	–	1	–	**563**
Total Students	9,812	–	1,532	–	130	–	**283,406**
Elementary Schools, Diocesan and Parish	74	9	26	10	29	8	**6,822**
Total Students	33,127	2,635	12,562	4,162	10,133	2,353	**1,960,274**
Elementary Schools, Private	6	–	–	–	2	–	**343**
Total Students	1,325	–	–	–	670	–	**93,545**
Non–residential Schools for the Disabled	1	–	–	–	–	–	**80**
Total Students	194	–	–	–	–	–	**19,198**
Religious Education High School Students	4,640	1,541	11,260	3,720	11,131	3,509	**804,759**
Religious Education Elementary Students	18,855	3,044	5,101	7,509	26,627	6,864	**3,445,153**
Priests Teaching	91	–	1	–	–	1	**2,174**
Scholastics Teaching	–	–	–	–	–	–	**51**
Brothers Teaching	38	2	4	7	3	1	**1,191**
Sisters Teaching	174	19	22	1	23	–	**11,217**
Lay Teachers	3,307	194	874	323	820	204	**152,165**
Infant Baptisms	7,353	751	2,985	1,827	6,084	1,543	**1,044,304**
Adult Baptisms	406	97	264	55	180	145	**75,645**
Received into Full Communion	390	131	406	113	205	199	**85,970**
First Communions	6,709	753	2,849	1,592	5,306	1,369	**846,104**
Confirmations	5,572	546	2,506	1,400	3,984	1,933	**592,399**
Marriages	2,609	281	1,192	563	1,967	512	**300,582**
Deaths	4,620	638	1,750	1,082	3,416	782	**472,126**
Totals Catholics	484,263	48,050	218,576	109,412	355,435	81,971	**61,207,914**
Total Population	1,330,855	393,880	798,343	208,185	540,001	259,425	**268,299,833**
Catholic Population Percentage	36	12	27	53	66	32	**23**

*Indicates Archdioceses.
†Certain Dioceses traverse state lines.

	Shreveport LA	LOUISIANA TOTAL	Portland (In Maine) ME	Marshall Islands	*Baltimore MD	*Boston MA	1997 U.S. GRAND TOTAL
Cardinals	–	–	–	–	1	1	**9**
Archbishops	–	3	–	–	1	–	**50**
Bishops	1	10	3	–	2	7	**358**
Abbots	–	1	–	–	–	1	**112**
Diocesan Priests	43	700	194	1	288	977	**31,977**
Religious Priests	11	377	54	5	257	752	**16,120**
Total Priests in Diocese	54	1,077	248	6	545	1,729	**48,097**
Newly Ordained Priests	2	19	2	–	4	10	**521**
Total Permanent Deacons	7	335	11	2	166	187	**11,788**
Total Brothers	–	205	26	2	121	183	**6,293**
Total Sisters	71	1,374	501	15	1,332	3,154	**87,644**
Number of Parishes	31	493	139	4	154	394	**19,677**
Missions	15	112	54	9	8	–	**3,051**
Pastoral Centers	2	4	–	1	3	–	**1,229**
New Parishes	–	–	1	–	1	–	**39**
Catholic Hospitals	2	6	3	–	5	8	**590**
Patients Assisted Annually	191,527	680,970	221,072	–	915,205	79,676	**61,489,163**
Health Care Centers	1	6	1	–	–	–	**366**
Patients Assisted Annually	30,163	47,622	83	–	–	–	**4,861,384**
Specialized Homes	3	43	12	–	23	18	**1,252**
Total Assisted Annually	152	9,921	1,025	–	3,156	1,630	**946,572**
Residential Care of Children (Orphanages)	–	3	–	–	2	2	**178**
Total Assisted Annually	–	318	–	–	251	469	**74,324**
Day Care and Extended Day Care Centers	1	21	4	–	10	9	**1,110**
Total Assisted Annually	100	1,381	530	–	1,544	1,917	**126,432**
Special Centers for Social Services	15	126	7	–	29	45	**2,014**
Total Assisted Annually	17,221	885,610	2,715	–	749,497	136,651	**18,262,444**
Diocesan Seminaries	–	2	–	–	2	3	**77**
Students	–	154	–	–	279	167	**3,149**
Religious Seminaries	–	5	–	–	–	3	**129**
Students	–	32	–	–	–	167	**1,496**
Colleges and Universities	–	4	1	–	3	9	**241**
Total Students	–	11,165	4,785	–	11,365	21,657	**690,826**
High Schools, Diocesan and Parish	2	34	1	2	9	17	**794**
Total Students	811	16,119	231	289	3,563	5,209	**369,281**
High Schools, Private	–	16	2	–	13	19	**563**
Total Students	–	11,474	574	–	7,020	9,749	**283,406**
Elementary Schools, Diocesan and Parish	11	167	18	6	68	119	**6,822**
Total Students	2,579	67,551	3,919	1,248	23,292	35,674	**1,960,274**
Elementary Schools, Private	–	8	1	–	6	11	**343**
Total Students	–	1,995	164	–	1,105	2,686	**93,545**
Non–residential Schools for the Disabled	–	1	–	–	2	–	**80**
Total Students	–	194	–	–	232	–	**19,198**
Religious Education High School Students	725	36,526	3,899	55	4,742	28,859	**804,759**
Religious Education Elementary Students	2,334	70,334	16,879	357	36,623	122,350	**3,445,153**
Priests Teaching	–	93	4	–	60	24	**2,174**
Scholastics Teaching	–	–	–	–	–	–	**51**
Brothers Teaching	–	55	–	2	22	37	**1,191**
Sisters Teaching	9	248	28	10	129	369	**11,217**
Lay Teachers	215	5,937	273	76	2,269	2,866	**152,165**
Infant Baptisms	527	21,070	3,141	95	8,435	26,728	**1,044,304**
Adult Baptisms	118	1,265	270	15	692	3,346	**75,645**
Received into Full Communion	185	1,629	513	21	1,261	316	**85,970**
First Communions	634	19,212	3,271	142	8,211	22,970	**846,104**
Confirmations	613	16,554	2,712	8	5,176	13,273	**592,399**
Marriages	227	7,351	1,377	11	2,926	9,373	**300,582**
Deaths	340	12,628	2,963	13	5,248	18,952	**472,126**
Totals Catholics	38,365	1,336,072	220,983	4,000	480,152	2,024,039	**61,207,914**
Total Population	785,635	4,316,324	1,227,927	50,000	2,862,671	3,793,058	**268,299,833**
Catholic Population Percentage	5	31	18	8	17	53	**23**

Archdioceses = 36; Dioceses = 164; Apostolates = 3

1997 GENERAL SUMMARY

	Fall River MA	Springfield in Massachusetts MA	Worcester MA	MASS. TOTAL	*Detroit MI	Gaylord MI	1997 U.S. GRAND TOTAL
Cardinals	–	–	–	1	1	–	**9**
Archbishops	–	–	–	–	–	–	**50**
Bishops	1	2	5	15	8	1	**358**
Abbots	–	–	3	4	–	–	**112**
Diocesan Priests	179	221	272	1,649	489	73	**31,977**
Religious Priests	113	58	116	1,039	230	15	**16,120**
Total Priests in Diocese	292	279	388	2,688	719	88	**48,097**
Newly Ordained Priests	4	2	2	18	7	2	**521**
Total Permanent Deacons	36	35	67	325	151	11	**11,788**
Total Brothers	39	10	78	310	71	3	**6,293**
Total Sisters	387	644	550	4,735	1,687	71	**87,644**
Number of Parishes	112	135	130	771	306	82	**19,677**
Missions	13	14	3	30	5	–	**3,051**
Pastoral Centers	–	1	–	1	6	–	**1,229**
New Parishes	–	–	–	–	1	–	**39**
Catholic Hospitals	1	2	1	12	11	3	**590**
Patients Assisted Annually	124,334	92,000	80,000	376,010	1,520,112	189,779	**61,489,163**
Health Care Centers	1	1	–	2	8	1	**366**
Patients Assisted Annually	120	140	–	260	9,391	774	**4,861,384**
Specialized Homes	5	6	9	38	21	2	**1,252**
Total Assisted Annually	969	596	25,280	28,475	3,776	30	**946,572**
Residential Care of Children (Orphanages)	1	1	1	5	8	–	**178**
Total Assisted Annually	130	125	16	740	1,477	–	**74,324**
Day Care and Extended Day Care Centers	2	1	3	15	2	–	**1,110**
Total Assisted Annually	56	85	450	2,508	499	–	**126,432**
Special Centers for Social Services	4	2	10	61	11	16	**2,014**
Total Assisted Annually	2,400	52,198	31,000	222,249	16,397	10,168	**18,262,444**
Diocesan Seminaries	–	–	1	4	2	–	**77**
Students	–	–	9	176	119	–	**3,149**
Religious Seminaries	–	1	–	4	2	–	**129**
Students	–	5	–	172	11	–	**1,496**
Colleges and Universities	1	1	3	14	4	–	**241**
Total Students	2,882	1,187	7,243	32,969	16,122	–	**690,826**
High Schools, Diocesan and Parish	4	4	4	29	18	4	**794**
Total Students	2,467	1,945	2,422	12,043	6,123	632	**369,281**
High Schools, Private	–	–	3	22	17	–	**563**
Total Students	–	–	1,313	11,062	8,009	–	**283,406**
Elementary Schools, Diocesan and Parish	24	30	20	193	134	18	**6,822**
Total Students	5,857	8,288	5,065	54,884	40,103	2,549	**1,960,274**
Elementary Schools, Private	1	–	3	15	6	–	**343**
Total Students	161	–	600	3,447	1,075	–	**93,545**
Non–residential Schools for the Disabled	–	1	1	2	–	–	**80**
Total Students	–	1,200	73	1,273	–	–	**19,198**
Religious Education High School Students	5,563	9,230	6,999	50,651	7,469	1,406	**804,759**
Religious Education Elementary Students	32,456	23,345	21,432	199,583	72,267	5,527	**3,445,153**
Priests Teaching	15	4	8	51	32	–	**2,174**
Scholastics Teaching	–	–	–	–	–	–	**51**
Brothers Teaching	4	–	13	54	25	–	**1,191**
Sisters Teaching	30	82	37	518	180	10	**11,217**
Lay Teachers	552	574	530	4,522	2,579	188	**152,165**
Infant Baptisms	5,695	4,465	5,096	41,984	17,215	1,170	**1,044,304**
Adult Baptisms	103	156	146	3,751	1,285	126	**75,645**
Received into Full Communion	125	233	264	938	1,642	226	**85,970**
First Communions	5,307	4,118	4,462	36,857	14,962	1,268	**846,104**
Confirmations	4,351	3,112	3,005	23,741	11,861	1,418	**592,399**
Marriages	2,087	1,610	1,467	14,537	6,287	577	**300,582**
Deaths	4,062	4,189	3,960	31,163	10,126	836	**472,126**
Totals Catholics	345,940	294,269	303,793	2,968,041	1,424,616	82,302	**61,207,914**
Total Population	715,000	802,611	709,705	6,020,374	4,266,654	437,375	**268,299,833**
Catholic Population Percentage	48	37	43	49	33	19	**23**

*Indicates Archdioceses.

†Certain Dioceses traverse state lines.

	Grand Rapids MI	Kalamazoo MI	Lansing MI	Marquette MI	Saginaw MI	MICHIGAN TOTAL	1997 U.S. GRAND TOTAL
Cardinals	–	–	–	–	–	1	**9**
Archbishops	–	–	–	–	–	–	**50**
Bishops	3	2	2	2	1	19	**358**
Abbots	–	–	–	–	–	–	**112**
Diocesan Priests	131	60	141	110	122	1,126	**31,977**
Religious Priests	23	14	28	6	15	331	**16,120**
Total Priests in Diocese	154	74	169	116	137	1,457	**48,097**
Newly Ordained Priests	3	1	–	1	–	14	**521**
Total Permanent Deacons	20	18	59	17	14	290	**11,788**
Total Brothers	3	4	9	–	2	92	**6,293**
Total Sisters	321	230	441	72	146	2,968	**87,644**
Number of Parishes	90	46	93	75	110	802	**19,677**
Missions	12	13	1	25	–	56	**3,051**
Pastoral Centers	–	1	1	–	–	8	**1,229**
New Parishes	–	–	–	–	–	1	**39**
Catholic Hospitals	2	3	7	1	1	28	**590**
Patients Assisted Annually	295,263	511,889	1,612 137	63,603	123,402	4,316,185	**61,489,163**
Health Care Centers	–	–	4	–	1	14	**366**
Patients Assisted Annually	–	–	7 518	–	10,325	28,008	**4,861,384**
Specialized Homes	2	7	2	1	2	37	**1,252**
Total Assisted Annually	406	1,136	258	123	143	5,872	**946,572**
Residential Care of Children (Orphanages)	–	–	3	–	3	14	**178**
Total Assisted Annually	–	–	270	–	96	1,843	**74,324**
Day Care and Extended Day Care Centers	–	2	2	–	7	13	**1,110**
Total Assisted Annually	–	75	267	–	138	979	**126,432**
Special Centers for Social Services	12	4	5	6	5	59	**2,014**
Total Assisted Annually	18,715	25,711	11,151	1,311	1,240	84,693	**18,262,444**
Diocesan Seminaries	1	–	–	–	–	3	**77**
Students	2	–	–	–	–	121	**3,149**
Religious Seminaries	–	–	–	–	–	2	**129**
Students	–	–	–	–	–	11	**1,496**
Colleges and Universities	1	–	1	–	–	6	**241**
Total Students	2,385	–	2,026	–	–	20,533	**690,826**
High Schools, Diocesan and Parish	4	3	4	–	3	36	**794**
Total Students	1,839	866	2,382	–	1,014	12,856	**369,281**
High Schools, Private	–	–	1	–	–	18	**563**
Total Students	–	–	136	–	–	8,145	**283,406**
Elementary Schools, Diocesan and Parish	41	21	38	10	32	294	**6,822**
Total Students	9,404	4,597	10,030	1,802	5,478	73,963	**1,960,274**
Elementary Schools, Private	–	–	1	–	–	7	**343**
Total Students	–	–	340	–	–	1,415	**93,545**
Non–residential Schools for the Disabled	–	–	–	–	–	–	**80**
Total Students	–	–	–	–	–	–	**19,198**
Religious Education High School Students	2,383	1,203	3,190	3,327	3,257	22,235	**804,759**
Religious Education Elementary Students	14,307	6,588	20,245	6,792	11,157	136,883	**3,445,153**
Priests Teaching	–	–	5	–	–	37	**2,174**
Scholastics Teaching	–	–	–	–	–	–	**51**
Brothers Teaching	1	–	1	–	–	27	**1,191**
Sisters Teaching	32	10	18	11	20	281	**11,217**
Lay Teachers	655	298	599	117	335	4,771	**152,165**
Infant Baptisms	3,006	1,620	4,222	1,209	2,300	30,742	**1,044,304**
Adult Baptisms	420	246	642	64	257	3,040	**75,645**
Received into Full Communion	547	197	851	130	224	3,817	**85,970**
First Communions	3,242	1,561	4,256	1,159	2,136	28,584	**846,104**
Confirmations	2,191	1,371	3,471	927	3,934	25,173	**592,399**
Marriages	1,130	607	1,693	546	985	11,825	**300,582**
Deaths	1,390	946	1,953	1,222	1,621	18,094	**472,126**
Totals Catholics	146,205	99,922	223,536	74,066	141,207	2,191,854	**61,207,914**
Total Population	1,167,900	909,236	1,670,223	318,705	685,532	9,455,625	**268,299,833**
Catholic Population Percentage	13	11	13	23	21	23	**23**

Archdioceses = 36; Dioceses = 164; Apostolates = 3

1997 GENERAL SUMMARY

	*St. Paul-Minneapolis MN	Crookston MN	Duluth MN	New Ulm MN	St. Cloud MN	Winona MN	1997 U.S. GRAND TOTAL
Cardinals	–	–	–	–	–	–	**9**
Archbishops	2	–	–	–	–	–	**50**
Bishops	3	1	1	1	2	2	**358**
Abbots	–	–	–	–	2	–	**112**
Diocesan Priests	345	49	83	95	145	129	**31,977**
Religious Priests	146	5	16	–	131	14	**16,120**
Total Priests in Diocese	491	54	99	95	276	143	**48,097**
Newly Ordained Priests	7	2	–	–	–	1	**521**
Total Permanent Deacons	166	8	19	3	32	2	**11,788**
Total Brothers	66	2	–	–	68	19	**6,293**
Total Sisters	1,189	214	178	99	595	518	**87,644**
Number of Parishes	222	76	95	81	141	122	**19,677**
Missions	5	–	3	2	–	1	**3,051**
Pastoral Centers	4	1	–	–	–	2	**1,229**
New Parishes	–	–	–	–	–	–	**39**
Catholic Hospitals	3	3	2	1	4	2	**590**
Patients Assisted Annually	132,555	48,118	171,785	7,314	156,327	113,761	**61,489,163**
Health Care Centers	–	–	–	2	–	1	**366**
Patients Assisted Annually	–	–	–	7,985	–	5,025	**4,861,384**
Specialized Homes	8	3	2	6	17	10	**1,252**
Total Assisted Annually	684	473	370	452	1,351	846	**946,572**
Residential Care of Children (Orphanages)	1	–	–	–	–	–	**178**
Total Assisted Annually	4,000	–	–	–	–	–	**74,324**
Day Care and Extended Day Care Centers	–	1	–	–	2	3	**1,110**
Total Assisted Annually	–	53	–	–	100	9,017	**126,432**
Special Centers for Social Services	5	–	1	–	6	5	**2,014**
Total Assisted Annually	–	–	700	–	22,644	10,938	**18,262,444**
Diocesan Seminaries	2	–	–	–	–	1	**77**
Students	143	–	–	–	–	39	**3,149**
Religious Seminaries	–	–	–	–	1	–	**129**
Students	–	–	–	–	7	–	**1,496**
Colleges and Universities	3	–	1	–	2	1	**241**
Total Students	14,324	–	2,000	–	3,689	7,387	**690,826**
High Schools, Diocesan and Parish	7	1	–	3	1	4	**794**
Total Students	4,302	150	–	669	536	1,228	**369,281**
High Schools, Private	4	–	–	–	1	–	**563**
Total Students	2,340	–	–	–	176	–	**283,406**
Elementary Schools, Diocesan and Parish	88	8	13	19	35	27	**6,822**
Total Students	27,133	1,165	1,689	3,498	6,149	5,511	**1,960,274**
Elementary Schools, Private	1	1	–	–	–	–	**343**
Total Students	259	85	–	–	–	–	**93,545**
Non-residential Schools for the Disabled	–	–	–	–	1	–	**80**
Total Students	–	–	–	–	25	–	**19,198**
Religious Education High School Students	21,404	2,726	4,605	4,070	7,877	5,636	**804,759**
Religious Education Elementary Students	63,595	3,614	5,385	8,687	17,783	12,921	**3,445,153**
Priests Teaching	6	–	1	–	43	3	**2,174**
Scholastics Teaching	–	–	–	–	–	–	**51**
Brothers Teaching	11	–	–	–	10	–	**1,191**
Sisters Teaching	107	6	8	12	60	14	**11,217**
Lay Teachers	2,324	95	136	247	612	348	**152,165**
Infant Baptisms	11,838	776	1,195	1,025	2,529	2,004	**1,044,304**
Adult Baptisms	439	15	43	60	73	68	**75,645**
Received into Full Communion	1,337	93	195	112	214	280	**85,970**
First Communions	10,305	696	1,243	1,426	2,980	2,065	**846,104**
Confirmations	7,294	756	1,135	1,320	2,702	1,926	**592,399**
Marriages	3,925	309	599	482	1,129	845	**300,582**
Deaths	4,860	440	1,564	759	1,417	1,146	**472,126**
Totals Catholics	733,961	42,934	82,175	71,272	147,415	148,445	**61,207,914**
Total Population	2,681,324	236,100	378,000	282,768	433,427	528,303	**268,299,833**
Catholic Population Percentage	27	18	22	25	34	28	**23**

*Indicates Archdioceses.
†Certain Dioceses traverse state lines.

	MINNESOTA TOTAL	Biloxi MS	Jackson MS	MISSISSIPPI TOTAL	*St. Louis MO	Jefferson City MO	1997 U.S. GRAND TOTAL
Cardinals	–	–	–	–	1	–	9
Archbishops	2	–	–	–	1	–	50
Bishops	10	1	1	2	4	1	358
Abbots	2	–	–	–	2	–	112
Diocesan Priests	846	56	71	127	481	114	31,977
Religious Priests	312	27	30	57	397	10	16,120
Total Priests in Diocese	1,158	83	101	184	878	124	48,097
Newly Ordained Priests	10	–	–	–	3	3	521
Total Permanent Deacons	230	19	11	30	196	61	11,788
Total Brothers	155	33	11	44	187	4	6,293
Total Sisters	2,793	59	286	345	2,340	101	87,644
Number of Parishes	737	44	74	118	227	95	19,677
Missions	11	12	27	39	9	16	3,051
Pastoral Centers	7	–	3	3	–	–	1,229
New Parishes	–	–	–	–	–	–	39
Catholic Hospitals	15	–	1	1	12	1	590
Patients Assisted Annually	629,860	–	65,812	65,812	1,144,665	99,202	61,489,163
Health Care Centers	3	–	1	1	–	15	366
Patients Assisted Annually	13,010	–	8,465	8,465	–	114,821	4,861,384
Specialized Homes	46	7	6	13	31	2	1,252
Total Assisted Annually	4,176	637	2,225	2,862	29,348	1,728	946,572
Residential Care of Children (Orphanages)	1	–	2	2	10	–	178
Total Assisted Annually	4,000	–	168	168	1,433	–	74,324
Day Care and Extended Day Care Centers	6	–	2	2	17	11	1,110
Total Assisted Annually	9,170	–	200	200	1,253	239	126,432
Special Centers for Social Services	17	6	2	8	24	–	2,014
Total Assisted Annually	34,282	81,224	8,050	89,274	128,650	–	18,262,444
Diocesan Seminaries	3	–	–	–	2	1	77
Students	182	–	–	–	72	25	3,149
Religious Seminaries	1	–	–	–	5	–	129
Students	7	–	–	–	49	–	1,496
Colleges and Universities	7	–	1	1	2	–	241
Total Students	27,400	–	28	28	12,462	–	690,826
High Schools, Diocesan and Parish	16	4	4	8	14	2	794
Total Students	6,885	1,204	815	2,019	6,509	984	369,281
High Schools, Private	5	1	–	1	15	–	563
Total Students	2,516	599	–	599	8,684	–	283,406
Elementary Schools, Diocesan and Parish	190	14	15	29	148	35	6,822
Total Students	45,145	2,245	4,380	6,625	41,532	6,027	1,960,274
Elementary Schools, Private	2	–	–	–	6	–	343
Total Students	344	–	–	–	2,328	–	93,545
Non–residential Schools for the Disabled	1	–	–	–	8	–	80
Total Students	25	–	–	–	270	–	19,198
Religious Education High School Students	46,318	2,481	1,295	3,776	631	2,878	804,759
Religious Education Elementary Students	111,985	3,890	4,166	8,056	22,504	4,979	3,445,153
Priests Teaching	53	1	–	1	40	6	2,174
Scholastics Teaching	–	–	–	–	–	–	51
Brothers Teaching	21	–	–	–	–	3	1,191
Sisters Teaching	207	17	23	40	210	32	11,217
Lay Teachers	3,762	278	325	603	3,378	417	152,165
Infant Baptisms	19,367	772	750	1,522	7,734	1,333	1,044,304
Adult Baptisms	698	586	103	689	906	247	75,645
Received into Full Communion	2,231	135	256	391	731	295	85,970
First Communions	18,715	1,168	685	1,853	7,772	1,542	846,104
Confirmations	15,133	564	455	1,019	7,284	1,477	592,399
Marriages	7,289	363	380	743	3,474	661	300,582
Deaths	10,186	688	466	1,154	4,520	752	472,126
Totals Catholics	1,226,202	64,556	44,340	108,896	568,300	84,308	61,207,914
Total Population	4,539,922	705,163	1,980,025	2,685,188	2,063,163	752,716	268,299,833
Catholic Population Percentage	27	9	2	4	28	11	23

Archdioceses = 36; Dioceses = 164; Apostolates = 3

1997 GENERAL SUMMARY

	Kansas City-St. Joseph MO	Springfield-Cape Girardeau MO	MISSOURI TOTAL	Great Falls - Billings MT	Helena MT	MONTANA TOTAL	1997 U.S. GRAND TOTAL
Cardinals	–	–	1	–	–	–	**9**
Archbishops	–	–	1	–	–	–	**50**
Bishops	2	1	8	2	1	3	**358**
Abbots	2	3	7	1	–	1	**112**
Diocesan Priests	132	76	803	78	89	167	**31,977**
Religious Priests	103	64	574	15	9	24	**16,120**
Total Priests in Diocese	235	140	1,377	93	98	191	**48,097**
Newly Ordained Priests	2	3	11	–	–	–	**521**
Total Permanent Deacons	54	5	316	3	29	32	**11,788**
Total Brothers	35	74	300	–	1	1	**6,293**
Total Sisters	329	135	2,905	78	70	148	**87,644**
Number of Parishes	84	64	470	54	58	112	**19,677**
Missions	15	21	61	72	39	111	**3,051**
Pastoral Centers	–	–	–	–	14	14	**1,229**
New Parishes	–	–	–	–	–	–	**39**
Catholic Hospitals	3	5	21	2	3	5	**590**
Patients Assisted Annually	161,692	341,018	1,746,577	106,271	173,111	279,382	**61,489,163**
Health Care Centers	–	–	15	1	–	1	**366**
Patients Assisted Annually	–	–	114,821	15,897	–	15,897	**4,861,384**
Specialized Homes	14	3	50	–	–	–	**1,252**
Total Assisted Annually	1,014	612	32,702	–	–	–	**946,572**
Residential Care of Children (Orphanages)	–	–	10	–	–	–	**178**
Total Assisted Annually	–	–	1,433	–	–	–	**74,324**
Day Care and Extended Day Care Centers	14	–	42	6	2	8	**1,110**
Total Assisted Annually	303	–	1,795	664	150	814	**126,432**
Special Centers for Social Services	–	1	25	2	–	2	**2,014**
Total Assisted Annually	–	1,666	130,316	63,350	–	63,350	**18,262,444**
Diocesan Seminaries	–	–	3	–	1	1	**77**
Students	–	–	97	–	3	3	**3,149**
Religious Seminaries	1	2	8	–	–	–	**129**
Students	9	20	78	–	–	–	**1,496**
Colleges and Universities	2	–	4	1	1	2	**241**
Total Students	3,850	–	16,312	1,299	1,418	2,717	**690,826**
High Schools, Diocesan and Parish	5	3	24	1	2	3	**794**
Total Students	1,531	788	9,812	393	396	789	**369,281**
High Schools, Private	3	–	18	1	–	1	**563**
Total Students	1,564	–	10,248	154	–	154	**283,406**
Elementary Schools, Diocesan and Parish	33	23	239	9	4	13	**6,822**
Total Students	10,090	3,801	61,450	1,889	784	2,673	**1,960,274**
Elementary Schools, Private	1	–	7	3	–	3	**343**
Total Students	265	–	2,593	576	–	576	**93,545**
Non-residential Schools for the Disabled	–	–	8	–	–	–	**80**
Total Students	–	–	270	–	–	–	**19,198**
Religious Education High School Students	1,039	1,784	6,332	2,505	1,650	4,155	**804,759**
Religious Education Elementary Students	10,028	3,786	41,297	4,667	6,100	10,767	**3,445,153**
Priests Teaching	4	–	50	4	10	14	**2,174**
Scholastics Teaching	–	–	–	–	–	–	**51**
Brothers Teaching	3	–	6	–	–	–	**1,191**
Sisters Teaching	33	15	290	6	10	16	**11,217**
Lay Teachers	1,020	224	5,039	273	196	469	**152,165**
Infant Baptisms	2,324	692	12,083	924	915	1,839	**1,044,304**
Adult Baptisms	514	234	1,901	115	203	318	**75,645**
Received into Full Communion	365	429	1,820	153	150	303	**85,970**
First Communions	2,582	1,263	13,159	1,045	1,050	2,095	**846,104**
Confirmations	1,454	841	11,056	638	850	1,488	**592,399**
Marriages	975	435	5,545	353	420	773	**300,582**
Deaths	1,202	542	7,016	743	820	1,563	**472,126**
Totals Catholics	150,106	54,525	857,239	56,384	66,500	122,884	**61,207,914**
Total Population	1,299,555	1,050,206	5,165,640	392,900	424,372	817,272	**268,299,833**
Catholic Population Percentage	12	5	17	14	16	15	**23**

*Indicates Archdioceses.

†Certain Dioceses traverse state lines.

	Chalan Kanoa MP	*Omaha NE	Grand Island NE	Lincoln NE	NEBRASKA TOTAL	Las Vegas NV	1997 U.S. GRAND TOTAL
Cardinals	–	–	–	–	–	–	**9**
Archbishops	–	2	–	–	2	–	**50**
Bishops	1	1	2	1	4	1	**358**
Abbots	–	2	–	–	2	–	**112**
Diocesan Priests	6	230	81	134	445	42	**31,977**
Religious Priests	1	127	1	12	140	20	**16,120**
Total Priests in Diocese	7	357	82	146	585	62	**48,097**
Newly Ordained Priests	1	10	1	4	15	–	**521**
Total Permanent Deacons	3	123	–	–	123	7	**11,788**
Total Brothers	–	25	–	11	36	6	**6,293**
Total Sisters	35	376	94	118	588	53	**87,644**
Number of Parishes	9	165	44	134	343	23	**19,677**
Missions	2	–	42	1	43	8	**3,051**
Pastoral Centers	–	–	–	–	–	–	**1,229**
New Parishes	1	1	–	–	1	–	**39**
Catholic Hospitals	–	5	–	3	8	1	**590**
Patients Assisted Annually	–	217,101	–	162,814	379,915	77,190	**61,489,163**
Health Care Centers	–	–	2	–	2	–	**366**
Patients Assisted Annually	–	–	142,646	–	142,646	–	**4,861,384**
Specialized Homes	–	9	1	3	13	–	**1,252**
Total Assisted Annually	–	594	79	292	965	–	**946,572**
Residential Care of Children (Orphanages)	–	–	–	–	–	–	**178**
Total Assisted Annually	–	–	–	–	–	–	**74,324**
Day Care and Extended Day Care Centers	–	5	–	–	5	–	**1,110**
Total Assisted Annually	–	3,128	–	–	3,128	–	**126,432**
Special Centers for Social Services	1	6	–	4	10	5	**2,014**
Total Assisted Annually	2,284	50,000	–	51,259	101,259	523,993	**18,262,444**
Diocesan Seminaries	–	–	–	–	–	–	**77**
Students	–	–	–	–	–	–	**3,149**
Religious Seminaries	–	–	–	–	–	–	**129**
Students	–	–	–	–	–	–	**1,496**
Colleges and Universities	–	2	–	–	2	–	**241**
Total Students	–	7,227	–	–	7,227	–	**690,826**
High Schools, Diocesan and Parish	1	12	4	6	22	1	**794**
Total Students	192	2,826	959	1,881	5,666	1,028	**369,281**
High Schools, Private	–	5	–	–	5	–	**563**
Total Students	–	2,216	–	–	2,216	–	**283,406**
Elementary Schools, Diocesan and Parish	2	61	7	25	93	7	**6,822**
Total Students	509	15,898	792	5,583	22,273	2,213	**1,960,274**
Elementary Schools, Private	–	1	–	–	1	1	**343**
Total Students	–	17	–	–	17	211	**93,545**
Non–residential Schools for the Disabled	–	1	–	1	2	–	**80**
Total Students	–	48	–	11	59	–	**19,198**
Religious Education High School Students	431	3,502	2,478	2,067	8,047	1,390	**804,759**
Religious Education Elementary Students	1,021	15,874	5,609	6,149	27,632	7,100	**3,445,153**
Priests Teaching	–	13	–	9	22	2	**2,174**
Scholastics Teaching	–	–	–	–	–	–	**51**
Brothers Teaching	–	3	–	–	3	3	**1,191**
Sisters Teaching	5	32	9	48	89	9	**11,217**
Lay Teachers	42	1,150	115	337	1,602	173	**152,165**
Infant Baptisms	850	4,500	1,012	1,377	6,889	3,351	**1,044,304**
Adult Baptisms	15	179	132	155	466	277	**75,645**
Received into Full Communion	1	427	189	219	835	279	**85,970**
First Communions	207	4,393	1,061	1,519	6,973	1,903	**846,104**
Confirmations	182	3,891	796	1,506	6,193	707	**592,399**
Marriages	49	1,510	432	479	2,421	562	**300,582**
Deaths	125	1,885	523	628	3,036	579	**472,126**
Totals Catholics	47,322	212,137	53,841	86,041	352,019	335,124	**61,207,914**
Total Population	56,189	808,076	290,429	516,662	1,615,167	1,155,600	**268,299,833**
Catholic Population Percentage	84	26	19	17	22	29	**23**

Archdioceses = 36; Dioceses = 164; Apostolates = 3

1997 GENERAL SUMMARY

	Reno NV	NEVADA TOTAL	Manchester NH	*Newark NJ	Camden NJ	Metuchen NJ	1997 U.S. GRAND TOTAL
Cardinals	–	–	–	–	–	–	**9**
Archbishops	–	–	–	2	–	–	**50**
Bishops	1	2	3	6	2	1	**358**
Abbots	–	–	2	1	–	–	**112**
Diocesan Priests	26	68	243	827	331	212	**31,977**
Religious Priests	12	32	84	250	42	45	**16,120**
Total Priests in Diocese	38	100	327	1,077	373	257	**48,097**
Newly Ordained Priests	–	–	4	17	–	4	**521**
Total Permanent Deacons	8	15	21	225	96	104	**11,788**
Total Brothers	3	9	41	124	14	24	**6,293**
Total Sisters	38	91	823	1,757	372	496	**87,644**
Number of Parishes	28	51	131	238	126	108	**19,677**
Missions	8	16	34	2	–	–	**3,051**
Pastoral Centers	–	–	–	172	31	–	**1,229**
New Parishes	2	2	–	–	–	–	**39**
Catholic Hospitals	1	2	2	8	1	1	**590**
Patients Assisted Annually	118,017	195,207	111,965	876,107	243,221	158,798	**61,489,163**
Health Care Centers	3	3	–	86	2	1	**366**
Patients Assisted Annually	9,539	9,539	–	24,970	9,320	1,723	**4,861,384**
Specialized Homes	–	–	7	11	5	6	**1,252**
Total Assisted Annually	–	–	433	663	1,020	353	**946,572**
Residential Care of Children (Orphanages)	–	–	3	–	2	–	**178**
Total Assisted Annually	–	–	354	–	11	–	**74,324**
Day Care and Extended Day Care Centers	1	1	1	126	1	8	**1,110**
Total Assisted Annually	215	215	309	3,000	60	1,878	**126,432**
Special Centers for Social Services	5	10	1	235	12	9	**2,014**
Total Assisted Annually	130,000	653,993	–	142,797	7,833	18,534	**18,262,444**
Diocesan Seminaries	–	–	–	3	–	–	**77**
Students	–	–	–	121	–	–	**3,149**
Religious Seminaries	–	–	–	1	–	–	**129**
Students	–	–	1	17	–	–	**1,496**
Colleges and Universities	–	–	6	4	–	–	**241**
Total Students	–	–	6,690	16,252	–	–	**690,826**
High Schools, Diocesan and Parish	1	2	3	18	8	4	**794**
Total Students	450	1,478	1,498	8,573	4,766	2,695	**369,281**
High Schools, Private	–	–	1	19	3	2	**563**
Total Students	–	–	782	7,371	1,071	1,107	**283,406**
Elementary Schools, Diocesan and Parish	4	11	23	142	61	42	**6,822**
Total Students	1,135	3,348	6,694	43,992	15,662	14,216	**1,960,274**
Elementary Schools, Private	–	1	3	6	–	1	**343**
Total Students	–	211	793	1,517	–	206	**93,545**
Non–residential Schools for the Disabled	–	–	–	4	–	1	**80**
Total Students	–	–	–	193	–	37	**19,198**
Religious Education High School Students	729	2,119	5,346	4,984	543	1,255	**804,759**
Religious Education Elementary Students	4,195	11,295	28,242	45,271	31,774	37,119	**3,445,153**
Priests Teaching	1	3	–	138	17	–	**2,174**
Scholastics Teaching	–	–	–	–	–	–	**51**
Brothers Teaching	1	4	8	49	3	11	**1,191**
Sisters Teaching	3	12	61	377	90	91	**11,217**
Lay Teachers	78	251	610	3,574	959	884	**152,165**
Infant Baptisms	1,651	5,002	5,530	17,656	7,305	7,407	**1,044,304**
Adult Baptisms	111	388	167	482	642	154	**75,645**
Received into Full Communion	168	447	184	753	540	280	**85,970**
First Communions	1,171	3,074	5,102	13,902	6,813	6,738	**846,104**
Confirmations	474	1,181	2,913	10,925	4,917	5,048	**592,399**
Marriages	308	870	1,541	5,525	2,128	2,110	**300,582**
Deaths	408	987	3,166	12,437	–	3,865	**472,126**
Totals Catholics	103,136	438,260	321,914	1,346,185	406,383	483,196	**61,207,914**
Total Population	515,419	1,671,019	1,148,000	2,656,348	1,286,240	1,177,058	**268,299,833**
Catholic Population Percentage	20	26	28	51	32	41	**23**

*Indicates Archdioceses.
†Certain Dioceses traverse state lines.

	Paterson NJ	Trenton NJ	NEW JERSEY TOTAL	*Santa Fe NM	† Gallup NM	Las Cruces NM	1997 U.S. GRAND TOTAL
Cardinals	–	–	–	–	–	–	**9**
Archbishops	–	–	2	2	–	–	**50**
Bishops	1	2	12	–	1	1	**358**
Abbots	6	–	7	2	–	–	**112**
Diocesan Priests	273	243	1,886	111	58	30	**31,977**
Religious Priests	201	94	632	106	31	47	**16,120**
Total Priests in Diocese	474	337	2,518	217	89	77	**48,097**
Newly Ordained Priests	2	3	26	3	–	2	**521**
Total Permanent Deacons	138	215	778	135	33	26	**11,788**
Total Brothers	42	57	261	91	12	–	**6,293**
Total Sisters	960	509	4,094	299	155	76	**87,644**
Number of Parishes	111	126	709	91	58	44	**19,677**
Missions	–	15	17	216	41	44	**3,051**
Pastoral Centers	5	–	208	4	38	–	**1,229**
New Parishes	–	–	–	–	–	–	**39**
Catholic Hospitals	3	1	14	4	–	–	**590**
Patients Assisted Annually	698,290	142,153	2,118,569	16,591	–	–	**61,489,163**
Health Care Centers	–	1	90	1	–	3	**366**
Patients Assisted Annually	–	3,687	39,700	5,000	–	141,420	**4,861,384**
Specialized Homes	11	10	43	6	3	–	**1,252**
Total Assisted Annually	16,471	7,190	25,697	829	222	–	**946,572**
Residential Care of Children (Orphanages)	2	9	13	–	–	–	**178**
Total Assisted Annually	56	14	81	–	–	–	**74,324**
Day Care and Extended Day Care Centers	20	2	157	2	–	1	**1,110**
Total Assisted Annually	900	230	6,068	133	–	40	**126,432**
Special Centers for Social Services	13	13	282	5	1	1	**2,014**
Total Assisted Annually	36,000	20,000	225,164	210,550	44,931	480	**18,262,444**
Diocesan Seminaries	–	–	3	1	–	–	**77**
Students	–	–	121	31	–	–	**3,149**
Religious Seminaries	4	–	5	–	–	–	**129**
Students	11	–	28	–	–	–	**1,496**
Colleges and Universities	2	1	7	1	–	–	**241**
Total Students	1,614	2,422	20,288	1,600	–	–	**690,826**
High Schools, Diocesan and Parish	5	8	43	1	–	–	**794**
Total Students	2,411	6,362	24,807	1,013	–	–	**369,281**
High Schools, Private	5	3	32	2	3	–	**563**
Total Students	1,576	1,116	12,241	883	201	–	**283,406**
Elementary Schools, Diocesan and Parish	58	54	357	18	2	5	**6,822**
Total Students	16,156	21,105	111,131	4,762	272	653	**1,960,274**
Elementary Schools, Private	3	2	12	–	8	–	**343**
Total Students	572	452	2,747	–	1,337	–	**93,545**
Non–residential Schools for the Disabled	–	7	12	–	–	–	**80**
Total Students	–	200	430	–	–	–	**19,198**
Religious Education High School Students	8,892	788	16,462	5,099	803	2,601	**804,759**
Religious Education Elementary Students	31,530	52,073	197,767	19,403	3,335	7,627	**3,445,153**
Priests Teaching	45	–	200	3	–	–	**2,174**
Scholastics Teaching	–	–	–	–	–	–	**51**
Brothers Teaching	20	23	106	5	–	–	**1,191**
Sisters Teaching	193	202	953	34	26	2	**11,217**
Lay Teachers	1,111	1,317	7,845	404	115	44	**152,165**
Infant Baptisms	8,887	10,724	51,979	6,404	886	2,433	**1,044,304**
Adult Baptisms	184	390	1,852	243	246	104	**75,645**
Received into Full Communion	372	862	2,807	331	69	115	**85,970**
First Communions	7,152	10,589	45,194	5,529	847	2,265	**846,104**
Confirmations	3,936	8,462	33,288	3,270	569	1,170	**592,399**
Marriages	2,215	3,110	15,088	1,356	214	494	**300,582**
Deaths	3,756	6,404	26,462	2,438	515	872	**472,126**
Totals Catholics	377,650	695,575	3,308,989	260,313	41,181	125,309	**61,207,914**
Total Population	1,048,018	1,763,149	7,930,813	979,742	355,640	453,500	**268,299,833**
Catholic Population Percentage	36	39	42	27	12	28	**23**

Archdioceses = 36; Dioceses = 164; Apostolates = 3

1997 GENERAL SUMMARY

	NEW MEXICO TOTAL	*New York NY	Albany NY	Brooklyn NY	Buffalo NY	Ogdensburg NY	1997 U.S. GRAND TOTAL
Cardinals	–	1	–	–	–	–	**9**
Archbishops	2	–	–	–	–	–	**50**
Bishops	2	8	2	6	4	2	**358**
Abbots	2	–	–	–	–	–	**112**
Diocesan Priests	199	911	324	685	450	178	**31,977**
Religious Priests	184	1,120	128	232	194	20	**16,120**
Total Priests in Diocese	383	2,031	452	917	644	198	**48,097**
Newly Ordained Priests	5	11	3	4	4	2	**521**
Total Permanent Deacons	194	307	91	164	85	58	**11,788**
Total Brothers	103	445	86	191	47	11	**6,293**
Total Sisters	530	4,020	980	1,572	1,489	193	**87,644**
Number of Parishes	193	413	188	219	266	121	**19,677**
Missions	301	–	37	–	10	28	**3,051**
Pastoral Centers	42	–	–	–	–	9	**1,229**
New Parishes	–	–	–	–	–	1	**39**
Catholic Hospitals	4	17	4	4	7	–	**590**
Patients Assisted Annually	16,591	1,893,420	560,000	186,831	908,267	–	**61,489,163**
Health Care Centers	4	3	10	22	–	2	**366**
Patients Assisted Annually	146,420	151,260	42,000	1,251,643	–	48,122	**4,861,384**
Specialized Homes	9	22	20	9	19	3	**1,252**
Total Assisted Annually	1,051	20,600	16,140	527,313	1,955	880	**946,572**
Residential Care of Children (Orphanages)	–	14	–	18	–	–	**178**
Total Assisted Annually	–	38,900	–	8,500	–	–	**74,324**
Day Care and Extended Day Care Centers	3	15	7	15	2	1	**1,110**
Total Assisted Annually	173	1,677	89	2,100	192	26	**126,432**
Special Centers for Social Services	7	148	22	50	4	8	**2,014**
Total Assisted Annually	255,961	635,000	149,260	38,000	2,893	15,407	**18,262,444**
Diocesan Seminaries	1	2	–	1	2	1	**77**
Students	31	84	–	17	30	23	**3,149**
Religious Seminaries	–	2	–	2	–	–	**129**
Students	–	3	–	16	–	–	**1,496**
Colleges and Universities	1	12	4	3	7	1	**241**
Total Students	1,600	60,500	4,550	20,739	13,298	335	**690,826**
High Schools, Diocesan and Parish	1	25	4	4	–	2	**794**
Total Students	1,013	13,685	1,923	1,933	–	649	**369,281**
High Schools, Private	5	30	3	18	17	–	**563**
Total Students	1,084	14,419	1,183	15,922	6,029	–	**283,406**
Elementary Schools, Diocesan and Parish	25	223	37	155	88	24	**6,822**
Total Students	5,687	75,172	9,328	55,067	22,896	4,476	**1,960,274**
Elementary Schools, Private	8	15	2	3	6	–	**343**
Total Students	1,337	3,680	418	509	1,763	–	**93,545**
Non–residential Schools for the Disabled	–	4	1	1	–	–	**80**
Total Students	–	195	50	91	–	–	**19,198**
Religious Education High School Students	8,503	13,050	8,237	9,650	12,433	3,100	**804,759**
Religious Education Elementary Students	30,365	98,300	22,653	46,000	42,328	10,109	**3,445,153**
Priests Teaching	3	50	6	10	18	2	**2,174**
Scholastics Teaching	–	–	–	–	–	–	**51**
Brothers Teaching	5	49	19	60	6	1	**1,191**
Sisters Teaching	62	269	86	310	127	31	**11,217**
Lay Teachers	563	4,177	817	3,065	1,812	306	**152,165**
Infant Baptisms	9,723	35,522	6,017	23,753	8,094	1,950	**1,044,304**
Adult Baptisms	593	898	353	835	501	167	**75,645**
Received into Full Communion	515	546	205	1,077	447	94	**85,970**
First Communions	8,641	25,492	5,249	15,456	8,588	1,890	**846,104**
Confirmations	5,009	18,345	3,264	11,779	5,964	1,473	**592,399**
Marriages	2,064	8,455	2,085	5,084	3,313	757	**300,582**
Deaths	3,825	16,956	4,844	12,744	7,268	1,698	**472,126**
Totals Catholics	426,803	2,327,300	403,403	1,603,110	753,117	138,865	**61,207,914**
Total Population	1,788,882	5,351,854	1,315,414	4,207,649	1,613,258	420,111	**268,299,833**
Catholic Population Percentage	24	43	31	38	47	33	**23**

*Indicates Archdioceses.

[†]Certain Dioceses traverse state lines.

	Rochester NY	Rockville Centre NY	Syracuse NY	NEW YORK TOTAL	Charlotte NC	Raleigh NC	1997 U.S. GRAND TOTAL
Cardinals	–	–	–	1	–	–	**9**
Archbishops	–	–	–	–	–	–	**50**
Bishops	3	4	4	33	2	2	**358**
Abbots	1	–	–	1	2	–	**112**
Diocesan Priests	277	458	300	3,583	82	71	**31,977**
Religious Priests	65	95	44	1,898	62	50	**16,120**
Total Priests in Diocese	342	553	344	5,481	144	121	**48,097**
Newly Ordained Priests	2	3	–	29	2	5	**521**
Total Permanent Deacons	106	196	69	1,076	60	22	**11,788**
Total Brothers	35	104	18	937	5	8	**6,293**
Total Sisters	675	1,543	514	10,986	192	82	**87,644**
Number of Parishes	161	134	172	1,674	66	70	**19,677**
Missions	20	–	18	113	24	13	**3,051**
Pastoral Centers	–	–	10	19	4	9	**1,229**
New Parishes	–	1	–	2	–	–	**39**
Catholic Hospitals	3	4	3	42	1	1	**590**
Patients Assisted Annually	450,000	611,462	650,000	5,259,980	82,452	6,000	**61,489,163**
Health Care Centers	4	–	–	41	8	–	**366**
Patients Assisted Annually	1,500	–	–	1,494,525	149,235	–	**4,861,384**
Specialized Homes	10	7	7	97	3	–	**1,252**
Total Assisted Annually	8,500	4,627	401	580,416	200	–	**946,572**
Residential Care of Children (Orphanages)	1	4	–	37	–	–	**178**
Total Assisted Annually	400	8,904	–	56,704	–	–	**74,324**
Day Care and Extended Day Care Centers	–	103	1	144	4	6	**1,110**
Total Assisted Annually	–	4,723	99	8,906	346	556	**126,432**
Special Centers for Social Services	3	38	8	281	1	10	**2,014**
Total Assisted Annually	120,000	194,219	56,616	1,211,395	75	30,890	**18,262,444**
Diocesan Seminaries	3	1	–	10	–	–	**77**
Students	3	41	–	198	–	–	**3,149**
Religious Seminaries	–	–	1	5	–	–	**129**
Students	–	5	14	38	–	–	**1,496**
Colleges and Universities	–	2	1	30	2	–	**241**
Total Students	12	4,586	2,800	106,820	902	–	**690,826**
High Schools, Diocesan and Parish	–	4	5	44	2	1	**794**
Total Students	–	3,754	2,618	24,562	1,084	439	**369,281**
High Schools, Private	7	9	1	85	–	–	**563**
Total Students	3,508	7,169	726	48,956	–	–	**283,406**
Elementary Schools, Diocesan and Parish	51	63	39	680	15	17	**6,822**
Total Students	15,574	27,675	9,024	219,212	5,462	4,833	**1,960,274**
Elementary Schools, Private	5	4	–	35	–	–	**343**
Total Students	780	1,110	–	8,260	–	–	**93,545**
Non–residential Schools for the Disabled	1	3	–	10	–	–	**80**
Total Students	97	210	–	643	–	–	**19,198**
Religious Education High School Students	3,600	4,599	7,544	62,213	3,888	2,964	**804,759**
Religious Education Elementary Students	32,153	105,134	38,967	395,644	10,639	12,147	**3,445,153**
Priests Teaching	12	10	12	120	3	–	**2,174**
Scholastics Teaching	–	–	–	–	–	–	**51**
Brothers Teaching	9	65	7	216	1	4	**1,191**
Sisters Teaching	69	236	100	1,228	16	12	**11,217**
Lay Teachers	971	1,729	825	13,702	380	268	**152,165**
Infant Baptisms	6,291	21,957	6,160	109,744	2,484	2,572	**1,044,304**
Adult Baptisms	329	545	374	4,002	574	202	**75,645**
Received into Full Communion	518	–	504	3,391	465	423	**85,970**
First Communions	5,420	17,641	6,029	85,765	2,402	2,519	**846,104**
Confirmations	4,958	15,199	4,129	65,111	1,219	1,164	**592,399**
Marriages	2,284	7,568	2,411	31,957	733	870	**300,582**
Deaths	4,236	11,564	4,609	63,919	631	669	**472,126**
Totals Catholics	363,672	1,347,096	372,665	7,309,228	110,302	125,652	**61,207,914**
Total Population	1,484,426	2,880,184	1,223,591	18,496,487	3,715,535	3,549,378	**268,299,833**
Catholic Population Percentage	25	47	30	40	3	4	**23**

Archdioceses = 36; Dioceses = 164; Apostolates = 3

1997 GENERAL SUMMARY

	NORTH CAROLINA TOTAL	Bismarck ND	Fargo ND	NORTH DAKOTA TOTAL	*Cincinnati OH	Cleveland OH	1997 U.S. GRAND TOTAL
Cardinals	–	–	–	–	–	–	**9**
Archbishops	–	–	–	–	1	–	**50**
Bishops	4	1	1	2	1	3	**358**
Abbots	2	3	–	3	–	1	**112**
Diocesan Priests	153	68	136	204	358	502	**31,977**
Religious Priests	112	28	10	38	281	147	**16,120**
Total Priests in Diocese	265	96	146	242	639	649	**48,097**
Newly Ordained Priests	7	1	4	5	1	2	**521**
Total Permanent Deacons	82	51	35	86	128	155	**11,788**
Total Brothers	13	23	15	38	179	74	**6,293**
Total Sisters	274	169	220	389	1,471	1,628	**87,644**
Number of Parishes	136	65	160	225	236	236	**19,677**
Missions	37	39	–	39	–	1	**3,051**
Pastoral Centers	13	–	–	–	1	3	**1,229**
New Parishes	–	–	–	–	–	–	**39**
Catholic Hospitals	2	6	8	14	11	2	**590**
Patients Assisted Annually	88,452	279,028	60,798	339,826	1,572,000	134,514	**61,489,163**
Health Care Centers	8	–	–	–	1	–	**366**
Patients Assisted Annually	149,235	–	–	–	265	–	**4,861,384**
Specialized Homes	3	5	8	13	14	29	**1,252**
Total Assisted Annually	200	527	662	1,189	1,834	4,290	**946,572**
Residential Care of Children (Orphanages)	–	–	–	–	4	1	**178**
Total Assisted Annually	–	–	–	–	740	248	**74,324**
Day Care and Extended Day Care Centers	10	–	–	–	2	6	**1,110**
Total Assisted Annually	902	–	–	–	201	1,204	**126,432**
Special Centers for Social Services	11	–	–	–	6	21	**2,014**
Total Assisted Annually	30,965	–	–	–	97,200	532,748	**18,262,444**
Diocesan Seminaries	–	–	1	1	1	2	**77**
Students	–	–	24	24	27	51	**3,149**
Religious Seminaries	–	–	1	1	–	–	**129**
Students	–	1	5	6	–	7	**1,496**
Colleges and Universities	2	1	1	2	4	3	**241**
Total Students	902	2,016	24	2,040	18,805	6,190	**690,826**
High Schools, Diocesan and Parish	3	3	1	4	18	7	**794**
Total Students	1,523	1,334	340	1,674	12,568	4,360	**369,281**
High Schools, Private	–	–	1	1	4	16	**563**
Total Students	–	–	19	19	2,816	10,087	**283,406**
Elementary Schools, Diocesan and Parish	32	16	12	28	111	134	**6,822**
Total Students	10,295	2,157	1,518	3,675	39,512	49,471	**1,960,274**
Elementary Schools, Private	–	–	–	–	2	7	**343**
Total Students	–	–	–	–	1,009	2,479	**93,545**
Non–residential Schools for the Disabled	–	–	–	–	–	1	**80**
Total Students	–	–	–	–	–	76	**19,198**
Religious Education High School Students	6,852	3,319	5,225	8,544	5,880	7,108	**804,759**
Religious Education Elementary Students	22,786	7,081	10,597	17,678	34,464	44,943	**3,445,153**
Priests Teaching	3	6	–	6	13	28	**2,174**
Scholastics Teaching	–	–	–	–	–	–	**51**
Brothers Teaching	5	1	4	5	28	29	**1,191**
Sisters Teaching	28	27	9	36	132	252	**11,217**
Lay Teachers	648	290	184	474	3,159	3,146	**152,165**
Infant Baptisms	5,056	1,153	1,570	2,723	8,476	11,294	**1,044,304**
Adult Baptisms	776	113	68	181	1,206	1,053	**75,645**
Received into Full Communion	888	114	107	221	865	930	**85,970**
First Communions	4,921	1,380	1,558	2,938	9,030	12,220	**846,104**
Confirmations	2,383	1,071	1,646	2,717	8,144	9,324	**592,399**
Marriages	1,603	539	587	1,126	3,333	4,921	**300,582**
Deaths	1,300	669	905	1,574	4,702	8,610	**472,126**
Totals Catholics	235,954	66,425	98,915	165,340	546,100	830,130	**61,207,914**
Total Population	7,264,913	253,552	390,400	643,952	2,892,000	2,811,515	**268,299,833**
Catholic Population Percentage	3	26	25	26	19	30	**23**

*Indicates Archdioceses.
†Certain Dioceses traverse state lines.

1997 GENERAL SUMMARY

	Columbus OH	Steubenville OH	Toledo OH	Youngstown OH	OHIO TOTAL	*Oklahoma City OK	1997 U.S. GRAND TOTAL
Cardinals	–	–	–	–	–	–	**9**
Archbishops	–	–	–	–	1	2	**50**
Bishops	3	2	3	3	15	–	**358**
Abbots	–	–	–	–	1	3	**112**
Diocesan Priests	203	125	217	203	1,608	86	**31,977**
Religious Priests	45	20	66	31	590	30	**16,120**
Total Priests in Diocese	248	145	283	234	2,198	116	**48,097**
Newly Ordained Priests	3	2	6	2	16	1	**521**
Total Permanent Deacons	48	5	190	51	577	52	**11,788**
Total Brothers	8	11	10	23	305	11	**6,293**
Total Sisters	411	89	377	284	4,760	151	**87,644**
Number of Parishes	108	74	163	115	932	73	**19,677**
Missions	8	3	–	2	14	45	**3,051**
Pastoral Centers	–	–	–	–	4	1	**1,229**
New Parishes	–	–	–	–	–	–	**39**
Catholic Hospitals	4	2	8	3	30	5	**590**
Patients Assisted Annually	906,461	237,074	820,465	587,465	4,257,979	468,767	**61,489,163**
Health Care Centers	–	–	–	–	1	–	**366**
Patients Assisted Annually	–	–	–	–	265	–	**4,861,384**
Specialized Homes	19	1	3	10	76	3	**1,252**
Total Assisted Annually	2,644	87	459	678	9,992	229	**946,572**
Residential Care of Children (Orphanages)	–	–	1	–	6	–	**178**
Total Assisted Annually	–	–	75	–	1,063	–	**74,324**
Day Care and Extended Day Care Centers	4	–	–	2	14	2	**1,110**
Total Assisted Annually	1,612	–	–	70	3,087	385	**126,432**
Special Centers for Social Services	13	1	13	5	59	–	**2,014**
Total Assisted Annually	375,723	11,057	5,502	37,560	1,059,790	–	**18,262,444**
Diocesan Seminaries	1	–	–	–	4	–	**77**
Students	103	–	–	–	181	–	**3,149**
Religious Seminaries	–	–	–	–	–	1	**129**
Students	7	–	5	–	19	–	**1,496**
Colleges and Universities	1	1	2	1	12	1	**241**
Total Students	1,883	1,936	1,838	1,447	32,099	335	**690,826**
High Schools, Diocesan and Parish	11	3	10	5	54	1	**794**
Total Students	4,819	728	4,100	2,933	29,508	648	**369,281**
High Schools, Private	–	–	4	1	25	1	**563**
Total Students	–	–	2,824	92	15,819	255	**283,406**
Elementary Schools, Diocesan and Parish	45	16	83	47	436	17	**6,822**
Total Students	15,161	2,899	22,231	12,242	141,516	3,311	**1,960,274**
Elementary Schools, Private	2	–	4	–	15	1	**343**
Total Students	232	–	803	–	4,523	4,214	**93,545**
Non–residential Schools for the Disabled	–	–	–	–	1	–	**80**
Total Students	–	–	–	–	76	–	**19,198**
Religious Education High School Students	1,548	1,056	3,041	4,547	23,180	2,700	**804,759**
Religious Education Elementary Students	14,832	2,809	15,555	15,362	127,965	7,814	**3,445,153**
Priests Teaching	3	1	24	6	75	2	**2,174**
Scholastics Teaching	–	–	–	–	–	–	**51**
Brothers Teaching	–	–	–	5	62	–	**1,191**
Sisters Teaching	23	10	145	65	627	14	**11,217**
Lay Teachers	844	242	1,761	859	10,011	228	**152,165**
Infant Baptisms	3,787	785	4,292	3,377	32,011	1,602	**1,044,304**
Adult Baptisms	448	350	467	382	3,906	294	**75,645**
Received into Full Communion	702	–	653	671	3,821	411	**85,970**
First Communions	3,857	1,622	5,667	3,587	35,983	1,712	**846,104**
Confirmations	3,063	1,383	5,106	2,409	29,429	1,430	**592,399**
Marriages	1,925	366	2,100	1,554	14,199	714	**300,582**
Deaths	1,562	729	3,045	3,138	21,786	708	**472,126**
Totals Catholics	216,676	46,015	328,623	260,541	2,228,085	92,080	**61,207,914**
Total Population	2,170,007	506,136	1,479,041	1,229,220	11,087,919	2,003,512	**268,299,833**
Catholic Population Percentage	10	9	22	21	20	5	**23**

Archdioceses = 36; Dioceses = 164; Apostolates = 3

	Tulsa OK	OKLAHOMA TOTAL	*Portland in Oregon OR	Baker OR	OREGON TOTAL	*Philadelphia PA	1997 U.S. GRAND TOTAL
Cardinals	–	–	–	–	–	1	**9**
Archbishops	–	2	2	–	2	–	**50**
Bishops	1	1	1	1	2	6	**358**
Abbots	–	3	3	–	3	2	**112**
Diocesan Priests	80	166	156	38	194	828	**31,977**
Religious Priests	17	47	184	9	193	407	**16,120**
Total Priests in Diocese	97	213	340	47	387	1,235	**48,097**
Newly Ordained Priests	3	4	5	1	6	14	**521**
Total Permanent Deacons	42	94	16	5	21	142	**11,788**
Total Brothers	5	16	77	–	77	141	**6,293**
Total Sisters	105	256	532	34	566	3,996	**87,644**
Number of Parishes	80	153	125	35	160	287	**19,677**
Missions	–	45	26	29	55	7	**3,051**
Pastoral Centers	–	1	1	–	1	17	**1,229**
New Parishes	–	–	–	–	–	–	**39**
Catholic Hospitals	2	7	9	4	13	7	**590**
Patients Assisted Annually	275,868	744,635	1,505,996	225,140	1,731,136	895,666	**61,489,163**
Health Care Centers	–	–	4	–	4	9	**366**
Patients Assisted Annually	–	–	1,068	–	1,068	–	**4,861,384**
Specialized Homes	3	6	12	1	13	22	**1,252**
Total Assisted Annually	215	444	7,618	140	7,758	7,608	**946,572**
Residential Care of Children (Orphanages)	–	–	–	–	–	5	**178**
Total Assisted Annually	–	–	–	–	–	1,078	**74,324**
Day Care and Extended Day Care Centers	–	2	4	3	7	1	**1,110**
Total Assisted Annually	–	385	1,614	155	1,769	91	**126,432**
Special Centers for Social Services	3	3	14	–	14	14	**2,014**
Total Assisted Annually	36,232	36,232	1,018,765	–	1,018,765	101,596	**18,262,444**
Diocesan Seminaries	–	–	1	–	1	1	**77**
Students	–	–	123	–	123	212	**3,149**
Religious Seminaries	–	1	–	–	–	1	**129**
Students	–	–	31	–	31	13	**1,496**
Colleges and Universities	–	1	2	–	2	11	**241**
Total Students	–	335	5,149	–	5,149	31,662	**690,826**
High Schools, Diocesan and Parish	1	2	3	–	3	25	**794**
Total Students	853	1,501	1,598	–	1,598	22,955	**369,281**
High Schools, Private	1	2	6	–	6	15	**563**
Total Students	567	822	3,045	–	3,045	6,705	**283,406**
Elementary Schools, Diocesan and Parish	10	27	41	3	44	221	**6,822**
Total Students	2,288	5,599	8,849	615	9,464	86,515	**1,960,274**
Elementary Schools, Private	1	2	1	–	1	21	**343**
Total Students	1,112	5,326	372	–	372	5,116	**93,545**
Non–residential Schools for the Disabled	–	–	–	–	–	5	**80**
Total Students	–	–	–	–	–	372	**19,198**
Religious Education High School Students	1,538	4,238	3,091	984	4,075	6,908	**804,759**
Religious Education Elementary Students	6,254	14,068	11,532	2,119	13,651	46,107	**3,445,153**
Priests Teaching	9	11	54	–	54	172	**2,174**
Scholastics Teaching	–	–	–	–	–	1	**51**
Brothers Teaching	3	3	7	–	7	46	**1,191**
Sisters Teaching	13	27	154	5	159	995	**11,217**
Lay Teachers	350	578	1,404	34	1,438	8,491	**152,165**
Infant Baptisms	1,005	2,607	4,918	876	5,794	17,559	**1,044,304**
Adult Baptisms	199	493	676	142	818	1,172	**75,645**
Received into Full Communion	298	709	703	115	818	714	**85,970**
First Communions	1,002	2,714	3,809	751	4,560	14,174	**846,104**
Confirmations	627	2,057	2,012	353	2,365	15,277	**592,399**
Marriages	391	1,105	1,394	210	1,604	7,599	**300,582**
Deaths	424	1,132	2,075	298	2,373	13,085	**472,126**
Totals Catholics	52,255	144,335	282,593	31,794	314,387	1,404,268	**61,207,914**
Total Population	1,447,927	3,451,439	2,725,200	406,800	3,132,000	3,737,583	**268,299,833**
Catholic Population Percentage	4	4	10	8	10	38	**23**

*Indicates Archdioceses.

†Certain Dioceses traverse state lines.

1997 GENERAL SUMMARY

	Allentown PA	Altoona-Johnstown PA	Erie PA	Greensburg PA	Harrisburg PA	Pittsburgh PA	1997 U.S. GRAND TOTAL
Cardinals	–	–	–	–	–	–	**9**
Archbishops	–	–	–	–	–	–	**50**
Bishops	1	2	2	1	1	4	**358**
Abbots	–	–	–	2	–	–	**112**
Diocesan Priests	250	158	251	154	168	520	**31,977**
Religious Priests	81	65	14	96	44	134	**16,120**
Total Priests in Diocese	331	223	265	250	212	654	**48,097**
Newly Ordained Priests	4	3	3	4	4	5	**521**
Total Permanent Deacons	84	16	2	1	59	22	**11,788**
Total Brothers	11	4	2	38	1	44	**6,293**
Total Sisters	690	155	570	322	571	1,909	**87,644**
Number of Parishes	153	113	127	107	89	218	**19,677**
Missions	13	5	27	–	7	–	**3,051**
Pastoral Centers	–	–	1	–	–	–	**1,229**
New Parishes	–	–	–	–	–	–	**39**
Catholic Hospitals	3	2	1	1	2	5	**590**
Patients Assisted Annually	632,592	204,995	225,000	79,287	212,530	644,305	**61,489,163**
Health Care Centers	–	–	–	–	–	5	**366**
Patients Assisted Annually	–	–	–	–	–	3,420	**4,861,384**
Specialized Homes	21	3	6	2	7	15	**1,252**
Total Assisted Annually	1,041	230	915	134	636	1,681	**946,572**
Residential Care of Children (Orphanages)	–	–	–	–	1	4	**178**
Total Assisted Annually	–	–	–	–	136	467	**74,324**
Day Care and Extended Day Care Centers	49	–	1	–	2	98	**1,110**
Total Assisted Annually	1,980	–	175	–	82	5,292	**126,432**
Special Centers for Social Services	14	2	9	–	9	5	**2,014**
Total Assisted Annually	78,872	43,844	114,651	–	4,857	54,825	**18,262,444**
Diocesan Seminaries	–	–	1	–	–	1	**77**
Students	–	–	13	–	–	14	**3,149**
Religious Seminaries	–	–	–	1	–	–	**129**
Students	–	–	–	11	–	–	**1,496**
Colleges and Universities	2	2	2	2	–	3	**241**
Total Students	3,001	6,083	6,027	2,144	–	13,380	**690,826**
High Schools, Diocesan and Parish	9	3	6	2	7	8	**794**
Total Students	4,129	1,230	1,779	837	3,693	3,796	**369,281**
High Schools, Private	–	–	2	–	1	3	**563**
Total Students	–	–	1,410	–	37	664	**283,406**
Elementary Schools, Diocesan and Parish	54	31	44	27	40	107	**6,822**
Total Students	14,288	5,336	10,801	5,804	10,751	29,560	**1,960,274**
Elementary Schools, Private	1	–	1	3	–	3	**343**
Total Students	13	–	380	229	–	760	**93,545**
Non–residential Schools for the Disabled	3	–	–	–	–	2	**80**
Total Students	128	–	–	–	–	163	**19,198**
Religious Education High School Students	2,364	4,807	7,398	1,242	2,247	8,509	**804,759**
Religious Education Elementary Students	16,336	8,803	13,467	10,183	20,724	50,541	**3,445,153**
Priests Teaching	22	6	10	2	2	5	**2,174**
Scholastics Teaching	–	–	–	–	–	–	**51**
Brothers Teaching	–	1	–	5	–	12	**1,191**
Sisters Teaching	100	29	36	39	105	158	**11,217**
Lay Teachers	817	707	777	366	924	1,966	**152,165**
Infant Baptisms	3,960	1,627	2,534	2,273	3,312	9,303	**1,044,304**
Adult Baptisms	193	127	275	115	350	454	**75,645**
Received into Full Communion	358	207	266	358	470	754	**85,970**
First Communions	–	1,922	3,027	2,306	3,565	9,204	**846,104**
Confirmations	3,259	1,810	2,567	2,460	2,170	9,181	**592,399**
Marriages	1,498	871	1,374	1,156	1,215	3,956	**300,582**
Deaths	3,130	1,563	2,583	2,518	1,890	9,230	**472,126**
Totals Catholics	258,527	114,914	235,195	195,582	230,000	753,090	**61,207,914**
Total Population	1,084,189	649,961	874,244	688,501	1,940,954	2,009,092	**268,299,833**
Catholic Population Percentage	24	18	27	28	12	37	**23**

Archdioceses = 36; Dioceses = 164; Apostolates = 3

1997 GENERAL SUMMARY

	Scranton PA	PENN. TOTAL	*San Juan, Puerto Rico	Arecibo, Puerto Rico	Caguas, Puerto Rico	Mayaguez, Puerto Rico	1997 U.S. GRAND TOTAL
Cardinals	–	1	1	–	–	–	**9**
Archbishops	–	–	1	–	–	–	**50**
Bishops	2	19	2	2	1	2	**358**
Abbots	1	5	–	–	1	–	**112**
Diocesan Priests	366	2,695	154	85	67	37	**31,977**
Religious Priests	101	942	145	43	53	32	**16,120**
Total Priests in Diocese	467	3,637	299	128	120	69	**48,097**
Newly Ordained Priests	5	42	2	4	3	–	**521**
Total Permanent Deacons	32	358	260	7	63	3	**11,788**
Total Brothers	9	250	36	7	1	5	**6,293**
Total Sisters	865	9,078	433	116	130	148	**87,644**
Number of Parishes	200	1,294	152	59	43	29	**19,677**
Missions	86	145	–	228	–	–	**3,051**
Pastoral Centers	25	43	150	1	–	152	**1,229**
New Parishes	–	–	–	–	–	–	**39**
Catholic Hospitals	7	28	2	–	–	1	**590**
Patients Assisted Annually	697,490	3,591,865	19,325	–	–	112,300	**61,489,163**
Health Care Centers	3	17	2	–	1	–	**366**
Patients Assisted Annually	98,256	101,676	381	–	100	–	**4,861,384**
Specialized Homes	17	93	7	4	–	1	**1,252**
Total Assisted Annually	3,280	15,525	1,014	755	–	150	**946,572**
Residential Care of Children (Orphanages)	7	17	3	2	–	–	**178**
Total Assisted Annually	962	2,643	110	45	–	–	**74,324**
Day Care and Extended Day Care Centers	2	153	37	–	–	–	**1,110**
Total Assisted Annually	148	7,768	1,295	–	–	–	**126,432**
Special Centers for Social Services	4	57	–	1	–	1	**2,014**
Total Assisted Annually	170,109	568,754	–	3,165	–	1,200	**18,262,444**
Diocesan Seminaries	1	4	2	1	1	–	**77**
Students	25	264	25	9	20	–	**3,149**
Religious Seminaries	2	4	6	–	–	–	**129**
Students	48	72	22	10	–	–	**1,496**
Colleges and Universities	4	26	2	1	–	1	**241**
Total Students	11,059	73,356	9,620	768	–	2,509	**690,826**
High Schools, Diocesan and Parish	9	69	20	14	1	3	**794**
Total Students	3,445	41,864	5,411	2,839	110	392	**369,281**
High Schools, Private	2	23	30	–	6	4	**563**
Total Students	738	9,554	6,780	–	2,851	896	**283,406**
Elementary Schools, Diocesan and Parish	60	584	27	14	4	5	**6,822**
Total Students	13,491	176,546	10,806	4,210	650	1,697	**1,960,274**
Elementary Schools, Private	4	33	42	–	13	7	**343**
Total Students	183	6,681	14,136	–	4,248	2,731	**93,545**
Non–residential Schools for the Disabled	1	11	–	–	–	–	**80**
Total Students	15	678	–	–	–	–	**19,198**
Religious Education High School Students	7,226	40,701	4,902	3,950	4,794	1,288	**804,759**
Religious Education Elementary Students	25,202	191,363	19,711	13,910	7,288	8,345	**3,445,153**
Priests Teaching	49	268	34	19	19	9	**2,174**
Scholastics Teaching	–	1	2	–	4	–	**51**
Brothers Teaching	2	66	20	5	4	3	**1,191**
Sisters Teaching	257	1,719	130	43	17	9	**11,217**
Lay Teachers	1,833	15,881	2,210	429	365	301	**152,165**
Infant Baptisms	4,911	45,479	12,642	4,780	7,670	5,022	**1,044,304**
Adult Baptisms	256	2,942	1,172	355	490	148	**75,645**
Received into Full Communion	289	3,416	–	839	8,160	213	**85,970**
First Communions	5,025	39,223	7,716	3,702	5,630	3,067	**846,104**
Confirmations	5,931	42,755	5,557	2,881	3,350	3,152	**592,399**
Marriages	2,334	20,003	2,546	1,094	1,204	1,049	**300,582**
Deaths	5,093	39,092	–	1,816	1,680	2,187	**472,126**
Totals Catholics	360,993	3,552,569	886,994	379,366	515,000	360,000	**61,207,914**
Total Population	1,036,320	12,020,844	1,233,743	550,678	653,012	451,000	**268,299,833**
Catholic Population Percentage	35	30	72	69	79	80	**23**

*Indicates Archdioceses.
†Certain Dioceses traverse state lines.

	Ponce, Puerto Rico	PUERTO RICO TOTAL	Providence RI	Charleston SC	Rapid City SD	Sioux Falls SD	1997 U.S. GRAND TOTAL
Cardinals	–	1	–	–	–	–	**9**
Archbishops	–	1	1	–	–	–	**50**
Bishops	2	9	3	1	–	2	**358**
Abbots	–	1	2	2	–	3	**112**
Diocesan Priests	83	426	317	95	40	128	**31,977**
Religious Priests	55	328	126	33	32	44	**16,120**
Total Priests in Diocese	138	754	443	128	72	172	**48,097**
Newly Ordained Priests	2	11	–	2	–	1	**521**
Total Permanent Deacons	59	392	83	62	31	24	**11,788**
Total Brothers	2	51	123	26	11	13	**6,293**
Total Sisters	229	1,056	759	164	82	461	**87,644**
Number of Parishes	40	323	159	86	68	156	**19,677**
Missions	2	230	8	27	38	–	**3,051**
Pastoral Centers	228	531	14	10	4	–	**1,229**
New Parishes	–	–	–	–	–	1	**39**
Catholic Hospitals	–	3	1	3	–	9	**590**
Patients Assisted Annually	–	131,625	201,000	302,548	–	485,000	**61,489,163**
Health Care Centers	–	3	–	1	–	–	**366**
Patients Assisted Annually	–	481	–	325	–	–	**4,861,384**
Specialized Homes	3	15	13	1	2	11	**1,252**
Total Assisted Annually	350	2,269	862	20	1,471	1,645	**946,572**
Residential Care of Children (Orphanages)	–	5	2	–	1	–	**178**
Total Assisted Annually	–	155	130	–	6	–	**74,324**
Day Care and Extended Day Care Centers	–	37	7	–	1	–	**1,110**
Total Assisted Annually	–	1,295	592	–	20	–	**126,432**
Special Centers for Social Services	1	3	10	8	2	5	**2,014**
Total Assisted Annually	3,538	7,903	68,222	199,500	2,377	112,000	**18,262,444**
Diocesan Seminaries	1	5	2	–	–	–	**77**
Students	11	65	9	–	–	–	**3,149**
Religious Seminaries	2	8	–	–	–	–	**129**
Students	9	41	–	–	–	–	**1,496**
Colleges and Universities	1	5	2	–	–	2	**241**
Total Students	11,462	24,359	7,731	–	–	2,350	**690,826**
High Schools, Diocesan and Parish	20	58	4	3	1	3	**794**
Total Students	2,424	11,176	1,752	1,416	265	1,120	**369,281**
High Schools, Private	–	40	7	–	1	–	**563**
Total Students	–	10,527	3,279	–	171	–	**283,406**
Elementary Schools, Diocesan and Parish	22	72	48	25	1	23	**6,822**
Total Students	7,674	25,037	11,735	6,449	535	4,352	**1,960,274**
Elementary Schools, Private	–	62	5	–	2	–	**343**
Total Students	–	21,115	1,362	–	371	–	**93,545**
Non–residential Schools for the Disabled	–	–	3	–	–	–	**80**
Total Students	–	–	1,500	–	–	–	**19,198**
Religious Education High School Students	–	14,934	9,986	1,942	1,986	8,283	**804,759**
Religious Education Elementary Students	–	49,254	31,174	9,311	4,280	12,047	**3,445,153**
Priests Teaching	16	97	55	1	3	2	**2,174**
Scholastics Teaching	–	6	–	–	–	–	**51**
Brothers Teaching	–	32	37	–	1	–	**1,191**
Sisters Teaching	47	246	133	12	9	11	**11,217**
Lay Teachers	1,155	4,460	1,405	538	91	259	**152,165**
Infant Baptisms	4,660	34,774	6,648	2,122	728	1,925	**1,044,304**
Adult Baptisms	3,585	5,750	169	239	51	64	**75,645**
Received into Full Communion	812	10,024	178	467	99	269	**85,970**
First Communions	5,574	25,689	6,398	2,405	761	2,111	**846,104**
Confirmations	5,175	20,115	4,763	3,881	521	1,885	**592,399**
Marriages	1,693	7,586	2,352	754	256	746	**300,582**
Deaths	–	5,683	5,630	904	439	1,129	**472,126**
Totals Catholics	442,000	2,583,360	637,554	109,629	42,320	118,596	**61,207,914**
Total Population	551,525	3,439,958	1,003,000	3,673,000	211,591	500,000	**268,299,833**
Catholic Population Percentage	80	75	64	3	20	24	**23**

Archdioceses = 36; Dioceses = 164; Apostolates = 3

1997 GENERAL SUMMARY

	SOUTH DAKOTA TOTAL	Knoxville TN	Memphis TN	Nashville TN	TENNESSEE TOTAL	*San Antonio TX	1997 U.S. GRAND TOTAL
Cardinals	–	–	–	–	–	–	**9**
Archbishops	–	–	–	–	–	1	**50**
Bishops	2	1	1	2	4	2	**358**
Abbots	3	–	–	–	–	–	**112**
Diocesan Priests	168	46	70	53	169	155	**31,977**
Religious Priests	76	15	11	20	46	230	**16,120**
Total Priests in Diocese	244	61	81	73	215	385	**48,097**
Newly Ordained Priests	1	1	–	–	1	8	**521**
Total Permanent Deacons	55	23	21	27	71	240	**11,788**
Total Brothers	24	16	26	2	44	96	**6,293**
Total Sisters	543	53	100	159	312	879	**87,644**
Number of Parishes	224	43	42	50	135	143	**19,677**
Missions	38	1	5	3	9	39	**3,051**
Pastoral Centers	4	–	1	–	1	3	**1,229**
New Parishes	1	–	–	–	–	–	**39**
Catholic Hospitals	9	2	1	1	4	5	**590**
Patients Assisted Annually	485,000	305,074	47,062	144,084	496,220	90,983	**61,489,163**
Health Care Centers	–	1	1	–	2	2	**366**
Patients Assisted Annually	–	105	64,505	–	64,610	14,476	**4,861,384**
Specialized Homes	13	2	9	4	15	13	**1,252**
Total Assisted Annually	3,116	777	1,012	731	2,520	3,035	**946,572**
Residential Care of Children (Orphanages)	1	–	–	–	–	2	**178**
Total Assisted Annually	6	–	–	–	–	180	**74,324**
Day Care and Extended Day Care Centers	1	–	8	3	11	13	**1,110**
Total Assisted Annually	20	–	1,442	307	1,749	1,496	**126,432**
Special Centers for Social Services	7	6	2	6	14	7	**2,014**
Total Assisted Annually	114,377	25,158	20,273	37,790	83,221	296,813	**18,262,444**
Diocesan Seminaries	–	–	–	–	–	1	**77**
Students	–	–	–	–	–	34	**3,149**
Religious Seminaries	–	–	–	–	–	11	**129**
Students	–	–	–	–	–	35	**1,496**
Colleges and Universities	2	–	1	1	2	4	**241**
Total Students	2,350	–	1,784	415	2,199	11,090	**690,826**
High Schools, Diocesan and Parish	4	2	4	1	7	3	**794**
Total Students	1,385	914	1,295	1,000	3,209	1,139	**369,281**
High Schools, Private	1	–	3	1	4	6	**563**
Total Students	171	–	1,109	190	1,299	2,262	**283,406**
Elementary Schools, Diocesan and Parish	24	7	11	13	31	38	**6,822**
Total Students	4,887	2,513	3,563	3,482	9,558	11,569	**1,960,274**
Elementary Schools, Private	2	–	2	2	4	4	**343**
Total Students	371	–	449	690	1,139	1,594	**93,545**
Non–residential Schools for the Disabled	–	–	1	–	1	–	**80**
Total Students	–	–	41	–	41	–	**19,198**
Religious Education High School Students	10,269	1,260	727	1,520	3,507	12,138	**804,759**
Religious Education Elementary Students	16,327	3,616	4,352	6,357	14,325	35,035	**3,445,153**
Priests Teaching	5	2	2	1	5	41	**2,174**
Scholastics Teaching	–	–	–	–	–	1	**51**
Brothers Teaching	1	–	10	–	10	26	**1,191**
Sisters Teaching	20	8	17	49	74	164	**11,217**
Lay Teachers	350	243	440	404	1,087	1,509	**152,165**
Infant Baptisms	2,653	777	1,071	1,352	3,200	13,709	**1,044,304**
Adult Baptisms	115	133	203	229	565	463	**75,645**
Received into Full Communion	368	269	279	504	1,052	735	**85,970**
First Communions	2,872	863	1,125	1,436	3,424	9,868	**846,104**
Confirmations	2,406	546	1,031	1,116	2,693	5,646	**592,399**
Marriages	1,002	222	411	422	1,055	2,840	**300,582**
Deaths	1,568	230	508	394	1,132	4,875	**472,126**
Totals Catholics	160,916	39,714	56,885	59,924	156,523	652,413	**61,207,914**
Total Population	711,591	1,860,218	1,426,923	1,782,729	5,069,870	1,828,740	**268,299,833**
Catholic Population Percentage	23	2	4	3	3	36	**23**

*Indicates Archdioceses.
†Certain Dioceses traverse state lines.

	Amarillo TX	Austin TX	Beaumont TX	Brownsville TX	Corpus Christi TX	Dallas TX	1997 U.S. GRAND TOTAL
Cardinals	–	–	–	–	–	–	**9**
Archbishops	–	–	–	–	–	–	**50**
Bishops	2	–	1	2	1	2	**358**
Abbots	–	–	–	–	2	1	**112**
Diocesan Priests	65	137	55	57	108	104	**31,977**
Religious Priests	8	56	25	51	62	84	**16,120**
Total Priests in Diocese	73	193	80	108	170	188	**48,097**
Newly Ordained Priests	2	3	1	3	5	6	**521**
Total Permanent Deacons	45	104	30	82	66	145	**11,788**
Total Brothers	1	41	3	18	22	4	**6,293**
Total Sisters	143	122	62	139	565	161	**87,644**
Number of Parishes	35	91	43	63	84	64	**19,677**
Missions	–	45	10	45	59	7	**3,051**
Pastoral Centers	–	–	2	1	11	–	**1,229**
New Parishes	1	1	–	2	–	1	**39**
Catholic Hospitals	1	4	2	–	5	1	**590**
Patients Assisted Annually	8,000	70,360	419,753	–	384,228	33,400	**61,489,163**
Health Care Centers	1	3	–	2	–	–	**366**
Patients Assisted Annually	720	82,000	–	177	–	–	**4,861,384**
Specialized Homes	3	3	1	3	4	1	**1,252**
Total Assisted Annually	606	837	8	13,992	1,267	45	**946,572**
Residential Care of Children (Orphanages)	–	1	–	–	1	–	**178**
Total Assisted Annually	–	250	–	–	64	–	**74,324**
Day Care and Extended Day Care Centers	8	3	–	1	3	7	**1,110**
Total Assisted Annually	300	190	–	53	210	695	**126,432**
Special Centers for Social Services	4	1	1	4	8	17	**2,014**
Total Assisted Annually	35,000	140	54,000	107,608	33,926	61,350	**18,262,444**
Diocesan Seminaries	–	–	–	–	1	1	**77**
Students	–	–	–	–	9	10	**3,149**
Religious Seminaries	–	–	–	–	1	–	**129**
Students	–	–	–	–	1	–	**1,496**
Colleges and Universities	–	1	–	–	–	1	**241**
Total Students	–	3,050	–	–	–	2,740	**690,826**
High Schools, Diocesan and Parish	1	2	1	–	2	3	**794**
Total Students	131	242	635	–	722	1,269	**369,281**
High Schools, Private	–	1	–	1	1	4	**563**
Total Students	–	345	–	673	315	1,794	**283,406**
Elementary Schools, Diocesan and Parish	8	15	7	6	23	29	**6,822**
Total Students	911	3,484	1,610	2,090	3,751	10,082	**1,960,274**
Elementary Schools, Private	–	1	–	2	5	3	**343**
Total Students	–	39	–	523	1,347	700	**93,545**
Non–residential Schools for the Disabled	–	–	–	–	–	1	**80**
Total Students	–	–	–	–	–	101	**19,198**
Religious Education High School Students	2,204	5,333	2,180	7,065	4,276	4,802	**804,759**
Religious Education Elementary Students	3,853	19,874	7,088	26,163	15,947	29,014	**3,445,153**
Priests Teaching	–	7	–	–	7	15	**2,174**
Scholastics Teaching	–	–	–	–	–	2	**51**
Brothers Teaching	–	1	1	6	–	2	**1,191**
Sisters Teaching	14	19	14	15	70	24	**11,217**
Lay Teachers	76	356	151	211	409	859	**152,165**
Infant Baptisms	1,014	5,540	1,380	9,280	5,989	10,266	**1,044,304**
Adult Baptisms	84	692	139	674	240	769	**75,645**
Received into Full Communion	106	464	242	448	504	637	**85,970**
First Communions	1,589	4,708	1,369	6,879	5,500	6,609	**846,104**
Confirmations	1,589	3,532	1,630	2,709	6,145	4,231	**592,399**
Marriages	269	1,617	395	1,568	1,252	2,004	**300,582**
Deaths	280	1,547	804	2,314	2,291	1,301	**472,126**
Totals Catholics	52,431	212,182	85,906	717,056	361,500	324,820	**61,207,914**
Total Population	386,574	1,638,245	561,605	888,112	792,300	2,733,974	**268,299,833**
Catholic Population Percentage	14	13	15	81	46	12	**23**

Archdioceses = 36; Dioceses = 164; Apostolates = 3

1997 GENERAL SUMMARY

	El Paso TX	Fort Worth TX	Galveston—Houston TX	Lubbock TX	San Angelo TX	Tyler TX	**1997 U.S. GRAND TOTAL**
Cardinals	–	–	–	–	–	–	**9**
Archbishops	–	–	–	–	–	–	**50**
Bishops	1	1	3	1	1	1	**358**
Abbots	–	–	–	–	–	–	**112**
Diocesan Priests	92	58	194	32	51	25	**31,977**
Religious Priests	43	53	223	9	17	21	**16,120**
Total Priests in Diocese	135	111	417	41	68	46	**48,097**
Newly Ordained Priests	1	1	6	1	–	–	**521**
Total Permanent Deacons	17	58	231	23	45	29	**11,788**
Total Brothers	16	14	17	–	–	1	**6,293**
Total Sisters	243	99	553	32	39	61	**87,644**
Number of Parishes	58	88	149	36	49	30	**19,677**
Missions	22	2	10	25	24	20	**3,051**
Pastoral Centers	–	–	8	–	–	3	**1,229**
New Parishes	–	2	–	–	–	3	**39**
Catholic Hospitals	–	1	4	1	–	3	**590**
Patients Assisted Annually	–	60,000	270,285	98,982	–	279,914	**61,489,163**
Health Care Centers	1	1	2	35	–	5	**366**
Patients Assisted Annually	18,500	622	60,463	292,665	–	8,313	**4,861,384**
Specialized Homes	3	4	8	–	–	–	**1,252**
Total Assisted Annually	156	801	5,994	–	–	–	**946,572**
Residential Care of Children (Orphanages)	–	–	2	–	–	–	**178**
Total Assisted Annually	–	–	215	–	–	–	**74,324**
Day Care and Extended Day Care Centers	2	6	30	–	–	–	**1,110**
Total Assisted Annually	185	221	2,656	–	–	–	**126,432**
Special Centers for Social Services	5	16	7	1	–	1	**2,014**
Total Assisted Annually	74,200	22,416	483,661	33,000	–	100	**18,262,444**
Diocesan Seminaries	1	–	1	–	–	–	**77**
Students	3	–	54	–	–	–	**3,149**
Religious Seminaries	2	–	3	–	–	–	**129**
Students	20	–	28	–	–	–	**1,496**
Colleges and Universities	–	–	1	–	–	–	**241**
Total Students	–	–	2,504	–	–	–	**690,826**
High Schools, Diocesan and Parish	1	4	2	1	–	1	**794**
Total Students	677	1,930	1,215	78	–	133	**369,281**
High Schools, Private	2	–	6	–	–	–	**563**
Total Students	325	–	2,300	–	–	–	**283,406**
Elementary Schools, Diocesan and Parish	9	15	45	2	3	5	**6,822**
Total Students	3,380	6,109	11,410	331	908	963	**1,960,274**
Elementary Schools, Private	3	1	6	–	–	–	**343**
Total Students	841	216	1,885	–	–	–	**93,545**
Non–residential Schools for the Disabled	–	–	–	–	–	–	**80**
Total Students	–	–	–	–	–	–	**19,198**
Religious Education High School Students	4,963	6,013	14,631	2,697	4,242	1,151	**804,759**
Religious Education Elementary Students	12,437	18,045	60,450	6,397	8,560	4,779	**3,445,153**
Priests Teaching	13	2	35	–	–	1	**2,174**
Scholastics Teaching	–	–	–	–	–	–	**51**
Brothers Teaching	10	9	4	–	–	–	**1,191**
Sisters Teaching	35	16	59	–	5	5	**11,217**
Lay Teachers	273	375	1,422	–	57	113	**152,165**
Infant Baptisms	8,307	4,663	16,913	1,910	2,212	1,387	**1,044,304**
Adult Baptisms	121	296	1,363	70	179	135	**75,645**
Received into Full Communion	250	650	885	58	255	170	**85,970**
First Communions	5,326	3,691	13,778	1,499	1,989	1,138	**846,104**
Confirmations	3,571	2,013	6,721	1,012	1,157	570	**592,399**
Marriages	1,237	1,198	3,759	340	442	253	**300,582**
Deaths	1,780	955	3,302	386	577	312	**472,126**
Totals Catholics	579,766	192,890	854,653	50,378	81,807	42,796	**61,207,914**
Total Population	776,724	2,263,399	4,231,599	451,995	675,907	1,185,155	**268,299,833**
Catholic Population Percentage	75	9	20	11	12	4	**23**

*Indicates Archdioceses.

†Certain Dioceses traverse state lines.

1997 GENERAL SUMMARY

	Victoria in Texas TX	TEXAS TOTAL	Salt Lake City UT	Burlington VT	St. Thomas Virgin Islands	Arlington VA	1997 U.S. GRAND TOTAL
Cardinals	–	–	–	–	–	–	9
Archbishops	–	1	–	–	–	–	50
Bishops	1	19	2	1	1	1	358
Abbots	–	3	1	–	–	–	112
Diocesan Priests	55	1,188	54	139	13	143	31,977
Religious Priests	13	895	32	48	7	74	16,120
Total Priests in Diocese	68	2,083	86	187	20	217	48,097
Newly Ordained Priests	2	39	–	2	–	13	521
Total Permanent Deacons	21	1,136	25	40	22	55	11,788
Total Brothers	1	234	12	21	2	17	6,293
Total Sisters	134	3,232	68	263	14	218	87,644
Number of Parishes	50	983	43	93	8	62	19,677
Missions	21	329	19	39	2	6	3,051
Pastoral Centers	–	28	–	1	–	–	1,229
New Parishes	–	10	–	–	–	2	39
Catholic Hospitals	–	27	–	1	–	–	590
Patients Assisted Annually	–	1,715,905	–	32,691	–	–	61,489,163
Health Care Centers	–	52	–	–	–	–	366
Patients Assisted Annually	–	477,936	–	–	–	–	4,861,384
Specialized Homes	1	44	1	4	–	–	1,252
Total Assisted Annually	59	26,800	449	143	–	–	946,572
Residential Care of Children (Orphanages)	–	6	–	1	–	–	178
Total Assisted Annually	–	709	–	14	–	–	74,324
Day Care and Extended Day Care Centers	–	73	6	–	4	–	1,110
Total Assisted Annually	–	6,006	291	–	76	–	126,432
Special Centers for Social Services	–	72	2	–	6	7	2,014
Total Assisted Annually	–	1,202,214	201,635	–	716	30,981	18,262,444
Diocesan Seminaries	–	5	–	–	–	–	77
Students	–	110	–	–	–	–	3,149
Religious Seminaries	–	17	–	–	–	1	129
Students	2	86	–	–	–	–	1,496
Colleges and Universities	–	7	–	3	–	2	241
Total Students	–	19,384	–	4,029	–	3,035	690,826
High Schools, Diocesan and Parish	2	23	2	2	2	3	794
Total Students	174	8,395	1,195	695	310	3,293	369,281
High Schools, Private	1	22	–	–	–	1	563
Total Students	431	8,445	–	–	–	156	283,406
Elementary Schools, Diocesan and Parish	12	217	10	9	3	31	6,822
Total Students	2,294	58,892	2,697	1,780	642	11,788	1,960,274
Elementary Schools, Private	1	26	–	2	–	2	343
Total Students	510	7,655	–	653	–	528	93,545
Non–residential Schools for the Disabled	–	1	–	–	–	1	80
Total Students	–	101	–	–	–	55	19,198
Religious Education High School Students	2,841	74,536	1,396	1,118	536	9,230	804,759
Religious Education Elementary Students	7,294	254,936	6,540	5,846	543	16,900	3,445,153
Priests Teaching	–	121	3	2	2	7	2,174
Scholastics Teaching	–	3	–	–	–	3	51
Brothers Teaching	–	59	2	2	1	1	1,191
Sisters Teaching	24	464	6	22	2	69	11,217
Lay Teachers	226	6,037	223	228	71	837	152,165
Infant Baptisms	1,642	84,212	2,328	2,012	480	5,194	1,044,304
Adult Baptisms	89	5,314	397	130	24	1,967	75,645
Received into Full Communion	127	5,531	314	157	10	–	85,970
First Communions	1,551	65,494	1,628	1,934	273	5,839	846,104
Confirmations	1,070	41,596	1,063	1,194	196	4,566	592,399
Marriages	491	17,665	510	753	86	1,874	300,582
Deaths	990	21,714	581	1,531	146	1,253	472,126
Totals Catholics	108,573	4,317,171	81,021	147,190	30,000	311,351	61,207,914
Total Population	255,276	18,669,605	1,964,000	584,771	101,809	2,115,700	268,299,833
Catholic Population Percentage	43	23	4	25	29	15	23

Archdioceses = 36; Dioceses = 164; Apostolates = 3

1997 GENERAL SUMMARY

	Richmond VA	VIRGINIA TOTAL	*Seattle WA	Spokane WA	Yakima WA	WASHINGTON TOTAL	1997 U.S. GRAND TOTAL
Cardinals	–	–	–	–	–	–	9
Archbishops	–	–	2	–	–	2	50
Bishops	1	2	–	1	1	2	358
Abbots	1	1	3	1	–	4	112
Diocesan Priests	161	304	189	84	56	329	31,977
Religious Priests	39	113	132	97	10	239	16,120
Total Priests in Diocese	200	417	321	181	66	568	48,097
Newly Ordained Priests	4	17	2	2	1	5	521
Total Permanent Deacons	22	77	82	37	25	144	11,788
Total Brothers	11	28	31	13	–	44	6,293
Total Sisters	269	487	674	299	53	1,026	87,644
Number of Parishes	141	203	138	78	41	257	19,677
Missions	13	19	30	5	5	40	3,051
Pastoral Centers	–	–	7	1	2	10	1,229
New Parishes	–	2	1	–	–	1	39
Catholic Hospitals	9	9	9	7	3	19	590
Patients Assisted Annually	438,670	438,670	1,068,576	323,693	291,781	1,684,050	61,489,163
Health Care Centers	1	1	3	2	–	5	366
Patients Assisted Annually	31,570	31,570	6,173	17,008	–	23,181	4,861,384
Specialized Homes	16	16	11	13	–	24	1,252
Total Assisted Annually	1,595	1,595	3,549	1,733	–	5,282	946,572
Residential Care of Children (Orphanages)	1	1	–	14	–	14	178
Total Assisted Annually	88	88	–	896	–	896	74,324
Day Care and Extended Day Care Centers	5	5	6	14	2	22	1,110
Total Assisted Annually	605	605	725	811	234	1,770	126,432
Special Centers for Social Services	4	11	22	4	6	32	2,014
Total Assisted Annually	9,938	40,919	98,538	14,032	14,998	127,568	18,262,444
Diocesan Seminaries	–	–	–	1	–	1	77
Students	–	–	–	17	–	17	3,149
Religious Seminaries	–	1	–	1	–	1	129
Students	–	–	–	17	–	17	1,496
Colleges and Universities	–	2	2	1	–	3	241
Total Students	–	3,035	7,503	4,416	–	11,919	690,826
High Schools, Diocesan and Parish	5	8	3	1	–	4	794
Total Students	995	4,288	2,189	881	–	3,070	369,281
High Schools, Private	4	5	6	1	1	8	563
Total Students	956	1,112	2,924	434	–	3,358	283,406
Elementary Schools, Diocesan and Parish	23	54	54	16	7	77	6,822
Total Students	5,102	16,890	15,641	3,206	1,928	20,775	1,960,274
Elementary Schools, Private	1	3	2	–	–	2	343
Total Students	412	940	674	–	–	674	93,545
Non–residential Schools for the Disabled	–	1	–	–	–	–	80
Total Students	–	55	–	–	–	–	19,198
Religious Education High School Students	4,850	14,080	6,530	1,846	1,777	10,153	804,759
Religious Education Elementary Students	17,818	34,718	27,580	4,536	5,255	37,371	3,445,153
Priests Teaching	3	10	40	17	–	57	2,174
Scholastics Teaching	–	3	–	3	–	3	51
Brothers Teaching	–	1	12	13	–	25	1,191
Sisters Teaching	26	95	45	4	7	56	11,217
Lay Teachers	588	1,425	1,527	81	95	1,703	152,165
Infant Baptisms	3,245	8,439	6,308	1,323	2,776	10,407	1,044,304
Adult Baptisms	152	2,119	1,129	321	154	1,604	75,645
Received into Full Communion	982	982	703	117	83	903	85,970
First Communions	3,377	9,216	5,562	787	1,943	8,292	846,104
Confirmations	1,500	6,066	2,687	384	650	3,721	592,399
Marriages	1,102	2,976	2,216	450	483	3,149	300,582
Deaths	1,458	2,711	2,853	1,631	519	5,003	472,126
Totals Catholics	183,304	494,655	369,050	80,102	69,978	519,130	61,207,914
Total Population	4,561,480	6,677,180	4,282,200	708,891	461,000	5,452,091	268,299,833
Catholic Population Percentage	4	7	9	11	15	10	23

*Indicates Archdioceses.
†Certain Dioceses traverse state lines.

1997 GENERAL SUMMARY

	Wheeling-Charleston WV	*Milwaukee WI	Green Bay WI	La Crosse WI	Madison WI	Superior WI	1997 U.S. GRAND TOTAL
Cardinals	–	–	–	–	–	–	**9**
Archbishops	–	1	–	–	–	–	**50**
Bishops	1	2	3	3	2	1	**358**
Abbots	–	3	3	1	–	–	**112**
Diocesan Priests	123	490	237	198	157	79	**31,977**
Religious Priests	64	345	143	27	23	16	**16,120**
Total Priests in Diocese	187	835	380	225	180	95	**48,097**
Newly Ordained Priests	1	8	1	4	–	1	**521**
Total Permanent Deacons	26	154	78	22	1	42	**11,788**
Total Brothers	8	96	49	11	9	2	**6,293**
Total Sisters	311	2,233	714	544	427	133	**87,644**
Number of Parishes	115	277	201	180	137	115	**19,677**
Missions	29	–	4	–	–	–	**3,051**
Pastoral Centers	18	21	19	2	–	2	**1,229**
New Parishes	1	–	1	–	–	–	**39**
Catholic Hospitals	3	11	8	9	4	4	**590**
Patients Assisted Annually	267,870	1,224,200	508,448	452,748	213,742	97,629	**61,489,163**
Health Care Centers	2	1	–	–	2	–	**366**
Patients Assisted Annually	–	14,000	–	–	308	–	**4,861,384**
Specialized Homes	5	25	15	18	6	2	**1,252**
Total Assisted Annually	–	4,135	1,798	12,050	780	357	**946,572**
Residential Care of Children (Orphanages)	1	–	–	–	–	–	**178**
Total Assisted Annually	–	–	–	–	–	–	**74,324**
Day Care and Extended Day Care Centers	–	7	2	1	14	5	**1,110**
Total Assisted Annually	–	1,070	100	150	878	275	**126,432**
Special Centers for Social Services	5	39	9	5	7	4	**2,014**
Total Assisted Annually	–	231,396	200,431	2,046	46,297	4,482	**18,262,444**
Diocesan Seminaries	–	1	–	1	–	–	**77**
Students	–	21	–	7	–	–	**3,149**
Religious Seminaries	–	1	1	–	–	–	**129**
Students	–	12	9	1	–	–	**1,496**
Colleges and Universities	1	5	2	1	1	–	**241**
Total Students	1,527	21,395	4,100	1,637	2,109	–	**690,826**
High Schools, Diocesan and Parish	7	7	5	7	1	–	**794**
Total Students	1,659	4,517	1,436	1,859	93	–	**369,281**
High Schools, Private	1	6	1	–	1	–	**563**
Total Students	58	3,187	820	–	594	–	**283,406**
Elementary Schools, Diocesan and Parish	27	145	80	78	44	18	**6,822**
Total Students	5,319	28,381	13,659	10,151	7,365	3,069	**1,960,274**
Elementary Schools, Private	2	1	–	–	1	–	**343**
Total Students	252	46	–	–	252	–	**93,545**
Non-residential Schools for the Disabled	–	2	–	–	–	–	**80**
Total Students	–	17	–	–	–	–	**19,198**
Religious Education High School Students	1,912	14,393	9,418	8,762	11,682	3,977	**804,759**
Religious Education Elementary Students	6,550	38,638	20,479	17,784	16,675	8,879	**3,445,153**
Priests Teaching	13	76	4	19	–	–	**2,174**
Scholastics Teaching	–	16	–	–	–	–	**51**
Brothers Teaching	1	10	1	2	1	–	**1,191**
Sisters Teaching	16	245	44	31	30	11	**11,217**
Lay Teachers	548	3,639	897	790	546	196	**152,165**
Infant Baptisms	1,291	9,417	9,262	3,239	3,211	1,183	**1,044,304**
Adult Baptisms	327	555	432	122	408	1,455	**75,645**
Received into Full Communion	303	537	705	359	–	125	**85,970**
First Communions	1,802	9,291	10,048	3,761	3,138	1,530	**846,104**
Confirmations	1,703	5,905	6,611	3,334	2,459	1,207	**592,399**
Marriages	718	3,704	4,147	2,042	1,311	587	**300,582**
Deaths	1,398	6,060	6,503	2,166	1,522	1,256	**472,126**
Totals Catholics	103,678	605,232	582,681	227,937	256,527	87,546	**61,207,914**
Total Population	1,793,477	2,080,883	836,600	817,382	866,227	381,350	**268,299,833**
Catholic Population Percentage	6	29	70	28	30	23	**23**

Archdioceses = 36; Dioceses = 164; Apostolates = 3

1997 GENERAL SUMMARY

			EASTERN RITE				
	WISCONSIN TOTAL	† Cheyenne WY	*Philadelphia	*Pittsburgh	Armenian	Lady of Deliverance	1997 U.S. GRAND TOTAL
Cardinals	–	–	–	–	–	–	9
Archbishops	1	–	1	1	–	–	50
Bishops	11	1	1	–	2	1	358
Abbots	7	–	–	1	–	–	112
Diocesan Priests	1,161	52	58	65	4	10	31,977
Religious Priests	554	11	6	9	8	1	16,120
Total Priests in Diocese	1,715	63	64	74	12	11	48,097
Newly Ordained Priests	14	1	–	–	–	2	521
Total Permanent Deacons	297	7	5	–	–	4	11,788
Total Brothers	167	1	3	4	–	–	6,293
Total Sisters	4,051	34	84	108	14	–	87,644
Number of Parishes	910	36	77	87	6	6	19,677
Missions	4	42	–	3	–	5	3,051
Pastoral Centers	44	–	–	–	–	–	1,229
New Parishes	1	–	–	–	–	–	39
Catholic Hospitals	36	–	–	–	–	–	590
Patients Assisted Annually	2,496,767	–	–	–	–	–	61,489,163
Health Care Centers	3	–	–	–	–	–	366
Patients Assisted Annually	14,308	–	–	–	–	–	4,861,384
Specialized Homes	66	3	1	3	–	–	1,252
Total Assisted Annually	19,120	201	45	322	–	–	946,572
Residential Care of Children (Orphanages)	–	–	–	–	–	–	178
Total Assisted Annually	–	–	–	–	–	–	74,324
Day Care and Extended Day Care Centers	29	5	2	3	–	–	1,110
Total Assisted Annually	2,473	200	68	90	–	–	126,432
Special Centers for Social Services	64	9	–	–	–	–	2,014
Total Assisted Annually	484,702	12,137	–	–	–	–	18,262,444
Diocesan Seminaries	2	–	1	1	–	–	77
Students	28	–	17	11	–	–	3,149
Religious Seminaries	2	–	–	–	–	–	129
Students	22	–	–	–	–	–	1,496
Colleges and Universities	9	–	1	–	–	–	241
Total Students	29,241	–	657	–	–	–	690,826
High Schools, Diocesan and Parish	20	–	–	–	–	–	794
Total Students	7,905	–	–	–	–	–	369,281
High Schools, Private	8	–	1	–	–	–	563
Total Students	4,601	–	350	–	–	–	283,406
Elementary Schools, Diocesan and Parish	365	7	7	3	4	–	6,822
Total Students	62,625	1,322	1,636	580	977	–	1,960,274
Elementary Schools, Private	2	–	–	–	–	–	343
Total Students	298	–	–	–	–	–	93,545
Non–residential Schools for the Disabled	2	–	–	–	–	–	80
Total Students	17	–	–	–	–	–	19,198
Religious Education High School Students	48,232	1,684	400	605	–	–	804,759
Religious Education Elementary Students	102,455	5,753	1,989	2,561	96	–	3,445,153
Priests Teaching	99	2	3	–	2	–	2,174
Scholastics Teaching	16	–	–	–	–	–	51
Brothers Teaching	14	–	–	–	–	–	1,191
Sisters Teaching	361	2	25	8	14	–	11,217
Lay Teachers	6,068	94	300	37	91	–	152,165
Infant Baptisms	26,312	1,071	345	521	77	74	1,044,304
Adult Baptisms	2,972	218	2	55	–	3	75,645
Received into Full Communion	1,726	265	5	75	–	–	85,970
First Communions	27,768	1,070	379	367	49	73	846,104
Confirmations	19,516	775	347	639	81	77	592,399
Marriages	11,791	297	195	308	15	23	300,582
Deaths	17,507	606	596	718	28	16	472,126
Totals Catholics	1,759,923	48,427	69,488	85,740	26,000	12,000	61,207,914
Total Population	4,982,442	480,184	–	–	–	–	268,299,833
Catholic Population Percentage	35	10	–	–	–	–	23

*Indicates Archdioceses.

†Certain Dioceses traverse state lines.

	EASTERN RITE (Cont.) Lady of Lebanon	Newton	Parma	Passaic	Romanian	St. Josaphat	1997 U.S. GRAND TOTAL
Cardinals	–	–	–	–	–	–	9
Archbishops	–	1	–	–	–	–	50
Bishops	1	2	1	2	2	1	358
Abbots	–	–	–	–	–	–	112
Diocesan Priests	33	45	41	93	15	38	31,977
Religious Priests	5	19	–	20	2	1	16,120
Total Priests in Diocese	38	64	41	113	17	39	48,097
Newly Ordained Priests	2	1	–	–	–	–	521
Total Permanent Deacons	6	28	–	18	–	9	11,788
Total Brothers	–	1	–	–	–	10	6,293
Total Sisters	–	3	12	13	–	10	87,644
Number of Parishes	25	35	39	102	15	35	19,677
Missions	9	7	2	6	3	2	3,051
Pastoral Centers	–	–	–	4	–	–	1,229
New Parishes	–	–	–	–	–	–	39
Catholic Hospitals	–	–	–	–	–	–	590
Patients Assisted Annually	–	–	–	–	–	–	61,489,163
Health Care Centers	–	–	–	–	–	–	366
Patients Assisted Annually	–	–	–	–	–	–	4,861,384
Specialized Homes	–	2	–	–	–	2	1,252
Total Assisted Annually	–	5,700	–	–	–	143	946,572
Residential Care of Children (Orphanages)	–	–	–	–	–	–	178
Total Assisted Annually	–	–	–	–	–	–	74,324
Day Care and Extended Day Care Centers	–	–	1	–	–	–	1,110
Total Assisted Annually	–	–	106	–	–	–	126,432
Special Centers for Social Services	–	1	1	–	–	–	2,014
Total Assisted Annually	–	5,400	9,100	–	–	–	18,262,444
Diocesan Seminaries	–	1	–	–	–	–	77
Students	–	2	–	–	–	–	3,149
Religious Seminaries	–	1	–	–	–	–	129
Students	–	1	–	–	–	–	1,496
Colleges and Universities	–	–	–	–	–	–	241
Total Students	–	–	–	–	–	–	690,826
High Schools, Diocesan and Parish	–	–	–	–	–	–	794
Total Students	–	–	–	–	–	–	369,281
High Schools, Private	–	–	–	–	–	–	563
Total Students	–	–	–	–	–	–	283,406
Elementary Schools, Diocesan and Parish	–	–	2	1	–	2	6,822
Total Students	–	–	342	1,055	–	262	1,960,274
Elementary Schools, Private	–	–	–	–	–	–	343
Total Students	–	–	–	–	–	–	93,545
Non–residential Schools for the Disabled	–	–	–	–	–	–	80
Total Students	–	–	–	–	–	–	19,198
Religious Education High School Students	–	298	217	814	5	105	804,759
Religious Education Elementary Students	–	1,306	1,104	2,676	50	232	3,445,153
Priests Teaching	–	–	–	1	–	–	2,174
Scholastics Teaching	–	–	–	–	–	–	51
Brothers Teaching	–	–	–	–	–	–	1,191
Sisters Teaching	–	–	5	13	–	2	11,217
Lay Teachers	–	–	18	33	–	26	152,165
Infant Baptisms	376	467	140	395	24	132	1,044,304
Adult Baptisms	27	21	13	21	1	4	75,645
Received into Full Communion	25	29	20	109	12	1	85,970
First Communions	186	527	142	309	12	110	846,104
Confirmations	238	594	138	447	25	–	592,399
Marriages	140	163	66	169	7	65	300,582
Deaths	156	182	227	579	39	267	472,126
Totals Catholics	21,790	27,730	12,714	66,965	5,300	11,629	61,207,914
Total Population	–	–	–	–	–	–	268,299,833
Catholic Population Percentage	–	–	–	–	–	–	23

Archdioceses = 36; Dioceses = 164; Apostolates = 3

1997 GENERAL SUMMARY

	EASTERN RITE (Cont.)					EASTERN RITE TOTAL	1997 U.S. GRAND TOTAL
	St. Maron	St. Nicholas	St. Thomas	Stamford	Van Nuys		
Cardinals	–	–	–	–	–	–	**9**
Archbishops	–	–	–	–	–	3	**50**
Bishops	1	3	1	1	1	20	**358**
Abbots	–	1	–	–	–	2	**112**
Diocesan Priests	62	37	18	38	18	575	**31,977**
Religious Priests	10	15	–	18	4	118	**16,120**
Total Priests in Diocese	72	52	18	56	22	693	**48,097**
Newly Ordained Priests	2	2	–	1	–	10	**521**
Total Permanent Deacons	10	14	–	5	3	102	**11,788**
Total Brothers	1	–	–	3	4	26	**6,293**
Total Sisters	12	–	–	42	4	302	**87,644**
Number of Parishes	33	33	12	49	16	570	**19,677**
Missions	3	4	–	5	–	49	**3,051**
Pastoral Centers	–	–	–	2	4	10	**1,229**
New Parishes	–	–	–	–	–	–	**39**
Catholic Hospitals	–	–	–	–	–	–	**590**
Patients Assisted Annually	–	–	–	–	–	–	**61,489,163**
Health Care Centers	–	–	–	–	–	–	**366**
Patients Assisted Annually	–	–	–	–		–	**4,861,384**
Specialized Homes	–	–	1	1	–	10	**1,252**
Total Assisted Annually	–	–	–	30	–	6,240	**946,572**
Residential Care of Children (Orphanages)	–	–	–	–	–	–	**178**
Total Assisted Annually	–	–	–	–	–	–	**74,324**
Day Care and Extended Day Care Centers	–	–	1	1	–	8	**1,110**
Total Assisted Annually	–	–	–	44	–	308	**126,432**
Special Centers for Social Services	–	–	–	1	–	3	**2,014**
Total Assisted Annually	–	–	–	100	–	14,600	**18,262,444**
Diocesan Seminaries	1	–	–	1	–	5	**77**
Students	4	–	1	48		83	**3,149**
Religious Seminaries	–	–	–	–	–	1	**129**
Students	–	–	–	–	–	1	**1,496**
Colleges and Universities	–	–	–	–	–	1	**241**
Total Students	–	–	–	–	–	657	**690,826**
High Schools, Diocesan and Parish	–	1	–	1	–	2	**794**
Total Students	–	80	–	140	–	220	**369,281**
High Schools, Private	–	–	–	–	–	1	**563**
Total Students	–	–	–	–	–	350	**283,406**
Elementary Schools, Diocesan and Parish	–	2	–	4	–	25	**6,822**
Total Students	–	465	–	463	–	5,780	**1,960,274**
Elementary Schools, Private	–	–	–	–	–	–	**343**
Total Students	–	–	–	–	–	–	**93,545**
Non–residential Schools for the Disabled	–	–	–	–	–	–	**80**
Total Students	–	–	–	–	–	–	**19,198**
Religious Education High School Students	131	50	–	23	76	2,724	**804,759**
Religious Education Elementary Students	890	180	–	848	336	12,268	**3,445,153**
Priests Teaching	–	1	–	–	–	7	**2,174**
Scholastics Teaching	–	–	–	–	–	–	**51**
Brothers Teaching	–	–	–	–	–	–	**1,191**
Sisters Teaching	–	3	–	6	–	76	**11,217**
Lay Teachers	–	48	–	28	–	581	**152,165**
Infant Baptisms	330	120	1,052	188	65	4,306	**1,044,304**
Adult Baptisms	9	3	17	18	7	201	**75,645**
Received into Full Communion	38	–	–	7	22	343	**85,970**
First Communions	184	158	865	184	128	3,673	**846,104**
Confirmations	269	–	1,069	196	140	4,260	**592,399**
Marriages	108	62	322	105	17	1,765	**300,582**
Deaths	171	138	126	385	28	3,656	**472,126**
Totals Catholics	30,000	10,000	63,150	32,117	2,951	477,574	**61,207,914**
Total Population	–	–	–	–	–	–	**268,299,833**
Catholic Population Percentage	–	–	–	–	–	–	**23**

*Indicates Archdioceses.

†Certain Dioceses traverse state lines.

	*Military Archdiocese				1987 GRAND TOTALS	1996 GRAND TOTALS	1997 U.S. GRAND TOTAL
Cardinals	–				8	10	**9**
Archbishops	2				46	48	**50**
Bishops	4				337	345	**358**
Abbots	–				109	120	**112**
Diocesan Priests	–				34,471	32,442	**31,977**
Religious Priests	–				18,911	16,629	**16,120**
Total Priests in Diocese	–				53,382	49,009	**48,097**
Newly Ordained Priests	–				670	520	**521**
Total Permanent Deacons	–				7,981	11,527	**11,788**
Total Brothers	–				7,418	6,357	**6,293**
Total Sisters	–				112,489	89,125	**87,644**
Number of Parishes	–				19,546	19,726	**19,677**
Missions	–				3,185	3,055	**3,051**
Pastoral Centers	–				830	1,262	**1,229**
New Parishes	–				46	59	**39**
Catholic Hospitals	–				645	603	**590**
Patients Assisted Annually	–				37,119,874	57,475,224	**61,489,163**
Health Care Centers	–				165	559	**366**
Patients Assisted Annually	–				1,246,820	3,868,551	**4,861,384**
Specialized Homes	–				487	1,383	**1,252**
Total Assisted Annually	–				114,070	671,453	**946,572**
Residential Care of Children (Orphanages)	–				743	173	**178**
Total Assisted Annually	–				63,782	77,140	**74,324**
Day Care and Extended Day Care Centers	–				217	1,060	**1,110**
Total Assisted Annually	–				19,047	144,623	**126,432**
Special Centers for Social Services	–				1,403	1,929	**2,014**
Total Assisted Annually	–				2,523,839	19,187,646	**18,262,444**
Diocesan Seminaries	–				76	72	**77**
Students	–				5,138	3,038	**3,149**
Religious Seminaries	–				163	126	**129**
Students	–				3,418	1,540	**1,496**
Colleges and Universities	–				238	237	**241**
Total Students	–				556,337	691,626	**690,826**
High Schools, Diocesan and Parish	–				850	790	**794**
Total Students	–				449,815	365,856	**369,281**
High Schools, Private	–				558	560	**563**
Total Students	–				304,899	281,757	**283,406**
Elementary Schools, Diocesan and Parish	–				7,485	6,677	**6,822**
Total Students	–				1,972,639	1,964,624	**1,960,274**
Elementary Schools, Private	–				287	334	**343**
Total Students	–				57,959	87,569	**93,545**
Non–residential Schools for the Disabled	–				–	80	**80**
Total Students	–				–	7,532	**19,198**
Religious Education High School Students	21,500				888,452	793,823	**804,759**
Religious Education Elementary Students	45,300				2,972,588	3,414,472	**3,445,153**
Priests Teaching	–				3,738	2,538	**2,174**
Scholastics Teaching	–				199	54	**51**
Brothers Teaching	–				2,265	1,394	**1,191**
Sisters Teaching	10				26,574	12,693	**11,217**
Lay Teachers	225				137,170	147,923	**152,165**
Infant Baptisms	6,389				941,898	1,029,281	**1,044,304**
Adult Baptisms	1,118				80,703	69,894	**75,645**
Received into Full Communion	485				–	92,155	**85,970**
First Communions	3,362				–	824,092	**846,104**
Confirmations	2,896				–	579,706	**592,399**
Marriages	1,421				342,440	302,919	**300,582**
Deaths	–				430,352	464,425	**472,126**
Totals Catholics	1,215,200				50,893,217	60,280,454	**61,207,914**
Total Population	–				233,152,397	268,784,851	**268,299,833**
Catholic Population Percentage	–				22	23	**23**

Archdioceses = 36; Dioceses = 164; Apostolates = 3

1. U.S. Census Bureau estimate of Total Population as of Jan.1, 1997: 266,490,000
2. U.S. Census Bureau estimate of Total Population as of Jan.1, 1996: 264,023,000
3. U.S. Census Bureau estimate of Total Population as of Jan.1, 1987: 242,085,811

CATHOLIC DIOCESAN AND PROVINCE BOUNDARIES
IN THE UNITED STATES

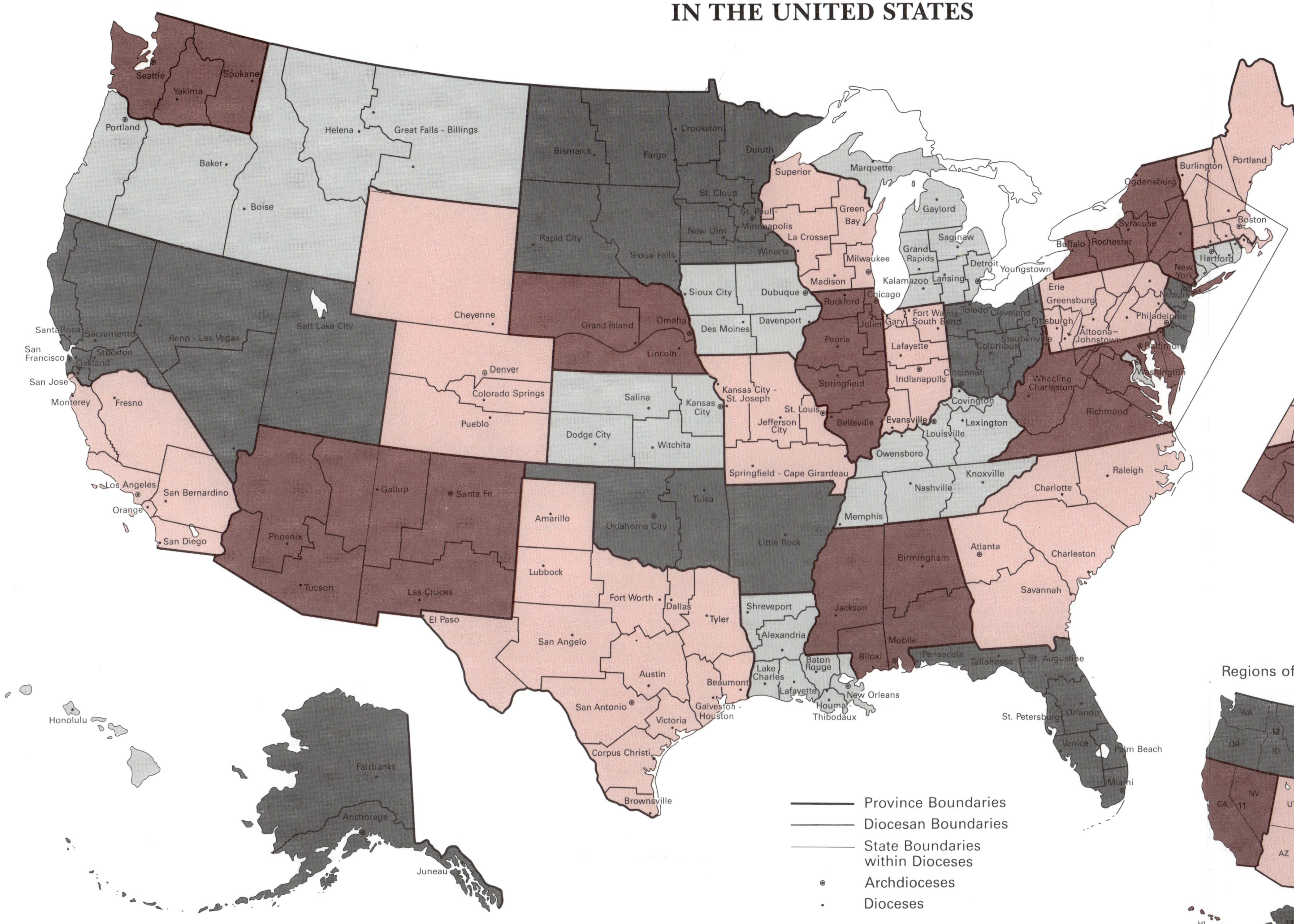

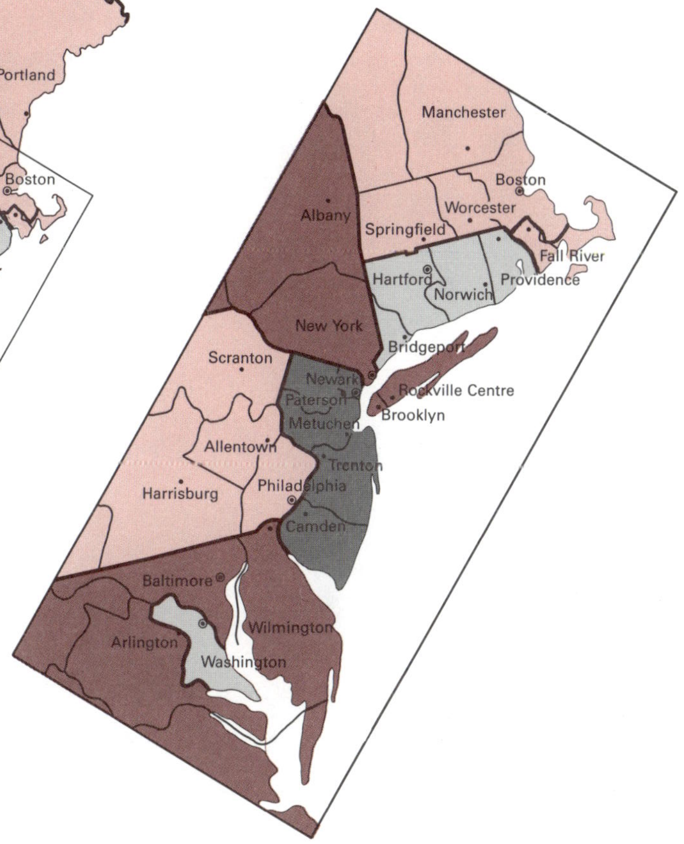

- Province Boundaries
- Diocesan Boundaries
- State Boundaries within Dioceses
- Archdioceses
- Dioceses

Regions of the National Conference of Catholic Bishops

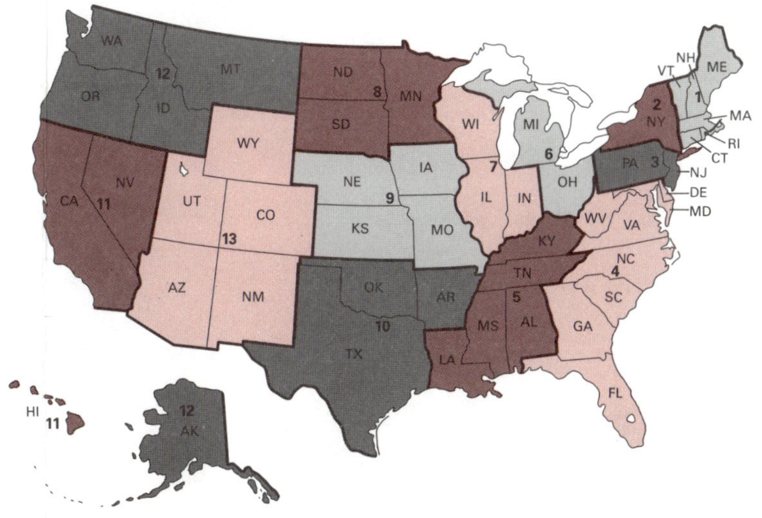

The Official Catholic Directory
P.J. Kenedy & Sons 1997

The Official Catholic Directory

Products & Services Guide

1997

P.J. Kenedy & Sons
121 Chanlon Road, New Providence, NJ 07974
(908) 665-3563

THE OFFICIAL CATHOLIC DIRECTORY PRODUCTS & SERVICES GUIDE TABLE OF CONTENTS

AUDIO & VIDEO

CASSETTES, AUDIO & VIDEO

Cathedral MUSIC PRESS

CATHEDRAL MUSIC PRESS
#4 Industrial Dr.
Pacific, MO 63069-0066
Tel.: 1-800-863-5229; 314-257-3970; FAX: 314-257-5062
Web: http://www.melbay.com; e-mail: email@melbay.com

Personnel:
William Bay . . . . Vice President
L. Dean Bye . . . . General Manager
Michael Entsminger . . . . Marketing Coordinator
Ginny Patterson . . . . Sales

Type of Business:
A leading music publisher specializing in instrumental and instructional material for the church. A complete line of piano, organ, flute, clarinet, trumpet, saxophone, guitar, and other fretted instruments along with beautifully recorded CDs and cassettes are available. Write or phone for our most recent catalog at 1-800-863-5229.

J.S. PALUCH COMPANY

J.S. PALUCH CO., INC.
3825 N. Willow Rd.
Schiller Park, IL 60176
Tel.: 800-621-5197; FAX: 847-671-5715

Personnel:
Liturgy and Music Resources Customer Service 1-800-566-6150
Parish Bulletins; Calendars; Computer Software: . . . 1-800-621-5197
. . . . Fax: 847-671-5715

Type of Business:
Serving the Church for over 80 years. Liturgy and Music Resources; Parish Sundays - Laser ComExpress; National Vocations Awareness and Religious Art Calendars; Computer Software for parish management.

LOUDSPEAKER SYSTEMS

PHONIC EAR INC.
3880 Cypress Dr.
Petaluma, CA 94954
Tel.: 800-227-0735; FAX: 707-769-9624

Personnel:
James Mulford . . . . President
Richard Pimentel . . . . Vice President, Marketing
Richard Steighner . . . . Vice President, Sales
Thomas Pelka . . . . Vice President

Type of Business:
With a 33-year history of quality, Phonic Ear helps build congregations by making worship services audible to seniors and others who may have difficulty hearing. The Easy Listener™ FM system's comfortable earphones help overcome the distance echo, or background noise that interferes with good hearing. Able to work either with or without your existing sound system it's the economical and easy way to open the full joys of worship to everyone.

PRE-RECORDED CASSETTES & VIDEO

PRE-RECORDED CASSETTES & VIDEO

credence cassettes®

CREDENCE CASSETTES
115 E. Armour Blvd.
Kansas City, MO 64111
Tel.: 816-531-0538; FAX: 816-931-5082

Personnel:
Clarence Thomson . . . . Director
Kathleen Madden . . . . Marketing Director
Holly Sparks, ... Production/Administrator Assistant

Type of Business:
Credence Cassettes is your premier source for religious audio and video cassettes in the Catholic tradition. We offer you more than 250 titles on scripture, prayer, spirituality, education, personal growth and music. We feature nationally known and loved speakers such as Richard Rohr, Joan Chittister, Gil Bailie, Gerald May, Jose Hobday, Eugene LaVerdiere and Megan McKenna. We are also the exclusive distributor of the talks of Thomas Merton.

RENEWAL MUSIC

RENEWAL MUSIC
1000 Cody Rd.
Mobile, AL 36695
Tel.: 800-223-7333; FAX: 334-633-0882

Type of Business:
Renewal Music's goal is to produce music and materials that enhances the Church liturgy. Songs include works by well-known Catholic songwriters along with other contemporary praise and worship songs. Songbooks will contain multiple arrangements along with suggestions for each song's seasonal and liturgical uses. Arrangements will be easy to use for choir and organ, or any size choir or instrumental group.
Watch for the two-volume set, entitled *We Will Meet You There,* coming in August 1997.

BUSINESS & FINANCE

The Catholic Software Co.

THE CATHOLIC SOFTWARE CO.
3768 Rocky River Dr., Suite 313
Cleveland, OH 44111-4050
Tel.: 800-428-3640; FAX: 216-671-1668

Personnel:
Rob Rhodes . . . . President
Peggy T.

Type of Business:
Offering software management solutions to Catholic parishes since 1991. Easy-to-use Window 95, Windows NT, Windows and Macintosh software products. Network ready at no additional cost! Software products available:
- Census, ministry, contribution & stewardship management
- Pledge campaign management
- Financial management: General Ledger with preloaded diocesan chart of accounts; Accounts Payable; Payroll
- School tuition and religious education management

CELEBRATING OUR 4TH ANNIVERSARY IN WINDOWS!

CHURCH REGISTERS & PARISH OFFICE FORMS

Serving Catholic Parishes since 1873.

D.P. MURPHY CO., INC.
1221 Walt Whitman Rd.
Melville, NY 11747
Tel: 516-673-9400; FAX: 516-673-1851

Personnel:
Peter Q. Murphy . . . . President

Type of Business:
Envelope mailing systems to meet every need . . . monthly, bi-monthly, quarterly, semi-annual, yearly sets. Free list maintenance. Census, tithing and fund-raising programs. Data processing and computer services, church stationery, registers, record books, mass cards and certificates. Quality printing and mailing services. Rebinding old church registers is our specialty. Serving Catholic parishes since 1873. Call 800-424-8724.

F.J. REMEY CO., INC.
121 Willis Ave.
Mineola, NY 11501-0589
Tel.: 516-741-5112; FAX: 516-741-0523

Type of Business:
Serving Catholic parishes since 1921 by providing the following products: Envelope Mailing Systems, Annual Offering Envelope Boxsets, Bulk Collection Envelopes, Computer Recording, Collection Baskets, Parish Census, Church Record Books, Parish Office Forms, Church Stationery, Mass Cards, Raffle Tickets and Tuition Supplies.

COMPUTERS & SOFTWARE

The Catholic Software Co.

THE CATHOLIC SOFTWARE CO.
3768 Rocky River Dr., Suite 313
Cleveland, OH 44111-4050
Tel.: 800-428-3640; FAX: 216-671-1668

Personnel:
Rob Rhodes . . . . President
Peggy T.

Type of Business:
Offering software management solutions to Catholic parishes since 1991. Easy-to-use Window 95, Windows NT, Windows and Macintosh software products. Network ready at no additional cost! Software products available:

- Census, ministry, contribution & stewardship management
- Pledge campaign management
- Financial management: General Ledger with preloaded diocesan chart of accounts; Accounts Payable; Payroll
- School tuition and religious education management

CELEBRATING OUR 4TH ANNIVERSARY IN WINDOWS!

NCS (National Computer Systems)
4401 West 76th St.
Edina, MN 55435
Tel.: 800-447-3269; FAX: 612-830-8564
e-mail: www@ncs.com

Personnel:
Mike Seeman. . . . . Marketing Manager, K-12
Fred Green . . . Marketing Mgr., Education Alternative Channels
For more information, contact NCS Telemarketing & Telesales

Type of Business:
For over 30 years, NCS has served the education market with optical mark reading (OMR) and imaging technology. NCS touches one of every two children in our nation's schools. NCS is the leading provider of scanning systems, software, and forms used to automate data collection and accurately report on assessment, instructional, and student records information. NCS scanners and forms are also compatible with most of the leading student administrative and testing software products on the market today.

J.S. PALUCH COMPANY

J.S. PALUCH CO., INC.
3825 N. Willow Rd.
Schiller Park, IL 60176
Tel.: 800-621-5197; FAX: 847-671-5715

Personnel:

Liturgy and Music Resources Customer Service 1-800-566-6150
Parish Bulletins; Calendars; Computer Software: . . . 1-800-621-5197
. . . . Fax: 847-671-5715

Type of Business:

Serving the Church for over 80 years. Liturgy and Music Resources; Parish Sundays - Laser ComExpress; National Vocations Awareness and Religious Art Calendars; Computer Software for parish management.

parish data system, inc.

PARISH DATA SYSTEM, INC.
14425 North 19th Ave.
Phoenix, AZ 85023-6702
Tel.: 800-999-7148; 602-789-0595; FAX: 602-789-0597

Type of Business:

Parish Data System has been providing computer programs and assistance to parishes and schools since 1978. Over 9,000 churches, schools and religious education offices are using PDS products and services.

Products Offered: *Census/Contribution for Windows™ and DOS,* DOS programs; *School Management & Grade Book, Religious Education, General Ledger/Accounts Payable, Payroll, Facility Scheduler, FOCCUS & more.*

Other Services: Data transfers, CASS Certification, Custom Reports, Training, Tuition Collection

RISO
IT IS NOT A COPIER!

RISO, INC.
300 Rosewood Dr.
Danvers, MA 01923
Tel.: 800-876-7476, ext. 705; 508-739-3553; FAX: 508-777-2517
website: http://www.riso.com

Personnel:

Mike Maki . . . . Church Market Specialist
Richard Grassis . . . . Vice President, Marketing

Type of Business:

RISO, Inc. presents the Risograph, incorporating breakthrough technology in enhanced imaging for superior print quality, and new paper handling features that contribute to increased reliability and ease of use. The Risograph offers cost effective printing on a wide range of paper stocks from 14 to 110 lbs., in sizes from 4″ x 6″ to 11″ x 17″ in 16 different colors. The Risograph is compatible with PC or Macintosh computers or function as a stand-alone duplicator.

SERVANT PC RESOURCES, INC.
RR5, P.O. Box 255
Jersey Shore, PA 17740
Tel.: 800-773-7570; FAX: 717-398-2501
website: www.servantpc.com

Type of Business:

Servant Keeper® is a powerful, flexible, yet extremely easy to use, Church Management Program for Windows® or Windows 95. Servant Keeper® handles membership lists, mailing labels, scheduling, attendance, pledges and contributions and includes the best searching tool on the market plus much more. Servant Keeper® linkes to Quicken/Quickbooks® for full accounting. Call today to find out why so many parishes are switching to Servant Keeper® or visit our website.

THE SOFTWARE LIBRARY
3300 Bass Lake Rd., #304
Brooklyn Center, MN 55429
Tel.: 800-247-8044; FAX: 612-566-2250
http://ourwold.compuserve.com/homepages/Software Library

Personnel:
- Charles Zimmer . . . . President
- Karen Johnson. . . . . Sales/Marketing
- Linda O'Brien, ... Product Specialist

Type of Business:
The Software Library provides computer consulting, CMS software products, and support services to over 1500 churches. The support services include education and training, toll free telephone assistance, and product upgrades. Client workshops are presented in the major cities annually. The CMS software products are a very good tool to help manage parish administration and communication. CMS also provides the data required by the various diocesan reports.

CONSULTANTS

CUNNEEN
PARISH
FUNDRAISING

CUNNEEN PARISH FUNDRAISING SERVICES, INC.
67 South Turnpike Rd.
Wallingford, CT 06492
Tel.: 203-265-0065; FAX: 203-284-3451

Personnel:
- Frank J. Cunneen . . . . President
- James F. Cunneen . . . . Director of Operations
- John F. Cunneen, ... Vice President
- Daniel J. Wendt, ... Director of Mid-West Operations

Type of Business:
The Cunneen Co. offers Catholic Parish's 16 years and 4,000 parish campaign's worth of expertise. Our Stewardship, Increased Weekly Giving, and Time, Talent & Treasure programs set the standard in our industry. The results are guaranteed in writing. Our Door to Door and In-Pew campaigns are unequalled. Our Directors are of outstanding quality, and will guide your parish through the campaign with the utmost professionalism. Our unique production, lettershop and printing capabilities also bring you an added advantage.

KELLY
PROFESSIONAL FUND RAISING CONSULTANTS
203 West Seventh St. • Traverse City, MI 49684 • 616/947-9636

KELLY-PROFESSIONAL FUND RAISING CONSULTANTS
203 W. Seventh St.
Traverse City, MI 49684
Tel.: 616-947-9636; FAX: 616-922-8120

Personnel:
- Joe Kelly . . . . President
- Al Kelly . . . . M.P.H., M.A., C.F.R.E.
- Ed Kelly . . . . M.P.H., M.A.
- Mike Kelly

Type of Business:
Establishment of Development Office with on-site training of a local person as Development Director.
- Capital Campaigns
- Stewardship Programs/Annual Renewals
- Major Gifts
- Planned Giving
- Feasibility Studies

Services to Dioceses, Parishes, Elementary & Secondary Schools. 28 YEARS EXPERIENCE.

Kirby Smith
Associates, Inc.
Ministry of Church Finance

KIRBY-SMITH ASSOCIATES, INC.
5 Fawn Dr.
Quarryville, PA 17566
Tel.: 1-800-762-3996; 717-284-3100; FAX: 717-284-3659
website: www.kirbysmith.com; e-mail: kirbysmith@aol.com

Personnel:
- C. Eugene Musser . . . . President
- Karl T. Frick . . . . Director Ministry Development

Type of Business:
Since our founding in 1938, we have served more than 5,000 Parishes, Christian Communities and schools, and have raised over two billion dollars. Kirby-Smith programs include detailed on-site counseling, organizational guidance, comprehensive materials, as well as long-term counsultation and stewardship training. We offer a full range of services to better meet the needs of your parish or school; Capital and Budget Campaigns, Feasibility Studies, Pre-Campaign Planning and Strategic Planning. Meeting the needs of The Christian Community we serve is our ministry and the service we bring to you.

John V. McCarthy and Associates

JOHN V. McCARTHY & ASSOCIATES INC.
16250 Northland Dr., Ste. 200
Southfield, MI 48075-5266
Tel.: 800-444-1840; FAX: 248-552-0857 (eff. 5/97)

Personnel:
John V. McCarthy . . . . (President
Joseph H. Schram . . . . Vice President
Frank J. Krajca . . . . Vice President Marketing
Thomas A. Parker . . . . Vice President Operations

Type of Business:
Specialists in fund-raising: exclusively for Catholic parishes, dioceses, schools and other institutions. Individual program timetables are designed to allow for the composition of the parish or institution. Established in 1954, we have completed over 4,100 programs. We charge a flat fee with no additional costs for travel or living expenses. Our assigned Account Executive is on site full-time, except for small parish programs which can be designed on a consultation basis. We provide unmatched follow-up service for all clients.

FINANCIAL SERVICES

THE ROGERS COMPANY
VISION FUNDING SPECIALISTS

THE ROGERS COMPANY
10713 Plano Rd.
Dallas, TX 75238
Tel.: 800-527-1354; FAX: 214-349-4741

Personnel:
Del Rogers, Sr. . . . . President
Del Rogers, Jr. . . . . Vice President of Sales & Marketing
Trevis Otey . . . . Budget Enhancement Specialist

Type of Business:
The Rogers Company programs, FORWARD IN FAITH and STEWARDSHIP ENRICHMENT, are scriptural responses to answer the financial needs of the church. FORWARD IN FAITH teaches faithful giving to the ongoing ministries of the church. STEWARDSHIP ENRICHMENT brings people to a point of spiritual growth that leads to gifts beyond regular giving. Since 1977, The Rogers Company has raised billions of dollars in churches across America for budgets, buildings, expansion, and other visions. Call today, 1-800-527-1354.

FUND-RAISING SERVICES

ACB
AMERICAN CITY BUREAU

AMERICAN CITY BUREAU
1721 Moon Lake Blvd.
Hoffman Estates, IL 60194
Tel.: 800-786-GOAL; FAX: 847-490-5860

Personnel:
James J. Biggins . . . . Chairman and CEO
Marcus T. Young . . . . President

Type of Business:
With eighty-four years of fund-raising success, American City Bureau is a national and international full service fund-raising counsel to not-for-profit organizations that has helped over 8900 clients raise more than $3 billion. Our fund-raising expertise has touched: archdioceses, dioceses and churches – healthcare related organizations • youth-related organizations • hospitals and medical centers • Catholic colleges and secondary schools – and social service agencies.

HANK BRANDT ASSOCIATES, INC
FUND RAISING
& Public Relations Specialists

HANK BRANDT ASSOCIATES, INC.
P.O. Box 12383
Tucson, AZ 85732
Tel.: 520-745-9905; FAX: 520-747-7774

Personnel:
Bruce Brandt . . . . Vice President

Type of Business:
Established in 1958, Hank Brandt Associates provides highly personalized service, which is essential in reaching fund-raising potential. Each Hank Brandt Associates campaign is tailor-made to suit the client's needs. For 38 years, the firm has continuously attained top-notch results in conducting Annual Appeals, Capital Fund Campaigns and Increased Giving Programs along with public relations services and feasibility studies. Hank Brandt Associates offers in-depth experience and the edge to meet the most challenging financial objectives.

Cathedral
CORPORATION
Church Services Division

CATHEDRAL CORPORATION
P.O. Box 1293
Buffalo, NY 14240
Tel.: 800-828-7455; FAX: 716-667-7309

Personnel:
Marianne Gaige . . . . President
Stephen L. Miller . . . . Director of Marketing
Maurie L. Jachimiak . . . . Sales/Service Manager

Type of Business:
Cathedral Corporation has been a full-service supplier of products and services designed to enhance the financial health of parishes for over 60 years, including:
- Mailed envelopes; monthly, bi-monthly, quarterly, Custom and money-saving Compuset envelopes
- Boxed sets; adult, youth and children's
- Cost-effective offering envelope recording and reporting
- Stewardship, Weekly renewal, and Capital campaigns
- Laser personalized mailings for improved parishioner communications
- Offset printing, addressing and mailing to fill a variety of parish and school needs.

The Catholic Software Co.

THE CATHOLIC SOFTWARE CO.
3768 Rocky River Dr., Suite 313
Cleveland, OH 44111-4050
Tel.: 800-428-3640; FAX: 216-671-1668

Personnel:
Rob Rhodes . . . . President
Peggy T.

Type of Business:
Offering software management solutions to Catholic parishes since 1991. Easy-to-use Window 95, Windows NT, Windows and Macintosh software products. Network ready at no additional cost! Software products available:
- Census, ministry, contribution & stewardship management
- Pledge campaign management
- Financial management: General Ledger with preloaded diocesan chart of accounts; Accounts Payable; Payroll
- School tuition and religious education management

CELEBRATING OUR 4TH ANNIVERSARY IN WINDOWS!

CCS
CELEBRATES 50 YEARS

COMMUNITY COUNSELLING SERVICE CO., INC.
350 Fifth Ave., Ste. 7210
New York, NY 10118
Tel.: 800-223-6733; FAX: 212-967-6451

Personnel:
William B. Hanrahan . . . . President
Robert Kissane . . . . Executive Vice President
Patrick W. Moughan . . . . Managing Director Midwest Division
Joseph F. X. Lee. . . . . Vice President

Type of Business:
CCS is celebrating its 50th year of service to the Church. We have become one of the largest, most widely recommended fund raising firms in the world. CCS has successfully planned and managed fund raising campaigns for a variety of Catholic dioceses, parishes, universities, colleges, high schools, hospitals, homes for the aged, social service agencies, seminaries and religious communities. Regional offices in Chicago, San Francisco, London and Toronto. Call 1-800-223-6733 for an estimate of your potential.

CUNNEEN
PARISH
FUNDRAISING

CUNNEEN PARISH FUNDRAISING SERVICES, INC.
67 South Turnpike Rd.
Wallingford, CT 06492
Tel.: 203-265-0065; FAX: 203-284-3451

Personnel:
Frank J. Cunneen . . . . President
James F. Cunneen . . . . Director of Operations
John F. Cunneen. . . . . Vice President
Daniel J. Wendt. . . . . Director of Mid-West Operations

Type of Business:
The Cunneen Co. offers Catholic Parish's 16 years and 4,000 parish campaign's worth of expertise. Our Stewardship, Increased Weekly Giving, and Time, Talent & Treasure programs set the standard in our industry. The results are guaranteed in writing. Our Door to Door and In-Pew campaigns are unequalled. Our Directors are of outstanding quality, and will guide your parish through the campaign with the utmost professionalism. Our unique production, lettershop and printing capabilities also bring you an added advantage.

DEVELOPMENT DIRECTION INC.
1539 Franklin Ave.
Mineola, NY 11501
Tel.: 516-747-0100; FAX: 516-747-0103
800-253-1305

Personnel:

William J. McGuire . . . . President
Charles P. McCormack. . . . . Vice President
Thomas P. Murphy. . . . . Vice President

Continued in Next Column

Continued from Previous Column

Type of Business:

DDI has been serving the Catholic market since 1961. It organizes and conducts campaigns of every type, with goals ranging from $50,000 to multi-million dollars. Fees are based on time and service. A financial analysis precedes a formal proposal. A resume of the assigned consultant is furnished prior to the signed agreement. A team concept assures the client of continuity and personalized attention. Geographically, DDI has worked in 49 of the 50 states, South America, Africa and India.

FCI

FIRST COUNSEL, INC

FIRST COUNSEL, INC.
Stewardship Counsel Div.
428 E. Fourth St., Ste. 100
Charlotte, NC 28202
Tel.: 800-313-1645; FAX: 704-342-1700
e-mail: Info@firstcounsel.com

Personnel:

Dallas Mackey . . . . Chairman, Executive Committee
Fred E. Beeson . . . . Chairman & CEO
Robert J. Simonds . . . . Chairman, FCI Northeast
James Glass . . . . Chairman, FCI West

Type of Business:

The STEWARDSHIP COUNSEL DIVISION was created by First Counsel, Inc. to meet the unique fundraising needs of churches and church-related organizations. First Counsel has helped these Catholic institutions achieve their fundraising objectives:

- St. Barnabas Health System — Gibsonia, PA
- St. Anthony Hospital Foundation — Oklahoma City, OK
- St. Mary's Hospital Foundation — Knoxville, TN
- St. Joseph's Hospital Foundation — Asheville, NC
- Diocese of Greensburg — Greensburg, PA
- Christ Church Cathedral — Louisville, KY
- St. Mary's Catholic Church — Greenville, SC
- Charlotte Catholic High School — Charlotte, NC

With six regional offices, FCI comprises a dynamic team of professionals dedicated to integrity and results. FCI offers preliminary advice without cost or obligation.

FCI New England, Brunswick, ME — FCI Northeast, New York, NY — FCI Southeast, Charlotte, NC — FCI South, Atlanta, GA —FCI Southwest, Dallas/Fort Worth, TX — FCI West, Los Angeles, CA

Ghiorse & Sorrenti INC.

FUND RAISING • MARKETING • PUBLIC RELATIONS

GHIORSE & SORRENTI, INC.
Cali Corporate Center
50 Tice Blvd.
Woodcliff Lake, NJ 07675
Tel.: 201-307-1970; FAX: 201-307-5632

Personnel:

Peter W. Ghiorse . . . . President & CEO
Dan Sorrenti . . . . Vice President & COO
Mary Ann Winters . . . . Senior Vice President
Glenn Vallach . . . . . VP for Public Relations & Communications

Continued in Next Column

Continued from Previous Column

Type of Business:

Ghiorse & Sorrenti, Inc., is a full-service fund-raising and public relations firm specializing in capital campaigns for religious, healthcare, education and social service organizations. GSI offers highly tailored services, the personal involvement of the principals, and a team of seasoned fund raising and public relations executives. Resident campaign management and consulting services are available.

HARVEST DEVELOPMENT, INC.

HARVEST DEVELOPMENT, INC.
200 Executive Way
Ponte Vedra Beach, FL 32082
Tel: (614) 263-7996; (904) 273-2108; FAX: (904) 285-1002

Personnel:

Paul D'Alessandro
John Patrick Alves
Jack Gibbons
Martin Alves
Greg Switaj

Type of Business:

A full service fund raising and development consulting firm dedicated to helping our Catholic clients successfully achieve their development and campaign goals.

KELLY

PROFESSIONAL FUND RAISING CONSULTANTS

203 West Seventh St. • Traverse City, MI 49684 • 616/947-9636

KELLY-PROFESSIONAL FUND RAISING CONSULTANTS
203 W. Seventh St.
Traverse City, MI 49684
Tel.: 616-947-9636; FAX: 616-922-8120

Personnel:

Joe Kelly . . . . President
Al Kelly . . . . M.P.H., M.A., C.F.R.E.
Ed Kelly . . . . M.P.H., M.A.
Mike Kelly

Type of Business:

Establishment of Development Office with on-site training of a local person as Development Director.

- Capital Campaigns
- Stewardship Programs/Annual Renewals
- Major Gifts
- Planned Giving
- Feasibility Studies

Services to Dioceses, Parishes, Elementary & Secondary Schools. 28 YEARS EXPERIENCE.

Kirby Smith
Associates, Inc.
Ministry of Church Finance

KIRBY-SMITH ASSOCIATES, INC.
5 Fawn Dr.
Quarryville, PA 17566
Tel.: 1-800-762-3996; 717-284-3100; FAX: 717-284-3659
website: www.kirbysmith.com; e-mail: kirbysmith@aol com

Personnel:
C. Eugene Musser . . . . President
Karl T. Frick . . . . Director Ministry Development

Type of Business:
Since our founding in 1938, we have served more than 5,000 Parishes, Christian Communities and schools, and have raised over two billion dollars. Kirby-Smith programs include detailed on-site counseling, organizational guidance, comprehensive materials, as well as long-term counsultation and stewardship training. We offer a full range of services to better meet the needs of your parish or school; Capital and Budget Campaigns, Feasibility Studies, Pre-Campaign Planning and Strategic Planning. Meeting the needs of The Christian Community we serve is our ministry and the service we bring to you.

John V. McCarthy
and Associates

JOHN V. McCARTHY & ASSOCIATES INC.
16250 Northland Dr., Ste. 200
Southfield, MI 48075-5266
Tel.: 800-444-1840; FAX: 810-552-0857 (eff. 5/97)

Personnel:
John V. McCarthy . . . . President
Joseph H. Schram . . . . Vice President
Frank J. Krajca . . . . Vice President Marketing
Thomas A. Parker . . . . Vice President Operations

Type of Business:
Specialists in fund-raising: exclusively for Catholic parishes, dioceses, schools and other institutions. Individual program timetables are designed to allow for the composition of the parish or institution. Established in 1954, we have completed over 4,100 programs. We charge a flat fee with no additional costs for travel or living expenses. Our assigned Account Executive is on site full-time, except for small parish programs which can be designed on a consultation basis. We provide unmatched follow-up service for all clients.

THE MARTIN J. MORAN CO.
Washington D.C. • San Diego • North Palm Beach • Boston
Catholic Fund-Raising Counsel

MARTIN J. MORAN CO.
One Pennsylvania Plaza
New York, NY 10119
Tel.: 212-736-9550

Type of Business:
The Moran Co. has been raising great amounts of money for its clients for a variety of needs. The key to success has been the design and conduct of a proven, time-tested Moran Co. Plan for generating both dollars and a high level of participation.

THE NATIONAL MUSEUM OF CATHOLIC ART & HISTORY

THE NATIONAL MUSEUM OF CATHOLIC ART & HISTORY
54 West 50th St. @ 30 Rockefeller Plaza
New York, NY 10020
Tel.: 212-957-8866; FAX: 212-957-5293

Personnel:
Christina Cox . . . . Executive Director
Larissa Van Duser . . . . Curator

Type of Business:
Exhibiting Religious Works of Old Masters and Contemporary Artists. Artists Available for Commissions. Collecting and Restoring Religious Art and Artifacts including Paintings, Sculpture, Crucifixes, Chalices, Monstrances, Bibles, Books, Photos, Altar Candlesticks, Vestments, Scapulars, Communion Bells, Madonnas, Church Interiors and Catholic Historical Items. Touring Exhibits. Cultural and Educational Programs.

THE ROGERS COMPANY
VISION FUNDING SPECIALISTS

THE ROGERS COMPANY
10713 Plano Rd.
Dallas, TX 75238
Tel.: 800-527-1354; FAX: 214-349-4741

Personnel:
Del Rogers, Sr. . . . . President
Del Rogers, Jr. . . . . Vice President of Sales & Marketing
Trevis Otey . . . . Budget Enhancement Specialist

Type of Business:
The Rogers Company programs, FORWARD IN FAITH and STEWARDSHIP ENRICHMENT, are scriptural responses to answer the financial needs of the church. FORWARD IN FAITH teaches faithful giving to the ongoing ministries of the church. STEWARDSHIP ENRICHMENT brings people to a point of spiritual growth that leads to gifts beyond regular giving. Since 1977, The Rogers Company has raised billions of dollars in churches across America for budgets, buildings, expansion, and other visions. Call today, 1-800-527-1354.

RUOTOLO ASSOCIATES INC.
Horizon Square
29 Broadway, Ste. 210
Cresskill, NJ 07626
Tel.: 201-568-3898; FAX: 201-568-8783

Personnel:
George C. Ruotolo, Jr. . . . . C.F.R.E., President

Type of Business:
Comprehensive development programs, capital campaigns, annual funds, planned giving, feasibility/planning studies, executive search, student recruitment, and marketing/public relations efforts. Specializing in service to Catholic institutions, including dioceses, schools, churches, religious orders, and social service and health organizations, serving the country through our four regional offices.

FUND RAISING SUPPLIES

AmericanChurch
a division of AmericanPaper Group, Inc.

AMERICAN CHURCH,
A DIVISION OF AMERICAN PAPER GROUP
8401 Southern Blvd.
Youngstown, OH 44512
Tel.: 800-228-6101; FAX: 330-758-9981

Personnel:
James P. Fitzgerald . . . . V.P. Sales & Marketing
Ron Blakeman . . . . Sales Manager
Rob Turnbull . . . . VP National Accounts

Type of Business:
World's largest supplier of offering envelopes
- Envelopes, Custom Printed
- Boxed Sets
- Mailing Programs
- Direct Banking

Honor The Gift........Honor The Giver

B&D ... CONTRIBUTOR RECOGNITION PRODUCTS
119 South Mansfield Blvd.
Cherry Hill, NJ 08034-3611
1-800-873-3180; FAX: 609-429-3772

Honor those who Give, and they are yours forever ... Contributor Recognition is a key fund raising element that increases response and levels of giving. Our products create a permanent bond between the giver and their Church. Impressive, awe-inspiring, and motivational they enhance Church decor in an understated elegant manner. Our products can accommodate Churches of all sizes. They are also expandable, of high quality and most economical.
We are as close as your telephone.

CARROLL ART, INC.
710 NE 26th St.
Fort Lauderdale, FL 33305
Tel.: 800-876-4569; FAX: 954-561-4098

Personnel:
David Nagle .... President Designer
Liza Palmer .... Sales Manager
Andrea Speier .... Sales Rep.
Robert Perkins .... Sales Rep.

Type of Business:
Carroll Art has been in business for 12 years. We design and custom build all types of plaques and memorials including the tree of life, plaques, recognition systems, church signs, donor plates, custom sculptures, and memorials are just a few of our products. We can provide you with the perfect fund raising tool.

HERSHEY

FUND RAISING

HERSHEY FUND RAISING
Hershey, Pennsylvania
Tel.: 800-217-8032

Type of Business:
Hershey's Fund Raising Products – Hershey's All American Candy Shoppe Assortment contains 40 assorted bars ($20 profit per box). Hershey's Candy Shoppe Max contains 50 assorted bars plus 2 free bars ($27 profit per box). Plus every box of $1.00 bars contains a free Hershey's All American Savings Card™ with discounts worth hundreds of dollars at national merchants and the chance to win $10,000 for your school. Contact your Fund Raising Distributor for information or call 800-217-8032.

JUMBO JACK'S COOKBOOKS
AUDUBON MEDIA CORPORATION
301 BROADWAY • AUDUBON IA 50025
1-800-798-2635

JUMBO JACK'S COOKBOOKS
301 Broadway
Audubon, IA 56025
Tel.: 712-563-2635; FAX: 712-563-3118

Personnel:
Michael J. Ruddy......................... Sales Manager

Type of Business:
Jumbo Jack's Cookbooks is a high quality fundraiser cookbook printer. We specialize in very competitive prices, liberal terms, no initial investment, and friendly professional service. We offer a variety of bindings and the flexibility to personalize your cookbook to suit your needs and wants, many times at no extra charge. Many groups have earned $500 to $50,000 and more on a successful cookbook project. Call 1-800-798-2635 today for our Complete Cookbook Planning Guide.

TREES•OF•LIFE

**A proven successful fund raiser
whose strong lines and rich colors
will enhance the space into which it is placed.**

DAVID KLASS ART STUDIOS
136 West 24th St.
New York, NY 10011
Tel.: 212-243-7633; FAX: 212-243-7633

Personnel:
David Klass . . . . Owner, Designer

Type of Business:
Since 1968 David Klass has created numerous Trees of Life. Each one is custom designed to meet your needs. The finest select hardwoods, brasses and bronze are used.
Our beautiful designs and workmanship are ideal for donor recognition and fund raising drives. Special symbols and imagery meaningful to your parish can be incorporated into the design.

MESSERSMITH PROMOTIONS, INC.
P.O. Box 247
New Hampton, IA 50659-0247
Tel.: 800-726-1206; FAX: 515-394-4556

Personnel:
Bob Messersmith

Type of Business:
For over 30 years supplying churches with keepsakes to commemorate anniversaries. A large selection of mugs, plates, ornaments, etc.

F. J. REMEY CO., INC.
121 Willis Ave.
Mineola, NY 11501-0589
Tel.: 516-741-5112; FAX: 516-741-0523

Type of Business:
Serving Catholic parishes since 1921 by providing the following products: Envelope Mailing Systems, Annual Offering Envelope Boxsets, Bulk Collection Envelopes, Computer Recording, Collection Baskets, Parish Census, Church Record Books, Parish Office Forms, Church Stationery, Mass Cards, Raffle Tickets and Tuition Supplies.

THE PRINTERY HOUSE
Conception Abbey · CONCEPTION · MISSOURI 64433

THE PRINTERY HOUSE
Conception Abbey
Conception, MO 64433
Tel.: 816-944-2632; FAX: 816-944-2582
e-mail: gnelson@msc-net.com

Personnel:
Gerald E. Nelson . . . . General Manager
Ron Riggs . . . . Director of Sales & Marketing

Type of Business:
The Printery House manufactures Christian greeting cards as a not-for-profit extension of the apostolic mission of Conception Abbey, a Benedictine community dedicated to a Christian life of work and prayer. We make our cards available to religious organizations to earn 50% with no risk, no prepayment. Call 800-889-0105 for your fund-raiser packet and more information.

THE ARTIST'S HAND MAKES THE DIFFERENCE

SANFORD WERFEL- ARTIST

SANFORD WERFEL - ARTIST
425 Old Georges Rd.,
North Brunswick, NJ 08902
Tel.: 800-443-3744; 908-297-1166; FAX: 908-297-7770

Type of Business:
Since 1968, Mr. Werfel's sculptures have been helping parishes to INSPIRE and MOTIVATE GIVING through the use of his original sculptures. Building drives, capital or endowment funds, sacrificial giving, and tithing programs all benefit from using Donor Recognition Sculptures. Call or write for FREE INFORMATION. Included will be costs and designs as well as a "HOW-TO-USE" guide that tells how your parish can use sculpture to raise funds. Good art is forever.

Sanford White

SANFORD WHITE CO. INC.
PO Box 157
Pawtucket, RI 02862-0157
Tel.: 800-245-7825; FAX: 401-728-3080

Personnel:
Stuart Aaronson
Michael Tally

Type of Business:
American designer and manufacturer of custom donor, volunteer and staff recognition products. For over forty years we have produced high quality recognition gifts at an affordable price. Our product line includes: Lapel pins, Medallions, Bookmarks, Key Chains, Letter Openers, Ornaments, Magnets, Wooden Gift Boxes and Desk Sets, Pewter Paperweights, Plaques and Lucite Embedments. Call our toll-free number and speak to an experienced member of our staff with your requirements or request our full color recognition catalog.

INSURANCE

CATHOLIC ORDER OF FORESTERS
355 Shuman Blvd., P.O. Box 3012
Naperville, IL 60555-7012
Tel.: 630-983-4920; 800-552-0145; FAX: 630-983-5113

Type of Business:
Catholic Order of Foresters, a fraternal benefit society with 135,000 members nationwide, has been providing Catholics with financial protection since 1883. In addition to quality life insurance and annuity products, COF offers added value through fraternal benefits—parish and diocese loans, college scholarships, student loans, orphan benefits, local youth and adult court activities, and benevolence that includes a matching funds program.

Personnel:
Robert Ciesla . . . . High Chief Ranger
Armand R. Lemire . . . . Vice High Chief Ranger
Leo J. Beranek . . . . High Sec.-Treas.

INVESTMENT ADVISORS

CBIS
Christian Brothers Investment Services, Inc.

CHRISTIAN BROTHERS INVESTMENT SERVICES
675 Third Ave., 31st Fl.
New York, NY 10017-5704
Tel.: 212-490-0800; FAX: 212-490-6092

Personnel:
Michael W. O'Hern, FSC . . . . President & CEO
Jessica W. Jennings. . . . . Vice President-Marketing

Type of Business:
Established in 1981, Christian Brothers Investment Services, Inc., (CBIS), acts as investment advisor exclusively to Catholic organizations throughout the world. As a registered investment advisor we currently work with over 850 organizations representing total assets under advisement of $1.5 billion. CBIS offers individually managed portfolios as well as nine pooled investment funds which provide a wide range of risk and return characteristics and a broad choice of investment management styles.
Our comprehensive advisory services include: needs analysis, policy consulting, custody and reporting, investment management and performance evaluation. In addition, all investments made on behalf of participants are guided by CBIS's socially responsible investment principles. CBIS's "Faith and Finance" standards define our belief that investing and maintaining our Catholic ethics are not incompatible activities; they are indeed, our moral obligation.

INVESTMENT MANAGEMENT

CATHOLIC VALUES INVESTMENT TRUST
1000 Lafayette Blvd.
Bridgeport, CT 06604
Tel.: 1-888-974-4486; 1-203-330-5197

Personnel:
Dr. Walter R. Miller, Ph.D. . . . . Secretary to the Board

Type of Business:
Catholic Values Investment Trust offers dioceses, parishes and other Catholic organizations and institutions a quality long-term growth mutual fund investment. What makes CVIT different from other investment options is that CVIT invests only in companies that conduct their business in a way consistent with the basic tenets and teachings of the Catholic Church.
The quality of the fund management and adherance to these Catholic views make this an investment you can put your faith in.

MINISTRY OF CHURCH FINANCE

KIRBY-SMITH ASSOCIATES, INC.
5 Fawn Dr.
Quarryville, PA 17566
Tel.: 1-800-762-3996; 717-284-3100; FAX: 717-284-3659
website: www.kirbysmith.com; e-mail: kirbysmith@aol.com

Personnel:
C. Eugene Musser . . . . President
Karl T. Frick . . . . Director Ministry Development

Type of Business:
Since our founding in 1938, we have served more than 5,000 Parishes, Christian Communities and schools, and have raised over two billion dollars. Kirby-Smith programs include detailed on-site counseling, organizational guidance, comprehensive materials, as well as long-term counsultation and stewardship training. We offer a full range of services to better meet the needs of your parish or school; Capital and Budget Campaigns, Feasibility Studies, Pre-Campaign Planning and Strategic Planning. Meeting the needs of The Christian Community we serve is our ministry and the service we bring to you.

OFFICE EQUIPMENT & SUPPLIES

AMERICAN CHURCH,
A DIVISION OF AMERICAN PAPER GROUP
8401 Southern Blvd.
Youngstown, OH 44512
Tel.: 800-228-6101; FAX: 330-758-9981

Personnel:
James P. Fitzgerald. . . . . V.P. Sales & Marketing
Ron Blakeman. . . . . Sales Manager
Rob Turnbull . . . . VP National Accounts

Type of Business:
World's largest supplier of offering envelopes
- Envelopes, Custom Printed
- Boxed Sets
- Mailing Programs
- Direct Banking

RISO, INC.
300 Rosewood Dr.
Danvers, MA 01923
Tel.: 800-876-7476, ext. 705; 508-739-3553; FAX: 508-777-2517
website: http://www.riso.com

Personnel:
Mike Maki . . . . Church Market Specialist
Richard Grassis . . . . Vice President, Marketing

Type of Business:
RISO, INc. presents the Risograph, incorporating breakthrough technology in enhanced imaging for superior print quality, and new paper handling features that contribute to increased reliability and ease of use. The Risograph offers cost effective printing on a wide range of paper stocks from 14 to 110 lbs., in sizes from 4″ x 6″ to 11″ x 17″ in 16 different colors. The Risograph is compatible with PC or Macintosh computers or function as a standalone duplicator.

He's outnumbered
2,500 to 1.
THE ARMY NEEDS PRIESTS.
The Catholic soldiers and families in the Army community share the same problems as civilians. Only more so. Most are young, have high pressure jobs, and many are away from home for the first time. But the ratio of parishioners to priests is more than twice as high in the Army as it is in the civilian world. So, if we're going to provide proper spiritual guidance and support, the Army Chaplain Corps needs reinforcements. For more information, call: 1-800-452-7617.
ARMY CHAPLAIN CORPS.
BE ALL YOU CAN BE.

ORGANIZATIONAL DEVELOPMENT

HARVEST DEVELOPMENT, INC.

HARVEST DEVELOPMENT, INC.
200 Executive Way
Ponte Vedra Beach, FL 32082
Tel: (614) 263-7996; (904) 273-2108; FAX: (904) 285-1002

Personnel:
Paul D'Alessandro
John Patrick Alves
Jack Gibbons
Martin Alves
Greg Switaj

Type of Business:
A full service fund raising and development consulting firm dedicated to helping our Catholic clients successfully achieve their development and campaign goals.

RECOGNITION GIFTS & AWARDS

SW Sanford White

SANFORD WHITE CO. INC.
PO Box 157
Pawtucket, RI 02862-0157
Tel.: 800-245-7825; FAX: 401-728-3080

Personnel:
Stuart Aaronson
Michael Tally

Type of Business:
American designer and manufacturer of custom donor, volunteer and staff recognition products. For over forty years we have produced high quality recognition gifts at an affordable price. Our product line includes: Lapel pins, Medallions, Bookmarks, Key Chains, Letter Openers, Ornaments, Magnets, Wooden Gift Boxes and Desk Sets, Pewter Paperweights, Plaques and Lucite Embedments. Call our toll-free number and speak to an experienced member of our staff with your requirements or request our full color recognition catalog.

STEWARDSHIP

R THE ROGERS COMPANY
VISION FUNDING SPECIALISTS

THE ROGERS COMPANY
10713 Plano Rd.
Dallas, TX 75238
Tel.: 800-527-1354; FAX: 214-349-4741

Personnel:
Del Rogers, Sr. . . . . President
Del Rogers, Jr. . . . . Vice President of Sales & Marketing
Trevis Otey . . . . Budget Enhancement Specialist

Type of Business:
The Rogers Company programs, FORWARD IN FAITH and STEWARDSHIP ENRICHMENT, are scriptural responses to answer the financial needs of the church. FORWARD IN FAITH teaches faithful giving to the ongoing ministries of the church. STEWARDSHIP ENRICHMENT brings people to a point of spiritual growth that leads to gifts beyond regular giving. Since 1977, The Rogers Company has raised billions of dollars in churches across America for budgets, buildings, expansion, and other visions. Call today, 1-800-527-1354.

STRATEGIC PLANNING

HARVEST DEVELOPMENT, INC.

HARVEST DEVELOPMENT, INC.
200 Executive Way
Ponte Vedra Beach, FL 32082
Tel: (614) 263-7996; (904) 273-2108; FAX: (904) 285-1002

Personnel:
Paul D'Alessandro
John Patrick Alves
Jack Gibbons
Martin Alves
Greg Switaj

Type of Business:
A full service fund raising and development consulting firm dedicated to helping our Catholic clients successfully achieve their development and campaign goals.

CHURCH FURNISHINGS

CHURCHORGANSYSTEMS

CHURCH ORGAN SYSTEMS
422 Wards Corner Rd.
Loveland, OH 45140-8390
Tel.: 513-576-4660; FAX: 513-576-6781

Personnel:
Dwane Kuhn . . . . Vice President
Darlene Davis. Administrative Assistant
Rodney Barbour . . . . Manager Sales & Service
David Wade . . . . Director Engrg.

Type of Business:
Church Organ Systems, a division of The Baldwin Piano and Organ Co., is dedicated to serving churches with products and programs designed to support music ministry.

THE MARSHALL CO.
620 N. 9th, P.O. Box 700
Payette, ID 83661
Tel.: 208-642-3344; 800-635-9026; FAX: 208-642-9537

Type of Business:
A commitment to solid wood quality, innovative design, value and service of distinctive church furniture. Special designs, fabrics and finishes. Custom fixed and portable pews. Chancel furniture and groupings. Marshallock chairs, wall crosses, carvings and accessories.

MORODER-INTERNATIONAL STATUARY & ALTAR, INC.
7406 N. Santa Monica Blvd.
Milwaukee, WI 53217
Tel.: 414-351-0130

Type of Business:
Over 88 years of ecclesiastic service: Designers, Sculptors, Manufacturers—marble, wood, mosaic, bronze.

NEW HOLLAND
Custom Woodwork Ltd.
Church Furniture

If You Can Imagine It ... We Can Build It!

NEW HOLLAND CUSTOM WOODWORK, LTD.
313 Prospect St., P.O. Box 217
New Holland, PA 17557-0217
Tel.: 800-648-9663; FAX: 717-354-2481
e-mail: nhcw@redrose.net
Website: http://www.newhollandwood.com

Personnel:
Jeff Lewis . . . . Director of Sales & Marketing

Type of Business:
Located in the heart of Pennsylvania Dutch Country, New Holland Church Furniture manufactures high quality standard and custom pews including "Radius" segmented and straight. Also a full line of stack chairs which may interlock and sanctuary furnishings. Specialize in solid wood construction.

RAMBUSCH

RAMBUSCH
40 West 13th St.
New York, NY 10011
Tel.: 212-675-0400; FAX: 212-620-4687

Personnel:
Viggo Bech Rambusch . . . . Senior Project Director
Martin V. Rambusch . . . . Stained Glass Director

Type of Business:
Since 1898, creating church interiors, liturgical furnishings, and art work. Fine restoration of church interiors. In-house studios and shops for designing and executing stained glass, church lighting systems, art metal work, and decorative painting

CONRAD SCHMITT STUDIOS, INC.
2405 S. 162nd St.
New Berlin, WI 53151
Tel.: 800-969-3033; 414-786-3030; FAX: 414-786-9036

Personnel:
Heidi Gruenke Emery . . . . Vice President & Marketing Director

Type of Business:
Since 1889, this family-owned Studio has restored and decorated hundreds of interiors across the country. Their scope of work includes the investigation and documentation of original decorative schemes; the restoration of those schemes through the application of various decorative techniques including gilding, glazing, marbleizing, stenciling, and graining, as well as the design, fabrication, conservation or replication of murals and stained glass. The Studio can assist projects in the early stages with architectural samples and rendering for fund-raising. Recently completed projects include St. Josaphat's Basilica, Milwaukee, WI; St. Ann's, Napoleanville, LA; and St. Bernard's, Akron, OH.

ALTARS, TABLERNACLES, ETC.

ANTHONY JOHN BELLOMO / THE BLACK FOREST CO.
310 Euclid
Mt. Clemens, MI 48043
Tel.: 810-954-4800; FAX: 810-954-4806

Personnel:
Anthony Bellomo . . . . President

Type of Business:
Anthony John Bellomo is a sculptor. He works in a wide variety of materials from wood and bronze to fibers, stone and living plant materials. Over the past twenty-five years he has developed the Black Forest Company. Black Forest is a group of artists and artisans, who along with Bellomo, design and build contemporary sculpture and furniture for liturgical spaces. He has developed a series of redwood sand carved exterior pieces for outdoor chapels and meditation gardens. Anthony, along with his team of dedicated crafts persons, pride themselves in listening to the individual community, designing and building pieces to help make their worship a deeper experience.

ECCLESIASTICAL ARTS, INC.
16 Herbert St.
Newark, NJ 07105
Tel: 201-491-0022; FAX: 201-491-0023

Personnel:
Joseph J. Zaky . . . . President

Type of Business:
Artists and Craftsmen specializing in custom designed and hand made furnishings in metal, wood, stone and glass. For interior design, fabrication, restoration and original sculpture, contact J.J. Zaky.

GRANDA LITURGICAL ARTS, INC.
2525 Eastwood Ave., Apt. 8A
Evanston, IL 60201
Tel.: 800-425-0828; FAX: 847-492-1374
www.hispacom.es/granda; e-mail: ruj4granda@aol.com

Personnel:
Monica Ruf

Type of Business:
GRANDA LITURGICAL ARTS, Inc. is the USA branch of the largest supplier of church goods in the world: TALLERES DE ARTE GRANDA, S.A.
With 65 employees and sales all over the world, we can offer our experience in the manufacture of:
— metalware: chalices, tabernacles, etc.
— vestments
— wood carvings
— church decoration, interior design
Since 1891, we have been serving the liturgy, combining modern techniques (design by computer, projects in 3D ...) with artistic values.
Special custom orders: our specialty, according to your needs, in style and price.

ADRIAN HAMERS®
CHURCH INTERIORS

ADRIAN HAMERS INC.
2 Madison Ave.
Larchmont, NY 10538
Tel.: 914-834-7780; FAX: 914-834-0712

Type of Business:
Since 1887, the Hamers name has been synonymous with expert silversmithing throughout the world in the field of Liturgical Art. We are also experts in: Church Interiors from design to execution, Renovations, Altars, Sacred Vessels, Appraisals, Gold and Silver Plating & Repairing, Tabernacles, Marble, Woodwork & Woodcarving, Statuary, Stained Glass, Pews & Chairs, Gold Leafing, Frescoes, Restoration, Trompe-l'oeuil, Wall Murals (repair and conservation cleaning), Ornamental Plaster, Heraldic Designs & Bishop Regalia.

RAMBUSCH

RAMBUSCH
40 West 13th St.
New York, NY 10011
Tel.: 212-675-0400; FAX: 212-620-4687

Personnel:
Viggo Bech Rambusch. . . . . Senior Project Director
Martin V. Rambusch. . . . . Stained Glass Director

Type of Business:
Since 1898, creating church interiors, liturgical furnishings, and art work. Fine restoration of church interiors. In-house studios and shops for designing and executing stained glass, church lighting systems, art metal work, and decorative painting.

Conrad Schmitt Studios Inc.

CONRAD SCHMITT STUDIOS, INC.
2405 S. 162nd St.
New Berlin, WI 53151
Tel.: 800-969-3033; 414-786-3030; FAX: 414-786-9036

Personnel:
Heidi Gruenke Emery . . . . Vice President & Marketing Director

Type of Business:
Since 1889, this family-owned Studio has restored and decorated hundreds of interiors across the country. Their scope of work includes the investigation and documentation of original decorative schemes; the restoration of those schemes through the application of various decorative techniques including gilding, glazing, marbleizing, stenciling, and graining, as well as the design, fabrication, conservation or replication of murals and stained glass. The Studio can assist projects in the early stages with architectural samples and rendering for fund-raising. Recently completed projects include St. Josaphat's Basilica, Milwaukee, WI; St. Ann's, Napoleanville, LA; and St. Bernard's, Akron, OH.

ANTIQUES, RELIGIOUS

ADRIAN HAMERS®
CHURCH INTERIORS

ADRIAN HAMERS INC.
2 Madison Ave.
Larchmont, NY 10538
Tel.: 914-834-7780; FAX: 914-834-0712

Type of Business:
Since 1887, the Hamers name has been synonymous with expert silversmithing throughout the world in the field of Liturgical Art. We are also experts in: Church Interiors from design to execution, Renovations, Altars, Sacred Vessels, Appraisals, Gold and Silver Plating & Repairing, Tabernacles, Marble, Woodwork & Woodcarving, Statuary, Stained Glass, Pews & Chairs, Gold Leafing, Frescoes, Restoration, Trompe-l'oeuil, Wall Murals (repair and conservation cleaning), Ornamental Plaster, Heraldic Designs & Bishop Regalia.

GREG SPIESS & CO.

SPIESS ARCHITECTURAL ANTIQUES
230 East Washington St.
Joliet, IL 60433
Tel.: 815-722-5639; FAX: 815-722-0171

Type of Business:
Specializing in older and antique church furniture. Gothic, Romanesque and Classical styles in marble, wood, bronze etc. Altars, pews, communion rails, stained glass, lecterns, baptismals, vestment cases, confessionals, Stations of the Cross statuary. Lighting. Pew and wood restoration available.

ART, STATUARY & DECORATIONS

ABBOTT CHURCH GOODS, INC.
1515 Route 38
Cherry Hill, NJ 08002
Tel.: 800-522-2688; 609-662-6959; FAX: 609-665-5109
website: http://www.abbottsinc.com
e-mail: ACG.INC@internetMCI.com

Personnel:
Daniel J. Castonguay . . . . President
Joseph F. McKeaney . . . . General Manager
Michael W. Wasyluk . . . . Customer Service

Type of Business:
Purveyors of the Finest Vesture, Paraments, Statuary & Metalware since 1962. Unique and original creations our specialty. Custom designs to complement your liturgical environment. Exclusive representatives of Slabbinck Master Collection & Original Collection.

Autom

AUTOM
5226 South 31st Pl.
Phoenix, AZ 85040
Tel.: 800-521-2914; FAX: 602-243-3878

Personnel:
Scott Evans . . . . Sales Manager

Type of Business:
Distributor of the complete line of Dolfi Church Statuary. Over 300 pieces in stock for immediate delivery. Serving over 25,000 churches since 1948. Custom Design Service available.

THE BLACK FOREST BUILDING COMPANY

ANTHONY JOHN BELLOMO / THE BLACK FOREST CO.
310 Euclid
Mt. Clemens, MI 48043
Tel.: 810-954-4800; FAX: 810-954-4806

Personnel:
Anthony Bellomo. . . . . President

Type of Business:
Anthony John Bellomo is a sculptor. He works in a wide variety of materials from wood and bronze to fibers, stone and living plant materials. Over the past twenty-five years he has developed the Black Forest Company. Black Forest is a group of artists and artisans, who along with Bellomo, design and build contemporary sculpture and furniture for liturgical spaces. He has developed a series of redwood sand carved exterior pieces for outdoor chapels and meditation gardens. Anthony, along with his team of dedicated crafts persons, pride themselves in listening to the individual community, designing and building pieces to help make their worship a deeper experience.

Berlinger Decorating Co. Inc.

BERLINGER DECORATING CO.
2605 N. Sheridan Rd.
Peoria, IL 61604
Tel.: 309-688-1771; FAX: 309-688-9240

Type of Business:
Church restoration specialists for 5 generations. Interior designing and decorating: Exterior Renovation; Professional artistry; Woodworking; Engineering service. We welcome inquiries from parishes of all sizes.

BOTTI STUDIO OF ARCHITECTURAL ARTS, INC.

BOTTI STUDIO OF ARCHITECTURAL ARTS, INC.
919 Grove St.
Evanston, IL 60201
Tel.: 800-524-7211; FAX: 847-869-5996
847-869-5933; e-mail: Boti@ix.netcom.com

East Coast Studio
1517 State St.
Sarasota, FL 33577
Tel.: 941-951-0978; FAX: 941-953-9078

West Coast Studio
1038 N Highway 101
Encinitas, CA 92024
Tel.: 619-753-0705; FAX: 619-753-0705

Personnel:
Staff includes internationlly recognized artists and designers working in conjunction with our highly skilled artisans and craftsmen.
Italo G. Botti . . . . President

Type of Business:
For generations Botti Studio has had a reputation for embodying all that is artistically creative in the traditional and contemporary ecclesiastical field. This field includes design and fabrication of stained and faceted glass windows, restoration of windows, church interiors, appointments, murals, sculpture, mosaic and marble. We are completely dedicated to both quality and satisfying our clients needs spiritually and liturgically. Botti Studio is nationwide, offering consultation and designs without obligation. Member Stained Glass Association of America.

DAPRATO RIGALI STUDIOS, INC.

DAPRATO RIGALI STUDIOS, INC.
7956 Oakton St.
Niles, IL 60714
Tel.: 847-692-6350; FAX: 847-692-3445

Personnel:
John Rigali
Robert Rigali
Lisa Rigali Galvin
Mike Rigali

Type of Business:
Daprato Rigali Studios Inc. has been beautifying Churches in America since 1860.
Today we find the Rigali Family restoring and renovating the churches originally decorated by their Great-Grandfather, John E. Rigali; aware of his reputation to create spiritually moving environments with quality material and craftsmanship.
Some of their most recent jobs include: decoration and stained glass restoration at St. Mary of the Lake Seminary, Mundelein, IL.; Marble renovation and decoration, St. Elizabeth's Mother House, Allegany, N.Y.; and General Contracting for complete renovation of St. Bernadette's Church, Rockford, IL.
The Daprato Rigali staff is equipped to take your project from start to finish. If you're interested in working with a fine interior design studio experienced in Ecclesiastical Artistries please call for consultation at no obligation. We deliver what we design.

Granda Liturgical Arts, Inc. TAC

GRANDA LITURGICAL ARTS, INC.
2525 Eastwood Ave., Apt. 8A
Evanston, IL 60201
Tel.: 800-425-0828; FAX: 847-492-1374
www.hispacom.es/granda; e-mail: ruj4granda@aol.com

Personnel:
Monica Ruf

Type of Business:
GRANDA LITURGICAL ARTS, Inc. is the USA branch of the largest supplier of church goods in the world: TALLERES DE ARTE GRANDA, S.A.
With 65 employees and sales all over the world, we can offer our experience in the manufacture of:
— metalware: chalices, tabernacles, etc.
— vestments
— wood carvings
— church decoration, interior design
Since 1891, we have been serving the liturgy, combining modern techniques (design by computer, projects in 3D ...) with artistic values.
Special custom orders: our specialty, according to your needs, in style and price.

INSTITUTIONAL STATUARY
637 E. 132nd St.
Bronx, NY 10450
Tel.: 718-665-1125; FAX: 718-665-0956

Type of Business:
Distinctive religious works of art: Designers-Sculptors-Manufacturers. Full color catalog available upon request.

RAMBUSCH

RAMBUSCH
40 West 13th St.
New York, NY 10011
Tel.: 212-675-0400; FAX: 212-620-4687

Personnel:
Viggo Bech Rambusch . . . . Senior Project Director
Martin V. Rambusch . . . . Stained Glass Director

Type of Business:
Since 1898, creating church interiors, liturgical furnishings, and art work. Fine restoration of church interiors. In-house studios and shops for designing and executing stained glass, church lighting systems, art metal work, and decorative painting.

Conrad Schmitt Studios Inc.

CONRAD SCHMITT STUDIOS, INC.
2405 S. 162nd St.
New Berlin, WI 53151
Tel.: 800-969-3033; 414-786-3030; FAX: 414-786-9036

Personnel:
Heidi Gruenke Emery . . . . Vice President & Marketing Director

Type of Business:
Since 1889, this family-owned Studio has restored and decorated hundreds of interiors across the country. Their scope of work includes the investigation and documentation of original decorative schemes; the restoration of those schemes through the application of various decorative techniques including gilding, glazing, marbleizing, stenciling, and graining, as well as the design, fabrication, conservation or replication of murals and stained glass. The Studio can assist projects in the early stages with architectural samples and rendering for fund-raising. Recently completed projects include St. Josaphat's Basilica, Milwaukee, WI; St. Ann's, Napoleanville, LA; and St. Bernard's, Akron, OH.

SERAPHIC RESTORATIONS SACRED ARTS STUDIO
P.O. Box 2712, 492 West St.
Bristol, CT 06011-2712
Tel.: 860-582-6759; FAX: 860-585-9611

Personnel:
Marek Czarnecki . . . . Artist

Type of Business:
This SACRED ARTS STUDIO specializes in custom hand-made ICONS of original design or from traditional prototypes, suitable for Catholic or Orthodox sanctuaries; inquiries are welcome regarding original commissioned works, paintings and murals. Dedicated to images of traditional piety in all formats, we are specialists in the sensitive restoration of indoor statuary and operate an active search service, locating refurbished fixtures no longer manufactured.

BAPTISMAL FONTS

THE BLACK FOREST BUILDING COMPANY

ANTHONY JOHN BELLOMO / THE BLACK FOREST CO.
310 Euclid
Mt. Clemens, MI 48043
Tel.: 810-954-4800; FAX: 810-954-4806

Personnel:
Anthony Bellomo. . . . . President

Type of Business:
Anthony John Bellomo is a sculptor. He works in a wide variety of materials from wood and bronze to fibers, stone and living plant materials. Over the past twenty-five years he has developed the Black Forest Company. Black Forest is a group of artists and artisans, who along with Bellomo, design and build contemporary sculpture and furniture for liturgical spaces. He has developed a series of redwood sand carved exterior pieces for outdoor chapels and meditation gardens. Anthony, along with his team of dedicated crafts persons, pride themselves in listening to the individual community, designing and building pieces to help make their worship a deeper experience.

Daprato Rigali Studios, Inc.

DAPRATO RIGALI STUDIOS, INC.
7956 Oakton St.
Niles, IL 60714
Tel.: 847-692-6350; FAX: 847-692-3445

Personnel:
John Rigali
Robert Rigali
Lisa Rigali Galvin
Mike Rigali

Type of Business:
Daprato Rigali Studios Inc. has been beautifying Churches in America since 1860.
Today we find the Rigali Family restoring and renovating the churches originally decorated by their Great-Grandfather, John E. Rigali; aware of his reputation to create spiritually moving environments with quality material and craftsmanship.
Some of their most recent jobs include: decoration and stained glass restoration at St. Mary of the Lake Seminary, Mundelein, IL.; Marble renovation and decoration, St. Elizabeth's Mother House, Allegany, N.Y.; and General Contracting for complete renovation of St. Bernadette's Church, Rockford, IL.
The Daprato Rigali staff is equipped to take your project from start to finish. If you're interested in working with a fine interior design studio experienced in Ecclesiastical Artistries please call for consultation at no obligation. We deliver what we design.

Conrad Schmitt Studios Inc.

CONRAD SCHMITT STUDIOS, INC.
2405 S. 162nd St.
New Berlin, WI 53151
Tel.: 800-969-3033; 414-786-3030; FAX: 414-786-9036

Personnel:
Heidi Gruenke Emery . . . . Vice President & Marketing Director

Type of Business:
Since 1889, this family-owned Studio has restored and decorated hundreds of interiors across the country. Their scope of work includes the investigation and documentation of original decorative schemes; the restoration of those schemes through the application of various decorative techniques including gilding, glazing, marbleizing, stenciling, and graining, as well as the design, fabrication, conservation or replication of murals and stained glass. The Studio can assist projects in the early stages with architectural samples and rendering for fund-raising. Recently completed projects include St. Josaphat's Basilica, Milwaukee, WI; St. Ann's, Napoleanville, LA; and St. Bernard's, Akron, OH.

BELLS, CARILLONS, ETC.

BELL INDUSTRIES
204 Washington Ave.
Hooven, OH 45033
Tel.: 800-343-0550; FAX: 513-353-2356

Type of Business:
Since 1933, Bell Industries remains the leader in electronic church bells and chimes. Today we offer a new line of digital carillon systems that produce the pure sounds of genuine cast bronze bells with no moving parts. Bell Industries uses the latest digital recording techniques to place all the bell sounds in permanent digital memory. The call to mass bells, angelus, tolling bells, pealing bells and time strikes can ring with a touch of a button or let the easy to program digital clock do it automatically. The systems also have the ability to play from thousands of standard and custom seasonal hymns. Optional equipment includes a MIDI keyboard and interface, auxiliary inputs, remote controls and larger amplifiers.

BROSAMER'S BELLS
207 Irwin St.
Brooklyn, MI 49230
Tel.: 517-592-9030; FAX: 517-592-4511

Personnel:
R.C. Brosamer and family

Type of Business:
We will purchase pre-owned bells and remove bells that are no longer needed by churches or other organizations. The bells will then be restored and kept until they are called on to serve someone else's needs. Our pre-owned cast bells are affordable. Check on new, then call us.

MAAS ROWE

MAAS-ROWE CARILLONS, INC.
2255 Meyers Ave.
Escondido, CA 92029
Tel.: 800-854-2023; FAX: 619-747-2677

Personnel:
Paul Rowe . . . . President
Craig Johnson . . . . National Sales Manager

Type of Business:
Established 1922. Manufacturers of automatic (computerized) Carillon and Church Bell Systems using compact discs for ultra high quality sound. Factory direct sales, service and installation. Sales—National and International. Upgrading of older carillon systems (any brand) to compact disc with computer control. Producers of compact discs featuring carillon and organ church music designed to play automatically or manually in computer controlled carillon equipment. Manufacturers of Musical Handbells. Importers of European Cast Bronze Church Bells and accessories.

McSHANE BELL FOUNDRY CO., INC.
400 C Arundel Corporation Rd.
Glen Burnie, MD 21060
Tel.: 410-636-4390; FAX: 410-636-7533

Type of Business:
Manufacturer of bells, chimes and electric ringing equipment for both swinging and stationary systems. Complete bell restoration and bell repairs to all makes.

Schulmerich Bells
Electronic Carillons • Handbells • Cast Bell Carillons
Carillon Hill • PO Box 903 • Sellersville, PA • 18960-0903
215/257-2771 • 800/772-3557 • Fax: 215/257-1910

SCHULMERICH CARILLONS INC.
Carillon Hill
Sellersville, PA 18960
Tel.: 215-257-2771; FAX: 215-257-1910

Personnel:
Ronald Beach . . . . Chmn. Bd.

Type of Business:
Design and manufacture church cast bronze bells, electronic carillons, hand bells and towers/cupolas, liturgical bells. Enhance your worship celebration easily and affordably with the inspiring sound of Schulmerich Bells, a leader in bell music technologies since 1935—and you can hear the difference.

VERDIN
V
SINCE 1842

THE VERDIN CO.
444 Reading Rd.
Cincinnati, OH 45202
Tel.: 800-543-0488; 513-241-4010; FAX: 513-241-1855

Personnel:
Thomas W. Reiring

Type of Business:
The Verdin Co.. In business since 1842, The Verdin Co. is the oldest and largest manufacturer of bells, carillons, street clocks and tower clocks. Verdin also provides bell ringing equipment, bell renovation and servicing.

BENCHES, LECTERNS, PEWS

Hamlin
ATWOOD-HAMLIN MANUFACTURING

ATWOOD-HAMLIN MFG., INC.
P.O. Box 150
Richmond, IL 60071
Tel.: 1-800-545-8964

Type of Business:
Since 1948, Atwood-Hamlin Manufacturing has been your source for church furnishing. Our products include the famous **Hamlin Folding Pew Kneeler** as well as their replacement upholstered pads and parts. For your pews we also offer our comfortable, non-slip **Pew-Form Cushions** that do not have to be fastened to your pews. All reversible styles available. Our solid oak, stacking pew-chairs top our line of seating products. All upholstered products are available in hundreds of colors and fabric choices. We also offer pew refinishing services. Call for free product information.

Serenity® CHURCH FURNITURE

WALTER JACOBI AND SONS, INC.
1400 Elmer St.
Belmont, CA 94002
Tel.: 800-522-6241; FAX: 415-592-2434
website: http://www.serenity-wjs.com

Type of Business:
Since 1921, MANUFACTURER: Devotional - Reverential - Furniture. MADE TO ORDER: Conducive to MEDITATION and PRAYER - ALL Wood, Cushion-loc, and Conventional Upholstered - Pews, Pewchairs, PewCHAR, Presider Chair, Clergy Chairs, Serenity Kneelers, Premium Kneelers, SKE Hydraulics, Kneeler Maintenance, Kneeler Parts and Repairs, Altar, Ambo, Lectern, Candlesticks, Crosses, Carvings. Seating Consultants to Church and/or Architect. Computer Layouts - send Plans or CAD Disk.

THE BLACK FOREST BUILDING COMPANY

ANTHONY JOHN BELLOMO / THE BLACK FOREST CO.
310 Euclid
Mt. Clemens, MI 48043
Tel.: 810-954-4800; FAX: 810-954-4806

Personnel:
Anthony Bellomo . . . . President

Type of Business:
Anthony John Bellomo is a sculptor. He works in a wide variety of materials from wood and bronze to fibers, stone and living plant materials. Over the past twenty-five years he has developed the Black Forest Company. Black Forest is a group of artists and artisans, who along with Bellomo, design and build contemporary sculpture and furniture for liturgical spaces. He has developed a series of redwood sand carved exterior pieces for outdoor chapels and meditation gardens. Anthony, along with his team of dedicated crafts persons, pride themselves in listening to the individual community, designing and building pieces to help make their worship a deeper experience.

BISHOP'S REGALIA

ADRIAN HAMERS®

CHURCH INTERIORS

ADRIAN HAMERS INC.
2 Madison Ave.
Larchmont, NY 10538
Tel.: 914-834-7780; FAX: 914-834-0712

Type of Business:

Since 1887, the Hamers name has been synonymous with expert silversmithing throughout the world in the field of Liturgical Art. We are also experts in: Church Interiors from design to execution, Renovations, Altars, Sacred Vessels, Appraisals, Gold and Silver Plating & Repairing, Tabernacles, Marble, Woodwork & Woodcarving, Statuary, Stained Glass, Pews & Chairs, Gold Leafing, Frescoes, Restoration, Trompe-l'oeuil, Wall Murals (repair and conservation cleaning), Ornamental Plaster, Heraldic Designs & Bishop Regalia.

P. J. McDERMOTT & CO.
P.O. Box 950101
Fort Tilden, NY 11695
Tel.: 718-634-5583

Personnel:

Patrick J. McDermott . . . . President

Type of Business:

We are a major supplier of Ready-made suits, coats, slacks, blazers, R.J. Toomey Co. shirt fronts, French-cuff shirts, clerical vests ... "Beau-Veste" and Gammarelli (Rome) albs, surplices and rochets ... Fully custom tailored cassocks ... We are considered the leader in the U.S. and specialize in Bishops and Monsignors robes, all of which are custom tailored here. We also supply all Episcopal accessories; mitres, zuchettos, birettas, rochets, albs, pectoral cross, chains and cross cords, bishops rings, croziers.
HAVE TAPE MEASURE — WILL TRAVEL

LAMPS & LIGHTING

CAPITOL LIGHTING & RESTORATION
500 W. Exchange St.
Spring Lake, MI 49456-2083
Tel.: 616-844-5000; FAX: 616-844-2228

Personnel:

Brenda Hoyt . . . . . . Managing Director — Sales and Marketing
John Fuchs . . . . Managing Director — Design

Type of Business:

CAPITOL LIGHTING & RESTORATION is a company whose two founders and senior business associates have a history in the lighting industry dating back to the 1950's. It is a company totally dedicated to supplying quality products and delivering them on schedule. Due to the background of its founders, CAPITOL LIGHTING is sensitive to the needs of its clients. Designers need accurate drawings and information on time. Owners and contractors need adherence to schedules with equipment delivered in good condition and in conformance with approved coordination drawings.

CAPITOL LIGHTING & RESTORATION is owned and operated by Brenda Hoyt and John Fuchs. Both bring their own unique talents to the organization making it unrivaled in the lighting industry. CAPITOL LIGHTING's associates include a metal sculptor with a Master of Fine Arts degree; another metal sculptor whose special interest is 19th century gas and oil lighting fixtures and their early conversion to electric usage; two foundry specialists, one for short custom production runs, the other for production runs using the traditional lost wax process. In this process, CAPITOL LIGHTING & RESTORATION is able to offer bronze chandeliers of extraordinary quality. CAPITOL LIGHTING & RESTORATION has also successfully modified existing and antique lighting equipment to make use of newly developed light sources. It has always been a corporate philosophy to restore old fixtures rather than discard them and supply new replacements — it is a philosophy much appreciated by sensitive clients.

In addition to restoring and supplying ornamental lighting equipment, CAPITOL LIGHTING & RESTORATION has carved a niche for itself in the design of special lighting equipment largely unavailable from other suppliers. Whether it is the design of ornamental exit signs or small accent lights to be installed in very limited spaces — CAPITOL LIGHTING & RESTORATION has always prevailed in the face of difficult design challenges.

It is safe to say that no other ornamental lighting fixture supplier can claim to have this type of expertise at its disposal or within its own corporate structure — it is a fertile environment conducive to the promotion and fulfillment of the design process.

RAMBUSCH

RAMBUSCH
40 West 13th St.
New York, NY 10011
Tel.: 212-675-0400; FAX: 212-620-4687

PersonneL:

Viggo Bech Rambusch .... Senior Project Director
Martin V. Rambusch .... Stained Glass Director

Type of Business:

Since 1898, creating church interiors, liturgical furnishings, and art work. Fine restoration of church interiors. In-house studios and shops for designing and executing stained glass, church lighting systems, art metal work, and decorative painting.

MOSAICS

ABBOTT CHURCH GOODS, INC.
1515 Route 38
Cherry Hill, NJ 08002
Tel.: 800-522-2688; 609-662-6959; FAX: 609-665-5109
website: http://www.abbottsinc.com
e-mail: ACG.INC@internetMCI.com

Personnel:

Daniel J. Castonguay .... President
Joseph F. McKeaney .... General Manager
Michael W. Wasyluk.................... Customer Service

Type of Business:

Purveyors of the Finest Vesture, Paraments, Statuary & Metalware since 1962. Unique and original creations our specialty. Custom designs to complement your liturgical environment. Exclusive representatives of Slabbinck Master Collection & Original Collection.

1847 **150** Years 1997

Franz Mayer of Munich, Inc.
F.X. Zettler

FRANZ MAYER OF MUNICH, INC.
25, Seidlstrasse
Munich, GER D-80335
Tel.: 011-49-89-595484; FAX: 011-49-89-593446

Personnel:

Gabriel Mayer, Ph.D. .... President
Konrad Mayer
Michael Mayer

Type of Business:

Founded 1847, Franz Mayer of Munich, still family owned and operated, is celebrating its 150th anniversary in 1997! Together with F.X.Zettler — the sister co. — they remain to be one of the international leading studios for **stained glass** and **mosaic**. More than 100 Cathedrals and thousands of churches worldwide — including St. Peter's in Rome (The Holy Spirit Window) — have windows, mosaics or — from earlier periods — altars or statuary from them. Your enquiry will be appreciated as a birthday present!

RAMBUSCH

RAMBUSCH
40 West 13th St.
New York, NY 10011
Tel.: 212-675-0400; FAX: 212-620-4687

Personnel:

Viggo Bech Rambusch .... Senior Project Director
Martin V. Rambusch .... Stained Glass Director

Type of Business:

Since 1898, creating church interiors, liturgical furnishings, and art work. Fine restoration of church interiors. In-house studios and shops for designing and executing stained glass, church lighting systems, art metal work, and decorative painting.

Conrad Schmitt Studios Inc.

CONRAD SCHMITT STUDIOS, INC.
2405 S. 162nd St.
New Berlin, WI 53151
Tel.: 800-969-3033; 414-786-3030; FAX: 414-786-9036

Personnel:
Heidi Gruenke Emery . . . . Vice President & Marketing Director

Type of Business:
Since 1889, this family-owned Studio has restored and decorated hundreds of interiors across the country. Their scope of work includes the investigation and documentation of original decorative schemes; the restoration of those schemes through the application of various decorative techniques including gilding, glazing, marbleizing, stenciling, and graining, as well as the design, fabrication, conservation or replication of murals and stained glass. The Studio can assist projects in the early stages with architectural samples and rendering for fund-raising. Recently completed projects include St. Josaphat's Basilica, Milwaukee, WI; St. Ann's, Napoleanville, LA; and St. Bernard's, Akron, OH.

ORGANS & PIANOS

Allen ORGAN COMPANY

ALLEN ORGAN CO.
P.O. Box 36
Macungie, PA 18062-0036
Tel.: 610-966-2202; FAX: 610-965-3098
e-mail: aosales@allenorgan.com
website: http://www.allenorgan.com

Personnel:
Barry Holben

Type of Business:
World's largest builder of church organs, with a variety of standard models and custom designs to meet every need.

ChurchOrganSystems

CHURCH ORGAN SYSTEMS
422 Wards Corner Rd.
Loveland, OH 45140-8390
Tel.: 513-576-4660; FAX: 513-576-6871

Personnel:
Duane Kuhn . . . . Vice President
Darlene Davis . . . . Administrative Assistant
Rodney Barbour . . . . Manager Sales & Svc.
David Wade . . . . Director Engrg.

Type of Business:
Church Organ Systems, a division of The Baldwin Piano and Organ Co., is dedicated to serving churches with products and programs designed to support music ministry.

ORGAN CLEARING HOUSE
P.O. Box 104-RC
Harrisville, NH 03450-0104
Tel.: 603-827-3055; FAX: 603-827-3750

Personnel:
Alan Miller Laufman . . . . Exec. Director

Type of Business:
Urban renewal and church closings/mergers frequently make pipe organs available for recycling. Since 1959, we have relocated nationwide hundreds of carefully renovated instruments to churches which could not afford new ones. We are now listing more than 300 pipe organs, large and small, old and new. Please send $6 in stamps for our current brochure. Or let us know if you have a pipe organ for sale; we may be able to help.

RODGERS®
INSTRUMENT CORPORATION
The sound choice!

RODGERS INSTRUMENT CORPORATION
1300 N.E. 25th Ave.
Hillsboro, OR 97124
Tel.: 503-648-4181; FAX: 503-681-0444

Personnel:
Dennis Houlihan . . . . President
Jonas Nordwall . . . . Product Marketing Manager
Donna Parker . . . . Marketing Administrator
David Tomb . . . . Sales & Marketing Development Manager

Type of Business:
Rodgers Instrument Corporation is respected worldwide for technical leadership in the manufacturing of digital electronic, pipe and electronic/pipe combination organs using PDI (Parallel Digital Imaging) technology for church, home, schools, and concert halls. Rodgers also builds digital keyboards, MIDI sound modules and sequencers.

WICKS PIPE ORGAN COMPANY

WICKS ORGAN CO.
1100 Fifth St.
Highland, IL 62249
Tel.: 618-654-2191; FAX: 618-654-3770

Personnel:

Martin Wick . . . . President
Scott Wick . . . . Vice President
Jack Jenkins. . . . . Sales Manager

Type of Business:

Custom designed pipe organs and combination instruments to fit your space and budget. 100+ years experience in over 6,000 churches worldwide. Free on-site evaluations and proposal drawings. Highest levels of professionalism from beginning to end. 10-year warranty. Specialists in DIRECT-ELECTRIC™ and Mechanical Action organs. Financially sound company, AAA-#1 Dunn & Bradstreet rating. Also, pre-designed compact models for limited space, time or budget. Some available for immediate delivery. Literature and video available for committees and individuals. Call Wicks Organ Co. at 800-444-WICK or 618-654-2191.

PEW CUSHIONS

Hamlin

ATWOOD-HAMLIN MANUFACTURING

ATWOOD-HAMLIN MFG., INC.
P.O. Box 150
Richmond, IL 60071
Tel.: 1-800-545-8964

Type of Business:

Since 1948, Atwood-Hamlin Manufacturing has been your source for church furnishing. Our products include the famous **Hamlin Folding Pew Kneeler** as well as their replacement upholstered pads and parts. For your pews we also offer our comfortable, non-slip **Pew-Form Cushions** that do not have to be fastened to your pews. All reversible styles available. All upholstered products are available in hundreds of colors and fabric choices. We also offer pew refinishing services. Call for free product information.

PLAQUES & MEMORIALS

Honor The Gift.........Honor The Giver

B&D ... CONTRIBUTOR RECOGNITION PRODUCTS
119 South Mansfield Blvd.
Cherry Hill, NJ 08034-3611
1-800-873-3180; FAX: 609-429-3772

Honor those who Give, and they are yours forever ... Contributor Recognition is a key fund raising element that increases response and levels of giving. Our products create a permanent bond between the giver and their Church. Impressive, awe-inspiring, and motivational they enhance Church decor in an understated elegant manner. Our products can accommodate Churches of all sizes. They are also expandable, of high quality and most economical.
We are as close as your telephone.

CARROLL ART INC.
710 NE 26th St.
Fort Lauderdale, FL 33305
Tel.: 800-876-4569; FAX: 954-561-4098

Personnel:

David Nagle . . . . President/Designer
Liza Palmer . . . . Sales Manager
Andrea Speier . . . . Sales Rep.
Robert Perkins . . . . Sales Rep.

Type of Business:

Carroll Art has been in business for 12 years. We design and custom build all types of plaques and memorials including the tree of life, plaques, recognition systems, church signs, donor plates, custom sculptures, and memorials are just a few of our products. We can provide you with the perfect fund raising tool.

TREES • OF • LIFE

A proven successful fund raiser whose strong lines and rich colors will enhance the space into which it is placed.

DAVID KLASS ART STUDIOS
136 West 24th St.
New York, NY 10011
Tel.: 212-243-7633; FAX: 212-243-7633

Personnel:
David Klass . . . . Owner, Designer

Type of Business:
Since 1968 David Klass has created numerous Trees of Life. Each one is custom designed to meet your needs. The finest select hardwoods, brasses and bronze are used.
Our beautiful designs and workmanship are ideal for donor recognition and fund raising drives. Special symbols and imagery meaningful to your parish can be incorporated into the design.

SANFORD WERFEL- ARTIST

SANFORD WERFEL - ARTIST
425 Old Georges Rd.,
North Brunswick, NJ 08902
Tel.: 800-443-3744; 908-297-1166; FAX: 908-297-7770

Type of Business:
Since 1968, Mr. Werfel's sculptures have been helping parishes to INSPIRE and MOTIVATE GIVING through the use of his original sculptures. Building drives, capital or endowment funds, sacrificial giving, and tithing programs all benefit from using Donor Recognition Sculptures. Call or write for FREE INFORMATION. Included will be costs and designs as well as a "HOW-TO-USE" guide that tells how your parish can use sculpture to raise funds. Good art is forever.

ZAX Recognition Products

Donor Wall

Tree of Life

Book of Memory

The fine art of gratitude.

Commemorate Your Donors with handsomely presented Plaques by Zax.

DONOR WALLS OF DISTINCTION
BOOK OF MEMORIES
TREES OF LIFE • MULTI-NAME PLAQUES
ADD-ON DONOR PLAQUES • MARBLEGRAPH PLAQUES
BRONZE TABLETS • AWARDS

zax
Recognition Products

Call TOLL FREE for an Estimate: 800/258-1566
or Write for Our Comprehensive New Catalog.

ZAX Corporation, 20 Otterson Street, Nashua, NH 03061
Telephone: (603) 889-4126 Fax: (603) 883-6395

SANFORD WHITE CO. INC.
PO Box 157
Pawtucket, RI 02862-0157
Tel.: 800-245-7825; FAX: 401-728-3080

Personnel:
Stuart Aaronson
Michael Tally

Type of Business:
American designer and manufacturer of custom donor, volunteer and staff recognition products. For over forty years we have produced high quality recognition gifts at an affordable price. Our product line includes: Lapel pins, Medallions, Bookmarks, Key Chains, Letter Openers, Ornaments, Magnets, Wooden Gift Boxes and Desk Sets, Pewter Paperweights, Plaques and Lucite Embedments. Call our toll-free number and speak to an experienced member of our staff with your requirements or request our full color recognition catalog.

ZAX CORPORATION
20 Otterson St.
Nashua, NH 03061
Tel.: 800-258-1566; 603-889-4126; FAX: 603-883-6395

Type of Business:
The Zax Corporation of Nashua, N.H. has a distinguished history of providing the highest quality recognition products throughout North America. Our recognition products represent not only fine materials and craftsmanship, but the highest standards of design excellence for meeting your specific needs.
Zax manufactures an array of products such as Donor Walls, Book of Memories, Trees of Life, Add-On Donor Plaques, MarbleGraph, ClassBrass Multi-Plate/Multi-Name Plaques, Bronze Tablets, Incentive Awards and Signage Products.
For detailed information on our product line, or help in designing a donor wall of distinction, our expert staff can help you with your donor recognition needs. Call us at 1-800-258-1566 for help or to request our recognition catalog.
We pledge ... Service, Value, Quality, and our Commitment to you, to help you express your gratitude to your donors, and at the same time ... increase donations.

TABLES & CHAIRS

CLARIN, A DIVISION OF GREENWICH INDUSTRIES, L.P.
927 North Shore Dr.
Lake Bluff, IL 60044
Tel.: 847-295-2200; FAX: 847-234-9001

Personnel:
William P. Peterson .... President
Richard H. Wagner .... Vice President, Clarin Sales
Kathleen J. Sobotta.......... Manager, Inside Sales

Type of Business:
The best choice in seating! Manufacturer of portable and fixed lecture room seating. Supplier of logo chairs and stools for athletic teams; correct pitch music chairs, tablet arm chairs and other seating products for all uses.

CLERICAL APPAREL

ROBERT GASPARD CO., INC.
200 N. Janacek Rd.,
Brookfield, WI 53045-6153
Tel.: 800-784-6868; 414-784-6800; FAX: 414-784-7567

Personnel:
Rose Gaspard .... President
Duane G. Buchholz .... General Manager

Type of Business:
The Robert Gaspard Co. was established in 1954. Over the past 40 years, we have grown to our present size, occupying a showroom and manufacturing facility in excess of 20,000 square feet and employing 44 full time employees. We pride ourselves on our ability to create original custom designs to enrich your worship needs. Our complete line consists of all ecclesiastical vesture as well as paraments, mass and altar linens, stoles, banners, chasubles, funeral palls, albs, cassocks, surplices, choir robes, acolyte robes and many accessories. Complimentary catalogs and fabric swatches sent on request.

ADAM KOCHLIN
DESIGNS

ADAM KOCHLIN DESIGNS
21 Ann St.
South Norwalk, CT 06854
Tel.: 800-886-4668; FAX: 203-838-8752

Personnel:
Adam Kochlin .... Design Director
Michael Kirshbaum.................... Executive Director
Regina Maguire .... Product Manager

Type of Business:
Adam Kochlin Designs creates a complete line of made to order vestments and hangings produced in our studio in Connecticut. Working with a number of artists we also create made to order sacred vessels and appointments including processional crosses, pacschal candlesticks, altar candlesticks, sanctuary lamps, incensors, chalices and patens, aumbrys, curets, and falgons in wood, ceramic, glass and metal. Call 800-886-4668 for free catalog and information.

P. J. McDERMOTT & CO.
P.O. Box 950101
Fort Tilden, NY 11695
Tel.: 718-634-5583

Personnel:
Patrick J. McDermott .... President

Type of Business:
We are a major supplier of Ready-made suits, coats, slacks, blazers, R.J. Toomey Co. shirt fronts, French-cuff shirts, clerical vests ... "Beau-Veste" and Gammarelli (Rome) albs, surplices and rochets ... Fully custom tailored cassocks ... We are considered the leader in the U.S. and specialize in Bishops and Monsignors robes, all of which are custom tailored here. We also supply all Episcopal accessories; mitres, zuchettos, birettas, rochets, albs, pectoral cross, chains and cross cords, bishops rings, croziers. HAVE TAPE MEASURE — WILL TRAVEL

MURPHY
ROBES

MURPHY CAP AND GOWN CO.
Murphy Vestments
4200 31st St. North
St. Petersburg, FL 33714
Tel.: 800-876-8774; 813-527-0696; FAX: 813-526-3528

Personnel:
Don Camp .... President
Howard Wright .... Sales Manager

Type of Business:
Manufacturer of vestments, albs, cassocks, choir and acolyte robes and accessories, value priced with guaranteed fit and quality. We supply a complete line of quality liturgical attire, custom tailored as well as many styles in stock and ready to ship within 24 hours of receipt of order. Available through your local church goods dealer, or call or write for more information.

ROBES, VESTMENTS, ETC.

ABBOTT CHURCH GOODS, INC.
1515 Route 38
Cherry Hill, NJ 08002
Tel.: 800-522-2688; 609-662-6959; FAX: 609-665-5109
website: http://www.abbottsinc.com
e-mail: ACG.INC@internetMCI.com

Personnel:
Daniel J. Castonguay . . . . President
Joseph F. McKeaney . . . . General Manager
Michael W. Wasyluk . . . . Customer Service

Type of Business:
Purveyors of the Finest Vesture, Paraments, Statuary & Metalware since 1962. Unique and original creations our specialty. Custom designs to complement your liturgical environment. Exclusive representatives of Slabbinck Master Collection & Original Collection.

C.M. ALMY & SON, INC.
10 Glenville St., P.O. Box 2644
Greenwich, CT 06836-2644
Tel.: 203-531-7600

Type of Business:
We make a complete line of eucharistic vestments, clerical haberdashery and choir robes; as well as sacred vessels worthy of the Lord's table. Chalices, ciboria and other metal appointments from ALMY are classic designs.

T.M.

Bringing the Art Back into the Craft

BRAMANTE STUDIO
321 Wellington St. N.
Kitchener, ON, Canada N2H 5K8
Tel.: 800-295-6902; FAX: 519-570-2706

Personnel:
Abraham Mathew. . . . . President

Type of Business:
Every parish is unique, not only in terms of the parishioners who make up the body of the church, but also in terms of the art and architectural elements that define the worship space. At Bramante Studio we endeavour to capture this individuality in each fabric art piece we make. Using exceptional fabrics and old world craftsmanship, we create custom made hangings, tapestries, vestments, and altar cloths that seek to recognize the uniqueness of each parish.

Chagall Design Limited

CHAGALL DESIGN LIMITED
910 S. Los Angeles St., 9th Fl.
Los Angeles, CA 90015
Tel.: 800-947-7923; 213-624-7656; FAX: 213-624-8036

Type of Business:
Chagall Design Limited is unique in its own right, its reputation stems from the custom designs created by the European Designer – Jacques de Groot, these creations were designed for the individual special needs of the Fathers and Parishes throughout the United States, Canada and Europe.
Working directly with the church, Chagall had created and custom-made the Chasubles, Banners, Altar Cloths, Stoles, and many other accessories. Chagall stands by the wide range of fine fabrics and excellent craftsmanship offered to you. With a full guarantee and low prices, Chagall stands second to none in the industry.
Call 1-800-947-7923 for more information or a catalog.

the symbol of
Regal Splendor

Robert Gaspard Co.

ROBERT GASPARD CO., INC.
200 N. Janacek Rd.
Brookfield, WI 53045-6153
Tel.: 800-784-6868; 414-784-6800; FAX: 414-784-7567

Personnel:
Rose Gaspard. . . . . President
Duane G. Buchholz . . . . Gen. Manager

Type of Business:
The Robert Gaspard Co. was established in 1954. Over the past 40 years, we have grown to our present size, occupying a showroom and manufacturing facility in excess of 20,000 square feet and employing 44 full time employees. We pride ourselves on our ability to create original custom designs to enrich your worship needs. Our complete line consists of all ecclesiastical vesture as well as paraments, mass and altar linens, stoles, banners, chasubles, funeral palls, albs, cassocks, surplices, choir robes, acolyte robes and many accessories. Complimentary catalogs and fabric swatches sent on request.

Granda Liturgical Arts, Inc.

GRANDA LITURGICAL ARTS, INC.
2525 Eastwood Ave., Apt. 8A
Evanston, IL 60201
Tel.: 800-425-0828; FAX: 847-492-1374
www.hispacom.es/granda; e-mail: ruj4granda@aol.com

Personnel:
Monica Ruf

Type of Business:
GRANDA LITURGICAL ARTS, Inc. is the USA branch of the largest supplier of church goods in the world: TALLERES DE ARTE GRANDA, S.A.
With 65 employees and sales all over the world, we can offer our experience in the manufacture of:
— metalware: chalices, tabernacles, etc.
— vestments
— wood carvings
— church decoration, interior design
Since 1891, we have been serving the liturgy, combining modern techniques (design by computer, projects in 3D ...) with artistic values.
Special custom orders: our specialty, according to your needs, in style and price.

HOUSE OF HANSEN
4223 W. Irving Park Rd.
Chicago, IL 60641
Tel.: 773-736-5858; FAX: 773-736-6715

Type of Business:
Clerical tailoring specialists for over 85 years. We specialize in Prelatial Appointments and Custom Tailored cassocks made by our professional staff. Custom tailored vestments and albs. A full line of ready-made clerical apparel. See our ad in the front section of this book.

THE HOLY+ROOD GUILD

THE HOLY ROOD GUILD
St. Joseph's Abbey
167 North Spencer Rd.
Spencer, MA 01562-1233
Tel.: 508-885-8750; FAX: 508-885-8701
(508) 885-8751

Type of Business:

Designers and crafters of ecclesiastical vesture for over 40 years. Inspired by our monastic tradition, we seek to unite in our work simplicity in design, quality in materials and excellence in craftsmanship. The result is vesture that enhances the liturgical celebration with visual grace and order. Our artists—both monks and laypersons—are available for custom design work and consultation. We also provide an extensive selection of ready made items.

ADAM KOCHLIN DESIGNS

ADAM KOCHLIN DESIGNS
21 Ann St.
South Norwalk, CT 06854
Tel.: 800-886-4668; FAX: 203-838-8752

Personnel:

Adam Kochlin . . . . Design Director
Michael Kirshbaum . . . . Executive Director
Regina Maguire . . . . Product Manager

Type of Business:

Adam Kochlin Designs creates a complete line of made to order vestments and hangings produced in our studio in Connecticut. Working with a number of artists we also create made to order sacred vessels and appointments including processional crosses, pacschal candlesticks, altar candlesticks, sanctuary lamps, incensors, chalices and patens, aumbrys, curets, and falgons in wood, ceramic, glass and metal. Call 800-886-4668 for free catalog and information.

P. J. McDERMOTT & CO.
P.O. Box 950101
Fort Tilden, NY 11695
Tel.: 718-634-5583

Personnel:

Patrick J. McDermott . . . . President

Type of Business:

We are a major supplier of Ready-made suits, coats, slacks, blazers, R.J. Toomey Co. shirt fronts, French-cuff shirts, clerical vests ... "Beau-Veste" and Gammarelli (Rome) albs, surplices and rochets ... Fully custom tailored cassocks ... We are considered the leader in the U.S. and specialize in Bishops and Monsignors robes, all of which are custom tailored here. We also supply all Episcopal accessories; mitres, zuchettos, birettas, rochets, albs, pectoral cross, chains and cross cords, bishops rings, croziers. HAVE TAPE MEASURE — WILL TRAVEL

SLABBINCK®

ART STUDIO SLABBINCK
Headquarters:
L. Bauwensstraat 18
8200 Brugge, Belgium
Tel.: 32-50-312557; FAX: 32-50-318358

Type of Business:

Belgian made vestments (chasubles, stoles, albs, copes, deacon-stoles, dalmatics, altar and lectern covers, altar linens and cloths, tapestries and banners). Chalices, ciboria, patens and pyxes also available. Slabbinck Speed Service offered for many items as advertised in our catalog. Also Dirk Slabbinck Master Collection, an exclusive collection of vestments and paraments created from the inspired imagination of master designer Dirk Slabbinck, or according to your own specifications. For information on the dealer nearest you, call 800-423-3224 or FAX 800-284-9000.

SN
STADELMAIER NIJMEGEN

STADELMAIER-NIJMEGEN-HOLLAND
Oranjesingel 65: P.O. Box 1011
Nijmegen, Holland 6501 BA
Tel.: 31-24-3224384; FAX: 31-24-3232255

Type of Business:

SN mighty mitres are visibly the best.
SN crosiers have the SN-signature, to match the total design.
Ben Stadelmaier Senior is the specialist.

CONSTRUCTION, MAINTENANCE & RENOVATION

ARTHUR
BUILDING SYSTEMS, INC.

ARTHUR BUILDING SYSTEMS
719 Middle St., P.O. Box 60
Bristol, CT 06011-0060
Tel.: 1-800-692-1234

Personnel:
David Welles . . . . V.P. Business Development

Type of Business:
Arthur Building Systems is a leader in modular and pre-engineered construction. We can design and construct your new facility in half the time required by traditional site-built methods with minimal site disruption. Our areas of expertise include classrooms, parish halls, day care, health and administrative facilities.

GERARD ROOFING TECHNOLOGIES, INC.
955 Columbia St.
Brea, CA 92821-2923
Tel.: 1-800-237-6637; FAX: 714-529-6643
website: http://www.gerardusa.com; e-mail: info@gerardusa.com

Personnel:
Matt Pritchard . . . . Product Manager

Type of Business:
The Gerard stone-coated steel roofing system is a durable, class "A" roof covering that has proven itself through nature's worst conditions. Manufactured to the strictest standards, Gerard has assembled a lightweight (1.4 lb/sq.ft.), interlocking roof system that won't dry up, burn, break, blow off, crack or curl ... offering a combination of properties that you can't get with other products. The Gerard panels are available in tile or shake profiles and in a variety of colors.

RAMBUSCH

RAMBUSCH
40 West 13th St.
New York, NY 10011
Tel.: 212-675-0400; FAX: 212-620-4687

Personnel:

Viggo Bech Rambusch . . . . Senior Project Director
Martin V. Rambusch . . . . Stained Glass Director

Type of Business:

Since 1898, creating church interiors, liturgical furnishings, and art work. Fine restoration of church interiors. In-house studios and shops for designing and executing stained glass, church lighting systems, art metal work, and decorative painting.

ARTISTS & DECORATORS

THE BLACK FOREST BUILDING COMPANY

ANTHONY JOHN BELLOMO / THE BLACK FOREST CO.
310 Euclid
Mt. Clemens, MI 48043
Tel.: 810-954-4800; FAX: 810-954-4806

Personnel:

Anthony Bellomo . . . . President

Type of Business:

Anthony John Bellomo is a sculptor. He works in a wide variety of materials from wood and bronze to fibers, stone and living plant materials. Over the past twenty-five years he has developed the Black Forest Company. Black Forest is a group of artists and artisans, who along with Bellomo, design and build contemporary sculpture and furniture for liturgical spaces. He has developed a series of redwood sand carved exterior pieces for outdoor chapels and meditation gardens. Anthony, along with his team of dedicated crafts persons, pride themselves in listening to the individual community, designing and building pieces to help make their worship a deeper experience.

BOTTI STUDIO OF ARCHITECTURAL ARTS, INC.

BOTTI STUDIO OF ARCHITECTURAL ARTS, INC.
919 Grove St.
Evanston, IL 60201
Tel.: 800-524-7211; FAX: 847-869-5996
847-869-5933; e-mail: Boti@ix.netcom.com

East Coast Studio
1517 State St.
Sarasota, FL 33577
Tel.: 941-951-0978; FAX: 941-953-9078

West Coast Studio
1038 N. Highway 101
Encinitas, CA 92024
Tel.: 619-753-0705; FAX: 619-753-0705

Personnel:

Staff includes internationlly recognized artists and designers working in conjunction with our highly skilled artisans and craftsmen.
Italo G. Botti . . . . President

Type of Business:

For generations Botti Studio has had a reputation for embodying all that is artistically creative in the traditional and contemporary ecclesiastical field. This field includes design and fabrication of stained and faceted glass windows, restoration of windows, church interiors, appointments, murals, sculpture, mosaic and marble. We are completely dedicated to both quality and satisfying our clients needs spiritually and liturgically. Botti Studio is nationwide, offering consultation and designs without obligation. Member Stained Glass Association of America.

Conrad Schmitt Studios Inc.

CONRAD SCHMITT STUDIOS, INC.
2405 S. 162nd St.
New Berlin, WI 53151
Tel.: 414-786-3030; 800-969-3033; FAX: 414-786-9036

Personnel:

Heidi Gruenke Emery . . . . Vice President & Marketing Director

Type of Business:

Since 1889, the Conrad Schmitt Studios has restored and decorated hundreds of interiors across the country. Their scope of work includes the investigation/documentation of original design schemes, the restoration of those schemes through the application of various decorative techniques including gilding, glazing, marbleizing, stencilling, and graining, as well as the conservation, restoration, and replication of murals and stained glass. Some of their recently completed projects include the Cathedral of the Assumption, Louisville, Kentucky; St. John's Cathedral, Shreveport, Louisiana; and Sacred Heart Church, New Philadelphia, Ohio.

Holy Land Art Company

For over seventy years, Holy Land Art Company has been a leader in design and fabrication of liturgical furnishings and artwork.

Holy Land Art Company offers a full array of services:

Liturgical Designs
Consultations
Custom Wood
Custom Metal
Stone
Fine Arts
Stained Glass
Seating
Ecclesiastical Painting

160 Chambers Street
New York, NY 10007
800-962-4659

12 Sullivan Street
Westwood, NJ 07675
800-334-3621

300 Prosperity Farm Road
North Palm Beach, FL 33408
800-526-1294

DAPRATO RIGALI STUDIOS, INC.

DAPRATO RIGALI STUDIOS, INC.
7956 Oakton St.
Niles, IL 60714
Tel.: 847-692-6350; FAX: 847-692-3445

Personnel:
John Rigali
Robert Rigali
Lisa Rigali Galvin
Mike Rigali

Type of Business:
Daprato Rigali Studios Inc. has been beautifying Churches in America since 1860.
Today we find the Rigali Family restoring and renovating the churches originally decorated by their Great-Grandfather, John E. Rigali; aware of his reputation to create spiritually moving environments with quality material and craftsmanship.
Some of their most recent jobs include: decoration and stained glass restoration at St. Mary of the Lake Seminary, Mundelein, IL.; Marble renovation and decoration, St. Elizabeth's Mother House, Allegany, N.Y.; and General Contracting for complete renovation of St. Bernadette's Church, Rockford, IL.
The Daprato Rigali staff is equipped to take your project from start to finish. If you're interested in working with a fine interior design studio experienced in Ecclesiastical Artistries please call for consultation at no obligation. We deliver what we design.

Holy Land Art Company

HOLY LAND ART CO.
160 Chambers St.
New York, NY 10007
Tel.: 212-962-2130

Type of Business:
For over 70 years, a leader in design and fabrication of liturgical furnishings and artwork.

RAMBUSCH

RAMBUSCH
40 West 13th St.
New York, NY 10011
Tel.: 212-675-0400; FAX: 212-620-4687

Personnel:
Viggo Bech Rambusch . . . . Senior Project Director
Martin V. Rambusch . . . . Stained Glass Director

Type of Business:
Since 1898, creating church interiors, liturgical furnishings, and art work. Fine restoration of church interiors. In-house studios and shops for designing and executing stained glass, church lighting systems, art metal work, and decorative painting.

WOODCARVING UNLIMITED
05340 U.S. 131 N.
Walloon Lake, MI 49796
Tel.: 616-535-2393

Personnel:
Pietro Vinotti . . . . President, Designer, Sculptor & Gild)
Riccardo Vinotti . . . . Sculptor & Casting Artist

Type of Business:
Religious art done with extreme dedication. Specialists in baroque, Gothic and contemporary art. Monuments, statues, altars, organs: ornaments in wood and bronze.

Winterich's

DESIGNERS AND CRAFTSMEN

JOHN W. WINTERICH & ASSOCIATES
9545 Midwest Ave., Ste. M
Cleveland, OH 44125
Tel.: 800-255-4544; FAX: 216-662-2509

Personnel:
John W. Winterich III
Greg M. Winterich
Bill O'Loughlin

Type of Business:
Founded in 1913, the Winterich Studio of Liturgical Art provides complete interior design and fabrication services for all aspects of new church projects and restoration and renovations. The award winning work of Winterich's is known nationwide. Our on-staff architect, liturgical consultants, designers and craftsmen are dedicated to excellence in Liturgical Art.

BELLTOWERS & STEEPLES

FIBERGLASS SPECIALTIES INCORPORATED

FIBERGLASS SPECIALTIES, INC.
P.O. Box 1340
Henderson, TX 75653
Tel.: 800-527-1459; FAX: 903-657-2318

Personnel:

Ben Bradshaw . . . . Sales Manager
Cloe York
Ellen Russell
Matt Pettigrew

Type of Business:

Fiberglass Specialties has been producing quality church steeples and cupolas for more than thirty years. They have the largest selection of standard designs in the industry, or they can custom build to your unique design. Their in-house sales staff combined with a nationwide network of local representatives are ready to assist you.

CHURCH SIGNS & BANNERS

THE BLACK FOREST BUILDING COMPANY

ANTHONY JOHN BELLOMO / THE BLACK FOREST CO.
310 Euclid
Mt. Clemens, MI 48043
Tel.: 810-954-4800; FAX: 810-954-4806

Personnel:

Anthony Bellomo. . . . . President

Type of Business:

Anthony John Bellomo is a sculptor. He works in a wide variety of materials from wood and bronze to fibers, stone and living plant materials. Over the past twenty-five years he has developed the Black Forest Company. Black Forest is a group of artists and artisans, who along with Bellomo, design and build contemporary sculpture and furniture for liturgical spaces. He has developed a series of redwood sand carved exterior pieces for outdoor chapels and meditation gardens. Anthony, along with his team of dedicated crafts persons, pride themselves in listening to the individual community, designing and building pieces to help make their worship a deeper experience.

CONSERVATION

ALBERT MICHAELS CONSERVATION, INC.
1116 North Third St.
Harrisburg, PA 17102
Tel.: 717-232-9592; FAX: 717-234-0311

Personnel:

John M. DiTonno . . . . Projects Manager
John A. Rita. . . . . Conservator
William W. Tull. . . . . General Manager

Type of Business:

Founded in 1971, we offer a range of art and architectural conservation and restoration services, including PROJECT PLANNING and collection assessment, ANALYTICAL INVESTIGATION to determine original and subsequent finishes including techniques and materials employed. CONSERVATION & RESTORATION OF original artwork, ornamental plaster, painted surfaces, interior wood finishes, marble surfaces historic furniture, metal light fixtures, leaded glass windows, and REPRODUCTION OF ornamental plaster, architectural woodwork, decorative paint finishes, faux finishes, historic furnishings and fixtures, historic window treatments and carpets.

Conrad Schmitt Studios Inc.

CONRAD SCHMITT STUDIOS, INC.
2405 S. 162nd St.
New Berlin, WI 53151
Tel.: 800-969-3033; 414-786-3030; FAX: 414-786-9036

Personnel:
Heidi Gruenke Emery . . . . Vice President & Marketing Director

Type of Business:
Since 1889, this family-owned Studio has restored and decorated hundreds of interiors across the country. Their scope of work includes the investigation and documentation of original decorative schemes; the restoration of those schemes through the application of various decorative techniques including gilding, glazing, marbleizing, stenciling, and graining, as well as the design, fabrication, conservation or replication of murals and stained glass. The Studio can assist projects in the early stages with architectural samples and rendering for fund-raising. Recently completed projects include St. Josaphat's Basilica, Milwaukee, WI; St. Ann's, Napoleanville, LA; and St. Bernard's, Akron, OH.

DOORS & PARTITIONS

THE BLACK FOREST BUILDING COMPANY

ANTHONY JOHN BELLOMO / THE BLACK FOREST CO.
310 Euclid
Mt. Clemens, MI 48043
Tel.: 810-954-4800; FAX: 810-954-4806

Personnel:
Anthony Bellomo . . . . President

Type of Business:
Anthony John Bellomo is a sculptor. He works in a wide variety of materials from wood and bronze to fibers, stone and living plant materials. Over the past twenty-five years he has developed the Black Forest Company. Black Forest is a group of artists and artisans, who along with Bellomo, design and build contemporary sculpture and furniture for liturgical spaces. He has developed a series of redwood sand carved exterior pieces for outdoor chapels and meditation gardens. Anthony, along with his team of dedicated crafts persons, pride themselves in listening to the individual community, designing and building pieces to help make their worship a deeper experience.

FACETED GLASS

Conrad Schmitt Studios Inc.

CONRAD SCHMITT STUDIOS, INC.
2405 S. 162nd St.
New Berlin, WI 53151
Tel.: 800-969-3033; 414-786-3030; FAX: 414-786-9036

Personnel:
Heidi Gruenke Emery . . . . Vice President & Marketing Director

Type of Business:
Since 1889, this family-owned Studio has restored and decorated hundreds of interiors across the country. Their scope of work includes the investigation and documentation of original decorative schemes; the restoration of those schemes through the application of various decorative techniques including gilding, glazing, marbleizing, stenciling, and graining, as well as the design, fabrication, conservation or replication of murals and stained glass. The Studio can assist projects in the early stages with architectural samples and rendering for fund-raising. Recently completed projects include St. Josaphat's Basilica, Milwaukee, WI; St. Ann's, Napoleanville, LA; and St. Bernard's, Akron, OH.

GENERAL CONTRACTORS

DAPRATO RIGALI STUDIOS, INC.

DAPRATO RIGALI STUDIOS, INC.
7956 Oakton St.
Niles, IL 60714
Tel.: 847-692-6350; FAX: 847-692-3445

Personnel:
John Rigali
Robert Rigali
Lisa Rigali Galvin
Mike Rigali

Type of Business:
Daprato Rigali Studios Inc. has been beautifying Churches in America since 1860.
Today we find the Rigali Family restoring and renovating the churches originally decorated by their Great-Grandfather, John E. Rigali; aware of his reputation to create spiritually moving environments with quality material and craftsmanship.
Some of their most recent jobs include: decoration and stained glass restoration at St. Mary of the Lake Seminary, Mundelein, IL.; Marble renovation and decoration, St. Elizabeth's Mother House, Allegany, N.Y.; and General Contracting for complete renovation of St. Bernadette's Church, Rockford, IL.
The Daprato Rigali staff is equipped to take your project from start to finish. If you're interested in working with a fine interior design studio experienced in Ecclesiastical Artistries please call for consultation at no obligation. We deliver what we design.

MONUMENTAL CHURCH ENTRANCES

THE BAUT STUDIOS, INC.
ECCLESIASTICAL CRAFTSMEN

THE BAUT STUDIOS, INC.
1095 Main St.
Swoyersville, PA 18704
Tel.: 800-326-9421; FAX: 717-288-0380

Personnel:

- Heide Marie Cebrick .... Artisan/Designer
- Conrad Dismas Baut .... President
- Gerhard Francis Baut..................... Master Sculptor

Type of Business:

The Baut Studios, Inc., established in 1927, is an ecclesiastical studio which has been manufacturing and installing their own door systems for over 18 years. Incorporating many outstanding features into their custom dies, Baut manufactures to any size and shape. Baut Studios has a high nationwide referral of new customers from its many existing satisfied customers. Innovative product know-how, modern plant facilities, in-house design staff and computerized drafting, design and manufacturing helps Baut build the most intricate doors with ease.

RESTORATION

DAPRATO RIGALI STUDIOS, INC.

DAPRATO RIGALI STUDIOS, INC.
7956 Oakton St.
Niles, IL 60714
Tel.: 847-692-6350; FAX: 847-692-3445

Personnel:

- John Rigali
- Robert Rigali
- Lisa Rigali Galvin
- Mike Rigali

Type of Business:

Daprato Rigali Studios Inc. has been beautifying Churches in America since 1860.

Today we find the Rigali Family restoring and renovating the churches originally decorated by their Great-Grandfather, John E. Rigali; aware of his reputation to create spiritually moving environments with quality material and craftsmanship.

Some of their most recent jobs include: decoration and stained glass restoration at St. Mary of the Lake Seminary, Mundelein, IL.; Marble renovation and decoration, St. Elizabeth's Mother House, Allegany, N.Y.; and General Contracting for complete renovation of St. Bernadette's Church, Rockford, IL.

The Daprato Rigali staff is equipped to take your project from start to finish. If you're interested in working with a fine interior design studio experienced in Ecclesiastical Artistries please call for consultation at no obligation. We deliver what we design.

ADRIAN HAMERS®
CHURCH INTERIORS
ONE HUNDRED YEARS SERVING THE CLERGY — TOUJOURS — 1887

ADRIAN HAMERS INC.
2 Madison Ave.
Larchmont, NY 10538
Tel.: 914-834-7780; FAX: 914-834-0712

Type of Business:

Since 1887, the Hamers name has been synonymous with expert silversmithing throughout the world in the field of Liturgical Art. We are also experts in: Church Interiors from design to execution, Renovations, Altars, Sacred Vessels, Appraisals, Gold and Silver Plating & Repairing, Tabernacles, Marble, Woodwork & Woodcarving, Statuary, Stained Glass, Pews & Chairs, Gold Leafing, Frescoes, Restoration, Trompe-l'oeuil, Wall Murals (repair and conservation cleaning), Ornamental Plaster, Heraldic Designs & Bishop Regalia.

KOLEY'S, INC.
2951 Harney St.
Omaha, NE 68131
Tel.: 402-341-9795; FAX: 402-341-5857

Personnel:
Tom Koley
Terry Goehring

Type of Business:
Quality, Care and Craftsmanship. For four generations these words have described Koley's, Inc. Since our very beginning in 1919, we have endeavored to serve the churches and clergy in repairing, polishing and replating of sacred vessels or other items of metal found in the Church. Our craftsmen strive to restore your cherished ecclesiastical items to its original condition whenever possible. We take pride in knowing that you have entrusted us with your items. Free estimates.

RAMBUSCH

RAMBUSCH
40 West 13th St.
New York, NY 10011
Tel.: 212-675-0400; FAX: 212-620-4687

Personnel:
Viggo Bech Rambusch .... Senior Project Director
Martin V. Rambusch .... Stained Glass Director

Type of Business:
Since 1898, creating church interiors, liturgical furnishings, and art work. Fine restoration of church interiors. In-house studios and shops for designing and executing stained glass, church lighting systems, art metal work, and decorative painting.

Conrad Schmitt Studios Inc.

CONRAD SCHMITT STUDIOS, INC.
2405 S. 162nd St.
New Berlin, WI 53151
Tel.: 800-969-3033; 414-786-3030; FAX: 414-786-9036

Personnel:
Heidi Gruenke Emery . . . . Vice President & Marketing Director

Type of Business:
Since 1889, this family-owned Studio has restored and decorated hundreds of interiors across the country. Their scope of work includes the investigation and documentation of original decorative schemes; the restoration of those schemes through the application of various decorative techniques including gilding, glazing, marbleizing, stenciling, and graining, as well as the design, fabrication, conservation or replication of murals and stained glass. The Studio can assist projects in the early stages with architectural samples and rendering for fund-raising. Recently completed projects include St. Josaphat's Basilica, Milwaukee, WI; St. Ann's, Napoleanville, LA; and St. Bernard's, Akron, OH.

Stained Glass Associates

STAINED GLASS ASSOCIATES
P.O. Box 1531
Raleigh, NC 27602-1531
Tel.: 919-266-2493

Personnel:
Robert J. Wysocki .... Owner

Type of Business:
- Design, Fabrication and Installation of:
  - Leaded, Faceted and Painted Glass
- Restoration and Repair
  - Replacement Frames
  - Fire Damage
- Appraisals

About SGA:
- Established in 1958
- Studio Member of Stained Glass Association of America
- 957 Installations Nationally and Internationally

Stained Glass Associates is committed to maintaining the highest of ecclesiastical standards and the complete satisfaction of every client.

ROOFING

GERARD ROOFING TECHNOLOGIES, INC.
955 Columbia St.
Brea, CA 92821-2923
Tel.: 800-237-6637; FAX: 714-529-6643
e-mail: info@gerardusa.com; website: http://www.gerardusa.com

Personnel:
Matt Pritchard. . . . . Product Manageri

Type of Business:
The Gerard stone-coated steel roofing system is a durable, class "A" roof covering that has proven itself through nature's worst conditions. Manufactued to the strictest standards, Gerard has assembled a lightweight (1.4 lb/sq.ft.), interlocking roof system that won't dry up, burn, break, blow off, crack or curl ... offering a combination of properties that you can't get with other products. The Gerard panels are available in tile or shake profiles and in a variety of colors.

STAINED GLASS

BOTTI STUDIO OF ARCHITECTURAL ARTS, INC.

BOTTI STUDIO OF ARCHITECTURAL ARTS, INC.
919 Grove St.
Evanston, IL 60201
Tel.: 800-524-7211; FAX: 847-869-5996
847-869-5933; e-mail: Boti@ix.netcom.com

East Coast Studio
1517 State St.
Sarasota, FL 33577
Tel.: 941-951-0978; FAX: 941-953-9078

West Coast Studio
1038 N Highway 101
Encinitas, CA 92024
Tel.: 619-753-0705; FAX: 619-753-0705

Personnel:
Staff includes internationlly recognized artists and designers working in conjunction with our highly skilled artisans and craftsmen.
Italo G. Botti . . . . President

Type of Business:
For generations Botti Studio has had a reputation for embodying all that is artistically creative in the traditional and contemporary ecclesiastical field. This field includes design and fabrication of stained and faceted glass windows, restoration of windows, church interiors, appointments, murals, sculpture, mosaic and marble. We are completely dedicated to both quality and satisfying our clients needs spiritually and liturgically. Botti Studio is nationwide, offering consultation and designs without obligation. Member Stained Glass Association of America.

DAPRATO RIGALI STUDIOS, INC.

DAPRATO RIGALI STUDIOS, INC.
7956 Oakton St.
Niles, IL 60714
Tel.: 847-692-6350; FAX: 847-692-3445

Personnel:
John Rigali
Robert Rigali
Lisa Rigali Galvin
Mike Rigali

Type of Business:
Daprato Rigali Studios Inc. has been beautifying Churches in America since 1860.
Today we find the Rigali Family restoring and renovating the churches originally decorated by their Great-Grandfather, John E. Rigali; aware of his reputation to create spiritually moving environments with quality material and craftsmanship.
Some of their most recent jobs include: decoration and stained glass restoration at St. Mary of the Lake Seminary, Mundelein, IL.; Marble renovation and decoration, St. Elizabeth's Mother House, Allegany, N.Y.; and General Contracting for complete renovation of St. Bernadette's Church, Rockford, IL.
The Daprato Rigali staff is equipped to take your project from start to finish. If you're interested in working with a fine interior design studio experienced in Ecclesiastical Artistries please call for consultation at no obligation. We deliver what we design.

DIETERICH SPAHN & ASSOCIATES, INC.
605 Bushaway Rd.
Wayzata, MN 55391
Tel.: 612-475-2601; FAX: 612-930-3930

Personnel:
Dieterich Spahn . . . . President

Type of Business:
Since 1961, creating new stained glass windows, mosaic icons & murals. Liturgical design for complete church interior with furnishings. Statues in wood or bronze. Fine restoration of early European stained glass, mosaic icons & murals. New frames — wood, metal — protective glazing — complete installations. References: completed church commissions in U.S. upon request. Inquiry appreciated.

Emmanuel Studios, Inc.
STAINED GLASS WINDOWS

EMMANUEL STUDIOS
410 Maple Ave.
Nashville, TN 37210
Tel.: 800-326-2228; 615-255-5446; FAX: 615-255-5447

Personnel:
Dennis R. Harmon . . . . President
William B. Brimm Jr. . . . . Vice President

Type of Business:
Emmanuel Studios has been designing, fabricating, and installing stained glass for over twenty-one years. We create designs that are sensitive to and compatible with any architectural style. Our leaded and faceted windows are constructed with quality craftsmanship and careful attention to detail. An installation by Emmanuel Studios can help your building convey an uplifting atmosphere.

Hiemer & Company
Stained Glass Studio

HIEMER & CO. STAINED GLASS STUDIO
403 Crooks Ave. at Wabash
Clifton, New Jersey 07011
Tel.: 973-772-5081; FAX: 973-772-0325

Personnel:
Gerhard E. Hiemer . . . . President
Judith Hiemer Van Wie . . . . Designer

Type of Business:
Designers, fabricators and installers of ecclesiastical stained glass since the 1880's. The permanent staff of certified journeymen specialize in traditional and contemporary liturgical design. Highly skilled and experienced with large scale restorations, artistic replications and window renovations. Works may be seen in over 1,060 North American churches.
*Portland, OR rep: Steven Closs 503-253-6343
*Anchorage, AK rep: Rita Hiemer Lammot 907-746-4948
Information and quotations submitted without obligation.
Member, National Glass Association

THE JUDSON STUDIOS
200 S. Ave. 66
Los Angeles, CA 90042
Tel.: 800-445-8376; FAX: 213-255-8529

Type of Business:
We listen to your needs and offer our expertise to design windows that will enhance your worship space. Call us with your repair or restoration concerns. We will work with you on the best solution for the care of your exiting windows. The Judson Studios have been family owned and operated since 1897. We have done this by serving people like yourself successfully and designing and crafting stained glass with time honored quality.

Personnel:
Walter Judson
Bill Judson

LSG

LYNCHBURG STAINED GLASS CO.
P.O. Box 4453
Lynchburg, VA 24502
Tel.: 800-237-6161; FAX: 804-525-6168

Type of Business:
Products Offered: Custom designed leaded and faceted stained glass windows. Aluminum frames and protective coverings.
Services Offered: On site design and consultation service. Complete delivery and installation. Repair and restoration service.
Recent Clients: Holy Spirit, Atlanta, GA; St. Joseph's, Cockeysville, MD; St. Andrew the Apostle, Silver Springs, MD; Immaculate Conception, Towson, MD; St. Anthonys, Atlanta, GA.
Free Information: Call for a free packet of information.

1847 — **150** Years — 1997
Franz Mayer of Munich, Inc.
F.X. Zettler

FRANZ MAYER OF MUNICH, INC.
25, Seidlstrasse
Munich, GER D-80335
Tel.: 011-49-89-595484; FAX: 011-49-89-593446

Personnel:
Gabriel Mayer, Ph.D. . . . . President
Konrad Mayer
Michael Mayer

Type of Business:
Founded 1847, Franz Mayer of Munich, still family owned and operated, is celebrating its 150th anniversary in 1997! Together with F.X.Zettler — the sister company — they remain to be one of the international leading studios for **stained glass** and **mosaic**. More than 100 Cathedrals and thousands of churches worldwide — including St. Peter's in Rome (The Holy Spirit Window) — have windows, mosaics or — from earlier periods — altars or statuary from them. Your enquiry will be appreciated as a birthday present!

RAMBUSCH

RAMBUSCH
40 West 13th St.
New York, NY 10011
Tel.: 212-675-0400; FAX: 212-620-4687

Personnel:
Viggo Bech Rambusch .... Senior Project Director
Martin V. Rambusch .... Stained Glass Director

Type of Business:
Since 1898, creating church interiors, liturgical furnishings, and art work. Fine restoration of church interiors. In-house studios and shops for designing and executing stained glass, church lighting systems, art metal work, and decorative painting.

Reinarts Stained Glass Studios Inc
Designers & Manufacturers

REINARTS STAINED GLASS STUDIOS
506 West 5th St.
Winona, MI 55987
Tel.: 507-452-4465; FAX: 507-452-4649

Personnel:
William A. Reinarts .... President
William H. Reinarts, Senior .... Vice President
Rebecca J. Reinarts .... Secretary Treasurer
Jim Reinarts............................ Studio Manager

Type of Business:
46 Years of continuous service of the church. New Stained Glass windows design and manufacture. Stained Glass window restoration. installation of protective covering. New frames and new ventilators. Repair of wood frames.

Conrad Schmitt Studios Inc.

CONRAD SCHMITT STUDIOS, INC.
2405 S. 162nd St.
New Berlin, WI 53151
Tel.: 800-969-3033; 414-786-3030; FAX: 414-786-9036

Personnel:
Heidi Gruenke Emery.... Vice President & Marketing Director

Type of Business:
Since 1889, this family-owned Studio has restored and decorated hundreds of interiors across the country. Their scope of work includes the investigation and documentation of original decorative schemes; the restoration of those schemes through the application of various decorative techniques including gilding, glazing, marbleizing, stenciling, and graining, as well as the design, fabrication, conservation or replication of murals and stained glass. The Studio can assist projects in the early stages with architectural samples and rendering for fund-raising. Recently completed projects include St. Josaphat's Basilica, Milwaukee, WI; St. Ann's, Napoleanville, LA; and St. Bernard's, Akron, OH.

GREG SPIESS & CO.

SPIESS ARCHITECTURAL ANTIQUES
230 East Washington St.
Joliet, IL 60433
Tel.: 815-722-5639; FAX: 815-722-0171

Type of Business:
Specializing in older and antique church furniture. Gothic, Romanesque and Classical styles in marble, wood, bronze etc. Altars, pews, communion rails, stained glass, lecterns, baptismals, vestment cases, confessionals, Stations of the Cross statuary. Lighting. Pew and wood restoration available.

Stained Glass Associates

STAINED GLASS ASSOCIATES
P.O. Box 1531
Raleigh, NC 27602-1531
Tel.: 919-266-2493

Personnel:
Robert J. Wysocki .... Owner

Type of Business:
- Design, Fabrication and Installation of:
  - Leaded, Faceted and Painted Glass
- Restoration and Repair
  - Replacement Frames
  - Fire Damage
- Appraisals

About SGA:
- Established in 1958
- Studio Member of Stained Glass Association of America
- 957 Installations Nationally and Internationally

Stained Glass Associates is committed to maintaining the highest of ecclesistical standards and the complete satisfaction of every client.

EDUCATION

THE NATIONAL MUSEUM OF CATHOLIC ART & HISTORY

THE NATIONAL MUSEUM OF CATHOLIC ART & HISTORY
54 West 50th St. @ 30 Rockefeller Plaza
New York, NY 10020
Tel.: 212-957-8866; FAX: 212-957-5293

Personnel:
Christina Cox .... Executive Director
Larissa Van Duser .... Curator

Type of Business:
Exhibiting Religious Works of Old Masters and Contemporary Artists. Artists Available for Commissions. Collecting and Restoring Religious Art and Artifacts including Paintings, Sculpture, Crucifixes, Chalices, Monstrances, Bibles, Books, Photos, Altar Candlesticks, Vestments, Scapulars, Communion Bells, Madonnas, Church Interiors and Catholic Historical Items. Touring Exhibits. Cultural and Educational Programs.

CHRISTIAN CONFERENCES

Franciscan University of Steubenville ©

FRANCISCAN UNIVERSITY OF STEUBENVILLE
University Blvd.
Steubenville, OH 43952-6701
Tel.: 614-283-3771

Personnel:
Fr. Michael Scanlan TOR .... President
Mr. Randall Cirner .... Dean of Students
Dr. Michael Healy .... Dean of Faculty
Miss Mary Kay Lacke .... Dean of Evangelization

Type of Business:
Founded in 1946 by Third Order Regular friars, Franciscan University is located in Steubenville, Ohio, 40 minutes west of Pittsburgh, Pennsylvania. The University offers over 30 undergraduate six master's degree programs to over 1960 students from all 50 states and over 40 countries. Committed to higher education based on Catholic teaching, Franciscan University has been named one of America's Best Colleges by *US News and World Report* and is listed in the Templeton Foundation's Honor Roll for Character Building Colleges.

COLLEGES & UNIVERSITIES

Franciscan University of Steubenville ©

FRANCISCAN UNIVERSITY OF STEUBENVILLE
University Blvd.
Steubenville, OH 43952-6701
Tel.: 614-283-3771

Personnel:
Fr. Michael Scanlan TOR .... President
Mr. Randall Cirner .... Dean of Students
Dr. Michael Healy .... Dean of Faculty
Miss Mary Kay Lacke .... Dean of Evangelization

Type of Business:
Founded in 1946 by Third Order Regular friars, Franciscan University is located in Steubenville, Ohio, 40 minutes west of Pittsburgh, Pennsylvania. The University offers over 30 undergraduate six master's degree programs to over 1960 students from all 50 states and over 40 countries. Committed to higher education based on Catholic teaching, Franciscan University has been named one of America's Best Colleges by *US News and World Report* and is listed in the Templeton Foundation's Honor Roll for Character Building Colleges.

EDUCATIONAL OPPORTUNITIES

GUEST HOUSE, INC.
1601 Joslyn Rd., P.O. Box 420
Lake Orion, MI 48361
Tel.: 800-626-6910; 810-391-4445; FAX: 810-391-021C

LAKE ORION CENTER
(For Women Religious)
P.O. Box 68
Lake Orion, MI 48361
Tel.: 800-626-6910; 810-391-3100; FAX: 810-391-1553

ROCHESTER TREATMENT CENTER
(For priests, deacons, brothers & seminarians)
P.O. Box 954
Rochester, MN 55903
Tel.: 800-634-4155; 507-288-4693; FAX: 507-288-1240

Personnel:
Richard K. Frisch, A.C.S.W. . . . . President & CEO
Danial A. Kidd. . . . . Chief Administrative Officer
Sr. Mae Kierans, C.S.J. . . . . Lake Orion Center
Bill Morgan, C.C.D.C.R.. . . . . Rochester Treatment Center
Daniel Webster. . . . . Director of Communications

Type of Business:
Guest House, Inc. is a lay-owned, lay-operated nonprofit corporation established in 1956. With the approbation of the Catholic hierarchy, it operates special residential treatment centers for alcoholic Catholic priests, deacons, brothers, sisters and seminarians from all over the world.
Catholic women religious are treated at Guest House in Lake Orion, Michigan. Our facility in Rochester, Minnesota has treatment programs for priests, deacons, brothers and seminarians.
Lovely buildings, spacious country landscape, comfortable rooms set in a serene, non-clinical setting all play an important role in reaffirming a sense of self-worth to a sick, chemically dependent priest or religious.
Accredited by JCAHO (Joint Commission on Accreditation of Healthcare Organizations) and licensed by the Department of Public Health in the states of Michigan and Minnesota respectively.

Weston Jesuit School of Theology

WESTON JESUIT SCHOOL OF THEOLOGY
3 Phillips Place
Cambridge, MA 02138
Tel.: 617-492-1960; FAX: 617-492-5833

Personnel:
Fr. Robert Wild, SJ. . . . . President
Fr. Brian McDermott, SJ . . . . Dean
Betty Smith, RSM,. . . . . Dean of Students
Mary Ellen Herx-Morrill . . . . Director. of Admissions

Type of Business:
Lay and religious men and women come to Weston Jesuit to study theology and prepare for ministry in the Roman Catholic church. A national Jesuit theological center, Weston offers the following degrees: Master of Theological Studies, Master of Divinity, Master of Theology, Licentiate in Sacred Theology, Doctorate in Sacred Theology, and the joint Weston/Boston College Ph.D. in Christian Ethics. At Weston Jesuit, theological and pastoral training by a world-renowned faculty is complemented by opportunities for spiritual formation.

EDUCATIONAL SYSTEMS & SOFTWARE

NCS (National Computer Systems)
4401 West 76th St.
Edina, MN 55435
Tel.: 800-447-3269; FAX: 612-830-8564
e-mail: www@ncs.com

Personnel:
Mike Seeman. . . . . Marketing Manager, K-12
Fred Green . . . Marketing Mgr., Education Alternative Channels
For more information, contact NCS Telemarketing & Telesales

Type of Business:
For over 30 years, NCS has served the education market with optical mark reading (OMR) and imaging technology. NCS touches one of every two children in our nation's schools. NCS is the leading provider of scanning systems, software, and forms used to automate data collection and accurately report on assessment, instructional, and student records information. NCS scanners and forms are also compatible with most of the leading student administrative and testing software products on the market today.

EDUCATIONAL TEST SCORING

NCS (National Computer Systems)
4401 West 76th St.
Edina, MN 55435
Tel.: 800-447-3269; FAX: 612-830-8564
e-mail: www@ncs.com

Personnel:
Mike Seeman . . . . Marketing Manager, K-12
Fred Green . . . Marketing Mgr., Education Alternative Channels
For more information, contact NCS Telemarketing & Telesales

Type of Business:
For over 30 years, NCS has served the education market with optical mark reading (OMR) and imaging technology. NCS touches one of every two children in our nation's schools. NCS is the leading provider of scanning systems, software, and forms used to automate data collection and accurately report on assessment, instructional, and student records information. NCS scanners and forms are also compatible with most of the leading student administrative and testing software products on the market today.

INSTRUCTIONAL MANAGEMENT & STUDENT RECORD SYSTEMS

NCS (National Computer Systems)
4401 West 76th St.
Edina, MN 55435
Tel.: 800-447-3269; FAX: 612-830-8564
e-mail: www@ncs.com

Personnel:
Mike Seeman . . . . Marketing Manager, K-12
Fred Green . . . Marketing Mgr., Education Alternative Channels
For more information, contact NCS Telemarketing & Telesales

Type of Business:
For over 30 years, NCS has served the education market with optical mark reading (OMR) and imaging technology. NCS touches one of every two children in our nation's schools. NCS is the leading provider of scanning systems, software, and forms used to automate data collection and accurately report on assessment, instructional, and student records information. NCS scanners and forms are also compatible with most of the leading student administrative and testing software products on the market today.

MINISTRY OPPORTUNITIES

CATHOLIC RELIEF SERVICES' OPERATION RICE BOWL
209 W. Fayette St.
Baltimore, MD 21201
Tel.: 410-625-2220; FAX: 410-234-2983

Personnel:
Fr. Brian McCullough . . . . Director Church Affairs
Bill O'Keefe . . . . Director Operation Rice Bowl
Lisa D'Ambrogi . . . . Materials Order Coordinator

Type of Business:
Catholic Relief Services' Operation Rice Bowl program draws Catholics into the unique spirit of the Lenten season. It is an opportunity for families, communities, parishes, and other groups to reflect on, pray for, and assist the poor in this country and in the developing world. The program provides a forum to understand the values of self-sacrifice and concern for the poor everywhere. Call 1-800-222-0025 to order free materials.

TUITION FINANCING

SMART TUITION MANAGEMENT SERVICES, INC.
95 Wall St., Ste. 2300
New York, NY 10005
Tel.: 1-800-762-7808; FAX: 212-858-8043

Personnel:
Sam Rosen . . . . President
Leonard Fine . . . . Executive Vice President
Gerald Login . . . . National Sales Manager

Type of Business:
A tuition management service that helps schools to reduce delinquencies, increase cash flow, decrease administrative workload and ensure financial stability. SMART presently serves over 1,000 schools nationwide and is the only tuition management company endorsed by the National Catholic Educational Association.
Complementing SMART is the Tuition Aid Analysis Service, an optional program designed to provide schools with an impartial and objective analysis of what families can afford to pay towards a private education for their children.

TUITION PROGRAM, INC.
521 S. Livingston Ave.
Livingston, NJ 07039-0571
Tel.: 1-800-828-9944; FAX: 1-800-432-9994

Personnel:

Brendon Devlin . . . . President
Cecilia Devlin . . . . Vice President
Brendan Devlin Jr. . . . . Assistant Vice President
Andi Devlin . . . . Assistant Vice President

Type of Business:

Founded in 1985 by Catholic Parents for Catholic Schools. The school receives 100% tuition on time. There is no cost to the school. There is no cost to those who pay on time. Call or Fax for list of schools using the program.

LITURGICAL & CHURCH GOOD S

THE HOLY ROOD GUILD
St. Joseph's Abbey
167 North Spencer Rd.
Spencer, MA 01562-1233
Tel.: 508-885-8750; FAX: 508-885-8701
(508) 885-8751

Type of Business:

Designers and crafters of ecclesiastical vesture for over 40 years. Inspired by our monastic tradition, we seek to unite in our work simplicity in design, quality in materials and excellence in craftsmanship. The result is vesture that enhances the liturgical celebration with visual grace and order. Our artists—both monks and laypersons—are available for custom design work and consultation. We also provide an extensive selection of ready made items.

ADAM KOCHLIN DESIGNS
21 Ann St.
South Norwalk, CT 06854
Tel.: 800-886-4668; FAX: 203-838-8752

Personnel:

Adam Kochlin . . . . Design Director
Michael Kirshbaum . . . . Executive Director
Regina Maguire . . . . Product Manager

Type of Business:

Adam Kochlin Designs creates a complete line of made to order vestments and hangings produced in our studio in Connecticut. Working with a number of artists we also create made to order sacred vessels and appointments including processional crosses, pacschal candlesticks, altar candlesticks, sanctuary lamps, incensors, chalices and patens, aumbrys, curets, and falgons in wood, ceramic, glass and metal. Call 800-886-4668 for free catalog and information.

THE LITURGICAL PRESS
St. John's Abbey, P.O. Box 7500
Collegeville, MN 56321
Tel.: 800-858-5450; 320-363-2213; FAX: 800-445-5899
e.mail: litpress@osb.org / homepage: www.osb.org/litpress

Personnel:

Ed Vessel . . . . Bookstore Sales
Carmen Donabauer . . . . Customer Service
Rita Groetsch . . . . Customer Service
Mary Ann Karasch . . . . Customer Service

Type of Business:

For over 70 years suppliers of liturgical, biblical, ritual, and instructional material to English-speaking countries. Products offered: *Celebrating the Eucharist* Mass Guide, *Bible and Liturgy Sunday Bulletins*, books, leaflets, video and audio cassettes, *Days of the Lord, Sacra Pagina, Collegeville Pastoral Dictionary of Biblical Theology,* and *The Bible Today, Sister's Today, Worship, New Theology Review, Liturgical Ministry,* and *Journal of Hispanic/Latino Theology* magazines. Call for a free catalog.

TERRA SANCTA GUILD®

TERRA SANCTA GUILD
P.O. Box 300, 858 Sussex Blvd.
Broomall, PA 19008
Tel.: 800-523-5155; 610-544-9900; FAX: 610-544-6994

Personnel:
Ade Bethune . . . . Liturgical Art Director
I.A. Serot . . . . President
Sharon Shore . . . . General Manager

Type of Business:
Custom design and manufacture of awards and recognition items for benefactors and volunteers; fundraising incentives; insignia for religious communities; commemoratives for church expansion and anniversaries. Your logo adapted or a new design created by world renowned liturgical artist, Ade Bethune. All lettering in original calligraphy.

ALTAR LINENS, LACES

the symbol of Regal Splendor

Robert Gaspard Co.

ROBERT GASPARD CO., INC.
200 N. Janacek Rd.,
Brookfield, WI 53045-6153
Tel.: 800-784-6868; 414-784-6800; FAX: 414-784-7567

Personnel:
Rose Gaspard . . . . President
Duane G. Buchholz . . . . Gen. Manager

Type of Business:
The Robert Gaspard Co. was established in 1954. Over the past 40 years, we have grown to our present size, occupying a showroom and manufacturing facility in excess of 20,000 square feet and employing 44 full time employees. We pride ourselves on our ability to create original custom designs to enrich your worship needs. Our complete line consists of all ecclesiastical vesture as well as paraments, mass and altar linens, stoles, banners, chasubles, funeral palls, albs, cassocks, surplices, choir robes, acolyte robes and many accessories. Complimentary catalogs and fabric swatches sent on request.

BIBLES, HYMNALS, MISSALETTES

GIA

GIA PUBLICATIONS, INC.
7404 S. Mason Ave.
Chicago, IL 60638
Tel.: 1-800-GIA-1358; 708-496-3800; FAX: 708-496-3828
website: www.giamusic.com; e-mail: custserv@giamusic.com

Personnel:
Robert J. Batastini . . . . Senior Editor, V.P.
Michael Cymbala . . . . Marketing Director
David Anderson . . . . Workshop Coordinator
Mike O'Connell . . . . Hymnal Sales

Type of Business:
GIA offers church music in all styles and forms for today's "eclectic" church. In addition to a broad range of hymnals, including *Worship, Gather, Gather Comprehensive, RitualSong,* and *Lead Me, Guide Me,* GIA also offers liturgical planning software, worship calendars and other music supplies, innovative music education products, excellent recordings, and the *GIA Quarterly,* a liturgical music journal.
Composers & distribution rights include:
John Bell and the Iona Community, Jacques Berthier and the Taizé Community, Rory Cooney, Jeanne Correr, Joseph Gelineau, David Haas, Marty Haugen, Howard Hughes, Michael Joncas, Alexander Peloquin, Donna Peña, and Richard Proulx.

J.S. PALUCH COMPANY

J.S. PALUCH CO., INC.
3825 N. Willow Rd.
Schiller Park, IL 60176
Tel.: 800-621-5197; FAX: 847-671-5715

Personnel:
Liturgy and Music Resources Customer Service 1-800-566-6150
Parish Bulletins 1-800 621-5197
Calendars Computer Software 1-800-621-5197

Type of Business:
Serving the church for over 80 years. Liturgy and Music Resources; Parish Sundays – Laser ComExpress; National Vocations Awareness and Religious Art Calendars; Computer Software for parish management.

THE LITURGICAL PRESS
St. John's Abbey, P.O. Box 7500
Collegeville, MN 56321
Tel.: 800-858-5450; 320-363-2213; FAX: 800-445-5899
e.mail: litpress@osb.org / homepage: www.osb.org/litpress

Personnel:

Ed Vessel . . . . Bookstore Sales
Carmen Donabauer . . . . Customer Service
Rita Groetsch . . . . Customer Service
Mary Ann Karasch . . . . Customer Service

Type of Business:

For over 70 years suppliers of liturgical, biblical, ritual, and instructional material to English-speaking countries. Products offered: *Celebrating the Eucharist* Mass Guide, *Bible and Liturgy Sunday Bulletins*, books, leaflets, video and audio cassettes, *Days of the Lord, Sacra Pagina, Collegeville Pastoral Dictionary of Biblical Theology,* and *The Bible Today, Sister's Today, Worship, New Theology Review, Liturgical Ministry,* and *Journal of Hispanic/Latino Theology* magazines. Call for a free catalog.

BULLETINS & CALENDARS

BARTON-COTTON

BARTON COTTON
1405 Parker Rd.
Baltimore, MD 21227
Tel.: 410-247-4800; FAX: 410-247-3681

Personnel:

Denise J. Payne . . . . Vice President Marketing and Sales

Type of Business:

For more than 65 years, Barton-Cotton, Inc. has been proud to supply the finest selection of quality religious stationery products for the Catholic Clergy and Religious. More than 300 products are available including Mass cards, Certificates, Christmas and Easter cards, Mother's and Father's Day sets, Ordination/Jubilee products, Way of the Cross booklets, Rosary folders. Holy cards, Bookmarks, bulletins and offering envelopes, and many other items. To request a FREE catalog, call toll-free today at 1-800-638-4652.

J.S. PALUCH COMPANY

J.S. PALUCH CO., INC.
3825 N. Willow Rd.
Schiller Park, IL 60176
Tel.: 800-621-5197; FAX: 847-671-5715

Personnel:

Liturgy and Music Resources Customer Service 1-800-566-6150
Parish Bulletins 1-800 621-5197
Calendars Computer Software 1-800-621-5197

Type of Business:

Serving the church for over 80 years. Liturgy and Music Resources; Parish Sundays – Laser ComExpress; National Vocations Awareness and Religious Art Calendars; Computer Software for parish management.

CANDLES, INCENSE

ROOT CANDLES

THE A.I. ROOT CANDLE CO.
623 W. Liberty St.
Medina, OH 44258
Tel.: 800-289-7668; FAX: 330-725-5624

Personnel:

John Holodnak . . . . Sales Manager

Type of Business:

• **Merchandise Handled:** Full line of altar candles, Advent, wedding and sacrament candles. Devotional lights, sanctuary lights, altar wine/bread, palms/ashes, and church supplies.
• **Services Offered**: Replating/refinishing services. Personalized sales representation in most states. Two factory locations: Medina, OH; San Antonio, TX.
• **Recent Clients:** Serving over 12,000 churches nationwide.
• **Statement:** Craftsmen in wax since 1869. Root Quality - Root Service.
• **Free Literature:** Free color catalog, 800-BUY-ROOT.

CATHEDRAL CANDLE CO.
Now in stock at your nearest Church Goods dealer.

Type of Business:

Classical symbolism and expressive liturgical design in the luxurious hand decorated artistry of SCULPTWAX ... created and mastercrafted here in the United States, exclusively at Cathedral Candle Co.

HELIOTRON CANDLE CO.
190 Bobby Jones Dr.
Etters, PA 17319
Tel.: 800-521-9838; FAX: 717-932-1942

Personnel:
Harold Shellenhamer . . . . President

Type of Business:
Importer and distributor of the finest German creafted liquid parrafin and polymer candle shells. Our patented product provides the safest, cleanest and most economical solution to alternative candles. A complete line of altar candles, votives, advent, paschal and sanctuary candles available. Call for our free catalog.

THE HOLY ROOD GUILD
St. Joseph's Abbey
167 N. Spencer Rd.
Spencer, MA 01562-1233
Tel.: 508-885-8750; 508-885-8751; FAX: 508-885-8701

Type of Business:
We offer hand-carved processional and hanging crosses in solid walnut which can be adorned with hand-painted icons, ordinarily images of the crucifixion and the Mother of God, or left with a plain varnished wood finish. Our complete line of vessels in pewter, porcelain and pottery include chalices, patens, cruets, trays, lavabo pitchers and bowls, flagons and candlesticks.

KERRY CANDLES
6070 Corte del Cedro
Carlsbad, CA 92009
Tel.: 619-931-0191

Type of Business:
So many churches have come to appreciate the cleanliness, safety, and beauty of Kerry Candles. The pure liquid inside lights their way without melted wax, smoke or odor. These handcrafted liquid candles are available in a variety of styles and sizes.

MUENCH KREUZER CANDLE CO.
P.O. Box 4969
Syracuse, NY 13221
Tel.: 315-471-4515; FAX: 315-471-4581

Type of Business:
Manufacturers of Church candles, altar, sanctuary, sacramental, votive & devotional candles of the highest quality. Emkay Candles ... available through your nearest Church Goods Dealer.

CHALICES, CROSSES & METAL WARE

ECCLESIASTICAL ARTS, INC.
16 Herbert St.
Newark, NJ 07105
Tel: 201-491-0022; FAX: 201-491-0023

Personnel:

Joseph J. Zaky . . . . President

Type of Business:

Artists and Craftsmen specializing in custom designed and hand made furnishings in metal, wood, stone and glass. For interior design, fabrication, restoration and original sculpture, contact J.J. Zaky.

Granda
Liturgical Arts, Inc.

GRANDA LITURGICAL ARTS, INC.
2525 Eastwood Ave., Apt. 8A
Evanston, IL 60201
Tel.: 800-425-0828; FAX: 847-492-1374
www.hispacom.es/granda; e-mail: ruj4granda@aol.com

Personnel:

Monica Ruf

Type of Business:

GRANDA LITURGICAL ARTS, Inc. is the USA branch of the largest supplier of church goods in the world: TALLERES DE ARTE GRANDA, S.A.

With 65 employees and sales all over the world, we can offer our experience in the manufacture of:

— metalware: chalices, tabernacles, etc.
— vestments
— wood carvings
— church decoration, interior design

Since 1891, we have been serving the liturgy, combining modern techniques (design by computer, projects in 3D ...) with artistic values.

Special custom orders: our specialty, according to your needs, in style and price.

ADRIAN HAMERS, INC.
2 Madison Ave.
Larchmont, NY 10538
Tel.: 914-834-7780; FAX: 914-834-0712

Type of Business:
Since 1887, the Hamers name has been synonymous with expert silversmithing throughout the world in the field of Liturgical Art. We are also experts in: Church Interiors from design to execution, Renovations, Altars, Sacred Vessels, Appraisals, Gold and Silver Plating & Repairing, Tabernacles, Marble, Woodwork & Woodcarving, Statuary, Stained Glass, Pews & Chairs, Gold Leafing, Frescoes, Restoration, Trompe-l'oeuil, Wall Murals (repair and conservation cleaning), Ornamental Plaster, Heraldic Designs & Bishop Regalia.

THE HOLY ROOD GUILD
St. Joseph's Abbey
167 N. Spencer Rd.
Spencer, MA 01562-1233
Tel.: 508-885-8750; 508-885-8751; FAX: 508-885-8701

Type of Business:
We offer hand-carved processional and hanging crosses in solid walnut which can be adorned with hand-painted icons, ordinarily images of the crucifixion and the Mother of God, or left with a plain varnished wood finish. Our complete line of vessels in pewter, porcelain and pottery include chalices, patens, cruets, trays, lavabo pitchers and bowls, flagons and candlesticks.

ADAM KOCHLIN DESIGNS
21 Ann St.
South Norwalk, CT 06854
Tel.: 800-886-4668; FAX: 203-838-8752

Personnel:
Adam Kochlin . . . . Design Director
Michael Kirshbaum . . . . Executive Director
Regina Maguire . . . . Product Manager

Type of Business:
Adam Kochlin Designs creates a complete line of made to order vestments and hangings produced in our studio in Connecticut. Working with a number of artists we also create made to order sacred vessels and appointments including processional crosses, pacschal candlesticks, altar candlesticks, sanctuary lamps, incensors, chalices and patens, aumbrys, curets, and falgons in wood, ceramic, glass and metal. Call 800-886-4668 for free catalog and information.

CHOIR ROBES

ROBERT GASPARD CO., INC.
200 N. Janacek Rd.,
Brookfield, WI 53045-6153
Tel.: 800-784-6868; 414-784-6800; FAX: 414-784-7567

Personnel:
Rose Gaspard . . . . President
Duane G. Buchholz . . . . Gen. Manager

Type of Business:
The Robert Gaspard Co. was established in 1954. Over the past 40 years, we have grown to our present size, occupying a showroom and manufacturing facility in excess of 20,000 square feet and employing 44 full time employees. We pride ourselves on our ability to create original custom designs to enrich your worship needs. Our complete line consists of all ecclesiastical vesture as well as paraments, mass and altar linens, stoles, banners, chasubles, funeral palls, albs, cassocks, surplices, choir robes, acolyte robes and many accessories. Complimentary catalogs and fabric swatches sent on request.

CHURCH REGISTERS

Serving Catholic Parishes since 1873.

D.P. MURPHY CO., INC.
1221 Walt Whitman Rd.
Melville, NY 11590-3090
Tel.: 516-673-9400; FAX: 516-673-1851
e-mail: dpmurphy@earthlink.net

Personnel:
Peter Q. Murphy .... President

Type of Business:
Envelope mailing systems specifically designd to meet the needs of your parish — available at any frequency ... monthly, bi-monthly, quarterly, semi-annual, yearly sets. FREE List Maintenance. Contribution recording via fax, phone, mail, diskette, modem or E-Mail. Census, stewardship, tithing, and fundraising programs. Church stationery, registers, record books, mass cards and certificates. Specialists in old register rebinding.

FABRIC ART HANGINGS & TAPESTRIES

ABBOTT CHURCH GOODS, INC.
1515 Route 38
Cherry Hill, NJ 08002
Tel.: 800-522-2688; 609-662-6959; FAX: 609-665-5109
website: http://www.abbottsinc.com
e-mail: ACG.INC@internetMCI.com

Personnel:
Daniel J. Castonguay .... President
Joseph F. McKeaney .... General Manager
Michael W. Wasyluk .... Customer Service

Type of Business:
Purveyors of the Finest Vesture, Paraments, Statuary & Metalware since 1962. Unique and original creations our specialty. Custom designs to complement your liturgical environment. Exclusive representatives of Slabbinck Master Collection & Original Collection.

T.M.

Bringing the Art Back into the Craft

BRAMANTE STUDIO
321 Wellington St. N.
Kitchener, ON, Canada N2H 5K8
Tel.: 800-295-6902; FAX: 519-570-2706

Personnel:
Abraham Mathew .... President

Type of Business:
Every parish is unique, not only in terms of the parishioners who make up the body of the church, but also in terms of the art and architectural elements that define the worship space. At Bramante Studio we endeavour to capture this individuality in each fabric art piece we make. Using exceptional fabrics and old world craftsmanship, we create custom made hangings, tapestries, vestments, and altar cloths that seek to recognize the uniqueness of each parish.

GOLD & SILVER PLATING, BRASS RESTORATION & REPAIRS

ADRIAN HAMERS®
CHURCH INTERIORS

ADRIAN HAMERS, INC.
2 Madison Ave.
Larchmont, NY 10538
Tel.: 914-834-7780; FAX: 914-834-0712

Type of Business:
Since 1887, the Hamers name has been synonymous with expert silversmithing throughout the world in the field of Liturgical Art. We are also experts in: Church Interiors from design to execution, Renovations, Altars, Sacred Vessels, Appraisals, Gold & Silver Plating and Repairing, Tabernacles, Marble, Woodwork & Woodcarving, Statuary, Stained Glass, Pews & Chairs, Gold Leafing, Frescoes, Restoration, Trompe-l'oeuil, Wall Murals (repair and conservation cleaning), Ornamental Plaster, Heraldic Designs & Bishop Regalia.

OFFERING ENVELOPES

AmericanChurch
a division of AmericanPaper Group, Inc.

AMERICAN CHURCH,
A DIVISION OF AMERICAN PAPER GROUP
8401 Southern Blvd.
Youngstown, OH 44512
Tel.: 800-228-6101; FAX: 330-758-9981

Personnel:
James P. Fitzgerald . . . . V.P. Sales & Marketing
Ron Blakeman . . . . Sales Manager
Rob Turnbull . . . . VP National Accounts

Type of Business:
World's largest supplier of offering envelopes
- Envelopes, Custom Printed
- Boxed Sets
- Mailing Programs
- Direct Banking

Cathedral
CORPORATION
Church Services Division

CATHEDRAL CORPORATION
P.O. Box 1293
Buffalo, NY 14240
Tel.: 800-828-7455; FAX: 716-667-7309

Personnel:
Marianne Gaige . . . . President
Stephen L. Miller . . . . Director of Marketing
Maurie L. Jachimiak . . . . Sales/Service Manager

Type of Business:
Cathedral Corporation has been a full-service supplier of products and services designed to enhance the financial health of parishes for over 60 years, including:

- Mailed envelopes; monthly, bi-monthly, quarterly, Custom and money-saving Compuset envelopes
- Boxed sets; adult, youth and children's
- Cost-effective offering envelope recording and reporting
- Stewardship, Weekly renewal, and Capital campaigns
- Laser personalized mailings for improved parishioner communications
- Offset printing, addressing and mailing to fill a variety of parish and school needs.

Serving Catholic Parishes since 1873.

D.P. MURPHY CO., INC.
1221 Walt Whitman Rd.
Melville, NY 11590-3090
Tel.: 516-673-9400; FAX: 516-673-1851
e-mail: dpmurphy@earthlink.net

Personnel:
Peter Q. Murphy . . . . President

Type of Business:
Envelope mailing systems specifically designd to meet the needs of your parish — available at any frequency ... monthly, bi-monthly, quarterly, semi-annual, yearly sets. FREE List Maintenance. Contribution recording via fax, phone, mail, diskette, modem or E-Mail. Census, stewardship, tithing, and fundraising programs. Church stationery, registers, record books, mass cards and certificates. Specialists in old register rebinding.

NATIONAL CHURCH SUPPLY CO.
P.O. Box 269
Chester, WV 26034
Tel.: 304-387-5200; FAX: 304-387-5266

Personnel:
Ms. Kathy Myers. . . . . Sales & Advertising Coordinator

Type of Business:
Nurturing Stewardship Growth in churches is a tradition at Catholic Envelope Service. A division of National Church Supply Co., we have been serving the Christian community for over 80 years. Every person in our family owned organization has the same goal: to help every church customer find the best possible solution to today's and tomorrow's stewardship challenges. Our innovative church offering envelopes and stewardship systems are geared to increase communications while improving parishioner commitment and response.

ONE-WRITE CO.
P.O. Box 310
Lancaster, OH 43130
Tel.: 1-800-268-6070; FAX: 800-504-2260

Type of Business:
Book Offering Envelopes, Tuition Payment Books, Mailing Plan for Offering Envelopes, and Contribution Report Forms. We invite you to compare the features and prices of the Book Offering Envelopes with your current system. The savings will be considerable. Write or call for a free catalog and quote today.

F.J. REMEY CO., INC.
121 Willis Ave.
Mineola, NY 11501-0589
Tel.: 516-741-5112; FAX: 516-741-0523

Type of Business:

Serving Catholic parishes since 1921 by providing the following products: Envelope Mailing Systems, Annual Offering Envelope Boxsets, Bulk Collection Envelopes, Computer Recording, Collection Baskets, Parish Census, Church Record Books, Parish Office Forms, Church Stationery, Mass Cards, Raffle Tickets and Tuition Supplies.

SACRED VESSELS

ADRIAN HAMERS®

CHURCH INTERIORS

ONE HUNDRED YEARS SERVING THE CLERGY TOUJOURS 1887

ADRIAN HAMERS INC.
2 Madison Ave.
Larchmont, NY 10538
Tel.: 914-834-7780; FAX: 914-834-0712

Type of Business:

Since 1887, the Hamers name has been synonymous with expert silversmithing throughout the world in the field of Liturgical Art. We are also experts in: Church Interiors from design to execution, Renovations, Altars, Sacred Vessels, Appraisals, Gold and Silver Plating & Repairing, Tabernacles, Marble, Woodwork & Woodcarving, Statuary, Stained Glass, Pews & Chairs, Gold Leafing, Frescoes, Restoration, Trompe-l'oeuil, Wall Murals (repair and conservation cleaning), Ornamental Plaster, Heraldic Designs & Bishop Regalia.

ADAM KOCHLIN
DESIGNS

ADAM KOCHLIN DESIGNS
21 Ann St.
South Norwalk, CT 06854
Tel.: 800-886-4668; FAX: 203-838-8752

Personnel:
Adam Kochlin . . . . Design Director
Michael Kirshbaum . . . . Executive Director
Regina Maguire . . . . Product Manager

Type of Business:
Adam Kochlin Designs creates a complete line of made to order vestments and hangings produced in our studio in Connecticut. Working with a number of artists we also create made to order sacred vessels and appointments including processional crosses, pacschal candlesticks, alter candlesticks, sanctuary lamps, incensors, chalices and patens, aumbrys, curets, and falgons in wood ceramic, glass and metal. Call 800-886-4668 for free catalog and information.

STATIONERY & GREETING CARDS

BC
BARTON-COTTON

BARTON COTTON
1405 Parker Rd.
Baltimore, MD 21227
Tel.: 410-247-4800; FAX: 410-247-3681

Personnel:
Denise J. Payne . . . . Vice President Marketing and Sales

Type of Business:
For more than 65 years, Barton-Cotton, Inc. has been proud to supply the finest selection of quality religious stationery products for the Catholic Clergy and Religious. More than 300 products are available including Mass cards, Certificates, Christmas and Easter cards, Mother's and Father's Day sets, Ordination/Jubilee products, Way of the Cross booklets, Rosary folders, Holy cards, Bookmarks, bulletins and offering envelopes, and many other items. To request a FREE catalog, call toll-free today at 1-800-638-4652.

THE PRINTERY HOUSE
Conception Abbey · CONCEPTION · MISSOURI 64433

THE PRINTERY HOUSE
Conception Abbey
Conception, MO 64433
Tel.: 816-944-2632; FAX: 816-944-2582
e-mail: gnelson@msc-net.com

Personnel:
Gerald E. Nelson . . . . General Manager
Ron Riggs . . . . Director of Sales & Marketing

Type of Business:
The Printery House manufactures Christian greeting cards as a not-for-profit extension of the apostolic mission of Conception Abbey, a Benedictine community dedicated to a Christian life of work and prayer. These high quality cards can be custom printed for quantity orders at quite reasonable prices. Call 800-889-0105 for your free catalog and more information.

PUBLISHERS

Augsburg Fortress
PUBLISHERS

AUGSBURG FORTRESS PUBLISHERS
426 S. 5th St., P.O. Box 1209
Minneapolis, MN 55440
Tel.: 800-328-4648; FAX: 612-330-3455

Personnel:
Joan Uselmann . . . . Representative Special Markets

Type of Business:
One stop shopping for award winning curriculum and books:
- Vacation Bible School
- GOOD NEWS EXPLORERS - Bible based interactive, child-centered religious education curriculum for ages 2 through 6th grade.
- YOUTH TALK - The resource that gets youth talking.
- INTERSECTIONS — Adult small group study materials connecting faith to life.
- ACTIVE CHRISTIAN PARENTING
- Media and print parish program designed to enhance Christian Parenting skills.
- Christian children's books for early childhood through teens.
- Books on prayer, spirituality, Christian living.
- Fortress Press academic books.
- A complete line of church supplies

BC

BARTON-COTTON

BARTON COTTON
1405 Parker Rd.
Baltimore, MD 21227
Tel.: 410-247-4800; FAX: 410-247-3681

Personnel:

Denise J. Payne . . . . Vice President Marketing and Sales

Type of Business:

For more than 65 years, Barton-Cotton, Inc. has been proud to supply the finest selection of quality religious stationery products for the Catholic Clergy and Religious. More than 300 products are available including Mass cards, Certificates, Christmas and Easter cards, Mother's and Father's Day sets, Ordination/Jubilee products, Way of the Cross booklets, Rosary folders, Holy cards, Bookmarks, bulletins and offering envelopes, and many other items. To request a FREE catalog, call toll-free today at 1-800-638-4652.

CHRISTENDOM PRESS

CHRISTENDOM PRESS
134 Christendom Dr.
Front Royal, VA 22630
Tel.: 540-636-2900; FAX: 540-636-1655
e-mail: christdm@shentel.net

Personnel:

John Janaro . . . . Director of the Press
Jennifer Dateno . . . . Managing Editor

Type of Business:

Christendom Press is committed to the defense of the Catholic faith and the development of the lay apostolate. Through our journal, *Faith & Reason*, and through books and audio-visuals, Christendom Press seeks to extend to a broader audience the kind of research and thought which Christendom College faculty bring to their classes. Christendom Press offers works in spirituality, theology, history, philosophy, and apologetics. For more information, or for a free catalog, call 1-800-877-5456.

THE LITURGICAL PRESS
St. John's Abbey, Box 7500
Collegeville, MN 56321
Tel.: 800-858-5450; 320-363-2213; FAX: 800-445-5899
e.mail: litpress@osb.org / homepage: www.osb.org/litpress

Personnel:

Ed Vessel . . . . Bookstore Sales
Carmen Donabauer . . . . Customer Service
Rita Groetsch . . . . Customer Service
Mary Ann Karasch . . . . Customer Service

Type of Business:

For over 70 years suppliers of liturgical, biblical, ritual, and instructional material to English-speaking countries. Products offered: *Celebrating the Eucharist* Mass Guide, *Bible and Liturgy Sunday Bulletins*, books, leaflets, video and audio cassettes, *Days of the Lord, Sacra Pagina, Collegeville Pastoral Dictionary of Biblical Theology,* and *The Bible Today, Sister's Today, Worship, New Theology Review, Liturgical Ministry,* and *Journal of Hispanic/Latino Theology* magazines. Call for a free catalog.

LTP

LITURGY TRAINING PUBLICATIONS

LITURGY TRAINING PUBLICATIONS
1800 N. Hermitage Ave.
Chicago, IL 60622-1101
Tel.: 800-933-1800; FAX: 800-933-7094
e-mail: orders@ltp.org

Personnel:

Gabe Huck . . . . Director
John D. Wright . . . . Marketing Director

Type of Business:

LTP provides materials that assist parishes, institutions and households in the preparation and celebration of liturgy in Christian life. In its products and its operation, LTP strives to express the justice and beauty that are fundamental to the church and to its liturgy. Publications include *Workbook for Lectors and Gospel Readers, Sourcebook for Sundays and Seasons, At Home with the Word, Children's Daily Prayer, The Sunday Mass Video Series, Catechumenate* magazine, *Liturgy 90, E&A Newsletter.*

PAULIST PRESS
997 Macarthur Blvd.
Mahwah, NJ 07430
Tel.: 201-825-7300; FAX: 201-825-8345

Personnel:

Kevin A. Lynch, CSP . . . . Publisher
Don Brophy . . . . Managing Editor
John A. Thomas . . . . Marketing Director
Jay R. McKee . . . . National Sales Manager

Type of Business:

- Publishes Ordo, religious books, catechetical programs, pastoral resources, liturgical desk and pocket calendars, Paulist Bible Study Program, The new wine program, and the Denver Catholic bible School Program.
- Produces religious video and audio cassettes.
- Provides Catholic books and magazines to parishes from a variety of Catholic publishers through its National Catholic Reading Distribution division.

Sheed & Ward
The Tradition Continues

SHEED & WARD
P.O. Box 419492
Kansas City, MO 64141
Tel.: 800-333-7373; FAX: 816-968-2280

Personnel:

Robert Heyer . . . . Editor-in-Chief
Chuck Blankenship. . . . . Marketing Director
Andy Apathy. . . . . Associate Editor
Sylvia Fox. . . . . Publicity Coordinator

Type of Business:

Publisher of resources for the ministering church, small-group resources, "Family Centered Intergenerational Religious Education," theology, spirituality, and a variety of video resources for ministry professionals. Publisher of the "Parish Sacrificial Giving" stewardship program for parishes and "The Stewardship Game" for grade school children.

MAGAZINES, JOURNALS

THE LITURGICAL PRESS
St. John's Abbey, P.O. Box 7500
Collegeville, MN 56321
Tel.: 800-858-5450; 320-363-2213; FAX: 800-445-5899
e.mail: litpress@osb.org / homepage: www.osb.org/litpress

Personnel:

Ed Vessel . . . . Bookstore Sales
Carmen Donabauer . . . . Customer Service
Rita Groetsch . . . . Customer Service
Mary Ann Karasch . . . . Customer Service

Type of Business:

For over 70 years suppliers of liturgical, biblical, ritual, and instructional material to English-speaking countries. Products offered: *Celebrating the Eucharist* Mass Guide, *Bible and Liturgy Sunday Bulletins*, books, leaflets, video and audio cassettes, *Days of the Lord, Sacra Pagina, Collegeville Pastoral Dictionary of Biblical Theology,* and *The Bible Today, Sister's Today, Worship, New Theology Review, Liturgical Ministry,* and *Journal of Hispanic/Latino Theology* magazines. Call for a free catalog.

MUSIC PUBLISHERS

CATHEDRAL MUSIC PRESS
#4 Industrial Dr.
Pacific, MO 63069-0066
Tel.: 1-800-863-5229; 314-257-3970; FAX: 314-257-5062
Web: http://www.melbay.com; e-mail: email@melbay.com

Personnel:

William Bay . . . . Vice President
L. Dean Bye . . . . General Manager
Michael Entsminger . . . . Marketing Coordinator
Ginny Patterson . . . . Sales

Type of Business:

A leading music publisher specializing in instrumental and instructional material for the church. A complete line of piano, organ, flute, clarinet, trumpet, saxophone, guitar, and other fretted instruments along with beautifully recorded CDs and cassettes are available. Write or phone for our most recent catalog at 1-800-863-5229.

RENEWAL MUSIC
1000 Cody Rd.
Mobile, AL 36695
Tel.: 800-223-7333; FAX: 334-633-0882

Type of Business:

Renewal Music's goal is to produce music and materials that enhances the Church liturgy. Songs include works by well-known Catholic songwriters along with other contemporary praise and worship songs. Songbooks will contain multiple arrangements along with suggestions for each song's seasonal and liturgical uses. Arrangements will be easy to use for choir and organ, or any size choir or instrumental group.
Watch for the two-volume set, entitled *We Will Meet You There,* coming in August 1997.

VOICE OF THE ROCKIES
P.O. Box 1043
Boulder, Colorado 80306
Tel.: 1-800-783-1223; 303-444-2475; FAX: 303-444-8334
e-mail: Voiceofroc@AOL.com

Personnel:

Patricia T. Holmberg . . . . President
Russell K. Holmberg . . . . V. President
April Seawell . . . . Office Manager

Type of Business:

A publisher of printed music, Voice of the Rockies has a steadily growing catalog of choral music, as well as piano, organ, instrumental, chamber, orchestral and vocal music. Please look for our products in music stores, call for our catalog or look for our presence on the Internet at the above address.

NEWS SERVICE

RNS
RELIGION NEWS SERVICE

RELIGION NEWS SERVICE
1101 Conn Ave. NW #350
Washington, DC 20036
Tel.: 202-463-8777; FAX: 202-463-0033

Personnel:
David Anderson . . . . Editor
Dale Hanson Bourke . . . . Publisher
Mike Paquette. . . . . Photo Editor

Type of Business:
RNS provides a daily and weekly news service as well as a daily photo and graphics service. For more information call 1-800-767-6781.

PARISH DIRECTORIES

Pictorial Family Albums for
The Catholic Community

OLAN MILLS
4325 Amnicola Hwy.
Chattanooga, TN 37422
Tel.: 800-952-2935; FAX: 615-622-5888

Personnel:
Olan Mills 1-800-952-2935

Type of Business:
Olan Mills is a pictoral directory co. that is endorsed by the Catholic Advisory Board. To help Catholic churches provide a pictoral directory for their parish.

Capturing Memories that will last a Lifetime...

UNITED
CHURCH DIRECTORIES
A Lifetouch Company

UNITED CHURCH DIRECTORIES
1371 Portland Way No.
Galion, OH 44833
Tel.: 1-800-521-4611; 419-468-4739; FAX: 419-468-2741

Personnel:
Sue Nigh . . . . Direct of Marketing

Type of Business:
Provider of no-cost ($0) outreach and communications tools/events for religious institutions since 1963. Products emphasize congregational participation with church while developing a "Faith & Family" bond. All printed outreach materials are quality controlled through digital layout processing and use of the world's finest presses — five 4-color Heidelbergs and one 5-color Heidelberg.

References:
"I would recommend your company to my colleagues. Your professionalism and kind cooperation made the process truly easy." Reverend Douglas J. Spina, Saint Anthony's Rectory, Woonsocket, Rhode Island.
"We were very pleased with United as an organization. They definitely delivered what they promised." Bernice Dziedzic, Administrative Secretary, St. Rita Parish, West Allis, Wisconsin.
"United is indeed a top-notch company. They will do whatever is necessary to meet your every need." Ms. Pauline Fink, Coordinator, Sacred Heart of Jesus Catholic Church, Anniston, Alabama.

PHOTOGRAPHY

Pictorial Family Albums for
The Catholic Community

OLAN MILLS
4325 Amnicola Hwy.
Chattanooga, TN 37422
Tel.: 800-952-2935; FAX: 615-622-5888

Personnel:
Olan Mills 1-800-952-2935

Type of Business:
Olan Mills is a pictoral directory co. that is endorsed by the Catholic Advisory Board. To help Catholic churches provide a pictoral directory for their parish.

TRANSLATIONS & EDITING

COME ALIVE
COMMUNICATIONS, INC.

A Catholic Translation & Editing Co.

COME ALIVE COMMUNICATIONS
50 Railrd. Ave., P.O. Box 436
West Grove, PA 19390-0436
Tel.: 610-869-3660; FAX: 610-869-7557

Personnel:
Bridget G. Hylak . . . . Chief of Translation & Editing

Type of Business:
- Expert Catholic Translators
- Guaranteed Lowest Rates
- State-of-the-Art Equipment

All types of translation, editing, desktop publishing and graphic design; books, movies, brochures, newsletters, etc. Most major languages available. Top quality staff of native linguists. Ample references within the Catholic Community.
Call/FAX for a free estimate.
Come Alive is dedicated to serving the Catholic Community with theologically sound and linguistically accurate documents in 12 languages. We work with skill, proper training, and love for our Church.

PROFESSIONAL ASSOCIATIONS & ORGANIZATIONS

FRATERNAL ORGANIZATIONS

CATHOLIC ORDER OF FORESTERS
355 Shuman Blvd., P.O. Box 3012
Naperville, IL 60555-7012
Tel.: 630-983-4920; 800-552-0145; FAX: 630-983-5113

Personnel:
Robert Ciesla . . . . High Chief Ranger
Armand R. Lemire . . . . Vice High Chief Ranger
Leo J. Beranek . . . . High Sec.-Treas.

Type of Business:
Catholic Order of Foresters, a fraternal benefit society with 135,000 members nationwide, has been providing Catholics with financial protection since 1883. In addition to quality life insurance and annuity products, COF offers added value through fraternal benefits—parish and diocese loans, college scholarships, student loans, orphan benefits, local youth and adult court activities, and benevolence that includes a matching funds program.

SCHOOL SUPPLIES & EQUIPMENT

CLASSROOM SEATING

CLARIN, A DIVISION OF GREENWICH INDUSTRIES, L.P.
927 North Shore Dr.
Lake Bluff, IL 60044
Tel.: 847-295-2200; FAX: 847-234-9001

Personnel:
William P. Peterson . . . . President
Richard H. Wagner . . . . Vice President, Clarin Sales
Kathleen J. Sobotta. . . . . Manager, Inside Sales

Continued in Next Column

Continued from Previous Column:

Type of Business:
The best choice in seating! Manufacturer of portable and fixed lecture room seating. Supplier of logo chairs and stools for athletic teams; correct pitch music chairs, tablet arm chairs and other seating products for all uses.

SPECIAL CARE FACILITIES

GUEST HOUSE, INC.
1601 Joslyn Rd., P.O. Box 420
Lake Orion, MI 48361
Tel.: 800-626-6910; 810-391-4445; FAX: 810-391-0210

LAKE ORION CENTER
(For Women Religious)
P.O. Box 68
Lake Orion, MI 48361
Tel.: 800-626-6910; 810-391-3100; FAX: 810-391-1553

ROCHESTER TREATMENT CENTER
(For priests, deacons, brothers & seminarians)
P.O. Box 954
Rochester, MN 55903
Tel.: 800-634-4155; 507-288-4693; FAX: 507-288-1240

Personnel:
Richard K. Frisch, A.C.S.W. . . . . President & CEO
Danial A. Kidd. . . . . Chief Administrative Officer
Sr. Mae Kierans, C.S.J. . . . . Lake Orion Center
Bill Morgan, C.C.D.C.R.. . . . . Rochester Treatment Center
Daniel Webster. . . . . Director of Communications

Type of Business:
Guest House, Inc. is a lay-owned, lay-operated nonprofit corporation established in 1956. With the approbation of the Catholic hierarchy, it operates special residential treatment centers for alcoholic Catholic priests, deacons, brothers, sisters and seminarians from all over the world.
Catholic women religious are treated at Guest House in Lake Orion, Michigan. Our facility in Rochester, Minnesota has treatment programs for priests, deacons, brothers and seminarians.
Lovely buildings, spacious country landscape, comfortable rooms set in a serene, non-clinical setting all play an important role in reaffirming a sense of self-worth to a sick, chemically dependent priest or religious.
Accredited by JCAHO (Joint Commission on Accreditation of Healthcare Organizations) and licensed by the Department of Public Health in the states of Michigan and Minnesota respectively.

TRAVEL & TOURISM

CONFERENCE CENTERS

SAN DAMIANO CONFERENCE AND RETREAT CENTER
Rt. 1, Box 106
Golconda, IL 62938
Tel.: 618-385-3507; FAX: 618-285-3507

Personnel:
Mark Migas . . . . Manager
Margie Douglas . . . . Reservationist
Reverend Robert Vonnahmen . . . . Director
Craig Simoneaux . . . . Assistant Director

Type of Business:
San Damiano Retreat Center and Shrine of the Good Shepherd is located in Southern Illinois' Shawnee National Forest high on the bluffs overlooking the Ohio River and Western Kentucky. The shrine hosts seminars, retreats, concerts, conferences, and workshops for groups of all faiths. Featured on the grounds are 26 cottages, 35 foot bronze Good Shepherd statue, XXIII Psalm, Meditation Garden, Stations of the Cross, book and video library as well as conference and visitor center.

PILGRIMAGES

BALTIC TOURS

BALTIC TOURS
368 West Broadway
Boston, MA 02127
Tel.: 800-216-5987; 617-268-7999; FAX: 617-268-7325
website: http://www.quikpage.com/B/baltictours

Personnel:
Kristin Mitkus . . . . President
Birute Mitkus . . . . Vice President
Albina Rudziunas . . . . Director of Operations

Type of Business:
Since our beginning in 1975, Baltic Tours has been a specialist in group and individual travel arrangements to Lithuania, Latvia and Estonia. Baltic Tours has also custom designed tours for organizations such as Church, Pilgrimages, social clubs, fraternal, university and special interest groups. We also have an office in Vilnius, Lithuania as well as representation in both Riga, Latvia and Tallinn, Estonia to take care of all our client's needs.

Catholic Travel Centre
Worldwide Tours and Pilgrimages

CATHOLIC TRAVEL CENTRE
7100 Hayvenhurst Ave., Ste. 107
Van Nuys, CA 91406
Tel.: 818-909-9910; FAX: 818-909-0486

Personnel:
J. Scott Scherer. . . . . President
Inga Duranovic . . . . Director of Operations
Yvonne Hanratty. . . . . Operations Assistant
Henry Nassim . . . . Business Manager

Type of Business:
Catholic Travel Centre's strong reputation derives from operating high quality, customized group tours and pilgrimages. Our President, Mr. J. Scott Scherer, has 13 years experience in leading and organizing religious group tours, part of that time in a development capacity for a Catholic diocese.
An intimate knowledge of Catholic sites permits us to design a one-of-a-kind itinerary that suits your group's unique interests. Our long list of repeat clientele includes parishes, religious orders, colleges, alumni associations, and schools of theology nationwide.

Central Holidays

CENTRAL HOLIDAYS
206 Central Ave.
Jersey City, NJ 09307
Tel.: 201-798-5777, X260; FAX: 201-222-7899

Personnel:
Sergio Bigini . . . . Vice President
Annette Lizzul . . . . Senior Account Executive
Roberta Jackson . . . . Account Executive

Type of Business:
CENTRAL HOLIDAYS, a group, convention and incentive program specialist, has been serving the traveling public for 25 years. Experts in Italy, Greece, Turkey, Spain, Portugal and Morocco, we can also customize itineraries for destinations throughout Europe and the Mediterranean. As an active member in the United States Tour Operators Association, we provide $1 million in passenger protection.

CROSSROADS TRAVEL, INC.

SPECIALIZING IN GROUP TRAVEL AND PILGRIMAGES

CROSSROADS TRAVEL
10906 E. Gary Rd.
Scottsdale, AZ 85259
Tel.: 602-661-8228; FAX: 602-860-2997

Personnel

Father Joseph Tye . . . . Vice President

Type of Business:

Crossroads Travel, Inc. is a network of Catholic priests from throughout the United States who have come together to form our own travel company. All of us have traveled extensively throughout Europe and the Middle East. Based on our collective experiences, we have established a network of clergy throughout the United States that uses our services and promotes our tour company.

Our Company's philosophy is: Clergy working with Clergy and Church ministers, providing the best services at the most reasonable cost.

As clergy, especially Pastors, the main concern is the *spiritual and fiscal responsibility* of a Parish community. A pilgrimage serves both purposes. Parishioners return spiritually renewed and you receive free trips or cash benefits or a combination of both.

We are a team of travel professionals and clergy with the experience and expertise to provide you with a richly rewarding and memorable tour wherever you choose to travel.

Design-A-Tour, Inc.

DESIGN-A-TOUR, INC.
5840 New England Woods Dr.
Burke, VA 22015
Tel.: 703-764-0355; FAX: 703-764-3776
Tel. Outside Metro Wash., DC area: 1-800-762-2256
website: http://pages.prodigy.com/designatour
e-mail: BXHG48A@prodigy.com

Personnel

Margaret M. Erner . . . . Tour Manager
Virginia M. (Gigi) Barbour . . . . Tour Director

Type of Business:

Design-A-Tour, Inc. specializes in travel to Italy. In addition to air, hotel and car rental reservations, we offer villas, farmhouses, castles and apartments in Italy, France, Spain, Portugal and London. Escorted tours to the Tuscan hill towns/Florence and the Umbrian hill towns/Rome are scheduled each year. Gigi and Margaret are personal travel planners, providing customized client service to individuals, families and groups.

DURGAN TRAVEL SERVICE
125 Main St.
Stoneham, MA 02180
Tel.: 800-234-9959-Toll Free; 617-438-2224; FAX: 617-438-6772

Personnel:
Richard Durgan . . . . President
Matthew Lordan . . . . Group Sales
Cathy Briggs . . . . Retail Sales Manager

Type of Business:
Full service travel agency planning custom group travel (jet, cruise & domestic & international motorcoach trips). Many group priced trips are available for the individual traveler. We specialize in Italy, Greece/Turkey, The Holy Land and the British Isles. Please call for a competitive bid on your next tour.

EDUCATIONAL OPPORTUNITIES
PO Box 6067
Lakeland, FL 33807
Tel.: 941-644-8485; FAX: 941-647-5789
web site: www.eo.travelwithus.com (expected operation date: 6/1/97)
e-mail: eo@travelwithus.com

Personnel:
James Ringway . . . . President

Type of Business:
EO is a not-for-profit Christian travel Organization established in 1974 and has grown into North America's **largest organizer of Christian groups to the Holy Land.** Our size gives you the best travel value at the lowest cost, the best guides and motor coaches, the best hotels. Despite our size, EO remains a traveler-friendly company. **Clergy and religious orders are eligible for a scholarship** on their first EO journey to the Holy Land. Group leaders can earn their trip. Contact us today for details.

ETT TOURS, INC.
198 E. Boston Post Rd.
Mamaronek, NY 10543
Tel.: 914-698-9426; FAX: 914-698-9516

Personnel:
Carmen Achermann . . . . Managing Director
Sandra R. Haas . . . . Office Manager

Type of Business:
ETT Tours, Inc. (aka Europe Train Tours) will customize any group request. They have been organizing trips to Europe for over 15 years. ETT Tours offers the lowest prices available. An experienced team of dedicated professionals will help you plan your trip to France, Italy, Spain, Portugal or other European countries. Transportation available on motorcoach or train. All classes of hotels can be offered. Tell ETT Tours you found them in the Official Catholic Directory!

GENESIS TOURS GROUP INT'L.
424 Madison Ave.
New York, NY 10017
Tel.: 212-750-6460; FAX: 212-750-6463

Personnel:
John E. Walsh. . . . . President
Jack Carley . . . . Vice President Sales
Gary Doyle . . . . Manager, System Development

Type of Business:
Genesis Tours was originally formed in 1983 for the express purpose of developing Christian tours to the Holy Land and other prominent Christian Holy places around the world. Mr. Walsh is a former airline executive who was deeply involved in the Holy Land, Syria and Jordan. Mr. Carley also was heavily involved in Turkey, Greece & Spain while Mr. Doyle was involved in the Irish, English and French Holy Shrines.

GEORGE'S INTERNATIONAL TOURS & TRAVEL, Inc.

GEORGE'S INTERNATIONAL TOURS & TRAVEL, INC.
9285 Dowdy Dr., Ste. 101
San Diego, CA 92126
Tel.: 800-566-7499; FAX: 619-271-6692

Personnel:
Garo Garabedian . . . . President
Steve Gureghian . . . . Director of Sales & Marketing
Ron Harris . . . . Operations Manager

Type of Business:
George's International Tours & Travel is a family owned and operated tour co.. For more than 65 years, we have been providing arrangements for Holy Land Pilgramages. Recently George's International has begun providing quality programs to other religious sites around the world, including the Marian Shrines of Europe, Betania, Medjugorje and more. Our reputation speaks for itself, references are available from the many thousands of Christian Pilgrims who have availed themselves of our service.

GLOBAL JOURNEYS
25 West 45th St., Ste. 1207
New York, NY 10036
Tel.: 212-768-8198; FAX: 212-869-0008

Type of Business:
Global Educational Journeys has been the leader of spiritual and educational pilgrimages around the world for over 12 years. Our experienced Christian guides take you to Israel to experience the home of Christ, Greece and Turkey to walk the steps of St. Paul, Egypt where Mary and Jesus took refuge and many other destinations.
Call us today and speak to one of our experienced and knowledgeable faculty members who will help you arrange your very special journey to the Holyland and beyond ...

GLOBE TRAVEL
YOU PACK • WE DO THE REST

GLOBE TRAVEL SERVICE
58 Perinton Hills Mall
Fairport, NY 14450
Tel.: 716-223-8330; FAX: 716-223-2736

Personnel:
Ann Marie Berner . . . . Owner/Agent
Karen DiFranco . . . . Disney Vacations
Sheldon Lopatin . . . . Cruises/Tours
Julie O'Dell . . . . Leisure Travel

Type of Business:
Globe Travel is a full service agency, providing travel arrangements for corporate, leisure and individual travel. The Agency specializes in vacation packages, cruises, Branson vacations and honeymoons.

GOLDEN FRONTIER
4100 North Illinois St.
Swansea, IL 62226-1834
Tel.: 618-234-1445; FAX: 618-234-9861

Personnel:
Linda Davinroy. Domestic Reservations
Patti Grindstaff. . . . . International Reservations
Reverend Robert Vonnahmen . . . . Director
Craig Simoneaux . . . . Assistant Director

Type of Business:
Golden Frontier has provided 19 years of spiritual renewal through travel to religious destinations throughout the world. A professional and knowledgeable staff are on hand here and at overseas destinations to assure your travel experience will be rewarding and uplifting. A priest chaplain accompanies each group to offer Holy Mass and spiritual guidance along the way. Customized group programs are available for parish groups and other religious organizations. See our accompanying ad.

Great Experiences, Inc.

GREAT EXPERIENCES, INC.
320 Kinderkamack Rd.
Oradell, NJ 07649
Tel: 201-261-8484; FAX: 201-262-8833

Personnel:

Anne Breslin . . . . President
Debra Costello . . . . Office Manager
Peggie Breslin . . . . Sales Consultant
Isabella Guisonni . . . . Bookkeeper

Type of Business:

Great Experiences is a Catholic office/ministry which provides parishes/organizations with the opportunity for personal/community growth, as well as fund-raising through travel experiences in the United States and in other lands. We have a reputation for quality, dependability and ethics. We custom design each program, taking into consideration the specific financial and other needs of each group. Sample brochures, suggested itineraries and letters of recommendation are available.

Inspirational Tours, Inc.

Religious Group Tour Wholesaler Since 1972!

INSPIRATIONAL TOURS INC.
5433 Westheimer, Ste. 600
Houston, TX 77056
Tel.: 1-800-231-6287; FAX: 713-961-7496

Type of Business:

Specializes in Pilgrimage Tours to the Holy Land, Shrines of Italy, Shrines of France and Shrines of Europe, Fatima. For any special request and customized itinerary, please contact Mr. Moses Khano, President at 1-800-231-6287.

Journeys Unlimited

JOURNEYS UNLIMITED
500 Eighth Ave.
New York, NY 10018
Tel.: 800-486-8359; 212-736-2028; FAX: 212-736-8959
e-mail: holytours@worldnet.att.net

Personnel:

Nicholas Mancino . . . . President
Raymond Masillo . . . . Vice President
Lucille Sciabarassi . . . . Travel Consultant
Everett Mansfield . . . . Group Sales
Total Staff 16

Type of Business:

Journeys Unlimited was founded by Raymond Masillo & Nicholas Mancino in 1990 in cooperation with four other travel professionals. The Management has been arranging Pilgrimages since 1969 and has over 100 years of professional experience. The company's philosophy is that each Pilgrimage be escorted by a spiritual leader in order to transform our tours into Pilgrimages. Our Pilgrimages have been designed to give each participant comfort for recreation and spiritual guidance for RENEWAL. Our staff is dedicated to personal, efficient and economical group travel. We also offer tours to Italy, Greece, Turkey, Egypt, Syria, Fatima, Lourdes, and other Marian Shrines.

All General Travel Services

MARIAN TRAVEL
3617 So. L St.
Tacoma, WA 98408
Tel.: 888-305-0774; 206-472-0963; FAX: 206-472-0473

3244 Hunter St.
Naples, FL 32703
Tel.: 800-458-6279; 407-774-2376; FAX: 407-774-2013

Personnel:

- Vern Barnes . . . . Washington
- Jon McMillan . . . . Florida

Type of Business:

We are a full service travel agent specializing in customized Catholic Pilgrimages. We work on a not-for-profit basis and all extra revenues are used to promote Perpetual Adoration. We can arrange deviations and/or extensions not available through other services. We consolidate and evaluate information on other pilgrimage companies to ensure you have the best choice and value for your money. The cheapest is not always the best. To Christ thank Mary.

NAWAS INTERNATIONAL
777 Post Rd., Third Floor
Darien, CT 06820-4721
Tel.: 800-221-4984; FAX: 203-655-1577

On the West Coast:
1100 Alma St., Ste. 100
Menlo Park, CA 94025-3344
Tel.: 800-288-2688; FAX: 415-322-6485

Personnel:

- Soli Nawas. . . . . President
- George Khoury. . . . . Executive Vice President (Darien, CT)
- Sami Nawas. . . . . Vice President
- Neil Dellis . . . . Vice President

Type of Business:

Nawas International has designed and operated pilgrimages to the Holy Land, Italy, Fatima, Lourdes, Shrines of Europe and more since 1949. With our dedication to delivering **high quality** programs at **very competitive** prices and on-site quality control via our local, Nawas-owned offices, we provide the finest pilgrimages available. We also offer **excellent tour host benefits** — you can travel **FREE** with **as few as five** paying passengers! Thousands of church leaders have organized their travel plans through Nawas. Call us toll-free and we'll show you how to do it, too!

NOTRE DAME TRAVEL
336 East Ripa Ave.
St. Louis, MO 63125-2836
Tel.: 800-761-7763; 314-638-7763
FAX: 800-761-7773; 314-638-7773

Personnel:

- Sister Elizabeth Lakin, SSND. . . . President, Dir. of Int'l. Travel
- Judy Brda . . . . Director of Leisure Sales
- Brian Hensley. . . . . Corporate Agent
- Sue Wood. . . . . Corporate/Leisure Agent

Type of Business:

NOTRE DAME TRAVEL is a full-service, non-profit travel agency benefiting the ministries of the SCHOOL SISTERS OF NOTRE DAME. Experienced agents in business, leisure and international travel provide excellent service in booking tours, pilgrimages and cruises for individuals and groups. Customized group travel, as well as car rentals, hotels and airline tickets can be yours with just a phone call to Notre Dame Travel. Commissions paid by the travel industry are shared with group clients who book more than $10,000 in a year

OUR PRECIOUS LEGACY TOURS
310 First Ave.
Needham, MA 02194
Tel.: 800-874-4445; FAX: 617-449-8988
website: www.catholic-legacytours.com
A division of the Interface Group

Type of Business:

"Our Precious Legacy Tours — Catholic Legacy Tours is committed to providing a special opportunity for all Catholics to share the beauty and legacy of the land of Israel. It is our goal and dream to allow each individual and family to experience the uniqueness of Israel's heritage in an atmosphere of sharing. As a company we stand behind the belief in the ability of a trip to Israel to foster the common bond that unites us all."

We specialize in providing the only deluxe, all-inclusive and personally guided tours of the Catholic sites in Israel, for individuals and small groups, with guaranteed weekly departures, available in the USA.

For Parish leaders we will create an educational, spiritual and fiscally rewarding pilgrimage to Israel, and other Catholic destinations upon request.

PEACE CENTER TOURS
558 Park Ave.
Elmhurst, IL 60126
Tel.: 800-233-0334; FAX: 630-941-7807

Personnel:

T. Malik . . . . Vice President

Type of Business:

Lois Malik, Catholic founded and editor since 1963, offers weekly international pilgrimages to the Shrines of Jesus and His Mother, Mary.

First in the U.S. to offer weekly pilgrimages to Medjugorje, Rome, the Land where Jesus Walked, Fatima, Lourdes, Lisieux, Garabandal, Santiago de Compostela as well as the first pilgrimages to Betania El Cajas and San Nicholas since 1990.

Your next pilgrimage travel free with only 5 people accompanying you.

PILGRIMAGE TOURS & TRAVEL INC.
39 Beechwood Ave.
Manhasset, NY 11030
Tel.: 516-627-2636; FAX: 516-365-1667

Personnel:

Mr. Misha Radulovic . . . . President
Mrs. Nina Jasic . . . . Vice President
Mr. Bo Radulovic . . . . Travel Consultant

Type of Business:

Pilgrimage Tours & Travel has been the leader for religious pilgrimages to Europe and Holyland for the past 70 years. Our 1997 program offers religious tour to: Fatima, Lourdes, Zaragoza, Santiago, Medjugorije, Nevers, Paris, Jerusalem, Bethlehem, Rome, Cracow, Oberammergau 2000 and Chestochowa. All inclusive programs with the best hotels, guides, transportation and excursions. For more information or bookings please call one of our travel counselors at 800-669-0757. We specialize in custom itineraries for religious groups.

PLATINUM TOURS
1341 Hamburg Turnpike, Ste. 7A
Wayne, NJ 07470
Tel.: 800-886-7528; FAX: 201-696-4177
e-mail: PLATEGYPT@aol.com

Personnel:

Tarek G. Sadek . . . . President
Magdalene Leong . . . . Vice President

Type of Business:

Tour specialist with several years of experience handling groups and individuals on Catholic pilgrimages to the Holy Land and the neighboring countries of Egypt, Jordan, Turkey and Greece. We want to provide you with the best of service and values in accommodation and air travel. But of greater importance is our goal to provide you with a visit-of-a-lifetime to a remarkable Land, filled with memorable and awe-inspiring experiences. No one will come away and not be moved by those experiences!

'QUEEN OF PEACE MINISTRY'
2120 Main St. #200
Huntington Beach, CA 92648
Tel.: 800-321-6279; FAX: 714-374-9490

Personnel:
Peter K. Miller . . . . Director
Jana Du Plantier . . . . Reservations Supervisor
Theresa Barcenas . . . . Book-Keeping Supervisor
Diane Cherry . . . . Air Dept. Supervisor

Type of Business:
Established in 1987, 'Queen of Peace' has rapidly become the Nation's Premier Catholic Pilgrimage Tour Operators, earning a reputation for 'Spirituality, Quality & Service.' 'QOP' offers the most comprehensive Schedule of Departures, covering virtually every major Catholic Shrine. Additionally 'QOP' can CUSTOMIZE Tours to suit every need. A Specialist in MARIAN SHRINES, especially MEDJUGORJre FATIMA, LOURDES & GUADALUPE plus a leader in Pilgrimage to the HOLYLAND.

SELECT International

SELECT INTERNATIONAL TOURS & CRUISES
116 US Highway 22 E.
North Plainfield, NJ 07060
Tel.: 800-571-0884; 908-412-0044; FAX: 908-412-0099

Personnel:
Edita Krunic . . . . President
Maryanna Kosorich . . . . Manager

Type of Business:
For the past 10 years, our company has created programs for Catholic churches, choirs, schools and organizations to Europe, Holy Land, and Latin America. In addition to the 40 page catalogue featuring over 45 different itineraries we also offer cruises for groups and custom designed itineraries, based on the group's interests and preferences.
Pilgrimages to special events such as the World Youth Day, Eucharistic Congress, Exposition of the Holy Shroud in Turin in 1998, Oberammergau Passion Play and the Great Jubilee, Celebration 2000 in Rome and Holy Land, are also planned. With affiliate offices throughout Europe, Holy Land and Latin America and with a staff that has visited each destination we feature, you will benefit by receiving assistance for your groups from an experienced and friendly staff, staying at excellent hotels, traveling with knowledgeable guides and all at a superior value.

TUCHMAN MEDITOURS

TUCHMAN MEDITOURS
7270 N.W. 12th Ave. #255
Miami, FL 33126
Tel.: 800-772-1010; 305-639-2500; FAX: 305-639-2599
e-mail: tuchman@netpoint.net

Personnel:
Mr. Eddy Tuchman . . . . President
Mrs. Aliza Tuchman . . . . Vice President
Ms. Joyce Schoonenberg-Reed . . . . . Dir. of Sales & Marketing
Ms. Martha Pérez . . . . Sales Executive

Type of Business:
Major wholesaler and tour operator to Israel and the Mediterranean countries, with 30 years of experience. Specializing in religious travel, we conduct Catholic tours once or twice a month.
Walk in the footsteps of Christ. Follow the steps of St. Paul or do a pilgrimage to Rome, Assisi, Santiago de Compostela, Fatima or Lourdes.
Church leaders travel for FREE when accompanying a group.
Todos estos programas los tenemos tambien en Español.

TURICUM INTERNATIONAL
306 Katherine Street, Englewood, New Jersey 07631
(201) 568-5967 Fax (201) 541-7682 1-(800) 451-4284

TURICUM INTERNATIONAL
306 Katherine St.
Englewood, NJ 07631
Tel.: 201-568-5967; FAX: 201-541-7682

Personnel:
Heidi Giger . . . . Owner

Type of Business:
Classic Christian Journeys by Turicum International.
Give us your ideas and we will put a well designed package together for you. If you prefer you may choose one of our standard tours.
Try us. Our reasonable rates will surprise you; and we offer attractive travel benefits to the host.
Our personalized service and vast experience will guarantee you a memorable pilgrimage.
We arrange for daily Mass at the place of your choice. Each group has its own bus and we do not charge extra for Massada, the Rabbinical Tunnel.
We also offer extensions to Egypt-Jordan-Greece-Turkey-Italy-Spain/Portugal.

1957/1997 - 40 YEARS OF QUALITY AND INTEGRITY
UNITOURS, inc.

UNITOURS, INC.
411 W. Putnam Ave.
Greenwich, CT 06830
Tel.: 800-777-7432; FAX: 203-629-1905
e-mail: unitoursus@aol.com

Personnel:
Larry Oliveri . . . . Sales Manager

Type of Business:
Unitours, Inc., a leader in Roman Catholic group travel since 1957, specializes in Israel travel and is a pioneer in Holy Land Pilgrimages. Unitours' experienced professionals lead travelers over the same paths and rocks that Jesus walked on, stirring feelings and inspiring memories that stay with you forever. Each touir is custom designed to satisfy your group's specific interests and priced to suit your budget. Holy Land, Rome, Fatima, Lourdes, Ireland, anywhere ... personal service, professionalism and quality give you the best value and the memorable experience of a lifetime. *SPECIAL HOLY YEAR 2000 TOURS AVAILABLE TO JERUSALEM, ITALY AND THE PASSION PLAY IN OBERAMMERGAU, GERMANY.* **Clergy that travel with their groups earn free travel and extra cash as well.**

Kitty Ward Travel Inc.
Kitty Ward Travel Agency Inc.
Showing the World for over 40 Years

KITTY WARD TRAVEL
146 Saxer Ave.
Springfield, PA 19064
Tel.: 610-543-0680; FAX: 610-543-0786

Personnel:
Thomas F. Ward . . . . President
Kathryn M. Ward . . . . Chairman of the Board
Thomas F. Ward Jr. . . . . Vice President
Maureen Rennie . . . . Vice President

Type of Business:
Kitty Ward Travel, Inc. was founded by Tom & Kitty Ward in 1973. Kitty Ward, herself has been in the travel business for over 40 years. Kitty has organized a staff of highly motivated professionals to assist you with your travel needs. Kitty Ward Travel has three locations: Springfield, PA — Havertown, PA — Newtown Square, PA.
Kitty Ward Travel, Inc. specializes in providing Fund Raising programs for both group travel and individual travel. These programs are very easy to promote and are monitored by our highly sophisticated tracking systems. Call 800-752-3718 for details.
Kitty Ward Travel, Inc. will do everything within our power to ensure a most pleasant vacation and a successful Fund Raising program.

WCTI

WCTI — WORLDWIDE CHRISTIAN TOURS INT'L.
13140 Coit Rd., Ste. 512, LB 134
Dallas, TX 75240
Tel.: 972-644-1822; FAX: 972-644-0204
e-mail: wcti@onramp.net

Personnel:
Robert J. Dorazil . . . . International Coordinator
Orlando Padron . . . . Director of Marketing
Merrilyn Long . . . . International Group Sales

Type of Business:
Specializing in Custom Group Tours & Pilgrimages throughout the world ... The travel management team with over 35 years experience in this field provides the most comprehensive programs, designed to meet the client's specific needs.
WCTI's travel business partners around the globe facilitate the most appropriate management for our client's itineraries, whatever destination is selected, we have it covered ... Offering exceptional Services and nothing but the highest of Quality are the primary factors in the formation of all programs.
For a FREE consultation on your next Journey abroad or Pilgrimage please call toll free 1-888-644-1822, experience what you deserve ... your satisfaction is our highest priority.

SHRINES

Blue Army Shrine

THE BLUE ARMY OF OUR LADY OF FATIMA, U.S.A.
Shrine of the Immaculate Heart of Mary
P.O. Box 976 - Mountainview Rd.
Washington, N.J. 07882 (Warren County)
Tel.: 908-689-1700; FAX: 908-689-6279
Internet: Website: http://www.ewtn.com/bluearmy
e-mail: bluearmy@ix.netcom.com

Personnel:
Most Rev. James S. Sullivan . . . . Blue Army President

Type of Business:
The Blue Army is a Church-approved non-profit Catholic organization with divisions in 70 United States dioceses. Our famous shrine honors Our Lady of Fatima. Perched upon a majestic country hillside, our shrine offers 72 acres of well-maintained countryside where you, or your group, can walk and pray. Mass is offered daily in our charming chapel. A unique Rosary garden allows an environment for outdoor prayer. Frequent exposition of the Blessed Sacrament. (Gift Shop.)

RAMBUSCH

RAMBUSCH
40 West 13th St.
New York, NY 10011
Tel.: 212-675-0400; FAX: 212-620-4687

PersonneL:
Viggo Bech Rambusch . . . . Senior Project Director
Martin V. Rambusch . . . . Stained Glass Director

Type of Business:
Since 1898, creating church interiors, liturgical furnishings, and art work. Fine restoration of church interiors. In-house studios and shops for designing and executing stained glass, church lighting systems, art metal work, and decorative painting.

On Target Assessment of your Financial Potential and the Experienced Personnel to Attain it!

How much can you raise? What's a realistic goal? How can you achieve maximum results? How can you best meet the need? When major funding is required for new construction or capital improvements or when the ordinary income needs to be increased, sometimes finding a starting point is difficult. **Call Hank Brandt Associates.** We will be pleased to provide a fund-raising proposal at no cost to you. Additionally, Hank Brandt Associates offers a complete range of pre-campaign planning including feasibility studies that pinpoint attitudinal factors, leadership and financial potential.

Experience Counts

Hank Brandt Associates has the expertise to motivate generous giving. Each campaign we undertake is tailor-made to the particular needs of that individual client. Our attention to planning and detail provides our clients with gratifying results.

Hank Brandt Associates has:

- Conducted more than 75 diocesan-wide appeals that have produced a participation of over **70%**! This is some 30% **ABOVE** the national average.
- Earned unprecedented loyalty by consistently producing results that meet or exceed campaign expectations. At the parish level, clients have used our services time and time again!
- A listing of references available upon request.

Bruce Brandt

Our Success is Measured in Dollars and Sense

Since 1958, Hank Brandt Associates, Inc. has raised millions upon millions of dollars for parishes and dioceses nationwide. However, our successes produce more than dollars. A fund raising effort should unite a faith community and engender a spirit of cooperation and caring that goes beyond the dollars raised. Hank Brandt Associates knows that results are not measured purely by numbers. The realization that the campaign was carried out in the proper manner, that everyone was given the opportunity to participate, and that the percent of participation was edifying are hallmarks of a Hank Brandt Associates campaign. Ours is a fund-raising philosophy that produces a level of support that is always generous and often sacrificial.

Hank Brandt Associates is Hands-On!

A principal of Hank Brandt Associates will be involved with your campaign in its entirety. From the planning to the actual on-site direction, our experience is one of the biggest factors in your success. There are larger firms, but they don't produce better results. Hank Brandt Associates has a proven track record. Since our inception, our personal and professional integrity has been unquestioned.

Full Service Professional Consultants for:

- CAPITAL FUND CAMPAIGNS
- ANNUAL DIOCESAN APPEALS
- INCREASED GIVING PROGRAMS
- DEBT REDUCTION
- FUND RAISING FOR EDUCATIONAL INSTITUTIONS
- DEVELOPMENT PROGRAMS
- FEASIBILITY STUDIES
- CAMPAIGNS FOR SOCIAL SERVICE AGENCIES
- PUBLIC RELATIONS

As simple as a single phone call...

For more information or to receive a copy of our company brochure, please call or write to:

HANK BRANDT ASSOCIATES, INC

FUND RAISING

& Public Relations Specialists

6675 E. 22nd St. • Tucson, AZ 85710 • Call collect **520-745-9905**/Fax: **520-747-7774**

INDEX OF DISPLAY ADVERTISERS

For Pages 1f to 46f see *front* advertising section.
For Pages 1r to 86r see *rear* advertising section.

Products & Services Section with company listings arranged by category begins on Page 1r.